THE UNIVERSAL REFERENCE SYSTEM

Economic Regulation: Business and Government

Volume VIII of the

POLITICAL SCIENCE, GOVERNMENT, AND PUBLIC POLICY SERIES

Included in this series:

Volume	I	*International Affairs (Second Edition)*
Volume	II	*Legislative Process, Representation, and Decision Making*
Volume	III	*Bibliography of Bibliographies in Political Science, Government, and Public Policy*
Volume	IV	*Administrative Management: Public and Private Bureaucracy*
Volume	V	*Current Events and Problems of Modern Society*
Volume	VI	*Public Opinion, Mass Behavior, and Political Psychology*
Volume	VII	*Law, Jurisprudence, and Judicial Process*
Volume	VIII	*Economic Regulation, Business, and Government*
Volume	IX	*Public Policy and the Management of Science*
Volume	X	*Comparative Government and Cultures*

POLITICAL SCIENCE, GOVERNMENT, & PUBLIC POLICY SERIES

Volume VIII

Economic Regulation: Business and Government

An annotated and intensively indexed compilation of significant books, pamphlets, and articles, selected and processed by The UNIVERSAL REFERENCE SYSTEM—a computerized information retrieval service in the social and behavioral sciences.

Prepared under the direction of

ALFRED DE GRAZIA, GENERAL EDITOR
Professor of Social Theory in Government, New York University, and Founder, *The American Behavioral Scientist*

CARL E. MARTINSON, MANAGING EDITOR

and

JOHN B. SIMEONE, CONSULTANT

Published by
PRINCETON RESEARCH PUBLISHING COMPANY
Princeton, New Jersey

For information, address:

UNIVERSAL REFERENCE SYSTEM
32 Nassau Street, Princeton, N.J. 08540

. . . and see the subscription information contained on the last page of this volume.

Standard Book No. 87635-008-2
Library of Congress Catalog Card No. 68-57824

Printed and Bound in the U.S.A. by
KINGSPORT PRESS, INC., KINGSPORT, TENN.

Contents

Advisory Committee* for the UNIVERSAL REFERENCE SYSTEM

*Not all members advise in all areas.

Introduction to the CODEX of Economic Regulation: Business, and Government

The UNIVERSAL REFERENCE SYSTEM CODEX on *Economic Regulation: Business, and Government* selects for annotation and analysis works that relate bargaining, production, consumption, and industry to political power. Both the internal governance of business activities—plants, companies, and associations—and the relations that all of these groups have to politics and governance come within scope. Formal structures—laws, regulations, sanctions—receive a prominent place in the selection of material. Methods of studying such subjects are watched for and identified, as in other UNIVERSAL REFERENCE SYSTEM collections. Political theory concerning the ownership and control of the means of production in the name of the state or public or social strata also is included. Agriculture is considered within the purview of these listings, along with all other branches of production, distribution, and marketing.

Approximately 2,960 documents and 33,200 index entries are to be found in this CODEX VIII on economics and government. The most frequent listings in the work, those containing 300 or more items, are as follows:

Entry	*Number of Works*
Economic Tactics and Measures (ECO/TAC)	1145
Finance (FINAN)	868
Economic System in Developing Countries (ECO/UNDEV)	859
Planning (PLAN)	832
Industry in General (INDUS)	743
Wealth (WEALTH)	671
Diplomacy—economic aspects (DIPLOM)	600
International Trade (INT/TRADE)	587
Technological Development (TEC/DEV)	449
Control (CONTROL)	449
Attitudes (ATTIT)	448
Labor Force (LABOR)	426
The Worker (WORKER)	402
Agriculture (AGRI)	400
Administration (ADMIN)	399
Foreign Aid (FOR/AID)	373
International Organization (INT/ORG)	370
Statistics (STAT)	354
Africa (AFR)	346
Marketing System (MARKET)	340
Capitalism (CAP/ISM)	339
Group Relations (GP/REL)	331
Power (PWR)	315
Education and Propaganda (EDU/PROP)	310
Bibliographies (BIBLIOG, BIBLIOG/A)	309
Trends, Projections (TREND)	301
Costs (COST)	301

These are most useful to consult in regard to course syllabi or general study projects. Usually the works included in them may be more easily located through the less frequent index entries referring to less common subject matters. This is explained in the instructions on how to use the CODEX. For instance, "MONEY" is more likely to produce relevant documents on the subject of the medium of exchange than "finance" with less time and trouble, for it is more specific and carries only 37 items.

This index term frequency list should not be used in disregard of the Grazian topical and methodological index system on which it is based. The logical classification system is often the quickest way to search ideas and processes, because it facilitates putting together and breaking into component parts the idea or process in hand.

How To Use This CODEX

(Hypothetical Example is Used)

1. Frame your need as specifically as possible. (Example: "I want articles written in 1968 that deal with the activities of labor leaders and small business owners in city politics in America.")
2. Scan the Dictionary of Descriptors in this Volume, page xv and following, for URS terms that match your subject. (Example: for cities you find MUNIC and LOC/G; for labor, LABOR; for small companies, SML/CO.) Find the number of titles each Descriptor carries. For rapidity select terms having few entries; for comprehensiveness, select terms having many entries.
3. Having identified terms that match your subject, enter the Index at one of them, say SML/CO, which heads a list of works on small business. For rapid identification of highly relevant titles, search the narrow right-hand column, which contains the Critical Descriptors; these index the primary facets of a work. Even if you read every title under a Descriptor, the critical column will help you identify works of high probable value. Titles are arranged by year of publication and within each year by format: books (B), long articles (L), short articles (S), and chapters (C). The designation "N" covers serials and titles lacking dates or published over several years. The Index entry carries author, title, secondary Descriptors (which index secondary facets of the work), page of the Catalog containing full citation and annotation, and Catalog accession number. Secondary Descriptors are always arranged in the order of the Topical and Methodological Index.
4. Listings of the document would be found in fourteen places in the Index, that is, under each of its numerous significant facets. One of them could be located in a search of "the small company in politics" as follows:

SAMPLE CATALOG LISTING

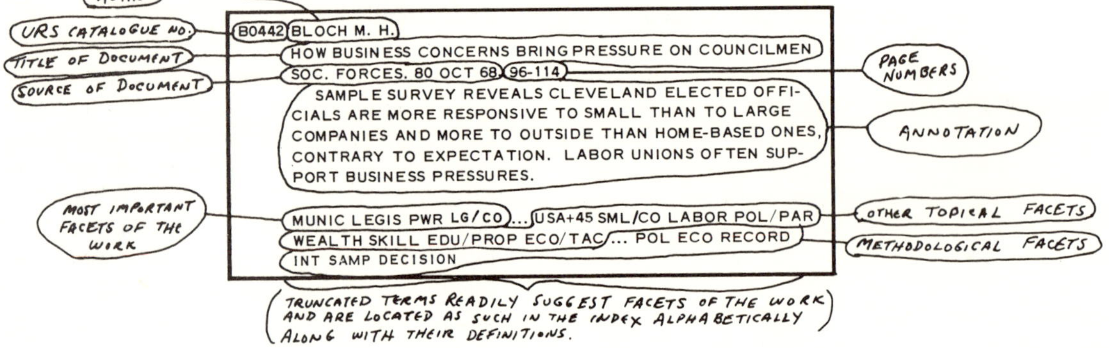

SAMPLE INDEX LISTING

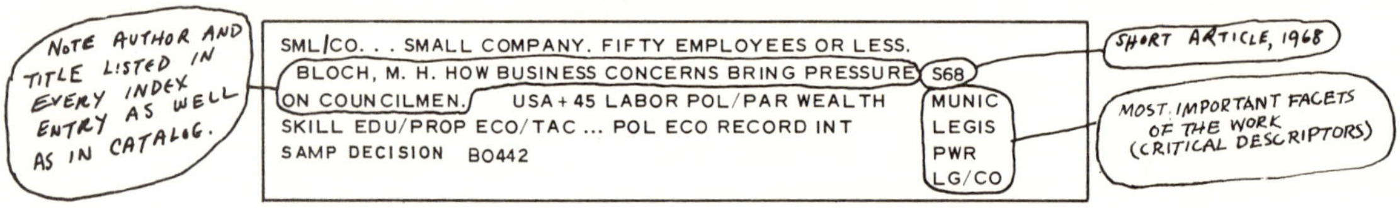

5. Jot down the page numbers and the accession numbers of items that interest you and look them up in the Catalog. There you will find the full citation and a brief annotation of each work.
6. You may locate information on methods authors employ, as well as topics they discuss. Survey the methodological Descriptors in the Grazian Index, pp. xiii-xiv, and locate the relevant Descriptors in the Index of Documents. (Example: if you wished to discover whether any studies of urban business politics had employed recorded interviews, you would look up the term INT [interviews]).
7. Read the Topical and Methodological classification of terms (Grazian Index System) once or twice to grasp the ways in which ideas and groups of related ideas are compressed. The truncated Descriptors, though obvious, are defined in the dictionary of the Index.
8. Although the Catalog is arranged alphabetically by author (except for Volumes II and III), accession numbers have been retained. The major exception to alphabetical arrangement is the group of journals and unsigned articles that begin the Catalog.
9. The Catalogs of Volumes I, IV, V, VI, VII, VIII, IX, and X do not carry Descriptors.
10. The Directory of Publishers pertains to all ten CODEXes.

Concerning the UNIVERSAL REFERENCE SYSTEM in General

The UNIVERSAL REFERENCE SYSTEM is a computerized documentation and information retrieval system employing citations of material above a modest level of quality, appearing in all social and behavioral sciences, annotated. It is indexed by author and employs a set of Standard Descriptors that are arranged according to a master system of topics and methodological techniques, plus various Unique Descriptors.

The flow chart on page x, entitled "The Universal Reference System," shows the numerous steps taken to process documents which come from the intellectual community until they cycle back into the same community as delivered instruments of improved scholarship.

Background of the Work

The many fields of social sciences have suffered for a long time from inadequate searching systems and information storage. The rate of development of periodical and book literature is well known to be far beyond the capacities of the existing book-form document retrieval services. Thousands of new books appear each year, dealing with society and man. Thousands of journals pour forth articles. Hundreds of periodicals are founded each year.

Countries outside of the United States have gone into the social sciences, so that the need for making available foreign publications in intelligible form is ever greater. If there is a light year's distance between present capabilities and the best available service in the social sciences, there is an even greater distance to be traversed in bringing into use the material being published in languages other than English.

A vicious economic cycle is at work in the matter of information retrieval, too: Scholars and students give up research because there are no tools to search with, and therefore their demand for searching tools decreases because they have learned to get along without the materials. Thus, the standards of all the social sciences are lowered because of an anticipated lack of success in handling the problem of information retrieval. The economic risk, therefore, of an information retrieval service has to be taken into account: Many professionals are like the Bengal peasant who cannot aid in his own economic development because he cannot conceive of the nature of the problem and has learned to live as a victim outside of it.

A study in the June, 1964, issue of *The American Behavioral Scientist* magazine showed what the need is today, even before the full capabilities of new systems are appreciated. One-half of a sample of social and behavioral scientists reported that, due to inadequate bibliographic aids, they had discovered significant information on some research too late to use it, and that this information would have significantly affected the scope and nature of their research. In a number of cases, the problem of the researcher was reported to be inadequate access to pre-existing materials, and in other cases was said to be insufficient means of addressing oneself to current material.

So the current ways of information retrieval, or lack thereof, are deficient with respect both to retrospective searching and to current material, not to mention the alarming problem of access to prospective material, in the form of current research project activities and current news of scientific development in relevant categories.

The international scholarly associations centered mainly in Paris have endeavored, with help of UNESCO and other sources of aid, to bring out bibliographies and abstracting services. These services are not fully used, because of their format, their incompleteness, their lack of selectivity, their formulation in traditional and conventional terms of the social sciences (slighting the so-called inter-disciplinary subject matters in methodology), and the simple indexing that they employ. Continuous efforts are being made to solve such problems. Lately, such solutions have been sought via computerized systems. The American Council of Learned Societies, for example, has funded projects at New York University to which the computer is integral.

The Universal Reference System is endeavoring to take an immediately practical view of the literature-access problem, while designing the system so that it will remain open to advances and permit a number of alterations. One must contemplate projects leading to automatic reading and indexing; retrieval of information in the form of propositions, historical dates, and other factual materials; encyclopedic information-providing services; movement into other scientific fields joining social and natural science materials; automatized printing and reproduction of a large variety of materials in quantities ranging from individual to thousands of copies, and provision for televised or other rapid-fire communication services from information retrieval centers.

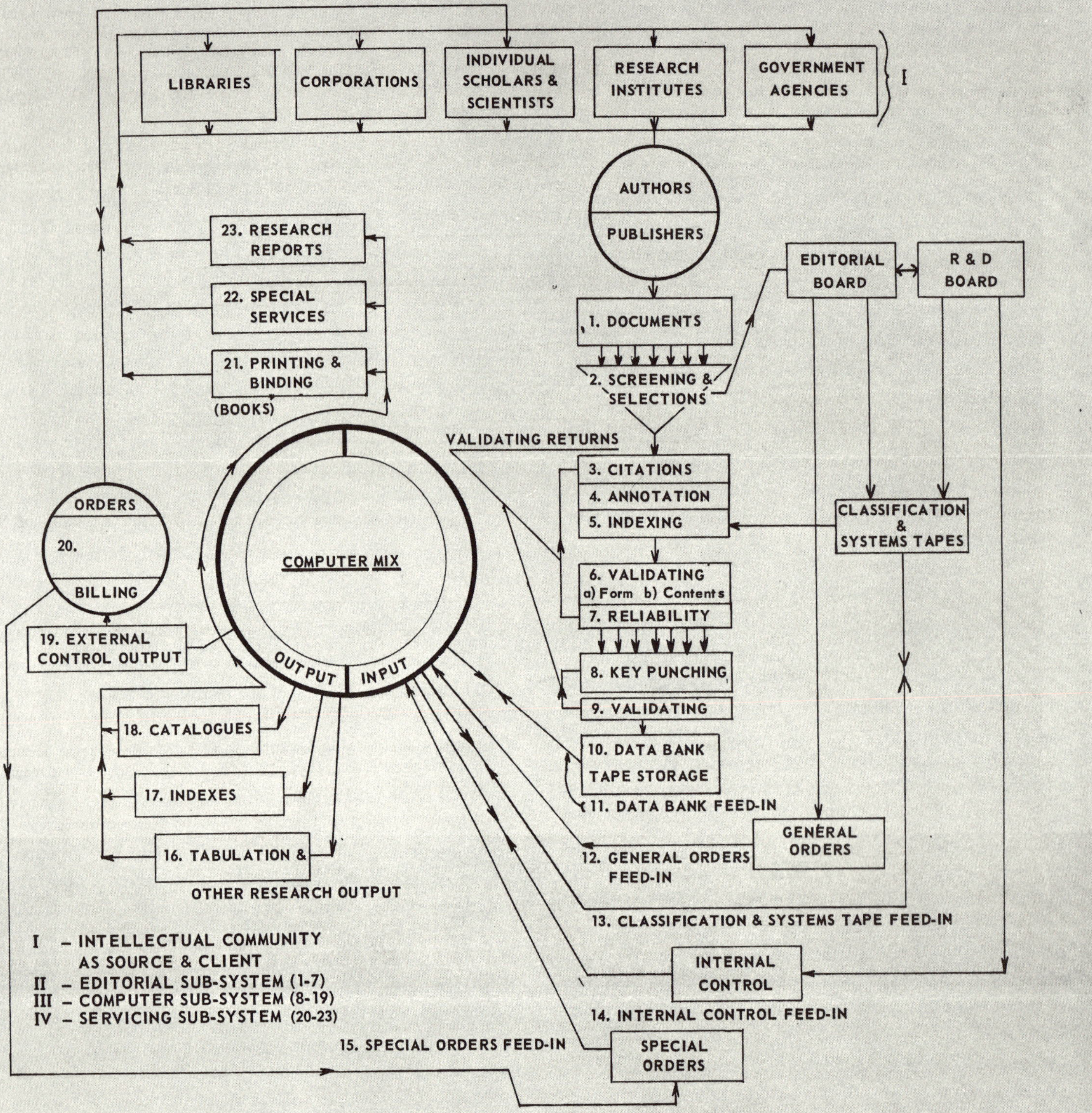

UNIVERSAL REFERENCE SYSTEM

A diagrammatic representation of the numerous steps taken to process documents which come from the intellectual community until they cycle back to the same community as pinpointed sources of information.

The Grazian Classification and Indexing System

The theory behind the URS Classification System is operational. It asks the question: *"Who says, 'Who does what with whom, where and when, by what means, why' and how does he know so?"* This question leads to the general categories and subcategories of the system, which is presented in its logical form on pages **xii-xiv**, along with the truncated terms used in the computerized Index of Documents. The advantage of reading the logical classification is that one will learn in a few minutes the general meaning of the truncated terms and can usually go directly and rapidly to the proper terms in the Index.

The Grazian classification cuts across various disciplines of social science to call attention to the methodological aspects of works which would appear to be important to scholars in the behavioral, instrumental, positivistic tradition of philosophy and science.

The constant recourse to method also serves as a screening device for eliminating numerous documents that are purely evaluative, journalistic, nonempirical, or of an intuitive type. The Grazian index contains some 351 Standard Descriptor categories at the present time. To them are added Unique Descriptors as they occur. Some additional categories logically subtending from the existing ones will be added as time goes on. These will be expanded as part of the original coding as the need is shown. (Several categories may be altered, too, on the same grounds.) From two to four of the Standard and Unique Descriptors are selected as most important facets of the work and are indicated as Critical Descriptors. These are printed apart in the Index of Documents.

The possibilities of utilizing cross-categories are immediate. Cross-categories can be used (both by the searcher and by the creator of the index) to provide a more specialized bibliography. This Cross-Faceting can permit adjusting to changes in the interests of scientists. An almost infinite number of cross-categories is possible, of course. The user of the system will find it set up beyond any existing system to facilitate this. In the future, and upon request, complicated cross-category or multi-faceted searches will be performed by the Universal Reference System's machinery. The ultimate instrumental goal is Controlled Faceting—contractible or expansible according to need and logic.

In practice, the Standard Descriptors, the Unique Descriptors, the Critical Descriptors, the Multiple Faceting, and the Cross-Faceting are interlaced in the operations of documentary analysis and control. Thus, to allow for gaps in the system, to go along with conventional practice, to employ more specialized terms, and to carry important proper nouns, the indexing rules permit the documentary analyst to add Unique Descriptors to the Standard Descriptors already taken from the master list. There are 63 of these in the *Codex of Legislative Process, Representation, and Decision-Making.* The total number of descriptors finally averaged 13 per item.

Some persons have inquired whether it might be useful to print out the whole descriptor rather than a truncated term. Several reasons arbitrate against this procedure, at least for the present. In most cases there is really no single term for which the printed-out truncated descriptor is the symbol. Most Standard Descriptors stand for several synonymous words and related ideas. Printing out the full descriptor *word* would be deluding in many cases, leading searchers to believe a word has only its face meaning.

Moreover, if all truncated descriptors were spelled out, the search time (after the first few searches) would be extended greatly since the eye would have to cover much more lettering and space. Furthermore, the size of the CODEX would be at least tripled, for the space provided for permuting would have to be open enough to carry the longest, not the average, words. There are other technical difficulties.

The repetition of numerous descriptors following each entry in the Index of Documents serves the purpose of targeting the search precisely. The richness of descriptors also postpones the moment of returning to the catalogue and thus enlarges the marginal utility of the first resort to the catalogue.

The intensive indexing of each document, which ranges from 10 to 20 entries, serves a purpose. Intensive indexing permits a document to exhibit all of its important facets to the searcher. The ratio of index carriage to title carriage is here termed the "carriage ratio." The carriage ratio of the URS is much higher than that of most bibliographies. The magnitude of the difference shows the meaning of high intensity indexing. Under other systems, unlike the URS CODEX, a topic is understated in the index. And, less obviously, topics other than the one carried as a flag in the title are sunk into oblivion; thus "Relations Between France and Indochina," which may be a valuable work on questions of economic development, would probably not be indexed on that question at all.

To sum up, the URS, when used as in this CODEX, thoroughly exposes the facets of a listed document. It makes the document thoroughly *retrievable.*

Also under consideration are suggestions to eliminate (or suppress) more of the descriptors. What is the optimal number? It is difficult to say, *a priori.* Experience and experiment will tell, over time. Meanwhile, the Critical Descriptors offer a researcher the "fast search," if he pleases. The more numerous group of descriptors in the final column offers a more complete faceting.

The search time of a researcher should be an important concern of a bibliographer. Search time begins to run, of course, with the knowledge of and access to a work that probably covers a searcher's need. It runs, too, with the ingenuity of the searcher's phrasing of his need. Then it runs with the presence of the works needed in the list searched; a missing document can be translated into lost time. An index saves time, too, when the term searched is the term under which a document is indexed; the need to compromise between detailed vocabularies and generalized ones is evident: it can reasonably be argued that more time is lost in research in social science in getting on the same semantic beam than in solving substantive problems of the "real world." Finally, the structure of an index should lessen search time while permitting a rich search.

Research and experimentation are in order, and it is hoped that a by-product of the initial publications of the Universal Reference System will be an increased stimulation of research into research procedures with respect to the URS' problems and to those of other reference systems.

Topical and Methodological Index (Grazian Index System)

The truncated descriptors (left of each column) and their expanded definitions (right of each column) that follow were employed in systematically computerizing the topics and methods of the Social and Behavioral Sciences. Truncated descriptors that are underscored in the listing that follows have not been carried in the left-hand index entry column of this CODEX; several others (denoted by a double underscore) have been entirely eliminated from this CODEX. Fuller definitions are included in the Index of Documents. So are proper names, place names, organization names, and incidents.

I. TOPICS

1. TIME—SPACE—CULTURE INDEX: Cultural-temporal location of subject.

Centuries covered (e.g., -4; 14-19; 20)

PREHIST	Prehistoric.
MEDIT-7	Mediterranean and Near East, pre-Islamic.
PRE/AMER	Pre-European Americas.
CHRIST-17C	Christendom to 1700.
AFR	Sub-Sahara Africa.
ASIA	China, Japan, Korea.
S/ASIA	India, Southeast Asia, Oceania, except European settlements.
ISLAM	Islamic world.
MOD/EUR	Europe, 1700 to 1918, including European settlements.
USA-45	USA, 1700 to 1945.
WOR-45	Worldwide to 1945.
L/A+17C	Latin America since 1700.
EUR+WWI	Europe, 1918 to present, including colonies, but excluding Communist countries.
COM	Communist countries.
USA+45	USA since 1945.
WOR+45	Worldwide since 1945.
FUT	Future.
SPACE	Outer space.
UNIV	Free of historical position.
SEA	Locale of activity is aquatic.
AIR	Locale of activity is aerial.

(Nations are readily identifiable.)

2. INSTITUTIONAL INDEX: (or subject treated).

A. General

SOCIETY	Society as a whole.
CULTURE	Cultural patterns.
STRUCT	Social structure.
CONSTN	Constitution. Basic group structure.
LAW	Sanctioned practices, enforced ethics in a community.
ELITES	A power-holding group.
INTELL	Intelligentsia.
SOC/INTEG	Social integration.
STRATA	Social strata.
CLIENT	Clients.

B. Economic type

ECO/UNDEV	Developing countries.
ECO/DEV	Developed countries.

C. Economic function

AGRI	Agriculture, including hunting.
R+D	Research and development organization.
FINAN	Financial services.
INDUS	All or most industry.
COM/IND	Communications industry.
CONSTRUC	Construction and building.
DIST/IND	Distributive system: Includes transportation, warehousing.
EXTR/IND	Extractive industry.
MARKET	Marketing system.
PROC/MFG	Processing or manufacturing.
SERV/IND	Service industry.

D. Organizations

SML/CO	Small company: 50 employees or less.
LG/CO	Company of more than 50 employees.
LABOR	Labor unions.
PROF/ORG	Professional organizations, including guilds.
PUB/INST	Habitational institutions: hospitals, prisons, sanitariums, etc.
POL/PAR	Political party.
SCHOOL	School (except University).
ACADEM	Higher learning.
PERF/ART	Performing arts groupings.
SECT	Church, sect, religious group.
FAM	Family.
KIN	Kinship groups.
NEIGH	Neighborhood.
LOC/G	Local governments.
MUNIC	Cities, villages, towns.
PROVS	State or province.
NAT/G	National governments.
FACE/GP	Acquaintance group: face-to-face association.
VOL/ASSN	Voluntary association.
INT/ORG	International organizations.

3. ORGANIC OR INTERNAL STRUCTURE INDEX: Subgroupings or substructures treated.

CONSULT	Consultants.
FORCES	Armed forces and police.
DELIB/GP	Conferences, committees, boards, cabinets.
LEGIS	Legislatures.
CT/SYS	Court systems.
EX/STRUC	Formal executive establishment.
TOP/EX	Individuals holding executive positions.
CHIEF	Chief officer of a government.
WORKER	Workers and work conditions.

4. PROCESSES AND PRACTICES: Procedures or tactics used by subject or discussed as subject.

A. Creating and Sciencing

CREATE	Creative and innovative processes.
ACT/RES	Combined research and social action.
COMPUTER	Computer techniques.
INSPECT	Inspecting quality, output, legality.
OP/RES	Operations research.
PLAN	Planning.
PROB/SOLV	Problem-solving and decision-making.
TEC/DEV	Development and change of technology.

B. Economizing

ACCT	Accounting, bookkeeping.
BAL/PWR	Balance of power.
BARGAIN	Bargaining, trade.
BUDGET	Budgeting, fiscal planning.
CAP/ISM	Enterprise, entrepreneurship.
DIPLOM	Diplomacy.
ECO/TAC	Economic measures or tactics.
FOR/AID	Foreign aid.
INT/TRADE	International trade.
RATION	Rationing, official control of goods or costs.
RENT	Renting.
TARIFFS	Tariffs.
TAX	Taxation.

C. Awarding

GIVE	Giving, philanthropy.
LICENSE	Legal permit.
PAY	Paying.
RECEIVE	Receiving of welfare.
REPAR	Reparations.
TRIBUTE	Payments to dominant by minor power, racketeering.
WORSHIP	Worship, ritual.

D. Symbolizing

DOMIN	Domination.
EDU/PROP	Education or propaganda.
LEGIT	Legitimacy.
PRESS	Printed media.
RUMOR	Rumor, gossip.
TV	Television.
WRITING	Writing.

E. Evaluating

CONFER	Group consultation.
DEBATE	Organized collective arguments.

ETIQUET	Etiquette, fashion, manners.
PRICE	Pricing.
SENIOR	Seniority.

F. Determining

ADJUD	Judicial behavior and personality.
ADMIN	Behavior of non-top executive personnel (except armed forces).
AGREE	Agreements, treaties, compacts.
AUTOMAT	Automation.
COLONIAL	Colonialism.
CONTROL	Specific ability of power to determine achievement.
EXEC	Executive, regularized management.
FEEDBACK	Feedback phenomena.
GAMBLE	Speculative activity.
LEAD	Leading.
LOBBY	Lobbying.
NEUTRAL	Neutralism, neutrality.
PARL/PROC	Parliamentary procedures (legislative).
PARTIC	Participation: civic apathy or activity.
REGION	Regionalism.
RISK	Risk, uncertainty, certainty.
ROUTINE	Procedural and work systems.
SANCTION	Sanctions of law and social law.
TASK	A specific operation within a work setting.
TIME	Timing, time-factor.

G. Forcing

ARMS/CONT	Arms control and disarmament.
COERCE	Force and violence.
CRIME	Criminal behavior.
CROWD	Mass behavior.
DEATH	Death-related behavior.
DETER	Military deterrence.
GUERRILLA	Guerrilla warfare.
MURDER	Murder, assassination.
NUC/PWR	All uses of nuclear energy.
REV	Revolution.
SUICIDE	Suicide.
WAR	War.
WEAPON	Conventional military weapons.

H. Choosing

APPORT	Apportionment of assemblies.
CHOOSE	Choice, election.
REPRESENT	Representation.
SUFF	Suffrage.

I. Consuming

DREAM	Dreaming.
LEISURE	Unobligated time expenditures.
SLEEP	Sleep-related behavior.
EATING	Eating, cuisine.

5. RELATIONS INDEX: Relationship of individuals and/or group under discussion.

CIVMIL/REL	Civil-military relation.
GOV/REL	Relations between local or state governments and governmental agencies.
GP/REL	Relations among groups, except nations.
~~INT/REL~~	~~Relations among sovereign states.~~
INGP/REL	Relations within groups.
PERS/REL	Relations between persons; interpersonal communication.
RACE/REL	Race relations.

6. CONDITIONS AND MEASURES (of activities being discussed).

ADJUST	Social adjustment, socialization.
BAL/PAY	Balance of payments.
CENTRAL	Centralization.
CONSEN	Consensus.
COST	Costs.
DEMAND	In economic sense, a demand.
DISCRIM	Social differentiation in support of inequalities.
EFFICIENCY	Effectiveness, measures.
EQUILIB	Equilibrium (technical).
FEDERAL	Federalism.
HAPPINESS	Satisfaction and unhappiness.
ILLEGIT	Bastardy.
INCOME	Income distribution, shares, earnings.
ISOLAT	Isolation and community.
LITERACY	Ability to read and write.
MAJORITY	Behavior of major parts of grouping.
MARRIAGE	Legal wedlock.
NAT/LISM	Nationalism.
OPTIMAL	Optimality in its economic usages.
OWN	Ownership.
PEACE	Freedom from conflict or termination of hostilities.
PRIVIL	Privilege, parliamentary.
PRODUC	Productivity.
PROFIT	Profit in economic sense.
RATIONAL	Instrumental rationality.
STRANGE	Estrangement or outsiders.
TOTALISM	Totalitarianism.
UTIL	Utility as in economics.
UTOPIA	Envisioned general social conditions.

7. PERSONALITY INDEX: Behavior of actors to their actions.

HABITAT	Ecology.
HEREDITY	Genetic influences on personality.
DRIVE	Drive, morale, or antithesis.
PERCEPT	Perception.
PERSON	Personality and human nature.
ROLE	Role, reference group feelings, cross-pressures.
AGE	Age factors in general.
AGE/C	Infants and children.
AGE/Y	Youth, adolescence.
AGE/A	Adults.
AGE/O	Old.
SEX	Sexual behavior.
SUPEGO	Conscience, superego, and responsibility.
RIGID/FLEX	Rigidity/flexibility; exclusive/inclusive.
ATTIT	Attitudes, opinions, ideology.
DISPL	Displacement and projection.
AUTHORIT	Authoritarianism, as personal behavior.
BIO/SOC	Bio-social processes: drugs, psychosomatic phenomena, etc.
ANOMIE	Alienation, anomie, generalized personal anxiety.

8. VALUES INDEX: Basically desired (or nondesired) conditions held or believed in by subjects.

HEALTH	Well-being, bodily and psychic integrity (sickness).
KNOWL	Enlightenment (ignorance).
LOVE	Affection, friendship (hatred).
MORAL	Rectitude, morality (immorality), goodness.
PWR	Power, participation in decision-making (impotence).
RESPECT	Respect, social class attitudes (contempt, disrespect).
SKILL	Skill, practical competence (incompetence).
WEALTH	Wealth, access to goods and services (poverty).
ALL/VALS	All, or six or more of above.
ORD/FREE	Security, order, restraint (change, experience, freedom).
SOVEREIGN	Sovereignty; home-rule.

9. IDEOLOGICAL TOPIC: Ideology discussed in work.

CATHISM	Roman Catholicism.
CONSERVE	Traditionalism.
FASCISM	Fascism.
LAISSEZ	Laissez-faire-ism (old liberal).
MARXISM	Marxism.
MYSTISM	Mysticism.
NEW/LIB	New Liberalism (welfare state).
OBJECTIVE	Value-free thought.
PACIFISM	Pacifism.
PLURISM	Socio-political order of autonomous groups.
POPULISM	Majoritarianism.
RELATISM	Relativism.
SOCISM	Socialism.
TECHRACY	Socio-political order dominated by technicians.
ALL/IDEOS	Three or more of above.

II. METHODOLOGY (What techniques are dealt with by the author and what techniques the document employs or describes).

10. ETHICAL STANDARDS APPLIED BY AUTHOR

~~ETHIC~~	~~Personal ethics (private and professional).~~
~~LAW/ETHIC~~	~~Ethics of laws and court processes.~~

POLICY	Treats ethics of public policies.

11. IDEOLOGY OF AUTHOR (where clear).

ANARCH	Anarchism.
CATH	Roman Catholic.
CONVNTL	Conventional: unsystematic acceptance of values in common currency.
FASCIST	Totalitarian with nonworker, upper class, or leader cult.
MAJORIT	Majoritarian, consensual.
MARXIST	Marxist Communist in viewpoint.
MYSTIC	Otherworldly, mystical.
OLD/LIB	Old liberal, laissez-faire.
PACIFIST	Pacifist.
PLURIST	Pluralist.
REALPOL	Realpolitik, Machiavellism.
RELATIV	Relativist.
SOCIALIST	Socialist (except Communist).
TECHNIC	Technocratic.
TRADIT	Traditional or aristocratic.
WELF/ST	Welfare state advocate.

12. FIELD INDEX: Fields, discipline, or methodological approach of document.

ART/METH	Fine Arts, Graphics, Performing Arts, Aesthetics.
CRIMLGY	Criminology.
DECISION	Decision-making and gaming (game theory).
ECO	Economics and economic enterprise.
ECOMETRIC	Econometrics, mathematical economics.
EPIST	Epistemology, sociology of knowledge.
GEOG	Demography and geography.
HEAL	Health sciences.
HIST	History (including current events).
HUM	Methods of the "Humanities." Literary analysis.
INT/LAW	International law. Uses legal approach.
JURID	Uses legal approach. Concerns largely the laws.
MGT	Administrative management.
PHIL/SCI	Scientific method and Philosophy of Science.
POL	Deals with political and power process.
PSY	Psychology.
SOC	Sociology.
SOC/WK	Social services.

13. CONCEPTS: Document is noteworthy for systematic and/or basic treatment of:

CONCPT	Subject-matter abstract concepts.
METH/CNCPT	Methodological concepts.
MYTH	Treats assumptions unconsciously accepted, fictions.
NEW/IDEA	Word inventions, new concepts and ideas.

14. LOGIC, MATHEMATICS, AND LANGUAGE

LOG	Logic: syntax, semantics, pragmatics.
MATH	Mathematics.
STAT	Statistics.
AVERAGE	Mean, average behaviors.
PROBABIL	Probability, chance.
MODAL	Modal types, fashions.
CORREL	Correlations (statistical).
REGRESS	Regression analysis.
QUANT	Nature and limits of quantification.
CLASSIF	Classification, typology, set theory.
INDICATOR	Numerical indicator, index weights.
LING	Linguistics.
STYLE	The styles and terminology of scientific communications.

15. DIRECT OBSERVATION

OBS	Trained or participant observation.
SELF/OBS	Self-observation, psycho-drama.
OBS/ENVIR	Social milieu of and resistances to observation.
CONT/OBS	Controlled direct observation.
RECORD	Recording direct observations. (But not content analysis, q.v.)

16. INTERVIEWS

INT	Interviews, short or long, in general.
STAND/INT	Standardized interviews.
DEEP/INT	Depth interviews.
UNPLAN/INT	Impromptu interview.
RESIST/INT	Social resistance to interviewing.
REC/INT	Recording, systematizing, and analyzing of interviews.

17. QUESTIONNAIRES

QU	Questionnaires in general, short or long.
DEEP/QU	Depth questionnaires, including projective or probing.
QU/SEMANT	Semantic and social problems of questionnaires.
SYS/QU	Systematizing and analyzing questionnaires.

18. TESTS AND SCALES

TESTS	Theory and uses of tests and scales.
APT/TEST	Aptitude tests.
KNO/TEST	Tests for factual knowledge, beliefs, or abilities.
PERS/TEST	Personality tests.
PROJ/TEST	Projective tests.

19. UNIVERSES AND SAMPLING

CENSUS	Census.
SAMP	Sample survey in general.
SAMP/SIZ	Sizes and techniques of sampling.
NET/THEORY	Systematic group-member connections analysis.

20. ANALYSIS OF TEMPORAL SEQUENCES

BIOG	Biography, personality development, and psychoanalysis.
HIST/WRIT	Historiography.
TIME/SEQ	Chronology and genetic series of men, institutions, processes, etc.
TREND	Projection of trends, individual and social.
PREDICT	Prediction of future events.

21. COMMUNICATION CONTENT ANALYSIS

CON/ANAL	Quantitative content analysis.
DOC/ANAL	Conventional analysis of records or documents.

22. INFORMATION STORAGE AND RETRIEVAL

OLD/STOR	Conventional libraries, books, records, tape, film.
THING/STOR	Artifacts and material evidence.
COMPUT/IR	Mechanical and electronic information retrieval.

23. GRAPHICS AND AUDIO-VISUAL TECHNIQUES: Used in the research and/or in the presentation.

AUD/VIS	Film and sound, photographs.
CHARTS	Graphs, charts, diagrams, maps.
EXHIBIT	Exhibits.
PROG/TEAC	Programmed instruction.

24. COMPARATIVE ANALYSIS INDEX

METH/COMP	Of methods, approaches, styles.
IDEA/COMP	Of ideas, methods, ideologies.
PERS/COMP	Of persons.
GP/COMP	Of groups.
GOV/COMP	Of governments.
NAT/COMP	Of nations.

25. EXPERIMENTATION

LAB/EXP	Laboratory or strictly controlled groups.
SOC/EXP	"Social" experimentation.
HYPO/EXP	Hypothetical, intellectual constructs.

26. MODELS: Intellectual representations of objects or processes.

SIMUL	Scientific models.
ORG/CHARTS	Blueprints and organization charts.
STERTYP	Stereotypes, ideologies, utopias.
GAME	Game or Decision Theory models.

27. GENERAL THEORY

GEN/LAWS	Systems based on substantive relations, such as idealism, economic determinism.
GEN/METH	Systems based on methodology, such as cycles, pragmatism, sociometry.

28. SPECIAL FORMATS

ANTHOL	Anthology, symposium, collection.
BIBLIOG	Bibliography over fifty items, or of rare utility.
BIBLIOG/A	Contains bibliography over fifty items or of rare utility, annotated.
DICTIONARY	Dictionary.
INDEX	List of names or subjects.
METH	Document heavily emphasizes methodology (Part II) rather than topics (Part I).
T	Textbook.

Dictionary of Descriptors in this Volume

(Incorporating List of Frequency of Descriptors in Index)

This Dictionary contains all Descriptors employed in this volume, and thus enables you to identify in a few minutes every Descriptor that may pertain to your subject. The frequency list calls your attention to the number of works carried under each Descriptor and assists you in determining the term at which you may most advantageously begin your search in the Index. A modest system of cross-references may be found in the Dictionary that appears in the Index.

DESCRIPTOR		*FREQUENCY*	*PAGE*
ABA	American Bar Association	1	153
ACADEM	University, graduate school	52	153
ACCT	Accounting, bookkeeping	1	154
ADENAUER/K	Konrad Adenauer	1	154
ADJUD	Judicial and adjudicative processes and behavior	154	154
ADJUST	Social adjustment, socialization	67	159
ADMIN	Behavior of non-top executive personnel in organizational structure	399	160
AEC	Atomic Energy Commission	1	171
AFGHANISTN	Afghanistan	3	171
AFL/CIO	American Federation of Labor, Congress of Industrial Organizations	8	171
AFR	Africa	346	171
AFRICA/E	East Africa	8	181
AFRICA/SW	South-West Africa	1	181
AFRICA/W	West Africa	3	181
AFTA	Atlantic Free Trade Area	1	181
AGE	Age factors	13	181
AGE/C	Infants and children	5	181
AGE/O	Old people	5	181
AGE/Y	Youth and adolescence	12	182
AGREE	Agreements, treaties, compacts	20	182
AGRI	Agriculture, including hunting	400	183
AID	U.S. Agency for International Development	20	193
AIR	Locale of activity is aerial	9	194
ALABAMA	Alabama	2	194
ALBANIA	Albania	3	194
ALGERIA	Algeria	2	194
ALL/IDEOS	Concerns three or more of the terms listed in the ideological topic index, p. xiii	26	194
ALL/PROG	Alliance for Progress	23	195
ALL/VALS	Concerns six or more of the terms listed in the values index, p. xiii	53	196
AMEND/I	First Amendment and related freedoms	1	197
ANARCH	Anarchist	4	198
ANGOLA	Angola	1	198
ANOMIE	Anomie, alienation, generalized personal anxiety	8	198
ANTHOL	Anthology, symposium	171	198
APPORT	Apportionment of assemblies	3	203
ARABS	Arab world and culture	5	203
ARGENTINA	Argentina	15	203
ARIZONA	Arizona	1	204
ARKANSAS	Arkansas	1	204
ARMS/CONT	Arms control, disarmament	18	204
ART/METH	Fine and performing arts	4	205
ASIA	China, Japan, Korea, Bhutan, Afghanistan, Taiwan	80	205
ASIANS	Asians, Asian minorities	1	207
ATATURK/MK	Mustafa Kemal Ataturk	1	207
ATLAN/ALL	Atlantic alliance	1	207
ATLANTA	Atlanta, Georgia	1	207
ATTIT	Attitudes, opinions, ideology	448	207
AUD/VIS	Film and sound, including photographs	8	219
AUST/HUNG	Austria-Hungary	1	220
AUSTRALIA	Australia	13	220
AUSTRIA	Austria	3	220
AUTHORIT	Authoritarianism, personal	6	220
AUTOMAT	Automation	34	220
AUTOMOBILE	Automobile	1	221
BAL/PAY	Balance of payments	235	222
BAL/PWR	Balance of power	71	228
BALKANS	Balkans	1	230
BARGAIN	Bargaining, trade	93	230
BEARD/CA	Charles A. Beard	1	233
BEHAVIORSM	Behaviorism	1	233
BELGIUM	Belgium	7	233
BERLIN/BLO	Berlin Blockade	1	234
BIBLIOG	Bibliography over 50 items	309	234
BIBLIOG/A	Annotated bibliography over 50 items	115	242
BIO/SOC	Bio-social processes: drugs, psychosomoatic phenomena	13	245
BIOG	Biography, personality development, psychoanalysis	17	245
BIRTH/CON	Birth control	2	246
BLACK/EUG	Eugene Black	1	246
BOLIVIA	Bolivia	7	246
BOLIVAR/S	Simon Bolivar	1	247
BOLSHEVISM	Bolshevism, Bolshevists, Bolsheviks	1	247
BOSTON	Boston, Massachusetts	2	247
BRAZIL	Brazil	25	247
BUDGET	Budgeting, fiscal planning	287	249
BUENOS/AIR	Buenos Aires, Argentina	1	256
BULGARIA	Bulgaria	5	256
BUR/BUDGET	Bureau of the Budget	4	256
BUR/STNDRD	Bureau of Standards	1	257
BURAGR/ECO	Bureau of Agricultural Economics	1	257
BUREAUCRCY	Bureaucracy	1	257
BURMA	Burma	8	257
CAB	Civil Aeronautics Board	2	257
CABINET	Cabinet	1	257
CALIFORNIA	California	2	257
CAMBODIA	Cambodia	1	257
CAMEROON	Cameroon	1	258
CANADA	Canada	38	258
CANON/LAW	Canon law	1	259
CAP/ISM	Capitalism, entrepreneurship	340	259
CARIBBEAN	Caribbean	2	268
CASEBOOK	Casebook (e.g., legal, sociological)	6	268
CASTRO/F	Fidel Castro	3	268
CATH	Roman Catholic	3	268
CATHISM	Roman Catholicism	12	269
CENSUS	Population enumeration	64	269
CENTO	Central Treaty Organization	2	271
CENTRAL	Centralization	69	271
CENTRAL/AM	Central America	1	273
CENTRL/AFR	Central African Republic	1	273
CEYLON	Ceylon	8	273
CHAD	Chad	1	273
CHAMBRLN/N	Neville Chamberlain	1	273
CHICAGO	Chicago, Illinois	4	273
CHIEF	Chief officer of government	60	274
CHILE	Chile	11	275
CHINA/COM	People's Republic of China	49	276
CHOOSE	Choice, election	69	277
CHRISTIAN	Christian belief, churches	4	279
CHRIST-17C	Christendom to 1700	9	279
CHURCH/STA	Church-state relations	2	279
CHURCHLL/W	Sir Winston Churchill	1	279
CIA	Central Intelligence Agency	3	279
CIV/DEFENS	Civil Defense	1	279
CIV/RIGHTS	Civil rights, including related movements	5	280
CIVIL/LIB	Civil liberties	2	280
CIVIL/SERV	Civil service	6	280
CIVMIL/REL	Civil-military relations	33	280

DESCRIPTOR		FREQUENCY	PAGE
CLARK/JB	John Bates Clark	1	281
CLASSIF	Classification, typology, set theory	28	281
CLEVELAND	Cleveland, Ohio	1	282
CLIENT	Clients	24	282
CMN/WLTH	British Commonwealth of Nations	22	283
COERCE	Coercion, violence	62	283
COL	Colorado	1	285
COLD/WAR	Cold war	1	285
COLOMBIA	Colombia	10	286
COLONIAL	Colonialism	160	286
COM	Communist countries, except China	142	290
COM/IND	Communications industry	40	294
COM/PARTY	Communist Party	4	295
COMECON	Council for Mutual Economic Assistance (Communist nations)	6	295
COMINFORM	Communist Information Bureau	1	295
COMMON/LAW	Common law	3	295
COMMONWLTH	British Commonwealth of Nations	1	295
COMMUN	Interpersonal communications	7	295
COMPNY/ACT	Companies Act (U.K., 1882)	1	296
COMPUT/IR	Mechanical and electronic information retrieval	13	296
COMPUTER	Computer technology and techniques	26	296
CON/ANAL	Quantitative content analysis	57	297
CONFER	Conference, group consultation	60	299
CONGO	Congo, pre-independence or general	2	300
CONGO/BRAZ	Congo, Brazzaville	5	300
CONGO/KINS	Congo, Kinshasa	4	301
CONGRESS	Congress	104	301
CONNECTICT	Connecticut	1	304
CONSCRIPTN	Conscription	1	304
CONSEN	Consensus	22	304
CONSERVE	Traditionalism	18	304
CONSRV/PAR	Conservative Party	1	305
CONSTN	Constitution; basic group structure	135	305
CONSTRUC	Construction and building	26	308
CONSULT	Consultants	124	309
CONT/OBS	Controlled direct observation	17	313
CONTROL	Power to determine achievement	449	313
CORN/LAWS	Corn Laws (U.K.)	1	325
CORREL	Statistical correlations	4	325
COST	Costs	304	325
COSTA/RICA	Costa Rica	1	333
COUNCL/EUR	Council of Europe	2	333
COUNTY/AGT	County agricultural agent	1	333
CREATE	Creative processes	150	334
CRIME	Criminal behavior	24	338
CRIMLGY	Criminology	2	338
CROWD	Mass behavior	7	338
CT/SYS	Court systems	62	339
CUBA	Cuba	12	340
CULTURE	Cultural patterns	168	341
CZECHOSLVK	Czechoslovakia	9	345
DARWIN/C	Charles Darwin	1	346
DEATH	Death	5	346
DEBATE	Organized collective argument	21	346
DEBT	Public debt	1	347
DECISION	Decision-making and game theory	202	347
DEEP/INT	Depth interviews	2	352
DEEP/QU	Depth questionnaires, including projective or probing	1	352
DEFINETT/B	Bruno Definetti	1	352
DEGAULLE/C	Charles de Gaulle	1	352
DELIB/GP	Conferences, committees, boards, cabinets	215	352
DEMAND	Economic demand	203	358
DEMOCRAT	Democratic Party	3	364
DENMARK	Denmark	3	364
DEPRESSION	Economic depression	12	364
DEPT/AGRI	U.S. Department of Agriculture	5	364
DEPT/DEFEN	U.S. Department of Defense	11	364
DEPT/HEW	U.S. Department of Health, Education, and Welfare	2	365
DEPT/LABOR	U.S. Department of Labor and Industry	7	365
DEPT/STATE	U.S. Department of State	9	365
DEPT/TREAS	U.S. Department of the Treasury	3	365
DETER	Deterrence	25	366
DEV/ASSIST	Development and Assistance Committee	1	366
DEWEY/THOM	Thomas Dewey	1	366
DICTIONARY	Dictionary, glossary	6	367
DIPLOM	Diplomacy	600	367
DIRKSEN/E	Everett Dirksen	1	383
DISCRIM	Discrimination, social differentiation in support of inequalities	72	383
DISPL	Displacement and projection	3	385
DIST/IND	Distributive system, including transportation, warehousing	163	385
DOMIN	Domination	101	389
DOMIN/REP	Dominican Republic	2	392
DOUGLAS/P	Paul Douglas	1	392
DREAM	Dreaming	1	392
DRIVE	Drive, morale, motivation	105	392
DUHRING/E	Eugen Duhring	1	395
EACM	East African Common Market	1	396
EATING	Eating, cuisine	12	396
ECAFE	UN Economic Commission for Asia and the Far East	1	396
ECO/TAC	Economic measurers	1145	396
ECO/UNDEV	Developing countries	859	426
ECOMETRIC	Mathematical economics, econometrics	66	449
ECSC	European Coal and Steel Community	12	451
ECUADOR	Ecuador	1	451
EDGEWORTH	Francis Ysidro Edgeworth	1	452
EDU/PROP	Education, propaganda, persuasion	310	452
EEC	European Economic Community	118	460
EFFICIENCY	Effectiveness	237	463
EFTA	European Free Trade Association	6	469
EIB	European Investment Bank	1	470
EISNHWR/DD	President Dwight David Eisenhower	10	470
ELITES	Power-dominant group	87	470
ENGLSH/LAW	English law	3	473
EPIST	Epistemology, sociology of knowledge	2	473
EQUILIB	Equibilibrium (technical)	106	473
ETHOPIA	Ethiopia	3	476
ETIQUET	Etiquette, styling, fashion	1	476
EURATOM	European Atomic Energy Community	5	476
EURCOALSTL	European Coal and Steel Community	2	476
EUROPE/E	Eastern Europe (all European Communist nations)	1	477
EUROPE/W	Western Europe (non-Communist Europe, excluding Greece, Turkey, Scandinavia, and the British Isles)	5	477
EX/STRUC	Formal executive establishment	142	477
EXEC	Executive process: regularized management	72	481
EXTR/IND	Extractive industry	77	483
FAA	U.S. Federal Aviation Agency	1	485
FABIAN	Fabians	1	485
FACE/GP	Acquaintance group: face-to-face association	10	485
FAIR/LABOR	Fair Labor Standard Act	1	485

DESCRIPTOR		FREQUENCY	PAGE
FAM	Family	45	485
FAO	Food and Agriculture Organization	5	487
FASCISM	Fascism	16	487
FBI	U.S. Federal Bureau of Investigation	1	487
FED/RESERV	U.S. Federal Reserve System	10	488
FEDERAL	Federalism	32	488
FEDERALIST	Federalist party	1	489
FEEDBACK	Feedback phenomena	8	489
FEMALE/SEX	Female sex	1	489
FEPC	Fair Employment Practices Commission	1	489
FIELD/SJ	Stephen J. Field	1	489
FILM	Film	1	489
FINAN	Financial services, e.g., banks, exchanges	868	489
FINLAND	Finland	3	512
FOOD/PEACE	Office of Food for Peace	1	513
FOR/AID	Foreign aid	373	513
FOR/TRADE	Foreign trade	70	523
FORCES	Armed forces and police	137	525
FRANCE	France	100	529
FRANK/PARL	Frankfurt Parliament	1	531
FRONTIER	Frontier	1	532
FTC	Federal Trade Commission	8	532
FUT	Future	195	532
GABON	Gabon	1	538
GAMBIA	Gambia	2	538
GAMBLE	Speculation on an uncertain event	2	538
GAME	Game theory, decision theory models	31	538
GANDHI/M	Mahatma Gandhi	4	539
GATT	General Agreement on Tariffs and Trade	16	539
GENACCOUNT	General Accounting Office	1	540
GEOG	Demography and geography	177	540
GEORGIA	Georgia	2	544
GER/CONFED	German Confederation	1	544
GERMANY	Germany in general	57	545
GERMANY/E	East Germany	4	546
GERMANY/W	West Germany	29	546
GHANA	Ghana	11	547
GIVE	Giving, philanthropy	75	547
GOLD/COAST	Gold Coast (pre-Ghana)	1	550
GOLD/STAND	Gold standard	1	550
GOV/COMP	Comparison of governments	49	550
GOV/REL	Relations between governments	181	551
GOVERNOR	Governor	1	556
GP/COMP	Comparison of groups	40	556
GP/REL	Intergroup relations	331	557
GRANGE	Grange and grangers	1	566
GRECO/ROMN	Greco-Roman civilization	1	566
GREECE	Modern Greece	6	566
GREECE/ANC	Ancient Greece	1	566
GREENBACK	Greenback Party	1	566
GUATEMALA	Guatemala	4	567
GUERRILLA	Guerrilla warfare	7	567
GUIANA/BR	British Guiana	1	567
GUINEA	Guinea	2	567
HABITAT	Ecology	85	567
HAIG	Robert Murray Haig	1	570
HAPPINESS	Satisfaction and happiness	13	570
HARRIMAN/A	Averill Harriman	1	571
HARTFORD	Hartford, Connecticut	1	571
HEAL	Health sciences	14	571
HEALTH	Bodily and psychic integrity	82	572
HEREDITY	Genetic influences on personality development and social growth	3	574
HIST/WRIT	Historiography	23	575
HITLER/A	Adolf Hitler	5	575
HOFFA/J	James Hoffa	2	576
HOLMES/OW	Oliver Wendell Holmes	1	576
HONDURAS	Honduras	5	576
HONG/KONG	Hong Kong	1	576
HOUSE/CMNS	House of Commons	2	576
HOUSE/LORD	House of Lords	1	577
HOUSE/REP	House of Representatives	7	577
HUM	Methods of the "Humanities." Literary analysis	4	577
HUME/D	David Hume	2	577
HUNGARY	Hungary	4	577
HYPO/EXP	Hypothetical intellectual constructs	35	578
IBRD	International Bank for Reconstruction and Development	6	579
ICELAND	Iceland	2	579
IDEA/COMP	Comparison of ideas	162	579
ILLEGIT	Bastardy	1	583
ILLINOIS	Illinois	4	583
ILO	International Labor Organization	13	583
IMF	International Monetary Fund	8	584
IN	Indiana	1	584
INCOME	Income distribution, shares, earnings	233	584
IND	Industry	7	590
INDIA	India	104	591
INDIAN/AM	American Indians	4	593
INDICATOR	Numerical indices and indicators	2	593
INDONESIA	Indonesia	8	594
INDUS	All or most industry	743	594
INDUS/REV	Industrial revolution	2	613
INGP/REL	Intragroup relations	146	614
INONU/I	Ismet Inonu	1	618
INSPECT	Examing for quality, output, legality	19	618
INT	Interviews	47	618
INT/AM/DEV	Inter-American Development Bank	1	619
INT/LAW	International law	33	620
INT/ORG	International organizations	370	620
INT/TRADE	International trade	587	630
INTELL	Intelligentsia	52	646
INTERVENT	Interference by a sovereign state or an international agency in the affairs of another sovereign state	3	648
INTL/DEV	International Development Association	2	648
INTL/ECON	International Economic Association	3	648
INTL/FINAN	International Finance Corporation	1	648
INTRVN/ECO	Governmental interference in domestic economy	7	648
IRAN	Iran	8	648
IRAQ	Iraq	3	649
IRELAND	Ireland	2	649
ISLAM	Islamic world	55	649
ISOLAT	Isolation and community	7	650
ISRAEL	Israel	14	651
ITALY	Italy	22	651
JAVA	Java, Indonesia	1	652
JEWS	Jews, Judaism	2	652
JOHNSON/LB	President Lyndon B. Johnson	5	652
JORDAN	Jordan	2	653
JUDGE	Judges	7	653
JURID	Jurisprudence. Uses legal approach	95	653
KENNEDY/JF	President John F. Kennedy	14	656
KENTUCKY	Kentucky	2	656
KEYNES/JM	John Maynard Keynes	33	657
KHRUSH/N	Nikita Khrushchev	8	658
KIN	Kinship, except nuclear family	16	658
KKK	Ku Klux Klan	1	658
KNO/TEST	Tests for factual knowledge, beliefs, or abilities	1	659
KNOWL	Enlightenment, knowledge	51	659
KOREA	Korea in general	10	660
KOREA/S	South Korea	2	660
KUWAIT	Kuwait	4	661
L/A+17C	Latin America since 1700	143	661

DESCRIPTOR		FREQUENCY	PAGE
LAB/EXP	Laboratory or strictly controlled experiments	1	665
LABOR	Labor unions	426	665
LABOR/PAR	Labor Party	6	676
LAFTA	Latin American Free Trade Association	7	676
LAISSEZ	Laissez-faire-ism (old liberal)	48	676
LAND/LEAG	Land League (Ireland)	1	678
LANDRAT	County chief executive (Germany)	1	678
LAOS	Laos	5	678
LAW	Law, ethical directives in a community	242	678
LEAD	Leading	156	685
LEAGUE/NAT	League of Nations	9	689
LEBANON	Lebanon	3	689
LEGIS	Legislatures	202	690
LEGIT	Legitimacy	47	695
LEISURE	Unobligated use of time	8	696
LENIN/VI	Vladimir Ilyich Lenin	8	697
LG/CO	Large company: more than 50 employees	189	697
LIB/PARTY	Liberal Party	1	702
LIBERIA	Liberia	1	702
LIBYA	Libya	1	702
LICENSE	Legal permit	10	702
LIECHTENST	Liechtenstein	1	703
LINDAHL/E	Erik Lindahl	1	703
LING	Linguistics, language	17	703
LITERACY	Ability to read and write	3	704
LITHUANIA	Lithuania	1	704
LOBBY	Pressure group, lobbying	96	704
LOC/G	Local government	131	706
LOG	Logic	4	710
LOS/ANG	Los Angeles	5	710
LOUISIANA	Louisiana	1	710
LOVE	Affection, friendship (hatred)	5	710
LOVESTN/J	Jay Lovestone	1	711
LUXEMBOURG	Luxembourg	2	711
MADAGASCAR	Madagascar	5	711
MAGHREB	Maghreb	1	711
MAJORIT	Majoritarian, consensual	40	711
MAJORITY	Behavior of major parts of a group	7	713
MALAYA	Malaya	2	713
MALAYSIA	Malaysia	5	713
MALI	Mali	2	713
MALTHUS	Thomas Robert Malthus	2	713
MANCHESTER	Manchester, England	1	713
MAO	Mao Tse-tung	6	713
MAPS	Maps and atlases	1	714
MARITIME	Maritime Provinces	2	714
MARKET	Marketing system	340	714
MARRIAGE	Wedlock	10	723
MARSHALL/A	Alfred Marshall	3	723
MARSHALL/J	John Marshall	1	723
MARSHL/PLN	Marshall Plan	4	723
MARX/KARL	Karl Marx	18	724
MARXISM	Marxism, Communism	193	724
MARXIST	Marxist	35	729
MARYLAND	Maryland	1	730
MATH	Mathematics	84	730
MATTEI/E	Enrico Mattei	1	733
MEDIT-7	Mediterranean and Near East, pre-Islamic	1	733
MERCANTLST	Mercantilist economic theory	4	734
MERTHYR	Merthyr, Wales	1	734
METH	Heavily emphasized methodology or technique of study	80	734
METH/COMP	Comparison of methods	195	736
MEXIC/AMER	Mexican-Americans	18	742
MGT	Management	271	742
MIAMI	Miami, Florida	1	750
MICHIGAN	Michigan	1	750
MID/EAST	Middle East	2	750
MIDWEST/US	Midwestern United Sstates	1	750
MIGRATION	Migration, immigration, and emigration	14	750
MILL/JS	John Stuart Mill	3	750
MINNESOTA	Minnesota	1	751
MOD/EUR	Europe, 1700-1918, including European settlements	51	751
MODAL	Modal types, fashions	4	752
MONEY	Money	37	753
MONOPOLY	Monopolies, oligopolies, and anti-trust actions	28	754
MORAL	Rectitude, morality, goodness (also immorality)	31	755
MOROCCO	Morocco	3	756
MOZAMBIQUE	Mozambique	1	756
MUNIC	Cities, towns, villages	165	756
MURDER	Murder, assassination	1	760
MUSLIM	Muslim people and religion	2	761
MYTH	Fiction	15	761
NAACP	National Association for the Advancement of Colored People	1	761
NAM	National Association of Manufacturers	1	761
NAPOLEON/B	Napoleon Bonaparte	1	761
NASA	National Aeronautic and Space Administration	1	761
NASSER/G	Gamal Abdul Nasser	3	762
NAT/COMP	Comparison of nations	136	762
NAT/FARMER	National Farmers' Union	1	765
NAT/LISM	Nationalism	107	765
NATO	North Atlantic Treaty Organization	22	769
NAVAL/RES	Office of Naval Research	1	769
NAVY	Navy	1	769
NAZI	Nazi movements	5	769
NEGRO	Negro	36	770
NEHRU/J	Jawaharlal Nehru	3	770
NEIGH	Neighborhood	45	771
NEPAL	Nepal	3	772
NET/THEORY	Network theory; systematic group member connections analysis	4	772
NETHERLAND	Netherlands	12	772
NEUTRAL	Neutralism, neutrality	9	772
NEW/BRUNS	New Brunswick, Canada	1	773
NEW/DEAL	New Deal	5	773
NEW/ENGLND	New England	1	773
NEW/GUINEA	New Guinea	3	773
NEW/JERSEY	New Jersey	8	773
NEW/LIB	New liberalism	39	773
NEW/YORK	New York State	5	774
NEW/ZEALND	New Zealand	3	775
NEWYORK/C	New York City	7	775
NICARAGUA	Nicaragua	1	775
NIGERIA	Nigeria	13	775
NKRUMAH/K	Kwame Nkrumah	3	776
NLRB	National Labor Relations Board	8	776
NORTH/CAR	North Carolina	1	776
NORWAY	Norway	3	776
NRA	National Recovery Administration	1	776
NSF	National Science Foundation	1	776
NUC/PWR	All uses of nuclear energy	55	777
NYASALAND	Nyasaland	1	778
OAS	Organization of American States	18	778
OBJECTIVE	Objective, objectivity	7	779
OBS	Observation	73	779
OBS/ENVIR	Social milieu of and resistances to observations	1	781
OECD	Organization for Economic Co-operation and Development	12	781
OEEC	Organization for European Economic Cooperation	36	782
OEO	Office of Economic Opportunity	1	783
OHLIN/HECK	Ohlin-Heckscher theory of commodity trade	1	783
OIL	Oil	4	783
OLD/LIB	Old Liberal	16	783
ONTARIO	Ontario, Canada	1	784
OP/RES	Operations research	103	784
OPA	Office of Price Administration	1	786

DESCRIPTOR		FREQUENCY	PAGE
OPEN/SPACE	Open space; town and country planning	1	786
OPTIMAL	Optimality	62	786
ORD/FREE	Security, order, restraint, liberty, freedom	293	788
OTTOMAN	Ottoman Empire	1	796
OUTER/MONG	Outer Mongolia	1	796
OVRSEA/DEV	Overseas Development Institute, London	2	796
OWN	Ownership, owner	94	796
PACIFISM	Pacifism	3	799
PACIFIST	Pacifist	2	799
PAKISTAN	Pakistan	23	799
PANAMA	Panama	1	800
PAPUA	Papua	1	800
PARAGUAY	Paraguay	1	800
PARETO/V	Vilfredo Pareto	1	800
PARL/PROC	Parliamentary processes	32	800
PARLIAMENT	Parliament	18	801
PARNELL/CS	Charles Stewart Parnell	1	802
PARTIC	Civic participation or apathy	101	802
PATENT/OFF	U.S. Patent Office	1	804
PAY	Paying	86	805
PEACE	Freedom from conflict or termination of hostilities	62	807
PEACE/CORP	Peace Corps	1	809
PENNSYLVAN	Pennsylvania	3	809
PERCEPT	Perception and cognition	26	809
PERF/ART	Performing arts groups	1	810
PERON/JUAN	Juan Peron	1	810
PERS/COMP	Comparison of persons	10	810
PERS/REL	Relations between persons, interpersonal communication	44	810
PERS/TEST	Personality tests	2	811
PERSON	Personality and human nature	64	811
PERU	Peru	5	813
PHIL/SCI	Scientific method and philosophy of science	54	813
PHILADELPH	Philadelphia, Pennsylvania	3	815
PHILIPPINE	Philippines	6	815
PLAN	Planning	832	815
PLURISM	Pluralism, socio-political order of autonomous groups	15	837
PLURIST	Pluralist	9	838
POL/PAR	Political party	196	838
POLAND	Poland	10	843
POLYNESIA	Polynesia	1	844
POPE	Pope	1	844
POPULISM	Majoritarianism	36	844
PORTUGAL	Portugal	6	845
POVRTY/WAR	War on poverty	3	845
PRE/AMER	Pre-European Americas	1	845
PRE/US/AM	Pre-1776 "United States"	2	846
PREDICT	Prediction of future events	59	846
PREHIST	Society before 3000 B.C.	2	847
PRESIDENT	Presidency	32	847
PRESS	Operations of printed media, journalism	32	848
PRICE	Pricing	271	849
PRIVIL	Parliamentary privilege; immunity	10	856
PROB/SOLV	Problem-solving process	402	856
PROBABIL	Probability, chance	13	867
PROC/MFG	Processing or manufacturing industries	55	867
PRODUC	Productivity	265	869
PROF/ORG	Professional organizations	45	876
PROFIT	Profit in economic sense	71	877
PROG/TEAC	Programmed instruction	2	879
PROGRSV/M	Progressive movement	1	879
PROJ/TEST	Projective tests	1	879
PROTESTANT	Protestants, Protestantism	2	879
PROVS	States and provinces	78	879
PRUSSIA	Prussia	3	881
PSY	Psychology	44	881
PUB/INST	Mental, correctional, and other habitational institutions	12	883
PUB/TRANS	Public transportation	7	883
PUERT/RICO	Puerto Rico	6	883
PWR	Power, participation in decision-making	315	883
QU	Questionnaires	23	892
QU/SEMANT	Semantic and social problems of questionnaires	1	892
QUANT	Quantification	15	893
R&D	Research and development organization	86	893
RACE/REL	Race relations	90	895
RAILROAD	Railroads and railway systems	9	898
RATION	Rationing, governmental control of costs and goods	43	898
RATIONAL	Rationality; behavior or thought in accord with stipulated logic of means and ends	18	899
REALPOL	Realpolitik, Machiavellism	1	900
REC/INT	Recording, systematizing, and analyzing of interviews	3	900
RECEIVE	Receiving of welfare	42	900
RECORD	Recording of direct observations	34	901
REDFIELD/R	Robert Redfield	1	902
REFORMERS	Reformers	6	902
REGION	Regionalism: process of integrating groups because of common political, economic, or social characteristics	145	903
REGRESS	Regression analysis	11	906
RELATIV	Relativist	11	907
RENT	Renting	19	907
REPAR	Reparations	7	908
REPRESENT	Representation, delegation, agency	94	908
REPUBLICAN	Republican Party	5	910
RESOURCE/N	Natural resources	24	911
RESPECT	Respect, social class attitudes (contempt)	12	911
REV	Revolution	99	912
RHODE/ISL	Rhode Island	1	914
RHODESIA	Rhodesia	7	914
RICARDO/D	David Ricardo	2	915
RICHARD/H	Henry Richard (19th Century Welsh politician)	1	915
RIGID/FLEX	Rigidity/flexibility: degree of responsiveness to novelty	81	915
RISK	Risk, uncertainty	21	917
RITCHIE/JM	Jess M. Ritchie	1	918
RITSCHL/H	Hans Ritschl	1	918
RODBRTUS/C	Carl Rodbertus	1	918
ROLE	Role, reference group feelings, cross-pressures	66	918
ROMANIA	Romania	3	920
ROOSEVLT/F	President Franklin D. Roosevelt	5	920
ROUTINE	Procedural and work systems	129	921
RUSSIA	Russia	7	924
RWANDA	Rwanda	1	924
S/ASIA	India, Pakistan, Southeast Asia, and Oceania, except European settlements	84	925
SAMP	Sample survey	19	927
SAMP/SIZ	Sizes and techniques of sampling	6	928
SAMUELSN/P	Paul Samuelson	1	928
SAN/FRAN	San Francisco	3	928
SAN/MARTIN	Jose de San Martin	1	928
SANCTION	Sanction of law and semi-legal private groups	30	928
SAO/PAULO	Sao Paulo, Brazil	1	929
SASKATCH	Saskatchewan, Canada	1	929
SAUDI/ARAB	Saudi Arabia	1	929
SAY/EMIL	Emil Say	1	929
SCHOOL	Schools, except universities	56	930
SCI/ADVSRY	Science Advisory Commission	1	931
SEA	Locale of activity is aquatic	12	931
SEATO	Southeast Asia Treaty Organization	2	932
SEATTLE	Seattle, Washington	1	932
SEC/STATE	U.S. Secretary of State	1	932
SECT	Church, sect, religious group	74	932
SELBORNE/W	William Selborne	1	934

DESCRIPTOR		FREQUENCY	PAGE
SELF/OBS	Self-observation	2	934
SENATE	Senate	14	934
SENEGAL	Senegal	2	935
SENIOR	Seniority	5	935
SERV/IND	Service industry	49	935
SEX	Sexual behavior	6	936
SHASTRI/LB	Lal Bahadur Shastri	1	937
SHRIVER/S	Sargent Shriver	1	937
SIER/LEONE	Sierra Leone	3	937
SILVER	Silver standard	10	937
SIMUL	Scientific models	94	938
SKILL	Skill, practical competence (incompetence)	58	940
SMITH/ADAM	Adam Smith	2	942
SMITH/LEVR	Smith-Lever Act	1	942
SML/CO	Small company: 50 employees or less	38	942
SOC	Sociology	248	943
SOC/DEMPAR	Social Democratic Party	1	950
SOC/EXP	"Social" experimentation under uncontrolled conditions	14	950
SOC/INTEG	Social integration	25	950
SOC/WK	Social work, social service organization	35	951
SOCDEM/PAR	Social Democratic Party	1	952
SOCIALIST	Non-Communist socialist	22	952
SOCISM	Socialism	160	953
SOUTH/AFR	Union of South Africa	31	957
SOUTH/AMER	South America	3	958
SOUTH/CAR	South Carolina	1	958
SOUTH/US	Southern United States	4	958
SOVEREIGN	Sovereignty, home rule	63	958
SPACE	Outer space, space law	7	960
SPAIN	Spain	9	960
STALIN/J	Joseph Stalin	10	961
STAND/INT	Standardized interviews	3	961
STAT	Statistics	354	961
STERTYP	Stereotype	29	971
STRANGE	Estrangement, alienation, impersonality	4	972
STRASBOURG	Strasbourg plan	1	972
STRATA	Social strata	184	972
STRIKE	Strike of workers	3	977
STRUCT	Social structure	161	977
STYLE	Styles and terminology of scientific communication	7	982
SUDAN	Sudan	1	982
SUEZ	Suez Canal	1	982
SUFF	Suffrage	7	982
SUPEGO	Superego, conscience, responsibility	25	982
SUPREME/CT	Supreme Court	15	983
SWEDEN	Sweden	18	984
SWITZERLND	Switzerland	7	984
SYRIA	Syria	2	984
SYS/QU	Systematizing and analyzing questionnaires	2	984
T	Textbook	66	984
TAFT/HART	Taft-Hartley Act	1	986
TAFT/RA	Robert A. Taft	1	986
TAIWAN	Taiwan, Republic of China	1	986
TANEY/RB	Roger B. Taney	1	986
TANGANYIKA	Tanganyika	2	986
TANZANIA	Tanzania	10	987
TARIFFS	Tariffs	86	987
TASK	A specific operation within a work setting	39	989
TAX	Taxation	196	990
TEC/DEV	Development of technology	449	995
TECHNIC	Technocratic	9	1007
TECHRACY	Socio-political order dominated by technicians	6	1008
TENNESSEE	Tennessee	1	1008
TESTS	Theory and uses of tests and scales	2	1009
THAILAND	Thailand	8	1009
THIRD/WRLD	Third world—nonaligned nations	13	1009
TIME	Timing, time factor	20	1010

DESCRIPTOR		FREQUENCY	PAGE
TIME/SEQ	Chronology and genetic series of men, institutions, processes	118	1011
TOGO	Togo	1	1014
TOP/EX	Individuals holding executive positions	59	1014
TORY/PARTY	Tory Party	1	1015
TOTALISM	Totalitarianism	34	1016
TRADIT	Traditional or aristocratic	2	1017
TRAVEL	Travel and tourism	1	1017
TREATY	Treaties; international agreements	29	1017
TREND	Projection of individual and social trends	301	1018
TRIBUTE	Formal payments to dominant power by minor power group; racketeering	3	1026
TROBRIAND	Trobriand Islands and Islanders	1	1026
TROTSKY/L	Leon Trotsky	1	1026
TRUMAN/HS	President Harry S. Truman	7	1026
TUNISIA	Tunisia	3	1026
TURKEY	Turkey	13	1027
TV	Television	4	1027
TVA	Tennessee Valley Authority	4	1027
UAR	United Arab Republic	18	1027
UGANDA	Uganda	13	1028
UK	United Kingdom	258	1028
UN	United Nations	79	1035
UNESCO	United Nations Educational, Scientific, and Cultural Organization	7	1037
UNIFICA	Geopolitical unification	2	1038
UNPLAN/INT	Impromptu interview	1	1038
UNSF	United Nations Special Fund	1	1038
URBAN/RNWL	Urban renewal	12	1038
URUGUAY	Uruguay	2	1039
USSR	Union of Soviet Socialist Republics	182	1040
UTIL	Economic utility, usefulness	44	1045
UTOPIA	Envisioned general social conditions	15	1046
VENEZUELA	Venezuela	3	1046
VERMONT	Vermont	1	1047
VIETNAM	Vietnam in general	12	1047
VIETNAM/N	North Vietnam	1	1047
VIETNAM/S	South Vietnam	4	1047
VINER/J	Jacob Viner	1	1047
VIRGINIA	Virginia	1	1047
VOL/ASSN	Voluntary association	136	1047
WAR	War	145	1052
WARRN/EARL	Earl Warren	1	1055
WARSAW/PCT	Warsaw Treaty Organization	1	1056
WASHING/DC	Washington, D.C.	1	1056
WATER	Non-salt water	3	1056
WEALTH	Wealth, access to goods and services (poverty)	671	1056
WEAPON	Non-nuclear weapons	22	1074
WEBER/MAX	Max Weber	3	1074
WEIMAR/REP	Weimar Republic	3	1075
WELF/ST	Welfare state advocate	34	1075
WHO	World Health Organization	1	1076
WILSON/J	James Wilson	1	1077
WILSON/W	President Woodrow Wilson	1	1077
WORKER	Worker, laborer	450	1078
WORLD/BANK	World bank	3	1089
WORSHIP	Worship ritual	12	1089
WPA	Work Projects Administration	1	1089
WRITING	Writing	12	1090
WWI	World War I	1	1090
YANKEE/C	Yankee City—location of W. L. Warner's study of same name	1	1090
YEMEN	Yemen	1	1090
YUGOSLAVIA	Yugoslavia	14	1090
ZAMBIA	Zambia	1	1091
ZONING	Zoning regulations	1	1091

CATALOGUE OF DOCUMENTS

0001 AMERICAN ECONOMIC REVIEW.
EVANSTON, ILL: AMER ECO ASSOC.
A QUARTERLY CONTAINING ANALYTICAL REVIEWS OF CURRENT ECONOMIC PROBLEMS, APPROXIMATELY SIXTY BOOK REVIEWS, AND AN EXTENSIVE BIBLIOGRAPHY OF RECENT BOOKS. CONCERNED WITH FOREIGN AND DOMESTIC ISSUES AND NEW MODES OF ECONOMIC THEORY. CONTAINS LARGE SECTION OF COMMUNICATIONS FROM READERS INCLUDING A DEBATE AND REBUTTAL FORUM. EMPHASIS ON DOMESTIC INDUSTRIAL AND FINANCIAL FUNCTIONS. PUBLISHED SINCE 1911.

0002 INTERNATIONAL BIBLIOGRAPHY OF ECONOMICS.
LONDON: TAVISTOCK.
ANNUAL PUBLICATION, BEGUN IN 1925, WHICH LISTS WORLDWIDE PUBLICATIONS PERTAINING TO ECONOMICS. ENTRIES CLASSIFIED BY SUBJECT; CONTAINS BOOKS, ARTICLES, REPORTS, AND ALL TYPES OF SOURCES EXCEPT UNPUBLISHED MATERIALS. AUTHOR INDEX. TOPICS INCLUDE ECONOMIC HISTORY AND THOUGHT, MONEY AND FINANCE, PUBLIC ECONOMY, INCOME AND INCOME DISTRIBUTION, SOCIAL ECONOMICS AND POLICY, AND PRODUCTION.

0003 TEXTBOOKS IN PRINT.
NEW YORK: RR BOWKER.
ANNUAL GUIDE TO TEXTBOOKS FOR ALL GRADES ISSUED BY MAJOR PUBLISHERS. ARRANGED BY SUBJECT AND BY GRADE LEVEL. TITLE AND SUBJECT INDEX. FIRST ISSUED IN 1872.

0004 DOCUMENTATION ECONOMIQUE: REVUE BIBLIOGRAPHIQUE DE SYNTHESE.
PARIS: PR UNIV DE FRANCE.
QUARTERLY JOURNAL FIRST PUBLISHED IN 1947 WHICH SYNTHESIZES AND CLASSIFIES BY CONTENT PRINCIPAL ECONOMIC REVIEWS AND FRENCH AND FOREIGN ECONOMIC STUDIES. CONTAINS ABSTRACTS OF WORKS IN FIELDS OF POLITICS AND ECONOMICS; DEMOGRAPHY, AND ON TYPES OF ECONOMIC ACTIVITY: FINANCES; COMMUNICATION AND TRANSPORT INDUSTRIES; SOCIAL ASPECTS OF ECONOMIC PROCESSES; AND INTERNATIONAL ECONOMIC RELATIONS.

0005 ECONOMIC ABSTRACTS.
THE HAGUE: MARTINUS NIJHOFF.
SEMI-MONTHLY REVIEW OF ABSTRACTS ON ECONOMICS, FINANCE, TRADE AND INDUSTRY, MANAGEMENT, AND LABOR. ABSTRACTS BOOKS AND REPORTS. ARTICLES WRITTEN IN MANY LANGUAGES. ARRANGES ABSTRACTS BY SUBJECT. ISSUES DETAILED SUBJECT INDEX ANNUALLY. FIRST PUBLISHED IN 1953.

0006 LONDON TIMES OFFICIAL INDEX.
LONDON: LONDON TIMES, INC.
QUARTERLY, DETAILED SUBJECT INDEX TO NEWSPAPER ARTICLES. CUMULATED ANNUALLY. FIRST PUBLISHED 1906.

0007 ECONOMIC LIBRARY SELECTIONS.
BALTIMORE: JOHNS HOPKINS PRESS.
QUARTERLY ANNOTATED LISTING OF ECONOMICS BOOKS PUBLISHED IN ENGLISH. FIRST ISSUED IN 1957. SELECTIONS LIST ABOUT 160 NEW PUBLICATIONS IN EACH ISSUE. TOPICALLY CLASSIFIED.

0008 THE MIDDLE EAST AND NORTH AFRICA.
LONDON: EUROPA PUBLICATIONS.
SURVEY AND DIRECTORY OF 29 MIDDLE EASTERN AND NORTH AFRICAN COUNTRIES WITH GEOGRAPHICAL, HISTORICAL, AND ECONOMIC SURVEYS; CONCISE INFORMATION ABOUT POLITICAL, INDUSTRIAL, FINANCIAL, CULTURAL, AND EDUCATIONAL ORGANIZATIONS; AND A BIOGRAPHICAL SECTION OF PROMINENT PERSONALITIES OF THE REGION. BIENNIAL PUBLICATION FIRST ISSUED IN 1948.

0009 SOUTH AFRICAN JOURNAL OF ECONOMICS.
JOHANNESBURG: ECO SOC OF S AFR.
QUARTERLY JOURNAL OF THE ECONOMIC SOCIETY OF SOUTH AFRICA. PUBLISHED IN MARCH, JUNE, SEPTEMBER, AND DECEMBER SINCE 1932. INTENDED TO REPRESENT ALL SHADES OF OPINION AND TO SERVE AS A FORUM FOR FREE DISCUSSION OF ALL ECONOMIC QUESTIONS. EACH ISSUE CONTAINS ABOUT FIVE ARTICLES IN ENGLISH AND AFRIKAANS, REVIEWS AND NOTES ON BOOKS RECEIVED, TABULATED OFFICIAL STATISTICS, AND REVIEWS OF NEW RELEASES.

0010 THE MIDDLE EAST.
LONDON: EUROPA PUBLICATIONS.
ENCYCLOPEDIA OF MIDDLE EAST. SURVEYS POLITICAL, INDUSTRIAL, SCIENTIFIC, FINANCIAL, CULTURAL, AND ECONOMIC ORGANIZATIONS. INCLUDES BIBLIOGRAPHIES. PUBLISHED ANNUALLY.

0011 HISTORICAL ABSTRACTS.
SANTA BARBARA: CLIO, 1956, LC#56-56304.
AN ANNOTATED QUARTERLY REVIEWING WORLDWIDE PERIODICAL LITERATURE ON POLITICAL, DIPLOMATIC, ECONOMIC, SOCIAL, CULTURAL, AND INTELLECTUAL HISTORY ON THE PERIOD 1775-1945. INDEXED BY COMPUTER FROM A CODE OF MAIN CUES, AND ABSTRACTS ARRANGED IN SEVEN SUBJECT TOPICS. ANNUAL INDEX DIVIDED INTO A SUBJECT INDEX AND A GENERAL NAMES INDEX. FIRST PUBLICATION 1956.

0012 DEFENSE AGAINST INFLATION.
NEW YORK: COMM FOR ECO DEV, 1958, 95 PP.
POLICY STATEMENTS BY RESEARCH AND POLICY COMMITTEE AS AID TO CLEARER UNDERSTANDING OF STEPS TO BE TAKEN IN ACHIEVING SUSTAINED GROWTH OF AMERICAN ECONOMY. CONCERNED WITH EFFECTS OF LONG-RUN INFLATION ON WELFARE OF IMPORTANT GROUPS IN POPULATION AND ON GROWTH OF ECONOMY.

0013 "THE EMERGING COMMON MARKETS IN LATIN AMERICA."
FED. RES. BANK N.Y. MON. REV., 42 (SEPT. 60), 154-60.
DISCUSSES ECONOMIC INTEGRATION PROGRAM IN LATIN AMERICA. ANALYZES AGREEMENT TO ELIMINATE BARRIERS. APPRAISES STEPS TAKEN TO COORDINATE INDUSTRIAL DEVELOPMENT. CONSIDERS SIGNIFICANCE OF MONTEVIDEO TREATY IN DEVELOPMENT OF LATIN AMERICAN COMMON MARKET. PREDICTS INCREASE IN INVESTMENTS IN LATIN AMERICA.

0014 MEXICO; CINCUENTA ANOS DE REVOLUCION VOL. II.
BUENOS AIRES: FONDS CULTURA ECON, 1961, 570 PP.
COLLECTION OF ARTICLES ON MEXICAN DEVELOPMENT IN 20TH CENTURY. DISCUSSES SOCIAL STRUCTURE, URBANIZATION, INDUSTRIAL DEVELOPMENT, POLITICAL PARTIES, LABOR GROUPS, WELFARE PROGRAMS, HEALTH IMPROVEMENT, AND YOUTH.

0015 "BIBLIOGRAPHY ON EDUCATION AND ECONOMIC AND SOCIAL DEVELOPMENT (AMERICAN SOURCES)"
EDUCATION IN THE AMERICAS, 2 (1962), 1-62.
ANNOTATED SELECTION OF 197 ENTRIES PUBLISHED IN AND HAVING SPECIFIC REFERENCE TO LATIN AMERICA. INCLUDES DIRECTORY OF JOURNALS.

0016 "HIGHER EDUCATION AND ECONOMIC AND SOCIAL DEVELOPMENT IN LATIN AMERICA: A BIBLIOGRAPHY."
EDUCATION IN THE AMERICAS, 1 (1962), 1-39.
ANNOTATED SELECTION OF BOOKS AND ARTICLES. TOPICS INCLUDE SOCIO-ECONOMIC BACKGROUND OF HIGHER EDUCATION, LATIN AMERICAN UNIVERSITIES, UNIVERSITY AND ECONOMIC AND SOCIAL DEVELOPMENT, UNIVERSITY ASSOCIATIONS, INTERNATIONAL COOPERATION, DISCIPLINES OF STUDY, CONFERENCES, AND DIRECTORIES.

0017 ROUND TABLE ON EUROPE'S ROLE IN LATIN AMERICAN DEVELOPMENT.
BUENOS AIRES: INTER-AM DEV BANK, 1962, 88 PP.
TEXTS OF STATEMENTS BY PANELISTS AND EXTRACTS OF COMMENTS BY OTHER PARTICIPANTS IN THIRD MEETING OF BOARD OF GOVERNORS OF INTER-AMERICAN DEVELOPMENT BANK. ASSESSES ROLE OF EUROPE IN ECONOMIC DEVELOPMENT OF LATIN AMERICA, STIMULATING EXCHANGE OF IDEAS ON BEST WAY TO STRENGTHEN RELATIONS AND INCREASE EUROPE'S CONTRIBUTION.

0018 BRITISH AID.
LONDON: MIN OF OVERSEAS DEVEL, 1963, 260 PP.
OVERSEAS DEVELOPMENT INSTITUTE SURVEY OF BRITISH AID TO DEVELOPING COUNTRIES. COVERS BOTH GOVERNMENT AID AND PRIVATE CONTRIBUTIONS. CONTAINS SECTIONS ON FIELDS OF FINANCE, EDUCATION, AND TECHNICAL ASSISTANCE. HISTORICAL BACKGROUND ALSO OUTLINED.

0019 THE SPECIAL COMMONWEALTH AFRICAN ASSISTANCE PLAN.
LONDON: COMMONWEALTH ECO COMM, 1964, 75 PP.
REPORTS THREE YEARS' OPERATIONS OF SPECIAL COMMONWEALTH AFRICAN ASSISTANCE PLAN. NOTES BROADENING BASIS OF UK ASSISTANCE. SHOWS TREND TOWARD INCREASE OF HELP IN DEVELOPING NATIONS, PARTICULARLY IN AFRICA.

0020 INTERNATIONAL MONETARY ARRANGEMENTS: THE PROBLEM OF CHOICE.
PRINCETON: PRIN U, DEPT OF ECO, 1964, 121 PP., LC#64-25535.
REPORT ON DELIBERATIONS OF AN INTERNATIONAL STUDY GROUP OF 32 ECONOMISTS. PRESENTS BRIEF STATEMENT OF MAJOR PROBLEMS CONFRONTONG WORLD CONCERNING INTERNATIONAL MONETARY ARRANGEMENTS. EXAMINES PROBLEMS AND TECHNICAL LINKS BETWEEN DIFFERENT MANIFESTATIONS OF PROBLEMS. DESCRIBES FOUR BASIC APPROACHES PROPOSED FOR SOLUTION, AND CONCLUDES WITH CONSENSUS ON POLICY.

0021 ANALYSIS AND ASSESSMENT OF THE ECONOMIC EFFECTS: PUBLIC LAW 480 TITLE I PROGRAM TURKEY.
ANKARA: UNIV OF ANKARA, 1965, 525 PP.
EVALUATES TITLE I PROGRAM BETWEEN US AND INDIA SINCE 1954. REVIEWS TURKISH ECONOMIC POLICY FOR 40 YEARS PRIOR. TITLE I DEALS PRIMARILY WITH US LOANS TO HELP TURKS SET UP INDUSTRIAL AND AGRICULTURAL PROGRAMS, AND PROVIDES CERTAIN FOOD PRODUCTS. STUDY EMPHASIZES CONTROL AND DISTRIBUTION OF MONEY FROM US. COVERS IMPACT OF PROGRAM ON CITIES, PEOPLE, AND INTERNATIONAL SCENE.

0022 PEACE RESEARCH ABSTRACTS.
ONTARIO: CANADIAN PEACE RES INST, 1965.
MONTHLY PUBLICATION SINCE 1965, WHICH CONTAINS ABSTRACTS OF BOOKS AND ARTICLES. INCLUDES SUCH TOPICS AS DISARMAMENT, FALLOUT, AND ECONOMIC AID. APPROXIMATELY 12,000 ABSTRACTS PER YEAR.

0023 BRITISH DEVELOPMENT POLICIES: 1966 (PAMPHLET)
LONDON: OVERSEAS DEVELOPMT INST, 1966, 85 PP.
FIRST OF OVERSEAS DEVELOPMENT INSTITUTE'S REVIEWS OF BRITISH POLICIES: AID, PRIVATE INVESTMENT, AND TRADE. SHOWS HOW BRITAIN'S PRESENT FINANCIAL DIFFICULTIES HAVE CAST A SHADOW OVER DEVELOPMENT OVERSEAS. PUTS FORWARD PRACTICAL STEPS THAT CAN BE TAKEN TO STRENGTHEN BRITISH CONTRIBUTIONS.

0024 "PROTEST AGAINST SOVIET INDUSTRIALIZATION ILLS IN LITHUANIA* A MEMORANDUM."

BALTIC REV., (JAN. 67), 22-31.
A MEMORANDUM FROM LITHUANIAN SCIENTISTS AND MEN OF LETTERS TO THE HEADS OF THE LITHUANIAN COMMUNIST PARTY AND LITHUANIAN GOVERNMENT. PROTESTS AGAINST MOSCOW-DIRECTED INDUSTRIALIZATION OF LITHUANIA, WHICH FAILS TO TAKE ANY ACCOUNT OF LITHUANIAN ECOLOGY, RESOURCES, OR NEEDS AND WHICH HAS ALREADY RESULTED IN THE POLLUTION AND DESTRUCTION OF MANY LITHUANIAN RESOURCES, ESPECIALLY SEACOASTS, FOREST.

0025 "THE FEDERAL AGRICULTURAL STABILIZATION PROGRAM AND THE NEGRO."
COLUMBIA LAW REV., 67 (JUNE 67), 1121-1136.
DISCUSSES INJUSTICE OF EXCLUDING NEGROES FROM PROGRAM WHICH DETERMINES NUMBER OF ACRES OF BASIC COMMODITIES THAT EVERY FARMER CAN PLANT OR SELL. PRLGRAM IS AGRICULTURAL STABILIZATION AND CONSERVATION SERVICE AND IS CONTROLLED BY PREJUDICED SOUTHERN WHITES WHO DISCOUNT ALL NEGRO FARMERS, AND DO NOT ALLOW NEGRO REPRESENTATIVES TO THE SERVICE. BELIEVES CONGRESS SHOULD CHANGE SYSTEM VIA COURTS.

0026 "GOVERNMENT CONTROL OF LAND: PROTECTING THE I-KNOW-IT-WHEN-I-SEE-IT INTEREST."
NORTHWESTERN U. TRI-Q., 62 (JULY-AUG. 67), 428-461.
EVALUATES VIABILITY OF EMINENT DOMAIN AND ZONING IN ILLINOIS AS MEANS OF GOVERNMENT LAND-USE CONTROL. EXAMINES THESE TOOLS IN TERMS OF ADAPTABILITY IN MEETING GOVERNMENTAL NEEDS AND CONSISTENCY WITH TRADITIONS OF PRIVATE LAND OWNERSHIP. SUGGESTS A NEW TECHNIQUE WHICH WILL INJECT NEEDED FLEXIBILITY INTO THE PROCESS.

0027 "THE SIERRA CLUB, POLITICAL ACTIVITY, AND TAX EXEMPT CHARITABLE STATUS."
GEORGETOWN LAW J., 55 (MAY 67), 1128-1143.
ANALYZES CHARGE OF POLITICAL ACTIVITY OF SIERRA CLUB, WHICH FUNCTIONS TO PRESERVE, EXPLORE, AND ENJOY US NATURAL RESOURCES. IN 1966 THEIR TAX-EXEMPT STATUS WAS REVOKED FOR VIOLATING SECTION 501 OF INTERNAL REVENUE CODE FORBIDDING INFLUENCE OF LEGISLATION. FINDS LAW BIASED BECAUSE IT DISTINGUISHES AMOUNT OF POLITICAL ACTIVITY GROUP PARTICIPATES IN TO DETERMINE EXEMPT STATUS.

0028 "ANTITRUST VENUE: TRANSACTING BUSINESS UNDER THE CLAYTON ACT."
GEORGETOWN LAW J., 55 (MAY 67), 1066-1082.
ANALYZES DEVELOPING INCONSISTENCY IN INTERPRETING CLAUSE OF CLAYTON ACT THAT SAYS SUIT MAY BE BROUGHT IN DISTRICT WHERE CORPORATION "TRANSACTS BUSINESS." ADVOCATES UNIFORMITY OF INTERPRETATION BY DETAILED IMPACT ANALYSIS, WITH CERTAIN CRITERIA FOR MEASURING IMPACT CORPORATION HAS ON AREA.

0029 "IMPORT-EXPORT CLAUSE: A BLANKET PROHIBITION MISAPPLIED."
SOUTH CALIFORNIA LAW REVIEW, 40 (SPRING 67), 528-539.
ANALYZES LAWS DETERMINING WHETHER GOODS ARE IN PROCESS OF BEING EXPORTED FOR FOREIGN CONSUMPTION. FINDS SOME GOODS ARE TRANSPORTED FROM ONE STATE TO ANOTHER WITH IDEA OF BEING EXPORTED, BUT NEVER ARE, AND THUS STATES ARE DEPRIVED OF VALUABLE SOURCE OF REVENUE SINCE THEY CANNOT TAX THEM. CITES SEVERAL CASES TO PROVE THEORY.

0030 AARON H.J., BIRD R.M. ET AL.
FINANCING URBAN DEVELOPMENT IN MEXICO CITY: A CASE STUDY OF PROPERTY TAX, LAND USE, HOUSING, AND URBAN PLANNING.
CAMBRIDGE: HARVARD U PR, 1967, 440 PP.
ANALYSIS OF PROBLEMS IN FINANCING URBAN DEVELOPMENT IN MEXICO CITY AS REFLECTED IN TAX LAWS AND OTHER REGULATIONS. MEXICO CITY SHARES WITH OTHER LATIN AMERICAN CITIES PROBLEM OF RAPID POPULATION GROWTH AND UNPLANNED DEVELOPMENT. SUGGESTS REFORMS AND IMPROVEMENTS.

0031 ABELS J.
THE TRUMAN SCANDALS.
CHICAGO: HENRY REGNERY CO, 1956, 329 PP., LC#56-8261.
ASSERTS THAT TRUMAN ADMINISTRATION WAS THE MOST CORRUPT IN AMERICAN HISTORY. REPORTS ON RECORDS OF COURTS AND CONGRESSIONAL INVESTIGATIONS. DISCUSSES TAX FIXING IN EXCHANGE FOR CAMPAIGN CONTRIBUTIONS, AND BILLIONS IN GOVERNMENT CONTRACTS AND SURPLUS PROPERTY LADLED OUT TO POLITICAL FRIENDS AND HACKS.

0032 ABSHIRE D.M. ED., ALLEN R.V. ED.
NATIONAL SECURITY: POLITICAL, MILITARY, AND ECONOMIC STRATEGIES IN THE DECADE AHEAD.
NEW YORK: PRAEGER, 1963, 1039 PP., $10.00.
A NUMBER OF SPECIALISTS IN INTERNATIONAL POLITICS AND SCIENCE ATTEMPT TO MAKE A SYSTEMATIC INQUIRY INTO CRITICAL CHOICES WHICH CONFRONT U.S. AND THE FREE WORLD IN THE NEXT TEN YEARS. COVERS SINO-SOVIET STRATEGY, POLITICAL REQUIREMENTS FOR U.S. STRATEGY, MILITARY STRATEGIES, ECONOMIC STRATEGIES, AND HOW STRATEGY REQUIREMENTS CAN BE MET WITHIN FRAMEWORK OF FREE ECONOMY. OUTLINES IN DETAIL THE RANGE OF ALTERNATIVES UPON WHICH OUR NATIONAL SECURITY MAY DEPEND.

0033 ACHTERBERG E.
BERLINER HOCHFINANZ - KAISER, FURSTEN, MILLIONARE UM 1900.
FRANKFURT: FRITZ KNAPP VERLAG, 1965, 240 PP.
DISCUSSES "HIGH FINANCE" OF BANKING AND INDUSTRIAL TYCOONS IN BERLIN AT TURN OF LAST CENTURY. EXAMINES THEIR POLITICAL, SOCIAL, AND CULTURAL ACTIVITIES.

0034 ACKLEY G.
MACROECONOMIC THEORY.
NEW YORK: MACMILLAN, 1961, 597 PP., LC#61-5091.
COLLEGE TEXT ON MACROECONOMICS. DISCUSSES CONCEPTS AND MEASUREMENT IN MACROECONOMICS, NATIONAL INCOME, NATIONAL PRODUCT, CLASSICAL THEORIES, KEYNESIAN MACROECONOMICS, EMPLOYMENT, THE CONSUMPTION FUNCTION, INFLATION, INVESTMENT, AND ECONOMIC GROWTH.

0035 ADAMS D.W., SCHULMAN S.
"MINIFUNDIA IN AGRARIAN REFORM: A COLOMBIAN EXAMPLE."
LAND ECONOMICS, 43 (AUG. 67), 274-283.
SUGGESTS A TYPOLOGY FOR CLASSIFYING MINIFUNDIA IN LATIN AMERICA SO THAT REMEDIAL ALTERNATIVES MAY BE MORE EASILY IDENTIFIED. DESCRIBES SOCIO-ECONOMIC CHARACTERISTICS OF SEVERAL PROMINENT FORMS.

0036 ADAMS E.S.
"THE EXPANDING ROLE OF BANKS IN PUBLIC AFFAIRS."
BANKING, 60 (AUG. 67), 33-36.
PRESENTS RESULTS OF SURVEY ON ACTIVITIES OF BANKS AND BANK PERSONNEL IN PUBLIC AFFAIRS. BANKS ENCOURAGE STAFF PARTICIPATION IN COMMUNITY ORGANIZATIONS, CONTRIBUTE TO CIVIC CAUSES, PROVIDE LEADERSHIP IN LOCAL PLANNING AND DEVELOPMENT PROGRAMS, CONCERN THEMSELVES WITH SOCIAL PROBLEMS, AND WORK FOR LEGISLATION.

0037 ADAMS F.G., GRAYSON L.E.
"ECONOMIC CONSIDERATIONS OF AN ATLANTIC ENERGY POLICY."
KYKLOS, 16 (NO.2 63), 228-46.
COMPARES ENERGY ECONOMICS AND POLICY IN WESTERN EUROPE AND IN US AND PROPOSES EVENTUAL COORDINATION OF EUROPEAN AND AMERICAN ENERGY POLICIES WHICH WILL SEEK AN OBJECTIVE OF LOW COST FUEL AND FACILITATE ECONOMIC ADJUSTMENTS INVOLVED.

0038 ADAMS G.P. JR.
"COMPETITIVE ECONOMIC SYSTEMS."
NEW YORK: THOMAS Y CROWELL, 1955.
EXTENSIVELY ANNOTATED COLLECTION OF ABOUT 120 ITEMS INCLUDING COMPARATIVE ECONOMIC SYSTEMS, CAPITALISM, INDUSTRIALISM, BUSINESS CYCLE, STAGNATION, SOCIALISM, MARXISM, FASCISM, BRITISH SOCIALISM, COMPETITION BETWEEN SYSTEMS. RANGES FROM 1920 TO 1952. BOOK IS DIVIDED IN SAME SECTIONS AS ABOVE, GIVING FUNCTION, ORGANIZATION, AND CHIEF CHARACTERISTICS OF EACH SYSTEM.

0039 ADAMS R.N.
"ETHICS AND THE SOCIAL ANTHROPOLOGIST IN LATIN AMERICA."
AMER. BEHAVIORAL SCIENTIST, 10 (JUNE 67), 16-21.
DISCUSSES CONFLICTS OF INTEREST AND RESPONSIBILITIES AS WELL AS WIDELY DIVERGENT KINDS OF PEOPLE INVOLVED IN POLICY-MAKING IN DEVELOPING NATIONS. RELATES THESE DIFFERENCES AND CONFLICTS TO THE DIFFERING NATURE OF DEVELOPMENT IN NORTH AND LATIN AMERICA. HOPES THAT ANTHROPOLOGICAL SCHOLARS OF US AND LATIN AMERICA CAN FORM A SCHOLARLY COMMUNITY TO SOLVE PROBLEMS OF HEMISPHERE.

0040 ADERBIGDE A. ET AL.
"SYMPOSIUM ON WEST AFRICA INTEGRATION."
NIGERIAN J. ECON. SOC. STUD., 5 (MARCH 63), 1-40.
AFRICAN ANALYSES OF THE ECONOMIC BASES, RATIONALES, AND PROBLEMS OF WEST AFRICAN INTEGRATION, INCLUDING N. A. COX-GEORGE, 'ECONOMIC STRUCTURES OF WEST AFRICAN COUNTRIES,' S. A. LUKO, 'PROBLEMS OF FINANCIAL AND MONETARY INTEGRATION,' J. H. GERVES, 'VERTICAL INTEGRATION WITH EUROPE.'

0041 ADISESHIAN M.
"EDUCATION AND DEVELOPMENT."
COUNCIL ON WORLD TENSIONS, 1962, 148-162.
DISCUSSES DIRECT AND INDIRECT EFFECTS OF LEVEL OF EDUCATION ON ECONOMIC DEVELOPMENT IN BOTH DEVELOPED AND UNDERDEVELOPED COUNTRIES. PROPOSES TECHNOLOGICAL, ORGANIZATIONAL, AND FINANCIAL ASSISTANCE BY STATES OF THE WORLD. SEES EDUCATION AS POTENTIAL KEY TO SOCIO-ECONOMIC AND POLITICAL UPLIFTING OF THE UNDERDEVELOPED NATIONS.

0042 ADLER J.H. ED.
CAPITAL MOVEMENTS AND ECONOMIC DEVELOPMENT.
NEW YORK: ST MARTIN'S PRESS, 1967, 498 PP., LC#67-13679.
COLLECTION OF PAPERS ON CAPITAL MOVEMENTS AND ECONOMIC DEVELOPMENT. CALLS FOR A RE-EVALUATION OF ECONOMIC THEORY DEALING WITH INTERNATIONAL CAPITAL MOVEMENTS. FINDS THAT NEO-CLASSICAL THEORY OF INTERNATIONAL CAPITAL MOVEMENTS ARE INADEQUATE TO EXPLAIN FLOW OF CAPITAL TO DEVELOPING COUNTRIES.

0043 ADMINISTRATIVE STAFF COLLEGE
THE ACCOUNTABILITY OF GOVERNMENT DEPARTMENTS (PAMPHLET) (REV. ED.)
HENLEY-ON-THAMES: ADMIN STAFF C, 1966, 49 PP.
DISCUSSES CONCEPT OF ACCOUNTABILITY OR PROCEDURE OF

MINISTER'S BEING CALLED UPON BY PARLIAMENT TO JUSTIFY HIS ACTIONS OR ADVICE. INCLUDES PERSONS ACCOUNTABLE AND PROCESS AS IT HAS DEVELOPED IN DIFFERENT DEPARTMENTS.

0044 ADORNO T.W.
THE AUTHORITARIAN PERSONALITY.
NEW YORK: HARPER & ROW, 1950, 989 PP.
STUDIES SOCIAL DISCRIMINATION AND ROLE OF A "NEW SPECIES" CALLED THE AUTHORITARIAN TYPE OF MAN. IN CONTRAST TO OLD-STYLE BIGOT, HE COMBINES SKILLS AND IDEAS TYPICAL OF HIGHLY INDUSTRIALIZED SOCIETY WITH IRRATIONAL OR ANTI-RATIONAL BELIEFS. STUDY APPROACHES PROBLEM THROUGH SOCIO-PSYCHOLOGICAL RESEARCH. SHOWS BEARING OF SEX, RELIGION, GENETICS, POLITICS, AND ECONOMICS UPON ATTITUDES.

0045 AFFELDT R.J.
"THE INDEPENDENT LABOR UNION AND THE GOOD LIFE."
G. WASH. LAW REV., 35 (JUNE 67), 869-906.
CALLS UPON COURTS TO VIEW POWER REALISTICALLY AS A PROCESS RATHER THAN A CONCEPT. ATTEMPTS TO DEMONSTRATE THAT THE LOCAL UNION IS INDEPENDENT IN NAME ONLY; THIS IN REALITY IT IS UNDER THE ABSOLUTE POWER OF THE INTERNATIONAL UNION; THAT MOST COURTS, BY APPLYING RESTRICTED COMMON LAW PRINCIPLES OF AGENCY IN MATTERS OF UNION JURISDICTION, HAVE ESTABLISHED A POWERFUL UNION OF IRRESPONSIBILITY.

0046 AFRICAN BIBLIOGRAPHIC CENTER
"AFRICAN ECONOMIC AFFAIRS: A SELECT BIBLIOGRAPHICAL SURVEY, 1965-1966."
AFR. BIBLIOG. CTR., SPEC. SERIES, 4 (AUG. 66), 1-46.
COMPILED AS A GUIDE FOR STUDY AND RESEARCH IN THE FIELD OF AFRICAN ECONOMICS AND RELATED SUBJECTS. BIBLIOGRAPHY OF 557 UNANNOTATED ENTRIES CONSISTING OF DOCUMENTS PUBLISHED BY GOVERNMENTS AND INTERNATIONAL ORGANIZATIONS, SCHOLARLY BOOKS ND ARTICLES, FROM 1965-1966. SOURCES IN ENGLISH, FRENCH, AND GERMAN COVER MAJOR TOPICS OF ECONOMIC DEVELOPMENT, ECONOMIC CONDITIONS AND POLICY, AND FOREIGN ASSISTANCE. AUTHOR INDEX.

0047 AFRICAN BIBLIOGRAPHIC CENTER
"AFRICAN ECONOMIC AFFAIRS: A SELECT BIBLIOGRAPHICAL SURVEY, 1965-1966; SUPPLEMENTS NUMBERS 1-3."
AFR. BIBLIOG. CTR., SPEC. SERIES, 4 (SEPT. 66), 1-32, 1-52.
THREE INDIVIDUAL SUPPLEMENTS ISSUED TO BIBLIOGRAPHY OF SAME TITLE. SUPPLEMENTS CONTAIN 388, 233, AND 459 ENTRIES, RESPECTIVELY. PARTIALLY ANNOTATED LISTINGS COVER FOREIGN AND DOMESTIC PUBLICATIONS FROM 1963-66 IN FIELD OF AFRICAN ECONOMICS. MATERIALS DIVIDED INTO A GENERAL AND A GEOGRAPHIC SECTION; ALL HAVE AUTHOR INDEXES. RUSSIAN TITLES TRANSLITERATED.

0048 AGARWAL R.C.
STATE ENTERPRISE IN INDIA.
ALLAHABAD: CHAITANYA PUBL HSE, 1961, 271 PP.
ANALYZES PROBLEMS RELATING TO PUBLIC ASPECTS OF INDIA'S CORPORATIONS, THEIR GROWTH AND OPERATIONS SINCE 1948. FEELS PUBLIC ENTERPRISE IS PERMANENT INSTITUTION IN INDIA, BUT CRITICIZES PROGRAM OF TOO RAPID INDUSTRIALIZATION. USES RR AND UTILITIES INDUSTRIES TO POINT OUT GAPS AND FLAWS IN DEVELOPMENT. BIBLIOGRAPHY OF SPECIFIC WORKS ON SUBJECT IN INDIA AND UK.

0049 AGGARWALA R.N.
FINANCIAL COMMITTEES OF THE INDIAN PARLIAMENT: A STUDY IN PARLIAMENTARY CONTROL OVER PUBLIC EXPENDITURE.
NEW DELHI: S CHAND AND CO, 1966, 490 PP.
DESCRIBES INDIAN SYSTEM OF PARLIAMENTARY CONTROL OVER PUBLIC EXPENDITURE THROUGH SPECIAL COMMITTEES FROM 1950 TO 1964. DISCUSSES RESULTS OF THEIR CONTROL AND COMPARES THEM TO RESULTS OF ENGLISH PARLIAMENTARY COMMITTEES.

0050 AGUILAR M.A.
"?UNA OEA MAS FUERTE O UNA AMERICA LATINA MAS DEBIL?"
CUADERNOS AMERICANOS, (MAY-JUNE 67), 7-26.
SURVEYS ACTIONS OF OAS SINCE 1965 CONCERNING SEVERAL LATIN AMERICAN COUNTRIES, ARGENTINA IN PARTICULAR. SEES US AS IMPERIALISTIC CONTROLLING FORCE. DISCUSSES NEED FOR ECONOMIC, CULTURAL, POLITICAL, AND MILITARY INTEGRATION WITH LATIN AMERICAN STATES. EXAMINES CHANGES IN US POLICY SINCE DEATH OF KENNEDY.

0051 AHMAD M.
THE CIVIL SERVANT IN PAKISTAN.
LONDON: OXFORD U PR, 1964, 288 PP.
SOCIOLOGICAL STUDY OF PUBLIC SERVANTS IN PAKISTAN. SEEKS TO FIND FROM WHICH SOCIAL CLASSES PUBLIC SERVANTS ARE MAINLY DRAWN. ATTEMPTS TO ASCERTAIN ATTITUDE OF PUBLIC SERVANTS. INVESTIGATES IN-SERVICE RELATIONS, STUDYING RELATIONSHIP BETWEEN SUPERIOR AND SUBORDINATE AT VARIOUS LEVELS.

0052 AHMED J.
NATURAL RESOURCES IN LOW INCOME COUNTRIES: AN ANALYTICAL SURVEY OF SOCIO-ECONOMIC RESEARCH (PAMPHLET)
PITTSBURGH: UNIVERSITY PR, 1960, 118 PP., LC#60-14674.
INVENTORY AND CRITICAL ANALYSIS OF RESEARCH DONE ON UTILIZATION OF NATURAL RESOURCES IN LOW-INCOME COUNTRIES ARRANGED BY TYPE OF RESOURCE AND COUNTRY. INCLUDES FIVE HUNDRED REPORTS FROM 1940 TO 1959 IN SEVERAL LANGUAGES.

0053 AHN L.A.
FUNFZIG JAHRE ZWISCHEN INFLATION UND DEFLATION.
TUBINGEN: J C B MOHR, 1963, 247 PP.
DISCUSSES INFLATIONARY AND DEFLATIONARY TENDENCIES IN GERMANY SINCE WWI. EXAMINES CRISIS IN 1929, CONFLICT OVER DOLLAR, AND GOLD CRISES IN RECENT YEARS.

0054 AITKEN H. ED.
THE STATE AND ECONOMIC GROWTH.
NEW YORK: SOC. SCI. RES. COUNCIL, 1959, 389 PP.
ANALYSIS OF NATION STATE'S PROMOTION OF ECONOMIC DEVELOPMENT. FRAMEWORK CONSISTS OF THREE CONTINUA: GRADIENT OF EXPANSIONISM; DEPENDENCE ON CAPITAL AND ON EXTERNAL MARKETS; AND ISTRIBUTION OF INDUCED OR AUTONOMOUS DECISION-MAKING POWERS.

0055 AITKEN H.G., DEUTSCH J.J., MAKINTOSH W.A.
THE AMERICAN ECONOMIC IMPACT ON CANADA.
DURHAM: DUKE U PR, 1959, 176 PP., LC#59-10916.
CONCERNED WITH ECONOMIC POLICIES OF US AND CANADA AND HOW THEY INFLUENCE EACH OTHER. DISCUSSES CANADIAN CONCERN OVER RISING FLOW OF INVESTMENT FUNDS FROM US AND RESULTING EFFECTS AND REPERCUSSIONS.

0056 ALBAUM G.
"INFORMATION FLOW AND DECENTRALIZED DECISION MAKING IN MARKETING."
CALIF. MANAGEMENT REV., 9 (SUMMER 67), 59-70.
DISCUSSES NECESSITY FOR INTERDEPARTMENTAL MARKETING INFORMATION SYSTEMS IN BUSINESSES WHERE DECISION-MAKING POWER IS NOT CENTRALIZED. NOTES IMPORTANT ASPECTS OF SYSTEM DESIGN AND GIVES SAMPLE SYSTEM. DISCUSSES INTEGRATION OF MARKETING INFORMATION SYSTEM WITH MASTER COMPANY FLOW SYSTEM HANDLING VARIOUS KINDS OF DATA.

0057 ALDERSON W.
DYNAMIC MARKETING BEHAVIOR.
HOMEWOOD: RICHARD IRWIN, 1965, 383 PP., LC#65-27839.
DISCUSSES FLOW OF INFORMATION, NEGOTIATED PRICES AND MARKET DETERMINED PRICES, ADVERTISING POLICIES, CONSUMER BEHAVIOR, RETAILING, COOPERATION AND CONFLICT IN MARKETING CHANNELS, TECHNOLOGICAL CHANGES, AND GENERAL METHODS IN MANAGEMENT SCIENCE.

0058 ALEXANDER G.J.
HONESTY AND COMPETITION: FALSE-ADVERTISING LAW AND POLICY UNDER FTC ADMINISTRATION.
SYRACUSE: SYRACUSE U PRESS, 1967, 315 PP., LC#67-26213.
STUDIES FEDERAL TRADE COMMISSION'S INTERDICTION OF DECEPTION IN ADVERTISING. EXAMINES COMMISSION'S ACTIONS FROM TWO PERSPECTIVES: AVOIDING CONSUMER DECEPTION AND ENHANCING COMPETITION. FINDS THAT FTC, WHILE OPPOSED TO FRAUD, OFTEN OVERLOOKS COMPLEX INTERRELATIONSHIP BETWEEN COMPETITION AND DECEPTION OF CONSUMER. FEELS THAT FTC SHOULD NOT DETERMINE AMOUNT OF INFORMATION NECESSARY FOR CONSUMERS' DECISIONS.

0059 ALEXANDER R.J.
ORGANIZED LABOR IN LATIN AMERICA.
NEW YORK: FREE PRESS OF GLENCOE, 1965, 274 PP., LC#65-23024.
SYMPATHETIC ACCOUNT OF DEVELOPMENT AND NATIONAL ROLE OF LATIN AMERICAN ORGANIZED LABOR. GENERAL STUDIES OF ECONOMIC AND SOCIAL BACKGROUND OF LABOR MOVEMENT, POLITICALIZATION OF MOVEMENT, AND COLLECTIVE BARGAINING AND ITS SUBSTITUTES. ANALYSES OF LABOR MOVEMENT IN 13 INDIVIDUAL COUNTRIES. SHORT BIBLIOGRAPHICAL NOTE.

0060 ALEXANDER R.J.
"'THIRD FORCE' IN WORLD COMMUNISM?"
NEW POLITICS, 6 (WINTER 67), 72-79.
MAINTAINS THAT THIRD BLOC OF COMMUNIST POWER IS DEVELOPING IN CUBA UNDER CASTRO. STATES REASONS WHY CUBAN COMMUNISM IS PART OF INTERNATIONAL MOVEMENT AND WHAT IT IS DOING TO ASSERT ITS LEADERSHIP. DISCUSSES CUBAN-INSPIRED REVOLUTIONARY MOVEMENTS IN LATIN AMERICA AND THROUGHOUT WORLD. POINTS OUT THAT CASTRO MAY BE VERY RELUCTANT TO GIVE UP HIS BID FOR WORLD POWER TO SOVIET CONTROL.

0061 ALEXANDER Y.
INTERNATIONAL TECHNICAL ASSISTANCE EXPERTS* A CASE STUDY OF THE U.N. EXPERIENCE.
NEW YORK: FREDERICK PRAEGER, 1966, 223 PP., LC#66-21767.
STUDY OF THE FUNCTIONS AND CHARACTERISTICS OF TECHNICAL ASSISTANCE AGENCIES, PROGRAMS AND PERSONNEL. FOCUS ON OBJECTIVES, FINANCING, MACHINERY, AND PLANNING OF UN PROGRAMS FOR TECHNICAL CO-OPERATION. FURTHER ANALYSIS OF PROBLEMS OF DETERMINING QUALIFICATIONS FOR ASSISTANCE PERSONNEL AND THEIR RECRUITMENT. INTERVIEWS WITHIN UN PERSONNEL, ND UN DOCUMENTS USED; DATA REPORTED IN APPENDICES.

0062 ALEXANDER Y.
INTERNATIONAL TECHNICAL ASSISTANCE EXPERTS: A CASE STUDY OF THE U.N. EXPERIENCE.
NEW YORK: FREDERICK PRAEGER, 1966, 223 PP., LC#66-21767.
EXAMINATION OF SPECIAL CHARACTERISTICS OF TECHNICAL

ASSISTANCE EXPERTS, STANDARDS APPLIED, AND MACHINERY AND PROCEDURES UTILIZED IN THEIR RECRUITMENT. CONCLUDES THAT VAST MAJORITY OF PERSONNEL HAVE PERFORMED THEIR ASSIGNMENTS SATISFACTORILY.

0063 ALEXANDROWICZ C.H.
INTERNATIONAL ECONOMIC ORGANIZATION.
LONDON: STEVENS, 1952, 263 PP.
VIEWS PERMANENT INTERNATIONAL ORGANIZATIONS FOR THEIR NATIONAL AND INTERNATIONAL PURPOSE. STRESSES THAT INTER-CONNECTED ACTIVITIES OF PRIVATE AND PUBLIC AGENCIES REQUIRE CONSIDERATION OF BOTH LAW AND ECONOMICS.

0064 ALEXANDROWICZ C.H.
WORLD ECONOMIC AGENCIES: LAW AND PRACTICE.
LONDON: STEVENS, 1962, 310 PP.
DISCUSSES FORMATION AND OPERATION OF WORLD ECONOMIC AGENCIES AS THEY INFLUENCE INTERNATIONAL LAW. EMPHASIZES INTERNAL STRUCTURE OF ORGANIZATIONS, DISTRIBUTION OF POWER, CONSEQUENCES OF UNIVERSAL MEMBERSHIP, LAW-PROMOTING FUNCTIONS, AND SIGNIFICANCE OF ADMINISTRATIVE PROCEDURES AND JUSTICE.

0065 ALFRED H. ED.
PUBLIC OWNERSHIP IN THE USA: GOALS AND PRIORITIES.
NEW YORK: PEACE PUBL, 1961, 238 PP., LC#61-14075.
ANALYZES DEVELOPMENT AND EFFECTIVENESS OF PUBLICLY OWNED PROJECTS IN US. ASSERTS PRIMACY OF SOCIAL SERVICES (THROUGH PUBLIC OWNERSHIP WHEN DESIRED BY VOTERS) AS GOAL OF CAPITALISTIC SYSTEM. CONSTITUTION SAID TO PROVIDE FOR NATIONAL PLANNING.

0066 ALI S., JONES G.N.
PLANNING, DEVELOPMENT AND CHANGE: AN ANNOTATED BIBLIOGRAPHY ON DEVELOPMENTAL ADMINISTRATION.
BALTIMORE: J HOPKINS SCHOOL HYG, 1966, 217 PP.
ANNOTATED BIBLIOGRAPHY OF 655 BOOKS, JOURNAL ARTICLES, AND GOVERNMENT PUBLICATIONS IN ENGLISH ON TOPICS OF PLANNING AND DEVELOPMENT IN EMERGING NATIONS, AND PROCESS OF CHANGE IN ALL SOCIETIES. ARRANGED ACCORDING TO TOPICS OF RESEARCH METHODOLOGY AND TYPES OF PLANNING; ECONOMIC, SOCIAL, POLITICAL, AND ADMINISTRATIVE DEVELOPMENT; AND ORGANIZATIONAL THEORY AND BEHAVIOR.

0067 ALIBER R.Z.
THE FUTURE OF THE DOLLAR AS AN INTERNATIONAL CURRENCY.
NEW YORK: FREDERICK PRAEGER, 1966, 169 PP., LC#65-24945.
TRACES DEVELOPMENT OF DOLLAR AS INTERNATIONAL CURRENCY. EXAMINES PROBLEMS IN INTERNATIONAL-RESERVE ARRANGEMENTS AND ALTERNATIVE APPROACHES TO INTERNATIONAL FINANCIAL ARRANGEMENTS.

0068 ALKHIMOV V.S.
"SOVIET FOREIGN TRADE CHANNELS."
A. AMER. POLIT. SOC. SCI., 324 (JULY 59), 30-36.
DISCUSSES RAPID GROWTH OF THE USSR AS THE TRADING POWER AND AS THE SOURCE OF CREDIT. REVEALS CHARACTERISTICS AND DIRECTION OF THE SOVIET FOREIGN TRADE AND EXPLORES POSSIBILITIES FOR FURTHER DEVELOPMENT OF TRADE WITH THE USA AND REST OF THE WORLD IN GENERAL.

0069 ALLEN G.
"NATIONAL FARMERS UNION AS A PRESSURE GROUP: II."
CONGRESSIONAL RECORD, 95 (JUNE 59), 321-329.
DISCUSSES ACCOMPLISHMENTS OF NATIONAL FARMERS' UNION SINCE 1939. CONCLUDES THAT FUTURE OF ORGANIZATION CANNOT EXPECT TO BE AS SUCCESSFUL BECAUSE NOW MINISTRY OF AGRICULTURE IS LESS KINDLY DISPOSED AND WILL SUBJECT IT TO RIGOROUS CRITICISM AND INVESTIGATION.

0070 ALLEN R.G.
MACRO-ECONOMIC THEORY: A MATHEMATICAL TREATMENT.
NEW YORK: ST MARTIN'S PRESS, 1967, 420 PP.
DISCUSSES SHORT AND LONG TERM MACRO-MODELS OF EQUILIBRIUM AND DISEQUILIBRIUM. TEXT IS GEARED TO ADVANCED UNDERGRADUATE AND FIRST-YEAR GRADUATE LEVEL.

0071 ALLEN R.L.
SOVIET INFLUENCE IN LATIN AMERICA.
WASHINGTON: PUBL. AFF. PR., 1959, 108 PP.
DURING THE POST-WAR PERIOD, THE INCREASED RUSSIAN-LATIN AMERICAN TRADE HAS LED TO INCREASED SOVIET INFLUENCE OVER LATIN AMERICAN NATIONS' AFFAIRS. WITHOUT EMPHASIZING THE POLITICAL ASPECTS OF THE RELATIONSHIP, GIVES A DETAILED ANALYSIS OF THE INCREASED TRADE OVER THE PAST DECADE.

0072 ALLEN R.L.
SOVIET ECONOMIC WARFARE.
WASHINGTON: PUB. AFF. PR., 1960, 293 PP., $5.00.
PRESENTS THE MAJOR FEATURES OF RUSSIAN ECONOMIC RELATIONS WITH FOREIGN COUNTRIES. GIVES A CONCEPTUAL FRAMEWORK FOR SYSTEMATIC ECONOMIC ANALYSIS OF GOVERNMENT TRADING, WITHIN THE PURVIEW OF ECONOMIC AND TECHNICAL ASSISTANCE. CONCLUDES THAT PRIVATE INVESTMENT IN FOREIGN TRADE PROMOTES HUMAN VALUES.

0073 ALLEN W.R. ED., ALLEN C.L. ED.
FOREIGN TRADE AND FINANCE.
NEW YORK: MACMILLAN, 1959, 500 PP., LC#59-7442.
ESSAYS DISCUSSING PROBLEMS IN INTERNATIONAL ECONOMIC EQUILIBRIUM AND THEIR RELATION TO GENERAL POLICY ISSUES IN TRADE AND FINANCE PROBLEMS. DISCUSS RELATIONSHIP BETWEEN DOMESTIC AND INTERNATIONAL EQUILIBRIUM AND MEANS OF ADJUSTMENT TO EQUILIBRIUM. EMPHASIZE ANALYTICAL APPROACH TO SPECIFIC PROBLEMS BUT ARE NOT TECHNICAL OR DETAILED. DIRECTED TOWARD STUDENTS AND NONSPECIALISTS.

0074 ALLEN W.R., E
INTERNATIONAL TRADE THEORY: HUME TO OHLIN.
NEW YORK: RANDOM HOUSE, INC, 1965, 210 PP., LC#65-23330.
EXCERPTS FROM MAJOR WRITINGS ON INTERNATIONAL, TRADE THEORY FROM DAVID HUME TO BERTIL OHLIN. EMPHASIZES BASSES OF AND GAINS DERIVED FROM INTERNATIONAL TRADE. INTRODUCTION PROVIDES DETAILED, TECHNICAL COMMENTARY ON THEORIES DISCUSSED IN EXCERPTS.

0075 ALLISON D.
"THE GROWTH OF IDEAS."
INT SCIENCE AND TECHNOLOGY, 67 (JULY 67), 24-32.
DISCUSSES TWO REPORTS RELATING TO ASPECTS OF THE PROCESS OF INVENTION AND INNOVATION. ONE STUDY EXAMINED WEAPONS SYSTEMS AND EVENTS WHICH CONTRIBUTED TO THEIR DEVELOPMENT. SECOND STUDY EXAMINED TEN TECHNOLOGICAL ACCOMPLISHMENTS, INCLUDING THE DEVELOPMENT OF SILICONES AND PYROCERAM GLASS, AND THE "RESEARCH-ENGINEERING INTERACTIONS" WHICH CONTRIBUTED TO THOSE DEVELOPMENTS.

0076 ALNASRAWI A.
FINANCING ECONOMIC DEVELOPMENT IN IRAQ.
NEW YORK: FREDERICK PRAEGER, 1967, 188 PP., LC#66-26557.
COMPLETE ANALYSIS OF IMPACT OF OIL PRODUCTION ON ECONOMY AND ECONOMIC PLANNING. CITES FIGURES TO SUPPORT ARGUMENTS, EVALUATES ECONOMIC POLICY FOLLOWED BY GOVERNMENT OF IRAQ. DISCUSSES TAXATION, AGRICULTURE, FINANCIAL SYSTEM, PROGNOSIS FOR INDUSTRIALIZATION.

0077 ALPANDER G.G.
"ENTREPRENEURS AND PRIVATE ENTERPRISE IN TURKEY."
BUSINESS TOPICS, 15 (SPRING 67), 59-68.
DISCUSSES DEVELOPMENT OF PRIVATE ENTERPRISE IN TURKEY, WHERE PRIVATE CORPORATE ENTERPRISE HAS HAD LITTLE RECEPTIVITY; EXAMINES REASONS WHY. FOCUSES ON FIRMS THAT DO EXIST AND TREATS GROWTH PATTERNS, GEOGRAPHICAL DISTRIBUTION, PUBLIC POLICY, WHOLESALING, AND RETAILING. ANALYZES SOCIOLOGICAL AND BEHAVIORAL CHARACTERISTICS OF ENTREPRENEURS.

0078 ALPERT P.
"ECONOMIC POLICIES AND PLANNING IN NEWLY INDEPENDENT AFRICA."
AMER. BEHAV. SCI., 5 (APRIL 62), 15-17.
ATTRIBUTES PRESENT SITUATION IN NEW AFRICAN STATES TO THEIR COLONIAL HERITAGE, WHICH HAS RESULTED IN A LACK OF QUALIFIED PERSONNEL. THERE IS, HOWEVER, PROGRESS IN THE FIELD OF ECONOMIC DEVELOPMENT.

0079 ALPERT P.
ECONOMIC DEVELOPMENT.
NEW YORK: FREE PRESS OF GLENCOE, 1963, 308 PP., LC#63-8412.
STUDIES ECONOMIC DEVELOPMENT VIEWED IN A BROAD CONTEXT. DISCUSSES CONCEPTS IN BOTH DOMESTIC AND INTERNATIONAL SETTINGS. INTERNATIONAL FACTORS SUCH AS TERMS OF TRADE, PRIVATE INVESTMENT, AND PUBLIC AID ARE SEEN AS CRUCIAL VARIABLES IN THE DEVELOPMENT PICTURE.

0080 ALTMAN G.T.
INVISIBLE BARRIER: THE OPTIMUM GROWTH CURVE.
NEW YORK TILDEN PRESS, 1962, 223 PP.
"TAX SPECIALIST'S ANALYSIS OF BUSINESS CYCLE" STUDIES ECONOMY WITH IDEA THAT INVESTMENT IS PRIME MOVER OF CAPITAL AND WHOLE ECONOMY. OUTLINES TAX SYSTEM TO COMPENSATE FOR BUSINESS FLUCTUATIONS. GIVES GENERAL ANALYSIS OF PAST US CYCLES AND DETAILED STUDY SINCE 1920'S.

0081 ALVES V.
"FOREIGN CAPITAL IN BRAZIL."
INTERNATIONAL SOCIALIST JOURN. 21 (JUNE 67), 367-381.
DISCUSSES FOREIGN ENTERPRISES INVESTING CAPITAL AND MAKING PROFITS WHICH, IF REINVESTED IN SAME COUNTRY, CAN BECOME IMPORTANT TO NATIONAL ECONOMY. SUCH INVESTORS, ONE BEING US, ARE PERMANENT THREATS TO UNDERDEVELOPED COUNTRIES. EXAMINES SITUATION IN BRAZIL CONCERNING FOREIGN INVESTMENT. MAINTAINS THAT LATIN AMERICA MUST GET AID FROM EUROPE TO STOP CAPITALIST EXPLOITATION.

0082 AMER ENTERPRISE INST FOR PUBL
INTERNATIONAL PAYMENTS PROBLEM.
WASHINGTON: AMER ENTERPRISE INST, 1966, 203 PP., LC#66-19601
COLLECTION OF ESSAYS AND DISCUSSIONS THEREOF ON INTERNATIONAL MONETARY SYSTEMS AND PROBLEM OF INTERNATIONAL ECONOMIC EQUILIBRIUM.

0083 AMER ENTERPRISE INST PUB POL

SIGNIFICANT ISSUES IN ECONOMIC AID TO DEVELOPING COUNTRIES.
MENLO PARK: STANFORD U RES INST, 1960, 75 PP., LC#60-1291.
DETAILED ANALYSIS OF PROGRAMS, TRENDS, AND ISSUES THAT HAVE BEEN CENTRALLY INVOLVED IN US POLICIES ON ECONOMIC AID TO PROMOTE PROGRESS IN UNDERDEVELOPED COUNTRIES. FOCUSES ON SEVERAL SPECIFIC SITUATIONS OCCURRING DURING POST-WWII ERA; CONSIDERS FOREIGN AID ACTIVITIES OF ALLIES OF US AND OF INTERNATIONAL AGENCIES.

0084 AMERASINGHE C.F.
"SOME LEGAL PROBLEMS OF STATE TRADING IN SOUTHEAST ASIA."
VANDERBILT LAW REV., 20 (MAR. 67), 257-277.
DISCUSSES LEGAL PROBLEMS OF STATE TRADING IN SOUTHEAST ASIA. CONCERNED WITH ASPECTS OF THE INTERNATIONAL LEGAL PROBLEMS WHICH ARISE WHERE ONE PARTY IN THE TRADING TRANSACTION IS THE STATE OR A STATE ENTITY.

0085 AMERICAN ASSEMBLY COLUMBIA U
THE UNITED STATES AND THE PHILIPPINES.
ENGLEWOOD CLIFFS: PRENTICE HALL, 1966, 179 PP., LC#66-22802.
SEVEN ESSAYS ANALYZING "SPECIAL RELATIONSHIP" EXISTING BETWEEN THE TWO NATIONS: COLONIAL RELATIONSHIP, PHILIPPINE SOCIETY IN TRANSITION, PHILIPPINE FOREIGN POLICY, MUTUAL SECURITY, ROLE OF AMERICAN INVESTMENT AND TRADE, AND THE PROBLEMS OF DECOLONIALIZATION.

0086 AMERICAN ECONOMIC ASSOCIATION
THE JOURNAL OF ECONOMIC ABSTRACTS.
EVANSTON, ILL: AMER ECO ASSOC.
FIRST PUBLISHED IN 1963, THIS JOURNAL IS DESIGNED TO ASSIST ECONOMISTS AROUND THE WORLD IN BECOMING ACQUAINTED WITH METHOD AND CONCLUSIONS OF RECENT RESEARCH REPORTED IN GENERAL ECONOMIC JOURNALS. PUBLISHED QUARTERLY. ABSTRACTS SELECTED ON AN INTERNATIONAL SCOPE. SUMMARY CLASSIFIED TOPICALLY.

0087 AMERICAN ECONOMIC ASSOCIATION
INDEX OF ECONOMIC JOURNALS 1886-1965 (7 VOLS.)
HOMEWOOD: RICHARD IRWIN, 1965, 2200 PP.
INDEX COVERING ENGLISH-LANGUAGE ARTICLES IN MAJOR ECONOMIC JOURNALS PUBLISHED BETWEEN 1886 AND 1965. INCLUDES CLASSIFIED INDEX IN WHICH MATERIAL IS ARRANGED BY SUBJECT; CONTAINS AN AUTHOR INDEX.

0088 AMERICAN ECONOMIC REVIEW
"SIXTY-THIRD LIST OF DOCTORAL DISSERTATIONS IN POLITICAL ECONOMY IN AMERICAN UNIVERSITIES AND COLLEGES."
AMER. ECO. REVIEW, 56 (SEPT. 66), 1024-1062.
THE ANNOTATED LIST SPECIFIES DOCTORAL DEGREES CONFERRED DURING THE ACADEMIC YEAR TERMINATING JUNE, 1966. ABSTRACTS OF MANY OF THE DISSERTATIONS ARE SUPPLIED. LIST EXCLUDES THESES UNDERTAKEN IN THE SAME PERIOD.

0089 AMERICAN FOREST PRODUCTS INDUS
GOVERNMENT LAND ACQUISITION: A SUMMARY OF LAND ACQUISITION BY FEDERAL, STATE, AND LOCAL GOVERNMENTS UP TO 1964.
WASHINGTON: AMER FOREST PROD IND, 1965, 127 PP.
GENERAL DESCRIPTION OF DEVELOPMENT OF GOVERNMENT LAND TENURE. COVERS GOVERNMENT LANDOWNERSHIP, HOW IT IS TAKEN CARE OF AND DISPOSED OF. AIMS TO INFORM PUBLIC OF SIZE OF GOVERNMENT PROPERTY TO INSURE WISE PLANNING FOR FUTURE OF US AS NATION OF EITHER PRIVATE OR PUBLIC LANDOWNERS.

0090 AMERICAN MANAGEMENT ASSN
SUPERIOR-SUBORDINATE COMMUNICATION IN MANAGEMENT.
NEW YORK: AMER MANAGEMENT ASSN, 1961, 96 PP., LC#61-18463.
ESSAYS ANALYZING PROBLEM OF COMMUNICATION BETWEEN SUPERIORS AND SUBORDINATES IN A BUSINESS SITUATION. SUGGESTS POSSIBLE WAYS OF OVERCOMING BARRIERS. ITEMS SELECTED FROM WORKS OF PSYCHOLOGIST, LINGUIST, EXECUTIVE, AND PERSONNEL DIRECTOR.

0091 AMERICAN U BEIRUT ECO RES INST
A SELECTED AND ANNOTATED BIBLIOGRAPHY OF ECONOMIC LITERATURE ON THE ARABIC SPEAKING COUNTRIES OF THE MIDDLE EAST.
BEIRUT: AMER U OF BEIRUT, 1960, 252 PP.
SUPPLEMENT TO SERIES WHICH COVERS MATERIAL PUBLISHED FROM 1938-1958. INCLUDES ONLY WORKS PUBLISHED IN 1958. COVERS ONLY A SELECTION OF ECONOMIC LITERATURE IN ARABIC, ENGLISH, AND FRENCH IN FIELD. MATERIAL IS CLASSIFIED BY COUNTRIES AND SUBJECTS, WITH BRIEF DESCRIPTIVE ANNOTATIONS. AUTHOR INDEX IS INCLUDED IN APPENDIX.

0092 ANDERSON C.A. ED., BOWMAN M.J. ED.
EDUCATION AND ECONOMIC DEVELOPMENT.
CHICAGO: ALDINE PUBLISHING CO, 1965, 436 PP., LC#65-12453.
HAS 22 ARTICLES ON INVESTMENT VIEW OF HUMAN RESOURCES: FORMATION OF HUMAN COMPETENCIES; DIFFUSION OF SCHOOLING, TECHNOLOGIES, AND EDUCATIONAL OPPORTUNITIES; AND HUMAN-FACTOR PRECONDITIONS, THE TIMING OF EMERGENCE, AND THE PACE OF CHANGE.

0093 ANDERSON C.W.
POLITICS AND ECONOMIC CHANGE IN LATIN AMERICA.
PRINCETON: VAN NOSTRAND, 1967, 388 PP.
ANALYSIS OF ECONOMIC CHANGE IN LATIN AMERICA THROUGH ITS RELATIONSHIP WITH POLITICAL ELEMENTS. ATTEMPTS TO SEE A SYSTEMATIC IMPACT OF POLITICAL FORCES ON DEVELOPMENT POLICY AND THUS CREATE OVER-ALL THEORETICAL STATEMENT ON DEVELOPMENTAL POLICY-MAKING IN LATIN AMERICA. DEMONSTRATES THAT "PRUDENCE MODEL" HAS BEEN APPROACH SINCE 1945 AND SUGGESTS, IN CONCLUSION, A CONSISTENT APPROACH TO DEVELOPMENT POLICY.

0094 ANDERSON C.W., VON DER MEHDEN F.R., YOUNG C.
ISSUES OF POLITICAL DEVELOPMENT.
ENGLEWOOD CLIFFS: PRENTICE HALL, 1967, 248 PP., LC#67-20651.
DISCUSS THREE MAJOR ASPIRATIONS OF EMERGING NATIONS--NATIONALISM, STABILITY, AND DEVELOPMENT. POSTULATE THAT AS FUNDAMENTAL PROBLEMS OF POLITICAL DEVELOPMENT, THEY DEAL WITH PURPOSE OF POLITICAL LIFE ITSELF. EACH AUTHOR SPECIALIZES IN DIFFERENT WORLD AREA AND BOOK ATTEMPTS TO ACHIEVE CROSS-FERTILIZATION OF APPROACH. SEE TREND TOWARD SOCIALIZATION AND STATE PLANNING IN EMERGING COUNTRIES.

0095 ANDERSON J.
THE ORGANIZATION OF ECONOMIC STUDIES IN RELATION TO THE PROBLEMS OF GOVERNMENT (PAMPHLET)
LONDON: OXFORD U PR, 1947, 25 PP.
EXAMINES PROGRESS MADE IN APPLICATION OF ECONOMIC THEORY TO PRACTICAL PROBLEMS DURING LAST 30 YEARS IN ENGLAND. PROPOSES THERE BE INCLUDED IN MACHINERY OF GOVERNMENT A CENTRAL ECONOMIC ORGANIZATION IN WHICH ALL DEPARTMENTS CONCERNED WITH ECONOMIC PROBLEMS COULD COLLABORATE EFFECTIVELY.

0096 ANDERSON J.E.
POLITICS AND THE ECONOMY.
BOSTON: LITTLE BROWN, 1966, 386 PP., LC#66-17720.
EXAMINES HOW AND BY WHOM PUBLIC ECONOMIC POLICY IS MADE, WITH CONCENTRATION ON ROLES OF PRESSURE GROUPS, POLITICAL PARTIES, GOVERNMENTAL ORGANIZATION, AND POLITICAL CULTURE.

0097 ANDERSON S.S.
"SOVIET RUSSIA AND THE TWO EUROPES."
CURRENT HISTORY, 53 (OCT. 67), 203-207, 241-242 .
EXAMINES SOVIET POLICY TOWARD TWO EUROPES, SOVIET EASTERN EUROPE AND WESTERN EUROPE. POLICY ENCOURAGES SELF-ASSERTION IN WESTERN PART WHILE MAINTAINING COHESIVENESS OF EASTERN SPHERE. TRACES DEVELOPMENT OF TWO EUROPES AND POLICY PROBLEMS THEY CREATE. SUGGESTS THAT EUROPE MAY BECOME A UNIFIED, MEDIATING FORCE BETWEEN US AND USSR.

0098 ANDERSON S.V.
THE NORDIC COUNCIL: A STUDY OF SCANDINAVIAN REGIONALISM.
SEATTLE: U OF WASHINGTON PR, 1967, 194 PP., LC#67-21202.
DESCRIBES SCANDINAVIAN REGIONALISM BY STUDYING NORDIC COUNCIL, CONSULTATIVE ASSEMBLY OF MEMBERS OF FIVE PARLIAMENTS. DISCUSSES NATIONAL ATTITUDES TOWARD REGIONALISM AND TRACES HISTORY OF INTERPARLIAMENTARY COOPERATION. EXAMINES ORGANS OF COUNCIL AND ITS LEGISLATIVE PROCEDURE. CHRONICLES NEGOTIATIONS FOR COMMON NORDIC MARKET.

0099 ANDERSON T.
RUSSIAN POLITICAL THOUGHT; AN INTRODUCTION.
ITHACA: CORNELL U PRESS, 1967, 444 PP., LC#67-12902.
STRESSES CONTINUITY AND EVOLUTION OF RUSSIAN POLITICAL ATTITUDES TOWARD AUTOCRACY, ISOLATIONISM, AND DOGMA FROM NINTH CENTURY TO REGIME OF BREZHNEV AND KOSYGIN. SEES GREEK-MONGOL-RUSSIAN TRADITION OF POLITICAL THOUGHT AS DISTINCT FROM WESTERN TRADITION. CONTAINS BIBLIOGRAPHY OF 550 BOOKS AND ARTICLES IN MODERN EUROPEAN LANGUAGES, ARRANGED UNDER TOPIC HEADINGS ALPHABETICALLY BY AUTHOR.

0100 ANDRESKI S.
PARASITISM AND SUBVERSION* THE CASE OF LATIN AMERICA.
NEW YORK: PANTHEON BOOKS, 1966, 303 PP., LC#67-12499.
DISCUSSES CAUSES AND PROBLEMS OF POLITICAL AND ECONOMIC STAGNATION AND INSTABILITY IN LATIN AMERICA. TOPICS COVERED INCLUDE THE PREDICAMENT OF TRADITIONAL SOCIETY, POVERTY, SOCIOLOGICAL STRUCTURE AND CULTURE, VARIETIES OF PARASITISM, ECONOMIC CONTORTIONS, FORMS OF GOVERNMENT, POLITICAL FORCES, REVOLUTIONS, AND CURES.

0101 ANDREWS F.E.
CORPORATION GIVING.
NEW YORK: RUSSELL SAGE FDN, 1952, 361 PP.
A BOOK DETAILING THE GROWTH AND HISTORY, POLICIES, BUDGETS, ADMINISTRATION OF CORPORATE GIVING AND THE USE OF FOUNDATIONS. THE BENEFICIARIES AND THE LEGAL AND TAX FACTORS ARE ALSO DISCUSSED IN DETAIL. DEALS WITH SPECIFIC PROBLEMS SUCH AS PREVENTION OF PROFIT DISCLOSURE BY GIVING FORMULAS AND THE STAKE OF BUSINESS IN EDUCATION.

0102 ANDREWS R.B.
"URBAN ECONOMICS: AN APPRAISAL OF PROGRESS."
LAND ECONOMICS, 37 (AUG. 61), 219-227.
APPRAISAL OF GROWTH OF URBAN ECONOMICS AS A DISCIPLINE. DISCUSSES DEFINITION OF THE DISCIPLINE, USE OF DATA, PROBLEMS IN PROCEDURE, AND PROPOSALS FOR THE IMPROVEMENT OF URBAN ECONOMIC STUDY TECHNIQUES. PRIMARILY CONCERNED WITH URBAN-ECONOMIC THEORY DEVELOPMENT.

0103 ANDREWS R.B.

"ECONOMIC PLANNING FOR SMALL AREAS: THE PLANNING PROCESS."
LAND ECONOMICS, 39 (AUG. 63), 253-264.
AN EXAMINATION OF THE PROCESS OF ECONOMIC PLANNING AS APPLIED TO CITIES AND TOWNS. DISCUSSES PLANNING OBJECTIVES, IMPLEMENTING HISTORICAL BACKGROUND MATERIALS PERTAINING TO INDUSTRIES INVOLVED IN THE AREA, PLANS INVOLVING INDUSTRIAL DEVELOPMENT, AND IMPROVING THE ADAPTATION OF AREA INDUSTRY. ARTICLE IS ORIENTED TOWARD THE PROBLEM OF OBTAINING OPTIMUM INDUSTRIAL DEVELOPMENT.

0104 ANGELL J.W.
"THE LONGER RUN PROSPECTS FOR THE US BALANCE OF PAYMENTS."
POLIT. SCI. QUART., 81 (SEPT. 66), 355-369.
WARNS OF FINANCIAL CRISIS CAUSED BY BALANCE OF PAYMENTS. CONTENDS THAT MAJOR US POLICIES OF HIGH GROWTH, FOREIGN AID, POLITICO-MILITARY SECURITY AND BALANCE OF PAYMENTS ARE CRUCIAL BUT INCOMPATIBLE. EXPLORES BALANCE OF PAYMENTS DEFICIT ITEMS AND AMELIORATIVE PROPOSALS. FINDS ALL REPUGNANT, BUT RESTRICTIONS ON TRAVEL AND CAPITAL EXPORTS MOST PROMISING. DEPRECIATION HIS "LAST RESORT".

0105 ANGERS F.A.
ESSAI SUR LA CENTRALISATION: ANALYSE DES PRINCIPES ET PERSPECTIVES CANADIENNES.
MONTREAL: PR L'ECOLE ETUD COMM, 1960, 331 PP.
EXAMINES GENERAL ASPECTS OF PROBLEM OF CENTRALIZATION IN CANADA: OVER-ALL ECONOMIC AND SOCIOLOGICAL PRINCIPLES THAT PROMPT ADMINISTRATION AND POLITICS. FIRST SECTION DEALS WITH WHOLE OF QUESTION AND ITS SOCIOLOGICAL, ECONOMIC, POLITICAL, AND ADMINISTRATIVE BASES. SECOND DEALS WITH CONTROL AND ECONOMIC STABILITY IN RELATION TO CENTRALIZATION. SPECIAL INTEREST IN THEORIES FROM 1945-55.

0106 ANSHEN M.
"BUSINESS, LAWYERS, AND ECONOMISTS."
HARVARD BUSINESS REV., 35 (MAR.-APR. 57), 107-114.
A STUDY OF MANAGEMENT PROBLEMS, THE PERSONNEL BEING ASSEMBELED TO SOLVE THEM, AND HOW THEY CAN WORK TOGETHER. DISCUSSES TECHNIQUES FOR SELECTING AND ASSIGNING PROBLEMS.

0107 APEL H.
"LES NOUVEAUX ASPECTS DE LA POLITIQUE ETRANGERE ALLEMANDE."
POLITIQUE ETRANGERE, 32 (1967), 5-21.
EXAMINATION OF GERMAN FOREIGN POLICY ON QUESTIONS OF EUROPEAN UNITY, FRANCO-GERMAN RELATIONS, AND EASTERN EUROPEAN COUNTRIES. ARGUES THAT EEC CONSTITUTES BASIS FOR POLITICAL SOLIDARITY OF WESTERN EUROPE. ENVISIONS EEC AS FOUNDATION OF DETENTE BETWEEN EAST AND WEST EUROPE. DENIES THAT HALLSTEIN DOCTRINE CONTRADICTS TRADE WITH EAST BUT SAYS DIPLOMATIC RELATIONS MUST BE EXTENDED TO EAST GERMANY.

0108 APPERT K.
"BERECHTIGE VORBEHALTE DER SCHWEIZERISCHEN ZUR INTEGRATION."
SCHWEIZ. MONATSH., 43 (NO.1, 63), 52-63.
EXAMINES SWISS INTEGRATION INTO EUROPEAN COMMON MARKET AND OPPOSITION TO ENGLISH CANDIDATURE. RELATES ECONOMIC INTERESTS OF NEUTRAL STATES TO POLITICAL ATTITUDES OF SIX NATIONS. GIVES INSIGHT INTO DOMESTIC PROBLEMS. OUTLINES POSITION OF SWISS PRICES.

0109 APTER D.E.
THE POLITICS OF MODERNIZATION.
CHICAGO: U OF CHICAGO PRESS, 1965, 481 PP., LC#65-24421.
ATTEMPT TO DEVELOP A THEORY OF POLITICAL MODERNIZATION UTILIZING EMPIRICAL DATA DRAWN FROM THE EXPERIENCES OF THE AFRICAN AND LATIN AMERICAN NATIONS. APPROACH IS COMPARATIVE, WITH COMPARISONS MADE BETWEEN THE EMERGING SOCIETIES AND TO THE WESTERN DEVELOPED SOCIETIES HELD AS A STANDARD. PROPOSES THAT MODERNIZING STATES MAY NECESSARILY PASS THROUGH A PRE-DEMOCRATIC POLITICAL STATE IN SEARCH FOR PROGRESS.

0110 APTHEKER H.
DISARMAMENT AND THE AMERICAN ECONOMY: A SYMPOSIUM.
NEW YORK: NEW CENTURY, 64 PP, 1960, $.75.
COLLECTION OF ARTICLES WITH MARXIST VIEWPOINT, ATTEMPTING TO DEMONSTRATE THAT DISARMAMENT WILL NOT CREATE SEVERE ECONOMIC CRISIS. ECONOMIC, POLITICAL AND IDEOLOGICAL FACTORS ARE CONSIDERED.

0111 APTHEKER H.
THE NATURE OF DEMOCRACY, FREEDOM AND REVOLUTION.
NEW YORK: INTERNATIONAL PUBL CO, 1967, 128 PP.
DISCUSSES HISTORICAL DEVELOPMENT OF BOURGEOIS CONCEPTS OF DEMOCRACY AND FREEDOM. SHOWS RELATION OF CONCEPTS AS USED BY MILTON, LOCKE, JEFFERSON, AND OTHERS TO PROBLEMS OF THEIR TIMES. DESCRIBES HOW MARXIST INTERPRETATIONS ENCOMPASS NEEDS OF REVOLUTIONARY AGE MOST COMPLETELY. EXAMINES NATURE OF REVOLUTION IN CONTEMPORARY WORLD, COSTS OF REVOLUTION, USE OF VIOLENCE, AND TYPES OF REVOLUTIONS.

0112 ARDANT G.
"A PLAN FOR FULL EMPLOYMENT IN THE DEVELOPING COUNTRIES."
INT. LABOUR REV., 87 (JAN. 63), 15-51.
OUTLINES A PLAN FOR PRODUCTIVE EMPLOYMENT OF UNEMPLOYED AND UNDEREMPLOYED MASSES OF DEVELOPING COUNTRIES. BASED LARGELY ON PRINCIPLE OF SELF-HELP AND MAKING RELATIVELY MODEST DEMANDS ON FINANCIAL OR SKILLED-MANPOWER RESOURCES. CONCLUSIONS ARE DERIVED MAINLY FROM THE AUTHOR'S EXPERIENCE WITH EMPLOYMENT PROJECTS IN MOROCCO AND TUNISIA.

0113 ARMENGALD A.
"ECONOMIE ET COEXISTENCE."
POLIT. ETRANG., 29 (64), 231-47.
ASKS IF THE CAPITALIST SYSTEM CAN SURVIVE THE INTERNATIONAL STRUGGLE OF ECONOMIES, AND QUESTIONS ITS ROLE IN THAT CONFLICT. SUGGESTS THAT TRADE BETWEEN THE SELLER'S MARKET OF THE WEST AND THE BUYERS MARKET OF THE EAST EUROPEAN NATIONS MIGHT PROVIDE AN AREA FOR FUTURE STABILIZATION OF INTERNATIONAL RELATIONS.

0114 ARNDT H.W.
AUSTRALIAN FOREIGN AID POLICY (PAMPHLET)
ADELAIDE: GRIFFIN PR, 1964, 20 PP.
LECTURE ON PROBLEMS FACING DONOR COUNTRY IN FOREIGN AID PROGRAMS. EMPHASIZES BEST AND MOST EFFECTIVE POLICY FOR AUSTRALIA. FEELS AID SHOULD BE GIVEN TO COUNTRIES THAT USE IT BEST RATHER THAN NEED IT MOST, ESPECIALLY SINCE AUSTRALIA IS ALSO OBLIGATED TO UNDEVELOPED DEPENDENTS, NEW GUINEA AND PAPUA.

0115 ARNOLD H.J.P.
AID FOR DEVELOPING COUNTRIES.
CHESTER SPRINGS: DEFOUR, 1962, 159 PP.
ANALYZES PATTERNS AND AMOUNT OF AID TO UNDERDEVELOPED NATIONS BY THE WEST, SOVIET BLOC AND INTERNATIONAL ORGANIZATIONS. SUGGESTS DESIGNING AID TO MEET SPECIFIC NEEDS OF INDIVIDUAL COUNTRIES CONSIDERING THEIR ECONOMIC NEEDS AND POLITICAL BACKGROUND.

0116 ARNOLD T.W.
THE FOLKLORE OF CAPITALISM.
NEW HAVEN: YALE U PR, 1962, 400 PP.
DESCRIBES FRUSTRATING EFFECTS, IN TIMES OF REVOLUTIONARY CHANGE, OF IDEALS AND SYMBOLS OF CAPITALISM INHERITED FROM PAST. STUDIES VIRTUES AND ABSURDITIES OF "GOSPELS" OF AMERICAN CAPITALISM. DISCUSSES CONSERVATISM OF "NORMAL" CITIZEN TOWARD SOCIAL CHANGE, RECONCILIATION OF LARGE COMPANY REALITY AND SMALL COMPANY IDEAL, EDUCATIONAL SYSTEM, EXECUTIVE STRUCTURE, DISTRIBUTION, AND PRIVATE PROPERTY.

0117 ARNOW K.
SELF-INSURANCE IN THE TREASURY (PAMPHLET)
INDIANAPOLIS: BOBBS-MERRILL, 1952, 52 PP.
CASE STUDY OF TWO "LOW TENSION" ADMINISTRATIVE PROBLEMS IN THE US TREASURY DEPARTMENT. COMPARES TWO INSTANCES OF ADMINISTERING TRANSFER OF SHIPPING METHODS TO A SELF-INSURANCE BASIS. ILLUMINATES NEED FOR REFORM IN BUREAUCRATIC PROCEDURE.

0118 ARON R. ET AL.
L'UNIFICATION ECONOMIQUE DE L'EUROPE.
NEUCHATEL: LA BACONNIERE, 1957, 162 PP.
COLLECTION OF ESSAYS WRITTEN BY OFFICIALS OF NATIONS WITHIN THE COMMON MARKET AND TWO SCHOLARS REPRESENTING GREAT BRITAIN AND SWITZERLAND. INDIVIDUAL AUTHORS PROBE ATTITUDES AND PROBLEMS OF THEIR COUNTRIES WITH REGARD TO EUROPEAN UNIFICATION. THOUGH UNITY ACHIEVED WOULD BE ECONOMIC, WRITERS RECOGNIZE POLITICAL ASPECTS OF PROBLEM.

0119 ARON R.
IMPERIALISM AND COLONIALISM (PAMPHLET)
LEEDS,ENGLAND: LEEDS U. PRESS, 1959, 18PP.
REVIEWS HISTORY OF IMPERIALISM AND COLONIALISM, TRACING POLITICAL AND ECONOMIC INTERPRETATIONS MOST COMMON IN RECENT THOUGHT. SHOWS THAT "COLONIAL PROBLEMS" EXIST ONLY IN TERRITORIES RULLED BY A FEARFUL EUROPEAN MINORITY. POINTS OUT INSIGNIFICANCE OF COLONIES AS PRESENT SOURCES OF INCOME. CALLS UPON EUROPEANS TO TREAT FORMER SUBJECTS AS EQUALS.

0120 ARON R.
COLLOQUES DE RHEINFELDEN.
PARIS: CALMAN-LEVY, 1960, 328 PP.
DISCUSSION OF THE CONFLICTING INDUSTRIALIZED SOCIETIES OF THE US AND THE USSR AND THE POSSIBILITY OF THE RESOLUTION OF THIS CONFLICT BY RAPPROCHEMENT AND DIPLOMATIC ACCOMMODATION. ALSO DISCUSSES ACCORDING TO WHICH MODEL WILL THE DEVELOPING COUNTRIES INDUSTRIALIZE.

0121 ARROW K.J.
"UTILITIES, ATTITUDES, CHOICES: A REVIEW NOTE."
ECONOMETRICA, 26 (JAN. 58), 1-23.
OUTLINES THE PURPOSE OF AN ECONOMIC THEORY OF CHOICE AS THE BACKGROUND FOR EMPERICAL DEMAND ANALYSIS OR A TOOL IN WELFARE ECONOMICS. BY CONTRAST TO THE BEHAVIORAL SCIENTIST, THE ECONOMIST IS CONCERNED WITH CHOICES NOT IN THEMSELVES BUT AS THE MEANS TO ACHIEVING AN OPTIMUM. THE DYNAMICS OF BEHAVIOR IS CONSIDERED THE ADAPTATION OR MOVEMENT TO THAT OPTIMUM.

0122 ARROW K.J., HURWICZ L.
"ON THE STABILITY OF THE COMPETITIVE EQUILIBRIUM: I."

ECONOMETRICA, 26 (OCT. 58), 522-552.
ASSESSES THE DYNAMIC STABILITY OF A PERFECTLY COMPETITIVE MARKET WITH PRICE ADJUSTMENT RATE PROPORTIONATE TO EXCESS DEMAND BY CONSTRUCTING A FORMAL DYNAMIC MODEL CHARACTERIZING THE COMPETITIVE PROCESS. CONCLUDES THAT THE SYSTEM WAS IN NO CASE UNSTABLE UNDER THE ADJUSTMENT PROCESS.

0123 ARROW K.J., NERLOVE M.
"A NOTE ON EXPECTATIONS AND STABILITY."
ECONOMETRICA, 26 (APR. 58), 297-305.
POSTULATES THAT DEMAND AND SUPPLY DEPEND ON CURRENT PRICES AND EXPECTATIONS. ASSUMES EXPECTATIONS BASED ON PREVIOUS PRICES IN ORDER TO PROVE THAT UNDER CERTAIN CIRCUMSTANCES THE RESULTING MARKET HAS DYNAMIC STABILITY. CONCLUDES THAT UNDER ADAPTIVE EXPECTATIONS THE DYNAMIC SYSTEM REMAINS STABLE DESPITE THE SYSTEM'S INERTIA OR THE ELASTICITY OF EXPECTATIONS.

0124 ARROW K.J., BLOCK H.D., HURWICZ L.
"ON THE STABILITY OF THE COMPETITIVE EQUILIBRIUM: II."
ECONOMETRICA, 27 (JAN. 59), 82-109.
PROVIDES A PROOF OF THE STABILITY IN LARGE MARKET WHEN ALL GOODS ARE GROSS SUBSTITUTES. TREATS MARKET SYSTEMS WHERE THE PREFERENCE COMMODITIES PLAY THE ROLE OF NUMERAIRE AND THOSE WHERE ALL COMMODITIES ARE TREATED SYMMETRICALLY. PROOF FOUND VALID FOR PROCESSES WHERE PRICE ADJUSTMENT RATE IS A CONTINUOUS SIGN-PRESERVING BUT NOT NECESSARILY PROPORTIONATE FUNCTION OF EXCESS DEMAND.

0125 ARTEL R.
THE STRUCTURE OF THE STOCKHOLM ECONOMY.
ITHACA: CORNELL U PRESS, 1965, 197 PP., LC#65-13640.
BASED ON FIRST LARGE-SCALE INPUT-OUTPUT STUDY EVER DONE OF A METROPOLITAN AREA, GIVES FRAMEWORK FOR PROJECTING METROPOLITAN COMMUNITY DEVELOPMENT. ASSESSES STOCKHOLM'S CONTRIBUTION TO SWEDISH NATIONAL INCOME AND TO THE REVENUES OF THE NATIONAL GOVERNMENT, ITS BLANCE-OF-PAYMENTS CONDITION, AND ITS INDUSTRIAL LABOR AND SPACE REQUIREMENTS. DISCUSSES EMPIRICAL METHODOLOGY IN DETAIL.

0126 ASCH P.
"CONGLOMERATE MERGERS AND PUBLIC POLICY."
BUSINESS TOPICS, 15 (WINTER 67), 61-67.
DISCUSSES VARIOUS LEGAL ASPECTS OF RECENT MERGER POLICY AS FORMULATED BY THE LEGAL SYSTEM OF THE COUNTRY. DIFFICULTIES ARISE AS A MATTER OF SEMANTICS, APPARENTLY, SINCE THE TERM "CONGLOMERATE" CANNOT BE ADEQUATELY HANDLED IN TERMS OF VERTICAL AND HORIZONTAL MERGERS OF TRADITIONAL METTLE.

0127 ASCHHEIM J.
TECHNIQUES OF MONETARY CONTROL.
BALTIMORE: JOHNS HOPKINS PRESS, 1961, 164 PP., LC#61-7804.
STUDY OF SCOPE AND METHOD OF CENTRAL BANKING IN FRAMEWORK OF CONTEMPORARY US MONETARY SYSTEM. EXAMINES NATURE AND USEFULNESS OF CONVENTIONAL CENTRAL BANKING INSTRUMENTS SUCH AS VARIATION OF CASH-RESERVE REQUIREMENTS, OPEN-MARKET OPERATIONS, REDISCOUNTING, AND MORAL SUASION. ALSO STUDIES SECONDARY REQUIREMENTS, POSITION OF FINANCIAL INTERMEDIARIES VS. COMMERCIAL BANKS, AND CONTROL OF TIME DEPOSITS.

0128 ASH W.
MARXISM AND MORAL CONCEPTS.
NEW YORK: MONTHLY REVIEW PR, 1964, 204 PP., LC#64-23146.
ATTEMPTS TO DERIVE CERTAIN BASIC MORAL CONCEPTS FROM THE MATERIAL CONDITIONS OF LIFE IN VARIOUS FORMS OF SOCIETY. ARGUES THAT DIFFERENCES IN CONTENT OF ETHICAL EXPRESSIONS LARGELY REFLECT DIFFERENCES IN ECONOMIC ORDERING OF SOCIETY OR DIFFERENCES IN ECONOMIC ROLE OF A GROUP IN SOCIETY.

0129 ASHER R.E., KOTSCHING W.M., BROWN W.A.
THE UNITED NATIONS AND ECONOMIC AND SOCIAL COOPERATION.
WASHINGTON: BROOKINGS INST, 1957, 561 PP., LC#57-9377.
CRITICAL ANALYSIS OF UN PROGRAMS IN ECONOMIC AND SOCIAL DEVELOPMENT WHICH EXAMINES STRUCTURE AND PROCEDURES OF SPECIALIZED UN AGENCIES AND EVALUATES EFFECTIVENESS OF PAST PROGRAMS. DISCUSSES LONG RANGE AID PROGRAMS ASSOCIATED WITH EXPANSION OF INTERNATIONAL TRADE AND IMPROVEMENT OF TRANSPORTATION AND COMMUNICATIONS. EMPHASIS IS ON PROBLEMS OF UNDERDEVELOPED COUNTRIES.

0130 ASHER R.E.
GRANTS, LOANS, AND LOCAL CURRENCIES: THEIR ROLE IN FOREIGN AID.
WASHINGTON: BROOKINGS INST, 1961, 142 PP., LC#61-13988.
DEALS WITH THEORY AND PRACTICE OF GRANTING, LENDING, AND SELLING AS THEY HAVE EVOLVED UNDER BILATERAL AND MULTILATERAL ASSISTANCE PROGRAMS DURING YEARS SINCE CLOSE OF WWII. DEFINES GRANTS, ETC., SHOWS MAGNITUDE AND AUTHORITY OF GOVERNMENT GIVING AND LENDING, DISCUSSES FOREIGN CURRENCY ACCUMULATION BY US, AND POINTS OUT HOW US GOES ABOUT PICKING RECIPIENTS.

0131 ASHWORTH W.
A SHORT HISTORY OF THE INTERNATIONAL ECONOMY 1850-1950.
LONDON: LONGMANS, 1952, 256 PP.
DEMONSTRATES RAPID EXPANSION OF PRODUCTIVE FORCES AFTER MID 19TH CENTURY, INDICATING TRENDS TOWARD SIMILAR FORMS OF ORGANIZATION AND PRODUCTION TECHNIQUES. NOTES INTERDEPENDFNCE OF INDUSTRY AND CONTEMPLATES EFFICACY OF GOVERNMENT PARTICIPATION AND/OR REGULATION.

0132 ASPREMONT-LYNDEN H.
RAPPORT SUR L'ADMINISTRATION BELGE DU RUANDA-URUNDI PENDANT L'ANNEE 1959.
BRUSSELS: IMPR VAN MUYSEWINKEL, 1960, 494 PP.
DOCUMENTS AND SUMMARIZES BELGIAN COLONIAL ADMINISTRATION OF RUANDA-URUNDI FOR 1959. INCLUDES DESCRIPTIVE DATA INDICATING GEOGRAPHY AND DEMOGRAPHY OF THE AREA; INDICATES LEGAL STATUS OF THE INHABITANTS; DESCRIBES EXTENT AND SCOPE OF COLONIAL COOPERATION WITH INTERNATIONAL AND REGIONAL AGENCIES; STRESSES SOCIAL, ECONOMIC, AND POLITICAL PROGRESS OF THE REGION.

0133 ASSN U BUREAUS BUS-ECO RES
INDEX OF PUBLICATIONS OF BUREAUS OF BUSINESS AND ECONOMIC RESEARCH 1950-56 AND YEARLY SUPPLEMENTS THROUGH 1967.
NY: ASSN UNIV BUR BUS & ECO RES, 1957, 115 PP.
BIBLIOGRAPHY OF ALL PUBLICATIONS ANNUALLY SINCE 1950 PUBLISHED BY THIS INSTITUTION. ABOUT 1,000 ENTRIES ARE ARRANGED ALPHABETICALLY, FIRST BY UNIVERSITY WHERE RESEARCH WAS DONE, AND SECOND BY SUBJECT. INCLUDES BOOKS, ARTICLES, RESEARCH MONOGRAPHS, AND OTHER.

0134 ATOMIC INDUSTRIAL FORUM
COMMENTARY ON LEGISLATION TO PERMIT PRIVATE OWNERSHIP OF SPECIAL NUCLEAR MATERIAL (PAMPHLET)
NEW YORK: ATOMIC INDUS FORUM, 1963, 63 PP.
DISCUSSES ATOMIC ENERGY COMMISSION'S BILL TO PERMIT PRIVATE OWNERSHIP OF SPECIAL NUCLEAR MATERIAL AND TO REVISE ATOMIC ENERGY ACT OF 1954 TO AUTHORIZE TRANSACTIONS BY AEC WITH PRIVATE PERSONS. PRESENTS ATOMIC ENERGY ACT AND TEXT OF BILL AND ANALYZES ADVISABILITY OF CHANGES. BASICALLY SUPPORTS BILL.

0135 ATOMIC INDUSTRIAL FORUM
PUBLIC RELATIONS FOR THE ATOMIC INDUSTRY.
NEW YORK: ATOMIC INDUS FORUM, 1956, 160 PP.
PAPERS ON USES OF ATOMIC ENERGY, ATOM AS NEWS, NEED TO INFORM PUBLIC, SOURCES OF INFORMATION, PUBLIC OPINION OF PEACEFUL USES OF ATOMIC ENERGY, SAFETY REQUIREMENTS NEEDED TO RECEIVE PUBLIC SUPPORT, AND TOOLS AND TECHNIQUES OF PUBLIC RELATIONS.

0136 ATOMIC INDUSTRIAL FORUM
MANAGEMENT AND ATOMIC ENERGY.
NEW YORK: ATOMIC INDUS FORUM, 1958, 460 PP.
PROCEEDINGS OF ATOMIC ENERGY MANAGEMENT CONFERENCE ON STATUS AND GROWTH OF ATOMIC INDUSTRY. CONSIDERS POLICY, HEALTH AND SAFETY, ASSESSMENT OF US POWER REACTOR PROGRAM, FEASIBILITY OF SMALL REACTORS, SALE OF NUCLEAR PRODUCTS OUTSIDE US, AMENDMENTS TO ATOMIC ENERGY ACT, NUCLEAR SHIPS, REDUCTION OF COST, INTERNATIONAL ACTIVITIES, PEACEFUL USES, INDEMNIFICATION LAW, AND RESEARCH DEVELOPMENTS.

0137 ATOMIC INDUSTRIAL FORUM
ATOMS FOR INDUSTRY: WORLD FORUM.
NEW YORK: ATOMIC INDUS FORUM, 1960, 160 PP.
DESCRIBES GROWTH OF INDUSTRIAL USES OF ATOMIC ENERGY, AND PROCEDURES. IDENTIFIES UNPRECEDENTED PROBLEMS OF USING ATOMS FOR SOCIAL PURPOSES, SUCH AS COST, SAFETY, FINANCES, LEGAL CONTROL, AND PUBLIC INTEREST.

0138 AUBERT DE LA RUE P.
"PERSPECTIVES ECONOMIQUES ENTRE LES ETATS-UNIS ET L'EUROPE."
POLITIQUE ETRANGERE, 32 (1967), 453-476, 4-5.
ANALYZES ECONOMIC PROBLEMS BETWEEN THE US AND THE EEC. DISCUSSES TRADE BENEFITS THAT WILL RESULT FROM CONCLUSION OF KENNEDY ROUND. EXAMINES ECONOMIC, POLITICAL, AND PSYCHOLOGICAL PROBLEMS BROUGHT ABOUT BY AMERICAN INDUSTRY IN EUROPE. AMERICAN INDUSTRY HAS ENCROACHED ON COMMON MARKET BY ESTABLISHING COMPANIES IN EUROPE AND BUYING CONTROL OF EUROPEAN COUNTRIES. DISCUSSES BALANCE OF PAYMENTS.

0139 AUBREY H.G.
COEXISTENCE: ECONOMIC CHALLENGE AND RESPONSE.
WASHINGTON: NATL PLANNING ASSN, 1961, 323 PP., LC#61-14482.
ORGANIZES MAIN THREADS OF SEVEN RELATED STUDIES ON COMPETITVE COEXISTENCE BETWEEN EAST AND WEST AND REVIEWS ENTIRE PROBLEM. CONSIDERS NEEDS AND ASPIRATIONS OF DEVELOPING COUNTRIES AND WEIGHS ABILITY OF EAST AND WEST TO MEET SUCH NEEDS. STUDIES POLITICAL IMPACT OF INSTITUTIONS, INSTRUMENTS, TECHNIQUES OF COMPETITION; LOOKS BEYOND COMPETITION TO LONG-RANGE RESPONSIBILITY OF THE WEST.

0140 AUBREY H.G.
THE DOLLAR IN WORLD AFFAIRS.
NEW YORK: HARPER & ROW, 1964, 295 PP., LC#63-21750.
ATTEMPTS TO ELUCIDATE ISSUES OF FOREIGN FINANCE AND TO PLACE THEM IN FOREIGN POLICY CONTEXT. INCLUDES FINANCIAL POLICY AND FOREIGN RELATIONS, DOLLAR STRENGTH, DOLLAR AS INTERNATIONAL MONEY, US AS INTERNATIONAL CAPITAL MARKET, AND OUTLOOK FOR AMERICAN FOREIGN FINANCIAL POLICY.

0141 AUSTIN D.A. ED.
"POLITICAL CONFLICT IN AFRICA."
GOVERNMENT AND OPPOSITION, 2 (JULY 67), 487-620.
STUDIES SINGLE-PARTY STATE IN TANZANIA, MOROCCO, AND SENEGAL. FINDS THAT SINGLE-PARTY IS INEFFECTIVE, UNSTABLE SYSTEM. EXAMINES FUNCTIONAL INDEPENDENCE OF POLITICAL SYSTEM OF NIGERIA AND EXAMPLES OF POLITICAL CONFLICT. STRESSES NOVELTY OF AFRICAN SITUATION, BRIEF HISTORY OF POLITICAL INSTITUTIONS, AND INSECURITY. NOTES DISSIMILARITIES AMONG AFRICAN POLITICAL SYSTEMS.

0142 AUSTRUY J.
STRUCTURE ECONOMIQUE ET CIVILISATION: L'EGYPTE ET LE DESTIN ECONOMIQUE DE L'ISLAM.
PARIS: SOC ED D'ENSEIGNEMENT SUP, 1960, 366 PP.
BELIEVES THAT IDEA OF "CIVILIZATION," RATHER THAN "NATION" GOVERNS ECONOMICS OF A PARTICULAR STATE. DISCUSSES STRUCTURE AND HISTORY, SOCIOLOGY, AND ECONOMICS; USES EGYPT TO ILLUSTRATE HIS THEORY. BELIEVES ISLAM HAS AN ECONOMIC VOCATION WHICH EGYPT FEELS AND WHICH IMPEDES ADOPTION OF WESTERN SYSTEM. EGYPT WILL PROBABLY DEVELOP OWN ORIGINAL TECHNIQUES SUITABLE TO HER DEVELOPMENT.

0143 AVRAMOVIC D.
POSTWAR GROWTH IN INTERNATIONAL INDEBTEDNESS.
BALTIMORE: JOHNS HOPKINS PRESS, 1958, 228 PP., LC#58-14424.
EXAMINES INTERNATIONAL LONG-TERM CAPITAL MOVEMENTS, CHANGES IN PATTERN OF EXPORTS, AND PROBLEM OF ADJUSTMENT TO CHANGES IN BALANCE OF PAYMENTS. TABLES ON ECONOMIC GROWTH, VOLUME OF EXPORT, GROWTH IN REAL INCOME, CAPITAL FORMATION, GROWTH RATES IN IMPORTS, ETC. OF SELECTED COUNTRIES.

0144 AVTORKHANOV A.
"A NEW AGRARIAN REVOLUTION."
INST. FOR STUDY OF USSR, 14 (JULY 67), 3-19.
COMPARES REFORMS IN SOVIET AGRICULTURE NOW CARRIED OUT BY KHRUSHCHEV'S SUCCESSORS AND ESSENTIAL FEATURES OF KOLKHOZ SYSTEM AS CREATED BY STALIN. BASES ARGUMENTS ON CONCEPT THAT FREE MARKETS ARE THE ONLY SOLUTION TO ECONOMIC PROBLEMS.

0145 AYAL E.B.
"VALUE SYSTEM AND ECONOMIC DEVELOPMENT IN JAPAN AND THAILAND."
J. SOC. ISSUES, 19 (JAN. 63), 35-57.
BY A COMPARATIVE STUDY OF JAPAN AND THAILAND, ESTABLISHES CAUSAL RELATIONSHIP BETWEEN VALUE SYSTEM AND MODES OF BEHAVIOR, ASSIGNING PROPER PLACE TO THE SYSTEM IN THE THEORY OF SOCIAL CHANGE BROUGHT ABOUT BY ECONOMIC DEVELOPMENT. CONCLUDES THAT VALUE SYSTEM IS A MAJOR COMPONENT OF THE DEVELOPMENT POTENTIAL OF A COUNTRY.

0146 AYRES C.E.
THE INDUSTRIAL ECONOMY.
BOSTON: HOUGHTON MIFFLIN, 1952, 433 PP.
STUDIES TECHNOLOGICAL BASIS AND INSTITUTIONAL FUTURE OF INDUSTRIAL ECONOMY, INCLUDING INSTITUTIONALIST APPROACH, ECONOMIC PROBLEMS AND PRINCIPLES, EVOLUTION OF INDUSTRIAL ECONOMY, PLANNING FOR STABILITY, MARKET MECHANISM, AND FUTURE PROSPECTS. BIBLIOGRAPHY OF 75 ENTRIES, PUBLISHED 1917-52 IN ENGLISH; ARRANGED BY CHAPTER.

0147 BACKMAN J.
THE ECONOMICS OF THE ELECTRICAL MACHINERY INDUSTRY.
NEW YORK: NEW YORK U PR, 1962, 374 PP., LC#62-18176.
STUDY OF ECONOMICS IN ELECTRICAL MACHINERY INDUSTRY EMPHASIZING QUANTITATIVE RECORDS RATHER THAN THEORY. DESCRIBES NATURE OF COMPONENT INDUSTRIES, PROBLEMS, GROWTH, PRODUCT COMPETITION, STRUCTURE, PRICE POLICIES, HISTORY, PRODUCTIVITY TRENDS, EMPLOYMENT AND UNIONISM, LABOR COST, FOREIGN COMPETITION, AND PERSPECTIVE ON FUTURE.

0148 BADGLEY R.F., WOLFE S.
DOCTORS' STRIKE; MEDICAL CARE AND CONFLICT IN SASKATCHEWAN.
NEW YORK: ATHERTON PRESS, 1967, 250 PP.
EXAMINES PLANNING AND IMPLEMENTATION OF NORTH AMERICA'S FIRST COMPREHENSIVE MEDICAL CARE PROGRAM, SETTING OF CONFLICT, AND ATTITUDES OF DOCTORS, GOVERNMENT, AND CITIZENS. TREATS MEDICAL CARE AS SOCIAL ISSUE AND ITS RELATION TO SOCIAL WELFARE. ANALYZES MEDICAL PROFESSION UNDER PRESSURE AND STUDIES MEDICAL CARE IN CONFLICT SITUATION FROM SOCIOLOGICAL VIEWPOINT.

0149 BAERRESEN D.W., CARNOY M., GRUNWALD J.
LATIN AMERICAN TRADE PATTERNS.
WASHINGTON: BROOKINGS INST, 1965, 329 PP., LC#65-27966.
TO ANALYZE THE EFFECTS OF ECONOMIC INTEGRATION IN LATIN AMERICA IT WAS FELT THAT ITS PRESENT ECONOMIC PICTURE MUST BE HISTORICALLY AND EMPIRICALLY DESCRIBED. THIS BOOK DOES BOTH WITH AN INTRODUCTORY VERBAL PICTURE FOLLOWED BY AN EXTENSIVE TABULATION OF HEMISPHERIC TRADE PATTERN DATA.

0150 BAERWALD F.
FUNDAMENTALS OF LABOR ECONOMICS.
NEW YORK: MC MULLEN BOOKS, INC, 1947, 464 PP.
STUDIES LABOR ECONOMICS, EMPHASIZING INTERRELATION OF CENTRAL TOPICS. STRESSES NEED FOR RECONCILING ADVANCING TECHNOLOGY WITH FULL EMPLOYMENT AND FOR BALANCING PRODUCTIVE POTENTIAL AND CONSUMER INCOME. DISCUSSES PROBLEM OF FREE SOCIETY FIGHTING TOTALITARIANISM OUTSIDE AND BUSINESS CONCENTRATION INSIDE. EXPLORES WAGE THEORIES, LABOR MARKET, EMPLOYMENT, SOCIAL SECURITY, AND LABOR RELATIONS.

0151 BAERWALD F.
ECONOMIC SYSTEM ANALYSIS: CONCEPTS AND PERSPECTIVES.
NEW YORK: FORDHAM U PR, 1960, 113 PP., LC#60-13937.
STUDY OF SCOPE AND PURPOSE OF SYSTEM ANALYSIS. PRESENTATION OF GROWTH ON MACRO-ECONOMIC SCALE; SPONTANEOUS ECONOMIC DEVELOPMENT; GROWTH-RATE; CONSUMER, INVESTMENT, AND PUBLIC SECTOR; ECONOMIC GROWTH AND PRICE STABILITY. PROPOSES, IN WIDER CONTEXT, THAT SYSTEM ANALYSIS CAN ACT AS DEFLATOR OF IDEOLOGICAL COMPONENTS IN ECONOMIC THOUGHT AND ANALYSIS.

0152 BAGDKIAN B.H.
"NEWS AS A BYPRODUCT: WHAT HAPPENS WHEN JOURNALISM IS HITCHED TO GREAT, DIVERSIFIED CORPORATIONS?"
COLUMBIA JOURNALISM REV., 6 (SPRING 67), 5-10.
FEELS THAT IF THE NEWS AND ITS INTERPRETATION ARE INCREASINGLY A BY-PRODUCT OF HUGE CORPORATIONS WHOSE PRIMARY CONCERN MUST BE CONVENTIONAL GAIN, THEN PUBLIC MUST QUICKLY ACT TO REVERSE THE TREND. OTHERWISE PUBLIC INFORMATION AND DEVELOPMENT OF SOCIAL AND FISCAL POLICIES WILL SUFFER.

0153 BAILY S.L.
"THE ITALIANS AND ORGANIZED LABOR IN THE UNITED STATES AND ARGENTINA: 1880-1910."
INTERNATIONAL MIGRATION REVIEW, 1 (SUMMER 67), 6-66.
ANALYZES ITALIAN IMMIGRATION TO US AND ARGENTINA AROUND TURN OF CENTURY TO DETERMINE CONTRIBUTION TO LABOR DEVELOPMENT AND ORGANIZATION AND EXTENT OF DIFFERENCE IN BOTH COUNTRIES.

0154 BAILY S.L.
LABOR, NATIONALISM, AND POLITICS IN ARGENTINA.
NEW BRUNSWICK: RUTGERS U PR, 1967, 241 PP., LC#67-23508.
EXAMINES DEVELOPMENT OF ARGENTINE LABOR MOVEMENT AND ITS RELATIONS WITH CENTRAL GOVERNMENT. COVERS PERIOD 1890-1957, HEAVILY EMPHASIZING PERON REGIME. ESTABLISHES TIE BETWEEN RISE OF ORGANIZED LABOR AND EMERGENCE OF COMPETING NATIONALIST GROUPS: "LIBERAL" EUROPEAN IMMIGRANTS, AND "ANTI-LIBERAL" CRIOLLOS. ANALYZES APPEAL OF PERON'S PERSONALISTIC RULE AND ITS CONTINUING INFLUENCE IN THE LABOR MOVEMENT.

0155 BAKKE E.W.
MUTUAL SURVIVAL; THE GOAL OF UNION AND MANAGEMENT (2ND ED.)
HAMDEN, CONN: ARCHON BOOKS, 1966, 116 PP.
ANALYSIS OF UNION-MANAGEMENT RELATIONS IN 1946 AND 1966, COMPARING STRUCTURE OF EACH AND THEIR SIGNIFICANCE TO US ECONOMY. INCLUDES ATTITUDES OF UNIONS AND MANAGEMENT TOWARD OTHER.

0156 BAKLANOFF E.N. ED.
NEW PERSPECTIVES ON BRAZIL.
NASHVILLE: VANDERBILT U PR, 1966, 328 PP., LC#66-10327.
ESSAYS EXAMINE SALIENT ASPECTS OF BRAZILIAN SOCIETY UNDERGOING TRANSFORMATION IN ITS ECONOMIC, POLITICAL, SOCIAL, DEMOGRAPHIC, PSYCHOLOGICAL, AND LINGUISTIC ELEMENTS. FOCUSES ON POST-WWII DEVELOPMENTS, CONTRIBUTING AUTHORS HAVE MADE, WHERE RELEVANT, INTERIM ASSESSMENTS OF MILITARY-CIVILIAN COUP OF MAR. 31, 1964.

0157 BALASSA B.
THE THEORY OF ECONOMIC INTEGRATION.
HOMEWOOD: IRWIN, 1961, 304 PP.
CONSIDERS THEORETICAL ISSUES CONCERNING INTEGRATION OF INDEPENDENT NATIONAL ECONOMIES, AND THE IMPACT OF INTEGRATION ON ECONOMIC GROWTH. SURVEYS VARIOUS FORMS SUCH AS FREE TRADE AREAS, CUSTOMS UNIONS, COMMON MARKET, ECONOMIC UNION, AND TOTAL INTEGRATION. PRESENTS DATA ON APPLICATION OF THEORETICAL PRINCIPLES TO EUROPEAN ECONOMIC MARKET, FREE TRADE ASSOCIATIONS, AND PROPOSED LATIN AMERICAN UNIONS.

0158 BALASSA B.
TRADE PROSPECTS FOR DEVELOPING COUNTRIES.
HOMEWOOD: RICHARD IRWIN, 1964, 450 PP., LC#64-17248.
PROJECTION OF GENERAL TRADE PATTERNS AND THE PROSPECTS FOR INDIVIDUAL COMMODITIES OF THE DEVELOPING WORLD TO 1975. ASSUMES THAT FURTHER GROWTH IN THE DEVELOPED COUNTRIES WILL AFFECT DEMAND SIDE OF PRICING WITH SUPPLY FLUCTUATIONS IN POOR LANDS AFFECTING OTHER SIDE. DISCUSSES ROLE OF POLITICAL TRADE POLICIES OF BOTH RICH AND POOR AND MAKES POLICY SUGGESTIONS. WEALTH OF EMPIRICAL MATERIAL.

0159 BALASSA B. ED.
CHANGING PATTERNS IN FOREIGN TRADE AND PAYMENTS.
NEW YORK: W W NORTON, 1964, 180 PP., LC#63-21515.
DISCUSSES THE RELATIONSHIPS BETWEEN THE US ECONOMY AND FOREIGN ECONOMIES. ANALYZES BALANCE OF PAYMENTS, BOOKKEEPING PROBLEMS, COMPETITION, AND VALUE OF THE DOLLAR. STUDIES TARIFFS AND TRADE, AND US POLICY AND WORLD POSITION. STUDIES THE DOLLAR AND INTERNATIONAL LIQUIDITY, ECONOMIC PROGRESS AND THE INTERNATIONAL MONETARY SYSTEM, AND THE BASIS FOR THE

GOLD SYSTEM.

0160 BALDWIN D.A.
"THE INTERNATIONAL BANK IN POLITICAL PERSPECTIVE"
WORLD POLITICS, 18 (OCT. 65), 68-81.
ANALYSIS OF INTERNATIONAL BANK FOR RECONSTRUCTION AND DEVELOPMENT ACTIVITIES FOR ITS POLITICAL CONTENT. CONCLUDES THAT IBRD ACTIVITIES ARE POLITICAL IN 3 RESPECTS: BANK CONSIDERS WILLINGNESS AND ABILITY OF BORROWER TO REPAY LOAN, LOAN AFFECTS DISTRIBUTION OF POWER AMONG AND WITHIN NATIONS, AND BANK SOMETIMES ATTEMPTS TO INFLUENCE BEHAVIOR OF GOVERNMENTS.

0161 BALDWIN D.A.
SOFT LOANS AND AMERICAN FOREIGN POLICY: 1943-1962 (THESIS)
PRINCETON: PRIN U, DEPT OF POL, 1965.
DISCUSSES SOFT LOANS AS WEAPON OF FOREIGN POLICY. EXAMINES IMPORTANCE OF SOFT LOANS TO US IN PROMOTING ECONOMIC DEVELOPMENT IN UNDERDEVELOPED NATIONS AND IN IMPROVING RELATIONSHIPS WITHOUT CAUSING DEPENDENCY.

0162 BALDWIN D.A.
FOREIGN AID AND AMERICAN FOREIGN POLICY; A DOCUMENTARY ANALYSIS.
NEW YORK: FREDERICK PRAEGER, 1966, 261 PP., LC#66-18888.
BALDWIN CONSIDERS FOREIGN AID TO BE AN INTEGRAL COMPONENT OF AMERICAN FOREIGN POLICY. WORK IS STRUCTURED TO PROVIDE AN INDEPENDENT LEARNING EXPERIENCE FOR THE STUDENT-READER. PRESENTS ALTERNATIVE FOREIGN-AID-POLICY THEORIES, STRUCTURES AND CAVEATS; FOLLOWS WITH EXTENSIVE 1945-1965 STATISTICS, PRESENTS BULK OF WORK, A CHRONOLOGICAL AND TOPICAL ORGANIZATION, WITH DOCUMENTS, REPORTS, RESOLUTIONS, STATEMENTS.

0163 BALDWIN D.A.
ECONOMIC DEVELOPMENT AND AMERICAN FOREIGN POLICY.
CHICAGO: U OF CHICAGO PRESS, 1966, 291 PP., LC#66-20597.
DISCUSSES US POLICY TOWARD UNDERDEVELOPED COUNTRIES IN PROMPTING ECONOMIC GROWTH. EXAMINES FOREIGN AID PROGRAMS, LOANS (SOFT LOAN EXPERIMENT), AND OTHER FOREIGN-POLICY MEASURES INTENDED TO FURTHER ECONOMIC DEVELOPMENT ABROAD (1940-62).

0164 BALDWIN G.B.
PLANNING AND DEVELOPMENT IN IRAN.
BALTIMORE: JOHNS HOPKINS PRESS, 1967, 213 PP., LC#67-18377.
DESCRIBES SUCCESS AND FAILURE OF IRANIAN DEVELOPMENT PLAN 1962-67. SHOWS HOW PLAN WAS FORMULATED AND HOW IRAN CONTINUES TO PROFIT FROM ORIGINAL PLANNING EFFORT, THOUGH NATIONAL DEVELOPMENT AGENCY FAILED IN 1957. RECONCILES ECONOMIC THEORY WITH POLITICAL, ECONOMIC, CULTURAL, AND INSTITUTIONAL PROBLEMS OF PLANNING IN DEVELOPING COUNTRY. POINTS OUT THAT PLANNING AND DEVELOPMENT DO NOT NECESSARILY GO HAND-IN-HAND.

0165 BALDWIN H.W.
THE PRICE OF POWER.
NEW YORK: HARPER & ROW, 1947, 361 PP.
EXAMINES PROBLEM OF AMERICAN POWER AND ITS USE IN ATOMIC AGE. DISCUSSES DILEMMA OF BUILDING MILITARY DEFENSE AND STILL MAINTAINING DEMOCRACY. PRESENTS CHANGES IN US POWER'S POLITICAL, MILITARY, ECONOMIC, AND PSYCHOLOGICAL POSITIONS. STUDIES REVISION MADE IN POLICIES AND COSTS OF SWITCHES. EXPLORES ALTERNATIVES OPEN IN FUTURE AND PRICE OF US POWER. STATES THAT COMMON IDEAL IS ONLY SOLUTION.

0166 BALDWIN R.E.
ECONOMIC DEVELOPMENT AND EXPORT GROWTH: A STUDY OF NORTHERN RHODESIA, 1920-1960.
NEW YORK: JOHN WILEY, 1966, 254 PP., LC#66-13091.
STUDY OF SIGNIFICANCE AND RELEVANCE OF EXPORT-TECHNOLOGY HYPOTHESIS AND OTHER GROWTH THEORIES IN 40 YEARS OF RHODESIAN GROWTH. INCLUDES STUDIES OF FACTOR COMBINATIONS IN THE COPPER INDUSTRY, AFRICAN WORKER, AND MARKET FOR AGRICULTURAL PRODUCTS. OFFERS DEVELOPMENT THEORY FOR INITIALLY BACKWARD SUBSISTENCE ECONOMY INTO WHICH FOREIGN-FINANCED AND DIRECTED EXPORT INDUSTRY IS INTRODUCED.

0167 BALL R.J.
INFLATION AND THE THEORY OF MONEY.
CHICAGO: ALDINE PUBLISHING CO, 1964, 313 PP.
THEORETICAL BACKGROUND TO ANALYSIS OF INFLATION FOR ADVANCED UNDERGRADUATE OR POSTGRADUATE STUDY. GENERAL PRICE LEVEL, EMPLOYMENT, KEYNESIAN THEORY OF INFLATION, ALTERNATIVE APPROACHES, BUSINESS BEHAVIOR, DEMAND FOR LABOR, ASSETS, INCOME, PROCESS OF INFLATION, AND ECONOMIC POLICY ARE AMONG SUBJECTS DISCUSSED.

0168 BALOGH T.
"L'INFLUENCE DES INSTITUTIONS MONETAIRES ET COMMERCIALES SUR LA STRUCTURE ECONOMIQUE AFRICAIN."
REV. ECON., 14 (NO. 2, 63), 177-95.
TRACES HISTORY OF ECONOMIC RELATIONS AMONG VARIOUS INTRANATIONAL AND INTERNATIONAL GROUPS. ANALYZES COMPARATIVE ECONOMIC DEVELOPMENT WITHIN EUROPEAN COMMON MARKET. CONSIDERS EFFECT OF THESE DEVELOPMENTS ON AFRICAN STATES.

0169 BALOGH T.
THE ECONOMIC IMPACT OF MONETARY AND COMMERCIAL INSTITUTIONS OF A EUROPEAN ORIGIN IN AFRICA.
CAIRO: NAT BANK OF EGYPT, 1964, 71 PP.
IN CONSIDERING THE ECONOMIC PROBLEMS OF EGYPT, AUTHOR SUBMITS VALUABLE ADVICE TO THE DEVELOPING COUNTRIES OF AFRICA FOR ACHIEVING A BALANCED AND RAPID GROWTH.

0170 BANCROFT G.
THE AMERICAN LABOR FORCE: ITS GROWTH AND CHANGING COMPOSITION.
NEW YORK: JOHN WILEY, 1958, 256 PP., LC#58-10795.
PRESENTS, SUMMARIZES, AND INTERPRETS FINDINGS OF US CENSUS BUREAU CONCERNING LABOR FORCE STATUS. EXAMINES TRENDS IN LABOR FORCE 1890-1955, CHANGING PATTERNS OF LABOR FORCE PARTICIPATION 1940-50, TRENDS IN PART-TIME LABOR FORCE, FAMILY EMPLOYMENT PATTERNS, AND PROJECTIONS OF LABOR FORCE TO 1975.

0171 BANERJI A.K.
INDIA'S BALANCE OF PAYMENTS.
NEW YORK: ASIA PUBL HOUSE, 1963, 255 PP.
DISCUSSES FOREIGN TRADE, NON-COMMERCIAL TRANSACTIONS (FOREIGN MISSIONARY AND CONSUL EXPENDITURES, GOVERNMENT TRANSACTIONS, ETC.), FOREIGN INVESTMENTS, AND BALANCE OF PAYMENTS IN INDIA BETWEEN 1920 AND PRESENT.

0172 BANFIELD E.C.
"CONGRESS AND THE BUDGET: A PLANNER'S CRITICISM"
AM. POL. SCI. REV., 43 (DEC. 49), 1217-1228.
CLAIMS THAT INSTEAD OF VIEWING THE BUDGET AS A MEANS OF EFFECTING A RATIONAL DISTRIBUTION OF LIMITED FUNDS AMONG ALTERNATIVES, CONGRESS SEES THE BUDGET AS AN INSTRUMENT FOR EXERTING MANAGERIAL CONTROL OVER THE EXECUTIVE AND AS A MEANS OF ESTABLISHING THE SUPREMACY OF PRIVATE AND LOCAL INTERESTS OVER THE NATIONAL INTEREST. PLANNING FOR THE GENERAL INTEREST IS NECESSARY.

0173 BANFIELD E.C.
THE MORAL BASIS OF A BACKWARD SOCIETY.
NEW YORK: MACMILLAN, 1967, 204 PP.
EXAMINATION OF BACKWARDNESS AND POVERTY OF AN ITALIAN VILLAGE. AUTHOR FINDS THAT THEY ARE PERPETUATED BY VILLAGERS' CULTURALLY DERIVED INABILITY TO GROUP TOGETHER FOR THEIR COMMON GOOD. BOOK PRESENTS IMPRESSIONS AND EXPLANATIONS AND DISCUSSES ECONOMY, CLASS RELATIONS, PREDICTIONS, AND ORIGINS AND PRINCIPLES OF ETHOS.

0174 BANK INTERNATIONAL SETTLEMENTS
AUSTRIA: MONETARY AND ECONOMIC SITUATION 1952-61 (PAMPHLET)
BASLE: BANK FOR INTL SETTLEMENTS, 1962, 26 PP.
REVIEW OF VARIOUS ASPECTS OF ECONOMY DURING THIS PERIOD BY MEANS OF GRAPHS, CHARTS, ETC.

0175 BANOVETZ J.M.
"METROPOLITAN SUBSIDIES: AN APPRAISAL."
PUBLIC ADMIN. REV., 25 (DEC. 65), 297-301.
THE QUESTION, "ARE SUBURBAN AREAS REALLY FREELOADERS?" IS EXAMINED. AFTER REVIEWING THE LIMITED RESEARCH DONE ON THE QUESTION, THE AUTHOR CONCLUDES THAT THE PROBLEM OF SUBSIDIZATION HAS BEEN "OVERRATED." FURTHERMORE, THE CITIES WOULD BE THE LOSERS IN ANY CONSOLIDATION OF GOVERNMENTS.

0176 BARALL M.
"THE UNITED STATES GOVERNMENT RESPONDS."
ANN. AMER. ACAD. POLIT. SOC. SCI., 334 (MARCH 61), 133-142.
USA CAN HELP DEVELOP LATIN AMERICAN POTENTIAL BY LENDING FINANCIAL AID AND ADVICE PERTAINING TO CAPITAL-FORMATION AS WELL AS CONTRIBUTING TO AGRICULTURAL AND EDUCATIONAL TRAINING. BUT LATIN AMERICA MUST HELP HERSELF BY REFORMING ITS ECONOMIC STRUCTURE AND DEVELOPING PLANS BASED ON SOLID PRIORITIES. ALTHOUGH WESTERN HEMISPHERE IS INTERDEPENDENT, LATIN AMERICA CAN ACHIEVE SELF-RELIANCE.

0177 BARAN P.
"THE FUTURE COMPUTER UTILITY."
PUBLIC INTEREST, 8 (SUMMER 67), 75-87.
DISCUSSES POSSIBILITY OF "NATIONAL COMPUTER PUBLIC UTILITY SYSTEM" IN FUTURE. FEELS IT WILL OPERATE ON PRINCIPLE OF "TIME-SHARING," ONLY WITH MANY MORE PEOPLE OWNING COMPUTERS THAN DO NOW. COVERS DEVELOPMENT OF COMPUTER OVER YEARS, ITS BENEFITS, ETC. CONCENTRATES ON PROBLEM OF REGULATING SUCH SYSTEM.

0178 BARAN P.A.
THE POLITICAL ECONOMY OF GROWTH.
NEW YORK: PROMETHEUS PRESS, 1957, 308 PP., LC#57-7953.
FOCUSES ON CONCEPTS OF ECONOMIC SURPLUS AND MONOPOLY CAPITALISM IN ANALYZING THE DIFFICULTY DEVELOPED CAPITALIST COUNTRIES HAVE IN RATIONALLY UTILIZING THEIR ECONOMIC RESOURCES. ALSO DISCUSSES THE PROBLEMS OF ECONOMIC GROWTH PECULIAR TO UNDERDEVELOPED SOCIETIES, REGARDLESS OF LOCATION OR CULTURE.

0179 BARAN P.A., SWEEZY P.M.
MONOPOLY CAPITAL; AN ESSAY ON THE AMERICAN ECONOMIC AND SOCIAL ORDER.

NEW YORK: MONTHLY REVIEW PR, 1966, 402 PP., LC#65-15269.
SYSTEMATIC ANALYSIS OF MONOPOLY CAPITALISM AS IT OPERATES IN AMERICA. IN ANALYZING PURELY ECONOMIC FUNCTIONING OF SYSTEM, ESSAY IS ORGANIZED AROUND THEME OF GENERATION AND ABSORPTION OF SURPLUS UNDER MONOPOLY CAPITALIST CONDITIONS. ARGUES THAT MODES OF SURPLUS UTILIZATION CONSTITUTE MECHANISM LINKING ECONOMIC FOUNDATION OF SOCIETY WITH MARXIAN POLITICAL, CULTURAL, AND IDEOLOGICAL SUPERSTRUCTURE.

0180 BARANSON J.
"ECONOMIC AND SOCIAL CONSIDERATIONS IN ADAPTING TECHNOLOGIES FOR DEVELOPING COUNTRIES."
TECHNOL. CULT., 4 (WINTER 63), 22-29.
'THE DEVELOPING ECONOMIES CALL FOR SMALL, EFFICIENT PROCESSING AND ASSEMBLY PLANTS DESIGNED TO FUNCTION WITH MODEST TRANSPORT AND POWER FACILITIES AND UTILIZING LOCAL MATERIAL AND SKILL.'

0181 BARANSON J.
TECHNOLOGY FOR UNDERDEVELOPED AREAS: AN ANNOTATED BIBLIOGRAPHY.
NEW YORK: PERGAMON PRESS, 1967, 81 PP., LC#67-14273.
INTERDISCIPLINARY BIBLIOGRAPHY OF 319 ITEMS FROM JOURNALS AND BOOKS SELECTED FROM 2,000 EUROPEAN AND AMERICAN SOURCES. ENTRIES, ARRANGED BY SUBJECT, TREAT SOCIO-CULTURAL INFLUENCES ON TECHNOLOGY, PRODUCTS AND SYSTEMS, INSTITUTIONAL ARRANGEMENTS, AND MAJOR ASPECTS OF ECONOMIC THEORY. ITEMS ARE ANNOTATED.

0182 BARBASH J.
THE PRACTICE OF UNIONISM.
NEW YORK: HARPER & ROW, 1956, 465 PP., LC#56-9325.
A WELL-WRITTEN BOOK ON THE INTERNAL AND EXTERNAL ASPECTS OF UNIONS, THEIR GOVERNANCE, ADMINISTRATION, AND RIVALRY BETWEEN THE AFL AND CIO FOR REPRESENTATION, AS WELL AS THE MACHINERY OF COLLECTIVE BARGAINING, STRIKES, THE UNION AS A LOBBY. SPECIFIC PROBLEMS SUCH AS RACKETEERING INFLUENCE IN UNIONS AND COMMUNISM ARE DISCUSSED.

0183 BARBASH J.
UNIONS AND UNION LEADERSHIP.
NEW YORK: HARPER & ROW, 1959, 348 PP.
A COLLECTION OF ESSAYS BY PROMINENT LABOR EXPERTS ON VARIOUS ASPECTS OF UNIONISM, SUCH AS UNION LEADERSHIP, ORGANIZERS, BUSINESS AGENTS, AND THE VARIOUS UNION "STYLES." INCLUDES QUESTIONS OF MEMBERSHIP CONTROL AND VARIOUS CONFLICT SITUATIONS, AS WELL AS SOME SPECIAL PROBLEMS (RACKETEERING, RACE RELATIONS, AND TECHNOLOGY) PRESENTED IN LIGHT OF A BROAD-RANGING GENERAL INTRODUCTION.

0184 BARBASH J.
LABOR'S GRASS ROOTS.
NEW YORK: HARPER & ROW, 1961, 250 PP., LC#61-14839.
FOCUSES ON INTERNAL GOVERNMENT OF LOCAL UNIONS, INCLUDING THE FUNCTION OF LOCAL UNIONS, THEIR RELATIONS TO THE INTERNATIONAL UNION, THEIR REGULATION BY COURTS AND LAW, INCLUDING UNION ASSOCIATIONAL "LAW." INTERESTING INSIGHTS ON CONFLICT, CONTROVERSY, FACTIONS, AND THE OPERATION OF DEMOCRACY WITHIN LOCAL UNIONS.

0185 BARBOUR V.
CAPITALISM IN AMSTERDAM IN THE 17TH CENTURY.
ANN ARBOR: U OF MICH PR, 1963, 171 PP.
STUDY ON ANGLO-DUTCH COMMERCIAL RIVALRY IN 17TH CENTURY. ANALYSIS OF ORGANIZATION OF CAPITALISTIC ENTERPRISES: AMSTERDAM MARKET, EXCHANGE BANKS, SPECULATIVE TRADING COMPANIES, LOANS AND INVESTMENT SYSTEMS. DISCUSSION OF CHARACTERISTICS OF AMSTERDAM CAPITALISM. SHORT BIBLIOGRAPHICAL NOTE.

0186 BARDENS D.
CHURCHILL IN PARLIAMENT.
LONDON: ROBERT HALE, 1967, 381 PP.
ANALYZES 60 YEARS DURING WHICH CHURCHILL WAS CENTRAL FIGURE OF "MOTHER PARLIAMENT." STRESSES AMAZING COMPLEX OF CHANGE (POLITICAL, SOCIAL, RELIGIOUS) THAT SWEPT ENGLAND SEVERAL TIMES DURING PERIOD, YET DID NOT FAZE CHURCHILL. STUDIES WAY HE ALWAYS LIVED AND ACTED IN PRESENT, FOR FUTURE.

0187 BARKSDALE H.C. ED.
MARKETING: CHANGE AND EXCHANGE.
NEW YORK: HOLT RINEHART WINSTON, 1964, 322 PP., LC#64-19809.
ARTICLES FROM "FORTUNE MAGAZINE" SELECTED TO DESCRIBE AND DEFINE CHANGES TAKING PLACE IN MARKETS AND PRODUCTS. REPORT ADJUSTMENTS BEING MADE IN MARKETING INSTITUTIONS AND DISTRIBUTION PROCESSES TO ADAPT TO NEW CONDITIONS. PRESENT PICTURE OF MARKETING IN FOUR DIMENSIONS: MARKETS, PRODUCTS, INSTITUTIONS, AND PROCESSES.

0188 BARNETT A.D.
COMMUNIST ECONOMIC STRATEGY: THE RISE OF MAINLAND CHINA.
WASHINGTON: NATL PLANNING ASSN, 1959, 106 PP., LC#59-14046.
ANALYSIS OF ECONOMIC GROWTH AND DEVELOPMENT IN COMMUNIST CHINA. DISCUSSES FIRST FIVE-YEAR-PLAN AS TO ITS EFFECTIVENESS, AND "LEAP FORWARD" INTENDED TO INCREASE INDUSTRIALIZATION AND IMPROVE AGRICULTURE. COVERS ECONOMIC RELATIONS WITH SOVIET BLOC AND FREE WORLD.

0189 BARNETT A.D.
CHINA AFTER MAO.
PRINCETON: PRINCETON U PRESS, 1967, 287 PP., LC#67-14406.
EXPOSITION OF RECENT TREND IN CHINESE POLITICAL AFFAIRS, EMPHASIZING THAT NEW ERA WITH PROFOUND CHANGES IS ABOUT TO BEGIN. DISCUSSES BASIC PROBLEMS IN MANY AREAS NOW FACING GOVERNMENT AND HOW THEY ARE BEING HANDLED BY MAO. MENTIONS PAST ACCOMPLISHMENTS AS SOURCE OF UNDERSTANDING. SEES A MAJOR PROBLEM IN ACHIEVING SUSTAINED ECONOMIC GROWTH.

0190 BARNETT H.J.
"RESEARCH AND DEVELOPMENT, ECONOMIC GROWTH, AND NATIONAL SECURITY."
ANN. AMER. ACAD. POLIT. SOC. SCI., 327 (JAN. 60), 36-49.
QUESTIONS THE PREVALENT BELIEF THAT GOVERNMENT-SPONSORED RESEARCH AND DEVELOPMENT CAN BE EQUATED WITH ECONOMIC GROWTH. CORRELATION BETWEEN THE TWO DOES EXIST BUT IT IS NECESSARY TO EXAMINE PATHS 'OPEN TO GOVERNMENT' IN SELECTING POLICY. ENDS BEST ACHIEVED IF GOVERNMENT INDICATES ONLY OBJECTIVES ALLOWING RESEARCH-DECISIONS TO BE MADE AT-LARGE.

0191 BARNETT H.J., MORSE C.
SCARCITY AND GROWTH: THE ECONOMICS OF NATURAL RESOURCE AVAILABILITY.
BALTIMORE: JOHNS HOPKINS PRESS, 1963, 288 PP., LC#63-9742.
APPLIES STATISTICAL INFORMATION AND MODERN ANALYTICAL TOOLS TO PROBLEM OF RESOURCE SCARCITY AND POPULATION GROWTH. EXAMINES THEORIES OF MALTHUS, RICARDO, AND J.S. MILL. DISCUSSES AMERICAN CONSERVATION MOVEMENT AND TRACES ITS ROOTS TO DARWIN AND GEORGE MARSH. DEVELOPS THEORY OF WELFARE IN A PROGRESSIVE WORLD, IN WHICH TECHNOLOGY CAN BE APPLIED TO RESOURCE PROBLEMS.

0192 BARRASH J.
LABOR'S GRASS ROOTS; A STUDY OF THE LOCAL UNION.
NEW YORK: HARPER & ROW, 1961, 250 PP., LC#61-14839.
STUDIES LOCAL US LABOR UNIONS IN RELATION TO NATIONAL LABOR MOVEMENT. DISCUSSES UNION GOVERNMENT, LEADERSHIP, INTERNAL CONFLICT, DEMOCRATIC OPERATION, AND CROSS SECTION OF LOCAL MEMBERSHIP.

0193 BARRERE A.
POLITIQUE FINANCIERE.
PARIS: LIBRAIRIE DALLOZ, 1958, 595 PP.
NATIONAL FINANCIAL POLICIES ARE NOW MORE ORIENTED TOWARD SATISFYING PUBLIC NEEDS. THE STATE, THEREFORE, IS INVOLVED IN PUBLIC ECONOMY AS WELL AS IN NATIONAL FINANCE, WITH POLITICAL IMPLICATIONS. EXTENSIVE WORK DIVIDES INTO THREE PARTS: FINANCIAL PLAN, FINANCIAL MANAGEMENT OF THE PUBLIC ECONOMY, AND ECONOMIC INTEGRATION OF PUBLIC FINANCES. INCLUDES BIBLIOGRAPHY OF ABOUT 130 ITEMS.

0194 BARRERE A.
ECONOMIE ET INSTITUTIONS FINANCIERES (VOL. I)
PARIS: DALLOZ, 1965, 460 PP.
EXAMINES FINANCIAL INSTITUTIONS IN THE AREA OF PUBLIC ECONOMY - SYYTEM AND STRUCTURE. STRESSES FINANCIAL PLANNING: BUDGET, RESOURCES, AND IMPLEMENTATION; FLOW OF FINANCES - FISCAL MATTERS; AND GROWTH POLICY IN THE FRENCH ECONOMY.

0195 BARRO S.
"ECONOMIC IMPACT OF SPACE EXPENDITURES: SOME BROAD ISSUES DEALING WITH COSTS AND BENEFITS."
BUSINESS HORIZONS, 10 (SUMMER 67) 71-80.
PROVIDES BACKGROUND ON HOW SPACE PROGRAM FUNDING DECISIONS MAY IMPINGE ON OVER-ALL ECONOMIC ACTIVITY AND ECONOMIC POLICY; SUGGESTS POSSIBILITY THAT SPACE OPERATIONS MAY MAKE MAJOR CONTRIBUTIONS TO ECONOMIC WELFARE.

0196 BARRON J.A.
"ACCESS TO THE PRESS."
HARVARD LAW REV., 80 (JUNE 67), 1641-1678.
STATES THAT 18TH-CENTURY VIEW OF FIRST AMENDMENT AS ENCOURAGEMENT TO "FULL AND FREE DISCUSSION" IN PRESS IS NO LONGER WORKING. EXAMINES NEW TECHNOLOGY OF COMMUNICATIONS INDUSTRY, WHICH LIMITS ACCESS TO MEDIA AND TYPES OF NEWS COVERED. EXAMINES SEVERAL COURT CASES AND URGES PASSAGE OF LAW THAT WOULD GUARANTEE FREE ACCESS TO ALL MEDIA FOR ALL POINTS OF VIEW.

0197 BARROW T.C.
TRADE AND EMPIRE: THE BRITISH CUSTOMS SERVICE IN COLONIAL AMERICA, 1660-1775.
CAMBRIDGE: HARVARD U PR, 1967, 352 PP., LC#67-11666.
ANALYSIS OF ORGANIZATION AND OPERATION OF BRITISH CUSTOMS SERVICE IN COLONIAL AMERICA. THE CUSTOMS SERVED TO IMPLEMENT BRITAIN'S POLICY FOR USE OF COLONIES PRIMARILY FOR THE ECONOMIC WELL-BEING OF THE MOTHER COUNTRY AND WERE THUS A NATURAL TARGET OF THE COLONIAL DISCONTENT WHICH LED TO REVOLUTION.

0198 BARRY E.E.
NATIONALISATION IN BRITISH POLITICS: THE HISTORICAL

BACKGROUND.
STANFORD: STANFORD U PRESS, 1965, 397 PP.
STUDIES HISTORICAL BACKGROUND TO NATIONALIZATION IN BRITAIN, THE SOCIALIST MOVEMENT ITSELF, AND LABOR POLITICS IN RECENT YEARS. COVERS ASPECTS OF NATIONALIZATION OF VARIOUS ACTIVITIES (INDUSTRY, RAILWAY, LAND, MINES), AND TRACES, CHRONOLOGICALLY, 20TH-CENTURY POLITICAL VIEWS AND ACTIONS IN RESPONSE TO NATIONALIZATION.

0199 BARTELS R.
THE DEVELOPMENT OF MARKETING THOUGHT.
HOMEWOOD: RICHARD IRWIN, 1962, 284 PP., LC#62-16521.
DISCUSSES EARLY THEORIES AND DEVELOPMENT OF MARKETING THOUGHT, AND EXAMINES SUCH BASIC ASPECTS AS ADVERTISING, SALES MANAGEMENT, MARKETING RESEARCH, RETAILING, AND WHOLESALING.

0200 BARTHELEMY G.
"LE NOUVEAU FRANC (CFA) ET LA BANQUE CENTRALE DES ETATS DE L'AFRIQUE DE L'OUEST."
TIERS-MONDE, 4 (NOS.13-14, 63), 275-77.
DISCUSSES STRUCTURE AND PURPOSES OF AFRICAN FINANCIAL COMMUNITY AND ADOPTION OF NEW AFRICAN FRANC. ANALYZES POSSIBLE FUTURE DEVELOPMENTS IN THE MONETARY DISTRIBUTION CENTERS. INDICATES THAT PRESENT SET-UP ENJOYS CONSIDERABLE AUTONOMY. CONSIDERS INTERRELATIONSHIP OF SIX STATES.

0201 BARTLETT J.L.
"AMERICAN BOND ISSUES IN THE EUROPEAN ECONOMIC COMMUNITY."
STANFORD LAW REV., 19 (JUNE 67), 1337-1357.
DISCUSSES RESULTS OF VOLUNTARY INVESTMENT GUIDELINES OF 1965 THAT FORCED AMERICAN BUSINESS TO SEEK FOREIGN SOURCES OF INVESTMENT CAPITAL FOR OVERSEAS OPERATIONS IN ORDER TO IMPROVE US BALANCE OF PAYMENTS. MAINTAINS THAT EUROPEAN CAPITAL MARKETS CAN MEET DEMAND AND SUGGESTS ESTABLISHMENT OF FINANCING SUBSIDIARIES IN US OR LUXEMBOURG TO OBTAIN FAVORABLE TAX TREATMENT FOR BOND FINANCING.

0202 BARZANSKI S.
"REGIONAL UNDERDEVELOPMENT IN THE EUROPEAN ECONOMIC COMMUNITY."
ORBIS, 7 (SPRING 63), 105-119.
EXAMINES UNBALANCED ECONOMIC GROWTH WITHIN EEC AND THREAT POSED TO EUROPEAN POLITICAL AND ECONOMIC UNION. CONFLICTING NATIONAL INTERESTS LIMIT EFFECTIVENESS OF NATIONAL PROGRAMS AS LONG-TERM SOLUTION. CONCLUDES THAT UNIFIED EUROPE DEPENDS ON PLANNED ECONOMY ACCORDING TO NEEDS OF WHOLE COMMUNITY UNDER A FORM OF CENTRALIZED CONTROL.

0203 BASCH A.
THE FUTURE OF FOREIGN LENDING FOR DEVELOPMENT (PAMPHLET)
ANN ARBOR: CTR RES ON ECO DEVEL, 1962, 45 PP., LC#62-63218.
ANALYZES EXTERNAL ASSISTANCE IN POSTWAR PERIOD, EXPORTS FROM UNDERDEVELOPED COUNTRIES, FLOW OF EXTERNAL ASSISTANCE IN RECENT YEARS, FUTURE REQUIREMENTS, AND RESPONSIBILITIES OF DEVELOPED NATIONS. PROPOSES A MOVE FROM CONVENTIONAL LOANS TO LENIENT TERM LOANS AND GRANTS.

0204 BASOV V.
"THE DEVELOPMENT OF PUBLIC EDUCATION AND THE BUDGET."
SOVIET EDUCATION, 9 (FEB. 67), 23-30.
DISCUSSES SOVIET FINANCING OF EDUCATION. STATES THAT FUNDS FOR MAINTENANCE OF CHILDREN'S PRESCHOOL INSTITUTIONS COME FROM STATE RESOURCES AND PARENTS' PAYMENTS, WHEREAS ALL OTHER EDUCATION IS PAID BY STATE. PRESENTS STATISTICS ON ENROLLMENT, EXPENDITURES, AND COMPARES FIGURES WITH PRE-REVOLUTIONARY DATA. DESCRIBES METHODS BEING DEVELOPED BY GOVERNMENT FOR DETERMING BUDGETS OF INSTITUTIONS.

0205 BASSIE V.L.
UNCERTAINTY IN FORECASTING AND POLICY FORMATION (PAMPHLET)
AUSTIN: U TEXAS, BUR OF BUS RES, 1959, 35 PP.
ANALYZES FLUCTUATIONS IN BUSINESS CYCLE AND EFFECTS ON MANAGEMENT DECISIONS; DISCUSSES ECONOMIC FORECASTING BY INVESTIGATION OF INTERACTIONS OF CYCLES.

0206 BASTIAT F.
ECONOMIC HARMONIES (1850)
PRINCETON: VAN NOSTRAND, 1964, 536 PP.
CENTRAL IDEA IS THAT THE INTERESTS OF MEN ARE HARMONIOUS AND ARE BEST REALIZED IN A COUNTRY WHERE THE GOVERNMENT MERELY APPLIES LAW AND ORDER. THUS THE AUTHOR ADVOCATES FREE TRADE AND IS AGAINST SUBSIDIES. AUTHOR ESSENTIALLY ADVOCATES "LAISSEZ-FAIRE" BUT IN THE SENCE THAT HUMAN FREEDOM AND INITIATIVE ARE TO BE RESPECTED. HE FEELS THAT IN A FREE MARKET WAGES AND PRICES WILL BALANCE OUT.

0207 BASTIAT F.
ECONOMIC SOPHISMS (1845)
PRINCETON: VAN NOSTRAND, 1964, 291 PP.
SERIES OF ESSAYS ATTACKING PROTECTIONISM, SUBSIDIES, AND TAXES INDICATES THAT THE LESS GOVERNMENT RESTRICTS THE FLOW OF MONEY THE BETTER OFF PEOPLE WILL BE. PRINCIPAL METHOD USED IS REDUCTIO AD ABSURDUM OF THE STAND TAKEN BY INDUSTRIALISTS, E.G., ADVOCATING CEMENTING OVER ALL OPENINGS THAT LET IN THE CHIEF FOREIGN COMPETITOR OF THE CANDLE-MAKERS, THE SUN.

0208 BATCHELOR B.
THE NEW OUTLOOK IN BUSINESS.
NEW YORK: HARPER & ROW, 1940, 317 PP.
A COLLECTION OF ESSAYS PROBING SUCH PROBLEMS AS GROUP INTERDEPENDENCE, BUSINESS LEADERSHIP, CORPORATIONS AS SOCIAL INSTRUMENT OF PROGRESS AND COOPERATION, GOVERNMENT REGULATION, AND CHALLENGES OF THE FUTURE.

0209 BATES J.L.
THE ORIGINS OF TEAPOT DOME: PROGRESSIVES, PARTIES, AND PETROLEUM, 1909-1921.
URBANA: U OF ILLINOIS PR, 1963, 278 PP., LC#63-17045.
STUDY OF ORIGINS OF TEAPOT DOME SCANDAL OF 1924, TRACING OIL PROBLEM IN INDUSTRY AND NAVY FROM TAFT TO HARDING. FEELS PROBLEM WAS ONE OF "CONSERVATION POLICY" AND TRIES TO ANALYZE VIEWS ON IT AT TIME. STUDIES PRESSURES ON GOVERNMENTAL POLICY, NEED FOR OIL SINCE WWI, URGE FOR REFORM OF BIG BUSINESS IN US, SECTIONALISM IN POLITICS, AND EFFECT OF ALL ON OIL POLICY. BIBLIOGRAPHY OF WORKS CITED IN TEXT.

0210 BATOR F.M.
QUESTION OF GOVERNMENT SPENDING.
NEW YORK: HARPER, 1960, 162 PP.
THREE PART STUDY OF PUBLIC SPENDING. PART ONE: QUANTITATIVE EXHAUSTIVE AND NON-EXHAUSTIVE STATE. PART TWO: SCARCITY AND ALLOCATION OF RESOURCES, INEFFICIENT MARKETS, INEFFICIENT GOVERNMENT, COST OF AVOIDING INFLATION. PART THREE: CHARTS, GRAPHS, AND STATISTICS ON GOVERNMENT SPENDING 1929-1957.

0211 BATTEN T.R.
PROBLEMS OF AFRICAN DEVELOPMENT (2ND ED.)
LONDON: OXFORD U PR, 1954, 358 PP.
SURVEY OF EMERGING AFRICA. FIRST PART DEALS WITH PROBLEMS OF ECONOMIC DEVELOPMENT, INCLUDING NATURAL RESOURCES, AGRICULTURE, INVESTMENT; SECOND PART DEALS WITH POLITICAL DEVELOPMENT, INCLUDING HEALTH, EDUCATION, TAXATION, LOCAL GOVERNMENT, AND LAW.

0212 BAUCHET P.
ECONOMIC PLANNING.
LONDON: HEINEMANN, 1964, 299 PP., LC#64-16665.
DESCRIBES THE FRENCH EXPERIENCE IN ECONOMIC PLANNING AS A MAJOR TRANSFORMATION OF CAPITALIST STRUCTURE. CONSIDERS PLANNING AND DEMOCRACY, BUSINESS FIRMS, AND SOCIAL CLASSES, AS WELL AS THE STRATEGY OF PLANNING FOR AN OPTIMUM.

0213 BAUER P.T., YAMEY B.S.
THE ECONOMICS OF UNDERDEVELOPED COUNTRIES.
DURHAM: DUKE U PR, 1957, 271 PP.
ANALYZES PROBLEMS OF MEASURING NATIONAL INCOME AND CAPITAL AND DISTRIBUTION OF LABOR IN UNDERDEVELOPED COUNTRIES. STUDIES NATURAL RESOURCES, EMPLOYMENT PROBLEMS, REMUNERATION, ENTREPRENEURSHIP, AND CAPITAL UTILIZATION. APPRAISES ROLE OF GOVERNMENT IN ECONOMIC DEVELOPMENT AND COMPARES DIFFERENT POLICIES AFFECTING AGRICULTURE AND MANUFACTURING.

0214 BAUER P.T.
ECONOMIC ANALYSIS AND POLICY IN UNDERDEVELOPED COUNTRIES.
DURHAM: DUKE U PR, 1957, 145 PP., LC#57-8814.
DESCRIBES SCOPE, METHOD, AND POSSIBILITIES OF ECONOMICS IN STUDY OF UNDERDEVELOPED NATIONS; AND REPERCUSSIONS OF INCREASED INTEREST IN FIELD. STUDIES CHARACTERISTIC FEATURES OF ECONOMIC LANDSCAPE AND ISSUES OF POLICY.

0215 BAUER P.T.
UNITED STATES AID AND INDIAN ECONOMIC DEVELOPMENT.
WASHINGTON: AMER ENTERPRISE INST, 1959, 119 PP., LC#59-14982
ANALYZES INDIA'S ECONOMIC SITUATION AND GOVERNMENT ECONOMIC POLICIES SINCE WWII. DISCUSSES INADEQUACY OF US AID. EMPHASIZES POLICY OF SOCIALIZING INDIAN ECONOMY AND POLITICAL AND SOCIAL PROBLEMS THIS CAUSES, ESPECIALLY SINCE IT IS BEING DONE WITH US MONEY.

0216 BAUER P.T.
INDIAN ECONOMIC POLICY AND DEVELOPMENT.
NEW YORK: FREDERICK PRAEGER, 1961, 152 PP., LC#61-8435.
ANALYZES INDIA'S ECONOMIC SITUATION SINCE WWII AND ITS GOVERNMENT ECONOMIC POLICIES. DISCUSSES PROS AND CONS OF GOVERNMENT'S ACTIONS DUE TO ITS POLITICAL BIAS. CRITICIZES VAGUENESS AND AMBIGUITY OF GOVERNMENT POLICIES. BRIEFLY SUGGESTS ALTERNATIVE POLICIES, EMPHASIZING VARIOUS EFFECTS ON POLITICAL AND SOCIAL SCENE RATHER THAN LONG-TERM RESULTS.

0217 BAUER R.A., POOL I., DEXTER L.A.
AMERICAN BUSINESS AND PUBLIC POLICY: THE POLITICS OF FOREIGN TRADE.
NEW YORK: ATHERTON, 1963, 499 PP., $8.95.
A DEFINITIVE CASE STUDY OF THE POLITICS OF FOREIGN TRADE FROM THE RENEWAL OF THE RECIPROCAL TRADE ACT OF 1953 TO THE PASSAGE OF KENNEDY'S TRADE EXPANSION ACT. EXAMINES THE CHANGING ATTITUDES OF THE GENERAL PUBLIC AND THE POLITICAL ACTIONS OF THE BUSINESS COMMUNITY, THE LOBBIES,

AND CONGRESS.

0218 BAUM M.
"THE CASE FOR BUSINESS CIVILIZATION."
HARVARD BUSINESS REV., 38 (NOV.-DEC. 60), 56-64.
AN ADMISSION OF MINOR FAULTS AND A DEFENSE AGAINST TWO MAJOR INDICTMENTS: THAT BUSINESS CULTURE CAUSES DRASTIC DAMAGE TO INDIVIDUAL CHARACTER AND CONDUCT, AND THAT IT DEBASES OUR PROFESSIONAL AND POLITICAL BEHAVIOR BY ITS COMPLETE DISREGARD FOR THE SOCIAL AND CULTURAL CONSEQUENCES OF BUSINESS ACTIVITIES. LARGE BUSINESSES HAVE BECOME SEMI-PUBLIC AND CANNOT OPERATE IN TERMS OF MERE EXPEDIENCY.

0219 BAUMOL W.J.
ECONOMIC THEORY AND OPERATIONS ANALYSIS (2ND ED.)
ENGLEWOOD CLIFFS: PRENTICE HALL, 1965, 606 PP., LC#65-13179.
DISCUSSION OF APPLICATIONS OF ECONOMIC THEORY TO TOOLS OF OPERATIONS RESEARCH AND BUSINESS ANALYSIS. OFFERS READER SYSTEMATIC EXPOSITION OF RECEIVED MICRO-ECONOMIC ANALYSIS, AND INTUITIVE GRASP OF RECENT DEVELOPMENTS IN MATHEMATICAL ECONOMICS.

0220 BAYER H. ED.
WIRTSCHAFTSPROGNOSE UND WIRTSCHAFTSGESTALTUNG.
BERLIN: DUNCKER & HUMBLOT, 1960, 318 PP.
COLLECTION OF ESSAYS ON ECONOMIC PLANNING, COOPERATIVE TRADING SYSTEM, FINANCIAL POLICY, PROGNOSIS AND PLANNING IN ECONOMY OF UNDERDEVELOPED NATIONS, AND ECONOMIC POLICY IN NETHERLANDS. INCLUDES DISCUSSION OF ESSAYS PRESENTED.

0221 BEAL E.F., WICKERSHAM E.D.
THE PRACTICE OF COLLECTIVE BARGAINING (3RD ED.)
HOMEWOOD: RICHARD IRWIN, 1967, 809 PP., LC#67-14355.
COVERS THEORETICAL AND PRACTICAL PROBLEMS AND TREATS PROFESSIONAL ASSOCIATIONS, MANAGEMENT ORGANIZATIONS, ACTIVITIES IN LABOR RELATIONS, ROLE OF GOVERNMENT, UNION SECURITY, AND RIGHTS OF INDIVIDUAL. PRESENTS MAJOR STATUTORY LAWS AND SPECIFIC CASE STUDIES ILLUSTRATING THE PRINCIPLES AND PRACTICE OF COLLECTIVE BARGAINING. EMPHASIZES US, BUT INCLUDES CHAPTER ON FOREIGN COUNTRIES.

0222 BEARD C.A.
AN ECONOMIC INTERPRETATION OF THE CONSTITUTION OF THE UNITED STATES.
NEW YORK: MACMILLAN, 1913, 330 PP.
ANALYSIS OF US CONSTITUTION BASED ON ECONOMIC ANALYSES (ECONOMIC BIOGRAPHIES) OF ITS AUTHORS, AND STUDY OF ECONOMIC CONDITIONS UNDER WHICH IT EVOLVED. INVOLVES STUDY AND INTERPRETATION OF POLITICAL DOCTRINES OF FOUNDING FATHERS; PROCESS OF RATIFICATION; POPULAR VOTE ON CONSTITUTION AND ECONOMICS OF THAT VOTE; THE ECONOMIC CONFLICT OVER RATIFICATION.

0223 BEARDSLEY R.K. ED.
STUDIES ON ECONOMIC LIFE IN JAPAN (OCCASIONAL PAPERS NO. 8)
ANN ARBOR: U OF MICH PR, 1964, 124 PP.
FOUR PAPERS ON JAPANESE ECONOMIC LIFE: A COMPARISON OF AMERICAN AND JAPANESE HOUSING; STUDY OF FINANCIAL COMBINE CENTERED IN OHARA FAMILY OF OKAYAMA; ANALYSIS OF MANUSCRIPT PUBLICATIONS IN JAPAN; AND A COMPARISON OF RURAL STANDARDS OF LIVING WITHIN JAPAN, ANALYZING FACTORS OF VILLAGE PROSPERITY.

0224 BEASLEY K.E.
STATE SUPERVISION OF MUNICIPAL DEBT IN KANSAS - A CASE STUDY
LAWRENCE: U KANSAS, GOV RES CTR, 1961, 220 PP.
TRACES DEVELOPMENT OF REGULATION OF MUNICIPAL DEBT IN KANSAS. FOCUSES ON LEGISLATIVE JUDICIAL, AND ADMINISTRATIVE SUPERVISION. INCLUDES STATISTICAL DATA AND TABLE OF CASES.

0225 BEATON L.
THE STRUGGLE FOR PEACE.
NEW YORK: FREDERICK PRAEGER, 1967, 118 PP., LC#66-29734.
STATES THE FACTS SURROUNDING TODAY'S ARMS RACE AND THE EXPENDITURE OF RESOURCES ON THE MAINTENANCE OF THE WAR MACHINE. DESCRIBES TODAY'S SYSTEM OF INTERNATIONAL POWER AND WHAT CAN BE EXPECTED OF IT.

0226 BEAUFRE A.
AN INTRODUCTION TO STRATEGY, WITH PARTICULAR REFERENCE TO PROBLEMS OF DEFENSE, POLITICS, ECONOMICS IN THE NUCLEAR AGE.
NEW YORK: FREDERICK PRAEGER, 1965, 138 PP.
SPEAKS OF STRATEGY AS A METHOD OF THOUGHT WHOSE OBJECT IS TO CODIFY EVENTS, SET THEM IN ORDER OF PRIORITY, THEN CHOOSE MOST EFFECTIVE COURSE OF ACTION. STRATEGY MUST BE EFFECTIVE AT ALL LEVELS FROM INTERNATIONAL PLANNING TO MILITARY TACTICS, AND MUST BE ORGANIZED ALONG LINES APPROPRIATE TO WORLD SITUATION TODAY.

0227 BECKER A.S.
"COMPARISIONS OF UNITED STATES AND USSR NATIONAL OUTPUT: SOME RULES OF THE GAME."
WORLD POLIT., 13 (OCT. 60), 99-111.
CONTENDS THAT SIGNIFICANT DIFFERENCES IN THE ECONOMIC STRUCTURES OF THE USA AND USSR MAKE COMPARISONS OF NATIONAL OUTPUTS ERRONEOUS AND MISLEADING. BELIEVES THAT AVERAGING INDEX-NUMBERS IS WRONG AND PROPOSES SOME 'RULES' WHICH SHOULD BE APPLIED IN PUBLIC DISCUSSION OF THIS VITAL MATTER.

0228 BEGUIN B.
"ILO AND THE TRIPARTITE SYSTEM."
INT. CONCIL., 523 (MAY 59), 401-48.
EACH NATION IN ILO REPRESENTED BY SPOKESMEN FOR WORKERS, EMPLOYERS, AND GOVERNMENTS. ILO FOUNDED IN 1919 AS MEANS OF CONCILIATION BETWEEN THE THREE BODIES. TRACES DEVELOPMENT OF SYSTEM, CHANGES, AND PROBLEMS WITH FASCIST AND COMMUNIST STATES. MAJOR CURRENT PROGRAM IS SOCIAL AND ECONOMIC DEVELOPMENT OF UNDERDEVELOPED NATIONS.

0229 BEGUIN H.
"ASPECTS STRUCTURELS DU COMMERCE EXTERIEUR DES PAYS SOUS-DEVELOPPES."
TIERS-MONDE, 4 (NOS.13-14, 63), 81-119.
COMPARISON AND ANALYSIS OF ECONOMIC ADVANCE IN UNDER-DEVELOPED COUNTRIES. ANALYZES FOREIGN TRADE AND POSSIBILITIES OF DEVELOPMENT. CONSIDERS IMPORTANT SOCIO-POLITICAL FACTORS INVOLVED. STUDY IS BASED ON STATISTICAL DATA.

0230 BEHRMAN J.N., SCHMIDT W.E.
INTERNATIONAL ECONOMICS: THEORY, PRACTICE, POLICY.
NEW YORK: RINEHART, 1957, 561 PP., LC#57-6447.
COMPREHENSIVE ANALYSIS OF PUBLIC POLICY ISSUES IN INTERNATIONAL ECONOMIC RELATIONS. COVERS WIDE RANGE OF THEORIES, TECHNIQUES, AND POLITICAL ISSUES WHICH CONSTITUTE AND AFFECT ECONOMIC POLICIES. EXAMINES HISTORY OF MAJOR MOVEMENTS IN ECONOMICS SUCH AS DEVELOPMENT OF MERCANTILISM AND FREE TRADE AND FORMATION OF INTERNATIONAL FINANCIAL INSTITUTIONS. ANALYZES AID, TRADE, AND INVESTMENT POLICIES IN POST-WWII US.

0231 BEIM D.
"THE COMMUNIST BLOC AND THE FOREIGN-AID GAME."
WEST. POLIT. QUART., 17 (DEC. 64), 784-799.
PROPOSING A MODEL OF FOREIGN AID AS A 3-PLAYER, NON-ZERO-SUM GAME, AUTHOR ASSERTS THAT SUCH A MODEL WOULD ENABLE ANALYSTS TO REVEAL NATURE OF THE INTEREST UNDERLYING A VARIETY OF GRANTS AND CREDITS AND TO DEDUCE THE MOTIVATIONS OF A COUNTRY DISPENSING SUCH ASSISTANCE LARGELY FROM ITS ACTIONS.

0232 BELASSA B.
ECONOMIC DEVELOPMENT AND INTEGRATION.
MEXICO CITY: CENTRO ESTUDIAS MONETARIOS LAT AM 1965, 157PP.
ANALYSIS OF APPLICATION OF THEORETICAL PRINCIPLES IN DETERMINING EFFECTS OF ECONOMIC INTEGRATION PROGRAMS ON ECONOMIC DEVELOPMENT. CENTERS ON ADAPTATION OF CUSTOMS UNION THEORY TO PROBLEMS OF ECONOMICALLY UNDERDEVELOPED COUNTRIES.

0233 BELISLE J.
"FOREIGN RESTRAINTS ON US BANKS ABROAD"
BANKING, 60 (AUG. 67), 45-46.
EXPLORES OVERSEAS EXPANSION OF US COMMERCIAL BANKS AND DISCUSSES RESTRAINTS PLACED ON THEIR ACTIVITIES BY FOREIGN GOVERNMENTS INVOLVED. REVEALS THAT LITTLE ACTUAL RESTRICTION IS ENFORCED.

0234 BELL D.E.
"THE QUALITY OF AID."
FOREIGN AFFAIRS, 44 (JULY 67), 601-607.
ADVOCATES PROGRAM OF FOREIGN AID BASED ON PARTNERSHIP AND SELF-HELP. URGES ACTION FROM BOTH PUBLIC AND PRIVATE SECTORS OF ECONOMY TO PROVIDE INITIATIVE FOR DEVELOPMENT. MAINTAINS THAT AGENCIES OF FOREIGN AID SHOULD DO MORE RESEARCH INTO AND EVALUATION OF THEIR PROGRAMS AND DESCRIBES AREAS IN NEED OF IMPROVEMENT AND TECHNIQUES TO BE USED.

0235 BELL P.W.
THE STERLING AREA IN THE POSTWAR WORLD.
NEW YORK: OXFORD U. PR., 1956, 479 PP.
STUDY OF INTERNAL DYNAMICS OF MONETARY UNION 'STERLING AREA' DURING POSTWAR PERIOD. CONSIDERATION GIVEN TO AREA'S RELATIONS WITH 'OUTSIDE WORLD' INCLUDING THE DOLLAR AREA. TRADE AND CAPITAL CONDITIONS INVESTIGATED ONLY WHEN RELEVANT TO PRESENT AND FUTURE PLANS OF MONETARY UNION.

0236 BELLAN R.C.
PRINCIPLES OF ECONOMICS AND THE CANADIAN ECONOMY (2ND ED.)
NEW YORK: MCGRAW HILL, 1960, 556 PP., LC#63-18129.
DESIGNED AS TEXTBOOK FOR CANADIAN STUDENTS TAKING INTRODUCTORY COURSE IN ECONOMICS. MUCH ATTENTION TO HISTORICAL BACKGROUND FOR PROPER APPRECIATION OF MODERN ECONOMIC INSTITUTIONS AND POLICIES. ECONOMIC PRINCIPLES DEVELOPED RIGOROUSLY IN STEP-BY-STEP PROCESS.

0237 BELLOC H.
THE SERVILE STATE (1912) (3RD ED.)
LONDON: CONSTABLE & CO, 1927, 189 PP.
AN ATTACK UPON EARLY 20TH-CENTURY CAPITALISM FROM A ROMAN CATHOLIC VIEWPOINT. CENTRAL THESIS IS THAT INDUSTRIAL SOCIETIES SUCH AS BRITAIN AND PRUSSIA, WHICH DEPARTED FROM 16TH-CENTURY CHRISTIAN TRADITIONS, WILL TEND TOWARD THE

RE-ESTABLISHMENT OF SLAVERY AS RESULT OF UNSTABLE BALANCE BETWEEN CLASSES CAUSED BY LEGALLY ENFORCED LABOR REGULATIONS AND FINANCIAL OPPRESSION. INCLUDES 1913 AND 1927 PREFACES.

0238 BELLOC H.
THE RESTORATION OF PROPERTY.
NEW YORK: SHEED AND WARD, 1936, 144 PP.
AN ASSAULT ON BRITISH ECONOMIC AND SOCIAL STRUCTURE. "PROPERTY" IS DEFINED AS CONTROL OVER MEANS OF PRODUCTION, WHICH THE INDIVIDUAL WAGE-EARNER HAS LOST TO MONOPOLISTIC INSTITUTIONS SANCTIONED BY GOVERNMENT. FREEDOM TO CONTROL THE OUTPUT OF HIS ENERGIES CAN BE RESTORED TO THE INDIVIDUAL ONLY THROUGH A LEGALLY ESTABLISHED GUILD SYSTEM, WHICH NEITHER CAPITALISM NOT SOCIALISM OFFERS.

0239 BELOFF M.
THE UNITED STATES AND THE UNITY OF EUROPE.
WASHINGTON: BROOKINGS INST., 1963, 124 PP.
TRACES THE DEVELOPMENT AND IMPLEMENTATION OF CONCEPT OF 'UNITED STATES OF EUROPE' AND DISCLOSES ITS INFLUENCE ON USA POLICY. EUROPEAN POST-WAR RECOVERY, DEFENSE, COMMON MARKET, ATLANTIC ALLIANCE AND ROLE OF GREAT BRITAIN ARE AMONG TOPICS DISCUSSED.

0240 BELOFF M.
"BRITAIN, EUROPE AND THE ATLANTIC COMMUNITY."
INT. ORGAN., 17 (SUMMER 63), 574-92 PP.
DISCUSSES BRITAIN'S RELATIONS WITH EUROPE IN THE DEVELOPMENT OF AN ATLANTIC COMMUNITY, AND THE PROBLEMS THAT SUCH AN ORGANIZATION WOULD POSE FOR HER OTHER INTERNATIONAL RELATIONS.

0242 BELSHAW D.G.R.
"PUBLIC INVESTMENT IN AGRICULTURE AND ECONOMIC DEVELOPMENT OF UGANDA"
J. OF EAST AFRICAN ECONOMIC REV., 9 (DEC. 62), 69-94.
CRITICISM OF 1960 ECONOMIC SURVEY MISSION OF WORLD BANK. SUGGESTS CENTRALIZED ECONOMIC PLANNING, APPLIED RESEARCH, AND A FLEXIBLE SYSTEM FOR REVIEWING PUBLIC EXPENDITURE.

0243 BENDIX R.
"INDUSTRIALIZATION, IDEOLOGIES, AND SOCIAL STRUCTURE" (BMR)"
AMER. SOCIOLOGICAL REV., 24 (OCT. 59), 613-623.
ILLUSTRATES BASIC DIFFERENCE BETWEEN MANAGERIAL IDEOLOGY IN ENGLAND AND RUSSIA, AND RELATES IT TO STRUCTURAL DIFFERENCES IN BUREAUCRACY. STUDIES EFFECTIVENESS OF IDEOLOGY PRESUPPOSING SELF-RELIANCE AND GOOD FAITH.

0244 BENHAM F.
ECONOMIC AID TO UNDERDEVELOPED COUNTRIES.
LONDON: OXFORD U PR, 1961, 121 PP.
EXAMINES FORMS AND CHANNELS THROUGH WHICH AID IS DISPENSED, AND WHO ARE CHIEF CONTRIBUTORS AND RECIPIENTS. EVALUATES VIEWS REGARDING TRADE VS. AID. CONSIDERS PART PLAYED BY FLOW OF PRIVATE CAPITAL. CONCLUDES GREATER AID IS NEEDED IN FORM OF OUTRIGHT GRANTS, NON-INTEREST BEARING AND NON-REPAYABLE.

0245 BEN-PORATH Y.
THE ARAB LABOR FORCE IN ISRAEL.
JERUSALEM: M FALK INST ECO RES, 1966, 96 PP.
ANALYZES STATUS OF ARAB LABOR FORCE IN ISRAEL, MAKING MUCH USE OF STATISTICS GATHERED MAINLY IN 1950'S. INCLUDES GEOGRAPHICAL DISTRIBUTION, EDUCATIONAL, OCCUPATIONAL, AND AGRICULTURAL INFORMATION ON ARAB COMMUNITY, PLUS STATISTICS ON COMPOSITION OF POPULATION. DISCUSSES LABOR MOBILITY, WAGES, INDUSTRIAL AND OCCUPATIONAL STRUCTURE OF EMPLOYMENT, AND MOBILITY REGRESSION ANALYSIS OF 1961.

0246 BENN W.
"TECHNOLOGY HAS AN INEXORABLE EFFECT."
SCIENCE AND TECHNOLOGY, 69 (SEPT. 67), 8-52.
DISCUSSES BRITISH ATTEMPT TO MERGE COMPETING COMPANIES SO THAT FOREIGN COMPETITION CAN BE MET. FEELS ONLY LARGE INDUSTRIES CAN EMPLOY TECHNOLOGY NEEDED TO MAKE BRITAIN TECHNOLOGICAL LEADER OF EUROPE. ANALYZES CHANGES NEEDED IN ADMINISTRATION, PRODUCTION, AND EDUCATIONAL SYSTEM. AUTHOR IS BRITAIN'S MINISTER OF TECHNOLOGY.

0247 BENNETT J.T.
"POLITICAL IMPLICATIONS OF ECONOMIC CHANGE: SOUTH VIETNAM."
ASIAN SURVEY, 7 (AUG. 67),581-591.
DISCUSSION BY OFFICIAL OF AGENCY FOR INTERNATIONAL DEVELOPMENT OF HIGHER LEVELS OF CONSUMPTION, DECLINE IN UNEMPLOYMENT, AND RISE IN WAGES IN SOUTH VIETNAMESE ECONOMY. EXAMINES GROWTH IN PRIVATE SERVICES, INDUSTRIAL PRODUCTION, AGRICULTURE, JOB MOBILITY, ETC. TRACES IMPACT OF ECONOMIC CONDITIONS UPON POLITICAL LIFE AND POPULAR DEMANDS.

0248 BENNION E.G.
"ECONOMETRICS FOR MANAGEMENT."
HARVARD BUSINESS REV., 39 (MAR. 61), 100-112.
INTRODUCES ECONOMETRIC AND PROGRAMMING MODELS AND SHOWS HOW THEY MAY BE USED TO THE COMPANY'S ADVANTAGE IN DECISION-MAKING. ASSESSES RELUCTANCE OF BUSINESS TO ADOPT THESE MODELS. ASSERTS VALUE OF SUCH MODELS IN AIDING CHOICE-MAKING ON COMPLEX ISSUES BY ENHANCING COMPREHENSION OF VARIABLES AND BY FACILITATING COMPREHENSIBLE, PRECISE ANALYSIS OF ALTERNATIVE ASSUMPTIONS.

0249 BENOIT E.
EUROPE AT SIXES AND SEVENS: THE COMMON MARKET, THE FREE TRADE ASSOCIATION AND THE UNITED STATES.
NEW YORK: COLUMBIA U. PR. 1961, 287 PP.
STATES THAT CREATION OF EUROPEAN COMMUNITY REPRESENTS ATTEMPT TO FIND NEW WAYS OF ORDERING RELATIONS BETWEEN STATES AUGMENTING MERE PROFESSIONS OF COOPERATION. EXAMINES STRUGGLE FOR INTEGRATION, DOLLAR CRISIS AND AMERICAN COMPETITIVENESS. STUDIES BUSINESS OPPORTUNITIES IN A CONSOLDATED EUROPEAN COMMUNITY.

0250 BENOIT E.
"THE PROPENSITY TO REDUCE THE NATIONAL DEBT OUT OF DEFENSE SAVINGS."
AMER. ECON. REV., 51 (MAY 61), 445-59.
EMPHASIZES DANGER OF ACHIEVING A BUDGET SURPLUS FOR PURPOSE OF DEBT REDUCTION. SUCH AN ATTEMPT COULD BE DANGEROUS BECAUSE A DECLINE IN GOVERNMENT ORDERS CAN SLOW DOWN THE NATIONAL ECONOMY AND BECOME A SERIOUS SOURCE OF WEAKNESS.

0251 BENOIT E.
"ECONOMIC ADJUSTMENTS TO ARMS CONTROL."
J. ARMS CONTR., 1 (APRIL 63), 105-111.
OUTLINES ECONOMIC EFFECTS OF DISARMAMENT AND MULTILATERAL ARMS STABILIZATION AND LIMITATION. CITES POSSIBILITY OF INCREASED DEFENSE EXPENDITURES IF LATTER OCCURS. THE ABILITY OF AMERICAN ECONOMY TO ADJUST TO LARGE-SCALE DISARMAMENT IS OPTIMISTICALLY APPRAISED.

0252 BENOIT E., BOULDING K.E.
DISARMAMENT AND THE ECONOMY.
NEW YORK: HARPER, 1963, 310 PP.
COSTS OF INSPECTION, IMPACT ON RESEARCH AND EFFECT PRODUCED ON USA FINANCIAL STRUCTURE ARE PROBLEMS DISCUSSED. AUTHORS REVIEW BALANCE OF PAYMENTS PLIGHT AND PROPOSE ALTERNATIVES TO DEFENSE PRODUCTION. REPORT SPONSORED BY UNIVERSITY OF MICHIGAN CENTER FOR RESEARCH ON CONFLICT RESOLUTION.

0253 BENOIT E.
"WORLD DEFENSE EXPENDITURES."
J. OF PHILOSOPHY, (1966), 7-113.
A COMPILATION AND ANALYSIS OF DEFENSE EXPENDITURES FOR 36 COUNTRIES IN US DOLLARS. EXPENDITURES, COVERING 1960-1965, ARE BROKEN DOWN INTO MILITARY PERSONNEL, R&D, MAJOR PROCUREMENTS, CONSTRUCTION, AND OPERATIONS AND MAINTENANCE CATEGORIES.

0254 BENTHAM J.
"THE RATIONALE OF REWARD" IN J. BOWRING, ED., THE WORKS OF JEREMY BENTHAM (VOL. 2)"
ORIGINAL PUBLISHER NOT AVAILABLE, 1843.
DISCUSSES SOURCES OF REWARD, SUCH AS POWER, MONEY, AND HONOR, AND CONSIDERS ADVANTAGES OF COMBINING USE OF POWER AND REWARD. SUGGESTS ESTABLISHMENT OF LAWS THAT WILL BE "SELF-EXECUTING" IN THAT INTEREST WILL BE COMBINED WITH DUTY. BELIEVES REWARD SHOULD BE USED FRUGALLY AND AS AN INSTRUMENT OF POWER. DISCUSSES SYSTEM OF REMUNERATION: SALARIES, AND REWARD TO ENCOURAGE PRODUCTION.

0255 BENTHAM J.
DEFENCE OF USURY (1787)
ORIGINAL PUBLISHER NOT AVAILABLE, 1788, 232 PP.
DENOUNCES PROHIBITORY USURY LAWS CONTROLLING RATE OF INTEREST ON LENDING MONEY; FEELS THAT IT BENEFITS PUBLIC TO HAVE UNLIMITED RATES. DISCIPLE OF ADAM SMITH INSISTS ON EXTREME LOGICAL APPLICATION OF PRINCIPLES AND ARGUES AGAINST SMITH'S APPROVAL OF FIVE-PER-CENT LIMITATION. ARGUES THAT LOANS ON SECURITY WOULD HELP TECHNOLOGICAL PROGRESS EVEN IF PROJECTS FAILED.

0256 BEQIRAJ M.
PEASANTRY IN REVOLUTION.
ITHACA: CORNELL U PRESS, 1966, 123 PP., LC#66-25067.
STUDIES SOCIAL CHANGE IN CONTEMPORARY PEASANT POPULATIONS. PRESENTS THE PEASANT AS A MAN INCAPABLE OF KNOWING HIS ENVIRONMENT, AND THUS INCAPABLE OF MASTERING IT. FOCUSES ON THIS FAILURE OF THE PEASANT TO MASTER THE PROBLEM OF KNOWLEDGE. THE PEASANT IS PART OF A ROUTINIZED PROCESS OF ACTIVITIES AND IS GUIDED IN HIS PERFORMANCE ONLY BY EMULATION.

0257 BERG E.J.
"ECONOMIC BASIS OF POLITICAL CHOICE IN FRENCH WEST AFRICA."
AMER. POLIT. SCI. REV., 54 (JUNE 60), 391-405.
ANALYZES ECONOMIC FACTORS WHICH HAVE PLAYED ROLE IN RELATIONS OF WEST AFRICAN STATES WITH ONE ANOTHER AND WITH FRENCH COMMUNITY. DISCUSSES ROLE OF TARIFF AND PRICE PROTECTION IN THEIR POLITICAL CONTEXT.

0258 BERGMANN D KAUN B.
STRUCTURAL UNEMPLOYMENT IN THE UNITED STATES.

WASHINGTON: US GOVERNMENT, 1967, 122 PP.
STUDY OF CAUSES OF UNEMPLOYMENT, UNDEREMPLOYMENT, AND UNDERDEVELOPMENT, PURSUANT TO PUBLIC WORKS AND ECONOMIC DEVELOPMENT ACT OF 1965. DISTINGUISHES STRUCTURE OF UNEMPLOYMENT FROM STRUCTURAL UNEMPLOYMENT, WHICH IS UNEMPLOYMENT THAT REMAINS AT LEVEL OF DEMAND CONSISTENT WITH PRICE STABILITY. ESTIMATES TARIFF UNEMPLOYMENT RATE.

0259 BERGSON A. ED.
ECONOMIC TRENDS IN THE SOVIET UNION.
CAMBRIDGE: HARVARD U PR, 1963, 392 PP., LC#63-9548.
ESSAYS PROVIDING DETAILED ANALYSIS OF MAJOR PROBLEM AREAS IN SOVIET ECONOMIC GROWTH. SEVERAL COMPARISONS WITH ECONOMIC PROGRESS IN OTHER COUNTRIES, PRINCIPALLY IN US.

0260 BERLE A.A. JR.
"THE 20TH CENTURY CAPITALIST REVOLUTION."
NEW YORK: HARCOURT BRACE, 1954.
STUDY OF THE MODERN CORPORATION FROM A QUASI-POLITICAL ANGLE. ARGUES THAT LARGE CORPORATION MANAGEMENTS HAVE REACHED A POSITION OF CONCENTRATED ECONOMIC POWER WHICH FORCES THEM TO CONSIDER AND PARTICIPATE IN POLITICAL, INTERNATIONAL, AND PHILOSOPHICAL CONSIDERATIONS. BRIEF ANNOTATED BIBLIOGRAPHY OF AMERICAN ECONOMIC WRITINGS PUBLISHED AFTER 1933.

0261 BERLE A.A. JR.
ECONOMIC POWER AND FREE SOCIETY (PAMPHLET)
NEW YORK: FUND FOR THE REPUBLIC, 1957, 20 PP.
BECAUSE OF WIDESPREAD OWNERSHIP OF STOCK, THE CORPORATE HOLDING OF PROPERTY HAS BEEN SPLIT INTO MANAGING AND CREATIVE FUNCTION AND PASSIVE RECEPTIVE FUNCTION. TREATS OF HISTORICAL LIMITS ON CORPORATION, THE THEORETICAL DEMOCRACY IN CORPORATIONS, AUTONOMY OF DIRECTORS, AND CHANGING CONCEPTS OF POSSESSORY PRIVATE PROPERTY. MENTIONS POSSIBLE CONSTITUTIONAL ARGUMENTS TO RESTRICT CORPORATION POWERS.

0262 BERLE A.A. JR.
THE AMERICAN ECONOMIC REPUBLIC.
NEW YORK: HARCOURT BRACE, 1963, 247 PP.
DISCUSSES AND REVIEWS OLD CONCEPTIONS, EXAMINES MAJOR ECONOMIC INSTITUTIONS AND THEIR OPERATION, AND DESCRIBES A NEW ECONOMIC THEORY OF "TRANSCENDENTAL MARGIN" (CF MORMONS). SEES END OF FREE MARKET AS A WAY OF ECONOMIC LIFE, AND EXPANSION OF PRODUCTIVITY BY NON-COMMERCIAL ROUTES, SUCH AS THE FINANCING OF EDUCATIONAL, CULTURAL, AND PHILANTHROPIC INSTITUTIONS, AND PROMOTING SOCIAL JUSTICE.

0263 BERLINER J.S.
SOVIET ECONOMIC AID: THE AID AND TRADE POLICY IN UNDERDEVELOPED COUNTRIES.
NEW YORK: PRAEGER, 1958, 232 PP., $4.25.
DENOTES PRINCIPAL OBJECTIVES OF RUSSIAN SUPPLY PROGRAMS, 1953-57. CONSIDERS COMMITMENTS AND TYPE OF ASSISTANCE RENDERED. APPRAISES BENEFITS OF TRADE AND AID PROGRAM TO DONOR AND RECIPIENTS, THE PROGRAMS' IMPACT ON SOVIET ECONOMY AND RUSSIAN ABILITY TO CONTINUE THIS UNDERTAKING.

0264 BERNAYS E.L. ED.
THE ENGINEERING OF CONSENT.
NORMAN: U OF OKLAHOMA PR, 1955, 246 PP., LC#55-9621.
EXAMINATION OF PUBLIC RELATIONS FROM A BROAD VIEWPOINT CONSIDERING WHAT IT IS, WHAT RELATION IT HAS TO SOCIETY, HOW IT APPROACHES A PROBLEM, AND HOW THAT APPROACH IS MADE. BERNAYS REVIEWS THE SUBJECT AS A WHOLE; SEVEN EXPERTS PRESENT THEIR THINKING ON VARIOUS ASPECTS. INCLUDES SUBJECT INDEX.

0265 BERNHARD R.C.
"COMPETITION IN LAW AND ECONOMICS."
ANTI-TRUST BULLETIN, 7 (WINTER 67), 1099-1165.
EXAMINES NOTION OF COMPETITION IN ECONOMIC AND LEGAL THEORY AND DECISION-MAKING, COMPARING DIFFERENCES AND SIMILARITIES IN ITS USE. DISCUSSES EFFECT OF AMBIGUITY ON VIEWS HELD BY COURTS, AND LEGAL AND POLICY RESULTS OF LACK OF CONCISENESS IN TERMS DEFINING COMPETITION.

0266 BERNSTEIN I.
ARBITRATION OF WAGES.
BERKELEY: U OF CALIF PR, 1954, 125 PP., LC#54-10437.
STUDY OF ARBITRATION WHICH REVOLVES ABOUT UNIFYING PROBLEM OF GENERAL WAGE CHANGE. EXAMINES INSTITUTIONAL SITUATIONS IN WHICH WAGE ARBITRATION FUNCTIONS; CRITICALLY ANALYZES PROCEDURAL QUESTIONS PECULIAR TO WAGE ARBITRATION; AND CODIFIES AND EVALUATES DISPOSITION OF CRITERIA OF WAGE DETERMINATION UNDER CIRCUMSTANCES THAT ARBITRATION AFFORDS. RESEARCH EMPHASIZES CASE STUDY OF DISPUTES.

0267 BERNSTEIN M.H.
"POLITICAL IDEAS OF SELECTED AMERICAN BUSINESS JOURNALS (BMR)"
PUBLIC OPINION QUART., 17 (SEPT. 53), 258-267.
EXAMINES VIEWS OF SELECTED BUSINESS JOURNALS CONCERNING RELATIONSHIP OF GOVERNMENT AND ECONOMIC LIFE. FIRST IDENTIFIES TYPICAL STATEMENTS ON PUBLIC AFFAIRS WHICH OCCUR FREQUENTLY, AND THEN NOTES CONTRADICTIONS AND DIFFERENCES OF OPINION. DISCUSSES APPROACHES TO GOVERNMENT-BUSINESS RELATIONS. HYPOTHESIZES ABOUT ATTITUDES ON ROLE OF STATE, CONCEPT OF FREEDOM, FLEXIBILITY OF GOALS AND VALUES.

0268 BERNSTEIN M.H.
REGULATING BUSINESS BY INDEPENDENT COMMISSION.
PRINCETON: PRINCETON U PRESS, 1955, 306 PP., LC#55-5001.
CRITICALLY EVALUATES SEVEN INDEPENDENT REGULATORY COMMISSIONS. EXAMINES ENVIRONMENT IN WHICH THEY DEVELOPED AND THEIR OBJECTIVES. ANALYZES RISE AND DECLINE OF COMMISSIONS AND APPRAISES COMMISSIONS' FUNCTIONS. FOCUSES ON RELATIONSHIP OF COMMISSIONS TO PRESIDENT AND CONGRESS AND OUTLINES PROBLEMS FACING COMMISSIONS IN DEVELOPING PUBLIC SUPPORT FOR THEIR PROGRAMS.

0269 BERNSTEIN P.L.
THE PRICE OF PROSPERITY.
GARDEN CITY: DOUBLEDAY, 1962, 273 PP.
APPRAISAL OF FUTURE OF NATIONAL ECONOMY. USES TOOLS OF ECONOMIC ANALYSIS; DISCUSSES STRUCTURAL AND CYCLICAL UNEMPLOYMENT AND "DYNAMICS OF DEMAND" TO BOLSTER THESIS THAT GOVERNMENT WILL BE SUPPORT OF EXPANDING ECONOMY.

0270 BERREBY J.J.
"IMPERATIFS STRATEGIQUES DU PETROLE."
POLITIQUE ETRANGERE, 30 (1965), 498-513.
DISCUSSES IMPORTANCE OF MIDDLE EASTERN OIL TO THE ECONOMIC DEVELOPMENT OF THE AREA, TO THE CONSUMER NATIONS AT WAR OR PEACE, AND HOW THE CONSUMER NATIONS HAVE INTERVENED IN MIDDLE EASTERN AFFAIRS TO HEIGHTEN POLITICAL CHAOS OF THE AREA.

0271 BERRILL K.
ECONOMIC DEVELOPMENT WITH SPECIAL REFERENCE TO EAST ASIA.
NEW YORK: ST MARTIN'S PRESS, 1964, 435 PP.
DISCUSSES FACTORS AND POLICIES AFFECTING ECONOMIC GROWTH, WITH EMPHASIS ON PROBLEMS IN EAST ASIA. PRIMARILY CONSIDERS RECENT DEVELOPMENTS AND CURRENT CONDITIONS IN JAPAN AND INDIA. CENTERS BOTH ON GENERAL TOPICS SUCH AS LABOR, CAPITAL, AND FISCAL PLANNING AND ON SPECIFIC SITUATIONS IN EAST ASIAN ECONOMICS.

0272 VAN DEN BEUGEL E.
FROM MARSHALL AID TO ATLANTIC PARTNERSHIP* EUROPEAN INTEGRATION AS A CONCERN OF AMERICAN FOREIGN POLICY.
LONDON: ELSEVIER, 1966, 480 PP., LC#66-16277.
COGENT ANALYSIS, FROM EUROPEAN VIEWPOINT, OF THE ROLE OF AMERICAN FOREIGN POLICY INITIATIVE IN WORKING TOWARDS ATLANTIC PARTNERSHIP THROUGH A STRENGTHENED AND INTEGRATED EUROPE. CHRONOLOGY PRESENTED STRESSING KEY ROLES OF INDIVIDUALS LIKE MARSHALL, HOFFMAN, DULLES, AND SCHUMANN IN DEVELOPING INTEGRATIVE INSTITUTIONS. FOREWARD BY KISSINGER. WELL DOCUMENTED.

0273 BEVAN A.
IN PLACE OF FEAR.
NEW YORK: SIMON AND SCHUSTER, 1952, 213 PP.
CONTENDS THAT THE ACTIVE FORCES IN SOCIETY ARE PRIVATE PROPERTY, POVERTY, AND DEMOCRACY; ARGUES THAT CONFLICT BETWEEN THESE FORCES RESULTS IN ISSUE WHETHER POVERTY WILL USE DEMOCRACY TO WIN STRUGGLE AGAINST PROPERTY, OR PROPERTY, IN FEAR OF POVERTY, WILL DESTROY DEMOCRACY. DISCUSSES INCOMPATIBILITY OF GREAT WEALTH, POVERTY, AND DEMOCRACY.

0274 BEVERIDGE W.H.
UNEMPLOYMENT: A PROBLEM OF INDUSTRY (1909-1930)
NEW YORK: LONGMANS, GREEN & CO, 1930, 514 PP.
TESTS THEORY OF UNEMPLOYMENT DEDUCED FROM FACTS OF 1909 AND DEMONSTRATES ITS CONTINUED APPLICABILITY. DISCUSSES RESULTS OF EMPLOYMENT POLICIES BASED ON THAT THEORY. DESCRIBES SOURCES OF UNEMPLOYMENT STATISTICS, FLUCTUATIONS IN SITUATION, LABOR RESERVES, AND QUALITY OF WORKERS. EXPLORES POLICY OF UNEMPLOYMENT INSURANCE, LABOR EXCHANGES, AND FUTURE POLICIES.

0275 BEYER G.H.
HOUSING AND SOCIETY.
LONDON: MACMILLAN, 1965, 595 PP., LC#65-12480.
PRACTICAL RATHER THAN THEORETICAL APPROACH TREATS HISTORICAL ASPECTS OF AMERICAN HOUSING. DISCUSSES MARKET, PRODUCTION, AND ACQUISITION AND CONSUMPTION. NEW AREAS TREATED INCLUDE COOPERATIVE HOUSING, INTERNATIONAL PROJECTS, AND EXPANDING PROGRAMS OF HOUSING FOR THE AGED.

0276 BHAGWATI J.
"THE PURE THEORY OF INTERNATIONAL TRADE: A SURVEY."
ECON. J., 74(MAR.64), 1-84.
AN ACCOUNT OF INTERNATIONAL TRADE BASED UPON THEORIES OF VALUE AND WELFARE. SUBJECTS KEY PREMISES TO EMPIRICAL VERIFICATION IN TERMS OF LABOR-PRODUCTIVITY RATIOS AND UNIT WAGE-COST RATIOS.

0277 BHAMBHRI C.P.
PARLIAMENTARY CONTROL OVER STATE ENTERPRISE IN INDIA.
NEW DELHI: METROPOLITAN BOOK, 1960, 115 PP.
STUDIES METHODS OF PARLIAMENTARY CONTROL OVER PUBLIC EN-

TERPRISE INCLUDING MINISTERIAL, FINANCIAL, AND AUDIT CONTROL AND CONTROL THROUGH COMMITTEES. ALSO DISCUSSES GENERAL RELATIONSHIP OF GOVERNMENT AND STATE ENTERPRISES. CONCLUDES THAT INDIAN PARLIAMENT HAS NEEDED CONTROLS AT ITS DISPOSAL, BUT THEY ARE NOT BEING FULLY UTILIZED.

0278 BIBBY J., DAVIDSON R.
ON CAPITOL HILL.
NEW YORK: HOLT RINEHART WINSTON, 1967, 280 PP., LC#67-11299.
NINE CASE STUDIES OF US GOVERNMENT COMMITTEE WORK AND POLICY-MAKING PRESENT UNIQUE FACTORS FROM WHICH AN ATTEMPT IS MADE TO DESCRIBE PATTERNS OF BEHAVIOR IN THE POLITICAL SYSTEM. IDENTIFIES RELEVANT VARIABLES. CONSCIOUSLY COMBINES METHODS OF QUANTIFICATION AND QUALIFICATION. BIBLIOGRAPHY ON BILLS, LAWS, PARTY POLITICS, INTEREST GROUPS, COMMITTEES, CAMPAIGNS AND ELECTIONS.

0279 BIDWELL P.W.
RAW MATERIALS: A STUDY OF AMERICAN POLICY.
NEW YORK: HARPER, 1958, 403 PP., $5.95.
EXAMINES U.S. POLICY AS IT AFFECTS SUPPLY OF RAW MATERIALS FOR AMERICAN INDUSTRIES. SUCCESSES AND FAILURES OF THIS POLICY ARE DISCUSSED AS WELL AS PROPOSED MEASURES FOR REFORM WHICH INCLUDE CHANGES IN NATIONAL POLICIES TO MAKE THEM MORE ADAPTABLE TO CHANGES IN TECHNOLOGY AND INTERNATIONAL RELATIONS.

0280 BIEL G.
TREATISE ON THE POWER AND UTILITY OF MONEY (1484)
PHILA: U OF PENN PR, 1930, 39 PP.
SEEKS TO ANSWER MORAL QUESTION ON ETHICALITY OF FALSIFYING MONEY. DISCUSSES MONEY AS A COMMODITY, CONCLUDING THAT IT IS A FORM OF THEFT TO ALTER IT IN EITHER INDIVIDUALS WHO POSSESS IT OR STATES THAT COIN IT. DOES ALLOW CERTAIN CONDITIONS UNDER WHICH IT MAY BE ALTERED: TO DRIVE OUT COUNTERFEITS, TO REPLACE OLD MONEY, AND IF THE SCARCITY OF METAL RAISES ITS PRICE.

0281 BIENSTOCK G., SCHWARZ S.M., ZUGOW A.
MANAGEMENT IN RUSSIAN INDUSTRY AND AGRICULTURE.
NEW YORK: OXFORD U PR, 1944, 198 PP.
STUDY OF SOVIET ECONOMIC SYSTEM FOCUSING ON MANAGERS OF SMALL INDUSTRIAL PLANTS AND OFFICERS OF COLLECTIVE FARMS. DESCRIBES MACHINERY OF SOVIET MANAGEMENT; DISTRIBUTION OF FUNCTIONS AND POWERS; AND STATUS, INCENTIVES, AND IDEOLOGY OF MANAGERIAL PERSONNEL. INCLUDES DISCUSSION OF PRODUCTION PLANNING, PROFITS, ORGANIZATION OF FARM WORKERS, ACCOUNTING METHODS, AND PRIVATE VERSUS COLLECTIVE SYSTEMS.

0282 BIERMAN H., SMIDT S.
THE CAPITAL BUDGETING DECISION.
NEW YORK: MACMILLAN, 1960, 246 PP., LC#60-6844.
ATTEMPTS TO "PRESENT FOR AN AUDIENCE, WHICH MAY BE COMPLETELY UNFAMILIAR WITH THE TECHNICAL LITERATURE ON ECONOMIC THEORY OR CAPITAL BUDGETING, A CLEAR CONCEPTION OF HOW TO EVALUATE INVESTMENT PROPOSALS." SURVEYS OVER-ALL METHOD OF ANALYSIS, BUT ELABORATES ENOUGH TO ASSIST A PERSON IN ACTUALLY PREPARING THE ANALYSIS OF INVESTMENTS. ARGUES IN FAVOR OF "PRESENT VALUE" APPROACH.

0283 BIERMAN H.
"PROBABILITY, STATISTICAL DECISION THEORY, AND ACCOUNTING."
ACCOUNTING REVIEW, 37 (JULY 62).
SUGGESTIONS TOWARD BETTER FINANCIAL INFORMATION AND BETTER DECISION-MAKING. ONE OF BEST TOOLS AVAILABLE IS QUANTITATIVE ANALYSIS, INCLUDING TOOL OF STATISTICAL DECISIONS. PAPER WAS BASIS OF TALK GIVEN AT NORTHEAST REGIONAL GROUP MEETING OF AAA BY PROFESSOR OF ACCOUNTING AT CORNELL UNIVERSITY.

0284 BILL J.A.
"THE SOCIAL AND ECONOMIC FOUNDATIONS OF POWER IN CONTEMPORARY IRAN."
MID. EAST J., 17 (AUTUMN 63), 400-18.
UTILIZING THE CLASS AS THE BASIC TOOL OF ANALYSIS, FOCUSES ATTENTION UPON THE CONCRETE ASPIRATIONS OF DEFINED GROUPS AND EXAMINES RELATIONSHIP BETWEEN SOCIO-POLITICAL PROCESSES AND SOCIAL STRUCTURE.

0285 BILLERBECK K.
SOVIET BLOC FOREIGN AID TO UNDERDEVELOPED COUNTRIES.
HAMBURG: HAMB WIRTSCHAFTS ARCHIV, 1960, 161 PP.
STUDIES PROBLEMS OF "SOVIET DEVELOPMENT AID" CONFRONTING NATIONS RECEIVING AID NOW AND THOSE THAT WILL RECEIVE IT IN FUTURE. EMPHASIZES INTRINSIC NATURE OF SOVIET AID, ITS UNIQUE METHODS AND TACTICS, AND CONSEQUENCES FOR RECEIVING NATIONS. STUDIES 1953-1960 AND PREDICTS DEVELOPMENTS THROUGH 1970. APPENDIX SUMMARIZES AID TO EACH NATION.

0286 BIRMINGHAM W. ED., NEUSTADT I. ED., OMABOE E.N. ED.
A STUDY OF CONTEMPORARY GHANA VOL I: THE ECONOMY OF GHANA.
EVANSTON: NORTHWESTERN U PRESS, 1966, 472 PP.
INTRODUCTORY SURVEY OF GHANA'S ECONOMY COLLECTS ESSAYS AND ANALYTIC TREATISES ON MACROECONOMIC STRUCTURE, FACTORS OF PRODUCTION, SECTORS OF THE ECONOMY, POLICY, AND PLANNING. INCLUDES COMPREHENSIVE CHARTS, MAPS, AND TABLES OF ECONOMIC STATISTICS.

0287 BIRMINGHAM W. ED., NEUSTADT I. ED., OMABOE E.N. ED.
A STUDY OF CONTEMPORARY GHANA VOL. I: SOME ASPECTS OF SOCIAL STRUCTURE.
EVANSTON: NORTHWESTERN U PRESS, 1967, 271 PP.
COLLECTS ESSAYS, TREATISES, AND STATISTICS ON GHANAIAN SOCIAL STRUCTURE. DISCUSSES GENERAL CHARACTERISTICS OF THE POPULATION AND ANALYZES RECENT ELEMENTS OF POPULATION CHANGE. DESCRIBES MIGRATION AND URBANIZATION, POPULATION PROSPECTS AND POLICY. STUDIES STRUCTURE OF MARRIAGE, FAMILY, AND HOUSEHOLD, AND ASPECTS OF EDUCATION, RELIGION, AND LAND TENURE.

0288 BIRNBAUM N.
"CONFLICTING INTERPRETATIONS OF THE RISE OF CAPITALISM: MARX AND WEBER" (BMR)"
BRIT. J. OF SOCIOLOGY, 4 (JUNE 53), 125-141.
ATTEMPTS TO RECALL SOME POLEMICAL ORIGINS OF MAJOR THEME IN WEBER'S WORK: FUNCTION OF IDEOLOGY AS AN INDEPENDENT VARIABLE IN SOCIAL DEVELOPMENT. COMPARES WEBER'S EXPLANATION OF EMERGENCE OF CAPITALISM WITH THAT OF MARX.

0289 BISSON A.
INSTITUTIONS FINANCIERES ET ECONOMIQUES EN FRANCE.
PARIS: EDITIONS BERGER-LEVRAULT, 1960, 311 PP.
STUDY OF FRENCH FINANCES FROM FOURTH REPUBLIC THROUGH 1959. ANALYZES AND CRITICIZES EFFORTS AT REFORMS. DISCUSSES BUDGETARY EQUILIBRIUM, MONEY, PRODUCTION, ETC.

0290 BLACK E.R.
THE DIPLOMACY OF ECONOMIC DEVELOPMENT.
CAMBRIDGE: HARVARD U. PR., 1960, 74 PP., $3.00.
INVESTIGATES THE 'REVOLUTION OF RISING EXPECTATIONS' IN UNDERDEVELOPED COUNTRIES, FOCUSING ATTENTION UPON THE IMPACT OF SCIENCE AND TECHNOLOGY AND QUALITY OF LEADERSHIP. DIPLOMACY IS VIEWED AS A CHALLENGE TO ILLUMINATE CHOICES RATHER THAN TO IMPOSE SOLUTIONS IN SHAPING ECONOMIC POLICIES.

0291 BLACK J.D.
ECONOMICS FOR AGRICULTURE.
CAMBRIDGE: HARVARD U PR, 1959, 719 PP., LC#59-12965.
ESSAYS EMPHASIZING PRODUCTION ECONOMICS, LAND USE, AND COOPERATION INCLUDING CONSUMPTION, FOOD SUPPLY, AND ECONOMIC THEORY.

0292 BLACKSTOCK P.W.
THE STRATEGY OF SUBVERSION.
CHICAGO: QUADRANGLE BOOKS, INC, 1964, 349 PP., LC#64-19620.
EXAMINES PROBLEMS OF MANAGEMENT AND CONTROL IN COVERT ESPIONAGE OPERATIONS. STUDIES EFFECTS UPON US STATE DEPARTMENT, MILITARY ESTABLISHMENT, AND INTELLIGENCE COMMUNITY. USES CASE STUDIES AND HISTORICAL ANALYSIS.

0293 BLAIR G.S., FLOURNOY H.I.
LEGISLATIVE BODIES IN CALIFORNIA.
BELMONT: DICKENSON PUBL CO, 1967, 120 PP., LC#67-14170.
DISCUSSES LEGISLATIVE SYSTEM IN CALIFORNIA. STUDIES STATE LEGISLATURE'S ORGANIZATION AND PROCEDURE; INFLUENCE OF PARTIES AND PRESSURE GROUPS; LOCAL LEGISLATIVE AUTHORITIES; SELECTION, ORGANIZATION, AND ACTIONS OF LOCAL LEGISLATURES; AND CITIZENS' RELATION TO LEGISLATURES. WRITTEN TO IMPROVE COMPULSORY COURSES IN CALIFORNIA GOVERNMENT FOR ALL STATE UNDERGRADUATES.

0294 BLAIR P.W.
THE MINISTATE DILEMMA.
NEW YORK: CARNEGIE ENDOWMENT, 1967, 98 PP.
DEFINES A MINISTATE OR MINITERRITORY AS AN AREA WITH A POPULATION UNDER 300,000. SOME ARE SELF-GOVERNING, OTHERS ARE ATTACHED TO A COLONIAL POWER. DISCUSSES CRITERIA FOR UN MEMBERSHIP, RIGHTS OF NON-MEMBERS, AND STATUS OF INTERMEDIATE MEMBERSHIP IN LEAGUE OF NATIONS, UN, AND OTHER INTERNATIONAL ORGANIZATIONS.

0295 BLAIR T.L.V.
AFRICA: A MARKET PROFILE.
LONDON: BUSINESS PUBLICATIONS, 1965, 260 PP.
SOCIOLOGICAL EXPLORATION AND GENERAL APPRAISAL OF THE MARKETING PROCESS IN CONTEMPORARY AFRICA. EXAMINES DATA ON THE GROWTH OF INDUSTRY, RISING NATIONAL PRODUCTIVITY, AND RESOLUTION OF SOCIAL PROBLEMS AS SOCIAL CORRELATES OF DECISION-MAKING FOR EUROPEAN AND AFRICAN INDUSTRY. RESEARCH BASED UPON FIELD STUDY AND CURRENT LITERATURE IN SOCIOLOGY, MARKET RESEARCH, ECONOMIC DEVELOPMENT, AND AFRICAN WORKS.

0296 BLAISDELL D.C.
GOVERNMENT AND AGRICULTURE; THE GROWTH OF FEDERAL FARM AID.
NEW YORK: FARRAR + RINEHART, 1940, 217 PP.
STUDIES ECONOMIC AND POLITICAL ISSUES FACING AMERICAN AGRICULTURE. EXAMINES GOVERNMENT'S RESPONSE TO AGRICULTURAL NEEDS WITH CREATION OF DEPARTMENT OF AGRICULTURE. INCLUDES AREAS OF MARKETS, SOIL CONSERVATION, USE OF TECHNOLOGY, AND FARM SECURITY. MAINTAINS THAT STUDY OF FEDERAL FARM AID AND STEPS TO HARMONIZE TECHNOLOGY WITH DEMOCRATIC INSTITUTIONS PRESENT GOOD EXAMPLE OF EFFICIENCY OF DEMOCRATIC SOLUTIONS.

0297 BLAKE R.R., SHEPARD H.A., MOUTON J.S.
MANAGING INTERGROUP CONFLICT IN INDUSTRY.
HOUSTON: GULF PUBL, 1964, 210 PP., LC#64-8696.
A WORKING MANUAL SUPPORTED BY ACTUAL CASE HISTORIES OF INDUSTRIAL CONFLICTS AND HOW THEY WERE SOLVED. SHOWS THAT THERE ARE 9 POSSIBLE METHODS FOR DEALING WITH CONFLICT, BUT THAT 8 HAVE INHERENT SIDE-EFFECTS WHICH ARE DETRIMENTAL TO OVERALL ORGANIZATIONAL OBJECTIVES AND GOALS. THE MOST COMMON OF THESE 8 IS THE WIN-LOOSE POWER STRUGGLE AMONG GROUPS. PRESENTS A PROBLEM-SOLVING METHOD THAT WORKS CREATIVELY.

0298 BLAUG M.
ECONOMICS OF EDUCATION: A SELECTED ANNOTATED BIBLIOGRAPHY.
LONDON: U OF LON, INST EDUC, 1967, 200 PP.
CONTAINS 800 PUBLISHED ITEMS IN ENGLISH, FRENCH, AND GERMAN, INCLUDING A LARGE NUMBER OF UNPUBLISHED PAPERS FROM INTERNATIONAL AGENCIES AND INSTITUTIONS. BOOK IS DIVIDED INTO TWO SECTIONS, DEALING SEPARATELY WITH DEVELOPED AND DEVELOPING COUNTRIES. BOTH SECTIONS INCLUDE A GENERAL SURVEY OF THE SUBJECT, ECONOMIC CONTRIBUTION OF EDUCATION, ECONOMIC ASPECTS OF EDUCATION, EDUCATIONAL PLANNING, AND MANPOWER.

0299 BLOOM G.F., NORTHRUP H.R.
ECONOMICS OF LABOR RELATIONS.
HOMEWOOD: RICHARD IRWIN, 1955, 784 PP.
SURVEY OF DEVELOPMENT OF LABOR UNIONS, THEIR RELATIONS WITH GOVERNMENT, KEY LABOR PROBLEMS IN CAPITALISTIC ECONOMY, AND CONFLICTING VIEWS CONCERNING SOLUTIONS. COVERS ALL POSSIBLE ASPECTS OF LABOR MOVEMENT ARRANGED FOR CLASSROOM STUDY AND DISCUSSION. ANALYZES TAFT-HARTLEY ACT IN DETAIL.

0300 BLOOMFIELD A.
MONETARY POLICY UNDER THE INTERNATIONAL GOLD STANDARD: 1880-1914 (PAMPHLET)
NEW YORK: FED RESERVE BANK OF NY, 1959, 62 PP.
ANALYZES AGAINST BACKGROUND OF WORKING OF PRE-1914 GOLD STANDARD SETTING IN WHICH CENTRAL BANKS FUNCTIONED IN PERIOD 1880-1914, THEIR OBJECTIVES, CRITERIA, AND NATURE OF OPERATIONS AND POLICIES. SHOWS HOW CENTRAL BANKS RESORTED TO VARIETY OF MONETARY TECHNIQUES, APART FROM TRADITIONAL DISCOUNT WEAPON, AND WERE ALREADY ENGAGING IN PRACTICES SERVING AS STEPPING STONES TO MORE ELABORATE TECHNIQUES OF TODAY.

0301 BLOUGH R.
"THE ROLE OF THE ECONOMIST IN FEDERAL POLICY MAKING."
U. ILLINOIS BULL., 5 (NOV. 53), 26 PP.
COUNCIL OF ECONOMIC ADVISERS HAS A DEFINITE ROLE IN THE FORMULATION OF FEDERAL POLICY. GIVES BRIEF ANALYSIS OF FUNCTIONS, ATTITUDES, QUALIFICATIONS AND DUTIES OF THE ECONOMIST IN GOVERNMENT AFFAIRS.

0302 BOARMAN P.M.
GERMANY'S ECONOMIC DILEMMA - INFLATION AND THE BALANCE OF PAYMENTS.
NEW HAVEN: YALE U PR, 1964, 344 PP., LC#64-20911.
EXAMINES CAUSES AND CONSEQUENCES OF BALANCE OF PAYMENTS SURPLUS IN WEST GERMANY'S ECONOMY BETWEEN 1950 AND 1961. ANALYZES INFLATIONARY TENDENCIES, EXPORT SURPLUSES, AND GENERAL PROBLEM OF INTERNATIONAL ECONOMIC DISEQUILIBRIUM.

0303 BOCK E. ED.
GOVERNMENT REGULATION OF BUSINESS.
ENGLEWOOD CLIFFS: PRENTICE HALL, 1965, 448 PP., LC#65-16944.
SEVEN CASE STUDIES DESCRIBE EVENTS AND FORCES AT WORK WHEN GOVERNMENTAL AGENCIES INITIATE REGULATORY ACTIONS IN BUSINESS. ANALYZES STRATEGY OF ONE OF THE MAJOR PARTICIPANTS INVOLVED IN EACH OF THE CASES.

0304 BOEKE J.H.
ECONOMICS AND ECONOMIC POLICY OF DUAL SOCIETIES AS EXEMPLIFIED BY INDONESIA.
NEW YORK: INST OF PACIFIC RELNS, 1953, 323 PP.
EXAMINES NATURE AND DEVELOPMENT OF DUALIST ECONOMIC THEORY AND ITS APPLICATION IN INDIA AND INDONESIA. STUDIES ECONOMIC CONTACT BETWEEN DUALISTIC GROUPS AND VITAL PROBLEMS IN INDONESIAN ECONOMICS. ANALYZES DUALISTIC ECONOMIC POLICY, DESCRIBING GOVERNMENT INTERVENTION IN EXPORTS, IMPORTS, HOME MARKETS, PRICE LEVEL, AND WELFARE.

0305 BOGARDUS J.
OUTLINE FOR THE COURSE IN BUSINESS AND ECONOMICS LITERATURE (REV. ED; PAMPHLET)
NEW YORK: COL U, SCH LIB SERV, 1962, 48 PP.
DEFINES FIELD OF BUSINESS AND GENERAL CHARACTERISTICS OF LITERATURE. STUDY OF GENERAL REFERENCE BOOKS, BASIC STATISTICAL SOURCES, PERIODICALS AND NEWSPAPERS, GOVERNMENTAL DOCUMENTS, ASSOCIATIONS AND ORGANIZATIONS. REFERENCE CHECKLIST HAS SOME DETAILED EXPLANATION.

0306 BOGEN J.I. ED., SHIPMAN S.S. ED.
FINANCIAL HANDBOOK (4TH ED.)
NEW YORK: RONALD PRESS, 1964, 1500 PP.
HANDBOOK OF LEADING PRINCIPLES AND PRACTICES IN FIELD OF FINANCE. EMPHASIZES EFFECTS OF CHANGES IN TAXATION, REGULATIONS, AND LAW, BUT COVERS ALL ASPECTS OF FINANCE.

0307 BOHM F.
REDEN UND SCHRIFTEN UBER DIE ORDNUNG EINER FREIEN GESELLSCHAFT, EINER FREIEN WIRTSCHAFT, UND UBER DIE WIEDERGUTMACH.
KARLSRUHE: VERL C F MULLER, 1960, 340 PP.
COLLECTION OF SPEECHES AND WRITINGS ON "RESPONSIBLE SOCIETY." DISCUSSES ECONOMY, STATE, AND REPARATION OF NAZI CRIMES.

0308 BOKOR-SZEGO H.
"LA CONVENTION DE BELGRADE ET LE REGIME DU DANUBE."
ANNU. FRANC. DR. INTER., 8 (1962), 192-205.
OUTLINES ECONOMIC GROWTH BORDERING DANUBE RIVER AND PRINCIPAL ARRANGEMENTS FOR ITS REGULATION ARRIVED AT BY BELGRADE CONVENTION OF 1948. DESCRIBES STRUCTURE AND FUNCTION OF DANUBE COMMISSION. SHOWS CHANGES EFFECTED BY COMMUNIST REGIME.

0309 BOLLENS J.C., SCHMANDT H.J.
THE METROPOLIS: ITS PEOPLE, POLITICS, AND ECONOMIC LIFE.
NEW YORK: HARPER & ROW, 1965, 643 PP., LC#65-19489.
PRESENTS MODERN US URBAN COMMUNITY AS A DYNAMIC SOCIAL, ECONOMIC, AND POLITICAL SYSTEM. ANALYSIS DEALS WITH VARIOUS ASPECTS OF THE METROPOLITAN COMMUNITY, INCLUDING SOCIAL CHARACTERISTICS AND TRENDS, PHYSICAL AND LAND-USE CONSIDERATIONS, ECONOMIC DEVELOPMENTS, AND GOVERNMENT AND POLITICS. ANALYZES PROBLEMS OF METROPOLITAN GROWTH. DISCUSSES POWER STRUCTURE, DECISION-MAKING PROCESS, AND THE CITIZEN'S ROLE.

0310 BOLTON R.E. ED.
DEFENSE AND DISARMAMENT: THE ECONOMICS OF TRANSITION.
ENGLEWOOD CLIFFS: PRENTICE HALL, 1966, 180 PP., LC#66-22609.
STUDIES ON ECONOMIC ASPECTS OF DEFENSE AND DISARMAMENT. DISCUSSES SCOPE OF DISARMAMENT; ECONOMIC IMPLICATIONS OF LARGE DEFENSE REDUCTIONS; PROBLEMS OF ECONOMIC TRANSITION FROM SWORD TO PLOWSHARE. ALSO STUDIES PUBLIC AND PRIVATE ARMS EXPENDITURES AND DANGERS OF POLITICAL PRESSURES.

0311 BONFIELD A.E.
"THE SUBSTANCE OF AMERICAN FAIR EMPLOYMENT PRACTICES LEGISLATION II - EMPLOYMENT AGENCIES, LABOR ORGANIZATIONS, ETC."
NORTHWESTERN U. LAW REVIEW,62(MAR-APR 67), 19-44.
GENERAL SURVEY OF THE SUBSTANTIVE PROVISIONS OF AMERICAN FAIR EMPLOYMENT STATUTES. EXAMINES EMPLOYMENT PRACTICES OF LABOR ORGANIZATIONS, EMPLOYMENT AGENCIES, AND OTHERS.

0312 BONILLA F.
"WHEN IS PETITION 'PRESSURE?'" (BMR)"
PUBLIC OPINION QUART., 20 (SPRING 56), 39-48.
EXAMINES EXTENSION OF RECIPROCAL TRADE ACT PASSED IN 1953 BY CONGRESS, AND EXTENT TO WHICH APPEALS FROM BUSINESSMEN SUPPORTING OR OPPOSING EXTENSION INFLUENCED CONGRESS. APPEALS CAME FROM INDUSTRIES AFFECTED BY FOREIGN TRADE AND LABOR GROUPS. MAINTAINS THAT CONGRESSMEN ANALYZED ISSUES AND MOTIVES OF BOTH SIDES IN SAME TERMS AS BUSINESSMEN, THUS MAKING APPEALS LEGITIMATE DEMANDS FROM CONSTITUENTS.

0313 BONINI C.P.
SIMULATION OF INFORMATION AND DECISION SYSTEMS IN THE FIRM.
ENGLEWOOD CLIFFS: PRENTICE HALL, 1963, 152 PP., LC#63-16585.
DESCRIBES SIMULATION MODEL OF HYPOTHETICAL BUSINESS FIRM. SYNTHESIS OF RELEVANT THEORY FROM DISCIPLINES OF ECONOMICS, ACCOUNTING, ORGANIZATION THEORY, AND BEHAVIORAL SCIENCE WITHIN SETTING OF TRADITIONAL CONCEPTS OF BUSINESS PRACTICE. STUDIES EFFECTS OF INFORMATIONAL, ORGANIZATIONAL, AND ENVIRONMENTAL FACTORS UPON DECISIONS OF BUSINESS FIRM.

0314 BONNEFOUS M.
EUROPE ET TIERS MONDE.
LEYDEN: SYTHOFF, 1961, 116 PP.
CONSIDERS EUROPE'S AID TO THE UNDERDEVELOPED COUNTRIES OF AFRICA AND QUESTIONS WHETHER THESE TECHNICAL CONNECTIONS WILL MORE FAVORABLY BIND THE COUNTRIES THAN THE FORMER HISTORICAL ONES.

0315 BONNETT C.E.
"THE EVOLUTION OF BUSINESS GROUPINGS."
ANN. POLITIQUE ECONOMIQUE, (MAY 35), 1-8.
A SHORT SURVEY OF THE HISTORY OF AMERICAN GUILDS AND MORE MODERN BUSINESS GROUPINGS, WITH COMMENTS ON PRESSURE TACTICS, PROPAGANDA, PRICE CONTROL, AND THE QUESTION OF SOCIAL CHANGE.

0316 BONNETT C.E.
HISTORY OF EMPLOYERS' ASSOCIATIONS IN THE UNITED STATES (1ST ED.)
NEW YORK: VANTAGE, 1956, 573 PP., LC#56-5520.
EXAMINES CLAIM THAT EMPLOYERS' ASSOCIATIONS ARE "BAD" AND THEIR FUNCTIONS NEGATIVE TO LABOR. TRACES THE HISTORY OF AMERICAN ASSOCIATIONS TO 1900. DISCUSSES "APPEASEMENT" OF WORKERS, BELLIGERENCY OF CORPORATIONS TO UNIONISM, THE ETHICS OF COLLUSION; CONCLUDES THAT THE REAL VICTIM IN THE SITUATION IS THE CONSUMER.

0317 BONNETT C.E.
LABOR-MANAGEMENT RELATIONS.

NEW YORK: EXPOSITION PRESS, 1959, 956 PP.
ANALYSIS OF BOTH SIDES OF THE UNION AND ASSOCIATION PROBLEM FROM PUBLIC VIEWPOINT. EXTENSIVE USE OF VISUAL AIDS IN FORM OF CARTOONS AND PICTURES FOUND IN LITERATURE OF SUBJECT. COORDINATED WITH DISCUSSION OF CENTRAL LABOR-MANAGEMENT RELATIONS PROBLEM - ITS SOCIAL IMPLICATIONS, ORGANIZED FORCES, INTERRELATIONS, AND PROPAGANDA ACTIVITIES.

0318 BOONE A.
"THE FOREIGN TRADE OF CHINA."
CHINA QUART., 11 (JUL.-SEP. 62), 169-183.
CONSIDERS COMMUNIST CHINA'S REORIENTATION OF TRADE SINCE 1950, ITS COMPOSITION AND PROBLEMS OF TRADE, AND TRACES ITS PROBLEM WITH AND DECLINE OF TRADE WITH UNITED KINGDOM. BELIEVES THAT ALTHOUGH CHINA'S TRADE WITH NON-COMMUNIST COUNTRIES HAS DECREASED GREATLY, IN THE FUTURE IT MIGHT INCREASE AS CHINA ATTEMPTS TO INDUSTRIALIZE.

0319 BOS H.C.
A DISCUSSION ON METHODS OF MONETARY ANALYSIS AND NORMS FOR MONETARY POLICY (PAMPHLET)
SCHIEDAM: ROYAL NETH PRINT OFF, 1956, 52 PP.
STUDY OF METHODS USED IN MONETARY POLICY AND MODELS EXAMINED AND COMPARED. DISCUSSES INFLATION, BALANCE OF PAYMENTS, AND SPENDING.

0320 BOSHER J.F.
"GOVERNMENT AND PRIVATE INTERESTS IN NEW FRANCE."
CAN. PUBLIC ADMIN., 10 (JUNE 67), 244-257.
DESCRIBES RELATIONSHIPS BETWEEN GOVERNMENT FINANCIAL ADMINISTRATION AND PRIVATE ENTERPRISE IN FRENCH CANADA IN 17TH AND 18TH CENTURIES. CRITICIZES TRADITIONAL HISTORICAL VIEW THAT SEES FRENCH COLONIAL GOVERNMENT AS A "LEVIATHAN" HAMPERING PRIVATE INTEREST. ARGUES THAT OPPOSITE WAS TRUE; "RAMPANT PRIVATE ENTERPRISE" OFTEN PREVENTED PROPER FUNCTIONING OF GOVERNMENT.

0321 BOULDING K.E.
THE ORGANIZATIONAL REVOLUTION.
NEW YORK: HARPER, 1953, 286 PP.
DEPICTS GREAT RISE IN THE NUMBER, SIZE, AND POWER OF ORGANIZATIONS, PARTICULARLY BUSINESS ESTABLISHMENTS. CASE-STUDIES ILLUSTRATE THE IMPACT ON PERSONAL CONDUCT AND ECONOMIC PROGRAMS OF NATIONS. COMMENTARY BY REINHOLD NIEBUHR WITH AUTHOR'S REPLY CONCLUDES TREATISE.

0322 BOULDING K.E.
ECONOMIC ANALYSIS (3RD ED.)
NEW YORK: HARPER & ROW, 1955, 905 PP., LC#55-06344.
TEXTBOOK DESCRIBES SOME PRINCIPAL ASPECTS OF ECONOMIC ANALYSIS, INCLUDING DEMAND AND SUPPLY, MACROECONOMICS, ELEMENTS OF MARGINAL ANALYSIS, AND ADVANCED ANALYTICAL TECHNIQUES.

0323 BOULDING K.E., SPIVEY W.A.
LINEAR PROGRAMMING AND THE THEORY OF THE FIRM.
NEW YORK: MACMILLAN, 1960, 227 PP.
REVIEW OF RECENT DEVELOPMENTS IN FIELD RELEVANT TO THE THEORY OF THE FIRM. DISCUSSES PRESENT CONCEPT OF THEORY AND ADAPTABILITY OF DATA TO LINEAR PROGRAMMING. PRESENTS STUDY OF RELATION OF OPERATIONS RESEARCH TO ECONOMIC APPLICATION, ESPECIALLY IN RELATION TO CYCLICAL CHANGES.

0324 BOURGOIGNIE G.E.
JEUNE AFRIQUE MOBILISABLE; LES PROBLEMES DE LA JEUNESSE DESOEUVREE EN AFRIQUE NOIRE.
PARIS: EDITIONS UNIVERSITAIRES, 1964, 213 PP.
ARGUES IN FAVOR OF "MOBILIZING" UNEMPLOYED YOUTHS OF AFRICA FOR ECONOMIC AND SOCIAL ACTION. REDEFINES THE TERMS "DEVELOPED," "UNDERDEVELOPED," AND "ANTI-DEVELOPED"; UNDERSCORES THE FORCES BEHIND AFRICA'S ECONOMIC HANDICAPS. ALSO STRESSES THE HUMAN FACTORS THAT CALL FOR SKILLS AND IDEAS OF AFRICAN YOUTHS. OFFERS ADVICE AND DISCUSSES EFFORTS TO "MOBILIZE" YOUTHS TO REBUILD DEVELOPING COUNTRIES.

0325 BOUSTEDT O., RANZ H.
REGIONALE STRUKTUR- UND WIRTSCHAFTSFORSCHUNG.
BREMEN: WALTER DOON VERLAG, 1957, 218 PP.
DISCUSSES RELATION BETWEEN REGIONAL GEOGRAPHIC AND CULTURAL CONDITIONS AND ECONOMICS. EXAMINES STRUCTURE OF REGIONS AND ECONOMIC DEVELOPMENT IN VARIOUS COUNTRIES.

0326 BOWEN H.R.
SOCIAL RESPONSIBILITIES OF THE BUSINESSMAN (FIRST EDITION)
NEW YORK: HARPER & ROW, 1953, 259 PP., LC#53-5434.
EXPLORES SOCIAL ROLE OF BUSINESSMAN IN FREE ENTERPRISE SYSTEM. SUGGESTS PRACTICAL STEPS TOWARD RECOGNITION OF BROADER SOCIAL GOALS IN BUSINESS DECISIONS; ANALYZES CURRENT RESEARCH DESIGNED TO STIMULATE EFFECTIVE SOCIAL RESPONSIBILITY IN BUSINESS COMMUNITY.

0327 US NATL COMN TECH, AUTOMAT, ECO
AUTOMATION AND ECONOMIC PROGRESS.
ENGLEWOOD CLIFFS: PRENTICE HALL, 1966, 170 PP., LC#66-28109.
STUDIES REPORT OF THE NATIONAL COMMISSION ON TECHNOLOGY, AUTOMATION, AND ECONOMIC PROGRESS. CONTAINS A SELECTION OF EIGHT EXPERT STUDIES AND PAPERS COMPRISING COMMISSION'S REPORT. THESE STUDIES COVER GENERAL OUTLOOK FOR TECHNOLOGICAL CHANGE, ITS PACE, AND EMPLOYMENT ASPECTS OF TECHNOLOGICAL CHANGE. INCLUDES ONE STUDY ON CHANGE IN WESTERN EUROPE; REMAINING ESSAYS CONCERN PROBLEM IN US.

0328 BOWEN R.H.
GERMAN THEORIES OF THE CORPORATIVE STATE, WITH SPECIAL REFERENCES TO THE PERIOD 1870-1919.
NEW YORK: MCGRAW HILL, 1947, 245 PP.
STUDIES THREE THEORIES OF CORPORATIVE STATE: SOCIAL CATHOLICISM, MONARCHICAL SOCIALISM, AND CARTEL CORPORATISM. ATTEMPTS TO ELUCIDATE THEORIES IN RELATION TO SOCIAL POLICIES OF PERIOD 1870-1919 IN GERMANY, AND IN RELATION TO TENDENCIES IN GERMAN SOCIAL THOUGHT. DISCUSSES ROOTS OF CORPORATIST TRADITION IN PRE-INDUSTRIAL ERA.

0329 BOWEN W.G.
ECONOMIC ASPECTS OF EDUCATION (NO. 104)
PRINCETON: PRIN U INDUS REL CTR, 1964, 121 PP.
CONTAINS THREE ESSAYS CONCERNING EDUCATION, MANPOWER, AND ECONOMIC GROWTH. FIRST DEALS WITH APPRAISING METHODS OF ECONOMISTS TO ESTIMATE RETURNS FROM EDUCATION. SECOND CONCERNS IMPLICATIONS OF ALTERNATIVE METHODS OF UNIVERSITY FINANCE FOR CERTAIN EDUCATIONAL POLICY ISSUES. THIRD DEALS WITH SALARY DIFFERENTIALS OF BRITISH UNIVERSITY TEACHERS IN FIELDS OF ART, SCIENCE, AND TECHNOLOGY.

0330 BOWEN W.G. ED., HARBISON F.H. ED.
UNEMPLOYMENT IN A PROSPEROUS ECONOMY.
PRINCETON: PRINCETON U PRESS, 1965, 173 PP.
PAPERS DISCUSS DIMENSIONS AND CHARACTERISTICS OF UNEMPLOYMENT PROBLEM, ROLE OF AGGREGATE DEMAND APPROACH TO ALLEVIATING UNEMPLOYMENT, AND SELECTIVE MANPOWER POLICIES. AUTHORS AGREE THAT UNEMPLOYMENT PROBLEM DESERVES ACTION; THAT NEW JOBS ARE CREATED ONLY WHEN ADDITIONAL SPENDING OCCURS; AND THAT THERE IS A NECESSITY FOR EXPANDING PROGRAMS OF TRAINING AND RETRAINING WORKERS.

0331 BOWIE R.R., ROSTOW E.V., BORK R.H.
GOVERNMENT REGULATION OF BUSINESS: CASES FROM THE NATIONAL REPORTER SYSTEM.
BROOKLYN: FOUNDATION PRESS, 1963, 1770 PP.
COLLECTION OF COURT CASES FROM 1897-1963 OF US SUPREME COURT AND FEDERAL COURTS ON GOVERNMENT REGULATION OF BUSINESS PROCEDURES. INCLUDES CASES INVOLVING ORDERS OF FEDERAL TRADE COMMISSION, MONOPOLY AND ANTITRUST LAWS, AND FAIR LABOR STANDARDS ACT.

0332 BOYD H.W. ED., IFFLAND C.P. ED., GIBSON D.M.T. ED.
MARKETING MANAGEMENT: CASES FROM EMERGING COUNTRIES.
READING, MASS: ADDISON-WESLEY, 1966, 424 PP., LC#66-25595.
COLLECTION OF FORTY-EIGHT CASE STUDIES OF EMERGING COUNRIES WITH CONSIDERATION OF MARKETING PROBLEMS THAT BUSINESS AND GOVERNMENT EXECUTIVES CONFRONT IN EMERGING ECONOMIES. CASES ORIGINATED IN SEVENTEEN COUNTRIES IN ARGENTINA, BRAZIL, CHILE, TAIWAN, COLUMBIA, GHANA, INDIA, INDONESIA, ISRAEL, SOUTH KOREA, MALAYSIA, MEXICO, NICARAGUA, PERU, PHILIPPINES, THAILAND, AND UAR.

0333 BRADLEY J.F.
THE ROLE OF TRADE ASSOCIATIONS AND PROFESSIONAL BUSINESS SOCIETIES IN AMERICA.
UNIVERSITY PARK: PENN STATE U PR, 1965, 166 PP., LC#64-8082.
CRITICAL INQUIRY INTO NATURE AND EVOLUTION OF BUSINESS ASSOCIATIONS IN THE US. DISCUSSES ORGANIZATIONAL ASPECTS, AND SEEKS TO DETERMINE IMPACT OF SUCH ASSOCIATIONS ON SOCIETY AT LARGE. ANALYZES EFFECTS RELATING TO ECONOMIC PROGRESS IN GENERAL.

0334 BRADY R.A.
BUSINESS AS A SYSTEM OF POWER.
NEW YORK: COLUMBIA U PRESS, 1943, 340 PP., LC#43-268.
AFTER NOTING INCREASE OF CHAMBERS OF COMMERCE, TRADE "PEAK" ASSOCIATIONS AND CONCENTRATIONS OF ECONOMIC POWER, THE DEVELOPMENTS IN SEVERAL COUNTRIES ARE EXAMINED IN THIS LIGHT. IN THE US, A "SELF-REGIMENTATION " OF BUSINESS IS NOTED AFTER WORLD WAR I, AND CENTRALIZATION OF CONTROL WITHIN THE NAM WITH USE OF "SCALAR" OR HIERARCHICAL POWER AS THE INVERSE OF "DEMOCRATIC" CONTROL.

0335 BRAFF A.J., MILLER R.F.
"WAGE-PRICE POLICIES UNDER PUBLIC PRESSURE."
SOUTHERN ECO. J., 27 (OCT. 61), 163-173.
HOW OPINION REACTS UPON WAGES AND PRICES, WITH POLICY IMPLICATIONS THEREOF.

0336 BRAIBANTI R.J.D. ED., SPENGLER J.J. ED.
TRADITION, VALUES AND SOCIO-ECONOMIC DEVELOPMENT.
DURHAM: DUKE U PR, 1961, 305 PP., LC#60-15267.
STUDY OF TRADITION, VALUES, AND SOCIO-ECONOMIC DEVELOPMENT, ENCOMPASSING A WIDE RANGE OF FIELDS. PROBLEMS ARE EXAMINED FROM BOTH THEORETICAL AND EMPIRICAL VIEWPOINTS. COVERS CONCEPTUAL AND METHODOLOGICAL PROBLEMS, AND CRITIQUES OF CONTEMPORARY POLICY.

0337 BRAIBANTI R.J.D., SPENGLER J.J.
ADMINISTRATION AND ECONOMIC DEVELOPMENT IN INDIA.
DURHAM: DUKE U. PR., 1963, 312 PP., $7.50.
INDIAN AND AMERICAN POLITICAL SCIENTISTS AND ECONOMISTS DISCUSS THE RELATIONSHIP OF ECONOMIC DEVELOPMENT AND ADMINISTRATION IN INDIA. ECONOMIC DEVELOPMENT 'HAS BEEN BLOCKED TO A LARGE EXTENT PRECISELY BECAUSE ITS IMPLEMENTATION DEPENDS ON A STRUCTURE AND DISPOSITION OF BUREAUCRACY, NEITHER OF WHICH CAN BE JARRED OUT OF THE LARGER SOCIETAL WHOLE.'

0338 BRANCH M.C.
THE CORPORATE PLANNING PROCESS.
NEW YORK: AMER MANAGEMENT ASSN, 1962, 253 PP., LC#62-15083.
STUDY OF CORPORATE PLANNING EMPHASIZING COMPLEX HUMAN, ORGANIZATIONAL, AND MECHANICAL PROCESSES THAT ARE CONTINGENT TO ANY PLANNING. INCLUDES SUPPLEMENTARY ESSAY ON TECHNIQUES OF ANALYSIS.

0339 BRANCO R.
"LAND REFORM* THE ANSWER TO LATIN AMERICA'S AGRICULTURAL DEVELOPMENT?"
J. INTER-AMER. STUDIES, 10 (APR. 67), 225-235.
ARGUES THAT SPLITTING UP HACIENDAS AND PLANTATIONS FOR RE-DISTRIBUTION HAS SERIOUS DRAWBACKS AND IS PROFITABLE ONLY IN AREAS WITH LOW CONCENTRATION OF HUMAN AND CAPITAL RESOURCES. CRASH PROGRAMS, AS IN MEXICO, BOLIVIA, AND CUBA, SHOULD BE AVOIDED. ADVOCATES INDIRECT METHODS SUCH AS LIMITING MAXIMUM SIZE OF HOLDINGS AND PROGRESSIVE LAND TAX. SUGGESTS "HIGHLY URGENT COMPLEMENTARY MEASURES."

0340 BRANDENBURG F.
"THE RELEVANCE OF MEXICAN EXPERIENCE TO LATIN AMERICAN DEVELOPMENT."
ORBIS, 9 (SPRING 65), 190-213.
AUTHOR BELIEVES THERE IS VERY LITTLE IN MEXICO'S BASIC POLITICAL AND ECONOMIC ORGANIZATION WORTHY OF DUPLICATION BY OTHER SOUTH AMERICAN NATIONS. MEXICO HAS FOUND THE KEY TO ITS OWN POLITICAL STABILITY ACCOMPANIED BY ECONOMIC GROWTH BASED ON ITS OWN INHERITANCE, NEEDS AND REALITIES. THE OTHER LA NATIONS MUST DO THE SAME.

0341 BRAUCHER R.
"RECLAMATION OF GOODS FROM A FRAUDULENT BUYER."
MICH. LAW REV., 65 (MAY 67), 1281-1298.
DISCUSSES SECTIONS OF UNIFORM COMMERCIAL CODE WHICH DEFINE RIGHT OF SELLER TO RECLAIM GOODS FROM AN INSOLVENT BUYER. TRACES PRE-CODE LAW AND HISTORY OF RECLAMATION SECTIONS. FINDS THAT LAWS IN CODE ARE NOT LEGALLY "TIGHT" AND PROPOSES AMENDMENT THAT WOULD SOLVE EXISTING PROBLEMS.

0342 BRAUN K.
LABOR DISPUTES AND THEIR SETTLEMENT.
BALTIMORE: JOHNS HOPKINS PRESS, 1955, 393 PP., LC#55-8425.
TRACES HISTORY OF LABOR MANAGEMENT DISPUTES AND PRINCIPLES OF CURRENT SETTLEMENT PRACTICES. THESE PRACTICES ARE CONCILIATION, ARBITRATION, AND LITIGATION. EACH IS ANALYZED ACCORDING TO PURPOSE AND SUCCESS UNDER SPECIFIC CIRCUMSTANCES. OPINIONS FOR AND AGAINST EACH ARE DISCUSSED, THOUGH NO ATTEMPT IS MADE TO GIVE RECOMMENDATIONS FOR OR AGAINST ANY SPECIFIC METHOD OF LABOR SETTLEMENT.

0343 BRAYBROOKE D., LINDBLOM C.E.
A STRATEGY OF DECISION: POLICY EVALUATION AS A SOCIAL PROCESS.
NEW YORK: FREE PRESS OF GLENCOE, 1963, 268 PP., LC#63-13537.
COMBINED STUDY OF THE ADAPTATIONS OF POLICY TO STRATEGIC DEMANDS OF SPECIFIC ECONOMIC SITUATIONS, AND RELATIONSHIP OF THIS PROCESS TO SOCIAL AND POLITICAL ETHICS. STRESSES PRIORITY OF "DISJOINTED INCREMENTALISM" IN ACTUAL DECISION-MAKING, ESPECIALLY IN EFFECTS OF CENSUS EVALUATION IN SHAPING OF POLICIES AND ALTERNATIVES.

0344 BREAK G.F.
FEDERAL LENDING AND ECONOMIC STABILITY.
WASHINGTON: BROOKINGS INST, 1965, 185 PP., LC#65-17865.
IN PROCESS OF EXPANSION, RECENT FEDERAL LOAN PROGRAMS BOTH HELPED AND HINDERED EFFORTS OF POLICY-MAKERS TO KEEP US ON STABLE PATH OF ECONOMIC GROWTH. NATURE OF THE CONFLICTING EFFECTS AND THEIR IMPLICATIONS ARE EXAMINED.

0345 BREAK G.F.
INTERGOVERNMENTAL FISCAL RELATIONS IN THE UNITED STATES.
WASHINGTON: BROOKINGS INST, 1967, 272 PP., LC#66-28890.
REVIEWS HISTORY OF US FEDERAL AID TO STATE AND LOCAL GOVERNMENTS AND NOTES LOCAL GOVERNMENTS' FISCAL OUTLOOK FOR 1970'S. DISCUSSES PROBLEMS OF COORDINATED INTERGOVERNMENTAL TAX SYSTEMS AND SPECIFIC FISCAL PROBLEMS OF LARGE CITIES. POSES POSSIBLE SOLUTIONS TO FUTURE FEDERAL AID PROBLEMS BASED ON GRANTS-IN-AID FOR SPECIFIC LOCAL GOVERNMENT PROGRAMS OR ON GRANTS MADE UNCONDITIONALLY.

0346 BRENNAN M.J. ED.
PATTERNS OF MARKET BEHAVIOR.
PROVIDENCE: BROWN U PRESS, 1965, 258 PP., LC#65-12932.
TREATS COMMODITIES, RESOURCES, MONEY, AND INTERNATIONAL MARKETS. COVERS CONTEMPORARY THEORY OF PRICE DETERMINATION, OCCUPATIONAL STRUCTURE, MONETARY POLICY, RESOURCE MIGRATION, DEVALUATION, AND GROWTH DIFFERENTIALS.

0347 BRESCIANI-TURRONI C
THE ECONOMICS OF INFLATION: A STUDY OF CURRENCY DEPRECIATION IN POST-WAR GERMANY.
LONDON: ALLEN & UNWIN, 1937, 450 PP.
STUDIES DEPRECIATION OF GERMAN MARK 1914-23, AND ANALYZES ITS WIDELY-FELT EFFECTS. SHOWS HOW IT DESTROYED WEALTH OF SOLID ELEMENTS OF GERMAN SOCIETY, FOSTERED HITLER, AND BROUGHT ABOUT MORAL AND ECONOMIC DISEQUILIBRIUM. DISCUSSES FOREIGN EXCHANGES AND INTERNAL PRICE MOVEMENTS IN GERMANY, INFLATION AND DEPRECIATION OF THE MARK, PROBLEMS IN INTERNATIONAL TRADE, AND SOCIAL EFFECTS.

0348 BREWIS T.N., ENGLISH H.E., SCOTT A.
CANADIAN ECONOMIC POLICY.
LONDON: MACMILLAN, 1961, 365 PP.
COMPREHENSIVE TREATMENT OF ROLE OF GOVERNMENT IN ECONOMY. TRACES EFFECTS OF GOVERNMENTAL POLICY ON SUPPLY, DEMAND, COMPETITION, RESOURCE ALLOCATION, CAPITAL FORMATION, AND EMPLOYMENT CONDITIONS. INDICATES RELATIONSHIPS OF FISCAL AND MONETARY POLICIES; DESCRIBES THEIR IMPACT UPON MARKET SITUATIONS.

0349 BRIEFS H.W.
PRICING POWER AND "ADMINISTRATIVE" INFLATION (PAMPHLET)
WASHINGTON: AMER ENTERPRISE INST, 1962, 63 PP., LC#62-21990.
ANALYSIS OF NATIONAL POLICY OF PRICE CONTROL AS MEANS TO REGULATE INFLATION. DISCUSSES CONCEPT OF ADMINISTERED PRICE AND OPINIONS ON ITS VALUE AND DEALS WITH STEEL INDUSTRY FOR UNDERSTANDING OF PRACTICE.

0350 BRIEFS H.W.
REGAINING BALANCE IN A HIGH EMPLOYMENT ECONOMY: UNRESOLVED ISSUES FOR 1967 AND BEYOND.
WASHINGTON: GEORGETOWN U PRESS, 1967, 55 PP., LC#67-23394.
ONE OF SERIES OF SUPPLEMENTARY PAPERS PUBLISHED BY THE CENTER FOR STRATEGIC STUDIES. ANALYZES LINK BETWEEN NATION'S ABILITY TO MAINTAIN COMMITMENTS ABROAD AND DOMESTIC ECONOMIC HEALTH. ANALYZES DETERMINANTS OF ADMINISTRATION'S STRATEGY SET FORTH IN 1967 ECONOMIC REPORT AND 1968 BUDGET, REGARDING INFLATION, FISCAL POLICY, MONETARY POLICY, AND BALANCE-OF-PAYMENTS COMPLICATIONS.

0351 BRIGHAM E.F.
"THE DETERMINANTS OF RESIDENTIAL LAND VALUES."
LAND ECONOMICS, 41 (NOV. 65), 325-334.
DESCRIBES AND TESTS A MODEL OF RESIDENTIAL LAND VALUES IN LOS ANGELES COUNTY. THE VALUE OF ANY PARTICULAR SITE IS ASSUMED TO BE RELATED TO AN INDEX OF ACCESSIBILITY, LEVEL OF AMENITY, TOPOGRAPHY, AND HISTORICAL FACTORS, INCLUDING THE WAY THE LAND IS BEING USED. ACCESSIBILITY TO EMPLOYMENT OPPORTUNITIES IS POSITIVELY RELATED TO VALUES.

0352 BRIGHT J.R.
RESEARCH, DEVELOPMENT AND TECHNOLOGICAL INNOVATION.
HOMEWOOD: RICHARD IRWIN, 1964, 764 PP., LC#64-11711.
DISCUSSION OF TECHNOLOGICAL INNOVATION AND ITS PROBLEMS. TYPICAL BUSINESS PROBLEMS ANALYZED IN ATTEMPT TO ILLUMINATE METHODS OF HANDLING ISSUES CONCERNING IDENTIFICATION OF, SUPPORT FOR, AND DEFENSE AGAINST RADICAL TECHNOLOGICAL CONCEPTS. CHANGE AND INNOVATION IN POPULATION, SOCIAL TRENDS, NATURAL RESOURCE POSITIONS, ETC. ARE CONSIDERED.

0353 BRIMMER A.F.
"EMPLOYMENT PATTERNS AND THE DILEMMA OF DESEGREGATION."
INTEGRATED EDUCATION, 5 (OCT. 67), 17-23.
TRACES RECENT TRENDS AND PATTERNS OF EMPLOYMENT AMONG NONWHITES, AND URGES EXPANSION OF TRAINING PROGRAMS. STUDIES ADVERSE IMPACT OF DESEGREGATION ON NEGRO MIDDLE CLASS AND THEIR RELIANCE ON EMPLOYMENT IN PUBLIC SECTOR. DISCUSSES TREND OF NEGRO EMPLOYMENT IN CLERICAL, TECHNICAL, AND MIDDLE GRADE WHITE COLLAR POSITIONS AND IMPLICATION FOR FUTURE LEADERSHIP.

0354 BRITISH COMMONWEALTH BUR AGRI
WORLD AGRICULTURAL ECONOMICS AND RURAL SOCIOLOGY ABSTRACTS.
LONDON: COMMONWEALTH AGRI BUR.
AN INTERNATIONAL ABSTRACT JOURNAL COVERING THE LITERATURE ON ECONOMIC AND SOCIAL ASPECTS OF AGRICULTURE. ENCOMPASSES ONLY NEWLY PUBLISHED MATERIAL OF INTEREST TO RESEARCH WORKERS, GOVERNMENT OFFICIALS, AND EXTENSION WORKERS. MATERIAL IS SYSTEMATICALLY ARRANGED BY SUBJECTS: GOVERNMENTAL POLICIES, LAND REFORM, FARM MANAGEMENT, MARKETING, ETC. SELECTIONS ARE INTERNATIONAL IN SCOPE.

0355 BRITT S.H., LOWRY R.L.
"CONFORMITY OF LABOR NEWSPAPERS WITH RESPECT TO THE AFL-CIO CONFLICT."
J. SOCIAL PSYCHOLOGY, 14 (NOV. 41), 375-387.
LABOR NEWSPAPERS ARE ANALYZED TO DETERMINE THE EXTENT OF CONFORMITY OF LOCAL UNION LEADERSHIP TO THE OFFICIAL ATTITUDE OF THE NATIONAL UNION. IT IS CONCLUDED THAT THERE WAS NO INSTITUTIONAL CONFORMITY TO THE PHILOSOPHY OF THE

NATIONAL GROUP. METHODOLOGY IS BASED ON ALLPORT'S J-CURVE.

0356 BROCKWAY A.F.
AFRICAN SOCIALISM.
CHESTER SPRINGS: DUFOUR, 1963, 126 PP., LC#63-21144.
TRACES HISTORICAL TRANSITION FROM EUROPEAN CAPITALISM TO AFRICAN SOCIALISM. DISCUSSES SOCIALISM OF NKRUMAH OF GHANA AND NASSER OF EGYPT. ATTEMPTS EVALUATION OF AFRICA'S POSSIBLE TURN TOWARD COMMUNISM.

0357 BRODERSEN A.
THE SOVIET WORKER: LABOR AND GOVERNMENT IN SOVIET SOCIETY.
NEW YORK: RANDOM HOUSE, INC, 1966, 278 PP., LC#66-10534.
DISCUSSES ROLE OF THE WORKING CLASS IN CONTEMPORARY SOVIET SOCIETY. SHOWS WORKER'S ROLE IN BOLSHEVIK, MARXIST, AND LENINIST THEORY AND IN BOLSHEVIK POLICY. ANALYZES THE WORKER WITHIN STALINIST INDUSTRIALIZATION AND DURING FORMATION OF THE LABOR FORCE. DESCRIBES NEW COURSE IN SOVIET LABOR POLICY SINCE KHRUSHCHEV. EXAMINES WORKER'S RELATIONS TO INTELLIGENTSIA AND POLITICS.

0358 BROEKMEIJER M.W.J.
FICTION AND TRUTH ABOUT THE "DECADE OF DEVELOPMENT"
NEW YORK: HUMANITIES PRESS, 1966, 151 PP., LC#66-25082.
CRITICAL ANALYSIS OF FOREIGN AID TO DEVELOPING NATIONS. DESCRIBES CHARACTERISTICS OF DEVELOPING WORLD. URGES BETTER UNDERSTANDING OF THEIR TRADITIONAL VALUES, INCREASED INVESTMENT IN EDUCATION, AND COOPERATION OF PUBLIC AND PRIVATE AID. DISCUSSES SEVERAL AID PROJECTS THAT WERE VERY SUCCESSFUL.

0359 BROGAN D.W.
THE PRICE OF REVOLUTION.
NEW YORK: HARPER & ROW, 1951, 280 PP.
CONCERNED WITH REVOLUTIONS, USE OF POLITICAL VIOLENCE TO TREAT SOCIAL AND ECONOMIC PROBLEMS. STATES THAT COSTS OF REVOLUTION SHOULD BE CONSIDERED ALONG WITH BENEFITS. STUDIES AMERICAN, FRENCH, AND RUSSIAN REVOLUTIONS, NATIONALISM AND IMPERIALISM, AND EFFECT OF REVOLUTIONS ON CHURCHES. MAINTAINS THAT PRESENT WORLD SITUATION IS ONE OF REVOLUTION INVOLVING US AND USSR'S OPPOSING IDEOLOGIES.

0360 BROMKE A.
POLAND'S POLITICS: IDEALISM VS. REALISM.
CAMBRIDGE: HARVARD U PR, 1967, 316 PP., LC#66-21331.
DISCUSSES CONFLICT BETWEEN POLITICAL IDEALISM AND POLITICAL REALISM IN POLAND. STATES THAT ROOT OF CONFLICT IS ANXIETY ABOUT NEIGHBORS' INTENTIONS. SHOWS THAT FOR 200 YEARS RIVALRY BETWEEN GERMANY AND RUSSIA HAS REPRESENTED A CONSTANT THREAD OF POLISH HISTORY. POINTS OUT THAT POLISH POLITICAL MOVEMENTS HAVE ALWAYS SPLIT, NOT OVER DOMESTIC ISSUES, BUT OVER FOREIGN POLICY.

0361 BROMWICH L.
UNION CONSTITUTIONS.
NEW YORK: FUND FOR THE REPUBLIC, 1959, 43 PP.
ANALYSIS OF PROCEDURAL INADEQUACIES IN SUCH AREAS OF UNION LIFE AS APPRENTICESHIP, RACIAL DISCRIMINATION, UNION CONVENTIONS, THE CONSTITUTION AMENDING PROCESS, CONCENTRATION OF POWER, NOMINATION OF OFFICERS, RECALL, UNION DUE PROCESS IN SOME CASES, SUSPENSION OF MEMBERS AND UNIONS, UNION PRESS AND DISCIPLINE. BASED ON SEVENTY UNIONS WITH MEMBERSHIP OF ALMOST 16 MILLION.

0362 BROOKINGS INSTITUTION
DEVELOPMENT OF THE EMERGING COUNTRIES; AN AGENDA FOR RESEARCH.
WASHINGTON: BROOKINGS INST, 1962, 239 PP., LC#62-12716.
SUGGESTS RESEARCH THAT MAY CONTRIBUTE TO REMEDYING PRESENT DEFICIENCY IN KNOWLEDGE OF ECONOMICS, POLITICS, SOCIOLOGY, AND PSYCHOLOGY OF DEVELOPMENT. EXAMINES COUNTRY PROGRAMMING, RURAL PROBLEMS, ECONOMIC AND POLITICAL CHANGE, TECHNOLOGICAL CHANGE, ROLE OF EDUCATION, AND FOREIGN AID.

0363 BROOKINGS INSTITUTION
BROOKINGS PAPERS ON PUBLIC POLICY.
WASHINGTON: BROOKINGS INST, 1965, 220 PP., LC#65-18919.
DISCUSSES FOREIGN POLICY, EDUCATION AND PUBLIC SERVICE, WAGE POLICY AND REGULATION OF COMPETITION, TAXATION AND FISCAL POLICY, AND CONGRESSIONAL CONTROL OF ADMINISTRATION.

0364 BROOKS R.R.
WHEN LABOR ORGANIZES.
NEW HAVEN: YALE U PR, 1937, 361 PP.
A SYSTEMATICL EXAMINATION OF UNIONS FROM ORGANIZATION, STRIKES, FINANCES, ADMINISTRATION AND LEADERSHIP, BENEFIT AND WELFARE POLICIES TO BROADER ISSUES OF POLITICAL ACTION, ANTI-UNIONISM AND BUSINESS POLICIES OF LABOR, WITH A HISTORICAL SECTION AND TRENDS FOR UNIONISM. REPRESENTATION, EXTERNAL AN INTERNAL, IS DISCUSSED THROUGHOUT THE WORK.

0365 BROUDE H.W.
STEEL DECISIONS AND THE NATIONAL ECONOMY.
NEW HAVEN: YALE U PR, 1963, 332 PP., LC#63-13958.
DISCUSSES PROBLEM OF US ECONOMIC DEPENDENCE ON STEEL AND THE INDUSTRY'S UNWILLINGNESS TO EXPAND AS GOVERNMENT POLICY DICTATES. ATTEMPTS TO DEFINE LIMITS OF DEPENDENCE, AND SUGGESTS THEORETICAL AND PRATICAL POLICIES WHICH MIGHT ALTER PRACTICES OF STEEL INDUSTRY.

0366 BROWN B., TATE J.H.
INCOME TRENDS IN THE UNITED STATES THROUGH 1975.
MENLO PARK: STANFORD U RES INST, 1958, 125 PP.
REPORT COVERS ESTIMATES OF PERSONAL INCOME, FEDERAL INDIVIDUAL INCOME TAXES, AND SPENDABLE INCOME, EXPECTED TO BE GENERATED, IN YEARS 1960, 1965, 1970, AND 1975, UNDER CONDITIONS OF VIRTUALLY FULL EMPLOYMENT. HISTORICAL DATA ON WHICH PROJECTIONS ARE BASED RELATES TO YEARS 1929-55. ESTIMATES REFER TO CONTINENTAL US, NINE CENSUS AREAS, AND 11 WESTERN STATES.

0367 BROWN C.V.
GOVERNMENT AND BANKING IN WESTERN NIGERIA.
LONDON: OXFORD U PR, 1964, 141 PP.
ANALYZES IMPLEMENTATION OF WESTERN NIGERIAN GOVERNMENT'S ECONOMIC POLICY OF AIDING INDIGENOUS BANKS. RELIES HEAVILY ON INFORMATION AND QUOTATIONS FROM COKER COMMISSION OF INQUIRY. SIGNIFICANT CASE STUDY MAY INDICATE TYPE OF RELATIONSHIP EXISTING AMONG POLITICIANS, CIVIL SERVANTS, AND PUBLIC CORPORATIONS IN WESTERN NIGERIA AND OTHER DEVELOPING AREAS.

0368 BROWN E.H.P., WISEMAN J.
A COURSE IN APPLIED ECONOMICS (2ND ED.)
NEW YORK: PITMAN PUBLISHING, 1964, 443 PP.
DESCRIBES PROCESS OF ECONOMIC POLICY-MAKING. DEFINES CONCEPTS AND CRITERIA OF WELFARE; DISCUSSES PROBLEMS OF RESOURCE ALLOCATION; EXAMINES SPECIFIC PROBLEMS ARISING IN MARKETS FOR PARTICULAR PRODUCTS; STUDIES GROWTH AND STABILITY; AND EXPLORES AREA OF INTERNATIONAL TRADE TO ILLUSTRATE PROCESS OF ECONOMIC ANALYSIS.

0369 BROWN J.F.
THE NEW EASTERN EUROPE.
NEW YORK: FREDERICK PRAEGER, 1966, 306 PP., LC#65-24939.
COVERS IMPORTANT POLITICAL, ECONOMIC, AND CULTURAL DEVELOPMENTS WITHIN EASTERN EUROPEAN STATES EXCLUDING ALBANIA AND YUGOSLAVIA. DISCUSSES INTRABLOC RELATIONS, EAST EUROPEAN RELATIONS WITH WESTERN POWERS, AND SUMMARY OF SITUATION AT TIME OF KHRUSHCHEV'S FALL.

0370 BROWN J.S.
"UNION SIZE AS A FUNCTION OF INTRA-UNION CONFLICT."
HUMAN RELATIONS, 9 (FEB. 56), 75-89.
THE DEGREE OF ABILITY OF A UNION TO CONDUCT BUSINESS PEACEFULLY AND CONTROL MEMBERS AFFECTS ITS SUCCESS IN SERVING MEMBERSHIP AND ATTRACTING NEW ADHERENTS. A STUDY OF THE ILGW UNION AND THE RELATION BETWEEN SIZE AND INTRA-GROUP CONFLICT IS PRESENTED ON THE BASIS OF JURISDICTIONAL AND CONSTITUTIONAL ISSUES AND LEADERSHIP TURNOVER.

0371 BROWN M.B.
"THE TRADE UNION QUESTION."
POLIT. QUART., 38 (APR.-JUNE 67), 156-164.
DISCUSSES CONTROVERSY OVER ENGLISH TRADE UNIONS' IMMUNITY FROM LEGAL PROCEEDINGS AS CORPORATE BODIES, AND IMMUNITY OF TRADE UNION OFFICIALS FROM LEGAL CHARGES OF "CONSPIRACY" AND "INTIMIDATION."

0372 BROWN R.E.
CHARLES BEARD AND THE CONSTITUTION.
PRINCETON: PRINCETON U PRESS, 1956, 219 PP., LC#56-08373.
CRITICAL ANALYSIS OF ECONOMIC INTERPRETATION OF THE CONSTITUTION AS PROPOSED BY BEARD IN 1913. IN STATING THAT CONSTITUTION WAS WORK OF CONSOLIDATED ECONOMIC GROUPS RATHER THAN PATRIOTS, THIS WORK OUTRAGED MANY. USING CHAPTER-BY-CHAPTER ANALYSIS, AUTHOR CRITICIZES BEARD FROM STANDPOINT OF HISTORICAL METHOD.

0373 BROWN R.T.
TRANSPORT AND THE ECONOMIC INTEGRATION OF SOUTH AMERICA.
WASHINGTON: BROOKINGS INST, 1966, 288 PP., LC#66-21327.
ANALYSIS OF GEOGRAPHIC, ECONOMIC, AND POLITICAL OBSTRUCTIONS TO SOUTH AMERICAN ECONOMIC DEVELOPMENT AND INTEGRATION. TRANSPORTATION SINGLED OUT MAJOR IMPEDIMENT TO NEEDED TRADE WITHIN SOUTH AMERICA AND AMELIORATING STRATEGY CALCULATED. EXTENSIVE DATA PRESENTED. ROLE OF LAFTA AND IMPORT OF MARITIME POLICY DISCUSSED.

0374 BROWN S.D.
STUDIES ON ASIA, 1962.
LINCOLN: U OF NEB PR, 1962, 87 PP., LC#60-15432.
STUDIES VARIOUS FACTORS SHAPING CONTEMPORARY ASIA: TAISHO CRISIS OF JAPAN, 1912-13; ISLAM AND MODERN WORLD; PRIVATE SECTOR IN INDIAN ECONOMY; BUDDHISM AND POLITICAL POWER IN BURMA; AND PARTY SYSTEM OF ISRAEL.

0375 BROWN W.M.
THE DESIGN AND PERFORMANCE OF "OPTIMUM" BLAST SHELTER PROGRAMS (PAMPHLET)
HARMON-ON-HUDSON: HUDSON INST, 1964, 38 PP.
RESEARCH REPORT ON BLAST SHELTERS, INCLUDING DESCRIPTION OF MODEL AND SUGGESTIONS FOR ITS IMPROVEMENT, ITS COST, AND

ITS EFFECTIVENESS.

0376 BROWN W.M.
THE EXTERNAL LIQUIDITY OF AN ADVANCED COUNTRY.
PRINCETON: PRIN U, DEPT OF ECO, 1964, 70 PP., LC#64-8379.
EXAMINES PROBLEM OF AVAILABILITY OF RESOURCES FOR FINANCING TEMPORARY DEFICITS IN BALANCE OF PAYMENTS. FOCUSES ON THEORETICAL DISCUSSION OF "ADEQUACY OF LIQUIDITY." ILLUSTRATED BY REFERENCE TO STATISTICAL DATA.

0377 BRUMBERG A. ED.
RUSSIA UNDER KHRUSHCHEV.
NEW YORK: FREDERICK PRAEGER, 1962, 660 PP.
PROVIDES CHRONOLOGICAL AND THEMATIC COMMENTARY ON INTERNAL DEVELOPMENTS IN USSR IN KHRUSHCHEV DECADE. THIRTY-FIVE ARTICLES DEAL WITH ECONOMIC, SOCIAL, AND ARTISTIC DEVELOPMENTS; IDEOLOGICAL SETTING; A LOOK INTO THE FUTURE.

0378 BRYCE M.D.
INDUSTRIAL DEVELOPMENT: A GUIDE FOR ACCELERATING ECONOMIC GROWTH.
NEW YORK: MCGRAW HILL, 1960, 282 PP., LC#60-10596.
DISCUSSES TECHNIQUES FOR PLANNING INDUSTRIAL PROJECTS. TELLS HOW TO ESTABLISH INDUSTRIAL DEVELOPMENT BANK, TO ATTRACT FOREIGN INVESTMENT, TO ANALYZE ECONOMIC AND MANAGEMENT PROBLEMS OF NATIONAL INDUSTRIES, AND TO APPRAISE INDUSTRIAL PROJECTS. GUIDE TO GOVERNMENT AND PRIVATE INDUSTRIAL DEVELOPMENT.

0379 BRYCE M.D.
POLICIES AND METHODS FOR INDUSTRIAL DEVELOPMENT.
NEW YORK: MCGRAW HILL, 1965, 301 PP., LC#64-66367.
DESCRIBES POLICIES AND METHODS FOR INDUSTRIAL DEVELOPMENT. EXPLAINS HOW REGION CAN SPEED INDUSTRIAL GROWTH. DISCUSSES INCENTIVES FOR INVESTMENT. TELLS WHAT NEW INDUSTRIES NEED TO BECOME SUCCESSFUL. DESIGNED AS GUIDEBOOK FOR GOVERNMENT OFFICIALS AND ADVISORS.

0380 BUCHANAN N.S., ELLIS H.S.
APPROACHES TO ECONOMIC DEVELOPMENT.
NEW YORK: TWENT. CENTURY, 1955, 494 PP.
AN ANALYSIS OF VARIOUS ECONOMIC PROBLEMS THAT FACE UNDERDEVELOPED COUNTRIES IN THEIR STRUGGLE TO ACHIEVE RAPID ECONOMIC DEVELOPMENT. SUGGESTS THAT INCREASED INTERNATIONAL TRADE WOULD BE THE BEST METHOD BY WHICH THE USA CAN HELP UNDERDEVELOPED NATIONS ATTAIN THEIR GOALS.

0381 BUCK S.J.
THE AGRARIAN CRUSADE: A CHRONICLE OF THE FARMER IN POLITICS.
NEW HAVEN: YALE U PR, 1920, 215 PP.
STUDIES MOVEMENTS AND AGITATIONS BY FARMERS TOWARD BETTERING THEIR LOT. SKETCHES COURSE AND REPRODUCES SPIRIT OF THIS CRUSADE FROM INCEPTION WITH GRANGER MOVEMENT, THROUGH GREENBACK AND POPULIST PHASES, TO A "CLIMAX IN THE BATTLE FOR FREE SILVER."

0382 BUGEDA LANZAS J.
A STATEMENT OF THE LAWS OF CUBA IN MATTERS AFFECTING BUSINESS (2ND ED. REV., ENLARGED)
WASHINGTON: PAN AMERICAN UNION, 1958, 333 PP.
SUMMARIZES BASIC CONSTITUTIONAL, STATUTORY, AND REGULATORY PROVISIONS OF CUBA UP TO 1958, CONCERNING BUSINESS MATTERS AND PERSONS INVOLVED IN THEM. EMPHASIZES COMMERCIAL, INDUSTRIAL, AND LABOR LAW, AND RELATED MATTERS. BASED UPON INFORMATION SUPPLIED BY PRACTICING CUBAN LAWYERS. ONE OF A SERIES.

0383 BUNZEL J.H.
"THE GENERAL IDEOLOGY OF AMERICAN SMALL BUSINESS"(BMR)"
POLIT. SCI. QUART., 70 (MAR. 55), 87-102.
DISCUSSES BELIEFS AND VALUES OF THE AMERICAN SMALL BUSINESSMAN. ARGUES THAT IDEOLOGY OF SMALL BUSINESS PARTAKES OF A GOOD DEAL OF WHAT WAS PREVALENT IN US PRIOR TO THE RISE OF INDUSTRY. PLACES IDEOLOGY IN CONTEXT OF "AGRARIAN SPIRIT" OF PRE-INDUSTRIAL AMERICA, SHOWING BELIEFS OF SMALL BUSINESS AND PERSONALITY OF SMALL BUSINESSMAN THAT PERSIST TODAY.

0384 BURDEN H.T.
THE NUREMBERG PARTY RALLIES 1923-39.
NEW YORK: FREDERICK PRAEGER, 1967, 420 PP.
DESCRIBES ROLE OF NUREMBERG PARTY RALLIES IN HISTORY OF NAZI GERMANY. NOTES THAT IN NUREMBERG, THE ABSOLUTE STATE PERFECTED ITS ABILITY TO DOMINATE MAN'S MIND. FINDS THAT RALLIES WERE PATTERNED AFTER PAGAN CULTS, CHURCH RITUALS, AND WAGNERIAN THEATER. RECREATES MOOD AND EVENTS OF RALLIES: RITUALS, PARADES, CHANTS, ETC. POINTS OUT THAT NAZIS RECOGNIZED PROPAGANDA VALUE OF FILM.

0385 BUREAU OF NATIONAL AFFAIRS
LABOR RELATIONS REFERENCE MANUAL VOL. 63.
WASHINGTON: BUREAU NATL AFFAIRS, 1967, 1592 PP.
COLLECTION OF DECISIONS OF NATIONAL LABOR RELATIONS BOARD AND STATE BOARDS AND DECISIONS OF STATE AND FEDERAL COURTS CONCERNING LAW OF LABOR RELATIONS FROM SEPTEMBER TO DECEMBER, 1966.

0386 BUREAU OF NATIONAL AFFAIRS
FEDERAL-STATE REGULATION OF WELFARE FUNDS (REV. ED.)
WASHINGTON: BUREAU NATL AFFAIRS, 1962, 265 PP., LC#62-16834.
EXAMINATION OF ORIGINAL WELFARE AND PENSION PLANS DISCLOSURE ACT OF 1958 AND CHANGES MADE BY 1962 AMENDMENTS. PROVIDES EDITORIAL ANALYSIS OF AMENDED ACT, INCLUDING CHECKLISTS FOR PLAN DESCRIPTIONS AND ANNUAL REPORTS. CONTAINS TEXT OF FEDERAL ACT AS AMENDED, LEGISLATIVE REPORTS ON ORIGINAL ACT AND AMENDMENTS, AND EXCERPTS FROM CONGRESSIONAL DEBATES ON SUBJECT.

0387 BURKE E.
"RESOLUTIONS FOR CONCILIATION WITH AMERICA" (1775), IN E. BURKE, COLLECTED WORKS, VOL. 2."
BOSTON: LITTLE BROWN, 1883.
ARGUES THAT SINCE WAR SELDOM SUBJECTS A POPULATION PERMANENTLY, AND SINCE TRADE WITH AMERICA IS SO GREAT, A PEACEFUL SOLUTION TO THE DISPUTE WITH THE AMERICAN COLONIES SHOULD BE FOUND. PROPOSES TO ALLOW COLONIES TO GOVERN THEMSELVES ON MATTERS OF TAXATION AND DEFENSE, WHILE ENGLAND WOULD LOOSELY CONTROL MATTERS OF TRADE.

0388 BURKHEAD J.
GOVERNMENT BUDGETING.
NEW YORK: JOHN WILEY, 1956, 498 PP., LC#56-8000.
FIRST DISCUSSES BUDGET AND MODERN GOVERNMENT: DEVELOPMENT AND BUDGET CYCLE; THEN BUDGET CLASSIFICATIONS. GOES OVER PHASES OF BUDGETING: AGENCIES, CENTRAL OFFICE, LEGISLATURE, EXECUTION, AND ACCOUNTING. LASTLY, EXAMINES SPECIALIZED BUDGET PROBLEMS: REVENUE ESTIMATING, BUDGETING OF PUBLIC ENTERPRISE, BALANCED BUDGET, AND BUDGETING FOR ECONOMIC DEVELOPMENT. COVERS BOTH NATIONAL AND STATE BUDGETING.

0389 BURNS A.E., NEAL A.C., WATSON D.S.
MODERN ECONOMICS.
NEW YORK: HARCOURT BRACE, 1953, 955 PP.
INTRODUCES KEYNESIAN ECONOMICS TO UNDERGRADUATE. STUDIES SCOPE OF ECONOMICS, NATIONAL INCOME AND EMPLOYMENT OF RESOURCES, MONETARY PROCESS, PRICE AND ALLOCATION OF RESOURCES. TREATS WORKINGS AND CYCLES IN MARKET ECONOMY, GOVERNMENT FINANCE, INTERNATIONAL FINANCE, AND PERSONAL DISTRIBUTION AND USES OF INCOME.

0390 BURNS A.R.
THE DECLINE OF COMPETITION.
NEW YORK: MCGRAW HILL, 1936, 563 PP.
ATTEMPTS TO BRIDGE ECONOMICS OF PERFECT AND IMPERFECT COMPETITION, CLAIMING THAT EVOLUTION OF INDUSTRIALIZATION IN US HAS MADE ECONOMIC CONSIDERATION OF PERFECTLY COMPETITIVE MARKETS NO LONGER USEFUL. GROWTH OF THEORY IN THIS AREA IS TOO ABSTRACT, AUTHOR STATES, AND WORK SEEKS TO BRING ABSTRACTIONS AND REALITIES TOGETHER. EXAMINES EFFECT OF NRA UPON US MARKET SYSTEM.

0391 BURNS T.G., STEIN H.A.
DEVELOPMENT BANKING BIBLIOGRAPHY (PAPER)
CAMBRIDGE: MIT, INDUSTRIAL MGT, 1963, 15 PP.
LISTS 109 BOOKS, ARTICLES, AND STUDIES ON DEVELOPMENT BANKING. ENTRIES ARRANGED ALPHABETICALLY BY AUTHOR. INCLUDES INDEX TO GEOGRAPHIC AREAS AND AGENCIES.

0392 BURRUS B.R.
ADMINSTRATIVE LAW AND LOCAL GOVERNMENT.
ANN ARBOR: U OF MICH LAW SCHOOL, 1963, 139 PP.
DISCUSSES CONSTITUTIONAL CONCEPTS OF LIMITATION, JUDICIAL REVIEW, AND STATE ADMINISTRATIVE PROCEDURES. EMPHASIZES ADMINISTRATIVE FUNCTIONS ON LOCAL LEVELS, SUCH AS GRANTING OF PERMITS, LICENSES, AND CERTIFICATES.

0393 BURTT E.J. JR.
LABOR MARKETS, UNIONS, AND GOVERNMENT POLICIES.
NEW YORK: ST MARTIN'S PRESS, 1963, 454 PP., LC#63-10686.
STUDY OF LABOR ECONOMICS, EMPHASIZING WAGES AND UNION ORGANIZATION; INCLUDES UNEMPLOYMENT, STRIKES, AND SOCIAL SECURITY IN AMERICA.

0394 BUSEY J.L.
NOTES ON COSTA RICAN DEMOCRACY.
BOULDER: U OF COLORADO PR, 1967, 84 PP.
EXAMINES POLITICAL FEATURES OF COSTA RICAN DEMOCRACY, REVIEWING THEM IN CONTEXT OF LATIN AMERICAN NORMS. SUGGESTS HYPOTHESES TO ILLUMINATE CAUSAL ELEMENTS IN COSTA RICAN HISTORICAL, PHYSICAL, AND ECONOMIC BACKGROUND, SUCH AS SOCIAL AND ECONOMIC HISTORY AND LAND DISTRIBUTION.

0395 BUSINESS ECONOMISTS' GROUP
INCOME POLICIES (PAMPHLET)
OXFORD: BUSINESS ECONOMISTS GP, 1963, 49 PP.
ANALYZES BRITISH INCOME POLICIES AND COMPARES THEM TO OTHER NATIONS. GIVES VIEWPOINTS OF INDUSTRIALIST, TRADE UNIONIST, AND GOVERNMENT REPRESENTATIVE OF FAIR WAGE AND INCOME DISTRIBUTION. ECONOMETRICIAN PROPOSES MODEL FOR DISTRIBUTION ANALYSIS.

0396 BUSSCHAU W.J.
GOLD AND INTERNATIONAL LIQUIDITY.

JOHANNESBURG: S AFR INST INT AFF, 1961, 102 PP.
TEXT OF LECTURES EXPLORING FLOW OF CREDIT IN RELATION TO GOLD IN INTERNATIONAL MONETARY SYSTEM. EXPLORES PRACTICAL AND THEORETICAL ASPECTS OF GOLD PROBLEM PRESENTING ARGUMENTS WITH STATISTICAL AND MONETARY BACKGROUND. EXPRESSES NEED FOR RESTORATION OF GOLD STANDARD.

0397 BUTLER W.F.
"ECONOMIC PROGRESS IN LATIN AMERICA."
SOC. SCI., 35 (OCT. 60), 225-30.
DEMONSTRATES THAT FORCES UNDERLYING LATIN AMERICAN ECONOMIC GROWTH ARE SLACKENING IN COMING DECADE AND ADVOCATES POLICIES FOR BOTH LATIN AND U.S. GOVERNMENTS WHICH WOULD CONTRIBUTE TO ECONOMIC DEVELOPMENT.

0398 BUTT R.
"THE COMMON MARKET AND CONSERVATIVE POLITICS, 1961-2."
GOVERNMENT AND OPPOSITION, 2 (APR-JULY 67), 372-386.
DISCUSSES HOW DECISION FOR BRITAIN TO SEEK ENTRY INTO EEC WAS TAKEN AND ARGUES THAT IT DID NOT ARISE FROM TRADITIONAL INFLUENCES IN CONSERVATIVE PARTY BUT OUT OF PERSONAL POLICY OF MACMILLAN. ANALYZES REACTION 6F CONSERVATIVES TO IDEA OF BRITISH MEMBERSHIP AND SIGNIFICANCE OF OPPOSITION TO IDEA IN TERMS OF EVENTUAL SUCCESS OF MEMBERSHIP ATTEMPT.

0399 CAIRNCROSS A.K.
FACTORS IN ECONOMIC DEVELOPMENT.
NEW YORK: PRAEGER, 1962, 346 PP., $6.60.
AMONG THE FACTORS THAT INFLUENCE DEVELOPMENT ARE INVESTMENT AND TECHNICAL PROGRESS, ADMINISTRATION AND PLANNING, AND THE GROWTH OF MARKETS. ALSO STRESSES EDUCATION.

0400 CALDER R.
TWO-WAY PASSAGE.
LONDON: HEINEMANN, 1964, 186 PP.
DISCUSSES VARIOUS ASPECTS OF MUTUAL AID PROGRAMS TO UNDERDEVELOPED NATIONS, POPULATION EXPLOSION, WASTE IN FOREIGN AID, AND FORMS OF IMAGINATIVE PLANNING. MAINTAINS THAT CENTRAL AIM OF FOREIGN AID SHOULD BE INVESTMENT IN HUMAN RESOURCES.

0401 CALKINS R.D.
ECONOMICS AS AN AID TO POLICY (PAMPHLET)
WASHINGTON: BROOKINGS INST, 1963, 28 PP.
THE ROLE OF ECONOMISTS IN HELPING TO SHAPE GOVERNMENTAL POLICY DECISIONS. SAYS THAT ECONOMISTS SHOULD HAVE A LARGER VOICE IN DECISION-MAKING PROCESS.

0402 CAMERON W.J.
NEW ZEALAND.
ENGLEWOOD CLIFFS: PRENTICE HALL, 1965, 180 PP.
STUDIES CHARACTER OF NEW ZEALAND'S POPULATION. DISCUSSES NATIVE GROUPS AND EUROPEAN COLONIZATION IN REGARD TO FORMATION OF PRESENT SOCIETY. EXPLAINS POLITICAL AND ECONOMIC STRUCTURE AND RELATION OF NEW ZEALAND TO OTHER COUNTRIES.

0403 CAMMETT J.M.
"COMMUNIST THEORIES OF FASCISM, 1920-35."
SCIENCE AND SOCIETY, 31 (SPRING 67), 49-163.
ARGUES THAT AFTER INITIAL CONFUSION, THE COMINTERN MADE A GOOD MANY IMPORTANT CONTRIBUTIONS TO THE THEORY OF FASCISM BUT THAT AFTER THE 6TH WORLD CONGRESS AND POPULAR FRONT, ITS WORK BECAME LESS CONCRETE AND ADAPTED TO POLITICAL DEMANDS. EXAMINES IMPERIALIST AND MIDDLE-CLASS THEORY ON THE SOCIAL FORCES BEHIND FASCISM. STRESSES ITALIAN FASCISM. EMPHASIZES NEED FOR SOCIALIST STUDY OF IDEOLOGY AND CULTURE.

0404 CAMPAIGNE J.G.
CHECK-OFF: LABOR BOSSES AND WORKING MEN.
CHICAGO: HENRY REGNERY CO, 1961, 248 PP., LC#61-17370.
A CONSERVATIVE AND FREE LIBERAL ATTACK UPON THE WAYS IN WHICH THE AMERICAN LABOR MOVEMENT HAS GONE IN RECENT YEARS TOWARD DICTATORIAL LEADERSHIP AND LOSS OF INDIVIDUAL RIGHTS FOR THE RANK-AND-FILE WORKER. HOFFA AND REUTHER ARE MAJOR FIGURES DISCUSSED. HOLDS THAT NO FREEDOM OF DISSENT, OF ASSOCIATION, OF REPRESENTATION, OR NON-ACTION EXISTS FOR THE LABORER.

0405 CAMPBELL A.K., SACKS S.
METROPOLITAN AMERICA* FISCAL PATTERNS AND GOVERNMENTAL SYSTEMS.
NEW YORK: MACMILLAN, 1967, 224 PP.
ANALYSIS OF LOCAL PUBLIC FINANCE AND THE INFLUENCE OF GOVERNMENTAL SYSTEMS ON FISCAL BEHAVIOR. EXAMINES FISCAL PATTERNS OF METROPOLITANISM, THEIR CAUSES, DETERMINANTS, AND IMPLICATIONS FOR PUBLIC POLICY. PRESENTS DIFFERENCES BETWEEN METROPOLITAN AND NONMETROPOLITAN FISCAL BEHAVIOR AND DIFFERENCES BETWEEN CENTRAL CITY AND SUBURBAN FISCAL BEHAVIOR.

0406 CAMPBELL J.C.
AMERICAN POLICY TOWARDS COMMUNIST EASTERN EUROPE* THE CHOICES AHEAD.
MINNEAPOLIS: U OF MINN PR, 1965, 136 PP., LC#65-15982.
ALTERNATIVES FOR AMERICAN FOREIGN POLICY TOWARDS THE COMMUNIST STATES OF EAST EUROPE ARE SUGGESTED AT THE CONCLUSION OF A DISCUSSION OF THE HISTORICAL BACKGROUND, AND RECENT POLITICAL AND ECONOMIC TRENDS IN POLAND AND YUGOSLAVIA.

0407 CAMPBELL J.C.
"SOVIET-AMERICAN RELATIONS: CONFLICT AND COOPERATION."
CURRENT HISTORY, 53 (OCT. 67), 193-202, 241.
EVALUATES USSR'S INTERNAL SITUATION AND FOREIGN RELATIONS WITH US AFTER 50 YEARS UNDER COMMUNISM. FINDS LITTLE CONSISTENCY IN KHRUSHCHEV'S FOREIGN POLICY. EXAMINES THAWING OF COLD WAR AFTER CUBAN CRISIS. DISCUSSES CHANGES IN POLICY UNDER BREZHNEV AND KOSYGIN. PRESENTS EFFECTS ON POLICY OF VIETNAM WAR AND MIDDLE EAST CRISIS. CONCLUDES THAT USSR MAY BE FACING BASIC FOREIGN POLICY DECISION.

0408 CAMPBELL P.
CONSUMER REPRESENTATION IN THE NEW DEAL.
NEW YORK: COLUMBIA U PRESS, 1940.
A BOOK ON FUNCTIONAL REPRESENTATION BY AN EXPERT ON CONSUMER AID, DESCRIBING A SEARCH FOR PROTECTING THE CONSUMER'S INTERESTS IN THE DAYS OF THE NRA AS A PART OF THE "PUBLIC INTEREST." CONSUMER REPRESENTATION IN INDUSTRIAL AND AGRICULTURAL REGULATION AND VARIOUS CONSUMER POLICIES AND DEMANDS ARE DISCUSSED.

0409 CAMPBELL R.W.
SOVIET ECONOMIC POWER.
CAMBRIDGE: HOUGHTON, 1960, 209 PP., $4.75.
EXAMINES FUNCTIONS AND OPERATIONS OF SOVIET ECONOMY. EVALUATES GROWTH, EFFICIENCY, AND OUTPUT. EXPLORES PROBLEMS IN COORDINATION AND OPTIMAL USE OF PLANNING PROCESS. CONCLUDES POTENTIAL PRODUCTIVITY OF SOVIET UNION POSES MAJOR CHALLENGE TO USA LEADERSHIP.

0410 CAMPOLONGO A.
"EUROPEAN INVESTMENT BANK* ACTIVITY AND PROSPECTS."
J. INT. AFFAIRS, 19 (1965), 276-285.
ORIGINS, STRUCTURE, ACTIVITIES, PROBLEMS, AND FUTURE PROSPECTS OF THE EUROPEAN INVESTMENT BANK ARE DISCUSSED.

0411 CANNING HOUSE LIBRARY
AUTHOR AND SUBJECT CATALOGUES OF THE CANNING HOUSE LIBRARY (5 VOLS.)
BOSTON: HALL, 1966.
BIBLIOGRAPHICAL LISTING OF BOOKS IN CANNING HOUSE LIBRARY IN LONDON PERTAINING TO LATIN AMERICA. OVER 30,000 ENTRIES OF 19TH- AND 20TH-CENTURY PUBLICATIONS. FOUR VOLUMES ON SPANISH-SPEAKING LATIN AMERICAN COUNTRIES AND ONE ON BRAZIL.

0412 CANNON M.
THE LAND BOOMERS.
MELBOURNE: MELBOURNE UNIV PRESS, 1966, 247 PP., LC#67-10259.
STORY OF MEN INVOLVED IN VICTORIA'S LAND BOOM OF 1880'S FROM OPTIMISM OF BOLD DISCOVERY TO SHATTERING DEPRESSION WHICH ENSUED. RECOUNTS TALES OF WELLKNOWN AUSTRALIAN FAMILES AND INSTITUTIONS.

0413 CANTERBERY E.R.
THE PRESIDENT'S COUNCIL OF ECONOMIC ADVISERS.
NEW YORK: EXPOSITION PRESS, 1961, 166 PP.
APPRAISAL OF THE COUNCIL AND ITS HANDLING OF SPECIFIC ECONOMIC PROBLEMS 1946-56. RELATIONSHIP OF COUNCIL TO PRESIDENTS TRUMAN AND EISENHOWER, RECESSION, INFLATION, AND KOREAN WAR ARE CONSIDERED.

0414 CARNEGIE ENDOWMENT INT. PEACE
"ECONOMIC AND SOCIAL QUESTION (ISSUES BEFORE THE NINETEENTH GENERAL ASSEMBLY)."
INT. CONCIL., 550 (NOV. 64), 117-87.
DISCUSSES PROBLEMS CONCERNING THE FOLLOWING WHICH WERE RAISED DURING NINETEENTH SESSION: GATT, COMMODITY TRADE, TECHNICAL COOPERATION, PATENTS, UN SPECIAL FUND, AND UN TRAINING AND RESEARCH INSTITUTE.

0415 CARNEGIE ENDOWMENT INT. PEACE
"ADMINISTRATION AND BUDGET (ISSUES BEFORE THE NINETEENTH GENERAL ASSEMBLY)."
INT. CONCIL., 550 (NOV. 64), 197-205.
DISCUSSES MONETARY AND ADMINISTRATIVE ISSUES WHICH WERE RAISED DURING THE NINETEENTH SESSION.

0416 CARNEY D.
PATTERNS AND MECHANICS OF ECONOMIC GROWTH: A GENERAL THEORETICAL APPROACH.
YELLOW SPRINGS: ANTIOCH, 1967, 154 PP., LC#67-13463.
INVESTIGATION OF DIFFERENT GROWTH PATTERNS OF AGGREGATE REAL OUTPUT, CONSUMPTION, AND INVESTMENT REVEALING THAT ALL ECONOMIES CONFORM TO ONE OF TWO MAIN PATTERNS OF GROWTH. BASED ON KEYNESIAN THEORY OF INCOME ANALYSIS. AUTHOR MAKES USE OF SIMPLE TOOL OF COMPOUND-INTEREST FORMULA AS WELL AS ELEMENTARY NOTIONS OF CALCULUS. HIGHLY TECHNICAL.

0417 CARNEY D.E.
GOVERNMENT AND ECONOMY IN BRITISH WEST AFRICA.
NEW YORK: BOOKMAN ASSOCIATES, 1961, 343 PP., LC#61-09845.
STUDY OF 1947-55 ECONOMIC PRACTICES OF BRITISH ADMINISTRATORS IN PREPARING COLONIES IN AFRICA FOR INDEPENDENCE.

COMPARISON OF ECONOMIC TACTICS OF GOVERNMENT OWNERSHIP AND PRIVATE INDUSTRY.

0418 CARPER E.T.
LOBBYING AND THE NATURAL GAS BILL (PAMPHLET)
INDIANAPOLIS: BOBBS-MERRILL, 1962, 39 PP.
STUDIES PRESSURES FROM CONFLICTING INTEREST GROUPS OF PRODUCERS AND CONSUMERS OVER PROPOSED AMENDMENTS TO NATURAL GAS ACT, 1955-56. "ARROGANT LOBBYING" COUPLED WITH DISCLOSURE OF BRIBERY PRECIPITATED EXECUTIVE VETO.

0419 CARPER E.T.
THE DEFENSE APPROPRIATIONS RIDER (PAMPHLET)
UNIVERSITY: U ALABAMA PR, 1960, 28 PP.
CASE STUDY OF 1955 RIDER TO DEFENSE BUDGET BILL, WHICH GAVE CONGRESSIONAL COMMITTEES RIGHT TO DISAPPROVE SHUTDOWN BY DEFENSE DEPARTMENT OF CERTAIN LOCAL INSTALLATIONS. CONGRESS FELT IT ILLEGAL, YET PRESIDENT COULD NOT VETO BILL. STUDY SHOWS FIGHT BETWEEN LEGISLATURE AND EXECUTIVE. ANALYZES LOCAL PRESSURE IN NATIONAL POLICY-MAKING, USING BOSTON NAVAL INSTALLATION AS EXAMPLE.

0420 CARPER E.T.
ILLINOIS GOES TO CONGRESS FOR ARMY LAND.
INDIANAPOLIS: BOBBS-MERRILL, 1962, 332 PP.
DESCRIBES SENATORS DOUGLAS'S AND DIRKSEN'S 2-YEAR OCCUPATION WITH REQUESTS FROM SPORTSMEN AND A BUSINESS SYNDICATE, EACH SEEKING SAME PIECE OF SURPLUS ARMY LAND. CONGRESSIONAL LEGISLATION ULTIMATELY TRANSFERRED THE LAND, IN LIEU OF FEDERAL AGENCY RESPONSIBLE, THE GENERAL SERVICE ADMINISTRATION.

0421 CARRINGTON C.E.
THE COMMONWEALTH IN AFRICA (PAMPHLET)
P1962 284 57 02840
REPORTS ON CONFERENCE HELD BY AFRICAN COMMONWEALTH NATIONS IN 1962. DEALS WITH COLD WAR AND AFRICA, PAN-AFRICANISM, COMMON MARKET AND BRITAIN'S DESIRE TO JOIN, ECONOMIC INDEPENDENCE, DEMOCRATIC INSTITUTIONS BEST SUITED FOR PLANNING AND DEVELOPMENT IN AFRICA, AND FUTURE OF COMMONWEALTH COOPERATION IN AFRICA.

0422 CARROTHERS A.W.R.
LABOR ARBITRATION IN CANADA.
TORONTO: BUTTERWORTHS, 1961, 190 PP.
EVALUATES ARBITRATION AS METHOD OF SETTLING GRIEVANCES IN LABOR DISPUTES. CONSIDERS RELEVANT SECTIONS OF ALL COLLECTIVE BARGAINING STATUTES IN CANADA AND ARBITRATION STATUTES OF COMMON LAW PROVINCES, WITH ILLUSTRATIVE CASE STUDIES IN BASIC AREAS.

0423 CARTER A.G.T.
"THE BALANCE OF PAYMENTS OF EAST AFRICA"
J. OF EAST AFRICAN ECONOMIC REV., 10 (DEC. 63), 75-87.
REVIEW OF BALANCE-OF-PAYMENTS SURVEYS OF EAST AFRICA STATISTICAL DEPARTMENT, 1956-61.

0424 CARVALHO C.M.
GEOGRAPHIA HUMANA; POLITICA E ECONOMICA (3RD ED.)
SAO PAULO: CO EDITORA NACIONAL, 1938, 358 PP.
TEXT DEALS WITH POLITICAL AND ECONOMIC GEOGRAPHY OF WORLD AND PARTICULARLY BRAZIL. DISCUSSES RACES, LANGUAGES, MIGRATION, URBANIZATION, PLUS ECONOMIC FACTORS OF AGRICULTURE, INDUSTRY, COMMUNICATIONS, AND RESOURCES.

0425 CASEY R.G.
THE FUTURE OF THE COMMONWEALTH.
LONDON: FREDERICK MULLER, 1964, 187 PP.
DISCUSSES FUTURE OF BRITISH COMMONWEALTH UNDER FORCES OF NATIONALISM AND INDEPENDENCE MOVEMENTS. SUGGESTS FORMS OF ECONOMIC AND TECHNICAL AID BY ENGLAND TO COMMONWEALTH COUNTRIES. EXAMINES IMPLICATIONS OF POSSIBLE BRITISH ENTRY INTO COMMON MARKET.

0426 CASSEL G., GREGORY T.E., KUCZYNSKI R.
FOREIGN INVESTMENTS.
CHICAGO: U. CHI. PR., 1928, 232 PP.
COLLECTION OF FOUR LECTURES ON ASPECTS OF FOREIGN INVESTMENTS IN THE POST W.W.1 PERIOD. ATTENTION IS GIVEN TO THE ECONOMIC AND POLITICAL CONSEQUENCES OF INTERNATIONAL MOVEMENTS OF CAPITAL AND TO PROBLEMS ARISING IN RELATION TO EXTENSIVE AMERICAN INVESTMENTS ABROAD, INTERALLIED WAR DEBT, AND REPARATIONS SETTLEMENT.

0427 CASSELL F. ED.
INTERNATIONAL MONETARY PROBLEMS (PAMPHLET)
LONDON: FED TRUST FOR ED & RES, 1965, 48 PP.
TRACES DEVELOPMENT OF PRESENT MONETARY SYSTEM AND SURVEYS PLANS FOR REFORM. ANALYZES POSSIBLE REPERCUSSION OF REVERSAL TO GOLD STANDARD OR CHANGE TO SYSTEM OF MAN-MADE MONEY. DISCUSSES FORMIDABLE POLITICAL PROBLEMS OF COMMON CURRENCY FOR EUROPEAN COMMUNITY AND INVESTIGATES IMPLICATIONS OF CRUCIAL CHOICE BETWEEN GOLD OR CREDIT AS BASIS OF INTERNATIONAL MONEY.

0428 CASSELL F.
GOLD OR CREDIT? THE ECONOMICS AND POLITICS OF INTERNATIONAL MONEY.
NEW YORK: FREDERICK PRAEGER, 1965, 216 PP.
EXAMINES TWO ALTERNATE BASES FOR MONETARY CONTROL, GOLD STANDARD OR INTERNATIONAL CREDIT. GIVES PROBLEM WITH BOTH METHODS AND SOLUTIONS. SACRIFICES NEEDED TO FACILITATE SOLUTIONS SUCH AS END TO ECONOMIC SOVEREIGNTY, COMMON MARKETS, AND COMMON CURRENCY ARE DISCUSSED. MAINTAINS THAT SYSTEM OF INTERNATIONAL CREDIT WOULD FURTHER WORLD ECONOMIES IN MOST EFFECTIVE MANNER.

0429 CASTILLO C.M.
GROWTH AND INTEGRATION IN CENTRAL AMERICA.
NEW YORK: FREDERICK PRAEGER, 1967, 188 PP., LC#66-18896.
STUDY OF ECONOMIC SYSTEMS OF 5 COUNTRIES, BASED UPON LONG TERM OBSERVATION. ANALYSIS OF ECONOMIC HISTORY BUT MAIN CONCERN IS WITH FUTURE DEVELOPMENT INTO AN INTEGRATED SYSTEM. COVERS INITIAL DEVELOPMENT INTO EXPORT STAGE, ATTEMPTS AT PROGRESS, REGIONAL APPROACHES, AND BALANCE. RELATES ECONOMIC QUESTIONS TO POLITICAL REQUIREMENTS AND CHANGES.

0430 CATTELL D.T.
"THE FIFTIETH ANNIVERSARY: A SOVIET WATERSHED?"
CURRENT HISTORY, 53 (OCT. 67), 224-229, 243.
DISCUSSES POST-KHRUSHCHEV REGIME IN USSR AND SUGGESTS THAT IT REPRESENTS ATTEMPT BY ELITE TO BRING END TO ONE-MAN, CHARISMATIC SYSTEM IN FAVOR OF COLLECTIVE RULE. STUDIES AULTS OF KHRUSHCHEV REGIME AND ADVOCATES NEED TO DEVELOP NEW METHODS OF POLICY-MAKING COMPATIBLE WITH DEVELOPED ECONOMY WHILE ADAPTING GOVERNMENT TO TRADITIONAL RUSSIAN VALUES.

0431 CECIL C.O.
"THE DETERMINANTS OF LIBYAN FOREIGN POLICY."
MIDDLE EAST J., 19 (WINTER 65), 20-34.
INTERESTING EXAMINATION OF THE EFFECTS A SUDDEN GROSS CHANGE IN MATERIAL WEALTH CAN HAVE ON THE FOREIGN POLICY OF A TRADITIONALIST STATE. LIBYA'S OIL BOOM HAS CREATED SOCIETAL PRESSURES OPERATING TO FORCE HAND OF LEADERS.

0432 CEFKIN J.L.
THE BACKGROUND OF CURRENT WORLD PROBLEMS.
NEW YORK: DAVID MCKAY, 1967, 436 PP., LC#67-15042.
DISCUSSES FIELD OF INTERNATIONAL RELATIONS, THE COLD WAR, RISE OF NATIONALISM IN UNDEVELOPED COUNTRIES, AND QUEST FOR ECONOMIC DEVELOPMENT.

0433 CENTRO ESTUDIOS MONETARIOS LAT
COOPERACION FINANCIERA EN AMERICA LATINA.
MEXICO CITY: CENT ESTUD MON L AM, 1963, 293 PP.
DOCUMENTS CONCERN CONTRIBUTION OF FINANCIAL SYSTEMS TO ECONOMIC INTEGRATION OF LATIN AMERICA. DEAL SPECIFICALLY WITH POSSIBLE FORMS OF FACILITATING EXPANSION OF ECONOMIC RELATIONS WITHIN LATIN AMERICA, AND DIFFICULTIES IN ESTABLISHING INTER-REGIONAL COMMERCE.

0434 CENTRO ESTUDIOS MONETARIOS LAT
PROBLEMAS DE PAGOS EN AMERICA LATINA.
MEXICO CITY: CENT ESTUD MON L AM, 1964, 299 PP.
THIRD IN A SERIES ON FINANCIAL COOPERATION AND REGIONAL MONETARY COORDINATION IN LATIN AMERICA. EXAMINES POSSIBILITY OF ESTABLISHING EFFECTIVE MECHANISMS OF COMPENSATION AND PAYMENTS TO PROMOTE FINANCIAL COORDINATION. DISCUSSES CENTRAL BANKS, PAYMENTS AND COMMERCE WITH CENTRAL AMERICA, REGIONAL COMMERCE AND MARKETS, ETC.

0435 CENTRO PARA EL DESARROLLO
LA ALIANZA PARA EL PROGRESO Y EL DESARROLLO SOCIAL DE AMERICA LATINA.
SANTIAGO: CEN PARAEL DESARROLLO, 1963, 104 PP.
CENTER FOR ECONOMIC AND SOCIAL DEVELOPMENT OF LATIN AMERICA ANALYZES ALLIANCE FOR PROGRESS. EXAMINES NEEDS OF LATIN AMERICAN NATIONS IN DRIVE FOR SOCIAL CHANGE, COVERING METHODS AND REQUIREMENTS FOR ECONOMIC GROWTH INCLUDED IN ALLIANCE FOR PROGRESS PROPOSALS.

0436 CEPEDE M., HOUTART F., GROND L.
POPULATION AND FOOD.
NEW YORK: SHEED AND WARD, 1964, 461 PP., LC#63-8546.
EXAMINES RATES OF POPULATION GROWTH, AVERAGE LIFE EXPECTANCIES, STANDARDS OF LIVING, AID TO UNDERDEVELOPED NATIONS, USE OF SURPLUS FOODS, AND FAMILY PLANNING. ARGUES THAT POOR SOCIAL AND ECONOMIC ORGANIZATION AND MANAGEMENT ARE TO BLAME FOR THE DIFFICULTIES BROUGHT ON BY RAPIDLY GROWING POPULATION, THAT US HAS THE TECHNOLOGY TO PRODUCE MORE THAN ENOUGH FOR A WORLD POPULATION OF OVER TEN BILLION.

0437 CERAMI C.A.
ALLIANCE BORN OF DANGER.
NEW YORK: HARCOURT BRACE, 1963, 181 PP., LC#63-13686.
DISCUSSES RELATIONS OF US, COMMON MARKET, AND ATLANTIC ALLIANCE: PROBLEMS OF UNITY, PROSPECTS FOR FUTURE INTEGRATION, UK'S RELATION TO CONTINENT, AND ROLE OF AMERICA IN WESTERN EUROPE.

0438 CERNY K.H. ED., BRIEFS H.W. ED.
NATO IN QUEST OF COHESION* A CONFRONTATION OF VIEWPOINTS.

NEW YORK: FREDERICK PRAEGER, 1965, 476 PP., LC#65-20045.
THIS COLLECTION INCLUDES THE TRANSCRIPTION OF A GEORGETOWN UNIVERSITY CONFERENCE ON NATO PROBLEMS, ALONG WITH ITS FORMAL STUDY PAPERS. AREAS DISCUSSED WERE: "THE NUCLEAR QUESTION, ECONOMIC PROBLEMS, AND THE POLITICAL DIMENSION." 20 PAPERS ARE INCLUDED BY SUCH SCHOLARS AS MORGENTHAU, KISSINGER, BEAUFRE, SLESSOR, URI, AND KLEIMAN AMONG OTHERS.

0439 CHADWELL J.T., RHODES R.S.
"ANTITRUST ASPECTS OF DEALER LICENSING AND FRANCHISING."
NORTHWESTERN U. TRI-Q., 62 (MAR.-APR. 67), 1-18.
EXPLORES ANTITRUST PROBLEMS CREATED BY CONTROLS OR CONTRACTUAL RESTRICTIONS PLACED UPON BUSINESS OPERATIONS OF A FRANCHISEE BY A FRANCHISOR.

0440 CHAMBER OF COMMERCE OF USA
ECONOMIC LESSONS OF POSTWAR RECESSIONS (PAMPHLET)
WASHINGTON: US CHAMBER OF COMM, 1959, 31 PP.
DISCUSSES POSTWAR RECESSIONS, PARTICULARLY THAT OF 1957-58, CAUSES, ATTEMPTS AT CONTROLLING IT, AND FINAL STOPPAGE. INCLUDES CONGRESSIONAL ACTION AND MOVEMENTS OF FEDERAL RESERVE SYSTEM. SUGGESTS METHODS TO PREVENT RECURRENCE.

0441 CHAMBERLAIN E.H.
THE ECONOMIC ANALYSIS OF LABOR UNION POWER (PAMPHLET)
WASHINGTON: AMER ENTERPRISE INST, 1963, 50 PP., LC#63-21935.
HOLDS THAT UNION POWER SHOULD BE USED NOT TO DISRUPT BUT TO CONTROL CONDITIONS OF THE ECONOMY, NOR SHOULD THE FREEDOM OF WORKERS TO ABSTAIN FROM UNIONS BE VIOLATED. THUS THE USE OF POWER MUST BE STRICTLY LIMITED, INVALID METHODS ELIMINATED, AND INSTITUTIONAL CHANGES MADE IN UNIONISM TO PROTECT AGAINST "IMPERSONAL MECHANISM OF ORGANIZATION AND THE HUMAN LUST FOR POWER."

0442 CHAMBERLAIN N.W.
"STRIKES IN CONTEMPORARY CONTEXT."
INDUST. LABOR REL. REV., 20 (JULY 67), 02-617.
EXAMINES ACTUAL NECESSITY FOR WORK STOPPAGES IN FUNCTIONING OF COLLECTIVE BARGAINING. DEFINES EMERGENCY CONDITIONS UNDER WHICH GOVERNMENT INTERVENTION SHOULD OCCUR. EXPLAINS "ARSENAL-OF-WEAPONS" LEGISLATIVE APPROACH, BENEFITS OF COMPULSORY ARBITRATION, AND "NON-STOPPAGE STRIKE" OR "STRIKE-WORK AGREEMENT" WHICH IMPOSES FINES ON BOTH WORKERS AND MANAGEMENT DURING NEGOTIATIONS, WHILE WORK CONTINUES.

0443 CHAMBERLIN E.
THE THEORY OF MONOPOLISTIC COMPETITION (1933)
CAMBRIDGE: HARVARD U PR, 1950, 314 PP.
CONTENDS THAT BOTH MONOPOLISTIC AND COMPETITIVE FORCES COMBINE IN PRICING MOST ARTICLES AND THAT A THEORY COMBINING BOTH WILL BE MORE USEFUL THAN ONE BASED ON PERFECT COMPETITION AND UTILIZING A SEPARATE THEORY FOR MONOPOLIES. DIFFERS FROM THEORIES OF IMPERFECT COMPETITION BY STATING THAT ALL COMPETITION IS IMPERFECT, BUT THAT REAL MONOPOLIES MAY EXIST IN IMPERFECT MARKETS.

0444 CHAMBERLIN E.H., BRADLEY P.H. ET AL.
LABOR UNIONS AND PUBLIC POLICY.
WASHINGTON: AMER ENTERPRISE INST, 1958, 177 PP., LC#58-10096
A NONPARTISAN RESEARCH ORGANIZATION'S STUDY, INCLUDING THE ECONOMIC POWER OF LABOR, COLLECTIVE BARGAINING, FREEDOM TO ORGANIZE AND INVOLUNTARY PARTICIPATION IN UNIONS, STATE REGULATION, AND A SECTION ON LABOR UNION IMMUNITIES BY DEAN ROSCOE POUND.

0445 CHAMPION J.M., BRIDGES F.J.
CRITICAL INCIDENTS IN MANAGEMENT.
HOMEWOOD: RICHARD IRWIN, 1963, 290 PP., LC#63-16884.
TEXT FOR MANAGEMENT-TRAINING PROGRAMS IN BUSINESS AND INDUSTRY. ANALYSIS OF 48 CRITICAL SITUATIONS INVOLVING PRINCIPLES AND PRACTICES OF MANAGEMENT. DESIGNED TO DEVELOP CRITICAL AND ANALYTIC POWERS IN VIEW OF FUTURE DECISION-MAKING SITUATIONS.

0446 CHANDLER A.D.
STRATEGY AND STRUCTURE: CHAPTERS IN THE HISTORY OF THE INDUSTRIAL ENTERPRISE.
CAMBRIDGE: M I T PRESS, 1962, 463 PP., LC#62-11990.
STUDY OF AMERICAN BIG BUSINESS: FINDS THAT DIFFERENT ORGANIZATIONAL FORMS RESULT FROM DIFFERENT TYPES OF GROWTH. MAINLY STUDIES DUPONT, GENERAL MOTORS, STANDARD OIL, AND SEARS, THEIR CHANGING STRUCTURE AND THE STRATEGY WHICH CREATES CHANGE.

0447 CHANDLER A.D. JR. ED.
GIANT ENTERPRISE: FORD, GENERAL MOTORS, AND THE AUTOMOBILE INDUSTRY; SOURCES AND READINGS.
NEW YORK: HARCOURT BRACE, 1964, 342 PP., LC#64-12560.
DOCUMENTS PRESENTED ARE INTENDED TO SHOW HOW NEW PATTERNS OF ECONOMIC ACTION OCCURRED AND HOW LABOR AND MANAGEMENT FUNCTIONED AT DIFFERENT PERIODS OF HISTORY.

0448 CHANDLER L.V.
INFLATION IN THE UNITED STATES 1940-1948.
NEW YORK: HARPER & ROW, 1951, 400 PP.
DESCRIBES PROCESS OF INFLATION IN US DURING AND AFTER WWII AND ANALYZES PRINCIPAL PUBLIC AND PRIVATE POLICIES RESPONSIBLE FOR IT. EMPHASIZES ROLE OF FISCAL AND MONETARY POLICIES, FINDING THAT FEDERAL DEFICITS DURING WAR GENERATED INFLATIONARY FORCES. FOCUSES ON REAL OUTPUT, DIRECT CONTROLS OVER PRICES, WAGES, AND PRODUCTION, PRIVATE CONTROVERSIES, AND FOREIGN CONDITIONS AFFECTING INFLATION.

0449 CHANDRASEKHAR S.
AMERICAN AID AND INDIA'S ECONOMIC DEVELOPMENT.
NEW YORK: FREDERICK PRAEGER, 1965, 243 PP., LC#65-24722.
FACTUAL SURVEY OF NONMILITARY US AID TO INDIA, 1951-64, DURING "FIRST EXPERIMENTAL PHASE." PHASE BEGAN WHEN US SENT FOOD TO END FAMINE AND ENDED WHEN US ADDED MILITARY AID 1962, WHEN COMMUNIST CHINESE ATTACKED. EMPHASIZES FEDERAL AID BECAUSE IT IS RECORDED AND ORGANIZED. CONSIDERS US TRUE FRIEND, FIGHTING FOR WORLD FREEDOM TODAY, HELPING POOR PEOPLES, AND NOT JUST FIGHTING COLD WAR.

0450 CHANDRASEKHAR S. ED., HULTMAN C.W. ED.
PROBLEMS OF ECONOMIC DEVELOPMENT.
BOSTON: D C HEATH, 1967, 382 PP., LC#67-12497.
SERIES OF ARTICLES CONCERNING EXPERIENCES OF SEVERAL DEVELOPING COUNTRIES' EFFORTS TO FIND SOLUTIONS TO SPECIFIC ECONOMIC PROBLEMS. PRESENTED IN FIVE SECTIONS, COVERS FOLLOWING MAJOR AREAS: SOCIAL CAPITAL, AGRICULTURE, INDUSTRIALIZATION, MANPOWER UTILIZATION, PLANNING AND ITS IMPLEMENTATION. SIZABLE LIST OF FURTHER SUGGESTED READINGS INCLUDED.

0451 CHANG C.
THE INFLATIONARY SPIRAL: THE EXPERIENCE IN CHINA 1939-50.
NEW YORK: JOHN WILEY, 1958, 394 PP., LC#58-6083.
ANALYZES ECONOMIC COLLAPSE OF CHINA AND CURRENCY AS RESULT OF POOR POLICY AND MISMANAGEMENT OF NATIONALISTS. HOPES TO WARN AND PREVENT OTHER ASIAN NATIONS FROM SAME ERRORS. DISCUSSES FAILURE OF NATIONALISTS TO HAVE SUPPLY MEET DEMAND, ESPECIALLY IN WARTIME SITUATION. REVEALS BASIC CONDITIONS THAT CAUSE INFLATIONARY SYMPTOMS AND SUGGESTS POLICY ALTERNATIVES TO COMBAT THEM.

0452 CHAO K.
THE RATE AND PATTERN OF INDUSTRIAL GROWTH IN COMMUNIST CHINA.
ANN ARBOR: U OF MICH PR, 1965, 188 PP., LC#65-11514.
CONSTRUCTS INDEPENDENT INDEX OF INDUSTRIAL OUTPUT PRODUCED BY COMMUNIST CHINA FROM 1949-59. PRIMARILY BASED ON OFFICIALLY PUBLISHED DATA OF INDUSTRIAL OUTPUT. BRIEF DISCUSSION OF STATISTICAL LOGIC OF CONSTRUCTING AN OUTPUT INDEX, AND THEORETICAL COMPARISON OF VARIOUS INDEXES. ANALYZES IMPLICATIONS DRAWN FROM RESULTING OUTPUT INDEXES; CHINA'S GROWTH IS COMPARED WITH OTHER NATIONS'.

0453 CHAPIN F.S., WEISS S.F.
URBAN GROWTH DYNAMICS IN A REGIONAL CLUSTER OF CITIES.
NEW YORK: JOHN WILEY, 1962, 484 PP.
A SERIES OF PAPERS ON THE PIEDMONT INDUSTRIAL CRESCENT OF NORTH AND SOUTH CAROLINA. THE PAPERS INVESTIGATE THE GROWTH POTENTIAL OF THE AREA, THE SOCIO-POLITICAL FACTORS INVOLVED, AND THE FACTORS AFFECTING PHYSICAL EXPANSION IN THE AREA.

0454 CHAPIN F.S. JR.
SELECTED REFERENCES ON URBAN PLANNING METHODS AND TECHNIQUES
CHAPEL HILL: U OF NC, CITY PLAN, 1967, 77 PP.
UNANNOTATED LISTING OF APPROXIMATELY 800 BOOKS AND PERIODICAL ARTICLES COMPILED FOR THE DEPARTMENT OF CITY AND REGIONAL PLANNING AT THE UNIVERSITY OF NORTH CAROLINA. INCLUDES SECTIONS ON PLANNING FOR INDUSTRIAL, COMMERCIAL, RESIDENTIAL, AND RECREATION AREAS, SCHOOL AND TRANSPORTATION PLANNING, LAND USE, ECONOMY, POPULATION STUDIES, AND HUMAN INTERACTION IN URBAN AREAS.

0455 CHASE S.B. JR. ED.
PROBLEMS IN PUBLIC EXPENDITURE ANALYSIS.
WASHINGTON: BROOKINGS INST, 1966, 269 PP., LC#67-30589.
A COLLECTION OF FIVE PAPERS, EACH FOLLOWED BY TWO CRITICAL COMMENTARIES, ON PROBLEMS OF BENEFIT AND COST MEASUREMENT IN GOVERNMENT FINANCE. SPECIFIC TOPICS INCLUDE USE OF SHADOW PRICES, VALUE OF TRAVEL TIME, CONSUMER INTEREST IN REDUCED RISK, INCOME REDISTRIBUTION AND BENEFIT COST, AND DISTRIBUTION OF BENEFITS FROM COTTON PRICE. EDITOR PROVIDES SUMMARY AND GENERAL OBSERVATIONS IN INTRODUCTION.

0456 CHATTERJEE I.K.
ECONOMIC DEVELOPMENT PAYMENTS DEFICIT AND PAYMENT RESTRICTION.
GENEVA: LIBRAIRIE DROZ, 1963, 168 PP.
ANALYZES AND EVALUATES IDEAS THAT INSPIRE POLICIES AND ACTIONS OF GOVERNMENTS IN FIELDS OF TRADE AND PAYMENTS. CONSIDERS PROS AND CONS OF RESTRICTING PAYMENTS, WHICH IN TURN LIMIT FREE TRAVEL AND TRADE. BIBLIOGRAPHY OF FURTHER READINGS ON SUBJECT.

0457 CHATTERS C.H.
NEW MUNICIPAL REVENUES FOR NEW MUNICIPAL EXPENDITURES (PAMPHLET)
WASHINGTON: AMER MUNICIPAL ASSOC, 1960, 14 PP.

ARGUES THAT CITIES CAN NO LONGER BE CONTENT TO BALANCE ANNUAL BUDGET BY INCREASING PROPERTY TAXES; NEW REVENUE SOURCES MUST BE DISCOVERED. WORTHWHILE ADJUSTMENTS CAN BE MADE IN FEES AND SERVICE CHARGES.

0458 CHECCHI V.
HONDURAS: A PROBLEM IN ECONOMIC DEVELOPMENT.
NEW YORK: TWENTIETH CENT FUND, 1959, 172 PP., LC#59-8020.
ANALYSIS OF ECONOMIC POSSIBILITIES OF HONDURAS AS ECONOMICALLY UNDERDEVELOPED COUNTRY. INCLUDES ECONOMIC AND POLITICAL BACKGROUND, ASPECTS OF COUNTRY AND PROMISING AREAS OF DEVELOPMENT, RECOMMENDED PROGRAM FOR DEVELOPMENT AND PREDICTION OF DEVELOPMENT AND PREDICTION OF FUTURE.

0459 CHEEK G.
ECONOMIC AND SOCIAL IMPLICATIONS OF AUTOMATION: A BIBLIOGRAPHIC REVIEW (PAMPHLET)
E LANSING: MSU LABOR & IND REL, 1958, 125 PP.
SOME 600 WELL-ANNOTATED BIBLIOGRAPHIES, BOOKS, ARTICLES, CONFERENCE REPORTS, CASE STUDIES, AND SPEECHES ARRANGED TOPICALLY AND PUBLISHED FROM 1948-57. SUBJECTS INCLUDE MANPOWER, SOCIETY AND GOVERNMENT, HUMAN RELATIONS, COLLECTIVE BARGAINING, AND MANAGEMENT ORGANIZATION. SUBJECT AND AUTHOR INDEX.

0460 CHEIT E.F. ED.
THE BUSINESS ESTABLISHMENT.
NEW YORK: JOHN WILEY, 1964, 240 PP., LC#64-23831.
EIGHT ESSAYS ON INTERPLAY OF BUSINESS AND SOCIETY. CONSIDERED ARE SUCH TOPICS AS CHANGING BUSINESS IDEOLOGY, INDIVIDUAL AND ORGANIZATION, MYTH OF AMERICAN BUSSNESSMAN, SOCIAL RESPONSIBILITY AND MANAGEMENT, AND EUROPEAN BUSINESS ENVIRONMENT.

0461 CHEN N-R.
THE ECONOMY OF MAINLAND CHINA, 1949-1963: A BIBLIOGRAPHY OF MATERIALS IN ENGLISH.
BERKELEY: SOC SCI RES COUNCIL, 1963, 297 PP.
ENGLISH-LANGUAGE BIBLIOGRAPHY INCLUDES TRANSLATIONS OF COMMUNIST CHINESE PUBLICATIONS AND BOOKS AND ARTICLES PUBLISHED IN ENGLISH IN AND OUTSIDE MAINLAND CHINA. PART I CONTAINS REFERENCES TO PRIMARY SOURCES ORIGINATING IN COMMUNIST CHINA: OFFICIAL DOCUMENTS; REPORTS AND SPEECHES; SEMI-OFFICIAL AND NONOFFICIAL PUBLICATIONS. PART II IS RESTRICTED TO SECONDARY SOURCE MATERIAL.

0462 CHENERY H.B.
"PATTERNS OF INDUSTRIAL GROWTH."
AMER. ECO. REVIEW, 50 (SEPT. 60), 624-654.
INCORPORATES CHANGES IN BOTH DEMAND AND SUPPLY CONDITIONS INTO GENERAL EXPLANATION OF GROWTH OF INDIVIDUAL SECTORS OF PRODUCTION. DERIVES "SECTOR GROWTH FUNCTIONS" FROM GENERAL EQUILIBRIUM MODEL AND USES THEM FOR REGRESSION ANALYSIS OF PRODUCTION AND IMPORT DATA. VARIABILITY IN GROWTH AMONG COUNTRIES IS INVESTIGATED IN TERMS OF IMPORTANCE OF SIZE, RESOURCES, AND OTHER FACTORS.

0463 CHENERY H.B.
"COMPARATIVE ADVANTAGE AND DEVELOPMENT POLICY."
AMER. ECO. REVIEW, 51 (MAR. 61), 18-51.
DISCUSSES ANALYSIS OF RESOURCE ALLOCATION IN LESS DEVELOPED ECONOMIES FROM THREE POINTS OF VIEW: STUDIES CONFLICT AND RECONCILIATION OF TRADE AND GROWTH THEORIES; COMPARES APPROACHES TO MEASUREMENT OF OPTIMAL RESOURCE ALLOCATION; AND EXAMINES PRACTICAL PROCEDURES OF INVESTMENT POLICY.

0464 CHENERY H.B., STROUT A.M.
"FOREIGN ASSISTANCE AND ECONOMIC DEVELOPMENT"
AMER. ECO. REVIEW, 56 (SEPT. 66), 679-733.
OUTLINES THEORETICAL FRAMEWORK DESIGNED TO ANALYZE THE PROCESS OF DEVELOPMENT WITH EXTERNAL ASSISTANCE IN QUANTITATIVE TERMS. USES THIS FRAMEWORK TO EVALUATE CURRENT PERFORMANCE OF DEVELOPING COUNTRIES AND TO ASSESS THEIR FUTURE NEEDS FOR ASSISTANCE UNDER VARIOUS ASSUMPTIONS.

0465 CHILCOTE R.H.
PORTUGUESE AFRICA.
ENGLEWOOD CLIFFS: PRENTICE HALL, 1967, 149 PP., LC#67-14849.
STUDIES DEVELOPMENTS IN PORTUGUESE POSSESSIONS IN AFRICA. DISCUSSES TRADITION OF EMPIRE AND HISTORY OF COLONIAL POLICY. DELINEATES PROBLEMS FACING PORTUGAL AND HER COLONIES TODAY AND EXAMINES INSTITUTIONAL FORCES THAT ALLOW PORTUGUESE DOMINANCE OR AFRICAN INDEPENDENCE. COMPARES AFRICAN AND PORTUGUESE CONCEPTS OF NATIONALISM AND EXAMINES POLITICAL, ECONOMIC, AND SOCIAL TRENDS IN EACH TERRITORY.

0466 CHILDS M.W., CATER D.
ETHICS IN A BUSINESS SOCIETY.
NEW YORK: HARPER & ROW, 1954, 180 PP.
ANALYSIS OF MODERN APPLICATIONS OF CHRISTIAN ETHICS. EXAMINES PROBLEM OF INDIVIDUAL CONSCIENCE IN RELATION TO ECONOMIC GOALS, AND THE DOCTRINES OF SPOKESMEN FOR CONSCIENCE, BUSINESSMEN, JUDGES, LABOR, COMMUNITY LEADERS, ETC.

0467 CHINITZ B. ED.
CITY AND SUBURB: THE ECONOMICS OF METROPOLITAN GROWTH.
ENGLEWOOD CLIFFS: PRENTICE HALL, 1964, 181 PP., LC#64-23569.
COLLECTED INDIVIDUAL ANALYSES OF ECONOMIC ASPECTS OF METROPOLITAN GROWTH. DEALS WITH ECONOMIC STRUCTURE OF URBAN AREAS SUCH AS PHILADELPHIA AND VIEWS LABOR MARKET IN NEW CITY. EXPLAINS URBAN TRANSPORTATION PROBLEMS, URBAN PLANNING AND FINANCIAL PROBLEMS, AND FUTURE DEVELOPMENTS.

0468 CHINOY E.
"THE TRADITION OF OPPORTUNITY AND THE ASPIRATIONS OF AUTOMOBILE WORKERS" (BMR)"
AMER. J. OF SOCIOLOGY, 57 (MAR. 52), 453-459.
EXAMINES THE PATENT DISPARITY INDUSTRIAL WORKERS FACE BETWEEN THE PROMISES OF THE TRADITION OF OPPORTUNITY AND THE REALITIES OF THEIR OWN EXPERIENCE. CAUGHT BETWEEN TRADITION AND REALITY, THE WORKERS INTERVIEWED CONFINE THEIR ASPIRATIONS TO THOSE ALTERNATIVES WHICH SEEM ATTAINABLE BY MEN WITH THEIR SKILLS AND RESOURCES. LIMITED ASPIRATIONS ARE RECONCILED WITH CULTURAL IMPERATIVE DIVERSE WAYS.

0469 CHO S.S.
KOREA IN WORLD POLITICS 1940-1950; AN EVALUATION OF AMERICAN RESPONSIBILITY.
BERKELEY: U OF CALIF PR, 1967, 338 PP., LC#67-14968.
TREATS AMERICAN POLICY TOWARD KOREA FROM CAIRO CONFERENCE IN 1943 TO KOREAN WAR IN 1950. FOCUSES ON MAKING OF POLICIES AND REASONS FOR FAILURE. DISCUSSES TRUSTEESHIP PROJECT AND DIVISION AT 38TH PARALLEL. STUDIES US-USSR RELATIONS AND BEGINNINGS OF AMERICAN MILITARY GOVERNMENT. EXAMINES IMPACT OF CONTAINMENT AND PRESENT PERMANENCE OF KOREAN DIVISION. ANALYZES AID PROGRAM AND FINDS IT VERY INADEQUATE.

0470 CHOJNACKI S. ED., PANKHURST R. ED., SHACK W.A. ED.
REGISTER ON CURRENT RESEARCH ON ETHIOPIA AND THE HORN OF AFRICA.
ADDIS ABABA: INST ETHIOPIAN STUD, 1963, 44 PP.
AN UNANNOTATED BIBLIOGRAPHY LISTING 341 PROJECTS OF CURRENT RESEARCH ON ETHIOPIA BEING CONDUCTED BOTH IN ETHIOPIA AND ABROAD. PROVIDES INFORMATION ON THE STATE OF RESEARCH AS OF 1963: STARTING DATE, DATE OF COMPLETION, PUBLICATIONS, SCHOLARSHIPS INVOLVED, AND NAMES OF SUPERVISORS AND ASSISTANTS. CLASSIFIED INTO 23 SUBJECT CATEGORIES.

0471 CHRISTENSON C.L.
ECONOMIC REDEVELOPMENT IN BITUMINOUS COAL: THE SPECIAL CASE OF TECHNOLOGICAL ADVANCE IN US COAL MINES 1930-1960.
CAMBRIDGE: HARVARD U PR, 1962, 312 PP., LC#62-8178.
ANALYSIS OF COAL INDUSTRY WITH PARTICULAR EMPHASIS ON ECONOMIC IMPLICATIONS OF PHYSICAL BASE AND ON VARIATIONS IN QUALITIES AND OTHER CHARACTERISTICS OF OUR COAL RESOURCES.

0472 CHU K., NAYLOR T.H.
"A DYNAMIC MODEL OF THE FIRM."
MANAGEMENT SCIENCE, 2 (MAY 65), 736-50.
UTILIZES TRADITIONAL MICRO-ECONOMIC THEORY AND ELEMENTARY QUEUING THEORY TO DEVELOP A COMPUTER SIMULATION MODEL OF A SINGLE-PRODUCT, MULTI-PROCESS FIRM. DEMONSTRATES "THEORY OF THE FIRM" MAY BE USED TO PROVIDE CONVENIENT FRAME OF REFERENCE IN APPLYING RECENTLY DEVELOPED ANALYTICAL TOOLS OF OPERATIONS RESEARCH AND COMPUTER TECHNOLOGY TO THE ANALYSIS OF THE BEHAVIOR OF THE FIRM.

0473 CLABAULT J.M.
"PRACTICALITIES IN COMPETITOR EXCHANGING PRICE INFORMATION."
ANTI-TRUST BULLETIN, 12 (SPRING 67), 49-63.
WARNS OF ANTITRUST ACTION ON THE BASIS OF ORAL COMMUNIATION BETWEEN COMPETITORS.SUGGESTS SAFEST COURSE IS INSTRUCTION TO EMPLOYEES NOT TO ENGAGE IN PRICE DISCUSSIONS AT ALL IN ORDER TO AVOID LEGAL PROBLEMS. CITES VARIOUS COURT CASES AND SUGGESTS NOT VIOLATING SHERMAN ACT. RECOGNIZES OCCASIONAL NEED FOR PRICE EXCHANGES.

0474 CLAIRBORN E.L.
FORECASTING THE BALANCE OF PAYMENTS: AN EVALUATION.
PRINCETON: PRIN U, DEPT OF ECO, 1964, 262 PP.
REVIEWS PAST BALANCE-OF-PAYMENTS FORECASTS TO EVALUATE THEIR DEGREE OF ACCURACY AND DETERMINE WHAT FUTURE MARGINS OF ERROR SHOULD BE ALLOWED. COVERS GENERAL PROBLEMS OF FORECASTING, SHORT-TERM FORECASTS IN US AND ENGLAND, AND LONG-TERM FORECASTS FOR FUTURE PROGRAMS. BIBLIOGRAPHY OF WORKS CITED IN TEXT.

0475 CLAIRMONTE F.
LE LIBERALISME ECONOMIQUE ET LES PAYS SOUS-DEVELOPPES: ETUDES SUR L'EVOLUTION D'UNE IDEE.
GENEVA: LIBRAIRIE DROZ, 1958, 361 PP.
PRINCIPAL IDEA OF WORK IS CONVICTION OF EXTREME IMPORTANCE OF THE INDUSTRIALIZATION OF UNDERDEVELOPED COUNTRIES. ATTEMPTS COMPLETELY NEUTRAL EXAMINATION OF THE EFFECT OF LIBERAL ECONOMIC THEORIES ON PROBLEMS OF DEVELOPMENT IN UNDERDEVELOPED COUNTRIES. BIBLIOGRAPHY OF APPROXIMATELY 560 ITEMS.

0476 CLAPHAN J.H.
THE ECONOMIC DEVELOPMENT OF FRANCE AND GERMANY 1815-1914.

NEW YORK: MACMILLAN, 1923, 420 PP.
PLACES ECONOMIC HISTORY OF FRANCE AND GERMANY FROM 1815 TO 1914 IN TOTAL WESTERN EUROPEAN SETTING. STUDIES RURAL LIFE BEFORE RAILROADS, INDUSTRIAL CONDITIONS FROM 1815-48, COMMUNICATIONS, COMMERCE, AND FINANCES BEFORE 1848, AND CHANGES IN ALL THESE FROM 1848-1914, THAT IS, AFTER RAILROADS.

0477 CLARK C.
THE CONDITIONS OF ECONOMIC PROGRESS.
LONDON: MACMILLAN, 1951, 584 PP.
CONSIDERING ECONOMIC PROGRESS PARTLY IN TERMS OF SATISFYING NEEDS AND JUST DISTRIBUTION OF WEALTH. COMPARES RELATIVE PURCHASING POWER AND REAL NATIONAL PRODUCT AND CONSEQUENTLY RELATIVE STANDARDS OF WELL BEING AMONG VARIOUS NATIONS PARTICULARLY IN EUROPE. CAPITAL RESOURCES AND ACCUMULATION, PRODUCTION, AND CONSUMPTION ARE CONSIDERED AS IS THE DISTRIBUTION OF INCOME AND OF LABOR BETWEEN INDUSTRIES AND PERSONS.

0478 CLARK J.B.
THE DISTRIBUTION OF WEALTH (1899)
NEW YORK: MACMILLAN, 1924, 445 PP.
PURPOSE IS TO SHOW THAT ALL INCOME IS CONTROLLED BY NATURAL LAW AND THAT IF THIS LAW OPERATED WITHOUT INTERFERENCE EVERYONE WOULD RECEIVE THE WEALTH HE CREATED IN PRODUCTION. HOWEVER, THIS LAW IS INTERFERED WITH BY STRIKES, TARIFFS, TAXES, AND SO ON. AUTHOR CLAIMS THAT THIS INTERFERENCE CANNOT BE UNDERSTOOD EXCEPT IN RELATION TO THE BASIC LAW, AND SHOWS HOW THIS LAW WOULD WORK IN PRACTICE.

0479 CLARK J.J. ED.
BUSINESS FLUCTUATIONS, GROWTH, AND ECONOMIC STABILIZATION.
NEW YORK: RANDOM HOUSE, INC, 1963, 682 PP., LC#63-08265.
EXAMINES BUSINESS FLUCTUATIONS, EMPIRICAL ANALYSIS OF BUSINESS CYCLES AND ITS THEORIES, STABILIZATION, GROWTH, AND INFLATION IN FREE MARKET. DISCUSSES GOVERNMENT ROLE IN BUSINESS AND STABILIZATION. BIBLIOGRAPHY LISTS 1,500 BOOKS AND ARTICLES, 1945-62, IN ENGLISH FOR FURTHER STUDY.

0480 CLARK J.M.
SOCIAL CONTROL OF BUSINESS (2ND ED.)
NEW YORK: MCGRAW HILL, 1939, 537 PP.
TREATS PROBLEM OF BALANCING CONTROL OVER BUSINESS TO MAINTAIN SOCIAL WELFARE AND INDIVIDUALISM. STATES THAT INDIVIDUALISM INVOLVES CONTROLS, TOO. COMPARES IDEAL AND REALISTIC INDIVIDUALISM TO DETERMINE AREAS IN NEED OF CHANGE AND OLD AND NEW CONTROLS TO SHOW DEVELOPMENT. DISCUSSES GROUP OF TANGIBLE PROBLEMS OF CONTROL. ADVOCATES REFORMS IN FREE ENTERPRISE SYSTEM SO IT WILL FUNCTION IN MODERN WORLD.

0481 CLARK J.M.
ALTERNATIVE TO SERFDOM.
NEW YORK: ALFRED KNOPF, 1950, 153 PP.
CLAIMS MAN'S NEED TO BELONG TO COMMUNITIES SMALLER THAN THE STATE BRINGS HIM INTO CONSTANT CONFLICTS. THESE SMALLER UNITS ARE CONSTANTLY WARRING. PROPOSES THAT IN ORDER TO RESOLVE THESE CONFLICTS WITHOUT DESTROYING LIBERTY, POWERS MUST BE BALANCED AND REASONABLY EXERCISED. PROVIDES EVALUATION OF ECONOMIC BEHAVIOR OF MEN WHICH GOES BEYOND ORDINARY DEMAND ANALYSIS.

0482 CLARK J.M.
ECONOMIC INSTITUTIONS AND HUMAN WELFARE.
NEW YORK: ALFRED KNOPF, 1957, 285 PP., LC#57-05796.
ESSAYS DEALING WITH ECONOMICS AND HUMAN AND COMMUNITY FACTORS WHICH UNDERLIE IT. INCLUDES ATTITUDES, INSTITUTIONS, MECHANISMS, ETHICAL STANDARDS, AND CONCEPTIONS OF WELFARE.

0483 CLARK J.M.
COMPETITION AS A DYNAMIC PROCESS.
WASHINGTON: BROOKINGS INST, 1961, 501 PP., LC#61-18475.
CRITICAL EXAMINATION OF DYNAMIC CHARACTER OF MODERN COMPETITION. APPRAISAL OF INADEQUACIES OF EQUILIBRIUM THEORY. SUGGESTS USE OF NEW DYNAMIC TOOLS OF ANALYSIS AND CONCEPTS OF TIME IN INTERPRETATION OF COMPETITIVE ACTIVITES IN ECONOMY.

0484 CLARK P.G.
"TOWARDS MORE COMPREHENSIVE PLANNING IN EAST AFRICA"
J. OF EAST AFRICAN ECONOMIC REV., 10 (DEC. 63), 65-74.
DISCUSSION OF FORMS OF QUANTITATIVE ECONOMIC ANALYSIS APPLICABLE TO EAST AFRICAN DEVELOPMENT - AGGREGATIVE PROJECTIONS AND PROJECT ANALYSIS.

0485 CLARK T.D.
THREE PATHS TO THE MODERN SOUTH: EDUCATION, AGRICULTURE, AND CONSERVATION.
ATHENS: U OF GEORGIA PRESS, 1965, 103 PP., LC#65-25288.
ANALYZES THREE ASPECTS OF LIFE IN SOUTHERN US WHICH AIDED REVIVAL AFTER CIVIL WAR. CONSIDERS FARMING ESSENTIAL TO RESTITUTION OF CAPITAL, AND EDUCATION ESSENTIAL TO ELEVATION OF FARMING FROM SUBSISTENCE TO PROFITABLE LEVEL. FUTURE ECONOMIC SUCCESS OF SOUTH DEPENDS ON ITS CONSERVATION PROGRAMS.

0486 CLAUNCH J.M. ED.
THE PROBLEM OF GOVERNMENT IN METROPOLITAN AREAS.
DALLAS: SMU, ARNOLD FOUNDATION, 1958, 55 PP.
DISCUSSIONS OF PROBLEMS RESULTING FROM INCREASED URBANIZATION AND EMERGENCE OF LARGE METROPOLITAN AREAS IN AMERICAN SOUTHWEST. EMPHASIS IS ON POLITICAL DIFFICULTIES RESULTING FROM COMBINATION OF ECONOMIC, SOCIAL, AND CULTURAL FACTORS. FOUR STATES DISCUSSED INCLUDE KANSAS, TEXAS, OKLAHOMA, AND NEW MEXICO.

0487 CLEGERN W.M.
BRITISH HONDURAS: COLONIAL DEAD END, 1859-1900.
BATON ROUGE: LOUISIANA ST U PR, 1967, 214 PP., LC#67-11686.
DEFINES POLITICAL DEVELOPMENTS IN BRITISH HONDURAS DURING LATE 19TH CENTURY. EMPHASIZES INTERNAL PROBLEMS OF THE COLONY AND BRITISH POLICY REGARDING BOUNDARIES. SHOWS HOW BRITISH USED THEIR POWER AND WAKNESSES OF NEIGHBORS OF HONDURAS TO PROMOTE BRITISH INTERESTS. DESCRIBES HOW BRITAIN CONVERTED COLONY FROM A TRADE CENTER INTO AN AGRICULTURAL SETTLEMENT.

0488 CLELLAND D.A., FORM W.H.
"ECONOMIC DOMINANTS AND COMMUNITY POWER: A COMPARATIVE ANALYSIS."
AMER. J. OF SOCIOLOGY, 69 (MAR. 64), 511-521.
ECONOMIC DOMINANTS IN BOTH A SATELLITE CITY AND AN INDEPENDENT CITY WITHDREW FROM ELECTIVE POLITICAL OFFICES AS BUSINESS BECAME INTEGRATED INTO NATIONAL MARKETS. DOMINANTS IN THE INDEPENDENT CITY WERE INVOLVED MORE FREQUENTLY IN LOCAL ISSUES AND PROJECTS AND WERE MORE OFTEN CITED AS TOP INDIVIDUALS.

0489 CLEMENT M.O., PFISTER R.L., ROTHWELL K.J.
THEORETICAL ISSUES IN INTERNATIONAL ECONOMICS.
BOSTON: HOUGHTON MIFFLIN, 1967, 449 PP.
NEW AND COMPLEX PROBLEMS IN INTERNATIONAL TRADE ARE TACKLED WITH RELEVANT ANALYTIC TOOLS TO IDENTIFY CLEARLY EFFECTS OF ALTERNATIVE POLICIES. EACH CHAPTER IS A "SURVEY ARTICLE" CONCERNED WITH ISSUES IN PURE TRADE THEORY AND INTERNATIONAL MONETARY THEORY. WRITTEN FOR ADVANCED STUDENTS.

0490 CLEMHOUT S.
"PRODUCTION FUNCTION ANALYSIS APPLIED TO THE LEONTIEF SCARCE-FACTOR PARADOX OF INTERNATIONAL TRADE."
MANCHESTER ECON. SOC. STUD., 31 (MAY 63), 103-114.
CONCLUDES THAT A COUNTRY WHICH HAS AN ABSOLUTE (OR COMPARATIVE) ADVANTAGE IN PRODUCTIVITY HAS 'PREPONDERANCE IN THE OPPORTUNITY-COSTS OF PRODUCTION' BESIDES THOSE RESULTING FROM NATURAL ENDOWMENTS. THE NATION SUPERIOR IN PRODUCTIVITY WILL EXPORT IN THESE LINES OF PRODUCTION AND MIGHT WELL DO SO REGARDLESS OF FACTOR-PROPORTIONS.

0491 CLEVELAND A.S.
"NAM: SPOKESMAN FOR INDUSTRY?"
HARVARD BUSINESS REV., 26 (MAY 48), 353-371.
A CRITICAL EVALUATION OF NAM, DISCUSSING ITS SELF-INTEREST, LIMITED APPROACH TO NATIONAL POLICY, INSISTENCE ON A UNITED FRONT, NONPARTICIPATION OF MEMBERSHIP, AND COMMENTS ON POSSIBLE CHANGE OF THE SITUATION.

0492 CLONER A., GABLE R.W.
"THE CALIFORNIA LEGISLATOR AND THE PROBLEM OF COMPENSATION."
WESTERN POLIT. QUART., 12 (SEPT. 59), 712-726.
SUMMARIZES THE REPORT OF FACULTY MEMBERS OF SCHOOL OF PUBLIC ADMINISTRATION AT THE UNIVERSITY OF SOUTHERN CALIFORNIA, WHO WERE COMMISSIONED TO INVESTIGATE FACTORS WHICH SHOULD DETERMINE THE SALARIES OF CALIFORNIA LAWMAKERS. EXAMINES THE DUTIES, RESPONSIBILITIES, AND THE CORRESPONDING WORK-LOAD. CONCLUDED THAT SALARIES SHOULD BE RAISED, TO INSURE FULL-TIME LEGISLATORS.

0493 CLOUGH S.B., COLE C.W.
ECONOMIC HISTORY OF EUROPE.
BOSTON: HEATH, 1946, 841 PP.
TRACES THE ECONOMIC HISTORY OF EUROPE FROM 600 AD TO THE BEGINNING OF THE SECOND WORLD WAR. SHOWS THE CONNECTION BETWEEN ECONOMIC DEVELOPMENT AND SOCIAL CONDITIONS, POLITICAL POWER, AND INTELLECTUAL LIFE.

0494 CLYDE P.H.
THE FAR EAST: A HISTORY OF THE IMPACT OF THE WEST ON EASTERN ASIA.
ENGLEWOOD CLIFFS: PRENTICE HALL, 1948, 868 PP.
ANALYSIS OF HISTORICAL CHANGE IN SINO-JAPANESE POLITICS, CULTURE, ECONOMICS, AND INTERNATIONAL RELATIONS RESULTING FROM CONTACT AND CONFLICT WITH THE WEST, 1860-1940.

0495 COALE A.J., HOOVER E.M.
POPULATION GROWTH AND ECONOMIC DEVELOPMENT IN LOW-INCOME COUNTRIES: A CASE STUDY OF INDIA'S PROSPECTS.
PRINCETON: PRINCETON U PRESS, 1958, 389 PP., LC#58-7124.
EXAMINES DIFFERENCES IN ECONOMIC TERMS THAT A DRASTIC REDUCTION IN BIRTH RATE WOULD EFFECT WITHIN A GENERATION. USING INDIA AS CASE STUDY, EXAMINES FINDINGS BY APPLYING THEM TO LESS POPULATED MEXICO. CONCLUDES THAT PACE OF

DEVELOPMENT DEPENDS ON DIVERSION OF RESOURCES FROM CONSUMPTION TO PROMOTING FUTURE OUTPUT. ITERATES BENEFITS OF REDUCTION IN FERTILITY TOWARD ECONOMIC ADVANTAGE.

0496 COHEN A.
"THE TECHNOLOGY/ELITE APPROACH TO THE DEVELOPMENTAL PROCESS* PERUVIAN CASE STUDY."
ECO. DEV. AND CULTURAL CHANGE, 14 (APR. 66), 323-333.
TECHNOLOGY/ELITE THEORY OF ECONOMIC GROWTH USING ONLY TWO VARIABLES PERMITS GENERALIZATIONS ABOUT NATURE AND DIRECTION OF DEVELOPMENTAL PROCESS. THE LESS VERTICAL MOBILITY AND THE SLOWER THE RATE OF GROWTH IN A PARTICULAR BACKWARD SOCIETY, THE MORE RELEVANT BECOMES TECHNOLOGY/ELITE EXPLANATION .IT IS FREQUENTLY APPLIED TO LATIN AMERICA.

0497 COHEN M.R.
LAW AND THE SOCIAL ORDER: ESSAYS IN LEGAL PHILOSOPHY.
HAMDEN, CONN: ARCHON BOOKS, 1967, 403 PP., LC#67-28552.
ORIGINALLY PUBLISHED IN 1933, THIS BOOK IS A RESULT OF THE DEPRESSION. ATTACKS ATTITUDE OF FEDERAL COURTS TOWARD LABOR LEGISLATION. FAVORS A "NEW DEAL" GOVERNMENT. SURVEYS LEGAL ATTITUDE TOWARD SOCIAL WELFARE AND CURRENT INSTITUTIONS THAT BLOCK PROGRESS. IN DISCUSSING LEADING EUROPEAN AND AMERICAN JURISTS, AUTHOR SIDES WITH THOSE WHO SUPPORT SOCIAL WELFARE MEASURES.

0498 COLBERG M.R.
HUMAN CAPITAL IN SOUTHERN DEVELOPMENT.
CHAPEL HILL: U OF N CAR PR, 1965, 136 PP., LC#65-23140.
STUDY OF SOUTHERN ECONOMIC DEVELOPMENT, HUMAN CAPITAL AS ECONOMIC RESOURCE, AND ECONOMIC ASPECTS OF RACIAL SEGREGATION AND DESEGREGATION.

0499 COLE A.B., TOTTEN G.O., UYEHARA C.H.
SOCIALIST PARTIES IN POSTWAR JAPAN.
NEW HAVEN: YALE U PR, 1966, 490 PP., LC#66-21511.
COMBINES HISTORICAL METHOD WITH POLITICAL DESCRIPTION AND ANALYSIS TO STUDY JAPAN'S NON-COMMUNIST SOCIAL DEMOCRATIC PARTIES FROM 1945-61. PROVIDES HISTORICAL SURVEY OF PARTY DEVELOPMENT; OUTLINES AND EVALUATES ECONOMIC POLICIES; AND CONSIDERS FOREIGN POLICIES OF SOCIALISTS. CONSIDERS PARTY ORGANIZATION AND LEADERSHIP, RELATIONS BETWEEN PARTY AND LABOR UNIONS, AND SUPPORT FROM VARIOUS SOCIAL STRATA.

0500 COLE G.D.H.
"NAZI ECONOMICS: HOW DO THEY MANAGE IT?"
POLIT. QUART., 10 (JAN. 39), 55-68.
CONSIDERS WORKING OF NAZI ECONOMY DURING PERIOD OF INTENSE ACTIVITY LEADING UP TO CRISIS OF SEPTEMBER, 1938. INVESTIGATES REASONS BEHIND SUCCESS OF ECONOMY THAT VIOLATES ALL LAWS OF ECONOMICS AND MANAGES "TO LEAVE THE DEMOCRATIC COUNTRIES TO GLORY IN THEIR OWN TRIUMPHS OF UNEMPLOYMENT." MAINTAINS THAT FORCE IS NECESSARY TO FASCIST ECONOMY AND WELFARE IS ANTITHESIS OF ITS AIMS.

0501 COLE G.D.H.
STUDIES IN CLASS STRUCTURE.
NEW YORK: HUMANITIES PRESS, 1955, 195 PP.
ANALYZES ECONOMIC ASPECTS OF CLASS STRUCTURE IN BRITAIN AND OTHER WESTERN SOCIETIES. MAINTAINS THAT CLASSES ARE NOT SHARPLY DEFINABLE GROUPS. STUDIES METHODS OF ASSIGNING PEOPLE TO A CLASS. EXAMINES INFLUENCE OF TECHNOLOGICAL CHANGE ON CLASS STRUCTURE AND DISCUSSES CONCEPT OF MIDDLE CLASS. EMPHASIZES POSITION OF SEVERAL KINDS OF ELITES IN BRITISH SOCIETY.

0502 COLE G.D.H.
COMMUNISM AND SOCIAL DEMOCRACY (VOL. IV OF "HISTORY OF SOCIAL THOUGHT")
LONDON: MACMILLAN, 1958, 940 PP.
BEGINS WITH RUSSIAN REVOLUTIONS OF 1917; FOLLOWS ADVANCE OF SOCIALISM FOLLOWING 18 YEARS. CONCERNED WITH DEVELOPMENTS IN RUSSIA, GERMANY, AUSTRIA, HUNGARY, BALKAN STATES, ITALY, AND UK.

0503 COLE W.E., CROWE H.P.
RECENT TRENDS IN RURAL PLANNING.
ENGLEWOOD CLIFFS: PRENTICE HALL, 1937, 579 PP.
COMPILATION OF VARIOUS ATTEMPTS MADE SYSTEMATICALLY TO ATTACK CERTAIN RURAL PROBLEMS AND TO PLAN FOR A RURAL LIFE DESIGNED TO ACHIEVE ADEQUACY AND SOCIAL EFFECTIVENESS IN US AND OTHER COUNTRIES.

0504 COLLERY A.
"A FULL EMPLOYMENT, KEYNESIAN THEORY OF INTERNATIONAL TRADE."
QUART. J. ECON., 77(AUG. 63), 438-58.
PRESENTS A THEORY OF INTERNATIONAL TRADE WITHIN A FULL EMPLOYMENT VERSION OF THE KEYNESIAN MODEL, AS OPPOSED TO A THEORY WHICH DEALS ONLY WITH ONE VERSION OF THE KEYNESIAN MODEL, NAMELY, THE CARE OF UNEMPLOYMENT AND PRICE STABILITY.

0505 COLLIER A.T.
MANAGEMENT, MEN, AND VALUES.
NEW YORK: HARPER & ROW, 1962, 235 PP., LC#62-14586.
ATTEMPTS TO IDENTIFY MAJOR PREMISES, PRINCIPLES, OR VALUES BY WHICH DECISIONS IN FORMAL ORGANIZATIONS ARE, CONSCIOUSLY OR UNCONSCIOUSLY, MADE. USES DIALOGUE METHOD TO ANSWER THE FOLLOWING: WHAT ARE PROFITS FOR? HOW IS MANAGEMENT TRAINED? WHAT IS THE KEY TO SELLING? WHAT SHOULD A BUSINESS SEEK? HOW SHOULD INDIVIDUALS BE JUDGED? HOW DESIRABLE IS RETIREMENT? AND, WHEN SHOULD CORPORATIONS MERGE?

0506 COLLINS H., ABRAMSKY C.
KARL MARX AND THE BRITISH LABOUR MOVEMENT; YEARS OF THE FIRST INTERNATIONAL.
NEW YORK: ST MARTIN'S PRESS, 1965, LC#65-11740.
AN ASSESSMENT OF THE FIRST INTERNATIONAL IN RELATION TO THE INDUSTRIAL AND POLITICAL MOVEMENT OF THE BRITISH WORKING CLASS. PROVIDES A NEW INTERPRETATION OF MARX'S "INAUGURAL ADDRESS," AND EVALUATES ITS SIGNIFICANCE IN THE DEVELOPMENT OF THE IDEOLOGY CONTAINED IN "DAS KAPITAL." CONTAINS A COMPREHENSIVE BIBLIOGRAPHY ON THE FIRST INTERNATIONAL: OFFICIAL STATEMENTS, MANUSCRIPTS, NEWSPAPERS, PAMPHLETS, AND BOOKS.

0507 COLLINS H., ABRAMSKY C.
KARL MARX AND THE BRITISH LABOR MOVEMENT, YEARS OF THE FIRST INTERNATIONAL.
LONDON: MACMILLAN, 1965, 356 PP.
INVESTIGATES ROLE PLAYED BY KARL MARX IN FOUNDING OF BRITAIN'S FIRST INTERNATIONAL LABOR UNION IN 1864. ASSESSES THE INTERNATIONAL IN RELATION TO INDUSTRIAL AND POLITICAL MOVEMENT OF BRITISH WORKING CLASS. NOTES IMPACT OF BRITISH TRADE UNIONS ON WORLD SOCIALISM AND DISCUSSES FOUNDING OF PARIS COMMUNE AS A STEP IN MARX'S EFFORTS TO ORGANIZE LABOR ON A WORLDWIDE SCALE.

0508 COLLOQUE SUR LA PLANIFICATION
LA PLANIFICATION COMME PROCESSUS DE DECISION.
PARIS: LIBRAIRIE ARMAND COLIN, 1965, 224PP.
COLLECTED ESSAYS CONCERNING FRENCH ECONOMIC PLANNING IN RELATION TO ITS ADMINISTRATIVE AND POLITICAL PROBLEMS, INCLUDING ECONOMIC STRUCTURES, INSTITUTIONS, AND PLANNERS.

0509 COLM G., GEIGER T.
THE ECONOMY OF THE AMERICAN PEOPLE: PROGRESS, PROBLEMS, PROSPECTS.
WASHINGTON: NATL PLANNING ASSN, 1958, 167 PP., LC#58-8790.
ANALYZES NATURE AND PROSPECTS OF AMERICAN ECONOMIC SYSTEM, HOW PRIVATE ENTERPRISE ECONOMY HAS ACHIEVED HIGH PRODUCTIVITY AND LIVING STANDARDS, AND ITS MAJOR ACHIEVEMENTS AND SHORTCOMINGS.

0510 COLSTON RESEARCH SOCIETY
ECONOMETRIC ANALYSIS FOR NATIONAL ECONOMIC PLANNING (PROCEEDINGS OF SIXTEENTH SYMPOSIUM OF COLSTON RESEARCH SOCIETY)
LONDON, WASH, DC: BUTTERWORTHS, 1964, 320 PP.
STUDIES ECONOMETRIC DEVELOPMENTS, INCLUDING TOPICS LIKE INFLATION, PRODUCTION FUNCTIONAL MODELS, CAPACITY AND SHORT-TERM MULTIPLIERS, AND INTERPRETATION OF SHADOW PRICES IN PARAMETRIC LINEAR ECONOMIC PROGRAMME.

0511 COLUMBIA U SCHOOL OF LAW
PUBLIC INTERNATIONAL DEVELOPMENT FINANCING IN SENEGAL.
NEW YORK: COLUMBIA U PRESS, 1963, 150 PP.
STUDIES PROGRAMS AND RELATIONS OF FOREIGN INSTITUTIONS INVOLVED IN PUBLIC FINANCING OF ECONOMIC DEVELOPMENT IN SENEGAL. INCLUDES SENEGAL'S ECONOMIC AND POLITICAL STRUCTURE, INTERNAL ECONOMIC PLANNING, SURVEY OF ALL EXTERNAL ASSISTANCE RECEIVED, CASE STUDIES OF SPECIAL AID PROGRAMS. EVALUATES PROGRAMS TO DEVELOP MORE EFFICIENT MEANS OF ORGANIZING PUBLIC AID FROM FOREIGN SOURCES.

0512 COLUMBIA U SCHOOL OF LAW
PUBLIC INTERNATIONAL DEVELOPMENT FINANCING IN INDIA.
NEW YORK: COLUMBIA U LAW SCHOOL, 1964, 256 PP.
EMPHASIZES INSTITUTIONAL ASPECTS OF PUBLIC INTERNATIONAL DEVELOPMENT FINANCING FOR ECONOMIC ADVANCEMENT OF LESS DEVELOPED REGIONS. CONCENTRATES ON FUNCTIONING AND INTERRELATIONSHIPS OF INSTITUTIONS CONCERNED - NATIONAL, REGIONAL, AND MULTILATERAL. GIVES ACCOUNT OF SUCCESSES AND FAILURES; CONSIDERS FEASIBILITY OF ALTERNATIVE ARRANGEMENTS FOR MORE EFFECTIVE ORGANIZATIONAL PROCEDURES IN INDIA.

0513 COMM ON FEDERAL TAX POLICY
FINANCING AMERICA'S FUTURE: TAXES, ECONOMIC STABILITY AND GROWTH (PAMPHLET)
NEW YORK: COMM ON FED TAX POLICY, 1963, 64 PP.
REPORT ON FEDERAL TAX STRUCTURE AND REFORM MEASURES FOR PRESENT AND FUTURE NEEDS. INCLUDES RECOMMENDATIONS, PROBLEMS OF REFORM, AND DISCUSSION OF CORPORATE AND BUSINESS INCOME TAX, PERSONAL INCOME TAX, PAYROLL, ESTATE, AND COMMODITY TAX, WITH POSSIBLE CHANGES IN EACH.

0514 COMMISSION ON MONEY AND CREDIT
INFLATION, GROWTH, AND EMPLOYMENT.
ENGLEWOOD CLIFFS: PRENTICE HALL, 1964, 470 PP., LC#63-14710.
CASE STUDIES EXPLORE EFFECTS OF ADMINISTERED PRICES AND RECENT INFLATION; CONCEPTS AND CAUSES OF GROWTH; CAPACITY EMPLOYMENT AND ITS EFFECTS ON INFLATION. AUTHORS INCLUDE J.W. CONARD AND J.W. MARKHAM.

0515 COMMITTEE ECONOMIC DEVELOPMENT
ECONOMIC DEVELOPMENT ASSISTANCE.
NEW YORK: COMM FOR ECO DEV, 1957, 37 PP., LC#57-10393.
STUDIES ASSISTANCE TO ECONOMICALLY DEVELOPING COUNTRIES, PAST AID PROGRAMS, PRINCIPLES TO GUIDE IMPROVED PROGRAM, ITS COST, REQUIREMENTS FOR AN EFFECTIVE PROGRAM SUCH AS LONG-TERM LOANS, UNIQUE PROGRAMS FOR EACH COUNTRY, MULTI- AND BILATERAL ASSISTANCE, ENCOURAGEMENT AND BETTER USE OF AGRICULTURAL SURPLUS. GOAL IS INCREASED FREEDOM IN WORLD.

0516 COMMITTEE ECONOMIC DEVELOPMENT
NATIONAL OBJECTIVES AND THE BALANCE OF PAYMENTS PROBLEM: A STATEMENT ON NATIONAL POLICY.
NEW YORK: COMM. ECON. DEVELOP., 1960, 32 PP., $1.00.
DEALS WITH THE CURRENT SITUATION (1960) AND OUTLINES IMMEDIATELY AVAILABLE AND APPROPRIATE POLICY RESPONSES. ADVOCATES ACTIONS CONSISTENT WITH ECONOMIC GROWTH AT HOME AND RECOMMENDS CONTINUED USA CONTRIBUTIONS TO MILITARY STRENGTH AND ECONOMIC DEVELOPMENT ABROAD.

0517 COMMITTEE ECONOMIC DEVELOPMENT
GUIDING METROPOLITAN GROWTH (PAMPHLET)
NEW YORK: COMM FOR ECO DEV, 1960, 47 PP., LC#60-15132.
DISCUSSES POPULATION GROWTH AND PATTERNS OF URBANIZATION IN US. EXAMINES PROBLEMS IN TRANSPORTATION, AIR AND WATER POLLUTION, AND INDUSTRIAL DEVELOPMENT. CITES NEED FOR STUDIES AND REORGANIZATION IN URBAN RENEWAL PROGRAMS.

0518 COMMITTEE ECONOMIC DEVELOPMENT
TAXES AND TRADE: 20 YEARS OF CED POLICY (PAMPHLET)
NEW YORK: COMM FOR ECO DEV, 1963, 53 PP.
DEALS WITH ROLE OF COMMITTEE FOR ECONOMIC DEVELOPMENT IN BUSINESS LEADERSHIP. DISCUSSES COMMITTEE'S FUNCTION IN MAINTAINING REALISM IN FISCAL AND MONETARY POLICY. ANALYZES IMPORTANCE OF TRADE POLICY AS A KEY TO ECONOMIC STRENGTH.

0519 COMMITTEE ECONOMIC DEVELOPMENT
COMMUNITY ECONOMIC DEVELOPMENT PROGRAMS.
NEW YORK: COMM FOR ECO DEV, 1964, 349 PP., LC#64-66259.
CASE STUDIES OF COMMUNITY DEVELOPMENT PROGRAMS IN NEW YORK AREA, VERMONT, PENNSYLVANIA, INDIANA, AND ARKANSAS. DISCUSSES PROBLEMS OF UNEMPLOYMENT, TRAINING PROGRAMS, PUBLIC PLANNING, INDUSTRIAL DEVELOPMENT, LABOR RELATIONS, EDUCATIONAL PROJECTS, ETC.

0520 CAMPOS R.O.
A MOEDA, O GOVERNO E O TEMPO.
RIO DE JANEIRO: APEC EDITORA, 1964, 232 PP.
ARTICLES BY LEADING BRAZILIAN ECONOMIST AND DIRECTOR OF PLANNING IN ADMINISTRATION OF CASTELLO BRANCO. DEAL WITH INFLATION, INTERNATIONAL RELATIONS, GOVERNMENT PLANNING, UNDERDEVELOPMENT, INTER-AMERICAN COOPERATION, AND FOREIGN AID.

0521 CONAN A.R.
THE PROBLEM OF STERLING.
NEW YORK: ST MARTIN'S PRESS, 1966, 122 PP., LC#66-21360.
ANALYZES STATUS OF UK AS WORLD'S STERLING RESERVE NATION, IN RELATION TO CRISIS CAUSED AFTER WWII WHEN UK CEASED TO BE "CREDITOR" NATION FOR WORLD. CONCENTRATES ON USE OF STERLING BY REST OF WORLD FOR PAYMENTS, ETC., AND ITS EFFECT ON BALANCE OF STERLING IN UK. COLLATES DATA ON UK'S PRESENT STATUS AND APPRAISES HER POLICIES, BUT GIVES NO ADVICE.

0522 CONF ON FUTURE OF COMMONWEALTH
THE FUTURE OF THE COMMONWEALTH.
LONDON: H M STATIONERY OFFICE, 1963, 51 PP.
GENERAL DISCUSSION OF ROLE OF BRITISH COMMONWEALTH IN RACE RELATIONS, MUTUAL DEFENSE, ECONOMIC PROGRESS, AND POLITICAL STABILITY. SUGGESTS TECHNICAL AID, TRAINING OF ADMINISTRATORS, COOPERATION IN AGRICULTURAL MATTERS, AND EDUCATION AS CHIEF MEASURES TO ACHIEVE ECONOMIC PROGRESS AND POLITICAL COHESION.

0523 CONFERENCE REGIONAL ACCOUNTS
REGIONAL ACCOUNTS FOR POLICY DECISIONS.
WASHINGTON: RESOURCES FOR FUTURE, 1966, 230 PP., LC#66-23000
PROPOSES NEED FOR REGIONAL INFORMATION SYSTEM, ORGANIZED BY GOVERNMENT TO COORDINATE ALL PAST DECISIONS ON REGIONAL POLICY AND ALL POSSIBLE METHODS OF DECISION-MAKING. AIM IS TO HAVE ONE REGIONAL MODEL FOR FUTURE TO UNITE ALL PLANS. REPRESENTATIVES DISCUSS POSSIBILITY AND NEED FOR SUCH SYSTEMS IN SPECIFIC AREAS, SUCH AS URBAN RENEWAL.

0524 CONGRES ECONOMISTES LANG FRAN
MONNAIE ET EXPANSION.
NEW YORK: JAMES H HEINEMAN, 1962, 136 PP.
TRANSCRIPTION OF MEETINGS OF CONGRESS IN MAY, 1961. CONCLUDES THAT SINCE THE LIBERATION, EUROPE HAS PASSED THROUGH A PERIOD OF DEPRECIATION AND MONETARY ANARCHY, AND HAS MOVED TOWARD A SYSTEM OF CONVERTIBILITY. HOWEVER THIS WILL INEVITABLY LEAD TOWARD GOLD-STANDARD SYSTEM. TO AVOID THIS, ONE MUST ESTABLISH INTERNATIONAL MONETARY SYSTEM UNDER FORM OF NARROW COOPERATION OF CENTRAL BANKS OR A SUPER-BANK.

0525 CONGRESSIONAL QUARTERLY SERV
FEDERAL ECONOMIC POLICY 1945-1965 (PAMPHLET)
WASHINGTON: US GOVERNMENT, 1966, 94 PP., LC#66-19945.
SUMMARY REPORT OF DEVELOPMENTS IN US FEDERAL ECONOMIC POLICY SINCE WWII. INCLUDES CHRONOLOGY OF ECONOMIC LEGISLATION, TEXTS OF PRESIDENTIAL ECONOMIC REPORTS AND BUDGETS, STATISTICS ON NATIONAL DEBT, AND CHARTS AND SUMMARIES IN MANY AREAS RELEVANT TO FEDERAL SPENDING.

0526 CONGRESSIONAL QUARTERLY SERV
FEDERAL ECONOMIC POLICY 1945-1965.
WASHINGTON: CONG QUARTERLY SERV, 1966, 94 PP., LC#66-19945.
SURVEY OF MAJOR ECONOMIC DEVELOPMENTS SINCE WWII, CHRONOLOGY OF ECONOMIC LEGISLATION, BUDGET BACKGROUND, US PUBLIC DEBT, THE PRESIDENT'S ECONOMIC REPORT AND 1967 BUDGET; CHARTS AND SUMMARIES.

0527 CONLEY R.W.
THE ECONOMICS OF VOCATIONAL REHABILITATION.
BALTIMORE: JOHNS HOPKINS PRESS, 1965, 177 PP., LC#65-22948.
DISCUSSES CHARACTERISTICS AND COSTS OF DISABILITY, REHABILITATION IN US, BENEFITS OF VOCATIONAL REHABILITATION, FACTORS IMPORTANT TO SUCCESS OF REHABILITATION, ETC. MAINTAINS THAT REHABILITATION PROGRAMS SHOULD BE EXTENDED TO AGED, UNEDUCATED, AND PARTIALLY DISABLED AS WELL.

0528 CONTY J.M.
PSYCHOLOGIE DE LA DECISION.
PARIS: LES EDITIONS D'ORGANISATION, 1959.
OFFERS A MEANS-END ANALYSIS AS AN ALTERNATIVE TO TRADITIONAL PROBLEM-SOLVING ANALYSES. ESTABLISHES SYSTEM OF CORRECTIVE CRITERIA AND PSYCHOLOGICAL VARIABLES FOR THE ORGANIZATION AND THOSE INVOLVED IN ITS PROCESSES. DERIVES DIRECTIONAL PRINCIPLES AND A MEANS OF ACTION FOR DECISIONS MADE BY BALANCING ALTERNATIVES.

0529 COOK P.L.
EFFECTS OF MERGERS: SIX STUDIES.
LONDON: ALLEN & UNWIN, 1958, 458 PP.
STUDIES OF SIX TYPES OF INDUSTRY (CEMENT, SOAP, GLASS, MOTOR, BREWING, TEXTILE) SHOWING IMMEDIATE AND LONG-RANGE CAUSES AND EFFECTS OF MERGERS ON INDIVIDUAL COMPANIES AND INDUSTRY AS A WHOLE. EVALUATES MERITS OF MERGER AND DEMONSTRATES WHAT MIGHT HAVE BEEN DONE ADMINISTRATIVELY TO IMPROVE THE EFFECTS.

0530 COOK P.W. JR. ED., VON PETERFRY G. ED.
PROBLEMS OF CORPORATE POWER.
HOMEWOOD: RICHARD IRWIN, 1966, 371 PP., LC#66-27457.
PRESENTS CASES DEALING WITH DEVELOPMENT AND USES OF CORPORATE POWER. MOST INVOLVE SITUATIONS WHERE DECISIONS WILL AFFECT WORLD OUTSIDE OF BUSINESS. MANY INVOLVE BARGAINS OR NEGOTIATIONS WITH COMPETING INTERESTS. STUDIES PROBLEMS THAT EXISTENCE OF ECONOMIC POWER PRESENTS TO SOCIETY.

0531 COOKE C.A.
CORPORATION TRUST AND COMPANY: AN ESSAY IN LEGAL HISTORY.
CAMBRIDGE: HARVARD U PR, 1951, 195 PP.
TRACES MINGLING OF LEGAL IDEAS AND ECONOMIC PURPOSES WHICH PRODUCED THE MODERN JOINT STOCK COMPANY IN ENGLAND, I.E., THE COMPANY WITH LIMITED LIABILITY AND TRANSFERABLE SHARES. ATTEMPTS TO SHOW THERE HAS BEEN NO NECESSARY CONNECTION BETWEEN CORPORATE FORM AND JOINT STOCK FUND. SHOWS HOW THESE TWO CONCEPTS COALESCED IN MID-19TH CENTURY. DISCUSSES COMPANIES ACT OF 1862.

0532 COOMBS P.H., BIGELOW K.W.
EDUCATION AND FOREIGN AID.
CAMBRIDGE: HARVARD U PR, 1965, 74 PP., LC#65-13840.
ANALYZES US EDUCATIONAL AID TO FOREIGN NATIONS AND SUGGESTS METHODS OF IMPROVEMENT. FEELS NEED FOR COOPERATIVE STRATEGY TO PLAN EDUCATIONAL PROJECTS AND SECURE MORE QUALIFIED PERSONNEL. ANALYZES SPECIFICALLY US POLICY IN AFRICA, ITS PROBLEMS, AND PROSPECTS FOR MORE PRACTICAL EDUCATIONAL PROGRAMS IN FUTURE.

0533 COPELAND M.A.
OUR FREE ENTERPRISE ECONOMY.
NEW YORK: MACMILLAN, 1965, 302 PP., LC#65-16562.
STUDIES ORGANIZATION BY INSTITUTIONS OF ECONOMIC ACTIVITY IN A FREE-ENTERPRISE, INDUSTRIALIZED COUNTRY SUCH AS THE US. FOCUSES ON PROBLEMS RELATING TO BUSINESS CYCLE AND THE ECONOMY'S OPERATION AT LESS THAN CAPACITY, AND RELEVANT PROBLEMS IN LABOR-MANAGEMENT RELATIONS.

0534 COPLAND D.
THE ADVENTURE OF GROWTH: ESSAYS ON THE AUSTRALIAN ECONOMY AND ITS INTERNATIONAL SETTING.
LONDON: F.W. CHESHIRE PTE, 1960, 148PP.
TRANSFORMATION OF AUSTRALIAN ECONOMY INTO MAJOR FACTOR IN INTERNATIONAL ECONOMICS. PROPOSES ESTABLISHMENT OF INTERNATIONAL FUND FOR DEVELOPMENT OF UNDERDEVELOPED NATIONS, TO WHICH NATIONS WOULD CONTRIBUTE SMALL PERCENTAGE OF NATIONAL INCOME AND REAP BENEFITS FROM INCREASED TRADE.

0535 COPPOCK J.D.
NORTH ATLANTIC POLICY - THE AGRICULTURAL GAP.

NEW YORK: TWENTIETH CENTURY FUND, 1963, 256 PP.
ANALYZES THE DIFFICULTIES IN THE FIELD OF AGRICULTURE ENCOUNTERED BY NATIONS ATTEMPTING TO CREATE AN ATLANTIC COMMUNITY. DISCUSSES THE STRENGTHS AND WEAKNESSES IN PRESENT AGRICULTURAL POLICIES WITH THIS END IN VIEW. UNDERSCORES THE NEED FOR REORGANIZATION OF THE STRUCTURE OF AGRICULTURE ALONG INDUSTRIAL LINES AND SETS FORTH AN ECONOMIC MODEL FOR 1970 BASED ON CONCLUSIONS.

0536 COPPOCK J.D.
INTERNATIONAL ECONOMIC INSTABILITY: THE EXPERIENCE AFTER WORLD WAR II.
NEW YORK: MCGRAW HILL, 1962, 184 PP., LC#62-15143.
DESCRIPTIVE AND ANALYTICAL STUDY OF ECONOMIC CONDITIONS 1946-58 DISCUSSES PROBLEMS AND MEASUREMENTS OF INSTABILITY, INSTABILITY OF INTERNATIONAL TRADE AND FOREIGN TRADE OF INDIVIDUAL COUNTRIES, AND STATISTICAL ANALYSIS OF INSTABILITY OF EXPORT PROCEEDS.

0537 CORLEY R.N., BLACK R.L.
THE LEGAL ENVIRONMENT OF BUSINESS.
NEW YORK: MCGRAW HILL, 1963, 378 PP., LC#63-15890.
TREATS LEGAL ENVIRONMENT IN WHICH BUSINESS DECISIONS OF TODAY ARE MADE. DISCUSSES GENERAL MEANING AND NATURE OF LAW AND THE ENVIRONMENT OF BUSINESS AS IT RESULTS FROM LAW. REVEALS ATTITUDE OF GOVERNMENT TOWARD BUSINESS AND PRESENTS TODAY'S MAJOR ISSUES IN LAW AND BUSINESS.

0538 COSGROVE C.A.
"AGRICULTURE, FINANCE AND POLITICS IN THE EUROPEAN COMMUNITY."
INTL. RELATIONS, 3 (APR. 67), 208-225.
DISCUSSES COMMON FARM POLICY AS SYMBOL OF INTEGRATION IN EEC. INTERACTION OF NATIONAL AND EEC INTERESTS NEGOTIATING FOR COMMON FARM POLICY ILLUSTRATES POLITICAL NATURE OF INTEGRATION. ANALYZES MAY-JULY 1966 DECISIONS TO DEMONSTRATE EFFECT OF INTERPLAY OF INTERESTS ON EEC DECISION-MAKING. ALTHOUGH COMMUNITY SPIRIT OVERPOWERED NATIONAL INTEREST IN MAY-JUNE, STILL DANGER NATIONAL INTEREST WILL DESTROY EEC.

0539 COSSA L.
SAGGI BIBLIOGRAFICI DI ECONOMIA POLITICA.
BOLOGNA: ARNOLD FORNI EDITORE, 1963, 452 PP.
BIBLIOGRAPHY OF ITALIAN ECONOMIC WRITINGS DATING FROM 1765 AND CONTINUING THROUGH 1849. IN ADDITION TO ITALIAN WRITINGS, CONTAINS EUROPEAN-LANGUAGE WRITINGS ON WORKER AND WAGES; DISTRIBUTION OF WEALTH; THEORY OF VALUE; AND ECONOMY OF NATIONAL MINORITIES. SECTIONS ON ENGLISH, GERMAN, AND FRENCH WORKS ON POLITICAL ECONOMY AND GENERAL THEORY OF FINANCES AND PUBLIC CREDIT.

0540 COSTANZA J.F.
"WHOLESOME NEUTRALITY: LAW AND EDUCATION."
NORTH DAKOTA LAW REVIEW, 43 (SUMMER 67), 605-658.
DETAILED STUDY OF RELATIONS BETWEEN CHURCH AND STATE IN AREA OF STATE AID TO CHURCH-RELATED COLLEGES. LOOKS AT PAST COURT DECISIONS ON ALL ASPECTS OF CHURCH AND STATE RELATIONSHIP. GIVES CRITERIA FOR SETTLEMENT OF PROBLEM AND ASSERTS THAT FACT THAT COLLEGES ARE EDUCATIONAL INSTITUTIONS SHOULD COME FIRST AND THAT MUTUAL ARRANGEMENT SHOULD BE FOUND SO EACH SIDE CAN REMAIN FREE OF OTHER'S CONTROL.

0541 COTTAM R.W.
COMPETITIVE INTERFERENCE AND TWENTIETH CENTURY DIPLOMACY.
PITTSBURGH: UNIVERSITY PR, 1967, 243 PP., LC#67-13925.
DESCRIBES MODERN ALTERNATIVE TO WAR, COUNTER-INSURGENCY, INVOLVING POLITICAL, ECONOMIC, AND PSYCHOLOGICAL MANIPULATIONS IN INTERNAL AFFAIRS OF OTHER NATIONS. EXPLORES US INSTITUTIONAL ADJUSTMENT TO THIS NEW DIPLOMACY. FINDS IT USED EXTENSIVELY, ESPECIALLY BY CIA, BUT IN HAPHAZARD WAY. CALLS FOR TRAINING OF DIPLOMATS IN NEW STYLE, AND FOR LONG-RANGE PLANNING, THEORETICAL COHERENCE. USES IDEAL MODEL.

0542 COUGHLIN B.J.
CHURCH AND STATE IN SOCIAL WELFARE.
NEW YORK: COLUMBIA U PRESS, 1965, 189 PP., LC#65-16309.
VOLUNTARY AGENCIES ARE INCREASINGLY THE BENEFICIARIES OF GOVERNMENT FUNDS. MANY AGENCIES ARE CHURCH-RELATED. EXAMINES WHETHER RECEIPT OF TAX FUNDS THREATENS AGENCY AUTONOMY, WHETHER THIS PRACTICE THREATENS SEPARATION OF CHURCH AND STATE, WHETHER DIFFERENT DENOMINATIONS DIFFER IN THEIR POLICIES TOWARD ACCEPTANCE OF GOVERNMENT FUNDS. MOST AGENCIES SEEM TO FEEL UNTHREATENED.

0543 COULANGES F D.E.
THE ORIGIN OF PROPERTY IN LAND.
ORIGINAL PUBLISHER NOT AVAILABLE, 1892, 153 PP.
AUTHOR ATTACKS SCHOLARLY VIEW OF PRIMITIVE COMMUNISM IN ENGLAND, ARGUING THAT THE SCHOLARSHIP ON THE SUBJECT HAS BEEN ERRONEOUS AND FULL OF MISTRANSLATION AND MISUNDERSTANDING. ADMITS TO THE POSSIBILITY OF PRIMITIVE COMMUNISM BUT FEELS THAT NO ONE HAS YET PROVED IT. BASIC FAULT IS THAT MEN LIKE MAUER AND VIOLLET HAVE CONFUSED FAMILY OWNERSHIP WITH COMMUNISM.

0544 COURNOT A.A.
RESEARCHES INTO THE MATHEMATICAL PRINCIPLES OF THE THEORY OF WEALTH (1838)
HOMEWOOD: RICHARD IRWIN, 1963, 174 PP., LC#63-14225.
ONE OF EARLIEST ATTEMPTS AT FORMULATION OF AN ECONOMETRIC SYSTEM. USES SILVER AS A MEASURE, MAKING COMPARISONS ON THE BASIS OF ITS WEIGHT REQUIRED FOR PURCHASE OF AN ITEM. APPLIES ALGEBRA TO AN ARBITRARY ANALYSIS OF WEALTH. CONSIDERS DEMAND, MONOPOLY, UNLIMITED COMPETITION, IMPERFECT COMPETITION, AND INCOME DISTRIBUTION.

0545 COWLING M.
1867 DISRAELI, GLADSTONE, AND REVOLUTION; THE PASSING OF THE SECOND REFORM BILL.
CAMBRIDGE: UNIVERSITY PRESS, 1967, 451 PP., LC#67-13801.
EXAMINES MID-VICTORIAN POLITICAL SYSTEM ATTACKED BY JOHN STUART MILL. DISCUSSES DECISION-MAKING PROCESS OF GOVERNMENT OF PERIOD AND EXPLAINS HOW DECISION FOR REFORM BILL OF 1867 WAS MADE NOT BY RADICAL LEADERS BUT BY HOUSE OF COMMONS. STUDIES FACTORS RELATED TO PASSAGE OF BILL: PARLIAMENTARY MANIPULATION AND CONSCIOUSNESS OF POPULAR PRESSURES AND TENSION BETWEEN, ACROSS, AND WITHIN PARTIES.

0546 COX D.W.
THE PERILS OF PEACE* CONVERSION TO WHAT?
NEW YORK: CHILTON BOOKS, 1965, 215 PP., LC#65-15993.
WITH TEN PERCENT OF AMERICAN LABOR FORCE INVOLVED IN DEFENSE WORK, DRASTIC DISLOCATIONS IN THE ECONOMY ARE LIKELY IF PEACE BRINGS SEVERE DEFENSE CUTBACKS. CALLS FOR ESTABLISHMENT OF NATIONAL PEACE-PLANNING "PENTAGON" WHICH WOULD PLAN FOR CONVERSION OF DEFENSE SPENDING TO OTHER DOMESTIC AND FOREIGN TASKS. PLOTS WASHINGTON'S PRESENT EFFORTS AT CONVERSION PLANNING AND SUGGESTS SPECIFIC IMPROVEMENTS.

0547 COX H.
ECONOMIC LIBERTY.
LONDON: LONGMANS, GREEN & CO, 1920, 263 PP.
ESSAYS DEFEND FREEDOM OF INDIVIDUAL FROM ECONOMIC CONTROL BY STATE OR OTHER BODY. FREE ENTERPRISE MUST EXIST FOR SOCIETY TO RUN SMOOTHLY; WHAT FEW GOVERNMENT CONTROLS SHOULD EXIST MUST MERELY PROTECT INDIVIDUALS FROM IMPINGING UPON EACH OTHER'S LIBERTY.

0548 COX O.C.
CAPITALISM AND AMERICAN LEADERSHIP.
NEW YORK: PHILOSOPHICAL LIB, 1962, 328 PP., LC#61-10606.
ANALYZES ORIGINS AND GROWTH OF CAPITALISM AS UNIQUE FORM OF SOCIAL ORGANIZATION. AUTHOR BELIEVES IT TO BE "SUPREME CULTURAL INVENTION OF MAN," WHICH HAS REPLACED FAITH AND REGION WITH RATIONAL "CULTURE BUILDING," I.E., MONEY-MAKING. ANALYZES TRANSFORMATION OF CAPITALISM IN US SOCIETY IN TERMS OF LEADERS' RELATIONS, RACE RELATIONS, FOREIGN TRADE, AND DEPENDENCE OF BACKWARD COUNTRIES.

0549 CRABB C.V. JR.
THE ELEPHANTS AND THE GRASS* A STUDY OF NONALIGNMENT.
NEW YORK: FREDERICK PRAEGER, 1965, 237 PP., LC#65-15653.
COMPARISON OF VARIOUS VERSIONS OF NONALIGNMENT. ANALYSIS OF THEIR ORGINS IN COLONIALISM AND IN RESPONSE TO COLD WAR PRESSURES. STUDIES BEHAVIOR OF NONALIGNED NATIONS IN THE UN CONCERNING ARMS CONTROL AND DISARMAMENT. COMPARES COMMUNIST BLOC AND AMERICAN RELATIONS WITH THE "NEUTRALIST MOVEMENT."

0550 CRAIG A.
"ARGENTINA: THE LATEST REVOLUTION."
WORLD TODAY, 23 (MAY 67),206-215.
SURVEYS CURRENT TRENDS IN ARGENTINE POLITICS: THE RISE OF PERONISMO, THE FAILURE OF ILLIA'S RADICAL GOVERNMENT TO ACCOMMODATE CHANGING ECONOMIC CONDITIONS, AND THE AFTERMATH OF LAST JUNE'S REVOLUTION. TRACES POLITICAL AND ECONOMIC FACTORS LEADING UP TO THE NEW ONGANIA REGIME. CONCLUDES THAT BITTER ANTI-PERONISTA FEELINGS OF MILITARY AND BLIND SUPPORT FOR PERON MAY DELAY ARGENTINE DEMOCRACY FOR SOME TIME.

0551 CRANE E.
MARKETING COMMUNICATION: A BEHAVIORAL APPROACH TO MEN, MESSAGES, AND MEDIA.
NEW YORK: JOHN WILEY, 1965, 569 PP., LC#65-21444.
DESCRIBES THE BEHAVIORAL APPROACH TO MARKETING COMMUNICATIONS* GOALS OF COMMUNICATIONS, MARKETS, AUDIENCES, SYMBOL SYSTEMS, MESSAGES AS TOOLS, AND CHANNELS OF COMMUNICATION. DISCUSSES THE BEHAVIOR OF MARKETS, AUDIENCES, AND INDIVIDUALS IN TERMS OF SENSES, PERCEPTION, HABIT, LEARNING, MEMORY, EMOTIONS, MOTIVES, PERSONALITY, ORGANIZATIONS, ROLE, AND STATUS. ANALYZES RESEARCH AS A FORM OF COMMUNICATIONS.

0552 CRAWFORD F.G.
"THE EXECUTIVE BUDGET DECISION IN NEW YORK."
AM. POL. SCI. REV., 24 (MAR. 30),403-408 .
TRACES DEVELOPMENT OF THE EXECUTIVE BUDGET IN NEW YORK, 1910-29. THE STRUGGLE FOR CONTROL OF THE FISCAL POLICIES BETWEEN THE GOVERNOR AND THE LEGISLATORS IS EXAMINED.

0553 CROKER F.P.U.
"ECONOMIC PEACEKEEPING."
ROYAL UNITED SERVICE INST. J., 62 (AUG. 67), 237-248.

DISCUSSES TECHNICAL AND STRATEGIC ASPECTS OF MAINTAINING A MILITARY FORCE, ATTEMPTING TO DETERMINE MOST ECONOMICAL WEAPONRY AND SUPPORT SYSTEM. DEALS BASICALLY WITH SEA-GOING, NONATOMIC FORCES, DRAWING HEAVILY ON WWII EXPERIENCES IN EVALUATING TACTICAL WEAPONRY.

0554 CROMER EARL OF
"STERLING AND THE COMMON MARKET."
WORLD TODAY, 23 (APR. 67), 131-146.
THERE ARE PEOPLE BOTH IN BRITAIN AND IN OTHER COUNTRIES WHO QUESTION THE COMPATIBILITY OF THE EXISTENCE OF WHAT IS USUALLY CALLED THE STERLING AREA WITH THE ENTRY OF THE UNITED KINGDOM INTO THE EEC. THE PURPOSE OF THE ARTICLE IS TO THROW LIGHT ON THE FACTS OF THE SUBJECT AND THE REAL ISSUES WHICH ARISE FROM THEM.

0555 CROOK W.H.
THE GENERAL STRIKE: A STUDY OF LABOR'S TRAGIC WEAPON IN THEORY AND PRACTICE.
CHAPEL HILL: U OF N CAR PR, 1931, 649 PP.
DISCUSSES GENERAL STRIKES BEFORE WWI IN BRITAIN, BELGIUM, FRANCE, SWEDEN, HOLLAND. ANALYZES THEORY OF GENERAL STRIKE FROM CHARTISM TO WWI. STUDIES PREPARATIONS FOR GENERAL STRIKES IN EUROPE AFTER WWI, NEGOTIATIONS WHICH PRECEDED THEM, AND SPECIFIC EVENTS OF BRITISH, GERMAN, AND AMERICAN STRIKES IN 1920'S.

0556 CROS L.
AFRIQUE FRANCAISE POUR TOUS.
PARIS: ALBIN MICHEL, 1928, 651 PP.
A DEFENSE OF COLONIZATION; GIVES PRACTICAL ADVICE FOR FRENCHMEN WHO CONTEMPLATED BECOMING COLONISTS. ARGUES IN FAVOR OF EXPLOITING THE EMPIRE AND CRITICIZES THE FRENCH PEOPLE FOR NOT SHOWING ENOUGH COLONIAL SPIRIT. AS PART OF A SERIES ENCOURAGING THIS SPIRIT, "AFRICA FOR ALL" PRESENTS THE VIEWS AND ENTHUSIASMS OF A FRENCH IMPERIALIST-MERCANTILIST.

0557 CROSSER P.K.
STATE CAPITALISM IN THE ECONOMY OF THE UNITED STATES.
NEW YORK: BOOKMAN ASSOCIATES, 1960, 158 PP., LC#60-12939.
THEORIZES THAT US PRACTICES STATE AND PRIVATE CAPITALISM, SINCE GOVERNMENT GIVES FUNDS TO CORPORATIONS, FARMERS, ETC., AND BUSINESS CONSTANTLY USES PUBLIC CONTROLS. ANALYZES US CAPITALISM IN ITS HISTORICAL CONTEXT, ITS IMPACT ON ECONOMY THROUGH SUBSIDIZATION, AND RELATION OF LABOR AND BUSINESS TO GOVERNMENT CONTROL.

0558 CROWDER M.
A SHORT HISTORY OF NIGERIA (REV.ED.)
NEW YORK: FREDERICK PRAEGER, 1966, 416 PP., LC#66-13679.
TRACES HISTORY OF NIGERIA FROM FIRST EXPLORATION BY EUROPEANS THROUGH NATIONAL INDEPENDENCE. INCLUDES GEOGRAPHY, SOCIAL GROUPS OF THE REGION, NATIVE CULTURE, SLAVE TRADE, ECONOMIC DEVELOPMENT, GOVERNMENT BY BRITAIN, RISE OF NATIONALISM, INTERNAL POLITICS, AND TRADE. PAYS PARTICULAR ATTENTION TO NATIVE WARRIOR GROUPS IN EARLY PERIODS, EARLY NATIVE RULERS, AND KEY FIGURES IN INDEPENDENCE MOVEMENT.

0559 CROWE S.
THE LANDSCAPE OF POWER.
LONDON: THE ARCHITECTURAL PRESS, 1958, 115 PP.
EXAMINES THE LANDSCAPE OF THE BRITISH ISLES AND THE CHALLENGE OF GIGANTIC CONSTRUCTIONS AND POWER LINES. STUDIES NATURAL, PRACTICAL METHODS FOR THE NEW INDUSTRIAL AGE. INCLUDES POWER, NATIONAL PARKS, NUCLEAR POWER STATIONS, HYDRO-ELECTRIC POWER, ELECTRIC AND OIL TRANSMISSION, AIRFIELDS, AND NEW INDUSTRIES IN OLD AREAS. CONCLUDES THAT MAN MUST REGAIN HIS SENSE OF VALUE AND BEAUTY, THEN ACT FOR THE FUTURE.

0560 CUCCORESE H.J.
HISTORIA DE LA CONVERSION DEL PAPEL MONEDA EN BUENOS AIRES, 1861-1867.
ARGENTINA: U NAC DE LA PLATA, 1959, 409 PP.
ATTEMPTS TO PRESENT HISTORY OF ECONOMIC ACTIONS, 1861-67, DEALING WITH MONETARY QUESTION AND CONVERSION OF PAPER MONEY. EXAMINES IMPORTANCE OF MONETARY POLICY AT THAT TIME, AND SUPPORT AND OPPOSITION TO CONVERSION.

0561 CUNNINGHAM E.M.
"THE BUSINESS MAN AND HIS LAWYER."
DUNS REV. AND MOD. IND., 70 (OCT. 57), 49-51.
SUGGESTS BUSINESS EXECUTIVES OFTEN MISUNDERSTAND THE ROLE OF THE LAWYER IN DECISION-MAKING. OFFERS GUIDE FOR SELECTING TYPE OF LEGAL SERVICES, WORKING WITH LAWYER, AND EVALUATING COST.

0562 CUNNINGHAM W.
THE GROWTH OF ENGLISH INDUSTRY AND COMMERCE.
NEW YORK: CAMBRIDGE U PRESS, 1882, 492 PP.
DISCUSSES RUDIMENTARY FORMS OF COMMERCE IN ENGLISH HISTORY: PROPERTY, COLLECTIVE INDUSTRY, AND BARTER. RELATES FEUDAL INDUSTRY TO CHRISTIAN MORALITY AND PAPAL POLICY. EXAMINES EARLY FORMS OF PRIVATE ENTERPRISE AND MERCANTILE SYSTEM. DISCUSSES MERCANTILE SYSTEM AND APPRAISES DIRECTION OF FUTURE ENGLISH COMMERCE.

0563 CUNNINGHAM W.B.
COMPULSORY CONCILIATION AND COLLECTIVE BARGAINING.
MONTREAL: MCGILL U PR, 1958, 123 PP.
EVALUATES COMPULSORY CONCILIATION IN PROVINCE OF NEW BRUNSWICK AS TO WHETHER IT EMASCULATES COLLECTIVE BARGAINING BY STUDYING CASES OF GOVERNMENT INTERVENTION, 1947-1956. DISCUSSES WHETHER ILLEGALIZING WORK STOPPAGES UNTIL CONCILIATION IS REQUESTED POSES MAJOR DIFFICULTY TO BARGAINING.

0564 CURRIE L.
ACCELERATING DEVELOPMENT: THE NECESSITY AND MEANS.
NEW YORK: MCGRAW HILL, 1966, 255 PP., LC#65-21573.
ANALYZES PROBLEM AND PROPOSES PROGRAM FOR CONTINUING UNDERDEVELOPMENT. DISCUSSES NEED FOR "BREAKTHROUGH" APPROACH AND STATES PREREQUISITES NECESSARY FOR SUCCESSFUL PROGRAM. DESCRIBES GOALS, DIAGNOSIS, AND STRATEGY APPLIED TO COLOMBIA AS TESTING GROUND FOR DEVELOPMENT POLICIES OF US.

0565 CURTIN W.J.
"NATIONAL EMERGENCY DISPUTES LEGISLATION* ITS NEED AND ITS PROSPECTS IN THE TRANSPORTATION INDUSTRIES."
GEORGETOWN LAW J., 55 (APR. 67), 786-811.
SKETCHES INCREASINGLY FAVORABLE PROSPECTS FOR NATIONAL EMERGENCY LABOR DISPUTES LEGISLATION. DISCUSSES SHORTCOMINGS OF EXISTING EMERGENCY PROCEDURES UNDER RAILWAY LABOR ACT LABOR MANAGEMENT RELATIONS ACT. OUTLINES MAJOR PROPOSALS FOR CHANGE: COMPULSORY ARBITRATION, ARSENAL OF WEAPONS APPROACH, ESTABLISHMENT OF INDUSTRIAL PEACE COMMISSION, & COMMON CONTRACT TERMINATION DATE WITHIN AN INDUSTRY.

0566 CYERT R.M., DILL W.R., MARCH J.G.
"THE ROLE OF EXPECTATIONS IN BUSINESS DECISION-MAKING."
ADMINISTRATIVE SCI. Q., 3 (DEC. 58), 307-40.
STUDY OF FOUR MAJOR DECISIONS IN THREE FIRMS. ANALYZES ROLE OF EXPECTATIONS IN DECISION-MAKING. QUESTIONS VALIDITY OF STANDARD THEORY OF PRICE IN INVESTMENT AND INTERNAL RESOURCE ALLOCATION DECISIONS.

0567 CYERT R.M., FEIGENBAUM E.A., MARCH J.G.
"MODELS IN A BEHAVIORAL THEORY OF THE FIRM."
BEHAVIORAL SCIENCE, 4 (APR. 59), 81-96.
PROPOSES A COMPLEX MODEL OF THE FIRM AS A DECISION-MAKING ORGANIZATION WHICH CAN YIELD ECONOMICALLY RELEVANT AND TESTABLE PREDICTIONS OF BUSINESS BEHAVIOR. EMPLOYS COMPUTER SIMULATION TECHNIQUES.

0568 CYERT R.M., MARCH J.G., STARBUCK W.H.
"TWO EXPERIMENTS ON BIAS AND CONFLICT IN ORGANIZATIONAL ESTIMATION."
MANAGEMENT SCIENCE, 7 (APR. 61), 254-264.
TWO EXPERIMENTS TESTING HYPOTHESES RELATING BIAS IN INTERNAL COMMUNICATION TO FINAL DECISIONS. ONE TESTS HYPOTHESIS THAT COST AND SALES ESTIMATIONS ARE MADE WITH IMPLICIT ASSUMPTION THAT A PAY-OFF STRUCTURE EXISTS. SECOND EXPLICITLY TESTS EFFECTS OF BIASED AND UNBIASED PAY-OFF STRUCTURES ON ESTIMATION WITHIN AN ORGANIZATION. INVOLVES DESCRIPTIVE STATISTICS. CONCLUSION: MICRO- BUT NO MACRO-LEVEL VARIATION.

0569 DAANE J.D., POLAK J.J., MACHLUP J.
"THE EVOLVING INTERNATIONAL MONETARY MECHANISM."
AMER. ECO. REVIEW, 55 (MAY 65), 150-186.
THREE PAPERS ON THE PROBLEMS AND PROSPECTS OF THE INTERNATIONAL MONETARY FUND AS WORLD FINANCIER. PAPERS PRESENTED BY "THE GROUP OF TEN," THE RICH NATIONS WHO SERVE THE IMF AS ITS POLICY PLANNING BOARD, BY THE IMF AS A WHOLE, AND BY A NON-GOVERNMENTAL STUDY GROUP OF ECONOMISTS.

0570 DAHL R.A.
"WORKERS' CONTROL OF INDUSTRY AND THE BRITISH LABOUR PARTY."
AM. POL. SCI. REV., 41 (OCT. 47), 875-900.
EXAMINES WORKERS' VERSUS PARLIAMENTARY CONTROL OF INDUSTRY UNDER BRITISH SOCIALISM. ANTECEDENT DOCTRINES OF FABIANISM, GUILD SOCIALISM, AND TRADE UNIONISM ARE TRACED UP TO LABOR PARTY VICTORY IN 1946, WHEN GOAL OF WORKERS' CONTROL WAS ABANDONED IN FAVOR OF CABINET CONTROL. CONCLUDES SOCIALISM CAN INCREASE WORKERS' BENEFITS, BUT NOT CHANGE THEIR INHERENTLY SUBORDINATE ROLE IN AN INTERDEPENDENT ECONOMY.

0571 DAHL R.A.
POLITICS, ECONOMICS AND WELFARE: PLANNING AND POLITICO-ECONOMIC SYSTEMS RESOLVED INTO BASIC SOCIAL PROCESSES.
NEW YORK: HARPER, 1953, 557 PP.
DESCRIBES VARIOUS POLITICO-ECONOMIC TECHNIQUES OF WHICH THERE IS AGREEMENT UPON BY SOCIAL SCIENCES. AS ANSWER TO FAILURE OF LIBERALISM AND SOCIALISM TO CONTROL MAN'S ENVIRONMENT, OFFERS RATIONAL SOCIAL ACTION THROUGH LARGE-SCALE PROCESSES SUCH AS BARGAINING AND PRICE SYSTEMS, RATIONAL CALCULATION AND CONTROL.

0572 DAHL R.A., LINDBLOM C.E.
POLITICS, ECONOMICS, AND WELFARE.
NEW YORK: HARPER & ROW, 1953, 550 PP., LC#53-5571.
SEEKS TO INCORPORATE CERTAIN ASPECTS OF POLITICS AND ECONOMICS INTO CONSISTENT BODY OF THEORY. ATTEMPTS TO IDENTIFY CONDITIONS UNDER WHICH INDIVIDUALS CAN MAXIMIZE ATTAINMENT OF GOALS THROUGH USE OF SOCIAL MECHANISMS.

FOCUSES ON THIS PROBLEM IN SOCIO-ECONOMIC PROCESSES.

0573 DALE W.B.
THE FOREIGN DEFICIT OF THE UNITED STATES.
MENLO PARK: STANFORD U RES INST, 1960, 48 PP.
PROVIDES FACTS AND BRIEF INTERPRETATION OF FOREIGN DEFICIT AND GOLD OUTFLOW OF US THROUGH 1959 AND RELATES THEM TO COMPETITIVE POSITIONS OF US COMPANIES. DISCUSSES COMMODITY COMPOSITION, COMPARATIVE COSTS OF PRODUCTION, AND PERFORMANCE OF US EXPORTS 1954-58. CONSIDERS ROLE OF GOVERNMENT AID IN ASSISTING EXPORT MARKETS.

0574 DALTON G.
"ECONOMIC THEORY AND PRIMITIVE SOCIETY" (BMR)"
AMERICAN ANTHROPOLOGIST, 63 (FEB. 61), 1-21.
PRESENTS REASONS WHY ECONOMIC THEORY CANNOT BE SUCCESSFULLY APPLIED TO STUDY OF PRIMITIVE COMMUNITIES. EXAMINES TECHNOLOGICAL PROCESSES, LEVEL OF MATERIAL SUBSISTANCE, ECOLOGICAL CONDITIONS, ETC. SUGGESTS ALTERNATIVE APPROACH TO ANALYTICAL TREATMENT OF PRIMITIVE ECONOMY.

0575 DALTON J.E.
SUGAR: A CASE STUDY OF GOVERNMENT CONTROL.
NEW YORK: MACMILLAN, 1937, 309 PP.
ATTEMPTS TO ASCERTAIN PAST AND PRESENT RELATIONSHIP OF ECONOMICS TO POLITICS IN MAJOR FOOD INDUSTRY, SUGAR, IN ORDER TO CHECK THESE FINDINGS AGAINST CONVICTIONS HELD BY BUSINESSMEN AND GOVERNMENT. EXAMINES HISTORICAL DEVELOPMENT OF PROBLEM SINCE CIVIL WAR, DESCRIBES BACKGROUND AGAINST WHICH SUGAR ACT WAS PASSED, RECOUNTS SOME OF ITS PROBLEMS, ANALYZES EFFECTS UPON SUGAR-PRODUCING AREAS AND CONSUMER.

0576 DALTON M.
"CONFLICTS BETWEEN STAFF AND LINE MANAGERIAL OFFICERS" (BMR)
AMER. SOCIOLOGICAL REV., 15 (JUNE 50), 342-351.
RESEARCH IN THREE INDUSTRIAL PLANTS SHOWING CONFLICT BETWEEN MANAGERIAL STAFF AND LINE GROUPS THAT HINDERED ATTAINMENT OF ORGANIZATIONAL GOALS. EXAMINES CAUSES OF CONFLICT AND PRESENTS POSSIBLE REMEDIAL MEASURES.

0577 DANIEL C.
"THE REGULATION OF PRIVATE ENTERPRISES AS PUBLIC UTILITIES."
SOCIAL RESEARCH, 34 (SUMMER 67), 347-354.
DETAILS AND ANALYZES ARGUMENT FOR UTILITY REGULATION CENTERING ON IDEA OF LACK OF SUITABLE SUBSTITUTES FOR CERTAIN ESSENTIAL SERVICES. NOTES ECONOMIC CONSIDERATIONS OBSERVED BY UNREGULATED UTILITY FIRMS.

0578 DANIEL C.
"FREEDOM, EQUITY, AND THE WAR ON POVERTY."
AMER. J. OF ECO. AND SOC., 26 (OCT. 67), 367-375.
STATES THAT IN ORDER FOR FREEDOM TO EXIST, MARKET COMPETITION AND POLITICAL SYSTEMS MUST BE FREE. DISCUSSES WAR ON POVERTY AS A MEANS WHEREBY EQUALITY OF OPPORTUNITY WILL BE PARTLY ATTAINED. MAINTAINS THAT THIS WAR REQUIRES A REDISTRIBUTION OF INCOME TO BRING ABOUT DISTRIBUTIVE JUSTICE.

0579 DANIELS R.V.
RUSSIA.
ENGLEWOOD CLIFFS: PRENTICE HALL, 1964, 152 PP., LC#64-23568.
ANALYSIS OF CZARIST RUSSIA AS NATION, THE REVOLUTION, AND EVOLUTION OF SOVIET SYSTEM IN ECONOMIC AND POLITICAL ASPECTS. EXAMINES PRESENT SOVIET SYSTEM.

0580 DANIELSON M.N.
FEDERAL-METROPOLITAN POLITICS AND THE COMMUTER CRISIS.
NEW YORK: COLUMBIA U PRESS, 1965, 244 PP., LC#65-16197.
THIS WORK ANALYZES FEDERAL-URBAN RELATIONS IN THE FIELD OF TRANSPORTATION BY EXAMINING ROLE ATTITUDES, CHANNELS OF INFLUENCE AND INFORMATION, AND THE IMPACT OF THE FEDERAL-URBAN INTERACTION AT BOTH LEVELS. THE NEW YORK AREA IS THE FOCUS OF THE STUDY.

0581 DAUGHERTY C.R.
LABOR PROBLEMS IN AMERICAN INDUSTRY (5TH ED.)
CAMBRIDGE: RIVERSIDE EDS, 1941, 1008 PP.
UNDERGRADUATE-LEVEL TEXT PRESENTS AREAS OF HUMAN MALADJUSTMENT IN LABOR PROBLEMS, SHOWING THAT THEY HAVE MANY INTERRELATIONSHIPS. EMPHASIZES ECONOMIC, SOCIAL, AND PSYCHOLOGICAL FACTORS OF SUPPLY AND DEMAND THAT OPERATE IN LABOR MARKET. PRESENTS EXISTING AND PROPOSED MEASURES FOR IMPROVING INDUSTRIAL RELATIONS.

0582 DAVENPORT H.J.
THE ECONOMICS OF ENTERPRISE.
NEW YORK: MACMILLAN, 1913, 543 PP.
STUDIES COMPETITIVE ECONOMICS AND IMPORTANCE OF PRICE. DISCUSSES SPECIALIZATION AND TRADE RELATED TO MONEY, THE ADJUSTMENT OF PRICE, SUPPLY AS DETERMINED BY COST OF PRODUCTION, NATURE OF PRODUCTION AND DISTRIBUTION, AND BASES OF COST. EXAMINES LAND RENT AND COST, TYPES OF RENTS, CAPITALIZATION VS. COST AS PRICE DETERMINANT, MONEY, BANKING, AND CREDIT.

0583 DAVIES E.
"NATIONAL" CAPITALISM: THE GOVERNMENT'S RECORD AS PROTECTOR OF PRIVATE MONOPOLY.
LONDON: VICTOR GOLLANCZ, 1938, 320 PP.
STUDIES GOVERNMENT CONTROL OF PRIVATE ENTERPRISE IN ENGLAND. STATES THAT CLASS THAT HAS CONTROLLED GOVERNMENT SINCE 1931 HAS IDENTIFIED ITS OWN INTEREST WITH NATION'S, THUS STRENGTHENING CAPITALIST STRUCTURE AND UTILIZING STATE RESOURCES FOR THE PROPERTIED CLASSES. FEELS COMMUNITY HAS THEREBY SUFFERED. HOPES TO RID ENGLAND OF CHAMBERLAIN GOVERNMENT AND INSTALL LABOUR PARTY.

0584 DAVIES E.
NATIONAL ENTERPRISE: THE DEVELOPMENT OF THE PUBLIC CORPORATION.
LONDON: VICTOR GOLLANCZ, 1946, 173 PP.
DISCUSSES ISSUES OF NATIONALIZATION OF BRITISH INDUSTRY, AND PROBLEMS THAT HAVE ARISEN IN REGARD TO ADMINISTRATION. ANALYZES THESE PROBLEMS IN RELATION TO PUBLIC CORPORATIONS ALREADY OPERATING, AND THOSE IN COURSE OF ESTABLISHMENT. ATTEMPTS TO DETERMINE GENERAL PRINCIPLES THAT CAN BE APPLIED TO NATIONAL ENTERPRISE TO ENSURE CONTINUED SUCCESS AND PUBLIC APPRECIATION OF ITS BENEFITS.

0585 DAVIES I.
AFRICAN TRADE UNIONS.
BALTIMORE: PENGUIN BOOKS, 1966, 256 PP.
SURVEY OF DEVELOPMENT OF TRADE UNIONISM IN AFRICA OVER PAST 30 YEARS. TAKES IN ENTIRE CONTINENT AND REVEALS ROOTS OF TRADE UNIONS IN STRUGGLE FOR INDEPENDENCE AGAINST COLONIAL RULE. DISCUSSES DEVELOPMENT OF RELATIONSHIP BETWEEN UNIONS AND VARIOUS AFRICAN GOVERNMENTS, AND EMERGENCE OF UNIONS AS CENTERS OF POLITICAL POWER.

0586 DAVIES JC I.I.I.
NEIGHBORHOOD GROUPS AND URBAN RENEWAL.
NEW YORK: COLUMBIA U PRESS, 1966, 235 PP.
AN ANALYSIS OF URBAN RENEWAL PROGRAMS IN NEW YORK CITY. PRESENTS POLITICAL BACKGROUND AND DEVELOPMENT OF RENEWAL IN NYC, STUDYING SEASIDE-HAMMELS, THE WEST VILLAGE, AND WEST SIDE URBAN RENEWAL AREA. INCLUDES FINANCIAL AND CONSTRUCTION DATA, AS WELL AS INTERVIEW INFORMATION. CONCLUDES THAT NEIGHBORHOOD POLITICAL GROUPS NEED TO BE INVOLVED IN THE PLANNING AND DECISION-MAKING PROCESS.

0587 DAVIS E.H.
OF THE PEOPLE, BY THE PEOPLE, FOR THE PEOPLE.
CHICAGO: JOHN NUVEEN + CO, 1958, 151 PP.
DESCRIBES MODERN CONCEPT OF TAX-FREE PUBLIC BONDS AND ANALYZES THEIR INVESTMENT CHARACTERISTICS. DISCUSSES EARLY ATTEMPTS AT ISSUANCE AND LEGAL PROBLEMS, SAFETY RECORD, AND TAX ADVANTAGES FOR PRIVATE INDIVIDUAL AND CORPORATIONS. COMPARES TO OTHER FORMS OF INVESTMENT.

0588 DAVIS F.M.
COME AS A CONQUEROR: THE UNITED STATES ARMY'S OCCUPATION OF GERMANY: 1945-1949.
NEW YORK: MACMILLAN, 1967, 271 PP., LC#67-10682.
CAREER ARMY OFFICER CHRONICLES US OCCUPATION OF GERMANY. DISCUSSES THE LACK OF UNDERSTANDING BETWEEN GOVERNMENT OFFICIALS AND THE MILITARY IN PLANNING OCCUPATION. EXAMINES EVENTS LEADING TO US'S ALLOWING RUSSIANS FIRST INTO BERLIN, AND SUPPORTING FOUR-PART DIVISION OF GERMANY. EXPLORES BLACK MARKET OPERATIONS AND CONTROLS. STUDIES SOCIO-POLITICAL AND PHYSICAL REBUILDING OF WEST GERMANY BY PEACETIME ARMY.

0589 DAVIS H.B.
NATIONALISM AND SOCIALISM: MARXIST AND LABOR THEORIES OF NATIONALISM TO 1917.
NEW YORK: MONTHLY REVIEW PR, 1967, 258 PP., LC#67-19255.
STUDY IN HISTORY OF MARXIST IDEAS,AND THEIR RELATIONSHIP TO SOCIETY FROM WHICH THEY CAME. EMPHASIS ON FORMULATION OF NEW THEORY OF NATIONALISM WITH DISCUSSION OF THEORIES OF MARX, ENGELS, BAKUNIN, LASSALLE, AND BAUER. DEVELOPMENT OF MARXIST NATIONALISM ON BROAD SCOPE IS DEPICTED FOR EASTERN EUROPE, WESTERN EUROPE, AND US.

0590 DAVIS J., CAMPBELL T.M., WRONG M.
AFRICA ADVANCING.
NEW YORK: FRIENDSHIP PRESS, 1945, 230 PP.
EVALUATION OF RURAL EDUCATION AND AGRICULTURE PROGRAMS IN WEST AFRICA AND BELGIAN CONGO. FOCUSES ON WORK BEING DONE BY VARIOUS AMERICAN AND EUROPEAN MISSIONARY ORGANIZATIONS.

0591 DAVIS K., BLOMSTROM R.L.
BUSINESS AND ITS ENVIRONMENT.
NEW YORK: MCGRAW HILL, 1966, 403 PP., LC#65-28234.
BUSINESS CULTURE AS A DYNAMIC SOCIAL SYSTEM. INTEGRATION OF ALL POINTS OF VIEW FROM MANY DISCIPLINES TO GIVE OVER-ALL PICTURE. PRO-BUSINESS, BUT RETAINS ACADEMIC INTEGRITY. HISTORICAL BACKGROUND SUPPLEMENTED BY DISCUSSIONS OF CURRENT ISSUES, RELATIONSHIPS TO OTHER SUBGROUPS OF SOCIETY, AND ACTUAL CASES OF BUSINESS PRACTICE. WRITTEN AS A TEXTBOOK FOR STUDENTS.

0592 DAVIS O.A., DEMPSTER M.A.H., WILDAVSKY A.

"A THEORY OF THE BUDGETARY PROCESS."
AM. POL. SCI. REV., 60 (SEPT. 66), 529-547.
ANALYTICAL SUMMARY OF NONDEFENSE FEDERAL AGENCY BUDGETS YIELDS THEORY THAT BUDGETARY PROCESS CAN BE REPRESENTED BY SIMPLE MODELS THAT ARE TEMPORARILY STABLE, LINEAR, AND STOCHASTIC. PROPOSES ALTERNATIVE SPECIFICATIONS FOR AGENCY: BUDGET BUREAU AND CONGRESSIONAL DECISION EQUATIONS. PRESENTS EMPIRICAL RESULTS AND EVIDENCE ON DEVIANT CASES. CONSIDERS PREDICTIONS AND PROBLEMS OF THIS FORM OF ANALYSIS.

0593 DAVIS O.A., WHINSTON A.B.
"ON THE DISTINCTION BETWEEN PUBLIC AND PRIVATE GOODS."
AMER. ECO. REVIEW, 57 (MAY 67), 360-373.
A CRITIQUE OF SAMUELSON'S POLAR DISTINCTION BETWEEN PUBLIC AND PRIVATE GOODS. CONTRASTS TO MINASIAN AND CONTROVERSY OVER SUBSCRIPTION TELEVISION. DISCUSSES INSTITUTIONAL ARRANGEMENTS, CONDITIONS FOR OPERATION OF A MARKET, MARKET ALLOCATION OF PUBLIC GOODS, AND HOW TO ASSIGN WHICH GOODS AS GOVERNMENTAL GOODS.

0594 DAY A.C.L.
OUTLINE OF MONETARY ECONOMICS.
LONDON: OXFORD U PR, 1957, 543 PP.
PROVIDES SYSTEMATIC PRESENTATION OF CONTEMPORARY MONETARY ECONOMICS. INCLUDES MACRO-ECONOMICS AS WELL AS MONETARY EVENTS AND INSTITUTIONS. DISCUSSES ECONOMIC SIGNIFICANCE OF MONEY, A SIMPLE MONETARY ECONOMICS MODEL, AND REASONS FOR HOLDING MONEY. INCLUDES INCOME, GOVERNMENT CONTROL, PRICE CHANGES, AND STABILITY.

0595 DE BARY W.T. ED., EMBREE A.T. ED.
APPROACHES TO ASIAN CIVILIZATIONS.
NEW YORK: COLUMBIA U PRESS, 1964, 293 PP., LC#63-20226.
PAPERS BY EXPERTS IN HISTORY, ECONOMICS, POLITICS, SOCIOLOGY, AND ANTHROPOLOGY EXPLAINING IMPORTANCE OF INDIAN, ISLAMIC, CHINESE, AND JAPANESE STUDIES IN THEIR DISCIPLINES. ADVOCATE ASIAN STUDIES IN LIBERAL ARTS EDUCATION, AND EXAMINE POSSIBLE ORGANIZATION OF COURSES IN ASIAN STUDIES.

0596 DE BLOCH J.
THE FUTURE OF WAR IN ITS TECHNICAL, ECONOMIC, AND POLITICAL RELATIONS (1899)
BOSTON: WORLD PEACE FOUNDATION, 1914, 380 PP.
SUMMARY FOR POPULAR USE OF ORIGINAL RUSSIAN AND FRENCH EDITIONS. THESIS IS THAT WAR IN EUROPE IS IMPOSSIBLE. THIS ASSUMPTION IS BASED ON THE FACT THAT THE INCREASED FIREPOWER AND ACCURACY OF RIFLES AND ARTILLERY WILL MEAN SUICIDE TO ANY ATTACKING ARMY. ALSO ARGUES THAT MODERN WAR WOULD BE SO COSTLY AS TO BANKRUPT ANY NATION. CONCLUDES THAT NATIONS WILL AVOID WAR.

0597 DE FOREST J.D.
"LOW LEVELS OF TECHNOLOGY AND ECONOMIC DEVELOPMENT PROSPECTS."
SOC. SCI., 38 (JUNE 63), 131-139.
DISCUSSES ROLE OF TECHNIQUE AND LEVEL OF PRODUCTIVE ARTS AS OBSTACLES TO ECONOMIC PROGRESS IN THE 'POOR' WORLD. CITES PROBLEMS OF TECHNOLOGICAL INNOVATION AS THEY RELATE TO GENERAL FACTORS. STRESSES THE VALUE OF LOCAL APPLIED RESEARCH ACTIVITY AS MEANS OF RAISING PRODUCTIVITY.

0598 DE GRAZIA A., GURR T.
AMERICAN WELFARE.
NEW YORK: NEW YORK U PR, 1961, 470 PP., LC#60-14432.
ASKS WHO GIVES WHAT, TO WHOM, BY WHAT MEANS, AND WITH WHAT EFFECT? DESCRIBES TYPES OF WELFARE ORGANIZATIONS IN NEIGHBORHOOD, COMMUNITY, STATE-WIDE AND NATION-WIDE. INCLUDES CHURCHES, BUSINESS, FOUNDATIONS, GOVERNMENTS -T VARIOUS LEVELS, FRATERNAL AND SERVICE ORGANIZATIONS, AND THEIR ACTIVITIES WITH EXPENDITURES. ALSO SHOWS AMOUNTS SPENT ON WELFARE PER MEMBER.

0599 DE GRAZIA S.
OF TIME, WORK, AND LEISURE.
NEW YORK: TWENTIETH CENT FUND, 1962, 559 PP.
ANALYZES LEISURE FROM 20TH-CENTURY AMERICAN VIEWPOINT. INCLUDES THE HISTORICAL CONTEXT FOR LEISURE; THE USE AND MISUSE OF TIME IN SOCIETY; AND THE GROWTH, POTENTIAL, AND DISADVANTAGES OF LEISURE IN US CULTURE. CONCLUDES WITH AN EXAMINATION OF PROBLEMS CONCERNING LEISURE: WORK WILL NOT BE POSSIBLE FOR ALL; IDEAS, BEAUTY, ART, PEACE CALL PEOPLE OPENLY TO FACE THE FUTURE OF LEISURE.

0600 DE JOUVENEL B.
THE ART OF CONJECTURE.
NEW YORK: BASIC BOOKS, 1967, 307 PP., LC#67-12649.
CONCERNS METHODS OF PREDICTING FUTURE SOCIAL, POLITICAL, AND ECONOMIC DEVELOPMENTS WITH ACCURACY. INCLUDES HISTORICAL AND SCIENTIFIC FORECASTING. OUTLINES WAYS OF CONCEIVING FUTURE, RELATION OF FUTURE TO PAST AND PRESENT, AND TERMINOLOGY. CONSIDERS RELATION OF CONJECTURE TO MAKING DECISIONS, PRINCIPLE OF UNCERTAINTY, FORECASTING OF IDEAS, AND PRAGMATISM OF CONJECTURE AND CONSEQUENCES.

0601 DE JOUVENEL B.
PROBLEMS OF SOCIALIST ENGLAND.
LONDON: BATCHWORTH PRESS, LTD, 1949, 221 PP.
AUTHOR SURVEYS ENGLAND IN THE IMMEDIATE POST-WAR PERIOD. HE FINDS THAT ENGLAND'S GREATEST PSYCHOLOGICAL ASSET IS THAT SHE HAS NOT EXPERIENCED FOREIGN OCCUPATION. BUT HE FINDS CONFUSION OVER THE FACT THAT ENGLAND STANDS ALONE BETWEEN THE US AND USSR. HE FEELS THAT THE LABOR GOVERNMENT IS APPLYING 19TH-CENTURY PRINCIPLES WITH 1930 TACTICS IN THE POSTWAR PERIOD. DISCUSSES BALANCE OF PAYMENTS DEFICIT.

0602 DE JOUVENEL B.
THE ETHICS OF REDISTRIBUTION.
NEW YORK: CAMBRIDGE U PRESS, 1952, 246 PP.
ATTACKS REDISTRIBUTION OF INCOME BY MEANS OF GRADUATED INCOME TAX. INEQUALITIES OF DISTRIBUTION ARE RELATED TO PSYCHOLOGICAL NEED OF MASSES TO ELEVATE SPECIAL PERSONS TO POSITIONS OF ADVANTAGE. DECLARES THAT ILL FEELING TOWARD BRITISH UPPER CLASSES IS DUE TO THEIR NO LONGER BEING CONSIDERED SUPERIOR BY MASSES.

0603 DE LAVALLE H.
A STATEMENT OF THE LAWS OF PERU IN MATTERS AFFECTING BUSINESS (3RD ED.)
WASHINGTON: PAN AMERICAN UNION, 1962, 234 PP.
SURVEY OF BASIC PERUVIAN LAW EMPHASIZING COMMERCIAL, INDUSTRIAL, AND LABOR LAW. EXAMINES STATUS OF FOREIGNERS AND THEIR INVESTMENTS AND NATURE OF CONTRACTS.

0604 DE MAN H.
THE PSYCHOLOGY OF SOCIALISM.
NEW YORK: HENRY HOLT & CO, 1928, 509 PP.
AUTHOR DISCUSSES THE PSYCHOLOGY OF THE WORKING CLASSES. HE FINDS THAT, ABOVE ALL, PEOPLE WANT DECENT LIVING CONDITIONS AND ARE GENERALLY LOYAL TO THE STATE. FOR THIS REASON HE REJECTS MARXISM AS PRACTICED IN RUSSIA, BECAUSE IT IS TOO CONCERNED WITH THEORY AND WILL SACRIFICE THE PEOPLE FOR THEORY. HE FEELS THAT SOCIAL DEMOCRACY IS MORE SOCIALLY AKIN TO THE WORKING-CLASS PSYCHOLOGY THAN MARXISM.

0605 DE MAN H.
JOY IN WORK.
NEW YORK: HENRY HOLT & CO, 1929, 224 PP.
AUTHOR EXAMINES FACTORS BY WHICH MEN ENJOY THEIR WORK IN A FACTORY SYSTEM. HE FINDS THE CHIEF ONES TO BE THE INSTINCT FOR WORK AND THE PRIDE A PERSON TAKES IN DOING A GOOD JOB. THE CHIEF OBSTACLES ARE LOW WAGES AND MONOTONY. AUTHOR FEELS THAT IF EMPLOYERS MADE WORKING CONDITIONS AS PLEASANT AS POSSIBLE AND GAVE GOOD WAGES, THEY COULD OBTAIN THE LOYALTY OF THEIR WORKERS AND THUS INCREASE PRODUCTION.

0606 DE TORRES J.
FINANCING LOCAL GOVERNMENT.
NEW YORK: NATL IND CONF BD, 1967, 146 PP.
REVIEWS IMPORTANT LOCAL GOVERNMENT EXPENDITURES, WITH EMPHASIS ON FORCES THAT HAVE SHAPED THEIR GROWTH DURING 20TH CENTURY. ANALYZES PROPERTY AND NONPROPERTY TAXES, SERVICE CHARGES, AND STATE AND FEDERAL "GRANTS-IN-AID" IN TERMS OF THEIR IMPACT ON LOCAL AUTONOMY. DISCUSSES PROBLEMS OF UNBALANCED COMMUNITIES AND DELAYING CITIES. REVEALS NEW ISSUES IN LOCAL FINANCES.

0607 DE VRIES E.
MAN IN RAPID SOCIAL CHANGE.
GARDEN CITY: DOUBLEDAY, 1961, 240 PP., LC#61-16774.
DISCUSSES IMPACT OF RAPID SOCIAL CHANGE IN MODERN TIMES ON VARIOUS SOCIETIES AND NATIONS. TREATS THE PHENOMENON OF CHANGE AND SPECIFIC ISSUES SUCH AS FAMILY LIFE, EDUCATION, AND RURAL DEVELOPMENT, AND THE CHALLENGE, ESPECIALLY TO CHRISTIANS, OF SUCH RAPID CHANGE.

0608 DE VRIES E. ED., ECHAVARRIA J.M. ED.
SOCIAL ASPECTS OF ECONOMIC DEVELOPMENT IN LATIN AMERICA.
PARIS: UNESCO, 1963, 401 PP., $5.00.
A COLLECTION OF PAPERS SUBMITTED TO EXPERT WORKING GROUP ON SOCIAL ASPECTS OF ECONOMIC DEVELOPMENT IN LATIN AMERICA IN DECEMBER 1960. VARIOUS SPECIALISTS IN ECONOMICS, SOCIOLOGY, POLITICAL SCIENCE, SOCIAL PSYCHOLOGY, AND PUBLIC ADMINISTRATION OFFER A MORE BALANCED VIEW OF ECONOMIC DEVELOPMENT PROBLEMS IN LATIN AMERICA.

0609 DEALEY S.
"MONETARY RECOVERY UNDER FEDERAL TRANSPORTATION STATUTES."
TEXAS LAW REVIEW, 45 (APR. 67), 984-1014.
ANALYZES IN DETAIL THREE STATUTES THAT PROVIDE FOR RECOVERY OF DAMAGES FOR PERSONAL INJURIES OR DEATH: FEDERAL EMPLOYEES LIABILITY ACT FOR RAILROAD WORKERS, JONES ACT FOR SEAMEN, AND DEATH ON HIGH SEAS ACT. DISCUSSES ASPECTS OF EACH ACT PERTAINING TO DETERMINATION OF INJURY, AMOUNT OF RECOVERY, AND SPECIAL CASES OF LOSS OF EARNING ABILITY.

0610 DEANE H.
THE WAR IN VIETNAM (PAMPHLET)
NEW YORK: MONTHLY REVIEW PR, 1963, 32 PP., LC#63-19862.
ANALYZES WAR IN VIETNAM SINCE 1954, SHOWING HOW US IS TRYING ONLY TO PROTECT ITS ECONOMIC INTERESTS AND RETAIN "FEUDAL REGIME" IN SOUTH. COMPARES US TACTICS TO NAZIS'.

STRESSES THAT ALL US SEEKS TO DO IS STOP COMMUNISM, OR ANY FORM OF SOCIALISM THAT THREATENS CAPITALISM, AT ANY PRICE. REFERS TO AVAILABLE DOCUMENTATION.

0611 DEBENKO E., KRISHNAN V.N.
RESEARCH SOURCES FOR SOUTH ASIAN STUDIES IN ECONOMIC DEVELOPMENT: A SELECT BIBLIOGRAPHY OF SERIAL PUBLICATIONS.
E LANSING: ASIAN STUD CTR, MSU, 1966, 97 PP., LC#66-63953.
BIBLIOGRAPHICAL LISTING OF PERIODICALS, MONOGRAPHS IN SERIES, PERIODICAL GOVERNMENT DOCUMENTS, AND ANNUALS ON NEPAL, INDIA, PAKISTAN, AND CEYLON. TREATS PLANNING, POLICIES, AND PROCESSES. INCLUDES POLITICAL SCIENCE AND RELATED AREAS. ENGLISH-LANGUAGE PUBLICATIONS. OVER 1,000 ENTRIES. (ASIAN STUDIES CENTER OCCASIONAL PAPER NO. 4)

0612 DEBUYST F.
LAS CLASES SOCIALES EN AMERICA LATINA.
MADRID: OFIC INVESTIG SOC FRERES, 1962, 217 PP.
EXAMINES PRESENT SOCIAL STRUCTURE OF COUNTRIES OF LATIN AMERICA. ANALYZES SOCIAL MOBILITY, ECONOMIC POWER, ETHNIC COMPOSITION, INCOME, AND EDUCATIONAL OPPORTUNITIES. COMPARES AND GROUPS COUNTRIES ACCORDING TO CHANCES FOR SOCIAL MOBILITY AND WORK.

0613 DELEFORTRIE-SOU N.
LES DIRIGEANTS DE L'INDUSTRIE FRANCAISE.
PARIS: COLIN (LIB ARMAND), 1961, 280 PP.
STUDY OF THE DIRECTORS OF FRENCH INDUSTRIES. ATTEMPTS TO ASSESS THEIR COMMON CHARACTERISTICS IN ORDER TO SITUATE THEM IN FRENCH SOCIETY. AUTHOR BELIEVES THAT BY ESTABLISHING CHARACTERISTICS OF LEADERS, REFORMS CAN BE MADE IN INDUSTRY.

0614 DELHI INSTITUTE OF ECO GROWTH
A STUDY IN THE WORKING OF THE INTENSIVE AREA SCHEME OF THE KHADI AND VILLAGE INDUSTRIES COMMISSION.
BOMBAY: KHADIAND VILL IND COMN, 1965, 332 PP.
EVALUATES INTENSIVE AREA SCHEME OF KHADI AND VILLAGE INDUSTRIES COMMISSION, INCLUDING BACKGROUND, PROGRESS, AIMS OF SCHEME, ITS ACTIVITIES IN 34 AREAS, AND ECONOMICS OF VILLAGE INDUSTRIES. EXAMINES WORKING OF VILLAGE PLANS IN EIGHT SPECIFIC AREAS, WORKING OF COOPERATIVE FARMS, CREDIT AND SERVICE SOCIETIES, INDUSTRY AND HOUSING, AND RECOMMENDATIONS FOR MORE EFFICIENT PROGRAM.

0615 DELL S.
TRADE BLOCS AND COMMON MARKETS.
NEW YORK: ALFRED KNOPF, 1963, 384 PP., LC#63-14165.
EXAMINES RECENT TRENDS TOWARD COMMON MARKETS THROUGHOUT WORLD. SHOWS THEIR RELATIONSHIP TO MAIN CONTEMPORARY ISSUES IN INTERNATIONAL ECONOMIC RELATIONS. EMPHASIZES ASPECTS OF PAST WHICH AFFORD POINTS OF COMPARISONS AND CONTRASTS WITH COMMON MARKET DEVELOPMENTS WHICH PREOCCUPY WORLD TODAY.

0616 DELLA PORT G.
"PROBLEMI E PROSPETTIVE DI COESISTENZA FRA ORIENTE ED OCCIDENTE, (PART 3)."
COMUN. INT., 16 (JULY 61), 503-26.
EFFECTS OF EAST-WEST RELATIONS ON UNCOMMITTED COUNTRIES. PROBLEMS OF INTERNATIONAL PAYMENTS, PRICES, FOREIGN AID TECHNIQUES.

0617 DELWERT J.
"L'ECONOMIE CAMBODGIENNE ET SON EVOLUTION ACTUELLE."
TIERS-MONDE, 4 (NOS.13-14, 63), 193-212.
POINTS OUT ECONOMIC WEAKNESSES OF CAMBODIA AND ITS INADEQUATE FINANCIAL POWER. REVIEWS RECENT SOCIO-ECONOMIC DEVELOPMENTS. MAKES RECOMMENDATIONS FOR IMPROVEMENT.

0618 DEMAS W.G.
THE ECONOMICS OF DEVELOPMENT IN SMALL COUNTRIES WITH SPECIAL REFERENCE TO THE CARIBBEAN.
MONTREAL: MCGILL U PR, 1965, 150 PP., LC#65-26563.
PROBES NATURE OF ECONOMIC GROWTH IN SMALL COUNTRIES, DISTINGUISHING ITS PROBLEMS FROM THOSE OF LARGER DEVELOPING NATIONS. COVERS SELF-SUSTAINED GROWTH IN UNDERDEVELOPED AREAS. DISCUSSES SPECIFIC SITUATION OF CARIBBEAN ECONOMIES CONCERNING THEIR SPECIAL CHARACTERISTICS AND PROBLEMS IN PLANNING.

0619 DEMUTH J.
"GE: PROFILE OF A CORPORATION."
DISSENT, 14 (JULY 67), 502-512.
INVESTIGATES GENERAL ELECTRIC'S PRICE-FIXING ACTIVITIES; LAW SUITS BY OTHER INDUSTRIES AGAINST GE; RONALD REAGAN AND HIS PROMOTION OF GE THEATER AND GENERAL ELECTRIC; GE'S TIES WITH HARDING COLLEGE, NAZISM, AND MCCARTHY. DISCUSSES TRUST BUILD-UP AND DEALINGS WITH UNIONS.

0620 DENISON E.F.
THE SOURCES OF ECONOMIC GROWTH IN THE UNITED STATES AND THE ALTERNATIVES BEFORE US.
NEW YORK: COMM FOR ECO DEV, 1962, 297 PP., LC#61-18717.
GIVES QUANTITATIVE APPRAISALS OF SOURCES OF ECONOMIC GROWTH IN THE US. FACTORS ANALYZED INCLUDE LAND, LABOR, CAPITAL INVESTMENT, EDUCATION, AND TECHNOLOGICAL ADVANCE. ATTEMPTS QUANTITATIVELY TO EVALUATE IMPORT OF EACH FOR FUTURE ECONOMIC GROWTH.

0621 DERBER M., CHALMERS W.E. ET AL.
PLANT UNION-MANAGEMENT RELATIONS: FROM PRACTICE TO THEORY.
URBANA: U ILLINOIS INST LABOR, 1965, 179 PP., LC#65-63564.
A SAMPLE OF 37 INDUSTRIAL ESTABLISHMENTS, FAIRLY SMALL AND LOCALLY ORIENTED, IS EXAMINED COMPREHENSIVELY ON SUCH REPRESENTATIONAL ISSUES AS DEPTH OF UNION PARTICIPATION IN DECISION-MAKING, THE USE OF PRESSURE IN GROUP INTERACTION AND ITS RELATIONSHIP TO LEADERSHIP CHANGE.

0622 DETAMBEL M.H., STOLUROW L.M.
"PROBABILITY AND WORK AS DETERMINERS OF MULTICHOICE BEHAVIOR."
J. EDUCATIONAL SOC., 53 (FEB. 57), 73-81.
CONCLUDES THROUGH EXPERIMENTS THAT IN CERTAIN PROBLEM-SOLVING SITUATIONS THE PROBABILITY FOR SUCCESS MORE STRONGLY DETERMINES BEHAVIOR THAN DOES THE AMOUNT OF WORK INVOLVED. SUGGESTS THAT PERSON PERFORMING A TASK DOES NOT NECESSARILY DISCOVER THE MOST EFFICIENT APPROACH.

0623 DETHINE P.
BIBLIOGRAPHIE DES ASPECTS ECONOMIQUES ET SOCIAUX DE L'INDUSTRIALISATION EN AFRIQUE.
BRUSSELS: CEN DOC ECO ET SOC AFR, 1961, 136 PP.
AN ANNOTATED BIBLIOGRAPHY OF 726 ENTRIES COVERING THE ECONOMIC AND SOCIAL FACTORS INVOLVED IN THE INDUSTRIALIZATION OF THE THIRD WORLD. SELECTIONS ARE INTERNATIONAL IN SCOPE AND WERE CHOSEN FROM 1940-60 PUBLICATIONS. ARRANGED IN ONE COMPREHENSIVE ALPHABETICAL LIST.

0624 DEUTSCH K.W., ECKSTEIN A.
"NATIONAL INDUSTRIALIZATION AND THE DECLINING SHARE OF THE INTERNATIONAL ECONOMIC SECTOR."
WORLD POLIT., 13 (JAN. 61), 267-99.
GIVES SOME REASONS THAT RENDER PLAUSIBLE THE THESIS THAT THE RATIO OF FOREIGN TRADE TO NATIONAL INCOME WILL CONTINUE TO DECLINE IN MANY COUNTRIES, AS WELL AS THE WORLD AS A WHOLE, FOR SOME TIME TO COME.

0625 DEUTSCH K.W., RUSSETT B.M.
THE POLITICAL ROLE OF LABOR IN DEVELOPING COUNTRIES.
WASHINGTON: BROOKINGS INSTIT., 1963, 148 PP., $3.50.
ANALYSIS OF LEADERSHIP, MEMBERSHIP, FINANCES AND OPERATING PRACTICES OF LABOR UNIONS IN ASIA AND AFRICA. SHOWS THAT U.S. POLICY CAN NO LONGER CONTINUE TO CONSIDER THESE UNIONS AS SIMILAR TO AMERICAN UNIONS. DESCRIBES THE NATURE OF THE NEW 'POLITICAL UNIONISM' IN THE DEVELOPING NATIONS.

0626 DEUTSCHE BUCHEREI
DEUTSCHES BUCHERVERZEICHNIS.
LEIPZIG: VEB VERL FUR BUCH-BIBL.
ANNUAL LISTING OF PRIMARY PUBLICATIONS IN BOTH EAST AND WEST GERMANY. ENTRIES ARRANGE ALPHABETICALLY BY AUTHOR WITH A SUBJECT INDEX. FIRST PUBLISHED 1911.

0627 DEWHURST A.
"THE WAGE MOVEMENT IN CANADA."
WORLD MARXIST REV., 10 (FEB. 67), 15-20.
DISCUSSES REASONS FOR GREATER NUMBER OF STRIKES AFFECTING MORE WORKERS AND INDUSTRIES IN CANADA IN SUMMER OF 1966. POINTS TO RISE IN COST OF LIVING AND IN PROFITS AND PRODUCTIVITY. IN ADDITION TO WAGE DEMANDS, WORKERS ARE SEEKING THE RIGHT OF A WORKER TO HIS JOB, THE RIGHT OF COLLECTIVE BARGAINING, AND RIGHT TO PICKET WITHOUT GOVERNMENT INTERFERENCE BY INJUNCTION.

0629 DEWITT N.
EDUCATION AND PROFESSIONAL EMPLOYMENT IN THE USSR.
WASHINGTON: NATL SCIENCE FDN, 1961, 856 PP.
FACTUAL STUDY OF SOVIET EDUCATIONAL SYSTEM. DESCRIBES PRIMARY AND SECONDARY GENERAL EDUCATION, AND SECONDARY SPECIALIZED, VOCATIONAL, AND SEMI-PROFESSIONAL EDUCATION. STUDIES SYSTEMS OF HIGHER PROFESSIONAL TRAINING AND OF ADVANCED DEGREES, AND SOVIET RESEARCH AND ACADEMIC PERSONNEL. SHOWS HOW USSR EMPLOYS ITS SPECIALIZED AND PROFESSIONAL MANPOWER.

0630 DEYRUP F.J.
"SOCIAL MOBILITY AS A MAJOR FACTOR IN ECONOMIC DEVELOPMENT."
SOCIAL RESEARCH, 34 (SUMMER 67),333-346.
NOTES THAT MOST CONSPICUOUS EXAMPLES OF FULL INDUSTRIALIZATION HAVE OCCURRED IN COUNTRIES WITH HIGH SOCIAL MOBILITY IN LARGE PART OF POPULATION. DISCUSSES SPECIFIC FACTORS ARISING FROM MOBILITY WHICH PROMOTE ECONOMIC DEVELOPMENT. MARSHALS HISTORICAL EVIDENCE TO SUPPORT THEORY. DISCUSSES IMPLICATIONS FOR UNDERDEVELOPED NATIONS.

0631 DIA M.
REFLEXIONS SUR L'ECONOMIE DE L'AFRIQUE NOIRE (REV. ED.)
PARIS: PRESENCE AFRIQUE, 1960, 210 PP.
PROVIDES INSIGHTS INTO DECOLONIZATION AND THE REBUILDING OF A DISTINCTLY AFRICAN ECONOMY. ADVISES HOW A BALANCED,

ORDERED, AND MODERN ECONOMY CAN BE FORGED ALONG SOCIALIST LINES. OUTLINES CONCEPTS, OBJECTIVES, AND MEANS FOR PLANNING AND DEVELOPING AFRICA'S CULTURAL, SOCIAL, AND ECONOMIC HERITAGE AND FOR INTEGRATING IT WITH GLOBAL ECONOMICS. CITES EVIDENCE AND GIVES DATA SUPPORTING THESE THESES.

0632 DICKINSON H.D.
INSTITUTIONAL REVENUE: A STUDY OF THE INFLUENCE OF SOCIAL INSTITUTIONS ON THE DISTRIBUTION OF WEALTH.
LONDON: WILLIAMS & VORGATE, LTD, 1932, 264 PP.
ATTEMPTS TO COMBINE ANALYTICAL METHOD OF MODERN MARGINAL SCHOOL WITH HISTORICAL ECONOMIST'S RECOGNITION OF EXISTENCE AND INFLUENCE OF SOCIAL INSTITUTIONS. CONTAINS OUTLINE OF THEORY OF DISTRIBUTION THAT DEMONSTRATES INFLUENCE OF SOCIAL INSTITUTIONS. ARGUES THAT THEORY OF MARGINAL VALUATION IS COMPATIBLE WITH VIEW OF DISTRIBUTION THAT TAKES INTO ACCOUNT PART PLAYED BY SOCIAL FRAMEWORK.

0633 DICKMAN A.B.
"SOUTH AFRICAN MONEY MARKET - PROGRESS AND PROBLEMS SINCE 1960."
S. AFR. J. OF ECONOMICS, 33 (SEPT. 65), 213-236.
DISCUSSION OF MONETARY SYSTEM, ITS INSTITUTIONAL GROWTH, CONTRIBUTION TO SHORT-TERM LOAN SYSTEM, AND PLACE IN COMPETITION OF MARKET. ALSO INCLUDES FUTURE OF MONETARY POLICY; ITS PROBLEMS AND SOLUTIONS DISCUSSED IN FOUR TIME PERIODS. SUGGESTS THAT ADJUSTMENTS BE MADE TO PLACE EMPHASIS ON LONG-RUN CAPACITY.

0634 DICKS-MIREAUX L.A.
"THE INTERRELATIONSHIP BETWEEN COST AND PRICE CHANGES 1946-1959: A STUDY OF INFLATION IN POST-WAR BRITAIN"
OXFORD ECONOMIC PAPERS, 13 (OCT. 61), 267-292.
CONCERNED WITH CHANGES IN GENERAL LEVEL OF WAGES AND PRICES. ATTEMPTS TO EXPLAIN, USING REGRESSION TECHNIQUES, WAY IN WHICH THEY WERE INFLUENCED BY PRESSURE OF DEMAND FOR LABOR AND CHANGES IN IMPORT PRICES. DESCRIBES MUTUAL REACTION OF PRICES ON WAGES AND OF WAGES ON PRICES.

0635 DIEBOLD W. JR.
THE SCHUMAN PLAN: A STUDY IN ECONOMIC COOPERATION, 1950-1959.
NEW YORK: PRAEGER, 1959, 750 PP.
RECOUNTS THE ORIGINS OF THE SCHUMAN PLAN AND EVENTS WHICH LED TO FORMATION OF THE EUROPEAN COAL AND STEEL COMMUNITY. CONSIDERS THE COMMUNITY'S OPERATIONS, DEVELOPMENTS, PROSPECTS, AND IMPLICATIONS FOR AMERICAN FOREIGN POLICY. DISCUSSES ITS RELATION TO PROSPECT OF EUROPEAN INTEGRATION.

0636 DIEBOLD W. JR.
"THE NEW SITUATION OF INTERNATIONAL TRADE POLICY."
INT. J., 18 (AUTUMN 63', 425-42.
CONSIDERS TRADE RELATIONS AMONG EUROPEAN COUNTRIES. EXAMINES COMMON MARKET AND ITS CHANGING DIRECTION AND TRADE EXPANSION ACT OF THE USA. COMMENTS ON COMMERCIAL QUESTIONS AND TRANSATLANTIC RELATIONS. SUGGESTS EQUAL TREATMENT OF ALL NATIONS IS THE ANSWER TO ECONOMIC BETTERMENT OF FREE WORLD.

0637 DIEGUES M. ED., WOOD B. ED.
SOCIAL SCIENCE IN LATIN AMERICA.
NEW YORK: COLUMBIA U PRESS, 1967, 335 PP., LC#67-15255.
ANTHOLOGY OF PAPERS PRESENTED AT CONFERENCE ON LATIN AMERICAN STUDIES, MARCH, 1965. EXAMINES STATE OF SOCIAL SCIENCE RESEARCH AND INSTRUCTION IN ECONOMICS, HISTORY, POLITICAL SCIENCE, SOCIOLOGY, ANTHROPOLOGY, AND LAW IN LATIN AMERICA.

0638 DIESING P.
"NONECONOMIC DECISION-MAKING" (BMR)"
ETHICS, 66 (OCT. 55), 18-35.
EXAMINES ECONOMIC MODEL OF DECISION-MAKING AND OFFERS ALTERNATIVE METHOD PURPOSELY CENTERED ON NONECONOMIC FACTORS OF SOCIAL LIFE. STUDIES GENERAL CHARACTERISTICS, PROBLEMS AND POSSIBILITIES, PRINCIPLES, AND LIMITATIONS OF PROPOSED METHOD.

0639 DILLEY M.R.
BRITISH POLICY IN KENYA COLONY (2ND ED.)
NEW YORK: BARNES AND NOBLE, 1966, 300 PP.
TREATS BRITISH COLONIAL POLICY IN KENYA FROM 1900-1965. PROVIDES BACKGROUND INFORMATION ON REGION AND PRESENTS DEVELOPMENT OF EUROPEAN COLONY AND ATTEMPTS BY COLONISTS TO GAIN ELECTIVE REPRESENTATION IN PARLIAMENT, HOME-RULE, AND FINANCIAL CONTROL. EXAMINES RELATIONS WITH INDIAN SETTLERS AND STUDIES PROBLEMS OF TRUSTEESHIPS, LAND, LABOR, AND TAXES.

0640 DIMOCK M.E.
FREE ENTERPRISE AND THE ADMINISTRATIVE STATE.
UNIVERSITY: U ALABAMA PR, 1951, 179 PP.
EXAMINES SYSTEM OF FREE ENTERPRISE FROM STANDPOINT OF INSTITUTIONS, THEIR ORGANIZATION AND FUNCTION. DISCUSSES ASPECTS OF MANAGEMENT, MONOPOLY, AND DECENTRALIZATION. MAINTAINS THAT DECENTRALIZATION IS NECESSARY TO PRESERVE SYSTEM.

0641 DIMOCK M.E.
BUSINESS AND GOVERNMENT (4TH ED.)
NEW YORK: HOLT RINEHART WINSTON, 1961, 505 PP., LC#61-7854.
ORIGINAL ANALYSIS OF WORKING RELATIONS BETWEEN ECONOMIC ORGANIZATIONS AND GOVERNMENT, SUPPLEMENTED BY CONSIDERATIONS OF NEW LABOR LEGISLATION; RECESSIONS; FOREIGN AID PROGRAMS; COMMUNIST BLOC EXPENDITURES; SPACE PROGRAM; FARM POLICIES; ANTI-TRUST ENFORCEMENT; PUBLIC UTILITY REGULATION AND PUBLIC POWER PROJECTS. SUGGESTIONS FOR SUPPLEMENTARY READINGS FOLLOW EACH CHAPTER.

0642 DIMOCK M.E.
THE NEW AMERICAN POLITICAL ECONOMY: A SYNTHESIS OF POLITICS AND ECONOMICS.
NEW YORK: HARPER & ROW, 1962, 306 PP., LC#62-7315.
BUSINESS AND GOVERNMENT MUST WORK TOGETHER IF MEN'S BASIC ASPIRATIONS ARE TO BE REACHED; POLICY MUST BE MADE BY BOTH PRIVATE AND PUBLIC GROUPS; BUSINESS WILL NOT THRIVE UNLESS GOVERNMENT IS ENTERPRISING; VALUES AND MORAL PHILOSOPHY ARE VERY IMPORTANT. ON THESE ASSUMPTIONS AUTHOR PROPOSES MASSIVE DECENTRALIZATION OF FEDERAL FUNCTIONS THAT COULD BE TURNED BACK TO STATE AND LOCAL OR VOLUNTARY GROUPS.

0643 DINERSTEIN H.S.
INTERVENTION AGAINST COMMUNISM (STUDIES IN INTERNATIONAL AFFAIRS NO. 1)
BALTIMORE: JOHNS HOPKINS PRESS, 1967, 53 PP., LC#67-18562.
HISTORICAL-ANALYTICAL EXAMINATION OF US INTERVENTION AGAINST COMMUNISM. GLOBAL AND DOMESTIC ISSUES CONTRIBUTING TO DEVELOPMENT OF AMERICAN POLICY ARE CONSIDERED AND SUCCESS OF THAT POLICY ASSESSED. FINDINGS INDICATE INTERVENTION DOES NOT CHECK SPREAD OF COMMUNISM, BUT INCREASES IT, DUE MAINLY TO ITS DIRECTION AGAINST NATIONAL ASPIRATIONS. AUTHOR PROPOSES GUIDELINES TO CORRECT NATURE OF SUCH INTERVENTION.

0644 DIXON W.
SOCIETY, SCHOOLS AND PROGRESS IN SCANDINAVIA.
NEW YORK: PERGAMON PRESS, 1967, 206 PP.
DESCRIBES EDUCATIONAL SYSTEMS OF NORWAY, DENMARK, AND SWEDEN SET AGAINST SOCIAL, ECONOMIC, AND POLITICAL BACKGROUNDS. DISCUSSES EFFECT OF CHANGES IN SCANDINAVIAN SOCIETY ON EDUCATION AND AIMS OF EDUCATIONAL SYSTEM.

0646 DOBB M.
CAPITALISM YESTERDAY AND TODAY.
NEW YORK: MONTHLY REVIEW PR, 1962, 89 PP., LC#62-13649.
DESCRIBES SYSTEM OF CAPITALISM AND PROCESS OUT OF WHICH CAPITALISM DEVELOPED. STUDIES COMPETITION AND MONOPOLY AS ASPECTS OF CAPITALISTIC SYSTEM. EXAMINES FALLING PROFIT-RATE AND LOWER SHARE OF PROFITS BELONGING TO LABOR AS CAPITALISM DEVELOPS. DISCUSSES CRISIS OF "ANARCHY OF PRODUCTION" AND EFFECTS OF WWII ON CAPITALISM.

0647 DOBB M.
SOVIET ECONOMIC DEVELOPMENT SINCE 1917.
NEW YORK: INTERNATIONAL PUBL CO, 1966, 515 PP.
BROAD AND DETAILED HISTORICAL REVIEW OF ECONOMIC DEVELOPMENT IN THE USSR. TREATS VARIOUS FIVE YEAR PLANS,INDUSTRIALIZATION, WAR DEVELOPMENTS, RECENT YEARS, PLANNING SYSTEM, TRADE UNIONS, LABOR CONDITIONS, SOCIAL INSURANCE. EXTENSIVE COVERAGE OF CURRENT SITUATION.

0648 DODD E.M. JR.
"FOR WHOM ARE CORPORATE MANAGERS TRUSTEES'."
HARVARD LAW REV., 45 (MAY 32), 1145-1163.
DISPUTES VIEW THAT BUSINESS CORPORATIONS EXIST FOR THE SOLE PURPOSE OF MAKING PROFITS FOR THEIR STOCKHOLDERS, AND EMPHASIZES SOCIAL SERVICE ROLE, SUCH AS PROVIDING ECONOMIC SECURITY TO WORKERS.

0649 DODDY F.S.
INTRODUCTION TO THE USE OF ECONOMIC INDICATORS.
NEW YORK: RANDOM HOUSE, INC, 1965, 173 PP., LC#64-14897.
EXAMINES TECHNIQUES OF PREPARATION AND USE OF ECONOMIC INDICATORS IN RELATION TO EMPLOYMENT, PRODUCTION, PRICES, AND FINANCE. DISCUSSES ANALYSIS OF INDICATORS AND LONG-TERM PROJECTIONS OF ECONOMIC GROWTH. PROVIDES SAMPLES AND CHARTS.

0650 DOE J.F.
"TROPICAL AFRICAN CONTRIBUTIONS TO FEDERAL FINANCE."
CAN. J. ECON. POLIT. SCI., 30 (FEB. 64), 49-61.
A REVIEW OF THE SOLUTIONS TO THE PROBLEM OF FEDERAL FINANCE ADOPTED BY THREE FEDERAL SYSTEMS IN BRITISH TROPICAL AFRICA. SUGGESTS THAT 'MANY OF THE MAJOR EVILS AND NUISANCE OF THE FISCAL ASPECTS OF FEDERALISM IN OLDER COUNTRIES CAN BE AVOIDED, BUT ONLY BY A MEASURE OF CENTRALIZATION THAT REDUCES THE FISCAL AUTONOMY OF THE TERRITORIES BELOW LEVELS REGARDED AS TOLERABLE.'

0651 DOERFER G.L.
"THE LIMITS ON TRADE SECRET LAW IMPOSED BY FEDERAL PATENT & ANTITRUST SUPREMACY."
HARVARD LAW REV., 80 (MAY 67), 1432-1462.
CONCERNS QUESTION OF COMPATIBILITY OF STATE BUSINESS PRACTICE REGULATORY MEASURES WITH FEDERAL POLICIES EMBODIED IN PATENT & ANTITRUST LAWS. SURVEYS ONE ASPECT OF STATE

MEASURES-TRADE SECRET LAWS. COMPARES PURPOSE OF THIS BODY OF LAW WITH OBJECTIVE OF FEDERAL PATENT & ANTITRUST POLICIES. CAUTIONS AGAINST ANALYSIS OF FEDERAL OBJECTIVES THAT DOES NOT ADEQUATELY WEIGH COMPETING STATE POLICIES.

0652 DOIG J.W.
THE POLITICS OF METROPOLITAN TRANSPORTATION.
PRINCETON: PRIN U, DEPT OF POL, 1961, 518 PP.
UNPUBLISHED THESIS DESCRIBING AND ANALYZING EFFORTS MADE IN NEW YORK CITY AREA TO SOLVE METROPOLITAN PROBLEM OF MASS TRANSPORTATION, WITH SPECIAL ATTENTION TO DEVELOPMENTS DURING YEARS 1954-59. FIRST PART OF STUDY TRACES DEVELOPMENT OF TRANSPORT IN REGION DURING PAST CENTURY, SECOND PART FOCUSES ON WORK OF NY AND NJ METROPOLITAN RAPID TRANSIT COMMISSION, AND CONCLUDES WITH RELEVANCE OF STUDY ELSEWHERE.

0653 DONALD A.G.
MANAGEMENT, INFORMATION, AND SYSTEMS.
NEW YORK: PERGAMON PRESS, 1967, 178 PP.
PROVIDES FRAMEWORK FOR NEW MANAGEMENT TECHNIQUES. OUTLINES CONCEPT OF SYSTEMS, FEEDBACK CONTROL, AND PROBLEMS IN CONTROLLING SYSTEMS. APPLIES CONCEPTS TO BUSINESS ENTERPRISES AND NON-PROFIT MAKING CONCERNS.

0654 DOSSER D.
"TOWARD A THEORY OF INTERNATIONAL PUBLIC FINANCE."
INT. REV. SOC. SCI., 16 (1963), 62-82.
APPLIES NATIONAL PUBLIC FINANCE THEORY TO DEVELOPMENT AID INSTITUTIONS, PARTICULARLY OF THE UN. DISCUSSES ASPECTS OF POLITICAL FEASIBILITY AND ECONOMIC EFFICIENCY.

0655 DOTSON A.
PRODUCTION PLANNING IN THE PATENT OFFICE (PAMPHLET)
INDIANAPOLIS: BOBBS-MERRILL, 1952, 13 PP.
DESCRIBES 1945 TROUBLES OF US PATENT OFFICE REGARDING DISTRIBUTION OF PATENT COPIES TO PUBLIC. ILLUSTRATES USE OF SCIENTIFIC MANAGEMENT TO EXPEDITE GOVERNMENT CLERICAL OPERATION.

0656 DOUGLAS A.
INDUSTRIAL PEACEMAKING.
NEW YORK: COLUMBIA U PRESS, 1962, 675 PP.
DISCUSSES METHODS OF ARBITRATION USED BY PROFESSIONAL MEDIATORS FOR RESOLVING DISPUTES IN INDUSTRY. USES CASE STUDIES OF GOVERNMENT BARGAINING AGENTS, SPECIFICALLY DISCUSSING TACTICS IN CONFERENCE.

0657 DOWD L.P.
PRINCIPLES OF WORLD BUSINESS.
NEW YORK: ALLYN AND BACON, 1965, 573 PP., LC#65-15936.
DISCUSSES SOURCES AND BASES FOR INTERNATIONAL TRADE, PRINCIPLES OF FOREIGN EXCHANGE, GOVERNMENTAL CONTROLS, MANAGEMENT OF INTERNATIONAL BUSINESS (MARKETING RESEARCH, ADVERTISING, FINANCING, ETC., AND EXPORT PROCEDURES.

0658 DOWNIE J.
THE COMPETITIVE PROCESS.
LONDON: DUCKWORTH, 1958, 197 PP.
CLAIMS NEO-CLASSICAL THEORIES OF COMPETITION AND THE FIRM HAVE BEEN OF LITTLE USE IN EITHER ECONOMIC OR JUDICIAL PROBLEM-SOLVING. BLAMING THIS ON THEIR UNYIELDING STAND ON NECESSITY FOR A PURE THEORY, AUTHOR FORMULATES HIS BODY OF THEORY TO BE MORE APPLICABLE IF NOT AS PRECISE. DISCUSSES EQUILIBRIUM IN MARKET ECONOMIES, EFFICIENCY, AND EFFECTS OF MONOPOLIES.

0659 DOWNS A.
AN ECONOMIC THEORY OF DEMOCRACY.
NEW YORK: HARPER & ROW, 1957, 300 PP., LC#57-10571.
ATTEMPTS TO PROVIDE GENERAL BEHAVIOR RULE FOR ROLE OF DEMOCRATIC GOVERNMENT IN FIELD OF ECONOMICS AND TRACE ITS IMPLICATIONS. PROPOSES THAT GOVERNMENTS ACT RATIONALLY TO MAXIMIZE POLITICAL SUPPORT. ECONOMIC THEORY OF GOVERNMENT DECISION-MAKING IN DEMOCRACY.

0660 DRAPER A.P.
"UNIONS AND THE WAR IN VIETNAM."
NEW POLITICS, 5 (1967), 7-12.
EXPOSES THE EFFORT OF MAJOR UNION LEADERS TO UNDERWRITE THE GOVERNMENT VIETNAM POLICY AND TO STIFLE DISSENT. MAINTAINS THAT UNDERLYING OFFICIAL UNION POLICY IS A LARGE PACIFIST ELEMENT WITH NO OUTLET FOR ITS OPINIONS. CALLS FOR THE FORMATION OF A TRADES UNION DIVISION OF SANE AS A UNITED FRONT FOR WORKERS OPPOSED TO WAR. CITES CRITICS OF ESCALATION AMONG UNIONISTS AS EVIDENCE.

0661 DREIER J.C.
THE ALLIANCE FOR PROGRESS.
BALTIMORE: JOHNS HOPKINS PRESS, 1962, 146 PP., LC#62-18508.
LECTURES ON ALLIANCE FOR PROGRESS: HISTORICAL BACKGROUND, ECONOMIC ASPECTS, POLITICAL GOALS, SOCIAL CHANGE, AND POSITION IN INTERNATIONAL AFFAIRS.

0662 DREYFUS S.
"THE INDUSTRIAL DESIGNER AND THE BUSINESSMAN."
HARVARD BUSINESS REV., 28 (NOV. 50), 77-85.
EXPLAINS WHY INDUSTRIAL DESIGNERS ARE USED BY INDUSTRY. DISCUSSES DESIGNER'S UNDERSTANDING OF BUSINESS'S POINT OF VIEW AND HIS KNOWLEDGE OF COSTS IN RELATION TO PROFITS. RELATES HOW DESIGNER CAN BOOST SALES FOR HIS CLIENT AND TELLS THE WAY IN WHICH DESIGNERS ARE SELECTED AND REMUNERATED.

0663 DROBNIG U.
"CONFLICT OF LAWS AND THE EUROPEAN ECONOMIC COMMUNITY."
AMER. J. OF COMPARATIVE LAW, 15 (JAN. 67), 204-229.
OUTLINES ROLE OF DOCTRINE OF CONFLICT-OF-LAWS IN DEVELOPMENT OF EUROPEAN COMMON MARKET. DISCUSSES ITS ADEQUACY IN NEW SITUATION AND CHANGES THAT WILL OCCUR BECAUSE OF STRAINS OF NEW ARRANGEMENT. SURVEYS SPECIFIC CONFLICT DOCTRINES OF PRIVATE LAW AND ANALYZES RULES ABOUT THEIR FUNCTIONS.

0664 DRUCKER P.F.
THE FUTURE OF INDUSTRIAL MAN; A CONSERVATIVE APPROACH.
NEW YORK: JOHN DAY, 1942, 298 PP.
INVESTIGATES MEANING AND PROBLEMS OF FREE, INDUSTRIAL SOCIETY. BELIEVES THAT US MUST MOVE FROM MERCANTILISM OF 19TH CENTURY TO "INDUSTRIAL REALITY" TO MEET CHALLENGE OF HITLER. MAINTAINS THAT RATIONALIST LIBERAL CANNOT FIGHT TOTALITARIANISM EFFECTIVELY. ANSWER TO FREE SOCIETY IS NOT IN TOTAL PLANNING OR LAISSEZ-FAIRE, BUT IN ORGANIZATION OF INDUSTRY ON BASIS OF LOCAL AND DECENTRALIZED GOVERNMENT.

0665 DRUCKER P.F.
CONCEPT OF CORPORATION.
LONDON: LONGMANS, GREEN & CO, 1946, 297 PP.
A CONSULTANT TO GENERAL MOTORS CORPORATION DEALS WITH THE "HUMAN EFFORT" IN CORPORATIONS (DECENTRALIZATION, DEALERS, AND LEADERSHIP), COMPANIES AS "SOCIAL INSTITUTIONS" (THE WORKER'S INDUSTRIAL CITIZENSHIP, UNIONS, AND THE INDIVIDUAL), AND ECONOMIC POLICY (REGULATION OF BIGNESS, PLANNING, LUST FOR POWER, AND FULL EMPLOYMENT).

0666 DRUCKER P.F.
"THE EMPLOYEE SOCIETY."
AMER. J. OF SOCIOLOGY, 58 (JAN. 53), 358-363.
EXPLORES AMERICAN SOCIETY AS AN "EMPLOYEE SOCIETY" WHERE THE BOSS HIMSELF IS USUALLY AN EMPLOYEE AND DEPENDS ON STATUS (CF. MAINE'S THESIS). CALLS FOR RESEARCH INTO IMPLICATIONS OF "MANAGEMENT" AND ITS ACCOUNTABILITY, THE REALIZATION OF HOPES AND BELIEFS THROUGH EMPLOYEE SOCIETY, RIGHTS AND DUTIES IN SUCH A SOCIETY RELATED TO POWER, EFFICIENCY, AND REDISTRIBUTION.

0667 DRUCKER P.F.
AMERICA'S NEXT TWENTY YEARS.
NEW YORK: HARPER & ROW, 1957, 114 PP., LC#57-7974.
EXAMINES LABOR SHORTAGES AND ENROLLMENT PRESSURES ON COLLEGES AND UNIVERSITIES IN US IN LIGHT OF POPULATION EXPLOSION. DISCUSSES ROLE OF AUTOMATION IN ECONOMY AND CONCLUDES WITH ANALYSIS OF FOREIGN AID ISSUES AND SOME PRESSING ISSUES IN DOMESTIC POLITICS (TRANSPORTATION, HOUSING, URBAN RENEWAL, MEDICAL CARE, ETC.).

0668 DUBIN R.
"POWER AND UNION-MANAGEMENT RELATIONS."
ADMINISTRATIVE SCI. Q., 2 (JUNE 57), 60-81.
STARTING FROM A DEFINITION OF POWER AND COLLECTIVE BARGAINING AS SYSTEMS, THE AUTHOR DESCRIBES UNION-MANAGEMENT RELATIONS AS THE INSTITUTIONALIZATION OF POWER RELATIONS AND DISCUSSES SIX ASPECTS OF INSTITUTIONALIZATION.

0669 DUBIN R.
WORKING UNION-MANAGEMENT RELATIONS.
ENGLEWOOD CLIFFS: PRENTICE HALL, 1958, 291 PP., LC#58-12403.
THIS BOOK IS VALUABLE ON MANAGEMENT GOALS, BUT MORE SO ON WORKER ORGANIZATIONS, UNION GOALS, UNION DECISION-MAKING, AND CONTRACT BARGAINING AS A POWER PROCESS.

0670 DUCROS B.
"MOBILISATION DES RESSOURCES PRODUCTIVES ET DEVELOPPEMENT."
REV. ECON. FRANC., 14 (NO.2, 63), 216-41.
APPRAISES PATTERNS OF DEVELOPMENT IN UNDERDEVELOPED COUNTRIES IN RELATION TO INVESTMENTS AND OTHER FACTORS OF PRODUCTION. FOCUSES ON PROBLEM OF MOBILIZATION OF UNSKILLED WORKERS. CRITICIZES IDEA OF ACCELERATED DEVELOPMENT.

0671 DUE J.F.
STATE SALES TAX ADMINISTRATION.
CHICAGO: PUBLIC ADMIN SERVICE, 1963, 259 PP., LC#63-20355.
REVIEW AND ANALYSIS OF SALES TAX STRUCTURE, ADMINISTRATION, AND OPERATION IN 33 STATES. AREAS COVERED INCLUDE: DEVELOPMENT, FORM, AND YIELDS; ADMINISTRATIVE AND PERSONNEL PRACTICE; PROCESSING OF TAX RETURNS; CONTROL OF DELINQUENTS; AUDIT; MEASURES OF LIABILITY AND TAX RATES; TREATMENT OF SERVICES AND REAL PROPERTY; EXEMPTIONS; USES; INFORMATION, COSTS, AND STUDIES; AND USE BY LOCAL GOVERNMENTS.

0672 DUESENBERRY J.S.
BUSINESS CYCLES AND ECONOMIC GROWTH.
NEW YORK: MCGRAW HILL, 1958, 341 PP., LC#57-13333.
ANALYZES EFFECTS OF FLUCTUATIONS IN ECONOMIC SYSTEM ON

RATE AND STABILITY OF GROWTH OF INCOME AND DISCUSSES SEVERITY OF 1930 DEPRESSION. INCLUDES DISCUSSION OF MANY ASPECTS OF ECONOMY SUCH AS CAPITAL, INVESTMENT, SAVINGS, CONSUMPTION, WAGES, INTEREST, AND CREDIT AS THEY AFFECT GROWTH OF INCOME, AND STATEMENT OF APPROPRIATE ASPECTS OF KEYNESIAN AND OTHER ECONOMIC THEORIES.

0673 DUGGAR G.S.
RENEWAL OF TOWN AND VILLAGE I: A WORLD-WIDE SURVEY OF LOCAL GOVERNMENT EXPERIENCE.
THE HAGUE: MARTINUS NIJHOFF, 1965, 95 PP.
COMPILATION AND ANALYSIS OF DATA RECEIVED IN ANSWER TO QUESTIONNAIRES SENT TO 31 COUNTRIES. FACTS DEAL WITH ECONOMIC, FINANCIAL, AND SOCIAL POLICIES OF URBAN RENEWAL, DISTRICT RENEWAL AND TOWN AND REGIONAL PLANNING, AND NATION'S GENERAL POLICY FOR RENEWAL ADMINISTRATION.

0674 DUKE UNIVERSITY
EXPULSION OR OPPRESSION OF BUSINESS ASSOCIATES: "SQUEEZE-OUTS" IN SMALL ENTERPRISES.
DURHAM: DUKE U PR, 1961, 263 PP., LC#61-16908.
A STUDY OF TECHNIQUES USED TO "SQUEEZE-OUT" SMALL BUSINESSMEN. THE MAJORITY OF SUCH CASES INVOLVE BASIC CONFLICT OF INTEREST AMONG ENTRENEURS, POLICY DISAGREEMENT FOR SOME TIME PRIOR TO SQUEEZE-PLAY, OR PROVEN DISABILITY OF PARTICIPANT TO CARRY FAIR SHARE OF BURDEN INVOLVED IN OPERATING BUSINESS. TACTICS AND RULES RECALL COMPARISONS TO POWER STRATEGIES IN OTHER AREAS. EDITED BY F.H. O'NEAL.

0675 DUMONT R.
"SURPEUPLEMENT CHINOIS ET SES CONSEQUENCES."
POLITIQUE ETRANGERE, 30 (1965), 486-497.
AUTHOR BELIEVES THAT IN TEN TO FIFTEEN YEARS, CHINA WILL BE IN DESPERATE NEED OF WESTERN AID TO FEED ITS STARVING POPULATION. COLD WAR TENSIONS MUST AND WILL FADE AS NOT ONLY CHINA, BUT ALL OF THE PRESENT UNDERDEVELOPED AREAS LOOK FOR ASSISTANCE FROM DEVELOPED WORLD IN MEETING FOOD SHORTAGES.

0676 DUN J.L. ED.
THE ESSENCE OF CHINESE CIVILIZATION.
PRINCETON: VAN NOSTRAND, 1967, 476 PP., LC#67-25328.
COLLECTION OF ABOUT 200 SKETCHES, OBSERVATIONS, LETTERS, SHORT STORIES, AND ESSAYS PORTRAYING FULL RANGE OF TRADITIONAL CHINESE CULTURE, THAT IS BEFORE IMPACT OF WESTERN INFLUENCE. SUBJECT HEADINGS INCLUDE PHILOSOPHY AND RELIGION, GOVERNMENT, ECONOMICS, AND FAMILY AND SOCIETY.

0677 DUNCAN O., SCOTT W.R. ET AL.
METROPOLIS AND REGION (PREPARED FOR RESOURCES FOR THE FUTURE INC., WASHINGTON, D.C.)
BALTIMORE: JOHNS HOPKINS PRESS, 1966, 587 PP., LC#60-10656.
PRIMARILY AN ECONOMIC DESCRIPTION OF AMERICA'S METROPOLISES AS THEY LOOKED AT MID-CENTURY. HEAVY USE IS MADE OF CENSUS AND DEMOGRAPHIC DATA. MANY METROPOLISES ARE DISCUSSED IN DETAIL.

0678 DUNCOMBE H.S.
COUNTY GOVERNMENT IN AMERICA.
WASHINGTN: NAT ASSN COUNTIES RES, 1966, 288 PP., LC#66-26090
STUDIES CURRENT TRENDS AND STATUS OF ORGANIZATION, FUNCTIONS, FINANCING, AND INTERGOVERNMENTAL RELATIONS OF COUNTY GOVERNMENT. DESCRIBES SERVICES AND FUNCTIONS OF COUNTIES COMPARATIVELY, AND DISCUSSES SIGNIFICANT DIFFERENCES BETWEEN THEM, STRESSING URBAN COUNTIES AND BREAKDOWN OF TRADITIONAL FUNCTIONS WITH GROWING URBANIZATION.

0679 DUNLOP J.T. ED.
THE THEORY OF WAGE DETERMINATION; PROCEEDINGS OF CONFERENCE HELD BY INTERNATIONAL ECONOMIC ASSOCIATION.
LONDON: MACMILLAN, 1957, 437 PP.
STUDIES REQUIREMENTS FOR THEORY OF WAGE DETERMINATION AND METHODS OF DETERMINING GENERAL LEVEL OF WAGE RATES AND WAGE POLICY AND FULL EMPLOYMENT IN SHORT AND LONG RUN. EXPLORES IMPACT OF BARGAINING ON WAGE LEVEL AND THEORY OF BARGAINING. DISCUSSES CONCEPT OF LABOR SUPPLY AND INSTITUTION OF LABOR UNIONS. EXAMINES RELATION BETWEEN WAGE RATE CHANGES AND INCOME DISTRIBUTION AND IMPACT OF INFLATION ON WAGE RATES.

0680 DUNN J.M.
"AMERICAN DEPENDENCE ON MATERIALS IMPORTS: THE WORLD-WIDE RESOURCE BASE."
J. CONFL. RESOLUT., 4 (MARCH 60), 106-122.
URGING AN ASSESSMENT OF OUR MATERIALS POLICY, AUTHOR CONCLUDES THAT DEPENDENCE OF AMERICA UPON IMPORTS LESSENS DRAIN ON DOMESTIC RESOURCES THEREBY SPURRING FOREIGN EXCHANGE WHICH COULD HASTEN PROGRESS IN UNDERDEVELOPED COUNTRIES. EMPHASIZES INTERDEPENDENCE OF NATIONS INVOLVED.

0681 DUNNING J.H.
"NON-PECUNIARY ELEMENTS AND BUSINESS BEHAVIOUR."
OXFORD ECONOMIC PAPERS, 11 (OCT. 59), 229-241.
ATTEMPTS TO INCORPORATE SUCH ELEMENTS INTO THE THEORY OF THE FIRM AND PROPOSES SEVERAL METHODS OF MEASURING THEM.

0682 DUPRE J.S., LAKOV S.A.
SCIENCE AND THE NATION: POLICY AND POLITICS.
ENGLEWOOD CLIFFS: PRENTICE HALL, 1962, 181 PP., LC#62-9307.
APPRAISAL OF HOW GOVERNMENT CONTRACTS FOR RESEARCH HAVE ALTERED SEPARATION OF PUBLIC AND PRIVATE SPHERES; HOW INDUSTRY, GOVERNMENT, AND UNIVERSITIES HAVE FORMED A NEW PARTNERSHIP; THE ROLE PLAYED BY SCIENTISTS IN SHAPING US MILITARY AND FOREIGN POLICY; AND SCIENCE ADVISORY COMMISSION.

0683 DURAND-REVILLE L., PAILLERE M.
"LE REGIME DES INVESTISSEMENTS DANS LES ETATS AFRICAINS D'EXPRESSION FRANCAISE ET A MADAGASCAR."
REV. JURID. POLIT. OUTREMER, 16 (OCT.-DEV. 62), 477-519.
ANALYZES INDUCEMENTS TO INVEST CAPITAL IN AFRICAN COUNTRIES. DISTINGUISHED BETWEEN STATES WITH AND STATES WITHOUT BENEFITS OF SPECIAL LAWS. DISCUSSES FISCAL ARRANGEMENTS. CLARIFIES HOW FINANCIAL MEASURES AFFECT ECONOMIC AND SOCIAL PROBLEMS.

0684 DURBIN E.F.M.
THE POLITICS OF DEMOCRATIC SOCIALISM; AN ESSAY ON SOCIAL POLICY.
LONDON: ROUTLEDGE & KEGAN PAUL, 1948, 384 PP.
EXAMINES REASONS FOR 20TH-CENTURY TRAGEDIES, SUCH AS TWO WORLD WARS AND ECONOMIC CRISIS. STUDIES AGGRESSIVE NATURE OF MAN, EXPLORES CAPITALISM AND SUGGESTS REFORMS, AND DISCUSSES MARXIST THEORY OF DISTRIBUTION OF ECONOMIC POWER AND SOCIAL PRIVILEGE. CONSIDERS SOCIALIST DEMOCRACY THE BEST SOLUTION. CONSTRUCTS PROGRAM FOR DEMOCRATIC SOCIALIST PARTY.

0685 DURIEZ P.
"THE IMPACT OF EX PARTE 230 (PIGGYBACKING) ON RAIL-MOTOR COMPETITION."
ROCKY MOUNTAIN SOCIAL SCIENCE J., 4 (OCT. 67), 52-59.
EXAMINES ATTEMPT OF US GOVERNMENT TO COORDINATE TRANSPORTATION, ESPECIALLY RAILROADS, THROUGH EX PARTE 230 WHICH CONTROLS PIGGYBACKING. DISCUSSES ACCEPTANCE AND REJECTION OF RULING BY COMPANIES INVOLVED. URGES CLOSER COOPERATION TO MAKE TRANSPORTATION LESS COSTLY AND MORE EFFICIENT.

0686 DUROSELLE J.B.
"THE FUTURE OF THE ATLANTIC COMMUNITY."
INTERNATIONAL JOURNAL, 21(FALL 66), 421-446.
DISCUSSES MYTHS OF UNITY AND INDEPENDENCE IN CONTEMPORARY ATLANTIC COMMUNITY, CLAIMING THAT WESTERN UNITY DOES NOT EXIST, NOR DOES WESTERN INDEPENDENCE, EITHER POLITICALLY OR ECONOMICALLY. ASSERTS THAT REASONS FOR WESTERN COOPERATION IN LATE 1940'S HAVE DISAPPEARED. LISTS SUGGESTIONS FOR RENEWED ATLANTIC COOPERATION.

0687 DUSCHA J.
ARMS, MONEY, AND POLITICS.
NEW YORK: IVES WASHBURN, INC, 1964, 210 PP., LC#65-20066.
EXAMINES POLITICS OF DEFENSE SPENDING, INCLUDING ATTITUDES OF CONGRESS, DEFENSE DEPARTMENT'S RELATION TO INDUSTRY. CONSIDERS SPENDING TOO GREAT. PROPOSES PLAN FOR PEACE AND FOR REDUCTION IN SPENDING.

0688 DWYER J.W.
YARDSTICKS FOR PERFORMANCE (PAMPHLET)
CHICAGO: MUNIC FIN OFFICERS ASSN, 1962, 16 PP.
EXAMINES ROLE OF MEASUREMENT IN BUDGETARY PROCESS AND SYSTEMS FOR DEVELOPING YARDSTICKS. DISCUSSES USEFULNESS OF YARDSTICKS IN REVIEWING BUDGET REQUESTS AND EXAMINES APPROACHES OF NEW YORK CITY TO MEASUREMENT SYSTEMS.

0689 EAST KENTUCKY REGIONAL PLAN
PROGRAM 60: A DECADE OF ACTION FOR PROGRESS IN EASTERN KENTUCKY (PAMPHLET)
FRANKFURT, KY: E KY ST PLAN COMN, 1960, 60 PP.
REPORT OF PLANS FOR REGIONAL DEVELOPMENT OF EASTERN KENTUCKY--PROPOSALS FOR ADMINISTRATIVE AGENCIES, HIGHWAYS, AIR SERVICE, ZONING, WATER DEVELOPMENT; IDEAS FOR IMPROVEMENT OF AGRICULTURE, FORESTRY, TOURIST TRAVEL, INDUSTRY, EDUCATION, HEALTH, AND WELFARE.

0690 EAST KENTUCKY REGIONAL PLAN
PROGRAM 60 REPORT: ACTION FOR PORGRESS IN EASTERN KENTUCKY (PAMPHLET)
FRANKFURT, KY: E KY ST PLAN COMN, 1962, 15 PP.
REPORT OUTLINING PROGRESS AND ACHIEVEMENTS OF KENTUCKY REGIONAL PLANNING COMMISSION IN FIRST QUARTER OF 1960 DECADE; INCLUDES KEY RECOMMENDATIONS FOR CONTINUING PROGRESS AND INDICATIONS OF OUTLOOK FOR NEAR FUTURE IN EASTERN KENTUCKY.

0691 EBENSTEIN W.
TODAY'S ISMS: COMMUNISM, FASCISM, CAPITALISM, SOCIALISM (5TH ED.)
ENGLEWOOD CLIFFS: PRENTICE HALL, 1967, 262 PP., LC#67-17373.
VIEWS WORLD SITUATION AS STRUGGLE BETWEEN TOTALITARIAN AND DEMOCRATIC IDEOLOGIES. APPROACH IS THROUGH GENERAL WAY OF LIFE INHERENT IN EACH SYSTEM. EXAMINES POLITICAL, ECONOMIC, AND SOCIAL ASPECTS DISTINGUISHING EACH SYSTEM PLUS BACKGROUNDS AND CURRENT OBJECTIVES. ANALYZES POWER RELATIONS

IN SOVIET ORBIT AND SOCIALISM IN NEW NATIONS. NOTES SPECIFIC FACTORS SEPARATING DEMOCRATIC AND TOTALITARIAN INSTITUTIONS.

0692 EBONY
THE NEGRO HANDBOOK.
CHICAGO: JOHNSON PUBL CO, 1966, 535 PP., LC#66-27272.
ATTEMPTS TO DOCUMENT PRESENT-DAY STATUS OF NEGRO. PRESENTS HISTORICAL EVENTS AND STATISTICS, WITH CONSIDERABLE COVERAGE OF EVENTS IN CIVIL RIGHTS, EDUCATION AND EMPLOYMENT OPPORTUNITIES, AND LEGAL DECISIONS. INCLUDES BIOGRAPHICAL SECTION, AND APPENDIXES WHICH LIST NEGRO-ORIENTED ORGANIZATIONS AND NEGROES HOLDING STATE ELECTIVE AND APPOINTIVE OFFICES.

0693 EBY K.
"RESEARCH IN LABOR UNIONS."
AMER. J. OF SOCIOLOGY, 56 (NOV. 50), 222-228.
SUGGESTS THAT THE PERSONAL, POLITICAL, AND DYNAMIC NATURE OF THE LABOR MOVEMENT MAKES A STUDY BASED SOLELY ON WRITTEN FORMAL RECORDS OFTEN INADEQUATE; NOR DOES THE USE OF QUESTIONNAIRES BRING OUT THE COMPLETE PICTURE. PARTICIPATION IN UNION ACTIVITIES AND ASSOCIATIONS WITH MEMBERS IS VITAL FOR THE STUDENT OF UNIONISM.

0694 ECKLER A.R., ZLOTNICK J.
"IMMIGRATION AND THE LABOR FORCE."
ANN. ACAD. POL. SOC. SCI., 262 (MAR. 49), 92-101.
MAINTAINS THAT IMMIGRATION INCREASES LABOR SUPPLY BECAUSE MOST IMMIGRANTS ARE YOUNG MALES. SEES IMMIGRATION FLUCTUATING WITH BUSINESS CYCLES. MOST IMMIGRANTS ARE UNSKILLED WORKERS, AND ENCOURAGE CAPITAL EXPANSION BECAUSE OF LOW WAGES. FINDS THAT MINING AND TEXTILE INDUSTRIES DRAW MOST HEAVILY ON IMMIGRANT LABOR SUPPLY.

0696 ECKSTEIN A.
COMMUNIST CHINA'S ECONOMIC GROWTH AND FOREIGN TRADE* IMPLICATIONS FOR US POLICY.
NEW YORK: MCGRAW HILL, 1966, 359 PP., LC#65-28588.
CAREFUL BREAKDOWN AND ANALYSIS OF THE FACTORS AFFECTING THE ECONOMIC DEVELOPMENT OF COMMUNIST CHINA, ESPECIALLY IN TERMS OF HER INFRASTRUCTURE AND TRADING PATTERNS. WEALTH OF DATA (ALL INCLUDE 1963, SOME 1964) IS ANALYZED IN TERMS OF CHINA'S INTERNATIONAL CAPABILITIES AND VULNERABILITIES TO ECONOMIC PRESSURE WITH REFERENCE TO US POLICY.

0697 ECONOMIC RESEARCH SERVICE
RESEARCH DATA ON MINORITY GROUPS: AN ANNOTATED BIBLIOGRAPHY OF ECONOMIC RESEARCH SERVICE REPORTS: 1955-1965 (PAMPHLET)
WASHINGTON: GOVT PR OFFICE, 1966, 25 PP.
COMPILATION OF PUBLICATIONS CONCERNING SOCIO-ECONOMIC PROBLEMS OF LOW-INCOME MINORITY GROUPS IN RURAL AREAS. REFERENCES GROUPED BY STATE.

0698 ECONOMIDES C.P.
LE POUVOIR DE DECISION DES ORGANISATIONS INTERNATIONALES EUROPEENNES.
LEYDEN: AW SIJTHOFF, 1964, 167 PP., LC#64-7605.
COMPARATIVE STUDY OF POWER OF DECISION. CONSIDERS EUROPEAN INTERNATIONAL AND INTERGOVERNMENTAL ORGANIZATIONS SUCH AS NATO, COUNCIL OF EUROPE, AND OEEC; AND SUPRANATIONAL ORGANIZATIONS SUCH AS EURATOM AND EEC. STUDIES POWER OF DECISION IN REFERENCE TO MEMBER STATES AND TO INTERNAL ORDER OF ORGANIZATIONS THEMSELVES.

0699 EDELMAN M., FLEMING R.W.
THE POLITICS OF WAGE-PRICE DECISIONS.
URBANA: U OF ILLINOIS PR, 1965, 321 PP., LC#65-10077.
ANALYSIS OF ATTEMPTS TO RESTRAIN PRICE AND WAGE LEVELS SINCE WWII. APPRAISES GAMUT OF INTERESTS, ORGANIZATIONAL AND POLITICAL PRESSURES THAT EXPLAIN WAGE-PRICE DECISION-MAKING IN POSTWAR EUROPE. EXAMINATION OF GOVERNMENTAL INSTITUTIONS AND PATTERNS OF INTERVENTION, PRIVATE AND PUBLIC ACTION, IDEOLOGIES, POLITICAL PARTIES, STRIKES, ETC.

0700 EDELMAN M.J.
"LABOR'S INFLUENCE IN FOREIGN POLICY."
LABOR LAW J., 5 (MAY 54), 323-329.
LABOR IS FORMALLY REPRESENTED IN AN ADVISORY CAPACITY IN LABOR SECTIONS OF STATE DEPARTMENT, DEFENSE DEPARTMENT, AND IN FOREIGN OPERATIONS ADMINISTRATION, BUT IT HAS LITTLE REAL INFLUENCE ON THE DECISIONS MADE BY THESE THREE AGENCIES.

0701 EDGEWORTH A.B. JR.
"CIVIL RIGHTS PLUS THREE YEARS: BANKS AND THE ANTI-DISCRIMINATION LAW"
BANKER'S MAGAZINE, 150 (SUMMER 67) 23-30.
EXAMINES EFFECTS OF 1964 CIVIL RIGHTS ACT ON EMPLOYMENT PRACTICES OF FINANCIAL INSTITUTIONS. INCLUDES REVIEW OF PROVISIONS OF ACT AND ENFORCEMENT PROCEDURES. DISCUSSES FUNCTION OF FEDERAL EQUAL EMPLOYMENT OPPORTUNITY COMMISSION. MAINTAINS THAT EQUAL EMPLOYMENT POLICIES IN FINANCIAL INSTITUTIONS WILL FURTHER EFFICIENCY AND HELP REDUCE SOCIAL TENSIONS WHICH IS ADVANTAGEOUS TO SUCH INSTITUTIONS.

0702 EDGEWORTH F.Y.
PAPERS RELATING TO POLITICAL ECONOMY.
LONDON: MACMILLAN, 1925, 3 VOLS., 1220 PP.
COMPILATION OF ARTICLES AND BOOK REVIEWS BY THE AUTHOR DEALING WITH FIELDS OF VALUE AND DISTRIBUTION, MONOPOLY, MONEY, INTERNATIONAL TRADE, TAXATION, AND MATHEMATICAL ECONOMICS. EXPRESSES THEORIES IN THESE FIELDS AND EXPLAINS HIS THEORETICAL DIFFERENCES WITH OTHER ECONOMISTS OF THE PERIOD.

0703 EDWARDS C.D.
TRADE REGULATIONS OVERSEAS.
NEW YORK: OCEANA PUBLISHING, 1966, 752 PP., LC#64-23357.
DISCUSSES POLICIES OF COMMON MARKET COUNTRIES, IRELAND, SOUTH AFRICA, NEW ZEALAND, AND JAPAN TOWARD MONOPOLIES, RESTRICTIVE AGREEMENTS, AND RESTRICTIVE BUSINESS PRACTICES.

0704 EDWARDS E.O. ED.
THE NATION'S ECONOMIC OBJECTIVES.
CHICAGO: U OF CHICAGO PRESS, 1964, 167 PP., LC#64-15816.
DISCUSSIONS OF DEVELOPMENT AND ACHIEVEMENT OF NATIONAL ECONOMIC GOALS. RANGE OF TOPICS INCLUDE ECONOMIC GROWTH, STABILITY, SOCIAL AND ECONOMIC SECURITY, ROLE OF PUBLIC POLICY IN ECONOMIC AFFAIRS, AND OTHER MAJOR ISSUES.

0705 EDWARDS N.
"EDUCATION IN THE FEDERAL-STATE STRUCTURE OF GOVERNMENT."
NORTH DAKOTA LAW REVIEW, 43 (SUMMER 67), 711-720.
EXAMINES DELEGATION OF CONTROL OVER EDUCATION BETWEEN STATE AND FEDERAL GOVERNMENTS. DISCUSSES EXPENDITURE OF PUBLIC FUNDS FOR SECTARIAN SCHOOLS AND RACIAL SEGREGATION. SUPPORTS VIEW THAT SYSTEM IN WHICH STATE AND LOCAL ADMINISTRATORS HAVE CONTROL OVER EDUCATIONAL POLICY HAS PREVENTED RIGID FEDERAL CONTROL, ALLOWED LOCAL EDUCATIONAL NEEDS TO BE MET, AND MADE EXPERIMENTATION POSSIBLE.

0706 EELLS R.S.F.
THE MEANING OF MODERN BUSINESS.
NEW YORK: COLUMBIA U PRESS, 1960, 427 PP., LC#60-8393.
TOWARD THE DEVELOPMENT OF CORPORATE PHILOSOPHY: THE ISSUES OF SOCIAL RESPONSIBILITY, CORPORATE GOALS AND DECISION-MAKING, AND THE ISSUES OF THE VARIOUS CLAIMANTS ON THE CORPORATIONS, BOTH DIRECT (CONTRIBUTORS, CUSTOMERS, EMPLOYEES, SUPPLIERS) AND INDIRECT (COMPETITORS, COMMUNITY, GENERAL PUBLIC, VARIOUS LEVELS OF GOVERNMENT), ALL LEADING TO THE "WELL-TEMPERED CORPORATION."

0707 EGGERT G.G.
RAILROAD LABOR DISPUTES.
ANN ARBOR: U OF MICH PR, 1967, 313 PP., LC#67-11984.
DESCRIBES THE FEDERAL GOVERNMENT'S METHODS OF DEALING WITH RAILROAD LABOR PROBLEMS IN THE LAST QUARTER OF THE 19TH CENTURY AND TRACES THE EVOLUTION OF FEDERAL STRIKE POLICY. TREATS QUESTIONS OF POLICY-MAKING IN CRISIS SITUATIONS, POWER ELITES, BARGAINING, AND EXPANDING ROLE OF THE COURTS.

0708 EGLE W.P.
ECONOMIC STABILIZATION.
PRINCETON: U. PR., 1952, 264 PP.
EXAMINES POSSIBILITIES OF ECONOMIC STABILIZATION WITHIN THE FRAMEWORK OF A PRIVATE ENTERPRISE SYSTEM. SUGGESTS THAT THIS CAN BE DONE THROUGH FIRM GOVERNMENTAL COMMITMENT TO ECONOMIC STABILIZATION, WHICH, AFTER YEARS OF ENFORCEMENT, WILL BECOME AN INCREASINGLY SELF-SUSTAINING ASPECT OF THE SYSTEM.

0709 EGLE W.P.
ECONOMIC STABILIZATION: OBJECTIVES, RULES, AND MECHANISMS.
PRINCETON: PRINCETON U PRESS, 1952, 264 PP., LC#52-5848.
EXAMINES POSSIBILITIES OF STABILIZATION WITHIN SYSTEM OF PRIVATE ENTERPRISE. ITS THEME IS THE SUBJECTION OF STABILIZING EFFORTS OF GOVERNMENT TO CLEARLY DEFINED AND BINDING OBJECTIVE.

0710 EHRHARD J.
LE DESTIN DU COLONIALISME.
PARIS: EDITIONS EYROLLES, 1958, 242 PP.
DISCUSSES PROBLEMS OF UNDERDEVELOPMENT IN AFRICAN NATIONS, FRENCH AID AND COMMERCE, LEVELS OF INDUSTRIALIZATION AND TECHNOLOGICAL PROGRESS, INTERNAL PRODUCTION AND EXPORTS, AGRICULTURE, AND NECESSITY OF LONG-TERM PLANNING AND PRICE STABILIZATION.

0711 EHRLICH S.
"INTERNATIONAL PRESSURE GROUPS: A CONTRIBUTION TO THE SOCIOLOGY OF INTERNATIONAL RELATIONS IN THE CAPITALIST WORLD."
CO-EXISTENCE, 4 (JULY 67),133-142
ANALYZES NATURE AND ACTIVITY OF INTERNATIONAL PRESSURE GROUPS SINCE WWII. DEFINES AND CLASSIFIES THESE "INTERNATIONAL GROUPS" BEFORE COVERING OPERATIONS AND METHODS OF GROUPS' ACTIVITIES ON NATIONAL GOVERNMENT AND WORLD DECISIONS. EMPHASIZES TACTICS USED BY GROUPS. FEELS THEY ARE SOURCE OF POWER FOR CAPITALISTIC WORLD.

0712 EHRMANN H.W.
ORGANIZED BUSINESS IN FRANCE.
PRINCETON: U. PR., 1957, 494 PP.

ANALYZES HISTORY OF FRENCH EMPLOYERS' ASSOCIATIONS' ACTIVITIES AS PRESSURE GROUPS FROM 1919 TO PRESENT. SUGGESTS FRANCE'S SLOW ECONOMIC GROWTH RATE MAY BE DUE TO INTERNAL STRIFE OF THESE ASSOCIATIONS. CONFLICT PREVENTS EFFECTIVE PRESSURE GROUP ACTIVITIES FOR BETTER ECONOMIC POLICY.

0713 EINZIG P.
A DYNAMIC THEORY OF FORWARD EXCHANGE.
NEW YORK: ST. MARTINS, 1961, 573 PP.
REVISION OF 1937 BOOK RE IMPORTANCE OF FORWARD MARGINS ON FOREIGN MONETARY EXCHANGE WITH NEW EMPHASIS ON HOW MUCH THE DYNAMISM OF FORWARD EXCHANGE IS LIABLE TO INFLUENCE THE ECONOMY FOR BETTER OR WORSE. HISTORY OF FORWARD EXCHANGE, AND ITS MOVEMENT BY VARIOUS CURRENCIES. SUGGESTS MINIMAL INTERFERENCE WITH FREE MARKET.

0714 EINZIG P.
THE HISTORY OF FOREIGN EXCHANGE.
LONDON: MACMILLAN, 1962, 319 PP.
COMPREHENSIVE DESCRIPTION OF ORIGIN AND EVOLUTION OF MARKETS, PRACTICES AND TECHNIQUES OF FOREIGN EXCHANGE. EXAMINES INFLUENCES THAT AFFECT EXCHANGE RATES. AIMS AT DISCERNING SOME THEORETICAL PATTERNS IN THE EVOLUTION OF FOREIGN EXCHANGE.

0715 EINZIG P.
MONETARY POLICY: ENDS AND MEANS.
BALTIMORE: PENGUIN BOOKS, 1964, 432 PP., LC#64-3215.
PRESENTS BROAD PICUTRE OF MONETARY POLICY WITHOUT ATTEMPTING TO GIVE DETAILED DESCRIPTION OF ANY PERIOD OR ASPECT IN PARTICULAR. SURVEYS POLICIES USED THROUGH THE AGES, POINTING OUT SIMILARITIES BETWEEN PAST AND PRESENT DEVICES. DISCUSSES MONEY, TRADE, BUSINESS CYCLES, CREDIT, FOREIGN EXCHANGE, AND INTERNATIONAL MONETARY POLICY.

0716 ELDREDGE H.W. ED.
TAMING MEGALOPOLIS; HOW TO MANAGE AN URBANIZED WORLD.
GARDEN CITY: DOUBLEDAY, 1967, 586 PP., LC#67-12878.
ESSAYS CONCERNED WITH METHODS AND WAYS TO MANAGE CITIES. BEGIN WITH PLANNING AS A PROFESSION, AND THEN DISCUSS DATA RESEARCH AND COMPUTER MODELS. TREAT GOVERNMENT STRUCTURE FOR PLANNING AND NEW TOOLS FOR ANALYSIS AND CONTROL. INCLUDE SOCIAL PLANNING, URBAN POVERTY, CITIZEN PARTICIPATION, AND URBANIZATION OF DEVELOPING NATIONS. CONCLUDE WITH FUNCTIONAL AND SPATIAL MACRO-PLANNING.

0717 ELDREDGE H.W. ED.
TAMING MEGALOPOLIS; WHAT IT IS AND WHAT COULD BE (VOL. I)
GARDEN CITY: DOUBLEDAY, 1967, 583 PP., LC#67-12878.
ESSAYS EXAMINE PROBLEMS OF MODERN URBAN DEVELOPMENT AND PLANNING. BEGIN WITH URBANIZATION AND MODERNIZATION IN US AND DISCUSS EXISTING CONDITIONS, THEN EXAMINE WHAT MUST BE DONE. INCLUDE AESTHETIC AND SOCIETAL GOALS, METROPOLITAN STRUCTURE AND FORM, ECONOMIC FUNCTION, AND TRANSPORTATION AND COMMUNICATION. CONSIDER TYPES OF HOUSING DEVELOPMENT AND PLANNING FOR RECREATION AND LEISURE.

0718 EL-NAGGAR S.
FOREIGN AID TO UNITED ARAB REPUBLIC.
CAIRO: INST OF NATIONAL PLANNING, 1963, 93 PP.
DISCUSSES AID TO UAR, TYPES AND ORGANIZATION OF PROGRAMS, AMERICAN AND SOVIET AID. PRESENTS STUDIES OF SPECIFIC AID PROGRAMS, SUCH AS SURPLUS AGRICULTURAL PRODUCTS, RURAL IMPROVEMENT, DAMS, INDUSTRIALIZATION, AND MILITARY AID. INCLUDES RESULTS AND PROBLEMS OF FOREIGN AID.

0719 ELKIN A.B.
"OEEC-ITS STRUCTURE AND POWERS."
EUROP. YRB., 4 (58), 96-149.
STUDIES POWER AND JURISDICTION OF OEEC VIS A VIS ITS MEMBER GOVERNMENTS. COUNCIL IS MAIN ORGAN WITH SUBORDINATE BODIES, SUCH AS STEERING BOARD FOR TRADE. ORIGINAL RULE OF UNANIMOUS VOTE HAS CHANGED TO MAJORITY RULE IN SUBORDINATE ORGANS.

0720 ELKOURI F., ELKOURI E.A.
HOW ARBITRATION WORKS (REV. ED.)
WASHINGTON: BUREAU NATL AFFAIRS, 1960, 498 PP., LC#60-11972.
THROUGH AN EXAMINATION OF ARBITRATION CASES, THE AUTHORS ANALYZE PROCEDURAL AND SUBSTANTIVE ASPECTS OF THE ARBITRATION PROCESS. DISCUSSION OF LEGAL STATUS, SCOPE, PRECEDENT, AND CUSTOMS ASSOCIATED WITH LABOR ARBITRATION IN AMERICA. EVALUATE ROLE OF ARBITRATION AS AN INDUSTRIAL INSTITUTION.

0721 ELLENDER A.J.
A REPORT ON UNITED STATES FOREIGN OPERATIONS IN AFRICA.
WASHINGTON: GOVT PR OFFICE, 1963, 803 PP.
SENATOR FROM LOUISIANA REPORTS ON RECENT AFRICAN TOUR, GIVING SHORT HISTORICAL BACKGROUND OF AFRICA, AND HIS OBSERVATIONS ON AND ENCOUNTERS WITH US MISSION HEADS AND STAFFS IN EACH COUNTRY VISITED. APPENDIX TO REPORT FURNISHES STATISTICAL DATA IN ANSWER TO QUESTIONNAIRES COVERING ALL ASPECTS OF US FOREIGN OPERATIONS.

0722 ELLIOTT J.R.
THE APPEAL OF COMMUNISM IN THE UNDERDEVELOPED NATIONS.
DUBUQUE: BROWN, 1962, 156 PP.
ATTEMPTS TO EXPLAIN WHY COMMUNISM HAS SUCH GREAT APPEAL IN UNDERDEVELOPED NATIONS, ESPECIALLY IN COMPARISON TO THE IDEAS EXPORTED FROM THE US. EXAMINES THEORY AND PRACTICE OF PRIVATE ENTERPRISE, THEORY AND PRACTICE OF COMMUNISM, BOTH MARXIST AND LENINIST, AND CONSIDERS THE ECONOMIC PROBLEMS AND NEEDS OF UNDERDEVELOPED NATIONS.

0723 ELLIS H.S. ED.
ECONOMIC DEVELOPMENT FOR LATIN AMERICA.
LONDON: MACMILLAN, 1961, 479 PP.
COLLECTS IDEAS ON LATIN AMERICAN ECONOMICS EXCHANGED AT CONFERENCE OF INTERNATIONAL ECONOMIC ASSOCIATION. TOPICS INCLUDE: LATIN AMERICAN ECONOMIC PLANNING, INFLATION, PRIVATE AND PUBLIC INVESTMENT, ROLE OF CAPITAL, FINANCIAL INSTITUTIONS, INTERNATIONAL TRADE, INVESTMENT PRIORITIES, AGRICULTURAL AND INDUSTRIAL DEVELOPMENT, AND EXCHANGE CONTROLS.

0724 ELLSWORTH P.T.
"INTERNATIONAL ECONOMY."
NEW YORK: MACMILLAN, 1950.
CONTAINS 400 ENTRIES FROM BOOKS AND ARTICLES WRITTEN FROM 1900-1950 IN ENGLISH ON INTERNATIONAL ECONOMICS. ARRANGED BY CHAPTER, SELECTIVE EMPHASIS ON HISTORICAL DEVELOPMENT.

0725 ELLSWORTH P.T.
THE INTERNATIONAL ECONOMY.
NEW YORK: MACMILLAN, 1958, 513 PP., LC#58-5211.
DESCRIBES GROWTH OF THEORY OF INTERNATIONAL ECONOMICS FROM RISE OF MERCANTILISM, INCLUDING INTERNATIONAL TRADE THEORY, TARIFFS, FOREIGN EXCHANGE, AND BALANCE OF PAYMENTS. ALSO CHRONICLES GROWTH OF INTERNATIONAL ECONOMY ITSELF.

0726 ELSNER H.
THE TECHNOCRATS, PROPHETS OF AUTOMATION.
SYRACUSE: SYRACUSE U PRESS, 1967, 252 PP., LC#67-14522.
STUDY OF THE TECHNOCRACY MOVEMENT FROM BEGINNING IN 1919, TO MOVEMENT AS IT EXISTS IN THE 1960'S. THE CONCLUDING CHAPTER IS A SOCIOLOGICAL-POLITICAL INTERPRETATION OF TECHNOCRACY.

0727 EMERSON F.D., LATCHAM F.C.
SHAREHOLDER DEMOCRACY: A BROADER OUTLOOK FOR CORPORATIONS.
CLEVELAND: WESTERN RESERVE U PR, 1954, 242 PP., LC#54-8779.
ALTHOUGH THE "TWO-PARTY SYSTEM" IS UNWORKABLE IN CORPORATE AFFAIRS, ANALOGIES TO POLITICAL LIFE CAN BE BASED ON CITY MANAGERS' ROLES AND ANNUAL REFERENDA. DEALS WITH SHAREHOLDERS' MEETINGS, THE SEARCH FOR EFFECTIVE PARTICIPATION, PROXY CONTESTS AND RIGHTS OF ECURITY HOLDERS TO MAKE PROPOSALS INCLUDED IN MANAGEMENT PROXY STATEMENTS, WITH SUPPORTING STUDIES, DATA, AND SUGGESTIONS.

0728 EMERSON F.D.
"THE ROLES OF MANAGEMENT AND SHAREHOLDERS IN CORPORATE GOVERNMENT."
LAW AND CONTEMPORARY PROB., 23 (SPRING 58), 231-238.
CONTEMPORARY CORPORATION STATUTES DO NOT "ACCORD WITH THE REALITIES AND NEEDS OF OUR SOCIETY"; THEY ARE, IN MANY CASES, OVERLY RESTRICTIVE ON RIGHTS OF SHAREHOLDERS TO PARTICIPATE DEMOCRATICALLY IN CORPORATE AFFAIRS. FAVORS ADOPTION OF UNIFORM BUSINESS CORPORATION ACT AS A MORE ADEQUATE APPROACH.

0729 EMERSON R.
"THE ATLANTIC COMMUNITY AND THE EMERGING COUNTRIES."
INT. ORGAN., 17 (SUMMER 63), 628-649.
EXAMINES DIVERSITY OF ATTITUDES LINKING OR DIVIDING THE EMERGING NATIONS AND THOSE WITHIN THE ATLANTIC COMMUNITY. EXPLORES RELATIONSHIPS BETWEEN THE GROUPS BY DRAWING ON EXPERIENCE OF COMMON MARKET AND REACTION TO IT BY NEWLY INDEPENDENT TERRITORIES. CONCLUDES THAT CONFLICT POSSIBLE BETWEEN INTERESTS OF EMERGING NATIONS AND ATLANTIC COMMUNITY NATIONS, BUT COOPERATION ALSO POSSIBLE FOR JOINT AND SEPARATE ENDS.

0730 ENGELS F.
THE BRITISH LABOUR MOVEMENT (PAMPHLET)
NEW YORK: INTERNATIONAL PUBLRS, 1940, 46 PP.
COLLECTION OF TEN ARTICLES BY ENGELS ON BRITISH LABOUR MOVEMENT WRITTEN FOR TRADE GROUPS IN ENGLAND. DEALS WITH WAGE SYSTEM, TRADE UNIONS, RELATIONS WITH US AND FRANCE, AND SIGNIFICANCE OF WORKING MAN'S PARTY IN GERMANY AND ENGLAND. FINALLY DISCUSSES EXISTENCE AND SIGNIFICANCE OF SOCIAL CLASSES.

0731 ENGELS F.
HERRN EUGEN DUHRING'S REVOLUTION IN SCIENCE (1878)
NEW YORK: INTERNATIONAL PUBLRS, 1939, 385 PP.
ATTACKS DUHRING'S CONCEPT OF SOCIETY AS POWER-BASED, WITH POLITICAL CONSIDERATIONS DOMINATING ECONOMIC ONES. GIVES POINT-BY-POINT REFUTATION OF THIS CONCEPT AS BASED ON PSEUDO-SCIENTIFIC MATERIALISM WHICH TOTALLY NEGLECTS ENERGY. DEFENDS MARXIAN ECONOMIC INTERPRETATION OF HISTORY AND BELIEF IN PREVALENCE OF STRUGGLE IN SOCIETY, ESPECIALLY CLASS CONFLICT.

0732 ENGELS F.
SOCIALISM: UTOPIAN AND SCIENTIFIC (2ND ED.)
MOSCOW: FOREIGN LANG PUBL HOUSE, 1959, 411 PP.
TRANSLATION OF ENGELS' "ANTI-DUHRING" MADE FROM THE THIRD GERMAN EDITION (1894). A CRITICAL EXAMINATION OF THE SOCIAL PHILOSOPHY OF DUHRING - NATURAL PHILOSOPHY, MORALITY AND LAW, DIALECTICS, AND POLITICAL ECONOMY. ABSTRACTS CONSCIOUS DIALECTICS FROM GERMAN IDEALIST PHILOSOPHY AND APPLIES IT TO MATERIALIST CONCEPTION OF NATURE AND HISTORY.

0733 ENGELS F.
THE CONDITION OF THE WORKING-CLASS IN ENGLAND (1848)
LONDON: SWAN SONNENSCHEIN, 1892, 298 PP.
DISCUSSES EFFECTS OF INDUSTRIAL CAPITALISM UPON WORKERS OF ENGLAND IN 1848. CLAIMS THAT BRIEF INCREASE IN THEIR STANDARD OF LIVING WAS SOON LOST DUE TO INHERENT NATURE OF CAPITALISM, WHICH MUST OPPRESS WORKERS TO SUPPORT CAPITALISTS. IT IS BY REDUCING AND CONTROLLING PRODUCTION THAT PRICES ARE MAINTAINED AT HIGH LEVELS. DESCRIBES POVERTY AND MISERY OF WORKERS IN INDUSTRIAL TOWNS.

0734 ENGLER R.
THE POLITICS OF OIL.
LONDON: MACMILLAN, 1961, 565 PP., LC#61-17192.
OIL IS A VAST AND WELL-ORGANIZED INDUSTRY WHICH ALWAYS GETS ITS WAY IN THE POLITICAL ARENA, OFTEN AT THE PUBLIC'S EXPENSE. THIS WAS ESPECIALLY TRUE DURING EISENHOWER'S ADMINISTRATION. TRUMAN DID RESIST OIL PRESSURES ON A FEW OCCASIONS.

0735 ENKE S., SALERA V.
INTERNATIONAL ECONOMICS.
ENGLEWOOD CLIFFS: PRENTICE HALL, 1947, 731 PP.
DISCUSSES PRINCIPLES OF INTERNATIONAL TRADE AND FINANCE. EXAMINES CLASSICAL THEORIES, TRADE CONTROL, CARTELS, COMMERCIAL TREATIES, TRADE POLICIES OF USSR, US, AND UK, MONETARY AND FINANCIAL POLICIES, ETC.

0736 ENKE S.
"THE ECONOMIES OF GOVERNMENT PAYMENTS TO LIMIT POPULATION."
ECON. DEV. CULT. CHANGE, 3 (JULY60), 339-348.
EXPLAINS REASONS FOR CERTAIN GOVERNMENTS SEEKING TO REDUCE BIRTH RATE AND HOW MONEY INCENTIVES CAN HELP DO THIS. PROPOSES BONUSES TO MEN WHO DO NOT HAVE CHILDREN OVER A CERTAIN AMOUNT OF TIME. INDIA CITED AS EXAMPLE OF A PLACE WHERE THIS HAS BEEN TRIED. HOW MANY SHOULD PARTICIPATE AND SOURCES OF MONEY PAYMENTS ARE TWO QUESTIONS POSED. ALTERNATIVE PROPOSALS ARE CITED.

0737 ENKE S.
ECONOMICS FOR DEVELOPMENT.
ENGLEWOOD CLIFFS: PRENTICE HALL, 1963, 616 PP., LC#63-9968.
EMPHASIZES PRINCIPLES OF ECONOMICS OF DEVELOPMENT. CONCLUDES FROM STUDY AND OBSERVATION THAT US IS UNSUCCESSFUL IN FOREIGN AID PROGRAMS BECAUSE IT IGNORES TRADITION AND VARIED INTERESTS THAT LIE AT ROOT OF ECONOMIC UNDERDEVELOPMENT. ARGUES POLICY-MAKERS ARE UNAWARE OF PRINCIPLES OF ECONOMIC THEORY. BIBLIOGRAPHY INCLUDED FOR EACH CHAPTER.

0738 ENKE S. ED.
DEFENSE MANAGEMENT.
ENGLEWOOD CLIFFS: PRENTICE HALL, 1967, 404 PP., LC#67-10540.
ESSAYS EXAMINING CHANGES IN DECISION-MAKING AT THE PENTAGON, APPLICATION OF COST-BENEFIT ANALYSIS TO SPECIFIC DEFENSE PROGRAMS, PROBLEMS IN RESEARCH AND DEVELOPMENT, AND ECONOMIC IMPACT OF DEFENSE SPENDING. ALSO DISCUSS PROBLEMS OTHER FEDERAL AGENCIES WILL FACE IN SHIFTING TO COST-EFFECTIVENESS TECHNIQUES.

0739 ENTHOVEN A.C.
"ECONOMIC ANALYSIS IN THE DEPARTMENT OF DEFENSE."
AMER. ECO. REVIEW, 53 (MAY 63), 413-423.
PROGRESS REPORT ON ECONOMISTS' WORK IN DEFENSE DEPARTMENT ON PROBLEMS OF DETERMINING REQUIREMENTS FOR WEAPON SYSTEMS AND FORCES. REDESIGNS PROGRAMMING SYSTEM TO HAVE COST AND BENEFITS PLANNED TOGETHER TO REDUCE BUDGET GAP. DEVISES PLAN FOR ALLOCATION OF RESOURCES FOR NUCLEAR AND CONVENTIONAL FORCE REQUIREMENTS. SUGGESTS WAYS OF DEALING WITH UNCERTAINTIES IN DEFENSE PLANNING.

0740 COMMITTEE ECONOMIC DEVELOPMENT
THE DOLLAR AND THE WORLD MONETARY SYSTEM: A STATEMENT ON NATIONAL POLICY (PAMPHLET)
NEW YORK: COMM FOR ECO DEV, 1966, 76 PP., LC#66-30658.
DETAILED STUDY OF POSSIBLE WAYS TO BRING US INTERNATIONAL ACCOUNTS INTO BALANCE. ANALYZES US AS WORLD BANKER AND PROBLEM ITS DEFICIT IS CREATING FOR ALL LONG-RANGE INTERNATIONAL MONETARY PLANS. SUGGESTS REDUCTION OF GOVERNMENT SPENDING, INCREASED FREEDOM FOR PRIVATE CAPITAL TRANSACTIONS, REDUCTION OF FOREIGN AID TO EUROPE, AND STRENGTHENING OF INTERNATIONAL MONETARY AGREEMENTS.

0741 ERASMUS C.J.
MAN TAKES CONTROL: CULTURAL DEVELOPMENT AND AMERICAN AID.
MINNEAPOLIS: U OF MINN PR, 1961, 365 PP., LC#61-8400.
CONCERNED WITH PRE-INDUSTRIAL PEOPLES OF UNDERDEVELOPED AREAS AND THEIR RELATION TO INDUSTRIALIZED SOCIETY. FORMULATES SIMPLE SCHEME OF CULTURAL CAUSALITY, CONGENIAL TO AN APPLIED INTEREST IN CULTURE CHANGE. ADVANCES GENERAL THEORY OF CULTURE DEVELOPMENT. INCLUDES CASE STUDY OF ECONOMIC DEVELOPMENT AND CULTURAL CHANGE IN NORTHWESTERN MEXICO.

0742 ERB GF
"THE UNITED NATIONS CONFERENCE ON TRADE AND DEVELOPMENT (UNCTAD): A SELECTED CURRENT READING LIST."
AFR. BIBLIOG. CTR., CUR. RDG., 4 (1966), 1-14.
A PARTIALLY ANNOTATED BIBLIOGRAPHY ON UNCTAD: PROCEEDINGS OF THE CONFERENCE; BACKGROUND AND CURRENT ACTIVITIES; DEVELOPMENT FINANCING; INTERNATIONAL MONETARY ISSUES AND THE DEVELOPING COUNTRIES. CONTAINS INTRODUCTION AND BRIEF DESCRIPTION OF UNCTAD. ALL SOURCES PUBLISHED IN ENGLISH, SPANISH, AND GERMAN BETWEEN 1958-65.

0743 ERDMAN P.E., BENVENISTE G., PRENTICE E.S.
COMMON MARKETS AND FREE TRADE AREAS (PAMPHLET)
MENLO PARK: STANFORD U RES INST, 1960, 37 PP.
OUTLINES WORLD-WIDE TREND TOWARD ECONOMIC REGIONAL GROUPINGS, FACTORS AND CAUSES CREATING TREND, NATURE OF PROPOSED SCHEMES, AND POTENTIAL PROBLEMS AND ISSUES THE US WILL FACE AS RESULT. FOCUSES UPON LATIN AMERICA, ASIA, AND AFRICA. ISSUES RELATE TO IMPACT OF EUROPEAN ECONOMIC COMMUNITY AND OTHER EUROPEAN ORGANIZATIONS UPON US.

0744 ERDMANN H.H. ED.
"ADMINISTRATIVE LAW AND FARM ECONOMICS."
JOURNAL OF FARM ECONOMICS, 44 (DEC. 62), 1627-1658.
ANTHOLOGY OF REPORTS AND DISCUSSIONS ON ADMINISTRATIVE PROCESSES ON NATIONAL AND LOCAL LEVEL AND ROLE OF JUDICIAL REVIEW IN ADMINISTRATIVE PROCESS. ALL REPORTS ARE RELATED TO IMPACT ON AGRICULTURAL INDUSTRY.

0745 ERHARD L.
THE ECONOMICS OF SUCCESS.
PRINCETON: VAN NOSTRAND, 1963, 412 PP.
ANALYSIS OF WEST GERMAN ECONOMIC DEVELOPMENT BY MINISTER OF ECONOMIC AFFAIRS RESPONSIBLE FOR ECONOMIC POLICY AND PLANNING. INCLUDES VARIOUS ARTICLES AND SPEECHES ON SPECIFIC ASPECTS OF GERMAN AND INTERNATIONAL ECONOMICS.

0746 ERNST M.L.
THE FIRST FREEDOM.
NEW YORK: MACMILLAN, 1946, 316 PP.
CONTENDS THAT AMERICAN FREEDOM OF THOUGHT IS BEING ERODED BY MONOPOLIES IN NEWSPAPER, BROADCASTING, AND MOTION PICTURE INDUSTRIES. PRESENTS STATISTICS ON CONTROL OF NEWS MEDIA BY A FEW LARGE CORPORATIONS TO SHOW THAT US HAS NO REAL SOURCE FOR COMPARISON OF VARYING POLITICAL IDEAS, THAT ALL THE POPULACE HEARS AND SEES CAN IN EFFECT BE CONTROLLED BY SMALL GROUPS.

0747 ESTEBAN J.C.
IMPERIALISMO Y DESARROLLO ECONOMICO.
BUENOS AIRES: EDITORIAL PALESTRA, 1961, 213 PP.
ANALYZES ECONOMIC DEVELOPMENT OF ARGENTINA REGARDING ROLE OF GOVERNMENT AND PRIVATE CAPITAL IN FURTHER IMPROVEMENT AND INDUSTRIALIZATION OF NATIONAL ECONOMY. DISCUSSES NEED TO REGULATE EXTENT OF FOREIGN CAPITAL INFLUENCE IN NATIONAL ECONOMY. EXAMINES INTERNATIONAL ECONOMIC OBLIGATIONS OF ARGENTINA AND STATE OF ITS BALANCE OF PAYMENTS.

0748 ESTEVEZ A., ELIA O.H.
ASPECTOS ECONOMICO-FINANCIEROS DE LA CAMPANA SANMARITANA.
BUENOS AIRES: COM NAC EJECUTIVA, 1961, 257 PP.
EXAMINES ECONOMIC SITUATION OF SOUTH AMERICA AT TIME OF ITS REVOLUTION FOR INDEPENDENCE FROM SPAIN. ANALYZES PLAN FOR POLITICAL AND ECONOMIC DEVELOPMENT UNDER REVOLUTIONARY LEADER SAN MARTIN. DISCUSSES ROLE OF GOVERNMENT IN FORMATION OF BANKING STRUCTURE AND STABILIZATION OF ECONOMY FOR NATIONAL DEVELOPMENT.

0749 ESTEY J.A.
BUSINESS CYCLES; THEIR NATURE, CAUSE, AND CONTROL.
ENGLEWOOD CLIFFS: PRENTICE HALL, 1941, 544 PP.
PART ONE DESCRIBES THE NATURE AND PATTERN OF BUSINESS CYCLES. PART TWO EXPLORES VARIOUS THEORIES AS TO CAUSE OF BUSINESS CYCLES, INCLUDING REAL CAUSES, PSYCHOLOGICAL THEORIES, MONETARY THEORIES, AND KEYNESIAN THEORY. PART THREE DISCUSSES STABILIZATION THROUGH MONETARY POLICIES, PUBLIC WORKS, AND WAGE AND PRICE POLICIES. PRAGMATIC RATHER THAN DOGMATIC APPROACH TO STABILIZATION.

0750 ESTEY M.
THE UNIONS: STRUCTURE, DEVELOPMENT, AND MANAGEMENT.
NEW YORK: HARCOURT BRACE, 1967, 125 PP., LC#67-14629.
INTRODUCTORY ANALYSIS OF WHAT UNIONS ARE, WHY THEY BEHAVE AS THEY DO, AND RULES THAT GOVERN THEM. COVERS PATTERNS OF UNION GROWTH IN RESPONSE TO CHANGING NEEDS, BUSINESS VS. DEMOCRATIC FUNCTIONS OF UNIONS, AND DECISION-MAKING PROCESS. EMPHASIZES NATURE OF UNIONS AS ORGANIZATIONS, AND DIFFERENCES BETWEEN UNIONS AND BUSINESSES THEY DEAL WITH.

0751 ESTHUS R.A.
FROM ENMITY TO ALLIANCE: US AUSTRALIAN RELATIONS.
SEATTLE: U OF WASHINGTON PR, 1964, 180 PP., LC#64-20486.
TRACES RISING IMPORTANCE OF AUSTRALIA IN PACIFIC AFFAIRS DURING 1930'S, NOTING OCASSIONAL BY ACRIMONIOUS US-AUSTRALIAN RELATIONS DURING THIS PERIOD. DISCUSSES ENMITY ARISING FROM TRADE AND SHIPPING COMPETITION. DESCRIBES ABRUPT CHANGES IN RELATIONS AFTER OUTBREAK OF WAR IN EUROPE AND EVENTUAL ALLIANCE IN PACIFIC WAR. ANALYZES COMMON INTERESTS REMAINING AFTER WWII AND SUBSEQUENT CHANGES IN RELATIONS.

0752 ETHERINGTON D.M.
"LAND RESETTLEMENT IN KENYA; POLICY AND PRACTICE"
J. OF EAST AFRICAN ECONOMIC REV., 10 (JUNE 63), 22-34.
SUGGESTS LAND REFORM IN KENYA MUST BE COUPLED WITH NEW TECHNIQUES IN AGRICULTURE TO BE SUCCESSFUL.

0753 ETSCHMANN R.
DIE WAHRUNGS- UND DEVISENPOLITIK DES OSTBLOCKS UND IHRE AUSWIRKUNGEN AUF DIE WIRTSCHAFTSBEZIEHUNGEN ZWISCHEN OST U WEST
BONN: UNIV OF BONN, 1959, 213 PP.
EXAMINES ECONOMIC AND FOREIGN TRADE POLICIES OF EASTERN COUNTRIES WITH EMPHASIS ON CURRENCY STANDARDS AND FOREIGN EXCHANGE. FOCUSES ON CZECHOSLOVAKIA, POLAND, HUNGARY, RUMANIA, BULGARIA, USSR, CHINA, AND EAST GERMANY.

0754 EUROPEAN COMM ECO-SOC PROG
EUROPEAN BUSINESS CYCLE POLICY (PAMPHLET)
MILAN: EUR COMM ECO & SOC PROG, 1958, 48 PP.
DISCUSSES RELATIONSHIP OF PROBLEMS OF FULL EMPLOYMENT, INFLATION, AND BALANCE OF PAYMENTS THAT ARE PART OF DIFFICULTY OF ECONOMIC GROWTH AND STABILITY OF BUSINESS CYCLE. PROPOSES PRINCIPLES TO COUNTER INFLATION AND RECESSIONS, AND TO IMPROVE INTERNATIONAL COOPERATION.

0755 EUROPEAN FREE TRADE ASSN
REGIONAL DEVELOPMENT POLICIES IN EFTA.
GENEVA: EUROPEAN FREE TRADE ASSN, 1965, 78 PP.
DETAILED DISCUSSION OF PRINCIPLES, OBJECTIVES, AND EXPERIENCES IN RELATION TO PROBLEMS OF REGIONAL DEVELOPMENT IN COUNTRIES OF AUSTRIA, DENMARK, FINLAND, NORWAY, PORTUGAL, SWEDEN, SWITZERLAND, AND UK. UNDEVELOPED, INDUSTRIALIZED, AND "OVERDEVELOPED" AREAS ARE DEFINED AND ANALYZED. INSTRUMENTS OF REGIONAL POLICIES ALSO DISCUSSED.

0756 EVANS R.H.
COEXISTENCE: COMMUNISM AND ITS PRACTICE IN BOLOGNA, 1945-1965.
SOUTH BEND: U OF NOTRE DAME, 1967, 225 PP.
ANALYZES BOLOGNA AS PARADIGM OF PEACEFUL COEXISTENCE OF COMMUNISM AND CAPITALISM. STUDIES MOTIVATION AND CONTENT OF SPECIFIC LOCAL BRAND OF COMMUNISM, AND REACTION AND RESPONSE TO IT BY SURROUNDING MIDDLE-CLASS MILIEU. EXAMINES STRENGTHS AND WEAKNESSES OF COMMUNIST ADMINISTRATION. ANALYZES REASONS FOR MODUS VIVENDI AND EXPOSTULATES ON FUTURE NEEDS.

0757 FABIAN SOCIETY
CAN PLANNING BE DEMOCRATIC?
LONDON: ROUTLEDGE & KEGAN PAUL, 1944, 118 PP.
ESSAYS ANALYZE IDEAS ON PLANNED ECONOMY, BUDGET, AND INDUSTRY IN DEMOCRATIC STATE. OPINIONS FAVOR PLANNING ECONOMY ON SOCIALISTIC LINES. FEEL THAT ANY TYPE OF GOVERNMENT CONTROL IN ECONOMY IS DESIRED STEP TOWARD SOCIALISM.

0758 FADDEYEV N.
"CMEA CO-OPERATION OF EQUAL NATIONS."
INTERNATIONAL AFFAIRS (USSR), 4 (APR 67).
DISCUSSION OF FIRST INTERNATIONAL ORGANIZATION OF SO CIALIST COUNTRIES WHICH EMBODIES PRINCIPLES OF SOCIALIST INTERNATIONALISM. PROVIDES SYSTEM OF MUTUAL ECONOMIC TIES TO PROMOTE SOCIAL PRODUCTION AND ECONOMIC DEVELOPMENT. TRACES HISTORY, FORMS OF ECONOMIC COOPERATION, AND PROCESSES OF SPECIALIZATION AND COMBINATION.

0759 FAHRNKOPF N. ED., LYNCH M.C. ED.
STATE AND LOCAL GOVERNMENT IN ILLINOIS (PAMPHLET)
URBANA: U OF ILLINOIS PR, 1965, 47 PP.
TOPICALLY ARRANGED, WORKS LISTED COVER 1954-64 IN FIELDS OF STATE, LOCAL, AND INTERGOVERNMENTAL PROCESSES. FIRST TWO SECTIONS INCLUDE CONSTITUTION, LEGISLATURE, COURT SYSTEMS, ADMINISTRATION, SERVICES, VOTING, AND ECONOMY. LAST SECTION LISTS WORKS IN INTERLOCAL, INTERSTATE, AND FEDERAL-STATE-LOCAL RELATIONSHIPS.

0760 FAINSOD M., GORDON L., PALAMOUNTAIN J.C.
"GOVERNMENT AND THE AMERICAN ECONOMY."
NEW YORK: W W NORTON, 1959.
AN EXAMINATION AND ANALYSIS OF GOVERNMENT'S ASSUMPTION OF MAJOR RESPONSIBILITY FOR GUIDANCE AND DIRECTION OF THE AMERICAN ECONOMY. EMPHASIS ON POLITICAL FORCES WHICH INFLUENCE FORMATION AND EXECUTION OF PUBLIC POLICY. UNANNOTATED BIBLIOGRAPHY OF GOVERNMENT PAMPHLETS, AND CONGRESSIONAL HEARINGS, BOOKS, AND PERIODICALS, ORGANIZED BY RELEVANCE TO CHAPTER HEADINGS.

0761 FALL B.B. ED.
HO CHI MINH ON REVOLUTION: SELECTED WRITINGS, 1920-66.
NEW YORK: FREDERICK PRAEGER, 1967, 389 PP., LC#67-20481.
BASIC WRITINGS OF HO CHI MINH BASED ON HIS VIEWS OF THE EVILS OF COLONIALISM AND HIS EFFORTS TO ELIMINATE THEM FROM VIETNAM. DISCUSSES PLACE OF COMMUNISM IN HIS REVOLUTIONARY MOVEMENT.

0762 FANON F.
TOWARD THE AFRICAN REVOLUTION.
NEW YORK: MONTHLY REVIEW PR, 1967, 197 PP., LC#67-19256.
POLITICAL ESSAYS, ARTICLES, AND NOTES PUBLISHED 1952-61. PRESENTS COMPLEXITY OF LIFE OF THE "COLONIZED", ITS DIVERSE ASPECTS AND INTERRELATIONS, AND YET ITS SAMENESS. EXPOSES CLOSE RELATIONSHIP BETWEEN COLONIZED AND COLONIZER AND DESCRIBES WORLD OF THE FORMER AS A "RESPONSE TO ALL FORMS OF OPPRESSION." DEALS ONLY WITH FRENCH COLONIES.

0763 FAO
FOOD AND AGRICULTURE ORG.
ROME: UN FAO, 1962, 168 PP.
SEEKS TO IDENTIFY AFRICAN RURAL PROBLEMS OBJECTIVELY, MARK OUT DIRECTIONS FOR INTERNATIONAL ACTION, AND POINT TO WAYS IT MAY BE MORE EFFECTIVE. REVEALS RISING STANDARD OF LIVING BUT NEED TO CHECK RURAL BACKWARDNESS. CALLS FOR INTEGRATED APPROACH TO SOCIAL AND ECONOMIC PROBLEMS. REPORT DIVIDED INTO THREE PARTS: SETTING, TECHNICAL CHANGE AND USE OF RESOURCES, PROBLEMS IN RURAL DEVELOPMENT.

0764 FARER T.J.
FINANCING AFRICAN DEVELOPMENT.
CAMBRIDGE: M I T PRESS, 1965, 245 PP., LC#65-28565.
COLLECTION OF ESSAYS BASED ON SELECTED PAPERS PRESENTED AT CONFERENCE AT UGANDA IN 1961 SPONSORED BY MIT'S AFRICA PROGRAM. IN ADDITION TO ECONOMIC AND MANAGERIAL QUESTIONS, ESSAYS FOCUS ON POLITICAL CONTEXT AND HUMAN COST OF FORCED-MARCH DEVELOPMENT. INCLUDES STUDIES OF FINANCIAL PLANNING OF ECONOMIC DEVELOPMENT, PRIVATE INVESTMENT AND FOREIGN AID.

0765 FARRIS M.T. ED., MCELHINEY P.T. ED.
MODERN TRANSPORTATION: SELECTED READINGS.
BOSTON: HOUGHTON MIFFLIN, 1967, 416 PP.
VARIOUS VIEWPOINTS ON GENERAL PRINCIPLES OF TRANSPROTATION: ECONOMICS, MANAGEMENT, REGULATION, AND PUBLIC POLICY. READINGS SELECTED FROM ACADEMIC AND TRADE JOURNALS. DESIGNED FOR USE IN BASIC TRANSPORTATION COURSE.

0766 FATEMI N.S., PHALLE T.D., KEEFE G.M.
THE DOLLAR CRISIS.
RUTHERFORD: FAIRLEIGH DICKEN PR, 1963, 317 PP., LC#63-23017.
ANALYSIS OF BALANCE OF PAYMENTS PROBLEM AND FACTORS CREATING IT. US FOREIGN PROGRAMS STUDIED WITH RECOMMENDATIONS DESIGNED TO PRESERVE GOOD OF PROGRAM AND REDUCE COST. ANALYSIS OF PRIVATE INVESTMENT AND STEPS TAKEN BY GOVERNMENT AND LEGISLATIVE ENACTMENT TO ENCOURAGE SUBSTITUTION OF PRIVATE INVESTMENT FOR GOVERNMENT AID.

0767 FATOUROS A.A.
GOVERNMENT GUARANTEES TO FOREIGN INVESTORS.
NEW YORK: COLUMBIA U PRESS, 1962, 411 PP., LC#62-12873.
ANALYZES VARIOUS FORMS AND MODALITIES BY WHICH STATES ENTER INTO ARRANGEMENTS WITH FOREIGN INVESTORS. ALSO STUDIES ASPECTS SUCH AS EXCHANGE RESTRICTIONS, EMPLOYMENT OF FOREIGN PERSONNEL, LEGAL EFFECTS OF TREATY PROMISES, AND STATE CONTRACTS.

0768 FATOUROS A.A., KELSON R N.
CANADA'S OVERSEAS AID.
TORONTO: CAN INST OF INTL AFF, 1964, 123 PP.
STUDY OF CANADIAN FOREIGN AID, 1950-62, BASED UPON CONFERENCE ON CANADIAN OVERSEAS AID, 1962. STUDIES TYPES, AIMS AND MOTIVES, DISTRIBUTION, AMOUNT AND FORMS, ADMINISTRATION OF AID. RECOMMENDS CONTINUED AID PROGRAM.

0769 FAULKNER H.U.
"AMERICAN ECONOMIC HISTORY (8TH ED.)"
NEW YORK: HARPER & ROW, 1960.
SURVEY OF AMERICAN ECONOMIC HISTORY SINCE COLONIAL TIMES. COMPREHENSIVE, CRITICALLY ANNOTATED BIBLIOGRAPHY OF PRIMARY AND SECONDARY SOURCES APPENDED TO TEXT. ARRANGED AS A CHAPTER-BY-CHAPTER SUPPLEMENT TO THE TEXTUAL ORGANIZATION. INCLUDES MUCH HISTORICALLY ORIENTED MATERIAL AND NO PUBLICATIONS MORE RECENT THAN 1953.

0770 FEARN H.
AN AFRICAN ECONOMY.
NEW YORK: OXFORD U. PR., 1961, 284 PP., $5.60.
DISCUSSES TRADITIONAL TOPICS AS RELATED TO DEVELOPMENT OF EMERGENT AFRICAN NATIONS. INCLUDES STUDY OF STRUCTURE, FUNCTIONS, AND ORGANIZATION OF PRIVATE AND GOVERNMENTAL GROUPS. BRIEF OUTLINE OF EUROPEAN ADMINISTRATION.

0771 FEDYSHYN O.S.
"KHRUSHCHEV'S 'LEAP FORWARD': NATIONAL ASSIMILATION IN THE USSR AFTER STALIN."
S.W. SOCIAL SCI. QUART., 48 (JUNE 67), 34-43.

ANALYZES KHRUSHCHEV'S NATIONALITIES POLICY IN LIGHT OF THE CONCESSIONS, RETREATS, RESTRICTIONS, AND PRESSURES THROUGH WHICH HE HOPED TO OVERCOME HUMAN OBSTACLES ON THE ROAD TO COMMUNIST CONSTRUCTION. DESCRIBES HIS METHODS AS MORE SUBTLE THAN STALIN'S, HIS GOALS MORE AMBITIOUS.

0772 FEI J.C.H., RANIS G.
DEVELOPMENT OF THE LABOR SURPLUS ECONOMY: THEORY AND POLICY.
HOMEWOOD: RICHARD IRWIN, 1964, 324 PP., LC#64-21024.
PRESENTS A THEORY OF DEVELOPMENT RELEVANT TO ORDINARY LABOR SURPLUS TYPE OF UNDERDEVELOPED ECONOMY, AND ATTEMPTS TO EXTRACT SOME POLICY CONCLUSIONS. APPROACHES PROBLEM FROM VIEWPOINTS OF ANALYTICAL ECONOMICS, INSTITUTIONAL ECONOMICS, AND STATISTICS. PRESENTS ANALYTICAL FRAMEWORK AT AGGREGATE LEVEL TO EXPLAIN GROWTH IN PARTICULAR TYPE OF UNDERDEVELOPED COUNTRY.

0773 FEIS H.
EUROPE, THE WORLD'S BANKER, 1871-1914.
NEW HAVEN: YALE U. PR., 1930, 469 PP.
ANALYZES THE PATTERNS OF FOREIGN INVESTMENT OF SURPLUS CAPITAL BY GREAT BRITAIN, FRANCE AND GERMANY BETWEEN 1870 AND 1914. ILLUSTRATES THE IMPORTANCE OF FOREIGN INVESTMENT AS AN INSTRUMENT OF NATIONAL FOREIGN POLICY.

0774 FEIS H.
THE DIPLOMACY OF THE DOLLAR: FIRST ERA 1919-32.
BALTIMORE: JOHNS HOPKINS PRESS, 1950, 81 PP.
DISCUSSES US "DOLLAR DIPLOMACY" PERIOD (1920'S) IN WHICH FEDERAL GOVERNMENT ENCOURAGED AND GUIDED PRIVATE CAPITAL SOURCES IN INVESTING IN FOREIGN SECURITIES TO EASE FINANCIAL STRAIN AFTER WWI. MAINTAINS THAT GOVERNMENT ACHIEVED FIRST PROXIMATE PURPOSES BUT NOTES NEGATION OF ALL DESIRED EFFECTS BY DEPRESSION. CONTENDS THAT OVER-ALL POLITICAL RESULTS WERE "LAMENTABLE," NOTING FAILURE OF LONG-RANGE PLANS.

0775 FEIS H.
FOREIGN AID AND FOREIGN POLICY.
NEW YORK: ST. MARTIN'S, 1964, 245 PP., $5.00.
REGARDS FOREIGN AID AS INTEGRAL PART OF FOREIGN POLICY. STRESSES IMPORTANCE OF PROGRAMMING FOR SOCIAL REFORM AND ECONOMIC CHANGE. COVERS OBSTACLES TO COOPERATION: AMERICAN RACE AND COLOR PREJUDICES, CLIMATE, MISUSE OF RESOURCES, LAND OWNERSHIP SYSTEMS, EXCESSIVE NATIONALISM, ETC. TREATS DILEMMAS OF AID ALLOTMENT.

0776 FELD W.
"EXTERNAL RELATIONS OF THE COMMON MARKET AND GROUP LEADERSHIP ATTITUDES IN THE MEMBER STATES."
ORBIS, 10 (SUMMER 66), 564-587.
INTERNATIONAL TRADE AND TARIFF POLICIES ARE AN IMPORTANT SET OF TOOLS IN A NATION'S FOREIGN POLICY KIT. THE SOVEREIGN CONTROL OF THEM IS USUALLY CLOSELY GUARDED BY NATIONAL GOVERNMENTS. AUTHOR ANALYZES CENTRAL COUNCIL ATTEMPTS TO BYPASS THE NATIONAL GOVERNMENTS TO CREATE AND IMPLEMENT COMMUNITY POLICY.

0777 FELD W.
"NATIONAL ECONOMIC INTEREST GROUPS AND POLICY FORMATION IN THE EEC."
POLIT. SCI. QUART., 81 (SEPT. 66), 392-411.
70 INTERVIEWS WITH INTEREST GROUP, POLITICAL PARTY, GOVERNMENT MINISTRY, AND EEC OFFICIALS ARE BASIS OF THIS STUDY OF THE ROUTES INTEREST GROUP DEMANDS TAKE. DISCERNS PREFERENCE FOR WORKING THROUGH OWN NATION'S GOVERNMENT AND PARTY OFFICIALS. RESULTS EVALUATED IN TERMS OF EASTON'S SYSTEM.

0778 FELKER J.L.
SOVIET ECONOMIC CONTROVERSIES.
CAMBRIDGE: M I T PRESS, 1966, 172 PP., LC#66-26017.
ANALYZES SOVIET UNION ECONOMIC SYSTEM, CONCENTRATING ON DEVELOPING MARKETING SYSTEM, POST-STALIN REFORMS, AND CHANGES IN TRADE, PRICING, AND PROFITS IN USSR. COVERS LENINIST AND STALINIST THEORY, ITS APPLICATION TO SOVIET INDUSTRIAL ORGANIZATION OVER YEARS, AND RESULTING CHANGES.

0779 FELLNER W.
TRENDS AND CYCLES IN ECONOMIC ACTIVITY: AN INTRODUCTION TO PROBLEMS OF ECONOMIC GROWTH.
NEW YORK: HOLT RINEHART WINSTON, 1956, 411 PP., LC#56-6059.
SHOWS HOW SUSTAINED ECONOMIC GROWTH REQUIRES QUALITATIVE ADEQUACY AS WELL AS QUANTITATIVE SUFFICIENCY OF TECHNOLOGICAL AND ORGANIZATIONAL IMPROVEMENTS. ATTEMPTS TO GAUGE ABILITY OF IMPROVEMENTS TO OFFSET CONSEQUENCES OF DIFFERENTIAL FACTOR SUPPLIES. BOOK IS PRIMARILY GROWTH-ORIENTED, OR TREND-ORIENTED TOWARD DYNAMIC ECONOMICS.

0780 FELLNER W., GILBERT M. ET AL.
THE PROBLEM OF RISING PRICES.
PARIS: ORG FOR ECO COOP AND DEV, 1961, 489 PP.
EXAMINES PROBLEMS OF RISING PRICES UNDER CONDITIONS OF ECONOMIC GROWTH AND HIGH EMPLOYMENT SINCE 1952. DISCUSSES ROLE OF DEMAND, WAGES, AND MONOPOLISTIC PRICING. APPENDED LIST OF ANTI-INFLATIONARY MEASURES AND WAGE DETERMINATION IN SELECTED COUNTRIES.

0781 FELLNER W., MACHLUP F. ET AL.
MAINTAINING AND RESTORING BALANCE IN INTERNATIONAL PAYMENTS.
PRINCETON: PRINCETON U PRESS, 1966, 259 PP., LC#66-23764.
STRESSES VARIETY OF CAUSES FOR IMBALANCES OF INTERNATIONAL PAYMENTS, DISCUSSES MEANS OF MEETING CRISES: FINANCING FROM ACCUMULATED RESERVES OR BORROWING, DEMAND OR EXCHANGE-RATE ADJUSTMENT, AND SELECTIVE MARKET INFLUENCING. EXAMINES DIFFERENCES IN MONETARY CRISES IN DEVELOPED AND UNDEVELOPED COUNTRIES.

0782 FELS R.
AMERICAN BUSINESS CYCLES 1865-1897.
CHAPEL HILL: U OF N CAR PR, 1959, 244 PP.
DISCUSSES METHOD AND THEORETICAL FRAMEWORK FOR STUDY OF BUSINESS CYCLES. FOR THE PERIOD DESIGNATED, EXAMINES PRICE AND WAGE FLEXIBILITY, AND THE CYCLES THEMSELVES, INCLUDING THE DEPRESSION OF THE NINETIES.

0783 FERBER R., VERDOORN P.J.
RESEARCH METHODS IN ECONOMICS AND BUSINESS.
NEW YORK: MACMILLAN, 1962, 573 PP., LC#62-7080.
RECOGNIZING SIMILARITIES BETWEEN PROBLEM-SOLVING TECHNIQUES USED FOR BUSINESS AND ECONOMIC ANALYSIS OF AGGREGATES, THIS STUDY PROVIDES GENERAL OUTLINE OF ORGANIZATION OF RESEARCH OPERATIONS, EXPOSITION OF MAIN APPROACHES TO RESEARCH PROBLEMS, AND DESCRIPTIONS OF SPECIFIC RESEARCH TECHNIQUES, WITH RELATIVE MERITS OF EACH.

0784 FERGUSON D.E.
"DETERMINING CAPACITY FOR CAPITAL EXPENDITURES."
MUNICIPAL FINANCE, 40 (AUG. 67), 59-64.
DISCUSSES ECONOMIC, ADMINISTRATIVE, ORGANIZATIONAL, AND METROPOLITAN FACTORS AS THEY RELATE TO DETERMINING CAPITAL EXPENDITURE LEVELS. COVERS FACTORS SUCH AS TAX BASE, SERVICES PROVIDED, AND TRENDS IN TAX ASSESSMENT.

0785 FERMAN L.A. ED., KORNBLUH J.L. ED., HABER A. ED.
POVERTY IN AMERICA: A BOOK OF READINGS.
ANN ARBOR: U OF MICH PR, 1965, 532 PP., LC#65-20351.
MULTI-FACETED STUDY OF POVERTY. COVERS ITS DEFINITION, PREVALENCE, STRUCTURE, AND RELATION TO ECONOMY, ALSO VALUES AND LIFE STYLES OF POOR. VARIOUS PROGRAMS AND PROPOSALS SUGGESTED TO MEET PROBLEMS OF SOCIAL, ECONOMIC, AND CULTURAL DEPRIVATION. SELECT BIBLIOGRAPHY ACCOMPANIES EACH SECTION.

0786 FERNANDES F.
MUDANCAS SOCIAIS NO BRASIL.
SAO PAULO: DIFUSAO EUROPEIA DO LIVRO, 1960, 401PP.
ANALYZES ECONOMIC AND SOCIAL OBSTACLES TO BRAZILIAN DEVELOPMENT. COMPARES AND EXPLAINS ROLE OF RACIAL AND ETHNIC GROUPS IN SOCIAL CHANGE AND INDUSTRIALIZATION. EXAMINES CONDITIONS IN MOST INDUSTRIALIZED STATE, SAO PAULO, AND COMPARES IT TO REST OF BRAZIL IN AGRICULTURAL STATES.

0787 FERRY W.H.
THE CORPORATION AND THE ECONOMY.
SANTA BARBARA: CTR DEMO INST, 1959, 122 PP.
NOTES ON THE PRESENT AND PAST USES OF CORPORATE POWER, WITH PROPOSALS FOR FUTURE CONTROL, FOLLOWED BY A TRANSCRIPT OF A DISCUSSION OF THE NOTES BY E. GOLDMAN, R. NIEBUHR, R. HUTCHINS, AND OTHERS. HOLDS THAT THE PRIVATE ORGANIZATION OF ECONOMIC ENTERPRISE, INVOLVING IMPORTANT PUBLIC INTEREST, MUST CONFORM TO JUSTICE AND FREEDOM, AS LABOR UNIONS SHOULD. DISCUSSES PLANNING IN MODERN SOCIETY.

0788 FERTIG L.
PROSPERITY THROUGH FREEDOM.
CHICAGO: HENRY REGNERY CO, 1961, 278 PP., LC#61-17367.
INTERPRETATIVE ANALYSES OF SEVERAL PHASES OF ECONOMIC AFFAIRS WITH EMPHASIS THROUGHOUT ON IMPORTANCE OF MAINTAINING FREE MARKETS AND FREE ECONOMIC SYSTEM TO PREVENT EMERGENCE OF COLLECTIVIST STATE. ARGUES AGAINST EXTENSION OF GOVERNMENT ECONOMIC ACITIVITY AND WELFARISM.

0789 FIELD G.C.
POLITICAL THEORY.
LONDON: METHUEN, 1956, 297 PP.
DISCUSSES VARIOUS ASPECTS OF POLITICAL THEORY AS CONCEPT OF SOVEREIGNTY, STATE, INDIVIDUAL LIBERTY, ETC. EXAMINES IN DETAIL MACHINERY OF DEMOCRACY AND RELATIONS BETWEEN STATES. CONCLUDES WITH ESSAY ON RELATION BETWEEN POLITICS, ECONOMICS, AND ETHICS.

0790 FIELD G.L.
COMPARATIVE POLITICAL DEVELOPMENT: THE PRECEDENT OF THE WEST
ITHACA: CORNELL U PRESS, 1967, 247 PP., LC#67-14082.
EXAMINES MAJOR EUROPEAN POWERS, ESPECIALLY THEIR LEVELS OF SOCIO-ECONOMIC DEVELOPMENT, AND SEEKS TO CLASSIFY THEM UNDER DEVELOPMENTAL FRAMEWORK. DISCUSSION CENTERS NOT ON VARIATIONS IN CONSTITUTIONAL STRUCTURES, BUT ON CONDITIONS WHICH PERMIT INSTITUTIONAL STABILITY.

0791 FIESER M.E.
ECONOMIC POLICY AND WAR POTENTIAL.

WASHINGTON: PUBLIC AFFAIRS PRESS, 1964, 136 PP., LC#64-18356
ANALYSIS OF ECONOMIC ASPECTS OF MILITARY PREPARATION DETAILING IMPACT OF STOCKPILING AND STRATEGIC IMPORTS ON MILITARY PRODUCTION AND NATIONAL SECURITY.

0792 FIKS M.
PUBLIC ADMINISTRATION IN ISRAEL (PAMPHLET)
NEW YORK: PERSONNEL RES ASSN, 1958, 29 PP.
ANALYSIS OF CIVIL SERVICE AND OTHER PUBLIC EMPLOYMENT IN ISRAEL, INCLUDING EDUCATIONAL SYSTEM. EXAMINES STRUCTURE AND PERSONNEL OF PUBLIC ADMINISTRATION AND BENEFITS OF PUBLIC EMPLOYMENT.

0793 FILENE P.G.
AMERICANS AND THE SOVIET EXPERIMENT, 1917-1933.
CAMBRIDGE: HARVARD U PR, 1967, 384 PP., LC#67-11669.
EXAMINES AMERICAN ATTITUDES TOWARD THE USSR FROM HER ESTABLISHMENT UNTIL US DIPLOMATIC RECOGNITION. TREATS VIEWS FROM ALL AREAS OF POLITICAL AND INTELLECTUAL SPECTRUM. CASE STUDIES OF FOUR US JOURNALISTS WHO WENT TO RUSSIA AS COMMUNISTS, THREE OF WHOM WERE DISILLUSIONED. ALSO TREATS AMERICAN ATTITUDES TOWARD CAPITALISM, SOCIALISM, AND AMERICAN SOCIETY.

0794 FILLOL T.R.
"SOCIAL FACTORS IN ECONOMIC DEVELOPMENT: THE ARGENTINE CASE"
CAMBRIDGE: M I T PRESS, 1961.
SHORT BIBLIOGRAPHY OF 80 BOOKS DEALING WITH ECONOMIC DEVELOPMENT IN GENERAL AND ARGENTINIAN PROBLEMS AND BACKGROUND IN PARTICULAR; ALSO US AND ARGENTINIAN WORKS ON LABOR AND LABOR LEGISLATION IN THAT COUNTRY. ENGLISH- AND SPANISH-LANGUAGE BOOKS, MOST PUBLISHED IN 1950'S.

0795 FILLOL T.R.
SOCIAL FACTORS IN ECONOMIC DEVELOPMENT: THE ARGENTINE CASE.
CAMBRIDGE: M I T PRESS, 1961, 118 PP., LC#61-10157.
MONOGRAPH SEEKS TO IMPROVE UNDERSTANDING OF RELATIONSHIP BETWEEN SOCIAL AND ECONOMIC CONDITIONS OF ARGENTINA AND TRENDS OF ITS DEVELOPING INDUSTRIAL ORGANIZATIONS. ANALYZES SOCIAL AND POLITICAL STRUCTURE INFLUENCING MANAGEMENT AND UNION LEADERSHIP. APPRAISES ARGENTINE INDUSTRIALIZATION AND LESS DEVELOPED ECONOMIES IN GENERAL.

0796 FINER H.
REPRESENTATIVE GOVERNMENT AND A PARLIAMENT OF INDUSTRY. A STUDY OF THE GERMAN FEDERAL ECONOMIC COUNCIL.
DUBUQUE: WC BROWN, 1923, 273 PP.
DISCUSSES GENESIS OF GERMAN ECONOMIC COUNCIL, ITS COMPOSITION, STATUS, AND PROCEDURE, AND ITS OPERATION IN WAR AND REVOLUTION. CONCLUDES WITH COMPARISON BETWEEN ENGLAND AND GERMANY.

0797 FINER S.E.
PRIVATE INDUSTRY AND POLITICAL POWER (PAMPHLET)
LONDON: PALL MALL PRESS, 1958, 22 PP.
THEORETICAL DISCUSSION OF INTERRELATIONSHIPS BETWEEN BUSINESS AND GOVERNMENT. SAYS GOVERNMENT SHOULD REPRESENT GENERAL PUBLIC AGAINST PRIVATE INTERESTS. LOOKS AT BUSINESS AS A KIND OF SURROGATE OF GOVERNMENT IN THE ECONOMIC SPHERE. IT SHOULD HAVE SOME RESPONSIBILITIES TOWARD PUBLIC AS THE GOVERNMENT.

0798 FINER S.E.
"THE ONE-PARTY REGIMES IN AFRICA: RECONSIDERATIONS."
GOVERNMENT AND OPPOSITION, 2 (JULY-OCT 67), 491-509.
PRESENTS TWO LINES OF ARGUMENT ASSERTING ADVANTAGES OF SINGLE-PARTY STATES IN AFRICA. FIRST, SINGLE-PARTY SYSTEM IS NECESSARY FOR ECONOMIC ADVANCE, POLITICAL STABILITY, AND NATION-BUILDING; IT ALSO FOLLOWS DESIRES OF PEOPLE. SECOND, SUCH SYSTEMS ARE ONLY AVAILABLE ALTERNATIVE TO MILITARY RULE. MAINTAINS THAT BOTH ARE UNTRUE AND THAT ONE-PARTY SYSTEM IS UNSTABLE AND UNCONSTRUCTIVE.

0799 FINKLE J.L.
THE PRESIDENT MAKES A DECISION: A STUDY OF DIXON-YATES.
ANN ARBOR: U MICH, INST PUB ADM, 1960, 204 PP.
INTENSIVE STUDY OF EFFECTS OF POLITICAL VALUES ON THE OPERATIONS OF THE EXECUTIVE BRANCH, AS OBSERVED IN THE DIXON-YATES CASE OF 1954. PRIMARY CONCERN OF STUDY IS WITH ATTEMPT OF EISENHOWER ADMINISTRATION TO ARRIVE AT SPECIFIC APPLICATION OF POLICY WITHIN FRAMEWORK ESTABLISHED IN PRESIDENT'S BUDGET MESSAGE. REVEALS POLITICAL DYNAMICS RESULTING IN SELECTION OF DIXON-YATES AND DECISION-MAKING PROCESS.

0800 FINLEY D.D.
"A POLITICAL PERSPECTIVE OF ECONOMIC RELATIONS IN THE COMMUNIST CAMP."
WEST. POLIT. QUART., 17 (JUNE 64), 294-316.
ASSERTS THAT USSR MANIPULATES ECONOMIC REGIONALISM AS INSTRUMENT TO STRENGTHEN AND MAINTAIN THREATENED POLITICAL PRIMACY IN COMMUNIST CAMP. EXPLORES EVOLUTION OF COMMUNIST POLICY ON ECONOMIC INTEGRATION SINCE 1945.

0801 FIRESTONE J.M.
FEDERAL RECEIPTS AND EXPENDITURES DURING BUSINESS CYCLES, 1879-1958.
PRINCETON: PRINCETON U PRESS, 1960, 176 PP., LC#60-8391.
FINDS SURPRISINGLY CONSISTENT PATTERN OF BEHAVIOR IN FEDERAL SPENDING AND REVENUE COLLECTIONS OVER 80 YEARS. SHOWS BUSINESS CYCLES HAVE CONSISTENTLY UPSET BUDGETARY BALANCE, TENDING TO CREATE SURPLUSES IN PROSPERITY AND DEFICITS IN DEPRESSION. ALSO FINDS THAT CYCLICAL SHIFT FROM SURPLUS TOWARD DEFICIT AND BACK HAS BEEN DUE TO REVENUE BEHAVIOR; TODAY, CYCLICAL SWING OF REVENUES AFFECTS BUSINESS CYCLE.

0802 FIRTH R.
PRIMITIVE POLYNESIAN ECONOMY.
LONDON: ROUTLEDGE & KEGAN PAUL, 1939, 385 PP.
DISCUSSES ECONOMY OF TIKOPIA, A MODERN PRIMITIVE POLYNESIAN SOCIETY. STUDIES AGRICULTURE AND POPULATION, KNOWLEDGE AND TECHNIQUES OF ECONOMICS, AND LABOR SITUATION. ANALYZES ROLE OF RITUAL IN PRODUCTIVE ACTIVITY, ECONOMIC FUNCTIONS OF CHIEFS, AND PROPERTY AND CAPITAL IN PRODUCTION. DESCRIBES POLYNESIAN PRINCIPLES OF DISTRIBUTION AND PAYMENT, EXCHANGE, AND VALUE.

0803 FIRTH R., YAMEY B.S.
CAPITAL, SAVING AND CREDIT IN PEASANT SOCIETIES.
CHICAGO: ALDINE, 1964, 399 PP., $8.95.
SEVENTEEN ESSAYS ON THE INTERACTION OF ECONOMIC AND SOCIAL FACTORS IN PEASANT LIFE, BASED ON STUDIES FROM ASIA, OCEANIA, THE CARIBBEAN, AND MIDDLE AMERICA. A PIONEERING WORK USING A COMBINATION OF ECONOMIC AND ANTHROPOLOGICAL TECHNIQUES OF INQUIRY.

0804 FISK E.K. ED.
NEW GUINEA ON THE THRESHOLD; ASPECTS OF SOCIAL, POLITICAL, AND ECONOMIC DEVELOPMENT.
LONDON: LONGMANS, GREEN & CO, 1966, 290 PP.
PAPERS ON ECONOMICS, SOCIAL PROBLEMS, AND POLITICS OF SITUATION IN PAPUA, NEW GUINEA, AT PRESENT AND DURING NEXT DECADE. COVERS HISTORICAL BACKGROUND, ECONOMIC STRUCTURE, RESOURCES, TRADE, DEMOGRAPHY, EDUCATION, LITERACY, SOCIAL CHANGE, ROLE OF WOMEN, EXPATRIATES, GROWTH OF TERRITORIAL ADMINISTRATION, AND ADVANCE TO RESPONSIBLE GOVERNMENT.

0805 FISK W.M.
ADMINISTRATIVE PROCEDURE IN A REGULATORY AGENCY: THE CAB AND THE NEW YORK-CHICAGO CASE (PAMPHLET)
INDIANAPOLIS: BOBBS-MERRILL, 1964.
STUDIES ECONOMIC REGULATION EXERCISED BY CIVIL AERONAUTICS BOARD OVER US AIR TRANSPORT INDUSTRY. EXAMINES CAB'S POWER IN DETERMINING AIR ROUTES, SERVICE POINTS, AND NATURE OF SERVICE. EMPHASIZES PROCEDURAL ASPECTS OF NEW YORK-CHICAGO CASE OF 1953 WHICH LED TO OVERHAUL OF STRUCTURE OF AIR ROUTES.

0806 FITCH L.C.
URBAN TRANSPORTATION AND PUBLIC POLICY.
SAN FRANCISCO: CHANDLER, 1964, 279 PP., LC#64-15743.
EXPLORES PRESENT DEFICIENCIES IN URBAN TRANSPORTATION FACILITIES AND POLICIES, AND FACTORS WHICH IMPEDE IMPROVEMENT. CONSIDERS QUESTIONS OF PRICING, SUBSIDIES, AND COST CHARACTERISTICS OF DIFFERENT MODES; ADEQUACY OF PRESENT ORGANIZATION FOR POLICY PLANNING, POLICY DECISIONS, AND POLICY IMPLEMENTATION; THE STATE OF TECHNOLOGY AND POSSIBLE LINES OF IMPROVEMENT; AND THE NEED FOR FEDERAL ASSISTANCE.

0807 FLACKS R.
"CONSCRIPTION IN A DEMOCRATIC SOCIETY."
NEW INDIVIDUALIST REVIEW, 4 (SPRING 67), 10-12.
PROPOSES WAYS TO LIMIT USES OF CONSCRIPTION AND TO RESIST ITS INTEGRATION INTO AMERICAN SOCIETY AS AN ACCEPTED INSTITUTION. SUGGESTS THAT DRAFTEES BE ALLOWED TO VOTE, THAT DRAFTEES BE USED ONLY FOR NATION'S DEFENSE AND NOT IN FOREIGN WARS, THAT BASE FOR CONSCIENTIOUS OBJECTION BE WIDENED, AND THAT FREEDOM AND OPPORTUNITY FOR SELF-DEVELOPMENT OF YOUTH BE ENLARGED.

0808 FLASH E.S. JR.
ECONOMIC ADVICE AND PRESIDENTIAL LEADERSHIP: THE COUNCIL OF ECONOMIC ADVISORS.
NEW YORK: COLUMBIA U PRESS, 1965, 382 PP., LC#65-24587.
DESCRIBES THE COUNCIL UNDER KEYSERLING, BURNS, AND HELLER EVALUATES ITS IMPACT ON ECONOMIC POLICY AND DESCRIBES ITS POLITICAL ROLE, ANALYZES ITS RELATIONS WITH CONGRESS AND AGENCIES.

0809 FLEMING R.W.
THE LABOR ARBITRATION PROCESS.
URBANA: U OF ILLINOIS PR, 1965, 227 PP., LC#65-19569.
DISCUSSES LABOR ARBITRATION, ITS PAST AND DEVELOPMENT; PROBLEMS OF COST, TIME-LAG AND FORMALITY, INDIVIDUAL RIGHTS, PROCEDURAL REGULARITY, EVIDENCE; AND STUDIES OF PREDICTABILITY IN ARBITRATION.

0810 FLEMING W.G.
"AUTHORITY, EFFICIENCY, AND ROLE STRESS: PROBLEMS IN THE DEVELOPMENT OF EAST AFRICAN BUREAUCRACIES."
ADMINISTRATIVE SCI. Q.,11 (DEC 66), 386-404.
AN ANALYSIS BY COUNTRY OF BRITISH EXPERIENCES IN EAST AFRICA IN ATTEMPTING TO IMPOSE BUREAUCRATIC STRUCTURES UPON

EXISTING POLITICAL SYSTEMS. STRESSES IMPOSSIBILITY OF MAXIMIZING BOTH EFFICIENCY AND AUTHORITY, AND EXPLORES CURRENT ATTEMPTS BY THESE NATIONS TO MODERNIZE THE NATIONAL POLITICAL STRUCTURE. INCLUDES BACKGROUND FOR RESEARCH INTO VARIOUS ASPECTS OF COLONIALISM, SOCIOLOGY, AND POLITICAL SYSTEMS.

0811 FLINN M.W.
AN ECONOMIC AND SOCIAL HISTORY OF BRITAIN, 1066-1939.
NEW YORK: ST MARTIN'S PRESS, 1961, 388 PP.
DISCUSSES BROAD SOCIETAL AND ECONOMIC SITUATION DURING THE VARIOUS STAGES OF DEVELOPMENT. INCLUDES MEDIEVAL ERA, RISE OF INDUSTRIALISM, REFORM PERIOD AND AFTER.

0812 FLOREA I.
"CU PRIVIRE LA OBIECTUL MATERIALISMULUI ISTORIC SI AL COMUNISMULUI STIINTIFIC SI LA RAPORTUL DINTRE ELE."
CERCET. FILOZOF., 10 (NO.2, 63), 733-54.
PRIME OBJECTIVE OF HISTORICAL MATERIALISM AND OF MARXIST SOCIOLOGY IS STUDY OF SOCIO-ECONOMIC FORMATIONS. ANALYZES SCIENTIFIC COMMUNISM AND PROLETARIAT ROLE IN ORDER TO FORMULATE REVOLUTIONARY POLICY. GIVES DIRECTIVE FOR WORLD-WIDE COMMUNIST EXPANSION.

0813 FLORENCE P.S.
THE LOGIC OF BRITISH AND AMERICAN INDUSTRY; A REALISTIC ANALYSIS OF ECONOMIC STRUCTURE AND GOVERNMENT.
LONDON: G ROUTLEDGE & SONS, 1953, 368 PP.
COMPARATIVE STUDY OF INDUSTRIAL SYSTEMS BEGINS BY DEFINING APPROACH. DISCUSSES INDUSTRIAL STRUCTURE, RELATIONS OF INDUSTRY AND CONSUMER, RELATIONS WITHIN FIRM, GOVERNMENT OF FREE ENTERPRISE CAPITALISM, AND NATIONALIZATION; INCLUDES LABOR RELATIONS. EXAMINES TREND OF INVESTMENT AND EMPLOYMENT, DELEGATION OF AUTHORITY, MEASURES OF EFFICIENCY, PATTERNS OF LOCATION, AND TYPES OF MANAGEMENT.

0814 FLORENCE P.S.
ECONOMICS AND SOCIOLOGY OF INDUSTRY; A REALISTIC ANALYSIS OF DEVELOPMENT.
NEW YORK: WATTS, 1964, 258 PP.
CONTAINS ANALYSIS OF INDUSTRIAL DEVELOPMENT AND RELATION OF SOCIOLOGY AND ECONOMICS TO ITS STUDY. EXAMINES INDUSTRY'S ECONOMIC AND SOCIAL MOBILITY, URBANIZATION AND INDUSTRIAL LOCATION, ORGANIZATIONAL SYSTEMS, INDUSTRIAL GOVERNMENT, INDUSTRIALIZATION IN UNDERDEVELOPED COUNTRIES, SOCIAL LIMITS ON ECONOMIC DEVELOPMENT, AND SOCIAL RESEARCH.

0815 FLORES E.
LAND REFORM AND THE ALLIANCE FOR PROGRESS (PAMPHLET)
PRINCETON: CTR OF INTL STUDIES, 1963, 14 PP.
DISCUSSES PROSPECTS OF ALLIANCE FOR PROGRESS, ARGUING THAT IT CAN SUCCEED ONLY IF IT ACCEPTS DRASTIC REVOLUTIONARY CHANGE IN LATIN AMERICA, EMPHASIZING IMPORTANCE OF LAND REFORM AS INTEGRAL PART OF CHANGE.

0816 FLORINSKY M.T.
INTEGRATED EUROPE.
NEW YORK: MACMILLAN, 1955, 182 PP.
SURVEYS ORIGINS AND NATURE OF MOVEMENTS PROMOTING THE INTEGRATION OF EUROPE. DISCUSSES ECONOMIC, MILITARY AND POLITICAL IMPLICATIONS OF INTEGRATION. AUTHOR REFLECTS ON RECENT EXPERIENCES AND CONCLUDES THAT WHILE ECONOMIC INTEGRATION IS FEASIBLE, POLITICAL AND MILITARY UNION IS DOUBTFUL.

0817 FLORINSKY M.T.
"TRENDS IN THE SOVIET ECONOMY."
CURR. HIST., 47 (NOV. 64), 266-271.
WHEN DEALING WITH USSR DIFFICULT TO RESIST TEMPTATION TO COMPARE WITH USA. POPULAR GROUND FOR COMPARISON IS RATE OF ECONOMIC GROWTH WHICH AUTHOR (AND OTHERS FAMILIAR WITH STATISTICAL METHODS) ASSERTS IS AN UNSOUND METHOD.

0818 FLOYD D.
"FIFTH AMENDMENT RIGHT TO COUNSEL IN FEDERAL INCOME TAX INVESTIGATIONS."
STANFORD LAW REV., 19 (MAY 67), 1014-1035.
EXAMINES ORDINARY TAX FRAUD INVESTIGATION IN FORMAL PRE-HEARING STAGES. OUTLINES ITS DANGERS FOR TAXPAYER AND CATALOGUES RECOGNIZED FIFTH AMENDMENT PROTECTIONS WITH FOCUS ON INADEQUACIES. DEFINES SCOPE OF RIGHTS ESTABLISHED IN MIRANDA VS. ARIZONA DECISION APPLICABLE TO RELATED CASES. PROVIDES GROUNDWORK FOR GENERAL APPROACH TO FIFTH AMENDMENT RIGHT-TO-COUNSEL QUESTIONS AT VARIOUS STAGES OF PROCEEDINGS.

0819 FOGARTY M.P.
ECONOMIC CONTROL.
LONDON: ROUTLEDGE & KEGAN PAUL, 1955, 324 PP.
DISCUSSES ISSUES OF GOVERNMENTAL CONTROL OF ECONOMY, ESPECIALLY IN BRITAIN, INCLUDING PRODUCTION DECISIONS, DECISIONS ABOUT OBJECTIVES, AND PROBLEMS OF CONTROL. STUDIES DIFFERENT ECONOMIC AREAS OF CONTROL. BIBLIOGRAPHY OF 300 ENTRIES IN ENGLISH, 1932-52, BOOKS, ARTICLES, DOCUMENTS, ARRANGED BY CHAPTER, THEN TOPOGRAPHICALLY.

0820 FOLDES L.
"UNCERTAINTY, PROBABILITY AND POTENTIAL SURPRISE."
ECONOMICA, 99 (AUG. 58), 246-254.
PRESENTS A REFUTATION OF KNIGHT'S DISTINCTION BETWEEN RISK AND UNCERTAINTY. ARGUES THAT THE CONCEPT OF "PROBABILITY" IS SUFFICIENT TO ANALYSE BUSINESS BEHAVIOR.

0821 FONER P.S. ED.
THE BOLSHEVIK REVOLUTION.
NEW YORK: INTERNATIONAL PUBL CO, 1967, 304 PP., LC#67-24548.
DOCUMENTARY STUDY OF IMPACT OF BOLSHEVIK REVOLUTION ON AMERICAN LABOR AND INTELLIGENTSIA FROM NOVEMBER, 1917-1921. CONSISTS OF PRIMARY SOURCE MATERIALS, LARGELY JOURNALS.

0822 FORBUSH D.R.
PROBLEMS OF CORPORATE POWER.
EVANSTON: NORTHWESTERN U PRESS, 1960, 250 PP.
DEALS LARGELY WITH THE QUESTION OF ECONOMIC COMPETITION, THE ROLE OF MONOPOLIES AND THE QUESTION OF REGULATION. POSES PROBLEM OF EXCESSIVE CORPORATE POWER AND REPRESENTATION OF PUBLIC INTERESTS WITH WIDE AREAS OF DISCRETION OPEN TO MANAGEMENT. ILLUSTRATES AMPLY BY COURT DECISIONS.

0823 FORD A.G.
THE GOLD STANDARD 1880-1914: BRITAIN AND ARGENTINA.
LONDON: OXFORD U PR, 1962, 200 PP.
STUDIES OPERATIONS OF GOLD STANDARD IN EACH COUNTRY PRIOR TO WWI. EMPHASIZES STRUCTURE OF INTERNATIONAL ACCOUNTS AND SYSTEMS, POINTING OUT TRADE, ETC., BETWEEN THESE NATIONS AS AN EXAMPLE. THEORIZES FROM NEW APPROACH BALANCE OF PAYMENTS' PROBLEMS AND THEIR SOLUTIONS WHICH LED TO SUCCESS OF GOLD STANDARD IN ENGLAND AND ITS FAILURE IN ARGENTINA.

0824 FORD J.L.
THE OHLIN-HECKSCHER THEORY OF THE BASIS AND EFFECTS OF COMMODITY TRADE.
NEW YORK: ASIA PUBL HOUSE, 1965, 88 PP.
ANALYSIS OF INTERNATIONAL TRADE THEORY FORMULATED BY OHLIN AND HECKSCHER. EXAMINES BASIC MODELS CREATED IN THEORY.

0825 FORD P.
CARDINAL MORAN AND THE A. L. P.
MELBOURNE: MELBOURNE UNIV PRESS, 1966, 319 PP., LC#66-17534.
ANALYZES ENCOUNTER BETWEEN CARDINAL AND SOCIALISM IN AUSTRALIA, AS IT DEVELOPED 1890-1907. CONCENTRATES ON EFFECTS ON AUSTRALIAN LABOR PARTY, AND FOUNDATIONS OF CATHOLIC SOCIAL THOUGHT AND ACTION IN MODERN AUSTRALIAN SOCIETY. FEELS MORAN'S FIGHT AGAINST SOCIALISM AS OBJECTIVE OF LABOR PARTY ILLUSTRATES NOT ONLY ERA INVOLVED, BUT IMPACT THAT AN ACTIVE CLERGYMAN CAN HAVE ON CIVIC LIFE.

0826 FORDE D. ED., KABERRY P.M. ED.
WEST AFRICAN KINGDOMS IN THE NINETEENTH CENTURY.
NEW YORK: OXFORD U PR, 1967, 289 PP.
DISCUSSES TEN WEST AFRICAN COUNTRIES THAT PLAYED A MAJOR PART IN THE POLITICAL, ECONOMIC, AND CULTURAL DEVELOPMENT OF THE REGION DURING THE 19TH CENTURY. DRAWS ON RECENT ANTHROPOLOGICAL FIELD WORK.

0827 FORM W.H.
"THE PLACE OF SOCIAL STRUCTURE IN THE DETERMINATION OF LAND USE: SOME IMPLICATIONS FOR A THEORY OF URBAN ECOLOGY" (BMR)"
SOCIAL FORCES, 32 (MAY 54), 317-323.
IN STUDYING LAND CHANGE USE, AUTHOR PROPOSES THAT ECOLOGY ABANDON ITS SUB-SOCIAL NON-ORGANIZATION ORIENTATIONS AND USE THE FRAME OF REFERENCE OF GENERAL SOCIOLOGY. FIRST STEP IS TO ANALYZE SOCIAL FORCES OPERATING ON LAND MARKET. FROM A STUDY OF THIS STRUCTURE ONE OBTAINS PICTURE OF PARAMETERS OF ECOLOGICAL BEHAVIOR, PATTERNS OF LAND CHANGE USE, AND INSTITUTIONAL PRESSURES ON ECOLOGICAL ORDER.

0828 FORM W.H., SAUER W.L.
INDUSTRY, LABOR, AND COMMUNITY.
NEW YORK: HARPER & ROW, 1960.
ANALYZES EXTERNAL RELATIONSHIPS AMONG SUCH ORGANIZATIONS. OUTLINES THEIR HISTORIC RELATIONS, CURRENT STRUCTURES, AND SUGGESTS FUTURE DEVELOPMENTS. DEALS EXTENSIVELY WITH ORGANIZATIONAL ROLE AND POWER AND COMMUNITY POWER PROBLEMS. A VERY COMPREHENSIVE TEXT.

0829 FORM W.H., SAUER W.L.
"ORGANIZED LABOR'S IMAGE OF COMMUNITY POWER STRUCTURE."
SOCIAL FORCES, 38 (MAY 60), 332-341.
INTERVIEWS OF INFLUENTIAL UNION REPRESENTATIVES SUGGEST THAT LABOR HAS LITTLE DESIRE FOR A DISTINCTIVE COMMUNITY PROGRAM BUT RATHER ENDORSES MANAGEMENT'S PRIORITIES AND WISHES GREATER REPRESENTATION IN THE SMALL "CLIQUE" WHICH LABOR LEADERS BELIEVE MEDIATES MOST COMMUNITY PROJECTS AND ISSUES. THUS LOCAL PARTICIPATION IS NOT VIEWED AS A CONTEST WITH MANAGEMENT.

0830 FORRESTER J.W.
"INDUSTRIAL DYNAMICS* A MAJOR BREAKTHROUGH FOR DECISION MAKERS."
HARVARD BUSINESS REV., 4 (JULY-AUG. 58), 37-66.
PROPOSES NEW STUDY METHODS AND TECHNIQUES, INCLUDING COMPUTER TECHNOLOGY, AS WELL AS NEW CONCEPTS IN ATTEMPT TO MAKE THE "ART OF MANAGEMENT" A PROFESSION.

0831 FORTE W.E.
"THE FOOD AND DRUG ADMINISTRATION, THE FEDERAL TRADE COMMISSION AND THE DECEPTIVE PACKAGING."
NYU LAW REV., 40 (NOV. 65), 860-904.
CASE STUDIES OF ACTIONS TAKEN AGAINST MANUFACTURERS BY FOOD AND DRUG ADMINISTRATION COMPARED WITH FTC ACTION ON SIMILAR MATTERS EMPHASIZING PROCEDURE AND EFFECTIVENESS.

0832 FOUAD M.
LE REGIME DE LA PRESSE EN EGYPTE: THESE POUR LE DOCTORAT.
PARIS: LIB SOC DU RECEUIL SIREY, 1912, 120 PP.
STUDY OF PRESS CENSORSHIP BY STATE. INCLUDES PRINTING, ADVERTISING, AND LEGAL DISPOSITIONS.

0833 FOURASTIE J., COURTHEOUX J.P.
"LES SCIENCES ECONOMIQUES ET SOCIALES EN EUROPE."
TABLE RONDE, 18 (FEB. 63), 59-71.
DISCUSSES NATURE AND EVOLUTION OF ECONOMICS AND THE SOCIAL SCIENCES IN EUROPE. RELATES THEIR DEVELOPMENT TO POLITICAL HISTORY, SOCIAL TRENDS, AND NATIONAL ATTITUDES. POINTS UP THEIR RELEVANCE TO HUMAN PROBLEMS.

0834 FOURIER C.
TRAITE DE L'ASSOCIATION DOMESTIQUE-AGRICOLE (2 VOLS.)
PARIS: BOSSANGE, 1822, 1240 PP.
EXPRESSES AUTHOR'S VIEWS ON DOMESTIC AND AGRICULTURAL ECONOMY AND HIS DOCTRINE OF UNIVERSAL SOCIAL HARMONY. BELIEVED THAT SOCIETY OF HIS DAY WAS ANARCHICAL. POLITICAL AND ECONOMIC FORCES AGGRAVATED DECOMPOSITION OF MASSES. SINCE INDIVIDUALS WORK BETTER IN GROUPS THAN ALONE, WANTED TO LINK ECONOMIC AND MORAL FORCES AND BENEFITS OF GROUPS BY FOUNDING SOCIETY ON "ASSOCIATIONS."

0835 FOURIER C.
SOCIAL DESTINIES, IN A. BRISBANE, GENERAL INTRODUCTION TO SOCIAL SCIENCE.
ORIGINAL PUBLISHER NOT AVAILABLE, 1876, 158 PP.
BELIEVES SOCIETY IS GOVERNED BY IMMUTABLE LAWS WHICH ARE SOURCE OF HARMONY AND ORDER IN UNIVERSE. MAN CAN DISCOVER THESE LAWS. WHEN MAN HAS DISCOVERED AND APPLIED THEM TO ORGANIZATION OF SOCIETY (THROUGH REGULATION OF MAN'S PASSIONS AND SOCIAL RELATIONS), SOCIAL HARMONY WILL REIGN ON EARTH. NEW SOCIETY WILL TAKE FORM OF ASSOCIATIONS, UNIFYING ACTION AND INTEREST IN AGRICULTURE, MANUFACTURE, INDUSTRY.

0836 FOUSEK P.G.
FOREIGN CENTRAL BANKING: THE INSTRUMENTS OF MONETARY POLICY.
NEW YORK: FED RESERVE BANK OF NY, 1957, 116 PP.
DESCRIBES TRENDS AND TECHNIQUES OF CENTRAL BANKING ABROAD AFTER WWII. STUDIES DISCOUNT POLICIES, THE OPEN MARKET, COMMERCIAL BANK'S CASH RESERVE REQUIREMENTS AND LIQUIDITY RATIOS, AND SELECTIVE AND DIRECT CREDIT CONTROLS TO REGULATE MONETARY POLICY. LAST CHAPTER DISCUSSES SEVERAL COUNTRIES' MONEY MARKETS AND MEASURES USED TO ENLARGE THEM.

0837 FOX K.A., SENGUPTA J.K., THORBECKE E.
THE THEORY OF QUANTITATIVE ECONOMIC POLICY WITH APPLICATIONS TO ECONOMIC GROWTH AND STABILIZATION.
NEW YORK: SIGNET BOOKS, 1966, 514 PP.
IN TEXTBOOK FORM PRESENTS BASIC THEORY OF QUANTITATIVE ECONOMIC POLICY AND SUPPLIES MOTIVATIONAL AND EMPIRICAL CONTENT FOR THEORY. DISCUSSES PARTICULAR ECONOMETRIC OR STABILIZATION MODELS FROM PERSPECTIVE OF POLICY-MAKING. SHOWS HOW THEORY MAY BE EXTENDED INTO REGIONAL SUBDIVISIONS OF A NATIONAL ECONOMY. DISCUSSES MODELS OF ECONOMIC GROWTH AND DEVELOPMENT PLANNING.

0838 FOX R.G.
"FAMILY, CASTE, AND COMMERCE IN A NORTH INDIAN MARKET TOWN."
ECO. DEV. AND CULTURAL CHANGE, 15 (APR. 67), 297-314.
ANALYZES HOW THE SOCIAL STRUCTURE OF TEZIBAZAR, A NORTH INDIAN MARKET TOWN, CREATES A COMMERCIAL CASTE, THE BANIYAS, WHO DETERMINE THE STYLE OF COMMERCIAL ACTIVITY. THE STEREOTYPED IMAGE OF THE BANIYAS INCLUDES MISERLINESS, PASSIVITY, ANONYMITY, AND ISOLATION, ATTITUDES REINFORCED BY THE CONTEMPT OF NON-BANIYAN CASTES TOWARD BUSINESS. SHOWS HOW PREJUDICES DELEGATE ECONOMIC CONTROL TO AN OUTGROUP.

0839 FOX S.
ECONOMIC CONTROL AND FREE ENTERPRISE.
NEW YORK: PHILOSOPHICAL LIB, 1963, 205 PP., LC#63-19700.
HYPOTHESIS ON OPERATION OF CONTROLLED ECONOMY. DISCUSSES BROAD PRINCIPLES AND PROPOSALS AND RELATES THEM TO CURRENT VIEWS IN ECONOMIC THOUGHT.

0840 FRANCIS R.G.
THE PREDICTIVE PROCESS.
RIO PIEDRAS: SOCIAL SCI RES CTR, 1960, 142 PP.
EXAMINES ROLE OF PREDICTION IN SCIENCE AND TRACES IDEA OF PROGRESS AS ADVANCED BY STATESMEN AND PHILOSOPHERS IN WESTERN SOCIETY, WITH PARTICULAR EMPHASIS ON ITS DEVELOPMENT IN US. DISCUSSES BRIEFLY PREDICTIVE PROCESS IN ECONOMIC SPHERE.

0841 FRANCK L.R.
LA POLITIQUE ECONOMIQUE DES ETATS-UNIS.
PARIS: EDITIONS SIREY, 1966, 374 PP.
A STUDY OF AMERICAN ECONOMIC POLICY FROM FRENCH VIEWPOINT PREPARED BY A MEMBER OF L'INSTITUT D'ETUDES POLITIQUES DE L'UNIVERSITE DE PARIS. COVERS HISTORICAL BACKGROUND, PRODUCTION, DISTRIBUTION, MASS CONSUMPTION, ECONOMIC CONCENTRATION AND ITS CONTROL, GOVERNMENTAL INTERVENTION, SYNDICATES, BANKING SYSTEM AND CREDIT CONTROL, ECONOMIC EXPANSION, US FOREIGN ECONOMIC POLICY.

0842 FRANCK P.G.
AFGHANISTAN BETWEEN EAST AND WEST: THE ECONOMICS OF COMPETITIVE COEXISTENCE (PAMPHLET)
WASHINGTON: NATL PLANNING ASSN, 1960, 86 PP., LC#60-14091.
STUDIES NATION VITALLY DEPENDENT ON TRADE, LANDLOCKED, AT MERCY OF TRANSIT RIGHTS ACCORDED BY ADJOINING COUNTRIES, AND POLITICALLY EXPOSED TO USSR ACROSS AN INDEFENSIBLE BORDER. ANALYZES HISTORY AND STATE OF USSR AND WESTERN AID, SHOWING FIERCE COMPETITION THAT HAS ARISEN. SUGGESTS THAT INTERNATIONAL ORGANIZATION (SUCH AS UN) SHOULD ADMINISTER AID TO REDUCE TENSION AND RELIEVE PRESSURES ON AFGHANISTAN.

0843 FRANCK P.G.
AFGHANISTAN: BETWEEN EAST AND WEST.
WASHINGTON: NAT. PLAN. ASSN., 1960, 183 PP.
SIXTH STUDY IN AREA OF THE ECONOMICS OF COMPETITIVE COEXISTENCE. PRESENTS ECONOMIC, POLITICAL, SOCIAL AND GEOGRAPHIC SITUATION OF AFGHANISTAN. CONCLUDES WITH ANALYSIS OF WESTERN AND SOVIET AID PROGRAMS WITH PARTICULAR EMPHASIS ON THEIR COMPETITIVE ASPECTS.

0844 FRANKEL P.H.
MATTEI; OIL AND POWER POLITICS.
NEW YORK: FREDERICK PRAEGER, 1966, 190 PP., LC#66-24529.
DISCUSSES "PROFILE OF SITUATION" IN WHICH ENRICO MATTEI WAS INVOLVED AS BUSINESS TYCOON AND POLITICIAN. HE CHALLENGED STATUS OF BIG BUSINESS IN ITALY, ESPECIALLY BIG INTERNATIONAL OIL COMPANIES. FOUGHT FOR ITALIAN NATIONAL CONTROL OVER FOREIGN OIL COMPANIES.

0845 FRANKEL S.H.
THE ECONOMIC IMPACT ON UNDERDEVELOPED SOCIETIES: ESSAYS ON INTERNATIONAL INVESTMENT AND SOCIAL CHANGE.
CAMBRIDGE: HARVARD U. PR., 1953, 179 PP.
RE-EXAMINES COMPARATIVE PROBLEMS OF ECONOMIC EVOLUTION AND SUMS UP THE CONCEPT OF COLONIZATION. STUDIES THEORIES OF INCOME, WELFARE, AND THE INTERCOMPARABILITY OF NATIONAL INCOME AGGREGATES. EVALUATES INVESTMENTS AND ECONOMIC DEVELOPMENT IN CONTINENTAL AFRICA.

0846 FRANKEL S.H.
"ECONOMIC ASPECTS OF POLITICAL INDEPENDENCE IN AFRICA."
INT. AFF., 36 (OCT. 60), 440-446.
RAISES SERIOUS DOUBTS REGARDING EFFECTS OF POLITICAL INDEPENDENCE ON ECONOMY OF EMERGENT AFRICAN STATES. EXPLAINS THEORY IN ECONOMIC TERMS OF ABSOLUTE INDEPENDENCE COUPLED WITH ABSOLUTE ISOLATION. SHOWS HOW NEW AFRICA IS ESTABLISHING ECONOMIC RELATIONSHIP WITH REST OF THE WORLD, BUT FEELS PRESENT CONDITIONS IN AFRICA OFFER LITTLE INDUCEMENT FOR CAPITAL AND SKILLED ASSISTANCE FROM ABROAD.

0847 FRANKEL T.
"ECONOMIC REFORM* A TENTATIVE APPRAISAL."
PROBLEMS OF COMMUNISM, 16 (MAY-JUNE 67), 29-41.
DISCUSSES RECENT SOVIET SHIFT TO GREATER OPERATIONAL CONTROL BY ENTERPRISE MANAGERS WHILE KEEPING PRINCIPLE OF CENTRAL PLANNING. REFORMS ALSO INCLUDED A SHIFT FROM INCENTIVE SYSTEM TO EFFICIENCY AND SATISFYING DEMAND. AUTHOR CONCLUDES THAT THESE REFORMS ARE TOO LIMITED TO CURE THE CURRENT MALAISE IN SOVIET ECONOMY, BUT MAY CLEAR THE WAY TOWARD A MORE RADICAL AND EFFECTIVE ECONOMIC REVOLUTION.

0848 FRANKFURTER F., LANDIS J.M.
THE BUSINESS OF THE SUPREME COURT; A STUDY IN THE FEDERAL JUDICIAL SYSTEM.
CAMBRIDGE: HARVARD LAW REV ASSN, 1928, 349 PP.
CONCERNED WITH POLITICAL SIGNIFICANCE OF SUPREME COURT'S JURISDICTION. SEEKS TO UNCOVER POLITICAL AND ECONOMIC POWER UNDER CONSTITUTIONAL TECHNICALITIES AND TO FIT MEANING OF SUCCESSIVE ACTS OF JUDICIARY INTO US HISTORY. INCLUDES ITS RELATIONS WITH LOWER COURTS. SKETCHES NATURE OF COURTS ESTABLISHED BY CONGRESS, VESTED POWERS, AND REVIEW OVER THEM. REVIEWING POWER AND PROBLEMS OF SUPREME COURT STUDIED.

0849 FRANKLIN N.N.
"THE CONCEPT AND MEASUREMENT OF 'MINIMUM LIVING STANDARDS'."
INTERNATIONAL LABOR REVIEW, 95 (APR. 67), 271-298.
DESCRIBES AND ASSESSES PREVIOUS ATTEMPTS TO DEFINE "MINIMUM LIVING STANDARDS." DISTINGUISHES BETWEEN NARROW PHYSICAL NEEDS AND SOCIAL DEMANDS, AND CONCLUDES THAT MINIMUM NEEDS ARE LITTLE HELP IN DETERMINING MINIMUM WAGES. SUGGESTS FURTHER RESEARCH IN DEFINING AREAS OF POVERTY STUDY.

0850 FREEMAN H.A., PAULLIN O.
COERCION OF STATES IN FEDERAL UNIONS (PAMPHLET)
PHILA: PACIFIST RESEARCH BUREAU, 1943, 67 PP.
EXAMINE HISTORICAL DEVELOPMENT OF NATIONAL FEDERATIONS,

WITH RESPECT TO INFLUENCES WORKING TOWARD OR FROM UNITY, GIVING SPECIAL ATTENTION TO USE OF FORCE. GIVE PACIFIST VIEW OF FEDERALISM AND MANNER OF ACHIEVING WORLD PEACE UTILIZING IT. CONSIDER COHESIVE FORCES PRESENT IN WORLD THAT COULD CONTRIBUTE TO NONVIOLENT SOLUTION TO WWII, WHICH AT TIME OF WRITING WAS IN SECOND YEAR OF US INVOLVEMENT.

0851 FREIDEL F. ED., POLLACK N. ED.
AMERICAN ISSUES IN THE TWENTIETH CENTURY.
SKOKIE: RAND MCNALLY & CO, 1966, 526 PP., LC#66-10803.
CONSIDER BASIC NATIONAL POLICY PROBLEMS OF EVERY DECADE OF 20TH CENTURY. SPECIALISTS IN VARIOUS FIELDS DISCUSS CRUCIAL DOMESTIC AND INTERNATIONAL ISSUES THAT THREATENED US SECURITY IN EACH PERIOD. RELEVANT PHILOSOPHIES OR PROGRAMS OF PRESIDENTS TREATED.

0852 FREITAG R.S. ED.
AGRICULTURAL DEVELOPMENT SCHEMES IN SUB-SAHARAN AFRICA.
WASHINGTON: LIBRARY OF CONGRESS, 1963, 189 PP., LC#63-60088.
COLLECTION OF 1,783 ITEMS PUBLISHED BETWEEN WWII AND 1962 CONCERNED WITH DEVELOPMENT ON SOCIAL LEVEL OF AWARENESS OF AGRICULTURAL ADVANCE. ALSO TREATS NATIONAL POLICY PLANNING. PROGRAMS ARE DESCRIBED AND EVALUATED IN THE INDEXED BOOKS, ARTICLES, AND REPORTS.

0853 FRENCH J.R.P. JR., ISRAEL J., AS D.
"AN EXPERIMENT ON PARTICIPATION IN A NORWEGIAN FACTORY:INTERPERSONAL DIMENSIONS OF DECISION-MAKING."
HUMAN RELATIONS, 13 (FEB. 60), 3-19.
A TEST OF THE COCH-FRENCH EXPERIMENT OF 1953. THEORY IS THAT INCREASES IN EMPLOYEE PARTICIPATION IN PLANNING TECHNOLOGICAL CHANGES LED TO INCREASES IN PRODUCTION AND TO FEWER SYMPTOMS OF RESISTANCE AND CONFLICT WITH MANAGEMENT. GIVES THEORY, HYPOTHESES AND METHODS OF EXPERIMENT AND RESULTS. FURTHER REFINES THE EARLIER COCH-FRENCH THEORY.

0854 FREYMOND J.
WESTERN EUROPE SINCE THE WAR.
NEW YORK: FREDERICK PRAEGER, 1964, 236 PP., LC#64-13495.
HISTORICAL ESSAY ON ATLANTIC EUROPE SINCE WWII, INCLUDING APPRAISAL OF POST-WAR OUTLOOK AND STRATEGY, ECONOMIC REDEVELOPMENT, CRISES OF 1950'S, AND DEBATE OF GRAND DESIGN, USUALLY FROM FRENCH POINT OF VIEW.

0855 FRIEDEN B.J.
THE FUTURE OF OLD NEIGHBORHOODS: REBUILDING FOR A CHANGING POPULATION.
CAMBRIDGE: M I T PRESS, 1964, 209 PP., LC#64-17322.
STUDY OF THREE US CITIES (NYC, LOS ANGELES, AND HARTFORD, CONNECTICUT), PORTRAYED AS COMMUNITIES IN DECLINE. ANALYZES THE CENTRAL CITY, REBUILDING IN DECLINING AREAS AND LOCATIONAL PREFERENCES FOR NEW HOUSING, THE ECONOMICS OF NEW HOUSING IN OLD NEIGHBORHOODS, AND REGIONAL FRAMEWORK. PROPOSES THAT RUNDOWN NEIGHBORHOODS NOT BE REBUILT UNTIL DWELLINGS ARE VIRTUALLY ABANDONED.

0856 FRIEDEN B.J.
"THE CHANGING PROSPECTS FOR SOCIAL PLANNING."
J. OF AM. INST. OF PLANNERS, 33 (SEPT. 67), 311-324.
EXAMINES PROSPECTS OF NEXT 50 YEARS IN CITY PLANNING, ESPECIALLY AS MEANS OF SOCIAL WELFARE AND COMBATING CONDITIONS OF POVERTY. DISCUSSES INFLUENCE OF CHANGING POLITICAL BASE, AS CITY POPULATIONS BECOME INCREASINGLY NEGRO, ON POLICY PLANNING.

0857 FRIEDENBERG D.M.
"THE US IN LATIN AMERICA; A RECKONING OF SHAME."
DISSENT, 14 (JULY 67), 400-420.
REVIEWS AMERICAN COLONIALISM IN WESTERN HEMISPHERE FROM LATIN AMERICAN POINT OF VIEW. INCLUDES CASES OF NICARAGUA, CUBAN SITUATION, CRISIS IN DOMINICAN REPUBLIC AND OTHER CONFLICTS. MAINTAINS THAT CONSERVATIVE CAPITALISTS CONTROL DOMESTIC AND HENCE FOREIGN AFFAIRS IN US, AND SUPPORT "PANTOMIME GOVERNMENTS" WHICH HAVE NO CONCERN FOR WELFARE OF PEOPLE BUT ONLY SELF INTEREST.

0858 FRIEDLANDER S.L.
LABOR MIGRATION AND ECONOMIC GROWTH: A CASE STUDY OF PUERTO RICO.
CAMBRIDGE: M I T PRESS, 1965, 181 PP., LC#65-27232.
DISCUSSES EFFECTS OF EMIGRATION ON ECONOMIC GROWTH OF AN UNDERDEVELOPED, DENSELY POPULATED COUNTRY. THEORETICAL ANALYSIS EXPLORES POTENTIAL BENEFICIAL EFFECT OF EMIGRATION ON UNEMPLOYMENT. INCLUDES EFFECT OF EMIGRATION ON SIZE, GROWTH, AND STRUCTURE OF THE POPULATION. CONCLUDES WITH POLICY RECOMMENDATIONS AND THE IMPLICATIONS OF THE ROLE OF MIGRATION IN FUTURE GROWTH.

0859 FRIEDMAN M.
CAPITALISM AND FREEDOM.
CHICAGO: U OF CHICAGO PRESS, 1962, 202 PP., LC#62-19619.
CONCERNED WITH ROLE OF COMPETITIVE CAPITALISM AS A SYSTEM OF ECONOMIC FREEDOM AND WITH ROLE OF GOVERNMENT IN A FREE SOCIETY. BEGINS WITH THEORETICAL PRINCIPLES OF POLITICAL AND ECONOMIC FREEDOM. DISCUSSES CONTROL OF MONEY, INTERNATIONAL FINANCIAL AND TRADE ARRANGEMENTS, FISCAL POLICY, AND ROLE OF GOVERNMENT IN EDUCATION. OTHER ISSUES INCLUDE DISTRIBUTION OF INCOME, SOCIAL WELFARE, AND ALLEVIATION OF POVERTY.

0860 FRIEDMAN M.
INFLATION: CAUSES AND CURES.
BOMBAY: ASIA PUBL HOUSE, 1963, 51 PP.
DISCUSSION OF RELATIONSHIP BETWEEN INFLATION AND ECONOMIC GROWTH. EXPLAINS INFLATION AS ONLY MONETARY SITUATION AND UNRELATED TO NATIONAL ECONOMIC GROWTH. EXAMINES INDIA'S ECONOMIC POLICY REGARDING CONTROL OF IMPORTS AND EXCHANGE RATE.

0861 FRIEDMAN W. ED.
THE PUBLIC CORPORATION: A COMPARATIVE SYMPOSIUM (UNIVERSITY OF TORONTO SCHOOL OF LAW COMPARATIVE LAW SERIES, VOL. I)
TORONTO: CARSWELL, 1954, 612 PP.
CONCERNS LEGAL STATUS AND ORGANIZATION OF THE PUBLIC CORPORATION. INCLUDES 14 ESSAYS ON THE PUBLIC CORPORATION IN AUSTRALIA, CANADA, FRANCE, GERMANY, ENGLAND, INDIA, ISRAEL, ITALY, NEW ZEALAND, SOUTH AFRICA, SWEDEN, US, USSR; STUDIES OF LEGAL RELATIONS OF A NATIONALIZED INDUSTRY (BRITAIN'S NATIONAL COAL BOARD) AND AN INTERNATIONAL PUBLIC CORPORATION; AND A FINAL COMPARATIVE ANALYSIS.

0862 FRIEDMANN G.
THE ANATOMY OF WORK.
NEW YORK: FREE PRESS OF GLENCOE, 1961, 203 PP., LC#61-9165.
ANALYZES PSYCHOLOGICAL AND SOCIOLOGICAL EFFECTS OF AUTOMATION AND INCREASED JOB SPECIALIZATION IN MODERN MECHANIZED INDUSTRY. DISCUSSES HOW HIGHLY REPETITIVE, FRAGMENTARY JOBS DESTROY WORKER'S INITIATIVE AND MOTIVATION, AND HOW THEY AFFECT WORKER'S BEHAVIOR AND MENTAL CONDITION DURING AND AFTER WORKING HOURS. MUCH DOCUMENTATION, WITH APPROACH MORE THEORETICAL THAN STATISTICAL.

0863 FRIEDMANN J. ED., ALONSO W. ED.
REGIONAL DEVELOPMENT AND PLANNING: A READER.
CAMBRIDGE: M I T PRESS, 1964, 722 PP., LC#64-25214.
DISCUSSES FIELD OF REGIONAL DEVELOPMENT, CONCEPTS USED IN DISCIPLINE, NATIONAL POLICY ISSUES THAT ARISE, ANATOMY OF SPACE AND ORGANIZATION OF REGIONS, THEORIES OF REGIONAL DEVELOPMENT AND OF GROWTH OR RETARDATION OF REGIONAL ECONOMIES, AND OBJECTIVE AND EVALUATION OF REGIONAL ECONOMIC PROGRESS.

0864 FRIEDMANN W. ED.
METHODS AND POLICIES OF PRINCIPAL DONOR COUNTRIES IN PUBLIC INTERNATIONAL DEVELOPMENT FINANCING: PRELIMINARY APPRAISAL.
NEW YORK: COLUMBIA U LAW SCHOOL, 1962, 49 PP.
ANALYZES FOREIGN AID MACHINERY IN US, UK, WEST GERMANY, AND FRANCE, AS WELL AS EEC, SHOWING THERE IS AGREEMENT ON PRE-EMINENCE OF NEED FOR TECHNICAL ASSISTANCE, BUT DISAGREEMENT ON CONCEPT AND PRINCIPLES OF CAPITAL AID FOR DEVELOPING COUNTRIES. POINTS OUT NATURE OF OTHER ISSUES UPON WHICH NATIONS AGREE AND DIFFER. SUGGESTS FURTHER TASKS FOR MULTILATERAL COORDINATION.

0865 FRIEDMANN W.G. ED., KALMANOFF G. ED.
JOINT INTERNATIONAL BUSINESS VENTURES.
NEW YORK: COLUMB. U. PR., 1961, 558 PP.
EXAMINES PROBLEMS AND PROSPECTS OF PARTNERSHIP IN BUSINESS ASSOCIATIONS BETWEEN DEVELOPED AND LESS DEVELOPED COUNTRIES. OUTLINES TYPES OF JOINT VENTURES, SURVEYS THEIR IMPORTANCE IN RELATION TO TOTAL FOREIGN INVESTMENTS, ANALYZES THEIR RESULTS IN INDIVIDUAL COUNTRIES, AND REVIEWS GOVERNMENTAL REGULATIONS AFFECTING THEM.

0866 FRIEDMANN W.G., KALMANOFF G., MEAGHER R.F.
INTERNATIONAL FINANCIAL AID.
NEW YORK: COLUMBIA U PRESS, 1966, 498 PP., LC#66-20494.
DESCRIBES MAGNITUDE AND CHARACTERISTICS OF INTERNATIONAL FINANCIAL AID: METHODS AND POLICIES OF DONOR COUNTRIES AND INTERNATIONAL INSTITUTIONS, CASE STUDIES OF RECIPIENT COUNTRIES AND MULTI-NATIONAL PROJECTS. POLICY ISSUES OF PLANNING REQUIREMENTS, LOANS VERSUS GRANTS, AND TIED AID, DISCUSSED. STATISTICS PRESENTED AND TRENDS PREDICTED.

0867 FRIEDRICH C.J.
MAN AND HIS GOVERNMENT: AN EMPIRICAL THEORY OF POLITICS.
NEW YORK: MCGRAW HILL, 1963, 737 PP., LC#63-15892.
LOOKS AT POLITICAL EXPERIENCE OF MANKIND IN ORDER TO SEE WHAT CONTRIBUTES TO POLITICAL ORDER AND THE GOOD LIFE AND WHAT DETRACTS. CONSIDERS POLITICAL PERSON AND POLITICAL ACT; DIMENSIONS OF POWER; JUSTICE; EQUALITY; FREEDOM; GOVERNING PROCESSES; MODES OF OPERATION; AND RANGE AND LEVELS OF GOVERNMENT.

0868 FRIEDRICH-EBERT-STIFTUNG
THE SOVIET BLOC AND DEVELOPING COUNTRIES.
HANNOVER: VERLAG FUR LITERATUR, 1962, 39 PP.
DESCRIBES FOREIGN AID POLICIES OF SOVIET BLOC NATIONS AS BEING PART OF POLITICAL PROGRAM TO GAIN ALLIES AMONG UNDERDEVELOPED NATIONS IN ECONOMIC COMPETITION WITH WEST. TAKES NOTE OF ORGANIZATIONS FOR THIS PURPOSE AND FOR CULTURAL AND SCIENTIFIC COOPERATION. FOCUSES PARTICULARLY ON USSR, COMMUNIST CHINA, AND EAST GERMANY.

0869 FROMM G.
"RECENT MONETARY POLICY: AN ECONOMETRIC VIEW"
NATIONAL BANKING REVIEW, 3 (MAR. 66), 299-306.
EXAMINES BROOKINGS QUARTERLY ECONOMETRIC MODEL OF US ECONOMY, DEVELOPED AFTER DEC., 1965. ATTEMPTS TO DETERMINE POTENTIAL IMPACT OF CHANGES IN POLICY MADE BY FEDERAL RESERVE BOARD IN 1965 ON GNP, CONSUMPTION, INDUSTRY OUTPUTS, WAGE RATES, PRICES, UNEMPLOYMENT, ETC. RESULTS PRESENTED TO ILLUSTRATE POTENTIALITIES OF USE OF LARGE-SCALE ECONOMETRIC MODEL IN ANALYZING EFFECTS OF POLICY ACTION.

0870 FRYE R.J.
GOVERNMENT AND LABOR: THE ALABAMA PROGRAM.
UNIVERSITY: U ALA, BUR PUBL ADM, 1960, 157 PP.
ANALYZES ADMINISTRATION OF SPECIFIC PUBLIC FUNCTIONS BY ALABAMA'S STATE GOVERNMENT. CHAPTERS DEVOTED TO CHILD LABOR, WORKMEN'S COMPENSATION, SAFETY AND INSPECTION, MEDIATION, STATE EMPLOYMENT SERVICE, AND UNEMPLOYMENT COMPENSATION. DISCUSSES HISTORY, PROGRAM, AND ORGANIZATION AND MANAGEMENT OF EACH.

0871 FRYE R.J.
HOUSING AND URBAN RENEWAL IN ALABAMA.
UNIVERSITY: U ALA, BUR PUBL ADM, 1965, 103 PP.
DISCUSSES RELATIONSHIPS BETWEEN FEDERAL AND CITY GOVERNMENTS IN SPHERE OF URBAN RENEWAL, EMPHASIZING HISTORICAL AND LEGAL FRAMEWORK OF PROGRAM, ORGANIZATIONAL ARRANGEMENTS AT BOTH LEVELS FOR IMPLEMENTATION OF PROGRAMS, PROGRAM CONTENT, AND PROCESSES THROUGH WHICH INTERGOVERNMENTAL ASPECTS OF THE PROGRAMS MANIFEST THEMSELVES.

0872 FUCHS R.F.
"FAIRNESS AND EFFECTIVENESS IN ADMINISTRATIVE AGENCY ORGANIZATION AND PROCEDURES."
INDIANA LAW J., 36 (FALL 60), 1-50.
REFORM OF ORGANIZATION AND PROCEDURES SHOULD BE MADE TO FURTHER PROTECT INDIVIDUAL RIGHTS AND THE PUBLIC INTEREST AND TO INCREASE EFFICIENCY. ON THE WHOLE, ADMINISTRATIVE AGENCIES HAVE GREATLY IMPROVED IN THESE AREAS IN RECENT YEARS.

0873 FUCHS V.R.
"REDEFINING POVERTY AND REDISTRIBUTING INCOME."
PUBLIC INTEREST, 8 (SUMMER 67), 88-95.
DEFINES POOR FAMILY IN TERMS OF MEDIAN INCOME OF US, RATHER THAN BY ABSOLUTE NUMBERS. ADVOCATES POLICY AIMED AT CHANGING INCOME DISTRIBUTION TO DECREASE POVERTY. CITES LACK OF ANY EFFECTIVE POLICY THROUGH TODAY. DISCUSSES COSTS AND PROBLEMS PERTINENT TO ANY POVERTY PROGRAM.

0874 FULLER G.H. ED., HELLMAN F.S. ED.
LIST OF REFERENCES ON PRIORITIES (MIMEOGRAPHED PAPER)
WASHINGTON: LIBRARY OF CONGRESS, 1940, 16 PP.
INCLUDES 158 ITEMS (BOOKS, ARTICLES, AND PAMPHLETS) DEALING WITH PRIORITIES, ECONOMIC PLANNING DURING WARTIME, ETC. ITEMS ALL DATE FROM LATE 1930'S. COMPILED FOR LIBRARY OF CONGRESS.

0875 FURASH E.A.
"PROBLEMS IN REVIEW: INDUSTRIAL ESPIONAGE."
HARVARD BUSINESS REV., 37 (NOV.-DEC. 59), 6-12, 148-174 .
DEALS WITH THE USE OF INDUSTRIAL ESPIONAGE AS A STRATEGY OF COMPETITION. GIVES RESULTS OF QUESTIONNAIRES SHOWING MAJORITY OF EXECUTIVES THINKING THAT SPYING DOES OCCUR BUT PREFERRING ABOVE-THE-BOARD METHODS. YOUNGER EXECUTIVES PREFER MORE AGGRESSIVE METHODS.

0876 FURNIVALL J.S.
NETHERLANDS INDIA.
NEW YORK: MACMILLAN, 1939, 502 PP.
STUDIES ECONOMIC AND SOCIAL DEVELOPMENT OF NETHERLANDS INDIA WITH SPECIAL REFERENCE TO ITS NATURE AS A PLURALISTIC SOCIETY. HISTORICALLY TRACES GENERAL POLITICAL AND ECONOMIC CHANGES IN ENVIRONMENT AND RELATES THEM TO VAST DIFFERENCES IN CULTURE AND RACE OF ITS INHABITANTS. FOLLOWS RISE OF LIBERALISM AND NOTES MAJOR CHANGES IN COLONIAL POLICY.

0877 FURTADO C.
THE ECONOMIC GROWTH OF BRAZIL: A SURVEY FROM COLONIAL TO MODERN TIMES.
BERKELEY: U OF CALIF PR, 1963, 285 PP., LC#63-12818.
INTRODUCTORY TEXT TO HISTORIC PROCESS OF BRAZIL'S ECONOMIC GROWTH. DISCUSSES ECONOMIC BASES OF TERRITORIAL OCCUPATION; SLAVERY ECONOMY OF TROPICAL AGRICULTURE (16TH AND 17TH CENTURIES); SLAVERY ECONOMY OF MINING (18TH CENTURY) AND ECONOMIC TRANSITION TO PAID LABOR; ECONOMY OF TRANSITION TO AN INDUSTRIAL SYSTEM.

0878 FUSFELD D.R.
THE AGE OF THE ECONOMIST.
GLENVIEW, ILL: SCOTT, FORESMAN, 1966, 157 PP.
PRESENTS DEVELOPMENT OF ECONOMICS IN ITS INTELLECTUAL AND HISTORICAL CONTEXT. DISCUSSES UTILITY OF ECONOMICS IN PUBLIC POLICY ISSUES, IDEOLOGICAL DISPUTES, AND SOCIAL PHILOSOPHIES.

0879 FYFE J.
"LIST OF CURRENT ACQUISITIONS OF PERIODICALS AND NEWSPAPERS DEALING WITH THE SOVIET UNION AND EAST EUROPEAN COUNTRIES."
ECONOMICS OF PLANNING, (1964), 85-199.
LISTS CURRENT ACQUISITIONS BY CERTAIN LIBRARIES IN NORWAY AND THE UNITED KINGDON. THESE PERIODICALS AND NEWSPAPERS ORIGINATE IN MANY COUNTRIES AND APPEAR IN MANY LANGUAGES. MOST OF THE PUBLICATIONS ARE FROM THE SOVIET UNION AND THE EAST EUROPEAN COUNTRIES AND ARE IN THEIR LANGUAGES. SOME PUBLICATIONS LISTED ARE BIBLIOGRAPHIES.

0880 GABLE R.W.
"NAM: INFLUENTIAL LOBBY OR KISS OF DEATH?" (BMR)"
J. OF POLITICS, 15 (MAY 53), 254-273.
DISCUSSES CHARGES MADE BY SEVERAL CONGRESSMEN THAT THE NATIONAL ASSOCIATION OF MANUFACTURERS WROTE THE TAFT-HARTLEY PROPOSAL. EXAMINES QUESTION OF THE GROUP'S POLITICAL POWER AS A LOBBY. CONSTRUCTS FRAME OF REFERENCE FOR STUDY OF POLITICAL INFLUENCE, AND ANALYZES NAM'S PUBLIC RELATIONS, PROPAGANDA, ACCESS TO CONGRESS. SHOWS EXTENT OF GROUP'S SUCCESS IN INFLUENCING CONGRESSIONAL DECISIONS.

0881 GALBRAITH J.K.
AMERICAN CAPITALISM: THE CONCEPT OF COUNTERVAILING POWER.
BOSTON: HOUGHTON MIFFLIN, 1952, 217 PP.
STATES THAT CAPITALISM IS BASICALLY AN ARRANGEMENT FOR GETTING A CONSIDERABLE DECENTRALIZATION IN DECISION. EXAMINES PROSPECTS FOR US ECONOMY. FINDS POTENTIAL FOR INFLATION IN 1950'S: AN EVENT THAT WOULD BRING ABOUT CENTRALIZED DECISION AND LOSS OF FREEDOM. HOPES PEACE, NOT WAR, IS ON HORIZON - PEACE WHICH WILL BRING PROSPERITY WITHOUT INFLATION.

0882 GALBRAITH J.K.
THE AFFLUENT SOCIETY.
BOSTON: HOUGHTON, 1958, 368 PP.
ANALYZES THE AMERICAN TENDANCY TO EQUATE INCREASED PRIVATELY PRODUCED GOODS WITH HAPPINESS. CONTENDS ECONOMIC ATTITUDES AND PRACTICES ROOTED IN PAST POVERTY AND ADVOCATES ATTITUDES CONSONANT WITH PRESENT AFFLUENCE. SUGGESTS GREATER INVESTMENT IN EDUCATION AND EXPANDED PUBLIC SERVICES AT STATE-LOCAL LEVEL THROUGH USE OF REVENUE FROM SALES TAX, NOT THROUGH INCREASED CONSUMER GOODS PRODUCTION.

0883 GALBRAITH J.K.
"A POSITIVE APPROACH TO ECONOMIC AID."
FOR. AFF., 39 (APRIL 61) 444-457.
PRESENTS REASONS FOR FAILURE OF FOREIGN AID: LACK OF EDUCATION, SOCIAL JUSTICE, RELIABLE GOVERNMENT AND UNDERSTANDING OF USE OF AID. ADVOCATES REALISTIC APPROACH BY AN INSTITUTE CONCERNED SOLELY WITH ELIMINATING ESSENTIAL PROBLEMS IN UNDERDEVELOPED NATIONS AND HELPING NATIONS USE AID EFFECTIVELY. AID SHOULD BE COMMENSURATE WITH RESOURCES.

0884 GALBRAITH J.K.
"ECONOMIC DEVELOPMENT IN PERSPECTIVE."
CAMBRIDGE: HARVARD U. PR., 1962, 76 PP.
EXPLORES WAYS OF AIDING UNDER-DEVELOPED NATIONS ATTAIN THEIR GOALS, I.E. ECONOMIC ADVANCEMENT AND STABILITY. PREFERS THEIR USE OF FREE ENTERPRISE SYSTEM AS CONTRASTED TO A SYSTEM OF FOREIGN OWNERSHIP OF INDUSTRY. OUTLINES PROGRAM FOR GROWTH.

0885 GALBRAITH V.
"JAPAN'S POSITION IN WORLD TRADE."
CURR. HIST., 46 (APRIL 64), 207-11.
BECAUSE JAPAN HAS ACCEPTED INEVITABILITY OF INCREASED COMPETITION BOTH AT HOME AND ABROAD FOR HER PRODUCTS, MERGERS AND MODERNIZATION OF PRODUCTION FACILITIES HAVE TAKEN PLACE. INDICATES THAT TRADING PATTERNS WILL CHANGE.

0886 GALENSON W.
TRADE UNION DEMOCRACY IN WESTERN EUROPE.
BERKELEY: U OF CALIF PR, 1961, 97 PP., LC#61-6779.
COMPARISON OF RIVAL OR DUAL UNIONISM WITH UNIFIED TRADE UNIONISM IN WESTERN EUROPE, RELATIVE ADVANTAGES AND DISADVANTAGES TO WORKERS DISCUSSED.

0887 GALENSON W. ED.
TRADE UNIONS MONOGRAPH SERIES (A SERIES OF NINE TEXTS)
NEW YORK: JOHN WILEY, 1962.
SERIES FOCUSING ON ASPECTS OF DEMOCRATIC GOVERNMENT WITHIN MAJOR LABOR UNIONS. EXAMINATION OF CONSTITUTIONS, VOTING PROCEDURES, CONVENTIONS, AND LEADERSHIP. SO FAR, NINE MONOGRAPHS, BY THE CENTER FOR THE STUDY OF DEMOCRATIC INSTITUTIONS.

0888 GALENSON W. ED.
LABOR IN DEVELOPING COUNTRIES.
BERKELEY: U OF CALIF PR, 1962, 299 PP., LC#62-16108.
FIVE ESSAYS ON LABOR RELATIONS IN VARIOUS ENVIRONMENTAL SETTINGS. EXAMINE TRADE UNION POWER IN UNDERDEVELOPED NATIONS, THE INFLUENCE OF UNIONS IN POLITICS, COLLECTIVE BARGAINING, AND WAGE DIFFERENTIALS. ANALYZE PROBLEMS INVOLVED IN CONVERSION OF A BACKWARD PEASANTRY TO AN INDUSTRIAL WORK FORCE.

0889 GALENSON W.
"ECONOMIC DEVELOPMENT AND THE SECTORAL EXPANSION OF EMPLOYMENT, INT."
LABOUR REV., 87 (JUNE 63), 506-19.
ANALYZES SIGNIFICANT CHANGES THAT HAVE TAKEN PLACE OVER THE LAST DECADE IN DISTRIBUTION OF EMPLOYMENT BY SECTORS OF ECONOMIC ACTIVITY IN 25 COUNTRIES REPRESENTATIVE OF DIFFERENT STANDARDS OF LIVING THROUGHOUT THE WORLD. EXAMINES RELATIONSHIPS BETWEEN EMPLOYMENT AND OUTPUT IN MANUFACTURING INDUSTRY, ON THE ONE HAND, DEVELOPMENT IN TERTIARY ACTIVITIES ON THE OTHER.

0890 GAMARNIKOW M.
"THE NEW ROLE OF PRIVATE ENTERPRISE."
EAST EUROPE, 16 (AUG. 67), 2-9.
RESURGENCE OF PRIVATE ENTERPRISE IN EASTERN EURPOE ALLOWS EMPLOYMENT OPPORTUNIES AND INDICATES A NEW PROFIT CONSCIOUSNESS. INCLUDES DISCUSSION OF PROBLEMS CONFRONTING FUTURE PRIVATE DEVELOPMENT.

0891 GAMBLE S.D.
NORTH CHINA VILLAGES: SOCIAL, POLITICAL, AND ECONOMIC ACTIVITIES BEFORE 1933.
BERKELEY: U OF CALIF PR, 1963, 352 PP., LC#63-21616.
STUDY OF VILLAGE LIFE IN HOPEI, SHANSI, HONAN, AND SHANTUNG. GENERAL SUMMARY OF FINDINGS AND RELATIONSHIP TO POLITICAL AND HISTORICAL EVENTS OF PERIOD. DESCRIPTION AND DISCUSSION OF VARIOUS PHASES OF VILLAGE LIFE AND ORGANIZATION. CONTAINS DETAILED STORIES OF 11 SAMPLE VILLAGES.

0892 GANDHI M.K.
THE WAY TO COMMUNAL HARMONY.
PORT WASHINGTON: KENNIKAT PRESS, 1963, 522 PP.
COLLECTION OF VARIOUS ESSAYS AND OTHER WRITINGS BY GANDHI ON GENERAL PROBLEMS POSED BY RACIAL, ECONOMIC, RELIGIOUS, AND POLITICAL DIVISIONS AMONG MEN, THOUGH WRITTEN WITH PARTICULAR REFERENCE TO INDIA. GANDHI SEEKS TO FIND WAYS OF BRIDGING SUCH GAPS IN SUCH A WAY AS TO PRODUCE A COMMUNAL SOCIETY. STRESSES NECESSITY OF OBJECTIVE CONSIDERATION OF SITUATIONS.

0893 GANDILHON J.
"LA SCIENCE ET LA TECHNIQUE A L'AIDE DES REGIONS PEU DEVELOPPEES."
POLIT. ETRANG., (NO.3, 63), 221-40.
RECOMMENDS CLOSER ECONOMIC RELATIONS WITH UNDERDEVELOPED REGIONS. SCIENTIFIC AID PROGRAMS SHOULD AIM TO APPLY RESEARCH TO TECHNOLOGY. GIVES INSIGHTS INTO FRENCH SCIENTIFIC SITUATION AND UN SCIENTIFIC AID PROGRAM.

0894 GANDOLFI A.
"LES ACCORDS DE COOPERATION EN MATIERE DE POLITIQUE ETRANGERE ENTRE LA FRANCE ET LES NOUVEAUX ETATS AFRICAINS ET." MALGACHE.
REV. JURID. POLIT. OUTREMER, 17 (APR.-JUNE 63), 202-19.
REVIEWS AGREEMENTS FOR COOPERATION BETWEEN FRANCE AND AFRICAN STATES AND MADAGASCAR. OUTLINES COMMON POLICY OBJECTIVES, RELATING THEM TO AFRICAN ECONOMIC PROBLEMS. INCLUDES LISTS OF DETAILED AGREEMENTS.

0895 GANGULI B.N.
ECONOMIC INTEGRATION.
BOMBAY: ASIA PUBL HOUSE, 1961, 13 PP.
DISCUSSION OF CONCEPT AND IMPLICATIONS OF ECONOMIC INTEGRATION ON REGIONAL, NATIONAL, AND INTERNATIONAL CHANGE. FOCUSES ON ECONOMIC GROUPS UNDERGOING CHANGES IN BEHAVIOR PATTERNS DUE TO PROCESS OF ECONOMIC CHANGE.

0896 GANGULI B.N.
ECONOMIC CONSEQUENCES OF DISARMAMENT.
BOMBAY: ASIA PUBL HOUSE, 1963, 85 PP.
ANALYZES ARMAMENT AND DISARMAMENT IN TERMS OF COSTS AND ALTERNATIVES SELECTED AND FOREGONE IN RATIONAL DECISION-MAKING. DISCUSSES "REAL COST OF DEFENCE, DISARMAMENT AND THE CONVERSION PROBLEM, DISARMAMENT AND EMPLOYMENT, AND DISARMAMENT AND INTERNATIONAL ECONOMIC RELATIONS."

0897 GANGULY D.S.
PUBLIC CORPORATIONS IN A NATIONAL ECONOMY.
CALCUTTA: BOOKLAND PRIVATE, 1963, 410 PP.
ANALYZES PRINCIPLES AND OPERATIONS OF PUBLIC CORPORATIONS SET UP BY STATUTES, PRIMARILY IN INDIA. CONCENTRATES ON NATIONAL LEVEL OPERATIONS AND STUDIES PRINCIPLES BORROWED FROM UK AND OTHER WESTERN NATIONS. INDIA ALONE HAS INTRODUCED PUBLIC CORPORATIONS IN INDUSTRIAL AND COMMERCIAL SPHERES OF GOVERNMENT AS WELL AS UTILITIES AND SOCIAL SERVICES.

0898 GANZ G.
"THE CONTROL OF INDUSTRY BY ADMINISTRATIVE PROCESS."
PUBLIC LAW, (SUMMER 67), 93-106.
ASSESSES SUITABILITY OF INDUSTRIAL DEVELOPMENT ACT OF 1966 AND LOCAL EMPLOYMENT ACT OF 1960 AND ADMINISTRATIVE MACHINERY THEY PROVIDE FOR IMPLEMENTING GOVERNMENT POLICY IN RELATION TO INDUSTRY. EXAMINES EXTENT OF PROTECTION OF INDIVIDUALS UNDER TWO LAWS. SHOWS MOVEMENT AWAY FROM LEGAL CONTROL OVER INDUSTRY TO ADMINISTRATIVE CONTROL.

0899 GARAUDY R.
KARL MARX: THE EVOLUTION OF HIS THOUGHT.
NEW YORK: INTERNATIONAL PUBL CO, 1967, 223 PP.
RE-EXAMINES GERMINAL IDEAS OF MARX IN LIGHT OF CENTURY OF SOCIAL UPHEAVAL AND CHANGE. WANTS TO EXPLAIN HOW "MARXIST THOUGHT HAS BECOME THE EFFECTIVE CONSCIOUSNESS OF A CENTURY." DISCUSSES INFLUENCES ON MARX AND DEVELOPMENT OF HIS PHILOSOPHY ON POLITICAL ECONOMY AND ACTIONS. SEEKS TO FREE MARXIST THOUGHT FROM REVISIONS AND STALIN'S DIDACTICISM.

0900 GARBARINO J.W.
HEALTH PLANS AND COLLECTIVE BARGAINING.
BERKELEY: U OF CALIF PR, 1960, 301 PP., LC#59-13460.
DISCUSSION AND ANALYSIS OF IMPACT OF NEGOTIATED PRIVATE HEALTH INSURANCE PLANS ON TERMS AND CONDITIONS UNDER WHICH MEDICARE IS PROVIDED. REVIEWS INFLUENCE OF COLLECTIVELY BARGAINED HEALTH PLANS ON HIGH COST OF MEDICAL CARE, HEALTH SERVICES, AND THE RELATIVE POSITION OF PRIVATE INSURANCE COMPANIES.

0901 GARDNER L.C.
ECONOMIC ASPECTS OF NEW DEAL DIPLOMACY.
MADISON: U. WISC. PR., 1964, 409 PP., $7.50.
INDICATES THAT THE NEW DEAL'S APPROACH TO FOREIGN POLICY WAS AS MUCH SHAPED BY OLDER PRINCIPLES AND TRADITIONS AS BY ANY INITIATED BY FDR. DISCUSSES THE ECONOMIC ORIENTATION OF THE GOOD NEIGHBOR POLICY, THE ROLE OF CORDELL HULL, AND THE INFLUENCE OF SUCH FINANCIERS AS THOMAS LAMONT, NORMAN H. DAVIS, AND WILL CLAYTON.

0902 GARDNER R.N.
STERLING-DOLLAR DIPLOMACY.
NEW YORK: OXFORD U. PR., 1956, 423 PP.
STUDY OF INTERNATIONAL ECONOMIC POLICY FORMULATION AND OF INSTITUTIONS FOR ITS IMPLEMENTATION. PLACES SPECIAL EMPHASIS ON INTERACTION OF OFFICIAL POLICY AND PUBLIC OPINION. DWELLS ON PROBLEM OF EXPLAINING COMPLEX ECONOMIC POLICIES TO A DEMOCRATIC ELECTORATE.

0903 GARDNER R.N.
"NEW DIRECTIONS IN UNITED STATES FOREIGN ECONOMIC POLICY."
NEW YORK: FOR. POL. ASSN., 1959, 77 PP.
ASSERTS THAT SOVIET ECONOMIC CHALLENGE HAS GENERATED CHANGE IN USA ECONOMIC STRATEGY. SUGGESTS INCREASED EMPHASIS ON FOREIGN AID PROGRAMS TO REACH POLICY OBJECTIVES. DECLARES THAT NATIONAL SURVIVAL DEPENDENT UPON READINESS OF USA TO COMPREHEND TEMPORARILY EXPEDIENT POLITICAL FACTS.

0904 GARDNER R.N.
LEGAL-ECONOMIC PROBLEMS OF INTERNATIONAL TRADE.
COLUMBIA LAW REV., 161 (MAR. 61), 3121-321.
ISSUE OFFERING COLLECTION OF ARTICLES BY LEADING EXPERTS ON A BROAD VARIETY OF INTERNATIONAL TRADE SUBJECTS. SUGGESTS THREE ESSENTIAL ELEMENTS IN A NEW APPROACH WHICH SHOULD BE ESPOUSED: OMNIBUS ECONOMIC PROGRAM, TARIFF REDUCTION AND RESOURCES ADJUSTMENTS.

0905 GARDNER R.N.
"GATT AND THE UNITED NATIONS CONFERENCE ON TRADE AND DEVELOPMENT."
INT. ORGAN., 18 (AUTUMN 64), 685-704.
NOTES UN'S ROLE IN HELPING TO DEFINE AND SOLVE PROBLEMS OF INTERNATIONAL TRADE BARRIERS AND SPECIFIC PROBLEMS FACING TRADE OF SMALL UNDER-DEVELOPED NATIONS. CITES AMBITIOUS GOALS OF KENNEDY ROUND ON TARIFFS, AND SHOWS GATT'S COMPLEX ROLE IN DEALING WITH THIS NEW POLICY OF ACROSS-THE-BOARD TRADE. POINTS TO NEED FOR POLICY OF SELF-DEVELOPMENT.

0906 GARFIELD PJ LOVEJOY WF
PUBLIC UTILITY ECONOMICS.
ENGLEWOOD CLIFFS: PRENTICE HALL, 1964, 503 PP., LC#64-10255.
TEXTBOOK DIFFERENTIATES PUBLIC OWNERSHIP, ADMINISTRATES PRICING, AND FINANCING OF UTILITIES FROM PRIVATE. DISCUSSES MARKETING AND DISTRIBUTION AS WELL AS LEGAL ASPECTS OF PUBLIC OWNERSHIP.

0907 GARNICK D.H.
"ON THE ECONOMIC FEASIBILITY OF A MIDDLE EASTERN COMMON MARKET."
MID. EAST. J., 14 (SUMMER 60), 265-276.
VIEWS PROSPECTS FOR FORMATION OF ECONOMIC UNION. ENUMERATES THREE MAJOR OBSTACLES: LACK OF (1)POLITICAL LIAISONS, (2)PARALLEL SYSTEMS OF ECONOMICS AND (3)SIMILAR LEVELS OF ECONOMIC STABILITY. EQUAL DISTRIBUTION OF RESOURCES, GROWTH POTENTIAL, REGIONAL COOPERATION AND STIMULATION OF TRADE CITED AS AIDS TO EVENTUAL ECONOMIC UNION.

0908 GATELL F.O.
"MONEY AND PARTY IN JACKSONIAN AMERICA* A QUANTITATIVE LOOK AT NEW YORK CITY'S MEN OF QUALITY."
POLIT. SCI. QUART., 82 (JUNE 67), 235-252.
AUTHOR EXAMINES DATA AND INFLUENTIAL MEN IN NEW YORK CITY DURING JACKSONIAN ERA TO DETERMINE WHETHER OR NOT POLITICAL

ALIGNMENT IS SYNONYMOUS WITH PARTISAN DIVISION OF RICH VS. POOR. HE CONCLUDES THAT THE WEALTHY HAPPENED TO SUPPORT THE WHIGS BECAUSE THAT PARTY AT THAT TIME HAPPENED TO SERVE THEIR INTERESTS BETTER, BUT IT WAS NOT A SIMPLE DICHOTOMY OF RICH FOR WHIGS AND POOR FOR DEMOCRATS.

0909 GAUS J.M., WOLCOTT L.O., LEWIS V.B.
PUBLIC ADMINISTRATION AND THE UNITED STATES DEPARTMENT OF AGRICULTURE.
CHICAGO: PUBLIC ADMIN SERVICE, 1940, 534 PP.
DESCRIBES EVOLUTION AND FUNCTION OF DEPARTMENT OF AGRICULTURE. SHOWS HOW IT INFLUENCES PRODUCTION, LAND USE, MARKETING AND DISTRIBUTION, RURAL LIFE, AND AGRICULTURAL CREDIT. DISCUSSES OVER-ALL FUNCTION AND ADMINISTRATIVE STRUCTURE OF DEPARTMENT, AND ANALYZES ITS POTENTIAL IN SOLUTION OF PROBLEMS OF 1940'S.

0910 GAUSE M.E.
"ELEMENTS OF FINANCE DEPARTMENT ORGANIZATION FOR SMALL GOVERNMENTAL UNITS."
MUNICIPAL FINANCE, 40 (AUG. 67), 7-50.
POINTS OUT FACTORS ESSENTIAL FOR AN EFFECTIVE ORGANIZATION IN SPITE OF DIFFICULTY IN SMALLER GOVERNMENTAL UNITS OF LIMITED FINANCE. DISCUSSES STAFFING, ORGANIZATION AND AUDITING SYSTEMS, AND PROMOTION METHODS.

0911 GAUSSENS J., BONNET R.
"THE APPLICATIONS OF NUCLEAR ENERGY - TECHNICAL, ECONOMIC AND SOCIAL ASPECTS."
IMPACT OF SCIENCE ON SOCIETY, 17 (1967), 75-99.
DISCUSSES THE NECESSARY DEVELOPMENT OF A NUCLEAR ECONOMY AND ITS TECHNICAL PROBLEMS, EXPLORING DIFFERENT NUCLEAR SYSTEMS AND TRAINING DEMANDS. CONCLUDES THAT THE SOCIAL CHANGES WILL BE POSITIVE, RAISING LIVING STANDARDS AND INDUSTRIAL CAPABILITY.

0912 GEARY R.C. ED.
EUROPE'S FUTURE IN FIGURES.
AMSTERDAM: NORTH HOLLAND PUBL CO, 1962, 343 PP.
FORECASTS OF GNP FOR 1970-75 IN NUMEROUS SMALL EUROPEAN NATIONS AS GIVEN BY A REPRESENTATIVE ECONOMIST WITH COMPARATIVE FIGURES FOR 1959-60. FEW REPORTS IN FRENCH HAVE ENGLISH SUMMARIES. EMPHASIS ON VARIOUS TECHNIQUES OF FORECASTING AND EACH IS ANALYZED AND CRITICIZED.

0913 GEERTZ C.
PEDDLERS AND PRINCES: SOCIAL DEVELOPMENT AND ECONOMIC CHANGE IN TWO INDONESIAN TOWNS.
CHICAGO: U. CHI. PR., 1963, 162 PP., $5.00.
CONCERNED WITH THE SOCIOLOGICAL CHANGES ALREADY UNDERWAY IN THE 'PRE-TAKE-OFF' PERIOD. COMPARES ENTREPRENEURIAL GROUPS IN TWO INDONESIAN TOWNS. AN ATTEMPT TO ANALYZE THE IMPORTANT STAGES AND VARIABLES INVOLVED IN THE PROCESS OF TRANSITION TO MODERN ECONOMIC GROWTH.

0914 GEISS I.
"THE GERMANS AND THE MIDDLE EAST CRISIS."
MIDSTREAM, 13 (NOV. 67), 3-9.
DISCUSSES WEST GERMAN ATTITUDES TOWARD ARAB-ISRAELI CRISIS OF JUNE, 1967. STATES THAT APPARENT SYMPATHIES WERE WITH ISRAEL, WHILE EXTREME LEFT AND RIGHT GROUPS WERE PRO-ARAB. FOCUSES ON HISTORICAL REASONS FOR GERMAN RIGHTIST ANTI-SEMITISM. MAINTAINS THAT CRISIS CAUSED LEFT TO LOSE CONFIDENCE IN SOVIET POLICY.

0915 GEORGE H.
PROGRESS AND POVERTY (1880)
NY: ROBERT SHALKENBACH FDN, 1955, 599 PP.
CLASSIC ECONOMIC WORK WHICH PROPOSES A SINGLE TAX SYSTEM BASED ON LAND HOLDINGS AS A PANACEA FOR UNJUST DISTRIBUTION OF WEALTH IN INDUSTRIAL SOCIETIES. BECAUSE PAUPERISM IS MOST EXTREME IN CENTERS OF GREATEST TECHNICAL PROGRESS, WHERE LAND VALUES INCREASE IN PROPORTION TO POPULATION GROWTH, GEORGE CONCLUDES ECONOMIC EQUILIBRIUM CAN BE ESTABLISHED ONLY BY ABOLISHING (I.E., TAXING) PRIVATE PROPERTY.

0916 GEORGIADIS H.G.
BALANCE OF PAYMENTS EQUILIBRIUM.
PITTSBURGH: U OF PITTSBURGH PR, 1964, 220 PP., LC#64-24967.
THEORETICAL AND EMPIRICAL STUDY OF BALANCE OF PAYMENTS EQUILIBRIUM. SUGGESTS THAT NO UNIQUE EQUILIBRIUM CONDITIONS CAN BE OBTAINED FROM KEYNESIAN MODELS; ATTEMPTS REFORMULATION OF CONDITIONS FOR BALANCE OF PAYMENTS EQUILIBRIUM; SHOWS THAT EQUILIBRIUM IN BALANCE OF PAYMENTS WITH FIXED EXCHANGE RATES CAN BE ACHIEVED ON A CONTINUING BASIS AND CAN BECOME A POLICY GOAL ONLY IN A PERFECTLY STATIC ECONOMY.

0917 GERBET P.
"LA MISE EN OEUVRE DU MARCHE COMMUN AGRICOLE."
REV. FRANCAISE SCI. POL., 4 (AUG 64), 761-73.
EVOLUTION AND ANALYSIS OF THE AGRICULTURAL POLICIES OF THE EUROPEAN COMMON MARKET, EXPLAINING ROLE OF VARIOUS PRESSURE GROUPS IN THEIR FORMULATION.

0918 GERHARD H.
"COMMODITY TRADE STABILIZATION THROUGH INTERNATIONAL AGREEMENTS."
LAW CONTEMP. PROBL., 28 (SPRING 63), 276-293.
ADVOCATES A STRONGER SYSTEM OF INTERNATIONAL AGREEMENTS TO STABILIZE COMMODITY TRADING SUGGESTING THE MULTILATERAL USE OF GOVERNMENT ACTION IN FORM OF BUFFER-STOCK SCHEMES AND LONG-RUN PURCHASE CONTRACTS. ALSO CONCERNED WITH PRICE STABILIZATION AND THE MEANS BY WHICH IT CAN BE ATTAINED.

0919 GERSCHENKRON A.
ECONOMIC BACKWARDNESS IN HISTORICAL PERSPECTIVE.
CAMBRIDGE: HARVARD U. PR., 1960, 456 PP.
ANALYZES PAST AND PRESENT ECONOMIC DEVELOPMENT THROUGHOUT THE WORLD PLACING EMPHASIS ON THE ECONOMIC SITUATION IN THE SOVIET UNION. DISCUSSES VARIOUS PROBLEMS, DIVERSIFICATION AND HISTORY IN FIELD OF MODERN INDUSTRIAL COMPLEXES AS RELATED TO ECONOMICS IN INDIVIDUAL COUNTRIES.

0920 GERWIG R.
"PUBLIC AUTHORITIES IN THE UNITED STATES."
LAW AND CONTEMPORARY PROB., 26 (FALL 61), 591-618.
DISCUSSES THE DEFINITION OF PUBLIC AUTHORITIES, THEIR HISTORICAL DEVELOPMENT, THEIR STRUCTURE, SOME LEGAL ASPECTS, THE FUNDING, BOND ISSUING AND TAXING POWERS OF AUTHORITIES, AND THEIR SOVEREIGN IMMUNITY AND TORT LIABILITY.

0921 GIAP V.N.
BIG VICTORY, GREAT TASK.
NEW YORK: FREDERICK PRAEGER, 1967, 250 PP.
NORTH VIETNAM'S MINISTER OF DEFENSE ASSESSES COURSE OF VIETNAM WAR. ADVOCATES LONG, DRAWN-OUT WAR AS BEST STRATEGY FOR NORTH TO THWART US BLITZKRIEG SCHEME. ASSERTS THAT US PACIFICATION PROGRAM IS FINISHED AND THAT US PROTESTORS HAVE DAMAGED US TROOPS' MORALE. CONSIDERS OPPOSITION TO WAR A "MARK OF SYMPATHY AND SUPPORT FOR OUR PEOPLE'S JUST RESISTANCE."

0922 GILBERT L.D.
DIVIDENDS AND DEMOCRACY.
LARCHMONT: AMER RESEACH COUNC, 1956, 242 PP., LC#56-7035.
THE THESIS OF THE BOOK IS THAT WHEN CORPORATE DEMOCRACY FLOURISHES, IN CONTRAST TO SECRECY AND AUTOCRACY, CORPORATE DIVIDENDS FLOURISH ALSO. CORPORATE DEMOCRACY INCLUDES DUE NOTICE TO SHAREHOLDERS BY MANAGEMENT ON SEVERAL MATTERS, WIDENING REGULATIONS APPLIED TO LISTED COMPANIES, AND KEEPING MANAGEMENT COMPENSATION WITHIN REASONABLE BOUNDS, AS WELL AS SEC RESPONSIVENESS TO SMALL INVESTORS.

0923 GILL P.J.
"FUTURE TAXATION POLICY IN AN INDEPENDENT EAST AFRICA"
J. OF EAST AFRICAN ECONOMIC REV., 9 (JUNE 62), 1-15.
CONTENDS PRESENT TAX STRUCTURE IN EAST AFRICAN NATIONS IS INADEQUATE. PROBLEMS OF LOCALIZED TAX-PAYING PUBLIC AND LACK OF PROFESSIONAL EXPERTS ARE SAID TO DEMAND SIMPLY ADMINISTERED PERSONAL INCOME AND CORPORATE TAX SYSTEM.

0924 GILMORE D.R.
DEVELOPING THE "LITTLE" ECONOMIES.
NEW YORK: COMM FOR ECO DEV, 1960, 200 PP., LC#60-11823.
DISCUSSES LOCAL ECONOMIC GROWTH IN US THROUGH PUBLICLY AND PRIVATELY FINANCED PROGRAMS. EXAMINES ROLE OF STATE PLANNING AGENCIES, LOCAL PLANNING ORGANIZATIONS, LOCAL CHAMBERS OF COMMERCE, INDUSTRIAL DEVELOPMENT GROUPS, DEVELOPMENT CREDIT CORPORATIONS, ETC.

0925 GILPATRICK T.V.
"PRICE SUPPORT POLICY AND THE MIDWEST FARM VOTE" (BMR)"
MIDWEST J. OF POLI. SCI., 3 (NOV. 59), 319-335.
STUDIES MIDWEST CONGRESSIONAL FARM VOTE IN 1954 WHEN THE ALTERNATIVE BETWEEN FLEXIBLE AND RIGID PRICE SUPPORTS WAS MOST SHARPLY DRAWN. FINDS THAT VOTERS WERE NOT GREATLY INFLUENCED BY CANDIDATES' POLICY STANDS. SUGGESTS THAT THE UNFAVORABLE IMAGE CREATED BY THE NATIONAL ADMINISTRATION IN THE EYES OF FARMERS OVERRODE PARTICULAR POLICY STANDS OF INDIVIDUAL REPUBLICANS.

0926 GITTELL M.
PARTICIPANTS AND PARTICIPATION: A STUDY OF SCHOOL POLICY IN NEW YORK.
NEW YORK: FREDERICK PRAEGER, 1967, 230 PP.
DESCRIBES ROLE OF PARTICIPANTS IN DECISION-MAKING IN NEW YORK CITY SCHOOL SYSTEM. EXAMINES HOW POLICY IS MADE IN MATTERS OF BUDGETING, CURRICULUM, INTEGRATION, SELECTION OF THE SUPERINTENDENT, AND TEACHERS' SALARIES. MAKES RECOMMENDATIONS DESIGNED TO INCREASE PUBLIC PARTICIPATION IN POLICY-MAKING BY DECENTRALIZING SCHOOL SYSTEM.

0927 GITTINGER J.P.
THE LITERATURE OF AGRICULTURAL PLANNING.
WASHINGTON: NATL PLANNING ASSN, 1966, 140 PP., LC#66-29351.
STUDIES CONTRIBUTORS TO AGRICULTURAL DEVELOPMENT AND PLANNING LITERATURE, PROBING THEIR ATTITUDES AND STYLISTIC APPROACHES. NOTES SHORTAGE OF CASE STUDIES AND TREATS SPECIFIC PROBLEMS. ALSO EXAMINES DATA GATHERING AND FORMAL PLANNING MODELS, AS WELL AS THE ECONOMIC ASPECTS OF AGRICULTURAL PROGRAM DESIGN. CONCLUDES WITH IDEAS ON MAKING THE LITERATURE AVAILABLE TO PLANNERS.

0928 GLADE W.P. JR., ANDERSON C.W.
THE POLITICAL ECONOMY OF MEXICO.
MADISON: U. WISC. PR., 1963, 242 PP., $5.00.
FIRST SECTION, 'REVOLUTION AND DEVELOPMENT: A MEXICAN REPRISE,' BY W.P. GLADE, IS AN ATTEMPT TO EXPLORE RELATIONS BETWEEN REVOLUTIONARY SOCIAL CHANGE AND SUCCESSFUL ECONOMIC GROWTH IN MEXICO. IN THE SECOND SECTION, 'BANKERS AS REVOLUTIONARIES: POLITICS AND DEVELOPMENT BANKING IN MEXICO,' C.W. ANDERSON GIVES A CASE STUDY OF MEXICO'S DEVELOPMENT BANKS, VIEWING THESE INSTITUTIONS PRIMARILY IN THEIR POLITICAL RATHER THAN THEIR ECONOMIC ROLE. BOTH ARE EXPERIMENTS IN THE USE OF INTER-DISCIPLINARY APPROACHES AS A WAY OF GETTING AT SOME BASIC PROBLEMS OF ECONOMIC DEVELOPMENT.

0929 GLAZER N.
"HOUSING PROBLEMS AND HOUSING POLICIES."
PUBLIC INTEREST, 7(SPRING 67),21-51.
ARGUES THAT US HOUSING POLICY PERMITS MAJORITY OF AMERICAN FAMILIES TO IMPROVE LIVING CONDITIONS & GAIN FAMILY SETTINGS SUPERIOR TO THOSE THEY LEFT. NECESSARY TO DEVISE INCOME MAINTENANCE POLICIES FOR THOSE WHO CAN'T ACHIEVE MINIMALLY DESIRABLE HOUSING AND PROVIDE RESOURCES FOR AESTHETICALLY DEPRIVED.

0930 GODFREY E.M.
"THE ECONOMICS OF AN AFRICAN UNIVERSITY."
S66 JOUS3 4 DEC- 435-455 4
EXAMINES EDUCATIONAL EXPENDITURES IN AFRICAN COUNTRIES, COMPARING RELATIVE COSTS OF RUNNING PRIMARY, SECONDARY, AND UNIVERSITY LEVEL INSTITUTIONS. CONCLUDES IT WOULD BE CHEAPER FOR AFRICAN GOVERNMENTS TO SEND CHILDREN ABROAD TO COLLEGES.

0931 GODWIN F.W., GOODWIN R.N., HADDAD W.F.
THE HIDDEN FORCE.
NEW YORK: HARPER & ROW, 1963, 203 PP., LC#63-17714.
"A REPORT OF THE INTERNATIONAL CONFERENCE ON MIDDLE LEVEL MANPOWER, SAN JUAN, PUERTO RICO, OCTOBER, 1962." DISCUSSES IMPORTANCE OF DEVELOPMENT OF SKILLED WORKERS IN DEVELOPING NATIONS, AND PLANS TO USE VOLUNTEERS AND INTERNATIONAL COOPERATION.

0932 GOETZ-GIREY R.
LE MOUVEMENT DES GREVES EN FRANCE.
PARIS: EDITIONS SIREY, 1965, 220 PP.
STUDY OF INDUSTRIAL CONFLICT IN FRANCE. DESCRIBES ENVIRONMENT IN WHICH STRIKES OCCUR. DISCUSSES COMPONENTS OF INDUSTRIAL CONFLICT IN WHOLE OF FRANCE, BY REGIONS AND INDUSTRIAL SECTORS. ATTEMPTS TO DETERMINE FACTORS THAT BRING ABOUT STRIKES. DISCUSSES INCIDENTS AND RESULTS OF STRIKES.

0933 GOLD J.
"INTERPRETATION BY THE INTERNATIONAL MONETARY FUND OF ITS ARTICLES OF AGREEMENT."
INT. AND COMP. LAW Q., 16 (APR. 67), 287-329.
DISCUSSION OF DEVELOPMENTS IN THE CHARTER OF THE FUND IN THE LAST TWELVE YEARS. VARIETY AND EXPANSIVENESS OF INTERPRETATION OF LEGAL DOCUMENT HAVE CONTRIBUTED TO CONTINUED VITALITY OF DOCUMENTS. DISCUSSES NUMBER OF INFLUENTIAL FORCES ON EVOLUTION OF DOCUMENT.

0934 GOLD N.L.
REGIONAL ECONOMIC DEVELOPMENT AND NUCLEAR POWER IN INDIA.
WASHINGTON: NATL PLANNING ASSN, 1957, 110 PP., LC#57-14761.
EXAMINES CASE STUDY IN INDIA OF USE OF ATOMIC ENERGY TO AID ECONOMIC DEVELOPMENT THROUGH INDUSTRIAL DEVELOPMENT. DISCUSSES POWER NEEDS, INDUSTRY EXPANSION EFFECTS ON TRADE, FINANCING, AND FUTURE USE OF IT.

0935 GOLDEN C.S.
"NEW PATTERNS OF DEMOCRACY."
ANTIOCH REV., 3 (SEPT. 43), 391-404.
THE PROBLEM OF WORKER DEPENDENCE ON AN IMPERSONAL MANAGEMENT IS STILLUNSOLVED; THE WAR PRODUCTION DRIVE COMMITTEES, HOWEVER, BUILT NEW PATTERNS OF DEMOCRACY. COOPERATION BASED ON PARTICIPATION IS HELD TO BE THE BEST WAY TO INTEGRATE SOCIAL FORCES.

0936 GOLDMAN M. ED.
CONTROLLING POLLUTION: THE ECONOMICS OF A CLEANER AMERICA.
ENGLEWOOD CLIFFS: PRENTICE HALL, 1967, 175 PP., LC#67-14840.
MAINTAINS THAT IMMEDIATE ECONOMIC ADVANTAGES OF CLEANLINESS MAY BE SLIGHT, BUT "LONG-RANGE FINANCIAL AND SOCIAL COSTS OF POLLUTION WILL BE ENORMOUS." CONTROL REQUIRES COMBINATION OF GOVERNMENTAL REGULATION, ECONOMIC INCENTIVE, AND SUBSIDIZATION, ALL SUPPORTED BY INFORMED PUBLIC.

0937 GOLDMAN M.I.
SOVIET MARKETING.
NEW YORK: FREE PRESS OF GLENCOE, 1963, 229 PP., LC#63-8417.
FUNCTIONING OF A CONTROLLED ECONOMY: ORGANIZATION, PRICING, FINANCES, DISTRIBUTION; ALSO STATE OWNERSHIP, ITS PROBLEMS AND TECHNIQUES.

0938 GOLDMAN M.I.
"COMPARATIVE ECONOMIC SYSTEMS: A READER."
NEW YORK: RANDOM HOUSE, INC, 1964.
A COLLECTION OF CLASSICAL AND CONTEMPORARY ARTICLES ON THE MAJOR ECONOMIC SYSTEMS OF THE 19TH AND 20TH CENTURIES: SYNDICALISM, CAPITALISM, SOCIALISM, FASCISM, AND COMMUNISM. EXTENSIVE SELECTED UNANNOTATED BIBLIOGRAPHY OF WORKS PUBLISHED IN ENGLISH BETWEEN 1919-62. SOME SOURCES EARLIER, BUT MOST FROM 1950-62. ENTRIES TOPICALLY ARRANGED ACCORDING TO THE ORGANIZATION OF THE BOOK.

0939 GOLDMAN M.I.
"A BALANCE SHEET OF SOVIET FOREIGN AID."
FOREIGN AFFAIRS, 43 (JAN. 65), 349-360.
ANALYSIS OF THE EFFECTS OF THE 3.5 BILLION DOLLARS OF FOREIGN AID PROVIDED BY THE SOVIETS OVER LAST DECADE. FOUND IMPRESSIVE TECHNICAL AND PROPAGANDA COUPS LIKE ASWAN AND BHILAI, BUT GENERALLY SOVIETS DISCOVERED SAME FRUSTRATIONS AND LACK OF COMMENSURATE POLITICO-ECONOMIC PAYOFFS AS US.

0940 GOLDSTEIN J.
THE GOVERNMENT OF BRITISH TRADE UNIONS.
LONDON: ALLEN & UNWIN, 1952, 300 PP.
DESCRIBES THE TRANSPORT AND GENERAL WORKERS UNION ON THREE LEVELS - THEORETICAL, NATIONAL, AND BRANCH. GREATEST EMPHASIS ON UNION ACTIVITY ON BRANCH LEVEL AND PROBLEMS OF ELICITING ACTIVE PARTICIPATION.

0941 GOLDSTEIN W.
"THE SCIENCE ESTABLISHMENT AND ITS POLITICAL CONTROL."
VIRGINIA QUART. REV., 43 (SUMMER 67), 353-371.
EXAMINES DIFFERENTIAL RATE OF CHANGE BETWEEN SCIENTIFIC INNOVATION AND POLITICAL ADJUSTMENT. CONSIDERS RESULTING NEED FOR NEW INSTITUTIONS OF POLITICAL CONTROL. DISCUSSES CONSEQUENCES OF SCIENTIFIC DEVELOPMENT AND MEASUREMENT OF SIZE OF SCIENTIFIC ESTABLISHMENT. ADVOCATES RATIONAL ORDERING OF SCIENTIFIC ACTIVITY TO ENCOURAGE ENLARGEMENT OF INDIVIDUAL FREEDOM AND OF SOCIAL WELFARE.

0942 GOLDWIN R.A. ED.
WHY FOREIGN AID? - TWO MESSAGES BY PRESIDENT KENNEDY AND ESSAYS.
SKOKIE: RAND MCNALLY & CO, 1962, 140 PP., LC#63-19359.
PRESENTS EIGHT ESSAYS TO CLARIFY QUESTION: WHY FOREIGN AID, WHILE DOUBTS AS TO ITS AIMS AND RESULTS SEEM TO PERSIST AND EVEN INCREASE. MOST AUTHORS ARGUE THAT, WHILE SUCH AID HAS BECOME A SOLID PART OF US PUBLIC POLICY SINCE WWII, PRESENT UNDERSTANDING OF BASIC TASK OF US AID TO UNDER-DEVELOPED NATIONS IS NOT CLEAR OR PROFOUND ENOUGH TO SERVE AS RELIABLE GUIDE TO POLICY.

0943 GOLEMBIEWSKI R.T.
ORGANIZING MEN AND POWER: PATTERNS OF BEHAVIOR AND LINE-STAFF MODELS.
NEW YORK: RAND MCNALLY & CO, 1967, 277 PP., LC#66-19446.
CHALLENGES NOTION THAT "STAFF" IN COOPERATIVE ENTERPRISES SHOULD BE OUTSIDE CHAIN OF COMMAND, AND THAT IT SHOULD AND DOES PROVIDE SERVICE RATHER THAN EXERT CONTROL. DEVELOPS NEW MODEL OF LINE-STAFF RELATIONS THAT WILL PERMIT EFFECTIVE MANAGERIAL ACTION.

0944 GOMES F.A.
OPERACAO MUNICIPIO.
RIO DE JAN: INST INTL CIEN ADMIN, 1955, 200 PP.
EXAMINES BRAZILIAN MUNICIPAL GOVERNMENT AND ITS IMPORTANCE FOR NATIONAL PROGRESS. COVERS EXTENT TO WHICH CITIES FULFILL THEIR FUNCTIONS OF PROVIDING SERVICES FOR PUBLIC AND CONNECTION OF CITIES AND FEDERAL GOVERNMENT PLANNING FOR FUTURE DEVELOPMENT. DISCUSSES ECONOMIC BASIS OF URBAN PROJECTS AND AMOUNT OF FEDERAL AID NEEDED.

0945 GOMEZ ROBLES J.
A STATEMENT OF THE LAWS OF GUATEMALA IN MATTERS AFFECTING BUSINESS (2ND ED. REV., ENLARGED)
WASHINGTON: PAN AMERICAN UNION, 1959, 323 PP.
SUMMARY OF BASIC CONSTITUTIONAL, STATUTORY, AND REGULATORY PROVISIONS OF GUATEMALA UP TO 1959, AS THEY CONCERN COMMERCIAL MATTERS AND THE PERSONS WHO TRANSACT THEM. ONE OF A SERIES, BASED UPON INFORMATION SUPPLIED BY PRACTICING GUATEMALAN LAWYERS. INCLUDES TREATIES.

0946 GONZALEZ M.P.
"CUBA, UNA REVOLUCION EN MARCHA."
CUADERNOS AMERICANOS, (JULY-AUG. 67), 7-24.
EXAMINES CUBAN REVOLUTION, COMPARING MANY ASPECTS WITH WAR IN VIETNAM. CRITICIZES US INVOLVEMENT AND POLICIES AS IMPERIALISTIC, AND MAINTAINS THAT US IS FOLLOWING SAME POLICIES WITH VIETNAM. CONTENDS CONDITIONS IMPROVED IN CUBA AFTER REVOLUTION. SPECULATES ON FUTURE OF CUBA AND VIETNAM.

0947 GONZALEZ NAVARRO M.
LA COLONIZACION EN MEXICO, 1877-1910.
MEXICO C: TALLERES DE IMPRESION, 1960, 160 PP.
EXAMINES PROGRAMS OF MEXICAN GOVERNMENT TO PROMOTE IMMIGRATION AND COLONIZATION OF LAND. DISCUSSES ATTEMPTS TO OFFER HOMESTEADING OPPORTUNITIES TO FOREIGNERS IN ORDER TO IMPROVE AGRICULTURE AND INCREASE POPULATION. EXPLAINS THE

PROBLEMS IN PROGRAM AND THE ENDING OF OFFICIAL METHOD, WHICH ADOPTED PRIVATE ACTIVITIES BY INDIVIDUALS WILLING TO HANDLE THEIR OWN AFFAIRS DESPITE TROUBLES OF CLIMATE AND LOW PAY.

0948 GOODMAN J.S.
THE DEMOCRATS AND LABOR IN RHODE ISLAND 9152-1962; CHANGES IN THE OLD ALLIANCE.
PROVIDENCE: BROWN U PRESS, 1967, 154 PP., LC#67-26817.
COMPARES AND ANLYZES RESULTS OF 76 INTERVIEWS WITH LABOR UNION AND POLITICAL PARTY ACTIVISTS TO TEST HYPOTHESIS THAT LABOR'S INFLUENCE IN DEMOCRATIC PARTY IN RHODE ISLAND DECLINED FROM 1952-62. HYPOTHESIS WAS SUPPORTED. DISCUSSES LEGISLATIVE RECRUITMENT, INTERNAL PARTY COMMUNICATION, ROLES OF LEGISLATIVE AND PARTY LEADERS, AND CRESS PRESSURES ON LEGISLATORS ASSOCIATED WITH BOTH THE PARTY AND LABOR.

0949 GOODMAN L.H. ED.
ECONOMIC PROGRESS AND SOCIAL WELFARE.
NEW YORK: COLUMBIA U PRESS, 1966, 233 PP., LC#66-20491.
COLLECTION OF ESSAYS ON SOCIAL WELFARE POLICIES AND NEED TO REVISE TRADITIONAL GOALS. EFFICIENCY IN PROGRAM OPERATION AND ADMINISTRATIVE IMPLEMENTATION IN AGE OF MATERIAL ABUNDANCE BASIC THEME OF ESSAYS.

0950 GOODMAN P.
LIKE A CONQUERED PROVINCE: THE MORAL AMBIGUITY OF AMERICA.
NEW YORK: RANDOM HOUSE, INC, 1967, 142 PP., LC#67-14466.
DISCUSSES EFFECT OF GENERATION OF COLD WAR TENSION ON ECONOMIC SYSTEM, SCIENTIFIC TECHNOLOGY, AND EDUCATION IN US ARGUES THAT TECHNOLOGICAL CHANGE DUE TO MILITANCE FAILS TO FILL NEEDS OF PEOPLE AND ACTS TO AGGRANDIZE PROFIT AND POWER. CRITICALLY EXPLORES MORAL ISSUES INVOLVED.

0951 GOODSELL C.T.
ADMINISTRATION OF A REVOLUTION.
CAMBRIDGE: HARVARD U PR, 1965, 254 PP., LC#65-16684.
DISCUSSES EXECUTIVE REFORM IN PUERTO RICO UNDER GOVERNOR TUGWELL, 1941-46. ANALYZES THE ECONOMIC REVOLUTION DURING WWII. DISCUSSES BUDGET PLANNING, THE LEGISLATURE, THE CIVIL SERVICE, MUNICIPAL IMPROVEMENT, AND THE LEADERSHIP FOR ECONOMIC REFORM THAT WAS GIVEN BY THE ADMINISTRATION.

0952 GOODWIN C.D.W.
CANADIAN ECONOMIC THOUGHT.
DURHAM: DUKE U PR, 1961, 214 PP., LC#61-6223.
QUESTIONS OF LAND SETTLEMENT, INTERNATIONAL TRADE, CURRENCY, AND BANKING ARE EXAMINED. DISCUSSES NATIONAL POLICY, AND ECONOMICS IN FRENCH CANADA, MARITIME PROVINCES, ONTARIO, AND WESTERN CANADA.

0953 GOODWIN C.D.W.
ECONOMIC INQUIRY IN AUSTRALIA.
DURHAM: DUKE U PR, 1966, 695 PP., LC#65-27768.
STUDY OF THE HISTORY OF ECONOMIC DOCTRINE. FOCUS ON ASPECTS OF AUSTRALIAN ECONOMY FROM FIRST SETTLEMENTS TO 1929. CONTENDS AUSTRALIA SELECTED AND MODIFIED EUROPEAN ECONOMIC THEORY TO MEET OWN NEEDS.

0954 GORDON B.
"ECONOMIC IMPEDIMENTS TO REGIONALISM IN SOUTH EAST ASIA."
ASIAN SURV., 3 (MAY 63), 235-44.
ANALYZES PAST AND PRESENT ECONOMIC ASPECTS OF REGION. PRESENT CONDITIONS AND FATE OF NEW PROPOSALS AFFECTED MAINLY BY TWO TOPICS: TRADE RELATIONSHIPS AND NATURE OF INDIVIDUAL DEVELOPMENT PROGRAMS. CONSIDERS FACTORS HINDERING INTER-REGIONAL TRADE. SCORES NEGLECT OF AGRICULTURAL DEVELOPMENT.

0955 GORDON D.L., DANGERFIELD R.
THE HIDDEN WEAPON: THE STORY OF ECONOMIC WARFARE.
NEW YORK: HARPER, 1947, 238 PP.
DESCRIBES BRITISH AND AMERICAN DEVICES OF ECONOMIC WARFARE DURING WW 2, DIRECTED TOWARDS CUTTING OF AXIS POWERS FROM FOREIGN SUPPLIES OF STRATEGIC MATERIALS. CONSIDERS NEUTRALITY AND INTERNATIONAL LAW GOVERNING RELATIONS OF NON-BELLIGERENTS AND BELLIGERENTS TO BE NOW EXTINCT DUE TO NATURE OF MODERN WAR. SEES NEED FOR ENFORCEABLE LAWS WHICH WILL ELIMINATE WAR.

0956 GORDON L.
"THE ORGANIZATION FOR EUROPEAN ECONOMIC COOPERATION."
INT. ORGAN., 10 (FEB. 56), 1-11.
CONTENDS OEEC HAS HAD INFLUENCE ON ATTITUDES AND ACTIONS OF MEMBER STATES. EXAMINES SUCCESSES IN ALLOCATION OF AID, TRADE AND PAYMENTS LIBERALIZATION, PRODUCTIVITY INCREASE, AND CURRENCY STABILIZATION. OEEC FAILED IN RECOVERY PROGRAMS, ECONOMIC INTEGRATION.

0957 GORDON L.
"ECONOMIC REGIONALISM RECONSIDERED."
WORLD POLIT., 13 (JAN. 61), 231-253.
ANY REAPPRAISAL OF ECONOMIC REGIONALISM MUST START WITH REVIEW OF PRESENT STRUCTURE OF WORLD ECONOMY. ANALYZES INDUSTRIALIZED AND NON-INDUSTRIALIZED FREE COUNTRIES, DEVELOPMENTAL REGIONALISM, INTERREGIONAL RELATIONS, AND AMERICAN FOREIGN ECONOMIC POLICY.

0958 GORDON L.
A NEW DEAL FOR LATIN AMERICA.
CAMBRIDGE: HARVARD U PR, 1963, 146 PP., LC#63-13812.
ADDRESSES BY US AMBASSADOR TO BRAZIL EXPLAINING PHILOSOPHY, PURPOSES, AND WORKING METHODS OF THE ALLIANCE FOR PROGRESS. ANALYZES DIFFICULTIES CONFRONTING THE PROGRAM. DISCUSSES ECONOMIC ASPECTS, DEMOCRATIC REVOLUTION, EDUCATIONAL FOUNDATIONS, AND FREE INITIATIVE.

0959 GORDON M.S.
THE ECONOMICS OF WELFARE POLICIES.
NEW YORK: COLUMBIA U PRESS, 1963, 159 PP., LC#63-14113.
DETAILED ANALYSIS OF PROBLEMS INVOLVED IN DEVELOPMENT OF WELFARE POLICIES WITH EMPHASIS ON RELATIONSHIP OF WELFARE TO ECONOMIC GROWTH. COMPARES WELFARE PROGRAMS IN US TO THOSE IN OTHER COUNTRIES AND DISCUSSES INCOME REDISTRIBUTION, UNEMPLOYMENT COMPENSATION, AND VARIOUS WELFARE INSURANCE PROGRAMS.

0960 GORDON R.A.
BUSINESS LEADERSHIP IN THE LARGE CORPORATION.
BERKELEY: U OF CALIF PR, 1961, 364 PP., LC#61-1574.
DOCUMENTS IMPORTANCE OF LARGE BUSINESS CORPORATION IN AMERICAN SOCIETY. INVESTIGATES WAYS IN WHICH LEADERSHIP ACTIVITIES ARE CARRIED ON IN LARGE FIRM. EVALUATES SOME OF ECONOMIC CONSEQUENCES OF ORGANIZATIONAL STRUCTURE AND THE INCENTIVE SYSTEM, AND THE POLITICAL RELATIONSHIPS CONDITIONING DECISION-MAKING PROCESS.

0961 GORDON R.A. ED., GORDON M.S. ED.
PROSPERITY AND UNEMPLOYMENT.
NEW YORK: JOHN WILEY, 1966, 353 PP., LC#66-16138.
EXAMINATION OF UNEMPLOYMENT IN THE FACE OF CURRENT BUSINESS EXPANSION. STUDIES THE RESPONSE OF LABOR SUPPLY TO THE DEMAND FOR LABOR, AND THE CHANGING LEVEL AND PATTERN OF EMPLOYMENT, 1961-65. DISCUSSES THE COMPOSITION OF UNEMPLOYMENT AND PUBLIC POLICY. CONCLUDES WITH ANALYSIS OF THE IMMEDIATE FUTURE. BELIEVES US MUST CONTINUE TO EXPAND ITS EDUCATION AND EMPLOYMENT POTENTIALS.

0962 GORDON W.
THE POLITICAL ECONOMY OF LATIN AMERICA.
NEW YORK: COLUMBIA U PRESS, 1965, 401 PP., LC#65-19444.
ANALYSIS OF ECONOMIC PROBLEMS OF LATIN AMERICA BY EXAMINING ECONOMIC SYSTEMS, MARKET ORGANIZATION, WELFARE, ECONOMIC DEVELOPMENT, AND TRADE AND FINANCE OF LATIN AMERICAN NATIONS.

0963 GORMAN W.
"ELLUL - A PROPHETIC VOICE."
CENTER MAGAZINE, 1 (OCT.-NOV. 67), 34-37.
DISCUSSES JACQUES ELLUL'S BOOK "POLITICAL ILLUSION," WHICH STATES THAT POLITICS IS NOW IN SERVITUDE TO TECHNICAL NECESSITY. EFFICIENCY, NOT MORALITY, IS THE SUPREME GOOD. FEELS RESISTANCE TO STATE IS REQUIRED TO CREATE TENSIONS WHICH WILL LIMIT STATE'S AUTONOMY. GORMAN HAS RESERVATIONS ON THIS.

0964 GORT M.
DIVERSIFICATION AND INTEGRATION IN AMERICAN INDUSTRY.
PRINCETON: PRINCETON U PRESS, 1962, 238 PP.
COMPREHENSIVE STUDY OF INTER-INDUSTRY STRUCTURE OF THE LARGE, DIVERSIFIED ENTERPRISE. DETAILED STATISTICAL ANALYSIS AND QUESTIONS ABOUT RELATIONSHIPS WITH OTHER ASPECTS OF THE ECONOMY. ONE CONSEQUENCE OF INCREASED DIVERSIFICATION IS FRAGMENTATION OF CONSUMER PRESSURE; AL INTEGRATION HAS WIDE EFFECTS ON COMPETITION AND AGAIN LESSENS THE CONSUMER IMPACT.

0965 GORZ A.
STRATEGY FOR LABOR: A RADICAL PROPOSAL (TRANS. BY MARTIN NICOLAUS AND VICTORIA ORTIZ)
BOSTON: BEACON PRESS, 1967, 199 PP., LC#67-14111.
STUDY OF SOCIETAL PROBLEMS OF WORKING CLASS, ADDRESSED PRIMARILY TO EUROPEAN SOCIALIST AND COMMUNIST LABOR UNIONS AND POLITICAL PARTIES, BUT ALSO RELEVANT TO AMERICAN PROBLEMS. CONCERNS LABOR'S LACK OF ECONOMIC OR POLITICAL POWER AND SUGGESTS STRATEGY FOR UNIONS TO REGAIN A HAND IN THE MAJOR CHANGES AFFECTING ADVANCED INDUSTRIAL SOCIETIES.

0966 GOSALVEZ R.B.
"PERFIL DEL GENERAL VINCENTE ROJO."
CUADERNOS AMERICANOS, (JULY-AUG. 67), 64-68.
DISCUSSES BOLIVIA AND HER RELATIONS WITH SPAIN DURING SPANISH CIVIL WAR. EXAMINES ROLE OF ROJO; PRAISES HIS LOYALTY AND MILITARY GENIUS, AND SENSE OF DUTY AND FIDELITY TOWARD REPUBLIC TO THE VERY END.

0967 GOULD J.M.
THE TECHNICAL ELITE.
NEW YORK: AUGUSTUS M KELLEY, 1966, 178 PP., LC#66-15566.
ANALYZES EMERGENCE AND SCOPE OF TECHNICIANS WHO INFLUENCE DECISION-MAKING IN GOVERNMENT AND BUSINESS TODAY. STUDIES THEIR CHARACTERISTICS AND THREAT THAT "PUBLIC POLICY CAN BE CAPTIVATED BY THEM IN FUTURE." CONCENTRATES ON MEN IN INDUSTRIAL FIELD WHO DETERMINE AMOUNT OF US PRODUCTIVITY.

0968 GOULD W.B.
"THE STATUS OF UNAUTHORIZED AND 'WILDCAT' STRIKES UNDER THE NATIONAL LABOR RELATIONS ACT."
CORNELL LAW Q., 52 (SPRING 67), 672-704.
EXAMINATION OF PROBLEMS THAT UNAUTHORIZED STRIKE PRESENTS FOR MANAGEMENT AND RESPONSIBLE UNION LEADERSHIP. OUTLINES PRESENT APPROACH TAKEN BY NATIONAL LABOR RELATIONS BOARD AND CIRCUIT COURTS. CONTENDS PRESENT METHODS OF HANDLING WORK STOPPAGES NEITHER WORKABLE NOR EFFECTIVE. SUGGESTS APPROACH MORE CONDUCIVE TO SECURING INDUSTRIAL PEACE AND EMPLOYEE JUSTICE TO BE FOUND IN DECISION OF CONGRESS.

0969 GOWDA K.V.
INTERNATIONAL CURRENCY PLANS AND EXPANSION OF WORLD TRADE.
BOMBAY: ASIA PUBL HOUSE, 1964, 216 PP.
ANALYSIS OF TRIFFIN PLAN AND OTHER RIVAL PLANS DESIGNED TO MAINTAIN INTERNATIONAL MONETARY STABILITY AS SECURE BASIS FOR WORLD TRADE AND FINANCE. DISCUSSES PROBLEMS OF ESTABLISHING SMOOTHLY FUNCTIONING INTERNATIONAL SYSTEM AND STRESSES IMPORTANCE OF MAINTAINING WORLD CONFIDENCE IN SYSTEM SUCH AS EXISTED IN 19TH CENTURY.

0970 GRAHAM F.D.
PROTECTIVE TARIFFS.
NEW YORK: HARPER, 1934, 176 PP.
ANALYSIS OF ARGUMENTS FOR AND AGAINST PROTECTION IN INTERNATIONAL TRADE AND SUGGESTIONS FOR FUTURE TRADE POLICIES FOR USA.

0971 GRAHAM F.D.
THE THEORY OF INTERNATIONAL VALUES.
PRINCETON: U. PR., 1948, 349 PP.
PRESENTS A THEORY WHICH IS A COMPLETE REFUTATION OF CLASSICAL DOCTRINES, AND DISCUSSES INTERNATION ECONOMICS AND TRADE IN THE LIGHT OF THIS NEW THEORY.

0972 GRAHAM R.
"BRAZIL'S DILEMMA."
CURRENT HISTORY, 53 (NOV. 67), 291-297, 308.
EXPLORES SUCCESS OF CASTELO BRANCO GOVERNMENT IN BRAZIL. NOTES THAT POLITICAL SYSTEM THIS GOVERNMENT INHERITED WAS BASED ON INCONGRUOUS POLICY OF MAINTAINING TRADITIONAL POLITICAL POWER BASE WHILE SUCCESSIVELY INCORPORATING NEWER FORCES. DISCUSSES PROSPECTS FOR FUTURE. FEELS NO NEW CRISES WILL OVERTAKE BRAZIL.

0973 GRAMPP W.D.
THE MANCHESTER SCHOOL OF ECONOMICS.
STANFORD: STANFORD U PRESS, 1960, 155 PP., LC#60-9050.
STUDIES NATURE, ACTIONS, AND THEORIES OF MANCHESTER SCHOOL. SHOWS REASONS WHY SCHOOL FORCED GREAT BRITAIN TO REPEAL CORN LAWS AND THEREBY COMMIT ITSELF FINALLY TO FREE TRADE. STATES THAT SCHOOL, UNLIKE CLASSICAL ONE, WAS A GROUP OF AGITATORS, AND ITS MEMBERS SPENT LESS TIME REASONING ABOUT THEIR PURPOSES THAN IN WINNING COUNTRY OVER TO THEM.

0974 GRAMPP W.D.
ECONOMIC LIBERALISM; THE BEGINNINGS (VOL. I)
NEW YORK: RANDOM HOUSE, INC, 1965, 186 PP., LC#65-13760.
CONCERNED WITH INTELLECTUAL ORIGINS OF ECONOMIC LIBERALISM. BEGINS WITH STOICS; THEN TREATS MERCANTILISTS AS LIBERALS; CONCLUDES WITH ORIGINS OF AMERICAN LIBERALISM. INCLUDES ECONOMIC PHILOSOPHIES OF ZENO AND EPICTETUS, POLITICAL IDEAS AND THEORIES OF MARKET AND FULL EMPLOYMENT OF THE MERCANTILISTS, AND ECONOMIC POLICIES OF REPUBLICAN AND FEDERALIST PARTIES IN US.

0975 GRAMPP W.D.
ECONOMIC LIBERALISM; THE CLASSICAL VIEW (VOL. II)
NEW YORK: RANDOM HOUSE, INC, 1965, 153 PP., LC#65-13760.
EXAMINES LIBERALISM AS EXPRESSED BY CLASSICAL SCHOOL OF ECONOMICS. BEGINS WITH CLASSICAL PSYCHOLOGY OF LIBERALISM, THEN DISCUSSES POLITICAL IDEAS OF CLASSICAL ECONOMIST. CONCLUDES WITH LIBERALISM IN 19TH CENTURY. INCLUDES THEORIES OF ADAM SMITH, HUME, AND MILL; NATIONALISM OF ECONOMISTS; ECONOMIC IMPROVEMENT AND SOCIAL PROGRESS; MEASURES PROMOTING AND RESTRICTING THE MARKET; AND THEORIES OF POLICY.

0976 GRANICK D.
THE RED EXECUTIVE.
NEW YORK: DOUBLEDAY, 1960, 334 PP.
SOVIET INDUSTRIAL SYSTEM RUN BY MANAGERIAL CLASS SIMILAR TO AMERICAN COUNTERPART. AMERICAN AND RED EXECUTIVES POSSESS SIMILAR EDUCATION AND EXPERIENTIAL BACKGROUNDS. RED EXECUTIVES ENJOYS GREATER STATUS AND WEALTH, BUT LACK DECISION MAKING POWER AND PERSONAL SECURITY.

0977 GRANICK D.
THE EUROPEAN EXECUTIVE.
GARDEN CITY: DOUBLEDAY, 1962, 384 PP., LC#62-07635.
ANALYZES EUROPEAN ECONOMIC MANAGEMENT, ESPECIALLY IN GREAT BRITAIN, BELGIUM, GERMANY, AND FRANCE. DISCUSSES THE TECHNOCRAT, ENTREPRENEURSHIP, LABOR PRACTICES, MANAGEMENT CONCEPTS, AND OWNER-MANAGER RELATIONS.

0978 GRANT J.A.C.
"THE GUILD RETURNS TO AMERICA."
J. OF POLITICS, 4 (AUG.-NOV. 42), 303-336, 458-477 .
HISTORY OF GUILDS IN AMERICA, INCLUDING HISTORICAL ANTECEDENTS, LABOR ORGANIZATIONS AND LAW IN US, REQUIREMENTS FOR PROFESSIONAL LICENSING, AND STATUTES CURBING SERVICES TO LICENSED PRACTICIONERS, EMPHASIZING SITUATION AT TIME OF WRITING.

0979 GRAYSON D.K.
"RISK ALLOCATIONS UNDER THE PERMITS AND RESPONSIBILITIES CLAUSE OF THE STANDARD GOVERNMENT CONSTRUCTION CONTRACT."
G. WASH. LAW REV., 35 (JUNE 67), 988-997.
DISCUSSES CLAUSE WHICH PLACES ON GOVERNMENT CONSTRUCTION CONTRACTOR THE RESPONSIBILITY FOR OBTAINING LICENSES, FOR COMPLYING WITH ALL APPLICABLE LAWS, AND GENERALLY FOR ALL MATERIALS DELIBERED AND WORK PERFORMED. SHOWS THAT IN PROVISIONS OF THIS CLAUSE, RISK ALLOCATION IS ESSENTIALLY THE SAME AS THAT OF COMMON LAW.

0980 GREAT BRITAIN CENTRAL OFF INF
THE COLOMBO PLAN (PAMPHLET)
LONDON: H M STATIONERY OFFICE, 1964, 79 PP.
DESCRIBES ORIGINS OF COLOMBO PLAN, ITS WORKINGS, RESOURCES OF REGION, PROGRESS IN AREAS OF EXTERNAL CAPITAL ASSISTANCE, TECHNICAL COOPERATION, AND AID FROM BRITAIN.

0981 GREBLER L.
URBAN RENEWAL IN EUROPEAN COUNTRIES: ITS EMERGENCE AND POTENTIALS.
PHILA: U OF PENN PR, 1964, 132 PP., LC#63-21714.
STUDY OF EUROPEAN EFFORTS, SUCCESSES, AND FAILURES AT URBAN RENEWAL. POINTS OUT THAT RENEWAL OFTEN GOES ON INDEPENDENTLY OF NATIONAL PROGRAMS. ALSO SHOWS THAT BRITISH EFFORTS HAVE BEEN FAR MORE SUSTAINED AND EFFECTIVE THAN THOSE OF NATIONS ON CONTINENT.

0982 GREEN C., LAMPMAN R.J.
"SCHEMES FOR TRANSFERRING INCOME TO THE POOR."
INDUSTRIAL RELATIONS, (FEB. 67), 121-137.
SURVEYS NINE VARIANTS OF THE FOLLOWING METHODS OF INCREASING INCOME OF THE POOR; NEGATIVE INCOME TAX, MODIFICATIONS OF PUBLIC ASSISTANCE AND SOCIAL INSURANCE, FAMILY ALLOWANCES, AND TAX CREDITS. CONCLUDES THAT BEST RESULTS PER DOLLAR SPENT WOULD COME FROM A COMBINATION OF CONTINUED SOCIAL INSURANCE PROGRAMS WITH NEGATIVE RATE ALLOWANCES. THE POVERTY-INCOME GAP WOULD BE THE BASIS FOR ELIGIBILITY.

0983 GREEN C.
NEGATIVE TAXES AND THE POVERTY PROBLEM.
WASHINGTON: BROOKINGS INST, 1967, 210 PP., LC#67-19191.
EXPLORES PROPOSAL OF DISTRIBUTING FUNDS TO POOR THROUGH "NEGATIVE TAXES." EVALUATES EQUITY AND EFFICIENCY OF VARIOUS METHODS AND ESTIMATES HOW WELL EACH CAN BE COORDINATED WITH "POSITIVE" TAX SYSTEM. CONSIDERS EFFECTS OF MINIMUN INCOME GUARANTEES ON INCENTIVES TO WORK AND ON BIRTH RATE.

0984 GREEN F.M.
CONSTITUTIONAL DEVELOPMENT IN THE SOUTH ATLANTIC STATES, 1776-1860; A STUDY IN THE EVOLUTION OF DEMOCRACY.
CHAPEL HILL: U OF N CAR PR, 1930, 328 PP.
ANALYZES SOCIAL, POLITICAL, AND ECONOMIC FACTORS INVOLVED IN FORMATION OF CONSTITUTIONS OF FIVE OLDEST SOUTHERN STATES. TRACES DEVELOPMENT, INFLUENCES LEADING TO REVISION AND AMENDMENT, AND DEMOCRATIC ELEMENTS; INCLUDES ROLE OF ELITE ARISTOCRATIC PLANTERS. DISCUSSES LEGISLATIVE, EXECUTIVE, AND JUDICIAL STRUCTURES; SOCIAL AND ECONOMIC SECTIONALISM; AND PARTY REPRESENTATION.

0985 GREEN J.L.
METROPOLITAN ECONOMIC REPUBLICS.
ATHENS: U OF GEORGIA PRESS, 1965, 206 PP., LC#65-25287.
PRESENTS STRUCTURAL MODEL FOR COMMUNITY ACTION IN URBAN AREAS. SUGGESTS METHODOLOGIES WHICH LEAD TOWARD "TOTAL SYSTEMS CONCEPT" IN COORDINATING COMMUNITY ACTION. ILLUSTRATES MODEL BY APPLYING IT TO ATLANTA, GEORGIA METROPOLITAN STRUCTURE.

0986 GREEN L.P.
"DEVELOPMENT IN AFRICA."
NEW YORK: INTL PUBLNS SERV, 1962.
REFERENCES PRIMARILY BRITISH WORKS WITH MAGAZINE ARTICLES AND ATLASES AS WELL AS BOOKS. SEVERAL REFERENCE WORKS ARE CONCERNED WITH ECONOMICS AND GEOGRAPHY OF VARIOUS AFRICAN NATIONS: SOUTH AFRICA, RHODESIA AND NYASALAND, NIGERIA, KENYA, AND UGANDA.

0987 GREEN L.P., FAIR T.J.D.
DEVELOPMENT IN AFRICA.
CAPETOWN: WITWATERSTRAND U PR, 1962, 203 PP.
STUDY PROMPTED BY AND DIRECTED TO CURRENT PROBLEMS ARISING IN AFRICA AS RADICAL SOCIAL, ECONOMIC, POLITICAL CHANGES MULTIPLY. OBJECTIVE IS TO ANALYZE PROCESSES AND PRINCIPLES CREATING EVOLVING PATTERN OF DEVELOPMENT AND PROVIDE FRAMEWORK FOR ANALYSIS OF ITS DETAILS SUCH AS POPULATION DISTRIBUTION AND URBANIZATION. BRIEFLY DISCUSSES RACE RELATIONS AND CONTEMPORARY POLITICAL PROBLEMS. BIBLIOGRAPHY INCLUDED.

0988 GREEN P.E.
"BAYESIAN DECISION THEORY IN PRICING STRATEGY."
J. OF MARKETING, 27 (JAN. 63), 5-14.
THE AUTHOR SHOWS HOW BAYESIAN STATISTICS CAN BE USED IN THE AREA OF PRICING ANALYSIS.

0989 GREENE L.E., AVERY R.S.
GOVERNMENT IN TENNESSEE (2ND ED.)
KNOXVILLE: U OF TENN PR, 1966, 371 PP., LC#66-21194.
CONTAINS MATERIAL ON STRUCTURE, FUNCTION, AND ADMINISTRATION OF TENNESSEE STATE GOVERNMENT. INCLUDES COPY OF STATE CONSTITUTION; DEALS WITH STATE POLITICS AND COURTS; COUNTY GOVERNMENT; BUSINESS AND INDUSTRY; PUBLIC HEALTH, EDUCATION, AND WELFARE; TRANSPORT FACILITIES, STATE REVENUES, AND STATE AND LOCAL PLANNING.

0990 GREENFIELD K.R.
ECONOMICS AND LIBERALISM IN THE RISORGIMENTO (REV. ED.)
BALTIMORE: JOHNS HOPKINS PRESS, 1965, 303 PP., LC#65-27721.
STUDY OF NATIONALISM IN LOMBARDY, 1814-48, INCLUDING DESCRIPTION OF PROVINCE'S ECONOMIC STRUCTURE, SURVEY OF NATIONAL JOURNALISM, EMERGENCE OF PROGRAM OF CIVIC ACTION, AND TRANSITION TO NATIONAL POLITICAL PROGRAM.

0991 GREENHUT M.L.
PLANT LOCATION IN THEORY AND PRACTICE; THE ECONOMICS OF SPACE.
CHAPEL HILL: U OF N CAR PR, 1956, 338 PP.
BEGINS WITH REVIEW OF VARIOUS THEORIES OF PLANT LOCATION. DISCUSSES FACTORS - SUCH AS DEMAND, COSTS, AND LABOR - THAT DETERMINE PLANT LOCATION IN A CAPITALISTIC STATE AND THEN INVESTIGATES ACTUAL SITE-SELECTIONS TO ASCERTAIN INFLUENCE OF THESE FACTORS ON PLANT LOCATIONS IN SMALL FIRMS. CONCLUDES WITH A GENERAL THEORY OF PLANT LOCATION AFTER EVALUATING BASIC POSTULATES OF PAST AND PRESENT THEORY.

0992 GREER S.
URBAN RENEWAL AND AMERICAN CITIES: THE DILEMMA OF DEMOCRATIC INTERVENTION.
INDIANAPOLIS: BOBBS-MERRILL, 1965, 201 PP., LC#65-26544.
SOCIOLOGICAL STUDY BASED UPON OBSERVATIONS OF AMERICAN CITIES AND INTERVIEWS WITH URBAN RENEWAL ADMINISTRATORS. ANALYZES RENEWAL AS PART OF US CULTURE; ORGANIZATIONAL ASPECTS, WITH EMPHASIS ON LOCAL PUBLIC AUTHORITY. STUDIES MASSIVE AND INTERTWINED SOCIAL TRENDS IN US CITIES. PROPOSES THAT GOVERNMENT SPEND MORE MONEY RESEARCHING NEEDS OF CITIES BEFORE MONEY IS PUMPED INTO URBAN RENEWAL PROJECTS.

0993 GREGORY A.J.
"AFRICAN SOCIALISM, SOCIALISM AND FASCISM: AN APPRAISAL."
REV. OF POLITICS, 29 (JULY 67), 324-353.
DISCUSSES LANGUAGE, IDEOLOGY, AND PROGRAMS OF CONTEMPORARY AFRICAN SOCIALISM. SHOWS IT IS NOT PART OF MARXIST "CLASS-STRUGGLE" DOCTRINES BUT IS CLOSER TO FASCIST IDEOLOGY. SUGGESTS THAT AFFINITIES BETWEEN FASCISM AND AFRICAN SOCIALISM HELP EXPLAIN RECURRENCE OF AFRICAN CHARISMATIC LEADERS AND POINT TO POSSIBLE APPEARANCE OF RACISM.

0994 GREGORY R.
"THE MINISTER'S LINE: OR, THE M4 COMES TO BERKSHIRE. PART I."
PUBLIC ADMINISTRATION, 45 (SUMMER 67), 113-128.
EXAMINES COMPLEX PROBLEMS BRITISH MINISTRY OF TRANSPORT ENCOUNTERED IN FIXING ROUTE FOR NEW HIGWAY M4. DISCUSSES CRITERIA FOR SETTLING "MOTORWAY" LINES AND DEALS WITH THE STATUTORY AND CONVENTIONAL PLANNING PROCEDURES FOLLOWED BY THE MINISTRY.

0995 GRENIEWSKI H.
"INTENTION AND PERFORMANCE: A PRIMER OF CYBERNETICS OF PLANNING."
MANAGEMENT SCIENCE, 11 (JULY 65), 263-282.
THE OBJECT OF A GOAL IS ALWAYS A RELATIVELY ISOLATED PROSPECTIVE SYSTEM; THE GOAL IS A CERTAIN STATE OF THE OUTPUT; THE MEANS ARE THE STATES OF THE CONTROLLED INPUTS. RELATIONS AMONG GOALS, MEANS, AND CIRCUMSTANCES ARE ANALYZED; PLANNING IS GIVEN A GAME THEORETICAL INTERPRETATION; THE IMPLEMENTATION OF A PLAN IS A 2 PERSON GAME, THE PLANNER AND THE CIRCUMSTANCES BEING THE TWO PLAYERS.

0996 GREY A.L. ED., ELLIOTT J.E. ED.
ECONOMIC ISSUES AND POLICIES; READINGS IN INTRODUCTORY ECONOMICS (2ND ED.)
BOSTON: HOUGHTON MIFFLIN, 1961, 548 PP.
TREATS ECONOMIC ISSUES OF 1960'S. EXPLORES HISTORY OF ECONOMIC THOUGHT IN US AND METHODOLOGICAL APPROACHES TO ECONOMICS. EXAMINES PROBLEMS OF EMPLOYMENT, OUTPUT, PRICES, COMPETITION AND MONOPOLIES, AGRICULTURE, LABOR, POVERTY, INCOME DISTRIBUTION, FOREIGN TRADE AND AID, AND ECONOMIC GROWTH. COMPARES SEVERAL ECONOMIC SYSTEMS TO STUDY THEIR POLICY SOLUTIONS.

0997 GRIER E., GRIER G.
PRIVATELY DEVELOPED INTERRACIAL HOUSING: AN ANALYSIS OF EXPERIENCE.
BERKELEY: U OF CALIF PR, 1960, 264 PP., LC#59-13463.
REPORT ON THE FINDINGS OF ONE PART OF A STUDY OF HOUSING PROBLEMS INVOLVING RACIAL AND ETHNIC GROUPS CARRIED OUT BY THE COMMISSION ON RACE AND HOUSING UNDER THE DIRECTORSHIP OF DAVIS MC ENTIRE AND FINANCED BY THE FUND FOR THE REPUBLIC. DISCUSSES PLANNING, FINANCING, AND MARKETING OF THE INTERRACIAL HOUSING DEVELOPMENT.

0998 GRIFFIN A.P.C. ED.
LISTS PUBLISHED 1902-03: GOVERNMENT OWNERSHIP OF RAILROADS (PAMPHLET)
WASHINGTON: LIBRARY OF CONGRESS, 1903, 14 PP.
ABOUT 90 ENTRIES OF BOOKS, PUBLICATIONS, AND ARTICLES IN PERIODICALS ON LEGALITY AND POSSIBILITY OF US GOVERNMENT'S OWNING RR. SOME ENTRIES ARE IN FRENCH AND GERMAN AND PUBLICATION RANGES FROM 1870-1903. ENTRIES ARE ALPHABETICAL BY AUTHOR, EXCEPT ARTICLES WHICH ARE CHRONOLOGICAL FROM 1871-1903.

0999 GRIFFIN C.E.
THE FREE SOCIETY.
WASHINGTON: AMER ENTERPRISE INST, 1965, 138 PP., LC#65-15709
PRESENTS PHILOSOPHY OF FREE SOCIETY OR FREE ENTERPRISE. STARTS WITH BASIC CONCEPTS OF GOOD SOCIETY, INTERDEPENDENCE AND FREEDOM, MARKET, LIBERALISM, INDIVIDUALISM, AND RATIONALITY. SHOWS THAT APPLICATIONS AND COROLLARIES, SUCH AS CIVIL LIBERTY, MAJORITY RULE, ECONOMIC FREEDOM, EQUALITY OF OPPORTUNITY, FEDERALISM, AND AFFLUENT SOCIETY FLOW OUT OF BASIC PREMISES.

1000 GRIFFITH W.E. ED.
COMMUNISM IN EUROPE (2 VOLS.)
CAMBRIDGE: M I T PRESS, 1964, 406 PP., LC#64-21409.
STUDY IS INTENDED TO RELATE IN DEPTH THE INTERACTION BETWEEN DOMESTIC DEVELOPMENTS AND SINO-SOVIET RIFT DEVELOPMENTS WITHIN MAJOR EUROPEAN COMMUNIST STATES. MAJOR ATTENTION IS GIVEN TO INTERNAL DEVELOPMENTS WITHIN THE SEVERAL PARTIES AND STATES.

1001 GRIFFITH W.E.
SINO-SOVIET RELATIONS, 1964-1965.
CAMBRIDGE: M I T PRESS, 1967, 504 PP., LC#66-29172.
ANALYZES SINO-SOVIET RELATIONS AND INCLUDES TEXT OF, OR EXCERPTS FROM, MAIN DOCUMENTS OF PERIOD 1964-65. REVIEWS POLICIES OF KHRUSHCHEV, BREZHNEV, AND KOSYGIN IN RELATION TO CHINESE COMMUNIST MOVEMENT. DISCUSSES IMPACT OF INTERNATIONAL CRISES ON SINO-SOVIET RELATIONS.

1002 GRIGSBY W.G.
HOUSING MARKETS AND PUBLIC POLICY.
PHILA: U OF PENN PR, 1963, 346 PP., LC#63-15010.
ANALYZES RELATIONSHIPS OF THE PRIVATE HOUSING MARKET AND PUBLIC RENEWAL AND OTHER PROGRAMS. INTRODUCES FLOW ANALYSIS INTO HOUSING MARKET STUDIES ON A SYSTEMATIC BASIS AND CONNECTS IT TO APPLICATIONS OF MATRIX ANALYSIS. EXAMINES CONFLICTS IN GOALS THAT MAY EMERGE WITHIN SUPERFICIALLY CONSISTENT PUBLIC POLICIES, AND ARGUES NECESSITY OF HOUSING MARKET FOR DEVELOPMENT OF RENEWAL.

1003 GRIPP R.C.
PATTERNS OF SOVIET POLITICS (REV. ED.)
HOMEWOOD: DORSEY, 1967, 386 PP., LC#67-21009.
ANALYZES PATTERNS OF POLITICS IN THE USSR. DESCRIBES POLITICAL ENVIRONMENT BY EXAMINING RUSSIAN HISTORY THROUGH TSARIST HERITAGE TO PRESENT DAY. STUDIES OGRANIZATION, LEADERSHIP, AND CONTROL OF COMMUNIST PARTY. EXAMINES STATE APPARATUS REGARDING RULE ADMINISTRATION AND ADJUDICATION. INCLUDES 1966 RULES OF COMMUNIST PARTY OF USSR, AND GLOSSARY.

1004 GROSECLOSE E.
THE DECAY OF MONEY; A SURVEY OF WESTERN CURRENCIES 1912-1962 (PAMPHLET)
WASHINGTON: INST MONETARY RES, 1962, 32 PP., LC#62-20029.
DISCUSSES 20TH-CENTURY CHANGES IN MONETARY SYSTEMS OF BRITAIN, FRANCE, GERMANY, AND US. COVERS MONETARY STANDARDS USED, IMPACT OF INFLATION, DEVALUATION, AND NATIONAL POLICY TO PROTECT CURRENCY.

1005 GROSS B.M. ED.
ACTION UNDER PLANNING: THE GUIDANCE OF ECONOMIC DEVELOPMENT.
NEW YORK: MCGRAW HILL, 1967, 314 PP., LC#66-29773.
DISCUSSION OF PLANNING POLICIES, THE INSTITUTIONAL AND CULTURAL CONTEXT OF IMPLEMENTATION, THE BIOPHYSICAL ENVIRONMENT, LIMITATIONS OF "PERFECT PLANNING," ETC. INCLUDES ARTICLES ON ECONOMIC ACTIVATION, PLANNING AND SOCIAL ORDER, ACTIVATING NATIONAL PLANS, DEVELOPING NATIONAL-PLANNING PERSONNEL, ETC.

1006 GROSS H.
MAKE OR BUY.
ENGLEWOOD CLIFFS: PRENTICE HALL, 1966, 231 PP., LC#66-14071.
EXAMINES CONDITIONS WHICH CONTROL MAKE-OR-BUY DECISIONS IN MODERN US BUSINESS. DISCUSSES ROLE OF ADMINISTRATIVE STAFF, COST ACCOUNTING ANALYSIS, AND TECHNIQUES FOR PLANNING IN MAKE-OR-BUY DECISIONS.

1007 GROSSMAN G.
"SOVIET GROWTH: ROUTINE, INERTIA, AND PRESSURE."
AMER. ECON. REV., 50 (MAY 60), 62-72.
STUDY SOURCE OF INITIATIVE IN SOVIET ECONOMIC GROWTH. POLITICAL LEADERSHIP ACKNOWLEDGED PRIME MOVER. RESISTANCE OF BUREAUCRACY TO NEW TECHNIQUES AND PRODUCTS IS SERIOUS OBSTACLE IN RACE WITH CAPITALISM. CHAIN OF COMMAND TRANSMITS PRESSURE FROM ABOVE, OVERCOMING OBSTACLES BY SANCTIONS AND INCENTIVES.

1008 GROVE J.W.
GOVERNMENT AND INDUSTRY IN BRITAIN.
LONDON: LONGMANS, GREEN & CO, 1962, 514 PP.
REVIEWS, SYSTEMATICALLY AND COMPREHENSIVELY, THE SUBJECT OF RELATIONS BETWEEN GOVERNMENT AND INDUSTRY. WRITTEN FROM VIEWPOINT OF CENTRAL ADMINISTRATION, SHOWS HOW DEPARTMENTS STAND IN CENTER OF "ENVIRONMENT" MADE UP OF VARIOUS AGENCIES THROUGH WHICH DEPARTMENTS WORK. DESCRIBES GOVERNMENT AS "REGULATOR, PROMOTER, ENTREPRENEUR, AND PLANNER."

1009 GRUBEL H.G. ED.
WORLD MONETARY REFORM: PLANS AND ISSUES.
STANFORD: U. PR., 1963, 446 PP., $10.00.
TWENTY-FOUR ESSAYS ON HOW WE CAN BEST ADAPT THE PRESENT INTERNATIONAL MONETARY SYSTEM TO MEET THE FUTURE NEEDS OF EXPANDING WORLD TRADE AND INTERNATIONAL PAYMENTS.

1010 GRUN C., MIRANDON S.
"DEUX ETUDES ALLEMANDES SUR LES PREJUGES NATIONAUX ET LES MOYENS DE LES COMBATTRE."
REV. PSYCH. PEUPLES, 22 (1967), 100-120.
SEPARATE STUDIES OF TWO GERMAN WORKS ON NATIONAL PREJUDICES. FIRST IS TEXTUAL EXPLICATION OF WORK ON ATTITUDES OF GERMAN YOUTH. EXAMINES BASES OF JUDGMENTS, HOW ARE THEY DEVELOPED, AND WHAT THEIR EFFECTS ARE. SECOND CONCERNS KNOWLEDGE THAT GERMANS AND FRENCH HAVE OF EACH OTHER. BOOK IS BASED ON INFORMATION GATHERED FROM PUBLIC OPINION POLLS. BOTH REVIEWS ARE FAVORABLE.

1011 GRUSHIN B.A., CHIKIN V.V.
"PROBLEMS OF THE MOVEMENT OF COMMUNIST LABOR IN THE USSR."
SOVIET REV., 4(FALL 63), 10-32.
PRESENTS POLICY STUDY OF UNRESOLVED PROBLEMS OF LABOR MOVEMENT AND OF SHORTCOMINGS IN ITS ORGANIZATION AND SPREAD, BASED ON A PUBLIC OPINION SURVEY BY KOMSOMALSKAIA PRAVDA.

1012 GUDIN E.
INFLACAO (2ND ED.)
RIO DE JAN: LIVRARIA AGIR EDIT, 1959, 262 PP.
EXAMINES BRAZILIAN INFLATION IN REGARD TO ECONOMIC GROWTH AND DEVELOPMENT. DISCUSSES INTERNATIONAL TRADE, COFFEE PRODUCTION, BALANCE OF PAYMENTS, AND INDUSTRIALIZATION. COVERS PLANNING BY NATIONAL GOVERNMENT TO LIMIT INFLATIONARY INCREASES.

1013 GUPTA S.
"FOREIGN POLICY IN THE 1967 MANIFESTOS."
INDIA Q., 23 (JAN.-MAR. 67), 28-46.
COMPARES STATEMENTS IN MANIFESTOS OF MAJOR INDIAN PARTIES ON ISSUE OF FOREIGN POLICY. DISCUSSED ARE: SWATANTRA, JANA SANGH, PRAJA SOCIALIST, COMMUNIST, AND MARXIST PARTY VIEWS ON DEFENSE, TAXES, FOREIGN AID, AND ECONOMIC RELATIONS.

1014 GURTOO D.H.N.
INDIA'S BALANCE OF PAYMENTS (1920-1960)
PRINCETON, NJ: PRINCETON UNIV, 1961, 241 PP.
STUDIES BALANCE-OF-PAYMENTS IN INDIA OVER 40-YEAR PERIOD. ESTIMATES INTEREST AND DIVIDENDS RECEIPTS AND PAYMENTS. DISCUSSES ANNUAL MOVEMENTS OF LONG-TERM INTERNATIONAL CAPITAL. ANALYZES MECHANISM OF ADJUSTMENT IN BALANCE-OF PAYMENTS ITEMS TO ECONOMICS, FINANCIAL, AND POLITICAL INSTABILITY OCCURRING BETWEEN 1920-60.

1015 GUTKIND E.A.
URBAN DEVELOPMENT IN SOUTHERN EUROPE* SPAIN AND PORTUGAL.
NEW YORK: FREE PRESS OF GLENCOE, 1967, 544 PP.
THIRD VOLUME IN SERIES, "THE INTERNATIONAL HISTORY OF CITY DEVELOPMENT," THIS TEXT DISCUSSES THE ECONOMIC, POLITICAL, HISTORICAL, SOCIOLOGICAL, AND CULTURAL DEVELOPMENT OVER THE LAST 5,000 YEARS. SURVEYS OF OVER 100 CITIES ARE INCLUDED, IN ADDITION TO EXTENSIVE COLLECTION OF MAPS, CITY PLANS, AND AERIAL VIEWS OF THE MAJOR URBAN AREAS.

1016 GUTMANN P.M. ED.
ECONOMIC GROWTH: AN AMERICAN PROBLEM.
ENGLEWOOD CLIFFS: PRENTICE HALL, 1964, 181 PP., LC#64-16246.
AMERICA'S ECONOMIC GROWTH IS COMPARED TO THAT OF OTHER COUNTRIES. INCLUDES ANALYSIS OF ANATOMY OF US ECONOMIC GROWTH. SPECIFIC ASPECTS OF ECONOMIC GROWTH COVERED INCLUDE: GOALS IN THIS DECADE; COMPARATIVE GROWTH RATES; CAUSES OF ECONOMIC GROWTH; IMPEDIMENTS TO IT; POLICIES FOR GROWTH.

1017 GWYN W.B.
DEMOCRACY AND THE COST OF POLITICS IN BRITAIN.
LONDON: ATHLONE PRESS, 1962, 256 PP.
TRACES FLUCTUATIONS IN COST OF RUNNING FOR OFFICE IN BRITAIN 1832-1959, WITH COMPARISONS OF EXPENDITURES BY MAJOR PARTIES. INCLUDES CORRUPT ELECTION EXPENSES, MEANS OF FINANCING, AND PAYMENT OF MEMBERS.

1018 GYORGY A.
ISSUES OF WORLD COMMUNISM.
PRINCETON: VAN NOSTRAND, 1966, 264 PP.
PRESENTS SERIES OF SELECTED ESSAYS ON VARIOUS FACETS AND ISSUES OF MARXISM-LENINISM. FOCUSES ON TWELVE SPECIFIC INCIDENTS IN INTERNATIONAL COMMUNISM. ANALYZES SITUATIONS IN HUNGARY, POLAND, RUMANIA, AND ALBANIA. DISCUSSES AREAS OF COMMUNIST STRENGTH AND WEAKNESS.

1019 HAAR C.M.
LAW AND LAND: ANGLO-AMERICAN PLANNING PRACTICE.
CAMBRIDGE: HARVARD U PR, 1964, 290 PP., LC#64-11129.
EXAMINES CITY PLANNING IN CONTEXT OF US AND BRITISH LEGAL SYSTEMS. HOPES TO INDICATE HOW INSTITUTIONS OF LAW AND PROPERTY CAN BE MOLDED INTO A MORE RATIONAL AND EFFECTIVE MEANS OF ORGANIZING LAND USE. TREATS THEORY AND FRAMEWORK OF PLANNING, FORMULATION OF PLANS, THE INDIVIDUAL'S RELATION TO MACHINERY OF PLANNING, AND FINANCIAL BASES OF PLANNING.

1020 HAAS E.B., SCHMITTER P.C.
"ECONOMICS AND DIFFERENTIAL PATTERNS OF POLITICAL INTEGRATION: PROJECTIONS ABOUT UNITY IN LATIN AMERICA."
INT. ORGAN., 18 (AUTUMN 64), 705-37.
PRESENTS THESIS THAT 'UNDER MODERN CONDITIONS THE RELATIONSHIP BETWEEN ECONOMIC AND POLITICAL UNION HAD BEST BE TREATED AS A CONTINUUM.... POLITICAL IMPLICATIONS CAN BE ASSOCIATED WITH MOST MOVEMENTS TOWARD ECONOMIC INTEGRATION EVEN WHEN THE CHIEF ACTORS THEMSELVES DO NOT ENTERTAIN SUCH NOTIONS AT THE TIME OF ADOPTING THEIR NEW CONSTUITIVE CHARTER.' CITES LAFTA AS EXAMPLE.

1021 HABERLER G.
INFLATION; ITS CAUSES AND CURES (PAMPHLET)
WASHINGTON: AMER ENTERPRISE INST, 1960, 85 PP.
ANALYSIS OF INFLATION IN US ECONOMY. EXAMINES CAUSES AND NATURE OF 1955-58 INFLATION IN US AND DEFICIT IN BALANCE OF PAYMENTS; DISCUSSES ANTI-INFLATIONARY POLICIES PROPOSED AND THEIR APPLICATION.

1022 HABERLER G.
A SURVEY OF INTERNATIONAL TRADE THEORY (PAMPHLET)
PRINCETON, NJ: PRIN U INTL FINAN, 1961, 78 PP.
PRESENTS OUTLINE OF INTERNATIONAL TRADE THEORY, INCLUDING SKETCH OF MONETARY THEORY OF BALANCE OF PAYMENTS. STUDIES CLASSICAL THEORY OF COMPARATIVE COSTS AND INTERNATIONAL VALUES FROM HUME TO MARSHALL AND MODERN DEVELOPMENTS OF PURE THEORY. EXAMINES TERMS OF TRADE AND MECHANISM OF BALANCE OF PAYMENTS, SINCE THEORIES MUST ACCOUNT FOR MONEYED ECONOMIES.

1023 HABERLER G.
"INTEGRATION AND GROWTH OF THE WORLD ECONOMY IN HISTORICAL PERSPECTIVE."
AMER. ECON. REV., 54 (MARCH 64), 1-22.
A BRIEF HISTORY OF CLOSER ECONOMIC RELATIONS AMONG DIFFERENT INTRANATIONAL AND INTERNATIONAL GROUPS, FOLLOWED BY DEEPER ANALYSIS OF THE COMPARATIVE RATES OF ECONOMIC GROWTH AROUND WORLD, SHOWING THAT POORER COUNTRIES HAVE BEEN IMPROVING AS RESULT OF RICHER COUNTRIES, GREATER IMPROVEMENT TRICKLING THROUGH WORLD TRADE. RECOMMENDS FREE ECONOMIC POLICIES.

1024 HABERLER G.
A SURVEY OF INTERNATIONAL TRADE THEORY.
LONDON: WM HODGE AND CO LTD, 1965, 386 PP.
ATTEMPTING SYSTEMATIC TREATMENT OF PROBLEMS OF FOREIGN TRADE, ADVOCATES FREE TRADE AS GENERAL POLICY. USES STATISTICAL AND HISTORICAL ANALYSIS TO CONSIDER MONETARY PROBLEMS, TARIFFS, MONOPOLY, AND TREATY EFFECTS IN SELECT CASES: FRANCE, 1871; CANADA, 1900-14; AND GERMANY, 1918-32.

1025 HACKER A. ED.
THE CORPORATION TAKE-OVER.
NEW YORK: HARPER & ROW, 1964, 280 PP., LC#63-20332.
COLLECTION OF ESSAYS ON THE CORPORATE FORM IN HISTORY, THE CORPORATE POWER, AND THE RELATION BETWEEN THE CORPORATION AND PEOPLE. MORE SPECIFICALLY, IT DEALS WITH COLLECTIVE CAPITALISM, IRRESPONSIBILITIES OF METRO-CORPORATE AMERICA, PRIVATE GOVERNMENTS AND THE CONSTITUTION, POLITICS AND THE CORPORATION, ECONOMIC POWER, AND FREE SOCIETY.

1026 HACKETT J.
ECONOMIC PLANNING IN FRANCE; ITS RELATION TO THE POLICIES OF THE DEVELOPED COUNTRIES OF WESTERN EUROPE (PAMPHLET)
NEW YORK: ASIA PUBL HOUSE, 1965, 55 PP.
DISCUSSES ECONOMIC PLANNING IN WESTERN EUROPE, ESPECIALLY FRANCE, IN ORDER TO APPLY SYSTEM TO PLANNING IN INDIA. EXAMINES REASONS FOR PLANNING IN MIXED ECONOMIES, CONSIDERATIONS THAT DETERMINE APPROACH, AND METHODS OF PLANNING. INVESTIGATES FRENCH SYSTEM, ITS OPERATION, AND

ITS RESULTS. EXPLORES PROBLEMS OF PLANNING AND METHODS TO DEAL WITH THEM.

1027 HACKETT J., HACKETT A.M.
L'ECONOMIE BRITANNIQUE: PROBLEMES ET PERSPECTIVES.
PARIS: COLIN (LIB ARMAND), 1966, 219 PP.
ATTEMPTS TO EXPLAIN TO THE FRENCH, ECONOMIC PROBLEMS AND POLITICAL ECONOMICS OF THE BRITISH. DISCUSSES KEY PROBLEMS 1950-60. ANALYZES NEW TENDENCIES SINCE 1961 AND INDICATES SOLUTIONS TO PROBLEMS.

1028 HADDAD W.F.
"MR. SHRIVER AND THE SAVAGE POLITICS OF POVERTY"
HARPER'S, 231 (DEC 65), 43-50.
DISCUSSION OF WAR ON POVERTY AND RELATIONS BETWEEN FEDERAL PROGRAMS AND STATE AND LOCAL SOCIAL AGENCIES. INCLUDES EXAMPLES OF CONFLICT, DESCRIPTIONS OF PROJECTS AND OF SARGENT SHRIVER, DIRECTOR OF PROGRAM.

1029 HADDOCK G.B.
"CORPORATE GROWTH AS AFFECTED BY THE FEDERAL ANTITRUST LAWS"
MICH. BUSINESS REV., 19 (MAR. 67), 9-14.
JUSTIFIES BUSINESSMAN'S AWARENESS OF ANTITRUST LAWS. GIVES BASIC INFORMATION AND REPORTS ON SEVERAL RECENT CASES. PURPOSE IS TO ACQUAINT BUSINES MAN WITH THE TOPIC. DISCUSSION OF GOVERNMENT'S POSITION ON VARIOUS AREAS COVERED BY ANTITRUST LAWS. PESSIMISTIC ABOUT ISSUANCE OF GUIDELINES BY COURT.

1030 HADWIGER D.F., TALBOTT R.B.
PRESSURES AND PROTEST.
SAN FRANCISCO: CHANDLER, 1965, 336 PP., LC#64-8160.
DISCUSSES THE KENNEDY FARM PROGRAM AND THE WHEAT REFERENDUM OF 1963 IN THE FORM OF A CASE STUDY. FARMER COMMITTEE SYSTEMS OF THE DEPT. OF AGRICULTURE, FARMER ORGANIZATIONS AND METHODS, AND THE DYNAMICS OF A FARM REFERENDUM ARE EXAMINED.

1031 HAEFELE E.T., STEINBERG E.B.
GOVERNMENT CONTROLS ON TRANSPORT.
WASHINGTON: BROOKINGS INST, 1965, 102 PP., LC#65-28379.
STUDIES NEED FOR TRANSPORT INVESTMENT IN EMERGING NATIONS OF AFRICA AND UTILIZATION OF EXISTING FACILITIES. PROBLEM OF CONTROL IS INTENSIFIED WHERE TWO NATIONS SHARE FACILITIES AS THEY DO ON MUCH OF CONTINENT. EXAMINES INSTITUTIONS, POLICIES, AND CONTROLS THAT DETERMINE TRANSPORT PATTERNS.

1032 HAGE J.
"AN AXIOMATIC THEORY OF ORGANIZATIONS"
ADMINISTRATIVE SCI. Q., 10 (JUNE-AUG. 65), 289-320.
EXAMINES ORGANIZATIONAL VARIABLES OF COMPLEXITY, CENTRALIZATION, PRODUCTION, EFFICIENCY, ETC., AND RELATES THEM TO SEVEN BASIC PROPOSITIONS AS FOUND IN WRITINGS OF WEBER, BARNARD, AND THOMPSON. DERIVES 21 COROLLARIES AND DEFINES TWO IDEAL TYPES OF ORGANIZATION.

1033 HAGEN E.E.
AN ANALYTICAL MODEL OF THE TRANSITION TO ECONOMIC GROWTH (PAMPHLET)
CAMBRIDGE: MIT CTR INTL STUDIES, 1957, 91 PP.
PRESENTS MODEL OF PROCESS OF SOCIAL CHANGE LEADING TO TECHNOLOGICAL PROGRESS; STATING ASSUMPTIONS AND STEPS IN ARGUMENT, EXPLAINS PARAMETERS, VARIABLES, FUNCTIONAL RELATIONSHIPS, AND PATH OF MOVEMENT OF MODEL. SURVEYS LITERATURE OF FIELD, EXPLAINS METHODOLOGY OF ANALYSIS, DISCUSSES VARIABLES IN PEASANT AND ADVANCED SOCIETIES, AND SKETCHES DYNAMICS OF CHANGE.

1035 HAGGER A.J.
THE THEORY OF INFLATION.
MELBOURNE: MELBOURNE UNIV PRESS, 1964, 238 PP.
ANALYSIS OF INFLATION AND POLICIES TO CONTROL IT. GENERAL VIEW OF PROBLEM OF INFLATION AS IT INFLUENCES DAILY LIFE.

1036 HAGUE D.C. ED.
INFLATION.
LONDON: MACMILLAN, 1962, 509 PP.
COLLECTION OF ESSAYS ON CAUSES OF INFLATION, MONETARY AND FISCAL POLICIES AS WEAPONS AGAINST INFLATION, TRADE UNIONS, INTERNATIONAL ASPECTS OF INFLATION, AND INFLATION IN UNDERDEVELOPED AND SOCIALIST COUNTRIES.

1037 HAGUE D.C. ED.
PRICE FORMATION IN VARIOUS ECONOMIES; PROCEEDINGS OF A CONFERENCE HELD BY THE INTERNATIONAL ECONOMIC ASSOCIATION.
NEW YORK: ST MARTIN'S PRESS, 1967, 281 PP., LC#66-13528.
COMPARES METHODS OF PRICE FORMATION IN VARYING CAPITALIST AND SOCIALIST ECONOMIES. INVESTIGATES RELATION BETWEEN PRICING AND INVESTMENT DECISIONS AS DETERMINED BY PLANNING MODELS AND FORECASTS. REPORTS ON PROCEEDINGS OF INTERNATIONAL ECONOMIC ASSOCIATION CONFERENCE.

1038 HAHN L.A.
DIE AMERIKANISCHE KONJUNKTURPOLITIK DER DOLLAR UND DIE D-MARK.
TUBINGEN: J C B MOHR, 1963, 37 PP.
EXAMINES UNEMPLOYMENT, WEAKNESS OF INVESTMENTS AND BALANCE-OF-PAYMENT DEFICITS IN US ECONOMY. INQUIRES WHETHER MONETARY EXPANSION WOULD RESULT IN INCREASED EMPLOYMENT ECONOMIC GROWTH, AND PRICE STABILITY. DISCUSSES BUDGET DEFICITS AND FOREIGN CREDITS AND IMPACT OF MONETARY EXPANSION ON ECONOMY OF WEST GERMANY.

1039 HAINES W.W.
MONEY PRICES AND POLICY.
NEW YORK: MCGRAW HILL, 1966, 854 PP., LC#65-26479.
ANALYZES ROLE OF MONEY IN MODERN ECONOMY, ITS HISTORY, AND INSTITUTIONS. EVALUATES POLICY IN TERMS OF ITS EFFECT ON NATIONAL INCOME AND INDIVIDUAL STANDARD OF LIVING. EMPHASIZES COMMERCIAL AND CENTRAL BANKING INSTITUTIONS. BIBLIOGRAPHY AFTER EACH CHAPTER WITH REVIEW QUESTIONS.

1040 HALD M.
A SELECTED BIBLIOGRAPHY ON ECONOMIC DEVELOPMENT AND FOREIGN AID.
NEW YORK: RAND CORP, 1957, 93 PP.
AN UNANNOTATED BIBLIOGRAPHY OF 1,500 WORKS RELATING TO ECONOMIC AND OTHER ASPECTS OF GROWTH AND DEVELOPMENT IN UNDERDEVELOPED AREAS AND POLICIES OF THE US AND OTHER AGENCIES IN FOSTERING DEVELOPMENT. PRIMARY EMPHASIS ON PUBLICATIONS ISSUED BETWEEN 1950-57; ONLY ENGLISH-LANGUAGE SOURCES INCLUDED. TOPICALLY CLASSIFIED AND GEOGRAPHICALLY INDEXED.

1041 HALE G.E., HALE R.D.
"EXPANDING ENTERPRISE: GEOGRAPHICAL CURBS ON MERGERS."
MINN. LAW REV., 51 (APR. 67), 857-875.
STUDIES COURT CASES AND LAWS CONCERNING "DISPERSION" OF INDUSTRIES THEOUGH MERGER. PRESENTS RATIONALE BEHIND LIMITATIONS ON DISPERSION AND CRITIQUE OF POLICY. MAINTAINS THAT MERGERS CHARACTERIZED BY DISPERSION DO NOT ALWAYS DECREASE COMPETITION AND MAY ACTUALLY INCREASE IT.

1042 HALEVY E.
IMPERIALISM AND THE RISE OF LABOR (2ND ED.)
LONDON: ERNEST BENN, LTD, 1951, 442 PP.
DISCUSSES IN DEPTH POLITICAL HISTORY OF BOER WAR AND ITS AFTERMATH - DOMINATION AND AGGRESSIVE IMPERIALISM OF LORD SALISBURY AND CHAMBERLAIN, WAR ITSELF, UNIONIST CABINET POLICIES, BIRTH OF LABOR PARTY, AND DECLINE OF UNIONISTS. TREATS PERIOD BETWEEN 1895-1914.

1043 HALL B.
"THE PAINTER'S UNION: A PARTIAL VICTORY."
NEW POLITICS, 6 (WINTER 67), 62-66.
DESCRIBES EFFORT OF MEMBERS OF PAINTERS' DISTRICT COUNCIL 19 IN NEW YORK CITY TO END CORRUPT RULE OF MARTIN RARBACK. DISCUSSES RESULTS OF ELECTION OF MEMBERS' CANDIDATE, FRANK SCHONFIELD, AND HIS SUBSEQUENT COURTING OF RARBACK AND HIS SUPPORTERS. URGES UNION MEMBERS TO CONSIDER ORIGINAL OVERTHROW AS VICTORY AND TO CONTINUE FIGHT AGAINST CORRUPTION.

1044 HALL B.
"THE COALITION AGAINST DISHWASHERS."
NEW POLITICS, 6 (WINTER 67), 23-32.
EXPLORES TRADE UNION BUREAUCRACIES AND THEIR EXTREME POWER OVER RANK-AND-FILE MEMBERS. DISCUSSES LAWS OF UNIONS PROHIBITING ELECTION OF WORKERS AS OFFICERS, LIMITING CRITICISM OF OFFICERS BY MEMBERS, AND MAKING REMOVAL OF UNION AS BARGAINING FORCE VERY DIFFICULT. MAINTAINS THAT RADICALS MUST CHOOSE BETWEEN COALITION WITH ANT-DEMOCRATIC BUREAUCRACY AND STRUGGLE AGAINST IT.

1045 HALL C.A. JR.
FISCAL POLICY FOR STABLE GROWTH.
NEW YORK: HOLT RINEHART WINSTON, 1960, 311 PP., LC#60-06490.
ANALYZES ACTION OF FISCAL POLICIES IN PROCESS OF ECONOMIC GROWTH, EMPHASIZING GOVERNMENTAL BUDGET, INCLUDING REVENUE, TECHNOLOGICAL PROGRESS, SAVINGS, INVESTMENT, AND TAX STRUCTURE, AND AUTOMATIC STABILIZERS. CONTAINS BIBLIOGRAPHY OF 100 BOOKS AND ARTICLES PUBLISHED IN ENGLISH 1938-58. ITEMS ARRANGED BY AUTHOR.

1046 HALL G.
MAIN STREET TO WALL STREET: END THE COLD WAR (PAMPHLET)
NEW YORK: NEW CENTURY PUBL, 1962, 48 PP.
ANALYSIS OF COLD WAR BY LEADING US COMMUNIST. DISCUSSES US POLICY TOWARD OTHER NATIONS AS PROGRAM TO CONTROL THEIR SOCIETIES. CLAIMS US ECONOMIC SYSTEM KEEPS MUCH OF POPULATION FROM SHARE OF WEALTH.

1047 HALL R.C.
"REPRESENTATION OF BIG BUSINESS IN THE HOUSE OF COMMONS."
PUBLIC OPINION QUART., 2 (JULY 38), 473-477.
DISCUSSES INFLUENCE OF INDUSTRIAL ORGANIZATIONS IN THE HOUSE OF COMMONS, NOTING REPRESENTATION, BY AN OFFICER OF NEARLY EVERY IMPORTANT NATIONAL BUSINESS ASSOCIATION, IN THE 1937 HOUSE OF COMMONS. ONE HUNDRED AND NINE MEMBERS OF PARLIAMENT WERE DIRECTORS OF TWO OR MORE CORPORATIONS. AUTHOR IS PRO-BIG-BUSINESS AND VIEWS INDUSTRY'S INFLUENCE IN PARLIAMENT AS ADVANTAGEOUS FOR DEMOCRACY.

1048 HALLE L.J.
THE COLD WAR AS HISTORY.
NEW YORK: HARPER & ROW, 1967, 434 PP.
INTERPRETATION OF COLD WAR AS CYCLICAL PHENOMENON IN HISTORY OF ALL INTERNATIONAL CONFLICTS. ANALYZES HISTORICAL CIRCUMSTANCES AND DIPLOMATIC RELATIONS OF EAST AND WEST FROM WWII THROUGH KENNEDY ADMINISTRATION AND CUBAN CRISIS.

1049 HALLER H.
DAS PROBLEM DER GELDWERTSTABILITAT.
STUTTGART: KOHLHAMMER VERLAG, 1966, 170 PP.
EXAMINES RELATION BETWEEN ECONOMIC GROWTH AND PRICE STABILITY. DISCUSSES CAUSES OF RISE IN PRICE LEVELS, FINANCIAL AND WAGE POLICIES, AND INHERENT LIMITS OF STABILIZATION.

1050 HALLET R.
PEOPLE AND PROGRESS IN WEST AFRICA: AN INTRODUCTION TO THE PROBLEMS OF DEVELOPMENT.
NEW YORK: PERGAMON PRESS, 1966, 161 PP., LC#65-27376.
DESCRIBES SITUATION OF WEST AFRICA TODAY: A DEVELOPING NATION FACED WITH INDUSTRIAL, ECONOMIC, AND SOCIAL PROBLEMS WHICH MUST BE SOLVED. GIVES AN OVER-ALL PICTURE OF ALMOST ALL FACETS OF LIFE AND SUGGESTS TRENDS AND POSSIBLE SOLUTIONS TO SOME OF THE PROBLEMS. EMPHASIZES ROLE DEVELOPED NATIONS MUST PLAY IN HELPING AFRICA ACHIEVE POTENTIAL. INCLUDES SUGGESTIONS FOR FURTHER READING.

1051 HALLETT D.
"THE HISTORY AND STRUCTURE OF OEEC."
EUROP. YRB., 1 (55), 62-70.
GIVES HISTORY OF 1948 CONVENTION FOUNDING OEEC. EARLY PURPOSE TO ADMINISTER MARSHALL PLAN. OUTLINES COMPOSITION AND FUNCTIONS OF AGENCIES. MAIN PRINCIPLES ARE: PROMOTION OF EUROPEAN ECONOMIC EXPANSION, CREATION OF CLOSE TIES BETWEEN US AND BRITISH COMMONWEALTH, AND COORDINATION OF NATIONAL POLICIES.

1052 HALLOWELL J.H. ED.
DEVELOPMENT: FOR WHAT.
DURHAM: DUKE U PR, 1964, 241 PP., LC#64-24990.
ESSAYS EXPLORING THE IMPLICATIONS OF ECONOMIC AND POLITICAL DEVELOPMENT IN THE NEWLY INDEPENDENT NATIONS. PROSPECTS FOR PLURALISM AND CONSTITUTIONALISM POSTULATED.

1053 HALLSTEIN W.
"THE EUROPEAN COMMUNITY AND ATLANTIC PARTNERSHIP."
INT. ORGAN., 17 (SUMMER 63)., 771-87.
ADAPTATION TO MODERN AGE MUST BE IMAGINATIVE RESPONSE TO CHANGE, COMBINING PRACTICALITY AND IDEALISM, DETERMINATION AND FLEXIBILITY. DISCUSSES EUROPEAN COMMUNITY AND ATLANTIC PARTNERSHIP IN REFERENCE TO THESE IDEAS. CONSIDERS USA AND BRITISH RESPONSES TO EEC.

1054 HAMBRIDGE G. ED.
DYNAMICS OF DEVELOPMENT.
NEW YORK: FREDERICK PRAEGER, 1964, 401 PP., LC#64-16678.
ARTICLES FROM INTERNATIONAL DEVELOPMENT REVIEW DEALING WITH PROBLEMS OF AGRICULTURE, INDUSTRY, EDUCATION, LEADERSHIP, ADMINISTRATION OF AID, AND HEALTH IN DEVELOPING NATIONS.

1055 HAMEROW T.S.
RESTORATION, REVOLUTION, REACTION: ECONOMICS AND POLITICS IN GERMANY, 1815-1871.
PRINCETON: PRINCETON U PRESS, 1958, 347 PP., LC#58-7117.
WELL-DOCUMENTED STUDY OF ORIGINS, EVENTS, AND AFTERMATH OF THE GERMAN REVOLUTION OF 1848, FOCUSING ON THE IMPACT ON GERMAN POLITICS OF THE PROFOUND SOCIAL ADJUSTMENT REQUIRED TO MEET THE NEW ECONOMIC CONDITIONS. REVEALS RELATION OF ECONOMICS AND NEEDS OF PEOPLE TO POLITICS, IDEOLOGY, AND CONSTITUTIONAL RIGHTS IN TRANSITION FROM AGRARIAN MANORIALISM TO INDUSTRIAL CAPITALISM IN CONFEDERATION PERIOD.

1056 HAMILTON W.H., ADAIR D.
THE POWER TO GOVERN.
NEW YORK: W W NORTON, 1937, 249 PP.
DISCUSSES CHARACTER, PARTICULARS, AND EFFECT ON COMMERCE OF THE CONSTITUTION WITH RESPECT TO PUBLIC OPINION, ECONOMY, PROBLEMS IN 1937, AND THE DOCUMENT ITSELF. EXAMINES ASPECTS OF SPECIFIC WARTIME POWERS, TREATIES, TAXES, TARIFFS, AND OTHER MEANS OF ENFORCEMENT. USES HISTORICAL LINGUISTICS TO DETERMINE WHAT CONSTITUTION'S FRAMERS INTENDED BY THEIR PHRASING.

1057 HAMMOND A.
"COMPREHENSIVE VERSUS INCREMENTAL BUDGETING IN THE DEPARTMENT OF AGRICULTURE"
ADMINISTRATIVE SCI. Q., 10 (JUNE-AUG. 65), 321-346.
DESCRIBES EXPERIMENT OF DEPARTMENT OF AGRICULTURE TO EVALUATE ALL DEPARTMENTAL PROGRAMS, ESPECIALLY ADOPTION OF "ZERO-BASE BUDGETING," WHICH ACCORDING TO AUTHOR ACHIEVED FEW SPECIFIC CHANGES OR IMPROVEMENTS. SHOWS THAT "ZERO-BASE BUDGETING" INSTEAD RESULTED IN "PSYCHIC BENEFITS" IN THAT TOP OFFICIALS COULD SHOW THEIR EXPERTISE TO BUREAU OFFICIALS.

1058 HANCE W.A.
AFRICAN ECONOMIC DEVELOPMENT.
NEW YORK: HARPER & ROW, 1958, 307 PP., LC#58-7060.
SERIES OF STUDIES WHOSE COMMON THEME IS ECONOMIC DEVELOPMENT IN AFRICA SOUTH OF THE SAHARA. INCLUDES CASES IN AGRICULTURAL AND INDUSTRIAL DEVELOPMENT, ANALYSIS OF TRANSPORT PROBLEMS IN TROPICAL AFRICA, AND PAPERS CONCERNED WITH INDIVIDUAL AFRICAN AREAS - LIBERIA, CENTRAL AFRICA, MADAGASCAR. INCLUDES SELECTED BIBLIOGRAPHY.

1059 HANCOCK J.L.
"PLANNERS IN THE CHANGING AMERICAN CITY, 1900-1940."
J. OF AM. INST. OF PLANNERS, 33 (SEPT. 67), 290-303.
TRACES GROWTH OF PLANNING PROFESSION IN US, 1900-1940, USING SPECIFIC CITIES AS EXAMPLES. RELATES RISE OF CITY PLANNING TO RISE OF SOCIAL WORK AND GROWING GENERAL CONCERN FOR AESTHETICS AND SOCIAL PROBLEMS.

1060 HANNAH H.W., CAUGHEY R.R.
THE LEGAL BASE FOR UNIVERSITIES IN DEVELOPING COUNTRIES.
URBANA: U OF ILLINOIS PR, 1967, 455 PP., LC#67-20151.
ANALYZES LEGAL STRUCTURE OF SELECTED UNIVERSITIES IN UNDERDEVELOPED COUNTRIES AND US, OFFERS IDEAS AND SUGGESTIONS FOR FORMULATION OF DESIRABLE STATUTES AND ACTS, AND SHOWS HOW LEGAL FRAMEWORK OF AN INSTITUTION RELATES TO ITS EDUCATIONAL PURPOSE AND ACHIEVEMENT OF GOALS. DISCUSSES CORPORATE NATURE OF THE UNIVERSITY, ITS ADMINISTRATION, LEGAL POWERS AND DUTIES, AND BUDGET AND FINANCE.

1061 HANRIEDER W.F.
WEST GERMAN FOREIGN POLICY 1949-1963: INTERNATIONAL PRESSURE AND DOMESTIC RESPONSE.
STANFORD: STANFORD U PRESS, 1967, 275 PP., LC#67-13657.
DISCUSSES RELATIONSHIP BETWEEN WEST GERMAN FOREIGN POLICY GOALS AND CONDITIONS OF EXTERNAL OPERATIONAL ENVIRONMENT IN WHICH THEY ARE PURSUED. EXAMINES RELATIONSHIPS BETWEEN FOREIGN POLICY GOALS AND INTERNATIONAL MOTIVATIONAL ENVIRONMENT, SHOWING ROLE OF GOVERNING COALITIONS AND PRESSURE GROUPS. RELATES EXTERNAL DIMENSIONS OF POLICY OBJECTIVES TO INTERNAL DIMENSIONS.

1062 HANSEN A.H.
FISCAL POLICY AND BUSINESS CYCLES.
NEW YORK: W W NORTON, 1941, 462 PP.
ANALYSIS OF AMERICAN BUSINESS CYCLES, BEGINNING WITH BACKGROUND OF THE DEPRESSION OF THE 1930'S. STUDIES INVESTMENT AND CONSUMPTION, MONETARY POLICY, AND FISCAL POLICY OF PREDEPRESSION AND RECOVERY YEARS. EXAMINES THE CHANGING ROLE OF GOVERNMENT, TAXES, PUBLIC DEBT, "PUMP-PRIMING," AND FULL EMPLOYMENT. CONCLUDES THAT INTERNATIONAL ECONOMIC COLLABORATION IS NEEDED IN FUTURE.

1063 HANSEN A.H.
MONETARY THEORY AND FISCAL POLICY.
NEW YORK: MCGRAW HILL, 1949, 236 PP.
COMPREHENSIVE ANALYSIS OF MONEY AND ITS ECONOMIC ROLE. BEGINS BY STUDYING THE HISTORICAL RATIO OF MONEY TO INCOME; EXPLAINS ROLE OF CENTRAL BANKING SYSTEM, INTEREST RATE, RELATION OF WAGES AND PRICES, EFFECT OF CURRENCY EXPANSION ON ECONOMIC GROWTH, AND INTERNATIONAL MONETARY DEVELOPMENTS. CONCLUDES WITH GOAL OF OPTIMUM INTERNATIONAL DIVISION OF LABOR TO BALANCE EXCHANGE RATES.

1065 HANSEN A.H.
BUSINESS CYCLES AND NATIONAL INCOME.
NEW YORK: W W NORTON, 1964, 720 PP., LC#63-21708.
ANALYZES RECESSIONS AND RECOVERIES IN AMERICAN ECONOMY IN 20TH CENTURY, AND GIVES INTRODUCTION TO MACRO-ECONOMICS AND KEYNESIAN THEORY. INCLUDES THEORIES OF INVESTMENT DETERMINATION, CONSUMPTION FUNCTION, INTERRELATIONS BETWEEN MULTIPLIER AND ACCELERATOR, AND ROLE OF GOVERNMENT OUTLAYS IN CONTRIBUTING TO CYCLES.

1066 HANSEN B.
INFLATION PROBLEMS IN SMALL COUNTRIES (PAMPHLET)
CAIRO: NAT BANK OF EGYPT, 1960, 39 PP.
DANGER OF FIXED EXCHANGE RATES FOR SMALL COUNTRIES IS SHOWN BY NEED FOR STABILIZATION OF DOMESTIC PRICE LEVEL IN SPITE OF WORLD INFLATION. THIS DANGER IS ALSO SHOWN BY NEED FOR NON-INFLATIONARY DEVELOPMENT POLICY BASED UPON FOREIGN BORROWING. CHOICE OF DOMESTIC POLICY IS ALSO INFLUENCED BY CHOICE OF EXCHANGE RATE POLICY.

1067 HANSEN B.
A STUDY IN THE THEORY OF INFLATION.
NEW YORK: RINEHART, 1951, 262 PP.
EMPHASIZING INTERDEPENDENCE OF COMMODITY AND FACTOR MARKETS, DEVELOPS MONETARY THEORY FOR REPRESSED INFLATION DURING WWII. DRAWS UP SOME CONDITIONS FOR MAINTENANCE OF EQUILIBRIUM WITH FULL EMPLOYMENT.

1068 HANSEN B.
INTERNATIONAL LIQUIDITY.
STOCKHOLM: NATL INST OF ECO RES, 1964, 48 PP.
DISCUSSES PROBLEM OF DOLLAR BECOMING INTERNATIONAL TRADE STANDARD OF PAYMENT WITH CONTINUING DRAIN UPON GOLD RESERVES

AND INABILITY OF GOLD PRODUCTION TO KEEP PACE WITH EXPANSION ON TRADE. PROPOSES INTERNATIONAL BANK TO OVERCOME THIS WITH ABILITY TO ISSUE CREDIT NOTES ON NONGOLD RESERVES.

1069 HANSER P.M.
"EXPLODING POPULATIONS: INTERNATIONAL AND REGIONAL ASPECTS."
SOC. SCI. 34 (JUNE 53) 144-48.
CONSIDERS MAIN PROBLEM HOW TO INCREASE AGGREGATE PRODUCTION SO WILL OUTPACE POPULATION GROWTH AND RAISE STANDARD OF LIVING. OUTPUT LEVELS TAKE ON POLITICAL SIGNIFICANCE, SINCE UNDERDEVELOPED COUNTRIES ARE PRONE TO COMMUNIST EXPLOITATION.

1070 HAPGOOD D.
AFRICA: FROM INDEPENDENCE TO TOMORROW.
NEW YORK: ATHENEUM PUBLISHERS, 1965, 221 PP., LC#65-15912.
STRESSES CURRENT THEMES OF INDEPENDENT BLACK AFRICA: PROBLEMS OF ECONOMY AND GOVERNMENT; EFFECTS OF FOREIGN AID; URBANIZATION; AND EDUCATION.

1071 HAQ M.
THE STRATEGY OF ECONOMIC PLANNING.
LONDON: OXFORD U PR, 1963, 266 PP.
DETAILED CASE STUDY OF ECONOMIC PLANNING AND DEVELOPMENT IN PAKISTAN, FOCUSING LARGELY ON THREE FIVE YEAR PLANS FROM 1955 TO 1965. DISCUSSES GENERAL CONCEPTS AND RATIONALE BEHIND KEY PLANNING DECISIONS AND PROVIDES THOROUGHLY DOCUMENTED ACCOUNTS OF PROGRESS MADE DURING FIVE YEAR PLANS.

1072 HARBERGER A.C. ED.
THE DEMAND FOR DURABLE GOODS.
CHICAGO: U CHI, CTR POLICY STUDY, 1960, 274 PP., LC#60-7236.
ANTHOLOGY PROVIDES ECONOMETRIC INSIGHTS INTO THE CYCLICAL ECONOMIC PROCESS IN THE US. DISCUSSES DEMAND FOR NONFARM HOUSING, REFRIGERATORS, AUTOMOBILES, AND FARM TRACTORS. ALSO ANALYZES THE DETERMINANTS OF CORPORATE INVESTMENT.

1073 HARBISON F.H., ED., MYERS C.A. ED.
MANPOWER AND EDUCATION.
NEW YORK: MCGRAW HILL, 1965, 343 PP., LC#64-20529.
CONCERNS PROCESSES OF HUMAN RESOURCE DEVELOPMENT AND THEIR RELATIONSHIP TO ECONOMIC GROWTH IN NEW DEVELOPING NATIONS. DETAILED PICTURE OF INDIVIDUAL COUNTRIES RATHER THAN GENERAL ANALYSIS; MAKES SUMMARY OF PRINCIPLES EVIDENT IN ALL CASES. EMPHASIS ON EFFECT OF EDUCATION.

1074 HARBISON F.H., COLEMAM J.R.
GOALS AND STRATEGY IN COLLECTIVE BARGAINING.
NEW YORK: HARPER & ROW, 1951, 172 PP.
WHAT ARE THE CRITERIA FOR JUDGING WHETHER UNION-MANAGEMENT RELATIONS ARE "CONSTRUCTIVE" OR "DESTRUCTIVE?" SEARCHES FOR GOALS TO BE REPRESENTED IN BARGAINING, BOTH IN TERMS OF A FREE SOCIETY AND MORE SPECIFIC GOALS OF UNIONS AND MANAGEMENT. IN WORKING HARMONY RELATIONSHIPS, UNIONS MAKE SOME MANAGERIAL GOALS THEIR OWN AND VICE-VERSA, WITH RESULTANT EFFECTS ON REPRESENTATIONAL QUESTIONS.

1075 HARBISON F.H., MYERS C.A.
EDUCATION, MANPOWER, AND ECONOMIC GROWTH.
NEW YORK: MCGRAW HILL, 1964, 229 PP., LC#63-20723.
ANALYSIS OF ECONOMIC, POLITICAL, AND SOCIAL DEVELOPMENT FROM PERSPECTIVE OF EDUCATION, TRAINING, AND ENERGIZING OF HUMAN RESOURCES. A POLICY-ORIENTED WORK, MORE CONCERNED WITH STUDYING APPROPRIATE POLICIES AND STRATEGIES OF HUMAN RESOURCE DEVELOPMENT THAN ESTIMATING THE RETURNS ON INVESTMENTS IN MAN. PROVIDES A GLOBAL ANALYSIS OF HUMAN RESOURCE DEVELOPMENT, QUANTITATIVELY AND QUALITATIVELY.

1076 HARBRECHT P.P., BERLE A.A. JR.
TOWARD THE PARAPROPRIETAL SOCIETY.
NEW YORK: TWENTIETH CENT FUND, 1960, 43 PP.
DETAILS PENSION FUNDS AS IMPORTANT HOLDERS OF STOCK IN AMERICAN CORPORATIONS, THEIR VOTING POWER, AND INFLUENCE OVER CORPORATION MANAGEMENT. NOTES THAT THIS DEVELOPMENT IS ANOTHER STEP WEAKENING DIRECT CONTROL BY "OWNERSHIP," AND ADVANCING POWERS OF ADMINISTRATION. ALSO DISCUSSES ROLE OF EMPLOYER AS FINANCIAL REPRESENTATIVE OF WORKERS IN THE OPERATION OF PENSION FUNDS.

1077 HARDIN C.M.
THE POLITICS OF AGRICULTURE.
NEW YORK: FREE PRESS OF GLENCOE, 1952, 282 PP., LC#52-08160.
DEFINES PUBLIC AND PRIVATE AGRICULTURAL INSTITUTIONS, DISCUSSES INTERACTION AT GOVERNMENT LEVEL, AND SURVEYS DEVELOPMENTS IN FIELD 1947-51.

1078 HARDIN C.M.
"REFLECTIONS ON AGRICULTURAL POLICY FORMATION IN THE UNITED STATES."
AM. POL. SCI. REV., 42 (OCT. 48), 881-905.
CRITICISM OF AGRICULTURAL ADMINISTRATION AND CONTENT OF AGRICULTURAL POLICY.

1079 HARDMAN J.B. ED.
AMERICAN LABOR DYNAMICS.
NEW YORK: HARCOURT BRACE, 1928, 432 PP.
THE RESULT OF A GROUP STUDY, IT EXAMINES VARIOUS EARLY 20TH CENTURY LABOR DEVELOPMENTS, A VIEW OF TRADE UNIONISM AS CONTENDER FOR SOCIAL POWER, LABOR POLICIES AND THEIR EFFECTIVENESS IN SELECTED TRADES, AS WELL AS A REVIEW OF LABOR'S LOBBYING ACTIVITIES AND A LONG SECTION ON LABOR IN-GROUP RELATIONSHIPS: ORGANIZATION, LEADERSHIP, MEMBERSHIP, FACTIONS, FOREIGN INFLUENCES ON AMERICAN LABOR.

1080 HARDMAN J.B.
THE HOUSE OF LABOR.
ENGLEWOOD CLIFFS: PRENTICE HALL, 1951, 555 PP.
A COMPREHENSIVE TREATMENT OF LABOR UNIONS AND THEIR FUNCTIONING, WITH SECTION ON UNION GOVERNMENT, PARTICIPATION IN THE COMMUNITY, UNION STAFF AND ADMINISTRATION, UNION RESEARCH AND SOCIAL ENGINEERING, THE LABOR PRESS, AND LOBBYING ACTIVITIES.

1081 HARDT J.P.
THE COLD WAR ECONOMIC GAP.
NEW YORK: FREDERICK PRAEGER, 1961, 112 PP., LC#61-10509.
DISCUSSION OF US AND SOVIET ECONOMIC STRENGTH; MAINTAINS THAT GAP BETWEEN TWO COUNTRIES HAS NARROWED CONSIDERABLY. OUTLINES POLICIES INTENDED TO INCREASE US ECONOMIC POWER.

1082 HARDT J.P., HOFFENBERG M. ET AL.
MATHEMATICS AND COMPUTERS IN SOVIET ECONOMIC PLANNING.
NEW HAVEN: YALE U PR, 1967, 320 PP., LC#67-13435.
AMERICAN ECONOMISTS DESCRIBE PROGRESS SOVIETS HAVE MADE IN DEVELOPING AND APPLYING MATHEMATICAL METHODS AND COMPUTER TECHNIQUES IN ACTUAL SOVIET PLANNING. DISCUSS PROBLEMS THAT WILL FACE THEM IN FUTURE. ANALYZE ASPECTS OF INFORMATION, CONTROL, LINEAR PROGRAMMING, AND USE OF OPTIMIZING MODELS IN PLANNING.

1083 HARING J.E.
"UTILITY THEORY, DECISION THEORY, AND PROFIT MAXIMIZATION."
AMER. ECO. REVIEW, 49 (SEPT. 59), 566-583.
AN ANALYSIS OF PROBABILITY IN CONNECTION WITH CHOICES IN AN ECONOMICALLY RISKY SITUATION. POINTS TO SPECIFIC INADEQUACIES OF EXISTING THEORIES, AND PRESENTS MODELS TO SUBSTANTIATE MODERN THEORY.

1084 HARLOW J.S.
FRENCH ECONOMIC PLANNING: A CHALLENGE TO REASON.
IOWA CITY: UNIVERSITY OF IOWA PR, 1966, 200 PP.
EXAMINES FRENCH ECONOMIC PLANNING PROCESS AND ITS RELATION TO POLITICAL STRUCTURE. STUDIES FIVE PLANS AND POLITICAL EVENTS OF EACH PERIOD TO EXPLORE QUESTION OF INDEPENDENT STRENGTH OF FRENCH ECONOMIC INSTITUTIONS. MAINTAINS THAT UNDERSTANDING OF FRENCH PLANNING IS NECESSARY TO COMPREHENSION OF POLITICAL AND ECONOMIC COURSE OF EUROPE.

1085 HARPER S.N.
THE GOVERNMENT OF THE SOVIET UNION.
PRINCETON: VAN NOSTRAND, 1938, 204 PP.
DISCUSSES SOVIET INSTITUTIONS, GOVERNMENTAL STRUCTURES, AND METHODS OF GOVERNING IMMEDIATELY PRECEDING AND AFTER BOLSHEVIK RISE TO POWER. INCLUDES ECONOMIC STRUCTURES AND PLANS, PARTY POLICY, LAW-MAKING, PUBLIC ADMINISTRATION, AND PUBLIC SERVICES. ALSO TREATS ROLE OF INDIVIDUAL IN A COLLECTIVIZED STATE, INTERNATIONAL RELATIONSHIPS, GOAL OF WORLD REVOLUTION, AND 1937-38 TREASON TRIALS.

1086 HARRINGTON M.
THE OTHER AMERICA: POVERTY IN THE UNITED STATES.
LONDON: MACMILLAN, 1962, 191 PP., LC#62-8555.
A STUDY OF THE ECONOMIC UNDERWORLD OF MIGRANT FARM WORKERS, THE AGED, MINORITY GROUPS, AND OTHER ECONOMICALLY UNDERPRIVILEGED CLASSES. OFFERS PROPOSITION THAT POVERTY FORMS A CULTURE, NECESSITATING NEW COMMUNITIES, AND OFFERS VALUABLE BACKGROUND FOR FUNCTIONAL REPRESENTATION DEVELOPING IN CONNECTION WITH THE ECONOMIC OPPORTUNITY ACT OF 1964.

1087 HARRINGTON M.
THE RETAIL CLERKS.
NEW YORK: JOHN WILEY, 1962, 99 PP., LC#62-20163.
ONE OF A SERIES ON COMPARATIVE UNION GOVERNMENTS, PRESENTS AN ANALYSIS OF RCIA STRUCTURE, BOTH ON THE INTERNATIONAL AND LOCAL UNION LEVEL, CONVENTIONS AND COMMITTEES, POLITICAL ACTION, AND RELATIONS WITH OTHER UNIONS.

1088 HARRIS S.E.
INTERNATIONAL AND INTERREGIONAL ECONOMICS.
NEW YORK: MCGRAW HILL, 1957, 564 PP., LC#57-6396.
CENTERS ON PROBLEMS OF DISEQUILIBRIUM. DISCUSSES CLASSICAL AND NEOCLASSICAL THEORIES OF ECONOMICS AND INTEGRATES MONETARY AND FISCAL POLICY WITH INTERNATIONAL ECONOMICS. CONSIDERS INSTITUTIONAL CHANGES WHICH DEVIATE FROM THE FREE MARKET AND WHICH REDUCE RELEVANCE OF CLASSICAL ECONOMICS. STUDIES POSTWAR ISSUES SUCH AS DOLLAR SHORTAGE, RESTRICTIONS, CAPITAL EXPORTS, AND EXCHANGE RATES.

1089 HARRIS S.E. ED.

THE DOLLAR IN CRISIS.
NEW YORK: HARCOURT BRACE, 1961, 311 PP., LC#61-11205.
COMPARES FOUR POSSIBLE MEANS TO STOP DOLLAR OUTFLOW AND LOSS OF GOLD RESERVES: RISE IN EXPORTS AND REDUCTION IN IMPORTS, REDUCTION IN NET OUTFLOW OF CAPITAL, CURTAILING US GOVERNMENT EXPENDITURES AND LOANS ABROAD, AND RISE OF INTERNATIONAL RESOURCES.

1090 HARRIS S.E.
THE ECONOMICS OF THE POLITICAL PARTIES.
NEW YORK: MACMILLAN, 1962, 382 PP., LC#62-11923.
STUDIES ECONOMIC POLICIES OF DEMOCRATIC AND REPUBLICAN PARTIES, FOCUSING ON PERIODS OF EISENHOWER AND KENNEDY ADMINISTRATIONS. EXAMINES PARTY IDEOLOGIES; POLITICAL ASPECTS OF ECONOMIC POLICY; INTERNATIONAL ECONOMICS; ETC. AUTHOR IDENTIFIES OWN POSITION AS DEMOCRATIC.

1091 HARRIS S.E.
ECONOMICS OF THE KENNEDY YEARS AND A LOOK AHEAD.
NEW YORK: HARPER & ROW, 1964, 273 PP., LC#64-18104.
ANALYZES NEW FRONTIER ECONOMICS, 1961-64, AND COMPARES POLICIES OF KENNEDY AND JOHNSON. STUDIES VARIETY OF ECONOMIC PROBLEMS, CONSIDERS KENNEDY'S ECONOMIC BACKGROUND, AND COMPARES AND CONTRASTS HIS APPROACH WITH THAT OF EISENHOWER.

1092 HARRISON S.M., ANDREWS F.E.
AMERICAN FOUNDATIONS FOR SOCIAL WELFARE.
NEW YORK: RUSSELL SAGE FDN, 1946, 249 PP.
DISCUSSES FOUNDATIONS IN THE US IN TERMS OF HISTORY, THEIR VARIOUS TYPES, METHODS OF ORGANIZATION AND OPERATION, FINANCES AND SOCIAL POLICY IN INVESTMENTS, VARIOUS FIELDS OF ACTIVITY, THE QUESTION OF PUBLIC CONTROL, FUTURE TRENDS, AS WELL AS VARIOUS IMPORTANT STATISTICAL DATA.

1093 HARROD R.F.
THE DOLLAR.
NEW YORK: HARCOURT BRACE, 1953, 156 PP.
TRACES RISE OF THE DOLLAR AS MEDIUM OF INTERNATIONAL EXCHANGE 1775-1950. DISCUSSES FEDERAL RESERVE SYSTEM AND ITS EFFECT ON MONETARY STABILITY, AND NEED FOR INTERNATIONAL COOPERATION IN PRESERVING STABILITY. DOLLAR GAP IS SAID NOT TO BE OF CONCERN BECAUSE COMMODITY VALUE IS MORE IMPORTANT THAN GOLD VALUE.

1094 HARROD R.F.
THE LIFE OF JOHN MAYNARD KEYNES.
NEW YORK: HARCOURT BRACE, 1951, 674 PP.
BIOGRAPHY OF KEYNES. DESCRIBES HIS FORMATIVE YEARS AT HOME, ETON, AND CAMBRIDGE. SHOWS ECONOMIST'S ROLE IN AND ATTITUDES TOWARD TWO WORLD WARS. DISCUSSES FACTORS THAT LED TO WRITING OF MAJOR TREATISES, AND PRESENTS BRIEFLY THEIR ESSENTIAL ELEMENTS.

1095 HARROD R.F. ED., HAGUE D.
INTERNATIONAL TRADE THEORY IN A DEVELOPING WORLD.
NEW YORK: ST MARTIN'S PRESS, 1963, 571 PP.
COLLECTION OF PAPERS ON THEORY AND PRACTICE OF INTERNATIONAL TRADE. DISCUSSES COST, MOVEMENT OF CAPITAL, TRADE CYCLES, COMMON MARKETS, INTERNATIONAL AID, FOREIGN TRADE OF SOCIALIST STATES, AND BALANCE OF PAYMENTS. PROCEEDINGS OF A CONFERENCE HELD BY THE INTERNATIONAL ECONOMIC ASSOCIATION.

1096 HARSANYI J.C.
"APPROACHES TO THE BARGAINING PROBLEM BEFORE AND AFTER THE THEORY OF GAMES."
ECONOMETRICA, 24 (APR. 56), 144-57.
DISCUSSION OF ZEUTHAN'S, HICK'S, AND NASH'S THEORIES. EQUATES ZEUTHAN'S WORK WITH THE LATER RESEARCH OF NASH WHICH COMPARES FAVORABLY WITH HICK'S THEORY OF COLLECTIVE BARGAINING. ECONOMIC SIGNIFICANCE OF ZEUTHAN-NASH THEORY OF BARGAINING IS CRITICALLY ANALYZED.

1097 HART A.G.
MONEY, DEBT, AND ECONOMIC ACTIVITY.
ENGLEWOOD CLIFFS: PRENTICE HALL, 1948, 558 PP.
BROAD STUDY OF MONEY AND ITS EFFECTS ON EMPLOYMENT, PRICING, INTERNATIONAL RELATIONS, AND ECONOMIC STABILITY. PREDOMINANTLY AN INSTITUTIONAL STUDY, ALSO THEORIZES ON POSSIBILITIES FOR FUTURE CONTROL OF ECONOMIC ACTIVITY AND CONSIDERS SYSTEMS OF AUTOMATIC AND DISCRETIONARY CONTROL.

1098 HART A.G.
DEFENSE WITHOUT INFLATION.
NEW YORK: TWENTIETH CENT FUND, 1951, 187 PP.
STUDIES CRISIS PRECIPITATED BY KOREAN WAR IN NATIONAL FISCAL POLICY. ANALYZES PROBLEM OF MOBILIZING FOR DEFENSE WITHOUT DISRUPTING INTERNAL MONETARY STRUCTURE. CONSIDERS EFFECTS OF MOBILIZATION ON UTILIZATION OF RESOURCES, AND METHODS OF COMBATING INFLATION, DIRECT AND INDIRECT.

1099 HART C.W.M.
"INDUSTRIAL RELATIONS RESEARCH AND SOCIAL THEORY."
CAN. J. OF ECO. AND POL. SCI., 15 (FEB. 49), 53-73.
EXAMINES CONNECTION BETWEEN SOCIAL THEORY AND INDUSTRIAL RELATIONS RESEARCH, DRAWING ON DATA OF SOCIOLOGICAL INVESTIGATION OF WINDSOR, ONTARIO. DISCUSSES TENDENCIES AT WORK IN HIGHLY UNIONIZED TOWN, AND SUGGESTS INADEQUACIES OF EXISTING THEORY TO EXPLAIN THESE TENDENCIES. PROPOSES A MORE ADEQUATE THEORETICAL BASIS FOR DISCUSSION.

1100 HART P.E. ED., MILLS G. ED., WHITAKER J.K. ED.
ECONOMETRIC ANALYSIS FOR NATIONAL ECONOMIC PLANNING.
LONDON, WASH, DC: BUTTERWORTHS, 1964, 320 PP.
ANTHOLOGY OF PRESENTATIONS HEARD AT 16TH SYMPOSIUM OF THE COLSTON RESEARCH SOCIETY, HELD IN THE UNIVERSITY OF BRISTOL APRIL 6-9, 1964. DISCUSSIONS ENUMERATE PARTICULAR PROBLEMS ENCOUNTERED IN ECONOMETRIC RESEARCH. INCLUDES ANALYSES OF VARIOUS POINTS OF ECONOMETRIC INTEREST EXCITED BY THE INFLATION PROBLEM; ILLUSTRATES RESEARCH DONE ON THE AGGREGATE GROWTH MODEL AND INDUSTRIAL PRODUCTION FUNCTIONS.

1101 HART W.R.
COLLECTIVE BARGAINING IN THE FEDERAL CIVIL SERVICE.
NEW YORK: HARPER & ROW, 1961, 302 PP., LC#61-7926.
STUDY OF LABOR-MANAGEMENT RELATIONS IN THE FEDERAL CIVIL SERVICE. CONSIDERS CRITICISMS AND DEFENSES OF REGULAR GOVERNMENT POLICY PROHIBITING COLLECTIVE BARGAINING. SUGGESTS COLLECTIVE BARGAINING BE TRIED, BUT SAYS IT ALONE CANNOT SOLVE ALL LABOR-MANAGEMENT PROBLEMS OF THE FEDERAL GOVERNMENT.

1102 HARTLAND P.C.
BALANCE OF INTERREGIONAL PAYMENTS OF NEW ENGLAND.
PROVIDENCE: BROWN U PRESS, 1950, 125 PP.
STUDY OF BALANCE-OF-PAYMENTS OF NEW ENGLAND WITH OTHER REGIONS OF COUNTRY IN RELATION TO DETERMINING SIZE OF BANK RESERVES. TREATS GOLD MOVEMENTS AND DEPOSITS IN NEW ENGLAND AS INDICATOR OF FUNCTION OF FEDERAL RESERVE SYSTEM IN ONE REGION AND ITS RELATION TO NATIONAL ECONOMY.

1103 HARTOG F.
EUROPEAN TRADE CYCLE POLICY.
LEYDEN: AW SIJTHOFF, 1959, 55 PP.
MAIN QUESTION OF STUDY IS HOW BEST TO ACHIEVE A PERMANENTLY HIGH LEVEL OF ECONOMIC ACTIVITY IN EUROPE. ANALYZES FACTUAL STRUCTURE OF EUROPEAN ECONOMIC PROCESS AND DISCUSSES AVAILABLE INSTRUMENTS OF STABILIZATION.

1105 HARVARD UNIVERSITY LAW SCHOOL
INTERNATIONAL PROBLEMS OF FINANCIAL PROTECTION AGAINST NUCLEAR RISK.
NEW YORK: ATOMIC INDUS FORUM, 1959, 96 PP.
STUDIES PROBLEMS DERIVING FROM POSSIBILITY OF SERIOUS NUCLEAR INDUSTRIAL ACCIDENT AS TO LIABILITY LIMITATIONS, INSURANCE, PROCESSING OF CLAIMS, COMPUTING PREMIUMS, AND ROLE OF GOVERNMENT. ALSO CONCERNED WITH PROBLEMS OF INTERNATIONAL COOPERATION IN THESE LAWSUITS.

1106 HARVEY O.L. ED., MILLER S.Q. ET AL.
THE ANVIL AND THE PLOW: A HISTORY OF THE UNITED STATES DEPARTMENT OF LABOR: 1913-1963.
WASHINGTON: GOVT PR OFFICE, 1963, 306 PP.
FAVORABLE ACCOUNT OF THE DEVELOPMENT OF THE DEPARTMENT TO INCLUDE ROLE IN INTERNATIONAL AFFAIRS, EMPLOYMENT AGENCIES AND PROGRAMS, SOCIAL WELFARE, AND COLLECTIVE BARGAINING. IMPLIES THAT WHILE AT FIRST DEPARTMENT REPRESENTED ONLY LABOR IT NOW REPRESENTS THE ENTIRE NATIONAL INTEREST AND BENEFITS ALL GROUPS AND INTERESTS.

1107 HARWOOD E.C.
CAUSE AND CONTROL OF THE BUSINESS CYCLE (5TH ED.)
GREAT BARRINGTON, MASS: INST ECO RES, 1957, 160PP
CHAPTERS BASED ON ELEMENTARY COURSE IN BUSINESS-CYCLE THEORY. TREATS PRODUCTION AND DISTRIBUTION, MONEY INCOME VERSUS PRODUCTION, INFLATION AND DEFLATION, ATTEMPTED EXPLANATION OF UNEMPLOYMENT AND INFLATION, THE GOLD STANDARD, AND CONTROL POSSIBILITIES.

1108 HASSON J.A.
THE ECONOMICS OF NUCLEAR POWER.
LONDON: LONGMANS, GREEN & CO, 1965, 160 PP.
DEVELOPMENT OF METHODOLOGICAL FRAMEWORK TO STUDY NEW INDUSTRY OF NUCLEAR POWER AND ITS EFFECT ON SOCIAL WELFARE INCLUDING NUCLEAR PROGRAMS IN US, UNITED KINGDOM, AND INDIA, AND ECONOMIC DECISIONS OF NUCLEAR DEVELOPMENT.

1109 HASTINGS P.G.
THE MANAGEMENT OF BUSINESS FINANCE.
PRINCETON: VAN NOSTRAND, 1966, 527 PP.
INTRODUCTORY SURVEY OF MANAGEMENT TECHNIQUES FUNDAMENTAL TO MAKING FINANCIAL DECISIONS IN BUSINESS. EMPHASIZES RELATION BETWEEN FINANCIAL ASPECTS OF FIRM AND MANAGEMENT'S POLICY-MAKING. WHICH DECISIONS MAKE MOST MONEY? COVERS ALL ASPECTS OF INVESTING AND BORROWING. BIBLIOGRAPHY AFTER EACH CHAPTER.

1110 HATANAKA M.
A SPECTRAL ANALYSIS OF BUSINESS CYCLE INDICATORS: LEAD-LAG IN TERMS OF ALL TIME POINTS (PAMPHLET)
PRINCETON: PRINCETON U PRESS, 1963, 65 PP.
EXPLANATION OF SPECTRAL ANALYSIS AND CROSS-SPECTRAL

ANALYSIS ON BASIS OF REGRESSION ANALYSIS, TIME SERIES DE-COMPOSITION, AND MACRO-DYNAMICS. COMPARES ESTIMATES OF LEAD-LAG AND STUDIES LEAD-LAG RELATIONSHIPS INVOLVED IN CYCLICAL ADJUSTMENT OF LABOR INPUTS TO MANUFACTURING OUTPUT. DERIVES GENERAL STATEMENTS AS TO SIGNIFICANCE OF CYCLICAL COMPONENT FROM SPECTRAL AND CROSS-SPECTRAL ANALYSIS OF TIME SERIES.

1111 HATHAWAY D.A.
GOVERNMENT AND AGRICULTURE: PUBLIC POLICY IN A DEMOCRATIC SOCIETY.
NEW YORK: MACMILLAN, 1963, 412 PP., LC#61-11797.
DISCUSSION OF THE ROLE OF GOVERNMENT IN DETERMINING FARM POLICY. SEES AGRICULTURAL POLICY AS PART OF A NATIONAL ATTEMPT AT DEVELOPING A UNIFORMLY PROSPEROUS, STABLE, CAPITALIST ECONOMY.

1112 HATHAWAY D.E.
PROBLEMS OF PROGRESS IN THE AGRICULTURAL ECONOMY.
GLENVIEW, ILL: SCOTT, FORESMAN, 1964, 168 PP.
DISCUSSES ECONOMIC STRUCTURE OF AGRICULTURE, EMPHASIZING ADVERSE EFFECT CREATED BY GENERAL STRUCTURAL GROWTH ON FAR-MER. EVALUATES PAST AND PRESENT GOVERNMENT REMEDIES WITH SUGGESTIONS FOR FUTURE.

1113 HATTERY L.H. ED., MCCORMICK E.M. ED.
INFORMATION RETRIEVAL MANAGEMENT.
DETROIT: AMER DATA PROCESSING, 1962, 151 PP., LC#62-18060.
SERIES OF 18 PAPERS BY DIFFERENT AUTHORS CONCERNING VARIOUS ASPECTS OF MANAGERIAL PROBLEMS IN SCIENCE INFORMATION PROCESSES. SOME DEAL WITH HISTORICAL, SOCIAL, AND CULTURAL BACKGROUNDS, OTHERS WITH QUESTIONS OF COST, ACCEPTANCE, AND COMMUNICATIONS. GENERAL TECHNIQUES AND SPECIFIC APPLICATION TO SCIENTIFIC AND INDUSTRIAL RESEARCH ARE DISCUSSED, INCLUDING EXAMPLES OF ACTUAL OPERATIONS.

1114 HAUSER M.
DIE URSACHEN DER FRANZOSISCHEN INFLATION IN DEN JAHREN 1946-1952.
WINTERTHUR: P G KELLER, 1961, 105 PP.
DISCUSSES THEORETICAL BASIS AND GENERAL DEVELOPMENT OF FRENCH INFLATION BETWEEN 1946 AND 1952. EXAMINES PRICE DE-VELOPMENTS, SUPPLY OF MONEY TO PRIVATE AND PUBLIC SECTOR OF ECONOMY, AND CHANGES IN GOLD AND CREDIT STANDARDS ABROAD.

1115 HAUSER P. ED., SCHNORE L.F. ED.
THE STUDY OF URBANIZATION.
NEW YORK: JOHN WILEY, 1965, 554 PP., LC#65-24223.
PRESENTS AN INVENTORY AND APPRAISAL OFTHE STUDY OF URBANIZATION IN SUCH FIELDS AS ECONOMICS, GEOGRAPHY, HISTO-RY, POLITICAL SCIENCE, SOCIOLOGY, AND ANTHROPOLOGY. POINTS OUT GAPS IN KNOWLEDGE IN BOTH ANTECEDENTS AND CONSEQUENCES OF URBANIZATION. INDICATES THE IMPORTANCE OF CROSS-CULTURAL RESEARCH, ESPECIALLY IN DEVELOPING AREAS. ESSAYS BY W. S. SAYRE AND N. POLSBY, O. LEWIS, G. SJOBERG, ET AL.

1116 HAUSMAN W.H. ED.
MANAGING ECONOMIC DEVELOPMENT IN AFRICA.
CAMBRIDGE: M I T PRESS, 1963, 253 PP., LC#63-16233.
ANTHOLOGY OF PAPERS ON MANAGEMENT OF AFRICAN ECONOMIC DE-VELOPMENT COVERING PLANNING, MANPOWER, TECHNICAL ASSISTANCE, CAPITAL, FOREIGN AID, LEGAL ASPECTS, AND US ROLE.

1117 HAWLEY A.H.
"METROPOLITAN POPULATION AND MUNICIPAL GOVERNMENT EXPENDITURES IN CENTRAL CITIES" (BMR)
J. SOCIAL ISSUES, 7 (1951), 100-108.
TESTS HYPOTHESIS ON INTERDEPENDENCE OF POPULATIONS LYING WITHIN AND OUTSIDE URBAN CENTERS. ARGUES THAT ANNUAL EXPENDITURES OF CITY GOVERNMENTS VARY WITH SIZE OF POPULATIONS OCCUPYING ADJOINING AREAS AND THE LARGER THE POPULATION LIVING OUTSIDE CITY, THE HEAVIER THE TAX BURDEN ON CENTRAL CITY'S POPULATION. AUTHOR USES CORRELATION ANALYSIS IN DETERMINING VARIABLES AFFECTING CITY BUDGET.

1118 HAWTREY R.G.
ECONOMIC ASPECTS OF SOVEREIGNTY.
LONDON: LONGMANS, 1930, 162 PP.
INDICATES THAT EACH GOVERNMENT POSSESSES BY VIRTUE OF ITS SOVEREIGNTY RIGHTS OVER ITS TERRITORY AND PROPERTY WITHIN. POINTS OUT THAT DISTINCTION BETWEEN ECONOMIC AND POLITICAL CAUSES OF WAR IS UNREAL AND THAT WARS ARE FOUGHT FOR PUR-POSES OF EXPANDING SOVEREIGNTY. STATES THAT ALL NATIONAL RIGHTS ARE SUBORDINATE TO COERCIVE FORCE BECAUSE THE USE OF FORCE IS PRINCIPAL TOOL OF NATIONAL POLICY.

1119 HAX K., OHM H. ET AL.
DIE HOCHSCHULLEHRER DER WIRTSCHAFTSWISSENSCHAFTEN IN DER BUNDESREPUBLIK DEUTSCHLAND EINSCHL. WESTBERLIN, OSTERREICH.
BERLIN: VEREIN FUR SOZIAL POL, 1959, 515 PP.
BIBLIOGRAPHY ON ORIGIN AND DEVELOPMENT OF PROFESSORSHIP IN ECONOMIC SCIENCE AND RELATED SUBJECTS IN HIGHER EDUCATION OF FEDERAL REPUBLIC OF WEST GERMANY INCLUDING WEST BERLIN, AUSTRIA, AND GERMAN-SPEAKING SWITZERLAND.

1120 VON HAYEK F.A.
THE PURE THEORY OF CAPITAL.
LONDON: MACMILLAN, 1941, 454 PP.
ATTEMPTS TO ESTABLISH A THEORY OF CAPITALIST PRODUCTION ADEQUATE FOR THE ANALYSIS OF DYNAMIC CHANGES. TREATS PROB-LEMS IN TERMS OF EQUILIBRIUM ANALYSIS RATHER THAN IN TERMS OF A THEORY OF CAPITAL AND INTEREST. BELIEVES THAT STUDY OF CAPITAL AS A SINGLE FACTOR WAS MISLEADING. DEFINES CAPITAL AS "A NAME FOR THE TOTAL STOCK OF THE NONPERMANENT FACTORS OF PRODUCTION."

1121 VON HAYEK F.A.
THE ROAD TO SERFDOM.
CHICAGO: U. CHI. PR., 1944, 249 PP.
CRITICISM OF THE SOCIALIST OR 'PLANNED ECONOMY' TENDENCIES THAT HAVE DEVELOPED AND BEEN ACCEPTED AS INEVIT-ABLE BY WESTERN DEMOCRACIES. SEES SOCIALISM ENDING IN EITHER CIVIL WAR OR EMERGENCE OF NATIONAL DICTATORSHIPS. ADVOCATES RETURN TO NINETEENTH CENTURY LIBERALISM WITH EMPHASIS ON INDIVIDUAL FREEDOM. ADVISES ADAPTATION OF THIS PHILOSOPHY TO TWENTIETH CENTURY.

1122 VON HAYEK F.A.
INDIVIDUALISM AND ECONOMIC ORDER.
CHICAGO: U OF CHICAGO PRESS, 1948, 272 PP.
ANALYSIS OF RELATIONSHIP BETWEEN APPROACHES TO INTERPRE-TATION OF SOCIAL PHENOMENA AND ATTITUDES TOWARD QUESTIONS OF SOCIAL POLICY. DISCUSSION OF MORAL ISSUES IN ECONOMICS, VA-LIDITY OF ECONOMIC THEORY, SOCIALIST PLANNING, PRINCIPLES OF MONETARY POLICY, AND FOUNDATION OF INTERNATIONAL ORDER. STRESSES DOMAIN OF REASON IN ORDERING SOCIAL AFFAIRS.

1123 VON HAYEK F.A.
FREEDOM AND THE ECONOMIC SYSTEM.
CHICAGO: U OF CHICAGO PRESS, 1939, 38 PP.
ATTEMPTS TO RELATE DECLINE OF FREE MARKET SYSTEM IN A COUNTRY'S ECONOMIC SYSTEM AND RISE OF ARBITRARY POWER IN ITS POLITY. POINTS TO GERMANY AND RUSSIA AS TOTALITARIAN STATES WHICH HAD CONTROLLED ECONOMIC SYSTEMS. CLAIMS THAT PLANNING ECONOMIC MATTERS PRESUPPOSES MORE COMPLETE AGREEMENT ON SOCIAL ENDS THAN GENERALLY EXISTS. WARNS AGAINST SOCIAL EXPERIMENTS WHICH MAY LEAD TO DESTRUCTION OF FREEDOMS.

1124 VON HAYEK F.A. ED.
CAPITALISM AND THE HISTORIANS.
CHICAGO: U OF CHICAGO PRESS, 1954, 188 PP.
ARTICLES EXAMINE THE BELIEF THAT INDUSTRIALIZATION INTRO-DUCED WIDESPREAD POVERTY AMONG THE MASSES. AUTHORS FIND THAT THIS IS NOT TRUE. IN GENERAL, THEY CLAIM, INDUSTRIALI-ZATION IMPROVED LIVING CONDITIONS, AND MOST EVILS WHICH DID EXIST ORIGINATED IN THE EARLIER, MONOPOLISTIC SYSTEM. THE FACT THAT THESE EVILS WERE REMEDIED BY LABOR'S AGITATION INDICATES THAT CAPITALISM GAVE LABOR A POLITICAL VOICE.

1125 HAYER T.
FRENCH AID.
LONDON: OVERSEAS DEVELOPMT INST, 1966, 230 PP.
DESCRIBES FRENCH AID IN CONTEXT BOTH OF FRANCE'S PAST COLONIAL POLICY AND FRENCH INTEREST IN THE THIRD WORLD. SIGNIFICANCE OF SIZE OF FRENCH PROGRAM IS FULLY DISCUSSED. EXAMINES CLOSENESS OF FRANCO-AFRICAN RELATIONS AND CONSIDERS ADVANTAGES AND DISADVANTAGES. STUDY IS ONE OF OVERSEAS DEVELOPMENT INSTITUTE'S.

1126 HAYS P.R.
LABOR ARBITRATION: A DISSENTING VIEW.
NEW HAVEN: YALE U PR, 1966, 125 PP., LC#66-12501.
DISCUSSES LAWS RELATING TO AND PRACTICE OF LABOR ARBITRATION. INCLUDES CHAPTER ON FUTURE OF SYSTEM AND AUTHOR'S SUGGESTION THAT ALL DECISIONS BE HANDLED IN REGULAR COURT SYSTEM IF COURTS ARE TO ENFORCE DECISIONS.

1127 HAYTER T.
"FRENCH AID TO AFRICA* ITS SCOPE AND ACHIEVEMENTS."
INTERNATIONAL AFFAIRS (UK), 41 (APR 65), 236-251.
THE BULK OF ALL FRENCH AID GOES TO HER FORMER COLONIES IN SUB-SAHARAN AFRICA. HAYTER TRACES DEVELOPMENT OF RELATIONAL CONCEPTS OF ASSIMILATION AND ASSOCIATION WHICH LED TO PEACE-FUL POLITICAL INDEPENDENCE, WITH FRANCE THEN THROUGH AID AND FAVORED TRADE POLICIES MAINTAINING OLD ECONOMIC STANDARDS. EEC POLICIES AND FRENCH CULTURAL PRIDE ARE SEEN AS INTER-ACTING TO CREATE AID POLICY AIMED AT ECONOMIC INDEPENDENCE.

1128 HAYTES W., TRUDEAU A.G., MUTTER C.
"THREE VIEWS ON THE SOVIET ECONOMIC THREAT."
MIL. REV., 41 (JAN. 61), 29-51.
SOVIET ECONOMY GEARED TO FAVOR TAKEOVER OF WORLD BY COMMUNISTS. ECONOMY IS CAPITALISM AT ITS WORST. RUSSIAN VIEWS OF USA ARE DISTORTED. ONLY A STRONG U.S. ECONOMY CAN PREVENT A COMMUNIST-DOMINATED WORLD.

1129 HAZLEWOOD A.
THE ECONOMICS OF "UNDER-DEVELOPED" AREAS.
LONDON: OXFORD U PR, 1959, 156 PP.
LIST OF 1,027 BOOKS, ARTICLES AND OFFICIAL PUBLICATIONS CONCERNED WITH ECONOMICS AND FINANCE, DEMOGRAPHY, RESOURCES, PLANNING, AND CONCEPTS OF ECONOMIC DEVELOPMENT. ARRANGED BY TOPIC WITH DETAILED TABLE OF CONTENTS.

1130 HAZLEWOOD A.
THE ECONOMICS OF DEVELOPMENT: AN ANNOTATED LIST OF BOOKS AND ARTICLES PUBLISHED 1958-1962.
LONDON: OXFORD U PR, 1964, 104 PP.
CONFINED TO ENGLISH-LANGUAGE PUBLICATIONS OF PERIOD 1958-1962. ORGANIZED BY CONTENT AND TYPE OF STUDY: THEORIES AND PROBLEMS; HISTORICAL STUDIES; AREA STUDIES; NATIONAL INCOME AND COMPONENTS; POPULATION, LABOR, AND MANAGEMENT; AGRICULTURE AND LAND; INDUSTRY; COMMERCE AND TRANSPORT; MONEY AND BANKING; GOVERNMENT; INTERNATIONAL ECONOMICS.

1131 HEADLEY J.C., LEWIS J.N.
PESTICIDE PROBLEM: AN ECONOMIC APPROACH TO PUBLIC POLICY.
BALTIMORE: JOHNS HOPKINS PRESS, 1967, 141 PP., LC#66-28503.
DEALS WITH STUDY OF ENVIRONMENTAL PROBLEMS TO DEVELOP ANALYSES AND INFORMATION AS BASIS FOR POLICY ON USE OF PESTICIDES. PROPOSES THAT USE MUST BE CONCERNED WITH COSTS AND RETURNS AND URGES "DEVELOPMENT OF REASONABLE POLICIES GOVERNING USE." GIVES BACKGROUND, ALTERNATIVES, PROBLEMS OF EFFECT AND DETERMINATION OF EFFECT, AND RESEARCH NEEDS.

1132 HEATH D.B.
"BOLIVIA UNDER BARRIENTOS."
CURRENT HISTORY, 53 (NOV. 67), 275-282, 307.
EXAMINES RECENT DEVELOPMENTS IN BOLIVIA, REVEALING THE INTRICATE INTERPLAY OF VALUES, PERSONALITIES, AND EVENTS THAT COMBINE TO SHAPE ITS CURRENT SITUATION. DISCUSSES RECENT REVOLUTIONARY MOVEMENTS AND BOLIVIA'S FOREIGN RELATIONS. NOTES THAT ALTHOUGH DOMESTIC UNREST CONTINUES TO PLAGUE THE COUNTRY, BOLIVIA'S ECONOMY IS BECOMING PROGRESSIVELY STRONGER.

1133 HEBERLE R.
"ON POLITICAL ECOLOGY" (BMR)"
SOCIAL FORCES, 31 (OCT. 52), 1-9.
CONTENDS THAT GUIDING PRINCIPLE IN SOCIOGRAPHIC STUDIES SHOULD BE THAT ALL EMPIRICAL PHENOMENA IN CONCRETE CONTEXTS ARE STUDIED ACCORDING TO THEIR SIGNIFICANCE FOR SOCIAL INTEGRATION OR DISINTEGRATION. DISCUSSES FOUR INDEXES OF SOCIAL SOLIDARITY OR DISINTEGRATION: GEOGRAPHIC CONDITIONS, ECONOMIC CONDITIONS, SOCIAL STRATIFICATION, AND VOTING BEHAVIOR.

1135 HEILBRONER R.L.
"DYNAMICS OF FOREIGN AID: PROBLEMS OF UNDERDEVELOPED NATIONS PLAGUE ASSISTANCE PROGRAM."
NEW LEADER, 44 (SEPT. 6), 18-21.
CAUTIONS AGAINST EXPECTATIONS OF QUICK RESULTS. ESTIMATES 20-30 YEARS FOR ACCUMULATION OF CAPITAL. FORESEES CLASS DISPLACEMENT LEADING TO SOCIAL TENSION, AND INCREASE IN ANTI-AMERICAN AND PRO-SOCIALIST SENTIMENTS.

1136 HEILBRONER R.L.
THE MAKING OF ECONOMIC SOCIETY.
ENGLEWOOD CLIFFS: PRENTICE HALL, 1962, 241 PP.
SYSTEMATIC ANALYSIS OF ECONOMICS AND FUNCTION OF SOCIAL ORGANIZATIONS IN TRYING TO SOLVE ECONOMIC PROBLEMS. HISTORICAL TREATMENT OF ECONOMICS CONCLUDES WITH OBSERVATIONS ON UNDERDEVELOPED AREAS. FORSEES PERIOD IN WHICH SOCIAL STRUGGLES ARE TERMINATED.

1137 HEILBRONER R.L.
THE LIMITS OF AMERICAN CAPITALISM.
NEW YORK: HARPER & ROW, 1967, 134 PP., LC#66-21708.
DISCUSSION OF IMPACT OF CORPORATE SYSTEM ON TOTAL ENVIRONMENT. CHANGES IN POWER, INFLUENCE, AND TECHNOLOGY AS THEY AFFECT CORPORATE SECTOR OF ECONOMY. HIGH MILITARY PRODUCTION HAS SLOWED DECLINE, BUT IN FUTURE CORPORATE STRUCTURE WILL BE MUCH LESS INFLUENTIAL.

1138 HEILBRONER R.L.
"BUILDING NEW NATIONS."
CURRENT, (JUNE 67), 19-27.
CONTENDS THAT THE "REVOLUTION OF RISING EXPECTATIONS" AND AVOWED US POLICY OF SUPPORTING THE ECONOMIC ASPIRATIONS OF DEVELOPING COUNTRIES MAY LEAD TO SOCIAL EXPERIMENTS AND DEVELOPMENTS WHICH US OPPOSES BUT WHICH ARE NECESSARY FOR SOCIO-ECONOMIC CHANGE. ARGUES THAT THE US MUST AVOID OVERTLY COUNTERREVOLUTIONARY POLICIES OR LOSE INFLUENCE AND PRESTIGE AMONGAMONG EMERGING NATIONS. (FROM COMMENTARY, APRIL 1967.)

1139 HEILPERIN M.A.
THE TRADE OF NATIONS.
NEW YORK: KNOPF, 1947, 234 PP.
ATTEMPT TO RE-EXAMINE THE PROBLEMS OF INTERNATIONAL TRADE, FINANCE, AND MONEY, WITH SPECIAL REFERENCE TO TASK OF PEACE AND TO THE PARTICULAR RESPONSIBILITIES AND OPPORTUNITIES OF THE UNITED STATES. ADVOCATES BUILDING A WORLD ECONOMY IN A HIGHLY NATIONALISTIC AND PROTECTIONIST WORLD.

1140 HEILPERIN M.A. ED.
STUDIES IN ECONOMIC NATIONALISM.
MOSCOW: SOVETSKAIA ROSSIIA, 1960, 230 PP.
STUDIES ECONOMIC NATIONALISM IN 20TH CENTURY (INCLUDING ITS DEFINITION AND HISTORY); ECONOMIC NATIONALISM OF KEYNES; COLLECTIVIST PLANNING SINCE WWII; AND US FOREIGN ECONOMIC POLICY.

1141 HEIMANN E.
COMMUNISM, FASCISM, OR DEMOCRACY?
NEW YORK: W W NORTON, 1938, 288 PP.
BEGINS WITH RELATION OF CAPITALISM TO DEMOCRACY AND DISCUSSES POLITICAL AND ECONOMIC INSTITUTIONS OF AN INDIVIDUALISTIC DEMOCRACY. COMPARES AND CONTRASTS CLASSICAL SOCIALISM, COMMUNISM, AND FASCISM TO DEMOCRACY. INCLUDES DISINTEGRATION OF HUMANISTIC PHILOSOPHY, PROBLEMS OF LIBERTY AND EQUALITY, ORGANIZATION AND INTEGRATION IN EACH TYPE OF POLITICAL SYSTEM, AND LOGIC MOTIVATING EACH SYSTEM.

1142 HEISS K.P.
GAME THEORY AND HUMAN CONFLICTS (RESEARCH MEMORANDUM)
PRINCETON: PRIN U ECONOMET RES, 1966, 34 PP.
REVIEW OF BRUNO DE FINETTI'S OUTLINE OF THE IMPACT OF GAME THEORY ON ECONOMIC, SOCIAL, AND POLITICAL PROBLEMS, INCLUDING HISTORICAL NOTES ON EVOLUTION OF GAME THEORY, AND EXPOSITION OF GAME THEORY PROBLEMS, AND RECOMMENDATIONS OF CORRECTIVE MEASURES WHEN THE MINIMAX FAILS.

1143 HEKHUIS D.J. ED., MCCLINTOCK C.G. ED., BURNS A.L. ED.
INTERNATIONAL STABILITY: MILITARY, ECONOMIC AND POLITICAL DIMENSIONS.
NEW YORK: WILEY, 1964, 296 PP., $6.00.
ESSAYS DEFINE STABILITY, ANALYZE THREATS TO STABILITY, AND STUDY MEANS FOR ALLEVIATING INSTABILITY. STUDY MUTUAL DETERRENCE, REGIONAL DEFENSE, DISARMAMENT, ARMS CONTROL.

1144 HELANDER S.
DAS AUTARKIEPROBLEM IN DER WELTWIRTSCHAFT.
BERLIN: DUNCKER & HUMBLOT, 1955, 684 PP.
DISCUSSES TRADE AND CREDIT POLICIES OF MAJOR POWERS IN RELATION TO PRINCIPLE OF ECONOMIC SELF-SUFFICIENCY. EXAMINES COLONIAL POLICIES AND COMPARES POLICY OF SMALL AND LARGE NATIONS.

1145 HELLMAN F.S.
THE NEW DEAL: SELECTED LIST OF REFERENCES.
WASHINGTON: LIBRARY OF CONGRESS, 1940, 71 PP.
INDEXED, ANNOTATED, AND CLASSIFIED BIBLIOGRAPHY INCLUDES 586 ITEMS RELATING TO 36 SEPARATE AGENCIES, AS WELL AS SPECIFIC POLICIES AND ISSUES OF THE NEW DEAL. CONCERNED WITH HOUSING, FINANCIAL, AND FOREIGN POLICY; COURT-PACKING; LABOR RELATIONS; REORGANIZATION OF EXECUTIVE DEPARTMENTS; THE TVA, WPA, SEC, SOCIAL SECURITY BOARD, NRA, CCC, AAA, ETC.

1146 HEMPSTONE S.
THE NEW AFRICA.
LONDON: FABER AND FABER, 1961, 664 PP.
JOURNALIST'S OBSERVATIONS OF AFRICA SOUTH OF SAHARA, NORTH OF CONGO. LAYMAN'S VIEW OF THE LAND, PEOPLE, AND INDEPENDENCE MOVEMENTS. INCLUDES HISTORICAL BACKGROUND AND PREDICTIONS FOR FUTURE ECONOMIC, POLITICAL, AND SOCIAL DEVELOPMENT. ANNOTATED BIBLIOGRAPHY INCLUDES WORKS OF GENERAL AND DETAILED NATURE IN RECENT US, EUROPEAN, AND AFRICAN PUBLICATIONS.

1147 HENDEL S. ED.
THE SOVIET CRUCIBLE.
PRINCETON: VAN NOSTRAND, 1959, 594 PP., LC#59-8657.
COLLECTION OF WRITINGS ON BACKGROUND OF USSR AND MARXIST DOCTRINE AND THEORY AS INCORPORATED BY BOLSHEVIK REVOLUTION. EXAMINES SOVIET SYSTEM IN RELATION TO THEORY UNDER LENIN, STALIN, AND POST-STALIN ERA. DEALS WITH THEIR INFLUENCE ON CHANGES IN POLICY AND DOCTRINE RELATED TO ECONOMY AND POLITICAL MATTERS.

1148 HENDERSON W.O.
THE INDUSTRIAL REVOLUTION IN EUROPE.
CHICAGO: QUADRANGLE BOOKS, INC, 1961, 288 PP., LC#61-13074.
ECONOMIC AND POLITICAL ANALYSIS OF GROWTH OF INDUSTRIALISM IN FRANCE, GERMANY, AND RUSSIA FROM 1800 TO 1914. EMPHASIZES EFFECTS OF INDUSTRIAL REVOLUTION ON WARS AND POLITICAL AFFAIRS OF 19TH-CENTURY EUROPE AND ON RISE OF INDUSTRIAL CAPITALISM IN 20TH CENTURY.

1149 HENDERSON W.O.
THE GENESIS OF THE COMMON MARKET.
CHICAGO: QUADRANGLE BOOKS, INC, 1962, 201 PP., LC#62-20924.
STUDIES EVOLUTION OF EUROPEAN ECONOMIC COOPERATION FROM ANGLO-FRENCH COMMERCIAL TREATY OF 1786 TO CREATION OF EEC AFTER WWII. DISCUSSES SUCH MATTERS AS THE SLAVE TRADE, FISHERIES, AND COMMUNICATIONS.

1150 HENNING C.N.
INTERNATIONAL FINANCING.
NEW YORK: HARPER & ROW, 1958, 481 PP., LC#57-9870.
DISCUSSION OF PRACTICES USED IN FINANCING FOREIGN TRADE AND OTHER INTERNATIONAL TRANSACTIONS. PRESENTS THEORY AND PROBLEMS OF INTERNATIONAL FINANCE. SPECIAL ATTENTION IS GIVEN TO BALANCE OF PAYMENTS, FINANCING OF COMMERCIAL TRANSACTIONS AND USE OF LETTERS OF CREDIT, OPERATIONS OF INTERNATIONAL FINANCE INSTITUTIONS, CHANGING NATURE OF

EXCHANGE DEALINGS SINCE WWII, LENDING, ETC.

1151 HERBERG W.
"BUREAUCRACY AND DEMOCRACY IN LABOR UNIONS."
ANTIOCH REV., 3 (SEPT. 43), 405-417.
DOES THE UNION WORKER ENJOY LESS FREEDOM IN RELATION TO HIS OWN UNION LEADER THAN HE DOES IN RELATION TO HIS EMPLOYER? IS THERE A RIGHT OF DISSENT IN UNIONS? THE ANSWERS INVOLVE ANALYSIS OF DUAL NATURE OF UNIONS AS BUSINESSLIKE SERVICE ORGANIZATIONS AND AS VEHICLES FOR DEMOCRATIC SELF-DETERMINATION. INDICATES NEED OF REFORM TO PRESERVE US CONSTITUTIONAL RIGHTS WITHIN THE UNIONS.

1152 HERMAN L.M.
"THE ECONOMIC CONTENT OF SOVIET TRADE WITH THE WEST."
LAW CONTEMP. PROBL., 29 (AUTUMN 64), 971-82.
ANALYSIS OF THE ECONOMIC REALITIES OF EAST-WEST TRADE, PARTICULARLY AS IT IS SIGNIFICANT TO SOCIAL AND ECONOMIC PROGRESS OF EACH SIDE.

1153 HERRERA F.
"THE INTER-AMERICAN DEVELOPMENT BANK."
SOC. SCI., 16 (1960), 216-21.
DISCUSSES MECHANISMS OF INTER-AMERICAN DEVELOPMENT BANK AND HOW IT WORKS TO PROVIDE NEEDED EXTERNAL CAPITAL FOR LATIN AMERICA, BY FURNISHING LOANS AND TECHNICAL ASSISTANCE.

1154 HERRERA F.
"EUROPEAN PARTICIPATION IN THE LATIN AMERICAN REGIONAL INTEGRATION"
CENTRO, 3 (FEB. 67), 30-36.
PRESENTS ARGUMENT FOR LATIN AMERICA'S DESIRE TO COOPERATE WITH EUROPEAN ECONOMIC COMMUNITIES ON MULTILATERAL BASIS. SEEKS SOLIDARITY THROUGH INTERDEPENDENCE AND MUTUAL PROTECTION. TRACES DEVELOPMENT OF LATIN AMERICA AS CULTURAL EXPANSION OF EUROPE, AND ENUMERATES FINANCIAL TIES WITH EUROPE.

1155 HERRESHOFF D.
AMERICAN DISCIPLES OF MARX: FROM THE AGE OF JACKSON TO THE PROGRESSIVE ERA.
DETROIT: WAYNE STATE U PR, 1967, 215 PP., LC#67-11584.
AN ACCOUNT OF RADICAL PHILOSOPHIES OF FIVE PRIMARY AMERICAN PROPONENTS OF MARXIAN IDEOLOGY--BROWNSON, KRIEGE, WEYDEMEYER, SORGE, AND DE LEON. ANALYZES THEIR EFFECT ON THE MARXIAN CREDO AND MARXIAN EFFECTS ON AMERICAN RADICALISM. ACCOUNT OF US INTERNATIONAL AND BRIEF HISTORY OF AMERICAN COMMUNIST PARTY IN 20TH CENTURY.

1156 HERRICK B.H.
URBAN MIGRATION AND ECONOMIC DEVELOPMENT IN CHILE.
CAMBRIDGE: M I T PRESS, 1965, 126 PP., LC#66-17754.
EXAMINATION OF CHILEAN ECONOMY DURING PERIOD 1940-60 AS AN EXAMPLE OF A COUNTRY IN WHICH INCIPIENT TENDENCIES TOWARD ECONOMIC DEVELOPMENT DECAYED INTO STAGNATION AND IN WHICH URBAN MIGRATION ASSUMED A FORM REFLECTING THE ECONOMIC AND DEMOGRAPHIC CONDITIONS SURROUNDING IT. COORDINATES RECORD OF CHILE'S ECONOMIC DEVELOPMENT WITH AN ACCOUNT OF ITS CONCOMITANT INTERNAL MIGRATION.

1157 HERSKOVITS M.J. ED., HARWITZ M. ED.
ECONOMIC TRANSITION IN AFRICA.
EVANSTON: NORTHWESTERN U PRESS, 1964, 444 PP.
COLLECTION OF PAPERS ANALYZING ECONOMIC GROWTH OF SUB-SAHARA AFRICA. DISCUSSES INDIGENOUS CHARACTER, DEVELOPMENT PLANNING, AND PROBLEMS.

1158 HERZ J.H.
"EAST GERMANY: PROGRESS AND PROSPECTS."
SOC. RES., 27 (SUMMER 60), 139-156.
CONTRASTS STALINISTIC DICTATORSHIP OF ULBRICHT REGIME WITH OTHER SOVIET SATELLITES. STRICT CONTROLS HAVE CONSOLIDATED REGIME THEREBY REDUCING CHANCES OF GERMAN REUNIFICATION. BRINGS TO LIGHT SWEEPING MEASURES FOR COLLECTIVIZED AGRICULTURE AND NATIONALIZATION OF COMMERCE AND INDUSTRY. SHOWS CLOSER TIES OF EAST GERMANY WITH EASTERN BLOC ECONOMY AS IMPORTANT STEP TOWARD ECONOMIC INTERGRATION.

1159 HERZBERG D.G., TILLETT P.
A BUDGET FOR NEW YORK STATE, 1956-1957 (PAMPHLET)
INDIANAPOLIS: BOBBS-MERRILL, 1962, 34 PP.
DESCRIBES BUDGET PROCESS CULMINATING IN ADOPTION BY REPUBLICAN-CONTROLLED NEW YORK STATE LEGISLATURE OF BUDGET PREPARED BY HARRIMAN'S DEMOCRATIC ADMINISTRATION. TOLD FROM PERSPECTIVE OF DIVISION OF THE BUDGET.

1160 HEVESY P.D.
THE UNIFICATION OF THE WORLD.
NEW YORK: PERGAMON PRESS, 1966, 356 PP., LC#65-14783.
ENVISIONS A UNIFIED WORLD AND PROPOSES MEANS TO ACHIEVE IT: WORLDWIDE AGRICULTURAL PROGRAM; CUSTOMS AND MONETARY UNION BETWEEN US AND COMMONWEALTH LEADING TOWARD UNIVERSAL CUSTOMS UNION; UNIFIED ECONOMIC SYSTEM; NEED FOR A NEW MARSHALL PLAN. HAS FAITH IN TODAY'S STATESMEN TO WORK FOR THIS IDEAL.

1161 HEYSE T.
PROBLEMS FONCIERS ET REGIME DES TERRES (ASPECTS ECONOMIQUES, JURIDIQUES ET SOCIAUX)
BRUSSELS: CEDESA, 1960, 163 PP.
BIBLIOGRAPHY OF 875 ITEMS COVERING PUBLISHED LITERATURE ON ECONOMIC, JUDICIAL, AND SOCIAL IMPLICATIONS OF TENURE OF LAND IN THE BELGIAN CONGO AND RUANDI-URANDI FOR PERIOD 1948-1959. EMPHASIZES PROBLEMS OF WATER AND HUNTING AND FISHING RIGHTS FOR ECONOMICALLY UNDERDEVELOPED COUNTRIES AND ROLE OF INTERNATIONAL ORGANIZATIONS IN SOLVING TERRITORIAL DISPUTES. INCLUDES AUTHOR AND SUBJECT INDEXES.

1162 HICKMAN B.G. ED.
QUANTITATIVE PLANNING OF ECONOMIC POLICY.
WASHINGTON: BROOKINGS INST, 1965, 266 PP., LC#65-18314.
SURVEY OF THEORETICAL AND EMPIRICAL DEVELOPMENTS IN QUANTITATIVE PLANNING OF ECONOMIC POLICY. APPRAISAL OF TECHNIQUES OF QUANTITATIVE POLICY ANALYSIS AND OF SPECIFIC APPLICATION IN NETHERLANDS, FRANCE, AND JAPAN. PROPOSALS FOR FUTURE RESEARCH INCLUDE METHODS OF DETERMINING POLICY ALTERNATIVES, AND PRACTICAL EXAMINATION OF POLITICAL DECISION-MAKING PROCESS. ECONOMETRIC MODELS INCLUDED.

1163 HICKMAN C.A., KUHN M.H.
INDIVIDUALS, GROUPS, AND ECONOMIC BEHAVIOR.
NEW YORK: THE DRYDEN PRESS, 1956, 216 PP.
SEEKS TO DEMONSTRATE USEFULNESS OF APPLYING SOCIAL PSYCHOLOGY TO ECONOMIC PROBLEMS. EXPLORES THREE BASIC ISSUES IN ECONOMICS: NATURE OF MANAGERIAL MOTIVATION, FEASIBILITY OF MAKING INTERPERSONAL COMPARISONS, AND RECONCILIATION OF PLANNING AND INDIVIDUAL FREEDOM.

1164 HICKS J.R.
THE THEORY OF WAGES.
LONDON: MACMILLAN, 1935, 247 PP.
ATTEMPTS TO RESTATE THEORY OF WAGES IN LIGHT OF RECENT (1930'S) ECONOMIC KNOWLEDGE. BASICALLY A REVISION OF MARSHALL'S "PRINCIPLES" AND CLARK'S "DISTRIBUTION OF WEALTH." MAJOR FACTORS AFFECTING LABOR WERE RISE IN TRADE UNIONS AND INCREASE IN GOVERNMENT CONTROL. WORK IS AMONG FIRST TO UTILIZE CONCEPT OF MARGINAL PRODUCTIVITY.

1165 HICKS J.R.
VALUE AND CAPITAL.
LONDON: OXFORD U PR, 1948, 341 PP.
ATTEMPT TO APPLY ALGEBRAIC METHODS TO ECONOMICS. ORIGINALLY PUBLISHED IN 1939, THIS IS A PIONEERING WORK IN THE FIELD OF ECONOMETRICS. DRAWS HEAVILY ON MARSHALL AND PARETO. SECOND EDITION ALSO REFERS TO SAMUELSON AS DIFFERING IN BASIC ASPECTS. ATTEMPTS TO FORMULATE STOCHASTIC SYSTEM OF ANALYSIS.

1166 HICKS J.R.
ESSAYS IN WORLD ECONOMICS.
NEW YORK: OXFORD U. PR., 1959, 274 PP.
EXAMINES POSITION OF GREAT BRITAIN IN WORLD ECONOMY. USING NIGERIA, CEYLON AND EAST AFRICA AS CASE STUDIES, REVIEWS PROBLEMS OF ECONOMIC DEVELOPMENT IN UNDERDEVELOPED COUNTRIES. CONCLUDES THAT ECONOMIC ACTIVITY LEADS TO ATTAINMENT OF EXTRA-ECONOMIC ENDS OF FREEDOM AND JUSTICE.

1167 HICKS U.K., CARNELL F.G. ET AL.
FEDERALISM AND ECONOMIC GROWTH IN UNDERDEVELOPED COUNTRIES.
NEW YORK: OXFORD U PR, 1961, 185 PP.
ANTHROPOLOGISTS, POLITICAL THEORISTS, AND ECONOMISTS DISCUSS ATTEMPTS OF UNDERDEVELOPED COUNTRIES TO ORGANIZE ECONOMY POLITICALLY WHEN THERE IS LITTLE REAL SENSE OF POLITICAL UNITY IN THESE NATIONS. ASSESSES PROBLEMS AND POSES SOLUTIONS. DESCRIBES CONDITIONS NECESSARY TO THEIR SUCCESS. SPECIAL ATTENTION GIVEN TO CONSTITUTIONAL ATTEMPTS TO CONTROL ECONOMY.

1168 HIGGINS B.
UNITED NATIONS AND U.S. FOREIGN ECONOMIC POLICY.
HOMEWOOD: IRWIN, 1962, 235 PP., $5.25.
CONSIDERS AMOUNT AND KINDS OF AID USA SHOULD GIVE THROUGH UN OR BILATERALLY TO MEET OBJECTIVES. REVIEWS USA AND UN AID ALLOCATION. RECOMMENDS IDEAL STRUCTURE FOR EXECUTING USA FOREIGN POLICY.

1169 HILDEBRAND G.H.
"SECOND THOUGHTS ON THE NEGATIVE INCOME TAX."
INDUSTRIAL RELATIONS, 6 (FEB. 67), 138-154.
THIS DISCUSSION, A RECONSIDERATION OF THE IDEA OF A NEGATIVE INCOME TAX, TRACES THE VARIOUS PROS AND CONS OF SUCH A DEVICE AS A SOLUTION TO POVERTY. WHILE TECHNICAL PROBLEMS ARE POSSIBLY SURMOUNTABLE, PROBLEMS OF COST AND IDEOLOGY SUGGEST THAT, AT LEAST FOR THE PRESENT, IT WOULD BETTER TO RECONSTRUCT EXISTING PUBLIC ASSISTANCE PROGRAMS, BASING THEM SOLELY ON NEED AND ACCEPTING THAT ASSISTANCE IS A RIGHT.

1170 HILDEBRAND J.R.
"THE CENTRAL AMERICAN COMMON MARKET: ECONOMIC AND POLITICAL INTEGRATION."
J. INTER-AMER. STUDIES, 9 (JULY 67), 383-395.
EXAMINES SOME ISSUES ARISING FROM STEPS TOWARD ECONOMIC

AND POLITICAL INTEGRATION ON A WIDE VARIETY OF REGIONAL AND LOBAL BASES. REVIEWS IN PARTICULAR, DEVELOPMENTS SUCH AS THE CENTRAL AMERICAN COMMON MARKET, SHOWING HOW IT IS RESULT OF CERTAIN CHANGES IN GENERAL CONCERN AND AWARENESS OF CURRENT PROBLEMS AND POSSIBILITIES.

1171 HILL L.W.
"FINANCING URBAN RENEWAL PROGRAMS."
MUNICIPAL FINANCE, 40 (AUG. 67), 10-16.
DISCUSSES MEANS OF RAISING MONEY FOR REBUILDING OF SLUM AREAS AND EXPANSION OF HOUSING FACILITIES TO MEET POPULATION GROWTH. INCLUDES FEDERAL GRANT, LOAN, LOCAL BOND, AND COOPERATIVE EFFORT.

1172 HILTON G.W.
"FEDERAL PARTICIPATION IN THE SUPERSONIC TRANSPORT PROGRAM."
BUSINESS HORIZONS, 10 (SUMMER 67), 21-28.
NQUIRY INTO TECHNOLOGICAL PROBLEMS AND ECONOMIC PROSPECTS OF SUPERSONIC TRANSPORT PLANE. EVALUATES QUESTION OF FEDERAL PARTICIPATION IN LIGHT OF PUBLIC EXPENDITURES. FEELS GOVERNMENT SHOULD GET INVOLVED.

1173 HINDLEY D.
"FOREIGN AID TO INDONESIA AND ITS POLITICAL IMPLICATIONS."
PACIFIC AFFAIRS, 36 (SUMMER 63), 107-119.
FEELS THAT FOREIGN AID IS PRIMARILY A TOOL WITH WHICH DONOR GOVERNMENTS SEEK TO PRODUCE POLITICAL RESULTS TO BENEFIT THEMSELVES. OUTLINES SOURCES, AMOUNTS, AND UTILIZATION OF AID RECEIVED BY INDONESIAN GOVERNMENT SINCE 1949. EXAMINES SHORT-TERM AND LONGER-TERM EFFECTS OF THIS AID ON POLITICAL SITUATION WITHIN INDONESIA.

1174 HINSHAW R.
THE EUROPEAN COMMUNITY AND AMERICAN TRADE: A STUDY IN ATLANTIC ECONOMICS AND POLICY.
NEW YORK: PRAEGER, 1964, 188 PP., $4.95.
EVALUATES COMMON MARKET AND RELATED ORGANIZATIONS IN TERMS OF AMERICAN INTERESTS. SHOWS HOW UNDERDEVELOPED NATIONS AFFECTED BY EUROPEAN MOVES TOWARD INTEGRATION. EXAMINES IMPLICATIONS FOR AMERICAN TRADE POLICY.

1175 HIRSCHFIELD R.S.
THE CONSTITUTION AND THE COURT.
NEW YORK: MCGRAW HILL, 1962, 257 PP., LC#62-10672.
DEALS WITH ESSENTIAL ELEMENT IN DYNAMISM OF AMERICAN GOVERNMENT: PROCESS OF CONSTITUTIONAL DEVELOPMENT THROUGH JUDICIAL INTERPRETATION OF LAW. STUDIES SUPREME COURT ACTION IN FOUR AREAS: ECONOMIC REGULATION, RACIAL EQUALITY, CIVIL LIBERTY, AND WARTIME GOVERNMENT.

1176 HIRSCHMAN A.O.
STRATEGY OF ECONOMIC DEVELOPMENT.
NEW HAVEN: YALE U. PR., 1958, 217 PP.
ASSERTS ECONOMIC GROWTH ARISES FROM ACHIEVING AN INDEPENDENT INTERLOCKING ADVANCE OF ALL NECESSARY GROWTH FACTORS, WITH SUCH ADVANCES CREATING NEEDS FOR OTHER ADVANCES. FAVORS THE PURPOSEFUL CREATION OF UNBALANCED GROWTH FACTORS WHICH WILL STIMULATE GROWTH BY CREATING RADIATING DEMANDS TO CORRECT THESE INBALANCES.

1177 HIRSCHMAN A.O.
JOURNEYS TOWARD PROGRESS: STUDIES OF ECONOMIC POLICY-MAKING IN LATIN AMERICA.
NEW YORK: TWENTIETH CENT. FUND, 1963, 308 PP., $4.00.
STUDIES PROBLEMS OF LAND REFORMS IN COLOMBIA, VARIOUS ATTEMPTS TO IMPROVE LIVING CONDITIONS IN NORTHEAST BRAZIL, AND INFLATIONS IN CHILE. SEES THE WHOLE SPECTRUM OF CHANGE IN NEW LIGHTS, AS COMING ABOUT NEITHER THROUGH CONVENTIONALLY PRESCRIBED METHODS, NOR THROUGH REVOLUTIONS, BUT THROUGH A PROCESS DESCRIBED AS 'REFORMMONGERING.'

1178 HIRSHLEIFER J.
"THE BAYESIAN APPROACH TO STATISTICAL DECISION: AN EXPOSITION."
J. OF BUSINESS, 34 (OCT. 61), 471-489.
A GUIDE TO RECENT DEVELOPMENTS IN DECISION THEORY KNOWN AS "THE BAYESIAN APPROACH" TO STATTSTICAL INFERENCE OR DECISION. DISCUSSES HOW THE NEW THEORY HAS EVOLVED FROM PROBLEMS OF BUSINESS DECISION UNDER UNCERTAINTY AND HOW IT REQUIRES A BASIC CHANGE IN STATISTICAL PRACTICE AT LEVELS OF "TESTS OF SIGNIFICANCE", "CONFIDENCE-INTERVAL ESTIMATION." CONTRASTS BAYESIAN APPROACH TO CURRENT OBJECTIVITST STANDARD PRACTICE.

1179 HITCH C.J., MCKEAN R.
THE ECONOMICS OF DEFENSE IN THE NUCLEAR AGE.
CAMBRIDGE: HARVARD U. PR., 1960, 442 PP., $9.50.
ESTABLISHES MUTUAL RELATIONS OF MILITARY AND ECONOMIC PROBLEMS, DEMONSTRATING CAUSAL CONNECTION BETWEEN AVAILABLE RESOURCES AND DEFENSE STRATEGY. DISCUSSES THE ECONOMICS OF MILITARY ALLIANCES, DISARMAMENT, AND MOBILIZATION. STRESS PLACED ON PROBLEMS ARISING FROM REVOLUTION IN TECHNOLOGY.

1180 HLA MYINT U.
THE ECONOMICS OF THE DEVELOPING COUNTRIES.
LONDON: HUTCHINSON & CO, 1965, 192 PP., LC#65-15656.
RELATES THE NATURE AND CAUSES OF THE POVERTY OF UNDERDEVELOPED COUNTRIES AND THE NEED TO DO SOMETHING ABOUT IT. USES ALTERNATIVE MODELS OF ANALYSIS TO ILLUSTRATE THE DIFFERENT TYPES OF UNDERDEVELOPED COUNTRY AT DIFFERENT STAGES OF DEVELOPMENT. MAINLY CONCERNED WITH THE THEORETICAL PROBLEMS OF LONG-TERM ECONOMIC DEVELOPMENT, AUTHOR OPPOSES ARBITRARY FOREIGN AID.

1181 HO YHI-MIN
AGRICULTURAL DEVELOPMENT OF TAIWAN: 1903-1960.
NASHVILLE: VANDERBILT U PR, 1966, 172 PP., LC#66-25966.
STUDIES AGRICULTURAL DEVELOPMENT, ANALYZING SOURCES AND PATTERNS OF CHANGE FROM 1901-60 AND MEASURING GROWTH IN OUTPUT FROM CHANGES IN INPUT AND OTHER GROWTH STATISTICS. DISCUSSES ROLE OF LABOR, CAPITAL, AND RURAL EDUCATION ON AGRICULTURAL DEVELOPMENT.

1182 HOAG M.W.
"ECONOMIC PROBLEMS OF ALLIANCE."
J. POLIT. ECON., 65 (DEC. 57), 522-34.
EVALUATES THE CUSTOMARY VIEW OF ALLIANCE AND ITS DRAWBACKS, THEN CONSIDERS ALTERNATE VIEWS IN TERMS OF RELEVANCY AND WORKABILITY. BELIEVES WE ARE LIVING IN AN AGE OF FERMENT IN MILITARY STRATEGY, AND USING NATO AS AN EXAMPLE, SHOWS THE UNDERLYING IMPORTANCE OF ECONOMICS.

1183 HOBBS E.H.
BEHIND THE PRESIDENT - A STUDY OF EXECUTIVE OFFICE AGENCIES.
WASHINGTON: PUBLIC AFFAIRS PRESS, 1954, 248 PP., LC#53-5789.
EXAMINES OPERATION OF VARIOUS EXECUTIVE OFFICE AGENCIES AND COUNCILS, SUCH AS BUREAU OF BUDGET, NATIONAL RESOURCES PLANNING BOARD, NATIONAL SECURITY COUNCIL, COUNCIL OF ECONOMIC ADVISERS, ETC.

1184 HOBSON J.A.
THE EVOLUTION OF MODERN CAPITALISM.
NEW YORK: CHAS SCRIBNER'S SONS, 1912, 449 PP.
TRACES DEVELOPMENT OF CAPITALISM FROM MEDIEVAL STATES TO 1900'S, EMPHASIZING EFFECTS OF MECHANIZATION UPON IT. DISCUSSES INDUSTRIALIZATION'S EFFECTS ON WELL-BEING OF VARIOUS CLASSES, DECIDING LOWER CLASSES BENEFIT LEAST. ATTEMPTS TO FIND HUMANISTIC SOLUTION TO THIS PROBLEM. CLAIMS MACHINE TENDING IS MAJOR DYSFUNCTION OF INDUSTRIALISM, SINCE WORK IS SO DULL THAT CONSUMPTION WILL NOT COMPENSATE FOR IT.

1185 HOBSON J.A.
WORK AND WEALTH.
NEW YORK: MACMILLAN, 1914, 367 PP.
SUPPORTS NOTION OF GOLD STANDARD AS STABLE MEASURE FOR PRICING GOODS, BUT SEEKS TO FIND MORE MEANINGFUL MEASURE IN COST OF LABOR NEEDED TO PRODUCE THEM. CONCERNED WITH WASTE OF MANPOWER BY MODERN INDUSTRY. ATTEMPTS A HUMANISTIC EVALUATION OF MODERN INDUSTRIAL PROCESSES. DISCUSSES INCOME, PRODUCTIVITY, CAPITALISM, DEMOCRACY, AND UTILITY TO DETERMINE VALUE OF SUCH A SOCIETY.

1186 HOBSON J.A.
INCENTIVES IN THE NEW INDUSTRIAL ORDER.
NEW YORK: THOMAS SELTZER, 1923, 160 PP.
DISCUSSES EFFECT OF INCREASING GOVERNMENT CONTROL OF INDUSTRY IN US, DEFENDING RESTRICTION OF PROFITEERING AND AUTOCRACY FROM CRITICS WHO CLAIM IT WILL HINDER PROGRESS AND CAUSE BREAKDOWN OF AUTHORITY IN SHOPS. ATTEMPTS POSTULATION OF PSYCHOLOGICAL REASONS WHY INCREASED WORKER WELFARE LEADS TO GREATER PRODUCTIVITY.

1187 HOBSON J.A.
IMPERIALISM.
LONDON: ALLEN UNWIN, 1938, 386 PP.
STUDY DESIGNED TO GIVE MORE PRECISION TO A TERM WHICH HAS BECOME A POWERFUL MOVEMENT IN THE CURRENT POLITICS OF THE CIVILIZED WORLD. IN PART ONE THE ECONOMIC ORIGINS OF IMPERIALISM ARE TRACED WITH STATISTICAL METHODS AND RESULTS PROVIDED. IN PART TWO THE THEORY AND PRACTICE OF IMPERIALISM ARE INVESTIGATED AS WELL AS ITS POLITICAL AND MORAL REACTIONS UPON THE WESTERN NATION ENGAGING IN IT.

1188 HODGKINS J.A.
SOVIET POWER: ENERGY RESOURCES, PRODUCTION AND POTENTIALS.
ENGLEWOOD CLIFFS: PRENTICE HALL, 1961, 189 PP., LC#61-12382.
RESEARCH INTO SOVIET ECONOMIC RESOURCES, ESPECIALLY MINERAL FUELS. DISCUSSES GEOGRAPHIC DISTRIBUTION; ENERGY POTENTIAL; PRODUCTION AND CONSUMPTION OF COAL, OIL SHALE, AND NATURAL GAS, EXTENSIVE STATISTICAL TABLES.

1189 HODGKINSON R.G.
THE ORIGINS OF THE NATIONAL HEALTH SERVICE: THE MEDICAL SERVICES OF THE NEW POOR LAW, 1834-1871.
BERKELEY: U OF CALIF PR, 1967, 725 PP.
STUDIES GROWTH OF BRITISH STATE MEDICAL SERVICES FROM POOR LAW OF 1834 TO 20TH-CENTURY WELFARE STATE. EXAMINES INADEQUACIES OF THIS LAW WHICH DETHRONED WEALTHY RISTOCRATS BUT OFFERED LITTLE MEDICAL RELIEF FOR POOR IN NEW RBAN SLUMS. REVIEWS LATER NATIONAL HEALTH SERVICE WHICH GREW OUT OF OMISSIONS OF POOR LAW AND GAVE RISE TO A NEW POLITICS OF POVERTY. DISCUSSES PRESENT FAILURES AND WEAKNESSES.

1190 HOFFMAN P.
"OPERATION BREAKTHROUGH."
FOR. AFF., 38, (OCT. 59), 31-45.
ESTIMATES RATES OF IMPROVEMENT IN LIVING STANDARDS IN UNDERDEVELOPED COUNTRIES. ATTRIBUTES FAILURE TO UNDERESTIMATION OF COMPLEXITY OF JOBS, LACK OF LONG-TERM PLANNING, INADEQUATE DEVELOPMENT PROGRAMS IN EDUCATION AND VOCATIONAL TRAINING, AND POLITICAL STRINGS ATTACHED TO ECONOMIC AID FROM INDUSTRIAL COUNTRIES. FEELS CORRECTION OF THESE DRAWBACKS NECESSARY FOR ECONOMIC STABILITY.

1191 HOFFMAN P.G.
ONE HUNDRED COUNTRIES, ONE AND ONE QUARTER BILLION PEOPLE.
WASHINGTON: A D + M LASKER FDN, 1960, 62 PP.
EXAMINES GROWTH OF GOVERNMENTAL ASSISTANCE TO UNDERDEVELOPED NATIONS. DISCUSSES MANPOWER NEEDS, WORK OF UN, TRADE POLICIES, AND GENERAL PURPOSES AND METHODS OF DISTRIBUTION OF ECONOMIC AID. CHARTS.

1192 HOGAN J.
THE US BALANCE OF PAYMENTS AND CAPITAL FLOWS.
NEW YORK: FREDERICK PRAEGER, 1967, 195 PP., LC#66-18904.
EXAMINES MONETARY EXCHANGE AND CREDIT SYSTEM OF WESTERN HEMISPHERE (BRETTON WOODS SYSTEM), TRACING ITS DEVELOPMENT FROM WWI TO PRESENT AND EMPHASIZING DISADVANTAGES TO US AND BRITAIN BECAUSE DOLLAR AND POUND ARE MOST IMPORTANT EXCHANGE CURRENCIES.

1193 HOGARTY R.A.
NEW JERSEY FARMERS AND MIGRANT HOUSING RULES (PAMPHLET)
INDIANAPOLIS: BOBBS-MERRILL, 1966, 19 PP.
DESCRIBES ATTEMPTS OF UNORGANIZED MIGRANT FARM LABOR GROUP TO OVERCOME RESISTANCE OF WELL-ORGANIZED, HIGHLY REPRESENTED NEW JERSEY GROWERS. ISSUE WAS TO CARRY OUT STATE REGULATION REQUIRING GROWERS TO PROVIDE HOT WATER IN MIGRANT HOUSING.

1194 HOLDSWORTH W.S.
A HISTORY OF ENGLISH LAW; THE COMMON LAW AND ITS RIVALS (VOL. VI)
LONDON: METHUEN, 1924, 763 PP.
CONCERNED WITH PUBLIC AND ENACTED LAW OF 17TH CENTURY. BEGINS WITH LAW UNDER STUART KINGS AND DISCUSSES PERIOD OF CIVIL WAR AND COMMONWEALTH. INCLUDES POLITICAL THEORIES, PRINCIPLES OF PUBLIC LAW, ROYAL PROCLAMATIONS, AND LAWS ON COMMERCE AND INDUSTRY, AGRICULTURE, PRESS, AND FRAUDS. ENDS WITH PROFESSIONAL DEVELOPMENT OF LAW - GROWTH OF LEGAL PROFESSION, LAWYERS, DIVISIONS, AND LITERATURE.

1195 HOLDSWORTH W.S.
A HISTORY OF ENGLISH LAW; THE COMMON LAW AND ITS RIVALS (VOL. IV)
LONDON: METHUEN, 1924, 600 PP.
CONCERNED WITH DEVELOPMENT OF MODERN ENGLISH LAW AND INFLUENCES SHAPING LEGAL STRUCTURE. BEGINS WITH PUBLIC LAW OF 16TH CENTURY AND CLOSES WITH ENACTED LAW OF 16TH AND EARLY 17TH CENTURIES. INCLUDES CRIMINAL LAW AND PROCEDURE, LAND LAW AND ECCLESIASTICAL LAW, CIVIL PROCEDURE, USE OF COMMON LAW, PROCLAMATIONS AND STATUTES, COMMERCIAL AND AGRICULTURAL POLICIES, AND LAW IN EUROPEAN COURTS.

1196 HOLLAND E.P., GILLESPIE R.W.
EXPERIMENTS ON A SIMULATED UNDERDEVELOPED ECONOMY: DEVELOPMENT PLANS AND BALANCE-OF-PAYMENTS POLICIES.
CAMBRIDGE: M.I.T. PR., 1963, 289 PP., $8.00.
A SIMULATION OF A NATIONAL ECONOMY MODEL FOR EXPLORING SOME OF THE COMPLEX PROBLEMS OF DEVELOPMENT. TESTS ALTERNATIVE POLICY COMBINATIONS. SUGGESTS METHODS FOR DESIGNING ECONOMIC STRATEGY.

1197 HOLLER J.E.
POPULATION TRENDS AND ECONOMIC DEVELOPMENT IN THE FAR EAST (PAMPHLET)
WASH,DC: G WASH U, POP RES PROJ, 1965, 56 PP., LC#65-23384.
EXAMINES POPULATION TRENDS AND ECONOMIC DEVELOPMENT IN EIGHT FAR EASTERN COUNTRIES: JAPAN, CHINA, TAIWAN, HONG KONG, NORTH AND SOUTH KOREA, OUTER MONGOLIA, AND THE PHILIPPINES. CONCLUDES THAT ECONOMIC GROWTH DEPENDS ON CONTROL OF POPULATION, THAT INDUSTRIALIZATION IS DEPENDENT ON SOLUTIONS TO AGRICULTURAL PROBLEMS, AND THAT TRADITIONAL BEHAVIOR MUST BE MADE MORE RATIONAL.

1198 HOLLEY I.B. JR.
US ARMY IN WORLD WAR II: SPECIAL STUDIES: BUYING AIRCRAFT: MATERIEL PROCUREMENT FOR THE ARMY AIR FORCES.
WASHINGTON: US GOVERNMENT, 1964, 643 PP., LC#64-60000.
STUDY OF PROBLEMS OF BUDGET, DESIGN, CONTRACT AND MANUFACTURE OF AIRCRAFT, ESPECIALLY IN MASS PRODUCTION IN AUTOMOBILE PLANTS. ANALYZES RELATIONSHIP BETWEEN GOVERNMENT AND INDUSTRY PLUS POLITICAL, LEGAL, AND ECONOMIC COMPLICATIONS IN OUR SOCIETY. AIMS TO EXPEDITE FUTURE PROCUREMENT OF COMPLICATED, EXPENSIVE WEAPONS.

1199 HOMAN A.G.
SOME MEASURES AND INTERPRETATIONS OF EFFECTS OF US FOREIGN ENTERPRISES ON US BALANCE OF PAYMENTS.
MENLO PARK: STANFORD U RES INST, 1962, 65 PP.
SHOWS HOW US PRIVATE FOREIGN INVESTMENTS AFFECT DEFICIT IN BALANCE OF PAYMENTS. VARIABLES OF DIRECT EFFECTS INCLUDE METHODS OF FINANCING AND EXPANDING FOREIGN ENTERPRISES, EARNINGS TRANSFERRED OR REINVESTED, AND NET EFFECT OF TRADE. RESULTS INDICATE THAT BALANCE OF PAYMENTS WAS POSITIVELY AFFECTED BY US FOREIGN INVESTMENTS DURING 1950-59.

1200 HOLMANS A.E.
UNITED STATES FISCAL POLICY 1945-1959.
LONDON: OXFORD U PR, 1961, 342 PP.
STUDIES CONTRIBUTION OF FISCAL POLICY TO ECONOMIC STABILITY, INCLUDING POLITICAL AND HISTORICAL BACKGROUND, COMPARISON OF REPUBLICAN AND DEMOCRATIC POLICIES, AND EFFECTS OF COLD WAR. DEALS WITH INFLATION AND RECESSION.

1201 HOLT R.T., TURNER J.E.
THE POLITICAL BASIS OF ECONOMIC DEVELOPMENT.
PRINCETON: VAN NOSTRAND, 1966, 411 PP.
ANALYZES ECONOMIC DEVELOPMENT AS A FUNCTION OF POLITICAL AND SOCIAL CHANGE, USING HISTORICAL EXAMPLES. COMPARES POLITICAL SYSTEMS AND THEIR RESPECTIVE EFFECTS ON CULTURE AND ECONOMIC GROWTH.

1202 HOMANS G.C.
"THE WESTERN ELECTRIC RESEARCHES" IN S. HOSLETT, ED., HUMAN FACTORS IN MANAGEMENT (BMR)"
NEW YORK: HARPER & ROW, 1951.
A DISCUSSION OF THE PROGRAM OF MANAGEMENT RESEARCH AND OF THE WORKER, CONDUCTED AT THE CHICAGO WORKS OF THE WESTERN ELECTRIC COMPANY. EXAMINES A NUMBER OF EXPERIMENTS TESTING THE HAPPINESS AND RESULTING PRODUCTIVITY OF THE WORKERS IN THIS PLANT. ANALYZES THE FAILURE AND SUCCESS OF THESE EXPERIMENTS.

1203 HONDURAS CONSEJO NAC DE ECO
PLAN NACIONAL DE DESARROLLO ECONOMICO Y SOCIAL DE HONDURAS 1965-69.
TEGUCIGALPA: SECRETAR NAC DE ECO, 1965, 1111 PP.
FOUR PART PLAN FOR ECONOMIC AND SOCIAL DEVELOPMENT OF HONDURAS FROM 1965 TO 1969 PREPARED BY HONDURAN NATIONAL COUNCIL OF ECONOMICS. COVERS GENERAL PROBLEMS OF ECONOMY AND PROGRAM METHOD, PUBLIC INVESTMENT, AGRICULTURAL DEVELOPMENT, AND INDUSTRIAL DEVELOPMENT.

1204 HOOD W.C.
FINANCING OF ECONOMIC ACTIVITY IN CANADA.
OTTAWA: ROYAL COMN CANADA'S ECO, 1958, 700 PP.
STUDIES FLOW OF FUNDS TO AND FROM MAJOR SECTORS AND FINANCIAL INSTITUTIONS OF CANADIAN ECONOMY CONTROLS EXERCISED OVER THESE FLOWS BY PRICES OF REAL AND FINANCIAL ASSETS, LAWS AND GOVERNMENT POLICY, AND PRIVATE PRACTICES AND TRADITIONS. SHOWS RESPECTS IN WHICH SYSTEM WORKS WELL AND THOSE IN WHICH ITS FUNCTIONING MIGHT BE IMPROVED.

1205 HOOPES R.
THE STEEL CRISIS.
NEW YORK: JOHN DAY, 1963, 314 PP., LC#63-10226.
ANALYSIS OF BACKGROUND AND DEVELOPMENTS OF CONFLICT BETWEEN KENNEDY ADMINISTRATION AND STEEL INDUSTRY OVER PRICE INCREASES AND PRESSURES APPLIED ON INDUSTRY TO REMOVE ITS PRICE INCREASE.

1206 HOOVER C.B.
THE ECONOMY, LIBERTY AND THE STATE.
BALTIMORE: LORD BALTIMORE PR., 1959, 445 PP.
STUDIES THE DIVERGENT ECONOMIC SYSTEMS OF THE WEST AND USSR INDICATING THE RELATIONSHIPS BETWEEN NATIONAL ECONOMIES, INDIVIDUAL LIBERTY AND STATE POWER. EXPLORES DEVELOPMENT OF MODIFIED CAPITALISM IN USA, 'MIXED' SYSTEMS OF EUROPE AND TOTALITARIANISM IN USSR.

1207 HOOVER C.B.
"NATIONAL POLICY AND RATES OF ECONOMIC GROWTH: THE US SOVIET RUSSIA AND WESTERN EUROPE."
S. ATLANT. QUART., 53 (SUMMER 60), 477-89.
SHOWS INTERDEPENDENCY OF NATIONAL POLICY AND RATES OF ECONOMIC GROWTH. COMPARES AND ANALYZES ECONOMIC TRENDS IN INDUSTRIALIZED COUNTRIES LIKE USA, USSR AND COUNTRIES OF WESTERN EUROPE. IMPLIES THAT RATES OF ECONOMIC GROWTH INFLUENCE NATIONAL POLICY.

1208 HOOVER C.B. ET AL.
ECONOMIC SYSTEMS OF THE COMMONWEALTH.
DURHAM: DUKE U PR, 1962, 538 PP., LC#62-18316.
TWELVE ESSAYS ANALYZING ECONOMIC SYSTEMS OF AUSTRALIA, CANADA, NEW ZEALAND, SOUTH AFRICA, UK, MALAYA, INDIA, PAKISTAN, CEYLON, GHANA, AND WEST INDIES BY SPECIALISTS ON EACH RESPECTIVE COUNTRY. FOCUS ON MODELS OF ECONOMIC SYSTEMS.

1209 HOOVER C.B.
"ECONOMIC REFORM VERSUS ECONOMIC GROWTH IN UNDERDEVELOPED COUNTRIES."
VIRGINIA QUART. REV., 39 (SUMMER 63), 369-384.
ASSERTS THAT EMERGING NATIONS SEEKING RAPID INDUSTRIALIZ-

ATION REPUDIATE CAPITALIST PRINCIPLE OF WITHHOLDING CONSUMER INCOME AND RE-INVESTING. PROPOSES METHODS OF SPEEDING INDUSTRIALIZATION AND CITES NEED FOR A FREE MARKET BUT WARNS AGAINST PROMOTING LOFTY EXPECTATIONS OF INCOME AND/OR ECONOMIC REFORM.

1210 HOOVER C.B.
"THE ROLE OF THE NATURAL AND DEVELOPED RESOURCES OF THE NATION STATES."
S. ATLAN. QUART., 63(SPRING 64), 154-65.
SEES THE ROLE OF NATURAL RESOURCES AS AN INDICATOR OF NATIONAL POWER, IN DECLINING USE, DUE, IN LARGE PART, TO THE UNLIKELIHOOD OF A FUTURE WAR BEING LONG AND DRAWN-OUT.

1211 HOOVER E.M.
THE LOCATION OF ECONOMIC ACTIVITY.
NEW YORK: MCGRAW HILL, 1948, 310 PP.
PRESENTS PROBLEMS OF SPATIAL RELATIONS OF ECONOMIC ACTIVITIES. TREATS FACTORS DETERMINING ADVANTAGES OF LOCATION, ACCESS TO SUPPLIERS AND MARKET AND PRODUCTION COST. DISCUSSES URBAN SITES AND ROLE OF ACCESSIBILITY IN DETERMINING LOCATION. ANALYZES CAUSES OF LOCATIONAL CHANGE, AND EFFECTS OF POLITICAL BOUNDARIES ON TRADE, LABOR, AND ADMINISTRATION. EXAMINES AIMS OF PUBLIC LOCATIONAL POLICY.

1212 HOOVER E.M., VERNON R.
ANATOMY OF A METROPOLIS.
GARDEN CITY: DOUBLEDAY, 1962, 338 PP.
ANALYZES THE CHANGING DISTRIBUTION OF PEOPLE AND JOBS WITHIN THE NEW YORK METROPOLITAN REGION. DISCUSSES EXODUS TO THE SUBURBS, WHY SOME JOBS REMAIN IN THE CITIES, WHY PEOPLE LIVE WHERE THEY DO, AND FUTURE PROSPECTS.

1213 HOOVER G.
TWENTIETH CENTURY ECONOMIC THOUGHT.
NEW YORK: PHILO/LIBRARY, 1950, 819 PP.
CONSIDERS MODERN ECONOMIC PROBLEMS CONFRONTING USA COVERING SUCH TOPICS AS SOCIAL SECURITY, GOVERNMENT CONTROL OF AGRICULTURAL PRICES, 'GURANTEED AND JUST WAGES,' LABOR UNIONS, IMMIGRATION, MONETARY FLUCTUATION, TAXATION AND INTERNATIONAL ECONOMIC POLICIES.

1214 HORECKY P.L.
"LIBRARY OF CONGRESS PUBLICATIONS IN AID OF USSR AND EAST EUROPEAN RESEARCH."
SLAVIC REVIEW, 23 (JAN. 64), 309-327.
AN ANNOTATED BIBLIOGRAPHY OF RESEARCH AIDS PUBLISHED BY THE LIBRARY OF CONGRESS TO ASSIST IN RESEARCHING USSR AND EAST EUROPEAN MATERIAL IN THE LIBRARY OF CONGRESS. CONTAINS ENTRIES IN ENGLISH, RANGING FROM 1929-1963.

1215 HOROWITZ D.
HEMISPHERES NORTH AND SOUTH: ECONOMIC DISPARITY AMONG NATIONS.
BALTIMORE: JOHNS HOPKINS PRESS, 1966, 118 PP., LC#66-23002.
ATTEMPTS TO CONSTRUCT BRIDGE BETWEEN NEW ECONOMICS AND REALITIES OF SITUATION IN WORLD DIVIDED BETWEEN HAVES AND HAVE-NOTS, AND TO JOIN ECONOMIC AND POLITICAL ACTION TOWARD IMPLEMENTATION OF A POLICY OF CHANGE. PROPOSES THAT INTERESTS OF DEVELOPING NATIONS RECEIVE PRIORITY IN POLICY EVEN AT PRICE OF SLIGHT SLOWING DOWN IN EXPANSION OF RICH NATIONS.

1216 HOROWITZ I.L.
THREE WORLDS OF DEVELOPMENT.
NEW YORK: OXFORD U PR, 1966, 475 PP., LC#66-15421.
QUALITATIVE STUDY OF THREE WORLDS OF DEVELOPMENT WHICH DESCRIBES AND EXPLAINS INTERACTION AND INTERPENETRATION OF THE THREE MAIN SOURCES OF ECONOMIC, POLITICAL, AND SOCIAL POWER IN WORLD TODAY. OFFERS A LANGUAGE FOR DEALING WITH INTERNATIONAL STRATIFICATION AND A STYLE OF HANDLING SOCIAL FACTS. INTENDED AS A CAUSAL AND INTERPRETATIVE STUDY IN SOCIOLOGICAL MEANINGS.

1217 HORVATH B.
THE CHARACTERISTICS OF YUGOSLAV ECONOMIC DEVELOPMENT.
SOCIALIST THOUGHT AND PRACTICE, (NO.1, 61), 83-97.
ANALYZES IN DETAIL FACTORS CONTRIBUTING TO HIGH RATE OF ECONOMIC GROWTH IN POSTWAR YUGOSLAVIA, EMPHASIZING REASONS FOR GROWTH AND FUTURE CAPABILITIES. THEORIZES AS TO PROJECTED PRODUCTIVITY OF LABOR AND CAPITAL INVESTMENT.

1218 HOSELITZ B.F.
"THE ROLE OF CITIES IN THE ECONOMIC GROWTH OF UNDERDEVELOPED COUNTRIES" IN "SOCIOLOGICAL ASPECTS OF ECONOMIC GROWTH"(BMR)
NEW YORK: FREE PRESS OF GLENCOE, 1960.
SUGGESTS VARIOUS PROBLEM AREAS THAT ARISE IN STUDYING THE PROCESS OF URBANIZATION AND IN THE STUDY OF TOWNS AND CITIES OF UNDERDEVELOPED AREAS. DISCUSSES IMPACT OF MEDIEVAL URBAN CENTERS ON WESTERN CULTURE, AND ENLARGES R. REDFIELD'S TYPOLOGY OF RURAL-URBAN RELATIONSHIPS. AUTHOR OFFERS A NUMBER OF POSSIBLE NEW APPROACHES TO STUDY OF INTERRELATION BETWEEN URBANIZATION AND INDUSTRIALIZATION.

1219 HOSELITZ B.F. ED.
THE PROGRESS OF UNDERDEVELOPED AREAS.
CHICAGO: U. CHI. PR., 1952, 297 PP.
SPECIALISTS IN VARIOUS SOCIAL SCIENCES CONSIDER PROBLEMS OF RENDERING ECONOMIC AID TO UNDERDEVELOPED COUNTRIES. INDICATE THAT ECONOMIC DEVELOPMENT IS A PROBLEM AREA WITH DIMENSIONS IN SEVERAL SOCIAL SCIENCE FIELDS. STRESS HUMAN IMPLICATIONS OF TECHNOLOGICAL AND ECONOMIC CHANGE.

1220 HOSELITZ B.F.
THEORIES OF ECONOMIC GROWTH.
GLENCOE: FREE PR., 1960, 344 PP.
RANGE OF SUBJECT MATTER INCLUDES CONTRIBUTIONS TO THE 'DISMAL SCIENCE' MADE BY MERCANTILISTS, CLASSICAL AND NEO-CLASSICIST ECONOMISTS AND JS MILLS. EMPHASIS ON THEORIES PRESCRIBING 'SERIES OF STAGES'

1221 HOSELITZ B.F.
SOCIOLOGICAL ASPECTS OF ECONOMIC GROWTH.
GLENCOE: FREE PR., 1960, 250 PP.
REVIEWS EXTENT OF ECONOMIC GROWTH THEORIES, POPULATION PRESSURES, INDUSTRIALIZATION AND SOCIAL MOBILITY. DISCUSSES URBANIZATION AND SUGGESTS TYPOLOGY OF CITIES WITH REGARD TO ECONOMIC EXPANSION. PROBES RELATIONSHIP OF SOCIAL DEVIANCE TO ECONOMIC INNOVATIONS.

1222 HOSELITZ B.F., WEINER M.
"ECONOMIC DEVELOPMENT AND POLITICAL STABILITY IN INDIA"
DISSENT, 8 (SPRING 61), 172-179.
THEORIZES THAT ECONOMIC DEVELOPMENT AND POLITICAL STABILITY IN INDIA ARE NOT POSITIVELY RELATED. MAINTAINS THAT DEVELOPMENT BENEFITS FROM POLITICAL ACTIVITY AND FOSTERS POLITICAL INSTABILITY. DEVELOPMENT POLICY OF INDIA WILL NOT HELP POLITICAL SITUATION; SOLUTION MUST COME FROM WITHIN POLITICS.

1223 HOSELITZ B.F. ED.
ECONOMICS AND THE IDEA OF MANKIND.
NEW YORK: COLUMB. U. PR., 1965, 277 PP., $6.95.
ESSAYS BASED ON ASSUMPTION THAT MANKIND INTERDEPENDENT. STUDY HOW MANKIND WOULD FUNCTION AS WHOLE IN PRODUCTION, DISTRIBUTION, AND CONSUMPTION OF GOODS AND WHAT WOULD CHARACTERIZE SUCH AN ECONOMY.

1224 HOSHII I.
"JAPAN'S STAKE IN ASIA."
ORIENT/WEST, 12 (1967), 89-143.
DISCUSSES RELATION OF JAPAN TO REST OF ASIA. HER AMBIGUOUS ROLE IN THE EAST HAS BEEN CAUSE FOR MUCH CONCERN. BASICALLY CAPITALISTIC, SHE CONFRONTS ONE OF THE LARGEST COMMUNIST COUNTRIES. ANALYZES POSSIBILITY OF JAPAN'S JOINING AFRO-ASIAN BLOC.

1225 HOWE M.
"THE TRANSPORT ACT, 1962, AND THE CONSUMERS' CONSULTATIVE COMMITTEES."
PUBLIC ADMINISTRATION, 42 (SPRING 64), 45-56.
REVIEW OF FUNCTIONS, PROCEDURES, AND POWERS CONSUMERS' COMMITTEES HAVE OVER STATE-CONTROLLED TRANSPORT SERVICES. IN FACT, CONSUMERS HAVE LITTLE POWER TO AFFECT POLICY EXCEPT WHERE COMPLETE CUT-OFF OF SERVICE IS PROPOSED.

1226 HOWE R.W.
BLACK AFRICA: FROM PRE-HISTORY TO THE EVE OF THE COLONIAL ERA.
NEW YORK: WALKER, 1966, 318 PP., LC#67-14265.
HISTORICAL NARRATIVE COVERS ALL TERRITORY SOUTH OF THE SAHARA, TRADE AND CONQUEST, AND DEVELOPMENT OF AGGRESSIVE AND PROGRESSIVE STATES. ALSO EXAMINES TRIBAL SOCIETIES, THE SPREAD OF RELIGION, COLONIZATION, AND INDEPENDENCE. PROVIDES A SURVEY OF AFRICAN HISTORY AND OFFERS A SELECT BIBLIOGRAPHY OF FRENCH AND ENGLISH TITLES.

1228 HUBBARD P.H.
"MONETARY RECOVERY UNDER THE COPYRIGHT, PATENT, AND TRADEMARK ACTS."
TEXAS LAW REVIEW, 45 (APR. 67), 953-983.
ANALYZES MONETARY AWARDS PROVIDED FOR RELIEF OF INFRINGEMENT OF COPYRIGHT, PATENT, AND TRADEMARK ACTS. INCLUDES DISCUSSION OF REMEDIES FOR INFRINGEMENT; INJUNCTION AGAINST FURTHER INFRINGEMENT, IMPOUNDING AND DESTRUCTION OF INFRINGEMENT ITEMS, AND MONETARY AWARDS. CONCENTRATES ON METHODS OF DETERMINING MONETARY SUMS UNDER EACH ACT.

1229 HUBBARD P.J.
ORIGINS OF THE TVA: THE MUSCLE SHOALS CONTROVERSY, 1920-1932
NASHVILLE: VANDERBILT U PR, 1961, 340 PP., LC#61-12300.
ATTEMPTS TO ASCERTAIN POLITICAL AND ECONOMIC ORIGINS OF TENNESSEE VALLEY AUTHORITY THROUGH INVESTIGATION OF STRUGGLE FOR CONTROL OF TENNESSEE RIVER SYSTEM. ANALYZES DISPUTE OVER PUBLIC VS. PRIVATE OPERATION OF IMPORTANT ALABAMA WATER POWER PLANT. INDICATES THAT TVA WAS HANDIWORK OF SMALL GROUP OF PROGRESSIVES IN CONGRESS WHO SOUGHT PLANNED MULTI-PURPOSE DEVELOPMENT OF NATION'S WATER RESOURCES.

1230 HUBERMAN L., SWEEZY P.M.
SOCIALISM IS THE ONLY ANSWER (PAMPHLET)
NEW YORK: MONTHLY REVIEW PR, 1961, 32 PP.

HUBERMAN ANALYZES BASIC DOCTRINES AND GOALS OF SOCIALISM AND POINTS OUT THEIR ROOTS IN CAPITALISTIC US SOCIETY. STRESSES RESPONSIBILITY OF ALL SOCIALISTS TO DEVELOP THESE ROOTS AND CULTIVATE WORLD SOCIALISM. SWEEZY PRESENTS, IN THEORY, ECONOMIC PROGRAM TO BRING US PEACEFULLY TO SOCIALISM.

1231 HUBERMAN L.
MAN'S WORLDLY GOODS: THE STORY OF THE WEALTH OF NATIONS.
NEW YORK: HARPER & ROW, 1936, 349 PP.
EXPLAINS, IN TERMS OF DEVELOPMENT OF ECONOMIC INSTITUTIONS, WHY CERTAIN DOCTRINES AROSE WHEN THEY DID, HOW THEY ORIGINATED IN FABRIC OF SOCIAL LIFE, HOW THEY WERE DEVELOPED, MODIFIED, AND REJECTED. DISCUSSES CLASSIC CYCLE OF FEUDALISM, CAPITALISM, AND MARXISM.

1232 HUELIN D.
"ECONOMIC INTEGRATION IN LATIN AMERICAN: PROGRESS AND PROBLEMS."
INT. AFF., 40 (JULY 64), 430-439.
LATIN AMERICA'S ECONOMIC AND SOCIAL PROBLEMS RELATED TO FAILURE OF REGION TO MAINTAIN SHARE IN WORLD TRADE. LATIN AMERICAN FREE TRADE ASSOCIATION REALIZES FUTURE OF ECONOMIC INTEGRATION LIES IN SIGNIFICANTLY EXPANDING MARKET OF MANUFACTURED GOODS.

1233 HUGHES J.
NATIONALISED INDUSTRIES IN THE MIXED ECONOMY (PAMPHLET)
LONDON: FABIAN SOCIETY, 1960, 40 PP.
ANALYZES RELATIONSHIP BETWEEN NATIONALIZED SECTOR AND PRIVATE SECTOR OF ECONOMY. CONCENTRATES ON PRESSURES EXERTED BY GOVERNMENT ACTION. CRITICIZES CAPITALISTIC ECONOMY FOR SUBORDINATING NATIONALIZED INDUSTRIES TO ITS OWN SHORT-TERM NEEDS. COVERS ORIGINS OF RELATIONSHIP AND SPECIAL PROBLEMS IT BRINGS TO OPERATING NATIONALIZED INDUSTRIES.

1234 HUGHES R.
THE CHINESE COMMUNES; A BACKGROUND BOOK.
NEW YORK: INST OF PACIFIC RELNS, 1960, 90 PP., LC#61-10602.
STUDIES "TOTAL AND RUTHLESS REGIMENTATION OF ALL LIFE, WORK, AND LIVING INSIDE CHINA," LIMITED TO CHINESE COMMUNE SYSTEM. EXPLORES ORIGINS AND DEVELOPMENT, OPERATION AND REVISION OF SYSTEM. MAINTAINS THAT COMMUNES STRENGTHEN COMMUNIST CONTROL OF CHINA AND THAT SYSTEM WILL PERSIST BECAUSE IT INCREASES PRODUCTION AND EFFICIENCY.

1235 HUHNE L.H.
FINANCING ECONOMIC DEVELOPMENT THROUGH NATIONAL AND INTERNATIONAL ORGANIZATIONS (THESIS; U OF WIS.)
MADISON: UNIV OF WISCONSIN, 1962, 199 PP.
EXAMINES POWT-WWII SHIFT FROM PRIVATE TO PUBLIC CAPITAL GOING TO UNDERDEVELOPED COUNTRIES. STRESSES NEED FOR CAPITAL IN THESE AREAS AND DESCRIBES RELATIVE MERITS OF KINDS OF CAPITAL AVAILABLE - SHORT AND LONG-TERM LOANS, INVESTMENTS, AND THE LIKE. ADVOCATES MORE OUTRIGHT GRANTS, ALTHOUGH WARNING AGAINST INFLATION.

1236 HUME D.
"OF TAXES" IN D. HUME, POLITICAL DISCOURSES (1752)"
ORIGINAL PUBLISHER NOT AVAILABLE, 1752.
CALLS FOR REASONABLE APPROACH TO TAXATION, CLAIMING THAT MODERATE TAXES INCREASE INDUSTRY OF THE POOR, RAISE PRODUCTION, LOWER PRICES, AND MAY EVEN IMPROVE LIVING STANDARD OF POOR. HUME WARNS OF HIGH TAXES, WHICH MIGHT FORCE POOR TO CALL FOR INCREASED WAGES, THEREBY MOVING BURDEN TO THE WEALTHY.

1237 HUME D.
"OF THE BALANCE OF TRADE" IN D. HUME, POLITICAL DISCOURSES (1752)"
ORIGINAL PUBLISHER NOT AVAILABLE, 1752.
DISCUSSES INTERNATIONAL TRADE AND THE EFFECTS OF TARIFFS AND CURRENCY UPON IT. SUGGESTS THAT LOWER CURRENCY SUPPLY WOULD INCREASE TRADE SINCE PRICES WOULD HAVE TO FALL. THIS IS BASED ON GOLD STANDARD CURRENCY. LAUDS TRADE AS MEANS FOR INSURING POWER AND WEALTH TO A STATE.

1238 HUME D.
"OF COMMERCE" IN D. HUME, POLITICAL DISCOURSES (1752)"
ORIGINAL PUBLISHER NOT AVAILABLE, 1752.
LINKS COMMERCE TO NATIONAL WELL-BEING. DIVIDING OCCUPATIONS INTO INDUSTRIAL AND AGRICULTURAL, DISCUSSES IMPORTANCE OF COMMERCE TO POSITION OF POWER OF NATION. ALLOWING THAT EXCESS RICHES MAY LEAD TO DEGENERACY, STILL MAINTAINS THAT COMMERCE, AND ESPECIALLY PROFIT, ARE FUNDAMENTAL DETERMINANTS OF A NATION'S POWER.

1239 HUME D.
"OF INTEREST" IN D. HUME, POLITICAL DISCOURSES (1752)"
ORIGINAL PUBLISHER NOT AVAILABLE, 1752.
TAKES ISSUE WITH IDEA THAT LOW INTEREST RATES INDICATE A PLENITUDE OF MONEY. DISCUSSES ARTIFICIALITY OF MONEY AND EFFECT OF DISCOVERY OF LARGE GOLD DEPOSITS IN AFRICA AND THE NEW WORLD UPON PRICES. MORE MONEY INCREASES COST OF LABOR; LOW INTEREST ONLY INDICATES LOW BORROWING DEMAND, GREAT BORROWING RESOURCES, OR LOW COMMERCIAL PROFITS.

1240 HUME D.
"OF MONEY" IN D. HUME, POLITICAL DISCOURSES (1752)"
ORIGINAL PUBLISHER NOT AVAILABLE, 1752.
DISCUSSES MONEY IN MODERN PERSPECTIVE. STATES THAT IT IS NOT A TRUE OBJECT OF COMMERCE, BUT MERELY A TOOL. ATTACKS MERCANTILIST THEORY THAT GOLD IS MEASURE OF WEALTH OF NATIONS, CLAIMING REAL WEALTH TO BE COMMERCE AND MEN IN THE STATE. SUPPORTS FREE CIRCULATION AND TOUCHES ON SUBJECT OF TIGHT CURRENCY.

1241 HUMPHREY D.D.
THE UNITED STATES AND THE COMMON MARKET.
NEW YORK: PRAEGER, 1962, 176 PP.
TRADE IS AN IMPORTANT MEANS OF SUPPORTING BASIC FOREIGN POLICY AND BUILDING INTERNATIONAL ORDER. THE COMMON MARKET HAS PRESENTED A PROBLEM TO OUR TRADE POLICY. USING AN ANALYTIC APPROACH, REFUTES U.S. PROTECTIVE ATTITUDE AND SUGGESTS TRADE EXPANSION THROUGH TARIFF REDUCTION. CONTENDS THAT, IN THIS WAY, USA WILL MAINTAIN INDUSTRIAL LEADERSHIP AND HIGH STANDARD OF LIVING.

1242 HUMPHREY R.A. ED.
UNIVERSITIES...AND DEVELOPMENT ASSISTANCE ABROAD.
WASHINGTON: AMER COUNCIL ON EDUC, 1967, 196 PP., LC#67-16127
ESSAYS FOCUSING ON AMERICAN HIGHER EDUCATION IN OVERSEAS DEVELOPMENT. ATTENTION GIVEN TO PROBLEMS AND POTENTIALITIES OF INSTITUTIONAL COMMITMENT ABROAD.

1243 HUNT C.L.
SOCIAL ASPECTS OF ECONOMIC DEVELOPMENT.
NEW YORK: MCGRAW HILL, 1966, 255 PP., LC#66-20718.
APPLIES SOCIOLOGICAL THEORY TO SPECIFIC DATA CONCERNING ECONOMIC AND SOCIAL CONDITIONS IN SOUTHEAST ASIA. EXAMINES PROBLEMS RELATING TO FAMILY ORGANIZATION; SOCIAL IMMOBILITY; ETHNIC DIVERSITY; EDUCATIONAL NEEDS; CONFLICT OF IDEOLOGIES AND SOCIAL REALITIES; THE RURAL VILLAGE; AGRARIAN REFORMS; AND POPULATION CONTROL.

1244 HUNT R.N.
THE THEORY AND PRACTICE OF COMMUNISM.
LONDON: GEOFFREY BLES, 1950, 231 PP.
EXAMINES MARXIST PHILOSOPHY, THE DEVELOPMENT OF EUROPEAN SOCIALISM, LENIN'S AND STALIN'S CONTRIBUTION TO MARXIST THEORY, AND IMPLEMENTATION OF THEORY IN RUSSIAN STATE.

1245 HUNTER A. ED.
THE ECONOMICS OF AUSTRALIAN INDUSTRY.
MELBOURNE: MELBOURNE UNIV PRESS, 1963, 543 PP.
SYMPOSIUM ON AUSTRALIAN INDUSTRY, WITH SPECIAL ATTENTION TO UNUSUAL FACTORS. PART I DEALS WITH EVNIRONMENT OF MANUFACTURING INDUSTRY--LOCATION, TRANSPORTATION, ELECTRICITY SUPPLY, OVERSEAS INVESTMENT, ETC. PART II STUDIES SPECIFIC INDUSTRIES--THEIR NUMBER AND SIZE, TECHNICAL AND ECONOMIC INTEGRATION WITHIN AN INDUSTRY, RELATIONSHIPS BETWEEN FIRMS, OVERSEAS COMPANIES, AND MONOPOLY.

1246 HUNTER R.
REVOLUTION: WHY, HOW, WHEN?
NEW YORK: HARPER & ROW, 1940, 383 PP.
SURVEYS CONDITIONS LEADING TO REVOLUTIONS 1776-1939, AND CONSIDERS IMPORTANCE OF LEADERSHIP, ECONOMIC UPHEAVAL, WAR, AND CYCLIC CHANGE IN GIVING THEM FORCE AND IMPETUS. CLAIMS THAT REVOLUTION IS AN EVIL, SOMETIMES NECESSARY BUT USUALLY LEADING TO UNREST AND INSTABILITY FOR EXTENDED PERIODS AFTER THEY OCCUR. DISCUSSES BASIC TECHNIQUES OF AGITATION.

1247 HUTCHINGS R.
"THE ENDING OF UNEMPLOYMENT IN THE USSR"
SOVIET STUDIES, 19 (JULY 67), 29-52.
EXAMINES ELIMINATION OF UNEMPLOYMENT IN USSR IN 1930. REASONS ARE INCREASED INDUSTRIALIZATION AND COLLECTIVIZATION OF ECONOMY. DISCUSSES ATTRACTIONS OF COLLECTIVE AGRICULTURAL EMPLOYMENT AND NOTES CORRESPONDENCE OF DATA ON UNEMPLOYMENT AND COLLECTIVIZATION. PROVIDES FIGURES ON LABOR MIGRATION AND REASONS FOR CHANGES IN RATE.

1248 HUTCHINSON E.C.
"AMERICAN AID TO AFRICA."
ANN. AMER. ACAD. POLIT. SOC. SCI., 354 (JULY 64), 65-74.
ARBITRARY BOUNDARIES, TRIBALISM, ILLITERACY, ABSENCE OF NECESSARY ECONOMIC AND SOCIAL INSTITUTIONS, AND CONTRASTING DEVELOPMENT POTENTIALS ARE SOME OBSTACLES TO ECONOMIC DEVELOPMENT. SUGGESTS USA CONCENTRATE ON INCREASING VOLUME AND DEVELOPMENT OF INTERNAL MARKET BY IMPROVED DISTRIBUTION OF PRODUCTS AND BY BUILDING UP LOCAL INDUSTRIES.

1249 HUTCHISON K.
THE DECLINE AND FALL OF BRITISH CAPITALISM.
NEW YORK: CHAS SCRIBNER'S SONS, 1950, 301 PP.
TRACES DEVELOPMENT OF ECONOMIC AND POLITICAL FACTORS THAT CHANGED EMPHASIS OF BRITISH ECONOMY FROM PRIVATE ENTERPRISE TO PLANNED AND SOCIALIZED BUSINESS. ARGUES THAT EVOLUTION IN THE ECONOMIC ORDER BROUGHT ABOUT TRANSFER OF POLITICAL POWER FROM SMALL RULING CLASS TO MASS OF WORKERS.

1250 HUTH A.G.
"COMMUNICATION AND ECONOMIC DEVELOPMENT."
INT. CONCIL., 477 (JAN. 52), 1-48.
DEFINES LACK OF PUBLIC INTEREST IN PROGRAMS OF TECHNOLOGICAL ADVANCEMENT AS PRINCIPLE OBSTACLE TO ECONOMIC DEVELOPMENT. ASSIGNS CAUSE TO SLOW DEVELOPMENT OF COMMUNICATIONS MEDIA FOR EDUCATION IN UNDERDEVELOPED COUNTRIES. CALLS FOR INTENSIFIED PROGRAMS OF COMMUNICATION DEVELOPMENT CITING EXAMPLES IN BRITISH COLONIES, COLOMBO PLAN, POINT 4 PROGRAM, AND THE UNITED NATIONS.

1251 HUTT W.H.
THE ECONOMICS OF THE COLOUR BAR.
LONDON: INST OF ECO AFFAIRS, 1964, 189 PP.
ANALYSIS OF ECONOMIC ASPECTS OF APARTHEID IN SOUTH AFRICA AS SEEN IN ORIGINS OF EUROPEAN DISCRIMINATION ON LEGAL BASIS AND RELATION OF RACIAL GROUPS TO ECONOMIC DEVELOPMENT OF NATION.

1252 HUTT W.H.
"KEYNESIAN REVISIONS"
S. AFR. J. OF ECONOMICS, 33 (JUNE 65), 101-113.
DISCUSSES SIGNIFICANCE OF NINE ARTICLES BY LEADING ECONOMISTS DEMONSTRATING GRADUAL ABANDONMENT OF CRITICAL ELEMENTS IN LOGIC OF KEYNESIAN ECONOMICS. CLAIMS THAT THESIS OF UNEMPLOYMENT EQUILIBRIUM DEPENDS ON ASSUMPTION OF WAGE RIGIDITY THAT IS NOT ALWAYS VALID. ALSO FINDS HIS CONCEPTIONS OF NATIONAL GOVERNMENT FISCAL POLICY OUTDATED.

1253 HUTTENBACK R.A.
BRITISH IMPERIAL EXPERIENCE.
NEW YORK: HARPER & ROW, 1966, 225 PP., LC#66-15671.
TRACES HISTORY OF BRITISH EMPIRE CHARTERING OF EAST INDIA COMPANY TO FOUNDATION OF COMMONWEALTH. DELINEATES TWO PERIODS OF IMPERIALISM: MERCANTILIST, ENDING ABOUT 1800, AND COMMERCIAL OR "SECOND BRITISH EMPIRE," FOUNDED ON AMBITIONS TO INCREASE FAR EASTERN TRADE. DISCUSSES HOW COURSE OF EVENTS THRUST EMPIRE INTO UNINTENTIONAL INVOLVEMENT.

1254 HUTTON D.G.
INFLATION AND SOCIETY.
LONDON: ALLEN & UNWIN, 1960, 161 PP.
GENERAL STUDY OF NATURE OF INFLATION PAST AND PRESENT. DISCUSSES MONEY AND NATIONAL POLICIES TO PREVENT LOSS OF CURRENCY VALUE WHILE MAINTAINING ECONOMIC GROWTH.

1255 HUZAR E.
"CONGRESS AND THE ARMY: APPROPRIATIONS."
AM. POL. SCI. REV., 37 (AUG. 43), 661-676.
DEALS WITH CONGRESSIONAL APPROPRIATIONS COMMITTEES IN RELATION TO MILITARY SPENDING. EXAMINES THEIR ORGANIZATION AND PROCEDURES; REVIEW OF ESTIMATES, THEIR INTERESTS IN MILITARY ADMINISTRATION, THEIR CONTROL OF MILITARY EXPENDITURES, AND THE ROLE OF CONGRESSMEN NOT ON APPROPRIATIONS COMMITTEES.

1256 HYDE D.
THE PEACEFUL ASSAULT.
CHESTER SPRINGS: DUFOUR, 1963, 127 PP., LC#63-21146.
STUDIES NEW TACTICS OF USSR TO EXPORT COMMUNISM THROUGH SUBVERSION AND ECONOMIC PENETRATION. EXAMINES RATIONALE OF PEACEFUL CO-EXISTENCE AND BURYING CAPITALISM. USES EGYPT AS A CASE STUDY.

1257 IANNI O.
INDUSTRIALIZACAO E DESENVOLVIMENTO SOCIAL NO BRASIL.
RIO DE JANEIRO: ED CIVIL BRASIL, 1963, 269 PP.
EXAMINES EFFECTS OF INDUSTRIALIZATION ON BRAZILIAN ECONOMIC AND POLITICAL LIFE. DISCUSSES RELATIONS BETWEEN CLASSES AND INCREASED INFLUENCE OF WORKING CLASS. EXPLAINS IMPORTANCE OF EDUCATION IN INDUSTRIAL SOCIETY AND GROWTH OF NATIONALISM THAT HAS FOLLOWED SHIFT FROM AGRICULTURE TO INDUSTRY.

1258 IANNI O.
ESTADO E CAPITALISMO.
RIO DE JANEIRO: ED CIVIL BRASIL, 1965, 270 PP.
ANALYZES ECONOMIC AND SOCIAL STRUCTURE OF BRAZIL SINCE INDUSTRIALIZATION IN 20TH CENTURY. EXAMINES ACTIONS OF PRIVATE SECTOR IN DEVELOPMENT AND TREATS ROLE OF NATIONAL GOVERNMENT IN PARTICIPATING IN AND ENCOURAGING DEVELOPMENT OF INDUSTRY.

1259 IBARRA J.
"EL EXPERIMENTO CUBANO."
CASA DE LAS AMERICAS, 7 (MAR.-APR. 67), 17-29.
SURVEYS ANTECEDENTS OF CUBAN EXPERIMENT--NORTH AMERICAN IMPERIALISM. DISCUSSES GOVERNMENT OF CUBA AFTER WAR WITH SPAIN, EXAMINING PLATT AMENDMENT, US POLICY IN GENERAL, RECIPROCAL TRADE AGREEMENT, ETC.

1260 ILLINOIS U BUR COMMUNITY PLAN
PROCEEDINGS OF ILLINOIS STATEWIDE PLANNING CONFERENCE 1960.
URBANA: U OF ILLINOIS PR, 1960, 97 PP.
IDENTIFIES SPECIAL PROBLEMS AND DEVELOPMENT OPPORTUNITIES PECULIAR TO ILLINOIS COMMUNITIES, INCLUDING INFORMATION ON CONCEPTS AND PROCEDURES OF PLANNING THAT WILL AID COMMUNITIES IN ORGANIZING OFFICIAL BODIES TO CARRY OUT THIS FUNCTION. ALSO HIGHLIGHTS WAYS IN WHICH BEST USE CAN BE MADE OF STATE AND FEDERAL FUNDS.

1261 IMAZ J.L.
LOS QUE MANDAN.
BUENOS AIRES: ED U BUENOS AIRES, 1964, 250 PP.
ANALYZES LEADERSHIP OF INFLUENTIAL SECTORS OF ARGENTINE SOCIETY AND GOVERNMENT SINCE 1936. DISCUSSES BACKGROUND AND ATTITUDES OF LEADERS OF ARMED FORCES, LAND OWNERS, CHURCH LEADERS, INDUSTRIALISTS, UNIONISTS, PROFESSIONAL POLITICIANS, AND NATIONAL AND PROVINCIAL OFFICIALS.

1262 INARRITU A.L.
EL PATRON CAMBIO-ORO Y SUS REFORMAS.
MEXICO CITY: QUEROMON EDITORES, 1966, 191 PP.
DEALS WITH TWO FUNDAMENTAL PROBLEMS OF INTERNATIONAL FLUIDITY: STRUCTURE OF INTERNATIONAL MONETARY SYSTEM, AND ELASTICITY OF FLOW. MAJOR EMPHASIS ON STRUCTURAL PROBLEM AND FUNCTIONING DEFECTS. EXAMINES BASIC CHANGES RELATIVE TO THE ORIGIN OF INTERNATIONAL RESERVE ACTIVITIES. PROPOSES FORMULA TO PERFECT REDISTRIBUTION OF LIMITED GOLD.

1263 INDIAN INST OF PUBLIC ADMIN
IMPROVING CITY GOVERNMENT.
NEW DELHI: INDIAN INST PUB ADMIN, 1958, 208 PP.
PAPERS FROM SEMINAR ON PROBLEMS OF LOCAL GOVERNMENT IN INDIA. DISCUSSES RELATIONS BETWEEN DELIBERATIVE AND EXECUTIVE AGENCIES IN CITY GOVERNMENT, TRENDS IN MUNICIPAL FINANCES, DEVELOPMENT AND REDEVELOPMENT OF CITIES. EXAMINES ASPECTS AND PROBLEMS OF PARTICIPATION OF CITIZENS IN MUNICIPAL GOVERNMENT.

1264 INDUSTRIAL COUN SOC-ECO STU
THE SWEDISH ECONOMY AND THE UNDERDEVELOPED COUNTRIES.
UPSALA: INDUS COUN SOC ECO STUD, 1961, 148 PP.
STUDIES PROBLEMS FACED BY SWEDEN AND UNDEVELOPED COUNTRIES. EXAMINES AID SWEDEN COULD OFFER, MOTIVES OF FOREIGN AID, PLANS AND RECOMMENDATIONS FOR PROGRAMS INCLUDING EXPORTS, INCREASED CAPITAL INVESTMENTS, TECHNICAL COOPERATION, TRADE, AND EDUCATION.

1265 INGRAM J.C.
INTERNATIONAL ECONOMIC PROBLEMS.
NEW YORK: JOHN WILEY, 1966, 180 PP., LC#66-16137.
SIMPLIFIED AND GENERAL DISCUSSION OF MAJOR PROBLEMS IN INTERNATIONAL ECONOMICS. EMPHASIZES GENERAL ECONOMIC PRINCIPLES IN RELATION TO THREE MAJOR PROBLEMS: TRADE BETWEEN DEVELOPED AND UNDERDEVELOPED COUNTRIES; EUROPEAN COMMON MARKET; AND INTERNATIONAL MONETARY REFORM. ADDRESSED TO STUDENT AND LAYMAN.

1266 INT. BANK RECONSTR. DEVELOP.
ECONOMIC DEVELOPMENT OF KUWAIT.
BALTIMORE: JOHNS HOPKINS PR., 1965, 194 PP.
KUWAIT IS FOURTH LARGEST OIL PRODUCER IN WORLD AND SECOND ONLY TO VENEZUELA AS AN OIL EXPORTER. SUMMARIZES RESULTS OF FINDINGS AND RECOMMENDATIONS OF TWO 'ECONOMIC MISSIONS' TO COUNTRY. DOMESTIC NEEDS AND INVESTMENT OPPORTUNITIES ARE EMPHASIZED WITH REVALUATION OF TARIFFS AND IMPORT RESTRICTIONS.

1267 INTERAMERICAN ECO AND SOC COUN
THE ALLIANCE FOR PROGRESS: ITS FIRST YEAR: 1961-1962.
WASHINGTON: PAN AMERICAN UNION, 1963, 198 PP.
REPORT ON PROGRESS OF ECONOMIC ANS SOCIAL DEVELOPMENT IN LATIN AMERICA FROM 1961 TO 1962 RESULTING FROM LONG-TERM DEVELOPMENT PLANS INSITUTED BY ALLIANCE FOR PROGRESS. PROVIDES OVER-ALL EVALUATION OF SOUTH AMERICAN PROGRESS AND PROSPECTS FOR FUTURE GAINS IN SOCIAL AND ECONOMIC AREAS, AND DISCUSSES SPECIFIC PROBLEMS AND ACHIEVEMENTS MADE IN EACH OF COUNTRIES INVOLVED.

1268 INTERAMERICAN ECO AND SOC COUN
THE ALLIANCE FOR PROGRESS: ITS THIRD YEAR 1963-1964.
WASHINGTON: PAN AMERICAN UNION, 1965, 149 PP.
REPORT OF ECONOMIC AND FINANCIAL STATUS OF LATIN AMERICA THROUGH 1964. ANALYSIS OF PLANS, REFORMS, AND SOCIAL PROGRAMS FOR 1965. APPENDIX INCLUDES REPORT OF DOMESTIC EFFORTS AND NEED FOR EXTERNAL FINANCING.

1269 INTERNAT CONGRESS OF JURISTS
EXECUTIVE ACTION AND THE RULE OF RULE: REPORTION PROCEEDINGS OF INT'T CONGRESS OF JURISTS,-RIO DE JANEIRO, BRAZIL.
RIO DE JANEIR: INTL CONG JURISTS, 1962, 187 PP.
CONGRESS RECOGNIZES ONE GREAT MODERN DILEMMA IS POWER OF EXECUTIVE VS RIGHTS OF INDIVIDUAL. EXAMINES ROLE OF JUDGES, LAWYERS, AND TEACHERS OF LAW IN STRIKING BALANCE BETWEEN THE TWO, THUS ADJUSTING RULE OF LAW TO NEEDS OF SOCIAL AND ECONOMIC DEVELOPMENT.

1270 INTERNATIONAL ASSOCIATION RES
AFRICAN STUDIES IN INCOME AND WEALTH.
CHICAGO: QUADRANGLE BOOKS, INC, 1963, 433 PP., LC#63-11846.
COLLECTION OF PAPERS ON DEVELOPING AFRICAN ECONOMY, DEALING WITH NATIONAL ACCOUNTS, PLANNING, INCOME ESTIMATION, AND

CALCULATION OF STATUS AND NEEDS OF NATIONAL ECONOMY IN AREA. PREPARED BY INTERNATIONAL ASSOCIATION FOR RESEARCH IN INCOME AND WEALTH.

1271 INTERNATIONAL BANK RECONST DEV
THE WORLD BANK IN AFRICA: SUMMARY OF ACTIVITIES.
WASHINGTON: INTL BANK REC & DEV, 1961, 61 PP.
SUMMARIZES LOANS MADE BY WORLD BANK TO AFRICAN MEMBER NATIONS CHIEFLY FOR DEVELOPMENT OF TRANSPORTATION, POWER, COMMUNICATIONS, AGRICULTURE, AND VARIOUS SEGMENTS OF INDUSTRY. DETAILS SPECIFIC PROJECTS AND NOTES EFFECTS OF WORLD BANK FINANCING ON GENERAL NATIONAL DEVELOPMENT. COVERS ENTIRE PERIOD OF EXISTENCE OF WORLD BANK.

1272 INTERNATIONAL BANK RECONST DEV
THE WORLD BANK AND IDA IN ASIA.
WASHINGTON: INTL BANK REC & DEV, 1962, 54 PP.
SUMMARIZES LOANS BY WORLD BANK, AND INTERNATIONAL DEVELOPMENT ASSOCIATION CREDITS TO 14 ASIAN NATIONS FOR DEVELOPMENT OF POWER, TRANSPORTATION, AGRICULTURE, INDUSTRY, AND OTHER USES. DETAILS PROJECTS SUPPORTED IN EACH COUNTRY AND NOTES OTHER ASSISTANCE. COMMENTS ON BANK AND ASSOCIATION POLICIES AND OPERATIONS IN ASIA.

1273 INTERNATIONAL BANK RECONST DEV
THE WORLD BANK GROUP IN ASIA.
WASHINGTON: INTL BANK REC & DEV, 1963, 90 PP.
DESCRIBES FUNCTIONS AND METHODS OF WORLD BANK AND ITS AFFILIATES. DISCUSSES IN DETAIL THEIR EFFORTS SINCE 1950 TO PROMOTE ECONOMIC DEVELOPMENT OF ASIA. LISTS NUMBER AND PURPOSE OF LOANS MADE BY BANK TO SEVERAL ASIAN COUNTRIES AND DESCRIBES PROJECTS FOR WHICH FUNDS WERE USED.

1274 INTERNATIONAL ECO POLICY ASSN
THE UNITED STATES BALANCE OF PAYMENTS.
WASHINGTON: INTL ECO POLICY ASSN, 1966, 200 PP., LC#66-23129
ANALYSIS OF US ECONOMIC STRATEGY, EMPHASIZING IMPACT OF DIRECT FOREIGN INVESTMENT AND OTHER ECONOMIC FACTORS ON US BALANCE OF PAYMENTS. ATTEMPTS TO DETERMINE CAUSE OF PERSISTENT US DEFICITS. CONSIDERS BOTH PUBLIC AND PRIVATE INTERNATIONAL TRANSACTIONS AND THEIR EFFECTS ON BALANCE OF PAYMENTS.

1275 INTERNATIONAL ECONOMIC ASSN
ECONOMICS OF INTERNATIONAL MIGRATION.
NEW YORK: ST MARTIN'S PRESS, 1958, 502 PP.
DEVELOPS ANALYTICAL TOOLS FOR INTERPRETING MIGRATION. COMPARATIVELY STUDIES EXPERIENCE OF REPRESENTATIVE COUNTRIES OF EMIGRATION AND IMMIGRATION, AND CHANGING GOVERNMENT POLICIES; SCALE AND FUTURE OF INTRA-CONTINENTAL MIGRATION IN EUROPE AND ASIA; SOCIAL PROBLEMS OF ASSIMILATION; EXTENT TO WHICH MIGRATION CAN HELP RELIEVE POPULATION PRESSURES AND CONTRIBUTE TO GROWTH OF UNDERDEVELOPED LANDS.

1276 INTERNATIONAL ECONOMIC ASSN
STABILITY AND PROGRESS IN THE WORLD ECONOMY: THE FIRST CONGRESS OF THE INTERNATIONAL ECONOMIC ASSOCIATION.
NEW YORK: ST. MARTIN'S, 1958, 266 PP.
RECORDS 1956 CONGRESS ON SUBJECT. FIVE ASPECTS COVERED: PROBLEMS OF RICHER AND POORER COUNTRIES, MONETARY FACTORS IN STABILITY, INTERNATIONAL STABILITY AND THE NATIONAL ECONOMY. CLOSING ADDRESS CONCLUDES THAT COMMONWEALTH TYPE OF DEVELOPMENT MORE FEASIBLE THAN WORLD ECONOMIC COORDINATION.

1277 INTERNATIONAL LABOUR OFF LIB
BIBLIOGRAPHY ON THE INTERNATIONAL LABOUR ORGANISATION.
GENEVA: INTL LABOUR OFFICE, 1954, 68 PP.
UNANNOTATED BIBLIOGRAPHY OF SELECTED WORKS IN ENGLISH, FRENCH, AND SPANISH PUBLISHED BETWEEN 1929-53. INCLUDES EARLIER BIBLIOGRAPHIES AND CATALOGS ON THE INTERNATIONAL LABOR ORGANIZATION; REPORTS AND MONOGRAPHS PREPARED BY THE ILO; COMMERCIALLY PUBLISHED BOOKS, THESES, AND OFFICIAL REPORTS ON THE ILO; AND A WIDE SELECTION OF PERIODICAL ARTICLES. TOPICALLY AND CHRONOLOGICALLY CLASSIFIED.

1278 INTERNATIONAL LABOUR OFFICE
EMPLOYMENT, UNEMPLOYMENT AND LABOUR FORCE STATISTICS (PAMPHLET)
GENEVA: INTL LABOUR OFFICE, 1948, 130 PP.
SEEKS TO ESTABLISH A COMPREHENSIVE SCHEME OF STATISTICAL DATA AND TO STATE AN IDEAL SYSTEM TOWARD WHICH DIFFERENT COUNTRIES SHOULD DEVELOP; PROVIDES COMMON GROUND OF DEFINITION, PROCEDURE, AND PRESENTATION. INCLUDES METHODS OF GATHERING DATA. COVERS TYPES OF EMPLOYMENT AND PROBLEMS, TYPES OF UNEMPLOYMENT AND PROBLEMS, AND INTERNATIONAL COMPARABILITY OF DATA. CLOSES WITH RESOLUTIONS FOR FUTURE.

1279 INTERNATIONAL LABOUR OFFICE
EMPLOYMENT AND ECONOMIC GROWTH.
GENEVA: INTL LABOUR OFFICE, 1964, 219 PP.
STUDIES UNEMPLOYMENT AND UNDEREMPLOYMENT AND MEASURES TO DEAL WITH THEM. GIVES STATISTICAL BACKGROUND IN VARIOUS COUNTRIES AND RELATES ECONOMIC DEVELOPMENT TO FULL EMPLOYMENT. ALSO CONSIDERS INTERNATIONAL TACTICS NECESSARY TO HELP UNDERDEVELOPED NATIONS TO RAISE EMPLOYMENT LEVELS.

1280 INTERNATIONAL LABOUR OFFICE
SUBJECT GUIDE TO PUBLICATIONS OF THE INTERNATIONAL LABOUR OFFICE, 1919-1964.
GENEVA: INTL LABOUR OFFICE, 1967, 478 PP.
SUBJECT GUIDE LISTS ITEMS UNDER SINGLE HEADING WITH CROSS-REFERENCES TO MORE SPECIFIC HEADINGS. INCLUDES ALPHABETICAL AUTHOR INDEX. IN ADDITION TO PRINTED SALES PUBLICATIONS, LIST INCLUDES IMPORTANT SERIES PRODUCED BY OFFSET PROCESSES.

1281 INTERNATIONAL MONETARY FUND
COMPENSATORY FINANCING OF EXPORT FLUCTUATIONS (PAMPHLET)
WASHINGTON: INTL MONETARY FUND, 1963, 27 PP.
REPORTS WAYS IN WHICH INTERNATIONAL MONETARY FUND MIGHT PLAY INCREASED PART IN COMPENSATORY FINANCING OF EXPORT FLUCTUATIONS OF PRIMARY EXPORTING COUNTRIES. FUND BELIEVES USE OF ITS FUNDS BY NATIONS EXPERIENCING DEFICITS ARISING OUT OF EXPORT SHORTFALLS IS LEGITIMATE, SINCE IT ENABLES NATIONS TO PURSUE DEVELOPMENT PROGRAMS DESPITE BALANCE-OF-PAYMENTS PROBLEMS.

1282 INTL BANKING SUMMER SCHOOL
RELATIONS BETWEEN THE CENTRAL BANKS AND COMMERCIAL BANKS.
FRANKFURT: FRITZ KNAPP VERLAG, 1957, 209 PP.
LECTURES DELIVERED BY PROMINENT BANKERS AND ECONOMISTS AT GARMISCH-PARTENKIRCHEN, GERMANY IN 1957. LARGEST PROPORTION OF ADDRESSES DEALS WITH RELATIONS BETWEEN CENTRAL BANKS OF GERMANY, ITALY, SWITZERLAND, AUSTRIA, FRANCE, BENELUX COUNTRIES, ENGLAND, AND THEIR RESPECTIVE COMMERCIAL BANKS. OTHER SUBJECTS COVERED ARE: IMPACT OF MONETARY MANAGEMENT ON US BANKS AND PROBLEMS OF FINANCING THROUGH SECURITIES.

1283 INTL BANKING SUMMER SCHOOL
TRENDS IN BANK CREDIT AND FINANCE.
THE HAGUE: MARTINUS NIJHOFF, 1961, 181 PP.
COLLECTION OF ADDRESSES DELIVERED IN NETHERLANDS. SUBJECTS TOUCHED UPON INCLUDE: MEDIUM-TERM CREDIT, FUNCTION OF AMSTERDAM STOCK EXCHANGE IN GOVERNMENT AND CORPORATE FINANCING, PRESENT-DAY PROBLEMS OF CAPITAL EXPORTS, FINANCIAL ASPECTS OF EEC, RELATIONSHIP BETWEEN GOVERNMENT CREDITS AND GUARANTEES AND CREDIT POLICY OF COMMERICAL BANKS. ALL SPEAKERS ARE PROMINENT BANKERS AND ECONOMISTS OF EUROPE.

1284 INTL CHAMBER OF COMMERCE
TERMS COMMONLY USED IN DISTRIBUTION AND ADVERTISING.
BASEL: VERLAG FUR RECHT & GES, 1944, 146 PP.
DICTIONARY OF COMMERCIAL TERMS IN SPANISH, PORTUGUESE, AND ENGLISH. ARRANGED IN THREE SECTIONS, EACH PRESENTS EQUIVALENT DEFINITIONS IN OTHER TWO LANGUAGES. INCLUDES GENERAL AND SPECIFIC TERMS USED IN THEORY AND PRACTICE OF ADVERTISING AND DISTRIBUTION.

1285 INTL INF CTR LOCAL CREDIT
GOVERNMENT MEASURES FOR THE PROMOTION OF REGIONAL ECONOMIC DEVELOPMENT.
THE HAGUE: MARTINUS NIJHOFF, 1964, 159 PP.
ANALYSIS OF UNEQUAL SOCIAL AND CULTURAL DEVELOPMENT OF SPECIFIC REGIONS IN NATIONS SINCE WWII. STUDIES NATURE AND CAUSES OF INEQUALITY IN EACH MEMBER NATION AND EVALUATES PROGRAMS IN PROGRESS TO RECTIFY SITUATION. ESTABLISHES CRITERIA FOR SPECIAL AREAS, SUGGESTS METHODS OF IMPROVING AREA, AND OFFERS AID IN ADMINISTERING REGION.

1286 INTL UNION LOCAL AUTHORITIES
METROPOLIS.
THE HAGUE: MARTINUS NIJHOFF, 1961, 45 PP.
NEARLY 1,000 ENTRIES IN FIELD OF CITY MANAGEMENT AND PUBLIC ADMINISTRATION, IN FRENCH, ENGLISH, AND GERMAN. MATERIAL ON NORTH AMERICA IS EXCLUDED. COVERS FINANCE, EDUCATION, WELFARE, HEALTH, HOUSING, PLANNING, TRANSPORTATION, AND CRIME.

1287 INTNTL COTTON ADVISORY COMMITT
GOVERNMENT REGULATIONS ON COTTON, 1962 (PAMPHLET)
WASHINGTON: INTL COTTON ADV COMM, 1962, 31 PP.
COLLECTION OF LAWS REGULATING COTTON INDUSTRY IN COUNTRIES THAT PRODUCE COTTON. INCLUDES CHANGES IN LAWS SINCE 1961 REGULATING PRODUCTION, EXPORTS, IMPORTS, CONSUMPTION, AND PRICES.

1288 IOVTCHOUK M.T., OSSIPOV G.
"ON SOME THEORETICAL PRINCIPLES AND METHODS OF SOCIOLOGICAL INVESTIGATIONS (IN RUSSIAN)."
VOP. FILOZOF., 16 (NO.12, 62), 23-34.
ANALYZES AND COMPARES ECONOMIC ADVANCE OF SOVIET UNION AND USA. DISCUSSES FUTURE PROBLEMS THAT MAY ARISE OUT OF CONFLICT BETWEEN COMMUNIST AND CAPITALIST ECONOMIC SYSTEMS. SUPPORTS THESIS OF SUPERIORITY OF MARXIST SYSTEM.

1289 ISAAC J.
ECONOMICS OF MIGRATION.
NEW YORK: OXFORD U PR, 1947, 285 PP.
DEALS WITH ECONOMIC AND SOCIAL ASPECTS OF THE MIGRATION OF FREE INDIVIDUALS. DISCUSSES HOW MIGRATION BECAME A DETERMINING FACTOR IN MOULDING THE SOCIAL STRUCTURE OF THE WEST-

ERN WORLD FROM THE NAPOLEONIC WARS TO WWI. EMPHASIZES THE EFFECTS OF MIGRATION ON CAPITAL DISPOSAL AND POPULATION DISTRIBUTION.

1290 ISARD W.
LOCATION AND SPACE-ECONOMY: GENERAL THEORY RELATING TO INDUSTRIAL LOCATION, MARKET AREAS, LAND USE, TRADE...
NEW YORK: JOHN WILEY, 1956, 350 PP., LC#56-11026.
ATTEMPTS TO IMPROVE SPATIAL AND REGIONAL FRAMEWORKS OF SOCIAL SCIENCE DISCIPLINES, PARTICULARLY OF ECONOMICS, THROUGH DEVELOPMENT OF AN ADEQUATE THEORY OF LOCATION AND SPACE-ECONOMY. ANALYZES TRANSPORT INPUTS AND RELATED SPATIAL CONCEPTS AND LOCATIONAL EQUILIBRIUM OF THE FIRM. STUDIES MARKET AND SUPPLY ANALYSIS AND COMPETITIVE LOCATIONAL EQUILIBRIUM, AND DEVELOPS A MATHEMATICAL FORMULATION.

1291 ISELIN J.J.
"THE TRUMAN DOCTRINE: ITS PASSAGE THROUGH CONGRESS AND THE AFTERMATH."
FOREIGN SERVICE J., 44 (MAY 67), 19-23.
ANALYZES REACTION OF CONGRESS TO TRUMAN DOCTRINE. OPPOSITION SUGGESTED UN INTERVENTION AS ALTERNATIVE TO US FOREIGN AID PROGRAM. AFTER CONVERSION OF TAFT AND BRIDGES THE PROGRAM PASSED WITH RELATIVE EASE. RATHER UNANALYTICAL HISTORICAL SKETCH TRACES EVOLUTION OF TRUMAN DOCTRINE INTO MARSHALL PLAN.

1292 ISSAWI C.
EGYPT IN REVOLUTION: AN ECONOMIC ANALYSIS.
NEW YORK: OXFORD U. PR., 1963, 343 PP.
OUTLINES EGYPTIAN HISTORY, RELIGION AND ECONOMIC EMERGENCE IN 1920 TO 1952 COUP D'GTAT OF NASSER. FOLLOWS WITH A THOROUGH DESCRIPTION OF MODERN EGYPT AS TO 'ARAB SOCIALISM', HUMAN RESOURCES AND POPULATION PROBLEMS, NATIONAL INCOME, AGRICULTURAL AND INDUSTRIAL SITUATUATION, FINANCIAL PICTURE AND POLICIES.

1293 JACKSON G.D.
COMINTERN AND PEASANT IN EAST EUROPE 1919-1930.
NEW YORK: COLUMBIA U PRESS, 1966, 339 PP., LC#66-15489.
ANALYSIS OF COMINTERN IN THEORY AND PRACTICE IN REGARD TO ITS POLICY TOWARD PEASANTRY AND PEASANT POLITICAL MOVEMENTS IN EASTERN EUROPE. EXPLAINS PROBLEMS OF PEASANT SOCIETIES IN TRANSITION AND MOVEMENTS THAT DEVELOPED IN EASTERN EUROPE. DISCUSSES IMPORTANCE OF PEASANT IN COMINTERN POLICY AND DETAILS RELATION OF COMINTERN TO BULGARIA, POLAND, YUGOSLAVIA, RUMANIA, AND CZECHOSLOVAKIA, AND TO THEIR PEASANT MOVEMENTS.

1294 JACKSON M.V.
EUROPEAN POWERS AND SOUTH-EAST AFRICA: A STUDY OF INTERNATIONAL RELATIONS ON SOUTH-EAST COAST OF AFRICA, 1796-1856.
LONDON: LONGMANS, GREEN & CO, 1942, 284 PP.
STUDIES EXPLOITATION, EMPHASIZING OCEAN STRATEGY, COMMERCE, AND FOREIGN POWER STRUGGLE TO GAIN TERRITORY AND ACCESS TO VITAL TRADE ROUTES.

1295 JACKSON R.G.A.
THE CASE FOR AN INTERNATIONAL DEVELOPMENT AUTHORITY (PAMPHLET)
SYRACUSE: SYRACUSE U PRESS, 1959, 67 PP., LC#59-9104.
LECTURES IN FAVOR OF THE ESTABLISHMENT OF A COOPERATING INTERNATIONAL ORGANIZATION WHICH WOULD CHANNEL FOREIGN AID OF ALL COUNTRIES TO ALL UNDERDEVELOPED AREAS. MEMBERSHIP WOULD BE OPEN TO ALL, INCLUDING COMMUNIST COUNTRIES THOUGH THEY WOULD BE IN MINORITY, AND VOTING WOULD BE WEIGHED IN RELATION TO CONTRIBUTION. THIS BODY WOULD FACILITATE ADMINISTRATION OF FOREIGN AID AND MAKE IT MORE EQUITABLE.

1296 JACOBS P.
STATE OF UNIONS.
NEW YORK: ATHENEUM PUBLISHERS, 1963, 303 PP., LC#63-17853.
STUDY OF PRESENT SITUATION OF LABOR UNIONS IN US ECONOMY. DEALS WITH JIMMY HOFFA AND OTHER LEADERS, CONGRESSIONAL INVESTIGATION, INTERNAL PROCESSES, STATUS OF NEGRO, AND CONDITION OF COLLECTIVE BARGAINING.

1297 JACOBS P.
"RE-RADICALIZING THE DE-RADICALIZED."
NEW POLITICS, 5 (FALL 66), 14-21.
DISCUSSES FORMATION OF ANTI-POVERTY PROGRAM ANS SHIFT BY MANY EX-RADICALS TO SUPPORT OF IT. MAINTAINS PROGRAM'S LACK OF REAL IMPACT IS RESULT OF NEED TO COMPROMISE FOR POLITICAL PURPOSES, INSUFFICIENT FUNDS, ADMINISTRATIVE INEFFICIENCY, AND MAINLY, INVALID BASIC ASSUMPTIONS. POVERTY IS VIEWED AS NATURAL PART OF SOCIAL SCENE, NOT A DYSFUNCTION. MUST FIND RADICAL PROGRAMS TO SOLVE DOMESTIC CRISES.

1298 JACOBSON H.K.
"THE USSR AND ILO."
INT. ORG. 14 (SUMMER 60), 402-428.
STATES THAT SOVIET UNION RE-ENTRY HAS BEEN A SHARP REVERSAL OF ITS PAST POLICIES. ANALYZES ILO POTENTIALITIES AS CONSTRUCTIVE FORCE FOR GUIDING DEVELOPMENT OF LABOR AND MANAGEMENT IN NEWLY INDEPENDENT COUNTRIES. CALLS FOR BETTER WAY OF MEETING PROBLEMS OF SOVIET PARTICIPATION.

1299 JACOBSSON P.
SOME MONETARY PROBLEMS, INTERNATIONAL AND NATIONAL.
NEW YORK: OXFORD U PR, 1958, 374 PP.
STUDIES ON MAJOR ECONOMIC PROBLEMS OF 1917-58, BOTH INTERNATIONAL AND NATIONAL. DISCUSSES ARMAMENTS EXPENDITURE, PLAN FOR INTERNATIONAL BANK, GOLD AND MONETARY PROBLEMS, INVESTMENT POLICIES, TRADE AND FINANCIAL RELATIONS AMONG COUNTRIES, AND EMPLOYMENT PROGRAMS IN DIFFERENT COUNTRIES.

1300 JACOBY N.H. ED.
UNITED STATES MONETARY POLICY.
NEW YORK: FREDERICK PRAEGER, 1964, 243 PP., LC#64-7956.
STUDY OF US MONETARY POLICY THROUGH ANALYSIS OF ISSUES AND MEANS INVOLVED. DISCUSSES MONEY SUPPLY AND ECONOMIC GROWTH; COMPARES US AND BRITISH POSTWAR MONETARY POLICY; AND DISCUSSES PRESENT LIMITATIONS AND IMPROVEMENTS.

1301 JACOBY N.H.
US AID TO TAIWAN.
NEW YORK: FREDERICK PRAEGER, 1967, 364 PP., LC#66-21784.
EVALUATION OF ALL ASPECTS OF US AID TO TAIWAN AS A REPORT TO AGENCY FOR INTERNATIONAL DEVELOPMENT, BASED ON INTERVIEWS OF ALL FACTIONS INVOLVED, OBSERVATION OF OPERATIONS, AND DISCUSSION OF POLICY. PURPOSE IS TO IDENTIFY THOSE ECONOMIC POLICIES WHICH RESULT IN MOST OPTIMAL IMPROVEMENT FOR UNDERDEVELOPED NATIONS.

1302 JACOBY S.B.
"THE 89TH CONGRESS AND GOVERNMENT LITIGATION."
COLUMBIA LAW REV., 77 (NOV. 67), 1212-1240.
DESCRIBES FOUR STATUTES ENACTED IN 89TH CONGRESS TREATING GOVERNMENT LITIGATION, WHICH INCREASE ADMINISTRATIVE SETTLEMENT OF TORT CLAIMS AGAINST GOVERNMENT, LIMIT CLAIMS OF GOVERNMENT, AND MAKE GOVERNMENT RESPONSIBLE FOR SOME COSTS OF LITIGATION. DISCUSSES INTERPRETATIONS OF THESE LAWS AND EXTENT OF THEIR APPLICATION. BELIEVES THAT GOVERNMENT'S UNFAIR ADVANTAGE THROUGH SOVEREIGN IMMUNITY WILL BE REDUCED.

1303 JAFFEE A.J.
"POPULATION TRENDS AND CONTROLS IN UNDERDEVELOPED COUNTRIES."
LAW CONTEMP. PROBL., 25 (SUMMER 60), 508-535.
OFFERS HISTORY OF POPULATION GROWTH, AND ANALYSIS OF POPULATION DISTRIBUTION AND BIRTH-DEATH RATES. COMPARES SOCIO-ECONOMIC FACTORS RELATED TO POPULATION GROWTH AND FERTILITY IN UNDERDEVELOPED COUNTRIES WITH THOSE IN DEVELOPED ONES. SPECULATES ON POSSIBLE FUTURE GROWTH OF POPULATION AND ITS EFFECT ON ECONOMIC DEVELOPMENT, EMPLOYMENT, AND STANDARD OF LIVING.

1304 JAIN S.C.
THE STATE AND AGRICULTURE.
ALLAHABAD, INDIA: KITAB MAHAL, 1965, 173 PP.
COMPARES AGRICULTURAL POLICIES OF CAPITALIST, MARXIST, AND MIXED ECONOMIES, AND EXAMINES THESE POLICIES AS CASE STUDY IN INDIAN EXPERIENCE, INCLUDING SURVEY OF MAIN PROBLEMS OF INDIAN AGRICULTURE AND PROCESS OF POLICY FORMATION FOR OVERCOMING THEM.

1305 JANSSEN P.
"NEA: THE RELUCTANT DRAGON."
SATURDAY REV., 50 (JUNE 67), 56-57, 72-73 .
A PERCEPTIVE ESSAY ON THE ROLE OF THE LARGEST PROFESSIONAL ORGANIZATION IN THE US. DEALS WITH ITS ORIENTATION TO "WHITE TEACHERS IN SMALL-CITY AND RURAL SCHOOL SYSTEMS," ADMINISTRATORS RATHER THAN TEACHERS, ANALYZING BOARD OF DIRECTORS AND TRUSTEES, SEGREGATION AND NEA SANCTIONS, THE POWER OF THE EXECUTIVE SECRETARY AHD LOBBYING WITH HEW UNDER VARIOUS FEDERAL ADMINISTRATIONS, WITH A PROGNOSIS.

1306 JASNY H.
KHRUSHCHEV'S CROP POLICY.
GLASGOW: GEORGE OUTRAM CO, LTD, 1965, 243 PP.
ANALYZES KHRUSHCHEV'S AGRICULTURAL PROGRAMS THAT BROUGHT ABOUT FAILURES IN ECONOMY. CONCLUDES THAT EXCESSIVE CONCERN WITH MAIZE, PULSE, AND SUGARBEET CAUSED FAILURE. COMPARES SOVIET CROP PRACTICES WITH THOSE OF OTHER NATIONS. FEELS KHRUSHCHEV MAY HAVE BEEN JUSTIFIED, OWING TO UNIQUENESS OF NATURAL RESOURCES.

1307 JAVITS B.A., KEYSERLING L.H.
THE PEACE BY INVESTMENT CORPORATION.
WASHINGTON: COMM PEACE INVESTMT, 1961, 63 PP.
DISCUSSION OF PURPOSE, AIMS, AND METHODS OF PEACE BY INVESTMENT CORPORATION WHICH STRIVES TO PROMOTE INTERNATIONAL ECONOMIC DEVELOPMENT THROUGH PEOPLE-TO-PEOPLE RELATIONS. CRITICIZES GOVERNMENT'S FAILURE TO MEET FOREIGN AND DOMESTIC ECONOMIC CHALLENGES. EXPLAINS NEW PROGRAMS SUCH AS PEACE CORPS AND FOOD FOR PEACE, WHICH USE VAST AMERICAN ECONOMIC POTENTIALS TO PROMOTE INTERNATIONAL ECONOMIC WELL-BEING.

1308 JAVITS J.K.
"POLITICAL ACTION VITAL FOR LATIN AMERICAN INTEGRATION."
CENTRO, 2 (JAN. 66), 11-15.
PROPOSES ESTABLISHMENT OF COMMITTEE FOR ECONOMIC UNION

OF AMERICAS. INVITES PARTICIPATION OF POLITICAL PARTIES, TRADE UNIONS, AND PRIVATE CORPORATIONS. ASSESSES PACE OF PRESENT PLAN FOR ECONOMIC INTEGRATION AS TOO SLOW.

1309 JAVITS J.K.
"THE USE OF AMERICAN PLURALISM."
COLORADO QUARTERLY, 16 (FALL 67), 119-126.
DISCUSSES "NEW DEAL THINKING" WHICH HOLDS THAT FEDERAL GOVERNMENT IS ONLY INSTRUMENT FOR DEFINING, DEVELOPING, DMINISTERING, AND FINANCING SOLUTIONS TO US PROBLEMS. FEELS PEOPLE OF US ARE GRADUALLY LOSING CONFIDENCE IN THIS THESIS AND BECOMING DISENCHANTED WITH DEPERSONALIZATION OF POLITICS. PROPOSES NEW PHILOSOPHY WHICH WILL MAKE USE OF PLURALISM THAT HAS PROVIDED AMERICAN FREEDOM AND WEALTH.

1310 JEDLICKI W.
"THE FREE SPEECH MOVEMENT IN WARSAW."
NEW POLITICS, 6 (WINTER 67), 49-56.
NARRATES EVENTS OF FREE-SPEECH MOVEMENT IN POLAND BEGINNING WITH FIRST ARREST OF KURON AND MODZELEWSKI IN 1964. DESCRIBES THEIR OPEN LETTER, SECOND ARRESTS, TRIALS OF LEADERS OF MOVEMENT, CAMPUS PROTESTS, AND POLICE ACTION. COMPARES POLISH MOVEMENT TO THAT OF STUDENT MOVEMENT IN US. STATES THAT PROTESTS ARE INDICATION OF FAILURE OF "OFFICIAL COMMUNISM."

1311 JENCKS C.E.
"COAL MINERS IN BRITAIN SINCE NATIONALIZATION."
AMER. J. OF COMPARATIVE LAW, 26 (JULY 67), 301-312.
MINEWORKERS' CONDITIONS GREATLY IMPROVED SINCE NATIONALIZATION, BUT MOST MINERS STILL FEEL THEY ARE RATED LOWER SOCIALLY THAN THEY DESERVE. THEIR APPRECIATION OF GAINS AND RESENTMENT OF SHORTCOMINGS EXERT AN INFLUENCE ON INDUSTRIAL RELATIONS.

1312 JENCKS C.E.
"SOCIAL STATUS OF COAL MINERS IN BRITAIN SINCE NATIONALIZATION."
AMER. J. OF ECO. AND SOC., 26 (JULY 67), 01-312.
FINDS COAL MINERS' WAGES, WORKING CONDITIONS, FRINGE BENEFITS, LABOR-MANAGEMENT REALTIONS, HOUSING, AND GENERAL WELFARE HAVE IMPROVED SINCE NATIONALIZATION. DISCUSSES MINERS' ATTITUDES TOWARD THEIR "LOW" SOCIAL POSITION, AND SHOWS HOW THESE ATTITUDES AFFECT INDUSTRIAL RELATIONS.

1313 JENKINS C.
POWER AT THE TOP: A CRITICAL SURVEY OF THE NATIONALIZED INDUSTRIES.
LONDON: MACGIBBON AND KEE, LTD, 1959, 292 PP.
INVESTIGATES NATIONALIZED INDUSTRY IN ENGLAND, ESPECIALLY SHORTCOMINGS OF SYSTEM SUCH AS EMPLOYING EXECUTIVES IN PRIVATE INDUSTRY TO HEAD PUBLIC INDUSTRIES. PUBLIC CORPORATIONS ARE BEING RUN TO HELP PRIVATE INTERESTS AND ARE NOT DIFFERENT ENOUGH FROM THE PRIVATE CORPORATIONS THEY REPLACED. ADVOCATES FURTHER ACTION BY LABOUR PARTY IN DEVELOPING TRUE PUBLIC ENTERPRISE.

1314 JENNINGS W.I.
PROBLEMS OF THE NEW COMMONWEALTH.
DURHAM: DUKE U PR, 1958, 114 PP., LC#58-6972.
REVISION OF THREE LECTURES DELIVERED BY AUTHOR AT COMMONWEALTH STUDIES CENTER, DUKE UNIVERSITY. FOCUS ON INFLUENCE OF INDIA, PAKISTAN, AND CEYLON ON STRUCTURE AND FUNCTION OF THE COMMONWEALTH. CONSIDER THE MANY ECONOMIC AND POLITICAL PROBLEMS FACING THE ORGANIZATION.

1315 JENNINGS W.I.
PARLIAMENT.
LONDON: CAMBRIDGE UNIV PRESS, 1939, 540 PP.
DESCRIBES AND ANALYZES WORKING OF PARLIAMENTARY PORTION OF MACHINERY OF GOVERNMENT. DISCUSSES COMPOSITION OF PARLIAMENT, MEMBERS AND THEIR INTERESTS, PARTIES AND OFFICIALS OF HOUSES. DESCRIBES FRAMEWORK OF ORATORY, ART OF MANAGEMENT, AND TECHNIQUE OF OPPOSITION. TREATS PROCESS OF LEGISLATION, FINANCIAL CONTROL, HOUSE OF LORDS, PRIVATE LEGISLATION, AND HOUSE OF COMMONS.

1316 JENNINGS W.I., YOUNG C.M.
CONSTITUTIONAL LAWS OF THE COMMONWEALTH.
LONDON: OXFORD U PR, 1952, 515 PP.
COMPILES SIGNIFICANT CASES IN BRITISH CONSTITUTIONAL LAW, 1702-1947, REGARDING RELATION OF COLONIES TO ENGLAND, LAND OWNERSHIP, INDUSTRIAL DEVELOPMENT, AND CIVIL LAW. ALSO GIVES SUMMARY OF CONSTITUTIONS OF CANADA, IRELAND, NEW ZEALAND, AND AUSTRALIA.

1317 JENSEN F.B. ED., WALTER I. ED.
READINGS IN INTERNATIONAL ECONOMIC RELATIONS.
NEW YORK: RONALD PRESS, 1966, 528 PP., LC#66-16846.
ESSAYS ON 12 MAJOR PROBLEM AREAS IN INTERNATIONAL ECONOMICS, WITH EXPLANATORY EDITORIAL COMMENTS. GENERAL APPROACH GEARED TO STUDENT AUDIENCE. SUBJECTS INCLUDE INTERNATIONAL ASPECTS OF TRADE, MONETARY SYSTEMS, BALANCE OF PAYMENTS, AND INVESTMENTS.

1318 JEVONS W.S.
THE THEORY OF POLITICAL ECONOMY (4TH ED.; 1ST ED. 1871)
LONDON: MACMILLAN, 1931, 339 PP.
TREATS ECONOMY AS A "CALCULUS OF PLEASURE AND PAIN" AND EVALUATES UTILITY, VALUE, LABOR, AND CAPITAL QUANTITATIVELY, DISTINGUISHING EMPIRICAL ELEMENTS FROM ABSTRACT THEORY AND FROM ART OF FINANCE AND ADMINISTRATION. RECOUNTS EARLIER ATTEMPTS TO APPLY MATHEMATICAL LANGUAGE TO POLITICAL ECONOMIC THEORY. DISCUSSES THEORY OF EXCHANGE AND OF RENT. EXTENDS BIBLIOGRAPHY OF MATHEMATICAL ECONOMIC WRITINGS.

1319 JEVONS W.S.
MONEY AND THE MECHANISM OF EXCHANGE.
NEW YORK: APPLETON, 1875, 341 PP.
PROPOSES SYSTEM OF CONSIDERING MONEY A QUASI-COMMODITY, SUBJECT TO SUPPLY AND DEMAND AND, THEREFORE, SELF-REGULATING. PAPER NOTES SHOULD BE STRICTLY MATCHED TO METALLIC CURRENCY. CLAIMS THAT IT IS FUTILE TO ATTEMPT TO CONTROL WAGES, PRICES, OR CURRENCY. SYSTEM IS COMPLETELY LAISSEZ-FAIRE, THOUGH RECOGNIZING THAT VALUE OF MONEY IS DETERMINED BY UTILITY AS WELL AS EXCHANGE.

1320 JHANGIANI M.A.
JANA SANGH AND SWATANTRA: A PROFILE OF THE RIGHTIST PARTIES IN INDIA.
BOMBAY: MANAKTALAS, 1967, 223PP.
STUDIES TWO NEW "RIGHTIST" PARTIES IN INDIA. JANA SANGH CLAIMS "LEFTISTS" ARE TOO WESTERN AND DERIVES INSPIRATION FROM VALUES OF BHARATIYA CULTURE. SWATANTRA OPPOSES SOCIALISM AND SEEKS TO MAINTAIN STATUS QUO OF FREE ENTERPRISE. DISCUSSES DEVELOPMENT, STRUCTURE, ORGANIZATION, AND IDEOLOGY OF TWO PARTIES, PLUS THEIR RESULTS IN ELECTIONS.

1321 JOHNSON D.G.
"GOVERNMENT AND AGRICULTURE: IS AGRICULTURE A SPECIAL CASE?"
JOURNAL OF LAW AND ECONOMICS, 1(OCT 58),122-136.
PROBES, AMONG OTHER ISSUES, THE ARGUMENT THAT SINCE INDUSTRY AND LABOR ARE ORGANIZED AND AGRICULTURE IS UNABLE TO REGULATE PRICES, GOVERNMENT INTERVENTION IS REQUIRED TO HELP THE FARMERS.

1322 JOHNSON D.G.
THE STRUGGLE AGAINST WORLD HUNGER (HEADLINE SERIES, NO. 184) (PAMPHLET)
NEW YORK: FOREIGN POLICY ASSN, 1967, 63 PP., LC#67-27423.
SUMMARIZES WORLD FOOD PROBLEM TODAY AND POSSIBLE FUTURE SITUATION. SUGGESTS IMPORTANCE OF PROGRAMS WHICH CAN EVENTUALLY MAKE DEVELOPING NATIONS AGRICULTURALLY SELF-SUFFICIENT, INSTEAD OF DEPENDENT ON US AID.

1323 JOHNSON H.G.
INTERNATIONAL TRADE AND ECONOMIC GROWTH.
CAMBRIDGE: HARVARD U PR, 1958, 204 PP.
DISCUSSES PRINCIPLES OF INTERNATIONAL TRADE AS OPTIMUM TARIFFS, TRADE BALANCE, EXCHANGE STABILITY, AND BALANCE-OF-PAYMENTS.

1324 JOHNSON H.G.
MONEY, TRADE AND ECONOMIC GROWTH.
CAMBRIDGE: HARVARD U PR, 1962, 197 PP.
SURVEYS KEYNESIAN ECONOMICS, WORLD TRADE, ECONOMIC GROWTH IN ADVANCED COUNTRIES, AND THE CONCEPT OF PLANNING ECONOMIC GROWTH. RELATES SOCIAL THEORY TO AFFLUENCE AND DISCUSSES NATURE OF POLICY IN OPULENT SOCIETY.

1325 JOHNSON H.G.
"A THEORETICAL MODEL OF ECONOMIC NATIONALISM IN NEW AND DEVELOPING STATES."
POLIT. SCI. QUART., 80 (JUNE 65), 169-185.
POSTULATES A MODEL RELATING THE DEMANDS OF NATIONALISM TO THE ECONOMIC CHOICES MADE IN DEVELOPING STATES. DERIVED FROM EARLIER THEORETIC WORK ON THE ECONOMICS OF DISCRIMINATION, APPLICATION OF ECONOMIC THEORY TO STUDY OF DEMOCRACY'S DEMANDS, AND BRETON'S HYPOTHESES ASSERTING THE PRIMACY OF MIDDLE CLASS GROUPS IN FORMULATING NATIONALIST ECONOMIC POLICY. "PSYCHIC SATISFACTION" IS KEY TO MODEL.

1326 JOHNSON H.G.
THE WORLD ECONOMY AT THE CROSSROADS.
LONDON: OXFORD U PR, 1965, 105 PP.
SURVEY OF CURRENT PROBLEMS OF INTERNATIONAL ECONOMIC ORGANIZATION INVOLVING FREE WORLD COUNTRIES. EMPHASIZES MONETARY, TRADE, AND ECONOMIC-DEVELOPMENT PROBLEMS ON INTERNATIONAL LEVEL. DISCUSSES FORMATION OF INTERNATIONAL ECONOMIC INSTITUTIONS UP TO POST-WWII ERA, NOTING SEVERE POLITICAL AND ECONOMIC CONFLICTS AMONG NATIONS COMPRISING THESE INSTITUTIONS.

1327 JOHNSON H.G.
ECONOMIC POLICY TOWARD LESS DEVELOPED COUNTRIES.
WASHINGTON: BROOKINGS INST, 1967, 212 PP., LC#67-14972.
COVERS MAIN ISSUES FACING US IN RELATION TO DEVELOPING NATIONS, GIVING BACKGROUND. DISCUSSES FOREIGN AID, ECONOMIC POLICY, DEVELOPMENT ECONOMICS. GIVES PICTURE OF POSSIBLE US POLICY CHOICES SUCH AS FREE TRADE, LOWER TARIFFS PREFERENTIAL TREATMENT, MONETARY REFORM. SOMEWHAT CRITICAL

OF PAST US POLICY.

1328 JOHNSON H.G. ED.
ECONOMIC NATIONALISM IN OLD AND NEW STATES.
CHICAGO: U OF CHICAGO PRESS, 1967, 145 PP., LC#67-20573.
PRESENTS MODEL FOR STUDY OF ECONOMIC NATIONALISM IN NEW STATES. STUDIES 19TH-CENTURY RELATIONSHIP BETWEEN NATIONALISM AND DEVELOPMENT, INFLUENCE OF NATIONALISM ON BRITISH ECONOMIC POLICY, AND ROLE OF NATIONALISM IN COMMUNIST CHINA, MEXICO, CANADA, AND MALI. FINDS THAT ROLE AND INFLUENCES DIFFER GREATLY. SURVEYS ECONOMIC THEORIES ABOUT DEVELOPMENT AND RELATIONS OF OLD AND NEW STATES.

1329 JOHNSON L.B.
"BULLETS DO NOT DISCRIMINATE-LANDLORDS DO."
CRISIS, 74 (MAR. 67), 61-67, 95-101 .
MESSAGE TO CONGRESS ON CIVIL RIGHTS, CALLS FOR EQUAL HOUSING OPPORTUNITY, NONDISCRIMINATE JURY SELECTION, FEDERAL PROTECTION FOR PURSUANCE OF CONSTITUTIONAL RIGHTS, INCREASED APPROPRIATIONS FOR COMMUNITY RELATIONS SERVICE, EMPOWERING EQUAL EMPLOYMENT OPPORTUNITY COMMISSION TO TAKE STRONGER ACTION, AND EXTENSION OF CIVIL RIGHTS COMMISSION.

1330 JOHNSON L.L.
"US BUSINESS INTERESTS IN CUBA AND THE RISE OF CASTRO."
WORLD POLITICS, 17 (APR. 65), 440-459.
ARGUES FROM THE CUBAN CASE, THAT SOME BUT NOT ALL PATTERNS OF PRIVATE INVESTMENT BY US CITIZENS IN LATIN AMERICA SERVE THE OVERALL OBJECTIVES OF THE AMERICAN FOREIGN ASSISTANCE PROGRAM. CONCLUSION RAISES A NUMBER OF POLITICAL ISSUES THAT MUST BE SEEN AS DEPENDENT ON ECONOMIC POLICIES OPEN TO MANIPULATION BY US POLICY-MAKERS.

1331 JOHNSON R.B.
FINANCING A SUBURBAN CITY.
MUNICIPAL FINANCE, 40 (AUG. 67), 56-58.
DISCUSSES AURORA, COLORADO'S SOLUTION TO PROBLEMS OF FINANCING, USING IT TO INDICATE MEANS APPLICABLE IN OTHER SMALL MUNICIPALITIES. INCLUDES UTILITIES, DIRECT CHARGING FOR PUBLIC SERVICES, AND PROPERTY TAXES.

1332 JOHNSTON B.F., MELLOR J.W.
"THE ROLE OF AGRICULTURE IN ECONOMIC DEVELOPMENT."
AMER. ECO. REVIEW, 51 (SEPT. 61), 566-593.
EXAMINES INTERRELATIONSHIPS BETWEEN AGRICULTURAL AND INDUSTRIAL DEVELOPMENT AND ANALYZES NATURE OF AGRICULTURE'S ROLE IN ECONOMIC GROWTH. MAINTAINS THAT AGRICULTURE'S CONTRIBUTION IS MOST SIGNIFICANT IN EARLY STAGES OF GROWTH WHEN ITS RESOURCE ALLOCATION MUST DECLINE IN FAVOR OF INDUSTRY. BELIEVES THAT BALANCED GROWTH IN BOTH SECTORS IS VITAL.

1333 JOHNSTON J.
ECONOMETRIC METHODS.
NEW YORK: MCGRAW HILL, 1963, 299 PP., LC#62-17369.
EXPLAINS ECONOMETRIC METHODS FOR STUDENTS WHO HAVE DONE A YEAR'S WORK IN STATISTICAL THEORY AND METHOD. CONTAINS EXPOSITION OF LINEAR NORMAL REGRESSION MODEL, AND EXPOUNDS MAIN STATISTICAL METHODS NOW AVAILABLE.

1334 JOHNSTON J.D. JR.
"CONSTITUTION OF SUBDIVISION CONTROL EXACTIONS: THE QUEST FOR A RATIONALE."
CORNELL LAW Q., 52 (SUMMER 67), 871-924.
ANALYZES THE "VOLUNTARINESS," "PRIVILEGE," AND "POLICE POWER" RATIONALES USED TO JUSTIFY SUBDIVISION CONTROL EXACTIONS. CONCLUDES THAT "POLICE POWER" RATIONALE IS THE MOST APPROPRIATE. EXAMINES CATEGORIES OF EXACTIONS AND ARGUES THAT MUNICIPALITIES SHOULD ESTABLISH LINK BETWEEN THEIR EXACTIONS AND PUBLIC NEEDS CREATED BY A SUBDIVISION DEVELOPMENT.

1335 JOHNSTONE A.
UNITED STATES DIRECT INVESTMENT IN FRANCE: AN INVESTIGATION OF THE FRENCH CHARGES.
CAMBRIDGE: M I T PRESS, 1965, 109 PP., LC#65-22005.
STUDIES FRENCH CLAIMS THAT US INVESTMENT PRESENTS THREAT TO ECONOMIC SOVEREIGNTY. POINTS OUT VIEWS OF BOTH AMERICAN BUSINESS AND FRENCH SOCIAL, POLITICAL, AND ECONOMIC INTERESTS. CONCLUSIONS GENERALLY SUPPORT FRENCH OFFICIALS. INCLUDES RECOMMENDATIONS FOR BOTH US AND FRENCH GOVERNMENTS.

1336 JOHR W.A., SINGER H.W.
THE ROLE OF THE ECONOMIST AS OFFICIAL ADVISER.
LONDON: ALLEN & UNWIN, 1955, 156 PP.
DISCUSSES "PROPER FUNCTION" OF ECONOMISTS IN FORMATION AND ADMINISTRATION OF ECONOMIC POLICY. CONCLUDES THAT, AS AN ADVISER, THE ECONOMIST SHOULD BE FREE TO ADVOCATE HIS OWN AIMS BY COMPARING THEIR CONSEQUENCES WITH THE CONSEQUENCES DESIRED BY THOSE HE ADVISES. ANALYZES PROBLEM OF ESTABLISHMENT OF AIMS, AND PROPOSES WORKING SYSTEM OF COORDINATION.

1337 JOINT ECONOMIC COMMITTEE
"DIMENSIONS OF SOVIET ECONOMIC POWER."
WASHINGTON: US GOVERNMENT, 1962.
COMPILATION OF STUDY PAPERS PREPARED BY A GROUP OF EXPERTS ON THE SOVIET ECONOMY FOR 87TH CONGRESS. ANALYZES SOVIET POLICY FRAMEWORK IN TERMS OF RESOURCE ALLOCATION, MILITARY ESTABLISHMENT, AND RECENT DEVELOPMENTS IN PLANNING. EXAMINES THE MEASURE AND STRATEGY OF PRODUCTION AND PRODUCTIVITY, DEVELOPMENT OF HUMAN RESOURCES, AND DEMOGRAPHY. SELECTED BIBLIOGRAPHY OF RECENT SOVIET ECONOMIC MONOGRAPHS.

1338 JONES J.H.
THE ECONOMICS OF WAR AND CONQUEST.
LONDON: KING, 1915, 160 PP.
REFUTES NORMAN ANGELL'S THESIS THAT WAR CAN RESULT IN PROFIT. ANALYZES ECONOMIC ASPECTS OF WORLD WAR I AND CONCLUDES WAR CANNOT RESULT IN NET MATERIAL GAIN. OUTLAY IS GREATER THAN VALUE OF EXPECTED RETURN. ECONOMIC GAIN MAY ACCRUE FROM WAR, BUT RETURN WILL NEVER EXCEED COST AND DAMAGE TO ECONOMIC SYSTEM. PRIMARY CONSIDERATION IN CAUSES OF WAR SHOULD BE POLITICAL, NOT ECONOMIC.

1339 JONES M.M.
CORPORATION CONTRIBUTIONS TO COMMUNITY WELFARE AGENCIES (PAMPHLET)
NEW YORK: AMER MANAGEMENT ASSN, 1929, 28 PP., LC#37-24434.
ADDRESSES ITSELF TO THE PROBLEM OF WORKING OUT A RATIONAL APPORTIONMENT, BETWEEN PRIMARY ELEMENTS OF A COMMUNITY, OF THE COST OF NECESSARY SOCIAL WELFARE WORK. LISTS CAUSES WHICH DO NOT RECEIVE ADEQUATE FINANCING FROM FAMILY, STATE, OR PRIMARY SUPPORTER, THE EXPECTATIONS OF CORPORATIONS AS PARTICIPANTS, CONTROL BY THE DONORS, AND TAX POLICY.

1340 JONES T.B., WARBURTON E.A. ET AL.
A BIBLIOGRAPHY ON SOUTH AMERICAN ECONOMIC AFFAIRS: ARTICLES IN NINETEENTH CENTURY PERIODICALS (PAMPHLET)
MINNEAPOLIS: U OF MINN PR, 1955, 146 PP., LC#55-7033.
UNANNOTATED LISTING BY NATION,SUBDIVIDED INTO SUBJECT HEADINGS. CHRONOLOGICALLY ARRANGED. ALL WESTERN EUROPEAN LANGUAGES WITH 6200 UNIQUE ITEMS. PERIODICALS USED ARE INDEXED.

1341 JORDAN A.A. JR.
FOREIGN AID AND THE DEFENSE OF SOUTHEAST ASIA.
NEW YORK: FREDERICK PRAEGER, 1962, 272 PP., LC#62-14862.
DIVIDES FOREIGN AID INTO MILITARY ASSISTANCE, STABILITY SUPPORT, AND ECONOMIC DEVELOPMENT AND DESCRIBES CLOSE INTERRELATION. PRESENTS RATIONALE BEHIND AND PLANS FOR EACH TYPE OF AID. DISCUSSES WARFARE IN SOUTHEAST ASIA, BUDGETARY AND FISCAL PROBLEMS, MILITARY DETERRENCE, AND OVERPOPULATION AS ASPECTS OF FOREIGN AID THAT MUST BE CONSIDERED IN POLICY-MAKING.

1342 JUAN T.L.
ECONOMIC AND SOCIAL DEVELOPMENT OF MODERN CHINA: A BIBLIOGRAPHICAL GUIDE.
NEW HAVEN: HUMAN REL AREA FILES, 1956, 87 PP.
BIBLIOGRAPHY OF MONOGRAPHS AND PAMPHLETS PUBLISHED IN ENGLISH, FRENCH, AND GERMAN FROM BEGINNING OF 20TH CENTURY THROUGH 1955. CONTAINS ITEMS ON STATISTICS, ECONOMIC HISTORY, BASIC ECONOMIC RESOURCES, AGRICULTURE, INDUSTRY, COMMERCE AND COMMUNICATION, TRANSPORTATION, MONEY AND BANKING, AND INTERNATIONAL ECONOMIC RELATIONS.

1343 JUCKER-FLEETWOOD E.
ECONOMIC THEORY AND POLICY IN FINLAND 1914-1925.
OXFORD: BLACKWELL, 1958, 109 PP.
TWO ESSAYS EXAMINING FINLAND'S ECONOMIC AND FINANCIAL PROBLEMS AND THE USE MADE OF ECONOMIC POLICY IN 12-YEAR PERIOD. EXAMINES POLICIES USING QUANTITATIVE THEORY OF MONEY. THEORY OF PURCHASING POWER PARITIES. STUDY OF STABILIZATION PERIOD GIVES DYNAMIC PICTURE OF HOW TO FORMULATE AND CARRY THROUGH A DESIRED POLICY. SHOWS HOW FINLAND MANAGED TO ESCAPE 1921 CRISIS AND RETURN TO GOLD STANDARD IN 1922.

1344 JUCKER-FLEETWOOD E.
MONEY AND FINANCE IN AFRICA.
NEW YORK: PRAEGER, 1964, 335 PP.
STUDIES FINANCIAL PROBLEMS OF EMERGING COUNTRIES IN AFRICA. NOTES ROLE OF CENTRAL BANKS IN LAYING FOUNDATIONS FOR CURRENCY EXCHANGE, FOREIGN EXCHANGE RESERVES, SUPPORT OF GOVERNMENT PROGRAMS. FOLLOWS ESTABLISHMENT OF COMMERCIAL BANKS AND OTHER FINANCIAL INSTITUTIONS. OUTLINES MODERN AFRICAN DEVELOPMENT PLANS AND THEIR FINANCING.

1345 JUSTER F.T.
ANTICIPATIONS AND PURCHASES; AN ANALYSIS OF CONSUMER BEHAVIOR.
PRINCETON: PRINCETON U PRESS, 1964, 298 PP., LC#63-23396.
CONCLUDES INVESTIGATION OF CONSUMER PURCHASE BEHAVIOR INITIATED BY NATIONAL BUREAU IN 1957. EVALUATES RELATION BETWEEN CONSUMER'S ATTITUDES ABOUT FUTURE AND PURCHASING. CRITICIZES PAST SURVEYS FOR FAILURE TO OBTAIN SUFFICIENTLY PRECISE MEASURE OF PURCHASE PROBABILITY.

1346 KAESTNER K.
GESAMTWIRTSCHAFTLICHE PLANUNG IN EINER GEMISCHTEN WIRTSCHAFTSORDNUNG (WIRTSCHAFTSPOLITISCHE STUDIEN 5)

GOTTINGEN: VAN DEN HOECK UND RUPRECHT, 1966,140PP.
PRESENTS CONCEPTS AND METHODS OF TOTAL ECONOMIC PLANNING; DISCUSSES SCOPE OF PLANNING (PUBLIC SECTOR, MANAGEMENT POLICY, PRIVATE SECTOR), TREATS PLANNING OF PRODUCTION IN THE PRIVATE SECTOR; CONSIDERS POSSIBILITIES OF TOTAL ECONOMIC PLANNING IN A MIXED ECONOMY. BIBLIOGRAPHY LISTS 146 BOOKS AND ARTICLES IN GERMAN, FRENCH, ENGLISH, 1883-1965.

1347 KAHN R.L., TANNENBAUM A.S.
"UNION PRACTICES AND MEMBER PARTICIPATION."
PERSONNEL PSYCHOLOGY, 10 (FALL 57), 277-292.
ATTEMPTS TO REPLICATE INDUSTRIAL FINDINGS TO SHOW THE IMPORTANCE OF LEADERS' INTERPERSONAL SKILLS IN DETERMINING THE ATTITUDES AND BEHAVIOR OF GROUP MEMBERS. SKILLS IN COMMUNICATION, INVOLVING MEN IN DECISION-MAKING AND PERSONAL INTEREST IN OTHERS, WERE NOTED.

1348 KALDOR N.
ESSAYS ON ECONOMIC POLICY (VOL. II)
LONDON: DUCKWORTH, 1964, 320 PP.
FIRST PART OF STUDY DISCUSSES ECONOMIC POLICIES FOR MAINTAINING INTERNATIONAL STABILITY WITH SPECIFIC REFERENCE TO PROBLEMS IN INTERNATIONAL TRADE AND PAYMENTS. SECOND PART DEVOTED TO DISCUSSIONS OF VARIED TOPICS IN ECONOMIC CONDITIONS OF FIVE DIFFERENT COUNTRIES.

1349 KANNER L. ED., MULLANEY T.E.
THE NEW YORK TIMES WORLD ECONOMIC REVIEW AND FORECAST: 1967.
NEW YORK: GROSSET AND DUNLAP, 1967, 256 PP., LC#65-17639.
REPORTORIAL SURVEY BY TIMES CORRESPONDENTS OF PREVIOUS FISCAL YEAR'S MOST IMPORTANT BUSINESS AND FINANCIAL EVENTS. COUNTRY BY COUNTRY SURVEY WITH MANY PHOTOGRAPHS, MAPS, GROWTH CHARTS, AND TABLES. GENERAL PREDICTION OF WORLD TRENDS ALSO INCLUDED.

1350 KANTOROVICH L.V.
THE BEST USE OF ECONOMIC RESOURCES.
CAMBRIDGE: HARVARD U PR, 1965, 349 PP., LC#64-21300.
DEMONSTRATES THE TECHNIQUES OF LINEAR PROGRAMMING. PRESENTS EVIDENCE THAT THIS TECHNIQUE, WITH ITS IMPLICATIONS FOR THE SETTING OF PRICES IN THE PRODUCER-GOODS MARKET, SHOULD BE MORE WIDELY ADOPTED IN THE PLANNING OF THE RUSSIAN ECONOMY. ILLUMINATES ASPECTS OF RUSSIAN ECONOMIC PLANNING AND SHOWS THAT MANAGERIAL PROBLEMS ARE ESSENTIALLY SIMILAR WHATEVER THE GENERAL ECONOMIC STRUCTURE OF THE COUNTRY.

1351 KAPLAN A.D.H.
BIG ENTERPRISE IN A COMPETITIVE SYSTEM (REV. ED.)
WASHINGTON: BROOKINGS INST, 1964, 240 PP., LC#64-8754.
DEALING WITH NONREGULATED SECTOR OF BIG BUSINESS, THIS IS A STUDY OF DEVELOPMENT OF PUBLIC OPINION AND POLICY TOWARD BIG BUSINESS. ANALYZES ROLE OF BUSINESS IN COMPETITIVE ENTERPRISE, IN THE BUSINESS POPULATION, IN INDUSTRIAL PRODUCTION, AND IN CONCENTRATION OF FINANCIAL POWER. ALSO STUDIES PRICE COMPETITION, COMPETITIVE PRESSURES, INTEGRATION, AND SIZE.

1352 KAPLAN J.J.
CHALLENGE OF FOREIGN AID.
NEW YORK: FREDERICK PRAEGER, 1967, 405 PP., LC#67-16681.
CRITICISM OF FOREIGN AID PROGRAM WITH SUGGESTED THEORY OF OPERATION AS WELL AS SPECIFIC RENOVATION PROPOSALS. MAKES NUMEROUS SUGGESTIONS AND ARGUES FOR THEM, IN AREAS SUCH AS BALANCE OF PAYMENTS, LOANS VS GRANTS, MILITARY ASSISTANCE. COVERS HISTORY OF PROGRAM, AND POLICY ISSUES. EXPLORES POSSIBILITIES OF MULTILATERAL AID.

1353 KAPP W.K.
HINDU CULTURE: ECONOMIC DEVELOPMENT AND ECONOMIC PLANNING IN INDIA.
NEW YORK: ASIA PUBL., 1963, 228 PP.
ANALYZES ECONOMIC DEVELOPMENT AND PLANNING IN TERMS OF 'HINDUISM, AS A RELIGION AND AS A SOCIAL SYSTEM...IN AN EFFORT TO DETERMINE THE EXTENT TO WHICH HINDU CULTURE SERVES OR CONTRADICTS THE SOCIAL PURPOSES OF INDIA'S DEVELOPMENT EFFORT. CONCLUDES THAT CERTAIN ASPECTS OF HINDU CULTURE, TOGETHER WITH THE RELATED ADMINISTRATIVE DEFECTS, HAVE RETARDED ECONOMIC GROWTH IN INDIA IN THE PAST AND ARE LIKELY TO FRUSTRATE THE AIMS OF ECONOMIC DEVELOPMENT IN THE FUTURE.'

1354 KAPP W.K.
SOCIAL COSTS OF BUSINESS ENTERPRISE.
BOMBAY: ASIA PUBL HOUSE, 1963, 311 PP.
STUDIES WAYS THAT PRIVATE ENTERPRISE UNDER CONDITIONS OF UNREGULATED COMPETITION GIVES RISE TO SOCIAL COSTS (WATER POLLUTION, RESOURCE EXHAUSTION, EFFECTS OF TECHNOLOGICAL CHANGE) THAT MUST BE BORNE BY THIRD PARTIES AND COMMUNITY AS A WHOLE. DEALS WITH SPECIFIC TECHNICAL QUESTION AND WITH BROAD ISSUES OF SOCIAL PHILOSOPY.

1355 KARDOUCHE G.K.
THE UAR IN DEVELOPMENT.
NEW YORK: FREDERICK PRAEGER, 1967, 170 PP., LC#67-14184.
COMPREHENSIVE COVERAGE OF EGYPTIAN ECONOMIC DEVELOPMENT, INCLUDING FOREIGN TRADE, BANKING, DEVELOPMENT, AND ALSO MONETARY DEVELOPMENT, INCLUDING FOREIGN ASSETS, CREDIT, BANKING CONTROL. DISCUSSES EFFECTS OF GOVERNMENT POLICY. WRITTEN FOR OTHER RESEARCHERS AS WELL AS ECONOMISTS.

1356 KAREFA-SMART J. ED., ADEBO S.O. ED.
AFRICA: PROGRESS THROUGH COOPERATION.
NEW YORK: DODD, MEAD, 1966, 288 PP., LC#66-12809.
SPEECHES AND PAPERS PREPARED FOR THE 1965 AFRICAN CONFERENCE ON PROGRESS THROUGH COOPERATION. STUDY WAYS IN WHICH AFRICAN NATIONS CAN HASTEN ECONOMIC AND SOCIAL DEVELOPMENT, MEET PRESSING NEEDS OF THEIR PEOPLE, RAISE THEIR STANDARDS OF LIVING, AND ESTABLISH ADVANTAGEOUS DOMESTIC AND INTERNATIONAL RELATIONS. INQUIRE INTO PRACTICAL WAYS FOR EFFECTIVE USE OF RESOURCES AND AID.

1357 KARLIN S.
MATHEMATICAL METHODS AND THEORY IN GAMES, PROGRAMMING, AND ECONOMICS.
READING, MASS: ADDISON-WESLEY, 1959, 819 PP., LC#60-5402.
EXPLANATION AND DISCUSSION OF METHODS AND PURPOSE OF GAME THEORY AND ORGANIZATION OF DATA FOR UNDERSTANDING OF STRATEGY AND DECISION MAKING.

1358 KARTUN D.
AFRICA, AFRICA: A CONTINENT RISES TO ITS FEET.
LONDON: LAWRENCE & WISHART, 1954, 99 PP.
STUDY OF EMERGENT AFRICA, THE INJUSTICE AND EXPLOITATION OF EUROPEAN IMPERIALISM, GOLD COAST, AND EARLY RESISTANCE TO DOMINATION.

1359 KASER M.
COMECON* INTEGRATION PROBLEMS OF THE PLANNED ECONOMIES.
LONDON: OXFORD U PR, 1965, 215 PP.
THE LACK OF AUTOMATIC REGULATION THROUGH THE PRICE MECHANISM HAS MADE TRADE A DIFFICULT PROBLEM WITHIN THE REGIONAL ECONOMIC ORGANIZATION OF THE EUROPEAN COMMUNIST STATES. INSTITUTIONAL HISTORY OF COMECON SHOWS INTERPLAY BETWEEN POLITICAL FACTORS LIKE NATIONALISM AND ECONOMIC PLANNING PARADOXES SUCH AS PROFITS. INTEGRATION PROBLEMS COMPARED TO THOSE FACING EEC.

1360 KATKOFF U.
SOVIET ECONOMY 1940-1965.
BALTIMORE: DANGARY, 1961, 559 PP. $6.50.
STUDY IS BASED ON OFFICIAL SOVIET STATISTICS. ANALYZES IMPACT ON ECONOMY OF MEASURES PROMULGATED BY STALIN AND KHRUSCHEV. REVEALS ADVERSE EFFECT OF RECENT AGRICULTURAL CRISES.

1361 KATZ S.M., MCGOWEN F.
A SELECTED LIST OF US READINGS ON DEVELOPMENT.
WASHINGTON: AGENCY FOR INTL DEV, 1963, 362 PP.
LIST OF SELECTED READINGS ON APPLICATION OF SCIENCE AND TECHNOLOGY TO PROBLEMS OF LESS-DEVELOPED NATIONS. REPRESENTATIVE SAMPLE OF CURRENT AMERICAN RESEARCH PAPERS, ACADEMIC STUDIES, AND OPERATIONAL REPORTS ON MAJOR AREAS OF SCIENCE AND TECHNOLOGY. CONTAINS FAIRLY EXTENSIVE ANNOTATIONS OF 1,195 ITEMS PUBLISHED AFTER 1950. MATERIAL ORGANIZED BY SUBJECT; INCLUDES AUTHOR INDEX.

1362 KAUFMAN R.H.
"THE ASIAN GOLD TRADE."
ASIAN SURVEY, 5 (MAY 65), 233-244.
REVIEWS KNOWN DATA AND MAKES ESTIMATES ON AMOUNTS OF ILLEGAL GOLD TRADE WITH PARTICULAR EMPHASIS ON HONG KONG, MACAO, LAOS, AND THAILAND. WITH THE LIMITED AVAILABLE DATA, RECORDS WHERE GOLD IS IMPORTED FROM AND EXPORTED TO AND HOW ITS FLOW IS AFFECTED BY INTERNATIONAL POLITICS. PREDICTS CONTINUED FLOW AS FUNCTION OF TRADITION AND INSTABILITY.

1363 KAUFMANN F.
METHODOLOGY OF THE SOCIAL SCIENCES.
LONDON: OXFORD U PR, 1944, 271 PP.
GENERAL CONSIDERATION OF PHILOSOPHY OF SCIENCE. ALSO DEALS WITH RELATION OF PRAGMATISM, RATIONALISM, AND RELATIVITY TO FORMULATION OF RESEARCH PARADIGMS. DISCUSSES APPLICATIONS IN SOCIAL SCIENCES AND DIFFICULTIES IN APPLICATION, ESPECIALLY IN ECONOMICS. ATTEMPTS TO GIVE BASIC FOUNDATION FOR CONSIDERATION OF BEHAVIOR.

1364 KAUN D.E.
"THE FAIR LABOUR STANDARDS ACT: AN EVALUATION IN TERMS OF ITS STATED GOALS."
S. AFR. J. OF ECONOMICS, 33 (JUNE 65), 131-145.
STATES BASIC AIMS OF FEDERAL MINIMUM WAGE LEGISLATION. DESCRIBES ACHIEVEMENTS, THEIR "DESIRABILITY," AND ALTERNATIVES TO MINIMUM WAGE.

1365 KAUTSKY J.H. ED.
POLITICAL CHANGE IN UNDERDEVELOPED COUNTRIES: NATIONALISM AND COMMUNISM.
NEW YORK: WILEY, 1962, 347 PP.
A COLLECTION OF WORKS CONCERNED WITH POLITICAL SITUATION IN A PREDOMINANTLY AGRARIAN SOCIETY AS EFFECTED BY INTRODUCTION OF INDUSTRIALIZATION.

1366 KEE W.S.
"CENTRAL CITY EXPENDITURES AND METROPOLITAN AREAS."
NATIONAL TAX J., 18 (1965), 337-353.
ANALYSIS OF THIRTY-SIX MAJOR CITIES INDICATES THAT THE CENTRAL-CITY EXPENDITURES MAY BE MORE PER CAPITA THAN IN THE SURROUNDING METROPOLITAN AREA BUT THAT SUBURBANITES ARE CHIEF BENEFICIARIES. ARGUES FOR WIDER ADOPTION OF CITY-COUNTY GOVERNMENTS.

1367 KEENLEYSIDE H.L.
INTERNATIONAL AID: A SUMMARY.
NEW YORK: JAMES H HEINEMAN, 1966, 343 PP., LC#66-22154.
ATTEMPTS TO REVIEW CONTEMPORARY CIRCUMSTANCES NECESSITATING AID PROGRAMS, TO PRESENT HISTORICAL SUMMARY OF INTERNATIONAL ASSISTANCE, DESCRIPTION OF CURRENT PROGRAMS, AND STEPS FOR FUTURE ACTION BASED ON PAST EXPERIENCE.

1368 KEIR D.L., LAWSON F.H.
CASES IN CONSTITUTIONAL LAW.
LONDON: OXFORD U PR, 1948, 530 PP.
COVERS 1606-1931, INCLUDING ALL IMPORTANT CASES DEALING WITH PREROGATIVE, PARLIAMENTARY PRIVILEGE, TAXATION, THE CROWN, PUBLIC AUTHORITIES, MARTIAL LAW, AND COLONIES. BRIEF INTRODUCTION RELATES EACH SECTION TO DEVELOPMENT OF BRITISH LEGAL SYSTEM.

1369 KELF-COHEN R.
NATIONALISATION IN BRITAIN: THE END OF DOGMA.
NEW YORK: ST MARTIN'S PRESS, 1959, 310 PP.
CRITICAL DISCUSSION OF THE NATIONALIZATION OF INDUSTRIES IN GREAT BRITAIN BY A FORMER SUPPORTER OF THIS ECONOMIC TACTIC. DISCUSSES WHICH INDUSTRIES ARE NATIONALIZED AND WHAT THE FUTURE IS FOR SUCH INDUSTRIES.

1370 KELLOGG C.E.
"TRANSFER OF BASIC SKILLS OF FOOD PRODUCTION."
ANN. AMER. ACAD. POLIT. SOC. SCI., 331 (SEPT. 60), 32-38.
REALIZES GROWING AWARENESS OF FOOD SURPLUSES IN ADVANCED COUNTRIES HAS STIRRED PEOPLE IN UNDERDEVELOPED COUNTRIES. ENUMERATES DIFFICULTIES ENCOUNTERED BY SCIENTISTS WORKING TO IMPROVE SKILLS OF PEOPLE. AMONG MAIN DIFFICULTIES THE PROMINENT ARE LOW SOCIAL STATUS OF CULTIVATORS, ADOPTION OF SHORT-RUN SINGLE PRACTICE PROGRAMS AND CLIMATIC CONDITIONS. TECHNICAL ASSISTANCE OF HIGHER CALIBRE IS NEEDED.

1371 KELLY F.K.
"A PROPOSAL FOR AN ANNUAL REPORT ON THE STATE OF MANKIND."
CENTER MAGAZINE, 1 (OCT.-NOV. 67), 38-41.
PROPOSES THAT UN SECRETARY GENERAL GIVE WORLD A FULL REPORT EVERY YEAR ON STATE OF MANKIND, TO EVALUATE MAN'S DEEPEST PROBLEMS AND MAKE RECOMMENDATIONS. PURPOSE: TO START GLOBAL DIALOGUE, INVITING SUGGESTIONS FOR DEVELOPING WORLD CIVILIZATION. PRINTS LETTERS OF REACTION FROM EUGENE CARSON BLAKE, REINHOLD NIEBUHR, PAUL HOFFMAN, AND MANY OTHERS.

1372 KELLY W.E.
"HOW SALES EXECUTIVES USE FACTORING TO BOOST SALES AND PROFITS TODAY."
SALES MANAGEMENT, 75 (AUG. 55), 08-114.
EXPLAINS WHAT FACTORING IS AND HOW IT WORKS. LINKS THEORY OF FACTORING TO GREATER CREDIT FLEXIBILITY. CONSIDERS FACTORING AS A SIGN OF STRENGTH. SHOWS USE OF FACTOR TO OBTAIN READY CASH AS WELL AS HIS USE AS A MARKET COUNSELOR. TELLS HOW ANALYSIS BY A FACTOR CAN INCREASE SALES AND PROFIT AND REDUCE EXPENDITURES, OR EXPLAINS HOW ECONOMICAL FACTORING REALLY IS.

1373 KELSO L.O., ADLER M.J.
THE NEW CAPITALISTS: A PROPOSAL TO FREE ECONOMIC GROWTH FROM THE SLAVERY OF SAVINGS.
NEW YORK: RANDOM HOUSE, INC, 1961, 109 PP., LC#61-6562.
THEORIZES THAT AS LABOR PROGRESSIVELY PRODUCES LESS AND CAPITAL PRODUCES MORE OF THE GNP, A GROWING PROPORTION OF HOUSEHOLDS MUST PARTICIPATE IN PRODUCTION THROUGH THEIR OWNERSHIP OF CAPITAL AND A DIMINISHING NUMBER MUST DEPEND UPON EARNINGS OF LABOR. STATES THAT OUR CONVENTIONAL METHODS OF FINANCING CORPORATE ENTERPRISES INEVITABLY LEAD TO SOCIALIZED OWNERSHIP OF CAPITAL.

1374 KEMP M.C.
THE PURE THEORY OF INTERNATIONAL TRADE.
ENGLEWOOD CLIFFS: PRENTICE-HALL, 1964, 324 PP., $7.95.
A COMPREHENSIVE REVIEW AND ANALYSIS OF THE TRADITIONAL THEORY OF BARTER TRADE, THE GAINS FROM TRADE AND INTERNATIONAL INVESTMENT, THE CONNECTION BETWEEN TRADE AND MONEY, AND THE EFFECTS OF TRADE BETWEEN UNDEREMPLOYED ECONOMIES.

1375 KENDALL R.J.
"CHANGED CONDITIONS AS MISREPRESENTATION IN GOVERNMENT CONSTRUCTION CONTRACTS."
G. WASH. LAW REV., 35 (JUNE 67), 978-987.
DISCUSSES "CHANGED CONDITIONS" CLAUSE OF MOST FIXED-PRICE CONSTRUCTION CONTRACTS. SHOWS THAT CONTRACTOR MUST DEPEND ON LAW TO CLAIM RECOVERY OF EXTRA COSTS IF GOVERNMENT MISREPRESENTS BUILDING CONDITIONS. SHOWS THAT THE DIFFERENCE BETWEEN GOVERNMENT AND COMMERCIAL CONTRACTS LIES IN THE ABSENCE OF REAL NEGOTIATION. URGES THAT THIS DISADVANTAGE TO CONTRACTOR BE REMEDIED.

1376 KENEN P.B.
GIANT AMONG NATIONS: PROBLEMS IN UNITED STATES FOREIGN ECONOMIC POLICY.
NEW YORK: HARCOURT BRACE, 1960, 232 PP., LC#60-9395.
ANALYZES US PROGRAMS OF FOREIGN AID AND TRADE AND PROPOSES RE-EVALUATION OF BOTH. ADVOCATES TRADE ADJUSTMENT LEGISLATION, INCREASED INVESTMENT ABROAD, MORE EFFICIENT USE OF FUNDS, INTERNATIONALIZATION OF AID EFFORTS, LESS POLITICAL INFLUENCE ON AID, ESPECIALLY CONNECTIONS TO COLD WAR.

1377 KENEN P.B.
BRITISH MONETARY POLICY AND THE BALANCE OF PAYMENTS 1951-57.
CAMBRIDGE: HARVARD U PR, 1960, 325 PP., LC#60-11556.
SURVEYS BRITAIN'S DOMESTIC ECONOMIC POLICIES, ESPECIALLY HER MONETARY POLICIES, IN THE LIGHT OF HER BALANCE-OF-PAYMENTS POSITION, FOCUSING ON GOVERNMENT'S ATTITUDE AND RESPONSE TO BALANCE-OF-PAYMENTS CRISIS. CONTENDS THAT ATTEMPTS TO MAINTAIN EXTERNAL BALANCE HAVE REVOLUTIONIZED BANK OF ENGLAND POLICIES, AFFECTING VOLUME PRICE OF CREDIT RATHER THAN CONDITIONS IN DISCOUNT MARKET.

1378 KENNY L.M.
"THE AFTERMATH OF DEFEAT IN EGYPT."
INT. J., 23 (WINTER 67), 97-108.
ANALYZES ECONOMIC EFFECTS OF EGYPTIAN DEFEAT BY ISRAELI FORCES, AND THE CONSEQUENCES OF THIS UPON GOOD WILL FOR US. ALSO DELVES INTO REASONS, MANIFEST AND LATENT, FOR MILITARY DEFEAT, BOTH AS GIVEN BY EGYPTIANS AND AS DERIVED FROM OBSERVATION. SEES CONTINUING ANIMOSITY BETWEEN EGYPT AND WEST AS LONG AS WEST SUPPORTS ISRAEL.

1379 KENT R.K.
FROM MADAGASCAR TO THE MALAGASY REPUBLIC.
NEW YORK: FREDERICK PRAEGER, 1962, 182 PP., LC#62-11772.
TRACES HISTORY OF MADAGASCAR FROM FRENCH COLONIAL ADMINISTRATION TO REVOLT IN 1947. ALSO DISCUSSES POLITICAL AND ECONOMIC PROBLEMS SINCE INDEPENDENCE.

1380 KENYA MINISTRY ECO PLAN DEV
AFRICAN SOCIALISM AND ITS APPLICATION TO PLANNING IN KENYA (PAMPHLET)
NAIROBI: KENYA MIN ECO PLAN DEV, 1964, 56 PP.
REPORTS ON CONFERENCE OF AFRICAN COMMONWEALTH NATIONS AFRICAN FORM OF SOCIALISM IN DEVELOPMENT SINCE INDEPENDENCE OF NATION. INDICATES AREAS AND METHOD OF GOVERNMENTAL ACTIVITY IN ECONOMY.

1381 KERR C., ET A.L.
INDUSTRIALISM AND INDUSTRIAL MAN.
CAMBRIDGE: HARVARD U PR, 1960, 331 PP., LC#60-15239.
EXAMINES PROCESS OF INDUSTRIALIZATION AND ITS EFFECT ON WORKERS AND SOCIETY IN VARIOUS COUNTRIES. APPROACH IS ABSTRACT RATHER THAN FACTUAL, AND AN ATTEMPT IS MADE TO FORMULATE PARADIGMS FOR PREDICTING OUTCOME OF INDUSTRIALIZATION ON SOCIETY AND ON MANKIND.

1382 KESSELMAN L.C.
THE SOCIAL POLITICS OF THE FEPC.
CHAPEL HILL: U OF N CAR PR, 1948, 253 PP.
EXAMINES EFFORT TO INFLUENCE PUBLIC POLICY INTO SUPPORT OF FAIR EMPLOYMENT PRACTICES COMMISSION AS MEANS TO ABOLISH DISCRIMINATION IN INDUSTRY. WORK DEALS WITH DISCRIMINATION IN EMPLOYMENT, IMPORTANCE OF SOCIAL COHESION AND IDEOLOGICAL OPPOSITION TO IT, AND USE OF COMMUNICATIONS MEDIA TO SECURE SUPPORT.

1383 KESTENBAUM L.
"PRIMARY JURISDICTION TO DECIDE ANTITRUST JURISDICTION* A PRACTICAL APPROACH TO THE ALLOCATION OF FUNCTIONS."
GEORGETOWN LAW J., 55 (APR. 67), 812-829.
EXPLORES CONFUSING JURISDICTION OF COURTS AND AGENCIES IN ANTITRUST LAW SUITS. EXEMPLIFIES PRACTICAL APPROACH TO PROBLEM IN JEWEL TEA CASE; UPHELD COURT'S ABILITY TO PROCEED ALONE WHILE AFFIRMING UTILITY OF AGENCY DECISION. ADVOCATES ALLOCATION OF JURISDICTION BETWEEN COURT & AGENCY BASED ON NATURE & ORIGIN OF ANTITRUST IMMUNITY ASSERTED TOGETHER WITH RELEVANCE OF THE REGULATIONS TO ULTIMATE ISSUES.

1384 KEWEN P.B.
INTERNATIONAL ECONOMICS (2ND ED.)
ENGLEWOOD CLIFFS: PRENTICE HALL, 1967, 117 PP., LC#67-19187.
AN ANALYTICAL AND EMPIRICAL SURVEY OF INTERNATIONAL ECONOMIC POLICY AND PROCEDURE. DISCUSSES THE NATION AS AN ECONOMIC UNIT IN TERMS OF FOREIGN AND DOMESTIC TRANSACTIONS AND IN TERMS OF AN ECONOMIST'S PERSPECTIVES AND CRITERIA OF APPROACH. EXAMINES TRADE AND RESOURCE ALLOCATION, PROBLEMS IN TRADE POLICY, BALANCE OF PAYMENTS, AND FOREIGN EXCHANGE MARKETS. INCLUDES A SELECTED BIBLIOGRAPHY.

1385 KEYNES J.M.

A TREATISE ON MONEY (2 VOLS.)
NEW YORK: HARCOURT BRACE, 1930, 750 PP.
DESCRIBES MOST IMPORTANT FEATURES OF MODERN BANKING AND MONETARY METHODS, AS DRAWN FROM EXPERIENCES OF US AND GREAT BRITAIN. DISCUSSES MONETARY MANAGEMENT THROUGH GOVERNMENT CONTROL OF CURRENCY, AS IN RAISING AND LOWERING OF INTEREST RATES. ATTEMPTS TO ANALYZE CHARACTERISTICS OF DISEQUILIBRIUM, EQUILIBRIUM, AND PASSAGE FROM ONE POSITION OF EQUILIBRIUM TO ANOTHER.

1386 KEYNES J.M.
THE GENERAL THEORY OF EMPLOYMENT, INTEREST, AND MONEY.
NEW YORK: HARCOURT BRACE, 1935, 406 PP.
STATES THAT INCREASES IN EMPLOYMENT ARE LINKED WITH THE DEMAND FOR MONEY IN SUCH A WAY THAT THEY TEND TO CAUSE RISES IN PRICE. DISPUTES NOTION THAT INCOME INCREASES RESULT IN PROPORTIONAL INCREASES IN CONSUMPTION. CLAIMS MONEY IS BOTH A TRANSACTION MEDIUM AND A METHOD OF STORING WEALTH, AND TAKES ISSUE WITH CLASSICISTS WHO FEEL MONEY IS OF VALUE ONLY IN RELATION TO PRESENT PURCHASING POWER.

1387 KILE O.M.
THE FARM BUREAU MOVEMENT: THE FARM BUREAU THROUGH THREE DECADES.
BALTIMORE: WAVERLY, 1948, 416 PP.
DESCRIBES THE RISE OF ORGANIZED AGRICULTURE, THE FOUNDING CONVENTION OF THE AFBF AND ITS ORGANIZATION, VARIOUS AFBF "ADMINISTRATIONS" MEMBERSHIP DRIVES, THE "FARM BLOC" AND LOBBYING, BUREAU FINANCING, PUBLICITY, PRESS, INTERGROUP CONFERENCES AND RELATIONSHIPS, AS WELL AS SERVICES FOR MEMBERS AND STRUCTURAL ANALYSIS.

1388 KILLOUGH H.B., KILLOUGH L.W.
INTERNATIONAL ECONOMICS.
PRINCETON: VAN NOSTRAND, 1960, 435 PP., LC#60-12865.
GENERAL STUDY OF CONCEPT OF INTERDEPENDENCE IN INTERNATIONAL ECONOMICS EMPHASIZING PRINCIPLES THAT ENABLE INTERNATIONAL INSTITUTIONS TO FUNCTION. DISCUSSES VARIATION IN ECONOMIC CIRCUMSTANCES OF COUNTRIES AND SEVERAL UNSOLVED PROBLEMS IN INTERNATIONAL ECONOMICS RESULTING FROM THESE VARIATIONS.

1389 KINDLEBERGER C.P.
BALANCE-OF-PAYMENTS DEFICITS AND THE INTERNATIONAL MARKET FOR LIQUIDITY (PAMPHLET)
PRINCETON: PRIN U, DEPT OF ECO, 1965, 30 PP.
CONTENDS THAT CONFUSION ABOUT US INTERNATIONAL-PAYMENTS POSITION IS RESULT OF MISTAKEN DEFINITION OF BALANCE-OF-PAYMENTS DISEQUILIBRIUM AND IS SOURCE OF FAULTY ECONOMIC ANALYSIS. REVIEWS DEFINITIONS AND DISCUSSES MISCONCEPTIONS. STUDIES LONG-TERM BORROWING FOR LIQUIDITY AND PRESENTS EXAMPLES. INCLUDES INTERNATIONAL MARKET LIQUIDITY, SEPARATION OF MARKETS, EUROPE'S COMPLAINTS, AND EQUILIBRIUM.

1390 KINDLEBERGER C.P.
THE TERMS OF TRADE: A EUROPEAN CASE-STUDY.
NEW YORK: WILEY, 1956, 382 PP.
DISCUSSES SHORT AND LONG-RUN INFLUENCES ON TERMS OF TRADE. APPLIES AN ANNUAL INDEX AND A MERCHANDISE INDEX OF EIGHT COUNTRIES IN INDUSTRIAL EUROPE TO EXAMINE SHORT-RUN FACTORS SUCH AS COMMERCIAL POLICY AND EXCHANGE RATES AND LONG-RUN FACTORS RELATED TO DEMAND AND SUPPLY. EVALUATES USEFULNESS OF TERMS OF TRADE CONCEPT AND OFFERS SOLUTIONS TO TRADE PROBLEMS.

1391 KINDLEBERGER C.P.
INTERNATIONAL ECONOMICS.
HOMEWOOD: IRWIN, 1958, 636 PP.
ANALYSIS OF THE FIELD, INCLUDING TRADE AND FINANCE, AND COVERS SUBJECT OF BALANCE OF PAYMENTS, TARIFFS, CARTELS, EXCHANGE CONTROL, AND INTERGOVERNMENTAL ECONOMIC ASSISTANCE.

1392 KINDLEBERGER C.P.
"UNITED STATES ECONOMIC FOREIGN POLICY: RESEARCH REQUIREMENTS FOR 1965."
WORLD POLIT., 11 (JULY 59), 588-613.
RESEARCH PROJECTION OF FUTURE ECONOMIC PROBLEMS STATED ACCORDING TO ALLOCATION, DISTRIBUTION AND ADJUSTMENT OF RESOURCES. DESCRIBES CURRENT AND POSSIBLE FUTURE TRENDS THAT THE USA MAY ENCOUNTER IN DEALING WITH DIFFERENT ECONOMIC AND MONETARY BLOCS.

1393 KINDLEBERGER C.P.
FOREIGN TRADE AND THE NATIONAL ECONOMY.
NEW HAVEN: YALE U PR, 1962, 265 PP., LC#62-16236.
STUDY OF FOREIGN TRADE TYPE AND QUANTITY OF A NATION'S IMPORTS AND EXPORTS AND IMPACT OF SUCH TRADE ON NATIONAL ECONOMY. DISCUSSES TRANSPORTATION, RESOURCES, CAPITAL, TECHNOLOGY, AND RELATIONSHIP BETWEEN PUBLIC AND PRIVATE SECTORS IN VARIOUS NATIONS.

1394 KINDLEBERGER C.P.
"MASS MIGRATION, THEN AND NOW."
FOREIGN AFFAIRS, 43 (JULY 65), 647-658.
COMPARISON OF THE MASS MIGRATION OF EUROPEANS TO THE US IN THE 19TH AND EARLY 20TH CENTURIES WITH THE MODERN MIGRATION OF WORKERS FROM SOUTHERN EUROPE AND AFRICA TO THE FULL EMPLOYMENT MARKETS OF NORTHERN EUROPE TODAY. MAIN DIFFERENCE FOUND IN THE ROLE OF EUROPEAN GOVERNMENTS IS IN CONTRACTING AND CARING FOR WORKERS. HAS BEEN FORCE FOR LABOR LAW AND ECONOMIC EQUALIZATION IN EUROPE.

1395 KINDLEBERGER C.P.
EUROPE AND THE DOLLAR.
CAMBRIDGE: M I T PRESS, 1966, 297 PP., LC#66-15568.
COLLECTION OF PAPERS THAT HAVE APPEARED OUTSIDE ROUTINE SCHOLARLY CHANNELS, DEALING WITH THEMES OF INTERNATIONAL FINANCE AMONG DEVELOPED COUNTRIES --THE DOLLAR, EUROPEAN CURRENCIES, WORLD LIQUIDITY, BALANCE-OF-PAYMENTS ADJUSTMENT. SEVERAL THREADS RUN THROUGHOUT: IMPORTANCE OF SUPPLY, NEED FOR INTERNATIONAL COOPERATION, SUPERIORITY OF UNWRITTEN TO FORMAL CONSTITUTIONS IN INSTITUTIONAL MACHINERY.

1396 KINGSLEY R.E.
"THE US BUSINESS IMAGE IN LATIN AMERICA."
BUSINESS TOPICS, 15 (1967), 74-80.
EXAMINES SIX AREAS OF ANTI-US BUSINESS OPINION: SEMANTIC, HISTORICAL, PRAGMATIC, POLITICAL, IDEOLOGICAL, AND INFERENTIAL. FEELS THAT PROBLEM IS BASICALLY ONE OF POOR COMMUNICATIONS; US MUST REVISE OWN THINKING FIRST, RATHER THAN THAT OF LATIN AMERICA. MUST FRAME COMMUNICATIONS FROM VIEWPOINT OF RECIPIENT, NOT OF COMMUNICATOR.

1397 KIRDAR U.
THE STRUCTURE OF UNITED NATIONS ECONOMIC AID TO UNDERDEVELOPED COUNTRIES.
THE HAGUE: MARTINUS NIJHOFF, 1966, 361 PP., LC#66-54220.
DETAILED STUDY OF VARIOUS FORMS OF FINANCIAL AND TECHNICAL ASSISTANCE TO UNDERDEVELOPED COUNTRIES, EMPHASIZING AID PROGRAMS THAT ARE MEDIATED AND ADMINISTERED BY UN AND OTHER INTERNATIONAL BODIES. STRESSES INTERNATIONAL NATURE OF ECONOMIC AID PROGRAMS IN RELATION TO BOTH ORGANIZATIONAL STRUCTURE AND POLITICAL IMPLICATIONS.

1398 KIRK R., MCCLELLAN J.
THE POLITICAL PRINCIPLES OF ROBERT A. TAFT.
NEW YORK: FLEET PUBL CORP, 1967, 213 PP., LC#67-24073.
ANALYZES IDEAS AND INFLUENCES OF SENATOR TAFT. EXAMINES HIS CONVICTIONS OF FREEDOM, JUSTICE, LABOR POLICY, SOCIAL REFORM, FOREIGN AFFAIRS, AND RESPONSIBILITIES OF POLITICAL PARTIES. SUPPORTS TAFT'S BELIEFS IN POLITICS, ORDER, AND FREEDOM. DESCRIBES HIS SOCIAL IMPROVEMENT PROGRAMS AS GENEROUS; CLAIMS THAT HE WAS NOT AN ISOLATIONIST.

1399 KIRKENDALL R.S.
SOCIAL SCIENTISTS AND FARM POLITICS IN THE AGE OF ROOSEVELT.
COLUMBIA: U OF MO PR, 1966, 358 PP., LC#66-14032.
STUDIES A SIGNIFICANT AND CONTROVERSIAL FEATURE OF NEW DEAL: ROLE OF INTELLECTUALS IN ITS DEVELOPMENT. FOCUSES ON ENTRY OF SOCIAL SCIENTISTS INTO POLITICS. EXAMINES CHARACTER AND ROLE OF THE "SERVICE INTELLECTUAL," ONE WHO FEELS HIS SERVICES ARE NEEDED BY SOCIETY. SHOWS SOCIAL SCIENTISTS' ACTIVITIES IN ELEVATING PRODUCTION CONTROL, PLANNING FOR RURAL POOR, AND ELEVATING BUREAU OF AGRICULTURAL ECONOMICS.

1400 KIRPICEVA I.K.
HANDBUCH DER RUSSISCHEN UND SOWJETISCHEN BIBLIOGRAPHIEN (5 VOLS.)
LEIPZIG: VEB VERL FUR BUCH BIBL, 1962.
ANNOTATED BIBLIOGRAPHICAL SURVEY OF SOVIET AND RUSSIAN BIBLIOGRAPHIES FROM 18TH CENTURY THROUGH 1959. INFORMATION GIVEN IN TABLE FORM; RUSSIAN CHARACTERS TRANSLITERATED AND FREQUENTLY TRANSLATED INTO GERMAN. TOPICALLY CLASSIFIED AND INDEXED BY AUTHOR. INCLUDES COMPREHENSIVE AND SPECIALIZED BIBLIOGRAPHIES, WORKS WITH APPENDED SUPPLEMENTARY READING LISTS, AND PERIODICALS.

1401 KISER M.
"ORGANIZATION OF AMERICAN STATES."
WASHINGTON: PAN AMER. UNION, 1955, 74 PP.
A HANDBOOK ABOUT ORGANIZATION DESCRIBING WHAT IT IS, HOW IT IS ORGANIZED, WHAT IT DOES, AND THE INTER-AMERICAN AGENCIES.

1402 KISSINGER H.A.
THE TROUBLED PARTNERSHIP* RE-APPRAISAL OF THE WESTERN ALLIANCE.
NEW YORK: MCGRAW HILL, 1965, 266 PP., LC#65-17493.
THE AUTHOR OF "NECESSITY FOR CHOICE," INQUIRES INTO THE POLITICAL, ECONOMIC, AND MILITARY PROBLEMS CONFRONTING THE ATLANTIC COMMUNITY. ATTACKS THE THEORY THAT ALL THE PROBLEMS ARE CAUSED BY DE GAULLE, SEEING THEM RATHER AS A FUNCTION OF FUNDAMENTAL CHANGES IN THE POLITICAL AND ECONOMIC POSITION OF EUROPE AND OF MODERN WEAPONS TECHNOLOGY.

1403 KITZINGER V.W.
THE CHALLENGE OF THE COMMON MARKET.
OXFORD: BLACKWELL, 1961, 168 PP.
EXAMINES HISTORIC AND ECONOMIC FACTORS ACTING AS STIMULUS TO COMMON MARKET ESTABLISHMENT. EXAMINES PROS AND CONS OF BRITISH CANDIDATURE. ANALYZES EFFECT OF BRITISH ENTRY ON HER INDUSTRY, WORLD POSITION AND COMMONWEALTH.

1404 KLASSEN L.H.
AREA ECONOMIC AND SOCIAL REDEVELOPMENT.
PARIS: ORG FOR ECO COOP AND DEV, 1965, 113 PP.
REDEVELOPMENT AND OPTIMALIZATION OF AREAS THAT LOSE INDUSTRY DISCUSSED AND SOLUTIONS PROPOSED. ECONOMETRIC ANALYSIS OF DAMAGE AS A RESULT OF LOSS OF INDUSTRY EXPLAINED AND ROLE OF GOVERNMENT IN REDEVELOPMENT DEFINED.

1405 KLEIN H.
"AMERICAN OIL COMPANIES IN LATIN AMERICA: THE BOLIVIAN EXPERIENCE."
INTER AMER. ECON. AFF., 18 (AUTUMN 64), 47-72.
TRACES RELATIONS BETWEEN BOLIVIA AND AMERICAN OIL COMPANIES 1936-52. ARGUES THAT BOLIVIAN NATIONALISTS OF RIGHT AND LEFT BOTH TAKE SIMILAR POSITIONS ON ISSUE OF FOREIGN EXPLOITATION OF NATIONAL PETROLEUM. WISH TO NATIONALIZE BUT REALIZE NEED FOR FOREIGN INVESTMENT TO DEVELOP. MUTUAL HOSTILITY HAS BEEN PATTERN OF BOLIVIAN EXPERIENCE.

1406 KLEIN J.J.
MONEY AND THE ECONOMY.
NEW YORK: HARCOURT BRACE, 1965, 436 PP., LC#65-17744.
ANALYSIS OF ROLE OF MONEY IN ECONOMY. EMPHASIS ON MONETARY POLICY AND WORKINGS OF PRIVATE INSTITUTIONS AND OPERATIONS OF FEDERAL RESERVE SYSTEM. INCLUDES HISTORICAL CRITIQUE OF MONETARY CONTROLS. DEVELOPS MODEL OF INCOME DETERMINATION AND DISCUSSES IN DETAIL PROBLEMS OF CURRENT MONETARY, FISCAL, AND INTERNATIONAL ECONOMIC POLICY.

1407 KLEIN L.R.
AN ECONOMETRIC MODEL OF THE UNITED KINGDOM.
OXFORD: BLACKWELL, 1961, 312 PP.
DISCUSSES ECONOMETRIC FORECASTS ABOUT ECONOMY OF UK THROUGH QUARTERLY AND ANNUAL PRELIMINARY MODELS. DETAILED DISCUSSION OF PROBLEMS AND PROCEDURES OF COMPUTATION.

1408 KLEIN L.R.
AN INTRODUCTION TO ECONOMETRICS.
ENGLEWOOD CLIFFS: PRENTICE HALL, 1962, 275 PP., LC#62-13244.
USES SECONDARY SCHOOL MATHEMATICS TO ACQUAINT READERS WITH ECONOMETRICS, THE GIVING OF EMPIRICAL CONTENT TO ABSTRACT GENERALIZATIONS IN ECONOMICS. COVERS ANALYSIS OF DEMAND, PRODUCTION, DISTRIBUTION, GROWTH, AND TRADE CYCLES; DISCUSSES PROBLEMS OF APPLYING MODELS IN THESE AREAS.

1409 KLEIN S.
"A SURVEY OF SINO-JAPANESE TRADE, 1950-1966"
CHINA MAINLAND REVIEW, 2 (DEC. 66), 185-191.
EXAMINES TRADE RELATIONS BETWEEN JAPAN AND CHINA FROM 1950 TO 1966. INCLUDES AGREEMENTS MADE AND POLITICAL ASPECTS OF TRADE. CONCLUDES THAT FRICTION IN RELATIONSHIP WILL CONTINUE TO INCREASE BECAUSE OF JAPANESE DESIRE TO REMAIN CLOSE TO US AND TAIWAN, POLITICAL PROPAGANDA OF CHINESE COMMUNISTS, AND POOR QUALITY OF CHINESE GOODS TRADED TO JAPAN.

1410 KLUMB S., VANDUSEN A.C.
"EMPLOYEE DETERMINATION OF MANAGERIAL FUNCTIONS AND CHARACTERISTICS."
PERSONNEL PSYCHOLOGY, 5 (WINTER 52), 263-279.
TO SELECT REPLACEMENTS FOR RETIRING SALES BRANCH MANAGERS, A COMPANY DETERMINED THE APPROPRIATE IMAGE BY SUBMITTING QUESTIONNAIRES TO PERSONNEL, AS WELL AS GROUP MEETINGS. THE ARTICLE DESCRIBES PROCEDURES, PRESENTS TABULATED RESULTS AND DISCUSSES EMPLOYEE REACTION TO PROCEDURES.

1411 KNAPP D.C.
"CONGRESSIONAL CONTROL OF AGRICULTURAL CONSERVATION POLICY: A CASE STUDY OF THE APPROPRIATIONS PROCESS."
POLIT. SCI. QUART., 71 (JUNE 56), 257-281.
EXAMINATION OF THE CONTROL WHICH CONGRESS EXERCISED OVER AGRICULTURAL CONSERVATION POLICY IN THE APPROPRIATIONS PROCESS 1940-50. ANALYSIS OF BOTH THE ADMINISTRATIVE ISSUES RAISED AND THE INFLUENCE IN THE SETTLEMENT. AIM IS TO PRESENT A COMPLETE PICTURE OF THE ROLE OF POLICY-MAKING IN THE APPROPRIATIONS PROCESS. GIVES DETAILED ANALYSIS OF THE AGRICULTURAL CONSERVATION PROGRAM.

1412 KNIGHT R.
BIBLIOGRAPHY ON INCOME AND WEALTH, 1957-1960 (VOL VIII)
NEW HAVEN:INTL. ASSN RES INCOMES, 1964, 304 PP.
BIBLIOGRAPHY CONSOLIDATES AND SUPPLEMENTS ANNUAL REPORTS OF INTERNATIONAL ASSOCIATION FOR RESEARCH ON INCOME AND WEALTH IN NATIONS. INCLUDES WORKS ON CONCEPTS AND METHODS RELATING TO INCOME AND WEALTH MEASUREMENT AND ON INTERNATIONAL COMPARISONS OF NATIONAL ESTIMATES. PARTICULAR ATTENTION IS GIVEN TO UNDERDEVELOPED COUNTRIES, LONG-TERM ECONOMIC GROWTH, AND FINANCIAL ACCOUNTING. ANNOTATED.

1413 KNORR K.E.
RUBLE DIPLOMACY: CHALLENGE TO AMERICAN FOREIGN AID(PAMPHLET)
PRINCETON: CTR OF INTL STUDIES, 1956, 42 PP.
EXAMINES SINO-SOVIET BLOC POLICY OF TRADE, LOANS, AND TECHNICAL ASSISTANCE TO UNDERDEVELOPED COUNTRIES. USSR MAINTAINS SUCH DEALINGS ARE BUSINESSLIKE AND WITHOUT POLITICAL STRINGS IMPOSED BY IMPERIALISTIC US AID. PRESENTS FACTS OF BLOC DRIVE SINCE 1955, DESCRIBES OBJECTIVES, EVALUATES EFFECTIVENESS OF ECONOMIC DIPLOMACY, AND SUGGESTS POINTS FOR AMERICAN DIPLOMACY.

1414 KOENIG L.W.
THE SALE OF THE TANKERS.
WASHINGTON: COMM ON PUBLIC ADMIN, 1950, 184 PP.
STUDY RELATES 1947-48 US GOVERNMENT SALE OF 83 TANKERS TO 13 FOREIGN NATIONS. EXAMINES ENSUING DIFFICULTIES AMONG PUBLIC AND PRIVATE GROUPS IN AMERICAN POLITICAL AND ADMINISTRATIVE LIFE. REVIEWS ATTITUDES AND ACTIONS OF ALL INVOLVED PARTIES.

1415 KOH S.J.
STAGES OF INDUSTRIAL DEVELOPMENT IN ASIA.
PHILA: U OF PENN PR, 1966, 461 PP., LC#65-22081.
STUDY OF COMPARATIVE HISTORY OF THE COTTON INDUSTRY IN JAPAN, INDIA, CHINA, AND KOREA. DISCUSSES THREE FACTORS WHICH HAD LIMITING EFFECT ON INDUSTRIALIZATION IN THESE COUNTRIES. PRIOR ECONOMIC EXPERIENCE, SOCIAL ORGANIZATION, AND POLITICAL INSTITUTIONS. CONTAINS NUMEROUS CHARTS AND TABLES.

1416 KOHLER E.L., WRIGHT H.W.
ACCOUNTING IN THE FEDERAL GOVERNMENT.
ENGLEWOOD CLIFFS: PRENTICE HALL, 1956, 291 PP., LC#56-13223.
STUDY DEALS PRIMARILY WITH ACCOUNTING PROBLEMS OF THE FEDERAL GOVERNMENT BUT ALSO BRIEFLY PRESENTS CHARACTERISTIC ACCOUNTING PRACTICES OF A MAJORITY OF STATE AND LOCAL GOVERNMENTS. EMPHASIZES ACCOUNTING METHODS OF FEDERAL AGENCIES, INTERNAL AUDITING, AND LIKE TASKS CONFRONTING ACCOUNTANTS OF FEDERAL AGENCIES. ALSO DESCRIBES FUNCTIONS OF GOVERNMENT AGENCIES CONCERNED WITH ACCOUNTING.

1417 KOHN W.S.G.
"THE SOVEREIGNTY OF LIECHTENSTEIN."
AMER. J. OF INT. LAW, 61 (APR. 67), 547-557.
EXAMINES SOVIET OBJECTION IN 1949 TO GRANTING MEMBERSHIP TO LIECHTENSTEIN IN INTERNATIONAL COURT OF JUSTICE. MAINTAINS LIECHTENSTEIN DOES POSSESS SOVEREIGNTY SINCE IT HAS UNLIMITED POWER OVER CITIZENS AND SUBJECTS, RESTRICTED ONLY BY CONSTITUTION. DISCUSSES PRINCIPALITY'S SIZE, HISTORY, GOVERNMENT, ETC., WHICH INDICATE THAT SHE IS NOT PART OF SWITZERLAND.

1418 KOHNSTAMM M.
THE EUROPEAN COMMUNITY AND ITS ROLE IN THE WORLD.
COLUMBIA: U OF MO PR, 1964, 82 PP., LC#64-20099.
THREE LECTURES DEALING WITH DEVELOPMENT OF CONTINENTAL EUROPEAN COMMUNITY, ITS RELATIONS WITH GREAT BRITAIN AND US, AND ITS PRESENT DIFFICULTIES AND FUTURE DECISIONS.

1419 KOJIMA K.
"THE PATTERN OF INTERNATIONAL TRADE AMONG ADVANCED COUNTRIES."
HITOTSUBASHI J. ECON., 5 (JUNE 64), 16-36.
ANALYZES TREND OF RAPIDLY INCREASING TRADE AMONG ADVANCED INDUSTRIAL COUNTRIES, WHICH HAS BEEN DEVELOPING SINCE WORLD WAR TWO. SEES THIS RAPID EXPANSION OF TRADE AMONG THEST COUNTRIES AS PRIMARILY IN 'HORIZONTAL TRADE', AMONG MANUFACTURERS AND SPECIFICALLY CONSIDERS INTRA-BLOC TRADE OF EEC AND TRADE AMONG USA, UK, EEC AND JAPAN IN LIGHT OF THIS.

1420 KOLKO G.
WEALTH AND POWER IN AMERICA.
NEW YORK: FREDERICK PRAEGER, 1962, 178 PP., LC#62-11584.
ANALYSIS OF SOCIAL CLASS AND INCOME DISTRIBUTION IN US, INCLUDING TAXATION AND INEQUALITY, CORPORATE POWER, CAUSES AND EXTENT OF POVERTY. AUTHOR CLAIMS NO SIGNIFICANT REDISTRIBUTION OF WEALTH SINCE DEPRESSION OR EVEN 1910.

1421 KOLKO G.
THE TRIUMPH OF CONSERVATISM.
NEW YORK: FREE PRESS OF GLENCOE, 1963, 280 PP., LC#63-16588.
ANALYSIS OF POLITICAL CAPITALISM AS IT OPERATED IN AMERICA BETWEEN 1900-16. DEFINES POLITICAL CAPITALISM AS UTILIZATION OF POLITICAL OUTLETS TO ATTAIN RATIONALIZATION IN THE ECONOMY. CONTENDS THAT BUSINESS CONTROLLED POLITICS IN PROGRESSIVE ERA IN ORDER TO ELIMINATE INTERNECINE COMPETITION AND ERRATIC FLUCTUATIONS IN THE ECONOMY. OUTLINES LEGISLATIVE STEPS TAKEN TO PERMIT THIS SECURITY.

1422 KOLLAI H.R.
DIE EINGLIEDERUNG DER VERTRIEBENEN UND ZUWANDERER IN NIEDERSACHSEN.
LONDON: CRESSET PRESS, 1959, 160 PP.
EXAMINES SOCIAL AND ECONOMIC STRUCTURE OF STATE OF NIEDERSACHSEN, WEST GERMANY. DISCUSSES IN DETAIL PROBLEM OF ASSIMILATION OF EAST GERMAN REFUGEES INTO ECONOMIC AND SOCIAL LIFE, AND RESULTING CHANGES IN SOCIAL STRUCTURE.

1423 KOLODZIEJ E.A.
"RATIONAL CONSENT AND DEFENSE BUDGETS: THE ROLE OF CONGRESS,

1945-1962."
ORBIS, 7 (WINTER 64), 748-777.
THROUGH AN ANALYSIS AND EVALUATION OF CONGRESSIONAL USE OF APPROPRIATIONS CONTROL TO INFLUENCE MILITARY POLICY, ARTICLE ATTEMPTS TO DETERMINE WHETHER US MILITARY POLICIES BALANCE SOCIETAL AND FOREIGN POLICY IMPERATIVES. PRESENTS SCALED MODEL OF WHAT CONGRESSIONAL ROLE SHOULD APPROXIMATE IN MILITARY POLICY-MAKING; EVALUATES PROCESS AND PRODUCT OF CONGRESSIONAL SECURITY AFFAIRS DECISIONS IN TERMS OF MODEL.

1424 KOMIYA R. ED.
POSTWAR ECONOMIC GROWTH IN JAPAN.
BERKELEY: U OF CALIF PR, 1966, 260 PP., LC#66-22705.
STUDY OF RAPID ECONOMIC PROGRESS MADE BY THE JAPANESE SINCE 1955 INCLUDES PUBLIC FINANCE AND MONETARY POLICY, TAX POLICY, PRICE PROBLEMS, ECONOMIC GROWTH AND THE BALANCE OF PAYMENTS, EMPLOYMENT AND LABOR, AND INCOME DISTRIBUTION. ALSO ANALYZES BUSINESS FLUCTUATIONS AND THE STABILIZATION POLICY, AND DEVELOPMENT OF POSTWAR JAPANESE EXECUTIVES.

1425 KORBONSKI A.
"COMECON."
INT. CONCIL. 549 (SEPT. 64), 1-62.
TRACES BROADLY THE DEVELOPMENT OF COMECON FROM ITS ORIGIN AND SKETCHES ITS CURRENT INSTITUTIONAL FRAMEWORK AND POLICIES FROM AN ECONOMIC AND POLITICAL VIEWPOINT. CONSIDERS RAPID ADVANCE IN ECONOMIC INTEGRATION IMPROBABLE.

1426 KORBONSKI A.
"USA POLICY IN EAST EUROPE."
CURR. HIST., 48 (MAR. 65), 129-134.
WHILE CHANGE IN USA ATTITUDE TOWARD EAST EUROPE HAS BEEN RATHER STRIKING, ITS PRESENT POLICY IS ESSENTIALLY STATIC AND SHORT-RUN. MOST MOVE ON FRONTS OTHER THAN BRIDGES OF AID, TRADE AND CULTURAL EXCHANGE EVEN AT COST OF ANTAGONIZING TEMPORARILY CLOSEST ALLIES.

1427 KOREAN MINISTRY RECONSTRUCTION
KOREAN ECONOMY AND ITS REQUIREMENTS.
SEOUL: KOREAN MIN RECONSTRUCTION, 1959, 55 PP.
EXAMINES AFTERMATH OF KOREAN WAR IN TERMS OF ECONOMIC EFFECT ON COUNTRY. SHOWS DECLINE IN GNP, PER CAPITA INCOME, AND RESULTS OF US FOREIGN AID IN RAISING LIVING STANDARDS. CUT IN AID IS REFLECTED BY CONCURRENT DROP IN OUTPUT AND ESTIMATION OF AID REQUIREMENTS IS GIVEN.

1428 KORNHAUSER W.
"THE NEGRO UNION OFFICIAL: A STUDY OF SPONSORSHIP AND CONTROL" (BMR)"
AMER. J. OF SOCIOLOGY, 57 (MAR. 52), 443-452.
CONCLUDES FROM 16 CASE STUDIES THAT A NEGRO CAN BE ELECTED TO UNION OFFICE ONLY WHERE THERE IS A SIZABLE NEGRO UNION MEMBERSHIP AND WHERE, TO AVOID CONFLICT, WHITE UNION OFFICIALS SPONSOR HIS ELECTION. TWO MAJOR ROLES PLAYED BY NEGRO, LIAISON AND SYMBOLIC, SUPPORT WHITE INTERESTS AND CONTROL. THEY PRESENT PROBLEMS FOR THE PERSONAL CAREER OF THE NEGRO WHO MAY TRY TO MODIFY THEM.

1429 KOTLER P.
"OPERATIONS RESEARCH IN MARKETING."
HARVARD BUSINESS REV., 45 (JAN. 67), 30-45, 187-188 .
REPORTS ON INCREASING USE OF MATHEMATICAL MODEL ANALYSIS INSTEAD OF TRADITIONAL INTUITION AND JUDGMENT IN MARKETING. DESCRIBES SPECIFIC MODELS IN SUCH DECISION AREAS AS NEW PRODUCTS, PRICING, DISTRIBUTION, ADVERTISING, AND SALES FORCE MANAGEMENT. NOTES THAT THESE DEVELOPMENTS, THOUGH JUST BEGINNING, MAY SIGNAL A TREND.

1430 KOVNER M.
THE CHALLENGE OF COEXISTENCE: A STUDY OF SOVIET ECONOMIC DIPLOMACY.
WASHINGTON: PUBL. AFF. PR., 1961, 130 PP. $3.25.
PURPOSE OF SOVIET FOREIGN POLICY IS TO DEPRIVE WEST OF MARKETS AND SOURCES, STRATEGIC MATERIALS AND TO EXACERBATE POLITICAL ANTAGONISM BETWEEN UNDERDEVELOPED AND DEVELOPED COUNTRIES.

1431 KRANZBERG M. ED., PURSELL G.W.E. ED.
TECHNOLOGY IN WESTERN CIVILIZATION VOLUME ONE.
NEW YORK: OXFORD U PR, 1967, 802 PP., LC#67-15129.
CONTAINS 45 ARTICLES WRITTEN IN DIRECTION OF EMPHASIZING IMPORTANCE OF TECHNOLOGY IN HUMAN AFFAIRS. COMMENCING WITH HISTORICAL PERSPECTIVES, CONTINUES ON TO INDUSTRIAL REVOLUTION, STEAM AGE, MECHANICAL AND ELECTRICAL ADVANCES, MASS PRODUCTION, AND PUBLIC POLICY.

1432 KRAUS J.
"A MARXIST IN GHANA."
PROBLEMS OF COMMUNISM, 16 (MAY-JUNE 67), 42-49.
PORTRAYS THE RISE AND FALL OF NKRUMAH, HIS EFFORTS TO ESTABLISH SOCIALIST STATE IN GHANA, HIS ATTEMPTS TO DISSEMMINATE MARXIST VIEWPOINT THROUGHOUT AFRICA, AND THE POLITTICAL AND IDEOLOGICAL FORCES BEHIND HIS IDEAS AND PROGRAMS. DESCRIBES EXTENT OF SOCIALIZATION, ITS ECONOMIC AND SOCIAL EFFECTS, ITS INTERNATIONAL REPERCUSSIONS. CONCLUDES THAT SOCIALISM HAS BEEN A "MANIPULATIVE MYTH" TO ADVANCE NKRUMAH.

1433 KRAUSE L.B. ED.
THE COMMON MARKET: PROGRESS AND CONTROVERSY.
ENGLEWOOD CLIFFS: PRENTICE HALL, 1964, 182 PP., LC#64-16427.
PROGRESS OF EEC AS DEPICTED BY STATESMEN, ECONOMISTS, AND SCHOLARS FROM BOTH EUROPE AND AMERICA. POSSIBLE CONSEQUENCES OF FRANCE'S VETO OF GREAT BRITAIN'S BID FOR MEMBERSHIP.

1434 KRAUSE W.
ECONOMIC DEVELOPMENT: THE UNDERDEVELOPED WORLD AND THE AMERICAN INTEREST.
BELMONT: WADSWORTH, 1961, 524 PP., LC#61-7374.
DISCUSSES ECONOMIC DEVELOPMENT IN UNDERDEVELOPED COUNTRIES, THEIR PROBLEMS, ATTEMPTS AT IMPROVEMENTS, AND AMERICAN INTEREST IN PROBLEMS OF DEVELOPMENT, AMERICAN SOLUTIONS, POSSIBILITIES FOR FURTHER AMERICAN AID, AND IMPLICATIONS FOR US AND WORLD OF ITS SUCCESSES AND FAILURES IN ASSISTING ECONOMICALLY UNDEVELOPED COUNTRIES.

1435 KRAVIS I.B.
DOMESTIC INTERESTS AND INTERNATIONAL OBLIGATIONS: SAFEGUARDS IN INTERNATIONAL TRADE ORGANIZATIONS.
PHILADELPHIA: U. PENN. PR., 1963, 448 PP.,$8.50.
AN EXAMINATION OF THE NATURE OF INTERNATIONAL COMMITMENTS AND OF THE MANNER IN WHICH DOMESTIC INTERESTS HAVE BEEN SAFEGUARDED IN THREE EUROPEAN ARRANGEMENTS-ORGANIZATION FOR EUROPEAN ECONOMIC COOPERATION'S CODE OF LIBERALIZATION, EUROPEAN COAL AND STEEL COMMUNITY, AND EUROPEAN ECONOMIC COMMUNITY.

1436 KREININ M.E.
"THE 'OUTER-SEVEN' AND EUROPEAN INTEGRATION."
AMER. ECON. REV., 50 (JUNE 60), 370-386.
EUROPEAN FREE-TRADE ASSOCIATION (EFTAA), A SCHEME DEVISED TO RIVAL EEC (WHICH DISCRIMINATES AGAINST NON-MEMBER NATIONS), SEEN AS TEMPORARY ARRANGEMENT TO PROVIDE SPUR TOWARDS A BROADER ALL-EUROPEAN AGREEMENT. COMPARISON DEMONSTRATES COMMON MARKET MUCH MORE LIKELY TO HAVE FAVORABLE IMPACT ON WORLD-PATTERN RESOURCE UTILIZATION. CONCLUSION THAT EFTAA'S CREATION WILL DEEPEN DIVISION IN EUROPE.

1437 KREININ M.E.
ALTERNATIVE COMMERCIAL POLICIES - THEIR EFFECT ON THE AMERICAN ECONOMY.
E LANSING: MICH STATE U SCHOOL OF BUS, 1967, 154PP., LC#67-64818
CONCERNED WITH QUANTITATIVE ESTIMATES OF EFFECTS OF COMMERCIAL POLICIES AND TRADE ARRANGEMENTS ON US DOMESTIC ECONOMY AND FOREIGN TRADE. PRIMARY EMPHASIS ON EFFECT OF AN ATLANTIC FREE TRADE AREA. DISCUSSES TRADE LEGISLATION, EFFECT OF AFTA ON US IMPORTS AND EXPORTS, MOTIVES FOR AND CONSIDERATIONS OF FOREIGN INVESTMENTS, AND EFFECTS ON GNP, EMPLOYMENT, AND WELFARE.

1438 KRESSBACH T.W.
HE MICHIGAN CITY MANAGER IN BUDGETARY PROCEEDINGS (PAMPHLET)
ANN ARBOR: MICH MUNICIPAL LEAGUE, 1962, 51 PP.
EXAMINES BUDGETARY ORGANIZATION, BUDGET MAKING, PRESENTATION, AND ADOPTION PROCESSES, AND CAPITAL BUDGETING OF MICHIGAN CITY AND VILLAGE OFFICES. FOCUSES ON MANAGER'S ROLE IN BUDGET PREPARATION AND PRESENTATION.

1439 KRIESBERG M.
CANCELLATION OF THE RATION STAMPS (PAMPHLET)
INDIANAPOLIS: BOBBS-MERRILL, 1952, 13 PP.
STUDY OF PROBLEMS RELATING TO ADMINISTRATIVE DECISION-MAKING AND PUBLIC RELATIONS IN SPECIFIC CASE OF FOOD RATION STAMPS CANCELLATION, 1944-45. INVOLVED QUESTION OF WHETHER OR NOT TO CANCEL RATIONING IN LIGHT OF SUDDEN FOOD CRISIS.

1440 KRIPALANI J.B.
CLASS STRUGGLE.
RAJGHAT: AKHIL BHARAT SARVA SEVA, 1959, 94 PP.
ESSAY BY FORMER CHAIRMAN OF PRAJA SOCIALIST PARTY, PREENTING AND ANALYZING MARXIAN THEORY OF CLASS CONFLICT. CRITICIZES IT AS INTRINSICALLY INVALID AND AS ERRONEOUS WHEN RELATED TO MODERN CAPITALISM. APPLIES HIS ANALYSIS TO CONTEMPORARY INDIA AND EXPLAINS HIS REASONS FOR NOT EMPHASIZING IDEA OF CLASS STRUGGLE.

1441 KRISHNA K.G.V.
"PLANNING AND ECONOMIC DEVELOPMENT"
J. OF EAST AFRICAN ECONOMIC REV., 9 (JUNE 62), 48-62.
ATTEMPTS TO APPLY INDIAN EXPERIENCE IN ECONOMIC PLANNING TO EAST AFRICA. SUGGESTS AFRICAN PLANNING COMMISSION FOR DEVELOPMENT OF THREE-NATION AREA.

1442 KRISTENSEN T.
THE ECONOMIC WORLD BALANCE.
COPENHAGEN: MUNKSGAARD, 1960, 377 PP.
CURRENT BALANCE OF ECONOMIC POWER BETWEEN EAST AND WEST AND FACTORS OF CHANGE SUCH AS INCREASED CONTACTS AND TRADE VOLUME ARE CONSIDERED. EXPORT OF CAPITAL AND TECHNICAL SKILLS TO UNDERDEVELOPED COUNTRIES ADVOCATED. EVALUATES FUTURE ECONOMIC GROWTH IN VARIOUS REGIONS AND GIVES PROPOSALS FOR FURTHER STUDY.

1443 KROOSS H.E.

AMERICAN ECONOMIC DEVELOPMENT (2ND ED.)
ENGLEWOOD CLIFFS: PRENTICE HALL, 1966, 498 PP., LC#66-10002.
TOPICAL APPROACH TO AMERICAN ECONOMIC HISTORY, EMPHASIZING ROLE OF BUSINESSMAN AS PROTAGONIST IN AMERICAN SOCIETY. INCLUDES NATIONAL INCOME, FARMER, CONTRIBUTION OF BUSINESS, FOREIGN TRADE, AND ECONOMIC ROLE OF GOVERNMENT.

1444 KROPOTKIN P.
THE CONQUEST OF BREAD.
LONDON: CHAPMAN AND HALL, 1913, 298 PP.
EXPRESSES AUTHOR'S IDEAS FOR ESTABLISHMENT OF SOCIALIST STATE, AND REVIEWS SOME PAST ATTEMPTS TO ESTABLISH SOCIALISM AND COMMUNAL LIVING. BELIEVES THAT MEANS OF PRODUCTION SHOULD BE COLLECTIVE PROPERTY. THERE MUST BE EXPROPRIATION TO INSURE WELL-BEING OF ALL. ONCE PROPERTY IS ABOLISHED, SOCIETY WILL BE ESTABLISHED IN FORM OF COMMUNISTIC ANARCHY, MADE UP OF FREE GROUPS ESTABLISHED THROUGH FREE AGREEMENTS.

1445 KROPOTKIN P.
FIELDS, FACTORIES, AND WORKSHOPS.
BOSTON: HOUGHTON MIFFLIN, 1899, 315 PP.
ADVOCATES COMBINATION OF INDUSTRIAL AND AGRICULTURAL PURSUITS AND OF THOUGHT AND MANUAL WORK. BELIEVES THAT SOCIETY SHOULD NOT BE MADE UP OF INDIVIDUALS WHO SPECIALIZE IN ONE OCCUPATION. NEEDED IS AN "INTEGRATED EDUCATION" THAT WILL GIVE EACH INDIVIDUAL KNOWLEDGE OF A SCIENCE AS WELL AS A HANDICRAFT. INDUSTRY MUST DECENTRALIZE SO THAT NATIONS CAN BECOME SELF-SUFFICIENT.

1446 KUENNE R.E.
THE POLARIS MISSILE STRIKE* A GENERAL ECONOMIC SYSTEMS ANALYSIS.
COLUMBUS: OHIO STATE U PR, 1966, 434 PP., LC#66-10715.
STUDY OF THE POLARIS DETERRENCE SYSTEM DEALING WITH ITS EFFECTIVENESS IN PREVENTING SOVIET UNION FROM LAUNCHING A THERMONUCLEAR ATTACK. OFFERS ECONOMIC SOLUTIONS AND PRESENTS A PROBABILISTIC MODEL SUSCEPTIBLE TO USE BY COMPUTER. HYPOTHESIZES ABOUT NATIONAL SECURITY AND ARMS CONTROL.

1447 KUHN T.E.
PUBLIC ENTERPRISES, PROJECT PLANNING AND ECONOMIC DEVELOPMENT (PAMPHLET)
HONDURAS: STANFORD RESEARCH INSTITUTE, 1962, 55PF.
COMPREHENSIVE ECONOMIC THEORY OF PUBLIC ENTERPRISE, ORGANIZATIONS WHOSE POLICIES AND MANAGEMENT ACTIONS ARE DIRECTLY OR INDIRECTLY DETERMINED BY PUBLIC DECISIONS. (INCLUDES PUBLIC UTILITIES OF US.) ANALYZES THESE CORPORATIONS IN TERMS OF THEIR IMPORTANCE TO ECONOMICALLY DEVELOPING NATIONS. TRIES TO ESTABLISH METHOD FOR PLANNING PROJECTS UNDER PUBLIC MANAGEMENT.

1448 KULSKI J.E.
LAND OF URBAN PROMISE* CONTINUING THE GREAT TRADITION* A SEARCH FOR SIGNIFICANT URBAN SPACE IN URBANIZED NORTHEAST.
SOUTH BEND: U OF NOTRE DAME, 1967, 282 PP., LC#66-24924.
A CRITICAL ANALYSIS OF THE DYNAMICS OF URBAN DESIGN AND THE SOCIAL AND ECONOMIC PROCESSES SHAPING THE ENVIRONMENT OF THE URBANIZED NORTHEAST REGION OF THE US. AUTHOR STRESSES IMPORTANCE OF A SYNOPTIC APPROACH, I.E., COMBINING IDEAS OF SOCIOLOGY, POLITICAL SCIENCE, ECONOMICS, AND URBAN DESIGN TO CREATE VIABLE, FUNCTIONAL, AND AESTHETIC CITIES.

1449 KUNKEL J.H.
"VALUES AND BEHAVIOR IN ECONOMIC DEVELOPMENT."
ECO. DEV. AND CULTURAL CHANGE, 13 (APR. 65), 257-277.
NEW ECONOMIC DEVELOPMENT AND SOCIAL CHANGE THEORIES ARE ATTEMPTING TO GIVE THE INDIVIDUAL A PROMINENT ROLE; ARTICLE PRESENTS MODEL USING EXPERIMENTAL PSYCHOLOGY PRINCIPLES. MODEL IS CONCERNED WITH OVERTLY EXPRESSED ACTIVITIES OF INDIVIDUALS AND THEIR RELATIONS TO PREVIOUSLY AND PRESENTLY SURROUNDING SOCIAL STRUCTURES AND PHYSICAL CONDITIONS.

1450 KURAKOV I.G.
SCIENCE, TECHNOLOGY AND COMMUNISM; SOME QUESTIONS OF DEVELOPMENT (TRANS. BY CARIN DEDIJER)
NEW YORK: PERGAMON PRESS, 1966, 126 PP., LC#66-12657.
IN LIGHT OF MARXIST SOCIAL THEORY AND METHODS OF MARXIST ECONOMICS, TREATS PROBLEMS OF ECONOMICS, RESEARCH POLICY, AND INDUSTRIAL MANAGEMENT. EMPHASIZES ACCOUNTING FOR RESEARCH WORK INPUTS IN COST BENEFIT ANALYSES. CRITICIZES SOVIET RESEARCH PLANNING AND USE OF MATERIAL INCENTIVES. SHOWS ROLE OF SCIENCE AND TECHNOLOGY IN SOVIET PRODUCTION AND EXPLAINS DIRECTION OF THEIR DEVELOPMENT.

1451 KURIHARA K.L.
"THE KEYNESIAN THEORY OF ECONOMIC DEVELOPMENT."
NEW YORK: COLUMBIA U PRESS, 1959.
ANALYZES TECHNICAL POSSIBILITIES AND LIMITATIONS OF ECONOMIC GROWTH IN GENERAL AND OF THE ECONOMIC DEVELOPMENT OF UNDERDEVELOPED COUNTRIES IN PARTICULAR. COMPARES GROWTH PROBLEMS OF UNDERDEVELOPED AND DEVELOPED ECONOMIES IN ORDER TO ELUCIDATE OPERATIONALLY SIGNIFICANT MECHANISMS OF ECONOMIC DEVELOPMENT IN GIVEN SOCIO-CULTURAL CONDITIONS. UNANNOTATED BIBLIOGRAPHY OF RECENT WORKS IN ENGLISH.

1452 KUWAIT ARABIA
KUWAIT FUND FOR ARAB ECONOMIC DEVELOPMENT (PAMPHLET)
KUWAIT: GOVERNMENT PRINTING PR, 1963, 17 PP.
LAW ESTABLISHING KUWAIT FUND, THE PURPOSE OF WHICH IS TO ASSIST ARAB STATES IN DEVELOPING THEIR ECONOMIES AND PROVIDE THEM WITH LOANS NECESSARY FOR THE EXECUTION OF THEIR PROGRAMS OF DEVELOPMENT. ALSO CONTAINS KUWAIT FUND'S CHARTER OUTLINING ADMINISTRATION, OPERATIONS, AND GENERAL PROVISIONS.

1453 KUWAIT FUND ARAB ECO DEVELOPMT
ANNUAL REPORTS 1962-65 (PAMPHLET)
KUWAIT: GOVERNMENT PRINTING PR, 1962, 60 PP.
REPORTS OF KUWAIT FUND FOR ARAB ECONOMIC DEVELOPMENT ON ITS LOAN ASSISTANCE TO ARAB NATIONS FOR ECONOMIC GROWTH. DISCUSSES LOAN POLICY AND SYSTEM, FINANCIAL POSITION OF FUND, AND PROJECTS IN PROGRESS.

1454 KUZNETS S.
"QUANTITATIVE ASPECTS OF THE ECONOMIC GROWTH OF NATIONS: DISTRIBUTION OF INCOME BY SIZE."
ECON. DEVELOP. CULT. CHANGE, 11 (JAN. 63), 1-80.
AN EXTENSIVE STUDY DEALING WITH RELATION BETWEEN ECONOMIC GROWTH AND DISTRIBUTION OF INCOME BY SIZE AMONG INDIVIDUALS AND HOUSEHOLDS IN A COUNTRY. ATTEMPTS TO ANSWER TWO CRUCIAL QUESTIONS: FIRST, DOES ECONOMIC DEVELOPMENT AFFECT DISTRIBUTION OF GROWING INCOME AMONG THE POPULATION. SECOND, DOES THE SIZE DISTRIBUTION OF INCOME, AFFECTED BY ECONOMIC GROWTH, HAVE IN TURN AN EFFECT ON THE LATTER.

1455 KUZNETS S.
POSTWAR ECONOMIC GROWTH: FOUR LECTURES.
CAMBRIDGE: BELKNAP PR, 1964, 148 PP., LC#64-25054.
REVIEWS RECENT ECONOMIC STRUCTURE OF WORLD. COOPERATION, COMPETITION, AND CONFLICT ARE EXAMINED AS RESULTING FROM DIVERSITY AND INTERDEPENDENCE OF WORLD STATES. EXAMINES ECONOMIC LOSSES OF WORLD WAR II AND RECENT TRENDS; ANALYZES CHARACTERISTICS OF MODERN ECONOMIC GROWTH.

1456 KUZNETS S.
MODERN ECONOMIC GROWTH.
NEW HAVEN: YALE U PR, 1966, 528 PP., LC#66-21524.
CONSIDERS RELEVANCE OF "WESTERN ECONOMICS" TO ANALYSIS OF STRUCTURE AND PROCESS IN OTHER COUNTRIES. DISCUSSES CYCLES IN ECONOMY AFFECTED BY TECHNOLOGICAL AND IDEOLOGICAL INNOVATION FROM HISTORICAL VIEWPOINT, AND EFFECTS OF POLITICAL SYSTEMS. REVIEWS AGGREGATE STRUCTURE OF GROWTH OF NATIONS IN MODERN TIMES.

1457 LAFEBER W.
THE NEW EMPIRE: AN INTERPRETATION OF AMERICAN EXPANSION, 1860-1898.
ITHACA: CORNELL U PRESS, 1963, 444 PP.
EXAMINES INDUSTRIAL REVOLUTION IN AMERICA, DEEMING IT CRUCIAL TO FOREIGN POLICY AND TRANSITION TO MODERN EMPIRE. STUDIES THE YEARS OF PREPARATION, THE INTELLECTUAL FORMULATION, THE FOREIGN STRATEGY, THE ECONOMIC GROWTH, AND US REACTION TO WORLD PROBLEMS. ALSO CONSIDERS DEPRESSION DIPLOMACY, VENEZUELAN CRISIS, CHANGING FRIENDS AND FOES, AND APPROACH TO WAR AS A STRONG WORLD POWER.

1458 LAFONT P.B.
BIBLIOGRAPHIE DU LAOS.
PARIS: ECOLE FRANC D'EXTR-ORIENT, 1964, 269 PP.
LIST OF 1,867 UNANNOTATED ITEMS IN FRENCH, RUSSIAN, VIETNAMESE, LAOTIAN AND THAI. INCLUDES SOME ENGLISH ITEMS ALSO. MATERIAL COVERS ONLY LAST FEW YEARS. IT IS ORGANIZED ALPHABETICALLY BY AUTHOR UNDER SUBJECT HEADING AND INCLUDES AUTHOR INDEX. REFERENCES TO HISTORY, DEMOGRAPHY, LAW, ETHNOGRAPHY, ECONOMY, AND EDUCATION.

1459 LAGOS G.
INTERNATIONAL STRATIFICATION AND UNDERDEVELOPED COUNTRIES.
CHAPEL HILL: U.N.C. PR., 1963, 302 PP., $7.50.
A STRATEGIC MODEL FOR UNDERDEVELOPED COUNTRIES ATTEMPTING TO IMPROVE THEIR LOW INTERNATIONAL STATUS. THEORY BASED ON EMPIRICAL DEVELOPMENT OF TYPOLOGIES OF INTERNATIONAL ACTION.

1460 LAHAYE R.
LES ENTREPRISES PUBLIQUES AU MAROC.
PARIS: LIBRAIRIE DE MEDICIS, 1961, 340 PP.
ANALYSIS OF STATE OWNERSHIP AND PARTICIPATION IN PUBLIC SERVICES AND INDUSTRY IN MOROCCO. DESCRIBES ENTERPRISES, ANALYZES THEIR STRUCTURE, AND DISCUSSES THEIR ECONOMIC AND ADMINISTRATIVE EVOLUTION. STATE PARTNERSHIP IN PRIVATE INDUSTRY IS IMPORTANT TO ECONOMIC DEVELOPMENT, AS WELL AS STATE OWNERSHIP WHERE INDUSTRY HAS NOT DEVELOPED SUCCESSFULLY. DISCUSSES GROWTH OF ADMINISTRATIVE JURISPRUDENCE.

1461 LAIRD R.D. ED.
SOVIET AGRICULTURAL AND PEASANT AFFAIRS.
LAWRENCE: U. KANSAS PR., 1963, 335 PP., $7.00.
A COLLECTION OF PAPERS ON THE PROBLEMS AND RECORD OF RUSSIAN AGRICULTURE BY AMERICAN SPECIALISTS. COMPARES THE SITUATION IN RURAL RUSSIA UNDER KHRUSHCHEV WITH THE SIT-

UATION UNDER STALIN, AND EXAMINES THE IMPACT OF THE NEW INCENTIVES, BOTH MATERIAL AND PSYCHIC, ON THE PEASANTS AND ON THE ADMINISTRATORS.

1462 LAMBERG R.F.
PRAG UND DIE DRITTE WELT.
HANNOVER: VERLAG FUR LITERATUR, 1966, 291 PP.
EXAMINES POLITICAL AND ECONOMIC RELATIONS BETWEEN CZECHOSLOVAKIA AND DEVELOPING NATIONS OF ASIA, AFRICA AND LATIN AMERICA. DISCUSSES FOREIGN TRADE, TECHNOLOGICAL ASSISTANCE, AND LOAN PROGRAMS.

1463 LAMBERT J.D.
"CORPORATE POLITICAL SPENDING AND CAMPAIGN FINANCE."
CORP. PRACTICE COMMENTATOR, 8 (FEB. 67), 363-419.
DISCUSSES RESOURCES POLITICAL PARTIES DRAW ON TO RAISE CAMPAIGN FUNDS. AS CAMPAIGN COSTS MOUNT - A RESULT OF INFLATION, INCREASING INCOME AND VOTING POPULATION, AND TECHNOLOGICAL CHANGE - BOTH PARTIES HAVE TO BROADEN BASE OF FINANCIAL SUPPORT. PRESENTS STATUTORY FRAMEWORK, CASES, LABOR AND CORPORATIONS AS RESOURCES, INDIRECT EXPENDITURES, AND CONSTITUTIONAL QUESTIONS.

1464 LAMFALUSSY A.
INVESTMENT AND GROWTH IN MATURE ECONOMIES.
NEW YORK: OCTAGON PUBL CO, 1961, 206 PP.
DETAILED ANALYSIS OF VARIOUS TYPES OF INVESTMENT POLICIES CONNECTED WITH PROBLEM OF DECLINING INDUSTRIES IN HIGHLY INDUSTRIALIZED COUNTRIES. DISCUSSES PROBLEMS INVOLVED IN TRANSFER OF LABOR AND CAPITAL FROM DECLINING TO EXPANDING INDUSTRIES. BASED ON STUDY OF BELGIAN INDUSTRIAL GROWTH FOLLOWING WWII. PRIMARILY DIRECTED TOWARD PROFESSIONAL ECONOMISTS.

1465 LANDAUER C.
THEORY OF NATIONAL ECONOMIC PLANNING.
BERKELEY: U OF CALIF PR, 1944, 191 PP.
DISCUSSES FORM AND EXTENT OF SOCIAL CONTROL NECESSARY TO ESTABLISH ECONOMIC STABILITY IN DEMOCRATIC SOCIETIES. ATTEMPTS TO DEFINE MINIMAL REQUIREMENTS FOR SUCH CONTROL AND TO FORMULATE INCREMENTAL PLAN FOR THEIR IMPLEMENTATION. CONSIDERS NONECONOMIC FACTORS AND INFLUENCE OF OTHER NATIONS ON ATTEMPTS TO ACHIEVE PLANNED ECONOMY.

1466 LANDAUER C.
"CONTEMPORARY ECONOMIC SYSTEMS."
PHILADELPHIA: J B LIPPINCOTT, 1964.
COMPARATIVE ANALYSIS OF ECONOMIC SYSTEMS IN TERMS OF STRUCTURE, ACHIEVEMENT, AND OPERATIONAL MECHANICS. ATTEMPTS TO ILLUSTRATE SIMILARITIES BETWEEN CAPITALISTIC AND COMMUNISTIC ECONOMIC SYSTEMS IN ORDER TO ANALYZE THEIR ALTERNATIVE METHODS TO BASICALLY COMMON GOALS. DISCUSSES PRIMITIVE AND UNDERDEVELOPED ECONOMIES IN CONTEXT OF CONVERGING DEVELOPMENT PATTERNS OF ECONOMIC SYSTEMS. BIBLIOGRAPHY APPENDED.

1467 LANDAUER J.D.
"PROFESSIONAL CONSULTANTS: A NEW FACTOR IN REAL ESTATE."
NAT. REAL ESTATE & BUILDING J., 57 (MAY 56), 31-37.
TREATS INCREASING DEMAND FOR REAL ESTATE CONSULTANTS. LISTS QUALIFICATIONS OF CONSULTANTS. ANALYZES HIS FUNCTIONS, HIS IMPORTANCE TO THE INDUSTRY, AND HIS FUTURE. ALSO RELATES THE SOURCE OF HIS SALARY TO HIS EFFICIENCY AND OBJECTIVENESS.

1468 LANDEN R.G.
OMAN SINCE 1856: DISRUPTIVE MODERNIZATION IN A TRADITIONAL ARAB SOCIETY.
PRINCETON: PRINCETON U PRESS, 1967, 488 PP.
STUDY OF EFFECTS OF ECONOMIC DEVELOPMENT IN OMAN POINTS OUT LATE 19TH CENTURY AS TIME OF IRREVOCABLE CHANGE IN CULTURE OF REGION. DESCRIBES PERSIAN GULF AREA BEFORE 19TH CENTURY AND TRACES HISTORY OF OMAN GOVERNMENT ALONG WITH ESTABLISHMENT OF BRITISH PREDOMINANCY. DISCUSSES EFFECTS OF OIL DEVELOPMENT ON CULTURLAND POLITICAL ESTABLISHMENTS.

1469 LANDERS D.S., E
RISE OF CAPITALISM.
NEW YORK: MACMILLAN, 1966, 150 PP., LC#66-17385.
COLLECTION OF TEN ESSAYS INTENDED TO DEMONSTRATE INTERRELATIONSHIP OF DIVERSE ASPECTS OF CAPITALISM. DISCUSSES ROLE OF RELIGIOUS AND CULTURAL AS WELL AS POLITICAL AND ECONOMIC FORCES IN DEVELOPMENT OF CAPITALISM. TRACES DEVELOPMENT IN EUROPE AND AMERICA TO ITS IMMENSE PROGRESS IN SEVERLA LEADING CAPITALIST COUNTRIES AFTER WWI. DIRECTED TOWARD GENERAL AUDIENCE.

1470 LANDES W.M.
"THE EFFECT OF STATE FAIR EMPLOYMENT LAWS ON THE ECONOMIC POSITION OF NONWHITES."
AMER. ECO. REVIEW, 57 (MAY 67), 578-590.
AUTHOR INVESTIGATES EFFECTS OF FAIR EMPLOYMENT LAW TO DETERMINE WHETHER OR NOT SUCH LEGISLATION HAS IMPROVED ECONOMIC POSITION OF RACIAL & RELIGIOUS MINORITIES IN REALITY. HE FIRST DEVELOPS A THEORETICAL MODEL TO ANALYZE IMPACT OF FAIR EMPLOYMENT LAWS, AND THEN TESTS HYPOTHESIS HE FINDS AGAINST EMPIRICAL EVIDENCE ON EFFECT OF STATE LAWS ON RATIO OF NONWHITE TO WHITE EARNINGS AND MARKET DISCRIMINATION.

1471 LANDSKROY W.A.
OFFICIAL SERIAL PUBLICATIONS RELATING TO ECONOMIC DEVELOPMENT IN AFRICA SOUTH OF THE SAHARA (PAMPHLET)
CAMBRIDGE: M I T PRESS, 1961, 44 PP.
LIST OF SERIAL REPORTS PUBLISHED IN ENGLISH COVERS BROAD RANGE OF SUBJECTS PERTAINING TO ECONOMIC DEVELOPMENT; ONLY REPORTS ON HEALTH AND EDUCATION HAVE BEEN EXCLUDED. INCLUDES STUDIES OF PRIVATE CORPORATIONS OPERATING UNDER GOVERNMENT APPROVAL AND OFFICIAL REPORTS ON UK'S COLONIES AND PROTECTORATES AND UN DOCUMENTS. REPORTS ARE ALL KNOWN TO BE AVAILABLE IN US. GEOGRAPHIC ARRANGEMENT.

1472 LANE F.C.
"ECONOMIC CONSEQUENCES OF ORGANIZED VIOLENCE."
J. ECO. HIST., 18 (DEC. 58), 401-17.
ENTERPRISES USING AND CONTROLLING VIOLENCE AFFECT AMOUNT AND DISTRIBUTION OF MATERIAL WEALTH BY INCURRING COSTS AND EXACTING LARGE SUMS. AS NATURAL MONOPOLIES, AFFECT MONOPOLIES IN OTHER FIELDS. THESE RELATIONSHIPS HAVE REPERCUSSIONS ON ENTIRE ECONOMIC ORGANIZATION.

1473 LANFALUSSY A.
"EUROPE'S PROGRESS: DUE TO COMMON MARKET."
LLOYD BANK REV., 62 (OCT. 61), 1-16.
REVIEWS DATA SHOWING THAT COMMON MARKET HAD NOT CAUSED GREAT ADVANCES. WARNS AGAINST LIMITS OF HIS FIGURES BECAUSE OF IMPONDERABLES OF MORALE AND POSSIBLE GROWING EFFECT NOT YET TOO APPARENT.

1474 LANG A.S., SOBERMAN R.M.
URBAN RAIL TRANSIT.
CAMBRIDGE: M I T PRESS, 1964, 139 PP., LC#63-23379.
DISCUSSES ECONOMICS AND TECHNOLOGY OF MASS RAIL-TRANSPORTATION SYSTEMS. DESCRIBES THE PHYSICAL COMPONENTS OF THESE SYSTEMS, THEIR OPERATIONAL REQUIREMENTS, AND THEIR COSTS. EMPHASIZES CHARACTERISTICS OF CAPACITY AND QUALITY OF SERVICE AND RELATES THESE FACTORS TO COST. ATTEMPTS TO RELATE RAIL TRANSIT TO THE ENTIRE URBAN TRANSPORTATION SCENE.

1475 LANGE O., TAYLOR F.Y.
ON THE ECONOMIC THEORY OF SOCIALISM.
MINNEAPOLIS: U. MINN. PR., 1938, 143 PP.
ANALYZES THE PROBLEM OF GOVERNMENT CONTROL OF ECONOMY. STUDIES REGULATION OF PRODUCTION IN SOCIALIST STATE. NOTES GENERAL APPLICATION OF TRIAL AND ERROR PROCEDURE. ALSO STUDIES DETERMINATION OF EQUILIBRIUM IN COMPETITIVE MARKET.

1476 LANGE O.
ECONOMIC DEVELOPMENT, PLANNING, AND INTERNATIONAL COOPERATION.
CAIRO: CENTRAL BANK OF EGYPT, 1963, 40 PP., LC#63-13434.
LECTURES DELIVERED AT THE CENTRAL BANK OF EGYPT IN 1961. EXAMINES PATTERNS OF ECONOMIC DEVELOPMENT; PLANNING ECONOMIC DEVELOPMENT; AND ASPECTS AND POSSIBILITIES FOR INTERNATIONAL COOPERATION. APPROACH IS MAINLY EMPIRICAL.

1477 LANGE O.R.
"DISARMAMENT ECONOMIC GROWTH AND INTERNATIONAL CO-OPERATION" (PAMPHLET)
LEEDS: LEEDS U PRESS, 1962, 11PP.
SOLUTION TO TWO MAJOR WORLD PROBLEMS OF DISARMAMENT AND ECONOMIC DEVELOPMENT LIES IN INTERNATIONAL COOPERATION. DISARMAMENT LEADS TO PROBLEMS OF CONVERSION AND ALTERNATIVE USES OF RESOURCES. SOCIALIST AND CAPITALIST SYSTEMS DIFFER IN CONVERSION ABILITY ACCORDING TO AMOUNT OF CENTRAL PLANNING. AFTER SUCCESSFUL CONVERSION THE UNUSED RESOURCES WOULD BE AVAILABLE TO AID IN ECONOMIC DEVELOPMENT.

1478 LANGHOFF P. ED.
MODELS, MEASUREMENT AND MARKETING.
ENGLEWOOD CLIFFS: PRENTICE HALL, 1964, 211 PP., LC#64-15211.
DESCRIBES IN NONMATHEMATICAL TERMS SIGNIFICANCE OF MODELS, DECISION THEORY, AND SIMULATION TO MARKETING. DISCUSSES SCIENTIFIC METHOD AND ITS APPLICABILITY TO SPECIFIC MARKETING PROBLEMS, PROS AND CONS OF MODEL-BUILDING AND TESTING, AND TRAINING OF MARKETING SPECIALISTS WHO COMMUNICATE WITH NEW MATHEMATICS.

1479 LANGLEY D.
"POSTSCRIPT ON THE COLONIZATION OF THE INTERNATIONAL TRADE UNION MOVEMENT"
NEW POLITICS, 5 (FALL 66), 66-69.
MAINTAINS LARGE-SCALE ATTEMPT TO SUBVERT INTERNATIONAL FREE TRADE UNION, BACKED BY UNLIMITED US GOVERNMENT FUNDS, HAS BEEN UNDERWAY AND HAS RESULTED IN PARTIAL OR TOTAL TAKEOVER OF SEVERAL INTERNATIONAL LABOR ORGANIZATIONS. JAY LOVESTONE REVEALED AS CHIEF ARCHITECT OF SUBJUGATION OF AFL-CIO FOREIGN POLICY TO CIA AND ATTEMPTED COLONIZATION BY CIA OF INTERNATIONAL FREE TRADE UNION MOVEMENT.

1480 LANGLEY L.D.
"THE DEMOCRATIC TRADITION AND MILITARY REFORM, 1878-1885."
S.W. SOCIAL SCI. QUART., 48 (SEPT. 67), 192-200.

STUDIES OPINION OF MILITARY REFORMERS OF 1878-85 THAT STRONG ARMY WAS NEEDED TO MAINTAIN DEMOCRACY. ADVOCATED EFFICIENCY IN MANAGEMENT, STRONGER MILITARY EDUCATION, AND FURTHERING OF NATIONAL PRESTIGE. SUGGESTED USE OF ARMY IN NATIONAL PROBLEMS OF RIOTS, INDIANS, MORMONS, AND DEFENSE. EFFORTS FAILED BUT AFFECTED POST-CIVIL WAR NATIONALISM.

1481 LANSING J.B.
TRANSPORTATION AND ECONOMIC POLICY.
NEW YORK: FREE PRESS OF GLENCOE, 1966, 409 PP., LC#66-18514.
USES FUNDAMENTAL ECONOMIC CONCEPTS, SUCH AS THEORY OF INVESTMENT AND RATE MAKING, IN AN ANALYTIC APPROACH TO THE PROBLEMS OF ECONOMIC POLICY IN THE FIELD OF TRANSPORTATION. EMPHASIZES PUBLIC ECONOMIC POLICY, OFTEN USING A COMPARATIVE AND HISTORICAL APPROACH TO PROBLEMS.

1482 LARY M.B.
PROBLEMS OF THE UNITED STATES AS WORLD TRADER AND BANKER.
NEW YORK: NATL BUREAU ECO RES, 1963, 175 PP., LC#63-11079.
FOCUSES ON PROBLEMS OF ASSESSING ELEMENTS OF STRENGTH AND WEAKNESS IN OUR INTERNATIONAL TRADE AND FINANCIAL POSITION OF IMPROVING ADJUSTMENT PROCESSES SO AS TO DIMINISH EXTERNAL CONSTRAINT OF DOMESTIC AND FOREIGN ECONOMIC POLICIES. ALSO DISCUSSES PROBLEM OF MAKING ADAPTATIONS IN OUR POLICIES TO PREVENT OUR INCREASED INTERNATIONAL EXPOSURE FROM HINDERING PURSUIT OF ECONOMIC STABILITY AND GROWTH.

1483 LASKI H.J.
THE STATE IN THEORY AND PRACTICE.
NEW YORK: VIKING PRESS, 1935, 366 PP.
ANALYZES EVOLUTION OF DEMOCRATIC FORMS OF CAPITALISM, HOW THE ECONOMICS OF 1800'S AFFECTED IT, AND PROBLEMS OF 20TH CENTURY. CLAIMS STATE IS ALWAYS INSTRUMENT OF DOMINANT ECONOMIC CLASS AND THAT ITS ESSENCE IS POWER TO COERCE. THEORY OF STATE CLOSELY PARALLELS MARX'S. APPLIES THIS THEORY TO 1930'S, PREDICTING DEMISE OF DEMOCRACY AS RESULT OF ACTIONS TO PROTECT CAPITALISTS' INTERESTS DURING ECONOMIC DISASTER.

1484 LASLETT J.H.M.
"SOCIALISM AND THE AMERICAN LABOR MOVEMENT* SOME NEW REFLECTIONS."
LABOR HISTORY, 8 (SPRING 67), 136-155.
DRAWS CONCLUSION FROM STUDY OF AFL IN POST-1900 ERA THAT SOCIALIST POLICIES FAILED TO ACHIEVE AS MUCH FOR LABOR AS MORE CONSERVATIVE PHILOSOPHIES DID. CITES FACTORS SUCH AS WORKING WITHIN THE MAJOR-PARTY SYSTEM, WHICH MAY BE MOST IMPORTANT, AND EXTENT OF CENTRALIZATION OF POWER. SPECIFIC REFERENCE MADE TO NUMEROUS UNIONS OF THIS PERIOD.

1485 LASSWELL H.D.
"THE GARRISON STATE" (BMR)
AMER. J. OF SOCIOLOGY, 46 (JAN. 41), 455-468.
EXAMINES POSSIBILITY THAT WORLD IS MOVING TOWARD CONDITION OF "GARRISON STATES," IN WHICH MILITARY IS MOST POWERFUL GROUP IN SOCIETY. EXAMINES TREND AWAY FROM SUPREMACY OF BUSINESSMEN. POSTULATES METHODS BY WHICH MILITARY GROUPS WILL GAIN SUPREMACY, SUCH AS ECONOMIC TACTICS AND MANIPULATION OF PUBLIC SYMBOLS.

1486 LATIFI D.
INDIA AND UNITED STATES AID.
BOMBAY: PUBLIC AFFAIRS FORUM, 1960, 135 PP.
HISTORICALLY ANALYZES EFFECTS OF US FOREIGN AID ON INDIAN ECONOMY AND RELATIONS. COMPARES US ASSISTANCE TO BRITISH COLONIALISM AND ITS EFFECTS ON INDIAN ECONOMY. TRACES ECONOMIC GROWTH 1949-60 WITH US AID. DISCUSSES EFFECTIVENESS OF WASHINGTON'S POLICIES IN ASIA IN GENERAL.

1487 LATTIN N.D.
"MINORITY AND DISSENTING SHAREHOLDERS' RIGHTS IN FUNDAMENTAL CHANGES."
LAW AND CONTEMPORARY PROB., 23 (SPRING 58), 307-324.
DEALS WITH CHANGES WHICH HAVE BEEN ANALYZED AS USURPATIONS OF STOCKHOLDERS' CONTRACTUAL RIGHTS AND THE COMPROMISE SOLUTION OFFERED BY APPRAISAL REMEDIES. MENTIONS DIFFERENT VOTING RIGHTS, APPRAISAL MACHINERY, AND ENDS ON AN OPTIMISTIC NOTE.

1488 LAURENS H.
"LES PAYS OCCIDENTAUX ET LE MARCHE CHINOIS."
POLITIQUE ETRANGERE, 31 (1966), 65-85.
PREDICTS CHINA WILL CONTINUE TO INCREASE TRADE WITH WESTERN NATIONS. LISTS AND DISCUSSES VOLUME OF TRADE OF EACH OF THE TWELVE WESTERN NATIONS THAT CHINA DEALS WITH.

1489 LAURSEN K., PEDERSEN J.
THE GERMAN INFLATION, 1918-23.
AMSTERDAM: NORTH HOLLAND PUBL CO, 1964, 138 PP.
ANALYZES GERMAN ECONOMY AFTER WWI. FEELS THAT POPULAR MONETARY THEORY OF INFLATION COULD NOT EXPLAIN WHAT HAPPENED THEN. THEORIZES THAT "SACRIFICIAL DEMANDS MADE ON GERMAN PEOPLE BY GOVERNMENT'S POLICIES WERE UNBEARABLE AND CAUSED INFLATION." THESE POLICIES WERE BASED ON MONETARY THEORIES. INCLUDES INDEX OF GRAPHS PLOTTING ECONOMY IN INFLATION.

1490 LAUTERBACH A.
ECONOMIC SECURITY AND INDIVIDUAL FREEDOM: CAN WE HAVE BOTH?
ITHACA: CORNELL U PRESS, 1948, 178 PP.
DISCUSSES RELATIONSHIP OF PLANNED ECONOMIC STABILITY TO BOTH TOTALITARIANISM AND DEMOCRACY. CONTRASTS LAISSEZ-FAIRE AND TOTALITARIAN SOLUTIONS TO ECONOMIC PROBLEMS IN SOCIETY. MAINTAINS THAT ECONOMIC WELFARE IS ESSENTIAL TO FREEDOM, BUT THAT ECONOMIC SECURITY SHOULD MEAN ONLY THE GUARANTEE THAT OPPORTUNITIES WILL ALWAYS BE AVAILABLE FOR THOSE WILLING TO WORK.

1491 LAVES W.H.C., THOMSON C.A.
UNESCO.
BLOOMINGTON: IND. U. PR., 1957, 469 PP.
HISTORY OF UNESCO CONTRASTING GOALS AND ACCOMPLISHMENTS AND CONCLUDING ORGANIZATION MOST SUCCESFUL IN ADVANCEMENT OF KNOWLEDGE THROUGH TECHNICAL ASSISTANCE AND LEAST SUCCESSFUL IN PROMOTION OF INTERNATIONAL UNDERSTANDING. URGES INCREASED EFFORTS ON THE PART OF THE MEMBER STATES.

1492 LAWLEY F.E.
THE GROWTH OF COLLECTIVE ECONOMY VOL. 1: NATIONAL.
LONDON: PS KING & SON, 1938, 520 PP.
ARGUES AGAINST "MENACE" OF PRIVATE PROPERTY, STATING THAT COLLECTIVIZATION IS PREREQUISITE TO DYNAMIC ECONOMY. COMPARES METHODS OF OBTAINING GOVERNMENT CONTROL OF PROPERTY IN VARIOUS COUNTRIES, USING WARTIME CONTROL AS EXEMPLAR OF EFFECTIVENESS. DEFENDS AGRARIAN REFORMS AND NATIONALIZATION OF MAJOR INDUSTRIES. ARGUMENT EXTENDED TO INTERNATIONAL SPHERE IN A SECOND VOLUME.

1493 LAWLEY F.E.
THE GROWTH OF COLLECTIVE ECONOMY VOL. 2: INTERNATIONAL.
LONDON: PS KING & SON, 1938, 501 PP.
FIRST VOLUME ARGUED THAT COLLECTIVIZATION IS NECESSARY FOR A DYNAMIC ECONOMY. SECOND VOLUME EXTENDS ARGUMENT TO INTERNATIONAL SPHERE, ARGUING THAT ECONOMIC NATIONALISM SHOULD BE SUPERSEDED BY INTERNATIONALISM. CLAIMS THAT FAULT OF FASCISM, NAZISM, COMMUNISM, AND NEW DEAL IS NATIONALISM RATHER THAN EXCESS CONTROL.

1494 LAWRENCE S.A.
THE BATTERY ADDITIVE CONTROVERSY (PAMPHLET)
UNIVERSITY: U ALABAMA PR, 1962, 34 PP.
RELATES EPISODE OF JESS M. RITCHIE, WHO SOUGHT TO MARKET A PREPARATION CLAIMING TO PROLONG BATTERY LIFE. CHARGED WITH MISLEADING ADVERTISING, HE ATTACKED FTC AND CHALLENGED SCIENTIFIC ACCURACY OF NATIONAL BUREAU OF STANDARD'S TEST FINDINGS. DESCRIBES TACTICS OF DIFFERENT GROUPS OF SCIENTISTS IN CASE.

1495 LAWTON F.J.
"LEGISLATIVE-EXECUTIVE RELATIONS IN BUDGETING AS VIEWED BY THE EXECUTIVE."
PUBLIC ADMIN. REV., 13 (SUMMER 53), 169-176.
LECTURE BY FORMER HEAD OF BUREAU OF BUDGET, CALLING FOR LESS CONGRESSIONAL INTERFERENCE IN DESIGNING FEDERAL BUDGET, IN ORDER TO INCREASE EFFICIENCY. SAYS EXECUTIVE BRANCH ADEQUATELY REPRESENTS THE PUBLIC.

1496 LAZARUS S., BRAY J.J. ET AL.
RESOLVING BUSINESS DISPUTES: THE POTENTIAL OF COMMERCIAL ARBITRATION.
NEW YORK: AMER MANAGEMENT ASSN, 1965, 208 PP., LC#65-24369.
AUTHORS REVIEW UTILITY OF COMMERCIAL ARBITRATION FOR SOLVING 20TH-CENTURY BUSINESS PROBLEMS. POINT OUT MOST LIKELY SITUATIONS WHERE IT CAN BE USED; EVALUATE LEGAL CRITICISMS OF THE PROCESS, RECOMMEND CERTAIN CHANGES IN CONDUCT OF PROCEEDINGS, AND PREDICT FUTURE COURSE OF ARBITRATION. APPROACH SUBJECT FROM DIVERSE VIEWPOINTS, INCLUDING THOSE OF BUSINESSMEN, LAWYERS, JUDGES, EDUCATORS, AND ARBITRATORS.

1497 LAZUTKIN Y.
"SOCIALISM AND SPARE TIME."
REPRINTS FROM THE SOVIET PRESS, 5 (AUG. 67), 31-37.
DISCUSSES ADVANTAGE OF SOCIALISM OVER CAPITALISM IN PROVIDING WORKING CLASS WITH SPARE TIME AND FREEDOM FROM EXPLOITATION. MAINTAINS THAT INCREASE IN LABOR PRODUCTIVITY DURING YEARS OF SOVIET POWER IS BOTH CAUSE AND EFFECT OF INCREASED SPARE TIME AND CONCERN FOR INDIVIDUAL'S DEVELOPMENT. EXAMINES INCREASED LABOR PRODUCTIVITY AND GREATER PROPORTION OF SPARE TIME SPENT ON INTELLECTUAL DEVELOPMENT.

1498 LEAGUE OF WOMEN VOTERS OF US
FOREIGN AID AT THE CROSSROADS.
WASHINGTON: LEAGUE WOMEN VOTERS, 1966, 78 PP.
INVESTIGATES FOREIGN AID FROM SEVERAL VIEWPOINTS. DISCUSSES PROBLEM OF POPULATION EXPLOSION, REVIEWS US AID EFFORTS PAST AND PRESENT, AND PRESENTS TOOLS FOR MORE EFFECTIVE AID. DISCUSSES ALLIANCE FOR PROGRESS AND OTHER EFFORTS AT MUTUAL AID, SUCH AS UN AND REGIONAL ORGANIZTIONS. REVEALS PROBLEMS IN GIVING AND IN RECEIVING, POLITICS OF AID, CURRENT PROBLEMS, AND NEW SOLUTIONS.

1499 LECHT L.
GOAL, PRIORITIES, AND DOLLARS: THE NEXT DECADE.

NEW YORK: FREE PRESS OF GLENCOE, 1966, 365 PP., LC#66-19798.
ATTEMPTS SYNTHESIS OF REQUIRED, DESIRED, AND FEASIBLE GOALS OF PUBLIC EXPENDITURE. SURVEYS THESE GOALS IN TERMS OF SOCIAL, ECONOMIC, AND POLITICAL OBJECTIVES: WELFARE, URBAN DEVELOPMENT, HEALTH, EDUCATION, TRANSPORTATION, DEFENSE, HOUSING, INTERNATIONAL AID, SPACE, AND AGRICULTURE.

1500 LECLERCQ H., WEST R.L.
"ECONOMIC RESEARCH AND DEVELOPMENT IN TROPICAL AFRICA."
SOCIAL RESEARCH, 32 (FALL 65), 299-320.
WHILE THE PRESENT CAPABILITY FOR RESEARCH IS DEFINITELY LOW BY STANDARDS OF INTERNATIONAL COMPARISON, A SHARP INCREASE OF RESEARCH ACTIVITY HAS OCCURRED SINCE 1960. ARTICLE COVERS THE STRUCTURE OF ECONOMIC RESEARCH FACILITIES THAT EXISTED IN COLONIAL AFRICA, AND THE GROWTH OF THE TEN MAJOR ACADEMIC RESEARCH CENTERS SINCE INDEPENDENCE.

1501 LEDEBUR L.C.
"THE PROBLEM OF SOCIAL COST."
AMER. J. OF ECO. AND SOC., 26 (OCT. 67), 399-415.
DISCUSSES ABILITY OF ANY SOCIO-ECONOMIC SYSTEM TO MAXIMIZE THE SOCIAL INCOME OF ITS MEMBERS. ADDRESSES PROBLEM OF SOCIAL SIGNIFICANCE OF EXISTENCE OF EXTERNAL DISECONOMIES. EXAMINES CORRECTIVE MEASURES UNDERTAKEN TO INSURE MAXIMIZATION OF THE NATIONAL DIVIDEND IN CASES INVOLVING SOCIAL COST.

1502 LEDERER W.
THE BALANCE ON FOREIGN TRANSACTIONS: PROBLEMS OF DEFINITION AND MEASUREMENT (PAMPHLET)
PRINCETON: PRIN U, DEPT OF ECO, 1963, 76 PP., LC#63-20994.
ATTEMPTS TO CLARIFY AND UNIFY PURPOSE FOR WHICH ANALYSIS OF DATA COMPILED ON INTERNATIONAL TRANSACTIONS IS INTENDED. TRIES TO DETERMINE FOCUS FOR ANALYSIS IN TERMS OF SPECIFIC KINDS OF TRANSACTIONS. ANALYZES DATA AND INSTITUTIONS IN US TO DECIDE WHICH TYPE OF DATA IS BEST FOR FORMULATING AND DISCUSSING PUBLIC POLICY.

1503 LEDUC G.
"L'AIDE INTERNATIONALE AU DEVELOPPEMENT."
TIERS-MONDE, 4 (NOS.13-14, 63), 237-60.
DESCRIBES GENERAL PRINCIPLES FOR ACHIEVING PROGRAM. CONSIDERS NATIONAL AND INTERNATIONAL FINANCIAL RESOURCES. CONCLUDES WITH EXAMINATION OF DIFFERENT FORMS OF ECONOMIC AID.

1504 LEE A.M., LEE E.B.
SOCIAL PROBLEMS IN AMERICA: A SOURCE BOOK.
NEW YORK: HOLT RINEHART WINSTON, 1949, 741 PP.
CASES IN SOCIOLOGY STUDYING PHYSICAL, POPULATION, URBAN, AND RURAL PROBLEMS: THOSE CAUSED BY PARTICULAR AGE IN LIFE; PROBLEMS OF EDUCATION, ECONOMICS, POLITICS, COMMUNICATION; INDIVIDUAL AND GROUP DEVIATIONS; PROBLEMS OF SOCIAL DIVISION AND SOCIAL CRISES; AND PROCESSES AND TECHNIQUES OF ADJUSTMENT.

1505 LEE M.W.
MACROECONOMICS: FLUCTUATIONS, GROWTH AND STABILITY (3RD ED.)
HOMEWOOD: RICHARD IRWIN, 1963, 646 PP., LC#63-10331.
EXPLORES VARIETY OF ECONOMIC FLUCTUATIONS AND MAKES ANALYTICAL SURVEY OF BUSINESS-CYCLE EXPERIENCE TO TIME OF GREAT DEPRESSION. ANALYZES THEORY OF ECONOMIC FLUCTUATIONS AND ECONOMIC STABILIZATION. SEEKS FINALLY TO FORECAST FUTURE TRENDS.

1506 LEE M.W.
TOWARD ECONOMIC STABILITY.
NEW YORK: JOHN WILEY, 1966, 177 PP., LC#66-25227.
HANDBOOK ON ECONOMIC STABILIZATION. INCLUDES CONSTANCY OF CHANGE, MACHANICS OF STABILIZATION, FISCAL POLICY, EMPLOYMENT, GROWTH, PRICE LEVELS, AND TWO DECADES OF STABILIZATION EXPERIENCE.

1507 LEE R.A.
TRUMAN AND TAFT-HARTLEY: A QUESTION OF MANDATE.
LEXINGTON: U OF KY PR, 1966, 254 PP., LC#66-26689.
ANALYZES POLITICAL HISTORY OF TAFT-HARLEY ACT. USES THIS NATIONAL LABOR POLICY ISSUE, IN POSTWAR YEARS, TO ILLUSTRATE CLEAVAGE THAT EXISTS BETWEEN EXECUTIVE AND LEGISLATIVE BRANCHES BECAUSE OF CONSTITUENCIES EACH REPRESENTS. SEES TRUMAN AS REPRESENTATIVE OF URBAN LABORERS, WHOSE POWER HE TRIED TO PROTECT BY VETOING ACT, WHILE CONSERVATIVE AND MIDDLE-CLASS CONGRESS OPPOSED LIBERAL-DEMOCRATIC MEASURES.

1508 LEE R.L.
"THE PARADOX OF EQUALITY: A THREAT TO INDIVIDUAL AND SYSTEM FUNCTIONING."
ROCKY MOUNTAIN SOCIAL SCIENCE J., 4 (OCT. 67), 120-130.
EXPLORES PARADOX IN COMMUNIST CHINA OF CLASSLESS SOCIETY OF UNEQUAL PEOPLE. STATES THAT EGALITARIAN MODEL OF SOCIETY IS NOT SUITABLE FOR RAPIDLY INDUSTRIALIZING SOCIETY. DISCUSSES PREMISES OF FUNCTIONALISM, DEVELOPS TWO FUNCTIONAL MODELS OF SOCIETY, EGALITARIAN AND STRATIFIED. COMPARES TWO MODELS TO DETERMINE REASON FOR MALFUNCTION OF EGALITARIAN SOCIETY: NEED FOR DIVISION OF LABOR FOR ECONOMIC GROWTH.

1509 LEE R.R., FLEISCHER G.A., ROGGEVEEN V.J.
ENGINEERING-ECONOMIC PLANNING MISCELLANEOUS SUBJECTS: A SELECTED BIBLIOGRAPHY (MIMEOGRAPHED)
STANFORD: STAN U PROJ ENG & ECO, 1961, 53 PP.
SELECTION OF REFERENCES TO CITY AND REGIONAL PLANNING. SPECIAL EMPHASIS ON ADMINISTRATIVE, ECONOMIC, LEGISLATIVE, AND POLITICAL ASPECTS. INCLUDES SECTIONS ON ENGINEERING ECONOMY THEORY, INVESTMENT DECISION-MAKING, LAND AND NATURAL RESOURCES, PUBLIC FINANCE, AND URBAN RENEWAL. INCLUDES BRIEF DESCRIPTIONS OF MANY BOOKS AND ARTICLES LISTED. STUDIES ARE BOTH GENERAL AND OF SPECIFIC TOPICS.

1510 LEFCOE G., SCHAFFER M.
"CONSTRUCTION LENDING AND THE EQUITABLE LIEN."
SOUTH CALIFORNIA LAW REVIEW, 40 (SPRING 67), 439-462.
ANALYZES PROCEDURE OF GAINING "EQUITABLE LIENS" ON UNDISPERSED LEAN FUNDS TO UNPAID MATERIALMEN IN CALIFORNIA, WHEN BUILDING PROJECTS FAIL. DISCUSSES CASES WHERE COURTS HAVE GRANTED LIENS OVER OBJECTIONS OF LENDERS. DEEMS THESE DECISIONS UNJUST AND RECOMMENDS IMPOSING LIENS ONLY WHEN LENDERS REALIZE LARGE GAIN, OR WHEN LOSS CAN BE MITIGATED ON UNCOMPLETED PROJECT.

1511 LEFF N.H.
"ECONOMIC DEVELOPMENT THROUGH BUREAUCRATIC CORRUPTION."
AMER. BEHAVIORAL SCIENTIST, 8 (NOV. 64), 8-14.
DISCUSSES GOVERNMENTAL CORRUPTION AS A POTENTIAL POSITIVE FORCE IN DEVELOPMENT. CORRUPTION GIVES REPRESENTATION TO NONGOVERNMENTAL ENTREPRENEURS WHO WOULD OTHERWISE HAVE NO MEANS OF IMPLEMENTING PROJECTS.

1512 LEHMAN R.L. ED., PRICE F.W. ED.
AFRICA SOUTH OF THE SAHARA (PAMPHLET)
NEW YORK: MISSIONARY RES LIB, 1961, 70 PP.
GEOGRAPHICAL ARRANGEMENT IS USED IN LISTING BOOKS IN THIS BIBLIOGRAPHY. AREAS DEALT WITH ARE: WEST AFRICA, EQUATORIAL AFRICA, SOUTH AFRICA, CENTRAL AFRICA, EAST AFRICA, AND MADAGASKAR. HAS SECTION ON REFERENCE AND BIBLIOGRAPHICAL WORKS AND GENERAL WORKS. A VARIETY OF FIELDS ARE COVERED. SOME WORKS ARE ANNOTATED.

1513 LEIBENSTEIN H.
ECONOMIC BACKWARDNESS AND ECONOMIC GROWTH.
NEW YORK: JOHN WILEY, 1957, 295 PP., LC#57-12296.
DESCRIBES NATURE OF UNDERDEVELOPED COUNTRIES, DISCUSSING THEORIES OF UNDEREMPLOYMENT, MINIMUM EFFORT, POPULATION GROWTH, AND OTHER ASPECTS OF ECONOMIC DEVELOPMENT SUCH AS PER CAPITA INCOME, GROWTH INCENTIVES, CAPITAL-OUTPUT RATIOS, AND INVESTMENT POLICIES.

1514 LEIBY J.
CHARITY AND CORRECTION IN JERSEY; A HISTORY OF STATE WELFARE INSTITUTIONS.
NEW BRUNSWICK: RUTGERS U PR, 1967, 500 PP., LC#67-13078.
NARRATES ESTABLISHMENT AND ORGANIZATION OF NEW JERSEY SERVICES FOR "DEPENDENT, DEFECTIVE, AND DELINQUENT CLASSES." RECOUNTS ORIGINS OF STATE WELFARE INSTITUTIONS BEFORE 1918 AND FOUNDING OF STATE DEPARTMENT TO OVERSEE THEM IN 1918. DISCUSSES PROBLEMS IN THEORY, POLICY, AND ADMINISTRATION AND PRESENTS SOLUTIONS AND REASONS FOR DEPARTMENT'S FAILURES.

1515 LEIFER M.
"ASTRIDE THE STRAITS OF JAHORE: THE BRITISH PRESENCE AND COMMONWEALTH RIVALRY IN SOUTHEAST ASIA."
MODERN ASIAN STUDIES, 1 (JULY 67), 283-296.
ANALYZES BRITISH ROLE IN MALAYSIA, DEFENDING IT FOR THE MOST PART. QUESTIONS IF, BY MAINTAINING ECONOMIC HEALTH IN AREA, BRITAIN IS NOT OVEREXTENDING HERSELF MILITARILY.

1516 LEISERSON W.
AMERICAN TRADE UNION DEMOCRACY.
NEW YORK: COLUMBIA U PRESS, 1959, 354 PP., LC#59-8112.
A CLASIC WORK ON THE GOVERNMENT OF LABOR UNIONS, IT DISCUSSES A NUMBER OF IMPORTANT REPRESENTATIONAL QUESTIONS SUCH AS AUTHORIZED EXTRAORDINARY POWERS OF UNION EXECUTIVES, A PRIMITIVE JUDICIAL SYSTEM, ATTITUDE OF RANK-AND-FILE MEMBERS, VARIOUS STRUCTURES, AND A COMPREHENSIVE REVIEW OF REPRESENTATION AND ITS FUNCTIONING IN UNION CONVENTIONS.

1517 LEKACHMAN R. ED.
KEYNES' GENERAL THEORY: REPORTS OF THREE DECADES.
NEW YORK: ST MARTIN'S PRESS, 1964, 347 PP., LC#64-11970.
ARTICLES BY P. A. SAMUELSON, P. M. SWEEZY, A. LERNER, R. HARROD, J. F. VINER, ET AL. LERNER WARNS AGAINST RESURGENCE OF PRE-KEYNESIAN ATTITUDES; REDDAWAY FITS FISCAL POLICY TO GENERAL THEORY. SWEEZY'S AND SAMUELSON'S EARLY AND PRESENT JUDGMENTS VARY CONSIDERABLY ON THEIR THEORETICAL ORIGINALITY AND USEFULNESS.

1518 LEMIEUX V.
"LA DIMENSION POLITIQUE DE L'ACTION RATIONNELLE."
CAN. J. OF ECO. AND POL. SCI., 33 (MAY 67), 190-204.
BELIEVES THAT THERE IS POLITICAL DIMENSION TO RATIONAL ACTION EXPRESSED IN TERMS OF POWER OF ONE MAN OVER ANOTHER. MAINTAINS THAT INTEGRATION OF DAHL'S FORMULA FOR MEASUREMENT OF POWER WITH THEORY OF POLITICAL RATIONALITY WILL LEAD TO

BETTER THEORY. EXTENDS THEORY TO COVER TWO-PERSON, TWO-ALTERNATIVE GAMES. DEFINES AND EXPLORES "MACRO-POLITICS," AND "MICRO POLITICS."

1519 LENCZOWSKI G.
OIL AND STATE IN THE MIDDLE EAST.
ITHACA: CORNELL U. PR., 1960, 360 PP.
BY EMPHASIZING AND EXPLAINING CERTAIN ASPECTS OF THE MIDDLE-EASTERN OIL COMPANIES (LEGAL STATUS, CONCESSION AGREEMENTS, METHOD OF HANDLING EMPLOYEES AND GOVERNMENT OFFICIALS, AND GENERAL RELATIONSHIP TO HOST NATION) ATTEMPTS TO PROJECT THEIR FUTURE POSITION IN THESE COUNTRIES.

1520 LENIN V.I.
SELECTED WORKS (12 VOLS.)
LONDON: LAWRENCE & WISHART, 1954, 3600 PP.
TWELVE-VOLUME WORK COVERS LENIN'S PHILOSOPHIES CONCERNING VARIOUS ASPECTS OF SOCIETY. INCLUDES WORKS ON CAPITALISM, POLITICS, AGRARIANISM, THE WORKER, THE INTELLIGENTSIA, ECONOMICS, WAR, NATIONAL GOVERNMENT, PARTY ORGANIZATION, THE REVOLUTIONS, AND SOCIAL STRUCTURE IN GENERAL.

1521 LENIN V.I.
THE DEVELOPMENT OF CAPITALISM IN RUSSIA.
LONDON: LAWRENCE & WISHART, 1957, 751 PP.
ANALYSIS OF FORMATION OF HOME MARKET FOR LARGE-SCALE INDUSTRY IN RUSSIA. DISCUSSION LIMITED TO ECONOMIC ASPECT OF PROCESS AND TO EVENTS AND CIRCUMSTANCES IN POST-REFORMATION ERA. FIRST CHAPTER PROVIDES BASIC THEORETICAL BACKGROUND OF POLITICAL ECONOMY. SUBSEQUENT CHAPTERS DISCUSS FACTUAL PROBLEMS IN EVOLUTION OF CAPITALISM IN RUSSIAN AGRICULTURE AND INDUSTRY.

1522 LENIN V.I.
WHAT IS TO BE DONE? (1902)
MOSCOW: FOREIGN LANG PUBL HOUSE, 1961, 183 PP.
DISCUSSES CHARACTER AND MAIN CONTENT OF POLITICAL AGITATION, AS SEEN BY LENIN IN 1901. CONSIDERS ORGANIZATIONAL TASKS OF THE PARTY, AND PLAN FOR BUILDING MILITANT, TOTALLY RUSSIAN ORGANIZATION. ATTACKS CURRENT ECONOMISTS FOR SUPPORTING OPPRESSION AND PROCLAIMS WORKING CLASS TO BE CAPABLE OF POWERFUL COLLECTIVE ACTION, PROPOSING USE OF NEWSPAPER "ISKA" AS ITS ORGAN.

1523 LENS S.
"WALTER REUTHER TRIES TO BUILD A FIRE."
COMMONWEAL, 86 (MAY 67), 253-254.
SUMMARY OF WALTER REUTHER'S PROPOSAL FOR UNION ORGANIZATION OF THE POOR, OVER WHICH HE SPLIT WITH THE AFL-CIO. PROGRAM WOULD CALL FOR ORGANIZATION ON BASIS OF COMMUNITIES RATHER THAN CRAFTS OR INDUSTRIES, AND WOULD AIM AT WIDESPREAD SOCIAL AND ECONOMIC CHANGE. ALSO, PRESENTLY UNORGANIZED CRAFTS AND TRADES WOULD BE ORGANIZED IN A MORE TRADITIONAL WAY. POSSIBLE NEW HOPE FOR STAGNANT LABOR MOVEMENT.

1524 LENSKI G.
THE RELIGIOUS FACTOR: A SOCIOLOGICAL STUDY OF RELIGION'S IMPACT ON POLITICS, ECONOMICS, AND FAMILY LIFE.
GARDEN CITY: DOUBLEDAY, 1961, 381 PP.
AN EXTENSIVE EMPIRICAL ANALYSIS OF IMPACT OF RELIGIOUS BELIEFS ON SOCIAL INSTITUTIONS. CARRIED OUT IN DETROIT, THIS STUDY DESCRIBES THE GROUP TIES AND PATTERNS OF FOUR SOCIO-RELIGIOUS GROUPS AND, AMONG OTHER ISSUES, THEIR FUNCTIONAL REPRESENTATION AND LOBBYING ACTIVITIES IN ECONOMIC AND POLITICAL LIFE, AS WELL AS THE EFFECT OF A CATHOLIC EDUCATION AND THE ROLE OF CLERGY GROUPS.

1525 LENSKI G.E.
POWER AND PRIVILEGE: A THEORY OF SOCIAL STRATIFICATION.
NEW YORK: MCGRAW HILL, 1966, 467 PP., LC#65-28594.
COMPARES, CONTRASTS, AND SYNTHESIZES THEORIES OF MOSCA, SPENCER, SUMNER, PARETO, VEBLEN, SOROKIN, PARSONS, DAHRENDORF, AND MARX WITH RELATION TO SOCIAL STRATIFICATION. AUTHOR CONCENTRATES ON CAUSES OF SOCIAL STRATIFICATION RATHER THAN THE CONSEQUENCES. CONSIDERS PROPOSITIONS ABOUT THE DISTRIBUTIVE SYSTEMS OF HUNTING AND GATHERING, SIMPLE AND ADVANCED HORTICULTURAL, AGRARIAN, AND INDUSTRIAL SOCIETIES.

1526 LENT G.E.
"TAX INCENTIVES FOR INVESTMENT IN DEVELOPING COUNTRIES"
INTL. MONETARY FUND STAFF BUL., 14 (JULY 67), 249-323.
COMPARES VARIETY OF METHODS FOR ESTABLISHING TAX-INCENTIVE PROGRAMS TO ENCOURAGE INVESTMENT. EVALUATES MERITS OF EACH SCHEME IN ATTEMPT TO ESTABLISH BETTER STANDARDS FOR INVESTMENT CODES. DEALS WITH HARMONIZATION OF TAX-INCENTIVE LAWS IN DIFFERENT COUNTRIES AND GIVES CONCLUSIONS ON FEATURES OF INVESTMENT-INCENTIVE PLANS.

1527 LEONARD L.L.
INTERNATIONAL ORGANIZATION.
NEW YORK: MCGRAW HILL, 1951, 600 PP.
TRACES HISTORY AND CHARACTERISTICS OF INTERNATIONAL ORGANIZATIONS AND DELINEATES BEGINNINGS OF LEAGUE OF NATIONS, UN. COMPARES PROCESSES OF DECISION-MAKING AND IMPLEMENTATION WITH THOSE OF SOVEREIGN STATES. EXAMINES POLITICAL, ECONOMIC,D SOCIAL, AND COLONIAL ACTIVITIES OF THE LEAGUE AND UN. DISCUSSES ORGANIZATION AND FUNCTION OF SEPARATE UN ORGANS AND RECOUNTS PAST ACTIONS OF UN AND LEAGUE.

1528 LEONTIEF W.
ESSAYS IN ECONOMICS.
NEW YORK: OXFORD U PR, 1966, 252 PP., LC#66-24437.
THREE-PART STUDY OF STRUCTURE AND APPLICATION OF ECONOMIC THEORY STRESSES ASPECTS OF NONMATHEMATICAL ECONOMICS. DISCUSSES GENERAL METHODS OF THEORIZING AND INVESTIGATES SPECIFIC ANALYTICAL PROBLEMS IN KEYNESIAN AND OTHER GENERAL ECONOMIC THEORY. EXAMINES IMPORTANT PROBLEMS IN SPECIFIC APPLICATIONS OF ECONOMIC THEORY IN SUCH AREAS AS AUTOMATION AND FOREIGN AID.

1529 LEONTYEV L.
"THE LENINIST PRINCIPLES OF SOCIALIST ECONOMIC MANAGEMENT."
REPRINTS FROM THE SOVIET PRESS, 5 (AUG. 67), 23-30.
DISCUSSES LENIN'S PLAN OF SOCIALIST CONSTRUCTION WHICH FORMED BASIS OF GENERAL LINE OF COMMUNIST PARTY. EXAMINES COMPETITION BETWEEN CAPITALISM AND SOCIALISM, AND MAINTAINS THAT SOCIALISM HAS OVERCOME ITS ADVERSARY WITH WEAPONS OF HIGHER PRODUCTIVITY OF SOCIAL LABOR. STUDIES LENIN'S PLANNED TYPE OF ECONOMIC DEVELOPMENT AND PLANNED MANAGEMENT OF ECONOMY.

1530 LERNER A.P.
THE ECONOMICS OF CONTROL.
NEW YORK: MACMILLAN, 1960, 428 PP.
STATES THAT PRINCIPAL PROBLEMS OF A CONTROLLED ECONOMY ARE EMPLOYMENT, MONOPOLY, AND DISTRIBUTION OF INCOME. ANALYZES BENEFITS OF BOTH CAPITALISTIC AND COLLECTIVIST ECONOMIES, AND WARNS AGAINST RIGHTIST OR LEFTIST POLITICAL DOGMATISM.

1531 LERNER E.M., CARLETON W.T.
A THEORY OF FINANCIAL ANALYSIS.
NEW YORK: HARCOURT BRACE, 1966, 281 PP., LC#66-18219.
APPROACHES QUESTIONS OF FINANCIAL THEORY THROUGH AN INTERRELATIONSHIP OF SECURITY ANALYSIS AND CORPORATION FINANCE. HIGHLY QUANTITATIVE EMPHASIS WITH BOTH MICRO- AND MACRO-ECONOMIC APPROACHES.

1532 LESTER R.A.
ECONOMICS OF LABOR.
NEW YORK: MACMILLAN, 1941, 913 PP.
DEALS WITH ECONOMIC ASPECTS OF LABOR PROBLEMS, INCLUDING WAGES, HOURS, AND UNEMPLOYMENT, THE GROWTH OF ORGANIZED LABOR, INCLUDING UNIONS AND MANAGEMENT-UNION RELATIONS, AND COLLECTIVE BARGAINING IN CERTAIN INDUSTRIES.

1533 LESTER R.A.
AS UNIONS MATURE.
PRINCETON: PRIN U INDUS REL CTR, 1958, 171 PP., LC#58-10048.
TRACES GROWTH OF US LABOR UNIONS, DEALING WITH MANAGEMENT RELATIONS, CENTRALIZATION OF POWER IN NATIONAL UNIONS, AND ECONOMIC ASPECTS OF UNIONISM. ALSO TREATS POLITICAL EFFECTS OF UNIONS AND THEIR ROLE IN AFFECTING PUBLIC POLICY. DISCUSSES TACTICS OF UNIONS IN HANDLING MANAGEMENT AND RELATIVE SUCCESS OF EACH.

1534 LETHBRIDGE H.J.
CHINA'S URBAN COMMUNES.
HONG KONG: DRAGONFLY BOOKS, 1961, 74 PP.
ANALYZES STRUCTURE OF THESE COMMUNES WHICH PROVIDE SOCIAL ORGANIZATION FOR ONE FOURTH OF WORLD'S PEOPLE. SEES SIGNIFICANCE OF THESE COMMUNES FOR REST OF WORLD SINCE CHINA FEELS US WILL BE ORGANIZED THIS WAY "WHEN WORKERS AND PEASANTS SEIZE POWER." COVERS ORIGIN OF COMMUNAL IDEA, ITS PLACE IN CHINESE IDEOLOGY, AND REASONS FOR ITS RAPID GROWTH SINCE 1960.

1535 LETHBRIDGE H.J.
THE PEASANT AND THE COMMUNES.
HONG KONG: GREEN PAGODA PR, 1963, 202 PP.
DESCRIBES ROLE OF CHINESE PEASANT IN COMMUNAL SYSTEM. EVALUATES COMMUNIST AGRARIAN POLICY, 1921-58. DISCUSSES SOCIAL ASPECTS OF COMMUNES AND SUGGESTS REASONS FOR THEIR FAILURE TO SOLVE ASIA'S FARM PROBLEM. REVIEWS ALTERNATIVE SOLUTIONS. COMPARES RUSSIA'S AND CHINA'S EXPERIENCES.

1536 LETICHE J.M. ED.
A HISTORY OF RUSSIAN ECONOMIC THOUGHT: NINTH THROUGH EIGHTEENTH CENTURIES.
BERKELEY: U OF CALIF PR, 1964, 690 PP., LC#64-18641.
DEVELOPMENT OF RUSSIAN ECONOMICS RELATED TO IDEOLOGICAL CHANGE. CONSIDERS ROLE OF CHURCH LAND OWNERSHIP, AGRICULTURAL TECHNIQUES, AND ECONOMIC THEORY IN DEVELOPING NATION, 900-1900.

1537 LETICHE J.M.
"EUROPEAN INTEGRATION: AN AMERICAN VIEW."
LLOYD BANK REV., 75 (JAN. 65), 1-23.
EXPLORES RELATIONSHIP OF COMMON MARKET TO DISUNITY BETWEEN FRANCE AND OTHER PARTICIPANTS. PROBES DIFFICULT ALTERNATIVES FACING WESTERN COUNTRIES REGARDING FURTHER INTEGRATION, CALCULATING EFFECT ON GROSS NATIONAL PRODUCT

OF MEMBERS. DISCUSSES BRITAIN'S ATTEMPT TO JOIN.

1538 LEVENSTEIN A.
WHY PEOPLE WORK; CHANGING INCENTIVES IN A TROUBLED WORLD.
NEW YORK: CROWELL COLLIER, 1962, 320 PP., LC#62-17493.
DISCUSSES PROBLEM OF CHANGING WORK INCENTIVES AND EXAMINES CHARGE THAT PEOPLE DO NOT CARE ANY MORE. STUDIES SENSE OF IMPOTENCE PRODUCED BY INCREASE IN POPULATION AND IN SOCIAL INSTITUTIONS THROUGH WHICH INCENTIVES ARE EXPRESSED, AND IN MASS COMMUNICATIONS SYSTEM. MAINTAINS THAT INCENTIVES ARE STILL PRESENT BUT ARE NOT CHANGING TO MEET NEW CIRCUMSTANCES OF WORK.

1539 LEVER E.A.
ADVERTISING AND ECONOMIC THEORY.
LONDON: OXFORD U PR, 1947, 132 PP.
BOOK APPEALS TO YOUNG ECONOMISTS TO THINK OUT PROPER PLACE OF ADVERTISING AND EMPHASIZES NECESSITY FOR A THEORY OF CONSUMPTION.

1540 LEVI M.
"LES RELATIONS ECONOMIQUES ENTRE L'EST ET L'OUEST EN EUROPE"
POLITIQUE ETRANGERE, 35 (1967), 477-492, 4-5.
EXAMINES TRADE BETWEEN THE OECD AND EAST EUROPEAN COUNTRIES. FINDS THAT IN LAST 17 YEARS TRADE WITH EAST EUROPE AS A WHOLE HAS NOT INCREASED MORE THAT TRADE WITH ANY OTHER AREA. HOWEVER, TRADE WITH THE USSR AND CZECHOSLOVAKIA HAS GREATLY INCREASED SINCE 1961. CONSIDERS EVOLUTION OF EXCHANGE BY COUNTRY AND BY PRODUCT. CONCLUDES THAT TYPES OF EXCHANGE MUST BE ALTERED.

1541 LEVIN T.
"PSYCHOANALYSIS AND SOCIAL CHANGE."
PSYCHOANALYTIC REVIEW, 54 (FALL 67), 66-76.
EXPLORES RELATIONSHIP OF SOCIAL ACTUALITY (SOCIAL ENVIRONMENT) TO THREE OF ERIKSON'S STAGES OF DEVELOPMENT: TRUST VS. MISTRUST, AUTONOMY VS. SHAME AND DOUBT, AND INITIATIVE VS. GUILT. INDICATES THAT CHARACTERISTICS OF POOR ARE APPROPRIATE, NOT DISTURBED, ADAPTATIONS TO THEIR ACTUALITY. URGES APPLICATION OF PSYCHOANALYTIC METHODS TO TECNIQUES OF SOCIAL CHANGE, SUCH AS GIVING POWER TO POOR.

1542 LEVINE L.
SYNDICALISM IN FRANCE (2ND ED.)
NEW YORK: COLUMBIA U PRESS, 1914, 229 PP.
CONCERNED WITH REVOLUTIONARY SYNDICALISM IN THEORY AND PRACTICE; TREATS IT AS FUSION OF REVOLUTIONARY SOCIALISM AND TRADE UNIONISM. REVIEWS LABOR MOVEMENT IN FRANCE, 1789-1871, TO COMMUNE AND ORIGIN OF GENERAL CONFEDERATION OF LABOR. EXPLICATES DOCTRINES OF THEORISTS AND DEVELOPMENTS SINCE 1902. SURVEYS CHARACTERISTICS AND CONDITIONS OF FRENCH SOCIETY MAKING FRANCE RECEPTIVE TO SYNDICALISM.

1543 LEVINSON E.
LABOR ON THE MARCH.
NEW YORK: HARPER & ROW, 1938, 325 PP.
THE CHALLENGES TO CRAFT UNIONISM OF THE AFL WITH THE PASSAGE OF THE NRA AND PARLIAMENTARY PROCEDURES TO MODERNIZE ITS ORGANIZATION ARE DESCRIBED, AS ARE ANTI-LABOR EFFECTS OF THE NRA, RANK-AND-FILE AND RECRUITMENT EFFORTS AGAINST OLD-LINE UNION LEADERS, THE CONTRAVERSIES OF THE 1935 ATLANTIC CITY CONVENTION, THE RISE OF THE CIO, AND THE DECLINE OF COMPANY UNIONS UNDER THE WAGNER ACT.

1544 LEVY H.V.
LIBERDADE E JUSTICA SOCIAL (2ND ED.)
SAO PAULO: LIVRARIA MARTINS EDITORA, 1962, 203PP.
DISCUSSION OF SOCIAL JUSTICE AND LIBERTY UNDER MARXISM, SOVIET SYSTEM, AND US CAPITALISM IN AUSTRIA, ENGLAND, AND BRAZIL. INCLUDES STUDY OF RELATED DOCUMENTS OF 20TH COMMUNIST PARTY CONGRESS OF USSR, UN, NEW CLASS BY DJILAS, AND BRAZILIAN DELEGATION TO 48TH WORLD INTER-PARLIAMENTARY CONFERENCE IN WARSAW.

1545 LEWIN J.
POLITICS AND LAW IN SOUTH AFRICA.
NEW YORK: MONTHLY REVIEW PR, 1963, 115 PP.
EXAMINATION OF RELATION OF AFRIKANER NATIONALISM, AFRICAN NATIONALISM, AND ENGLISH ECONOMIC INTERESTS TO PRESENT FORM OF GOVERNMENT IN SOUTH AFRICA. EXPLAINS DEVELOPMENT OF SEPARATE NATIONALISM OF WHITE AFRICAN AND ATTAINMENT OF POWER DESPITE LARGER BLACK AFRICAN POPULATION AND MORE POWERFUL BRITISH ECONOMIC INFLUENCE.

1546 LEWIN P.
THE FOREIGN TRADE OF COMMUNIST CHINA* ITS IMPACT ON THE FREE WORLD.
NEW YORK: FREDERICK PRAEGER, 1964, 128 PP., LC#64-16671.
IN THE FUTURE ANY MAJOR CHANGES IN CHINA'S BEHAVIOR AS A BUYER OR SELLER IN THE INTERNATIONAL MARKETS COULD HAVE IMPORTANT CONSEQUENCES. THEREFORE, LEWIN PRESENTS A HISTORY OF CHINESE TRADING PRACTICES (PRE & POST REVOLUTION), DEVELOPMENTAL EXPERIENCES UNDER COMMUNISM, HER MODEST FOREIGN AID PROGRAM, AND THE REACTIONS OF TRADE PATTERNS TO SINO-SOVIET SPLIT. WEALTH OF DATA ON ALL OF ABOVE.

1547 LEWIS E.G.
"PARLIAMENTARY CONTROL OF NATIONALIZED INDUSTRY IN FRANCE."
AM. POL. SCI. REV., 51 (SEPT. 57), 669-684.
STUDIES METHODS USED BY PARLIAMENT, AND NOTES THAT WHILE PARLIAMENT MAINTAINS LITTLE INFLUENCE ON MAJOR DECISIONS IT RETAINS POTENTIALLY ENORMOUS POWERS AND HAS DEVELOPED EFFECTIVE CONTROL OVER THE NATIONALIZED INDUSTRIES. CITES INCREASING CONTROL THROUGH USE OF COMMITTEES CREATED TO STUDY AND CHECK ABUSES.

1548 LEWIS G.K.
PUERTO RICO: FREEDOM AND POWER IN THE CARIBBEAN.
NEW YORK: MONTHLY REVIEW PR, 1963, 626 PP., LC#63-20065.
EXAMINES THE GENERAL EXPERIENCE OF PUERTO RICAN LIFE AND THOUGHT WITHIN A PAN-CARIBBEAN WORLD. FINDS THAT PUERTO RICO IS A NEOCOLONIAL SOCIETY UNDER THE INFLUENCE OF US, A NEOCOLONIAL POWER. DISCUSSES ECONOMIC, SOCIAL, AND POLITICAL EFFECTS OF THIS RELATIONSHIP.

1549 LEWIS J.P.
BUSINESS CONDITIONS ANALYSIS.
NEW YORK: MCGRAW HILL, 1959, 602 PP., LC#58-13882.
CONSIDERS THEORY OF AGGREGATIVE ECONOMIC BEHAVIOR WHICH MODERN ECONOMICS OFFERS. FIRST TREATS SOCIAL ACCOUNTING, ESPECIALLY STRUCTURE AND CHARACTER OF NATIONAL INCOME ACCOUNTING IN US. ANALYZES MODERN MACROECONOMIC THEORY. DISCUSSES RECENT HISTORY OF US BUSINESS CONDITIONS AND CONTRIBUTIONS OF ECONOMIC ANALYSIS TO DIAGNOSES OF NATION'S LONG-TERM PROSPECTS.

1550 LEWIS L.J.
SOCIETY, SCHOOLS AND PROGRESS IN NIGERIA.
NEW YORK: PERGAMON PRESS, 1967, 176 PP.
DESCRIBES EDUCATION IN NIGERIA IN CONTEXT OF NATION'S ATTAINING SELF-SUSTAINING SOCIAL AND ECONOMIC GROWTH. MAINTAINS THAT AIMS OF EDUCATION ARE TO PROVIDE PEOPLE WITH SKILLS TO CARRY OUT PROGRAMS OF DEVELOPMENT AND TO ASSIST YOUNG PEOPLE IN ADAPTING TO CHANGING SOCIAL AND ECONOMIC SYSTEMS.

1551 LEWIS V.B.
"TOWARD A THEORY OF BUDGETING" (BMR)"
PUBLIC ADMIN. REV., 12 (WINTER 52), 42-54.
ANALYZES PRINCIPLES FROM GENERAL ECONOMIC THEORY WHICH WOULD BE APPLICABLE TO A THEORY OF PUBLIC BUDGETING, AND OUTLINES A BUDGET PROCEDURE. INCLUDES APPLICABILITY OF VARIOUS CONCEPTS BY ECONOMISTS TO A METHODOLOGY OF ANALYZING BUDGET ESTIMATES. CONCERNED PRIMARILY WITH PROBLEMS OF FEDERAL GOVERNMENT. DISCUSSES THEORIES OF RELATIVE VALUE, INCREMENTAL ANALYSIS, AND RELATIVE EFFECTIVENESS.

1552 LEWIS W.A.
DEVELOPMENT PLANNING; THE ESSENTIALS OF ECONOMIC POLICY.
NEW YORK: HARPER & ROW, 1966, 278 PP., LC#66-10655.
CONCERNED WITH TECHNIQUES AND ECONOMICS OF DEVELOPMENT PLANNING; EMPHASIZES POLICY. BEGINS WITH PATTERNS OF PLANNING, THEN EXAMINES STRATEGY. ARITHMETIC AND STATISTICAL FRAMEWORK OF A PLAN EXPLAINED IN DETAIL. CLOSES WITH PROCESS OF PLANNING. AREAS COVERED INCLUDE ADMINISTRATIVE STRUCTURE OF FEDERAL AND PRIVATE PLANNING AGENCIES AND COMMITTEES, FOREIGN TRADE AND AID, LINEAR PROGRAMMING, CAPITAL.

1553 LEWIS W.A.
"THE STATUTORY LANGUAGE OF LABOR DISQUALIFICATION IN STATE EMPLOYMENT SECURITY LAWS."
POLIT. SCI. QUART., 82 (MAR. 67), 72-87.
STUDIES RELATION AND SOURCES OF FOUR TYPES OF LANGUAGE IN STATE LAWS GOVERNING UNEMPLOYMENT COMPENSATION DISQUALIFICATION IN LABOR DISPUTES AND SHOWS PATTERN IN ESCAPE CLAUSES IN SUCH LAWS. BOTH SIMILARITIES AND DIFFERENCES OF VARIOUS STATE LAWS ARE SHOWN.

1554 LEYS C.T. ED., ROBSON P. ED.
FEDERATION IN EAST AFRICA.
LONDON: OXFORD U PR, 1965, 244 PP.
ANTHOLOGY OF PAPERS ON EAST AFRICAN FEDERATION DEALING WITH TRADE, ADMINISTRATION, FINANCE, LABOR, AGRICULTURE, TRANSPORTATION, LAW, AND COOPERATION IN REGION.

1555 LHOSTE-LACHAUME P.
OU GIT LE DESACCORD ENTRE LIBERAUX ET SOCIALISTES.
PARIS: EDITIONS SEDIF, 1961, 77 PP.
DESCRIBES WESTERN POLITICAL AND ECONOMIC MALAISE, ANALYZING HISTORICAL ANTECEDENTS AND CONSEQUENCES OF THE DEPRESSION AND INCLUDES DICUSSION OF CURRENCY, KEYNES, AND THE NEW DEAL.

1556 LI C.M. ED.
INDUSTRIAL DEVELOPMENT IN COMMUNIST CHINA.
NEW YORK: PRAEGER, 1964, 205 PP., $5.00.
PRESENTS UP TO DATE INFORMATION AND CRITICAL ANALYSES ON CAPITAL FORMATION, WORK-INCENTIVE POLICY, ECONOMIC PLANNING, CHANGES IN THE STEEL INDUSTRY, HANDICRAFTS AND AGRICULTURE, SINO-SOVIET TRADE AND EXCHANGE RATES, AND THE DIFFICULTIES IN MEASURING CHINESE INDUSTRIAL OUTPUT.

1557 LI CHOH-MING
ECONOMIC DEVELOPMENT OF COMMUNIST CHINA.
BERKELEY: U CAL BUR BUS ECON RES, 1959, 284 PP., LC#58-1330.
ECONOMIC ANALYSIS OF GROWTH OF COMMUNIST CHINA FROM 1952-57. USING DATA DERIVED FROM CHINESE-LANGUAGE SOURCES PUBLISHED IN PEKING UP TO 1957. MAY ALSO BE VIEWED AS A CASE STUDY OF HOW ADOPTION OF A PROGRAM OF HEAVY AND RAPID INDUSTRIALIZATION AFFECTS ECONOMIC GROWTH OF A LOW-INCOME, AGRICULTURAL NATION.

1558 LICHFIELD N.
COST-BENEFIT ANALYSIS IN URBAN REDEVELOPMENT.
BERKELEY: U CAL BUR BUS ECON RES, 1962, 52 PP.
DISCUSSES THE APPLICATION OF DECISION-MAKING THEORY TO CITY PLANNING AND DESCRIBES TECHNIQUE OF COST-BENEFIT ANALYSIS. COST-BENEFIT ANALYSIS DEALS WITH THE RELATIONSHIP BETWEEN SOCIAL AND ECONOMIC COSTS AND BENEFITS, SUCH AS THE RELATIVE MERITS OF USING A VACANT LOT TO BUILD A GARAGE OR A PLAYGROUND.

1559 LICHTHEIM G.
MARXISM.
NEW YORK: FREDERICK PRAEGER, 1961, 410 PP., LC#61-08694.
EXAMINES CULTURAL EVOLUTION OF MARXISM, ITS PHILOSOPHIC, ECONOMIC, AND POLITICAL FOUNDATIONS. CONSIDERS INFLUENCE ON AND BY OTHER THEORIES OF ITS PERIOD, COMPARING IT TO NATIONALISM, DEMOCRACY, ANARCHISM, AND VICTORIAN BOURGEOIS SOCIETY.

1560 LICHTHEIM G.
THE NEW EUROPE: TODAY AND TOMORROW.
NEW YORK: FREDERICK PRAEGER, 1963, 232 PP., LC#63-11152.
ARGUMENTS UNDERLYING CURRENT DEBATE OVER WESTERN EUROPE'S FUTURE ROLE WITHIN THE EMERGING ATLANTIC COMMUNITY. TECHNICAL QUESTIONS REGARDING ECONOMICS OF EUROPEAN INTEGRATION. MOSTLY POLITICAL BUT PARTLY DEVOTED TO ANALYSIS OF FACTS AND FIGURES RELATING TO ECONOMICS.

1561 LICHTMAN R.
TOWARD COMMUNITY (PAPER)
SANTA BARBARA: CTR DEMO INST, 1966, 58 PP.
EXPLORES THEORY AND PRACTICE OF WELFARE LIBERALISM AS CURRENT FORM OF CAPITALISM. CONTENDS THAT IT IS ILL-SUITED TO DEMANDS OF HUMANE SOCIETY. OFFERS SUGGESTIONS TOWARD ESTABLISHMENT OF RESPONSIBLE COMMUNITY.

1562 LIEFMANN-KEIL E.
OKONOMISCHE THEORIE DER SOZIALPOLITIK.
GOTTINGEN: SPRINGER VERLAG, 1961, 424 PP.
EXAMINES ECONOMIC BASIS OF SOCIAL POLITICS AND SEEKS TO ESTABLISH RELEVANCE OF ECONOMIC JUDGMENTS ABOUT REALIZED POLITICAL DEMANDS. DISCUSSES DISTRIBUTION OF INCOME, PUBLIC EXPENDITURES, WORKING CONDITIONS AND MINIMUM WAGES, AND CONCLUDES WITH EXAMINATION OF INTERNATIONAL SOCIAL POLITICS THROUGH INTERNATIONAL ORGANIZATIONS.

1563 LIFLAND W.T.
"BANKING PRACTICE AND THE ANTITRUST LAWS."
NOTRE DAME LAWYER, 42 (APR. 67), 465-478.
COVERS APPLICATION OF FEDERAL ANTITRUST LAWS TO BANKING. SPECIFIC DISCUSSION OF PRACTICES WHICH HAVE BEEN AND WOULD BE CONSTRUED AS VIOLATING FEDERAL LAW. WRITTEN FROM LEGAL POINT OF VIEW AS A SUMMARY OF POSSIBLE PRACTICES EXCEEDING LIMITS OF FAIR COMPETION AND INSTIGATING ANTITRUST ACTION.

1564 LILLEY S.
MEN, MACHINES AND HISTORY: THE STORY OF TOOLS AND MACHINES IN RELATION TO SOCIAL PROGRESS.
NEW YORK: INTERNATIONAL PUBLRS, 1966, 352 PP., LC#66-21951.
SURVEYS HISTORY OF TECHNOLOGY AND SOCIAL EFFECTS OF SCIENTIFIC DISCOVERY AND INVENTION FROM BEGINNINGS OF AGRICULTURE IN 8,000 BC TO SPACE AGE. DETAILS EFFORTS OF INNOVATIONS - FROM PRIMITIVE TOOLS TO THE MOTOR - AND DESCRIBES DEVELOPMENTS IN NEW FIELDS OF NUCLEAR POWER, COMPUTERS, AUTOMATION, AND CONQUEST OF SPACE. EXPLORES POLICY PROBLEMS ARISING FROM NEW FIELDS.

1565 LINCOLN G.
ECONOMICS OF NATIONAL SECURITY.
NEW YORK: PRENTICE-HALL, 1950, 567 PP.
ANALYZES ECONOMIC REQUIREMENTS OF NATIONAL SECURITY AND EXAMINES PRESENT READINESS OF THE U.S. ECONOMY TO ACHIEVE RAPID AND EFFICIENT MOBILIZATION AGAINST COMMUNIST THREAT, INDICATING STRENGTHS AND WEAKNESSES AND POSSIBLE REMEDIES ALONG THE LINES OF INCREASED GOVERNMENTAL CONTROL AND DIRECTION OF THE NATIONAL ECONOMY.

1566 LINCOLN G.
"FACTORS DETERMINING ARMS AID."
PROC. ACAD. POLIT. SCI., 25 (MAY 53) 263-72.
THE MAIN FACTOR DETERMINING QUANTITY AND DIRECTION OF FUTURE ARMS AID IS SOVIET TANGIBLE REACTION TO AMERICAN PROPOSED POINTS FOR ACHIEVING PEACE. BY SEEKING NATIONAL SECURITY THROUGH COLLECTIVE ACTION USA MUST PROVIDE AID, ACCORDING TO NEEDS OF EACH PARTICULAR ALLY AT THE PARTICULAR TIME, ADEQUATE FOR PURPOSE OF HALTING COMMUNIST EXPANSION IN THE AREA.

1567 LINDBERG L.
POLITICAL DYNAMICS OF EUROPEAN ECONOMIC INTEGRATION.
STANFORD: U. PR., 1963, 295 PP.
ATTEMPTS TO EXAMINE THE EEC AS AN INSTITUTIONAL SYSTEM AND ASSESS ITS IMPACT ON DECISION-MAKING PATTERNS OF THE COMMON MARKET COUNTRIES. RELATES THIS TO PROBLEM OF EUROPEAN INTEGRATION.

1568 LINDBLOM C.E.
"HAS INDIA AN ECONOMIC FUTURE?"
FOREIGN AFFAIRS, 44 (JAN. 66), 239-252.
MAINTAINS THAT INDIA'S ECONOMIC DEVELOPMENT DEPENDS ON FOOD-GRAIN OUTPUT. STUDIES RECORD OF PAST PRODUCTIVITY AND PROSPECT FOR FUTURE. INVESTIGATES FERTILIZERS, IRRIGATION, EXTENSION WORK, AND PRICE AS SOLUTIONS. URGES GOVERNMENT POLICY FOR ACCELERATION AND STATES THAT PROBLEM OF FOOD SHORTAGE COULD BE EASILY SOLVED IF THOUGHT OF AS SHORT-TERM PROBLEM.

1569 LINDER S.B.
TRADE AND TRADE POLICY FOR DEVELOPMENT.
NEW YORK: FREDERICK PRAEGER, 1967, 179 PP., LC#66-26552.
DETAILS FOREIGN TRADE PROBLEMS OF UNDERDEVELOPED NATIONS COVERING IMPORT-EXPORT DIFFERENCES, FOREIGN-EXCHANGE POLICY AND DIFFICULTIES, TARIFF AGREEMENTS. SUGGESTS CORRECTIVE THEORY TO SOLVE THESE PROBLEMS OF DEVELOPMENT. BLAMES POLITICAL EXPEDIENCY FOR UNPROFITABLE POLICIES NOW EMPLOYED BY THESE NATIONS.

1570 LINDHOLM R.W.
"ACCELERATED DEVELOPMENT WITH A MINIMUM OF FOREIGN AID AND ECONOMIC CONTROLS."
SOC. ECON. STUD., 9 (MAR. 60), 57-67.
A POLICY PROPOSAL WHOSE MAIN POINTS ARE: A MONEY SUPPLY INCREASING LESS RAPIDLY THAN PRODUCTIVITY, GOVERNMENT INVESTMENT IN POWER, TRANSPORTATION, AND EDUCATION, EMPHASIS ON LAND AND GROSS RECEIPTS TAXES TO REDUCE IMPACT ON PRICES, AND SIPHONING OFF OF PROFITS.

1571 LINDHOLM R.W.
ECONOMIC DEVELOPMENT POLICY WITH EMPHASIS ON VIET-NAM.
EUGENE: U OREGON PR, 1964, 139 PP.
DISCUSSES GENERAL PROBLEMS OF DEVELOPMENT IN EMERGING NATIONS, PROBLEMS OF TAXATION, LAND REFORM, AND FINANCE IN VIETNAM, AND ROLE OF ECONOMIC ADVISER IN FINDING SOLUTIONS TO THESE PROBLEMS. INCLUDES BRIEF DISCUSSION OF PROBLEMS ENCOUNTERED IN PAKISTAN AND KOREA.

1572 LINDSAY F.A.
"PLANNING IN FOREIGN AFFAIRS: THE MISSING ELEMENT."
FOR. AFF. 39 (JAN. 61), 271-78.
PRESSURE OF OPERATING NEEDS FORCES USA DIPLOMACY TO FACE PROBLEMS OF CONFLICTING GROUPS WITHIN POWER STRUCTURE. RECOMMENDS REORGANIZATION OF PROGRAMS AND OF MUTUALLY DEPENDENT PLANS.

1573 LINEBERRY R.L., FOWLER E.P.
"REFORMISM AND PUBLIC POLICIES IN AMERICAN CITIES."
AM. POL. SCI. REV., 61 (SEPT. 67), 701-716.
TREATS TWO POLICY OUTPUTS, TAXATION AND EXPENDITURE LEVELS OF CITIES, AS VARIABLES. RELATES THESE TO SOCIO-ECONOMIC CHARACTERISTICS OF CITIES AND TO STRUCTURAL CHARACTERISTICS OF THEIR GOVERNMENT. EXAMINES IMPACT OF POLITICAL STRUCTURES, REFORMED AND UNREFORMED, ON POLICY-MAKING IN US CITIES.

1574 LINK R.G.
ENGLISH THEORIES OF ECONOMIC FLUCTUATIONS: 1815-1848.
NEW YORK: COLUMBIA U PRESS, 1959, 226 PP., LC#58-11901.
STUDY IN HISTORY OF ECONOMIC THOUGHT FROM END OF NAPOLEONIC WARS THROUGH 1848. WORKS OF SIX ECONOMISTS ARE EXAMINED: MALTHUS, TOOKE, MILL, ATTWOOD, JOPLIN, AND JAMES WILSON. USES TO WHICH THEORIES WERE PUT IN ANALYZING CONTEMPORARY ECONOMIC FLUCTUATIONS ALSO DESCRIBED.

1575 LIPPMANN W.
WESTERN UNITY AND THE COMMON MARKET.
BOSTON: LITTLE BROWN, 1962, 51 PP., LC#62-18624.
PRESENTS AUTHOR'S VIEWS CONCERNING THE WESTERN ALLIANCE: THE COMMON MARKET, ENLARGED BY THE ADMISSION OF GREAT BRITAIN AND JOINED WITH THE US IN A WIDE FREE-TRADING AREA. DISCUSSES THE RELATIONSHIP BETWEEN THE WESTERN ECONOMIC COMMUNITY AND THE NUCLEAR STALEMATE, THE SUCCESS OF THE COMMON MARKET, THE LACK OF ANY KNOWN AND CLEAR SUCCESSION IN FRANCE AND GERMANY, AND THE FADING US ECONOMIC PRE-EMINENCE.

1576 LIPSET S.M.
AGRARIAN SOCIALISM.
BERKELEY: U OF CALIF PR, 1950, 315 PP.
RISE AND EFFECTS OF SOCIALISM AMONG FARMERS IN SASKATCHEWAN. SOCIAL, POLITICAL, AND ECONOMIC EFFECTS OF COOPERATIVE COMMONWEALTH FEDERATION IN CANADA.

1577 LIPSET S.M., TROW M.A., COLEMAN J.S.

UNION DEMOCRACY.
NEW YORK: FREE PRESS OF GLENCOE, 1956, 455 PP., LC#56-6202.
A STUDY OF THE INTERNATIONAL TYPOGRAPHICAL UNION, IT DEALS WITH ASPECTS OF ITU POLITICAL LIFE: ORGANIZATION, MEMBERSHIP CONTROL, IDEOLOGY, LEADERSHIP, LEGITIMACY OF OPPOSITION AND A TWO-PARTY SYSTEM, SOURCES OF DIVERSITY AMONG MEMBERS, AND THE QUESTION OF LOCALS' AUTONOMY.

1578 LIPSON H.A.
"FORMAL REASONING AND MARKETING STRATEGY."
J. OF MARKETING, (OCT. 62), 1-5.
DESCRIBES MAJOR NEW FORMAL APPROACHES TO DECISION (E.G. ORGANIZATION THEORY AND GAME THEORY) IN RELATION TO NEEDS OF MARKETING MEN.

1579 LISKA G.
EUROPE ASCENDANT.
BALTIMORE: JOHNS HOPKINS PRESS, 1964, 182 PP., LC#64-16189.
STUDIES CONDITIONS NECESSARY FOR A UNIFIED EUROPE. SUGGESTS STRATEGY OF REGIONAL ECONOMIC COOPERATION THAT WILL EVENTUALLY INCLUDE A COMMUNIST CENTRAL EUROPE.

1580 LISS S.B.
THE CANAL, ASPECTS OF UNITED STATES-PANAMANIAN RELATIONS.
SOUTH BEND: U OF NOTRE DAME, 1967, 310 PP., LC#67-22147.
HISTORY OF US-PANAMANIAN RELATIONS FROM 1903-66. CLOSE EXAMINATION OF POST-WWII SITUATION AND RISE OF COMMUNISM IN PANAMA UNDER IMPACT OF CASTRO. ANALYZES KENNEDY S AND JOHNSON'S POLICIES TO DETERMINE CAUSES OF 1964 CRISIS. EXPLORES POSSIBILITIES OF NEW CANAL OR ENLARGING PRESENT ONE. STATES THAT US PRESENCE IS VIEWED AS IMPERIALISM AND THAT CONCESSIONS TO PANAMA WOULD ENHANCE US IMAGE.

1581 LIST F.
NATIONAL SYSTEM OF POLITICAL ECONOMY.
PHILADELPHIA: LIPPINCOTT, 1856, 197 PP.
FOCUSES ON THE THEORY OF PRODUCTIVE FORCES AND VALUES. ANALYZES: (1) MANUFACTURING PROCESS AS RELATED TO CAPITAL, (2) AGRICULTURAL INTERESTS, AND (3) METHODS OF DISTRIBUTION OF FINISHED PRODUCTS. CONCLUDES WITH ANALYSIS OF MERCANTILISM.

1582 LISTER L.
EUROPE'S COAL AND STEEL COMMUNITY.
NEW YORK: TWENTIETH CENTURY FUND, 1960, 495 PP.
TRACES THE DEVELOPMENT OF THE ECSC DURING ITS FIRST SIX YEARS OF EXISTENCE. TREATS ECSC AS A STEP TOWARDS EUROPEAN INTEGRATION. VIEWING ITS PROBLEMS IN ECONOMIC TERMS, OFFERS SUGGESTIONS FOR IMPROVING EFFICIENCY THROUGH GREATER INTERNATIONAL SPECIALIZATION.

1583 LITTLE I.M.D.
AID TO AFRICA.
NEW YORK: MACMILLAN, 1964, 76 PP., LC#64-22219.
STUDIES AID TO UNDERDEVELOPED COUNTRIES WITH PARTICULAR REFERENCE TO BRITISH AID POLICY, ESPECIALLY THOSE IN SUB-SAHARAN AFRICA, EXCLUDING REPUBLIC OF SOUTH AFRICA. CONSIDERS REASONS FOR GIVING AID, PROBLEM OF ADMINISTERING IT, ROLE OF PRIVATE CAPITAL, AND IMPORTANCE OF TECHNICAL DEVELOPMENT IN ASSISTING THESE COUNTRIES.

1584 LITTLE I.M.D., CLIFFORD J.M.
INTERNATIONAL AID.
LONDON: ALLEN & UNWIN, 1965, 360 PP.
DETAILED ANALYSIS OF INTERNATIONAL PROGRAMS OF PUBLIC NONMILITARY AID TO UNDERDEVELOPED COUNTRIES. DISCUSSES HISTORY, QUANTITY, AND FUNDAMENTAL PRINCIPLES OF AID PROGRAMS IN US AND EUROPEAN COUNTRIES. DISCUSSES VARIOUS POLITICAL AND ECONOMIC CONDITIONS CREATED BY AID PROGRAMS IN DONOR AND RECIPIENT COUNTRIES. EMPHASIS IS ON BRITISH AID POLICY.

1585 LITTLE AD, INC.
COMMUNITY RENEWAL PROGRAMMING.
NEW YORK: FREDERICK PRAEGER, 1967, 235 PP., LC#66-18906.
EXTENSIVE EXPLANATION OF MASSIVE PROGRAM TO REHABILITATE SAN FRANCISCO. COVERS POPULATION, HOUSING, AND INCOME CHANGE. SETS UP GOALS, EXPLAINS BARRIERS, DEVELOPS LONG-RANGE POLICY. SPECIFIC PROGRAM DISCUSSED, INCLUDING PROCEDURES, COSTS, FINANCING, MODEL SIMULATION.

1586 LITTLEFIELD N.
METROPOLITAN AREA PROBLEMS AND MUNICIPAL HOME RULE.
ANN ARBOR: U OF MICH LAW SCHOOL, 1962, 83 PP.
EXAMINES LAW OF MUNICIPAL HOME RULE IN RELATION TO METROPOLITAN AREA PROBLEMS. REEXAMINES JURISPRUDENCE OF HOME RULE IN THE LIGHT OF INCREASING DOMINANCE OF AREA INTERESTS. EXAMINES POWERS OF ANNEXATION, STATE ADMINISTRATIVE CONTROL OVER LOCAL RULE, AND SOME MODEL HOME RULE PROVISIONS.

1587 LITVAK I.A. ED., MALLEN B.E. ED.
MARKETING: CANADA.
NEW YORK: MCGRAW HILL, 1964, 344 PP., LC#64-25687.
SELECTIONS REFLECTING PECULIARITIES OF CANADIAN MARKETING ENVIRONMENT. BLENDS CURRENT RELEVANCY, DESCRIPTIVE AND ANALYTICAL MERIT, WITH MAJOR AREAS OF MARKETING: PRODUCTS, RETAILING, PERSONAL SELLING, ADVERTISING AND SALES PROMOTION, AND INTERNATIONAL MARKETING.

1588 LITWACK L.
THE AMERICAN LABOR MOVEMENT.
ENGLEWOOD CLIFFS: PRENTICE HALL, 1962, 176 PP., LC#62-13726.
HISTORICAL READINGS DIRECTED TOWARD BETTER UNDERSTANDING OF HERITAGE OF ORGANIZED AMERICAN LABOR: CONDITIONS PROMPTING RISE AND FREQUENT ERUPTIONS, MEN, PRINCIPLES, TACTICS, IDEOLOGY, AND OPPOSITION. MUCH MATERIAL FOCUSES UPON 1930'S FOR AUTHOR SEES HERE ABILITY OF MOVEMENT TO MEET CHALLENGES OF ORGANIZATION AUTOMATION, CORRUPTION, AND APATHY WHICH ABILITY MUST BE RECAPTURED.

1589 LIVERNASH E.R.
"THE RELATION OF POWER TO THE STRUCTURE AND PROCESS OF COLLECTIVE BARGAINING."
J. OF LATIN AM. RES. REV., 6 (OCT. 63), 10-40.
A TENATIVE ANALYSIS OF COLLECTIVE BARGAINING, ITS MULTI-EMPLOYER AND SINGLE EMPLOYER TYPES, DECENTRALIZATION OF THE PROCESS AND ITS CAUSES, STRIKE FUNDS AND TACTICS, THE RELATION OF STRIKES AND ORGANIZATIONAL STRUCTURE, PROCESSES OF NEGOTATION AND CONSIDERATIONS OF PUBLIC POLICY SUCH AS PARTIAL INJUNCTIONS AND PARTIAL OPERATION DURING STRIKES AND THE QUESTION OF RESTRICTIVE PRACTICES.

1590 LLOYD H.D.
THE SWISS DEMOCRACY.
LONDON: ALLEN & UNWIN, 1908, 273 PP.
DISCUSSES SUCCESS OF SWISS IN COMBINING SOCIALISM WITH DEMOCRACY, ESPECIALLY IN TREATMENT OF WORKERS, IN NATIONALIZATION OF CERTAIN INDUSTRIES, IN MAINTENANCE OF CANTONS' INDIVIDUALITY, IN CONTROL OF MONOPOLIES, AND IN INDIVIDUAL LIBERTY. SUGGESTS EXAMPLES TO BE FOLLOWED IN US.

1591 LOCKE J.
FURTHER CONSIDERATIONS CONCERNING RAISING THE VALUE OF MONEY
ORIGINAL PUBLISHER NOT AVAILABLE, 1644, 111 PP.
ARGUES FOR SILVER STANDARD, CALLING GOLD A COMMODITY AND CLAIMING THAT USING TWO STANDARDS FOR MONEY IS NOT A FEASIBLE MEASURE. CLAIMS SILVER TO BE INSTRUMENT OF COMMERCE BY ITS INTRINSIC VALUE, AND A UNIVERSAL INSTRUMENT OF TRADE IN CIVILIZATION. DISCUSSES TECHNICAL ASPECTS OF COINING, SINCE INEXACT COINAGE COULD BE MELTED, INCREASING CURRENCY SUPPLY AND THUS INFLATING PRICES.

1592 LOCKLIN D.P.
ECONOMICS OF TRANSPORTATION (4TH ED.)
HOMEWOOD: RICHARD IRWIN, 1954, 916 PP.
EXTENSIVE ANALYSIS OF ORGANIZATION OF TRANSPORTATION SYSTEM IN US. BEGINS WITH OVER-ALL LOOK AT VARIOUS MODES OF TRANSPORTATION; NOTES SIGNIFICANT DIFFERENCES IN THEIR ORGANIZATION AND DEVELOPMENT. COVERS GOVERNMENTAL CONTROLS, MAJOR PROBLEMS, FINANCING, AND SERVICES. MAJOR PORTION DEVOTED TO RAILROADS; INCLUDES HIGHWAY, WATER, AND AIR TRANSPORTATION. ENDS WITH TRANSPORT COMPETITION.

1593 LOCKWOOD W.W.
"THE SOCIALISTIC SOCIETY: INDIA AND JAPAN."
FOREIGN AFFAIRS, 37 (OCT. 58), 117-130.
CONTRASTS INDIAN AND JAPANESE PHILOSOPHY AND PRACTICE OF INDUSTRIAL ENTERPRISE. POINTS OUT CONTRAST BETWEEN BUSINESS LEADERSHIP AND CAPITALISTIC ORIENTATION OF JAPAN, AND POLITICAL INITIATIVE AND SOCIALIST ORIENTATION OF INDIA. SHOWS DIFFERENCES IN EACH GOVERNMENT'S ACTIONS TO INFLUENCE RATE OF CAPITAL FORMATION AND INVESTMENT. COMPARES BANKING SYSTEMS IN TWO COUNTRIES.

1594 LOCKWOOD W.W. ED.
THE STATE AND ECONOMIC ENTERPRISE IN JAPAN; ESSAYS IN THE POLITICAL ECONOMY OF GROWTH.
PRINCETON: PRINCETON U PRESS, 1965, 753 PP., LC#65-15386.
EXAMINES RAPID ECONOMIC MODERNIZATION OF JAPAN SINCE 1868. SUGGESTS THAT JAPAN'S UNIQUENESS IN ECONOMIC GROWTH CAN BE ATTRIBUTED TO INTERPLAY OF INITIATIVES ENERGIZING INDUSTRIALIZATION. DISCUSSES PHASES OF GROWTH, ROLE OF AGRICULTURE, SOURCES OF ENTREPRENEURSHIP, GOALS OF PROGRESS AND POSSIBILITIES OF CONTINUENCE, RELATIONS OF ECONOMY WITH POLITICAL DEMOCRACY, AND PARALLELS WITH EUROPE.

1595 LOEWENSTEIN L.K.
"THE LOCATION OF URBAN LAND USES."
LANGUAGE, 39 (NOV. 63), 407-420.
SUGGESTS A TECHNIQUE FOR STUDY OF LAND USE. FOCUSES ON CHARACTERISTICS OF EACH TYPE OF LAND USE. EMPLOYS VISUAL AND STATISTICAL TOOLS TO SHOW THAT THERE IS MORE VARIATION IN SPATIAL DISTRIBUTION OF LAND USES BETWEEN DIFFERENT CATEGORIES THAN WITHIN THE SAME CATEGORY.

1596 LOFTUS M.L.
"INTERNATIONAL MONETARY FUND, 1962-1965: A SELECTED BIBLIOGRAPHY."
INTL. MONETARY FUND STAFF BUL., 12 (NOV. 65), 470-524.
AN UNANNOTATED BIBLIOGRAPHY OF MATERIALS WHICH DESCRIBE THE FUNCTIONS, ORGANIZATION, AND ACTIVITIES OF INTERNATIONAL MONETARY FUND. MATERIAL RANGES FROM 1962-65 IN

ENGLISH, FRENCH, GERMAN, SPANISH, NORWEGIAN, AND RUSSIAN LANGUAGES. 648 ENTRIES.

1597 LONDON K. ED.
EASTERN EUROPE IN TRANSITION.
BALTIMORE: JOHNS HOPKINS PRESS, 1966, 364 PP., LC#66-24409.
STUDIES POLITICAL, SOCIAL, AND ECONOMIC CHANGES IN EASTERN EUROPE SINCE KHRUSHCHEV ERA. EXAMINES TRANSITION FROM SYSTEM OF RIGID CONTROL BY USSR TO ONE OF LOOSELY CONNECTED SEMI-INDEPENDENT NATIONS. COVERS NATURE OF NATIONALISM AND EFFECT OF SINO-SOVIET SPLIT.

1598 LONG T.G.
"THE ADMINISTRATIVE PROCESS: AGONIZING REAPPRAISAL IN THE FTC."
G. WASH. LAW REV., 33 (MAR. 65), 671-691.
COMMISSIONER ELMAN'S DRIVE TO MAKE CEASE AND DESIST ORDERS MORE SPECIFIC HAS RESULTED IN MUCH MORE ACTIVE INTERST GROUP PARTICIPATION IN FTC DECISION-MAKING.

1599 LONGRIGG S.H.
OIL IN THE MIDDLE EAST: ITS DISCOVERY AND DEVELOPMENT.
LONDON: OXFORD U. PR., 1961.
TRACES HISTORY OF INDUSTRY FROM ITS FORMATION. EVALUATES ACTUAL AND PROBABLE EFFECT OF OIL ON ECONOMICALLY BACKWARD AND POLITICALLY UNSTABLE SOCIETIES. DESCRIBES LOCAL GOVERNMENT AND RELATIONS WITH FOREIGN OIL COMPANIES.

1600 LOPEZ VILLAMIL H.
A STATEMENT OF THE LAWS OF THE HONDURAS IN MATTERS AFFECTING BUSINESS (2ND ED.)
WASHINGTON: PAN AMERICAN UNION, 1959, 233 PP.
SURVEY OF BASIC LEGISLATION, INCLUDING NATIONALITY AND IMMIGRATION, CONTRACTS, INSURANCE, PATENTS, TRADEMARKS, AND COPYRIGHT.

1601 LORWIN L.L.
ADVISORY ECONOMIC COUNCILS.
WASHINGTON: BROOKINGS INST, 1931, 84 PP.
SKETCHES SOURCES OF THE IDEA OF ECONOMIC COUNCILS AND OUTLINES VARIOUS TYPES OF THEM. STUDIES GERMAN AND FRENCH COUNCILS, SUMMARIZING WESTERN WORLD'S MOST SIGNIFICANT EXPERIENCE WITH ONE TYPE OF COUNCIL. DESCRIBES MAIN PROBLEMS RELATING TO GROWTH OF ADVISORY ECONOMIC COUNCILS AND INDICATES THEIR POSSIBILITIES.

1602 LOSMAN D.L.
"FOREIGN AID, SOCIALISM AND THE EMERGING COUNTRIES"
DUQUESNE REVIEW, 12 (SPRING 67), 47-65.
EXPLAINS CAUSES OF EXPANSION OF GOVERNMENT POWERS AND PROGRAMS IN UNDERDEVELOPED COUNTRIES ASSISTED BY US FOREIGN AID. CONTENDS THAT SOCIAL, POLITICAL, AND ECONOMIC FACTORS EXISTING TODAY IN UNDERDEVELOPED COUNTRIES HAVE FORCED GOVERNMENTS TO ASSUME MORE POWERS, AND SUCH INCREASED GOVERNMENT ACTIVITIES WILL SPEED THE LONG-DELAYED DEVELOPMENT.

1603 LOUCKS W.N.
COMPARATIVE ECONOMIC SYSTEMS (5TH ED.)
NEW YORK: HARPER & ROW, 1957, 862 PP., LC#57-8333.
COMPARATIVE STUDY OF ALTERNATIVE FORMS OF ECONOMIC ORGANIZATION WITH EMPHASIS ON ECONOMIC SYSTEMS IN ACTION. DISCUSSES EXPANDING FACETS OF SOCIALISM IN BRITAIN, RECENT DEVELOPMENTS IN SOVIET ECONOMY, AND NEWLY PROMINENT POTENTIALITIES OF CAPITALISM. UNANNOTATED BIBLIOGRAPHY RELATING TO POLITICO-ECONOMIC MATERIALS APPENDED TO EACH CHAPTER.

1604 LOUFTY A.
"LA PLANIFICATION DE L'ECONOMIE."
GENEVA: LIBRAIRIE DROZ, 1964.
AUTHOR BELIEVES ECONOMIC PLANNING IS NECESSARY FOR ALL AREAS OF THE WORLD. PLAN MUST INCLUDE COORDINATION OF POLICY IN SUCH AREAS AS SALARIES, INVESTMENTS AND FISCAL POLICY, PREPLANNING TO DETERMINE CONSUMPTION, AND CENTRALIZATION. AUTHOR REVIEWS SOVIET PLANNING, MORE SUPPLE PLANNING OF WEST, AND PLANNING IN UNDERDEVELOPED COUNTRIES. INCLUDES BIBLIOGRAPHY OF APPROXIMATELY 500 ITEMS.

1605 LOWELL A.L.
"THE INFLUENCE OF PARTY UPON LEGISLATION IN ENGLAND AND AMERICA" IN ANNUAL REPORT OF AMER HISTORICAL ASSN."
NEW YORK: AMER HISTORICAL SOCIETY, 1901.
DETAILED EXAMINATION OF PARTY CONTROL OVER WORK OF LEGISLATIVE BODIES. A STUDY OF THE BRITISH PARLIAMENT, US CONGRESS, AND SEVERAL STATE LEGISLATURES, COMPILING THE VOTING RECORDS OF ALL MEMBERS OF EACH PARTY AND TABULATING AMOUNT OF PARTY VOTING AT ANY ONE MOMENT AND TENDENCIES TO CHANGE WITH THE COURSE OF TIME. MARGINAL REFERENCES TO PAGES IN "PARLIAMENTARY DIVISION" AND "CONGRESSIONAL JOURNAL."

1606 LUGO-MARENCO J.J.
A STATEMENT OF THE LAWS OF NICARAGUA IN MATTERS AFFECTING BUSINESS.
WASHINGTON: PAN AMERICAN UNION, 1965, 312 PP.
SUMMARY OF BASIC LEGISLATION CONCERNING NATIONALITY AND IMMIGRATION, CONTRACTS, SOCIAL LEGISLATION, AND NATURAL RESOURCES. ALSO TREATS SUCCESSION, ADMINISTRATION OF JUSTICE, AND COPYRIGHT.

1607 LUNDBERG E.
BUSINESS CYCLES AND ECONOMIC POLICY (TRANS. BY J. POTTER)
CAMBRIDGE: HARVARD U PR, 1957, 346 PP.
STUDY OF SWEDISH ECONOMIC DEVELOPMENT AND PLANNING POLICIES FROM END OF WWI TO PRESENT. DISCUSSES FOREIGN TRADE, BALANCE OF PAYMENTS, METHODS OF GOVERNMENTAL INTERVENTION, FISCAL POLICY, PREPARATION OF BUDGETS, AND FUNCTIONING OF THE PRICE SYSTEM.

1608 LUTHULI A., KAUNDA K., MBOYA T.
AFRICA'S FREEDOM.
NEW YORK: BARNES AND NOBLE, 1964, 94 PP.
ESSAYS BY LEADING AFRICAN STATESMEN ON ECONOMIC, POLITICAL, AND SOCIAL PROBLEMS; TREAT COLONIALISM AND PAN-AFRICANISM IN DETAIL. DISCUSS ROLES OF PRESS, LABOR UNIONS, YOUTH GROUPS, ETC., IN CONTEXT OF MODERNIZATION.

1609 LUTZ F.A.
THE PROBLEM OF INTERNATIONAL LIQUIDITY AND THE MULTIPLE-CURRENCY STANDARD (PAMPHLET)
PRINCETON, NJ: PRIN U INTL FINAN, 1963, 20 PP.
PRESENTS THREE SOLUTIONS TO PROBLEM OF WEAKNESS OF GOLD STANDARD AND SCARCITY OF INTERNATIONAL RESERVES: FLEXIBLE EXCHANGE RATES, INCREASE IN GOLD PRICE, AND WIDENING FOREIGN BORROWING POTENTIAL. DEVELOPS SOLUTION OF MULTIPLE-CURRENCY STANDARD AS MOST ADVANTAGEOUS AND DISCUSSES INTERNATIONAL MONETARY FUND'S ROLE IN SOLUTION.

1610 LUTZ F.A.
GELD UND WAHRUNG.
TUBINGEN: J C B MOHR, 1962, 267 PP.
EXAMINES CURRENCY PROBLEMS AND POLICIES IN RELATION TO ECONOMIC GROWTH, INFLATION, AND INTERNATIONAL ECONOMIC BALANCE. DISCUSSES GOLD STANDARD, EUROPEAN CURRENCY PROBLEMS BETWEEN 1946-50, AND IMPORTANCE OF INVESTMENTS TO ECONOMIC DEVELOPMENT.

1611 LUTZ F.A.
THE PROBLEM OF INTERNATIONAL ECONOMIC EQUILIBRIUM.
AMSTERDAM: NORTH HOLLAND PUBL CO, 1962, 75 PP.
LECTURES EXPLORING COMPLEX PROBLEMS MONETARY AUTHORITIES ARE FACING IN INTERNATIONAL FIELD. INVESTIGATES CAUSES OF BALANCE-OF-PAYMENTS DISEQUILIBRIUM, PURCHASING-POWER-PARITY THEORY, INFLATION, PRODUCTIVITY, INTERNATIONAL CAPITAL MOVEMENTS, AND PROBLEMS OF INTERNATIONAL LIQUIDITY.

1612 LUTZ F.A.
DAS PROBLEM DES INTERNATIONALEN WIRTSCHAFTLICHEN GLEICHGEWICHTS.
TUBINGEN: J C B MOHR, 1963, 59 PP.
DISCUSSES PROBLEM OF INTERNATIONAL ECONOMIC EQUILIBRIUM IN RELATION TO DIFFERENCES IN INFLATIONARY TENDENCIES, PRODUCTIVITY, AND INTERNATIONAL EXCHANGE OF CAPITAL.

1613 LUTZ V.
FRENCH PLANNING.
WASHINGTON: AMER ENTERPRISE INST, 1965, 105 PP., LC#65-22084
FINDS IMPOSSIBLE TO ASCERTAIN EFFECT OF FRENCH ECONOMIC PLANNING ON POSTWAR ECONOMIC GROWTH OR TO DISCOVER WHETHER PLAN WILL BECOME AN INSTRUMENT OF REGIMENTATION. DESCRIBES PLAN AS IN AN UNSTABLE POSITION. DETAILS ITS ADMINISTRATIVE MACHINERY, PREPARATION, OBJECTIVES, OPTIONS, INSTRUMENTS, AND RECORD OF PAREDICTIVE SUCCESSES.

1614 LUXEMBORG R.
THE ACCUMULATION OF CAPITAL (TRANS. BY AGNES SCHWARZSCHILD)
NEW HAVEN: YALE U PR, 1951, 475 PP.
FAMOUS AND HIGHLY COMPETENT MARXIST ANALYZES ECONOMIC AND SOCIAL FACTORS BEHIND THE ACCUMULATION OF CAPITAL. USES MARXIST TERMS AND APPROACHES BUT DEVELOPS OWN ECONOMIC THESES. DEALS WITH REPRODUCTION AND CIRCULATION OF MONEY, HISTORICAL CONDITIONS FOR ITS ACCUMULATION, AND SURVEYS ARGUMENTS OF THE PAST CENTURY.

1615 LUZ N.V.
A LUTA PELA INDUSTRIALIZACAO DO BRAZIL.
SAO PAULO: DIFUSAO EUROPEIA DO LIVRO, 1961, 216PP.
ANALYZES INDUSTRIALIZATION OF BRAZIL FROM 1808 AS COLONY TO 1930 WHEN ECONOMIC NATIONALISM AND AGRICULTURAL DECLINE LED BRAZIL TO PUBLIC POLICY OF ENDORSING AND SUPPORTING NATIONAL INDUSTRIES.

1616 LYND S. ED.
RECONSTRUCTION.
NEW YORK: HARPER & ROW, 1967, 181 PP., LC#67-10796.
SELECTED WRITINGS ON RECONSTRUCTION TO PROVIDE VARIETY OF HISTORICAL INTERPRETATIONS AS TO REASONS FOR FAILURE OF RECONSTRUCTION. EXPRESS OPINIONS THAT NEGRO SUFFRAGE, LACK OF NEGRO SUFFRAGE, ECONOMIC CONFLICT, AND POLITICAL INACTION CONTRIBUTED TO FAILURE OF RECONSTRUCTION.

1617 LYONS G.M. ED.
AMERICA: PURPOSE AND POWER.
CHICAGO: QUADRANGLE BOOKS, INC, 1965, 384 PP., LC#65-18243.

ESSAYS PUBLISHED BY PUBLIC AFFAIRS CENTER AT DARTMOUTH COLLEGE. DEALS WITH RELATIONSHIP OF POWER AND PURPOSE IN DESCRIBING DEVELOPMENT OF US SOCIETY AND ANALYZING MILITARY DEFENSE, ECONOMIC AID, URBANIZATION, WORLD TRADE, TECHNOLOGICAL INNOVATION, AND CIVIL RIGHTS.

1618 LYTLE C.M.
THE WARREN COURT AND ITS CRITICS.
TUCSON: U OF ARIZONA PR, 1967, 200 PP., LC#66-28788.
EXAMINES REASONS WHY SUPREME COURT HAS RECENTLY BEEN FOCAL POINT OF CONTROVERSY. ATTEMPTS TO EXPLAIN WHY AND IN WHAT MANNER THE WARREN COURT HAS BECOME TARGET OF CRITICISM FROM CONGRESSMEN, INTEREST GROUPS OF FAR AND MIDDLE RIGHT, SPOKESMEN FOR STATES, LAW ENFORCEMENT AGENCIES, AND "PROFESSIONAL CRITICS."

1619 MACARTHUR D.
REVITALIZING A NATION.
CHICAGO: HERITAGE FOUNDATION, 1952, 141 PP.
STATES BELIEFS AND OPINIONS OF MACARTHUR AND THE POLICY THEY EMBODY, GLEANED FROM PUBLIC PRONOUNCEMENTS ON SUCH SUBJECTS AS: JAPAN'S ROLE IN THE FUTURE OF ASIA, PROBLEMS OF KOREA AND COMMUNISM, AID TO EUROPE, TAXES, AND POSSIBILITIES FOR WWIII.

1620 MACAVOY P.W.
THE ECONOMIC EFFECTS OF REGULATION: THE TRUNK-LINE RAILROAD CARTELS AND THE INTERSTATE COMMERCE COMMISSION BEFORE 1900.
CAMBRIDGE: M I T PRESS, 1965, 275 PP., LC#65-23542.
ANALYZES EFFECTS OF CARTEL AGREEMENTS ON RATES, TONNAGE SHARES, AND PROFITS OF MAJOR RAILROADS EAST OF MISSISSIPPI RIVER AND NORTH OF OHIO RIVER, 1871-1899. FOCUSES ON CONSEQUENCES OF REGULATION BY INTERSTATE COMMERCE COMMISSION FOR SUCCESS OF CARTEL. REVIEWS THEORIES OF CARTEL STABILITY.

1621 MACAVOY P.W., SLOSS J.
REGULATION OF TRANSPORT INNOVATION.
NEW YORK: RANDOM HOUSE, INC, 1967, 143 PP., LC#67-10910.
INVESTIGATES PROBLEM OF LONG DELAY IN ADOPTION OF UNIT TRAIN SERVICE TO EASTERN SEABOARD. DESCRIBES UNIT TRAIN AS AN INNOVATION AND EXAMINES LEGAL CONSTRAINTS WHICH AFFECTED ITS ADOPTION. INDICATES EXTENT TO WHICH LEGAL DECISIONS RESULTED IN NEGATIVE ECONOMIC ATTITUDE TOWARD ADOPTION OF NEW TRANSPORT SYSTEM.

1622 MACBEAN A.I.
EXPORT INSTABILITY AND ECONOMIC DEVELOPMENT.
CAMBRIDGE: HARVARD U PR, 1966, 367 PP.
ECONOMETRIC INVESTIGATION INTO FACTS OF INFLUENCE OF EXPORT FLUCTUATIONS ON ECONOMIC DEVELOPMENT. TESTS THEORIES OF EXPORT INSTABILITY BY CROSS-COUNTRY REGRESSION AND TIME-SERIES ANALYSIS. EXAMINES NATIONAL AND INTERNATIONAL POLICIES OF STABILIZATION. MAINTAINS THAT IMPORTANCE OF SHORT-TERM EXPORT INSTABILITY HAS BEEN EXAGGERATED.

1623 MACCLOSKEY M.
PACTS FOR PEACE: UN, NATO, SEATO, CENTO, OAS.
NEW YORK: RICHARDS ROSEN PR, 1967, 192 PP., LC#67-10036.
DESCRIBES, UN, NATO, SEATO, CENTO, OAS, AND THEIR ORIGINS STRUCTURE, FUCTIONS, AND ACHIEVEMENTS. REPORTS ON PROBLEMS ENCOUNTERED BY THESE ORGANIZATIONS IN ESTABLISHING WORLD PEACE AND SECURITY. MAINTAINS THAT US SHOULD RE-EXAMINE HER ROLE AS WORLD POLICEMAN AND HER COMMITMENTS TO ALLIANCES.

1624 MACDONALD R.M.
"COLLECTIVE BARGAINING IN THE POSTWAR PERIOD."
INDUST. LABOR REL. REV., 20 (JULY 67),553-578.
REVIEWS EVOLUTION OF BARGAINING INSTITUTIONS AND PRACTICES; EXAMINES CURRENT EFFECTIVENESS AND PROSPECTS FOR CHANGE. SUGGESTS THAT UNIONS HAVE LITTLE INFLUENCE OVER FRINGE BENEFITS, WHICH EFFECTIVE MANPOWER MANAGEMENT ITSELF INITIATES. CHIEF BENEFITS ARE INCOME-MAINTENANCE AND JOB SECURITY, PLUS WORKER'S COMMITMENT TO FREE ENTERPRISE. CONSIDERS UNION IMPEDIMENTS TO ECONOMY'S GROWTH.

1625 MACDONALD R.S.J.
"THE RESORT TO ECONOMIC COERCION BY INTERNATIONAL POLITICAL ORGANIZATIONS."
U. TORONTO LAW J., 17 (1967), 85-169.
SURVEYS FOUR SPECIFIC ETHIOPIAN CASES OF 1935, DOMINICAN CASE OF 1960, AND THE CURRENT SOUTH AFRICAN AND CUBAN CASES - WHICH HAVE BEEN HANDLED BY THREE PRINCIPAL INTERNATIONAL ORGANIZATIONS, AND REVIEWS VARIETIES OF ECONOMIC MEASURES EMPLOYED TO MAKE THESE STATES CONFORM TO THE ORGANIZATIONS' POLICIES.

1626 MACDONALD R.W.
THE LEAGUE OF ARAB STATES: A STUDY IN THE DYNAMICS OF REGIONAL ORGANIZATION.
PRINCETON: PRINCETON U PRESS, 1965, 407 PP., LC#65-10832.
ANALYZES STRUCTURAL AND OPERATIONAL ASPECTS OF ARAB LEAGUE INCLUDING TREATIES, BALANCE OF POWER, AND AMERICAN INVOLVEMENT. INCLUDES BIBLIOGRAPHY CITING DOCUMENTS, BOOKS, ARTICLES, PERIODICALS, AND NEWSPAPERS CONTAINING MATERIAL ON SUBJECT. ARRANGED BY NATURE OF SOURCE AND ALPHABETICALLY. INCLUDES FOREIGN-LANGUAGE MATERIAL.

1627 MACESICH G.
COMMERCIAL BANKING AND REGIONAL DEVELOPMENT IN THE US, 1950-1960.
TALLAHASSEE: FLORIDA STATE U, 1965, 160 PP.
ANALYSIS OF ROLE OF COMMERCIAL BANKING IN ECONOMIC DEVELOPMENT, PARTICULARLY IN SOUTHERN US. EXAMINES ROLE OF MONETARY FORCES, FEDERAL RESERVE OPERATIONS, PRESENT COMMERCIAL BANKING, AND INCOME AND EXPENSES OF MEMBER BANKS.

1628 MACFARQUHAR R. ED.
CHINA UNDER MAO: POLITICS TAKES COMMAND.
CAMBRIDGE: M I T PRESS, 1966, 525 PP., LC#66-25630.
ESSAYS FROM "CHINA QUARTERLY" SINCE 1960 DEAL WITH POLITICS AND ORGANIZATION, ECONOMIC DEVELOPMENT, CULTURE, SOCIETY, FOREIGN RELATIONS, AND RECENT CHINESE HISTORY, WITH ATTENTION TO ABIDING THEORIES AND PRACTICES OF CHINESE COMMUNISM.

1629 MACGREGOR D.H.
ECONOMIC THOUGHT AND POLICY.
NEW YORK: OXFORD U PR, 1949, 180 PP.
CONCERNED WITH ECONOMICS AS EFFECTUAL DEMAND FOR EFFECTUAL SUPPLY; INTERPRETS MAJOR ECONOMIC THEORIES, EMPHASIZING PERIOD 1850-1948. BEGINS WITH SUPPLY AND SCARCITY; COVERS REPRESENTATION OF SUPPLY, LAISSEZ-FAIRE DOCTRINE, EFFECTUAL DEMAND, AND EMPLOYMENT. CLOSING SECTIONS TREAT ECONOMIC POLICY OF DEMOCRATIC SOCIALISM AND ECONOMIC ASPECTS OF WAR.

1630 MACHLUP F.
THE POLITICAL ECONOMY OF MONOPOLY: BUSINESS, LABOR AND GOVERNMENT POLICIES.
BALTIMORE: JOHNS HOPKINS PRESS, 1952, 545 PP.
DEFINES FUNDAMENTAL CONCEPTS, EFFECTS, AND MANIFESTATIONS OF MONOPOLY, WITH ECONOMIC AND POLITICAL APPRAISALS. EXPLAINS SUCH MONOPOLISTIC PRACTICES AS COLLUSION, MERGER, AND EXCLUSION; TREATS PRICE LEADERSHIP, DISCRIMINATION, AND UNFAIR COMPETITION. STUDIES GOVERNMENTAL AIDS TO, AND RESTRAINTS ON, MONOPOLY, AND EXAMINES ROLE OF ORGANIZED LABOR. CONCLUDES WITH METHODS OF MEASUREMENT.

1631 MACHLUP F.
"PLANS FOR REFORM OF THE INTERNATIONAL MONETARY SYSTEM.
PRINCETON: U. PR., 1962, 70 PP., $0.25."
PAPER.
DISCUSSES THE PRESENT INTERNATIONAL MONETARY SYSTEM AND THREE PROBLEMS CONNECTED WITH IT: DIFFICULTIES WITH THE BALANCE OF PAYMENTS OF INDIVIDUAL COUNTRIES, THE INADEQUACY OF THE GROWTH OF MONETARY RESERVES, THE FRAGILITY OF THE GOLD-EXCHANGE STANDARD. SURVEYS RECENT PLANS FOR REFORM AND EXPLORES THE PRECONDITIONS FOR ADOPTING THESE PLANS, THE WAYS IN WHICH THEY MIGHT WORK IF ADOPTED, AND THEIR MOST PROBABLE CONSEQUENCES. VALUE JUDGEMENTS ON PARTICULAR PLANS ARE AVOIDED.

1632 MACHLUP F., MILLER M.H. ED.
ESSAYS ON ECONOMIC SEMANTICS.
ENGLEWOOD CLIFFS: PRENTICE HALL, 1963, 301 PP., LC#63-8621.
CONCERNED WITH NECESSITY FOR PRECISE AND CLEAR LANGUAGE IN ECONOMICS. BEGINS WITH REVIEW OF THEORISTS CONCERNED WITH SEMANTICS; EXAMINES SEMANTIC ISSUES IN ECONOMIC METHODOLOGY, IN VALUE THEORY, AND IN MACRO-ECONOMICS AND ECONOMIC POLICY. DISCUSSES SYNONYMS AND HOMONYMS OF INDUCED SAVING, MEANING OF MARGINAL PRODUCT, AND DISGUISED POLITICS. CLOSES WITH DISPUTES AND PARADOXES OF ECONOMIC DEVELOPMENT.

1633 MACHLUP F.
"THEORIES OF THE FIRM* MARGINALIST, BEHAVIORALIST, MANAGERIAL."
AMER. ECO. REVIEW, 57 (MAR. 67), 1-33.
A REVIEW AND UPDATE ON THE "MARGINALIST THEORY OF THE FIRM" CONTROVERSY, BY A PARTICIPANT. DISCUSSES MARGINALISM, BEHAVIORALIST STUDIES OF ECONOMIC ACTIVITY, AND "MANAGERIAL THEORIES OF THE FIRM," SUGGESTING THAT THE MARGINALISTS AND MANAGERIALISTS HAVE AT PRESENT COALESCED. AN ATTEMPT TO INDICATE THE LIMITS OF VARIOUS APPROACHES TO THE THEORY OF THE FIRM

1634 MACK R.W.
"ECOLOGICAL PATTERNS IN AN INDUSTRIAL SHOP" (BMR)"
SOCIAL FORCES, 32 (MAY 54), 351-356.
DISCUSSES INDUSTRIAL AND RESIDENTIAL SEGREGATION SYSTEMS WHICH ARE BASED PRIMARILY ON CULTURAL DIFFERENCES. FINDS SEGREGATION INTO SEPARATE WORK COMMUNITIES ON ETHNIC LINES TO BE MECHANISM FOR AVOIDING CONFLICTS BETWEEN MEMBERS OF VARIANT CULTURES.

1635 MACKENZIE F. ED.
PLANNED SOCIETY: YESTERDAY, TODAY, AND TOMORROW.
ENGLEWOOD CLIFFS: PRENTICE HALL, 1937, 989 PP.
SYMPOSIUM BY 35 ECONOMISTS, SOCIOLOGISTS, AND STATESMEN COVERING VARIETY OF FORMS OF ECONOMIC CONTROL. STUDIES DEAL WITH PRIMITIVE AND EARLIER SOCIETIES, NATIONALISM, USE OF NATURAL RESOURCES, INDUSTRY AND PUBLIC SERVICE, GOVERNMENT

CONTROL, INNOVATIONS, POLITICAL CONSEQUENCES, FASCIST AND COMMUNIST CONTROL, PHILOSOPHICAL IMPLICATIONS, TYPES AND POTENTIALITIES, PROSPECTS, AND THE LIKE.

1636 MACMAHON A.W., MILLETT J.D., OGDEN G.
THE ADMINISTRATION OF FEDERAL WORK RELIEF.
CHICAGO: PUBLIC ADMIN SERVICE, 1941, 407 PP.
REPORT APPRAISING STRUCTURE AND EFFECTIVENESS OF FEDERAL WORK RELIEF. TRACES ORIGINS OF WORK PROGRAM, SHOWING HOW ADMINISTRATIVE PATTERN WAS SET UP. DISCUSSES CENTRAL MANAGEMENT OF WORKS PROGRAM, AND MANAGEMENT WITHIN THE WPA. DESCRIBES COLLABORATIVE RELATIONSHIPS IN PROJECT, EMPLOYMENT, AND FISCAL ADMINISTRATION.

1637 MACMAHON A.W.
DELEGATION AND AUTONOMY.
BOMBAY: ASIA PUBL HOUSE, 1961, 170 PP.
DISCUSSES USES AND LIMITS OF AUTONOMOUS ELEMENTS IN MODERN ADMINISTRATION WITH EMPHASIS ON ECONOMIC REGULATION AND COMPATIBILITY BETWEEN THESE ELEMENTS AND INTEGRATIVE IDEALS OF PUBLIC ADMINISTRATION. CONSIDERS PROBLEMS OF STRUCTURE AND RELATIONSHIPS ARISING FROM DIRECT CONTACT BETWEEN GOVERNMENT AND MARKETPLACE.

1638 MADAN G.R.
ECONOMIC THINKING IN INDIA.
NEW DELHI: S CHAND AND CO, 1966.
SURVEYS INDIAN ECONOMIC THOUGHT FROM ANCIENT TIMES. CHAPTERS ON MOST INFLUENTIAL INDIVIDUALS, AND EMPHASIZING CURRENT ECONOMIC POLICIES OF GOVERNMENT AND POLITICAL GROUPS.

1639 MADHOK B.
POLITICAL TRENDS IN INDIA.
NEW DELHI: S CHAND AND CO, 1959, 162 PP.
STUDY OF INDIAN POLITICS, WITH REFERENCE TO THE CONFLICT BETWEEN COMMUNISM AND CAPITALISM. DISCUSSES POLITICAL PARTIES, ELECTION RESULTS, AND THE CASTE STRUCTURE. EMPHASIZES INTERNAL AND EXTERNAL DANGERS OF COMMUNISM. CONCLUDES WITH DISCUSSION OF THE FUTURE OF DEMOCRACY IN INDIA.

1640 MAGALHAES S.
PRATICA DA EMANCIPACAO NACIONAL.
RIO DE JANEIRO: ED CIVIL BRASIL, 1964, 221 PP.
STUDY OF ECONOMIC PROBLEMS REGARDING IMPORTATION AND ACTIVITIES OF FOREIGN COMPANIES IN BRAZIL. PRESENTS NATIONALISTIC PROGRAM TO IMPROVE BALANCE OF PAYMENTS. EXPLAINS PLANS TO LIMIT ECONOMIC POWER OF FOREIGN COMPANIES AND MAKE BRAZIL ECONOMICALLY INDEPENDENT.

1641 MAIR L.P.
"SOCIAL CHANGE IN SOUTH AFRICA."
INT. AFF., 136 (OCT. 60), 447-57.
DEPICTS INDIGENOUS ECONOMIC AND POLITICAL SYSTEMS. COMPARES CHANGES WHICH AFRICANS ARE GOING THROUGH WITH THOSE EXPERIENCED BY EUROPE SINCE INDUSTRIAL REVOLUTION. ANALYZES AFRICAN CONCEPTS OF GOVERNMENT, FREEDOM AND DEMOCRACY.

1642 MAIZELS A.
INDUSTRIAL GROWTH AND WORLD TRADE.
NEW YORK: CAMBRIDGE U. PR., 1963, 563 PP., $14.00.
'AN EMPIRICAL STUDY OF TRENDS IN PRODUCTION, CONSUMPTION AND TRADE IN MANUFACTURES FROM 1899-1959 WITH A DISCUSSION OF PROBABLE FUTURE TRENDS.' ATTEMPTS TO ANSWER THE IMPORTANT QUESTION OF WHETHER INDUSTRIALIZATION OF LESS-DEVELOPED COUNTRIES WOULD ULTIMATELY RESULT IN AN EXPANSION OR A CONTRACTION IN DEMAND FOR MANUFACTURED EXPORTS OF INDUSTRIAL COUNTRIES.

1643 MAJSTRENKO I.W.
"PROBLEMS CONFRONTING SOVIET AGRICULTURE."
INST. FOR STUDY OF USSR, 14 (JULY 67), 29-34.
EXAMINES EFFECT OF BAD WEATHER ON 1967'S CROP OUTPUT, ITS RELATION TO ECONOMY AS A WHOLE, AND CORRECTIVE STEPS BEING ATTEMPTED. DISCUSSES CROP PRICE SUPPORT, COLLECTIVIZATION, AND INTER-FARM COOPERATION.

1644 MALASSIS L.
ECONOMIC DEVELOPMENT AND THE PROGRAMMING OF RURAL EDUCATION.
PARIS: UNESCO, 1966, 59 PP.
STUDY OF EDUCATION IN RURAL AREAS AND THE APPLICATION OF SCIENCE TO RURAL AND AGRICULTURAL DEVELOPMENT. EMPHASIZES THE METHODOLOGY OF SUCH STUDIES AND IS BASED ON THE ANALYSIS OF PREVIOUS WORK IN EDUCATIONAL PLANNING FOR AGRICULTURE IN VARIOUS COUNTRIES, AND ON A SYSTEMATIC INVESTIGATION OF THE METHODOLOGY AT PRESENT BEING APPLIED.

1645 MALENBAUM W.
"GOVERNMENT, ENTREPRENEURSHIP, AND ECONOMIC GROWTH IN POOR LANDS."
WORLD POLITICS, 19 (OCT. 66), 52-68.
DEVELOPMENT PROJECTS IN THE LAST DECADE HAVE SPURRED SOME GROWTH, BUT TOO LITTLE TO REDUCE THE DIFFERENTIAL BETWEEN RICH AND POOR NATIONS, AND BETWEEN THE MODERN AND TRADITIONAL ELEMENTS IN THE STRUCTURE OF THE DEVELOPING NATIONS. DEVELOPMENT PLANS MUST RELATE GROWTH IN MODERN SECTORS TO CHANGE IN THE TRADITIONAL. THIS REQUIRES ENTERPRENEURSHIP WHICH ONLY GOVERNMENT CAN PROVIDE IN THE POOR NATIONS

1646 MALHERBE E.G.
"MANPOWER TRAINING: EDUCATIONAL REQUIREMENTS FOR ECONOMIC EXPANSION."
S. AFR. J. OF ECONOMICS, 33 (MAR. 65), 29-51.
DISCUSSES SOUTH AFRICA'S RAPIDLY EXPANDING ECONOMY, PARTICULARLY ITS INDUSTRIAL DEVELOPMENT, IN RELATION TO REST OF AFRICA. EXAMINES MANPOWER REQUIRED, CHIEFLY AT MANAGEMENT LEVEL, TO MAINTAIN RATE OF EXPANSION; INDICATES PRESENT MANPOWER AT VARIOUS OCCUPATIONAL LEVELS WHICH REQUIRE FORMAL TRAINING. ANALYZES OUTPUT OF EDUCATIONAL INSTITUTIONS IN SOUTH AFRICA AND LEAKAGES OF TALENT IN EDUCATION SYSTEM.

1647 MALINOWSKI B.
"THE PRIMITIVE ECONOMICS OF THE TROBRIAND ISLANDERS" (BMR)"
ECO. J., 31 (MAR. 21), 1-16.
DISCUSSES NATURAL RESOURCES OF TROBRIANDERS AND SURVEYS MANNER IN WHICH THEY ARE USED. CONSIDERS AGRICULTURE, LAND TENURE, PRODUCTION, AND ORGANIZATION. RELATES ELEMENTS OF MAGIC, SOCIAL STRUCTURE, CULTURE, AND INFLUENCE OF CHIEF. CONCLUDES THAT ECONOMY OF PRIMITIVE CULTURE IS VERY COMPLEX AND DIVERSIFIED.

1648 MALINVAUD E. ED., BACHARACH M.O. ED.
ACTIVITY ANALYSIS IN THE THEORY OF GROWTH AND PLANNING.
NEW YORK: ST MARTIN'S PRESS, 1967, 334 PP.
AN EXTREMELY TECHNICAL COLLECTION OF CASE STUDIES ILLUSTRATING THE APPLICATION OF NEW METHODS FOR SPECIALISTS AND GENERAL ECONOMISTS IN THE ANALYSIS OF GROWTH AND PLANNING. DISCUSSES DEVELOPMENT IN US, WESTERN EUROPE, ASIA, AND EASTERN EUROPE.

1649 MALKIN A.
"BUSINESS BOOKS OF 1966."
LIBRARY JOURNAL, 92 (MAR. 67), 976-978.
AN ANNOTATED BIBLIOGRAPHY ON VARIOUS ASPECTS OF BUSINESS. 70 ENGLISH-LANGUAGE ENTRIES. BIBLIOGRAPHY IS OF BOOKS PERTAINING TO ASPECTS OF THE BUSINESS WORLD, SUCH AS BANKING, CONSUMER CREDIT, INDUSTRIAL RELATIONS, LABOR, MARKETING, PLANNING, AND PRODUCTION CONTROL. LISTING COVERS THOSE BOOKS PUBLISHED IN 1966.

1650 MALTHUS T.R.
PRINCIPLES OF POLITICAL ECONOMY.
ORIGINAL PUBLISHER NOT AVAILABLE, 1820, 599 PP.
BASICALLY A LAISSEZ-FAIRE THEORIST, BUT CONTENDS THAT SOME FORM OF GOVERNMENT INFLUENCE ON ECONOMY IS DESIRABLE. TAKES ISSUE WITH ADAM SMITH ON CONCEPT OF SAVING AS MEANS OF INCREASING WEALTH, STATING THAT THIS TENDS TO DECREASE PRODUCTION. DISCUSSES EFFECT OF DEMAND UPON WEALTH AND LAUDS RICARDO'S DISCUSSION OF IT. PROPOSES COMMERCE AS MEASURE OF WEALTH.

1651 MANGER W. ED.
THE ALLIANCE FOR PROGRESS: A CRITICAL APPRAISAL.
WASHINGTON: PUBLIC AFFAIRS PRESS, 1963, 131 PP.
ARTICLES DISCUSSING OBJECTIVES, PROBLEMS, AND FUTURE OF ALLIANCE FOR PROGRESS, INCLUDING ECONOMIC ASPECTS, RELATION TO CULTURAL VALUES, ROLE OF EDUCATION, POLITICAL IMPLICATIONS, AND RELATION TO OAS.

1652 MANGLAPUS R.S.
"ASIAN REVOLUTION AND AMERICAN IDEOLOGY."
FOREIGN AFFAIRS, 45 (JAN. 67), 344-352.
DISCUSSES CHANGE IN ASIAN SOCIETY FROM STABILITY TO REVOLUTION. EMPHASIZES INAPPLICABILITY OF AMERICAN IDEALS TO ASIAN SITUATION. COMPARES CHARACTERISTICS OF AMERICAN REVOLUTION: TRADITION OF DISSENT, FRONTIERS, AND RICH LAND TO ASIAN REVOLUTION. ADVOCATES SOCIAL REVOLUTION TO CLOSE CLASS GAP AND TO RELEASE PEOPLE FROM BONDS OF CENTRALIZED POWER BUT URGES THAT REVOLUTION BE UNIQUE TO EACH COUNTRY.

1653 MANGONE G.J.
UN ADMINISTRATION OF ECONOMIC AND AOCIAL PROGRAMS.
NEW YORK: COLUMBIA U PRESS, 1966, 291 PP., LC#66-20490.
COLLECTION OF ESSAYS ON PROGRAMMING, IMPLEMENTATION, AND ADMINISTRATION OF UN ECONOMIC AND SOCIAL ACTIVITIES. DISCUSSES FUNCTION OF SECRETARIAT, BUDGETARY COORDINATION BY GENERAL ASSEMBLY, FIELD ADMINISTRATION, AND TASK OF REGIONAL COMMISSIONS.

1654 MANN B.
STATE CONSTITUTIONAL RESTRICTIONS ON LOCAL BORROWING AND PROPERTY TAXING POWERS.
ALBANY: GOVERNMENT AFFAIRS FDN, 1964, 318 PP., LC#64-66404.
"DIGEST OF CONSTITUTIONAL PROVISIONS AND DISCUSSION OF LEADING COURT DECISIONS IN THE FIFTY STATES" INVOLVING BORROWING AND PROPERTY TAXING POWERS OF LOCAL GOVERNMENTS.

1655 MANN D.E.
THE POLITICS OF WATER IN ARIZONA.
TUCSON: U OF ARIZONA PR, 1963, 317 PP., LC#62-17991.
ANALYZES ECONOMIC ISSUES OF WATER RESOURCE POLICIES IN ARIZONA. EMPLOYS ECONOMIC ANALYSIS TO INDICATE THE ALTERNA-

TIVES THAT ARE POSED BY PUBLIC VERSUS PRIVATE INVESTMENT IN WATER RESOURCE DEVELOPMENT. SURVEYS THE GENERAL PICTURE OF WATER MANAGEMENT IN ARIZONA.

1656 MANN S.Z.
"POLICY FORMULATION IN THE EXECUTIVE BRANCH: THE TAFT-HARTLEY EXPERIENCE."
WESTERN POLIT. QUART., 13 (SEPT. 60), 597-608.
DISCUSSION OF CONFLICT BETWEEN NLRB, DEPARTMENT OF LABOR, AND BUREAU OF BUDGET ON PROPOSED CHANGES IN WAGNER ACT. SINCE THE EXECUTIVE BRANCH COULD NOT AGREE, CONGRESS PASSED A BILL REPUGNANT TO PRESIDENT TRUMAN.

1657 MANNE H.G.
"OUR TWO CORPORATION SYSTEMS* LAW AND ECONOMICS."
VIRGINIA LAW REV, 53 (MAR 67), 259-284.
DEVELOPMENT OF AMERICAN CORPORATIONS IN 19TH CENTURY BECAUSE ENTREPRENEURS NEEDED SOME DEVICE TO RAISE CAPITAL FROM A RELATIVELY LARGE NUMBER OF INVESTORS. CONCEPT OF LIMITED LIABILITY DISCUSSED. INTERRELATION BETWEEN LAW AND BUSINESS TRACED AND DEVELOPED. MANAGEMENT OR "BOARD OF DIRECTORS" AND SHAREHOLDERS' RIGHTS AND DUTIES ARE DISCUSSED. INTERESTS OF THE CLOSED CORPORATION ARE MAINLY UNCHALLENGED.

1658 MANSFIELD E., WEIN H.H.
"A STUDY OF DECISION-MAKING WITHIN THE FIRM."
J. ABNORMAL SOC. PSYCH., 72 (NOV. 58), 515-536.
AUTHOR EXPLAINS SOME DECISIONS OF A MANAGER AT AN INTERMEDIATE LEVEL IN A RAILROAD AND LINKS THESE DECISIONS TO THE SHORT-RUN FLUCTUATIONS IN OUTPUT AND COST OF INDIVIDUAL FREIGHT YARDS. CONTAINS INTRODUCTORY MATERIAL CONCERNING FREIGHT YARDS, DESCRIPTION OF THE MODEL, AND TEST OF THE MODEL.

1659 MANSFIELD E. ED.
MONOPOLY POWER AND ECONOMIC PERFORMANCE: AN INTRODUCTION TO A CURRENT ISSUE OF PUBLIC POLICY.
NEW YORK: W W NORTON, 1964, 174 PP., LC#63-21710.
COLLECTION OF ARTICLES DEALS WITH THE EFFICIENCY OF MONOPOLIES IN THE US. SUBJECTS CONSIDERED ARE: MARKET STRUCTURE, RESOURCE ALLOCATION, AND ECONOMIC PROGRESS; INDUSTRIAL CONCENTRATION, COLLUSION, AND THE SOCIAL RESPONSIBILITY OF BIG BUSINESS; AND THE ANTITRUST LAWS - THEIR PROVISIONS, EFFECTIVENESS, AND STANDARDS.

1660 MANSFIELD E. ED.
MANAGERIAL ECONOMICS AND OPERATIONS RESEARCH; A NONMATHEMATICAL INTRODUCTION.
NEW YORK: W W NORTON, 1966, 244 PP., LC#65-23036.
ANALYZES THE DECISION-MAKING PROCESS IN INDUSTRIAL ORGANIZATIONS, EMPHASIZING NECESSITY OF SCIENTIFIC METHODS. INCLUDES STUDY OF CONCEPTS, TECHNIQUES, AND PROBLEMS IN MANAGERIAL ECONOMICS, I.E., PROFITS, PRICE, DEMAND, CAPITAL, AND FORECASTING. ALSO INTRODUCES TECHNIQUES OF OPERATIONS RESEARCH, SUCH AS PROGRAM SCHEDULING, LINEAR PROGRAMMING, GAME THEORY, AND ROLE OF COMPUTER IN INDUSTRIAL MANAGEMENT.

1661 MANSFIELD H.C.
"THE CONGRESS AND ECONOMIC POLICY" IN C. TRUMAN ED., THE CONGRESS AND AMERICA'S FUTURE."
ENGLEWOOD CLIFFS: PRENTICE HALL, 1965.
DESCRIBES THE WAYS IN WHICH CONGRESS AND ITS COMPONENT PARTS GO ABOUT THEIR VARIED ACTIVITIES IN THE FIELD OF ECONOMIC POLICY AND ATTEMPTS TO ACCOUNT FOR SOME OF THE WHATS AND HOWS AND WHYS OF THEIR ACTIONS. DISTINGUISHES BETWEEN MICRO- AND MARCO- ECONOMIC POLICIES.

1662 MAO J.C.T.
EFFICIENCY IN PUBLIC URBAN RENEWAL EXPENDITURES THROUGH CAPITAL BUDGETING.
BERKELEY: U CAL, INST URBAN DEV, 1965, 117 PP.
DEVISES A TECHNIQUE FOR MEASURING EFFICIENCY OF GOVERNMENT EXPENDITURES WHEN SUCH EXPENDITURES ABSORB SCARCE RESOURCES, USING TECHNIQUES OF CAPITAL BUDGETING. TOUCHES ON RELATION BETWEEN CAPITAL BUDGETING AND CERTAIN SIMULATION MODELS OF URBAN RENEWAL. INCLUDES CASE STUDY TO ILLUSTRATE APPLICABILITY OF TECHNIQUES.

1663 MARCHAL J.
EXPANSION ET RECESSION.
PARIS: EDITIONS CUJAS, 1963, 221PP.
NONTECHNICAL WORK ON SHORT-TERM EXPANSION AND RECESSION IN FRANCE. INDICATES CHAIN OF EVENTS CAUSING CHANGE IN ECONOMY. AUTHOR BELIEVES THAT INSTEAD OF CONSTRUCTING RIGID ECONOMIC MODELS, ECONOMISTS' JOB IS TO INDICATE WHAT HAS HAPPENED SO THAT PARTICIPANTS CAN BETTER JUDGE FUTURE ACTIONS.

1664 MARCUS E., MARCUS M.R.
INTERNATIONAL TRADE AND FINANCE.
NEW YORK: PITMAN PUBLISHING, 1965, 616 PP., LC#65-10464.
ATTEMPTS TO EXPLAIN OPERATIONS OF INTERNATIONAL TRADE, PAYMENTS, AND CAPITAL MOVEMENTS. FOCUSES ON PROBLEMS OF DEVELOPING AND POVERTY-STRICKEN COUNTRIES.

1665 MARCUS S.
COMPETITION AND THE LAW.
BELMONT: WADSWORTH, 1967, 161 PP., LC#67-11933.
ADDRESSED TO BUSINESS STUDENTS PRIMARILY, EXAMINES ISSUES STEMMING FROM DIFFERENCES IN RATIONALE OF LAW AND ITS IMPACT ON BUSINESS PRACTICES. FINDS "LAW IS OFTEN IMPRECISE, DYNAIC, AND SEEMINGLY GROPING TOWARD A RELATIVELY UNDEFINED GOAL."

1666 MARCUS W.
US PRIVATE INVESTMENT AND ECONOMIC AID IN UNDERDEVELOPED COUNTRIES (PAMPHLET)
WASHINGTON: PUBLIC AFFAIRS PRESS, 1959, 42 PP.
DISCUSSES PRESENT INVESTMENT AND FOREIGN AID PROGRAMS AND NEED FOR NEW ONES. SHOWS ROLES OF PRIVATE AND PUBLIC EFFORTS TO MOBILIZE CAPITAL, NEED FOR EDUCATED PUBLIC TO PUSH BETTER POLICY INTO ACTION. CONCLUSIONS ARE THAT PRIVATE INVESTMENT MUST BE INCREASED, AIDED BY LIBERAL GOVERNMENT LOAN POLICY, AND THAT PRIVATE AND PUBLIC ACTIONS SHOULD BE CONSOLIDATED UNDER REVOLUTIONARY PLAN.

1667 MARGOLIS J.
"ON MUNICIPAL LAND POLICY FOR FISCAL GAINS."
NATIONAL TAX J., 9 (SEPT. 56), 247-257.
STATES THAT A RECENT LAND-USE POLICY OF CITIES HAS BEEN THE ENCOURAGEMENT OF SPECIFIC USES IN ORDER TO IMPROVE FISCAL CONDITION OF LOCAL GOVERNMENT. EVALUATES THIS PROGRAM FROM ASPECT OF ITS GOALS, EFFECTIVENESS OF THE POLICY, AND LEVEL OF SCIENTIFIC KNOWLEDGE AND MANAGERIAL ABILITIES NECESSARY TO USE POLICIES EFFECTIVELY. EMPHASIZES PROBLEM OF ALLOCATION OF PUBLIC COSTS AMONG TYPES OF LAND USES.

1668 MARGOLIS J. ED.
THE PUBLIC ECONOMY OF URBAN COMMUNITIES.
WASHINGTON: RESOURCES FOR FUTURE, 1965, 264 PP., LC#65-26179
COLLECTION OF PAPERS PRESENTED AT CONFERENCE ON URBAN PUBLIC EXPENDITURES. DISCUSSES MODELS OF ECONOMIC AND POLITICAL DECISION-MAKING, VOTING BEHAVIOR, URBAN TRANSPORTATION, POLITICAL INFLUENCE ON EXPENDITURE POLICIES, ETC.

1669 MARITANO N., OBAID A.H.
AN ALLIANCE FOR PROGRESS.
MINNEAPOLIS: T S DENISON + CO, 1963, 205 PP., LC#63-21948.
DISCUSSES ALLIANCE FOR PROGRESS: HISTORICAL BACKGROUND, NUMBER AND NATURE OF OBSTACLES CONFRONTING IT, INCLUDING COLTURAL AND PSVCHOLOGICAL OBSTACLES, CONDITIONS FOR ECONOMIC GROWTH AND SOCIAL PROGRESS, DIRECTION OF FOREIGN AID, AND FUTURE PROSPECTS.

1670 MARK S.M. ED.
ECONOMICS IN ACTION (3RD ED.)
BELMONT: WADSWORTH, 1965, 522 PP., LC#65-2111.
COLLECTION OF ESSAYS ON ECONOMIC POLICY FORMATION IN RELATION TO MAJOR ECONOMIC GOALS OF EFFICIENCY, EQUALITY, STABILITY, PROGRESS, AND FREEDOM. EXAMINES RESOURCE ALLOCATION, PRICE DETERMINATION, ECONOMIC SECTORS, INTERNATIONAL TRADE AND PAYMENTS, AND PROMOTION OF ECONOMIC DEVELOPMENT IN UNDERDEVELOPED COUNTRIES.

1671 MARKHAM J.W. ET AL.
THE COMMON MARKET: FRIEND OR COMPETITOR.
NEW YORK: N.Y.U. PR., 1964, 123 PP., $3.00.
THREE ESSAYS ADDRESSED TO 1) WHY THE EEC HAS ENCOURAGED A SYSTEM OF PRIVATE ENTERPRISE THAT HAS NOT REQUIRED THE TRANSFER OF NATIONAL POLITICAL PREROGATIVES FROM MEMBER GOVERNMENTS, 2) THE ROLE OF DIRECT AMERICAN INVESTMENT IN EUROPE, AND 3) EFFECTS ON AMERICAN EXPORTS AND IMPORTS OF EEC TARIFFS.

1672 MARKSHAK J.
"ECONOMIC PLANNING AND THE COST OF THINKING."
SOCIAL RESEARCH, 33 (SUMMER 66), 151-159.
CENTRALIZATION, OR ECONOMIC PLANNING, HAS AN ADVANTAGE OVER THE DECENTRALIZED MARKET SYSTEM, IN THAT ALL INFORMATION AS TO NEEDS OF THE SOCIETY IS COLLECTED FROM ALL SOURCES BEFORE PRODUCTION IS BEGUN. THE COST OF THIS CENTRALIZATION IS, A LOSS OF LIBERTY, INCENTIVES, AND LOWERED UTILITY TO ALMOST ALL CITIZENS.

1673 MARQUAND H.A., PHILIP A. ET AL.
ORGANIZED LABOUR IN FOUR CONTINENTS.
LONDON: LONGMANS, GREEN & CO, 1939, 518 PP.
ELEVEN ESSAYS BY DIFFERENT AUTHORS COVERING THE STATE OF ORGANIZED LABOR IN FRANCE, GERMANY, BRITAIN, ITALY, SCANDINAVIA, USSR, US, CANADA, MEXICO, AUSTRALIA, AND JAPAN. EACH TRACES THE DEVELOPMENT OF UNIONISM FROM 1919 TO 1937 AND ITS RELATION TO THE ECONOMIC, POLITICAL, AND SOCIAL CLIMATE IN EACH COUNTRY. EFFECTS OF GLOBAL AND INTERNAL EVENTS ON LABOR MOVEMENTS ARE ALSO EXAMINED.

1674 MARRIS P., REIN M.
DILEMMAS OF SOCIAL REFORM: POVERTY AND COMMUNITY ACTION IN THE UNITED STATES.
NEW YORK: ATHERTON PRESS, 1967, 248 PP., LC#67-17146.
DISCUSSION OF THE PROBLEMS SOCIAL REFORM FACES IN US. PHASIS IS ON STRATEGIES OF REFORM, ADMINISTRATIVE-POLITICAL CONFLICT, BUREAUCRATIC IMPEDIMENTS, AND EXISTENT POVERTY

PROGRAM. MOST STRESS IS ON PRACTICAL ASPECTS AND OVER-ALL ACHIEVEMENTS OF OBJECTIVES. CONCLUDES THAT NO REFORM MOVEMENT IN US CAN SUPPLANT CONFLICTS OF INTEREST FROM WHICH POLICY EVOLVED.

1675 MARRIS R.
THE ECONOMIC THEORY OF "MANAGERIAL" CAPITALISM.
NEW YORK: FREE PRESS OF GLENCOE, 1964, 346 PP., LC#64-10371.
STUDIES SEPARATION OF MANAGEMENT CONTROL FROM OWNERSHIP IN FIRMS, INCLUDING INSTITUTIONAL FRAMEWORK, SUPPLY AND DEMAND, AND BEHAVIOR AND EVIDENCE. BIBLIOGRAPHY OF ENGLISH BOOKS AND ARTICLES, LISTED ALPHABETICALLY BY AUTHOR, 1932-1962; 125 ENTRIES.

1676 MARSH D.C.
THE FUTURE OF THE WELFARE STATE.
BALTIMORE: PENGUIN BOOKS, 1964, 140 PP.
EXAMINES ASSUMPTIONS ON WHICH BRITISH SOCIAL POLICIES ARE BASED, WAYS BRITAIN HAS ATTEMPTED TO ACHIEVE POST-WWII AIMS, AND APPLICABILITY OF TITLE "WELFARE STATE." ARGUES THAT WELFARE STATE MUST SERVE NEEDS OF CITIZENS AND THAT 20TH-CENTURY CONCEPT HAS BEEN RESTRAINED BY 19TH-CENTURY SYSTEM OF ADMINISTRATION. WARNS THAT LARGEST DANGER IS IN INERTIA OF MACHINE ITSELF AND ADVOCATES REMODELING.

1677 MARSH J.F. JR.
THE FBI RETIREMENT BILL (PAMPHLET)
INDIANAPOLIS: BOBBS-MERRILL, 1949, 26 PP.
CASE STUDY OF FBI RETIREMENT BILL. ILLUMINATES CONTROVERSY BETWEEN FBI AND BUDGET BUREAU. CONTRASTS SMOOTH FUNCTIONING OF EXECUTIVE-LEGISLATIVE RELATIONS WITH DIFFICULTIES OF EXECUTIVE POLICY COORDINATION.

1678 MARSHALL A.
PRINCIPLES OF ECONOMICS.
LONDON: MACMILLAN, 1898, 819 PP.
PRESENTS SYSTEMATIC INTERPRETATION OF RICARDIAN CLASSICAL ECONOMICS, WHICH HAS AS BASIC TENETS RELATION OF PRICE TO COST AND EXPLANATIONS BASED UPON FREELY REPRODUCIBLE COMMODITIES. CLAIMS THAT PRICE OF AN ITEM IS DETERMINED BY LABOR COST TO PRODUCE IT, ASSUMING NONMONOPOLISTIC MARKET. ALSO TRACES DEVELOPMENT OF MODERN MARKET SYSTEM. COVERS DEMAND, PRODUCTION, DISTRIBUTION, AND EQUILIBRIUM.

1679 MARSHALL A.H.
FINANCIAL ADMINISTRATION IN LOCAL GOVERNMENT.
LONDON: ALLEN & UNWIN, 1960, 391 PP.
DISCUSSES INTERNAL ORGANIZATION AND PRINCIPLES OF FINANCIAL ADMINISTRATION IN LOCAL GOVERNMENTS IN ENGLAND. EXAMINES BUDGETARY PROCEDURES, COLLECTION OF INCOME, ROLE OF COUNTY, TOWN, OR DISTRICT COUNCIL CLERK, AND ROLE OF CHIEF FINANCIAL OFFICER.

1680 MARTHELOT P.
"PROGRES DE LA REFORME AGRAIRE."
TIERS-MONDE, 4 (NOS.13-14, 63), 261-64.
CRITICIZES THIRD PUBLIC REPORT MADE BY UN COUNCIL OF ECONOMY AND SOCIOLOGY ON APRIL 5, 1962 ON SUBJECT OF AGRARIAN REFORM. EMPHASIZES ITS LACK OF CLARITY AND ITS TREATMENT OF THE QUESTION OF PRODUCTIVITY.

1681 MARTIN D.D.
MERGERS AND THE CLAYTON ACT.
LOS ANGELES: UNIV OF CALIF PR, 1959, 351 PP.
STUDIES CLAYTON ACT OF 1914 AS SUPPLEMENT TO SHERMAN ACT. CLAYTON ACT PROHIBITED PURCHASE OF STOCK IN ANOTHER CORPORATION; IN 1950 THIS PROHIBITION WAS EXTENDED TO ASSETS. EXAMINES HISTORY, JUDICIAL INTERPRETATION, ADMINISTRATION, AND LEGISLATIVE REVISION OF THE ACT. CONSIDERS CASES BEFORE AND AFTER CHANGES, IMPLICATIONS, AND MEANING FOR FUTURE MERGERS.

1682 MARTIN E.M.
"NEW TRENDS IN UNITED STATES ECONOMIC FOREIGN POLICY."
ANN. AMER. ACAD. POLIT. SOC. SCI., 330 (JULY 60).
POINTS OUT DIFFICULTY OF REACHING TOTAL ACCORD ON ANY FOREIGN POLICY DECISION DUE TO THE VAST ECONOMIC INTERESTS OF AMERICAN BUSINESS. IN SPITE OF THIS FACTOR, MANY DECISIONS ON FOREIGN AID, FOREIGN TRADE AND GENERAL FOREIGN POLICY ARE REACHED. DISCUSSES THE BACKGROUND OF SOME OF THESE DECISIONS.

1683 MARTIN K.
WAR, HISTORY, AND HUMAN NATURE.
BOMBAY: ASIA PUBL HOUSE, 1959, 109 PP.
ANALYSIS OF THEORIES, PRINCIPLES, AND ABSURDITIES OF WAR. DISCUSSES LENINIST THEORY OF WAR, THE ECONOMIC BASIS OF MODERN WAR, AND THEORIES OF DETERRENCE. DEALS WITH PSYCHOLOGY OF WARLIKE ATTITUDES AND PACIFISM. ANALYZES GANDHI'S TEACHINGS AND THEIR RELEVANCE FOR PRESENT-DAY POLITICS. SHOWS HOW DIFFERENT ATTITUDES HAVE INFLUENCED BRITISH, FRENCH, AND GERMAN HISTORY.

1684 MARTIN P.
CANADA AND THE QUEST FOR PEACE.
NEW YORK: COLUMBIA U PRESS, 1967, 93 PP., LC#67-27409.
EXAMINES CANADA'S EFFORTS AND POLICIES IN INTERNATIONAL AFFAIRS SINCE WWII. STUDIES ROLE IN UN AND CONTRIBUTIONS TO ITS PEACEKEEPING EFFORTS. DESCRIBES CANADA'S ATTEMPTS AT FINDING SOLUTION TO VIETNAM WAR WHICH TAKE INTO ACCOUNT LONG-RANGE INTERESTS OF VIETNAMESE AND PRESENT FOUR-STAGE PROPOSAL FOR CEASE FIRE. EXPLORES EXTENSIVE FOREIGN AID PROGRAM TO UNDERDEVELOPED NATIONS.

1685 MARTINS A.F.
REVOLUCAO BRANCA NO CAMPO.
SAO PAULO: EDITORA BRASILIENSE, 1962, 202 PP.
EXAMINES RURAL AGRICULTURAL ECONOMY OF BRAZIL, EXPLAINING IMPORTANCE OF MODERNIZATION OF PRODUCTION BY MORE EXTENSIVE ELECTRICAL FACILITIES AND USE OF MODERN MACHINERY. COMPARES DEVELOPMENT OF US AGRICULTURE THROUGH APPLICATION OF MODERN ELECTRICAL POWER TO THE SLOW DEVELOPMENT OF BRAZILIAN RURAL AREAS.

1686 MARX H.L. ED.
THE WELFARE STATE.
NEW YORK: H W WILSON, 1950, 212 PP.
CONSIDERS SOCIAL WELFARE IN US AS OF 1950: DOES WELFARE STATE EXIST? IS IT COMPATIBLE WITH FREE ENTERPRISE? HOW DOES IT AFFECT INDIVIDUAL FREEDOM? DISCUSSES MEANING OF TERM "WELFARE," AND ITS APPLICATION IN US. EXAMINES MERITS, DANGERS, TRENDS, AND ITS EXISTENCE ELSEWHERE, AS IT IS DISCUSSED IN ESSAYS BY LEADING AMERICAN POLITICIANS, HISTORIANS, AND SOCIAL PHILOSOPHERS.

1687 MARX K.
A CONTRIBUTION TO THE CRITIQUE OF POLITICAL ECONOMY (TRANS. FROM 2ND ED. BY N.I. STONE)
CHICAGO: CHARLES H KERR, 1904, 314 PP.
PRELIMINARY STUDY OF POLITICAL ECONOMY LATER SUPERSEDED BY "CAPITAL." TWO CHAPTERS (ON COMMODITIES AND MONEY OR SIMPLE CIRCULATION) COMPRISE THIS VOLUME, WHICH THE PREFACE INDICATES WAS TO BE PART OF AN EXTENSIVE TREATISE. INTRODUCTION, PUBLISHED POSTHUMOUSLY, EXPOUNDS MARX'S GENERAL THEORY OF POLITICAL ECONOMY. PREFACE INCLUDES AUTOBIOGRAPHICAL NOTES.

1688 MARX K.
CAPITAL.
LONDON: SWAN SONNENSCHEIN, 1918, 868 PP.
PRESENTS AN EVALUATION OF CAPITALIST PRODUCTION PLACING EMPHASIS ON THE STRICT MEANING OF THE TERM PRODUCTION. MARX CONTENDS THAT AS SOON AS SOCIETY HAS OUTLIVED A GIVEN PERIOD OF DEVELOPMENT, IT IS PASSING OVER FROM ONE STAGE TO ANOTHER AND IS SUBJECT TO OTHER LAWS. ECONOMIC LIFE IS ANALOGOUS TO THE HISTORY OF EVOLUTION IN OTHER BRANCHES OF BIOLOGY.

1689 MARX K.
THE CLASS STRUGGLES IN FRANCE.
NEW YORK: INTERNATIONAL PUBLRS, 1934, 159 PP.
EXPLANATION OF THE REVOLUTIONARY MOVEMENTS IN FRANCE FROM 1848 TO 1850 IN TERMS OF ECONOMIC CONDITIONS. MAINTAINS THAT WORLD TRADE CRISIS CAUSED OUTBREAKS, AND THAT RETURN OF PROSPERITY IN 1849 RESULTED IN CRUSHING OF REVOLUTION AND RETURN OF REACTIONARY GOVERNMENTS.

1690 MARX K.
WAGE-LABOR AND CAPITAL -- VALUE, PRICE AND PROFIT.
NEW YORK: INTERNATIONAL PUBLRS, 1935, 110 PP., LC#37-13364.
TWO MARXIAN CLASSICS THAT HAVE SERVED AS WELL-KNOWN INTRODUCTIONS TO STUDIES IN POLITICAL ECONOMY APPEAR IN THIS VOLUME, NUMBER 34, OF "MARXIST LIBRARY: WORKS OF MARXISM-LENINISM." FIRST IS BASED ON LECTURES DELIVERED IN BRUSSELS IN 1847. SECOND IS AN ADDRESS DELIVERED BY MARX IN 1865.

1691 MARX K., ENGELS F.
THE COMMUNIST MANIFESTO.
IN (MENDEL A. ESSENTIAL WORKS OF MARXISM, NEW YORK: BANTAM. BOOKS, 1961, CHAPTER 1, PAGES 13-44).
SETS FORTH THE DOCTRINE OF CLASS STRUGGLE BETWEEN THE RULING BOURGEOISIE AND THE PROLETARIAT, AND DESCRIBES HOW THE LATTER WILL RISE UP AND CONQUER ITS OPPRESSORS. UNTIL THE COMPLETE SUPPRESSION OF THE BOURGEOISIE, THE DICTATORSHIP OF THE PROLETARIAT WOULD PREVAIL. EVENTUALLY, IT WOULD WITHER AWAY, ALONG WITH THE STATE, A CLASSLESS SOCIETY EMERGING.

1692 MARX K.
THE POVERTY OF PHILOSOPHY (1847)
NEW YORK: INTERNATIONAL PUBLRS, 1963, 233 PP., LC#63-10632.
WRITTEN IN CONTRADICTION OF PROUDHON'S "THE PHILOSOPHY OF MISERY." CRITICIZES PROUDHON'S RESORTING TO PHILOSOPHY AS "FEEBLE HEGELIANISM." MAINTAINS THAT PROUDHON DOES NOT UNDERSTAND ECONOMIC DEVELOPMENT. BELIEVES THAT FORM OF SOCIETY IS A "PRODUCT OF MEN'S RECIPROCAL ACTION." MEN ARE NOT FREE TO CHOOSE PRODUCTIVE FORCES. PROUDHON'S THEORY OF ECONOMIC CONTRADICTIONS SERVES THE "PETTY BOURGEOIS."

1693 MARX K.
REVOLUTION AND COUNTER-REVOLUTION.
ORIGINAL PUBLISHER NOT AVAILABLE, 1896, 148 PP.
REPORTS AND INTERPRETS GERMAN REVOLUTION OF 1848 AS A

CLASS STRUGGLE. LINKS UPRISING TO GERMANY'S INABILITY TO COMPETE WITH REST OF EUROPE INDUSTRIALLY, AND SUFFERING OF LOWER CLASSES WHICH RESULTED. DECLINE OF MIDDLE CLASS IS SEEN AS BASIC CAUSE OF DEFEAT OF GOVERNMENT. ATTACKS MIDDLE-CLASS RISE TO POWER AS INCREASING POVERTY AND SUPPRESSION OF THE LOWER CLASSES.

1694 MASCHLER M.
STABLE PAYOFF CONFIGURATIONS FOR QUOTA GAMES (PAMPHLET)
PRINCETON: PRINCETON U PRESS, 1961, 25 PP.
ANALYSIS OF GAME THEORY AND APPROACHES AS RELATED TO DECISION-MAKING IN STABLE PAYOFF SITUATION AND COALITION FORMATION.

1695 MASON E.S.
THE DIPLOMACY OF ECONOMIC ASSISTANCE (PAMPHLET)
MIDDLEBURY: MIDDLEBURY COLLEGE, 1966, 26 PP.
EXAMINES EXTENT TO WHICH IT IS DESIRABLE FOR US TO ATTACH CONDITIONS TO FOREIGN AID, PARTICULARLY IN RELATION TO SOUTHERN ASIA (INDIA, PAKISTAN). CONCLUDES THAT "POLITICAL STRINGS" ARE LIKELY TO BE INEFFECTIVE BUT THAT ECONOMIC CONDITIONS ARE OFTEN WARRANTED AS EXPRESSION OF INTIMATE INVOLVEMENT IN ECONOMIC DEVELOPMENT OF AID-RECEIVING COUNTRIES.

1696 MASON E.S.
ECONOMIC CONCENTRATION AND THE MONOPOLY PROBLEM.
CAMBRIDGE: HARVARD U PR, 1957, 411 PP., LC#57-6351.
STUDIES MONOPOLY AND LARGE FIRM IN SUCH AREAS AS MARKET; WAGE-PRICE CONTROVERSY; RAW MATERIALS, NATIONAL SECURITY, AND ECONOMIC GROWTH; ALSO PUBLIC ANTITRUST POLICY, BY DISCUSSION AND ANALYSIS OF OTHER EXPERTS' OPINIONS.

1697 MASON E.S.
"ECONOMIC PLANNING IN UNDERDEVELOPED AREAS."
NEW YORK: FORDHAM U. PR., 1958, 89 PP.
DISCUSSES ROLE OF GOVERNMENT IN ECONOMIC DEVELOPMENT. STATES THAT GROWTH VARIES FROM COUNTRY TO COUNTRY DEPENDING ON PREVAILING ECONOMIC AND SOCIAL CONDITIONS.

1698 MASON E.S.
"INTERESTS, IDEOLOGIES AND THE PROBLEM OF STABILITY AND GROWTH."
AMER. ECON. REV., 53 (MAR. 63), 1-18.
EXAMINES RELATIONSHIP BETWEEN AMERICAN GOVERNMENT AND BUSINESS-LABOR INTERESTS. SUGGESTS THAT BUSINESS AND LABOR HAVE PREVENTED FORMULATION OF OVERALL PLAN TO PREVENT UNEMPLOYMENT AND INBALANCE OF PAYMENTS. LEAVES ECONOMIC DEVELOPMENT TO FATE.

1699 MASON E.S.
FOREIGN AID AND FOREIGN POLICY.
NEW YORK: HARPER, 1964, 118 PP.
AID FROM LARGE COUNTRIES IS PREDOMINANTLY BILATERAL. GEOGRAPHICAL DISTRIBUTION OF AID SUGGESTS PRIMARY INTEREST IN MUTUAL SECURITY. 'AS AN INSTRUMENT OF FOREIGN POLICY... AID IS A USELESS TOOL UNLESS IT CAN BE ASSUMED THAT THERE IS A STRONG OCMMUNITY OF INTEREST BETWEEN AID-GIVING AND AID-RECEIVING COUNTRIES.'

1700 MASON E.S.
ECONOMIC DEVELOPMENT IN INDIA AND PAKISTAN.
CAMBRIDGE: HARV CTR INTL AFFAIRS, 1966, 67 PP., LC#66-28532.
EXAMINES DIVERGENT TRENDS OBSERVABLE IN INDIAN AND PAKISTANI ECONOMIES, 1960-65. ANALYZES NATURE AND AMOUNT OF FOREIGN ASSISTANCE RECEIVED BY BOTH NATIONS, SHOWING HOW EACH MANAGED FOREIGN EXCHANGE. DESCRIBES METHODS OF EXPORT PROMOTION AND IMPORT REPLACEMENT. DISCUSSES AGRICULTURAL PRIORITIES AND POLICIES.

1701 MASON J.B. ED., PARISH H.C. ED.
THAILAND BIBLIOGRAPHY.
GAINESVILLE: U OF FLORIDA LIB, 1958, 245 PP.
CONTAINS MORE THAN 2,300 ENTRIES, MANY ANNOTATED, TO BOOKS, ARTICLES, AND DOCUMENTS IN NINE WESTERN LANGUAGES. WORKS ON HISTORY, GOVERNMENT, INTERNATIONAL RELATIONS, PUBLIC ADMINISTRATION, ECONOMICS, ARCHEOLOGY, GEOGRAPHY, SOCIOLOGY, EDUCATION, ART, LANGUAGE STUDY, AND THE NATURAL SCIENCES. HAS A LIST OF BIBLIOGRAPHIES.

1702 MASS. INST. TECH.
"THE CENTER FOR INTERNATIONAL STUDIES."
MIT, SIXTH ANNUAL REPORT, 6 (1957), 1-38.
DESCRIBES PROJECTS IN FOUR MAJOR RESEARCH PROGRAMS: INTERNATIONAL COMMUNICATIONS, ECONOMIC AND POLITICAL DEVELOPMENT, USA-SOVIET RELATIONS AND AMERICAN SOCIETY IN ITS WORLD SETTING.

1703 MATHEWS J.M.
AMERICAN STATE GOVERNMENT.
NEW YORK: APPLETON, 1925, 660 PP.
SURVEYS AMERICAN SYSTEM OF STATE GOVERNMENT. DISCUSSES POSITION OF STATES IN FEDERAL SYSTEM, STATE CONSTITUTIONS, LEGISLATURES, COURTS, AND EXECUTIVES. EXAMINES STATE POWERS, ADMINISTRATIVE ORGANIZATION, ELECTIONS AND POLITICS, AND CONTROL OVER TAXES, FINANCE, BUSINESS, AND UNIONS. DESCRIBES RELATIONSHIP BETWEEN STATE AND LOCAL GOVERNMENTS.

1704 MATHUR P.N.
"GAINS IN ECONOMIC GROWTH FROM INTERNATIONAL TRADE."
KYKLOS, 16 (FALL 63), 609-23.
INTERNATIONAL TRADE OPERATES TO CHANGE STRUCTURE OF PRODUCTION WITHIN A COUNTRY. EFFECTS A REDUCTION IN AVERAGE CAPITAL OUT-PUT RATIO BY IMPORTATION OF HIGH-COST MATERIALS AND GOODS.

1705 MATTHEWS R.C.O.
THE BUSINESS CYCLE.
CHICAGO: U OF CHICAGO PRESS, 1959, 300 PP., LC#59-10286.
PRESENTS THEORETICAL FRAMEWORK WITHIN WHICH ANY PARTICULAR PHASE OF HISTORICAL EXPERIENCE OF FLUCTUATIONS CAN USEFULLY BE STUDIED. EXPLAINS VARIOUS MODELS OF BUSINESS CYCLE, INVESTMENT, CONSUMPTION, MONEY AND FINANCE, THE CEILING, INTERNATIONAL FACTORS, AND POLICY TO CONTROL CYCLE.

1706 MAYER H.M. ED., KOHN C.F. ED.
READINGS IN URBAN GEOGRAPHY.
CHICAGO: U OF CHICAGO PRESS, 1959, 625 PP., LC#59-11973.
PRESENTS GEOGRAPHIC THEORIES AND RESEARCH TREATING URBAN GROWTH, FUNCTIONS, AND FORMS. SUPPLIES DEFINITIONS; STUDIES ECONOMICS OF CITIES, METHODS OF CLASSIFICATION, AND CITY GROWTH. DISCUSSES URBAN POPULATION STUDIES, LAND-USE SURVEYS AND MAPPING, AND CITY STRUCTURE. EXAMINES SPACING, INDUSTRY, TRANSPORTATION, COMMERCE, WATER SUPPLY, AND RESIDENTIAL PATTERNS OF CITIES.

1707 MAYNE A.
DESIGNING AND ADMINISTERING A REGIONAL ECONOMIC DEVELOPMENT PLAN WITH SPECIFIC REFERENCE TO PUERTO RICO (PAMPHLET)
PARIS: ORG FOR ECO COOP AND DEV, 1961, 62 PP.
STUDIES METHODS OF DESIGNING REGIONAL ECONOMIC DEVELOPMENT PLANS STRESSING NEED TO EVALUATE POTENTIALS, TRANSLATE OBJECTIVES INTO PROGRAMS, CHOOSE ALTERNATIVE PROGRAMS, AND COORDINATE PLANS. MAINTAINS THAT ONE REASON FOR PROGRAM FAILURES IS NEGLECT OF PUBLIC ADMINISTRATION PROCEDURE AND GOVERNMENT DECISION-MAKING PROCESS. LOOKS AT SOCIAL AND ECONOMIC DEVELOPMENT SINCE 1940.

1708 MAYO H.B.
DEMOCRACY AND MARXISM.
NEW YORK: OXFORD U PR, 1955, 364 PP., LC#55-7539.
PRESENTS A SURVEY AND ASSESSMENT OF MARXISM, AS CONCEIVED BY LENIN AND STALIN AND AS MANIFESTED IN CONTEMPORARY USSR. ANALYZES AND ASSESSES DEMOCRACY. AUTHOR BELIEVES THAT THE DEMOCRAT OUGHT TO UNDERSTAND BOTH COMMUNISM AND DEMOCRACY. DISCUSSES DIALECTICAL MATERIALISM, THE ECONOMIC INTERPRETATION OF HISTORY, THE CLASS STRUGGLE, REVOLUTION, AND MORALITY AND RELIGION.

1709 MAYO H.B.
INTRODUCTION TO MARXIST THEORY.
NEW YORK: OXFORD U PR, 1960, 334 PP., LC#60-5276.
EXPLAINS IT, ITS APPLICATIONS, CLASS STRUGGLE, COMPARISON TO DEMOCRACY. DIALECTICAL MATERIALISM DISCUSSED, ALSO MARXISM AS PHILOSOPHY OF LIFE, HISTORY, SCIENTIFIC METHOD.

1710 MAZA ZAVALA D.F.
VENEZUELA; UNA ECONOMIA DEPENDIENTE.
CARACAS: U CENTRAL DE VENEZUELA, 1964, 378 PP.
ANALYZES INTERNATIONAL ASPECTS OF VENEZUELAN ECONOMY AND PRESENT STATUS OF VENEZUELA IN WORLD TRADE. DISCUSSES BALANCE OF PAYMENTS, INDUSTRIALIZATION, MAJOR IMPORTS AND EXPORTS, AND PRICE TRENDS.

1711 MAZOUR A.G.
SOVIET ECONOMIC DEVELOPMENT: OPERATION OUTSTRIP: 1921-1965.
PRINCETON: VAN NOSTRAND, 1967, 191 PP.
SIMPLE HISTORICAL ANALYSIS OF SOVIET ECONOMIC PROGRESS FROM 1921 TO 1965 INITIATION OF KHRUSHCHEV-KOSYGIN CO-EXISTENCE POLICY. EMPHASIS ON NEP AND FIVE-YEAR PLANS WITH ABOUT HALF OF BOOK DEVOTED TO EXCERPTED READINGS FROM RUSSIAN GOVERNMENT DOCUMENTS AND COMMENTARY SOURCES.

1712 MC CLELLAN G.S. ED.
INDIA.
NEW YORK: H W WILSON, 1960, 164 PP., LC#60-8238.
ESSAYS ON SOCIO-ECONOMIC AND POLITICAL PROBLEMS, DISCUSSING NEUTRALITY, TIBET, KASHMIR, AND RELATIONS WITH THE US. GANDHI AND NEHRU ARE ALSO CONSIDERED.

1713 MC CONNELL J.P.
LAW AND BUSINESS: PATTERNS AND ISSUES IN COMMERCIAL LAW.
NEW YORK: MACMILLAN, 1966, 656 PP., LC#66-18768.
EXPLAINS AMERICAN LEGAL SYSTEM AND BUSINESS LAW WITH EMPHASIS ON INTANGIBLE RIGHTS, TORTS, AND CONTRACTS.

1714 MC GOVERN G.S.
WAR AGAINST WANT.
NEW YORK: WALKER, 1964, 148 PP., LC#64-23992.
STUDY OF DEVELOPMENT OF OFFICE OF FOOD FOR PEACE UNDER KENNEDY ADMINISTRATION AND ITS PRESENT STATUS AND IMPORTANCE IN US FOREIGN AID POLICY.

1715 MC WILLIAM M.
"THE WORLD BANK AND THE TRANSFER OF POWER IN KENYA."
J. COMMONWEALTH POLIT. STUD., 2 (MAY 64), 141-160.
EVALUATES STUDY MADE IN 1961 BY WORLD BANK COMMISSION, WHICH ANALYZED KENYA'S ECONOMIC CRISIS, PROBLEMS CONNECTED WITH TRANSFER OF POWER, GOVERNMENT'S DEVELOPMENT PROGRAM AND KENYA'S ECONOMIC POLICIES.

1716 MCALLISTER J.T. JR.
"THE POSSIBILITIES FOR DIPLOMACY IN SOUTHEAST ASIA."
WORLD POLITICS, 19 (JAN. 67), 258-305.
REVIEWS EIGHT BOOKS RELATING TO DIPLOMATIC HISTORY AND PRESENT SITUATION OF DIPLOMACY IN SOUTHEAST ASIA. BEGINS WITH ANGLO-FRENCH RIVALRY, COLONIALISM, AND INTERREGIONAL WARS. DISCUSSES DIFFICULTY OF SUCCESSFUL DIPLOMACY IN CONFLICT BETWEEN STRONG INTERNATIONAL POWER AND INTENSE LOCAL POER. EXAMINES RESULTS OF 1954 GENEVA AGREEMENTS, LAOTIAN CRISIS, AND VIETNAM WAR.

1717 MCCABE D.A., LESTER R.A.
LABOR AND SOCIAL ORGANIZATION.
BOSTON: D C HEATH, 1948, 373 PP., LC#48-4817.
DISCUSSES LABOR ORGANIZATION, LABOR LEGISLATION, SOCIAL SECURITY, AND SOCIAL REORGANIZATION IN RELATION TO THE WAGE SYSTEM. DESCRIBES RISE OF ORGANIZED LABOR, GOVERNMENT INTERVENTION AND REGULATION, AND ATTACKS ON WAGE SYSTEM.

1718 MCCLELLAN J.L.
CRIME WITHOUT PUNISHMENT.
NEW YORK: DUELL, SLOAN & PEARCE, 1962, 300 PP., LC#62-8523.
PRESENTATION OF EVIDENCE BEFORE AND REPORTS OF SENATE SELECT COMMITTEE ON IMPROPER ACTIVITIES IN THE LABOR OR MANAGEMENT FIELD AND SENATE PERMANENT SUBCOMMITTEE ON INVESTIGATIONS WITH PURPOSE OF INFORMING PUBLIC OF DANGEROUS CORRUPTION IN LABOR UNIONS AND AFFILIATED ORGANIZED CRIME.

1719 MCCOLL G.D.
THE AUSTRALIAN BALANCE OF PAYMENTS.
MELBOURNE: MELBOURNE UNIV PRESS, 1965, 180 PP., LC#65-21859.
DISCUSSES HOME AND INTERNATIONAL ASPECTS OF AUSTRALIAN BALANCE OF PAYMENTS. TREATS IMPORTS AND EXPORTS OF GOODS AND SERVICES, CAPITAL FLOW AND SERVICING COSTS, DIRECTION OF TRADE AND PAYMENTS, EXTERNAL IMBALANCE, AND OFFICIAL POLICY.

1720 MCCOLL R.W.
"A POLITICAL GEOGRAPHY OF REVOLUTION: CHINA, VIETNAM, AND THAILAND."
J. OF CONFLICT RESOLUTION, 11 (JUNE 67), 153-167.
DISCUSSES STRATEGIC CONSIDERATIONS OF IMPORTANCE OF BASE AREAS AND THEIR LOCATIONS. ALSO COVERS IMPORTANCE OF POLITICAL VIEWS HELD IN MAJORITY OF SURROUNDING NATIONS AND NECESSITY FOR THEIR LACK OF POLITICAL STABILITY TO PREVENT THEIR INTERFERING WITH REVOLUTION.

1721 MCCONNELL G.
THE STEEL SEIZURE OF 1952 (PAMPHLET)
UNIVERSITY: U ALABAMA PR, 1960, 53 PP.
DESCRIBES EVENTS OF 1952 NATIONAL CRISIS IN STEEL INDUSTRY. BREAKDOWN OF NEGOTIATIONS THREATENED STRIKE. ATTEMPTS TO EVALUATE GOVERNMENTAL SEIZURE OF CONTROL IN NATIONAL INTEREST.

1722 MCCONNELL G.
STEEL AND THE PRESIDENCY, 1962.
NEW YORK: W W NORTON, 1963, 119 PP., LC#62-19026.
CASE STUDY, WITH BACKGROUND MATERIAL, OF PRESIDENT KENNEDY'S FORCING STEEL COMPANIES TO RESCIND PRICE RISE IN 1962.

1723 MCCORD W.
"ARMIES AND POLITICS: A PROBLEM IN THE THIRD WORLD."
DISSENT, 14 (JULY-AUG. 67), 440-452.
EXAMINES MILITARY GOVERNMENTS IN COUNTRIES OF AFRICA AND NEAR EAST. DISCUSSES POSSIBILITIES OF LIBERAL OR SOCIAL DEMOCRACY AND OF ECONOMIC DEVELOPMENT AND SOCIAL REFORM UNDER MILITARY RULE. CONCLUDES THAT MILITARY RULE SELDOM AIDS GROWTH OF DEMOCRACY AND PARALYZES ECONOMY. QUESTIONS AMERICAN MILITARY ASSISTANCE AND FOREIGN AID POLICY.

1724 MCCRACKEN H.L.
KEYNESIAN ECONOMICS IN THE STREAM OF ECONOMIC THOUGHT.
BATON ROUGE: LOUISIANA ST U PR, 1961, 205 PP., LC#61-13012.
ANALYZES AND EVALUATES KEYNES'S SYSTEM OF ECONOMICS, WITH SPECIAL EMPHASIS ON PLACING IT INTO CONTEXT OF EVOLVING ECONOMIC THOUGHT, RELATING IT TO, AND SHOWING CONTRIBUTIONS FROM, PREVIOUS ECONOMIC THEORIES.

1725 MCCRONE G.
THE ECONOMICS OF SUBSIDING AGRICULTURE.
TORONTO: U OF TORONTO PRESS, 1962, 189 PP.
DISCUSSES AGRICULTURE IN BRITISH ECONOMY SINCE 1939. EXAMINES GOVERNMENTAL SUPPORT AND BALANCE OF PAYMENTS PROBLEM. ALSO EXAMINES LARGER PROBLEMS OF INTERNATIONAL SPECIALIZATION, GROWTH OF WORLD POPULATION, RELATION OF BRITISH AGRICULTURE TO COMMON MARKET, AND THREAT TO BRITAIN'S FOOD SUPPLY AS RESULT OF DEVELOPMENTS IN OTHER COUNTRIES.

1726 MCDONOUGH A.M.
INFORMATION ECONOMICS AND MANAGEMENT SYSTEMS.
NEW YORK: MCGRAW HILL, 1963, 321 PP., LC#63-15459.
EXAMINES STUDIES IN INFORMATION FIELD, ESTABLISHES THEORETICAL FRAMEWORK UNDER WHICH VALUES PLACED ON KNOWLEDGE AND INFORMATION ARE DISCUSSED, AND PROBES INTO INFORMATION-RETRIEVAL SYSTEMS IN CONTEXT OF MANAGEMENT SYSTEMS.

1727 MCDOUGAL M.S., LASSWELL H.D., MILLER J.C.
THE INTERPRETATION OF AGREEMENTS AND WORLD PUBLIC ORDER: PRINCIPLES OF CONTENT AND PROCEDURE.
NEW HAVEN: YALE U PR, 1967, 448 PP., LC#67-13442.
RELATES INTERNATIONAL AGREEMENTS TO PROCESS OF COMMUNICATION, AND DISCUSSES NEW APPROACHES TO THEORY OF COMMUNICATION AND PARTICIPATION OF NEW NATIONS. APPRAISES ADEQUACY OF TRADITIONAL PRINCIPLES OF INTERPRETATION AND SUGGESTS A SYSTEMIZATION AND MODERIZATION OF THESE PRINCIPLES.

1728 MCFADYEAN A.
GOVERNMENT AND INDUSTRY (PAMPHLET)
LONDON: BRIT LIB PARTY ORG, 1944, 23 PP.
STATEMENT OF BRITISH LIBERAL PARTY THAT STATE OWNERSHIP OF INDUSTRY OR OTHER INTERFERENCE IN THE ECONOMY CAN ONLY BE JUSTIFIED WHEN THE GENERAL PUBLIC WILL CLEARLY BENEFIT.

1729 MCIVOR R.C.
CANADIAN MONETARY, BANKING, AND FISCAL DEVELOPMENT.
TORONTO: MACMILLAN CO OF CANADA, 1958, 263 PP.
HISTORICAL APPROACH TO DEVELOPMENTS, INSTITUTIONAL AND THEORETICAL, WITHIN CANADIAN ECONOMY SINCE 17TH CENTURY, FOCUSING ON EVOLUTION OF COMMERICAL BANKING. IN ANALYZING ECONOMY OF TODAY, AUTHOR FINDS THAT COMPLEMENTARY USE OF MONETARY AND FISCAL INSTRUMENTS IS ESSENTIAL FOR ECONOMIC STABILITY.

1730 MCKEE J.B.
"STATUS AND POWER IN THE INDUSTRIAL COMMUNITY: A COMMENT ON DRUCKER'S THESIS."
AMER. J. OF SOCIOLOGY, 58 (JAN. 53), 364-370.
CRITICIZES STRATIFICATION OF SOCIETY BY A SINGLE DIMENSION, I.E. DRUCKER'S EMPLOYEESHIP, DETERMINING STATUS AND POWER. POINTS TO OTHER DIMENSIONS OF STATUS IN A COMMUNITY, IN ADDITION TO FUNCTIONAL POSITION OF CORPORATE ORGANIZATION AND THE PARTICIPATION OF LABOR GROUPS IN COMMUNITY CHEST LEADERSHIP. SEARCHES FOR LEGITIMIZATION OF POWER THROUGH PARTICIPATION IN COMMUNITY ACTIVITIES.

1731 MCKEE J.B.
"THE POWER TO DECIDE" IN M. WEINBERG AND O. SHABET, SOCIETY AND MAN."
ENGLEWOOD CLIFFS: PRENTICE HALL, 1956.
THIS STUDY OF STEELPORT, AN INDUSTRIAL CITY OF 50,000 IN THE GREAT LAKES AREA, TRACES THE RISE OF LABOR TO A POSITION OF POWER IN THE COMMUNITY. THE EFFECTS OF THIS RISE WERE TO REDISTRIBUTE COMMUNITY POWER AND LEADERSHIP AND TO EQUALIZE THE OPPORTUNITIES FOR ACQUIRING STATUS. A GENERAL LESSENING OF CONFLICT IN THE COMMUNITY WAS SEEN AS A CONCOMITANT OF LABOR'S RISE.

1732 MCKERSIE R.B., BROWN M.
"NONPROFESSIONAL HOSPITAL WORKERS AND A UNION ORGANIZING DRIVE."
QUART. J. OF ECO., 77 (AUG. 63), 372-404.
CASE STUDY, ATTEMPTING THE DEVELOPMENT OF A MODEL TO EXPLAIN SUCH BEHAVIOR AS JOINING A UNION, PARTICIPATING IN A STRIKE, AND SUPPORTING A PICKET LINE. OPPOSITION TACTICS OF HOSPITAL MANAGEMENT, RACIAL OVERTONES, GROUP COHESIVENESS, AND MORALE ARE ALSO ANALYZED.

1733 MCNELLY T. ED.
SOURCES IN MODERN EAST ASIAN HISTORY AND POLITICS.
NEW YORK: APPLETON, 1967, 422 PP., LC#67-18502.
PROVIDES SUPPLEMENTARY READING FOR COURSES IN HISTORY, POLITICS, AND IDEOLOGIES OF MODERN CHINA, JAPAN, KOREA, AND VIETNAM. EDITORIAL NOTES SUMMARIZE RECENT POLITICAL HISTORY OF EAST ASIA AND SUGGEST SIGNIFICANCE AND INTERRELATIONS OF SELECTIONS. DOCUMENTS COVER REFORM AND REVOLUTION IN CHINA, EMERGENCE OF JAPANESE EMPIRE WWI AND WWII IN FAR EAST, COMMUNIST RULE IN CHINA, AND WAR IN VIETNAM.

1734 MCNULTY J.E.
SOME ECONOMIC ASPECTS OF BUSINESS ORGANIZATION.
PHILA: U OF PENN PR, 1964, 122 PP., LC#64-18620.
APPLIES ECONOMIC THEORY TO BUREAUCRATIC ORGANIZATION OF BUSINESS. EXAMINES EVOLUTION OF THOUGHT AND RESEARCH IN ECONOMICS CONCERNING NATURE AND SIGNIFICANCE OF ORGANIZED FIRM. DISCUSSES TESTING PROCEDURES FOR HYPOTHESES USED IN THESE THEORIES. FINDS THAT ADJUSTMENTS TO ORGANIZATIONAL UTILITY FUNCTION ARE NECESSARY TO UNDERSTAND RELATIONSHIP.

1735 MCPHEE A.
THE ECONOMIC REVOLUTION IN BRITISH WEST AFRICA.
LONDON: ROUTLEDGE & KEGAN PAUL, 1926, 322 PP.
ANALYSIS OF ECONOMIC SITUATION IN WEST AFRICA AS RELATED

TO BRITISH EMPIRE. COVERS GEOGRAPHY, TRADE, TRANSPORTATION, FINANCE, AND NATIVE POPULATION IN THEIR ECONOMIC EFFECTS ON ECONOMY OF WEST AFRICA.

1736 MEAD W.
"SOME POLITICAL-ECONOMIC ISSUES DETERMINING USA TARIFF POLICY."
AMER. J. ECON. SOCIOL, 21 (APRIL 62), 131-144.
FACTORS SUCH AS THE SOUTH'S NEW INDUSTRIALISM AND THE BALANCE OF PAYMENTS SITUATION LEAD TO PROTECTIONISM. A PERIOD OF VACILLATION IN TARIFF POLICY IS PREDICTED, TAKING THE FORM OF SUPPORT OF FREE TRADE IN PRINCIPLE BUT 'DE FACTO' PROTECTION THROUGH ESCAPE CLAUSES, AS INDICATED IN CURRENT LEGISLATION.

1737 MEADE J.E.
AN INTRODUCTION TO ECONOMIC ANALYSIS AND POLICY (AMERICAN EDITION EDITED BY C.J. HITCH)
NEW YORK: OXFORD U PR, 1938, 428 PP.
DISCUSSES ECONOMIC THEORY WITH DIRECT REFERENCE TO ECONOMIC PROBLEMS OF THE MODERN WORLD. STRESSES COMPREHENSION OF TOOLS OF ANALYSIS AND THE ECONOMIC CONSEQUENCES OF CERTAIN LINES OF ACTION. ADAPTED FROM ENGLISH EDITION FOR APPLICATION TO US. AREAS COVERED INCLUDE: UNEMPLOYMENT, COMPETITION AND MONOPOLY, INCOME DISTRIBUTION, SUPPLY AND PRODUCTION, AND INTERNATIONAL PROBLEMS.

1738 MEADE J.E., WELLS S.J., LIESNER H.H.
CASE STUDIES IN EUROPEAN ECONOMIC UNION.
LONDON: OXFORD U. PR., 1962, 424 PP.
CONSIDER ECONOMIC MECHANISMS AND ARRANGEMENTS NECESSARY TO EFFECTIVE ECONOMIC UNION. BASE ANALYSIS ON STUDY OF BELGIUM-LUXEMBOURG UNION, BENELUX, AND EUROPEAN COAL AND STEEL COMMUNITY.

1739 MEADE J.E.
"POPULATION EXPLOSION, THE STANDARD OF LIVING AND SOCIAL CONFLICT."
ECO. J., 77 (JUNE 67), 233-255.
EXAMINES POPULATION GROWTH OF WORLD AND ANALYZES TRENDS TO PREDICT FUTURE POPULATION. DISCUSSES IMPOSSIBILITY OF DEVELOPED NATIONS CONTINUING TO SUSTAIN UNDERDEVELOPED ONES AND SPECULATES ON EFFECT OF THIS UPON INTERNATIONAL RELATIONS.

1740 MEAGHER R.F.
PUBLIC INTERNATIONAL DEVELOPMENT FINANCING IN SUDAN.
NEW YORK: COLUMBIA U LAW SCHOOL, 1965, 127 PP.
STUDIES PROGRAMS AND RELATIONS OF FOREIGN INSTITUTIONS INVOLVED IN PUBLIC FINANCING OF ECONOMIC DEVELOPMENT IN SUDAN. INCLUDES SUDAN'S ECONOMIC AND POLITICAL STRUCTURE, TEN YEAR PLAN, PUBLIC FINANCIAL INSTITUTIONS; NEED FOR EXTERNAL ASSISTANCE, ITS SOURCES AND AMOUNT; CASE STUDIES OF IMPORTANT AID IN TRANSPORTATION, IRRIGATION, AND INDUSTRY.

1741 MEANS G.C.
PRICING POWER AND THE PUBLIC INTEREST.
NEW YORK: HARPER & ROW, 1962, 359 PP.
TO MAKE STEEL AND SIMILAR INDUSTRIES RESPONSIVE TO THE PUBLIC INTEREST, A SYSTEM CALLED "TARGET PRICING," ALREADY TRIED IN SOME AREAS OF BUSINESS, IS ADVOCATED, CONSISTING OF A PLANNED RATE OF RETURN ON CAPITAL CONSISTENT WITH CORPORATE GROWTH. APPLIED THROUGHOUT LARGE CORPORATIONS, THIS METHOD WOULD PUT A PREMIUM ON PERFORMANCE BY MANAGEMENT.

1742 MEANS G.C.
THE CORPORATE REVOLUTION IN AMERICA: ECONOMIC REALITY VS. ECONOMIC THEORY.
NEW YORK: CROWELL COLLIER, 1962, 191 PP., LC#62-15809.
COLLECTION OF ESSAYS ON SUBJECT OF BIG BUSINESS AND ADMINISTERED PRICES; MOST OF MATERIAL WAS TESTIMONY BEFORE CONGRESSIONAL SUBCOMMITTEES. EACH ESSAY IS CONCERNED WITH ASPECT OF PROBLEM CREATED BY BIG BUSINESS. SOME FOCUS ON FACTS OF BIGNESS AND OF PRICE ADMINISTRATION, SOME DEAL WITH IMPLICATIONS OF THESE FACTS FOR ECONOMIC POLICY, AND SOME ARE CONCERNED WITH IMPLICATIONS FOR PUBLIC POLICY.

1743 MEEK C.K., MACMILLAN W.M., HUSSEY E.R.
EUROPE AND WEST AFRICA.
LONDON: OXFORD U PR, 1940, 143 PP.
ANALYSIS OF CULTURAL CHANGE AND ADMINISTRATION IN WEST AFRICA. PRIMARILY CONCERNED WITH AFRICAN ECONOMIC, SOCIAL, AND POLITICAL DEVELOPMENTS; TREATS RELATION TO EUROPE, ADJUSTMENT TO CHANGING CONDITIONS AS RESULT OF WESTERNIZATION, AND ROLE OF EDUCATION.

1744 MEEK R.L.
THE ECONOMICS OF PHYSIOCRACY.
CAMBRIDGE: HARVARD U PR, 1963, 432 PP.
AIM IS TO PRESENT MAIN ELEMENTS OF BASIC ECONOMIC DOCTRINES OF FRENCH PHYSIOCRATS IN THEIR OWN WORDS AND TO ASSIST IN UNDERSTANDING DOCTRINES BY NOTES. FINAL SECTION CONSISTS OF FIVE LENGTHY ESSAYS DEALING WITH CERTAIN ASPECTS OF PHYSIOCRATIC DOCTRINE, HISTORY, AND INFLUENCE.

1745 MEERHAEGHE M.
INTERNATIONAL ECONOMIC INSTITUTIONS.
LONDON: LONGMANS, GREEN & CO, 1966, 404 PP.
PART I PRESENTS THEORY OF INTERNATIONAL ECONOMIC RELATIONS, INCLUDING TRADE, BALANCE-OF-PAYMENTS EQUILIBRIUM, AND POLICY. PART II DESCRIBES AND APPRAISES WORLD ORGANIZATIONS: INTERNATIONAL MONETARY FUND, INTERNATIONAL BANK FOR RECONSTRUCTION AND DEVELOPMENT, GATT, COMMODITY AGREEMENTS. PART III FOCUSES ON EUROPEAN ORGANIZATIONS: BENELUX, ORGANIZATION FOR ECONOMIC CO-OPERATION AND DEVELOPMENT.

1746 MEHTA A.
"INDIA* POVERTY AND CHANGE."
DISSENT, (MAR.-APR. 67), 191-199.
INDIAN SOCIETY AS IT FACES MODERNIZATION. BREAKUP OF TRADITIONAL SOCIETY BECAUSE OF SCIENCE, INDUSTRY, AGRICULTURAL TECHNOLOGY. SOCIAL SCIENCES READY TO CHANGE MOTIVATION AND ATTITUDES. GOAL FOR INDIA IS NOW ECONOMIC FREEDOM. COVERS CASTE, NATIONAL INCOME, INDUSTRY, TECHNOLOGY, RESEARCH, AND FOREIGN AID. CONSIDERS SOCIAL CHANGE AND ECONOMIC DEVELOPMENT AS INTERDEPENDENT.

1747 MEIER G.
INTERNATIONAL TRADE AND DEVELOPMENT.
NEW YORK: HARPER & ROW, 1963, 208 PP., LC#63-7147.
FROM THE PERSPECTIVE OF INTERNATIONAL ECONOMIC DEVELOPMENT, RECONSIDERS MAIN TOPICS IN PURE THEORY AND MONETARY THEORY OF INTERNATIONAL TRADE. MODIFIES CLASSICAL TRADE THEORY BY RELAYING ASSUMPTIONS ABOUT STATIC EQUILIBRIUM AND BY ADDING VARIABLES. STUDIES COMPARATIVE COSTS IN DEVELOPMENT, TERMS OF TRADE, AND DEVELOPMENT THROUGH TRADE.

1748 MEIER G.M., BALDWIN R.
ECONOMIC DEVELOPMENT: THEORY, HISTORY, AND POLICY.
NEW YORK: WILEY, 1957, 588 PP.
EXAMINES PROBLEMS OF ACCELERATING DEVELOPMENT IN UNDERDEVELOPED COUNTRIES AND MAINTAINING DEVELOPMENT IN INDUSTRIALIZED COUNTRIES. EXPLAINS IMPETUS FOR ECONOMIC GROWTH IN TERMS OF ECONOMIC THEORY, HISTORY, AND CURRENT PRACTICES.

1749 MEIER G.M.
"UNCTAD PROPOSALS FOR INTERNATIONAL ECONOMIC REFORM."
STANFORD LAW REV., 19 (JUNE 67), 1173-1216.
PRESENTS PROPOSALS OF UNITED NATIONS CONFERENCE ON TRADE AND DEVELOPMENT TO REFORM INTERNATIONAL CODE OF ECONOMIC CONDUCT AS ESTABLISHED BY GATT AND IMF. EXAMINES BACKGROUND AND ACTIONS OF IMF AND GATT AND PROPOSES THAT LAWS BECOME MORE FAVORABLE TO LESS DEVELOPED COUNTRIES THROUGH INTERNATIONAL COMMODITY AGREEMENTS, PREFERENCES, AND INTERNATIONAL MONETARY REFORM.

1751 MEISEL J. ED.
PAPERS ON THE 1962 ELECTION.
TORONTO: U OF TORONTO PRESS, 1964, 288 PP.
FIFTEEN ESSAYS DEALING WITH VARIOUS ASPECTS OF CANADIAN GENERAL ELECTION OF 1962. RECOGNIZES FAILURE OF POLITICAL PARTIES TO PROMOTE SENSE OF NATIONAL COMMUNITY. ELECTION RESULTS IN ALL PARTS OF CANADA ANALYZED WITH ATTEMPT TO INTERPRET RESULTS.

1752 MELADY T.
FACES OF AFRICA.
NEW YORK: MACMILLAN, 1964, 338 PP., $7.50.
COUNTRY BY COUNTRY STUDY OF HISTORY AND POLITICAL, ECONOMIC, SOCIAL, AND EDUCATIONAL PROBLEMS OF AFRICAN TERRITORIES AS WELL AS A PROJECTION OF TRENDS AND PREDICTION OF POSSIBLE FUTURE DEVELOPMENTS. MORE DESCRIPTIVE THAN ANALYTICAL.

1753 MELMAN S.
OUR DEPLETED SOCIETY.
NEW YORK: HOLT RINEHART WINSTON, 1965, 366 PP., LC#65-14453.
EFFECT OF COLD WAR MILITARY EXPENDITURES ON ECONOMIC CONDITIONS OF US. DEFENSE RESEARCH AND DEVELOPMENT CONTRACTS; SPACE PROGRAM PRIORITIES AND ARMS SALE BUSINESS SEEN AS DESTRUCTIVE TO THE SOCIAL WELFARE OF THE AMERICAN PEOPLE.

1754 MELTZER B.D.
"RUMINATIONS ABOUT IDEOLOGY, LAW, AND LABOR ARBITRATION."
UNIV. CHICAGO LAW REV., 34 (SPRING 67), 545-561.
INQUIRES INTO VULNERABILITY OF ARBITRATION SYSTEM TO PRESSURES INCOMPATIBLE WITH FAIR DISPUTE-SETTLING MECHANISM. DISCUSSES APPROPRIATE ROLE OF COURTS IN CHALLENGING AWARD AS INCOMPATIBLE WITH GOVERNMENT AGREEMENT. EXPLAINS ROLE OF ARBITRATOR WITH RESPECT TO POLICY ISSUES CONCERNED WITH INTERPRETING COLLECTIVE BARGAINING AGREEMENT. DESIRES ARBITRATORS TO SOLVE PROBLEM WITHIN REGULATORY FRAMEWORK.

1755 MENCHER S.
"THE PROBLEM OF MEASURING POVERTY."
BRIT. J. OF SOCIOLOGY, 18 (MAR. 67), 1-12.
DEALS WITH CONCEPTUAL PROBLEMS OF MEASURING POVERTY AND DETERMINATION OF POVERTY BY ABSOLUTE OR RELATIVE STANDARDS. FEELS A MODERN DEFINITION OF POVERTY IS NEEDED WHICH DOES NOT DEPEND ON STANDARDS OF MINIMAL SUBSISTENCE FOR THE

LOWEST CLASSES.

1756 MENDE T.
WORLD POWER IN THE BALANCE.
NEW YORK: NOONDAY, 1953, 188 PP.
PROBES POWER SHIFT FROM EUROPE TO AMERICA SINCE 1900. ADVOCATES REVIVAL OF WESTERN UTOPIANISM ON HUMANISTIC BASIS. DEFINES POWER AS BEING NON-PERMANENT AND AS CONSISTING OF MATERIAL AND IMMATERIAL ELEMENTS. FORSEES FUTURE CONFLICTS BETWEEN WEST AND NEW WORLD POWERS LIKE RUSSIA, BUT FEELS COMPROMISE CAN PRODUCE IDEAL WORLD.

1757 MENDEL A.P. ED.
POLITICAL MEMOIRS 1905-1917 BY PAUL MILIUKOV (TRANS. BY CARL GOLDBERG)
ANN ARBOR: U OF MICH PR, 1967, 508 PP., LC#67-25341.
PRESENTSPERSONAL ACCOUNT OF STRUGGLE OF LIBERALS TO ESTABLISH CONSTITUTIONAL, REPRESENTATIVE GOVERNMENT IN RUSSIA FROM 1905-17. DISCUSSES MILIUKOV'S ROLE IN ATTEMPT, FOREIGN AFFAIRS DURING PERIOD, PROCESS OF MODERNIZING RURAL ECONOMY, AND ESTABLISHMENT OF PROVISIONAL GOVERNMENT IN 1917. PROVIDES PORTRAITS OF OTHER LEADERS OF PERIOD.

1758 MENDELSON W.
CAPITALISM, DEMOCRACY, AND THE SUPREME COURT.
NEW YORK: APPLETON, 1960, 137 PP., LC#60-10146.
ANALYZES RECORD OF SIX SUPREME COURT JUSTICES TO SUPPORT IMPORTANCE OF SUPREME COURT IN DETERMINING PUBLIC ATTITUDES AND GOVERNMENT POLICY THROUGHOUT US HISTORY. CITES CHIEF JUSTICE MARSHALL AND MERCANTILISM, CHIEF JUSTICE TANEY AND JACKSONIAN DEMOCRACY, AND JUSTICE FIELD AND LAISSEZ-FAIRE; ALSO THE RECORD OF HOLMES MARKED BY HUMILITY AND SKEPTICISM, AND THE "NEW FREEDOM" WITH JUSTICES BLACK AND FRANKFURTER.

1759 MENEZES A.J.
SUBDESENVOLVIMENTO E POLITICA INTERNACIONAL.
RIO DE JANEIRO: EDICIONES GRD, 1963, 223 PP.
STUDY OF UNDERDEVELOPED WORLD IN FIELD OF INTERNATIONAL POLITICS. DISCUSSES NATIONALISM AND WORLD WIDE POLITICAL AND ECONOMIC COMPETITION AMONG NATIONS. DEALS WITH POSITION OF BRAZIL AND ITS PLANS FOR INDEPENDENT GROWTH IN POWER AND INFLUENCE.

1760 MERIKOSKI V.
"BASIC PROBLEMS OF UNIVERSITY ADMINISTRATION."
INT. REV. OF ADMIN. SCI., 33 (JAN. 67), 17-30.
DESCRIBES CATEGORIES OF UNIVERSITY ADMINISTRATIONS, SUCH AS PRIVATE, STATE, AND DENOMINATIONAL, AND COMPARES SYSTEMS. ASSERTS IMPORTANCE OF AUTONOMY FOR EFFICIENT UNIVERSITY ADMINISTRATION AND DISCUSSES AREAS IN WHICH AUTONOMY IS VITAL, SUCH AS ADMISSIONS, EXAMINATIONS, CURRICULA, RESEARCH, AND FINANCES.

1761 MERON T.
"THE UN'S 'COMMON SYSTEM' OF SALARY, ALLOWANCE, AND BENEFITS: CRITICAL APPR'SAL OF COORD IN PERSONNEL MATTERS."
INTL. ORGANIZATION, 21 (SPRING 67), 284-305.
ANALYZES SYSTEM OF AGREEMENTS MADE BETWEEN UN AND ITS AGENCIES, IN 1945, TO PROVIDE SALARIES AND OTHER BENEFITS FOR MEMBERS. FEELS AGREEMENTS SHOULD BE RE-EVALUATED AND RE-JUSTIFIED AFTER 20 YEARS. SEES NEED FOR MORE STABLE, COMPETENT SYSTEM. STUDIES AGREEMENTS THEMSELVES AND PROCESS BY WHICH THEY WERE ESTABLISHED.

1762 MERRIAM C.E.
PUBLIC AND PRIVATE GOVERNMENT.
NEW HAVEN: YALE U PR, 1944, 78 PP.
LECTURES DEALING WITH PRIVATE GOVERNMENT, NOTING THE CONTRIBUTIONS OF GIERKE, DUGNIT, AND GUILD SOCIALISTS, AS WELL AS INDUSTRIAL SELF-GOVERNMENT, THE PROBLEMS OF PUBLIC AND PRIVATE INTERDEPENDENCE, PLURALISM, POLITICAL ORGANIZATION, AND DEMOCRACY.

1763 MERRIAM R.E.
"THE BUREAU OF THE BUDGET AS PART OF THE PRESIDENT'S STAFF."
ANN. ACAD. POL. SOC. SCI., (SEPT. 56), 15-23.
BUREAU OF THE BUDGET IS A MOST VALUABLE STAFF AGENCY, PROVIDING THE PRESIDENT WITH INFORMATION ENABLING HIM TO EXERCISE SOME REAL CONTROL OVER THE ADMINISTRATIVE AGENCIES AND DEPARTMENTS IN LINE WITH HIS GREAT RESPONSIBILITY TO THE NATION.

1764 MESTMACKER E.J.
"STATE TRADING MONOPOLIES IN THE EUROPEAN ECONOMIC COMMUNITY
VANDERBILT LAW REV., 20 (MAR. 67), 321-353.
EXAMINES POSITION OF STATETRADING MONOPOLIES WITHIN THE EEC, ANALYZING IN DETAIL THE INTERPRETATION AND APPLICATION OF ART. 37 OF THE ROME TREATY, WHICH REQUIRES MEMBERS TO "GRADUALLY ADJUST STATE TRADING MONOPOLIES TO ENSURE THAT, WHEN THE TRANSITIONAL PERIOD EXPIRES, NO DISCRIMINATION EXISTS BETWEEN NATIONALS OF MEMBER STATES AS REGARDS THE SUPPLY OR MARKETING OF GOODS."

1765 METZLER L.A., ET A.L.
INCOME, EMPLOYMENT, AND PUBLIC POLICY.
NEW YORK: W W NORTON, 1948, 381 PP.
DISCUSSES RELATIONSHIP OF DETERMINANTS OF INCOME: INVESTMENT, REDISTRIBUTION, PRODUCTIVITY, EMPLOYMENT. CONSIDERS SOCIAL SETTING AND EFFECTS OF PUBLIC POLICY ON INCOME. EXAMINES CREDIT CONTROLS, INTEREST RATES, PUBLIC EXPENDITURES, AND EXPANSIONISTIC FISCAL POLICIES. RELATION OF PRODUCTIVITY TO WAGES IS ALSO STUDIED.

1766 MEYER A.G.
MARXISM.
CAMBRIDGE: HARVARD U PR, 1954, 181 PP., LC#54-07063.
CRITICAL ESSAY ON THEORY AND PRACTICE OF MARXISM, INCLUDING ITS CONTRIBUTION TO SOCIAL SCIENCE. DISCUSSES MARX AS RADICAL CRITIC OF CIVILIZATION, FAITH IN PROGRESS, AND DISINTEGRATION OF MARXISM.

1767 MEYER A.J.
MIDDLE EASTERN CAPITALISM: NINE ESSAYS.
CAMBRIDGE: HARVARD U. PR., 1959, 161 PP.
SYSTEMATIC ANALYSIS OF ECONOMIC GROWTH OF IRAQ, KUWAIT, CYPRUS, ISRAEL, ET AL. CONSIDERS WHETHER ECONOMIC PROSPERITY WILL CONTINUE. SUGGESTS THAT WEST IMPROVE UNDERSTANDING OF ECONOMICS OF MIDDLE EAST WITHOUT DELAY.

1768 MEYER F.V.
INFLATION AND CAPITAL.
CAMBRIDGE: BOWES AND BOWES, LTD, 1954, 75 PP.
STUDY OF RELATION BETWEEN INFLATION AND VOLUME OF CAPITAL AVAILABLE. ANALYZES DEFINITIONS OF INFLATION AND ITS ECONOMIC FUNCTION. VIEWS INFLATION AS SYMPTOM OF UNDER-PRODUCING ECONOMY IN RELATION TO DEMANDS MADE ON IT, AND DISCUSSES ANTI-INFLATIONARY TACTICS OF ENGLAND, 1945-52, WITH CURRENT ESTIMATE OF CAPITAL BASIS OF BRITISH ECONOMY.

1769 MEYER F.V.
THE TERMS OF TRADE.
COPENHAGEN: MUNKSGAARD INTL, 1962, 160 PP., LC#63-46723.
STUDY OF THEORY OF INTERNATIONAL TRADE BALANCE BETWEEN MANUFACTURES AND PRIMARY PRODUCTS. ESPECIALLY DISCUSSES EXPANSION OF TRADE IN 1950'S AND ITS FAILURE TO FOLLOW THEORY OF ADJUSTMENT OF DEMAND AND PRICE.

1770 MEYER J.R.
"REGIONAL ECONOMICS: A SURVEY."
AMER. ECO. REVIEW, 53 (MAR. 63), 19-54.
DISCUSSES RISE OF A NEW ACADEMIC FIELD: REGIONAL ANALYSIS IN ECONOMICS. ATTEMPTS TO DEFINE NEW FIELD. OUTLINES PROBLEMS, THEORETICAL FOUNDATIONS, AND TYPES OF APPROACHES.

1771 MEYER J.R., GLAUBER R.R.
INVESTMENT DECISIONS, ECONOMIC FORECASTING, AND PUBLIC POLICY.
CAMBRIDGE: HARVARD U PR, 1964, 280 PP., LC#64-12399.
STUDIES DETERMINANTS OF INVESTMENT OUTLAYS OF BUSINESS AND QUESTIONS INVOLVED IN DECISION-MAKING. INCORPORATES STUDY INTO SYSTEMATIC FORECASTING MODEL. HYPOTHESIZES THAT INVESTMENT DEMANDS ARE GREATER THAN SUPPLY OF INTERNAL FUNDS DURING BUSINESS UPSWINGS AND LESS DURING DOWNSWINGS. COMPARES FORECASTING RESULTS OF DIFFERENT INVESTMENT MODELS.

1772 MEYERS M. ED., CAWELTI J.G. ED., KERN A. ED.
SOURCES OF THE AMERICAN REPUBLIC; A DOCUMENTARY HISTORY OF POLITICS, SOCIETY, AND THOUGHT (VOL. I, REV. ED.)
CHICAGO: SCOTT, FORESMAN & CO, 1967, 498 PP., LC#67-22300.
SELECTED READINGS ON AMERICAN HISTORY FROM 1607-1865, DIVIDED INTO THREE SECTIONS: COLONIAL PERIOD, 1607-1763; REVOLUTIONARY PERIOD, 1763-1828; AND CIVIL WAR ERA, 1828-65. INCLUDES EXCERPTS FROM EMINENT LEADERS, POLITICIANS, AND THINKERS OF EACH PERIOD AND CONCLUDES WITH MODERN INTERPRETATIONS OF HISTORICAL EVENTS AND IDEAS. TREATS POLITICAL, SOCIAL, ECONOMIC, AND CULTURAL DEVELOPMENTS.

1773 MEYNAUD J.
PLANIFICATION ET POLITIQUE.
LAUSANNE: ETUDES DE SCIENCE POL, 1963, 190 PP.
EXAMINES THE MOTIVATION OF ECONOMIC PLANNING, ITS VALUE, AND CHARACTERISTICS INCLUDING JURISDICTION, TECHNIQUES, THE POLITICS OF PLANNING AND ITS PROBLEMS.

1774 MEYNAUD J., BEY A.S.
TRADE UNIONISM IN AFRICA; A STUDY OF ITS GROWTH AND ORIENTATION (TRANS. BY ANGELA BRENCH)
LONDON: METHUEN, 1967, 242 PP.
PRESENTS SOCIO-ECONOMIC AND EXTERNAL FACTORS RESPONSIBLE FOR FORMATION OF AFRICAN TRADE UNIONS AND DIRECTION OF THEIR DEVELOPMENT. EMPHASIZES EMERGENCE OF POLITICAL FACTORS, ESPECIALLY NATIONALISM, DURING AND AFTER DEMANDS FOR INDEPENDENCE. DISCUSSES PROBLEMS CONFRONTING UNIONS IN INDEPENDENT NATIONS AND PAN-AFRICAN FORCE URGING INTERNATIONAL RECOGNITION.

1775 MEZERIK A.G. ED.
ECONOMIC AID FOR UNDERDEVELOPED COUNTRIES (PAMPHLET)
NEW YORK: INTL REVIEW SERVICE, 1957, 29 PP.
DISCUSSES TECHNICAL ASSISTANCE FOR DEVELOPING NATIONS THROUGH UN AND OTHER AGENCIES, COLD WAR AS MOTIVATION FOR INCREASED AID EFFORTS, US AND USSR AID POLICIES, IMPORTANCE

OF ATOMIC AID, NEED FOR PRIVATE INVESTMENT, AND COMPLICATIONS OF POPULATION GROWTH.

1776 MEZERIK A.G.
ECONOMIC DEVELOPMENT AIDS FOR UNDERDEVELOPED COUNTRIES.
NEW YORK: INTL REVIEW SERVICE, 1961, 108 PP., LC#61-2436.
SUMMARY OF POST-WWII ECONOMIC AID TO UNDERDEVELOPED COUNTRIES DERIVED PRIMARILY FROM UN SOURCES AND CONSISTING OF FINANCIAL AND TECHNICAL ASSISTANCE.

1777 MEZERIK A.G. ED.
TRADE, AID AND ECONOMIC DEVELOPMENT.
NEW YORK: INTL REVIEW SERVICE, 1964, 79 PP.
REVIEWS VARIOUS PROBLEMS OF ECONOMIC DEVELOPMENT, APPROACH TO PROBLEMS, AND ORGANIZATIONS. NOTES POLITICAL TECHNIQUES USED TO OVERCOME ECONOMIC UNDERDEVELOPMENT. APPENDIXES CONTAIN HISTORY OF POSTWAR TRADE ORGANIZATIONS: GATT, HAVANA CHARTER, AND KENNEDY ROUND; BACKGROUND ON INTERNATIONAL MONETARY FUND, INTERNATIONAL BANK FOR RECONSTRUCTION AND DEVELOPMENT, AND INTERNATIONAL FINANCE CORP.

1778 MEZERIK A.G. ED.
FINANCIAL ASSISTANCE FOR ECONOMIC DEVELOPMENT.
NEW YORK: INTL REVIEW SERVICE, 1959, 71 PP.
REVIEW OF EXCHANGES OF WORLD-WIDE FINANCIAL ASSISTANCE SINCE 1950. CHRONOLOGY OF UNRRA'S ACTIVITIES 1943-59. INCLUDES ANALYSES OF POLICIES AND DEVELOPMENTS IN INTERNATIONAL FINANCIAL RELATIONS.

1779 MICHAELY M.
CONCENTRATION IN INTERNATIONAL TRADE.
AMSTERDAM: NORTH HOLLAND PUBL CO, 1962.
EMPIRICAL STUDY OF COMMODITY AND GEOGRAPHIC CONCENTRATION IN INTERNATIONAL TRADE IN GOODS. SEEKS TO DETERMINE MAGNITUDE OF THIS CONCENTRATION, TO DISTINGUISH MAJOR FACTORS WHICH CONTRIBUTE TO IT, AND TO EXPLORE A FEW OF ITS MOST IMPORTANT EFFECTS. DEFINES MAIN ATTRIBUTES OF COUNTRIES WHOSE TRADE TENDS TO BE HIGHLY CONCENTRATED, AND THUS SUGGESTS CAUSES FOR CONCENTRATION.

1780 MIKESELL R.F., BEHRMAN J.N.
FINANCING FREE WORLD TRADE WITH THE SINO-SOVIET BLOC.
PRINCETON: U. PR., 1958, 101 PP.
SYSTEMATIC INQUIRY INTO FOREIGN ECONOMIC RELATIONS OF SOVIET UNION, EASTERN EUROPE AND CHINA. EXAMINES MOTIVATIONS FOR TRADE, PAYMENT ARRANGEMENTS AND BANKING PRACTICES. ROLE OF GOLD AND FREE CURRENCIES EVALUATED.

1781 MIKESELL R.F.
"AMERICA'S ECONOMIC RESPONSIBILITY AS A GREAT POWER."
AMER. ECON. REV., 50 (MAY 60), 258-71.
STATES ONLY USA HAS ECONOMIC AND MILITARY CAPABILITY TO OPPOSE COMMUNISM. CHALLENGE COMPLICATED BY RAPID CHANGES IN RELATIVE POWER POSITION. DEFINES OBSTACLES IN LESS DEVELOPED AREAS. COUNSELS MEANINGFUL DOMESTIC ECONOMIC GROWTH.

1782 MIKESELL R.F.
"COMMODITY AGREEMENTS AND AID TO DEVELOPING COUNTRIES."
LAW CONTEMP. PROBL., 28 (SPRING 63), 294-312.
CITES INSTABILITY OF PROCEEDS FROM COMMODITY EXPORT AS A BASIC PROBLEM OF UNDERDEVELOPED COUNTRIES. PROBABLE FAILURE TO ACHIEVE RATE OF GROWTH IN FOREIGN EXCHANGE HINDERS LONG-TERM DEVELOPMENT GOALS. SUGGESTS COORDINATING TRADE POLICIES AND ASSISTANCE PROGRAMS OF INDUSTRIALIZED COUNTRIES AND INTERNATIONAL AGENCIES.

1783 MIKESELL R.F.
PUBLIC INTERNATIONAL LENDING FOR DEVELOPMENT.
NEW YORK: RANDOM HOUSE, INC, 1966, 244 PP., LC#66-10538.
EXPLORES POLICIES AND PROBLEMS OF PUBLIC INTERNATIONAL LENDING AGENCIES AIDING SOCIAL AND ECONOMIC PROGRESS IN DEVELOPING NATIONS. EMPHASIZES PROBLEMS OF RELATIONSHIP OF THEORIES OF ECONOMIC DEVELOPMENT AND APPROACHES OF LENDING AGENCIES. ALSO TRACES DEVELOPMENT OF INTERNATIONAL LENDING AGENCIES, TYPES OF LOANS AND INVESTMENT, AND INTERNATIONAL MEETINGS TO FOUND ORGANIZATIONS.

1784 MILIBAND R. ED., SAVILLE J. ED.
THE SOCIALIST REGISTER: 1964.
NEW YORK: MONTHLY REVIEW PR, 1964, 308 PP.
SOME 18 ESSAYS ON CURRENT SOCIALIST AND COMMUNIST THEORY, POLITICS, ECONOMICS, AND BEHAVIOR. EMPHASIS IS ON EVENTS AND PROGRESS IN ENGLAND, BUT 1964 EDITION INCLUDES COMMENTARY ON NASSER, MAOISM, WEST GERMANY, ALLIANCE FOR PROGRESS, AND OTHER ITEMS OF INTERNATIONAL SIGNIFICANCE. ALSO INCLUDES REVIEWS OF PERTINENT BOOKS AND ARTICLES.

1785 MILL J.
ELEMENTS OF POLITICAL ECONOMY.
ORIGINAL PUBLISHER NOT AVAILABLE, 1884, 304 PP.
ANALYZES POLITICAL ECONOMY, BEGINNING WITH PRODUCTION, DISTRIBUTION, AND CONSUMPTION AS FACTUAL BASIS. CONSIDERS EFFECTS OF GOVERNMENT UPON ECONOMY, MAINLY CONCENTRATING ON TAXATION. SUPPORTS PROPORTIONAL INCOME TAX AS MEANS OF EQUALIZING BURDEN OF TAXATION, THOUGH OPPOSING USE OF TAXATION TO EQUALIZE INCOME DISTRIBUTION ITSELF. DISCUSSES MOST MODERN FORMS OF TAXATION.

1786 MILL J.S.
PRINCIPLES OF POLITICAL ECONOMY.
NEW YORK: APPLETON, 1885, 658 PP.
DEALS WITH CIRCULATION OF CAPITAL, FACTORS AFFECTING THE EFFICIENCY OF PRODUCTION, LAWS OF THE INCREASE OF LABOR, AND THE THEORY OF WAGES, PROFITS AND RENTS. ANALYZES MONETARY SYSTEMS AND COMPETITION WITHIN MARKETS. SURVEYS THE INFLUENCE OF SOCIAL CHANGE UPON PRODUCTION AND DISTRIBUTION.

1787 MILL J.S.
SOCIALISM (1859)
ORIGINAL PUBLISHER NOT AVAILABLE, 1891, 214 PP.
CLASSIFYING HIMSELF AS A DEMOCRATIC SOCIALIST, MILL ADVOCATED COMMON OWNERSHIP IN THE RAW MATERIALS OF THE WORLD AND EQUAL PARTICIPATION IN ALL BENEFITS OF COMBINED LABOR. HOWEVER, HE FELT THAT THESE THINGS WERE FAR AWAY AND SHOULD BE ACHIEVED THROUGH EVOLUTIONARY RATHER THAN REVOLUTIONARY MEANS. NOT A STATE BUT AN INDIVIDUAL FORM OF SOCIALISM IS FAVORED, AND PRIVATE OWNERSHIP IS NOT EXCLUDED.

1788 MILLEN B.H.
"INTERNATIONAL TRADE AND POLITICAL INDEPENDENCE."
AMER. BEHAV. SCI., 6 (MARCH 63), 18-20.
THE CURRENT ACHIEVEMENT OF POLITICAL INDEPENDENCE BY FORMER COLONIES MAY TEND TO DIMINISH THE ROLE OF FOREIGN TRADE IN THEIR ECONOMIES, AND LIKEWISE DIMINISH THAT OF INTERNATIONAL TRADE IN THE WORLD ECONOMY.

1789 MILLER A.S.
"CONSTITUTIONALIZING THE CORPORATION."
PROD, 3 (SEPT. 59), 10-12.
A LAW PROFESSOR'S VIEW THAT PRIVATE POWER CENTERS WITHIN THE AMBIT OF CONSTITUTIONAL STATE ACTION, E.G. APPLYING THE FOURTEENTH AMENDMENT TO CORPORATE DECISION-MAKING, IMPOSE DUTIES ON CORPORATIONS BY A POSITIVE APPLICATION OF THE FIRST AMENDMENT TO THE "FACTORY COMMUNITY" CONSISTING OF SHAREHOLDERS, MANAGEMENT, EMPLOYEES, AND UNION MANAGEMENT.

1790 MILLER A.S.
"SOME OBSERVATIONS ON THE POLITICAL ECONOMY OF POPULATION GROWTH."
LAW CONTEMP. PROBL., 25 (SUMMER 60), 614-29.
NOTES PARTICULARLY THE DANGER OF UNCONTROLLED POPULATION GROWTH AND ITS RELATION TO SUCH PROBLEMS AS BIRTH CONTROL. USING SUPPORTING DATA, CONCLUDES THAT CONSCIOUS APPLICATION OF SCIENTIFIC METHOD IS NECESSARY IN ACHIEVING POPULATION CONTROL.

1791 MILLER C.H.
"B. TRAVEN Y EL 'PROBLEMA PETROLERO'."
CUADERNOS AMERICANOS, (JULY-AUG. 67), 225-229.
DISCUSSES B. TRAVEN AND TREATMENT OF MEXICAN PETROLEUM PROBLEM IN HIS NOVEL "LA ROSA BLANCA." STUDIES EXPLOITATION OF MEXICAN OIL RESOURCES BY IMPERIALISTIC US, MAINTAINING THAT US IS DENYING MEXICO HER LAND AND LIBERTY. EXAMINES ATTITUDES AND REACTIONS TO BOOK IN US AND MEXICO.

1792 MILLER W.
REVENUE-COST RATIOS OF RURAL TOWNSHIPS WITH CHANGING LAND USES.
TRENTON: NJ DEPT AGRI, RURAL ADV, 1963, 92 PP.
ANALYZES MUNICIPAL SERVICES AND ASSOCIATED TAX COSTS IN SIX REPRESENTATIVE NEW JERSEY TOWNSHIPS AS THEY PROCEED FROM RURAL TOWARD URBAN CONDITION. EMPHASIZES RELATIONSHIP BETWEEN REVENUES AND COSTS UNDER PRESENT LAND USE AND TAXATION POLICIES, ESPECIALLY AS THEY AFFECT AGRICULTURE. CONCLUDES THAT FARMS PAY GREATER PERCENTAGE OF TOTAL LEVY THAN THEIR PERCENTAGE OF SERVICE COSTS.

1793 MILLETT J.D.
THE PROCESS AND ORGANIZATION OF GOVERNMENT PLANNING.
NEW YORK: COLUMBIA U PRESS, 1947, 187 PP.
DISCUSSES PROCEDURES BY WHICH GOVERNMENTAL POLICY GOALS ARE ACHIEVED. ANALYZES ACTIVITIES OF NATIONAL RESOURCES PLANNING BOARD. INDICATES PROCESS OF FIXING GOALS, MEASURING EXISTING SITUATION, AND DESIGNING POSITIVE ACTION. DESCRIBES IMPORTANCE OF TIME FACTOR, GEOGRAPHICAL FACTOR, AND RESEARCH.

1794 MILLIKAN M.F. ED.
INCOME STABILIZATION FOR A DEVELOPING DEMOCRACY.
NEW HAVEN: YALE U PR, 1953, 730 PP., LC#52-12073.
ESSAYS WRITTEN DURING POST WWII RECESSION AND POST-KOREAN INFLATION. AUTHORS AVOID COMMENT ON CURRENT SCENE BUT PRESENT RELEVANT ANALYSIS IN VARIOUS PROBLEM AREAS. SOME RETREAT TO FUNDAMENTAL PRINCIPLES WHILE OTHERS PRESENT ORIGINAL ANALYSES.

1795 MILLIKAN M.F., ROSTOW W.W.
A PROPOSAL: KEY TO AN EFFECTIVE FOREIGN POLICY.
NEW YORK: HARPER & ROW, 1957, 170 PP., LC#56-12227.
PROPOSES NEW PROGRAM OF AMERICAN FOREIGN POLICY THAT CALLS FOR INCREASE IN FOREIGN AID SPENDING FOR ECONOMIC

DEVELOPMENT OF UNDERDEVELOPED AREAS TO ACHIEVE GREATER AWARENESS THAT AMERICA'S GOAL IS THAT OF ALL COUNTRIES: DEVELOPMENT OF VIABLE DEMOCRATIC SOCIETIES AND THEREFORE A MORE SECURE WORLD. CRITICIZES PREVIOUS FOREIGN AID PROGRAMS.

1796 MILLIKEN M.
"NEW AND OLD CRITERIA FOR AID."
PROC. ACAD. POLIT. SCI., 27 (JAN 62), 112-24.
DISCUSSES CRITERIA FOR USA AID PROGRAMS. ANALYZES INFLUENCE OF USA ON ECONOMIC SITUATIONS IN OTHER COUNTRIES. SETS FORTH CONDITIONS FOR SUCCESSFUL UTILIZATION OF USA RESOURCES OF INFLUENCE.

1797 MILLIS H.A., MONTGOMERY R.E.
ORGANIZED LABOR (FIRST ED.)
NEW YORK: MCGRAW HILL, 1945, 930 PP.
AN EXHAUSTIVE TREATMENT BY TWO ECONOMISTS OF AMERICAN UNIONISM. SECTIONS RELEVANT TO REPRESENTATION INCLUDE TRADE-UNION STRUCTURE, GOVERNMENT, GROUP RELATIONS, TRADE UNION POLICIES AND PRACTICES, EMPLOYEE-REPRESENTATION PLANS, AND UNIONS' USE OF COOPERATIVES. AN EXAMINATION OF THE RELATIONSHIP BETWEEN TRADE UNIONS, THE LAW, AND COURTS IS INCLUDED.

1798 MILLS C.W., ATKINSON M.
"THE TRADE UNION LEADER: A COLLECTIVE PORTRAIT."
PUBLIC OPINION QUART., 9 (SUMMER 45), 158-175.
A QUESTION RELEVANT TO REPRESENTATION IN THE INFORMAL SENSE IS DISCUSSED, NAMELY THE QUALIFICATIONS AND BACKGROUND OF TOP LABOR EXECUTIVES GLEANED FROM DETAILED QUESTIONNAIRES. FIVE FACTS EMERGE: I.E., THE LEADERS' EXPERIENCE AS WORKERS, WORK IN THE LOCALS, TOP PAY, IDENTIFICATION WITH EITHER NATIONAL OR STATE UNION HIERARCHY, WITH MOBILITY BETWEEN LOCAL AND OTHER HIERARCHIES.

1799 MILLS C.W.
THE NEW MEN OF POWER.
NEW YORK: HARCOURT BRACE, 1948, 323 PP.
DESCRIBES UNION MACHINES, THE PARALLELS OF POLITICAL MACHINES, THE UNION LEADER, AND THE POLITICAL AND MASS PUBLICS; DESCRIBES ORGANIZATIONAL ARRANGEMENTS OF UNION LEADERSHIP, RELATIONS BETWEEN LOCAL AND INTERNATIONAL UNIONS, MEMBERSHIP, LABOR'S POLITICAL ROLE, ITS IMAGE OF BUSINESS, INSTITUTIONALIZATION, AND PROGRAMS.

1800 MILNE R.S.
"CONTROL OF GOVERNMENT CORPORATIONS IN THE UNITED STATES."
PUBLIC ADMINISTRATION, 34 (WINTER 56), 355-364.
CONTROL OF ALL FORMS OF GOVERNMENT CORPORATIONS IS SHARED BY THE PRESIDENT AND VARIOUS CONGRESSIONAL COMMITTEES, WITH A VERY IMPORTANT ROLE BEING PLAYED BY THE GENERAL ACCOUNTING OFFICE.

1801 MINER J.
SOCIAL AND ECONOMIC FACTORS IN SPENDING FOR PUBLIC EDUCATION
SYRACUSE: SYRACUSE U PRESS, 1963, 158 PP., LC#63-11011.
EXAMINES CRITERIA FOR DETERMINING LEVEL OF PUBLIC EXPENDITURE FOR PUBLIC EDUCATION AND DEVELOPS EMPIRICAL MODEL TO STUDY REGULARITIES OF EXPENDITURE PATTERSN. RESULTS GIVE OPTIMUM LEVEL AND ALLOW A FORECAST OF FUTURE POLICY.

1802 MINGAY G.E.
ENGLISH LANDED SOCIETY IN THE EIGHTEENTH CENTURY.
TORONTO: TORONTO UNIV PRESS, 1963, 292 PP.
HISTORY OF BRITAIN'S LANDED SOCIETY IN EIGHTEENTH CENTURY. INCLUDES CLASS STRUCTURE; GROWTH OF GREAT ESTATES; LANDLORDS' RELATION TO POLITICS, SOCIETY, AGRICULTURE, AND INDUSTRY; AND COUNTRY LIFE.

1803 GT BRIT MIN OVERSEAS DEV LIB
TECHNICAL CO-OPERATION -- A BIBLIOGRAPHY.
LONDON: MIN OF OVERSEAS DEVEL.
MONTHLY LISTING, FIRST PUBLISHED 1964, OF CURRENT OFFICIAL PUBLICATIONS OF THE COMMONWEALTH, DOCUMENTS, PROCESSED AND UNPUBLISHED MATERIALS, AND OTHER REPORTS AND BULLETINS FROM FOREIGN INSTITUTIONS. ENTRIES PERTAIN TO ECONOMIC, SOCIAL, LEGAL, AND STATISTICAL ASPECTS OF TECHNICAL DEVELOPMENT.

1804 MINTZ S.W.
"INTERNAL MARKET SYS AS MECHANISMS OF SOCIAL ARTIC," IN V.F. RAY, INTERMED SOCIETIES, SOCIAL MOBILITY, AND COMMUNIC (BMR)
SEATTLE: U OF WASHINGTON PR, 1959.
DESCRIBES INTERNAL MARKET SYSTEM (DEFINED AS AN "ORGANIZED FRAMEWORK FOR THE CONDUCT OF ECONOMIC EXCHANGES") AS A MECHANISM TO FACILITATE THE EXCHANGE OF GOODS AND SERVICES AND SOCIAL RELATIONSHIPS. EXAMINES VARIOUS PEASANT SOCIETIES.

1805 MIT CENTER INTERNATIONAL STU
BIBLIOGRAPHY OF THE ECONOMIC AND POLITICAL DEVELOPMENT OF INDONESIA.
CAMBRIDGE: M I T PRESS, 1953, 169 PP.
BIBLIOGRAPHY INTENDED PRIMARILY FOR USE OF STAFF MEMBERS OF PROJECT ON ECONOMIC AND POLITICAL DEVELOPMENT OF INDONESIA AT CENTER FOR INTERNATIONAL STUDIES, MIT. CONTAINS 2353 ITEMS IN DUTCH, ENGLISH, AND INDONESIAN AVAILABLE IN THE US. INCLUDES SECTIONS ON BASIC REFERENCE AND STATISTICAL WORKS; HISTORICAL AND DESCRIPTIVE WORKS.

1806 MIT CENTER INTERNATIONAL STU
OFFICIAL SERIAL PUBLICATIONS RELATING TO ECONOMIC DEVELOPMENT IN AFRICA SOUTH OF THE SAHARA.
CAMBRIDGE: M I T PRESS, 1961, 44 PP.
LISTS ALL ENGLISH-LANGUAGE REPORTS ON ECONOMIC DEVELOPMENT AVAILABLE IN US UP TO DECEMBER 1960; MOST ARE OFFICIAL GOVERNMENT PUBLICATIONS, THOUGH SOME MAJOR PRIVATE CORPORATIONS ARE INCLUDED; ARRANGED BY COUNTRY.

1807 MITAU G.T. ED., CHASE H.W. ED.
INSOLUBLE PROBLEMS: CASE PROBLEMS ON THE FUNCTIONS OF STATE AND LOCAL GOVERNMENT.
NEW YORK: CHAS SCRIBNER'S SONS, 1964, 351 PP., LC#64-10217.
CASE STUDIES OF PROBLEMS INVOLVING IMPORTANT FUNCTIONS OF STATE AND LOCAL GOVERNMENT: GOVERNMENT REGULATION OF POLITICAL PARTIES; TAXING AND LICENSING, WELFARE, EDUCATION AND HOUSING; BUSINESS AND LABOR RELATIONS; LOCAL ISSUES INVOLVING AIRPORTS, ZONING, AND TORT LIABILITY. EXPLANATORY ESSAYS RAISE QUESTIONS IN EACH GROUP OF CASES.

1808 MITCHELL J.D.B.
"THE CONSTITUTIONAL IMPLICATIONS OF JUDICIAL CONTROL OF THE ADMINISTRATION IN THE UNITED KINGDOM."
CAMBRIDGE LAW JOURNAL, (APR. 67), 46-61.
ANALYZES RELATIONSHIP BETWEEN ADMINISTRATION OR PRIME MINISTER, PARLIAMENT, AND COURTS IN ENGLAND. SEES NEED FOR ONE TO CONTROL OTHER (FORM OF CHECKS AND BALANCES), PROVES THEORY BY DISCUSSING FUNCTIONS OF ALL, AS LAID DOWN IN CONSTITUTION. SUGGESTS NEED FOR CONFORMING TO LAW IN COMPLEX SOCIETIES.

1809 MITCHELL W.G.
BUSINESS CYCLES.
NEW YORK: NATL BUREAU ECO RES, 1954, 485 PP.
COMPARES METHODOLOGIES AND THEORIES IN STUDY OF BUSINESS CYCLES, INCLUDING THOSE DENYING THEIR EXISTENCE. CLAIMS THAT THEY DO EXIST AND THAT THEY ARE INTERNATIONAL IN SCOPE. CONSIDERS THEIR RELATION TO ECONOMIC ORGANIZATION TYPES. ADVOCATES USE OF STATISTICAL SURVEYS AND COMPARISONS FOR DETERMINING THE NATURE OF CYCLICAL FLUCTUATIONS IN BUSINESS.

1810 MIXON J.
"JANE JACOBS AND THE LAW - ZONING FOR DIVERSITY EXAMINED."
NORTHWESTERN U LAW REVIEW, 62 (JULY-AUG 67), 314-356.
DISCUSSES PROS AND CONS OF TWO TYPES OF CITY PLANNING: "GARDEN CITY" PLANNING WHICH CREATES IDEALIZED RURAL ATMOSPHERE, LOW DENSITY, AND SINGLE USE, AND (2) DIVERSE USE POLICY AS ADVOCATED BY JANE JACOBS. FEELS PROTOTYPES SHOULD BE BUILT BASED ON BOTH APPROACHES. REVIEWS ZONING LAWS, CONSTITUTIONAL CLAIMS, ANTICIPATED CLAIMS BY AGGRIEVED LANDOWNERS, AND TRADITIONAL DOCTRINES OF COURTS.

1811 MIYASAWA K.
AN ECONOMIC SURVIVAL GAME (PAMPHLET)
PRINCETON: PRINCETON U PRESS, 1961, 27 PP.
RESEARCH STUDY OF ECONOMIC GAME THEORY OF CORPORATE POLICY. ECONOMETRIC EXAMINATION OF DECISION-MAKING PROCESS IN REGARD TO COMPANY INCOME.

1812 MOAK L.L., KILLIAN K.W.
A MANUAL OF SUGGESTED PRACTICE FOR THE PREPARATION AND ADOPTION OF CAPITAL PROGRAMS AND CAPITAL BUDGETS BY LOCAL GOVERN
CHICAGO: MUNIC FIN OFFICERS ASSN, 1964, 152 PP., LC#64-18473
DISCUSSES PLANNING BACKGROUND FOR CAPITAL PROGRAMMING AND PREPARATION AND PRESENTATION OF CAPITAL PROGRAM AND CAPITAL BUDGET. EXAMINES LEGISLATIVE PROCEDURES IN CONSIDERING BUDGET PROPOSALS FOR LOCAL GOVERNMENT.

1813 MODESITT L.E.
"THE MUTUAL FUND - A CORPORATE ANOMALY."
UCLA LAW REV, 14 (AUG 67), 1252-1271.
DESCRIBES CORPORATE STRUCTURE OF MUTUAL INVESTMENT FUNDS. COMPARES MUTUAL FUND TO OTHER CORPORATIONS AND PRESENTS COMMON AND SINGULAR CHARACTERISTICS. ILLUSTRATES REGULATION OF MANAGEMENT COMPENSATION AND UNDERWRITING COMMISSIONS WITH EXAMPLES FROM COURT CASES. EXAMINES PROPOSED AMENDMENTS TO SECURITIES EXCHANGE ACT OF 1934 AND CONCLUDES THAT PROPOSALS ONLY CREATE NEW CONFUSION.

1814 MOHL R.V.
DIE GESCHICHTE UND LITERATUR DER STAATSWISSENSCHAFTEN (3 VOLS.)
BONN: FERDINAND ENKE VERLAG, 1855, 2053 PP.
SURVEYS HISTORY OF, AND LITERATURE ON, POLITICAL SCIENCE AND POLITICAL ECONOMY. NOT FORMALLY A BIBLIOGRAPHY, BUT AN EXTENDED TREATMENT OF MAJOR WORKS AND DEVELOPMENTS IN THE SCIENCE OF GOVERNMENT.

1815 MOLTMANN G.
"ZUR FORMULIERUNG DER AMERIKANISCHEN BESATZUNGSPOLITIK IN DEUTSCHLAND AM ENDE DES ZWEITEN WELTKRIEGES"

VIERTELJAHRSCHR ZEITGESCHICHTE, 15 (JULY 67), 299-322.
DISCUSSES FORMULATION OF US OCCUPATION POLICY IN GERMANY AFTER WWII. INCLUDES DOCUMENTARY APPENDIX OF PRESIDENTIAL MEMORANDA AND DIRECTIVES ON ELIMINATION OF HEAVY INDUSTRY, CONTROLS OVER ECONOMY, AND IMPOSITION OF MILITARY GOVERNMENT.

1816 MONCRIEFF A. ED.
SECOND THOUGHTS ON AID.
LONDON: BRITISH BROADCAST CORP, 1965, 138 PP.
BEGINS WITH ESSENTIAL BROAD POLITICAL AND PHILOSOPHICAL ISSUES FROM POINTS OF VIEW OF DONORS AND RECIPIENTS. ARGUES URGENCY OF ECONOMIC PROBLEM AND EXAMINES PRACTICES OF PRIVATE INVESTMENT AND INTERNATIONAL INSTITUTIONS. USING FACTS ABOUT AGRICULTURE, TECHNICAL ASSISTANCE, AND EDUCATION STATES THAT ROLE OF ECONOMICS MAY BE LIMITED. CONSIDERS POSSIBLE CONTRIBUTION FROM OTHER SOCIAL SCIENCE DISCIPLINES.

1817 MONROE A.D.
"BRITAIN AND THE EUROPEAN COMMUNITY."
CURR. HIST., 45 (NOV. 63), 271-275.
EFTA TOO SMALL, UNBALANCED, TOO LITTLE NATURAL COHESION TO OFFER A REAL ALTERNATIVE TO EEC. LIKE EFTA, COMMONWEALTH PRESENTS NO VIABLE ALTERNATIVE. BRITAIN MUST SEEK EITHER CLOSER ASSOCIATION WITH EEC OR DEVELOP GREATER FREEDOM IN WORLD AFFAIRS.

1818 MONTGOMERY J.D.
FOREIGN AID IN INTERNATIONAL POLITICS.
ENGLEWOOD CLIFFS: PRENTICE HALL, 1967, 118 PP., LC#67-10171.
TRACES BACKGROUND OF US FOREIGN AID IN ITS MILITARY, CAPITAL, ECONOMIC, AND TECHNOLOGICAL FORMS. ORGANIZES AID ACCORDING TO DIPLOMATIC, COMPENSATORY, AND STRATEGIC PURPOSES AND NOTES DEVELOPMENT, REFORM, AND STABILITY AS TACTICAL OBJECTIVES. CONTENDS THAT FOREIGN AID PROGRAM MUST BE JUDGED ONLY IN VIEW OF SPECIFIC OBJECTIVES. OVERALL ASSESSMENT IS NOT POSSIBLE. NOTES FUTURE OUTLOOK FOR US AID.

1820 MOONEY J.D.
"URBAN POVERTY AND LABOR FORCE PARTICIPATION."
AMER. ECO. REVIEW, 57 (MAR. 67), 104-119.
THIS STUDY TREATS THE RELATION BETWEEN UNEMPLOYMENT AND LABOR FORCE PARTICIPATION BY THE POOR. IT PROPOSES TO COMBINE CURRENT CONCERN WITH INCOME DISTRIBUTION WITH STUDIES OF THE FACTORS INFLUENCING LABOR SUPPLY. THE CONCLUSION IS THAT AS UNEMPLOYMENT FALLS THE WIFE IN AN AVERAGE NON-WHITE FAMILY GETS A JOB, THUS RAISING THE FAMILY INCOME, AND THE HUSBAND'S WAGES TEND TO RISE.

1821 MOONEY R.E. ED., DALE E.L. ED.
INFLATION AND RECESSION?
GARDEN CITY: DOUBLEDAY, 1958, 96 PP., LC#58-7577.
ANALYSIS FOR THE GENERAL PUBLIC OF DOMESTIC ECONOMIC SITUATION IN 1958, PREDICTING THAT PRICES WOULD RISE MODERATELY DURING TEMPORARY RECESSIONARY LULL. A COLLECTION OF STATEMENTS BY PUBLIC FIGURES AND ECONOMISTS, REPRESENTING DIFFERING VIEWPOINTS OF SITUATION.

1822 MOORE G.H. ED.
BUSINESS CYCLE INDICATORS (TWO VOLS.)
PRINCETON: PRINCETON U PRESS, 1961, LC#60-14062.
ESSAYS DEALING WITH GENERAL PROBLEM OF SELECTING, TESTING, AND INTERPRETING BUSINESS CYCLE INDICATORS. BEHAVIOR OF PARTICULAR TYPES OR CLOSELY RELATED GROUPS ALSO DISCUSSED. STUDY PRESENTED IN TWO VOLUMES.

1823 MOORE W.E. ED., FELDMAN A.S. ED.
LABOR COMMITMENT AND SOCIAL CHANGE IN DEVELOPING AREAS.
NEW YORK: SOCIAL SCI RES COUNCIL, 1960, 378 PP., LC#60-53440
ANALYTICAL STUDY OF NEWLY DEVELOPING AREAS, WITH PARTICULAR EMPHASIS ON PROBLEM OF LABOR MOTIVATION IN UNFAMILIAR TASKS. EXAMINES COMMITMENT OF INDUSTRIAL LABOR BOTH IN SHORT-RUN OBJECTIVE PERFORMANCE OF MODERN ECONOMIC ACTIVITY AND LONG-RUN AND DEEP-SEATED ACCEPTANCE OF ATTITUDES AND BELIEFS APPROPRIATE TO A MODERNIZED ECONOMY.

1824 MOORE W.E.
THE IMPACT OF INDUSTRY.
ENGLEWOOD CLIFFS: PRENTICE HALL, 1965, 117 PP., LC#65-23228.
INTRODUCTION TO SERIES OF STUDIES ON "MODERNIZATION OF TRADITIONAL SOCIETIES."ATTEMPTS TO PRESENT OVER-ALL VIEW OF INTERPLAY OF PROCESSES OF CHANGE. DISCUSSES WORLD INDUSTRIAL REVOLUTION; CREATION OF A COMMON CULTURE; CONDITIONS FOR INDUSTRIALIZATION; INDUSTRIAL ORGANIZATION; AND THE FUTURE OF INDUSTRIAL SOCIETY.

1825 MORALES C.J.
"TRADE AND ECONOMIC INTEGRATION IN LATIN AMERICA."
SOC. SCI., 35 (OCT. 60), 231-37.
ILLUSTRATES ARRANGEMENTS FOR ECONOMIC INTEGRATION BY LATIN AMERICAN COUNTRIES, BUT CONSIDERS ECONOMIC FOUNDATIONS NOT FAVORABLE FOR SUCH PLANS AND INDUSTRIAL DEVELOPMENT NOT SUFFICIENTLY ADVANCED. PROPOSES A TRADE FREE ZONE AS AN ALTERNATIVE SCHEME. LAFTA COUNTRIES' PLANS TO ELIMINATE TARIFFS AND OTHER TRADE BARRIERS MAY PROMOTE INTRA-REGIONAL TRADE.

1826 MOREL E.D.
AFFAIRS OF WEST AFRICA.
LONDON: HEINEMANN, 1902, 381 PP.
CONSIDERS THE RACIAL, POLITICAL, AND COMMERCIAL PROBLEMS, AND THEIR YEARLY INCREASE IN MAGNITUDE, CONNECTED WITH THE ADMINISTRATION OF WEST AFRICA BY GREAT BRITAIN AND OTHER POWERS OF WESTERN EUROPE THAT PARTICIPATED IN THE SCRAMBLE FOR AFRICAN TERRITORY. INCLUDES STUDIES OF TRIBES, PLANTATIONS, TRADE, FINANCE, AND GOVERNMENT. HAS MANY INTERESTING OLD PHOTOGRAPHS.

1827 MOREL E.D.
THE BRITISH CASE IN FRENCH CONGO.
LONDON: HEINEMANN, 1903, 215 PP.
CRITICISM OF DRASTIC MEASURES TAKEN BY FRENCH GOVERNMENT IN FRENCH CONGO TO INTERFERE WITH BRITISH TRADE AND ABUSE RIGHTS OF BRITISH MERCHANTS. ARGUES THAT CONCESSIONS DECREE OF 1899 , WHICH AUTHORIZED MEASURES, VIOLATED BERLIN ACT OF 1885 THAT ESTABLISHED RIGHT OF FREE TRADE FOR ALL NATIONS IN CONGO BASIN. ASSESSES DAMAGE DONE TO FRENCH AND BRITISH INTERESTS BY ACTIONS OF THE CONCESSIONNAIRE REGIME.

1828 MOREL E.D.
THE BLACK MAN'S BURDEN.
LONDON: NAT LABOUR PRESS, 1920, 241 PP.
EXAMINATION OF EXPLOITATION AND RACIAL RESPONSIBILITY, EMPHASIZING SLAVE TRADE AND NATIVE LAND TENURE. GIVES EXAMPLES OF SEVERAL TERRITORIES AND DISCUSSES LEAGUE OF NATIONS AS TROUBLE SHOOTER IN AFRICA.

1829 MORGAN C.A.
LABOR ECONOMICS.
HOMEWOOD: DORSEY, 1962, 657 PP., LC#62-9135.
ANALYZES MAJOR PROBLEMS OF LABOR AS THEY EMERGE IN FREE-ENTERPRISE NATION LIKE US. COVERS IMPACT OF INDUSTRIALIZATION ON LABOR MARKETS, EMPHASIZING PROBLEMS RESULTING. REVIEWS LABOR MARKET INSTITUTIONS ESTABLISHED TO SOLVE THESE PROBLEMS, INCLUDING THEIR FUNCTIONS AND LEGAL RELATIONS. DISCUSSES ROLES OF THESE INSTITUTIONS IN WHOLE SOCIETY, STRESSING NEED FOR RESPONSIBILITY.

1830 MORGAN H.W. ED.
AMERICAN SOCIALISM 1900-1960.
ENGLEWOOD CLIFFS: PRENTICE HALL, 1964, 146 PP., LC#64-14978.
STUDY OF 20TH-CENTURY SOCIALISM IN US, INCLUDING ITS ACTIVITIES IN POLITICS AND RELATION TO EXISTING ORDER. EXAMINES ITS CONNECTION WITH NEGRO, IMMIGRANT, FARMER, YOUNG INTELLECTUALS, LABOR, DEPRESSION, AND CONTEMPORARY WORLD.

1831 MORGENSTERN O.
A NEW LOOK AT ECONOMIC TIMES SERIES ANALYSIS (PAMPHLET)
PRINCETON: PRIN U ECONOMET RES, 1961, 18 PP.
STUDY SUPPORTED JOINTLY BY NATIONAL SCIENCE FOUNDATION AND OFFICE OF NAVAL RESEARCH. BRIEF ANALYSES OF RECENT WRITERS ON BUSINESS CYCLES AND DISCUSSION OF THEIR DEFICIENCIES. NOTES ADVANCEMENTS OF SPECTRAL ANALYSIS.

1832 MORGENSTERN O.
INTERNATIONAL FINANCIAL TRANSACTIONS AND BUSINESS CYCLES.
PRINCETON: U. PR., 1959, 536 PP.
DISCUSSES AND SEEKS TO EXPLAIN SPREAD OF INTERNATIONAL BUSINESS CYCLES, 1870-1938. EXPLORES INTERACTION OF INTERNATIONAL MONEY MARKETS. ANALYZES INTEREST AND EXCHANGE RATES AND THEIR EFFECTS ON FINANCE.

1833 MORGENTHAU H.J.
"A POLITICAL THEORY OF FOREIGN AID."
AMER. POLIT. SCI. REV., 56 (JUNE 62), 301-309.
SEES NEED TO DEVELOPE INTELLIGIBLE THEORY OF FOREIGN AID, SO TO PROVIDE STANDARDS FOR DISCUSSION. CLASSIFIES AID INTO 6 TYPES AND PARTICULARY DISCUSSES THE ASPECTS AND SUCCESSES OF AID 'FOR ECONOMIC DEVELOPMENT.' CONCLUDES THAT US MUST LEARN TO CHOOSE QUANTITY AND QUALITY OF AID APPROPRIATE TO SITUATION, TO ATTUNE DIFFERENT TYPES OF AID TO EACH OTHER, AND TREAT FOREIGN AID AS INTEGRAL PART OF POLITICAL POLICY.

1834 MORLEY L., MORLEY F.
THE PATCHWORK HISTORY OF FOREIGN AID.
WASHINGTON: AMER ENTERPRISE INST, 1961, 55 PP., LC#61-11619.
DISCUSSION OF AMERICAN FOREIGN AID DEVELOPMENT AND HISTORICAL SETTING AFTER WWII: AID FOR RELIEF AND RECONSTRUCTION; MARSHALL PLAN AND ECONOMIC COOPERATION ACT OF 1948; AID FOR MILITARY ALLIANCES WITH KOREA, NATIONALIST CHINA, ASIA; AID FOR ECONOMIC DEVELOPMENT; AND RIVALRY BETWEEN US AND USSR.

1835 MORRIS A.J.A.
PARLIAMENTARY DEMOCRACY IN THE NINETEENTH CENTURY.
NEW YORK: PERGAMON PRESS, 1967, 200 PP., LC#67-21276.
TRACES EVOLUTION OF BRITISH CONSTITUTION FROM TENUOUS BEGINNINGS OF PARLIAMENTARY DEMOCRACY TO EMERGENCE OF INDUSTRY AND TRADE IN 19TH CENTURY. CONSIDERS ENLARGEMENT OF FRANCHISE IN 1832 AS START OF ACTUAL DEMOCRACY STRESSES DYNAMIC NATURE OF BRITISH CONSTITUTION. DISCUSSES PARTIES, PARLIAMENT, ROYALTY, CABINET MINISTERS, CIVIL SERVICE, LOCAL GOVERNMENT, AND POLITICAL SOVEREIGNTY.

1836 MORRIS B.R.
PROBLEMS OF AMERICAN ECONOMIC GROWTH.
NEW YORK: OXFORD U PR, 1961, 279 PP., LC#61-6297.
ANALYSIS OF PROBLEMS AND ISSUES IN US ECONOMIC DEVELOPMENT. DISCUSSES LABOR FORCE, RESOURCES, INVESTMENT, TECHNOLOGY, CONSUMPTION, FOREIGN TRADE, AND GOVERNMENTAL ROLE.

1837 MORRIS M.D.
THE EMERGENCE OF AN INDUSTRIAL LABOR FORCE IN INDIA: A STUDY OF THE BOMBAY COTTON MILLS, 1854-1947.
BERKELEY: U OF CALIF PR, 1965, 263 PP., LC#65-13143.
DISCUSSES PROBLEM OF HOW A LABOR FORCE IS MOBILIZED AND ORGANIZED FOR FACTORY EMPLOYMENT DURING EARLY STAGES OF INDUSTRIALIZATION. ARGUES THAT IN PARTICULAR STUDY SUPPLY OF LABOR FOR INDUSTRIAL REQUIREMENTS WAS NOT HARD TO GET AND THAT THE LEVEL OF LABOR FORCE'S PERFORMANCE WAS ALMOST ENTIRELY SET BY NATURE OF INDUSTRIAL ORGANIZATION AND DEVELOPMENT.

1838 MORRIS W.T.
ENGINEERING ECONOMY.
HOMEWOOD: RICHARD IRWIN, 1960, 506 PP., LC#60-12922.
A PRESENTATION OF ENGINEERING ECONOMY WITHIN THE LARGER CONTEXT OF MANAGEMENT DECISION ANALYSIS. DISCUSSES FUNDAMENTALS OF ENGINEERING DECISIONS IN TERMS OF APPROACHES, GOALS, MODELS, AND CASES UNDER CERTAINTY, UNCERTAINTY, AND RISK. EXAMINES SOURCES OF INFORMATION, PREDICTION AND JUDGMENT, EVALUATION OF INTANGIBLES, REPLACEMENT POLICY, AND PROBABILITY THEORY. ANALYZES ECONOMICS OF AUTOMATION IN MANAGEMENT.

1839 MORRISSENS L., BESTERS H. ET AL.
ECONOMIC POLICY IN OUR TIME: COUNTRY STUDIES.
AMSTERDAM: NORTH HOLLAND PUBL CO, 1964, 482 PP.
DETAILED DESCRIPTION OF ECONOMIC SYSTEMS IN BELGIUM, NETHERALNDS, ITALY, FRANCE, AND WEST GERMANY IN COMPARABLE TERMS. INCLUDES DESCRIPTION OF ECONOMIC POLICIES AND BACKGROUND, 1949-61; ANALYSIS OF POLICIES FOR SHORT RANGE OBJECTIVES, I.E., EMPLOYMENT, PRICE FIXING, AND POLICIES FOR LONG-TERM OBJECTIVES OF NATIONS.

1840 MORTON H.C.
BROOKINGS PAPERS ON PUBLIC POLICY.
WASHINGTON: BROOKINGS INST, 1965, 220 PP., LC#65-18919.
HIGHLIGHTS OF 26 STUDIES ON ECONOMICS, FOREIGN POLICY, GOVERNMENTAL AFFAIRS, CONGRESS, TAXATION AND FISCAL POLICY, EDUCATION AND PUBLIC SERVICE, COMPETITION, LABOR, THE BALANCE OF PAYMENTS, AND ECONOMIC AND POLITICAL DEVELOPMENT.

1841 MORTON J.A.
"A SYSTEMS APPROACH TO THE INNOVATION PROCESS: ITS USE IN THE BELL SYSTEM."
BUSINESS HORIZONS, 10 (SUMMER 67), 27-36.
AS A PROCESS, INNOVATION CAN BE STUDIED AND MANAGED FROM SYSTEMS VIEWPOINT; IN LAB STAGE, SPECIALIZED FUNCTIONS OF BASIC RESEARCH, APPLIED RESEARCH, AND DEVELOPMENT DESIGN CAN BE PROVIDED WITH OVER-ALL GUIDANCE, JUDGMENTS, AND CATALYSIS BY SYSTEMS ENGINEERING.

1842 MOSELY P.E.
"EASTERN EUROPE IN WORLD POWER POLITICS: WHERE DE-STALINIZATION HAS LED."
MODERN AGE, 11 (SPRING 67), 119-130.
ALTHOUGH EASTERN EUROPEAN SATELLITE COUNTRIES CAN BOAST A DEFINITE NATIONAL IDENTITY AND INCREASED ECONOMIC OPPORTUNITIES, THE NECESSARY PRE-CONDITION FOR THIS FREEDOM REMAINS ALLEGIANCE TO THE BASIC TENETS OF MARXISM-LENINISM. AN ATTEMPT IS MADE TO ASSESS THE EFFECT OF KHRUSHCHEV'S DE-STALINIZATION POLICY ON MAOIST CHINA.

1843 MOSK S.A.
INDUSTRIAL REVOLUTION IN MEXICO.
BERKELEY: U OF CALIF PR, 1954, 331 PP.
ANALYZES REVOLUTION IN MEXICAN ECONOMY SINCE 1940, BASIC ATTITUDES OF INDUSTRIAL DRIVE, AND PERSPECTIVES OF BUSINESS, GOVERNMENT, AND LABOR. DISCUSSES GOVERNMENTAL POLICIES ENCOURAGING INDUSTRIAL DEVELOPMENT. SURVEYS DEVELOPMENTS IN PRINCIPAL INDUSTRIAL FIELDS.

1844 MOSKOW M.H.
TEACHERS AND UNIONS.
PHILA: U OF PENN PR, 1966, 288 PP.
STUDIES RELATIONSHIP OF US TEACHER TO ORGANIZED LABOR. DISCUSSES REASON FOR TEACHER MILITANCY AND PUBLIC ATTITUDES TOWARD TEACHERS' LOBBYING AND BARGAINING. COVERS LEGAL LIMITATION AND GENERAL POLICIES OF EDUCATIONAL ORGANIZATIONS.

1845 MOSKOWITZ M.
HUMAN RIGHTS AND WORLD ORDER.
NEW YORK: OCEANA PUBLISHING, 1958, 239 PP., LC#58-14333.
DISCUSSES STRUGGLE FOR HUMAN RIGHTS IN UN. EXAMINES PROGRAMS FOR PROMOTION OF HUMAN RIGHTS, AND MEANING AND PURPOSE OF THEIR IMPLEMENTATION.

1846 MOSS F.M.
THE WATER CRISIS.
NEW YORK: FREDERICK PRAEGER, 1967.
EXAMINES WATER PROBLEMS THE US FACES TODAY - POLLUTION, SHORTAGE, VARIABILITY, DEPLETION, AND WASTE. PROPOSES SOLUTIONS - STEPS TO REORGANIZE OUR WATER MANAGEMENT ACTIVITIES AND ACHIEVE A FUNDAMENTAL NATIONAL WATER POLICY. SUGGESTS THE CREATION OF A DEPT. OF NATURAL RESOURCES.

1847 MOULTON H.G.
CAN INFLATION BE CONTROLLED?
WASHINGTN: ANDERSON KRAMER ASSOC, 1958, 302 PP., LC#58-13970
ANALYSIS OF ALL FORCES RESPONSIBLE FOR CHANGE IN PRICE LEVEL OF COMMODITIES IN CAPITALISTIC SYSTEM. INCLUDES STUDY OF CIRCULATION OF MONEY, INTEREST RATES, INCOME, AND ANALYSIS OF WAR-TIME PRICES IN WWI AND WWII. CRITICIZES TRADITIONAL MONETARY THEORIES OF INFLATION AND SHOWS INEVITABILITY OF INFLATION FROM MONETARY VIEW. APPENDIX ANALYZES "LOGICAL AND EVIDENTIAL BASES" OF OLD THEORIES.

1848 MOUNTJOY A.B.
INDUSTRIALIZATION AND UNDER-DEVELOPED COUNTRIES (2ND REV. ED.)
LONDON: HUTCHINSON & CO, 1966, 200 PP.
GEOGRAPHER EXAMINES SOCIAL, ECONOMIC, POLITICAL, AND GEOGRAPHICAL PROBLEMS ASSOCIATED WITH INDUSTRIALIZATION. DISCUSSES DEMOGRAPHY OF UNDERDEVELOPED NATIONS, ENVIRONMENTAL PROBLEMS OF DEVELOPMENT, FORMS OF INDUSTRIALIZATION, AND PROGRESS IN GHANA, NIGERIA, CHILE, HONG KONG, INDIA, AND EGYPT. STATES THAT ALL AREAS OF SOCIETY, INCLUDING DEMOGRAPHY, MUST BE STUDIED.

1849 MOUSKHELY M.
"LE BLOC COMMUNISTE ET LA COMMUNAUTE ECONOMIQUE EUROPEENNE."
REV. ECON. POLIT., 73 (NO.3, 63), 406-38.
EXAMINES SOURCES OF USSR HOSTILITY TOWARD EEC. EXPOSES SOVIET BLOC ECONOMIC MYTHS AND EUROPEAN REALITIES. RELATES QUESTION TO LABOR PROBLEMS AND TO ECONOMIES OF AFRICAN UNDERDEVELOPED COUNTRIES.

1850 MOUSSA P.
THE UNDERPRIVILEGED NATIONS.
LONDON: SIDGWICK + JACKSON, 1962, 198 PP.
ANALYSIS OF INTERNATIONAL IMPLICATIONS OF POLITICAL AND ECONOMIC GROWTH OF UNDERDEVELOPED COUNTRIES THROUGHOUT WORLD. VIEWS PROBLEMS OF UNDERDEVELOPED COUNTRIES ON COMPARATIVE BASIS WITH CONDITIONS OF INDUSTRIALIZED, PROSPEROUS COUNTRIES. STRESSES IMPORTANCE OF POLICIES OF WORLD POWERS TOWARD POORER NATIONS IN MAINTAINING INTERNATIONAL POLITICAL STABILITY.

1851 MOWITZ R.J., WRIGHT D.S.
PROFILE OF A METROPOLIS: A CASE BOOK.
DETROIT: WAYNE STATE U PR, 1962, 688 PP., LC#62-14069.
COLLECTION OF TEN CASE STUDIES WHICH EXAMINE DECISIONS AND EVENTS TAKING PLACE IN DETROIT IN THE YEARS 1945-60. FOCUSES UPON DECISIONS IN PROBLEM AREAS CAUSED BY SLUM CLEARANCE, URBAN RENEWAL, WATER PROBLEMS, INDUSTRIAL CONSTRUCTION, EXPANSION OF PORT AND TRANSPORTATION FACILITIES.

1852 MUELLER E., MORGAN J.N.
"LOCATION DECISIONS OF MANUFACTURERS."
AMER. ECO. REVIEW, 92 (MAY 62), 204-217.
ANALYZES FACTORS GOVERNING LOCATION DECISIONS IN MANUFACTURING SECTOR OF ECONOMY, USING DATA FROM SURVEY OF "LOCATION DECISIONS AND INDUSTRIAL MOBILITY IN MICHIGAN" CONDUCTED BY SURVEY RESEARCH CENTER IN SPRING OF 1961. STUDY BASED ON PERSONAL INTERVIEWS OF TOP EXECUTIVES OF 239 MICHIGAN MANUFACTURING PLANTS.

1853 MUHAMMAD A.C.
THE EMERGENCE OF PAKISTAN.
NEW YORK: COLUMBIA U PRESS, 1967, 418 PP., LC#67-12535.
ACCOUNT OF LAST DAYS OF BRITISH EMPIRE IN INDIA AND UPHEAVALS THAT ATTENDED PARTITION OF SUBCONTINENT INTO UNION OF INDIA AND PAKISTAN. SPECIFIC PROBLEMS OF PAKISTAN IN ESTABLISHING POLITICAL AND ECONOMIC SYSTEM. RESULTING RELATION BETWEEN SECTS, STATES, AND BRITISH COMMONWEALTH.

1854 MUKERJEE R.
"POPULATION THEORY AND POLITICS (BMR)"
AMER. SOCIOLOGICAL REV., 6 (DEC. 41), 784-793.
DISCUSSES POLITICAL DEFINITION OF OPTIMUM POPULATION AND CONCEPT OF INTEGRAL OPTIMUM BASED ON COORDINATION OF LEVELS OF ECOLOGY, ECONOMY, AND GOVERNMENT. EXAMINES EFFECT OF OPTIMUM POPULATION IN ONE AREA ON ECONOMY OF SURROUNDING COUNTRIES AND RESULTING POSSIBILITIES OF WAR. STUDIES IMBALANCE OF WORLD POPULATION AND RESOURCES, FREE TRADE, AND BIRTH CONTROL AS SOLUTIONS FOR WORLD PEACE.

1855 MULLENBACH P.
CIVILIAN NUCLEAR POWER: ECONOMIC ISSUES AND POLICY FORMATION.
NEW YORK: TWENTIETH CENT. FUND, 1963, 406 PP., $8.50.
CONCERNED WITH THE EXTENT TO WHICH THE U.S. CAN MAINTAIN WORLD LEADERSHIP IN PEACETIME DEVELOPMENT OF NUCLEAR ENERGY. EVALUATES POLICY FORMATION, BASED ON ECONOMIC ANALYSIS OF THE ISSUES UNDERLYING POWER REACTOR DEVELOPMENT DURING THE

PERIOD 1953-1961.

1856 MULLER A.L.
"THE ECONOMIC POSITION OF THE ASIANS IN AFRICA."
S. AFR. J. OF ECONOMICS, 33 (JUNE 65), 114-130.
DISCUSSION OF ASIANS AS A MINORITY GROUP IN AFRICA AND THEIR CONTRIBUTION AS A LABOR FORCE IN COMMERCE, MANUAL LABOR, AND INDUSTRIES. CONDITIONS OF UNEMPLOYMENT AND INCOME ARE INCLUDED. ASIANS ARE BEING DEPRIVED OF NEAR-MONOPOLY IN CERTAIN AREAS BY AFRICANIZATION. HOPE LIES IN CLOSER TIES TO BLACK AFRICANS.

1857 MULLER A.L.
"ECONOMIC GROWTH AND MINORITIES."
AMER. J. OF ECO. AND SOC., 26 (JULY 67), 25-230.
EXAMINES RELATIONSHIP BETWEEN IMPROVEMENT OF NEGRO'S ECONOMIC POSITION AND DEVELOPMENT OF US ECONOMY. FINDS THAT NEGRO'S FINANCIAL POSITION HAS IMPROVED FASTER THAN WHITE'S, BUT IMPROVEMENT OF OCCUPATIONAL POSITION HAS PROGRESSED MORE SLOWLY THAN INCOME RATE.

1858 MULLER E.
DIE HEIMATVERTRIEBENEN IN BADEN-WURTTEMBERG.
BERLIN: DUNCKER & HUMBLOT, 1962, 185 PP.
EXAMINES SOCIAL STRUCTURE AND PROBLEMS OF ASSIMILATION INTO ECONOMY OF EAST GERMAN REFUGEES IN BADEN-WURTTEMBERG, WEST GERMANY. DISCUSSES PROBLEMS OF RELOCATION AND ASSIMILATION INTO AGRICULTURAL ECONOMY AND NATURE AND EXTENT OF PUBLIC AID.

1859 MUNBY D. ED.
ECONOMIC GROWTH IN WORLD PERSPECTIVE.
NEW YORK: ASSN OF COLLEGE PR, 1966, 380 PP., LC#66-11796.
DISCUSSES ISSUES THAT TECHNOLOGY, TRADE, FOREIGN AID, PLANNING, AND WELFARE IN INDUSTRIALIZED AND DEVELOPING COUNTRIES RAISE FOR CHRISTIAN CHURCH. EXAMINES DIFFERENT AND SIMILAR PROBLEMS IN ECONOMIC GROWTH IN AFRICA, WESTERN EUROPE, AND AMERICA. STUDIES ETHICAL ISSUES INVOLVED IN DEVELOPMENT, SUCH AS SOCIAL COST, AND ACTIVITIES OF ROMAN CATHOLIC CHURCH IN ECONOMIC PLANNING.

1860 MUND V.A.
GOVERNMENT AND BUSINESS (4TH ED.)
NEW YORK: HARPER & ROW, 1965, 385 PP., LC#65-11139.
ANALYZES WAYS IN WHICH BUSINESS AND ECONOMIC LIFE ARE SHAPED AND DIRECTED BY GOVERNMENT. STUDIES ACTION WHICH GOVERNMENT TAKES TO PROMOTE AND ENHANCE ECONOMIC WELL-BEING OF ITS CITIZENS THROUGH MEASURES DESIGNED TO ACHIEVE GROWING OUTPUT OF DESIRED GOODS AND SERVICES, AND TO PROVIDE FOR DISTRIBUTION OF THIS INCOME IN HARMONY WITH THE GENERAL WELFARE.

1861 MUNDHEIM R.H.
"SOME THOUGHTS ON THE DUTIES AND RESPONSIBILITIES OF UNAFFILIATED DIRECTORS OF MUTUAL FUNDS."
U. PENN. LAW REV., 115 (MAY 67), 1058-1072.
DISCUSSES OPINIONS THAT UNAFFILIATED DIRECTORS OF MUTUAL FUNDS HAVE NOT SAFEGUARDED INTERESTS OF SHAREHOLDERS. SUGGESTS THAT DIRECTORS BE MADE MORE AWARE OF THEIR ROLES, AND ACQUIRE SOPHISTICATED KNOWLEDGE OF SECURITIES BUSINESS. FEELS DIRECTORS SHOULD RELY ON EXPERTS AVAILABLE TO THE FUND.

1862 MUNZI U.
"THE EUROPEAN SOCIAL FUND IN THE DEVELOPMENT OF THE MEDITERRANEAN REGIONS OF THE EEC."
J. INT. AFFAIRS, 19 (1965), 286-296.
EUROPEAN SOCIAL FUND'S PURPOSE IS TO TRAIN OR RETRAIN UNSKILLED LABORERS AND/OR RELOCATE THEM IN ANOTHER REGION. FUND HAS OPERATED SATISFACTORILY HERE, BUT IT NOW MUST TURN ATTENTION TO PROBLEM OF IMPROPER UTILIZATION OF LABOR WHICH IS BRINGING ABOUT A DISSIPATION OF RESOURCES. THE LABORER WHOSE SKILLS ARE BECOMING OBSOLETE HAS THUS FAR NOT BEEN GIVEN ENOUGH AID.

1863 MURDESHWAR A.K.
ADMINISTRATIVE PROBLEMS RELATING TO NATIONALISATION: WITH SPECIAL REFERENCE TO INDIAN STATE ENTERPRISES.
BOMBAY: POPULAR BOOK DEPOT, 1957, 330 PP.
DEVELOPS THEORY REGARDING ORGANIZATION AND ADMINISTRATION OF NATIONALIZED UNDERTAKINGS BASED ON EXPERIENCE OF NATIONALIZED CONCERNS AND STATE ENTERPRISES IN BRITAIN, FRANCE, CZECHOSLOVAKIA AND US. DISCUSSES VARIOUS PROBLEMS OF ALL NATIONALIZED ENTERPRISES AND INDIA'S IN PARTICULAR; THOSE OF LABOR, COMPOSITION OF GOVERNING BOARD, PARLIAMENTARY CONTROL, VOICE OF CONSUMER, STAFF, FINANCE, PRICE, POLICY.

1864 MURPHEY R.
"ECONOMIC CONFLICTS IN SOUTH ASIA."
J. CONFL. RESOLUT., 4 (MAR. 60), 83-95.
DISCUSSES AREA'S ECONOMIC SITUATION INCLUDING PROSPECTS FOR INDUSTRIALIZATION, ECONOMIC INDEPENDENCE, INCREASING PER CAPITA INCOME, AND THE GENERATION AND CONTROL OF CAPITAL. CONCLUDES CONFLICTS ARISE FROM THE FRUSTRATION OF ASIAN AMBITIONS, DERIVED FROM WESTERN MODELS, WHICH DO NOT COINCIDE WITH CIRCUMSTANCES.

1865 MURPHY G.G.
SOVIET MONGOLIA: A STUDY OF THE OLDEST POLITICAL SATELLITE.
BERKELEY: U OF CALIF PR, 1966, 224 PP., LC#66-22455.
DISCUSSES RELATIONSHIP BETWEEN OUTER MONGOLIA AND USSR FROM 1921-1960. EXAMINES SOCIAL, POLITICAL, AND ECONOMIC CONDITIONS AND TRANSITION TO PLANNED ECONOMY. DISCUSSES COSTS AND BENEFITS OF SATELLITESHIP.

1866 MURPHY J.C.
"SOME IMPLICATIONS OF EUROPE'S COMMON MARKET.
IN (COOK P, ECONOMIC DEVELOPMENT AND INTERNATIONAL TRADE,."
DALLAS: SOUTHERN METHODIST U. PR., 1959, P. 33-49).
RAISES TWO QUESTIONS: 1)WILL GEOGRAPHIC DISTRIBUTION OF PRODUCTION AND PATTERN OF TRADE BENEFIT EUROPE AND FREE WORLD, AND 2)WILL COMMON MARKET LEAD TO LARGER SCALE ECONOMIC PRODUCTION. SUPPORTS AFFIRMATIVE ANSWER TO BOTH QUESTIONS.

1867 MURPHY J.C.
"INTERNATIONAL INVESTMENT AND THE NATIONAL INTEREST."
S. ECON. J., 22 (JULY 60), 11-17.
SINCE NATIONAL AND PRIVATE INTERESTS DIVERGE IN MATTER OF FOREIGN INVESTMENT, QUESTIONS THESIS THAT NATIONAL ECONOMIC INTEREST JUSTIFIES STIMULATING PRIVATE FOREIGN INVESTMENT. CONCLUDES THAT PRIVATE COMPARISON OF RATE OF RETURN ON INVESTMENT AT HOME AND ABROAD INADEQUATE GUIDE TO INVESTING IN THE NATIONAL INTEREST.

1868 MURTY B.S.
PROPAGANDA AND WORLD PUBLIC ORDER.
NEW HAVEN: YALE U PR, 1967, 320 PP., LC#68-24505.
EMPLOYS A POLICY-ORIENTED JURISPRUDENTIAL APPROACH TO SEEK SOLUTIONS TO PROBLEMS OF REGULATION OF PROPAGANDA. SUGGESTS THAT NEW POLICIES MUST AIM AT PROMOTING FREEDOM OF INFORMATION AND MAINTAINING WORLD PUBLIC ORDER. EMPHASIZES PRESENT AND POTENTIAL ROLE OF UN IN REGULATING USE OF PROPAGANDA.

1869 MURUMBI J., NEWMAN P.K. ET AL.
PROBLEMS OF ECONOMIC DEVELOPMENT IN EAST AFRICA.
NAIROBI: EAST AFRICA PUBL HOUSE, 1965, 107 PP.
INCLUDES TEN PAPERS ON ECONOMIC PLANNING, MANPOWER UTILIZATION, AND REGIONAL DEVELOPMENT. PUBLISHED AS SECOND IN SERIES BY EAST AFRICAN INSTITUTE OF SOCIAL AND CULTURAL AFFAIRS. ECONOMIC PROBLEMS, TRENDS, SOCIALISM, AGRICULTURAL DEVELOPMENT, INDUSTRIAL LOCATION, TAX STRUCTURE, ROLE OF CENTRAL BANK, WAGES, AND EMPLOYMENT ARE TOPICS TREATED.

1870 MUSGRAVE R.A. ED., PEACOCK A.T. ED.
CLASSICS IN THE THEORY OF PUBLIC FINANCE.
LONDON: MACMILLAN, 1958, 244 PP.
CHRONOLOGICALLY ARRANGED SELECTIONS FROM LITERATURE ON PUBLIC FINANCE CONCENTRATING ON PROBLEM OF OPTIMUM DISTRIBUTION OF RESOURCES BETWEEN GOVERNMENT AND PRIVATE SECTOR. INCLUDES WORKS OF EMIL SAY, EDGEWORTH, ERIK LINDAHL, AND HANS RITSCHL.

1871 MUSHKIN S.J.
LOCAL SCHOOL EXPENDITURES: 1970 PROJECTIONS (PAMPHLET)
CHICAGO: COUNCIL OF STATE GOVTS, 1965, 84 PP.
SEEKS TO ESTIMATE THE REVENUES IN THE 50 STATES AND THE DISTRICT OF COLUMBIA, AND TO PROJECT EXPENDITURES IN PUBLIC EDUCATION UNDER ASSUMED ECONOMIC AND DEMOGRAPHIC CONDITIONS. ESTIMATES NUMBER OF SCHOOL CHILDREN AND TEACHERS, TEACHERS' PAY, AND NON-INSTRUCTIONAL SCHOOL COSTS SUCH AS MAINTENANCE AND BUILDING.

1872 MUSHKIN S.J.
PROPERTY TAXES: THE 1970 OUTLOOK (PAMPHLET)
CHICAGO: COUNCIL OF STATE GOVTS, 1965, 62 PP.
STUDY OF STATE AND LOCAL FINANCES ESTIMATES REVENUES IN 50 STATES AND D.C. FOR 1970, AND PROJECTS EXPENDITURES FOR MAJOR PROGRAM AREAS WITHIN A PATTERN OF DEMOGRAPHIC AND ECONOMIC ASSUMPTIONS. PROJECTS SPENDING AND TAXING UNDER ASSUMED CONDITIONS OF HIGH EMPLOYMENT AND GROWTH OF NATIONAL OUTPUT. SECTIONS DIVIDED INTO BACKGROUND AND ISSUES, SUMMARY OF FINDINGS, AND METHOD OF PROJECTIONS.

1873 MUSOLF L.D.
PUBLIC OWNERSHIP AND ACCOUNTABILITY: THE CANADIAN EXPERIENCE
CAMBRIDGE: HARVARD U PR, 1959, 174 PP., LC#59-10319.
DISCUSSION OF PUBLIC CORPORATIONS IN CANADA: THEIR ORGANIZATION, MANAGEMENT, AND MEANS OF HOLDING THEM ACCOUNTABLE TO THE GOVERNMENT.

1874 MUSOLF L.D.
PROMOTING THE GENERAL WELFARE: GOVERNMENT AND THE ECONOMY.
GLENVIEW, ILL: SCOTT, FORESMAN, 1965, 204 PP.
EXPLORATION OF ECONOMIC ACTIVITIES OF FEDERAL GOVERNMENT AS PROMOTER, REGULATOR, BUYER, AND MANAGER. DISCUSSES HOW THESE OPERATIONS PROMOTE GENERAL WELFARE.

1875 MYRDAL G.
THE POLITICAL ELEMENT IN THE DEVELOPMENT OF ECONOMIC THEORY.
LONDON: ROUTLEDGE & KEGAN PAUL, 1961, 248 PP.
ANALYZES ECONOMIC THEORY OF PAST AS EVOLVING BODY OF

IDEAS THAT CANNOT BE TAKEN OUT OF CONTEXT OF SOCIETY'S VALUES AND GOALS THAT CREATED THEM. IN ANALYSIS HE POINTS OUT FALLACIES BETWEEN THEORY AND FACTS OF SOCIETY THAT DEVELOPED THEORY. FEELS POLITICAL CONCLUSIONS CAN BE DRAWN FROM ECONOMIC THEORY BY ADDING VALUES OF SOCIETY TO FACTUAL DATA.

1876 MYERS C.A., TURNBULL J.G.
"LINE AND STAFF IN INDUSTRIAL RELATIONS."
HARVARD BUSINESS REV., 34 (JULY-AUG. 56), 113-124.
RESULTS OF STUDY ON PLACE OF INDUSTRIAL RELATIONS DIRECTOR IN INDUSTRY, HIS VIEW OF OWN ROLE, HIS CONTROL OVER PERSONNEL POLICIES AND DECISIONS, HIS PART IN CONTRACT NEGOTIATIONS, HIS PROBLEMS. CONCLUSIONS ARE THAT ROLE SHOULD BE LIMITED TO THAT OF ADVICE AND CONTROL IN SITUATIONS WHICH INVOLVE LINE SUPERVISOR, VARYING ACCORDING TO COMPANY NEED.

1877 MYERS S.
"TECHNOLOGY AND URBAN TRANSIT: THE ENORMOUS POTENTIAL OF BUS AND RAIL SYSTEMS."
BUSINESS HORIZONS, 10 (SUMMER 67),63-70.
SUGGESTS THAT EXISTING RAIL AND BUS SYSTEMS CAN BE GREATLY IMPROVED USING TODAY'S TECHNOLOGY, WHILE RESEARCH GOES ON SEEKING NEW FORMS. TRANSPORTATION IMPROVEMENT SHOULD BE MADE IN QUALITY RATHER THAN QUANTITY OF TRANSPORT SYSTEMS; USE OF ELECTRONIC HIGHWAY CONTROL AND OFF-PEAK PRICING IS SUGGESTED.

1878 HLA MYINT U.
THE ECONOMICS OF THE DEVELOPING COUNTRIES.
LONDON: HUTCHINSON & CO, 1964, 192 PP.
ANALYZES POST-WAR ECONOMIC STATUS OF DEVELOPING NATIONS. EXAMINES EXPORTS, MONETARY SYSTEM, MINING, AGRICULTURE, POPULATION GROWTH, ECONOMIC PROGRAMS, AND PATTERNS OF DEVELOPMENT POLICY.

1879 MYRDAL G.
AN INTERNATIONAL ECONOMY.
NEW YORK: HARPER, 1956, 335 PP.
EXAMINES PROBLEMS OF ACHIEVING WORLD-WIDE ECONOMIC INTEGRATION. NOTES THAT PRESENT TREND IS TOWARDS GREATER INEQUALITY. DEALS WITH ECONOMIC EFFECTS OF THE COLD WAR ON NON-SOVIET WORLD.

1880 MYRDAL G.
RICH LANDS AND POOR: THE ROAD TO WORLD PROSPERITY.
NEW YORK: HARPER, 1958, 168 PP.
FOCUSING ON ECONOMIC INEQUALITIES BETWEEN DEVELOPED AND UNDERDEVELOPED COUNTRIES, INQUIRES HOW AND WHY INEQUALITIES ORIGINATE, WHY THEY PERSIST AND TEND TO INCREASE. PRESENTS PHILOSOPHICAL BASIS OF ECONOMIC THEORY.

1881 MYRDAL G.
BEYOND THE WELFARE STATE: ECONOMIC PLANNING AND ITS IMPLICATIONS.
NEW HAVEN: YALE U. PR., 1960, 287 PP.
PLANNING PROBLEMS, GOALS, AND PROGRAMS IN WEST, SOVIET UNION, AND UNDERDEVELOPED COUNTRIES REVIEWED, COMPARED AND CONTRASTED. CAUSES OF INTERNATIONAL INSTABILITY EXAMINED. INDIVIDUAL NATIONS CRITICIZED FOR REFUSING LIMITS ON FREEDOM IN ECONOMIC PLANNING.

1882 MYRDAL G.
CHALLENGE TO AFFLUENCE.
LONDON: VICTOR GOLLANCZ, 1963, 172 PP., LC#63-19684.
AUTHOR FEELS THAT AMERICAN ECONOMIC STAGNATION IS PRINCIPAL WORLD PROBLEM. DESCRIBES THE DYNAMICS OF THAT STAGNATION AND ITS INTERNATIONAL IMPLICATIONS, ESPECIALLY REGARDING THE SOVIET BLOC AND WESTERN EUROPE.

1883 MYRDAL G.
"ECONOMIC DEVELOPMENT IN THE BACKWARD COUNTRIES."
DISSENT, (MAR.-APR. 67), 180-190.
UNDERDEVELOPED COUNTRIES MUST INDUSTRIALIZE AS FAST AS POSSIBLE TO PREVENT REGRESSION IN LIVING STANDARDS. LARGE GROWTH OF LABOR FORCE NECESSITATES THAT THERE ARE ALSO CREATED NUMEROUS AGRICULTURAL JOBS. POPULATION PLANNING CANNOT IN LESS THAN 20 YEARS AFFECT FANTASTIC RISE IN LABOR POPULATION. DISCUSSION OF INTERNATIONAL ECONOMICS AS USEFUL TO GROWTH OF THESE NATIONS.

1884 MINNESOTA LAW REVIEW EDITORS
"UNION INVESTMENT IN BUSINESS: A SOURCE OF UNION CONFLICT OF INTEREST."
MINN. LAW REV., 46 (JAN. 62), 573-598.
UNIONS NOW CONTROL OVER FOUR BILLION DOLLARS IN INVESTMENT CAPITAL; PRESENT LEGISLATION AND INTERNAL UNION CONTROLS ARE INEFFECTIVE IN COPING WITH THE RESULTANT PROBLEMS. UNION FUNDS CAN BE USED TO EXPAND MARKETS FOR A UNIONIZED EMPLOYER AN A CONFLICT OF INTEREST IS CREATED. FUNDS CAN ALSO BE INVESTED IN A COMPETITOR FIRM ON A DECISION TAKEN MOSTLY BY THE INTERNATIONAL UNION.

1885 COLUMBIA LAW REVIEW EDITORS
"QUASI-LEGISLATIVE ARBITRATION AGREEMENTS."
COLUMBIA LAW REV., 64 (JAN. 64), 109-126.
RE-EVALUATES THE ATTITUDES OF MANAGEMENT, LABOR, AND THE COURTS TOWARD ARBITRATION AS A MEANS OF RESOLVING DISPUTES AND AS A SUBSTITUTE FOR ECONOMIC FORCE. PROBES LETHAL EFFECTS OF CLOSING AN ESSENTIAL INDUSTRY AND ARGUES USE OF AGREEMENTS IN ADVANCE TO ARBITRATE FUTURE DISPUTES NOT SETTLED DURING NEGOTIATIONS AS A BETTER REPRESENTATIONAL TECHNIQUE THAN FORCE OR COSTLY STRIKES.

1886 NADLER E.B.
"SOME ECONOMIC DISADVANTAGES OF THE ARMS RACE."
J. CONFL. RESOLUT., 7 (SEPT. 63), 503-09.
STUDIES WAYS IN WHICH GROWTH OF MILITARY-INDUSTRIAL COMPLEX PREVENTS EFFECTIVE CONTROL OF AMERICAN ECONOMY. PROBLEM CONTRIBUTES TO BUSINESS STAGNATION AND UNEMPLOYMENT. OFFERS SOLUTIONS.

1887 NAGEL P.C.
ONE NATION INDIVISIBLE: THE UNION IN AMERICAN THOUGHT 1776-1861.
NEW YORK: OXFORD U PR, 1964, 328 PP., LC#64-11235.
EXAMINES ONE CENTURY OF PUBLIC FEELING TOWARD IDEA OF THE UNION; FINDS PATTERN OF PERSISTING CULT: AMERICA, UNEASY IN MIDST OF POLITICAL AND TECHNOLOGICAL CHANGE, STRUGGLED TO MAINTAIN AGREEMENT ON TACTICS AND GOALS OF MAN IN POLITICAL SOCIETY. THE UNION BECAME SUPREME IDEAL AND PROVED A REASSURING SYMBOL OF THE AMERICAN DREAM.

1888 NAMBOODIRIPAD E.M.
ECONOMICS AND POLITICS OF INDIA'S SOCIALIST PATTERN.
NEW DELHI: PEOPLE'S PUBL HOUSE, 1966, 419 PP.
DISCUSSES AND ASSESSES PLANNED ECONOMY IN INDIA SINCE INDEPENDENCE. MAINTAINS THAT INDIA HAS FAILED TO BUILD A SOCIALIST SOCIETY AND THAT CAPITALIST FORMS OF EXPLOITATION ARE PERPETUATED ON EVER-INCREASING SCALE.

1889 NANES A., EFRON R.
"THE EUROPEAN COMMUNITY AND THE UNITED STATES: EVOLVING RELATIONS."
REV. POLIT., 22 (APR. 60), 175-86.
TRACES DEVELOPMENT OF EUROPEAN ECONOMIC INTEGRATION, FOCUSING ON COMMON MARKET AND EURATOM. REVIEW USA POSITIONS ON UNILATERAL INSPECTION AND DISCUSS 1960 DILLON PROPOSALS FOR ECONOMIC REORGANIZATION AND AID TO UNDERDEVELOPED COUNTRIES.

1890 NANIWADA H.
STAAT UND WIRTSCHAFT; GRUNDLEGUNG DER NATIONALOEKONOMIE ALS DER LOGIK DER BURGERLICHEN GESELLSCHAFT.
TOKYO: SCIENCE COUN OF JAPAN, 1957, 76 PP.
THEORETICAL STUDY OF RELATIONS BETWEEN STATE AND BOURGEOIS ECONOMY, CONSIDERING FREE ECONOMY; CONSTITUTIONAL STATE; CYCLICAL ASPECTS OF BOURGEOIS ECONOMY; KEYNES AND MARX; MARXISM AND LENINISM; ECONOMY AND POLITICAL SYSTEM IN SOCIALISM. TRUTH LIES BETWEEN CAPITALISM AND SOCIALISM.

1891 NARASIMHAN V.K.
DEMOCRACY AND MIXED ECONOMY.
BOMBAY: POPULAR PRAKASHAN, 1965, 84 PP.
CONCERNED WITH PRESERVATION OF VALUES OF FREE SOCIETY IN COUNTRY UNDERGOING INCREASED STATE CONTROL. DISCUSSES BEGINNINGS OF AND CHANGES IN RELATIONSHIP BETWEEN COMMUNISM CAPITALISM, BASIS, JUSTIFICATION, AND LIMITS LIMITS OF STATE INTERFERENCE AND PRESSURES OF POPULATION GROWTH ON NATURAL RESOURCES. MAINTAINS THAT STATE INTERVENTION MUST BE CONTROLLED AND PRIVATE ENTERPRISE INCLUDED IN DEVELOPMENT.

1892 NARVER J.C.
CONGLOMERATE MERGERS AND MARKET COMPETITION.
BERKELEY: U OF CALIF PR, 1967, 155 PP., LC#67-11444.
AUTHOR DEFINES CONGLOMERATE FIRM AS "A MARKET DIVERSIFIED FIRM" OPERATING IN "TWO OR MORE SEPARATE PRODUCT AND/OR GEOGRAPHIC MARKETS," AND HE DISCUSSES THE SEVERAL FACTORS IN CONGLOMERATE MERGERS LEADING TO THEIR ABILITY TO AFFECT COMPETITION. ANALYZES UNDER WHAT CONDITIONS MERGERS INCREASE OR LESSEN COMPETITION IN A MARKET, MARKET STRUCTURE, AND MANAGERIAL BEHAVIOR.

1893 NASH M. ED., CHIN R. ED.
"PSYCHO-CULTURAL FACTORS IN ASIAN ECONOMIC GROWTH."
J. SOC. ISSUES, 19 (JAN. 63), 1-87.
ARTICLES ON CHARACTERISTICS OF ASIAN ECONOMIC GROWTH, BY VARIOUS EXPERTS. ATTEMPTS TO DEMONSTRATE THAT PSYCHOLOGY, SOCIOLOGY, AND ANTHROPOLOGY SHOULD PLAY AN IMPORTANT ROLE IN SHAPING ECONOMIC POLICY AND IN CONDUCTING ECONOMIC RESEARCH FOR ASIA.

1894 NASH M.
"SOCIAL PREREQUISITES TO ECONOMIC GROWTH IN LATIN AMERICA AND SOUTHEAST ASIA."
ECON. DEVELOP. CULT. CHANGE, 12(APR 64), 225-42.
COMPARATIVE STUDY OF MODERNIZING NATION IN LATIN AMERICA AND A NEWLY INDEPENDENT NATION OF SOUTHEAST ASIA. EMPLOYS MACRO-STRUCTURAL ANALYSIS AND MICRO-ANALYSIS TO FIT ROLE PERCEPTIONS IN THEIR INSTUTIONAL CONTEXT.

1895 NATIONAL BUREAU ECONOMIC RES
THE RATE AND DIRECTION OF INVENTIVE ACTIVITY: ECONOMIC AND SOCIAL FACTORS.
PRINCETON: PRINCETON U PRESS, 1962, 626 PP., LC#62-7044.
SELECTION OF PAPERS FROM CONFERENCE OF UNIVERSITIES-NATTIONAL BUREAU COMMITTEE FOR ECONOMIC RESEARCH AND COMMITTEE ON ECONOMIC GROWTH OF SOCIAL SCIENCE RESEARCH COUNCIL. DEALS WITH RECENT RESEARCH INTO PROCESS OF INVENTION IN ECONOMIC GROWTH, INDUSTRIAL ORGANIZATION, DEFENSE ECONOMICS, AND MANAGEMENT SCIENCE.

1897 NATIONAL CENTRAL LIBRARY
LATIN AMERICAN ECONOMIC AND SOCIAL SERIALS.
LONDON: NATIONAL CENTRAL LIBRARY, 1965.
LIST OF SERIALS IN LIBRARIES OF LONDON PERTAINING TO LATIN AMERICAN SOCIAL AND ECONOMIC DEVELOPMENT.

1898 NATIONAL COMN COMMUNITY HEALTH
ACTION - PLANNING FOR COMMUNITY HEALTH SERVICES (PAMPHLET)
WASHINGTON: PUBLIC AFFAIRS PRESS, 1967, 67 PP., LC#67-19824.
REPORTS ON COMMUNITY ACTION STUDIES PROJECT TO STUDY COMMUNITY-SUPPORTED IMPROVEMENTS IN HEALTH SERVICES. PRESENTS FINDINGS ON FUNCTIONING OF COMMUNITY ACTION PROGRAMS, STEPS IN PROCESS, AND RESULTS IN INCREASED SERVICES. DISCUSSES NEED FOR DEFINITION OF AREA INVOLVED, COOPERATION OF HEALTH ASSOCIATIONS, DEFINITE BUDGET, CORRECT TIMING, AND FAVORABLE PUBLIC OPINION.

1899 NATIONAL CONF SOCIAL WELFARE
THE SOCIAL WELFARE FORUM, 1965.
NEW YORK: COLUMBIA U PRESS, 1965, 292 PP., LC#08-85377.
A SERIES OF PAPERS PRESENTED AT THE CONFERENCE ON SUCH TOPICS AS CIVIL RIGHTS, POVERTY, SOCIAL CHANGE COMMUNITY SERVICES AND COMMUNITY ACTION, AND THE ROLE OF RELIGIOUSLY SPONSORED SOCIAL WELFARE AGENCIES, REPLETE WITH REFERENCES TO VOLUNTARY AGENCIES AND ORGANIZATIONAL CHANGE.

1900 NATIONAL COUN APPLIED ECO RES
A STRATEGY FOR THE FOURTH PLAN.
NEW DELHI: NATL COUN APPL ECO RES, 1964, 85 PP.
DECRIBES FOURTH PLAN TO PROVIDE EMPLOYMENT, ENSURE MINIMUM LEVEL OF LIVING, AND NARROW ECONOMIC AND SOCIAL DISPARITIES. CALLS FOR RATIONING AND EQUAL DISTRIBUTION OF FOOD, INCREASED RURAL WORKS PROGRAM, AND TRAINING OF WORKERS IN VARIETY OF SKILLS.

1901 NATIONAL COUN APPLIED ECO RES
DEVELOPMENT WITHOUT AID.
NEW DELHI: NATL COUN APPL ECO RES, 1966, 95 PP.
DISCUSSES PROBLEMS FOR INDIA RESULTING FROM LITTLE OR NO ECONOMIC AID. PROPOSES INCREASED FOREIGN AID AND USE OF OPPORTUNITIES FOR SELF-RELIANCE. AID SHOULD BE PLANNED TOWARD GRADUAL REDUCTION AS ECONOMY BECOMES MORE SELF-SUSTAINING. DEPENDS ON SAVINGS, EXPORTS, EFFECTIVE UTILIZATION OF AID, IMPORT SUBSTITUTES, AND TECHNOLOGICAL DEVELOPMENT.

1902 NATIONAL INDUSTRIAL CONF BOARD
GOLD AND WORLD MONETARY PROBLEMS.
NEW YORK: NATL IND CONF BD, 1966, 240 PP., LC#66-29051.
ANALYSES AND EVALUATIONS OF FUNCTION OF GOLD IN INTERNATIONAL FINANCIAL SYSTEM. COVERS CHANGING ROLE OF GOLD IN WORLD'S EVOLVING MONETARY SYSTEMS. FEELS MORE GOLD SHOULD BE KEPT FOR OFFICIAL RESERVES TO MEET LIQUIDITY NEEDS OF FUTURE ESPECIALLY SINCE US HAS INCURRED LARGE BALANCE-OF-PAYMENTS DEFICITS IN PAST EIGHT YEARS.

1903 NAUMANN R.
THEORIE UND PRAXIS DES NEOLIBERALISMUS; DAS MAERCHEN VON DER FREIEN ODER SOZIALEN MARKTWIRTSCHAFT.
BERLIN: VERLAG DER WIRTSCHAFT, 1957, 414 PP.
EXPOSES THE "MYTH" OF THE FREE OR SOCIAL MARKET-ECONOMY, ESPOUSED BY THE ADENAUER REGIME. SEES NEOLIBERALISM AS IDEOLOGICAL WEAPON OF DECLINING CAPITALISM; DESCRIBES THEORY AND PRACTICE OF NEOLIBERALISM; CONSIDERS IT A WAR ECONOMY AND ASOCIAL.

1904 NEAL A.C.
"NEW ECONOMIC POLICIES FOR THE WEST."
FOR. AFF., 39 (JAN. 61), 247-58.
RECOMMENDS RE-EXAMINATION OF USA FOREIGN ECONOMIC POLICY IN DEVELOPING COUNTRIES. MOST IMPORTANT GOALS ARE TO PROMOTE MAXIMUM UNITY AMONG OUR STRONGEST ALLIES, INFLUENCE DEVELOPING COUNTRIES TOWARD LIBERAL ECONOMIC SYSTEMS, AND FRUSTRATE USSR BLOC PLANS TO EXPAND INFLUENCE.

1905 NEALE A.D.
THE FLOW OF RESOURCES FROM RICH TO POOR.
CAMBRIDGE: HARV CTR INTL AFFAIRS, 1960, 83 PP.
DISCUSSES PROBLEMS ENCOUNTERED BY HEALTHY NATIONS IN MOBILIZING AND TRANSFERRING RESOURCES TO POORER NATIONS. ADVOCATES INCREASE IN SPEED AND AMOUNT OF FLOW OF RESOURCES FROM RICH TO POOR NATIONS AND ATTRIBUTES LIMITATIONS OF VOLUME OF AID TO POOR NATIONS TO POLITICAL RATHER THAN ECONOMIC FACTORS.

1906 NEALE R.S.
"WORKING CLASS WOMEN AND WOMEN'S SUFFRAGE."
LABOR HISTORY, (MAY 67), 16-34.
EXAMINES WOMEN'S DEMAND FOR FRANCHISE AND PART PLAYED BY WORKING-CLASS WOMEN IN ORIGIN OF MILITANT, SUFFRAGETTE PHASE OF DEMAND. DISCUSSES WAGE DIFFERENTIATION, TRADE UNIONISM AMONG WOMEN. EMPHASIZES INCIDENT INVOLVING ANNIE KENNEDY'S QUESTION TO SIR EDWARD GREY ABOUT LIBERAL GOVERNMENT GIVING VOTES TO WOMEN. SAYS WORKING-CLASS WOMEN'S PARTICIPATION WAS SLIGHT AND INEFFECTIVE.

1907 NEHEMKIS P.
LATIN AMERICA: MYTH AND REALITY.
NEW YORK: ALFRED KNOPF, 1964, 286 PP.
ATTEMPTS TO EXPOSE IMMENSITY OF FALSE INFORMATION CONCERNING LATIN AMERICA WHICH PREVENTS MUTUAL UNDERSTANDING BETWEEN LATIN AND NORTH AMERICANS CONCERNING THEIR RESPECTIVE POLITICAL AND CULTURAL HERITAGES. EMPHASIS IS ON LATIN AMERICAN POLITICAL DISORDERS AND ECONOMIC PROBLEMS.

1908 NEISSER H., MODIGLIANI
NATIONAL INCOMES AND INTERNATIONAL TRADE.
URBANA: U OF ILLINOIS PR, 1953, 396 PP., LC#52-12404.
STUDY AIMS TO ESTABLISH IN QUANTITATIVE TERMS THE RELATION BETWEEN FOREIGN TRADE AND LEVEL OF DOMESTIC ECONOMIC ACTIVITIES OF VARIOUS COUNTRIES PARTICIPATING IN INTERNATIONAL EXCHANGE. PERIOD COVERED IS ROUGHLY YEARS BETWEEN WWI AND WWII.

1909 NEISSER H.
"ECONOMIC IMPERIALISM RECONSIDERED."
SOC. RES., 27 (MAR. 60), 63-82.
REVIEWING MAJOR THEORIES OF ECONOMIC IMPERIALISM, REJECTS THESIS THAT FOREIGN INVESTMENT IS A NECESSARY CONCOMITANT OF DEVELOPED CAPITALISM. REFUTING CRITICISM OF CAPITALISM, THAT UNDERCONSUMPTION OR OVERSAVING INHERENT IN SYSTEM, CONCLUDES THAT RESTORING CYCLICAL PROSPERITY NOT DEPENDENT ON CAPITAL EXPORTS.

1910 NEISSER H.
"THE EXTERNAL EQUILIBRIUM OF THE UNITED STATES ECONOMY."
SOC. RES., 31 (SUMMER 64), 214-233.
DISCUSSION OF AMERICAN BALANCE OF PAYMENTS PROBLEM. FAVORS SOME LIMITATION OF OVERSEAS CAPITAL INVESTMENT. FEELS A HIGHER DOMESTIC INTEREST RATE WOULD HELP WITHOUT RETARDING INDUSTRIAL INVESTMENT. SEES FAVORABLE OUTLOOK FOR IMPROVEMENT OF UNITED STATES POSITION IN THE LATE SIXTIES.

1911 NELSON J.R., PALMER D.K.
"UNITED STATES FOREIGN ECONOMIC POLICY AND THE STERLING AREA."
PRINCETON: CENT. INT. STUD., 1953, 44 PP.
PRESENTS PROBLEMS OF STERLING AREA, PARTICULARLY THOSE DEVELOPED DURING OR AFTER 1939. INCLUDES BRIEF STUDY OF ITS BACKGROUND AND OFFERS APPRAISAL OF STERLING AREA ITSELF. SUGGESTS NEW DIRECTIONS FOR US FOREIGN ECONOMIC POLICY IN THIS AREA.

1912 NELSON R.R., PECK M.J., KALACHEK E.D.
TECHNOLOGY, ECONOMIC GROWTH, AND PUBLIC POLICY.
WASHINGTON: BROOKINGS INST, 1967, 238 PP., LC#67-14973.
RELATES ECONOMY TO TECHNOLOGICAL ADVANCE, UNEMPLOYMENT, INTEGRATION OF DEVELOPMENT INTO ECONOMY. RESEARCH AND INNOVATION ARE TIED TO GROWTH. ANALYZES IMPACT UPON ECONOMY, GOVERNMENT POLICY, AND PUBLIC. PROPOSES CHANGES IN PUBLIC POLICY. CREATES UNDERSTANDING BASIC TO COMPREHENSION OF PUBLIC POLICY.

1913 NENAROKOV A.P.
RUSSIA IN THE 20TH CENTURY: THE OFFICIAL SOVIET HISTORY.
NEW YORK: WILLIAM MORROW, 1968, 350 PP.
FROM SOVIET POINT OF VIEW PORTRAYS EVENTS OF 20TH CENTURY THAT TRANSFORMED RUSSIA. COMPARES IMPERIAL RUSSIA AS PRESENTED AT FIRST WORLD EXHIBITION IN PARIS IN 1900 TO REAL RUSSIA. STUDIES REVOLUTION OF 1917 AND CHANGES IN ECONOMIC AND SOCIAL LIFE. EXAMINES USSR AND ITS ACHIEVEMENTS ON ITS 50TH ANNIVERSARY IN 1967.

1914 NEUFIELD M.F.
A REPRESENTATIVE BIBLIOGRAPHY OF AMERICAN LABOR HISTORY.
ITHACA: NY STATE SCH IND & LABOR, 1964, 146 PP., LC#64-63608
BIBLIOGRAPHY CONTAINS APPROXIMATELY 2,000 BOOKS, ARTICLES, AND GOVERNMENT PUBLICATIONS FROM 1910-63 ON HISTORY OF AMERICAN LABOR. ENTRIES ARE ARRANGED UNDER TOPICS OF PERIODS OF DEVELOPMENT, LABOR MOVEMENTS, INFLUENCE ON INTERNATIONAL AFFAIRS, THEORIES OF MOVEMENTS, AND OCCUPATIONS AND INDUSTRIES INVOLVED.

1915 NEUMARK S.D.
ECONOMIC INFLUENCES ON THE SOUTH AFRICAN FRONTIER, 1652-1836
STANFORD: STANFORD U PRESS, 1957, 195 PP., LC#56-7273.
DEALS WITH ECONOMIC FACTORS BEHIND EXPANSION MOVEMENT IN SOUTH AFRICAN HISTORY. USING COMMODITY APPROACH, ANALYZES DEMAND, PRICES, AND PRODUCTION. HYPOTHESIZES THAT REMOTE PARTS OF FRONTIER AND WHOLE ECONOMY WERE CLOSELY TIED TO MARKET OF CAPETOWN, AND THEREFORE TO MILITARY AND COMMERICAL

MARITIME TRAFFIC AND TRADE. PROVIDES HISTORICAL BACKGROUND; INCLUDES AGRICULTURAL MARKET AND LABOR PROBLEMS.

1916 NEUMARK S.D.
FOREIGN TRADE AND ECONOMIC DEVELOPMENT IN AFRICA: A HISTORICAL PERSPECTIVE.
STANFORD: U. PR. (FOOD RES. INST.), 222 PP., $6.95.
ANALYSIS OF THE CUMULATIVE EFFECTS OF EXTERNAL TRADE ON THE INTERNAL DEVELOPMENT OF AFRICA, AND THE COURSE OF DEVELOPMENT IN TRANSPORT, MINING, AND AGRICULTURE. EVIDENCE IN SUPPORT OF SOME 'UNCOMMON' HYPOTHESES, E.G., THAT FOREIGN TRADE HAS BEEN THE MOST IMPORTANT SINGLE FACTOR IN AFRICAN ECONOMIC DEVELOPMENT.

1917 NEVITT A.A. ED.
THE ECONOMIC PROBLEMS OF HOUSING.
NEW YORK: ST MARTIN'S PRESS, 1966, 350 PP.
CONFERENCE PAPERS OF INTERNATIONAL ECONOMIC ASSOCIATION. INCLUDES COMMENTS ON POLITICAL ECONOMY OF HOUSING, SLUMS, GOVERNMENTAL RESPONSIBILITIES, RENT CONTROL, HOUSE-BUILDING, FINANCING, FEDERAL HOUSING POLICY IN USA, SOCIALIST HOUSING POLICY, AS WELL AS SPECIFIC REPORTS BY COUNTRY CONCENTRATING ON HOUSING QUESTION.

1918 NEVITT A.A.
HOUSING, TAXATION AND SUBSIDIES: A STUDY OF HOUSING IN THE UNITED KINGDOM.
LONDON: THOMAS NELSON & SONS, 1966, 185 PP.
STUDIES HOUSING PROBLEM THROUGH HOUSING ECONOMY. GIVES ACCOUNT OF LAND TENURE SINCE 16TH CENTURY AND DISCUSSES TAXES ON RENTAL INCOME, TAX RELIEF, SUBSIDIES, EFFECTS OF CONTROLLING AND DECONTROLLING RENTS, AND RELATION OF INCOME TO PRICE OF HOUSES. PROPOSES RECONSTRUCTION OF HOUSING COSTS, CREATION OF FINANCIAL INSTITUTION TO PROVIDE LOANS, AND TAXATION OF REVENUE FROM HOUSES.

1919 NEW JERSEY LEGISLATURE-SENATE
PUBLIC HEARINGS BEFORE COMMITTEE ON REVISION AND AMENDMENT OF LAWS ON SENATE BILL NO. 8.
TRENTON: NJ STATE LEGISLATURE, 1961, 300 PP.
HEARINGS HELD FEBRUARY, 1961, ON "URBAN RENEWAL CORPORATION LAW OF 1961," A BILL PROPOSING TAX RELIEF TO INCOMING BUSINESSES IN HOPES THAT INCREASED INDUSTRIALIZATION WILL ALLEVIATE SOME OF THE POWERTY, DISEASE, AND DELINQUENCY OF THE CITIES. SOME DISAGREEMENT AMONG SPEAKERS AS TO HOW BEST TO IMPLEMENT TAX RELIEF; A FEW SUGGEST SUBSIDIZING RENEWAL; ALL AGREE RENEWAL IS NECESSARY BY SOME METHOD.

1920 NEW JERSEY STATE OF
SECOND REPORT TO GOVERNOR, SENATE, ASSEMBLY BY UNIFORM COMMERCIAL CODE STUDY COMMISSION.
NEWARK: SOMERY AND SAGE CO, 1960, 806 PP.
REPORT OF COMMISSION WHICH ANALYZED EXISTING COMMERCIAL LAW IN NEW JERSEY. SHOWS EFFECTS UNIFORM COMMERCIAL CODE WOULD HAVE ON NJ LAW, IF CODE IS ADOPTED. INCLUDES COMPREHENSIVE RECORD OF STATE COMMERCIAL LAW AND PRACTICE.

1921 NEWCOMER H.A.
INTERNATIONAL AIDS TO OVERSEAS INVESTMENTS AND TRADE.
KENT: KENT ST U BUR ECO BUS RES, 1964, 67 PP.
TREATISE WHICH COLLATES FACTUAL INFORMATION CONCERNING DEVELOPMENT OF INTERNATIONAL PRIVATE INVESTMENT AND TRADE. EXAMINES INVESTMENT PROCEDURE AND DISCUSSES COOPERATIVE TREATIES AND CONVENTIONS BETWEEN AGENCIES OF THE UN AND NATIONAL GOVERNMENTS. CONTAINS BRIEF UNANNOTATED BIBLIOGRAPHIES FOR EACH CHAPTER. EMPHASIZES ROLE OF UN INTERNATIONAL AGENCIES IN WORLD ECONOMIC DEVELOPMENT AND RECONSTRUCTION.

1922 NEWLYN W.T.
"MONETARY SYSTEMS AND INTEGRATION"
J. OF EAST AFRICAN ECONOMIC REV., 11 (JUNE 64), 41-58.
DISCUSSION OF RELATIONSHIP BETWEEN POLITICAL INTEGRATION AND ECONOMIC INTEGRATION, WITH SPECIAL REFERENCE TO MONETARY SYSTEMS. ANALYSIS APPLIED TO EAST AFRICA.

1923 NEWLYN W.T.
"MONEY MARKETS IN EAST AFRICA."
J. OF MOD. AFR. STUD., 4 (DEC. 66), 472-478.
DISCUSSES CHANGE IN BORROWING PATTERNS OF EAST AFRICAN NATIONS AS THEY SHIFT FROM NAIROBI TO LONDON AS SOURCE OF FUNDS DURING PEAK INDEBTEDNESS PERIODS.

1924 NICHOLS J.P.
"HAZARDS OF AMERICAN PRIVATE INVESTMENT IN UNDERDEVELOPED COUNTRIES."
ORBIS, 4 (SUMMER 60), 174-191.
SURVEYS DEVELOPMENT OF AMERICAN INVESTMENT IN THE UNDERDEVELOPED NATIONS FROM EARLIER AGE OF EXPLOITATION TO THE PRESENT AGE OF NATIONALIZATION. CONCLUDES THAT ALTHOUGH SOME COMPANIES HAVE CREATED GOOD FEELING BY CONTRIBUTING TO LOCAL WELFARE, RISKS TO PRIVATE INVESTMENT ARE INCREASING DUE TO INDIGENOUS POLITICAL AND ECONOMIC FACTORS AND COMMUNISM.

1925 NICOSIA F.N.
CONSUMER DECISION PROCESSES* MARKETING AND ADVERTISING IMPLICATIONS.
ENGLEWOOD CLIFFS: PRENTICE HALL, 1966, 281 PP., LC#66-22092.
INQUIRY INTO LITERATURE OF MARKETING, ECONOMIC THEORY OF DEMAND, AND BEHAVIORAL SCIENCES. RESULTS OF ANALYZING THESE PROBLEMS. CONSUMER BEHAVIOR STUDIED.

1926 NICOSIA M.N.
CONSUMER DECISION PROCESSES: MARKETING AND ADVERTISING IMPLICATIONS.
ENGLEWOOD CLIFFS: PRENTICE HALL, 1966, 284 PP., LC#66-22092.
PRESENTS A STRUCTURAL VIEW OF CONSUMER BEHAVIOR AS A DECISION PROCESS AND EXAMINES THE VARIOUS FACTORS INFLUENCING THE CONSUMER IN THE FIELDS OF MARKETING, ECONOMICS, AND THE BEHAVIORAL SCIENCES. RESULTS INTENDED FOR APPLICATION BY ADMINISTRATORS TO SPECIFIC PROBLEMS OF CONSUMER BEHAVIOR. SURVEYS PREVIOUS THEORIES AND WORK IN THE FIELD.

1927 NICULESCU B.
COLONIAL PLANNING: A COMPARATIVE STUDY.
NEW YORK: MACMILLAN, 1958, 208 PP.
CONSIDERS PROCESSES OF DEVELOPMENTAL PLANNING IN AFRICAN NATIONS. SHOWS GROWTH OF IDEA WITH COLONIAL EMPIRES AND MACHINERY OF PLANNING IN FORMER COLONIES. ANALYZES SEVERAL PLANS NOW IN USE AND APPRAISES THEIR ACHIEVEMENTS.

1928 NILES J.G.
"CIVIL ACTIONS FOR DAMAGES UNDER THE FEDERAL CIVIL RIGHTS STATUTES."
TEXAS LAW REVIEW, 45 (APR. 67), 1015-1035.
ANALYZES PARTICULAR CONSTITUTIONAL RIGHTS THAT HAVE BEEN SUBJECT OF FEDERAL CIVIL ACTIONS FOR DAMAGES. CONCENTRATES ON DEFINING EXTENT AND NATURE OF THESE RIGHTS IN SPECIFIC STATUTES AVAILABLE, AND ON PROBLEMS THAT ARISE IN TRYING TO ASSIGN MONETARY VALUE TO MAGAGES OF INFRINGEMENT. FINDS PRESENT CIVIL ACTION PROVISIONS DO NOT PREVENT RACIAL DISCRIMINATION, LACKING INCENTIVE TO BE USED OFTEN.

1929 NKRUMAH K.
NEO-COLONIALISM: THE LAST STAGE OF IMPERIALISM.
LONDON: THOMAS NELSON & SONS, 1965, 280 PP.
NKRUMAH'S NOTED ATTACK ON THE "WORST FORM OF IMPERIALISM" SHOWS HOW FOREIGN INVESTMENTS IN AN UNDERDEVELOPED COUNTRY LEAD TO DANGEROUS CONTROL BY CAPITALIST POWER AND TO TOTAL SUBJUGATION AND PUPPET GOVERNMENTS.

1930 NKRUMAH K.
CHALLENGE OF THE CONGO.
LONDON: THOMAS NELSON & SONS, 1967, 304 PP.
REVEALS WORKINGS OF POLITICAL AND ECONOMIC FOREIGN PRESSURES WHICH MADE PEACEFUL PROGRESS IN THE CONGO IMPOSSIBLE. NOTES THAT SINCE 1961 THERE HAS BEEN NO TRULY REPRESENTATIVE GOVERNMENT THERE. DISCUSSES KATANGA'S SECESSION, FAILURE OF THE UN OPERATION, MURDER OF LUMUMBA, FOREIGN MILITARY INTERVENTION AT STANLEYVILLE, AND MOBUTU'S SO-CALLED COUP D'ETAT.

1931 NOMAD M.
POLITICAL HERETICS: FROM PLATO TO MAO TSE-TUNG.
ANN ARBOR: U OF MICH PR, 1963, 367 PP., LC#63-9895.
BRIEF DISCUSSION OF LIVES AND THEORIES OF MANY "LEFTISTS" FROM PLATO TO MAO. EMPHASIS ON UTOPIANS, NIHILISTS, SOCIAL AND ECONOMIC MARXISTS, SOCIALISTS, SYNDICALISTS, AND ANARCHISTS.

1932 NORGREN P.H., HILL S.E.
"TOWARD FAIR EMPLOYMENT."
NEW YORK: COLUMBIA U PRESS, 1964.
CRITICAL STUDY AND APPRAISAL OF GOVERNMENTAL FAIR EMPLOYMENT AGENCIES AT FEDERAL, STATE, AND LOCAL LEVELS. CONTENDS THAT ALTHOUGH GOVERNMENT FAIR EMPLOYMENT MEASURES CAN EXPEDITE THE PROCESS, THE ESSENTIAL KEY TO FULL EMPLOYMENT EQUALITY FOR RACIAL MINORITIES IS TO BE FOUND IN CHANGING LABOR MARKET BEHAVIOR AND EQUALIZATION OF EDUCATIONAL OPPORTUNITIES. BIBLIOGRAPHY OF WORKS PUBLISHED FROM 1943-63.

1933 NORTH D.C.
THE ECONOMIC GROWTH OF THE UNITED STATES 1790-1860.
ENGLEWOOD CLIFFS: PRENTICE HALL, 1961, 304 PP., LC#61-6358.
DESCRIBES DETERMINANTS AND INTERRELATIONSHIPS INVOLVED IN ECONOMIC EXPANSION. HYPOTHESIS IS THAT US GROWTH WAS THE EVOLUTION OF A MARKET ECONOMY IN WHICH THE BEHAVIOR OF PRICES OF GOODS, SERVICES, AND PRODUCTIVE FACTORS WAS THE MAJOR ELEMENT IN ANY EXPLANATION OF ECONOMIC CHANGE. AUTHOR CONSIDERS INSTITUTIONAL AND POLITICAL FACTORS AS SECONDARY.

1934 NORTH CAROLINA U INST GOVT
COSTING URBAN DEVELOPMENT AND REDEVELOPMENT (PAMPHLET)
CHAPEL HILL: INST INTL STUDIES, 1963, 17 PP.
SHORT BIBLIOGRAPHY OF MATERIALS PUBLISHED IN US IN LAST 30 YEARS RELATING TO LAND USE: COST-BENEFIT AND COST-REVENUE ANALYSIS, PROPERTY TAX REVENUES, ANNEXATION, LAND USES IN URBAN AND SUBURBAN COMMUNITIES, SLUMS, URBAN REDEVELOPMENT, RENEWAL. INCLUDES LIST OF FIVE RESEARCH WORKS IN PROGRESS AS OF JULY, 1963.

1935 NORTON H.S.
NATIONAL TRANSPORTATION POLICY: FORMATION AND IMPLEMENTATION

BERKELEY: MCCUTCHAN PUBL CORP, 1967, 249 PP.
TRACES DEVELOPMENT AND FUNCTIONING OF NATIONAL TRANSPORTATION POLICY AS ATTEMPT TO INTEGRATE PRIVATE ENTERPRISE AND PUBLIC UTILITY. EXAMINES INSTITUTIONS INVOLVED IN POLICY-MAKING AND MEN WHO CONTROL THEM. STUDIES ECONOMIC AND SOCIAL FACTORS INFLUENCING POLICY, SUCH AS EXPANSION OF POPULATION AND NEW FORMS OF TRANSPORTATION. EVALUATES PRESENT PROBLEM AND PROSPECTS FOR FUTURE.

1936 NORTON P.L. ED.
URBAN PROBLEMS AND TECHNIQUES.
LEXINGTON, MASS: CHANDLER-DAVIS, 1959, 249 PP., LC#59-11407.
THIS SERIES OF ESSAYS EXAMINES THE TECHNICAL ASPECTS OF URBAN PLANNING. DISCUSSED ARE ZONING AND SMOG CONTROL, THE ARGUMENTS FOR AND AGAINST "GREENBELTS," THE PURPOSE AND ACHIEVEMENTS OF FEDERAL AID, AND RECREATION.

1937 NOSSITER B.D.
THE MYTHMAKERS: AN ESSAY ON POWER AND WEALTH.
BOSTON: HOUGHTON MIFFLIN, 1964, 244 PP., LC#64-10542.
DISCUSSES WHETHER FREE, COMPETITIVE MARKETS GOVERN AMERICAN BUSINESS. FINDS THAT ATTEMPTS TO DEAL DEMOCRATICALLY WITH ECONOMIC AND POLITICAL ILLS ARE OFTEN THWARTED. SYSTEM OF "PLANNING BY ASSENT" TO UNITE POLITICS AND ECONOMICS IS SUGGESTED.

1938 NOURSE E.G., GROSS B.H.
"THE ROLE OF THE COUNCIL OF ECONOMIC ADVISERS."
AM. POL. SCI. REV., 42 (APR. 48), 283-295.
DISCUSSES THE COUNCIL'S FUNCTIONS AND NATURE AS WELL AS THE GAP THAT IT WAS DESIGNED TO FILL AS AN ORGANIZATIONAL UNIT "CAPABLE OF MOBILIZING ALL GOVERNMENT RESOURCES AND EFFORTS TO THE ACHIEVEMENT OF AN ACCEPTED END."

1939 NOURSE E.G.
"EARLY FLOWERING OF THE EMPLOYMENT ACT"
VIRGINIA QUART. REV., 43 (SPRING 67), 233-247.
DISCUSSES MATURING OF POLICIES UNDER 1946 EMPLOYMENT ACT. ANALYZES QUESTIONS OF WHETHER ACT EXPRESSED A NATIONAL INTENTION TO CURTAIL INDEPENDENCE OF PRIVATE BUSINESS, AND WHETHER FURTHER GOVERNMENT CONTROLS ARE NECESSARY. SUGGESTS THAT GOVERNMENT ADVISERS, AGENCIES, AND CONGRESSIONAL COMMITTEES MUST COORDINATE THEIR ACTIVITIES IN FUTURE YEARS IN ORDER TO ATTAIN FULL USE OF NATIONAL RESOURCES.

1940 NOVACK D.E. ED., LEKACHMAN R. ED.
DEVELOPMENT AND SOCIETY; THE DYNAMICS OF ECONOMIC CHANGE.
NEW YORK: ST MARTIN'S PRESS, 1964, 433 PP., LC#64-11972.
TOPICS INCLUDE THE MEANING OF DEVELOPMENT, THEORIES OF ECONOMIC DEVELOPMENT, OBSTACLES, SOCIETY PERSONALITY AND ENTREPRENEURSHIP, THE CLASH OF CULTURES, STATUS AND MOBILITY, CITIES AND SAVINGS, MAKING SOCIAL CHANGE POSSIBLE, THE RICH AND THE POOR, AND ELITES AND DEVELOPMENT. AUTHORS INCLUDE SHILS, BENDA, ECKSTEIN, MORGENTHAU, LINTON, MEAD, MYRDAL, ROLSTOW, VINER, AUBREY, LETWIN, COALE, ET AL.

1941 NOVE A.
COMMUNIST ECONOMIC STRATEGY: SOVIET GROWTH AND CAPABILITIES.
WASHINGTON: NATL PLANNING ASSN, 1959, 82 PP., LC#59-15078.
DISCUSSES RESOURCES AND INTERNAL ECONOMIC ORGANIZATION OF USSR IN RELATION TO "COMPETITIVE COEXISTENCE." EXAMINES MANPOWER, SCIENTIFIC PROGRESS, MATERIAL RESOURCES, PLANNING EFFICIENCY, AGRICULTURE, AND GENERAL COMMUNIST BLOC GROWTH. MAINTAINS THAT WEST "WILL CONTINUE TO BE THE PRINCIPAL TRADING PARTNER" OF "UNCOMMITTED COUNTRIES."

1942 NOVE A.
"THE SOVIET MODEL AND UNDERDEVELOPED COUNTRIES."
INT. AFF., 37 (JAN. 61), 29-38.
ANALYZES FACTORS WEAKENING GROWTH OF ECONOMIC ACTIVITY RELATING TO PARTICULAR COUNTRIES. COMPARES COMMUNIST AND WESTERN PROPAGANDA METHODS, AND THEIR PURPOSE OF MOBILIZING PEOPLE TO CARRY OUT DIFFICULT TASKS. WARNS THAT WEST'S ALTERNATIVE SUGGESTIONS ARE NOT ALWAYS ATTUNED TO GOALS.

1943 NOVE A.
THE SOVIET ECONOMY.
NEW YORK: FREDERICK PRAEGER, 1961, 328 PP., LC#61-16579.
INTRODUCTION SURVEY OF SOVIET ECONOMY, INCLUDING ITS PRODUCTIVE ENTERPRISES, ADMINISTRATION, CHANGING NATURE OF ITS PROBLEMS, AND BASIC CONCEPTS OF SOVIET ECONOMICS.

1944 NOYES C.R.
ECONOMIC MAN IN RELATION TO HIS NATURAL ENVIRONMENT (2 VOLS.)
NEW YORK: COLUMBIA U PRESS, 1948, 1443 PP.
COMPREHENSIVE STUDY OF MAN AS CONSUMER AND PRODUCER WITHIN A BIOLOGICAL ENVIRONMENT. PART I ANLAYZES MAN'S WANTS AND THEIR SATISFACTION. PART II DEALS WITH MAN'S WORKING EFFORTS AND SACRIFICES. PART III EXAMINES ENVIRONMENT IN ITS ECONOMIC RELATION TO THE HUMAN BEING. PART IV SYNTHESIZES THE FOREGOING. EMPHASIS THROUGHOUT IS ON A BIOLOGICAL APPROACH TO ECONOMICS.

1945 NUNEZ JIMENEZ A.
LA LIBERACION DE LAS ISLAS.
HAVANA: EDITORIAL LEX, 1959, 623 PP.
DESCRIBES FIRST YEAR OF FIDEL CASTRO'S POWER IN CUBA. EXPLAINS LAWS AND PROGRAMS BEGUN BY REVOLUTIONARY GOVERNMENT AND DIPLOMATIC MISSIONS TO EUROPE AND US IN SEARCH OF AID AND SUPPORT FOR NEW REGIME. DEVOTES LARGE SECTION TO PLAN AND PROCESS OF AGRARIAN REFORM AND LAWS OF ENACTMENT.

1946 NUSENBAUM A.A.
"ON THE QUESTION OF TENDENCIES IN AMERICAN EDUCATION."
SOVIET EDUCATION, 9 (APR. 67), 3-10.
REPRINT FROM SOVIET PEDAGOGICAL PERIODICAL DISCUSSING CURRENTS OF AMERICAN THOUGHT IN PHILOSOPHY OF EDUCATION. ATTEMPTS TO CLASSIFY AMERICAN -PHILOSOPHIES OF EDUCATION," AND TO DESCRIBE THEIR MAIN CHARACTERISTICS AND PROPONENTS. FOCUSES ON SCHOOLS OF PRAGMATISM AND "CONNECTIONISM." STATES THAT QUESTIONS RAISED BY THESE SCHOOLS CAN BE ANSWERED ONLY ON BASIS OF MARXIST IDEOLOGY.

1947 NYANZI S.
"THE EAST AFRICAN MARKET: FOR BETTER OF FOR WORSE."
TRANSACTIONS, 1 (DEC. 61), 18-20.
PROPOSES SETUP OF INTERTERRITORIAL POOL OF CAPITAL, FINANCED BY INCOME TAX TO PROMOTE INDUSTRIAL DEVELOPMENT AND INSURE BALANCE OF TRADE.

1948 NYE J.
"TANGANYIKA'S SELF-HELP."
TRANSACTIONS, 3 (NOV. 63), 35-39.
TANGANYIKA'S PROGRAM OF USING VOLUNTARY LABOR TO INCREASE VALUE OF CAPITAL IN COUNTRY CRITICIZED AND EVALUATED. DECLINE IN NATIONALISTIC SPIRIT AND CONFLICT BETWEEN GOVERNMENT AND LABOR BLAMED FOR INEFFICIENCY; BIPARTISAN POLITICAL SYSTEM SUGGESTED AS REMEDY.

1949 NYOMARKAY J.
CHARISMA AND FACTIONALISM IN THE NAZI PARTY.
MINNEAPOLIS: U OF MINN PR, 1967, 161 PP., LC#67-21015.
STUDIES INTRAPARTY FACTIONALISM OF GERMAN NAZI PARTY. CONCERNED WITH ISSUES, ATTITUDES, MOTIVATIONS, AND ACTIONS OF VARIOUS FACTIONS. EXAMINES ROLE OF HITLER'S CHARISMA IN ELEVATING HIM ABOVE DISPUTES. COMPARES NAZI FACTIONALISM TO COMMUNIST, IN WHICH AUTHORITY RESTS ON IDEOLOGY, NOT ON CHARISMA. THEORIZES ON RELATIONSHIP BETWEEN CONFLICT AND LEGITIMACY OF POWER AND GROUP COHESION.

1950 O.E.E.C.
PRIVATE UNITED STATES INVESTMENT IN EUROPE AND THE OVERSEAS TERRITORIES.
PARIS: ORG FOR EUROP ECON COOP AND DEV, 1961,47PP.
SHOWS AMOUNT AND DISTRIBUTION OF USA INVESTMENTS AS WELL AS NEEDS FOR US CAPITAL AND AMERICAN MOTIVATION. SCRUTINIZES EACH COUNTRY AS TO EXCHANGE CONTROLS, LOCAL FISCAL SYSTEMS AND RESPONSIVENESS TO FOREIGN INVESTMENT. ALSO NOTES PRIVATE INVESTMENT AND US LOANS TO WORLD BANK.

1951 O'BRIEN F.
CRISIS IN WORLD COMMUNISM* MARXISM IN SEARCH OF EFFICIENCY.
NEW YORK: FREE PRESS OF GLENCOE, 1965, 191 PP., LC#65-16439.
GRANTS THAT TECHNOLOGISTS LIKE BREZHNEV NOW RUN USSR BUT CLAIMS THEY STILL OPERATE IN AMBIENCE OF MARXISM AND THAT THEREFORE THE WAYS IN WHICH DOCTRINAL MARXISM INSPIRE AND IMPINGE ON DOMESTIC AND INTERNATIONAL POLICIES -- AIMED AT CREATING THE SOVIET STATE AS A TECHNOLOGICAL IDEAL, FRATERNAL COMMUNISM AS A MODEL INTERNATIONAL SYSTEM, AND PEACEFUL COEXISTENCE AS WORLD'S BEST POLICY-- SHOULD BE ANALYZED.

1952 O'CONNELL D.P.
INTERNATIONAL LAW (2 VOLS.)
NEW YORK: OCEANA PUBLISHING, 1965, 1213 PP.
EXAMINES INTERNATIONAL LAW AS A SYSTEM OF LAW RATHER THAN A BRANCH OF DIPLOMACY OR POLITICAL SCIENCE. APPLIES CRITICAL STANDARDS OF LAWYER. INCLUDES VAST DOCUMENTATION AND VARIETY OF SOURCE MATERIALS. ATTEMPTS TO AVOID NATIONAL APPROACH AND EMPHASIZES UNIVERSALITY OF SCOPE AND APPEAL. PARTICULAR ATTENTION IS GIVEN TO ECONOMIC PROBLEMS AND DISPUTES.

1953 O'CONNOR A.M.
AN ECONOMIC GEOGRAPHY OF EAST AFRICA.
NEW YORK: FREDERICK PRAEGER, 1966, 292 PP., LC#66-22358.
CONCERNED WITH ECONOMIC ACTIVITIES IN EAST AFRICA, INDICATING MAIN FACTORS AFFECTING BOTH EXISTENCE AND DISTRIBUTION OF ACTIVITIES. BACKGROUND PICTURE OF GEOGRAPHY AND ECONOMY OF REGION.

1954 O'CONNOR H.
REVOLUTION IN SEATTLE.
NEW YORK: MONTHLY REVIEW PR, 1964, 300 PP., LC#64-16129.
PRESENTS DETAILED AND DOCUMENTED HISTORICAL ACCOUNT OF AN EPISODE IN THE HISTORY OF MARXISM IN US AND THE SOCIAL FORCES BEHIND IT. PEPPERS ACCOUNT WITH PERSONAL REMINISCENCES, ANECDOTES, ETC., AND PRESENTS VIVID PICTURE (DRAWN FROM LABOR NEWSPAPERS AND MEMOIRS) OF SUBVERSION TRIAL THAT FOLLOWED THE SEATTLE GENERAL STRIKE. COVERS PERIOD FROM 1900 TO EARLY TWENTIES.

1955 O'CONNOR H.
THE EMPIRE OF OIL.
NEW YORK: MONTHLY REVIEW PR, 1955, 272 PP., LC#55-12156.
EXPOSES AND ANALYZES THE SCOPE AND IMPLICATIONS OF US OIL INDUSTRY, GOVERNMENT POLICIES, AND THE WORLD MARKET. ATTEMPTS TO ASSESS THE "GLOBAL IMPLICATIONS OF OIL PRODUCTION AND DISTRIBUTION." TAKES MARXIST STAND AND SEES THE FREE WORLD "STRADDLED BY AN INTERNATIONAL OIL CARTEL."

1956 O'CONNOR H.
WORLD CRISES IN OIL (BMR)
LONDON: ELEK BOOKS, 1962, 433 PP.
SURVEY OF OIL INDUSTRY, CENTERED MAINLY ON STANDARD OIL, ROYAL DUTCH, SHELL, AND THE OTHER FIVE INTERNATIONAL COMPANIES. VIEWS RISE OF NATIONAL COMPANIES IN LATIN AMERICA, ASIA, AND SEVERAL SOCIALIST COUNTRIES, AND RESULTING CHALLENGE TO THE WORLD PETROLEUM CARTEL'S DOMINATION OF THE MARKET. SEVERAL PAGES OF REFERENCES INCLUDED.

1957 O'CONNOR T.P.
THE PARNELL MOVEMENT: WITH A SKETCH OF IRISH PARTIES FROM 1843.
NEW YORK: BENZIGER BROS, 1886, 574 PP.
EXAMINES BRITISH INTIMIDATION OF IRELAND, EMPHASIZING RESULTANT FAMINES AND THE ACTIVITIES OF PARNELL. INCLUDES ULSTER COUNTY, THE LAND LEAGUE, AND LANDLORDS.

1958 O'LEARY M.K.
THE POLITICS OF AMERICAN FOREIGN AID.
NEW YORK: ATHERTON, 1967, 172 PP., LC#67-18274.
EXAMINES PROCESS OF ALLOCATION OF US BUDGET FOR FOREIGN AID. DISCUSSES PRESIDENTIAL AND CONGRESSIONAL ACTIONS AND OPINION OF PUBLIC AND POLITICAL PARTIES ON VALUE OF AID.

1959 O'NEAL F.H.
"RECENT LEGISLATION AFFECTING CLOSE CORPORATIONS."
LAW AND CONTEMPORARY PROB., 23 (SPRING 58), 341-362.
STATUS SINCE 1945 HAVE PERMITTED INCREASED FLEXIBILITY TO PERMIT MOLDING OF THE CORPORATE DEVICE TO THE NEEDS OF CLOSELY-HELD ENTERPRISES. TECHNIQUES INCLUDE AUTHORIZATION OF SPECIAL BYLAWS, HIGH-VOTE REQUIREMENTS FOR STOCKHOLDER AND DIRECTOR ACTION, IRREVOCABLE PROXIES, RELAXED REQUIREMENTS OF FORMALITY, AND DISSOLUTION IN CASE OF DEADLOCK.

1960 OBERER W.E.
"VOLUNTARY IMPARTIAL REVIEW OF LABOR: SOME REFLECTIONS."
MICH. LAW REV., 58 (NOV. 59), 55-88.
DISCUSSES CHARACTER, FUNCTIONS, AND PROBLEMS OF VOLUNTARY REVIEW BODIES IN LABOR UNIONS. WRITTEN JUST PRIOR TO PASSAGE OF LANDRUM-GRIFFIN ACT, BOOK CONSIDERS UAW PUBLIC REVIEW BOARD AS A SUPREME COURT, DISCUSSES ACLU'S LABOR UNION BILL OF RIGHTS AND ADVANTAGES OF SUCH VOLUNTARY TRTBUNALS AND RE-VIEW BOARDS.
ADVANTAGES OF SUCH VOLUNTARY TRIBUNALS AND REVIEW BOARDS.

1961 OCHENG D.
"ECONOMIC FORCES AND UGANDA'S FOREIGN POLICY."
TRANSACTIONS, 2 (OCT. 62), 27-29.
EXAMINES NEED FOR DIPLOMATIC UNITY OF UGANDA WITH TANGAN-YIKA AND KENYA TO DEAL WITH THEIR ECONOMIC PROBLEMS. WEIGHS BENEFITS OF JOINING EEC AND PROPOSES ESTABLISHMENT OF OVER-SEAS MISSIONS IN THE NAME OF ALL THREE RATHER THAN SEPARATELY.

1962 ODEGARD P.H.
POLITICAL POWER AND SOCIAL CHANGE.
NEW BRUNSWICK: RUTGERS U PR, 1966, 111 PP., LC#62-28215.
ETHICS OF GOVERNMENT, PAST, PRESENT, AND FUTURE, COMPARED AND RELATED TO ECONOMIC, HISTORICAL, AND SOCIAL EVOLUTION. SKETCHES EFFECT OF TECHNOLOGY AND POPULATION ON POWER AND GIVES BRIEF HISTORY OF ITS ABUSE.

1963 ODEH H.S.
THE IMPACT OF INFLATION ON THE LEVEL OF ECONOMIC ACTIVITY.
ROTTERDAM: ROTTERDAM U PRESS, 1964, 101 PP.
STUDY OF PROBLEM OF INFLATION IN DEVELOPING NATIONS OF BRAZIL AND CHILE ON LEVEL OF ECONOMIC ACTIVITY, I.E., "DECI-SIONS TO INVEST OR CONSUME." ANALYZES BY ECONOMETRICS "WHETHER INFLATION IN TWO COUNTRIES IS CAUSED BY MONETARY MISMANAGEMENT OR INHERENT STRUCTURAL DEFICIENCIES." EXCEL-LENT METHODOLOGICAL STUDY INCLUDING APPENDIX OF STATISTICS USED.

1964 OECD
MARSHALL PLAN IN TURKEY.
PARIS: ORG FOR ECO COOP AND DEV, 1955, 40 PP.
REPORT ON OPERATION OF MARSHALL PLAN IN TURKISH ECONOMY. COLLECTION OF STATISTICAL DATA ON EXPENDITURES IN AGRICUL-TURE, NATIONAL DEFENSE, PUBLIC WORKS, COMMUNICATIONS, AND INDUSTRY.

1965 OECD
STATISTICS OF BALANCE OF PAYMENTS 1950-61.
PARIS: ORG FOR ECO COOP AND DEV, 1961, 134 PP.
PRESENTS AND COMPARES STATISTICS FOR NATIONS IN OECD EACH YEAR REGARDING THEIR BALANCE OF PAYMENTS. INCLUDES SEPARATE LISTS FOR EACH MEMBER NATION IN ALPHABETICAL ORDER.

1966 OECD
FOOD AID: ITS ROLE IN ECONOMIC DEVELOPMENT.
PARIS: ORG FOR ECO COOP AND DEV, 1963, 85 PP.
SURVEY OF ECONOMIC IMPLICATIONS OF FOOD AID PROGRAMS IN-STITUTED BY MEMBER NATIONS OF ORGANIZATION FOR ECONOMIC CO-OPERATION AND DEVELOPMENT. EMPHASIS ON CONTRIBUTION OF FOOD AID TO ECONOMIC IMPROVEMENT IN UNDERDEVELOPED COUNTRIES.

1967 OECD
DEVELOPMENT ASSISTANCE EFFORTS - POLICIES OF THE MEMBERS.
PARIS: ORG FOR ECO COOP AND DEV, 1964, 114 PP.
REPORT BY DEVELOPMENT ASSISTANCE COMMITTEE OF OECD ON VOLUME OF AID, GEOGRAPHIC DISTRIBUTION, CONDITIONS FOR ASSISTANCE, COORDINATION EFFORTS, TECHNICAL AID, AND PROPO-SALS ON STRENGTHENING ASSISTANCE EFFORTS OF OECD.

1968 OECD
THE FLOW OF FINANCIAL RESOURCES TO LESS DEVELOPED COUNTRIES 1956-1963.
PARIS: ORG FOR ECO COOP AND DEV, 1964, 165 PP.
PROVIDES FACTUAL INFORMATION ON FLOW OF FINANCIAL RE-SOURCES AS REPORTED BY INDIVIDUAL DONOR COUNTRIES TO LESS DEVELOPED NATIONS BETWEEN 1956-63. INCLUDES CONTRIBU-TIONS OF MULTILATERAL AGENCIES AND FOCUSES ON SIZE OF AID, FEATURES OF POLICIES OF COUNTRY EXTENDING AID, AND INSTITU-TIONAL METHODS BY WHICH FINANCIAL AID IS GRANTED.

1969 OECD
MEDITERRANEAN REGIONAL PROJECT: TURKEY; EDUCATION AND DEVELOPMENT.
PARIS: ORG FOR ECO COOP AND DEV, 1965, 189 PP.
REVIEWS PRESENT EDUCATIONAL STRUCTURE AND POLICY IN TURKEY; TREATS ROLE OF EDUCATION IN SOCIAL AND ECONOMIC DEVELOPMENT. DISCUSSES FACILITIES, TEACHER TRAINING AND SUPPLY, AND ADMINISTRATION. EXAMINES COST OF EDUCATIONAL DEVELOPMENT, PRESENT EXPENDITURES, AND FUTURE NEEDS. COVERS ECONOMIC TARGETS AND MANPOWER, OCCUPATIONAL CLASSIFICATIONS, DEMAND AND SUPPLY, AND PARTICIPATION.

1970 OECD
THE MEDITERRANEAN REGIONAL PROJECT: PORTUGAL; EDUCATION AND DEVELOPMENT.
PARIS: ORG FOR ECO COOP AND DEV, 1965, 225 PP.
ECONOMIC ANALYSIS OF EDUCATIONAL DEVELOPMENT. BEGINS WITH METHODOLOGY AND FUTURE REQUIREMENTS FOR SKILLED PERSONNEL; INCLUDES BREAKDOWN OF EMPLOYMENT BY EDUCATIONAL LEVEL. ANALYZES PRESENT STRUCTURE AND ESTIMATES GROWTH OF SCHOOL ENROLLMENT; DISCUSSES FACILITIES AND TEACHERS, PRESENT AND FUTURE, ACCORDING TO TYPE OF EDUCATIONAL INSTITUTION. CLOSES WITH EXPENDITURES ON EDUCATION.

1971 OECD
THE MEDITERRANEAN REGIONAL PROJECT: ITALY; EDUCATION AND DEVELOPMENT.
PARIS: ORG FOR ECO COOP AND DEV, 1965, 216 PP.
CONCERNED WITH RELATION OF EDUCATIONAL PLANNING TO ECONOMIC DEVELOPMENT AND SOCIAL ADVANCEMENT. OPENS WITH SURVEY OF TRENDS IN PAST AND TARGETS FOR 1975; EXAMINES OCCUPATIONAL STRUCTURE OF EMPLOYMENT AND TRAINING FACILITIES IN PAST DECADE. DISCUSSES WAYS OF ACHIEVING PROPOSED GOALS, STRUCTURE OF SYSTEM, FINANCING. ENDS WITH METHODOLOGY FOR ESTIMATING OCCUPATIONAL STRUCTURE IN 1951, 1961, AND 1975.

1972 OECD
THE MEDITERRANEAN REGIONAL PROJECT: GREECE; EDUCATION AND DEVELOPMENT.
PARIS: ORG FOR ECO COOP AND DEV, 1965, 195 PP.
BEGINS WITH ECONOMIC FRAMEWORK AND ROLE OF EDUCATION. RELATES EDUCATIONAL PLANNING TO ECONOMIC GROWTH AND SOCIAL ADVANCEMENT; DISCUSSES EXISTING SYSTEM AND GOAL FOR 1974. EXAMINES ADJUSTMENTS THAT WILL HAVE TO BE MADE, RESOURCES FOR EXPANSION, AND OUTLINE OF PLAN; INCLUDES STRUCTURE OF SYSTEM, MANPOWER NEEDS, AND EDUCATIONAL NEEDS IN AGRICULTURE. CLOSES WITH EXPENDITURES FOR EDUCATION TO 1974.

1973 OECD
THE MEDITERRANEAN REGIONAL PROJECT: SPAIN; EDUCATION AND DEVELOPMENT.
PARIS: ORG FOR ECO COOP AND DEV, 1965, 135 PP.
SURVEYS PRESENT EDUCATIONAL SYSTEM, ASSESSES LONG-TERM EDUCATIONAL NEEDS, AND FORMULATES PLANS AND FINANCIAL ESTIMATES TO MEET NEEDS. BEGINS WITH SUMMARY OF PRESENT EDUCATIONAL POLICY; DISCUSSES ORGANIZATION AND ADMINISTRATION OF EDUCATION, COST, QUALITY, OCCUPATIONAL STRUCTURE OF LABOR FORCE, AND EDUCATIONAL LEVELS. CLOSES WITH EXPENDITURES ON EDUCATION.

1974 OECD
TECHNIQUES OF ECONOMIC FORECASTING.
PARIS: ORG FOR ECO COOP AND DEV, 1965, 173 PP.
ACCOUNT OF METHODS OF SHORT-TERM ECONOMIC FORECASTING USED IN SEVERAL NATIONS TO FORMULATE ECONOMIC POLICIES THAT

WOULD AVOID SUDDEN FLUCTUATIONS IN ECONOMIC ACTIVITY. DISCUSSES PROCESS OF FORECASTING, CONCEPTUAL AND METHODOLOGICAL ISSUES, AND USEFULNESS OF FORECASTS. MAINTAINS THAT FORECASTS ARE NECESSARY FOR EFFICIENT ECONOMIC POLICY.

1975 OECD
THE BALANCE OF PAYMENTS ADJUSTMENT PROCESS (PAMPHLET)
PARIS: ORG FOR ECO COOP AND DEV, 1966, 29 PP.
STUDY OF THE PROCESS OF INTERNATIONAL LIQUIDITY, WITH SUGGESTIONS FOR IMPROVING THE BALANCE-OF-PAYMENT PROCESS. ASPECTS DISCUSSED INCLUDE: CLEARER FORMULATION OF AIMS, RESPONSIBILITIES OF DEFICIT AND SURPLUS COUNTRIES, USE OF MEASURES DIRECTLY AFFECTING INTERNATIONAL TRANSACTIONS, AND THE IMPORTANCE OF INCREASED INTERGOVERNMENTAL CONSULTATION.

1976 OECD DEVELOPMENT CENTRE
CATALOGUE OF SOCIAL AND ECONOMIC DEVELOPMENT INSTITUTES AND PROGRAMMES* RESEARCH.
PARIS: ORG FOR ECO COOP AND DEV, 1966, 452 PP.
LISTING OF RESEARCH INSTITUTES AND THEIR ACTIVITIES IN FIELD OF SOCIAL AND ECONOMIC DEVELOPMENT. THIRTY NON-IRON-CURTAIN NATIONS SURVEYED. ALL DATA IN ENGLISH.

1977 OEEC
THE INDUSTRIAL CHALLENGE OF NUCLEAR ENERGY.
PARIS: ORG FOR EUROP ECON COOP AND DEV, 1958, 301PP.
COLLECTION OF PAPERS ON EUROPE AND NUCLEAR ENERGY: ITS RESEARCH, USES, AND SOCIAL PROBLEMS, INCLUDING NUCLEAR FUELS, PRODUCTION OF ENERGY, AND RISKS OF RADIATION.

1978 OEEC
STATISTICS OF SOURCES AND USES OF FINANCE.
PARIS: ORG FOR EUROP ECON COOP AND DEV, 1960, 195PP.
STATISTICAL SURVEY OF MONEY AND CREDIT DEVELOPMENTS OF OEEC COUNTRIES BETWEEN 1948 AND 1958. LISTS PRICE INCREASES, WAGES AND SALARIES, FOREIGN ASSETS, PRODUCTION RATES, MONEY IN CIRCULATION, ETC.

1979 OFER G.
THE SERVICE INDUSTRIES IN A DEVELOPING ECONOMY: ISRAEL AS A CASE STUDY.
NEW YORK: FREDERICK PRAEGER, 1967, 168 PP., LC#66-27961.
DISCUSSES ISRAELI ECONOMIC DEVELOPMENT WITH SPECIAL ATTENTION GIVEN TO SERVICE INDUSTRIES. INTERNATIONAL COMPARISONS ARE MADE. ATTENTION ALSO GIVEN TO THE ISRAELI PROBLEM OF EXCESS SERVICES.

1980 OFFICE OF ECONOMIC OPPORTUNITY
CATALOG OF FEDERAL PROGRAMS FOR INDIVIDUAL AND COMMUNITY IMPROVEMENT.
WASHINGTON: US GOVERNMENT, 1965, 414 PP.
A DESCRIPTION OF GOVERNMENTAL PROGRAMS TO HELP INDIVIDUALS AND COMMUNITIES MEET THEIR OWN GOALS FOR ECONOMIC AND SOCIAL DEVELOPMENT. EXPLAINS NATURE AND PURPOSE OF PROGRAMS AND SPECIFIES MAJOR ELIGIBILITY REQUIREMENTS. LISTS PRINTED INFORMATION AVAILABLE. INCLUDES INDEX OF PROGRAMS AND ALPHABETICAL SUBJECT INDEX.

1981 OGBURN C.
ECONOMIC PLAN AND ACTION.
NEW YORK: HARPER & ROW, 1959, 287 PP., LC#59-7051.
STUDY OF US POSTWAR ECONOMY AND ITS GROWTH. EXAMINES RELATION OF US ECONOMY TO EXPORTS AND FOREIGN INVESTMENT IN SPECIFIC COUNTRIES.

1982 OGDEN F.D.
THE POLL TAX IN THE SOUTH.
UNIVERSITY: U ALABAMA PR, 1958, 301 PP., LC#58-08773.
STUDIES WHAT POLL TAX IS, HOW IT OPERATES, AND ITS VALUE AS VOTING PREREQUISITE. PRESENTS HISTORICAL SUMMARY, MEANS OF ADMINISTERING IT, ITS EFFECTS ON VOTER PARTICIPATION AND RELATION BETWEEN TAX AND CORRUPTION.

1983 OGLESBY C., SHAULL R.
CONTAINMENT AND CHANGE.
NEW YORK: MACMILLAN, 1967, 248 PP., LC#67-13593.
FIRST OF TWO ANALYSES OF PRESENT WORLD TURMOIL IS BASED ON DENIAL OF POPULAR BELIEF THAT STALIN STARTED COLD WAR AND THAT US HAS NOTHING TO GAIN FROM IT. CONTENDS THAT IDEAL OF FREE ENTERPRISE DICTATES IMPERIALISM WHICH COMMUNIST BLOC ATTEMPTS TO CONTAIN. SECOND COMMENTARY MAINTAINS THAT INTERNAL AND WORLD TURMOIL IS SIGN OF CONFLICT BETWEEN NEW TECHNOLOGY-BASED SOCIAL ORDER AND TRADITIONAL INFLUENCES.

1984 OHLIN G.
AID AND INDEBTEDNESS.
PARIS: ORG FOR ECO COOP AND DEV, 1966, 55 PP.
ANALYSIS OF CURRENT INTERNATIONAL ECONOMIC AID SITUATION FOCUSING ON RELATIONSHIPS BETWEEN AID REQUIREMENTS, TERMS OF ASSISTANCE, AND PROBLEMS OF INDEBTEDNESS OF UNDERDEVELOPED COUNTRIES.

1985 OHLIN G.
FOREIGN AID POLICIES RECONSIDERED.
PARIS: ORG FOR ECO COOP AND DEV, 1966, 120 PP.
STUDY AND EVALUATION OF AID PROGRAMS IN DEVELOPED COUNTRIES. EXAMINES EVOLUTION OF AID DOCTRINE, PUBLIC OPINION ON FOREIGN AID, VOLUME OF AID AND ITS MEASUREMENT, FORMS OF FINANCIAL AID, AND IDEAS ON FORMULATION OF CODE FOR DEVELOPMENT ASSISTANCE. CONCLUDES THAT KEY TO AID EFFECTIVENESS IS UNDERSTANDING RELATIONSHIP BETWEEN NATION GIVING AND PEOPLE RECEIVING THE AID.

1986 OLIVECRONA K.
THE PROBLEM OF THE MONETARY UNIT.
NEW YORK: MACMILLAN, 1957, 185 PP.
ANALYZES NATURE OF MONEY AS UNIT OF VALUE. PROVIDES DEFINITION, THEN DISCUSSES MONEY AS MEDIUM OF PAYMENT AND AS UNIT OF CALCULATION.

1987 OLIVER H.M. JR.
ECONOMIC OPINION AND POLICY IN CEYLON.
DURHAM: DUKE U PR, 1957, 145 PP., LC#57-13023.
STUDIES EFFECTS OF NATIONALIST SENTIMENT ON ECONOMIC OPINION AND POLICY IN CEYLON. EXAMINES MAIN FEATURES OF DEVELOPMENT THEORY AND POLICY, AND THEIR EFFECTS UPON CEYLONESE INCOMES. COVERS PERIOD 1916-56, DURING WHICH SUBSTANTIAL POLITICAL AND ECONOMIC CHANGE BOTH RESULTED FROM AND CAUSED INTELLECTUAL CURRENTS.

1988 OLIVIER G.
"ASPECTS JURIDIQUES DE L'ADOPTION DU TRAITE CECA A LA CRISE CHARBONNIERE (SUITE ET FIN)"
CAHIERS DU DROIT EUR., 2 (1967), 163-177.
DISCUSSION OF USE OF ARTICLE 95, AL. 1 & 2 OF ECSC CHARTER DURING COAL CRISES. ARGUES THAT FUNDAMENTAL CHANGES IN EUROPEAN FUEL SITUATION NECESSITATE CHANGES IN ECSC TREATY. ARGUES THAT GREATER ATTENTION SHOULD BE PAID TO PROBLEMS OF FIXING QUOTAS IN CRISES THAN TO QUESTIONS OF ORGANIZATION OF INTERNATIONAL TREATY.

1989 OLSON M. JR.
"RAPID ECONOMIC GROWTH AS A DESTABILIZING FORCE."
J. ECON. HIST., 23 (DEC. 63), 529-552.
CITING HISTORICAL EXAMPLES AS TO ITS DISRUPTIVE EFFECT UPON VARIOUS CLASSES OF SOCIETY, SHOWS HOW RAPID ECONOMIC GROWTH CAN BE A SOURCE OF SOCIAL INSTABILITY RATHER THAN VICE VERSA. SUBMITS THAT ANY POLICY OF RAPID ECONOMIC GROWTH MUST BE PRECEDED BY A DEFINITE PROGRAM OF EDUCATION TO PREPARE FOR AND CONTROL THE ENSUING INSTABILITY.

1990 OLSON M. JR.
THE ECONOMICS OF WARTIME SHORTAGE.
DURHAM: DUKE U PR, 1963, 152 PP., LC#63-17328.
INVESTIGATES HISTORICALLY THE EFFECTS OF WAR UPON A NATION AND TO WHAT EXTENT THAT NATION CAN ADJUST PHYSICALLY AND ECONOMICALLY. SHOWS BRITAIN'S PROBLEMS IN REVOLUTIONARY AND NAPOLEONIC WARS. THEN CONSIDERS POSITION OF UK IN WWI AND COMPARES IT WITH GERMANY. FINALLY CONSIDERS BRITAIN'S LOSSES IN FOOD IMPORTS DURING WWII AND DRAWS THEORETICAL SPECULATIONS FROM RESULTS OF STUDY.

1991 ONSLOW C. ED.
ASIAN ECONOMIC DEVELOPMENT.
NEW YORK: FREDERICK PRAEGER, 1965, 243 PP.
STUDIES OF ECONOMIC DEVELOPMENT IN SIX ASIAN COUNTRIES, INCLUDING BURMA, CEYLON, INDIA, MALAYA, PAKISTAN, AND THAILAND, LISTED BY COUNTRY, AND SUMMARIZED BY A COMPARATIVE ANALYSIS BY THE EDITOR.

1992 ONUOHA B.
THE ELEMENTS OF AFRICAN SOCIALISM.
LONDON: ANDRE DEUTSCH, 1965, 139 PP.
SUBMITS ELEMENTS OF AFRICAN NEO-SOCIALISM DESIGNED TO PRESERVE SOCIAL AND SPIRITUAL VALUES IGNORED BY EUROPEANS AND TO ESTABLISH ECONOMIC SYSTEM FITTED TO AFRICAN SOCIETY. REJECTS INJUSTICES OF LAISSEZ-FAIRE OR MARXISM. DESCRIBES SOCIALIST STRUCTURE AND INSTITUTIONS AND RELATIONSHIP WITH RELIGIOUS BODIES. DEFINES IDEOLOGICAL CONCEPTS PERTINENT TO PURSUIT OF SOCIALISM.

1993 OPLER M.E.
"SOCIAL ASPECTS OF TECHNICAL ASSISTANCE IN OPERATION."
PARIS: UNESCO, 1954, 79 PP.
REPORT OF JOINT CONFERENCE OF U.N. AGENCIES ON PROBLEMS OF ADMINISTRATION OF TECHNICAL ASSISTANCE. DEALS WITH SOCIAL, CULTURAL, ECONOMIC, AND POLITICAL IMPEDIMENTS TO EXECUTION OF TECHNICAL ASSISTANCE MISSIONS AND POSSIBLE SOLUTIONS.

1994 ORAZEM F.
"THE NEW SOVIET PLAN FOR AGRICULTURE (1960-1970)"
ROCKY MOUNTAIN SOCIAL SCIENCE J., 4 (OCT. 67), 60-64.
DISCUSSES FAILURE OF FOOD PRODUCTION IN USSR AND NEW PLAN FOR AGRICULTURAL DEVELOPMENT. DESCRIBES MODEST AIMS OF PROGRAM AND ITS ACCEPTANCE OF LIMITED PRIVATE OWNERSHIP. STUDIES INCENTIVES OF INCREASED PRICES, NEW LAND, AND GUARANTEED WAGES. MAINTAINS THAT REALISTIC PLAN SHOWS THAT SOVIET GOVERNMENT IS WILLING TO INVEST IN AGRICULTURE TO FURTHER ECONOMIC GROWTH.

1995 ORG FOR ECO COOP AND DEVEL
THE MEDITERRANEAN REGIONAL PROJECT: AN EXPERIMENT IN PLANNING BY SIX COUNTRIES.
PARIS: ORG FOR ECO COOP AND DEV, 1965, 39 PP.
RELATES EDUCATION TO ECONOMIC GROWTH AND SOCIAL ADVANCEMENT IN GREECE, YUGOSLAVIA, SPAIN, TURKEY, PORTUGAL, AND ITALY. ESTIMATES FUTURE EDUCATIONAL NEEDS ACCORDING TO ECONOMIC CRITERIA, SOCIAL AND CULTURAL OBJECTIVES, AND DEMOGRAPHIC TRENDS. FORMULATES PROPOSALS FOR 1961-75. ANALYZES COSTS, ADMINISTRATION, EDUCATIONAL STRUCTURE, DEMAND AND SUPPLY, MANPOWER, AND ROLE OF TEACHERS.

1996 ORG FOR ECO COOP AND DEVEL
THE MEDITERRANEAN REGIONAL PROJECT: YUGOSLAVIA; EDUCATION AND DEVELOPMENT.
PARIS: ORG FOR ECO COOP AND DEV, 1965, 143 PP.
REVIEWS ECONOMIC AND SOCIAL DEVELOPMENTS, PAST AND PRESENT, AND SURVEYS YUGOSLAV EDUCATIONAL SYSTEM. DISCUSSES ECONOMIC AND MANPOWER PROJECTIONS, 1961-75, AND SKILL STRUCTURE; INCLUDES PROSPECTIVE VERSUS REQUIRED OUTPUTS OF EDUCATIONAL SYSTEM FOR 1961-75 AND PRESENTS METHODOLOGICAL APPROACH. CLOSING SECTION DEALS WITH TEACHING STAFF AND FINANCIAL EXPENDITURE.

1997 ORG FOR ECO COOP AND DEVEL
GEOGRAPHICAL DISTRIBUTION OF FINANCIAL FLOWS TO LESS DEVELOPED COUNTRIES.
PARIS: ORG FOR ECO COOP AND DEV, 1966, 179 PP.
PROVIDES DATA ON FINANCIAL AID TO UNDERDEVELOPED COUNTRIES FROM DEVELOPED OECD MEMBERS AND MULTI-LATERAL AGENCIES. DATA ARRANGED BY RECIPIENT COUNTRY OR AREA. SPECIFIES AMOUNTS RECEIVED BY EACH UNDERDEVELOPED COUNTRY, SOURCE OF FUNDS, AND TYPE OF ASSISTANCE.

1998 ORGANIZATION AMERICAN STATES
ECONOMIC SURVEY OF LATIN AMERICA, 1962.
BALTIMORE: JOHNS HOPKINS PR., 1964, 444 PP.
DEMONSTRATES IMPACT OF ALLIANCE OR PROGRESS ON LATIN-AMERICAN ECONOMY, ASSESSING CAPACITY TO IMPORT AND DEVELOPMENT OF PRODUCTIVE STRUCTURE. EVALUATES EXECUTION OF ECONOMIC PROGRAMS UNDER ALLIANCE FOR PROGRESS.

1999 ORLANS H.
CONTRACTING FOR ATOMS.
WASHINGTON: BROOKINGS INST, 1967, 242 PP., LC#67-17131.
DISCUSSES CURRENT ATOMIC ENERGY COMMISSION CONTRACT POLICIES AND PROBLEMS, MEN INVOLVED, AND COMMISSION'S FUTURE ROLE. RECOMMENDS DEFINITION OF AIMS, COMPETITION FOR GROWTH, AND CLARIFICATION OF MISSION OF AEC.

2000 ORTON W.A.
THE ECONOMIC ROLE OF THE STATE.
CHICAGO: U OF CHICAGO PRESS, 1950, 192 PP.
HISTORICAL STUDY OF ACTIVITIES OF GOVERNMENT IN ECONOMY OF NATION. ANALYZES POWERS OF STATE AND HOW APPLIED TO CONTROL OR REGULATE ECONOMIC DEVELOPMENT.

2001 OSBORN F.
OUR PLUNDERED PLANET.
BOSTON: LITTLE BROWN, 1948, 217 PP.
BELIEVES THAT MAN, IN SPITE OF HIS ADVANCED CIVILIZATION, IS STILL A PART OF NATURE'S PROCESSES. ATTEMPTS TO SHOW HOW MAN IS MISUSING THE EARTH, AND ASSERTS THAT IF HE CONTINUES AT HIS PRESENT RATE, HIS LIFE SOURCES WILL BE DESTROYED. BELIEVES MISUSE HELPED TO BRING ON WWI AND II, AND MAY THREATEN MAN'S SURVIVAL.

2002 OSGOOD H.L.
"SCIENTIFIC SOCIALISM: RODBERTUS"
POLIT. SCI. QUART., 1 (DEC. 86), 560-594.
HISTORY OF POLITICAL THEORY OF CARL RODBERTUS, BELIEVED TO BE SOCIALISTIC ECONOMIC THEORIST BETTER THAN MARX. INDICATES SIMILARITIES TO AND IMPROVEMENTS ON MARXIST VIEWS.

2003 OTERO L.M.
HONDURAS.
MADRID: ED CULTURA HISPANICA, 1963, 399 PP.
DISCUSSION OF PRESENT-DAY HONDURAS, INCLUDING SOCIAL STRUCTURE, POPULATION, ECONOMY, CULTURAL INTEGRATION, AND RELIGION. EMPHASIZES EVOLUTION OF HONDURAN NATIONAL IDENTITY.

2004 OVERSEAS DEVELOPMENT INST
EFFECTIVE AID.
LONDON: MIN OF OVERSEAS DEVEL, 1967, 129 PP.
EXAMINES AID ADMINISTRATION, TERMS AND CONDITIONS OF FOREIGN AID, AND TECHNICAL ASSISTANCE TO UNDERDEVELOPED NATIONS. DISCUSSES PRACTICES IN GERMANY, FRANCE, UK, AND US.

2005 OWEN C.F.
"US AND SOVIET RELATIONS WITH UNDERDEVELOPED COUNTRIES: LATIN AMERICA-A CASE STUDY."
INTER-AMER. ECON. AFF., 14 (WINTER 60), 85-116.
ILLUSTRATES COMPATIBILITY OF NATIONAL ASPIRATIONS WITH ECONOMIC INTERNATIONALISM. AS OUTSTANDING EXAMPLE, CITES CASE OF ARGENTINA, WHERE STATE OIL MONOPOLY, YPF, SUCCESSFULLY NEGOTIATED WITH USA OIL INTERESTS. CONSIDERS NATIONALISM AS FORCE DRIVING LATIN AMERICAN AND AFRICAN COUNTRIES TO TRADE WITH SOVIET UNION.

2006 OWENS R.N.
BUSINESS, ORGANIZATION, AND COMBINATION.
ENGLEWOOD CLIFFS: PRENTICE HALL, 1951, 555 PP.
STUDY OF SIMPLE OR INDEPENDENT TYPES OF BUSINESS ENTERPRISE, AND OF INTERRELATED AND MORE COMPLEX FORMS IN WHICH SIMPLER TYPES ARE CONSTITUENT UNITS. TREATS ECONOMIC AND LEGAL ASPECTS OF ENTERPRISES. DISCUSSES COMBINATION MOVEMENT AND ECONOMICS AND REGULATION OF COMBINATION. REVIEWS ACCOMPLISHMENTS OF NEW DEAL LEGISLATION.

2007 OXENFELDT A.R., HOLUMNYCHY V.
ECONOMIC SYSTEMS IN ACTION.
NEW YORK: HOLT RINEHART WINSTON, 1965, 264 PP., LC#65-14872.
COMPARES OPERATIONS AND ECONOMIC PLANNING IN US, USSR, AND FRANCE. BRIEF DISCUSSION OF STRENGTHS AND WEAKNESSES OF EACH AND RELATIONS TO CULTURAL BACKGROUND PRESENTED.

2008 OZGA S.A.
EXPECTATIONS IN ECONOMIC THEORY.
LONDON: WEIDENFIELD & NICOLSON, 1965, 303 PP., LC#65-25578.
EXAMINES NOTION OF EXPECTATIONS IN ECONOMIC THEORY WITH EMPHASIS ON METHODOLOGICAL CONSIDERATIONS. DISCUSSES THEORY OF GAMES, OF "MORAL EXPECTATION," AND "SURE-PROSPECT EQUIVALENTS."

2009 PAARLBERG D.
AMERICAN FARM POLICY: A CASE STUDY IN CENTRALIZED DECISION-MAKING.
NEW YORK: JOHN WILEY, 1964, 375 PP., LC#64-14996.
DETAILED DISCUSSION OF FARM PROBLEM IN US, AND HOW CONGRESS, FARMERS' GROUPS, AND EXECUTIVE AGENCIES VIE FOR POWER TO CONTROL POLICY: THE DEPARTMENT OF AGRICULTURE IS THE SINGLE MOST POWERFUL ORGANIZATION. CONCLUDES THAT GOVERNMENT INTERVENTION SHOULD CEASE AND US SHOULD RETURN TO A FREE MARKET ECONOMY IN AGRICULTURE.

2010 PAAUW D.S.
"ECONOMIC PROGRESS IN SOUTHEAST ASIA."
J. ASIAN STUD., 23 (NOV. 63), 69-92.
'SOUTHEAST ASIA SHARES WITH OTHER UNDERDEVELOPED AREAS PROBLEMS OF STATISTICAL RELIABILITY OF AGGREGATIVE ECONOMIC DATA. DIFFICULTIES IN MEASURING AND COMPARING DIMENSIONS OF GROWTH ARE COMPOUNDED BY UNRESOLVED CONCEPTUAL PROBLEMS.' IT IS NEVERTHELESS CLEAR THAT THERE HAS BEEN A PERCEPTIBLE RETARDATION OF GROWTH RATES IN ALL SOUTHEAST ASIAN COUNTRIES, AND WHERE NEW GROWTH HAS OCCURRED, IT APPEARS THAT INCREMENTAL CAPITAL-OUTPUT RATIOS HAVE RISEN SHARPLY.

2011 PACKENHAM R.A.
"POLITICAL-DEVELOPMENT DOCTRINES IN THE AMERICAN FOREIGN AID PROGRAM."
WORLD POLITICS, 18 (JAN. 66), 194-235.
AUTHOR GIVES BRIEF, BUT SUBSTANTIAL COVERAGE OF IMPORTANT THEORISTS VIEWS ON FIVE CONDITIONS OF POLITICAL DEVELOPMEMT AND DISCUSSES LACK OF ATTENTION SPENT ON THE DEPENDENT VARIABLE, POLITICAL DEVELOPMENT ITSELF. HE THEN SHOWS THAT U.S. A.I.D. ADMINISTRATORS AND DOCTRINES PAY LITTLE ATTENTION TO POLITICAL DEVELOPMENT BECAUSE IT IS BELIEVED LITTLE POLITICAL CHANGE CAN BE EFFECTED BY AID.

2012 PADELFORD N.J.
"FINANCIAL CRISIS AND THE UNITED NATIONS."
WORLD POLIT., 15 (JULY 63), 531-568.
DETAILED ANALYSIS OF UNITED NATIONS' ASSESSMENTS. FINANCIAL CRISIS DUE TO MEMBERS WHO, FOR POLITICAL NOT ECONOMIC REASONS, DO NOT PAY THEIR BILLS. IF UN IS TO SURVIVE, ADEQUATE MEANS OF FINANCING MUST BE FOUND.

2013 PADELFORD N.J.
"THE ORGANIZATION OF AFRICAN UNITY."
INT. ORGAN., 18 (SUMMER 64), 521-42.
CONSIDERS MAJOR PROBLEMS OF FUNCTIONAL COOPERATION AND GRADUALISM AS OPPOSED TO UNITY AND CENTRALIZATION IN THE HISTORICAL DEVELOPMENT OF AFRICAN UNITY. EXAMINES PRINCIPLE ORGANS ESTABLISHED BY THE ORGANIZATION'S CHARTER AND THE RESOLUTIONS THUS FAR ADOPTED.

2014 PAENSON I. ED.
SYSTEMATIC GLOSSARY ENGLISH, FRENCH, SPANISH, RUSSIAN OF SELECTED ECONOMIC AND SOCIAL TERMS.
NEW YORK: PERGAMON PRESS, 1963, 414 PP., LC#63-10029.
DICTIONARY OF TERMS FROM ECONOMICS AND SOCIAL SCIENCES IN ENGLISH, FRENCH, SPANISH AND RUSSIAN, ARRANGED ACCORDING TO SUBJECT. TRANSLATIONS ARE CAREFUL AND COMPLETE.

2015 PAI G.A.
"TAXATION AND PLANNING IN INDIA: A BIRDS-EYE VIEW."
UNITED ASIA, 19 (MAR.-APR. 67), 112-118.
ANALYZES POSSIBILITIES OF DIRECT OR INDIRECT TAXATION AS "EGALITARIAN" MEASURES IN INDIA. FINDS TAXES HAVE WIDENED INCOME GAP, SHOWING THAT CONGRESS GOVERNMENT FAVORS WEALTHY

CLASS. PROPOSES GOVERNMENT REDUCE BURDEN OF INDIRECT TAXATION ON COMMON MAN BY ENFORCING COLLECTION OF ASSESSED DIRECT TAXES. RECOMMENDS INCREASE OF DIRECT TAXATION TO LEVEL OF INDIRECT.

2016 PAKISTAN MINISTRY OF FINANCE
FOREIGN ECONOMIC AID: A REVIEW OF FOREIGN ECONOMIC AID TO PAKISTAN.
RAWALPINDI: PAKISTAN MIN FINANCE, 1962, 118 PP.
DETAILED REPORT PRESENTING IN RETROSPECT THE POSITION OF ECONOMIC ASSISTANCE TO PAKISTAN BY FRIENDLY COUNTRIES AND AGENCIES. STUDY GROUPED UNDER HEADINGS OF US AID; AID RECEIVED UNDER COLOMBO PLAN FROM COMMONWEALTH COUNTRIES AND JAPAN; AID FROM UN, FORD FOUNDATION, AND EUROPEAN COUNTRIES; AND FOREIGN LOANS AND CREDITS FROM EIGHT COUNTRIES.

2017 PALACIOS A.L.
PETROLEO, MONOPOLIOS, Y LATIFUNDIOS.
BUENOS AIRES: GUILLERMO KRAFT, 1957, 405 PP.
EXAMINES ECONOMIC STRUCTURE OF OIL, MONOPOLY, AND LAND IN ARGENTINA. EXPLAINS NEED FOR NATIONALIZATION OF RESOURCES AND ELIMINATION OF ECONOMIC CONTROL BY FOREIGN CAPITAL. DISCUSSES NEED FOR NATIONAL GOVERNMENT TO HELP IMPROVE INDUSTRIAL OUTPUT AND TO END UNFAIR OPERATIONS.

2018 PALAMOUNTAIN JC J.R.
THE DOLCIN CASE AND THE FEDERAL TRADE COMMISSION (PAMPHLET)
UNIVERSITY: U ALABAMA PR, 1963, 64 PP.
STUDIES PROCESS OF INVESTIGATION, LITIGATION, AND REVIEW OF DRUG MANUFACTURER'S ADVERTISING CLAIMS ABOUT AN ASPIRIN PRODUCT. DEPICTS FTC'S DIFFICULTIES IN DISTINGUISHING BETWEEN DECEPTIVE ADVERTISING AND HARMLESS EXAGGERATION OF PRODUCT'S MERITS.

2019 PALAMOUNTAIN JC J.R.
THE POLITICS OF DISTRIBUTION.
CAMBRIDGE: HARVARD U PR, 1955, 270 PP., LC#55-11952.
THESIS IS THAT STRUCTURE OF ECONOMIC SYSTEM OF DISTRIBUTION INHERENTLY CREATES ECONOMIC POWER STRUGGLES WHICH AFFECT POLITICAL PROCESSES. EXPLORES INTERACTION OF CONSUMERS, DISTRIBUTORS, MANUFACTURERS, AND GOVERNMENT. GIVES GOVERNMENT ROLE OF HOLDING POWER BALANCE. FOOD, DRUG, AND AUTOMOBILE INDUSTRIES SERVE FOR EXAMPLES.

2020 PALMER E.E. ED.
INDUSTRIAL MAN.
SYRACUSE: SYR U, MAXWELL SCHOOL, 1958, 139 PP.
EXPLORES NATURE OF INDUSTRIALISM, ITS EFFECTS ON WORKERS, WAYS IN WHICH SOCIETY HAS MET INDUSTRIAL DEMANDS AND THE NATURE OF INDUSTRIAL PROBLEMS. DISCUSSES EXISTENCE OF MASS SOCIETY IN INDUSTRIALIZED STATES, AFFLUENCE IN INDUSTRIAL SOCIETIES, AND THE EFFECT OF INDUSTRIALISM ON CULTURE.

2021 PALMER E.E. ED.
THE ECONOMY AND THE DEMOCRATIC IDEAL.
SYRACUSE: SYR U, MAXWELL SCHOOL, 1958, 138 PP.
DISCUSSES NATURE, POSSIBLE DEVELOPMENTS, AND PITFALLS OF US ECONOMY. PRESENTS ECONOMIC AND POLITICAL PHILOSOPHY; DEALS WITH AMERICAN ECONOMICS AND HOW FOREIGN NATIONS VIEW US. INCLUDES WRITINGS BY PAINE, SUMNER, WILSON, FDR, TRUMAN, GALBRAITH, AND THOMAS.

2022 PALYI M.
MANAGED MONEY AT THE CROSSROADS: THE EUROPEAN EXPERIENCE.
NOTRE DAME: U OF NOTRE DAME, 1958, 196 PP., LC#57-11375.
SURVEY OF FINANCIAL CENTERS OF EUROPE. ANALYZES METHODS OF MANAGING AND CONVERTING MONEY SINCE 1900'S. COVERS POSTWAR RECOVERY METHODS, INFLATIONARY CONTROLS, AND DEVALUATION TACTICS. BIBLIOGRAPHY OF SELECTED READINGS ON SUBJECT.

2023 PAN AMERICAN UNION
REPERTORIO DE PUBLICACIONES PERIODICAS ACTUALES LATINO-AMERICANAS.
PARIS: UNESCO, 1958.
DIRECTORY OF LATIN AMERICAN PERIODICALS ARRANGED BY DEWEY DECIMAL SYSTEM.

2024 PAN AMERICAN UNION
THE EFFECTS OF THE EUROPEAN ECONOMIC COMMUNITY ON THE LATIN AMERICAN ECONOMIES (BMR)
WASHINGTON: PAN AMERICAN UNION, 1963, 93 PP.
ANALYSIS OF EEC'S IMPACT ON LATIN AMERICAN EXPORTS. REPORT SUMMARIZES POLICY IMPLICATIONS OF EEC'S CHARTER, EXAMINES CHARACTER OF LATIN AMERICA'S TRADE, AND DISCUSSES THE TREATY OF ROME AND ITS IMPLEMENTATION. LATIN AMERICAN-EEC TRADE PATTERNS ARE ANALYZED THROUGH EXPORTS AND IMPORTS AND PROSPECTS FOR MAJOR COMMODITIES TRADE ARE REVIEWED FOR INDIVIDUAL COMMODITIES.

2025 PANIKKAR K.M.
THE AFRO-ASIAN STATES AND THEIR PROBLEMS.
NEW YORK: JOHN DAY, 1959, 104 PP.
OUTLINE OF PROBLEMS OF EMERGENT NATION, POLITICAL, ECONOMIC, AND SOCIAL. NECESSITY FOR NEW GOVERNMENT, EDUCATIONAL FAILINGS, BREAKDOWN OF EXISTING SOCIAL STRUCTURE, AND ECONOMIC DEPENDENCE ARE EXAMINED.

2026 PANT Y.P.
PLANNING IN UNDERDEVELOPED ECONOMIES.
ALLAHABAD: INDIAN PRESS, LTD, 1955, 160 PP.
DESCRIPTION OF PLANNING IN INDIA UNDER VARIOUS FOREIGN RULERS. EXPLAINS ECONOMIC PLANNING AT PRESENT, DESCRIBING FIRST FIVE YEAR PLAN, AND MAKES SUGGESTIONS FOR NEPAL.

2027 PARKER G.P. JR.
"MONETARY RECOVERY UNDER THE FEDERAL LABOR STATUTES."
TEXAS LAW REVIEW, 45 (APR. 67), 881-920.
DISCUSSES FOUR FEDERAL ACTS BY WHICH LABOR CAN SUE FOR DAMAGES: WAGNER ACT WHICH ESTABLISHED LABOR RELATIONS BOARD, RAILWAY LABOR ACT, TAFT-HARTLEY ACT, AND LABOR-MANAGEMENT REPORTING AND DISCLOSURE ACT. COVERS METHOD OF DETERMINING, PROVING, AND COMPUTING DAMAGES, AND POINTS OUT VARIOUS SECTIONS OF EACH ACT THAT CAN BE CALLED ON. CITES CASES IN ILLUSTRATION.

2028 PARMELEE M.
GEO-ECONOMIC REGIONAL AND WORLD FEDERATION.
NEW YORK: EXPOSITION, 1949, 137 PP., $2.50.
ATTEMPT AT DELINEATION OF REGIONS ACCORDING TO GEOGRAPHIC AND ECONOMIC PRINCIPLES. REGIONALISM AS BASIS FOR WORLD FEDERATION ANALYZED IN TERMS OF THE FORCES FOR AND AGAINST IT, ITS NATURE, BASES, AND FUNCTIONS. GEOGRAPHIC, ECONOMIC, AND GEO-ECONOMIC REGIONS ARE DISCUSSED AND RELATED. CLASSIFICATIONS ARE PROPOSED.

2029 PARRIS H.W.
GOVERNMENT AND THE RAILWAYS IN NINETEENTH-CENTURY BRITAIN.
LONDON: ROUTLEDGE & KEGAN PAUL, 1965, 244 PP.
DESCRIBES NEW FUNCTION OF CENTRAL GOVERNMENT IN 19TH CENTURY, THAT OF CONTROLLING RAILWAYS ON BEHALF OF PUBLIC. DISCUSSES NEW AGENCIES INSTITUTED TO DEAL WITH RAILWAYS, THEIR INFLUENCE ON POLICIES, THEIR FUNCTIONS, AND THEIR ROLE IN IMPROVING SERVICE. EXAMINES RAILWAYS' EFFECTS ON GOVERNMENTAL POLICIES, IMPACT OF LEADERS ON RAILWAY COMPANIES, AND INTERCOMPANY RELATIONS.

2030 PARSONS T.
THE SOCIAL SYSTEM.
GLENCOE: FREE PR., 1951, 575 PP.
BRINGS TOGETHER VARIOUS CONCEPTUAL APPROACHES TO ANALYSIS OF SOCIAL SYSTEMS. ASSESSES FUNCTIONS AND MOTIVATIONS OF ROLE WITHIN SOCIAL SYSTEM.

2031 PARSONS T., SMELSER N.J.
ECONOMY AND SOCIETY: A STUDY IN THE INTEGRATION OF ECONOMIC AND SOCIAL THEORY.
LONDON: ROUTLEDGE & KEGAN PAUL, 1956, 322 PP.
AN ATTEMPT TO ATTAIN A SYNTHESIS OF ECONOMIC AND SOCIAL THEORY BY FIRST POINTING OUT CERTAIN CONGRUENCES, SECOND, DELINEATING THE SOCIAL NATURE OF ECONOMIC THEORY, AND LAST, RELATING GROWTH AND PROBLEM OF INSTITUTIONAL CHANGE IN THE ECONOMY. SEES ADVANTAGES IN COMBINATION OF BOTH DISCIPLINES.

2032 PASSIN H. ED.
THE UNITED STATES AND JAPAN.
ENGLEWOOD CLIFFS: PRENTICE HALL, 1966, 174 PP., LC#66-14703.
COLLECTION OF ESSAYS DISCUSSING POLITICAL AND ECONOMIC RELATIONS BETWEEN US AND JAPAN. MAINTAINS THAT INTERNAL POLITICAL STRIFE IN JAPAN REFLECTS IN LARGE MEASURE THE MEMORY OF DEFEAT AND OCCUPATION BY US. DISCUSSES ECONOMIC RELATIONS IN LIGHT OF COMMON OBJECTIVES AND CONCLUDES WITH PROJECTION OF FUTURE TRENDS.

2033 PASTOR R.S., BRUGADA R.S.
A STATEMENT OF THE LAWS OF PARAGUAY IN MATTERS AFFECTING BUSINESS (2ND ED.)
WASHINGTON: PAN AMERICAN UNION, 1962, 284 PP.
SUMMARY IN ENGLISH OF CONSTITUTIONAL, STATUTORY, AND REGULATORY PROVISIONS OF PARAGUAY (IN 1962) RELEVANT TO COMMERCIAL, INDUSTRIAL, AND LABOR CONCERNS AND THE PERSONS THEY INVOLVE.

2034 PATAI R.
JORDAN, LEBANON AND SYRIA: AN ANNOTATED BIBLIOGRAPHY.
NEW HAVEN: HUMAN REL AREA FILES, 1957, 289 PP., LC#57-13286.
BIBLIOGRAPHY OF 1605, ITEMS LISTING IMPORTANT BOOKS AND ARTICLES DEALING WITH SOCIAL SCIENCES, INCLUDING ANTHROPOLOGY, ECONOMICS, POLITICS, SOCIOLOGY AND HUMAN GEOGRAPHY. CONTAINS SOME MATERIAL PERTAINING TO ARAB POPULATION OF MANDATORY AND PALESTINE BUT EMPHASIS IS ON PRESENT-DAY JORDAN, LEBANON, AND SYRIA. INCLUDES HANDBOOKS, GUIDES, AND MAPS.

2035 PATEL S.J.
"THE ECONOMIC DISTANCE BETWEEN NATIONS: ITS ORIGIN, MEASUREMENT AND OUTLOOK."
ECON. J., 74 (MAR 64), 119-31.
ANALYZES ECONOMIC DISPARITY AMONG NATIONS IN TERMS OF ORIGIN, SCOPE AND PROCESS. TO BRIDGE THE EXISTING GAP, A SUSTAINED (50 YEARS) RATE OF GROWTH OF 5 PER CENT MUST BE

PLANNED FOR, BY THE UNDEVELOPED COUNTRIES.

2036 PATRICK H.T.
CYCLICAL INSTABILITY AND FISCAL-MONETARY POLICY IN POST-WAR JAPAN (PAMPHLET)
COLO: CONF ECO ENTERPR MOD JAPAN, 1963, 58PP.
ANALYZES CYCLICAL NATURE IN GROWTH RATE OF GROSS NATIONAL PRODUCT, INDUSTRIAL OUTPUT, AND OTHER ASPECTS OF POSTWAR JAPANESE ECONOMY. NOTES NATURE AND EFFECTIVENESS OF FISCAL AND MONETARY POLICIES TAKEN TO DAMP THEM. TIME PERIOD CONSIDERED IS 1951-62.

2038 PATTON R., WARNE C.
THE DEVELOPMENT OF THE AMERICAN ECONOMY: REVISED.
GLENVIEW, ILL: SCOTT, FORESMAN, 1963, 464 PP.
INTERPRETATIVE ACCOUNT OF US ECONOMIC DEVELOPMENT AND MODERN ECONOMIC INSTITUTIONS. BEGINS WITH EUROPEAN ANTECEDENTS AND COVERS COLONIAL PERIOD, INDUSTRIALIZATION, WARS, LABOR, CRISES, AND CURRENT NATIONAL AND INTERNATIONAL PROBLEMS.

2039 PAULY M.V.
"MIXED PUBLIC AND PRIVATE FINANCING OF EDUCATION."
AMER. ECO. REVIEW, 57 (MAR. 67), 120-130.
DISCUSSION OF METHODS FOR OBTAINING OPTIMAL EDUCATIONAL BENEFITS MOST EFFICIENTLY THROUGH MIXED PUBLIC AND INDIVIDUAL FAMILY CONTRIBUTIONS. PUBLIC CONTRIBUTIONS MAY HAVE TO BE UNEQUAL, IF EFFICIENCY RATHER THAN ETHICAL CONSIDERATIONS IS PRIMARY. DIFFERENT INCOME LEVELS MAY REQUIRE DIFFERENT AMOUNTS OF PUBLIC AID.

2040 PAUNIO J.J.
A STUDY IN THE THEORY OF OPEN INFLATION.
HELSINKI: BANK FIN, INST ECO RES, 1961, 141 PP.
ABSTRACT STUDY ANALYZING COURSE OF INFLATIONARY PROCESS AND FACTORS THAT INFLUENCE IT, INCLUDING BASIC MODEL, PRICING PROCESS, AND DEMAND EQUATIONS.

2041 PAWERA J.C.
ALGERIA'S INFRASTRUCTURE.
NEW YORK: FREDERICK PRAEGER, 1964, 234 PP., LC#64-23511.
ECONOMIC SURVEY OF RECENT DEVELOPMENTS IN AREAS OF TRANSPORTATION, COMMUNICATIONS, AND ENERGY RESOURCES IN ALGERIA. FOCUSES ON DEVELOPMENT OF INTEGRATED INDUSTRIALIZATION IN ALGERIA.

2042 PAYNE J.L.
LABOR AND POLITICS IN PERU; THE SYSTEM OF POLITICAL BARGAINING.
NEW HAVEN: YALE U PR, 1965, 292 PP., LC#65-22335.
DISCUSSES LABOR RELATIONS AND LABOR POLITICS AS ONE AREA. COLLECTIVE BARGAINING IS MORE ACCURATELY POLITICAL BARGAINING IN PERU WHERE POLITICS AND UNIONS ARE CLOSELY TIED. EXAMINES RELATIONS BETWEEN LABOR AND EXTREMIST AND MODERATE PARTIES, STRUCTURE AND LEADERSHIP OF LABOR MOVEMENT, AND SYSTEM OF POLITICAL BARGAINING.

2043 PAYNO M.
LA REFORMA SOCIAL EN ESPANA Y MEXICO.
MEXICO CITY: U NAC INST HIST MEX, 1958, 127 PP.
ANALYZES SPANISH AND MEXICAN SOCIAL REFORM REGARDING CHURCH PROPERTY IN 19TH AND 20TH CENTURIES. EXAMINES LEGAL POSITION OF CATHOLIC CHURCH AS LARGEST LANDOWNER IN BOTH COUNTRIES AND BENEFICIAL ADVANTAGES OF FREEDOM FROM TAXES. ALSO DISCUSSES TIGHT LEGAL RESTRICTIONS ON CHURCH ACTIVITY AS REVOLUTION BROUGHT ANTI-CLERICAL LIBERALS TO POWER.

2044 PEARL A., RIESSMAN F.
NEW CAREERS FOR THE POOR: THE NON-PROFESSIONAL IN HUMAN SERVICE.
NEW YORK: FREE PRESS OF GLENCOE, 1965, 272 PP., LC#65-14910.
TAKES THESIS FROM HARYOU PROPOSAL AND ARGUES THAT "HIRING THE POOR TO SERVE THE POOR IS A FUNDAMENTAL APPROACH TO POVERTY IN AN AUTOMATED AGE." MAINTAINS THAT THIS APPROACH PROVIDES JOBS FOR THE POOR, IMPROVES QUALITY OF WELFARE SERVICES, AND RELIEVES SHORTAGES OF TRAINED PROFESSIONALS. EVALUATES EFFORTS TO OVERCOME POVERTY AND DISCUSSES EMPLOYMENT AND TRAINING OF NONPROFESSIONALS TO AID POOR.

2045 PECCEI A.
"DEVELOPED-UNDERDEVELOPED AND EAST-WEST RELATIONS."
ATLANTIC COMMUNITY QUART., 5 (SPRING 67), 71-86.
FOR THE WEST ADEQUATELY TO EXERCISE WORLD LEADERSHIP, THE OUTMODED EAST-WEST AND NORTH-SOUTH SCHEMA SHOULD BE REPLACED BY AN "ONION LAYERS CONCEPT" WITH THE ATLANTIC COMMUNITY AS CORE. LAYERS THEN WOULD BE SPECIAL RELATIONSHIP AREAS, OUTSIDE DEVELOPING REGIONS, AND AREAS TO BE DEVELOPED LATER, E.G., SUB-SAHARAN AFRICA. THE LATTER CANNOT NOW USE MASSIVE COMMITMENT, THOUGH PRESENT AID SHOULD CONTINUE.

2046 PEDLER F.J.
ECONOMIC GEOGRAPHY OF WEST AFRICA.
LONDON: LONGMANS, GREEN & CO, 1955, 232 PP.
DETAILED DISCUSSION OF ECONOMIC FACTORS IN WEST AFRICA WITH ATTENTION TO ECONOMIC THEORY. TREATS GEOGRAPHY, POPULATION, PRODUCTS, TRANSPORTATION, IMPORTS, DISTRIBUTION, LABOR, CAPITAL AND INVESTMENT, ETC. ATTEMPTS TO PRESENT FACTS AND ESTABLISH CAUSE-EFFECT RELATIONSHIP BY USING ECONOMIST'S ANALYSIS AND REASONING.

2047 PEDLEY F.H.
EDUCATION AND SOCIAL WORK.
NEW YORK: PERGAMON PRESS, 1967, 170 PP.
SURVEYS VARIOUS ASPECTS OF COORDINATION BETWEEN EDUCATION AND SOCIAL WORK. ANALYZES GROWING AWARENESS AMONG EDUCATIONISTS AND SOCIAL WORKERS OF NEED TO INTERRELATE THEIR DISCIPLINES SO THAT MAXIMUM VALUE CAN BE OBTAINED FROM EDUCATIONAL RESOURCES.

2048 PEGRUM D.E.
"PUBLIC REGULATION OF BUSINESS (REV ED)"
HOMEWOOD: RICHARD IRWIN, 1965.
ECONOMIC ANALYSIS OF REGULATION. ANALYZES PRINCIPLES OF PRICING DECISIONS, BASIC FACTS OF INSTITUTIONAL AND GOVERNMENTAL ARRANGEMENTS, ORGANIZATIONAL STRUCTURE OF BUSINESS, ANTI-TRUST LAWS AND THEIR ADMINISTRATION, TRANSPORTATION AND PUBLIC UTILITIES. EXAMINES RELATIONSHIPS OF ECONOMIC POLICY TO POLITICAL AND SOCIAL OBJECTIVES. EXTENSIVE BIBLIOGRAPHY INCLUDED.

2049 PEGRUM D.F.
URBAN TRANSPORT AND THE LOCATION OF INDUSTRY IN METROPOLITAN LOS ANGELES (PAMPHLET)
LOS ANGELES: UCLA BUR GOVT RES, 1963, 46 PP.
AUTHOR FINDS THAT INDUSTRIAL LOCATION IN LOS ANGELES AREA FOLLOWS ROUTES LAID OUT BY PRE-AUTOMOBILE RAILROAD LINES. IN LAST 40 YEARS INDUSTRIAL GROWTH HAS BEEN EXPANDING FROM CENTRAL CITY AREA IN ALL DIRECTIONS INDEPENDENT OF AUTO ROUTES; BUT RAIL TRANSPORTATION FOR PEOPLE HAS ALMOST BEEN ELIMINATED, THUS PRESENT-DAY RELIANCE ON AUTO TRANSPORT.

2050 PEIRCE W.S.
SELECTIVE MANPOWER POLICIES AND THE TRADE-OFF BETWEEN RISING PRICES AND UNEMPLOYMENT (DISSERTATION)
PRINCETON: PRIN U, DEPT OF ECO, 1966, 207 PP.
CONCEPTUAL CONSIDERATIONS ON DILEMMA OF APPARENT INCOMPATIBILITY OF FULL EMPLOYMENT WITH STABLE PRICES, ESTABLISHING CONDITIONS UNDER WHICH SELECTIVE MANPOWER POLICIES CAN DEAL WITH PROBLEM IN PARTICULAR MODELS OF LABOR MARKETS.

2051 PELLING H.M.
A HISTORY OF BRITISH TRADE UNIONISM.
BALTIMORE: PENGUIN BOOKS, 1963, 287 PP.
TRACES ORIGINS OF BRITISH TRADE UNIONISM IN EARLY 1800'S COVERS ITS DEVELOPMENT THROUGH WWI AND WWII. RELATES ITS STATUS IN EARLY 1960'S AND IMPORTANCE OF ITS EFFECT UPON BRITISH GOVERNMENT.

2052 PELTASON J.W. ED., BURNS J.M. ED.
FUNCTIONS AND POLICIES OF AMERICAN GOVERNMENT (3RD ED.)
ENGLEWOOD CLIFFS: PRENTICE HALL, 1967, 447 PP., LC#67-17594.
INTRODUCTORY STUDY OF US GOVERNMENT, ITS STRUCTURE, FUNCTIONS, AND PROGRAMS. CONCENTRATES ON GOVERNMENT'S PUBLIC POLICIES AND PROGRAMS FOR PUBLIC WELFARE. EACH AUTHOR DISCUSSES HIS PARTICULAR FIELD OF POLICY, AND RELATIONSHIP BETWEEN STATE AND FEDERAL GOVERNMENT IN CARRYING OUT POLICIES OF "GREAT SOCIETY."

2053 PELZER K.J.
SELECTED BIBLIOGRAPHY ON THE GEOGRAPHY OF SOUTHEAST ASIA (3 VOLS., 1949-1956)
NEW HAVEN: YALE U, SE ASIA STUD, 1949.
INTENDED AS REFERENCE AND READING LIST FOR STUDENTS OF PHYSICAL, CULTURAL, ECONOMIC, AND POLITICAL GEOGRAPHY OF SOUTHEAST ASIA. VOLUME I REFERS TO GENERAL STUDIES AND VOLUME II TO PHILIPPINES IN PARTICULAR. VOLUME III, PUBLISHED IN 1956, HAS BEEN EXPANDED TO DEVOTE GREATER ATTENTION TO ANTHROPOLOGY IN MALAYA. ORGANIZED BY CONTENT OF GENERAL DISCIPLINES.

2054 PEMBERTON J., JR.
"CONSTITUTIONAL PROBLEMS IN RESTRAINT ON THE MEDIA."
NOTRE DAME LAWYER, 42 (1967), 881-887.
INVESTIGATES CONSTITUTIONAL PROBLEMS IN AMERICAN BAR ASSOCIATIONS'S PROPOSALS FOR RESTRAINT OF PRESS BEFORE AND DURING COURT PROCEDURES. FINDS THAT CONSTITUTION GUARANTEES RIGHT OF PROTECTION AGAINST PARTIALITY IN TRIAL AND DOES NOT GIVE GOVERNMENT POWER TO CONTROL PRESS. BELIEVES THAT SUCH LAWS SHOULD NOT BE PASSED UNTIL NEED FOR THEM IS FULLY ESTABLISHED.

2055 PEN I.
PRIMER ON INTERNATIONAL TRADE.
NEW YORK: RANDOM HOUSE, INC, 1967, 146 PP., LC#67-12749.
DESCRIBES BASIC PRINCIPLES OF INTERNATIONAL TRADE. DEALS WITH PROBLEM OF EQUILIBRIUM AND BALANCE OF PAYMENTS; DISCUSSES FUNCTION OF TRADE BLOCS; TAKES STAND ON NUMBER OF CURRENT ISSUES.

2056 PENNEY N.

"BANK STATEMENTS, CANCELLED CHECKS, AND ARTICLE FOUR IN THE ELECTRONIC AGE."
MICH. LAW REV., 65 (MAY 67), 1341-1360.
EXAMINES EFFECT OF ACCELERATING OPERATIONAL AND TECHNOLOGICAL CHANGES IN BANKING INDUSTRY ON ARTICLE FOUR OF UNIFORM COMMERCIAL CODE. MEASURES WORKABILITY OF CODE FOR PRESENT AND CONTEMPLATED OPERATIONAL INNOVATIONS. FOCUSES ON BANKS' PROCEDURE OF ISSUING CHECKING-ACCOUNT STATEMENTS.

2057 PENNOCK J.R.
"PARTY AND CONSTITUENCY IN POSTWAR AGRICULTURAL PRICE SUPPORT LEGISLATION."
J. OF POLITICS, 18 (MAY 56), 167-210.
EXAMINES THE RELATIVE IMPORTANCE OF PARTY LOYALTY AND CONSTITUENTS' PREFERENCES IN DETERMINING VOTES IN CONGRESS, BY CONSIDERING VOTES ON ONE PARTICULAR SUBJECT, NAMELY, ON AGRICULTURAL PRICE SUPPORT IN THE POSTWAR PERIOD. IN GENERAL THERE WAS MORE PARTY COHESION AMONG REPUBLICANS, WHEREAS DEMOCRATS RESPONDED MORE TO CONSTITUENCY INTERESTS.

2058 PENNOCK J.R. ED.
SELF-GOVERNMENT IN MODERNIZING NATIONS.
ENGLEWOOD CLIFFS: PRENTICE HALL, 1964, 118 PP., LC#64-23554.
DISCUSSES PROBLEMS OF EMERGING NATIONS IN MODERNIZING THEIR WORKINGS. TREATS DIFFICULTIES IN SOCIAL, POLITICAL, AND ECONOMIC DEVELOPMENT FROM BOTH INTERNAL AND EXTERNAL VIEWPOINTS. COVERS INSTABILITY, CRISIS MANAGEMENT, ONE-PARTY SYSTEM, COMMUNISM, AND US POLICY TOWARD EMERGING NATIONS.

2059 PENNSYLVANIA ECONOMY LEAGUE
URBAN RENEWAL IMPACT STUDY: ADMINISTRATIVE-LEGAL-FISCAL.
PITTSBURGH: ACTION HOUSING, INC, 1960, 300 PP.
ATTEMPTS TO PLACE MAJOR PHYSCIAL, SOCIAL, ECONOMIC, AND ADMINISTRATIVE DIMENSIONS ON A COMPREHENSIVE RENEWAL PROGRAM FOR ALLEGHENY COUNTY, PENNSYLVANIA. IDENTIFIES BASIC PROBLEMS AND ISSUES AND POINTS WAY TOWARD MORE EFFECTIVELY OVERCOMING BLIGHT AND DECAY. AMONG SUGGESTIONS ARE THOSE FOR GREATER COOPERATION IN ADMINISTRATION, AND COMMUNITY PROGRAM FINANCING SOCIAL AND ECONOMIC AS WELL AS PHYSICAL PLANNING.

2060 PENTONY D.E. ED.
UNITED STATES FOREIGN AID.
SAN FRANCISCO: CHANDLER, 1960, 147 PP., LC#60-07597.
DISCUSSES OBJECTIVES OF US FOREIGN AID, MILITARY, ECONOMIC, AND HUMANITARIAN. GIVES BACKGROUND OF FOREIGN AID PROGRAM AND EXAMINES VARYING METHODS OF AID IN ITS ADMINISTRATION. USES TWO CASE STUDIES OF AID TO ANALYZE ITS EFFECTIVENESS.

2061 PERKINS D.
THE UNITED STATES AND LATIN AMERICA.
BATON ROUGE: LOUISIANA ST U PR, 1961, 124 PP., LC#61-7544.
DISCUSSES POLITICAL AND ECONOMIC RELATIONS BETWEEN US AND LATIN AMERICA FROM MONROE DOCTRINE TO PRESENT. EXAMINES HISTORY IN TERMS OF HEMISPHERIC INTEGRITY AND NATIONAL SECURITY.

2062 PERKINS D.H.
"ECONOMIC GROWTH IN CHINA AND THE CULTURAL REVOLUTION(1960-APRIL 1967)"
CHINA Q., 30 (APR.-JUNE 67), 33-48.
QUESTIONS DEGREE TO WHICH ECONOMIC ISSUES HAVE BEEN MAJOR SOURCE OF CONFLICT WITHIN CHINESE COMMUNIST LEADERSHIP, AND WHETHER IMPACT OF EVENTS OF EARLY 1967 ON ECONOMY HAS BEEN GREAT ENOUGH TO REDUCE CHINA'S FUTURE RATE OF GROWTH. ANALYZES ECONOMIC GROWTH AND POLICY, 1958-65, AND FINDS THAT EXPERIENCES OF THOSE YEARS CONVINCED MANY PARTY LEADERS THAT SUSTAINED GROWTH WAS POSSIBLE.

2063 PERLO V.
EL IMPERIALISMO NORTHEAMERICANO.
BUENOS AIRES: EDITORIAL PLATINA, 1961, 338 PP.
ANALYSIS OF US ECONOMIC POLICY AND INTERNATIONAL TRADE JUDGED AD ECONOMIC IMPERIALISM. EXTREMELY SOCIALISTIC OUTLOOK OF US INVESTMENT AND EXPORT PROGRAMS AROUND WORLD. DISCUSSES RACIAL DISCRIMINATION AND MILITARY POLICY BESIDES INTERNATIONAL ECONOMIC RELATIONS.

2064 PERLO V.
MILITARISM AND INDUSTRY.
NEW YORK: INTERNATIONAL PUBLRS, 1963, 63-8584 PP.
SUGGESTS THAT MUNITIONS AND AIRCRAFT INDUSTRIES ARE LARGELY RESPONSIBLE FOR CONTINUATION OF ARMS RACE. SHOWS HOW COMPANIES HOLDING FOREIGN INVESTMENTS STAND TO LOSE MONEY IF DISARMAMENT OCCURS. SUPPORTING DOCUMENTATION SHOWS HOW BUSINESS INFLUENCES GOVERNMENT POLICY.

2065 PERROUX F.
L'ECONOMIE DES JEUNES NATIONS.
PARIS: PR UNIV DE FRANCE, 1962, 252 PP.
DISCUSSES PROBLEMS OF INDUSTRIALIZATION IN DEVELOPING COUNTRIES OF AFRICA; EXAMINES FOREIGN INVESTMENT AND TECHNICAL ASSISTANCE. CENTERS ON DISCUSSIONS OF EUROPEAN-AFRICAN RELATIONS, WITH EMPHASIS ON FRENCH INVESTMENTS AND RESPONSIBILITIES.

2066 PERSALL E.S.
AN ECONOMETRIC STUDY OF FINANCIAL MARKETS.
PRINCETON: PRIN U, DEPT OF ECO, 1966, 313 PP.
ANALYZES TECHNICAL PROBLEMS OF "SPECIFYING AND ESTIMATING MODELS OF FINANCIAL MARKETS USING FLOW-OF-FUNDS DATA AND AN APPROPRIATE SIMULTANEOUS-EQUATION ESTIMATOR." ATTEMPTS TO TEST RECENT HYPOTHESES ON FINANCIAL MARKET ACTIVITY WITH STATISTICAL METHODS. FINDS RELATIONSHIP BETWEEN ACTIVITIES OF ALL TYPES OF MARKETS.

2067 PESELT B.M.
"COMMUNIST ECONOMIC OFFENSIVE."
LAW CONTEMP. PROBL., 29 (AUTUMN 64), 983-99.
TRACES EVOLUTION OF SOVIET VIEW TOWARDS POLICY AND PROBLEMS OF FOREIGN AID TO UNDERDEVELOPED NATIONS. MOTIVES AND AIMS OF SUCH AID IS ASSESSED AND THE FORMS OF SOVIET BILATERAL AGREEMENTS IS ANALYZED.

2068 PETCH G.A.
ECONOMIC DEVELOPMENT AND MODERN WEST AFRICA.
LONDON: U OF LONDON PRESS, 1961, 224 PP.
STUDY OF ECONOMIC DEVELOPMENT AND POSSIBILITIES OF WEST AFRICA. INTENDS TO CLARIFY ECONOMIC ACTIVITY, ECONOMIC AND POLITICAL FACTORS INVOLVED, PROBLEMS, AND POLICIES.

2069 PETERSON F.
SURVEY OF LABOR ECONOMICS (REV. ED.)
NEW YORK: HARPER & ROW, 1951, 871 PP.
ANALYZES BASIC DATA AND MAJOR THEORIES PERTAINING TO ECONOMIC PHENOMENA RELATING TO LABOR. EMPHASIZES HISTORICAL DEVELOPMENT OF CURRENT THEORIES, PRACTICES, AND INSTITUTIONAL ARRANGEMENTS. COVERS EMPLOYMENT AND UNEMPLOYMENT, WAGES AND HOURS, LABOR UNIONS AND LABOR-MANAGEMENT RELATIONS, AND SOCIAL SECURITY. REVISED EDITION IS UPDATED AND CONTAINS MANY CHANGES AND ADDITIONS.

2070 PETERSON W.C.
THE WELFARE STATE IN FRANCE.
LINCOLN: U OF NEB PR, 1960, 115 PP., LC#60-61504.
ANALYZES EXTENT TO WHICH FRANCE SINCE WWII HAS BECOME WELFARE STATE OR HAS ATTEMPTED TO ALTER PATTERN OF INCOME DISTRIBUTION TO GIVE MORE PEOPLE EQUAL SHARE AND MINIMUM STANDARD OF LIVING. CONCENTRATES ON SHOWING HOW SOCIAL SECURITY SYSTEM HAS BECOME INSTRUMENT FOR REDISTRIBUTION OF INCOME. SHOWS HOW PATTERNS OF DISTRIBUTION ARE ALTERED AS RESULT OF GOVERNMENTAL WELFARE EXPENDITURES.

2071 PETRAS J.
"U.S. HEGEMONY AND LATIN AMERICAN RULING CLASSES."
INTERNATIONAL SOCIALIST J., 21 (JUNE 67), 382-388.
STUDIES OCCASIONALLY AMBIGUOUS ATTITUDES OF LATIN AMERICAN GOVERNMENTS VIS-A-VIS CURRENT US POLICIES TOWARD THEM. ASSERTS UNDERSTANDING DEPENDS ON THREE FACTORS: LATIN AMERICAN DEPENDENCE ON US ECONOMIC-MILITARY SUPPORT; FEAR OF INTERNAL POPULAR REVOLTS; AND DESIRE TO EMULATE WESTERN SOCIO-POLITICAL PATTERNS OF BEHAVIOR. INTERRELATIONSHIP OF THESE FACTORS DETERMINES INTER-AMERICAN RELATIONS.

2072 PETRAS J.
"GUERRILLA MOVEMENTS IN LATIN AMERICA - I."
NEW POLITICS, 6 (WINTER 67), 80-94.
EXPLORES PARTICULAR HISTORICAL EXPERIENCES WHICH UNDERLIE GUERRILLA MOVEMENTS IN GUATEMALA, COLOMBIA, VENEZUELA, AND PERU. EXPLAINS EFFECT OF BREAKDOWN OF GOVERNMENT'S AUTHORITY ON SUCCESS OF MOVEMENTS AND CAUSES OF BREAKDOWNS. FINDS EACH GUERRILLA REVOLUTION HAS UNIQUE ASPECTS THAT REQUIRE SPECIAL CONSIDERATION.

2073 PETRAS J., ZEITLIN M.
"MINERS AND AGRARIAN RADICALISM."
AMER. SOCIOLOGICAL REV., 32 (AUG. 67), 578-586.
STUDIES RELATIONSHIP OF CHILEAN MINERS TO THEIR NEIGHBORING COMMUNITIES. DUE TO THEIR ORGANIZATIONAL SKILLS AND POLITICAL COMPETENCE, PROXIMITY OF MINES TO COUNTRYSIDE, SHARING OF EXPLOITED POSITIONS, AND ACTIVE POLITICAL CHOICE, THE MINERS POLITICIZE AND RADICALIZE THE RURAL COMMUNITIES.

2074 PETRO S.
THE KINGSPORT STRIKE.
NEW ROCHELLE: ARLINGTON HOUSE, 1967, 238 PP., LC#67-13408.
JOURNALISTIC APPROACH, WITH HUMAN INTEREST AS MAJOR DEVICE. ON-THE-SCENE COVERAGE OF PRESS STRIKE IN APPALACHIA. AIMS TO STIMULATE RE-EXAMINATION OF US LABOR POLICIES. HOLDS NLRB ACCOUNTABLE FOR DISTORTION OF CONGRESSIONAL POLICY WHICH RESULTED IN GROWING ARROGANCE OF UNIONS. CITES UNION MISUSE OF COLLECTIVE BARGAINING AND LOBBY AS TRAVESTY OF JUSTICE.

2075 PETROVICH M.B.
"UNITED STATES POLICY IN EAST EUROPE."
CURRENT HISTORY, 52 (APR. 67), 113-199, 243-244 .
EXPLAINS CURRENT POLITICAL RELATIONSHIP BETWEEN USSR AND EASTERN EUROPE. CURRENT US POLICY IS AIMED AT FOSTERING EVOLUTIONARY CHANGE. JOHNSON SEES GOAL AS BETTER ECONOMIC RELATIONS, SECURITY, AND "COMMON GOOD." EXPANSION OF TRADE HAS BEEN ENCOURAGED, AS WELL AS CULTURAL EXCHANGE.

2076 PFEFFER K.H.
WELT IM UMBRUCH.
GUTERSLOH: GUTERSLOHER VERL, 1966, 258 PP.
DISCUSSES ECONOMIC, SOCIAL, POLITICAL, AND INTELLECTUAL CHANGES WHICH HAVE OCCURRED WITH RISE OF MODERN INDUSTRIAL SOCIETY. EXAMINES MODERNIZATION AND NATIONALIZATION OF ECONOMY, PROFESSIONAL TRAINING, SECULARIZATION OF THINKING, AND SOCIAL MOBILITY. CONCLUDES BY EXAMINING TASKS OF CHRISTIANITY AND POSSIBILITIES OF CHRISTIAN ACTION.

2077 PFEFFERMANN G.
"TRADE UNIONS AND POLITICS IN FRENCH WEST AFRICA DURING THE FOURTH REPUBLIC."
AFRICAN AFFAIRS, 66 (JULY 67), 213-230.
ANALYZES POLITICAL MOTIVATION AND ORIENTATION OF TRADE UNIONS, SEEKING TO ASCERTAIN WHAT WERE LIMITING FACTORS WITHIN UNIONS WHICH PREVENTED DEEPER INVOLVEMENT IN POLITICS OR DIFFERENT COURSE FROM BEING FOLLOWED. BELIEVES MAIN ECONOMIC INTERESTS OF TRADE UNIONS DEPENDED ON PERPETUATION OF COLONIAL STRUCTURE. THIS HELPS EXPLAIN LACK OF POLITICAL ACTIVISM IN COLONIES.

2078 PFOUTS R.W. ED.
THE TECHNIQUES OF URBAN ECONOMIC ANALYSIS.
TRENTON: CHANDLER-DAVIS PUBLG, 1960, 410 PP., LC#59-11409.
PRESENTS SOME RECENT WRITINGS ON ECONOMICS OF URBAN DEVELOPMENT, INCLUDING AT LEAST THREE DIFFERENT AND CONFLICTING VIEWPOINTS. EXAMINES ECONOMIC BASE THEORY AND ITS IMPLICATIONS, OBJECTIONS TO THE THEORY AND AN ALTERNATIVE ONE, AND INPUT-OUTPUT APPROACH.

2079 PHELPS E.S. ED.
THE GOAL OF ECONOMIC GROWTH: SOURCES, COSTS, BENEFITS.
NEW YORK: W W NORTON, 1962, 176 PP., LC#62-20921.
ESSAYS ON WISDOM OF US GROWTH POLICIES, POSSIBILITY OF ACHIEVING GOALS THROUGH USE OF EXISTING RESOURCES, AND GOVERNMENT CONTROL OF GROWTH. VIEW PAST GROWTH IN US, AND ANALYZE POSSIBILITIES FOR THE FUTURE. COMPARE SOVIET AND US ECONOMIES. DESCRIBE METHODS THROUGH WHICH GROWTH IS ACHIEVED.

2080 PHELPS E.S.
FISCAL NEUTRALITY TOWARD ECONOMIC GROWTH.
NEW YORK: MCGRAW HILL, 1965, 113 PP., LC#65-21575.
ANALYSIS OF GOVERNMENT ACTIVITY IN ECONOMY AND HOW IT INFLUENCES ECONOMIC GROWTH. DISCUSSES TAX POLICY CONDUCTED ON BASIS OF FISCAL NEUTRALITY, NOT DIRECT PLANNING OR CONTROL OF INVESTMENT.

2081 PHELPS E.S. ED.
PRIVATE WANTS AND PUBLIC NEEDS - AN INTRODUCTION TO A CURRENT ISSUE OF PUBLIC POLICY (REV. ED.)
NEW YORK: W W NORTON, 1965, 178 PP., LC#65-12517.
PRESENTS 14 ESSAYS DEALING WITH QUESTION OF GOVERNMENT EXPENDITURE (EXCLUDING "TRANSFER PAYMENTS" AND PURCHASES FOR ANTI-CYCLICAL PURPOSES), WHICH HAS BEEN MADE CENTRAL ISSUE CONCERNING ROLE OF GOVERNMENT AND PUBLIC POLICY DUE TO INCREASING EXPANSION OF PUBLIC SECTOR AND POPULAR PRESSURES SURROUNDING IT. CONTRASTS ECONOMIC AND POLITICAL VIEWPOINTS, TRACING THE THEORETICAL DEVELOPMENTS.

2082 PHILLIPS C.
"THE HIGH COST OF OUR LOW-PAID CONGRESS" (NYT MAG. 2/24/52)"
N.Y. TIMES MAGAZINE, (FEB. 52), 7, 41-42.
DEALS WITH THE ANNUAL DEFICIT INCURRED BY THE AVERAGE CONGRESSMAN. ESTIMATES THAT GIGURED EITHER ON THE IMPORTANCE AND RESPONSIBILITY OF THE JOB OR ON WHAT IT ACTUALLY COSTS A MEMBER OF CONGRESS TO LIVE IN REASONABLE COMFORT, HIS PAY AND PERQUISITES FALL SHORT BY AT LEAST THREE THOUSAND A YEAR. QUESTIONS HOW MUCH THESE FINANCIAL WORRIES ACTUALLY HAMPER THE EFFICIENCY OF CONGRESS.

2083 PIERPONT J.R.
"NEW STAGE IN THE LONGSHORE STRUGGLE."
NEW POLITICS, 6 (WINTER 67), 67-71.
NARRATES FIRING OF 82 SAN FRANCISCO LONGSHOREMEN AND THEIR LAW SUITS AGAINST HARRY BRIDGES, PRESIDENT OF ILWU. DESCRIBES BRIDGES' CONTROL OVER LOCAL TEN'S PROMOTION AND FIRING POLICIES. MAINTAINS THAT GROUP OF 51 WILL CONTINUE TO FIGHT AGAINST BRIDGES, PARTLY BECAUSE OF RACIAL DISCRIMINATION, SINCE 90 PER CENT OF MEN ARE NEGRO.

2084 PIERSON J.H.
INSURING FULL EMPLOYMENT.
NEW YORK: VIKING PRESS, 1964, 305 PP., LC#64-11194.
ANALYSIS OF QUESTION OF FULL EMPLOYMENT IN US ECONOMY AND MEANS AND REASONS FOR ATTAINING IT. DISCUSSES POLICIES NEEDED TO GAIN FULL EMPLOYMENT AND ITS SIGNIFICANCE FOR US AND INTERNATIONAL ECONOMICS.

2085 PIGOU A.C.
THE ECONOMICS OF WELFARE.
NEW YORK: MACMILLAN, 1920, 976 PP.
WELL-KNOWN TREATISE ADVOCATING SHARING NATIONAL DIVIDEND WITH THE POOR; COMPLICATED ECONOMIC THEORY BY WHICH MEN MUST COME TO UNDERSTAND HOW TO BETTER LIFE OF POOR. ANALYZES VARIABILITY OF INCOME, DISTRIBUTION OF PRODUCTIVE RESOURCES, ORGANIZATION OF LABOR, AND GOVERNMENT FINANCE.

2086 PIKE F.B. ED.
FREEDOM AND REFORM IN LATIN AMERICA.
SOUTH BEND: U OF NOTRE DAME, 1967, 308 PP., LC#59-10417.
EXAMINES CHANGES SHAPING TRENDS IN LATIN AMERICA: DESIRE FOR INDIVIDUAL FREEDOM, SOCIAL AND ECONOMIC REFORM, AND RISE OF ARTICULATE MIDDLE CLASS. POINTS UP NECESSITY FOR FASTER ECONOMIC PROGRESS WITHIN FRAMEWORK OF TRADITIONAL WESTERN VALUES. DEFENDS FIGHTERS FOR FREEDOM. COVERS POPULATION PROBLEM AND ROLES OF CATHOLIC CHURCH AND US IN LATIN AMERICAN FREEDOMS AND REFORMS.

2087 PINCUS J.
"THE COST OF FOREIGN AID."
REV. ECON. STAT., 23 (NOV. 63), 360-68.
DISCUSSION OF DEFINITIONS OF DONOR NATIONS FOR VALUING ECONOMIC AID AND HOW MORE APPROPRIATE CRITERIA MIGHT BE ESTABLISHED. ON THE BASIS OF THESE CRITERIA, COMPUTES THE REAL COST OF U.S. BILATERAL AID TO UNDERDEVELOPED CONTRIES IN 1961, CONCLUDING THAT REAL COST WAS MUCH LESS THAN OFFICIAL TOTALS IMPLY.

2088 PINCUS J.A.
ECONOMIC AID AND INTERNATIONAL COST SHARING* A RAND CORPORATION RESEARCH STUDY.
BALTIMORE: JOHNS HOPKINS PRESS, 1965, 221 PP., LC#65-19539.
PRESENTATION OF THE FACTORS INVOLVED IN WORKING OUT INTERNATIONAL COST-SHARING ARRANGEMENTS, ESPECIALLY FOR FINANCING ECONOMIC ASSISTANCE TO POOR NATIONS. ALSO TREATS HISTORICAL CASES INVOLVING SUCH ARRANGEMENTS. EMPIRICAL MATERIAL ON RELATIONSHIP OF EXTERNAL ASSISTANCE AND ECONOMIC GROWTH, MEASUREMENT OF AID COSTS, AND RELATION BETWEEN COMMODITY POLICY AND AID CLAIMS. AID MUST BE INCREASED.

2089 PIQUEMAL M.
"LA COOPERATION FINANCIERE ENTRE LA FRANCE ET LES ETATS AFRICAINS ET MALGACHE."
REV. JURID. POLIT. OUTREMER, 16 (OCT.-DEC. 62), 437-54.
DESCRIBES GENERAL POLITICAL CHARACTERISTICS OF FINANCIAL COOPERATION BETWEEN FRANCE AND AFRICAN STATES. FOCUSES ON PROBLEMS OF PUBLIC FINANCE AND BUDGET CONTROL. DISCUSSES METHODS OF MINTING CURRENCY. REVEALS INSTITUTIONAL RULES OF MULTILATERAL AFRICAN COOPERATION.

2090 PIQUET H.S.
THE US BALANCE OF PAYMENTS AND INTERNATIONAL MONETARY RESERVES.
WASHINGTON: AMER ENTERPRISE INST, 1966, 98 PP., LC#66-17531.
ANALYZES US PROBLEM OF INTERNATIONAL PAYMENTS WHICH HAVE BEEN INCURRING DEFICITS SINCE 1950. FEELS THIS IS NO CRISIS, FOR AMOUNT OF DEFICIT IS DECREASING ANNUALLY. EMPHASIZES PROBLEM IN RELATION TO WORLD, AS US IS CENTRAL BANKER FOR WORLD. FEELS CRITICISM OF US FAILURE TO CHECK OUTFLOW OF GOLD IN EXCHANGE FOR DOLLAR IS NOT JUSTIFIED.

2091 PITCHER G.M. ED.
BIBLIOGRAPHY OF GHANA.
KUMASI: LIBRARY, KUMASI COL OF TECHN, 1960, 177PP
LISTING OF PUBLICATIONS ABOUT GHANA ISSUED BETWEEN 1957-59. ENTRIES ARRANGED UNDER BROAD HEADINGS; MANY HAVE BRIEF ANNOTATIONS. THE SOCIAL SCIENCES, HUMANITIES, AND NATURAL AND PHYSICAL SCIENCES ARE COVERED.

2092 PLAZA G.
"FOR A REGIONAL MARKET IN LATIN AMERICA."
FOR. AFF., 34 (JULY 59), 607-16.
EVALUATES NEEDS OF GROWING MIDDLE CLASS AND EXPECTATIONS OF MASSES IN LATIN AMERICAN SOCIAL REVOLUTION NOW BEGINNING. SUGGESTS THAT ONLY ECONOMIC INTEGRATION WILL ALLOW EFFICIENT USE OF ECONOMIC AND POLITICAL RESOURCES.

2093 PLOSS S.I.
CONFLICT AND DECISION-MAKING IN SOVIET RUSSIA - A CASE STUDY OF AGRICULTURAL POLICY - 1953-1963.
PRINCETON: PRINCETON U PRESS, 1965, 312 PP., LC#65-12992.
AIMS AT FURTHERING "OUR UNDERSTANDING OF CONTEMPORARY SOVIET POLITICS BY RECONSTRUCTING FROM THE OFFICIAL RECORD DISPUTES OVER AGRICULTURE IN THE POST-STALIN PERIOD. SEEKS TO ANSWER THE QUESTIONS: WHO MAKES IMPORTANT DECISIONS? WHO PARTICIPATES IN THE DECISION-MAKING PROCESS? WHAT ARE THEIR POSITIONS AND ATTITUDES? TO UNDERSTAND PARTY DECISIONS ONE MUST TAKE INTO ACCOUNT - WHEN, WHY AND FOR WHAT PURPOSE?"

2094 PLOTT C.R.
"A NOTION OF EQUILIBRIUM AND ITS POSSIBILITY UNDER MAJORITY RULE."
AMER. ECO. REVIEW, 57 (SEPT. 67), 787-806.
DESCRIBES STATE OF EQUILIBRIUM IN WHICH VOTE ON CHANGES IN VARIABLES DOES NOT RECEIVE MAJORITY VOTE SO VARIABLES EMAIN IN EXISITING STATE. SETS FORTH SETTING AND DEFINITIONS AND DISCUSSES SITUATIONS IN WHICH THERE IS NO OR ONLY ONE CONSTRAINT ON MAGNITUDES OF VARIABLES. PRESENTS APPLICATIONS OF PROCEDURE AND PROBLEMS.

2095 POLARIS J.
"THE SINO-SOVIET DISPUTE: ITS ECONOMIC IMPACT ON CHINA."
INT. AFF., 40 (OCT. 64), 647-658.
SUGGESTS THAT CHINA WILL BE REMOVED FROM ISOLATION AND THAT IT IS TO THE ADVANTAGE OF THE WEST TO ENCOURAGE THIS 'ECONOMIC DETENTE'.

2096 POLK J., MEISTER I.W., VEIT L.A.
U S PRODUCTION ABROAD AND THE BALANCE OF PAYMENTS* A SURVEY OF CORPORATE INVESTMENT EXPERIENCE.
NEW YORK: NATL IND CONF BD, 1966, 200 PP.
100 OF UNITED STATES LEADING MANUFACTURING ENTERPRISES WERE EXAMINED IN TERMS OF THEIR INDIVIDUAL CORPORATE BALANCE OF PAYMENTS SITUATION AND THEIR CHIEF INTERNATIONAL EXECUTIVES WERE INTERVIEWED. COMPARES GOVERNMENT AND CORPORATE BALANCE OF PAYMENTS PHILOSOPHIES AND ACCOUNTING TECHNIQUES.

2097 POLLACK N. ED.
THE POPULIST MIND.
INDIANAPOLIS: BOBBS-MERRILL, 1967, 539 PP., LC#66-16752.
SERIES OF PRIMARY SOURCES SUPPORTING SYMPATHETIC VIEW OF POPULISTS AS EMBODIMENT OF TRUTH AND JUSTICE IN THEIR TIME. WORKS CENTER ON INDIVIDUAL OPPRESSION AND DEGRADATION; POLITICAL INEQUALITY; INJUSTICE TO THE UNEMPLOYED AND NEGROES; AND POPULIST SUPPORT FOR THE WORKING CLASS, ALL IN 1890'S. DEPICT POPULIST MOVEMENT AS QUEST FOR A JUST SOCIAL SYSTEM. REJECT IDEA OF PETTY AGRARIAN CAPITALISM.

2098 POLLARD J.A.
"EMERGING PATTERNS OF CORPORATE GIVING."
HARVARD BUSINESS REV., 38 (MAY-JUNE 60), 103-112.
DEALS WITH NEW MECHANISMS THAT ENCOURAGE THE GROWTH OF CORPORATE CONTRIBUTIONS, ESPECIALLY TO EDUCATION. POINTS OUT DECLINE OF SPONTANEOUS GIVING AND RISE OF CENTRALIZED RESPONSIBILITY, CITING CASE-STUDIES, DESCRIBES DELIBERATIVE GROUPS AND PERSONNEL FOR CORPORATE GIVING AS WELL AS TYPES OF AID AND DISTRIBUTION PATTERNS.

2099 POLLOCK F.
AUTOMATION: A STUDY OF ITS ECONOMIC AND SOCIAL CONSEQUENCES.
NEW YORK: PRAEGER, 1958, 276 PP.
HISTORICAL SURVEY AND DISCUSSION OF SUBJECT BASED ON USA EXPERIENCE. SEES BOTH POSITIVE AND NEGATIVE CONSEQUENCES. URGES AUTOMATION TO MINIMIZE HUMAN EXPENDITURE.

2100 POLYANOV N.
"THE DOLLAR'S VENTURES IN EUROPE."
INT. AFF., 10 (OCT. 63), 61-6.
COMMUNIST PARTISAN VIEWS USA FINANCIAL VENTURES IN WESTERN EUROPE. DESCRIBES USA AS UNSCRUPULOUS AND AGGRESSIVE. HOLDS USA CAPITAL EXPLOITS EUROPEAN FINANCIAL WEAKNESS, UNDERCUTS COMMON MARKET, WAR INDUSTRY.

2101 PONCET J.
LA COLONISATION ET L'AGRICULTURE EUROPEENNES EN TUNISIE DEPUIS 1881.
PARIS: MOUTON & CO, 1962, 706 PP.
ANALYZES EFFECT OF EUROPEAN COLONIZATION ON TUNISIA'S AGRICULTURAL ECONOMY. EXPLAINS SYSTEM OF LAND OWNERSHIP AND EXPLOITATION USED BY FRENCH. DISCUSSES FINANCING OF MODERN METHODS OF AGRICULTURAL PRODUCTION. ALSO DISCUSSES ROLE OF TUNISIAN WORKER IN THIS SYSTEM.

2102 POOLE K.E. ED.
FISCAL POLICIES AND THE AMERICAN ECONOMY.
ENGLEWOOD CLIFFS: PRENTICE HALL, 1951, 468 PP.
NINE ESSAYS BY DIFFERENT AUTHORS COVER THE FOLLOWING: BACKGROUND AND SCOPE OF US FISCAL POLICIES; MONETARY ASPECT; EMPLOYMENT AND PRICE LEVEL; DEBT MANAGEMENT; GOVERNMENT EXPENDITURES; FINANCIAL INSTITUTIONS; THE TAX SYSTEM AND BUSINESS; DISTRIBUTION OF INCOME AND PUBLIC WELFARE; AND INTERNATIONAL ASPECTS.

2103 POOLE K.E.
PUBLIC FINANCE AND ECONOMIC WELFARE.
NEW YORK: RINEHART, 1956, 640 PP., LC#56-7949.
EXAMINES WELFARE ASPECTS OF PUBLIC FINANCE AND EFFECTS OF FISCAL MEASURES ON INDIVIDUALS AND GROUPS. DISCUSSES FISCAL AND MONETARY THEORY, RELATION OF PUBLIC FINANCE AND INCOME DISTRIBUTION, TECHNIQUE OF BUDGETING, PROBLEMS FACING USE OF FISCAL MEASURES FOR FULL EMPLOYMENT WITHOUT INFLATION, THE MEANING OF ECONOMIC EQUILIBRIUM AS A BASIS FOR ECONOMIC CONTROL, THE ECONOMICS OF SOCIAL SECURITY, ETC.

2104 POOLEY B.J.
THE EVOLUTION OF BRITISH PLANNING LEGISLATION.
ANN ARBOR: U OF MICH LAW SCHOOL, 1960, 100 PP., LC#60-63300.
STUDIES HISTORY OF PLANNING IN GREAT BRITAIN; ANALYZES STRUCTURE OF STATE AND LOCAL GOVERNMENT; AND DESCRIBES IN DETAIL TOWN AND COUNTRY PLANNING ACTS OF 1947, 1953, AND 1954, SHOWING SOME OF BRITAIN'S STARTLING SOLUTIONS TO METROPOLITAN PROBLEMS.

2105 POPPINO R.E.
"IMBALANCE IN BRAZIL."
CURR. HIST., 44 (FEB. 63), 100-105.
CHRONIC POLITICAL INDECISION AND CONTINUED RAMPANT INFLATION HAS SERVED TO OBSCURE FACT THAT BRAZIL HAS PRESERVED OPEN POLITICAL SYSTEM AND BASICALLY FREE ECONOMY. OBSERVES THAT, DESPITE STRONG PRESSURES FROM LEFT AND RIGHT, EXTREMES OF MILITARY COUP D'ETAT AND SOCIAL REVOLUTION AVERTED.

2106 PORWIT K.
CENTRAL PLANNING: EVALUATION OF VARIANTS.
NEW YORK: PERGAMON PRESS, 1967, 200 PP., LC#66-17808.
ANALYSIS OF CIRCUMSTANCES UNDER WHICH PLANNING CALCULATIONS CAN BECOME A REAL BASIS FOR IMPLEMENTATION OF THE PRINCIPLE OF RATIONAL MANAGEMENT. DEALS WITH THE TYPE OF CALCULATIONS IN WHICH MAIN ATTENTION IS FOCUSED ON MATERIAL, REAL-TERMSRELATIONSHIPS IN THE ECONOMY. CONSIDERS THEM PRIMARILY FROM THE POINT OF VIEW OF THE CENTRAL PLAN COVERING THE WHOLE ECONOMY.

2107 POSEN G.S.
"RECENT TRENDS IN SOVIET ECONOMIC THOUGHT."
INT. J., 21 (FALL 66), 491-507.
DISCUSSES CHANGING SOVIET ECONOMIC POLICY, INCLUDING DECENTRALIZATION SCHEME USING PROFIT AS SUCCESS CRITERION, AND GIVING SOME CONSUMER INDUSTRIES SUPPLY CONTROL.

2108 POTTER D.M.
PEOPLE OF PLENTY: ECONOMIC ABUNDANCE AND THE AMERICAN CHARACTER.
CHICAGO: U. CHI. PR., 1954, 219 PP.
THEORETICAL STUDY OF NATIONAL CHARACTER, DRAWING ON VIEWS OF BEHAVIORAL SCIENTISTS AND HISTORIANS. ALSO STUDIES EFFECT OF PROSPERITY ON AMERICAN SOCIAL STRUCTURE, ON SOCIAL MOBILITY, ON POLITICAL BEHAVIOR, AND ON AMERICAN CONCEPT OF DEMOCRACY.

2109 POWELL D.
"THE EFFECTIVENESS OF SOVIET ANTI-RELIGIOUS PROPAGANDA."
PUBLIC OPINION QUART., 31 (FALL 67), 366-380.
DISCUSSES VALUE OF SOVIET PROPAGANDA, STATING IT TO BE OF LITTLE OR NO USE IN AFFECTING CHANGES IN DEISTIC GROUPS. PROPOSES THAT ITS MAJOR VALUE IS IN REINFORCING BELIEFS OF ATHEISTS AND THEREBY INSURING THEIR SUPPORT. CLAIMS THAT RELIGION IS NO LONGER MAJOR TARGET OF THE PARTY.

2110 POWELSON J.P.
LATIN AMERICA: TODAY'S ECONOMIC AND SOCIAL REVOLUTION.
NEW YORK: MCGRAW HILL, 1964, 303 PP., LC#63-20719.
DISCUSSION OF LATIN AMERICAN ECONOMICS BY LATIN AND NORTH AMERICANS. STUDIES THE ECONOMIC REVOLUTION; INDIVIDUAL AND COLLECTIVE APPROACHES TO DEVELOPMENT; AGRARIAN REFORM; MONOPOLY; PRIMARY PRODUCTS; EXPERIENCES WITH COPPER, SUGAR, OIL, AND COFFEE; INFLATION; ECONOMIC INTEGRATION; FOREIGN AID; NATIONAL ECONOMIC PLANNING; AND REVOLUTION - OLD AND NEW.

2111 POWLEDGE F.
BLACK POWER WHITE RESISTANCE.
CLEVELAND: WORLD, 1967, 282 PP., LC#67-15224.
EXAMINES RACIAL CONFLICT IN NORTH AND SOUTH OF US IN RECENT TIMES. CONSIDERS LEGISLATIVE POLICY, FAILURE OF INTEGRATION, AND SOCIAL ATTITUDES AND THEIR CONSEQUENCES FOR POSSIBLITIES OF RESOLUTION. ASSERTS THAT SOUTHERN ECONOMIC INSTITUTIONS SERVE WHITES BY PERMITTING TOKEN INTEGRATION AND BY WITHHHOLDING POWER FROM NEGROES. NEGROES SWITCH GOALS FROM INTEGRATION TO NEGRO POWER.

2112 PRAKASH O.M.
THE THEORY AND WORKING OF STATE CORPORATIONS: WITH SPECIAL REFERENCE TO INDIA.
LONDON: ALLEN & UNWIN, 1962, 272 PP.
ANALYZES GENERAL CHARACTERISTICS AND OPERATIONS OF STATE CORPORATIONS, WHICH INCLUDE PUBLIC CORPORATIONS AND GOVERNMENT COMPANIES, IN INDIA, UK, AND US. CRITICALLY EXAMINES SPECIFIC ISSUES RELATING TO FUNCTIONING OF THESE CORPORATIONS, ONE US, AND ONE ENGLISH.

2113 PRASOW P., PETERS E.
"THE DEVELOPMENT OF JUDICIAL ARBITRATION IN LABOR-MANAGEMENT DISPUTES."
CALIF. MANAGEMENT REV., 9 (SPRING 67), 7-16.
SINCE THE RISE OF "BIG LABOR" IN THE LATE 1930'S, COLLECTIVE BARGAINING IN THE US HAS DEVELOPED TWO UNIQUE FEATURES WITHOUT COUNTERPART IN THE WORLD - THE DETAILED COLLECTIVE AGREEMENT AND A "COMMON LAW" OF ARBITRATION.

2114 PRATT R.C.
"THE ADMINISTRATION OF ECONOMIC PLANNING IN A NEWLY INDEPEND ENT STATE* THE TANZANIAN EXPERIENCE 1963-1966."
J. COMMONWEALTH POL. ST., 5 (MAR. 67), 38-59.
PRAISES FIVE YEAR PLAN IN TANZANIA AS HIGHLY PROFESSIONAL AND USEFUL OUTLINE FOR ALL ASPECTS OF DEVELOPMENT. RELATES IT TO POLITICAL SITUATION, AND EXPLAINS FAILURE OF GOVERNMENT TO GIVE TOP PRIORITY TO PLAN IN ADMINISTRATIVE PROGRAM. DISCUSSES REASONS AND POSSIBLE CORRECTIONS.

2115 PREST A.R.
PUBLIC FINANCE IN UNDERDEVELOPED COUNTRIES.
NEW YORK: PRAEGER, 1963, 164 PP., $4.50.
TWO MAJOR PROBLEMS OF SUBJECT ARE LONG-TERM PRESSURE FOR INCREASED GOVERNMENT SPENDING AND CONCURRENT INSTABILITY OF GOVERNMENT FINANCES. RELATES PROBLEMS TO TAX SYSTEMS OF SUCH COUNTRIES AND SUGGESTS DESIRABLE FEATURES.

2116 PRESTHUS R.
MEN AT THE TOP; A STUDY IN COMMUNITY POWER.
NEW YORK: OXFORD U PR, 1964, 485 PP., LC#64-11236.
CONSIDERATION OF VIABILITY OF POLITICAL PLURALISM IN AN ERA OF LARGE-SCALE ORGANIZATION AND CONCENTRATION OF POLITICAL AND ECONOMIC POWER. PROVIDES THEORETICAL FRAMEWORK FOR POWER STRUCTURE ANALYSIS AND APPLIES THIS FRAMEWORK TO SEVERAL SPECIFIC COMMUNITIES. OFFERS A SYSTEMATIC ANALYSIS OF CONDITIONS UNDER WHICH PLURALISM EXISTS; CONTENDS THAT DEMOCRATIC IDEOLOGY MUST BE ALIGNED TO REALITY.

2117 PRINCE C.E.
NEW JERSEY'S JEFFERSONIAN REPUBLICANS; THE GENESIS OF AN EARLY PARTY MACHINE (1789-1817)
CHAPEL HILL: U OF N CAR PR, 1967, 266 PP., LC#67-15103.
STUDIES CONTRIBUTIONS TO POLITICAL PARTY MACHINERY MADE BY NEW JERSEY'S JEFFERSONIAN REPUBLICANS. STATES THAT PARTY MANAGERS USED NEWSPAPER PROPAGANDA, PATRONAGE CONTROL, AND OTHER TECHNIQUES TO GAIN ASCENDENCE. DISCUSSES FIRST STATE NOMINATING COVENTION IN 1800 AND LOCAL ORGANIZATIONS AS EVIDENCE OF POLITICAL SOPHISTICATION. TRACES ADVANCE OF MACHINE TO ELECTION OF 1812 AND FOLLOWING DECLINE.

2118 PRINCETON U INDUSTRIAL REL SEC
COMPULSORY ARBITRATION OF UTILITY DISPUTES IN NEW JERSEY AND PENNSYLVANIA.
PRINCETON: PRIN U INDUS REL CTR, 1951, 90 PP.
DISCUSSES PROBLEM OF RETAINING FREEDOM IN COLLECTIVE BARGAINING WHILE ASSURING MAINTENANCE OF ESSENTIAL PUBLIC SERVICES. USING CASE STUDIES FROM TWO STATES, COMPARES METHODS OF COMPULSORY BARGAINING, OFFERING THEM AS EXAMPLES OF FAIR PRACTICE.

2119 PRINCETON U INDUSTRIAL REL SEC
PUBLIC PROGRAMS TO CREATE JOBS (PAMPHLET NO. 125)
PRINCETON: PRIN U INDUS REL CTR, 1966, 4 PP.
ANNOTATED BIBLIOGRAPHY OF BOOKS, ARTICLES, AND DOCUMENTS PUBLISHED IN ENGLISH, 1941-65; LISTED TOPICALLY.

2120 PRINCETON U INDUSTRIAL REL SEC
RECENT MATERIAL ON COLLECTIVE BARGAINING IN GOVERNMENT (PAMPHLET NO. 130)
PRINCETON: PRIN U INDUS REL CTR, 1966, 4 PP.
ANNOTATED BIBLIOGRAPHY OF BOOKS, ARTICLES, AND DOCUMENTS PUBLISHED IN ENGLISH, 1962-66; LISTED TOPICALLY.

2121 PRINCETON U INDUSTRIAL REL SEC
THE ROLE OF THE PUBLIC EMPLOYMENT SERVICE (PAMPHLET NO. 129)
PRINCETON: PRIN U INDUS REL CTR, 1966, 4 PP.
ANNOTATED BIBLIOGRAPHY OF BOOKS, ARTICLES, AND DOCUMENTS PUBLISHED IN ENGLISH, 1964-66; LISTED ALPHABETICALLY BY AUTHOR.

2122 PRITCHETT C.H. ED., WESTIN A.F. ED.
THE THIRD BRANCH OF GOVERNMENT.
NEW YORK: HARCOURT BRACE, 1963, 308 PP., LC#63-13250.
SURVEYS ACTIVITIES OF SUPREME COURT SINCE 1937, AND CONSISTS OF EIGHT ARTICLES DEALING WITH A VARIETY OF CASES, FROM SEPARATION OF CHURCH AND STATE, TO LOYALTY-SECURITY PROGRAMS, TO INDUSTRIAL RELATIONS.

2123 PROBERT J.R.
"STREAMLINING THE FOREIGN POLICY MACHINE."
PUBLIC ADMIN. REV., 27 (SEPT. 67), 229-236.
DESCRIBES STATE DEPARTMENT'S NEW STRUCTURAL ORGANIZATION, WHICH IS NOW SUBDIVIDED INTO SENIOR INTERDEPARTMENTAL GROUP, INTERDEPARTMENTAL REGIONAL GROUP, AND OFFICE OF COUNTRY DIRECTOR. EVALUATES IMPROVEMENTS IN ADMINISTRATIVE EFFICIENCY.

2124 PROCHNOW H.V. ED.
WORLD ECONOMIC PROBLEMS AND POLICIES.
NEW YORK: HARPER & ROW, 1965, 382 PP., LC#64-18107.
SEEKS TO ANALYZE NUMBER OF SIGNIFICANT WORLD ECONOMIC PROBLEMS AND REALISTICALLY ASSESS POLICIES BEING FOLLOWED TO SOLVE PROBLEMS. MAKES ANALYSES OF UNDERLYING ECONOMIC TRENDS AND IMPLICATIONS. FIFTEEN INTERNATIONALLY COMPETENT AUTHORS EXPRESS THEIR VIEWS.

2125 PROUDHON P.J.
LA GUERRE ET LA PAIX (2 VOLS.)
ORIGINAL PUBLISHER NOT AVAILABLE, 1861, 824 PP.
BELIEVES THAT WAR ONCE SERVED A PURPOSE IN SOCIAL EVOLUTION, BUT THAT IT NO LONGER DOES. IMPULSES UNDERLYING WAR MUST BE POSITIVELY DIRECTED, AND THE END OF MILITARISM IS THE GOAL OF THE NINETEENTH CENTURY. DEPRAVITY OF WAR IS CAUSED BY PAUPERISM. STATES INDULGE IN WAR TO AVOID CONSEQUENCES OF DISEQUILIBRIUM OF WEALTH. REMEDY IS TO BRING ABOUT ECONOMIC EQUILIBRIUM, WHICH WILL BRING PEACE.

2126 PROUDHON P.J.
SYSTEME DES CONTRADICTIONS ECONOMIQUES, OU PHILOSOPHIE DA LA MISERE (2 VOLS.) (1846)
ORIGINAL PUBLISHER NOT AVAILABLE, 1868, 796 PP.
ATTEMPT TO ANALYZE ENTIRE ECONOMIC BASIS OF SOCIETY. SEES IT IN TERMS OF CONTRADICTIONS. NON-PRODUCER SHOULD OBEY, BUT COMMANDS. CREDIT SHOULD BE PROVIDER OF WORK, BUT KILLS IT. PROPERTY IS THE EARTH MADE AVAILABLE, BUT IN FACT IS EARTH DENIED. CONTRADICTIONS DISCUSSED IN TERMS OF THEIR POTENTIAL VALUE AND ACTUAL MALIGNANCY. MAINTAINS THAT RELIGION PERPETUATES CONTRADICTIONS.

2127 PROUDHON P.J.
WHAT IS PROPERTY? (TRANS. BY B.R. TUCKER)
ORIGINAL PUBLISHER NOT AVAILABLE, 1876, 457 PP.
MAINTAINS THAT "PROPERTY IS THEFT." REFERENCE TO PROPERTY CONCERNS THOSE WHO OWN BUT DO NOT LABOR. DISPOSES OF JUSTIFICATIONS FOR PROPERTY. THEN DEVELOPS THEORY OF "SURPLUS VALUE," OF WHICH, HE MAINTAINS, THE CAPITALIST HAS A DISPROPORTIONATE SHARE. PROPERTY IS INCOMPATIBLE WITH JUSTICE, AND SINCE PRESENT SOCIAL SYSTEM IS BASED ON PROPERTY, THERE MUST BE AN ALTERNATIVE. ANARCHY PROVIDES ONLY JUST SOCIETY.

2128 PRYBYLA J.
"THE QUEST FOR ECONOMIC RATIONALITY IN THE SOVIET BLOC."
SOC. RES., 30 (AUTUMN 63), 343-66.
COMMENTS ON DIRECTIONS AND SCOPE OF ECONOMIC DEBATE IN RUSSIA. CONTENDS USSR WILL INTRODUCE SYSTEMATIC MATHEMATICAL METHODS, SUBSTITUTE VALUE ECONOMICS FOR COMMAND ECONOMICS.

2129 PRYOR F.L.
"FOREIGN TRADE IN THE COMMUNIST BLOC."
SOV. STUD., 15 (JULY 62), 41-61.
BLOC'S ANALYSIS OF FOREIGN-TRADE PROFITABILITY FOR A SINGLE NATION IS CRITICALLY EXAMINED AS IS THE 'PURE FOREIGN TRADE THEORY' AND THE ISSUE OF INTRA-BLOC PRICING. AUTHOR FINDS COMMUNIST THEORISTS DEFICIENT IN THAT THEY ARE UNABLE TO ANALYZE THE PROBLEMS OF A FOREIGN-TRADE EQUILIBRIUM, OF AN INTRA-BLOC DIVISION OF LABOR AND RELATED ISSUES.

2130 PRYOR F.L.
THE COMMUNIST FOREIGN TRADE SYSTEM.
LONDON: ALLEN UNWIN, 1963, 234 PP.
SINCE ALL 'SYSTEMS' (DEFINED AS TOTAL NETWORK OF FOREIGN-TRADE DECISIONS) OPERATE FUNDAMENTALLY THE SAME, THE DDR (EAST GERMANY) CHOSEN AS CASE-STUDY TO ILLUSTRATE MAIN PROBLEMS FACING PLANNERS AND POLICY-MAKERS. TRADITIONAL METHODS OF ANALYSIS BY WESTERNER INAPPLICABLE BECAUSE PRIMARY ORIENTATION TOWARDS FULFILLMENT PLAN AND CERTAIN POLITICAL-IDEOLOGICAL GOALS.

2131 PURCELL T.V.
THE WORKER SPEAKS HIS MIND ON COMPANY AND UNION.
CAMBRIDGE: HARVARD U PR, 1953, 344 PP., LC#53-9040.
A DETAILED AND THOROUGH EMPIRICAL INVESTIGATION OF WORKER ATTITUDES IN A CHICAGO MEAT- PACKING PLANT. REACTION TO THE COMPANY BY UNION LEADERS AND MEN, WORKERS' VIEWS ON RACE RELATIONS, FOREMEN, UNION ALLEGIANCE, UNION LEADERS, UNION PARTICIPATION, GRIEVANCE PROCEDURES, WAGE-INCENTIVE SYSTEMS,AND COMMUNISM ARE DISCUSSED.

2132 PYE L.W.
"SOVIET AND AMERICAN STYLES IN FOREIGN AID."
ORBIS, 4 (JULY 60), 159-73.
SOVIETS CONSIDER ECONOMIC AID TO BE MORE BLUNT AND LIMITED INSTRUMENT OF FOREIGN POLICY THAN WE DO. SOVIETS THROUGH LOGIC OF POLITICS ARE ABLE TO RECONCILE GOALS AMD TECHNIQUES, WHILE USA, IN DENYING USE OF POLITICS, IS WITHOUT AN EXPLICIT METHOD FOR DEALING WITH RELATIONSHIP BETWEEN GOALS AND TECHNIQUES OF FOREIGN AID. PRESENTS EIGHT MOST IMPORTANT DIFFERENCES OF VIEW ABOUT FOREIGN AID BETWEEN USA AND USSR.

2133 PYE L.W.
"THE POLITICAL IMPULSES AND FANTASIES BEHIND FOREIGN AID."
PROC. ACAD. POLIT. SCI., 27 (JAN. 62), 92-111.
ILLUSIONS THAT USA AID IS NON-POLITICAL, THAT UNDERDEVELOPED COUNTRIES ARE ALL MORAL AND THE BELIEFS IN CULTURAL RELATIVISM AND MISSIONARY ZEAL HAVE ADVERSE EFFECTS ON FOREIGN-AID PROGRAMS. FOREGOING FACTORS LEAD TO AMBIVALENCE. RELATION BETWEEN AID AND EVOLUTION OF WORLD ORDER IS PRESENTED AND SUGGESTIONS MADE TO FACILITATE CHANGE FROM A COLONIAL INTERNATIONAL SYSTEM TO A NEW WORLD ORDER.

2134 QURESHI S.
INCENTIVES IN AMERICAN EMPLOYMENT (THESIS, UNIVERSITY OF PENNSYLVANIA)
PHILA: UNIV OF PENNSYLVANIA, 1961, 188 PP.
DISCUSSES USE OF INCENTIVES IN FEDERAL CIVILIAN EMPLOYMENT. ANALYSIS OF HEALTH AND RETIREMENT PLANS, OVERTIME PAY, AND IDEA AWARDS LEADS TO CONCLUSION THAT THE GENERAL MONETARY LEVEL OF INCENTIVES SHOULD BE INCREASED AND THAT SPECIAL SERVICES SHOULD BE PROVIDED TO UPPER LEVEL ADMINISTRATORS.

2135 RAFUSE R.W. JR.
STATE AND LOCAL FISCAL BEHAVIOR OVER THE POSTWAR CYCLES (DISSERTATION)
PRINCETON: PRIN U, DEPT OF ECO, 1963, 241 PP.
EXAMINES CYCLICAL BEHAVIOR OF STATE AND LOCAL GOVERNMENT IN INFLATION AND RECESSION, OVER-ALL IMPACT ON ECONOMY, EXTENT TO WHICH BEHAVIOR HAS BEEN STABILIZING, AND EXTENT TO WHICH IT HAS BEEN THE RESULT OF DISCRETIONARY RATHER THAN AUTOMATIC FACTORS.

2136 RAGAN S.
"THE ABA RECOMMENDATIONS: A NEWSPAPERMAN'S CRITIQUE."
NOTRE DAME LAWYER, 42 (1967), 888-895.
NEWSPAPERMAN CRITICIZES AMERICAN BAR ASSOCIATION'S PROPOSALS REGULATING PRESS BEFORE AND DURING TRIAL. MAINTAINS THAT FIRST AND SIXTH AMENDMENTS ARE COMPATIBLE AND INTERDEPENDENT. LIMITATIONS SHOULD BE BASED ON JOINT AGREEMENT OF BAR AND PRESS AND ON MUTUAL TRUST.

2137 RAISON T.
WHY CONSERVATIVE?
BALTIMORE: PENGUIN BOOKS, 1964, 144 PP.
DISCUSSES TORY PARTY IN ENGLAND AND POLICIES WHICH ARE OPEN TO IT IN DEALING WITH CONTEMPORARY SOCIAL PROBLEMS. COVERS WELFARE, EDUCATION, DIPLOMACY, DEFENSE, AND ECONOMY, DEFENDING CONSERVATISM AS VIABLE ALTERNATIVE AND AS THE ONE WHICH WILL RESULT IN MOST SUCCESSFUL FORM OF DEMOCRACY.

2138 RAMA C.M.
LAS CLASES SOCIALES EN EL URUGUAY.
MONTEVIDEO: ED NUESTRO TIEMPO, 1960, 249 PP.
ANALYZES CLASS STRUCTURE OF URUGUAY AND EXTENT OF PARTICIPATION OF EACH CLASS IN POLITICAL, ECONOMIC, AND SOCIAL LIFE OF COUNTRY. COMPARES RURAL AND URBAN SOCIETY AND INFLUENCE OF URBANIZATION ON POWER STRUCTURE.

2139 RAMA C.M.
"PASADO Y PRESENTE DE LA RELIGION EN AMERICA LATINA."
CUADERNOS AMERICANOS, (JULY-AUG. 67), 25-43.
ASSERTS CHRISTIANITY OF LATIN AMERICA AND IMPORTANCE OF HER RESISTANCE OF WESTERN RELIGIONS. PRESENTS STATISTICS ON NUMBER OF CATHOLICS AND PROTESTANTS IN VARIOUS LATIN AMERICAN COUNTRIES. REVIEWS HISTORY OF CATHOLIC CHURCH IN LATIN AMERICA, STRUCTURE OF RELIGIOUS SOCIETY, AND EFFECTS OF POLITICS ON POLICIES OF CHURCH.

2140 RAMANADHAM V.V.
PROBLEMS OF PUBLIC ENTERPRISE: THOUGHTS ON BRITISH EXPERIENCE.
CHICAGO: QUADRANGLE BOOKS, INC, 1959, 176 PP., LC#59-15513.
ANALYZES PERTINENT PROBLEMS OF NATIONALIZATION IN FIELDS OF MANAGEMENT, RESOURCE ALLOCATION, AND PUBLIC CONTROL. TRIES TO DETERMINE BEST STATUS OF CORPORATION WITH GOVERNMENT, BEST FORM OF CENTRAL ORGANIZATION, AND BEST FORM OF CONSUMER ORGANIZATION. USES UK AS EXAMPLE TO HELP OTHER NATIONS OVERCOME SIMILAR PROBLEMS.

2141 RAMAZANI R.K.
THE MIDDLE EAST AND THE EUROPEAN COMMON MARKET.
CHARLOTTESVILLE: U. VA. PR., 1964, 152 PP., $3.75.
STUDIES ADVERSE EFFECT OF EEC ON MAJOR MIDDLE EASTERN EXPORTS: PETROLEUM, GRAINS, FRUIT, ETC. ALSO EXPLORES POSITIVE AND NEGATIVE REACTIONS TOWARD EEC: ATTEMPTS AT COOPERATION BY NON-ARAB COUNTRIES, OPPOSITION BY ARAB COUNTRIES.

2142 RAMERIE L.
"TENSION AU SEIN DU COMECON: LE CAS ROUMAIN."
POLIT. ENTRANG., 28 (NO. 3, 63), 249-57.
NOTES TENSION WITHIN COMECON. SINCE COMECON FAVORS RUSSIAN ECONOMY, SOME COUNTRIES IN COMMUNIST BLOC MUST TURN TO WESTERN GOVERNMENTS TO ACHIEVE ECONOMIC GOALS. RUSSIAN SUPPLIES ARE OF UNSATISFACTORY QUANTITY AND QUALITY.

2143 RAND SCHOOL OF SOCIAL SCIENCE
INDEX TO LABOR ARTICLES.
LONDON: MEYER LONDON MEM LIB.
MONTHLY UNANNOTATED GUIDE TO ARTICLES CURRENTLY APPEARING IN SELECTED PERIODICALS. COVERS BUSINESS AND LABOR CONDITIONS, TRADE UNIONISM, LABOR LEGISLATION, DISPUTES AND ARBITRATION, AND INTERNATIONAL ORGANIZATIONS. FIRST ISSUED IN 1926.

2144 RANGEL I.
A INFLACAO BRASILEIRA (2ND ED.)
RIO DE JANEIRO: ED. TEMPO BRASILEIRO, 1963, 138PP.
ANALYSIS OF INFLATION IN BRAZIL. EXAMINES AGRICULTURAL STRUCTURE, PROPENSITY TO CONSUME, CAPITAL FORMATION, TAX, PRICING, AND PREFERENCE FOR LIQUIDITY DURING INFLATION.

2145 RANIS G. ED.
THE UNITED STATES AND THE DEVELOPING ECONOMIES.
NEW YORK: W W NORTON, 1964, 174 PP., LC#63-21712.
DISCUSSES VALUE AND ROLE OF US FOREIGN AID IN CONTRIBUTING TO ECONOMIC ADVANCE OF BACKWARD NATIONS, IMPORTANCE TO TRADE DEVELOPMENT, AND USE AS TOOL TO PREVENT COMMUNIST DOMINATION. ANALYZES INSTRUMENTS OF FOREIGN AID AND EFFECT ON INTERNAL ECONOMY OF DONOR NATION.

2146 RANSOM H.H. ED.
AN AMERICAN FOREIGN POLICY READER.
NEW YORK: THOMAS Y CROWELL, 1965, 690 PP., LC#65-16871.
ASSEMBLES VARIED MATERIAL THAT ILLUSTRATES THE ISSUES AND CHOICES FACED BY AMERICAN FOREIGN POLICY MAKERS PRINCIPALLY SINCE WWII. ASSUMES THAT IMPLICIT AND EXPLICIT POWER OF US FOREIGN POLICY CAN BE ANALYZED IN TERMS OF ITS INSTRUMENTAL MEANS, APPLIED AT VARIOUS DEGREES IN CONCRETE SITUATIONS. THESE INSTRUMENTS ARE MILITARY, ECONOMIC, PROPAGANDISTIC, AND DIPLOMATIC; ESSAYS CENTER ON THEM.

2147 RAO V.K.R.
INTERNATIONAL AID FOR ECONOMIC DEVELOPMENT - POSSIBILITIES AND LIMITATIONS.
CAMBRIDGE: LEEDS U PRESS, 1960, 29 PP.
DETAILED CRITICAL ANALYSIS OF INTERNATIONAL ECONOMIC AID PROGRAMS EMPHASIZING OBLIGATIONS AND VITAL IMPORTANCE OF INCREASED AID FROM DEVELOPED NATIONS. STRESSES LIMITATIONS IMPOSED ON VOLUME AND EFFECTIVENESS OF ECONOMIC AID BY NUMEROUS POLITICAL AND SOCIAL AS WELL AS ECONOMIC FACTORS IN DEVELOPED AND UNDERDEVELOPED COUNTRIES. EXAMINES ACTIVITIES OF UN AGENCIES AND OTHER INTERNATIONAL ECONOMIC BODIES.

2148 RAO V.K.R., NARAIN D.
FOREIGN AID AND INDIA'S ECONOMIC DEVELOPMENT.
NEW YORK: ASIA PUBL HOUSE, 1963, 111 PP.
DEALS WITH CHARACTER, MAGNITUDE, AND ORGANIZATION OF FOREIGN AID, CONDITIONS ON WHICH INDIA HAS RECEIVED IT, IMPACT IT HAS MADE ON ECONOMY, AND PROBLEMS THAT HAVE ARISEN. ALSO TOUCHES UPON WHAT INFLUENCE AID HAS HAD ON RELATIONS BETWEEN INDIA AND AID-GIVING COUNTRIES. MAKES SUGGESTIONS REGARDING GIVING AND RECEIVING OF FOREIGN AID IN FUTURE IN THE LIGHT OF INDIA'S EXPERIENCE.

2149 RAO Y.V.L.
COMMUNICATION AND DEVELOPMENT.
MINNEAPOLIS: U OF MINN PR, 1966, 145 PP., LC#66-21940.
STUDIES RELATIONSHIP IN DEVELOPING COUNTRIES BETWEEN COMMUNICATION LEADING TO INFORMED, LITERATE POPULACE ON THE ONE HAND, AND DEVELOPMENT LEADING TO BROAD ECONOMIC, POLITICAL, AND SOCIAL CHANGES ON THE OTHER. BASED ON TWO INDIAN VILLAGES.

2150 RAPHAEL J.S.
GOVERNMENTAL REGULATION OF BUSINESS.
NEW YORK: FREE PRESS OF GLENCOE, 1966, 260 PP., LC#66-12081.
SURVEYS LEGAL BACKGROUND OF GOVERNMENT CONTROL OF BUSINESS. ANALYZES SOURCES OF POWER, SUCH AS CONSTITUTION. EXAMINES ADMINISTRATIVE AGENCIES THAT ARE INSTRUMENTAL IN ENFORCING LAWS. REVEALS DEVICES AVAILABLE TO COMPANIES IF GOVERNMENT BECOMES TOO POWERFUL.

2151 RAPKIN C., GRIGSBY W.G.
THE DEMAND FOR HOUSING IN RACIALLY MIXED AREAS: A STUDY OF THE NATURE OF NEIGHBORHOOD CHANGE.
BERKELEY: U OF CALIF PR, 1960, 177 PP., LC#60-10360.
ANALYSIS OF THE PROCESS OF NEIGHBORHOOD RACIAL CHANGE FROM STANDPOINT OF HOUSING MARKET, INCLUDING CONDITIONS OF SUPPLY, DEMAND, PRICE, FINANCING, AND RELATED FACTORS. SPECIFIC AREAS STUDIED ARE IN PHILADELPHIA.

2152 RATNAM K.J.
COMMUNALISM AND THE POLITICAL PROCESS IN MALAYA.
KUALALUMPUR: U OF MALAYA, 1965, 248 PP.
ANALYZES ADVERSE POLITICAL RESULTS OF DIVISIONS OF FEDERATION OF MALAYA AFTER WWII. FEELS DIVISIONS ARE RESULT OF POLITICAL GROWTH CAUSED BY WAR. EMPHASIZES LACK OF MEANS OF EXPRESSION OR INFLUENCE OF EACH SECTOR ON BASIC ASPECTS OF GOVERNMENT PROCESS AS CAUSE OF MUCH DISAGREEMENT ON ISSUES.

2153 RAVKIN A.
THE NEW STATES OF AFRICA (HEADLINE SERIES, NO. 183((PAMPHLET)
NEW YORK: FOREIGN POLICY ASSN, 1967, 63 PP., LC#67-25598.
INTRODUCTION TO SITUATION AND PROBLEMS OF NEWLY-INDEPENDENT AFRICAN STATES, INCLUDING POLITICAL, ECONOMIC, AND SOCIAL ASPECTS. AFRICA EQUIPPED NEITHER TO ACCEPT MODERN WORLD ORDER NOR TO CHANGE IT.

2154 RAY D.D.
ACCOUNTING AND BUSINESS FLUCTUATIONS.
GAINESVILLE: U OF FLA PR, 1960, 184 PP., LC#60-6718.
CRITICALLY EXAMINES THEORY ASCRIBING TO ACCOUNTING METHODS THE POWER OF CREATING BUSINESS FLUCTUATIONS. CONSIDERS VARIABLES SUCH AS SIZE AND OWNERSHIP OF FIRM, COMPETITION, INVESTMENT INCENTIVES, SUPPLY AND DEMAND, AND RELATION OF SALES TO PROFITS. MAINTAINS THEORY IS NOT SUPPORTED BY EVIDENCE.

2155 RAY J.
"THE EUROPEAN FREE-TRADE ASSOCIATION AND ITS IMPACT ON INDIA'S TRADE."
INT. STUDIES, 3 (JULY 61), 25-44.
TRACES EVENTS LEADING UP TO THE FORMATION OF THE EUROPEAN

FREE TRADE AREA. HISTORY OF INDIA'S TRADE WITH COUNTRIES OF THE PACT IS ANALYZED WITH STRESS ON HER EXPORTS TO ENGLAND. SURVEYS EFFECTS ON INDIA'S FUTURE TRADE WITH THESE NATIONS FROM POINT OF VIEW OF TARIFF, INCREASED PRODUCTIVITY AND INCOME OF THE MEMBER NATIONS.

2156 RAYBACK J.G.
A HISTORY OF AMERICAN LABOR.
NEW YORK: FREE PRESS OF GLENCOE, 1966, 491 PP., LC#59-5344.
ANALYZES HISTORY AND DEVELOPMENT OF LABOR MOVEMENT IN US. DISCUSSES COLONIAL ECONOMY, EMERGENCE OF US AS NATION, AND MODERN ERA. DISCUSSES ACTIONS BY LABOR IN AND OUTSIDE GOVERNMENT TO ATTAIN POWER AND INFLUENCE.

2157 RAZA M.A.
"EMERGING TRENDS IN PUBLIC LABOR POLICIES AND UNION - GOVERNMENT RELATIONS IN ASIA AND AFRICA."
CALIF. MANAGEMENT REV., 9 (SPRING 67), 25-38.
NEW PATTERNS OF UNION-GOVERNMENT RELATIONSHIPS ARE EMERGING IN AFRICA AND ASIA WHICH RANGE FROM OUTRIGHT CONTROL OF LABOR MOVEMENTS (AND REPRESSION OF "UNCOOPERATIVE UNIONS") TO ELICITING UNION SUPPORT OF GOVERNMENT BY MORE SUBTLE MEANS.

2158 RAZAFIMBAHINY J.
"L'ORGANISATION AFRICAINE ET MALGACHE DE COOPERATION ECONOMIQUE."
REV. JURID. POLIT., 17 (APR.-JUNE 1962), 177-201.
STUDIES STRUCTURE OF ORGANIZATION OF AFRICAN STATES AND MADAGASCAR FOR ECONOMIC COOPERATION. STUDIES ITS METHODS OF ACHIEVING ECONOMIC, TECHNICAL, SCIENTIFIC AND CULTURAL COOPERATION BETWEEN DEVELOPING AFRICAN COUNTRIES. EVALUATES CURRENT PROGRAMS AND ACHIEVEMENTS TO DATE.

2159 READ W.H.
"UPWARD COMMUNICATION IN INDUSTRIAL HIERARCHIES."
HUMAN RELATIONS, 15 (1962), 3-15.
CONCERNS COMMUNICATION IN LARGE ORGANIZATIONS. PARTICULAR FOCUS IS UPON MOTIVATIONAL AND ATTITUDINAL FACTORS THAT AFFECT THE ACCURACY WITH WHICH MEMBERS AT ONE ADMINISTRATIVE LEVEL COMMUNICATE TO A HIGHER LEVEL. SIGNIFICANTLY NEGATIVE RELATIONSHIP BETWEEN UPWARD-MOBILITY AND UPWARD-COMMUNICATION WAS FOUND, A RELATIONSHIP MODIFIED BY THE TRUST THESE EXECUTIVES HAD IN THEIR SUPERIORS.

2160 READER D.H.
"A SURVEY OF CATEGORIES OF ECONOMIC ACTIVITIES AMONG THE PEOPLES OF AFRICA."
AFRICA, 34 (JAN. 64), 28-45.
GRAPHICALLY AND TEXTUALLY OUTLINES REPORTED ECONOMIC DEVELOPMENT WITHIN AND OUTSIDE THE SUBSISTENCE SECTOR IN TRADITIONAL AFRICAN SOCIETIES. ASSESSES TRIBAL ECONOMIC ATTITUDES DISCLOSED, ON THIS BASIS APPRAISES PROBABLE REACTIONS TOWARD FURTHER ECONOMIC DEVELOPMENT WITH REFERENCE TO THE TECHNOLOGICAL, INDUSTRIAL, AND COMMERCIAL DIMENSIONS OF URBANIZATION. IDENTIFIES AND MAPS FOUR SETS OF ECONOMIC AREAS: A SUBSISTENCE AREA, NON-MONETARY TRADING AREAS, MIXED MONEY-EARNING AREAS, AND AN INDUSTRIAL AREA.

2161 REAGAN M.D.
THE MANAGED ECONOMY.
NEW YORK: OXFORD U PR, 1963, 288 PP., LC#63-19946.
STUDY OF ROLE OF GOVERNMENT IN PLANNING AND OPERATION OF NATIONAL ECONOMY. ANALYZES AMERICAN POLITICAL THOUGHT AND CONCEPT OF GOVERNMENTAL RELATIONSHIP TO ECONOMY; DISCUSSES POWER AND INFLUENCE OF PRIVATE CORPORATION.

2162 REAGAN M.D. ED.
POLITICS, ECONOMICS, AND THE GENERAL WELFARE.
GLENVIEW, ILL: SCOTT, FORESMAN, 1965, 151 PP.
EXAMINES EXTENT OF NATIONAL GOVERNMENT INTERACTION WITH ECONOMY AND BUSINESS, SCIENTIFIC RESEARCH, AND EDUCATION. AUTHORS INCLUDE MEN IN BUSINESS, GOVERNMENT, AND ACADEMICS.

2163 REAGAN M.O.
"THE POLITICAL STRUCTURE OF THE FEDERAL RESERVE SYSTEM."
AM. POL. SCI. REV., 55 (MAR. 61), 64-76.
HISTORY AND STRUCTURE OF THE FEDERAL RESERVE SYSTEM AND WHERE ITS AUTHORITY LIES. FORMAL ROLES DO NOT REFLECT ACTUAL DISTRIBUTION OF POWER IN THE SYSTEM.

2164 RECK D.
GOVERNMENT PURCHASING AND COMPETITION.
BERKELEY: U OF CALIF PR, 1954, 215 PP., LC#54-12093.
STUDY OF POLICIES ESTABLISHED BY CONGRESS TO GUIDE PURCHASING OPERATIONS OF CIVILIAN AGENCIES OF FEDERAL GOVERNMENT: LEGAL REQUIREMENT THAT SEALED BIDS BE USED IN CONTRACTING, AND DELEGATION OF AUTHORITY TO CENTRALIZE PURCHASES AND POLICIES TO GENERAL SERVICES ADMINISTRATION. STUDY IS DESIGNED TO CONTRIBUTE TO UNDERSTANDING OF POLICIES PURSUED BY OTHER LARGE-QUANTITY BUYERS.

2165 REDDAWAY W.B.
"THE ECONOMICS OF UNDERDEVELOPED COUNTRIES."
ECON. J., 73 (MARCH 63), 1-12.
INDIA CITED AS EXAMPLE OF UNDERDEVELOPED COUNTRY. AUTHOR PROVIDES INSIGHTS FOR UNDERSTANDING ECONOMIC PROBLEMS PECULIAR TO UNDERDEVELOPED COUNTRIES AND ALSO SUGGESTS WHAT SHOULD BE DONE AND BY WHOM TO TRANSFORM THESE NATIONS INTO ONES OF HIGHER PRODUCTIVITY AND HIGHER REAL INCOME.

2166 REDFORD E.S.
ADMINISTRATION OF NATIONAL ECONOMIC CONTROL.
NEW YORK: MACMILLAN, 1952, 403 PP.
FEATURES OF ADMINISTRATIVE SYSTEM IN USE IN ECONOMIC CONTROL AND PROBLEMS OF ADMINISTERING ECONOMIC CONTROLS, COURTS AND ADMINISTRATIVE PROCESS, INTEREST GROUPS AND ADMINISTRATIVE DECISION-MAKING.

2167 REDFORD E.S. ED.
PUBLIC ADMINISTRATION AND POLICY FORMATION: STUDIES IN OIL, GAS, BANKING, RIVER DEVELOPMENT AND CORPORATE INVESTIGATIONS
AUSTIN: U OF TEXAS PR, 1956, 319 PP., LC#56-7507.
FIVE CASE STUDIES OF ADMINISTRATIVE REGULATION EMPHASIZE RELATIONSHIP BETWEEN CONTROL, EFFICIENCY, AND PUBLIC INTEREST. DISCUSSES INTERRELATIONSHIPS BETWEEN AGENCIES, CLIENTELE, AND SPECIFIC INDIVIDUALS.

2168 REDFORD E.S.
AMERICAN GOVERNMENT AND THE ECONOMY.
NEW YORK: MACMILLAN, 1965, 674 PP., LC#65-10959.
EXAMINES GOVERNMENT'S ROLE IN US ECONOMY - PAST, PRESENT, AND FUTURE. INCLUDES STUDY OF THE ROLE AND PROCESS OF GOVERNMENT, OF THE CONSTITUTION AND THE ECONOMY, OF POLITICS AFFECTING THE ECONOMY GENERALLY, THE REGULATION AND PROMOTION OF INDUSTRIES, THE REGULATORY SYSTEM, AND THE PUBLIC ENTERPRISE. CONCLUDES THAT HUMAN NEEDS ARE NOW REGARDED AS SOCIAL PROBLEMS REQUIRING ORGANIZED SOLUTIONS.

2169 REDFORD E.S.
THE ROLE OF GOVERNMENT IN THE AMERICAN ECONOMY.
NEW YORK: MACMILLAN, 1966, 148 PP., LC#66-25280.
ANALYSIS OF INTERRELATIONSHIP BETWEEN US GOVERNMENT AND AMERICAN ECONOMIC SYSTEM. EVOLUTION OF EFFECT THAT GOVERNMENT HAS HAD IN DEVELOPMENT, REGULATION, AND ADMINISTRATION OF ECONOMY. BASIC SYSTEM OF PRESENT DAY OF THIS INTERACTION AND PERCEIVED FUTURE PROBLEMS.

2170 REDLICH F.
THE GERMAN MILITARY ENTERPRISER AND HIS WORK FORCE.
WIESBADEN: FRANK STEINER VERLAG, 1964, 532 PP.
A STUDY IN THE BORDER AREA BETWEEN MILITARY AND ECONOMIC HISTORY, FOCUSING ON MILITARY OFFICER-ENTERPRISER, WHO BOTH LED AND RAISED HIS ARMY. EXAMINES DEVELOPMENT OF THIS SOCIAL AND OCCUPATIONAL TYPE AND VARIOUS SPECIFIC QUESTIONS: ORGANIZATION OF BUSINESS, FINANCING OF IT, SOCIAL ASPECTS, HUMAN RELATIONS AND MOTIVATION, SOLDIER-CIVILIAN RELATIONS. A WORK IN COMPARATIVE HISTORIOGRAPHY.

2171 REES A.
"DO UNIONS CAUSE INFLATION?"
JOURNAL OF LAW AND ECONOMICS, 2 (OCT. 59), 84-94.
DISCUSSION OF EFFECTS UNIONS HAVE ON MEMBERS' WAGES, THE CONCEPT OF WAGE-PRICE SPIRAL, AND RELATION OF INCREASE IN PRICES TO UNEMPLOYMENT. AUTHOR DISAGREES WITH WAGE-PRICE POSITION.

2172 REES A.
THE ECONOMICS OF TRADE UNIONS.
CHICAGO: U OF CHICAGO PRESS, 1962, 208 PP., LC#62-9741.
EMPHASIZES ECONOMIC ASPECTS OF AMERICAN UNIONS. ALSO DISCUSSES UNION POLITICAL POWER, MEMBERSHIP PROCEDURES, SENIORITY, GRIEVANCE PROCEDURES, AND CORRUPTION. CONCLUDES WITH A SUMMARY OF THE ROLE OF UNIONS, AND A PREDICTION OF THE FUTURE GROWTH OF UNIONS.

2173 REES A.
"THE EFFECTS OF UNIONS ON RESOURCE ALLOCATION."
JOURNAL OF LAW AND ECONOMICS, 6 (OCT. 63), 69-78.
DISCUSSES EFFECTS OF LABOR UNIONS ON RESOURCE ALLOCATION THROUGH CONTROL OVER WAGE INCREASES. EXAMINES RESULTS OF COLLECTIVE BARGAINING ON INTER- AND INTRA-INDUSTRY WAGE STRUCTURES. COMPARES WAGES AND EMPLOYMENT DISTRIBUTION UNDER UNION AND OPEN COMPETITIVE MARKET SYSTEMS. MAINTAINS THAT BENEFICIAL ASPECTS OF BARGAINING ARE MORE IMPORTANT THAN ITS EFFECT ON RESOURCE ALLOCATION.

2175 REHMUS C.M. ED., MCLAUGHLIN D.B. ED.
LABOR AND AMERICAN POLITICS.
ANN ARBOR: U OF MICH PR, 1967, 461 PP., LC#67-11983.
BOOK OF READINGS EXPLORING AMERICAN LABOR MOVEMENT'S INVOLVEMENT IN POLITICS FROM COLONIAL TIME TO PRESENT. RECOUNTS PRESSURE GROUP ACTIVITIES OF WORKINGMEN'S PARTIES, KNIGHTS OF LABOR, IWW, AND EMERGENCE OF AFL AND CIO AS POLITICAL FORCES. DEALS WITH FACETS OF LABOR'S CONTEMPORARY ROLE: LOBBYING AND ELECTORAL PARTICIPATION, LABOR'S MONEY IN POLITICS, AND VOTING BEHAVIOR OF UNION MEMBERS.

2176 REICH N.
LABOR RELATIONS IN REPUBLICAN GERMANY.
NEW YORK: OXFORD U PR, 1938, 292 PP.

TREATS EMPLOYER-EMPLOYEE RELATIONSHIPS, 1918-1933, IN WEIMAR REPUBLIC. STUDIES COLLECTIVE ORGANIZATION OF INDUSTRIAL RELATIONS WITHIN FRAMEWORK OF TRADITIONAL POLITICAL DEMOCRACY. ANALYZES ECONOMIC PROVISIONS OF WEIMAR CONSTITUTION, ROLE OF LABOR IN THE REPUBLIC, ARBITRATION METHODS, ORGANIZATION WITHIN THE SHOPS, AND ULTIMATE FAILURE OF THE REPUBLIC.

2177 REILLY T.J.
"FREEZING AND CONFISCATION OF CUBAN PROPERTY."
STANFORD LAW REV., 19 (JUNE 67), 1358-1368.
QUESTIONS US ACTIONS OF FREEZING AND CONFISCATING CUBAN NATIONALISTS' PROPERTY IN US, AND POLICY BEHIND IT, THROUGH STUDY OF COURT CASE OF SARDINO V. FEDERAL RESERVE BANK. MAINTAINS THAT POLICY IS IRRECONCILABLE WITH POLICY OF PROMOTING US INVESTMENT ABROAD.

2178 RENO P.
THE ORDEAL OF BRITISH GUIANA.
NEW YORK: MONTHLY REVIEW PR, 1964, 132 PP., LC#64-23143.
PORTRAYS LAND AND PEOPLES OF AN EMERGING, UNDERDEVELOPED NATION STRUGGLING TO MAKE SOCIALISM WORK. CRITICIZES AMERICAN EFFORTS AT INTERVENTION.

2179 RESOURCES FOR THE FUTURE
URBAN AND REGIONAL STUDIES AT US UNIVERSITIES; A REPORT BASED ON A 1963 SURVEY OF URBAN AND REGIONAL RESEARCH.
WASHINGTON: US GOVERNMENT, 1964, 127 PP., LC#64-22156.
ANNOTATED CATALOG OF RESEARCH STUDIES IN PROGRESS IN FIELDS OF URBAN AND REGIONAL PLANNING. ONLY COVERS WORK GOING ON IN MAJOR UNIVERSITIES OVER FIVE-YEAR PERIOD PRIOR TO 1963. BROKEN DOWN INTO CATEGORIES OF ECONOMIC STUDIES, SOCIAL AND DEMOGRAPHIC, STUDIES OF LAND USE AND TRANSPORTATION, AND GOVERNMENTAL STUDIES.

2180 REUBENS E.D.
"THE BASIS FOR REORIENATION OF AMERICAN FOREIGN AID POLICY."
SOC. SCI., 34 (OCT. 59), 218-22.
ANALYZES MAJOR FOREIGN AID PROBLEMS FACED BY UNITED STATES. ASSISTANCE TO UNDERDEVELOPED COUNTRIES BECOMES A MORAL RESPONSIBILITY RATHER THAN ECONOMIC NECESSITY SINCE AMERICAN ECONOMY IS INDEPENDENT OF TRADE WITH UNDERDEVELOPED NATIONS. COMPARES RELATIVE ADVANTAGES ENJOYED BY USSR IN FOREIGN AID PROGRAM. STRESSES NEED FOR INTERNATIONAL ADMINISTRATION OF ECONOMIC AID FOR DEVELOPMENT.

2181 REUSS H.S.
THE CRITICAL DECADE - AN ECONOMIC POLICY FOR AMERICA AND THE FREE WORLD.
NEW YORK: MCGRAW HILL, 1964, 227 PP., LC#63-23048.
EXAMINES US TRADE AND FOREIGN AID POLICIES, PROBLEMS OF UNEMPLOYMENT, BALANCE OF PAYMENTS, ROLE OF CONGRESS IN SHAPING EFFECTIVE AID PROGRAMS, FOREIGN TRADE POLICIES, AND INTERNAL ECONOMIC STABILITY.

2182 REYNOLDS P.A.
BRITISH FOREIGN POLICY IN THE INTER-WAR YEARS.
LONDON: LONGMANS, GREEN & CO, 1954, 182 PP.
TRACES COURSE OF POLICY DEVELOPMENT, 1919-39, DISCUSSING CHANGES BY RELATING THEM TO POLITICAL PRESSURES, ECONOMIC INFLUENCES, PUBLIC OPINION, AND NEGOTIATIONS. ALSO DISCUSSES RELATIONS WITH US AND EFFECT ON BRITISH POLICY.

2183 RICARDO D.
THE PRINCIPLES OF POLITICAL ECONOMY AND TAXATION (1817)
ORIGINAL PUBLISHER NOT AVAILABLE, 1963, 300 PP.
DEFENDS LAISSEZ-FAIRE THEORIES IN ECONOMICS, ATTACKING ALL FORMS OF PRICE CONTROLS AND REGULATORY TAXATION. GIVES JUSTIFICATION FOR STATUS QUO IN ENGLAND AT TIME OF WRITING. DISCUSSES ALL FORMS OF ECONOMIC TACTICS AND ESTABLISHES A BASIC STRUCTURE IN WHICH THEY MAY BE CONSIDERED. COVERS VALUE, RENT, TAXES, TARIFFS, TRADE, AND DEMAND.

2184 RICHARDSON G.B.
INFORMATION AND INVESTMENT.
LONDON: OXFORD U PR, 1960, 226 PP.
DISCUSSES THEORY OF ECONOMIC EQUILIBRIUM, FORMATION OF ENTREPRENEURIAL EXPECTATIONS AND INVESTMENT DECISIONS, AND DEPENDENCY OF INFORMATION ON MARKET STRUCTURE, INCLUDING ROLE OF MARKET IMPERFECTIONS AND CONDITIONS OF PLANNING.

2185 RICHMAN B.M.
"CAPITALISTS & MANAGERS IN COMMUNIST CHINA."
HARVARD BUSINESS REV., 45 (JAN. 67), 57-78.
AUTHOR REPORTS ON PERSONAL VISIT TO COMMUNIST CHINA IN 1966. ARTICLE COMMENTS ON MANY AREAS OF CHINESE PRODUCTION. CONCLUDES THAT CHINESE IDEOLOGY, THOUGH MORE FLEXIBLE THAN SOVIET POLICY IN PAST, STILL OBSTRUCTS PROGRESS, AND THAT CHINESE ECONOMY MUST SUPPLY MANAGERS WITH EFFECTIVE PERSONAL INCENTIVES. ESPECIALLY INTERESTING IS THE REPORT ON THE 300,000 CAPITALIST MANAGERS PERMITTED TO SUPERVISE INDUSTRY.

2186 RICHMAN B.M.
"SOVIET MANAGEMENT IN TRANSITION."
BUSINESS TOPICS, 15 (SPRING 67), 27-41.
CONCERNED WITH PROBLEMS FACING MANAGEMENT AS SOVIET INDUSTRIAL ECONOMY EXPANDS AND GROWS MORE COMPLEX. DISCUSSES LIBERMAN PLAN, DECENTRALIZATION OF AUTHORITY, NEED FOR OVERHAUL OF PRICING SYSTEM, MARKETING PRACTICES, USE OF SCIENTIFIC TOOLS AND TECHNIQUES FOR PLANNING AND CONTROL FINANCING, REFORMS UNDER KOSYGIN, INCENTIVE PLANS, SKILLS, AND ESTABLISHMENT OF NEW MINISTRIES.

2187 RICHTER J.H.
"TOWARDS AN INTERNATIONAL POLICY ON AGRICULTURAL TRADE."
KYKLOS, 16 (NO.2, 60), 203-27.
DISCUSSES PROBLEMS OF 'TRADE IN AGRICULTURAL PRODUCTS OF TEMPERATE ZONE.' ANALYZES PROBLEM OF MAINTAINING INTERNATIONAL TRADE AND NEED FOR 'PROGRAMS OF AGRICULTURAL SUPPORT IN BOTH IMPORTING AND EXPORTING COUNTRIES.' MAKES RECOMMENDATIONS FOR RECONCILING THESE ISSUES.

2188 RICHTER R.
DAS KONKURRENZ PROBLEM IM OLIGOPOL.
BERLIN: DUNCKER & HUMBLOT, 1954, 112 PP.
DISCUSSES PROBLEM OF "COMPETITION AMONG THE FEW"; SEEKS TO APPLY THEORY OF GAMES TO INTERPRETATION OF COMPANIES WHICH COMMAND SIZABLE PORTIONS OF MARKET.

2189 RIDAH A.
"LE NEO-DESTOUR DEPUIS L'INDEPENDANCE."
REV. JURID. POLIT. OUTREMER, 17 (OCT.-DEC. 63), 573-657.
EXPLORES ISSUES OF SOUSSE CONGRESS HELD IN MARCH 1959. SURVEYS INSTITUTIONAL FRAMEWORK WITHIN WHICH PARTY MUST FUNCTION. ANALYZES TUNISIAN ECONOMIC BACKGROUNDS. EXAMINES ALL EFFORTS TO CONSTRUCT NEW POLITICAL STRUCTURE.

2190 RIDKER R.G.
ECONOMIC COSTS OF AIR POLLUTION* STUDIES IN MEASUREMENT.
NEW YORK: FREDERICK PRAEGER, 1967, 214 PP., LC#66-26571.
SETS UP MEASUREMENT SYSTEM FOR ECONOMIC COST OF AIR POLLUTION. INCLUDES AS RELEVANT MEDICAL COSTS, DAMAGE TO MATERIALS, EFFECT ON MARKETS. PROVIDES CASE STUDY GIVING TECHNIQUES, DATA ANALYSIS. CONSIDERS PROPERTY VALUES, BOTH IN CROSSSECTION AND TIME-SERIES STUDIES. ADVISES FOR FUTURE RESEARCH.

2191 RIDLEY C.E., SIMON H.A.
MEASURING MUNICIPAL ACTIVITIES (PAMPHLET)
CHICAGO: INT CITY MANAGER'S ASSN, 1943, 75 PP.
DEFINES CRITERIA BY WHICH MUNICIPAL SERVICES MAY BE MEASURED AND PURPOSES OF SUCH MEASUREMENT. SERVICES CONSIDERED ARE PUBLIC HEALTH, LIBRARIES, POLICE AND FIRE PROTECTION, PLAYGROUNDS, WELFARE, AND SO ON. DIFFERENT CRITERIA MUST BE EXAMINED FOR THEIR USEFULNESS IF A CITY IS TO KNOW IT IS GETTING THE MOST BENEFIT FROM EACH TAX DOLLAR.

2192 RIGBY P.H.
CONCEPTUAL FOUNDATIONS OF BUSINESS RESEARCH.
NEW YORK: JOHN WILEY, 1965, 215 PP., LC#65-12701.
EXPLORES RESEARCH PROCESS AND ITS RELATIONSHIP TO DECISION-MAKING AND THE DEVELOPMENT OF KNOWLEDGE. EMPHASIZES RESEARCH STRATEGY LEADING TO EFFICIENT AND PRODUCTIVE DEPLOYMENT OF TECHNIQUES.

2193 RILEY J.W. JR. ED., LEVY M.F. ED.
THE CORPORATION AND ITS PUBLICS. ESSAYS ON THE CORPORATE IMAGE.
NEW YORK: JOHN WILEY, 1963, 195 PP.
SYMPOSIUM DEVOTED TO RE-EXAMINATION OF THE CORPORATE IMAGE. RESEARCH DEVELOPMENTS SHOW A DEFINITE INCREASE IN THE USE OF EMPIRICAL METHODS IN THE NEGLECTED WORLD OF BUSINESS. CHAPTERS ON MEASUREMENT AND THE CULTURAL CONTEXT ARE OF PARTICULAR INTEREST. IT MAY BE, HOWEVER, THAT REPRESENTATION BY VARIOUS PUBLICS RELATES MORE TO PRODUCT REPUTATION THAN SERVICE, BUT THE FORMER MAY RELATE TO EXECUTIVE IMAGE.

2194 RIMALOV V.V.
ECONOMIC COOPERATION BETWEEN USSR AND UNDERDEVELOPED COUNTRIES.
MOSCOW: FOREIGN LANG PUBL HOUSE, 1962, 162 PP.
EXPLAINS SOVIET POLICY OF SUPPORT FOR NATIONAL-LIBERATION MOVEMENT, AIMS AND CHARACTER OF SOVIET ECONOMIC AID, AND PROGRAMS IN VARIOUS AREAS OF WORLD.

2195 RIVKIN A.
"AFRICAN ECONOMIC DEVELOPMENT: ADVANCED TECHNOLOGY AND THE STAGES OF GROWTH."
J. HUM. REL., 8 (SUMMER 60), 617-645.
CONCERNED WITH BASIC PROBLEM AREAS OF AFRICAN ECONOMIC DEVELOPMENT (INCLUDING AGRICULTURE, MINING, TRANSPORTATION, AND LABOR), AND ROLE ADVANCED FREE WORLD TECHNOLOGY CAN PLAY IN ENSURING FREEDOM AND INDEPENDENCE OF AFRICAN STATES. POINTS OUT DANGERS OF EXCESSIVE RAPIDITY IN GROWTH, AND INCORPORATING TECHNOLOGY INTO CULTURAL PROCESSES OF AFRICA.

2196 RIVKIN A.
AFRICA AND THE EUROPEAN COMMON MARKET (PAMPHLET)
DENVER: U OF DENVER, 1964, 61 PP.
ANALYSIS OF RELATION TO EUROPEAN COMMON MARKET OF AFRICAN

STATES. INCLUDES AFRICAN NATIONS ACCEPTED AS ASSOCIATE MEMBERS BY 1963 CONVENTION OF ASSOCIATION AND THOSE NOT PART OF CONVENTION. EXAMINES DEVELOPMENT OF AFRICAN COMMON MARKET AS ADDITION OR ALTERNATIVE TO EEC.

2197 RIVKIN M.D.
AREA DEVELOPMENT FOR NATIONAL GROWTH; THE TURKISH PRECEDENT.
NEW YORK: FREDERICK PRAEGER, 1965, 228 PP., LC#65-21104.
EXAMINES PROBLEMS OF ECONOMICALLY DEVELOPING COUNTRIES IN LIGHT OF AREA DEVELOPMENTS IN TURKEY UNDER ATATURK, INONU, AND MULTI-PARTY DEMOCRACY. CONSIDERS CONCENTRATION OF DEVELOPMENT AT URBAN CENTERS, ASSESSES NEW PATTERNS OF DEVELOPMENT, TREATS PUBLIC POLICY CREATING GROWTH AREAS OUTSIDE ESTABLISHED NATIONAL CENTERS. STUDIES ECONOMY OF ZONGULDAK REGION AS CASE EXAMPLE.

2198 RIZK C.
LE REGIME POLITIQUE LIBANAIS.
PARIS: PICHON ET DURAND-AUZIAS, 1966, 170PP.
ANALYZED MODERN ECONOMIC, POLITICAL, AND SOCIAL STRUCTURE OF LEBANON. DISCUSSES COMBINATION OF ARAB AND WESTERN CULTURES AND OUTLOOKS IN FORMATION OF PRESENT ECONOMY AND POLITICAL ORGANIZATION. EXAMINES POLITICAL PARTIES AND ADMINISTRATIVE PATTERNS IN ACTION TODAY. ALSO COVERS RELATIONSHIP OF MOSLEM AND CHRISTIAN GROUPS IN MAINTAINING FUNCTIONING NATIONAL GOVERNMENT.

2199 ROACH J.R. ED.
THE UNITED STATES AND THE ATLANTIC COMMUNITY; ISSUES AND PROSPECTS.
AUSTIN: U OF TEXAS PR, 1967, 87 PP., LC#67-27782.
STUDIES PRESENT PLACE OF NATO AS PEACE-KEEPING FORCE. ADVOCATES REVISION OF POLICIES AND FUNCTIONS OF NATO TO MEET CHANGES IN WORLD SITUATION PARTIALLY CAUSED BY NATO ITSELF. CONSIDERS IMPLICATIONS OF ECONOMIC RECOVERY OF EUROPE, END OF COLONIALISM, LESSENING OF SOVIET THREAT, ADVANTAGES IN MODERN TECHNOLOGY, AND UNIFICATION OF EUROPE FOR US POSITION IN NATO AND FOREIGN POLICY.

2200 ROBBINS J.J.
THE GOVERNMENT OF LABOR RELATIONS IN SWEDEN.
CHAPEL HILL: U OF N CAR PR, 1942, 361 PP.
STUDIES METHODS OF SETTLING LABOR DISPUTES BEFORE WWII IN SWEDEN AND RELATIONSHIP OF GOVERNMENT TO LABOR AND INDUSTRY DISPUTES, ADVANCING FROM SIMPLE ADVISORY BARGAINING IN CONTRACT SETTLEMENTS TO JURISPRUDENCE OF LABOR COURT. ALSO DISCUSSES PROBLEMS OF INSTITUTIONAL AUTONOMY IN DEMOCRACY WITHOUT DENYING PROTECTION OF LAW.

2201 ROBBINS L.
AN ESSAY ON THE NATURE AND SIGNIFICANCE OF ECONOMIC SCIENCE.
LONDON: MACMILLAN, 1932, 141 PP.
SEEKS TO DETERMINE SUBJECT MATTER OF ECONOMICS AND NATURE OF ITS GENERALIZATIONS. EXPLAINS LIMITATIONS AND SIGNIFICANCE OF THESE GENERALIZATIONS. COMPARES MATERIALIST AND SCARCITY DEFINITIONS OF ECONOMICS. DISCUSSES RELATIVITY OF ECONOMIC QUANTITIES AND ADVANTAGES AND DISADVANTAGES OF PRODUCTION-DISTRIBUTION AND EQUILIBRIUM ANALYSIS.

2202 ROBBINS L.
ECONOMIC PLANNING AND INTERNATIONAL ORDER.
NEW YORK: MACMILLAN, 1937, 330 PP.
VIEWS VARIOUS TYPES OF PLANNING: INDEPENDENT NATIONAL PLANNING, PARTIAL INTERNATION AND COMPLETE INTERNATIONAL PLANNING. POINTS OUT CHARACTERISTICS OF EACH TYPE. CONCLUDES WITH ANALYSIS OF KEYNESIAN DOCTRINE.

2203 ROBBINS L.
ECONOMIC CAUSES OF WAR.
LONDON: CAPE, 1939, 124 PP.
ATTEMPTS TO CONTRIBUTE TO THE DISCOVERY OF THE CAUSES OF WAR 'BY INQUIRING TO WHAT EXTENT WAR CAN BE REGARDED AS BEING DUE TO ECONOMIC CAUSES.'

2204 ROBBINS L.
POLITICS AND ECONOMICS.
NEW YORK: ST MARTIN'S PRESS, 1963, 231 PP.
EXPLORES RELATIONS BETWEEN POLITICS AND ECONOMICS, GENERAL THEORY OF STATE, AND RELATIONS BETWEEN STATES, WITH SPECIAL REFERENCE TO PRINCIPLES OF ECONOMIC POLICY AND PROBLEMS OF HIGH FINANCE.

2205 ROBERTS B.C.
NATIONAL WAGES POLICY IN WAR AND PEACE.
NEW YORK: MACMILLAN, 1958, 180 PP.
STUDY OF ATTEMPTS IN VARIOUS COUNTRIES TO CONTROL INFLATION THROUGH GOVERNMENT WAGE CONTROL. CHALLENGES EFFECTIVENESS OF THESE POLICIES. PROPOSES INSTEAD FREE COLLECTIVE BARGAINING WITH MINIMUM OF GOVERNMENT INTERFERENCE IF PARTIES ACT WITH RESTRAINT AND RESPONSIBILITY.

2206 ROBERTS B.C., DE BELLECOMBE L.G.
COLLECTIVE BARGAINING IN AFRICAN COUNTRIES.
NEW YORK: ST MARTIN'S PRESS, 1967, 158 PP., LC#67-14192.
COVERS ENGLISH AND FRENCH SUB-SAHARA COLONIES. EXAMINES EXTENT OF COLLECTIVE BARGAINING COVERAGE, TRADE UNIONISM, EMPLOYER ORGANIZATIONS, LEGAL FRAMEWORK OF LABOR LAW, AND RANGE OF EFFECT OF AGREEMENTS. EFFECT OF PRE-COLONIAL AND COLONIAL POWER STRUCTURES ON CURRENT DEVELOPMENTS.

2207 ROBERTS E.F.
"THE CASE OF THE UNWARY HOME BUYER: THE HOUSING MERCHANT DID IT."
CORNELL LAW Q., 52 (SUMMER 67), 835-870.
SHOWS DECLINE OF "CAVEAT EMPTOR" AS VIABLE DOCTRINE GOVERNING SALE OF NEW HOMES. ANALYZES EMERGENCE OF IMPLIED WARRANTY AS REMEDY FOR STRUCTURAL DEFICIENCIES AND PERSONAL INJURIES. ARGUES THAT WARRANTY CONCEPT BLURS DISTINCTION BETWEEN BUILDER-VENDOR'S RESPONSIBILITY FOR STRUCTURAL INTEGRITY OF NEW HOMES AND FOR PERSONAL INJURIES CAUSED BY DEFECTS THEREIN. CALLS FOR LEGISLATION TO SOLVE IMPASSE.

2208 ROBERTSON A.H.
EUROPEAN INSTITUTIONS: COOPERATION, INTEGRATION, UNIFICATION
NEW YORK: FREDERICK PRAEGER, 1959, 371 PP., LC#59-8407.
DISCUSSES PROBLEMS OF EUROPEAN POLITICAL AND ECONOMIC UNIFICATION, FROM FORMATIVE PERIOD (1947-49) TO DEVELOPMENT OF EUROPEAN ECONOMIC COMMUNITY AND EURATOM. INCLUDES DOCUMENTARY APPENDIX.

2209 ROBERTSON B.C.
REGIONAL DEVELOPMENT IN THE EUROPEAN ECONOMIC COMMUNITY.
LONDON: ALLEN & UNWIN, 1962, 95 PP.
CONSIDERS PRINCIPLES BASIC TO REGIONAL PLANNING IN GENERAL; ANALYZES DEVELOPMENT SCHEMES OF SOUTHERN ITALY AND SOUTHWEST FRANCE AND ASSESSES THEIR SUCCESS IN BRINGING PROSPERITY. GIVES AN ACCOUNT OF WAYS IN WHICH EEC IS CONCERNED WITH REGIONAL DEVELOPMENT THROUGH READAPTATION PROVISIONS OF COAL AND STEEL COMMUNITY. SUMS UP ACHIEVEMENTS AND INDICATES FUTURE OF REGIONAL POLICIES OF EEC.

2210 ROBERTSON D. H.
GROWTH, WAGES, MONEY (PAMPHLET)
NEW YORK: CAMBRIDGE U PRESS, 1961, 64 PP.
THREE LECTURES COVERING CLASSICAL ORIGINS OF CONCEPT OF MONEY AND INVESTMENT. CONCENTRATES ON GROWTH OF OUTPUT, POPULATION, AND THEIR RELATIONSHIPS TO VALUE OF MONEY. FEELS IDEA THAT FULL EMPLOYMENT LEADS TO FULL PRODUCTION AND INCREASED INVESTING IS FALLACIOUS.

2211 ROBERTSON D. H., DENNISON S.
CONTROLS OF INDUSTRY
LONDON: JAMES NISBET & CO, 1960, 158 PP.
DISCUSSES PROBLEMS OF PRODUCTION, DISTRIBUTION, AND GOVERNMENT CONTROL IN CONTEMPORARY SOCIETY. EXAMINES STRUCTURE OF ECONOMIC ORGANIZATION FOR UTILIZING RESOURCES, ATTEMPTING TO FIND OUT HOW IT WORKS TO ASCERTAIN HOW BEST IT MAY BE CONTROLLED. SPECIFIES DISTINQUISHING CHARACTERISTICS OF MODERN INDUSTRY AND ANALYZES THEM FUNCTIONALLY.

2212 ROBERTSON D.H.
MONEY.
LONDON: JAMES NISBET & CO, 1948, 220 PP.
ANALYZES MONEY FROM 1928 STANDPOINT, THUS HAVING HISTORICAL INTEREST FOR ITS PRE-DEPRESSION EXAMINATION OF VALUE, QUANTITY, BASES, AND CONSERVATION OF MONEY. DISCUSSES GOLD STANDARD AND ASPECTS OF CIRCULATION, EXCHANGE, ITS RELATION TO VALUE OF MONEY, EFFECT OF MONEY ON TRADE CYCLES, AND GOVERNMENT CONTROL OF CURRENCY.

2213 ROBERTSON D.J. ED.
THE BRITISH BALANCE OF PAYMENTS.
LONDON: OLIVER & BOYD, 1966, 187 PP.
SYMPOSIUM CONSIDERING PERFORMANCE OF EXPORTS AND BURDEN OF IMPORT, WITH SPECIAL ATTENTION ON EUROPEAN PROSPECTS AND INVISABLE EARNINGS. EXAMINES MONETARY ASPECTS OF BALANCE OF PAYMENTS IN TERMS OF CAPITAL MOVEMENTS, AND IN RELATION TO MULTIPLE FUNCTIONS OF STERLING AND ROLE OF FISCAL POLICY.

2214 ROBERTSON H.M.
SOUTH AFRICA, ECONOMIC AND POLITICAL ASPECTS.
DURHAM: DUKE U PR, 1957, 192 PP., LC#57-08817.
VIEWS EFFECT OF APARTHEID ON ECONOMIC DEVELOPMENT, POLITICAL PARTIES, DEVELOPMENT OF CONSTITUTIONALISM, AND LEGISLATION. INCLUDES BACKGROUND FOR SOCIO-ECONOMIC ANALYSIS OF RACE RELATIONS IN PARTICULAR CASE STUDIES.

2215 ROBINSON A.D.
DUTCH ORGANIZED AGRICULTURE IN INTERNATIONAL POLITICS, 1945-1960.
THE HAGUE: NIJHOFF, 1962, 192 PP.
AN ANALYSIS OF THE NATURE AND PARTICIPATION OF PRESSURE GROUPS IN SEVERAL FOREIGN ISSUES OF EUROPEAN UNITY.

2216 ROBINSON E.A. ED., VAIZEY J.E. ED.
THE ECONOMICS OF EDUCATION.
NEW YORK: ST MARTIN'S PRESS, 1966, 782 PP., LC#66-10672.
COLLECTION OF ARTICLES ON INTERRELATION OF EDUCATION AND ECONOMIC SYSTEM; CONTRIBUTIONS OF EDUCATION TO ECONOMIC GROWTH; COST OF AND DEMAND FOR EDUCATION; EDUCATION IN DEVELOPING COUNTRIES; INTERNATIONAL AID; NEED FOR EDUCATIONAL

STATISTICS; AND BALANCE OF DIFFERENT FORMS OF EDUCATION.

2217 ROBINSON E.A.G.
THE STRUCTURE OF COMPETITIVE INDUSTRY.
NEW YORK: CAMBRIDGE U PRESS, 1953, 179 PP.
DISCUSSES MEANS AVAILABLE TO GREAT BRITAIN FOR INCREASING ITS NATIONAL PRODUCT, THROUGH CONSIDERATION OF INDUSTRIAL EFFICIENCY. DEFENDS FREE MARKET SYSTEM AS MOST EFFICIENT BECAUSE IT ADJUSTS TO DEMANDS OF CONSUMER. ATTEMPTS TO DEFINE AND DESCRIBE WORKINGS OF FREE MARKET SYSTEM.

2218 ROBINSON E.A.G.
ECONOMIC CONSEQUENCES OF THE SIZE OF NATIONS.
NEW YORK: ST MARTIN'S PRESS, 1960, 447 PP.
ANALYSIS OF RELATION OF SIZE OF NATIONS TO THEIR ECONOMIC PROSPERITY. DISCUSSES SIZE IN RELATION TO ECONOMIC EFFICIENCY, ADAPTABILITY, AND STABILITY AND TO PROBLEMS OF EXECUTIVE ADMINISTRATION AND TO FOREIGN AID POLICIES.

2219 ROBINSON E.A.G. ED.
ECONOMIC DEVELOPMENT FOR AFRICA SOUTH OF THE SAHARA.
NEW YORK: ST MARTIN'S PRESS, 1964, 744 PP.
PROCEEDINGS OF CONFERENCE HELD BY INTERNATIONAL ECONOMIC ASSOCIATION. ARTICLES COVER WIDE RANGE OF TOPICS, INCLUDING REGIONAL ANALYSES, PROBLEMS OF GEOGRAPHY, LABOR, PRICES, CAPITAL, AGRICULTURE, INDUSTRY, AND FISCAL POLICY.

2220 ROBINSON E.A.G.
ECONOMIC PLANNING IN THE UNITED KINGDOM.
NEW YORK: CAMBRIDGE U PRESS, 1967, 46 PP., LC#67-12142.
GIVES AN HISTORICAL ACCOUNT OF THE FIRST ATTEMPTS AT ECONOMIC PLANNING IN THE UNITED KINGDOM. TRIES TO DRAW SOME LESSONS FROM EARLIER ATTEMPTS TO PLAN AND ASKS HOW FAR THESE LESSONS HAVE LED IN RECENT YEARS TO IMPROVEMENT IN PLANNING OR HOW FAR THOSE RESPONSIBLE HAVE FAILED TO LEARN FROM EARLIER EXPERIENCE.

2221 ROBINSON J.
THE ECONOMICS OF IMPERFECT COMPETITION.
LONDON: MACMILLAN, 1934, 344 PP.
PROPOSES TECHNIQUES FOR USE IN ECONOMIC ANALYSIS THAT PRESENT AN ACCOUNT NOT DEPENDENT ON PERFECT COMPETITION, BUT DO NOT BASICALLY REFLECT A PRAGMATIC THEORY. THIS WORK PIONEERED IN FIELD OF MONOPOLIES AND THEIR ECONOMIC ROLE, USING IMPERFECT COMPETITION. CONSIDERS MONOPOLY AND COMPETITIVE EQUILIBRIUM, DEMAND, PRICE, AND COMPETITIVE LABOR DEMAND.

2222 ROBINSON J.
AN ESSAY ON MARXIAN ECONOMICS.
NEW YORK: ST MARTIN'S PRESS, 1960, 104 PP.
COMPARES ECONOMIC ANALYSIS OF MARX'S "CAPITAL" WITH CURRENT ACADEMIC TEACHING. DISCUSSES MARX'S ECONOMIC VIEWS ONLY, NOT HIS SOCIAL OR HISTORICAL OPINIONS.

2223 ROBINSON M.A., MORTON H.C., CALDERWOOD J.D.
AN INTRODUCTION TO ECONOMIC REASONING.
GARDEN CITY: DOUBLEDAY, 1962, 298 PP., LC#62-18650.
INTRODUCTORY EXPOSITION OF FUNDAMENTALS OF ECONOMIC ANALYSIS DESIGNED TO TEACH LAYMEN TO UNDERSTAND AND MAKE INTELLIGENT JUDGMENTS ABOUT ECONOMIC EVENTS AND ISSUES. EMPHASIZES ANALYTICAL METHOD RATHER THAN GENERAL CONCEPTS.

2224 ROBINSON R.D.
INTERNATIONAL BUSINESS POLICY.
NEW YORK: HOLT RINEHART WINSTON, 1964, 252 PP., LC#64-11210.
ATTEMPT TO DEVELOP CALCULUS WHICH, IF USED IN SELECTING OVERSEAS PROJECTS, IN STRUCTURING INTERNATIONAL ENTERPRISES, AND IN RESOLVING OPERATIONAL PROBLEMS, WOULD BECOME A VIABLE INTERNATIONAL CONCEPT AND ENABLE BUSINESS TO REDUCE CONFLICT.

2225 ROBINSON R.D.
INTERNATIONAL MANAGEMENT.
NEW YORK: HOLT RINEHART WINSTON, 1967, 178 PP., LC#67-11817.
A TEXT ON INTERNATIONAL MANAGEMENT. INTENT IS TO PROVIDE A THEORETICAL STRUCTURE FOR THE INTERNAT. MANAGEMENT FIELD, AND TO PROVIDE THE TEACHER WITH A FRAMEWORK INTO WHICH HE MAY FEED RELEVANT DETAILS AND CASE MATERIAL. INCLUDES CHAPTERS ON STRATEGY OF MARKETING, SUPPLY, LABOR, MANAGEMENT, OWNERSHIP, FINANCE, LEGAL ASPECTS, AND CONTROL.

2226 ROBINSON R.I. ED.
FINANCIAL INSTITUTIONS.
HOMEWOOD: RICHARD IRWIN, 1960, 729 PP., LC#60-11208.
INTRODUCTORY STUDY OF MONEY AND ITS VARIOUS FORMS AND FUNCTION IN US FINANCIAL SYSTEM SINCE 1958. COVERS COMMERCIAL AND INSTITUTIONAL BANKING IN DETAIL PLUS ALL ASPECTS OF FUNCTIONS, SUCH AS CREDIT. DISCUSSES PUBLIC AND CONSUMER FINANCE PLUS VARIOUS FORMS OF PRIVATE FINANCIAL INTERMEDIARIES.

2227 ROBSON W.A.
NATIONALIZED INDUSTRY AND PUBLIC OWNERSHIP.
LONDON: ALLEN & UNWIN, 1960, 544 PP.
ANALYZES AND DISCUSSES SOME OF THE THEORIES AND CONCEPTIONS WHICH HAVE EMERGED IN RECENT YEARS FROM SEVERAL DIFFERENT QUARTERS IN BRITAIN AS TO THE MANNER IN WHICH PUBLIC ENTERPRISE SHOULD BE RUN AND PURPOSES IT SHOULD PURSUE. EXAMINES IN PARTICULAR SOME VIEWS AND PROPOSALS WHICH HAVE EEN AGITATING LABOR PARTY, TRADE UNIONS, AND THE COOPERATIVE MOVEMENT.

2228 ROCHE J.
LA COLONISATION ALLEMANDE ET LE RIO GRANDE DO SUL.
RIO DE JANEIRO: INST ETUD AM LAT, 1959, 683 PP.
EXAMINES GERMAN IMMIGRATION TO AND COLONIZATION OF SOUTHERN BRAZIL, SPECIFICALLY STATE OF RIO GRANDE DO SUL. COVERS EARLY COLONISTS FROM 1824 TO POSTWAR GERMAN REFUGEES. ANALYZES THEIR INFLUENCE ON ECONOMIC AND POLITICAL CHANGE AND DEVELOPMENT IN SOUTH AND ON NATIONAL LEVEL.

2229 ROCKE J.R.M.
"THE BRITISH EXPORT BATTLE FOR THE CARIBBEAN"
BOARD OF TRADE JOURNAL, (SEPT. 67), 507-513.
AFTER INDEPENDENCE CARIBBEAN TRADE WAS NO LONGER LIMITED TO ENGLAND. SITUATION OF COMPETITION FORCED ENGLAND TO CHANGE TRADE POLICIES AND METHODS. DESCRIBES AREAS IN WHICH ENGLAND SHOULD INCREASE ACTIVITIES INCLUDING PERSONAL VISITS, DESIGN AND STYLING, AND MARKET RESEARCH. EMPHASIZES NEED FOR INCREASED COOPERATION BETWEEN BRITISH GOVERNMENT POSTS AND MANUFACTURERS.

2230 ROELOFS H.M.
THE LANGUAGE OF MODERN POLITICS: AN INTRODUCTION TO THE STUDY OF GOVERNMENT.
HOMEWOOD: DORSEY, 1967, 380 PP., LC#67-21006.
INTRODUCTORY TEXT STUDIES POLITICS AS THE ACTIVITY OF POLITICIANS TALKING TO ONE ANOTHER RATHER THAN AS DECISION-MAKING PROCESS OR INSTITUTIONAL ARRANGEMENT. DEFINES NATURE OF POLITICAL TALK AND DISCUSSES NATION-STATE, WORK OF JUDGES AND ADMINISTRATORS, AND VARIATIONS IN STYLE AND DIRECTION. COMPARES DIFFERENT STATES AND CLOSES WITH TALK OF INTERNATIONAL POLITICS.

2231 ROEPKE W.
THE PROBLEM OF ECONOMIC ORDER.
CAIRO: NAT BANK OF EGYPT, 1951, 38 PP.
FOUR LECTURES ON LACK OF ECONOMIC PRINCIPLES AND WORKING ECONOMIC ORDER IN WORLD. DEFINES PROBLEM AS "MARKET VS. OFFICE ECONOMY," I.E., ORDER VS. INCENTIVE. PRESENTS POSSIBLE SOLUTIONS AND DISCUSSES BEST CHOICE IN TERMS OF LIBERTY, EFFICIENCY, AND CONTROL OF POWER.

2232 ROEPKE W.
A HUMANE ECONOMY: THE SOCIAL FRAMEWORK OF THE FREE MARKET.
CHICAGO: REGNERY, 1960, 261 PP.
IMPASSIONED STATEMENT WITH REFERENCE TO TRIUMPH OF FREE-MARKET ECONOMY AND CORRESPONDING FAILURE OF SOCIALIST TECHNIQUES IN PAST 15 YEARS. ASSERTS THAT IT IS A PRECEPT OF ETHICAL AND HUMANE BEHAVIOR AS WELL AS POLITICAL WISDOM TO ADAPT ECONOMIC POLICY TO MAN INSTEAD OF CONVERSE. ADDS, HOWEVER, THAT THE FREE-MARKET ECONOMY MUST ALSO FIND A PLACE 'WITHIN THE HIGHER ORDER'.

2233 ROEPKE W.
JENSEITS VON ANGEBOT UND NACHFRAGE (DRITTE VERAENDERTE AUFLAGE)
STUTTGART: EUGEN RENTSCH VERL, 1961, 403 PP.
CONSIDERS MODERN MASS SOCIETY; MARKET ECONOMY AND COLLECTIVISM; PRESUPPOSITIONS AND BOUNDARIES OF THE MARKET; THE WELFARE STATE AND INFLATION; AND CENTRALIZATION AND DECENTRALIZATION. TOPICS TREATED AS PART OF PROBLEM OF CONTEMPORARY CRISIS OF SOCIETY, IN WHICH A FRAGMENTARY, DISINTEGRATED PERSON IS EMERGING UNDER THE IMPACT OF TECHNOLOGY.

2234 ROLFE S.E.
GOLD AND WORLD POWER.
NEW YORK: HARPER & ROW, 1965, 276 PP., LC#66-10658.
EXAMINES DATA CONSTITUTING BALANCE-OF-PAYMENTS STATISTICS. INVESTIGATES VARIOUS POSSIBLE TYPES OF EQUILIBRATING ADJUSTMENTS IN ORDER TO PROVIDE ANALYTIC FRAMEWORK OF PROTOTYPES OF ADJUSTMENT MECHANISMS AVAILABLE TO FREE NATIONS. TREATS ROOTS OF CURRENT SYSTEM.

2235 RONNING C.
"NANKING: 1950."
INTERNATIONAL JOURNAL, 22 (SUMMER 67), 441-456.
REPORT OF CANADIAN POLICY IN CHINA 1945-51, DURING AUTHOR'S SERVICE AS CANADIAN AMBASSADOR TO CHINA. BELIEVES CANADA SHOULD RECOGNIZE THE PEKING GOVERNMENT TO CONTINUE CANADA'S IMPORTANT PEACE-KEEPING ROLE.

2236 RONY V.
"HEARTBREAK IN TENNESSEE* POOR WHITES AND THE UNIONS."
DISSENT, (MAR.-APR. 67), 159-171.
EXPOSITION OF MODERN ANTI-UNION ACTIVITY IN SEMI-APPALACHIAN AREAS. HISTORY OF UAW ORGANIZING, UNION BUSTING, CORPORATE CHICANERY, TEAMSTER ACTIVITIES. SEMI-VIOLENT STRIKE AND ARRESTS RESULTED. NLRB EVENTUALLY RULED AGAINST UNION IN GENERAL. HOFFA ACCUSED OF SELLING OUT.

2237 ROOSA R.V.
MONETARY REFORM FOR THE WORLD ECONOMY.
NEW YORK: HARPER & ROW, 1965, 167 PP., LC#65-24990.
ANALYZES INTERNATIONAL MONETARY POLICY OVER THE PAST TWO DECADES FOR CONTINUING PROCESSES MAKING FOR MONETARY ORDER AND FOR AREAS OF INSTABILITY NEEDING REFORM. IN LIGHT OF CONTINUING LIQUIDITY PROBLEMS HE OUTLINES THE CREATION OF A NEW INTERNATIONAL MONETARY UNIT TO SERVE AS PRIMARY RESERVE ASSET. MEANS OF CREATING A SECONDARY RESERVE ASSET ALSO DISCUSSED. HAS 1964 MINISTERIAL STATEMENT OF THE GROUP OF TEN.

2238 ROPKE W.
INTERNATIONAL ORDER AND ECONOMIC INTEGRATION.
DORDRECHT: D REIDEL PUBL CO, 1959, 280 PP.
EVALUATES RELATION BETWEEN ECONOMICS AND PEACE. TRACES HISTORY OF IDEOLOGICAL CONFLICTS IN EUROPE AND OTHER AREAS. PROPOSES IDEAS FOR ECONOMIC UNIFICATION AS A MEANS FOR ACHIEVING STABILITY IN INTERNATIONAL RELATIONS.

2239 ROPKE W.
A HUMANE ECONOMY.
CHICAGO: HENRY REGNERY CO, 1960, 312 PP., LC#60-09661.
ATTEMPTS TO SHOW NECESSITY FOR CHANGE IN ECONOMIC SYSTEMS OF TODAY BY HISTORICAL EXAMPLES, NEED FOR INTERNATIONAL ORGANIZATION TO STABILIZE WORLD, AND SOCIAL CHANGES POSSIBLE IN UNIFIED ECONOMIC ASSOCIATIONS. COMPARES ECONOMIC IDEAS.

2240 ROPKE W.
ECONOMICS OF THE FREE SOCIETY.
CHICAGO: HENRY REGNERY CO, 1963, 273 PP., LC#63-10948.
SCIENTIFIC STUDY OF ECONOMIC SYSTEM AND PROCESS OF WESTERN SOCIETY. ANALYZES VARIOUS THEORIES ON LABOR, CAPITAL, TRADE, AND THEIR DISTRIBUTION. INCLUDES ALTERNATIVE ECONOMIC SYSTEMS OF TOTALITARIAN NATURE EMPHASIZING THEIR INSTABILITY. EXTENSIVE NOTES ON ECONOMIC THEORY AFTER EACH CHAPTER.

2241 ROSE A.M.
UNION SOLIDARITY: THE INTERNAL COHESION OF A LABOR UNION.
MINNEAPOLIS: U OF MINN PR, 1952, 209 PP., LC#52-5322.
A STUDY OF TEAMSTER LOCAL 866 IN ST. LOUIS, WITH OVER 8,500 MEMBERS. PROBES QUESTIONS OF PARTICIPATION, AGREEMENT ON UNION POLICIES, VARIOUS ATTITUDES ON ISSUES BY VARIOUS GROUPS OF MEMBERS, WORKERS' CONCEPTION OF THE UNION'S ROLE AS WELL AS AN EXAMINATION OF RELATIONSHIPS WITH RACIAL AND RELIGIOUS GROUPS.

2242 ROSS A.M. ED.
EMPLOYMENT POLICY AND THE LABOR MARKET.
BERKELEY: U OF CALIF PR, 1965, 406 PP., LC#65-12596.
COLLECTION OF PAPERS ON ECONOMIC POLICIES AND MANPOWER PROGRAMS ANALYZES UNEMPLOYEMENT, LABOR PARTICIPATION, AND PROCESS OF TRAINING AS RELATED TO FULL-EMPLOYMENT POLICY GOAL.

2243 ROSS A.M. ED.
INDUSTRIAL RELATIONS AND ECONOMIC DEVELOPMENT.
NEW YORK: ST MARTIN'S PRESS, 1966, 413 PP., LC#66-28213.
PAPERS PRESENTED AT RESEARCH CONFERENCE OF INTERNATIONAL INSTITUTE FOR LABOUR STUDIES. DISCUSS ROLES OF STATE AND POLITICAL PARTIES IN INDUSTRIAL RELATIONS OF DEVELOPING COUNTRIES, SOURCES AND FUNCTIONS OF UNION LEADERSHIP, DISTRIBUTION OF DECISION-MAKING POWER IN WAGE DETERMINATION, ROLES OF COLLECTIVE BARGAINING AND LEGISLATION IN INCOME POLICY, AND PARTICIPATION OF INTEREST GROUPS IN PLANNING.

2244 ROSS A.M. ED., HILL H. ED.
EMPLOYMENT, RACE, AND POVERTY.
NEW YORK: HARCOURT BRACE, 1967, 598 PP., LC#65-23537.
TREATS ECONOMIC DISABILITIES OF NEGRO WORKERS AND STAKES AND POSSIBILITIES INVOLVED IN ECONOMIC INTEGRATION. DISCUSSES NEGRO'S POSITION IN LABOR MARKET, SOCIAL EFFECTS (SUCH AS DISTURBED STATUS AND FAMILY LIFE) OF NEGRO UNEMPLOYMENT, AND MEANS OF PROTEST. EXAMINES MANAGEMENT'S AND UNIONS' RESPONSIBILITIES, EDUCATION AND TRAINING OF NEGRO, AND LAWS RELATING TO JOB DISCRIMINATION.

2245 ROSS P.
THE GOVERNMENT AS A SOURCE OF UNION POWER.
PROVIDENCE: BROWN U PRESS, 1965, 320 PP., LC#65-10155.
ANALYSIS OF GOVERNMENT INFLUENCE AND ACTIVITY IN LABOR-MANAGEMENT COLLECTIVE BARGAINING. DISCUSSES LEGISLATION REGARDING DUTY OF BOTH GROUPS TO BARGAIN IN GOOD FAITH.

2246 ROSTOW W.W.
THE STAGES OF ECONOMIC GROWTH.
CAMBRIDGE, ENGLAND: U. PR., 1962, 178 PP.
AN ATTEMPT TO BRING MODERN ECONOMIC THEORY TO BEAR ON ECONOMIC HISTORY AND TO RELATE ECONOMIC TO SOCIAL AND POLITICAL FORCES. TRACES ECONOMIC GROWTH THROUGH FIVE STAGES AND SPECIFICALLY REJECTS MARX'S SOLUTION TO THE PROBLEM OF LINKING ECONOMIC AND NON-ECONOMIC BEHAVIOR DURING THESE STAGES OF GROWTH. AUTHOR CONTENDS HIS CONCEPT WILL HELP USA TO COPE WITH ARMS RACE AND DEVELOPING 'MATURE NATIONS'.

2247 ROTHBARD M.N.
THE PANIC OF 1819; REACTIONS AND POLICIES.
NEW YORK: COLUMBIA U PRESS, 1962, 261 PP., LC#62-9975.
STUDY OF EVENTS LEADING TO DEPRESSION OF 1819 AND PROPOSALS AND POLICIES THAT DEVELOPED AFTERWARD. EXAMINES MONETARY CONTROLS AND ATTEMPTS TO EASE STRAIN OF DISRUPTED SEGMENTS OF ECONOMY.

2248 ROTHBARD M.N.
AMERICA'S GREAT DEPRESSION.
PRINCETON: VAN NOSTRAND, 1963, 361 PP.
EXAMINES THEORY OF BUSINESS CYCLES AGAINST DEPRESSION OF 1930'S. MAINTAINS THAT CYCLES AND DEPRESSIONS STEM FROM DISTURBANCES GENERATED BY MONETARY INTERVENTION IN MARKET. SETS FORTH THEORY, REFUTES CONFLICTING IDEAS, AND FINDS THEORY APPLICABLE TO CAUSES OF 1929 DEPRESSION.

2249 ROTHCHILD D.
"EAST AFRICAN FEDERATION."
TRANSACTIONS, 3 (JAN. 64), 39-42.
REPORTS ON NAIROBI CONFERENCE WHICH DISCUSSED FEDERATION OF KENYA, UGANDA, AND TANGANYIKA, CONCENTRATING ON ECONOMIC ADVANTAGES OF UNITY.

2250 ROTHCHILD D.
"THE LIMITS OF FEDERALISM: AN EXAMINATION OF POLITICAL INSTITUTIONAL TRANSFER IN AFRICA."
J. OF MOD. AFR. STUD., 4 (NOV. 66), 275-293.
DISCUSSES FAILURE OF CLASSICAL FEDERALISM AS EMPLOYED IN EUROPE TO ACHIEVE REGIONAL AND CONTINENTAL UNITY IN AFRICA. EXAMINES MAIN FACTORS CONTRIBUTING TO FAILURE: ATTITUDE OF LEADERS, AND PREVAILING POLITICAL, ECONOMIC, AND SOCIAL CONDITIONS. SEES NEW NATIONS FACING EXTREMES OF UNITARY GOVERNMENT AND LOOSE INTER-UNIT ARRANGEMENTS, AND NEEDING TO FIND CONSTITUTIONAL SYSTEMS TO RECONCILE THESE EXTREMES.

2251 ROURKE F.E.
"THE POLITICS OF ADMINISTRATIVE ORGANIZATION: A CASE HISTORY."
J. OF POLITICS, 19 (AUG. 57), 461-478.
CASE STUDY IN DEVELOPMENT OF NATIONAL EMPLOYMENT SECURITY POLICY DEMONSTRATING THAT, CONTRARY TO EXPECTATIONS, INFLUENCE OF GROUPS ALIGNING THEMSELVES IN OPPOSITION TO REORGANIZATION PLAN NO. 2 OF 1949 HAS INCREASED RATHER THAN DIMINISHED SINCE ITS APPROVAL.

2252 ROUSSEAU J.J.
"A DISCOURSE ON POLITICAL ECONOMY" (1755) IN THE SOCIAL CONTRACT AND DISCOURSES."
NEW YORK: EP DUTTON, 1950.
ESSAY ON JUST AND LEGITIMATE MANAGEMENT OF ECONOMY IN GOVERNMENT FOR THE COMMON GOOD OF SOCIETY. THE IDEAL STATE IS DESCRIBED AS CONSISTING OF THE GENERAL WILL OF SOCIETY, WITH THE WELL-BEING OF ALL ITS MEMBERS AS ITS PRINCIPAL AIM. TAXES, THEREFORE, SHOULD BE LEVIED ACCORDINGLY, WITH HEAVY IMPOSTS ON ALL LUXURIES AND EXEMPTIONS FOR THOSE WHO HAVE ONLY THE NECESSITIES FOR SUSTAINING LIFE.

2253 ROWE J.W.
PRIMARY COMMODITIES IN INTERNATIONAL TRADE.
NEW YORK: CAMBRIDGE U PRESS, 1965, 223 PP., LC#65-18930.
DISCUSSES PRINCIPAL PRIMARY COMMODITIES, CONSUMING MARKETS, PROCESSES OF MARKETING, PRICE CONTROL, FLUCTUATIONS IN INTER-WAR PERIOD, AND NEW CONTROL SCHEMES SINCE WWII.

2254 ROY E.V.
"AN INTERPRETATION OF NORTHERN THAI PEASANT ECONOMY."
J. OF ASIAN STUDIES, 26 (MAY 67), 421-433.
ANALYSIS OF "MIANG" ECONOMIC COMMUNITY AS REFLECTION OF GREATER PEASANT ECONOMIC SYSTEM OF NORTHERN THAILAND. SYSTEM OF PATRON-CLIENT RELATIONSHIPS IN NONSUBSISTENCE MONETARY ECONOMY FORMS RECIPROCATIVE-HIERARCHIC STRUCTURE. ARGUES THAT DESPITE ELEMENTS OF COMPETITION AND MONETARY SYSTEM PEASANT ECONOMY IS NOT AN INSTANCE OF PRIMITIVE CAPITALISM.

2255 RUBIN B.
PUBLIC RELATIONS AND THE STATE, A CASE STUDY OF NEW YORK STATE ADMINISTRATION, 1943-54.
NEW BRUNSWICK: RUTGERS U PR, 1958, 357 PP., LC#58-9104.
STUDY OF PUBLIC RELATIONS PROGRAM OF DEWEY ADMINISTRATION IN NEW YORK. CONCLUDES THAT PUBLIC RELATIONS IS HIGHLY BENEFICIAL AREA OF GOVERNMENT ENDEAVOR. DISCUSSES REASONS FOR PUBLIC RELATIONS IN GOVERNMENT. DESCRIBES NEW YORK PROGRAMS, POLICIES, AND PERSONNEL. OUTLINES PROMOTIONAL AND INFORMATION PROGRAMS OF VARIOUS BRANCHES OF ADMINISTRATION AND OUTLINES NEW PROSPECTS FOR GOVERNMENT PUBLIC RELATIONS.

2256 RUBIN S.J.
THE CONSCIENCE OF THE RICH NATIONS: THE DEVELOPMENT ASSISTANCE COMMITTEE AND THE COMMON AID EFFORT.
NEW YORK: HARPER & ROW, 1966, 161 PP., LC#66-21712.
PERSONAL ACCOUNT OF HOW THE DEVELOPMENT ASSISTANCE COMMITTEE OF THE ORGANIZATION FOR ECONOMIC COOPERATION AND DEVELOPMENT FUNCTIONS AS THE COORDINATING AGENCY FOR THE FORMULATION OF A COMMON AID STRATEGY BY THE RICH NATIONS AND THE PATTERN OF AID-GIVING WHICH HAS DEVELOPED. EXAMINES ROLE OF MOTIVES AND PROBLEM OF COORDINATING GENERAL AND

SPECIFIC INTERESTS, AND BILATERAL AND MULTILATERAL AID.

2257 RUEDA B.
A STATEMENT OF THE LAWS OF COLOMBIA IN MATTERS AFFECTING BUSINESS (3RD ED.)
WASHINGTON: PAN AMERICAN UNION, 1961, 303 PP.
SUMMARY IN ENGLISH OF CONSTITUTIONAL, STATUTORY, AND REGULATORY PROVISIONS OF COLOMBIA RELEVANT TO COMMERCIAL CONCERNS. COVERS LAWS IN FORCE IN SPRING, 1961, BOTH CIVIL AND CRIMINAL.

2258 RUEFF J., HIRSCH F.
THE ROLE AND THE RULE OF GOLD: AN ARGUMENT (PAMPHLET)
PRINCETON: PRIN U, DEPT OF ECO, 1965, 22 PP.
INTERVIEW CONCERNING DE GAULLE'S STATEMENT IN 1965 THAT INTERNATIONAL EXCHANGES MUST USE GOLD AS SINGLE STANDARD TO REPLACE SUPREMACY OF US DOLLAR. TWO ECONOMISTS DEBATE PROS AND CONS; DISCUSS DE GAULLE'S ECONOMIC POLICIES AND REFORMS, REASONS FOR GOLD STANDARD, ITS SHORTCOMINGS, DEFICIT IN BALANCE OF PAYMENTS, POSSIBILITIES OF INFLATION AND DEFLATION, LIQUIDITY, AND FUTURE OF US DOLLAR.

2259 RUEFF J.
BALANCE OF PAYMENTS: PROPOSALS FOR RESOLVING THE CRITICAL WORLD ECONOMIC PROBLEM OF OUR TIME.
NEW YORK: MACMILLAN, 1967, 215 PP., LC#67-20735.
TRACES BACKGROUND OF BALANCE OF PAYMENTS PROBLEM INCLUDING GERMAN WWI REPARATIONS, LATE 40'S DOLLAR SCARCITY, TRENDS IN INTERNATIONAL TRADE, AND SPECIFIC FACTORS INVOLVED IN US BALANCE OF PAYMENTS DEFICIT IN 1960'S. ADVANCES GENERAL THEORY TO DEAL WITH PROBLEM CENTERING ON DIVERGENT WORLD MONETARY SYSTEMS, REGULATION OF INTERNATIONAL CURRENCY LEVELS, AND CONTROL OF FEDERAL RESERVE DISCOUNT RATE.

2260 RUMMEL J.F., BALLAINE W.C.
RESEARCH METHODOLOGY IN BUSINESS.
NEW YORK: HARPER & ROW, 1963, 359 PP., LC#63-14051.
DISCUSSION OF RESEARCH TECHNIQUES INCLUDING DESIGNING OF PROJECT, DATA COLLECTION AND ANALYSIS, AND REPORT WRITING.

2261 RUPPENTHAL K.M. ED., MCKINNELL H.A. JR. ED.
TRANSPORTATION AND TOMORROW.
STANFORD: STANFORD U, BUS ADMIN, 1966, 180 PP., LC#66-23037.
DISCUSSES SEVERAL TYPES OF TRANSPORTATION: RAILROADS, TRUCKING, PIPELINES, SHIPPPING, AIR, AND SPACE. STUDIES CHANGES NECESSARY TO MEET INDUSTRIAL AND MILITARY NEEDS, SUCH AS MORE EFFICIENT ORGANIZATION AND CLOSER COOPERATION AMONG TYPES. PREDICTS TYPES OF TRANSPORTATION IN 2000.

2262 RUSINOW D.I.
"YUGOSLAV DEVELOPMENT BETWEEN EAST AND WEST."
J. INT. AFFAIRS, 19 (1965), 181-193.
HISTORY, PROBLEMS AND SUCCESS OF YUGOSLAVIA'S RECORD OF DEVELOPMENT AS A "NON-ALIGNED" COMMUNIST NATION. FEATURES OF ITS UNIQUE WORKERS' SELF- MANAGEMENT AND MARKET SOCIALISM EXPLAINED, PLUS FOREIGN AID, TRADE AND DELICATE RELATIONS WITH BOTH EAST AND WEST DISCUSSED.

2263 RUSSETT B.M.
"INEQUALITY AND INSTABILITY: THE RELATION OF LAND TENURE TO POLITICS."
WORLD POLIT., 16 (APRIL 64), 442-54.
ATTEMPTS TO CLARIFY CONCEPTUALLY THE PROBLEM OF THE RELATION BETWEEN ECONOMIC INEQUALITY AND POLITICS, PRESENTS DATA ON DISTRIBUTION OF LAND, AND CONCLUDES THAT RELATIVE EQUALITY OF LAND TENURE IS NOT NECESSARILY A GUARANTEE OF DEMOCRATIC DEVELOPMENT.

2264 RUSTAMJI R.F.
THE LAW OF INDUSTRIAL DISPUTES IN INDIA.
NEW YORK: ASIA PUBL HOUSE, 1964, 878 PP.
DEALS WITH INCREASING PROBLEMS IN LABOR RELATIONS BY ATTEMPTING TO GIVE BASIC FRAMEWORK FOR SOCIAL LEGISLATION AND BY CATEGORICALLY LISTING EXISTING STATUTES OF INDIAN LAW APPLYING TO LABOR AND INDUSTRY IN MATTERS OF STRIKES, LAYOFFS, LOCK-OUTS, AND INDUSTRIAL DISPUTES ACT OF 1947.

2265 RUSTOW D.A.
THE POLITICS OF COMPROMISE.
PRINCETON: PRINCETON U PRESS, 1955, 257 PP., LC#55-6702.
STUDY OF PARTIES AND CABINET GOVERNMENT IN SWEDEN EMPHASIZING NECESSITY AND EFFECTUALITY OF COMPROMISE POLICY IN SWEDISH POLITICS. DISCUSSES SEVERAL SUCCESSFUL PROGRAMS IN SOCIAL AND ECONOMIC PLANNING. PROVIDES CURSORY ACCOUNT OF SOCIAL WELFARE, LABOR RELATIONS, AND FOREIGN POLICY. TRACES DEVELOPMENT OF SWEDISH DEMOCRACY.

2266 SABLE M.H.
PERIODICALS FOR LATIN AMERICAN ECONOMIC DEVELOPMENT, TRADE, AND FINANCE: AN ANNOTATED BIBLIOGRAPHY (A PAMPHLET)
LOS ANGELES: U CAL LAT AM CTR, 1965, 72 PP.
LIST OF ENGLISH AND FOREIGN LANGUAGE PERIODICALS DEALING WITH FIELDS OF ECONOMICS AS RELATED TO LATIN AMERICA IN GENERAL AND INDIVIDUAL LATIN AMERICAN NATIONS. INCLUDES TITLE, SUBJECT, AND GEOGRAPHIC INDEXES. CONTAINS 220 PERIODICALS ANNOTATED.

2267 SACHS E.S.
THE CHOICE BEFORE SOUTH AFRICA.
LONDON: TURNSTILE PR, 1952, 220 PP.
DISCUSSES AFRIKANER NATIONALISM, POLICY OF APARTHEID, POLITICAL PARTIES, ECONOMIC DEVELOPMENT IN AGRICULTURE AND INDUSTRY (MINING/MANUFACTURING), AND TRADE UNION AND LABOR MOVEMENT. ARGUES FOR MOBILIZATION OF DEMOCRATIC FORCES TO REMOVE THE NATIONALIST GOVERNMENT.

2268 SACKS B.
SOUTH AFRICA: AN IMPERIAL DILEMMA.
ALBUQUERQUE: U OF N MEX PR, 1967, 356 PP., LC#66-29015.
EXAMINES WHETHER BRITISH TRUSTEESHIP AT BEGINNING OF 20TH CENTURY COULD HAVE AVERTED MODERN-DAY DILEMMA. MAINTAINS THAT BRITISH COLONIAL OFFICE STRESSED PROTECTION OF NATIVE PEOPLES FROM PREDATORY COLONIALISM, BUT DUE TO INTERNATIONAL RELATIONS WITH GERMANY, WAS FORCED TO GRANT WHITE COLONIALS A FREE HAND IN DEALING WITH BANTU. CONSISTS OF DEBATES BETWEEN SOUTH AFRICAN OFFICIALS AND UK, 1902-14.

2269 SACKS S., HELLMUTH W.F.
FINANCING GOVERNMENT IN A METROPOLITAN GOVERNMENT.
NEW YORK: FREE PRESS OF GLENCOE, 1961, 387 PP., LC#60-10900.
DISCUSSES OPERATING EXPENDITURES OF METROPOLITAN CLEVELAND, ITS REVENUES, DEBTS, AND CAPITAL OUTLAY, AS AN EXAMPLE OF IMPACT OF METROPOLIS ON LOCAL GOVERNMENT FINANCING. INCLUDES SUMMARY AND RECOMMENDATIONS.

2270 SAKAI R.K. ED.
STUDIES ON ASIA, 1960.
LINCOLN: U OF NEB PR, 1960, 97 PP., LC#60-15432.
STUDIES VARIOUS SOCIAL FORCES OF EMERGENT ASIA AND AREA'S HISTORY: A RURAL COMMUNITY IN MALAYA, LABOR PRODUCTIVITY IN COMMUNIST CHINA, AND VOICE OF AMERICA IN ASIA.

2271 SAKAI R.K. ED.
STUDIES ON ASIA, 1961.
LINCOLN: U OF NEB PR, 1961, 85 PP., LC#60-15432.
STUDIES FORCES SHAPING CONTEMPORARY ASIA AND AREA'S HISTORY: NATIONALISM, INVESTMENT IN INDIA, JAPANESE IMPERIALISM, AND RELIGION AND POLITICS IN BURMA.

2272 SAKAI R.K.
STUDIES ON ASIA, 1964.
LINCOLN: U OF NEB PR, 1964, 186 PP., LC#60-15432.
ASIAN HISTORY AND POLITICAL FORCES SHAPING CONTEMPORARY ASIA, EMPHASIZING CHINA AND JAPAN. INCLUDES SINO-SOVIET-BRITISH RESPONSES TO INDIAN NATIONALISM; POSTWAR JAPAN-KOREA RELATIONS; AND POLITICAL IDEOLOGY IN MALAYSIA.

2273 SALANT W.S. ET AL.
THE UNITED STATES BALANCE OF PAYMENTS IN 1968.
WASHINGTON: BROOKINGS INST., 1963, 298 PP., $2.95.
REVISED VERSION OF REPORT SUBMITTED TO COUNCIL OF ECONOMIC ADVISORS IN JANUARY 1963, WITH SOME POLICY RECOMMENDATIONS ADDED LATER. REVIEWS CAUSES OF DIFFICULTY IN U.S. BALANCE OF PAYMENTS AND EXAMINES OUTLOOK OVER THE NEXT SEVERAL YEARS.

2274 SALANT W.S., ET A.L.
THE UNITED STATES BALANCE OF PAYMENTS IN 1968.
WASHINGTON: BROOKINGS INST, 1963, 298 PP., LC#63-21038.
REVISED VERSION OF REPORT SUBMITTED TO COUNCIL OF ECONOMIC ADVISERS, INCLUDING FINAL CHARTER ON POLICY RECOMMENDATIONS. CITES US WORLD PAYMENTS, PROBABLE CHANGES IN DEMAND AND OUTPUT, US BALANCE OF PAYMENTS, EEC, PRIVATE FOREIGN INVESTMENT, DEFENSE TRANSACTIONS, AND FOREIGN ECONOMIC ASSISTANCE.

2275 SALVADORI M.
"EL CAPITALISMO EN LA EUROPA DE LA POSGUERRA."
REV. INST. CIENC. SOC., (NO.3, 64), 211-30.
ANALYZES DEVELOPMENT OF THEORY AND PRACTICE OF CAPITALISM IN WESTERN EUROPE AFTER WW 2 AND ITS RELATION TO INDIVIDUALISM, RATIONALISM, AND MATERIALISM. DISCUSSES STATE CAPITALISM AND LIBERAL PRIVATE CAPITALISM IN RELATION TO ECONOMIC REBIRTH OF WESTERN EUROPE.

2276 SAMUELSON P.A.
FOUNDATIONS OF ECONOMIC ANALYSIS.
CAMBRIDGE: HARVARD U PR, 1948, 447 PP.
EXAMINES IMPLICATIONS FOR THEORETICAL AND APPLIED ECONOMICS. STATES THAT MEANINGFUL THEOREMS DO EXIST IN ECONOMICS. EXPLORES CONDITIONS FOR EQUILIBRIUM AND DYNAMIC BEHAVIOR OF ECONOMIC SYSTEMS. DISCUSSES THEORIES OF COST AND PRODUCTION, CONSUMER'S BEHAVIOR, RATIONING, WELFARE ECONOMICS, AND SYSTEMS TO MEASURE STABILITY OF EQUILIBRIUM.

2277 SANDEE J.
EUROPE'S FUTURE CONSUMPTION.
AMSTERDAM: NORTH HOLLAND PUBL CO, 1964, 363 PP.
STUDY IN PURPOSE AND APPLICATION OF CONSUMPTION ANALYSIS: 13 ESSAYS (4 IN FOREIGN LANGUAGES) PREDICTING FUTURE CONSUMPTION IN EUROPEAN COUNTRIES. MAIN CONCLUSION IS THAT CONSUMPTION FUNCTIONS ARE NEARLY THE SAME ALL OVER

EUROPE.

2278 SANDMEYER R.L., WARNER L.
"METHODOLOGICAL ISSUES IN THE STUDY OF LABOR FORCE PARTICIPATION RATES."
ROCKY MOUNTAIN SOCIAL SCIENCE J., 4 (OCT. 67), 32-51.
EXAMINES METHODOLOGICAL APPROACHES USED IN STUDIES OF LABOR FORCE PARTICIPATION RATES, EMPHASIZING ECONOMIC POLICY ISSUES THAT STIMULATE SUCH ANALYSES. DESCRIBES CROSS-CLASSIFICATIONS OF DATA AND MULTIPLE REGRESSION ANALYSIS. ADVOCATES NEW SYSTEM OF REGRESSION RUNS BASED ON SPECIFIC MODEL.

2279 SANNWALD R.E., STOHLER J.
ECONOMIC INTEGRATION: THEORETICAL ASSUMPTIONS AND CONSEQUENCES OF EUROPEAN UNIFICATION.
PRINCETON: U. PR., 1959, 260 PP.
DISCUSSES THE COMMON MARKET'S ECONOMIC INTEGRATION. PUTS SPECIAL EMPHASIS ON THE METHOD OF INTEGRATION, CURRENCY SYSTEM, ENONOMIC STABILIZATION POLICY, FISCAL POLICY, AND FACTOR MOBILITY.

2280 SANTHANAM K.
UNION-STATE RELATIONS IN INDIA.
NEW YORK: ASIA PUBL HOUSE, 1960, 71 PP.
EXAMINATION OF INDIAN FEDERAL SYSTEM. DISCUSSES CONSTITUTION, RELATIONS OF THREE BRANCHES, PLANNING IN REGARD TO FEDERAL-STATE RELATIONS, FINANCIAL RELATIONS, AND POLITICAL AND LINGUISTIC INFLUENCES ON FEDERAL STRUCTURE.

2281 SAPARINA Y.
CYBERNETICS WITHIN US.
HOLLYWOOD: WILSHIRE BOOK CO, 1967, 315 PP., LC#66-30621.
EXAMINES CYBERNETICS, SCIENCE OF CONTROL AND COMMUNICATION. LOOKS AT BIOLOGICAL SELF-REGULATORY SYSTEMS IN HUMAN BODY AND COMPARES THESE TO ELECTRONIC REGULATORY SYSTEMS DEVELOPED BY MAN. INVESTIGATES SYSTEM OF HUMAN THINKING AND DISCUSSES SIMILAR SYSTEMS OF THOUGHT, LEARNING, AND PERCEPTION IN MACHINES.

2282 SAPIR H.M.
JAPAN, CHINA, AND THE WEST (PAMPHLET)
WASHINGTON: NATL PLANNING ASSN, 1959, 79 PP., LC#59-11126.
ANALYSIS OF ECONOMY OF JAPAN AS TO POSTWAR GROWTH AND IMPORTANCE IN COLD WAR PERIOD. COVERS POLICY-MAKING, ECONOMIC STRUCTURE, TRADE WITH WEST, SINO-SOVIET BLOC, AND FREE NATIONS OF ASIA.

2283 SASTRI K.V.S.
FEDERAL-STATE FISCAL RELATIONS IN INDIA: A STUDY OF THE FINANCE COMMISSION AND TECHNIQUES OF FINANCIAL ADJUSTMENT.
LONDON: OXFORD U PR, 1966, 142 PP.
STUDIES INDIAN FINANCE COMMISSION, ITS ROLE IN FEDERAL-STATE STRUCTURE, ITS PRINCIPLES, AND PROCEDURES. ANALYZES PROBLEM OF RELATED TAX EFFORTS OF STATES IN FEDERATION. PROPOSES DISTRIBUTABLE POOLS OF UNION TAX-REVENUES AND DISCUSSES PROCEDURES FOR DISTRIBUTING THEM.

2284 SAYLES L.R., STRAUSS G.
THE LOCAL UNION.
NEW YORK: HARPER & ROW, 1953, 269 PP., LC#53-5477.
BOOK STUDIES LOCAL INDUSTRIAL UNIONS, GRIEVANCE PROCEDURES AND GROUP PRESSURES, THE ROLES OF OFFICERS AND STEWARDS, MEMBERSHIP AND UNION DEMOCRACY AND THUS PRESENTS A VALUABLE SOURCE FOR STUDENTS OF REPRESENTATION. GRIEVANCE PROCEDURES, THE DECLINE OF THE STEWARDS' COMMUNICATION FUNCTION, CROSS-PRESSURES, UNION ELECTIONS, AND UPWARD COMMUNICATIONS FROM MEMBERS AT UNION MEETINGS ARE DISCUSSED.

2285 SCALAPINO R.A. ED.
"A SURVEY OF ASIA IN 1966."
ASIAN SURVEY, 7 (JAN.-FEB. 67), 1-80, 83-150 .
ESSAYS ON EVENTS AND CONDITIONS IN ASIA IN 1966. STUDIES CULTURAL REVOLUTION IN CHINA, GROWTH OF MONGOLIAN PEOPLE'S REPUBLIC, EFFORTS BY KOREA TO IMPROVE GOVERNMENT AND SOCIAL SYSTEM, AND SOUTH VIETNAM'S POLITICS. DISCUSSES POLITICAL AND DIPLOMATIC SITUATION IN TAIWAN, PHILIPPINES, CAMBODIA, LAOS, JAPAN, INDIA, NEPAL, PAKISTAN, CEYLON, BURMA, THAILAND, MALAYSIA, AND INDONESIA.

2286 SCAMMEL W.M.
INTERNATIONAL MONETARY POLICY.
NEW YORK: MACMILLAN, 1961, 417 PP.
SURVEY ON POLICY SINCE 1915 FOCUSES ON EXPERIMENTS IN INTERNATIONAL MONETARY COOPERATION OF LAST 20 YEARS. ONE SUCH EXPERIMENT DISCUSSED IS UN MONETARY AND FINANCE CONFERENCE AT BRETTON WOODS THAT PLANNED ADJUSTMENTS OF DEFICITS AND SURPLUSES IN BALANCE OF PAYMENTS.

2287 SCHACHTER G.
"REGIONAL DEVELOPMENT IN THE ITALIAN DUAL ECONOMY"
ECO. DEV. AND CULTURAL CHANGE, 15 (JULY 67), 398-407.
EXAMINES REGIONAL DUALISM IN ITALIAN ECONOMY AND EFFECTS ON ECONOMIC DEVELOPMENT. OBSTACLES TO DEVELOPMENT ARE DEPENDENCY OF ONE REGION ON ANOTHER, MARKET PROBLEMS, AND MASS MIGRATION. STUDIES ROLE OF GOVERNMENT IN EQUALIZING DEVELOPMENT IN EACH REGION THROUGH MIXED GOVERNMENT ENTERPRISES AND PLANNED INDUSTRIAL DEVELOPMENT OF AGRICULTURAL REGIONS.

2288 SCHAEFER W.V.
THE SUSPECT AND SOCIETY: CRIMINAL PROCEDURE AND CONVERGING CONSTITUTIONAL DOCTRINES.
EVANSTON: NORTHWESTERN U PRESS, 1967, 99 PP.
DEALS WITH LEGAL PROBLEMS CENTERING ON POLICE INTERROGATION OF PERSONS SUSPECTED OF HAVING COMMITTED CRIMES. CONSIDERS CONSTITUTIONAL DOCTRINES THAT BEAR UPON POLICE INTERROGATION AS IT HAS BEEN CONDUCTED IN THE PAST. DISCUSSES MODEL CODE OF PROCEDURE ADVANCED BY AMERICAN LAW INSTITUTE TO REGULATE POLICE CONDUCT IN TREATMENT OF CRIMINAL.

2289 SCHALLER H.G. ED.
PUBLIC EXPENDITURE DECISIONS IN THE URBAN COMMUNITY: PREPARED FOR RESOURCES FOR THE FUTURE, INC.
BALTIMORE: JOHNS HOPKINS PRESS, 1962, 198 PP., LC#63-22774.
FIRST THREE PAPERS EXAMINE THE NEED FOR THE PUBLIC PRODUCTION OF GOODS AND SERVICES AND HOW RECENT CHANGES IN THE PRIVATE SECTOR HAVE AFFECTED THE NEED FOR EXPANSION OF THE PUBLIC SECTOR OF URBAN ECONOMY. NEXT FOUR PAPERS DEAL WITH THE APPLICATION OF THEORETICAL TOOLS TO DECISION-MAKING IN THE PUBLIC SECTOR OF URBAN ECONOMY. THE REST EXPLORE QUESTION OF HOW TO MEASURE QUALITY OF LOCAL GOVERNMENT OUTPUT.

2290 SCHATTSCHNEIDER E.E.
POLITICS, PRESSURES AND THE TARIFF: A STUDY OF FREE PRIVATE ENTERPRISE IN PRESSURE POLITICS IN TARIFF REVISION 1929-1930
ENGLEWOOD CLIFFS: PRENTICE HALL, 1935, 301 PP., LC#35-29634.
DESCRIBES POLITICAL BEHAVIOR OF ECONOMIC GROUPS IN TARIFF REVISION OF 1929-30; HOW TARIFFS ARE MADE: PUBLIC HEARINGS AND COLLECTION OF EVIDENCE; POLITICAL BEHAVIOR OF PRESSURE GROUPS: THEIR VARIOUE ACTIVITIES, AND INSIDERS, OUTSIDERS, AND CONGRESS; INTERNAL POLITICS OF PRESSURE GROUPS: THEIR REPRESENTATIVE CHARACTER.

2291 SCHECHTER A.
THE BUSINESSMAN IN GOVERNMENT (THESIS, COLUMBIA UNIVERSITY)
NEW YORK: COLUMBIA UNIVERSITY, 1965, 360 PP.
ANALYZES THE BACKGROUNDS OF 112 BUSINESSMEN WHO SERVED IN CABINET OR SUB-CABINET POSTS UNDER PRESIDENTS TRUMAN AND EISENHOWER. FINDS THAT THE MAJORITY, BEFORE APPOINTMENT, HAD BEEN POLITICALLY INACTIVE BANKERS, AND THAT AFTER LEAVING OFFICE, THEY TRUSTED BIG GOVERNMENT MORE THAN DO MOST BUSINESSMEN. CONCLUDES THAT USE OF BUSINESSMEN IN GOVERNMENT OFFICE GREATLY HELPS GOVERNMENT-BUSINESS UNDERSTANDING.

2292 SCHECTER J.
THE NEW FACE OF BUDDHA: BUDDHISM AND POLITICAL POWER IN SOUTHEAST ASIA.
NEW YORK: COWARD-MCMANN, 1967, 300 PP., LC#67-10560.
DESCRIBES NEW BUDDHISM AS MORE THAN RELIGION AND PHILOSOPHY; IT IS NATIONALISM, IDEOLOGY, AND ULTIMATE SOURCE OF ASIAN VALUES. SHOWS THAT IN TRADITIONAL BUDDHISM, CHURCH AND STATE WERE UNITED AND THIS FORCE OF RELIGION AS JUSTIFICATION FOR RULE REMAINS. DISCUSSES PERSONALITIES IN FOREFRONT OF NEW BUDDHISM: PRINCE SIHANOUK AND VIETNAM'S THICH TRI QUANG.

2293 SHEEHAN D.
"PUBLIC AND PRIVATE GROUPS AS IDENTIFIED IN THE FIELD OF TRADE REGULATIONS."
RUTGERS LAW REV., 13 (SPRING 59), 577-588.
DISCUSSES GROUP INTERESTS IN TRADE REGULATION IN THREE FIELDS: PATENT AND ANTI-TRUST LAW, DOMESTIC ADMINISTRATIVE LAW, AND INTERNATIONAL LAW.

2294 SCHELLING T.C.
"AN ESSAY ON BARGAINING" (BMR)"
AMER. ECO. REVIEW, 46 (JUNE 56), 281-306.
PRESENTS A TACTICAL APPROACH TO BARGAINING ON THE TACIT AND EXPLICIT LEVELS. EMPHASIZES THE LOGICAL OUTCOME OF THE SITUATION AS FOUND IN THE CLASS OF TACTICS EMPLOYED. ANALYZES TACTICS PECULIARLY APPROPRIATE TO THE LOGIC OF INDETERMINATE SITUATIONS; THESE TACTICS REST ON ASSUMPTION THAT POWER TO CONSTRAIN AN ADVERSARY MAY DEPEND ON THE POWER TO BIND ONESELF. ILLUSTRATED WITH GAME THEORY AND MODELS.

2295 SCHELLING T.C.
"ECONOMICS AND CRIMINAL ENTERPRISE."
PUBLIC INTEREST, 7 (SPRING 63), 465-486.
ECONOMIC ANALYSIS OF CRIMINAL UNDERWORLD. SUGGESTS TENTATIVE TYPOLOGY OF UNDERWORLD BUSINESS AND EXAMINES INCENTIVES TO CRIMINAL ORGANIZATION. ARGUES FOR ANALYSIS OF MARKET ADJUSTMENTS TO COMPARE THE COSTS OF SOCIETY TO THE GAINS OF CRIMINALS AND BETTER UNDERSTANDING OF INSTITUTIONAL PRACTICES. EXAMINES RELATION OF ORGANIZED CRIME TO ENFORCEMENT, AND SOCIAL ADVANTAGES OF ORGANIZED CRIME.

2296 SCHER S.
"REGULATORY AGENCY CONTROL THROUGH APPOINTMENT: THE CASE OF THE EISENHOWER ADMINISTRATION AND THE NLRB."
J. OF POLITICS, 23 (NOV. 61), 667-688.

"THIS PAPER FOCUSES ON EFFORTS OF THE REGULATED CLIENTELE OF OUR INDEPENDENT COMMISSION, THE NATIONAL LABOR RELATIONS BOARD, TO INVOKE IN THEIR BEHALF THE PRESIDENTIAL APPOINTIVE POWER IN THE EISENHOWER YEARS."

2297 SCHILLING W.R., HAMMOND P.Y., SNYDER G.H.
STRATEGY, POLITICS, AND DEFENSE BUDGETS.
NEW YORK: COLUMBIA U PRESS, 1962, 532 PP.
PROBLEM OF SECURITY POLICY IN US, ITS CLOSE RELATION TO DOMESTIC POLITICS IN THREE STUDIES COVERING CRITICAL TRANSITIONAL PERIOD AFTER WWII, ESPECIALLY POLICY OF EISENHOWER ADMINISTRATION.

2299 SCHLEIFFER H. ED., CRANDALL R. ED.
INDEX TO ECONOMIC HISTORY ESSAYS IN FESTSCHRIFTEN (PAMPHLET)
CAMBRIDGE: HARVARD U PR, 1953, 68 PP., LC#53-11201.
COVERS FESTSCHRIFTEN PUBLISHED IN THE COUNTRIES IN WHICH THIS TYPE OF PUBLICATION IS MOST COMMON. ARRANGED UNDER TIME PERIOD AS WELL AS INDIVIDUAL COUNTRY HEADINGS. AN INDEX OF AUTHORS AND OF PROPER NAMES IN THE TITLES OF ESSAYS HAS BEEN INCLUDED.

2300 SCHMITT H.A.
THE PATH TO EUROPEAN UNITY.
BATON ROUGE: LOUISIANA ST U PR, 1962, 272 PP., LC#62-18669.
ANALYSIS OF EUROPEAN PLAN FOR UNION FROM POSTWAR DRIVE OF MARSHALL PLAN TO FORMATION OF COMMON MARKET. STUDIES US AID AND POLICY REGARDING EUROPEAN UNION AND STRUCTURE AND OPERATION OF EUROPEAN COAL AND STEEL COMMUNITY'S ECONOMIC AND POLITICAL EFFECTS TOWARD UNITY.

2301 SCHMITT H.O.
"POLITICAL CONDITIONS FOR INTERNATIONAL CURRENCY REFORM."
INT. ORGAN., 18 (SUMMER 64), 543-57.
APPRAISES THE CORRELATIONS EXISTING BETWEEN POLITICAL INTEGRATION AND SCHEMES FOR INTERNATIONAL CURRENCY REFORM.

2302 SCHMOLLER G.
THE MERCANTILE SYSTEM AND ITS HISTORICAL SIGNIFICANCE: ILLUSTRATED CHIEFLY FROM PRUSSIAN HISTORY (TRANS.)
NEW YORK: MACMILLAN, 1896, 95 PP.
ANALYSIS OF THE DEVELOPMENT OF MERCANTILISM AND ECONOMIC EVOLUTION FROM SIMPLE TRIBAL SUBSISTENCE TO COMPLEX NATIONAL AND INTERNATIONAL ECONOMIC SYSTEMS. ARGUES THAT ECONOMIC FORCES, WHILE PURSUING THEIR OWN ENDS, SHOULD SERVE THE STATE AND CONVERSELY THE STATE SHOULD PLACE ITS POWER IN THE SERVICE OF NATIONAL ECONOMY. SPECIFIC EXAMPLE OF THIS IDEAL IS GIVEN IN AN EXAMINATION OF PRUSSIA'S SILK INDUSTRY.

2303 SCHNAPPER B.
LA POLITIQUE ET LE COMMERCE FRANCAIS DANS LE GOLFE DE GUINEE DE 1838 A 1871.
HAGUE: MOUTON & CO, 1961, 286 PP.
STUDY OF FRENCH POLITICAL AND COMMERCIAL IMPERIALISM ON THE GULF OF GUINEA, EMPHASIZING FORTIFIED COMMERCIAL INSTALLATIONS, COLONIZATION, AND TRADE PRODUCTS.

2304 SCHNEIDER C.W.
"REFORM OF THE FEDERAL SECURITIES LAWS."
U. PENN. LAW REV., 115 (MAY 67), 1023-1057.
PROPOSES ADMINISTRATIVE ACTION TO REFORM FEDERAL SECURITIES LAWS. REFORM SHOULD BE ADMINISTRATIVELY EFFECTED WITHIN EXISTING STATUTORY FRAMEWORK BY SECURITIES AND EXCHANGE COMMISSION. SUGGESTS UPDATING 1934 ACT (CONTINUOUS DISCLOSURE SYSTEM) AND GENERAL ADMINISTRATIVE REFORM OF THE DISCLOSURE SYSTEM.

2305 SCHNEIDER E.
MONEY, INCOME AND EMPLOYMENT.
NEW YORK: HUMANITIES PRESS, 1962, 290 PP., LC#62-52970.
DISCUSSES THE MEANS OF PAYMENT IN CONTEMPORARY ECONOMY IN TERMS OF THE CREATION AND DESTRUCTION OF MONEY AND THE DETERMINANTS OF NATIONAL INCOME. BIBLIOGRAPHY IN ENGLISH, GERMAN, BOOKS AND ARTICLES, 1913-57, LISTED IN ORDER OF APPEARANCE AS FOOTNOTES; 115 ENTRIES.

2306 SCHNEIDER E. ED.
WIRTSCHAFTSKREISLAUF UND WIRTSCHAFTSWACHSTUM.
TUBINGEN: J C B MOHR, 1966, 224 PP.
COLLECTION OF ESSAYS ON PUBLIC FINANCE, ECONOMIC GROWTH, CAPITAL ACCUMULATION, WORLD ECONOMIC MONEY CYCLES, INCOME AND PROPERTY DISTRIBUTION, AND PUBLIC AND PRIVATE INVESTMENT.

2307 SCHNEIDER E.
"DIE ENTPOLITISIERUNG DES DEUTSCHEN OSTHANDELS."
AUSSENPOLITIK, 18 (JULY 67),389-397.
ARGUES FOR TRADE POLICY OF COUNTRIES OF EUROPEAN ECONOMIC COMMUNITY TOWARD EASTERN EUROPE FREE OF IDEOLOGICAL AND BILATERAL IMPLICATIONS. TRACES DEVELOPMENT OF IDEOLOGICAL BARRIERS AND SUGGESTS THAT ECONOMIC EXCHANGE WOULD AID IN DECREASING POLITICAL TENSIONS BETWEEN EAST AND WEST.

2308 SCHNEIDER E.V.
INDUSTRIAL SOCIOLOGY: THE SOCIAL RELATIONS OF INDUSTRY AND COMMUNITY.
NEW YORK: MCGRAW HILL, 1957, 559 PP., LC#57-7242.
AN OVER-ALL VIEW OF INDUSTRIAL INSTITUTIONS, PAST AND PRESENT, AND THEIR INFLUENCE ON THE FAMILY, THE COMMUNITY, AND THE GOVERNMENT AS WELL AS INDUSTRY'S GENERAL ROLE IN SOCIAL CHANGE. DEALS WITH ROLE, STRATIFICATION, MINORITY GROUPS, AND GOVERNMENT REGULATION, AS WELL AS THE SOCIAL STRUCTURE AND FUNCTIONS OF TRADE UNIONISM.

2309 SCHOECK H. ED., WIGGINS J.W. ED.
THE NEW ARGUMENT IN ECONOMICS.
PRINCETON: VAN NOSTRAND, 1963, 264 PP.
ESSAYS PRESENTING VARIOUS VIEWS ON ECONOMIC ISSUES SUCH AS NEOMERCANTILISM, ECONOMIC ROLE OF STATE, PRIVATE AND PUBLIC EXPENDITURES, AND TRADE UNIONISM. ALSO DISCUSSES NATURAL RESOURCES, FOREIGN AID PROGRAM IN BOLIVIA, GROWTH OF BUREAUCRATIC POWER, AND PUBLIC VS. PRIVATE SECTOR IN BRITAIN.

2310 SCHOFLING J.A.
"EFTA: THE OTHER EUROPE."
J. COMMONWEALTH POLIT. STUD., 40 (OCT. 64), 674-684.
EXAMINES HISTORICAL BACKGROUND OF DEVELOPMENT OF EUROPEAN FREE TRADE ASSOCIATION, GIVING ATTENTION TO ITS PRESENT POLITICAL SIGNIFICANCE, ITS INTERNAL ORGANIZATION, AND ITS EXTERNAL RELATIONS. GIVES SPECIAL CONSIDERATION TO ITS RELATIONS WITH EEC.

2311 SCHON D.A.
TECHNOLOGY AND CHANGE* THE NEW HERACLITUS.
NEW YORK: DELACORTE PRESS, 1967, 248 PP.
THESIS: TODAY'S LARGE BUSINESS CORPORATIONS, ENTIRE INDUSTRIES, AND GOVERNMENT AGENCIES, CANNOT LIVE WITHOUT A STREAM OF NEW INVENTIONS AND INNOVATIONS - BUT THEY CANNOT LIVE WITH THEM OR READILY RESPOND TO THEM. BOOK DISCUSSES MATTERS THAT HELP OR HINDER CHANGE, AND OFFERS REMEDIES TO INDUSTRY'S CURRENT RESPONSE TO INNOVATION.

2313 SCHROEDER G.
"LABOR PLANNING IN THE USSR."
SOVIET EDUCATION, 32 (JULY 65), 63-72.
ATTENTION GIVEN TO THE SOVIET'S FIVE AND SEVEN YEAR PLANS AND THE RESULTS DURING THE FIRST FIVE YEARS OF THE NEW PLAN. DISCUSSES POPULATION PROJECTIONS VERSUS ACTUAL GROWTH AND LABOR FORCE SIZE, AND PRODUCTIVITY PROJECTIONS AND REALITIES. ALSO DISCUSSES SOVIET PREDICTIONS OF SCHOOL ENROLLMENTS AND GRADUATIONS AS COMPARED TO REALITIES. ESTIMATES HAVE GENERALLY BEEN TOO GREAT.

2314 SCHULER E.A.
THE PAKISTAN ACADEMIES FOR RURAL DEVELOPMENT COMILLA AND PESHAWAR 1959-1964.
E LANSING: ASIAN STUD CTR, MSU, 1965, 116 PP.
BIBLIOGRAPHY OF MATERIALS ON PAKISTAN ACADEMIES FOR RURAL DEVELOPMENT ESTABLISHED SINCE 1959. LISTS TRAINING MATERIALS (MANUALS), REPORTS FOR GOVERNMENT OFFICIALS OF PAKISTAN, AND PROFESSIONAL LITERATURE ON DEVELOPMENT AND NATION-BUILDING PRODUCED BY ACADEMIES. ARRANGED ALPHABETICALLY AND BY ACADEMY. ENGLISH-LANGUAGE SOURCES PUBLISHED 1959-64.

2315 SCHULTZ T.W. ED.
"INVESTMENT IN HUMAN BEINGS."
J. OF POLITICAL ECONOMY, 70 (OCT. 62), 1-157.
PAPERS PRESENTED AT EXPLORATORY CONFERENCE ON CAPITAL INVESTMENT IN HUMAN BEINGS. HYPOTHESIZES THAT RATIO OF ALL CAPITAL TO INCOME IS NOT DECLINING, ECONOMIC CAPABILITIES OF MAN ARE PRODUCED MEANS OF PRODUCTION, AND HUMAN CAPITAL REDUCES INEQUALITY OF INCOME DISTRIBUTION. STUDIES COSTS AND RETURNS OF ON-THE-JOB TRAINING AND OF MIGRATION. DISCUSSES LABOR MARKET AND EDUCATION AND HEALTH AS INVESTMENTS.

2316 SCHULTZ T.W.
TRANSFORMING TRADITIONAL AGRICULTURE.
NEW HAVEN: YALE U. PR., 1964, 212 PP., $6.00.
PRESENTS A THEORETICAL APPROACH LEADING TO NEW HYPOTHESES THAT EXPLAIN ECONOMIC STAGNATION OF TRADITIONAL AGRICULTURE, AND THEN TESTS HIS HYPOTHESES EMPIRICALLY. DISCUSSES INVESTMENT COMPREHENSIVELY, INCLUDING BOTH NEW MATERIAL INPUTS AND INVESTMENT IN FARM PEOPLE.

2317 SCHULTZ T.W.
ECONOMIC CRISES IN WORLD AGRICULTURE.
ANN ARBOR: U OF MICH PR, 1965, 114 PP., LC#65-11465.
SURVEY OF EFFECTS OF INDUSTRIALIZATION UPON AGRICULTURE THROUGHOUT THE WORLD. CONCLUDES THAT FOR WANT OF ATTENTION TO AGRICULTURAL PRODUCTION, THE VERY COURSE OF INDUSTRIALIZATION IS THREATENED IN THE US, USSR, CHINA, AND INDIA. SUGGESTS INCREASED ECONOMIC INCENTIVES TO FARMERS AND GOVERNMENT WELFARE SERVICES EQUAL TO THOSE EXTENDED TO URBAN POPULATIONS.

2318 SCHULTZ W.J., HARRIS C.L.
AMERICAN PUBLIC FINANCE.
ENGLEWOOD CLIFFS: PRENTICE HALL, 1949, 798 PP.
STUDY OF US PUBLIC FINANCE DEALING WITH GOVERNMENTAL EX-

PENDITURE, TAXATION, GOVERNMENTAL BORROWING, FISCAL INTERRELATIONSHIPS ON ALL GOVERNMENTAL LEVELS, AND OVER-ALL FISCAL POLICY.

2319 SCHULZE R.O.
"THE ROLE OF ECONOMIC DOMINANTS IN COMMUNITY POWER STRUCTURE."
AMER. SOCIOLOGICAL REV., 23 (FEB. 58), 3-9.
SHOWS "NO NEAT, CONSTANT, AND DIRECT RELATIONSHIP BETWEEN POWER AS A POTENTIAL FOR DETERMINATIVE ACTION, AND POWER AS DETERMINATIVE ACTION ITSELF." HISTORICAL TREND SHOWS WITHDRAWAL OF ECONOMIC DOMINANTS FROM ACTIVE AND OVERT PARTICIPATION IN THE PUBLIC LIFE OF CIBOLA - A MIDWESTERN INDUSTRIAL CITY OF 20,000.

2320 SCHUMM S.
"INTEREST REPRESENTATION IN FRANCE AND GERMANY."
CAHIERS DE BRUGES, 3 (1958), 139-147.
DISCUSSES METHODS OF ORGANIZING ECONOMIC PRESSURE GROUPS INTO GOVERNMENT STRUCTURE. QUESTIONS THAT SUCH UNION WILL BRING ABOUT COMPROMISES OF DIFFERENT ASPECTS OF ECONOMY FOR NATIONAL INTEREST. EXAMINES GERMAN NATIONAL ECONOMIC COUNCIL UNDER WEIMAR CONSTITUTION AND FRENCH NATIONAL ECONOMIC COUNCIL. MAINTAINS THAT ECONOMIC COUNCIL AND PARLIAMENTARY GOVERNMENT ARE INCOMPATIBLE.

2321 SCHUMPETER J.A.
CAPITALISM, SOCIALISM, AND DEMOCRACY (3RD ED.)
NEW YORK: HARPER & ROW, 1950, 431 PP.
DISCUSSES MARXIST DOCTRINE IN NONTECHNICAL MANNER. PROCEEDS TO CAPITALISM, AND TRIES TO SHOW THAT SOCIALIST FORM OF SOCIETY WILL EMERGE FROM INEVITABLE DECOMPOSITION OF CAPITALIST SOCIETY. EXAMINES PROBLEMS THAT BEAR UPON CONDITIONS IN WHICH SOCIALISM MAY BE EXPECTED TO BE AN ECONOMIC SUCCESS.

2322 SCHUMPETER J.A.
HISTORY OF ECONOMIC ANALYSIS.
NEW YORK: OXFORD U PR, 1954, 1260 PP., LC#52-9434.
DESCRIBES DEVELOPMENT AND FORTUNES OF SCIENTIFIC ANALYSIS IN FIELD OF ECONOMICS FROM GRAECO-ROMAN TIMES TO PRESENT. SHOWS GROWTH OF HISTORICAL, STATISTICAL, AND THEORETICAL KNOWLEDGE OF ECONOMIC PHENOMENA. CONSIDERS METHODOLOGICAL QUESTIONS RAISED BY THIS APPROACH AND WEIGHS QUESTION OF HOW FAR DISTINCTION BETWEEN SCIENTIFIC ECONOMIC ANALYSIS AND ECONOMIC THOUGHT IS VALID IN LIGHT OF THEIR INTERACTION.

2323 SCHURMANN F.
"ECONOMIC POLICY AND POLITICAL POWER IN COMMUNIST CHINA."
ANN. AMER. ACAD. POLIT. SOC. SCI., 349 (SEPT. 63), 49-69.
SCRUTINIZES WITHIN HISTORICAL CONTEXT THE TWO MAJOR STRATEGIES BEHIND CHINESE DEVELOPMENT AND DISCLOSES THEIR ULTIMATE SHORTCOMINGS. RELATES THE DECISIONS INVOLVED IN STRATEGY-DEVELOPMENT TO A COMPLEX OF IDEOLOGICAL, POLITICAL, AND SOCIAL VARIABLES. SUGGESTS THAT THE NON-ECONOMIC VARIABLES WILL BE AS IMPORTANT TO CHINA AS PURELY ECONOMIC.

2324 SCHWARTZ G. ED.
SCIENCE IN MARKETING.
NEW YORK: JOHN WILEY, 1965, 512 PP., LC#65-14245.
SEVERAL AUTHORS SEEK TO CONTRIBUTE TO DEVELOPMENT OF MARKETING SCIENCE THROUGH APPRAISAL OF CURRENT STATE OF MARKETING KNOWLEDGE AND SUGGEST AREAS NEEDING FURTHER STUDY. TREAT NATURE AND GOALS OF MARKETING SCIENCE AND DIVIDE VARIOUS ASPECTS OF MARKETING INTO CONVENTIONAL SEGMENTS, LIKE PRICING, PERSONAL SELLING, TRADING AREAS, AND MARKETING CHANNELS.

2325 SCHWARTZ H.
THE RED PHOENIX: RUSSIA SINCE WORLD WAR II.
NEW YORK: FREDERICK PRAEGER, 1961, 417 PP., LC#61-11062.
TRACES INTERNAL POLITICAL DEVELOPMENT, ECONOMIC GROWTH, SCIENTIFIC ADVANCES, AND FOREIGN RELATIONS OF USSR SINCE WWII. DISCUSSES US-SOVIET RELATIONS AND COMPETITION AS WELL AS RELATIONS WITH RED CHINA.

2326 SCHWARZWELLER H.K., BROWN J.S.
"SOCIAL CLASS ORIGINS, RURAL-URBAN MIGRATION, AND ECONOMIC LIFE CHANGES."
RURAL SOCIOLOGY, 32 (MAR. 67), 5-19.
EXPLORES THESIS THAT IN A RURAL LOW-INCOME AREA WITH A HIGH RATE OF OUT-MIGRATION, THE SOCIAL CLASS POSITION OF A FAMILY INFLUENCES THE PATTERN OF OUT-MIGRATION, THE STRUCTURE OF THE MIGRATION PROCESS, AND ECONOMIC LIFE CHANGES OF INDIVIDUAL MIGRANTS AND FAMILIES. CASE STUDY OF PERSON IN 3 ISOLATED MOUNTAIN NEIGHBORHOODS IN KENTUCKY.

2327 SCIENTIFIC COUNCIL FOR AFRICA
INVENTORY OF ECONOMIC STUDIES CONCERNING AFRICA SOUTH OF THE SAHARA.
JAHORE: COMM FOR TECHNICAL COOP.
ANNOTATED READING LIST OF BOOKS, ARTICLES, AND OFFICIAL PUBLICATIONS ON AFRICA SOUTH OF THE SAHARA PUBLISHED SINCE 1945. LIST CONFINED ALMOST ENTIRELY TO WORKS DEALING SPECIFICALLY WITH AFRICA. INCLUDES SEPARATE SECTIONS ON ECONOMIC HISTORY AND GEOGRAPHY. CONTAINS 1,377 EXTENSIVELY ANNOTATED ITEMS IN WEST EUROPEAN LANGUAGES.

2328 SCITOUSKY T.
ECONOMIC THEORY AND WESTERN EUROPEAN INTEGRATION.
STANFORD: U. PR., 1958, 154 PP.
RANGE OF SUBJECT MATTER INCLUDES: THE CURRENCY UNION, COAL AND STEEL COMMUNITY, EMPLOYMENT, PRODUCTIVITY AND THE BALANCE OF PAYMENTS PROBLEM. REJECTS THE TRADITIONAL FREE-TRADE ARGUMENT AND POINTS OUT THAT INCREASED COMPETITION WOULD ONLY RESULT IN INDIRECT BENEFITS TO UNION.

2329 SCITOVSKY T.
"TWO CONCEPTS OF EXTERNAL ECONOMIES."
J. OF POLITICAL ECONOMY, 62 (APR. 54), 143-151.
DISCUSSES TWO DIFFERENT DEFINITIONS OF EXTERNAL ECONOMIES AS FOUND IN INDUSTRIALIZATION AND EQUILIBRIUM THEORY. STATES THAT EQUILIBRIUM THEORY IS STATIC AND NOT AS COMPLETE AS INDUSTRIALIZATION THEORY, WHICH ENCOMPASSES AND GOES BEYOND EQUILIBRIUM DEFINITION.

2330 SCITOVSKY T.
REQUIREMENTS OF AN INTERNATIONAL RESERVE SYSTEM.
PRINCETON: PRINCETON U PRESS, 1965, 18 PP., LC#65-28274.
DISCUSSES ESTABLISHMENT AND EFFECT OF MONETARY RESERVE SYSTEM TO PROVIDE STABILITY IN PAYMENTS FOR INTERNATIONAL TRADE WITHOUT DEPENDENCY ON STERLING OR DOLLAR.

2331 SCOTT A.M.
THE REVOLUTION IN STATECRAFT: INFORMAL PENETRATION.
NEW YORK: RANDOM HOUSE, INC, 1965, 194 PP., LC#65-23340.
COMPREHENSIVE ANALYSIS OF A DEVELOPMENT THAT HAS REVOLUTIONIZED MODERN STATECRAFT: ADVENT OF INFORMAL RELATIONS BETWEEN NATIONS. DISCUSSES EVOLUTION OF INFORMAL ACCESS TECHNIQUES, INCLUDING ECONOMIC AID, INFORMATION PROGRAMS, POLITICAL WARFARE, MILITARY TRAINING OPERATIONS, AND CULTURAL EXCHANGE PROGRAMS.

2332 SCOTT D.J.R.
RUSSIAN POLITICAL INSTITUTIONS.
NEW YORK: RINEHART, 1958, 265 PP., LC#58-4632.
STUDIES INTERNAL GOVERNMENT STRUCTURE AND ORGANIZATION, POLITICAL PERIODS, THE UNION, COLLECTIVE ADMINISTRATION, REPRESENTATIVE BODIES, AND METHODS USED TO SECURE COOPERATION. BIBLIOGRAPHY OF 50 ENTRIES, 1902-65, IN ENGLISH, LISTED TOPICALLY: TEXTBOOKS, STUDIES OF SOVIET POLITICS, SPECIAL ASPECTS OF POLITICS, BACKGROUND, AND JOURNALS.

2333 SCOTT J.B.
"ANGLO-SOVIET TRADE AND ITS EFFECTS ON THE COMMONWEALTH."
ROYAL CENT. ASIAN J., 49 (JAN. 62), 40-46.
DISCUSSES PROBLEMS CREATED BY SOVIET SHIFT IN TRADE AND PURCHASE PRACTICES FROM LONDON COMMONWEALTH TRADE OFFICES TO DIRECT AND BILATERAL TRADE WITH COMMONWEALTH COUNTRIES. WARNS THAT INCREASED SOVIET EXPORTS MAY ENDANGER ALREADY DIFFICULT BRITISH TRADE SITUATION.

2334 SCOTT J.C., ROCKEFELLER E.S.
ANTITRUST AND TRADE REGULATION TODAY: 1967.
WASHINGTON: BUREAU NATL AFFAIRS, 1967, 419 PP., LC#67-25865.
PRESENTS CURRENT LEGISLATION AND FEDERAL REGULATIONS BEARING ON TRADE AND CORPORATIONS. OFFERS WARNINGS AND SUGGESTIONS ON RECENT KEY DEVELOPMENTS IN TRADE REGULATION. INCLUDES GOVERNMENT PRACTICES, LEGISLATION, AND SPECIFIC CASES PERTINENT TO MONOPOLIES, DEALERSHIPS, AND FRANCHISES, MERGERS, PATENTS, PRICES, FOREIGN LAWS, CERTAIN REGULATED INDUSTRIES. INCLUDES SECTIONS ON SUPREME COURT AND FTC.

2335 SCOTT R.
"TRADE UNIONS IN AFRICA."
TRANSITION, 7 (OCT.-NOV. 67), 27-36.
ATTEMPTS TO EVALUATE PRESENT POLITICAL ROLE OF TRADE UNIONS IN AFRICA AND TO FORESEE THEIR PLACE IN POSTINDEPENDENCE NATIONS. EMPHASIZES ATTEMPTS TO FORM SUPERTERRITORIAL UNION ORGANIZATION. DISCUSSES WHETHER UNIONS SHOULD SERVE A SOCIAL AS WELL AS AN ECONOMIC FUNCTION. COMPARES AFRICAN UNIONS TO AMERICAN AND EUROPEAN UNIONS.

2336 SCOTT W.D.
INFLUENCING MEN IN BUSINESS: THE PSYCHOLOGY OF ARGUMENT AND SUGGESTION.
NEW YORK: RONALD PRESS, 1911, 168 PP.
SETS FORTH PRINCIPLES AND FACTS OF THE PSYCHOLOGY OF INFLUENCING MEN IN BUSINESS WORLD. SHOWS HOW BUSINESSMAN CAN INDUCE EMPLOYEES TO IMPROVE THEIR WORK, AND INDUCE PARTICULAR MEN TO ENTER EMPLOY. DISCUSSES METHODS OF SELLING GOODS BY PERSONAL APPEAL AND BY PRINTED ADVERTISING.

2337 SCOVILLE W.J.
"GOVERNMENT REGULATION AND GROWTH IN THE FRENCH PAPER INDUSTRY DURING THE EIGHTEENTH CENTURY."
AMER. ECO. REVIEW, 57 (MAY 67), 283-293.
EXAMINATION OF ECONOMIC HISTORY OF PAPER INDUSTRY. AUTHOR FINDS DIRECT CORRELATION BETWEEN THE INDUSTRY'S EXPANSION AND RELAXATION OF DIRECT GOVERNMENTAL CONTROLS. IN THIS PERIOD LARGE-SCALE CAPITALISTIC ENTERPRISE BECAME MORE COMMON. EXPLORES CHANGING ROLE OF GOVERNMENT, METHODS IT USED TO RE-

LAX CONTROL AND ENCOURAGE INDIVIDUALS, AND AREAS WHERE GOVERNMENT CONTROL SHOULD HAVE BEEN RELAXED BUT WASN'T.

2338 SCRIPP J.
"CONTROLLING PREJUDICIAL PUBLICITY BY THE CONTEMPT POWER: THE BRITISH PRACTICE AND ITS PROSPECT IN AMERICAN LAW."
NOTRE DAME LAWYER, 42 (1967), 957-968.
DISCUSSES BRITISH USE OF CONTEMPT POWER TO CONTROL PRETRIAL PUBLICITY, AND ITS SUCCESS. EXAMINES OBSTACLE OF FIRST AMENDMENT INVOLVING FREEDOM OF PRESS TO AMERICAN ADOPTION OF POWER OF CONTEMPT. MAINTAINS THAT NEWSPAPER'S ROLE AS "WATCHDOG" ON CORRUPTION AND AS SOCIAL REFORMER WOULD BE JEOPARDIZED BY ADOPTION OF SUCH SYSTEM.

2339 SEABERG G.P.
"THE DRUG ABUSE PROBLEMS AND SOME PROPOSALS."
J. CRIM. LAW CRIM. POLICE SCI., 58 (SEPT. 67), 349-375.
DISCUSSES COMMON DRUGS INVOLVED IN DRUG ABUSE AND ASPECTS OF DEPENDENCE, TOLERATION, AND HABITUATION. PRESENTS LAWS RELATING TO DRUG USE AND PROBLEMS OF INTERPRETATION AND ENFORCEMENT. URGES LAWS PROVIDING HUMANE TREATMENT FOR ADDICTS AND PUNISHMENT FOR PROFITEERS. ADVOCATES BETTER AFTER-CARE PROGRAMS, RETRIAL OF DISPENSARY TECHNIQUE, AND REVISION OF LAWS IN ACCORD WITH DIFFERENCES IN DRUGS.

2340 COUNCIL OF EUROPE, SECRETARIAT
THE STRASBOURG PLAN.
STRASBOURG: COUNCIL OF EUROPE, 1952, 197 PP.
PRESENTS STRASBOURG PLAN REGARDING ECONOMIC RELATIONS AMONG MEMBERS OF COUNCIL OF EUROPE AND COUNTRIES WITH WHICH THEY MAINTAIN CONSTITUTIONAL TIES. DISCUSSES TRADE POLICIES AND STATUS OF OVERSEAS TERRITORIES. INCLUDES SPEECHES OF CONSULTATIVE ASSEMBLY MEETING SEPTEMBER, 1952.

2341 SEERS D. ED.
CUBA: THE ECONOMIC AND SOCIAL REVOLUTION.
CHAPEL HILL: U.N.C. PR., 1964, 432 PP., $7.50.
COMPARES THE POST-REVOLUTIONARY SITUATION IN CUBA WITH THAT BEFORE 1959. REVIEWS THE PROBLEMS INHERITED BY THE CASTRO GOVERNMENT AND HOW THEY DIFFERED FROM THE PROBLEMS ENCOUNTERED BY OTHER 20TH-CENTURY REVOLUTIONS, SUCH AS THOSE OF YUGOSLAVIA AND THE SOVIET UNION.

2342 SEGAL R.
SANCTIONS AGAINST SOUTH AFRICA.
BALTIMORE: PENGUIN BOOKS, 1964, 272 PP.
TWENTY-TWO ARTICLES FROM INTERNATIONAL CONFERENCE ON ECONOMIC SANCTIONS AGAINST SOUTH AFRICA OF 1964, DESCRIBING ECONOMIC, RACIAL, POLITICAL, LEGAL, AND STRATEGIC ASPECTS OF SANCTIONS.

2343 SEIDLER G.L.
"MARXIST LEGAL THOUGHT IN POLAND."
SLAVIC REVIEW, 26 (SEPT. 67), 382-394.
SINCE WWII, POLISH LEGAL THEORY HAS FOCUSED PRIMARILY ON SOCIOLOGICAL ASPECTS OF THE LAW. RESEARCH INDICATES THAT THIS FOCUS BENEFITED INTEREST GROUPS. AS A RESULT NEW PROBLEMS ARE BEING CONSIDERED. THOSE RECEIVING SPECIAL ATTENTION ARE: EVALUATION OF POSITIVE LAW; RELATIONSHIP BETWEEN LEGAL AND SOCIALIST CONSCIOUSNESS; AND COMPREHENSIVE LEGAL RESEARCH. ARTICLE IS CONFINED TO PRESENTATION OF PROBLEMS.

2344 SEIDMAN H.
"THE GOVERNMENT CORPORATION IN THE UNITED STATES."
PUBLIC ADMINISTRATION, 37 (SUMMER 59), 103-109.
GOVERNMENT CORPORATIONS IN THE US ARE SET UP TO HELP PRIVATE ENTERPRISE. CONTROL OVER THESE CORPORATIONS IS LESS SPECIFIC THAN IN BRITAIN, BUT CONGRESS AND THE PRESIDENT DO HAVE SUFFICIENT CONTROL.

2345 SEIDMAN J.I.
DEMOCRACY IN THE LABOR MOVEMENT (PAMPHLET)
ITHACA: NY STATE SCH IND & LABOR, 1958, 55 PP.
SUGGESTS PROBLEMS OF DEMOCRACY WITHIN THE LABOR MOVEMENT ESPECIALLY AT NATIONAL UNION LEVELS, SUCH AS DISCIPLINE AGAINST DEMOCRACY, UNITY AND FACTIONALISM, OPPOSITION CANDIDATES FOR UNION OFFICES. SEES ACTUAL RESPONSIVENESS OF LEADERS TO MEMBERS FOR THE SAKE OF PRESTIGE. DISCUSSES CONTROL OF EXECUTIVE POWER AND OTHER FACTORS AFFECTING UNION DEMOCRACY.

2346 SELF P., STORING H.J.
THE STATE AND THE FARMER.
BERKELEY: U OF CALIF PR, 1963, 251 PP.
DISCUSSES AGRICULTURAL POLICIES AND POLITICS IN GREAT BRITAIN BETWEEN 1945-61. ANALYZES THE CLOSE AND PERVASIVE COOPERATION BETWEEN GOVERNMENT AND PRINCIPAL AGRICULTURAL ORGANIZATIONS. EXPLORES CHARACTER AND HISTORY OF PARTNERSHIP AND REVIEWS PROBLEMS AND CONFLICTS OVER THE ADMINISTRATION OF PUBLIC POLICY.

2347 SELIGMAN B.B. ED.
POVERTY AS A PUBLIC ISSUE.
NEW YORK: MACMILLAN, 1965, 354 PP., LC#65-23026.
FOURTEEN ARTICLES ON POVERTY IN THE UNITED STATES, EIGHT DEFINING THE POOR AND SIX DEALING WITH POVERTY IN THE CONTEXT OF CONTEMPORARY GOVERNMENT.

2348 SELIGMAN E.R.
THE ECONOMIC INTERPRETATION OF HISTORY.
NEW YORK: COLUMBIA U PRESS, 1902, 166 PP.
ANALYSIS OF THEORY OF ECONOMIC INTERPRETATION OF HISTORY. DISCUSSES PHILOSOPHY OF HISTORY AND CONCEPTS OF IMPORTANT WRITERS ON ECONOMICS AND PHILOSOPHY. EXAMINES BASIS OF ECONOMIC INTERPRETATION AND VALUE OF THEORY FOR FUTURE STUDY.

2349 SELIGMAN E.R.A.
ESSAYS IN TAXATION.
LONDON: MACMILLAN, 1895, 418 PP.
DISCUSSES TAXATION, PRIMARILY IN US: ITS DEVELOPMENT, FORMS, PROLIFERATION, AND THEORY. PREDATING INCOME TAX, CONSIDERS TYPES OF TAXES AND DEFECTS OF EACH - FISCAL, POLITICAL, ETHICAL, AND ECONOMIC. BASIC TYPES INCLUDE: SINGLE, INHERITANCE, CORPORATION, PROPERTY, AND TARIFFS. ALSO EXAMINES REFORMS IN ENGLAND, NEW ZEALAND, AND PRUSSIA.

2350 SELIGSOHN I.J.
"USING COMPUTER SERVICES IN SMALL BUSINESS" MANAGEMENT AIDS FOR SMALL MANUFACTURERS 109 (PAMPHLET)
WASHINGTON: GOVT PR OFFICE, 1959, 4 PP.
THOUGH HIGH-SPEED DIGITAL COMPUTERS ARE TOO EXPENSIVE FOR PURCHASE BY SMALL BUSINESSMEN, THESE MACHINES CAN SOLVE MANY PROBLEMS. SOLUTION: RENT USE OF COMPUTER ON HOURLY BASIS FROM COMPUTER SERVICE ORGANIZATIONS, THUS GETTING DATA UNTIL NOW AVAILABLE ONLY TO BIG ORGANIZATIONS. CAN BE USED FOR PROBLEMS OF ENGINEERING, DATA-PROCESSING, PRODUCTION, TRANSPORTATION AND DISTRIBUTION. GIVES COST ESTIMATES.

2351 SELLERS C.
"THE EQUILIBRIUM CYCLE IN TWO-PARTY POLITICS."
PUBLIC OPINION QUART., 29 (1965), 16-38.
SEEKS TO INFER UNDERLYING DISTRIBUTION OF PARTY IDENTIFICATIONS FROM THE ELECTION RETURNS OVER THE WHOLE PERIOD OF PRESIDENTIAL AND CONGRESSIONAL ELECTIONS, AND TO EXPLAIN THE PATTERN OF REGULAR OSCILLATIONS THAT APPEARS TO EMERGE.

2352 SELOSOEMARDJAN O.
SOCIAL CHANGES IN JOGJAKARTA.
ITHACA: CORNELL U PRESS, 1962, 447 PP., LC#62-14114.
VIEWS SOCIAL, ECONOMIC, POLITICAL CHANGE IN INDONESIA, RESULT OF 1958 REVOLUTION. EFFECT OF DUTCH AND JAPANESE OCCUPATIONS ON JAVANESE CULTURE AND THE ROLE OF JAVA AS A LEADER IN ECONOMIC AND SOCIAL PROGRESS IN THE AREA ARE CONSIDERED.

2353 SELZNICK P.
TVA AND THE GRASS ROOTS: A STUDY IN THE SOCIOLOGY OF FORMAL ORGANIZATION.
BERKELEY: U OF CALIF PR, 1949, 274 PP.
STUDY OF TVA IN 1942-43, ATTEMPTING TO DESCRIBE AND UNDERSTNAD IT AS A DEMOCRATIC ORGANIZATION SEEKING SUPPORT FROM ALL ORGANIZATIONS AFFECTED BY IT.

2354 SEN S.R.
THE STRATEGY FOR AGRICULTURAL DEVELOPMENT AND OTHER ESSAYS ON ECONOMIC POLICY AND PLANNING.
BOMBAY: ASIA PUBL HOUSE, 1962, 244 PP.
ESSAYS ON AGRICULTURAL PLANNING, TECHNIQUES OF PLANNING, AND COMMODITY PROBLEMS AND POLICIES IN INDIA. ALSO INCLUDES SEVERAL LECTURES ON OBJECTIVES, MACHINERY, AND TECHNIQUES OF PLANNING, INVESTMENT CRITERIA, PRICE POLICY, USE OF STATISTICS, ECONOMIC RESEARCH, AND SO ON.

2355 SENGHOR L.S.
AFRICAN SOCIALISM (PAMPHLET)
NEW YORK: AMER SOC AFR CULTURE, 1959, 49 PP.
DESCRIBES MALI FEDERATION, PLOTS COURSE OF MALI'S ECONOMIC, POLITICAL, EDUCATIONAL, AND SOCIAL PROGRESS TOWARD INDEPENDENCE, AND EXAMINES MALI ATTITUDES TOWARD OTHER AFRICAN STATES, FRANCE, US, AND USSR. PRESENTS A CRITICAL ANALYSIS OF MARXISM IN AFRICAN NEGRO LIGHT.

2356 SEPULVEDA C.
A STATEMENT OF THE LAWS OF MEXICO IN MATTERS AFFECTING BUSINESS (3RD ED.)
WASHINGTON: PAN AMERICAN UNION, 1961, 268 PP.
SUMMARY OF BASIC LEGISLATION THAT COVERS NATIONALITY AND IMMIGRATION, CONTRACTS AND OBLIGATIONS, AND MONOPOLIES. ALSO INCLUDES COPYRIGHT, INSURANCE, AND ADMINISTRATION OF JUSTICE.

2357 SERAPHIM H.J. ED.
PROBLEME DER WILLENSBILDUNG UND DER WIRTSCHAFTSPOLITISCHEN FUEHRUNG.
BERLIN: VERL DUNCKER AND HUM, 1959, 161 PP.
SCIENTIFIC ECONOMIC POLICY DEALING WITH MEANS AND ENDS IS TIED TO TWO QUESTIONS DEALT WITH HERE: WHO DETERMINES ENDS AND WHO APPLIES MEANS? TO WHOM ARE THE MEANS RELATED? CONCERNS INFLUENCING PERSONS AND THEIR PURPOSES IN VARIOUS ECONOMIC, SOCIAL, POLITICAL SETTINGS, USING VARIOUS

MEANS.

2358 SERAPHIM H.J. ED.
ZUR GRUNDLEGUNG WIRTSCHAFTSPOLITISCHER KONZEPTIONEN (SCHRIFTEN DES VEREINS FUR SOZIALPOLITIK, N.F. BAND 18)
BERLIN: VERL DUNCKER AND HUM, 1960, 291 PP.
ESSAYS TREAT NEGLECTED GROUP OF QUESTIONS, DECISIVE FOR A FAR-SIGHTED ECONOMIC POLICY: CONCEPTS OF ECONOMIC POLICY. PRESENT ESSENCE AND THEORETICAL CHARACTER OF THE ECONOMIC-POLICY CONCEPT; CONSIDER PROBLEMS AND PRINCIPLES OF ESTABLISHMENT OF GOALS IN ECONOMIC POLICY; DISCUSS CONFORMITY OF ECONOMIC MEASURES TO A SYSTEM; TREAT COMPETITION AS A PRINCIPLE OF ORDER.

2359 SERRANO MOSCOSO E.
A STATEMENT OF THE LAWS OF ECUADOR IN MATTERS AFFECTING BUSINESS (2ND ED.)
WASHINGTON: PAN AMERICAN UNION, 1955, 191 PP.
SUMMARY IN ENGLISH OF CONSTITUTIONAL, STATUTORY, AND REGULATORY PROVISIONS OF ECUADOR RELEVANT TO COMMERCIAL CONCERNS; COVERS LAWS IN FORCE IN 1955. INCLUDES LAWS ON MARRIAGE, TAXATION, AND COMMERCE.

2360 SEWELL J.P.
FUNCTIONALISM AND WORLD POLITICS* A STUDY BASED ON UNITED NATIONS PROGRAMS FINANCING ECONOMICAL DEVELOPMENT.
PRINCETON: PRINCETON U PRESS, 1966, 359 PP., LC#63-18650.
FUNCTIONALIST THEORIES OF INTERNATIONAL RELATIONS DISCUSSED IN BOTH EXPLANATORY AND PRESCRIPTIVE ASPECTS. ATTEMPT MADE TO EVALUATE THESE "THEORIES" THROUGH A DEPTH ANALYSIS OF UN FINANCIAL PROGRAMS. PARTICULAR ATTENTION PAID TO WORKS OF MITRANY, CLAUDE AND HAAS. QUESTION ASKED IS FUNCTIONALISM AN INDEPENDENT OR DEPENDENT VARIABLE IN WORLD POLITICS?

2361 SHACKLE G.L.S.
ECONOMICS FOR PLEASURE.
CAMBRIDGE: CAMBRIDGE UNIV PRESS, 1959, 268 PP.
INTRODUCES BASIC ECONOMIC THEORY, METHODOLOGY, AND HISTORY COVERING PRODUCTIVITY, INCOME, EMPLOYMENT, FINANCE, AND GOVERNMENT EXPENDITURES AND PLANNING.

2362 SHAFFER H.G.
THE SOVIET SYSTEM IN THEORY AND PRACTICE: SELECTED WESTERN AND SOVIET VIEWS.
NEW YORK: APPLETON, 1965, 470 PP., LC#65-11530.
WESTERN AND SOVIET WRITINGS COLLECTED TO GIVE READER WIDE PICTURE OF IMPORTANT PHILOSOPHICAL, HISTORICAL, POLITICAL, ECONOMIC, AND SOCIAL ASPECTS OF SOVIET SYSTEM. SHOWS ROLE OF PRESS, FUNCTION OF EDUCATION, AND POLICY-MAKING PROCESSES IN USSR.

2363 SHAFFER H.G.
THE COMMUNIST WORLD: MARXIST AND NON-MARXIST VIEWS.
NEW YORK: APPLETON, 1967, 558 PP., LC#67-21993.
INTRODUCES GENERAL PHILOSOPHY OF COMMUNIST WORLD, POINTING OUT ASPECTS OF HOMOGENEITY AND HETEROGENEITY. GROUPS INDIVIDUAL COMMUNIST NATIONS BY GEORGRAPHICAL AREAS, PRESENTING NATIVE AND FOREIGN VIEWS OF MARXIST IDEOLOGY. MOST MARXIST VIEWS REFLECT OFFICIAL EXPRESSIONS FROM COMMUNIST NATIONS.

2364 SHANKS M. ED.
THE LESSONS OF PUBLIC ENTERPRISE.
LONDON: JONATHAN CAPE, 1963, 313 PP.
EXAMINES STATE OF PUBLIC ENTERPRISE IN ENGLAND IN 1963, EVALUATING RELATIONSHIP WITH GOVERNMENT, THE PUBLIC, CUSTOMERS, WORKERS, AND PRIVATE INDUSTRIES. DISCUSSES PROBLEM OF WHO DECIDES PUBLIC INTEREST, PROBLEMS OF PARLIAMENTARY CONTROL; COMPARES WITH CASES ON CONTINENT.

2365 SHANNON D.A. ED.
THE GREAT DEPRESSION.
ENGLEWOOD CLIFFS: PRENTICE HALL, 1960, 171 PP., LC#60-8764.
NEWSPAPER ARTICLES, CONGRESSIONAL STATEMENTS, AND ESSAYS TRACE EFFECTS OF 1930'S DEPRESSION ON FARMING, INDUSTRY, AND EDUCATION. DISCUSSES PERSONAL EFFECTS OF JOBLESSNESS, INCLUDING SPECIFIC CASE HISTORIES, AND NOTES GOVERNMENT RELIEF EFFORTS. EXAMINES SPECIFIC PARTS OF NATIONAL FINANCIAL PROBLEMS. INCLUDES PROBLEMS OF WANDERING CHILDREN, POSSIBLE REVOLUTION IN PLAINS STATES, AND EFFECTS OF HUNGER.

2366 SHANNON I.
THE ECONOMIC FUNCTIONS OF GOLD.
LONDON: FW CHESHIRE, 1962, 139PP. 139 PP.
ANALYZES INTERNATIONAL MONETARY HISTORY OF WORLD SINCE WWI. CRITICIZES WEST FOR NOT COOPERATING OR AIDING PROGRESS OF WORLD MONETARY SYSTEM SINCE 1913. OFFERS COMPROMISE SOLUTIONS TO MONETARY PROBLEMS TO APPEASE BOTH EAST AND WEST, WHOSE VIOLENT DISAGREEMENTS HAVE PRODUCED STALEMATE. SEES SOLUTION URGENT FOR WORLD PEACE.

2367 SHANNON I.
INTERNATIONAL LIQUIDITY.
LONDON: F W CHESIRE, 1964, 143 PP.
ANALYZES PRESENT FUNCTIONS OF INTERNATIONAL MONETARY SYSTEM IN TERMS OF FUTURE OBJECTIVES. DOES NOT FEEL SYSTEM INADEQUATE FOR FUTURE NEEDS BUT THAT WORLD IS NOT FOCUSING ON CRUCIAL ISSUE, WHICH IS FAILURE OF US DOLLAR TO BE CONVERTIBLE TO GOLD. COVERS BASIC ECONOMIC FUNCTIONS OF GOLD AS MONETARY UNIT.

2368 SHARIF A.
THE BALANCE OF PAYMENTS OF PAKISTAN, 1948-1958 (THESIS, UNIVERSITY OF TORONTO)
TORONTO: UNIV OF TORONTO, 1965, 278 PP.
STUDIES RELATION OF EXPORTS AND IMPORTS ON BALANCE OF PAYMENTS. FINDS THAT PAKISTANI EXPORTS FLUCTUATED IN VOLUME THOUGH PRICE REMAINED STABLE AND THAT IMPORTS INCREASED HEAVILY, OWING TO DOMESTIC INFLATION. CONCLUDES THAT THE BALANCE OF PAYMENTS DEFICIT HAS INCREASED IN THE PERIOD STUDIED.

2369 SHARP W.R.
FIELD ADMINISTRATION IN THE UNITED NATION SYSTEM: THE CONDUCT OF INTERNATIONAL ECONOMIC AND SOCIAL PROGRAMS.
NEW YORK: PRAEGER, 1961, 570 PP.
CLASSIFIES AND DESCRIBES THE VARIOUS FORMS OF FIELD ORGANIZATIONS WITHIN THE U.N., AND ANALYZES THEIR ADMINISTRATIVE AND PLANNING PROBLEMS. ALSO DISCUSSES THE FUTURE DEVELOPMENT OF THESE ORGANIZATIONS.

2370 SHAW E.S.
MONEY, INCOME, AND MONETARY POLICY.
HOMEWOOD: RICHARD IRWIN, 1950, 661 PP.
MAKING INTENSIVE USE OF MONETARY SYSTEM'S FINANCIAL STATEMENTS, DESCRIBES MONEY AND HOW ITS SUPPLY CHANGES. EMPHASIZES THAT ECONOMICS OF MONEY IS INSEPARABLE FROM THAT OF OTHER SCARCE GOODS. DISCUSSES ROLE OF TREASURY, FEDERAL RESERVE SYSTEM, AND COMMERCIAL BANKS IN MANIPULATING ITS SUPPLY. LINKS PRODUCTIVITY TO PRICING; CONSIDERS INTERNATIONAL ASPECTS.

2371 SHAW S.J.
THE FINANCIAL AND ADMINISTRATIVE ORGANIZATION AND DEVELOPMENT OF OTTOMAN EGYPT 1517-1798.
PRINCETON: PRIN U ORIENTAL STUD, 1958.
EXAMINES TOTAL ADMINISTRATIVE SYSTEM OF EGYPT FROM OTTOMAN CONQUEST TO NAPOLEON'S EXPEDITION. CONCENTRATES ON OBJECTIVES OF REGIME AND DEGREE TO WHICH THEY WERE FULFILLED. COVERS REVENUES OF EMPIRE AND METHOD OF COLLECTING MORE FULLY THAN SPENDING. BIBLIOGRAPHY OF WORKS CITED AND REFERENCES USED.

2372 SHEEHAN D.
"PUBLIC CORPORATIONS AND PUBLIC ACTION."
POLIT. QUART., 35 (JAN.-MAR. 64), 58-68.
PUBLIC CORPORATIONS IN GREAT BRITAIN, DESPITE SOME FAILINGS, HAVE SERVED THE NATIONAL ECONOMY AND THE PUBLIC WELL AS SHOWN BY ECONOMIC GROWTH RATE AND HIGH EMPLOYMENT.

2373 SHEFFTZ M.C.
"THE TRADE DISPUTES AND TRADE UNIONS ACT OF 1927: THE AFTERMATH OF THE GENERAL STRIKE."
REV. OF POLITICS, 29 (JULY 67), 387-406.
EXAMINES BRITISH GENERAL STRIKE OF 1926 WHICH SHUT DOWN THE WHOLE ECONOMY. DISCUSSES TRADE UNIONS ACT OF 1927 WHICH CONSERVATIVE PARTY PASSED IN RESPONSE TO STRIKE. SHOWS THAT IT WAS NEVER PUT INTO EFFECT BUT INFLUENCED GOVERNMENT AND PUBLIC ATTITUDES TO A GREAT DEGREE. ANALYZES SHORT- AND LONG-TERM EFFECTS OF THE ACT.

2374 SHEPARD H.A.
"DEMOCRATIC CONTROL IN A LABOR UNION."
AMER. J. OF SOCIOLOGY, 54 (JAN. 49), 311-316.
A STUDY OF THE TORONTO DISTRICT OF AMALGAMATED CLOTHING WORKERS OF AMERICA (CCL-CIO) AND DEMOCRATIC CONTROL OF UNION BASED ON COMMUNICATIONS IN THE GROUP, LEADER SENSITIVITY, AND MEMBER ABILITY TO REMOVE OFFICERS. DISTRICT ORGANIZATION BASED ON SHOP AND LOCAL, THE CAUSES OF BUSINESS AGENT MOTIVATIONS, THE ROLE OF JEWISH WORKERS AND THE CHALLENGES OF NEW TYPES OF MEMBERS ARE DISCUSSED.

2375 SHEPHERD W.G.
ECONOMIC PERFORMANCE UNDER PUBLIC OWNERSHIP: BRITISH FUEL AND POWER.
NEW HAVEN: YALE U PR, 1965, 161 PP., LC#65-12546.
REVIEWS SOME LESSONS THAT HAVE BEEN DRAWN FROM EXPERIENCE OF BRITISH NATIONALIZED INDUSTRY. TESTS BOTH LOGICAL CONSISTENCY THAT CRITERIA OF "LESSONS" ARE BASED ON AND CORRECTNESS OF THEIR FACTUAL CONCLUSIONS. STUDY CENTERS ON QUESTION OF EFFICIENT RESOURCE ALLOCATION IN BRITISH FUEL AND POWER INDUSTRIES.

2376 SHEPPARD H.L., MASTERS N.A.
"THE POLITICAL ATTITUDES AND PREFERENCES OF UNION MEMBERS: THE CASE OF THE DETROIT AUTO WORKERS."
AM. POL. SCI. REV., 53 (JUNE 59), 437-446.
COMPARES 1952 AND 1956 SURVEYS OF UAW UNION MEMBERS; THE UNION PLAYS A SIGNIFICANT PART IN THE POLITICAL THINKING OF MOST OF THEM. ENDORSEMENTS, IN TURN, POINT TO THE STATE OF INTERNAL SOLIDARITY IN UNIONS. CLASSIFIES UNION MEMBERS BY POLITICAL ACTIVITY.

2377 SHERIF M. ED.
INTERGROUP RELATIONS AND LEADERSHIP: APPROACHES AND RESEARCH IN INDUSTRIAL, ETHNIC, CULTURAL AND POLITICAL AREAS
NEW YORK: JOHN WILEY, 1962, 284 PP., LC#62-17470.
AN EXAMINATION OF FRIENDSHIP AND ENMITY, COOPERATION AND COMPETITION, ALLIANCE AND CONFLICT AMONG HUMAN GROUPS. THE ROLE OF LEADERSHIP AS IT CONTRIBUTES TO AND IS AFFECTED BY SUCH RELATIONSHIPS. AN "INTERDISCIPLINARY STOCKTAKING AND EXCHANGE OF NOTES ON THEORY, RESEARCH, AND POSSIBLE PRACTICAL IMPLICATIONS IN THIS COMPLEX AREA:" DEALS WITH REPRESENTATIVE'S LOYALTY TO HIS GROUP, AND COMPROMISE.

2378 SHERWOOD W.B.
"THE RISE OF THE JUSTICE PARTY IN TURKEY."
WORLD POLITICS, 20 (OCT. 67), 54-65.
STUDIES DEVELOPMENT AND NATURE OF WHAT MAY BE THE NEAR EAST'S ONLY GRASS-ROOTS POLITICAL PARTY. SHOWS JUSTICE PARTY'S ROOTS IN TURKEY'S SOCIAL STRUCTURE AND DESCRIBES ITS YOUNG LEADERS. DISCUSSES TURKEY'S PRESENT AND FUTURE ECONOMIC, POLITICAL, AND SOCIAL STRUCTURE, AND THE PROBABLE ROLE OF THE JUSTICE PARTY.

2380 SHINOHARA M.
GROWTH AND CYCLES IN THE JAPANESE ECONOMY.
TOKYO: KINO KUNIYA BOOKSTORE, 1962, 249 PP.
ANALYZES POSTWAR RECOVERY FACTORS, EXPORT GROWTH POTENTIALS, EFFECT OF CONCENTRATION OF CAPITAL IN LARGE INDUSTRY AND EXISTENCE OF SO-CALLED KUZNETS CYCLE, A 20-YEAR CYCLE IN JAPAN'S GROWTH RATE. DISCUSSES POSSIBILITY OF TEN PERCENT GROWTH RATE AND IMPORTANCE OF TECHNICAL DEVELOPMENT TO GROWTH.

2381 SHISTER J.
ECONOMICS OF THE LABOR MARKET.
NEW YORK: J B LIPPINCOTT, 1949, 590 PP.
ANALYZES NATURE AND OPERATION OF THE LABOR MARKET. EXAMINES GROWTH OF TRADE UNIONS, THEIR LOCAL AND NATIONAL STRUCTURES AND BARGAINING POLICIES, MANAGEMENT'S RELATIONS WITH ORGANIZED AND UNORGANIZED LABOR, AND GOVERNMENT POLICY. DISCUSSES OPERATION OF THE LABOR MARKET WITH RESPECT TO WAGES; SEASONAL, CYCLICAL, AND TECHNOLOGICAL ASPECTS OF VOLUME OF EMPLOYMENT; AND DISTRIBUTION OF INCOME.

2382 SHISTER J.
"THE DIRECTION OF UNIONISM 1947-1967: THRUST OF DRIFT?"
INDUST. LABOR REL. REV., 20 (JULY 67),578-602.
CONSIDERS CHANGES IN GROWTH PATTERNS, STRUCTURE, PHILOSOPHY, INTERNAL AFFAIRS, POLITICAL ACTIVITY, MEMBERSHIP, LEADERSHIP. PREDICTS GROWTH OF WHITE-COLLAR UNIONISM AND FURTHER PENETRATION OF BLUE- AND WHITE-COLLAR UNIONS IN SOUTH. EXAMINES PROBABILITY OF FUTURE SOCIAL UNIONISM. REVIEWS THE NEW PSYCHOLOGY, PUBLIC ACCEPTANCE OF UNIONS, AND CENTRALIZATION.

2383 SHONFIELD A.
THE ATTACK ON WORLD POVERTY.
NEW YORK: RANDOM, 1960, 269 PP.
NEED AID YIELDING MAXIMUM RESULTS. MOST ATTEMPTS POORLY ORGANIZED, MAKE LITTLE USE OF NATURAL RESOURCES. EXAMINES PART TO BE PLAYED BY INTERNATIONAL ORGANIZATIONS, SUCH AS THE WORLD BANK.

2384 SHONFIELD A.
ECONOMIC GROWTH AND INFLATION; A STUDY OF INDIAN PLANNING.
BOMBAY: COUNCIL FOR ECO ED, 1961, 49 PP.
SPEECH ON PROBLEM OF INFLATION IN INDIA. DISCUSSES PLANS TO CONTROL INFLATION AND THEIR EFFECT. EXAMINES RESOURCES AVAILABLE AND POLICIES MOST EFFICIENTLY TO FILL NATIONAL NEEDS.

2385 SHONFIELD A.
"AFTER BRUSSELS."
FOR. AFF., 41 (JULY 63), 721-731.
DISCUSSES EUROPEAN ECONOMIC COMMUNITY AND FREE-TRADE AREA, FOCUSING ATTENTION ON BRITAIN'S UNSUCCESSFUL ATTEMPT TO ENTER EEC IN 1962. ALSO EXAMINES PROSPECT OF GREATER COHESION AND INTEGRATION IN COMMON MARKET. BELIEVES BRITAIN WILL TRY TO USE EFTA TO GET COMPENSATORY TRADE ADVANTAGES FOR INCREASED DISCRIMINATION THAT IS EXPECTED TO BE EXERCISED AGAINST HER BY EEC.

2386 SHONFIELD A.
MODERN CAPITALISM: THE CHANGING BALANCE OF PUBLIC AND PRIVATE POWER.
NEW YORK: OXFORD U PR, 1965, 456 PP.
ANALYSIS OF THE ECONOMIC ORDER WHICH HAS DEVELOPED IN THE WEST SINCE WWII. PRESENTS THE OUTSTANDING FACTORS IN THE GROWTH OF CAPITALISM, AND THEN EXAMINES THE APPROACH TO THE FUTURE. INCLUDES STUDY OF INTERNATIONAL AND GOVERNMENTAL PLANNING, OF THE CHANGING ROLE AND STYLE OF PRIVATE ENTERPRISE, AND OF THE IMPLICATIONS FOR FUTURE. CONCLUDES THAT INDIVIDUAL-STATE RELATIONSHIP IS KEY TO POWER BALANCE.

2387 SHORTE F.C.
"THE APPLICATION OF DEVELOPMENT HYPOTHESES IN MIDDLE EASTERN STUDIES."
ECO. DEV. AND CULTURAL CHANGE, 14 (APR. 66), 340-354.
BY USE OF SOCIOLOGISTS, DEMOGRAPHIC TRANSITION HYPOTHESIS, AND THE TRANSFORMATION OF THE PRODUCTION STRUCTURE HYPOTHESIS, AUTHOR SHOWS HOW MAJOR HYPOTHESES CONCERNING SOCIAL EVOLUTION PROVIDE VALUABLE FRAMEWORK FOR REGIONAL STUDIES.

2388 SHOSTAK A.B. ED., GOMBERG W. ED.
NEW PERSPECTIVES ON POVERTY.
ENGLEWOOD CLIFFS: PRENTICE HALL, 1965, 185 PP., LC#65-15149.
ATTEMPTS TO PRESENT COMPLETE AND OBJECTIVE VIEW OF POVERTY CONDITIONS IN US. DISCUSSES FACTORS FOSTERING POVERTY SUCH AS LACK OF BIRTH CONTROL INFORMATION, GOVERNMENT STIPENDS FOR BABIES, POOR EDUCATION, LACK OF JOB-FINDING AGENCIES, AND POOR MEDICAL CARE. PRAISES WAR ON POVERTY AND GIVES OVERVIEW OF JOHNSON POVERTY POLICY. DISCUSSES RACIAL ATTITUDES.

2389 SHUBIK M.
STRATEGY AND MARKET STRUCTURE: COMPETITION, OLIGOPOLY, AND THE THEORY OF GAMES.
NEW YORK: JOHN WILEY, 1959, 387 PP., LC#58-14221.
EXAMINATION OF OLIGOPOLISTIC COMPETITION, USING METHODS OF GAME THEORY. DISCUSSES CURRENT THEORIES OF COMPETITION AND VIEWS OF MONOPOLY. PRESENTS THE MATHEMATICS OF INSTITUTIONAL ECONOMICS AND THE GAME STRUCTURES USEFUL. SEVERAL FACTORS ARE INCLUDED: INFORMATION, ADVERTISING, PRICE, MARKET, AND THE LAW. EXPLAINS ECONOMIC THEORY OF ACTIONS TAKEN BY FIRMS UNDER VARIOUS MARKET FORMS.

2390 SHUBIK M.
"APPROACHES TO THE STUDY OF DECISION-MAKING RELEVANT TO THE FIRM."
J. OF BUSINESS, 34 (APR. 61), 101-118.
A REVIEW OF SELECTED DIFFICULTIES IN UTILIZING ECONOMIC THEORY AS AID TO STUDY OF DECISION-MAKING AT THE BUSINESS FIRM LEVEL. PROVIDES GENERAL INDICATION OF TYPE OF WORK IN PRORESS, (NEW THEORIES, TECHNIQUES, AND EXPERIMENTATION), AND NATURE OF PROBLEM TO WHICH THEY ARE ADDRESSED. OUTLINES NECESSITY FOR GROWTH OF SCIENTIFIC AND EMPIRICAL ATTITUDES IO GATHERING OF STATISTICS AND INFORMATION PROCESSES.

2391 SHULTZ G.P., WEBER A.R.
STRATEGIES FOR THE DISPLACED WORKER.
NEW YORK: HARPER & ROW, 1966, 221 PP., LC#66-13925.
DISCUSSES PROBLEMS OF AUTOMATION FOR LABOR AND METHODS CREATED TO DEAL WITH JOB LOSS. EXAMINES PROPOSALS FOR PAYMENTS, RETRAINING, TRANSFER, AND COLLECTIVE BARGAINING DISCUSSIONS OF PROBLEM BY UNIONS AND MANAGEMENT.

2392 SHULTZ G.P. ED., ALIBER R.Z. ED.
GUIDELINES, INFORMAL CONTROLS, AND THE MARKET PLACE: POLICY CHOICES IN A FULL EMPLOYMENT ECONOMY.
CHICAGO: U OF CHICAGO PRESS, 1966, 357 PP., LC#66-23699.
ANALYZES GOVERNMENTAL CONTROLS ON BEHAVIOR OF BUSINESS, BANKS, AND LABOR UNIONS AS NEW EXECUTIVE POLICY TO CONTROL AND PREVENT DOMESTIC AND INTERNATIONAL INFLATION. REPORTS GIVEN AT UNIVERSITY OF CHICAGO'S CENTER FOR STUDIES IN BUSINESS. INCLUDES DISCUSSION OF WORKSHOPS AND APPENDIX OF US DOCUMENTS ON WAGE-PRICE CONTROL AND BANKING ABROAD.

2393 SHWADRAN B.
"MIDDLE EAST OIL, 1962."
MID. EAST AFF., 14 (AUG-SEPT. 63), 194-200.
EXPLORES RELATIONS BETWEEN OIL-PRODUCING GOVERNMENTS AND INTERNATIONAL CONCESSIONAIRE OIL COMPANIES. INDICATES THAT COMPANIES ARE RESTRICTING AREAS OF EXPLOITATION FOR SELFISH REASONS THUS DEPRIVING COUNTRIES OF IMPORTANT REVENUE. ORGANIZATIONAL ISSUES IN PETROLEUM-EXPORTING COUNTRIES AND PRODUCTION RATES ANALYZED.

2394 SHWADRAN B.
"MIDDLE EAST OIL, 1962."
MID. EAST AFF., 14 (OCT. 63), 226-235.
VOICES CONCERN OVER SOVIET OIL ENTERING NON-COMMUNIST COUNTRIES. INVESTIGATED FROM VIEW-POINT OF COMMON MARKET, THE MIDDLE EAST AND WESTERN OIL COMPANIES.

2395 SIDDIQ M.M.
"LOCAL GOVERNMENT IN PAKISTAN."
J. OF ADMINISTRATION OVERSEAS, 6 (JULY 67), 179-191.
EXAMINES STRUCTURE, FUNCTIONS, AND FINANCIAL RESOURCES OF LOCAL GOVERNMENT IN PAKISTAN. SHOWS ADMINISTRATIVE DIVISIONS, ROLE OF RURAL AND MUNICIPAL COMMITTEES, AND TAX SYSTEMS. STATES THAT REFORM OF REVENUE COLLECTION METHODS WOULD GIVE IMPETUS TO ADVANCEMENT OF LOCAL GOVERNMENT.

2396 SIEGEL B.N.
AGGREGATE ECONOMICS AND PUBLIC POLICY.
HOMEWOOD: RICHARD IRWIN, 1960, 337 PP., LC#60-14051.
UNIVERSITY OF UTAH PROFESSOR'S COURSE NOTES DESIRING TO BRING STUDENTS TO SOPHISTICATED INTERMEDIATE UNDERSTANDING OF ECONOMICS. BEGINS WITH ELEMENTARY ANALYSIS OF INCOME FLOWS, PROCEDES TO COVER EXPENDITURE MODELS, DISCUSSES CONSUMPTION AND INVESTMENT, AGGREGATE DEMAND, AGGREGATE SUPPLY, INFLATION AND ECONOMIC GROWTH, AND BASIC ECONOMIC

POLICY.

2397 SIEGEL S., FOURAKER L.E.
BARGAINING AND GROUP DECISION-MAKING: EXPERIMENTS IN BILATERAL MONOPOLY.
NEW YORK: MCGRAW HILL, 1960, 132 PP., LC#60-8844.
PSYCHOLOGIST AND ECONOMIST STUDY DECISIONS REACHED BY GROUPS OF TWO, THE MODEL FOR THE DECISION PROCESS OF BARGAINERS UNDER BILATERAL MONOPOLY, AND DEMONSTRATE THE FEASIBILITY AND FRUITFULNESS OF THE STUDY OF BARGAINING AND GROUP DECISION-MAKING.

2398 SIEGFRIED A.
AMERICA COMES OF AGE: A FRENCH ANALYSIS (TRANS. BY H.H. HEMMING AND DORIS HEMMING)
NEW YORK: HARCOURT BRACE, 1927, 358 PP.
AN EXAMINATION OF US SOCIETY AND CULTURE IN THE EARLY 20TH CENTURY. DISCUSSES ORIGINS OF THE POPULATION AND MAJOR RELIGIOUS AND RACIAL TRENDS. DESCRIBES EFFECTS OF INDUSTRIALIZATION ON STANDARD OF LIVING AND WORLD TRADE. EXPLAINS NATURE OF US POLITICAL SYSTEM AND AMERICA'S EMERGENCE AS A WORLD POWER, WITH SPECIAL ATTENTION TO RELATIONS WITH BRITAIN AND FRANCE.

2399 SIEVERS A.M.
REVOLUTION, EVOLUTION AND THE ECONOMIC ORDER.
ENGLEWOOD CLIFFS: PRENTICE HALL, 1962, 173 PP., LC#62-7449.
EXAMINATION OF VIEWS OF JOHN MAYNARD KEYNES, AND FOUR LEADING POST-KEYNESIAN POLITICAL ECONOMISTS. REPRESENTATIVE BOOKS OF AUTHORS ANALYZED, INTERPRETED, AND COMPARED. CONCLUDES THAT REVOLUTION HAS STOPPED SHORT OF GOALS AND FURTHER INSTITUTIONAL CHANGES ARE NECESSARY FOR ECONOMIC EFFICIENCY AND NATIONAL SURVIVAL.

2400 SIKES E.R.
CONTEMPORARY ECONOMIC SYSTEMS: THEIR ANALYSIS AND SOCIAL BACKGROUND.
NEW YORK: HOLT RINEHART WINSTON, 1940, 690 PP.
ATTEMPTS TO SHOW HOW HISTORICAL ECONOMIC SYSTEMS SOLVE PROBLEMS OF PRODUCTION, DISTRIBUTION, EXCHANGE, AND CONSUMPTION OF GOODS AND SERVICES. COMPARES AND EVALUATES THESE SYSTEMS. TRACES DEVELOPMENTS LEADING UP TO INTRODUCTION OF NEW SYSTEMS. BIBLIOGRAPHICAL REFERENCES FOLLOW EACH CHAPTER.

2401 SILCOCK T.H.
THE COMMONWEALTH ECONOMY IN SOUTHEAST ASIA.
DURHAM: DUKE U PR, 1959, 259 PP., LC#59-7085.
CONTRASTS THE PATTERNS OF ECONOMIC DEVELOPMENT OF SOUTHEAST ASIA IN THE COLONIAL AND COMMONWEALTH CONTEXTS. DISCUSSES THE IMPACT OF FREE TRADE UPON THESE NATIONS. SEES NEED FOR ACCOMMODATION WITH MINORITY GROUPS IN MALAY AND INDIA.

2402 SILK L.S.
THE RESEARCH REVOLUTION.
NEW YORK: MCGRAW HILL, 1960, 244 PP., LC#60-15866.
SEES HOW TO ACHIEVE SATISFACTORY RATE OF GROWTH AS MAIN US ECONOMIC PROBLEM TODAY. DESCRIBES INCESSANT TECHNOLOGICAL INNOVATION THROUGH SCIENTIFIC ADVANCE AS NEW FORCE WHICH ENABLES OUR ECONOMIC ENGINE TO INCREASE ITS SPEED. MAINTAINS THAT DEPENDENCE ON PERPETUAL FLOW OF INNOVATION CREATES NEW PROBLEMS FOR BUSINESS AND GOVERNMENT.

2403 SILOW R.A.
THE POTENTIAL CONTRIBUTION OF ATOMIC ENERGY TO DEVELOPMENT IN AGRICULTURE AND RELATED INDUSTRIES (PAMPHLET)
J OF APPLIED BEHAVIORAL SCIENCE, 1 (JAN.-MAR. 65), 25-57.
EVALUATES POTENTIAL CONTRIBUTIONS OF ATOMIC ENERGY TO FOOD PRESERVATION AND PROCESSING, PLANT BREEDING, AND AGRICULTURAL RESEARCH. INDICATES PRIORITIES OF THESE USES UNTIL NUCLEAR POWER CAN BE GENERATED EFFICIENTLY. SUGGESTS THAT RADIATION MAY HELP SOLVE PROBLEM OF FOOD SHORTAGE.

2404 SILVERMAN C.
THE PRESIDENT'S ECONOMIC ADVISERS (PAMPHLET)
UNIVERSITY: U ALABAMA PR, 1959, 18 PP.
DESCRIBES PROBLEMS OF FIRST THREE MEMBERS OF PRESIDENT'S COUNCIL OF ECONOMIC ADVISERS. EXAMINES SCOPE OF ROLE OF PROFESSIONAL EXPERTISE IN THE MAKING OF MAJOR POLICY DECISIONS.

2405 SIMMS R.P.
URBANIZATION IN WEST AFRICA; A REVIEW OF CURRENT LITERATURE.
EVANSTON: NORTHWESTERN U PRESS, 1965, 109 PP., LC#65-19464.
REVIEW OF PUBLICATIONS DATED FROM 1950 TO AUGUST 1962, BASICALLY FOCUSED ON SOCIAL ASPECTS OF URBANIZATION. CLASSIFIED INTO FOUR CATEGORIES: SUBSTANTIVE, METHODOLOGICAL, EMPIRICAL AND THEORETICAL, AND BIBLIOGRPHICAL WORKS. ONE CHAPTER DEVOTED TO ANNOTATED BIBLIOGRPHY OF 234 PERIODICALS, BOOKS, AND MONOGRAPHS. SUPPLEMENTARY BIBLIOGRAPHY COVERING PERIOD 1962-64 APPENDED TO REGULAR LISTING.

2406 SIMON B.
EDUCATION AND THE LABOR MOVEMENT, 1870-1920.
LONDON: LAWRENCE & WISHART, 1965, 387 PP.
DISCUSSES EDUCATIONAL DEVELOPMENT AFTER EDUCATION ACT OF 1870 TO END OF WWI, ACHIEVED THROUGH NEW POLITICAL AND SOCIAL REFORM ACTIVITIES OF WORKING CLASS.

2408 SIMON H.A.
"BIRTH OF AN ORGANIZATION: THE ECONOMIC COOPERATION ADMINISTRATION."
PUBLIC ADMIN. REV., 13 (FALL 53), 227-236.
EARLY HISTORY OF THE GROWTH OF THE INTERNAL ORGANIZATION OF ECA, ON A DISORGANIZED, "AD HOC" BASIS.

2409 SIMON H.A.
"THEORIES OF DECISION-MAKING IN ECONOMICS AND BEHAVIORAL SCIENCE" (BMR)"
AMER. ECO. REVIEW, 49 (JUNE 59), 253-283.
DISCUSSES RECENT EXPLORATIONS IN THEORY, MODEL-BUILDING, AND EMPIRICAL TESTING OF INTERRELATIONSHIP OF ECONOMICS AND PSYCHOLOGY. EXAMINES DEVELOPMENTS IN THEORY OF UTILITY AND CONSUMER CHOICE, CONSIDERS MANAGER MOTIVATION, AND TREATS CONFLICT OF GOALS AND PHENOMENA OF BARGAINING. SURVEYS WORK DONE ON UNCERTAINTY AND FORMATION OF EXPECTATIONS. APPLIES THEORY OF HUMAN PROBLEM-SOLVING TO ECONOMIC DECISION-MAKING.

2410 SIMONE A.J.
"SCIENTIFIC PUBLIC POLICY, MARKET PERFORMANCE, AND SIZE OF FIRM."
ANTI-TRUST BULLETIN, 12 (SPRING 67), 99-108.
ARGUES THAT BASIC PROBLEM FACING ANTITRUST POLICY IS THE MARKET PERFORMANCE OF THE INDUSTRY, AND NOT THE SIZE OF THE FIRM. THE QUESTION OF SIZE IS RELATIVE, THAT IS, THE SIZE OF THE FIRM MUST ALWAYS BE CONSIDERED IN RELATION TO ITS MARKET.

2411 SIMOONS F.J.
NORTHWEST ETHIOPIA; PEOPLES AND ECONOMY.
MADISON: U OF WISCONSIN PR, 1960, 250 PP., LC#60-5660.
DISCUSSES PEOPLE, SOCIAL LIFE, POLITICAL ORGANIZATION, AGRICULTURE, ANIMAL HUSBANDRY, CRAFTS AND INDUSTRIES AND MARKETS AND TRADING IN NORTHWEST ETHIOPIA.

2412 SINGER H.W.
INTERNATIONAL DEVELOPMENT: GROWTH AND CHANGE.
NEW YORK: MCGRAW HILL, 1964, 295 PP., $7.50.
ANALYZES TRENDS IN ECONOMIC THEORY ON UNDERDEVELOPED ECONOMIES. STRESSES NEED FOR PREINVESTMENT WORK AND FOR PLANS UTILIZING TOTAL RESOURCES OF COUNTRIES. RELATES EDUCATION AND POPULATION TO ECONOMIC DEVELOPMENTS. TREATS OBSTACLES TO AFRICAN AND BRAZILIAN GROWTH.

2413 SINGH D.B.
INFLATIONARY PRICE TRENDS IN INDIA SINCE 1939.
BOMBAY: ASIA PUBL HOUSE, 1957, 184 PP.
ANALYSIS OF PRICE PATTERNS SINCE BEGINNING OF WWII AND INFLUENCE OF FACTORS OF WAR FINANCE, DEVELOPMENTAL OUTLAYS, BALANCE OF PAYMENTS, AND PRODUCTION TRENDS ON PRICE LEVELS. TREATS EFFECT OF HIGH PRICES ON CONSUMPTION HABITS OF PEOPLE AND ON SOCIETY. STUDIES METHODS OF GOVERNMENT PRICE CONTROL AND NEW PRICE POLICY IN INDIA.

2414 SINGH L.P.
THE POLITICS OF ECONOMIC COOPERATION IN ASIA; A STUDY OF ASIAN INTERNATIONAL ORGANIZATIONS.
COLUMBIA: U OF MO PR, 1966, 271 PP., LC#66-17956.
STUDIES ASIAN ECONOMIC ORGANIZATIONS AND THE POLITICS OF AND INITIATIVES FOR ECONOMIC COOPERATION AND INTEGRATION IN ASIA. CONSIDERS ECONOMIC AND NONECONOMIC FACTORS AFFECTING REGIONAL ECONOMIC COOPERATION; ASSESSES EFFORTS TOWARD INTEGRATION. STUDIES UN'S ECONOMIC COMMISSION FOR ASIA AND THE FAR EAST, COLOMBO PLAN, SEATO, AND COOPERATION OUTSIDE OF INTERNATIONAL ORGANIZATIONS.

2415 SINHA M.R. ED.
THE ECONOMICS OF MANPOWER PLANNING.
BOMBAY: ASIAN STUDIES PRESS, 1965, 194 PP.
ARTICLES ON UTILIZATION OF LABOR-INTENSIVE METHODS IN DEVELOPING COUNTRIES.

2416 SIPPEL D.
"INDIENS UNSICHERE ZUKUNFT."
NEUE POLITISCHE LITERATUR, 12 (1967), 200-220.
CRITICAL REVIEW OF MAJOR WORKS ON INDIAN POLITICS, SOCIETY, AND ECONOMY. POINTS TO ESTABLISHMENT OF SOUTH ASIA INSTITUTE AT HEIDELBERG UNIVERSITY WHERE INTERDISCIPLINARY APPROACHES TO ETHNOLOGY, ECONOMICS, TROPICAL HYGIENE, GEOGRAPHY, AND AGRARIAN POLITICS SEEK TO MAKE CONTRIBUTIONS TO UNDERSTANDING OF PROBLEMS OF SOUTH ASIA. SUGGESTS OPPORTUNITIES FOR RESEARCH.

2417 SIRUGO F. ED.
L'ECONOMIA DEGLI STAT' ITALIANI PRIMA DELL' UNIFICAZIONE (10 VOLS.)
MILAN: FETRINELLI EDITORE, 1962.
TEN-VOLUME BIBLIOGRAPHY ON ECONOMY OF ITALIAN STATES FROM 1700 THROUGH 1860-70. INCLUDES ALL PUBLICATIONS (INCLUDING PERIODICALS) PUBLISHED IN RESPECTIVE STATES DURING PERIOD AND SELECTED PUBLICATIONS PRINTED ELSEWHERE. LEGISLATION AND NEWSPAPERS ARE EXCLUDED FROM COLLECTION.

MATERIAL IS ORGANIZED CHRONOLOGICALLY. EACH VOLUME IS DEVOTED TO SEPARATE REGION.

2418 SKILTON R.M., HELSTAD O.L.
"PROTECTION OF THE INSTALLMENT BUYER OF GOODS UNDER THE UNIFORM COMMERCIAL CODE."
MICH. LAW REV., 65 (MAY 67), 1465-1488.
DISCUSSES PROTECTION OF INSTALLMENT BUYER PROVIDED BY UNIFORM COMMERCIAL CODE. ANALYZES PROVISIONS OF PROPOSED UNIFORM CONSUMER CREDIT CODE. FINDS THAT IT WOULD AFFORD MORE EFFECTIVE BUYER PROTECTION THAN DOES UNIFORM COMMERCIAL CODE.

2419 SKOLNICK J.H.
"SOCIAL CONTROL IN THE ADVERSARY SYSTEM."
J. OF CONFLICT RESOLUTION, 11 (MAR. 67), 52-70.
DESCRIBES AND ANALYZES OUTSTANDING FEATURES OF THE ADVERSARY SYSTEM, AS OBSERVED IN OPERATION, THAT ARE RELEVANT TO SOCIAL CONTROL PROBLEM OF CONFLICT MAINTENANCE IN THE SYSTEM. EXAMINES PRESSURES ON PROSECUTOR TO REDUCE CONFLICT. ANALYZES CONFLICT MODEL FOR VARYING CATEGORIES OF DEFENSE ATTORNEY.

2420 SLICHTER S.H.
UNION POLICIES AND INDUSTRIAL MANAGEMENT.
WASHINGTON: BROOKINGS INST, 1941, 597 PP.
FOCUSES ON COLLECTIVE BARGAINING, ITS CONTENT AND PROCESS, TO PROVIDE WIDE-RANGE ANALYSIS OF RELATIONSHIPS BETWEEN TRADE UNIONISTS AND EMPLOYERS. CONSIDERS EFFECTS OF MODERN UNION UPON PRODUCTION IN HIRING, LAYOFFS, WORK RULES, AND WAGE PAYMENT. ALSO EXAMINES RELATION OF UNION AND NON-UNION PLANTS AND EMPLOYEES.

2421 SLICHTER S.H.
THE CHALLENGE OF INDUSTRIAL RELATIONS: TRADE UNIONS, MANAGEMENT AND THE PUBLIC INTEREST.
ITHACA: CORNELL U PRESS, 1947, 196 PP.
DEALS WITH SIX PRINCIPAL GROUPS OF PROBLEMS CREATED BY THE RISE OF UNIONS SUCH AS EFFECTS ON MANAGEMENT, THE ECONOMY, INDUSTRIAL PEACE, THE PUBLIC INTEREST AND POLITICAL LIFE, AS WELL AS THE GOVERNMENT OF TRADE UNIONS, MEMBERS' RIGHTS AND DUTIES, THEIR OPPORTUNITIES TO PARTICIPATE, AND UNION DISCIPLINE, WITH HELPFUL POLICY SUGGESTIONS.

2422 SLICHTER S.H.
ECONOMIC GROWTH IN THE UNITED STATES.
BATON ROUGE: LOUISIANA ST U PR, 1961, 195 PP., LC#61-17301.
LOOKS PRINCIPALLY AHEAD TO FUTURE OF AMERICAN ECONOMIC INSTITUTIONS WHILE ACCOUNTING FOR PAST GROWTH, ESPECIALLY GROWTH IN OUTPUT PER MAN-HOUR.

2423 SLOTKIN J.S.
FROM FIELD TO FACTORY; NEW INDUSTRIAL EMPLOYEES.
NEW YORK: FREE PRESS OF GLENCOE, 1960, 156 PP., LC#59-15921.
DEVELOPS A THEORY ON THE RECRUITMENT AND COMMITMENT OF LABOR FORCE IN UNDERDEVELOPED AREAS. APPROACHES PROBLEM AS A SOCIAL ANTHROPOLOGIST AND CONTENDS THAT, CULTURALLY SPEAKING, UNDERDEVELOPED AREAS ARE THOSE WHICH HAVE NOT ADOPTED THE BODY OF CUSTOMS CONSTITUTING INDUSTRIALISM. DISCUSSES HOW NEW INDUSTRIAL LABOR FORCE IS CONFRONTED BY NOVEL CULTURAL AND SOCIAL SITUATIONS IN PROCESS OF ADAPTATION.

2424 SMALL A.H.
"THE EFFECT OF TARIFF REDUCTIONS ON US IMPORT VOLUME."
BUSINESS TOPICS, 15 (SPRING 67), 43-53.
ATTEMPTS TO ANSWER QUESTION OF WHETHER TARIFF REDUCTIONS INCREASE TRADE. EXAMINES EFFECTS OF GATT CONFERENCES AND AGREEMENTS TO REDUCE TARIFFS. DISCUSSES THE "DILLON ROUND" AND "KENNEDY ROUND," POINTING OUT MAJOR DIFFERENCES; COVERS TRADE GROWTH OF 1964 OVER 1961, TARIFF CLASSIFICATION ACT OF 1963, AND DOLLAR VOLUME OF US IMPORTS. CONCLUDES TARIFF REDUCTIONS INCREASE SOME IMPORTS, DECREASE OTHERS.

2425 SMELSER N.J.
THE SOCIOLOGY OF ECONOMIC LIFE.
ENGLEWOOD CLIFFS: PRENTICE HALL, 1963, 120 PP., LC#63-18024.
TRACES INTERRELATION OF SOCIOLOGY AND ECONOMICS THROUGH HISTORY OF BOTH. COMPARES METHODOLOGIES AND COMMON ASPECTS EACH HAS IN ITS CROSSING WITH PSYCHOLOGY. DISCUSSES RELATION OF SOCIAL SUBSYSTEMS WITH ECONOMY OF CULTURE; SOCIOLOGICAL ANALYSIS OF ECONOMIC PROCESSES; AND SOCIAL FACTORS AS DETERMINANTS OF ECONOMIC CHANGE AND GROWTH.

2426 SMERK G.M.
URBAN TRANSPORTATION; THE FEDERAL ROLE.
BLOOMINGTON: INDIANA U PR, 1965, 336 PP., LC#65-10035.
PROVIDES BROAD BACKGROUND AND ANALYSIS OF URBAN TRANSPORTATION PROBLEM AND ITS CAUSES; EXAMINES ROLE OF GOVERNMENT - STATE, LOCAL, FEDERAL AND THEIR INTERRELATIONSHIPS. SUGGESTS SOLUTIONS FOR CONGESTION: USE OF ALTERNATIVE MODES OF TRANSPORT, TRAFFIC REGULATORY DEVICES, DEVELOPMENT OF NEW URBAN CENTERS. ALSO SUGGESTS PROGRAM OF FEDERAL REMEDIAL ACTION AIMED AT COORDINATION OF GOVERNMENT RESOURCES.

2427 SMET G.
BIBLIOGRAPHIE DE LA CONTRIBUTION A L'ETUDE DE LA PROGRESSION ECONOMIQUE DE L'AFRIQUE.
BRUSSELS: CEDESA, 1960, 217 PP.
BIBLIOGRAPHY COVERS DIVERSE MATERIAL ON AFRICA APPEARING IN MAGAZINES AND BOOKS DURING PERIOD 1957-1959. INCLUDES SECTIONS ON POLITICAL ECONOMY. ECONOMIC SITUATION OF DIFFERENT AFRICAN COUNTRIES; INDUSTRIAL EXPLOITATION OF AGRICULTURE AND FORESTS; MINING AND INDUSTRY; FUEL; TRANSPORTATION AND COMMERCE; AND SUBSTANCE ECONOMIES. CONTAINS 1,532 ITEMS WITH AUTHOR INDEX. TOPICAL ARRANGEMENT.

2428 SMITH A.
THE WEALTH OF NATIONS.
ORIGINAL PUBLISHER NOT AVAILABLE, 1776, 486 PP.
ASSUMES PRIMARY PSYCHOLOGICAL DRIVE IN MAN IS SELF-INTEREST AND THAT THERE IS A NATURAL ORDER IN THE UNIVERSE WHICH MAKES INDIVIDUAL STRIVINGS RESULT IN SOCIAL GOOD. CONCLUDES THAT BEST PROGRAM IS TO LEAVE ECONOMIC PROCESS ALONE. JUSTIFIES SELF-INTEREST AND BUSINESS ENTERPRISE. PRESENTS FIRST FORMULATION OF IDEA THAT SOURCE OF VALUE IN COMMODITIES IS LABOR.

2429 SMITH A.
LECTURES ON JUSTICE, POLICE, REVENUE AND ARMS (1763)
LONDON: OXFORD U PR, 1896, 293 PP.
DISCUSSES THEORIES OF JURISPRUDENCE FROM LAISSEZ-FAIRE STANDPOINT. CONSIDERS JUSTICE TO BE SECURITY FROM INJURY; PRICE CEILINGS AN OBJECTIVE OF LAW ENFORCEMENT; AND PREFERRED MEANS OF TAXATION TO BE THAT WHICH IS LEAST DISCOMFITING. CONCENTRATES ON ENGLISH JUDICIAL SYSTEM FOR EXAMPLES. ALSO EXAMINES POSSIBILITY OF EXISTENCE OF NATURAL LAW'S AFFECTING INTERNATIONAL RELATIONS.

2430 SMITH G.A. JR., CHRISTENSEN C.R.
POLICY FORMULATION AND ADMINISTRATION: A CASEBOOK OF TOP-MANAGEMENT PROBLEMS IN BUSINESS.
HOMEWOOD: RICHARD IRWIN, 1962, 811 PP., LC#55-7391.
THIRTY-FIVE CASES DESCRIBING SITUATIONS IN MANAGEMENT THAT REQUIRE DECISION-MAKING. CASES ARE DRAWN FROM OVER 30 INDUSTRIES. BOOK IS NOT AN INTRODUCTION BUT IS FOR THE ADVANCED STUDENT OF MANAGEMENT. CASES DEAL WITH SIZING UP SITUATIONS, PLANNING PROGRAMS, ORGANIZING PERSONNEL, EXECUTING PLANS, FOLLOW-UP AND REAPPRAISAL, DAY-TO-DAY ADMINISTRATIVE PROBLEMS, AND PUBLIC RESPONSIBILITY AND THE EXECUTIVE.

2431 SMITH H.E. ED.
READINGS IN ECONOMIC DEVELOPMENT AND ADMINISTRATION IN TANZANIA.
DAR SALAAM: U SALAAM PUB ADMIN, 1966, 598 PP.
CREATES HEREWITH FIRST SOURCE BOOK FOR TANZANIAN ECONOMY, INCLUDING GOVERNMENT DOCUMENTS, RESEARCH REPORTS, AND JOURNALISTIC CONTRIBUTIONS. BRIEFLY DESCRIBES HISTORY AND SPECIFIC PROBLEMS, THEN DEALS WITH MONETARY SYSTEM, FINANCE, LABOR, INDUSTRIALIZATION, PLANNING, INTERNATIONAL TRADE, AND MUCH-DESIRED INTEGRATION OF EAST AFRICA.

2432 SMITH R.A.
CORPORATIONS IN CRISIS.
GARDEN CITY: DOUBLEDAY, 1963, 214 PP.
DISCUSSES MEN, CHANGES, FATE, AND PROBLEMS OF BIG BUSINESS IN SITUATIONS OF CRISIS. INCLUDES STUDY OF OLIN MATHIESON, RKO, GENERAL DYNAMICS, GENERAL ELECTRIC, INGALLS, US STEEL, AND BOEING WHEN THEY FACED AND SOLVED PROBLEMS OR ELSE WENT UNDER. CONCLUDES THAT FUTURE PROSPERITY DEPENDS ON THE ABILITY OF CORPORATION MANAGEMENT TO FORESEE CRISES AND TO SOLVE PROBLEMS IMMEDIATELY.

2433 SMITH R.M.
"THE NATIONAL BUREAU OF LABOR AND INDUSTRIAL DEPRESSIONS"
POLIT. SCI. QUART., 1 (SEPT. 86), 437-448.
ILLUSTRATES VALUE OF CREATING BUREAU TO GATHER ACCURATE NATIONAL STATISTICS NOW THAT THEY ARE VALUABLE IN ALL TYPES OF RESEARCH. CRITICIZES CHOICE OF SUBJECT OF INDUSTRIAL DEPRESSIONS AS TOO WIDE AND DIVERSE IN ORIGIN. ANALYZES DEPRESSIONS AND THEIR ROOTS THROUGH 19TH CENTURY FROM PRACTICAL AND THEORETICAL VIEWPOINTS.

2434 SMITH T.L.
THE PROCESS OF RURAL DEVELOPMENT IN LATIN AMERICA (A MONOGRAPH)
GAINESVILLE: U OF FLA PR, 1967, 85 PP., LC#67-22199.
SIX ARTICLES PERTINENT TO RURAL DEVELOPMENT IN LATIN AMERICA. INCLUDES SOCIOLOGY OF PERSONAL AND COMMUNITY DEVELOPMENT, ANALYSIS OF SOCIAL AND ECONOMIC ASPECTS OF RURAL SYSTEMS BASED ON FAMILY SIZED FARMS AND ON LARGE ESTATES, AND COMMENTS ON PROBLEMS OF LATIN AMERICAN RURAL COMMUNITY PLANNING. ANALYZES PRESENT COLOMBIAN AGRICULTURAL SYSTEM AND SUGGESTS MEASURES FOR IMPROVEMENT.

2435 SMITH W.H.T.
"THE IMPLICATIONS OF THE AMERICAN BAR ASSOCIATION ADVISORY COMMITTEE RECOMMENDATIONS FOR POLICE ADMINISTRATION."
NOTRE DAME LAWYER, 42 (1967), 907-914.
DISCUSSES EXTENT OF PRESS INFLUENCE ON FREE TRIALS,
STATING THAT IN NEW YORK STATE LESS THAN 10 PER CENT OF CRIMINAL DEFENDANTS EVER COME TO TRIAL. INVESTIGATES EXTENT OF POLICE RESTRICTION OF INFORMATION ABOUT DEFENDANT.

MAINTAINS THAT AMERICAN BAR ASSOCIATION RECOMMENDATIONS ARE NOT SOLUTION AND SUGGESTS VOLUNTARY CODE OF ETHICS.
PRESS FORCES ADJUD ETHIC

2436 SMITHIES A.
THE BUDGETARY PROCESS IN THE UNITED STATES.
NEW YORK: MCGRAW HILL, 1955, 486 PP., LC#54-11767.
HOW FEDERAL GOVERNMENT MAKES EXPENDITURE DECISIONS, INCLUDING PARTS PLAYED BY PRESIDENT, CONGRESS, AND DEPARTMENTAL BUREAUS. MAKES RECOMMENDATIONS, STARTING WITH IDEA THAT DECISION-MAKING CAN BE IMPROVED BY CLEAR FORMULATION OF ALTERNATIVES. COVERS DEFENSE AND NON-DEFENSE BUDGETS, ECONOMIC IMPACT OF BUDGET, HISTORY OF BUDGETARY PROCESS, RELATION TO NATIONAL POLICY, FORMULATION, EXECUTION, REVIEW OF BUDGET.

2437 SOCIAL SCIENCE RESEARCH COUN
BIBLIOGRAPHY OF RESEARCH IN THE SOCIAL SCIENCES IN AUSTRALIA 1957-1960.
SYDNEY: SOC SCI RES COUN AUSTRAL, 1961, 102 PP.
COVERS UNIVERSITY-SPONSORED, GOVERNMENTAL AND NONUNIVERSITY AGENCY PUBLICATIONS ISSUED FROM 1957-1960.

2438 SOLDATI A.
"EOCNOMIC DISINTEGRATION IN EUROPE."
FOR. AFF., 38 (OCT. 59), 715-83.
RECOMMENDS ECONOMIC TIES AMONG ALL EUROPEAN COUNTRIES. DELINEATES DEVELOPMENTS NECESSARY TO ACHIEVE COMMON AGREEMENT.

2439 SOLOW R.M.
THE NATURE AND SOURCES OF UNEMPLOYMENT IN THE UNITED STATES (PAMPHLET)
UPPSALA: ALMQUIST & WIKSELL, 1964, 51 PP.
CONTAINS WICKSELL LECTURES OF 1964 CONCERNING QUESTION OF UNEMPLOYMENT. DISCUSSES THEORY OF AUTOMATION AND ABUNDANCE IN RELATION TO US ECONOMY. MAINTAINS THAT STATISTICS SHOW NO APPROACH TO SATIATION WITH CONSUMPTION, NOR ANY SPECTACULAR ACCELERATION OF PRODUCTIVITY. OUTPUT PER MANHOUR IN US MANUFACTURING HAS RISEN ONLY SLIGHTLY FASTER SINCE WWII THAN IT DID BEFORE.

2440 SOLT L.F.
"PURITANISM, CAPITALISM, DEMOCRACY, AND THE NEW SCIENCE."
AMER. HISTORICAL REVIEW, 73 (OCT. 67), 18-29.
RELATES PROTESTANT INDIVIDUALISTIC, NON-TRADITIONAL PHILOSOPHIES TO REJECTION OF CLASSICAL SCIENTIFIC AUTHORITY. LINKS DOWNFALL OF SCHOLASTICISM TO INCREASING ATTEMPTS TO CONTROL MATERIAL WORLD. PARALLELING THIS IN POLITICS WERE REJECTION OF DIVINE RIGHT AND RISE OF DEMOCRATIC THEORIES OF THE STATE.

2442 SOMMERFELD R.M.
TAX REFORM AND THE ALLIANCE FOR PROGRESS.
AUSTIN: U OF TEXAS PR, 1966, 217 PP., LC#65-21300.
ANALYZES TAX REFORMS NECESSARY IN RECIPIENT NATIONS OF ALLIANCE FOR PROGRESS, IF IT IS TO SUCCEED. STUDIES PRESENT TAX REFORMS IN EACH NATIONA AND SUGGESTS CHANGES IN PRESENT PROGRAMS.

2443 SOPER T.
"THE EEC AND AID TO AFRICA."
INTERNATIONAL AFFAIRS (UK), 41 (JULY 65), 463-477.
THE DEVELOPMENT FUND AND SPECIAL TRADING RELATIONS CREATED BY THE EEC FOR THOSE AFRICAN STATES WHICH CHOSE TO REMAIN ASSOCIATED AFTER INDEPENDENCE ARE ANALYZED FOR EFFECT THEY HAVE HAD ON DEVELOPMENT, EFFECTS OF POLICY ON NON-ASSOCIATE STATES, AND EFFECTS ON AFRICAN UNITY.

2444 SOREL G.
LES ILLUSIONS DU PROGRES (1906)
PARIS: RIVIERE PUBLISHING CO, 1911, 340 PP.
BELIEVES THAT HISTORIAN MUST RETURN TO CONSIDERATION OF REAL IDEAS AND PERSONS, WHICH WILL LEAD HIM TO CONSIDERATION OF CLASS. DEMOCRACY IS FOUNDED ON IDEAS AND FORMULAS OF UNKNOWN ORIGIN RATHER THAN ON DOCTRINES BASED ON OBSERVATION. ATTEMPTS TO EXPOSE DEMOCRATIC "CHARLATANISME" THROUGH A HISTORICAL STUDY OF CLASS RELATIONS. EXAMINES IDEAS OF PROGRESS BEGINNING WITH SEVENTEENTH CENTURY.

2445 SOREL G.
REFLECTIONS ON VIOLENCE (1908) (TRANS. BY T.E. HULME AND J. ROTH)
NEW YORK: FREE PRESS OF GLENCOE, 1950.
REJECTS ANY IDEA OF PARLIAMENTARY SOCIALISM OR DEMOCRATIC COMPROMISE. BELIEVES THAT PROLETARIAN VIOLENCE, IN FORM OF GENERAL STRIKES BY UNIONS, IS ONLY WAY TO SAVE SOCIALISM AND MAINTAIN ITS REVOLUTIONARY IDEOLOGY. DOES NOT WANT TO REFORM STATE, BUT TO DESTROY IT. VIOLENCE IS MORAL AND NOT SAME AS BRUTALITY. WORKERS CALLED TO REVOLT THROUGH "MYTH" OF GENERAL STRIKE - IMAGES CAPABLE OF PRODUCING ACTION.

2446 SOVERN M.I.
LEGAL RESTRAINTS ON RACIAL DISCRIMINATION IN EMPLOYMENT.
NEW YORK: TWENTIETH CENT FUND, 1966, 270 PP., LC#66-19437.
DISCUSSES ABUSES OF EQUAL OPPORTUNITY IN EMPLOYMENT, AND PRESENTS LEGAL REMEDIES FOR RACIAL DISCRIMINATION. FOCUSES ON RECENT STATE FAIR EMPLOYMENT PRACTICES LEGISLATION AND ON CIVIL RIGHTS ACT OF 1964. EXAMINES VARIOUS EXECUTIVE ORDERS AND NATIONAL LABOR RELATIONS AND RAILWAY LABOR ACTS. OUTLINES MAIN PROVISIONS OF A MODEL FAIR EMPLOYMENT PRACTICES LAW.

2447 SPAAK P.H.
"THE SEARCH FOR CONSENSUS: A NEW EFFORT TO BUILD EUROPE."
FOR. AFF., 43 (JAN. 62), 199-209.
ANALYZES PROBLEMS OF COMMON MARKET AND ATLANTIC ALLIANCE, SEEING THEM AS CLOSELY INTERRELATED. CONSIDERS NATIONALISM AND ITS RECENT UPSURGE TO BE 'INTEGRATED', EUROPE'S BASIC PROBLEM AND STUDIES POSITION OF FRANCE AND GERMANY IN THIS LIGHT.

2448 SPECTOR S.D.
CHECKLIST OF ITEMS IN THE NDEA INSTITUTE LIBRARY (PAMPHLET)
TROY: RUSSELL SAGE, NDEA INST, 1967, 58 PP.
ANNOTATED BIBLIOGRAPHY OF APPROXIMATELY 850 BOOKS, ARTICLES, AND GOVERNMENT PUBLICATIONS FROM 1960-66 IN ENGLISH THAT WERE ADDED TO NDEA CIVICS INSTITUTE LIBRARY AT RUSSELL SAGE COLLEGE. REFERENCES ARE ARRANGED ALPHABETICALLY BY AUTHOR UNDER SEVERAL TOPICS AS THEY RELATE TO COMMUNIST COUNTRIES.

2449 SPENCE J.E.
REPUBLIC UNDER PRESSURE: A STUDY OF SOUTH AFRICAN FOREIGN POLICY.
LONDON: OXFORD U PR, 1965, 132 PP.
STRESSES LINK BETWEEN DOMESTIC AND FOREIGN POLICY AND DISCUSSES PROBABLE EFFECT OF EXTERNAL PRESSURES ON SOUTH AFRICAN GOVERNMENT; EXAMINES ITS ROLE IN INTERNATIONAL ORGANIZATIONS, ITS ECONOMIC POSITION, ITS VULNERABILITY TO CONCERTED UN ECONOMIC ACTION, AND ITS PROSPECTS FOR PEACEFUL CO-EXISTENCE WITH NEIGHBORS. OFFERS TENTATIVE CONCLUSIONS ON ABILITY TO KEEP PRESENT COURSE IN INTERNATIONAL AFFAIRS.

2450 SPENCER H.
THE MAN VS. THE STATE (1892)
CALDWELL: CAXTON PRINTERS, 1940, 211 PP.
WARNS AGAINST RISE OF "STATISM," THE THEORY OF STATE SUPREMACY OVER INDIVIDUAL RIGHTS. CONTENDS THAT STATES SHOULD CONFINE ACTIONS TO PUNISHING CRIMES AGAINST PERSON OR PROPERTY AS RECOGNIZED BY "COMMON SENSE OF MANKIND." THESE INCLUDE MURDER, ARSON, ROBBERY, AND ASSAULT. DISCUSSES TENDENCY OF BRITISH LIBERAL PARTY TO BECOME MORE AND MORE SOCIALISTIC, THEREBY APPROACHING DANGER OF FASCISM.

2451 SPENGLER J.J.
"POPULATION THREATENS PROSPERITY" (BMR)"
HARVARD BUSINESS REV., (JAN. 56), 85-94.
MAINTAINS THAT POPULATION GROWTH ABSORBS CAPITAL AND RESOURCES THAT MAY BE USED TO INCREASE EQUIPMENT PER WORKER AND CONSUMPTION PER HEAD, AND INCREASES COST OF RAW MATERIALS. "POPULATION GROWTH IS REALLY INCOME-DEPRESSING." EXAMINES TRENDS IN US POPULATION AND ARGUMENTS FOR INCREASED GROWTH. ARGUES THAT NEW POVERTY WILL RESULT FROM POPULATION PRESSURE THAT WILL INTENSIFY SOCIAL AND ECONOMIC PROBLEMS.

2452 SPENGLER J.J.
"ECONOMIC DEVELOPMENT: POLITICAL PRECONDITIONS AND POLITICAL CONSEQUENCE."
J. POLIT., 22 (AUGUST 60), 387-416.
HOLDS THAT POLITICAL AND SOCIAL FOUNDATIONS FOR ECONOMIC DEVELOPMENT BASED MORE ON IMPLEMENTING VALUES, ENCOURAGING INVESTMENT AND MAINTAINING STABILITY THAN ON ANY SPECIFIC STRUCTURES. LISTS FACTORS WHICH LIMIT AND ENCOURAGE DEVELOPMENT, INCLUDING CURTAILMENT OF WELFARE STATE PHILOSOPHY.

2453 SPERO S.D.
GOVERNMENT AS EMPLOYER.
NEW YORK: REMSEN PR, 1948, 497 PP.
DISCUSSION OF ATTEMPTS AND RIGHTS OF CIVIL SERVANTS TO ORGANIZE FOR COLLECTIVE BARGAINING AND THE US GOVERNMENT'S CLAIM THAT RECOGNITION OF CIVIL SERVANTS' BARGAINING ORGANIZATION WOULD BE A DEROGATION OF THE SOVEREIGNTY OF THE GOVERNMENT.

2454 SPICER G.W.
THE SUPREME COURT AND FUNDAMENTAL FREEDOMS (2ND ED.)
NEW YORK: APPLETON, 1967, 280 PP., LC#67-10891.
ANALYZES ROLE OF SUPREME COURT IN US AS GUARDIAN OF THOSE FUNDAMENTAL CONSTITUTIONAL LIBERTIES WHICH ARE ASSUMED TO BE ESSENTIAL TO EFFECTIVE OPERATION OF FREE INSTITUTIONS. SHOWS HOW FREEDOM OF PRESS, SPEECH, ASSEMBLY, AND RELIGION FURNISHES FOUNDATION OF DEMOCRATIC POLITICAL SOCIETY. DTSCUSSES SUPREME COURT'S RESPONSE TO ANTISUBVERSION PROGRAMS PUT FORTH IN RECENT YEARS.

2455 SPICER K.
A SAMARITAN STATE?
TORONTO: TORONTO UNIV PRESS, 1966, 272 PP.
DETAILED RECORDS OF CANADA'S AID PROGRAM IN PAST SIX FORMATIVE YEARS. PREFACED BY FIRST CHAPTER WHICH POSES MAJOR ISSUES OF POLICY FOR CANADIANS, THEN MOVES INTO HISTORY OF CANADIAN AID.

2456 SPINRAD W.
"CORRELATES OF TRADE UNION PARTICIPATION: A SUMMARY OF LITERATURE."
AMER. SOCIOLOGICAL REV., 25 (APR. 60), 237-244.
A DIGEST OF RESEARCH FINDINGS ON TRADE UNIONS ATTEMPTS TO "EXTRICATE THE VARIABLES ASSOCIATED WITH PARTICIPATION OR LACK OF PARTICIPATION." FACTORS ALLOWING FOR GREATER IDENTIFICATION WITH WORKING ROLE AND COMMUNITY MAKE FOR GREATEST PARTICIPATION. NEGLECT IN THEORY OF ROLE OF UNION ACTIVISTS WITH A SOCIAL ORIENTATION (LOOKING BEYOND ECONOMIC AND POLITICAL ROLE OF UNIONS) IS NOTED.

2457 SPIRO H.S. ED.
PATTERNS OF AFRICAN DEVLOPMENT: FIVE COMPARISONS.
ENGLEWOOD CLIFFS: PRENTICE HALL, 1967, 144 PP., LC#67-14837.
FIVE ESSAYS BY POLITICAL THEORISTS (ONE AFRICAN AND FOUR AMERICAN) ON PROBABLE DIRECTIONS OF AFRICAN POLITICAL DEVELOPMENT. CENTER ON QUESTION OF WHETHER AFRICAN DEVELOPMENT WILL BE REPETITIOUS, ESPECIALLY RELATIVE TO THE LATIN AMERICAN EXAMPLE, OR INNOVATORY.

2458 SPITTMANN I.
"EAST GERMANY: THE SWINGING PENDULUM."
PROBLEMS OF COMMUNISM, 16 (JULY-AUG. 67), 14-20.
EXAMINES RISE AND FALL OF BOTH MAJOR POLITICAL PARTIES IN EAST GERMANY SINCE CONSTRUCTION OF BERLIN WALL. DECLARES TENDENCIES IN GOVERNMENT TO BE NEO-STALINISTIC.

2459 SPOONER F.P.
SOUTH AFRICAN PREDICAMENT.
NEW YORK: FREDERICK PRAEGER, 1961, 288 PP., LC#61-11021.
DESCRIBES ECONOMICS OF APARTHEID. INCLUDES HISTORICAL BACKGROUND, RACE RELATIONSHIPS, POLITICAL SITUATION, RECENT PROSPERITY, INCOME OF RACE GROUPS, VULNERABILITY OF ECONOMY, ECONOMIC CONSEQUENCES OF APARTHEID, AND FUTURE PROSPECTS.

2460 SPULBER N.
THE STATE AND ECONOMIC DEVELOPMENT IN EASTERN EUROPE.
NEW YORK: RANDOM HOUSE, INC, 1966, 179 PP., LC#66-14883.
EXAMINES ROLE OF STATE IN ECONOMIC DEVELOPMENT OF SOVIET TYPE OF COUNTRY. STUDIES HISTORY OF STATE WITH RESPECT TO INDUSTRIALIZATION, CITING THE BALKAN COUNTRIES 1860-1960 IN THEIR CHANGE OF ECONOMIC STRUCTURE - CHANGE ACCOMPANIED BY EXPANSION OF STATE OWNERSHIP AND ECONOMIC ACTIVITY. COMPARES CAPITALISM TO STRUCTURED DEVELOPMENT WITH ITS CONCOMITANT DISCRIMINATION AND SELF-STYLED SUCCESS.

2461 SPURRIER R.B.
THE OVERPOPULATED SOCIETY.
NEW YORK: EXPOSITION PRESS, 1967, 88 PP.
AN ATTEMPT TO APPLY THE OBSERVATIONS AND RECOMMENDATIONS OF MALTHUS TO CURRENT POPULATION PROBLEMS. AUTHOR QUESTIONS FOREIGN AID AND WELFARE EXPENDITURES AND SEES THE POOR AS "PARASITES ON THE BODY OF SOCIETY."

2462 SRIVASTAVA G.L.
COLLECTIVE BARGAINING AND LABOR-MANAGEMENT RELATIONS IN INDIA.
LONDON: BOOKLAND PRIVATE, LTD, 1962, 405 PP.
COMPARES COLLECTIVE BARGAINING METHODS AND THEORIES IN INDIA, GREAT BRITAIN, AND US, USING CASE STUDIES FOR ILLUSTRATION. EVALUATES RELATIVE MERITS OF VOLUNTARY VS. COMPULSORY ARBITRATION AND RESULTS OF BOTH AFFECTING LABOR AND INDUSTRY.

2463 STALEY E., FULTON D.C.
SCIENTIFIC RESEARCH AND PROGRESS IN NEWLY DEVELOPING COUNTRIES (PAMPHLET)
MENLO PARK: STANFORD U RES INST, 1961, 48 PP.
EXPLORES WAYS IN WHICH BASIC AND APPLIED RESEARCH CAN BE USED MORE EFFECTIVELY TO SPEED SOCIO-ECONOMIC DEVELOPMENT IN AFRICA, ASIA, AND LATIN AMERICA.

2464 STALEY E.
WAR AND THE PRIVATE INVESTOR.
CHICAGO: U. CHI. PR., 1935, 562 PP.
DOCUMENTED STUDY OF RELATIONSHIP BETWEEN PRIVATE INVESTMENTS AND INTERNATIONAL POLITICS, PARTICULARLY AS THEY BEAR ON INTERNATIONAL POLITICAL TENSIONS. OBSERVES TYPES OF COMFLICT THAT MAY ARISE BETWEEN COUNTRIES WITH TRADE RELATIONS.

2465 STALEY E.
WORLD ECONOMY IN TRANSITION.
NEW YORK: COUNCIL FOR. REL., 1939, 333 PP.
EXPLORES HOW CONFLICTING TENDENCIES OF TECHNOLOGY AND POLITICS AFFECT HUMAN WELFARE. NOTES CONSEQUENCES OF CHANGES IN STRUCTURE OF ECONOMIC ORGANIZATION ON INTERNATIONAL ECONOMIC RELATIONS AND POLICIES.

2466 STALEY E.
THE FUTURE OF UNDERDEVELOPED COUNTRIES: POLITICAL IMPLICATIONS OF ECONOMIC DEVELOPMENT.
NEW YORK: HARPER, 1954, 410 PP., $5.00.
DEFINES SUCCESSFUL DEVELOPMENT AND CONTRASTS COMMUNIST METHODS FOR ACHIEVING IT WITH THOSE OF THE WESTERN WORLD. CRITICAL ESTIMATE OF PROPAGANDA, AGRARIAN REFORM AND VARIOUS PROBLEMS ACCOMPANYING INDUSTRIALIZATION. ALTHOUGH A PREREQUISITE TO POLITICAL STABILITY, ECONOMIC DEVELOPMENT MAY NOT SUFFICE AND 'DOES NOT NECESSARILY MAKE NICE PEOPLE.'

2467 STANFORD RESEARCH INSTITUTE
AFRICAN DEVELOPMENT: A TEST FOR INTERNATIONAL COOPERATION.
MENLO PARK: STANFORD U RES INST, 1960, 170 PP.
COVERING ALL OF AFRICA BUT UAR AND UNION OF SOUTH AFRICA, THIS STUDY EXAMINES CHARACTER OF AFRICAN DEVELOPMENT IN LIGHT OF PAST ROLES OF ASSISTANCE, INVESTMENT, AND TRADE; STEPS TAKEN TO MODIFY THESE EXTERNAL FACTORS, AND THOSE SUGGESTED. EXAMINES EFFECTIVENESS OF MEASURES IN LIGHT OF AFRICAN ATTITUDES AND ASPIRATIONS. INDICATES PROBLEMS IMPEDING DEVELOPMENT OF AN EFFECTIVE WESTERN APPROACH.

2468 STANFORD U, BOARD OF TRUSTEES
THE ALLOCATION OF ECONOMIC RESOURCES.
STANFORD: STANFORD U PRESS, 1959, 244 PP., LC#59-7420.
ESSAYS CONCERN ALLOCATION AND DISTRIBUTION OF GOODS AND SERVICES. DISCUSS WELFARE, COSTS AND OUTPUT, THEORIES OF PRICES, EMPLOYMENT, INVESTMENT, TAXES, ECONOMIC GROWTH, MONETARY STABILITY, AND INTERNATIONAL PRICE COMPARISONS. INCLUDE SEVERAL ECONOMIC MODELS AND THEORY COMPARISONS.

2469 STANLEY C.J.
LATE CH'ING FINANCE: HU KUANG-YUNG AS AN INNOVATOR.
CAMBRIDGE: HARVARD U PR, 1961, 117 PP.
STUDY OF FINANCIAL CAREER OF HU 1860-1880, A MERCHANT-BANKER IN CHINA. ANALYZES HIS FUNCTIONS AS PURCHASING AGENT FOR GOVERNMENT DURING TAIPING REBELLION. CONCENTRATES ON POLICY OF CONTRACTING FOREIGN LOANS TO SUPPORT ARMIES SINCE TAXATION WAS INADEQUATE. HU SERVED DURING TRANSITIONAL PERIOD OF DECENTRALIZATION OF GOVERNMENT BUDGET SYSTEM.

2470 STARK H.
SOCIAL AND ECONOMIC FRONTIERS IN LATIN AMERICA (2ND ED.)
DUBUQUE: WC BROWN, 1961, 427 PP., LC#61-13707.
TEXTBOOK COVERING SOCIAL, ECONOMIC, AND POLITICAL CONDITIONS IN LATIN AMERICA. DISCUSSES CONTINENT AS A WHOLE: LANDS AND PEOPLES, POLITICO-MILITARY ORGANIZATION, COMMUNISM, ANTI-YANKEEISM, ECONOMIC PROGRAMS, PRODUCTION ACTIVITIES, AND INTERNATIONAL RELATIONSHIPS. OFFERS PREDICTIONS FOR FUTURE DEVELOPMENT AND ROLE OF LATIN AMERICA.

2471 STARNER F.L., LEUTHOLD D.A., MCCARTY J.F.
GENERAL OBLIGATION BOND FINANCING BY LOCAL GOVERNMENTS: A SURVEY OF STATE CONTROLS.
BERKELEY: U CALIF, BUR PUB ADMIN, 1961, 117 PP.
PRESENTS COMPILATION OF LAWS AND REGULATIONS GOVERNING LOCAL GENERAL-OBLIGATION-BOND-FINANCING IN US. HISTORY AND GROWTH IS BRIEFLY TRACED AND EXPERIENCE OF CERTAIN CALIFORNIA LOCAL GOVERNMENTS IS SAMPLED. LOCAL FINANCING POLICIES OF CANADA, GREAT BRITAIN, AND WESTERN EUROPE ARE SUMMARIZED TO PROVIDE PERSPECTIVE.

2472 STEARNS P.N.
EUROPEAN SOCIETY IN UPHEAVAL* SOCIAL HISTORY SINCE 1800.
NEW YORK: MACMILLAN, 1967, 400 PP.
AUTHOR USES SUPRA-NATIONAL APPROACH AND CONCENTRATES ON ASPECTS COMMON TO EUROPEAN SOCIAL STRUCTURE AS A WHOLE WHILE RETAINING NATIONAL DIFFERENCES. EMPHASIS IS PLACED ON SOCIAL IMPACT OF INDUSTRIALIZATION IN TERMS OF MAJOR SOCIAL CLASSES. DEALS WITH ECONOMIC DEVELOPMENT, RELIGION, RISE OF MIDDLE CLASS, SOCIAL PROTEST, WELFARE STATE, AND EFFECTS OF THE WORLD WARS.

2473 STEENKAMP W.F.J.
"THE PROBLEM OF WAGE REGULATION."
S. AFR. J. OF ECONOMICS, 33 (JUNE 65), 87-100.
STUDY OF WAGE REGULATION IN FREE ENTERPRISE AND UNDEVELOPED ECONOMIES AS APPLIED TO SOUTH AFRICAN ECONOMY. COOPERATION BETWEEN GOVERNMENT AND COLLECTIVE BARGAINING GROUPS AND INCREASED ECONOMIC DEVELOPMENT UNDER A SYSTEM OF "BENEVOLENT PATERNALISM" SUGGESTED.

2474 STEFANIAK N.J.
"A REFINEMENT OF HAIG'S THEORY."
LAND ECONOMICS, 39 (NOV. 63), 429-433.
DISCUSSES HAIG'S THEORY OF LOCATIONAL ANALYSIS. SHOWS HOW THIS THEORY OF "COSTS OF FRICTION" HAS BEEN APPLIED TO LAND-USE STUDIES. SUGGESTS AN APPLICATION AND EXTENSION OF HAIG'S THEORY TO INDUSTRIAL PLANT LOCATION. PROPOSES A MOVE TOWARD SYNTHESIS OF UNCOORDINATED URBAN ANALYTICAL APPROACHES THAT WILL PRODUCE A BETTER CONCEPTION OF BASIC LOCATION FORCES THAT FORM US CITIES.

2475 STEIN E. ED., NICHOLSON T.L. ED.
AMERICAN ENTERPRISE IN THE EUROPEAN COMMON MARKET: A LEGAL PROFILE.
ANN ARBOR: U. MICH. PR., 1960 2 VOLS., 1242 PP.
PROFESSORS AND INTERNATIONAL CIVIL SERVANTS IN USA AND EUROPE CONTRIBUTE TO TREATISE ON THE SUBJECT. DOCUMENTED EXTENSIVELY BY GOVERNING TREATIES AND INTERNATIONAL LAWS. FIRST VOLUME SURVEYS EUROPEAN INTEGRATION AND SECOND VOLUME

PRESENTS VARIOUS LEGAL FORMS AVAILABLE TO AN ENTERPRISE IN BUSINESS OPERATIONS.

2476 STEINER G.A. ED.
THE CREATIVE ORGANIZATION.
CHICAGO: U OF CHICAGO PRESS, 1965, 267 PP., LC#65-17301.
COLLECTION OF ARTICLES ADDRESSES ITSELF TO PROBLEMS ARISING FROM THE INCREASING NEED FOR, AND EMPHASIS ON, CREATIVITY IN BUSINESS OPERATIONS. DEALS WITH DEFINING, MEASURING, AND FOSTERING CREATIVITY, AS WELL AS METHODS OF DISCOVERING CREATIVE INDIVIDUALS IN MANAGEMENT SPHERES.

2477 STEINHEIMER R.L. JR.
"THE UNIFORM COMMERCIAL CODE COMES OF AGE."
MICH. LAW REV., 65 (MAY 67), 1275-1280.
TRACES LEGAL DEVELOPMENTS WHICH LED TO ADOPTION OF UNIFORM COMMERCIAL CODE. CALLS FOR ORDERLY PERIODIC REVIEW OF CODE'S OPERATIONAL EFFECTIVENESS BY NATIONAL CONFERENCE OF COMMISSIONERS ON UNIFORM STATE LAWS. FEELS THAT IF BOARD'S ACTIVITIES ARE WELL PUBLICIZED, NEEDLESS AMENDMENT BY LEGISLATORS WILL BE AVOIDED.

2478 STEINMETZ H.
"THE PROBLEMS OF THE LANDRAT: A STUDY OF COUNTY GOVERNMENT IN THE US ZONE OF GERMANY."
J. OF POLITICS, 11 (MAY 49), 318-334.
DISCUSSES ROLE AND PROBLEMS OF COUNTY GOVERNMENT IN AMERICAN OCCUPIED ZONES OF GERMANY AFTER WWII. MENTIONS HOUSING, HEALTH, WELFARE, AND PRICE CONTROLS INITIATED AFTER WWII, AND PROBLEM CREATED BY HITLER'S PLANNED, WARTIME ECONOMY.

2479 STEMPEL G.H.
"A NEW ANALYSIS OF MONOPOLY AND COMPETITION."
COLUMBIA JOURNALISM REV., 6 (SPRING 67), 11-12.
ANALYZES DECLINE IN COMPETITION BETWEEN LOCAL DAILY NEWSPAPERS IN US CITIES. FINDS THAT COMPETITION FROM LOCAL RADIO AND TELEVISION STATIONS HAS REPLACED NEWSPAPER COMPETITION WHICH IS VITAL TO MAINTENANCE OF HIGH STANDARDS OF JOURNALISM.

2480 STERN R.M.
"POLICIES FOR TRADE AND DEVELOPMENT."
INT. CONCIL., 548 (MAY 64), 3-63.
WARNS AGAINST UNDUE RELIANCE ON TRADE TO SOLVE THE PROBLEMS OF GROWTH AND AGAINST THE DANGER OF CONFUSING SHORT-TERM AND LONG-TERM OBJECTIVES. GIVES PRIORITY TO TRADE LIBERALIZATION AND INCREASED MARKET ACCESS FOR THE EXPORTS OF DEVELOPING COUNTRIES. STRESSES THE CRITICAL ROLE OF THE DEVELOPING COUNTRIES THEMSELVES IN THE ORDERING OF THEIR DOMESTIC POLICIES.

2481 STERNBERG F.
THE MILITARY AND INDUSTRIAL REVOLUTION OF OUR TIME.
NEW YORK: FREDERICK PRAEGER, 1959, 359 PP., LC#59-7948.
ANALYSIS OF MAJOR CHANGES AND DEVELOPMENTS IN MILITARY AND INDUSTRIAL TECHNIQUES IN POSTWAR WORLD. EXAMINES US AND SOVIET MILITARY STRENGTH, NUCLEAR WEAPONS, AND RELATIONSHIP BETWEEN MILITARY AND INDUSTRY IN NEW INDUSTRIAL REVOLUTION.

2482 STEUBER F.A.
THE CONTRIBUTION OF SWITZERLAND TO THE ECONOMIC AND SOCIAL DEVELOPMENT OF LOW-INCOME COUNTRIES (PAMPHLET)
WINTERTHUR: P G KELLER, 1961, 62 PP.
DISCUSSES SWITZERLAND'S ROLE IN ECONOMIC AID TO LOW-INCOME COUNTRIES, INCLUDING MOTIVES FOR AID, TRADE, INVESTMENT, LOANS, CONTRIBUTIONS OF FEDERAL AND VOLUNTARY ORGANIZATIONS, EXPANSION OF PROGRAM, AND BILATERAL APPROACH TO AID.

2483 STEVENSON A.E.
PUTTING FIRST THINGS FIRST.
NEW YORK: RANDOM HOUSE, INC, 1960, 115 PP., LC#60-10097.
COLLECTION OF SPEECHES BY ADLAI STEVENSON IN 1959. DISCUSSES INTERNATIONAL AFFAIRS, ECONOMIC DEVELOPMENT, PUBLIC RESPONSIBILITY, EDUCATION, URBAN DEVELOPMENT, AND INDIVIDUAL RIGHTS AND RESPONSIBILITIES TO SOCIETY.

2484 STEWART C.F., SIMMONS G.B.
A BIBLIOGRAPHY OF INTERNATIONAL BUSINESS.
NEW YORK: COLUMBIA U PRESS, 1964, 603 PP., LC#64-19445.
UNANNOTATED BIBLIOGRAPHY CONTAINING 8,000 ENTRIES FROM BOOKS AND ARTICLES PUBLISHED IN ENGLISH AFTER 1950. COVERS MATERIALS ON COMPARATIVE BUSINESS SYSTEMS, GOVERNMENT AND INTERNATIONAL OPERATIONS, THE FIRM IN INTERNATIONAL OPERATIONS, AND INDIVIDUAL NATIONAL AND REGIONAL STUDIES. PROVIDES EXTENSIVE CROSS-REFERENCING.

2485 STEWART I.G. ED., ORD H.W., E
AFRICAN PRIMARY PRODUCTS AND INTERNATIONAL TRADE.
EDINBURGH: EDINBURGH U PR, 1965, 218 PP.
A COLLECTION OF ESSAYS DISCUSSING THE RELATION OF INTERNATIONAL TRADE TO "STRUCTURAL CHANGE AND GROWTH IN TROPICAL AFRICA." LARGELY A STUDY OF TRANSFORMATIONS IN TRADING SYSTEMS AND THE EXPORT OF PRIMARY GOODS AS MEANS TO ACHIEVING ECONOMIC STABILITY.

2486 STIFEL L.D.
THE TEXTILE INDUSTRY - A CASE STUDY OF INDUSTRIAL DEVELOPMENT IN THE PHILIPPINES (PAPER)
ITHACA: CORNELL U, DEPT ASIAN ST, 1963, 193 PP.
REPORTS ON RAPID DEVELOPMENT OF PHILIPPINE TEXTILE INDUSTRY CAUSED BY GOVERNMENT IMPORT CONTROLS, AN ABUNDANCE OF US SURPLUS COTTON, PLUS AMPLE SUPPLY OF CAPITAL, SOME FROM US FOREIGN AID. NOTES THAT SHORTAGES OF MANAGERIAL RESOURCES AND SKILLED LABOR ARE CONCEALED BY LACK OF EMPHASIS ON EFFICIENCY AND THAT COSTS OF ENCOURAGING TEXTILE INDUSTRY ARE HIGH IN RELATION TO BENEFITS ACCRUING TO THE ECONOMY.

2487 STILL C.H.
"MONETARY RECOVERY UNDER THE FAIR LABOR STANDARDS ACT."
TEXAS LAW REVIEW, 45 (APR. 67), 921-952.
ANALYZES PART OF FLSA THAT REQUIRES THAT COMPENSATION PAID TO AN EMPLOYEE MEET MINIMUM STANDARDS. IF IT DOES NOT MEET STANDARDS, EMPLOYER IS LIABLE FOR AMOUNT UNDERPAID. CONCENTRATES ON METHOD OF COMPUTING AMOUNT DUE UNDER FLSA. INCLUDES DETAILED DISCUSSION OF PROCEDURE OF FLSA AND RECOVERY OF SPECIAL DAMAGES UNDER ACT.

2488 STILL J.F.
"THE FUTURE OF METROPOLITAN GOVERNMENT ORGANIZATION."
MUNICIPAL FINANCE, 40 (AUG. 67), 51-55.
NOTES DEVELOPMENTS TAKING PLACE IN GOVERNING METROPOLITAN AREAS AND EVALUATES THEM, CRITICIZING TREND TOWARD RISING COSTS AND ATTITUDE THAT PUBLIC FUNDS ARE UNLIMITED.

2489 STILLMAN C.W. ED.
AFRICA IN THE MODERN WORLD.
CHICAGO: U OF CHICAGO PRESS, 1955, 342 PP., LC#55-5147.
COLLECTION OF BACKGROUND INFORMATION ON AFRICA CONCERNING ITS HISTORY, RESOURCES, ECONOMIC DEVELOPMENT, AND ITS RELATIONS WITH WESTERN NATIONS. ANALYZES STATUS OF REGIONS OF AFRICA, THEIR IMPACT IN WORLD, AND RELATION TO US.

2490 STINCHCOMBE A.L.
"BUREAUCRATIC AND CRAFT ADMINISTRATION OF PRODUCTION: A COMPARATIVE STUDY" (BMR)"
ADMINISTRATIVE SCI. Q., 4 (SEPT. 59), 168-187.
COMPARES MASS PRODUCTION AND CONSTRUCTION INDUSTRIES WITH RESPECT TO SOCIAL LOCATION OF WORK PLANNING, ADMINISTRATIVE STATUS STRUCTURE, AND CONTENT OF ADMINISTRATIVE COMMUNICATION. EXPLAINS LACK OF BUREAUCRACY IN CONSTRUCTION BY ECONOMIC INSTABILITY. REVISES MAX WEBER'S IDEAL TYPE OF BUREAUCRACY TO INCLUDE ONLY THOSE ELEMENTS PRESENT IN MASS PRODUCTION AND ABSENT IN CONSTRUCTION.

2491 STOCKING G.W.
WORKABLE COMPETITION AND ANTITRUST POLICY.
NASHVILLE: VANDERBILT U PR, 1961, 451 PP.
COLLECTION OF ARTICLES ON COMPETITIVE AND MONOPOLISTIC TRENDS IN BUSINESS AND THEIR RELATION TO GOVERNMENTAL CONTROL. STUDY OF WORKABLE COMPETITION, SAVING FREE ENTERPRISE FROM ITS FRIENDS, ROLE OF THE ATTORNEY GENERAL, THE SHERMAN ACT, AND THE ECONOMIC MARKET. INCLUDES DUPONT-GENERAL MOTORS CASE. CONCLUDES THAT A FLEXIBLE BALANCE IS ADVANTAGEOUS TO ALL.

2492 STOCKWELL E.G.
"THE MEASUREMENT OF ECONOMIC DEVELOPMENT."
ECON. DEVELOP. CULT. CHANGE, 8 (JULY 60), 419-432.
DEMOSTRATES THAT POPULATION STATISTICS CAN PROVIDE A CONVENIENT SET OF DATA FOR CONSTRUCTING INDICES OF ECONOMIC DEVELOPMENT. CONSIDERS THE INFANT MORTALITY RATE AS PROVIDING THE BEST INDIRECT MEASURE OF NATION'S DEVELOPMENTAL LEVEL, DUE TO ITS HIGH CORRELATION WITH PER-CAPITA INCOME. ALSO ANALYZES USEFULLNESS OF OTHER DEMOGRAPHIC INDICES AS SUBSTITUTE FOR DIRECT MEASUREMENTS PRESENTLY UNAVAILABLE.

2493 STOESSINGER J.G. ET AL.
FINANCING THE UNITED NATIONS SYSTEM.
WASHINGTON: BROOKINGS INST., 1964, 348 PP., $6.75.
COMPLETE SURVEY OF THE FINANCIAL HISTORY AND BACKGROUND OF THE UN AND OTHER PAST AND PRESENT INTERNATIONAL BODIES MEMBERSHIP COSTS BUDGETARY AND ASSESSMENT PROCEDURES AND POSSIBLE SOURCES OF FUTURE REVENUES. ALL ASPECTS SET WITHIN THE POLITICAL CONTEXT OF THE UN.

2494 STOLPER W.
"SOCIAL FACTORS IN ECONOMIC PLANNING, WITH SPECIAL REFERENCE TO NIGERIA"
EAST AFRICAN ECONOMIC REV, 11 (JUNE 64), 1-17. 00110
DISCUSSION OF NEED TO INCLUDE SOCIAL VARIABLES - LOCAL CUSTOMS, HISTORIES, MANNERS - IN ECONOMIC PLANNING.

2495 STOLPER W.F.
GERMANY BETWEEN EAST AND WEST: THE ECONOMICS OF COMPETITIVE COEXISTENCE.
WASHINGTON: NATL PLANNING ASSN, 1960, 80 PP., LC#60-15350.
COMPARISON OF ECONOMIC DEVELOPMENT AND POLITICAL SITUATIONS IN EAST AND WEST GERMANY SINCE WWII. ANALYZES "ECONOMIC PROSPECTS OF EAST AND WEST GERMANY IN NEXT 15 YEARS." STUDIES RELATION BETWEEN ECONOMIC MOVES AND POLITICAL ROLE OF WEST GERMANY IN THE COLD WAR STRUGGLE FOR CONTROL OF

UNDEVELOPED NATIONS.

2496 STOLTE S.C.
"THREE PROBLEMS FACING THE SOVIET BLOC."
INST. FOR STUDY OF USSR, 14 (JULY 67), 20-28.
ENUMERATES FIRST THREE STRATEGIC ADVANTAGES OF WARSAW PACT NATIONS OVER NATO NATIONS: COMMON SOCIO-POLITICAL VIEWS BASED ON MARXISM, COMPACT TERRITORY OF GREAT DEPTH, HIGHLY DEVELOPED MILITARY CAPABILITIES. RELATES THESE FACTORS TO PROBLEMS OF COMMON ECONOMIC POLICY, COMMON POLICY TOWARD WEST, AND COMMON POLICY TOWARD CHINA.

2497 STONE P.A.
"DECISION TECHNIQUES FOR TOWN DEVELOPMENT."
OPERATIONAL RESEARCH Q., 15 (SEPT. 64), 185-205.
QUANTITATIVE ANALYSIS OF CONSEQUENCES OF TOWN DEVELOPMENT WITH PURPOSE OF REDUCING MASS OF PROBLEMS TO COMPREHENSIBLE STATISTICS. DRAWS DISTINCTION BETWEEN COST-BENEFIT ANALYSIS, COST-BENEFIT CRITERIA AND COSTS-IN-USE CRITERIA. CONTENDS CONSEQUENCES CAN ONLY BE MEASURED BY TRACING THEIR INCIDENCE BEYOND EFFECTS ON MARKET AND LOOKING AT THEIR TOTAL SOCIO-ECONOMIC IMPACT BY EVALUATING THEIR COSTS AND BENEFITS.

2498 STONIER A.W., HAGUE D.C.
EXERCISES IN ECONOMICS.
LONDON: LONGMANS, GREEN & CO, 1964, 574 PP.
INTRODUCES ECONOMICS TO NOVICES BY DEALING GENERALLY WITH CONCEPTS AND THEORY. COVERS PRICE, EMPLOYMENT AND GROWTH THEORY, COMPETITION, AND CONSUMPTION, AND COMPARES CLASSICAL AND KEYNESIAN SYSTEMS.

2499 STOVEL J.A.
CANADA IN THE WORLD ECONOMY.
CAMBRIDGE: HARVARD U PR, 1959, 364 PP., LC#59-7663.
DISCUSSES CANADIAN BALANCE OF TRADE, THEORIES OF BALANCE-OF-PAYMENTS, AND ECONOMIC DEVELOPMENTS PRIOR TO WWI. INCLUDES ANALYTICAL CRITIQUE OF VINER'S ANALYSIS OF ECONOMIC EVENTS FROM 1900-13. ALSO STUDIES ECONOMIC DEVELOPMENT, COMMERCIAL POLICY, BALANCE-OF-PAYMENTS, AND PROBLEMS OF ADJUSTMENT DURING INTERWAR PERIOD.

2500 STRANGE S.
"DEBTS, DEFAULTERS AND DEVELOPMENT."
INTERNATIONAL AFFAIRS (UK), 43 (JULY 67), 516-529.
SUGGESTS THAT PROBLEM OF DEFAULT ON DEBTS BY FOREIGN COUNTRIES STILL EXISTS AND IS SUPPRESSED BY CREATION OF CREDIT PLANS AND RESCHEDULING OF DEBTS TO KEEP ECONOMICALLY UNDERDEVELOPED COUNTRIES SOLVENT. EVENTUALLY REPAYMENTS ON OLD LOANS WILL EXCEED PROCEEDS OF NEW ONES. STUDIES DEBT CRISES IN SEVERAL COUNTRIES. PROPOSES CHANGES IN AID AND TRADE POLICIES AS SOLUTION.

2501 STREAT R.
"GOVERNMENT CONSULTATION WITH INDUSTRY."
PUBLIC ADMINISTRATION, 37 (SPRING 59), 1-8.
AS A RESULT OF WORLD WAR II, RELATIONS BETWEEN INDUSTRY AND GOVERNMENT HAVE BECOME CLOSE: THERE IS CONSTANT CONSULTATION ON ALL TOPICS BETWEEN BUREAUCRATS AND INDUSTRIALISTS.

2502 STREETEN P.
"UNBALANCED GROWTH"
OXFORD ECONOMIC PAPERS, (JUNE 59), 1-8.
PRESENTS GENERAL DEFINITION OF BALANCED GROWTH AND COMPARES THEORIES OF SEVERAL ECONOMISTS. EXAMINES ASPECTS OF UNBALANCE AND CONSUMPTION, UNBALANCE AND PRODUCTION, FOREIGN TRADE AND LENDING, AND SAVINGS AND INVESTMENT. MAINTAINS IN SOME CONDITIONS LACK OF BALANCE PROMOTES GROWTH. IN ORDER TO GET GROWTH, ONE MAY HAVE TO SACRIFICE BALANCE.

2503 STRONG A.L.
THE RISE OF THE CHINESE PEOPLE'S COMMUNES - AND SIX YEARS AFTER (2ND ED.)
NEW YORK: NEW WORLD PRESS, 1964, 228 PP.
DESCRIBES HOW COMMUNES ROSE IN CHINA IN 1958. TELLS HOW THEY DIFFERED ECONOMICALLY AND POLITICALLY FROM PAST ORGANIZATIONS CALLED COMMUNES. DISCUSSES HOW COMMUNES HANDLE FARMING, INDUSTRY, COMMERCE, EDUCATION, AND MILITARY AFFAIRS IN THEIR TERRITORY. COVERS FIGHT AGAINST NATURAL DISASTERS AND REVIEWS THEIR FORM AND CONDITION IN 1964.

2504 STROUD G.S.
LABOR HISTORY IN THE UNITED STATES: A GENERAL BIBLIOGRAPHY.
URBANA: INST LABOR & INDUS REL, 1961, 167 PP., LC#61-9096.
AN UNANNOTATED BIBLIOGRAPHY OF LABOR HISTORY IN THE UNITED STATES. MATERIAL IN ENGLISH. CONTAINS 2,022 ENTRIES. PUBLICATION OF MATERIAL RANGES FROM 1874 TO 1959.

2505 STRUVE G.M.
"THE LESS-RESTRICTIVE-ALTERNATIVE PRINCIPLE AND ECONOMIC DUE PROCESS."
HARVARD LAW REV., 80 (MAY 67), 1463-1488.
SEPARATES COMPONENTS OF LESS-RESTRICTIVE-ALTERNATIVE PRINCIPLE. DOCUMENTS ITS POWER IN STATE AND CONTINENTAL JURISDICTIONS TO VALIDATE ECONOMIC REGULATIONS. ADVOCATES RETURN OF ITS USE BY SUPREME COURT AS INDEPENDENT GROUND FOR INVALIDATING OVERBROAD REGULATIONS. SHOWS ROLE IN STRIKING DOWN LAWS THAT RESTRICT ENTRY INTO CHOSEN OCCUPATION OR BUSINESS, THUS PRESERVING ECONOMIC LIBERTY.

2506 STUCKI C.W. ED.
AMERICAN DOCTORAL DISSERTATIONS ON ASIA 1933-62 (A PAPER)
ITHACA: CORNELL U, DEPT ASIAN ST, 1963, 175 PP.
BIBLIOGRAPHY OF DISSERTATIONS ON ASIA. INCLUDES PHILOSOPHY AND RELIGION, CULTURE, EDUCATION, ECONOMICS, GEOGRAPHY, HISTORY, SOCIOLOGY, ANTHROPOLOGY, GOVERNMENT AND POLITICS, AND LANGUAGE FOR ALL ASIAN, SOUTH, AND SOUTHEASTERN NATIONS. APPROXIMATELY 2,300 LISTINGS INDEXED BY TOPIC AND AUTHOR.

2507 STUDY GP CREATE RESERVE ASSETS
REPORT TO DEPUTIES (PAMPHLET)
ROME: BANK OF ITALY, 1965, 113 PP.
ANALYSIS OF SEVERAL BROAD PRACTICAL PROPOSALS FOR CREATING INTERNATIONAL SYSTEM OF RESERVE ASSETS. FEELS SUPPLY OF GOLD AND FOREIGN EXCHANGE RESERVES WILL BE INADEQUATE FOR WORLD IN FUTURE. EXPERTS ANALYZE EACH POSSIBILITY OBJECTIVELY AND WITHOUT DECISIONS.

2508 STUTZ R.L.
COLLECTIVE DEALING BY UNITS OF LOCAL GOVERNMENT IN CONNECTICUT (PAMPHLET)
STORRS: U CONN INST PUBLIC SERV, 1960, 55 PP.
ANALYSIS OF NATURE AND EXTENT OF EMPLOYEE ORGANIZATIONS IN LOCAL GOVERNMENT JURISDICTIONS; PRESENTS FIGURES ON NUMBER OF MUNICIPAL EMPLOYEES WHO ARE EMPLOYED IN CONNECTICUT AND ON NUMBER WHO ARE MEMBERS OF EMPLOYEE ORGANIZATIONS.

2509 STYCOS J.M.
"POLITICS AND POPULATION CONTROL IN LATIN AMERICA."
WORLD POLITICS, 20 (OCT. 67), 66-82.
STUDIES LATIN AMERICAN ATTITUDES TOWARD POPULATION CONTROL. SHOWS INFLUENTIAL POLICIES OF CATHOLIC CHURCH, NATIONAL GOVERNMENTS, AND MARXIST MINORITIES. FORESEES THAT US SPONSORSHIP TOGETHER WITH HELP FROM UN AND A CHANGE IN CATHOLIC ATTITUDES WILL EVENTUALLY CREATE A FAVORABLE ENVIRONMENT FOR INTRODUCTION OF NATIONAL FAMILY-PLANNING PROGRAMS IN LATIN AMERICA.

2510 SUFRIN S.C.
A BRIEF ANNOTATED BIBLIOGRAPHY ON LABOR IN EMERGING SOCIETIES.
SYRACUSE: SYR U, MAXWELL SCHOOL, 1961, 64 PP.
AN ANNOTATED BIBLIOGRAPHY ON LABOR IN EMERGING SOCIETIES. MATERIAL IN ENGLISH. PUBLICATION OF MATERIAL RANGES FROM 1950 TO 1960. CONTAINS 352 ENTRIES.

2511 SULLIVAN G.
THE STORY OF THE PEACE CORPS.
NEW YORK: FLEET, 1964, 156 PP.
DISCUSSES HISTORY AND ORGANIZATION OF PEACE CORPS, WITH EMPHASIS ON PROJECTS AND PROGRAMS.

2512 SULTAN P.E.
THE DISENCHANTED UNIONIST.
NEW YORK: HARPER & ROW, 1964, 272 PP., LC#63-16548.
A PSYCHOLOGIST AND EXPERT IN LABOR RELATIONS ANALYZES THE VIEWS AND MOTIVATIONS OF THE UNION DISSENTER. FIFTY "INDIVIDUALISTS" ARE INTERVIEWED, CAUSES OF DISSENT LISTED, AND SANCTIONS FOR ANOMIE DISCUSSED. IN-GROUP CONFLICTS, DISSENTER STRUGGLE WITH UNIONS' POLICY AND CONTROL ARE DETAILED AGAINST AN EVALUATION OF UNION DEMOCRACY AND THE ROLE OF THE LAW.

2513 SUMMERS C.W.
"UNION POWERS AND WORKERS RIGHTS."
MICH. LAW REV., 49 (APR. 51), 805-838.
AN EXAMINATION OF THE RELATIONSHIP BETWEEN UNIONS AND INDIVIDUAL WORKERS, WITH SUGGESTIONS OF INDIVIDUAL RIGHTS DEMANDED BY THAT RELATIONSHIP. CRITICIZES PRESENT STATE OF UNION GOVERNMENT, THE COMPLETENESS OF THE UNIONS' POWER TO BIND INDIVIDUALS IN REPRESENTATIVE PROCESSES, AND RESTRICTIONS ON MEMBERS' RIGHTS.

2514 SUMNER W.G.
WAR AND OTHER ESSAYS.
NEW HAVEN: YALE U PR, 1919, 381 PP.
SERIES OF ESSAYS IN WHICH AUTHOR ARGUES FOR FREE TRADE, AN END TO AMERICAN IMPERIALISM, AND AGAINST WAR. HE ARGUES FROM A SOCIOLOGICAL VIEWPOINT AND FEELS THAT IF MEN COULD FREELY TRADE WITH ONE ANOTHER THEY WOULD FIND PACIFIC MEANS FOR SETTLING THEIR DISPUTES. ALSO FEELS THAT THE PRINCIPLES OF AMERICAN DEMOCRACY DEMAND NOT ONLY FREEDOM AND EQUALITY BUT THE WILL TO LET OTHER NATIONS DETERMINE THEIR PATHS.

2516 SURANYI-UNGER T.
PRIVATE ENTERPRISE AND GOVERNMENTAL PLANNING.
NEW YORK: MCGRAW HILL, 1950, 389 PP.
STARTING WITH A DISCUSSION OF INDIVIDUAL AND GROUP "WANTS" AND A HIERARCHY OF "WANTS," THEIR SATISFACTION THROUGH PRIVATE OR SEMI-PUBLIC GROUP, AND PARTIAL COLLECTIVE PLANNING, AUTHOR ASKS QUESTIONS ABOUT OPTIMAL EXTENT OF

COLLECTIVE PLANNING, STRUCTURAL TRANSFORMATIONS, COORDINATION OF PRIVATE AND PUBLIC PLANNING REPRIVATIZATION OF WELFARE WITH STATISTICAL, ECONOMIC, AND MATHEMATICAL ANALYSIS.

2517 SURANYI-UNGER T.
COMPARATIVE ECONOMIC SYSTEMS.
NEW YORK: MCGRAW HILL, 1952, 628 PP., LC#52-7446.
STRESSES INTERMEDIATE ECONOMIC SYSTEMS AND TRANSITIONS AMONG THEM RATHER THAN EXTREME CASES. EXAMINES RELATION OF WESTERN FREEDOM TO EASTERN PLANNING AND COORDINATION OF FREEDOM AND PLANNING; DISCUSSES APPROACHES TO STUDY OF ECONOMIC SYSTEMS, THE SOCIAL PREMISES OF ECONOMIC SYSTEMS. CONCLUDES WITH ANALYSIS OF ECONOMIC CONCEPTS AND FUNCTIONS. SUGGESTED READINGS FOLLOW EACH CHAPTER.

2518 SURREY S.S.
"THE CONGRESS AND THE TAX LOBBYIST - HOW SPECIAL TAX PROVISIONS GET ENACTED."
HARVARD LAW REV., 7 (MAY 57), 1145-1182.
THE INSTITUTIONAL FACTORS IN THE TAX LEGISLATIVE PROCESS DIFFER FROM THOSE IN OTHER LEGISLATIVE PROCESSES. THE CONGRESSMAN'S DESIRE TO BE HELPFUL CAUSES DEPARTURES FROM FAIRNESS. THE TREASURY DEPARTMENT DOES NOT RESPOND EFFECTIVELY TO DEMANDS FOR SPECIAL TREATMENT ALTHOUGH IT IS THE ONLY CHAMPION OF TAX FAIRNESS.

2519 SWEEZY P.M.
THE THEORY OF CAPITALIST DEVELOPMENT.
NEW YORK: OXFORD U PR, 1942, 398 PP.
ANALYTICAL STUDY OF MARXIAN POLITICAL ECONOMY, INCLUDING SECTIONS ON VALUE, ACCUMULATION PROCESS, CRISES AND DEPRESSIONS, AND IMPERIALISM.

2520 SYMONS L.
AGRICULTURAL GEOGRAPHY.
NEW YORK: FREDERICK PRAEGER, 1967, 283 PP., LC#67-12296.
CONSIDERATION OF PHYSICAL, SOCIAL, AND ECONOMIC FACTORS WHICH INFLUENCE THE DEVELOPMENT OF AGRICULTURE. SOME REGIONAL ANALYSIS, AND ILLUSTRATIONS OF PRINCIPLES BY TYPES OF AGRICULTURE.

2521 TABORSKY E.
"THE CLASS STRUGGLE, THE PROLETARIAT, AND THE DEVELOPING NATIONS."
REV. OF POLITICS, 29 (JULY 67), 371-386.
DISCUSSES MARXIST-LENINIST IDEOLOGY AND STRATEGY OF CLASS STRUGGLE AND LEADERSHIP OF THE PROLETARIAT. SHOWS THAT SOVIET THEORETICIANS DEEM THESE PRINCIPLES MOST APPLICABLE TO DEVELOPING NATIONS. DESCRIBES METHODS SOVIETS ARE EMPLOYING IN ENCOURAGING "THIRD WORLD" CLASS STRUGGLE.

2522 TAEUBER I.B.
POPULATION TRENDS IN THE UNITED STATES: 1900 TO 1960.
WASHINGTON: US GOVERNMENT, 1964, 416 PP., LC#64-7759.
TECHNICAL PAPER PROVIDES DATA ON THE GROWTH AND CHARACTERISTICS OF US POPULATION FROM THE SEVEN DECENNIAL CENSUSES OF THE 20TH CENTURY. GIVES DATA ON US POPULATION BY SIZE OF PLACE, METROPOLITAN STATUS, AND DEMOGRAPHIC, SOCIAL, AND ECONOMIC CHARACTERISTICS. POPULATION DIVIDED BY AGE, URBAN-RURAL AND FARM-NONFARM RESIDENCE, RACE AND COLOR, NATIVITY AND PARENTAGE, OCCUPATION, EDUCATION, INCOME, ETC.

2524 TAFT P.
THE STRUCTURE AND GOVERNMENT OF LABOR UNIONS.
CAMBRIDGE: HARVARD U PR, 1954, 312 PP., LC#54-8633.
A WELL-KNOWN TEXT ON UNION GOVERNMENT, DEALING WITH INITIATION FEES AND DUES, CONTESTED ELECTIONS FOR OFFICES, DISCIPLINARY PENALTIES FOR RULE INFRACTION, AND APPEALS THEREFROM, AS WELL AS SPECIFIC STUDIES OF FOUR MAJOR UNIONS AND AN EVALUATION OF THE PRESENT STATE OF AMERICAN LABOR UNIONS IN TERMS OF FREEDOM AND UNION MANAGEMENT, CONTRIBUTIONS, FEARS OF DISCIPLINE, AND CONTROL BY COMMUNISTS.

2525 TAFT P.
CORRUPTION AND RACKETEERING IN THE LABOR MOVEMENT (PAMPHLET)
ITHACA: NY STATE SCH IND & LABOR, 1958, 58 PP.
EXAMINES THE CHARGES BEFORE 1900, THE ROLE OF IDEALISM AND UNION DEMOCRACY, CENTRALIZATION, TYPE OF INDUSTRY, AND SIZE IN FOSTERING OR CURBING CORRUPTION AND DESCRIBES MACHINERY FOR CORRECTIVE ACTION, WITH SUGGESTIONS FOR REMEDYING ABUSES SUCH AS REGULATION OF CONFLICT OF INTEREST AND THE ADMINISTRATION OF HEALTH AND WELFARE FUNDS.

2526 TAGLIACOZZO D.L.
"TRADE-UNION GOVERNMENT, ITS NATURE AND ITS PROBLEMS: A BIBLIOGRAPHICAL REVIEW, 1945-1955."
AMER. J. OF SOCIOLOGY, 61 (MAY 56), 554-581.
A CLASSIFICATION OF THE LITERATURE INTO THEORY AND METHOD, TRADE-UNION GOVERNMENT (INCLUDING THE QUESTION OF DEMOCRACY, FACTIONALISM, DISCIPLINE, ADMISSION TO MEMBERSHIP), RANK AND FILE (INCLUDING PARTICIPATION), UNION LEADERSHIP, AND COLLECTIVE BARGAINING. GIVES 429 ITEMS.

2527 TAINE H.A.
THE ANCIENT REGIME.
ORIGINAL PUBLISHER NOT AVAILABLE, 1876, 421 PP.
AUTHOR EXAMINES CONTEMPORARY FRANCE IN LIGHT OF PRE-REVOLUTIONARY FRANCE. UTILIZING TAX RECORDS, DIARIES, AND GOVERNMENT DOCUMENTS, HE SHOWS THE SOCIAL, POLITICAL, AND ECONOMIC FABRIC OF THE OLD REGIME. HE POINTS OUT THE WEAK SPOTS, SUCH AS THE UNBALANCED TAX STRUCTURE AND DISAFFECTION IN THE ARMY. HIS PORTRAYALS OF PEASANT LIFE AND THE FLIRTATION WITH LIBERALISM SHOW WHY REVOLUTION WAS INEVITABLE.

2528 TANDON Y.
"CONSENSUS AND AUTHORITY BEHIND UNITED NATIONS PEACEKEEPING OPERATIONS."
INTL. ORGANIZATION, 21 (SPRING 67), 254-283.
REVIEWS NATURE OF CONSENSUS AND BASIS FOR PEACEKEEPING OPERATIONS OF UN BY ANALYZING ALL PEACEKEEPING SUBORGANS SET UP SINCE ½(:'. RESOLVES FINANCIAL CRISIS THAT OCCURRED AT 1964-65 SESSION WHEN SEVERAL MEMBERS REFUSED TO PAY FOR PEACEKEEPING OPERATIONS IN WORLD, THEREBY CHALLENGING LEGITIMACY OF ENTIRE PROGRAM.

2529 TANNENBAUM A.S.
"CONTROL OF STRUCTURE AND UNION FUNCTIONS."
AMER. J. OF SOCIOLOGY, 61 (MAY 56), 536-545.
ONE OF FIVE PAPERS ON UNION DEMOCRACY IN MAY, 1956, ISSUE. BASED ON A STUDY OF FOUR UNIONS OF INDUSTRIAL TYPE IN MICHIGAN, IT DISCUSSES CONTROL, EMPLOYING FOUR HIERARCHICAL LEVELS, RELATING IT TO IDEOLOGY, UNION-MANAGEMENT CONFLICT, AND MEMBERSHIP LOYALTY.

2530 TANNENBAUM A.S., KAHN R.L.
"ORGANIZATIONAL CONTROL STRUCTURE: A GENERAL DESCRIPTIVE TECHNIQUE AS APPLIED TO FOUR LOCAL UNIONS."
HUMAN RELATIONS, 10 (1957), 127-140.
AN ELABORATION OF "CONTROL GRAPHS" AND DISTRIBUTION OF CONTROL IN FOUR LOCAL UNIONS, SPECIALTIES OF TANNENBAUM. DESCRIBES FOUR TYPES OF CONTROL GRAPHS DEALING WITH VARIOUS HIERARCHICAL LEVELS, AND THEIR APPLICATION TO RESULTS OBTAINED BY QUESTIONNAIRES. SUGGESTS FURTHER USES SUCH AS THE GAUGING OF MEMBER ATTITUDES BY PLOTTING ACTUAL AND DESIRED AMOUNT OF CONTROL OVER HIERARCHICAL STRUCTURE.

2531 TANNENBAUM A.S., KAHN R.L.
PARTICIPATION IN UNION LOCALS.
EVANSTON: ROW-PETERSON, 1958, 275 PP., LC#58-10219.
STUDY OF FOUR UNION LOCALS TO DETERMINE BEHAVIOR OF ACTIVE AND INACTIVE MEMBERS; FACTORS OF SOCIAL LIFE; LOYALTY; TIME; LEISURE; STATUS; ORIENTATION TOWARD MANAGEMENT; IDEOLOGY; AND LEADERSHIP. ANALYZES CONTROL FACTORS BOTH WITHIN AND OUTSIDE LOCAL UNION, AND HOW THESE HELP DETERMINE PARTICIPATION.

2532 TANNENBAUM F.
PEACE BY REVOLUTION.
NEW YORK: COLUMBIA U PRESS, 1933, 310 PP.
DEVELOPMENT OF MEXICAN REVOLUTION, ANALYZING ITS BACKGROUND IN CULTURE, RACE RELATIONS, ECONOMIC NECESSITY, EDUCATION, AND POLITICS, AND ITS HERITAGE IN MODERN MEXICO'S GOVERNMENT, POLICIES, AND POLITICS. IMPORTANCE OF THE INDIAN IN MEXICAN HISTORY IS DISCUSSED.

2533 TANNENBAUM F.
A PHILOSOPHY OF LABOR.
NEW YORK: ALFRED KNOPF, 1952, 199 PP.
CONTENDS THAT TRADE-UNIONISM IS CONSERVATIVE AND COUNTERREVOLUTIONARY. IMPORTANT ROLE OF UNIONS HAS BEEN IN HELPING WORKERS TO MAKE THE TRANSITION FROM A SIMPLE SOCIETY TO A COMPLEX, INDUSTRIAL, URBAN SOCIETY. UNIONS ARE COUNTERREVOLUTIONARY AND CONSERVATIVE BECAUSE THEIR EMPHASIS IS ON GROUP IDENTITY, NOT INDIVIDUALISM; AND THEY ARE CONCERNED WITH VALUES RATHER THAN IDEOLOGIES.

2534 TANSKY L.
US AND USSR AID TO DEVELOPING COUNTRIES.
NEW YORK: FREDERICK PRAEGER, 1967, 192 PP., LC#66-26574.
COMPARISION OF FOREIGN AID PROGRAMS OF US AND USSR COVERING OBJECTIVES, MAGNITUDE, DISTRIBUTION, TYPES OF AID PROVIDED. SPECIFIC CASES OF 3 COUNTRIES AND DETAILED INFORMATION ON AID RECEIVED, WHERE ONE COUNTRY WAS US SATELLITE, ONE USSR SATELLITE, AND THE OTHER NEUTRAL. DISCUSSION OF IDEOLOGICAL ATTACHMENTS.

2535 TANSKY L.
US AND USSR AID TO DEVELOPING COUNTRIES.
NEW YORK: FREDERICK PRAEGER, 1966, 192 PP., LC#66-26574.
COMPARES ALL AREAS OF RUSSIAN AND US FOREIGN AID: MAGNITUDE AND GEOGRAPHIC DISTRIBUTION, OBJECTIVES, FINANCIAL DISTRIBUTION METHODS, CREDIT SYSTEMS. CASE STUDIES OF TURKEY, INDIA, AND UAR SHOW DIFFERENCES IN METHODS, IMPACT, AND EFFECT. DISCUSSES TRENDS OF AID PROGRAMS IN BOTH COUNTRIES.

2536 TAWNEY R.H.
THE ACQUISITIVE SOCIETY.
NEW YORK: HARCOURT BRACE, 1920, 188 PP.
BELIEVES THAT ANY SOCIETAL REFORMS MUST BE BASED UPON PRINCIPLES, BUT SOCIETY BASED UPON INDUSTRIAL ACQUISITION DOES NOT WANT TO HAVE RECOURSE TO MORALS. BELIEVES PRINCIPLES OF INDUSTRY COULD BE SIMPLE BECAUSE ITS FUNCTION IS A

SERVICE. INDUSTRY SHOULD BE SUBORDINATED TO THE COMMUNITY SO AS TO RENDER BEST SERVICE POSSIBLE. ITS DIRECTION SHOULD BE IN HANDS OF PERSONS RESPONSIBLE TO CITIZENRY.

2537 TAWNEY R.H.
RELIGION AND THE RISE OF CAPITALISM.
NEW YORK: HARCOURT BRACE, 1926, 336 PP.
TRACES DEVELOPMENT OF RELIGIOUS THOUGHT ON SOCIAL AND ECONOMIC MATTERS IN PERIOD OF TRANSITION FROM FEUDALISM TO INDUSTRIALISM. DISCUSSES MEDIEVAL BACKGROUND, REFORMS ON THE CONTINENT, CHURCH OF ENGLAND, AND PURITAN MOVEMENT AS INFLUENTIAL IN AFFECTING CAPITALISM.

2538 TAWNEY R.H.
EQUALITY.
LONDON: ALLEN & UNWIN, 1964, 248 PP.
ATTACKS NOTION OF BRITISH EQUALITY, CLAIMING THAT INSTEAD OF BECOMING LESS STRATIFIED, BRITISH SOCIETY HAS BECOME EVEN MORE SO. POINTS TO INHERITED WEALTH AND EDUCATIONAL SYSTEM AS MAJOR FLAWS IN ATTEMPTS AT IMPLEMENTING EQUALITY. ADVOCATES REMOVAL OF SOCIAL AND ECONOMIC INEQUALITIES, EQUAL EDUCATION FOR ALL CHILDREN, AND EQUALIZING ACCESS TO IMPORTANT GOODS AND SERVICES.

2539 TAX S.
EL CAPITALISMO DEL CENTAVO; UNA ECONOMIA INDIGENA DE GUATEMALA (2 VOLS.)
GUATEMALA CITY: CENTRO EDITORIAL, 1964, 579 PP.
COMPARES STRUCTURE AND OPERATION OF PRIMITIVE RURAL ECONOMY IN RELATION TO MODERN SYSTEM IN URBAN GUATEMALA. DISCUSSES AGRICULTURAL BASIS OF SOCIETY AND FORM OF EXCHANGE AND CONSUMPTION OF MAINLY INDIAN POPULATION OF BACKLANDS. EXAMINES BASIS OF WEALTH AND LEVEL AND COST OF LIVING OF AREA.

2540 TAYLOR P.E.
THE ECONOMICS OF PUBLIC FINANCE.
NEW YORK: MACMILLAN, 1948, 617 PP.
CONCERNED WITH THEORY AND POLICY OF FINANCING BY US GOVERNMENT SINCE WWI. STUDY FOCUSES ON TAXES AS PRIMARY SOURCE OF REVENUE. AFTER INTRODUCTORY SURVEY OF FIELD, EXAMINES BUDGETING, PUBLIC EXPENDITURES, PUBLIC DEBT, AND SOURCES OF REVENUE. STUDY OF TAXATION INCLUDES OBJECTIVES AND ALLOCATION, PERSONAL, PROPERTY, AND SALES TAXES. CLOSES WITH CASE FOR AND AGAINST COMPENSATORY FISCAL POLICY.

2541 TEITSWORTH C.S.
"GROWING ROLE OF THE COMPANY ECONOMIST."
HARVARD BUSINESS REV., 37 (JAN.-FEB. 59), 97-104.
EXPLORES THE EXTENT TO WHICH THE ECONOMIST HAS INSERTED HIMSELF INTO LARGE CORPORATIONS. DEVELOPS THE INCREASING INFLUENCE OF ECONOMISTS ON THE DECISION-MAKING OF MANAGEMENT. CONCLUDES THAT IN ORDER TO RETAIN THE HIGH STANDARD OF LIVING IN THE US, BIG BUSINESS WILL HAVE TO USE MORE ECONOMISTS TO AID IT IN PLANNING FOR THE FUTURE.

2542 TELLADO A.
A STATEMENT OF THE LAWS OF THE DOMINICAN REPUBLIC IN MATTERS AFFECTING BUSINESS (3RD ED.)
WASHINGTON: PAN AMERICAN UNION, 1964.
SURVEY OF BASIC LEGISLATION EMPHASIZING NATIONALITY AND IMMIGRATION, CONTRACTS, AND ADMINISTRATION OF JUSTICE. ALSO INCLUDES PATENTS, TRADEMARKS, AND COPYRIGHT.

2543 TELLER A.
"AIR-POLLUTION ABATEMENT: ECONOMIC RATIONALITY AND REALITY."
DAEDALUS, 96 (FALL 67), 1082-1098.
DISCUSSES COST OF AIR-POLLUTION ABATEMENT AND PROBLEM OF WEIGHING COST AGAINST EFFECTIVENESS OF VARIOUS METHODS. STUDIES DISEASES BELIEVED TO BE CAUSED BY POLLUTION. STATES THAT EACH CITY MUST DECIDE ON ITS OWN METHODS, BUT FEDERAL GOVERNMENT CAN SERVE AS CENTER FOR INFORMATION AND CAN ASSIST IN ORGANIZING INTERSTATE AIR-POLLUTION COMMISSIONS.

2544 TENDLER J.D.
"TECHNOLOGY AND ECONOMIC DEVELOPMENT* THE CASE OF HYDRO VS THERMAL POWER."
POLIT. SCI. QUART., 80 (JUNE 65), 236-253.
A COMPARISON OF ARGENTINE AND BRAZILIAN EXPERIENCES IN THE DEVELOPMENT OF PUBLIC POWER FACILITIES OVER THE LAST TWO DECADES. ADVISES THAT THE DEVELOPMENT OF ELECTRIC CAPACITY THROUGH HYDRO POWER, WHILE ORIGINALLY MORE EXPENSIVE, IS IN LONG RUN BETTER FOR THE DEVELOPING COUNTRY BECAUSE IT PROMOTES LOCAL INDUSTRY, SKILLS AND INTEGRATION RATHER THAN HIGH TECHNOLOGY IMPORTS NECESSITATED BY THERMAL SYSTEMS.

2545 TENNYSON L.B.
"THE USA IN ATLANTIC COMMUNITY."
CURR. HIST., 45 (NOV. 63), 264-270.
USA POLICY APPRAISED AS BEING BASICALLY SOUND. POINTS OUT THAT STRATEGY REMAINS THE SAME - ONLY TACTICS HAVE CHANGED. USA HAS WISELY RESISTED THE TEMPTATIONS TO: MAKE DE GAULLE THE SCAPEGOAT, RENEW MUTUALLY EXCLUSIVE USA-BRITISH POLICIES AND 'PLAYING OFF' THE 5 NATIONS OF EEC AGAINST FRANCE.

2546 TEW B.
WEALTH AND INCOME.
MELBOURNE: MELBOURNE UNIV PRESS, 1965, 223 PP.
ANALYZES ECONOMIC AND FINANCIAL SYSTEMS OF BRITAIN AND AUSTRALIA. EMPHASIZES CONTEMPORARY PROBLEMS SUCH AS INFLATION, UNEMPLOYMENT, AND RELATIONS BETWEEN "MOTHER COUNTRY AND WORLD." SETS UP SYSTEM OF PAPER MONEY AND NOTES AS BASIS FOR ALL EXCHANGES AND APPLIES SYSTEM TO CURRENT FUNCTIONS BETWEEN TWO NATIONS.

2547 THAILAND NATIONAL ECO DEV
THE NATIONAL ECONOMIC DEVELOPMENT PLAN: 1961-66: SECOND PHASE 1964-66.
BANGKOK: THAINATL ECO DEV BOARD, 1964, 214 PP.
REPORT OF PROPOSED PLAN FOR ECONOMY FOR 1964-66. COVERS PROGRESS OF PHASE ONE OF PLAN AND REVISIONS NECESSARY FOR PHASE TWO. STUDIES SPECIFIC SECTOR PROGRAMS THAT WILL BE CARRIED OUT IN PERIOD, IN FIELDS OF TRANSPORTATION, WELFARE, EDUCATION ETC. GOAL IS TO RAISE PER CAPITA INCOME THREE PER CENT PER YEAR. STRESSES GOVERNMENT SPENDING IN PRIVATE SECTORS OF ECONOMY.

2548 THAYER F.C. JR.
AIR TRANSPORT POLICY AND NATIONAL SECURITY: A POLITICAL, ECONOMIC, AND MILITARY ANALYSIS.
CHAPEL HILL: U OF N CAR PR, 1965, 352 PP., LC#65-25600.
HISTORICAL ACCOUNT OF NATURE AND DEVELOPMENT OF MILITARY AND COMMERCIAL LONG-HAUL AIRLIFT SYSTEMS. DISCUSSES NATIONAL AND INTERNATIONAL POLICY BEFORE WORLD WAR II TO PRESENT, AND RELATIONS BETWEEN MILITARY AND PRIVATE USE FROM ECONOMIC AND DEFENSE VIEWPOINTS. SUGGESTS VARIOUS REVISIONS TO AIRLINE REGULATORY PROCESS AND REFINEMENTS OF ECONOMIC THEORY. COMMENTS ON SPECIFIC MILITARY STRATEGIES FOR 1960'S.

2549 THE BROOKINGS INSTITUTION
ECONOMICS AND THE POLICY MAKER.
WASHINGTON: BROOKINGS INST, 1959, 209 PP., LC#59-15669.
SERIES OF LECTURES ON USE OF ECONOMIC ANALYSIS BY POLICY MAKERS TO SOLVE PROBLEMS OF PUBLIC AND PRIVATE ORGANIZATIONS SUCH AS STABILIZATION, INFLATION, TAX AND CREDIT POLICIES, COLLECTIVE BARGAINING, COMPETITION AND MONOPOLY, AND ECONOMIC DEVELOPMENT.

2550 THE ECONOMIST (LONDON)
THE COMMONWEALTH AND EUROPE.
LONDON: ECONOMIST INTELLIG UNIT, 1960, 606 PP.
COLLECTION AND ANALYSIS OF FACTS RELEVANT TO PATTERNS OF TRADE IN COMMONWEALTH AND EEC. INCLUDES CHAPTERS ON PRODUCTION AND TRADE OF FOODSTUFFS, RAW MATERIALS, MANUFACTURES. ANALYZES TRADE SYSTEMS IN "OLDER DOMINIONS" OF THE COMMONWEALTH, ASIAN MEMBERS, TROPICAL AFRICA, AND WEST INDIES.

2551 THEIL H.
ECONOMIC FORECASTS AND POLICY.
AMSTERDAM: NORTH HOLLAND PUBL CO, 1958, 562 PP.
DEALS WITH THREE ISSUES IN ECONOMETRIC MODEL-BUILDING: THAT OF PREDICTIVE QUALITY OF MODELS, THAT OF RELATIONSHIP BETWEEN DECISION-MAKING AND ECONOMETRIC MODEL USED TO FORMULATE PREDICTIVE STATEMENTS, AND THAT OF STATISTICAL NATURE, CONCERNED WITH ESTIMATIONS OF SYSTEMS OF SIMULTANEOUS EQUATIONS.

2552 THEIL H.
APPLIED ECONOMIC FORECASTING.
SKOKIE: RAND MCNALLY & CO, 1966, 474 PP.
SURVEY OF RESULTS OF ECONOMIC PREDICTION METHODS. STUDY INCLUDES METHODS OF MEASURING ACCURACY OF POINT PREDICTIONS, COMPARISON OF CONDITIONAL AND UNCONDITIONAL PREDICTIONS, PREDICTING THE FUTURE AND ESTIMATING THE PAST, INPUT-OUTPUT PREDICTIONS OF IMMEDIATE DEMAND, BASICS OF INFORMATION APPROACH, ANALYSIS OF NO-CHANGE AND OF QUANTIFICATION, AND ECONOMETRIC ANALYSIS BASED ON SURVEY DATA.

2553 THEOBALD R.
THE RICH AND THE POOR: A STUDY OF THE ECONOMICS OF RISING EXPECTATIONS.
NEW YORK: POTTER, 1960, 196 PP.
EXAMINES DIFFERENT PROBLEMS ENCOUNTERED IN RAISING LIVING STANDARDS AND HOW THESE PROBLEMS COMPLICATE WORLD TRADE. ANALYZES ECONOMIC SYSTEMS OF MODERN WORLD AND THEIR THEORETICAL BASES.

2554 THEOBALD R.
THE CHALLENGE OF ABUNDANCE.
NEW YORK: CLARKSON N POTTER, 1961, 235 PP., LC#61-11426.
SETS OUT IMPLICATIONS OF CONTINUING ECONOMIC AND SOCIAL REVOLUTIONS AND SUGGESTS NECESSARY CHANGES IN POLICY. THE US AS DEVELOPED NATION MUST RECOGNIZE NEEDS OF POOR COUNTRIES. RECOGNIZES NECESSITY OF WORLD CITIZENSHIP.

2555 THEOBALD R.
NATIONAL DEVELOPMENT EFFORTS (PAMPHLET)
NEW YORK: UNITED NATIONS, 1962, 67 PP.
EXAMINES PLANS AND ACTIONS OF UNDERDEVELOPED NATIONS TO IMPROVE THEIR ECONOMIC CONDITIONS. DISCUSSES PLANNING, ED-

UCATION, INDUSTRY, AGRICULTURE, INFLATION, BALANCE-OF-PAYMENTS, INVESTMENT, AND TAXATION.

2556 THEOBALD R.
FREE MEN AND FREE MARKETS.
NEW YORK: CLARKSON N POTTER, 1963, 207 PP., LC#63-18879.
RELATES DEVELOPMENT OF FREE MARKETING TO PERSONAL FREEDOM IN AFFLUENT AMERICA AND PREDICTS FUTURE OF FREE MARKETING IN EVER-INCREASING INTERACTION OF WORLD ECONOMIES. TRACES PROGRESS AND ANALYZES BEGINNINGS OF ECONOMIC CONTROL IN US.

2557 THEROUX P.
"HATING THE ASIANS."
TRANSITION, 7 (OCT.-NOV. 67), 46-52.
EXAMINES ROLE OF ASIANS IN AFRICA AND SOURCES OF DEEP HATRED THAT NATIVES BEAR TOWARD THEM. DECRIES RACISM THAT IS RESULTING IN MASS EXODUS OF ASIANS FROM KENYA, UGANDA, AND TANZANIA. POINTS OUT CONTRIBUTIONS OF ASIANS IN POLITICAL, ECONOMIC, AND CULTURAL AREAS. CRITICIZES GROWING ANTI-ASIAN FEELINGS.

2558 THIESENHUSEN W.C.
CHILE'S EXPERIMENTS IN AGRARIAN REFORM.
MADISON: U OF WISCONSIN PR, 1966, 230 PP., LC#66-29119.
ANALYZES LAND REFORM EXPERIMENTS IN CHILE, WHERE TRADITIONAL AGRARIAN STRUGGLE STILL DOMINATES. CONSIDERING FOUR LARGE FARMS THAT WERE COLONIZED, ISOLATES MAJOR FACTORS FOR THE SUCCESS OR FAILURE OF THE SHARECROPPER COLONISTS. STUDY IS PREDICATED ON THE IDEA THAT WHEN A MORE INCLUSIVE REFORM COMES, TECHNICIANS WILL BE AIDED BY STUDIES OF HOW SMALL-SCALE REFORM WORKS.

2559 THOMAN R.S., CONKLING E.C.
GEOGRAPHY OF INTERNATIONAL TRADE.
ENGLEWOOD CLIFFS: PRENTICE HALL, 1967, 186 PP., LC#67-18931.
TRENDS, PATTERNS, AND PROBLEMS OF INTERNATIONAL TRADE WITH RELATIVELY LITTLE EMPHASIS ON GEOGRAPHIC ASPECTS OF THIS TRADE. EXTENSIVE USE OF CHARTS BUT MOST ARE DESCRIPTIVE IN NATURE. EMPHASIS ON TRADE PATTERNS OF IDEOLOGICALLY OR ECONOMICALLY RELATED NATIONS AND ON LOGISTICS OF TRADING CONCERNS, COMMERCIAL CENTERS, COUNTRIES, AND INTERNATIONAL ORGANIZATIONS.

2560 THOMAS D.S.
"AGE AND ECONOMIC DIFFERENTIALS IN INTERSTATE MIGRATION."
POPULATION INDEX, 24 (OCT. 58), 313-325.
PRESENTS UNPUBLISHED SUMMARIES OF DATA PREPARED BY THE UNIV. OF PENN. STUDY OF POPULATION REDISTRIBUTION AND GROWTH TOGETHER WITH DATA OBTAINED FROM 1940 CENSUS AND FROM VARIOUS CURRENT POPULATION SURVEYS. DATA PERTAIN TO AGE DIFFERENTIALS BY SEX IN INTERSTATE MIGRATION. THEY ARE LIMITED TO NATIONAL SUMMARIES AND GIVE NO REGIONAL DETAIL.

2561 THOMAS J.A.
THE HOUSE OF COMMONS, 1832-1901; A STUDY OF ITS ECONOMIC AND FUNCTIONAL CHARACTER.
CARDIFF: U OF WALES PRESS, 1939, 176 PP.
ANALYZES FUNCTIONS OF HOUSE OF COMMONS, ITS STRUCTURE, AND COMPOSITION. DISCUSSES ITS LAW-MAKING POWER, DOMESTIC AND INTERNATIONAL POLICY, LEADERSHIP, AND SEGMENTS OF SOCIETY IT REPRESENTS. EXAMINES THEORY AND BEHAVIOR OF ITS MEMBERS, SIGNIFICANT LEGISLATION, AND ECONOMIC POLICY AND POWERS. CONCENTRATES ON MEASURES TO INCREASE STATE CONTROL OVER INDIVIDUALS AND PROPERTY.

2562 THOMAS M.J. ED.
PRESIDENTIAL STATEMENTS ON EDUCATION: EXCERPTS FROM INAUGURAL AND STATE OF THE UNION MESSAGES 1789-1967.
PITTSBURGH: UNIVERSITY PR, 1967, 155 PP., LC#67-18695.
COLLECTS AND DISCUSSES PRESIDENTIAL STATEMENTS ON EDUCATION. SHOWS THAT FIRST SIX PRESIDENTS CALLED UPON FEDERAL AUTHORITY TO SUPPORT ESTABLISHMENT OF SCHOOLS "IN ORDER TO FORM A MORE PERFECT UNION AND TO PROMOTE GENERAL WELFARE." LATE 19TH-CENTURY PRESIDENTS UNSUCCESSFULLY APPEALED TO CONGRESS. FEELS THAT PRESIDENT JOHNSON IS REALIZING DREAM OF FOUNDING FATHERS.

2563 THOMAS R.G.
OUR MODERN BANKING AND MONETARY SYSTEM (3RD ED.)
ENGLEWOOD CLIFFS: PRENTICE HALL, 1957, 644 PP., LC#57-6256.
DESCRIBES THEORY AND PRACTICE OF OUR MONEY AND BANKING SYSTEMS. APPLIES MONETARY AND BANKING THEORY TO CURRENT DOMESTIC AND INTERNATIONAL PROBLEMS. PROVIDES INSTITUTIONAL BACKGROUND FOR STUDY OF CENTRAL BANK AND MONETARY THEORY. DISCUSSES MONEY SUPPLY AND DEMAND, AND EFFECT ON INCOME, OUTPUT, AND PRICES. EXPLORES MONETARY POLICY; DISCUSSES BALANCE OF PAYMENTS AND PROBLEMS OF DOMESTIC STABILITY.

2564 THOMPSON C.D.
CONFESSIONS OF THE POWER TRUST.
NEW YORK: EP DUTTON, 1932, 670 PP.
A REVIEW OF THE HEARINGS OF THE FEDERAL TRADE COMMISSION ON UTILITY CORPORATIONS PURSUANT TO RESOLUTION NO. 83 OF THE US SENATE, APPROVED FEBRUARY 15, 1928. AUTHOR ATTEMPTS TO SUMMARIZE AND ORGANIZE INTO CHAPTERS FOUR YEARS OF TESTIMONY. ATTEMPTS TO GIVE A COMPLETE PICTURE OF THE METHODS, OPERATIONS, AND ACTIVITIES OF THE UTILITIES COMPANIES. ALSO SHOWS FINANCIAL METHODS AND OPERATIONS.

2565 THOMPSON J.H. ED., REISCHAUER R.D. ED.
MODERNIZATION OF THE ARAB WORLD.
PRINCETON: VAN NOSTRAND, 1966, 249 PP.
DIVERSE OPINIONS ON AND APPROACHES TO STUDY OF MODERN ARAB WORLD. EXAMINES INTERACTIONS OF TRADITIONAL PAST, CURRENT REALITIES, AND FUTURE EXPECTATIONS. EXPLORES IMPEDING AND POSITIVE ELEMENTS OF PAST, PROBLEMS OF ECONOMIC GROWTH, INTRA-ARAB AND ARAB-ISRAELI RELATIONS, POPULATION, AND SOCIAL INSTABILITY. COMPARES PROCESS OF MODERNIZATION IN ARAB COUNTRIES AND GIVES REASONS FOR DIFFERENCES.

2566 THOMPSON V.A.
THE REGULATORY PROCESS IN OPA RATIONING.
NEW YORK: KINGS CROWN PR, 1960, 466 PP.
STUDY OF HOW OPA MADE RATIONING RULES. DISCUSSES ROLES OF COMMITTEES, PRESSURE GROUPS, AND CONGRESS.

2567 THOMPSON W.R.
POPULATION PROBLEMS.
NEW YORK: MCGRAW HILL, 1930, 471 PP.
STUDIES POPULATION CONTROLS OF PRECEDING GENERATIONS. DISCUSSES THE COMPOSITION OF POPULATION AND CITIES FACTORS INHERENT IN DECLINE OF BIRTH RATE. ENJOINS LEADERS TO BASE POLICIES ON MODEL ANALOGOUS TO ECONOMIC EFFICIENCY.

2568 THOMPSON W.S.
"POPULATION AND PROGRESS IN THE FAR EAST."
CHICAGO: U. CHI. PR., 1959, 443 PP.
INCREASED LIFE EXPECTANCY HAS LED TO UNPRECEDENTED GROWTH OF POPULATION WHICH HINDERS ECONOMIC EFFICIENCY. POLITICAL IMPLICATIONS ARE REFLECTED IN INTERNATIONAL TENSIONS ROOTED IN ECONOMIC PRESSURES. CONVERSELY, INTENSITY OF POVERTY TENDS TO BECOME A CAUSAL FACTOR OF WAR.

2569 THORBECKE E.
THE TENDENCY TOWARDS REGIONALIZATION IN INTERNATIONAL TRADE, 1928-1956.
GENEVA: NIJHOFF, 1960, 223 PP.
ANALYSIS AND INTERPRETATION OF STATISTICS ON STRUCTURE OF WORLD TRADE. POINTS OUT POLITICAL CONTROLS OF PAYMENTS HAVE RESTRICTED TRADE. DISCUSSES GEOGRAPHIC, MONETARY, ECONOMIC, AND POLITICAL FACTORS THAT HAVE EFFECTED TREND TOWARDS TRADE REGIONALIZATION.

2570 THORKELSON H.
"FOOD STAMPS AND HUNGER IN AMERICA."
DISSENT, 14 (JULY-AUG. 67), 479-484.
DESCRIBES CHANGES IN FEDERAL FOOD SUBSIDIES TO POOR FROM SURPLUS FOOD PROGRAM TO FOOD STAMPS, ADMINISTRATION OF NEW PROGRAM, ITS FAILURES AND WEAK POINTS, AND ITS DETRIMENTAL EFFECTS SUCH AS RAISING FOOD COSTS.

2571 THORNTON A.P.
DOCTRINES OF IMPERIALISM.
NEW YORK: JOHN WILEY, 1965, 246 PP., LC#65-27652.
HISTORIAN OUTLINES THE BELIEFS THAT UNDERLIE THE DOCTRINES OF POWER, PROFIT, AND CIVILIZATION WHICH HAVE BEEN THE MOTIVATING DRIVES FOR IMPERIALISM. THE THOUGHT OF THE WORLD'S IMPERIALISTS FROM ROME TO THE US AND USSR ARE PRESENTED, AS WELL AS THE CRITICS OF IMPERIALISM.

2572 TIEBOUT C.M.
THE COMMUNITY ECONOMIC BASE STUDY (PAMPHLET)
NEW YORK: COMM FOR ECO DEV, 1962, 84 PP., LC#62-22333.
EXPLANATION OF ECONOMIC BASE STUDY AS ANALYSIS OF BASIC SOURCES OF EMPLOYMENT AND INCOME ON WHICH LOCAL ECONOMY DEPENDS. DISCUSSES VALUE OF SUCH STUDY FOR COMMUNITIES AND TECHNIQUES OF RESEARCH.

2573 TILLION G.
ALGERIA: THE REALITIES.
NEW YORK: ALFRED KNOPF, 1958, 115 PP., LC#58-10980.
BASED ON AUTHOR'S FIELD WORK IN ALGERIA, DESCRIBES OVERPOPULATED CONDITIONS, ECONOMIC DEGRADATION, AND SOCIAL DECAY OF THE COUNTRY. DISCUSSES COMPARATIVE PROBLEMS OF OVERPOPULATION, COLONIALISM, AND CONSERVATION. PROPOSES A FRANCO-ALGERIAN UNION IN ORDER TO SOLVE ECONOMIC PROBLEMS.

2574 TINBERGEN J.
INTERNATIONAL ECONOMIC INTEGRATION.
AMSTERDAM: ELSEVIER, 1954, 191 PP.
DISCUSSES PRESENT ECONOMIC RELATIONS OF GOVERNMENTS OF DIFFERING ECONOMIC STATUS. ADVOCATES INTERNATIONAL AGENCIES AIDING ECONOMIC INTEGRATION BY REGULATING PUBLIC FINANCE, EMPLOYMENT, RAW MATERIAL MARKETS, TRADE RESTRICTIONS, ETC.

2576 TINBERGEN J.
CENTRAL PLANNING.
NEW HAVEN: YALE U PR, 1964, 150 PP., LC#64-20938.
CENTRAL PLANNING IS A FEATURE OF EVERY INDUSTRIALIZED STATE. PLANNING PROCESS CONFRONTS PROBLEMS OF CENTRALIZATION OF DECISION-MAKING, OF DETERMINING THE ROLES OF INTEREST GROUPS IN DRAWING UP PLAN, OF UTILITY OF FORECASTS.

PRESENTS DATA ON PLANNING PROGRAMS COLLECTED BY QUESTIONNAIRES TO WESTERN,, DEVELOPING, AND COMMUNIST NATIONS. POLICY SHOULD BE CARRIED OUT PARTLY BY SUPERNATIONAL ORGANS.

2577 TIPTON J.B.
"PARTICIPATION OF THE UNITED STATES IN THE INTERNATIONAL LABOR ORGANIZATION."
URBANA: INST. LABOR INDUS. REL./U. ILL., 1959, 150 PP.
ENVISAGES CONSTRUCTIVE ROLE FOR USA IN ILO. RAPID INDUSTRIAL DEVELOPMENT IN EMERGING NATIONS PRESENTS NEW PROBLEMS TO WHICH THE US CAN CONTRIBUTE TO THE SOLUTION FROM HER OWN EXPERIENCE. TREATS SUBJECT OF AUTOMATION AND ITS IMPACT ON LABOR RELATIONS.

2578 TIVEY L.J.
NATIONALISATION IN BRITISH INDUSTRY.
LONDON: JONATHAN CAPE, 1966, 219 PP.
DESCRIBES DEVELOPMENT OF IDEAS ABOUT NATIONALIZATION IN BRITAIN, CIRCUMSTANCES IN WHICH NATIONALIZATION FIRST TOOK PLACE, PARLIAMENTARY PROCESS OF LEGISLATION, AND BASIC STRUCTURE OF PUBLIC CORPORATIONS AS THEY HAVE EMERGED. PICTURES NATIONALIZATION IN PRACTICE AND INDUSTRIAL RECORD OF CORPORATIONS. EXAMINES PROBLEMS OF INTERNAL ORGANIZATION, EXTERNAL RELATIONS, AND CONTROVERSIES OVER NATIONALIZATION.

2579 TOBIN J.
"ECONOMIC GROWTH AS AN OBJECTIVE OF GOVERNMENT POLICY."
AMER. ECO. REVIEW, 54 (MAY 64), 1-20.
DISCUSSES WISDOM OF GROWTH AS AN OBJECTIVE OF GOVERNMENT POLICY. BELIEVES IT SHOULD BE POSSIBLE TO OPPOSE AS WELL AS SUPPORT GROWTH DEPENDING ON JUDGMENTS OF SOCIAL PRIORITIES. ANALYZES ISSUE OF GROWTH VERSUS FULL EMPLOYMENT. PROPOSES THAT STRONGEST REASON FOR ADVOCATING GROWTH POLICY SHOULD BE POSITIVE RETURNS TO A HIGHER SAVING AND INVESTMENT RATIO.

2580 TOMA P.A.
THE POLITICS OF FOOD FOR PEACE; EXECUTIVE-LEGISLATIVE INTERACTION.
TUCSON: U OF ARIZONA PR, 1967, 195 PP., LC#67-20091.
DISCUSSES 1964 SWING IN CONGRESSIONAL ATTITUDES AWAY FROM EXPANSION OF FOOD FOR PEACE PROGRAM. PRESENTS POSSIBLE TRENDS IN US FOREIGN AID POLICY ON QUESTION OF FOOD AID. INVESTIGATES LARGE GOVERNMENT SURPLUSES AND RISING WORLDWIDE FOOD DEFICIT. ANALYZES CONGRESSIONAL DEBATE AND VOTING PATTERNS TO DETERMINE FACTORS AFFECTING CONGRESSIONAL DECISIONS AND RESULTS OF EXECUTIVE SUGGESTIONS ON POLICY.

2581 TONG T.
UNITED STATES DIPLOMACY IN CHINA, 1844-1860.
SEATTLE: U OF WASHINGTON PR, 1964, 332 PP., LC#64-11051.
ANALYSIS OF DIPLOMATIC RELATIONS BETWEEN CHINA AND US IN SPECIFIC PERIOD BEGINNING WITH TREATY OF WANGHIA. DEALS WITH IMPERIALISM IN CHINA AND US ACTIVITIES IN POLITICAL AND TRADE EVENTS DURING PERIOD.

2582 TOWLE L.W.
INTERNATIONAL TRADE AND COMMERCIAL POLICY.
NEW YORK: HARPER, 1947, 780 PP.
STUDIES ECONOMIC BASES OF INTERNATIONAL RELATIONS AND EFFECT ON NATIONAL INCOMES AND NATIONAL PROSPERITY. PRESENTS MAJOR ISSUES OF INTERNATIONAL ECONOMICS AND EXAMINES THEIR EFFECTS ON POLITICS. DISCUSSES METHODOLOGY OF ECONOMIC ANALYSIS.

2583 TRAGER F.N.
"A SELECTED AND ANNOTATED BIBLIOGRAPHY ON ECONOMIC DEVELOPMENT, 1953-1957."
ECO. DEV. AND CULTURAL CHANGE, 6 (JULY 58), 257-329.
AN ANNOTATED BIBLIOGRAPHY OF ECONOMIC DEVELOPMENT. MATERIAL IN ENGLISH-LANGUAGE; RANGING FROM 1953 TO 1957. 409 ENTRIES. BIBLIOGRAPHY DIVIDED INTO SEVEN CLASSES: COUNTRY AND AREA STUDIES, CHARACTERISTICS AND INSTITUTIONAL ORGANIZATION OF UNDERDEVELOPED COUNTRIES, MEASUREMENT AND THEORY OF ECONOMIC GROWTH, POPULATION, LABOR AND URBANIZATION, CAPITAL ACCUMULATION, INVESTMENT, AND PRODUCTIVITY.

2584 TRAVERS H. JR.
"AN EXAMINATION OF THE CAB'S MERGER POLICY."
U. KANSAS LAW J., 15 (MAR. 67), 227-263.
EXAMINES 3 RECENT CASES TO DETERMINE CAB'S POLICY AND STANDARDS FOR DECISION REGARDING AIRLINE MERGERS. DISCUSSES POLICY PRIOR TO 1938, CIVIL AERONAUTICS ACT, ECONOMIC DETERMINANTS OF POLICY, STRUCTURE OF AIRLINES INDUSTRY, COMPETITION, IMPACT OF MERGERS, AND ANTI-MONOPOLY PROVISO. AUTHOR PRESENTS IDEAS FOR REFORM.

2585 TREVES G.
GOVERNMENT ORGANIZATION FOR ECONOMIC DEVELOPMENT (PAMPHLET)
BRUSSELS: INTL INST OF ADMIN SCI, 1963, 82 PP.
ANALYSIS OF REPORTS BY VARIOUS NATIONS ON ECONOMIC DEVELOPMENT POLICY. EXAMINES PLANNING SYSTEMS, INSTRUMENTS, POLICY-MAKING AUTHORITIES, LEGAL BASES, PARLIAMENTARY CONTROLS, AND ADMINISTRATIVE AND FINANCIAL SUPERVISION OF IMPLEMENTATION.

2586 TRIFFIN R.
MONOPOLISTIC COMPETITION AND GENERAL EQUILIBRIUM THEORY.
CAMBRIDGE: HARVARD U PR, 1940, 197 PP.
CONSOLIDATES CURRENT THEORIES ON MONOPOLY AND PRICE-AND-DEMAND. CONCLUDES THAT PRESENT (1940) THEORY IS NOT ADEQUATE FOR THE DEMANDS OF INCREASED INTERNATIONAL TRADE AND THE PROLIFERATION OF GOODS AND SERVICES. ADVOCATES TREATMENT OF ECONOMIC CIRCUMSTANCES AS UNIQUE RATHER THAN AS FITTING A PRESCRIBED SET OF RULES.

2587 TRIFFIN R.
EUROPE AND THE MONEY MUDDLE.
NEW HAVEN: YALE U. PR., 1957, 351 PP.
ANALYZES THREE ASPECTS OF EUROPEAN MONETARY RECOVERY AFTER WORLD WAR TWO: EXISTING PROBLEMS, THE EUROPEAN PAYMENTS UNION, AND PROSPECTS OF CONVERTIBILITY. FAVORS CLOSE REGIONAL COOPERATION.

2588 TRIFFIN R.
GOLD AND THE DOLLAR CRISIS: THE FUTURE OF CONVERTIBILITY.
NEW HAVEN: YALE U PR, 1961, 181 PP., LC#61-11398.
ANALYZES SUCCESS OF 19TH-CENTURY SYSTEM OF "INTERNATIONAL CONVERTIBILITY" AND FAILURE OF SAME SYSTEM IN 1920'S. POINTS OUT REASONS WHY 20TH CENTURY CANNOT REVERT TO 19TH-CENTURY SYSTEM WITHOUT CERTAIN RADICAL INSTITUTIONAL REFORMS.

2589 TRIFFIN R.
THE WORLD MONEY MAZE.
NEW HAVEN: YALE U PR, 1966, 585 PP., LC#66-12516.
ANALYZES INTERNATIONAL MONEY PROBLEMS 1938-64, DOLLAR SHORTAGE, FAILURE OF INTERNATIONAL MONETARY ORGANIZATIONS, AND RECURRENT CRISES IN KEY CURRENCIES: STERLING AND DOLLAR. CRITICIZES MAINTENANCE OF GOLD EXCHANGE STANDARD AND ADVOCATES SYSTEM OF GOVERNMENT CONTROL SUCH AS OEEC, EPU, AND EEC.

2590 TRIFFIN R.
THE BALANCE OF PAYMENTS AND THE FOREIGN INVESTMENT POSITION OF THE UNITED STATES.
PRINCETON: PRINCETON U PRESS, 1966, 34 PP., LC#66-28512.
ANALYZES PROBLEM OF LIQUIDITY IN FOREIGN EXCHANGE ASSETS, ROLE OF DOLLAR AS INTERMEDIARY IN EUROPEAN EXCHANGE, AND METHOD OF DEALING WITH PROBLEM THROUGH INTERNATIONAL ORGANIZATION. DUE TO GOLD STANDARD IN FOREIGN EXCHANGE AND INABILITY OF GOLD PRODUCTION TO KEEP PACE, IT BECOMES NECESSARY TO FIND CREDIT BASE SUCH AS PROPOSED.

2591 TRUE A.C.
A HISTORY OF AGRICULTURAL EXTENSION WORK IN THE UNITED STATES, 1785-1923.
WASHINGTON: US DEPT OF AGRI, 1928, 220 PP.
HISTORY OF MOVEMENT THAT RESULTED IN ESTABLISHMENT OF NATIONAL SYSTEM OF COOPERATIVE AGRICULTURAL EXTENSION WORK FROM 1785-1923. DISCUSSES EARLY FARMERS' INSTITUTES AND OTHER EDUCATIONAL WORKS, FORMATION OF CLUBS FOR YOUTH AND WIVES, AND DEVELOPMENT OF COUNTY-AGENT GROUPS. STUDIES SMITH-LEVER ACT AND OTHER LAWS. DESCRIBES WARTIME AND POSTWAR PROGRAMS.

2592 TUMIN M.M.
SOCIAL STRATIFICATION; THE FORMS AND FUNCTIONS OF INEQUALITY
ENGLEWOOD CLIFFS: PRENTICE HALL, 1967, 118 PP., LC#67-25909.
ANALYZES SOCIAL CONDITIONS WHICH GIVE RISE TO AND SUSTAIN DIFFERENT FORMS AND DEGREES OF SOCIO-ECONOMIC INEQUALITY. STUDIES CONSEQUENCES OF INEQUALITY FOR SOCIETIES. DEFINES BASIC CONCEPTS OF "EVALUATION" AND "REWARD." TREATS FOUR PROCESSES OF STRATIFICATION: DIFFERENTIATION, RANKING, EVALUATION, AND REWARD. DISCUSSES SOCIAL MOBILITY AND SUGGESTS METHODS FOR STUDY OF STRATIFICATION.

2593 TURNER H.A., ZOETEWEIJ H.
PRICES, WAGES, AND INCOME POLICIES IN INDUSTRIALIZED MARKET ECONOMIES.
GENEVA: INTL LABOUR OFFICE, 1966, 172 PP.
DISCUSSES INCOME POLICIES AND PRICE AND WAGE CONTROL AS ANTI-INFLATIONARY DEVICES. STUDIES BACKGROUND OF WAGE DETERMINATION, ADVOCATES CAREFUL USE OF PRICE CONTROL, AND STATES THAT SOME MEASURES MAY ACTUALLY INCREASE PROBLEM. ATTEMPTS TO DECIDE HOW CAUSES OF INFLATION CAN BE DETERMINED AND ANALYZES SEVERAL ATTEMPTS TO DEAL WITH STEADY INFLATION. PRESENTS SOLUTIONS TO WAGE INFLATION PROBLEM.

2594 TYBOUT R.A.
ECONOMICS OF RESEARCH AND DEVELOPMENT.
COLUMBUS: OHIO STATE U PR, 1965, 458 PP., LC#65-18734.
TOPICS INCLUDE& HISTORY OF SCIENCE, INDUSTRIAL R&D, INTERNATIONAL ORGANIZATION, PUBLIC POLICY, MILITARY R&D, INTERNATIONAL COLLABORATION, AND THE EMERGENT NATIONS. RESULTS OF A CONFERENCE, INCLUDES COMMENTS ON PAPERS.

2595 TYLER G.
"THE PRESIDENCY AND LABOR."
ANN. ACAD. POL. SOC. SCI., 307 (SEPT. 56), 82-91.
"FROM 1932 TO 1952 LABOR LOOKED TO THE PRESIDENT TO BE THE MOST CONSISTENT SPOKESMAN FOR ITS POINT OF VIEW IN GOVERNMENT VIS-A-VIS BOTH CONGRESS AND THE COURTS.:

2596 U OF MICHIGAN LAW SCHOOL
ATOMS AND THE LAW.
ANN ARBOR: U OF MICH LAW SCHOOL, 1959, 1512 PP.
CONCERNS LEGAL PROBLEMS INVOLVED IN PEACEFUL USES OF ATOMIC ENERGY. CONCENTRATES ON TORT LIABILITY FOR RADIATION INJURIES, WORKMEN'S COMPENSATION, FEDERAL STATUTORY AND ADMINISTRATIVE PROVISIONS REGULATING ATOMIC ACTIVITIES, AND STATE REGULATION OF ATOMIC ENERGY. INCLUDES ESSAYS ON INTERNATIONAL ASPECTS OF THE SUBJECT.

2597 U WISCONSIN BUREAU OF GOVT
SERVICE SALES OF THE CITY OF MADISON TO METROPOLITAN COMMUNITIES AND NONRESIDENTS (PAMPHLET)
MADISON: U OF WISCONSIN PR, 1957, 37 PP.
DESCRIPTION OF THE SERVICES WHICH THE CITY OF MADISON SELLS TO SURROUNDING COMMUNITIES. FOUND THAT MADISON WAS NOT RECOVERING ITS UNIT COST OF THE SERVICES IN SEVERAL AREAS. ALSO CONCLUDED THAT THE FRINGE AREAS PROBABLY COULD NOT PROVIDE THE SERVICES AT AS LOW A UNIT COST AS THE CITY.

2598 UDY S.H. JR.
THE ORGANIZATION OF PRODUCTION IN NONINDUSTRIAL CULTURE.
PRINCETON: PRIN U, DEPT OF ECO, 1957, 300 PP.
COMPARATIVE ANALYSIS OF 320 NONINDUSTRIAL PRODUCTION ORGANIZATIONS. TESTS HYPOTHESIS THAT NATURE OF THESE ORGANIZATIONS IS DEFINED BY THE TECHNOLOGICAL PROCESS EACH DIRECTS, BY ITS INSTITUTIONAL SETTING, AND BY THE EFFECT UPON THE REWARD SYSTEM OF ALL THESE DETERMINING FACTORS. THE EVIDENCE SUPPORTS THE HYPOTHESIS.

2599 ULMAN L. ED.
CHALLENGES TO COLLECTIVE BARGAINING.
ENGLEWOOD CLIFFS: PRENTICE HALL, 1967, 180 PP., LC#67-14836.
A COLLECTION OF ESSAYS ON CURRENT AND FUTURE PROBLEMS OF COLLECTIVE BARGAINING. THE NINE CONTRIBUTORS TREAT SUCH PROBLEMS AS RACIAL DISCRIMINATION, DISREGARD OF THE PUBLIC INTEREST IN STRIKES, AND THE INTERNAL ORGANIZATION OF UNIONS. IF COLLECTIVE BARGAINING IS TO REMAIN FREE OF GOVERNMENT CONTROL, THEN UNIONS MUST REFLECT PUBLIC POLICY AND CONSIDER THE WIDER IMPLICATIONS OF THEIR ACTIVITIES.

2600 UN ECONOMIC COMN ASIA & FAR E
ECONOMIC SURVEY OF ASIA AND THE FAR EAST, 1954.
BANGKOK: UN ECAFE, 1955, 223 PP.
SURVEYS RECENT ECONOMIC DEVELOPMENTS IN INDIVIDUAL ASIAN COUNTRIES AND IN REGION AS A WHOLE. GIVES STATISTICAL DATA ON PRODUCTION, MONEY AND PRICE MOVEMENTS, VALUE OF IMPORTS AND EXPORTS, AND MONETARY AND FINANCIAL INDICATORS IN EACH COUNTRY.

2601 UN FAO
BIBLIOGRAPHY ON THE ANALYSIS AND PROJECTION OF DEMAND AND PRODUCTION, 1963.
ROME: UN FAO, 1963, 279 PP.
ABOUT 1200 ITEMS PUBLISHED BETWEEN 1950 AND 1963 IN MANY LANGUAGES, DEALING WITH PRODUCTION OF COMMODITIES, METHODOLOGY OF THE STUDY, PROJECTIONS BY COUNTRY, AND STATISTICAL SOURCES BY COUNTRY. ANNOTATIONS ARE ALL IN ENGLISH.

2602 UN HEADQUARTERS LIBRARY
BIBLIOGRAPHY OF INDUSTRIALIZATION IN UNDERDEVELOPED COUNTRIES (BIBLIOGRAPHICAL SERIES NO. 6)
NEW YORK: UNITED NATIONS, 1956, 216 PP.
LISTS PUBLICATIONS OF UN AND SPECIALIZED AGENCIES ON SUBJECT OF INDUSTRIALIZATION AND INFORMATION ON PERTINENT RESEARCH PROJECTS BEING CARRIED OUT BY GOVERNMENTS, UNIVERSITIES, AND SCIENTIFIC INSTITUTIONS. RECORDS ALSO RELEVANT PUBLICATIONS AND UNPUBLISHED RESEARCH. ITEMS ARRANGED BY GEOGRAPHY. WRITTEN IN SPANISH, ENGLISH, AND FRENCH. ITEMS IN ALL RELEVANT LANGUAGES, INCLUDING ORIENTAL.

2603 UN SECRETARY GENERAL
PLANNING FOR ECONOMIC DEVELOPMENT.
NEW YORK: UNITED NATIONS, 1963, 156 PP.
REPORTS ON ECONOMIC PLANNING AND TECHNIQUES USED IN SEVERAL COUNTRIES. EXAMINES ORGANIZATION AND MANAGEMENT OF PLANS, AS WELL AS NATIONAL AND INTERNATIONAL POLICIES.

2604 UN STATISTICAL OFFICE
STATISTICAL YEARBOOK (17TH ED.)
NEW YORK: UNITED NATIONS, 1966, 747 PP.
INTERNATIONAL STATISTICAL COMPILATION OF THE ECONOMIC, SOCIAL, AND EDUCATIONAL ACTIVITIES OF ABOUT 200 NATIONS. STATISTICAL TABLES GROUPED INTO TWO SECTIONS: A WORLD SUMMARY, AND MORE DETAILED SUBJECT-COUNTRY INFORMATION GUIDE. WORLD SUMMARY ATTEMPTS TO SUMMARIZE GLOBAL AGGREGATES DIVIDED INTO GEOGRAPHIC AND ECONOMIC AREAS; CORRELATES BROAD ECONOMIC ASPECTS TO POPULATION, NATIONAL INCOME, AND TRADE.

2605 UNECA LIBRARY
BOOKS ON AFRICA IN THE UNECA LIBRARY.
NEW YORK: UNITED NATIONS, 1962, 318 PP.
SELECTED LIST OF MONOGRAPHS CONCERNING ECONOMIC AND SOCIAL CONDITIONS OF AFRICA AND AFRICAN COUNTRIES. MAJORITY OF TITLES ARE GOVERNMENTAL PUBLICATIONS. TITLES ARE DIVIDED FIRST BY REGION, THEN BY GROUP OF COUNTRIES SPEAKING SAME LANGUAGE. CONTAINS AUTHOR, TITLE, AND SUBJECT INDEXES. INCLUDES 2,031 ENTRIES

2606 UNECA LIBRARY
NEW ACQUISITIONS IN THE UNECA LIBRARY.
NEW YORK: UNITED NATIONS, 1962.
PERIODICAL LISTING OF RECENT BOOKS, MONOGRAPHS, SERIAL PUBLICATIONS AND PERIODICALS COVERING CURRENT SOCIAL, ECONOMIC, CULTURAL, AND TECHNICAL PROBLEMS OF WORLD WITH SPECIAL ATTENTION TO AFRICA AND DEVELOPING NATIONS. FIRST PUBLISHED 1962. ITEMS, IN ALL LANGUAGES, ARRANGED BY SUBJECT.

2607 UNESCO
INTERNATIONAL BIBLIOGRAPHY OF ECONOMICS (VOLUMES 1-8)
PARIS: UNESCO.
AN UNANNOTATED BIBLIOGRAPHY OF INTERNATIONAL SCOPE LISTING CURRENT BOOKS AND PERIODICAL ARTICLES DEALING WITH ALL PHASES OF ECONOMIC ACTIVITY. CLASSIFIED ARRANGEMENT WITH AUTHOR AND SUBJECT INDEX AND A LIST OF PERIODICALS CONSULTED. VOLUMES 1-8, COVERING THE PERIOD 1952-59, PUBLISHED BY UNESCO; BEGINNING WITH VOLUME 9, PUBLISHED IN LONDON BY STEVENS & SONS AND IN CHICAGO BY ALDINE PUBLISHING CO.

2608 UNESCO
SOUTH ASIA SOCIAL SCIENCES ABSTRACTS.
PARIS: UNESCO.
ABSTRACTS OF ARTICLES PUBLISHED IN ENGLISH IN BURMA, CEYLON, AND INDIA. BEGAN PUBLICATION ANNUALLY IN 1952 AND LIMITED TO ITEMS PUBLISHED IN CURRENT YEAR. SCIENTIFIC VALUE OF ARTICLE IS CRITERION STRESSED IN SELECTION. LIMITED TO SOCIAL SCIENCES.

2609 UNESCO
SOUTHERN ASIA SOCIAL SCIENCE BIBLIOGRAPHY (WITH ANNOTATIONS AND ABSTRACTS), 1959 (PAMPHLET)
PARIS: UNESCO, 1960, 230 PP.
INCLUDES BOOKS, PAMPHLETS, AND ARTICLES FROM PERIODICALS IN REGION IN SOCIAL SCIENCE PUBLISHED IN ENGLISH AND, FOR CASE OF VIETNAM, IN FRENCH. THE 1,413 ITEMS HAVE BEEN ANNOTATED WHERE TITLE IS VAGUE AND ABSTRACTS MADE OF IMPORTANT ARTICLES ON SOCIAL AND ECONOMIC DEVELOPMENT AND THOSE ON THEME OF "SOCIAL IMPLICATIONS OF INDUSTRIALIZATION IN SOUTHERN ASIA." ANNUAL PUBLICATION CONTINUES FORMAT.

2610 UNION OF SOUTH AFRICA
REPORT CONCERNING ADMINISTRATION OF SOUTH WEST AFRICA (6 VOLS.)
PRETORIA: U OF SOUTH AFRICA, 1937, 3000 PP.
YEARLY REPORTS, 1922-37, BY GOVERNMENT OF UNION OF SOUTH AFRICA TO COUNCIL OF LEAGUE OF NATIONS CONCERNING ADMINISTRATION OF SOUTH WEST AFRICA. COVERS TOPICS OF LEGISLATION, INTERNATIONAL RELATIONS, CONSTITUTION, COURT SYSTEM, PRISONS, ARMS AND POLICE, DEMOGRAPHY, FINANCE AND TAXES, INDUSTRY, AGRICULTURE, NATIVE AFFAIRS, HEALTH, TRADE, MISSIONS, AND ECONOMY.

2611 UNITED NATIONS
OFFICIAL RECORDS OF THE ECONOMIC AND SOCIAL COUNCIL OF THE UNITED NATIONS.
NEW YORK: UNITED NATIONS.
OFFICIAL UN ECONOMIC AND SOCIAL COUNCIL RECORDS INCLUDE SUMMARIES OF PLENARY MEETINGS, ANNEXED ESSENTIAL DOCUMENTS, AND SUPPLEMENTS CONSISTING OF RESOLUTIONS AND COMMISSION REPORTS. ANNUAL PUBLICATION.

2612 UNITED NATIONS
BIBLIOGRAPHY ON INDUSTRIALIZATION IN UNDER-DEVELOPED COUNTRIES.
NEW YORK: UNITED NATIONS, 1956, 216 PP.
A BIBLIOGRAPHY IN ENGLISH, FRENCH, AND SPANISH COVERING PUBLICATIONS OF THE UNITED NATIONS, OTHER PUBLICATIONS, AND UNPUBLISHED RESEARCH. BESIDES GENERAL WORKS, IT INCLUDES MATERIAL ON AFRICA, THE MIDDLE EAST, ASIA AND THE FAR EAST, EUROPE, AND LATIN AMERICA AND THE CARIBBEAN. HAS INDEXES OF PERSONAL AND GENERAL NAMES.

2613 UNITED NATIONS
THE GROWTH OF WORLD INDUSTRY, 1938-1961: NATIONAL TABLES.
NEW YORK: UNITED NATIONS, 1963, 849 PP.
INTERNATIONALLY COMPARABLE DATA ON THE INDUSTRIAL SECTOR IN RELATION TO OTHER ASPECTS OF ECONOMY, FOR 100 NATIONS AND TERRITORIES. STATISTICS INDICATE ROLE OF INDUSTRIAL SECTOR IN ECONOMY, DELINEATE CHARACTER AND STRUCTURE OF SECTOR, AND MEASURE OUTPUT RESULTING FROM AND KEY RESOURCES EMPLOYED IN INDUSTRIAL ACTIVITIES. ALSO CONTAINS DATA ON ECONOMIC RELATIONS.

2614 UNITED NATIONS
YEARBOOK OF INTERNATIONAL TRADE STATISTICS, 1964 (15TH ISSUE)
NEW YORK: UNITED NATIONS, 1966, 832 PP.
DETAILED ANNUAL STATISTICS FOR 144 COUNTRIES COVERING 98 PER CENT OF 1964 AGGREGATE TRADE. INCLUDES, FOR EACH COUNTRY, AN HISTORICAL TABLE, SHOWING FOR YEARS 1934-64, IMPORT AND EXPORT SERIES. FURTHER TABLES DISPLAY

QUANTITY AND VALUE OF IMPORTS AND EXPORTS IN RECENT YEARS ANALYZED BY COMMODITIES; AND TABLES OF VALUE OF TRADE ANALYZED BY COUNTRIES OF PROVENANCE AND DESTINATION.

2615 UNIVERSAL REFERENCE SYSTEM
BIBLIOGRAPHY OF BIBLIOGRAPHIES IN POLITICAL SCIENCE, GOVERNMENT, AND PUBLIC POLICY (VOLUME III)
PRINCETON* UNIV. REF. SYSTEM, 1967, 1200 PP.
COMPUTERIZED INFORMATION RETRIEVAL SYSTEM FOR THE SOCIAL AND BEHAVIORAL SCIENCES. ANNOTATED AND EXTENSIVELY INDEXED, UTILIZING "TOPICAL-METHODOLOGICAL INDEX" DEVELOPED BY PROFESSOR ALFRED DE GRAZIA. APPROXIMATELY 3,000 CITATIONS FROM SCHOLARLY JOURNALS, BOOKS, GOVERNMENT DOCUMENTS IN ENGLISH AND EUROPEAN LANGUAGES. INCLUDES CLASSICAL SOURCES THROUGH 1967. TO BE PUBLISHED EARLY 1968 WITH QUARTERLY GAZETTES.

2616 UNIVERSAL REFERENCE SYSTEM
ADMINISTRATIVE MANAGEMENT: PUBLIC AND PRIVATE BUREAUCRACY (VOLUME IV)
PRINCETON* UNIV. REF. SYSTEM, 1967, 1200 PP.
COMPUTERIZED INFORMATION RETRIEVAL SYSTEM. ANNOTATED AND EXTENSIVELY INDEXED, UTILIZING "TOPICAL-METHODOLOGICAL INDEX" DEVELOPED BY PROFESSOR ALFRED DE GRAZIA. APPROXIMATELY 3,000 CITATIONS FROM BOOKS, GOVERNMENT PUBLICATIONS, AND JOURNALS. ENGLISH AND EUROPEAN LANGUAGES. MATERIALS SELECTED FROM CLASSICAL SOURCES THROUGH 1967. TO BE PUBLISHED EARLY 1968, WITH SUBSEQUENT QUARTERLY GAZETTES.

2617 UNIVERSAL REFERENCE SYSTEM
ECONOMIC REGULATION, BUSINESS, AND GOVERNMENT (VOLUME VIII)
PRINCETON* UNIV. REF. SYSTEM, 1967, 1200 PP.
COMPUTERIZED INFORMATION RETRIEVAL SYSTEM DEALING WITH VARIOUS FACETS OF INTERNAL GOVERNANCE OF BUSINESS ACTIVITIES AND THEIR RELATION TO POLITICS. ABOUT 3000 ANNOTATIONS FROM ALL TYPES OF PUBLICATIONS IN ENGLISH AND EUROPEAN LANGUAGES. SOURCES RANGE FROM CLASSICS WITH EMPHASIS ON MATERIALS OF 1960'S. TO BE PUBLISHED EARLY 1968. QUARTERLY GAZETTES BEGAN AUG., 1967.

2618 UNIVERSAL REFERENCE SYSTEM
PUBLIC POLICY AND THE MANAGEMENT OF SCIENCE (VOLUME IX)
PRINCETON* UNIV. REF. SYSTEM, 1967, 1200 PP.
ABOUT 3000 SELECTED BOOKS, ARTICLES, AND DOCUMENTS CONCERNED WITH INSTITUTIONAL AND BEHAVIORAL PROCESS OF SCIENTIFIC DECISION-MAKING. MAJORITY OF ITEMS FROM 1960'S; INCLUDES ENGLISH-LANGUAGE AND EUROPEAN SOURCES. USES PROFESSOR ALFRED DE GRAZIA'S "TOPICAL-METHODOLOGICAL INDEX." TO BE PUBLISHED EARLY 1968. QUARTERLY GAZETTES BEGAN AUG., 1967.

2619 UNIVERSITY OF CHICAGO
BIBLIOGRAPHY OF UKRAINE (PAMPHLET)
NEW HAVEN: HUMAN REL AREA FILES, 1956, 20 PP.
ANNOTATED BIBLIOGRAPHY OF 145 ITEMS IN RUSSIAN AND ENGLISH ON HISTORY AND POLITICS OF UKRAINE. REFERENCES ALSO TO ECONOMIC AND SOCIAL SITUATION OF REGION. MATERIAL PUBLISHED MAINLY AFTER 1935.

2620 UNIVERSITY OF FLORIDA
CARIBBEAN ACQUISITIONS: MATERIALS ACQUIRED BY THE UNIVERSITY OF FLORIDA 1957-1960.
GAINESVILLE: U OF FLORIDA LIB.
LIST OF MATERIALS ACQUIRED BY THE UNIVERSITY OF FLORIDA UNDER THE FARMINGTON PLAN AND THE UNIVERSITY'S EMPHASIS ON LATIN AMERICAN STUDIES. ANNUAL SUPPLEMENTS UPDATE LIST.

2621 UNIVERSITY OF LONDON
THE FAR EAST AND SOUTH-EAST ASIA: A CUMULATED LIST OF PERIODICAL ARTICLES, MAY 1956-APRIL 1957.
LONDON: U LON, ORIENT + AFR STUD, 1958, 123 PP.
THIRD ANNUAL CUMULATION OF PERIODICAL ARTICLES IN WESTERN LANGUAGES. CONTAINS 2,000 ITEMS ON ANTHROPOLOGY, SOCIOLOGY AND FOLKLORE; GEOGRAPHY AND HISTORY; AND SOCIAL SCIENCES. MATERIAL IS CLASSIFIED BY GEOGRAPHIC REGION. INCLUDES AUTHOR INDEX.

2622 UNIVERSITY OF TENNESSEE
GOVERNMENT AND WORLD CRISIS.
KNOXVILLE: U OF TENN PR, 1962, 85 PP., LC#62-21409.
EXAMINES US EXPERIENCE IN DEMOCRATIC GOVERNMENT. DEALS WITH RELATION OF UN TO ECONOMIC DEVELOPMENT; DISCUSSES AIMS OF ALLIANCE FOR PROGRESS AND ROLE OF US IN BUILDING WORLD COMMUNITY.

2623 UNIVS-NATL BUR COMM ECO RES
PUBLIC FINANCES: NEEDS, SOURCES, AND UTILIZATION.
PRINCETON: PRINCETON U PRESS, 1961, 512 PP., LC#60-12235.
COLLECTION OF PAPERS DEALING WITH PUBLIC FINANCE ALL EMPHASIZING COLLECTIVE DECISION-MAKING ABOUT FISCAL AFFAIRS. MAINTAINS THAT EXAMINATION OF DECISION-MAKING INSTITUTIONS IS NECESSARY TO IMPROVE PROCESS. DISCUSSES AREAS OF TAXATION, METROPOLITAN FINANCE, FEDERALISM, DECENTRALIZATION, FINANCIAL NEEDS AND RESOURCES, DEFENSE, CONSUMER PRICE, AND ALTERNATIVE EXPENDITURE PROGRAMS.

2624 UPHOFF W.H., DUNETTE M.D.
UNDERSTANDING THE UNION MEMBER (PAMPHLET)
MINNEAPLIS: U MINN INDUS REL CTR, 1956, 45 PP.
DESCRIBES RESEARCH AT THE UNIVERSITY OF MINNESOTA INDUSTRIAL RELATIONS CENTER ON THE BASIS OF AN EMPLOYEE ATTITUDE QUESTIONNAIRE. PROBES UNION MEMBER ATTITUDES, THE ROLE OF LOCAL UNIONS IN MEMBERS' LIVES, AND OFFICERS VERSUS RANK-AND-FILE MEMBERS' RELATIONSHIP. PRESENTS RESEARCH FINDINGS.

2625 UREN P.E. ED.
EAST - WEST TRADE* A SYMPOSIUM.
TORONTO: CAN INST OF INTL AFF, 1966, 181 PP.
COLLECTION OF ESSAYS CONCERNING WAYS IN WHICH EAST-WEST COLD WAR SUSPICIONS HAVE COLORED EVEN INNOCUOUS EAST-WEST TRADE CONTACTS WITH BALANCE OF POWER MEANINGS. ARTICLES DISCUSS POLITICAL, STRATEGIC, LEGAL, AND ECONOMIC ASPECTS OF EAST-WEST TRADE. BASICALLY PRESENTED FROM CANADIAN VANTAGE POINT.

2626 URQUIDI C.W.
A STATEMENT OF THE LAWS OF BOLIVIA IN MATTERS AFFECTING BUSINESS (3RD ED. REV., ENLARGED)
WASHINGTON: PAN AMERICAN UNION, 1962, 286 PP.
SUMMARIZES RELEVANT CONSTITUTIONAL, STATUTORY, AND REGULATORY PROVISIONS OF BOLIVIA UP TO 1962, AS THEY CONCERN COMMERCIAL MATTERS AND THE PERSONS WHO TRANSACT THEM. BASED UPON INFORMATION SUPPLIED BY PRACTICING BOLIVIAN LAWYERS. APPENDIX LISTS RELEVANT TREATIES.

2627 URQUIDI V.L.
FREE TRADE AND ECONOMIC INTEGRATION IN LATIN AMERICA: THE EVOLUTION OF A COMMON MARKET POLICY.
BERKELEY: U OF CALIF PR, 1962, 190 PP., LC#62-9167.
EXPLAINS RECENT EVOLUTION OF CONCEPT OF FREE TRADE IN LATIN AMERICA AND THE MANNER IN WHICH IT HAS BEEN AGREED TO CARRY OUT LATIN AMERICAN INTEGRATION IN GENERAL AND THE INTEGRATION OF SOME GROUPS IN PARTICULAR. DISCUSSES EFFECT OF ECONOMIC DEVELOPMENT ON COMPOSITION OF LATIN AMERICAN IMPORTS, NATURE OF SMALL VOLUME OF INTERNAL TRADE IN PAST, ETC.

2628 URQUIDI V.L.
THE CHALLENGE OF DEVELOPMENT IN LATIN AMERICA.
NEW YORK: FREDERICK PRAEGER, 1964, 209 PP., LC#64-16692.
EXAMINES OVER-ALL CONDITION AND PROSPECTS OF THE LATIN AMERICAN ECONOMY. SINGLES OUT SPECIFIC ECONOMIC ASPECTS SUCH AS TRADE TRENDS, MONETARY PROBLEMS, PRIMARY PRODUCTS PRICES, AND FOREIGN CAPITAL.

2629 US ADVISORY COMM INTERGOV REL
STATE AND LOCAL TAXATION ON PRIVATELY OWNED PROPERTY LOCATED ON FEDERAL AREAS: PROPOSED AMENDMENT OF BUCK ACT (PAMPHLET)
WASHINGTON: US GOVERNMENT, 1961, 34 PP.
STUDIES PROBLEM OF PROPERTY TAX STATUS OF PRIVATELY OWNED PROPERTIES LOCATED IN AREAS UNDER EXCLUSIVE JURISDICTION OF US GOVERNMENT. PRESENTS "ESSENTIAL FACTS AND POLICY CONSIDERATIONS"; RECOMMENDS END TO IMMUNITY FROM TAXATION ENJOYED BY OWNERS OF THESE PROPERTIES AND STRESSES NEED TO INSURE THAT THEY RECEIVE EQUAL TREATMENT WITH REGARD TO SERVICES AND PRIVILEGES.

2630 US ADVISORY COMN INTERGOV REL
THE COMMISSION ON INTERGOVERNMENTAL RELATIONS; A REPORT TO THE PRESIDENT FOR TRANSMITTAL TO THE CONGRESS.
WASHINGTON: US GOVERNMENT, 1955, 311 PP.
EXAMINES ROLE OF NATIONAL GOVERNMENT IN RELATION TO STATES AND POLITICAL SUBDIVISIONS; CENTERS ON FUNCTIONAL AND FISCAL RELATIONSHIPS BETWEEN LEVELS OF GOVERNMENT. BEGINS WITH EVOLUTION OF AMERICAN FEDERAL SYSTEM, THEN DISCUSSES RESPONSIBILITIES IN AREAS SUCH AS AGRICULTURE, EDUCATION, HOUSING AND URBAN RENEWAL, PUBLIC HEALTH AND WELFARE, CIVIL DEFENSE, AND HIGHWAYS.

2631 US ADVISORY COMN INTERGOV REL
STATE CONSTITUTIONAL AND STATUTORY RESTRICTIONS ON LOCAL GOVERNMENT DEBT (PAMPHLET)
WASHINGTON: US GOVERNMENT, 1961, 98 PP.
REPORT FOCUSES ON STATE RESTRICTIONS ON THE BORROWING POWERS OF LOCAL GOVERNMENT. FINDS THAT SUCH PROVISIONS ARE "CRITICALLY IN NEED OF INTENSIVE REVIEW AND MAJOR CHANGE." MAKES A SERIES OF RECOMMENDATIONS.

2632 US ADVISORY COMN INTERGOV REL
STATE CONSTITUTIONAL AND STATUTORY RESTRICTIONS ON LOCAL TAXING POWERS.
WASHINGTON: US GOVERNMENT, 1962, 122 PP.
STUDIES POWERS OF LOCAL GOVERNMENTS TO FINANCE THEMSELVES BY TAXATION. TRACES HISTORY BEHIND STATE CONSTITUTIONAL AND STATUTORY RESTRICTIONS ON VARIOUS LOCAL TAXES, ASSESSES EFFECTS OF PROPERTY TAX LIMITATIONS ON LOCAL GOVERNMENT, SUBMITS TO GOVERNORS AND STATE LEGISLATURES GUIDELINES FOR ENHANCING ABILITY OF LOCAL GOVERNMENTS TO MEET LOCAL REVENUE NEEDS THROUGH TAXATION OF LOCAL RESOURCES.

2633 US ADVISORY COMN INTERGOV REL
PERFORMANCE OF URBAN FUNCTIONS: LOCAL AND AREAWIDE.

WASHINGTON: US GOVERNMENT, 1963, 281 PP.
STUDY TO DETERMINE WHICH FUNCTIONS ARE BEST PERFORMED ON A LOCAL BASIS AND WHICH ON AN AREAWIDE BASIS CONSIDERS ECONOMIC AND POLITICAL CRITERIA IN THE ANALYSIS.

2634 US ADVISORY COMN INTERGOV REL
METROPOLITAN SOCIAL AND ECONOMIC DISPARITIES: IMPLICATIONS FOR INTERGOVERNMENTAL RELATIONS IN CENT'L CITIES AND SUBURBS
WASHINGTON: US GOVERNMENT, 1965, 253 PP.
THIS REPORT CONCLUDES "THAT VERY FEW MEANINGFUL GENERALIZATIONS ABOUT ECONOMIC, SOCIAL AND RACIAL DISPARITIES CAN BE APPLIED TO ALL METROPOLITAN AREAS."

2635 US ADVISORY COMN INTERGOV REL
CATALOGS AND OTHER INFORMATION SOURCES ON FEDERAL AND STATE AID PROGRAMS: A SECTED BIBLIOGRAPHY (PAPER)
WASHINGTON: ADV COMM INTGOV REL, 1966, 13 PP.
ANNOTATED LISTING OF CATALOGS PUBLISHED BY FEDERAL AGENCIES AND BY ORGANIZATIONS OF PUBLIC OFFICIALS, STATE CATALOGS ON FEDERAL GRANTS TO STATES AND STATE GRANTS TO LOCALITIES, AND PUBLICATIONS OF ADVISORY COMMITTEE ON INTERGOVERNMENTAL RELATIONS. ALL ENTRIES PERTAIN TO FEDERAL AND STATE PROGRAMS OF FINANCIAL AND TECHNICAL ASSISTANCE. ABOUT 50 ENTRIES ALL PUBLISHED 1962 THROUGH 1966.

2636 US AGENCY INTERNATIONAL DEV
OPERATIONS REPORT - 1962
(PAMPHLET)
WASHINGTON: AGENCY FOR INTL DEV, 1962, 270 PP.
GRAPHIC PRESENTATIONS AND STATISTICAL TABLES ON US FOREIGN COMMITMENTS IN ASIA, AFRICA, AND LATIN AMERICA FOR FISCAL 1962. LISTS DEVELOPMENT LOANS, SUPPORTING ASSISTANCE, CONTRIBUTIONS TO INTERNATIONAL ORGANIZATIONS, CASH TRANSFERS, AND DEVELOPMENT GRANTS.

2637 US AGENCY INTERNATIONAL DEV
OPERATIONS REPORT - 1963.
WASHINGTON: AGENCY FOR INTL DEV, 1963, 289 PP.
GRAPHIC PRESENTATIONS AND STATISTICAL TABLES ON US FOREIGN AID COMMITMENTS IN ASIA, AFRICA, AND LATIN-AMERICA FOR FISCAL 1963. LISTS DEVELOPMENT LOANS, SUPPORTING ASSISTANCE, CONTRIBUTIONS TO INTERNATIONAL AGENCIES, ETC.

2638 US AGENCY INTERNATIONAL DEV
PRINCIPLES OF FOREIGN ECONOMIC ASSISTANCE (PAMPHLET)
WASHINGTON: AGENCY FOR INTL DEV, 1963, 49 PP.
SUMMARIZES PRINCIPLES THAT GUIDE US ECONOMIC ASSISTANCE PROGRAMS. DISCUSSES PROCESS OF PROGRAMMING ASSISTANCE; AVAILABLE RESOURCES SUCH AS LOANS, FOOD SURPLUS, LOCAL CURRENCY, AND PRIVATE ENTERPRISE; INTERNAL DEVELOPMENT PROGRAMS AND SELF-HELP; AID AS SOURCE OF FOREIGN EXCHANGE; AND COORDINATION OF VARIOUS AID PROGRAMS.

2639 US AGENCY INTERNATIONAL DEV
A.I.D. PROJECTS IN FISCAL YEAR 1963: BY COUNTRY AND FIELD OF ACTIVITY.
WASHINGTON: AGENCY FOR INTL DEV, 1964, 186 PP.
LIST OF ALL PROJECTS AND AMOUNT OF FUNDS OBLIGATED DURING YEAR, TOTALLY AND BY CATEGORY. COVERS SPECIFIC REGIONS OF WORLD, BROKEN DOWN BY COUNTRIES AND SPECIAL NONREGIONAL PROGRAMS.

2640 US AGENCY INTERNATIONAL DEV
PROPOSED FOREIGN AID PROGRAM FOR 1968: SUMMARY PRESENTATION TO THE CONGRESS.
WASHINGTON: US GOVERNMENT, 1967, 297 PP.
FOREIGN AID BUDGET REQUESTS CITE AGRICULTURE, HEALTH, AND EDUCATION AS MAIN NEEDS. STRESSES SELF-HELP AND DEVELOPMENT AND USE OF PRIVATE RESOURCES. PROPOSES AID LARGELY IN FORM OF COMMODITIES AND SERVICES. SPECIFIES THAT 90 PER CENT OF BUDGET BE SPENT IN US TO MAINTAIN BALANCE OF PAYMENTS. GIVES FIRST PRIORITY TO PROGRAMS FOSTERING COOPERATION AMONG NEIGHBORING NATIONS WITH COMMON DEVELOPMENT PROBLEMS.

2641 US BD GOVERNORS FEDL RESRV
THE FEDERAL RESERVE AND THE TREASURY.
ENGLEWOOD CLIFFS: PRENTICE HALL, 1963, 275 PP., LC#63-12487.
ANSWERS TO QUESTIONS BY COMMISSION ON MONEY AND CREDIT, BY TREASURY DEPARTMENT, AND BY FEDERAL RESERVE BOARD, SEPARATELY. STUDIES INFLUENCE OF MONEY AND CREDIT ON JOBS, PRICES, AND GROWTH OF ECONOMY. INCLUDES QUESTIONS.

2642 US BOARD GOVERNORS FEDL RESRV
SELECTED BIBLIOGRAPHY ON MONETARY POLICY AND MANAGEMENT OF THE PUBLIC DEBT 1947-1960 AND 1961-1963 SUPPLEMENT (PAMPH.)
WASHINGTON: US GOVERNMENT, 1964, 20 PP.
BIBLIOGRAPHY OF APPROXIMATELY 200 BOOKS, ARTICLES, AND GOVERNMENT PUBLICATIONS IN ENGLISH; ARRANGED ALPHABETICALLY BY AUTHOR ON TOPICS OF MONETARY POLICY AND MANAGEMENT OF PUBLIC DEBT FROM 1947-63.

2643 US BUREAU EDUC CULTURAL AFF
RESOURCES SURVEY FOR LATIN AMERICAN COUNTRIES.
WASHINGTON: DEPT OF STATE, 1965, 640 PP.
RECORD OF US PUBLIC AND PRIVATE EFFORTS TO DEVELOP HUMAN RESOURCES ESSENTIAL TO EDUCATION, CULTURE, ECONOMY, AND SOCIETY OF LATIN AMERICA. MENTIONS MORE THAN 1,200 PRIVATE ORGANIZATIONS INVOLVED IN PROJECT ALONG WITH US GOVERNMENT.

2644 US BUREAU OF THE BUDGET
THE BALANCE OF PAYMENTS STATISTICS OF THE UNITED STATES: A REVIEW AND APPRAISAL.
WASHINGTON: US GOVERNMENT, 1965, 194 PP.
REVIEWS IN DETAIL THE PURPOSES FOR WHICH BALANCE-OF-PAYMENTS STATISTICS ARE NEEDED. EXAMINES SCOPE AND QUALITY OF STATISTICS AND WAYS IN WHICH THEY ARE COLLECTED, PROCESSED, AND PRESENTED TO PUBLIC. CONSIDERS CONCEPTUAL PROBLEM OF DEFINING A BALANCE-OF-PAYMENTS DEFICIT WHICH AFFECTS BOTH PRESENTATION AND INTERPRETATION OF STATISTICS.

2645 US BUREAU OF THE CENSUS
THE PROPORTION OF THE SHIPMENTS (OR EMPLOYEES) OF EACH INDUSTRY... (PAMPHLET)
WASHINGTON: GOVT PR OFFICE, 1957, 109 PP.
REPORT OF 1954 CENSUS OF MANUFACTURERS AND MINERS TO SENATE. DATA ON TOTAL YEARLY SHIPMENTS OF LARGEST FIRMS IN EACH INDUSTRY; VALUES TO BE USED FOR HEARINGS ON MONOPOLIES.

2646 US BUREAU OF THE CENSUS
REPORT FOR SUBCOMMITTEE ON ANTITRUST AND MONOPOLY: CONCENTRATION RATIOS IN MANUFACTURING INDUSTRY 1958.
WASHINGTON: GOVT PR OFFICE, 1962, 452 PP.
PRESENTATION OF RATIOS OR DATA OF COMPANIES' SHARE OF TOTAL ACTIVITY OF CERTAIN SEGMENT OF ECONOMY. TREATS ONLY LARGEST COMPANIES AND PRESENTS DATA IN GROUPS OF FOUR, ACCORDING TO SIZE.

2647 US CHAMBER OF COMMERCE
THE SIGNIFICANCE OF CONCENTRATION RATIOS (PAMPHLET)
WASHINGTON: US CHAMBER OF COMM, 1957, 8 PP.
CLOSE LOOK AT GAUGE BEING USED TO MEASURE ECONOMIC CONCENTRATION, IN ORDER TO DETERMINE WHETHER CONCENTRATION RATIOS ARE CONCEPTUALLY VALID MEASURES, AND WHETHER THEY ARE STATISTICALLY ACCURATE. MAINTAINS THAT CONCENTRATION RATIOS ARE CONCEPTUALLY INVALID AS MEASURES OF INDUSTRIAL CONCENTRATION OR MARKET POWER.

2648 US COMM STRENG SEC FREE WORLD
THE SCOPE AND DISTRIBUTION OF UNITED STATES MILITARY AND ECONOMIC ASSISTANCE PROGRAMS (PAMPHLET)
WASHINGTON: DEPT OF STATE, 1963, 25 PP.
ANALYSIS OF US AID PROGRAMS TO ADVISE AND RECOMMEND NECESSARY CHANGES FOR US SECURITY. SUGGEST REDUCTION OF US MILITARY RATHER THAN ANY FOREIGN-SUPPORTED ONES. FAVORS CONTINUED ECONOMIC AID TO ASIA AND LIMITED AMOUNT TO AFRICA. GIVES GENERAL VIEWS ON US POLICY, NOT SPECIFIC PROGRAMS. DOES NOT COVER BANKING POLICIES.

2649 US CONG INTERNAL REV TAX JT COMM
LEGISLATIVE HISTORY OF UNITED STATES TAX CONVENTIONS(VOL. 1)
WASHINGTON: GOVT PR OFFICE, 1962, 1501 PP.
COMPILATION OF LEGISLATIVE HISTORY MATERIALS RELATING TO INCOME TAX CONVENTIONS, INCLUDING INFORMATION ABOUT CONVENTIONS AND VERBATIM TEXT OF AGREEMENTS WITH SEVERAL COUNTRIES.

2650 US CONGRESS JOINT ECO COMM
THE RELATIONSHIP OF PRICES TO ECONOMIC STABILITY AND GROWTH.
WASHINGTON: GOVT PR OFFICE, 1958, 712 PP.
COMPENDIUM OF PAPERS SUBMITTED BY PANELISTS APPEARING BEFORE US JOINT ECONOMIC COMMITTEE. COMMITTEE'S MAJOR GOAL IS OBJECTIVE AND AUTHORITATIVE EXPLORATION OF GENERAL ECONOMIC PROCESSES WHICH INVOLVE PRICES, PRICE RELATIONSHIPS, COSTS, AND PRICE POLICIES IN EXPECTATION IT WILL REVEAL WAYS IN WHICH PUBLIC AND PRIVATE POLICIES CAN CONTRIBUTE TO ATTAINMENT OF EMPLOYMENT ACT.

2651 US CONGRESS JOINT ECO COMM
INTERNATIONAL PAYMENTS IMBALANCES AND NEED FOR STRENGTHENING INTERNATIONAL FINANCIAL ARRANGEMENTS.
WASHINGTON: US GOVERNMENT, 1961, 340 PP.
HEARINGS BEFORE SUBCOMMITTEE ON INTERNATIONAL EXCHANGE AND PAYMENTS OF JOINT ECONOMIC COMMITTEE HEADED BY HENRY S. REUSS ON INTERNATIONAL FINANCIAL ARRANGEMENTS THAT WOULD REDUCE PROBLEM OF BALANCE OF PAYMENTS. INCLUDES TESTIMONY BY DR. REINHARD KAMITZ, PRESIDENT OF AUSTRIAN NATIONAL BANK, AND OTHER PROMINENT PEOPLE IN WORLD ECONOMIC AFFAIRS.

2652 US CONGRESS JOINT ECO COMM
INVENTORY FLUCTUATIONS AND ECONOMIC STABILIZATION.
WASHINGTON: GOVT PR OFFICE, 1962, 263 PP.
HEARINGS BEFORE SUBCOMMITTEE ON ECONOMIC STABILIZATION, AUTOMATION, AND ENERGY RESOURCES OF JOINT ECONOMIC COMMITTEE HEADED BY WRIGHT PATMAN, ON ROLE OF INVENTORY FLUCTUATION IN ECONOMIC RECESSIONS AND BOOMS AND IN INFLUENCING TURNING POINTS IN BUSINESS CYCLE.

2653 US CONGRESS JOINT ECO COMM
FACTORS AFFECTING THE UNITED STATES BALANCE OF PAYMENTS.
WASHINGTON: US GOVERNMENT, 1962, 561 PP.
COLLECTION OF STUDIES PREPARED FOR SUBCOMMITTEE ON INTER-

NATIONAL EXCHANGE AND PAYMENTS OF JOINT ECONOMIC COMMITTEE HEADED BY HENRY S. REUSS ON COMPETITIVE POSITION OF US; COMMON MARKET'S EFFECT ON US EXPORTS; INTERNATIONAL MONETARY SYSTEM; EXCHANGE RATE; NEW US BALANCE OF PAYMENTS POLICY; US CAPITAL INVESTMENT IN FOREIGN COUNTRIES; AND PROBLEMS OF "KEY CURRENCY."

2654 US CONGRESS JOINT ECO COMM
ECONOMIC DEVELOPMENTS IN SOUTH AMERICA.
WASHINGTON: GOVT PR OFFICE, 1962, 151 PP.
HEARINGS BEFORE SUBCOMMITTEE ON INTER-AMERICAN ECONOMIC RELATIONSHIPS OF JOINT ECONOMIC COMMITTEE OF CONGRESS. CONSIDER HOW INTER-AMERICAN POLICIES CAN BE IMPROVED AND ALLIANCE FOR PROGRESS MADE MORE EFFECTIVE. SEEK TO IDENTIFY CHIEF DETERRENTS TO PRIVATE INVESTMENT, FIND HOPE FOR DIVERSIFIED PRODUCTION, SPECIFY TYPES OF AID, AND ASCERTAIN WILLINGNESS OF LATIN AMERICA TO BRING ABOUT PROGRESS.

2655 US CONGRESS JOINT ECO COMM
THE UNITED STATES BALANCE OF PAYMENTS.
WASHINGTON: US GOVERNMENT, 1963, 406 PP.
HEARINGS BEFORE JOINT ECONOMIC COMMITTEE HEADED BY PAUL H. DOUGLAS ON OUTLOOK FOR US BALANCE OF PAYMENTS, AND FUNCTION AND REFORM OF INTERNATIONAL MONETARY SYSTEM. INCLUDES DISCUSSIONS ON GOLD EXCHANGE STANDARD, INTERNATIONAL LIQUIDITY, FOREIGN INVESTMENT, AND TRADE.

2656 US CONGRESS JOINT ECO COMM
THE UNITED STATES BALANCE OF PAYMENTS.
WASHINGTON: US GOVERNMENT, 1963, 587 PP.
"STATEMENTS BY ECONOMISTS, BANKERS AND OTHERS ON BROOKINGS INSTITUTION STUDY OF US BALANCE OF PAYMENTS IN 1968." SUBMITTED TO JOINT ECONOMIC COMMITTEE. INCLUDES ASSUMPTIONS, METHODS, INFERENCES, AND FINDINGS OF STUDY; PROBLEMS IT PRESENTS; AND POSSIBILITY OF PREDICTION OF MORE FAVORABLE BALANCE OF PAYMENTS IN 1968 BEING REALIZED.

2657 US CONGRESS JOINT ECO COMM
OUTLOOK FOR UNITED STATES BALANCE OF PAYMENTS.
WASHINGTON: GOVT PR OFFICE, 1963, 264 PP.
HEARINGS BEFORE SUBCOMMITTEE ON INTERNATIONAL EXCHANGE AND PAYMENTS OF JOINT ECONOMIC COMMITTEE OF CONGRESS. CONCERN WAYS TO IMPROVE US BALANCE OF PAYMENTS AND TO REDUCE DEFICIT; CONCENTRATE ON US COMPETITIVE POSITION AND CHALLENGE OF COMMON MARKET TO US EXPORTS. CONSIDER DEFENSE, FOREIGN AID, EXPANDING TOURISM, EXCHANGE RATES, CAPITAL, DEFECTS AND REFORMS OF INTERNATIONAL MONETARY SYSTEM.

2658 US CONGRESS JOINT ECO COMM
PRIVATE INVESTMENT IN LATIN AMERICA.
WASHINGTON: GOVT PR OFFICE, 1964, 492 PP.
RECORD OF HEARING BEFORE SUBCOMMITTEE ON INTER-AMERICAN ECONOMIC RELATIONSHIPS ON PRIVATE INVESTMENT IN LATIN AMERICA, INCLUDING TESTIMONY OF WITNESSES, ADDITIONAL TEXTS, AND EXHIBITS.

2659 US CONGRESS JOINT ECO COMM
GUIDELINES FOR INTERNATIONAL MONETARY REFORM.
WASHINGTON: US GOVERNMENT, 1965, 601 PP.
HEARINGS BEFORE SUBCOMMITTEE ON INTERNATIONAL EXCHANGE AND PAYMENTS OF JOINT ECONOMIC COMMITTEE HEADED BY HENRY S. REUSS ON DEVELOPMENT OF GUIDELINES FOR INTERNATIONAL MONETARY REFORM AND PARTICULAR CHARACTERISTICS OF FUTURE SYSTEM. DISCUSSES QUESTION OF EXPANDED ROLE OF INTERNATIONAL MONETARY FUND.

2660 US CONGRESS JOINT ECO COMM
NEW APPROACH TO UNITED STATES INTERNATIONAL ECONOMIC POLICY.
WASHINGTON: US GOVERNMENT, 1966, 44 PP.
HEARING BEFORE SUBCOMMITTEE ON INTERNATIONAL EXCHANGE AND PAYMENTS OF JOINT ECONOMIC COMMITTEE HEADED BY HENRY S. REUSS ON POSSIBILITY OF INTERNATIONAL CONFERENCE FOR HEADS OF STATE TO FURTHER POLITICAL MECHANISMS OF SOLUTIONS TO WORLD ECONOMIC PROBLEMS NOW THAT TECHNICAL MECHANISMS HAVE BEEN OBTAINED. DISCUSSES BALANCE OF PAYMENTS AND INTERNATIONAL MONETARY REFORM.

2661 US CONGRESS JOINT ECO COMM
MAINLAND CHINA IN THE WORLD ECONOMY (PAMPHLET)
WASHINGTON: US GOVERNMENT, 1967, 25 PP.
REPORT OF JOINT ECONOMIC COMMITTEE SUMMARIZES RESULTS OF HEARINGS ON ECONOMY OF MAINLAND CHINA. FINDINGS CONCERN IDEOLOGICAL IMPACT, RESOURCES, INTERNATIONAL TRADE PARTICIPATION, AND EFFECT OF US EMBARGO.

2662 US CONGRESS JOINT ECO COMM
ECONOMY IN GOVERNMENT (PAMPHLET)
WASHINGTON: US GOVERNMENT, 1967, 54 PP.
REPORT BY SUBCOMMITTEE ON ECONOMY IN GOVERNMENT. DESCRIBES PERSISTING PROBLEMS IN PROCUREMENT POLICIES, AND IN INVENTORY AND REAL ESTATE MANAGEMENT. SETS FORTH RECOMMENDATIONS TO CORRECT DEFICIENCIES.

2663 US CONGRESS JOINT ECO COMM
REPORT ON JANUARY 1967 ECONOMIC REPORT OF THE PRESIDENT.
WASHINGTON: US GOVERNMENT, 1967, 107 PP.
STATES MAJORITY AND MINORITY MEMBERS' CONCLUSIONS ABOUT PRESIDENT'S ECONOMIC REPORT. SURVEYS ECONOMIC OUTLOOK; FISCAL POLICY; MONETARY POLICY; GROWTH AND UNEMPLOYMENT; PRICES, COSTS, AND INCOME; COMPETITION; EMPLOYMENT AND HUMAN RESOURCES; INCOME MAINTENANCE; INTERNATIONAL TRADE AND FINANCE. REPORTS; COMMITTEE AND SUBCOMMITTEE ACTIVITIES.

2664 US CONGRESS JOINT ECO COMM
AN ECONOMIC PROFILE OF MAINLAND CHINA, VOLUMES I AND II.
WASHINGTON: US GOVERNMENT, 1967, 684 PP.
SYMPOSIUM BY AUTHORITIES ON COMMUNIST CHINA FOR CONGRESS' JOINT ECONOMIC COMMITTEE. FURNISHES CURRENT DATA AND INTERPRETATION ON DOMESTIC ECONOMY OF CHINA: ECONOMIC POLICY, TEMPO OF ECONOMIC DEVELOPMENT, CAPITAL FORMATION, DEFENSE, ECONOMIC SECTORS. VOLUME II TREATS POPULATION AND MANPOWER RESOURCES, EXTERNAL ECONOMIC RELATIONS.

2665 US CONGRESS JOINT ECO COMM
BACKGROUND MATERIAL ON ECONOMY IN GOVERNMENT 1967 (PAMPHLET)
WASHINGTON: US GOVERNMENT, 1967, 229 PP.
ANALYSIS OF FEDERAL PROPERTY HOLDINGS AND PROPERTY MANAGEMENT ACTIVITIES IN ORDER TO IMPROVE OPERATIONS AND LOWER COSTS. LISTS AMOUNT AND COST OF REAL PROPERTY HOLDINGS AND EXTENT OF DEFENSE DEPARTMENT PROPERTY ACTIVITIES AND YEARLY EXPENDITURES.

2666 US CONGRESS SENATE
SURVEY OF THE ALLIANCE FOR PROGRESS; INFLATION IN LATIN AMERICA (PAMPHLET)
WASHINGTON: US GOVERNMENT, 1967, 46 PP.
STUDY FOR SUBCOMMITTEE ON AMERICAN REPUBLICS AFFAIRS OF COMMITTEE ON FOREIGN RELATIONS TREATING INFLATION IN LATIN AMERICA AND QUESTIONS IT RAISES FOR US FOREIGN AID POLICY. DESCRIBES CAUSES AND CONSEQUENCES OF INFLATION, MEASURES FOR AVOIDING OR ELIMINATING IT, AND ROLE OF US IN LIMITING INFLATION. SUBCOMMITTEE WAS HEADED BY WAYNE MORSE.

2667 US DEPARTMENT OF LABOR
THE ANVIL AND THE PLOW.
WASHINGTON: US GOVERNMENT, 1963, 306 PP.
HISTORY OF DEPARTMENT OF LABOR, 1913-1963. INCLUDES ENTIRE RANGE OF ITS ACTIVITIES THROUGH THREE WARS, BULL MARKET OF 1920'S, GREAT DEPRESSION, POSTWAR RECOVERY, AND PEACETIME ECONOMY AFTER KOREA.

2668 US DEPARTMENT OF LABOR
PRODUCTIVITY: A BIBLIOGRAPHY.
WASHINGTON: US GOVERNMENT, 1966, 129 PP.
ANNOTATED BIBLIOGRAPHY OF 454 PUBLICATIONS ISSUED BETWEEN 1957-64. COVERS MATERIAL ON PRODUCTIVITY RATIOS, WITH EMPHASIS ON LABOR INPUT; EXCLUDES MATERIAL RELATED TO TIME AND MOTION STUDIES AT THE JOB LEVEL AND MATERIAL IN FIELD OF PSYCHOLOGY. ITEMS DIVIDED INTO SIX SUBJECT CLASSIFICATIONS, INCLUDING CONCEPTS, FACTORS, PRODUCTIVITY LEVELS, INTERNATIONAL WORKS, AND BIBLIOGRAPHIES.

2669 US DEPARTMENT OF LABOR
TECHNOLOGICAL TRENDS IN MAJOR AMERICAN INDUSTRIES.
WASHINGTON: US GOVERNMENT, 1966, 269 PP.
APPRAISES SOME OF MAJOR TECHNOLOGICAL CHANGES EMERGING AMONG AMERICAN INDUSTRIES AND PROJECTS THE IMPACT OF THESE CHANGES OVER NEXT 5-10 YEARS. EVALUATES GENERAL EFFECTS OF TECHNOLOGICAL PROGRESS ON FUTURE PATTERNS OF EMPLOYMENT, OCCUPATION, AND ISSUE OF LABOR-MANAGEMENT ADJUSTMENT. INCLUDES LENGTHY UNANNOTATED BIBLIOGRAPHY PRIMARILY CONSISTING OF POST-1962 PUBLICATIONS ON THE SUBJECT.

2670 US DEPARTMENT OF STATE
SOVIET BIBLIOGRAPHY (PAMPHLET)
WASHINGTON: DEPT OF STATE, 1949.
SERIES OF SOME 110 SEPARATE BIBLIOGRAPHIES PUBLISHED FROM 1949 TO 1953, AVERAGING ABOUT 18 PAGES EACH, AND CONTAINING MORE THAN 10,000 ITEMS. PUBLISHED BIMONTHLY AND INCLUDES ONLY ENGLISH-LANGUAGE WORKS SELECTED FROM SCHOLARLY JOURNALS, SPEECHES, GOVERNMENT DOCUMENTS, AND BOOKS. ARRANGED TOPICALLY AND ANNOTATED. ALL MATERIALS ARE CURRENT TO DATE OF BIBLIOGRAPHY. SUBJECT INDEX.

2671 US DEPARTMENT OF STATE
POINT FOUR: COOPERATIVE PROGRAM FOR AID IN THE DEVELOPMENT OF ECONOMICALLY UNDERDEVELOPED AREAS.
WASHINGTON: GOVT PR OFFICE, 1950, 167 PP.
EXPLAINS NATURE, PURPOSE, SCOPE, AND OPERATING ARRANGEMENTS OF POINT FOUR PROGRAM AND ITS RELATION TO UN PROGRAM OF ECONOMIC ASSISTANCE. DISCUSSES PROMOTION OF PEACE AND ECONOMIC PROGRESS, US INTEREST, AGRICULTURE, EDUCATION, AND HOUSING. STUDIES DEVELOPMENT OF INDUSTRY, NEED FOR ASSISTANCE, FINANCING OF PROGRAM THROUGH CAPITAL INVESTMENT AND TECHNICAL COOPERATION, AND LIVING STANDARDS.

2672 US DEPARTMENT OF STATE
POINT FOUR, NEAR EAST AND AFRICA, A SELECTED BIBLIOGRAPHY OF STUDIES ON ECONOMICALLY UNDERDEVELOPED COUNTRIES.
WASHINGTON: DEPT OF STATE, 1951, 136 PP.
ANNOTATED BIBLIOGRAPHY INCLUDES WORKS IN FRENCH AND ENGLISH DEALING PRIMARILY WITH ECONOMIC STUDIES OF VARIOUS

COUNTRIES AND REGIONS OF THE NEAR EAST, SOUTH ASIA, AND AFRICA MOSTLY WRITTEN IN THE PERIOD 1940-50. COMPILED AS REFERENCE GUIDE FOR PRESIDENT'S POINT FOUR PROGRAM. CONTAINS APPROXIMATELY 1,500 LISTINGS.

2673 US DEPARTMENT OF STATE
ECONOMIC PROBLEMS OF UNDERDEVELOPED AREAS (PAMPHLET)
WASHINGTON: US GOVERNMENT, 1956, 59 PP.
SHOWS CURRENT STATUS OF RESEARCH ON PROBLEMS OF ECONOMIC CHANGE AND DEVELOPMENT IN UNDERDEVELOPED AREAS UNDERTAKEN BY UNIVERSITIES AND RESEARCH INSTITUTES. PROJECTS ARE LISTED BY COUNTRY WITH WHICH CONCERNED. DESIGNED TO INDICATE STATUS AND AVAILABILITY OF RESEARCH REPORTED.

2674 US DEPARTMENT OF STATE
THE UNITED STATES ECONOMY AND THE MUTUAL SECURITY PROGRAM.
WASHINGTON: DEPT OF STATE, 1959, 130 PP.
DISCUSSES EFFECT OF MUTUAL SECURITY PROGRAM, AND ECONOMIC GROWTH OF OTHER NATIONS RECEIVING US AID ON US ECONOMY. EXTENSIVE APPENDIX ON DEVELOPMENT LOAN FUND, MILITARY ASSISTANCE, AND INTERNATIONAL TRADE.

2675 US DEPARTMENT OF STATE
RESEARCH ON THE USSR AND EASTERN EUROPE (EXTERNAL RESEARCH LIST NO 1-25)
WASHINGTON: DEPT OF STATE, 1966, 63 PP.
LIST OF SOCIAL SCIENCE RESEARCH SUBMITTED BY PRIVATE US SCHOLARS AND RESEARCH CENTERS TO DEPT OF STATE ON COMMUNIST COUNTRIES OF EASTERN EUROPE CURRENTLY "IN PROGRESS" OR "COMPLETED" BUT UNPUBLISHED AS OF LATTER DATE FOR PERIOD AUGUST 1965 THROUGH FEBRUARY 1966. MAJORITY OF ENTRIES ANNOTATED. ANNUAL PUBLICATION SINCE 1965.

2676 US DEPARTMENT OF STATE
RESEARCH ON WESTERN EUROPE, GREAT BRITAIN, AND CANADA (EXTERNAL RESEARCH LIST NO 3-25)
WASHINGTON: DEPT OF STATE, 1966, 120 PP.
SERIAL PUBLICATION OF DEPT OF STATE RECORDING SOCIAL SCIENCE RESEARCH SUBMITTED BY SCHOLARS IN US FOR PERIOD AUGUST 1965 THROUGH FEBRUARY 1966. ENTRIES ARRANGED BY SUBJECT AND CLASSIFIED AS "IN PROGRESS" OR "COMPLETED." APPEARS ANNUALLY SINCE 1965. MAJORITY OF ENTRIES ANNOTATED.

2677 US DEPT LABOR OFF SOLICITOR
LEGISLATIVE HISTORY OF THE LABOR-MANAGEMENT AND DISCLOSURE ACT OF 1959.
WASHINGTON: GOVT PR OFFICE, 1964, 1138 PP.
TEXT OF ACT, INCLUDING EXCERPTS ON CONGRESSIONAL DEBATE. ARRANGEMENT BY TITLE OF BILL; BILL OF RIGHTS OF MEMBERS OF LABOR ORGANIZATIONS, TRUSTEESHIPS, ELECTIONS.

2678 US ECON SURVEY TEAM INDONESIA
INDONESIA - PERSPECTIVE AND PROPOSALS FOR UNITED STATES ECONOMIC AID.
NEW HAVEN: YALE U, SE ASIA STUD, 1963, 205 PP.
EXAMINES ECONOMIC CONDITION, OPERATION OF LONG-TERM ECONOMIC PLANNING, PROGRESS OF ECONOMY IN AGRICULTURE, INDUSTRY, AND INTERNATIONAL TRADE, AND OBJECTIVES OF US AID IN INDONESIA. MAKES RECOMMENDATIONS FOR NEW AID PROGRAMS IN EDUCATION, INDUSTRY, AND TECHNOLOGICAL RESEARCH.

2679 US GENERAL ACCOUNTING OFFICE
EXAM OF ECONOMIC AND TECHNICAL ASSISTANCE PROGRAM FOR INDIA INT'NAT'L COOP ADMIN REPORT TO CONGRESS 1955-1958.
WASHINGTON: US GOVERNMENT, 1959, 93 PP.
REVIEWS USE OF US CAPITAL AND GOODS GIVEN INDIA TO AID HER FIVE-YEAR ECONOMIC PLAN. EMPHASIS ON ADEQUACY OF FINANCIAL AND ADMINISTRATIVE PROCEDURES. REVIEWED ALL PROGRAMS AND FOUND PROJECTS UNDERSTAFFED, "OVER PROGRAMMED," AND LACKING IN CONTROL OF DISTRIBUTION OF SUPPLIES AND CAPITAL. RECOMMENDATIONS ARE GIVEN TO SPEED UP EACH PROJECT.

2680 US GENERAL ACCOUNTING OFFICE
EXAMINATION OF ECONOMIC AND TECHNICAL ASSISTANCE PROGRAM FOR GUATEMALA.
WASHINGTON: US GOVERNMENT, 1960, 59 PP.
REPORT TO US CONGRESS BY COMPTROLLER GENERAL, 1960, ON PROGRAM AS ADMINISTERED BY ICA OF DEPARTMENT OF STATE FOR FISCAL YEARS 1955-59. SHOWS MOST OF MAJOR DEVELOPMENT PROJECTS BEHIND SCHEDULE. MAINTAINS PROGRESS HAS BEEN MADE IN SPITE OF POLITICAL UNREST IN GUATEMALA THAT CAUSED MANY PROJECT DELAYS.

2681 US GENERAL ACCOUNTING OFFICE
EXAMINATION OF ECONOMIC AND TECHNICAL ASSISTANCE PROGRAM FOR IRAN.
WASHINGTON: US GOVERNMENT, 1961, 80 PP.
REPORTS ON ADMINISTRATION OF FOREIGN AID TO IRAN, BREAKING DOWN NATURE AND AMOUNT OF AID, SPENDING PRACTICES, WASTAGE, AND PROBLEMS OF CONTROL. CASE STUDIES GIVE SPECIFIC ILLUSTRATIONS OF USAGE AND EFFECT OF US AID.

2682 UNITED STATES
REPORT TO INTER-AMERICAN ECONOMIC AND SOCIAL COUNCIL AT SECOND ANNUAL MEETING.
WASHINGTON: US GOVERNMENT, 1963, 183 PP.
REVIEW OF US ROLE AND RESPONSIBILITY IN ALLIANCE FOR PROGRESS. STUDIES ECONOMIES OF US AND LA SEPARATELY AND REVIEWS AND EVALUATES ALL US PROGRAMS FOR ECONOMIC AND FINANCIAL AID. LA RECIEVES MORE US AID THAN ANY NATION. NOTES INCREASE IN LONG-TERM LOW INTEREST LOANS. SUGGESTS WAYS TO IMPROVE PROGRAMS FOR FUTURE.

2683 US HOUSE COMM FOREIGN AFFAIRS
SECTION-BY-SECTION ANALYSIS OF THE PROPOSED FOREIGN ASSISTANCE ACT OF 1967 (PAMPHLET)
WASHINGTON: US GOVERNMENT, 1967, 24 PP.
REPORT RECOMMENDS FURTHER AMENDMENT OF FOREIGN ASSISTANCE ACT OF 1961. PURPOSE OF PROPOSED 1967 BILL IS TO CLEARLY STATE OBJECTIVES, STANDARDS, AND PROGRAM TECHNIQUES OF FOREIGN ASSISTANCE, CODIFYING EXPERIENCE GATHERED SINCE ENACTMENT OF EARLIER BILL. INCLUDES COMPLETE ANALYSIS OF PROPOSED ACT.

2684 US HOUSE
URBAN RENEWAL: HOUSE COMMITTEE ON BANKING AND CURRENCY.
WASHINGTON: GOVT PR OFFICE, 1963, 527 PP.
HEARINGS HELD OCTOBER, 1963, BEFORE SUBCOMMITTEE ON HOUSING TO FIND OUT FACTS OF OPERATIONS OF URBAN RENEWAL PROJECTS AND TO CORRECT ANY LEGISLATIVE FAULTS THAT MIGHT BE HAMPERING THE PROGRAM. AMONG THOSE WHO TESTIFIED WERE MAYORS OF FIVE AMERICAN CITIES, URBAN RENEWAL EXPERTS, AND PROMINENT BUSINESS AND CIVIC LEADERS INVOLVED IN THE PROGRAM.

2685 US HOUSE
MESSAGE FROM THE PRESIDENT OF THE UNITED STATES: URBAN AND RURAL POVERTY (PAMPHLET)
WASHINGTON: US GOVERNMENT, 1967, 16 PP.
RECOMMENDATIONS FOR AMENDING ECONOMIC OPPORTUNITY ACT OF 1967 TO "GIVE NEW DIRECTION AND MOMENTUM TO THE PROGRAMS IN RURAL AREAS." DISCUSSES LEGAL SERVICES AND NEIGHBORHOOD CENTERS AND YOUTH CORPS, JOB CORPS, VISTA, RURAL LOAN PROGRAMS, RENT SUPPLEMENTS, MODEL CITIES, URBAN TRANSPORTATION, ETC. RECOMMENDS LEGISLATION TO PROVIDE FOR INCREASED SERVICE IN ALL AREAS.

2686 US HOUSE COMM APPROPRIATIONS
MUTUAL SECURITY PROGRAM APPROPRIATIONS FOR 1952: HEARINGS BEFORE A SUBCOMMITTEE OF THE COMMITTEE ON APPROPRIATIONS.
WASHINGTON: US GOVERNMENT, 1951, 798 PP.
HEARINGS BEFORE SUBCOMMITTEE ON ECONOMIC COOPERATION ADMINISTRATION. TESTIMONY COVERS PROGRAMS FOR MILITARY ASSISTANCE TO NORTH ATLANTIC TREATY AREA OF WESTERN EUROPE, MIDDLE EAST (GREECE, TURKEY, IRAN), SOUTHEASTERN ASIA, AND LATIN AMERICA. TOTAL REQUEST OF SIX BILLION WEIGHED AGAINST COMMUNIST THREAT IN GENERAL AND KOREAN CONFLICT IN PARTICULAR.

2687 US HOUSE COMM BANKING CURRENCY
HEARINGS BEFORE HOUSE COMMITTEE ON BANKING AND CURRENCY: SALE OF SBA LOAN POOL PARTICIPATIONS.
WASHINGTON: US GOVERNMENT, 1966, 300 PP.
DISCUSSION AND TESTIMONY ON PROPOSAL TO AMEND SMALL BUSINESS ACT TO AUTHORIZE ISSUANCE AND SALE OF PARTICIPATION INTERESTS, BASED ON CERTAIN POOLS OF LOANS TO BE HELD BY SMALL BUSINESS ADMINISTRATION.

2688 US HOUSE COMM BANKING-CURR
RECENT CHANGES IN MONETARY POLICY AND BALANCE OF PAYMENTS PROBLEMS.
WASHINGTON: US GOVERNMENT, 1963, 412 PP.
HEARINGS BEFORE HOUSE COMMITTEE ON BANKING AND CURRENCY HEADED BY WRIGHT PATMAN ON POLICY ACTIONS OTHER THAN RAISING SHORT-TERM INTEREST RATES THAT WOULD POSITIVELY AFFECT BALANCE OF PAYMENTS. ALSO INCLUDES INVESTIGATION OF EFFECTS THIS MOVE HAS HAD ON EUROPEAN CENTRAL BANKS.

2689 US HOUSE COMM BANKING-CURR
INTERNATIONAL DEVELOPMENT ASSOCIATION ACT AMENDMENT.
WASHINGTON: GOVT PR OFFICE, 1964, 104 PP.
COMMITTEE REPORT ON ACT TO AMEND INTERNATIONAL ASSOCIATION ACT IN ORDER THAT US MAY BE AUTHORIZED TO PARTICIPATE IN INCREASE OF RESOURCES OF INTERNATIONAL DEVELOPMENT ASSOCIATION. STATEMENTS BY SENATORS HARVEY, PATMAN, RUESS, AND SECRETARY OF STATE RUSK.

2690 US HOUSE COMM BANKING-CURR
INTERNATIONAL TRAVEL IN RELATION TO THE BALANCE OF PAYMENTS DEFICIT.
WASHINGTON: US GOVERNMENT, 1965, 413 PP.
HEARINGS BEFORE SPECIAL SUBCOMMITTEE ON TOURISM OF HOUSE COMMITTEE ON BANKING AND CURRENCY ON METHODS OF ELIMINATING TWO BILLION DOLLAR BALANCE OF PAYMENTS DEFICIT CAUSED BY TOURISTS' SPENDING ABROAD. SUGGESTS MAKING TRAVEL OF EUROPEANS IN US EASIER, CHEAPER, AND MORE ATTRACTIVE.

2691 US HOUSE COMM FOREIGN AFFAIRS
REPORT OF THE SPECIAL STUDY MISSION TO AFRICA, SOUTH AND EAST OF THE SAHARA (PAMPHLET)
WASHINGTON: GOVT PR OFFICE, 1956, 151 PP.
SURVEY OF CONGRESSIONAL VISIT TO SOUTHERN AFRICA DESCRIB-

ING CONDITIONS IN EACH COUNTRY OR TERRITORY. EXPLAINS MEDICAL PROBLEMS IN AFRICA AND FACILITIES AVAILABLE. DEALS WITH US POLICY, AID PROGRAMS, AND COLONIAL SITUATION.

2692 US HOUSE COMM FOREIGN AFFAIRS
HEARINGS ON HR 12449 A BILL TO AMEND FURTHER THE FOREIGN ASSISTANCE ACT OF 1961.
WASHINGTON: GOVT PR OFFICE, 1966, 1092 PP.
TESTIMONIES AND STATEMENTS BY PUBLIC OFFICIALS ON US FOREIGN AID PROGRAMS WITH EMPHASIS ON ACTIVITIES OF AGENCY FOR INTERNATIONAL DEVELOPMENT. INCLUDES AID MEMORANDA ON CONTINGENCY FUNDS, AID PERSONNEL REQUIREMENTS IN VIETNAM, BRAZILIAN PURCHASE OF EAST GERMAN LOCOMOTIVES, ANTI-AMERICAN STUDENT DEMONSTRATIONS, AFRICAN ATTITUDE TOWARDS US AID, ETC.

2693 US HOUSE COMM FOREIGN AFFAIRS
THE FOREIGN POLICY ASPECTS OF THE KENNEDY ROUND (PAMPHLET)
WASHINGTON: US GOVERNMENT, 1967, 11 PP.
REPORT OF SUBCOMMITTEE OF FOREIGN ECONOMIC POLICY ON THE KENNEDY ROUND, 1966-67. URGES LOWERING OF BARRIERS TO INTERNATIONAL COMMERCE WITHIN FRAMEWORK OF ADJUSTMENT ASSISTANCE TO INJURED DOMESTIC FIRMS AND WORKERS.

2694 US HOUSE COMM FOREIGN AFFAIRS
REPORT OF SPECIAL STUDY MISSION TO THE NEAR EAST (PAMPHLET)
WASHINGTON: US GOVERNMENT, 1967, 70 PP.
REPORT TO COMMITTEE ON FOREIGN AFFAIRS GIVES FINDINGS OF SPECIAL STUDY MISSION TO NEAR EAST, NOVEMBER-DECEMBER, 1966. MEMBERS EXAMINED UN PEACEKEEPING AND OTHER ACTIVITIES; MILITARY AND POLITICAL SIGNIFICANCE OF DIPLOMATIC ACTIVITIES; YEMEN WAR; ASSISTANCE PROGRAMS; WATER DEVELOPMENT IN ISRAEL; EXPROPRIATION AND NATIONALIZATION OF AMERICAN FIRMS AND PROPERTY; AND THE ARMS RACE.

2695 US HOUSE COMM FOREIGN AFFAIRS
FOREIGN ASSISTANCE ACT OF 1967 (PAMPHLET)
WASHINGTON: US GOVERNMENT, 1967, 137 PP.
REPORT OF COMMITTEE ON FOREIGN AFFAIRS RECOMMENDS PASSAGE OF FOREIGN ASSISTANCE ACT OF 1967. INCLUDES AUTHORIZATIONS THROUGH 1969. DISCUSSES IMPORTANCE AND OBJECTIVES OF FOREIGN AID. REPRODUCES IN ENTIRETY PROVISIONS OF BILL.

2696 US HOUSE COMM FOREIGN AFFAIRS
COMMUNIST ACTIVITIES IN LATIN AMERICA 1967 (PAMPHLET)
WASHINGTON: US GOVERNMENT, 1967, 24 PP.
REPORT OF SUBCOMMITTEE ON INTER-AMERICAN AFFAIRS OF COMMITTEE ON FOREIGN AFFAIRS. GIVES FINDINGS AND RECOMMENDATIONS WITH REGARD TO COMMUNIST ACTIVITIES IN LATIN AMERICA, 1967. URGES PLANNING TO ELIMINATE GUERRILLA ACTIVITIES; CUTTING OFF FREE-WORLD TRADE WITH CUBA; INVESTIGATION OF LATIN AMERICAN SOLIDARITY CONFERENCE; STRENGTHENING OAS MEASURES; AND INCREASING US PROPAGANDA EFFORTS.

2697 US HOUSE COMM GOVT OPERATIONS
UNITED STATES AID OPERATIONS IN LAOS.
WASHINGTON: US GOVERNMENT, 1959, 983 PP.
HEARINGS ON US AID TO LAOS. INVESTIGATES EFFECT OF MILITARY AID ON ECONOMIC AND POLITICAL STABILITY AND METHODS OF IMPROVING ADMINISTRATION OF PROGRAM TO FURTHER POLITICAL OBJECTIVES.

2698 US HOUSE COMM GOVT OPERATIONS
OPERATIONS OF THE DEVELOPMENT LOAN FUND: HEARINGS (COMMITTEE ON GOVERNMENT OPERATIONS)
WASHINGTON: GOVT PR OFFICE, 1960, 636 PP.
INQUIRY INTO OPERATIONS AND ADMINISTRATION OF FUND. REPORT IN DIALOGUE FORM ONLY. QUESTIONS MEN HANDLING RECORDS AND MEN DISPERSING MONEY TO NATIONS. FEELS MONEY IS BEING WASTED OR NOT USED FOR WELFARE AND SECURITY OF US. RECOMMENDS CENTRALIZING FUND AND CONTROLLING PROJECTS AS WELL AS GIVING FAIR LOAN TERMS, ETC. FEELS NEED FOR OFFICIAL POLICY STATEMENT OF RULES.

2699 US HOUSE COMM GOVT OPERATIONS
US OWNED FOREIGN CURRENCIES: HEARINGS (COMMITTEE ON GOVERNMENT OPERATIONS)
WASHINGTON: GOVT PR OFFICE, 1964, 260 PP.
REVIEW OF EIGHT FOREIGN NATIONS WHERE US HAS EXCESS AMOUNTS OF FOREIGN CURRENCY FOR FUTURE NEEDS. EMPHASIS ON INDIA WHERE US HAS 20-YEAR SUPPLY OF RUPEES. SUGGESTIONS MADE TO HELP AID PROJECTS UTILIZE THIS EXCESS IN PLACE OF APPROPRIATED US DOLLARS OR TO USE EXCESS TO PAY OFF FOREIGN DEBTS.

2700 US HOUSE COMM GOVT OPERATIONS
FEDERALLY FINANCED SOCIAL RESEARCH, EXPENDITURES, STATUS, AND OBJECTIVES (PAMPHLET)
WASHINGTON: US GOVERNMENT, 1967.
PART I OF REPORT ON USE OF SOCIAL RESEARCH IN FEDERAL DOMESTIC PROGRAMS. DISCUSSES FEDERAL RESPONSIBILITIES, ACTIVITIES, AND AID IN FIELD OF SOCIAL RESEARCH.

2701 US HOUSE COMM ON COMMERCE
PARTNERSHIP FOR HEALTH AMENDMENTS FOR 1967 (PAMPHLET)
WASHINGTON: GOVT PR OFFICE, 1967, 89 PP.
INTERSTATE AND FOREIGN COMMERCE COMMITTEE REPORT ON HR 6418, 90TH CONGRESS, AMENDING PUBLIC HEALTH SERVICE ACT TO PROVIDE INCREASED FINANCING FOR COMPREHENSIVE HEALTH PLANNING, TO REGULATE CLINICAL LABORATORIES, AND FOR OTHER PURPOSES. INCLUDES MINOR OBJECTIONS OF MINORITY.

2702 US HOUSE COMM POST OFFICE
MANPOWER UTILIZATION IN THE FEDERAL GOVERNMENT.
WASHINGTON: GOVT PR OFFICE, 1958, 401 PP.
HEARINGS BEFORE SUBCOMMITTEE ON MANPOWER UTILIZATION, OF THE HOUSE COMMITTEE ON POST OFFICE AND CIVIL SERVICE OF THE 85TH CONGRESS. HEARINGS HELD DECEMBER, 1958, WEIGHED ACTIONS TAKEN ON VARIOUS EXECUTIVE ORDERS; HEARD REPORTS OF SPECIAL STUDIES OF WASTE AND INEFFICIENCY IN FEDERAL EMPLOYMENT. RECOMMENDATIONS MADE FOR MORE EFFICIENCY IN CIVIL SERVICE PROGRAMS.

2703 US HOUSE COMM POST OFFICE
MANPOWER UTILIZATION IN THE FEDERAL GOVERNMENT.
WASHINGTON: GOVT PR OFFICE, 1958, 200 PP.
HEARINGS BEFORE SUBCOMMITTEE ON MANPOWER UTILIZATION, OF THE HOUSE COMMITTEE ON POST OFFICE AND CIVIL SERVICE OF THE 85TH CONGRESS. HEARINGS HELD APRIL AND MAY, 1958, CONSIDERED PROPOSAL THAT A CAREER EXECUTIVE PROGRAM BE SET UP TO TRAIN CAREER CIVIL SERVANTS FOR SERVICE IN ADMINISTRATIVE AND MANAGERIAL POSITIONS.

2704 US HOUSE COMM SCI ASTRONAUT
AUTHORIZING APPROPRIATIONS TO THE NATIONAL AERONAUTICS AND SPACE ADMINISTRATION (PAMPHLET)
WASHINGTON: US GOVERNMENT, 1967, 194 PP.
AUTHORIZES 1968 NASA APPROPRIATIONS. FUNDS ALLOCATED FOR RESEARCH AND DEVELOPMENT, CONSTRUCTION OF FACILITIES, ADMINISTRATIVE OPERATIONS, AND OTHER USES. EXPLAINS AUTHORIZATIONS OF FUNDS FOR SEPARATE NASA PROGRAMS.

2705 US HOUSE COMM SCI ASTRONAUT
GOVERNMENT, SCIENCE, AND INTERNATIONAL POLICY (PAMPHLET)
WASHINGTON: US GOVERNMENT, 1967, 81 PP.
SIX PAPERS, BY SCIENTISTS FROM VARIOUS NATIONS, PRESENTED TO PANEL ON SCIENCE AND TECHNOLOGY OF SCIENCE AND ASTRONAUTICS COMMITTEE. MOST DEAL PRIMARILY WITH BACKGROUND OF SCIENTIFIC RESEARCH, GOVERNMENT SCIENCE POLICIES, AND SCIENCE-INDUSTRY RELATION IN SPECIFIC COUNTRIES. SI LESS CONCERNED WITH SCIENCE AND FOREIGN AFFAIRS THAN TITLE INDICATES, BUT SOME ATTENTION IS GIVEN TO THIS SUBJECT.

2706 US LIBRARY OF CONGRESS
SELECTED AND ANNOTATED BIBLIOGRAPHY ON AGRICULTURAL PROBLEMS AND POLICIES IN A WARTIME ECONOMY (PAMPHLET)
WASHINGTON: LIBRARY OF CONGRESS.
SERIES OF THREE PAMPHLETS (APRIL, 1941-MARCH 1942; APRIL-DECEMBER, 1942; JANUARY-MAY 1943), EACH OF WHICH INCLUDES 415 TO 800 ANNOTATED ITEMS. BOOKS, ARTICLES, JOURNALS AND GOVERNMENT DOCUMENTS (BOTH FOREIGN AND US) ARE ARRANGED TOPICALLY AND THEN BY COUNTRY. MATERIALS ARE CURRENT: 1941-1943 WITH SOME IN FOREIGN LANGUAGES. TONE IS DESCRIPTIVE AS WELL AS STATISTICAL. INCLUDES ENEMY NATIONS.

2707 US LIBRARY OF CONGRESS
SELECTED AND ANNOTATED BIBLIOGRAPHY ON INDUSTRIAL PROBLEMS AND POLICIES IN WARTIME (PAMPHLET)
WASHINGTON: LIBRARY OF CONGRESS.
SERIES OF THREE PAMPHLETS (APRIL, 1941-MARCH 1942; APRIL-DECEMBER 1942; JANUARY-MAY, 1943), EACH OF WHICH INCLUDES 650 TO 1,400 ANNOTATED ITEMS. BOOKS, ARTICLES, JOURNALS, AND GOVERNMENT DOCUMENTS (BOTH FOREIGN AND US) ARE ARRANGED TOPICALLY BY INDUSTRY AND THEN BY COUNTRY. MOST MATERIALS ARE CURRENT: 1941-43. TONE IS DESCRIPTIVE AS WELL AS STATISTICAL. INCLUDES ENEMY NATIONS.

2708 US LIBRARY OF CONGRESS
SELECTED AND ANNOTATED BIBLIOGRAPHY ON LABOR PROBLEMS AND POLICIES IN A WARTIME ECONOMY (PAMPHLET)
WASHINGTON: LIBRARY OF CONGRESS.
SERIES OF THREE PAMPHLETS (APRIL, 1941-MARCH 1942; APRIL-DECEMBER, 1942; JANUARY-MAY 1943), EACH OF WHICH INCLUDES 450 TO 760 ANNOTATED ITEMS. BOOKS, ARTICLES, JOURNALS AND GOVERNMENT DOCUMENTS (BOTH FOREIGN AND US) ARE ARRANGED TOPICALLY AND THEN BY COUNTRY. MATERIALS ARE CURRENT: 1941-1943 WITH SOME IN FOREIGN LANGUAGES. TONE IS DESCRIPTIVE AS WELL AS STATISTICAL. INCLUDES ENEMY NATIONS.

2709 US LIBRARY OF CONGRESS
SELECTED AND ANNOTATED BIBLIOGRAPHY ON RAW MATERIALS IN A WARTIME ECONOMY (PAMPHLET)
WASHINGTON: LIBRARY OF CONGRESS.
SERIES OF THREE PAMPHLETS (APRIL, 1941-MARCH 1942; APRIL-DECEMBER, 1942; JANUARY-MAY 1943), EACH OF WHICH INCLUDES 450 TO 700 ANNOTATED ITEMS. THESE ARE ARTICLES, YEARBOOKS, GOVERNMENT DOCUMENTS, AND REPORTS (BOTH FOREIGN AND DOMESTIC) ARRANGED BY WORLD AREA AND TYPE OF RAW MATERIAL. MOST MATERIALS ARE CURRENT: 1941-43. TONE IS DESCRIPTIVE AS WELL AS STATISTICAL. INCLUDES ENEMY NATIONS.

2710 US LIBRARY OF CONGRESS

SOUTHERN ASIA ACCESSIONS LIST.
WASHINGTON: LIBRARY OF CONGRESS.
PERIODICAL PUBLISHED QUARTERLY THROUGH 1956 UNDER TITLE "SOUTHERN ASIA: PUBLICATIONS IN WESTERN LANGUAGES, A QUARTERLY ACCESSION LIST." FROM 1956 TO DECEMBER, 1960, PUBLISHED MONTHLY UNDER CURRENT TITLE AT WHICH TIME DISCONTINUED. EACH POST-1956 VOLUME ARRANGED BY COUNTRY AND SUBJECT (FOR WESTERN LANGUAGES) AND SIMILAR SEPARATE LISTING FOR EASTERN-LANGUAGE PUBLICATIONS. ITEMS CURRENT TO PUBLICATION OF LISTING.

2711 US LIBRARY OF CONGRESS
EAST EUROPEAN ACCESSIONS INDEX.
WASHINGTON: LIBRARY OF CONGRESS.
MONTHLY LIST OF PUBLICATIONS RECEIVED FROM IRON CURTAIN COUNTRIES. ENTRIES ARE ARRANGED MONTHLY BY COUNTRY AND GROUPED UNDER 17 SUBJECTS LISTED IN CONTENTS. ABOUT 15,000 ENTRIES ARE RECEIVED MONTHLY IN ALL EASTERN LANGUAGES PLUS ENGLISH.

2712 US LIBRARY OF CONGRESS
ECONOMICS OF WAR (APRIL 1941-MARCH 1942)
WASHINGTON: LIBRARY OF CONGRESS, 1942, 120 PP.
ANNOTATED BIBLIOGRAPHY ON ECONOMIC PROBLEMS AND POLICIES IN WARTIME INCLUDES 913 ITEMS ARRANGED BY SUBJECT AND INDEXED BY AUTHOR. LISTS REFERENCES ON GENERAL ECONOMIC CONDITIONS; INCOME, CONSUMPTION, AND EXPENDITURE; PRICES, WAGES, COST OF LIVING; INTERNATIONAL TRADE; BANKING; STATE AND MUNICIPAL FINANCE; ETC. ALSO LISTS ITEMS RELATING TO WARTIME FINANCE, POLICIES, RATIONING, LEND-LEASE ETC.

2713 US LIBRARY OF CONGRESS
THE WAR PRODUCTION PROGRAM: SELECTED DOCUMENTATION ON THE ECONOMICS OF WAR (PAMPHLET)
WASHINGTON: LIBRARY OF CONGRESS, 1942, 31 PP.
ANNOTATED MATERIALS, TOPICALLY ARRANGED, ON US WAR PRODUCTION PROGRAM. SOME 150 ARTICLES, GOVERNMENT DOCUMENTS, PAMPHLETS, AND REPORTS FROM 1939-42 ON ASPECTS OF PROGRAM. ALL US SOURCES.

2714 US LIBRARY OF CONGRESS
POSTWAR PLANNING AND RECONSTRUCTION: JANUARY-MARCH 1943.
WASHINGTON: LIBRARY OF CONGRESS, 1947, 135 PP.
ANNOTATED BIBLIOGRAPHY ON POSTWAR PLANS AND PROBLEMS. CONTAINS 862 ITEMS (INCLUDING BOOKS, ARTICLES, AND PAMPHLETS) AND COVERS JANUARY-DECEMBER, 1943. ARRANGED BY SUBJECT; TREATS POLITICAL, SOCIAL, ECONOMIC ASPECTS OF WORLD WAR II. LISTS BIBLIOGRAPHIC AND REFERENCE MATERIALS. PART OF LIBRARY OF CONGRESS SERIES OF "BIBLIOGRAPHIES OF THE WORLD AT WAR."

2715 US LIBRARY OF CONGRESS
EAST EUROPEAN ACCESSIONS LIST (VOL. I)
WASHINGTON: LIBRARY OF CONGRESS, 1951, 1500 PP., LC#51-60032
RECORD OF EASTERN EUROPEAN MONOGRAPHS AND PERIODICALS SINCE 1939 IN ENGLISH AND LANGUAGE OF ORIGINAL COUNTRY; ARRANGED BY COUNTRY AND DIVIDED INTO PERIODICALS AND MONOGRAPHS WHICH ARE FURTHER DIVIDED INTO SUBJECTS.

2716 US LIBRARY OF CONGRESS
UNITED STATES DIRECT ECONOMIC AID TO FOREIGN COUNTRIES: A COLLECTION OF EXCERPTS AND A BIBLIOGRAPHY (PAMPHLET)
WASHINGTON: LIBRARY OF CONGRESS, 1956, 60 PP.
PROVIDES BACKGROUND TO DEBATE ON FOREIGN AID AND SAMPLING OF VIEWS ON CONTINUANCE OF FOREIGN ECONOMIC ASSISTANCE. BIBLIOGRAPHY APPENDED AS GUIDE TO EXTENSIVE PUBLISHED MATERIAL ON SUBJECT. SHORT BIBLIOGRAPHY IS ANNOTATED.

2717 US LIBRARY OF CONGRESS
A LIST OF AMERICAN DOCTORAL DISSERTATIONS ON AFRICA.
WASHINGTON: LIBRARY OF CONGRESS, 1962, 69 PP., LC#62-60088.
700 THESES, ON SUBJECTS RELATING TO AFRICA, WHICH HAVE BEEN ACCEPTED BY US AND CANADIAN UNIVERSITIES FROM LATE 19TH CENTURY TO 1961. ARRANGED ALPHABETICALLY BY AUTHOR.

2718 US LIBRARY OF CONGRESS
SOUTHEAST ASIA.
WASHINGTON: LIBRARY OF CONGRESS, 1964, 180 PP., LC#63-60089.
AN UPDATED VERSION OF 1952 LIBRARY OF CONGRESS PUBLICATION "SOUTHEAST ASIA: AN ANNOTATED BIBLIOGRAPHY OF SELECTED REFERENCE SOURCES." CONTAINS 535 ENTRIES, EACH WITH A CRITICAL APPRAISAL IN SUBSTANTIVE LANGUAGE OF THE TEXT, BIBLIOGRAPHY, MAPS, ILLUSTRATIONS, STATISTICAL TABLES, AND DOCUMENTS. COVERS HISTORY, GOVERNMENT, ECONOMICS, SOCIAL CONDITIONS, AND CULTURAL LIFE OF THE AREA.

2719 US MARITIME ADMINISTRATION
CONTRIBUTION OF FEDERAL AID PROGRAMS TO THE OCEANBORNE FOREIGN TRADE OF THE UNITED STATES: 1959-62 (PAMPHLET)
WASHINGTON: US GOVERNMENT, 1964, 15 PP.
GIVES BREAKDOWN OF FEDERAL SPENDING TO SUPPORT US SHIPPING INDUSTRY IN DOLLAR PER TON. DISCUSSES OBJECTIONS OF FOREIGN MARITIME NATIONS TO US GOVERNMENT-SPONSORED CARGOES.

2720 US NATIONAL LABOR RELATIONS BD
LEGISLATIVE HISTORY OF THE LABOR-MANAGEMENT REPORTING AND DISCLOSURE ACT OF 1959 (2 VOLS.)
WASHINGTON: GOVT PR OFFICE, 1959, 1927 PP.
COLLECTION OF DOCUMENTS DEALING WITH LABOR-MANAGEMENT REPORTING AND DISCLOSURE ACT OF 1959, ITS LEGISLATIVE HISTORY, AMENDMENTS TO LABOR MANAGEMENT RELATIONS ACT OF 1947, CONGRESSIONAL BILLS, AND PROCEEDINGS ON SUBJECT.

2721 US OFFICE ECONOMIC OPPORTUNITY
CATALOG OF FEDERAL PROGRAMS FOR INDIVIDUAL AND COMMUNITY IMPROVEMENT.
WASHINGTON: US GOVERNMENT, 1965, 414 PP.
DESCRIBES NATURE AND PURPOSES OF GOVERNMENTAL PROGRAMS TO HELP INDIVIDUALS AND COMMUNITIES. NOTES MAJOR ELIGIBILITY REQUIREMENTS AND HOW TO APPLY. LISTS PRINTED MATERIAL AVAILABLE ON PROGRAM. NOTES AUTHORIZING LEGISLATION AND ADMINISTERING AGENCY.

2722 US OFFICE OF THE PRESIDENT
REPORT TO CONGRESS ON THE MUTUAL SECURITY PROGRAM FOR THE SIX MONTHS ENDED JUNE 30, 1955.
WASHINGTON: US GOVERNMENT, 1955, 60 PP.
PROGRESS REPORT ON OPERATIONS AND EXPENDITURES DURING FIRST HALF OF 1955. MAJOR PORTION OF MILITARY AID SHIPMENTS WENT TO EUROPE. LARGEST INVESTMENT IN NONMILITARY FUNDS WAS IN ASIA. DETAILED ANALYSES OF PROGRAMS IN FREE ASIA, NEAR EAST, AFRICA, LATIN AMERICA, AND EUROPE COVER 70 COUNTRIES. INTERNATIONAL COOPERATION ADMINISTRATION WAS ESTABLISHED IN STATE DEPARTMENT TO DIRECT MUTUAL SECURITY PROGRAMS.

2723 US OFFICE OF THE PRESIDENT
REPORT TO CONGRESS ON THE MUTUAL SECURITY PROGRAM FOR THE SIX MONTHS ENDED DECEMBER 31, 1955.
WASHINGTON: US GOVERNMENT, 1956, 37 PP.
PROGRESS REPORT ON OPERATIONS AND EXPENDITURES DURING SECOND HALF OF 1955 AND ANTICIPATED NEEDS FOR 1956. USSR'S AID TO COUNTRIES OUTSIDE COMMUNIST BLOC SEEN AS MAJOR THREAT. BUDGET OF $2.9 BILLION NEEDED PRIMARILY FOR MILITARY AID AND DEFENSE SUPPORT WITH 52% OF FUNDS EARMARKED FOR ASIA. USE OF ECONOMIC RESOURCES ABROAD AND SHARING TECHNICAL SKILLS EMPHASIZED.

2724 US OPERATIONS MISSION - TURKEY
SOME POSSIBILITIES FOR ACCELERATING TURKEY'S ECONOMIC GROWTH.
WASHINGTON: US GOVERNMENT, 1960, 75 PP.
SUMMARIZES CURRENT PROBLEMS IN EXPANDING THE TURKISH GROSS NATIONAL PRODUCT AND OFFERS SUGGESTIONS AS TO ACTION THAT WOULD HELP ACHIEVE HIGHER GROWTH RATE WHILE MAINTAINING A STABLE ECONOMY. PROPOSES INCREASED RELIANCE ON DOMESTIC PRODUCTS, IMPROVEMENT OF COMPOSITION OF INVESTMENT, AND INTRODUCTION OF PRIVATE FOREIGN CAPITAL AND LOANS.

2725 US OPERATIONS MISSION TO VIET
BUILDING ECONOMIC STRENGTH (PAMPHLET)
WASHINGTON: US OPER MISS VIET, 1958, 80 PP.
REPORT ON US ECONOMIC AID OPERATIONS IN SOUTH VIETNAM FOR FISCAL 1958. GIVES STATISTICAL DATA ON FOOD PRODUCTION, EDUCATION, HEALTH SERVICES, INDUSTRIAL GROWTH, PUBLIC ADMINISTRATION, AND TRAINING FOR PUBLIC SERVICE ABROAD.

2726 US PRES COMM ECO IMPACT DEFENS
REPORT* JULY 1965.
WASHINGTON: GOVT PR OFFICE, 1966, 92 PP., LC#66-60269.
BASIC CONCENTRATION ON INTERNAL IMPACT OF CHANGING DEFENSE EXPENDITURES, ALSO A CONCERN FOR EFFECTS ON BALANCE OF PAYMENTS. MOST VALUABLE FOR INCLUSIVECOLLECTION OF ALL DEFENSE-RELATED EXPENDITURE DATA.

2727 US SENATE COMM APPROPRIATIONS
FOREIGN ASSISTANCE AND RELATED AGENCIES APPROPRIATIONS FOR FISCAL YEAR 1967: HEARINGS... ON H. R. 17788.
WASHINGTON: US GOVERNMENT, 1966, 396 PP.
PRESENTATION OF BUDGET REQUESTS FROM DEFENSE DEPARTMENT; AGENCY FOR INTERNATIONAL DEVELOPMENT; PEACE CORPS; ARMY; DEPARTMENT OF HEALTH, EDUCATION, AND WELFARE (REFUGEE AID); EXPORT-IMPORT BANK; INTERNATIONAL DEVELOPMENT ASSOCIATION; INTER-AMERICAN DEVELOPMENT BANK; AND STATE DEPARTMENT. TOTAL REQUEST: $3.385 BILLION; $2.469 BILLION FOR ECONOMIC AND $917 MILLION FOR MILITARY ASSISTANCE (EXCLUDING VIETNAM).

2728 US SENATE COMM GOVT OPERATIONS
REPORT OF A STUDY OF US FOREIGN AID IN TEN MIDDLE EASTERN AND AFRICAN COUNTRIES.
WASHINGTON: GOVT PR OFFICE, 1963, 472 PP.
REVIEW OF US MILITARY AND ECONOMIC PROGRAMS, AND AGREEMENTS FOR THEM IN THESE NATIONS. FINDS NEED FOR RE-EVALUATION OF ESTABLISHED MEANS OF DISPERSING AND ACCOUNTING FOR MONEY SPENT ON PROJECTS, AND METHOD OF SELECTING NATIONS TO RECEIVE AID. GIVES RECOMMENDATIONS AND CRITICISMS OF ALL PROJECTS STUDIED.

2729 US SENATE COMM GOVT OPERATIONS
HEARINGS BEFORE SUBCOMMITTEE ON FOREIGN AID EXPENDITURES: POPULATION CRISIS VOLUMES 1-5 JUNE-SEPT 1965.
WASHINGTON: US GOVERNMENT, 1966, 2620 PP.

REPORT ON WORLD PROBLEM OF FERTILITY AND ITS CONTROL IN US. DISCUSSES INCREASED POPULATION AND RELATION BETWEEN HIGH FERTILITY AND LOW INCOME, AS BARRIER TO SOCIAL MOBILITY. REPORTS OF RESEARCH AND PROJECTS UNDERWAY IN US AND FUTURE PLANS. INCLUDES US AND FOREIGN EXPERTS' OPINIONS. VOL. 4 IS APPENDIX OF FAMILY-PLANNING PROJECTS IN STATES AND NATIONS; VOL. 5 IS INDEX AND LIST OF WITNESSES.

2730 US SENATE COMM GOVT OPERATIONS
INTERGOVERNMENTAL PERSONNEL ACT OF 1966.
WASHINGTON: GOVT PR OFFICE, 1966, 277 PP.
HEARINGS BEFORE SENATE SUBCOMMITTEE ON INTERGOVERNMENTAL RELATIONS, OF COMMITTEE ON GOVERNMENT OPERATIONS, APRIL, 1966.CONCERNS BILL TO STRENGTHEN COOPERATION AND ADMINISTRATION OF GRANT-IN-AID PROGRAMS, TO EXTEND STATE MERIT SYSTEMS (FINANCED FEDERALLY), AND TO PROVIDE FUNDS FOR IMPROVEMENT OF PERSONNEL ADMINISTRATION.

2731 US SENATE COMM LABOR-PUB WELF
AMEND THE RAILWAY LABOR ACT.
WASHINGTON: GOVT PR OFFICE, 1966, 317 PP.
HEARINGS BEFORE SENATE SUBCOMMITTEE ON LABOR OF COMMITTEE ON LABOR AND PUBLIC WELFARE HEADED BY PAT MCNAMARA ON HR 706, A BILL TO AMEND RAILWAY LABOR ACT TO ESTABLISH SPECIAL ADJUSTMENT BOARDS ON REQUEST OF LABOR OR MANAGEMENT TO SETTLE DISPUTES PREVIOUSLY SETTLED BY NATIONAL RAILROAD ADJUSTMENT BOARD.

2732 US SENATE COMM ON COMMERCE
URBAN MASS TRANSPORTATION.
WASHINGTON: GOVT PR OFFICE, 1960, 308 PP.
HEARING BEFORE SUBCOMMITTEE ON SURFACE TRANSPORTATION OF US SENATE COMMITTEE ON COMMERCE. DISCUSSES THREE PROPOSED BILLS ON URBAN MASS TRANSPORTATION. FIRST BILL PROVIDES FINANCIAL ASSISTANCE FOR PUBLIC AND PRIVATE SYSTEMS; SECOND ENCOURAGES STATE AND LOCAL INITIATIVE IN URBAN TRANSIT DEVELOPMENT; THIRD ALSO PROVIDES FUNDS. ALL PROVIDE FOR LONG-RANGE PROGRAMS AND FOR RESEARCH PROJECTS.

2733 US SENATE COMM ON FOREIGN REL
HEARING ON BILLS RELATING TO FOREIGN ASSISTANCE.
WASHINGTON: GOVT PR OFFICE, 1964, 628 PP.
STATEMENTS AND MEMORANDA ON TECHNICAL COOPERATION AND DEVELOPMENT GRANTS, INVESTMENT GUARANTEES AND SURVEYS OF INVESTMENT OPPORTUNITIES, AND UN TECHNICAL ASSISTANCE PROGRAMS.

2734 US SENATE COMM ON FOREIGN REL
HEARINGS ON THE FOREIGN ASSISTANCE PROGRAM.
WASHINGTON: GOVT PR OFFICE, 1965, 772 PP.
STATEMENTS AND MEMORANDA BY SECRETARY OF STATE, ADMINISTRATOR OF AGENCY FOR INTERNATIONAL DEVELOPMENT, AND OTHER PUBLIC OFFICIALS ON DEVELOPMENT FUNDS, US OBJECTIVES, WORK OF INTERNATIONAL ORGANIZATIONS, SELF-HELP PROJECTS, AND OTHER ASPECTS OF US FOREIGN AID PROGRAM IN ASIA, AFRICA, AND LATIN AMERICA.

2735 US SENATE COMM ON FOREIGN REL
HEARINGS ON S 2859 AND S 2861.
WASHINGTON: GOVT PR OFFICE, 1966, 752 PP.
STATEMENTS BY PUBLIC AND PRIVATE OFFICIALS ON MILITARY AND ECONOMIC AID, NATURE AND EXTENT OF SOVIET AID, DEVELOPMENT LOANS, ROLE OF PRIVATE ENTERPRISE, VALUE OF MILITARY ASSISTANCE, AND GENERAL ASPECTS OF INTERNATIONAL SECURITY.

2736 US SENATE COMM ON FOREIGN REL
ASIAN DEVELOPMENT BANK ACT.
WASHINGTON: US GOVERNMENT, 1966, 138 PP.
HEARINGS BEFORE COMMITTEE ON FOREIGN RELATIONS ON ASIAN DEVELOPMENT BANK ACT. INCLUDES TESTIMONY BY EUGENE BLACK, PRESIDENTIAL ADVISER ON SOUTHEASTERN ASIAN ECONOMIC AND SOCIAL DEVELOPMENT.

2737 US SENATE COMM ON FOREIGN REL
ARMS SALES AND FOREIGN POLICY (PAMPHLET)
WASHINGTON: US GOVERNMENT, 1967, 13 PP.
STAFF STUDY OF COMMITTEE ON FOREIGN POLICY. CONCLUDES THAT SALE OF ARMS HAS REPLACED GIVING ARMS AS PREDOMINANT FORM OF US MILITARY ASSISTANCE. BELIEVES THAT US MUST REAPPRAISE ADEQUACY OF PRESENT MACHINERY OF POLICY CONTROL AND LEGISLATIVE OVERSIGHT GOVERNING SALE OF ARMS. MAKES SPECIFIC RECOMMENDATIONS FOR IMPROVEMENT.

2738 US SENATE COMM ON FOREIGN REL
THE UNITED NATIONS AT TWENTY-ONE (PAMPHLET)
WASHINGTON: US GOVERNMENT, 1967, 46 PP.
REPORT ON UN BY SENATOR FRANK CHURCH TO SENATE COMMITTEE ON FOREIGN RELATIONS. DISCUSSES FOUNDING OF UN, CHANGES IN WORLD SITUATION SINCE THEN, AND FUNCTIONING OF UN AS PEACEKEEPING FORCE. MAINTAINS NEED FOR GREATER UNDERSTANDING IN CONGRESS OF POTENTIAL AND LIMITS OF UN AS PEACEKEEPER.

2739 US SENATE COMM ON FOREIGN REL
WAR OR PEACE IN THE MIDDLE EAST (PAMPHLET)
WASHINGTON: US GOVERNMENT, 1967, 17 PP.
REPORT TO SENATE COMMITTEE ON FOREIGN RELATIONS BY SENATOR JOSEPH S. CLARK ON STUDY MISSION TO GREECE, UNITED ARAB REPUBLIC, JORDAN, AND ISRAEL DURING NOVEMBER AND DECEMBER. DISCUSSES GREEK POLITICS, ECONOMY, AND MILITARY; CYPRUS; NASSER'S AMBITIONS AND POWER POLITICS; USSR AND US AID; JORDAN'S AND ISRAEL'S POLITICS AND ECONOMY; EGYPT'S ECONOMY; AND MILITARY SITUATION OF ISRAEL AND HER NEIGHBORS.

2740 US SENATE COMM ON FOREIGN REL
LATIN AMERICAN SUMMIT CONFERENCE.
WASHINGTON: US GOVERNMENT, 1967, 161 PP.
HEARINGS BEFORE SENATE COMMITTEE ON FOREIGN RELATIONS ON JOINT RESOLUTION TO SUPPORT OTHER AMERICAN REPUBLICS BY PLEDGING INCREASED FINANCIAL ASSISTANCE FOR PROJECTS IN AGRICULTURE, EDUCATION, HEALTH, LATIN AMERICAN COMMON MARKET, AND MULTINATIONAL PROJECTS IN COMMUNICATIONS, ROADS, AND RIVERS. SECRETARY OF STATE DEAN RUSK TESTIFIED. AID IS THROUGH ALLIANCE FOR PROGRESS.

2741 US SENATE COMM ON FOREIGN REL
INTER-AMERICAN DEVELOPMENT BANK ACT AMENDMENT.
WASHINGTON: US GOVERNMENT, 1967, 143 PP.
HEARINGS BEFORE SENATE COMMITTEE ON FOREIGN RELATIONS, HEADED BY J. W. FULBRIGHT ON BILL TO AMEND INTER-AMERICAN DEVELOPMENT BANK ACT. PURPOSE OF AMENDMENT IS TO AUTHORIZE US PARTICIPATION IN INCREASING FUNDS AVAILABLE TO BANK.

2742 US SENATE COMM ON FOREIGN REL
ARMS SALES TO NEAR EAST AND SOUTH ASIAN COUNTRIES.
WASHINGTON: US GOVERNMENT, 1967, 102 PP.
HEARINGS BEFORE SUBCOMMITTEE ON NEAR EASTERN AND SOUTH ASIAN AFFAIRS OF SENATE COMMITTEE ON FOREIGN RELATIONS HEADED BY STUART SYMINGTON ON US ARMS SALES TO IRAN. INVESTIGATES COORDINATION OF GOVERNMENT MACHINERY IN SALES; ASKS WHETHER OR NOT CONGRESS IS PROPERLY CONSULTED AND INFORMED ABOUT SALE DECISIONS. ALSO DEALS WITH SALES TO INDIA AND PAKISTAN AND ROLE OF COMMERCIAL ARMS SUPPLIERS.

2743 US SENATE COMM ON FOREIGN REL
HARRISON E. SALISBURY'S TRIP TO NORTH VIETNAM.
WASHINGTON: US GOVERNMENT, 1967, 159 PP.
STATEMENTS BY HARRISON E. SALISBURY BEFORE SENATE FOREIGN RELATIONS COMMITTEE ON HIS OBSERVATIONS IN NORTH VIETNAM. INCLUDES HIS TESTIMONY ON BOMBING, CIVILIAN CASUALTIES, AND WAR SPIRIT OF NORTH VIETNAMESE. SUPPLIES TEXT OF HIS NEWSPAPER ARTICLES.

2744 US SENATE COMM ON FOREIGN REL
FOREIGN ASSISTANCE ACT OF 1967.
WASHINGTON: US GOVERNMENT, 1967, 393 PP.
HEARINGS BEFORE SENATE COMMITTEE ON FOREIGN RELATIONS ON FOREIGN ASSISTANCE BILL OF 1967. WITNESSES INCLUDE SECRETARY OF DEFENSE ROBERT MC NAMARA, SECRETARY OF STATE DEAN RUSK, AND WILLIAM E. MORAN OF INTERNATIONAL ECONOMIC POLICY ASSOCIATION. COVERS ALL AREAS OF FOREIGN AID IN SEVERAL PARTS OF WORLD.

2745 US SENATE COMM ON FOREIGN REL
THE RIM OF ASIA (PAMPHLET)
WASHINGTON: US GOVERNMENT, 1967, 15 PP.
REPORT OF SENATOR MIKE MANSFIELD TO COMMITTEE ON FOREIGN RELATIONS ON STUDY MISSION TO WESTERN PACIFIC IN SEPTEMBER, 1967. DISCUSSES WESTERN PACIFIC'S ROLE IN VIETNAM WAR; CULTURAL REVOLUTION IN CHINA AND ITS EXTENSION INTO AREA STUDIED; JAPAN'S INFLUENCE; AND PROBLEMS OF HONG KONG AND MACAO, PHILIPPINES, KOREA, AND REPUBLIC OF CHINA. ADVOCATES FREEDOM FOR THEM TO CHOOSE DIRECTION OF THEIR OWN DESTINY.

2746 US SENATE COMM ON FOREIGN REL
SURVEY OF THE ALLIANCE FOR PROGRESS: THE LATIN AMERICAN MILITARY (PAMPHLET)
WASHINGTON: US GOVERNMENT, 1967, 36 PP.
DEALS WITH ROLE OF LATIN AMERICAN MILITARY AND THE QUESTIONS IT RAISES FOR US FOREIGN POLICY. DISCUSSES EXTRAMILITARY FUNCTIONS AND CAPABILITIES. STUDIES POLITICAL ROLE OF MILITARY IN LATIN AMERICAN MILITARY REGIMES, COUNTRIES WITH HEAVY INDIRECT MILITARY INFLUENCE UPON POLITICS, AND THOSE WITH NON-POLITICAL MILITARY. DISCUSSES EXTERNAL AND INTERNAL DEFENCE, FACTIONALISM AND CIVIC ORDER.

2747 US SENATE COMM ON FOREIGN RELS
INTERNATIONAL DEVELOPMENT AND SECURITY: HEARINGS ON BILL (2 VOLS.)
WASHINGTON: GOVT PR OFFICE, 1961, 1221 PP.
REQUEST TO INCLUDE AS PART OF US FOREIGN AID PROGRAM A FLEXIBLE MILITARY STRATEGY TO PREVENT AGGRESSION AND PROVIDE SECURITY FOR DEVELOPING NATIONS. INCLUDES STATEMENTS OF OPINION, PRO AND CON, AND PROPOSED METHOD FOR SETTING UP SPECIAL POLICY FORCES, ETC., AND GIVING PRESIDENT SPECIAL POWERS.

2748 US SENATE COMM ON JUDICIARY
LEGISLATION TO STRENGTHEN PENALTIES UNDER THE ANTITRUST LAWS (PAMPHLET)
WASHINGTON: GOVT PR OFFICE, 1962, 218 PP.
COLLECTION OF STATEMENTS AND WITNESS TESTIMONIES FROM INVESTIGATION OF SUBCOMMITTEE ON ANTITRUST AND MONOPOLY OF

SENATE COMMITTEE ON JUDICIARY INTO EXISTING MONOPOLY LAW AND PROPOSED CHANGES.

2749 US SENATE COMM ON JUDICIARY
HEARINGS BEFORE SUBCOMMITTEE ON ANTITRUST AND MONOPOLY: ECONOMIC CONCENTRATION VOLUMES 1-5 JULY 1964-SEPT 1966.
WASHINGTON: US GOVERNMENT, 1964, 2163 PP.
TESTIMONIES FOR AND AGAINST EXISTING OR VIRTUAL MONOPOLIES IN US. GIVES OVER-ALL ASPECTS, COVERS MERGERS AND OTHER LEGAL FORMS OF CONCENTRATING, AS WELL AS NEW INNOVATIONS. DISCUSSES EFFICIENCY OF CONCENTRATING AS OPPOSED TO DIVIDING AND GIVES REPORTS OF COMPANIES THAT HAVE DONE BOTH.

2750 US SENATE COMM ON JUDICIARY
ANTITRUST EXEMPTIONS FOR AGREEMENTS RELATING TO BALANCE OF PAYMENTS.
WASHINGTON: US GOVERNMENT, 1965, 248 PP.
REPORT OF HEARINGS ON H RES 40, AN ACT TO PROVIDE FOR EXEMPTIONS FROM ANTITRUST LAWS FOR COMPANIES IN INTERNATIONAL TRADING TO ASSIST US IN MAINTAINING FAVORABLE BALANCE OF PAYMENTS. DEBATES WHETHER ANTI-MONOPOLY LAWS OR INTERNATIONAL MONETARY POSITION IS MORE INPORTANT.

2751 US SUPERINTENDENT OF DOCUMENTS
CENSUS PUBLICATIONS (PRICE LIST 70)
WASHINGTON: GOVT PR OFFICE.
STATISTICS OF AGRICULTURE, BUSINESS, GOVERNMENTS, HOUSING, MANUFACTURES, MINERALS, POPULATION, AND MAPS. SERIALS PUBLICATION LISTING US GOVERNMENT PUBLICATIONS CURRENTLY AVAILABLE FOR SALE, 39 EDITIONS TO DATE; LATEST EDITION INCLUDES MATERIALS PUBLISHED 1960 THROUGH 1966. ENTRIES GROUPED BY SUBJECT. MAJORITY OF ITEMS ANNOTATED.

2752 US SUPERINTENDENT OF DOCUMENTS
INTERSTATE COMMERCE (PRICE LIST 59)
WASHINGTON: GOVT PR OFFICE.
SERIES PUBLICATION OF US GOVERNMENT LISTING GOVERNMENT PUBLICATIONS CURRENTLY AVAILABLE FOR SALE. 48 EDITIONS TO DATE. LATEST ISSUE CONTAINS PUBLICATIONS FROM 1949 THROUGH 1966. MAJORITY OF ENTRIES ANNOTATED; GROUPED BY SUBJECTS SUCH AS ACCIDENTS AND SAFETY, INTERSTATE COMMERCE COMMISSION, LOCOMOTIVES AND RAILROADS, LEGISLATION, STATE TAXATION, AND TARIFF CIRCULARS.

2753 US SUPERINTENDENT OF DOCUMENTS
LABOR (PRICE LIST 33)
WASHINGTON: GOVT PR OFFICE.
SERIES PUBLICATION OF US GOVERNMENT LISTING GOVERNMENT PUBLICATIONS CURRENTLY AVAILABLE FOR SALE. ENTRIES GROUPED BY SUBJECT: INCLUDE TOPICS SUCH AS COLLECTIVE BARGAINING, LABOR DEPARTMENT, NATIONAL LABOR RELATIONS ACT AND BOARD, PUBLIC WORKS, UNIONS, WAGES, EMPLOYMENT AND UNEMPLOYMENT, PRODUCTIVITY, AND PUBLIC WORKS. 45 EDITIONS TO DATE. MATERIALS IN LATEST ISSUE PUBLISHED 1958 THROUGH 1966.

2754 US SUPERINTENDENT OF DOCUMENTS
TARIFF AND TAXATION (PRICE LIST 37)
WASHINGTON: GOVT PR OFFICE.
SERIES PUBLICATION OF US GOVERNMENT PUBLICATIONS CURRENTLY AVAILABLE FOR SALE LISTING ITEMS BY SUBJECT. TOPICS INCLUDE US CUSTOMS COURT REPORTS, REPORT OF CASES ADJUDGED BEFORE CUSTOMS AND PATENT APPEALS COURT, INTERNAL REVENUE BUREAU, TARIFF AND TRADE, TAX COURT, TARIFF COMMISSION, PROPERTY TAX, ETC. 46 EDITIONS TO DATE. LATEST ISSUE COVERS MATERIALS PUBLISHED FROM 1951 THROUGH 1966.

2755 UYEHARA C.H., ROYAMA M. ET AL.
COMPARATIVE PLATFORMS OF JAPAN'S MAJOR PARTIES...
BOSTON: FLETCHER SCH LAW, DIPL, 1955, 65 PP.
EXCERPTS FROM PARTY STATEMENTS INCLUDE COMMENTS ON REARMAMENT, SOCIAL WELFARE, PARTY FUNCTION AND COMPOSITION.

2756 VACCARO J.R., MONTENEGRO C.V.
A STATEMENT OF THE LAWS OF CHILE IN MATTERS AFFECTING BUSINESS (3RD ED.)
WASHINGTON: PAN AMERICAN UNION, 1962, 242 PP.
SUMMARIZES CONSTITUTIONAL, STATUTORY, AND REGULATORY PROVISIONS OF CHILE IN 1962 DEALING WITH NUMEROUS ASPECTS OF BUSINESS. INCLUDES CONSTITUTION AND FORM OF GOVERNMENT OF CHILE.

2757 VAID K.N.
STATE AND LABOR IN INDIA.
NEW YORK: ASIA PUBL HOUSE, 1965, 279 PP.
TREATS ROLE OF STATE IN GUIDING EMPLOYER-EMPLOYEE RELATIONSHIP AND IN SETTING STANDARDS FOR WORKING CONDITIONS AND WAGES. EXAMINES LEGISLATION RELATING TO HOURS, WELFARE, SOCIAL SECURITY, WAGES, DISPUTES, AND UNIONS.

2758 VAIZEY J.
THE ECONOMICS OF EDUCATION.
NEW YORK: FREE PRESS OF GLENCOE, 1962, 165 PP.
ECONOMIC ANALYSIS OF EDUCATION: ITS ECONOMIC ROLE, COMPARISON WITH CONSUMPTION AND INVESTMENT, MEASURE OF ECONOMIC RETURNS OF INVESTMENT, ITS RELATION TO ECONOMIC GROWTH, AND ITS PRODUCTIVITY.

2759 VAKIL C.N., BRAHMANAND P.R.
PLANNING FOR AN EXPANDING ECONOMY.
BOMBAY: VORA & CO, 1956, 404 PP.
DISCUSSES OPERATION OF INDIAN ECONOMY UNDER FIRST PLAN. EXAMINES METHODOLOGY OF SECOND PLAN, AND STUDIES PROBLEMS OF CAPITAL ACCUMULATION, TECHNICAL PROGRESS, INVESTMENT, AND UNEMPLOYMENT.
ECO/UNDEV PLAN ECO/TAC FINAN

2760 VALLET R.
"IRAN: KEY TO THE MIDDLE EAST."
MIL. REV., 14 (NOV. 61), 54-61.
IRAN'S MEMBERSHIP IN CENTRAL TREATY ORGANIZATION, THE ALLIANCE WHICH REPLACED THE BAGHDAD PACT AFTER IRAQ'S DEFECTION, MIGHT BE IMPAIRED BECAUSE OF DEVELOPMENTS IN ECONOMIC AND POLITICAL FIELD. SITUATION EVALUATED IN LIGHT OF CONDITIONS IN NEIGHBORING COUNTRIES OF IRAQ, TURKEY, SAUDI ARABIA, KUWAIT AND LEBANON.

2761 VAN DER HORST S.T.
"THE ECONOMICS OF DECENTRALISATION OF INDUSTRY."
S. AFR. J. OF ECONOMICS, 33 (MAR. 65), 17-28.
DISCUSSION OF ECONOMICS OF INDUSTRIAL DECENTRALIZATION IN TERMS OF FORCES DETERMINING INDUSTRIAL LOCATION AND ECONOMIES CONNECTED WITH INDUSTRIAL SIZE. PROMOTES POLICIES WHICH REMOVE RESTRICTIONS ON USE OF HUMAN MATERIAL RESOURCES; ARGUES THAT RESTRICTIVE POLICIES RETARD ECONOMIC DEVELOPMENT. MAINTAINS DELIBERATE DISPERSAL OF INDUSTRY EMPLOYED TO RESOLVE POLITICAL, RATHER THAN ECONOMIC, CONFLICT.

2762 VAN KLAVEREN J.
"DIE WIRTSCHAFTLICHEN AUSWIRKUNGEN DES SCHWARZEN TODES"
VIERTELJSCHR. SOZIAL U WIRTSCHAFTSGES, 54 (JULY 67), 187-202.
RELATES ECONOMIC DEPRESSION IN AGRICULTURE IN GERMANY IN 15TH CENTURY TO EPIDEMIC (BLACK DEATH) WHICH SWEPT EUROPE IN 1348. MAINTAINS THAT CHANGES IN VOLUME OF MONEY SUPPLY AND DEMAND FOR MONEY RESULTING FROM EPIDEMIC WERE CHIEF FACTORS PRODUCING ECONOMIC DEPRESSION. FOCUSES ON DECLINE OF POPULATION AND RESULTING ECONOMIC CONDITIONS IN CITIES.

2763 VAN RENSBURG P.
GUILTY LAND: THE HISTORY OF APARTHEID.
NEW YORK: FREDERICK PRAEGER, 1962, 224 PP., LC#62-9588.
AN ANTI-APARTHEID SOUTH AFRICAN DISCUSSES NATION'S RACIAL POLICIES. ANALYZES MAJOR SOCIAL, ECONOMIC, AND POLITICAL FORCES THAT DOMINATE SOUTH AFRICA. SHOWS THAT AFRIKANER NATIONALISM MAY HAVE PROVIDED PATTERN FOR AFRICAN NATIONALISM. HOPES COLOR REVOLUTION WILL COME SOON AND DESTROY EVILS OF WHITE DOMINATION.

2764 VAN SLYKE L.P.
ENEMIES AND FRIENDS; THE UNITED FRONT IN CHINESE COMMUNIST HISTORY.
STANFORD: STANFORD U PRESS, 1967, 320 PP.
TRACES THEORY AND PRACTICE OF UNITED FRONT IN CHINA SINCE 1922, EMPHASIZING KUO-MINTANG-COMMUNIST ALLIANCE IN 1920'S, MILITARY ALLIANCE AGAINST JAPAN DURING 1937-45, AND PARTY'S POST-1949 CAMPAIGNS TO TRANSFORM CHINA'S SOCIETY AND ECONOMY. SHOWS IMPORTANCE OF UNITED FRONT TO MAO'S STRATEGY. EXAMINES CONTEMPORARY MANIFESTATIONS OF UNITED FRONT.

2765 VANEK J.
INTERNATIONAL TRADE - THEORY AND ECONOMIC POLICY.
CAMBRIDGE: M I T PRESS, 1962, 426 PP., LC#62-9131.
GENERAL DISCUSSION OF PRINCIPLES OF INTERNATIONAL TRADE. EXAMINES FOREIGN-EXCHANGE MARKET, BALANCE OF PAYMENTS, TRADE EQUILIBRIUM, TARIFF POLICY, AND THEORY OF CUSTOMS UNIONS.

2766 VANEK J.
THE BALANCE OF PAYMENTS, LEVEL OF ECONOMIC ACTIVITY AND THE VALUE OF CURRENCY: THEORY AND SOME RECENT EXPERIENCES.
GENEVA: LIBRAIRIE DROZ, 1962, 36 PP.
SURVEYS KEYNESIAN THEORY OF INTERNATIONAL PAYMENTS. SYNTHESIZES PRICE AND INCOME APPROACHES TO PROBLEM, APPLYING NEW THEORY TO ACTUAL CASES. PRIMARY VARIABLES ARE LEVEL OF ECONOMIC ACTIVITY, RATE OF EXCHANGE, AND BALANCE OF PAYMENTS.

2767 VANEK J.
GENERAL EQUILIBRIUM OF INTERNATIONAL DISCRIMINATION; THE CASE OF CUSTOMS UNIONS.
CAMBRIDGE: HARVARD U PR, 1965, 234 PP., LC#65-11593.
EXAMINES EFFECTS OF DISCRIMINATORY TRADE ARRANGEMENTS ON GENERAL EQUILIBRIUM OF WORLD ECONOMY, EMPHASIZING CUSTOMS UNIONS. BRIEFLY ANALYZES CUSTOM UNIONS TO DETERMINE BENEFITS OF UNIONS. USES GENERAL EQUILIBRIUM AND ORDINAL PREFERENCE FUNCTIONS IN STUDY. DESCRIBES UNIONS OF SIMILAR AND DISSIMILAR ECONOMIES, WORLD INCOME, AND GAINS FROM UNIONS BY INDIVIDUAL COUNTRIES.

2768 VEBLEN T.
THE INSTINCT OF WORKMANSHIP.

NEW YORK: MACMILLAN, 1914, 355 PP.
ANALYZES INSTITUTIONAL STRUCTURE OF CIVILIZATION AT ANY GIVEN STAGE OF DEVELOPMENT. CREDITS INSTINCT OF WORKMANSHIP WITH ADVANCING MAN FROM CAVEMAN TO CIVILIZED BEING.

2769 VEBLEN T.
IMPERIAL GERMANY AND THE INDUSTRIAL REVOLUTION.
NEW YORK: VIKING PRESS, 1915, 343 PP.
DESCRIBES RAPID STRIDES IN MACHINE TECHNOLOGY MADE BY DYNASTIC GERMANY. CONTRASTS ITS EMERGENT SYSTEM WITH THAT OF ENGLAND. POINTS TO FUTURE OF DYNASTIC STATES AND WESTERN DEMOCRACIES.

2770 VEBLEN T.B.
THE THEORY OF BUSINESS ENTERPRISE.
NEW YORK: CHAS SCRIBNER'S SONS, 1904, 250 PP.
CONTAINS VEBLEN'S BASIC ECONOMIC THEORY, CLAIMING THAT THE MACHINE IS ALL-IMPORTANT IN MODERN SOCIETY AND THAT TO SURVIVE, SOCIETY MUST ADAPT ITSELF TO SATISFY THE MACHINE. CONTRASTS BUSINESS AND INDUSTRY IN AIMS. POINTS OUT CONSTANT CHANGE AND REAL INSTABILITY OF INSTITUTIONS. FEELS BUSINESS-MEN ARE LESS SUITED TO HANDLE PRODUCTION THAN GOVERNMENT, BUT IMPLIES BOTH WILL INEVITABLY FAIL.

2771 VEBLEN T.B.
THE VESTED INTERESTS AND THE STATE OF THE INDUSTRIAL ARTS.
NEW YORK: VIKING PRESS, 1919, 225 PP.
ATTACKS US FREE ENTERPRISE SYSTEM AS A GROUP OF INTERESTS WITH "A MARKETABLE RIGHT TO GET SOMETHING FOR NOTHING." CLAIMS PURPOSE OF BUSINESS IS TO MAXIMIZE PROFITS BY RE-STRICTING PRODUCTION AND RAISING PRICES. OPPOSES THE IDEAS OF BUSINESS AND INDUSTRY, SAYING THEY SEEK DIFFERENT ENDS. DISCUSSES EFFECTS OF MACHINE PROCESS, NATURE OF CORPORATE PROMOTION, AND INFLUENCE OF BUSINESS UPON POLITICS.

2772 VEBLEN T.B.
THE THEORY OF THE LEISURE CLASS.
NEW YORK: VIKING PRESS, 1924, 261 PP.
CLAIMS UNPRODUCTIVENESS AND INUTILITY TO BE VALUES OF LEISURE CLASS AND ATTACKS MIDDLE-CLASS STRIVINGS TO SIMULATE THIS BEHAVIOR. EXAMINES PSYCHOLOGICAL ASPECTS AND RESULTS OF THESE VALUES: CONSPICUOUS CONSUMPTION, WASTEFUL CONSUMPTION, AND VICARIOUS LEISURE. STRIVES TO DEMONSTRATE INFLUENCE OF THESE PECUNIARY VALUES UPON RELIGION, ART, GOVERNMENT, AND EDUCATION.

2773 VEIT O.
GRUNDRISS DER WAHRUNGSPOLITIK.
FRANKFURT: FRITZ KNAPP VERLAG, 1961, 844 PP.
EXAMINES CENTRAL CONCEPTS OF POLITICS OF CURRENCY STANDARDS. DISCUSSES FOREIGN EXCHANGE, CREDIT, GOLD AND SILVER STANDARDS, AND MONEY ECONOMY IN GERMANY SINCE 1857. ANALYZES POLICIES OF OTHER EUROPEAN COUNTRIES, USSR, AND US.

2774 VELEZ GARCIA J. ED.
DEVALUACION 1962; HISTORIA DOCUMENTAL DE UN PROCESO ECONOMICO.
BOGOTA: EDICIONES TERCER MUNDO, 1963, 517 PP.
DOCUMENTS, SPEECHES, ARTICLES, AND LETTERS DEALING WITH VARIOUS ASPECTS OF COLOMBIAN ECONOMY. TREATS ECONOMIC PLANS PUT INTO EFFECT, FOREIGN AID, LAWS, PRODUCTION AND UTILIZATION OF RESOURCES, ETC.

2775 VELYAMINOV G.
AFRICA AND THE COMMON MARKET (PAMPHLET)
NEW YORK: G VELYAMINOV, 1964, 20 PP.
MAINTAINS THAT CHANGE FROM COLONIAL TO NATIONAL ECONOMY IS NECESSARY FOR ECONOMIC PROGRESS IN AFRICA. TRADE IS KEY FACTOR IN GROWTH. QUESTIONS EQUALITY AND BENEFITS OF AFFILIATION WITH EUROPEAN COMMON MARKET, STATING THAT IT IS MORE LIKE SITUATION OF NEO-COLONIALISM. ADVOCATES AFRICA'S SEPARATION FROM COMMON MARKET AND CLOSER ALLIANCES WITH SOCIALIST COUNTRIES.

2776 VENKATESWARAN R.J.
CABINET GOVERNMENT IN INDIA.
NEW YORK: HILLARY HOUSE PUBL, 1967, 200 PP.
ANALYZES CONSTITUTIONAL POSITION AND DAY-TO-DAY OPERATION OF INDIAN CENTRAL CABINET SINCE INDEPENDENCE. ALSO STUDIES EXTENT TO WHICH CABINET SYSTEM, MODELED ON THAT OF BRITAIN, HAS TAKEN ROOT IN INDIA AND HOW FAR INDIA HAS FOLLOWED BRITISH PRECEDENTS AND CONVENTIONS. POINTS OUT STRONG AND WEAK POINTS OF CABINET SYSTEM.

2777 VENTRE F.T.
"LOCAL INITIATIVES IN URBAN INDUSTRIAL DEVELOPMENT."
URBAN AFFAIRS Q., 2 (DEC. 66), 53-67.
TRACES HISTORY OF LOCAL GOVERNMENT SUBSIDIES TO NEW COM-MERCIAL INDUSTRY. FINDS THAT METROPOLITAN GOVERNMENTS ARE ADOPTING THESE INDUCEMENTS IN ORDER TO ATTRACT TO CITY THE EXECUTIVE OFFICES OF INDUSTRY AND SERVICES. REASONS: 1) THESE BUSINESSES REQUIRE LITTLE SPACE, 2) THEY ARE ECONOMICALLY SOUND, AND 3) THEY ARE NOT LIKELY TO BLIGHT A CITY.

2778 VERNEY D.V.
PUBLIC ENTERPRISE IN SWEDEN.
LIVERPOOL: LIVERPOOL U PRESS, 1959, 132 PP.
EXPLAINS SWEDISH ECONOMIC SYSTEM, PAYING PARTICULAR ATTENTION TO PUBLIC ACCOUNTABILITY. BEGINS WITH PUBLIC ENTERPRISE WITHOUT NATIONALIZATION AND COMPARES WITH UK. DISCUSSES GROWTH OF TRADING AGENCIES AND STATE COMPANIES, FORM OF SWEDISH PUBLIC ENTERPRISE, AND PROBLEM OF ACCOUNTABILITY. INCLUDES CIVIL SERVICE FORMALISM, SOCIAL DEMOCRATIC PARTY, ALTERNATIVES, AND FUTURE REFORMS.

2779 VERNON R.
"PRODUCTION AND DISTRIBUTION IN THE LARGE METROPOLIS" (BMR)"
ANN. ACAD. POL. SOC. SCI., (NOV. 57), 15-29.
EXAMINES PRESENT AND FUTURE ROLE OF METROPOLITAN AREAS IN FIELD OF PRODUCTION AND DISTRIBUTION AND PROBLEMS THAT FUTURE GROWTH WILL BRING. EMPHASIZES IMPLICATIONS OF MOVEMENT OF MANUFACTURING ACTIVITIES OUT OF CENTRAL CITIES. EXPLORES CONSEQUENCES OF RELATIVE GROWTH OF BUSINESS SERVICES IN METROPOLITAN AREAS AND RELATES BUSINESS TRENDS TO OUTWARD SHIFT OF POPULATIONS.

2780 VERNON R.
METROPOLIS 1985.
CAMBRIDGE: HARVARD U PR, 1960, 228 PP.
ANALYSIS OF THE FINDINGS OF STUDIES ON THE PROBABLE DEVELOPMENT OF THE NEW YORK METROPOLITAN REGION. THE MULTIPLICITY OF LOCAL GOVERNMENTS IN THE REGION HAS HAMPERED PROGRESS TOWARD SOLUTION OF METROPOLITAN PROBLEMS.

2781 VERNON R.
"A TRADE POLICY FOR THE 1960'S."
FOR. AFF., 39 (APR. 61), 458-70.
BELIEVES PRINCIPAL CONTRIBUTION OF AN APPROPIATE US TRADE POLICY IN THE NEXT DECADE IS POLITICAL RATHER THAN ECONOMIC, AND THAT GOVERNMENT ENCOURAGEMENT OF INCREASED INTERNATIONAL TRADE IS THE NECESSARY FIRST OBJECTIVE.

2782 VERSLUYS J.D.N.
"SOME NOTES ON THE SOCIAL AND ECONOMIC EFFECTS OF RURAL ELECTRIFICATION IN BURMA"
J OF ASIAN AND AFRICAN STUDIES, 1 (JULY 66), 220-236.
INVESTIGATES SOCIAL AND ECONOMIC CHANGES RESULTING FROM ELECTRIFICATION OF SEVERAL BURMESE VILLAGES. VILLAGERS STATE THAT IT ADDS SECURITY; ENABLES VILLAGERS TO MOVE FREELY IN VILLAGE; CHANGES AVAILABLE TIME FOR WORK, RECREATION, AND EDUCATION; BRINGS RADIO TO VILLAGE TO BROADCAST PRICES OF GOODS; AND IMPROVES PRODUCTION TECHNIQUES.

2783 VIA J.W. JR.
"ANTITRUST AND THE AMENDED BANK MERGER AND HOLDING COMPANY ACTS: THE SEARCH FOR STANDARDS."
VIRGINIA LAW REV., 53 (JUNE 67), 1115-1132.
DESCRIBES ANALYTICAL TECHNIQUE EMPLOYED BY SUPREME COURT IN JUDGING EFFECT OF BANK MERGERS ON COMPETITION. FOCUSES ON COURT'S TREATMENT OF BANKING AS DISTINCT LINE OF COMMERCE AND ON ALTERNATIVES OPEN TO DEAL WITH CONTROL. STUDIES PROB-LEM OF WEIGHING EFFECTS OF ANTICOMPETITIVE ASPECTS OF MERGER AGAINST IMPACT ON CONVENIENCE TO COMMUNITY AS PRESENTED IN AMENDED MERGER ACT AND HOLDING COMPANY ACT.

2784 VIET J.
INTERNATIONAL COOPERATION AND PROGRAMMES OF ECONOMIC AND SOCIAL DEVELOPMENT.
PARIS: UNESCO, 1962, 107 PP.
ANNOTATED BIBLIOGRAPHY OF 1,141 BOOKS, ARTICLES, AND PA-PERS CONCERNED WITH QUESTIONS OF INTERNATIONAL COOPERATION PROGRAMS RELATING TO THEIR DEFINITION, FORMULATION, AND EXE-CUTION. ENTRIES ORGANIZED BY THEIR CLASSIFICATION INTO BI-LATERAL, MULTILATERAL, AND REGIONAL ASSISTANCE PROGRAMS. TITLES OF DOCUMENTS PUBLISHED BY UN QUOTED IN FRENCH AND ENGLISH. COVERS MATERIAL ISSUED FROM 1944 THROUGH 1960.

2785 VINCENT W.S.
ROLES OF THE CITIZENS: PRINCIPLES AND PRACTICES.
EVANSTON: ROW-PETERSON, 1959, 256 PP., LC#59-11829.
DISCUSSES ROLE OF CITIZEN IN FREE GOVERNMENT AND FIVE TECHNIQUES TO INFLUENCE PUBLIC AFFAIRS: SECURING AND SPREAD-ING FACTS, SETTLING DISPUTES AND JOINING VOLUNTARY ORGANIZA-TIONS TO INFLUENCE DECISIONS, VOTING INTELLIGENTLY, PARTICI-PATING IN JUDICIAL PROCESS, AND UNDERSTANDING MACHINERY OF GOVERNMENT TO INFLUENCE POLICIES.

2786 VINER J.
"ECONOMIC FOREIGN POLICY ON THE NEW FRONTIER."
FOR. AFF., 39 (JULY 61), 560-77.
SCORES KENNEDY ON PROTECTIONIST COMMERCIAL POLICY TO PROMOTE TARIFF REDUCTION AND FOR CONTINUING ILLOGICAL FARM PROGRAM. COMMENDS KENNEDY ON PROPOSALS REORGANIZING FOREIGN AID PROGRAM. ANALYZES REMEDIES TO BALANCE-OF-PAYMENT DEFICIT.

2787 VINER J.
THE INTELLECTUAL HISTORY OF LAISSEZ FAIRE (PAMPHLET)
CHICAGO: U OF CHICAGO LAW SCHOOL, 1961, 24 PP.
DISCUSSES LOGICAL AND RHETORICAL NATURE OF THE ARGUMENTS

BY WHICH EXPONENTS OF LAISSEZ-FAIRE ATTEMPTED TO WIN CONVERTS TO THEIR CAUSE. OBSERVES ART OF PERSUASION AS USED IN SOCIAL THOUGHT. STATES THAT DOCTRINE HAS LEGAL, ETHICAL, AND POLITICAL ASPECTS AS WELL AS ECONOMIC ONES.

2788 VINER J.
"REPORT OF THE CLAY COMMITTEE ON FOREIGN AID: A SYMPOSIUM."
POLIT. SCI. QUART., 78 (SEPT. 63), 321-61.
REPORT ON FOREIGN AID. STATES THAT THERE ARE REASONS FOR CONCERN WITH BOTH THE OBJECTIVES OF THE CURRENT PROGRAM OF FOREIGN AID AND WITH ITS ADMINISTRATION. ALMOST UNANIMOUS RECOMMENDATION OF DECREASE OR ABOLITION OF AID IN A NUMBER OF COUNTRIES.

2789 VON BECKERATH E. ED., GIERSCH H. ED.
PROBLEME DER NORMATIVEN OEKONOMIK UND DER WIRTSCHAFTSPOLITI - SCHEN BERATUNG.
BERLIN: DUNCKER & HUMBLOT, 1963, 611 PP.
DISCUSSES BASIS AND LIMITATIONS OF "NORMATIVE ECONOMICS" AND ROLE OF ECONOMIC EXPERTS IN INSTITUTIONS AND POLICY-MAKING.

2790 VON DER MEHDEN F.R.
POLITICS OF THE DEVELOPING NATIONS.
ENGLEWOOD CLIFFS: PRENTICE HALL, 1964, 142 PP., LC#64-16041.
ISOLATES AND INTERPRETS THE FORCES WHICH UNDERMINE STABLE UNIFIED POLITICAL SYSTEMS IN EMERGENT COUNTRIES. TAKES DATA FROM FAILURES AND SUCCESSES OF 84 STATES, ASSESSES THE IMPACT OF COLONIAL HERITAGES AND OUTWORN TRADITIONS ON THE DEVELOPMENT OF COMPETITIVE POLITICS IN THE NEW NATIONS. ASSERTS THAT RELATIVELY FEW AFRO-ASIAN COUNTRIES HAVE DEEP IDEOLOGICAL FRICTIONS.

2791 VON ENGELIN O.D.
INHERITING THE EARTH, THE GEOGRAPHICAL FACTOR IN NATIONAL DEVELOPMENT.
NEW YORK: MACMILLAN, 1922, 417 PP.
SUBMITS THAT GEOGRAPHICAL ENVIRONMENT IS PRINCIPAL BASIS OF ALL HUMAN ASSOCIATION. DISCUSSES INTERACTION BETWEEN MAN AND ENVIRONMENT AS FACTOR IN NATIONAL DEVELOPMENT AND NOTES RELATIONSHIP OF MAN TO NATION. CONTENDS THAT GEOGRAPHY DICTATES INTERDEPENDENCE OF NATIONS, IS NECESSARY FOR COMPLETE ECONOMIC DEVELOPMENT. TRACES RELATION OF ENVIRONMENT TO CULTURAL DEVELOPMENT IN TROPICAL AND TEMPERATE AREAS.

2792 VON HAYEK F.A.
MONETARY NATIONALISM AND INTERNATIONAL STABILITY.
NEW YORK: LONGMANS, GREEN & CO, 1937, 94 PP.
CONCENTRATES ON THEORETICAL ISSUES RESPONSIBLE FOR RISE OF MONETARY NATIONALISM; EXAMINES POLICIES AND PRACTICES EMPLOYED BY NATIONS. DISCUSSES INTERNATIONAL STANDARD VERSUS NATIONAL CURRENCIES, MERITS OF VARIOUS POLITICAL SYSTEMS, FUNCTION AND MECHANISM OF INTERNATIONAL FLOWS OF MONEY, AND CAPITAL MOVEMENTS. CLOSES WITH GOLD AS STANDARD, EXCHANGE RATES, AND CREDIT.

2793 VON HAYEK F.A.
INDIVIDUALISM AND ECONOMIC ORDER.
CHICAGO: U OF CHICAGO PRESS, 1948, 271 PP.
SUPPORTS FREE MARKET SYSTEM OF ECONOMIC ORDER, ATTACKING ALL FORMS OF SOCIALISM AND OTHER MARKET-CONTROLLING SYSTEMS. PROPOSES SYSTEM OF INTERNATIONAL FEDERALISM SIMILAR TO COMMON MARKET, BUT MORE EXTENSIVE AND ENTERING INTO POLITICAL AS WELL AS ECONOMIC MATTERS. DISCUSSES ECONOMIC TYPES THEN IN PRACTICE IN RUSSIA, GERMANY, AND US. CLAIMS EVALUATIONS MUST BE MADE IN TERMS OF HOW WELL INDIVIDUALS ARE SERVED.

2794 VON MISES L.
HUMAN ACTION: A TREATISE ON ECONOMICS (2ND ED.)
NEW HAVEN: YALE U PR, 1963, 907 PP., LC#62-17874.
GENERAL DISCUSSION OF HUMAN ABILITY TO UNDERSTAND MAN'S MOTIVES AND ACTIONS REGARDING ECONOMICS. ATTEMPTS TO ELUCIDATE HUMAN IMPACT ON VARIOUS ELEMENTS OF SOCIETY AND CONTRIBUTION TO ECONOMIC EQUILIBRIUM.

2795 VON RENESSE E.A., KRAWIETZ W., BIERKAEMPER C.
UNVOLLENDETE DEMOKRATIEN.
COLOGNE: WESTDEUTSCHER VERLAG, 1965, 429 PP.
EXAMINES FORMS OF ORGANIZATION AND STRUCTURES OF POWER IN NON-COMMUNIST DEVELOPING NATIONS IN ASIA, AFRICA, AND NEAR EAST. STUDIES LEGAL AND POLITICAL STATUS OF THESE LANDS AND THEIR SOCIAL AND ECONOMIC BACKGROUNDS. EMPIRICAL-INDUCTIVE APPROACH.

2796 VOSE C.E.
CAUCASIANS ONLY: THE SUPREME COURT, THE NAACP, AND THE RESTRICTIVE COVENANT CASES.
BERKELEY: U OF CALIF PR, 1959, 296 PP., LC#59-8758.
DESCRIBES SOCIOLOGICAL AND POLITICAL EVENTS LEADING TO SUPREME COURT'S DECISION IN "RESTRICTIVE COVENANT CASES." APPRAISES PRACTICAL RESULT OF RULING. FOCUSES ON ROLE OF INTEREST GROUPS IN DECISION-MAKING PROCESS AND INTERPLAY OF HISTORICAL FORCES IN RECENT CONSTITUTIONAL DEVELOPMENT.

2797 WADE J.
HISTORY OF THE MIDDLE AND WORKING CLASSES; WITH A POPULAR EXPOSITION OF THE ECONOMICAL AND POLITICAL PRINCIPLES....
LONDON: EFFINGHAM WILSON PUBLRS, 1835, 604 PP.
GIVES HISTORY OF THESE CLASSES, TRACING ORIGINS AND PROGRESS, AND INDICATING CIRCUMSTANCES WHICH DETERMINE THEIR SOCIAL CONDITION. DISCUSSES POLITICAL ECONOMY, INCLUDING EMPLOYMENT FLUCTUATIONS, OVER-POPULATION, WAGES AND PROFITS, UNIONS, CURRENCY, POOR LAWS, ETC. CRITICIZES EIGHTEENTH-CENTURY POLITICAL THEORISTS, AND BELIEVES THAT FRENCH REVOLUTION HAS MADE GOVERNMENT A "PRODUCTIVE MACHINE."

2798 WAGLE S.S.
TECHNIQUE OF PLANNING FOR ACCELERATED ECONOMIC GROWTH OF UNDERDEVELOPED COUNTRIES.
BOMBAY: VORA & CO, 1961, 296 PP.
STUDY OF ECONOMIC PLANNING IN DEVELOPING NATIONS WITH REGARD TO BALANCING ECONOMIC GROWTH AND INCREASING INDUSTRIALIZATION.

2799 WAGLEY C.
INTRODUCTION TO BRAZIL.
NEW YORK: COLUMBIA U PRESS, 1963, 322 PP., LC#63-17538.
GENERAL ANALYSIS OF BRAZILIAN SOCIAL, ECONOMIC, AND POLITICAL LIFE. DISCUSSES GEOGRAPHY, SOCIAL CLASSES, EDUCATIONAL SYSTEM, FAMILY AND COMMUNITY LIFE, AND RELATIONSHIP BETWEEN RELIGION AND STATE.

2800 WAHLKE J.C. ED., EULAU H. ED.
LEGISLATIVE BEHAVIOR: A READER IN THEORY AND RESEARCH.
NEW YORK: FREE PRESS OF GLENCOE, 1959, 413 PP., LC#59-6814.
PRESENTS, IN COMPACT AND CONVENIENT FORM, SIGNIFICANT THEORETICAL AND RESEARCH CONTRIBUTIONS DEALING WITH IMPORTANT PROBLEMS OF BEHAVIOR OF LEGISLATURES AND LEGISLATORS. CONSIDERS ROLE OF PARTISANSHIP, PRESSURE GROUPS, CONSTITUENCY RELATIONS AND FACTIONAL ALIGNMENTS; RECRUITMENT AND COMPOSITION OF LEGISLATURES; CONCEPTIONS OF LEGISLATOR'S OFFICE AND ROLE; PERSONAL AND INTERPERSONAL ORIENTATION.

2801 WAITS C.R.
"CRAFT GILDS AS AN INSTITUTIONAL BARRIER TO THE INDUSTRIAL REVOLUTION."
S.W. SOCIAL SCI. QUART., 48 (JUNE 67), 61-67.
STUDIES EFFECTS OF CRAFT GILDS ON INDUSTRIAL REVOLUTION. CONTRASTS MEDIEVAL PERIOD WITH ITS PREJUDIECS AGAINST EXPANSION AND INNOVATION TO EARLY MODERN PERIOD WITH ITS EMPHASIS ON EXPANSION AND FOCUSES ON THE NATURE OF THE INTERVENING PERIOD: INTERACTIONS BETWEEN THE OLD INSTITUTIONS WHICH HINDERED INDUSTRIALIZATION AND THE NEW ONEW WHICH ENCOURAGED DEVELOPMENT.

2802 WALINSKY L.J.
PLANNING AND EXECUTION OF ECONOMIC DEVELOPMENT.
NEW YORK: MCGRAW HILL, 1963, 248 PP., LC#63-15897.
DEALS WITH PROBLEMS IN PLANNING AND IN ORGANIZATION AND EXECUTION OF EFFECTIVE ECONOMIC PROGRAM. ESTABLISHES OPERATIONAL GUIDELINES AND EMPHASIZES IMPORTANCE OF SELF-HELP, AS WELL AS NEED FOR REALISM AND DETERMINATION.

2803 WALKER F.V.
GROWTH, EMPLOYMENT, AND THE PRICE LEVEL.
ENGLEWOOD CLIFFS: PRENTICE HALL, 1963, 342 PP., LC#63-12751.
COVERS MACROECONOMIC MEASUREMENT, THEORY, AND POLICY. EMPHASIZES NEED FOR THEORY OF AGGREGATE DEMAND IN DEALING WITH PROBLEMS IN US GROWTH. SHOWS WHY GROWTH EQUILIBRIUM, THOUGH ULTIMATELY UNSTABLE, DEMONSTRATES CONSIDERABLE RESILIENCY IN FACE OF TEMPORARY DEPARTURES FROM STEADY EXPANSION IN INVESTMENT.

2804 WALKER H.
"THE INTERNATIONAL LAW OF COMMODITY AGREEMENTS."
LAW CONTEMP. PROBL., 28 (SPRING 63), 392-415.
DISCUSSES GATT PROVISIONS, OBLIGATIONS TOWARD NON-MEMBERS, PRIMARY COMMODITY AND COTTON TEXTILE AGREEMENTS, AND THE HAVANA CHARTER. SUGGESTS THAT GENERAL AGREEMENTS ARE FRAMED TO PROMOTE INTERNATIONAL TRADE AND EFFICIENT DISTRIBUTION OF PRODUCTION BY REMOVING ARTIFICIAL BARRIERS THAT PREVENT MARKET DETERMINATION OF FREE TRADE.

2805 WALKER R.L.
"THE WEST AND THE 'NEW ASIA'."
MODERN AGE, 11 (SPRING 67),153-161.
CONTRASTS ANTI-COLONIALIST ATTITUDES OF ASIA IN 1950'S WITH DEPENDENCE ON FORMER EUROPEAN COLONIAL POWERS FOR TRADE IN 1960'S. GENERAL REJECTION BY ASIA OF MAO'S METHODS. DIFFICULTIES REMAINING ARE: US PRESENCE, DIVIDED COUNTRIES, AND THREAT OF COMMUNISM. YET TREND IS TOWARD ECONOMIC EFFICIENCY: ASIAN DEVELOPMENT BANK,ASPAC. POLITICAL CHANGES MAY RESULT FROM CHINESE TRADE WITH NON-COMMUNIST NATIONS.

2806 WALLACE H.M., EISNER V., DOOLEY S.
"AVAILABILITY AND USEFULNESS OF SELECTED HEALTH AND SOCIO-ECONOMIC DATA FOR COMMUNITY PLANNING."
AMER. J. PUBLIC HEALTH, 57 (MAY 67), 762-771.
A STUDY OF THE AVAILABILITY AND USEFULNESS OF HEALTH AND SOCIAL INDEXES IN IDENTIFYING GEOGRAPHICAL AREAS OF HIGH PRIORITY FOR HEALTH AND SOCIAL SERVICES. BASED ON A SAN FRANCISCO SURVEY. DISCUSSES THE MOST USEFUL HEALTH AND SOC-

IO-ECONOMIC INDEXES, AND THE METHODOLOGY OF USING THEM.

2807 WALLACE R.A.
"CONGRESSIONAL CONTROL OF THE BUDGET."
MIDWEST J. OF POLI. SCI., 3 (MAY 59), 151-167.
ARTICLE IS BASED ON THE PREMISE THAT CONGRESS HOLDS THE CONSTITUTIONAL POWER OVER SPENDING AND IT OUGHT TO EXERCISE THAT POWER. THE PROBLEMS BETWEEN EXECUTIVE AND PRESIDENTIAL CONTROL ARE DISCUSSED.

2808 WALLACE R.A.
CONGRESSIONAL CONTROL OF FEDERAL SPENDING.
DETROIT: WAYNE STATE U PR, 1960, 188 PP., LC#60-16509.
AN ATTEMPT TO CLARIFY THE CONGRESSIONAL APPROPRIATIONS PROCESS. IT OUTLINES CONGRESSIONAL PREPARATIONS FOR CONTROL, THE TECHNIQUES EMPLOYED, AND SUGGESTS SOME POTENTIAL IMPROVEMENTS.

2809 WALLBANK T.W., TAYLOR A.M., BAILKEY N.M.
CIVILIZATION PAST AND PRESENT (3RD ED.)
CHICAGO: SCOTT, FORESMAN & CO, 1967, 856 PP., LC#67-12014.
GENERAL INTRODUCTORY TEXT DEALING WITH ECONOMIC, SOCIAL, CULTURAL, POLITICAL, RELIGIOUS, AND INTELLECTUAL HISTORY OF WORLD. TREATS HISTORY AS A GLOBAL EXPERIENCE THROUGH WHICH ALL CULTURAL SYSTEMS HAVE INTERACTED TO PRODUCE PRESENT-DAY WORLD; NOT CONFINED TO WESTERN EXPERIENCE ALONE. INCLUDES INTERCHAPTERS INTRODUCING MATERIAL, BIBLIOGRAPHIES, COLOR PLATES, CHRONOLOGICAL CHARTS, AND MAPS.

2810 WALLICH H.C.
THE COST OF FREEDOM: A NEW LOOK AT CAPITALISM.
NEW YORK: HARPER & ROW, 1960, 178 PP., LC#60-12974.
DISCUSSES PRINCIPLE OF FREEDOM ON WHICH AMERICAN ECONOMIC SYSTEM IS BASED, ITS DEFINITION, IMPORTANCE, RELATION TO SOCIALISM, SYSTEM OF INITIATIVE, INCENTIVES, AND EQUALITY. FREE ECONOMY MEANS SLOWER GROWTH, BUT THAT IS PRICE PAID FOR FREEDOM.

2811 WALSTON H.
AGRICULTURE UNDER COMMUNISM.
CHESTER SPRINGS: DUFOUR, 1962, 108 PP., LC#62-10661.
DESCRIBES AGRARIAN HISTORY OF COMMUNIST COUNTRIES AND METHODS USED TO SOLVE PROBLEM OF AGRICULTURAL WORKERS' RESISTANCE TO GOVERNMENT INTERFERENCE. EVALUATES SUCCESS OF COMMUNIST CHANGES. MAINTAINS INNOVATOR MUST SEE THAT CHANGE BRINGS "BETTER AND HAPPIER LIFE" TO CULTIVATORS.

2812 WALTON R.E., MCKERSIE R.B.
A BEHAVIORAL THEORY OF LABOR NEGOTIATIONS: AN ANALYSIS OF A SOCIAL INTERACTION SYSTEM.
NEW YORK: MCGRAW HILL, 1965, 437 PP., LC#64-66050.
BEHAVIORAL THEORY OF LABOR-MANAGEMENT BARGAINING APPLIED TO FOUR SYSTEMS OF ACTIVITIES: DISTRIBUTIVE BARGAINING, INTEGRATIVE BARGAINING, ATTITUDINAL STRUCTURING, AND INTRAORGANIZATIONAL BARGAINING; HOW NEGOTIATOR MUST BALANCE HIS SEPARATE CONCERNS AND ACHIEVE GREATEST GOOD FOR GREATEST NUMBER.

2813 WALTON S.D.
AMERICAN BUSINESS AND ITS ENVIRONMENT.
NEW YORK: MACMILLAN, 1966, 654 PP., LC#66-14694.
ANALYZES EXTERNAL INFLUENCES ON AMERICAN BUSINESS AND EXTENT TO WHICH A FIRM'S MARKET AND NONMARKET ENVIRONMENT AFFECTS ITS DECISIONS, POLICIES, AND RESULTS. SEPARATE DISCUSSIONS OF ECONOMIC, POLITICAL.,AND SOCIAL BUSINESS ENVIRONMENTS WITH LITTLE ENPHASIS ON PHYSICAL, SCIENTIFIC, AND TECHNICAL ELEMENTS OF ENVIRONMENT. CHAPTERS INCLUDE SUPPLEMENTARY READINGS. INTENDED AS GENERAL TEXTBOOK.

2814 WALZER M.
"THE CONDITION OF GREECE; TWENTY YEARS AFTER THE TRUMAN DOCTRINE."
DISSENT, 14 (JULY 67), 421-431.
EXAMINES EFFECTS OF AMERICAN INTERVENTION IN GREECE UNDER TRUMAN DOCTRINE. DISCUSSES ECONOMIC, MILITARY, AND POLITICAL ASPECTS OF US INTERVENTION. STATES THAT SUCH POLICIES ENCOURAGE RIGHT-WING MILITARY DICTATORSHIPS BY PROMOTING ECONOMIC GROWTH WITHOUT APPROPRIATE SOCIAL CHANGE.

2815 JACKSON, BARBARA (WARD)
5 IDEAS THAT CHANGE THE WORLD.
NEW YORK: NORTON, 1959, 188 PP.
TRACES HISTORY OF THEORY AND PRACTICE OF NATIONALISM AND SHOWS HOW IT CHANGES AND IS CHANGED BY FOUR OTHER BASIC IDEAS: INDUSTRIALISM, COLONIALISM, COMMUNISM AND INTERNATIONALISM.

2816 JACKSON, BARBARA (WARD)
THE RICH NATIONS AND THE POOR NATIONS.
NEW YORK: NORTON, 1962, 159 PP., $3.75.
RICH NATIONS BECOME RICHER AND POOR NATIONS POORER. ATLANTIC NATIONS HAVE SPECIAL RESPONSIBILITY TO HELP UNDERDEVELOPED COUNTRIES SINCE IT WAS IN THE 'ATLANTIC ARENA' THAT THE FOUR REVOLUTIONS OCCURRED: EQUALITY, MATERIAL PROGRESS, SCIENCE AND TECHNOLOGY AND POPULATION-GROWTH, ALL OF WHICH ARE NOW SHAKING THE EMERGING NATIONS.

2817 JACKSON, BARBARA (WARD)
INDIA AND THE WEST.
NEW YORK: W W NORTON, 1961, 256 PP., LC#61-5713.
INDIA'S EXPERIMENTS IN ECONOMIC DEVELOPMENT HAVE CREATED IN HER SOCIETY AN AMBIVALENCE WHICH MAY OPEN A DOOR FOR COMMUNISTS TO STEP INTO. GIVES GENERAL HISTORICAL BACKGROUND OF INDIAN PLANS, AND STRONGLY SUGGESTS THAT TIME HAS COME FOR US TO RESTORE MARSHALL APPROACH TO FOREIGN POLICY. US SHOULD SAVE STARVING MASSES AND HELP INDIA REALIZE HER POTENTIAL BY INSURING SUCCESS OF INDIA'S THIRD PLAN.

2818 WARD R.
BACKGROUND MATERIAL ON ECONOMIC IMPACT OF FEDERAL PROCUREMENT - 1965: FOR JOINT ECONOMIC COMMITTEE US CONGRESS.
WASHINGTON: US GOVERNMENT, 1965, 251 PP.
DESCRIPTION OF AND STATISTICS ON US PROCUREMENT AND PROPERTY MANAGEMENT IN AREAS OF MOST WASTE IN PAST FIVE YEARS. PREPARED FOR HEARINGS TO REDUCE WASTE AND INCREASE EFFICIENCY IN AREAS WHERE GOVERNMENT HAS GREATEST MONETARY OBLIGATIONS, PRIMARILY MILITARY. EMPHASIZES ECONOMIC ASPECTS OF PROCUREMENT AND RELATED SUPPLY MANAGEMENT MATTERS.

2819 WARD R.J.
INTERNATIONAL FINANCE.
ENGLEWOOD CLIFFS: PRENTICE HALL, 1965, 213 PP., LC#65-21172.
STUDY OF OPERATION OF INTERNATIONAL FINANCE. COVERS MEANS OF PAYMENT, PRIVATE AND GOVERNMENTAL INVESTMENT, FOREIGN EXCHANGE, INTERNATIONAL RESERVES, NATIONAL INCOME, AND BALANCE OF PAYMENTS.

2820 WARNER A.W., FUCHS V.R.
CONCEPTS AND CASES IN ECONOMIC ANALYSIS.
NEW YORK: HARCOURT BRACE, 1958, 288 PP., LC#58-9446.
ATTEMPTS TO DEFINE BASIC ECONOMIC THEORY THROUGH USE OF CONCEPTS AND METHODS OF ECONOMIC ANALYSIS. FOCUSES ON ACTUAL ECONOMIC SITUATIONS RATHER THAN BROAD PROBLEM AREAS. SOME CONCEPTS DISCUSSED INCLUDE DEMAND, ELASTICITY, EQUILIBRIUM, AND MARGINAL ANALYSIS. EACH SECTION INCLUDES SEVERAL REAL CASE PROBLEMS TAKEN FROM PUBLISHED SOURCES WHICH REQUIRE APPLICATION OF ONE OF THE CONCEPTUAL TOOLS DISCUSSED.

2821 WARNER A.W. ED., MORSE D. ED., EICHNER A.S. ED.
THE IMPACT OF SCIENCE ON TECHNOLOGY.
NEW YORK: COLUMBIA U PRESS, 1965, 218 PP., LC#65-19945.
ARTICLES BY LEADING SCIENTISTS AND PUBLIC OFFICIALS. C. WRIGHT NOTES THAT INTERACTION OF SCIENCE AND TECHNOLOGY IS INCREASING, SUBJECT TO POLICY CHOICES. PROBES FACTORS MOST PRODUCTIVE OF SCIENTIFIC ADVANCE. ASKS: CAN TECHNOLOGY ACCELERATE GROWTH IN THE CIVILIAN SECTOR OF ECONOMY.

2822 WARNER G.
"FRANCE, BRITAIN AND THE EEC."
WORLD TODAY, 23 (MAR. 67), 115-122.
BRITAIN'S ENTRY INTO THE EEC HINGES ON WHETHER WILSON CAN WIN OVER DE GAULLE. THE FRENCH ARE CONCERNED ABOUT THREE AREAS. THEY ARE THE BRITISH ACCEPTANCE OF THE ROME TREATY AS IT STANDS, BRITAIN'S VIEW OF THE ROLE EUROPE SHOULD PLAY IN WORLD AFFAIRS, AND THE CHANGED BALANCE OF POWER WHICH WOULD RESULT IF BRITAIN WERE TO JOIN.

2823 WARNER K.O.
"FINANCIAL IMPLICATION OF EMPLOYEE BARGAINING IN THE PUBLIC SERVICE."
MUNICIPAL FINANCE, 40 (AUG. 67), 34-39.
EXAMINES COST DIFFERENCE AND IMPACT ON ADMINISTRATORS OF COLLECTIVE BARGAINING IN PUBLIC AGENCIES. USES CANADA AS EXAMPLE FROM WHICH TO DRAW BASIC GUIDELINES FOR US ADMINISTRATORS. CANADIAN EMPLOYEES HAVE FAR GREATER BARGAINING POWER THAN US COUNTERPARTS.

2824 WARNER W.L., LOW J.O.
THE SOCIAL SYSTEM OF THE MODERN FACTORY; THE STRIKE: AN ANALYSIS.
NEW HAVEN: YALE U PR, 1947, 245 PP.
STUDIES SOCIAL ORGANIZATION OF FACTORY. SHOWS LABOR'S RELATIONS WITH MANAGEMENT AND POSITION OF FACTORY AND WORKERS IN COMMUNITY BY EXAMPLE OF STRIKE IN SHOE FACTORY. EXAMINES CAUSES OF STRIKE AND REASONS FOR ITS SUCCESS. DESCRIBES FOUNDATION OF STRONG UNION AGAINST ALL EFFORTS OF MANAGEMENT, AND CHANGE OF YANKEE CITY FROM NONUNION TO UNION TOWN.

2825 WARRINER D.
LAND REFORM AND DEVELOPMENT IN THE MIDDLE EAST: A STUDY OF EGYPT, SYRIA AND IRAQ.
LONDON: ROYAL INST. INT. AFF., 1957, 196 PP.
PROFESSES NEED FOR AGRARIAN REFORM AS A MEANS OF RAISING STANDARDS OF LIVING WITH REFERENCE TO ECONOMIC DEVELOPMENT OF EGYPT, SYRIA AND IRAQ. VIEWS AGRARIAN REFORM AS BEING A POINT OF INTERSECTION BETWEEN ECONOMIC DEVELOPMENT AND SOCIAL CHANGE. FOCUSES ATTENTION ON THREE DYNAMICS OF CHANGE: REVOLUTION, PRIVATE ENTERPRISE AND MONEY.

2826 WASHBURNE N.F.
INTERPRETING SOCIAL CHANGE IN AMERICA.
NEW YORK: RANDOM HOUSE, INC, 1954, 50 PP., LC#54-10158.

TREATS EFFECT OF SOCIAL STRUCTURE ON CHANGE, INTERCONNECTIONS AMONG INSTITUTIONAL FUNCTIONS, SOCIAL PROCESSES, AND SOCIAL MOVEMENTS. EMPHASIZES TRENDS IN URBANIZATION, BUREAUCRATIZATION, AND TECHNOLOGICAL DEVELOPMENTS.

2827 WASSERMAN M.
"BEYOND TOKENISM: REVERSE INTEGRATION IN ALBANY, GEORGIA."
INTEGRATED EDUCATION, 5 (JUNE-JULY 67), 16-22.
DESCRIBES PROGRESS OF RACIAL INTEGRATION IN ALBANY, GEORGIA. STATES THAT PROGRAMS HAVE ACCOMPLISHED MANY OF THEIR AIMS, AND HOPES THAT INTEGRATED EDUCATION WILL ERASE REMAINING PREJUDICES IN SOUTH. DISCUSSES PLANS AND EFFECTS OF HEADSTART AND TUTORIAL PROGRAMS, USE OF FEDERAL FUNDS, AND GENERAL INADEQUACY OF SOUTHERN SCHOOLS COMPARED TO NORTHERN.

2828 WASSERMAN M.J., WARE R.M.
THE BALANCE OF PAYMENTS: HISTORY, METHODOLOGY, THEORY.
NEW YORK: SIMMONS-BOARDMAN PUB, 1965, 481 PP., LC#65-19624.
TRACES DEVELOPMENT OF THE BALANCE OF PAYMENTS. SHOWS DISCOVERY OF PROCEDURES FOR GATHERING NECESSARY DATA. INDICATES EVOLUTION TOWARD A PRESENTATION USEFUL IN POLICY-MAKING DECISIONS. ANALYZES ACCURACY OF BALANCE OF PAYMENTS, DISCUSSING MEANS EMPLOYED TO MEASURE SURPLUSES AND DEFICITS.

2829 WATERSTON A.
"PLANNING IN MOROCCO, ORGANIZATION AND IMPLEMENTATION.
BALTIMORE: HOPKINS ECON. DEVELOP. INT. BANK FOR."
RECON. AND DEV., 1962, 72 PP., $2.50.
DISCUSSES THE ORGANIZATIONAL AND ADMINISTRATIVE ASPECTS OF PLANNING AND THE DESIGN OF POLICIES, PROCEDURES AND INSTITUTIONAL ARRANGEMENTS FOR IMPLEMENTING DEVELOPMENT PLANS IN MOROCCO.

2830 WATERSTON A.
DEVELOPMENT PLANNING* LESSONS OF EXPERIENCE.
BALTIMORE: JOHNS HOPKINS PRESS, 1965, 706 PP., LC#65-26180.
A COMPARISON OF A NUMBER OF TYPES OF NATIONAL ECONOMIC PLANS, THEIR MACHINERY AND IMPLEMENTATION. PLANNING AS ECONOMIC FUNCTION DISCUSSED AND ITS HISTORY TRACED. MANY CASES EXAMINED, WEALTH OF INTERACTING DETAILS PRESENTED IN ORGANIZED FASHION, WITH GOOD INDEX AND BIBLIOGRAPHY.

2831 WATKINS J.B.
"MONETARY RECOVERY UNDER FEDERAL ANTITRUST STATUTES."
TEXAS LAW REVIEW, 45 (APR. 67), 856-880.
ANALYZES SECTION OF CLAYTON ACT THAT PROVIDES FOR TRIPLE DAMAGE SUIT OF ANY PERSON WHO, BY VIOLATING ANTITRUST ACT, HAS INJURED ANOTHER'S BUSINESS OR PROPERTY. CATEGORIZES DAMAGES FOR WHICH PRIVATE PLAINTIFF MAY FILE SUIT. DISCUSSES PROVING DEFENDANT'S VIOLATION AND PLAINTIFF'S INJURY.

2832 WATSON D.S.
ECONOMIC POLICY: BUSINESS AND GOVERNMENT.
BOSTON: HOUGHTON MIFFLIN, 1960, 829 PP.
SURVEY OF GOVERNMENT'S ROLE IN REGULATION OF ECONOMY, INCLUDING VARIOUS ECONOMIC PHILOSOPHIES, GENERAL INFORMATION ON ECONOMIC POLICY, AND DETAILED DISCUSSIONS OF AREAS IN WHICH GOVERNMENT DETERMINES POLICY.

2833 WATSON G.
THE UNSERVILE STATE: ESSAYS IN LIBERTY AND WELFARE.
NEW YORK: MACMILLAN, 1957, 324 PP.
DISCUSSES ATTITUDES AND POLICIES OF BRITISH LIBERALISM SINCE 1928. SHOWS THAT LIBERAL PARTY OF 1950'S IS MOST MYSTERIOUS ELEMENT IN BRITISH POLITICAL LIFE; IT APPEALS TO GENERATIONS WHO HAVE NEVER KNOWN A LIBERAL GOVERNMENT. ANALYZES THE "LIBERAL OUTLOOK," CONCEPTS OF LIBERTY IN A WELFARE STATE, ECONOMICS OF LIBERALISM, AND ROLE OF BRITAIN IN INTERNATIONAL POLITICS.

2834 WATT A.
THE EVOLUTION OF AUSTRALIAN FOREIGN POLICY 1938-65.
NEW YORK: CAMBRIDGE U PRESS, 1967, 387 PP., LC#67-10782.
TRACES HISTORY OF AUSTRALIAN FOREIGN POLICY BEGINNING WITH PREWAR DIVERGENCE FROM BRITAIN THROUGH 1965. DISCUSSES ESTABLISHMENT OF AUSTRALIAN RELATIONS IN AMERICA AND ASIA AT BEGINNING OF WWII AND SUBSEQUENT POSTWAR INTERNATIONAL RELATIONS AND AGREEMENTS. INCLUDES ACTION IN KOREA, RELATIONS WITH INDONESIA, COMMUNIST CHINA, AND MALAYSIA. DISSECTS AND CRITICIZES PRINCIPLES UNDERLYING AUSTRALIAN FOREIGN POLICY.

2835 WATT D.C.
BRITAIN AND THE SUEZ CANAL.
LONDON: ROYAL INST OF INTL AFF, 1956, 51 PP.
DOCUMENTARY ANALYSIS OF THE EXTENT OF BRITISH INTEREST IN THE NATURE AND EFFICIENCY OF MANAGEMENT OF THE SUEZ CANAL. INCLUDES SEVEN DOCUMENTS VITAL TO THE ISSUE: TEXT OF EGYPTIAN DECREE NATIONALIZING THE CANAL; TEXT OF 1888 CONVENTION OF FREE NAVIGATION OF THE SUEZ; ANGLO-EGYPTIAN TREATY OF 1936; SUEZ CANAL BASE AGREEMENT OF 1954; EXTRACTS FROM VARIOUS SUEZ COMPANY CONCESSIONS; AND SEVERAL TABLES.

2836 WEAVER J.H.
THE INTERNATIONAL DEVELOPMENT ASSOCIATION: A NEW APPROACH TO FOREIGN AID.
NEW YORK: FREDERICK PRAEGER, 1965, 286 PP., LC#65-19792.
TRACES HISTORY OF INTERNATIONAL DEVELOPMENT ASSOCIATION BY EXAMINING THREE ISSUES: SOFT LOANS, LOCAL CURRENCY, AND BILATERAL VS MULTILATERAL AID. OUTLINES ORGANIZATION OF THE ASSOCIATION, ITS RELATIONSHIP WITH INTERNATIONAL BANK, AND PROBLEMS OF ALLOCATION IN DISBURSING THE FUNDS. CONTAINS BIBLIOGRAPHY OF PUBLISHED AND UNPUBLISHED MATERIAL WRITTEN IN ENGLISH SINCE 1949.

2837 WEBB S., WEBB B.
THE HISTORY OF TRADE UNIONISM.
LONDON: LONGMANS, GREEN & CO, 1902, 558 PP.
EXAMINES FACTORS INVOLVED IN DEVELOPMENT OF TRADE UNIONS IN UNITED KINGDOM. OUTLINES HISTORY OF UNIONS FROM THE BEGINNINGS IN THE MIDDLE AGES; THROUGH STRUGGLE TO SURVIVE, REVOLUTION, AND NEW FORMS, TO GROWTH TOWARD A TRADE UNION WORLD. AUTHORS PRESENT CASES AND INDICATE SECTIONAL DEVELOPMENTS.

2838 WEBB S., WEBB B.
INDUSTRIAL DEMOCRACY.
LONDON: LONGMANS, GREEN & CO, 1920, 899 PP.
ANALYZES THE TRADE UNION IN THE UNITED KINGDOM. INTERNAL STRUCTURE OF VOLUNTARY UNIONS AS CLASS DEMOCRACIES; FUNCTIONS, METHODS, AND POLICY OF THE TRADE UNION; AND BASIC THEORY ARE THE MAJOR TOPICS DISCUSSED. PERSONAL INVESTIGATION BY AUTHORS CONTRIBUTES TO THEIR ANALYSIS. CONCLUDES THAT THE TRADE UNION HAS A POSITIVE INFLUENCE ON NATIONAL GOVERNMENT.

2839 WEBER M.
GENERAL ECONOMIC HISTORY.
GREENBERG, NY: ADELPHI, 1927, 401 PP.
GENERAL ECONOMIC HISTORY OF THE WEST, ANALYZING ECONOMIC LIFE WITH SPECIAL REFERENCE TO THE PREPARATION FOR AND DEVELOPMENT OF MODERN CAPITALISM. NEVER COMPLETED BY AUTHOR BUT PIECED TOGETHER FROM NOTES BY HIS STUDENTS.

2840 WEBER M.
THE THEORY OF SOCIAL AND ECONOMIC ORGANIZATION.
NEW YORK: OXFORD U PR, 1947, 436 PP.
TRANSLATION OF WEBER'S WORK, WITH INTRODUCTION THAT COVERS FUNDAMENTAL CONCEPTS OF SOCIOLOGY, SOCIOLOGICAL CATEGORIES OF ECONOMIC ACTION, AND TYPES OF AUTHORITY.

2841 WEBER M.
WIRTSCHAFT UND GESELLSCHAFT (2ND VOL.)
TUBINGEN: J C B MOHR, 1956, 840 PP.
DISCUSSES LAW, POLITICAL COMMUNITIES, AND CONCEPTS OF POLITICAL POWER FROM SOCIOLOGICAL POINT OF VIEW. EMPHASIZES QUESTION OF LEGITIMACY.

2842 WECHSBERG J.
THE MERCHANT BANKERS.
BOSTON: LITTLE BROWN, 1966, 365 PP., LC#66-16558.
STUDY OF SEVEN GREAT MERCHANT-BANKER FAMILIES OF EUROPE: THE HAMBROS, BARINGS, WARBURGS, MATTOLI, ABS, LEHMANS, AND ROTHSCHILDS. DESCRIBES HOW EACH FAMILY WAS FOUNDED BY A MAN WHO BEGAN WITH NOTHING AND DIED RICH; HOW WEALTH ACCUMULATED; AND HOW ABILITY, IMAGINATION, AND DARING PLAYED LARGE PART IN FAMILIES' RISE.

2843 WEIDENBAUM M.L., SALOMA JS I.I.I.
CONGRESS AND THE FEDERAL BUDGET: FEDERAL BUDGETING AND THE RESPONSIBLE USE OF POWER.
WASHINGTON: AMER ENTERPRISE INST, 1964, 99 PP.
DISCUSSES THE PRESSURES FOR GOVERNMENT SPENDING, FEDERAL SPENDING AND THE LOCALITY, THE MECHANICS OF GOVERNMENT SPENDING, BUILT-IN RIGIDITIES IN THE FEDERAL BUDGET, THE CONGRESSIONAL BUDGET PROCESS, AND ATTEMPTS AT ITS REFORM.

2844 WEIDENBAUM M.L., SALOMA J.S.
CONGRESS AND THE FEDERAL BUDGET.
CHICAGO: AMER LIB ASSN, 1965, 203 PP., LC#65-18227.
TWO STUDIES ON BUDGET PREPARATION, EXPLANATION, AND HANDLING IN CONGRESS. SUGGESTS A FRAMEWORK FOR PREPARATION THAT WOULD PERMIT GREATER CHOICE AMONG VARIOUS ALTERNATIVE PROGRAMS. ANALYZES CONGRESSIONAL ROLE IN BUDGET PROCESS FOCUSING ON AUTHORIZATION-APPROPRIATIONS PHASE.

2845 WEIGERT H.W., BRODIE H. ET AL.
PRINCIPLES OF POLITICAL GEOGRAPHY.
NEW YORK: APPLETON, 1957, 723 PP., LC#56-9859.
INTRODUCTION TO SUBJECT, EMPHASIZING FACTS AND PROBLEMS OF POLITICAL GEOGRAPHY BUT AVOIDING ANSWERS TO PROBLEMS. ORGANIZED FUNCTIONALLY RATHER THAN REGIONALLY, EXCEPT IN SECTION ON ECONOMIC FACTOR IN POLITICAL GEOGRAPHY, WHERE REGIONAL APPROACH IS USED TO PROVIDE ASSESSMENT OF CAPABILITIES OF SOME MAJOR REGIONS. OTHER SECTIONS DEAL WITH SPATIAL FACTOR AND HUMAN AND CULTURAL FACTORS.

2846 WEIL G.L. ED.
A HANDBOOK ON THE EUROPEAN ECONOMIC COMMUNITY.
NEW YORK: FREDERICK PRAEGER, 1965, 480 PP., LC#65-25594.
COMPILATION OF BASIC DOCUMENTS ON HISTORY AND DEVELOPMENT

OF THE EEC. INCLUDES BACKGROUND DATA ON ITS INSTITUTIONS, ASSOCIATION WITH EUROPEAN STATES, EXTERNAL RELATIONS, AND ECONOMIC AND FINANCIAL AFFAIRS. CONSIDERS THE INTERNAL MARKET, LABOR REGULATIONS, FAIR COMPETITION, AGRICULTURE, TRANSPORT, AND OVERSEAS TRADE. SUMS UP PAST PROGRESS AND LOOKS AT FUTURE GOALS.

2847 WEIL G.L.
"THE MERGER OF THE INSTITUTIONS OF THE EUROPEAN COMMUNITIES"
AMER. J. OF INT. LAW, 61 (JAN. 67), 57-65.
REPORTS ON NATURE AND SIGNIFICANCE OF MERGER TREATY OF 1965 WHICH REPLACED EEC, EURATOM, AND ECSC WITH A SINGLE COUNCIL AND COMMISSION. THIS SINGLE COMMISSION DEALING WITH EUROPEAN NATURAL POWER CONTROL IS CONSIDERED AS A MAJOR CONSTITUTIONAL DEVELOPMENT IN PROGRESS TOWARD EUROPEAN UNITY.

2848 WEILER J.
L'ECONOMIE INTERNATIONALE DEPUIS 1950.
PARIS: PR UNIV DE FRANCE, 1965, 250 PP.
STUDY OF INTERNATIONAL ECONOMICS SINCE 1950. EXAMINES RECONSTRUCTION OF WAR TORN ECONOMIES BY MARSHALL PLAN AND DEVELOPMENT OF EUROPEAN COMMUNITY. COVERS INTERNATIONAL ECONOMIC NEGOTIATIONS ON TARIFFS AND MONETARY SYSTEMS.

2849 WEINBERG M. ED.
SCHOOL INTEGRATION: A COMPREHENSIVE CLASSIFIED BIBLIOGRAPHY OF 3,100 REFERENCES.
CHICAGO: INTEGRATED EDUC ASSOC, 1967, 137 PP., LC#67-29000.
LISTS BOOKS, ARTICLES, AND GOVERNMENT PUBLICATIONS IN ENGLISH FROM 1954-67 ON SCHOOL INTEGRATION. REFERENCES ARRANGED ALPHABETICALLY UNDER TOPICS, INCLUDING PRACTICES, NEW APPROACHES, DEPRIVATION, AND SPANISH-AMERICANS.

2850 WEINER H.E.
BRITISH LABOR AND PUBLIC OWNERSHIP.
WASHINGTON: PUBLIC AFFAIRS PRESS, 1960, 111 PP., LC#59-15840
TRACES THROUGH THE BRITISH TRADE UNION CONGRESS THE EVOLUTION OF IDEA OF NATIONALIZATION AS AN OBJECTIVE OF BRITISH TRADE UNIONISM. ANALYZES ENVIRONMENT AND IDEAS THAT HAVE GOVERNED UNIONISM'S ATTITUDES TOWARD PUBLIC OWNERSHIP OF CERTAIN INDUSTRIES AND SERVICES.

2851 WEISBROD B.A.
ECONOMICS OF PUBLIC HEALTH.
PHILA: U OF PENN PR, 1961, 127 PP., LC#61-5545.
ANALYSIS OF PUBLIC HEALTH AS FACTOR IN ECONOMY AND ITS IMPORTANCE TO OVER-ALL SOCIETY. EXAMINES LOSS TO US DUE TO MAJOR DISEASES AND BENEFITS OBTAINABLE BY IMPROVED HEALTH.

2852 WEISBROD B.A. ED.
THE ECONOMICS OF POVERTY: AN AMERICAN PARADOX.
ENGLEWOOD CLIFFS: PRENTICE HALL, 1965, 180 PP., LC#65-26859.
COLLECTION OF PAPERS ON POVERTY IN US TODAY. ANALYZES WHAT CONSTITUTES POVERTY IN US AND RELATION OF POOR TO OVER-ALL ECONOMIC GROWTH OF NATION. EXAMINES GOVERNMENT ACTIVITY AND RESPONSIBILITY IN ALLEVIATION OF POVERTY.

2853 WEISSKOPF W.A.
"THE DIALECTICS OF ABUNDANCE."
DIOGENES, 57 (SPRING 67), 1-15.
DISCUSSES CHANGES IN VALUE SYSTEM BROUGHT ABOUT BY MOVEMENT FROM ECONOMIC SCARCITY TO ABUNDANCE. ECONOMY BEGAN TO BE REGULATED BY "CORPORATE AND GOVERNMENTAL BUREAUCRACY." CONFLICT BETWEEN "QUALITY OF LIFE AND QUANTITY OF PRODUCTION" DEVELOPED. AFTER MERGER OF ECONOMIC AND PSYCHOLOGICAL VALUES NEW SET OF NONTECHNICAL VALUES DEVELOPS AND STRUGGLES WITH OLD VALUES.

2854 WELLISZ S.
THE ECONOMICS OF THE SOVIET BLOC.
NEW YORK: MCGRAW HILL, 1964, 245 PP., LC#63-1762.
STUDY OF SOVIET ECONOMICS AIMING TO SHOW HOW SYSTEM WORKS AND ANALYZING HOW ECONOMIC DECISIONS ARE REACHED AND PUT INTO PRACTICE. SHOWS HOW SOVIET-TYPE ECONOMY ALLOCATES RESOURCES AND DECIDES UPON PRODUCT MIX, METHOD OF PRODUCTION, AND DISTRIBUTION.

2855 WELTON H.
THE THIRD WORLD WAR; TRADE AND INDUSTRY, THE NEW BATTLEGROUND.
NEW YORK: PHILOSOPHICAL LIB, 1959, 330 PP.
CLAIMS NO MILITARY CONFLICT WILL DEVELOP BETWEEN COMMUNIST AND WESTERN NATIONS, SINCE WAR, ALREADY IN PROGRESS IN TRADE AND INDUSTRY, WILL ITSELF DETERMINE FUTURE OF WORLD. DEFEAT IS BASED ON ECONOMIC DESTRUCTION BY DISPLACEMENT OF EXPORTS IN WORLD MARKETS.

2856 WENDT P.F.
HOUSING POLICY - THE SEARCH FOR SOLUTIONS.
BERKELEY: U CAL BUR BUS ECON RES, 1962, 283 PP., LC#62-11497
EVALUATES NATIONAL HOUSING PROGRAMS AND POLICIES IN UK, SWEDEN, WEST GERMANY, AND US SINCE WWII. COMPARES POSTWAR POLICIES, PRODUCTION, AND RELATIVE IMPROVEMENT IN HOUSING STANDARDS AMONG ALTERNATIVE POLICIES. EXAMINES RELATION BETWEEN HOUSING AND GENERAL ECONOMIC POLICIES.

2857 WENTHOLT W.
SOME COMMENTS ON THE LIQUIDATION OF THE EUROPEAN PAYMENT UNION AND RELATED PROBLEMS (PAMPHLET)
AMSTERDAM: AMST STOCK EX REPORT, 1959, 23 PP.
DISCUSSES EACH NATION'S DEBTS AND FOREIGN EXCHANGE OR GOLD RESERVES LEFT AS RESULT OF LIQUIDATION. STUDIES CREDIT TERMS, ETC., IN NEW EUROPEAN MONETARY AGREEMENT, SET UP TO SETTLE LEFT-OVER DEBTS. LIQUIDATION OF EPU SPRANG FROM CONFLICT BETWEEN FRANCE AND ENGLAND WHEN US REFUSED TO MAKE DOLLAR CONVERTIBLE TO GOLD.

2858 WENTHOLT W.
INFLATION OR SECURITY?
AMSTERDAM: BUIJTEN & SCHIPPERHEIJN, 1960, 103PP.
"WILL THE US JEOPARDIZE AN ATLANTIC ECONOMIC COOPERATION AND THUS UNWITTINGLY REDUCE THE WORLD TO CHAOS? THE WEST SHOULD ENFORCE THE EUROPEAN MONETARY AGREEMENT IN CONSULTATION WITH THE INTERNATIONAL MONETARY FUND."

2859 WERNETTE J.P.
GOVERNMENT AND BUSINESS.
NEW YORK: MACMILLAN, 1964, 534 PP., LC#64-12864.
STUDY OF RELATIONSHIPS BETWEEN GOVERNMENT AND BUSINESS, ENABLING THE "THOUGHTFUL CITIZEN" TO BETTER UNDERSTAND PUBLIC PROBLEMS AND GOVERNMENT ACTION. COVERS SUCH TOPICS AS COMPETITION AND MONOPOLY, ECONOMIC GROWTH, PROTECTIVE LABOR LEGISLATION, CONSERVATION, INTERNATIONAL TRADE POLICIES, AND REGULATION OF PRIVATE FINANCIAL ACTIVITIES.

2860 WERTHEIM W.F.
EAST-WEST PARALLELS.
CHICAGO: QUADRANGLE BOOKS, INC, 1964, 284 PP.
A SOCIOLOGICAL STUDY OF ECONOMIC AND CULTURAL GROWTH OF SOUTHEAST ASIA, EMPHASIZING CONDITIONS AND CHANGES IN INDONESIA. CONCLUDES WITH "SOCIOLOGICAL APPROACH TO INDONESIAN HISTORY." DEPICTS NATIONALISM, RELIGIOUS REFORM MOVEMENTS, AND CORRUPTION.

2861 WESSON R.G.
THE IMPERIAL ORDER.
BERKELEY: U OF CALIF PR, 1967, 547 PP., LC#67-11938.
DISCUSSES THEORY OF POLITICAL POWER. ARGUES THAT THE DEGREE TO WHICH POWER OR POLITICAL MOTIVATION DOMINATES SOCIETY DEPENDS LARGELY UPON THE DEGREE TO WHICH IT IS CHECKED BY CONTRARY POWER, THAT IS, THE DEGREE TO WHICH POWER IS DIVIDED. DESCRIBES IMPERIAL SYSTEMS THROUGHOUT HISTORY, WHERE A SINGLE WILL MOBILIZES THE POTENCY OF THE MASSES WHO ARE OTHERWISE UNABLE TO GOVERN THEMSEVLES.

2862 WESTON J.F.
THE ROLE OF MERGERS IN THE GROWTH OF LARGE FIRMS.
BERKELEY: U OF CALIF PR, 1961, 159 PP.
TREATS HISTORICAL ORIGINS OF CONCENTRATION AND SUPPLIES ADDITIONAL DATA FOR APPRAISING ALTERNATIVE PUBLIC POLICIES TOWARD OLIGOPOLY GATHERED FROM STUDIES OF 74 COMPANIES. ANALYZES EFFECTS OF MERGERS ON INDUSTRIAL CONCENTRATION AND REVIEWS ECONOMIC THEORY OF MERGERS IN LIGHT OF EMPIRICAL FINDINGS. CONSIDERS IMPLICATIONS OF THE RESULT FOR DECISIONS INVOLVING PUBLIC POLICY.

2863 WESTON J.F.
THE SCOPE AND METHODOLOGY OF FINANCE.
ENGLEWOOD CLIFFS: PRENTICE HALL, 1966, 143 PP., LC#66-19883.
STUDIES CHANGE IN FIELD OF FINANCE FROM CONCERN WITH PROCUREMENT OF FUNDS TO ANALYSIS OF MOST VALUABLE USE OF THESE FUNDS FOR FIRM. EXPLAINS CHANGES IN WHOLE ECONOMY SINCE WWII, ALONG WITH NEW METHODS AND TOOLS OF ANALYSIS THAT HAVE CAUSED CHANGES. EMPHASIZES NEED FOR FINANCIAL MANAGERS TO SELECT RIGHT TYPE OF METHODS OF ANALYSIS BECAUSE OF VARIETY OF RESULTS POSSIBLE.

2864 WETTER G.A.
SOVIET IDEOLOGY TODAY.
LONDON: HEINEMANN, 1966, 334 PP.
PROVIDES COMPACT STATEMENT AND CRITICAL DISCUSSION OF PHILOSOPHICAL DOCTRINES OF SOVIET IDEOLOGY. POLITICAL THEORY NOT TREATED. FIRST TREATS DIALECTICAL MATERIALISM, THEN HISTORICAL MATERIALISM, CONCLUDING WITH DISCUSSION OF POLITICAL ECONOMY OF CAPITALISM.

2865 WHEARE K.C.
THE CONSTITUTIONAL STRUCTURE OF THE COMMONWEALTH.
LONDON: OXFORD U PR, 1960, 201 PP.
DESCRIBES CONSTITUTIONAL STRUCTURE OF COMMONWEALTH AS OF MARCH, 1960; PRESENTS CONCEPTS AND CASES OF AUTONOMY, AUTOCHTHONY, EQUALITY, AND COOPERATION AMONG MEMBER STATES. DETAILS PSYCHOLOGY AND PRACTICE OF LOYALTY TO QUEEN, AND OTHER SYMBOLIC EXPRESSIONS OF UNITY.

2866 WHEARE K.C.
FEDERAL GOVERNMENT (4TH ED.)
NEW YORK: OXFORD U PR, 1964, 266 PP.
COMPARES AND CONTRASTS ORGANIZATION, INSTITUTIONS, DIVISION OF POWERS, BASIC PRINCIPLES, CONSTITUTIONS, ROLE OF

GOVERNMENT IN ECONOMY, AND DEVELOPMENT OF COUNTRIES IN WORLD WITH FEDERAL SYSTEM OF GOVERNMENT. ESTABLISHES REQUIREMENTS FOR A FEDERAL SYSTEM.

2867 WHITAKER A.P.
"ARGENTINA: STRUGGLE FOR RECOVERY."
CURR. HIST., 48 (JAN. 65), 16-20.
'LOOKING UP FOR ARGENTINA IN POLITICAL AND ECONOMIC LIFE. PRESIDENT ILLIA IS AN ARDENT NATIONALIST AND DIFFICULTIES WITH USA WILL CONTINUE.'

2868 WHITE C.L., RENNER G.T.
HUMAN GEOGRAPHY: AN ECOLOGICAL STUDY OF GEOGRAPHY.
NEW YORK: APPLETON, 1948, 692 PP.
AUTHORS HOLD THAT GEOGRAPHY IS PRIMARILY HUMAN ECOLOGY, OR THE STUDY OF HUMAN SOCIETY IN RELATION TO THE EARTH BACKGROUND. TEXT TREATS THE CONTENT, POINT OF VIEW, AND TOOLS OF GEOGRAPHY. DISCUSSES CLIMATIC AND MINERAL FACTORS OF THE NATURAL ENVIRONMENT. ANALYZES THE RACE, CULTURE, DISTRIBUTION, AND POPULATION DENSITY OF MAN AS MODIFIERS OF THE GEOGRAPHIC EQUATION.

2869 WHITE J.
"WEST GERMAN AID TO DEVELOPING COUNTRIES."
INTERNATIONAL AFFAIRS (UK), 41 (JAN.65), 74-88
THE HISTORY AND GOALS OF WEST GERMAN AID TO THE DEVELOPING COUNTRIES IS ILLUSTRATIVE OF GENERAL PROBLEMS FACED BY ALL DONORS AND THOSE PECULIAR TO GERMANY. INTERESTINGLY, POLITICAL CONSIDERATIONS (OTHER THAN HALLSTEIN DOCTRINE) ARE OF LITTLE IMPORT COMPARED TO DESIRE TO PROMOTE GROWTH, FREE ENTERPRISE, AND TRADE. UK- GERMAN DATA COMPARED.

2870 WHITE J.
GERMAN AID.
LONDON: MIN OF OVERSEAS DEVEL, 1965, 217 PP.
SURVEYS SOURCES, POLICY, AND STRUCTURE OF GERMAN AID AND ATTITUDE OF GERMAN PEOPLE TOWARD IT. DISCUSSES THEORETICAL RESULTS OF FOREIGN AID, ROLE OF TECHNICAL DEVELOPMENT, AND ITS IMPORTANCE TO TRADE FOR DONOR AND RECEIVER.

2871 WHITE W.L., STRICK J.C.
"THE TREASURY BOARD AND PARLIAMENT."
CAN. PUBLIC ADMIN., 10 (JUNE 67), 209-222.
DISCUSSES LITTLE-KNOWN CANADIAN TREASURY BOARD AND PRESENT SECRETARIAT ADVISING IT. EXPLAINS POLITICAL DIMENSIONS OF BOARD AND THE WAY THESE ARE RELATED TO ITS CENTRAL POSITION IN OVERSEEING GOVERNMENT FINANCIAL ACTIVITIES. SUGGESTS MEANS OF IMPROVING BOARD'S ADMINISTRATIVE PROCEDURES.

2872 WHITEHEAD T.N.
LEADERSHIP IN A FREE SOCIETY; A STUDY IN HUMAN RELATIONS BASED ON AN ANALYSIS OF PRESENT-DAY INDUSTRIAL CIVILIZATION.
CAMBRIDGE: HARVARD U PR, 1947, 266 PP.
CONCERNED WITH IMPACT OF BUSINESS AND INDUSTRIAL INSTITUTIONS ON SOCIETY AND WITH TYPE OF SOCIAL STRUCTURE WHICH CAN MAINTAIN ITSELF BEST IN TECHNOLOGICALLY DEVELOPING WORLD. STUDIES FUNCTIONING OF WORKING GROUPS AND ROLE OF LEADERSHIP IN COLLECTIVE ACTION; INVESTIGATES INTERACTION BETWEEN HUMAN MOTIVES AND SHAPE AND DEVELOPMENT OF ORGANIZED INSTITUTIONS. REVIEWS TYPES OF SOCIAL SYSTEMS.

2873 WHITNEY S.N.
"MERGERS, CONGLOMERATES, AND OLIGOPOLIES* A WIDENING OF ANTI TRUST TARGETS."
RUTGERS LAW REV., 21 (WINTER 67), 187-261.
COVERS HISTORY AND IMPORTANCE OF MERGERS AND PASSAGE OF ANTIMERGER LAW, EFFECT OF SUPREME COURT DECISIONS OF RECENT YEARS, ECONOMIC PROBLEMS OF COMPETITION AND CONCENTRATION ARISING FROM CONGLOMERATE MERGERS, AND PLANNED GOVERNMENT ATTACK ON NON-COMPETITIVE OLIGOPOLIES. EXTENSIVE REFERENCES TO LEGAL PRECEDENTS.

2874 WHYTE W.F.
HUMAN RELATIONS IN THE RESTAURANT INDUSTRY (1ST ED)
NEW YORK: MCGRAW HILL, 1948, 378 PP.
AN INTERESTING STUDY OF A SOCIAL SYSTEM, SUPPORTED BY THE NATIONAL RESTAURANT ASSOCIATION, MADE DURING WARTIME. IT DETAILS VARIOUS WORKER, MANAGEMENT, AND PUBLIC ATTITUDES AS WELL AS THE ROLE OF UNIONS IN THE RESTAURANT INDUSTRY, BASED ON OBSERVATIONS AND INTERVIEWS.

2875 WHYTE W.H. JR.
THE ORGANIZATION MAN.
NEW YORK: SIMON AND SCHUSTER, 1956, 429 PP., LC#56-9926.
A CRITIQUE OF "EMPLOYEESHIP" APPLICABLE TO THOSE IN ANY LARGE COLLECTIVE ORGANIZATION, IT DESCRIBES THE NEW ETHIC OF BELIEVING IN GROUP BELONGINGNESS AND MAKING IT THE SOURCE OF CREATIVITY, AND MAKES A PLEA FOR THE PRESERVATION OF THE INDIVIDUAL. DESCRIBES FASHIONABLE TONING-DOWN OF LEADERSHIP FUNCTIONS AMBITION, OVERWORK, AND GENIUS WITH RESULTING BUREAUCRATIZATION, AND COMMONALITY.

2876 WIBBERLEY G.P.
AGRICULTURE AND URBAN GROWTH.
LONDON: MICHAEL JOSEPH, LTD, 1959, 240 PP.
STUDY OF THE COMPETITION FOR RURAL LAND IN UK. FACTUAL ACCOUNT OF LAND USE AND THE EFFECTS OF THE COMPETITION FOR LAND. (METHOD IS SUGGESTED FOR ASSESSING THE VALUE OF LAND USED FOR AGRICULTURE AS COMPARED TO ITS PROBABLE VALUE IF IT WERE USED FOR URBAN REDEVELOPMENT PROJECTS.) DISCUSSES POSSIBILITIES OF IMPORTING FOOD TO MAKE RURAL LAND AVAILABLE FOR THE CITIES.

2877 WIGHTMAN D.
TOWARD ECONOMIC CO-OPERATION IN ASIA.
NEW HAVEN: YALE U. PR., 1963, 400 PP.
INDEPENDENT HISTORY AS WELL AS AN APPRAISAL OF THE WORK OF THE U.N. ECONOMIC COMMISSION FOR ASIA AND THE FAR EAST 'ECAFE). INCLUDES APPROACHES TO ECONOMIC DEVELOPMENT COMMONLY PROPOUNDED AND ACCEPTED IN THE REGION. CITES ABILITY OF ECAFE TO INFLUENCE AND SHAPE THE POLICIES AND ACTIONS OF THE INDIVIDUAL GOVERNMENTS.

2878 WILCOX C., WEATHERFORD W.D. JR. ET AL.
ECONOMIES OF THE WORLD TODAY: THEIR ORGANIZATION, DEVELOPMENT, AND PERFORMANCE (2ND ED.)
NEW YORK: HARCOURT BRACE, 1966, 171 PP., LC#65-28576.
STUDY OF GROWTH IN COUNTRIES AT VARIOUS STAGES OF MATURITY, INCLUDING UNITED STATES AND SOVIET UNION. INTRODUCTION EXPLAINS ECONOMIC ORGANIZATION, PERFORMANCE RATES, AND STANDARDS.

2879 WILCOX W.A.
ASIA AND UNITED STATES POLICY.
ENGLEWOOD CLIFFS: PRENTICE HALL, 1967, 116 PP., LC#67-24901.
EXAMINES TRADITIONAL US ATTITUDES TOWARD ASIA. DISCUSSES DIVERSITY OF COUNTRIES AND GROUPS THEM BY CATEGORY AND NATURE OF THEIR POLICY PROBLEMS. MAINTAINS THAT US POLICY MUST TAKE DIFFERENCES AMONG COUNTRIES AND BETWEEN US AND ASIA INTO ACCOUNT. EXPLORES TWO MAJOR DIPLOMATIC PROBLEMS: STABLE, SECURE NATIONS SURROUNDING CHINA, AND INTEGRATION OF ALL NATIONS INTO COMPETITIVE WORLD ECONOMY.

2880 WILCOX W.W.
SOCIAL RESPONSIBILITY IN FARM LEADERSHIP.
NEW YORK: HARPER & ROW, 1956, 194 PP., LC#56-6438.
HAS EXTENSIVE COVERAGE ON FARM ORGANIZATIONS, FARM LEADERSHIP IN ACTION, RESPONSIBILITIES TO LOW-INCOME RURAL GROUPS IN ADDITION TO AID TO FORMAL MEMBERSHIP, AND VARIOUS FARM "LEADERSHIP OPPORTUNITIES" IN THE LEGISLATIVE AND EXECUTIVE PROCESS.

2881 WILDAVSKY A.
"POLITICAL IMPLICATIONS OF BUDGETARY REFORM."
PUBLIC ADMIN. REV., 21 (FALL 61), 183-190.
DISCUSSES MAJOR IMPLICATIONS OF BUDGETARY REFORM AND ILLUSTRATES WHERE TO LOOK TO LEARN HOW THE BUDGET IS MADE. DEVELOPS A NORMATIVE THEORY OF BUDGETING THAT PROVIDES FOR ALLOCATING FUNDS AMONG COMPETING ACTIVITIES. RELATES BUDGET REFORM TO POLITICS. VIEWS STUDY OF BUDGETING AS ANOTHER EXPRESSION FOR STUDY OF POLITICS.

2882 WILDAVSKY A.
"TVA AND POWER POLITICS."
AM. POL. SCI. REV., 55 (SEPT. 65), 576-590.
REVIEW OF POLITICAL STRUGGLES OVER FUNDS AND PROGRAMS FOR TVA. INDICATES THAT CONFLICT IN POLITICAL ARENA MAY BE BEST WAY TO INSURE REPRESENTATION OF ALL POINTS OF VIEW.

2883 WILES P.J. D.
"THE POLITICAL AND SOCIAL PREREQUISITES FOR A SOVIET-TYPE ECONOMY."
ECONOMICA, 34 (FEB. 67), 1-19.
RELATES THEORY TO PRACTICE IN SOVIET ECONOMY. DISCUSSES PHILOSOPHY OF ECONOMIC MANAGEMENT. GIVES CHARACTERISTICS OF STALIN'S ECONOMIC SYSTEM AND RELATES THEM TO MARXISM. COMMAND ECONOMY CRITICIZED FROM MANY ASPECTS BUT PRAISED FOR ACHIEVEMENTS DESPITE DRAWBACKS. HISTORICAL DEVELOPMENT OF SOVIET SYSTEM.

2885 WILES P.J.D.
"WILL CAPITALISM AND COMMUNISM SPONTANEOUSLY CONVERGE."
ENCOUNTER, 20 (JUNE 63), 86-90.
DISCOUNTS BELIEF THAT CAPITALISM AND COMMUNISM WILL CONVERGE. POINTS OUT THAT NEW MATHEMATICAL TECHNIQUES AND USE OF COMPUTERS WILL MAKE POSSIBLE MORE EFFICIENT CONTROL OF RUSSIA'S COMMAND-ECONOMY.

2886 WILKINSON J.H. JR.
"THE NET OPERATING LOSS DEDUCTION AND RELATED INCOME TAX DEVICES."
TEXAS LAW REVIEW, 45 (APR. 67), 809-841.
ANALYZES MECHANICS OF LAW THAT PROVIDES FOR PERSON WHO HAS NET OPERATING LOSS ONE YEAR, TO CARRY LOSSES TO OTHER YEARS ON HIS INCOME TAX AND DEDUCT THEM. COVERS MEANS OF COMPUTING AMOUNT OF DEDUCTION, ITS ADVANTAGES AND DISADVANTAGES, AND PROBLEMS ARISING FROM STATUTES OF LIMITATIONS. SUGGESTS DEVICES TO SHIFT INCOME FROM PROFIT YEAR TO LOSS YEAR, ON PAPER, TO AVOID LOSS OF DEDUCTIONS.

2887 WILKINSON T.O.

THE URBANIZATION OF JAPANESE LABOR, 1868-1955.
AMHERST: U OF MASS PRESS, 1965, 243 PP., LC#65-26242.
SOCIOLOGICAL AND DEMOGRAPHIC ANALYSIS OF URBAN AND INDUSTRIAL GROWTH IN MAJOR JAPANESE METROPOLITAN AREAS SINCE 1868. CLASSIFIES CITIES ON FUNCTIONAL BASIS TO DELINEATE PATTERN OF DEVELOPMENT FROM RURAL TO URBAN AND FROM AGRICULTURAL TO INDUSTRIAL LABOR ORIENTATION.

2888 WILLIAMS B. ED.
THE SELBORNE MEMORANDUM.
LONDON: OXFORD U PR, 1925, 184 PP.
COLLECTION OF OFFICIAL DOCUMENTS, KNOWN COLLECTIVELY AS SELBORNE MEMORANDUM, REVIEWING MUTUAL RELATIONS OF BRITISH SOUTH AFRICAN COLONIES IN 1907 LEADING TO UNION. LONG INTRODUCTION. CORRESPONDENCE CONCERNS CAUSE OF SOUTH AFRICAN DISUNION, ITS EFFECTS ON RAILWAY DEVELOPMENT, FISCAL POLICY, AND ECONOMIC POSITION.

2889 WILLIAMS C.
"REGIONAL MANAGEMENT OVERSEAS."
HARVARD BUSINESS REV., 45 (JAN. 67), 87-91.
CONSIDERS THE ADVANTAGES OF REGIONAL MANAGEMENT AND THE COMPANIES IN WHICH IT WORKS BEST. ADVISES BRUSSELS, LONDON, GENEVA, ZURICH, AND PARIS AS HQ SITES FOR EXPANDING EUROPEAN MARKETS. CONCLUDES THAT INCREASE IN OVERHEAD AND COMPLEXITY OF COMMUNICATION IS OFFSET BY ADVANTAGES OF ON-THE-SPOT DECISION-MAKING.

2890 WILLIAMS E.J.
LATIN AMERICAN CHRISTIAN DEMOCRATIC PARTIES.
KNOXVILLE: U OF TENN PR, 1967, 305 PP., LC#67-13159.
TENTATIVE ANALYSIS AND DESCRIPTION OF RISING ANTI-COMMUNIST MOVEMENT IN LATIN AMERICA. DISTINGUISHES CHRISTIAN DEMOCRATS FROM TRADITIONAL CATHOLIC PARTIES. CONSIDERS ORIGINS, TENETS, ORGANIZATION, DOMESTIC POLICIES (LABOR, FAMILY, AGRARIAN REFORM), ECONOMIC AND INTERNATIONAL POLICIES. SEES RELATION WITH CATHOLIC CHURCH AND MILITARY AS STRATEGIC TO SUCCESS. ASSESSES FUTURE. SPANISH-ENGLISH BIBLIOGRAPHY.

2891 WILLIAMS G. ED.
MERTHYR POLITICS: THE MAKING OF A WORKING-CLASS TRADITION.
CARDIFF: U OF WALES PRESS, 1966, 109 PP.
TRACES FOUR MAIN PHASES OF POLITICS OF MERTHYR, WELSH INDUSTRIAL TOWN. BEGINS WITH HENRY RICHARD'S REIGN IN 1868, AND ESTABLISHMENT OF LIBERAL ASCENDENCY. DISCUSSES SUPERSESSION OF LIBERALISM BY SOCIALIST ALLEGIANCE AND IMPACT ON POLITICS OF ECONOMIC EVENTS IN TOWN.

2892 WILLIAMS J.H.
ECONOMIC STABILITY IN A CHANGING WORLD.
NEW YORK: OXFORD U PR, 1953, 284 PP., LC#52-14155.
CONCERNS RELATION OF ECONOMIC THEORY TO PUBLIC POLITY. FIRST DISCUSSES ECONOMIC THEORY AND POLICY WITH BIAS TO KEYNESIAN ECONOMICS. FOLLOWS WITH STUDY OF MARSHALL PAPERS, ESSAYS ON FREE ENTERPRISE AND FULL EMPLOYMENT, AND KEYNES MONETARY DOCTRINES.

2893 WILLIAMS M.
THE EAST IS RED: THE VIEW INSIDE CHINA.
NEW YORK: WILLIAM MORROW, 1967, 267 PP., LC#67-29845.
PRESENTS ACCOUNT OF AUTHOR'S TEN-WEEK TRIP INTO RED CHINA IN 1966. ATTEMPTS TO QUALIFY VIEW HE FEELS MOST AMERICANS HAVE OF EVENTS IN CHINA. SEES IN MAO AND HIS SUPPORTERS A DETERMINED RESISTANCE TO THE "RAPE OF CHINA" BY PRIVILEGED RESISTANCE-CHINESE AND WESTERNERS. SEES IN THE MILITANT ACTIVITIES OF RED GUARDS THE MOPPING UP OF DISSIDENTS INEVITABLE IN THE WAKE OF REVOLUTION.

2894 WILLIAMS S.
"NEGOTIATING INVESTMENT IN EMERGING COUNTRIES."
HARVARD BUS. REV., 43 (JAN. - FEB. 65), 89 PP.
NOTES PRESSURES AND TENSIONS IN THE DECISION TO INVEST IN UNDERDEVELOPED AREAS. ASSERTS THAT 'THE ART OF POLITICS AND THE CONCEPTS OF SOCIAL SCIENCE CAN BECOME AS IMPORTANT AS HARDHEADED TECHNICAL AND FINANCIAL CALCULATIONS....'

2895 WILLIAMSON H.F. ED., BUTTRICK J.A.
ECONOMIC DEVELOPMENT - PRINCIPLES AND PATTERNS.
ENGLEWOOD CLIFFS: PRENTICE HALL, 1954, 576 PP., LC#54-9455.
COLLECTION OF ESSAYS ON FACTORS AND MEASURES IMPORTANT TO ECONOMIC GROWTH. EXAMINES ROLE OF NATURAL RESOURCES, DEMOGRAPHIC PATTERNS, LABOR FORCE, TECHNOLOGY, FOREIGN TRADE AND CAPITAL TRANSFERS, AND CULTURAL FACTORS. INCLUDES CASE STUDIES IN ECONOMIC DEVELOPMENT (JAPAN, KOREA, INDIA, MEXICO).

2896 WILLIAMSON J.G.
AMERICAN GROWTH AND THE BALANCE OF PAYMENTS, 1820-1913: A STUDY OF THE LONG SWING.
CHAPEL HILL: U.N.C. PR., 1964, 298 PP., $7.50.
STUDY OF THE EFFECT OF LONG SWINGS IN THE DOMESTIC ECONOMY ON U.S. FOREIGN TRADE AND BALANCE OF PAYMENTS. SUGGESTS THAT RAPID GROWTH AND PRICE INFLATION HAVE TENDED TO GENERATE A SURPLUS OF PAYMENTS, WHEREAS POOR GROWTH PERFORMANCE AND PRICE DEFLATION HAVE TENDED TO GENERATE DEFICITS. ALSO COMPARES AMERICAN EXPERIENCE WITH THAT OF THE BRITISH.

2897 WILLIAMSON O.E.
THE ECONOMICS OF DISCRETIONARY BEHAVIOR: MANAGERIAL OBJECTIVES IN A THEORY OF THE FIRM.
ENGLEWOOD CLIFFS: PRENTICE HALL, 1964, 182 PP., LC#64-18412.
FORD FOUNDATION DOCTORAL DISSERTATION. CENTERS ATTENTION ON DISCRETIONARY BEHAVIOR OF MANAGERS IN THEIR OPERATION OF BUSINESS FIRMS. OBJECTIVES: TO INDICATE IN WHAT WAY MANAGERS ARE MOTIVATED TO ATTEND TO OTHER THAN PROFIT GOALS, TO TRANSLATE MOTIVATION OF MANAGERS TO ANALYSIS OF OPERATIONS CONTEXT, TO IDENTIFY CONDITIONS FOR DISCRETIONARY BEHAVIOR TO BE OF QUANTITATIVE IMPORTANCE, AND TO DEVELOP A THEORY.

2898 WILLMANN J.
"LA COMMUNAUTE EUROPEENNE ET LA GRANDE-BRETAGNE."
POLITIQUE ENTRANGERE, 32 (1967), 35-47.
EXAMINES PROBLEM OF BRITISH ENTRANCE TO EEC IN TERMS OF COMMUNITY INTERESTS OF PARTICIPANT NATIONS. EXAMINES MOTIVES AND OBJECTIVES OF BRITISH ENTRANCE AND THEIR ACCORDANCE WITH INTERESTS OF EEC. SETS UP CONDITIONS TO WHICH BRITAIN MUST AGREE BEFORE ENTRANCE TO COMMON MARKET.

2899 WILLS A.J.
AN INTRODUCTION TO THE HISTORY OF CENTRAL AFRICA.
LONDON: OXFORD U PR, 1967, 412 PP.
VIEWS EARLY INVASIONS OF EUROPEAN TRADERS THROUGHOUT THE CONTINENT, GROWTH OF SLAVE TRADE AND DISRUPTION OF AFRICAN LIFE, AND MISSIONS. THEN CONFINES ITSELF TO BRITISH COLONIZATION ALONG ZAMBEZI AND ESTABLISHMENT OF TERRITORIES, DESCRIBING POLICIES AND CHARACTERISTICS OF TERRITORIES UP TO END OF COLONIAL PHASE.

2900 WILMERDING L. JR.
THE SPENDING POWER: A HISTORY OF THE EFFORTS OF CONGRESS TO CONTROL EXPENDITURES.
NEW HAVEN: YALE U PR, 1943, 316 PP.
AFTER DISCUSSING WHETHER CIRCUMSTANCES SOMETIMES OCCUR WHICH MAKE IT A DUTY TO ASSUME AUTHORITY BEYOND THE APPROPRIATION LAWS, EIGHT STAGES OF AMERICAN HISTORY ARE COVERED FROM VIEWPOINT OF EFFORTS TO CONTROL BEFORE EXPENDITURE. IT SHOWS THAT DOCTRINE OF SPECIFIC APPROPRIATION IS ALWAYS PRESENT BUT NOT AFFECTED. LAST CHAPTERS DESCRIBE EFFORT TO CONTROL AFTER EXPENDITURE DURING FOUR STAGES OF US HISTORY.

2901 WILSON C.E.
"AMERICAN INVESTMENT IN PORTUGUESE AFRICA: A PROBLEM OF "DEMOCRATIC" COLONIALISM."
FREEDOMWAYS, 7 (SUMMER 67), 14-225.
TRACES DEVELOPMENT OF PORTUGUESE COLONIES IN SOUTHERN AFRICA, ESPECIALLY ANGOLA AND MOZAMBIQUE, FROM FOUNDING THROUGH SALAZAR'S ERA TO INDEPENDENCE. EMPHASIZES INFLUENCE OF AMERICAN "DEMOCRATIC" IMPERIALISM AND MAINTAINS THAT US IS "MORALLY BANKRUPT" DUE TO SERVING DEMOCRACY AND FREEDOM PLUS COLONIALISM AND HER BUSINESS INTERESTS, TWO INCOMPATIBLE AIMS.

2902 WILSON T.
FINANCIAL ASSISTANCE WITH REGIONAL DEVELOPMENT (PAMPHLET)
FREDERICKTON, N.B., CANADA: U OF GLASGOW, 1964, 75 PP.
ANALYZES TYPES OF POLICY ACTION THAT WILL CAUSE GREATEST RATE OF ECONOMIC GROWTH IN ATLANTIC PROVINCES. CONCENTRATES ON STUDYING TAX INCENTIVES TO PROMOTE ECONOMIC AND INDUSTRIAL GROWTH. CONSIDERS COSTS OF GOVERNMENT AND METHODS OF APPLYING NEW POLICIES.

2903 WILSON T.
INFLATION.
CAMBRIDGE: HARVARD U PR, 1961, 280 PP.
DISCUSSES VARIOUS IMPLICATIONS OF ECONOMIC INFLATION; ITS DIFFERENT TYPES, ITS RELATION TO DEFLATION AND RECESSION, AND POLICIES TO COPE WITH IT.

2904 WILSON T.
POLICIES FOR REGIONAL DEVELOPMENT.
LONDON: OLIVER & BOYD, 1964, 93 PP.
COMPARES OFFICIAL MEASURES FOR REGIONAL DEVELOPMENT ADOPTED BY CANADA AND ENGLAND. FOCUSES ON USE OF TAX INCENTIVES AND OTHER BUDGETARY INDUCEMENTS. DESCRIBES EFFECTS OF MOBILITY ON CENTERS OF GROWTH, FINANCIAL ASSISTANCE TO INDUSTRY, AND COST TO GOVERNMENT.

2905 WILTZ J.E.
IN SEARCH OF PEACE: THE SENATE MUNITIONS INQUIRY, 1934-36.
BATON ROUGE: LOUISIANA ST U PR, 1963, 277 PP., LC#63-16656.
ILLUSTRATED STUDY OF SENATE INVESTIGATION ATTEMPTING TO PROVE THAT INDUSTRIES WHICH PROFITED FROM THE WAR WERE RESPONSIBLE FOR WAR. INCLUDES MUNITIONS MANUFACTURE, ARMS EMBARGO, AND CONSCRIPTION.

2906 WINSLOW E.M.
THE PATTERN OF IMPERIALISM; A STUDY IN THE THEORIES OF POWER.
NEW YORK: COLUMBIA U PRESS, 1948, 278 PP.
PRESENTS MAIN POINTS IN CONTROVERSY BETWEEN SOCIALISTS AND COMMUNISTS REGARDING PRECISE RELATION OF CAPITALISM TO IMPERIALISM AND WAR. DISCUSSES EACH SIDE'S THEORY AND THEIR AGREEMENT ON ECONOMIC BASIS OF IMPERIALISM. MAINTAINS THAT

IMPERIALISM AND WAR ARE NOT ECONOMIC BUT POLITICAL PHENOMENA IN WHICH BOTH CAPITALISM AND SOCIALISM PARTICIPATE.

2907 WINT G. ED.
ASIA: A HANDBOOK.
NEW YORK: FREDERICK PRAEGER, 1965, 856 PP., LC#65-13263.
ARTICLES ABOUT RELATIONS BETWEEN THE ASIAN STATES AND THE REST OF THE WORLD, FOCUSING ON THE GROWTH IN WORLD POWER EXERCISED BY THESE COUNTRIES. GIVE BASIC COUNTRY-BY-COUNTRY INFORMATION AND SURVEYS, EMPHASIZING POLITICAL, SOCIAL, ECONOMIC, CULTURAL, AND RELIGIOUS ASPECTS OF ASIA, WITH MAPS AND EXTRACTS FROM TREATIES AND AGREEMENTS SIGNED SINCE WWII.

2908 WINT G. ED.
"ASIA: A HANDBOOK."
NEW YORK: FREDERICK PRAEGER, 1966.
COMPREHENSIVE REFERENCE WORK ON ASIA CONTAINING ESSAYS ON POLITICAL, SOCIAL, ECONOMIC, CULTURAL, AND RELIGIOUS ASPECTS OF ASIA; MAPS; EXTRACTS FROM TREATIES AND AGREEMENTS SIGNED SINCE 1945; AND BASIC INFORMATION AND SURVEYS ON EACH NATION. UNANNOTATED BIBLIOGRAPHY OF AMERICAN PUBLICATIONS RELEASED SINCE 1952, WITH EMPHASIS ON POST-1960 WORKS.

2909 WIONCZEK M.
"LATIN AMERICA FREE TRADE ASSOCIATION."
INT. CONCIL., 551 (JAN. 65), 80 PP.
CRITIQUE OF LATIN AMERICAN NATIONALISM AS A STRUCTURE ON TRADE AND ECONOMIC DEVELOPMENT IN THAT AREA. CITES UTILITY OF LAFTA IN REGIONAL COOPERATION.

2910 WISCONSIN HISTORICAL SOCIETY
LABOR PAPERS ON MICROFILM: A COMBINED LIST.
MADISON: WISC STATE HIST SOC, 1965, 66 PP., LC#65-63011.
LIST OF CONTENTS OF US MICROFILM LIBRARIES. ENTRIES PROVIDE MINIMUM OF BIBLIOGRAPHIC INFORMATION. ALL LABOR PAPERS ARE PRINTED IN US.

2911 WISEMAN H.V.
BRITAIN AND THE COMMONWEALTH.
NEW YORK: BARNES AND NOBLE, 1967, 157 PP., LC#67-16629.
DISCUSSES COMMONWEALTH IN WORLD CONTEXT WITH EMPHASIS ON BRITISH INFLUENCE. COMPARES SOCIAL AND POLITICAL SYSTEMS OF MEMBER NATIONS WITH BRITISH MODEL. INCLUDES FORMAL AND INFORMAL TIES WITHIN COMMONWEALTH, AND EXAMINES MEANING OF MEMBERSHIP. PROJECTS FUTURE POLITICAL AND ECONOMIC RELATIONSHIPS AMONG MEMBERS AND COMMENTS ON FUTURE ROLE IN WORLD AFFAIRS. SUGGESTS THAT TIES AMONG MEMBERS MAY BE WEAKENING.

2912 WISH J.R.
ECONOMIC DEVELOPMENT IN LATIN AMERICA: AN ANNOTATED BIBLIOGRAPHY.
NEW YORK: FREDERICK PRAEGER, 1965, 144 PP., LC#65-21105.
ANNOTATED BIBLIOGRAPHY EMPHASIZING ITEMS PUBLISHED SINCE 1955 AND RELEVANT TO OBJECTIVE OF MAKING OPERATIVE ROSTOW'S "NATIONAL MARKET" CONCEPT. FOCUSES ON MARKETING AND COMMUNICATION IN AGRICULTURAL RESEARCH. INCLUDES SECTIONS DEALING WITH WRITINGS AND ISSUES OF SOCIAL SCIENCE RESEARCH, AND ECONOMIC DEVELOPMENT. APPENDEXES CONTAIN SHORT LISTING OF INFORMATION SOURCES AND SHORT BIBLIOGRAPHY OF KEY SOURCES.

2913 WITHERELL J.W.
OFFICIAL PUBLICATIONS OF FRENCH EQUATORIAL AFRICA, FRENCH CAMEROONS, AND TOGO, 1946-1958 (PAMPHLET)
WASHINGTON: LIBRARY OF CONGRESS, 1964, 78 PP., LC#64-60029.
AN ANNOTATED BIBLIOGRAPHY OF 405 PUBLICATIONS CONCERNED WITH AFRIQUE EQUATORIALE FRANCAISE AND THE TRUST TERRITORIES WHICH WERE ISSUED DURING THE TERM OF THE FOURTH REPUBLIC. COVERS PUBLICATIONS OF GOVERNMENT GENERAL OF FRENCH EQUATORIAL AFRICA, GOVERNMENTS OF FOUR TERRITORIES WHICH COMPRISED AEF, AND THE ADMINISTRATIONS IN THE CAMEROONS AND TOGO FROM 1946-58. SOURCES IN FRENCH AND ENGLISH.

2914 WITHERS W.
THE ECONOMIC CRISIS IN LATIN AMERICA.
NEW YORK: FREE PRESS OF GLENCOE, 1964, 307 PP., LC#64-21208.
SURVEYS ECONOMIC CONDITIONS AND PROBLEMS IN LATIN AMERICA, AS A WHOLE AND IN SPECIFIC COUNTRIES. BELIEVES RESISTANCE TO COMMUNISM DEPENDS ON MIDDLE CLASSES' RETENTION OF POLITICAL POWER. URGES GREATER AWARENESS BY US OF BASIC PROBLEM OF ECONOMIC DEVELOPMENT IN FORM OF SOCIALIZED CAPITALISM AS FORMULATED UNDER LEADERSHIP OF MEXICO.

2915 WODDIS J.
AFRICA: THE ROOTS OF REVOLT.
LONDON: LAWRENCE & WISHART, 1960, 285 PP.
DISCUSSES IMPACT OF IMPERIALISM ON AFRICA, SOCIAL AND ECONOMIC CHANGES CAUSING REVOLT, AND METHODS EMPLOYED TO ELIMINATE MISERY AND OPPRESSION. ATTEMPTS TO SEE PROBLEMS OF AFRICA THROUGH EYES OF AFRICANS IN POLITICS AND ECONOMY.

2916 WOLF C. JR.
UNITED STATES POLICY AND THE THIRD WORLD.
BOSTON: LITTLE BROWN, 1967, 204 PP., LC#67-14078.
DISCUSSES RELATIONS BETWEEN US AND NON-COMMUNIST UNDERDEVELOPED COUNTRIES, EMPHASIZING FORMULATION AND UNDERSTANDING OF THIRD WORLD PROBLEMS, INCLUDING INTERPLAY OF POLITICAL, ECONOMIC, AND MILITARY PROBLEMS.

2917 WOLFE T.W.
"SOVIET MILITARY POLICY AT THE FIFTY YEAR MARK."
CURRENT HISTORY, 53 (OCT. 67), 208-216.
STUDIES BACKGROUND OF SOVIET MILITARY POLICY INHERITED BY BREZHNEV AND KOSYGIN. BELIEVES THAT PRESENT POLICY IS ATTEMPT AT BROADENING MILITARY CAPACITIES IN NEGLECTED AREAS, WITH BASIC POLICY REMAINING. EXAMINES RESOURCE ALLOCATION ISSUE, QUESTION OF PREPARATION FOR LIMITED WAR, AND POLITICAL-MILITARY RELATIONS. DESCRIBES EFFECTS OF WARSAW PACT AND VIETNAM WAR.

2918 WOLFERS A.
"INTEGRATION IN THE WEST: THE CONFLICT OF PERSPECTIVES."
INT. ORGAN., 17 (SUMMER 63), 753-771.
BELIEVES USA MUST TURN TO THE ECONOMIC FIELD TO APPRECIATE THE SUCCESS OF EUROPEAN MOVEMENT AND TO DISCOVER (FROM THE PERSPECTIVE OF EUROPEAN NATIONS) CHIEF PREREQUISITES OF CONTINUED PROGRESS TOWARD GOAL OF COMPLETE INTEGRATION.

2919 WOLFF R.L.
THE BALKANS IN OUR TIME.
CAMBRIDGE: HARVARD U PR, 1956, 618 PP., LC#56-6529.
INTRODUCTORY STUDY OF BALKAN COUNTRIES - YUGOSLAVIA, RUMANIA, BULGARIA, AND ALBANIA. DESCRIBES COUNTRIES AND PEOPLE, GIVING HISTORY FROM FOURTH CENTURY TO WWII. ANALYZES BALKAN ECONOMY SINCE WWII. STUDIES WAR YEARS, COMMUNIST TAKE-OVER, SOVIET-YUGOSLAV DISPUTE, YUGOSLAVIA SINCE BREAK WITH COMINFORM, POLITICAL LIFE IN BALKANS SINCE 1948, BALKAN ECONOMIES SINCE 1948, BALKAN RELIGION, EDUCATION, CULTURE.

2920 WOLFSON M.
"GOVERNMENT'S ROLE IN TOURISM DEVELOPMENT."
DEVELOPMENT DIGEST, 5 (JULY 67), 50-56.
DISCUSSES IMPORTANT ROLE OF NATIONAL GOVERNMENT IN GUIDING TOURIST INDUSTRY IN ALL COUNTRIES. POINTS OUT THAT BASIC MARKET RESEARCH, AREA DEVELOPMENT PLANNING, PROMOTION, AND PROPAGANDA ARE VITAL TO SUCCESSFUL TOURIST INDUSTRY. SUGGESTS GOVERNMENT SET UP STANDARDS OF QUALITY AND SERVICE, AND PROVIDE NEEDED FUNDS FOR PRIVATE INVESTMENT.

2921 WOOD N.
"THE FAMILY FIRM - BASE OF JAPAN'S GROWING ECONOMY."
J. ECON. SOC., 23(JULY 64), 315-24.
THE FAMILY FIRM CONTINUES TO PLAY AN IMPORTANT ROLE IN JAPAN'S RAPIDLY EXPANDING ECONOMY. THE ROLE IS BECOMING MORE CREATIVE THAN IT HAS BEEN. IT IS SUGGESTED THAT THE EMERGING ECONOMIES ADOPT THIS TYPE OF FREE ECONOMIC FRAMEWORK AS AN ALTERNATIVE TO STATE PLANNING.

2922 WOODMAN H.D. ED.
SLAVERY AND THE SOUTHERN ECONOMY: SOURCES AND READINGS.
NEW YORK: HARCOURT BRACE, 1966, 261 PP., LC#66-18864.
PART OF THE "FORCES IN AMERICAN ECONOMIC GROWTH" SERIES, WHICH PRESENTS DOCUMENTARY RECORD OF THE BUILDING OF AMERICAN ECONOMY. BOOK DEALS WITH SLAVERY AND THE PLANTER, SLAVERY AND THE NONSLAVEHOLDER, SLAVERY AND ITS EFFECTS ON THE SLAVES, AND THE ECONOMIC DEVELOPMENT INVOLVED. DOCUMENTS ARE NOT ANALYZED OR INTERPRETED.

2923 WOODS H.D. ED.
PATTERNS OF INDUSTRIAL DISPUTE SETTLEMENT IN FIVE CANADIAN INDUSTRIES.
MONTREAL: MCGILL U, IND REL SEC, 1958, 395 PP.
STUDIES GOVERNMENT INTERVENTION IN SETTLEMENT OF LABOR DISPUTES AND ROLE OF CANADIAN LABOR RELATIONS LAW IN SETTLING THEM. COMPARES MEDIATION, ARBITRATION, AND LABOR LAW IN CANADA AND US. GIVES GENERAL INTERPRETATION OF CONTEMPORARY ACCOMMODATION THEORY.

2924 WOODS H.D., OSTRY S.
LABOUR POLICY AND LABOUR ECONOMICS IN CANADA.
TORONTO: MACMILLAN CO OF CANADA, 1962, 534 PP.
EXPLORES LABOR POLICY AND ECONOMICS IN CANADA, CONSIDERING ROLE OF GOVERNMENT IN LABOR RELATIONS, LABOR-RELATIONS BOARDS, ARBITRATION AND NEGOTIATIONS, LABOR FORCE, UNEMPLOYMENT, WAGES, AND FUTURE OF LABOR IN CANADIAN ECONOMY.

2925 WOOTON G.
WORKERS, UNIONS, AND THE STATE.
NEW YORK: SCHOCKEN BOOKS, 1967, 173 PP., LC#67-12612.
DISCUSSES THE OBLIGATION OF WORKERS IN THEIR TRADE (OR LABOR) UNIONS TO THE COMMUNITY-AT-LARGE, AS REPRESENTED BY THE STATE. TAKES THE PERSPECTIVE OF THE ORDINARY WORKER AND SKETCHES THE PROBLEM OF CIVIC OBLIGATION AS IT TOUCHES HIM. THEN TRIES TO TRACE THE CIVIC OBLIGATION OF THE WORKER TO ITS SOCIOLOGICAL AND SOCIAL-PSYCHOLOGICAL ROOTS.

2926 WOOTTON B.
FREEDOM UNDER PLANNING.
CHAPEL HILL: U OF N CAR PR, 1945, 180 PP.
DISCUSSES FUNCTION AND POSSIBILITIES OF FREEDOM UNDER

ECONOMIC PLANNING. ANALYZES EFFECTS ON FREEDOM WHICH MAY RESULT FROM WELL-INTENTIONED PLANNING. FEELS THAT THE JUSTIFICATION OF PLANNING, IN TERMS OF FREEDOM, MUST BE THAT BY CONSCIOUS COLLECTIVE DECISION OF ECONOMIC PRIORITIES, MAN'S FRUSTRATIONS ARE DIMINISHED AND FREEDOMS ENLARGED.

2927 WORTHY J.C.
BIG BUSINESS AND FREE MEN.
NEW YORK: HARPER & ROW, 1959, 205 PP., LC#59-9941.
STUDIES ROLE OF BUSINESSMEN AS CIVIC LEADERS IN DEMOCRATIC SOCIETY. FEELS THEIR VALUES SAME AS INDIVIDUAL'S, AND AIMS TO OFFER CONSTRUCTIVE ADVICE FOR CIVIC LEADERS FROM PERSONAL EXPERIENCE IN BUSINESS AND GOVERNMENT. CONCENTRATES ON BUSINESS AS A "HUMAN AND SOCIALLY VALUABLE INSTITUTION."

2928 WOYTINSKY W.S., WOYTINSKY E.S.
WORLD POPULATION AND PRODUCTION: TRENDS AND OUTLOOK.
NEW YORK: TWENTIETH CENTURY FUND, 1953, 1268 PP.
BROAD STATISTICAL SURVEY OF COLLECTIVE RESOURCES AND ECONOMIC PERFORMANCES AND PROMISE OF NATIONS OF THE WORLD. TRACES MAN AND HIS ENVIRONMENT THEN OUTLINES TOPICS SUCH AS WORLD NEEDS AND RESOURCES, ENERGY AND MINING, AND FARMING.

2929 WOYTINSKY W.S., WOYTINSKY E.S.
WORLD COMMERCE AND GOVERNMENTS: TRENDS AND OUTLOOK.
NEW YORK: TWENTIETH CENT FUND, 1955, 907 PP., LC#55-8797.
EXTENSIVE SURVEY OF WORLD TRANSPORTATION, TRADE, AND POLITICAL SYSTEMS, INCLUDING BALANCE OF PAYMENTS AND INTERNATIONAL INVESTMENT, TARIFFS, RAILROADS, AVIATION, AND PUBLIC DEBTS.

2930 WRIGHT D.M.
THE CREATION OF PURCHASING POWER.
CAMBRIDGE: HARVARD U PR, 1942, 251 PP.
EXAMINES CREATION OF PURCHASING POWER AS STIMULUS TO STOP DEPRESSIONS. CONSIDERS PURCHASING POWER AS PROBLEM OF PRODUCTION, AS MONEY, IN TERMS OF PRICES AND INCOME, AND AS ABILITY AND WILLINGNESS TO BUY. DEFINES INFLATION AND EVALUATES THEORIES OF BANK CREDIT AND POLICY, VELOCITY STIMULATORS, AND PURCHASING POWER INJECTORS. INCLUDES DEFICIT FINANCING, DISTRIBUTION, AND ADMINISTRATION.

2931 WRIGHT D.M.
THE KEYNESIAN SYSTEM.
NEW YORK: FORDHAM U PR, 1962, 90 PP., LC#62-15667.
EXAMINES BASIC TENETS OF KEYNESIAN THEORY AND EXPLORES SHORTCOMINGS. DISCUSSES ECONOMIC PROBLEMS OF POSTWAR ERA - PARTICULARLY INFLATION AND ECONOMIC GROWTH - WITHIN KEYNESIAN FRAMEWORK, BUT PRESENTS NEW MODELS TO MEET CHANGED SITUATION. CONSIDERS THEORIES OF EMPLOYMENT, INVESTMENT, AND CONSUMPTION. MARGINAL EFFICIENCY AS A TOOL OF ANALYSIS, SPECULATION, AND SATURATION ARE INCLUDED.

2932 WRIGHT G.
RURAL REVOLUTION IN FRANCE: THE PEASANTRY IN THE TWENTIETH CENTURY.
STANFORD: U. PR., 1964, 271 PP., $6.00.
TRACES GRADUAL AWAKENING OF FRENCH PEASANTRY--AT FIRST TO A NEW SELF-CONSCIOUSNESS, AND LATER TO SYNDICALIST ORGANIZATION AND POLITICAL ACTION. DISCUSSES RIVAL EFFORTS OF THE COMMUNISTS AND CATHOLICS IN THE COUNTRYSIDE. CONCLUDES WITH AN ANALYSIS AND TENTATIVE ASSESSMENT OF THE FIFTH REPUBLIC'S NEW COURSE IN THE AREA OF RURAL REFORM.

2933 WRIGHT H.M.
THE "NEW IMPERIALISM": ANALYSIS OF LATE NINETEENTH-CENTURY EXPANSION.
BOSTON: D C HEATH, 1961, 110 PP., LC#61-9906.
COLLECTION OF HISTORICAL ESSAYS CONSIDERING ORIGINS, NATURE, AND IMPLICATIONS OF LATE-19TH-CENTURY EXPANSION. EACH ESSAY IS REPRESENTATIVE OF PARTICULAR HISTORICAL POINT OF VIEW. INCLUDES SEVERAL ECONOMIC INTERPRETATIONS, OTHERS WHICH CLAIM EUROPE SUFFERED FROM "ATAVISM," DISCONTENT, OR EXCESSIVE NATIONALISM.

2934 WRIGHT L.B.
THE DREAM OF PROSPERITY IN COLONIAL AMERICA.
NEW YORK: NEW YORK U PR, 1965, 96 PP., LC#64-22263.
FOR NEARLY 500 YEARS EUROPEANS HAVE LOOKED ACROSS THE ATLANTIC AND DREAMED OF WEALTH AND PLEANTY. THIS BOOK TRACES THE SOURCES AND EFFECTS OF THAT DREAM AND SUGGESTS HOW TODAY IT REMAINS PART OF THE AMERICAN INHERITANCE. QUOTES EXTENSIVELY FROM LETTERS AND DOCUMENTS OF THE PERIOD.

2935 WRIGHT Q. ED.
GOLD AND MONETARY STABILIZATION.
CHICAGO: U. CHI. PR., 1932, 174 PP.
SERIES OF LECTURES COVERS INTERNATIONAL ASPECTS OF THE GOLD STANDARD, MONEY AND BUSINESS CYCLE, FEDERAL RESERVE POLICY IN DEPRESSION, THE FUTURE OF GOLD STANDARD, AND MONETARY STABILITY AND THE GOLD STANDARD.

2936 WRONG D.H.
AMERICAN AND CANADIAN VIEWPOINTS.
WASHINGTON: AMER COUNCIL ON EDUC, 1955, 62 PP., LC#55-12179.
PRESENTS BRIEF SUMMARY OF NATIONAL VALUE SYSTEMS OF AMERICANS AND CANADIANS. COMPARES ATTITUDES ON FAMILY, RELIGION, EDUCATION, ECONOMIC ACTIVITIES, GOVERNMENT, SOCIAL CLASSES, AND LAW. COMPARES TWO SIMILAR INDUSTRIAL NATIONS TO DISCOVER DIFFERENCES.

2937 WU YUAN-LI
ECONOMIC WARFARE.
ENGLEWOOD CLIFFS: PRENTICE HALL, 1952, 403 PP., LC#52-10552.
STUDY OF ECONOMICS OF WAR GIVING SPECIAL CONSIDERATION TO INTERNATIONAL TRADE. DISCUSSES PROBLEMS OF REGULATION AND CONTROL OF TRADE WITH ENEMY. DESCRIBES ECONOMIC WARFARE DURING WWII. PRESENTS HYPOTHETICAL SITUATIONS TO EXPLAIN IDEAS AND THEORIES.

2938 WU YUAN-LI
"CHINA'S ECONOMY AND ITS PROSPECTS."
CURR. HIST., 47 (SEPT. 64), 166-172.
'PROSPECT OF COMMUNIST CHINESE CONTINUED ECONOMIC RECOVERY MUST BE PREDICATED UPON WESTERN CO-OPERATION... RESUMPTION OF EXPANSION ON SELF-RELIANT BASIS DEPENDS ON CO-OPERATION OF SOME, ACQUIESCENCE OF OTHERS.'

2939 WU YUAN-LI
THE ECONOMY OF COMMUNIST CHINA.
NEW YORK: FREDERICK PRAEGER, 1965, 225 PP., LC#65-18082.
ANALYZES MODERN CHINA'S ECONOMIC GROWTH, EMPHASIZING NATIONAL GROWTH AND THE COMMUNE SYSTEM, WITH DISCUSSION OF THE ACCOUNTING SYSTEM, RESOURCE ALLOCATION, GROSS DOMESTIC PRODUCT, AND STATISTICAL REPORTING.

2940 WUERTHNER J.J.
THE BUSINESSMAN'S GUIDE TO PRACTICAL POLITICS.
CHICAGO: HENRY REGNERY CO, 1959, 235 PP., LC#59-7768.
PARTISAN TREATIES CLAIMING BUSINESS INTERESTS ARE NOT REPRESENTED IN THE FEDERAL GOVERNMENT, AND THAT LABOR IS OVER REPRESENTED. SUGGESTS METHODS OF POLITICAL ACTIVITY TO ELECT PRO-BUSINESS OFFICIALS.

2941 WUNDERLICH F.
LABOR UNDER GERMAN DEMOCRACY, ARBITRATION 1918-1933.
NEW YORK: NEW SCHOOL SOC RES, 1940, 100 PP.
DESCRIBES CONFLICT BETWEEN LABOR AND CAPITAL AS INFLATION SOARED AND ECONOMY RECOILED UNDER REPARATIONS PAYMENTS. MAIN BATTLEFIELD WAS ARBITRATION AND HEREIN ARE DESCRIBED METHODS AND ACHIEVEMENTS OF BOTH SIDES.

2942 WUORINEN J.H.
"SCANDINAVIA."
ENGLEWOOD CLIFFS: PRENTICE HALL, 1965.
BIBLIOGRAPHICAL ESSAY OF ENGLISH BOOKS AND PERIODICALS FROM 1929-1964. ARRANGED BY GROUP TOPICS INCLUDING GENERAL HISTORIES, OFFICIAL PUBLICATIONS, ECONOMIC AND SOCIAL DEVELOPMENTS, FOREIGN POLICY AND AFFAIRS, AND SCANDINAVIAN COOPERATION. APPROXIMATELY 200 ENTRIES.

2943 WURFEL D.
"FOREIGN AID AND SOCIAL REFORM IN POLITICAL DEVELOPMENT" (BMR)
AM. POL. SCI. REV., 53 (JUNE 59), 456-482.
PRESENTS SOME GENERAL CONSIDERATIONS IN SUPPORT OF A PROPOSAL THAT US ATTEMPT TO STIMULATE SOCIAL CHANGE WITHIN CONTEXT OF A FOREIGN AID PROGRAM. DESCRIBES NATURE AND TECHNIQUES OF REFORM THROUGH ECONOMIC AID. REPORTS A PHILIPPINE PROGRAM AS CASE STUDY TO ILLUSTRATE EFFECTIVENESS OF SUCH AN AID ARRANGEMENT.

2944 WURFEL S.W.
FOREIGN ENTERPRISE IN COLOMBIA.
CHAPEL HILL: U OF N CAR PR, 1965, 563 PP.
DISCUSSES LEGAL ENVIRONMENT FOR FOREIGN INVESTMENT IN COLOMBIA IN CONTEXT OF POLITICAL, ECONOMIC, AND SOCIAL DEVELOPMENT. COVERS ASSETS AND LIABILITIES OF COLOMBIA, DEVELOPMENT PROGRAMS NOW UNDER WAY, AND LEGAL INSTITUTIONS AND THEIR IMPACT ON INVESTMENT.

2945 YABUKI K.
JAPAN BIBLIOGRAPHIC ANNUAL, 1956: THE LATEST LIST OF OLD AND NEW BOOKS ON JAPAN IN ENGLISH.
TOKYO: HOKUSEIDO PR OF JAPAN, 1956, 318 PP.
ANNUAL PUBLICATION INCLUDES ENGLISH MATERIAL ARRANGED IN ALPHABETICAL ORDER AND AN APPENDIX, A CLASSIFIED LIST OF POSTWAR ARTICLES IN "CONTEMPORARY JAPAN" (1946-1955) AND "JAPAN QUARTERLY" (1954-1955). THE LATTER MATERIAL IS ARRANGED BY SUBJECT: ECONOMICS, HISTORY, POLITICS, SOCIOLOGY, AND ETHNOLOGY.

2946 YAMAMURA K.
ECONOMIC POLICY IN POSTWAR JAPAN.
BERKELEY: U OF CALIF PR, 1967, 320 PP.
EXAMINES TWO POSTWAR ECONOMIC POLICIES - DEMOCRATIZATION IMPOSED BY "ALLIED POWERS" AND SUBSEQUENT REACTION OF DE-DEMOCRATIZATION PURSUED AND FORMULATED BY THE INDEPENDENT GOVERNMENT. CONSIDERS BOTH POLICIES IN TERMS OF WHAT, WHY, AND HOW. INCLUDES EXAMINATION OF JAPANESE ECONOMIC INSTITUTIONS AND POSTWAR GROWTH.

2947 YEAGER L.B.
INTERNATIONAL MONETARY RELATIONS: THEORY, HISTORY, AND POLICY.
NEW YORK: HARPER & ROW, 1966, 504 PP., LC#66-10055.
INVESTIGATES THEORY OF HOW THE SEVERAL ALTERNATIVE SYSTEMS OF INTERNATIONAL MONETARY RELATIONS OPERATE, INCLUDING SOME ABSTRACT ANALYSIS OF POLICY MEASURES. SURVEYS POLICIES PURSUED BY WORLD GOVERNMENTS OVER PAST THREE CENTURIES, AND DISCUSSES SOME PRESENT-DAY PROPOSALS FOR INTERNATIONAL MONETARY POLICY CHANGES.

2948 YLVISAKER P.N.
THE NATURAL CEMENT ISSUE (PAMPHLET)
INDIANAPOLIS: BOBBS-MERRILL, 1950, 62 PP.
STUDY OF NATURAL CEMENT MANUFACTURER'S ATTEMPTS TO GET MINNESOTA STATE COMMISSIONER OF HIGHWAYS TO SPECIFY HIS PRODUCT FOR HIGHWAY CONSTRUCTION. TWELVE-YEAR CONTROVERSY (1939-47) PROVOKED DEFINITION OF FEDERAL POLICY ON ISSUE. SUGGESTS COMPLEXITY OF RELATIONS BETWEEN PRIVATE AND PUBLIC AGENCIES.

2949 YOUNG A.N.
CHINA'S WARTIME FINANCE AND INFLATION.
CAMBRIDGE: HARVARD U PR, 1965, 421 PP., LC#65-22049.
DISCUSSES CHINA'S FINANCIAL POLICIES FROM JAPAN'S INVASION IN 1937 TO END OF WWII. EXAMINES REVENUE AND EXPENDITURE, FOREIGN FINANCIAL AID, CURRENCY MANAGEMENT, AND INFLATION.

2950 YOUNG G.B.
FEDERALISM AND FREEDOM.
LONDON: OXFORD U. PR., 1941, 204 PP.
BRIEF HISTORY OF POLITICAL TRENDS OF EUROPEAN COUNTRIES. EVALUATES GROWTH OF GERMAN INDUSTRIAL STRENGTH, THE WORKING OF AMERICAN FEDERATION AND THE RUSSIAN PROBLEM. SURVEYS RELATIONSHIP BETWEEN ETHICS AND ECONOMICS. CONCLUDES WITH DIAGNOSIS OF ECONOMIC DISORDERS.

2951 YOUNG J.M.
THE BRAZILIAN REVOLUTION OF 1930 AND THE AFTERMATH.
NEW BRUNSWICK: RUTGERS U PR, 1967, 156 PP., LC#66-25171.
A STUDY OF RECENT BRAZILIAN HISTORY, INCLUDING BRIEF SKETCH OF COLONIAL BACKGROUND. ILLUSTRATES EFFECTS OF REVOLUTION OF 1930 HEADED BY GETULIO VARGAS, ITS PLANNING, EXECUTION, AND ECONOMIC AND POLITICAL POWER RELATIONSHIPS WHICH STEMMED FROM IT AND WHICH STILL AFFECT CONTEMPORARY AFFAIRS THERE.

2952 YOUNG S.
MANAGEMENT: A SYSTEMS ANALYSIS.
GLENVIEW, ILL: SCOTT, FORESMAN, 1966, 445 PP.
DESIGN, IMPLEMENTATION, OPERATION, AND CONTROL OF A MANAGEMENT SYSTEM IS DISCUSSED, WITH EMPHASIS ON ORGANIZATIONAL PROBLEM-SOLVING. SYSTEMS APPROACH UTILIZED TO CONSIDER MANAGERIAL DECISION-MAKING AS A TOTAL OPERATING SYSTEM; THE RELATIONSHIP OF PARTS TO WHOLE IS ALSO ANALYZED. INCLUDES CASES.

2953 YRARRAZAVAL E.
AMERICA LATINE EN LA GUERRA FRIA.
SANTIAGO: EDITORIAL NASCIMENTO, 1959, 295 PP.
ANALYSIS OF POSITION OF LATIN AMERICA IN COLD WAR. DISCUSSES REGIONAL ECONOMIC DEVELOPMENT AND RELATIONS WITH US, EUROPE, AND USSR IN ECONOMIC AND POLITICAL MATTERS.

2954 YUAN TUNG-LI
ECONOMIC AND SOCIAL DEVELOPMENT OF MODERN CHINA: A BIBLIOGRAPHIC GUIDE.
NEW HAVEN: HUMAN REL AREA FILES, 1956, 217 PP.
BIBLIOGRAPHY OF MONOGRAPHS AND PAMPHLETS PUBLISHED IN ENGLISH, FRENCH, AND GERMAN, LIMITED TO PERIOD FROM 1900 TO 1955. LISTINGS ARRANGED BY SUBJECT: STATISTICS, ECONOMIC HISTORY, AGRICULTURE, INDUSTRY, COMMERCE, TRANSPORTATION, COMMUNICATION, ETC. SECTION ON SOCIAL DEVELOPMENT WHICH INCLUDES SOCIOLOGICAL AND ETHNOLOGICAL STUDIES. AUTHOR INDEX INCLUDED.

2955 YUDELMAN M.
AFRICANS ON THE LAND.
CAMBRIDGE: HARVARD U PR, 1964, 288 PP., LC#63-21929.
PROBLEMS OF AGRICULTURAL DEVELOPMENT IN SOUTHERN, CENTRAL, AND EAST AFRICA WITH SPECIAL EMPHASIS ON SOUTHERN RHODESIA. LABOR, LAND APPORTIONMENT, MARKETING, AND FINANCE, APPENDICES OF METHODS, OUTPUT, AND ECONOMETRIC RELIABICITY ARE COVERED.

2956 ZACK A.M.
"ARE STRIKES OF PUBLIC EMPLOYEES NECESSARY?"
AMER BAR ASSN., 53 (SEPT. 67), 808-810.
EXAMINES ACTIVITIES OF AMERICAN ARBITRATION ASSOCIATION'S LABOR MANAGEMENT INSTITUTE IN FORESTALLING AND RESOLVING LABOR DISPUTES OF PUBLIC EMPLOYEES. EMPHASIZES RIGHT OF PUBLIC EMPLOYEES TO EXPRESS GRIEVANCES BUT MAINTAINS NEED FOR PROTECTING PUBLIC FROM CONSEQUENCES OF WORK STOPPAGE.

2957 ZALESKI E.
PLANNING REFORMS IN THE SOVIET UNION 1962-1966.
CHAPEL HILL: U OF N CAR PR, 1967, 203 PP., LC#67-17035.
EXAMINES SOVIET ECONOMIC PLANNING AND ADMINISTRATION SPECIFICALLY DEALING WITH CHANGES AND REFORMS IN PERIOD 1962-66. DISCUSSES STRUCTURE OF NATIONAL PLANNING AND DECISION-MAKING ON ECONOMIC POLICY AND EXTENT OF CENTRAL CONTROL AND UNIT INDEPENDENCE. COVERS DIFFERENCE IN CHANGES SINCE REMOVAL OF KHRUSHCHEV.

2958 ZAUBERMAN A.
"SOVIET BLOC ECONOMIC INTEGRATION."
PROBL. COMMUNISM, 8 (JULY-AUG. 59) 23-29.
ASSERTS THAT BLOCK ECONOMIC INTEGRATION HAS FAR-REACHING POLITICAL IMPLICATIONS. INDICATES THAT IT MAY COMMEND ITSELF TO SOVIET POLICY-MAKERS AS MEANS OF STRENGTHENING INTRA-BLOC TIES AND THEREBY CONSOLIDATING SOVIET POLITICAL HEGEMONY OVER EASTERN EUROPE.

2959 ZAUBERMAN A.
"SOVIET AND CHINESE STRATEGY FOR ECONOMIC GROWTH."
INT. AFF., 38 (1962), 339-352.
TRACES PATH CHINESE GOVERNMENT HAS PURSUED WITH REGARD TO CONTROLLED AND PLANNED ECONOMIES USING THE RUSSIAN ECONOMY AS A PROTOTYPE. DESCRIBES AIMS OF CHINESE REPUBLIC, SIMILARITIES AND DIFFERENCES TO SOVIET ECONOMY, AND EXPLORES RESULTS CLAIMED AFTER THE 'FIRST DECADE'.

2960 ZAWADZKI K.K.F.
THE ECONOMICS OF INFLATIONARY PROCESSES.
LONDON: WEIDENFIELD & NICOLSON, 1965, 288 PP.
STUDIES ECONOMIC INFLATION AND ITS VARIOUS IMPLICATIONS, INCLUDING ITS NATURE, PROCESSES, STABILIZATION, EFFECT ON PRICES, TRADE, EXPANSION, SAVING, AND RATE OF GROWTH.

2961 ZEBOT C.A.
THE ECONOMICS OF COMPETITIVE COEXISTENCE.
NEW YORK: FREDERICK PRAEGER, 1964, 262 PP., LC#64-16695.
PRESENTS COMPARATIVE STUDY OF ROOT PROBLEMS OF ECONOMIC GROWTH IN EACH OF THREE SUBDIVISIONS IN CONTEMPORARY WORLD: NEWLY DEVELOPING COUNTRIES, SOVIET COUNTRIES, AND THE WEST. DEALS WITH UNRESOLVED PROBLEMS OF INTERDEPENDENCE AND INTERPLAY BETWEEN ECONOMIC DEVELOPMENT AND GROWTH AND VARIOUS SOCIAL SYSTEMS OF ORGANIZATION.

2962 ZEIDBERG L.D., ET A.L.
"THE NASHVILLE AIR POLLUTION STUDY" (PARTS V-VII)"
ARCH. OF ENVIRONMENTAL HEALTH, 15 (AUG. 67), 214-247.
STUDIES RELATIONSHIP BETWEEN AIR POLLUTION AND MORTALITY FROM EACH OF THE THREE FOLLOWING DISEASES: RESPIRATORY DISEASES, CARDIOVASCULAR DISEASES, AND CANCER. CONSIDERS SPECIFIC POLLUTANTS, SOCIOECONOMIC AND DEMOGRAPHIC CHARACTERISTICS OF NASHVILLE, AND DEGREE OF EXPOSURE TO AIR POLLUTION. RESEARCH BEGAN IN 1957. INVESTIGATION INOT EFFECTS OF POLLUTION ON HEALTH IS CONTINUING.

2963 ZEIGLER H.
THE POLITICS OF SMALL BUSINESS.
WASHINGTON: PUBLIC AFFAIRS PRESS, 1961, 150 PP.
HISTORY OF THE ATTEMPTED POLITICAL ORGANIZATION AND REPRESENTATION THROUGH THE SMALL BUSINESS ADMINISTRATION OF SMALL BUSINESS, WHICH THE AUTHOR SAYS IS NTO A UNIFIED INTEREST GROUP.

2964 ZINKIN T.
CHALLENGES IN INDIA.
NEW YORK: WALKER, 1966, 248 PP.
DISCUSSES INDIAN DOMESTIC ISSUES AND EVENTS SINCE THE DEATH OF NEHRU. ANALYZES EFFECTS OF HIS ADMINISTRATION AND CHANGES SHASTRI INTRODUCED. CONSIDERS PROBLEMS OF AGRICULTURAL SELF-SUFFICIENCY AND INDUSTRIALIZATION FROM PRE-INDEPENDENCE TO SHASTRI. RELATED PROBLEMS OF CIVIL SERVICE CORRUPTION AND INDIAN-PAKISTANI RELATIONS ARE ALSO INCLUDED.

2965 ZISCHKA A.
WAR ES EIN WUNDER?
HAMBURG: MOSAIK VERLAG, 1966, 607 PP.
DISCUSSES GERMAN ECONOMIC RECOVERY AFTER WWII. EXAMINES LIMITATIONS PLACED ON INDUSTRIAL EXPANSION BY ALLIED POWERS, IMPACT OF MARSHALL PLAN, RISE OF AUTO INDUSTRY AND EXPORTS, AND CONCLUDES WITH DISCUSSION OF BEGINNINGS OF REPUBLIC AND REARMAMENT.

2966 ZOBER M.
MARKETING MANAGEMENT.
NEW YORK: JOHN WILEY, 1964, 483 PP., LC#64-15002.
MARKETING TEXTBOOK FOR THE UNDERGRADUATE CONCERNED WITH THEORY AND BODY OF KNOWLEDGE SUPPORTING MARKETING. DIVIDED INTO FOUR PARTS: FIRST, INTRODUCES CONCEPT OF MARKETING AND MARKETING MANAGEMENT; SECOND, REVIEWS PROBLEM AREAS IN MARKETING; THIRD, EXPLORES TECHNIQUES FOR SOLVING MARKETING PROBLEMS; AND FOURTH, STUDIES ROLE OF ORGANIZATION AND ANTI-TRUST LAWS.

2967 ZOETEWEIJ B.
"INCOME POLICIES ABROAD: AN INTERIM REPORT."

INDUST. LABOR REL. REV., 20 (JULY 67),650-664.
COMPARES PURPOSES AND METHODS OF SEVERAL WESTERN EUROPEAN COUNTRIES IN SETTING NORMS FOR WAGE AND PRICE ADJUSTMENTS. EVALUATES EFFECTIVENESS OF VARIOUS TECHNIQUES. CONSIDERS INCOME POLICY AS INSTRUMENT FOR AVOIDING INFLATION AS DISTINCT FROM CHANGING OVER-ALL INCOME OR INCREASING INVESTMENTS. FINDS LONG-TERM CENTRAL COORDINATION OF WAGE CLAIMS IMPOSSIBLE. SUGGESTS COMPROMISE ALTERNATIVES.

2968 ZOLLSCHAN G.K. ED., HIRSCH W. ED.
EXPLORATIONS IN SOCIAL CHANGE.
BOSTON: HOUGHTON MIFFLIN, 1964, 832 PP.
ESSAYS ON GENERAL PERSPECTIVES OF SOCIAL CHANGE AND SOCIAL SYSTEM MODELS OF CHANGE. INCLUDES WORKING PAPERS IN THEORY OF INSTITUTIONALIZATION. GENERAL STUDIES DEAL WITH ASPECTS OF PSYCHO-SOCIAL MODELS OF CHANGE, HISTORICAL PERSPECTIVES, CULTURAL CHANGE AND CONTACT, SOCIAL MOBILITY, AND ECONOMIC CHANGE.

2969 ZONDAG C.H.
THE BOLIVIAN ECONOMY 1952-65.
NEW YORK: FREDERICK PRAEGER, 1967, 262 PP., LC#66-14090.
DISCUSSES ECONOMIC EFFECTS OF SOCIAL REVOLUTION. INCLUDES DESCRIPTION OF SITUATION CAUSING REVOLUTION. INFLATION, PUBLIC ADMINISTRATION, INDUSTRY, FOREIGN TRADE ARE EXTENSIVELY ANALYZED. EXPOSITION OF FUTURE PROSPECTS AND POLICIES OF BOLIVIAN GOVERNMENT.

2970 ZOOK P.D. ED.
FOREIGN TRADE AND HUMAN CAPITAL.
DALLAS: SOUTHERN METHODIST U PR, 1962, 103 PP., LC#62-13276.
RELATION OF ECONOMIC DEVELOPMENT, INTERNATIONAL RELATIONS, FOREIGN AID, AND PRODUCTIVITY EXAMINED. US FOREIGN AID PROGRAM EVALUATED, ESPECIALLY IN SOUTH AMERICA, AND RESULTANT EFFECTS ON BALANCE OF PAYMENTS AND ECONOMIC DEVELOPMENT APPRAISED.

2971 ZUPNICK E.
UNDERSTANDING THE INTERNATIONAL MONEY SYSTEM (HEADLINE SERIES, NO. 182) (PAMPHLET)
NEW YORK: FOREIGN POLICY ASSN, 1967, 62 PP., LC#67-18100.
INTRODUCTION TO THE PRESENT SYSTEM, INCLUDING EVOLUTION BEFORE AND AFTER WWII, PROBLEMS WHICH MAY SOON LEAD TO BREAKDOWN, AND VARIOUS SUGGESTED REFORMS.

INDEX OF DOCUMENTS

A

AARON H.J. F0030

ABA....AMERICAN BAR ASSOCIATION

S67
RAGAN S.,"THE ABA RECOMMENDATIONS: A NEWSPAPERMAN'S CRITIQUE." EDU/PROP CONTROL GP/REL...JURID ABA. PAGE 109 F2136 — LAW PRESS ADJUD ORD/FREE

ABELS J. F0031

ABILITY TESTS....SEE KNO/TEST

ABM/DEFSYS....ANTI-BALLISTIC MISSILE DEFENSE SYSTEMS

ABORIGINES....ABORIGINES (AUSTRALIA)

ABORTION....ABORTION

ABRAMSKY C. F0506,F0507

ABRIKOSSOV, DIMITRI....SEE ABRIKSSV/D

ABRIKSSV/D....DIMITRI ABRIKOSSOV

ABSHIRE D.M. F0032

ACAD/ASST....ACADEMIC ASSISTANCE COUNCIL (U.K.)

ACADEM....UNIVERSITY, COLLEGE, GRADUATE SCHOOL, HIGHER EDUCATION

N
SOUTH AFRICAN JOURNAL OF ECONOMICS. SOUTH/AFR FINAN MARKET ACT/RES OP/RES...PHIL/SCI STAT CON/ANAL METH/COMP BIBLIOG/A 20. PAGE 1 F0009 — ECO/UNDEV ACADEM INTELL R+D

LCA
GODFREY E.M.,"THE ECONOMICS OF AN AFRICAN UNIVERSITY." AFR SCHOOL PRICE EFFICIENCY INCOME WEALTH...ECOMETRIC CHARTS 20. PAGE 48 F0930 — ACADEM ECO/TAC COST EDU/PROP

B56
UN HEADQUARTERS LIBRARY,BIBLIOGRAPHY OF INDUSTRIALIZATION IN UNDERDEVELOPED COUNTRIES (BIBLIOGRAPHICAL SERIES NO. 6). WOR+45 R+D ACADEM INT/ORG NAT/G. PAGE 132 F2602 — BIBLIOG ECO/UNDEV TEC/DEV

B57
DRUCKER P.F.,AMERICA'S NEXT TWENTY YEARS. USA+45 DIST/IND ACADEM SCHOOL DIPLOM ECO/TAC AUTOMAT HABITAT HEALTH...SOC/WK TREND MUNICH 20 URBAN/RNWL PUB/TRANS. PAGE 34 F0667 — WORKER FOR/AID CENSUS GEOG

B59
HAX K.,DIE HOCHSCHULLEHRER DER WIRTSCHAFTSWISSENSCHAFTEN IN DER BUNDESREPUBLIK DEUTSCHLAND EINSCHL. WESTBERLIN, OSTERREICH. AUSTRIA GERMANY/W SWITZERLND FINAN MARKET PROF/ORG BUDGET ECO/TAC INT/TRADE PRICE COST 20. PAGE 57 F1119 — BIBLIOG ACADEM INTELL

B60
COPLAND D.,THE ADVENTURE OF GROWTH: ESSAYS ON THE AUSTRALIAN ECONOMY AND ITS INTERNATIONAL SETTING. WOR+45 DIST/IND ACADEM EDU/PROP ADMIN INCOME 20 AUSTRAL. PAGE 27 F0534 — ECO/DEV ECO/UNDEV ECO/TAC INT/TRADE

B60
ROBINSON J.,AN ESSAY ON MARXIAN ECONOMICS. USA+45 STRATA INDUS MARKET CAP/ISM...METH/COMP 19/20 MARX/KARL. PAGE 113 F2222 — IDEA/COMP MARXISM ACADEM

B61
DEWITT N.,EDUCATION AND PROFESSIONAL EMPLOYMENT IN THE USSR. USSR PROF/ORG WORKER PLAN ADMIN UTIL AGE/C AGE/Y MARXISM...STAT CHARTS 20. PAGE 32 F0629 — EDU/PROP ACADEM SCHOOL INTELL

B62
DUPRE J.S.,SCIENCE AND THE NATION: POLICY AND POLITICS. USA+45 LAW ACADEM FORCES ADMIN CIVMIL/REL GOV/REL EFFICIENCY PEACE...TREND 20 SCI/ADVSRY. PAGE 35 F0682 — R+D INDUS TEC/DEV NUC/PWR

B62
INTERNAT CONGRESS OF JURISTS,EXECUTIVE ACTION AND THE RULE OF RULE: REPORTION PROCEEDINGS OF INT'T CONGRESS OF JURISTS,-RIO DE JANEIRO, BRAZIL. WOR+45 ACADEM CONSULT JUDGE EDU/PROP ADJUD CT/SYS INGP/REL PERSON DEPT/DEFEN. PAGE 64 F1269 — JURID EXEC ORD/FREE CONTROL

B62
US LIBRARY OF CONGRESS,A LIST OF AMERICAN DOCTORAL DISSERTATIONS ON AFRICA. SOCIETY SECT DIPLOM EDU/PROP ADMIN...GEOG 19/20. PAGE 138 F2717 — BIBLIOG AFR ACADEM CULTURE

B62
VAIZEY J.,THE ECONOMICS OF EDUCATION. INTELL ECO/TAC PAY COST PRODUC 20. PAGE 140 F2758 — ECO/DEV SCHOOL ACADEM PROFIT

L62
"BIBLIOGRAPHY ON EDUCATION AND ECONOMIC AND SOCIAL DEVELOPMENT (AMERICAN SOURCES)" L/A+17C ECO/UNDEV PROB/SOLV...SOC 20. PAGE 1 F0015 — BIBLIOG/A ACADEM EDU/PROP INTELL

L62
"HIGHER EDUCATION AND ECONOMIC AND SOCIAL DEVELOPMENT IN LATIN AMERICA: A BIBLIOGRAPHY." L/A+17C SOCIETY ECO/UNDEV PROF/ORG DIPLOM CONFER ...SOC 20. PAGE 1 F0016 — BIBLIOG/A ACADEM INTELL EDU/PROP

S62
BIERMAN H.,"PROBABILITY, STATISTICAL DECISION THEORY, AND ACCOUNTING." ACADEM TASK EFFICIENCY ...METH/CNCPT GEN/METH 20. PAGE 15 F0283 — FINAN QUANT DECISION STAT

B63
CHOJNACKI S.,REGISTER ON CURRENT RESEARCH ON ETHIOPIA AND THE HORN OF AFRICA. ETHIOPIA LAW CULTURE AGRI SECT EDU/PROP ADMIN...GEOG HEAL LING 20. PAGE 24 F0470 — BIBLIOG ACT/RES INTELL ACADEM

B63
MANGER W.,THE ALLIANCE FOR PROGRESS: A CRITICAL APPRAISAL. FUT L/A+17C USA+45 CULTURE ECO/UNDEV ACADEM NAT/G SCHOOL PLAN FOR/AID...POLICY OAS ALL/PROG. PAGE 84 F1651 — DIPLOM INT/ORG ECO/TAC REGION

L63
MEYER J.R.,"REGIONAL ECONOMICS: A SURVEY." INTELL ACADEM CREATE...IDEA/COMP BIBLIOG. PAGE 90 F1770 — REGION ECO/TAC GEN/LAWS PROB/SOLV

B64
BARKSDALE H.C.,MARKETING: CHANGE AND EXCHANGE. USA+45 FINAN ACADEM TEC/DEV PRICE AUTOMAT WEALTH ...CHARTS 20. PAGE 10 F0187 — MARKET ECO/DEV DEMAND TREND

B64
BOWEN W.G.,ECONOMIC ASPECTS OF EDUCATION (NO. 104). EUR+WWI UK USA+45 PROF/ORG PLAN TEC/DEV PAY ...POLICY STAT 20. PAGE 17 F0329 — EDU/PROP ACADEM FINAN METH/COMP

B64
DE BARY W.T.,APPROACHES TO ASIAN CIVILIZATIONS. INDIA ISLAM USA+45 CULTURE ACADEM...SOC ANTHOL 20 CHINJAP ARABS. PAGE 31 F0595 — ASIA EDU/PROP SOCIETY

B64
HARBISON F.H.,EDUCATION, MANPOWER, AND ECONOMIC GROWTH. WOR+45 ECO/DEV ECO/UNDEV ACADEM LABOR SCHOOL WORKER UTIL...IDEA/COMP NAT/COMP. PAGE 55 F1075 — PLAN TEC/DEV EDU/PROP SKILL

B64
RESOURCES FOR THE FUTURE,URBAN AND REGIONAL STUDIES AT US UNIVERSITIES; A REPORT BASED ON A 1963 SURVEY OF URBAN AND REGIONAL RESEARCH. USA+45 SOCIETY CONSTRUC DIST/IND ACADEM NAT/G ACT/RES ECO/TAC ...CENSUS IDEA/COMP MUNICH. PAGE 111 F2179 — BIBLIOG/A REGION PLAN

B65
COLBERG M.R.,HUMAN CAPITAL IN SOUTHERN DEVELOPMENT. USA+45 AGRI ACADEM LABOR SCHOOL WORKER CAP/ISM DISCRIM. PAGE 26 F0498 — PROVS RACE/REL GP/REL

B65
MORTON H.C.,BROOKINGS PAPERS ON PUBLIC POLICY. USA+45 WOR+45 INDUS ACADEM INT/ORG LOC/G PROVS EDU/PROP MUNICH. PAGE 94 F1840 — FINAN ECO/DEV TOP/EX NAT/G

B65
OECD,MEDITERRANEAN REGIONAL PROJECT: TURKEY; EDUCATION AND DEVELOPMENT. FUT TURKEY SOCIETY STRATA FINAN NAT/G PROF/ORG PLAN PROB/SOLV ADMIN COST...STAT CHARTS 20 OECD. PAGE 100 F1969 — EDU/PROP ACADEM SCHOOL ECO/UNDEV

B65
OECD,THE MEDITERRANEAN REGIONAL PROJECT: PORTUGAL; EDUCATION AND DEVELOPMENT. PORTUGAL SOCIETY STRATA FINAN PROF/ORG WORKER PLAN PROB/SOLV ADMIN...POLICY STAT CHARTS METH 20 OECD. PAGE 100 F1970 — EDU/PROP SCHOOL ACADEM ECO/UNDEV

B65
OECD,THE MEDITERRANEAN REGIONAL PROJECT: ITALY; EDUCATION AND DEVELOPMENT. ITALY SOCIETY STRATA FINAN NAT/G PROF/ORG WORKER PLAN PROB/SOLV ADMIN ...STAT CHARTS METH 20 OECD. PAGE 100 F1971 — SCHOOL EDU/PROP ECO/UNDEV ACADEM

B65
OECD,THE MEDITERRANEAN REGIONAL PROJECT: GREECE; EDUCATION AND DEVELOPMENT. FUT GREECE SOCIETY AGRI FINAN NAT/G PROF/ORG WORKER PLAN PROB/SOLV ADMIN DEMAND ATTIT 20 OECD. PAGE 100 F1972 — EDU/PROP SCHOOL ACADEM ECO/UNDEV

B65
OECD,THE MEDITERRANEAN REGIONAL PROJECT: SPAIN; EDUCATION AND DEVELOPMENT. FUT SPAIN STRATA FINAN NAT/G WORKER PLAN PROB/SOLV ADMIN COST...POLICY STAT CHARTS 20 OECD. PAGE 100 F1973 — ECO/UNDEV EDU/PROP ACADEM SCHOOL

B65
ORG FOR ECO COOP AND DEVEL,THE MEDITERRANEAN REGIONAL PROJECT: AN EXPERIMENT IN PLANNING BY SIX COUNTRIES. FUT GREECE SPAIN TURKEY YUGOSLAVIA SOCIETY FINAN NAT/G PROF/ORG EDU/PROP ADMIN REGION COST...POLICY STAT CHARTS 20 OECD. PAGE 102 F1995 — PLAN ECO/UNDEV ACADEM SCHOOL

B65
ORG FOR ECO COOP AND DEVEL,THE MEDITERRANEAN REGIONAL PROJECT: YUGOSLAVIA; EDUCATION AND DEVELOPMENT. YUGOSLAVIA SOCIETY FINAN PROF/ORG PLAN ADMIN COST DEMAND MARXISM...STAT TREND CHARTS METH 20 OECD. PAGE 102 F1996
EDU/PROP ACADEM SCHOOL ECO/UNDEV

B65
REAGAN M.D.,POLITICS, ECONOMICS, AND THE GENERAL WELFARE. USA+45 INDUS ECO/TAC TAX WEALTH...POLICY IDEA/COMP ANTHOL 20. PAGE 110 F2162
NAT/G ECO/DEV R+D ACADEM

S65
LECLERCQ H.,"ECONOMIC RESEARCH AND DEVELOPMENT IN TROPICAL AFRICA." ECO/UNDEV INT/ORG CREATE PLAN UN. PAGE 77 F1500
AFR R+D ACADEM ECO/TAC

S65
MALHERBE E.G.,"MANPOWER TRAINING: EDUCATIONAL REQUIREMENTS FOR ECONOMIC EXPANSION." SOUTH/AFR ECO/DEV INDUS EDU/PROP...MGT STAT CHARTS 20. PAGE 84 F1646
LABOR SKILL SCHOOL ACADEM

B66
EBONY,THE NEGRO HANDBOOK. ACADEM LABOR LOC/G SECT FORCES WORKER CT/SYS CRIME DISCRIM ORD/FREE...BIOG SOC/INTEG 19/20 NEGRO CIV/RIGHTS. PAGE 36 F0692
RACE/REL EDU/PROP LAW STAT

B66
GOODWIN C.D.W.,ECONOMIC INQUIRY IN AUSTRALIA. ECO/DEV ECO/UNDEV ACADEM INT/TRADE RENT TARIFFS TAX PRESS GOV/REL SOCISM 18/20 AUSTRAL. PAGE 49 F0953
ECO/TAC IDEA/COMP BUDGET COLONIAL

B66
KIRKENDALL R.S.,SOCIAL SCIENTISTS AND FARM POLITICS IN THE AGE OF ROOSEVELT. ACADEM PLAN ECO/TAC GIVE ADMIN CONTROL PRODUC...SOC 20 NEW/DEAL ROOSEVLT/F BURAGR/ECO. PAGE 71 F1399
AGRI INTELL POLICY NAT/G

B66
OECD DEVELOPMENT CENTRE,CATALOGUE OF SOCIAL AND ECONOMIC DEVELOPMENT INSTITUTES AND PROGRAMMES* RESEARCH. ACT/RES PLAN TEC/DEV EDU/PROP...SOC GP/COMP NAT/COMP. PAGE 101 F1976
ECO/UNDEV ECO/DEV R+D ACADEM

L66
AMERICAN ECONOMIC REVIEW,"SIXTY-THIRD LIST OF DOCTORAL DISSERTATIONS IN POLITICAL ECONOMY IN AMERICAN UNIVERSITIES AND COLLEGES." ECO/DEV AGRI FINAN LABOR WORKER PLAN BUDGET INT/TRADE ADMIN DEMAND...MGT STAT 20. PAGE 5 F0088
BIBLIOG/A CONCPT ACADEM

B67
BLAUG M.,ECONOMICS OF EDUCATION: A SELECTED ANNOTATED BIBLIOGRAPHY. EUR+WWI INTELL ECO/DEV ECO/UNDEV ACADEM INT/ORG NAT/G CREATE ADMIN EFFICIENCY ROLE PREDICT. PAGE 16 F0298
BIBLIOG/A EDU/PROP FINAN PLAN

B67
DIEGUES M.,SOCIAL SCIENCE IN LATIN AMERICA. L/A+17C ...JURID SOC ANTHOL 20. PAGE 33 F0637
METH ACADEM EDU/PROP ACT/RES

B67
HANNAH H.W.,THE LEGAL BASE FOR UNIVERSITIES IN DEVELOPING COUNTRIES. AFR ASIA L/A+17C S/ASIA USA+45 FINAN CREATE EDU/PROP TASK EFFICIENCY ...JURID METH/COMP 20. PAGE 54 F1060
ADMIN LAW ACADEM LEGIS

B67
HUMPHREY R.A.,UNIVERSITIES...AND DEVELOPMENT ASSISTANCE ABROAD. USA+45 OP/RES ECO/TAC FOR/AID ...ANTHOL 20. PAGE 63 F1242
ACADEM DIPLOM KNOWL ECO/UNDEV

B67
ORLANS H.,CONTRACTING FOR ATOMS. AFR USA+45 LAW INTELL ACADEM LG/CO NAT/G PLAN TEC/DEV CONTROL DETER...TREND 20. PAGE 102 F1999
NUC/PWR R+D PRODUC PEACE

L67
COSTANZA J.F.,"WHOLESOME NEUTRALITY: LAW AND EDUCATION." USA+45 GIVE EDU/PROP ADJUD CONTROL GP/REL...DECISION JURID. PAGE 28 F0540
SECT PROVS ACADEM

S67
JEDLICKI W.,"THE FREE SPEECH MOVEMENT IN WARSAW." POLAND FORCES EDU/PROP LEAD ATTIT MARXISM ...IDEA/COMP 20. PAGE 67 F1310
COERCE CROWD ORD/FREE ACADEM

S67
MERIKOSKI V.,"BASIC PROBLEMS OF UNIVERSITY ADMINISTRATION." PROVS SECT CONTROL...CLASSIF 20. PAGE 90 F1760
ACADEM ADMIN SOVEREIGN METH/COMP

S67
SIPPEL D.,"INDIENS UNSICHERE ZUKUNFT." INDIA CULTURE ACADEM POL/PAR LEGIS COLONIAL CHOOSE SOVEREIGN...JURID 20. PAGE 122 F2416
SOCIETY STRUCT ECO/UNDEV NAT/G

S67
STEINHEIMER R.L. JR.,"THE UNIFORM COMMERCIAL CODE COMES OF AGE." USA+45 FINAN ACADEM JUDGE. PAGE 126 F2477
ADJUD LEGIS INT/TRADE GOV/REL

N67
US HOUSE COMM SCI ASTRONAUT,GOVERNMENT, SCIENCE, AND INTERNATIONAL POLICY (PAMPHLET). INDIA NETHERLAND ECO/DEV ECO/UNDEV R+D ACADEM PLAN DIPLOM FOR/AID CONFER...PREDICT 20 CHINJAP. PAGE 137 F2705
NAT/G POLICY CREATE TEC/DEV

B92
COULANGES F D.E.,THE ORIGIN OF PROPERTY IN LAND. LAW STRATA AGRI ACADEM EDU/PROP ORD/FREE 19. PAGE 28 F0543
OWN HIST/WRIT IDEA/COMP SOCISM

ACADEM/SCI....ACADEMY OF SCIENCES (U.S.S.R.)

ACBC....ACTION COUNCIL FOR BETTER CITIES

ACCOUNTING....SEE ACCT

ACCT....ACCOUNTING, BOOKKEEPING

B44
BIENSTOCK G.,MANAGEMENT IN RUSSIAN INDUSTRY AND AGRICULTURE. USSR CONSULT WORKER LEAD COST PROFIT ATTIT DRIVE PWR...MGT METH/COMP DICTIONARY ACCT 20. PAGE 15 F0281
ADMIN MARXISM SML/CO AGRI

ACCULTURATION....SEE CULTURE

ACD....UNITED STATES ARMS CONTROL AND DISARMAMENT AGENCY

ACHESON/D....DEAN ACHESON

ACHTERBERG E. F0033

ACKLEY G. F0034

ACLU....AMERICAN CIVIL LIBERTIES UNION

ACQUAINTANCE GROUP....SEE FACE/GP

ACT/RES....RESEARCH FACILITATING SOCIAL ACTION

ACTION COUNCIL FOR BETTER CITIES....SEE ACBC

ACTION....ALLEGHENY COUNCIL TO IMPROVE OUR NEIGHBORHOODS

ACTON/LORD....LORD ACTON

ADA....AMERICANS FOR DEMOCRATIC ACTION

ADAIR D. F1056

ADAMS D.W. F0035

ADAMS E.S. F0036

ADAMS F.G. F0037

ADAMS G.P. F0038

ADAMS R.N. F0039

ADAMS/J....PRESIDENT JOHN ADAMS

ADAMS/JQ....PRESIDENT JOHN QUINCY ADAMS

ADAMS/SAM....SAMUEL ADAMS

ADDICTION....ADDICTION

ADEBO S.O. F1356

ADENAUER/K....KONRAD ADENAUER

B57
NAUMANN R.,THEORIE UND PRAXIS DES NEOLIBERALISMUS; DAS MAERCHEN VON DER FREIEN ODER SOZIALEN MARKTWIRTSCHAFT. GERMANY/W FORCES PLAN EDU/PROP SOCISM...POLICY MARXIST IDEA/COMP BIBLIOG 18/20 ADENAUER/K. PAGE 97 F1903
MARXISM NEW/LIB ECO/TAC CAP/ISM

ADERBIGDE A. F0040

ADISESHIAN M. F0041

ADJUD....JUDICIAL AND ADJUDICATIVE PROCESSES

N
RAND SCHOOL OF SOCIAL SCIENCE,INDEX TO LABOR ARTICLES. ECO/DEV INT/ORG LEGIS DIPLOM GP/REL ...NAT/COMP 20. PAGE 109 F2143
BIBLIOG LABOR MGT ADJUD

N
US SUPERINTENDENT OF DOCUMENTS,TARIFF AND TAXATION (PRICE LIST 37). USA+45 LAW INT/TRADE ADJUD ADMIN CT/SYS INCOME OWN...DECISION GATT. PAGE 140 F2754
BIBLIOG/A TAX TARIFFS NAT/G

B03
GRIFFIN A.P.C.,LISTS PUBLISHED 1902-03: GOVERNMENT OWNERSHIP OF RAILROADS (PAMPHLET). USA-45 LAW NAT/G RATION GOV/REL CENTRAL SOCISM...POLICY 19/20. PAGE 51 F0998
BIBLIOG DIST/IND CONTROL ADJUD

N19
CARPER E.T.,LOBBYING AND THE NATURAL GAS BILL (PAMPHLET). USA+45 SERV/IND BARGAIN PAY DRIVE ROLE WEALTH 20 CONGRESS SENATE EISNHWR/DD. PAGE 22 F0418
LOBBY ADJUD TRIBUTE NAT/G

N19
MCCONNELL G.,THE STEEL SEIZURE OF 1952 (PAMPHLET). USA+45 FINAN INDUS PROC/MFG LG/CO EX/STRUC ADJUD CONTROL GP/REL ORD/FREE PWR 20 TRUMAN/HS PRESIDENT CONGRESS. PAGE 88 F1721
DELIB/GP LABOR PROB/SOLV NAT/G

N19
PALAMOUNTAIN JC J.R.,THE DOLCIN CASE AND THE FEDERAL TRADE COMMISSION (PAMPHLET). USA+45 LAW MARKET SERV/IND LG/CO NAT/G BIO/SOC 20 FTC. PAGE 103 F2018
ADJUD PROB/SOLV EDU/PROP HEALTH

B24
HOLDSWORTH W.S.,A HISTORY OF ENGLISH LAW; THE COMMON LAW AND ITS RIVALS (VOL. VI). AFR UK STRATA EX/STRUC ADJUD ADMIN CONTROL CT/SYS...JURID CONCPT GEN/LAWS 17 PARLIAMENT ENGLSH/LAW COMMON/LAW. PAGE 61 F1194
LAW CONSTN LEGIS CHIEF

B24
HOLDSWORTH W.S.,A HISTORY OF ENGLISH LAW; THE COMMON LAW AND ITS RIVALS (VOL. IV). UK SEA AGRI CHIEF ADJUD CONTROL CRIME GOV/REL...INT/LAW JURID NAT/COMP 16/17 PARLIAMENT COMMON/LAW CANON/LAW ENGLSH/LAW. PAGE 61 F1195
LAW LEGIS CT/SYS CONSTN

B25
MATHEWS J.M.,AMERICAN STATE GOVERNMENT. USA-45 LOC/G CHIEF EX/STRUC LEGIS ADJUD CONTROL CT/SYS ROUTINE GOV/REL PWR 20 GOVERNOR. PAGE 87 F1703
PROVS ADMIN FEDERAL CONSTN

B28
FRANKFURTER F.,THE BUSINESS OF THE SUPREME COURT; A STUDY IN THE FEDERAL JUDICIAL SYSTEM. USA-45 CONSTN EX/STRUC PROB/SOLV GP/REL ATTIT PWR...POLICY JURID 18/20 SUPREME/CT CONGRESS. PAGE 43 F0848
CT/SYS ADJUD LAW FEDERAL

B28
HARDMAN J.B.,AMERICAN LABOR DYNAMICS. WORKER ECO/TAC DOMIN ADJUD LEAD LOBBY PWR...POLICY MGT. PAGE 55 F1079
LABOR INGP/REL ATTIT GP/REL

B37
UNION OF SOUTH AFRICA,REPORT CONCERNING ADMINISTRATION OF SOUTH WEST AFRICA (6 VOLS.). SOUTH/AFR INDUS PUB/INST FORCES LEGIS BUDGET DIPLOM EDU/PROP ADJUD CT/SYS...GEOG CHARTS 20 AFRICA/SW LEAGUE/NAT. PAGE 132 F2610
NAT/G ADMIN COLONIAL CONSTN

B38
LEVINSON E.,LABOR ON THE MARCH. WORKER CREATE ECO/TAC ADJUD LEAD PARL/PROC PARTIC INGP/REL SKILL POLICY. PAGE 79 F1543
LABOR INCOME NAT/G PLAN

B40
WUNDERLICH F.,LABOR UNDER GERMAN DEMOCRACY, ARBITRATION 1918-1933. GERMANY NAT/G PAY REPAR ADJUD CT/SYS GP/REL...MAJORIT 20. PAGE 149 F2941
LABOR WORKER INDUS BARGAIN

B42
ROBBINS J.J.,THE GOVERNMENT OF LABOR RELATIONS IN SWEDEN. SWEDEN LAW CONSTN ADJUD CT/SYS GP/REL ...JURID 20. PAGE 112 F2200
NAT/G BARGAIN LABOR INDUS

L42
GRANT J.A.C.,"THE GUILD RETURNS TO AMERICA." CHRIST-17C USA-45 LEGIS LICENSE ADJUD CONTROL GP/REL. PAGE 50 F0978
PROF/ORG JURID LABOR PWR

B45
MILLIS H.A.,ORGANIZED LABOR (FIRST ED.). LAW STRUCT DELIB/GP WORKER ECO/TAC ADJUD CONTROL REPRESENT INGP/REL INCOME MGT. PAGE 92 F1797
LABOR POLICY ROUTINE GP/REL

B47
SLICHTER S.H.,THE CHALLENGE OF INDUSTRIAL RELATIONS: TRADE UNIONS, MANAGEMENT AND THE PUBLIC INTEREST. PLAN ECO/TAC ADJUD CONTROL LEAD SANCTION GP/REL INGP/REL INCOME. PAGE 123 F2421
LABOR MGT CLIENT POLICY

B48
KEIR D.L.,CASES IN CONSTITUTIONAL LAW. UK CHIEF LEGIS DIPLOM TAX PARL/PROC CRIME GOV/REL...INT/LAW JURID 17/20. PAGE 70 F1368
CONSTN LAW ADJUD CT/SYS

B51
PRINCETON U INDUSTRIAL REL SEC,COMPULSORY ARBITRATION OF UTILITY DISPUTES IN NEW JERSEY AND PENNSYLVANIA. USA+45 LEGIS WORKER ADJUD ORD/FREE ...POLICY MGT METH/COMP 20 NEW/JERSEY PENNSYLVAN. PAGE 108 F2118
BARGAIN PROVS INDUS LABOR

B52
JENNINGS W.I.,CONSTITUTIONAL LAWS OF THE COMMONWEALTH. AFR UK LAW CHIEF LEGIS TAX CT/SYS PARL/PROC GOV/REL...INT/LAW 18/20 ENGLSH/LAW COMMON/LAW. PAGE 67 F1316
CONSTN JURID ADJUD COLONIAL

B52
REDFORD E.S.,ADMINISTRATION OF NATIONAL ECONOMIC CONTROL. ECO/DEV DELIB/GP ADJUD CONTROL EQUILIB 20. PAGE 110 F2166
ADMIN ROUTINE GOV/REL LOBBY

B53
PURCELL T.V.,THE WORKER SPEAKS HIS MIND ON COMPANY AND UNION. WORKER ADJUD LEAD RACE/REL ATTIT DRIVE MARXISM...MGT CLASSIF STAT OBS INT SAMP BIBLIOG. PAGE 108 F2131
LABOR PARTIC INGP/REL HAPPINESS

B53
SAYLES L.R.,THE LOCAL UNION. CONSTN CULTURE DELIB/GP PARTIC CHOOSE GP/REL INGP/REL ATTIT ROLE ...MAJORIT DECISION MGT. PAGE 116 F2284
LABOR LEAD ADJUD ROUTINE

B54
EMERSON F.D.,SHAREHOLDER DEMOCRACY: A BROADER OUTLOOK FOR CORPORATIONS. DELIB/GP EX/STRUC LEGIS ADJUD CONTROL REPRESENT INGP/REL OWN PWR...POLICY STAT RECORD. PAGE 37 F0727
LG/CO PARTIC MAJORIT TREND

B54
TAFT P.,THE STRUCTURE AND GOVERNMENT OF LABOR UNIONS. SANCTION INGP/REL ORD/FREE PWR MARXISM ...MAJORIT STAT TREND. PAGE 128 F2524
LABOR ADJUD WORKER FINAN

B55
BERNSTEIN M.H.,REGULATING BUSINESS BY INDEPENDENT COMMISSION. USA+45 USA-45 LG/CO CHIEF LEGIS PROB/SOLV ADJUD SANCTION GP/REL ATTIT...TIME/SEQ 19/20 MONOPOLY PRESIDENT CONGRESS. PAGE 14 F0268
DELIB/GP CONTROL CONSULT

B55
BLOOM G.F.,ECONOMICS OF LABOR RELATIONS. USA+45 LAW CONSULT WORKER CAP/ISM PAY ADJUD CONTROL EFFICIENCY ORD/FREE...CHARTS 19/20 AFL/CIO NLRB DEPT/LABOR. PAGE 16 F0299
ECO/DEV ECO/TAC LABOR GOV/REL

B55
BRAUN K.,LABOR DISPUTES AND THEIR SETTLEMENT. ECO/TAC ROUTINE TASK GP/REL...DECISION GEN/LAWS. PAGE 18 F0342
INDUS LABOR BARGAIN ADJUD

B55
WRONG D.H.,AMERICAN AND CANADIAN VIEWPOINTS. CANADA USA+45 CONSTN STRATA FAM SECT WORKER ECO/TAC EDU/PROP ADJUD MARRIAGE...IDEA/COMP 20. PAGE 149 F2936
DIPLOM ATTIT NAT/COMP CULTURE

B56
GILBERT L.D.,DIVIDENDS AND DEMOCRACY. DELIB/GP LEGIS CAP/ISM ADJUD LOBBY OWN PWR LAISSEZ MAJORIT. PAGE 47 F0922
LG/CO INGP/REL CONTROL PARTIC

S57
DUBIN R.,"POWER AND UNION-MANAGEMENT RELATIONS." PROB/SOLV ADJUD ROUTINE ATTIT ORD/FREE...MGT STERTYP. PAGE 34 F0668
PWR LABOR BARGAIN GP/REL

B58
CUNNINGHAM W.B.,COMPULSORY CONCILIATION AND COLLECTIVE BARGAINING. CANADA NAT/G LEGIS ADJUD CT/SYS GP/REL...MGT 20 NEW/BRUNS STRIKE CASEBOOK. PAGE 29 F0563
POLICY BARGAIN LABOR INDUS

B58
HOOD W.C.,FINANCING OF ECONOMIC ACTIVITY IN CANADA. CANADA FUT VOL/ASSN WORKER ECO/TAC ADJUD ADMIN ...CHARTS 20. PAGE 61 F1204
BUDGET FINAN GP/REL ECO/DEV

B58
OGDEN F.D.,THE POLL TAX IN THE SOUTH. USA+45 USA-45 CONSTN ADJUD ADMIN PARTIC CRIME...TIME/SEQ GOV/COMP METH/COMP 18/20 SOUTH/US. PAGE 101 F1982
TAX CHOOSE RACE/REL DISCRIM

B58
SEIDMAN J.I.,DEMOCRACY IN THE LABOR MOVEMENT (PAMPHLET). LAW CONSTN STRUCT DELIB/GP WORKER ADJUD PARTIC SANCTION POLICY. PAGE 119 F2345
LABOR INGP/REL PWR MAJORIT

B58
WOODS H.D.,PATTERNS OF INDUSTRIAL DISPUTE SETTLEMENT IN FIVE CANADIAN INDUSTRIES. CANADA USA+45 CONSULT ADJUD GP/REL...JURID GOV/COMP METH/COMP ANTHOL 20. PAGE 148 F2923
BARGAIN INDUS LABOR NAT/G

S58
LATTIN N.D.,"MINORITY AND DISSENTING SHAREHOLDERS' RIGHTS IN FUNDAMENTAL CHANGES." FINAN LEGIS ADJUD PARTIC ROUTINE CHOOSE REPRESENT INGP/REL TREND. PAGE 76 F1487
MAJORIT LG/CO LAW CREATE

B59
BROMWICH L.,UNION CONSTITUTIONS. CONSTN EX/STRUC PRESS ADJUD CONTROL CHOOSE REPRESENT PWR SAMP.
LABOR ROUTINE

PAGE 19 F0361 — INGP/REL RACE/REL

B59
GOMEZ ROBLES J.,A STATEMENT OF THE LAWS OF GUATEMALA IN MATTERS AFFECTING BUSINESS (2ND ED. REV., ENLARGED). GUATEMALA L/A+17C LAW FINAN FAM WORKER ACT/RES DIPLOM ADJUD ADMIN GP/REL 20 OAS. PAGE 48 F0945 — JURID NAT/G INDUS LEGIT

B59
HARVARD UNIVERSITY LAW SCHOOL,INTERNATIONAL PROBLEMS OF FINANCIAL PROTECTION AGAINST NUCLEAR RISK. WOR+45 NAT/G DELIB/GP PROB/SOLV DIPLOM CONTROL ATTIT...POLICY INT/LAW MATH 20. PAGE 56 F1105 — NUC/PWR ADJUD INDUS FINAN

B59
LEISERSON W.,AMERICAN TRADE UNION DEMOCRACY. CONSTN STRUCT ADJUD EXEC REPRESENT GP/REL INGP/REL MAJORITY ATTIT PWR. PAGE 77 F1516 — LABOR LEAD PARTIC DELIB/GP

L59
OBERER W.E.,"VOLUNTARY IMPARTIAL REVIEW OF LABOR: SOME REFLECTIONS." DELIB/GP LEGIS PROB/SOLV ADJUD CONTROL COERCE PWR PLURISM POLICY. PAGE 100 F1960 — LABOR LAW PARTIC INGP/REL

S59
SCHEEHAN D.,"PUBLIC AND PRIVATE GROUPS AS IDENTIFIED IN THE FIELD OF TRADE REGULATIONS." USA+45 ADMIN REPRESENT GOV/REL. PAGE 116 F2293 — LAW CONTROL ADJUD LOBBY

B60
CARPER E.T.,THE DEFENSE APPROPRIATIONS RIDER (PAMPHLET). USA+45 CONSTN CHIEF DELIB/GP LEGIS BUDGET LOBBY CIVMIL/REL...POLICY 20 CONGRESS EISNHWR/DD DEPT/DEFEN PRESIDENT BOSTON. PAGE 22 F0419 — GOV/REL ADJUD LAW CONTROL

B60
ELKOURI F.,HOW ARBITRATION WORKS (REV. ED.). LAW INDUS BARGAIN 20. PAGE 37 F0720 — MGT LABOR ADJUD GP/REL

B60
FORBUSH D.R.,PROBLEMS OF CORPORATE POWER. CLIENT LAW ELITES ADJUD...DECISION MGT. PAGE 42 F0822 — LG/CO PWR CONTROL GP/REL

B60
PENNSYLVANIA ECONOMY LEAGUE,URBAN RENEWAL IMPACT STUDY: ADMINISTRATIVE-LEGAL-FISCAL. USA+45 FINAN LOC/G NEIGH ADMIN EFFICIENCY...CENSUS CHARTS MUNICH 20 PENNSYLVAN. PAGE 105 F2059 — PLAN BUDGET ADJUD

B60
STEIN E.,AMERICAN ENTERPRISE IN THE EUROPEAN COMMON MARKET: A LEGAL PROFILE. EUR+WWI FUT USA+45 SOCIETY STRUCT ECO/DEV NAT/G VOL/ASSN CONSULT PLAN TEC/DEV ECO/TAC INT/TRADE ADMIN ATTIT RIGID/FLEX PWR...MGT NEW/IDEA STAT TREND COMPUT/IR SIMUL EEC 20. PAGE 125 F2475 — MARKET ADJUD INT/LAW

L60
FUCHS R.F.,"FAIRNESS AND EFFECTIVENESS IN ADMINISTRATIVE AGENCY ORGANIZATION AND PROCEDURES." USA+45 ADJUD ADMIN REPRESENT. PAGE 45 F0872 — EFFICIENCY EX/STRUC EXEC POLICY

S60
NICHOLS J.P.,"HAZARDS OF AMERICAN PRIVATE INVESTMENT IN UNDERDEVELOPED COUNTRIES." FUT L/A+17C USA+45 USA-45 EXTR/IND CONSULT BAL/PWR ECO/TAC DOMIN ADJUD ATTIT SOVEREIGN WEALTH ...HIST/WRIT TIME/SEQ TREND TERR/GP VAL/FREE 20. PAGE 98 F1924 — FINAN ECO/UNDEV CAP/ISM NAT/LISM

B61
ALFRED H.,PUBLIC OWNERSHIP IN THE USA: GOALS AND PRIORITIES. LAW INDUS INT/TRADE ADJUD GOV/REL EFFICIENCY PEACE SOCISM...POLICY ANTHOL 20 TVA. PAGE 4 F0065 — CONTROL OWN ECO/DEV ECO/TAC

B61
BEASLEY K.E.,STATE SUPERVISION OF MUNICIPAL DEBT IN KANSAS - A CASE STUDY. USA+45 USA-45 FINAN PROVS BUDGET TAX ADJUD ADMIN CONTROL SUPEGO MUNICH. PAGE 12 F0224 — LOC/G LEGIS JURID

B61
CARROTHERS A.W.R.,LABOR ARBITRATION IN CANADA. CANADA LAW NAT/G CONSULT LEGIS WORKER ADJUD ADMIN CT/SYS 20. PAGE 22 F0422 — LABOR MGT GP/REL BARGAIN

B61
STARNER F.L.,GENERAL OBLIGATION BOND FINANCING BY LOCAL GOVERNMENTS: A SURVEY OF STATE CONTROLS. CANADA UK USA+45 CONSTN PROVS...POLICY JURID METH/COMP 20 EUROPE CALIFORNIA. PAGE 125 F2471 — FINAN LOC/G GOV/REL ADJUD

B62
ALEXANDROWICZ C.H.,WORLD ECONOMIC AGENCIES: LAW AND PRACTICE. WOR+45 DIST/IND FINAN LABOR CONSULT INT/TRADE TARIFFS REPRESENT HEALTH...JURID 20 UN GATT EEC OAS ECSC. PAGE 4 F0064 — INT/LAW INT/ORG DIPLOM ADJUD

B62
FATOUROS A.A.,GOVERNMENT GUARANTEES TO FOREIGN INVESTORS. WOR+45 ECO/UNDEV INDUS WORKER ADJUD ...NAT/COMP BIBLIOG TREATY. PAGE 39 F0767 — NAT/G FINAN INT/TRADE ECO/DEV

B62
HIRSCHFIELD R.S.,THE CONSTITUTION AND THE COURT. AFR SCHOOL WAR RACE/REL EQUILIB ORD/FREE...POLICY MAJORIT DECISION JURID 18/20 PRESIDENT CIVIL/LIB SUPREME/CT CONGRESS. PAGE 60 F1175 — ADJUD PWR CONSTN LAW

B62
INTERNAT CONGRESS OF JURISTS,EXECUTIVE ACTION AND THE RULE OF RULE: REPORTION PROCEEDINGS OF INT'T CONGRESS OF JURISTS,-RIO DE JANEIRO, BRAZIL. WOR+45 ACADEM CONSULT JUDGE EDU/PROP ADJUD CT/SYS INGP/REL PERSON DEPT/DEFEN. PAGE 64 F1269 — JURID EXEC ORD/FREE CONTROL

B62
LITWACK L.,THE AMERICAN LABOR MOVEMENT. USA-45 NAT/G CREATE TEC/DEV CAP/ISM ECO/TAC ADJUD AUTOMAT SKILL...TREND ANTHOL 19/20. PAGE 81 F1588 — INDUS LABOR GP/REL METH/COMP

B62
SRIVASTAVA G.L.,COLLECTIVE BARGAINING AND LABOR-MANAGEMENT RELATIONS IN INDIA. INDIA UK USA+45 INDUS LEGIS WORKER ADJUD EFFICIENCY PRODUC ...METH/COMP 20. PAGE 125 F2462 — LABOR MGT BARGAIN GP/REL

B62
URQUIDI C.W.,A STATEMENT OF THE LAWS OF BOLIVIA IN MATTERS AFFECTING BUSINESS (3RD ED. REV., ENLARGED). L/A+17C LAW FINAN FAM WORKER ACT/RES DIPLOM ADJUD ADMIN GP/REL 20 BOLIV OAS. PAGE 133 F2626 — JURID INDUS NAT/G LEGIT

B62
VACCARO J.R.,A STATEMENT OF THE LAWS OF CHILE IN MATTERS AFFECTING BUSINESS (3RD ED.). CHILE AGRI FINAN FAM LABOR ECO/TAC FOR/AID TAX ADJUD CONTROL MARRIAGE STRANGE...BIBLIOG 20. PAGE 140 F2756 — CONSTN LAW INDUS MGT

L62
ERDMANN H.H.,"ADMINISTRATIVE LAW AND FARM ECONOMICS." USA+45 LOC/G NAT/G PLAN PROB/SOLV LOBBY ...DECISION ANTHOL 20. PAGE 38 F0744 — AGRI ADMIN ADJUD POLICY

N62
US SENATE COMM ON JUDICIARY,LEGISLATION TO STRENGTHEN PENALTIES UNDER THE ANTITRUST LAWS (PAMPHLET). USA+45 LG/CO CONFER CONTROL SANCTION ORD/FREE 20 SENATE MONOPOLY. PAGE 139 F2748 — LEAD ADJUD INDUS ECO/TAC

B63
BOWIE R.R.,GOVERNMENT REGULATION OF BUSINESS: CASES FROM THE NATIONAL REPORTER SYSTEM. USA+45 USA-45 NAT/G ECO/TAC ADJUD...ANTHOL 19/20 SUPREME/CT FTC FAIR/LABOR MONOPOLY. PAGE 17 F0331 — LAW CONTROL INDUS CT/SYS

B63
BURRUS B.R.,ADMINSTRATIVE LAW AND LOCAL GOVERNMENT. USA+45 PROVS LEGIS LICENSE ADJUD ORD/FREE 20. PAGE 20 F0392 — EX/STRUC LOC/G JURID CONSTN

B63
FRIEDRICH C.J.,MAN AND HIS GOVERNMENT: AN EMPIRICAL THEORY OF POLITICS. UNIV LOC/G NAT/G ADJUD REV INGP/REL DISCRIM PWR BIBLIOG. PAGE 44 F0867 — PERSON ORD/FREE PARTIC CONTROL

B63
PRITCHETT C.H.,THE THIRD BRANCH OF GOVERNMENT. USA+45 USA-45 CONSTN SOCIETY INDUS SECT LEGIS JUDGE PROB/SOLV GOV/REL 20 SUPREME/CT CHURCH/STA. PAGE 108 F2122 — JURID NAT/G ADJUD CT/SYS

L63
LIVERNASH E.R.,"THE RELATION OF POWER TO THE STRUCTURE AND PROCESS OF COLLECTIVE BARGAINING." ADJUD ORD/FREE...POLICY MGT CLASSIF GP/COMP. PAGE 81 F1589 — LABOR GP/REL PWR ECO/TAC

B64
BLAKE R.R.,MANAGING INTERGROUP CONFLICT IN INDUSTRY. INDUS DELIB/GP EX/STRUC GP/REL PERS/REL GAME. PAGE 16 F0297 — CREATE PROB/SOLV OP/RES ADJUD

B64
HUTT W.H.,THE ECONOMICS OF THE COLOUR BAR. SOUTH/AFR EXTR/IND LABOR ADJUD NEGRO. PAGE 64 F1251 — INDUS DISCRIM RACE/REL ECO/UNDEV

B64
KAPLAN A.D.H.,BIG ENTERPRISE IN A COMPETITIVE SYSTEM (REV. ED.). USA+45 INDUS MARKET WORKER TEC/DEV ECO/TAC PRICE ADJUD ADMIN CONTROL...MGT CHARTS 20 MONOPOLY. PAGE 69 F1351 — FINAN GP/REL NAT/G LG/CO

B64
MITAU G.T.,INSOLUBLE PROBLEMS: CASE PROBLEMS ON THE FUNCTIONS OF STATE AND LOCAL GOVERNMENT. USA+45 AIR FINAN LABOR POL/PAR PROB/SOLV TAX RECEIVE CONTROL GP/REL 20 CASEBOOK ZONING. PAGE 92 F1807 — ADJUD LOC/G PROVS

B64
RUSTAMJI R.F.,THE LAW OF INDUSTRIAL DISPUTES IN INDIA. INDIA LEGIS WORKER CONTROL GP/REL...JURID MGT TIME/SEQ 20. PAGE 115 F2264 — INDUS ADJUD BARGAIN LABOR

B64
SULTAN P.E.,THE DISENCHANTED UNIONIST. NAT/G ADJUD CONTROL SANCTION RACE/REL ANOMIE ATTIT ROLE ...METH/CNCPT INT. PAGE 127 F2512 LABOR INGP/REL CHARTS MAJORIT

B64
US SENATE COMM ON JUDICIARY,HEARINGS BEFORE SUBCOMMITTEE ON ANTITRUST AND MONOPOLY: ECONOMIC CONCENTRATION VOLUMES 1-5 JULY 1964-SEPT 1966. USA+45 LAW FINAN ECO/TAC ADJUD COST EFFICIENCY PRODUC...STAT CHARTS 20 CONGRESS MONOPOLY. PAGE 140 F2749 ECO/DEV CONTROL MARKET LG/CO

S64
N,"QUASI-LEGISLATIVE ARBITRATION AGREEMENTS." LAW LG/CO ECO/TAC SANCTION ATTIT POLICY. PAGE 96 F1885 ADJUD ADJUST LABOR GP/REL

B65
FLEMING R.W.,THE LABOR ARBITRATION PROCESS. USA+45 LAW BARGAIN ADJUD ROUTINE SANCTION COST...PREDICT CHARTS TIME 20. PAGE 41 F0809 GP/REL LABOR CONSULT DELIB/GP

B65
FRYE R.J.,HOUSING AND URBAN RENEWAL IN ALABAMA. USA+45 NEIGH LEGIS BUDGET ADJUD ADMIN PARTIC...MGT MUNICH 20 ALABAMA URBAN/RNWL. PAGE 45 F0871 PROB/SOLV PLAN GOV/REL

B65
HAEFELE E.T.,GOVERNMENT CONTROLS ON TRANSPORT. AFR RHODESIA TANZANIA DIPLOM ECO/TAC TARIFFS PRICE ADJUD CONTROL REGION EFFICIENCY...POLICY 20 CONGO. PAGE 53 F1031 ECO/UNDEV DIST/IND FINAN NAT/G

B65
LAZARUS S.,RESOLVING BUSINESS DISPUTES: THE POTENTIAL OF COMMERCIAL ARBITRATION. USA+45 INDUS LG/CO ACT/RES PROB/SOLV EDU/PROP CONSEN UTIL ...TREND 20. PAGE 76 F1496 FINAN DELIB/GP CONSULT ADJUD

B65
MUND V.A.,GOVERNMENT AND BUSINESS (4TH ED.). USA+45 INDUS LG/CO SML/CO LEGIS INT/TRADE LICENSE PRICE ADJUD. PAGE 95 F1860 NAT/G ECO/TAC BUDGET CONTROL

B65
US SENATE COMM ON JUDICIARY,ANTITRUST EXEMPTIONS FOR AGREEMENTS RELATING TO BALANCE OF PAYMENTS. FINAN ECO/TAC CONTROL WEALTH...POLICY 20 CONGRESS. PAGE 140 F2750 BAL/PAY ADJUD MARKET INT/TRADE

B65
VAID K.N.,STATE AND LABOR IN INDIA. INDIA INDUS WORKER PAY PRICE ADJUD CONTROL PARL/PROC GP/REL ORD/FREE 20. PAGE 140 F2757 LAW LABOR MGT NEW/LIB

L65
FORTE W.E.,"THE FOOD AND DRUG ADMINISTRATION, THE FEDERAL TRADE COMMISSION AND THE DECEPTIVE PACKAGING." ROUTINE...JURID 20 FTC. PAGE 43 F0831 CONTROL HEALTH ADJUD INDUS

S65
LONG T.G.,"THE ADMINISTRATIVE PROCESS: AGONIZING REAPPRAISAL IN THE FTC." NAT/G REPRESENT 20 FTC. PAGE 82 F1598 ADJUD LOBBY ADMIN EX/STRUC

B66
HAYS P.R.,LABOR ARBITRATION: A DISSENTING VIEW. USA+45 LAW DELIB/GP BARGAIN ADJUD...PREDICT 20. PAGE 57 F1126 GP/REL LABOR CONSULT CT/SYS

B66
LEE R.A.,TRUMAN AND TAFT-HARTLEY: A QUESTION OF MANDATE. USA+45 LAW CONSTN LG/CO CONTROL LOBBY GOV/REL PEACE NEW/LIB 20 TRUMAN/HS CONGRESS. PAGE 77 F1507 LEGIS TOP/EX ADJUD LABOR

B66
MC CONNELL J.P.,LAW AND BUSINESS: PATTERNS AND ISSUES IN COMMERCIAL LAW. USA+45 USA-45 LOC/G WORKER LICENSE CRIME REPRESENT GP/REL 20. PAGE 87 F1713 ECO/DEV JURID ADJUD MGT

B66
MOSKOW M.H.,TEACHERS AND UNIONS. SCHOOL WORKER ADJUD LOBBY ATTIT ORD/FREE 20. PAGE 94 F1844 EDU/PROP PROF/ORG LABOR BARGAIN

B66
RAPHAEL J.S.,GOVERNMENTAL REGULATION OF BUSINESS. USA+45 LAW CONSTN TAX ADJUD ADMIN EFFICIENCY PWR 20. PAGE 109 F2150 LG/CO GOV/REL CONTROL ECO/DEV

B66
US HOUSE COMM BANKING CURRENCY,HEARINGS BEFORE HOUSE COMMITTEE ON BANKING AND CURRENCY: SALE OF SBA LOAN POOL PARTICIPATIONS. USA+45 LAW LEGIS ECO/TAC RATION 20 CONGRESS. PAGE 136 F2687 FINAN SML/CO ADJUD GOV/REL

B66
US SENATE COMM LABOR-PUB WELF,AMEND THE RAILWAY LABOR ACT. USA+45 CONSTN CONSULT DELIB/GP ADJUD CONGRESS RAILROAD. PAGE 139 F2731 GP/REL LABOR DIST/IND LAW

B67
BARDENS D.,CHURCHILL IN PARLIAMENT. UK DIPLOM ADJUD CONTROL AUTHORIT PERSON ORD/FREE 20 CHURCHLL/W PARLIAMENT. PAGE 10 F0186 TOP/EX LEGIS GOV/REL

B67
BEAL E.F.,THE PRACTICE OF COLLECTIVE BARGAINING (3RD ED.). USA+45 WOR+45 ECO/DEV INDUS LG/CO PROF/ORG WORKER ECO/TAC GP/REL WEALTH...JURID METH/CNCPT. PAGE 12 F0221 BARGAIN MGT LABOR ADJUD

B67
BLAIR G.S.,LEGISLATIVE BODIES IN CALIFORNIA. USA+45 LAW POL/PAR LOBBY APPORT CHOOSE REPRESENT GP/REL ...T CALIFORNIA. PAGE 15 F0293 LEGIS PROVS LOC/G ADJUD

B67
BUREAU NATIONAL AFFAIRS,LABOR RELATIONS REFERENCE MANUAL VOL. 63. USA+45 CONSTN ECO/DEV PROVS WORKER DEBATE INGP/REL...DECISION 20. PAGE 20 F0385 LABOR ADJUD CT/SYS NAT/G

B67
ESTEY M.,THE UNIONS: STRUCTURE, DEVELOPMENT, AND MANAGEMENT. FUT USA+45 ADJUD CONTROL INGP/REL DRIVE ...DECISION T 20 AFL/CIO. PAGE 38 F0750 LABOR EX/STRUC ADMIN GOV/REL

B67
GRIPP R.C.,PATTERNS OF SOVIET POLITICS (REV. ED.). USSR LAW ELITES LOC/G PLAN CONTROL CT/SYS CHOOSE ...POLICY BIBLIOG/A DICTIONARY 9/20. PAGE 51 F1003 COM ADJUD POL/PAR

B67
KIRK R.,THE POLITICAL PRINCIPLES OF ROBERT A. TAFT. USA+45 LABOR DIPLOM ADJUD ADJUST ORD/FREE TAFT/RA. PAGE 71 F1398 POL/PAR LEAD LEGIS ATTIT

B67
LYTLE C.M.,THE WARREN COURT AND ITS CRITICS. USA+45 NAT/G PROVS FORCES LOBBY RACE/REL DISCRIM SOVEREIGN 20 SUPREME/CT WARRN/EARL. PAGE 83 F1618 CT/SYS ADJUD PROB/SOLV ATTIT

B67
MACAVOY P.W.,REGULATION OF TRANSPORT INNOVATION. ACT/RES ADJUD COST DEMAND...POLICY CHARTS 20. PAGE 83 F1621 DIST/IND CONTROL PRICE PROFIT

B67
ULMAN L.,CHALLENGES TO COLLECTIVE BARGAINING. ECO/TAC DISCRIM EQUILIB ATTIT...JURID SOC/WK. PAGE 132 F2599 LABOR BARGAIN ADJUD POLICY

L67
"GOVERNMENT CONTROL OF LAND: PROTECTING THE I-KNOW-IT-WHENI-SEE-IT INTEREST." USA+45 LAW CONSTN DELIB/GP CT/SYS HABITAT ILLINOIS. PAGE 2 F0026 PLAN LOC/G CONTROL ADJUD

L67
AFFELDT R.J.,"THE INDEPENDENT LABOR UNION AND THE GOOD LIFE." USA+45 ADJUD CONTROL SANCTION GP/REL ORD/FREE JURID. PAGE 3 F0045 LABOR CT/SYS PWR SOVEREIGN

L67
BARRON J.A.,"ACCESS TO THE PRESS." USA+45 TEC/DEV PRESS TV ADJUD AUD/VIS. PAGE 10 F0196 ORD/FREE COM/IND EDU/PROP LAW

L67
COSTANZA J.F.,"WHOLESOME NEUTRALITY: LAW AND EDUCATION." USA+45 GIVE EDU/PROP ADJUD CONTROL GP/REL...DECISION JURID. PAGE 28 F0540 SECT PROVS ACADEM

L67
DEALEY S.,"MONETARY RECOVERY UNDER FEDERAL TRANSPORTATION STATUTES." USA+45 SEA WORKER TAX PAY ADJUD DEATH GOV/REL OWN HEALTH ORD/FREE 20. PAGE 31 F0609 DIST/IND LAW CONTROL FINAN

L67
DROBNIG U.,"CONFLICT OF LAWS AND THE EUROPEAN ECONOMIC COMMUNITY." EUR+WWI PROB/SOLV DIPLOM ...JURID EEC. PAGE 34 F0663 INT/LAW ADJUD INT/ORG MARKET

L67
GOLD J.,"INTERPRETATION BY THE INTERNATIONAL MONETARY FUND OF ITS ARTICLES OF AGREEMENT." INT/TRADE ADJUD ATTIT...POLICY JURID. PAGE 48 F0933 CONSTN INT/ORG LAW DIPLOM

L67
GOULD W.B.,"THE STATUS OF UNAUTHORIZED AND 'WILDCAT' STRIKES UNDER THE NATIONAL LABOR RELATIONS ACT." USA+45 ACT/RES BARGAIN ECO/TAC LEGIT ADJUD ADMIN GP/REL MGT. PAGE 50 F0968 ECO/DEV INDUS LABOR POLICY

L67
HUBBARD P.H.,"MONETARY RECOVERY UNDER THE COPYRIGHT, PATENT, AND TRADEMARK ACTS." PROC/MFG TAX PAY LEGIT ADJUD GOV/REL OWN ORD/FREE 20. PAGE 62 F1228 CREATE LAW CONTROL FINAN

L67
JACOBY S.B.,"THE 89TH CONGRESS AND GOVERNMENT LITIGATION." USA+45 ADMIN COST...JURID 20 CONGRESS. PAGE 66 F1302 LAW NAT/G ADJUD

SANCTION
L67

JOHNSTON J.D. JR.,"CONSTITUTION OF SUBDIVISION CONTROL EXACTIONS: THE QUEST FOR A RATIONALE." USA+45 PROVS PUB/INST ADJUD CT/SYS GP/REL MUNICH. PAGE 68 F1334
PLAN CONTROL LOC/G FORCES
L67

LAMBERT J.D.,"CORPORATE POLITICAL SPENDING AND CAMPAIGN FINANCE." LAW CONSTN FINAN LABOR LG/CO LOC/G NAT/G VOL/ASSN TEC/DEV ADJUD ADMIN PARTIC. PAGE 75 F1463
USA+45 POL/PAR CHOOSE COST
L67

MESTMACKER E.J.,"STATE TRADING MONOPOLIES IN THE EUROPEAN ECONOMIC COMMUNITY. DIPLOM ECO/TAC ADJUD CONTROL DISCRIM 20 EEC. PAGE 90 F1764
INT/TRADE INT/ORG LAW TARIFFS
L67

PARKER G.P. JR.,"MONETARY RECOVERY UNDER THE FEDERAL LABOR STATUTES." USA+45 USA-45 INDUS ADJUD CT/SYS GOV/REL HEALTH ORD/FREE 20 DEPT/LABOR NLRB. PAGE 103 F2027
LABOR CONTROL LAW FINAN
L67

ROBERTS E.F.,"THE CASE OF THE UNWARY HOME BUYER: THE HOUSING MERCHANT DID IT." USA+45 CLIENT DIST/IND MARKET LG/CO SML/CO PROB/SOLV LEGIT COST PROFIT. PAGE 112 F2207
ADJUD CONSTRUC OWN LAW
L67

SEABERG G.P.,"THE DRUG ABUSE PROBLEMS AND SOME PROPOSALS." UK USA+45 MARKET SANCTION CRIME ...POLICY NEW/IDEA. PAGE 119 F2339
BIO/SOC LAW ADJUD PROB/SOLV
L67

STILL C.H.,"MONETARY RECOVERY UNDER THE FAIR LABOR STANDARDS ACT." USA+45 USA-45 WORKER PAY ADJUD GOV/REL HEALTH ORD/FREE...MATH 20 NLRB. PAGE 126 F2487
LABOR CONTROL LAW FINAN
L67

TRAVERS H. JR.,"AN EXAMINATION OF THE CAB'S MERGER POLICY." USA+45 USA-45 LAW NAT/G LEGIS PLAN ADMIN ...DECISION 20 CONGRESS. PAGE 131 F2584
ADJUD LG/CO POLICY DIST/IND
L67

WATKINS J.B.,"MONETARY RECOVERY UNDER FEDERAL ANTITRUST STATUTES." USA+45 PROB/SOLV ADJUD CT/SYS GOV/REL ORD/FREE 20. PAGE 144 F2831
LG/CO CONTROL LAW FINAN
L67

WILKINSON J.H. JR.,"THE NET OPERATING LOSS DEDUCTION AND RELATED INCOME TAX DEVICES." PROB/SOLV BUDGET PAY GOV/REL ORD/FREE...MATH CHARTS METH 20. PAGE 146 F2886
TAX FINAN LAW ADJUD
S67

"THE SIERRA CLUB, POLITICAL ACTIVITY, AND TAX EXEMPT CHARITABLE STATUS." USA+45 LAW VOL/ASSN TAX PAY ADJUD LOBBY INGP/REL HABITAT 20. PAGE 2 F0027
ELITES GOV/REL FACE/GP ORD/FREE
S67

"ANTITRUST VENUE: TRANSACTING BUSINESS UNDER THE CLAYTON ACT." USA+45 DIST/IND PROB/SOLV ECO/TAC ADJUD CT/SYS 20. PAGE 2 F0028
LAW LG/CO CONTROL NAT/G
S67

"IMPORT-EXPORT CLAUSE: A BLANKET PROHIBITION MISAPPLIED." USA+45 INT/TRADE ADJUD INCOME PWR 20. PAGE 2 F0029
CONSTN TAX PROVS LAW
S67

AMERASINGHE C.F.,"SOME LEGAL PROBLEMS OF STATE TRADING IN SOUTHEAST ASIA." PROB/SOLV ADJUD CONTROL CT/SYS GP/REL 20. PAGE 5 F0084
INT/TRADE NAT/G INT/LAW PRIVIL
S67

ASCH P.,"CONGLOMERATE MERGERS AND PUBLIC POLICY." USA+45 ECO/DEV LG/CO NAT/G ECO/TAC ADJUD CENTRAL 20. PAGE 7 F0126
INDUS CAP/ISM BARGAIN
S67

BRAUCHER R.,"RECLAMATION OF GOODS FROM A FRAUDULENT BUYER." USA+45 CLIENT FINAN CT/SYS PERS/REL COST WEALTH. PAGE 18 F0341
LAW ADJUD GOV/REL INT/TRADE
S67

CHADWELL J.T.,"ANTITRUST ASPECTS OF DEALER LICENSING AND FRANCHISING." ACT/RES LICENSE ADJUD CONTROL OWN. PAGE 23 F0439
LAW PRIVIL INDUS
S67

CURTIN W.J.,"NATIONAL EMERGENCY DISPUTES LEGISLATION* ITS NEED AND ITS PROSPECTS IN THE TRANSPORTATION INDUSTRIES." USA+45 ECO/DEV INDUS NAT/G LEGIS ACT/RES BARGAIN POLICY. PAGE 29 F0565
JURID LABOR ADJUD DIST/IND
S67

DEMUTH J.,"GE: PROFILE OF A CORPORATION." USA+45 USA-45 LABOR ACT/RES RATION EDU/PROP ADJUD CT/SYS FASCISM 20. PAGE 32 F0619
LG/CO CONSERVE PRICE
S67

GREGORY R.,"THE MINISTER'S LINE: OR, THE M4 COMES TO BERKSHIRE. PART I." UK CONSTN DIST/IND LEGIS TOP/EX PLAN ADJUD...GEOG 20. PAGE 51 F0994
DECISION CONSTRUC NAT/G DELIB/GP
S67

HADDOCK G.B.,"CORPORATE GROWTH AS AFFECTED BY THE FEDERAL ANTITRUST LAWS" ECO/DEV NAT/G PLAN TEC/DEV CAP/ISM ECO/TAC 20. PAGE 53 F1029
INDUS JURID ADJUD
S67

HALE G.E.,"EXPANDING ENTERPRISE: GEOGRAPHICAL CURBS ON MERGERS." USA+45 MARKET LG/CO ADJUD CONTROL GP/REL 20. PAGE 53 F1041
LAW HABITAT INDUS EX/STRUC
S67

KENDALL R.J.,"CHANGED CONDITIONS AS MISREPRESENTATION IN GOVERNMENT CONSTRUCTION CONTRACTS." USA+45 BARGAIN ADJUD COST. PAGE 70 F1375
CONTROL CONSTRUC NAT/G LAW
S67

KESTENBAUM L.,"PRIMARY JURISDICTION TO DECIDE ANTITRUST JURISDICTION* A PRACTICAL APPROACH TO THE ALLOCATION OF FUNCTIONS." USA+45 ECO/DEV INDUS VOL/ASSN ECO/TAC. PAGE 70 F1383
JURID CT/SYS LABOR ADJUD
S67

LEFCOE G.,"CONSTRUCTION LENDING AND THE EQUITABLE LIEN." LICENSE CT/SYS OWN...STAT 20. PAGE 77 F1510
CONSTRUC RENT ADJUD
S67

MELTZER B.D.,"RUMINATIONS ABOUT IDEOLOGY, LAW, AND LABOR ARBITRATION." USA+45 ECO/DEV PROB/SOLV CONFER MGT. PAGE 89 F1754
JURID ADJUD LABOR CONSULT
S67

MITCHELL J.D.B.,"THE CONSTITUTIONAL IMPLICATIONS OF JUDICIAL CONTROL OF THE ADMINISTRATION IN THE UNITED KINGDOM." UK LAW ADJUD ADMIN GOV/REL ROLE ...GP/COMP 20. PAGE 92 F1808
CONSTN CT/SYS CONTROL EX/STRUC
S67

NILES J.G.,"CIVIL ACTIONS FOR DAMAGES UNDER THE FEDERAL CIVIL RIGHTS STATUTES." CONSTN FINAN ADJUD CT/SYS GOV/REL RACE/REL 20. PAGE 98 F1928
DISCRIM LAW CONTROL ORD/FREE
S67

PENNEY N.,"BANK STATEMENTS, CANCELLED CHECKS, AND ARTICLE FOUR IN THE ELECTRONIC AGE." USA+45 TEC/DEV COST EFFICIENCY WEALTH. PAGE 104 F2056
CREATE LAW ADJUD FINAN
S67

PIERPONT J.R.,"NEW STAGE IN THE LONGSHORE STRUGGLE." USA+45 SENIOR ADJUD RACE/REL...JURID 20 NEGRO. PAGE 106 F2083
LABOR DISCRIM WORKER CT/SYS
S67

PRASOW P.,"THE DEVELOPMENT OF JUDICIAL ARBITRATION IN LABOR-MANAGEMENT DISPUTES." LAW INDUS WORKER GP/REL ROLE...HIST/WRIT 20. PAGE 107 F2113
LABOR BARGAIN ADJUD TREND
S67

RAGAN S.,"THE ABA RECOMMENDATIONS: A NEWSPAPERMAN'S CRITIQUE." EDU/PROP CONTROL GP/REL...JURID ABA. PAGE 109 F2136
LAW PRESS ADJUD ORD/FREE
S67

REILLY T.J.,"FREEZING AND CONFISCATION OF CUBAN PROPERTY." CUBA USA+45 LAW DIPLOM LEGIT ADJUD CONTROL. PAGE 111 F2177
STRANGE OWN ECO/TAC
S67

RONY V.,"HEARTBREAK IN TENNESSEE* POOR WHITES AND THE UNIONS." LAW STRUCT CAP/ISM ADJUD GP/REL. PAGE 113 F2236
LABOR LOC/G WORKER PWR
S67

SCRIPP J.,"CONTROLLING PREJUDICIAL PUBLICITY BY THE CONTEMPT POWER: THE BRITISH PRACTICE AND ITS PROSPECT IN AMERICAN LAW." UK USA+45 EDU/PROP CONTROL GP/REL ORD/FREE JURID. PAGE 119 F2338
METH/COMP LAW PRESS ADJUD
S67

SEIDLER G.L.,"MARXIST LEGAL THOUGHT IN POLAND." POLAND SOCIETY R+D LOC/G NAT/G ACT/RES ADJUD CT/SYS SUPEGO PWR...SOC TREND 20 MARX/KARL. PAGE 119 F2343
MARXISM LAW CONCPT EFFICIENCY
S67

SHEFFTZ M.C.,"THE TRADE DISPUTES AND TRADE UNIONS ACT OF 1927: THE AFTERMATH OF THE GENERAL STRIKE." UK FINAN WORKER ADJUD LEAD PARL/PROC 20. PAGE 120 F2373
LEGIS ATTIT LABOR GP/REL
S67

SKILTON R.M.,"PROTECTION OF THE INSTALLMENT BUYER OF GOODS UNDER THE UNIFORM COMMERCIAL CODE." USA+45 NAT/G COST. PAGE 123 F2418
LAW ADJUD LEGIT FINAN
S67

SKOLNICK J.H.,"SOCIAL CONTROL IN THE ADVERSARY SYSTEM." USA+45 CONSULT OP/RES ADMIN CONTROL. PAGE 123 F2419
PROB/SOLV PERS/REL ADJUD CT/SYS
S67

STEINHEIMER R.L. JR.,"THE UNIFORM COMMERCIAL CODE
ADJUD

COMES OF AGE." USA+45 FINAN ACADEM JUDGE. PAGE 126 F2477
LEGIS INT/TRADE GOV/REL

ADJUST....SOCIAL ADJUSTMENT, SOCIALIZATION. SEE ALSO INGP/REL

NCO
STOLPER W.,"SOCIAL FACTORS IN ECONOMIC PLANNING, WITH SPECIAL REFERENCE TO NIGERIA" AFR NIGER CULTURE FAM SECT RECEIVE ETIQUET ADMIN DEMAND 20. PAGE 126 F2494
ECO/UNDEV PLAN ADJUST RISK

N19
HATANAKA M.,A SPECTRAL ANALYSIS OF BUSINESS CYCLE INDICATORS: LEAD-LAG IN TERMS OF ALL TIME POINTS (PAMPHLET). UNIV WORKER EFFICIENCY...REGRESS STAT CHARTS TIME 20. PAGE 56 F1110
ECOMETRIC ADJUST PRODUC CON/ANAL

B27
SIEGFRIED A.,AMERICA COMES OF AGE: A FRENCH ANALYSIS (TRANS. BY H.H. HEMMING AND DORIS HEMMING). FRANCE UK POL/PAR WORKER TEC/DEV DIPLOM REGION RACE/REL ADJUST PRODUC HEREDITY...TIME/SEQ GP/COMP SOC/INTEG 20 DEMOCRAT REPUBLICAN KKK. PAGE 122 F2398
USA-45 CULTURE ECO/DEV SOC

B28
TRUE A.C.,A HISTORY OF AGRICULTURAL EXTENSION WORK IN THE UNITED STATES, 1785-1923. USA-45 LAW SCHOOL WAR ADJUST...CHARTS BIBLIOG 18/20 SMITH/LEVR COUNTY/AGT. PAGE 131 F2591
EDU/PROP AGRI VOL/ASSN PLAN

B40
BLAISDELL D.C.,GOVERNMENT AND AGRICULTURE; THE GROWTH OF FEDERAL FARM AID. USA-45 MARKET PLAN PROB/SOLV TEC/DEV ECO/TAC GOV/REL ADJUST ATTIT ...CHARTS 20 DEPT/AGRI. PAGE 15 F0296
NAT/G GIVE AGRI DELIB/GP

B47
BALDWIN H.W.,THE PRICE OF POWER. USA+45 FORCES PLAN NUC/PWR ADJUST COST ORD/FREE...POLICY PSY BIBLIOG 20. PAGE 9 F0165
PROB/SOLV PWR POPULISM PRICE

B48
OSBORN F.,OUR PLUNDERED PLANET. UNIV DEATH WAR ...BIBLIOG RESOURCE/N. PAGE 102 F2001
HABITAT GEOG ADJUST AGRI

B52
TANNENBAUM F.,A PHILOSOPHY OF LABOR. SOCIETY STRATA INDUS LG/CO AGREE ADJUST OWN ORD/FREE PWR...CONCPT 20. PAGE 128 F2533
LABOR PHIL/SCI WORKER CREATE

B53
MILLIKAN M.F.,INCOME STABILIZATION FOR A DEVELOPING DEMOCRACY. USA+45 ECO/DEV LABOR BUDGET ECO/TAC TAX ADMIN ADJUST PRODUC WEALTH...POLICY TREND 20. PAGE 91 F1794
ANTHOL MARKET EQUILIB EFFICIENCY

S54
MACK R.W.,"ECOLOGICAL PATTERNS IN AN INDUSTRIAL SHOP" (BMR)" USA+45 CULTURE SOCIETY STRATA STRUCT LABOR NEIGH GP/REL ADJUST HABITAT...SOC SOC/INTEG 20. PAGE 83 F1634
INDUS DISCRIM WORKER

B55
BERNAYS E.L.,THE ENGINEERING OF CONSENT. VOL/ASSN OP/RES ROUTINE INGP/REL ATTIT RESPECT...POLICY METH/CNCPT METH/COMP 20. PAGE 14 F0264
GP/REL PLAN ACT/RES ADJUST

B56
BONNETT C.E.,HISTORY OF EMPLOYERS' ASSOCIATIONS IN THE UNITED STATES (1ST ED.). MARKET DETER GP/REL ADJUST. PAGE 16 F0316
LABOR VOL/ASSN LG/CO

B58
HAMEROW T.S.,RESTORATION, REVOLUTION, REACTION: ECONOMICS AND POLITICS IN GERMANY, 1815-1871. CAP/ISM ADJUST ATTIT PWR...BIBLIOG/A 19 GER/CONFED FRANK/PARL. PAGE 54 F1055
REV ORD/FREE ECO/DEV

B58
US CONGRESS JOINT ECO COMM,THE RELATIONSHIP OF PRICES TO ECONOMIC STABILITY AND GROWTH. USA+45 MARKET TAX ADJUST COST DEMAND INCOME PRODUC ...POLICY TREND CHARTS ANTHOL 20 CONGRESS. PAGE 134 F2650
ECO/DEV PLAN EQUILIB PRICE

B59
MATTHEWS R.C.O.,THE BUSINESS CYCLE. AFR LABOR INT/TRADE TAX PRICE RISK ADJUST WEALTH...POLICY ECOMETRIC CHARTS SIMUL TIME 20. PAGE 87 F1705
FINAN DEMAND TASK

B60
HUGHES R.,THE CHINESE COMMUNES; A BACKGROUND BOOK. CHINA/COM SOCIETY CONTROL ROUTINE ADJUST EFFICIENCY PRODUC 20. PAGE 63 F1234
AGRI INDUS STRUCT MARXISM

B62
ARNOLD T.W.,THE FOLKLORE OF CAPITALISM. USA+45 USA-45 SOCIETY LG/CO SML/CO EX/STRUC ECO/TAC EDU/PROP ADJUST INCOME...MYTH CHARTS 20. PAGE 6 F0116
CAP/ISM ATTIT STERTYP ECO/DEV

B62
BROOKINGS INSTITUTION,DEVELOPMENT OF THE EMERGING COUNTRIES; AN AGENDA FOR RESEARCH. WOR+45 AGRI TEC/DEV FOR/AID EDU/PROP ADJUST HABITAT KNOWL...PSY SOC ANTHOL 20 THIRD/WRLD. PAGE 19 F0362
ECO/UNDEV R+D SOCIETY PROB/SOLV

B62
LEVENSTEIN A.,WHY PEOPLE WORK; CHANGING INCENTIVES IN A TROUBLED WORLD. USA+45 SOCIETY PROB/SOLV TEC/DEV EDU/PROP ADJUST...CENSUS BIBLIOG 20. PAGE 79 F1538
DRIVE WORKER ECO/DEV ANOMIE

B63
GANDHI M.K.,THE WAY TO COMMUNAL HARMONY. INDIA MAJORITY RIGID/FLEX ROLE RESPECT 20 GANDHI/M. PAGE 46 F0892
RACE/REL DISCRIM ATTIT ADJUST

B63
LETHBRIDGE H.J.,THE PEASANT AND THE COMMUNES. CHINA/COM COM USSR NEIGH PROB/SOLV ADJUST EFFICIENCY...POLICY METH/COMP NAT/COMP 20. PAGE 78 F1535
MARXISM ECO/TAC AGRI WORKER

B63
OLSON M. JR.,THE ECONOMICS OF WARTIME SHORTAGE. FRANCE GERMANY MOD/EUR UK AGRI PROB/SOLV ADMIN DEMAND WEALTH...POLICY OLD/LIB FOR/TRADE 17/20. PAGE 101 F1990
WAR ADJUST ECO/TAC NAT/COMP

B64
INTERNATIONAL MONETARY ARRANGEMENTS: THE PROBLEM OF CHOICE. PLAN PROB/SOLV INT/TRADE ADJUST COST EQUILIB 20. PAGE 1 F0020
POLICY DIPLOM FINAN ECO/DEV

B64
BALL R.J.,INFLATION AND THE THEORY OF MONEY. MARKET TAX PAY PRICE TASK ADJUST BAL/PAY COST INCOME PRODUC WEALTH...METH/COMP 20 KEYNES/JM MONEY. PAGE 9 F0167
EQUILIB DEMAND POLICY

B64
NOVACK D.E.,DEVELOPMENT AND SOCIETY; THE DYNAMICS OF ECONOMIC CHANGE. WOR+45 STRATA STRUCT ECO/TAC CONTROL CROWD REV GP/REL ADJUST PRODUC WEALTH PSY. PAGE 99 F1940
SOCIETY CULTURE SOC ECO/UNDEV

B64
POWELSON J.P.,LATIN AMERICA: TODAY'S ECONOMIC AND SOCIAL REVOLUTION. L/A+17C INTELL SOCIETY STRUCT AGRI INDUS NAT/G DIPLOM ECO/TAC REV...POLICY 20. PAGE 107 F2110
ECO/UNDEV WEALTH ADJUST PLAN

S64
CLELLAND D.A.,"ECONOMIC DOMINANTS AND COMMUNITY POWER: A COMPARATIVE ANALYSIS." ELITES ADJUST ATTIT WEALTH...DECISION MUNICH. PAGE 25 F0488
LEAD MGT PWR

S64
N,"QUASI-LEGISLATIVE ARBITRATION AGREEMENTS." LAW LG/CO ECO/TAC SANCTION ATTIT POLICY. PAGE 96 F1885
ADJUD ADJUST LABOR GP/REL

B65
HARBISON F.,MANPOWER AND EDUCATION. AFR CHINA/COM IRAN L/A+17C S/ASIA TEC/DEV ADJUST OPTIMAL SKILL ...ANTHOL 20. PAGE 55 F1073
ECO/UNDEV EDU/PROP WORKER NAT/COMP

B65
INTERAMERICAN ECO AND SOC COUN,THE ALLIANCE FOR PROGRESS: ITS THIRD YEAR 1963-1964. FUT L/A+17C WOR+45 ECO/DEV INT/ORG PLAN CONTROL ADJUST...STAT ANTHOL SOC/INTEG 20 ALL/PROG. PAGE 64 F1268
ECO/UNDEV ECO/TAC FINAN FOR/AID

B65
KASER M.,COMECON* INTEGRATION PROBLEMS OF THE PLANNED ECONOMIES. INT/ORG TEC/DEV INT/TRADE PRICE ADMIN ADJUST CENTRAL...STAT TIME/SEQ ORG/CHARTS COMECON. PAGE 69 F1359
PLAN ECO/DEV COM REGION

B65
NATIONAL CONF SOCIAL WELFARE,THE SOCIAL WELFARE FORUM, 1965. LAW CULTURE VOL/ASSN CONTROL PERS/REL ADJUST POLICY. PAGE 97 F1899
CONSTN WEALTH ORD/FREE NEIGH

B65
O'BRIEN F.,CRISIS IN WORLD COMMUNISM* MARXISM IN SEARCH OF EFFICIENCY. AFR COM ECO/DEV PLAN INT/TRADE WAR ADJUST PEACE...STAT TIME/SEQ GOV/COMP NAT/COMP. PAGE 99 F1951
MARXISM USSR DRIVE EFFICIENCY

B65
SCHWARTZ G.,SCIENCE IN MARKETING. OP/RES PROB/SOLV INT/TRADE PRICE CONTROL ADJUST PRODUC...CONCPT 20. PAGE 118 F2324
PHIL/SCI TREND ECO/DEV MARKET

B65
SIMON B.,EDUCATION AND THE LABOR MOVEMENT, 1870-1920. UK SOCIETY STRATA LABOR POL/PAR SCHOOL CONTROL PARTIC SOCISM...BIBLIOG 19/20. PAGE 122 F2406
EDU/PROP WORKER ADJUST LAW

B66
FISK E.K.,NEW GUINEA ON THE THRESHOLD; ASPECTS OF SOCIAL, POLITICAL, AND ECONOMIC DEVELOPMENT. AGRI NAT/G INT/TRADE ADMIN ADJUST LITERACY ROLE...CHARTS ANTHOL 20 NEW/GUINEA. PAGE 41 F0804
ECO/UNDEV SOCIETY

B66
GORDON R.A.,PROSPERITY AND UNEMPLOYMENT. USA+45 PLAN ECO/TAC ADJUST DEMAND ALL/VALS...POLICY DECISION TREND CHARTS ANTHOL 20. PAGE 49 F0961
WORKER INDUS ECO/DEV WEALTH

B66
KOMIYA R.,POSTWAR ECONOMIC GROWTH IN JAPAN. ELITES NAT/G EX/STRUC TEC/DEV BUDGET DIPLOM CONTROL BAL/PAY PRODUC...BIBLIOG 20 CHINJAP. PAGE 73 F1424
ECO/DEV POLICY PLAN ADJUST

B66
LICHTMAN R.,TOWARD COMMUNITY (PAPER). PLAN PROB/SOLV WEALTH MARXISM...HEAL CONCPT 20. PAGE 80 F1561
NEW/LIB EFFICIENCY CAP/ISM ADJUST

B66
MACFARQUHAR R.,CHINA UNDER MAO: POLITICS TAKES COMMAND. CHINA/COM COM AGRI INDUS CHIEF FORCES DIPLOM INT/TRADE EDU/PROP TASK REV ADJUST...ANTHOL 20 MAO. PAGE 83 F1628
ECO/UNDEV TEC/DEV ECO/TAC ADMIN

B66
ROBERTSON D.J.,THE BRITISH BALANCE OF PAYMENTS. UK WOR+45 INDUS BUDGET TAX ADJUST...CHARTS ANTHOL 20. PAGE 112 F2213
FINAN BAL/PAY ECO/DEV INT/TRADE

B66
ROBINSON E.A.,THE ECONOMICS OF EDUCATION. WOR+45 CULTURE ECO/UNDEV FINAN SCHOOL DIPLOM PRICE COST DEMAND...CHARTS METH/COMP 20. PAGE 112 F2216
EDU/PROP ADJUST CONFER

B66
SEWELL J.P.,FUNCTIONALISM AND WORLD POLITICS* A STUDY BASED ON UNITED NATIONS PROGRAMS FINANCING ECONOMICAL DEVELOPMENT. ECO/UNDEV FINAN PROB/SOLV DIPLOM ECO/TAC FEEDBACK REGION ADJUST ATTIT UN IBRD INTL/FINAN INTL/DEV UNSF. PAGE 120 F2360
TASK INT/ORG IDEA/COMP GEN/LAWS

B66
THOMPSON J.H.,MODERNIZATION OF THE ARAB WORLD. FUT ISRAEL STRUCT ECO/UNDEV DIPLOM INGP/REL ATTIT ...CENSUS ANTHOL 20 ARABS. PAGE 130 F2565
ADJUST ISLAM PROB/SOLV NAT/COMP

B67
BADGLEY R.F.,DOCTORS' STRIKE; MEDICAL CARE AND CONFLICT IN SASKATCHEWAN. CANADA NAT/G PROF/ORG GP/REL ADJUST ATTIT...HEAL SOC 20. PAGE 8 F0148
HEALTH PLAN LABOR BARGAIN

B67
DE TORRES J.,FINANCING LOCAL GOVERNMENT. USA+45 USA-45 NAT/G PROVS GIVE ADJUST PWR...TIME/SEQ CHARTS MUNICH 20. PAGE 31 F0606
LOC/G BUDGET TAX TREND

B67
DIXON W.,SOCIETY, SCHOOLS AND PROGRESS IN SCANDINAVIA. DENMARK NORWAY SWEDEN 20. PAGE 33 F0644
EDU/PROP SOCIETY ADJUST PLAN

B67
GOODMAN P.,LIKE A CONQUERED PROVINCE: THE MORAL AMBIGUITY OF AMERICA. AFR USA+45 NAT/G PROB/SOLV EDU/PROP ADJUST EFFICIENCY 20. PAGE 49 F0950
SOCIETY TEC/DEV WAR MORAL

B67
KIRK R.,THE POLITICAL PRINCIPLES OF ROBERT A. TAFT. USA+45 LABOR DIPLOM ADJUD ADJUST ORD/FREE TAFT/RA. PAGE 71 F1398
POL/PAR LEAD LEGIS ATTIT

B67
LEIBY J.,CHARITY AND CORRECTION IN JERSEY; A HISTORY OF STATE WELFARE INSTITUTIONS. DELIB/GP EX/STRUC PROB/SOLV INSPECT LEAD ADJUST HEALTH ...POLICY PSY NEW/JERSEY. PAGE 77 F1514
PROVS PUB/INST ADMIN

B67
LEWIS L.J.,SOCIETY, SCHOOLS AND PROGRESS IN NIGERIA. NIGERIA WORKER ECO/TAC ADJUST 20. PAGE 79 F1550
EDU/PROP ECO/UNDEV SKILL SOCIETY

B67
LYND S.,RECONSTRUCTION. USA-45 PROB/SOLV RACE/REL ...IDEA/COMP ANTHOL 19. PAGE 82 F1616
SUFF ECO/TAC ADJUST

B67
ROACH J.R.,THE UNITED STATES AND THE ATLANTIC COMMUNITY; ISSUES AND PROSPECTS. AFR WOR+45 TEC/DEV ECO/TAC COLONIAL REGION PEACE ROLE...ANTHOL NATO EEC. PAGE 112 F2199
INT/ORG POLICY ADJUST DIPLOM

B67
VAN SLYKE L.P.,ENEMIES AND FRIENDS; THE UNITED FRONT IN CHINESE COMMUNIST HISTORY. CHINA/COM SOCIETY FORCES PLAN ADJUST 20 MAO. PAGE 140 F2764
INGP/REL MARXISM ATTIT GP/REL

L67
GLAZER N.,"HOUSING PROBLEMS AND HOUSING POLICIES." USA+45 PLAN RENT ADJUST CONSEN DEMAND DISCRIM AGE ATTIT HEALTH WEALTH MUNICH NEGRO. PAGE 48 F0929
POLICY CONSTRUC CREATE HABITAT

S67
CATTELL D.T.,"THE FIFTIETH ANNIVERSARY: A SOVIET WATERSHED?" USSR CONSTN ECO/DEV NAT/G LEAD TOTALISM 20 KHRUSH/N. PAGE 22 F0430
MARXISM CHIEF POLICY ADJUST

S67
GAUSSENS J.,"THE APPLICATIONS OF NUCLEAR ENERGY - TECHNICAL, ECONOMIC AND SOCIAL ASPECTS." WOR+45 INDUS R+D ACT/RES EFFICIENCY PRODUC SKILL PREDICT. PAGE 47 F0911
NUC/PWR TEC/DEV ECO/DEV ADJUST

S67
GOLDSTEIN W.,"THE SCIENCE ESTABLISHMENT AND ITS POLITICAL CONTROL." WOR+45 SOCIETY GP/REL RATIONAL ORD/FREE. PAGE 48 F0941
CREATE ADJUST CONTROL

S67
HEILBRONER R.L.,"BUILDING NEW NATIONS." AFR STRUCT PLAN TEC/DEV ADJUST MARXISM...POLICY 20. PAGE 58 F1138
PROB/SOLV REV NAT/LISM ECO/UNDEV

S67
JENCKS C.E.,"COAL MINERS IN BRITAIN SINCE NATIONALIZATION." UK LABOR GP/REL ADJUST SOCISM ...INT 20. PAGE 67 F1311
EXTR/IND WORKER STRATA ATTIT

S67
LEVIN T.,"PSYCHOANALYSIS AND SOCIAL CHANGE." SOCIETY ANOMIE DRIVE PWR 20. PAGE 79 F1541
PSY PHIL/SCI ADJUST WEALTH

S67
MANGLAPUS R.S.,"ASIAN REVOLUTION AND AMERICAN IDEOLOGY." USA+45 SOCIETY CAP/ISM DIPLOM ADJUST CENTRAL...NAT/COMP 20. PAGE 84 F1652
REV POPULISM ATTIT ASIA

S67
MEHTA A.,"INDIA* POVERTY AND CHANGE." STRATA INDUS CREATE ECO/TAC FOR/AID NEUTRAL GP/REL ADJUST INCOME ...NEW/IDEA 20. PAGE 89 F1746
INDIA SOCIETY ECO/UNDEV TEC/DEV

S67
RONNING C.,"NANKING: 1950." ASIA CANADA CHINA/COM NAT/G PLAN ECO/TAC REV ADJUST 20. PAGE 113 F2235
DIPLOM ROLE PEACE

S67
SCHELLING T.C.,"ECONOMICS AND CRIMINAL ENTERPRISE." LAW FORCES BARGAIN ECO/TAC CONTROL GAMBLE ROUTINE ADJUST DEMAND INCOME PROFIT CRIMLGY. PAGE 116 F2295
CRIME PROB/SOLV CONCPT

N67
NATIONAL COMN COMMUNITY HEALTH,ACTION - PLANNING FOR COMMUNITY HEALTH SERVICES (PAMPHLET). USA+45 PROF/ORG DELIB/GP BUDGET ROUTINE GP/REL ATTIT ...HEAL SOC SOC/WK CHARTS MUNICH TIME 20. PAGE 97 F1898
PLAN HEALTH ADJUST

B68
NENAROKOV A.P.,RUSSIA IN THE 20TH CENTURY: THE OFFICIAL SOVIET HISTORY. USSR SOCIETY REV...AUD/VIS 20. PAGE 97 F1913
COM ADJUST MARXISM

ADJUSTMENT, SOCIAL....SEE ADJUST

ADLER J.H. F0042

ADLER M.J. F1373

ADLER/A....ALFRED ADLER

ADMIN....ORGANIZATIONAL BEHAVIOR, NONEXECUTIVE; SEE ALSO GP/ADMIN

N
INTERNATIONAL BIBLIOGRAPHY OF ECONOMICS. WOR+45 FINAN MARKET ADMIN DEMAND INCOME PRODUC...POLICY IDEA/COMP METH. PAGE 1 F0002
BIBLIOG ECO/DEV ECO/UNDEV INT/TRADE

N
ECONOMIC LIBRARY SELECTIONS. AGRI INDUS MARKET ADMIN...STAT NAT/COMP 20. PAGE 1 F0007
BIBLIOG/A WRITING FINAN

N
DEUTSCHE BUCHEREI,DEUTSCHES BUCHERVERZEICHNIS. GERMANY LAW CULTURE POL/PAR ADMIN LEAD ATTIT PERSON ...SOC 20. PAGE 32 F0626
BIBLIOG NAT/G DIPLOM ECO/DEV

N
US SUPERINTENDENT OF DOCUMENTS,INTERSTATE COMMERCE (PRICE LIST 59). USA+45 LAW LOC/G NAT/G LEGIS TARIFFS TAX ADMIN CONTROL HEALTH DECISION. PAGE 140 F2752
BIBLIOG/A DIST/IND GOV/REL PROVS

N
US SUPERINTENDENT OF DOCUMENTS,LABOR (PRICE LIST 33). USA+45 LAW AGRI CONSTRUC INDUS NAT/G BARGAIN PRICE ADMIN AUTOMAT PRODUC MGT. PAGE 140 F2753
BIBLIOG/A WORKER LABOR LEGIS

N
US SUPERINTENDENT OF DOCUMENTS,TARIFF AND TAXATION (PRICE LIST 37). USA+45 LAW INT/TRADE ADJUD ADMIN CT/SYS INCOME OWN...DECISION GATT. PAGE 140 F2754
BIBLIOG/A TAX TARIFFS NAT/G

NCO
STOLPER W.,"SOCIAL FACTORS IN ECONOMIC PLANNING, WITH SPECIAL REFERENCE TO NIGERIA" AFR NIGER CULTURE FAM SECT RECEIVE ETIQUET ADMIN DEMAND 20. PAGE 126 F2494
ECO/UNDEV PLAN ADJUST RISK

B02
MOREL E.D.,AFFAIRS OF WEST AFRICA. UK FINAN INDUS FAM KIN SECT CHIEF WORKER DIPLOM RACE/REL LITERACY HEALTH...CHARTS 18/20 AFRICA/W NEGRO. PAGE 93 F1826
COLONIAL ADMIN AFR

B12
FOUAD M.,LE REGIME DE LA PRESSE EN EGYPTE: THESE POUR LE DOCTORAT. UAR LICENSE EDU/PROP ADMIN SANCTION CRIME SUPEGO PWR...ART/METH JURID 19/20. PAGE 43 F0832
ORD/FREE LEGIS CONTROL PRESS

N19
ADMINISTRATIVE STAFF COLLEGE,THE ACCOUNTABILITY OF GOVERNMENT DEPARTMENTS (PAMPHLET) (REV. ED.). UK CONSTN FINAN NAT/G CONSULT ADMIN INGP/REL CONSEN PRIVIL 20 PARLIAMENT. PAGE 2 F0043
PARL/PROC ELITES SANCTION PROB/SOLV

N19
ANDERSON J.,THE ORGANIZATION OF ECONOMIC STUDIES IN RELATION TO THE PROBLEMS OF GOVERNMENT (PAMPHLET). UK FINAN INDUS DELIB/GP PLAN PROB/SOLV ADMIN 20. PAGE 5 F0095
ECO/TAC ACT/RES NAT/G CENTRAL

N19
ARNOW K.,SELF-INSURANCE IN THE TREASURY (PAMPHLET). USA+45 LAW RIGID/FLEX...POLICY METH/COMP 20 DEPT/TREAS. PAGE 6 F0117
ADMIN PLAN EFFICIENCY NAT/G

N19
DOTSON A.,PRODUCTION PLANNING IN THE PATENT OFFICE (PAMPHLET). USA+45 DIST/IND PROB/SOLV PRODUC...MGT PHIL/SCI 20 BUR/BUDGET PATENT/OFF. PAGE 34 F0655
EFFICIENCY PLAN NAT/G ADMIN

N19
EAST KENTUCKY REGIONAL PLAN,PROGRAM 60: A DECADE OF ACTION FOR PROGRESS IN EASTERN KENTUCKY (PAMPHLET). USA+45 AGRI CONSTRUC INDUS CONSULT ACT/RES PROB/SOLV EDU/PROP GOV/REL HEALTH KENTUCKY. PAGE 35 F0689
REGION ADMIN PLAN ECO/UNDEV

N19
EAST KENTUCKY REGIONAL PLAN,PROGRAM 60 REPORT: ACTION FOR PORGRESS IN EASTERN KENTUCKY (PAMPHLET). USA+45 CONSTRUC INDUS ACT/RES PROB/SOLV EDU/PROP ADMIN GOV/REL KENTUCKY. PAGE 35 F0690
REGION PLAN ECO/UNDEV CONSULT

N19
FAHRNKOPF N.,STATE AND LOCAL GOVERNMENT IN ILLINOIS (PAMPHLET). CONSTN ADMIN PARTIC CHOOSE REPRESENT GOV/REL...JURID MGT 20 ILLINOIS. PAGE 39 F0759
BIBLIOG LOC/G LEGIS CT/SYS

N19
FIKS M.,PUBLIC ADMINISTRATION IN ISRAEL (PAMPHLET). ISRAEL SCHOOL EX/STRUC BUDGET PAY INGP/REL ...DECISION 20 CIVIL/SERV. PAGE 41 F0792
EDU/PROP NAT/G ADMIN WORKER

N19
HERZBERG D.G.,A BUDGET FOR NEW YORK STATE, 1956-1957 (PAMPHLET). USA+45 ADMIN GOV/REL 20 NEW/YORK HARRIMAN/A. PAGE 59 F1159
POL/PAR PROVS BUDGET LEGIS

N19
JACKSON R.G.A.,THE CASE FOR AN INTERNATIONAL DEVELOPMENT AUTHORITY (PAMPHLET). WOR+45 ECO/DEV DIPLOM GIVE CONTROL GP/REL EFFICIENCY NAT/LISM SOVEREIGN 20. PAGE 66 F1295
FOR/AID INT/ORG ECO/UNDEV ADMIN

N19
KRIESBERG M.,CANCELLATION OF THE RATION STAMPS (PAMPHLET). USA+45 USA-45 MARKET PROB/SOLV PRICE GOV/REL RIGID/FLEX 20 OPA. PAGE 73 F1439
RATION DECISION ADMIN NAT/G

N19
KUWAIT ARABIA,KUWAIT FUND FOR ARAB ECONOMIC DEVELOPMENT (PAMPHLET). ISLAM KUWAIT UAR ECO/UNDEV LEGIS ECO/TAC WEALTH 20. PAGE 74 F1452
FOR/AID DIPLOM FINAN ADMIN

N19
MARSH J.F. JR.,THE FBI RETIREMENT BILL (PAMPHLET). USA+45 EX/STRUC WORKER PLAN PROB/SOLV BUDGET LEAD LOBBY PARL/PROC PERS/REL RIGID/FLEX...POLICY 20 FBI PRESIDENT BUR/BUDGET. PAGE 86 F1677
ADMIN NAT/G SENIOR GOV/REL

N19
SILVERMAN C.,THE PRESIDENT'S ECONOMIC ADVISERS (PAMPHLET). USA+45 LAW ELITES ECO/DEV EX/STRUC ADMIN LEAD GOV/REL PERS/REL ROLE...POLICY DECISION 20 PRESIDENT CONGRESS EISNHWR/DD. PAGE 122 F2404
CONSULT PROB/SOLV NAT/G PLAN

N19
US CHAMBER OF COMMERCE,THE SIGNIFICANCE OF CONCENTRATION RATIOS (PAMPHLET). USA+45 FINAN INDUS ADMIN...METH/CNCPT SAMP CHARTS 20. PAGE 134 F2647
MARKET PREDICT LG/CO CONTROL

N19
YLVISAKER P.N.,THE NATURAL CEMENT ISSUE (PAMPHLET). USA+45 USA-45 CONSTRUC PROVS CAP/ISM ADMIN LOBBY PERS/REL OWN RIGID/FLEX ROLE 20 MINNESOTA. PAGE 150 F2948
POLICY NAT/G PLAN GOV/REL

B20
MOREL E.D.,THE BLACK MAN'S BURDEN. AFR MOD/EUR AGRI EXTR/IND PROB/SOLV INT/TRADE ADMIN CONTROL COERCE DISCRIM...POLICY 19/20 NEGRO LEAGUE/NAT. PAGE 93 F1828
ORD/FREE CAP/ISM RACE/REL DOMIN

B24
HOLDSWORTH W.S.,A HISTORY OF ENGLISH LAW; THE COMMON LAW AND ITS RIVALS (VOL. VI). AFR UK STRATA EX/STRUC ADJUD ADMIN CONTROL CT/SYS...JURID CONCPT GEN/LAWS 17 PARLIAMENT ENGLSH/LAW COMMON/LAW. PAGE 61 F1194
LAW CONSTN LEGIS CHIEF

B25
MATHEWS J.M.,AMERICAN STATE GOVERNMENT. USA-45 LOC/G CHIEF EX/STRUC LEGIS ADJUD CONTROL CT/SYS ROUTINE GOV/REL PWR 20 GOVERNOR. PAGE 87 F1703
PROVS ADMIN FEDERAL CONSTN

B32
WRIGHT Q.,GOLD AND MONETARY STABILIZATION. FUT USA-45 WOR-45 INTELL ECO/DEV INT/ORG NAT/G CONSULT PLAN ECO/TAC ADMIN ATTIT WEALTH...CONCPT TREND 20. PAGE 149 F2935
FINAN POLICY

B37
BROOKS R.R.,WHEN LABOR ORGANIZES. FINAN EDU/PROP ADMIN LOBBY PARTIC REPRESENT WEALTH TREND. PAGE 19 F0364
LABOR GP/REL POLICY

B37
UNION OF SOUTH AFRICA,REPORT CONCERNING ADMINISTRATION OF SOUTH WEST AFRICA (6 VOLS.). SOUTH/AFR INDUS PUB/INST FORCES LEGIS BUDGET DIPLOM EDU/PROP ADJUD CT/SYS...GEOG CHARTS 20 AFRICA/SW LEAGUE/NAT. PAGE 132 F2610
NAT/G ADMIN COLONIAL CONSTN

B38
HARPER S.N.,THE GOVERNMENT OF THE SOVIET UNION. COM USSR LAW CONSTN ECO/DEV PLAN TEC/DEV DIPLOM INT/TRADE ADMIN REV NAT/LISM...POLICY 20. PAGE 55 F1085
MARXISM NAT/G LEAD POL/PAR

B38
REICH N.,LABOR RELATIONS IN REPUBLICAN GERMANY. GERMANY CONSTN ECO/DEV INDUS NAT/G ADMIN CONTROL GP/REL FASCISM POPULISM 20 WEIMAR/REP. PAGE 110 F2176
WORKER MGT LABOR BARGAIN

B39
FURNIVALL J.S.,NETHERLANDS INDIA. INDIA NETHERLAND CULTURE INDUS NAT/G DIPLOM ADMIN WEALTH...POLICY CHARTS 17/20. PAGE 45 F0876
COLONIAL ECO/UNDEV SOVEREIGN PLURISM

B40
GAUS J.M.,PUBLIC ADMINISTRATION AND THE UNITED STATES DEPARTMENT OF AGRICULTURE. USA-45 STRUCT DIST/IND FINAN MARKET EX/STRUC PROB/SOLV GIVE PRODUC...POLICY GEOG CHARTS 20 DEPT/AGRI. PAGE 47 F0909
ADMIN AGRI DELIB/GP OP/RES

B40
HELLMAN F.S.,THE NEW DEAL: SELECTED LIST OF REFERENCES. USA-45 FINAN LABOR EX/STRUC CREATE INT/TRADE ADMIN CT/SYS 20 SUPREME/CT. PAGE 58 F1145
BIBLIOG/A ECO/TAC PLAN POLICY

B41
MACMAHON A.W.,THE ADMINISTRATION OF FEDERAL WORK RELIEF. USA-45 EX/STRUC WORKER BUDGET EFFICIENCY ...CONT/OBS CHARTS 20 WPA. PAGE 84 F1636
ADMIN NAT/G MGT GIVE

B42
WRIGHT D.M.,THE CREATION OF PURCHASING POWER. USA-45 NAT/G PRICE ADMIN WAR INCOME PRODUC...POLICY CONCPT IDEA/COMP BIBLIOG 20 MONEY. PAGE 149 F2930
FINAN ECO/TAC ECO/DEV CREATE

B43
WILMERDING L. JR.,THE SPENDING POWER: A HISTORY OF THE EFFORTS OF CONGRESS TO CONTROL EXPENDITURES. USA-45 POL/PAR DELIB/GP EX/STRUC TOP/EX TARIFFS ADMIN GOV/REL...TIME/SEQ SENATE HOUSE/REP. PAGE 147 F2900
LEGIS BUDGET CONTROL

S43
HERBERG W.,"BUREAUCRACY AND DEMOCRACY IN LABOR UNIONS." LAW CONSTN STRUCT WORKER ADMIN CONTROL PARTIC RIGID/FLEX PWR TREND. PAGE 59 F1151
LABOR REPRESENT ROUTINE INGP/REL

B44
BIENSTOCK G.,MANAGEMENT IN RUSSIAN INDUSTRY AND AGRICULTURE. USSR CONSULT WORKER LEAD COST PROFIT ATTIT DRIVE PWR...MGT METH/COMP DICTIONARY ACCT 20. PAGE 15 F0281
ADMIN MARXISM SML/CO AGRI

B44
MERRIAM C.E.,PUBLIC AND PRIVATE GOVERNMENT. VOL/ASSN EDU/PROP ADMIN REPRESENT EFFICIENCY PWR PLURISM...MAJORIT CONCPT. PAGE 90 F1762
NAT/G NEIGH MGT POLICY

B46
DAVIES E.,NATIONAL ENTERPRISE: THE DEVELOPMENT OF THE PUBLIC CORPORATION. UK LG/CO EX/STRUC WORKER PROB/SOLV COST ATTIT SOCISM 20. PAGE 30 F0584
ADMIN NAT/G CONTROL INDUS

B46
HARRISON S.M.,AMERICAN FOUNDATIONS FOR SOCIAL WELFARE. OP/RES CONTROL...POLICY MGT METH/CNCPT STAT TREND BIBLIOG. PAGE 56 F1092
GIVE FINAN CLASSIF ADMIN

B47
MILLETT J.D.,THE PROCESS AND ORGANIZATION OF GOVERNMENT PLANNING. USA+45 DELIB/GP ACT/RES LEAD
ADMIN NAT/G

LOBBY TASK...POLICY GEOG TIME 20 RESOURCE/N. PAGE 91 F1793
PLAN CONSULT

B48
HOOVER E.M.,THE LOCATION OF ECONOMIC ACTIVITY. WOR+45 MARKET WORKER PROB/SOLV INT/TRADE ADMIN COST ...POLICY CHARTS T MUNICH 20. PAGE 62 F1211
HABITAT INDUS ECO/TAC GEOG

B48
KESSELMAN L.C.,THE SOCIAL POLITICS OF THE FEPC. INDUS WORKER EDU/PROP GP/REL RACE/REL 20 NEGRO JEWS FEPC. PAGE 70 F1382
POLICY NAT/G ADMIN DISCRIM

B48
SPERO S.D.,GOVERNMENT AS EMPLOYER. USA+45 NAT/G EX/STRUC ADMIN CONTROL EXEC 20. PAGE 124 F2453
SOVEREIGN INGP/REL REPRESENT CONFER

S48
HARDIN L.M.,"REFLECTIONS ON AGRICULTURAL POLICY FORMATION IN THE UNITED STATES." LEGIS PLAN BUDGET ECO/TAC LEAD CENTRAL...MGT SOC NEW/IDEA STAT FAO. PAGE 55 F1078
AGRI POLICY ADMIN NEW/LIB

B49
SCHULTZ W.J.,AMERICAN PUBLIC FINANCE. USA+45 ECO/TAC TAX ADMIN GOV/REL GP/REL INCOME 20. PAGE 117 F2318
FINAN POLICY ECO/DEV NAT/G

B50
KOENIG L.W.,THE SALE OF THE TANKERS. USA+45 SEA DIST/IND POL/PAR DIPLOM ADMIN CIVMIL/REL ATTIT ...DECISION 20 PRESIDENT DEPT/STATE. PAGE 72 F1414
NAT/G POLICY PLAN GOV/REL

B50
LIPSET S.M.,AGRARIAN SOCIALISM. CANADA POL/PAR OP/RES ECO/TAC ADMIN ATTIT...TIME/SEQ NAT/COMP SOC/EXP 20 SASKATCH. PAGE 80 F1576
SOCISM AGRI METH/COMP STRUCT

B50
US DEPARTMENT OF STATE,POINT FOUR: COOPERATIVE PROGRAM FOR AID IN THE DEVELOPMENT OF ECONOMICALLY UNDERDEVELOPED AREAS. WOR+45 AGRI INDUS INT/ORG PLAN TEC/DEV DIPLOM EDU/PROP ADMIN PEACE PRODUC WEALTH 20 CONGRESS UN. PAGE 135 F2671
ECO/UNDEV FOR/AID FINAN INT/TRADE

S50
DALTON M.,"CONFLICTS BETWEEN STAFF AND LINE MANAGERIAL OFFICERS" (BMR). USA+45 USA-45 ELITES LG/CO WORKER PROB/SOLV ADMIN EXEC EFFICIENCY PRODUC ...GP/COMP 20. PAGE 30 F0576
MGT ATTIT GP/REL INDUS

B51
DIMOCK M.E.,FREE ENTERPRISE AND THE ADMINISTRATIVE STATE. FINAN LG/CO BARGAIN BUDGET DOMIN CONTROL INGP/REL EFFICIENCY 20. PAGE 33 F0640
CAP/ISM ADMIN MGT MARKET

B51
HARBISON F.H.,GOALS AND STRATEGY IN COLLECTIVE BARGAINING. WORKER BAL/PWR PARTIC DRIVE...POLICY MGT. PAGE 55 F1074
LABOR BARGAIN GP/REL ADMIN

B51
HARDMAN J.B.,THE HOUSE OF LABOR. LAW R+D NEIGH EDU/PROP LEAD ROUTINE REPRESENT GP/REL...POLICY STAT. PAGE 55 F1080
LABOR LOBBY ADMIN PRESS

B51
US LIBRARY OF CONGRESS,EAST EUROPEAN ACCESSIONS LIST (VOL. I). POL/PAR DIPLOM ADMIN LEAD 20. PAGE 138 F2715
BIBLIOG/A COM SOCIETY NAT/G

B52
ANDREWS F.E.,CORPORATION GIVING. LAW TAX EDU/PROP ADMIN...POLICY STAT CHARTS. PAGE 5 F0101
LG/CO GIVE SML/CO FINAN

B52
REDFORD E.S.,ADMINISTRATION OF NATIONAL ECONOMIC CONTROL. ECO/DEV DELIB/GP ADJUD CONTROL EQUILIB 20. PAGE 110 F2166
ADMIN ROUTINE GOV/REL LOBBY

B53
MILLIKAN M.F.,INCOME STABILIZATION FOR A DEVELOPING DEMOCRACY. USA+45 ECO/DEV LABOR BUDGET ECO/TAC TAX ADMIN ADJUST PRODUC WEALTH...POLICY TREND 20. PAGE 91 F1794
ANTHOL MARKET EQUILIB EFFICIENCY

B53
ROBINSON E.A.G.,THE STRUCTURE OF COMPETITIVE INDUSTRY. UK ECO/DEV DIST/IND MARKET TEC/DEV DIPLOM EDU/PROP ADMIN EFFICIENCY WEALTH...MGT 19/20. PAGE 113 F2217
INDUS PRODUC WORKER OPTIMAL

S53
GABLE R.W.,"NAM: INFLUENTIAL LOBBY OR KISS OF DEATH?" (BMR)" USA+45 LAW INSPECT EDU/PROP ADMIN CONTROL INGP/REL EFFICIENCY PWR 20 CONGRESS NAM TAFT/HART. PAGE 45 F0880
LOBBY LEGIS INDUS LG/CO

S53
LAWTON F.J.,"LEGISLATIVE-EXECUTIVE RELATIONS IN BUDGETING AS VIEWED BY THE EXECUTIVE." NAT/G LEGIS ADMIN REPRESENT EFFICIENCY 20. PAGE 76 F1495
BUDGET EX/STRUC EXEC CONTROL

S53
SIMON H.A.,"BIRTH OF AN ORGANIZATION: THE ECONOMIC COOPERATION ADMINISTRATION." USA+45 PROB/SOLV INGP/REL EFFICIENCY 20. PAGE 122 F2408
ADMIN EX/STRUC EXEC MGT

B54
LOCKLIN D.P.,ECONOMICS OF TRANSPORTATION (4TH ED.). USA+45 USA-45 SEA AIR LAW FINAN LG/CO EX/STRUC ADMIN CONTROL...STAT CHARTS 19/20 RAILROAD PUB/TRANS. PAGE 81 F1592
ECO/DEV DIST/IND ECO/TAC TEC/DEV

B54
MOSK S.A.,INDUSTRIAL REVOLUTION IN MEXICO. MARKET LABOR CREATE CAP/ISM ADMIN ATTIT SOCISM...POLICY 20 MEXIC/AMER. PAGE 94 F1843
INDUS TEC/DEV ECO/UNDEV NAT/G

B55
SMITHIES A.,THE BUDGETARY PROCESS IN THE UNITED STATES. AFR ECO/DEV AGRI EX/STRUC FORCES LEGIS PROB/SOLV TAX ROUTINE EFFICIENCY...MGT CONGRESS PRESIDENT. PAGE 124 F2436
NAT/G ADMIN BUDGET GOV/REL

L55
KISER M.,"ORGANIZATION OF AMERICAN STATES." L/A+17C USA+45 ECO/UNDEV INT/ORG NAT/G PLAN TEC/DEV DIPLOM ECO/TAC INT/TRADE EDU/PROP ADMIN ALL/VALS...POLICY MGT RECORD ORG/CHARTS OAS COMMUN 20. PAGE 71 F1401
VOL/ASSN ECO/DEV REGION

B56
ABELS J.,THE TRUMAN SCANDALS. USA+45 USA-45 POL/PAR TAX LEGIT CT/SYS CHOOSE PRIVIL MORAL WEALTH 20 TRUMAN/HS PRESIDENT CONGRESS. PAGE 2 F0031
CRIME ADMIN CHIEF TRIBUTE

B56
BARBASH J.,THE PRACTICE OF UNIONISM. ECO/TAC LEAD LOBBY GP/REL INGP/REL DRIVE MARXISM BIBLIOG. PAGE 10 F0182
LABOR REPRESENT CONTROL ADMIN

B56
BURKHEAD J.,GOVERNMENT BUDGETING. ECO/DEV PROB/SOLV ECO/TAC ADMIN ROUTINE GOV/REL EFFICIENCY...DECISION MGT. PAGE 20 F0388
BUDGET NAT/G PROVS EX/STRUC

B56
GARDNER R.N.,STERLING-DOLLAR DIPLOMACY. EUR+WWI USA+45 INT/ORG NAT/G PLAN INT/TRADE EDU/PROP ADMIN KNOWL PWR WEALTH...POLICY SOC METH/CNCPT STAT CHARTS SIMUL GEN/LAWS 20. PAGE 46 F0902
ECO/DEV DIPLOM

B56
HICKMAN C.A.,INDIVIDUALS, GROUPS, AND ECONOMIC BEHAVIOR. WORKER PAY CONTROL EXEC GP/REL INGP/REL PERSON ROLE...PSY SOC PERS/COMP METH 20. PAGE 59 F1163
MGT ADMIN ECO/TAC PLAN

B56
REDFORD E.S.,PUBLIC ADMINISTRATION AND POLICY FORMATION: STUDIES IN OIL, GAS, BANKING, RIVER DEVELOPMENT AND CORPORATE INVESTIGATIONS. USA+45 CLIENT NAT/G ADMIN LOBBY REPRESENT GOV/REL INGP/REL 20. PAGE 110 F2167
EX/STRUC PROB/SOLV CONTROL EXEC

B56
UNITED NATIONS,BIBLIOGRAPHY ON INDUSTRIALIZATION IN UNDER-DEVELOPED COUNTRIES. WOR+45 R+D INT/ORG NAT/G FOR/AID ADMIN LEAD 20 UN. PAGE 132 F2612
BIBLIOG ECO/UNDEV INDUS TEC/DEV

B56
WHYTE W.H. JR.,THE ORGANIZATION MAN. CULTURE FINAN VOL/ASSN DOMIN EDU/PROP EXEC DISPL HABITAT ROLE ...PERS/TEST STERTYP. PAGE 146 F2875
ADMIN LG/CO PERSON CONSEN

S56
MYERS C.A.,"LINE AND STAFF IN INDUSTRIAL RELATIONS." INDUS LABOR GP/REL PWR...MGT INT. PAGE 96 F1876
ROLE PROB/SOLV ADMIN CONSULT

B57
MURDESHWAR A.K.,ADMINISTRATIVE PROBLEMS RELATING TO NATIONALISATION: WITH SPECIAL REFERENCE TO INDIAN STATE ENTERPRISES. CZECHOSLVK FRANCE INDIA UK USA+45 LEGIS WORKER PROB/SOLV BUDGET PRICE CONTROL ...MGT GEN/LAWS 20 PARLIAMENT. PAGE 95 F1863
NAT/G OWN INDUS ADMIN

B57
SCHNEIDER E.V.,INDUSTRIAL SOCIOLOGY: THE SOCIAL RELATIONS OF INDUSTRY AND COMMUNITY. STRATA INDUS NAT/G NEIGH CREATE ADMIN PARTIC GP/REL RACE/REL ROLE PWR...POLICY BIBLIOG. PAGE 117 F2308
LABOR MGT INGP/REL STRUCT

B57
UDY S.H. JR.,THE ORGANIZATION OF PRODUCTION IN NONINDUSTRIAL CULTURE. VOL/ASSN DELIB/GP TEC/DEV ...CHARTS BIBLIOG. PAGE 132 F2598
METH/COMP ECO/UNDEV PRODUC ADMIN

S57
ROURKE F.E.,"THE POLITICS OF ADMINISTRATIVE ORGANIZATION: A CASE HISTORY." USA+45 LABOR WORKER PLAN ADMIN TASK EFFICIENCY 20 DEPT/LABOR CONGRESS. PAGE 114 F2251
POLICY ATTIT MGT GP/COMP

N57
U WISCONSIN BUREAU OF GOVT,SERVICE SALES OF THE
REGION

CITY OF MADISON TO METROPOLITAN COMMUNITIES AND NONRESIDENTS (PAMPHLET). DIST/IND LOC/G ADMIN ...DECISION GOV/COMP MUNICH. PAGE 132 F2597 ECO/TAC PLAN

B58
BUGEDA LANZAS J.,A STATEMENT OF THE LAWS OF CUBA IN MATTERS AFFECTING BUSINESS (2ND ED. REV., ENLARGED). CUBA L/A+17C LAW FINAN FAM LEGIS ACT/RES ADMIN GP/REL...BIBLIOG 20 OAS. PAGE 20 F0382 JURID NAT/G INDUS WORKER

B58
CHANG C.,THE INFLATIONARY SPIRAL: THE EXPERIENCE IN CHINA 1939-50. CHINA/COM BUDGET INT/TRADE PRICE ADMIN CONTROL WAR DEMAND...POLICY CHARTS 20. PAGE 23 F0451 FINAN ECO/TAC BAL/PAY GOV/REL

B58
COOK P.L.,EFFECTS OF MERGERS: SIX STUDIES. USA+45 ECO/DEV LABOR LG/CO SML/CO VOL/ASSN ADMIN EFFICIENCY 20 CASEBOOK. PAGE 27 F0529 INDUS FINAN EX/STRUC GP/REL

B58
HOOD W.C.,FINANCING OF ECONOMIC ACTIVITY IN CANADA. CANADA FUT VOL/ASSN WORKER ECO/TAC ADJUD ADMIN ...CHARTS 20. PAGE 61 F1204 BUDGET FINAN GP/REL ECO/DEV

B58
INDIAN INST OF PUBLIC ADMIN,IMPROVING CITY GOVERNMENT. INDIA ECO/UNDEV PLAN BUDGET PARTIC GP/REL MUNICH 20. PAGE 64 F1263 LOC/G PROB/SOLV ADMIN

B58
MASON J.B.,THAILAND BIBLIOGRAPHY. S/ASIA THAILAND CULTURE EDU/PROP ADMIN...GEOG SOC LING 20. PAGE 87 F1701 BIBLIOG/A ECO/UNDEV DIPLOM NAT/G

B58
OGDEN F.D.,THE POLL TAX IN THE SOUTH. USA+45 USA-45 CONSTN ADJUD ADMIN PARTIC CRIME...TIME/SEQ GOV/COMP METH/COMP 18/20 SOUTH/US. PAGE 101 F1982 TAX CHOOSE RACE/REL DISCRIM

B58
PAN AMERICAN UNION,REPERTORIO DE PUBLICACIONES PERIODICAS ACTUALES LATINO-AMERICANAS. CULTURE ECO/UNDEV ADMIN LEAD GOV/REL 20 OAS. PAGE 103 F2023 BIBLIOG L/A+17C NAT/G DIPLOM

B58
SCOTT D.J.R.,RUSSIAN POLITICAL INSTITUTIONS. RUSSIA USSR CONSTN AGRI DELIB/GP PLAN EDU/PROP CONTROL CHOOSE EFFICIENCY ATTIT MARXISM...BIBLIOG/A IND 13/20. PAGE 118 F2332 NAT/G POL/PAR ADMIN DECISION

B58
SHAW S.J.,THE FINANCIAL AND ADMINISTRATIVE ORGANIZATION AND DEVELOPMENT OF OTTOMAN EGYPT 1517-1798. UAR LOC/G FORCES BUDGET INT/TRADE TAX EATING INCOME WEALTH...CHARTS BIBLIOG 16/18 OTTOMAN NAPOLEON/B. PAGE 120 F2371 FINAN ADMIN GOV/REL CULTURE

B58
TAFT P.,CORRUPTION AND RACKETEERING IN THE LABOR MOVEMENT (PAMPHLET). ADMIN SANCTION CENTRAL ROLE WEALTH...POLICY CLASSIF. PAGE 128 F2525 LABOR INGP/REL GP/REL CRIME

B58
UNIVERSITY OF LONDON,THE FAR EAST AND SOUTH-EAST ASIA: A CUMULATED LIST OF PERIODICAL ARTICLES, MAY 1956-APRIL 1957. ASIA S/ASIA LAW ADMIN...LING 20. PAGE 133 F2621 BIBLIOG SOC

B58
US HOUSE COMM POST OFFICE,MANPOWER UTILIZATION IN THE FEDERAL GOVERNMENT. USA+45 DIST/IND EX/STRUC LEGIS CONFER EFFICIENCY 20 CONGRESS CIVIL/SERV. PAGE 137 F2702 ADMIN WORKER DELIB/GP NAT/G

B58
US HOUSE COMM POST OFFICE,MANPOWER UTILIZATION IN THE FEDERAL GOVERNMENT. USA+45 DIST/IND EX/STRUC LEGIS CONFER EFFICIENCY 20 CONGRESS CIVIL/SERV. PAGE 137 F2703 ADMIN WORKER DELIB/GP NAT/G

B58
US OPERATIONS MISSION TO VIET,BUILDING ECONOMIC STRENGTH (PAMPHLET). USA+45 VIETNAM/S INDUS TEC/DEV BUDGET ADMIN EATING HEALTH...STAT 20. PAGE 138 F2725 FOR/AID ECO/UNDEV AGRI EDU/PROP

S58
EMERSON F.D.,"THE ROLES OF MANAGEMENT AND SHAREHOLDERS IN CORPORATE GOVERNMENT." CLIENT DELIB/GP CREATE ADMIN EXEC PARTIC PERS/REL PWR. PAGE 37 F0728 LG/CO LAW INGP/REL REPRESENT

S58
FOLDES L.,"UNCERTAINTY, PROBABILITY AND POTENTIAL SURPRISE." MARKET PROB/SOLV RISK PERSON...DECISION MGT HYPO/EXP GAME. PAGE 42 F0820 PROBABIL ADMIN ROUTINE

B59
GOMEZ ROBLES J.,A STATEMENT OF THE LAWS OF GUATEMALA IN MATTERS AFFECTING BUSINESS (2ND ED. REV., ENLARGED). GUATEMALA L/A+17C LAW FINAN FAM WORKER ACT/RES DIPLOM ADJUD ADMIN GP/REL 20 OAS. PAGE 48 F0945 JURID NAT/G INDUS LEGIT

B59
U OF MICHIGAN LAW SCHOOL,ATOMS AND THE LAW. USA+45 PROVS WORKER PROB/SOLV DIPLOM ADMIN GOV/REL ANTHOL. PAGE 132 F2596 NUC/PWR NAT/G CONTROL LAW

B59
US HOUSE COMM GOVT OPERATIONS,UNITED STATES AID OPERATIONS IN LAOS. LAOS USA+45 PLAN INSPECT HOUSE/REP. PAGE 137 F2697 FOR/AID ADMIN FORCES ECO/UNDEV

S59
BENDIX R.,"INDUSTRIALIZATION, IDEOLOGIES, AND SOCIAL STRUCTURE" (BMR)" UK USA-45 USSR STRUCT WORKER GP/REL EFFICIENCY...IDEA/COMP 20. PAGE 13 F0243 INDUS ATTIT MGT ADMIN

S59
REUBENS E.D.,"THE BASIS FOR REORIENATION OF AMERICAN FOREIGN AID POLICY." USA+45 USSR STRUCT INT/ORG CONSULT ECO/TAC ADMIN DRIVE MORAL ORD/FREE PWR WEALTH...RELATIV MATH STAT TREND GEN/LAWS VAL/FREE 20. PAGE 111 F2180 ECO/UNDEV PLAN FOR/AID DIPLOM

S59
SCHEEHAN D.,"PUBLIC AND PRIVATE GROUPS AS IDENTIFIED IN THE FIELD OF TRADE REGULATIONS." USA+45 ADMIN REPRESENT GOV/REL. PAGE 116 F2293 LAW CONTROL ADJUD LOBBY

S59
SEIDMAN H.,"THE GOVERNMENT CORPORATION IN THE UNITED STATES." USA+45 LEGIS ADMIN PLURISM 20. PAGE 119 F2344 CONTROL GOV/REL EX/STRUC EXEC

S59
SHEENAN D.,"PUBLIC CORPORATIONS AND PUBLIC ACTION." UK ADMIN CONTROL REPRESENT SOCISM 20. PAGE 120 F2372 ECO/DEV EFFICIENCY EX/STRUC EXEC

S59
STINCHCOMBE A.L.,"BUREAUCRATIC AND CRAFT ADMINISTRATION OF PRODUCTION: A COMPARATIVE STUDY" (BMR)" USA+45 STRUCT EX/STRUC ECO/TAC GP/REL ...CLASSIF GP/COMP IDEA/COMP GEN/LAWS 20 WEBER/MAX. PAGE 126 F2490 CONSTRUC PROC/MFG ADMIN PLAN

S59
STREAT R.,"GOVERNMENT CONSULTATION WITH INDUSTRY." UK 20. PAGE 127 F2501 REPRESENT ADMIN EX/STRUC INDUS

S59
TEITSWORTH C.S.,"GROWING ROLE OF THE COMPANY ECONOMIST." USA+45 PLAN PROB/SOLV CAP/ISM ECO/TAC ADMIN ATTIT MGT. PAGE 129 F2541 INDUS CONSULT UTIL DECISION

S59
TIPTON J.B.,"PARTICIPATION OF THE UNITED STATES IN THE INTERNATIONAL LABOR ORGANIZATION." USA+45 LAW STRUCT ECO/DEV ECO/UNDEV INDUS TEC/DEV ECO/TAC ADMIN PERCEPT ORD/FREE SKILL...STAT HIST/WRIT GEN/METH ILO WORK 20. PAGE 131 F2577 LABOR INT/ORG

B60
ANGERS F.A.,ESSAI SUR LA CENTRALISATION: ANALYSE DES PRINCIPES ET PERSPECTIVES CANADIENNES. CANADA ECO/TAC CONTROL...SOC IDEA/COMP BIBLIOG 20. PAGE 6 F0105 CENTRAL ADMIN

B60
ASPREMONT-LYNDEN H.,RAPPORT SUR L'ADMINISTRATION BELGE DU RUANDA-URUNDI PENDANT L'ANNEE 1959. BELGIUM RWANDA AGRI INDUS DIPLOM ECO/TAC INT/TRADE DOMIN ADMIN RACE/REL...GEOG CENSUS 20 UN. PAGE 7 F0132 AFR COLONIAL ECO/UNDEV INT/ORG

B60
BHAMBHRI C.P.,PARLIAMENTARY CONTROL OVER STATE ENTERPRISE IN INDIA. INDIA DELIB/GP ADMIN CONTROL INGP/REL EFFICIENCY 20 PARLIAMENT. PAGE 14 F0277 NAT/G OWN INDUS PARL/PROC

B60
CAMPBELL R.W.,SOVIET ECONOMIC POWER. COM USA+45 DIST/IND MARKET TOP/EX ACT/RES CAP/ISM ECO/TAC DOMIN EDU/PROP ADMIN ROUTINE DRIVE...MATH TIME/SEQ CHARTS WORK 20. PAGE 21 F0409 ECO/DEV PLAN SOCISM USSR

B60
COPLAND D.,THE ADVENTURE OF GROWTH: ESSAYS ON THE AUSTRALIAN ECONOMY AND ITS INTERNATIONAL SETTING. WOR+45 DIST/IND ACADEM EDU/PROP ADMIN INCOME 20 AUSTRAL. PAGE 27 F0534 ECO/DEV ECO/UNDEV ECO/TAC INT/TRADE

B60
FINKLE J.L.,THE PRESIDENT MAKES A DECISION: A STUDY OF DIXON-YATES. OP/RES PROB/SOLV BUDGET ADMIN GOV/REL...POLICY BIBLIOG/A 20 PRESIDENT. PAGE 41 F0799 DECISION CHIEF PWR POL/PAR

B60
FRANCK P.G.,AFGHANISTAN: BETWEEN EAST AND WEST. AFGHANISTN AFR USA+45 USSR ECO/UNDEV PLAN ADMIN ROUTINE ATTIT PWR...STAT OBS CHARTS TOT/POP FOR/TRADE 20. PAGE 43 F0843 ECO/TAC TREND FOR/AID

B60
FRYE R.J.,GOVERNMENT AND LABOR: THE ALABAMA PROGRAM. USA+45 INDUS R+D LABOR WORKER BUDGET EFFICIENCY AGE/Y HEALTH...CHARTS 20 ALABAMA. PAGE 45 F0870 ADMIN LEGIS LOC/G PROVS

B60
GILMORE D.R.,DEVELOPING THE "LITTLE" ECONOMIES. USA+45 FINAN LG/CO PROF/ORG VOL/ASSN CREATE ADMIN. PAGE 47 F0924 ECO/TAC LOC/G PROVS PLAN

B60
GRANICK D.,THE RED EXECUTIVE. COM USA+45 SOCIETY ECO/DEV INDUS NAT/G POL/PAR EX/STRUC PLAN ECO/TAC EDU/PROP ADMIN EXEC ATTIT DRIVE...GP/COMP 20. PAGE 50 F0976 PWR STRATA USSR ELITES

B60
HARBRECHT P.P.,TOWARD THE PARAPROPRIETAL SOCIETY. REPRESENT INCOME OWN PROFIT AGE/O. PAGE 55 F1076 PWR ADMIN ELITES CONTROL

B60
KERR C.,INDUSTRIALISM AND INDUSTRIAL MAN. CULTURE SOCIETY ECO/UNDEV NAT/G ADMIN PRODUC WEALTH ...PREDICT TREND NAT/COMP 19/20. PAGE 70 F1381 WORKER MGT ECO/DEV INDUS

B60
LENCZOWSKI G.,OIL AND STATE IN THE MIDDLE EAST. FUT IRAN LAW ECO/UNDEV EXTR/IND NAT/G TOP/EX PLAN TEC/DEV ECO/TAC LEGIT ADMIN COERCE ATTIT ALL/VALS PWR...CHARTS 20. PAGE 78 F1519 ISLAM INDUS NAT/LISM

B60
MARSHALL A.H.,FINANCIAL ADMINISTRATION IN LOCAL GOVERNMENT. UK DELIB/GP CONFER COST INCOME PERSON ...JURID 20. PAGE 86 F1679 FINAN LOC/G BUDGET ADMIN

B60
PENNSYLVANIA ECONOMY LEAGUE,URBAN RENEWAL IMPACT STUDY: ADMINISTRATIVE-LEGAL-FISCAL. USA+45 FINAN LOC/G NEIGH ADMIN EFFICIENCY...CENSUS CHARTS MUNICH 20 PENNSYLVAN. PAGE 105 F2059 PLAN BUDGET ADJUD

B60
PENTONY D.E.,UNITED STATES FOREIGN AID. INDIA LAOS USA+45 ECO/UNDEV INT/TRADE ADMIN PEACE ATTIT ...POLICY METH/COMP ANTHOL 20. PAGE 105 F2060 FOR/AID DIPLOM ECO/TAC

B60
POOLEY B.J.,THE EVOLUTION OF BRITISH PLANNING LEGISLATION. UK ECO/DEV LOC/G CONSULT DELIB/GP ADMIN MUNICH 20 URBAN/RNWL. PAGE 107 F2104 PLAN LEGIS PROB/SOLV

B60
RAO V.K.R.,INTERNATIONAL AID FOR ECONOMIC DEVELOPMENT - POSSIBILITIES AND LIMITATIONS. FINAN PLAN TEC/DEV ADMIN TASK EFFICIENCY...POLICY SOC METH/CNCPT CHARTS 20 UN. PAGE 109 F2147 FOR/AID DIPLOM INT/ORG ECO/UNDEV

B60
ROBINSON E.A.G.,ECONOMIC CONSEQUENCES OF THE SIZE OF NATIONS. AGRI INDUS DELIB/GP FOR/AID ADMIN EFFICIENCY...METH/COMP 20. PAGE 113 F2218 CONCPT INT/ORG NAT/COMP

B60
ROEPKE W.,A HUMANE ECONOMY: THE SOCIAL FRAMEWORK OF THE FREE MARKET. FUT USSR WOR+45 CULTURE SOCIETY ECO/DEV PLAN ECO/TAC ADMIN ATTIT PERSON RIGID/FLEX SUPEGO MORAL WEALTH SOCISM...POLICY OLD/LIB CONCPT TREND GEN/LAWS 20. PAGE 113 F2232 DRIVE EDU/PROP CAP/ISM

B60
STANFORD RESEARCH INSTITUTE,AFRICAN DEVELOPMENT: A TEST FOR INTERNATIONAL COOPERATION. AFR USA+45 WOR+45 FINAN INT/ORG PLAN PROB/SOLV ECO/TAC INT/TRADE ADMIN...CHARTS 20. PAGE 125 F2467 FOR/AID ECO/UNDEV ATTIT DIPLOM

B60
STEIN E.,AMERICAN ENTERPRISE IN THE EUROPEAN COMMON MARKET: A LEGAL PROFILE. EUR+WWI FUT USA+45 SOCIETY STRUCT ECO/DEV NAT/G VOL/ASSN CONSULT PLAN TEC/DEV ECO/TAC INT/TRADE ADMIN ATTIT RIGID/FLEX PWR...MGT NEW/IDEA STAT TREND COMPUT/IR SIMUL EEC 20. PAGE 125 F2475 MARKET ADJUD INT/LAW

B60
THOMPSON V.A.,THE REGULATORY PROCESS IN OPA RATIONING. USA-45 CLIENT PROB/SOLV ADMIN LOBBY REPRESENT 20. PAGE 130 F2566 EX/STRUC GOV/REL INGP/REL

B60
WHEARE K.C.,THE CONSTITUTIONAL STRUCTURE OF THE COMMONWEALTH. UK EX/STRUC DIPLOM DOMIN ADMIN COLONIAL CONTROL LEAD INGP/REL SUPEGO 20 CMN/WLTH. PAGE 145 F2865 CONSTN INT/ORG VOL/ASSN SOVEREIGN

L60
FUCHS R.F.,"FAIRNESS AND EFFECTIVENESS IN ADMINISTRATIVE AGENCY ORGANIZATION AND PROCEDURES." USA+45 ADJUD ADMIN REPRESENT. PAGE 45 F0872 EFFICIENCY EX/STRUC EXEC POLICY

S60
"THE EMERGING COMMON MARKETS IN LATIN AMERICA." FUT L/A+17C STRATA DIST/IND INDUS LABOR NAT/G LEGIS ECO/TAC ADMIN RIGID/FLEX HEALTH...NEW/IDEA TIME/SEQ OAS 20. PAGE 1 F0013 FINAN ECO/UNDEV INT/TRADE

S60
BUTLER W.F.,"ECONOMIC PROGRESS IN LATIN AMERICA." L/A+17C USA+45 ECO/UNDEV AGRI FINAN NAT/G PLAN ECO/TAC FOR/AID ADMIN WEALTH...OLD/LIB TOT/POP 20. PAGE 21 F0397 INDUS ACT/RES

S60
FRANKEL S.H.,"ECONOMIC ASPECTS OF POLITICAL INDEPENDENCE IN AFRICA." AFR FUT SOCIETY ECO/UNDEV COM/IND FINAN LEGIS PLAN TEC/DEV CAP/ISM ECO/TAC INT/TRADE ADMIN ATTIT DRIVE RIGID/FLEX PWR WEALTH ...MGT NEW/IDEA MATH TIME/SEQ VAL/FREE 20. PAGE 43 F0846 NAT/G FOR/AID

S60
GARNICK D.H.,"ON THE ECONOMIC FEASIBILITY OF A MIDDLE EASTERN COMMON MARKET." AFR ISLAM CULTURE INDUS NAT/G PLAN TEC/DEV ECO/TAC ADMIN ATTIT DRIVE RIGID/FLEX...PLURIST STAT TREND GEN/LAWS 20. PAGE 46 F0907 MARKET INT/TRADE

S60
GROSSMAN G.,"SOVIET GROWTH: ROUTINE, INERTIA, AND PRESSURE." COM STRATA NAT/G DELIB/GP PLAN TEC/DEV ECO/TAC EDU/PROP ADMIN ROUTINE DRIVE WEALTH 20. PAGE 52 F1007 POL/PAR ECO/DEV AFR USSR

S60
HERZ J.H.,"EAST GERMANY: PROGRESS AND PROSPECTS." COM AGRI FINAN INDUS LOC/G NAT/G FORCES PLAN TEC/DEV DOMIN ADMIN COERCE DRIVE PERCEPT RIGID/FLEX MORAL ORD/FREE PWR...MARXIST PSY SOC RECORD STERTYP WORK. PAGE 59 F1158 POL/PAR STRUCT GERMANY

S60
MORALES C.J.,"TRADE AND ECONOMIC INTEGRATION IN LATIN AMERICA." FUT L/A+17C LAW STRATA ECO/UNDEV DIST/IND INDUS LABOR NAT/G LEGIS ECO/TAC ADMIN RIGID/FLEX WEALTH...CONCPT NEW/IDEA CONT/OBS TIME/SEQ WORK 20. PAGE 93 F1825 FINAN INT/TRADE REGION

S60
POLLARD J.A.,"EMERGING PATTERNS OF CORPORATE GIVING." FINAN DELIB/GP PLAN EDU/PROP CENTRAL TREND. PAGE 107 F2098 GIVE LG/CO ADMIN MGT

B61
AGARWAL R.C.,STATE ENTERPRISE IN INDIA. FUT INDIA UK FINAN INDUS ADMIN CONTROL OWN...POLICY CHARTS BIBLIOG 20 RAILROAD. PAGE 3 F0048 ECO/UNDEV SOCISM GOV/REL LG/CO

B61
BEASLEY K.E.,STATE SUPERVISION OF MUNICIPAL DEBT IN KANSAS - A CASE STUDY. USA+45 USA-45 FINAN PROVS BUDGET TAX ADJUD ADMIN CONTROL SUPEGO MUNICH. PAGE 12 F0224 LOC/G LEGIS JURID

B61
CANTERBERY E.R.,THE PRESIDENT'S COUNCIL OF ECONOMIC ADVISERS. AFR USA+45 FINAN LABOR NAT/G PLAN ADMIN OPTIMAL WEALTH 20 EISNHWR/DD PRESIDENT TRUMAN/HS KEYNES/JM. PAGE 21 F0413 ECO/TAC OP/RES EXEC CHIEF

B61
CARNEY D.E.,GOVERNMENT AND ECONOMY IN BRITISH WEST AFRICA. GAMBIA GHANA NIGERIA SIER/LEONE DOMIN ADMIN GOV/REL SOVEREIGN WEALTH LAISSEZ...BIBLIOG 20 CMN/WLTH. PAGE 21 F0417 METH/COMP COLONIAL ECO/TAC ECO/UNDEV

B61
CARROTHERS A.W.R.,LABOR ARBITRATION IN CANADA. CANADA LAW NAT/G CONSULT LEGIS WORKER ADJUD ADMIN CT/SYS 20. PAGE 22 F0422 LABOR MGT GP/REL BARGAIN

B61
DEWITT N.,EDUCATION AND PROFESSIONAL EMPLOYMENT IN THE USSR. USSR PROF/ORG WORKER PLAN ADMIN UTIL AGE/C AGE/Y MARXISM...STAT CHARTS 20. PAGE 32 F0629 EDU/PROP ACADEM SCHOOL INTELL

B61
FRIEDMANN W.G.,JOINT INTERNATIONAL BUSINESS VENTURES. ASIA ISLAM L/A+17C ECO/DEV DIST/IND FINAN PROC/MFG FACE/GP LG/CO NAT/G VOL/ASSN CONSULT EX/STRUC PLAN ADMIN ROUTINE WEALTH...OLD/LIB FOR/TRADE WORK 20. PAGE 44 F0865 ECO/UNDEV INT/TRADE

B61
GORDON R.A.,BUSINESS LEADERSHIP IN THE LARGE CORPORATION. USA+45 SOCIETY EX/STRUC ADMIN CONTROL ROUTINE GP/REL PWR...MGT 20. PAGE 49 F0960 LG/CO LEAD DECISION LOBBY

B61
HART W.R.,COLLECTIVE BARGAINING IN THE FEDERAL CIVIL SERVICE. NAT/G EX/STRUC ADMIN EXEC 20. PAGE 56 F1101 INGP/REL MGT REPRESENT LABOR

B61
LAHAYE R.,LES ENTREPRISES PUBLIQUES AU MAROC. FRANCE MOROCCO LAW DIST/IND EXTR/IND FINAN CONSULT PLAN TEC/DEV ADMIN AGREE CONTROL OWN...POLICY 20. PAGE 74 F1460 NAT/G INDUS ECO/UNDEV ECO/TAC

B61
LEE R.R.,ENGINEERING-ECONOMIC PLANNING MISCELLANEOUS SUBJECTS: A SELECTED BIBLIOGRAPHY (MIMEOGRAPHED). FINAN LOC/G NEIGH ADMIN CONTROL INGP/REL HABITAT...GEOG MGT SOC/WK MUNICH 20 RESOURCE/N. PAGE 77 F1509 BIBLIOG/A PLAN REGION

B61
LENIN V.I.,WHAT IS TO BE DONE? (1902). RUSSIA LABOR NAT/G POL/PAR WORKER CAP/ISM ECO/TAC ADMIN PARTIC ...MARXIST IDEA/COMP GEN/LAWS 19/20. PAGE 78 F1522 EDU/PROP PRESS MARXISM METH/COMP

B61
MACMAHON A.W.,DELEGATION AND AUTONOMY. INDIA STRUCT LEGIS BARGAIN BUDGET ECO/TAC LEGIT EXEC REPRESENT GOV/REL CENTRAL DEMAND EFFICIENCY PRODUC. PAGE 84 F1637
ADMIN PLAN FEDERAL

B61
MARX K.,THE COMMUNIST MANIFESTO. IN (MENDEL A. ESSENTIAL WORKS OF MARXISM, NEW YORK: BANTAM. FUT MOD/EUR CULTURE ECO/DEV ECO/UNDEV AGRI FINAN INDUS MARKET PROC/MFG LABOR POL/PAR CONSULT FORCES CREATE PLAN ADMIN ATTIT DRIVE RIGID/FLEX ORD/FREE PWR RESPECT MARX/KARL MUNICH WORK. PAGE 86 F1691
COM NEW/IDEA CAP/ISM REV

B61
MAYNE A.,DESIGNING AND ADMINISTERING A REGIONAL ECONOMIC DEVELOPMENT PLAN WITH SPECIFIC REFERENCE TO PUERTO RICO (PAMPHLET). PUERT/RICO SOCIETY NAT/G DELIB/GP REGION...DECISION 20. PAGE 87 F1707
ECO/UNDEV PLAN CREATE ADMIN

B61
MIT CENTER INTERNATIONAL STU,OFFICIAL SERIAL PUBLICATIONS RELATING TO ECONOMIC DEVELOPMENT IN AFRICA SOUTH OF THE SAHARA. AFR SOCIETY AGRI FINAN INDUS LG/CO ADMIN 20. PAGE 92 F1806
BIBLIOG ECO/UNDEV ECO/TAC NAT/G

B61
NOVE A.,THE SOVIET ECONOMY. USSR ECO/DEV FINAN NAT/G ECO/TAC PRICE ADMIN EFFICIENCY MARXISM ...TREND BIBLIOG 20. PAGE 99 F1943
PLAN PRODUC POLICY

B61
QURESHI S.,INCENTIVES IN AMERICAN EMPLOYMENT (THESIS, UNIVERSITY OF PENNSYLVANIA). DELIB/GP TOP/EX BUDGET ROUTINE SANCTION COST TECHRACY MGT. PAGE 108 F2134
SERV/IND ADMIN PAY EX/STRUC

B61
SCHNAPPER B.,LA POLITIQUE ET LE COMMERCE FRANCAIS DANS LE GOLFE DE GUINEE DE 1838 A 1871. FRANCE GUINEA UK SEA EXTR/IND NAT/G DELIB/GP LEGIS ADMIN ORD/FREE...POLICY GEOG CENSUS CHARTS BIBLIOG 19. PAGE 117 F2303
COLONIAL INT/TRADE DOMIN AFR

B61
STANLEY C.J.,LATE CH'ING FINANCE: HU KUANG-YUNG AS AN INNOVATOR. ASIA NAT/G FORCES BUDGET TAX WAR GOV/REL COST...POLICY BIOG CHARTS BIBLIOG 19. PAGE 125 F2469
FINAN ECO/TAC CIVMIL/REL ADMIN

B61
US GENERAL ACCOUNTING OFFICE,EXAMINATION OF ECONOMIC AND TECHNICAL ASSISTANCE PROGRAM FOR IRAN. IRAN USA+45 AGRI INDUS DIPLOM CONTROL COST 20. PAGE 136 F2681
FOR/AID ADMIN TEC/DEV ECO/UNDEV

B61
ZEIGLER H.,THE POLITICS OF SMALL BUSINESS. USA+45 EX/STRUC ADMIN 20. PAGE 150 F2963
LOBBY REPRESENT EXEC VOL/ASSN

L61
GERWIG R.,"PUBLIC AUTHORITIES IN THE UNITED STATES." LAW CONSTN PROVS TAX ADMIN FEDERAL MUNICH. PAGE 47 F0920
LOC/G GOV/REL PWR

S61
CYERT R.M.,"TWO EXPERIMENTS ON BIAS AND CONFLICT IN ORGANIZATIONAL ESTIMATION." WORKER PROB/SOLV EFFICIENCY...MGT PSY STAT CHARTS. PAGE 29 F0568
LAB/EXP ROUTINE ADMIN DECISION

S61
NOVE A.,"THE SOVIET MODEL AND UNDERDEVELOPED COUNTRIES." COM FUT USSR WOR+45 CULTURE ECO/DEV POL/PAR FOR/AID EDU/PROP ADMIN MORAL WEALTH ...POLICY RECORD HIST/WRIT 20. PAGE 99 F1942
ECO/UNDEV PLAN

S61
REAGAN M.D.,"THE POLITICAL STRUCTURE OF THE FEDERAL RESERVE SYSTEM." USA+45 FINAN NAT/G ADMIN 20. PAGE 110 F2163
PWR EX/STRUC EXEC LEAD

S61
VINER J.,"ECONOMIC FOREIGN POLICY ON THE NEW FRONTIER." USA+45 ECO/UNDEV AGRI FINAN INDUS MARKET INT/ORG NAT/G FOR/AID INT/TRADE ADMIN ATTIT PWR 20 KENNEDY/JF. PAGE 141 F2786
TOP/EX ECO/TAC BAL/PAY TARIFFS

B62
CARPER E.T.,ILLINOIS GOES TO CONGRESS FOR ARMY LAND. USA+45 LAW EXTR/IND PROVS REGION CIVMIL/REL GOV/REL FEDERAL ATTIT 20 ILLINOIS SENATE CONGRESS DIRKSEN/E DOUGLAS/P. PAGE 22 F0420
ADMIN LOBBY GEOG LEGIS

B62
CHANDLER A.D.,STRATEGY AND STRUCTURE: CHAPTERS IN THE HISTORY OF THE INDUSTRIAL ENTERPRISE. USA+45 USA-45 ECO/DEV EX/STRUC ECO/TAC EXEC...DECISION 20. PAGE 23 F0446
LG/CO PLAN ADMIN FINAN

B62
COLLIER A.T.,MANAGEMENT, MEN, AND VALUES. INDUS FACE/GP EX/STRUC PLAN PROB/SOLV DEBATE SENIOR ADMIN PROFIT PERSON...PSY SOC 20. PAGE 26 F0505
MGT ATTIT PERS/REL DECISION

B62
DIMOCK M.E.,THE NEW AMERICAN POLITICAL ECONOMY: A SYNTHESIS OF POLITICS AND ECONOMICS. USA+45 FINAN LG/CO PLAN ADMIN REGION GP/REL CENTRAL MORAL 20. PAGE 33 F0642
FEDERAL ECO/TAC NAT/G PARTIC

B62
DUPRE J.S.,SCIENCE AND THE NATION: POLICY AND POLITICS. USA+45 LAW ACADEM FORCES ADMIN CIVMIL/REL GOV/REL EFFICIENCY PEACE...TREND 20 SCI/ADVSRY. PAGE 35 F0682
R+D INDUS TEC/DEV NUC/PWR

B62
FORD A.G.,THE GOLD STANDARD 1880-1914: BRITAIN AND ARGENTINA. AFR UK ECO/UNDEV INT/TRADE ADMIN GOV/REL DEMAND EFFICIENCY...STAT CHARTS 19/20 ARGEN. PAGE 42 F0823
FINAN ECO/TAC BUDGET BAL/PAY

B62
FRIEDMANN W.,METHODS AND POLICIES OF PRINCIPAL DONOR COUNTRIES IN PUBLIC INTERNATIONAL DEVELOPMENT FINANCING: PRELIMINARY APPRAISAL. FRANCE GERMANY/W UK USA+45 USSR WOR+45 FINAN TEC/DEV CAP/ISM DIPLOM ECO/TAC ATTIT 20 EEC. PAGE 44 F0864
INT/ORG FOR/AID NAT/COMP ADMIN

B62
GROVE J.W.,GOVERNMENT AND INDUSTRY IN BRITAIN. UK FINAN LOC/G CONSULT DELIB/GP INT/TRADE ADMIN CONTROL...BIBLIOG 20. PAGE 52 F1008
ECO/TAC INDUS NAT/G GP/REL

B62
KUHN T.E.,PUBLIC ENTERPRISES, PROJECT PLANNING AND ECONOMIC DEVELOPMENT (PAMPHLET). ECO/UNDEV FINAN PLAN ADMIN EFFICIENCY OWN...MGT STAT CHARTS ANTHOL 20. PAGE 74 F1447
ECO/DEV ECO/TAC LG/CO NAT/G

B62
LITTLEFIELD N.,METROPOLITAN AREA PROBLEMS AND MUNICIPAL HOME RULE. USA+45 PROVS ADMIN CONTROL GP/REL PWR. PAGE 81 F1586
LOC/G SOVEREIGN JURID LEGIS

B62
MEANS G.C.,THE CORPORATE REVOLUTION IN AMERICA: ECONOMIC REALITY VS. ECONOMIC THEORY. USA+45 USA-45 INDUS WORKER PLAN CAP/ISM ADMIN...IDEA/COMP 20. PAGE 89 F1742
LG/CO MARKET CONTROL PRICE

B62
MOWITZ R.J.,PROFILE OF A METROPOLIS: A CASE BOOK. COM/IND CONSTRUC INDUS PUB/INST PLAN TEC/DEV LEAD GP/REL...POLICY TECHNIC WELF/ST MUNICH. PAGE 94 F1851
DECISION ADMIN

B62
PRAKASH O.M.,THE THEORY AND WORKING OF STATE CORPORATIONS: WITH SPECIAL REFERENCE TO INDIA. INDIA UK USA+45 TOP/EX PRICE ADMIN EFFICIENCY...MGT METH/COMP 20 TVA. PAGE 107 F2112
LG/CO ECO/UNDEV GOV/REL SOCISM

B62
SELOSOEMARDJAN O.,SOCIAL CHANGES IN JOGJAKARTA. INDONESIA NETHERLAND ELITES STRATA STRUCT FAM POL/PAR CREATE DIPLOM INT/TRADE EDU/PROP ADMIN GOV/REL...SOC 20 JAVA CHINJAP. PAGE 119 F2352
ECO/UNDEV CULTURE REV COLONIAL

B62
SMITH G.A. JR.,POLICY FORMULATION AND ADMINISTRATION: A CASEBOOK OF TOPMANAGEMENT PROBLEMS IN BUSINESS. EX/STRUC PLAN PROB/SOLV ADMIN CONTROL EXEC LEAD ROUTINE EFFICIENCY ATTIT MGT. PAGE 123 F2430
INDUS SOC/EXP TOP/EX DECISION

B62
UNECA LIBRARY,NEW ACQUISITIONS IN THE UNECA LIBRARY. LAW NAT/G PLAN PROB/SOLV TEC/DEV ADMIN REGION...GEOG SOC 20 UN. PAGE 132 F2606
BIBLIOG AFR ECO/UNDEV INT/ORG

B62
URQUIDI C.W.,A STATEMENT OF THE LAWS OF BOLIVIA IN MATTERS AFFECTING BUSINESS (3RD ED. REV., ENLARGED). L/A+17C LAW FINAN FAM WORKER ACT/RES DIPLOM ADJUD ADMIN GP/REL 20 BOLIV OAS. PAGE 133 F2626
JURID INDUS NAT/G LEGIT

B62
US LIBRARY OF CONGRESS,A LIST OF AMERICAN DOCTORAL DISSERTATIONS ON AFRICA. SOCIETY SECT DIPLOM EDU/PROP ADMIN...GEOG 19/20. PAGE 138 F2717
BIBLIOG AFR ACADEM CULTURE

B62
WENDT P.F.,HOUSING POLICY - THE SEARCH FOR SOLUTIONS. GERMANY/W SWEDEN UK USA+45 OP/RES HABITAT WEALTH...SOC/WK CHARTS 20. PAGE 145 F2856
PLAN ADMIN METH/COMP NAT/G

L62
BELSHAW D.G.R.,"PUBLIC INVESTMENT IN AGRICULTURE AND ECONOMIC DEVELOPMENT OF UGANDA" UGANDA AGRI INDUS R+D ECO/TAC RATION TAX PAY COLONIAL 20 WORLD/BANK. PAGE 13 F0242
ECO/UNDEV PLAN ADMIN CENTRAL

L62
ERDMANN H.H.,"ADMINISTRATIVE LAW AND FARM ECONOMICS." USA+45 LOC/G NAT/G PLAN PROB/SOLV LOBBY ...DECISION ANTHOL 20. PAGE 38 F0744
AGRI ADMIN ADJUD POLICY

S62
GILL P.J.,"FUTURE TAXATION POLICY IN AN INDEPENDENT EAST AFRICA" UGANDA LOC/G ECO/TAC ADMIN EFFICIENCY INCOME PRODUC...CHARTS 20. PAGE 47 F0923
ECO/UNDEV TAX AFR COLONIAL

S62
READ W.H.,"UPWARD COMMUNICATION IN INDUSTRIAL HIERARCHIES." LG/CO TOP/EX PROB/SOLV DOMIN EXEC
ADMIN INGP/REL

PERS/REL ATTIT DRIVE PERCEPT...CORREL STAT CHARTS 20. PAGE 110 F2159
PSY MGT

B63
BONINI C.P.,SIMULATION OF INFORMATION AND DECISION SYSTEMS IN THE FIRM. MARKET BUDGET DOMIN EDU/PROP ADMIN COST ATTIT HABITAT PERCEPT PWR...CONCPT PROBABIL QUANT PREDICT HYPO/EXP BIBLIOG. PAGE 16 F0313
INDUS SIMUL DECISION MGT

B63
BRAIBANTI R.J.D.,ADMINISTRATION AND ECONOMIC DEVELOPMENT IN INDIA. INDIA S/ASIA SOCIETY STRATA ECO/TAC PERSON WEALTH...MGT GEN/LAWS TOT/POP VAL/FREE 20. PAGE 18 F0337
ECO/UNDEV ADMIN

B63
BROUDE H.W.,STEEL DECISIONS AND THE NATIONAL ECONOMY. USA+45 LG/CO PLAN ADMIN COST DECISION. PAGE 19 F0365
PROC/MFG NAT/G CONTROL ECO/TAC

B63
CHAMPION J.M.,CRITICAL INCIDENTS IN MANAGEMENT. MARKET LG/CO SML/CO OP/RES ADMIN CONTROL LEAD GP/REL PERS/REL COST ATTIT SUPEGO ALL/VALS...PSY PERS/TEST BIBLIOG. PAGE 23 F0445
MGT DECISION EX/STRUC INDUS

B63
CHOJNACKI S.,REGISTER ON CURRENT RESEARCH ON ETHIOPIA AND THE HORN OF AFRICA. ETHIOPIA LAW CULTURE AGRI SECT EDU/PROP ADMIN...GEOG HEAL LING 20. PAGE 24 F0470
BIBLIOG ACT/RES INTELL ACADEM

B63
CONF ON FUTURE OF COMMONWEALTH,THE FUTURE OF THE COMMONWEALTH. AFR UK ECO/UNDEV AGRI EDU/PROP ADMIN SOC/INTEG 20. PAGE 27 F0522
DIPLOM RACE/REL ORD/FREE TEC/DEV

B63
CORLEY R.N.,THE LEGAL ENVIRONMENT OF BUSINESS. CONSTN LEGIS TAX ADMIN CT/SYS DISCRIM ATTIT PWR ...TREND 18/20. PAGE 28 F0537
NAT/G INDUS JURID DECISION

B63
DE VRIES E.,SOCIAL ASPECTS OF ECONOMIC DEVELOPMENT IN LATIN AMERICA. CULTURE SOCIETY STRATA FINAN INDUS INT/ORG DELIB/GP ACT/RES ECO/TAC EDU/PROP ADMIN ATTIT SUPEGO HEALTH KNOWL ORD/FREE...SOC STAT TREND ANTHOL TOT/POP VAL/FREE. PAGE 31 F0608
L/A+17C ECO/UNDEV

B63
DUE J.F.,STATE SALES TAX ADMINISTRATION. OP/RES BUDGET PAY ADMIN EXEC ROUTINE COST EFFICIENCY PROFIT...CHARTS METH/COMP 20. PAGE 34 F0671
PROVS TAX STAT GOV/COMP

B63
HATHAWAY D.A.,GOVERNMENT AND AGRICULTURE: PUBLIC POLICY IN A DEMOCRATIC SOCIETY. USA+45 LEGIS ADMIN EXEC LOBBY REPRESENT PWR 20. PAGE 57 F1111
AGRI GOV/REL PROB/SOLV EX/STRUC

B63
INTERAMERICAN ECO AND SOC COUN,THE ALLIANCE FOR PROGRESS: ITS FIRST YEAR: 1961-1962. AGRI SCHOOL PLAN TEC/DEV INT/TRADE TAX GIVE ADMIN WEALTH...SOC 20 ALL/PROG SOUTH/AMER. PAGE 64 F1267
INT/ORG PROB/SOLV ECO/TAC L/A+17C

B63
KAPP W.K.,HINDU CULTURE: ECONOMIC DEVELOPMENT AND ECONOMIC PLANNING IN INDIA. INDIA S/ASIA CULTURE ECO/TAC EDU/PROP ADMIN ALL/VALS...POLICY MGT TIME/SEQ TRUE/GP VAL/FREE 20. PAGE 69 F1353
SECT ECO/UNDEV

B63
LINDBERG L.,POLITICAL DYNAMICS OF EUROPEAN ECONOMIC INTEGRATION. EUR+WWI ECO/DEV INT/ORG VOL/ASSN DELIB/GP ADMIN WEALTH...DECISION EEC TERR/GP 20. PAGE 80 F1567
MARKET ECO/TAC

B63
MEYNAUD J.,PLANIFICATION ET POLITIQUE. FRANCE ITALY FINAN LABOR DELIB/GP LEGIS ADMIN EFFICIENCY ...MAJORIT DECISION 20. PAGE 90 F1773
PLAN ECO/TAC PROB/SOLV

B63
OLSON M. JR.,THE ECONOMICS OF WARTIME SHORTAGE. FRANCE GERMANY MOD/EUR UK AGRI PROB/SOLV ADMIN DEMAND WEALTH...POLICY OLD/LIB FOR/TRADE 17/20. PAGE 101 F1990
WAR ADJUST ECO/TAC NAT/COMP

B63
PREST A.R.,PUBLIC FINANCE IN UNDERDEVELOPED COUNTRIES. UK WOR+45 WOR-45 SOCIETY INT/ORG NAT/G LEGIS ACT/RES PLAN ECO/TAC ADMIN ROUTINE...CHARTS 20. PAGE 108 F2115
FINAN ECO/UNDEV NIGERIA

B63
SCHOECK H.,THE NEW ARGUMENT IN ECONOMICS. UK USA+45 INDUS MARKET LABOR NAT/G ECO/TAC ADMIN ROUTINE BAL/PAY PWR...POLICY BOLIV. PAGE 117 F2309
WELF/ST FOR/AID ECO/DEV ALL/IDEOS

B63
SELF P.,THE STATE AND THE FARMER. UK ECO/DEV MARKET WORKER PRICE CONTROL GP/REL...WELF/ST 20 DEPT/AGRI. PAGE 119 F2346
AGRI NAT/G ADMIN VOL/ASSN

B63
SHANKS M.,THE LESSONS OF PUBLIC ENTERPRISE. UK LEGIS WORKER ECO/TAC ADMIN PARL/PROC GOV/REL ATTIT ...POLICY MGT METH/COMP NAT/COMP ANTHOL 20 PARLIAMENT. PAGE 120 F2364
SOCISM OWN NAT/G INDUS

B63
STIFEL L.D.,THE TEXTILE INDUSTRY - A CASE STUDY OF INDUSTRIAL DEVELOPMENT IN THE PHILIPPINES (PAPER). PHILIPPINE WORKER CAP/ISM INT/TRADE TARIFFS RECEIVE PRICE ADMIN COST EFFICIENCY WEALTH...BIBLIOG 20. PAGE 126 F2486
S/ASIA ECO/UNDEV PROC/MFG NAT/G

B63
UN SECRETARY GENERAL,PLANNING FOR ECONOMIC DEVELOPMENT. ECO/UNDEV FINAN BUDGET INT/TRADE TARIFFS TAX ADMIN 20 UN. PAGE 132 F2603
PLAN ECO/TAC MGT NAT/COMP

S63
CARTER A.G.T.,"THE BALANCE OF PAYMENTS OF EAST AFRICA" AFR ECO/TAC FOR/AID RATION TARIFFS TAX ADMIN...STAT 20 AFRICA/E. PAGE 22 F0423
BUDGET ECO/UNDEV BAL/PAY INT/TRADE

S63
MARTHELOT P.,"PROGRES DE LA REFORME AGRAIRE." INTELL ECO/DEV R+D FOR/AID ADMIN KNOWL...OBS VAL/FREE UN 20. PAGE 86 F1680
AGRI INT/ORG

S63
SCHURMANN F.,"ECONOMIC POLICY AND POLITICAL POWER IN COMMUNIST CHINA." ASIA CHINA/COM USSR SOCIETY ECO/UNDEV AGRI INDUS CREATE ADMIN ROUTINE ATTIT DRIVE RIGID/FLEX PWR WEALTH...HIST/WRIT TREND CHARTS WORK 20. PAGE 118 F2323
PLAN ECO/TAC

B64
THE SPECIAL COMMONWEALTH AFRICAN ASSISTANCE PLAN. AFR CANADA INDIA NIGERIA UK FINAN SCHOOL...CHARTS 20 COMMONWLTH. PAGE 1 F0019
ECO/UNDEV TREND FOR/AID ADMIN

B64
AHMAD M.,THE CIVIL SERVANT IN PAKISTAN. PAKISTAN ECO/UNDEV COLONIAL INGP/REL...SOC CHARTS BIBLIOG 20 CIVIL/SERV. PAGE 3 F0051
WELF/ST ADMIN ATTIT STRATA

B64
BAUCHET P.,ECONOMIC PLANNING. FRANCE STRATA LG/CO CAP/ISM ADMIN PARL/PROC DEMAND OPTIMAL ATTIT PWR SOCISM...POLICY CHARTS 20. PAGE 11 F0212
ECO/DEV NAT/G PLAN ECO/TAC

B64
BLACKSTOCK P.W.,THE STRATEGY OF SUBVERSION. USA+45 FORCES EDU/PROP ADMIN COERCE GOV/REL...DECISION MGT 20 DEPT/DEFEN CIA DEPT/STATE. PAGE 15 F0292
ORD/FREE DIPLOM CONTROL

B64
BROWN C.V.,GOVERNMENT AND BANKING IN WESTERN NIGERIA. AFR NIGERIA GOV/REL GP/REL...POLICY 20. PAGE 19 F0367
ADMIN ECO/UNDEV FINAN NAT/G

B64
CHANDLER A.D. JR.,GIANT ENTERPRISE: FORD, GENERAL MOTORS, AND THE AUTOMOBILE INDUSTRY; SOURCES AND READINGS. USA+45 USA-45 FINAN MARKET CREATE ADMIN ...TIME/SEQ ANTHOL 20 AUTOMOBILE. PAGE 23 F0447
LG/CO DIST/IND LABOR MGT

B64
CHEIT E.F.,THE BUSINESS ESTABLISHMENT. FRANCE WOR+45 PROF/ORG TOP/EX PROB/SOLV CAP/ISM ADMIN SUPEGO MORAL PWR...METH/CNCPT MYTH NEW/IDEA 20. PAGE 24 F0460
PERSON EX/STRUC MGT INDUS

B64
COLUMBIA U SCHOOL OF LAW,PUBLIC INTERNATIONAL DEVELOPMENT FINANCING IN INDIA. GERMANY/W INDIA UK USA+45 INDUS PLAN TEC/DEV DIPLOM ECO/TAC GIVE ADMIN UTIL ATTIT 20. PAGE 26 F0512
ECO/UNDEV FINAN FOR/AID INT/ORG

B64
FATOUROS A.A.,CANADA'S OVERSEAS AID. CANADA WOR+45 ECO/DEV FINAN NAT/G BUDGET ECO/TAC CONFER ADMIN 20. PAGE 39 F0768
FOR/AID DIPLOM ECO/UNDEV POLICY

B64
FISK W.M.,ADMINISTRATIVE PROCEDURE IN A REGULATORY AGENCY: THE CAB AND THE NEW YORK-CHICAGO CASE (PAMPHLET). USA+45 DIST/IND ADMIN CONTROL LOBBY GP/REL ROLE ORD/FREE NEWYORK/C CHICAGO CAB. PAGE 41 F0805
SERV/IND ECO/DEV AIR JURID

B64
FLORENCE P.S.,ECONOMICS AND SOCIOLOGY OF INDUSTRY; A REALISTIC ANALYSIS OF DEVELOPMENT. ECO/UNDEV LG/CO NAT/G PLAN...GEOG MGT BIBLIOG 20. PAGE 42 F0814
INDUS SOC ADMIN

B64
GARFIELD PJ LOVEJOY WF,PUBLIC UTILITY ECONOMICS. DIST/IND FINAN MARKET ADMIN COST DEMAND ...TECHNIC JURID MUNICH 20 MONOPOLY. PAGE 46 F0906
T ECO/TAC OWN SERV/IND

B64
GREBLER L.,URBAN RENEWAL IN EUROPEAN COUNTRIES: ITS EMERGENCE AND POTENTIALS. EUR+WWI UK ECO/DEV LOC/G NEIGH CREATE ADMIN ATTIT...TREND NAT/COMP MUNICH 20 URBAN/RNWL. PAGE 50 F0981
PLAN CONSTRUC NAT/G

B64
HAMBRIDGE G.,DYNAMICS OF DEVELOPMENT. AGRI FINAN INDUS LABOR INT/TRADE EDU/PROP ADMIN LEAD OWN
ECO/UNDEV ECO/TAC

HEALTH...ANTHOL BIBLIOG 20. PAGE 54 F1054 — OP/RES ACT/RES

B64
HERSKOVITS M.J.,ECONOMIC TRANSITION IN AFRICA. FUT INT/ORG NAT/G WORKER PROB/SOLV TEC/DEV INT/TRADE EQUILIB INCOME...ANTHOL 20. PAGE 59 F1157 — AFR ECO/UNDEV PLAN ADMIN

B64
KAPLAN A.D.H.,BIG ENTERPRISE IN A COMPETITIVE SYSTEM (REV. ED.). USA+45 INDUS MARKET WORKER TEC/DEV ECO/TAC PRICE ADJUD ADMIN CONTROL...MGT CHARTS 20 MONOPOLY. PAGE 69 F1351 — FINAN GP/REL NAT/G LG/CO

B64
LITTLE I.M.D.,AID TO AFRICA. AFR UK TEC/DEV DIPLOM ECO/TAC INCOME WEALTH 20. PAGE 81 F1583 — FOR/AID ECO/UNDEV ADMIN POLICY

B64
MARSH D.C.,THE FUTURE OF THE WELFARE STATE. UK CONSTN NAT/G POL/PAR...POLICY WELF/ST 20. PAGE 86 F1676 — NEW/LIB ADMIN CONCPT INSPECT

B64
MCNULTY J.E.,SOME ECONOMIC ASPECTS OF BUSINESS ORGANIZATION. ECO/DEV UTIL...MGT CHARTS BIBLIOG METH 20. PAGE 88 F1734 — ADMIN LG/CO GEN/LAWS

B64
NOSSITER B.D.,THE MYTHMAKERS: AN ESSAY ON POWER AND WEALTH. USA+45 LG/CO NAT/G TOP/EX PROB/SOLV ADMIN GP/REL ORD/FREE 20. PAGE 99 F1937 — ECO/TAC WEALTH FINAN PLAN

B64
PRESTHUS R.,MEN AT THE TOP; A STUDY IN COMMUNITY POWER. USA+45 STRUCT ACT/RES REPRESENT CONSEN ALL/VALS ORD/FREE...SAMP/SIZ 20. PAGE 108 F2116 — PLURISM LG/CO PWR ADMIN

B64
SULLIVAN G.,THE STORY OF THE PEACE CORPS. USA+45 WOR+45 INTELL FACE/GP NAT/G SCHOOL VOL/ASSN CONSULT EX/STRUC PLAN EDU/PROP ADMIN ATTIT DRIVE ALL/VALS ...POLICY HEAL SOC CONCPT INT QU BIOG TREND SOC/EXP WORK. PAGE 127 F2511 — INT/ORG ECO/UNDEV FOR/AID PEACE

B64
US DEPT LABOR OFF SOLICITOR,LEGISLATIVE HISTORY OF THE LABOR-MANAGEMENT AND DISCLOSURE ACT OF 1959. DELIB/GP WORKER ADMIN LOBBY PARL/PROC SANCTION CHOOSE GOV/REL 20 CONGRESS PRESIDENT. PAGE 136 F2677 — LABOR LEGIS DEBATE POLICY

B64
WEIDENBAUM M.L.,CONGRESS AND THE FEDERAL BUDGET: FEDERAL BUDGETING AND THE RESPONSIBLE USE OF POWER. LOC/G PLAN TAX CONGRESS. PAGE 144 F2843 — LEGIS EX/STRUC BUDGET ADMIN

B64
WELLISZ S.,THE ECONOMICS OF THE SOVIET BLOC. COM USSR INDUS WORKER PLAN BUDGET INT/TRADE TAX PRICE PRODUC WEALTH MARXISM...METH/COMP 20. PAGE 145 F2854 — EFFICIENCY ADMIN MARKET

B64
WERNETTE J.P.,GOVERNMENT AND BUSINESS. LABOR CAP/ISM ECO/TAC INT/TRADE TAX ADMIN AUTOMAT NUC/PWR CIVMIL/REL DEMAND...MGT 20 MONOPOLY. PAGE 145 F2859 — NAT/G FINAN ECO/DEV CONTROL

B64
WITHERELL J.W.,OFFICIAL PUBLICATIONS OF FRENCH EQUATORIAL AFRICA, FRENCH CAMEROONS, AND TOGO, 1946-1958 (PAMPHLET). CAMEROON CHAD FRANCE GABON TOGO LAW ECO/UNDEV EXTR/IND INT/TRADE...GEOG HEAL 20. PAGE 148 F2913 — BIBLIOG/A AFR NAT/G ADMIN

S64
CARNEGIE ENDOWMENT INT. PEACE,"ADMINISTRATION AND BUDGET (ISSUES BEFORE THE NINETEENTH GENERAL ASSEMBLY)." WOR+45 FINAN BUDGET ECO/TAC ROUTINE COST...STAT RECORD UN. PAGE 21 F0415 — INT/ORG ADMIN

S64
HORECKY P.L.,"LIBRARY OF CONGRESS PUBLICATIONS IN AID OF USSR AND EAST EUROPEAN RESEARCH." BULGARIA CZECHOSLVK POLAND USSR YUGOSLAVIA NAT/G POL/PAR DIPLOM ADMIN GOV/REL...CLASSIF 20. PAGE 62 F1214 — BIBLIOG/A COM MARXISM

S64
NEWLYN W.T.,"MONETARY SYSTEMS AND INTEGRATION" AFR BUDGET ADMIN FEDERAL PRODUC PROFIT UTIL...CHARTS 20 AFRICA/E. PAGE 98 F1922 — ECO/UNDEV REGION METH/COMP FINAN

S64
STONE P.A.,"DECISION TECHNIQUES FOR TOWN DEVELOPMENT." PLAN COST PROFIT...DECISION MGT CON/ANAL CHARTS METH/COMP BIBLIOG MUNICH 20. PAGE 127 F2497 — OP/RES ADMIN PROB/SOLV

C64
GOLDMAN M.I.,"COMPARATIVE ECONOMIC SYSTEMS: A READER." COM ECO/UNDEV NAT/G BUDGET CAP/ISM ADMIN TOTALISM MARXISM SOCISM...MGT ANTHOL BIBLIOG 19/20. PAGE 48 F0938 — NAT/COMP CONTROL IDEA/COMP

C64
NORGREN P.H.,"TOWARD FAIR EMPLOYMENT." USA+45 LAW — RACE/REL

STRATA LABOR NAT/G FORCES ACT/RES ADMIN ATTIT ...POLICY BIBLIOG 20 NEGRO. PAGE 98 F1932 — DISCRIM WORKER MGT

B65
AMERICAN ECONOMIC ASSOCIATION,INDEX OF ECONOMIC JOURNALS 1886-1965 (7 VOLS.). UK USA+45 USA-45 AGRI FINAN PLAN ECO/TAC INT/TRADE ADMIN...STAT CENSUS 19/20. PAGE 5 F0087 — BIBLIOG WRITING INDUS

B65
APTER D.E.,THE POLITICS OF MODERNIZATION. AFR L/A+17C CULTURE NAT/G POL/PAR ADMIN COLONIAL NAT/LISM ATTIT RIGID/FLEX PWR...SOC CONCPT. PAGE 6 F0109 — ECO/UNDEV GEN/LAWS STRATA CREATE

B65
BOCK E.,GOVERNMENT REGULATION OF BUSINESS. USA+45 LAW EX/STRUC LEGIS EXEC ORD/FREE PWR...ANTHOL CONGRESS. PAGE 16 F0303 — MGT ADMIN NAT/G CONTROL

B65
COPELAND M.A.,OUR FREE ENTERPRISE ECONOMY. USA+45 INDUS LABOR ADMIN CONTROL GP/REL MGT. PAGE 27 F0533 — CAP/ISM PLAN FINAN ECO/DEV

B65
DUGGAR G.S.,RENEWAL OF TOWN AND VILLAGE I: A WORLD-WIDE SURVEY OF LOCAL GOVERNMENT EXPERIENCE. WOR+45 CONSTRUC INDUS CREATE BUDGET REGION GOV/REL...QU NAT/COMP MUNICH 20 URBAN/RNWL. PAGE 35 F0673 — NEIGH PLAN ADMIN

B65
FLASH E.S. JR.,ECONOMIC ADVICE AND PRESIDENTIAL LEADERSHIP: THE COUNCIL OF ECONOMIC ADVISORS. USA+45 NAT/G EX/STRUC LEGIS TOP/EX ACT/RES ADMIN PRESIDENT CONGRESS. PAGE 41 F0808 — PLAN CONSULT CHIEF

B65
FRYE R.J.,HOUSING AND URBAN RENEWAL IN ALABAMA. USA+45 NEIGH LEGIS BUDGET ADJUD ADMIN PARTIC...MGT MUNICH 20 ALABAMA URBAN/RNWL. PAGE 45 F0871 — PROB/SOLV PLAN GOV/REL

B65
GOODSELL C.T.,ADMINISTRATION OF A REVOLUTION. PUERT/RICO ECO/UNDEV FINAN POL/PAR PROVS LEGIS PLAN BUDGET RECEIVE ADMIN COLONIAL LEAD MUNICH 20 ROOSEVLT/F. PAGE 49 F0951 — EXEC SOC

B65
GORDON W.,THE POLITICAL ECONOMY OF LATIN AMERICA. L/A+17C FINAN MARKET PROB/SOLV TEC/DEV RECEIVE ADMIN WEALTH 20. PAGE 49 F0962 — ECO/UNDEV INT/TRADE REGION POLICY

B65
GREER S.,URBAN RENEWAL AND AMERICAN CITIES: THE DILEMMA OF DEMOCRATIC INTERVENTION. USA+45 R+D LOC/G VOL/ASSN ACT/RES BUDGET ADMIN GOV/REL...SOC INT SAMP MUNICH 20 BOSTON CHICAGO LOS/ANG MIAMI URBAN/RNWL. PAGE 51 F0992 — PROB/SOLV PLAN NAT/G

B65
INT. BANK RECONSTR. DEVELOP.,ECONOMIC DEVELOPMENT OF KUWAIT. ISLAM KUWAIT AGRI FINAN MARKET EX/STRUC TEC/DEV ECO/TAC ADMIN WEALTH...OBS CON/ANAL CHARTS 20. PAGE 64 F1266 — INDUS NAT/G

B65
KASER M.,COMECON* INTEGRATION PROBLEMS OF THE PLANNED ECONOMIES. INT/ORG TEC/DEV INT/TRADE PRICE ADMIN ADJUST CENTRAL...STAT TIME/SEQ ORG/CHARTS COMECON. PAGE 69 F1359 — PLAN ECO/DEV COM REGION

B65
LEYS C.T.,FEDERATION IN EAST AFRICA. LAW AGRI DIST/IND FINAN INT/ORG LABOR INT/TRADE CONFER ADMIN CONTROL GP/REL...ANTHOL 20 AFRICA/E. PAGE 79 F1554 — FEDERAL REGION ECO/UNDEV PLAN

B65
LUTZ V.,FRENCH PLANNING. FRANCE TEC/DEV RIGID/FLEX ORD/FREE 20. PAGE 82 F1613 — PLAN ADMIN FUT

B65
MACDONALD R.W.,THE LEAGUE OF ARAB STATES: A STUDY IN THE DYNAMICS OF REGIONAL ORGANIZATION. ISRAEL UAR USSR FINAN INT/ORG DELIB/GP ECO/TAC AGREE NEUTRAL ORD/FREE PWR...DECISION BIBLIOG 20 TREATY UN. PAGE 83 F1626 — ISLAM REGION DIPLOM ADMIN

B65
MELMANS S.,OUR DEPLETED SOCIETY. AFR SPACE USA+45 ECO/DEV FORCES BUDGET ECO/TAC ADMIN WEAPON EFFICIENCY 20. PAGE 89 F1753 — CIVMIL/REL INDUS EDU/PROP CONTROL

B65
MORRIS M.D.,THE EMERGENCE OF AN INDUSTRIAL LABOR FORCE IN INDIA: A STUDY OF THE BOMBAY COTTON MILLS, 1854-1947. INDIA WORKER OP/RES ADMIN 19/20. PAGE 94 F1837 — INDUS LABOR ECO/UNDEV CAP/ISM

B65
OECD,MEDITERRANEAN REGIONAL PROJECT: TURKEY; EDUCATION AND DEVELOPMENT. FUT TURKEY SOCIETY STRATA FINAN NAT/G PROF/ORG PLAN PROB/SOLV ADMIN COST...STAT CHARTS 20 OECD. PAGE 100 F1969 — EDU/PROP ACADEM SCHOOL ECO/UNDEV

B65
OECD,THE MEDITERRANEAN REGIONAL PROJECT: PORTUGAL; EDUCATION AND DEVELOPMENT. PORTUGAL SOCIETY STRATA — EDU/PROP SCHOOL

FINAN PROF/ORG WORKER PLAN PROB/SOLV ADMIN...POLICY STAT CHARTS METH 20 OECD. PAGE 100 F1970
ACADEM ECO/UNDEV

B65
OECD,THE MEDITERRANEAN REGIONAL PROJECT: ITALY; EDUCATION AND DEVELOPMENT. ITALY SOCIETY STRATA FINAN NAT/G PROF/ORG WORKER PLAN PROB/SOLV ADMIN ...STAT CHARTS METH 20 OECD. PAGE 100 F1971
SCHOOL EDU/PROP ECO/UNDEV ACADEM

B65
OECD,THE MEDITERRANEAN REGIONAL PROJECT: GREECE; EDUCATION AND DEVELOPMENT. FUT GREECE SOCIETY AGRI FINAN NAT/G PROF/ORG WORKER PLAN PROB/SOLV ADMIN DEMAND ATTIT 20 OECD. PAGE 100 F1972
EDU/PROP SCHOOL ACADEM ECO/UNDEV

B65
OECD,THE MEDITERRANEAN REGIONAL PROJECT: SPAIN; EDUCATION AND DEVELOPMENT. FUT SPAIN STRATA FINAN NAT/G WORKER PLAN PROB/SOLV ADMIN COST...POLICY STAT CHARTS 20 OECD. PAGE 100 F1973
ECO/UNDEV EDU/PROP ACADEM SCHOOL

B65
ORG FOR ECO COOP AND DEVEL,THE MEDITERRANEAN REGIONAL PROJECT: AN EXPERIMENT IN PLANNING BY SIX COUNTRIES. FUT GREECE SPAIN TURKEY YUGOSLAVIA SOCIETY FINAN NAT/G PROF/ORG EDU/PROP ADMIN REGION COST...POLICY STAT CHARTS 20 OECD. PAGE 102 F1995
PLAN ECO/UNDEV ACADEM SCHOOL

B65
ORG FOR ECO COOP AND DEVEL,THE MEDITERRANEAN REGIONAL PROJECT: YUGOSLAVIA; EDUCATION AND DEVELOPMENT. YUGOSLAVIA SOCIETY FINAN PROF/ORG PLAN ADMIN COST DEMAND MARXISM...STAT TREND CHARTS METH 20 OECD. PAGE 102 F1996
EDU/PROP ACADEM SCHOOL ECO/UNDEV

B65
SPENCE J.E.,REPUBLIC UNDER PRESSURE: A STUDY OF SOUTH AFRICAN FOREIGN POLICY. SOUTH/AFR ADMIN COLONIAL GOV/REL RACE/REL DISCRIM NAT/LISM ATTIT ROLE...TREND 20 NEGRO. PAGE 124 F2449
DIPLOM POLICY AFR

B65
STEINER G.A.,THE CREATIVE ORGANIZATION. ELITES LG/CO PLAN PROB/SOLV TEC/DEV INSPECT CAP/ISM CONTROL EXEC PERSON...METH/COMP HYPO/EXP 20. PAGE 126 F2476
CREATE MGT ADMIN SOC

B65
TYBOUT R.A.,ECONOMICS OF RESEARCH AND DEVELOPMENT. ECO/DEV ECO/UNDEV INDUS PROFIT DECISION. PAGE 131 F2594
R+D FORCES ADMIN DIPLOM

B65
US OFFICE ECONOMIC OPPORTUNITY,CATALOG OF FEDERAL PROGRAMS FOR INDIVIDUAL AND COMMUNITY IMPROVEMENT. USA+45 GIVE RECEIVE ADMIN HEALTH KNOWL SKILL WEALTH ...CHARTS MUNICH. PAGE 138 F2721
BIBLIOG CLIENT ECO/TAC

B65
WALTON R.E.,A BEHAVIORAL THEORY OF LABOR NEGOTIATIONS: AN ANALYSIS OF A SOCIAL INTERACTION SYSTEM. USA+45 FINAN PROB/SOLV ECO/TAC GP/REL INGP/REL...DECISION BIBLIOG. PAGE 143 F2812
SOC LABOR BARGAIN ADMIN

B65
WATERSTON A.,DEVELOPMENT PLANNING* LESSONS OF EXPERIENCE. ECO/TAC CENTRAL...MGT QUANT BIBLIOG. PAGE 144 F2830
ECO/UNDEV CREATE PLAN ADMIN

B65
WHITE J.,GERMAN AID. GERMANY/W FINAN PLAN TEC/DEV INT/TRADE ADMIN ATTIT...POLICY 20. PAGE 146 F2870
FOR/AID ECO/UNDEV DIPLOM ECO/TAC

L65
WILLIAMS S.,"NEGOTIATING INVESTMENT IN EMERGING COUNTRIES." USA+45 WOR+45 INDUS MARKET NAT/G TOP/EX TEC/DEV CAP/ISM ECO/TAC ADMIN SKILL WEALTH...POLICY RELATIV MGT WORK 20. PAGE 147 F2894
FINAN ECO/UNDEV

S65
HAYTER T.,"FRENCH AID TO AFRICA* ITS SCOPE AND ACHIEVEMENTS." CULTURE ECO/TAC INT/TRADE ADMIN REGION CENTRAL FEDERAL LOVE PWR SOVEREIGN EEC. PAGE 57 F1127
AFR FRANCE FOR/AID COLONIAL

S65
LONG T.G.,"THE ADMINISTRATIVE PROCESS: AGONIZING REAPPRAISAL IN THE FTC." NAT/G REPRESENT 20 FTC. PAGE 82 F1598
ADJUD LOBBY ADMIN EX/STRUC

C65
MANSFIELD H.C.,"THE CONGRESS AND ECONOMIC POLICY" IN C. TRUMAN ED., THE CONGRESS AND AMERICA'S FUTURE." USA+45 USA-45 CONSTN NAT/G BUDGET ADMIN CONTROL EXEC LOBBY. PAGE 85 F1661
POLICY ECO/TAC PWR LEGIS

B66
ALEXANDER Y.,INTERNATIONAL TECHNICAL ASSISTANCE EXPERTS* A CASE STUDY OF THE U.N. EXPERIENCE. ECO/UNDEV CONSULT EX/STRUC CREATE PLAN DIPLOM FOR/AID TASK EFFICIENCY...ORG/CHARTS UN. PAGE 3 F0061
ECO/TAC INT/ORG ADMIN MGT

B66
ALI S.,PLANNING, DEVELOPMENT AND CHANGE: AN ANNOTATED BIBLIOGRAPHY ON DEVELOPMENTAL ADMINISTRATION. PAKISTAN SOCIETY ORD/FREE 20. PAGE 4 F0066
BIBLIOG/A ADMIN ECO/UNDEV PLAN

B66
BAKKE E.W.,MUTUAL SURVIVAL; THE GOAL OF UNION AND MANAGEMENT (2ND ED.). USA+45 ELITES ECO/DEV ECO/TAC CONFER ADMIN REPRESENT GP/REL INGP/REL ATTIT ...GP/COMP 20. PAGE 8 F0155
MGT LABOR BARGAIN INDUS

B66
BALDWIN D.A.,FOREIGN AID AND AMERICAN FOREIGN POLICY; A DOCUMENTARY ANALYSIS. USA+45 ECO/UNDEV ADMIN...ECOMETRIC STAT STYLE CHARTS PROG/TEAC GEN/LAWS ANTHOL. PAGE 9 F0162
FOR/AID DIPLOM IDEA/COMP

B66
BOYD H.W.,MARKETING MANAGEMENT: CASES FROM EMERGING COUNTRIES. BRAZIL GHANA ISRAEL WOR+45 ADMIN PERS/REL ATTIT HABITAT WEALTH...ANTHOL 20 ARGEN CASEBOOK. PAGE 17 F0332
MGT ECO/UNDEV PROB/SOLV MARKET

B66
COOK P.W. JR.,PROBLEMS OF CORPORATE POWER. WOR+45 FINAN INDUS BARGAIN GP/REL...MGT ANTHOL. PAGE 27 F0530
ADMIN LG/CO PWR ECO/TAC

B66
DAVIS K.,BUSINESS AND ITS ENVIRONMENT. LAW ECO/DEV INDUS OP/RES ADMIN CONTROL ROUTINE GP/REL PROFIT POLICY. PAGE 30 F0591
EX/STRUC PROB/SOLV CAP/ISM EXEC

B66
DEBENKO E.,RESEARCH SOURCES FOR SOUTH ASIAN STUDIES IN ECONOMIC DEVELOPMENT: A SELECT BIBLIOGRAPHY OF SERIAL PUBLICATIONS. CEYLON INDIA NEPAL PAKISTAN PROB/SOLV ADMIN...POLICY 20. PAGE 32 F0611
BIBLIOG ECO/UNDEV S/ASIA PLAN

B66
DILLEY M.R.,BRITISH POLICY IN KENYA COLONY (2ND ED.). AFR INDIA UK LABOR BUDGET TAX ADMIN PARL/PROC GP/REL...BIBLIOG 20 PARLIAMENT. PAGE 33 F0639
COLONIAL REPRESENT SOVEREIGN

B66
DUNCOMBE H.S.,COUNTY GOVERNMENT IN AMERICA. USA+45 FINAN ADMIN ROUTINE GOV/REL...GOV/COMP MUNICH 20. PAGE 35 F0678
LOC/G PROVS CT/SYS TOP/EX

B66
FISK E.K.,NEW GUINEA ON THE THRESHOLD; ASPECTS OF SOCIAL, POLITICAL, AND ECONOMIC DEVELOPMENT. AGRI NAT/G INT/TRADE ADMIN ADJUST LITERACY ROLE...CHARTS ANTHOL 20 NEW/GUINEA. PAGE 41 F0804
ECO/UNDEV SOCIETY

B66
FOX K.A.,THE THEORY OF QUANTITATIVE ECONOMIC POLICY WITH APPLICATIONS TO ECONOMIC GROWTH AND STABILIZATION. ECO/DEV AGRI NAT/G PLAN ADMIN RISK ...DECISION IDEA/COMP SIMUL T. PAGE 43 F0837
ECO/TAC ECOMETRIC EQUILIB GEN/LAWS

B66
GREENE L.E.,GOVERNMENT IN TENNESSEE (2ND ED.). USA+45 DIST/IND INDUS POL/PAR EX/STRUC LEGIS PLAN BUDGET GIVE CT/SYS...MGT T 20 TENNESSEE. PAGE 51 F0989
PROVS LOC/G CONSTN ADMIN

B66
HAYER T.,FRENCH AID. AFR FRANCE AGRI FINAN BUDGET ADMIN WAR PRODUC...CHARTS 18/20 THIRD/WRLD OVRSEA/DEV. PAGE 57 F1125
TEC/DEV COLONIAL FOR/AID ECO/UNDEV

B66
HOLT R.T.,THE POLITICAL BASIS OF ECONOMIC DEVELOPMENT. STRATA STRUCT NAT/G DIPLOM ADMIN...SOC NAT/COMP BIBLIOG 20. PAGE 61 F1201
ECO/TAC GOV/COMP CONSTN EX/STRUC

B66
KEENLEYSIDE H.L.,INTERNATIONAL AID: A SUMMARY. AFR INDIA S/ASIA UK STRATA EXTR/IND TEC/DEV ADMIN RACE/REL DEMAND NAT/LISM WEALTH...TREND CHINJAP. PAGE 70 F1367
ECO/UNDEV FOR/AID DIPLOM TASK

B66
KIRDAR U.,THE STRUCTURE OF UNITED NATIONS ECONOMIC AID TO UNDERDEVELOPED COUNTRIES. AGRI FINAN INDUS NAT/G EX/STRUC PLAN GIVE TASK...POLICY 20 UN. PAGE 71 F1397
INT/ORG FOR/AID ECO/UNDEV ADMIN

B66
KIRKENDALL R.S.,SOCIAL SCIENTISTS AND FARM POLITICS IN THE AGE OF ROOSEVELT. ACADEM PLAN ECO/TAC GIVE ADMIN CONTROL PRODUC...SOC 20 NEW/DEAL ROOSEVLT/F BURAGR/ECO. PAGE 71 F1399
AGRI INTELL POLICY NAT/G

B66
LEWIS W.A.,DEVELOPMENT PLANNING; THE ESSENTIALS OF ECONOMIC POLICY. USA+45 FINAN INDUS NAT/G WORKER FOR/AID INT/TRADE ADMIN ROUTINE WEALTH...CONCPT STAT. PAGE 79 F1552
PLAN ECO/DEV POLICY CREATE

B66
MACFARQUHAR R.,CHINA UNDER MAO: POLITICS TAKES COMMAND. CHINA/COM COM AGRI INDUS CHIEF FORCES DIPLOM INT/TRADE EDU/PROP TASK REV ADJUST...ANTHOL 20 MAO. PAGE 83 F1628
ECO/UNDEV TEC/DEV ECO/TAC ADMIN

B66
MANGONE G.J.,UN ADMINISTRATION OF ECONOMIC AND AOCIAL PROGRAMS. CONSULT BUDGET INT/TRADE REGION 20 UN. PAGE 84 F1653
ADMIN MGT ECO/TAC DELIB/GP

B66
OHLIN G.,AID AND INDEBTEDNESS. AUSTRIA FINAN
FOR/AID

INT/ORG PLAN DIPLOM GIVE...POLICY MATH CHARTS 20. PAGE 101 F1984
ECO/UNDEV ADMIN WEALTH

B66
RAPHAEL J.S.,GOVERNMENTAL REGULATION OF BUSINESS. USA+45 LAW CONSTN TAX ADJUD ADMIN EFFICIENCY PWR 20. PAGE 109 F2150
LG/CO GOV/REL CONTROL ECO/DEV

B66
REDFORD E.S.,THE ROLE OF GOVERNMENT IN THE AMERICAN ECONOMY. USA+45 USA-45 FINAN INDUS LG/CO PROB/SOLV ADMIN INGP/REL INCOME PRODUC 18/20. PAGE 110 F2169
NAT/G ECO/DEV CAP/ISM ECO/TAC

B66
SMITH H.E.,READINGS IN ECONOMIC DEVELOPMENT AND ADMINISTRATION IN TANZANIA. TANZANIA FINAN INDUS LABOR NAT/G PLAN PROB/SOLV INT/TRADE COLONIAL REGION...ANTHOL BIBLIOG 20 AFRICA/E. PAGE 123 F2431
TEC/DEV ADMIN GOV/REL

B66
SPICER K.,A SAMARITAN STATE? AFR CANADA INDIA PAKISTAN UK USA+45 FINAN INDUS PRODUC...CHARTS 20 NATO. PAGE 124 F2455
DIPLOM FOR/AID ECO/DEV ADMIN

B66
US SENATE COMM GOVT OPERATIONS,INTERGOVERNMENTAL PERSONNEL ACT OF 1966. USA+45 NAT/G CONSULT DELIB/GP WORKER TEC/DEV PAY AUTOMAT UTIL 20 CONGRESS. PAGE 139 F2730
ADMIN LEGIS EFFICIENCY EDU/PROP

B66
US SENATE COMM ON FOREIGN REL,HEARINGS ON S 2859 AND S 2861. USA+45 WOR+45 FORCES BUDGET CAP/ISM ADMIN DETER WEAPON TOTALISM...NAT/COMP 20 UN CONGRESS. PAGE 139 F2735
FOR/AID DIPLOM ORD/FREE ECO/UNDEV

B66
ZINKIN T.,CHALLENGES IN INDIA. INDIA PAKISTAN LAW AGRI FINAN INDUS TOP/EX TEC/DEV CONTROL ROUTINE ORD/FREE PWR 20 NEHRU/J SHASTRI/LB CIVIL/SERV. PAGE 150 F2964
NAT/G ECO/TAC POLICY ADMIN

L66
AFRICAN BIBLIOGRAPHIC CENTER,"AFRICAN ECONOMIC AFFAIRS: A SELECT BIBLIOGRAPHICAL SURVEY, 1965-1966." AFR FINAN INDUS INT/ORG LABOR PLAN BUDGET DIPLOM INT/TRADE ADMIN EFFICIENCY WEALTH 20. PAGE 3 F0046
BIBLIOG ECO/UNDEV TEC/DEV FOR/AID

L66
AFRICAN BIBLIOGRAPHIC CENTER,"AFRICAN ECONOMIC AFFAIRS: A SELECT BIBLIOGRAPHICAL SURVEY, 1965-1966; SUPPLEMENTS NUMBERS 1-3." AFR FINAN INDUS LABOR PLAN BUDGET CAP/ISM DIPLOM INT/TRADE ADMIN...GEOG 20. PAGE 3 F0047
BIBLIOG/A ECO/UNDEV FOR/AID TEC/DEV

L66
AMERICAN ECONOMIC REVIEW,"SIXTY-THIRD LIST OF DOCTORAL DISSERTATIONS IN POLITICAL ECONOMY IN AMERICAN UNIVERSITIES AND COLLEGES." ECO/DEV AGRI FINAN LABOR WORKER PLAN BUDGET INT/TRADE ADMIN DEMAND...MGT STAT 20. PAGE 5 F0088
BIBLIOG/A CONCPT ACADEM

S66
FLEMING W.G.,"AUTHORITY, EFFICIENCY, AND ROLE STRESS: PROBLEMS IN THE DEVELOPMENT OF EAST AFRICAN BUREAUCRACIES." AFR UGANDA STRUCT PROB/SOLV ROUTINE INGP/REL ROLE...MGT SOC GP/COMP GOV/COMP 20 TANGANYIKA AFRICA/E. PAGE 41 F0810
DOMIN EFFICIENCY COLONIAL ADMIN

S66
JACOBS P.,"RE-RADICALIZING THE DE-RADICALIZED." USA+45 SOCIETY STRUCT FINAN PLAN PROB/SOLV CAP/ISM WEALTH CONSERVE NEW/LIB 20. PAGE 66 F1297
NAT/G POLICY MARXIST ADMIN

S66
LANGLEY D.,"POSTSCRIPT ON THE COLONIZATION OF THE INTERNATIONAL TRADE UNION MOVEMENT" USA+45 ELITES FINAN DOMIN LEGIT ADMIN PWR...SOCIALIST 20 AFL/CIO CIA LOVESTN/J. PAGE 75 F1479
INT/TRADE LABOR NAT/G CONTROL

S66
ROTHCHILD D.,"THE LIMITS OF FEDERALISM: AN EXAMINATION OF POLITICAL INSTITUTIONAL TRANSFER IN AFRICA." AFR CONSTN CULTURE ELITES ECO/UNDEV KIN PROB/SOLV ADMIN ORD/FREE PWR...POLICY 20. PAGE 114 F2250
FEDERAL NAT/G NAT/LISM COLONIAL

N66
US ADVISORY COMN INTERGOV REL,CATALOGS AND OTHER INFORMATION SOURCES ON FEDERAL AND STATE AID PROGRAMS: A SECTED BIBLIOGRAPHY (PAPER). USA+45 LAW LOC/G NAT/G PROVS VOL/ASSN TEC/DEV ADMIN HEALTH ...WELF/ST SOC/WK MUNICH. PAGE 134 F2635
BIBLIOG/A GOV/REL FINAN ECO/DEV

B67
ANDERSON C.W.,POLITICS AND ECONOMIC CHANGE IN LATIN AMERICA. L/A+17C INDUS NAT/G OP/RES ADMIN DEMAND ...POLICY STAT CHARTS NAT/COMP 20. PAGE 5 F0093
ECO/UNDEV PROB/SOLV PLAN ECO/TAC

B67
BALDWIN G.B.,PLANNING AND DEVELOPMENT IN IRAN. IRAN AGRI INDUS CONSULT WORKER EDU/PROP BAL/PAY...CHARTS 20. PAGE 9 F0164
PLAN ECO/UNDEV ADMIN PROB/SOLV

B67
BARROW T.C.,TRADE AND EMPIRE: THE BRITISH CUSTOMS SERVICE IN COLONIAL AMERICA, 1660-1775. UK USA-45 ECO/UNDEV NAT/G ECO/TAC DOMIN REV 17/18. PAGE 10 F0197
COLONIAL TARIFFS ADMIN EX/STRUC

B67
BERGMANN D KAUN B.,STRUCTURAL UNEMPLOYMENT IN THE UNITED STATES. USA+45 ECO/DEV PRICE ADMIN INGP/REL DEMAND EQUILIB WEALTH...MATH REGRESS STAT 20 NEGRO. PAGE 13 F0258
ECOMETRIC METH WORKER ECO/TAC

B67
BLAUG M.,ECONOMICS OF EDUCATION: A SELECTED ANNOTATED BIBLIOGRAPHY. EUR+WWI INTELL ECO/DEV ECO/UNDEV ACADEM INT/ORG NAT/G CREATE ADMIN EFFICIENCY ROLE PREDICT. PAGE 16 F0298
BIBLIOG/A EDU/PROP FINAN PLAN

B67
DONALD A.G.,MANAGEMENT, INFORMATION, AND SYSTEMS. WOR+45 LG/CO PROB/SOLV CONTROL FEEDBACK KNOWL MGT. PAGE 34 F0653
ROUTINE TEC/DEV CONCPT ADMIN

B67
DUN J.L.,THE ESSENCE OF CHINESE CIVILIZATION. ASIA FAM NAT/G TEC/DEV ADMIN SANCTION WAR HABITAT ...ANTHOL WORSHIP. PAGE 35 F0676
CULTURE SOCIETY

B67
ENKE S.,DEFENSE MANAGEMENT. USA+45 R+D FORCES WORKER PLAN ECO/TAC ADMIN NUC/PWR BAL/PAY UTIL WEALTH...MGT DEPT/DEFEN. PAGE 38 F0738
DECISION DELIB/GP EFFICIENCY BUDGET

B67
ESTEY M.,THE UNIONS: STRUCTURE, DEVELOPMENT, AND MANAGEMENT. FUT USA+45 ADJUD CONTROL INGP/REL DRIVE ...DECISION T 20 AFL/CIO. PAGE 38 F0750
LABOR EX/STRUC ADMIN GOV/REL

B67
EVANS R.H.,COEXISTENCE: COMMUNISM AND ITS PRACTICE IN BOLOGNA, 1945-1965. ITALY CAP/ISM ADMIN CHOOSE PEACE ORD/FREE...SOC STAT DEEP/INT SAMP CHARTS BIBLIOG MUNICH 20. PAGE 39 F0756
MARXISM CULTURE POL/PAR

B67
GITTELL M.,PARTICIPANTS AND PARTICIPATION: A STUDY OF SCHOOL POLICY IN NEW YORK. USA+45 EX/STRUC BUDGET PAY ATTIT...POLICY MUNICH 20 NEWYORK/C. PAGE 47 F0926
SCHOOL DECISION PARTIC ADMIN

B67
GOLEMBIEWSKI R.T.,ORGANIZING MEN AND POWER: PATTERNS OF BEHAVIOR AND LINESTAFF MODELS. WOR+45 EX/STRUC ACT/RES DOMIN PERS/REL...NEW/IDEA 20. PAGE 48 F0943
ADMIN CONTROL SIMUL MGT

B67
GROSS B.M.,ACTION UNDER PLANNING: THE GUIDANCE OF ECONOMIC DEVELOPMENT. STRUCT R+D NAT/G ACT/RES HABITAT...DECISION 20. PAGE 51 F1005
ECO/UNDEV PLAN ADMIN MGT

B67
HANNAH H.W.,THE LEGAL BASE FOR UNIVERSITIES IN DEVELOPING COUNTRIES. AFR ASIA L/A+17C S/ASIA USA+45 FINAN CREATE EDU/PROP TASK EFFICIENCY ...JURID METH/COMP 20. PAGE 54 F1060
ADMIN LAW ACADEM LEGIS

B67
JHANGIANI M.A.,JANA SANGH AND SWATANTRA: A PROFILE OF THE RIGHTIST PARTIES IN INDIA. INDIA ADMIN CHOOSE MARXISM SOCISM...INT CHARTS BIBLIOG 20. PAGE 67 F1320
POL/PAR LAISSEZ NAT/LISM ATTIT

B67
LEIBY J.,CHARITY AND CORRECTION IN JERSEY; A HISTORY OF STATE WELFARE INSTITUTIONS. DELIB/GP EX/STRUC PROB/SOLV INSPECT LEAD ADJUST HEALTH ...POLICY PSY NEW/JERSEY. PAGE 77 F1514
PROVS PUB/INST ADMIN

B67
MARRIS P.,DILEMMAS OF SOCIAL REFORM: POVERTY AND COMMUNITY ACTION IN THE UNITED STATES. USA+45 NAT/G OP/RES ADMIN PARTIC EFFICIENCY WEALTH...SOC METH/COMP T MUNICH 20 REFORMERS. PAGE 85 F1674
STRUCT PROB/SOLV COST

B67
MORRIS A.J.A.,PARLIAMENTARY DEMOCRACY IN THE NINETEENTH CENTURY. UK INDUS LOC/G NAT/G POL/PAR CONSULT LEGIS INT/TRADE ADMIN CHOOSE SUFF SOVEREIGN 19 PARLIAMENT. PAGE 93 F1835
TIME/SEQ CONSTN PARL/PROC POPULISM

B67
NARVER J.C.,CONGLOMERATE MERGERS AND MARKET COMPETITION. USA+45 LAW STRUCT ADMIN LEAD RISK COST PROFIT WEALTH...POLICY CHARTS BIBLIOG. PAGE 96 F1892
DEMAND LG/CO MARKET MGT

B67
OVERSEAS DEVELOPMENT INSTIT,EFFECTIVE AID. WOR+45 INT/ORG TEC/DEV DIPLOM INT/TRADE ADMIN. PAGE 102 F2004
FOR/AID ECO/UNDEV ECO/TAC NAT/COMP

B67
PRINCE C.E.,NEW JERSEY'S JEFFERSONIAN REPUBLICANS; THE GENESIS OF AN EARLY PARTY MACHINE (1789-1817). USA-45 LOC/G EDU/PROP PRESS CONTROL CHOOSE...CHARTS 18/19 NEW/JERSEY REPUBLICAN. PAGE 108 F2117
POL/PAR CONSTN ADMIN PROVS

B67
RAVKIN A.,THE NEW STATES OF AFRICA (HEADLINE SERIES, NO. 183((PAMPHLET). CULTURE STRUCT INDUS COLONIAL NAT/LISM...SOC 20. PAGE 109 F2153
AFR ECO/UNDEV SOCIETY

ADMIN

B67
ROELOFS H.M.,THE LANGUAGE OF MODERN POLITICS: AN INTRODUCTION TO THE STUDY OF GOVERNMENT. DIPLOM ADMIN MARXISM NEW/LIB...JURID CONCPT METH/COMP T 20. PAGE 113 F2230
LEAD NAT/COMP PERS/REL NAT/G

B67
TANSKY L.,US AND USSR AID TO DEVELOPING COUNTRIES. INDIA TURKEY UAR USA+45 USSR FINAN PLAN TEC/DEV ADMIN WEALTH...TREND METH/COMP 20. PAGE 128 F2535
FOR/AID ECO/UNDEV MARXISM CAP/ISM

B67
UNIVERSAL REFERENCE SYSTEM,BIBLIOGRAPHY OF BIBLIOGRAPHIES IN POLITICAL SCIENCE, GOVERNMENT, AND PUBLIC POLICY (VOLUME III). WOR+45 WOR-45 LAW ADMIN...SOC CON/ANAL COMPUT/IR GEN/METH. PAGE 133 F2615
BIBLIOG/A NAT/G DIPLOM POLICY

B67
UNIVERSAL REFERENCE SYSTEM,ADMINISTRATIVE MANAGEMENT: PUBLIC AND PRIVATE BUREAUCRACY (VOLUME IV). WOR+45 WOR-45 ECO/DEV LG/CO LOC/G PUB/INST VOL/ASSN GOV/REL...COMPUT/IR GEN/METH. PAGE 133 F2616
BIBLIOG/A MGT ADMIN NAT/G

B67
VENKATESWARAN R.J.,CABINET GOVERNMENT IN INDIA. INDIA UK SOCIETY OP/RES COLONIAL LEAD EFFICIENCY ORD/FREE 20. PAGE 141 F2776
DELIB/GP ADMIN CONSTN NAT/G

B67
WESSON R.G.,THE IMPERIAL ORDER. WOR-45 STRUCT SECT DOMIN ADMIN COLONIAL LEAD CONSERVE...CONCPT BIBLIOG 20. PAGE 145 F2861
PWR CHIEF CONTROL SOCIETY

B67
ZALESKI E.,PLANNING REFORMS IN THE SOVIET UNION 1962-1966. COM USSR NAT/G CONFER CONTROL EFFICIENCY MARXISM...POLICY DECISION 20. PAGE 150 F2957
ECO/DEV PLAN ADMIN CENTRAL

B67
ZONDAG C.H.,THE BOLIVIAN ECONOMY 1952-65. L/A+17C TEC/DEV FOR/AID ADMIN...OBS TREND CHARTS BIBLIOG 20 BOLIV. PAGE 151 F2969
ECO/UNDEV INDUS PRODUC

L67
AUSTIN D.A.,"POLITICAL CONFLICT IN AFRICA." CONSTN NAT/G CREATE ADMIN COLONIAL ORD/FREE MARXISM POPULISM SOCISM...NAT/COMP ANTHOL 20. PAGE 8 F0141
ANOMIE AFR POL/PAR

L67
GOULD W.B.,"THE STATUS OF UNAUTHORIZED AND 'WILDCAT' STRIKES UNDER THE NATIONAL LABOR RELATIONS ACT." USA+45 ACT/RES BARGAIN ECO/TAC LEGIT ADJUD ADMIN GP/REL MGT. PAGE 50 F0968
ECO/DEV INDUS LABOR POLICY

L67
JACOBY S.B.,"THE 89TH CONGRESS AND GOVERNMENT LITIGATION." USA+45 ADMIN COST...JURID 20 CONGRESS. PAGE 66 F1302
LAW NAT/G ADJUD SANCTION

L67
LAMBERT J.D.,"CORPORATE POLITICAL SPENDING AND CAMPAIGN FINANCE." LAW CONSTN FINAN LABOR LG/CO LOC/G NAT/G VOL/ASSN TEC/DEV ADJUD ADMIN PARTIC. PAGE 75 F1463
USA+45 POL/PAR CHOOSE COST

L67
LENT G.E.,"TAX INCENTIVES FOR INVESTMENT IN DEVELOPING COUNTRIES" WOR+45 LAW INDUS PLAN BUDGET TARIFFS ADMIN...METH/COMP 20. PAGE 78 F1526
ECO/UNDEV TAX FINAN ECO/TAC

L67
MACHLUP F.,"THEORIES OF THE FIRM* MARGINALIST, BEHAVIORALIST, MANAGERIAL." ADMIN EXEC EFFICIENCY PROFIT METH/CNCPT. PAGE 83 F1633
METH/COMP GEN/LAWS INDUS

L67
MANNE H.G.,"OUR TWO CORPORATION SYSTEMS* LAW AND ECONOMICS." LAW CONTROL SANCTION GP/REL...JURID 20. PAGE 85 F1657
INDUS ELITES CAP/ISM ADMIN

L67
SCHNEIDER C.W.,"REFORM OF THE FEDERAL SECURITIES LAWS." FUT USA+45 LAW FINAN INDUS DELIB/GP ACT/RES PROB/SOLV GP/REL. PAGE 117 F2304
NAT/G LG/CO ADMIN CONTROL

L67
TRAVERS H. JR.,"AN EXAMINATION OF THE CAB'S MERGER POLICY." USA+45 USA-45 LAW NAT/G LEGIS PLAN ADMIN ...DECISION 20 CONGRESS. PAGE 131 F2584
ADJUD LG/CO POLICY DIST/IND

S67
ALLISON D.,"THE GROWTH OF IDEAS." USA+45 LG/CO ADMIN. PAGE 4 F0075
R+D OP/RES INDUS TEC/DEV

S67
AVTORKHANOV A.,"A NEW AGRARIAN REVOLUTION." COM USSR ECO/DEV PLAN TEC/DEV ADMIN CONTROL OPTIMAL WEALTH SOCISM 20 KHRUSH/N STALIN/J. PAGE 8 F0144
AGRI METH/COMP MARXISM OWN

S67
BENN W.,"TECHNOLOGY HAS AN INEXORABLE EFFECT." FUT UK ECO/DEV INT/ORG CONSULT PLAN EDU/PROP ADMIN LEAD GP/REL PRODUC...INT 20 EEC. PAGE 13 F0246
R+D LG/CO TEC/DEV INDUS

S67
BOSHER J.F.,"GOVERNMENT AND PRIVATE INTERESTS IN NEW FRANCE." CANADA FRANCE INDUS LG/CO SML/CO CAP/ISM INT/TRADE COLONIAL GP/REL...HIST/WRIT 17/18. PAGE 17 F0320
NAT/G FINAN ADMIN CONTROL

S67
DAVIS O.A.,"ON THE DISTINCTION BETWEEN PUBLIC AND PRIVATE GOODS." USA+45 COM/IND LG/CO NAT/G TV DEBATE PRICE ADMIN ROLE...MATH IDEA/COMP. PAGE 31 F0593
MARKET OWN CONCPT

S67
DRAPER A.P.,"UNIONS AND THE WAR IN VIETNAM." USA+45 CONFER ADMIN LEAD WAR ORD/FREE PACIFIST 20. PAGE 34 F0660
LABOR PACIFISM ATTIT ELITES

S67
FERGUSON D.E.,"DETERMINING CAPACITY FOR CAPITAL EXPENDITURES." USA+45 LOC/G BUDGET TAX ADMIN CONTROL...TREND MUNICH 20. PAGE 40 F0784
FINAN PAY COST

S67
FOX R.G.,"FAMILY, CASTE, AND COMMERCE IN A NORTH INDIAN MARKET TOWN." INDIA STRATA AGRI FACE/GP FAM NEIGH OP/RES BARGAIN ADMIN ROUTINE WEALTH...SOC CHARTS 20. PAGE 43 F0838
CULTURE GP/REL ECO/UNDEV DIST/IND

S67
GANZ G.,"THE CONTROL OF INDUSTRY BY ADMINISTRATIVE PROCESS." UK DELIB/GP WORKER 20. PAGE 46 F0898
INDUS LAW ADMIN CONTROL

S67
GAUSE M.E.,"ELEMENTS OF FINANCE DEPARTMENT ORGANIZATION FOR SMALL GOVERNMENTAL UNITS." USA+45 PROB/SOLV CONTROL CENTRAL...METH MUNICH. PAGE 47 F0910
ADMIN LOC/G FINAN

S67
HALL B.,"THE PAINTER'S UNION: A PARTIAL VICTORY." USA+45 PROB/SOLV LEGIT ADMIN REPRESENT 20. PAGE 53 F1043
LABOR CHIEF CHOOSE CRIME

S67
HALL B.,"THE COALITION AGAINST DISHWASHERS." USA+45 POL/PAR PROB/SOLV BARGAIN LEAD CHOOSE REPRESENT GP/REL ORD/FREE PWR...POLICY 20. PAGE 53 F1044
LABOR ADMIN DOMIN WORKER

S67
JAVITS J.K.,"THE USE OF AMERICAN PLURALISM." USA+45 ECO/DEV BUDGET ADMIN ALL/IDEOS...DECISION TREND. PAGE 67 F1309
CENTRAL ATTIT POLICY NAT/G

S67
LANDES W.M.,"THE EFFECT OF STATE FAIR EMPLOYMENT LAWS ON THE ECONOMIC POSITION OF NONWHITES." USA+45 PROVS SECT LEGIS ADMIN GP/REL RACE/REL...JURID CONCPT CHARTS HYPO/EXP NEGRO. PAGE 75 F1470
DISCRIM LAW WORKER

S67
LOSMAN D.L.,"FOREIGN AID, SOCIALISM AND THE EMERGING COUNTRIES" WOR+45 ADMIN CONTROL PWR 20. PAGE 82 F1602
ECO/UNDEV FOR/AID SOC

S67
MERIKOSKI V.,"BASIC PROBLEMS OF UNIVERSITY ADMINISTRATION." PROVS SECT CONTROL...CLASSIF 20. PAGE 90 F1760
ACADEM ADMIN SOVEREIGN METH/COMP

S67
MERON T.,"THE UN'S 'COMMON SYSTEM' OF SALARY, ALLOWANCE, AND BENEFITS: CRITICAL APPR'SAL OF COORD IN PERSONNEL MATTERS." VOL/ASSN PAY EFFICIENCY ...CHARTS 20 UN. PAGE 90 F1761
ADMIN EX/STRUC INT/ORG BUDGET

S67
MITCHELL J.D.B.,"THE CONSTITUTIONAL IMPLICATIONS OF JUDICIAL CONTROL OF THE ADMINISTRATION IN THE UNITED KINGDOM." UK LAW ADJUD ADMIN GOV/REL ROLE ...GP/COMP 20. PAGE 92 F1808
CONSTN CT/SYS CONTROL EX/STRUC

S67
MODESITT L.E.,"THE MUTUAL FUND - A CORPORATE ANOMALY." USA+45 CONTROL...MGT 20. PAGE 92 F1813
SERV/IND FINAN ADMIN LAW

S67
MOLTMANN G.,"ZUR FORMULIERUNG DER AMERIKANISCHEN BESATZUNGSPOLITIK IN DEUTSCHLAND AM ENDE DES ZWEITEN WELTKRIEGES" GERMANY ECO/TAC ADMIN WAR CIVMIL/REL ORD/FREE FASCISM 20. PAGE 92 F1815
FORCES CONTROL POLICY INDUS

S67
MUNDHEIM R.H.,"SOME THOUGHTS ON THE DUTIES AND RESPONSIBILITIES OF UNAFFILIATED DIRECTORS OF MUTUAL FUNDS." USA+45 LG/CO SML/CO CONSULT LEAD PARTIC. PAGE 95 F1861
FINAN WEALTH ECO/TAC ADMIN

S67
OLIVIER G.,"ASPECTS JURIDIQUES DE L'ADOPTION DU TRAITE CECA A LA CRISE CHARBONNIERE (SUITE ET FIN)"
INT/TRADE INT/ORG

LAW DIST/IND PLAN DIPLOM RATION PRICE ADMIN COST DEMAND...POLICY CON/ANAL ECSC TREATY. PAGE 101 F1988 — EXTR/IND CONSTN

S67
PRATT R.C.,"THE ADMINISTRATION OF ECONOMIC PLANNING IN A NEWLY INDEPEND ENT STATE* THE TANZANIAN EXPERIENCE 1963-1966." AFR TANZANIA ECO/UNDEV PLAN CONTROL ROUTINE TASK EFFICIENCY 20. PAGE 107 F2114 — NAT/G DELIB/GP ADMIN TEC/DEV

S67
PROBERT J.R.,"STREAMLINING THE FOREIGN POLICY MACHINE." USA+45 EFFICIENCY DEPT/STATE. PAGE 108 F2123 — DIPLOM ADMIN EXEC GOV/REL

S67
SCOVILLE W.J.,"GOVERNMENT REGULATION AND GROWTH IN THE FRENCH PAPER INDUSTRY DURING THE EIGHTEENTH CENTURY." FRANCE MOD/EUR FINAN CAP/ISM TAX ADMIN CONTROL PRIVIL LAISSEZ...POLICY 18. PAGE 118 F2337 — NAT/G PROC/MFG ECO/DEV INGP/REL

S67
SIDDIQ M.M.,"LOCAL GOVERNMENT IN PAKISTAN." PAKISTAN PROB/SOLV TAX COLONIAL GOV/REL MUNICH 20. PAGE 121 F2395 — ADMIN LOC/G DELIB/GP BUDGET

S67
SKOLNICK J.H.,"SOCIAL CONTROL IN THE ADVERSARY SYSTEM." USA+45 CONSULT OP/RES ADMIN CONTROL. PAGE 123 F2419 — PROB/SOLV PERS/REL ADJUD CT/SYS

S67
SMITH W.H.T.,"THE IMPLICATIONS OF THE AMERICAN BAR ASSOCIATION ADVISORY COMMITTEE RECOMMENDATIONS FOR POLICE ADMINISTRATION." AFR ADMIN...JURID 20. PAGE 123 F2435 — EDU/PROP CONTROL GP/REL ORD/FREE

S67
STILL J.F.,"THE FUTURE OF METROPOLITAN GOVERNMENT ORGANIZATION." USA+45 LOC/G BUDGET COST ATTIT MUNICH 20. PAGE 126 F2488 — ADMIN FINAN CONTROL

S67
THORKELSON H.,"FOOD STAMPS AND HUNGER IN AMERICA." USA+45 LAW DELIB/GP ADMIN COST DEMAND POLICY. PAGE 130 F2570 — WEALTH RECEIVE EATING PLAN

S67
WARNER K.O.,"FINANCIAL IMPLICATION OF EMPLOYEE BARGAINING IN THE PUBLIC SERVICE." CANADA USA+45 FINAN ADMIN...MGT 20. PAGE 143 F2823 — BARGAIN LABOR COST LOC/G

S67
WHITE W.L.,"THE TREASURY BOARD AND PARLIAMENT." CANADA CONSTN CONSULT LEGIS LEAD PARL/PROC GP/REL ...DECISION 20. PAGE 146 F2871 — FINAN DELIB/GP NAT/G ADMIN

S67
WILES P.J.,"THE POLITICAL AND SOCIAL PREREQUISITES FOR A SOVIET-TYPE ECONOMY." COM USSR LAW CULTURE CREATE ADMIN FEEDBACK ROUTINE COST OPTIMAL TOTALISM MARXISM 20. PAGE 146 F2883 — ECO/DEV PLAN EX/STRUC EFFICIENCY

S67
WILLIAMS C.,"REGIONAL MANAGEMENT OVERSEAS." USA+45 WOR+45 DIST/IND LG/CO EX/STRUC INT/TRADE TARIFFS ADMIN TASK CENTRAL. PAGE 147 F2889 — MGT EUR+WWI ECO/DEV PLAN

N67
US SENATE COMM ON FOREIGN REL,ARMS SALES AND FOREIGN POLICY (PAMPHLET). FINAN FOR/AID CONTROL 20. PAGE 139 F2737 — ARMS/CONT ADMIN OP/RES DIPLOM

N67
US SENATE COMM ON FOREIGN REL,THE UNITED NATIONS AT TWENTY-ONE (PAMPHLET). WOR+45 BUDGET ADMIN SENATE UN. PAGE 139 F2738 — INT/ORG DIPLOM PEACE

ADMINISTRATIVE STAFF COLLEGE F0043

ADMINISTRATIVE MANAGEMENT....SEE MGT

ADOLESCENCE....SEE AGE/Y

ADORNO T.W. F0044

ADVERT/ADV....ADVERTISING ADVISORY COMMISSION

ADVERTISING....SEE SERV/IND+EDU/PROP; SEE ALSO TV, PRESS

AEA....ATOMIC ENERGY AUTHORITY OF UN; SEE ALSO NUC/PWR

AEC....ATOMIC ENERGY COMMISSION; SEE ALSO NUC/PWR

N19
ATOMIC INDUSTRIAL FORUM,COMMENTARY ON LEGISLATION TO PERMIT PRIVATE OWNERSHIP OF SPECIAL NUCLEAR MATERIAL (PAMPHLET). USA+45 DELIB/GP LEGIS PLAN OWN ...POLICY 20 AEC CONGRESS. PAGE 7 F0134 — NUC/PWR MARKET INDUS LAW

AFFELDT R.J. F0045

AFGHANISTN....SEE ALSO ISLAM, ASIA

N19
FRANCK P.G.,AFGHANISTAN BETWEEN EAST AND WEST: THE ECONOMICS OF COMPETITIVE COEXISTENCE (PAMPHLET). AFGHANISTN USA+45 USA-45 USSR INDUS ECO/TAC INT/TRADE CONTROL NEUTRAL ORD/FREE MARXISM...GEOG 20 UN. PAGE 43 F0842 — FOR/AID PLAN DIPLOM ECO/UNDEV

B55
UN ECONOMIC COMN ASIA & FAR E,ECONOMIC SURVEY OF ASIA AND THE FAR EAST, 1954. AFGHANISTN CEYLON INDIA PHILIPPINE S/ASIA ECO/DEV FINAN INDUS INT/TRADE PRODUC WEALTH...STAT CHARTS 20 CHINJAP. PAGE 132 F2600 — ECO/UNDEV PRICE NAT/COMP ASIA

B60
FRANCK P.G.,AFGHANISTAN: BETWEEN EAST AND WEST. AFGHANISTN AFR USA+45 USSR ECO/UNDEV PLAN ADMIN ROUTINE ATTIT PWR...STAT OBS CHARTS TOT/POP FOR/TRADE 20. PAGE 43 F0843 — ECO/TAC TREND FOR/AID

AFL/CIO....AMERICAN FEDERATION OF LABOR, CONGRESS OF INDUSTRIAL ORGANIZATIONS

B39
MARQUAND H.A.,ORGANIZED LABOUR IN FOUR CONTINENTS. EUR+WWI USA-45 INDUS NAT/G PAY GP/REL TOTALISM ATTIT WEALTH ALL/IDEOS...TREND NAT/COMP 20 ILO AFL/CIO EUROPE CHINJAP MEXIC/AMER. PAGE 85 F1673 — LABOR WORKER CONCPT ANTHOL

B51
PETERSON F.,SURVEY OF LABOR ECONOMICS (REV. ED.). STRATA ECO/DEV LABOR INSPECT BARGAIN PAY PRICE EXEC ROUTINE GP/REL ALL/VALS ORD/FREE 20 AFL/CIO DEPT/LABOR. PAGE 105 F2069 — WORKER DEMAND IDEA/COMP T

B55
BLOOM G.F.,ECONOMICS OF LABOR RELATIONS. USA+45 LAW CONSULT WORKER CAP/ISM PAY ADJUD CONTROL EFFICIENCY ORD/FREE...CHARTS 19/20 AFL/CIO NLRB DEPT/LABOR. PAGE 16 F0299 — ECO/DEV ECO/TAC LABOR GOV/REL

B62
REES A.,THE ECONOMICS OF TRADE UNIONS. FUT ECO/DEV INDUS BARGAIN CAP/ISM PRICE SENIOR CONTROL GP/REL COST...TREND 20 AFL/CIO. PAGE 110 F2172 — LABOR WORKER ECO/TAC

B63
BURTT E.J. JR.,LABOR MARKETS, UNIONS, AND GOVERNMENT POLICIES. USA+45 MARKET NAT/G DELIB/GP CREATE BARGAIN GP/REL ORD/FREE PWR...POLICY CHARTS 20 AFL/CIO. PAGE 20 F0393 — LABOR ECO/DEV CONTROL WORKER

S66
LANGLEY D.,"POSTSCRIPT ON THE COLONIZATION OF THE INTERNATIONAL TRADE UNION MOVEMENT" USA+45 ELITES FINAN DOMIN LEGIT ADMIN PWR...SOCIALIST 20 AFL/CIO CIA LOVESTN/J. PAGE 75 F1479 — INT/TRADE LABOR NAT/G CONTROL

B67
ESTEY M.,THE UNIONS: STRUCTURE, DEVELOPMENT, AND MANAGEMENT. FUT USA+45 ADJUD CONTROL INGP/REL DRIVE ...DECISION T 20 AFL/CIO. PAGE 38 F0750 — LABOR EX/STRUC ADMIN GOV/REL

S67
SHISTER J.,"THE DIRECTION OF UNIONISM 1947-1967: THRUST OF DRIFT?" INDUS CENTRAL EFFICIENCY INCOME ATTIT SOCISM...POLICY TREND 20 AFL/CIO. PAGE 121 F2382 — LABOR PROF/ORG LEAD LAW

AFLAK/M....MICHEL AFLAK

AFR....AFRICA

N
BROCKWAY A.F.,AFRICAN SOCIALISM. EUR+WWI GHANA ISLAM UAR ECO/UNDEV CAP/ISM INT/TRADE COLONIAL COERCE GOV/REL DISCRIM 20 NEGRO NKRUMAH/K NASSER/G. PAGE 19 F0356 — AFR SOCISM MARXISM

N
THE MIDDLE EAST AND NORTH AFRICA. AFR ISLAM CULTURE ECO/UNDEV AGRI NAT/G TEC/DEV FOR/AID INT/TRADE EDU/PROP...CHARTS 20. PAGE 1 F0008 — INDEX INDUS FINAN STAT

N
SCIENTIFIC COUNCIL FOR AFRICA,INVENTORY OF ECONOMIC STUDIES CONCERNING AFRICA SOUTH OF THE SAHARA. AFR ...PHIL/SCI 20. PAGE 118 F2327 — BIBLIOG/A GEOG ECO/UNDEV

LCA
GODFREY E.M.,"THE ECONOMICS OF AN AFRICAN UNIVERSITY." AFR SCHOOL PRICE EFFICIENCY INCOME WEALTH...ECOMETRIC CHARTS 20. PAGE 48 F0930 — ACADEM ECO/TAC COST EDU/PROP

NCO
CARRINGTON C.E.,THE COMMONWEALTH IN AFRICA (PAMPHLET). UK STRUCT NAT/G COLONIAL REPRESENT GOV/REL RACE/REL NAT/LISM...MAJORIT 20 EEC NEGRO. PAGE 22 F0421 — ECO/UNDEV AFR DIPLOM PLAN

NCO
STOLPER W.,"SOCIAL FACTORS IN ECONOMIC PLANNING, WITH SPECIAL REFERENCE TO NIGERIA" AFR NIGER — ECO/UNDEV PLAN

CULTURE FAM SECT RECEIVE ETIQUET ADMIN DEMAND 20. PAGE 126 F2494
ADJUST RISK

B02
MOREL E.D.,AFFAIRS OF WEST AFRICA. UK FINAN INDUS FAM KIN SECT CHIEF WORKER DIPLOM RACE/REL LITERACY HEALTH...CHARTS 18/20 AFRICA/W NEGRO. PAGE 93 F1826
COLONIAL ADMIN AFR

B03
MOREL E.D.,THE BRITISH CASE IN FRENCH CONGO. CONGO/BRAZ FRANCE UK COERCE MORAL WEALTH...POLICY INT/LAW 20 CONGO/LEOP. PAGE 93 F1827
DIPLOM INT/TRADE COLONIAL AFR

N19
BLOOMFIELD A.,MONETARY POLICY UNDER THE INTERNATIONAL GOLD STANDARD: 18801914 (PAMPHLET). AFR USA-45 DIPLOM CONTROL...POLICY 19. PAGE 16 F0300
FINAN ROLE EFFICIENCY

N19
CASSELL F.,INTERNATIONAL MONETARY PROBLEMS (PAMPHLET). AFR BAL/PWR CONTROL EFFICIENCY WEALTH 20 EEC. PAGE 22 F0427
INT/TRADE FINAN DIPLOM TREND

N19
DEANE H.,THE WAR IN VIETNAM (PAMPHLET). AFR CHINA/COM VIETNAM BAL/PWR DIPLOM ECO/TAC SOCISM INTERVENT INTERVENT. PAGE 31 F0610
WAR SOCIALIST MORAL CAP/ISM

N19
GROSECLOSE E.,THE DECAY OF MONEY; A SURVEY OF WESTERN CURRENCIES 1912-1962 (PAMPHLET). AFR FRANCE GERMANY UK LAW INT/TRADE BAL/PAY COST EQUILIB ...POLICY 20 DEPRESSION. PAGE 51 F1004
FINAN NAT/G ECO/DEV ECO/TAC

N19
HABERLER G.,INFLATION; ITS CAUSES AND CURES (PAMPHLET). AFR USA+45 FINAN BUDGET PAY PRICE COST DEMAND 20. PAGE 52 F1021
ECO/DEV BAL/PAY POLICY NAT/G

N19
HALL G.,MAIN STREET TO WALL STREET: END THE COLD WAR (PAMPHLET). AFR USA+45 LAW STRUCT POL/PAR WORKER INT/TRADE DOMIN INCOME...POLICY 20 COM/PARTY. PAGE 53 F1046
MARXIST CAP/ISM DIPLOM NAT/G

N19
HANSEN B.,INFLATION PROBLEMS IN SMALL COUNTRIES (PAMPHLET). AFR UNIV FOR/AID CONTROL BAL/PAY DEMAND PRODUC 20. PAGE 54 F1066
PRICE FINAN ECO/UNDEV ECO/TAC

N19
MEZERIK A.G.,ECONOMIC AID FOR UNDERDEVELOPED COUNTRIES (PAMPHLET). AFR USSR WOR+45 FINAN LG/CO DELIB/GP NUC/PWR...GEOG CENSUS CHARTS 20 UN THIRD/WRLD. PAGE 90 F1775
FOR/AID ECO/UNDEV DIPLOM POLICY

N19
SAPIR H.M.,JAPAN, CHINA, AND THE WEST (PAMPHLET). AFR ASIA CHINA/COM PROB/SOLV GOV/REL 20 CHINJAP. PAGE 116 F2282
ECO/UNDEV INT/TRADE DECISION PLAN

N19
SENGHOR L.S.,AFRICAN SOCIALISM (PAMPHLET). AFR FRANCE MALI USSR ELITES ECO/UNDEV NAT/G DIPLOM DOMIN EDU/PROP ATTIT 20 NEGRO. PAGE 119 F2355
SOCISM MARXISM ORD/FREE NAT/LISM

N19
STALEY E.,SCIENTIFIC RESEARCH AND PROGRESS IN NEWLY DEVELOPING COUNTRIES (PAMPHLET). AFR ASIA L/A+17C CONSULT DIPLOM...METH/COMP 20. PAGE 125 F2463
ECO/UNDEV ACT/RES FOR/AID TEC/DEV

N19
VELYAMINOV G.,AFRICA AND THE COMMON MARKET (PAMPHLET). AFR MARKET VOL/ASSN ECO/TAC COLONIAL ORD/FREE...SOCIALIST 20 THIRD/WRLD. PAGE 141 F2775
INT/ORG INT/TRADE SOVEREIGN ECO/UNDEV

B20
MOREL E.D.,THE BLACK MAN'S BURDEN. AFR MOD/EUR AGRI EXTR/IND PROB/SOLV INT/TRADE ADMIN CONTROL COERCE DISCRIM...POLICY 19/20 NEGRO LEAGUE/NAT. PAGE 93 F1823
ORD/FREE CAP/ISM RACE/REL DOMIN

B24
HOLDSWORTH W.S.,A HISTORY OF ENGLISH LAW; THE COMMON LAW AND ITS RIVALS (VOL. VI). AFR UK STRATA EX/STRUC ADJUD ADMIN CONTROL CT/SYS...JURID CONCPT GEN/LAWS 17 PARLIAMENT ENGLSH/LAW COMMON/LAW. PAGE 61 F1194
LAW CONSTN LEGIS CHIEF

B25
WILLIAMS B.,THE SELBORNE MEMORANDUM. AFR FUT SOUTH/AFR UK NAT/G BUDGET DIPLOM REGION GOV/REL SOVEREIGN...POLICY CHARTS 20 UNIFICA SELBORNE/W. PAGE 147 F2888
COLONIAL PROVS

B26
MCPHEE A.,THE ECONOMIC REVOLUTION IN BRITISH WEST AFRICA. AFR UK CULTURE DIST/IND FINAN INDUS PLAN GP/REL RACE/REL 20 AFRICA/W. PAGE 88 F1735
ECO/UNDEV INT/TRADE COLONIAL GEOG

B28
CROS L.,AFRIQUE FRANCAISE POUR TOUS. EUR+WWI FRANCE PLAN TEC/DEV ATTIT 20. PAGE 29 F0556
COLONIAL DOMIN ECO/TAC AFR

B37
BRESCIANI-TURRONI C,THE ECONOMICS OF INFLATION: A STUDY OF CURRENCY DEPRECIATION IN POST-WAR GERMANY. AFR GERMANY FINAN INT/TRADE PRICE TOTALISM...POLICY TIME/SEQ CHARTS GEN/LAWS 20 HITLER/A. PAGE 18 F0347
ECO/TAC WEALTH SOCIETY

B40
MEEK C.K.,EUROPE AND WEST AFRICA. AFR EUR+WWI EXTR/IND DIPLOM INT/TRADE EDU/PROP GP/REL...SOC 20. PAGE 89 F1743
CULTURE TEC/DEV ECO/UNDEV COLONIAL

B42
JACKSON M.V.,EUROPEAN POWERS AND SOUTH-EAST AFRICA: A STUDY OF INTERNATIONAL RELATIONS ON SOUTH-EAST COAST OF AFRICA, 1796-1856. AFR FRANCE PORTUGAL SOUTH/AFR UK USA-45 FORCES INT/TRADE PWR...CHARTS BIBLIOG 18/19 TREATY. PAGE 66 F1294
DOMIN POLICY ORD/FREE DIPLOM

B44
LOCKE J.,FURTHER CONSIDERATIONS CONCERNING RAISING THE VALUE OF MONEY. AFR UK NAT/G ECO/TAC INCOME WEALTH...METH/COMP GEN/LAWS 17 SILVER. PAGE 81 F1591
COST FINAN PRICE CONTROL

B45
DAVIS J.,AFRICA ADVANCING. AFR CONGO/BRAZ LIBERIA NIGER INT/ORG SCHOOL DIPLOM GIVE KNOWL SKILL 20. PAGE 30 F0590
SECT COLONIAL AGRI ECO/UNDEV

B48
HART A.G.,MONEY, DEBT, AND ECONOMIC ACTIVITY. AFR WORKER DIPLOM PRICE CONTROL BAL/PAY COST OWN PRODUC ...METH/COMP 20 FED/RESERV. PAGE 56 F1097
FINAN WEALTH ECO/TAC NAT/G

B48
ROBERTSON D.H.,MONEY. AFR ECO/DEV NAT/G DIPLOM INT/TRADE BAL/PAY INCOME WEALTH...TIME/SEQ 20 DEPRESSION. PAGE 112 F2212
FINAN MARKET COST PRICE

B49
DE JOUVENEL B.,PROBLEMS OF SOCIALIST ENGLAND. AFR UK USSR BAL/PWR ECO/TAC INT/TRADE PRICE WAR BAL/PAY PEACE 20. PAGE 31 F0601
SOCISM NEW/LIB PROB/SOLV PLAN

B50
LINCOLN G.,ECONOMICS OF NATIONAL SECURITY. USA+45 ELITES COM/IND DIST/IND INDUS NAT/G VOL/ASSN DELIB/GP EX/STRUC FOR/AID EDU/PROP COERCE NUC/PWR WAR ATTIT KNOWL ORD/FREE PWR TOT/POP VAL/FREE 20. PAGE 80 F1565
FORCES ECO/TAC AFR

B50
SHAW E.S.,MONEY, INCOME, AND MONETARY POLICY. AFR USA-45 NAT/G DIPLOM PAY CONTROL COST INCOME PRODUC WEALTH...T 20 FED/RESERV DEPT/TREAS. PAGE 120 F2370
FINAN ECO/TAC ECO/DEV PRICE

B51
CHANDLER L.V.,INFLATION IN THE UNITED STATES 1940-1948. AFR NAT/G BUDGET PAY PRICE CONTROL WAR INCOME PRODUC...POLICY BIBLIOG 20. PAGE 23 F0448
ECO/TAC FINAN PROB/SOLV WEALTH

B51
HART A.G.,DEFENSE WITHOUT INFLATION. AFR KOREA FINAN INDUS NAT/G WORKER DIPLOM RATION TAX PRICE COST OPTIMAL 20 RESOURCE/N. PAGE 56 F1098
ECO/TAC CONTROL WAR PLAN

B51
POOLE K.,FISCAL POLICIES AND THE AMERICAN ECONOMY. AFR ECO/DEV FINAN INDUS WORKER OP/RES INT/TRADE TAX COST INCOME PROFIT WEALTH...GP/COMP 20. PAGE 107 F2102
NAT/G POLICY ANTHOL

B51
US DEPARTMENT OF STATE,POINT FOUR, NEAR EAST AND AFRICA, A SELECTED BIBLIOGRAPHY OF STUDIES ON ECONOMICALLY UNDERDEVELOPED COUNTRIES. AGRI COM/IND FINAN INDUS PLAN INT/TRADE...SOC TREND 20. PAGE 135 F2672
BIBLIOG/A AFR S/ASIA ISLAM

B51
US HOUSE COMM APPROPRIATIONS,MUTUAL SECURITY PROGRAM APPROPRIATIONS FOR 1952: HEARINGS BEFORE A SUBCOMMITTEE OF THE COMMITTEE ON APPROPRIATIONS. AFR KOREA L/A+17C ECO/DEV ECO/UNDEV INT/ORG INSPECT BAL/PWR DIPLOM DEBATE WAR...POLICY STAT ASIA/S 20 CONGRESS NATO MID/EAST. PAGE 136 F2686
LEGIS FORCES BUDGET FOR/AID

B52
GALBRAITH J.K.,AMERICAN CAPITALISM: THE CONCEPT OF COUNTERVAILING POWER. AFR FUT USA+45 FINAN PRICE CENTRAL INCOME PEACE WEALTH...POLICY DECISION 20. PAGE 45 F0881
ECO/TAC CAP/ISM TREND NAT/G

B52
HOSELITZ B.F.,THE PROGRESS OF UNDERDEVELOPED AREAS. AFR FUT WOR+45 WOR-45 ECO/DEV ECO/TAC INT/TRADE WEALTH...SOC TREND GEN/LAWS TOT/POP VAL/FREE FOR/TRADE 20. PAGE 62 F1219
ECO/UNDEV PLAN FOR/AID

B52
JENNINGS W.I.,CONSTITUTIONAL LAWS OF THE COMMONWEALTH. AFR UK LAW CHIEF LEGIS TAX CT/SYS PARL/PROC GOV/REL...INT/LAW 18/20 ENGLSH/LAW COMMON/LAW. PAGE 67 F1316
CONSTN JURID ADJUD COLONIAL

B53
FRANKEL S.H.,THE ECONOMIC IMPACT ON UNDERDEVELOPED SOCIETIES: ESSAYS ON INTERNATIONAL INVESTMENT AND SOCIAL CHANGE. AFR WOR+45 ECO/DEV FINAN INDUS NAT/G ACT/RES TEC/DEV COLONIAL ATTIT...CONCPT OBS TREND 20. PAGE 43 F0845
ECO/UNDEV FOR/AID INT/TRADE

B53
HARROD R.,THE DOLLAR. AFR USA+45 USA-45 ECO/DEV OPTIMAL WEALTH 18/20 FED/RESERV. PAGE 56 F1093
FINAN DIPLOM BAL/PAY

B53
MENDE T.,WORLD POWER IN THE BALANCE. FUT USA+45 USSR WOR-45 ECO/DEV ECO/TAC INT/TRADE EDU/PROP UTOPIA ATTIT...HUM CONCPT TREND TOT/POP 20. PAGE 90 F1756
WOR+45 PWR BAL/PWR AFR

S53
HANSER P.M.,"EXPLODING POPULATIONS: INTERNATIONAL AND REGIONAL ASPECTS." AFR S/ASIA ECO/TAC WEAPON BIO/SOC LOVE ORD/FREE...NEW/IDEA CENSUS TOT/POP 20. PAGE 55 F1069
ECO/UNDEV GEOG

B54
BATTEN T.R.,PROBLEMS OF AFRICAN DEVELOPMENT (2ND ED.). AFR LAW SOCIETY SCHOOL ECO/TAC TAX...GEOG HEAL SOC 20. PAGE 11 F0211
ECO/UNDEV AGRI LOC/G PROB/SOLV

B54
FRIEDMAN W.,THE PUBLIC CORPORATION: A COMPARATIVE SYMPOSIUM (UNIVERSITY OF TORONTO SCHOOL OF LAW COMPARATIVE LAW SERIES, VOL. I). AFR SWEDEN USA+45 INDUS INT/ORG NAT/G REGION CENTRAL FEDERAL...POLICY JURID IDEA/COMP NAT/COMP ANTHOL 20 MONOPOLY EUROPE. PAGE 44 F0861
LAW SOCISM LG/CO OWN

B54
KARTUN D.,AFRICA, AFRICA: A CONTINENT RISES TO ITS FEET. AFR SOUTH/AFR UK ELITES AGRI LABOR LOC/G POL/PAR EDU/PROP CONTROL COERCE DISCRIM AGE/Y NEGRO THIRD/WRLD GOLD/COAST. PAGE 69 F1358
COLONIAL ORD/FREE PROFIT EXTR/IND

B54
MEYER F.V.,INFLATION AND CAPITAL. AFR UK WOR+45 BUDGET GOV/REL INCOME PRODUC PROFIT WEALTH...CONCPT CHARTS 20. PAGE 90 F1768
ECO/DEV FINAN ECO/TAC DEMAND

B54
STALEY E.,THE FUTURE OF UNDERDEVELOPED COUNTRIES: POLITICAL IMPLICATIONS OF ECONOMIC DEVELOPMENT. AFR COM FUT USA+45 SOCIETY ECO/UNDEV CREATE PLAN CAP/ISM ATTIT DRIVE MARXISM SOCISM...POLICY CONCPT CHARTS 20. PAGE 125 F2466
EDU/PROP ECO/TAC FOR/AID

B55
SMITHIES A.,THE BUDGETARY PROCESS IN THE UNITED STATES. AFR ECO/DEV AGRI EX/STRUC FORCES LEGIS PROB/SOLV TAX ROUTINE EFFICIENCY...MGT CONGRESS PRESIDENT. PAGE 124 F2436
NAT/G ADMIN BUDGET GOV/REL

B55
STILLMAN C.W.,AFRICA IN THE MODERN WORLD. AFR USA+45 WOR+45 INT/TRADE COLONIAL PARTIC REGION GOV/REL RACE/REL 20. PAGE 126 F2489
ECO/UNDEV DIPLOM POLICY STRUCT

B56
KNORR K.E.,RUBLE DIPLOMACY: CHALLENGE TO AMERICAN FOREIGN AID(PAMPHLET). AFR CHINA/COM USA+45 USSR PLAN TEC/DEV CAP/ISM INT/TRADE DOMIN EDU/PROP CONTROL LEAD 20. PAGE 72 F1413
ECO/UNDEV COM DIPLOM FOR/AID

B56
KOHLER E.L.,ACCOUNTING IN THE FEDERAL GOVERNMENT. USA+45 LOC/G PLAN TAX CONTROL COST 20. PAGE 72 F1416
BUDGET AFR NAT/G FINAN

B56
MYRDAL G.,AN INTERNATIONAL ECONOMY. EUR+WWI USA+45 WOR+45 WOR-45 NAT/G DIPLOM ECO/TAC BAL/PAY...PSY CONCPT OEEC TOT/POP 20. PAGE 96 F1879
VOL/ASSN AFR

B56
US DEPARTMENT OF STATE,ECONOMIC PROBLEMS OF UNDERDEVELOPED AREAS (PAMPHLET). AFR ASIA ISLAM L/A+17C AGRI FINAN INDUS INT/ORG LABOR INT/TRADE ...PSY SOC 20. PAGE 136 F2673
BIBLIOG ECO/UNDEV TEC/DEV R+D

N56
US HOUSE COMM FOREIGN AFFAIRS,REPORT OF THE SPECIAL STUDY MISSION TO AFRICA, SOUTH AND EAST OF THE SAHARA (PAMPHLET). AFR SOUTH/AFR USA+45 STRUCT INT/TRADE PARL/PROC NAT/LISM ATTIT ALL/VALS HEALTH ...POLICY 20 CONGRESS. PAGE 136 F2691
FOR/AID COLONIAL ECO/UNDEV DIPLOM

B57
BAUER P.T.,ECONOMIC ANALYSIS AND POLICY IN UNDERDEVELOPED COUNTRIES. AFR WOR+45 AGRI INT/TRADE TAX PRICE...GEN/METH BIBLIOG/A 20. PAGE 11 F0214
ECO/UNDEV METH/COMP POLICY

B57
DAY A.C.L.,OUTLINE OF MONETARY ECONOMICS. AFR WOR-45 INT/ORG WORKER DIPLOM BAL/PAY COST INCOME WEALTH...TIME/SEQ SIMUL 20. PAGE 31 F0594
FINAN NAT/G EQUILIB PRICE

B57
DUNLOP J.T.,THE THEORY OF WAGE DETERMINATION; PROCEEDINGS OF CONFERENCE HELD BY INTERNATIONAL ECONOMIC ASSOCIATION. AFR ECO/DEV LABOR BARGAIN PAY CONFER...CHARTS ANTHOL 20. PAGE 35 F0679
PRICE WORKER GEN/LAWS INCOME

B57
HARRIS S.E.,INTERNATIONAL AND INTERREGIONAL ECONOMICS. AFR WOR+45 WOR-45 NAT/G TARIFFS BAL/PAY EQUILIB...POLICY CONCPT STAT CHARTS IDEA/COMP 19/20. PAGE 55 F1088
INT/TRADE ECO/DEV MARKET FINAN

B57
HARWOOD E.C.,CAUSE AND CONTROL OF THE BUSINESS CYCLE (5TH ED.). AFR USA-45 PRICE CONTROL WAR DEMAND INCOME WEALTH...TREND CHARTS 19. PAGE 56 F1107
PRODUC MARKET FINAN

B57
HUTTON D.G.,INFLATION AND SOCIETY. AFR FINAN PLAN COST DEMAND EQUILIB...CONCPT 20. PAGE 64 F1254
ECO/DEV POLICY NAT/G ECO/TAC

B57
OLIVECRONA K.,THE PROBLEM OF THE MONETARY UNIT. AFR UNIV PAY PRICE UTIL...MATH 20 MONEY SILVER. PAGE 101 F1986
FINAN ECO/TAC ECO/DEV CONCPT

B57
SINGH D.B.,INFLATIONARY PRICE TRENDS IN INDIA SINCE 1939. AFR INDIA ECO/TAC RATION CONTROL WAR GOV/REL BAL/PAY DEMAND INCOME PEACE PRODUC...POLICY CHARTS 20. PAGE 122 F2413
BUDGET ECO/UNDEV PRICE FINAN

B57
THOMAS R.G.,OUR MODERN BANKING AND MONETARY SYSTEM (3RD ED.). AFR USA+45 USA-45 ACT/RES PLAN PROB/SOLV INT/TRADE PRICE WAR BAL/PAY INCOME...POLICY METH/CNCPT 20 DEPRESSION. PAGE 130 F2563
FINAN SERV/IND ECO/TAC

L57
MASS. INST. TECH.,"THE CENTER FOR INTERNATIONAL STUDIES." AFR ASIA COM EUR+WWI ISLAM L/A+17C S/ASIA USA+45 USA-45 DIST/IND CONSULT FORCES ACT/RES TEC/DEV DIPLOM REV ATTIT WEALTH...CONCPT FOR/TRADE 20. PAGE 87 F1702
R+D ECO/UNDEV

S57
HOAG M.W.,"ECONOMIC PROBLEMS OF ALLIANCE." AFR COM EUR+WWI WOR+45 ECO/DEV ECO/UNDEV NAT/G VOL/ASSN FORCES PLAN TEC/DEV DIPLOM COERCE ORD/FREE PWR WEALTH...DECISION GEN/LAWS NATO TERR/GP. PAGE 60 F1182
INT/ORG ECO/TAC

B58
AVRAMOVIC D.,POSTWAR GROWTH IN INTERNATIONAL INDEBTEDNESS. AFR WOR+45 AGRI INDUS CAP/ISM PRICE INCOME...NAT/COMP 20 SILVER. PAGE 8 F0143
INT/TRADE FINAN COST BAL/PAY

B58
BERLINER J.S.,SOVIET ECONOMIC AID: THE AID AND TRADE POLICY IN UNDERDEVELOPED COUNTRIES. AFR COM ISLAM L/A+17C S/ASIA USSR ECO/DEV DIST/IND FINAN MARKET INT/ORG ACT/RES PLAN BAL/PWR WEAPON PWR WEALTH...CHARTS FOR/TRADE 20. PAGE 14 F0263
ECO/UNDEV ECO/TAC FOR/AID

B58
EHRHARD J.,LE DESTIN DU COLONIALISME. AFR FRANCE ECO/UNDEV AGRI FINAN MARKET CREATE PLAN TEC/DEV BUDGET DIPLOM PRICE 20. PAGE 36 F0710
COLONIAL FOR/AID INT/TRADE INDUS

B58
HANCE W.A.,AFRICAN ECONOMIC DEVELOPMENT. AGRI DIST/IND INDUS R+D ACT/RES PLAN CAP/ISM FOR/AID ...GOV/COMP BIBLIOG 20. PAGE 54 F1058
AFR ECO/UNDEV PROB/SOLV TEC/DEV

B58
JENNINGS I.,PROBLEMS OF THE NEW COMMONWEALTH. AFR CEYLON INDIA PAKISTAN S/ASIA ECO/UNDEV INT/ORG LOC/G DIPLOM ECO/TAC INT/TRADE COLONIAL RACE/REL DISCRIM 20 PARLIAMENT. PAGE 67 F1314
NAT/LISM NEUTRAL FOR/AID POL/PAR

B58
MOONEY R.E.,INFLATION AND RECESSION? AFR USA+45 LABOR LG/CO PRESS LEAD...IDEA/COMP ANTHOL 20. PAGE 93 F1821
PRICE ECO/TAC NAT/G PRODUC

B58
NICULESCU B.,COLONIAL PLANNING: A COMPARATIVE STUDY. AFR AGRI LOC/G NAT/G DELIB/GP COLONIAL MUNICH 20. PAGE 98 F1927
PLAN ECO/UNDEV TEC/DEV NAT/COMP

B58
PALYI M.,MANAGED MONEY AT THE CROSSROADS: THE EUROPEAN EXPERIENCE. AFR WOR+45 WOR-45 TEC/DEV DIPLOM INT/TRADE DEMAND WEALTH...CHARTS BIBLIOG 19/20 EUROPE SILVER. PAGE 103 F2022
FINAN ECO/TAC ECO/DEV PRODUC

N58
EUROPEAN COMM ECO-SOC PROG,EUROPEAN BUSINESS CYCLE POLICY (PAMPHLET). AFR EUR+WWI MARKET WORKER DIPLOM PRICE BAL/PAY 20 EUROPE. PAGE 39 F0754
ECO/DEV FINAN ECO/TAC PROB/SOLV

B59
CUCCORESE H.J.,HISTORIA DE LA CONVERSION DEL PAPEL MONEDA EN BUENOS AIRES, 1861-1867. AFR LAW LOC/G NAT/G ATTIT...POLICY BIBLIOG 19 ARGEN BUENOS/AIR. PAGE 29 F0560
FINAN PLAN LEGIS

B59
HICKS J.R.,ESSAYS IN WORLD ECONOMICS. AFR CEYLON
ECO/UNDEV

NIGERIA WOR+45 SOCIETY ECO/DEV ORD/FREE WEALTH ...GEN/LAWS TOT/POP 20. PAGE 59 F1166 ECO/TAC UK

B59
MATTHEWS R.C.O.,THE BUSINESS CYCLE. AFR LABOR INT/TRADE TAX PRICE RISK ADJUST WEALTH...POLICY ECOMETRIC CHARTS SIMUL TIME 20. PAGE 87 F1705 FINAN DEMAND TASK

B59
PANIKKAR K.M.,THE AFRO-ASIAN STATES AND THEIR PROBLEMS. COM CULTURE KIN POL/PAR SECT DIPLOM EDU/PROP COLONIAL SOVEREIGN...TECHNIC GOV/COMP 20. PAGE 103 F2025 AFR S/ASIA ECO/UNDEV

B59
SILCOCK T.H.,THE COMMONWEALTH ECONOMY IN SOUTHEAST ASIA. AFR INDIA MALAYSIA S/ASIA ECO/DEV AGRI LOC/G PLAN TARIFFS COLONIAL BAL/PAY DEMAND...BIBLIOG/A 20 GATT. PAGE 122 F2401 ECO/TAC INT/TRADE RACE/REL DIPLOM

B59
WELTON H.,THE THIRD WORLD WAR; TRADE AND INDUSTRY, THE NEW BATTLEGROUND. AFR WOR+45 ECO/DEV INDUS MARKET TASK...MGT IDEA/COMP. PAGE 145 F2855 INT/TRADE PLAN DIPLOM

B59
WENTHOLT W.,SOME COMMENTS ON THE LIQUIDATION OF THE EUROPEAN PAYMENT UNION AND RELATED PROBLEMS (PAMPHLET). AFR WOR+45 PLAN BUDGET PRICE CONTROL 20 EEC. PAGE 145 F2857 FINAN ECO/DEV INT/ORG ECO/TAC

B59
YRARRAZAVAL E.,AMERICA LATINE EN LA GUERRA FRIA. AFR EUR+WWI L/A+17C USA+45 USSR WOR+45 INDUS INT/ORG NAT/LISM POLICY. PAGE 150 F2953 REGION DIPLOM ECO/UNDEV INT/TRADE

L59
GARDNER R.N.,"NEW DIRECTIONS IN UNITED STATES FOREIGN ECONOMIC POLICY." AFR USA+45 CONSULT ...GEN/LAWS GEN/METH FOR/TRADE 20. PAGE 46 F0903 ECO/UNDEV ECO/TAC FOR/AID DIPLOM

S59
HOFFMAN P.,"OPERATION BREAKTHROUGH." AFR S/ASIA STRUCT INDUS CONSULT TEC/DEV ATTIT RIGID/FLEX SKILL WEALTH...TECHNIC CONCPT STYLE RECORD CHARTS ORG/CHARTS GEN/METH VAL/FREE 20. PAGE 61 F1190 ECO/UNDEV EDU/PROP FOR/AID

N59
CHAMBER OF COMMERCE OF USA,ECONOMIC LESSONS OF POSTWAR RECESSIONS (PAMPHLET). AFR USA+45 LAW LEGIS WORKER TAX...CHARTS 20 CONGRESS FED/RESERV. PAGE 23 F0440 ECO/DEV PROB/SOLV FINAN ECO/TAC

B60
ARON R.,COLLOQUES DE RHEINFELDEN. AFR USA+45 USSR WOR+45 WOR-45 CULTURE ECO/UNDEV NAT/G POL/PAR DIPLOM NAT/LISM TOTALISM ATTIT DRIVE ALL/VALS ...PLURIST CONCPT STERTYP GEN/LAWS TOT/POP 20. PAGE 6 F0120 ECO/DEV SOCIETY CAP/ISM SOCISM

B60
ASPREMONT-LYNDEN H.,RAPPORT SUR L'ADMINISTRATION BELGE DU RUANDA-URUNDI PENDANT L'ANNEE 1959. BELGIUM RWANDA AGRI INDUS DIPLOM ECO/TAC INT/TRADE DOMIN ADMIN RACE/REL...GEOG CENSUS 20 UN. PAGE 7 F0132 AFR COLONIAL ECO/UNDEV INT/ORG

B60
BIERMAN H.,THE CAPITAL BUDGETING DECISION. AFR ECO/DEV MARKET TAX PRICE RISK COST INCOME TIME 20. PAGE 15 F0282 FINAN OPTIMAL BUDGET PROFIT

B60
DIA M.,REFLEXIONS SUR L'ECONOMIE DE L'AFRIQUE NOIRE (REV. ED.). CULTURE ECO/UNDEV CREATE TEC/DEV DIPLOM INT/TRADE OPTIMAL ATTIT...POLICY 20. PAGE 32 F0631 AFR ECO/TAC SOCISM PLAN

B60
FRANCK P.G.,AFGHANISTAN: BETWEEN EAST AND WEST. AFGHANISTN AFR USA+45 USSR ECO/UNDEV PLAN ADMIN ROUTINE ATTIT PWR...STAT OBS CHARTS TOT/POP FOR/TRADE 20. PAGE 43 F0843 ECO/TAC TREND FOR/AID

B60
HEYSE T.,PROBLEMS FONCIERS ET REGIME DES TERRES (ASPECTS ECONOMIQUES, JURIDIQUES ET SOCIAUX). AFR CONGO/BRAZ INT/ORG DIPLOM SOVEREIGN...GEOG TREATY 20. PAGE 59 F1161 BIBLIOG AGRI ECO/UNDEV LEGIS

B60
KENEN P.B.,GIANT AMONG NATIONS: PROBLEMS IN UNITED STATES FOREIGN ECONOMIC POLICY. AFR USA+45 FINAN DIPLOM TARIFFS BAL/PAY WEALTH 20. PAGE 70 F1376 FOR/AID ECO/UNDEV INT/TRADE PLAN

B60
MC CLELLAN G.S.,INDIA. AFR CHINA/COM INDIA CONSTN ELITES STRATA AGRI POL/PAR FOR/AID ARMS/CONT REV MARXISM...CENSUS BIBLIOG 20 GANDHI/M NEHRU/J. PAGE 87 F1712 DIPLOM NAT/G SOCIETY ECO/UNDEV

B60
PITCHER G.M.,BIBLIOGRAPHY OF GHANA. AFR GHANA NAT/G 20. PAGE 106 F2091 BIBLIOG/A SOC

B60
RAY D.D.,ACCOUNTING AND BUSINESS FLUCTUATIONS. LG/CO SML/CO FEEDBACK DEMAND...CHARTS IDEA/COMP BIBLIOG 20. PAGE 109 F2154 FINAN AFR CONTROL

B60
SMET G.,BIBLIOGRAPHIE DE LA CONTRIBUTION A L'ETUDE DE LA PROGRESSION ECONOMIQUE DE L'AFRIQUE. AFR DIST/IND EXTR/IND TEC/DEV 20. PAGE 123 F2427 BIBLIOG ECO/UNDEV INDUS AGRI

B60
STANFORD RESEARCH INSTITUTE,AFRICAN DEVELOPMENT: A TEST FOR INTERNATIONAL COOPERATION. AFR USA+45 WOR+45 FINAN INT/ORG PLAN PROB/SOLV ECO/TAC INT/TRADE ADMIN...CHARTS 20. PAGE 125 F2467 FOR/AID ECO/UNDEV ATTIT DIPLOM

B60
STOLPER W.F.,GERMANY BETWEEN EAST AND WEST: THE ECONOMICS OF COMPETITIVE COEXISTENCE. AFR FUT GERMANY/E GERMANY/W WOR+45 FINAN POL/PAR BUDGET ECO/TAC FOR/AID INT/TRADE...STAT CHARTS METH/COMP 20. PAGE 126 F2495 ECO/DEV DIPLOM GOV/COMP BAL/PWR

S60
BARNETT H.J.,"RESEARCH AND DEVELOPMENT, ECONOMIC GROWTH, AND NATIONAL SECURITY." AFR USA+45 R+D CREATE ECO/TAC ATTIT DRIVE PWR...POLICY SOC METH/CNCPT QUANT STAT TIME/SEQ ORG/CHARTS LOG/LING 20. PAGE 10 F0190 ACT/RES PLAN

S60
BERG E.J.,"ECONOMIC BASIS OF POLITICAL CHOICE IN FRENCH WEST AFRICA." FRANCE ECO/UNDEV AGRI INDUS NAT/G PLAN LEGIT COLONIAL REGION ATTIT PWR WEALTH ...CONCPT FOR/TRADE 20. PAGE 13 F0257 AFR ECO/TAC

S60
FRANKEL S.H.,"ECONOMIC ASPECTS OF POLITICAL INDEPENDENCE IN AFRICA." AFR FUT SOCIETY ECO/UNDEV COM/IND FINAN LEGIS PLAN TEC/DEV CAP/ISM ECO/TAC INT/TRADE ADMIN ATTIT DRIVE RIGID/FLEX PWR WEALTH ...MGT NEW/IDEA MATH TIME/SEQ VAL/FREE 20. PAGE 43 F0846 NAT/G FOR/AID

S60
GARNICK D.H.,"ON THE ECONOMIC FEASIBILITY OF A MIDDLE EASTERN COMMON MARKET." AFR ISLAM CULTURE INDUS NAT/G PLAN TEC/DEV ECO/TAC ADMIN ATTIT DRIVE RIGID/FLEX...PLURIST STAT TREND GEN/LAWS 20. PAGE 46 F0907 MARKET INT/TRADE

S60
GROSSMAN G.,"SOVIET GROWTH: ROUTINE, INERTIA, AND PRESSURE." COM STRATA NAT/G DELIB/GP PLAN TEC/DEV ECO/TAC EDU/PROP ADMIN ROUTINE DRIVE WEALTH 20. PAGE 52 F1007 POL/PAR ECO/DEV AFR USSR

S60
JACOBSON H.K.,"THE USSR AND ILO." AFR COM STRUCT ECO/DEV ECO/UNDEV CONSULT DELIB/GP ECO/TAC ILO WORK 20. PAGE 66 F1298 INT/ORG LABOR USSR

S60
JAFFEE A.J.,"POPULATION TRENDS AND CONTROLS IN UNDERDEVELOPED COUNTRIES." AFR FUT ISLAM L/A+17C S/ASIA CULTURE R+D FAM ACT/RES PLAN EDU/PROP BIO/SOC RIGID/FLEX HEALTH...SOC STAT OBS CHARTS 20. PAGE 66 F1303 ECO/UNDEV GEOG

S60
KELLOGG C.E.,"TRANSFER OF BASIC SKILLS OF FOOD PRODUCTION." AFR FUT S/ASIA STRATA ECO/UNDEV LABOR VOL/ASSN RIGID/FLEX...OLD/LIB SOCIALIST NEW/IDEA STAT PROJ/TEST GEN/LAWS 20. PAGE 70 F1370 AGRI PLAN

S60
MAIR L.P.,"SOCIAL CHANGE IN SOUTH AFRICA." MOD/EUR SOUTH/AFR WOR+45 ECO/UNDEV EX/STRUC TEC/DEV ATTIT DRIVE PERCEPT ORD/FREE...MGT CONCPT TIME/SEQ IND 20. PAGE 84 F1641 AFR NAT/G REV SOVEREIGN

S60
MURPHY J.C.,"INTERNATIONAL INVESTMENT AND THE NATIONAL INTEREST." AFR WOR+45 WOR-45 ECO/DEV ECO/UNDEV NAT/G ACT/RES...CHARTS TOT/POP FOR/TRADE 20. PAGE 95 F1867 FINAN WEALTH FOR/AID

S60
OWEN C.F.,"US AND SOVIET RELATIONS WITH UNDERDEVELOPED COUNTRIES: LATIN AMERICA-A CASE STUDY." AFR COM L/A+17C USA+45 USSR EXTR/IND MARKET TEC/DEV DIPLOM ECO/TAC NAT/LISM ORD/FREE PWR ...TREND WORK 20. PAGE 102 F2005 ECO/UNDEV DRIVE INT/TRADE

S60
RIVKIN A.,"AFRICAN ECONOMIC DEVELOPMENT: ADVANCED TECHNOLOGY AND THE STAGES OF GROWTH." CULTURE ECO/UNDEV AGRI COM/IND EXTR/IND PLAN ECO/TAC ATTIT DRIVE RIGID/FLEX SKILL WEALTH...MGT SOC GEN/LAWS FOR/TRADE WORK TOT/POP 20. PAGE 111 F2195 AFR TEC/DEV FOR/AID

B61
ACKLEY G.,MACROECONOMIC THEORY. AFR FINAN WORKER ECO/TAC PRICE COST INCOME PRODUC...MATH TREND CHARTS IDEA/COMP T KEYNES/JM. PAGE 2 F0034 SIMUL ECOMETRIC WEALTH

B61
ASHER R.E.,GRANTS, LOANS, AND LOCAL CURRENCIES; THEIR ROLE IN FOREIGN AID. AFR USA+45 ECO/UNDEV INT/ORG ACT/RES PLAN ECO/TAC GIVE CONTROL WEALTH 20. PAGE 7 F0130 FOR/AID FINAN NAT/G BUDGET

B61
AUBREY H.G.,COEXISTENCE: ECONOMIC CHALLENGE AND RESPONSE. AFR USSR WOR+45 ACT/RES BAL/PWR CAP/ISM DIPLOM ECO/TAC FOR/AID INT/TRADE PEACE SOCISM ...METH/COMP NAT/COMP. PAGE 7 F0139 POLICY ECO/UNDEV PLAN COM

B61
BONNEFOUS M.,EUROPE ET TIERS MONDE. EUR+WWI SOCIETY AFR

INT/ORG NAT/G VOL/ASSN ACT/RES TEC/DEV CAP/ISM ECO/TAC ATTIT ORD/FREE SOVEREIGN...POLICY CONCPT TREND TERR/GP COMMUN 20. PAGE 16 F0314 — ECO/UNDEV FOR/AID INT/TRADE

B61
BREWIS T.N.,CANADIAN ECONOMIC POLICY. AFR CANADA BUDGET CAP/ISM INT/TRADE RATION TARIFFS TAX PRICE CONTROL ROUTINE FEDERAL INCOME PRODUC 20. PAGE 18 F0348 — ECO/DEV ECO/TAC NAT/G PLAN

B61
BUSSCHAU W.J.,GOLD AND INTERNATIONAL LIQUIDITY. AFR WOR+45 PRICE EQUILIB WEALTH...CHARTS 20. PAGE 20 F0396 — FINAN DIPLOM PROB/SOLV

B61
CANTERBERY E.R.,THE PRESIDENT'S COUNCIL OF ECONOMIC ADVISERS. AFR USA+45 FINAN LABOR NAT/G PLAN ADMIN OPTIMAL WEALTH 20 EISNHWR/DD PRESIDENT TRUMAN/HS KEYNES/JM. PAGE 21 F0413 — ECO/TAC OP/RES EXEC CHIEF

B61
DETHINE P.,BIBLIOGRAPHIE DES ASPECTS ECONOMIQUES ET SOCIAUX DE L'INDUSTRIALISATION EN AFRIQUE. AFR FINAN LABOR FOR/AID...SOC 20. PAGE 32 F0623 — BIBLIOG/A ECO/UNDEV INDUS TEC/DEV

B61
FEARN H.,AN AFRICAN ECONOMY. AFR EUR+WWI PLAN COLONIAL WEALTH...CONT/OBS TREND EEC VAL/FREE 20. PAGE 39 F0770 — ECO/UNDEV

B61
HARDT J.P.,THE COLD WAR ECONOMIC GAP. AFR USA+45 USSR ECO/DEV FORCES INT/TRADE NUC/PWR PWR 20. PAGE 55 F1081 — DIPLOM ECO/TAC NAT/COMP POLICY

B61
HARRIS S.E.,THE DOLLAR IN CRISIS. AFR USA+45 MARKET INT/ORG ECO/TAC PRICE CONTROL WEALTH...METH/COMP ANTHOL 20. PAGE 55 F1089 — BAL/PAY DIPLOM FINAN INT/TRADE

B61
HAUSER M.,DIE URSACHEN DER FRANZOSISCHEN INFLATION IN DEN JAHREN 1946-1952. AFR FRANCE INDUS NAT/G BUDGET DIPLOM ECO/TAC FOR/AID COST MONEY 20. PAGE 57 F1114 — ECO/DEV FINAN PRICE

B61
HEMPSTONE S.,THE NEW AFRICA. AGRI INDUS KIN NAT/G COLONIAL MARXISM...SOC INT TREND NAT/COMP BIBLIOG/A 20. PAGE 58 F1146 — AFR ORD/FREE PERSON CULTURE

B61
HOLMANS A.E.,UNITED STATES FISCAL POLICY 1945-1959. AFR USA+45 USA-45 ECO/DEV TAX PRICE WAR...BIBLIOG 20 DEMOCRAT REPUBLICAN. PAGE 61 F1200 — POLICY BUDGET NAT/G ECO/TAC

B61
INTERNATIONAL BANK RECONST DEV,THE WORLD BANK IN AFRICA: SUMMARY OF ACTIVITIES. AGRI COM/IND DIST/IND EXTR/IND INDUS TAX COST...CHARTS 20. PAGE 65 F1271 — FINAN ECO/UNDEV INT/ORG AFR

B61
KOVNER M.,THE CHALLENGE OF COEXISTENCE: A STUDY OF SOVIET ECONOMIC DIPLOMACY. COM FUT ECO/DEV ECO/UNDEV PLAN EDU/PROP DETER SKILL...OBS VAL/FREE 20. PAGE 73 F1430 — PWR DIPLOM USSR AFR

B61
LANDSKROY W.A.,OFFICIAL SERIAL PUBLICATIONS RELATING TO ECONOMIC DEVELOPMENT IN AFRICA SOUTH OF THE SAHARA (PAMPHLET). AFR UK R+D ACT/RES 20 UN. PAGE 75 F1471 — BIBLIOG ECO/UNDEV COLONIAL INT/ORG

B61
LEHMAN R.L.,AFRICA SOUTH OF THE SAHARA (PAMPHLET). DIPLOM COLONIAL NAT/LISM. PAGE 77 F1512 — BIBLIOG/A AFR CULTURE NAT/G

B61
MIT CENTER INTERNATIONAL STU,OFFICIAL SERIAL PUBLICATIONS RELATING TO ECONOMIC DEVELOPMENT IN AFRICA SOUTH OF THE SAHARA. AFR SOCIETY AGRI FINAN INDUS LG/CO ADMIN 20. PAGE 92 F1806 — BIBLIOG ECO/UNDEV ECO/TAC NAT/G

B61
MORLEY L.,THE PATCHWORK HISTORY OF FOREIGN AID. AFR KOREA/S USA+45 USSR LAW FINAN INT/ORG TEC/DEV BAL/PWR GIVE 20 NATO. PAGE 93 F1834 — FOR/AID ECO/UNDEV FORCES DIPLOM

B61
PAUNIO J.J.,A STUDY IN THE THEORY OF OPEN INFLATION. AFR FINAN CAP/ISM PRICE DEMAND INCOME ...CHARTS BIBLIOG 20. PAGE 104 F2040 — ACT/RES ECO/DEV ECO/TAC COST

B61
PETCH G.A.,ECONOMIC DEVELOPMENT AND MODERN WEST AFRICA. AFR CONGO/BRAZ GHANA NIGER SIER/LEONE AGRI MARKET LABOR FOR/AID TAX COST EFFICIENCY EQUILIB PRODUC...GEOG TREND 20. PAGE 105 F2068 — ECO/UNDEV TEC/DEV EXTR/IND ECO/TAC

B61
SCHNAPPER B.,LA POLITIQUE ET LE COMMERCE FRANCAIS DANS LE GOLFE DE GUINEE DE 1838 A 1871. FRANCE GUINEA UK SEA EXTR/IND NAT/G DELIB/GP LEGIS ADMIN ORD/FREE...POLICY GEOG CENSUS CHARTS BIBLIOG 19. PAGE 117 F2303 — COLONIAL INT/TRADE DOMIN AFR

B61
SHONFIELD A.,ECONOMIC GROWTH AND INFLATION; A STUDY OF INDIAN PLANNING. AFR INDIA AGRI INDUS TEC/DEV CONTROL DEMAND UTIL 20. PAGE 121 F2384 — ECO/UNDEV PRICE PLAN BUDGET

B61
TRIFFIN R.,GOLD AND THE DOLLAR CRISIS: THE FUTURE OF CONVERTIBILITY. AFR USA+45 USA-45 INT/ORG PROB/SOLV BUDGET INT/TRADE PRICE...STAT CHARTS 19/20. PAGE 131 F2588 — FINAN ECO/DEV ECO/TAC BAL/PAY

B61
VEIT O.,GRUNDRISS DER WAHRUNGSPOLITIK. AFR FRANCE GERMANY USSR DIPLOM INT/TRADE...NAT/COMP 19/20 SILVER. PAGE 141 F2773 — FINAN POLICY ECO/TAC CAP/ISM

S61
DELLA PORT G.,"PROBLEMI E PROSPETTIVE DI COESISTENZA FRA ORIENTE ED OCCIDENTE, (PART 3)." COM FUT WOR+45 NAT/G BAL/PWR FOR/AID BAL/PAY PWR WEALTH...SOC CONCPT GEN/LAWS 20. PAGE 32 F0616 — AFR INT/TRADE

S61
DICKS-MIREAUX L.A.,"THE INTERRELATIONSHIP BETWEEN COST AND PRICE CHANGES 19461959: A STUDY OF INFLATION IN POST-WAR BRITAIN" AFR UK ECO/DEV INDUS WORKER ECO/TAC ORD/FREE WEALTH...ECOMETRIC REGRESS STAT TREND CHARTS 20. PAGE 33 F0634 — PRICE PAY DEMAND

S61
HAYTES W.,"THREE VIEWS ON THE SOVIET ECONOMIC THREAT." AFR COM USA+45 USA-45 USSR WOR+45 WOR-45 INDUS TEC/DEV ECO/TAC DOMIN ATTIT PERCEPT PWR FOR/TRADE 20. PAGE 57 F1128 — ECO/DEV PLAN TOTALISM

S61
NYANZI S.,"THE EAST AFRICAN MARKET: FOR BETTER OF FOR WORSE." AFR TANZANIA UGANDA PROB/SOLV TARIFFS TAX BAL/PAY. PAGE 99 F1947 — ECO/TAC ECO/UNDEV INT/ORG INT/TRADE

S61
OCHENG D.,"ECONOMIC FORCES AND UGANDA'S FOREIGN POLICY." AFR UGANDA INT/TRADE TARIFFS INCOME SOVEREIGN WEALTH 20 EACM EEC TANGANYIKA. PAGE 100 F1961 — ECO/TAC DIPLOM ECO/UNDEV INT/ORG

S61
WILDAVSKY A.,"POLITICAL IMPLICATIONS OF BUDGETARY REFORM." AFR NAT/G POL/PAR DELIB/GP EX/STRUC ATTIT PWR CONGRESS. PAGE 146 F2881 — BUDGET PLAN LEGIS

B62
BRIEFS H.W.,PRICING POWER AND "ADMINISTRATIVE" INFLATION (PAMPHLET). AFR USA+45 PROC/MFG CONTROL EFFICIENCY MONEY. PAGE 18 F0349 — ECO/DEV PRICE POLICY EXEC

B62
CONGRES ECONOMISTES LANG FRAN,MONNAIE ET EXPANSION. AFR FRANCE PROB/SOLV BUDGET CENTRAL COST OPTIMAL PRODUC WEALTH 20. PAGE 27 F0524 — FINAN PLAN EUR+WWI

B62
ELLIOTT J.R.,THE APPEAL OF COMMUNISM IN THE UNDERDEVELOPED NATIONS. AFR USSR WOR+45 INT/ORG NAT/G DIPLOM DOMIN EDU/PROP ROUTINE ATTIT RIGID/FLEX ORD/FREE PWR WEALTH MARXISM...POLICY SOC METH/CNCPT MYTH TOT/POP METH/GP 20. PAGE 37 F0722 — COM ECO/UNDEV

B62
FAO,FOOD AND AGRICULTURE ORGANIZATION AFRICAN SURVEY. AFR CONGO/BRAZ GHANA STRATA AGRI INT/ORG TEC/DEV FOR/AID INT/TRADE RACE/REL DEMAND EFFICIENCY PRODUC...GEOG 20 UN CONGO/LEOP. PAGE 39 F0763 — ECO/TAC WEALTH EXTR/IND ECO/UNDEV

B62
FERBER R.,RESEARCH METHODS IN ECONOMICS AND BUSINESS. AFR ECO/DEV FINAN MARKET LG/CO SML/CO CONSULT CONTROL COST...STAT METH/COMP 20. PAGE 40 F0783 — ACT/RES PROB/SOLV ECO/TAC MGT

B62
FORD A.G.,THE GOLD STANDARD 1880-1914: BRITAIN AND ARGENTINA. AFR UK ECO/UNDEV INT/TRADE ADMIN GOV/REL DEMAND EFFICIENCY...STAT CHARTS 19/20 ARGEN. PAGE 42 F0823 — FINAN ECO/TAC BUDGET BAL/PAY

B62
GREEN L.P.,DEVELOPMENT IN AFRICA. AFR CENTRL/AFR GHANA RHODESIA SOUTH/AFR AGRI PROC/MFG INT/TRADE DEMAND NAT/LISM PRODUC WEALTH...GEOG METH/CNCPT CHARTS BIBLIOG 20. PAGE 50 F0987 — CULTURE ECO/UNDEV GOV/REL TREND

B62
HAGUE D.C.,INFLATION. AFR ECO/DEV ECO/UNDEV LABOR BUDGET CAP/ISM INT/TRADE TARIFFS SOCISM 20. PAGE 53 F1036 — FINAN NAT/COMP BARGAIN ECO/TAC

B62
HIRSCHFIELD R.S.,THE CONSTITUTION AND THE COURT. AFR SCHOOL WAR RACE/REL EQUILIB ORD/FREE...POLICY MAJORIT DECISION JURID 18/20 PRESIDENT CIVIL/LIB SUPREME/CT CONGRESS. PAGE 60 F1175 — ADJUD PWR CONSTN LAW

B62
HOOVER C.B.,ECONOMIC SYSTEMS OF THE COMMONWEALTH. AFR CANADA INDIA UK ECO/DEV ECO/UNDEV AGRI INDUS TEC/DEV TARIFFS PRICE BAL/PAY DEMAND...SIMUL 20 — CAP/ISM SOCISM ECO/TAC

AUSTRAL. PAGE 61 F1208 — PLAN

B62
LUTZ F.A.,GELD UND WAHRUNG. AFR MARKET LABOR BUDGET 20 EUROPE. PAGE 82 F1610 — ECO/TAC FINAN DIPLOM POLICY

B62
ROTHBARD M.N.,THE PANIC OF 1819; REACTIONS AND POLICIES. AFR USA-45 LAW FINAN BUDGET TARIFFS DEMAND 19 DEPRESSION. PAGE 114 F2247 — ECO/UNDEV POLICY ATTIT ECO/TAC

B62
SCHILLING W.R.,STRATEGY, POLITICS, AND DEFENSE BUDGETS. AFR USA+45 CHIEF LEGIS PLAN TEC/DEV BAL/PWR BUDGET NUC/PWR WAR CIVMIL/REL GOV/REL PWR 20 EISNHWR/DD. PAGE 117 F2297 — NAT/G POLICY FORCES DETER

B62
SHANNON I.,THE ECONOMIC FUNCTIONS OF GOLD. AFR FUT WOR+45 WOR-45 INT/ORG BUDGET INT/TRADE BAL/PAY DEMAND PEACE 20 MONEY. PAGE 120 F2366 — FINAN PRICE ECO/DEV ECO/TAC

B62
UNECA LIBRARY,BOOKS ON AFRICA IN THE UNECA LIBRARY. WOR+45 AGRI INT/ORG NAT/G PLAN WRITING REGION...SOC STAT UN. PAGE 132 F2605 — BIBLIOG AFR ECO/UNDEV TEC/DEV

B62
UNECA LIBRARY,NEW ACQUISITIONS IN THE UNECA LIBRARY. LAW NAT/G PLAN PROB/SOLV TEC/DEV ADMIN REGION...GEOG SOC 20 UN. PAGE 132 F2606 — BIBLIOG AFR ECO/UNDEV INT/ORG

B62
US AGENCY INTERNATIONAL DEV,OPERATIONS REPORT - 1962 (PAMPHLET). AFR ASIA L/A+17C USA+45 ECO/UNDEV FINAN INT/ORG NAT/G 20 MICHIGAN. PAGE 134 F2636 — FOR/AID CHARTS STAT BUDGET

B62
US LIBRARY OF CONGRESS,A LIST OF AMERICAN DOCTORAL DISSERTATIONS ON AFRICA. SOCIETY SECT DIPLOM EDU/PROP ADMIN...GEOG 19/20. PAGE 138 F2717 — BIBLIOG AFR ACADEM CULTURE

L62
DURAND-REVILLE L.,"LE REGIME DES INVESTISSEMENTS DANS LES ETATS AFRICAINS D'EXPRESSION FRANCAISE ET A MADAGASCAR." MADAGASCAR ECO/UNDEV CAP/ISM ECO/TAC WEALTH...SOC TREND CHARTS 20. PAGE 35 F0683 — AFR FINAN

S62
ALPERT P.,"ECONOMIC POLICIES AND PLANNING IN NEWLY INDEPENDENT AFRICA." PLAN ATTIT PWR WEALTH ...STERTYP GEN/LAWS VAL/FREE 20. PAGE 4 F0078 — AFR ECO/DEV NAT/LISM COLONIAL

S62
BOONE A.,"THE FOREIGN TRADE OF CHINA." AFR ECO/DEV ECO/UNDEV INDUS MARKET NAT/G TEC/DEV WEALTH ...POLICY STAT TREND CHARTS FOR/TRADE. PAGE 17 F0318 — ASIA ECO/TAC

S62
GILL P.J.,"FUTURE TAXATION POLICY IN AN INDEPENDENT EAST AFRICA" UGANDA LOC/G ECO/TAC ADMIN EFFICIENCY INCOME PRODUC...CHARTS 20. PAGE 47 F0923 — ECO/UNDEV TAX AFR COLONIAL

S62
KRISHNA K.G.V.,"PLANNING AND ECONOMIC DEVELOPMENT" AFR UGANDA AGRI INDUS R+D BUDGET RATION TAX COLONIAL 20. PAGE 73 F1441 — ECO/UNDEV ECO/TAC NAT/LISM PLAN

S62
PIQUEMAL M.,"LA COOPERATION FINANCIERE ENTRE LA FRANCE ET LES ETATS AFRICAINS ET MALGACHE." ISLAM INT/ORG TOP/EX ECO/TAC...JURID CHARTS 20. PAGE 106 F2089 — AFR FINAN FRANCE MADAGASCAR

S62
RAZAFIMBAHINY J.,"L'ORGANISATION AFRICAINE ET MALGACHE DE COOPERATION ECONOMIQUE." AFR ISLAM MADAGASCAR NAT/G ACT/RES ECO/TAC ALL/VALS ...TIME/SEQ 20. PAGE 110 F2158 — INT/ORG ECO/UNDEV

C62
GREEN L.P.,"DEVELOPMENT IN AFRICA." RHODESIA SOUTH/AFR UGANDA MARKET PROC/MFG PRODUC WEALTH ...GEOG 20. PAGE 50 F0986 — BIBLIOG ECO/UNDEV AFR AGRI

B63
AHN L.A.,FUNFZIG JAHRE ZWISCHEN INFLATION UND DEFLATION. AFR GERMANY DIPLOM PRICE...CONCPT 20. PAGE 3 F0053 — FINAN CAP/ISM NAT/COMP ECO/TAC

B63
CONF ON FUTURE OF COMMONWEALTH,THE FUTURE OF THE COMMONWEALTH. AFR UK ECO/UNDEV AGRI EDU/PROP ADMIN SOC/INTEG 20. PAGE 27 F0522 — DIPLOM RACE/REL ORD/FREE TEC/DEV

B63
DEUTSCH K.W.,THE POLITICAL ROLE OF LABOR IN DEVELOPING COUNTRIES. AFR ASIA S/ASIA USA+45 WOR+45 ECO/UNDEV POL/PAR ECO/TAC EDU/PROP LEGIT COERCE ORD/FREE PWR WEALTH...OBS INT TREND VAL/FREE 20. PAGE 32 F0625 — LABOR NAT/LISM

B63
FREITAG R.S.,AGRICULTURAL DEVELOPMENT SCHEMES IN SUB-SAHARAN AFRICA. AFR EDU/PROP 20. PAGE 44 F0852 — BIBLIOG/A AGRI TEC/DEV KNOWL

B63
FRIEDMAN M.,INFLATION: CAUSES AND CURES. AFR INDIA ECO/DEV ECO/TAC INT/TRADE RATION PRICE DEMAND ...POLICY 20. PAGE 44 F0860 — ECO/UNDEV PLAN FINAN EQUILIB

B63
HAUSMAN W.H.,MANAGING ECONOMIC DEVELOPMENT IN AFRICA. AFR USA+45 LAW FINAN WORKER TEC/DEV WEALTH ...ANTHOL 20. PAGE 57 F1116 — ECO/UNDEV PLAN FOR/AID MGT

B63
HOLLAND E.P.,EXPERIMENTS ON A SIMULATED UNDERDEVELOPED ECONOMY: DEVELOPMENT PLANS AND BALANCE-OF-PAYMENTS POLICIES. WOR+45 ECO/UNDEV FINAN PLAN ECO/TAC...MATH STAT CHARTS SIMUL VAL/FREE. PAGE 61 F1196 — AFR BAL/PAY

B63
INTERNATIONAL ASSOCIATION RES,AFRICAN STUDIES IN INCOME AND WEALTH. AFR NAT/G PROB/SOLV DEMAND INCOME...ECOMETRIC METH/COMP 20. PAGE 64 F1270 — WEALTH PLAN ECO/UNDEV BUDGET

B63
MULLENBACH P.,CIVILIAN NUCLEAR POWER: ECONOMIC ISSUES AND POLICY FORMATION. AFR FINAN INT/ORG DELIB/GP ACT/RES ECO/TAC ATTIT SUPEGO HEALTH ORD/FREE PWR...POLICY CONCPT MATH STAT CHARTS VAL/FREE 20. PAGE 94 F1855 — USA+45 ECO/DEV NUC/PWR

B63
NEUMARK S.D.,FOREIGN TRADE AND ECONOMIC DEVELOPMENT IN AFRICA: A HISTORICAL PERSPECTIVE. EUR+WWI MOD/EUR ECO/UNDEV AGRI COM/IND EXTR/IND PROC/MFG SKILL WEALTH...CONCPT TIME/SEQ TREND SIMUL FOR/TRADE WORK TOT/POP TERR/GP VAL/FREE 19/20. PAGE 98 F1916 — AFR

B63
RANGEL I.,A INFLACAO BRASILEIRA (2ND ED.). AFR BRAZIL AGRI INDUS MARKET INT/TRADE DEMAND EQUILIB ATTIT 20. PAGE 109 F2144 — ECO/UNDEV FINAN PRICE TAX

B63
US AGENCY INTERNATIONAL DEV,OPERATIONS REPORT - 1963. AFR ASIA L/A+17C USA+45 ECO/UNDEV FINAN INT/ORG NAT/G. PAGE 134 F2637 — FOR/AID CHARTS STAT BUDGET

B63
US CONGRESS JOINT ECO COMM,THE UNITED STATES BALANCE OF PAYMENTS. AFR USA+45 DELIB/GP BUDGET PRICE PRODUC 20 CONGRESS MONEY. PAGE 135 F2655 — BAL/PAY INT/TRADE FINAN ECO/TAC

B63
US CONGRESS JOINT ECO COMM,OUTLOOK FOR UNITED STATES BALANCE OF PAYMENTS. AFR USA+45 ECO/DEV NAT/G FORCES DIPLOM FOR/AID COST EFFICIENCY ...POLICY CONGRESS EEC. PAGE 135 F2657 — BAL/PAY FINAN INT/TRADE PROB/SOLV

B63
US SENATE COMM GOVT OPERATIONS,REPORT OF A STUDY OF US FOREIGN AID IN TEN MIDDLE EASTERN AND AFRICAN COUNTRIES. AFR ISLAM USA+45 FORCES PLAN BUDGET DIPLOM TAX DETER WEALTH...STAT CHARTS 20 CONGRESS AID MID/EAST. PAGE 138 F2728 — FOR/AID EFFICIENCY ECO/TAC FINAN

B63
VELEZ GARCIA J.,DEVALUACION 1962; HISTORIA DOCUMENTAL DE UN PROCESO ECONOMICO. AFR L/A+17C USA+45 FINAN FOR/AID PRODUC WEALTH...POLICY STAT CHARTS ANTHOL 20 COLOMB. PAGE 141 F2774 — ECO/UNDEV ECO/TAC PLAN NAT/G

L63
ADERBIGDE A.,"SYMPOSIUM ON WEST AFRICA INTEGRATION." AFR EUR+WWI FUT CULTURE SOCIETY STRATA DIST/IND INDUS MARKET SERV/IND DELIB/GP PLAN TEC/DEV DOMIN EDU/PROP LEGIT COERCE ATTIT ALL/VALS ...POLICY STAT TREND CHARTS VAL/FREE. PAGE 2 F0040 — FINAN ECO/TAC REGION

L63
MOUSKHELY M.,"LE BLOC COMMUNISTE ET LA COMMUNAUTE ECONOMIQUE EUROPEENNE." AFR COM EUR+WWI FUT USSR WOR+45 INTELL ECO/UNDEV LABOR POL/PAR NUC/PWR RIGID/FLEX...TIME/SEQ ORG/CHARTS EEC TOT/POP 20. PAGE 94 F1849 — INT/ORG ECO/DEV

S63
ARDANT G.,"A PLAN FOR FULL EMPLOYMENT IN THE DEVELOPING COUNTRIES." AFR FUT WOR+45 DELIB/GP ACT/RES PLAN ECO/TAC ATTIT ALL/VALS...POLICY STAT CHARTS TUNIS VAL/FREE 20. PAGE 6 F0112 — ECO/UNDEV SOCIETY MOROCCO

S63
BALOGH T.,"L'INFLUENCE DES INSTITUTIONS MONETAIRES ET COMMERCIALES SUR LA STRUCTURE ECONOMIQUE AFRICAIN." AFR EUR+WWI FUT USA+45 USA-45 WOR+45 SERV/IND INT/ORG NAT/G TOP/EX ROUTINE...INDEX EEC METH/GP 20. PAGE 9 F0168 — FINAN

S63
BARTHELEMY G.,"LE NOUVEAU FRANC (CFA) ET LA BANQUE — AFR

CENTRALE DES ETATS DE L'AFRIQUE DE L'OUEST." FUT STRUCT INT/ORG PLAN ATTIT ALL/VALS FOR/TRADE 20. PAGE 11 F0200
FINAN

S63
CARTER A.G.T.,"THE BALANCE OF PAYMENTS OF EAST AFRICA" AFR ECO/TAC FOR/AID RATION TARIFFS TAX ADMIN...STAT 20 AFRICA/E. PAGE 22 F0423
BUDGET ECO/UNDEV BAL/PAY INT/TRADE

S63
CLARK P.G.,"TOWARDS MORE COMPREHENSIVE PLANNING IN EAST AFRICA" AFR OP/RES ECO/TAC RATION TAX EFFICIENCY INCOME...MATH TREND CHARTS 20 AFRICA/E. PAGE 25 F0484
ECO/UNDEV PLAN STAT METH/COMP

S63
ETHERINGTON D.M.,"LAND RESETTLEMENT IN KENYA; POLICY AND PRACTICE" AFR TEC/DEV ECO/TAC FOR/AID TAX PRODUC...CHARTS 20. PAGE 39 F0752
ECO/UNDEV AGRI WORKER PLAN

S63
GANDOLFI A.,"LES ACCORDS DE COOPERATION EN MATIERE DE POLITIQUE ETRANGERE ENTRE LA FRANCE ET LES NOUVEAUX ETATS AFRICAINS ET." AFR ISLAM MADAGASCAR WOR+45 ECO/DEV INT/ORG NAT/G DELIB/GP ECO/TAC ALL/VALS...CON/ANAL 20. PAGE 46 F0894
VOL/ASSN ECO/UNDEV DIPLOM FRANCE

S63
NADLER E.B.,"SOME ECONOMIC DISADVANTAGES OF THE ARMS RACE." AFR USA+45 INDUS R+D FORCES PLAN TEC/DEV ECO/TAC FOR/AID EDU/PROP PWR WEALTH...TREND FOR/TRADE 20. PAGE 96 F1886
ECO/DEV MGT BAL/PAY

S63
WOLFERS A.,"INTEGRATION IN THE WEST: THE CONFLICT OF PERSPECTIVES." AFR EUR+WWI USA+45 ECO/DEV INT/ORG DELIB/GP CREATE TEC/DEV DIPLOM ATTIT PWR ...CONCPT HIST/WRIT TREND GEN/LAWS EEC 20. PAGE 148 F2918
RIGID/FLEX ECO/TAC

B64
THE SPECIAL COMMONWEALTH AFRICAN ASSISTANCE PLAN. AFR CANADA INDIA NIGERIA UK FINAN SCHOOL...CHARTS 20 COMMONWLTH. PAGE 1 F0019
ECO/UNDEV TREND FOR/AID ADMIN

B64
BALASSA B.,CHANGING PATTERNS IN FOREIGN TRADE AND PAYMENTS. AFR USA+45 USA-45 ECO/DEV NAT/G PLAN BAL/PWR...POLICY ANTHOL BIBLIOG 20. PAGE 8 F0159
ECO/TAC INT/TRADE BAL/PAY WEALTH

B64
BALOGH T.,THE ECONOMIC IMPACT OF MONETARY AND COMMERCIAL INSTITUTIONS OF A EUROPEAN ORIGIN IN AFRICA. AFR UAR INDUS FOR/AID COLONIAL CONTROL ...NAT/COMP 20. PAGE 9 F0169
TEC/DEV FINAN ECO/UNDEV ECO/TAC

B64
BOARMAN P.M.,GERMANY'S ECONOMIC DILEMMA - INFLATION AND THE BALANCE OF PAYMENTS. AFR GERMANY/W LABOR CAP/ISM PRICE BAL/PAY COST INCOME 20. PAGE 16 F0302
ECO/DEV FINAN INT/TRADE BUDGET

B64
BOURGOIGNIE G.E.,JEUNE AFRIQUE MOBILISABLE; LES PROBLEMES DE LA JEUNESSE DESOEUVREE EN AFRIQUE NOIRE. INT/ORG VOL/ASSN ECO/TAC ROUTINE UTIL ATTIT 20. PAGE 17 F0324
AGE/Y AFR CREATE ECO/UNDEV

B64
BROWN C.V.,GOVERNMENT AND BANKING IN WESTERN NIGERIA. AFR NIGERIA GOV/REL GP/REL...POLICY 20. PAGE 19 F0367
ADMIN ECO/UNDEV FINAN NAT/G

B64
CLAIRBORN E.L.,FORECASTING THE BALANCE OF PAYMENTS: AN EVALUATION. AFR FUT UK USA+45 WOR+45 FINAN PLAN BUDGET PAY CONTROL...STAT CHARTS BIBLIOG 20. PAGE 24 F0474
PREDICT BAL/PAY ECO/DEV ECO/TAC

B64
COMMISSION ON MONEY AND CREDIT,INFLATION, GROWTH, AND EMPLOYMENT. AFR USA+45 PLAN PROB/SOLV PAY PRICE EFFICIENCY PRODUC WEALTH 20. PAGE 26 F0514
WORKER ECO/TAC OPTIMAL

B64
COMPOS R.O.,A MOEDA, O GOVERNO E O TEMPO. AFR BRAZIL WOR+45 FINAN TEC/DEV FOR/AID REGION DEMAND ...ANTHOL 20. PAGE 27 F0520
ECO/UNDEV PLAN DIPLOM INT/TRADE

B64
EINZIG P.,MONETARY POLICY: ENDS AND MEANS. AFR UK INDUS WORKER PLAN DIPLOM PRICE BAL/PAY COST WEALTH ...DECISION TIME/SEQ 20. PAGE 37 F0715
FINAN POLICY ECO/TAC BUDGET

B64
FIESER M.E.,ECONOMIC POLICY AND WAR POTENTIAL. AFR WOR+45 ECO/DEV INDUS NAT/G FORCES TEC/DEV NUC/PWR CIVMIL/REL ORD/FREE 20. PAGE 40 F0791
INT/TRADE POLICY ECO/TAC DETER

B64
HAGGER A.J.,THE THEORY OF INFLATION. AFR PLAN PROB/SOLV PAY COST INCOME 20. PAGE 53 F1035
DEMAND TEC/DEV FINAN

B64
HERSKOVITS M.J.,ECONOMIC TRANSITION IN AFRICA. FUT INT/ORG NAT/G WORKER PROB/SOLV TEC/DEV INT/TRADE EQUILIB INCOME...ANTHOL 20. PAGE 59 F1157
AFR ECO/UNDEV PLAN ADMIN

B64
JUCKER-FLEETWOOD E.,MONEY AND FINANCE IN AFRICA. ISLAM ECO/UNDEV SERV/IND NAT/G EX/STRUC PLAN ECO/TAC ROUTINE WEALTH...MGT TOT/POP 20. PAGE 68 F1344
AFR FINAN

B64
LEWIN P.,THE FOREIGN TRADE OF COMMUNIST CHINA* ITS IMPACT ON THE FREE WORLD. AFR EUR+WWI L/A+17C S/ASIA ECO/UNDEV CREATE FOR/AID...STAT NET/THEORY TREND CHARTS. PAGE 79 F1546
ASIA INT/TRADE NAT/COMP USSR

B64
LITTLE I.M.D.,AID TO AFRICA. AFR UK TEC/DEV DIPLOM ECO/TAC INCOME WEALTH 20. PAGE 81 F1583
FOR/AID ECO/UNDEV ADMIN POLICY

B64
LUTHULI A.,AFRICA'S FREEDOM. KIN LABOR POL/PAR SCHOOL DIPLOM NEUTRAL REGION REV NAT/LISM PWR WEALTH SOCISM SOC/INTEG 20. PAGE 82 F1608
AFR ECO/UNDEV COLONIAL

B64
MARKHAM J.W.,THE COMMON MARKET: FRIEND OR COMPETITOR. AFR EUR+WWI FUT USA+45 INT/ORG LG/CO NAT/G VOL/ASSN DELIB/GP EX/STRUC PLAN TARIFFS ORD/FREE PWR WEALTH...POLICY STAT TREND EEC VAL/FREE 20. PAGE 85 F1671
ECO/DEV ECO/TAC

B64
MELADY T.,FACES OF AFRICA. AFR FUT ISLAM NAT/G POL/PAR SCHOOL DELIB/GP PLAN ECO/TAC EDU/PROP ATTIT ALL/VALS...CHARTS TOT/POP TERR/GP VAL/FREE 20. PAGE 89 F1752
ECO/UNDEV TREND NAT/LISM

B64
MORGAN H.W.,AMERICAN SOCIALISM 1900-1960. AFR USA+45 USA-45 INTELL AGRI LABOR WORKER BARGAIN ECO/TAC GP/REL RACE/REL 20 NEGRO MIGRATION. PAGE 93 F1830
SOCISM POL/PAR ECO/DEV STRATA

B64
ODEH H.S.,THE IMPACT OF INFLATION ON THE LEVEL OF ECONOMIC ACTIVITY. AFR BRAZIL CHILE BUDGET GOV/REL COST DEMAND INCOME WEALTH...STAT METH 20 MONEY. PAGE 100 F1963
ECOMETRIC ECO/TAC ECO/UNDEV FINAN

B64
PENNOCK J.R.,SELF-GOVERNMENT IN MODERNIZING NATIONS. AFR COM USA+45 ECO/DEV POL/PAR PROB/SOLV DIPLOM ECO/TAC COLONIAL REV POPULISM SOCISM 20. PAGE 105 F2058
ECO/UNDEV POLICY SOVEREIGN NAT/G

B64
REUSS H.S.,THE CRITICAL DECADE - AN ECONOMIC POLICY FOR AMERICA AND THE FREE WORLD. AFR USA+45 FINAN POL/PAR WORKER PLAN DIPLOM ECO/TAC TARIFFS BAL/PAY ...POLICY 20 CONGRESS. PAGE 111 F2181
FOR/AID INT/TRADE LABOR LEGIS

B64
RIVKIN A.,AFRICA AND THE EUROPEAN COMMON MARKET (PAMPHLET). AFR MOD/EUR WOR+45 TEC/DEV FOR/AID TARIFFS BAL/PAY...POLICY 20 EEC. PAGE 111 F2196
INT/ORG INT/TRADE ECO/TAC ECO/UNDEV

B64
ROBINSON E.A.G.,ECONOMIC DEVELOPMENT FOR AFRICA SOUTH OF THE SAHARA. AFR AGRI INDUS LABOR BUDGET INT/TRADE PRICE...POLICY GEOG ANTHOL 20. PAGE 113 F2219
ECO/UNDEV ECO/TAC ACT/RES PLAN

B64
ROBINSON R.D.,INTERNATIONAL BUSINESS POLICY. AFR INDIA L/A+17C USA+45 ELITES AGRI FOR/AID COERCE BAL/PAY...DECISION INT/LAW MGT 20. PAGE 113 F2224
ECO/TAC DIST/IND COLONIAL FINAN

B64
SEGAL R.,SANCTIONS AGAINST SOUTH AFRICA. AFR SOUTH/AFR NAT/G INT/TRADE RACE/REL PEACE PWR ...INT/LAW ANTHOL 20 UN. PAGE 119 F2342
SANCTION DISCRIM ECO/TAC POLICY

B64
SHANNON I.,INTERNATIONAL LIQUIDITY. AFR FUT USA+45 WOR+45 ECO/TAC PRICE DEMAND WEALTH...CONCPT 20. PAGE 120 F2367
FINAN DIPLOM BAL/PAY ECO/DEV

B64
SINGER H.W.,INTERNATIONAL DEVELOPMENT: GROWTH AND CHANGE. AFR BRAZIL L/A+17C WOR+45 CULTURE AGRI INDUS NAT/G ACT/RES ECO/TAC EDU/PROP WEALTH...GEOG CONCPT METH/CNCPT STAT HYPO/EXP WORK TOT/POP 20. PAGE 122 F2412
FINAN ECO/UNDEV FOR/AID INT/TRADE

B64
WITHERELL J.W.,OFFICIAL PUBLICATIONS OF FRENCH EQUATORIAL AFRICA, FRENCH CAMEROONS, AND TOGO, 1946-1958 (PAMPHLET). CAMEROON CHAD FRANCE GABON TOGO LAW ECO/UNDEV EXTR/IND INT/TRADE...GEOG HEAL 20. PAGE 148 F2913
BIBLIOG/A AFR NAT/G ADMIN

B64
YUDELMAN M.,AFRICANS ON THE LAND. RHODESIA MARKET LABOR OWN...ECOMETRIC TREND 20. PAGE 150 F2955
ECO/DEV AFR AGRI ECO/TAC

L64
ARMENGALD A.,"ECONOMIE ET COEXISTENCE." COM EUR+WWI
MARKET

FUT USA+45 WOR+45 ECO/DEV ECO/UNDEV FINAN INT/ORG NAT/G EXEC CHOOSE ATTIT ALL/VALS...POLICY RELATIV DECISION TREND SOC/EXP WORK 20. PAGE 6 F0113
ECO/TAC AFR CAP/ISM

L64

STERN R.M.,"POLICIES FOR TRADE AND DEVELOPMENT." AFR FUT WOR+45 DIST/IND FINAN NAT/G DELIB/GP PLAN ECO/TAC ORD/FREE WEALTH...POLICY STAT TIME/SEQ CHARTS METH/GP 20. PAGE 126 F2480
MARKET ECO/UNDEV INT/TRADE

S64

BEIM D.,"THE COMMUNIST BLOC AND THE FOREIGN-AID GAME." AFR WOR+45 NAT/G PLAN ROUTINE ATTIT KNOWL ORD/FREE...DECISION QUANT CONT/OBS TIME/SEQ CHARTS GAME SIMUL LOG/LING 20. PAGE 12 F0231
COM ECO/UNDEV ECO/TAC FOR/AID

S64

DOE J.F.,"TROPICAL AFRICAN CONTRIBUTIONS TO FEDERAL FINANCE." AFR NAT/G PROVS CENTRAL RIGID/FLEX PWR WEALTH...STAT VAL/FREE 20 CMN/WLTH. PAGE 33 F0650
FINAN ECO/TAC

S64

HUTCHINSON E.C.,"AMERICAN AID TO AFRICA." FUT USA+45 MARKET INT/ORG LOC/G NAT/G PUB/INST PLAN ECO/TAC ATTIT RIGID/FLEX...POLICY CONCPT TREND TERR/GP 20. PAGE 63 F1248
AFR ECO/UNDEV FOR/AID

S64

MC WILLIAM M.,"THE WORLD BANK AND THE TRANSFER OF POWER IN KENYA." AFR ECO/UNDEV CONSULT ACT/RES TEC/DEV PERCEPT PWR SKILL WEALTH...CONCPT OBS TREND 20. PAGE 88 F1715
NAT/G ECO/TAC

S64

NEWLYN W.T.,"MONETARY SYSTEMS AND INTEGRATION" AFR BUDGET ADMIN FEDERAL PRODUC PROFIT UTIL...CHARTS 20 AFRICA/E. PAGE 98 F1922
ECO/UNDEV REGION METH/COMP FINAN

S64

PADELFORD N.J.,"THE ORGANIZATION OF AFRICAN UNITY." ECO/UNDEV INT/ORG PLAN BAL/PWR DIPLOM ECO/TAC NAT/LISM ORD/FREE PWR WEALTH...CONCPT TREND STERTYP TERR/GP VAL/FREE 20. PAGE 102 F2013
AFR VOL/ASSN REGION

S64

READER D.H.,"A SURVEY OF CATEGORIES OF ECONOMIC ACTIVITIES AMONG THE PEOPLES OF AFRICA." AGRI INDUS MARKET KIN HEALTH SKILL WEALTH...GEOG METH/CNCPT CHARTS TERR/GP WORK TOT/POP VAL/FREE 20. PAGE 110 F2160
TEC/DEV ECO/UNDEV AFR

S64

ROTHCHILD D.,"EAST AFRICAN FEDERATION." AFR TANZANIA UGANDA INDUS REGION 20. PAGE 114 F2249
INT/ORG DIPLOM ECO/UNDEV ECO/TAC

S64

SALVADORI M.,"EL CAPITALISMO EN LA EUROPA DE LA POSGUERRA." AFR INT/ORG NAT/G POL/PAR PLAN ECO/TAC ATTIT ORD/FREE WEALTH...HIST/WRIT EEC 20. PAGE 115 F2275
EUR+WWI ECO/DEV CAP/ISM

N64

GREAT BRITAIN CENTRAL OFF INF,THE COLOMBO PLAN (PAMPHLET). AFR ASIA S/ASIA USA+45 VOL/ASSN ...CHARTS 20 RESOURCE/N. PAGE 50 F0980
FOR/AID PLAN INT/ORG ECO/UNDEV

N64

KENYA MINISTRY ECO PLAN DEV,AFRICAN SOCIALISM AND ITS APPLICATION TO PLANNING IN KENYA (PAMPHLET). AFR AGRI INDUS WORKER TAX COLONIAL WEALTH 20. PAGE 70 F1380
NAT/G SOCISM PLAN ECO/UNDEV

B65

APTER D.E.,THE POLITICS OF MODERNIZATION. AFR L/A+17C CULTURE NAT/G POL/PAR ADMIN COLONIAL NAT/LISM ATTIT RIGID/FLEX PWR...SOC CONCPT. PAGE 6 F0109
ECO/UNDEV GEN/LAWS STRATA CREATE

B65

BARRERE A.,ECONOMIE ET INSTITUTIONS FINANCIERES (VOL. I). AFR FRANCE PLAN...BIBLIOG T 20. PAGE 10 F0194
ECO/DEV BUDGET NAT/G FINAN

B65

BLAIR T.L.V.,AFRICA: A MARKET PROFILE. AFR COM/IND DIST/IND FINAN UTIL...DECISION CHARTS BIBLIOG 20. PAGE 15 F0295
MARKET OP/RES ECO/UNDEV INDUS

B65

BRENNAN M.J.,PATTERNS OF MARKET BEHAVIOR. AFR USA+45 OP/RES CAP/ISM ECO/TAC INT/TRADE...CHARTS METH/COMP ANTHOL TIME 20. PAGE 18 F0346
MARKET LABOR FINAN ECOMETRIC

B65

CAMPBELL J.C.,AMERICAN POLICY TOWARDS COMMUNIST EASTERN EUROPE* THE CHOICES AHEAD. AFR USA+45 ECO/DEV BAL/PWR MARXISM TREND. PAGE 21 F0406
POLAND YUGOSLAVIA DIPLOM COM

B65

CASSELL F.,GOLD OR CREDIT? THE ECONOMICS AND POLITICS OF INTERNATIONAL MONEY. AFR WOR+45 PLAN PROB/SOLV BAL/PAY SOVEREIGN WEALTH 20 OEEC. PAGE 22 F0428
FINAN INT/ORG DIPLOM ECO/TAC

B65

CHANDRASEKHAR S.,AMERICAN AID AND INDIA'S ECONOMIC DEVELOPMENT. AFR CHINA/COM INDIA USA+45 GIVE EDU/PROP EATING HEALTH ORD/FREE 20 AID. PAGE 23 F0449
FOR/AID PEACE DIPLOM ECO/UNDEV

B65

COOMBS P.H.,EDUCATION AND FOREIGN AID. AFR USA+45 DIPLOM EFFICIENCY KNOWL ORD/FREE...ANTHOL 20 AID. PAGE 27 F0532
EDU/PROP FOR/AID SCHOOL ECO/UNDEV

B65

CRABB C.V. JR.,THE ELEPHANTS AND THE GRASS* A STUDY OF NONALIGNMENT. ASIA INDIA S/ASIA USA+45 USSR BAL/PWR NEUTRAL ATTIT...TREND NAT/COMP. PAGE 28 F0549
ECO/UNDEV AFR DIPLOM CONCPT

B65

FARER T.J.,FINANCING AFRICAN DEVELOPMENT. AFR ECO/TAC FOR/AID SOCISM 20. PAGE 39 F0764
ECO/UNDEV FINAN CAP/ISM PLAN

B65

HAEFELE E.T.,GOVERNMENT CONTROLS ON TRANSPORT. AFR RHODESIA TANZANIA DIPLOM ECO/TAC TARIFFS PRICE ADJUD CONTROL REGION EFFICIENCY...POLICY 20 CONGO. PAGE 53 F1031
ECO/UNDEV DIST/IND FINAN NAT/G

B65

HAPGOOD D.,AFRICA: FROM INDEPENDENCE TO TOMARROW. AFR GUINEA SENEGAL CULTURE ELITES ECO/UNDEV AGRI SCHOOL FOR/AID COLONIAL MARXISM...TREND 20. PAGE 55 F1070
ECO/TAC SOCIETY NAT/G

B65

HARBISON F.,MANPOWER AND EDUCATION. AFR CHINA/COM IRAN L/A+17C S/ASIA TEC/DEV ADJUST OPTIMAL SKILL ...ANTHOL 20. PAGE 55 F1073
ECO/UNDEV EDU/PROP WORKER NAT/COMP

B65

MELMANS S.,OUR DEPLETED SOCIETY. AFR SPACE USA+45 ECO/DEV FORCES BUDGET ECO/TAC ADMIN WEAPON EFFICIENCY 20. PAGE 89 F1753
CIVMIL/REL INDUS EDU/PROP CONTROL

B65

NKRUMAH K.,NEO-COLONIALISM: THE LAST STAGE OF IMPERIALISM. AFR INT/ORG WORKER FOR/AID INT/TRADE EDU/PROP GOV/REL NAT/LISM SOVEREIGN POPULISM SOCISM ...SOCIALIST 20 THIRD/WRLD INTRVN/ECO. PAGE 98 F1929
COLONIAL DIPLOM ECO/UNDEV ECO/TAC

B65

O'BRIEN F.,CRISIS IN WORLD COMMUNISM* MARXISM IN SEARCH OF EFFICIENCY. AFR COM ECO/DEV PLAN INT/TRADE WAR ADJUST PEACE...STAT TIME/SEQ GOV/COMP NAT/COMP. PAGE 99 F1951
MARXISM USSR DRIVE EFFICIENCY

B65

ONUOHA B.,THE ELEMENTS OF AFRICAN SOCIALISM. AFR FINAN SECT TEC/DEV FOR/AID GP/REL OWN LAISSEZ MARXISM...CONCPT BIBLIOG 20. PAGE 101 F1992
SOCISM ECO/UNDEV NAT/G EX/STRUC

B65

ROLFE S.E.,GOLD AND WORLD POWER. AFR UK USA+45 WOR-45 INDUS WORKER INT/TRADE DEMAND...MGT CHARTS 20. PAGE 113 F2234
BAL/PAY EQUILIB ECO/TAC DIPLOM

B65

ROOSA R.V.,MONETARY REFORM FOR THE WORLD ECONOMY. AFR EUR+WWI USA+45 WOR+45 CREATE BUDGET DIPLOM FOR/AID EQUILIB WEALTH IMF. PAGE 114 F2237
FINAN INT/ORG INT/TRADE BAL/PAY

B65

RUEFF J.,THE ROLE AND THE RULE OF GOLD: AN ARGUMENT (PAMPHLET). AFR FRANCE USA+45 WOR+45 MARKET NAT/G PLAN DIPLOM ATTIT...POLICY INT 20 DEGAULLE/C. PAGE 115 F2258
FINAN ECO/DEV INT/TRADE BAL/PAY

B65

SCITOVSKY T.,REQUIREMENTS OF AN INTERNATIONAL RESERVE SYSTEM. AFR ECO/TAC...PREDICT 20 SILVER MONEY. PAGE 118 F2330
BAL/PAY FINAN EQUILIB INT/TRADE

B65

SIMMS R.P.,URBANIZATION IN WEST AFRICA; A REVIEW OF CURRENT LITERATURE. AFR PLAN TEC/DEV...SOC OBS NAT/COMP MUNICH 20. PAGE 122 F2405
BIBLIOG/A ECO/DEV ECO/UNDEV

B65

SPENCE J.E.,REPUBLIC UNDER PRESSURE: A STUDY OF SOUTH AFRICAN FOREIGN POLICY. SOUTH/AFR ADMIN COLONIAL GOV/REL RACE/REL DISCRIM NAT/LISM ATTIT ROLE...TREND 20 NEGRO. PAGE 124 F2449
DIPLOM POLICY AFR

B65

STEWART I.G.,AFRICAN PRIMARY PRODUCTS AND INTERNATIONAL TRADE. ECO/UNDEV AGRI FINAN DIPLOM CONTROL 20. PAGE 126 F2485
AFR INT/TRADE INT/ORG

B65

US SENATE COMM ON FOREIGN REL,HEARINGS ON THE FOREIGN ASSISTANCE PROGRAM. AFR ASIA L/A+17C USA+45 WOR+45 FORCES TEC/DEV BUDGET CONTROL WEAPON ORD/FREE 20 UN CONGRESS SEC/STATE. PAGE 139 F2734
FOR/AID DIPLOM INT/ORG ECO/UNDEV

B65

VON RENESSE E.A.,UNVOLLENDETE DEMOKRATIEN. AFR ISLAM S/ASIA SOCIETY ACT/RES COLONIAL...JURID CHARTS BIBLIOG METH 13/20. PAGE 142 F2795
ECO/UNDEV NAT/COMP SOVEREIGN

S65
CECIL C.O.,"THE DETERMINANTS OF LIBYAN FOREIGN POLICY." AFR INTELL ECO/UNDEV EXTR/IND POL/PAR CREATE REGION SOVEREIGN CONSERVE MAGHREB NASSER/G. PAGE 22 F0431 — LIBYA DIPLOM WEALTH ISLAM

S65
DUMONT R.,"SURPEUPLEMENT CHINOIS ET SES CONSEQUENCES." AFR ECO/UNDEV AGRI PLAN PROB/SOLV ECO/TAC FOR/AID NUC/PWR...OBS INT PREDICT. PAGE 35 F0675 — GEOG ASIA STAT

S65
HAYTER T.,"FRENCH AID TO AFRICA* ITS SCOPE AND ACHIEVEMENTS." CULTURE ECO/TAC INT/TRADE ADMIN REGION CENTRAL FEDERAL LOVE PWR SOVEREIGN EEC. PAGE 57 F1127 — AFR FRANCE FOR/AID COLONIAL

S65
LECLERCQ H.,"ECONOMIC RESEARCH AND DEVELOPMENT IN TROPICAL AFRICA." ECO/UNDEV INT/ORG CREATE PLAN UN. PAGE 77 F1500 — AFR R+D ACADEM ECO/TAC

S65
MULLER A.L.,"THE ECONOMIC POSITION OF THE ASIANS IN AFRICA." AFR SOUTH/AFR ECO/UNDEV MARKET ECO/TAC GP/REL INCOME...CHARTS IND 20 MONOPOLY ASIANS. PAGE 95 F1856 — WORKER RACE/REL CAP/ISM DISCRIM

S65
SOPER T.,"THE EEC AND AID TO AFRICA." FRANCE UK ECO/UNDEV INT/TRADE TARIFFS REGION ROUTINE CENTRAL DISCRIM...DECISION RECORD EEC. PAGE 124 F2443 — AFR FOR/AID COLONIAL

S65
WHITE J.,"WEST GERMAN AID TO DEVELOPING COUNTRIES." AFR INT/ORG OP/RES GIVE CENTRAL ATTIT DRIVE...STAT NAT/COMP. PAGE 146 F2869 — GERMANY FOR/AID ECO/UNDEV CAP/ISM

N65
STUDY GP CREATE RESERVE ASSETS,REPORT TO DEPUTIES (PAMPHLET). AFR FUT PLAN CONTROL DEMAND WEALTH ...ANTHOL METH 20. PAGE 127 F2507 — INT/ORG INT/TRADE FINAN BUDGET

B66
ALIBER R.Z.,THE FUTURE OF THE DOLLAR AS AN INTERNATIONAL CURRENCY. AFR USA+45 USA-45 ECO/DEV PRICE COST INCOME...POLICY 20. PAGE 4 F0067 — FINAN DIPLOM INT/ORG INT/TRADE

B66
BALDWIN R.E.,ECONOMIC DEVELOPMENT AND EXPORT GROWTH: A STUDY OF NORTHERN RHODESIA, 1920-1960. AFR RHODESIA AGRI EXTR/IND FINAN MARKET LABOR WORKER ECO/TAC...CONCPT NEW/IDEA MUNICH 20. PAGE 9 F0166 — ECO/UNDEV TEC/DEV INT/TRADE CAP/ISM

B66
BIRMINGHAM W.,A STUDY OF CONTEMPORARY GHANA VOL I: THE ECONOMY OF GHANA. AFR GHANA PLAN...POLICY STAT CHARTS ANTHOL BIBLIOG 20. PAGE 15 F0286 — ECO/UNDEV ECO/TAC NAT/G PRODUC

B66
CROWDER M.,A SHORT HISTORY OF NIGERIA. AFR NIGERIA UK ECO/UNDEV CHIEF INT/TRADE RACE/REL NAT/LISM ORD/FREE...GEOG SOC CHARTS BIBLIOG 14/20. PAGE 29 F0558 — COLONIAL NAT/G CULTURE

B66
DAVIES I.,AFRICAN TRADE UNIONS. AFR ECO/UNDEV INT/ORG GP/REL ORD/FREE SOVEREIGN SOCISM 20. PAGE 30 F0585 — LABOR COLONIAL PWR INDUS

B66
DILLEY M.R.,BRITISH POLICY IN KENYA COLONY (2ND ED.). AFR INDIA UK LABOR BUDGET TAX ADMIN PARL/PROC GP/REL...BIBLIOG 20 PARLIAMENT. PAGE 33 F0639 — COLONIAL REPRESENT SOVEREIGN

B66
GROSS H.,MAKE OR BUY. AFR USA+45 FINAN INDUS CREATE PRICE PRODUC 20. PAGE 51 F1006 — ECO/TAC PLAN MGT COST

B66
HALLET R.,PEOPLE AND PROGRESS IN WEST AFRICA: AN INTRODUCTION TO THE PROBLEMS OF DEVELOPMENT. COM/IND INDUS KIN DIPLOM FOR/AID INT/TRADE HEALTH ...GEOG TREND CHARTS BIBLIOG/A 20 AFRICA/W. PAGE 54 F1050 — AFR SOCIETY ECO/UNDEV ECO/TAC

B66
HAYER T.,FRENCH AID. AFR FRANCE AGRI FINAN BUDGET ADMIN WAR PRODUC...CHARTS 18/20 THIRD/WRLD OVRSEA/DEV. PAGE 57 F1125 — TEC/DEV COLONIAL FOR/AID ECO/UNDEV

B66
HOWE R.W.,BLACK AFRICA: FROM PRE-HISTORY TO THE EVE OF THE COLONIAL ERA. ECO/UNDEV KIN PROVS SECT INT/TRADE EDU/PROP COLONIAL...BIBLIOG WORSHIP. PAGE 62 F1226 — AFR CULTURE SOC

B66
HUTTENBACH R.A.,BRITISH IMPERIAL EXPERIENCE. AFR S/ASIA UK WOR-45 INT/ORG TEC/DEV...CHARTS 16/20 MERCANTLST. PAGE 64 F1253 — COLONIAL TIME/SEQ INT/TRADE

B66
INARRITU A.L.,EL PATRON CAMBIO-ORO Y SUS REFORMAS. AFR L/A+17C WOR+45 PLAN PROB/SOLV BUDGET ECO/TAC INT/TRADE EFFICIENCY ORD/FREE 20 MEXIC/AMER. PAGE 64 F1262 — ECO/UNDEV FINAN DIPLOM POLICY

B66
KAREFA-SMART J.,AFRICA: PROGRESS THROUGH COOPERATION. AFR FINAN TEC/DEV DIPLOM FOR/AID EDU/PROP CONFER REGION GP/REL WEALTH...HEAL SOC/INTEG 20. PAGE 69 F1356 — ORD/FREE ECO/UNDEV VOL/ASSN PLAN

B66
KEENLEYSIDE H.L.,INTERNATIONAL AID: A SUMMARY. AFR INDIA S/ASIA UK STRATA EXTR/IND TEC/DEV ADMIN RACE/REL DEMAND NAT/LISM WEALTH...TREND CHINJAP. PAGE 70 F1367 — ECO/UNDEV FOR/AID DIPLOM TASK

B66
KINDLEBERGER C.P.,EUROPE AND THE DOLLAR. AFR EUR+WWI FRANCE GERMANY/W USA+45 CONSTN INT/ORG DIPLOM INT/TRADE...ANTHOL 20. PAGE 71 F1395 — BAL/PAY BUDGET FINAN ECO/DEV

B66
LAMBERG R.F.,PRAG UND DIE DRITTE WELT. AFR ASIA CZECHOSLVK L/A+17C MARKET TEC/DEV ECO/TAC REV ATTIT 20 TREATY. PAGE 75 F1462 — DIPLOM ECO/UNDEV INT/TRADE FOR/AID

B66
MUNBY D.,ECONOMIC GROWTH IN WORLD PERSPECTIVE. AFR WOR+45 SOCIETY INDUS PLAN TEC/DEV ECO/TAC FOR/AID INT/TRADE COST CATHISM...ANTHOL 20 EUROPE/W CHURCH/STA. PAGE 95 F1859 — SECT ECO/UNDEV ECO/DEV

B66
NATIONAL INDUSTRIAL CONF BOARD,GOLD AND WORLD MONETARY PROBLEMS. AFR FUT WOR+45 PROB/SOLV BUDGET INT/TRADE PAY GOV/REL...POLICY ANTHOL 20. PAGE 97 F1902 — FINAN ECO/TAC PRICE BAL/PAY

B66
O'CONNER A.M.,AN ECONOMIC GEOGRAPHY OF EAST AFRICA. AFR TANZANIA UGANDA AGRI WORKER INT/TRADE COLONIAL GOV/REL...CHARTS METH/COMP 20 AFRICA/E. PAGE 99 F1953 — ECO/UNDEV EXTR/IND GEOG HABITAT

B66
PIQUET H.S.,THE US BALANCE OF PAYMENTS AND INTERNATIONAL MONETARY RESERVES. AFR USA+45 PROB/SOLV INT/TRADE GOV/REL EQUILIB...POLICY STAT CHARTS 20. PAGE 106 F2090 — BAL/PAY DIPLOM FINAN ECO/TAC

B66
SPICER K.,A SAMARITAN STATE? AFR CANADA INDIA PAKISTAN UK USA+45 FINAN INDUS PRODUC...CHARTS 20 NATO. PAGE 124 F2455 — DIPLOM FOR/AID ECO/DEV ADMIN

B66
TRIFFIN R.,THE WORLD MONEY MAZE. AFR INT/ORG ECO/TAC PRICE OPTIMAL WEALTH...METH/COMP 20 EEC OEEC SILVER. PAGE 131 F2589 — BAL/PAY FINAN INT/TRADE DIPLOM

B66
TRIFFIN R.,THE BALANCE OF PAYMENTS AND THE FOREIGN INVESTMENT POSITION OF THE UNITED STATES. AFR USA+45 INT/ORG INT/TRADE PRICE CONTROL...POLICY 20. PAGE 131 F2590 — BAL/PAY DIPLOM FINAN ECO/TAC

B66
TURNER H.A.,PRICES, WAGES, AND INCOME POLICIES IN INDUSTRIALIZED MARKET ECONOMIES. AFR WOR+45 ECO/DEV INDUS PROB/SOLV ECO/TAC CONTROL WEALTH...CHARTS 20 INTRVN/ECO. PAGE 131 F2593 — PRICE PAY MARKET INCOME

B66
UREN P.E.,EAST - WEST TRADE* A SYMPOSIUM. COM AGRI INT/ORG PRICE HABITAT RIGID/FLEX...GEOG INT/LAW ANTHOL NATO. PAGE 133 F2625 — INT/TRADE BAL/PWR AFR CANADA

B66
US HOUSE COMM FOREIGN AFFAIRS,HEARINGS ON HR 12449 A BILL TO AMEND FURTHER THE FOREIGN ASSISTANCE ACT OF 1961. AFR ASIA L/A+17C USA+45 VIETNAM INT/ORG TEC/DEV INT/TRADE ATTIT ORD/FREE 20 UN NATO CONGRESS AID. PAGE 137 F2692 — FOR/AID ECO/TAC ECO/UNDEV DIPLOM

L66
AFRICAN BIBLIOGRAPHIC CENTER,"AFRICAN ECONOMIC AFFAIRS: A SELECT BIBLIOGRAPHICAL SURVEY, 1965-1966." AFR FINAN INDUS INT/ORG LABOR PLAN BUDGET DIPLOM INT/TRADE ADMIN EFFICIENCY WEALTH 20. PAGE 3 F0046 — BIBLIOG ECO/UNDEV TEC/DEV FOR/AID

L66
AFRICAN BIBLIOGRAPHIC CENTER,"AFRICAN ECONOMIC AFFAIRS: A SELECT BIBLIOGRAPHICAL SURVEY, 1965-1966; SUPPLEMENTS NUMBERS 1-3." AFR FINAN INDUS LABOR PLAN BUDGET CAP/ISM DIPLOM INT/TRADE ADMIN...GEOG 20. PAGE 3 F0047 — BIBLIOG/A ECO/UNDEV FOR/AID TEC/DEV

S66
FLEMING W.G.,"AUTHORITY, EFFICIENCY, AND ROLE STRESS: PROBLEMS IN THE DEVELOPMENT OF EAST AFRICAN BUREAUCRACIES." AFR UGANDA STRUCT PROB/SOLV ROUTINE INGP/REL ROLE...MGT SOC GP/COMP GOV/COMP 20 TANGANYIKA AFRICA/E. PAGE 41 F0810 — DOMIN EFFICIENCY COLONIAL ADMIN

S66
NEWLYN W.T.,"MONEY MARKETS IN EAST AFRICA." AFR TANZANIA UGANDA UK DIPLOM CENTRAL 20. PAGE 98 F1923 — FINAN WEALTH BAL/PAY

ECO/UNDEV

S66 ROTHCHILD D.,"THE LIMITS OF FEDERALISM: AN EXAMINATION OF POLITICAL INSTITUTIONAL TRANSFER IN AFRICA." AFR CONSTN CULTURE ELITES ECO/UNDEV KIN PROB/SOLV ADMIN ORD/FREE PWR...POLICY 20. PAGE 114 F2250 — FEDERAL NAT/G NAT/LISM COLONIAL

N66 EOMMITTEE ECONOMIC DEVELOPMENT,THE DOLLAR AND THE WORLD MONETARY SYSTEM: A STATEMENT ON NATIONAL POLICY (PAMPHLET). AFR USA+45 NAT/G PLAN PROB/SOLV BUDGET ECO/TAC FOR/AID INCOME...POLICY 20 EUROPE. PAGE 38 F0740 — FINAN BAL/PAY DIPLOM ECO/DEV

B67 BIRMINGHAM W.,A STUDY OF CONTEMPORARY GHANA VOL. I: SOME ASPECTS OF SOCIAL STRUCTURE. AFR GHANA AGRI FAM SECT PLAN EDU/PROP MARRIAGE OWN...POLICY STAT CHARTS MUNICH 20. PAGE 15 F0287 — SOCIETY STRUCT CENSUS ECO/UNDEV

B67 CEFKIN J.L.,THE BACKGROUND OF CURRENT WORLD PROBLEMS. AFR NAT/G MARXISM...T 20 UN. PAGE 22 F0432 — DIPLOM NAT/LISM ECO/UNDEV

B67 CHANDRASEKHAR S.,PROBLEMS OF ECONOMIC DEVELOPMENT. AFR INDIA PHILIPPINE UAR WOR+45 INDUS...GEOG SOC ANTHOL BIBLIOG 20 CHINJAP. PAGE 23 F0450 — ECO/UNDEV PLAN AGRI PROB/SOLV

B67 CHILCOTE R.H.,PORTUGUESE AFRICA. PORTUGAL CULTURE SOCIETY ECO/UNDEV DOMIN NAT/LISM...TREND IDEA/COMP NAT/COMP BIBLIOG 15/20. PAGE 24 F0465 — AFR COLONIAL ORD/FREE PROB/SOLV

B67 FANON F.,TOWARD THE AFRICAN REVOLUTION. AFR FRANCE CULTURE ELITES LEAD REV GP/REL ORD/FREE SOVEREIGN 20. PAGE 39 F0762 — COLONIAL DOMIN ECO/UNDEV RACE/REL

B67 FORDE D.,WEST AFRICAN KINGDOMS IN THE NINETEENTH CENTURY. ECO/UNDEV AGRI KIN...SOC CHARTS NAT/COMP 19. PAGE 42 F0826 — AFR REGION CULTURE

B67 GOODMAN P.,LIKE A CONQUERED PROVINCE: THE MORAL AMBIGUITY OF AMERICA. AFR USA+45 NAT/G PROB/SOLV EDU/PROP ADJUST EFFICIENCY 20. PAGE 49 F0950 — SOCIETY TEC/DEV WAR MORAL

B67 HALLE L.J.,THE COLD WAR AS HISTORY. AFR USSR WOR+45 ECO/TAC FOR/AID NUC/PWR WAR PEACE ORD/FREE ...MAJORIT TREND 20 KENNEDY/JF KHRUSH/N BERLIN/BLO. PAGE 54 F1048 — DIPLOM BAL/PWR

B67 HANNAH H.W.,THE LEGAL BASE FOR UNIVERSITIES IN DEVELOPING COUNTRIES. AFR ASIA L/A+17C S/ASIA USA+45 FINAN CREATE EDU/PROP TASK EFFICIENCY ...JURID METH/COMP 20. PAGE 54 F1060 — ADMIN LAW ACADEM LEGIS

B67 LISS S.B.,THE CANAL, ASPECTS OF UNITED STATES-PANAMANIAN RELATIONS. AFR FUT PANAMA DOMIN COERCE ATTIT SOVEREIGN MARXISM 20 JOHNSON/LB KENNEDY/JF. PAGE 81 F1580 — DIPLOM POLICY

B67 MEYNAUD J.,TRADE UNIONISM IN AFRICA; A STUDY OF ITS GROWTH AND ORIENTATION (TRANS. BY ANGELA BRENCH). INT/ORG PROB/SOLV COLONIAL PWR...TIME/SEQ TREND ILO. PAGE 90 F1774 — LABOR AFR NAT/LISM ORD/FREE

B67 OGLESBY C.,CONTAINMENT AND CHANGE. AFR COM USA+45 ECO/UNDEV TEC/DEV ECO/TAC FOR/AID INT/TRADE DOMIN GUERRILLA REV PEACE 20 STALIN/J. PAGE 101 F1983 — DIPLOM BAL/PWR MARXISM CULTURE

B67 ORLANS H.,CONTRACTING FOR ATOMS. AFR USA+45 LAW INTELL ACADEM LG/CO NAT/G PLAN TEC/DEV CONTROL DETER...TREND 20. PAGE 102 F1999 — NUC/PWR R+D PRODUC PEACE

B67 RAVKIN A.,THE NEW STATES OF AFRICA (HEADLINE SERIES, NO. 183((PAMPHLET). CULTURE STRUCT INDUS COLONIAL NAT/LISM...SOC 20. PAGE 109 F2153 — AFR ECO/UNDEV SOCIETY ADMIN

B67 ROACH J.R.,THE UNITED STATES AND THE ATLANTIC COMMUNITY; ISSUES AND PROSPECTS. AFR WOR+45 TEC/DEV ECO/TAC COLONIAL REGION PEACE ROLE...ANTHOL NATO EEC. PAGE 112 F2199 — INT/ORG POLICY ADJUST DIPLOM

B67 ROBERTS B.C.,COLLECTIVE BARGAINING IN AFRICAN COUNTRIES. AFR LAW ECO/UNDEV BARGAIN GP/REL ...DECISION METH/COMP 20. PAGE 112 F2206 — LABOR MGT PLAN ECO/TAC

B67 SPIRO H.S.,PATTERNS OF AFRICAN DEVLOPMENT: FIVE COMPARISONS. STRUCT ECO/UNDEV NAT/G CONSERVE SOCISM ...PREDICT NAT/COMP 20 CHINJAP. PAGE 125 F2457 — AFR CONSTN NAT/LISM TREND

B67 US AGENCY INTERNATIONAL DEV,PROPOSED FOREIGN AID PROGRAM FOR 1968: SUMMARY PRESENTATION TO THE CONGRESS. AFR S/ASIA USA+45 AGRI TEC/DEV DIPLOM ECO/TAC BAL/PAY COST HEALTH KNOWL SKILL 20 AID CONGRESS ALL/PROG. PAGE 134 F2640 — ECO/UNDEV BUDGET FOR/AID STAT

B67 WILLS A.J.,AN INTRODUCTION TO THE HISTORY OF CENTRAL AFRICA. RHODESIA ZAMBIA CULTURE SOCIETY ECO/UNDEV TEC/DEV DOMIN WAR ALL/VALS...POLICY TREND BIBLIOG T 14/20 NYASALAND. PAGE 147 F2899 — AFR COLONIAL ORD/FREE

L67 AUSTIN D.A.,"POLITICAL CONFLICT IN AFRICA." CONSTN NAT/G CREATE ADMIN COLONIAL ORD/FREE MARXISM POPULISM SOCISM...NAT/COMP ANTHOL 20. PAGE 8 F0141 — ANOMIE AFR POL/PAR

L67 GREGORY A.J.,"AFRICAN SOCIALISM, SOCIALISM AND FASCISM: AN APPRAISAL." FUT LEAD REV GP/REL RACE/REL NAT/LISM ATTIT...IDEA/COMP STERTYP 20. PAGE 51 F0993 — FASCISM MARXISM SOCISM AFR

S67 ANDERSON S.S.,"SOVIET RUSSIA AND THE TWO EUROPES." AFR USSR PROB/SOLV CENTRAL SOVEREIGN 20. PAGE 5 F0097 — DIPLOM POLICY MARXISM

S67 APEL H.,"LES NOUVEAUX ASPECTS DE LA POLITIQUE ETRANGERE ALLEMANDE." AFR EUR+WWI GERMANY POL/PAR BAL/PWR ECO/TAC INT/TRADE NUC/PWR NAT/LISM PEACE ...POLICY 20 EEC. PAGE 6 F0107 — DIPLOM INT/ORG FEDERAL

S67 CAMPBELL J.C.,"SOVIET-AMERICAN RELATIONS: CONFLICT AND COOPERATION." AFR USA+45 USSR AGREE WAR PEACE 20 KHRUSH/N KENNEDY/JF. PAGE 21 F0407 — DIPLOM POLICY

S67 FINER S.E.,"THE ONE-PARTY REGIMES IN AFRICA: RECONSIDERATIONS." AFR DOMIN CONSEN ORD/FREE 20. PAGE 41 F0798 — ELITES POL/PAR CONSTN ECO/UNDEV

S67 HEILBRONER R.L.,"BUILDING NEW NATIONS." AFR STRUCT PLAN TEC/DEV ADJUST MARXISM...POLICY 20. PAGE 58 F1138 — PROB/SOLV REV NAT/LISM ECO/UNDEV

S67 ISELIN J.J.,"THE TRUMAN DOCTRINE: ITS PASSAGE THROUGH CONGRESS AND THE AFTERMATH." USA+45 ECO/UNDEV R+D INT/ORG DELIB/GP BAL/PWR REV PEACE ...POLICY UN. PAGE 66 F1291 — DIPLOM COM FOR/AID AFR

S67 MCCORD W.,"ARMIES AND POLITICS; A PROBLEM IN THE THIRD WORLD." AFR ISLAM USA+45 ECO/UNDEV TOTALISM 20. PAGE 88 F1723 — FOR/AID POLICY NAT/G FORCES

S67 PFEFFERMANN G.,"TRADE UNIONS AND POLITICS IN FRENCH WEST AFRICA DURING THE FOURTH REPUBLIC." AFR INDUS POL/PAR COLONIAL ATTIT PWR 20. PAGE 106 F2077 — PARTIC DRIVE INT/TRADE LABOR

S67 PRATT R.C.,"THE ADMINISTRATION OF ECONOMIC PLANNING IN A NEWLY INDEPEND ENT STATE* THE TANZANIAN EXPERIENCE 1963-1966." AFR TANZANIA ECO/UNDEV PLAN CONTROL ROUTINE TASK EFFICIENCY 20. PAGE 107 F2114 — NAT/G DELIB/GP ADMIN TEC/DEV

S67 SCHNEIDER E.,"DIE ENTPOLITISIERUNG DES DEUTSCHEN OSTHANDELS." AFR MARKET TEC/DEV OBJECTIVE 20. PAGE 117 F2307 — ATTIT INT/TRADE ECO/TAC DIPLOM

S67 SCOTT R.,"TRADE UNIONS IN AFRICA." AFR UGANDA USA-45 ECO/UNDEV INDUS INT/ORG POL/PAR ECO/TAC WEALTH...GP/COMP 20 NKRUMAH/K. PAGE 118 F2335 — LABOR WORKER NAT/G

S67 SMITH W.H.T.,"THE IMPLICATIONS OF THE AMERICAN BAR ASSOCIATION ADVISORY COMMITTEE RECOMMENDATIONS FOR POLICE ADMINISTRATION." AFR ADMIN...JURID 20. PAGE 123 F2435 — EDU/PROP CONTROL GP/REL ORD/FREE

S67 THEROUX P.,"HATING THE ASIANS." TANZANIA UGANDA CONSTN INDUS NAT/G POL/PAR WORKER ECO/TAC HABITAT LOVE...POLICY GEOG 20 MIGRATION. PAGE 130 F2557 — AFR RACE/REL SOVEREIGN ATTIT

S67 WALZER M.,"THE CONDITION OF GREECE; TWENTY YEARS AFTER THE TRUMAN DOCTRINE." AFR GREECE FORCES CAP/ISM 20 TRUMAN/HS. PAGE 143 F2814 — DIPLOM POLICY FOR/AID TOTALISM

S67 WILSON C.E.,"AMERICAN INVESTMENT IN PORTUGUESE AFRICA: A PROBLEM OF "DEMOCRATIC" COLONIALISM." AFR ECO/UNDEV DIPLOM MORAL...IDEA/COMP 20 ANGOLA MOZAMBIQUE. PAGE 147 F2901 — COLONIAL DOMIN ORD/FREE POLICY

AFR/STATES....ORGANIZATION OF AFRICAN STATES

AFRICA/CEN....CENTRAL AFRICA

AFRICA/E....EAST AFRICA

S63
CARTER A.G.T.,"THE BALANCE OF PAYMENTS OF EAST AFRICA" AFR ECO/TAC FOR/AID RATION TARIFFS TAX ADMIN...STAT 20 AFRICA/E. PAGE 22 F0423 BUDGET ECO/UNDEV BAL/PAY INT/TRADE

S63
CLARK P.G.,"TOWARDS MORE COMPREHENSIVE PLANNING IN EAST AFRICA" AFR OP/RES ECO/TAC RATION TAX EFFICIENCY INCOME...MATH TREND CHARTS 20 AFRICA/E. PAGE 25 F0484 ECO/UNDEV PLAN STAT METH/COMP

S64
NEWLYN W.T.,"MONETARY SYSTEMS AND INTEGRATION" AFR BUDGET ADMIN FEDERAL PRODUC PROFIT UTIL...CHARTS 20 AFRICA/E. PAGE 98 F1922 ECO/UNDEV REGION METH/COMP FINAN

B65
LEYS C.T.,FEDERATION IN EAST AFRICA. LAW AGRI DIST/IND FINAN INT/ORG LABOR INT/TRADE CONFER ADMIN CONTROL GP/REL...ANTHOL 20 AFRICA/E. PAGE 79 F1554 FEDERAL REGION ECO/UNDEV PLAN

B65
MURUMBI J.,PROBLEMS OF ECONOMIC DEVELOPMENT IN EAST AFRICA. FINAN INDUS WORKER TEC/DEV INT/TRADE TAX DEMAND EFFICIENCY PRODUC SOCISM...TREND CHARTS 20 AFRICA/E. PAGE 95 F1869 AGRI ECO/TAC ECO/UNDEV PROC/MFG

B66
O'CONNER A.M.,AN ECONOMIC GEOGRAPHY OF EAST AFRICA. AFR TANZANIA UGANDA AGRI WORKER INT/TRADE COLONIAL GOV/REL...CHARTS METH/COMP 20 AFRICA/E. PAGE 99 F1953 ECO/UNDEV EXTR/IND GEOG HABITAT

B66
SMITH H.E.,READINGS IN ECONOMIC DEVELOPMENT AND ADMINISTRATION IN TANZANIA. TANZANIA FINAN INDUS LABOR NAT/G PLAN PROB/SOLV INT/TRADE COLONIAL REGION...ANTHOL BIBLIOG 20 AFRICA/E. PAGE 123 F2431 TEC/DEV ADMIN GOV/REL

S66
FLEMING W.G.,"AUTHORITY, EFFICIENCY, AND ROLE STRESS: PROBLEMS IN THE DEVELOPMENT OF EAST AFRICAN BUREAUCRACIES." AFR UGANDA STRUCT PROB/SOLV ROUTINE INGP/REL ROLE...MGT SOC GP/COMP GOV/COMP 20 TANGANYIKA AFRICA/E. PAGE 41 F0810 DOMIN EFFICIENCY COLONIAL ADMIN

AFRICA/N....NORTH AFRICA

AFRICA/SW....SOUTH WEST AFRICA

B37
UNION OF SOUTH AFRICA,REPORT CONCERNING ADMINISTRATION OF SOUTH WEST AFRICA (6 VOLS.). SOUTH/AFR INDUS PUB/INST FORCES LEGIS BUDGET DIPLOM EDU/PROP ADJUD CT/SYS...GEOG CHARTS 20 AFRICA/SW LEAGUE/NAT. PAGE 132 F2610 NAT/G ADMIN COLONIAL CONSTN

AFRICA/W....WEST AFRICA

B02
MOREL E.D.,AFFAIRS OF WEST AFRICA. UK FINAN INDUS FAM KIN SECT CHIEF WORKER DIPLOM RACE/REL LITERACY HEALTH...CHARTS 18/20 AFRICA/W NEGRO. PAGE 93 F1826 COLONIAL ADMIN AFR

B26
MCPHEE A.,THE ECONOMIC REVOLUTION IN BRITISH WEST AFRICA. AFR UK CULTURE DIST/IND FINAN INDUS PLAN GP/REL RACE/REL 20 AFRICA/W. PAGE 88 F1735 ECO/UNDEV INT/TRADE COLONIAL GEOG

B66
HALLET R.,PEOPLE AND PROGRESS IN WEST AFRICA: AN INTRODUCTION TO THE PROBLEMS OF DEVELOPMENT. COM/IND INDUS KIN DIPLOM FOR/AID INT/TRADE HEALTH ...GEOG TREND CHARTS BIBLIOG/A 20 AFRICA/W. PAGE 54 F1050 AFR SOCIETY ECO/UNDEV ECO/TAC

AFRICAN BIBLIOGRAPHIC CENTER F0046,F0047

AFTA....ATLANTIC FREE TRADE AREA

B67
KREININ M.E.,ALTERNATIVE COMMERCIAL POLICIES - THEIR EFFECT ON THE AMERICAN ECONOMY. USA+45 LAW ECO/DEV MARKET INT/ORG DIPLOM ECO/TAC TARIFFS PRICE DEMAND WEALTH...QUANT EEC AFTA. PAGE 73 F1437 INT/TRADE BAL/PAY NAT/G POLICY

AGARWAL R.C. F0048

AGE....AGE FACTORS

N19
INTERNATIONAL LABOUR OFFICE,EMPLOYMENT, UNEMPLOYMENT AND LABOUR FORCE STATISTICS (PAMPHLET). EUR+WWI STRATA AGRI INDUS NAT/G PROB/SOLV PAY AGE SEX...SAMP NAT/COMP METH 20 ILO. PAGE 65 F1278 WORKER LABOR STAT ECO/DEV

B49
LEE A.M.,SOCIAL PROBLEMS IN AMERICA: A SOURCE BOOK. STRATA STRUCT KIN NEIGH VOL/ASSN ACT/RES LEAD CRIME AGE SEX 20. PAGE 77 F1504 SOC SOCIETY PERSON EDU/PROP

B57
ASSN U BUREAUS BUS-ECO RES,INDEX OF PUBLICATIONS OF BUREAUS OF BUSINESS AND ECONOMIC RESEARCH 1950-56 AND YEARLY SUPPLEMENTS THROUGH 1967. FINAN OP/RES PLAN GOV/REL INCOME AGE...POLICY 20. PAGE 7 F0133 BIBLIOG ECO/DEV ECO/TAC LG/CO

B58
COALE A.J.,POPULATION GROWTH AND ECONOMIC DEVELOPMENT IN LOW-INCOME COUNTRIES: A CASE STUDY OF INDIA'S PROSPECTS. INDIA AGRI WORKER INCOME AGE WEALTH...CHARTS 20 MEXIC/AMER. PAGE 25 F0495 ECO/UNDEV GEOG CENSUS SEX

S58
THOMAS D.S.,"AGE AND ECONOMIC DIFFERENTIALS IN INTERSTATE MIGRATION." SEX...GEOG SAMP/SIZ TREND CON/ANAL CHARTS BIBLIOG. PAGE 130 F2560 AGE WEALTH HABITAT CENSUS

L59
FURASH E.A.,"PROBLEMS IN REVIEW: INDUSTRIAL ESPIONAGE." WORKER ECO/TAC PERS/REL OPTIMAL AGE ATTIT KNOWL...MGT DEEP/INT DEEP/QU GP/COMP IDEA/COMP. PAGE 45 F0875 INDUS TOP/EX MAJORITY

B63
RILEY J.W. JR.,THE CORPORATION AND ITS PUBLICS. ESSAYS ON THE CORPORATE IMAGE. CLIENT ISOLAT AGE ATTIT...POLICY SOC METH/CNCPT INT. PAGE 111 F2193 LG/CO CLASSIF GP/REL NEIGH

B64
TAEUBER I.B.,POPULATION TRENDS IN THE UNITED STATES: 1900 TO 1960. USA+45 USA-45 PROVS INCOME AGE...SOC TIME/SEQ TREND CHARTS MUNICH TIME 20 NEGRO. PAGE 128 F2522 CENSUS GEOG STRATA STRUCT

B65
ANDERSON C.A.,EDUCATION AND ECONOMIC DEVELOPMENT. INDUS R+D SCHOOL TEC/DEV ECO/TAC EDU/PROP AGE HEREDITY PERCEPT SKILL 20. PAGE 5 F0092 ANTHOL ECO/DEV ECO/UNDEV WORKER

L67
GLAZER N.,"HOUSING PROBLEMS AND HOUSING POLICIES." USA+45 PLAN RENT ADJUST CONSEN DEMAND DISCRIM AGE ATTIT HEALTH WEALTH MUNICH NEGRO. PAGE 48 F0929 POLICY CONSTRUC CREATE HABITAT

L67
ZEIDBERG L.D.,"THE NASHVILLE AIR POLLUTION STUDY" (PARTS V-VII)" USA+45 PLAN AGE HEALTH...GEOG STAT CENSUS SAMP/SIZ CHARTS BIBLIOG MUNICH. PAGE 150 F2962 DEATH HABITAT AIR BIO/SOC

S67
BASOV V.,"THE DEVELOPMENT OF PUBLIC EDUCATION AND THE BUDGET." USSR NAT/G CONTROL REV COST AGE...STAT 20. PAGE 11 F0204 BUDGET GIVE EDU/PROP SCHOOL

S67
LENS S.,"WALTER REUTHER TRIES TO BUILD A FIRE." WORKER LEAD DISCRIM AGE ORD/FREE NEW/LIB SOC. PAGE 78 F1523 LABOR PARTIC NEIGH PLAN

AGE/A....ADULTS

AGE/C....INFANTS AND CHILDREN

B61
DEWITT N.,EDUCATION AND PROFESSIONAL EMPLOYMENT IN THE USSR. USSR PROF/ORG WORKER PLAN ADMIN UTIL AGE/C AGE/Y MARXISM...STAT CHARTS 20. PAGE 32 F0629 EDU/PROP ACADEM SCHOOL INTELL

B65
SHOSTAK A.B.,NEW PERSPECTIVES ON POVERTY. USA+45 SCHOOL WORKER INGP/REL RACE/REL AGE/C AGE/Y ATTIT HEALTH...ANTHOL BIBLIOG 20 JOHNSON/LB POVRTY/WAR. PAGE 121 F2388 WEALTH NAT/G RECEIVE INCOME

B67
WEINBERG M.,SCHOOL INTEGRATION: A COMPREHENSIVE CLASSIFIED BIBLIOGRAPHY OF 3,100 REFERENCES. USA+45 LAW NAT/G NEIGH SECT PLAN ROUTINE AGE/C WEALTH SOC/INTEG INDIAN/AM. PAGE 145 F2849 BIBLIOG SCHOOL DISCRIM RACE/REL

S67
STYCOS J.M.,"POLITICS AND POPULATION CONTROL IN LATIN AMERICA." USA+45 FAM NAT/G GP/REL AGE/C ATTIT CATHISM MARXISM...POLICY UN WHO. PAGE 127 F2509 PLAN CENSUS CONTROL L/A+17C

S67
WASSERMAN M.,"BEYOND TOKENISM: REVERSE INTEGRATION IN ALBANY, GEORGIA." USA+45 PLAN BUDGET EDU/PROP LEAD AGE/C AGE/Y GEORGIA NEGRO. PAGE 144 F2827 REGION RACE/REL DISCRIM SCHOOL

AGE/O....OLD PEOPLE

B60
HARBRECHT P.P.,TOWARD THE PARAPROPRIETAL SOCIETY. REPRESENT INCOME OWN PROFIT AGE/O. PAGE 55 F1076 PWR ADMIN ELITES CONTROL

B62
BUREAU OF NATIONAL AFFAIRS,FEDERAL-STATE REGULATION OF WELFARE FUNDS (REV. ED.). USA+45 LAW LEGIS DEBATE AGE/O 20 CONGRESS. PAGE 20 F0386 — WELF/ST WEALTH PLAN SOC/WK

B62
HARRINGTON M.,THE OTHER AMERICA: POVERTY IN THE UNITED STATES. WORKER CREATE REPRESENT RACE/REL AGE/O DRIVE POLICY. PAGE 55 F1086 — WEALTH WELF/ST INCOME CULTURE

B63
GORDON M.S.,THE ECONOMICS OF WELFARE POLICIES. INDUS LOC/G NAT/G LEGIS WORKER INCOME AGE/O SKILL WEALTH...METH/COMP NAT/COMP 20. PAGE 49 F0959 — METH/CNCPT ECO/TAC POLICY

B65
BEYER G.H.,HOUSING AND SOCIETY. USA+45 ECO/DEV FAM NAT/G PLAN RENT...CHARTS BIBLIOG MUNICH 20. PAGE 14 F0275 — HABITAT AGE/O CONSTRUC

AGE/Y....YOUTH AND ADOLESCENCE

B37
COLE W.E.,RECENT TRENDS IN RURAL PLANNING. USA-45 LAW ECO/DEV LOC/G SECT EDU/PROP CRIME LEISURE AGE/Y HABITAT...SOC/WK MUNICH 20. PAGE 26 F0503 — AGRI NEIGH PLAN ACT/RES

S49
ECKLER A.R.,"IMMIGRATION AND THE LABOR FORCE." USA+45 USA-45 EXTR/IND FINAN PROC/MFG AGE/Y SKILL ...CHARTS 19/20 MIGRATION. PAGE 36 F0694 — WORKER STRANGE INDUS ECO/TAC

B54
KARTUN D.,AFRICA, AFRICA: A CONTINENT RISES TO ITS FEET. AFR SOUTH/AFR UK ELITES AGRI LABOR LOC/G POL/PAR EDU/PROP CONTROL COERCE DISCRIM AGE/Y NEGRO THIRD/WRLD GOLD/COAST. PAGE 69 F1358 — COLONIAL ORD/FREE PROFIT EXTR/IND

B60
FRYE R.J.,GOVERNMENT AND LABOR: THE ALABAMA PROGRAM. USA+45 INDUS R+D LABOR WORKER BUDGET EFFICIENCY AGE/Y HEALTH...CHARTS 20 ALABAMA. PAGE 45 F0870 — ADMIN LEGIS LOC/G PROVS

B61
MEXICO; CINCUENTA ANOS DE REVOLUCION VOL. II. L/A+17C SOCIETY LABOR RECEIVE GP/REL AGE/Y HEALTH ...SOC/WK ANTHOL MUNICH 20 MEXIC/AMER. PAGE 1 F0014 — ECO/UNDEV STRUCT INDUS POL/PAR

B61
DEWITT N.,EDUCATION AND PROFESSIONAL EMPLOYMENT IN THE USSR. USSR PROF/ORG WORKER PLAN ADMIN UTIL AGE/C AGE/Y MARXISM...STAT CHARTS 20. PAGE 32 F0629 — EDU/PROP ACADEM SCHOOL INTELL

B64
BOURGOIGNIE G.E.,JEUNE AFRIQUE MOBILISABLE; LES PROBLEMES DE LA JEUNESSE DESOEUVREE EN AFRIQUE NOIRE. INT/ORG VOL/ASSN ECO/TAC ROUTINE UTIL ATTIT 20. PAGE 17 F0324 — AGE/Y AFR CREATE ECO/UNDEV

B65
SHOSTAK A.B.,NEW PERSPECTIVES ON POVERTY. USA+45 SCHOOL WORKER INGP/REL RACE/REL AGE/C AGE/Y ATTIT HEALTH...ANTHOL BIBLIOG 20 JOHNSON/LB POVRTY/WAR. PAGE 121 F2388 — WEALTH NAT/G RECEIVE INCOME

N66
PRINCETON U INDUSTRIAL REL SEC,PUBLIC PROGRAMS TO CREATE JOBS (PAMPHLET NO. 125). USA+45 ECO/DEV INDUS PLAN ECO/TAC AGE/Y 20. PAGE 108 F2119 — BIBLIOG/A NAT/G POLICY WORKER

B67
WILLIAMS M.,THE EAST IS RED: THE VIEW INSIDE CHINA. CHINA/COM CONSTN COERCE AGE/Y ATTIT PERSON...OBS 20 MAO. PAGE 147 F2893 — REV MARXIST GP/REL DIPLOM

S67
GRUN C.,"DEUX ETUDES ALLEMANDES SUR LES PREJUGES NATIONAUX ET LES MOYENS DE LES COMBATTRE." FRANCE GERMANY DIST/IND PROB/SOLV GP/REL AGE/Y RIGID/FLEX ...PSY STAT INT SAMP. PAGE 52 F1010 — ATTIT REGION DISCRIM STERTYP

S67
WASSERMAN M.,"BEYOND TOKENISM: REVERSE INTEGRATION IN ALBANY, GEORGIA." USA+45 PLAN BUDGET EDU/PROP LEAD AGE/C AGE/Y GEORGIA NEGRO. PAGE 144 F2827 — REGION RACE/REL DISCRIM SCHOOL

AGGARWALA R.N. F0049

AGGRESSION....SEE WAR, COERCE+INT/REL

AGGRESSION, PHYSICAL....SEE COERCE, DRIVE

AGREE....AGREEMENTS, CONTRACTS, TREATIES, CONCORDATS, INTERSTATE COMPACTS

B13
KROPOTKIN P.,THE CONQUEST OF BREAD. SOCIETY STRATA AGRI INDUS WORKER REV HAPPINESS INCOME PRODUC HEALTH MORAL ORD/FREE. PAGE 74 F1444 — ANARCH SOCIALIST OWN AGREE

B36
BURNS A.R.,THE DECLINE OF COMPETITION. LAW LG/CO NAT/G SML/CO LEGIS PRICE AGREE CONTROL GP/REL INCOME PRODUC...POLICY 19/20 NRA. PAGE 20 F0390 — MARKET GEN/LAWS INDUS

B52
TANNENBAUM F.,A PHILOSOPHY OF LABOR. SOCIETY STRATA INDUS LG/CO AGREE ADJUST OWN ORD/FREE PWR...CONCPT 20. PAGE 128 F2533 — LABOR PHIL/SCI WORKER CREATE

B55
US OFFICE OF THE PRESIDENT,REPORT TO CONGRESS ON THE MUTUAL SECURITY PROGRAM FOR THE SIX MONTHS ENDED JUNE 30, 1955. ECO/DEV INT/ORG NAT/G CREATE TEC/DEV BAL/PWR ECO/TAC AGREE DETER COST ORD/FREE 20 DEPT/STATE DEPT/DEFEN. PAGE 138 F2722 — DIPLOM FORCES PLAN FOR/AID

B56
US OFFICE OF THE PRESIDENT,REPORT TO CONGRESS ON THE MUTUAL SECURITY PROGRAM FOR THE SIX MONTHS ENDED DECEMBER 31, 1955. ASIA USSR ECO/DEV ECO/UNDEV INT/ORG CREATE TEC/DEV BAL/PWR ECO/TAC AGREE DETER COST ORD/FREE 20 DEPT/STATE DEPT/DEFEN EISNHWR/DD. PAGE 138 F2723 — DIPLOM FORCES PLAN FOR/AID

B61
LAHAYE R.,LES ENTREPRISES PUBLIQUES AU MAROC. FRANCE MOROCCO LAW DIST/IND EXTR/IND FINAN CONSULT PLAN TEC/DEV ADMIN AGREE CONTROL OWN...POLICY 20. PAGE 74 F1460 — NAT/G INDUS ECO/UNDEV ECO/TAC

B62
LIPPMANN W.,WESTERN UNITY AND THE COMMON MARKET. EUR+WWI FRANCE GERMANY/W UK USA+45 ECO/DEV AGRI FINAN MARKET INT/ORG NAT/G FOR/AID AGREE WEALTH 20 EEC. PAGE 80 F1575 — DIPLOM INT/TRADE VOL/ASSN

B63
PAN AMERICAN UNION,THE EFFECTS OF THE EUROPEAN ECONOMIC COMMUNITY ON THE LATIN AMERICAN ECONOMIES (BMR). EUR+WWI L/A+17C ECO/UNDEV AGRI INDUS MARKET REGION 20 EEC TREATY. PAGE 103 F2024 — INT/TRADE INT/ORG AGREE POLICY

B65
HABERLER G.,A SURVEY OF INTERNATIONAL TRADE THEORY. CANADA FRANCE GERMANY ECO/TAC TARIFFS AGREE COST DEMAND WEALTH...ECOMETRIC 19/20 MONOPOLY TREATY. PAGE 52 F1024 — INT/TRADE BAL/PAY DIPLOM POLICY

B65
MACDONALD R.W.,THE LEAGUE OF ARAB STATES: A STUDY IN THE DYNAMICS OF REGIONAL ORGANIZATION. ISRAEL UAR USSR FINAN INT/ORG DELIB/GP ECO/TAC AGREE NEUTRAL ORD/FREE PWR...DECISION BIBLIOG 20 TREATY UN. PAGE 83 F1626 — ISLAM REGION DIPLOM ADMIN

B65
O'CONNELL D.P.,INTERNATIONAL LAW (2 VOLS.). WOR+45 WOR-45 ECO/DEV ECO/UNDEV INT/ORG NAT/G AGREE ...POLICY JURID CONCPT NAT/COMP 20 TREATY. PAGE 99 F1952 — INT/LAW DIPLOM CT/SYS

B66
COLE A.B.,SOCIALIST PARTIES IN POSTWAR JAPAN. STRATA AGRI LABOR PLAN DIPLOM ECO/TAC AGREE LEAD CHOOSE ATTIT...CHARTS 20 CHINJAP SOC/DEMPAR. PAGE 26 F0499 — POL/PAR POLICY SOCISM NAT/G

B67
BLAIR P.W.,THE MINISTATE DILEMMA. WOR+45 AGREE COLONIAL ORD/FREE...GEOG CHARTS MUNICH LEAGUE/NAT UN. PAGE 15 F0294 — INT/ORG NAT/G CENSUS

L67
MCALLISTER J.T. JR.,"THE POSSIBILITIES FOR DIPLOMACY IN SOUTHEAST ASIA." LAOS VIETNAM INT/ORG NAT/G PROVS BAL/PWR DOMIN AGREE COLONIAL WAR PWR 17/20 TREATY. PAGE 88 F1716 — DIPLOM S/ASIA

S67
AUBERT DE LA RUE P.,"PERSPECTIVES ECONOMIQUES ENTRE LES ETATS-UNIS ET L'EUROPE." FUT INDUS R+D INT/ORG ACT/RES ECO/TAC AGREE BAL/PAY PRODUC...CHARTS 20 EEC GATT WORLD/BANK. PAGE 7 F0138 — INT/TRADE ECO/DEV FINAN TARIFFS

S67
CAMPBELL J.C.,"SOVIET-AMERICAN RELATIONS: CONFLICT AND COOPERATION." AFR USA+45 USSR AGREE WAR PEACE 20 KHRUSH/N KENNEDY/JF. PAGE 21 F0407 — DIPLOM POLICY

S67
DURIEZ P.,"THE IMPACT OF EX PARTE 230 (PIGGYBACKING) ON RAIL-MOTOR COMPETITION." USA+45 USA-45 LG/CO COST EFFICIENCY...CHARTS 20. PAGE 35 F0685 — DIST/IND LAW CONTROL AGREE

S67
WOLFE T.W.,"SOVIET MILITARY POLICY AT THE FIFTY YEAR MARK." USSR VIETNAM WOR+45 RATION AGREE WAR WEAPON CIVMIL/REL TREATY. PAGE 148 F2917 — FORCES POLICY TIME/SEQ PLAN

N67
US SENATE COMM ON FOREIGN REL,SURVEY OF THE ALLIANCE FOR PROGRESS: THE LATIN AMERICAN MILITARY (PAMPHLET). USA+45 INT/ORG POL/PAR DIPLOM AGREE GP/REL ROLE ORD/FREE 20. PAGE 139 F2746 — L/A+17C FORCES CIVMIL/REL POLICY

B96
SMITH A.,LECTURES ON JUSTICE, POLICE, REVENUE AND ARMS (1763). UK LAW FAM FORCES TARIFFS AGREE COERCE INCOME OWN WEALTH LAISSEZ...GEN/LAWS 17/18. PAGE 123 F2429 — DIPLOM JURID OLD/LIB TAX

AGRI....AGRICULTURE (INCLUDING HUNTING AND GATHERING)

B
BRITISH COMMONWEALTH BUR AGRI,WORLD AGRICULTURAL ECONOMICS AND RURAL SOCIOLOGY ABSTRACTS. NAT/G OP/RES PLAN TEC/DEV LEAD PRODUC...GEOG MGT NAT/COMP 20. PAGE 18 F0354
BIBLIOG/A AGRI SOC WORKER

N
ECONOMIC LIBRARY SELECTIONS. AGRI INDUS MARKET ADMIN...STAT NAT/COMP 20. PAGE 1 F0007
BIBLIOG/A WRITING FINAN

N
THE MIDDLE EAST AND NORTH AFRICA. AFR ISLAM CULTURE ECO/UNDEV AGRI NAT/G TEC/DEV FOR/AID INT/TRADE EDU/PROP...CHARTS 20. PAGE 1 F0008
INDEX INDUS FINAN STAT

N
UNESCO,INTERNATIONAL BIBLIOGRAPHY OF ECONOMICS (VOLUMES 1-8). WOR+45 AGRI INDUS LABOR PLAN TEC/DEV 20. PAGE 132 F2607
BIBLIOG ECO/DEV ECO/UNDEV

N
US LIBRARY OF CONGRESS,SELECTED AND ANNOTATED BIBLIOGRAPHY ON AGRICULTURAL PROBLEMS AND POLICIES IN A WARTIME ECONOMY (PAMPHLET). R+D WORKER PRODUC 20. PAGE 137 F2706
BIBLIOG/A WAR AGRI EXTR/IND

N
US LIBRARY OF CONGRESS,SOUTHERN ASIA ACCESSIONS LIST. BURMA CEYLON INDIA NEPAL PAKISTAN S/ASIA THAILAND AGRI INDUS SCHOOL WORKER...ART/METH GEOG HEAL PHIL/SCI LING 20. PAGE 137 F2710
BIBLIOG/A SOCIETY CULTURE ECO/UNDEV

N
US SUPERINTENDENT OF DOCUMENTS,CENSUS PUBLICATIONS (PRICE LIST 70). AGRI CONSTRUC DIST/IND FINAN LOC/G NAT/G PROVS INT/TRADE APPORT INCOME. PAGE 140 F2751
BIBLIOG/A CENSUS STAT USA+45

N
US SUPERINTENDENT OF DOCUMENTS,LABOR (PRICE LIST 33). USA+45 LAW AGRI CONSTRUC INDUS NAT/G BARGAIN PRICE ADMIN AUTOMAT PRODUC MGT. PAGE 140 F2753
BIBLIOG/A WORKER LABOR LEGIS

B00
LIST F.,NATIONAL SYSTEM OF POLITICAL ECONOMY. ECO/DEV AGRI EXTR/IND FINAN INDUS TEC/DEV ECO/TAC ATTIT WEALTH...TREND GEN/LAWS FOR/TRADE 19. PAGE 81 F1581
MOD/EUR MARKET

B00
MILL J.S.,PRINCIPLES OF POLITICAL ECONOMY. WOR-45 CULTURE SOCIETY STRATA ECO/DEV AGRI EXTR/IND FINAN INDUS DELIB/GP ECO/TAC WEALTH...CONCPT MATH TREND 20. PAGE 91 F1786
MARKET INT/ORG INT/TRADE

B13
BEARD C.A.,AN ECONOMIC INTERPRETATION OF THE CONSTITUTION OF THE UNITED STATES. USA-45 AGRI INT/TRADE SUFF OWN ATTIT...CONCPT MYTH BIOG HIST/WRIT 18. PAGE 12 F0222
CONSTN ECO/TAC CHOOSE

B13
KROPOTKIN P.,THE CONQUEST OF BREAD. SOCIETY STRATA AGRI INDUS WORKER REV HAPPINESS INCOME PRODUC HEALTH MORAL ORD/FREE. PAGE 74 F1444
ANARCH SOCIALIST OWN AGREE

N19
EAST KENTUCKY REGIONAL PLAN,PROGRAM 60: A DECADE OF ACTION FOR PROGRESS IN EASTERN KENTUCKY (PAMPHLET). USA+45 AGRI CONSTRUC INDUS CONSULT ACT/RES PROB/SOLV EDU/PROP GOV/REL HEALTH KENTUCKY. PAGE 35 F0689
REGION ADMIN PLAN ECO/UNDEV

N19
HOGARTY R.A.,NEW JERSEY FARMERS AND MIGRANT HOUSING RULES (PAMPHLET). USA+45 LAW ELITES FACE/GP LABOR PROF/ORG LOBBY PERS/REL RIGID/FLEX ROLE 20 NEW/JERSEY. PAGE 61 F1193
AGRI PROVS WORKER HEALTH

N19
INTERNATIONAL LABOUR OFFICE,EMPLOYMENT, UNEMPLOYMENT AND LABOUR FORCE STATISTICS (PAMPHLET). EUR+WWI STRATA AGRI INDUS NAT/G PROB/SOLV PAY AGE SEX...SAMP NAT/COMP METH 20 ILO. PAGE 65 F1278
WORKER LABOR STAT ECO/DEV

B20
BUCK S.J.,THE AGRARIAN CRUSADE: A CHRONICLE OF THE FARMER IN POLITICS. USA-45 INDUS PROB/SOLV PWR WEALTH...GEOG CENSUS 19/20 GREENBACK GRANGE SILVER. PAGE 20 F0381
AGRI POPULISM VOL/ASSN POL/PAR

B20
MALTHUS T.R.,PRINCIPLES OF POLITICAL ECONOMY. UK AGRI INDUS MARKET NAT/G DIPLOM PRICE CONTROL BAL/PAY COST OWN PWR LAISSEZ 18/19. PAGE 84 F1650
GEN/LAWS DEMAND WEALTH

B20
MOREL E.D.,THE BLACK MAN'S BURDEN. AFR MOD/EUR AGRI EXTR/IND PROB/SOLV INT/TRADE ADMIN CONTROL COERCE DISCRIM...POLICY 19/20 NEGRO LEAGUE/NAT. PAGE 93 F1828
ORD/FREE CAP/ISM RACE/REL DOMIN

B21
CLAPHAN J.H.,THE ECONOMIC DEVELOPMENT OF FRANCE AND GERMANY 1815-1914. FRANCE GERMANY MOD/EUR COM/IND DIST/IND FINAN INT/TRADE EDU/PROP 19/20. PAGE 24 F0476
ECO/UNDEV ECO/DEV AGRI INDUS

S21
MALINOWSKI B.,"THE PRIMITIVE ECONOMICS OF THE TROBRIAND ISLANDERS" (BMR)" CULTURE SOCIETY NAT/G CHIEF LEAD OWN...SOC MYTH WORSHIP 20 NEW/GUINEA TROBRIAND RESOURCE/N. PAGE 84 F1647
ECO/UNDEV AGRI PRODUC STRUCT

B22
FOURIER C.,TRAITE DE L'ASSOCIATION DOMESTIQUE-AGRICOLE (2 VOLS.). UNIV SOCIETY INDUS ECO/TAC PERSON MORAL ANARCH. PAGE 43 F0834
VOL/ASSN AGRI UTOPIA CONCPT

B24
HOLDSWORTH W.S.,A HISTORY OF ENGLISH LAW; THE COMMON LAW AND ITS RIVALS (VOL. IV). UK SEA AGRI CHIEF ADJUD CONTROL CRIME GOV/REL...INT/LAW JURID NAT/COMP 16/17 PARLIAMENT COMMON/LAW CANON/LAW ENGLSH/LAW. PAGE 61 F1195
LAW LEGIS CT/SYS CONSTN

B27
WEBER M.,GENERAL ECONOMIC HISTORY. CHRIST-17C MOD/EUR STRUCT AGRI EXTR/IND FINAN INDUS MARKET FAM NAT/G PROF/ORG SECT ECO/TAC MUNICH 8/20. PAGE 144 F2839
ECO/DEV CAP/ISM

B28
TRUE A.C.,A HISTORY OF AGRICULTURAL EXTENSION WORK IN THE UNITED STATES, 1785-1923. USA-45 LAW SCHOOL WAR ADJUST...CHARTS BIBLIOG 18/20 SMITH/LEVR COUNTY/AGT. PAGE 131 F2591
EDU/PROP AGRI VOL/ASSN PLAN

B30
GREEN F.M.,CONSTITUTIONAL DEVELOPMENT IN THE SOUTH ATLANTIC STATES, 1776-1860; A STUDY IN THE EVOLUTION OF DEMOCRACY. USA-45 ELITES SOCIETY STRATA ECO/DEV AGRI POL/PAR EX/STRUC LEGIS CT/SYS REGION...BIBLIOG 18/19 MARYLAND VIRGINIA GEORGIA NORTH/CAR SOUTH/CAR. PAGE 50 F0984
CONSTN PROVS PLURISM REPRESENT

B30
HAWTREY R.G.,ECONOMIC ASPECTS OF SOVEREIGNTY. UNIV WOR+45 WOR-45 ECO/DEV ECO/UNDEV AGRI COM/IND INDUS MARKET NAT/G TEC/DEV ECO/TAC EDU/PROP COERCE ATTIT KNOWL WEALTH...CONCPT CON/ANAL GEN/LAWS 20. PAGE 57 F1118
FORCES PWR SOVEREIGN WAR

B33
TANNENBAUM F.,PEACE BY REVOLUTION. ECO/UNDEV AGRI SECT WORKER DIPLOM EDU/PROP DISCRIM OWN WEALTH POPULISM 17/20 MEXIC/AMER INDIAN/AM. PAGE 128 F2532
CULTURE COLONIAL RACE/REL REV

B35
KEYNES J.M.,THE GENERAL THEORY OF EMPLOYMENT, INTEREST, AND MONEY. AGRI INDUS WORKER ECO/TAC DEMAND EQUILIB INCOME PRODUC PROFIT ATTIT WEALTH 20. PAGE 71 F1386
FINAN GEN/LAWS MARKET PRICE

B37
COLE W.E.,RECENT TRENDS IN RURAL PLANNING. USA-45 LAW ECO/DEV LOC/G SECT EDU/PROP CRIME LEISURE AGE/Y HABITAT...SOC/WK MUNICH 20. PAGE 26 F0503
AGRI NEIGH PLAN ACT/RES

B37
DALTON J.E.,SUGAR: A CASE STUDY OF GOVERNMENT CONTROL. USA-45 AGRI PROC/MFG LG/CO LEGIS PROB/SOLV ECO/TAC GP/REL...CHARTS 19/20. PAGE 30 F0575
CONTROL NAT/G INDUS POLICY

B37
MACKENZIE F.,PLANNED SOCIETY: YESTERDAY, TODAY, AND TOMORROW. ECO/DEV ECO/UNDEV AGRI FINAN INDUS PLAN INSPECT CONTROL ALL/IDEOS...TREND METH/COMP BIBLIOG 20 RESOURCE/N. PAGE 83 F1635
SOC CONCPT ANTHOL

B38
CARVALHO C.M.,GEOGRAPHIA HUMANA; POLITICA E ECONOMICA (3RD ED.). BRAZIL CULTURE AGRI INDUS DIPLOM COLONIAL GP/REL RACE/REL...LING 20 RESOURCE/N. PAGE 22 F0424
GEOG HABITAT

B38
HEIMANN E.,COMMUNISM, FASCISM, OR DEMOCRACY? WOR-45 CONSTN SOCIETY STRATA AGRI CAP/ISM MORAL ORD/FREE ...MAJORIT METH/COMP NAT/COMP 19/20. PAGE 58 F1141
SOCISM MARXISM FASCISM PLURISM

B38
LAWLEY F.E.,THE GROWTH OF COLLECTIVE ECONOMY VOL. 1: NATIONAL. EUR+WWI AGRI INDUS NAT/G BARGAIN CAP/ISM ECO/TAC WAR OPTIMAL WEALTH...GOV/COMP METH/COMP 19/20 MONOPOLY. PAGE 76 F1492
SOCISM PRICE CONTROL OWN

B38
LAWLEY F.E.,THE GROWTH OF COLLECTIVE ECONOMY VOL. 2: INTERNATIONAL. WOR-45 AGRI INDUS EQUILIB OPTIMAL OWN WEALTH...NAT/COMP 19/20 NAZI NEW/DEAL MONOPOLY. PAGE 76 F1493
ECO/TAC SOCISM NAT/LISM CONTROL

B39
FIRTH R.,PRIMITIVE POLYNESIAN ECONOMY. SOCIETY DIST/IND SECT CHIEF CAP/ISM PRODUC WEALTH...SOC OBS METH WORSHIP 20 POLYNESIA. PAGE 41 F0802
ECO/UNDEV CULTURE AGRI ECO/TAC

B40
BLAISDELL D.C.,GOVERNMENT AND AGRICULTURE; THE GROWTH OF FEDERAL FARM AID. USA-45 MARKET PLAN PROB/SOLV TEC/DEV ECO/TAC GOV/REL ADJUST ATTIT ...CHARTS 20 DEPT/AGRI. PAGE 15 F0296
NAT/G GIVE AGRI DELIB/GP

B40
CAMPBELL P.,CONSUMER REPRESENTATION IN THE NEW
CLIENT

DEAL. AGRI INDUS MARKET EX/STRUC PLAN CAP/ISM CONTROL GP/REL DEMAND POLICY. PAGE 21 F0408
REPRESENT NAT/G

B40
GAUS J.M.,PUBLIC ADMINISTRATION AND THE UNITED STATES DEPARTMENT OF AGRICULTURE. USA-45 STRUCT DIST/IND FINAN MARKET EX/STRUC PROB/SOLV GIVE PRODUC...POLICY GEOG CHARTS 20 DEPT/AGRI. PAGE 47 F0909
ADMIN AGRI DELIB/GP OP/RES

B40
SIKES E.R.,CONTEMPORARY ECONOMIC SYSTEMS: THEIR ANALYSIS AND SOCIAL BACKGROUND. GERMANY ITALY USSR AGRI INDUS PLAN CAP/ISM ROUTINE TOTALISM FASCISM ...POLICY CON/ANAL BIBLIOG 20. PAGE 122 F2400
COM SOCISM CONCPT

B42
US LIBRARY OF CONGRESS,THE WAR PRODUCTION PROGRAM: SELECTED DOCUMENTATION ON THE ECONOMICS OF WAR (PAMPHLET). USA-45 ECO/DEV AGRI FINAN NAT/G ECO/TAC RATION PRICE EFFICIENCY 20. PAGE 138 F2713
BIBLIOG/A WAR PRODUC INDUS

B44
BIENSTOCK G.,MANAGEMENT IN RUSSIAN INDUSTRY AND AGRICULTURE. USSR CONSULT WORKER LEAD COST PROFIT ATTIT DRIVE PWR...MGT METH/COMP DICTIONARY ACCT 20. PAGE 15 F0281
ADMIN MARXISM SML/CO AGRI

B45
DAVIS J.,AFRICA ADVANCING. AFR CONGO/BRAZ LIBERIA NIGER INT/ORG SCHOOL DIPLOM GIVE KNOWL SKILL 20. PAGE 30 F0590
SECT COLONIAL AGRI ECO/UNDEV

B48
KILE O.M.,THE FARM BUREAU MOVEMENT: THE FARM BUREAU THROUGH THREE DECADES. NAT/G LEGIS LEAD LOBBY GP/REL INCOME POLICY. PAGE 71 F1387
AGRI STRUCT VOL/ASSN DOMIN

B48
OSBORN F.,OUR PLUNDERED PLANET. UNIV DEATH WAR ...BIBLIOG RESOURCE/N. PAGE 102 F2001
HABITAT GEOG ADJUST AGRI

B48
WHITE C.L.,HUMAN GEOGRAPHY: AN ECOLOGICAL STUDY OF GEOGRAPHY. UNIV SEA CULTURE AGRI EXTR/IND RACE/REL PRODUC...CHARTS HYPO/EXP SIMUL GEN/LAWS T. PAGE 146 F2868
SOC HABITAT GEOG SOCIETY

S48
HARDIN L.M.,"REFLECTIONS ON AGRICULTURAL POLICY FORMATION IN THE UNITED STATES." LEGIS PLAN BUDGET ECO/TAC LEAD CENTRAL...MGT SOC NEW/IDEA STAT FAO. PAGE 55 F1078
AGRI POLICY ADMIN NEW/LIB

B49
US DEPARTMENT OF STATE,SOVIET BIBLIOGRAPHY (PAMPHLET). CHINA/COM COM USSR LAW AGRI INT/ORG ECO/TAC EDU/PROP...POLICY GEOG IND 20. PAGE 135 F2670
BIBLIOG/A MARXISM CULTURE DIPLOM

B50
HOOVER G.,TWENTIETH CENTURY ECONOMIC THOUGHT. USA+45 ECO/DEV AGRI FINAN INDUS MARKET SERV/IND LABOR NAT/G...STAT 20. PAGE 62 F1213
ECO/TAC CAP/ISM INT/TRADE

B50
LIPSET S.M.,AGRARIAN SOCIALISM. CANADA POL/PAR OP/RES ECO/TAC ADMIN ATTIT...TIME/SEQ NAT/COMP SOC/EXP 20 SASKATCH. PAGE 80 F1576
SOCISM AGRI METH/COMP STRUCT

B50
US DEPARTMENT OF STATE,POINT FOUR: COOPERATIVE PROGRAM FOR AID IN THE DEVELOPMENT OF ECONOMICALLY UNDERDEVELOPED AREAS. WOR+45 AGRI INDUS INT/ORG PLAN TEC/DEV DIPLOM EDU/PROP ADMIN PEACE PRODUC WEALTH 20 CONGRESS UN. PAGE 135 F2671
ECO/UNDEV FOR/AID FINAN INT/TRADE

B51
US DEPARTMENT OF STATE,POINT FOUR, NEAR EAST AND AFRICA, A SELECTED BIBLIOGRAPHY OF STUDIES ON ECONOMICALLY UNDERDEVELOPED COUNTRIES. AGRI COM/IND FINAN INDUS PLAN INT/TRADE...SOC TREND 20. PAGE 135 F2672
BIBLIOG/A AFR S/ASIA ISLAM

B52
ASHWORTH W.,A SHORT HISTORY OF THE INTERNATIONAL ECONOMY 1850-1950. WOR+45 WOR-45 AGRI FINAN INDUS MARKET LABOR ECO/TAC...CONCPT STAT HIST/WRIT FOR/TRADE ILO 19/20. PAGE 7 F0131
ECO/DEV TEC/DEV INT/TRADE

B52
HARDIN C.M.,THE POLITICS OF AGRICULTURE. USA+45 NAT/G PROF/ORG LEGIS LOBBY 20 DEPT/AGRI. PAGE 55 F1077
AGRI POLICY ECO/TAC GOV/REL

B52
SACHS E.S.,THE CHOICE BEFORE SOUTH AFRICA. SOUTH/AFR AGRI EXTR/IND PROC/MFG PROB/SOLV ORD/FREE SOVEREIGN 20 NEGRO. PAGE 115 F2267
NAT/LISM DISCRIM RACE/REL LABOR

C52
HUME D.,"OF COMMERCE" IN D. HUME, POLITICAL DISCOURSES (1752)" UK FINAN DIPLOM WEALTH ...GEN/LAWS 18 MONEY. PAGE 63 F1238
INDUS INT/TRADE PWR AGRI

B53
WILLIAMS J.H.,ECONOMIC STABILITY IN A CHANGING WORLD. FRANCE USA+45 USSR AGRI WORKER BUDGET INT/TRADE TAX WAR BAL/PAY COST EFFICIENCY ALL/IDEOS EQULIB 20 KEYNES/JM. PAGE 147 F2892
POLICY FINAN ECO/TAC WEALTH

B53
WOYTINSKY W.S.,WORLD POPULATION AND PRODUCTION: TRENDS AND OUTLOOK. FUT WOR+45 WOR-45 CULTURE SOCIETY ECO/DEV AGRI INDUS TEC/DEV EDU/PROP SKILL WEALTH...SOC TREND. PAGE 149 F2928
ECO/UNDEV METH/CNCPT GEOG PERSON

B54
BATTEN T.R.,PROBLEMS OF AFRICAN DEVELOPMENT (2ND ED.). AFR LAW SOCIETY SCHOOL ECO/TAC TAX...GEOG HEAL SOC 20. PAGE 11 F0211
ECO/UNDEV AGRI LOC/G PROB/SOLV

B54
KARTUN D.,AFRICA, AFRICA: A CONTINENT RISES TO ITS FEET. AFR SOUTH/AFR UK ELITES AGRI LABOR LOC/G POL/PAR EDU/PROP CONTROL COERCE DISCRIM AGE/Y NEGRO THIRD/WRLD GOLD/COAST. PAGE 69 F1358
COLONIAL ORD/FREE PROFIT EXTR/IND

B55
JONES T.B.,A BIBLIOGRAPHY ON SOUTH AMERICAN ECONOMIC AFFAIRS: ARTICLES IN NINETEENTH CENTURY PERIODICALS (PAMPHLET). AGRI COM/IND DIST/IND EXTR/IND FINAN INDUS LABOR NAT/G 19. PAGE 68 F1340
BIBLIOG ECO/UNDEV L/A+17C TEC/DEV

B55
OECD,MARSHALL PLAN IN TURKEY. TURKEY USA+45 COM/IND CONSTRUC SERV/IND FORCES BUDGET...STAT 20 MARSHL/PLN. PAGE 100 F1964
FOR/AID ECO/UNDEV AGRI INDUS

B55
SMITHIES A.,THE BUDGETARY PROCESS IN THE UNITED STATES. AFR ECO/DEV AGRI EX/STRUC FORCES LEGIS PROB/SOLV TAX ROUTINE EFFICIENCY...MGT CONGRESS PRESIDENT. PAGE 124 F2436
NAT/G ADMIN BUDGET GOV/REL

B55
US ADVISORY COMN INTERGOV REL,THE COMMISSION ON INTERGOVERNMENTAL RELATIONS; A REPORT TO THE PRESIDENT FOR TRANSMITTAL TO THE CONGRESS. USA+45 ECO/DEV AGRI COM/IND FINAN FORCES PLAN EDU/PROP HEALTH WEALTH...STAT MUNICH 20 CIV/DEFENS. PAGE 133 F2630
GOV/REL NAT/G LOC/G PROVS

B55
UYEHARA C.H.,COMPARATIVE PLATFORMS OF JAPAN'S MAJOR PARTIES... USA+45 AGRI LEGIS WORKER CAP/ISM ORD/FREE MARXISM SOCISM...IDEA/COMP 20 CHINJAP. PAGE 140 F2755
POLICY POL/PAR DIPLOM NAT/G

S55
BUNZEL J.H.,"THE GENERAL IDEOLOGY OF AMERICAN SMALL BUSINESS"(BMR)" USA+45 USA-45 AGRI GP/REL INGP/REL PERSON...MGT IDEA/COMP 18/20. PAGE 20 F0383
ALL/IDEOS ATTIT SML/CO INDUS

B56
JUAN T.L.,ECONOMIC AND SOCIAL DEVELOPMENT OF MODERN CHINA: A BIBLIOGRAPHICAL GUIDE. ASIA AGRI COM/IND DIST/IND FINAN INDUS DIPLOM...STAT 20. PAGE 68 F1342
BIBLIOG SOC

B56
KINDLEBERGER C.P.,THE TERMS OF TRADE: A EUROPEAN CASE-STUDY. EUR+WWI MOD/EUR ECO/DEV ECO/UNDEV AGRI INDUS BAL/PAY...METH/CNCPT STAT CONT/OBS CON/ANAL SOC/EXP SIMUL FOR/TRADE 20. PAGE 71 F1390
PLAN ECO/TAC

B56
US DEPARTMENT OF STATE,ECONOMIC PROBLEMS OF UNDERDEVELOPED AREAS (PAMPHLET). AFR ASIA ISLAM L/A+17C AGRI FINAN INDUS INT/ORG LABOR INT/TRADE ...PSY SOC 20. PAGE 136 F2673
BIBLIOG ECO/UNDEV TEC/DEV R+D

B56
WILCOX W.W.,SOCIAL RESPONSIBILITY IN FARM LEADERSHIP. CLIENT LEGIS EXEC LOBBY GP/REL ATTIT WEALTH. PAGE 146 F2880
AGRI LEAD VOL/ASSN WORKER

L56
PENNOCK J.R.,"PARTY AND CONSTITUENCY IN POSTWAR AGRICULTURAL PRICE SUPPORT LEGISLATION." USA+45 LEGIS DEBATE LOBBY RIGID/FLEX. PAGE 105 F2057
POL/PAR REPRESENT AGRI CHOOSE

S56
KNAPP D.C.,"CONGRESSIONAL CONTROL OF AGRICULTURAL CONSERVATION POLICY: A CASE STUDY OF THE APPROPRIATIONS PROCESS." DELIB/GP PLAN PROB/SOLV CONFER PARL/PROC...POLICY INT CONGRESS. PAGE 72 F1411
LEGIS AGRI BUDGET CONTROL

B57
BAUER P.T.,THE ECONOMICS OF UNDERDEVELOPED COUNTRIES. WOR+45 AGRI FINAN INDUS PROC/MFG WORKER CAP/ISM PAY PRICE INCOME MARXISM...METH/COMP 20 RESOURCE/N. PAGE 11 F0213
ECO/UNDEV ECO/TAC PROB/SOLV NAT/G

B57
BAUER P.T.,ECONOMIC ANALYSIS AND POLICY IN UNDERDEVELOPED COUNTRIES. AFR WOR+45 AGRI INT/TRADE TAX PRICE...GEN/METH BIBLIOG/A 20. PAGE 11 F0214
ECO/UNDEV METH/COMP POLICY

B57
BEHRMAN J.N.,INTERNATIONAL ECONOMICS: THEORY, PRACTICE, POLICY. AGRI INDUS NAT/G TARIFFS CONTROL BAL/PAY...POLICY METH/CNCPT T 19/20. PAGE 12 F0230
INT/TRADE FINAN DIPLOM FOR/AID

B57
COMMITTEE ECONOMIC DEVELOPMENT,ECONOMIC DEVELOPMENT ASSISTANCE. USA+45 WOR+45 AGRI CONFER ORD/FREE ...MGT CHARTS 20. PAGE 27 F0515 FOR/AID ECO/UNDEV FINAN PLAN

B57
LEIBENSTEIN H.,ECONOMIC BACKWARDNESS AND ECONOMIC GROWTH. WOR+45 SOCIETY AGRI INDUS TEC/DEV CAP/ISM FOR/AID COST DEMAND WEALTH...CHARTS IDEA/COMP 20. PAGE 77 F1513 ECO/UNDEV ECO/TAC PRODUC POLICY

B57
LENIN V.I.,THE DEVELOPMENT OF CAPITALISM IN RUSSIA. MOD/EUR USSR AGRI MARKET POL/PAR TEC/DEV...CONCPT 19/20. PAGE 78 F1521 COM INDUS CAP/ISM

B57
MILLIKAN M.F.,A PROPOSAL: KEY TO AN EFFECTIVE FOREIGN POLICY. USA+45 AGRI FINAN DELIB/GP DIPLOM REPRESENT MAJORITY...NEW/IDEA CHARTS. PAGE 91 F1795 FOR/AID GIVE ECO/UNDEV PLAN

B57
NEUMARK S.D.,ECONOMIC INFLUENCES ON THE SOUTH AFRICAN FRONTIER, 1652-1836. SOUTH/AFR SEA AGRI NAT/G FORCES WORKER DIPLOM INT/TRADE PRICE DEMAND PRODUC...STAT CHARTS 17/19 FRONTIER. PAGE 97 F1915 COLONIAL ECO/UNDEV ECO/TAC MARKET

B57
PALACIOS A.L.,PETROLEO, MONOPOLIOS, Y LATIFUNDIOS. L/A+17C EXTR/IND NAT/G TEC/DEV ECO/TAC CONTROL PRODUC 20 ARGEN MONOPOLY RESOURCE/N. PAGE 103 F2017 ECO/UNDEV NAT/LISM INDUS AGRI

B57
WARRINER D.,LAND REFORM AND DEVELOPMENT IN THE MIDDLE EAST: A STUDY OF EGYPT, SYRIA AND IRAQ. IRAQ ISLAM SYRIA UAR AGRI DIST/IND PLAN TEC/DEV DOMIN REV ATTIT WEALTH...SOC METH/CNCPT STAT OBS RECORD HIST/WRIT TREND GEN/LAWS FAO 20. PAGE 143 F2825 ECO/UNDEV CONCPT

B58
AVRAMOVIC D.,POSTWAR GROWTH IN INTERNATIONAL INDEBTEDNESS. AFR WOR+45 AGRI INDUS CAP/ISM PRICE INCOME...NAT/COMP 20 SILVER. PAGE 8 F0143 INT/TRADE FINAN COST BAL/PAY

B58
BIDWELL P.W.,RAW MATERIALS: A STUDY OF AMERICAN POLICY. USA+45 USA-45 ECO/UNDEV AGRI INDUS KIN CREATE PLAN ECO/TAC WAR PEACE ATTIT DRIVE WEALTH ...STAT CHARTS CONGRESS FOR/TRADE VAL/FREE. PAGE 15 F0279 EXTR/IND ECO/DEV

B58
COALE A.J.,POPULATION GROWTH AND ECONOMIC DEVELOPMENT IN LOW-INCOME COUNTRIES: A CASE STUDY OF INDIA'S PROSPECTS. INDIA AGRI WORKER INCOME AGE WEALTH...CHARTS 20 MEXIC/AMER. PAGE 25 F0495 ECO/UNDEV GEOG CENSUS SEX

B58
COLE G.D.H.,COMMUNISM AND SOCIAL DEMOCRACY (VOL. IV OF "HISTORY OF SOCIAL THOUGHT"). COM GERMANY ITALY UK AGRI INT/ORG WORKER DIPLOM COLONIAL NAT/LISM ALL/IDEOS...BIBLIOG 20 LEAGUE/NAT AUST/HUNG. PAGE 26 F0502 MARXISM REV POL/PAR SOCISM

B58
EHRHARD J.,LE DESTIN DU COLONIALISME. AFR FRANCE ECO/UNDEV AGRI FINAN MARKET CREATE PLAN TEC/DEV BUDGET DIPLOM PRICE 20. PAGE 36 F0710 COLONIAL FOR/AID INT/TRADE INDUS

B58
HANCE W.A.,AFRICAN ECONOMIC DEVELOPMENT. AGRI DIST/IND INDUS R+D ACT/RES PLAN CAP/ISM FOR/AID ...GOV/COMP BIBLIOG 20. PAGE 54 F1058 AFR ECO/UNDEV PROB/SOLV TEC/DEV

B58
MIKESELL R.F.,FINANCING FREE WORLD TRADE WITH THE SINO-SOVIET BLOC. CHINA/COM COM USSR WOR+45 ECO/DEV AGRI DIST/IND EXTR/IND FINAN INDUS MARKET PROC/MFG NAT/G PLAN TEC/DEV ECO/TAC...CHARTS METH/GP EEC FOR/TRADE 20. PAGE 91 F1780 STAT BAL/PAY

B58
NICULESCU B.,COLONIAL PLANNING: A COMPARATIVE STUDY. AFR AGRI LOC/G NAT/G DELIB/GP COLONIAL MUNICH 20. PAGE 98 F1927 PLAN ECO/UNDEV TEC/DEV NAT/COMP

B58
SCOTT D.J.R.,RUSSIAN POLITICAL INSTITUTIONS. RUSSIA USSR CONSTN AGRI DELIB/GP PLAN EDU/PROP CONTROL CHOOSE EFFICIENCY ATTIT MARXISM...BIBLIOG/A IND 13/20. PAGE 118 F2332 NAT/G POL/PAR ADMIN DECISION

B58
SILOW R.A.,THE POTENTIAL CONTRIBUTION OF ATOMIC ENERGY TO DEVELOPMENT IN AGRICULTURE AND RELATED INDUSTRIES (PAMPHLET). WOR+45 R+D TEC/DEV EFFICIENCY 20 UN. PAGE 122 F2403 NUC/PWR ECO/UNDEV AGRI

B58
US OPERATIONS MISSION TO VIET,BUILDING ECONOMIC STRENGTH (PAMPHLET). USA+45 VIETNAM/S INDUS TEC/DEV BUDGET ADMIN EATING HEALTH...STAT 20. PAGE 138 F2725 FOR/AID ECO/UNDEV AGRI EDU/PROP

L58
TRAGER F.N.,"A SELECTED AND ANNOTATED BIBLIOGRAPHY ON ECONOMIC DEVELOPMENT, 1953-1957." WOR+45 AGRI FINAN INDUS MARKET LABOR WORKER PLAN INT/TRADE PRODUC...CENSUS MUNICH. PAGE 131 F2583 BIBLIOG/A ECO/UNDEV ECO/DEV

B59
AITKEN H.G.,THE AMERICAN ECONOMIC IMPACT ON CANADA. CANADA USA+45 AGRI FINAN INDUS LABOR INT/TRADE BAL/PAY...INT/LAW TREND 20. PAGE 3 F0055 DIPLOM ECO/TAC POLICY NAT/G

B59
BARNETT A.D.,COMMUNIST ECONOMIC STRATEGY: THE RISE OF MAINLAND CHINA. CHINA/COM USSR WOR+45 AGRI INDUS FOR/AID INGP/REL ATTIT. PAGE 10 F0188 ECO/UNDEV INT/TRADE TOTALISM BAL/PWR

B59
BLACK J.D.,ECONOMICS FOR AGRICULTURE. USA+45 EXTR/IND FAM WORKER ACT/RES PLAN PRICE EATING INCOME...CENSUS BIBLIOG 20. PAGE 15 F0291 AGRI ECO/TAC MARKET POLICY

B59
CHECCHI V.,HONDURAS: A PROBLEM IN ECONOMIC DEVELOPMENT. HONDURAS AGRI FINAN INDUS LABOR WORKER INT/TRADE EDU/PROP PRICE HEALTH...GEOG CHARTS BIBLIOG 20. PAGE 24 F0458 ECO/UNDEV ECO/TAC PROB/SOLV PLAN

B59
HAZLEWOOD A.,THE ECONOMICS OF "UNDER-DEVELOPED" AREAS. WOR+45 DIST/IND EXTR/IND FINAN INDUS MARKET PLAN FOR/AID...GEOG 20. PAGE 57 F1129 BIBLIOG/A ECO/UNDEV AGRI INT/TRADE

B59
LI CHOH-MING,ECONOMIC DEVELOPMENT OF COMMUNIST CHINA. ASIA CHINA/COM AGRI FINAN TAX INCOME MARXISM ...MGT 20. PAGE 80 F1557 ECO/UNDEV INDUS ORD/FREE TEC/DEV

B59
LINK R.G.,ENGLISH THEORIES OF ECONOMIC FLUCTUATIONS: 1815-1848. FRANCE UK AGRI WORKER DIPLOM PRICE TASK WAR DEMAND PRODUC...POLICY BIBLIOG 18 MALTHUS MILL/JS WILSON/J. PAGE 80 F1574 IDEA/COMP ECO/DEV WEALTH EQUILIB

B59
NORTON P.L.,URBAN PROBLEMS AND TECHNIQUES. AIR AGRI INDUS MARKET TEC/DEV BUDGET LEISURE ALL/VALS ...ANTHOL MUNICH 20 URBAN/RNWL. PAGE 99 F1936 PLAN LOC/G HABITAT

B59
NOVE A.,COMMUNIST ECONOMIC STRATEGY: SOVIET GROWTH AND CAPABILITIES. USSR AGRI LABOR PLAN TEC/DEV CAP/ISM INT/TRADE EFFICIENCY MARXISM 20 THIRD/WRLD. PAGE 99 F1941 FOR/AID ECO/TAC DIPLOM INDUS

B59
NUNEZ JIMENEZ A.,LA LIBERACION DE LAS ISLAS. CUBA L/A+17C USA+45 LAW CHIEF PLAN DIPLOM FOR/AID OWN WEALTH 20 CASTRO/F. PAGE 99 F1945 AGRI REV ECO/UNDEV NAT/G

B59
ROPKE W.,INTERNATIONAL ORDER AND ECONOMIC INTEGRATION. ECO/DEV ECO/UNDEV AGRI FINAN INDUS INT/ORG WAR PEACE ORD/FREE...SOC METH/COMP 20 EEC. PAGE 114 F2238 INT/TRADE DIPLOM BAL/PAY ALL/IDEOS

B59
SILCOCK T.H.,THE COMMONWEALTH ECONOMY IN SOUTHEAST ASIA. AFR INDIA MALAYSIA S/ASIA ECO/DEV AGRI LOC/G PLAN TARIFFS COLONIAL BAL/PAY DEMAND...BIBLIOG/A 20 GATT. PAGE 122 F2401 ECO/TAC INT/TRADE RACE/REL DIPLOM

B59
WARD B.,5 IDEAS THAT CHANGE THE WORLD. WOR+45 WOR-45 SOCIETY STRUCT AGRI INDUS INT/ORG NAT/G FORCES ACT/RES ARMS/CONT TOTALISM ATTIT DRIVE GEN/LAWS. PAGE 143 F2815 ECO/UNDEV ALL/VALS NAT/LISM COLONIAL

B59
WIBBERLEY G.P.,AGRICULTURE AND URBAN GROWTH. UK USA+45 ECO/DEV FINAN PROB/SOLV INT/TRADE COST ...GEOG STAT CHARTS METH/COMP HYPO/EXP METH MUNICH 20. PAGE 146 F2876 AGRI PLAN

S59
ALLEN G.,"NATIONAL FARMERS UNION AS A PRESSURE GROUP: II." UK ECO/DEV MARKET POL/PAR DELIB/GP PROB/SOLV ECO/TAC LOBBY INCOME...POLICY METH/COMP 19/20 NAT/FARMER. PAGE 4 F0069 DIST/IND AGRI PROF/ORG TREND

S59
GILPATRICK T.V.,"PRICE SUPPORT POLICY AND THE MIDWEST FARM VOTE" (BMR)" NAT/G PRICE CONTROL REGION...POLICY CHARTS 440 20 MIDWEST/US CONGRESS REPUBLICAN EISNHWR/DD 20. PAGE 47 F0925 POL/PAR AGRI ATTIT CHOOSE

S59
STREETEN P.,"UNBALANCED GROWTH" UK ECO/DEV AGRI MARKET TEC/DEV CAP/ISM ECO/TAC FOR/AID INT/TRADE DEMAND ORD/FREE...CONCPT 20. PAGE 127 F2502 IDEA/COMP FINAN PRODUC EQUILIB

B60
AHMED J.,NATURAL RESOURCES IN LOW INCOME COUNTRIES: AN ANALYTICAL SURVEY OF SOCIO-ECONOMIC RESEARCH (PAMPHLET). WOR+45 20. PAGE 3 F0052 BIBLIOG/A ECO/UNDEV INDUS AGRI

B60
AMERICAN U BEIRUT ECO RES INST,A SELECTED AND ANNOTATED BIBLIOGRAPHY OF ECONOMIC LITERATURE ON THE ARABIC SPEAKING COUNTRIES OF THE MIDDLE EAST. ISLAM AGRI COM/IND DIST/IND FINAN INDUS LABOR BIBLIOG/A ECO/UNDEV STAT

...GEOG 20. PAGE 5 F0091

B60
ASPREMONT-LYNDEN H.,RAPPORT SUR L'ADMINISTRATION BELGE DU RUANDA-URUNDI PENDANT L'ANNEE 1959. BELGIUM RWANDA AGRI INDUS DIPLOM ECO/TAC INT/TRADE DOMIN ADMIN RACE/REL...GEOG CENSUS 20 UN. PAGE 7 F0132
AFR COLONIAL ECO/UNDEV INT/ORG

B60
CROSSER P.K.,STATE CAPITALISM IN THE ECONOMY OF THE UNITED STATES. USA+45 USA-45 AGRI FINAN INDUS LABOR WORKER RATION CONTROL GOV/REL DEMAND...NEW/IDEA 20. PAGE 29 F0557
CAP/ISM ECO/DEV ECO/TAC NAT/G

B60
FERNANDES F.,MUDANCAS SOCIAIS NO BRASIL. BRAZIL L/A+17C SOCIETY AGRI PROVS LEAD GP/REL RACE/REL ORD/FREE...SOC SOC/INTEG 20 SAO/PAULO. PAGE 40 F0786
ECO/UNDEV STRATA INDUS

B60
GONZALEZ NAVARRO M.,LA COLONIZACION EN MEXICO, 1877-1910. AGRI NAT/G PLAN PROB/SOLV INCOME ...POLICY JURID CENSUS 19/20 MEXIC/AMER MIGRATION. PAGE 48 F0947
ECO/UNDEV GEOG HABITAT COLONIAL

B60
HARBERGER A.C.,THE DEMAND FOR DURABLE GOODS. AGRI FINAN COST EQUILIB...MATH STAT TIME/SEQ TREND CON/ANAL CHARTS SIMUL ANTHOL 20. PAGE 55 F1072
ECOMETRIC DEMAND PRICE

B60
HEYSE T.,PROBLEMS FONCIERS ET REGIME DES TERRES (ASPECTS ECONOMIQUES, JURIDIQUES ET SOCIAUX). AFR CONGO/BRAZ INT/ORG DIPLOM SOVEREIGN...GEOG TREATY 20. PAGE 59 F1161
BIBLIOG AGRI ECO/UNDEV LEGIS

B60
HUGHES R.,THE CHINESE COMMUNES; A BACKGROUND BOOK. CHINA/COM SOCIETY CONTROL ROUTINE ADJUST EFFICIENCY PRODUC 20. PAGE 63 F1234
AGRI INDUS STRUCT MARXISM

B60
LATIFI D.,INDIA AND UNITED STATES AID. ASIA INDIA UK USA+45 AGRI FINAN INDUS COLONIAL ORD/FREE SOVEREIGN WEALTH...METH/COMP 20. PAGE 76 F1486
FOR/AID DIPLOM ECO/UNDEV

B60
MC CLELLAN G.S.,INDIA. AFR CHINA/COM INDIA CONSTN ELITES STRATA AGRI POL/PAR FOR/AID ARMS/CONT REV MARXISM...CENSUS BIBLIOG 20 GANDHI/M NEHRU/J. PAGE 87 F1712
DIPLOM NAT/G SOCIETY ECO/UNDEV

B60
ROBINSON E.A.G.,ECONOMIC CONSEQUENCES OF THE SIZE OF NATIONS. AGRI INDUS DELIB/GP FOR/AID ADMIN EFFICIENCY...METH/COMP 20. PAGE 113 F2218
CONCPT INT/ORG NAT/COMP

B60
SHANNON D.A.,THE GREAT DEPRESSION. USA-45 FINAN LG/CO SCHOOL SML/CO DELIB/GP RECEIVE REV EATING INCOME...ANTHOL MUNICH 20 ROOSEVLT/F CONGRESS. PAGE 120 F2365
WEALTH NAT/G AGRI INDUS

B60
SIMOONS F.J.,NORTHWEST ETHIOPIA; PEOPLES AND ECONOMY. ETHIOPIA MARKET CREATE 20. PAGE 122 F2411
SOCIETY STRUCT AGRI INDUS

B60
SMET G.,BIBLIOGRAPHIE DE LA CONTRIBUTION A L'ETUDE DE LA PROGRESSION ECONOMIQUE DE L'AFRIQUE. AFR DIST/IND EXTR/IND TEC/DEV 20. PAGE 123 F2427
BIBLIOG ECO/UNDEV INDUS AGRI

B60
THE ECONOMIST (LONDON),THE COMMONWEALTH AND EUROPE. EUR+WWI WOR+45 AGRI FINAN INCOME...STAT CENSUS CHARTS CMN/WLTH EEC. PAGE 129 F2550
INT/TRADE INDUS INT/ORG NAT/COMP

B60
US OPERATIONS MISSION - TURKEY,SOME POSSIBILITIES FOR ACCELERATING TURKEY'S ECONOMIC GROWTH. TURKEY USA+45 AGRI FINAN INDUS NAT/G ACT/RES BUDGET COST ...CHARTS 20. PAGE 138 F2724
ECO/UNDEV ECO/TAC FOR/AID PRODUC

S60
BECKER A.S.,"COMPARISIONS OF UNITED STATES AND USSR NATIONAL OUTPUT: SOME RULES OF THE GAME." COM USA+45 ECO/DEV AGRI DIST/IND INDUS R+D CONSULT PLAN ECO/TAC RIGID/FLEX KNOWL...METH/CNCPT CHARTS 20. PAGE 12 F0227
STAT USSR

S60
BERG E.J.,"ECONOMIC BASIS OF POLITICAL CHOICE IN FRENCH WEST AFRICA." FRANCE ECO/UNDEV AGRI INDUS NAT/G PLAN LEGIT COLONIAL REGION ATTIT PWR WEALTH ...CONCPT FOR/TRADE 20. PAGE 13 F0257
AFR ECO/TAC

S60
BUTLER W.F.,"ECONOMIC PROGRESS IN LATIN AMERICA." L/A+17C USA+45 ECO/UNDEV AGRI FINAN NAT/G PLAN ECO/TAC FOR/AID ADMIN WEALTH...OLD/LIB TOT/POP 20. PAGE 21 F0397
INDUS ACT/RES

S60
HERZ J.H.,"EAST GERMANY: PROGRESS AND PROSPECTS." COM AGRI FINAN INDUS LOC/G NAT/G FORCES PLAN TEC/DEV DOMIN ADMIN COERCE DRIVE PERCEPT RIGID/FLEX MORAL ORD/FREE PWR...MARXIST PSY SOC RECORD STERTYP WORK. PAGE 59 F1158
POL/PAR STRUCT GERMANY

S60
KELLOGG C.E.,"TRANSFER OF BASIC SKILLS OF FOOD PRODUCTION." AFR FUT S/ASIA STRATA ECO/UNDEV LABOR VOL/ASSN RIGID/FLEX...OLD/LIB SOCIALIST NEW/IDEA STAT PROJ/TEST GEN/LAWS 20. PAGE 70 F1370
AGRI PLAN

S60
RICHTER J.H.,"TOWARDS AN INTERNATIONAL POLICY ON AGRICULTURAL TRADE." EUR+WWI USA+45 ECO/DEV NAT/G PLAN ECO/TAC ATTIT PWR WEALTH...CONCPT GEN/LAWS 20. PAGE 111 F2187
AGRI INT/ORG

S60
RIVKIN A.,"AFRICAN ECONOMIC DEVELOPMENT: ADVANCED TECHNOLOGY AND THE STAGES OF GROWTH." CULTURE ECO/UNDEV AGRI COM/IND EXTR/IND PLAN ECO/TAC ATTIT DRIVE RIGID/FLEX SKILL WEALTH...MGT SOC GEN/LAWS FOR/TRADE WORK TOT/POP 20. PAGE 111 F2195
AFR TEC/DEV FOR/AID

C60
FAULKNER H.U.,"AMERICAN ECONOMIC HISTORY (8TH ED.)" USA+45 USA-45 FINAN...CHARTS BIBLIOG/A T 17/20. PAGE 39 F0769
AGRI INDUS ECO/DEV CAP/ISM

B61
BAUER P.T.,INDIAN ECONOMIC POLICY AND DEVELOPMENT. INDIA STRATA AGRI FINAN POL/PAR BUDGET FOR/AID GOV/REL EFFICIENCY...CENSUS 20. PAGE 11 F0216
ECO/UNDEV ECO/TAC POLICY PLAN

B61
DE VRIES E.,MAN IN RAPID SOCIAL CHANGE. WOR+45 SOCIETY ECO/DEV ECO/UNDEV AGRI INDUS FAM SECT TEC/DEV ATTIT...RECORD 20 CHRISTIAN. PAGE 31 F0607
CULTURE ALL/VALS SOC TASK

B61
DIMOCK M.E.,BUSINESS AND GOVERNMENT (4TH ED.). AGRI FINAN OP/RES PLAN BUDGET DIPLOM LOBBY NUC/PWR NEW/LIB SOCISM...POLICY BIBLIOG 20. PAGE 33 F0641
NAT/G INDUS LABOR ECO/TAC

B61
ELLIS H.S.,ECONOMIC DEVELOPMENT FOR LATIN AMERICA. L/A+17C AGRI FINAN INDUS FOR/AID GP/REL BAL/PAY DEMAND...ANTHOL 20 INTL/ECON. PAGE 37 F0723
ECO/UNDEV ECO/TAC PLAN INT/TRADE

B61
FELLNER W.,THE PROBLEM OF RISING PRICES. AGRI INDUS WORKER BUDGET CAP/ISM ECO/TAC INT/TRADE PAY DEMAND ...POLICY 20 EEC. PAGE 40 F0780
PRICE MARKET ECO/DEV COST

B61
FLINN M.W.,AN ECONOMIC AND SOCIAL HISTORY OF BRITAIN, 1066-1939. UK LAW STRATA STRUCT AGRI DIST/IND INDUS WORKER INT/TRADE WAR...CENSUS 11/20. PAGE 42 F0811
SOCIETY SOC

B61
HEMPSTONE S.,THE NEW AFRICA. AGRI INDUS KIN NAT/G COLONIAL MARXISM...SOC INT TREND NAT/COMP BIBLIOG/A 20. PAGE 58 F1146
AFR ORD/FREE PERSON CULTURE

B61
HORVATH B.,THE CHARACTERISTICS OF YUGOSLAV ECONOMIC DEVELOPMENT. COM ECO/UNDEV AGRI INDUS PLAN CAP/ISM ECO/TAC ROUTINE WEALTH...SOCIALIST STAT CHARTS STERTYP WORK 20. PAGE 62 F1217
ACT/RES YUGOSLAVIA

B61
INTERNATIONAL BANK RECONST DEV,THE WORLD BANK IN AFRICA: SUMMARY OF ACTIVITIES. AGRI COM/IND DIST/IND EXTR/IND INDUS TAX COST...CHARTS 20. PAGE 65 F1271
FINAN ECO/UNDEV INT/ORG AFR

B61
KATKOFF U.,SOVIET ECONOMY 1940-1965. COM WOR+45 WOR-45 INTELL NAT/G POL/PAR TOP/EX ATTIT PWR ...POLICY TIME/SEQ VAL/FREE 20. PAGE 69 F1360
AGRI PERSON TOTALISM USSR

B61
LUZ N.V.,A LUTA PELA INDUSTRIALIZACAO DO BRAZIL. BRAZIL L/A+17C AGRI NAT/G TEC/DEV COLONIAL 19/20. PAGE 82 F1615
ECO/UNDEV INDUS NAT/LISM POLICY

B61
MARX K.,THE COMMUNIST MANIFESTO. IN (MENDEL A. ESSENTIAL WORKS OF MARXISM, NEW YORK: BANTAM. FUT MOD/EUR CULTURE ECO/DEV ECO/UNDEV AGRI FINAN INDUS MARKET PROC/MFG LABOR POL/PAR CONSULT FORCES CREATE PLAN ADMIN ATTIT DRIVE RIGID/FLEX ORD/FREE PWR RESPECT MARX/KARL MUNICH WORK. PAGE 86 F1691
COM NEW/IDEA CAP/ISM REV

B61
MIT CENTER INTERNATIONAL STU,OFFICIAL SERIAL PUBLICATIONS RELATING TO ECONOMIC DEVELOPMENT IN AFRICA SOUTH OF THE SAHARA. AFR SOCIETY AGRI FINAN INDUS LG/CO ADMIN 20. PAGE 92 F1806
BIBLIOG ECO/UNDEV ECO/TAC NAT/G

B61
NORTH D.C.,THE ECONOMIC GROWTH OF THE UNITED STATES 1790-1860. USA-45 INDUS TEC/DEV CAP/ISM ECO/TAC PRICE COST DEMAND LAISSEZ...ECOMETRIC STAT TREND 19. PAGE 98 F1933
AGRI ECO/UNDEV

B61
PETCH G.A.,ECONOMIC DEVELOPMENT AND MODERN WEST AFRICA. AFR CONGO/BRAZ GHANA NIGER SIER/LEONE AGRI
ECO/UNDEV TEC/DEV

MARKET LABOR FOR/AID TAX COST EFFICIENCY EQUILIB PRODUC...GEOG TREND 20. PAGE 105 F2068
EXTR/IND ECO/TAC

B61

SEPULVEDA C.,A STATEMENT OF THE LAWS OF MEXICO IN MATTERS AFFECTING BUSINESS (3RD ED.). AGRI DIST/IND EXTR/IND FINAN INDUS WORKER TAX MARRIAGE OWN ORD/FREE...BIBLIOG 20 MEXIC/AMER TREATY MIGRATION MONOPOLY. PAGE 119 F2356
CONSTN NAT/G JURID LEGIS

B61

SHONFIELD A.,ECONOMIC GROWTH AND INFLATION; A STUDY OF INDIAN PLANNING. AFR INDIA AGRI INDUS TEC/DEV CONTROL DEMAND UTIL 20. PAGE 121 F2384
ECO/UNDEV PRICE PLAN BUDGET

B61

STARK H.,SOCIAL AND ECONOMIC FRONTIERS IN LATIN AMERICA (2ND ED.). CUBA FUT CULTURE AGRI INDUS ECO/TAC PRODUC ATTIT MARXISM...NAT/COMP BIBLIOG T 20. PAGE 125 F2470
L/A+17C SOCIETY DIPLOM ECO/UNDEV

B61

US GENERAL ACCOUNTING OFFICE,EXAMINATION OF ECONOMIC AND TECHNICAL ASSISTANCE PROGRAM FOR IRAN. IRAN USA+45 AGRI INDUS DIPLOM CONTROL COST 20. PAGE 136 F2681
FOR/AID ADMIN TEC/DEV ECO/UNDEV

L61

JOHNSTON B.F.,"THE ROLE OF AGRICULTURE IN ECONOMIC DEVELOPMENT." FINAN PRODUC ROLE BIBLIOG. PAGE 68 F1332
AGRI ECO/UNDEV PLAN INDUS

S61

DALTON G.,"ECONOMIC THEORY AND PRIMITIVE SOCIETY" (BMR)" UNIV AGRI KIN TEC/DEV ECO/TAC REGION HABITAT SKILL...METH/COMP BIBLIOG. PAGE 30 F0574
ECO/UNDEV METH PHIL/SCI SOC

S61

VINER J.,"ECONOMIC FOREIGN POLICY ON THE NEW FRONTIER." USA+45 ECO/UNDEV AGRI FINAN INDUS MARKET INT/ORG NAT/G FOR/AID INT/TRADE ADMIN ATTIT PWR 20 KENNEDY/JF. PAGE 141 F2786
TOP/EX ECO/TAC BAL/PAY TARIFFS

B62

BROOKINGS INSTITUTION,DEVELOPMENT OF THE EMERGING COUNTRIES; AN AGENDA FOR RESEARCH. WOR+45 AGRI TEC/DEV FOR/AID EDU/PROP ADJUST HABITAT KNOWL...PSY SOC ANTHOL 20 THIRD/WRLD. PAGE 19 F0362
ECO/UNDEV R+D SOCIETY PROB/SOLV

B62

BRUMBERG A.,RUSSIA UNDER KHRUSHCHEV. FUT USSR SOCIETY ECO/DEV AGRI PERF/ART WORKER PWR...SOC ANTHOL 20 KHRUSH/N. PAGE 20 F0377
COM MARXISM NAT/G CHIEF

B62

DENISON E.F.,THE SOURCES OF ECONOMIC GROWTH IN THE UNITED STATES AND THE ALTERNATIVES BEFORE US. AGRI INDUS SCHOOL TEC/DEV CAP/ISM ECO/TAC PRICE COST WEALTH...STAT TREND CHARTS 20. PAGE 32 F0620
ECO/DEV WORKER PRODUC

B62

FAO,FOOD AND AGRICULTURE ORGANIZATION AFRICAN SURVEY. AFR CONGO/BRAZ GHANA STRATA AGRI INT/ORG TEC/DEV FOR/AID INT/TRADE RACE/REL DEMAND EFFICIENCY PRODUC...GEOG 20 UN CONGO/LEOP. PAGE 39 F0763
ECO/TAC WEALTH EXTR/IND ECO/UNDEV

B62

GALENSON W.,LABOR IN DEVELOPING COUNTRIES. BRAZIL INDONESIA ISRAEL PAKISTAN TURKEY AGRI INDUS WORKER PAY PRICE GP/REL WEALTH...MGT CHARTS METH/COMP NAT/COMP 20. PAGE 45 F0888
LABOR ECO/UNDEV BARGAIN POL/PAR

B62

GREEN L.P.,DEVELOPMENT IN AFRICA. AFR CENTRL/AFR GHANA RHODESIA SOUTH/AFR AGRI PROC/MFG INT/TRADE DEMAND NAT/LISM PRODUC WEALTH...GEOG METH/CNCPT CHARTS BIBLIOG 20. PAGE 50 F0987
CULTURE ECO/UNDEV GOV/REL TREND

B62

HOOVER C.B.,ECONOMIC SYSTEMS OF THE COMMONWEALTH. AFR CANADA INDIA UK ECO/DEV ECO/UNDEV AGRI INDUS TEC/DEV TARIFFS PRICE BAL/PAY DEMAND...SIMUL 20 AUSTRAL. PAGE 61 F1208
CAP/ISM SOCISM ECO/TAC PLAN

B62

INTERNATIONAL BANK RECONST DEV,THE WORLD BANK AND IDA IN ASIA. ASIA S/ASIA COM/IND DIST/IND...CHARTS 20. PAGE 65 F1272
FINAN ECO/UNDEV AGRI INDUS

B62

INTNTL COTTON ADVISORY COMMITT,GOVERNMENT REGULATIONS ON COTTON, 1962 (PAMPHLET). WOR+45 RATION PRODUC...CHARTS 20. PAGE 65 F1287
ECO/TAC LAW CONTROL AGRI

B62

KAUTSKY J.H.,POLITICAL CHANGE IN UNDERDEVELOPED COUNTRIES: NATIONALISM AND COMMUNISM. WOR+45 AGRI TEC/DEV EDU/PROP ATTIT...POLICY METH/CNCPT STYLE INT QU CENSUS TREND SOC/EXP GEN/LAWS 20. PAGE 69 F1365
ECO/UNDEV SOCIETY CAP/ISM REV

B62

LIPPMANN W.,WESTERN UNITY AND THE COMMON MARKET. EUR+WWI FRANCE GERMANY/W UK USA+45 ECO/DEV AGRI FINAN MARKET INT/ORG NAT/G FOR/AID AGREE WEALTH 20 EEC. PAGE 80 F1575
DIPLOM INT/TRADE VOL/ASSN

B62

MARTINS A.F.,REVOLUCAO BRANCA NO CAMPO. L/A+17C SERV/IND DEMAND EFFICIENCY PRODUC...POLICY METH/COMP. PAGE 86 F1685
AGRI ECO/UNDEV TEC/DEV NAT/COMP

B62

MCCRONE G.,THE ECONOMICS OF SUBSIDING AGRICULTURE. UK ECO/DEV MARKET PLAN TARIFFS PROFIT 20 EEC. PAGE 88 F1725
AGRI BAL/PAY INT/TRADE LABOR

B62

MEYER F.V.,THE TERMS OF TRADE. WOR+45 AGRI MARKET PROC/MFG DIPLOM PRICE DEMAND PRODUC 20. PAGE 90 F1769
INT/TRADE BAL/PAY SIMUL EQUILIB

B62

MULLER E.,DIE HEIMATVERTRIEBENEN IN BADEN-WURTTEMBERG. GERMANY/W AGRI INDUS LABOR PROVS SOC/INTEG 20 MIGRATION. PAGE 95 F1858
GP/REL INGP/REL

B62

PONCET J.,LA COLONISATION ET L'AGRICULTURE EUROPEENNES EN TUNISIE DEPUIS 1881. FRANCE WORKER TEC/DEV ECO/TAC CONTROL EFFICIENCY ROLE WEALTH 19/20 TUNIS. PAGE 107 F2101
ECO/UNDEV AGRI COLONIAL FINAN

B62

ROBINSON A.D.,DUTCH ORGANIZED AGRICULTURE IN INTERNATIONAL POLITICS, 1945-1960. EUR+WWI NETHERLAND STRUCT ECO/DEV NAT/G VOL/ASSN CONSULT DELIB/GP PLAN TEC/DEV INT/TRADE EDU/PROP ATTIT RIGID/FLEX ALL/VALS...NEW/IDEA TREND EEC COMMUN 20. PAGE 112 F2215
AGRI INT/ORG

B62

SEN S.R.,THE STRATEGY FOR AGRICULTURAL DEVELOPMENT AND OTHER ESSAYS ON ECONOMIC POLICY AND PLANNING. INDIA FINAN ACT/RES TEC/DEV CAP/ISM PRICE...STAT 20. PAGE 119 F2354
ECO/UNDEV PLAN AGRI POLICY

B62

THEOBALD R.,NATIONAL DEVELOPMENT EFFORTS (PAMPHLET). WOR+45 AGRI BUDGET FOR/AID INT/TRADE TAX 20. PAGE 129 F2555
ECO/UNDEV PLAN BAL/PAY WEALTH

B62

UNECA LIBRARY,BOOKS ON AFRICA IN THE UNECA LIBRARY. WOR+45 AGRI INT/ORG NAT/G PLAN WRITING REGION...SOC STAT UN. PAGE 132 F2605
BIBLIOG AFR ECO/UNDEV TEC/DEV

B62

VACCARO J.R.,A STATEMENT OF THE LAWS OF CHILE IN MATTERS AFFECTING BUSINESS (3RD ED.). CHILE AGRI FINAN FAM LABOR ECO/TAC FOR/AID TAX ADJUD CONTROL MARRIAGE STRANGE...BIBLIOG 20. PAGE 140 F2756
CONSTN LAW INDUS MGT

B62

WALSTON H.,AGRICULTURE UNDER COMMUNISM. CHINA/COM COM PROB/SOLV HAPPINESS RIGID/FLEX...POLICY METH/COMP 20. PAGE 143 F2811
AGRI MARXISM PLAN CREATE

L62

BELSHAW D.G.R.,"PUBLIC INVESTMENT IN AGRICULTURE AND ECONOMIC DEVELOPMENT OF UGANDA" UGANDA AGRI INDUS R+D ECO/TAC RATION TAX PAY COLONIAL 20 WORLD/BANK. PAGE 13 F0242
ECO/UNDEV PLAN ADMIN CENTRAL

L62

ERDMANN H.H.,"ADMINISTRATIVE LAW AND FARM ECONOMICS." USA+45 LOC/G NAT/G PLAN PROB/SOLV LOBBY ...DECISION ANTHOL 20. PAGE 38 F0744
AGRI ADMIN ADJUD POLICY

L62

WATERSTON A.,"PLANNING IN MOROCCO, ORGANIZATION AND IMPLEMENTATION. BALTIMORE: HOPKINS ECON. DEVELOP. INT. BANK FOR." ISLAM ECO/DEV AGRI DIST/IND INDUS PROC/MFG SERV/IND LOC/G EX/STRUC ECO/TAC PWR WEALTH TOT/POP TRUE/GP METH/GP TERR/GP VAL/FREE 20. PAGE 144 F2829
NAT/G PLAN MOROCCO

S62

KRISHNA K.G.V.,"PLANNING AND ECONOMIC DEVELOPMENT" AFR UGANDA AGRI INDUS R+D BUDGET RATION TAX COLONIAL 20. PAGE 73 F1441
ECO/UNDEV ECO/TAC NAT/LISM PLAN

C62

GREEN L.P.,"DEVELOPMENT IN AFRICA." RHODESIA SOUTH/AFR UGANDA MARKET PROC/MFG PRODUC WEALTH ...GEOG 20. PAGE 50 F0986
BIBLIOG ECO/UNDEV AFR AGRI

B63

BRITISH AID. UK AGRI DIST/IND INDUS SCHOOL TEC/DEV INT/TRADE COLONIAL DEMAND...TREND CHARTS 20. PAGE 1 F0018
FOR/AID ECO/UNDEV NAT/G FINAN

B63

BARNETT H.J.,SCARCITY AND GROWTH: THE ECONOMICS OF NATURAL RESOURCE AVAILABILITY. FUT WOR+45 AGRI INDUS PROB/SOLV TEC/DEV CONTROL PRODUC...SOC/WK IDEA/COMP METH/COMP SIMUL 20 RESOURCE/N MALTHUS RICARDO/D MILL/JS DARWIN/C. PAGE 10 F0191
DEMAND HABITAT CENSUS GEOG

B63

BERGSON A.,ECONOMIC TRENDS IN THE SOVIET UNION.
ECO/DEV

USSR ECO/UNDEV AGRI NAT/G FORCES PLAN TEC/DEV INT/TRADE BAL/PAY...POLICY ANTHOL 20. PAGE 14 F0259
NAT/COMP INDUS LABOR

B63
CHOJNACKI S.,REGISTER ON CURRENT RESEARCH ON ETHIOPIA AND THE HORN OF AFRICA. ETHIOPIA LAW CULTURE AGRI SECT EDU/PROP ADMIN...GEOG HEAL LING 20. PAGE 24 F0470
BIBLIOG ACT/RES INTELL ACADEM

B63
CONF ON FUTURE OF COMMONWEALTH,THE FUTURE OF THE COMMONWEALTH. AFR UK ECO/UNDEV AGRI EDU/PROP ADMIN SOC/INTEG 20. PAGE 27 F0522
DIPLOM RACE/REL ORD/FREE TEC/DEV

B63
COPPOCK J.,NORTH ATLANTIC POLICY - THE AGRICULTURAL GAP. EUR+WWI ELITES ECO/DEV DIST/IND MARKET PLAN WEALTH...STAT TREND GEN/LAWS OEEC TOT/POP VAL/FREE FAO 20. PAGE 27 F0535
AGRI TEC/DEV INT/TRADE

B63
COURNOT A.A.,RESEARCHES INTO THE MATHEMATICAL PRINCIPLES OF THE THEORY OF WEALTH (1838). UNIV ECO/DEV ECO/UNDEV AGRI INDUS MARKET PAY CONTROL COST INCOME 19. PAGE 28 F0544
ECOMETRIC GEN/LAWS WEALTH

B63
EL-NAGGAR S.,FOREIGN AID TO UNITED ARAB REPUBLIC. UAR USA+45 USSR AGRI FINAN INDUS FORCES EATING DEMAND...CHARTS METH/COMP 20 RESOURCE/N AID. PAGE 37 F0718
FOR/AID ECO/UNDEV RECEIVE PLAN

B63
ENKE S.,ECONOMICS FOR DEVELOPMENT. AGRI TEC/DEV CAP/ISM DIPLOM ECO/TAC TAX ATTIT DRIVE HABITAT WEALTH...GOV/COMP BIBLIOG 20. PAGE 38 F0737
ECO/UNDEV PHIL/SCI CON/ANAL

B63
FLORES E.,LAND REFORM AND THE ALLIANCE FOR PROGRESS (PAMPHLET). L/A+17C USA+45 STRUCT ECO/UNDEV NAT/G WORKER CREATE PLAN ECO/TAC COERCE REV 20 ALL/PROG. PAGE 42 F0815
AGRI INT/ORG DIPLOM POLICY

B63
FREITAG R.S.,AGRICULTURAL DEVELOPMENT SCHEMES IN SUB-SAHARAN AFRICA. AFR EDU/PROP 20. PAGE 44 F0852
BIBLIOG/A AGRI TEC/DEV KNOWL

B63
FURTADO C.,THE ECONOMIC GROWTH OF BRAZIL: A SURVEY FROM COLONIAL TO MODERN TIMES. L/A+17C AGRI DIST/IND EXTR/IND INDUS WORKER COLONIAL RACE/REL OWN GOV/COMP. PAGE 45 F0877
ECO/UNDEV TEC/DEV LABOR DOMIN

B63
GAMBLE S.D.,NORTH CHINA VILLAGES: SOCIAL, POLITICAL, AND ECONOMIC ACTIVITIES BEFORE 1933. ASIA CULTURE STRUCT FAM DOMIN EDU/PROP MUNICH WORSHIP 20. PAGE 46 F0891
AGRI LEAD FINAN

B63
GLADE W.P. JR.,THE POLITICAL ECONOMY OF MEXICO. FUT L/A+17C CULTURE SOCIETY AGRI INDUS DELIB/GP ACT/RES ECO/TAC ATTIT HEALTH ORD/FREE...STAT TIME/SEQ TREND MEXIC/AMER TOT/POP VAL/FREE 20. PAGE 48 F0928
FINAN ECO/UNDEV

B63
HAQ M.,THE STRATEGY OF ECONOMIC PLANNING. PAKISTAN AGRI FINAN INDUS NAT/G FOR/AID TAX CONTROL REGION PRODUC...POLICY CHARTS 20. PAGE 55 F1071
ECO/TAC ECO/UNDEV PLAN PROB/SOLV

B63
HATHAWAY D.A.,GOVERNMENT AND AGRICULTURE: PUBLIC POLICY IN A DEMOCRATIC SOCIETY. USA+45 LEGIS ADMIN EXEC LOBBY REPRESENT PWR 20. PAGE 57 F1111
AGRI GOV/REL PROB/SOLV EX/STRUC

B63
HIRSCHMAN A.O.,JOURNEYS TOWARD PROGRESS: STUDIES OF ECONOMIC POLICYMAKING IN LATIN AMERICA. CHILE FUT ECO/UNDEV AGRI FINAN INDUS CONSULT DELIB/GP PLAN ATTIT HEALTH ORD/FREE WEALTH...POLICY STAT VAL/FREE COLOMB 20. PAGE 60 F1177
L/A+17C ECO/TAC BRAZIL

B63
INTERAMERICAN ECO AND SOC COUN,THE ALLIANCE FOR PROGRESS: ITS FIRST YEAR: 1961-1962. AGRI SCHOOL PLAN TEC/DEV INT/TRADE TAX GIVE ADMIN WEALTH...SOC 20 ALL/PROG SOUTH/AMER. PAGE 64 F1267
INT/ORG PROB/SOLV ECO/TAC L/A+17C

B63
ISSAWI C.,EGYPT IN REVOLUTION: AN ECONOMIC ANALYSIS. ISLAM STRUCT ECO/UNDEV AGRI FINAN INDUS PLAN EXEC REV NAT/LISM ATTIT RIGID/FLEX WEALTH SOCISM...STAT FOR/TRADE WORK 20. PAGE 66 F1292
NAT/G UAR

B63
KATZ S.M.,A SELECTED LIST OF US READINGS ON DEVELOPMENT. AGRI COM/IND DIST/IND INDUS LABOR PLAN FOR/AID EDU/PROP HEALTH...POLICY SOC/WK 20. PAGE 69 F1361
BIBLIOG/A ECO/UNDEV TEC/DEV ACT/RES

B63
LAIRD R.D.,SOVIET AGRICULTURAL AND PEASANT AFFAIRS. FUT STRATA LOC/G DELIB/GP ACT/RES TEC/DEV ECO/TAC EDU/PROP ATTIT RIGID/FLEX ORD/FREE SKILL WEALTH ...STAT CON/ANAL ANTHOL MUNICH WORK VAL/FREE 20. PAGE 74 F1461
COM AGRI POLICY

B63
LETHBRIDGE H.J.,THE PEASANT AND THE COMMUNES.
MARXISM

CHINA/COM COM USSR NEIGH PROB/SOLV ADJUST EFFICIENCY...POLICY METH/COMP NAT/COMP 20. PAGE 78 F1535
ECO/TAC AGRI WORKER

B63
MANN D.E.,THE POLITICS OF WATER IN ARIZONA. AGRI EXTR/IND PROVS ACT/RES CREATE PLAN GOV/REL COST HABITAT...MGT CHARTS 20 ARIZONA WATER. PAGE 84 F1655
POLICY ECO/TAC TEC/DEV

B63
MEEK R.L.,THE ECONOMICS OF PHYSIOCRACY. FRANCE UK AGRI FINAN WORKER CAP/ISM TAX DEMAND EQUILIB INCOME HABITAT...CHARTS ANTHOL 17. PAGE 89 F1744
PRODUC WEALTH MARKET

B63
MILLER W.,REVENUE-COST RATIOS OF RURAL TOWNSHIPS WITH CHANGING LAND USES. USA+45 INDUS SERV/IND PROVS GP/REL HABITAT...CHARTS GP/COMP MUNICH 20 NEW/JERSEY. PAGE 91 F1792
TAX COST AGRI

B63
MINGAY G.E.,ENGLISH LANDED SOCIETY IN THE EIGHTEENTH CENTURY. UK ELITES STRUCT AGRI INDUS CONTROL WEALTH 18. PAGE 92 F1802
OWN STRATA PWR

B63
NEUMARK S.D.,FOREIGN TRADE AND ECONOMIC DEVELOPMENT IN AFRICA: A HISTORICAL PERSPECTIVE. EUR+WWI MOD/EUR ECO/UNDEV AGRI COM/IND EXTR/IND PROC/MFG SKILL WEALTH...CONCPT TIME/SEQ TREND SIMUL FOR/TRADE WORK TOT/POP TERR/GP VAL/FREE 19/20. PAGE 98 F1916
AFR

B63
OLSON M. JR.,THE ECONOMICS OF WARTIME SHORTAGE. FRANCE GERMANY MOD/EUR UK AGRI PROB/SOLV ADMIN DEMAND WEALTH...POLICY OLD/LIB FOR/TRADE 17/20. PAGE 101 F1990
WAR ADJUST ECO/TAC NAT/COMP

B63
PAN AMERICAN UNION,THE EFFECTS OF THE EUROPEAN ECONOMIC COMMUNITY ON THE LATIN AMERICAN ECONOMIES (BMR). EUR+WWI L/A+17C ECO/UNDEV AGRI INDUS MARKET REGION 20 EEC TREATY. PAGE 103 F2024
INT/TRADE INT/ORG AGREE POLICY

B63
RANGEL I.,A INFLACAO BRASILEIRA (2ND ED.). AFR BRAZIL AGRI INDUS MARKET INT/TRADE DEMAND EQUILIB ATTIT 20. PAGE 109 F2144
ECO/UNDEV FINAN PRICE TAX

B63
SALENT W.S.,THE UNITED STATES BALANCE OF PAYMENTS IN 1968. EUR+WWI UK USA+45 AGRI R+D LABOR FORCES PRODUC...GEOG CONCPT CHARTS 20 CHINJAP EEC. PAGE 115 F2274
BAL/PAY DEMAND FINAN INT/TRADE

B63
SELF P.,THE STATE AND THE FARMER. UK ECO/DEV MARKET WORKER PRICE CONTROL GP/REL...WELF/ST 20 DEPT/AGRI. PAGE 119 F2346
AGRI NAT/G ADMIN VOL/ASSN

B63
UN FAO,BIBLIOGRAPHY ON THE ANALYSIS AND PROJECTION OF DEMAND AND PRODUCTION, 1963. WOR+45 ECO/DEV ECO/UNDEV...PREDICT TREND 20. PAGE 132 F2601
BIBLIOG/A AGRI INDUS

B63
US ECON SURVEY TEAM INDONESIA,INDONESIA - PERSPECTIVE AND PROPOSALS FOR UNITED STATES ECONOMIC AID. INDONESIA AGRI MARKET TEC/DEV DIPLOM INT/TRADE EDU/PROP 20. PAGE 136 F2678
FOR/AID ECO/UNDEV PLAN INDUS

S63
ETHERINGTON D.M.,"LAND RESETTLEMENT IN KENYA: POLICY AND PRACTICE" AFR TEC/DEV ECO/TAC FOR/AID TAX PRODUC...CHARTS 20. PAGE 39 F0752
ECO/UNDEV AGRI WORKER PLAN

S63
GORDON B.,"ECONOMIC IMPEDIMENTS TO REGIONALISM IN SOUTH EAST ASIA." BURMA FUT S/ASIA THAILAND USA+45 AGRI INDUS R+D NAT/G PLAN ECO/TAC WEALTH...STAT CONT/OBS 20. PAGE 49 F0954
VOL/ASSN ECO/UNDEV INT/TRADE REGION

S63
MARTHELOT P.,"PROGRES DE LA REFORME AGRAIRE." INTELL ECO/DEV R+D FOR/AID ADMIN KNOWL...OBS VAL/FREE UN 20. PAGE 86 F1680
AGRI INT/ORG

S63
PAAUW D.S.,"ECONOMIC PROGRESS IN SOUTHEAST ASIA." S/ASIA AGRI INDUS PROC/MFG ACT/RES ECO/TAC...CHARTS VAL/FREE 20. PAGE 102 F2010
ECO/UNDEV STAT

S63
REDDAWAY W.B.,"THE ECONOMICS OF UNDERDEVELOPED COUNTRIES." S/ASIA WOR+45 WOR-45 STRATA AGRI COM/IND DIST/IND MARKET PROC/MFG PLAN TEC/DEV FOR/AID BAL/PAY ATTIT DRIVE SKILL WORK FOR/TRADE 20. PAGE 110 F2165
ECO/TAC ECO/UNDEV INDIA

S63
SCHURMANN F.,"ECONOMIC POLICY AND POLITICAL POWER IN COMMUNIST CHINA." ASIA CHINA/COM USSR SOCIETY ECO/UNDEV AGRI INDUS CREATE ADMIN ROUTINE ATTIT DRIVE RIGID/FLEX PWR WEALTH...HIST/WRIT TREND CHARTS WORK 20. PAGE 118 F2323
PLAN ECO/TAC

B64
BALASSA B.,TRADE PROSPECTS FOR DEVELOPING COUNTRIES. WOR+45 ECO/DEV AGRI EXTR/IND INDUS CREATE PLAN PRICE...ECOMETRIC CLASSIF TIME/SEQ
INT/TRADE ECO/UNDEV TREND

GEN/METH. PAGE 8 F0158 — STAT

B64
BERRILL K.,ECONOMIC DEVELOPMENT WITH SPECIAL REFERENCE TO EAST ASIA. ASIA INDIA S/ASIA AGRI INDUS LABOR DELIB/GP PLAN INT/TRADE COST PRODUC 20 CHINJAP. PAGE 14 F0271 — FINAN ECO/UNDEV INT/ORG CAP/ISM

B64
CEPEDE M.,POPULATION AND FOOD. USA+45 STRUCT ECO/UNDEV FAM PLAN TEC/DEV FOR/AID CONTROL...CATH SOC TREND 19/20. PAGE 22 F0436 — FUT GEOG AGRI CENSUS

B64
FEI J.C.H.,DEVELOPMENT OF THE LABOR SURPLUS ECONOMY: THEORY AND POLICY. WOR+45 AGRI INDUS MARKET PROB/SOLV TEC/DEV...STAT CHARTS GEN/LAWS METH 20 THIRD/WRLD. PAGE 40 F0772 — ECO/TAC POLICY WORKER ECO/UNDEV

B64
FIRTH R.,CAPITAL, SAVING AND CREDIT IN PEASANT SOCIETIES. WOR+45 WOR-45 FAM ACT/RES ECO/TAC HEALTH ...SOC CONCPT STAT CHARTS ANTHOL CARIBBEAN VAL/FREE 20. PAGE 41 F0803 — AGRI FINAN

B64
FRIEDMANN J.,REGIONAL DEVELOPMENT AND PLANNING: A READER. AGRI MARKET NAT/G ECO/TAC INCOME...GEOG STAT CENSUS CHARTS ANTHOL BIBLIOG MUNICH 20 OPEN/SPACE. PAGE 44 F0863 — PLAN REGION INDUS ECO/DEV

B64
HAMBRIDGE G.,DYNAMICS OF DEVELOPMENT. AGRI FINAN INDUS LABOR INT/TRADE EDU/PROP ADMIN LEAD OWN HEALTH...ANTHOL BIBLIOG 20. PAGE 54 F1054 — ECO/UNDEV ECO/TAC OP/RES ACT/RES

B64
HATHAWAY D.E.,PROBLEMS OF PROGRESS IN THE AGRICULTURAL ECONOMY. USA+45 USA-45 ECO/DEV NAT/G INT/TRADE PRICE DEMAND EFFICIENCY OPTIMAL 20. PAGE 57 F1112 — AGRI ECO/TAC MARKET PLAN

B64
HAZLEWOOD A.,THE ECONOMICS OF DEVELOPMENT: AN ANNOTATED LIST OF BOOKS AND ARTICLES PUBLISHED 1958-1962. AGRI FINAN INDUS LABOR NAT/G DIPLOM INT/TRADE INCOME...MGT 20. PAGE 58 F1130 — BIBLIOG/A ECO/UNDEV TEC/DEV

B64
HINSHAW R.,THE EUROPEAN COMMUNITY AND AMERICAN TRADE: A STUDY IN ATLANTIC ECONOMICS AND POLICY. EUR+WWI UK USA+45 ECO/DEV ECO/UNDEV AGRI INDUS INT/ORG NAT/G ECO/TAC TARIFFS REGION...STAT CHARTS EEC 20. PAGE 60 F1174 — MARKET TREND INT/TRADE

B64
LI C.M.,INDUSTRIAL DEVELOPMENT IN COMMUNIST CHINA. CHINA/COM ECO/DEV ECO/UNDEV AGRI FINAN INDUS MARKET LABOR NAT/G ECO/TAC INT/TRADE EXEC ALL/VALS ...POLICY RELATIV TREND WORK TOT/POP VAL/FREE 20. PAGE 79 F1556 — ASIA TEC/DEV

B64
LINDHOLM R.W.,ECONOMIC DEVELOPMENT POLICY WITH EMPHASIS ON VIET-NAM. KOREA/S PAKISTAN VIETNAM/S AGRI INDUS CONSULT DELIB/GP FOR/AID...METH 20. PAGE 80 F1571 — ECO/UNDEV TAX FINAN ECO/TAC

B64
MASON E.S.,FOREIGN AID AND FOREIGN POLICY. USA+45 AGRI INDUS NAT/G EX/STRUC ACT/RES RIGID/FLEX ALL/VALS...POLICY GEN/LAWS MARSHL/PLN ALL/PROG CONGRESS 20. PAGE 87 F1699 — ECO/UNDEV ECO/TAC FOR/AID DIPLOM

B64
MC GOVERN G.S.,WAR AGAINST WANT. USA+45 AGRI DIPLOM INT/TRADE GIVE RECEIVE DEMAND HEALTH 20 KENNEDY/JF FOOD/PEACE. PAGE 87 F1714 — FOR/AID ECO/DEV POLICY EATING

B64
MORGAN H.W.,AMERICAN SOCIALISM 1900-1960. AFR USA+45 USA-45 INTELL AGRI LABOR WORKER BARGAIN ECO/TAC GP/REL RACE/REL 20 NEGRO MIGRATION. PAGE 93 F1830 — SOCISM POL/PAR ECO/DEV STRATA

B64
MYINT H.,THE ECONOMICS OF THE DEVELOPING COUNTRIES. WOR+45 AGRI PLAN COST...POLICY GEOG 20 MONEY. PAGE 96 F1878 — ECO/UNDEV INT/TRADE EXTR/IND FINAN

B64
NATIONAL COUN APPLIED ECO RES,A STRATEGY FOR THE FOURTH PLAN. INDIA DIST/IND EXTR/IND SERV/IND ECO/TAC RATION EDU/PROP EATING HEALTH...CHARTS 20. PAGE 97 F1900 — ECO/UNDEV PLAN AGRI WORKER

B64
OECD,DEVELOPMENT ASSISTANCE EFFORTS - POLICIES OF THE MEMBERS. AGRI INDUS BUDGET...GEOG NAT/COMP 20 OECD. PAGE 100 F1967 — INT/ORG FOR/AID ECO/UNDEV TEC/DEV

B64
ORGANIZATION AMERICAN STATES,ECONOMIC SURVEY OF LATIN AMERICA, 1962. L/A+17C AGRI DIST/IND INDUS MARKET PROC/MFG R+D PLAN TEC/DEV ECO/TAC REGION BAL/PAY ALL/VALS...CON/ANAL ORG/CHARTS GEN/METH OAS ALL/PROG 20 ALL/PROG. PAGE 102 F1998 — ECO/UNDEV CHARTS

B64
PAARLBERG D.,AMERICAN FARM POLICY: A CASE STUDY IN CENTRALIZED DECISION-MAKING. USA+45 NAT/G LEGIS LOBBY REPRESENT GOV/REL PWR LAISSEZ 20. PAGE 102 F2009 — PROB/SOLV EX/STRUC AGRI

B64
POWELSON J.P.,LATIN AMERICA: TODAY'S ECONOMIC AND SOCIAL REVOLUTION. L/A+17C INTELL SOCIETY STRUCT AGRI INDUS NAT/G DIPLOM ECO/TAC REV...POLICY 20. PAGE 107 F2110 — ECO/UNDEV WEALTH ADJUST PLAN

B64
RANIS G.,THE UNITED STATES AND THE DEVELOPING ECONOMIES. COM USA+45 AGRI FINAN TEC/DEV CAP/ISM ECO/TAC INT/TRADE...POLICY METH/COMP ANTHOL 20 AID. PAGE 109 F2145 — ECO/UNDEV DIPLOM FOR/AID

B64
RENO P.,THE ORDEAL OF BRITISH GUIANA. L/A+17C USA+45 STRUCT AGRI EXTR/IND INDUS NAT/G FOR/AID ORD/FREE...GEOG 20 GUIANA/BR INTRVN/ECO. PAGE 111 F2178 — COLONIAL ECO/UNDEV SOCISM PWR

B64
ROBINSON E.A.G.,ECONOMIC DEVELOPMENT FOR AFRICA SOUTH OF THE SAHARA. AFR AGRI INDUS LABOR BUDGET INT/TRADE PRICE...POLICY GEOG ANTHOL 20. PAGE 113 F2219 — ECO/UNDEV ECO/TAC ACT/RES PLAN

B64
ROBINSON R.D.,INTERNATIONAL BUSINESS POLICY. AFR INDIA L/A+17C USA+45 ELITES AGRI FOR/AID COERCE BAL/PAY...DECISION INT/LAW MGT 20. PAGE 113 F2224 — ECO/TAC DIST/IND COLONIAL FINAN

B64
SCHULTZ T.W.,TRANSFORMING TRADITIONAL AGRICULTURE. WOR+45 WOR-45 CULTURE STRATA FINAN ACT/RES ECO/TAC ATTIT KNOWL SKILL...MATH STAT TIME/SEQ GEN/LAWS VAL/FREE. PAGE 117 F2316 — AGRI ECO/UNDEV

B64
SEERS D.,CUBA: THE ECONOMIC AND SOCIAL REVOLUTION. L/A+17C USSR YUGOSLAVIA STRATA AGRI INDUS SCHOOL DELIB/GP PLAN ECO/TAC DOMIN EDU/PROP ATTIT RIGID/FLEX ALL/VALS...STAT OBS TIME/SEQ WORK VAL/FREE 20. PAGE 119 F2341 — ACT/RES COERCE CUBA REV

B64
SINGER H.W.,INTERNATIONAL DEVELOPMENT: GROWTH AND CHANGE. AFR BRAZIL L/A+17C WOR+45 CULTURE AGRI INDUS NAT/G ACT/RES ECO/TAC EDU/PROP WEALTH...GEOG CONCPT METH/CNCPT STAT HYPO/EXP WORK TOT/POP 20. PAGE 122 F2412 — FINAN ECO/UNDEV FOR/AID INT/TRADE

B64
STRONG A.L.,THE RISE OF THE CHINESE PEOPLE'S COMMUNES - AND SIX YEARS AFTER (2ND ED.). CHINA/COM AGRI INDUS FORCES WORKER PROB/SOLV EDU/PROP EFFICIENCY ISOLAT 20. PAGE 127 F2503 — NEIGH ECO/TAC MARXISM METH/COMP

B64
TAX S.,EL CAPITALISMO DEL CENTAVO; UNA ECONOMIA INDIGENA DE GUATEMALA (2 VOLS.). GUATEMALA L/A+17C SOCIETY GP/REL DEMAND INCOME HABITAT...SOC MUNICH 20 INDIAN/AM. PAGE 129 F2539 — ECO/UNDEV AGRI WEALTH COST

B64
TELLADO A.,A STATEMENT OF THE LAWS OF THE DOMINICAN REPUBLIC IN MATTERS AFFECTING BUSINESS (3RD ED.). DOMIN/REP AGRI DIST/IND EXTR/IND FINAN FAM WORKER ECO/TAC TAX CT/SYS MARRIAGE OWN...BIBLIOG 20 MIGRATION. PAGE 129 F2542 — CONSTN LEGIS NAT/G INDUS

B64
THAILAND NATIONAL ECO DEV,THE NATIONAL ECONOMIC DEVELOPMENT PLAN: 1961-66: SECOND PHASE 1964-66. THAILAND AGRI FINAN BUDGET EFFICIENCY INCOME...STAT CHARTS 20. PAGE 129 F2547 — ECO/UNDEV ECO/TAC PLAN NAT/G

B64
WITHERS W.,THE ECONOMIC CRISIS IN LATIN AMERICA. BRAZIL CHILE STRATA AGRI DIPLOM FOR/AID PWR SOCISM ...POLICY 20 MEXIC/AMER ARGEN ALL/PROG. PAGE 148 F2914 — L/A+17C ECO/UNDEV CAP/ISM ALL/IDEOS

B64
WRIGHT G.,RURAL REVOLUTION IN FRANCE: THE PEASANTRY IN THE TWENTIETH CENTURY. EUR+WWI MOD/EUR LAW CULTURE AGRI POL/PAR DELIB/GP LEGIS ECO/TAC EDU/PROP COERCE CHOOSE ATTIT RIGID/FLEX HEALTH ...STAT CENSUS CHARTS VAL/FREE 20. PAGE 149 F2932 — PWR STRATA FRANCE REV

B64
YUDELMAN M.,AFRICANS ON THE LAND. RHODESIA MARKET LABOR OWN...ECOMETRIC TREND 20. PAGE 150 F2955 — ECO/DEV AFR AGRI ECO/TAC

S64
FLORINSKY M.T.,"TRENDS IN THE SOVIET ECONOMY." COM USA+45 USSR INDUS LABOR NAT/G PLAN TEC/DEV ECO/TAC ALL/VALS SOCISM...MGT METH/CNCPT STYLE CON/ANAL GEN/METH WORK 20. PAGE 42 F0817 — ECO/DEV AGRI

S64
GALBRAITH V.,"JAPAN'S POSITION IN WORLD TRADE." ASIA AGRI INDUS CREATE ECO/TAC LEGIT DRIVE WEALTH ...TREND EEC GATT FOR/TRADE 20 CHINJAP. PAGE 45 F0885 — ECO/DEV DELIB/GP

S64
GERBET P.,"LA MISE EN OEUVRE DU MARCHE COMMUN AGRICOLE." ECO/DEV MARKET INT/ORG NAT/G PLAN EDU/PROP NAT/LISM WEALTH...OBS EEC VAL/FREE 20. — EUR+WWI AGRI REGION

PAGE 47 F0917

S64
HERMAN L.M.,"THE ECONOMIC CONTENT OF SOVIET TRADE COM
WITH THE WEST." WOR+45 ECO/DEV ECO/UNDEV AGRI MARKET
COM/IND INDUS CAP/ISM ECO/TAC ATTIT RIGID/FLEX INT/TRADE
WEALTH...OBS TREND VAL/FREE MARX/KARL 20. PAGE 59 USSR
F1152

S64
HUELIN D.,"ECONOMIC INTEGRATION IN LATIN AMERICAN: MARKET
PROGRESS AND PROBLEMS." L/A+17C ECO/DEV AGRI ECO/UNDEV
DIST/IND FINAN INDUS NAT/G VOL/ASSN CONSULT INT/TRADE
DELIB/GP EX/STRUC ACT/RES PLAN TEC/DEV ECO/TAC
ROUTINE BAL/PAY WEALTH FOR/TRADE WORK TERR/GP 20.
PAGE 63 F1232

S64
NASH M.,"SOCIAL PREREQUISITES TO ECONOMIC GROWTH IN ECO/DEV
LATIN AMERICA AND SOUTHEAST ASIA." L/A+17C S/ASIA PERCEPT
CULTURE SOCIETY ECO/UNDEV AGRI INDUS NAT/G PLAN
TEC/DEV EDU/PROP ROUTINE ALL/VALS...POLICY RELATIV
SOC NAT/COMP WORK TOT/POP 20. PAGE 96 F1894

S64
PATEL S.J.,"THE ECONOMIC DISTANCE BETWEEN NATIONS: ECO/UNDEV
ITS ORIGIN, MEASUREMENT AND OUTLOOK." WOR+45 PLAN
ECO/DEV AGRI FINAN INDUS MARKET LABOR NAT/G CONSULT
TEC/DEV ECO/TAC WEALTH...POLICY RELATIV MGT TREND
WORK 20. PAGE 103 F2035

S64
READER D.H.,"A SURVEY OF CATEGORIES OF ECONOMIC TEC/DEV
ACTIVITIES AMONG THE PEOPLES OF AFRICA." AGRI INDUS ECO/UNDEV
MARKET KIN HEALTH SKILL WEALTH...GEOG METH/CNCPT AFR
CHARTS TERR/GP WORK TOT/POP VAL/FREE 20. PAGE 110
F2160

S64
RUSSETT B.M.,"INEQUALITY AND INSTABILITY: THE WEALTH
RELATION OF LAND TENURE TO POLITICS." WOR+45 GEOG
ECO/DEV ECO/UNDEV AGRI NAT/G COERCE PWR...MATH STAT ECO/TAC
CHARTS GEN/LAWS TERR/GP TRUE/GP METH/GP VAL/FREE ORD/FREE
20. PAGE 115 F2263

S64
WU Y.,"CHINA'S ECONOMY AND ITS PROSPECTS." ASIA ECO/DEV
CHINA/COM FUT USSR AGRI INDUS PLAN ECO/TAC LEGIT
WEALTH...STAT CON/ANAL CHARTS GEN/LAWS FOR/TRADE
20. PAGE 149 F2938

N64
KENYA MINISTRY ECO PLAN DEV,AFRICAN SOCIALISM AND NAT/G
ITS APPLICATION TO PLANNING IN KENYA (PAMPHLET). SOCISM
AFR AGRI INDUS WORKER TAX COLONIAL WEALTH 20. PLAN
PAGE 70 F1380 ECO/UNDEV

B65
ANALYSIS AND ASSESSMENT OF THE ECONOMIC EFFECTS: ECO/TAC
PUBLIC LAW 480 TITLE I PROGRAM TURKEY. INDIA TURKEY FOR/AID
USA+45 AGRI NAT/G PLAN BUDGET DIPLOM COST FINAN
EFFICIENCY...CHARTS 20. PAGE 1 F0021 ECO/UNDEV

B65
AMERICAN ECONOMIC ASSOCIATION,INDEX OF ECONOMIC BIBLIOG
JOURNALS 1886-1965 (7 VOLS.). UK USA+45 USA-45 AGRI WRITING
FINAN PLAN ECO/TAC INT/TRADE ADMIN...STAT CENSUS INDUS
19/20. PAGE 5 F0087

B65
BAERRESEN D.W.,LATIN AMERICAN TRADE PATTERNS. INT/TRADE
L/A+17C ECO/UNDEV AGRI INDUS MARKET CREATE STAT
...NET/THEORY CHARTS LAFTA. PAGE 8 F0149 REGION

B65
BARRY E.E.,NATIONALISATION IN BRITISH POLITICS: THE NAT/G
HISTORICAL BACKGROUND. UK AGRI DIST/IND EXTR/IND OWN
LABOR LG/CO ATTIT CONSERVE SOCISM 19/20 LABOR/PAR. INDUS
PAGE 10 F0198 POL/PAR

B65
CLARK T.D.,THREE PATHS TO THE MODERN SOUTH: AGRI
EDUCATION, AGRICULTURE, AND CONSERVATION. FUT EDU/PROP
USA-45 ECO/DEV ECO/TAC PEACE WEALTH...POLICY 20 GOV/REL
SOUTH/US. PAGE 25 F0485 REGION

B65
COLBERG M.R.,HUMAN CAPITAL IN SOUTHERN DEVELOPMENT. PROVS
USA+45 AGRI ACADEM LABOR SCHOOL WORKER CAP/ISM RACE/REL
DISCRIM. PAGE 26 F0498 GP/REL

B65
DELHI INSTITUTE OF ECO GROWTH,A STUDY IN THE PLAN
WORKING OF THE INTENSIVE AREA SCHEME OF THE KHADI INDUS
AND VILLAGE INDUSTRIES COMMISSION. INDIA AGRI FINAN ECO/UNDEV
DELIB/GP ECO/TAC EFFICIENCY...QU CHARTS MUNICH 20.
PAGE 32 F0614

B65
FRIEDLANDER S.L.,LABOR MIGRATION AND ECONOMIC CENSUS
GROWTH: A CASE STUDY OF PUERTO RICO. PUERT/RICO GEOG
AGRI WORKER PLAN PROB/SOLV...ECOMETRIC STAT PREDICT ECO/UNDEV
CHARTS HYPO/EXP SIMUL 20. PAGE 44 F0858 WEALTH

B65
GREENFIELD K.R.,ECONOMICS AND LIBERALISM IN THE NAT/LISM
RISORGIMENTO (REV. ED.). ITALY AGRI FINAN PROC/MFG PRESS
PLAN INT/TRADE CONTROL PWR 19. PAGE 51 F0990 POLICY

B65
HADWIGER D.F.,PRESSURES AND PROTEST. NAT/G LEGIS AGRI
PLAN LEAD PARTIC ROUTINE ATTIT POLICY. PAGE 53 GP/REL
F1030 LOBBY
CHOOSE

B65
HAPGOOD D.,AFRICA: FROM INDEPENDENCE TO TOMARROW. ECO/TAC
AFR GUINEA SENEGAL CULTURE ELITES ECO/UNDEV AGRI SOCIETY
SCHOOL FOR/AID COLONIAL MARXISM...TREND 20. PAGE 55 NAT/G
F1070

B65
HERRICK B.H.,URBAN MIGRATION AND ECONOMIC HABITAT
DEVELOPMENT IN CHILE. CHILE AGRI INDUS LABOR NAT/G GEOG
CENTRAL PRODUC...STAT SAMP CHARTS BIBLIOG/A MUNICH ECO/UNDEV
20 MIGRATION. PAGE 59 F1156

B65
HLA MYINT U.,THE ECONOMICS OF THE DEVELOPING ECO/UNDEV
COUNTRIES. USA+45 WOR+45 AGRI FINAN NAT/G INT/TRADE FOR/AID
...CLASSIF CENSUS TREND NAT/COMP SIMUL GEN/LAWS. GEOG
PAGE 60 F1180

B65
HOLLER J.E.,POPULATION TRENDS AND ECONOMIC CENSUS
DEVELOPMENT IN THE FAR EAST (PAMPHLET). KOREA TREND
S/ASIA AGRI INDUS DELIB/GP PROB/SOLV RATIONAL ECO/UNDEV
...POLICY CHARTS BIBLIOG 20 OUTER/MONG CHINJAP ASIA
HONG/KONG. PAGE 61 F1197

B65
HONDURAS CONSEJO NAC DE ECO,PLAN NACIONAL DE ECO/UNDEV
DESARROLLO ECONOMICO Y SOCIAL DE HONDURAS 1965-69. NAT/G
HONDURAS AGRI INDUS BAL/PAY INCOME 20. PAGE 61 PLAN
F1203 POLICY

B65
INT. BANK RECONSTR. DEVELOP.,ECONOMIC DEVELOPMENT INDUS
OF KUWAIT. ISLAM KUWAIT AGRI FINAN MARKET EX/STRUC NAT/G
TEC/DEV ECO/TAC ADMIN WEALTH...OBS CON/ANAL CHARTS
20. PAGE 64 F1266

B65
JAIN S.C.,THE STATE AND AGRICULTURE. INDIA S/ASIA NAT/G
ECO/UNDEV PROB/SOLV CAP/ISM MARXISM SOCISM 20. POLICY
PAGE 66 F1304 AGRI
ECO/TAC

B65
JASNY H.,KHRUSHCHEV'S CROP POLICY. USSR ECO/DEV AGRI
PLAN MARXISM...STAT 20 KHRUSH/N RESOURCE/N. PAGE 66 NAT/G
F1306 POLICY
ECO/TAC

B65
JOHNSON H.G.,THE WORLD ECONOMY AT THE CROSSROADS. FINAN
COM WOR-45 ECO/DEV AGRI INDUS INT/TRADE REGION DIPLOM
NAT/LISM 20. PAGE 67 F1326 INT/ORG
ECO/UNDEV

B65
KRAUSE W.,ECONOMIC DEVELOPMENT: THE UNDERDEVELOPED FOR/AID
WORLD AND THE AMERICAN INTEREST. USA+45 AGRI PLAN ECO/UNDEV
MARXISM...CHARTS 20. PAGE 73 F1434 FINAN
PROB/SOLV

B65
LEYS C.T.,FEDERATION IN EAST AFRICA. LAW AGRI FEDERAL
DIST/IND FINAN INT/ORG LABOR INT/TRADE CONFER ADMIN REGION
CONTROL GP/REL...ANTHOL 20 AFRICA/E. PAGE 79 F1554 ECO/UNDEV
PLAN

B65
LITTLE I.M.D.,INTERNATIONAL AID. UK WOR+45 AGRI FOR/AID
INDUS GIVE RECEIVE COLONIAL BAL/PAY WEALTH...POLICY DIPLOM
GOV/COMP METH/COMP 20. PAGE 81 F1584 ECO/UNDEV
NAT/G

B65
THE STATE AND ECONOMIC ENTERPRISE IN JAPAN; ESSAYS ECO/UNDEV
IN THE POLITICAL ECONOMY OF GROWTH. AGRI INDUS ECO/DEV
DRIVE POPULISM...CHARTS NAT/COMP ANTHOL 19/20 CAP/ISM
CHINJAP. PAGE 81 F1594 ECO/TAC

B65
LUGO-MARENCO J.J.,A STATEMENT OF THE LAWS OF CONSTN
NICARAGUA IN MATTERS AFFECTING BUSINESS. NICARAGUA NAT/G
AGRI DIST/IND EXTR/IND FINAN INDUS FAM WORKER LEGIS
INT/TRADE TAX MARRIAGE OWN BIO/SOC 20 TREATY JURID
RESOURCE/N MIGRATION. PAGE 82 F1606

B65
MARK S.M.,ECONOMICS IN ACTION (3RD ED.). USA+45 POLICY
ECO/UNDEV AGRI INDUS FOR/AID INT/TRADE BAL/PAY COST ECO/TAC
ORD/FREE...ANTHOL 20 RESOURCE/N. PAGE 85 F1670 EFFICIENCY
PRICE

B65
MCCOLL G.D.,THE AUSTRALIAN BALANCE OF PAYMENTS. UK ECO/DEV
USA+45 AGRI WORKER DIPLOM EQUILIB PRODUC...STAT BAL/PAY
TREND CHARTS BIBLIOG/A 20 AUSTRAL. PAGE 88 F1719 INT/TRADE
COST

B65
MONCRIEFF A.,SECOND THOUGHTS ON AID. WOR+45 FOR/AID
ECO/UNDEV AGRI FINAN VOL/ASSN PLAN TEC/DEV GIVE ECO/TAC
EDU/PROP ROLE WEALTH 20. PAGE 93 F1816 INT/ORG
IDEA/COMP

B65
MURUMBI J.,PROBLEMS OF ECONOMIC DEVELOPMENT IN EAST AGRI
AFRICA. FINAN INDUS WORKER TEC/DEV INT/TRADE TAX ECO/TAC
DEMAND EFFICIENCY PRODUC SOCISM...TREND CHARTS 20 ECO/UNDEV
AFRICA/E. PAGE 95 F1869 PROC/MFG

B65
OECD,THE MEDITERRANEAN REGIONAL PROJECT: GREECE; EDU/PROP
EDUCATION AND DEVELOPMENT. FUT GREECE SOCIETY AGRI SCHOOL
FINAN NAT/G PROF/ORG WORKER PLAN PROB/SOLV ADMIN ACADEM

DEMAND ATTIT 20 OECD. PAGE 100 F1972
ECO/UNDEV

B65
ONSLOW C.,ASIAN ECONOMIC DEVELOPMENT. BURMA CEYLON INDIA MALAYSIA PAKISTAN S/ASIA AGRI INDUS MARKET PROB/SOLV CAP/ISM FOR/AID INT/TRADE DEMAND WEALTH ...POLICY ANTHOL 20. PAGE 101 F1991
ECO/UNDEV ECO/TAC PLAN NAT/G

B65
PLOSS S.I.,CONFLICT AND DECISION-MAKING IN SOVIET RUSSIA - A CASE STUDY OF AGRICULTURAL POLICY - 1953-1963. USSR DELIB/GP INGP/REL PWR MARXISM. PAGE 106 F2093
AGRI DECISION ATTIT

B65
PROCHNOW H.V.,WORLD ECONOMIC PROBLEMS AND POLICIES. INDIA ISRAEL WOR+45 AGRI LABOR PROB/SOLV FOR/AID TARIFFS CONTROL BAL/PAY NAT/LISM WEALTH...TREND CHARTS 20 CHINJAP EEC. PAGE 108 F2124
MARKET ECO/TAC PRODUC IDEA/COMP

B65
ROWE J.W.,PRIMARY COMMODITIES IN INTERNATIONAL TRADE. MARKET CAP/ISM ECO/TAC DEMAND...NAT/COMP 20. PAGE 114 F2253
INT/TRADE AGRI RATION PRICE

B65
SCHULER E.A.,THE PAKISTAN ACADEMIES FOR RURAL DEVELOPMENT COMILLA AND PESHAWAR 1959-1964. PAKISTAN S/ASIA SOCIETY STRUCT AGRI NAT/G TEC/DEV EDU/PROP 20. PAGE 117 F2314
BIBLIOG PLAN ECO/TAC ECO/UNDEV

B65
SCHULTZ T.W.,ECONOMIC CRISES IN WORLD AGRICULTURE. ASIA INDIA USSR ECO/DEV ECO/UNDEV INDUS VOL/ASSN CAP/ISM RATION COLONIAL 20. PAGE 117 F2317
AGRI ECO/TAC INCOME WORKER

B65
STEWART I.G.,AFRICAN PRIMARY PRODUCTS AND INTERNATIONAL TRADE. ECO/UNDEV AGRI FINAN DIPLOM CONTROL 20. PAGE 126 F2485
AFR INT/TRADE INT/ORG

B65
WILKINSON T.O.,THE URBANIZATION OF JAPANESE LABOR, 1868-1955. AGRI PROC/MFG CAP/ISM PRODUC PROFIT ...SOC CLASSIF CENSUS CHARTS MUNICH 19/20 CHINJAP. PAGE 146 F2887
LABOR INDUS GEOG

B65
WISH J.R.,ECONOMIC DEVELOPMENT IN LATIN AMERICA: AN ANNOTATED BIBLIOGRAPHY. L/A+17C COM/IND MARKET R+D CREATE CAP/ISM ATTIT...STAT METH 20. PAGE 148 F2912
BIBLIOG/A ECO/UNDEV TEC/DEV AGRI

B65
WRIGHT L.B.,THE DREAM OF PROSPERITY IN COLONIAL AMERICA. USA-45 ECO/UNDEV AGRI EXTR/IND PARLIAMENT 17/18. PAGE 149 F2934
PROVS WEALTH MOD/EUR

B65
WU YUAN-LI,THE ECONOMY OF COMMUNIST CHINA. CHINA/COM USSR AGRI FINAN INDUS POL/PAR WORKER PROB/SOLV INT/TRADE PRICE EATING INCOME OWN WEALTH 20. PAGE 149 F2939
ECO/TAC MARXISM PLAN EFFICIENCY

B65
YOUNG A.N.,CHINA'S WARTIME FINANCE AND INFLATION. ASIA AGRI INDUS NAT/G ECO/TAC CONFER PRICE WAR COST 20. PAGE 150 F2949
FINAN FOR/AID TAX BUDGET

L65
HAMMOND A.,"COMPREHENSIVE VERSUS INCREMENTAL BUDGETING IN THE DEPARTMENT OF AGRICULTURE" USA+45 GP/REL ATTIT...PSY INT 20 DEPT/AGRI. PAGE 54 F1057
TOP/EX EX/STRUC AGRI BUDGET

L65
LETICHE J.M.,"EUROPEAN INTEGRATION: AN AMERICAN VIEW." EUR+WWI FRANCE WOR+45 ECO/DEV DIST/IND EXTR/IND NAT/G DELIB/GP TOP/EX PLAN ECO/TAC ATTIT ...STAT CON/ANAL CHARTS EEC 20. PAGE 78 F1537
INDUS AGRI

L65
WIONCZEK M.,"LATIN AMERICA FREE TRADE ASSOCIATION." AGRI DIST/IND FINAN INDUS INT/ORG LABOR NAT/G TEC/DEV ECO/TAC HEALTH SKILL WEALTH...POLICY RELATIV MGT LAFTA 20. PAGE 148 F2909
L/A+17C MARKET REGION

S65
BRANDENBURG F.,"THE RELEVANCE OF MEXICAN EXPERIENCE TO LATIN AMERICAN DEVELOPMENT." BRAZIL CHILE VENEZUELA STRUCT ECO/UNDEV AGRI CREATE ECO/TAC ...STAT RECORD MEXIC/AMER ARGEN COLOMB. PAGE 18 F0340
L/A+17C GOV/COMP

S65
DUMONT R.,"SURPEUPLEMENT CHINOIS ET SES CONSEQUENCES." AFR ECO/UNDEV AGRI PLAN PROB/SOLV ECO/TAC FOR/AID NUC/PWR...OBS INT PREDICT. PAGE 35 F0675
GEOG ASIA STAT

S65
RUSINOW D.I.,"YUGOSLAV DEVELOPMENT BETWEEN EAST AND WEST." AGRI VOL/ASSN PLAN CAP/ISM ECO/TAC FOR/AID INT/TRADE BAL/PAY...MARXIST EEC COMECON. PAGE 115 F2262
YUGOSLAVIA ECO/UNDEV STAT

C65
WUORINEN J.H.,"SCANDINAVIA." DENMARK FINLAND ICELAND NORWAY SWEDEN SOCIETY AGRI POL/PAR DELIB/GP DIPLOM INT/TRADE NEUTRAL WAR...CHARTS IND TREATY 20. PAGE 149 F2942
BIBLIOG NAT/G POLICY

B66
BALDWIN R.E.,ECONOMIC DEVELOPMENT AND EXPORT GROWTH: A STUDY OF NORTHERN RHODESIA, 1920-1960. AFR RHODESIA AGRI EXTR/IND FINAN MARKET LABOR WORKER ECO/TAC...CONCPT NEW/IDEA MUNICH 20. PAGE 9 F0166
ECO/UNDEV TEC/DEV INT/TRADE CAP/ISM

B66
BEN-PORATH Y.,THE ARAB LABOR FORCE IN ISRAEL. ISLAM ISRAEL AGRI INDUS SCHOOL CAP/ISM PAY DEMAND...GEOG REGRESS STAT CHARTS 20 ARABS. PAGE 13 F0245
WORKER CENSUS GP/REL STRUCT

B66
BEQIRAJ M.,PEASANTRY IN REVOLUTION. STRATA ECO/UNDEV AGRI ROUTINE REV HABITAT RIGID/FLEX ...EPIST GEOG NEW/IDEA TREND MUNICH 20. PAGE 13 F0256
WORKER KNOWL NAT/LISM SOC

B66
BROEKMEIJER M.W.J.,FICTION AND TRUTH ABOUT THE "DECADE OF DEVELOPMENT" WOR+45 AGRI FINAN INDUS NAT/G TEC/DEV DIPLOM EDU/PROP LEAD SKILL 20 THIRD/WRLD. PAGE 19 F0358
FOR/AID POLICY ECO/UNDEV PLAN

B66
BROWN J.F.,THE NEW EASTERN EUROPE. ALBANIA BULGARIA HUNGARY POLAND ROMANIA CULTURE AGRI POL/PAR WAR NAT/LISM MARXISM...CHARTS BIBLIOG 20. PAGE 19 F0369
DIPLOM COM NAT/G ECO/UNDEV

B66
COLE A.B.,SOCIALIST PARTIES IN POSTWAR JAPAN. STRATA AGRI LABOR PLAN DIPLOM ECO/TAC AGREE LEAD CHOOSE ATTIT...CHARTS 20 CHINJAP SOC/DEMPAR. PAGE 26 F0499
POL/PAR POLICY SOCISM NAT/G

B66
ECONOMIC RESEARCH SERVICE,RESEARCH DATA ON MINORITY GROUPS: AN ANNOTATED BIBLIOGRAPHY OF ECONOMIC RESEARCH SERVICE REPORTS: 1955-1965 (PAMPHLET). USA+45 STRATA ECO/DEV AGRI SCHOOL WORKER EDU/PROP HEALTH NEW/LIB SOC. PAGE 36 F0697
BIBLIOG/A DISCRIM WEALTH RACE/REL

B66
FISK E.K.,NEW GUINEA ON THE THRESHOLD; ASPECTS OF SOCIAL, POLITICAL, AND ECONOMIC DEVELOPMENT. AGRI NAT/G INT/TRADE ADMIN ADJUST LITERACY ROLE...CHARTS ANTHOL 20 NEW/GUINEA. PAGE 41 F0804
ECO/UNDEV SOCIETY

B66
FOX K.A.,THE THEORY OF QUANTITATIVE ECONOMIC POLICY WITH APPLICATIONS TO ECONOMIC GROWTH AND STABILIZATION. ECO/DEV AGRI NAT/G PLAN ADMIN RISK ...DECISION IDEA/COMP SIMUL T. PAGE 43 F0837
ECO/TAC ECOMETRIC EQUILIB GEN/LAWS

B66
GITTINGER J.P.,THE LITERATURE OF AGRICULTURAL PLANNING. UNIV INT/ORG CONSULT WORKER TEC/DEV ECO/TAC OPTIMAL...POLICY METH/COMP BIBLIOG/A 20. PAGE 47 F0927
ECO/UNDEV AGRI PLAN WRITING

B66
GYORGY A.,ISSUES OF WORLD COMMUNISM. ALBANIA CHINA/COM COM USSR YUGOSLAVIA STRATA AGRI INT/ORG CHIEF FORCES WORKER WAR ALL/IDEOS...GEOG 20 MAO. PAGE 52 F1018
ECO/UNDEV REV MARXISM CON/ANAL

B66
HAYER T.,FRENCH AID. AFR FRANCE AGRI FINAN BUDGET ADMIN WAR PRODUC...CHARTS 18/20 THIRD/WRLD OVRSEA/DEV. PAGE 57 F1125
TEC/DEV COLONIAL FOR/AID ECO/UNDEV

B66
HO YHI-MIN,AGRICULTURAL DEVELOPMENT OF TAIWAN: 1903-1960. FINAN WORKER EDU/PROP...STAT CHARTS BIBLIOG 20. PAGE 60 F1181
ECO/UNDEV AGRI PRODUC PLAN

B66
HUNT C.L.,SOCIAL ASPECTS OF ECONOMIC DEVELOPMENT. S/ASIA AGRI FAM TEC/DEV RECEIVE EDU/PROP OWN...GEOG MUNICH 20. PAGE 63 F1243
SOC STRATA ATTIT ECO/UNDEV

B66
JACKSON G.D.,COMINTERN AND PEASANT IN EAST EUROPE 1919-1930. BULGARIA COM CZECHOSLVK EUR+WWI POLAND ROMANIA YUGOSLAVIA STRATA AGRI VOL/ASSN DIPLOM CONTROL CROWD WEALTH...POLICY NAT/COMP 20. PAGE 66 F1293
MARXISM ECO/UNDEV WORKER INT/ORG

B66
KIRDAR U.,THE STRUCTURE OF UNITED NATIONS ECONOMIC AID TO UNDERDEVELOPED COUNTRIES. AGRI FINAN INDUS NAT/G EX/STRUC PLAN GIVE TASK...POLICY 20 UN. PAGE 71 F1397
INT/ORG FOR/AID ECO/UNDEV ADMIN

B66
KIRKENDALL R.S.,SOCIAL SCIENTISTS AND FARM POLITICS IN THE AGE OF ROOSEVELT. ACADEM PLAN ECO/TAC GIVE ADMIN CONTROL PRODUC...SOC 20 NEW/DEAL ROOSEVLT/F BURAGR/ECO. PAGE 71 F1399
AGRI INTELL POLICY NAT/G

B66
KROOSS H.E.,AMERICAN ECONOMIC DEVELOPMENT (2ND ED.). USA+45 USA-45 AGRI INDUS LABOR WORKER INT/TRADE TAX WAR...CHARTS 18/20. PAGE 73 F1443
ECO/TAC NAT/G CAP/ISM ECO/DEV

B66
KUZNETS S.,MODERN ECONOMIC GROWTH. WOR+45 WOR-45 ECO/DEV ECO/UNDEV AGRI FINAN INDUS TEC/DEV
TIME/SEQ WEALTH

EFFICIENCY INCOME...NAT/COMP 19/20. PAGE 74 F1456
PRODUC

B66
LANDERS D.S.,RISE OF CAPITALISM. LABOR AUTOMAT GP/REL CENTRAL COST PROFIT...SOC CONCPT ANTHOL 19/20. PAGE 75 F1469
CAP/ISM INDUS AGRI

B66
LECHT L.,GOAL, PRIORITIES, AND DOLLARS: THE NEXT DECADE. SPACE USA+45 SOCIETY AGRI BUDGET FOR/AID ...HEAL SOC/WK STAT CHARTS 20 URBAN/RNWL PUB/TRANS. PAGE 76 F1499
IDEA/COMP POLICY CONSEN PLAN

B66
LILLEY S.,MEN, MACHINES AND HISTORY: THE STORY OF TOOLS AND MACHINES IN RELATION TO SOCIAL PROGRESS. PREHIST SPACE STRUCT COMPUTER AUTOMAT NUC/PWR ...POLICY SOC. PAGE 80 F1564
AGRI TEC/DEV SOCIETY

B66
MACFARQUHAR R.,CHINA UNDER MAO: POLITICS TAKES COMMAND. CHINA/COM COM AGRI INDUS CHIEF FORCES DIPLOM INT/TRADE EDU/PROP TASK REV ADJUST...ANTHOL 20 MAO. PAGE 83 F1628
ECO/UNDEV TEC/DEV ECO/TAC ADMIN

B66
MADAN G.R.,ECONOMIC THINKING IN INDIA. INDIA ECO/UNDEV AGRI FINAN INDUS LABOR PLAN CAP/ISM INT/TRADE MARXISM SOCISM...POLICY 1/20. PAGE 84 F1638
ECO/TAC PHIL/SCI NAT/G POL/PAR

B66
MALASSIS L.,ECONOMIC DEVELOPMENT AND THE PROGRAMMING OF RURAL EDUCATION. CONSULT PROB/SOLV LITERACY KNOWL...CHARTS GEN/METH 20. PAGE 84 F1644
AGRI ECO/UNDEV SCHOOL PLAN

B66
MASON E.S.,ECONOMIC DEVELOPMENT IN INDIA AND PAKISTAN. INDIA PAKISTAN AGRI FINAN PLAN BUDGET INT/TRADE WEALTH...POLICY STAT TREND CHARTS 20. PAGE 87 F1700
NAT/COMP ECO/UNDEV ECO/TAC FOR/AID

B66
NAMBOODIRIPAD E.M.,ECONOMICS AND POLITICS OF INDIA'S SOCIALIST PATTERN. INDIA STRATA AGRI INDUS NAT/G PRICE ORD/FREE SOVEREIGN 20. PAGE 96 F1888
ECO/UNDEV PLAN SOCISM CAP/ISM

B66
O'CONNER A.M.,AN ECONOMIC GEOGRAPHY OF EAST AFRICA. AFR TANZANIA UGANDA AGRI WORKER INT/TRADE COLONIAL GOV/REL...CHARTS METH/COMP 20 AFRICA/E. PAGE 99 F1953
ECO/UNDEV EXTR/IND GEOG HABITAT

B66
THIESENHUSEN W.C.,CHILE'S EXPERIMENTS IN AGRARIAN REFORM. CHILE STRUCT NAT/G ACT/RES ECO/TAC GOV/REL COST SOCISM...TREND CHARTS SOC/EXP 20. PAGE 130 F2558
AGRI ECO/UNDEV SOC TEC/DEV

B66
UN STATISTICAL OFFICE,STATISTICAL YEARBOOK (17TH ED.). WOR+45 AGRI...GEOG CHARTS 20. PAGE 132 F2604
STAT INDEX SOCIETY INDUS

B66
UREN P.E.,EAST - WEST TRADE* A SYMPOSIUM. COM AGRI INT/ORG PRICE HABITAT RIGID/FLEX...GEOG INT/LAW ANTHOL NATO. PAGE 133 F2625
INT/TRADE BAL/PWR AFR CANADA

B66
WOODMAN H.D.,SLAVERY AND THE SOUTHERN ECONOMY: SOURCES AND READINGS. USA-45 CULTURE STRUCT AGRI ECO/TAC LEAD RACE/REL DISCRIM EFFICIENCY...CHARTS ANTHOL MUNICH 18/19 NEGRO SOUTH/US. PAGE 148 F2922
ECO/DEV STRATA WORKER UTIL

B66
ZINKIN T.,CHALLENGES IN INDIA. INDIA PAKISTAN LAW AGRI FINAN INDUS TOP/EX TEC/DEV CONTROL ROUTINE ORD/FREE PWR 20 NEHRU/J SHASTRI/LB CIVIL/SERV. PAGE 150 F2964
NAT/G ECO/TAC POLICY ADMIN

L66
AMERICAN ECONOMIC REVIEW,"SIXTY-THIRD LIST OF DOCTORAL DISSERTATIONS IN POLITICAL ECONOMY IN AMERICAN UNIVERSITIES AND COLLEGES." ECO/DEV AGRI FINAN LABOR WORKER PLAN BUDGET INT/TRADE ADMIN DEMAND...MGT STAT 20. PAGE 5 F0088
BIBLIOG/A CONCPT ACADEM

S66
FELD W.,"EXTERNAL RELATIONS OF THE COMMON MARKET AND GROUP LEADERSHIP ATTITUDES IN THE MEMBER STATES." COM USA+45 ELITES AGRI NAT/G ATTIT...OBS EEC GATT. PAGE 40 F0776
DIPLOM CENTRAL TARIFFS INT/TRADE

S66
LAURENS H.,"LES PAYS OCCIDENTAUX ET LE MARCHE CHINOIS." EUR+WWI FUT S/ASIA AGRI INDUS VOL/ASSN ECO/TAC BAL/PAY...RECORD PREDICT TREATY. PAGE 76 F1488
ASIA INT/TRADE TREND STAT

S66
LINDBLOOM C.E.,"HAS INDIA AN ECONOMIC FUTURE?" FUT INDIA NAT/G PROB/SOLV...POLICY 20. PAGE 80 F1568
AGRI PRODUC PLAN ECO/UNDEV

S66
SHORTE F.C.,"THE APPLICATION OF DEVELOPMENT HYPOTHESES IN MIDDLE EASTERN STUDIES." STRUCT AGRI CREATE DEMAND...GEOG STAT CON/ANAL CHARTS. PAGE 121 F2387
ECO/UNDEV ISLAM SOC HYPO/EXP

N66
BRITISH DEVELOPMENT POLICIES: 1966 (PAMPHLET). UK AGRI TARIFFS BAL/PAY...TREND CHARTS 20 OVRSEA/DEV. PAGE 1 F0023
WEALTH DIPLOM INT/TRADE FOR/AID

B67
BALDWIN G.B.,PLANNING AND DEVELOPMENT IN IRAN. IRAN AGRI INDUS CONSULT WORKER EDU/PROP BAL/PAY...CHARTS 20. PAGE 9 F0164
PLAN ECO/UNDEV ADMIN PROB/SOLV

B67
BIRMINGHAM W.,A STUDY OF CONTEMPORARY GHANA VOL. I: SOME ASPECTS OF SOCIAL STRUCTURE. AFR GHANA AGRI FAM SECT PLAN EDU/PROP MARRIAGE OWN...POLICY STAT CHARTS MUNICH 20. PAGE 15 F0287
SOCIETY STRUCT CENSUS ECO/UNDEV

B67
CHANDRASEKHAR S.,PROBLEMS OF ECONOMIC DEVELOPMENT. AFR INDIA PHILIPPINE UAR WOR+45 INDUS...GEOG SOC ANTHOL BIBLIOG 20 CHINJAP. PAGE 23 F0450
ECO/UNDEV PLAN AGRI PROB/SOLV

B67
CLEGERN W.M.,BRITISH HONDURAS: COLONIAL DEAD END, 1859-1900. HONDURAS AGRI FINAN PROB/SOLV INT/TRADE PWR WEALTH...BIBLIOG/A 19. PAGE 25 F0487
COLONIAL POLICY ECO/UNDEV DOMIN

B67
FORDE D.,WEST AFRICAN KINGDOMS IN THE NINETEENTH CENTURY. ECO/UNDEV AGRI KIN...SOC CHARTS NAT/COMP 19. PAGE 42 F0826
AFR REGION CULTURE

B67
GUTKIND E.A.,URBAN DEVELOPMENT IN SOUTHERN EUROPE* SPAIN AND PORTUGAL. CHRIST-17C EUR+WWI MOD/EUR PORTUGAL SPAIN CULTURE AGRI...SOC SAMP/SIZ BIBLIOG MUNICH. PAGE 52 F1015
TEC/DEV ECO/DEV

B67
HEADLEY J.C.,PESTICIDE PROBLEM: AN ECONOMIC APPROACH TO PUBLIC POLICY. AGRI TEC/DEV GOV/REL COST ATTIT CHARTS. PAGE 58 F1131
HABITAT POLICY BIO/SOC CONTROL

B67
HERRESHOFF D.,AMERICAN DISCIPLES OF MARX: FROM THE AGE OF JACKSON TO THE PROGRESSIVE ERA. USA-45 AGRI POL/PAR 19/20. PAGE 59 F1155
MARXISM ATTIT WORKER CONCPT

B67
JOHNSON D.G.,THE STRUGGLE AGAINST WORLD HUNGER (HEADLINE SERIES, NO. 184) (PAMPHLET). PLAN TEC/DEV FOR/AID...CHARTS 20 FAO MEXIC/AMER. PAGE 67 F1322
AGRI PROB/SOLV ECO/UNDEV HEALTH

B67
MALINVAUD E.,ACTIVITY ANALYSIS IN THE THEORY OF GROWTH AND PLANNING. UNIV AGRI COMPUTER OP/RES REGION...CHARTS ANTHOL METH. PAGE 84 F1648
MATH GAME SIMUL

B67
MAZOUR A.G.,SOVIET ECONOMIC DEVELOPMENT: OPERATION OUTSTRIP: 1921-1965. USSR ECO/UNDEV FINAN CHIEF WORKER PROB/SOLV CONTROL PRODUC MARXISM...CHARTS ORG/CHARTS 20 STALIN/J. PAGE 87 F1711
ECO/TAC AGRI INDUS PLAN

B67
MENDEL A.P.,POLITICAL MEMOIRS 1905-1917 BY PAUL MILIUKOV (TRANS. BY CARL GOLDBERG). USSR AGRI DIPLOM ECO/TAC POPULISM...MAJORIT 20. PAGE 90 F1757
BIOG LEAD NAT/G CONSTN

B67
POLLACK N.,THE POPULIST MIND. USA-45 STRATA AGRI NAT/G POL/PAR LEGIS WORKER RACE/REL WEALTH...ANTHOL BIBLIOG 19 NEGRO. PAGE 107 F2097
POPULISM HIST/WRIT ATTIT INGP/REL

B67
SMITH T.L.,THE PROCESS OF RURAL DEVELOPMENT IN LATIN AMERICA (A MONOGRAPH). L/A+17C STRATA INDUS PLAN GP/REL PERS/REL RIGID/FLEX WEALTH...OBS CHARTS ORG/CHARTS ANTHOL 20 COLOMB. PAGE 123 F2434
IDEA/COMP SOC AGRI ECO/UNDEV

B67
SYMONS L.,AGRICULTURAL GEOGRAPHY. OP/RES SKILL ...CONCPT CHARTS BIBLIOG T 20. PAGE 128 F2520
AGRI GEOG METH/COMP OBS

B67
TOMA P.A.,THE POLITICS OF FOOD FOR PEACE; EXECUTIVE-LEGISLATIVE INTERACTION. USA+45 ECO/UNDEV POL/PAR DEBATE EXEC LOBBY CHOOSE PEACE...DECISION CHARTS. PAGE 131 F2580
FOR/AID POLICY LEGIS AGRI

B67
US AGENCY INTERNATIONAL DEV,PROPOSED FOREIGN AID PROGRAM FOR 1968: SUMMARY PRESENTATION TO THE CONGRESS. AFR S/ASIA USA+45 AGRI TEC/DEV DIPLOM ECO/TAC BAL/PAY COST HEALTH KNOWL SKILL 20 AID CONGRESS ALL/PROG. PAGE 134 F2640
ECO/UNDEV BUDGET FOR/AID STAT

B67
US CONGRESS JOINT ECO COMM,AN ECONOMIC PROFILE OF MAINLAND CHINA, VOLUMES I AND II. CHINA/COM AGRI DIST/IND FINAN INDUS LABOR FORCES ACT/RES PLAN INT/TRADE INGP/REL BAL/PAY 20 CONGRESS. PAGE 135 F2664
ECO/UNDEV WEALTH ECO/TAC DELIB/GP

S67
"THE FEDERAL AGRICULTURAL STABILIZATION PROGRAM AND THE NEGRO." LAW CONSTN PLAN REPRESENT DISCRIM ORD/FREE 20 NEGRO CONGRESS. PAGE 2 F0025
AGRI CONTROL NAT/G RACE/REL

S67
ADAMS D.W.,"MINIFUNDIA IN AGRARIAN REFORM: A COLOMBIAN EXAMPLE."...SOC CLASSIF 20 COLOMB. PAGE 2 F0035
AGRI METH/COMP OWN PRODUC

S67
AVTORKHANOV A.,"A NEW AGRARIAN REVOLUTION." COM USSR ECO/DEV PLAN TEC/DEV ADMIN CONTROL OPTIMAL WEALTH SOCISM 20 KHRUSH/N STALIN/J. PAGE 8 F0144
AGRI METH/COMP MARXISM OWN

S67
BENNETT J.T.,"POLITICAL IMPLICATIONS OF ECONOMIC CHANGE: SOUTH VIETNAM." VIETNAM/S INGP/REL INCOME ATTIT 20 AID. PAGE 13 F0247
ECO/UNDEV INDUS AGRI PRODUC

S67
BRANCO R.,"LAND REFORM* THE ANSWER TO LATIN AMERICA'S AGRICULTURAL DEVELOPMENT?" L/A+17C NAT/G PLAN TEC/DEV BUDGET RENT EFFICIENCY 20. PAGE 18 F0339
ECO/UNDEV AGRI TAX OWN

S67
COSGROVE C.A.,"AGRICULTURE, FINANCE AND POLITICS IN THE EUROPEAN COMMUNITY." EUR+WWI DIST/IND MARKET INT/ORG VOL/ASSN DELIB/GP TEC/DEV BAL/PWR BARGAIN ECO/TAC RATION CONFER 20 EEC. PAGE 28 F0538
ECO/DEV DIPLOM AGRI INT/TRADE

S67
DEWHURST A.,"THE WAGE MOVEMENT IN CANADA." CANADA AGRI NAT/G PARTIC COST PRODUC PROFIT 20. PAGE 32 F0627
WORKER MARXIST INDUS LABOR

S67
FOX R.G.,"FAMILY, CASTE, AND COMMERCE IN A NORTH INDIAN MARKET TOWN." INDIA STRATA AGRI FACE/GP FAM NEIGH OP/RES BARGAIN ADMIN ROUTINE WEALTH...SOC CHARTS 20. PAGE 43 F0838
CULTURE GP/REL ECO/UNDEV DIST/IND

S67
HILDEBRAND J.R.,"THE CENTRAL AMERICAN COMMON MARKET: ECONOMIC AND POLITICAL INTEGRATION." L/A+17C USA+45 ECO/DEV ECO/UNDEV AGRI SOVEREIGN. PAGE 59 F1170
DIPLOM ECO/TAC INT/TRADE INT/ORG

S67
HUTCHINGS R.,"THE ENDING OF UNEMPLOYMENT IN THE USSR" USSR PLAN ECO/TAC PRICE INGP/REL...GEOG STAT CHARTS 20 MIGRATION. PAGE 63 F1247
WORKER AGRI INDUS MARXISM

S67
MAJSTRENKO I.W.,"PROBLEMS CONFRONTING SOVIET AGRICULTURE." COM USSR ECO/DEV ECO/TAC EFFICIENCY OPTIMAL WEALTH MARXISM 20. PAGE 84 F1643
AGRI PROB/SOLV CENTRAL TEC/DEV

S67
ORAZEM F.,"THE NEW SOVIET PLAN FOR AGRICULTURE (1960-1970)" USSR WORKER CAP/ISM ECO/TAC PRICE OWN HABITAT MARXISM...CHARTS 20. PAGE 101 F1994
AGRI PLAN COM ECO/DEV

S67
PERKINS D.H.,"ECONOMIC GROWTH IN CHINA AND THE CULTURAL REVOLUTION(1960APRIL 1967)" CHINA/COM FUT AGRI INDUS PLAN LEAD MARXISM...CHARTS 20 MAO. PAGE 105 F2062
ECO/TAC CULTURE REV ECO/UNDEV

S67
PETRAS J.,"MINERS AND AGRARIAN RADICALISM." CHILE AGRI EXTR/IND WORKER CHOOSE ATTIT SOCISM MUNICH 20. PAGE 105 F2073
PARTIC EDU/PROP LABOR

S67
ROY E.V.,"AN INTERPRETATION OF NORTHERN THAI PEASANT ECONOMY." THAILAND CLIENT CULTURE AGRI PROC/MFG FACE/GP DEMAND INCOME 20. PAGE 114 F2254
STRUCT STRATA ECO/UNDEV INGP/REL

S67
SCHACHTER G.,"REGIONAL DEVELOPMENT IN THE ITALIAN DUAL ECONOMY" ITALY AGRI INDUS MARKET WORKER ECO/TAC CONTROL INCOME PRODUC 20. PAGE 116 F2287
REGION ECO/UNDEV NAT/G PROB/SOLV

S67
SCHWARZWELLER H.K.,"SOCIAL CLASS ORIGINS, RURAL-URBAN MIGRATION, AND ECONOMIC LIFE CHANGES." USA+45 SOCIETY STRUCT FAM NEIGH INCOME...SOC RECORD CHARTS MUNICH. PAGE 118 F2326
CLASSIF WEALTH AGRI

S67
VAN KLAVEREN J.,"DIE WIRTSCHAFTLICHEN AUSWIRKUNGEN DES SCHWARZEN TODES" GERMANY PRICE DEMAND PRODUC MUNICH 14/15 DEPRESSION. PAGE 140 F2762
HEALTH AGRI GEOG

N67
US CONGRESS JOINT ECO COMM,MAINLAND CHINA IN THE WORLD ECONOMY (PAMPHLET). CHINA/COM USA+45 AGRI CHIEF MARXISM CONGRESS. PAGE 135 F2661
ECO/UNDEV POLICY ECO/TAC INT/TRADE

B76
FOURIER C.,SOCIAL DESTINIES, IN A. BRISBANE, GENERAL INTRODUCTION TO SOCIAL SCIENCE. UNIV AGRI INDUS SECT PRODUC...PHIL/SCI CONCPT. PAGE 43 F0835
UTOPIA SOCIETY PERSON VOL/ASSN

B76
PROUDHON P.J.,WHAT IS PROPERTY? (TRANS. BY B.R. TUCKER). SOCIETY AGRI CAP/ISM CRIME GP/REL PERSON MORAL ORD/FREE WEALTH. PAGE 108 F2127
OWN WORKER PRODUC ANARCH

B91
MILL J.S.,SOCIALISM (1859). MOD/EUR AGRI INDUS NAT/G REV INCOME PRODUC ORD/FREE POPULISM SOCISM ...GOV/COMP METH/COMP 19. PAGE 91 F1787
WEALTH SOCIALIST ECO/TAC OWN

B92
COULANGES F D.E.,THE ORIGIN OF PROPERTY IN LAND. LAW STRATA AGRI ACADEM EDU/PROP ORD/FREE 19. PAGE 28 F0543
OWN HIST/WRIT IDEA/COMP SOCISM

B99
KROPOTKIN P.,FIELDS, FACTORIES, AND WORKSHOPS. UNIV INTELL ECO/DEV LG/CO SCHOOL SML/CO ECO/TAC PRODUC UTOPIA...NEW/IDEA MUNICH. PAGE 74 F1445
SOCIETY WORKER AGRI INDUS

AGRICULTURE....SEE AGRI

AGUILAR M.A. F0050

AHMAD M. F0051

AHMED J. F0052

AHN L.A. F0053

AHRCO....ALLEGHENY HOUSING REHABILITATION CORPORATION

AID....US AGENCY FOR INTERNATIONAL DEVELOPMENT

B59
BAUER P.T.,UNITED STATES AID AND INDIAN ECONOMIC DEVELOPMENT. INDIA STRATA FINAN PLAN BUDGET DIPLOM INGP/REL EFFICIENCY SOCISM 20 AID. PAGE 11 F0215
FOR/AID ECO/UNDEV ECO/TAC POLICY

B59
US GENERAL ACCOUNTING OFFICE,EXAM OF ECONOMIC AND TECHNICAL ASSISTANCE PROGRAM FOR INDIA INT'NAT'L COOP ADMIN REPORT TO CONGRESS 1955-1958. INDIA USA+45 ECO/UNDEV FINAN PLAN DIPLOM COST UTIL WEALTH ...CHARTS 20 CONGRESS AID. PAGE 136 F2679
FOR/AID EFFICIENCY ECO/TAC TEC/DEV

B60
US HOUSE COMM GOVT OPERATIONS,OPERATIONS OF THE DEVELOPMENT LOAN FUND: HEARINGS (COMMITTEE ON GOVERNMENT OPERATIONS). USA+45 PLAN BUDGET DIPLOM GOV/REL COST...CHARTS 20 CONGRESS DEPT/STATE AID. PAGE 137 F2698
FINAN FOR/AID ECO/TAC EFFICIENCY

B61
US SENATE COMM ON FOREIGN RELS,INTERNATIONAL DEVELOPMENT AND SECURITY: HEARINGS ON BILL (2 VOLS.). ECO/UNDEV FINAN FORCES REV COST WEALTH ...CHARTS 20 AID PRESIDENT. PAGE 139 F2747
FOR/AID CIVMIL/REL ORD/FREE ECO/TAC

B63
EL-NAGGAR S.,FOREIGN AID TO UNITED ARAB REPUBLIC. UAR USA+45 USSR AGRI FINAN INDUS FORCES EATING DEMAND...CHARTS METH/COMP 20 RESOURCE/N AID. PAGE 37 F0718
FOR/AID ECO/UNDEV RECEIVE PLAN

B63
US GOVERNMENT,REPORT TO INTER-AMERICAN ECONOMIC AND SOCIAL COUNCIL AT SECOND ANNUAL MEETING. L/A+17C USA+45 VOL/ASSN TEC/DEV DIPLOM TAX EATING EFFICIENCY HEALTH...STAT CHARTS 20 AID. PAGE 136 F2682
ECO/TAC FOR/AID FINAN PLAN

B63
US SENATE COMM GOVT OPERATIONS,REPORT OF A STUDY OF US FOREIGN AID IN TEN MIDDLE EASTERN AND AFRICAN COUNTRIES. AFR ISLAM USA+45 FORCES PLAN BUDGET DIPLOM TAX DETER WEALTH...STAT CHARTS 20 CONGRESS AID MID/EAST. PAGE 138 F2728
FOR/AID EFFICIENCY ECO/TAC FINAN

N63
US AGENCY INTERNATIONAL DEV,PRINCIPLES OF FOREIGN ECONOMIC ASSISTANCE (PAMPHLET). USA+45 FINAN GP/REL BAL/PAY EFFICIENCY 20 AID. PAGE 134 F2638
FOR/AID PLAN ECO/UNDEV ATTIT

B64
RANIS G.,THE UNITED STATES AND THE DEVELOPING ECONOMIES. COM USA+45 AGRI FINAN TEC/DEV CAP/ISM ECO/TAC INT/TRADE...POLICY METH/COMP ANTHOL 20 AID. PAGE 109 F2145
ECO/UNDEV DIPLOM FOR/AID

B64
US AGENCY INTERNATIONAL DEV,A.I.D. PROJECTS IN FISCAL YEAR 1963: BY COUNTRY AND FIELD OF ACTIVITY. USA+45 ECO/UNDEV ECO/TAC EDU/PROP GOV/REL...CHARTS 20 AID. PAGE 134 F2639
FINAN FOR/AID COST STAT

B64
US HOUSE COMM GOVT OPERATIONS,US OWNED FOREIGN CURRENCIES: HEARINGS (COMMITTEE ON GOVERNMENT OPERATIONS). INDIA ECO/DEV PLAN BUDGET TAX DEMAND EFFICIENCY 20 AID CONGRESS. PAGE 137 F2699
FINAN ECO/TAC FOR/AID OWN

B65
CHANDRASEKHAR S.,AMERICAN AID AND INDIA'S ECONOMIC DEVELOPMENT. AFR CHINA/COM INDIA USA+45 GIVE EDU/PROP EATING HEALTH ORD/FREE 20 AID. PAGE 23 F0449
FOR/AID PEACE DIPLOM ECO/UNDEV

B65
COOMBS P.H.,EDUCATION AND FOREIGN AID. AFR USA+45 DIPLOM EFFICIENCY KNOWL ORD/FREE...ANTHOL 20 AID. PAGE 27 F0532
EDU/PROP FOR/AID SCHOOL ECO/UNDEV

B66
RUBIN S.J.,THE CONSCIENCE OF THE RICH NATIONS: THE DEVELOPMENT ASSISTANCE COMMITTEE AND THE COMMON AID EFFORT. EUR+WWI USA+45 ECO/UNDEV INT/ORG NAT/G VOL/ASSN ECO/TAC INT/TRADE...OBS UN AID DEV/ASSIST IBRD OECD. PAGE 114 F2256
FOR/AID ECO/DEV CONFER CENTRAL

B66
US HOUSE COMM FOREIGN AFFAIRS,HEARINGS ON HR 12449 A BILL TO AMEND FURTHER THE FOREIGN ASSISTANCE ACT OF 1961. AFR ASIA L/A+17C USA+45 VIETNAM INT/ORG TEC/DEV INT/TRADE ATTIT ORD/FREE 20 UN NATO CONGRESS AID. PAGE 137 F2692
FOR/AID ECO/TAC ECO/UNDEV DIPLOM

B66
US SENATE COMM APPROPRIATIONS,FOREIGN ASSISTANCE AND RELATED AGENCIES APPROPRIATIONS FOR FISCAL YEAR 1967: HEARINGS... ON H. R. 17788. ECO/UNDEV INT/ORG FORCES INSPECT ECO/TAC GIVE DEBATE WEAPON CIVMIL/REL WEALTH...INT 20 CONGRESS DEPT/DEFEN DEPT/STATE DEPT/HEW AID. PAGE 138 F2727
BUDGET FOR/AID DIPLOM COST

L66
PACKENHAM R.A.,"POLITICAL-DEVELOPMENT DOCTRINES IN THE AMERICAN FOREIGN AID PROGRAM." STRUCT R+D CREATE DIPLOM AID. PAGE 102 F2011
FOR/AID ECO/UNDEV GEN/LAWS

B67
MONTGOMERY J.D.,FOREIGN AID IN INTERNATIONAL POLITICS. USA+45 USA-45 WOR+45 ECO/TAC EFFICIENCY ...SOC TREND CHARTS BIBLIOG/A 20 AID. PAGE 93 F1818
DIPLOM FOR/AID

B67
US AGENCY INTERNATIONAL DEV,PROPOSED FOREIGN AID PROGRAM FOR 1968: SUMMARY PRESENTATION TO THE CONGRESS. AFR S/ASIA USA+45 AGRI TEC/DEV DIPLOM ECO/TAC BAL/PAY COST HEALTH KNOWL SKILL 20 AID CONGRESS ALL/PROG. PAGE 134 F2640
ECO/UNDEV BUDGET FOR/AID STAT

S67
BENNETT J.T.,"POLITICAL IMPLICATIONS OF ECONOMIC CHANGE: SOUTH VIETNAM." VIETNAM/S INGP/REL INCOME ATTIT 20 AID. PAGE 13 F0247
ECO/UNDEV INDUS AGRI PRODUC

AIR POLLUTION....SEE POLLUTION

AIR....LOCALE OF SUBJECT ACTIVITY IS AERIAL

B54
LOCKLIN D.P.,ECONOMICS OF TRANSPORTATION (4TH ED.). USA+45 USA-45 SEA AIR LAW FINAN LG/CO EX/STRUC ADMIN CONTROL...STAT CHARTS 19/20 RAILROAD PUB/TRANS. PAGE 81 F1592
ECO/DEV DIST/IND ECO/TAC TEC/DEV

B59
NORTON P.L.,URBAN PROBLEMS AND TECHNIQUES. AIR AGRI INDUS MARKET TEC/DEV BUDGET LEISURE ALL/VALS ...ANTHOL MUNICH 20 URBAN/RNWL. PAGE 99 F1936
PLAN LOC/G HABITAT

B60
US SENATE COMM ON COMMERCE,URBAN MASS TRANSPORTATION. FUT USA+45 AIR ECO/DEV FINAN LOC/G LEGIS CREATE PROB/SOLV TEC/DEV MUNICH 20 PUB/TRANS. PAGE 139 F2732
DIST/IND PLAN NAT/G LAW

B64
FISK W.M.,ADMINISTRATIVE PROCEDURE IN A REGULATORY AGENCY: THE CAB AND THE NEW YORK-CHICAGO CASE (PAMPHLET). USA+45 DIST/IND ADMIN CONTROL LOBBY GP/REL ROLE ORD/FREE NEWYORK/C CHICAGO CAB. PAGE 41 F0805
SERV/IND ECO/DEV AIR JURID

B64
MITAU G.T.,INSOLUBLE PROBLEMS: CASE PROBLEMS ON THE FUNCTIONS OF STATE AND LOCAL GOVERNMENT. USA+45 AIR FINAN LABOR POL/PAR PROB/SOLV TAX RECEIVE CONTROL GP/REL 20 CASEBOOK ZONING. PAGE 92 F1807
ADJUD LOC/G PROVS

B65
THAYER F.C. JR.,AIR TRANSPORT POLICY AND NATIONAL SECURITY: A POLITICAL, ECONOMIC, AND MILITARY ANALYSIS. DIST/IND OP/RES PLAN TEC/DEV DIPLOM DETER WAR COST EFFICIENCY...POLICY BIBLIOG 20 DEPT/DEFEN FAA CAB. PAGE 129 F2548
AIR FORCES CIVMIL/REL ORD/FREE

B66
RUPPENTHAL K.M.,TRANSPORTATION AND TOMORROW. FUT SPACE USA+45 SEA AIR FORCES TEC/DEV INT/TRADE ...ANTHOL 20 RAILROAD. PAGE 115 F2261
DIST/IND PLAN CIVMIL/REL PREDICT

L67
ZEIDBERG L.D.,"THE NASHVILLE AIR POLLUTION STUDY" (PARTS V-VII)" USA+45 PLAN AGE HEALTH...GEOG STAT CENSUS SAMP/SIZ CHARTS BIBLIOG MUNICH. PAGE 150 F2962
DEATH HABITAT AIR BIO/SOC

S67
TELLER A.,"AIR-POLLUTION ABATEMENT: ECONOMIC RATIONALITY AND REALITY." NAT/G DELIB/GP ECO/TAC GOV/REL CENTRAL EFFICIENCY HEALTH...CHARTS METH MUNICH. PAGE 129 F2543
PROB/SOLV CONTROL COST AIR

AITKEN H. F0054

AITKEN H.G. F0055

AJAO/A....ADEROGBA AJAO

ALABAMA....ALABAMA

B60
FRYE R.J.,GOVERNMENT AND LABOR: THE ALABAMA PROGRAM. USA+45 INDUS R+D LABOR WORKER BUDGET EFFICIENCY AGE/Y HEALTH...CHARTS 20 ALABAMA. PAGE 45 F0870
ADMIN LEGIS LOC/G PROVS

B65
FRYE R.J.,HOUSING AND URBAN RENEWAL IN ALABAMA. USA+45 NEIGH LEGIS BUDGET ADJUD ADMIN PARTIC...MGT MUNICH 20 ALABAMA URBAN/RNWL. PAGE 45 F0871
PROB/SOLV PLAN GOV/REL

ALASKA....ALASKA

ALBANIA....SEE ALSO COM

B56
WOLFF R.L.,THE BALKANS IN OUR TIME. ALBANIA FUT MOD/EUR USSR YUGOSLAVIA CULTURE INT/ORG SECT DIPLOM EDU/PROP COERCE WAR ORD/FREE...CHARTS 4/20 BALKANS COMINFORM. PAGE 148 F2919
GEOG COM

B66
BROWN J.F.,THE NEW EASTERN EUROPE. ALBANIA BULGARIA HUNGARY POLAND ROMANIA CULTURE AGRI POL/PAR WAR NAT/LISM MARXISM...CHARTS BIBLIOG 20. PAGE 19 F0369
DIPLOM COM NAT/G ECO/UNDEV

B66
GYORGY A.,ISSUES OF WORLD COMMUNISM. ALBANIA CHINA/COM COM USSR YUGOSLAVIA STRATA AGRI INT/ORG CHIEF FORCES WORKER WAR ALL/IDEOS...GEOG 20 MAO. PAGE 52 F1018
ECO/UNDEV REV MARXISM CON/ANAL

ALBAUM G. F0056

ALBERTA....ALBERTA

ALCOHOLISM....SEE BIO/SOC

ALDERSON W. F0057

ALEMBERT/J....JEAN LE ROND D'ALEMBERT

ALEXANDER G.J. F0058

ALEXANDER R.J. F0059,F0060

ALEXANDER Y. F0061,F0062

ALEXANDROWICZ C.H. F0063,F0064

ALFRED H. F0065

ALGERIA....SEE ALSO ISLAM

B58
TILLION G.,ALGERIA: THE REALITIES. ALGERIA FRANCE ISLAM CULTURE STRATA PROB/SOLV DOMIN REV NAT/LISM WEALTH MARXISM...GEOG 20. PAGE 130 F2573
ECO/UNDEV SOC COLONIAL DIPLOM

B64
PAWERA J.C.,ALGERIA'S INFRASTRUCTURE. ALGERIA PLAN WEALTH...METH/CNCPT 20. PAGE 104 F2041
ECO/UNDEV INDUS TEC/DEV COM/IND

ALGIER/CHR....CHARTER OF ALGIERS

ALI S. F0066

ALIBER R.Z. F0067,F2392

ALIENATION....SEE STRANGE

ALKHIMOV V.S. F0068

ALL/IDEOS....CONCERNS THREE OR MORE OF THE TERMS LISTED IN THE IDEOLOGICAL TOPIC INDEX, P. XIII

N
TEXTBOOKS IN PRINT. WOR+45 WOR-45 LAW DIPLOM ALL/VALS ALL/IDEOS...SOC T 19/20. PAGE 1 F0003
BIBLIOG SCHOOL KNOWL

B37
MACKENZIE F.,PLANNED SOCIETY: YESTERDAY, TODAY, AND
SOC

TOMORROW. ECO/DEV ECO/UNDEV AGRI FINAN INDUS PLAN INSPECT CONTROL ALL/IDEOS...TREND METH/COMP BIBLIOG 20 RESOURCE/N. PAGE 83 F1635
CONCPT ANTHOL

B39
MARQUAND H.A.,ORGANIZED LABOUR IN FOUR CONTINENTS. EUR+WWI USA-45 INDUS NAT/G PAY GP/REL TOTALISM ATTIT WEALTH ALL/IDEOS...TREND NAT/COMP 20 ILO AFL/CIO EUROPE CHINJAP MEXIC/AMER. PAGE 85 F1673
LABOR WORKER CONCPT ANTHOL

B50
ADORNO T.W.,THE AUTHORITARIAN PERSONALITY. STRATA SECT PROB/SOLV ECO/TAC DISCRIM ATTIT SEX...SOC INT CHARTS METH 20. PAGE 3 F0044
AUTHORIT PERSON ALL/IDEOS SOCIETY

B53
WILLIAMS J.H.,ECONOMIC STABILITY IN A CHANGING WORLD. FRANCE USA+45 USSR AGRI WORKER BUDGET INT/TRADE TAX WAR BAL/PAY COST EFFICIENCY ALL/IDEOS EQULIB 20 KEYNES/JM. PAGE 147 F2892
POLICY FINAN ECO/TAC WEALTH

B54
MEYER A.G.,MARXISM. INTELL ECO/DEV WORKER CAP/ISM LEAD WAR ATTIT ALL/IDEOS...SOC 19/20 MARX/KARL. PAGE 90 F1766
MARXISM CONCPT ECO/TAC STRUCT

B55
PANT Y.P.,PLANNING IN UNDERDEVELOPED ECONOMIES. INDIA NEPAL INT/TRADE COLONIAL SOVEREIGN ALL/IDEOS ...TIME/SEQ METH/COMP 20. PAGE 103 F2026
ECO/UNDEV PLAN ECO/TAC DIPLOM

S55
BUNZEL J.H.,"THE GENERAL IDEOLOGY OF AMERICAN SMALL BUSINESS"(BMR)" USA+45 USA-45 AGRI GP/REL INGP/REL PERSON...MGT IDEA/COMP 18/20. PAGE 20 F0383
ALL/IDEOS ATTIT SML/CO INDUS

B57
NANIWADA H.,STAAT UND WIRTSCHAFT; GRUNDLEGUNG DER NATIONALOEKONOMIE ALS DER LOGIK DER BURGERLICHEN GESELLSCHAFT. WOR+45 WOR-45 STRATA MARKET WORKER INGP/REL DEMAND EQUILIB WEALTH...POLICY IDEA/COMP GEN/LAWS 17/20 MARX/KARL KEYNES/JM LENIN/VI. PAGE 96 F1890
ALL/IDEOS ECO/TAC SOCIETY NAT/G

B58
COLE G.D.H.,COMMUNISM AND SOCIAL DEMOCRACY (VOL. IV OF "HISTORY OF SOCIAL THOUGHT"). COM GERMANY ITALY UK AGRI INT/ORG WORKER DIPLOM COLONIAL NAT/LISM ALL/IDEOS...BIBLIOG 20 LEAGUE/NAT AUST/HUNG. PAGE 26 F0502
MARXISM REV POL/PAR SOCISM

B59
ROPKE W.,INTERNATIONAL ORDER AND ECONOMIC INTEGRATION. ECO/DEV ECO/UNDEV AGRI FINAN INDUS INT/ORG WAR PEACE ORD/FREE...SOC METH/COMP 20 EEC. PAGE 114 F2238
INT/TRADE DIPLOM BAL/PAY ALL/IDEOS

B60
BELLAN R.C.,PRINCIPLES OF ECONOMICS AND THE CANADIAN ECONOMY (2ND ED.). CANADA UK USA+45 LABOR WORKER CAP/ISM INT/TRADE RISK BAL/PAY EQUILIB ALL/IDEOS 20. PAGE 12 F0236
ECO/DEV PRODUC WEALTH FINAN

B62
SIEVERS A.M.,REVOLUTION, EVOLUTION AND THE ECONOMIC ORDER. INDUS LABOR TAX CONTROL REV WAR DEMAND PRODUC WEALTH...IDEA/COMP 19/20 KEYNES/JM. PAGE 122 F2399
EFFICIENCY ALL/IDEOS ECO/DEV WELF/ST

B63
NOMAD M.,POLITICAL HERETICS: FROM PLATO TO MAO TSE-TUNG. UNIV INGP/REL...SOC IDEA/COMP. PAGE 98 F1931
SOCIETY UTOPIA ALL/IDEOS CONCPT

B63
SCHOECK H.,THE NEW ARGUMENT IN ECONOMICS. UK USA+45 INDUS MARKET LABOR NAT/G ECO/TAC ADMIN ROUTINE BAL/PAY PWR...POLICY BOLIV. PAGE 117 F2309
WELF/ST FOR/AID ECO/DEV ALL/IDEOS

B63
STUCKI C.W.,AMERICAN DOCTORAL DISSERTATIONS ON ASIA 1933-62 (A PAPER). PREHIST INDUS NAT/G GOV/REL ALL/IDEOS...ART/METH GEOG SOC LING 20. PAGE 127 F2506
BIBLIOG ASIA SOCIETY S/ASIA

B64
WITHERS W.,THE ECONOMIC CRISIS IN LATIN AMERICA. BRAZIL CHILE STRATA AGRI DIPLOM FOR/AID PWR SOCISM ...POLICY 20 MEXIC/AMER ARGEN ALL/PROG. PAGE 148 F2914
L/A+17C ECO/UNDEV CAP/ISM ALL/IDEOS

B64
ZEBOT C.A.,THE ECONOMICS OF COMPETITIVE COEXISTENCE. CHINA/COM USSR WOR+45 FINAN MARKET FOR/AID PRICE DEMAND EQUILIB WEALTH ALL/IDEOS 20. PAGE 150 F2961
TEC/DEV DIPLOM METH/COMP

B66
ANDRESKI S.,PARASITISM AND SUBVERSION* THE CASE OF LATIN AMERICA. CULTURE ECO/UNDEV LABOR NAT/G SECT PROB/SOLV RACE/REL TOTALISM ATTIT WEALTH ALL/IDEOS. PAGE 5 F0100
L/A+17C GOV/COMP STRATA REV

B66
GYORGY A.,ISSUES OF WORLD COMMUNISM. ALBANIA CHINA/COM COM USSR YUGOSLAVIA STRATA AGRI INT/ORG CHIEF FORCES WORKER WAR ALL/IDEOS...GEOG 20 MAO. PAGE 52 F1018
ECO/UNDEV REV MARXISM CON/ANAL

B66
ODEGARD P.H.,POLITICAL POWER AND SOCIAL CHANGE. UNIV NAT/G CREATE ALL/IDEOS...POLICY GEOG SOC CENSUS TREND. PAGE 100 F1962
PWR TEC/DEV IDEA/COMP

B66
WETTER G.A.,SOVIET IDEOLOGY TODAY. USSR ECO/UNDEV SECT WORKER CAP/ISM CONTROL TASK EFFICIENCY TOTALISM DRIVE WEALTH...TREND 18/20. PAGE 145 F2864
ALL/IDEOS MARXISM REV

B67
GORZ A.,STRATEGY FOR LABOR: A RADICAL PROPOSAL (TRANS. BY MARTIN NICOLAUS AND VICTORIA ORTIZ). EUR+WWI FRANCE ITALY ECO/DEV POL/PAR OP/RES PLAN GP/REL ALL/IDEOS...SOC 20 EEC. PAGE 49 F0965
LABOR PWR STRUCT ECO/TAC

B67
MCNELLY T.,SOURCES IN MODERN EAST ASIAN HISTORY AND POLITICS. KOREA VIETNAM CULTURE DIPLOM COLONIAL REV WAR PWR ALL/IDEOS MARXISM...ANTHOL 20 CHINJAP. PAGE 88 F1733
NAT/COMP ASIA S/ASIA SOCIETY

B67
SPECTOR S.D.,CHECKLIST OF ITEMS IN THE NDEA INSTITUTE LIBRARY (PAMPHLET). USA+45 NAT/G SECT EDU/PROP ATTIT ALL/IDEOS...SOC BIOG. PAGE 124 F2448
BIBLIOG/A COM MARXISM

S67
JAVITS J.K.,"THE USE OF AMERICAN PLURALISM." USA+45 ECO/DEV BUDGET ADMIN ALL/IDEOS...DECISION TREND. PAGE 67 F1309
CENTRAL ATTIT POLICY NAT/G

ALL/PROG....ALLIANCE FOR PROGRESS

B62
DREIER J.C.,THE ALLIANCE FOR PROGRESS. L/A+17C USA+45 CULTURE ECO/DEV ECO/UNDEV NAT/G PLAN DIPLOM PWR 20 OAS ALL/PROG. PAGE 34 F0661
FOR/AID INT/ORG ECO/TAC POLICY

B62
UNIVERSITY OF TENNESSEE,GOVERNMENT AND WORLD CRISIS. USA+45 FOR/AID ORD/FREE...ANTHOL 20 UN ALL/PROG. PAGE 133 F2622
ECO/DEV DIPLOM NAT/G INT/ORG

B62
US CONGRESS JOINT ECO COMM,ECONOMIC DEVELOPMENTS IN SOUTH AMERICA. USA+45 SOCIETY FINAN NAT/G PROB/SOLV TEC/DEV INT/TRADE TAX EFFICIENCY PRODUC ATTIT ...POLICY 20 ALL/PROG CONGRESS SOUTH/AMER. PAGE 135 F2654
L/A+17C ECO/UNDEV FOR/AID DIPLOM

B63
CENTRO PARA EL DESARROLLO,LA ALIANZA PARA EL PROGRESO Y EL DESARROLLO SOCIAL DE AMERICA LATINA. L/A+17C INT/ORG DIPLOM ECO/TAC INT/TRADE ATTIT 20 ALL/PROG. PAGE 22 F0435
ECO/UNDEV FOR/AID PLAN REGION

B63
FLORES E.,LAND REFORM AND THE ALLIANCE FOR PROGRESS (PAMPHLET). L/A+17C USA+45 STRUCT ECO/UNDEV NAT/G WORKER CREATE PLAN ECO/TAC COERCE REV 20 ALL/PROG. PAGE 42 F0815
AGRI INT/ORG DIPLOM POLICY

B63
GORDON L.,A NEW DEAL FOR LATIN AMERICA. L/A+17C USA+45 CULTURE NAT/G TEC/DEV DIPLOM FOR/AID REGION TASK...POLICY 20 ALL/PROG DEPT/STATE. PAGE 49 F0958
ECO/UNDEV ECO/TAC INT/ORG PLAN

B63
INTERAMERICAN ECO AND SOC COUN,THE ALLIANCE FOR PROGRESS: ITS FIRST YEAR: 1961-1962. AGRI SCHOOL PLAN TEC/DEV INT/TRADE TAX GIVE ADMIN WEALTH...SOC 20 ALL/PROG SOUTH/AMER. PAGE 64 F1267
INT/ORG PROB/SOLV ECO/TAC L/A+17C

B63
MANGER W.,THE ALLIANCE FOR PROGRESS: A CRITICAL APPRAISAL. FUT L/A+17C USA+45 CULTURE ECO/UNDEV ACADEM NAT/G SCHOOL PLAN FOR/AID...POLICY OAS ALL/PROG. PAGE 84 F1651
DIPLOM INT/ORG ECO/TAC REGION

B63
MARITANO N.,AN ALLIANCE FOR PROGRESS. FUT L/A+17C USA+45 CULTURE ECO/UNDEV NAT/G PLAN CONTROL ...POLICY ALL/PROG. PAGE 85 F1669
DIPLOM INT/ORG ECO/TAC FOR/AID

B64
MASON E.S.,FOREIGN AID AND FOREIGN POLICY. USA+45 AGRI INDUS NAT/G EX/STRUC ACT/RES RIGID/FLEX ALL/VALS...POLICY GEN/LAWS MARSHL/PLN ALL/PROG CONGRESS 20. PAGE 87 F1699
ECO/UNDEV ECO/TAC FOR/AID DIPLOM

B64
ORGANIZATION AMERICAN STATES,ECONOMIC SURVEY OF LATIN AMERICA, 1962. L/A+17C AGRI DIST/IND INDUS MARKET PROC/MFG R+D PLAN TEC/DEV ECO/TAC REGION BAL/PAY ALL/VALS...CON/ANAL ORG/CHARTS GEN/METH OAS ALL/PROG 20 ALL/PROG. PAGE 102 F1998
ECO/UNDEV CHARTS

B64
ORGANIZATION AMERICAN STATES,ECONOMIC SURVEY OF LATIN AMERICA, 1962. L/A+17C AGRI DIST/IND INDUS MARKET PROC/MFG R+D PLAN TEC/DEV ECO/TAC REGION BAL/PAY ALL/VALS...CON/ANAL ORG/CHARTS GEN/METH OAS ALL/PROG 20 ALL/PROG. PAGE 102 F1998
ECO/UNDEV CHARTS

B64
URQUIDI V.L.,THE CHALLENGE OF DEVELOPMENT IN LATIN AMERICA. L/A+17C FINAN INT/ORG TEC/DEV DIPLOM
ECO/UNDEV ECO/TAC

INT/TRADE PRICE REGION PRODUC...CHARTS 20 ALL/PROG. PAGE 133 F2628
NAT/G TREND

B64
WITHERS W.,THE ECONOMIC CRISIS IN LATIN AMERICA. BRAZIL CHILE STRATA AGRI DIPLOM FOR/AID PWR SOCISM ...POLICY 20 MEXIC/AMER ARGEN ALL/PROG. PAGE 148 F2914
L/A+17C ECO/UNDEV CAP/ISM ALL/IDEOS

B65
INTERAMERICAN ECO AND SOC COUN,THE ALLIANCE FOR PROGRESS: ITS THIRD YEAR 1963-1964. FUT L/A+17C WOR+45 ECO/DEV INT/ORG PLAN CONTROL ADJUST...STAT ANTHOL SOC/INTEG 20 ALL/PROG. PAGE 64 F1268
ECO/UNDEV ECO/TAC FINAN FOR/AID

S65
JOHNSON L.L.,"US BUSINESS INTERESTS IN CUBA AND THE RISE OF CASTRO." L/A+17C USA+45 ECO/UNDEV INDUS NAT/G VOL/ASSN ATTIT ORD/FREE PWR WEALTH ALL/PROG. PAGE 68 F1330
DIPLOM CUBA ECO/TAC INT/TRADE

S65
WHITAKER A.P.,"ARGENTINA: STRUGGLE FOR RECOVERY." L/A+17C USA+45 NAT/G TOP/EX PLAN LEGIT COERCE REV RIGID/FLEX PWR WEALTH...RECORD ALL/PROG ARGEN FOR/TRADE 20. PAGE 146 F2867
POL/PAR ECO/TAC NAT/LISM

B66
LEAGUE OF WOMEN VOTERS OF US,FOREIGN AID AT THE CROSSROADS. USA+45 WOR+45 DELIB/GP PROB/SOLV DIPLOM INT/TRADE RECEIVE BAL/PAY...CHARTS 20 UN ALL/PROG. PAGE 76 F1498
FOR/AID GIVE ECO/UNDEV PLAN

B66
SOMMERFELD R.M.,TAX REFORM AND THE ALLIANCE FOR PROGRESS. USA+45 ECO/DEV ECO/UNDEV FINAN NAT/G INCOME ORD/FREE WEALTH...STAT CHARTS 20 ALL/PROG. PAGE 124 F2442
TAX INT/ORG L/A+17C FOR/AID

S66
JAVITS J.K.,"POLITICAL ACTION VITAL FOR LATIN AMERICAN INTEGRATION." ECO/UNDEV INT/ORG POL/PAR VOL/ASSN PLAN PROB/SOLV INT/TRADE EFFICIENCY 20 OAS LAFTA ALL/PROG. PAGE 66 F1308
L/A+17C ECO/TAC REGION

B67
US AGENCY INTERNATIONAL DEV,PROPOSED FOREIGN AID PROGRAM FOR 1968: SUMMARY PRESENTATION TO THE CONGRESS. AFR S/ASIA USA+45 AGRI TEC/DEV DIPLOM ECO/TAC BAL/PAY COST HEALTH KNOWL SKILL 20 AID CONGRESS ALL/PROG. PAGE 134 F2640
ECO/UNDEV BUDGET FOR/AID STAT

B67
US CONGRESS SENATE,SURVEY OF THE ALLIANCE FOR PROGRESS; INFLATION IN LATIN AMERICA (PAMPHLET). USA+45 MARKET INT/ORG DIPLOM INT/TRADE BAL/PAY SENATE ALL/PROG. PAGE 135 F2666
L/A+17C FINAN POLICY FOR/AID

B67
US SENATE COMM ON FOREIGN REL,LATIN AMERICAN SUMMIT CONFERENCE. L/A+17C USA+45 FINAN PLAN SENATE ALL/PROG. PAGE 139 F2740
FOR/AID BUDGET DIPLOM INT/ORG

ALL/VALS....CONCERNS SIX OR MORE OF THE TERMS LISTED IN THE VALUES INDEX, P. XIII

N
TEXTBOOKS IN PRINT. WOR+45 WOR-45 LAW DIPLOM ALL/VALS ALL/IDEOS...SOC T 19/20. PAGE 1 F0003
BIBLIOG SCHOOL KNOWL

B35
STALEY E.,WAR AND THE PRIVATE INVESTOR. UNIV WOR-45 INTELL SOCIETY INT/ORG NAT/G TOP/EX CAP/ISM ECO/TAC WAR ATTIT ALL/VALS...INT TIME/SEQ TREND CON/ANAL WORK TOT/POP 20. PAGE 125 F2464
FINAN INT/TRADE DIPLOM

B38
LANGE O.,ON THE ECONOMIC THEORY OF SOCIALISM. UNIV ECO/DEV FINAN INDUS INT/ORG PUB/INST ROUTINE ATTIT ALL/VALS...SOC CONCPT STAT TREND 20. PAGE 75 F1475
MARKET ECO/TAC INT/TRADE SOCISM

B41
YOUNG G.,FEDERALISM AND FREEDOM. EUR+WWI MOD/EUR RUSSIA USA-45 WOR-45 SOCIETY STRUCT ECO/DEV INT/ORG EXEC FEDERAL ATTIT PERSON ALL/VALS...OLD/LIB CONCPT OBS TREND LEAGUE/NAT TOT/POP. PAGE 150 F2950
NAT/G WAR

B48
LAUTERBACH A.,ECONOMIC SECURITY AND INDIVIDUAL FREEDOM: CAN WE HAVE BOTH? COM EUR+WWI MOD/EUR UNIV WOR+45 CAP/ISM TOTALISM ALL/VALS...GOV/COMP BIBLIOG 20. PAGE 76 F1490
ORD/FREE ECO/DEV DECISION INGP/REL

B51
PETERSON F.,SURVEY OF LABOR ECONOMICS (REV. ED.). STRATA ECO/DEV LABOR INSPECT BARGAIN PAY PRICE EXEC ROUTINE GP/REL ALL/VALS ORD/FREE 20 AFL/CIO DEPT/LABOR. PAGE 105 F2069
WORKER DEMAND IDEA/COMP T

S52
CHINOY E.,"THE TRADITION OF OPPORTUNITY AND THE ASPIRATIONS OF AUTOMOBILE WORKERS" (BMR)" STRATA ACT/RES ALL/VALS SKILL...INT 20. PAGE 24 F0468
WORKER ECO/DEV DRIVE INDUS

L54
OPLER M.E.,"SOCIAL ASPECTS OF TECHNICAL ASSISTANCE IN OPERATION." WOR+45 VOL/ASSN CREATE PLAN TEC/DEV EDU/PROP ALL/VALS...METH/CNCPT OBS RECORD TREND UN 20. PAGE 101 F1993
INT/ORG CONSULT FOR/AID

L55
KISER M.,"ORGANIZATION OF AMERICAN STATES." L/A+17C USA+45 ECO/UNDEV INT/ORG NAT/G PLAN TEC/DEV DIPLOM ECO/TAC INT/TRADE EDU/PROP ADMIN ALL/VALS...POLICY MGT RECORD ORG/CHARTS OAS COMMUN 20. PAGE 71 F1401
VOL/ASSN ECO/DEV REGION

N56
US HOUSE COMM FOREIGN AFFAIRS,REPORT OF THE SPECIAL STUDY MISSION TO AFRICA, SOUTH AND EAST OF THE SAHARA (PAMPHLET). AFR SOUTH/AFR USA+45 STRUCT INT/TRADE PARL/PROC NAT/LISM ATTIT ALL/VALS HEALTH ...POLICY 20 CONGRESS. PAGE 136 F2691
FOR/AID COLONIAL ECO/UNDEV DIPLOM

B58
POLLOCK F.,AUTOMATION: A STUDY OF ITS ECONOMIC AND SOCIAL CONSEQUENCES. FUT USA+45 USA-45 SOCIETY ECO/DEV LABOR ACT/RES PLAN ECO/TAC AUTOMAT ROUTINE ALL/VALS...STAT TREND COMPUT/IR CHARTS SOC/EXP WORK 20. PAGE 107 F2099
TEC/DEV SOC CAP/ISM

B59
ALLEN R.L.,SOVIET INFLUENCE IN LATIN AMERICA. ECO/UNDEV FINAN PROC/MFG NAT/G TEC/DEV EDU/PROP EXEC ROUTINE ATTIT DRIVE PERSON ALL/VALS PWR...STAT CHARTS WORK FOR/TRADE 20. PAGE 4 F0071
L/A+17C ECO/TAC INT/TRADE USSR

B59
NORTON P.L.,URBAN PROBLEMS AND TECHNIQUES. AIR AGRI INDUS MARKET TEC/DEV BUDGET LEISURE ALL/VALS ...ANTHOL MUNICH 20 URBAN/RNWL. PAGE 99 F1936
PLAN LOC/G HABITAT

B59
WARD B.,5 IDEAS THAT CHANGE THE WORLD. WOR+45 WOR-45 SOCIETY STRUCT AGRI INDUS INT/ORG NAT/G FORCES ACT/RES ARMS/CONT TOTALISM ATTIT DRIVE GEN/LAWS. PAGE 143 F2815
ECO/UNDEV ALL/VALS NAT/LISM COLONIAL

B60
ARON R.,COLLOQUES DE RHEINFELDEN. AFR USA+45 USSR WOR+45 WOR-45 CULTURE ECO/UNDEV NAT/G POL/PAR DIPLOM NAT/LISM TOTALISM ATTIT DRIVE ALL/VALS ...PLURIST CONCPT STERTYP GEN/LAWS TOT/POP 20. PAGE 6 F0120
ECO/DEV SOCIETY CAP/ISM SOCISM

B60
LENCZOWSKI G.,OIL AND STATE IN THE MIDDLE EAST. FUT IRAN LAW ECO/UNDEV EXTR/IND NAT/G TOP/EX PLAN TEC/DEV ECO/TAC LEGIT ADMIN COERCE ATTIT ALL/VALS PWR...CHARTS 20. PAGE 78 F1519
ISLAM INDUS NAT/LISM

B61
BENHAM F.,ECONOMIC AID TO UNDERDEVELOPED COUNTRIES. WOR+45 INDUS BAL/PAY ALL/VALS 20. PAGE 13 F0244
ECO/UNDEV FOR/AID INT/TRADE FINAN

B61
BRAIBANTI R.,TRADITION, VALUES AND SOCIO-ECONOMIC DEVELOPMENT. WOR+45 ACT/RES TEC/DEV ATTIT ORD/FREE CONSERVE...POLICY SOC ANTHOL. PAGE 17 F0336
ALL/VALS ECO/UNDEV CONCPT METH/CNCPT

B61
DE VRIES E.,MAN IN RAPID SOCIAL CHANGE. WOR+45 SOCIETY ECO/DEV ECO/UNDEV AGRI INDUS FAM SECT TEC/DEV ATTIT...RECORD 20 CHRISTIAN. PAGE 31 F0607
CULTURE ALL/VALS SOC TASK

S61
VALLET R.,"IRAN: KEY TO THE MIDDLE EAST." COM IRAQ ISLAM KUWAIT LEBANON SAUDI/ARAB TURKEY ELITES SOCIETY INDUS PROC/MFG POL/PAR TOP/EX PLAN BAL/PWR DIPLOM ECO/TAC ALL/VALS...TREND FOR/TRADE CENTO 20. PAGE 140 F2760
NAT/G ECO/UNDEV IRAN

B62
DE GRAZIA S.,OF TIME, WORK, AND LEISURE. USA+45 ECO/DEV WORKER HAPPINESS UTOPIA ALL/VALS...SOC NEW/IDEA TIME. PAGE 31 F0599
CULTURE LEISURE CONCPT

B62
ROBINSON A.D.,DUTCH ORGANIZED AGRICULTURE IN INTERNATIONAL POLITICS, 1945-1960. EUR+WWI NETHERLAND STRUCT ECO/DEV NAT/G VOL/ASSN CONSULT DELIB/GP PLAN TEC/DEV INT/TRADE EDU/PROP ATTIT RIGID/FLEX ALL/VALS...NEW/IDEA TREND EEC COMMUN 20. PAGE 112 F2215
AGRI INT/ORG

S62
LIPSON H.A.,"FORMAL REASONING AND MARKETING STRATEGY." ECO/DEV PROB/SOLV PRICE ALL/VALS CONT/OBS. PAGE 81 F1578
MARKET DECISION GAME ECO/TAC

S62
RAZAFIMBAHINY J.,"L'ORGANISATION AFRICAINE ET MALGACHE DE COOPERATION ECONOMIQUE." AFR ISLAM MADAGASCAR NAT/G ACT/RES ECO/TAC ALL/VALS ...TIME/SEQ 20. PAGE 110 F2158
INT/ORG ECO/UNDEV

B63
CHAMPION J.M.,CRITICAL INCIDENTS IN MANAGEMENT. MARKET LG/CO SML/CO OP/RES ADMIN CONTROL LEAD GP/REL PERS/REL COST ATTIT SUPEGO ALL/VALS...PSY PERS/TEST BIBLIOG. PAGE 23 F0445
MGT DECISION EX/STRUC INDUS

B63
KAPP W.K.,HINDU CULTURE: ECONOMIC DEVELOPMENT AND ECONOMIC PLANNING IN INDIA. INDIA S/ASIA CULTURE ECO/TAC EDU/PROP ADMIN ALL/VALS...POLICY MGT TIME/SEQ TRUE/GP VAL/FREE 20. PAGE 69 F1353
SECT ECO/UNDEV

L63
ADERBIGDE A.,"SYMPOSIUM ON WEST AFRICA
FINAN

INTEGRATION." AFR EUR+WWI FUT CULTURE SOCIETY STRATA DIST/IND INDUS MARKET SERV/IND DELIB/GP PLAN TEC/DEV DOMIN EDU/PROP LEGIT COERCE ATTIT ALL/VALS ...POLICY STAT TREND CHARTS VAL/FREE. PAGE 2 F0040
ECO/TAC REGION

L63
RIDAH A.,"LE NEO-DESTOUR DEPUIS L'INDEPENDANCE." FUT ISLAM WOR+45 ECO/UNDEV INT/ORG SCHOOL DELIB/GP TOP/EX ACT/RES EDU/PROP LEGIT ATTIT ALL/VALS 20 TUNIS. PAGE 111 F2189
NAT/G CONSTN

S63
ARDANT G.,"A PLAN FOR FULL EMPLOYMENT IN THE DEVELOPING COUNTRIES." AFR FUT WOR+45 DELIB/GP ACT/RES PLAN ECO/TAC ATTIT ALL/VALS...POLICY STAT CHARTS TUNIS VAL/FREE 20. PAGE 6 F0112
ECO/UNDEV SOCIETY MOROCCO

S63
AYAL E.B.,"VALUE SYSTEM AND ECONOMIC DEVELOPMENT IN JAPAN AND THAILAND." ASIA S/ASIA THAILAND CULTURE ECO/DEV CAP/ISM DOMIN NAT/LISM DRIVE RIGID/FLEX SOCISM...WELF/ST OBS TREND CON/ANAL GEN/LAWS TERR/GP 20 CHINJAP. PAGE 8 F0145
ECO/UNDEV ALL/VALS

S63
BARTHELEMY G.,"LE NOUVEAU FRANC (CFA) ET LA BANQUE CENTRALE DES ETATS DE L'AFRIQUE DE L'OUEST." FUT STRUCT INT/ORG PLAN ATTIT ALL/VALS FOR/TRADE 20. PAGE 11 F0200
AFR FINAN

S63
GANDOLFI A.,"LES ACCORDS DE COOPERATION EN MATIERE DE POLITIQUE ETRANGERE ENTRE LA FRANCE ET LES NOUVEAUX ETATS AFRICAINS ET." AFR ISLAM MADAGASCAR WOR+45 ECO/DEV INT/ORG NAT/G DELIB/GP ECO/TAC ALL/VALS...CON/ANAL 20. PAGE 46 F0894
VOL/ASSN ECO/UNDEV DIPLOM FRANCE

S63
LEDUC G.,"L'AIDE INTERNATIONALE AU DEVELOPPEMENT." FUT WOR+45 ECO/DEV ECO/UNDEV R+D PROF/ORG TEC/DEV ECO/TAC ROUTINE ATTIT ALL/VALS...MGT TIME/SEQ FOR/TRADE TOT/POP 20. PAGE 77 F1503
FINAN PLAN FOR/AID

B64
LI C.M.,INDUSTRIAL DEVELOPMENT IN COMMUNIST CHINA. CHINA/COM ECO/DEV ECO/UNDEV AGRI FINAN INDUS MARKET LABOR NAT/G ECO/TAC INT/TRADE EXEC ALL/VALS ...POLICY RELATIV TREND WORK TOT/POP VAL/FREE 20. PAGE 79 F1556
ASIA TEC/DEV

B64
MASON E.S.,FOREIGN AID AND FOREIGN POLICY. USA+45 AGRI INDUS NAT/G EX/STRUC ACT/RES RIGID/FLEX ALL/VALS...POLICY GEN/LAWS MARSHL/PLN ALL/PROG CONGRESS 20. PAGE 87 F1699
ECO/UNDEV ECO/TAC FOR/AID DIPLOM

B64
MELADY T.,FACES OF AFRICA. AFR FUT ISLAM NAT/G POL/PAR SCHOOL DELIB/GP PLAN ECO/TAC EDU/PROP ATTIT ALL/VALS...CHARTS TOT/POP TERR/GP VAL/FREE 20. PAGE 89 F1752
ECO/UNDEV TREND NAT/LISM

B64
ORGANIZATION AMERICAN STATES,ECONOMIC SURVEY OF LATIN AMERICA, 1962. L/A+17C AGRI DIST/IND INDUS MARKET PROC/MFG R+D PLAN TEC/DEV ECO/TAC REGION BAL/PAY ALL/VALS...CON/ANAL ORG/CHARTS GEN/METH OAS ALL/PROG 20 ALL/PROG. PAGE 102 F1998
ECO/UNDEV CHARTS

B64
PRESTHUS R.,MEN AT THE TOP; A STUDY IN COMMUNITY POWER. USA+45 STRUCT ACT/RES REPRESENT CONSEN ALL/VALS ORD/FREE...SAMP/SIZ 20. PAGE 108 F2116
PLURISM LG/CO PWR ADMIN

B64
SEERS D.,CUBA: THE ECONOMIC AND SOCIAL REVOLUTION. L/A+17C USSR YUGOSLAVIA STRATA AGRI INDUS SCHOOL DELIB/GP PLAN ECO/TAC DOMIN EDU/PROP ATTIT RIGID/FLEX ALL/VALS...STAT OBS TIME/SEQ WORK VAL/FREE 20. PAGE 119 F2341
ACT/RES COERCE CUBA REV

B64
SULLIVAN G.,THE STORY OF THE PEACE CORPS. USA+45 WOR+45 INTELL FACE/GP NAT/G SCHOOL VOL/ASSN CONSULT EX/STRUC PLAN EDU/PROP ADMIN ATTIT DRIVE ALL/VALS ...POLICY HEAL SOC CONCPT INT QU BIOG TREND SOC/EXP WORK. PAGE 127 F2511
INT/ORG ECO/UNDEV FOR/AID PEACE

L64
ARMENGALD A.,"ECONOMIE ET COEXISTENCE." COM EUR+WWI FUT USA+45 WOR+45 ECO/DEV ECO/UNDEV FINAN INT/ORG NAT/G EXEC CHOOSE ATTIT ALL/VALS...POLICY RELATIV DECISION TREND SOC/EXP WORK 20. PAGE 6 F0113
MARKET ECO/TAC AFR CAP/ISM

S64
FLORINSKY M.T.,"TRENDS IN THE SOVIET ECONOMY." COM USA+45 USSR INDUS LABOR NAT/G PLAN TEC/DEV ECO/TAC ALL/VALS SOCISM...MGT METH/CNCPT STYLE CON/ANAL GEN/METH WORK 20. PAGE 42 F0817
ECO/DEV AGRI

S64
NASH M.,"SOCIAL PREREQUISITES TO ECONOMIC GROWTH IN LATIN AMERICA AND SOUTHEAST ASIA." L/A+17C S/ASIA CULTURE SOCIETY ECO/UNDEV AGRI INDUS NAT/G PLAN TEC/DEV EDU/PROP ROUTINE ALL/VALS...POLICY RELATIV SOC NAT/COMP WORK TOT/POP 20. PAGE 96 F1894
ECO/DEV PERCEPT

B65
FERMAN L.A.,POVERTY IN AMERICA: A BOOK OF READINGS. USA+45 CULTURE ECO/DEV PROB/SOLV ALL/VALS...POLICY ANTHOL BIBLIOG 20 POVRTY/WAR. PAGE 40 F0785
WEALTH TEC/DEV CONCPT RECEIVE

B66
GORDON R.A.,PROSPERITY AND UNEMPLOYMENT. USA+45 PLAN ECO/TAC ADJUST DEMAND ALL/VALS...POLICY DECISION TREND CHARTS ANTHOL 20. PAGE 49 F0961
WORKER INDUS ECO/DEV WEALTH

B67
KAPLAN J.J.,CHALLENGE OF FOREIGN AID. USA+45 CONTROL BAL/PAY COST ATTIT ALL/VALS...METH/COMP 20. PAGE 69 F1352
FOR/AID PLAN GIVE POLICY

B67
PETRO S.,THE KINGSPORT STRIKE. USA+45 PROC/MFG NAT/G JUDGE PRESS PARTIC PERS/REL...OLD/LIB OBS INT 20 NLRB. PAGE 105 F2074
LABOR COERCE SANCTION ALL/VALS

B67
PIKE F.B.,FREEDOM AND REFORM IN LATIN AMERICA. BRAZIL URUGUAY CONSTN CULTURE SECT DIPLOM EDU/PROP PARTIC DRIVE ALL/VALS CATHISM...GEOG ANTHOL BIBLIOG REFORMERS BOLIV. PAGE 106 F2086
L/A+17C ORD/FREE ECO/UNDEV REV

B67
WILLIAMS E.J.,LATIN AMERICAN CHRISTIAN DEMOCRATIC PARTIES. L/A+17C FAM LABOR FORCES...CATH TREND BIBLIOG 20. PAGE 147 F2890
POL/PAR GP/COMP CATHISM ALL/VALS

B67
WILLS A.J.,AN INTRODUCTION TO THE HISTORY OF CENTRAL AFRICA. RHODESIA ZAMBIA CULTURE SOCIETY ECO/UNDEV TEC/DEV DOMIN WAR ALL/VALS...POLICY TREND BIBLIOG T 14/20 NYASALAND. PAGE 147 F2899
AFR COLONIAL ORD/FREE

S67
FRANKLIN N.N.,"THE CONCEPT AND MEASUREMENT OF 'MINIMUM LIVING STANDARDS'." UNIV OP/RES PAY INGP/REL DEMAND INCOME DRIVE WEALTH...SOC CHARTS METH/COMP. PAGE 43 F0849
CONCPT PHIL/SCI ALL/VALS HAPPINESS

S67
LASLETT J.H.M.,"SOCIALISM AND THE AMERICAN LABOR MOVEMENT* SOME NEW REFLECTIONS." USA-45 VOL/ASSN LOBBY PARTIC CENTRAL ALL/VALS SOCISM...GP/COMP 20. PAGE 76 F1484
LABOR ROUTINE ATTIT GP/REL

S67
WEISSKOPF W.A.,"THE DIALECTICS OF ABUNDANCE." UNIV CAP/ISM ATTIT MARXISM...CONCPT 20. PAGE 145 F2853
INDUS SOCIETY IDEA/COMP ALL/VALS

ALLEN C.L. F0073

ALLEN G. F0069

ALLEN R.G. F0070

ALLEN R.L. F0071,F0072

ALLEN R.V. F0032

ALLEN W.R. F0073,F0074

ALLIANCE FOR PROGRESS....SEE ALL/PROG

ALLIANCES, MILITARY....SEE FORCES+INT/REL

ALLISON D. F0075

ALNASRAWI A. F0076

ALONSO W. F0863

ALPANDER G.G. F0077

ALPERT P. F0078,F0079

ALTMAN G.T. F0080

ALTO/ADIGE....ALTO-ADIGE REGION OF ITALY

ALVES V. F0081

AM/LEGION....AMERICAN LEGION

AMA....AMERICAN MEDICAL ASSOCIATION

AMBITION....SEE DRIVE

AMEND/I....CONCERNED WITH FREEDOMS GRANTED IN THE FIRST AMENDMENT

B46
ERNST M.L.,THE FIRST FREEDOM. USA-45 CONSTN PRESS PRIVIL...CHARTS IDEA/COMP BIBLIOG 20 AMEND/I. PAGE 38 F0746
EDU/PROP COM/IND ORD/FREE

CONTROL

AMEND/IV....CONCERNED WITH FREEDOMS GRANTED IN THE FOURTH AMENDMENT

AMEND/V....CONCERNED WITH FREEDOMS GRANTED IN THE FIFTH AMENDMENT

AMEND/VI....CONCERNED WITH FREEDOMS GRANTED IN THE SIXTH AMENDMENT

AMEND/XIV....CONCERNED WITH FREEDOMS GRANTED IN THE FOURTEENTH AMENDMENT

AMER ENTERPRISE INST FOR PUBL F0082

AMER ENTERPRISE INST PUB POL F0083

AMERASINGHE C.F. F0084

AMERICAN BAR ASSOCIATION....SEE ABA

AMERICAN FARM BUREAU FEDERATION....SEE FARM/BUR

AMERICAN FEDERATION OF LABOR, CONGRESS OF INDUSTRIAL ORGANIZATIONS....SEE AFL/CIO, LABOR

AMERICAN INDIANS....SEE INDIAN/AM

AMERICAN LEGION....SEE AM/LEGION

AMERICAN POLITICAL SCIENCE ASSOCIATION....SEE APSA

AMERICAN TELEPHONE AND TELEGRAPH....SEE AT+T

AMERICAN ASSEMBLY COLUMBIA U F0085

AMERICAN ECONOMIC ASSOCIATION F0086,F0087

AMERICAN ECONOMIC REVIEW F0088

AMERICAN FOREST PRODUCTS INDUS F0089

AMERICAN MANAGEMENT ASSN F0090

AMERICAN U BEIRUT ECO RES INST F0091

AMERICAS, PRE/EUROPEAN....SEE PRE/AMER

AMMAN/MAX....MAX AMMAN

ANARCH....ANARCHISM; SEE ALSO ATTIT, VALUES INDEX

B13
KROPOTKIN P.,THE CONQUEST OF BREAD. SOCIETY STRATA AGRI INDUS WORKER REV HAPPINESS INCOME PRODUC HEALTH MORAL ORD/FREE. PAGE 74 F1444
ANARCH SOCIALIST OWN AGREE

B22
FOURIER C.,TRAITE DE L'ASSOCIATION DOMESTIQUE-AGRICOLE (2 VOLS.). UNIV SOCIETY INDUS ECO/TAC PERSON MORAL ANARCH. PAGE 43 F0834
VOL/ASSN AGRI UTOPIA CONCPT

B50
SOREL G.,REFLECTIONS ON VIOLENCE (1908) (TRANS. BY T.E. HULME AND J. ROTH). UNIV SOCIETY LABOR UTOPIA MORAL SOCISM...ANARCH SOCIALIST CONCPT 20. PAGE 124 F2445
COERCE REV WORKER MYTH

B76
PROUDHON P.J.,WHAT IS PROPERTY? (TRANS. BY B.R. TUCKER). SOCIETY AGRI CAP/ISM CRIME GP/REL PERSON MORAL ORD/FREE WEALTH. PAGE 108 F2127
OWN WORKER PRODUC ANARCH

ANARCHISM....SEE ANARCH

ANCIENT GREECE....SEE GREECE/ANC

ANDALUSIA....SEE ALSO SPAIN

ANDERSON C.A. F0092

ANDERSON C.W. F0093,F0094,F0928

ANDERSON J. F0095

ANDERSON J.E. F0096

ANDERSON S.S. F0097

ANDERSON S.V. F0098

ANDERSON T. F0099

ANDORRA....SEE ALSO APPROPRIATE TIME/SPACE/CULTURE INDEX

ANDRESKI S. F0100

ANDREWS F.E. F0101,F1092

ANDREWS R.B. F0102,F0103

ANGELL J.W. F0104

ANGERS F.A. F0105

ANGLO/SAX....ANGLO-SAXON

ANGOLA....ANGOLA

S67
WILSON C.E.,"AMERICAN INVESTMENT IN PORTUGUESE AFRICA: A PROBLEM OF "DEMOCRATIC" COLONIALISM." AFR ECO/UNDEV DIPLOM MORAL...IDEA/COMP 20 ANGOLA MOZAMBIQUE. PAGE 147 F2901
COLONIAL DOMIN ORD/FREE POLICY

ANNEXATION....ANNEXATION

ANOMIE....GENERALIZED PERSONAL ANXIETY; SEE DISPL

B29
DE MAN H.,JOY IN WORK. STRATA ECO/DEV ECO/TAC PRODUC ANOMIE ROLE SOCISM...IDEA/COMP 20. PAGE 31 F0605
SOC WORKER HAPPINESS RESPECT

B48
MILLS C.W.,THE NEW MEN OF POWER. ELITES INTELL STRUCT WORKER ANOMIE ATTIT PWR POLICY. PAGE 92 F1799
LABOR LEAD PLAN

B62
LEVENSTEIN A.,WHY PEOPLE WORK; CHANGING INCENTIVES IN A TROUBLED WORLD. USA+45 SOCIETY PROB/SOLV TEC/DEV EDU/PROP ADJUST...CENSUS BIBLIOG 20. PAGE 79 F1538
DRIVE WORKER ECO/DEV ANOMIE

B62
MCCLELLAN J.L.,CRIME WITHOUT PUNISHMENT. USA+45 LAW SOCIETY DELIB/GP TRIBUTE CONTROL LOBBY COERCE GP/REL ANOMIE MORAL...CRIMLGY 20 CONGRESS HOFFA/J. PAGE 88 F1718
CRIME ACT/RES LABOR PWR

B64
SULTAN P.E.,THE DISENCHANTED UNIONIST. NAT/G ADJUD CONTROL SANCTION RACE/REL ANOMIE ATTIT ROLE ...METH/CNCPT INT. PAGE 127 F2512
LABOR INGP/REL CHARTS MAJORIT

B67
CHO S.S.,KOREA IN WORLD POLITICS 1940-1950; AN EVALUATION OF AMERICAN RESPONSIBILITY. KOREA USA+45 USSR CONSTN INT/ORG NAT/G FORCES FOR/AID ANOMIE SUPEGO MARXISM...DECISION BIBLIOG 20. PAGE 24 F0469
POLICY DIPLOM PROB/SOLV WAR

L67
AUSTIN D.A.,"POLITICAL CONFLICT IN AFRICA." CONSTN NAT/G CREATE ADMIN COLONIAL ORD/FREE MARXISM POPULISM SOCISM...NAT/COMP ANTHOL 20. PAGE 8 F0141
ANOMIE AFR POL/PAR

S67
LEVIN T.,"PSYCHOANALYSIS AND SOCIAL CHANGE." SOCIETY ANOMIE DRIVE PWR 20. PAGE 79 F1541
PSY PHIL/SCI ADJUST WEALTH

ANSHEN M. F0106

ANTHOL....ANTHOLOGY, SYMPOSIUM, PANEL OF WRITERS

N19
BUSINESS ECONOMISTS' GROUP,INCOME POLICIES (PAMPHLET). UK INDUS LABOR TOP/EX PAY COST PRODUC ...ECOMETRIC GOV/COMP SIMUL ANTHOL 20. PAGE 20 F0395
INCOME WORKER WEALTH POLICY

N19
HUBERMAN L.,SOCIALISM IS THE ONLY ANSWER (PAMPHLET). CREATE ECO/TAC EDU/PROP CONTROL ...SOCIALIST GEN/LAWS ANTHOL 20. PAGE 62 F1230
SOCISM ECO/DEV CAP/ISM PLAN

B28
CASSEL G.,FOREIGN INVESTMENTS. GERMANY UK USA-45 WOR-45 ECO/DEV NAT/G VOL/ASSN CAP/ISM REPAR ATTIT WEALTH...METH/CNCPT STAT SIMUL STERTYP ANTHOL FOR/TRADE TOT/POP VAL/FREE 20. PAGE 22 F0426
FINAN ECO/TAC BAL/PAY

B37
MACKENZIE F.,PLANNED SOCIETY: YESTERDAY, TODAY, AND TOMORROW. ECO/DEV ECO/UNDEV AGRI FINAN INDUS PLAN INSPECT CONTROL ALL/IDEOS...TREND METH/COMP BIBLIOG 20 RESOURCE/N. PAGE 83 F1635
SOC CONCPT ANTHOL

B39
MARQUAND H.A.,ORGANIZED LABOUR IN FOUR CONTINENTS. EUR+WWI USA-45 INDUS NAT/G PAY GP/REL TOTALISM
LABOR WORKER

ATTIT WEALTH ALL/IDEOS...TREND NAT/COMP 20 ILO AFL/CIO EUROPE CHINJAP MEXIC/AMER. PAGE 85 F1673
CONCPT ANTHOL

B44
FABIAN SOCIETY,CAN PLANNING BE DEMOCRATIC? UK CULTURE INDUS NAT/G BUDGET ORD/FREE...GEN/LAWS ANTHOL 20. PAGE 39 F0757
PLAN MAJORIT SOCIALIST ECO/DEV

B50
MARX H.L.,THE WELFARE STATE. USA+45 USA-45 CHIEF CAP/ISM CENTRAL ORD/FREE LAISSEZ...SOC ANTHOL 20. PAGE 86 F1686
ECO/DEV INDUS WEALTH WELF/ST

B51
POOLE K.,FISCAL POLICIES AND THE AMERICAN ECONOMY. AFR ECO/DEV FINAN INDUS WORKER OP/RES INT/TRADE TAX COST INCOME PROFIT WEALTH...GP/COMP 20. PAGE 107 F2102
NAT/G POLICY ANTHOL

B53
MILLIKAN M.F.,INCOME STABILIZATION FOR A DEVELOPING DEMOCRACY. USA+45 ECO/DEV LABOR BUDGET ECO/TAC TAX ADMIN ADJUST PRODUC WEALTH...POLICY TREND 20. PAGE 91 F1794
ANTHOL MARKET EQUILIB EFFICIENCY

B53
SCHLEIFFER H.,INDEX TO ECONOMIC HISTORY ESSAYS IN FESTSCHRIFTEN (PAMPHLET). WOR+45 WOR-45...CONCPT IDEA/COMP ANTHOL. PAGE 117 F2299
BIBLIOG NAT/G

B54
FRIEDMAN W.,THE PUBLIC CORPORATION: A COMPARATIVE SYMPOSIUM (UNIVERSITY OF TORONTO SCHOOL OF LAW COMPARATIVE LAW SERIES, VOL. I). AFR SWEDEN USA+45 INDUS INT/ORG NAT/G REGION CENTRAL FEDERAL...POLICY JURID IDEA/COMP NAT/COMP ANTHOL 20 MONOPOLY EUROPE. PAGE 44 F0861
LAW SOCISM LG/CO OWN

B54
HAYEK FA V.O.N.,CAPITALISM AND THE HISTORIANS. MOD/EUR TEC/DEV GP/REL WEALTH...HIST/WRIT ANTHOL 19. PAGE 57 F1124
CAP/ISM LABOR STRATA ECO/TAC

B56
ATOMIC INDUSTRIAL FORUM,PUBLIC RELATIONS FOR THE ATOMIC INDUSTRY. WOR+45 PLAN PROB/SOLV EDU/PROP PRESS CONFER...AUD/VIS ANTHOL 20. PAGE 7 F0135
NUC/PWR INDUS GP/REL ATTIT

B56
US LIBRARY OF CONGRESS,UNITED STATES DIRECT ECONOMIC AID TO FOREIGN COUNTRIES: A COLLECTION OF EXCERPTS AND A BIBLIOGRAPHY (PAMPHLET). USA+45 PRESS DEBATE...ANTHOL BIBLIOG/A CONGRESS. PAGE 138 F2716
FOR/AID POLICY DIPLOM ECO/UNDEV

B57
DUNLOP J.T.,THE THEORY OF WAGE DETERMINATION; PROCEEDINGS OF CONFERENCE HELD BY INTERNATIONAL ECONOMIC ASSOCIATION. AFR ECO/DEV LABOR BARGAIN PAY CONFER...CHARTS ANTHOL 20. PAGE 35 F0679
PRICE WORKER GEN/LAWS INCOME

B58
ATOMIC INDUSTRIAL FORUM,MANAGEMENT AND ATOMIC ENERGY. WOR+45 SEA LAW MARKET NAT/G TEC/DEV INSPECT INT/TRADE CONFER PEACE HEALTH...ANTHOL 20. PAGE 7 F0136
NUC/PWR INDUS MGT ECO/TAC

B58
CLAUNCH J.M.,THE PROBLEM OF GOVERNMENT IN METROPOLITAN AREAS. CULTURE INDUS POL/PAR PLAN REGION GP/REL...CENSUS ANTHOL MUNICH 20. PAGE 25 F0486
PROB/SOLV SOC

B58
JACOBSSON P.,SOME MONETARY PROBLEMS, INTERNATIONAL AND NATIONAL. WOR+45 WOR-45 ECO/DEV FORCES WORKER PROB/SOLV DIPLOM INT/TRADE...ANTHOL 20. PAGE 66 F1299
FINAN PLAN ECO/TAC NAT/COMP

B58
MOONEY R.E.,INFLATION AND RECESSION? AFR USA+45 LABOR LG/CO PRESS LEAD...IDEA/COMP ANTHOL 20. PAGE 93 F1821
PRICE ECO/TAC NAT/G PRODUC

B58
MUSGRAVE R.A.,CLASSICS IN THE THEORY OF PUBLIC FINANCE. UNIV MARKET LG/CO NAT/G CAP/ISM PRICE OPTIMAL...IDEA/COMP ANTHOL 19/20 SAY/EMIL EDGEWORTH LINDAHL/E RITSCHL/H. PAGE 95 F1870
TAX FINAN ECO/TAC GP/REL

B58
OEEC,THE INDUSTRIAL CHALLENGE OF NUCLEAR ENERGY. EUR+WWI ECO/DEV INDUS OP/RES CONFER RISK PWR ...AUD/VIS CHARTS ANTHOL 20 OEEC. PAGE 101 F1977
NUC/PWR ACT/RES ECO/TAC INT/ORG

B58
PALMER E.E.,INDUSTRIAL MAN. USA+45 PERSON ORD/FREE POPULISM...PREDICT TREND ANTHOL 20. PAGE 103 F2020
INDUS ECO/UNDEV CULTURE WEALTH

B58
PALMER E.E.,THE ECONOMY AND THE DEMOCRATIC IDEAL. USA+45 USA-45 STRATA CHIEF CT/SYS ORD/FREE SOCISM ...MAJORIT CONCPT ANTHOL 18/20 PRESIDENT. PAGE 103 F2021
ECO/DEV POPULISM METH/COMP ECO/TAC

B58
US CONGRESS JOINT ECO COMM,THE RELATIONSHIP OF PRICES TO ECONOMIC STABILITY AND GROWTH. USA+45 MARKET TAX ADJUST COST DEMAND INCOME PRODUC ...POLICY TREND CHARTS ANTHOL 20 CONGRESS. PAGE 134 F2650
ECO/DEV PLAN EQUILIB PRICE

B58
WOODS H.D.,PATTERNS OF INDUSTRIAL DISPUTE SETTLEMENT IN FIVE CANADIAN INDUSTRIES. CANADA USA+45 CONSULT ADJUD GP/REL...JURID GOV/COMP METH/COMP ANTHOL 20. PAGE 148 F2923
BARGAIN INDUS LABOR NAT/G

B59
ALLEN W.R.,FOREIGN TRADE AND FINANCE. ECO/DEV DIPLOM BAL/PAY...POLICY CONCPT ANTHOL 20. PAGE 4 F0073
INT/TRADE EQUILIB FINAN

B59
HENDEL S.,THE SOVIET CRUCIBLE. USSR LEAD COERCE NAT/LISM UTOPIA PWR...POLICY CONCPT ANTHOL 20 STALIN/J LENIN/VI MARX/KARL BOLSHEVIK. PAGE 58 F1147
COM MARXISM REV TOTALISM

B59
MAYER H.M.,READINGS IN URBAN GEOGRAPHY. WOR+45 SOCIETY DIST/IND INDUS MARKET HABITAT...CLASSIF CENSUS CHARTS ANTHOL MUNICH 20 WATER. PAGE 87 F1706
GEOG STRUCT

B59
MEYER A.J.,MIDDLE EASTERN CAPITALISM: NINE ESSAYS. ISLAM CULTURE ECO/UNDEV INDUS MARKET NAT/G PLAN ATTIT RIGID/FLEX...STAT OBS TREND GEN/LAWS. PAGE 90 F1767
TEC/DEV ECO/TAC ANTHOL

B59
NORTON P.L.,URBAN PROBLEMS AND TECHNIQUES. AIR AGRI INDUS MARKET TEC/DEV BUDGET LEISURE ALL/VALS ...ANTHOL MUNICH 20 URBAN/RNWL. PAGE 99 F1936
PLAN LOC/G HABITAT

B59
STANFORD U, BOARD OF TRUSTEES,THE ALLOCATION OF ECONOMIC RESOURCES. WORKER PLAN BUDGET ECO/TAC TAX RECEIVE COST PRODUC...POLICY IDEA/COMP SIMUL ANTHOL 20. PAGE 125 F2468
INCOME PRICE FINAN

B59
THE BROOKINGS INSTITUTION,ECONOMICS AND THE POLICY MAKER. USA+45 CREATE...ANTHOL 20. PAGE 129 F2549
ELITES ECO/TAC PROB/SOLV ECO/DEV

B59
U OF MICHIGAN LAW SCHOOL,ATOMS AND THE LAW. USA+45 PROVS WORKER PROB/SOLV DIPLOM ADMIN GOV/REL ANTHOL. PAGE 132 F2596
NUC/PWR NAT/G CONTROL LAW

B60
ATOMIC INDUSTRIAL FORUM,ATOMS FOR INDUSTRY: WORLD FORUM. WOR+45 FINAN COST UTIL...JURID ANTHOL 20. PAGE 7 F0137
NUC/PWR INDUS PLAN PROB/SOLV

B60
HARBERGER A.C.,THE DEMAND FOR DURABLE GOODS. AGRI FINAN COST EQUILIB...MATH STAT TIME/SEQ TREND CON/ANAL CHARTS SIMUL ANTHOL 20. PAGE 55 F1072
ECOMETRIC DEMAND PRICE

B60
PENTONY D.E.,UNITED STATES FOREIGN AID. INDIA LAOS USA+45 ECO/UNDEV INT/TRADE ADMIN PEACE ATTIT ...POLICY METH/COMP ANTHOL 20. PAGE 105 F2060
FOR/AID DIPLOM ECO/TAC

B60
PFOUTS R.W.,THE TECHNIQUES OF URBAN ECONOMIC ANALYSIS. USA+45...ECOMETRIC CONCPT CHARTS IDEA/COMP ANTHOL MUNICH 20. PAGE 106 F2078
METH ECO/DEV METH/COMP

B60
SAKAI R.K.,STUDIES ON ASIA, 1960. ASIA CHINA/COM S/ASIA COM/IND ECO/TAC...ANTHOL 17/20 MALAYA. PAGE 115 F2270
ECO/UNDEV SOC

B60
SHANNON D.A.,THE GREAT DEPRESSION. USA-45 FINAN LG/CO SCHOOL SML/CO DELIB/GP RECEIVE REV EATING INCOME...ANTHOL MUNICH 20 ROOSEVLT/F CONGRESS. PAGE 120 F2365
WEALTH NAT/G AGRI INDUS

B60
STEVENSON A.E.,PUTTING FIRST THINGS FIRST. USA+45 INT/ORG NEIGH FOR/AID DISCRIM...ANTHOL 20. PAGE 126 F2483
DIPLOM ECO/UNDEV ORD/FREE EDU/PROP

B61
MEXICO; CINCUENTA ANOS DE REVOLUCION VOL. II. L/A+17C SOCIETY LABOR RECEIVE GP/REL AGE/Y HEALTH ...SOC/WK ANTHOL MUNICH 20 MEXIC/AMER. PAGE 1 F0014
ECO/UNDEV STRUCT INDUS POL/PAR

B61
ALFRED H.,PUBLIC OWNERSHIP IN THE USA: GOALS AND PRIORITIES. LAW INDUS INT/TRADE ADJUD GOV/REL EFFICIENCY PEACE SOCISM...POLICY ANTHOL 20 TVA. PAGE 4 F0065
CONTROL OWN ECO/DEV ECO/TAC

B61
BRAIBANTI R.,TRADITION, VALUES AND SOCIO-ECONOMIC DEVELOPMENT. WOR+45 ACT/RES TEC/DEV ATTIT ORD/FREE CONSERVE...POLICY SOC ANTHOL. PAGE 17 F0336
ALL/VALS ECO/UNDEV CONCPT METH/CNCPT

B61
ELLIS H.S.,ECONOMIC DEVELOPMENT FOR LATIN AMERICA. L/A+17C AGRI FINAN INDUS FOR/AID GP/REL BAL/PAY DEMAND...ANTHOL 20 INTL/ECON. PAGE 37 F0723
ECO/UNDEV ECO/TAC PLAN

INT/TRADE
B61

GARDNER R.N.,LEGAL-ECONOMIC PROBLEMS OF INTERNATIONAL TRADE. FUT WOR+45 INTELL ECO/DEV EX/STRUC INT/TRADE ROUTINE ATTIT WEALTH...GEN/LAWS ANTHOL FOR/TRADE 20. PAGE 46 F0904 FINAN ACT/RES
B61

GREY A.L.,ECONOMIC ISSUES AND POLICIES; READINGS IN INTRODUCTORY ECONOMICS (2ND ED.). WOR+45 ECO/UNDEV FINAN MARKET LABOR LG/CO INT/TRADE BAL/PAY WEALTH ...ANTHOL T. PAGE 51 F0996 ECO/TAC PROB/SOLV METH/COMP
B61

HARRIS S.E.,THE DOLLAR IN CRISIS. AFR USA+45 MARKET INT/ORG ECO/TAC PRICE CONTROL WEALTH...METH/COMP ANTHOL 20. PAGE 55 F1089 BAL/PAY DIPLOM FINAN INT/TRADE
B61

HICKS U.K.,FEDERALISM AND ECONOMIC GROWTH IN UNDERDEVELOPED COUNTRIES. WOR+45 WOR-45 FINAN NAT/G PLAN BUDGET DIPLOM INT/TRADE DEMAND WEALTH...ANTHOL 20. PAGE 59 F1167 ECO/UNDEV ECO/TAC FEDERAL CONSTN
B61

SAKAI R.K.,STUDIES ON ASIA, 1961. ASIA BURMA INDIA S/ASIA FINAN ECO/TAC NAT/LISM SOCISM...POLICY ANTHOL 19/20 CHINJAP. PAGE 115 F2271 ECO/UNDEV SECT
B61

UNIVS-NATL BUR COMM ECO RES,PUBLIC FINANCES: NEEDS, SOURCES, AND UTILIZATION. USA+45 FORCES PLAN TAX CONFER PRICE FEDERAL UTIL...ANTHOL MUNICH 20. PAGE 133 F2623 NAT/G FINAN DECISION BUDGET
B61

WRIGHT H.M.,THE "NEW IMPERIALISM": ANALYSIS OF LATE NINETEENTH-CENTURY EXPANSION. MOD/EUR WOR-45 SOCIETY FINAN ECO/TAC INT/TRADE NAT/LISM...ANTHOL BIBLIOG/A 19. PAGE 149 F2933 HIST/WRIT IDEA/COMP COLONIAL DOMIN
B62

ROUND TABLE ON EUROPE'S ROLE IN LATIN AMERICAN DEVELOPMENT. EUR+WWI L/A+17C PLAN BAL/PAY UTIL ROLE WEALTH...CHARTS ANTHOL 20 UN INT/AM/DEV. PAGE 1 F0017 ECO/UNDEV FINAN TEC/DEV FOR/AID
B62

BROOKINGS INSTITUTION,DEVELOPMENT OF THE EMERGING COUNTRIES; AN AGENDA FOR RESEARCH. WOR+45 AGRI TEC/DEV FOR/AID EDU/PROP ADJUST HABITAT KNOWL...PSY SOC ANTHOL 20 THIRD/WRLD. PAGE 19 F0362 ECO/UNDEV R+D SOCIETY PROB/SOLV
B62

BROWN S.D.,STUDIES ON ASIA, 1962. ASIA BURMA INDIA ISLAM ISRAEL S/ASIA ECO/UNDEV POL/PAR SECT ECO/TAC ...ANTHOL 20 CHINJAP. PAGE 19 F0374 PWR PARL/PROC
B62

BRUMBERG A.,RUSSIA UNDER KHRUSHCHEV. FUT USSR SOCIETY ECO/DEV AGRI PERF/ART WORKER PWR...SOC ANTHOL 20 KHRUSH/N. PAGE 20 F0377 COM MARXISM NAT/G CHIEF
B62

GEARY R.C.,EUROPE'S FUTURE IN FIGURES. FUT GOV/REL DEMAND PRODUC...STAT CHARTS METH/COMP ANTHOL METH 20 EUROPE. PAGE 47 F0912 FINAN ECO/DEV PREDICT WEALTH
B62

HATTERY L.H.,INFORMATION RETRIEVAL MANAGEMENT. CLIENT INDUS TOP/EX COMPUTER OP/RES TEC/DEV ROUTINE COST EFFICIENCY RIGID/FLEX...METH/COMP ANTHOL 20. PAGE 57 F1113 R+D COMPUT/IR MGT CREATE
B62

KUHN T.E.,PUBLIC ENTERPRISES, PROJECT PLANNING AND ECONOMIC DEVELOPMENT (PAMPHLET). ECO/UNDEV FINAN PLAN ADMIN EFFICIENCY OWN...MGT STAT CHARTS ANTHOL 20. PAGE 74 F1447 ECO/DEV ECO/TAC LG/CO NAT/G
B62

LITWACK L.,THE AMERICAN LABOR MOVEMENT. USA-45 NAT/G CREATE TEC/DEV CAP/ISM ECO/TAC ADJUD AUTOMAT SKILL...TREND ANTHOL 19/20. PAGE 81 F1588 INDUS LABOR GP/REL METH/COMP
B62

PHELPS E.S.,THE GOAL OF ECONOMIC GROWTH: SOURCES, COSTS, BENEFITS. USA+45 USSR FINAN TAX CONTROL DEMAND WEALTH...POLICY NAT/COMP ANTHOL BIBLIOG 20. PAGE 106 F2079 ECO/TAC ECO/DEV NAT/G FUT
B62

UNIVERSITY OF TENNESSEE,GOVERNMENT AND WORLD CRISIS. USA+45 FOR/AID ORD/FREE...ANTHOL 20 UN ALL/PROG. PAGE 133 F2622 ECO/DEV DIPLOM NAT/G INT/ORG
L62

ERDMANN H.H.,"ADMINISTRATIVE LAW AND FARM ECONOMICS." USA+45 LOC/G NAT/G PLAN PROB/SOLV LOBBY ...DECISION ANTHOL 20. PAGE 38 F0744 AGRI ADMIN ADJUD POLICY
L62

SCHULTZ T.W.,"INVESTMENT IN HUMAN BEINGS." ECO/DEV ECO/TAC CONFER COST INCOME PRODUC HEALTH...GEOG ANTHOL. PAGE 117 F2315 FINAN WORKER EDU/PROP SKILL
B63

ABSHIRE D.M.,NATIONAL SECURITY: POLITICAL, MILITARY, AND ECONOMIC STRATEGIES IN THE DECADE AHEAD. ASIA COM USA+45 WOR+45 ECO/DEV ECO/UNDEV INT/ORG DELIB/GP FORCES ECO/TAC COERCE ATTIT RIGID/FLEX HEALTH ORD/FREE PWR WEALTH...POLICY STAT CHARTS ANTHOL COLD/WAR VAL/FREE APP/SCI. PAGE 2 F0032 FUT ACT/RES BAL/PWR
B63

BERGSON A.,ECONOMIC TRENDS IN THE SOVIET UNION. USSR ECO/UNDEV AGRI NAT/G FORCES PLAN TEC/DEV INT/TRADE BAL/PAY...POLICY ANTHOL 20. PAGE 14 F0259 ECO/DEV NAT/COMP INDUS LABOR
B63

BOWIE R.R.,GOVERNMENT REGULATION OF BUSINESS: CASES FROM THE NATIONAL REPORTER SYSTEM. USA+45 USA-45 NAT/G ECO/TAC ADJUD...ANTHOL 19/20 SUPREME/CT FTC FAIR/LABOR MONOPOLY. PAGE 17 F0331 LAW CONTROL INDUS CT/SYS
B63

CENTRO ESTUDIOS MONETARIOS LAT,COOPERACION FINANCIERA EN AMERICA LATINA. L/A+17C PLAN PROB/SOLV CONTROL REGION DEMAND...POLICY ANTHOL 20. PAGE 22 F0433 ECO/UNDEV INT/TRADE MARKET FINAN
B63

CLARK J.J.,BUSINESS FLUCTUATIONS, GROWTH, AND ECONOMIC STABILIZATION. USA+45 FINAN INT/TRADE OPTIMAL...METH/CNCPT ANTHOL BIBLIOG 20. PAGE 25 F0479 CAP/ISM ECO/TAC EQUILIB POLICY
B63

COLUMBIA U SCHOOL OF LAW,PUBLIC INTERNATIONAL DEVELOPMENT FINANCING IN SENEGAL. SENEGAL FINAN DELIB/GP GIVE EFFICIENCY...CHARTS GOV/COMP ANTHOL 20. PAGE 26 F0511 FOR/AID PLAN RECEIVE ECO/UNDEV
B63

DE VRIES E.,SOCIAL ASPECTS OF ECONOMIC DEVELOPMENT IN LATIN AMERICA. CULTURE SOCIETY STRATA FINAN INDUS INT/ORG DELIB/GP ACT/RES ECO/TAC EDU/PROP ADMIN ATTIT SUPEGO HEALTH KNOWL ORD/FREE...SOC STAT TREND ANTHOL TOT/POP VAL/FREE. PAGE 31 F0608 L/A+17C ECO/UNDEV
B63

ERHARD L.,THE ECONOMICS OF SUCCESS. GERMANY/W WOR+45 LABOR CHIEF TAX REGION COST DEMAND ANTHOL. PAGE 38 F0745 ECO/DEV INT/TRADE PLAN DIPLOM
B63

GRUBEL H.G.,WORLD MONETARY REFORM: PLANS AND ISSUES. FUT WOR+45 ECO/DEV ECO/UNDEV R+D DELIB/GP CREATE ECO/TAC ATTIT RIGID/FLEX WEALTH...STAT ANTHOL VAL/FREE 20. PAGE 52 F1009 FINAN INT/ORG BAL/PAY INT/TRADE
B63

HAUSMAN W.H.,MANAGING ECONOMIC DEVELOPMENT IN AFRICA. AFR USA+45 LAW FINAN WORKER TEC/DEV WEALTH ...ANTHOL 20. PAGE 57 F1116 ECO/UNDEV PLAN FOR/AID MGT
B63

LAIRD R.D.,SOVIET AGRICULTURAL AND PEASANT AFFAIRS. FUT STRATA LOC/G DELIB/GP ACT/RES TEC/DEV ECO/TAC EDU/PROP ATTIT RIGID/FLEX ORD/FREE SKILL WEALTH ...STAT CON/ANAL ANTHOL MUNICH WORK VAL/FREE 20. PAGE 74 F1461 COM AGRI POLICY
B63

MEEK R.L.,THE ECONOMICS OF PHYSIOCRACY. FRANCE UK AGRI FINAN WORKER CAP/ISM TAX DEMAND EQUILIB INCOME HABITAT...CHARTS ANTHOL 17. PAGE 89 F1744 PRODUC WEALTH MARKET
B63

SHANKS M.,THE LESSONS OF PUBLIC ENTERPRISE. UK LEGIS WORKER ECO/TAC ADMIN PARL/PROC GOV/REL ATTIT ...POLICY MGT METH/COMP NAT/COMP ANTHOL 20 PARLIAMENT. PAGE 120 F2364 SOCISM OWN NAT/G INDUS
B63

VELEZ GARCIA J.,DEVALUACION 1962; HISTORIA DOCUMENTAL DE UN PROCESO ECONOMICO. AFR L/A+17C USA+45 FINAN FOR/AID PRODUC WEALTH...POLICY STAT CHARTS ANTHOL 20 COLOMB. PAGE 141 F2774 ECO/UNDEV ECO/TAC PLAN NAT/G
L63

NASH M.,"PSYCHO-CULTURAL FACTORS IN ASIAN ECONOMIC GROWTH." ASIA ISLAM S/ASIA CULTURE ECO/UNDEV DELIB/GP EDU/PROP COERCE ATTIT PERSON HEALTH KNOWL ORD/FREE...PSY SOC STAT TREND ANTHOL VAL/FREE 20. PAGE 96 F1893 SOCIETY ECO/TAC
B64

BALASSA B.,CHANGING PATTERNS IN FOREIGN TRADE AND PAYMENTS. AFR USA+45 USA-45 ECO/DEV NAT/G PLAN BAL/PWR...POLICY ANTHOL BIBLIOG 20. PAGE 8 F0159 ECO/TAC INT/TRADE BAL/PAY WEALTH
B64

CHANDLER A.D. JR.,GIANT ENTERPRISE: FORD, GENERAL MOTORS, AND THE AUTOMOBILE INDUSTRY; SOURCES AND READINGS. USA+45 USA-45 FINAN MARKET CREATE ADMIN ...TIME/SEQ ANTHOL 20 AUTOMOBILE. PAGE 23 F0447 LG/CO DIST/IND LABOR MGT
B64

COMPOS R.O.,A MOEDA, O GOVERNO E O TEMPO. AFR BRAZIL WOR+45 FINAN TEC/DEV FOR/AID REGION DEMAND ...ANTHOL 20. PAGE 27 F0520 ECO/UNDEV PLAN DIPLOM INT/TRADE
B64

DE BARY W.T.,APPROACHES TO ASIAN CIVILIZATIONS. INDIA ISLAM USA+45 CULTURE ACADEM...SOC ANTHOL 20 ASIA EDU/PROP

CHINJAP ARABS. PAGE 31 F0595 SOCIETY

B64
EDWARDS E.O.,THE NATION'S ECONOMIC OBJECTIVES. INDUS WORKER BUDGET DIPLOM CONTROL ORD/FREE ...POLICY SOC METH/CNCPT ANTHOL 20. PAGE 36 F0704 NAT/G ECO/TAC

B64
FIRTH R.,CAPITAL, SAVING AND CREDIT IN PEASANT SOCIETIES. WOR+45 WOR-45 FAM ACT/RES ECO/TAC HEALTH ...SOC CONCPT STAT CHARTS ANTHOL CARIBBEAN VAL/FREE 20. PAGE 41 F0803 AGRI FINAN

B64
FRIEDMANN J.,REGIONAL DEVELOPMENT AND PLANNING: A READER. AGRI MARKET NAT/G ECO/TAC INCOME...GEOG STAT CENSUS CHARTS ANTHOL BIBLIOG MUNICH 20 OPEN/SPACE. PAGE 44 F0863 PLAN REGION INDUS ECO/DEV

B64
GRIFFITH W.E.,COMMUNISM IN EUROPE (2 VOLS.). CZECHOSLVK USSR WOR+45 WOR-45 YUGOSLAVIA INGP/REL MARXISM SOCISM...ANTHOL 20 EUROPE/E. PAGE 51 F1000 COM POL/PAR DIPLOM GOV/COMP

B64
GUTMANN P.M.,ECONOMIC GROWTH: AN AMERICAN PROBLEM. USA+45 FINAN R+D...POLICY NAT/COMP ANTHOL BIBLIOG 20. PAGE 52 F1016 WEALTH ECO/DEV CAP/ISM ORD/FREE

B64
HAMBRIDGE G.,DYNAMICS OF DEVELOPMENT. AGRI FINAN INDUS LABOR INT/TRADE EDU/PROP ADMIN LEAD OWN HEALTH...ANTHOL BIBLIOG 20. PAGE 54 F1054 ECO/UNDEV ECO/TAC OP/RES ACT/RES

B64
HART P.E.,ECONOMETRIC ANALYSIS FOR NATIONAL ECONOMIC PLANNING. INDUS OP/RES PRICE PRODUC ...SIMUL ANTHOL MODELS 20. PAGE 56 F1100 PLAN ECOMETRIC STAT

B64
HERSKOVITS M.J.,ECONOMIC TRANSITION IN AFRICA. FUT INT/ORG NAT/G WORKER PROB/SOLV TEC/DEV INT/TRADE EQUILIB INCOME...ANTHOL 20. PAGE 59 F1157 AFR ECO/UNDEV PLAN ADMIN

B64
KRAUSE L.B.,THE COMMON MARKET: PROGRESS AND CONTROVERSY. EUR+WWI UK ECO/DEV REGION...ANTHOL NATO EEC. PAGE 73 F1433 DIPLOM MARKET INT/TRADE INT/ORG

B64
LETICHE J.M.,A HISTORY OF RUSSIAN ECONOMIC THOUGHT: NINTH THROUGH EIGHTEENTH CENTURIES. RUSSIA FINAN SECT CAP/ISM DOMIN DEMAND EFFICIENCY OWN MARXISM ...TECHNIC ANTHOL BIBLIOG 9/18. PAGE 78 F1536 ECO/TAC TIME/SEQ IDEA/COMP ECO/UNDEV

B64
LITVAK I.A.,MARKETING: CANADA. CANADA STRATA PROC/MFG LEGIS TEC/DEV DIPLOM INT/TRADE PRICE AUTOMAT ATTIT WEALTH...ANTHOL 20. PAGE 81 F1587 ECO/TAC MARKET ECO/DEV EFFICIENCY

B64
RANIS G.,THE UNITED STATES AND THE DEVELOPING ECONOMIES. COM USA+45 AGRI FINAN TEC/DEV CAP/ISM ECO/TAC INT/TRADE...POLICY METH/COMP ANTHOL 20 AID. PAGE 109 F2145 ECO/UNDEV DIPLOM FOR/AID

B64
ROBINSON E.A.G.,ECONOMIC DEVELOPMENT FOR AFRICA SOUTH OF THE SAHARA. AFR AGRI INDUS LABOR BUDGET INT/TRADE PRICE...POLICY GEOG ANTHOL 20. PAGE 113 F2219 ECO/UNDEV ECO/TAC ACT/RES PLAN

B64
SANDEE J.,EUROPE'S FUTURE CONSUMPTION. EUR+WWI FUT EDU/PROP...IDEA/COMP NAT/COMP ANTHOL 20 EUROPE. PAGE 115 F2277 MARKET ECO/DEV PREDICT PRICE

B64
SEGAL R.,SANCTIONS AGAINST SOUTH AFRICA. AFR SOUTH/AFR NAT/G INT/TRADE RACE/REL PEACE PWR ...INT/LAW ANTHOL 20 UN. PAGE 119 F2342 SANCTION DISCRIM ECO/TAC POLICY

B64
ZOLLSCHAN G.K.,EXPLORATIONS IN SOCIAL CHANGE. SOCIETY STRATA STRUCT ECO/UNDEV EX/STRUC...PSY ANTHOL 20. PAGE 151 F2968 ORD/FREE SIMUL CONCPT CULTURE

C64
GOLDMAN M.I.,"COMPARATIVE ECONOMIC SYSTEMS: A READER." COM ECO/UNDEV NAT/G BUDGET CAP/ISM ADMIN TOTALISM MARXISM SOCISM...MGT ANTHOL BIBLIOG 19/20. PAGE 48 F0938 NAT/COMP CONTROL IDEA/COMP

B65
ALLEN W.R.,INTERNATIONAL TRADE THEORY: HUME TO OHLIN. FINAN LABOR TARIFFS TAX PRICE DEMAND PRODUC PROFIT...ANTHOL 18/20. PAGE 4 F0074 INT/TRADE WEALTH METH/CNCPT

B65
ANDERSON C.A.,EDUCATION AND ECONOMIC DEVELOPMENT. INDUS R+D SCHOOL TEC/DEV ECO/TAC EDU/PROP AGE HEREDITY PERCEPT SKILL 20. PAGE 5 F0092 ANTHOL ECO/DEV ECO/UNDEV WORKER

B65
BOCK E.,GOVERNMENT REGULATION OF BUSINESS. USA+45 LAW EX/STRUC LEGIS EXEC ORD/FREE PWR...ANTHOL CONGRESS. PAGE 16 F0303 MGT ADMIN NAT/G CONTROL

B65
BOWEN W.G.,UNEMPLOYMENT IN A PROSPEROUS ECONOMY. USA+45 ECO/DEV NAT/G ACT/RES PLAN PAY EDU/PROP DEMAND...POLICY IDEA/COMP ANTHOL 20. PAGE 17 F0330 WORKER ECO/TAC WEALTH PROB/SOLV

B65
BRENNAN M.J.,PATTERNS OF MARKET BEHAVIOR. AFR USA+45 OP/RES CAP/ISM ECO/TAC INT/TRADE...CHARTS METH/COMP ANTHOL TIME 20. PAGE 18 F0346 MARKET LABOR FINAN ECOMETRIC

B65
CERNY K.H.,NATO IN QUEST OF COHESION* A CONFRONTATION OF VIEWPOINTS. COM EUR+WWI USA+45 FORCES LEAD REGION DETER...ANTHOL NATO. PAGE 22 F0438 CENTRAL NUC/PWR VOL/ASSN

B65
COOMBS P.H.,EDUCATION AND FOREIGN AID. AFR USA+45 DIPLOM EFFICIENCY KNOWL ORD/FREE...ANTHOL 20 AID. PAGE 27 F0532 EDU/PROP FOR/AID SCHOOL ECO/UNDEV

B65
FERMAN L.A.,POVERTY IN AMERICA: A BOOK OF READINGS. USA+45 CULTURE ECO/DEV PROB/SOLV ALL/VALS...POLICY ANTHOL BIBLIOG 20 POVRTY/WAR. PAGE 40 F0785 WEALTH TEC/DEV CONCPT RECEIVE

B65
HARBISON F.,MANPOWER AND EDUCATION. AFR CHINA/COM IRAN L/A+17C S/ASIA TEC/DEV ADJUST OPTIMAL SKILL ...ANTHOL 20. PAGE 55 F1073 ECO/UNDEV EDU/PROP WORKER NAT/COMP

B65
INTERAMERICAN ECO AND SOC COUN,THE ALLIANCE FOR PROGRESS: ITS THIRD YEAR 1963-1964. FUT L/A+17C WOR+45 ECO/DEV INT/ORG PLAN CONTROL ADJUST...STAT ANTHOL SOC/INTEG 20 ALL/PROG. PAGE 64 F1268 ECO/UNDEV ECO/TAC FINAN FOR/AID

B65
LEYS C.T.,FEDERATION IN EAST AFRICA. LAW AGRI DIST/IND FINAN INT/ORG LABOR INT/TRADE CONFER ADMIN CONTROL GP/REL...ANTHOL 20 AFRICA/E. PAGE 79 F1554 FEDERAL REGION ECO/UNDEV PLAN

B65
THE STATE AND ECONOMIC ENTERPRISE IN JAPAN; ESSAYS IN THE POLITICAL ECONOMY OF GROWTH. AGRI INDUS DRIVE POPULISM...CHARTS NAT/COMP ANTHOL 19/20 CHINJAP. PAGE 81 F1594 ECO/UNDEV ECO/DEV CAP/ISM ECO/TAC

B65
MARK S.M.,ECONOMICS IN ACTION (3RD ED.). USA+45 ECO/UNDEV AGRI INDUS FOR/AID INT/TRADE BAL/PAY COST ORD/FREE...ANTHOL 20 RESOURCE/N. PAGE 85 F1670 POLICY ECO/TAC EFFICIENCY PRICE

B65
ONSLOW C.,ASIAN ECONOMIC DEVELOPMENT. BURMA CEYLON INDIA MALAYSIA PAKISTAN S/ASIA AGRI INDUS MARKET PROB/SOLV CAP/ISM FOR/AID INT/TRADE DEMAND WEALTH ...POLICY ANTHOL 20. PAGE 101 F1991 ECO/UNDEV ECO/TAC PLAN NAT/G

B65
REAGAN M.D.,POLITICS, ECONOMICS, AND THE GENERAL WELFARE. USA+45 INDUS ECO/TAC TAX WEALTH...POLICY IDEA/COMP ANTHOL 20. PAGE 110 F2162 NAT/G ECO/DEV R+D ACADEM

B65
SHAFFER H.G.,THE SOVIET SYSTEM IN THEORY AND PRACTICE: SELECTED WESTERN AND SOVIET VIEWS. USSR LAW SOCIETY CREATE FOR/AID EDU/PROP PRESS CHOOSE PEACE ORD/FREE...ANTHOL 20 STALIN/J. PAGE 120 F2362 MARXISM SOCISM IDEA/COMP

B65
SHOSTAK A.B.,NEW PERSPECTIVES ON POVERTY. USA+45 SCHOOL WORKER INGP/REL RACE/REL AGE/C AGE/Y ATTIT HEALTH...ANTHOL BIBLIOG 20 JOHNSON/LB POVRTY/WAR. PAGE 121 F2388 WEALTH NAT/G RECEIVE INCOME

B65
SINHA M.R.,THE ECONOMICS OF MANPOWER PLANNING. FUT HUNGARY NAT/G CONTROL...POLICY GEOG ANTHOL 20 CHINJAP. PAGE 122 F2415 ECO/UNDEV PLAN WORKER ECO/TAC

N65
STUDY GP CREATE RESERVE ASSETS,REPORT TO DEPUTIES (PAMPHLET). AFR FUT PLAN CONTROL DEMAND WEALTH ...ANTHOL METH 20. PAGE 127 F2507 INT/ORG INT/TRADE FINAN BUDGET

B66
BAKLANOFF E.N.,NEW PERSPECTIVES ON BRAZIL. BRAZIL SOCIETY INDUS DOMIN LEAD REV CIVMIL/REL...GEOG PSY LING ANTHOL 20. PAGE 8 F0156 ECO/UNDEV TEC/DEV DIPLOM ORD/FREE

B66
BALDWIN D.A.,FOREIGN AID AND AMERICAN FOREIGN POLICY; A DOCUMENTARY ANALYSIS. USA+45 ECO/UNDEV ADMIN...ECOMETRIC STAT STYLE CHARTS PROG/TEAC GEN/LAWS ANTHOL. PAGE 9 F0162 FOR/AID DIPLOM IDEA/COMP

B66
BIRMINGHAM W.,A STUDY OF CONTEMPORARY GHANA VOL I: THE ECONOMY OF GHANA. AFR GHANA PLAN...POLICY STAT CHARTS ANTHOL BIBLIOG 20. PAGE 15 F0286 ECO/UNDEV ECO/TAC NAT/G

PRODUC

B66
BOLTON R.E.,DEFENSE AND DISARMAMENT: THE ECONOMICS OF TRANSITION. USA+45 R+D FORCES PLAN LOBBY DETER WAR COST PEACE...ANTHOL BIBLIOG 20. PAGE 16 F0310
ARMS/CONT POLICY INDUS

B66
BOWEN H.R.,AUTOMATION AND ECONOMIC PROGRESS. EUR+WWI USA+45 ECO/DEV INCOME ORD/FREE WEALTH ...POLICY ANTHOL 20. PAGE 17 F0327
AUTOMAT TEC/DEV WORKER LEISURE

B66
BOYD H.W.,MARKETING MANAGEMENT: CASES FROM EMERGING COUNTRIES. BRAZIL GHANA ISRAEL WOR+45 ADMIN PERS/REL ATTIT HABITAT WEALTH...ANTHOL 20 ARGEN CASEBOOK. PAGE 17 F0332
MGT ECO/UNDEV PROB/SOLV MARKET

B66
CHASE S.B. JR.,PROBLEMS IN PUBLIC EXPENDITURE ANALYSIS. DIST/IND INDUS OP/RES PLAN BUDGET RECEIVE PRICE RISK COST INCOME...CHARTS ANTHOL 20. PAGE 23 F0455
ECO/DEV FINAN NAT/G INSPECT

B66
CONFERENCE REGIONAL ACCOUNTS,REGIONAL ACCOUNTS FOR POLICY DECISIONS. PROB/SOLV CONTROL RATIONAL KNOWL ORD/FREE...POLICY DECISION MATH STAT ANTHOL 20. PAGE 27 F0523
GOV/REL REGION PLAN ECO/TAC

B66
COOK P.W. JR.,PROBLEMS OF CORPORATE POWER. WOR+45 FINAN INDUS BARGAIN GP/REL...MGT ANTHOL. PAGE 27 F0530
ADMIN LG/CO PWR ECO/TAC

B66
FISK E.K.,NEW GUINEA ON THE THRESHOLD; ASPECTS OF SOCIAL, POLITICAL, AND ECONOMIC DEVELOPMENT. AGRI NAT/G INT/TRADE ADMIN ADJUST LITERACY ROLE...CHARTS ANTHOL 20 NEW/GUINEA. PAGE 41 F0804
ECO/UNDEV SOCIETY

B66
FREIDEL F.,AMERICAN ISSUES IN THE TWENTIETH CENTURY. SOCIETY FINAN ECO/TAC FOR/AID CONTROL NUC/PWR WAR RACE/REL PEACE ATTIT...ANTHOL T 20 WILSON/W ROOSEVLT/F KENNEDY/JF TRUMAN/HS. PAGE 44 F0851
DIPLOM POLICY NAT/G ORD/FREE

B66
GORDON R.A.,PROSPERITY AND UNEMPLOYMENT. USA+45 PLAN ECO/TAC ADJUST DEMAND ALL/VALS...POLICY DECISION TREND CHARTS ANTHOL 20. PAGE 49 F0961
WORKER INDUS ECO/DEV WEALTH

B66
JENSEN F.B.,READINGS IN INTERNATIONAL ECONOMIC RELATIONS. COM ECO/UNDEV MARKET NAT/G FOR/AID ...ANTHOL 20. PAGE 67 F1317
BAL/PAY INT/TRADE FINAN

B66
KINDLEBERGER C.P.,EUROPE AND THE DOLLAR. AFR EUR+WWI FRANCE GERMANY/W USA+45 CONSTN INT/ORG DIPLOM INT/TRADE...ANTHOL 20. PAGE 71 F1395
BAL/PAY BUDGET FINAN ECO/DEV

B66
LANDERS D.S.,RISE OF CAPITALISM. LABOR AUTOMAT GP/REL CENTRAL COST PROFIT...SOC CONCPT ANTHOL 19/20. PAGE 75 F1469
CAP/ISM INDUS AGRI

B66
LEONTIEF W.,ESSAYS IN ECONOMICS. ECO/UNDEV INDUS NAT/G CAP/ISM FOR/AID AUTOMAT MARXISM...ECOMETRIC CHARTS ANTHOL METH 20 KEYNES/JM. PAGE 78 F1528
CONCPT METH/CNCPT METH/COMP

B66
LONDON K.,EASTERN EUROPE IN TRANSITION. CHINA/COM USSR DOMIN COLONIAL CENTRAL RIGID/FLEX PWR...SOC ANTHOL 20. PAGE 82 F1597
SOVEREIGN COM NAT/LISM DIPLOM

B66
MACFARQUHAR R.,CHINA UNDER MAO: POLITICS TAKES COMMAND. CHINA/COM COM AGRI INDUS CHIEF FORCES DIPLOM INT/TRADE EDU/PROP TASK REV ADJUST...ANTHOL 20 MAO. PAGE 83 F1628
ECO/UNDEV TEC/DEV ECO/TAC ADMIN

B66
MUNBY D.,ECONOMIC GROWTH IN WORLD PERSPECTIVE. AFR WOR+45 SOCIETY INDUS PLAN TEC/DEV ECO/TAC FOR/AID INT/TRADE COST CATHISM...ANTHOL 20 EUROPE/W CHURCH/STA. PAGE 95 F1859
SECT ECO/UNDEV ECO/DEV

B66
NATIONAL COUN APPLIED ECO RES,DEVELOPMENT WITHOUT AID. INDIA FINAN TEC/DEV EFFICIENCY...ANTHOL 20. PAGE 97 F1901
FOR/AID PLAN SOVEREIGN ECO/UNDEV

B66
NATIONAL INDUSTRIAL CONF BOARD,GOLD AND WORLD MONETARY PROBLEMS. AFR FUT WOR+45 PROB/SOLV BUDGET INT/TRADE PAY GOV/REL...POLICY ANTHOL 20. PAGE 97 F1902
FINAN ECO/TAC PRICE BAL/PAY

B66
ROBERTSON D.J.,THE BRITISH BALANCE OF PAYMENTS. UK WOR+45 INDUS BUDGET TAX ADJUST...CHARTS ANTHOL 20. PAGE 112 F2213
FINAN BAL/PAY ECO/DEV INT/TRADE

B66
ROSS A.M.,INDUSTRIAL RELATIONS AND ECONOMIC DEVELOPMENT. POL/PAR LEGIS WORKER BARGAIN PRICE EXEC LOBBY INCOME PWR...DECISION ANTHOL BIBLIOG 20. PAGE 114 F2243
ECO/UNDEV LABOR NAT/G GP/REL

B66
RUPPENTHAL K.M.,TRANSPORTATION AND TOMORROW. FUT SPACE USA+45 SEA AIR FORCES TEC/DEV INT/TRADE ...ANTHOL 20 RAILROAD. PAGE 115 F2261
DIST/IND PLAN CIVMIL/REL PREDICT

B66
SHULTZ G.P.,GUIDELINES, INFORMAL CONTROLS, AND THE MARKET PLACE: POLICY CHOICES IN A FULL EMPLOYMENT ECONOMY. UK ECO/DEV LABOR INT/TRADE CONFER GOV/REL BAL/PAY DEMAND INCOME...POLICY ANTHOL 20 PRESIDENT. PAGE 121 F2392
ECO/TAC CONTROL FINAN RATION

B66
SMITH H.E.,READINGS IN ECONOMIC DEVELOPMENT AND ADMINISTRATION IN TANZANIA. TANZANIA FINAN INDUS LABOR NAT/G PLAN PROB/SOLV INT/TRADE COLONIAL REGION...ANTHOL BIBLIOG 20 AFRICA/E. PAGE 123 F2431
TEC/DEV ADMIN GOV/REL

B66
THOMPSON J.H.,MODERNIZATION OF THE ARAB WORLD. FUT ISRAEL STRUCT ECO/UNDEV DIPLOM INGP/REL ATTIT ...CENSUS ANTHOL 20 ARABS. PAGE 130 F2565
ADJUST ISLAM PROB/SOLV NAT/COMP

B66
UREN P.E.,EAST - WEST TRADE* A SYMPOSIUM. COM AGRI INT/ORG PRICE HABITAT RIGID/FLEX...GEOG INT/LAW ANTHOL NATO. PAGE 133 F2625
INT/TRADE BAL/PWR AFR CANADA

B66
WILLIAMS G.,MERTHYR POLITICS: THE MAKING OF A WORKING-CLASS TRADITION. UK CHIEF WORKER LEAD SOCISM...ANTHOL MUNICH 19/20 MERTHYR RICHARD/H. PAGE 147 F2891
LOC/G POL/PAR INDUS

B66
WOODMAN H.D.,SLAVERY AND THE SOUTHERN ECONOMY: SOURCES AND READINGS. USA-45 CULTURE STRUCT AGRI ECO/TAC LEAD RACE/REL DISCRIM EFFICIENCY...CHARTS ANTHOL MUNICH 18/19 NEGRO SOUTH/US. PAGE 148 F2922
ECO/DEV STRATA WORKER UTIL

B67
ADLER J.H.,CAPITAL MOVEMENTS AND ECONOMIC DEVELOPMENT. WOR+45 FINAN NAT/G BARGAIN ECO/TAC FOR/AID INT/TRADE ANTHOL. PAGE 2 F0042
DIPLOM ECO/DEV ECO/UNDEV

B67
CHANDRASEKHAR S.,PROBLEMS OF ECONOMIC DEVELOPMENT. AFR INDIA PHILIPPINE UAR WOR+45 INDUS...GEOG SOC ANTHOL BIBLIOG 20 CHINJAP. PAGE 23 F0450
ECO/UNDEV PLAN AGRI PROB/SOLV

B67
DIEGUES M.,SOCIAL SCIENCE IN LATIN AMERICA. L/A+17C ...JURID SOC ANTHOL 20. PAGE 33 F0637
METH ACADEM EDU/PROP ACT/RES

B67
DUN J.L.,THE ESSENCE OF CHINESE CIVILIZATION. ASIA FAM NAT/G TEC/DEV ADMIN SANCTION WAR HABITAT ...ANTHOL WORSHIP. PAGE 35 F0676
CULTURE SOCIETY

B67
ELDREDGE H.W.,TAMING MEGALOPOLIS; HOW TO MANAGE AN URBANIZED WORLD. WOR+45 SOCIETY ECO/DEV ECO/UNDEV NAT/G COMPUTER CREATE PARTIC EFFICIENCY WEALTH ...MGT ANTHOL MUNICH. PAGE 37 F0716
TEC/DEV PLAN PROB/SOLV

B67
ELDREDGE H.W.,TAMING MEGALOPOLIS; WHAT IT IS AND WHAT COULD BE (VOL. I). FUT USA+45 WOR+45 SOCIETY STRUCT ECO/DEV INDUS LEISURE WEALTH...ANTHOL MUNICH. PAGE 37 F0717
PROB/SOLV PLAN TEC/DEV

B67
FALL B.B.,HO CHI MINH ON REVOLUTION: SELECTED WRITINGS, 1920-66. COM VIETNAM ELITES NAT/G COERCE GUERRILLA RACE/REL MARXISM...MARXIST ANTHOL 20. PAGE 39 F0761
REV COLONIAL ECO/UNDEV S/ASIA

B67
FARRIS M.T.,MODERN TRANSPORTATION: SELECTED READINGS. UNIV CONTROL...POLICY ANTHOL T 20. PAGE 39 F0765
DIST/IND MGT COST

B67
GOLDMAN M.,CONTROLLING POLLUTION: THE ECONOMICS OF A CLEANER AMERICA. USA+45 SOCIETY PROB/SOLV CONTROL COST ANTHOL. PAGE 48 F0936
HEALTH ECO/DEV NAT/G FINAN

B67
HUMPHREY R.A.,UNIVERSITIES...AND DEVELOPMENT ASSISTANCE ABROAD. USA+45 OP/RES ECO/TAC FOR/AID ...ANTHOL 20. PAGE 63 F1242
ACADEM DIPLOM KNOWL ECO/UNDEV

B67
LYND S.,RECONSTRUCTION. USA-45 PROB/SOLV RACE/REL ...IDEA/COMP ANTHOL 19. PAGE 82 F1616
SUFF ECO/TAC ADJUST

B67
MALINVAUD E.,ACTIVITY ANALYSIS IN THE THEORY OF GROWTH AND PLANNING. UNIV AGRI COMPUTER OP/RES REGION...CHARTS ANTHOL METH. PAGE 84 F1648
MATH GAME SIMUL

B67
MCNELLY T.,SOURCES IN MODERN EAST ASIAN HISTORY AND POLITICS. KOREA VIETNAM CULTURE DIPLOM COLONIAL REV
NAT/COMP ASIA

WAR PWR ALL/IDEOS MARXISM...ANTHOL 20 CHINJAP. PAGE 88 F1733
S/ASIA SOCIETY

B67
MEYERS M.,SOURCES OF THE AMERICAN REPUBLIC; A DOCUMENTARY HISTORY OF POLITICS, SOCIETY, AND THOUGHT (VOL. I, REV. ED.). USA-45 CULTURE STRUCT NAT/G LEGIS LEAD ATTIT...JURID SOC ANTHOL 17/19 PRESIDENT. PAGE 90 F1772
COLONIAL REV WAR

B67
PELTASON J.W.,FUNCTIONS AND POLICIES OF AMERICAN GOVERNMENT (3RD ED.). USA+45 FINAN INDUS EDU/PROP CIVMIL/REL RACE/REL ORD/FREE...ANTHOL T 20 JOHNSON/LB. PAGE 104 F2052
NAT/G GOV/REL POLICY PLAN

B67
PIKE F.B.,FREEDOM AND REFORM IN LATIN AMERICA. BRAZIL URUGUAY CONSTN CULTURE SECT DIPLOM EDU/PROP PARTIC DRIVE ALL/VALS CATHISM...GEOG ANTHOL BIBLIOG REFORMERS BOLIV. PAGE 106 F2086
L/A+17C ORD/FREE ECO/UNDEV REV

B67
POLLACK N.,THE POPULIST MIND. USA-45 STRATA AGRI NAT/G POL/PAR LEGIS WORKER RACE/REL WEALTH...ANTHOL BIBLIOG 19 NEGRO. PAGE 107 F2097
POPULISM HIST/WRIT ATTIT INGP/REL

B67
ROACH J.R.,THE UNITED STATES AND THE ATLANTIC COMMUNITY; ISSUES AND PROSPECTS. AFR WOR+45 TEC/DEV ECO/TAC COLONIAL REGION PEACE ROLE...ANTHOL NATO EEC. PAGE 112 F2199
INT/ORG POLICY ADJUST DIPLOM

B67
ROSS A.M.,EMPLOYMENT, RACE, AND POVERTY. USA+45 LAW STRATA MARKET LABOR EDU/PROP ISOLAT SKILL...MGT ANTHOL 20 NEGRO. PAGE 114 F2244
RACE/REL WORKER WEALTH DISCRIM

B67
SHAFFER H.G.,THE COMMUNIST WORLD: MARXIST AND NON-MARXIST VIEWS. WOR+45 SOCIETY DIPLOM ECO/TAC CONTROL SOCISM...MARXIST ANTHOL BIBLIOG/A 20. PAGE 120 F2363
MARXISM NAT/COMP IDEA/COMP COM

B67
SMITH T.L.,THE PROCESS OF RURAL DEVELOPMENT IN LATIN AMERICA (A MONOGRAPH). L/A+17C STRATA INDUS PLAN GP/REL PERS/REL RIGID/FLEX WEALTH...OBS CHARTS ORG/CHARTS ANTHOL 20 COLOMB. PAGE 123 F2434
IDEA/COMP SOC AGRI ECO/UNDEV

L67
AUSTIN D.A.,"POLITICAL CONFLICT IN AFRICA." CONSTN NAT/G CREATE ADMIN COLONIAL ORD/FREE MARXISM POPULISM SOCISM...NAT/COMP ANTHOL 20. PAGE 8 F0141
ANOMIE AFR POL/PAR

L67
SCALAPINO R.A.,"A SURVEY OF ASIA IN 1966." ASIA S/ASIA CONSTN SOCIETY POL/PAR CHIEF WAR...ANTHOL 20. PAGE 116 F2285
DIPLOM

ANTHROPOLOGY, CULTURAL....SEE SOC

ANTHROPOLOGY, PSYCHOLOGICAL....SEE PSY

ANTI/SEMIT....ANTI-SEMITISM; SEE ALSO JEWS, GP/REL

ANTIBALLISTIC MISSILE DEFENSE SYSTEMS....SEE ABM/DEFSYS

ANTI-SEMITISM....SEE JEWS, GP/REL

ANTI-TRUST ACTIONS....SEE MONOPOLY, INDUS, CONTROL

ANXIETY....SEE ANOMIE

APACHE....APACHE INDIANS

APARTHEID....APARTHEID

APEL H. F0107

APP/SCI ....APPLIED SCIENCE

B63
ABSHIRE D.M.,NATIONAL SECURITY: POLITICAL, MILITARY, AND ECONOMIC STRATEGIES IN THE DECADE AHEAD. ASIA COM USA+45 WOR+45 ECO/DEV ECO/UNDEV INT/ORG DELIB/GP FORCES ECO/TAC COERCE ATTIT RIGID/FLEX HEALTH ORD/FREE PWR WEALTH...POLICY STAT CHARTS ANTHOL COLD/WAR VAL/FREE APP/SCI. PAGE 2 F0032
FUT ACT/RES BAL/PWR

APPALACHIA

APPELLATE COURT SYSTEM....SEE CT/APPEALS, CT/SYS

APPERT K. F0108

APPLIC

L62
MACHLUP F.,"PLANS FOR REFORM OF THE INTERNATIONAL MONETARY SYSTEM. PRINCETON: U. PR., 1962, 70 PP., $0.25." WOR+45 INT/ORG ECO/TAC BAL/PAY HEALTH ORD/FREE WEALTH MID/EX TERR/GP VAL/FREE APPLIC 20. PAGE 83 F1631
ECO/DEV STAT

S62
ADISESHIAN M.,"EDUCATION AND DEVELOPMENT." FUT WOR+45 SOCIETY ACT/RES INT/TRADE EDU/PROP KNOWL SKILL WEALTH...POLICY CONCPT CONT/OBS CENSUS CHARTS TOT/POP VAL/FREE APPLIC FAO FOR/TRADE 20. PAGE 2 F0041
SCHOOL ECO/UNDEV

S63
DIEBOLD W. JR.,"THE NEW SITUATION OF INTERNATIONAL TRADE POLICY." EUR+WWI FRANCE FUT UK USA+45 WOR+45 DIST/IND PLAN INT/TRADE EDU/PROP PWR WEALTH ...RECORD TREND GEN/LAWS EEC TRUE/GP VAL/FREE APPLIC 20. PAGE 33 F0636
MARKET ECO/TAC

APPORT....DELINEATION OF LEGISLATIVE DISTRICTS

N
US SUPERINTENDENT OF DOCUMENTS,CENSUS PUBLICATIONS (PRICE LIST 70). AGRI CONSTRUC DIST/IND FINAN LOC/G NAT/G PROVS INT/TRADE APPORT INCOME. PAGE 140 F2751
BIBLIOG/A CENSUS STAT USA+45

B65
BROOKINGS INSTITUTION,BROOKINGS PAPERS ON PUBLIC POLICY. USA+45 ECO/UNDEV LEGIS CAP/ISM ECO/TAC TAX EDU/PROP CONTROL APPORT 20. PAGE 19 F0363
DIPLOM FOR/AID POLICY FINAN

B67
BLAIR G.S.,LEGISLATIVE BODIES IN CALIFORNIA. USA+45 LAW POL/PAR LOBBY APPORT CHOOSE REPRESENT GP/REL ...T CALIFORNIA. PAGE 15 F0293
LEGIS PROVS LOC/G ADJUD

APRA....ALIANZA POPULAR REVOLUCIONARIA AMERICANA, A PERUVIAN POLITICAL PARTY

APSA....AMERICAN POLITICAL SCIENCE ASSOCIATION

APT/TEST....APTITUDE TESTS

APTER D.E. F0109

APTHEKER H. F0110,F0111

AQUINAS/T....SAINT THOMAS AQUINAS

ARA....AREA REDEVELOPMENT ACT

ARABIA/SOU....SOUTH ARABIA

ARABS....ARAB WORLD, INCLUDING ITS CULTURE

N19
KUWAIT FUND ARAB ECO DEVELOPMT,ANNUAL REPORTS 1962-65 (PAMPHLET). KUWAIT ECO/UNDEV DIPLOM ...POLICY 20 ARABS. PAGE 74 F1453
FOR/AID DELIB/GP FINAN ISLAM

B64
DE BARY W.T.,APPROACHES TO ASIAN CIVILIZATIONS. INDIA ISLAM USA+45 CULTURE ACADEM...SOC ANTHOL 20 CHINJAP ARABS. PAGE 31 F0595
ASIA EDU/PROP SOCIETY

B66
BEN-PORATH Y.,THE ARAB LABOR FORCE IN ISRAEL. ISLAM ISRAEL AGRI INDUS SCHOOL CAP/ISM PAY DEMAND...GEOG REGRESS STAT CHARTS 20 ARABS. PAGE 13 F0245
WORKER CENSUS GP/REL STRUCT

B66
RIZK C.,LE REGIME POLITIQUE LIBANAIS. ISLAM LEBANON STRUCT POL/PAR SECT LOBBY GP/REL 20 ARABS MUSLIM CHRISTIAN. PAGE 112 F2198
ECO/UNDEV NAT/G CULTURE

B66
THOMPSON J.H.,MODERNIZATION OF THE ARAB WORLD. FUT ISRAEL STRUCT ECO/UNDEV DIPLOM INGP/REL ATTIT ...CENSUS ANTHOL 20 ARABS. PAGE 130 F2565
ADJUST ISLAM PROB/SOLV NAT/COMP

ARBITRATION....SEE DELIB/GP, CONSULT, AND FUNCTIONAL GROUP CONCERNED (E.G., LABOR)

ARDANT G. F0112

AREA STUDIES....SEE NAT/COMP

ARGENTINA....SEE ALSO L/A&17C

B57
PALACIOS A.L.,PETROLEO, MONOPOLIOS, Y LATIFUNDIOS. L/A+17C EXTR/IND NAT/G TEC/DEV ECO/TAC CONTROL PRODUC 20 ARGEN MONOPOLY RESOURCE/N. PAGE 103 F2017
ECO/UNDEV NAT/LISM INDUS AGRI

B59
CUCCORESE H.J.,HISTORIA DE LA CONVERSION DEL PAPEL MONEDA EN BUENOS AIRES, 1861-1867. AFR LAW LOC/G NAT/G ATTIT...POLICY BIBLIOG 19 ARGEN BUENOS/AIR. PAGE 29 F0560
FINAN PLAN LEGIS

B61
FILLOL T.R.,SOCIAL FACTORS IN ECONOMIC DEVELOPMENT: THE ARGENTINE CASE. STRUCT INDUS LABOR CREATE TEC/DEV EFFICIENCY PRODUC DRIVE...METH/CNCPT METH/COMP BIBLIOG/A 20 ARGEN. PAGE 41 F0795
ECO/UNDEV MGT PERS/REL TREND

C61
FILLOL T.R.,"SOCIAL FACTORS IN ECONOMIC DEVELOPMENT: THE ARGENTINE CASE" INDUS LABOR CREATE TEC/DEV PERS/REL EFFICIENCY PRODUC DRIVE ...METH/CNCPT METH/COMP 20 ARGEN. PAGE 41 F0794
BIBLIOG ECO/UNDEV MGT TREND

B62
FORD A.G.,THE GOLD STANDARD 1880-1914: BRITAIN AND ARGENTINA. AFR UK ECO/UNDEV INT/TRADE ADMIN GOV/REL DEMAND EFFICIENCY...STAT CHARTS 19/20 ARGEN. PAGE 42 F0823
FINAN ECO/TAC BUDGET BAL/PAY

B64
IMAZ J.L.,LOS QUE MANDAN. INDUS LABOR NAT/G POL/PAR PROVS SECT CHIEF TOP/EX CONTROL 20 ARGEN. PAGE 64 F1261
LEAD FORCES ELITES ATTIT

B64
WITHERS W.,THE ECONOMIC CRISIS IN LATIN AMERICA. BRAZIL CHILE STRATA AGRI DIPLOM FOR/AID PWR SOCISM ...POLICY 20 MEXIC/AMER ARGEN ALL/PROG. PAGE 148 F2914
L/A+17C ECO/UNDEV CAP/ISM ALL/IDEOS

S65
BRANDENBURG F.,"THE RELEVANCE OF MEXICAN EXPERIENCE TO LATIN AMERICAN DEVELOPMENT." BRAZIL CHILE VENEZUELA STRUCT ECO/UNDEV AGRI CREATE ECO/TAC ...STAT RECORD MEXIC/AMER ARGEN COLOMB. PAGE 18 F0340
L/A+17C GOV/COMP

S65
KUNKEL J.H.,"VALUES AND BEHAVIOR IN ECONOMIC DEVELOPMENT." INDIA PERU CULTURE STRUCT CREATE PERS/REL ATTIT PERSON...CHARTS HYPO/EXP ARGEN. PAGE 74 F1449
SIMUL ECO/UNDEV PSY STERTYP

S65
TENDLER J.D.,"TECHNOLOGY AND ECONOMIC DEVELOPMENT* THE CASE OF HYDRO VS THERMAL POWER." CONSTRUC DIST/IND CREATE TEC/DEV INT/TRADE CENTRAL PWR SKILL WEALTH...MGT NAT/COMP ARGEN. PAGE 129 F2544
BRAZIL INDUS ECO/UNDEV

S65
WHITAKER A.P.,"ARGENTINA: STRUGGLE FOR RECOVERY." L/A+17C USA+45 NAT/G TOP/EX PLAN LEGIT COERCE REV RIGID/FLEX PWR WEALTH...RECORD ALL/PROG ARGEN FOR/TRADE 20. PAGE 146 F2867
POL/PAR ECO/TAC NAT/LISM

B66
BOYD H.W.,MARKETING MANAGEMENT: CASES FROM EMERGING COUNTRIES. BRAZIL GHANA ISRAEL WOR+45 ADMIN PERS/REL ATTIT HABITAT WEALTH...ANTHOL 20 ARGEN CASEBOOK. PAGE 17 F0332
MGT ECO/UNDEV PROB/SOLV MARKET

B67
BAILY S.L.,LABOR, NATIONALISM, AND POLITICS IN ARGENTINA. POL/PAR TOP/EX GP/REL...BIBLIOG/A 19/20 MIGRATION PERON/JUAN ARGEN. PAGE 8 F0154
LABOR NAT/LISM

S67
BAILEY S.L.,"THE ITALIANS AND ORGANIZED LABOR IN THE UNITED STATES AND ARGENTINA: 1880-1910." ITALY USA-45 PARTIC HABITAT PWR...GEOG GP/COMP 19/20 ARGEN. PAGE 8 F0153
LABOR LEAD WEALTH GP/REL

S67
CRAIG A.,"ARGENTINA: THE LATEST REVOLUTION." ELITES NAT/G CHIEF FORCES ECO/TAC CIVMIL/REL GOV/REL EQUILIB PRIVIL 20 ARGEN. PAGE 28 F0550
ECO/UNDEV FINAN ATTIT REV

ARISTOCRATIC....SEE TRADIT, STRATA, ELITES

ARISTOTLE....ARISTOTLE

ARIZONA....ARIZONA

B63
MANN D.E.,THE POLITICS OF WATER IN ARIZONA. AGRI EXTR/IND PROVS ACT/RES CREATE PLAN GOV/REL COST HABITAT...MGT CHARTS 20 ARIZONA WATER. PAGE 84 F1655
POLICY ECO/TAC TEC/DEV

ARKANSAS....ARKANSAS

B64
COMMITTEE ECONOMIC DEVELOPMENT,COMMUNITY ECONOMIC DEVELOPMENT PROGRAMS. USA+45 FINAN INDUS LG/CO PROF/ORG CREATE GP/REL MUNICH NEW/YORK VERMONT PENNSYLVAN IN ARKANSAS. PAGE 27 F0519
LOC/G LABOR PLAN

ARMED FORCES....SEE FORCES

ARMENGALD A. F0113

ARMS CONTROL....SEE ARMS/CONT

ARMS/CONT....ARMS CONTROL, DISARMAMENT

N19
LANGE O.R.,"DISARMAMENT ECONOMIC GROWTH AND INTERNATIONAL CO-OPERATION" (PAMPHLET). WOR+45 DIST/IND PLAN INT/TRADE GIVE TASK DETER WEALTH SOCISM 18/19 BOLIVAR/S. PAGE 75 F1477
ARMS/CONT DIPLOM ECO/DEV ECO/UNDEV

B51
LEONARD L.L.,INTERNATIONAL ORGANIZATION. WOR+45 WOR-45 EX/STRUC FORCES LEGIS ECO/TAC INT/TRADE COLONIAL ARMS/CONT...SOC/WK GOV/COMP BIBLIOG. PAGE 78 F1527
NAT/G DIPLOM INT/ORG DELIB/GP

B54
REYNOLDS P.A.,BRITISH FOREIGN POLICY IN THE INTER-WAR YEARS. CZECHOSLVK GERMANY POLAND UK USA-45 POL/PAR FORCES ECO/TAC ARMS/CONT WAR ATTIT 20. PAGE 111 F2182
DIPLOM POLICY NAT/G

B59
WARD B.,5 IDEAS THAT CHANGE THE WORLD. WOR+45 WOR-45 SOCIETY STRUCT AGRI INDUS INT/ORG NAT/G FORCES ACT/RES ARMS/CONT TOTALISM ATTIT DRIVE GEN/LAWS. PAGE 143 F2815
ECO/UNDEV ALL/VALS NAT/LISM COLONIAL

B60
APTHEKER H.,DISARMAMENT AND THE AMERICAN ECONOMY: A SYMPOSIUM. FUT USA+45 ECO/DEV DIST/IND FINAN INDUS PROC/MFG LABOR NAT/G POL/PAR CONSULT PLAN CAP/ISM INT/TRADE PEACE ATTIT MORAL WEALTH...TREND GEN/LAWS TOT/POP 20. PAGE 6 F0110
MARXIST ARMS/CONT

B60
MC CLELLAN G.S.,INDIA. AFR CHINA/COM INDIA CONSTN ELITES STRATA AGRI POL/PAR FOR/AID ARMS/CONT REV MARXISM...CENSUS BIBLIOG 20 GANDHI/M NEHRU/J. PAGE 87 F1712
DIPLOM NAT/G SOCIETY ECO/UNDEV

B63
BENOIT E.,DISARMAMENT AND THE ECONOMY. USA+45 NAT/G ACT/RES ECO/TAC BAL/PAY...STAT CON/ANAL GEN/LAWS 20. PAGE 13 F0252
ECO/DEV ARMS/CONT

B63
GANGULI B.N.,ECONOMIC CONSEQUENCES OF DISARMAMENT. EUR+WWI ECO/DEV ECO/UNDEV FORCES ACT/RES BUDGET DIPLOM INT/TRADE...STAT CHARTS NAT/COMP. PAGE 46 F0896
ECOMETRIC ARMS/CONT COST HYPO/EXP

B63
PERLO V.,MILITARISM AND INDUSTRY. USA+45 INT/TRADE EDU/PROP DETER KNOWL...CHARTS MAPS 20. PAGE 105 F2064
CIVMIL/REL INDUS LOBBY ARMS/CONT

B63
WILTZ J.E.,IN SEARCH OF PEACE: THE SENATE MUNITIONS INQUIRY, 1934-36. EUR+WWI USA-45 ELITES INDUS LG/CO LEGIS INT/TRADE LOBBY NEUTRAL ARMS/CONT...POLICY CONGRESS 20 LEAGUE/NAT PRESIDENT SENATE CONSCRIPTN. PAGE 147 F2905
DELIB/GP PROFIT WAR WEAPON

S63
BENOIT E.,"ECONOMIC ADJUSTMENTS TO ARMS CONTROL." FUT USA+45 NAT/G NUC/PWR WAR WEAPON 20. PAGE 13 F0251
ECO/DEV PWR ARMS/CONT

S63
HALLSTEIN W.,"THE EUROPEAN COMMUNITY AND ATLANTIC PARTNERSHIP." EUR+WWI USA+45 MARKET NAT/G VOL/ASSN DELIB/GP ARMS/CONT NUC/PWR ATTIT PWR...CONCPT STAT TIME/SEQ TREND OEEC 20 EEC. PAGE 54 F1053
INT/ORG ECO/TAC UK

B65
PEACE RESEARCH ABSTRACTS. FUT WOR+45 R+D INT/ORG NAT/G PLAN TEC/DEV BAL/PWR DIPLOM FOR/AID NUC/PWR HEALTH. PAGE 1 F0022
BIBLIOG/A PEACE ARMS/CONT WAR

B66
BOLTON R.E.,DEFENSE AND DISARMAMENT: THE ECONOMICS OF TRANSITION. USA+45 R+D FORCES PLAN LOBBY DETER WAR COST PEACE...ANTHOL BIBLIOG 20. PAGE 16 F0310
ARMS/CONT POLICY INDUS

B66
KUENNE R.E.,THE POLARIS MISSILE STRIKE* A GENERAL ECONOMIC SYSTEMS ANALYSIS. USA+45 USSR NAT/G BAL/PWR ARMS/CONT WAR...MATH PROBABIL COMPUT/IR CHARTS HYPO/EXP SIMUL. PAGE 74 F1446
NUC/PWR FORCES DETER DIPLOM

B66
US PRES COMM ECO IMPACT DEFENS,REPORT* JULY 1965. USA+45 ECO/DEV INDUS DELIB/GP FORCES OP/RES ARMS/CONT NUC/PWR WEAPON BAL/PAY...PREDICT SIMUL. PAGE 138 F2726
ACT/RES STAT WAR BUDGET

N67
US HOUSE COMM FOREIGN AFFAIRS,REPORT OF SPECIAL STUDY MISSION TO THE NEAR EAST (PAMPHLET). ISRAEL USA+45 YEMEN ECO/UNDEV INT/ORG FOR/AID ARMS/CONT WAR WEAPON NAT/LISM PEACE...GEOG 20 UN HOUSE/REP. PAGE 137 F2694
ISLAM DIPLOM FORCES

N67
US SENATE COMM ON FOREIGN REL,ARMS SALES AND FOREIGN POLICY (PAMPHLET). FINAN FOR/AID CONTROL 20. PAGE 139 F2737
ARMS/CONT ADMIN OP/RES DIPLOM

ARMY....ARMY (ALL NATIONS)

ARNDT H.W. F0114

ARNOLD H.J.P. F0115

ARNOLD T.W. F0116

ARNOLD/M....MATTHEW ARNOLD

ARNOW K. F0117

ARON R. F0118,F0119,F0120

ARROW K.J. F0121,F0122,F0123,F0124

ART/METH....FINE AND PERFORMING ARTS

N
UNIVERSITY OF FLORIDA,CARIBBEAN ACQUISITIONS: MATERIALS ACQUIRED BY THE UNIVERSITY OF FLORIDA 1957-1960. L/A+17C...ART/METH GEOG MGT 20. PAGE 133 F2620
BIBLIOG ECO/UNDEV EDU/PROP JURID

N
US LIBRARY OF CONGRESS,SOUTHERN ASIA ACCESSIONS LIST. BURMA CEYLON INDIA NEPAL PAKISTAN S/ASIA THAILAND AGRI INDUS SCHOOL WORKER...ART/METH GEOG HEAL PHIL/SCI LING 20. PAGE 137 F2710
BIBLIOG/A SOCIETY CULTURE ECO/UNDEV

B12
FOUAD M.,LE REGIME DE LA PRESSE EN EGYPTE: THESE POUR LE DOCTORAT. UAR LICENSE EDU/PROP ADMIN SANCTION CRIME SUPEGO PWR...ART/METH JURID 19/20. PAGE 43 F0832
ORD/FREE LEGIS CONTROL PRESS

B63
STUCKI C.W.,AMERICAN DOCTORAL DISSERTATIONS ON ASIA 1933-62 (A PAPER). PREHIST INDUS NAT/G GOV/REL ALL/IDEOS...ART/METH GEOG SOC LING 20. PAGE 127 F2506
BIBLIOG ASIA SOCIETY S/ASIA

ARTEL R. F0125

ARTHUR/CA....PRESIDENT CHESTER ALAN ARTHUR

ARTIFACTS....SEE THING/STOR

ARTISTIC ACHIEVEMENT....SEE CREATE

AS D. F0853

ASCH P. F0126

ASCHHEIM J. F0127

ASH W. F0128

ASHER R.E. F0129,F0130

ASHWORTH W. F0131

ASIA....SEE ALSO APPROPRIATE TIME/SPACE/CULTURE INDEX

N19
SAPIR H.M.,JAPAN, CHINA, AND THE WEST (PAMPHLET). AFR ASIA CHINA/COM PROB/SOLV GOV/REL 20 CHINJAP. PAGE 116 F2282
ECO/UNDEV INT/TRADE DECISION PLAN

N19
STALEY E.,SCIENTIFIC RESEARCH AND PROGRESS IN NEWLY DEVELOPING COUNTRIES (PAMPHLET). AFR ASIA L/A+17C CONSULT DIPLOM...METH/COMP 20. PAGE 125 F2463
ECO/UNDEV ACT/RES FOR/AID TEC/DEV

B48
CLYDE P.H.,THE FAR EAST: A HISTORY OF THE IMPACT OF THE WEST ON EASTERN ASIA. CHINA/COM CULTURE INT/TRADE DOMIN COLONIAL WAR PWR...CHARTS BIBLIOG 19/20 CHINJAP. PAGE 25 F0494
DIPLOM ASIA

B52
MACARTHUR D.,REVITALIZING A NATION. ASIA COM FUT KOREA WOR+45 NAT/G FOR/AID TAX GIVE WAR ATTIT SOCISM 20 CHINJAP EUROPE. PAGE 83 F1619
LEAD FORCES TOP/EX POLICY

B55
UN ECONOMIC COMN ASIA & FAR E,ECONOMIC SURVEY OF ASIA AND THE FAR EAST, 1954. AFGHANISTN CEYLON INDIA PHILIPPINE S/ASIA ECO/DEV FINAN INDUS INT/TRADE PRODUC WEALTH...STAT CHARTS 20 CHINJAP. PAGE 132 F2600
ECO/UNDEV PRICE NAT/COMP ASIA

B56
JUAN T.L.,ECONOMIC AND SOCIAL DEVELOPMENT OF MODERN CHINA: A BIBLIOGRAPHICAL GUIDE. ASIA AGRI COM/IND DIST/IND FINAN INDUS DIPLOM...STAT 20. PAGE 68 F1342
BIBLIOG SOC

B56
US DEPARTMENT OF STATE,ECONOMIC PROBLEMS OF UNDERDEVELOPED AREAS (PAMPHLET). AFR ASIA ISLAM L/A+17C AGRI FINAN INDUS INT/ORG LABOR INT/TRADE ...PSY SOC 20. PAGE 136 F2673
BIBLIOG ECO/UNDEV TEC/DEV R+D

B56
US OFFICE OF THE PRESIDENT,REPORT TO CONGRESS ON THE MUTUAL SECURITY PROGRAM FOR THE SIX MONTHS ENDED DECEMBER 31, 1955. ASIA USSR ECO/DEV ECO/UNDEV INT/ORG CREATE TEC/DEV BAL/PWR ECO/TAC AGREE DETER COST ORD/FREE 20 DEPT/STATE DEPT/DEFEN EISNHWR/DD. PAGE 138 F2723
DIPLOM FORCES PLAN FOR/AID

B56
YUAN TUNG-LI,ECONOMIC AND SOCIAL DEVELOPMENT OF MODERN CHINA: A BIBLIOGRAPHIC GUIDE. COM/IND FINAN FAM LABOR SECT CRIME INCOME...STAT SAMP CON/ANAL. PAGE 150 F2954
BIBLIOG ASIA ECO/UNDEV SOC

L57
MASS. INST. TECH.,"THE CENTER FOR INTERNATIONAL STUDIES." AFR ASIA COM EUR+WWI ISLAM L/A+17C S/ASIA USA+45 USA-45 DIST/IND CONSULT FORCES ACT/RES TEC/DEV DIPLOM REV ATTIT WEALTH...CONCPT FOR/TRADE 20. PAGE 87 F1702
R+D ECO/UNDEV

B58
CLAIRMONTE F.,LE LIBERALISME ECONOMIQUE ET LES PAYS SOUS-DEVELOPPES: ETUDES SUR L'EVOLUTION D'UNE IDEE. ASIA INDIA UK FINAN INDUS PLAN CAP/ISM ECO/TAC COLONIAL NEW/LIB...BIBLIOG 20 THIRD/WRLD. PAGE 24 F0475
LAISSEZ ECO/UNDEV

B58
UNIVERSITY OF LONDON,THE FAR EAST AND SOUTH-EAST ASIA: A CUMULATED LIST OF PERIODICAL ARTICLES, MAY 1956-APRIL 1957. ASIA S/ASIA LAW ADMIN...LING 20. PAGE 133 F2621
BIBLIOG SOC

B59
LI CHOH-MING,ECONOMIC DEVELOPMENT OF COMMUNIST CHINA. ASIA CHINA/COM AGRI FINAN TAX INCOME MARXISM ...MGT 20. PAGE 80 F1557
ECO/UNDEV INDUS ORD/FREE TEC/DEV

S59
THOMPSON W.S.,"POPULATION AND PROGRESS IN THE FAR EAST." ASIA S/ASIA DIST/IND CREATE ECO/TAC WAR LOVE SKILL WEALTH...CONT/OBS TOT/POP 20. PAGE 130 F2568
ECO/UNDEV BIO/SOC GEOG

B60
LATIFI D.,INDIA AND UNITED STATES AID. ASIA INDIA UK USA+45 AGRI FINAN INDUS COLONIAL ORD/FREE SOVEREIGN WEALTH...METH/COMP 20. PAGE 76 F1486
FOR/AID DIPLOM ECO/UNDEV

B60
SAKAI R.K.,STUDIES ON ASIA, 1960. ASIA CHINA/COM S/ASIA COM/IND ECO/TAC...ANTHOL 17/20 MALAYA. PAGE 115 F2270
ECO/UNDEV SOC

S60
MURPHEY R.,"ECONOMIC CONFLICTS IN SOUTH ASIA." ASIA CULTURE INTELL ECO/TAC REGION ATTIT DRIVE KNOWL ...METH/CNCPT TIME/SEQ STERTYP TOT/POP METH/GP VAL/FREE 20. PAGE 95 F1864
S/ASIA ECO/UNDEV

B61
FRIEDMANN W.G.,JOINT INTERNATIONAL BUSINESS VENTURES. ASIA ISLAM L/A+17C ECO/DEV DIST/IND FINAN PROC/MFG FACE/GP LG/CO NAT/G VOL/ASSN CONSULT EX/STRUC PLAN ADMIN ROUTINE WEALTH...OLD/LIB FOR/TRADE WORK 20. PAGE 44 F0865
ECO/UNDEV INT/TRADE

B61
SAKAI R.K.,STUDIES ON ASIA, 1961. ASIA BURMA INDIA S/ASIA FINAN ECO/TAC NAT/LISM SOCISM...POLICY ANTHOL 19/20 CHINJAP. PAGE 115 F2271
ECO/UNDEV SECT

B61
STANLEY C.J.,LATE CH'ING FINANCE: HU KUANG-YUNG AS AN INNOVATOR. ASIA NAT/G FORCES BUDGET TAX WAR GOV/REL COST...POLICY BIOG CHARTS BIBLIOG 19. PAGE 125 F2469
FINAN ECO/TAC CIVMIL/REL ADMIN

B62
BROWN S.D.,STUDIES ON ASIA, 1962. ASIA BURMA INDIA ISLAM ISRAEL S/ASIA ECO/UNDEV POL/PAR SECT ECO/TAC ...ANTHOL 20 CHINJAP. PAGE 19 F0374
PWR PARL/PROC

B62
INTERNATIONAL BANK RECONST DEV,THE WORLD BANK AND IDA IN ASIA. ASIA S/ASIA COM/IND DIST/IND...CHARTS 20. PAGE 65 F1272
FINAN ECO/UNDEV AGRI INDUS

B62
US AGENCY INTERNATIONAL DEV,OPERATIONS REPORT - 1962 (PAMPHLET). AFR ASIA L/A+17C USA+45 ECO/UNDEV FINAN INT/ORG NAT/G 20 MICHIGAN. PAGE 134 F2636
FOR/AID CHARTS STAT BUDGET

S62
BOONE A.,"THE FOREIGN TRADE OF CHINA." AFR ECO/DEV ECO/UNDEV INDUS MARKET NAT/G TEC/DEV WEALTH ...POLICY STAT TREND CHARTS FOR/TRADE. PAGE 17 F0318
ASIA ECO/TAC

S62
ZAUBERMAN A.,"SOVIET AND CHINESE STRATEGY FOR ECONOMIC GROWTH." ASIA CHINA/COM COM USSR STRATA VOL/ASSN PLAN ATTIT PWR...METH/CNCPT GEN/LAWS WORK TERR/GP 20. PAGE 150 F2959
ECO/DEV EDU/PROP

B63
ABSHIRE D.M.,NATIONAL SECURITY: POLITICAL, MILITARY, AND ECONOMIC STRATEGIES IN THE DECADE AHEAD. ASIA COM USA+45 WOR+45 ECO/DEV ECO/UNDEV INT/ORG DELIB/GP FORCES ECO/TAC COERCE ATTIT RIGID/FLEX HEALTH ORD/FREE PWR WEALTH...POLICY STAT CHARTS ANTHOL COLD/WAR VAL/FREE APP/SCI. PAGE 2 F0032
FUT ACT/RES BAL/PWR

B63
CHEN N.-.R.,THE ECONOMY OF MAINLAND CHINA, 1949-1963: A BIBLIOGRAPHY OF MATERIALS IN ENGLISH. CHINA/COM ECO/UNDEV PRESS 20. PAGE 24 F0461
BIBLIOG MARXISM NAT/G ASIA

B63
DEUTSCH K.W.,THE POLITICAL ROLE OF LABOR IN DEVELOPING COUNTRIES. AFR ASIA S/ASIA USA+45 WOR+45 ECO/UNDEV POL/PAR ECO/TAC EDU/PROP LEGIT COERCE ORD/FREE PWR WEALTH...OBS INT TREND VAL/FREE 20. PAGE 32 F0625
LABOR NAT/LISM

B63
GAMBLE S.D.,NORTH CHINA VILLAGES: SOCIAL, POLITICAL, AND ECONOMIC ACTIVITIES BEFORE 1933. ASIA CULTURE STRUCT FAM DOMIN EDU/PROP MUNICH WORSHIP 20. PAGE 46 F0891
AGRI LEAD FINAN

B63
INTERNATIONAL BANK RECONST DEV,THE WORLD BANK GROUP IN ASIA. ASIA S/ASIA INDUS TEC/DEV ECO/TAC...RECORD 20 IBRD WORLD/BANK. PAGE 65 F1273
INT/ORG DIPLOM ECO/UNDEV FINAN

B63
STUCKI C.W.,AMERICAN DOCTORAL DISSERTATIONS ON ASIA 1933-62 (A PAPER). PREHIST INDUS NAT/G GOV/REL ALL/IDEOS...ART/METH GEOG SOC LING 20. PAGE 127 F2506
BIBLIOG ASIA SOCIETY S/ASIA

B63
US AGENCY INTERNATIONAL DEV,OPERATIONS REPORT 1963. AFR ASIA L/A+17C USA+45 ECO/UNDEV FINAN INT/ORG NAT/G. PAGE 134 F2637
FOR/AID CHARTS STAT BUDGET

B63
WIGHTMAN D.,TOWARD ECONOMIC CO-OPERATION IN ASIA. ASIA S/ASIA VOL/ASSN ACT/RES PLAN TEC/DEV ECO/TAC EDU/PROP RIGID/FLEX SKILL...POLICY METH/CNCPT OBS INT GEN/LAWS UN 20 ECAFE. PAGE 146 F2877
ECO/UNDEV CREATE

L63
NASH M.,"PSYCHO-CULTURAL FACTORS IN ASIAN ECONOMIC GROWTH." ASIA ISLAM S/ASIA CULTURE ECO/UNDEV DELIB/GP EDU/PROP COERCE ATTIT PERSON HEALTH KNOWL ORD/FREE...PSY SOC STAT TREND ANTHOL VAL/FREE 20. PAGE 96 F1893
SOCIETY ECO/TAC

S63
AYAL E.B.,"VALUE SYSTEM AND ECONOMIC DEVELOPMENT IN JAPAN AND THAILAND." ASIA S/ASIA THAILAND CULTURE ECO/DEV CAP/ISM DOMIN NAT/LISM DRIVE RIGID/FLEX SOCISM...WELF/ST OBS TREND CON/ANAL GEN/LAWS TERR/GP 20 CHINJAP. PAGE 8 F0145
ECO/UNDEV ALL/VALS

S63
SCHURMANN F.,"ECONOMIC POLICY AND POLITICAL POWER IN COMMUNIST CHINA." ASIA CHINA/COM USSR SOCIETY ECO/UNDEV AGRI INDUS CREATE ADMIN ROUTINE ATTIT DRIVE RIGID/FLEX PWR WEALTH...HIST/WRIT TREND CHARTS WORK 20. PAGE 118 F2323
PLAN ECO/TAC

B64
BERRILL K.,ECONOMIC DEVELOPMENT WITH SPECIAL REFERENCE TO EAST ASIA. ASIA INDIA S/ASIA AGRI INDUS LABOR DELIB/GP PLAN INT/TRADE COST PRODUC 20 CHINJAP. PAGE 14 F0271
FINAN ECO/UNDEV INT/ORG CAP/ISM

B64
DE BARY W.T.,APPROACHES TO ASIAN CIVILIZATIONS. INDIA ISLAM USA+45 CULTURE ACADEM...SOC ANTHOL 20 CHINJAP ARABS. PAGE 31 F0595
ASIA EDU/PROP SOCIETY

B64
LEWIN P.,THE FOREIGN TRADE OF COMMUNIST CHINA* ITS IMPACT ON THE FREE WORLD. AFR EUR+WWI L/A+17C S/ASIA ECO/UNDEV CREATE FOR/AID...STAT NET/THEORY TREND CHARTS. PAGE 79 F1546
ASIA INT/TRADE NAT/COMP USSR

B64
LI C.M.,INDUSTRIAL DEVELOPMENT IN COMMUNIST CHINA. CHINA/COM ECO/DEV ECO/UNDEV AGRI FINAN INDUS MARKET LABOR NAT/G ECO/TAC INT/TRADE EXEC ALL/VALS ...POLICY RELATIV TREND WORK TOT/POP VAL/FREE 20. PAGE 79 F1556
ASIA TEC/DEV

B64
SAKAI R.K.,STUDIES ON ASIA, 1964. ASIA CHINA/COM ISRAEL MALAYSIA S/ASIA USA+45 USSR ECO/UNDEV FAM POL/PAR SECT CONSULT NAT/LISM...POLICY SOC 20 CHINJAP. PAGE 115 F2272
PWR DIPLOM

B64
TONG T.,UNITED STATES DIPLOMACY IN CHINA, 1844-1860. ASIA USA-45 ECO/UNDEV ECO/TAC COERCE GP/REL...INT/LAW 19 TREATY. PAGE 131 F2581
DIPLOM INT/TRADE COLONIAL

L64
KORBONSKI A.,"COMECON." ASIA ECO/DEV ECO/UNDEV ECO/TAC BAL/PAY NAT/LISM FOR/TRADE 20 COMECON. PAGE 73 F1425
COM INT/ORG INT/TRADE

S64
GALBRAITH V.,"JAPAN'S POSITION IN WORLD TRADE." ASIA AGRI INDUS CREATE ECO/TAC LEGIT DRIVE WEALTH ...TREND EEC GATT FOR/TRADE 20 CHINJAP. PAGE 45 F0885
ECO/DEV DELIB/GP

S64
POLARIS J.,"THE SINO-SOVIET DISPUTE: ITS ECONOMIC IMPACT ON CHINA." ASIA CHINA/COM COM WOR+45 NAT/G ATTIT PWR WEALTH...STAT TREND FOR/TRADE 20. PAGE 107 F2095
ECO/UNDEV ECO/TAC

S64
WOOD N.,"THE FAMILY FIRM - BASE OF JAPAN'S GROWING ECONOMY." ECO/DEV ECO/UNDEV ECO/TAC WEALTH...POLICY TRADIT BIOG TREND 20 CHINJAP. PAGE 148 F2921
ASIA SML/CO FAM

S64
WU Y.,"CHINA'S ECONOMY AND ITS PROSPECTS." ASIA CHINA/COM FUT USSR AGRI INDUS PLAN ECO/TAC LEGIT WEALTH...STAT CON/ANAL CHARTS GEN/LAWS FOR/TRADE 20. PAGE 149 F2938
ECO/DEV

N64
GREAT BRITAIN CENTRAL OFF INF,THE COLOMBO PLAN (PAMPHLET). AFR ASIA S/ASIA USA+45 VOL/ASSN ...CHARTS 20 RESOURCE/N. PAGE 50 F0980
FOR/AID PLAN INT/ORG ECO/UNDEV

B65
CRABB C.V. JR.,THE ELEPHANTS AND THE GRASS* A STUDY OF NONALIGNMENT. ASIA INDIA S/ASIA USA+45 USSR BAL/PWR NEUTRAL ATTIT...TREND NAT/COMP. PAGE 28 F0549
ECO/UNDEV AFR DIPLOM CONCPT

B65
HOLLER J.E.,POPULATION TRENDS AND ECONOMIC DEVELOPMENT IN THE FAR EAST (PAMPHLET). KOREA S/ASIA AGRI INDUS DELIB/GP PROB/SOLV RATIONAL ...POLICY CHARTS BIBLIOG 20 OUTER/MONG CHINJAP HONG/KONG. PAGE 61 F1197
CENSUS TREND ECO/UNDEV ASIA

B65
SCHULTZ T.W.,ECONOMIC CRISES IN WORLD AGRICULTURE. ASIA INDIA USSR ECO/DEV ECO/UNDEV INDUS VOL/ASSN CAP/ISM RATION COLONIAL 20. PAGE 117 F2317
AGRI ECO/TAC INCOME WORKER

B65
US SENATE COMM ON FOREIGN REL,HEARINGS ON THE FOREIGN ASSISTANCE PROGRAM. AFR ASIA L/A+17C USA+45 WOR+45 FORCES TEC/DEV BUDGET CONTROL WEAPON ORD/FREE 20 UN CONGRESS SEC/STATE. PAGE 139 F2734
FOR/AID DIPLOM INT/ORG ECO/UNDEV

B65
WINT G.,ASIA: A HANDBOOK. ASIA COM INDIA USSR CULTURE INTELL NAT/G...GEOG STAT CENSUS NAT/COMP WORSHIP 20 TREATY CHINJAP. PAGE 148 F2907
DIPLOM SOC

B65
YOUNG A.N.,CHINA'S WARTIME FINANCE AND INFLATION. ASIA AGRI INDUS NAT/G ECO/TAC CONFER PRICE WAR COST 20. PAGE 150 F2949
FINAN FOR/AID TAX BUDGET

S65
DUMONT R.,"SURPEUPLEMENT CHINOIS ET SES CONSEQUENCES." AFR ECO/UNDEV AGRI PLAN PROB/SOLV ECO/TAC FOR/AID NUC/PWR...OBS INT PREDICT. PAGE 35 F0675
GEOG ASIA STAT

S65
KAUFMAN R.H.,"THE ASIAN GOLD TRADE." ASIA LAOS THAILAND UK CHARTS. PAGE 69 F1362
S/ASIA FINAN STAT INT/TRADE

B66
ECKSTEIN A.,COMMUNIST CHINA'S ECONOMIC GROWTH AND FOREIGN TRADE* IMPLICATIONS FOR US POLICY. COM USA+45 USSR STRUCT INDUS MARKET DIPLOM ECO/TAC FOR/AID INT/TRADE...STAT CHARTS. PAGE 36 F0696
ASIA ECO/UNDEV CREATE PWR

B66
KOH S.J.,STAGES OF INDUSTRIAL DEVELOPMENT IN ASIA. ASIA INDIA KOREA STRATA STRUCT NAT/G INT/TRADE ...CHARTS 19/20 CHINJAP. PAGE 72 F1415
INDUS ECO/UNDEV ECO/DEV LABOR

B66
LAMBERG R.F.,PRAG UND DIE DRITTE WELT. AFR ASIA CZECHOSLVK L/A+17C MARKET TEC/DEV ECO/TAC REV ATTIT 20 TREATY. PAGE 75 F1462
DIPLOM ECO/UNDEV INT/TRADE FOR/AID

B66
SINGH L.P.,THE POLITICS OF ECONOMIC COOPERATION IN ASIA; A STUDY OF ASIAN INTERNATIONAL ORGANIZATIONS. ASIA INT/ORG ACT/RES PLAN GP/REL...POLICY GP/COMP BIBLIOG 20 UN SEATO. PAGE 122 F2414
ECO/UNDEV ECO/TAC REGION DIPLOM

B66
US HOUSE COMM FOREIGN AFFAIRS,HEARINGS ON HR 12449 A BILL TO AMEND FURTHER THE FOREIGN ASSISTANCE ACT OF 1961. AFR ASIA L/A+17C USA+45 VIETNAM INT/ORG TEC/DEV INT/TRADE ATTIT ORD/FREE 20 UN NATO CONGRESS AID. PAGE 137 F2692
FOR/AID ECO/TAC ECO/UNDEV DIPLOM

S66
LAURENS H.,"LES PAYS OCCIDENTAUX ET LE MARCHE CHINOIS." EUR+WWI FUT S/ASIA AGRI INDUS VOL/ASSN ECO/TAC BAL/PAY...RECORD PREDICT TREATY. PAGE 76 F1488
ASIA INT/TRADE TREND STAT

C66
WINT G.,"ASIA: A HANDBOOK." ASIA S/ASIA INDUS LABOR SECT PRESS RACE/REL MARXISM...STAT CHARTS BIBLIOG 20. PAGE 148 F2908
ECO/UNDEV DIPLOM NAT/G SOCIETY

B67
BARNETT A.D.,CHINA AFTER MAO. ASIA CHINA/COM CULTURE ECO/UNDEV ECO/TAC CONTROL EFFICIENCY NAT/LISM MARXISM 20. PAGE 10 F0189
POL/PAR NAT/G TEC/DEV GP/REL

B67
DUN J.L.,THE ESSENCE OF CHINESE CIVILIZATION. ASIA FAM NAT/G TEC/DEV ADMIN SANCTION WAR HABITAT ...ANTHOL WORSHIP. PAGE 35 F0676
CULTURE SOCIETY

B67
HANNAH H.W.,THE LEGAL BASE FOR UNIVERSITIES IN DEVELOPING COUNTRIES. AFR ASIA L/A+17C S/ASIA USA+45 FINAN CREATE EDU/PROP TASK EFFICIENCY ...JURID METH/COMP 20. PAGE 54 F1060
ADMIN LAW ACADEM LEGIS

B67
MCNELLY T.,SOURCES IN MODERN EAST ASIAN HISTORY AND POLITICS. KOREA VIETNAM CULTURE DIPLOM COLONIAL REV WAR PWR ALL/IDEOS MARXISM...ANTHOL 20 CHINJAP. PAGE 88 F1733
NAT/COMP ASIA S/ASIA SOCIETY

B67
WATT A.,THE EVOLUTION OF AUSTRALIAN FOREIGN POLICY 1938-65. ASIA S/ASIA USA+45 USA-45 INT/ORG NAT/G FORCES FOR/AID TREATY 20 AUSTRAL. PAGE 144 F2834
DIPLOM WAR

B67
WILCOX W.A.,ASIA AND UNITED STATES POLICY. CHINA/COM USA+45. PAGE 146 F2879
ASIA S/ASIA DIPLOM POLICY

B67
YAMAMURA K.,ECONOMIC POLICY IN POSTWAR JAPAN. ASIA FINAN POL/PAR DIPLOM LEAD NAT/LISM ATTIT NEW/LIB POPULISM 20 CHINJAP. PAGE 149 F2946
ECO/DEV POLICY NAT/G TEC/DEV

L67
HOSHII I.,"JAPAN'S STAKE IN ASIA." ASIA S/ASIA CAP/ISM ECO/TAC ROLE...GEOG 20 CHINJAP. PAGE 62 F1224
DIPLOM REGION NAT/G INT/ORG

L67
SCALAPINO R.A.,"A SURVEY OF ASIA IN 1966." ASIA S/ASIA CONSTN SOCIETY POL/PAR CHIEF WAR...ANTHOL 20. PAGE 116 F2285
DIPLOM

S67
GUPTA S.,"FOREIGN POLICY IN THE 1967 MANIFESTOS." ASIA COM INDIA USA+45 FORCES FOR/AID TAX ATTIT ...DECISION 20. PAGE 52 F1013
IDEA/COMP POL/PAR POLICY DIPLOM

S67
MCCOLL R.W.,"A POLITICAL GEOGRAPHY OF REVOLUTION: CHINA, VIETNAM, AND THAILAND." ASIA THAILAND VIETNAM FORCES CONTROL 20. PAGE 88 F1720
REV GEOG PLAN DECISION

S67
MANGLAPUS R.S.,"ASIAN REVOLUTION AND AMERICAN IDEOLOGY." USA+45 SOCIETY CAP/ISM DIPLOM ADJUST CENTRAL...NAT/COMP 20. PAGE 84 F1652
REV POPULISM ATTIT ASIA

S67
RICHMAN B.M.,"CAPITALISTS & MANAGERS IN COMMUNIST CHINA." ASIA CHINA/COM ECO/UNDEV NAT/G CONSULT EX/STRUC PLAN EFFICIENCY PRODUC WEALTH MARXISM ...MGT CHARTS 20. PAGE 111 F2185
CAP/ISM INDUS

S67
RONNING C.,"NANKING: 1950." ASIA CANADA CHINA/COM NAT/G PLAN ECO/TAC REV ADJUST 20. PAGE 113 F2235
DIPLOM ROLE PEACE

S67
STOLTE S.C.,"THREE PROBLEMS FACING THE SOVIET BLOC." ASIA COM USA+45 USSR FORCES MARXISM ...IDEA/COMP METH/COMP 20 NATO WARSAW/P. PAGE 127 F2496
ECO/TAC DIPLOM INT/ORG POLICY

S67
WALKER R.L.,"THE WEST AND THE 'NEW ASIA'." CHINA/COM ECO/UNDEV DIPLOM...PREDICT 20. PAGE 142 F2805
ASIA INT/TRADE COLONIAL REGION

N67
US SENATE COMM ON FOREIGN REL,THE RIM OF ASIA (PAMPHLET). WAR MARXISM 20. PAGE 139 F2745
ASIA PROB/SOLV SOVEREIGN POLICY

ASIANS....ASIANS, ASIAN MINORITIES

S65
MULLER A.L.,"THE ECONOMIC POSITION OF THE ASIANS IN AFRICA." AFR SOUTH/AFR ECO/UNDEV MARKET ECO/TAC GP/REL INCOME...CHARTS IND 20 MONOPOLY ASIANS. PAGE 95 F1856
WORKER RACE/REL CAP/ISM DISCRIM

ASPREMONT-LYNDEN H. F0132

ASQUITH/HH....HERBERT HENRY ASQUITH

ASSASSINATION....SEE MURDER

ASSIMILATION....SEE GP/REL+INGP/REL

ASSN U BUREAUS BUS-ECO RES F0133

ASSOCIATIONS....SEE VOL/ASSN

AT+T....AMERICAN TELEPHONE AND TELEGRAPH

ATATURK/MK....MUSTAFA KEMAL ATATURK

B65
RIVKIN M.D.,AREA DEVELOPMENT FOR NATIONAL GROWTH; THE TURKISH PRECEDENT. ISLAM TURKEY ACT/RES INGP/REL...POLICY CHARTS GP/COMP MUNICH 20 ATATURK/MK INONU/I. PAGE 112 F2197
ECO/UNDEV REGION ECO/TAC PLAN

ATHENS....ATHENS, GREECE

ATKINSON M. F1798

ATLAN/ALL....ATLANTIC ALLIANCE

B63
CERAMI C.A.,ALLIANCE BORN OF DANGER. EUR+WWI USA+45 USSR ECO/DEV INDUS VOL/ASSN ECO/TAC REGION ATTIT MARXISM ATLAN/ALL 20 NATO EEC. PAGE 22 F0437
DIPLOM INT/ORG NAT/G POLICY

ATLANTA....ATLANTA, GEORGIA

B65
GREEN J.L.,METROPOLITAN ECONOMIC REPUBLICS. USA+45 ECO/TAC INCOME...GEOG SOC CONCPT SIMUL MUNICH 20 ATLANTA. PAGE 50 F0985
SOC/WK PLAN LABOR

ATLANTIC ALLIANCE....SEE ATLAN/ALL

ATLANTIC FREE TRADE AREA....SEE AFTA

ATLASES....SEE MAPS

ATOM BOMB....SEE NUC/PWR

ATOMIC ENERGY AUTHORITY OF UN....SEE AEA

ATOMIC ENERGY COMMISSION....SEE AEC + COUNTRY'S NAME

ATOMIC INDUSTRIAL FORUM F0134,F0135,F0136,F0137

ATTENTION....SEE PERCEPT

ATTIT....ATTITUDES, OPINIONS, IDEOLOGY

N
NEW JERSEY STATE OF,SECOND REPORT TO GOVERNOR, SENATE, ASSEMBLY BY UNIFORM COMMERCIAL CODE STUDY COMMISSION. USA+45 INDUS LOC/G NAT/G PROF/ORG CONSULT ACT/RES LEGIT CT/SYS ATTIT NEW/JERSEY. PAGE 98 F1920
LAW FINAN CENTRAL PROVS

N
LONDON TIMES OFFICIAL INDEX. UK LAW ECO/DEV NAT/G DIPLOM LEAD ATTIT 20. PAGE 1 F0006
BIBLIOG INDEX PRESS WRITING

N
DEUTSCHE BUCHEREI,DEUTSCHES BUCHERVERZEICHNIS. GERMANY LAW CULTURE POL/PAR ADMIN LEAD ATTIT PERSON ...SOC 20. PAGE 32 F0626
BIBLIOG NAT/G DIPLOM ECO/DEV

N
US LIBRARY OF CONGRESS,EAST EUROPEAN ACCESSIONS INDEX. NAT/G ISOLAT ATTIT KNOWL...POLICY 20. PAGE 138 F2711
BIBLIOG COM MARXIST DIPLOM

B00
LIST F.,NATIONAL SYSTEM OF POLITICAL ECONOMY. ECO/DEV AGRI EXTR/IND FINAN INDUS TEC/DEV ECO/TAC ATTIT WEALTH...TREND GEN/LAWS FOR/TRADE 19. PAGE 81 F1581
MOD/EUR MARKET

B04
MARX K.,A CONTRIBUTION TO THE CRITIQUE OF POLITICAL ECONOMY (TRANS. FROM 2ND ED. BY N.I. STONE). UK STRATA ECO/DEV FINAN MARKET PLAN BARGAIN CAP/ISM ECO/TAC ATTIT WEALTH...METH/CNCPT BIOG 19. PAGE 86 F1687
MARXIST NEW/IDEA MARXISM

B11
SCOTT W.D.,INFLUENCING MEN IN BUSINESS: THE PSYCHOLOGY OF ARGUMENT AND SUGGESTION. WOR-45 WORKER EDU/PROP DEMAND ATTIT PERSON 20. PAGE 118 F2336
PSY MARKET SML/CO TOP/EX

B11
SOREL G.,LES ILLUSIONS DU PROGRES (1906). UNIV
WORKER

SOCIETY STRATA INDUS GP/REL OWN PRODUC SOCISM 17/20. PAGE 124 F2444
POPULISM ECO/DEV ATTIT

B13
BEARD C.A.,AN ECONOMIC INTERPRETATION OF THE CONSTITUTION OF THE UNITED STATES. USA-45 AGRI INT/TRADE SUFF OWN ATTIT...CONCPT MYTH BIOG HIST/WRIT 18. PAGE 12 F0222
CONSTN ECO/TAC CHOOSE

B14
LEVINE L.,SYNDICALISM IN FRANCE (2ND ED.). FRANCE LAW SOCIETY ECO/DEV NAT/G ECO/TAC LEAD ATTIT ...POLICY CONCPT STAT BIBLIOG 18/20 REFORMERS. PAGE 79 F1542
LABOR INDUS SOCISM REV

N19
BASCH A.,THE FUTURE OF FOREIGN LENDING FOR DEVELOPMENT (PAMPHLET). WOR+45 ECO/UNDEV FINAN INT/ORG ECO/TAC ATTIT...PREDICT 20. PAGE 11 F0203
FOR/AID ECO/DEV DIPLOM GIVE

N19
MASON E.S.,THE DIPLOMACY OF ECONOMIC ASSISTANCE (PAMPHLET). INDIA PAKISTAN USA+45 ECO/UNDEV NAT/G BUDGET ATTIT...POLICY 20. PAGE 87 F1695
FOR/AID DIPLOM FINAN

N19
SENGHOR L.S.,AFRICAN SOCIALISM (PAMPHLET). AFR FRANCE MALI USSR ELITES ECO/UNDEV NAT/G DIPLOM DOMIN EDU/PROP ATTIT 20 NEGRO. PAGE 119 F2355
SOCISM MARXISM ORD/FREE NAT/LISM

B20
TAWNEY R.H.,THE ACQUISITIVE SOCIETY. STRATA WORKER PROB/SOLV CAP/ISM ECO/TAC CONTROL GP/REL OWN PRIVIL ATTIT ORD/FREE WEALTH 20. PAGE 128 F2536
INDUS SOCIETY PRODUC MORAL

B28
CASSEL G.,FOREIGN INVESTMENTS. GERMANY UK USA-45 WOR-45 ECO/DEV NAT/G VOL/ASSN CAP/ISM REPAR ATTIT WEALTH...METH/CNCPT STAT SIMUL STERTYP ANTHOL FOR/TRADE TOT/POP VAL/FREE 20. PAGE 22 F0426
FINAN ECO/TAC BAL/PAY

B28
CROS L.,AFRIQUE FRANCAISE POUR TOUS. EUR+WWI FRANCE PLAN TEC/DEV ATTIT 20. PAGE 29 F0556
COLONIAL DOMIN ECO/TAC AFR

B28
DE MAN H.,THE PSYCHOLOGY OF SOCIALISM. EUR+WWI USSR LABOR NAT/LISM PERSON WEALTH MARXISM...METH/COMP 20. PAGE 31 F0604
WORKER ATTIT SOC SOCISM

B28
FRANKFURTER F.,THE BUSINESS OF THE SUPREME COURT; A STUDY IN THE FEDERAL JUDICIAL SYSTEM. USA-45 CONSTN EX/STRUC PROB/SOLV GP/REL ATTIT PWR...POLICY JURID 18/20 SUPREME/CT CONGRESS. PAGE 43 F0848
CT/SYS ADJUD LAW FEDERAL

B28
HARDMAN J.B.,AMERICAN LABOR DYNAMICS. WORKER ECO/TAC DOMIN ADJUD LEAD LOBBY PWR...POLICY MGT. PAGE 55 F1079
LABOR INGP/REL ATTIT GP/REL

B30
FEIS H.,EUROPE, THE WORLD'S BANKER, 1871-1914. FRANCE GERMANY MOD/EUR UK WOR-45 NAT/G PLAN ECO/TAC EXEC ATTIT PWR WEALTH...CONCPT HIST/WRIT GEN/LAWS VAL/FREE 19/20. PAGE 40 F0773
FINAN DIPLOM INT/TRADE

B30
HAWTREY R.G.,ECONOMIC ASPECTS OF SOVEREIGNTY. UNIV WOR+45 WOR-45 ECO/DEV ECO/UNDEV AGRI COM/IND INDUS MARKET NAT/G TEC/DEV ECO/TAC EDU/PROP COERCE ATTIT KNOWL WEALTH...CONCPT CON/ANAL GEN/LAWS 20. PAGE 57 F1118
FORCES PWR SOVEREIGN WAR

B32
WRIGHT Q.,GOLD AND MONETARY STABILIZATION. FUT USA-45 WOR-45 INTELL ECO/DEV INT/ORG NAT/G CONSULT PLAN ECO/TAC ADMIN ATTIT WEALTH...CONCPT TREND 20. PAGE 149 F2935
FINAN POLICY

B34
GRAHAM F.D.,PROTECTIVE TARIFFS. FUT USA+45 WOR-45 INDUS MARKET VOL/ASSN PLAN CAP/ISM ECO/TAC PEACE ATTIT DRIVE HEALTH ORD/FREE...OBS TREND GEN/LAWS FOR/TRADE 20. PAGE 50 F0970
INT/ORG TARIFFS

B35
KEYNES J.M.,THE GENERAL THEORY OF EMPLOYMENT, INTEREST, AND MONEY. AGRI INDUS WORKER ECO/TAC DEMAND EQUILIB INCOME PRODUC PROFIT ATTIT WEALTH 20. PAGE 71 F1386
FINAN GEN/LAWS MARKET PRICE

B35
O'CONNOR H.,REVOLUTION IN SEATTLE. USA-45 STRATA WORKER GP/REL ATTIT SOCISM...OBS BIBLIOG/A 20 SEATTLE STRIKE COM/PARTY. PAGE 99 F1954
REV EDU/PROP LABOR MARXISM

B35
STALEY E.,WAR AND THE PRIVATE INVESTOR. UNIV WOR-45 INTELL SOCIETY INT/ORG NAT/G TOP/EX CAP/ISM ECO/TAC WAR ATTIT ALL/VALS...INT TIME/SEQ TREND CON/ANAL WORK TOT/POP 20. PAGE 125 F2464
FINAN INT/TRADE DIPLOM

B38
HOBSON J.A.,IMPERIALISM. MOD/EUR UK WOR-45 CULTURE ECO/UNDEV NAT/G VOL/ASSN PLAN EDU/PROP LEGIT REGION COERCE ATTIT PWR...POLICY PLURIST TIME/SEQ GEN/LAWS TERR/GP 19/20. PAGE 60 F1187
DOMIN ECO/TAC BAL/PWR COLONIAL

B38
LANGE O.,ON THE ECONOMIC THEORY OF SOCIALISM. UNIV ECO/DEV FINAN INDUS INT/ORG PUB/INST ROUTINE ATTIT ALL/VALS...SOC CONCPT STAT TREND 20. PAGE 75 F1475
MARKET ECO/TAC INT/TRADE SOCISM

B39
MARQUAND H.A.,ORGANIZED LABOUR IN FOUR CONTINENTS. EUR+WWI USA-45 INDUS NAT/G PAY GP/REL TOTALISM ATTIT WEALTH ALL/IDEOS...TREND NAT/COMP 20 ILO AFL/CIO EUROPE CHINJAP MEXIC/AMER. PAGE 85 F1673
LABOR WORKER CONCPT ANTHOL

B39
ROBBINS L.,ECONOMIC CAUSES OF WAR. WOR-45 ECO/DEV ECO/UNDEV INT/ORG NAT/G TEC/DEV DIPLOM DOMIN COLONIAL ATTIT DRIVE PWR WEALTH...POLICY CONCPT OBS SAMP TREND CON/ANAL GEN/LAWS MARX/KARL 20. PAGE 112 F2203
COERCE ECO/TAC WAR

B39
STALEY E.,WORLD ECONOMY IN TRANSITION. WOR-45 SOCIETY INT/ORG PROF/ORG ECO/TAC ATTIT WEALTH ...METH/CNCPT TREND GEN/LAWS 20. PAGE 125 F2465
TEC/DEV INT/TRADE

S39
COLE G.D.H.,"NAZI ECONOMICS: HOW DO THEY MANAGE IT?" GERMANY FORCES WORKER BUDGET INT/TRADE ROUTINE COERCE WAR 20 HITLER/A NAZI. PAGE 26 F0500
FASCISM ECO/TAC ATTIT PLAN

B40
BLAISDELL D.C.,GOVERNMENT AND AGRICULTURE; THE GROWTH OF FEDERAL FARM AID. USA-45 MARKET PLAN PROB/SOLV TEC/DEV ECO/TAC GOV/REL ADJUST ATTIT ...CHARTS 20 DEPT/AGRI. PAGE 15 F0296
NAT/G GIVE AGRI DELIB/GP

B41
YOUNG G.,FEDERALISM AND FREEDOM. EUR+WWI MOD/EUR RUSSIA USA-45 WOR-45 SOCIETY STRUCT ECO/DEV INT/ORG EXEC FEDERAL ATTIT PERSON ALL/VALS...OLD/LIB CONCPT OBS TREND LEAGUE/NAT TOT/POP. PAGE 150 F2950
NAT/G WAR

S41
BRITT S.H.,"CONFORMITY OF LABOR NEWSPAPERS WITH RESPECT TO THE AFL-CIO CONFLICT." BAL/PWR CONSEN ATTIT. PAGE 18 F0355
LABOR PRESS DOMIN GP/REL

B42
VEBLEN T.B.,THE THEORY OF THE LEISURE CLASS. USA-45 SOCIETY STRATA STRUCT NAT/G SECT WORKER CREATE EDU/PROP ATTIT...SOC GEN/LAWS 19. PAGE 141 F2772
WEALTH ELITES LEISURE PRODUC

S43
HUZAR E.,"CONGRESS AND THE ARMY: APPROPRIATIONS." USA-45 CONFER CONTROL ATTIT SUPEGO SKILL CONGRESS. PAGE 64 F1255
LEGIS FORCES BUDGET DELIB/GP

B44
BIENSTOCK G.,MANAGEMENT IN RUSSIAN INDUSTRY AND AGRICULTURE. USSR CONSULT WORKER LEAD COST PROFIT ATTIT DRIVE PWR...MGT METH/COMP DICTIONARY ACCT 20. PAGE 15 F0281
ADMIN MARXISM SML/CO AGRI

B44
HAYEK F.A.,THE ROAD TO SERFDOM. NAT/G POL/PAR CREATE EDU/PROP ATTIT WEALTH LAISSEZ...OLD/LIB CONCPT TREND 20. PAGE 57 F1121
FUT PLAN ECO/TAC SOCISM

B45
WOOTTON B.,FREEDOM UNDER PLANNING. UNIV ROUTINE ATTIT AUTHORIT DECISION. PAGE 148 F2926
PLAN ORD/FREE ECO/TAC CONTROL

B46
CLOUGH S.B.,ECONOMIC HISTORY OF EUROPE. CHRIST-17C EUR+WWI MOD/EUR WOR-45 SOCIETY EXEC ATTIT WEALTH ...CONCPT GEN/LAWS WORK TOT/POP VAL/FREE 7/20. PAGE 25 F0493
ECO/TAC CAP/ISM

B46
DAVIES E.,NATIONAL ENTERPRISE: THE DEVELOPMENT OF THE PUBLIC CORPORATION. UK LG/CO EX/STRUC WORKER PROB/SOLV COST ATTIT SOCISM 20. PAGE 30 F0584
ADMIN NAT/G CONTROL INDUS

B47
HEILPERIN M.A.,THE TRADE OF NATIONS. USA+45 USA-45 WOR+45 WOR-45 CULTURE ECO/DEV NAT/G DELIB/GP EDU/PROP ATTIT DISPL ORD/FREE PWR WEALTH TOT/POP 20. PAGE 58 F1139
MARKET INT/ORG INT/TRADE PEACE

B47
LEVER E.A.,ADVERTISING AND ECONOMIC THEORY. FINAN ECO/TAC DEMAND EFFICIENCY ATTIT...MGT PSY SAMP/SIZ CHARTS 20. PAGE 79 F1539
EDU/PROP MARKET COM/IND ECO/DEV

S47
DAHL R.A.,"WORKERS' CONTROL OF INDUSTRY AND THE BRITISH LABOUR PARTY." UK STRATA STRUCT DELIB/GP BARGAIN CAP/ISM DEBATE CONTROL CHOOSE GP/REL ATTIT ROLE PWR 19/20 PARLIAMENT LABOR/PAR FABIAN. PAGE 29 F0570
INDUS LABOR WORKER SOCISM

B48
MILLS C.W.,THE NEW MEN OF POWER. ELITES INTELL STRUCT WORKER ANOMIE ATTIT PWR POLICY. PAGE 92
LABOR LEAD

F1799 — PLAN

B48
WHYTE W.F.,HUMAN RELATIONS IN THE RESTAURANT INDUSTRY (1ST ED). CLIENT WORKER WAR ATTIT...MGT OBS INT. PAGE 146 F2874
INGP/REL GP/REL SERV/IND LABOR

S48
CLEVELAND A.S.,"NAM: SPOKESMAN FOR INDUSTRY?" LEGIS PLAN LEAD LOBBY PARTIC CONSEN INCOME ATTIT ROLE ORD/FREE POLICY. PAGE 25 F0491
VOL/ASSN CLIENT REPRESENT INDUS

B50
ADORNO T.W.,THE AUTHORITARIAN PERSONALITY. STRATA SECT PROB/SOLV ECO/TAC DISCRIM ATTIT SEX...SOC INT CHARTS METH 20. PAGE 3 F0044
AUTHORIT PERSON ALL/IDEOS SOCIETY

B50
FEIS H.,THE DIPLOMACY OF THE DOLLAR: FIRST ERA 1919-32. EUR+WWI USA-45 FOR/AID REPAR ATTIT ...POLICY 20. PAGE 40 F0774
FINAN NAT/G DIPLOM ECO/TAC

B50
KOENIG L.W.,THE SALE OF THE TANKERS. USA+45 SEA DIST/IND POL/PAR DIPLOM ADMIN CIVMIL/REL ATTIT ...DECISION 20 PRESIDENT DEPT/STATE. PAGE 72 F1414
NAT/G POLICY PLAN GOV/REL

B50
LINCOLN G.,ECONOMICS OF NATIONAL SECURITY. USA+45 ELITES COM/IND DIST/IND INDUS NAT/G VOL/ASSN DELIB/GP EX/STRUC FOR/AID EDU/PROP COERCE NUC/PWR WAR ATTIT KNOWL ORD/FREE PWR TOT/POP VAL/FREE 20. PAGE 80 F1565
FORCES ECO/TAC AFR

B50
LIPSET S.M.,AGRARIAN SOCIALISM. CANADA POL/PAR OP/RES ECO/TAC ADMIN ATTIT...TIME/SEQ NAT/COMP SOC/EXP 20 SASKATCH. PAGE 80 F1576
SOCISM AGRI METH/COMP STRUCT

S50
DALTON M.,"CONFLICTS BETWEEN STAFF AND LINE MANAGERIAL OFFICERS" (BMR). USA+45 USA-45 ELITES LG/CO WORKER PROB/SOLV ADMIN EXEC EFFICIENCY PRODUC ...GP/COMP 20. PAGE 30 F0576
MGT ATTIT GP/REL INDUS

B51
HALEVY E.,IMPERIALISM AND THE RISE OF LABOR (2ND ED.). UK NAT/G POL/PAR TOP/EX ATTIT ORD/FREE PWR 19/20 PARLIAMENT LABOR/PAR. PAGE 53 F1042
COLONIAL LABOR POLICY WAR

B51
HARROD R.F.,THE LIFE OF JOHN MAYNARD KEYNES. UK INTELL FAM CAP/ISM DIPLOM ECO/TAC WAR ATTIT PERSON ROLE 20 KEYNES/JM WWI. PAGE 56 F1094
BIOG FINAN GEN/LAWS

B51
LUXEMBORG R.,THE ACCUMULATION OF CAPITAL (TRANS. BY AGNES SCHWARZSCHILD). ECO/TAC DOMIN COLONIAL ATTIT LAISSEZ 19 MONEY. PAGE 82 F1614
MARXIST INT/TRADE CAP/ISM FINAN

B52
MACARTHUR D.,REVITALIZING A NATION. ASIA COM FUT KOREA WOR+45 NAT/G FOR/AID TAX GIVE WAR ATTIT SOCISM 20 CHINJAP EUROPE. PAGE 83 F1619
LEAD FORCES TOP/EX POLICY

B52
ROSE A.M.,UNION SOLIDARITY: THE INTERNAL COHESION OF A LABOR UNION. SECT GP/REL RACE/REL ATTIT ROLE HEALTH WEALTH...INT QU. PAGE 114 F2241
LABOR INGP/REL PARTIC SUPEGO

S52
HEBERLE R.,"ON POLITICAL ECOLOGY" (BMR)" INCOME ATTIT WEALTH...GEOG METH SOC/INTEG 20. PAGE 58 F1133
HABITAT STRATA CHOOSE

B53
FRANKEL S.H.,THE ECONOMIC IMPACT ON UNDERDEVELOPED SOCIETIES: ESSAYS ON INTERNATIONAL INVESTMENT AND SOCIAL CHANGE. AFR WOR+45 ECO/DEV FINAN INDUS NAT/G ACT/RES TEC/DEV COLONIAL ATTIT...CONCPT OBS TREND 20. PAGE 43 F0845
ECO/UNDEV FOR/AID INT/TRADE

B53
MENDE T.,WORLD POWER IN THE BALANCE. FUT USA+45 USSR WOR-45 ECO/DEV ECO/TAC INT/TRADE EDU/PROP UTOPIA ATTIT...HUM CONCPT TREND TOT/POP 20. PAGE 90 F1756
WOR+45 PWR BAL/PWR AFR

B53
PURCELL T.V.,THE WORKER SPEAKS HIS MIND ON COMPANY AND UNION. WORKER ADJUD LEAD RACE/REL ATTIT DRIVE MARXISM...MGT CLASSIF STAT OBS INT SAMP BIBLIOG. PAGE 108 F2131
LABOR PARTIC INGP/REL HAPPINESS

B53
SAYLES L.R.,THE LOCAL UNION. CONSTN CULTURE DELIB/GP PARTIC CHOOSE GP/REL INGP/REL ATTIT ROLE ...MAJORIT DECISION MGT. PAGE 116 F2284
LABOR LEAD ADJUD ROUTINE

S53
BERNSTEIN M.H.,"POLITICAL IDEAS OF SELECTED AMERICAN BUSINESS JOURNALS (BMR)" USA+45 GP/REL ATTIT RIGID/FLEX ROLE ORD/FREE POLICY. PAGE 14 F0267
IDEA/COMP NAT/G LEAD

B54
CHILDS M.W.,ETHICS IN A BUSINESS SOCIETY. PROF/ORG LEAD WAR GP/REL ATTIT DRIVE PERSON KNOWL MORAL PWR ...WELF/ST BIBLIOG. PAGE 24 F0466
MGT SOCIETY

B54
MEYER A.G.,MARXISM. INTELL ECO/DEV WORKER CAP/ISM LEAD WAR ATTIT ALL/IDEOS...SOC 19/20 MARX/KARL. PAGE 90 F1766
MARXISM CONCPT ECO/TAC STRUCT

B54
MOSK S.A.,INDUSTRIAL REVOLUTION IN MEXICO. MARKET LABOR CREATE CAP/ISM ADMIN ATTIT SOCISM...POLICY 20 MEXIC/AMER. PAGE 94 F1843
INDUS TEC/DEV ECO/UNDEV NAT/G

B54
O.E.E.C.,PRIVATE UNITED STATES INVESTMENT IN EUROPE AND THE OVERSEAS TERRITORIES. EUR+WWI WOR+45 ECO/DEV ECO/UNDEV INT/ORG NAT/G VOL/ASSN ECO/TAC ATTIT WEALTH...GEOG STAT SYS/QU CHARTS VAL/FREE 20. PAGE 99 F1950
USA+45 FINAN BAL/PAY FOR/AID

B54
POTTER D.M.,PEOPLE OF PLENTY: ECONOMIC ABUNDANCE AND THE AMERICAN CHARACTER. USA+45 USA-45 ECO/DEV ATTIT PERSON...PSY SOC CONCPT TREND GEN/METH TOT/POP 20. PAGE 107 F2108
CULTURE WEALTH

B54
REYNOLDS P.A.,BRITISH FOREIGN POLICY IN THE INTER-WAR YEARS. CZECHOSLVK GERMANY POLAND UK USA-45 POL/PAR FORCES ECO/TAC ARMS/CONT WAR ATTIT 20. PAGE 111 F2182
DIPLOM POLICY NAT/G

B54
STALEY E.,THE FUTURE OF UNDERDEVELOPED COUNTRIES: POLITICAL IMPLICATIONS OF ECONOMIC DEVELOPMENT. AFR COM FUT USA+45 SOCIETY ECO/UNDEV CREATE PLAN CAP/ISM ATTIT DRIVE MARXISM SOCISM...POLICY CONCPT CHARTS 20. PAGE 125 F2466
EDU/PROP ECO/TAC FOR/AID

C54
BERLE A.A. JR.,"THE 20TH CENTURY CAPITALIST REVOLUTION." ECO/DEV NAT/G DIPLOM PRICE CONTROL ATTIT...BIBLIOG/A 20. PAGE 14 F0260
LG/CO CAP/ISM MGT PWR

B55
BERNAYS E.L.,THE ENGINEERING OF CONSENT. VOL/ASSN OP/RES ROUTINE INGP/REL ATTIT RESPECT...POLICY METH/CNCPT METH/COMP 20. PAGE 14 F0264
GP/REL PLAN ACT/RES ADJUST

B55
BERNSTEIN M.H.,REGULATING BUSINESS BY INDEPENDENT COMMISSION. USA+45 USA-45 LG/CO CHIEF LEGIS PROB/SOLV ADJUD SANCTION GP/REL ATTIT...TIME/SEQ 19/20 MONOPOLY PRESIDENT CONGRESS. PAGE 14 F0268
DELIB/GP CONTROL CONSULT

B55
BUCHANAN N.S.,APPROACHES TO ECONOMIC DEVELOPMENT. FUT USA+45 WOR+45 STRATA ECO/DEV INT/ORG NAT/G TEC/DEV DIPLOM FOR/AID ATTIT KNOWL PWR WEALTH ...RELATIV METH/CNCPT SELF/OBS TREND CON/ANAL STERTYP GEN/LAWS FOR/TRADE COMMUN 20. PAGE 20 F0380
ECO/UNDEV ECO/TAC INT/TRADE

B55
FLORINSKY M.T.,INTEGRATED EUROPE. EUR+WWI FRANCE ITALY NETHERLAND UK ECO/DEV INT/ORG FORCES LEGIT FEDERAL ATTIT PWR WEALTH...POLICY GEOG CONCPT GEN/LAWS TOT/POP EEC OEEC 20. PAGE 42 F0816
FUT ECO/TAC REGION

B55
WRONG D.H.,AMERICAN AND CANADIAN VIEWPOINTS. CANADA USA+45 CONSTN STRATA FAM SECT WORKER ECO/TAC EDU/PROP ADJUD MARRIAGE...IDEA/COMP 20. PAGE 149 F2936
DIPLOM ATTIT NAT/COMP CULTURE

S55
BUNZEL J.H.,"THE GENERAL IDEOLOGY OF AMERICAN SMALL BUSINESS"(BMR)" USA+45 USA-45 AGRI GP/REL INGP/REL PERSON...MGT IDEA/COMP 18/20. PAGE 20 F0383
ALL/IDEOS ATTIT SML/CO INDUS

B56
HISTORICAL ABSTRACTS. NAT/G CREATE DIPLOM ATTIT ...SOC DICTIONARY INDEX 18/20. PAGE 1 F0011
WOR-45 COMPUT/IR BIBLIOG/A

B56
ATOMIC INDUSTRIAL FORUM,PUBLIC RELATIONS FOR THE ATOMIC INDUSTRY. WOR+45 PLAN PROB/SOLV EDU/PROP PRESS CONFER...AUD/VIS ANTHOL 20. PAGE 7 F0135
NUC/PWR INDUS GP/REL ATTIT

B56
LIPSET S.M.,UNION DEMOCRACY. STRUCT INDUS FACE/GP WORKER CONTROL LEAD PARTIC GP/REL ATTIT LAISSEZ ...INT QU CHARTS. PAGE 80 F1577
LABOR INGP/REL MAJORIT

B56
UPHOFF W.H.,UNDERSTANDING THE UNION MEMBER (PAMPHLET). STRATA R+D LEAD PARTIC...METH/CNCPT STAT QU. PAGE 133 F2624
LABOR WORKER ATTIT DRIVE

B56
WILCOX W.W.,SOCIAL RESPONSIBILITY IN FARM LEADERSHIP. CLIENT LEGIS EXEC LOBBY GP/REL ATTIT WEALTH. PAGE 146 F2880
AGRI LEAD VOL/ASSN WORKER

L56
TAGLIACOZZO D.L.,"TRADE-UNION GOVERNMENT, ITS NATURE AND ITS PROBLEMS: A BIBLIOGRAPHICAL REVIEW, 1945-1955." STRUCT LEAD PARTIC CHOOSE ATTIT ...MAJORIT METH/CNCPT BIBLIOG. PAGE 128 F2526 CLASSIF LABOR INGP/REL GP/REL

S56
BONILLA F.,"WHEN IS PETITION 'PRESSURE?'" (BMR)" USA+45 ELITES INDUS LABOR CHIEF EDU/PROP LEGIT ATTIT...INT CHARTS 20 CONGRESS PRESIDENT EISNHWR/DD. PAGE 16 F0312 LEGIS EX/STRUC INT/TRADE TARIFFS

S56
BROWN J.S.,"UNION SIZE AS A FUNCTION OF INTRA-UNION CONFLICT." CLIENT CONTROL CHOOSE EFFICIENCY ATTIT TREND. PAGE 19 F0370 LABOR INGP/REL CONSEN DRIVE

S56
TANNENBAUM A.S.,"CONTROL OF STRUCTURE AND UNION FUNCTIONS." PARTIC GP/REL INGP/REL CONSEN ATTIT PWR ...QU SAMP. PAGE 128 F2529 LABOR STRUCT CONTROL LEAD

C56
MCKEE J.B.,"THE POWER TO DECIDE" IN M. WEINBERG AND O. SHABET, SOCIETY AND MAN." ELITES STRATA REPRESENT GP/REL ATTIT PWR MUNICH BUSINESS. PAGE 88 F1731 LABOR DECISION LEAD

N56
US HOUSE COMM FOREIGN AFFAIRS,REPORT OF THE SPECIAL STUDY MISSION TO AFRICA, SOUTH AND EAST OF THE SAHARA (PAMPHLET). AFR SOUTH/AFR USA+45 STRUCT INT/TRADE PARL/PROC NAT/LISM ATTIT ALL/VALS HEALTH ...POLICY 20 CONGRESS. PAGE 136 F2691 FOR/AID COLONIAL ECO/UNDEV DIPLOM

B57
EHRMANN H.W.,ORGANIZED BUSINESS IN FRANCE. EUR+WWI MOD/EUR ECO/DEV VOL/ASSN LEGIT ATTIT PERCEPT PWR RESPECT...PLURIST SOC INT TOT/POP 20. PAGE 36 F0712 PROF/ORG ECO/TAC FRANCE

B57
MEIER G.M.,ECONOMIC DEVELOPMENT: THEORY, HISTORY, AND POLICY. WOR+45 WOR-45 ECO/DEV ECO/UNDEV PLAN CAP/ISM BAL/PAY ATTIT PWR WEALTH SOCISM...CHARTS TOT/POP FOR/TRADE 20. PAGE 89 F1748 ECO/TAC GEN/LAWS

B57
WARRINER D.,LAND REFORM AND DEVELOPMENT IN THE MIDDLE EAST: A STUDY OF EGYPT, SYRIA AND IRAQ. IRAQ ISLAM SYRIA UAR AGRI DIST/IND PLAN TEC/DEV DOMIN REV ATTIT WEALTH...SOC METH/CNCPT STAT OBS RECORD HIST/WRIT TREND GEN/LAWS FAO 20. PAGE 143 F2825 ECO/UNDEV CONCPT

L57
MASS. INST. TECH.,"THE CENTER FOR INTERNATIONAL STUDIES." AFR ASIA COM EUR+WWI ISLAM L/A+17C S/ASIA USA+45 USA-45 DIST/IND CONSULT FORCES ACT/RES TEC/DEV DIPLOM REV ATTIT WEALTH...CONCPT FOR/TRADE 20. PAGE 87 F1702 R+D ECO/UNDEV

S57
DUBIN R.,"POWER AND UNION-MANAGEMENT RELATIONS." PROB/SOLV ADJUD ROUTINE ATTIT ORD/FREE...MGT STERTYP. PAGE 34 F0668 PWR LABOR BARGAIN GP/REL

S57
KAHN R.L.,"UNION PRACTICES AND MEMBER PARTICIPATION." PARTIC CHOOSE REPRESENT PERS/REL PERSON SKILL...DECISION METH/CNCPT QU. PAGE 69 F1347 INGP/REL LABOR ATTIT LEAD

S57
ROURKE F.E.,"THE POLITICS OF ADMINISTRATIVE ORGANIZATION: A CASE HISTORY." USA+45 LABOR WORKER PLAN ADMIN TASK EFFICIENCY 20 DEPT/LABOR CONGRESS. PAGE 114 F2251 POLICY ATTIT MGT GP/COMP

B58
BIDWELL P.W.,RAW MATERIALS: A STUDY OF AMERICAN POLICY. USA+45 USA-45 ECO/UNDEV AGRI INDUS KIN CREATE PLAN ECO/TAC WAR PEACE ATTIT DRIVE WEALTH ...STAT CHARTS CONGRESS FOR/TRADE VAL/FREE. PAGE 15 F0279 EXTR/IND ECO/DEV

B58
GALBRAITH J.K.,THE AFFLUENT SOCIETY. EUR+WWI FUT USA+45 USSR CULTURE SERV/IND PEACE WEALTH SOCISM ...NEW/IDEA TREND VAL/FREE 20. PAGE 45 F0882 ATTIT ECO/TAC CAP/ISM

B58
HAMEROW T.S.,RESTORATION, REVOLUTION, REACTION: ECONOMICS AND POLITICS IN GERMANY, 1815-1871. CAP/ISM ADJUST ATTIT PWR...BIBLIOG/A 19 GER/CONFED FRANK/PARL. PAGE 54 F1055 REV ORD/FREE ECO/DEV

B58
HIRSCHMAN A.O.,STRATEGY OF ECONOMIC DEVELOPMENT. WOR+45 WOR-45 CULTURE ECO/DEV NAT/G PLAN TEC/DEV INT/TRADE BAL/PAY ATTIT DRIVE RIGID/FLEX WEALTH ...CONCPT METH/CNCPT OBS CHARTS SIMUL GEN/LAWS TOT/POP VAL/FREE. PAGE 60 F1176 ECO/UNDEV ECO/TAC CAP/ISM

B58
KINDLEBERGER C.P.,INTERNATIONAL ECONOMICS. WOR+45 WOR-45 ECO/DEV ECO/UNDEV FINAN VOL/ASSN ACT/RES DIPLOM ECO/TAC LEGIT REGION ATTIT DRIVE ORD/FREE WEALTH...POLICY STAT TREND GEN/LAWS EEC ECSC OEEC 20. PAGE 71 F1391 INT/ORG BAL/PWR TARIFFS

B58
SCOTT D.J.R.,RUSSIAN POLITICAL INSTITUTIONS. RUSSIA USSR CONSTN AGRI DELIB/GP PLAN EDU/PROP CONTROL CHOOSE EFFICIENCY ATTIT MARXISM...BIBLIOG/A IND 13/20. PAGE 118 F2332 NAT/G POL/PAR ADMIN DECISION

L58
MASON E.S.,"ECONOMIC PLANNING IN UNDERDEVELOPED AREAS." FUT WOR+45 PLAN TEC/DEV EDU/PROP ATTIT RIGID/FLEX KNOWL...SOC CONCPT GEN/LAWS TOT/POP 20. PAGE 87 F1697 NAT/G ECO/UNDEV

S58
SCHULZE R.O.,"THE ROLE OF ECONOMIC DOMINANTS IN COMMUNITY POWER STRUCTURE." ECO/TAC ROUTINE ATTIT OBJECTIVE...SOC RECORD CENSUS. PAGE 118 F2319 SOCIETY STRUCT PROB/SOLV

B59
ALLEN R.L.,SOVIET INFLUENCE IN LATIN AMERICA. ECO/UNDEV FINAN PROC/MFG NAT/G TEC/DEV EDU/PROP EXEC ROUTINE ATTIT DRIVE PERSON ALL/VALS PWR...STAT CHARTS WORK FOR/TRADE 20. PAGE 4 F0071 L/A+17C ECO/TAC INT/TRADE USSR

B59
BARNETT A.D.,COMMUNIST ECONOMIC STRATEGY: THE RISE OF MAINLAND CHINA. CHINA/COM USSR WOR+45 AGRI INDUS FOR/AID INGP/REL ATTIT. PAGE 10 F0188 ECO/UNDEV INT/TRADE TOTALISM BAL/PWR

B59
CUCCORESE H.J.,HISTORIA DE LA CONVERSION DEL PAPEL MONEDA EN BUENOS AIRES, 1861-1867. AFR LAW LOC/G NAT/G ATTIT...POLICY BIBLIOG 19 ARGEN BUENOS/AIR. PAGE 29 F0560 FINAN PLAN LEGIS

B59
HARVARD UNIVERSITY LAW SCHOOL,INTERNATIONAL PROBLEMS OF FINANCIAL PROTECTION AGAINST NUCLEAR RISK. WOR+45 NAT/G DELIB/GP PROB/SOLV DIPLOM CONTROL ATTIT...POLICY INT/LAW MATH 20. PAGE 56 F1105 NUC/PWR ADJUD INDUS FINAN

B59
LEISERSON W.,AMERICAN TRADE UNION DEMOCRACY. CONSTN STRUCT ADJUD EXEC REPRESENT GP/REL INGP/REL MAJORITY ATTIT PWR. PAGE 77 F1516 LABOR LEAD PARTIC DELIB/GP

B59
MARTIN K.,WAR, HISTORY, AND HUMAN NATURE. FRANCE GERMANY INDIA UK UNIV POL/PAR COLONIAL DETER REV MARXISM PACIFISM...PSY CONCPT PREDICT LENIN/VI GANDHI/M. PAGE 86 F1683 PERSON WAR ATTIT IDEA/COMP

B59
MEYER A.J.,MIDDLE EASTERN CAPITALISM: NINE ESSAYS. ISLAM CULTURE ECO/UNDEV INDUS MARKET NAT/G PLAN ATTIT RIGID/FLEX...STAT OBS TREND GEN/LAWS. PAGE 90 F1767 TEC/DEV ECO/TAC ANTHOL

B59
ROCHE J.,LA COLONISATION ALLEMANDE ET LE RIO GRANDE DO SUL. BRAZIL L/A+17C NAT/G PROVS INGP/REL RACE/REL DISCRIM HABITAT...GEOG SOC/INTEG 19/20 MIGRATION. PAGE 113 F2228 ECO/UNDEV GP/REL ATTIT

B59
WAHLKE J.C.,LEGISLATIVE BEHAVIOR: A READER IN THEORY AND RESEARCH. USA+45 CONSTN ELITES POL/PAR LOBBY REPRESENT PERS/REL PERSON ROLE...IDEA/COMP METH/COMP SIMUL. PAGE 142 F2800 LEGIS CHOOSE INGP/REL ATTIT

B59
WARD B.,5 IDEAS THAT CHANGE THE WORLD. WOR+45 WOR-45 SOCIETY STRUCT AGRI INDUS INT/ORG NAT/G FORCES ACT/RES ARMS/CONT TOTALISM ATTIT DRIVE GEN/LAWS. PAGE 143 F2815 ECO/UNDEV ALL/VALS NAT/LISM COLONIAL

B59
WORTHY J.C.,BIG BUSINESS AND FREE MEN. LG/CO EX/STRUC EDU/PROP LEAD CHOOSE GP/REL ATTIT DRIVE ROLE ORD/FREE...MAJORIT 20. PAGE 149 F2927 ELITES LOC/G TOP/EX PARTIC

L59
FURASH E.A.,"PROBLEMS IN REVIEW: INDUSTRIAL ESPIONAGE." WORKER ECO/TAC PERS/REL OPTIMAL AGE ATTIT KNOWL...MGT DEEP/INT DEEP/QU GP/COMP IDEA/COMP. PAGE 45 F0875 INDUS TOP/EX MAJORITY

S59
BENDIX R.,"INDUSTRIALIZATION, IDEOLOGIES, AND SOCIAL STRUCTURE" (BMR)" UK USA-45 USSR STRUCT WORKER GP/REL EFFICIENCY...IDEA/COMP 20. PAGE 13 F0243 INDUS ATTIT MGT ADMIN

S59
GILPATRICK T.V.,"PRICE SUPPORT POLICY AND THE MIDWEST FARM VOTE" (BMR)" NAT/G PRICE CONTROL REGION...POLICY CHARTS 440 20 MIDWEST/US CONGRESS REPUBLICAN EISNHWR/DD 20. PAGE 47 F0925 POL/PAR AGRI ATTIT CHOOSE

S59
HOFFMAN P.,"OPERATION BREAKTHROUGH." AFR S/ASIA STRUCT INDUS CONSULT TEC/DEV ATTIT RIGID/FLEX SKILL WEALTH...TECHNIC CONCPT STYLE RECORD CHARTS ORG/CHARTS GEN/METH VAL/FREE 20. PAGE 61 F1190 ECO/UNDEV EDU/PROP FOR/AID

S59
PLAZA G.,"FOR A REGIONAL MARKET IN LATIN AMERICA." FUT L/A+17C CULTURE INDUS NAT/G ECO/TAC INT/TRADE ATTIT WEALTH...NEW/IDEA TREND OAS 20. PAGE 106 F2092 MARKET INT/ORG REGION

S59
SHEPPARD H.L.,"THE POLITICAL ATTITUDES AND PREFERENCES OF UNION MEMBERS: THE CASE OF THE LABOR ATTIT

DETROIT AUTO WORKERS." LOBBY CHOOSE ROLE...CLASSIF QU SAMP TREND. PAGE 120 F2376 — WORKER

S59
TEITSWORTH C.S.,"GROWING ROLE OF THE COMPANY ECONOMIST." USA+45 PLAN PROB/SOLV CAP/ISM ECO/TAC ADMIN ATTIT MGT. PAGE 129 F2541 — INDUS CONSULT UTIL DECISION

S59
ZAUBERMAN A.,"SOVIET BLOC ECONOMIC INTEGRATION." COM CULTURE INTELL ECO/DEV INDUS TOP/EX ACT/RES PLAN ECO/TAC INT/TRADE ROUTINE CHOOSE ATTIT ...TIME/SEQ 20. PAGE 150 F2958 — MARKET INT/ORG USSR TOTALISM

B60
APTHEKER H.,DISARMAMENT AND THE AMERICAN ECONOMY: A SYMPOSIUM. FUT USA+45 ECO/DEV DIST/IND FINAN INDUS PROC/MFG LABOR NAT/G POL/PAR CONSULT PLAN CAP/ISM INT/TRADE PEACE ATTIT MORAL WEALTH...TREND GEN/LAWS TOT/POP 20. PAGE 6 F0110 — MARXIST ARMS/CONT

B60
ARON R.,COLLOQUES DE RHEINFELDEN. AFR USA+45 USSR WOR+45 WOR-45 CULTURE ECO/UNDEV NAT/G POL/PAR DIPLOM NAT/LISM TOTALISM ATTIT DRIVE ALL/VALS ...PLURIST CONCPT STERTYP GEN/LAWS TOT/POP 20. PAGE 6 F0120 — ECO/DEV SOCIETY CAP/ISM SOCISM

B60
BAERWALD F.,ECONOMIC SYSTEM ANALYSIS: CONCEPTS AND PERSPECTIVES. USA+45 ECO/DEV NAT/G COMPUTER EQUILIB INCOME ATTIT...DECISION CONCPT IDEA/COMP. PAGE 8 F0151 — ACT/RES ECO/TAC ROUTINE FINAN

B60
DIA M.,REFLEXIONS SUR L'ECONOMIE DE L'AFRIQUE NOIRE (REV. ED.). CULTURE ECO/UNDEV CREATE TEC/DEV DIPLOM INT/TRADE OPTIMAL ATTIT...POLICY 20. PAGE 32 F0631 — AFR ECO/TAC SOCISM PLAN

B60
FORM W.H.,INDUSTRY, LABOR, AND COMMUNITY. STRUCT NEIGH SECT BAL/PWR EDU/PROP PARTIC ATTIT ROLE PWR WEALTH...METH/CNCPT CHARTS. PAGE 42 F0828 — LABOR MGT GP/REL CONTROL

B60
FRANCK P.G.,AFGHANISTAN: BETWEEN EAST AND WEST. AFGHANISTN AFR USA+45 USSR ECO/UNDEV PLAN ADMIN ROUTINE ATTIT PWR...STAT OBS CHARTS TOT/POP FOR/TRADE 20. PAGE 43 F0843 — ECO/TAC TREND FOR/AID

B60
GRAMPP W.D.,THE MANCHESTER SCHOOL OF ECONOMICS. UK LAW ECO/DEV COERCE ATTIT ORD/FREE LAISSEZ ...PHIL/SCI IDEA/COMP 19/20 MANCHESTER CORN/LAWS. PAGE 50 F0973 — ECO/TAC VOL/ASSN LOBBY NAT/G

B60
GRANICK D.,THE RED EXECUTIVE. COM USA+45 SOCIETY ECO/DEV INDUS NAT/G POL/PAR EX/STRUC PLAN ECO/TAC EDU/PROP ADMIN EXEC ATTIT DRIVE...GP/COMP 20. PAGE 50 F0976 — PWR STRATA USSR ELITES

B60
HITCH C.J.,THE ECONOMICS OF DEFENSE IN THE NUCLEAR AGE. USA+45 WOR+45 CREATE PLAN NUC/PWR ATTIT ...CON/ANAL CHARTS HYPO/EXP NATO 20. PAGE 60 F1179 — R+D FORCES

B60
KENEN P.B.,BRITISH MONETARY POLICY AND THE BALANCE OF PAYMENTS 1951-57. UK PLAN BUDGET ECO/TAC INT/TRADE PAY PRICE COST ATTIT 20. PAGE 70 F1377 — BAL/PAY PROB/SOLV FINAN NAT/G

B60
LENCZOWSKI G.,OIL AND STATE IN THE MIDDLE EAST. FUT IRAN LAW ECO/UNDEV EXTR/IND NAT/G TOP/EX PLAN TEC/DEV ECO/TAC LEGIT ADMIN COERCE ATTIT ALL/VALS PWR...CHARTS 20. PAGE 78 F1519 — ISLAM INDUS NAT/LISM

B60
LERNER A.P.,THE ECONOMICS OF CONTROL. USA+45 ECO/UNDEV INT/ORG ACT/RES PLAN CAP/ISM INT/TRADE ATTIT WEALTH...SOC MATH STAT GEN/LAWS INDEX 20. PAGE 78 F1530 — ECO/DEV ROUTINE ECO/TAC SOCISM

B60
LISTER L.,EUROPE'S COAL AND STEEL COMMUNITY. FRANCE GERMANY STRUCT ECO/DEV EXTR/IND INDUS MARKET NAT/G DELIB/GP ECO/TAC INT/TRADE EDU/PROP ATTIT RIGID/FLEX ORD/FREE PWR WEALTH...CONCPT STAT TIME/SEQ CHARTS ECSC TERR/GP 20. PAGE 81 F1582 — EUR+WWI INT/ORG REGION

B60
MENDELSON W.,CAPITALISM, DEMOCRACY, AND THE SUPREME COURT. USA+45 USA-45 CONSTN DIPLOM GOV/REL ATTIT ORD/FREE LAISSEZ...POLICY CHARTS PERS/COMP 18/20 SUPREME/CT MARSHALL/J HOLMES/OW TANEY/RB FIELD/JJ. PAGE 90 F1758 — JUDGE CT/SYS JURID NAT/G

B60
MOORE W.E.,LABOR COMMITMENT AND SOCIAL CHANGE IN DEVELOPING AREAS. SOCIETY STRATA ECO/UNDEV MARKET VOL/ASSN WORKER AUTHORIT SKILL...MGT NAT/COMP SOC/INTEG 20. PAGE 93 F1823 — LABOR ORD/FREE ATTIT INDUS

B60
PENTONY D.E.,UNITED STATES FOREIGN AID. INDIA LAOS USA+45 ECO/UNDEV INT/TRADE ADMIN PEACE ATTIT ...POLICY METH/COMP ANTHOL 20. PAGE 105 F2060 — FOR/AID DIPLOM ECO/TAC

B60
RAMA C.M.,LAS CLASES SOCIALES EN EL URUGUAY. L/A+17C URUGUAY ELITES SOCIETY STRATA INDUS ATTIT HABITAT PWR...GEOG SOC/INTEG MUNICH 20. PAGE 109 F2138 — ECO/UNDEV STRUCT PARTIC

B60
ROBSON W.A.,NATIONALIZED INDUSTRY AND PUBLIC OWNERSHIP. UK ECO/DEV FINAN LABOR LG/CO POL/PAR LEGIS ACT/RES GP/REL...TREND IDEA/COMP 20. PAGE 113 F2227 — NAT/G OWN INDUS ATTIT

B60
ROEPKE W.,A HUMANE ECONOMY: THE SOCIAL FRAMEWORK OF THE FREE MARKET. FUT USSR WOR+45 CULTURE SOCIETY ECO/DEV PLAN ECO/TAC ADMIN ATTIT PERSON RIGID/FLEX SUPEGO MORAL WEALTH SOCISM...POLICY OLD/LIB CONCPT TREND GEN/LAWS 20. PAGE 113 F2232 — DRIVE EDU/PROP CAP/ISM

B60
STANFORD RESEARCH INSTITUTE,AFRICAN DEVELOPMENT: A TEST FOR INTERNATIONAL COOPERATION. AFR USA+45 WOR+45 FINAN INT/ORG PLAN PROB/SOLV ECO/TAC INT/TRADE ADMIN...CHARTS 20. PAGE 125 F2467 — FOR/AID ECO/UNDEV ATTIT DIPLOM

B60
STEIN E.,AMERICAN ENTERPRISE IN THE EUROPEAN COMMON MARKET: A LEGAL PROFILE. EUR+WWI FUT USA+45 SOCIETY STRUCT ECO/DEV NAT/G VOL/ASSN CONSULT PLAN TEC/DEV ECO/TAC INT/TRADE ADMIN ATTIT RIGID/FLEX PWR...MGT NEW/IDEA STAT TREND COMPUT/IR SIMUL EEC 20. PAGE 125 F2475 — MARKET ADJUD INT/LAW

B60
WEINER H.E.,BRITISH LABOR AND PUBLIC OWNERSHIP. UK SERV/IND LG/CO WORKER CONTROL OWN 20. PAGE 145 F2850 — LABOR NAT/G INDUS ATTIT

L60
SPENGLER J.J.,"ECONOMIC DEVELOPMENT: POLITICAL PRECONDITIONS AND POLITICAL CONSEQUENCE." WOR+45 STRUCT ECO/UNDEV NAT/G PLAN ECO/TAC EDU/PROP ATTIT ORD/FREE WEALTH SOCISM...SOC CONCPT TREND SIMUL GEN/METH WORK 20. PAGE 124 F2452 — TEC/DEV METH/CNCPT CAP/ISM

S60
BARNETT H.J.,"RESEARCH AND DEVELOPMENT, ECONOMIC GROWTH, AND NATIONAL SECURITY." AFR USA+45 R+D CREATE ECO/TAC ATTIT DRIVE PWR...POLICY SOC METH/CNCPT QUANT STAT TIME/SEQ ORG/CHARTS LOG/LING 20. PAGE 10 F0190 — ACT/RES PLAN

S60
BERG E.J.,"ECONOMIC BASIS OF POLITICAL CHOICE IN FRENCH WEST AFRICA." FRANCE ECO/UNDEV AGRI INDUS NAT/G PLAN LEGIT COLONIAL REGION ATTIT PWR WEALTH ...CONCPT FOR/TRADE 20. PAGE 13 F0257 — AFR ECO/TAC

S60
DUNN J.M.,"AMERICAN DEPENDENCE ON MATERIALS IMPORTS: THE WORLD-WIDE RESOURCE BASE." USA+45 WOR+45 NAT/G ATTIT WEALTH...RECORD TIME/SEQ CHARTS FOR/TRADE 20. PAGE 35 F0680 — ACT/RES ECO/TAC

S60
ENKE S.,"THE ECONOMIES OF GOVERNMENT PAYMENTS TO LIMIT POPULATION." FUT INDIA WOR+45 CULTURE FINAN NAT/G CONSULT PLAN LEGIT CONTROL COST ATTIT RIGID/FLEX HEALTH WEALTH...STAT OBS CHARTS TOT/POP VAL/FREE 20. PAGE 38 F0736 — FAM ACT/RES

S60
FRANKEL S.H.,"ECONOMIC ASPECTS OF POLITICAL INDEPENDENCE IN AFRICA." AFR FUT SOCIETY ECO/UNDEV COM/IND FINAN LEGIS PLAN TEC/DEV CAP/ISM ECO/TAC INT/TRADE ADMIN ATTIT DRIVE RIGID/FLEX PWR WEALTH ...MGT NEW/IDEA MATH TIME/SEQ VAL/FREE 20. PAGE 43 F0846 — NAT/G FOR/AID

S60
GARNICK D.H.,"ON THE ECONOMIC FEASIBILITY OF A MIDDLE EASTERN COMMON MARKET." AFR ISLAM CULTURE INDUS NAT/G PLAN TEC/DEV ECO/TAC ADMIN ATTIT DRIVE RIGID/FLEX...PLURIST STAT TREND GEN/LAWS 20. PAGE 46 F0907 — MARKET INT/TRADE

S60
MAIR L.P.,"SOCIAL CHANGE IN SOUTH AFRICA." MOD/EUR SOUTH/AFR WOR+45 ECO/UNDEV EX/STRUC TEC/DEV ATTIT DRIVE PERCEPT ORD/FREE...MGT CONCPT TIME/SEQ IND 20. PAGE 84 F1641 — AFR NAT/G REV SOVEREIGN

S60
MURPHEY R.,"ECONOMIC CONFLICTS IN SOUTH ASIA." ASIA CULTURE INTELL ECO/TAC REGION ATTIT DRIVE KNOWL ...METH/CNCPT TIME/SEQ STERTYP TOT/POP METH/GP VAL/FREE 20. PAGE 95 F1864 — S/ASIA ECO/UNDEV

S60
NANES A.,"THE EUROPEAN COMMUNITY AND THE UNITED STATES: EVOLVING RELATIONS." EUR+WWI USA+45 WOR+45 ECO/UNDEV MARKET NAT/G DELIB/GP PLAN LEGIT ATTIT PWR WEALTH...CONCPT STAT TIME/SEQ CON/ANAL EEC METH/GP OEEC 20 EURATOM. PAGE 96 F1889 — INT/ORG REGION

S60
NICHOLS J.P.,"HAZARDS OF AMERICAN PRIVATE INVESTMENT IN UNDERDEVELOPED COUNTRIES." FUT L/A+17C USA+45 USA-45 EXTR/IND CONSULT BAL/PWR ECO/TAC DOMIN ADJUD ATTIT SOVEREIGN WEALTH ...HIST/WRIT TIME/SEQ TREND TERR/GP VAL/FREE 20. PAGE 98 F1924 — FINAN ECO/UNDEV CAP/ISM NAT/LISM

S60
PYE L.W.,"SOVIET AND AMERICAN STYLES IN FOREIGN AID." COM USA+45 USSR WOR+45 NAT/G PLAN ECO/TAC ROUTINE RIGID/FLEX...POLICY CONCPT TREND GEN/LAWS TOT/POP 20. PAGE 108 F2132
ECO/UNDEV ATTIT FOR/AID

S60
RICHTER J.H.,"TOWARDS AN INTERNATIONAL POLICY ON AGRICULTURAL TRADE." EUR+WWI USA+45 ECO/DEV NAT/G PLAN ECO/TAC ATTIT PWR WEALTH...CONCPT GEN/LAWS 20. PAGE 111 F2187
AGRI INT/ORG

S60
RIVKIN A.,"AFRICAN ECONOMIC DEVELOPMENT: ADVANCED TECHNOLOGY AND THE STAGES OF GROWTH." CULTURE ECO/UNDEV AGRI COM/IND EXTR/IND PLAN ECO/TAC ATTIT DRIVE RIGID/FLEX SKILL WEALTH...MGT SOC GEN/LAWS FOR/TRADE WORK TOT/POP 20. PAGE 111 F2195
AFR TEC/DEV FOR/AID

B61
AMERICAN MANAGEMENT ASSN,SUPERIOR-SUBORDINATE COMMUNICATION IN MANAGEMENT. STRATA FINAN INDUS SML/CO WORKER CONTROL EXEC ATTIT 20. PAGE 5 F0090
MGT ACT/RES PERS/REL LG/CO

B61
BARRASH J.,LABOR'S GRASS ROOTS; A STUDY OF THE LOCAL UNION. STRATA BARGAIN LEAD REPRESENT DEMAND ATTIT PWR. PAGE 10 F0192
LABOR USA+45 INGP/REL EXEC

B61
BONNEFOUS M.,EUROPE ET TIERS MONDE. EUR+WWI SOCIETY INT/ORG NAT/G VOL/ASSN ACT/RES TEC/DEV CAP/ISM ECO/TAC ATTIT ORD/FREE SOVEREIGN...POLICY CONCPT TREND TERR/GP COMMUN 20. PAGE 16 F0314
AFR ECO/UNDEV FOR/AID INT/TRADE

B61
BRAIBANTI R.,TRADITION, VALUES AND SOCIO-ECONOMIC DEVELOPMENT. WOR+45 ACT/RES TEC/DEV ATTIT ORD/FREE CONSERVE...POLICY SOC ANTHOL. PAGE 17 F0336
ALL/VALS ECO/UNDEV CONCPT METH/CNCPT

B61
DE VRIES E.,MAN IN RAPID SOCIAL CHANGE. WOR+45 SOCIETY ECO/DEV ECO/UNDEV AGRI INDUS FAM SECT TEC/DEV ATTIT...RECORD 20 CHRISTIAN. PAGE 31 F0607
CULTURE ALL/VALS SOC TASK

B61
GARDNER R.N.,LEGAL-ECONOMIC PROBLEMS OF INTERNATIONAL TRADE. FUT WOR+45 INTELL ECO/DEV EX/STRUC INT/TRADE ROUTINE ATTIT WEALTH...GEN/LAWS ANTHOL FOR/TRADE 20. PAGE 46 F0904
FINAN ACT/RES

B61
KATKOFF U.,SOVIET ECONOMY 1940-1965. COM WOR+45 WOR-45 INTELL NAT/G POL/PAR TOP/EX ATTIT PWR ...POLICY TIME/SEQ VAL/FREE 20. PAGE 69 F1360
AGRI PERSON TOTALISM USSR

B61
KITZINGER V.W.,THE CHALLENGE OF THE COMMON MARKET. EUR+WWI ECO/DEV DIST/IND PLAN ECO/TAC INT/TRADE LEGIT ATTIT PWR WEALTH...TIME/SEQ TREND CHARTS EEC 20. PAGE 71 F1403
MARKET INT/ORG UK

B61
MARX K.,THE COMMUNIST MANIFESTO. IN (MENDEL A. ESSENTIAL WORKS OF MARXISM, NEW YORK: BANTAM. FUT MOD/EUR CULTURE ECO/DEV ECO/UNDEV AGRI FINAN INDUS MARKET PROC/MFG LABOR POL/PAR CONSULT FORCES CREATE PLAN ADMIN ATTIT DRIVE RIGID/FLEX ORD/FREE PWR RESPECT MARX/KARL MUNICH WORK. PAGE 86 F1691
COM NEW/IDEA CAP/ISM REV

B61
MYBDAL G.,THE POLITICAL ELEMENT IN THE DEVELOPMENT OF ECONOMIC THEORY. FINAN LOBBY ATTIT...WELF/ST CONCPT IDEA/COMP GEN/LAWS 20. PAGE 95 F1875
ECO/DEV ECO/TAC SOCIETY

B61
PROUDHON P.J.,LA GUERRE ET LA PAIX (2 VOLS.). UNIV STRATA PROB/SOLV EQUILIB INCOME ATTIT...CONCPT 19. PAGE 108 F2125
WAR PEACE WEALTH

B61
STARK H.,SOCIAL AND ECONOMIC FRONTIERS IN LATIN AMERICA (2ND ED.). CUBA FUT CULTURE AGRI INDUS ECO/TAC PRODUC ATTIT MARXISM...NAT/COMP BIBLIOG T 20. PAGE 125 F2470
L/A+17C SOCIETY DIPLOM ECO/UNDEV

B61
STROUD G.S.,LABOR HISTORY IN THE UNITED STATES: A GENERAL BIBLIOGRAPHY. USA+45 USA-45 STRATA VOL/ASSN AUTOMAT GP/REL INGP/REL ATTIT HEALTH 18/20. PAGE 127 F2504
BIBLIOG WORKER LABOR

B61
WARD B.J.,INDIA AND THE WEST. INDIA UK USA+45 INT/TRADE GIVE COLONIAL ATTIT MARXISM 19/20. PAGE 143 F2817
PLAN ECO/UNDEV ECO/TAC FOR/AID

S61
BARALL M.,"THE UNITED STATES GOVERNMENT RESPONDS." L/A+17C USA+45 SOCIETY NAT/G CREATE PLAN DIPLOM ECO/TAC ATTIT DRIVE RIGID/FLEX KNOWL SKILL WEALTH ...METH/CNCPT TIME/SEQ GEN/METH 20. PAGE 9 F0176
ECO/UNDEV ACT/RES FOR/AID

S61
BRAFF A.J.,"WAGE-PRICE POLICIES UNDER PUBLIC PRESSURE." USA+45 EX/STRUC LOBBY REPRESENT PWR 20. PAGE 17 F0335
ATTIT PARTIC PROB/SOLV

S61
GALBRAITH J.K.,"A POSITIVE APPROACH TO ECONOMIC AID." FUT USA+45 INTELL NAT/G CONSULT ACT/RES DIPLOM ECO/TAC EDU/PROP ATTIT KNOWL PWR WEALTH ...SOC STERTYP MID/EX METH/GP 20. PAGE 45 F0883
ECO/UNDEV ROUTINE FOR/AID

S61
GORDON L.,"ECONOMIC REGIONALISM RECONSIDERED." FUT USA+45 WOR+45 INDUS NAT/G TEC/DEV DIPLOM ROUTINE PERCEPT WEALTH...WELF/ST METH/CNCPT WORK 20. PAGE 49 F0957
ECO/DEV ATTIT CAP/ISM REGION

S61
HAYTES W.,"THREE VIEWS ON THE SOVIET ECONOMIC THREAT." AFR COM USA+45 USA-45 USSR WOR+45 WOR-45 INDUS TEC/DEV ECO/TAC DOMIN ATTIT PERCEPT PWR FOR/TRADE 20. PAGE 57 F1128
ECO/DEV PLAN TOTALISM

S61
HEILBRONER R.L.,"DYNAMICS OF FOREIGN AID: PROBLEMS OF UNDERDEVELOPED NATIONS PLAGUE ASSISTANCE PROGRAM." FUT USA+45 WOR+45 STRATA NAT/G PLAN TEC/DEV ATTIT DRIVE WEALTH WORK 20. PAGE 58 F1135
ECO/UNDEV ECO/TAC FOR/AID

S61
VINER J.,"ECONOMIC FOREIGN POLICY ON THE NEW FRONTIER." USA+45 ECO/UNDEV AGRI FINAN INDUS MARKET INT/ORG NAT/G FOR/AID INT/TRADE ADMIN ATTIT PWR 20 KENNEDY/JF. PAGE 141 F2786
TOP/EX ECO/TAC BAL/PAY TARIFFS

S61
WILDAVSKY A.,"POLITICAL IMPLICATIONS OF BUDGETARY REFORM." AFR NAT/G POL/PAR DELIB/GP EX/STRUC ATTIT PWR CONGRESS. PAGE 146 F2881
BUDGET PLAN LEGIS

N61
VINER J.,THE INTELLECTUAL HISTORY OF LAISSEZ FAIRE (PAMPHLET). WOR+45 WOR-45 LAW INTELL...POLICY LING LOG 19/20. PAGE 141 F2787
ATTIT EDU/PROP LAISSEZ ECO/TAC

B62
ARNOLD H.J.P.,AID FOR DEVELOPING COUNTRIES. COM EUR+WWI USA+45 USSR WOR+45 EDU/PROP ATTIT DRIVE PWR WEALTH...TREND CHARTS STERTYP NAT/ 20. PAGE 6 F0115
ECO/UNDEV ECO/TAC FOR/AID

B62
ARNOLD T.W.,THE FOLKLORE OF CAPITALISM. USA+45 USA-45 SOCIETY LG/CO SML/CO EX/STRUC ECO/TAC EDU/PROP ADJUST INCOME...MYTH CHARTS 20. PAGE 6 F0116
CAP/ISM ATTIT STERTYP ECO/DEV

B62
CAIRNCROSS A.K.,FACTORS IN ECONOMIC DEVELOPMENT. WOR+45 ECO/UNDEV INDUS R+D LG/CO NAT/G EX/STRUC PLAN TEC/DEV ECO/TAC ATTIT HEALTH KNOWL PWR WEALTH ...TIME/SEQ GEN/LAWS TOT/POP TRUE/GP VAL/FREE 20. PAGE 21 F0399
MARKET ECO/DEV

B62
CARPER E.T.,ILLINOIS GOES TO CONGRESS FOR ARMY LAND. USA+45 LAW EXTR/IND PROVS REGION CIVMIL/REL GOV/REL FEDERAL ATTIT 20 ILLINOIS SENATE CONGRESS DIRKSEN/E DOUGLAS/P. PAGE 22 F0420
ADMIN LOBBY GEOG LEGIS

B62
COLLIER A.T.,MANAGEMENT, MEN, AND VALUES. INDUS FACE/GP EX/STRUC PLAN PROB/SOLV DEBATE SENIOR ADMIN PROFIT PERSON...PSY SOC 20. PAGE 26 F0505
MGT ATTIT PERS/REL DECISION

B62
DEBUYST F.,LAS CLASES SOCIALES EN AMERICA LATINA. L/A+17C SOCIETY STRUCT WORKER EDU/PROP RACE/REL ATTIT HABITAT ROLE...GEOG SOC NAT/COMP SOC/INTEG 20. PAGE 32 F0612
STRATA GP/REL WEALTH

B62
EINZIG P.,THE HISTORY OF FOREIGN EXCHANGE. CHRIST-17C ISLAM MEDIT-7 PRE/AMER WOR+45 ECO/DEV FINAN PLAN ECO/TAC ATTIT KNOWL WEALTH...SIMUL GEN/LAWS. PAGE 37 F0714
MARKET TIME/SEQ INT/TRADE

B62
ELLIOTT J.R.,THE APPEAL OF COMMUNISM IN THE UNDERDEVELOPED NATIONS. AFR USSR WOR+45 INT/ORG NAT/G DIPLOM DOMIN EDU/PROP ROUTINE ATTIT RIGID/FLEX ORD/FREE PWR WEALTH MARXISM...POLICY SOC METH/CNCPT MYTH TOT/POP METH/GP 20. PAGE 37 F0722
COM ECO/UNDEV

B62
FRIEDMANN W.,METHODS AND POLICIES OF PRINCIPAL DONOR COUNTRIES IN PUBLIC INTERNATIONAL DEVELOPMENT FINANCING: PRELIMINARY APPRAISAL. FRANCE GERMANY/W UK USA+45 USSR WOR+45 FINAN TEC/DEV CAP/ISM DIPLOM ECO/TAC ATTIT 20 EEC. PAGE 44 F0864
INT/ORG FOR/AID NAT/COMP ADMIN

B62
HUMPHREY D.D.,THE UNITED STATES AND THE COMMON MARKET. USA+45 INDUS MARKET INT/ORG PLAN EDU/PROP BAL/PAY DRIVE PWR WEALTH...TREND STERTYP FOR/TRADE EEC 20. PAGE 63 F1241
ATTIT ECO/TAC

B62
KAUTSKY J.H.,POLITICAL CHANGE IN UNDERDEVELOPED COUNTRIES: NATIONALISM AND COMMUNISM. WOR+45 AGRI TEC/DEV EDU/PROP ATTIT...POLICY METH/CNCPT STYLE INT QU CENSUS TREND SOC/EXP GEN/LAWS 20. PAGE 69 F1365
ECO/UNDEV SOCIETY CAP/ISM REV

B62
KIRPICEVA I.K.,HANDBUCH DER RUSSISCHEN UND SOWJETISCHEN BIBLIOGRAPHIEN (5 VOLS.). USSR STRUCT ECO/DEV DIPLOM LEAD ATTIT 18/20. PAGE 71 F1400
BIBLIOG/A NAT/G MARXISM

COM

B62
ROBINSON A.D.,DUTCH ORGANIZED AGRICULTURE IN INTERNATIONAL POLITICS, 1945-1960. EUR+WWI NETHERLAND STRUCT ECO/DEV NAT/G VOL/ASSN CONSULT DELIB/GP PLAN TEC/DEV INT/TRADE EDU/PROP ATTIT RIGID/FLEX ALL/VALS...NEW/IDEA TREND EEC COMMUN 20. PAGE 112 F2215
AGRI INT/ORG

B62
ROTHBARD M.N.,THE PANIC OF 1819; REACTIONS AND POLICIES. AFR USA-45 LAW FINAN BUDGET TARIFFS DEMAND 19 DEPRESSION. PAGE 114 F2247
ECO/UNDEV POLICY ATTIT ECO/TAC

B62
SMITH G.A. JR.,POLICY FORMULATION AND ADMINISTRATION: A CASEBOOK OF TOPMANAGEMENT PROBLEMS IN BUSINESS. EX/STRUC PLAN PROB/SOLV ADMIN CONTROL EXEC LEAD ROUTINE EFFICIENCY ATTIT MGT. PAGE 123 F2430
INDUS SOC/EXP TOP/EX DECISION

B62
US CONGRESS JOINT ECO COMM,ECONOMIC DEVELOPMENTS IN SOUTH AMERICA. USA+45 SOCIETY FINAN NAT/G PROB/SOLV TEC/DEV INT/TRADE TAX EFFICIENCY PRODUC ATTIT ...POLICY 20 ALL/PROG CONGRESS SOUTH/AMER. PAGE 135 F2654
L/A+17C ECO/UNDEV FOR/AID DIPLOM

B62
WARD B.,THE RICH NATIONS AND THE POOR NATIONS. FUT WOR+45 CULTURE ECO/DEV ECO/UNDEV PLAN CAP/ISM EDU/PROP REV NAT/LISM ATTIT DRIVE SOCISM...POLICY CONCPT TIME/SEQ 20. PAGE 143 F2816
ECO/TAC GEN/LAWS

L62
GALBRAITH J.K.,"ECONOMIC DEVELOPMENT IN PERSPECTIVE." CAP/ISM ECO/TAC ROUTINE ATTIT WEALTH ...TREND CHARTS SOC/EXP WORK TERR/GP 20. PAGE 45 F0884
ECO/UNDEV PLAN

S62
ALPERT P.,"ECONOMIC POLICIES AND PLANNING IN NEWLY INDEPENDENT AFRICA." PLAN ATTIT PWR WEALTH ...STERTYP GEN/LAWS VAL/FREE 20. PAGE 4 F0078
AFR ECO/DEV NAT/LISM COLONIAL

S62
IOVTCHOUK M.T.,"ON SOME THEORETICAL PRINCIPLES AND METHODS OF SOCIOLOGICAL INVESTIGATIONS (IN RUSSIAN)." FUT USA+45 STRATA R+D NAT/G POL/PAR TOP/EX ACT/RES PLAN ECO/TAC EDU/PROP ROUTINE ATTIT RIGID/FLEX MARXISM SOCISM...MARXIST METH/CNCPT OBS TREND NAT/COMP GEN/LAWS 20. PAGE 65 F1288
COM ECO/DEV CAP/ISM USSR

S62
MEAD W.,"SOME POLITICAL-ECONOMIC ISSUES DETERMINING USA TARIFF POLICY." USA+45 USA-45 ECO/DEV NAT/G TARIFFS ATTIT...TIME/SEQ TREND CHARTS 19/20. PAGE 89 F1736
ECO/TAC METH/CNCPT BAL/PAY

S62
MILLIKEN M.,"NEW AND OLD CRITERIA FOR AID." WOR+45 ECO/DEV ECO/UNDEV ACT/RES PLAN ATTIT KNOWL...TREND CON/ANAL SIMUL GEN/METH TERR/GP 20. PAGE 92 F1796
USA+45 ECO/TAC FOR/AID

S62
MUELLER E.,"LOCATION DECISIONS OF MANUFACTURERS." USA+45 MARKET ATTIT...POLICY STAT INT CHARTS 20. PAGE 94 F1852
DECISION PROC/MFG GEOG TOP/EX

S62
PYE L.W.,"THE POLITICAL IMPULSES AND FANTASIES BEHIND FOREIGN AID." FUT USA+45 ECO/UNDEV DIPLOM ECO/TAC ROUTINE DRIVE KNOWL...SOC METH/CNCPT NEW/IDEA TREND HYPO/EXP STERTYP GEN/METH 20. PAGE 108 F2133
ACT/RES ATTIT FOR/AID

S62
READ W.H.,"UPWARD COMMUNICATION IN INDUSTRIAL HIERARCHIES." LG/CO TOP/EX PROB/SOLV DOMIN EXEC PERS/REL ATTIT DRIVE PERCEPT...CORREL STAT CHARTS 20. PAGE 110 F2159
ADMIN INGP/REL PSY MGT

S62
ZAUBERMAN A.,"SOVIET AND CHINESE STRATEGY FOR ECONOMIC GROWTH." ASIA CHINA/COM COM USSR STRATA VOL/ASSN PLAN ATTIT PWR...METH/CNCPT GEN/LAWS WORK TERR/GP 20. PAGE 150 F2959
ECO/DEV EDU/PROP

B63
ABSHIRE D.M.,NATIONAL SECURITY: POLITICAL, MILITARY, AND ECONOMIC STRATEGIES IN THE DECADE AHEAD. ASIA COM USA+45 WOR+45 ECO/DEV ECO/UNDEV INT/ORG DELIB/GP FORCES ECO/TAC COERCE ATTIT RIGID/FLEX HEALTH ORD/FREE PWR WEALTH...POLICY STAT CHARTS ANTHOL COLD/WAR VAL/FREE APP/SCI. PAGE 2 F0032
FUT ACT/RES BAL/PWR

B63
BAUER R.A.,AMERICAN BUSINESS AND PUBLIC POLICY: THE POLITICS OF FOREIGN TRADE. USA+45 COM/IND LG/CO NAT/G PROF/ORG SML/CO VOL/ASSN LEGIS TOP/EX ECO/TAC EDU/PROP CHOOSE HEALTH PWR WEALTH...CONCPT METH/CNCPT OBS INT QU SAMP FOR/TRADE TRUE/GP VAL/FREE HI. PAGE 11 F0217
ECO/DEV ATTIT

B63
BELOFF M.,THE UNITED STATES AND THE UNITY OF EUROPE. EUR+WWI UK USA+45 WOR+45 VOL/ASSN DIPLOM REGION ATTIT PWR...CONCPT EEC OEEC 20 NATO. PAGE 13 F0239
ECO/DEV INT/ORG

B63
BONINI C.P.,SIMULATION OF INFORMATION AND DECISION SYSTEMS IN THE FIRM. MARKET BUDGET DOMIN EDU/PROP ADMIN COST ATTIT HABITAT PERCEPT PWR...CONCPT PROBABIL QUANT PREDICT HYPO/EXP BIBLIOG. PAGE 16 F0313
INDUS SIMUL DECISION MGT

B63
CENTRO PARA EL DESARROLLO,LA ALIANZA PARA EL PROGRESO Y EL DESARROLLO SOCIAL DE AMERICA LATINA. L/A+17C INT/ORG DIPLOM ECO/TAC INT/TRADE ATTIT 20 ALL/PROG. PAGE 22 F0435
ECO/UNDEV FOR/AID PLAN REGION

B63
CERAMI C.A.,ALLIANCE BORN OF DANGER. EUR+WWI USA+45 USSR ECO/DEV INDUS VOL/ASSN ECO/TAC REGION ATTIT MARXISM ATLAN/ALL 20 NATO EEC. PAGE 22 F0437
DIPLOM INT/ORG NAT/G POLICY

B63
CHAMPION J.M.,CRITICAL INCIDENTS IN MANAGEMENT. MARKET LG/CO SML/CO OP/RES ADMIN CONTROL LEAD GP/REL PERS/REL COST ATTIT SUPEGO ALL/VALS...PSY PERS/TEST BIBLIOG. PAGE 23 F0445
MGT DECISION EX/STRUC INDUS

B63
CORLEY R.N.,THE LEGAL ENVIRONMENT OF BUSINESS. CONSTN LEGIS TAX ADMIN CT/SYS DISCRIM ATTIT PWR ...TREND 18/20. PAGE 28 F0537
NAT/G INDUS JURID DECISION

B63
DE VRIES E.,SOCIAL ASPECTS OF ECONOMIC DEVELOPMENT IN LATIN AMERICA. CULTURE SOCIETY STRATA FINAN INDUS INT/ORG DELIB/GP ACT/RES ECO/TAC EDU/PROP ADMIN ATTIT SUPEGO HEALTH KNOWL ORD/FREE...SOC STAT TREND ANTHOL TOT/POP VAL/FREE. PAGE 31 F0608
L/A+17C ECO/UNDEV

B63
ENKE S.,ECONOMICS FOR DEVELOPMENT. AGRI TEC/DEV CAP/ISM DIPLOM ECO/TAC TAX ATTIT DRIVE HABITAT WEALTH...GOV/COMP BIBLIOG 20. PAGE 38 F0737
ECO/UNDEV PHIL/SCI CON/ANAL

B63
GANDHI M.K.,THE WAY TO COMMUNAL HARMONY. INDIA MAJORITY RIGID/FLEX ROLE RESPECT 20 GANDHI/M. PAGE 46 F0892
RACE/REL DISCRIM ATTIT ADJUST

B63
GLADE W.P. JR.,THE POLITICAL ECONOMY OF MEXICO. FUT L/A+17C CULTURE SOCIETY AGRI INDUS DELIB/GP ACT/RES ECO/TAC ATTIT HEALTH ORD/FREE...STAT TIME/SEQ TREND MEXIC/AMER TOT/POP VAL/FREE 20. PAGE 48 F0928
FINAN ECO/UNDEV

B63
GRUBEL H.G.,WORLD MONETARY REFORM: PLANS AND ISSUES. FUT WOR+45 ECO/DEV ECO/UNDEV R+D DELIB/GP CREATE ECO/TAC ATTIT RIGID/FLEX WEALTH...STAT ANTHOL VAL/FREE 20. PAGE 52 F1009
FINAN INT/ORG BAL/PAY INT/TRADE

B63
HIRSCHMAN A.O.,JOURNEYS TOWARD PROGRESS: STUDIES OF ECONOMIC POLICYMAKING IN LATIN AMERICA. CHILE FUT ECO/UNDEV AGRI FINAN INDUS CONSULT DELIB/GP PLAN ATTIT HEALTH ORD/FREE WEALTH...POLICY STAT VAL/FREE COLOMB 20. PAGE 60 F1177
L/A+17C ECO/TAC BRAZIL

B63
HOOPES R.,THE STEEL CRISIS. USA+45 INDUS ECO/TAC EDU/PROP PRICE CONTROL ATTIT...POLICY 20 KENNEDY/JF. PAGE 61 F1205
PROC/MFG NAT/G RATION CHIEF

B63
ISSAWI C.,EGYPT IN REVOLUTION: AN ECONOMIC ANALYSIS. ISLAM STRUCT ECO/UNDEV AGRI FINAN INDUS PLAN EXEC REV NAT/LISM ATTIT RIGID/FLEX WEALTH SOCISM...STAT FOR/TRADE WORK 20. PAGE 66 F1292
NAT/G UAR

B63
JACOBS P.,STATE OF UNIONS. USA+45 STRATA TOP/EX GP/REL RACE/REL DEMAND DISCRIM ATTIT PWR 20 CONGRESS NEGRO HOFFA/J. PAGE 66 F1296
LABOR ECO/TAC BARGAIN DECISION

B63
KRAVIS I.B.,DOMESTIC INTERESTS AND INTERNATIONAL OBLIGATIONS: SAFEGUARDS IN INTERNATIONAL TRADE ORGANIZATIONS. EUR+WWI USA+45 WOR+45 FINAN DELIB/GP ATTIT RIGID/FLEX HEALTH...STAT EEC VAL/FREE OEEC ECSC 20. PAGE 73 F1435
INT/ORG ECO/TAC INT/TRADE

B63
LAIRD R.D.,SOVIET AGRICULTURAL AND PEASANT AFFAIRS. FUT STRATA LOC/G DELIB/GP ACT/RES TEC/DEV ECO/TAC EDU/PROP ATTIT RIGID/FLEX ORD/FREE SKILL WEALTH ...STAT CON/ANAL ANTHOL MUNICH WORK VAL/FREE 20. PAGE 74 F1461
COM AGRI POLICY

B63
MULLENBACH P.,CIVILIAN NUCLEAR POWER: ECONOMIC ISSUES AND POLICY FORMATION. AFR FINAN INT/ORG DELIB/GP ACT/RES ECO/TAC ATTIT SUPEGO HEALTH ORD/FREE PWR...POLICY CONCPT MATH STAT CHARTS VAL/FREE 20. PAGE 94 F1855
USA+45 ECO/DEV NUC/PWR

B63
OTERO L.M.,HONDURAS. HONDURAS SPAIN STRUCT SECT COLONIAL REV WAR ATTIT PWR...GEOG WORSHIP 16/20. PAGE 102 F2003
NAT/G SOCIETY NAT/LISM ECO/UNDEV

B63
PRYOR F.L.,THE COMMUNIST FOREIGN TRADE SYSTEM. COM CZECHOSLVK GERMANY YUGOSLAVIA LAW ECO/DEV DIST/IND POL/PAR PLAN DOMIN TOTALISM DRIVE RIGID/FLEX WEALTH ...STAT STAND/INT CHARTS FOR/TRADE 20. PAGE 108 F2130
ATTIT ECO/TAC

B63
RAFUSE R.W. JR.,STATE AND LOCAL FISCAL BEHAVIOR OVER THE POSTWAR CYCLES (DISSERTATION). USA+45 TAX PRICE ATTIT...POLICY TIME/SEQ TREND CHARTS BIBLIOG 20. PAGE 109 F2135
BUDGET LOC/G ECO/TAC PROVS

B63
RANGEL I.,A INFLACAO BRASILEIRA (2ND ED.). AFR BRAZIL AGRI INDUS MARKET INT/TRADE DEMAND EQUILIB ATTIT 20. PAGE 109 F2144
ECO/UNDEV FINAN PRICE TAX

B63
RILEY J.W. JR.,THE CORPORATION AND ITS PUBLICS. ESSAYS ON THE CORPORATE IMAGE. CLIENT ISOLAT AGE ATTIT...POLICY SOC METH/CNCPT INT. PAGE 111 F2193
LG/CO CLASSIF GP/REL NEIGH

B63
ROBBINS L.,POLITICS AND ECONOMICS. ECO/DEV FINAN BUDGET DIPLOM BAL/PAY ORD/FREE 20. PAGE 112 F2204
NAT/G ATTIT

B63
SHANKS M.,THE LESSONS OF PUBLIC ENTERPRISE. UK LEGIS WORKER ECO/TAC ADMIN PARL/PROC GOV/REL ATTIT ...POLICY MGT METH/COMP NAT/COMP ANTHOL 20 PARLIAMENT. PAGE 120 F2364
SOCISM OWN NAT/G INDUS

B63
VON MISES L.,HUMAN ACTION: A TREATISE ON ECONOMICS (2ND ED.). SOCIETY MARKET TAX PAY PRICE DEMAND EQUILIB RATIONAL...PSY 20. PAGE 142 F2794
PLAN DRIVE ATTIT

B63
WAGLEY C.,INTRODUCTION TO BRAZIL. BRAZIL L/A+17C FAM KIN SCHOOL SECT ATTIT WEALTH...GEOG SOC. PAGE 142 F2799
ECO/UNDEV ELITES HABITAT STRATA

L63
ADERBIGDE A.,"SYMPOSIUM ON WEST AFRICA INTEGRATION." AFR EUR+WWI FUT CULTURE SOCIETY STRATA DIST/IND INDUS MARKET SERV/IND DELIB/GP PLAN TEC/DEV DOMIN EDU/PROP LEGIT COERCE ATTIT ALL/VALS ...POLICY STAT TREND CHARTS VAL/FREE. PAGE 2 F0040
FINAN ECO/TAC REGION

L63
MCKERSIE R.B.,"NONPROFESSIONAL HOSPITAL WORKERS AND A UNION ORGANIZING DRIVE." PLAN GP/REL RACE/REL ATTIT DRIVE...CORREL STAT INT GP/COMP. PAGE 88 F1732
VOL/ASSN HEALTH INGP/REL LABOR

L63
NASH M.,"PSYCHO-CULTURAL FACTORS IN ASIAN ECONOMIC GROWTH." ASIA ISLAM S/ASIA CULTURE ECO/UNDEV DELIB/GP EDU/PROP COERCE ATTIT PERSON HEALTH KNOWL ORD/FREE...PSY SOC STAT TREND ANTHOL VAL/FREE 20. PAGE 96 F1893
SOCIETY ECO/TAC

L63
OLSON M. JR.,"RAPID ECONOMIC GROWTH AS A DESTABILIZING FORCE." WOR+45 WOR-45 STRATA ECO/UNDEV FAM KIN CREATE TEC/DEV DIPLOM PEACE ATTIT PERSON RIGID/FLEX PWR RESPECT WEALTH...SOC 20. PAGE 101 F1989
SOCIETY FOR/AID

L63
RIDAH A.,"LE NEO-DESTOUR DEPUIS L'INDEPENDANCE." FUT ISLAM WOR+45 ECO/UNDEV INT/ORG SCHOOL DELIB/GP TOP/EX ACT/RES EDU/PROP LEGIT ATTIT ALL/VALS 20 TUNIS. PAGE 111 F2189
NAT/G CONSTN

S63
APPERT K.,"BERECHTIGE VORBEHALTE DER SCHWEIZERISCHEN ZUR INTEGRATION." EUR+WWI UK MARKET SERV/IND NAT/G PLAN RIGID/FLEX OEEC 20 EEC. PAGE 6 F0108
FINAN ATTIT SWITZERLND

S63
ARDANT G.,"A PLAN FOR FULL EMPLOYMENT IN THE DEVELOPING COUNTRIES." AFR FUT WOR+45 DELIB/GP ACT/RES PLAN ECO/TAC ATTIT ALL/VALS...POLICY STAT CHARTS TUNIS VAL/FREE 20. PAGE 6 F0112
ECO/UNDEV SOCIETY MOROCCO

S63
BARTHELEMY G.,"LE NOUVEAU FRANC (CFA) ET LA BANQUE CENTRALE DES ETATS DE L'AFRIQUE DE L'OUEST." FUT STRUCT INT/ORG PLAN ATTIT ALL/VALS FOR/TRADE 20. PAGE 11 F0200
AFR FINAN

S63
BELOFF M.,"BRITAIN, EUROPE AND THE ATLANTIC COMMUNITY." EUR+WWI ELITES NAT/G VOL/ASSN TOP/EX ATTIT ORD/FREE PWR SOVEREIGN WEALTH EEC TOT/POP VAL/FREE CMN/WLTH 20. PAGE 13 F0240
INT/ORG ECO/DEV UK

S63
BILL J.A.,"THE SOCIAL AND ECONOMIC FOUNDATIONS OF POWER IN CONTEMPORARY IRAN." ISLAM CULTURE NAT/G ECO/TAC DOMIN COERCE ATTIT PWR WEALTH...TREND VAL/FREE 20. PAGE 15 F0284
SOCIETY STRATA IRAN

S63
DELWERT J.,"L'ECONOMIE CAMBODGIENNE ET SON EVOLUTION ACTUELLE." FUT S/ASIA ECO/UNDEV ACT/RES PLAN WEALTH...CONCPT OBS TIME/SEQ TREND 20. PAGE 32 F0617
FINAN ATTIT CAMBODIA

S63
EMERSON R.,"THE ATLANTIC COMMUNITY AND THE EMERGING COUNTRIES." FUT WOR+45 ECO/DEV ECO/UNDEV R+D NAT/G DELIB/GP BAL/PWR ECO/TAC EDU/PROP ROUTINE ORD/FREE PWR WEALTH...POLICY CONCPT TREND GEN/METH EEC 20 NATO. PAGE 37 F0729
ATTIT INT/TRADE

S63
FLOREA I.,"CU PRIVIRE LA OBIECTUL MATERIALISMULUI ISTORIC SI AL COMUNISMULUI STIINTIFIC SI LA RAPORTUL DINTRE ELE." EUR+WWI WOR+45 WOR-45 INTELL NAT/G POL/PAR WORKER EDU/PROP PERCEPT MARXISM ...MARXIST PHIL/SCI CONCPT TOT/POP 20. PAGE 42 F0812
COM ATTIT TOTALISM

S63
FOURASTIE J.,"LES SCIENCES ECONOMIQUES ET SOCIALES EN EUROPE." EUR+WWI FUT MOD/EUR WOR+45 WOR-45 INTELL SOCIETY R+D PLAN ROUTINE ATTIT RIGID/FLEX KNOWL...OBS TREND. PAGE 43 F0833
ACT/RES CULTURE

S63
GRUSHIN B.A.,"PROBLEMS OF THE MOVEMENT OF COMMUNIST LABOR IN THE USSR." COM SOCIETY LABOR ECO/TAC EDU/PROP COERCE RIGID/FLEX ORD/FREE...POLICY MARXIST STAT QU WORK 20. PAGE 52 F1011
ATTIT USSR

S63
HALLSTEIN W.,"THE EUROPEAN COMMUNITY AND ATLANTIC PARTNERSHIP." EUR+WWI USA+45 MARKET NAT/G VOL/ASSN DELIB/GP ARMS/CONT NUC/PWR ATTIT PWR...CONCPT STAT TIME/SEQ TREND OEEC 20 EEC. PAGE 54 F1053
INT/ORG ECO/TAC UK

S63
HINDLEY D.,"FOREIGN AID TO INDONESIA AND ITS POLITICAL IMPLICATIONS." INDONESIA POL/PAR ATTIT SOVEREIGN...CHARTS 20. PAGE 60 F1173
FOR/AID NAT/G WEALTH ECO/TAC

S63
HOOVER C.B.,"ECONOMIC REFORM VERSUS ECONOMIC GROWTH IN UNDERDEVELOPED COUNTRIES." FUT WOR+45 ELITES STRATA ECO/UNDEV DIST/IND INDUS TEC/DEV CAP/ISM FOR/AID INT/TRADE ATTIT WEALTH...MYTH TREND STERTYP GEN/LAWS WORK 20. PAGE 61 F1209
ECO/DEV ECO/TAC

S63
LEDUC G.,"L'AIDE INTERNATIONALE AU DEVELOPPEMENT." FUT WOR+45 ECO/DEV ECO/UNDEV R+D PROF/ORG TEC/DEV ECO/TAC ROUTINE ATTIT ALL/VALS...MGT TIME/SEQ FOR/TRADE TOT/POP 20. PAGE 77 F1503
FINAN PLAN FOR/AID

S63
MASON E.S.,"INTERESTS, IDEOLOGIES AND THE PROBLEM OF STABILITY AND GROWTH." EUR+WWI USA+45 DELIB/GP CREATE PLAN EXEC ROUTINE BAL/PAY ATTIT PWR...MGT CONCPT OEEC 20. PAGE 87 F1698
NAT/G ECO/DEV

S63
MATHUR P.N.,"GAINS IN ECONOMIC GROWTH FROM INTERNATIONAL TRADE." USA-45 ECO/DEV FINAN INDUS ATTIT WEALTH...MATH QUANT STAT BIOG TREND GEN/LAWS WORK 20. PAGE 87 F1704
MARKET ECO/TAC CAP/ISM INT/TRADE

S63
MIKESELL R.F.,"COMMODITY AGREEMENTS AND AID TO DEVELOPING COUNTRIES." WOR+45 WOR-45 INT/ORG ECO/TAC ATTIT WEALTH WORK FOR/TRADE 20. PAGE 91 F1782
FINAN ECO/UNDEV BAL/PAY FOR/AID

S63
MONROE A.D.,"BRITAIN AND THE EUROPEAN COMMUNITY." EUR+WWI FRANCE NAT/G DELIB/GP TOP/EX ECO/TAC DOMIN PWR...POLICY RECORD GEN/LAWS EEC EFTA 20 EFTA CMN/WLTH. PAGE 93 F1817
VOL/ASSN ATTIT UK

S63
PRYBYLA J.,"THE QUEST FOR ECONOMIC RATIONALITY IN THE SOVIET BLOC." COM FUT WOR+45 WOR-45 DIST/IND MARKET PLAN ECO/TAC ATTIT...METH/CNCPT TOT/POP 20. PAGE 108 F2128
ECO/DEV TREND USSR

S63
RAMERIE L.,"TENSION AU SEIN DU COMECON: LE CAS ROUMAIN." COM EUR+WWI USSR WOR+45 ECO/DEV DIST/IND NAT/G POL/PAR VOL/ASSN EDU/PROP TOTALISM ATTIT WEALTH...TIME/SEQ 20 COMECON. PAGE 109 F2142
INT/ORG ECO/TAC INT/TRADE ROMANIA

S63
REDDAWAY W.B.,"THE ECONOMICS OF UNDERDEVELOPED COUNTRIES." S/ASIA WOR+45 WOR-45 STRATA AGRI COM/IND DIST/IND MARKET PROC/MFG PLAN TEC/DEV FOR/AID BAL/PAY ATTIT DRIVE SKILL WORK FOR/TRADE 20. PAGE 110 F2165
ECO/TAC ECO/UNDEV INDIA

S63
SCHURMANN F.,"ECONOMIC POLICY AND POLITICAL POWER IN COMMUNIST CHINA." ASIA CHINA/COM USSR SOCIETY ECO/UNDEV AGRI INDUS CREATE ADMIN ROUTINE ATTIT DRIVE RIGID/FLEX PWR WEALTH...HIST/WRIT TREND CHARTS WORK 20. PAGE 118 F2323
PLAN ECO/TAC

S63
SHONFIELD A.,"AFTER BRUSSELS." EUR+WWI FRANCE GERMANY UK ECO/DEV DIST/IND MARKET VOL/ASSN DELIB/GP CREATE INT/TRADE ATTIT RIGID/FLEX...RECORD TREND GEN/LAWS EEC COMMUN CMN/WLTH 20. PAGE 121 F2385
PLAN ECO/TAC

S63
SHWADRAN B.,"MIDDLE EAST OIL, 1962." ISLAM DIST/IND INDUS PLAN ATTIT DRIVE WEALTH...POLICY STAT CONT/OBS TREND CHARTS GEN/LAWS TERR/GP METH/GP 20
PROC/MFG ECO/TAC ELITES

OIL. PAGE 121 F2393 REGION

S63
TENNYSON L.B.,"THE USA IN ATLANTIC COMMUNITY." ATTIT
EUR+WWI FRANCE UK USA+45 ECO/UNDEV VOL/ASSN ECO/TAC
DELIB/GP TOP/EX DIPLOM DOMIN PWR...POLICY CONCPT BAL/PWR
TREND GEN/LAWS EEC 20. PAGE 129 F2545

S63
VINER J.,"REPORT OF THE CLAY COMMITTEE ON FOREIGN ACT/RES
AID: A SYMPOSIUM." USA+45 WOR+45 NAT/G CONSULT PLAN ECO/TAC
BAL/PWR ATTIT WEALTH...MGT CONCPT TOT/POP 20. FOR/AID
PAGE 142 F2788

S63
WALKER H.,"THE INTERNATIONAL LAW OF COMMODITY MARKET
AGREEMENTS." FUT WOR+45 ECO/DEV ECO/UNDEV FINAN VOL/ASSN
INT/ORG NAT/G CONSULT CREATE PLAN ECO/TAC ATTIT INT/LAW
PERCEPT...CONCPT GEN/LAWS TOT/POP GATT 20. PAGE 142 INT/TRADE
F2804

S63
WOLFERS A.,"INTEGRATION IN THE WEST: THE CONFLICT RIGID/FLEX
OF PERSPECTIVES." AFR EUR+WWI USA+45 ECO/DEV ECO/TAC
INT/ORG DELIB/GP CREATE TEC/DEV DIPLOM ATTIT PWR
...CONCPT HIST/WRIT TREND GEN/LAWS EEC 20. PAGE 148
F2918

N63
US AGENCY INTERNATIONAL DEV,PRINCIPLES OF FOREIGN FOR/AID
ECONOMIC ASSISTANCE (PAMPHLET). USA+45 FINAN GP/REL PLAN
BAL/PAY EFFICIENCY 20 AID. PAGE 134 F2638 ECO/UNDEV
ATTIT

N63
US COMM STRENG SEC FREE WORLD,THE SCOPE AND DELIB/GP
DISTRIBUTION OF UNITED STATES MILITARY AND ECONOMIC POLICY
ASSISTANCE PROGRAMS (PAMPHLET). USA+45 PLAN BAL/PWR FOR/AID
BUDGET DIPLOM CONTROL CIVMIL/REL ATTIT. PAGE 134 ORD/FREE
F2648

B64
AHMAD M.,THE CIVIL SERVANT IN PAKISTAN. PAKISTAN WELF/ST
ECO/UNDEV COLONIAL INGP/REL...SOC CHARTS BIBLIOG 20 ADMIN
CIVIL/SERV. PAGE 3 F0051 ATTIT
STRATA

B64
BAUCHET P.,ECONOMIC PLANNING. FRANCE STRATA LG/CO ECO/DEV
CAP/ISM ADMIN PARL/PROC DEMAND OPTIMAL ATTIT PWR NAT/G
SOCISM...POLICY CHARTS 20. PAGE 11 F0212 PLAN
ECO/TAC

B64
BOURGOIGNIE G.E.,JEUNE AFRIQUE MOBILISABLE; LES AGE/Y
PROBLEMES DE LA JEUNESSE DESOEUVREE EN AFRIQUE AFR
NOIRE. INT/ORG VOL/ASSN ECO/TAC ROUTINE UTIL ATTIT CREATE
20. PAGE 17 F0324 ECO/UNDEV

B64
CHINITZ B.,CITY AND SUBURB: THE ECONOMICS OF TEC/DEV
METROPOLITAN GROWTH. DIST/IND BUDGET GOV/REL DEMAND PLAN
ATTIT HABITAT MUNICH PHILADELPH. PAGE 24 F0467

B64
COLUMBIA U SCHOOL OF LAW,PUBLIC INTERNATIONAL ECO/UNDEV
DEVELOPMENT FINANCING IN INDIA. GERMANY/W INDIA UK FINAN
USA+45 INDUS PLAN TEC/DEV DIPLOM ECO/TAC GIVE ADMIN FOR/AID
UTIL ATTIT 20. PAGE 26 F0512 INT/ORG

B64
DUSCHA J.,ARMS, MONEY, AND POLITICS. USA+45 INDUS NAT/G
POL/PAR ECO/TAC TAX DETER NUC/PWR WAR WEAPON FORCES
GOV/REL ATTIT...BIBLIOG/A 20 CONGRESS MONEY POLICY
DEPT/DEFEN. PAGE 35 F0687 BUDGET

B64
ESTHUS R.A.,FROM ENMITY TO ALLIANCE: US AUSTRALIAN DIPLOM
RELATIONS. S/ASIA DIST/IND VOL/ASSN FORCES ATTIT 20 WAR
AUSTRAL TREATY CMN/WLTH. PAGE 39 F0751 INT/TRADE
FOR/AID

B64
FEIS H.,FOREIGN AID AND FOREIGN POLICY. USA+45 ECO/UNDEV
WOR+45 NAT/G VOL/ASSN ACT/RES TEC/DEV ATTIT HEALTH ECO/TAC
WEALTH...SOC GEN/LAWS 20. PAGE 40 F0775 FOR/AID
DIPLOM

B64
FRIEDEN B.J.,THE FUTURE OF OLD NEIGHBORHOODS: NEIGH
REBUILDING FOR A CHANGING POPULATION. CONSTRUC PROB/SOLV
LOC/G NAT/G ACT/RES ECO/TAC REGION ATTIT...INT SAMP PLAN
MUNICH 20 NEWYORK/C LOS/ANG HARTFORD URBAN/RNWL. BUDGET
PAGE 44 F0855

B64
GREBLER L.,URBAN RENEWAL IN EUROPEAN COUNTRIES: ITS PLAN
EMERGENCE AND POTENTIALS. EUR+WWI UK ECO/DEV LOC/G CONSTRUC
NEIGH CREATE ADMIN ATTIT...TREND NAT/COMP MUNICH 20 NAT/G
URBAN/RNWL. PAGE 50 F0981

B64
IMAZ J.L.,LOS QUE MANDAN. INDUS LABOR NAT/G POL/PAR LEAD
PROVS SECT CHIEF TOP/EX CONTROL 20 ARGEN. PAGE 64 FORCES
F1261 ELITES
ATTIT

B64
LEKACHMAN R.,KEYNES' GENERAL THEORY: REPORTS OF PHIL/SCI
THREE DECADES. FINAN ATTIT...POLICY 20 KEYNES/JM. GEN/METH
PAGE 77 F1517 IDEA/COMP

B64
LITVAK I.A.,MARKETING: CANADA. CANADA STRATA ECO/TAC
PROC/MFG LEGIS TEC/DEV DIPLOM INT/TRADE PRICE MARKET

AUTOMAT ATTIT WEALTH...ANTHOL 20. PAGE 81 F1587 ECO/DEV
EFFICIENCY

B64
MELADY T.,FACES OF AFRICA. AFR FUT ISLAM NAT/G ECO/UNDEV
POL/PAR SCHOOL DELIB/GP PLAN ECO/TAC EDU/PROP ATTIT TREND
ALL/VALS...CHARTS TOT/POP TERR/GP VAL/FREE 20. NAT/LISM
PAGE 89 F1752

B64
NAGEL P.C.,ONE NATION INDIVISIBLE: THE UNION IN FEDERAL
AMERICAN THOUGHT 1776-1861. USA-45 INDUS TEC/DEV NAT/G
EDU/PROP DREAM...IDEA/COMP 18/19. PAGE 96 F1887 ATTIT
INGP/REL

B64
RAMAZANI R.K.,THE MIDDLE EAST AND THE EUROPEAN ECO/UNDEV
COMMON MARKET. EUR+WWI ISLAM ECO/DEV EXTR/IND ATTIT
MARKET PROC/MFG INT/ORG NAT/G TEC/DEV ECO/TAC INT/TRADE
REGION DRIVE WEALTH...STAT CHARTS EEC TOT/POP 20.
PAGE 109 F2141

B64
SCHULTZ T.W.,TRANSFORMING TRADITIONAL AGRICULTURE. AGRI
WOR+45 WOR-45 CULTURE STRATA FINAN ACT/RES ECO/TAC ECO/UNDEV
ATTIT KNOWL SKILL...MATH STAT TIME/SEQ GEN/LAWS
VAL/FREE. PAGE 117 F2316

B64
SEERS D.,CUBA: THE ECONOMIC AND SOCIAL REVOLUTION. ACT/RES
L/A+17C USSR YUGOSLAVIA STRATA AGRI INDUS SCHOOL COERCE
DELIB/GP PLAN ECO/TAC DOMIN EDU/PROP ATTIT CUBA
RIGID/FLEX ALL/VALS...STAT OBS TIME/SEQ WORK REV
VAL/FREE 20. PAGE 119 F2341

B64
SULLIVAN G.,THE STORY OF THE PEACE CORPS. USA+45 INT/ORG
WOR+45 INTELL FACE/GP NAT/G SCHOOL VOL/ASSN CONSULT ECO/UNDEV
EX/STRUC PLAN EDU/PROP ADMIN ATTIT DRIVE ALL/VALS FOR/AID
...POLICY HEAL SOC CONCPT INT QU BIOG TREND SOC/EXP PEACE
WORK. PAGE 127 F2511

B64
SULTAN P.E.,THE DISENCHANTED UNIONIST. NAT/G ADJUD LABOR
CONTROL SANCTION RACE/REL ANOMIE ATTIT ROLE INGP/REL
...METH/CNCPT INT. PAGE 127 F2512 CHARTS
MAJORIT

B64
US CONGRESS JOINT ECO COMM,PRIVATE INVESTMENT IN FINAN
LATIN AMERICA. L/A+17C USA+45 INT/ORG PROB/SOLV ECO/UNDEV
ECO/TAC ATTIT...INT 20 CONGRESS. PAGE 135 F2658 PARL/PROC
LEGIS

B64
WRIGHT G.,RURAL REVOLUTION IN FRANCE: THE PEASANTRY PWR
IN THE TWENTIETH CENTURY. EUR+WWI MOD/EUR LAW STRATA
CULTURE AGRI POL/PAR DELIB/GP LEGIS ECO/TAC FRANCE
EDU/PROP COERCE CHOOSE ATTIT RIGID/FLEX HEALTH REV
...STAT CENSUS CHARTS VAL/FREE 20. PAGE 149 F2932

B64
ZOBER M.,MARKETING MANAGEMENT. FINAN BUDGET ECO/DEV
EDU/PROP PRICE PRODUC ATTIT...POLICY TREND CHARTS MGT
METH/COMP EQULIB 20. PAGE 150 F2966 CONTROL
MARKET

L64
ARMENGALD A.,"ECONOMIE ET COEXISTENCE." COM EUR+WWI MARKET
FUT USA+45 WOR+45 ECO/DEV ECO/UNDEV FINAN INT/ORG ECO/TAC
NAT/G EXEC CHOOSE ATTIT ALL/VALS...POLICY RELATIV AFR
DECISION TREND SOC/EXP WORK 20. PAGE 6 F0113 CAP/ISM

L64
HAAS E.B.,"ECONOMICS AND DIFFERENTIAL PATTERNS OF L/A+17C
POLITICAL INTEGRATION: PROJECTIONS ABOUT UNITY IN INT/ORG
LATIN AMERICA." SOCIETY NAT/G DELIB/GP ACT/RES MARKET
CREATE PLAN ECO/TAC REGION ROUTINE ATTIT DRIVE PWR
WEALTH...CONCPT TREND CHARTS LAFTA TERR/GP 20.
PAGE 52 F1020

S64
BEIM D.,"THE COMMUNIST BLOC AND THE FOREIGN-AID COM
GAME." AFR WOR+45 NAT/G PLAN ROUTINE ATTIT KNOWL ECO/UNDEV
ORD/FREE...DECISION QUANT CONT/OBS TIME/SEQ CHARTS ECO/TAC
GAME SIMUL LOG/LING 20. PAGE 12 F0231 FOR/AID

S64
CLELLAND D.A.,"ECONOMIC DOMINANTS AND COMMUNITY LEAD
POWER: A COMPARATIVE ANALYSIS." ELITES ADJUST ATTIT MGT
WEALTH...DECISION MUNICH. PAGE 25 F0488 PWR

S64
FINLEY D.D.,"A POLITICAL PERSPECTIVE OF ECONOMIC VOL/ASSN
RELATIONS IN THE COMMUNIST CAMP." COM USSR FACE/GP ECO/TAC
NAT/G ACT/RES PLAN DOMIN COERCE ATTIT ORD/FREE DIPLOM
WEALTH...TIME/SEQ 20. PAGE 41 F0800 REGION

S64
HERMAN L.M.,"THE ECONOMIC CONTENT OF SOVIET TRADE COM
WITH THE WEST." WOR+45 ECO/DEV ECO/UNDEV AGRI MARKET
COM/IND INDUS CAP/ISM ECO/TAC ATTIT RIGID/FLEX INT/TRADE
WEALTH...OBS TREND VAL/FREE MARX/KARL 20. PAGE 59 USSR
F1152

S64
HUTCHINSON E.C.,"AMERICAN AID TO AFRICA." FUT AFR
USA+45 MARKET INT/ORG LOC/G NAT/G PUB/INST PLAN ECO/UNDEV
ECO/TAC ATTIT RIGID/FLEX...POLICY CONCPT TREND FOR/AID
TERR/GP 20. PAGE 63 F1248

S64
N,"QUASI-LEGISLATIVE ARBITRATION AGREEMENTS." LAW ADJUD
LG/CO ECO/TAC SANCTION ATTIT POLICY. PAGE 96 F1885 ADJUST

LABOR
GP/REL

S64
NEISSER H.,"THE EXTERNAL EQUILIBRIUM OF THE UNITED STATES ECONOMY." FUT USA+45 NAT/G ACT/RES PLAN ECO/TAC ATTIT WEALTH...METH/CNCPT GEN/METH VAL/FREE FOR/TRADE 20. PAGE 97 F1910 — FINAN ECO/DEV BAL/PAY INT/TRADE

S64
PESELT B.M.,"COMMUNIST ECONOMIC OFFENSIVE." WOR+45 SOCIETY INT/ORG PLAN ECO/TAC DOMIN EDU/PROP ATTIT PERSON PWR WEALTH...TREND CHARTS METH/GP 20. PAGE 105 F2067 — COM ECO/UNDEV FOR/AID USSR

S64
POLARIS J.,"THE SINO-SOVIET DISPUTE: ITS ECONOMIC IMPACT ON CHINA." ASIA CHINA/COM COM WOR+45 NAT/G ATTIT PWR WEALTH...STAT TREND FOR/TRADE 20. PAGE 107 F2095 — ECO/UNDEV ECO/TAC

S64
SALVADORI M.,"EL CAPITALISMO EN LA EUROPA DE LA POSGUERRA." AFR INT/ORG NAT/G POL/PAR PLAN ECO/TAC ATTIT ORD/FREE WEALTH...HIST/WRIT EEC 20. PAGE 115 F2275 — EUR+WWI ECO/DEV CAP/ISM

S64
SCHMITT H.D.,"POLITICAL CONDITIONS FOR INTERNATIONAL CURRENCY REFORM." WOR+45 SOCIETY ECO/DEV PLAN ECO/TAC BAL/PAY ATTIT ORD/FREE WEALTH ...SOC CONCPT OBS TREND EEC VAL/FREE ECSC 20. PAGE 117 F2301 — FINAN VOL/ASSN REGION

C64
NORGREN P.H.,"TOWARD FAIR EMPLOYMENT." USA+45 LAW STRATA LABOR NAT/G FORCES ACT/RES ADMIN ATTIT ...POLICY BIBLIOG 20 NEGRO. PAGE 98 F1932 — RACE/REL DISCRIM WORKER MGT

B65
ALDERSON W.,DYNAMIC MARKETING BEHAVIOR. USA+45 FINAN CREATE TEC/DEV EDU/PROP PRICE COST 20. PAGE 3 F0057 — MGT MARKET ATTIT CAP/ISM

B65
APTER D.E.,THE POLITICS OF MODERNIZATION. AFR L/A+17C CULTURE NAT/G POL/PAR ADMIN COLONIAL NAT/LISM ATTIT RIGID/FLEX PWR...SOC CONCPT. PAGE 6 F0109 — ECO/UNDEV GEN/LAWS STRATA CREATE

B65
BALDWIN D.A.,SOFT LOANS AND AMERICAN FOREIGN POLICY: 1943-1962 (THESIS). USA+45 WOR+45 FINAN NAT/G FOR/AID BAL/PAY ATTIT...POLICY METH/COMP 20 UN CONGRESS. PAGE 9 F0161 — DIPLOM ECO/TAC ECO/UNDEV

B65
BARRY E.E.,NATIONALISATION IN BRITISH POLITICS: THE HISTORICAL BACKGROUND. UK AGRI DIST/IND EXTR/IND LABOR LG/CO ATTIT CONSERVE SOCISM 19/20 LABOR/PAR. PAGE 10 F0198 — NAT/G OWN INDUS POL/PAR

B65
COLLOQUE SUR LA PLANIFICATION,LA PLANIFICATION COMME PROCESSUS DE DECISION. FRANCE SOCIETY MARKET LABOR LEGIS GP/REL EFFICIENCY INCOME ATTIT TECHRACY ...MYTH IDEA/COMP 20. PAGE 26 F0508 — PLAN ECO/TAC PROB/SOLV

B65
CRABB C.V. JR.,THE ELEPHANTS AND THE GRASS* A STUDY OF NONALIGNMENT. ASIA INDIA S/ASIA USA+45 USSR BAL/PWR NEUTRAL ATTIT...TREND NAT/COMP. PAGE 28 F0549 — ECO/UNDEV AFR DIPLOM CONCPT

B65
CRANE E.,MARKETING COMMUNICATION: A BEHAVIORAL APPROACH TO MEN, MESSAGES, AND MEDIA. STRATA R+D VOL/ASSN CROWD DRIVE PERSON SKILL WEALTH. PAGE 28 F0551 — EDU/PROP MARKET PERCEPT ATTIT

B65
DERBER M.,PLANT UNION-MANAGEMENT RELATIONS: FROM PRACTICE TO THEORY. PROC/MFG NEIGH PROB/SOLV ORD/FREE...DECISION MGT OBS QU SAMP. PAGE 32 F0621 — LG/CO LABOR GP/REL ATTIT

B65
GRAMPP W.D.,ECONOMIC LIBERALISM; THE BEGINNINGS (VOL. I). USA-45 WOR-45 MARKET LABOR ATTIT WEALTH ...POLICY CONCPT BIBLIOG GREECE/ANC MERCANTLST REPUBLICAN FEDERALIST. PAGE 50 F0974 — ECO/DEV CAP/ISM IDEA/COMP ECO/TAC

B65
HADWIGER D.F.,PRESSURES AND PROTEST. NAT/G LEGIS PLAN LEAD PARTIC ROUTINE ATTIT POLICY. PAGE 53 F1030 — AGRI GP/REL LOBBY CHOOSE

B65
MARGOLIS J.,THE PUBLIC ECONOMY OF URBAN COMMUNITIES. USA+45 LEGIS PROB/SOLV TAX LOBBY CHOOSE ATTIT MUNICH. PAGE 85 F1668 — LOC/G DECISION FINAN

B65
OECD,THE MEDITERRANEAN REGIONAL PROJECT: GREECE; EDUCATION AND DEVELOPMENT. FUT GREECE SOCIETY AGRI FINAN NAT/G PROF/ORG WORKER PLAN PROB/SOLV ADMIN DEMAND ATTIT 20 OECD. PAGE 100 F1972 — EDU/PROP SCHOOL ACADEM ECO/UNDEV

B65
PLOSS S.I.,CONFLICT AND DECISION-MAKING IN SOVIET RUSSIA - A CASE STUDY OF AGRICULTURAL POLICY - 1953-1963. USSR DELIB/GP INGP/REL PWR MARXISM. PAGE 106 F2093 — AGRI DECISION ATTIT

B65
RATNAM K.J.,COMMUNALISM AND THE POLITICAL PROCESS IN MALAYA. MALAYSIA WOR+45 ECO/UNDEV PARTIC CHOOSE REPRESENT GP/REL CENTRAL ATTIT...CHARTS WORSHIP 20. PAGE 109 F2152 — CONSTN GOV/REL REGION

B65
RUEFF J.,THE ROLE AND THE RULE OF GOLD: AN ARGUMENT (PAMPHLET). AFR FRANCE USA+45 WOR+45 MARKET NAT/G PLAN DIPLOM ATTIT...POLICY INT 20 DEGAULLE/C. PAGE 115 F2258 — FINAN ECO/DEV INT/TRADE BAL/PAY

B65
SHOSTAK A.B.,NEW PERSPECTIVES ON POVERTY. USA+45 SCHOOL WORKER INGP/REL RACE/REL AGE/C AGE/Y ATTIT HEALTH...ANTHOL BIBLIOG 20 JOHNSON/LB POVRTY/WAR. PAGE 121 F2388 — WEALTH NAT/G RECEIVE INCOME

B65
SPENCE J.E.,REPUBLIC UNDER PRESSURE: A STUDY OF SOUTH AFRICAN FOREIGN POLICY. SOUTH/AFR ADMIN COLONIAL GOV/REL RACE/REL DISCRIM NAT/LISM ATTIT ROLE...TREND 20 NEGRO. PAGE 124 F2449 — DIPLOM POLICY AFR

B65
THORNTON A.P.,DOCTRINES OF IMPERIALISM. WOR+45 WOR-45 DOMIN NAT/LISM PROFIT ATTIT PERSON PWR RESPECT SOVEREIGN...CONCPT STERTYP. PAGE 130 F2571 — IDEA/COMP COLONIAL DRIVE

B65
WHITE J.,GERMAN AID. GERMANY/W FINAN PLAN TEC/DEV INT/TRADE ADMIN ATTIT...POLICY 20. PAGE 146 F2870 — FOR/AID ECO/UNDEV DIPLOM ECO/TAC

B65
WISH J.R.,ECONOMIC DEVELOPMENT IN LATIN AMERICA: AN ANNOTATED BIBLIOGRAPHY. L/A+17C COM/IND MARKET R+D CREATE CAP/ISM ATTIT...STAT METH 20. PAGE 148 F2912 — BIBLIOG/A ECO/UNDEV TEC/DEV AGRI

L65
HAGE J.,"AN AXIOMATIC THEORY OF ORGANIZATIONS" USA+45 STRUCT LABOR PRODUC DRIVE PERSON RIGID/FLEX 20 WEBER/MAX. PAGE 53 F1032 — GP/REL EFFICIENCY PROF/ORG ATTIT

L65
HAMMOND A.,"COMPREHENSIVE VERSUS INCREMENTAL BUDGETING IN THE DEPARTMENT OF AGRICULTURE" USA+45 GP/REL ATTIT...PSY INT 20 DEPT/AGRI. PAGE 54 F1057 — TOP/EX EX/STRUC AGRI BUDGET

L65
LETICHE J.M.,"EUROPEAN INTEGRATION: AN AMERICAN VIEW." EUR+WWI FRANCE WOR+45 ECO/DEV DIST/IND EXTR/IND NAT/G DELIB/GP TOP/EX PLAN ECO/TAC ATTIT ...STAT CON/ANAL CHARTS EEC 20. PAGE 78 F1537 — INDUS AGRI

S65
JOHNSON L.L.,"US BUSINESS INTERESTS IN CUBA AND THE RISE OF CASTRO." L/A+17C USA+45 ECO/UNDEV INDUS NAT/G VOL/ASSN ATTIT ORD/FREE PWR WEALTH ALL/PROG. PAGE 68 F1330 — DIPLOM CUBA ECO/TAC INT/TRADE

S65
KUNKEL J.H.,"VALUES AND BEHAVIOR IN ECONOMIC DEVELOPMENT." INDIA PERU CULTURE STRUCT CREATE PERS/REL ATTIT PERSON...CHARTS HYPO/EXP ARGEN. PAGE 74 F1449 — SIMUL ECO/UNDEV PSY STERTYP

S65
SPAAK P.H.,"THE SEARCH FOR CONSENSUS: A NEW EFFORT TO BUILD EUROPE." FRANCE GERMANY ECO/DEV NAT/G CONSULT FORCES PLAN EDU/PROP REGION CONSEN ATTIT ...SOC METH/CNCPT OBS TREND EEC NATO WORK TERR/GP METH/GP 20. PAGE 124 F2447 — EUR+WWI INT/ORG

S65
WHITE J.,"WEST GERMAN AID TO DEVELOPING COUNTRIES." AFR INT/ORG OP/RES GIVE CENTRAL ATTIT DRIVE...STAT NAT/COMP. PAGE 146 F2869 — GERMANY FOR/AID ECO/UNDEV CAP/ISM

B66
ANDRESKI S.,PARASITISM AND SUBVERSION* THE CASE OF LATIN AMERICA. CULTURE ECO/UNDEV LABOR NAT/G SECT PROB/SOLV RACE/REL TOTALISM ATTIT WEALTH ALL/IDEOS. PAGE 5 F0100 — L/A+17C GOV/COMP STRATA REV

B66
BAKKE E.W.,MUTUAL SURVIVAL; THE GOAL OF UNION AND MANAGEMENT (2ND ED.). USA+45 ELITES ECO/DEV ECO/TAC CONFER ADMIN REPRESENT GP/REL INGP/REL ATTIT ...GP/COMP 20. PAGE 8 F0155 — MGT LABOR BARGAIN INDUS

B66
BOYD H.W.,MARKETING MANAGEMENT: CASES FROM EMERGING COUNTRIES. BRAZIL GHANA ISRAEL WOR+45 ADMIN PERS/REL ATTIT HABITAT WEALTH...ANTHOL 20 ARGEN CASEBOOK. PAGE 17 F0332 — MGT ECO/UNDEV PROB/SOLV MARKET

B66
COLE A.B.,SOCIALIST PARTIES IN POSTWAR JAPAN. STRATA AGRI LABOR PLAN DIPLOM ECO/TAC AGREE LEAD CHOOSE ATTIT...CHARTS 20 CHINJAP SOC/DEMPAR. PAGE 26 F0499 — POL/PAR POLICY SOCISM NAT/G

B66
FREIDEL F.,AMERICAN ISSUES IN THE TWENTIETH CENTURY. SOCIETY FINAN ECO/TAC FOR/AID CONTROL NUC/PWR WAR RACE/REL PEACE ATTIT...ANTHOL T 20 WILSON/W ROOSEVLT/F KENNEDY/JF TRUMAN/HS. PAGE 44 — DIPLOM POLICY NAT/G ORD/FREE

F0851

B66
HUNT C.L.,SOCIAL ASPECTS OF ECONOMIC DEVELOPMENT. S/ASIA AGRI FAM TEC/DEV RECEIVE EDU/PROP OWN...GEOG MUNICH 20. PAGE 63 F1243
SOC STRATA ATTIT ECO/UNDEV

B66
LAMBERG R.F.,PRAG UND DIE DRITTE WELT. AFR ASIA CZECHOSLVK L/A+17C MARKET TEC/DEV ECO/TAC REV ATTIT 20 TREATY. PAGE 75 F1462
DIPLOM ECO/UNDEV INT/TRADE FOR/AID

B66
MOSKOW M.H.,TEACHERS AND UNIONS. SCHOOL WORKER ADJUD LOBBY ATTIT ORD/FREE 20. PAGE 94 F1844
EDU/PROP PROF/ORG LABOR BARGAIN

B66
MURPHY G.G.,SOVIET MONGOLIA: A STUDY OF THE OLDEST POLITICAL SATELLITE. USSR STRATA STRUCT COST INCOME ATTIT SOCISM 20. PAGE 95 F1865
DIPLOM ECO/TAC PLAN DOMIN

B66
NICOSIA F.N.,CONSUMER DECISION PROCESSES* MARKETING AND ADVERTISING IMPLICATIONS. DIST/IND INDUS CONSULT EDU/PROP ATTIT. PAGE 98 F1925
MARKET PROB/SOLV SERV/IND

B66
NICOSIA M.N.,CONSUMER DECISION PROCESSES: MARKETING AND ADVERTISING IMPLICATIONS. ECO/TAC ATTIT PERSON ...DECISION MGT SOC. PAGE 98 F1926
MARKET SOCIETY CREATE ACT/RES

B66
OHLIN G.,FOREIGN AID POLICIES RECONSIDERED. ECO/DEV ECO/UNDEV VOL/ASSN CONSULT PLAN CONTROL ATTIT ...CONCPT CHARTS BIBLIOG 20. PAGE 101 F1985
FOR/AID DIPLOM GIVE

B66
POLK J.,U S PRODUCTION ABROAD AND THE BALANCE OF PAYMENTS* A SURVEY OF CORPORATE INVESTMENT EXPERIENCE. USA+45 SERV/IND NAT/G OP/RES COST PROFIT ATTIT...ECOMETRIC STAT INT QU GEN/METH. PAGE 107 F2096
BAL/PAY FINAN INT/TRADE INDUS

B66
RAO Y.V.L.,COMMUNICATION AND DEVELOPMENT. INDIA S/ASIA SOCIETY ACT/RES EDU/PROP PARTIC ATTIT...SOC GP/COMP BIBLIOG MUNICH MUNICH 20. PAGE 109 F2149
COM/IND ECO/UNDEV OBS

B66
SEWELL J.P.,FUNCTIONALISM AND WORLD POLITICS* A STUDY BASED ON UNITED NATIONS PROGRAMS FINANCING ECONOMICAL DEVELOPMENT. ECO/UNDEV FINAN PROB/SOLV DIPLOM ECO/TAC FEEDBACK REGION ADJUST ATTIT UN IBRD INTL/FINAN INTL/DEV UNSF. PAGE 120 F2360
TASK INT/ORG IDEA/COMP GEN/LAWS

B66
THOMPSON J.H.,MODERNIZATION OF THE ARAB WORLD. FUT ISRAEL STRUCT ECO/UNDEV DIPLOM INGP/REL ATTIT ...CENSUS ANTHOL 20 ARABS. PAGE 130 F2565
ADJUST ISLAM PROB/SOLV NAT/COMP

B66
TIVEY L.J.,NATIONALISATION IN BRITISH INDUSTRY. UK LEGIS PARL/PROC GP/REL OWN ATTIT SOCISM 20. PAGE 131 F2578
NAT/G INDUS CONTROL LG/CO

B66
US HOUSE COMM FOREIGN AFFAIRS,HEARINGS ON HR 12449 A BILL TO AMEND FURTHER THE FOREIGN ASSISTANCE ACT OF 1961. AFR ASIA L/A+17C USA+45 VIETNAM INT/ORG TEC/DEV INT/TRADE ATTIT ORD/FREE 20 UN NATO CONGRESS AID. PAGE 137 F2692
FOR/AID ECO/TAC ECO/UNDEV DIPLOM

B66
US SENATE COMM GOVT OPERATIONS,HEARINGS BEFORE SUBCOMMITTEE ON FOREIGN AID EXPENDITURES: POPULATION CRISIS VOLUMES 1-5 JUNE-SEPT 1965. STRATA ECO/UNDEV PLAN TEC/DEV EDU/PROP ATTIT HEALTH ...GEOG CHARTS 20 CONGRESS BIRTH/CON CASEBOOK. PAGE 138 F2729
ECO/DEV CENSUS FAM CONTROL

S66
DUROSELLE J.B.,"THE FUTURE OF THE ATLANTIC COMMUNITY." EUR+WWI USA+45 USSR NAT/G CAP/ISM REGION DETER NUC/PWR ATTIT MARXISM...INT/LAW 20 NATO. PAGE 35 F0686
FUT DIPLOM MYTH POLICY

S66
FELD W.,"EXTERNAL RELATIONS OF THE COMMON MARKET AND GROUP LEADERSHIP ATTITUDES IN THE MEMBER STATES." COM USA+45 ELITES AGRI NAT/G ATTIT...OBS EEC GATT. PAGE 40 F0776
DIPLOM CENTRAL TARIFFS INT/TRADE

B67
ANDERSON S.V.,THE NORDIC COUNCIL: A STUDY OF SCANDINAVIAN REGIONALISM. DENMARK FINLAND ICELAND NORWAY SWEDEN MARKET NAT/G VOL/ASSN CONSULT PARL/PROC ATTIT...TIME/SEQ BIBLIOG 20. PAGE 5 F0098
INT/ORG REGION DIPLOM LEGIS

B67
ANDERSON T.,RUSSIAN POLITICAL THOUGHT; AN INTRODUCTION. USSR NAT/G POL/PAR CHIEF MARXISM ...TIME/SEQ BIBLIOG 9/20. PAGE 5 F0099
TREND CONSTN ATTIT

B67
BADGLEY R.F.,DOCTORS' STRIKE; MEDICAL CARE AND CONFLICT IN SASKATCHEWAN. CANADA NAT/G PROF/ORG GP/REL ADJUST ATTIT...HEAL SOC 20. PAGE 8 F0148
HEALTH PLAN LABOR

BARGAIN

B67
BANFIELD E.C.,THE MORAL BASIS OF A BACKWARD SOCIETY. EUR+WWI ITALY STRATA NEIGH PARTIC INGP/REL ...SOC QU PREDICT TREND HYPO/EXP MUNICH 20. PAGE 9 F0173
MORAL WEALTH ATTIT

B67
BURDEN H.T.,THE NUREMBERG PARTY RALLIES 1923-39. GERMANY POL/PAR SECT CREATE DOMIN WAR ATTIT ...AUD/VIS FILM 20. PAGE 20 F0384
EDU/PROP CONTROL CROWD TOTALISM

B67
BUSEY J.L.,NOTES ON COSTA RICAN DEMOCRACY. COSTA/RICA L/A+17C NAT/G POL/PAR LEGIS CHOOSE OWN ATTIT...BIBLIOG 20. PAGE 20 F0394
CONSTN MAJORIT SOCIETY ECO/UNDEV

B67
COHEN M.R.,LAW AND THE SOCIAL ORDER: ESSAYS IN LEGAL PHILOSOPHY. USA-45 CONSULT WORKER ECO/TAC ATTIT WEALTH...POLICY WELF/ST SOC 20 NEW/DEAL DEPRESSION. PAGE 26 F0497
JURID LABOR IDEA/COMP

B67
COTTAM R.W.,COMPETITIVE INTERFERENCE AND TWENTIETH CENTURY DIPLOMACY. IRAN ACT/RES CREATE PLAN ECO/TAC EFFICIENCY ATTIT...DECISION NEW/IDEA TREND 20 CIA. PAGE 28 F0541
DIPLOM DOMIN GAME

B67
COWLING M.,1867 DISRAELI, GLADSTONE, AND REVOLUTION; THE PASSING OF THE SECOND REFORM BILL. UK LEGIS LEAD LOBBY GP/REL INGP/REL...DECISION BIBLIOG 19 REFORMERS. PAGE 28 F0545
PARL/PROC POL/PAR ATTIT LAW

B67
DAVIS H.B.,NATIONALISM AND SOCIALISM: MARXIST AND LABOR THEORIES OF NATIONALISM TO 1917. WOR-45 PROB/SOLV SOVEREIGN...CONCPT IDEA/COMP 19/20. PAGE 30 F0589
MARXISM ATTIT NAT/LISM SOCISM

B67
ELSNER H.,THE TECHNOCRATS, PROPHETS OF AUTOMATION. SOCIETY INDUS VOL/ASSN COST INCOME ATTIT 20. PAGE 37 F0726
AUTOMAT TECHRACY PRODUC HIST/WRIT

B67
FILENE P.G.,AMERICANS AND THE SOVIET EXPERIMENT, 1917-1933. USA-45 USSR INTELL NAT/G CAP/ISM DIPLOM EDU/PROP PRESS REV SOCISM...PSY 20. PAGE 41 F0793
ATTIT RIGID/FLEX MARXISM SOCIETY

B67
GIAP V.N.,BIG VICTORY, GREAT TASK. VIETNAM WOR+45 FORCES PLAN DOMIN LEGIT RISK PEACE 20. PAGE 47 F0921
WAR LEAD ATTIT INSPECT

B67
GITTELL M.,PARTICIPANTS AND PARTICIPATION: A STUDY OF SCHOOL POLICY IN NEW YORK. USA+45 EX/STRUC BUDGET PAY ATTIT...POLICY MUNICH 20 NEWYORK/C. PAGE 47 F0926
SCHOOL DECISION PARTIC ADMIN

B67
HANRIEDER W.F.,WEST GERMAN FOREIGN POLICY 1949-1963: INTERNATIONAL PRESSURE AND DOMESTIC RESPONSE. EUR+WWI GERMANY/W POL/PAR LOBBY CONSEN 20. PAGE 54 F1061
DIPLOM POLICY NAT/G ATTIT

B67
HEADLEY J.C.,PESTICIDE PROBLEM: AN ECONOMIC APPROACH TO PUBLIC POLICY. AGRI TEC/DEV GOV/REL COST ATTIT CHARTS. PAGE 58 F1131
HABITAT POLICY BIO/SOC CONTROL

B67
HERRESHOFF D.,AMERICAN DISCIPLES OF MARX: FROM THE AGE OF JACKSON TO THE PROGRESSIVE ERA. USA-45 AGRI POL/PAR 19/20. PAGE 59 F1155
MARXISM ATTIT WORKER CONCPT

B67
HODGKINSON R.G.,THE ORIGINS OF THE NATIONAL HEALTH SERVICE: THE MEDICAL SERVICES OF THE NEW POOR LAW, 1834-1871. UK INDUS WORKER PROB/SOLV EFFICIENCY ATTIT HEALTH WEALTH SOCISM...JURID SOC/WK MUNICH 19/20. PAGE 60 F1189
HEAL NAT/G POLICY LAW

B67
JHANGIANI M.A.,JANA SANGH AND SWATANTRA: A PROFILE OF THE RIGHTIST PARTIES IN INDIA. INDIA ADMIN CHOOSE MARXISM SOCISM...INT CHARTS BIBLIOG 20. PAGE 67 F1320
POL/PAR LAISSEZ NAT/LISM ATTIT

B67
KAPLAN J.J.,CHALLENGE OF FOREIGN AID. USA+45 CONTROL BAL/PAY COST ATTIT ALL/VALS...METH/COMP 20. PAGE 69 F1352
FOR/AID PLAN GIVE POLICY

B67
KIRK R.,THE POLITICAL PRINCIPLES OF ROBERT A. TAFT. USA+45 LABOR DIPLOM ADJUD ADJUST ORD/FREE TAFT/RA. PAGE 71 F1398
POL/PAR LEAD LEGIS ATTIT

B67
LISS S.B.,THE CANAL, ASPECTS OF UNITED STATES-PANAMANIAN RELATIONS. AFR FUT PANAMA DOMIN COERCE ATTIT SOVEREIGN MARXISM 20 JOHNSON/LB KENNEDY/JF.
DIPLOM POLICY

PAGE 81 F1580

B67
LITTLE AD, INC.,COMMUNITY RENEWAL PROGRAMMING. CULTURE LOC/G ACT/RES TASK COST ATTIT...SOC/WK MODAL STAT STAND/INT CHARTS 20 SAN/FRAN. PAGE 81 F1585
STRATA NEIGH PLAN CREATE

B67
LYTLE C.M.,THE WARREN COURT AND ITS CRITICS. USA+45 NAT/G PROVS FORCES LOBBY RACE/REL DISCRIM SOVEREIGN 20 SUPREME/CT WARRN/EARL. PAGE 83 F1618
CT/SYS ADJUD PROB/SOLV ATTIT

B67
MEYERS M.,SOURCES OF THE AMERICAN REPUBLIC; A DOCUMENTARY HISTORY OF POLITICS, SOCIETY, AND THOUGHT (VOL. I, REV. ED.). USA-45 CULTURE STRUCT NAT/G LEGIS LEAD ATTIT...JURID SOC ANTHOL 17/19 PRESIDENT. PAGE 90 F1772
COLONIAL REV WAR

B67
MURTY B.S.,PROPAGANDA AND WORLD PUBLIC ORDER. FUT WOR+45 COM/IND INT/ORG PROB/SOLV ATTIT KNOWL ORD/FREE...POLICY UN. PAGE 95 F1868
EDU/PROP DIPLOM CONTROL JURID

B67
O'LEARY M.K.,THE POLITICS OF AMERICAN FOREIGN AID. USA+45 POL/PAR CHIEF BUDGET EDU/PROP LOBBY CONGRESS. PAGE 100 F1958
FOR/AID DIPLOM PARL/PROC ATTIT

B67
POLLACK N.,THE POPULIST MIND. USA-45 STRATA AGRI NAT/G POL/PAR LEGIS WORKER RACE/REL WEALTH...ANTHOL BIBLIOG 19 NEGRO. PAGE 107 F2097
POPULISM HIST/WRIT ATTIT INGP/REL

B67
POWLEDGE F.,BLACK POWER WHITE RESISTANCE. USA+45 STRUCT PLAN GP/REL DISCRIM HABITAT ORD/FREE WEALTH ...METH/COMP SOC/INTEG NEGRO. PAGE 107 F2111
RACE/REL ATTIT PWR

B67
REHMUS C.M.,LABOR AND AMERICAN POLITICS. POL/PAR WORKER EDU/PROP PARTIC ATTIT PWR. PAGE 110 F2175
LABOR ROLE LOBBY

B67
SCHECTER J.,THE NEW FACE OF BUDDHA: BUDDHISM AND POLITICAL POWER IN SOUTHEAST ASIA. S/ASIA NAT/G POL/PAR NAT/LISM ATTIT MARXISM...BIBLIOG 20. PAGE 116 F2292
SECT POLICY PWR LEAD

B67
SPECTOR S.D.,CHECKLIST OF ITEMS IN THE NDEA INSTITUTE LIBRARY (PAMPHLET). USA+45 NAT/G SECT EDU/PROP ATTIT ALL/IDEOS...SOC BIOG. PAGE 124 F2448
BIBLIOG/A COM MARXISM

B67
SPICER G.W.,THE SUPREME COURT AND FUNDAMENTAL FREEDOMS (2ND ED.). USA+45 CONSTN SOCIETY ATTIT 20 SUPREME/CT. PAGE 124 F2454
CT/SYS JURID CONTROL ORD/FREE

B67
ULMAN L.,CHALLENGES TO COLLECTIVE BARGAINING. ECO/TAC DISCRIM EQUILIB ATTIT...JURID SOC/WK. PAGE 132 F2599
LABOR BARGAIN ADJUD POLICY

B67
US SENATE COMM ON FOREIGN REL,HARRISON E. SALISBURY'S TRIP TO NORTH VIETNAM. CHINA/COM USA+45 VIETNAM/N PRESS TASK GUERRILLA CONSEN EFFICIENCY PEACE DRIVE...OBS SENATE. PAGE 139 F2743
DIPLOM WAR FORCES ATTIT

B67
VAN SLYKE L.P.,ENEMIES AND FRIENDS; THE UNITED FRONT IN CHINESE COMMUNIST HISTORY. CHINA/COM SOCIETY FORCES PLAN ADJUST 20 MAO. PAGE 140 F2764
INGP/REL MARXISM ATTIT GP/REL

B67
WILLIAMS M.,THE EAST IS RED: THE VIEW INSIDE CHINA. CHINA/COM CONSTN COERCE AGE/Y ATTIT PERSON...OBS 20 MAO. PAGE 147 F2893
REV MARXIST GP/REL DIPLOM

B67
YAMAMURA K.,ECONOMIC POLICY IN POSTWAR JAPAN. ASIA FINAN POL/PAR DIPLOM LEAD NAT/LISM ATTIT NEW/LIB POPULISM 20 CHINJAP. PAGE 149 F2946
ECO/DEV POLICY NAT/G TEC/DEV

L67
GLAZER N.,"HOUSING PROBLEMS AND HOUSING POLICIES." USA+45 PLAN RENT ADJUST CONSEN DEMAND DISCRIM AGE ATTIT HEALTH WEALTH MUNICH NEGRO. PAGE 48 F0929
POLICY CONSTRUC CREATE HABITAT

L67
GOLD J.,"INTERPRETATION BY THE INTERNATIONAL MONETARY FUND OF ITS ARTICLES OF AGREEMENT." INT/TRADE ADJUD ATTIT...POLICY JURID. PAGE 48 F0933
CONSTN INT/ORG LAW DIPLOM

L67
GREGORY A.J.,"AFRICAN SOCIALISM, SOCIALISM AND FASCISM: AN APPRAISAL." FUT LEAD REV GP/REL RACE/REL NAT/LISM ATTIT...IDEA/COMP STERTYP 20. PAGE 51 F0993
FASCISM MARXISM SOCISM AFR

L67
MIXON J.,"JANE JACOBS AND THE LAW - ZONING FOR DIVERSITY EXAMINED." FUT USA+45 CONSTN NEIGH PROB/SOLV CONTROL CT/SYS PARTIC ATTIT...POLICY CENSUS METH/COMP MUNICH. PAGE 92 F1810
IDEA/COMP PLAN LAW

S67
ADAMS E.S.,"THE EXPANDING ROLE OF BANKS IN PUBLIC AFFAIRS." USA+45 GIVE LEAD ROLE...QU 20. PAGE 2 F0036
PARTIC FINAN LOC/G ATTIT

S67
ALEXANDER R.J.,"'THIRD FORCE' IN WORLD COMMUNISM?" CHINA/COM CUBA USSR INT/ORG DIPLOM TASK INGP/REL ATTIT PWR 20 CASTRO/F. PAGE 3 F0060
CHIEF MARXISM LEAD REV

S67
ALPANDER G.G.,"ENTREPRENEURS AND PRIVATE ENTERPRISE IN TURKEY." TURKEY INDUS PROC/MFG EDU/PROP ATTIT DRIVE WEALTH...GEOG MGT SOC STAT TREND CHARTS 20. PAGE 4 F0077
ECO/UNDEV LG/CO NAT/G POLICY

S67
BAGDKIAN B.H.,"NEWS AS A BYPRODUCT: WHAT HAPPENS WHEN JOURNALISM IS HITCHED TO GREAT, DIVERSIFIED CORPORATIONS?" USA+45 INDUS EDU/PROP PARTIC PROFIT ATTIT. PAGE 8 F0152
COM/IND PRESS CONTROL LG/CO

S67
BENNETT J.T.,"POLITICAL IMPLICATIONS OF ECONOMIC CHANGE: SOUTH VIETNAM." VIETNAM/S INGP/REL INCOME ATTIT 20 AID. PAGE 13 F0247
ECO/UNDEV INDUS AGRI PRODUC

S67
BUTT R.,"THE COMMON MARKET AND CONSERVATIVE POLITICS, 1961-2." UK CHIEF DIPLOM ECO/TAC INT/TRADE CONFER DEBATE REGION ATTIT...POLICY 20 EEC. PAGE 21 F0398
EUR+WWI INT/ORG POL/PAR

S67
CAMMETT J.M.,"COMMUNIST THEORIES OF FASCISM, 1920-35." ITALY POL/PAR PROF/ORG VOL/ASSN WORKER COLONIAL TOTALISM...SOCIALIST 20. PAGE 21 F0403
MARXISM FASCISM ATTIT

S67
CHAMBERLAIN N.W.,"STRIKES IN CONTEMPORARY CONTEXT." LAW INDUS NAT/G CHIEF CONFER COST ATTIT ORD/FREE ...POLICY MGT 20. PAGE 23 F0442
LABOR BARGAIN EFFICIENCY PROB/SOLV

S67
CRAIG A.,"ARGENTINA: THE LATEST REVOLUTION." ELITES NAT/G CHIEF FORCES ECO/TAC CIVMIL/REL GOV/REL EQUILIB PRIVIL 20 ARGEN. PAGE 28 F0550
ECO/UNDEV FINAN ATTIT REV

S67
DRAPER A.P.,"UNIONS AND THE WAR IN VIETNAM." USA+45 CONFER ADMIN LEAD WAR ORD/FREE PACIFIST 20. PAGE 34 F0660
LABOR PACIFISM ATTIT ELITES

S67
GAMARNIKOW M.,"THE NEW ROLE OF PRIVATE ENTERPRISE." ECO/DEV INDUS NAT/G SML/CO CREATE PROB/SOLV MARXISM ...POLICY TREND IDEA/COMP 20. PAGE 46 F0890
ECO/TAC ATTIT CAP/ISM COM

S67
GATELL F.O.,"MONEY AND PARTY IN JACKSONIAN AMERICA* A QUANTITATIVE LOOK AT NEW YORK CITY'S MEN OF QUALITY." USA-45 STRATA SECT SUFF CONSEN MAJORITY ATTIT...CHARTS HYPO/EXP 19. PAGE 46 F0908
WEALTH POL/PAR PERSON IDEA/COMP

S67
GEISS I.,"THE GERMANS AND THE MIDDLE EAST CRISIS." GERMANY/W ISLAM ISRAEL USSR POL/PAR RACE/REL MARXISM...GP/COMP 20 JEWS. PAGE 47 F0914
ATTIT DIPLOM WAR POLICY

S67
GRUN C.,"DEUX ETUDES ALLEMANDES SUR LES PREJUGES NATIONAUX ET LES MOYENS DE LES COMBATTRE." FRANCE GERMANY DIST/IND PROB/SOLV GP/REL AGE/Y RIGID/FLEX ...PSY STAT INT SAMP. PAGE 52 F1010
ATTIT REGION DISCRIM STERTYP

S67
GUPTA S.,"FOREIGN POLICY IN THE 1967 MANIFESTOS." ASIA COM INDIA USA+45 FORCES FOR/AID TAX ATTIT ...DECISION 20. PAGE 52 F1013
IDEA/COMP POL/PAR POLICY DIPLOM

S67
HILTON G.W.,"FEDERAL PARTICIPATION IN THE SUPERSONIC TRANSPORT PROGRAM." USA+45 LEGIS PROB/SOLV BUDGET ATTIT 20. PAGE 60 F1172
DIST/IND TEC/DEV FINAN NAT/G

S67
JAVITS J.K.,"THE USE OF AMERICAN PLURALISM." USA+45 ECO/DEV BUDGET ADMIN ALL/IDEOS...DECISION TREND. PAGE 67 F1309
CENTRAL ATTIT POLICY NAT/G

S67
JEDLICKI W.,"THE FREE SPEECH MOVEMENT IN WARSAW." POLAND FORCES EDU/PROP LEAD ATTIT MARXISM ...IDEA/COMP 20. PAGE 67 F1310
COERCE CROWD ORD/FREE ACADEM

S67
JENCKS C.E.,"COAL MINERS IN BRITAIN SINCE NATIONALIZATION." UK LABOR GP/REL ADJUST SOCISM ...INT 20. PAGE 67 F1311
EXTR/IND WORKER STRATA

ATTIT

S67
JENCKS C.E.,"SOCIAL STATUS OF COAL MINERS IN BRITAIN SINCE NATIONALIZATION." UK STRATA STRUCT LABOR RECEIVE GP/REL INCOME OWN ATTIT HABITAT...MGT T 20. PAGE 67 F1312
EXTR/IND WORKER CONTROL NAT/G

S67
KELLY F.K.,"A PROPOSAL FOR AN ANNUAL REPORT ON THE STATE OF MANKIND." FUT INTELL COM/IND INT/ORG CREATE PROB/SOLV PERS/REL...CONCPT 20 UN. PAGE 70 F1371
SOCIETY UNIV ATTIT NEW/IDEA

S67
KENNY L.M.,"THE AFTERMATH OF DEFEAT IN EGYPT." ISLAM ISRAEL UAR UK USA+45 USSR INDUS FORCES ECO/TAC PRICE COERCE WEAPON COST ATTIT. PAGE 70 F1378
WAR ECO/UNDEV DIPLOM POLICY

S67
KINGSLEY R.E.,"THE US BUSINESS IMAGE IN LATIN AMERICA." L/A+17C USA+45 NAT/G TEC/DEV CAP/ISM FOR/AID DOMIN EDU/PROP...CONCPT LING IDEA/COMP 20. PAGE 71 F1396
ATTIT LOVE DIPLOM ECO/UNDEV

S67
KRAUS J.,"A MARXIST IN GHANA." GHANA ELITES CHIEF PROB/SOLV TEC/DEV DIPLOM ECO/TAC COLONIAL PARTIC PWR 20 NKRUMAH/K. PAGE 73 F1432
MARXISM PLAN ATTIT CREATE

S67
LANGLEY L.D.,"THE DEMOCRATIC TRADITION AND MILITARY REFORM, 1878-1885." USA-45 SECT EDU/PROP CROWD EFFICIENCY NAT/LISM 19 INDIAN/AM. PAGE 75 F1480
ATTIT FORCES POPULISM

S67
LASLETT J.H.M.,"SOCIALISM AND THE AMERICAN LABOR MOVEMENT* SOME NEW REFLECTIONS." USA-45 VOL/ASSN LOBBY PARTIC CENTRAL ALL/VALS SOCISM...GP/COMP 20. PAGE 76 F1484
LABOR ROUTINE ATTIT GP/REL

S67
MANGLAPUS R.S.,"ASIAN REVOLUTION AND AMERICAN IDEOLOGY." USA+45 SOCIETY CAP/ISM DIPLOM ADJUST CENTRAL...NAT/COMP 20. PAGE 84 F1652
REV POPULISM ATTIT ASIA

S67
MILLER C.H.,"B. TRAVEN Y EL 'PROBLEMA PETROLERO'." USA-45 ECO/UNDEV INDUS TEC/DEV INT/TRADE ATTIT ORD/FREE SOVEREIGN 20 MEXIC/AMER. PAGE 91 F1791
EXTR/IND DIPLOM ECO/TAC DOMIN

S67
PETRAS J.,"U.S. HEGEMONY AND LATIN AMERICAN RULING CLASSES." L/A+17C USA+45 ECO/UNDEV FOR/AID REV SOC. PAGE 105 F2071
NAT/G ATTIT DIPLOM POLICY

S67
PETRAS J.,"GUERRILLA MOVEMENTS IN LATIN AMERICA - I." GUATEMALA PERU VENEZUELA NAT/G COLONIAL LEAD ATTIT PWR...TIME/SEQ METH/COMP 20 COLOMB. PAGE 105 F2072
GUERRILLA REV L/A+17C MARXISM

S67
PETRAS J.,"MINERS AND AGRARIAN RADICALISM." CHILE AGRI EXTR/IND WORKER CHOOSE ATTIT SOCISM MUNICH 20. PAGE 105 F2073
PARTIC EDU/PROP LABOR

S67
PFEFFERMANN G.,"TRADE UNIONS AND POLITICS IN FRENCH WEST AFRICA DURING THE FOURTH REPUBLIC." AFR INDUS POL/PAR COLONIAL ATTIT PWR 20. PAGE 106 F2077
PARTIC DRIVE INT/TRADE LABOR

S67
POWELL D.,"THE EFFECTIVENESS OF SOVIET ANTI-RELIGIOUS PROPAGANDA." USSR NAT/G DOMIN LEGIT NAT/LISM 20. PAGE 107 F2109
EDU/PROP ATTIT SECT CONTROL

S67
RAZA M.A.,"EMERGING TRENDS IN PUBLIC LABOR POLICIES AND UNION - GOVERN MENT RELATIONS IN ASIA AND AFRICA." LAW NAT/G POL/PAR COLONIAL COERCE GP/REL ATTIT 20. PAGE 110 F2157
LABOR CONTROL TREND

S67
SCHNEIDER E.,"DIE ENTPOLITISIERUNG DES DEUTSCHEN OSTHANDELS." AFR MARKET TEC/DEV OBJECTIVE 20. PAGE 117 F2307
ATTIT INT/TRADE ECO/TAC DIPLOM

S67
SHEFFTZ M.C.,"THE TRADE DISPUTES AND TRADE UNIONS ACT OF 1927: THE AFTERMATH OF THE GENERAL STRIKE." UK FINAN WORKER ADJUD LEAD PARL/PROC 20. PAGE 120 F2373
LEGIS ATTIT LABOR GP/REL

S67
SHERWOOD W.B.,"THE RISE OF THE JUSTICE PARTY IN TURKEY." FUT TURKEY LEAD ATTIT 20. PAGE 121 F2378
POL/PAR ECO/UNDEV STRUCT SOCIETY

S67
SHISTER J.,"THE DIRECTION OF UNIONISM 1947-1967: THRUST OF DRIFT?" INDUS CENTRAL EFFICIENCY INCOME ATTIT SOCISM...POLICY TREND 20 AFL/CIO. PAGE 121 F2382
LABOR PROF/ORG LEAD LAW

S67
SPITTMANN I.,"EAST GERMANY: THE SWINGING PENDULUM." COM GERMANY/E NAT/G EFFICIENCY MARXISM 20. PAGE 125 F2458
PRODUC POL/PAR WEALTH ATTIT

S67
STEMPEL GH I.I.I.,"A NEW ANALYSIS OF MONOPOLY AND COMPETITION." USA+45 INDUS TV ATTIT MUNICH. PAGE 126 F2479
PRESS COM/IND GP/REL

S67
STILL J.F.,"THE FUTURE OF METROPOLITAN GOVERNMENT ORGANIZATION." USA+45 LOC/G BUDGET COST ATTIT MUNICH 20. PAGE 126 F2488
ADMIN FINAN CONTROL

S67
STYCOS J.M.,"POLITICS AND POPULATION CONTROL IN LATIN AMERICA." USA+45 FAM NAT/G GP/REL AGE/C ATTIT CATHISM MARXISM...POLICY UN WHO. PAGE 127 F2509
PLAN CENSUS CONTROL L/A+17C

S67
THEROUX P.,"HATING THE ASIANS." TANZANIA UGANDA CONSTN INDUS NAT/G POL/PAR WORKER ECO/TAC HABITAT LOVE...POLICY GEOG 20 MIGRATION. PAGE 130 F2557
AFR RACE/REL SOVEREIGN ATTIT

S67
WAITS C.R.,"CRAFT GILDS AS AN INSTITUTIONAL BARRIER TO THE INDUSTRIAL REVOLUTION." CHRIST-17C MOD/EUR ECO/UNDEV CONTROL GP/REL ATTIT 16/19. PAGE 142 F2801
TEC/DEV INDUS REV PROF/ORG

S67
WEISSKOPF W.A.,"THE DIALECTICS OF ABUNDANCE." UNIV CAP/ISM ATTIT MARXISM...CONCPT 20. PAGE 145 F2853
INDUS SOCIETY IDEA/COMP ALL/VALS

N67
NATIONAL COMN COMMUNITY HEALTH,ACTION - PLANNING FOR COMMUNITY HEALTH SERVICES (PAMPHLET). USA+45 PROF/ORG DELIB/GP BUDGET ROUTINE GP/REL ATTIT ...HEAL SOC SOC/WK CHARTS MUNICH TIME 20. PAGE 97 F1898
PLAN HEALTH ADJUST

N67
US HOUSE COMM GOVT OPERATIONS,FEDERALLY FINANCED SOCIAL RESEARCH, EXPENDITURES, STATUS, AND OBJECTIVES (PAMPHLET). WOR+45 CREATE LEAD GP/REL ATTIT...GEOG PSY SOC. PAGE 137 F2700
ACT/RES NAT/G GIVE BUDGET

B88
BENTHAM J.,DEFENCE OF USURY (1787). UK LAW NAT/G TEC/DEV ECO/TAC CONTROL ATTIT...CONCPT IDEA/COMP 18 SMITH/ADAM. PAGE 13 F0255
TAX FINAN ECO/DEV POLICY

ATTLEE/C....CLEMENT ATLEE

ATTRNY/GEN....ATTORNEY GENERAL

AUBERT DE LA RUE P. F0138

AUBREY H.G. F0139,F0140

AUD/VIS....FILM AND SOUND (INCLUDING PHOTOGRAPHY)

B56
ATOMIC INDUSTRIAL FORUM,PUBLIC RELATIONS FOR THE ATOMIC INDUSTRY. WOR+45 PLAN PROB/SOLV EDU/PROP PRESS CONFER...AUD/VIS ANTHOL 20. PAGE 7 F0135
NUC/PWR INDUS GP/REL ATTIT

B58
OEEC,THE INDUSTRIAL CHALLENGE OF NUCLEAR ENERGY. EUR+WWI ECO/DEV INDUS OP/RES CONFER RISK PWR ...AUD/VIS CHARTS ANTHOL 20 OEEC. PAGE 101 F1977
NUC/PWR ACT/RES ECO/TAC INT/ORG

B59
BONNETT C.E.,LABOR-MANAGEMENT RELATIONS. USA+45 OP/RES PROB/SOLV EDU/PROP...AUD/VIS CHARTS 20. PAGE 16 F0317
MGT LABOR INDUS GP/REL

B62
RIMALOV V.V.,ECONOMIC COOPERATION BETWEEN USSR AND UNDERDEVELOPED COUNTRIES. USSR FINAN TEC/DEV INT/TRADE DOMIN EDU/PROP COLONIAL NAT/LISM DRIVE SOVEREIGN...AUD/VIS 20. PAGE 111 F2194
FOR/AID PLAN ECO/UNDEV DIPLOM

B63
US DEPARTMENT OF LABOR,THE ANVIL AND THE PLOW. KOREA USA+45 USA-45 INDUS WORKER BUDGET WAR ...POLICY AUD/VIS CHARTS 20 DEPT/LABOR. PAGE 135 F2667
ECO/DEV LABOR ECO/TAC NAT/G

B67
BURDEN H.T.,THE NUREMBERG PARTY RALLIES 1923-39. GERMANY POL/PAR SECT CREATE DOMIN WAR ATTIT ...AUD/VIS FILM 20. PAGE 20 F0384
EDU/PROP CONTROL CROWD TOTALISM

L67
BARRON J.A.,"ACCESS TO THE PRESS." USA+45 TEC/DEV PRESS TV ADJUD AUD/VIS. PAGE 10 F0196
ORD/FREE COM/IND EDU/PROP LAW

B68
NENAROKOV A.P.,RUSSIA IN THE 20TH CENTURY: THE OFFICIAL SOVIET HISTORY. USSR SOCIETY REV...AUD/VIS 20. PAGE 97 F1913 — COM ADJUST MARXISM

AUGUSTINE....SAINT AUGUSTINE

AUST/HUNG....AUSTRIA-HUNGARY

B58
COLE G.D.H.,COMMUNISM AND SOCIAL DEMOCRACY (VOL. IV OF "HISTORY OF SOCIAL THOUGHT"). COM GERMANY ITALY UK AGRI INT/ORG WORKER DIPLOM COLONIAL NAT/LISM ALL/IDEOS...BIBLIOG 20 LEAGUE/NAT AUST/HUNG. PAGE 26 F0502 — MARXISM REV POL/PAR SOCISM

AUSTIN D.A. F0141

AUSTRALIA....SEE ALSO S/ASIA, COMMONWLTH

N19
ARNDT H.W.,AUSTRALIAN FOREIGN AID POLICY (PAMPHLET). ECO/UNDEV DIPLOM GIVE GOV/REL COST UTIL PWR...CHARTS 20 AUSTRAL PAPUA NEW/GUINEA. PAGE 6 F0114 — FOR/AID POLICY ECO/TAC EFFICIENCY

B60
COPLAND D.,THE ADVENTURE OF GROWTH: ESSAYS ON THE AUSTRALIAN ECONOMY AND ITS INTERNATIONAL SETTING. WOR+45 DIST/IND ACADEM EDU/PROP ADMIN INCOME 20 AUSTRAL. PAGE 27 F0534 — ECO/DEV ECO/UNDEV ECO/TAC INT/TRADE

B62
HOOVER C.B.,ECONOMIC SYSTEMS OF THE COMMONWEALTH. AFR CANADA INDIA UK ECO/DEV ECO/UNDEV AGRI INDUS TEC/DEV TARIFFS PRICE BAL/PAY DEMAND...SIMUL 20 AUSTRAL. PAGE 61 F1208 — CAP/ISM SOCISM ECO/TAC PLAN

B63
HUNTER A.,THE ECONOMICS OF AUSTRALIAN INDUSTRY. DIST/IND EXTR/IND FINAN PROC/MFG SERV/IND ACT/RES PLAN TARIFFS GP/REL INGP/REL 20 AUSTRAL. PAGE 63 F1245 — INDUS ECO/DEV HABITAT GP/COMP

B64
CASEY R.G.,THE FUTURE OF THE COMMONWEALTH. INDIA PAKISTAN UK ECO/UNDEV INT/ORG TEC/DEV COLONIAL SUPEGO 20 EEC AUSTRAL. PAGE 22 F0425 — DIPLOM SOVEREIGN NAT/LISM FOR/AID

B64
ESTHUS R.A.,FROM ENMITY TO ALLIANCE: US AUSTRALIAN RELATIONS. S/ASIA DIST/IND VOL/ASSN FORCES ATTIT 20 AUSTRAL TREATY CMN/WLTH. PAGE 39 F0751 — DIPLOM WAR INT/TRADE FOR/AID

B65
MCCOLL G.D.,THE AUSTRALIAN BALANCE OF PAYMENTS. UK USA+45 AGRI WORKER DIPLOM EQUILIB PRODUC...STAT TREND CHARTS BIBLIOG/A 20 AUSTRAL. PAGE 88 F1719 — ECO/DEV BAL/PAY INT/TRADE COST

B65
TEW B.,WEALTH AND INCOME. UK BUDGET INT/TRADE PRICE BAL/PAY DEMAND...CHARTS GOV/COMP 20 AUSTRAL. PAGE 129 F2546 — FINAN ECO/DEV WEALTH INCOME

B66
CANNON M.,THE LAND BOOMERS....BIBLIOG/A 19 AUSTRAL. PAGE 21 F0412 — FINAN HABITAT LAISSEZ ECO/UNDEV

B66
FORD P.,CARDINAL MORAN AND THE A. L. P. NAT/G POL/PAR SECT DELIB/GP LOBBY REV CHOOSE ORD/FREE MARXISM 19/20 AUSTRAL PROTESTANT LABOR/PAR. PAGE 42 F0825 — CATHISM SOCISM LABOR SOCIETY

B66
GOODWIN C.D.W.,ECONOMIC INQUIRY IN AUSTRALIA. ECO/DEV ECO/UNDEV ACADEM INT/TRADE RENT TARIFFS TAX PRESS GOV/REL SOCISM 18/20 AUSTRAL. PAGE 49 F0953 — ECO/TAC IDEA/COMP BUDGET COLONIAL

B66
SOCIAL SCIENCE RESEARCH COUN,BIBLIOGRAPHY OF RESEARCH IN THE SOCIAL SCIENCES IN AUSTRALIA 1957-1960. LAW R+D DIPLOM 20 AUSTRAL. PAGE 124 F2437 — BIBLIOG SOC PSY

B67
WATT A.,THE EVOLUTION OF AUSTRALIAN FOREIGN POLICY 1938-65. ASIA S/ASIA USA+45 USA-45 INT/ORG NAT/G FORCES FOR/AID TREATY 20 AUSTRAL. PAGE 144 F2834 — DIPLOM WAR

AUSTRIA....SEE ALSO APPROPRIATE TIME/SPACE/CULTURE INDEX

B59
HAX K.,DIE HOCHSCHULLEHRER DER WIRTSCHAFTSWISSENSCHAFTEN IN DER BUNDESREPUBLIK DEUTSCHLAND EINSCHL. WESTBERLIN, OSTERREICH. AUSTRIA GERMANY/W SWITZERLND FINAN MARKET PROF/ORG BUDGET ECO/TAC INT/TRADE PRICE COST 20. PAGE 57 F1119 — BIBLIOG ACADEM INTELL

N62
BANK INTERNATIONAL SETTLEMENTS,AUSTRIA: MONETARY AND ECONOMIC SITUATION 1952-61 (PAMPHLET). AUSTRIA WORKER BUDGET INT/TRADE PRICE BAL/PAY DEMAND EFFICIENCY INCOME PRODUC...STAT 20 SILVER. PAGE 9 F0174 — FINAN ECO/DEV CHARTS WEALTH

B66
OHLIN G.,AID AND INDEBTEDNESS. AUSTRIA FINAN INT/ORG PLAN DIPLOM GIVE...POLICY MATH CHARTS 20. PAGE 101 F1984 — FOR/AID ECO/UNDEV ADMIN WEALTH

AUSTRIA-HUNGARY....SEE AUST/HUNG

AUSTRUY J. F0142

AUTHORIT....AUTHORITARIANISM, PERSONAL; SEE ALSO DOMIN

B45
WOOTTON B.,FREEDOM UNDER PLANNING. UNIV ROUTINE ATTIT AUTHORIT DECISION. PAGE 148 F2926 — PLAN ORD/FREE ECO/TAC CONTROL

B50
ADORNO T.W.,THE AUTHORITARIAN PERSONALITY. STRATA SECT PROB/SOLV ECO/TAC DISCRIM ATTIT SEX...SOC INT CHARTS METH 20. PAGE 3 F0044 — AUTHORIT PERSON ALL/IDEOS SOCIETY

B58
DUBIN R.,WORKING UNION-MANAGEMENT RELATIONS. LAW PLAN ECO/TAC CHOOSE REPRESENT INGP/REL PWR...POLICY SOC BIBLIOG. PAGE 34 F0669 — LABOR MGT AUTHORIT GP/REL

B60
MOORE W.E.,LABOR COMMITMENT AND SOCIAL CHANGE IN DEVELOPING AREAS. SOCIETY STRATA ECO/UNDEV MARKET VOL/ASSN WORKER AUTHORIT SKILL...MGT NAT/COMP SOC/INTEG 20. PAGE 93 F1823 — LABOR ORD/FREE ATTIT INDUS

B67
BARDENS D.,CHURCHILL IN PARLIAMENT. UK DIPLOM ADJUD CONTROL AUTHORIT PERSON ORD/FREE 20 CHURCHLL/W PARLIAMENT. PAGE 10 F0186 — TOP/EX LEGIS GOV/REL

S67
RICHMAN B.M.,"SOVIET MANAGEMENT IN TRANSITION." USSR FINAN MARKET EX/STRUC PLAN PROB/SOLV TEC/DEV CONTROL LEAD CENTRAL EFFICIENCY...METH/COMP 20 REFORMERS. PAGE 111 F2186 — MGT MARXISM POLICY AUTHORIT

AUTHORITY....SEE DOMIN

AUTOMAT....AUTOMATION; SEE ALSO COMPUTER, PLAN

N
US SUPERINTENDENT OF DOCUMENTS,LABOR (PRICE LIST 33). USA+45 LAW AGRI CONSTRUC INDUS NAT/G BARGAIN PRICE ADMIN AUTOMAT PRODUC MGT. PAGE 140 F2753 — BIBLIOG/A WORKER LABOR LEGIS

B57
DRUCKER P.F.,AMERICA'S NEXT TWENTY YEARS. USA+45 DIST/IND ACADEM SCHOOL DIPLOM ECO/TAC AUTOMAT HABITAT HEALTH...SOC/WK TREND MUNICH 20 URBAN/RNWL PUB/TRANS. PAGE 34 F0667 — WORKER FOR/AID CENSUS GEOG

B58
CHEEK G.,ECONOMIC AND SOCIAL IMPLICATIONS OF AUTOMATION: A BIBLIOGRAPHIC REVIEW (PAMPHLET). USA+45 LG/CO WORKER CREATE PLAN CONTROL ROUTINE PERS/REL EFFICIENCY PRODUC...METH/COMP 20. PAGE 24 F0459 — BIBLIOG/A SOCIETY INDUS AUTOMAT

B58
POLLOCK F.,AUTOMATION: A STUDY OF ITS ECONOMIC AND SOCIAL CONSEQUENCES. FUT USA+45 USA-45 SOCIETY ECO/DEV LABOR ACT/RES PLAN ECO/TAC AUTOMAT ROUTINE ALL/VALS...STAT TREND COMPUT/IR CHARTS SOC/EXP WORK 20. PAGE 107 F2099 — TEC/DEV SOC CAP/ISM

S58
MANSFIELD E.,"A STUDY OF DECISION-MAKING WITHIN THE FIRM." LG/CO WORKER INGP/REL COST EFFICIENCY PRODUC ...CHARTS 20. PAGE 85 F1658 — OP/RES PROB/SOLV AUTOMAT ROUTINE

B59
LEWIS J.P.,BUSINESS CONDITIONS ANALYSIS. USA+45 MARKET LABOR BUDGET TAX AUTOMAT WAR DEMAND PRODUC ...ECOMETRIC CHARTS BIBLIOG 19/20. PAGE 79 F1549 — FINAN PRICE TREND

B60
MORRIS W.T.,ENGINEERING ECONOMY. AUTOMAT RISK RATIONAL...PROBABIL STAT CHARTS GAME SIMUL BIBLIOG T 20. PAGE 94 F1838 — OP/RES DECISION MGT PROB/SOLV

B61
FRIEDMANN G.,THE ANATOMY OF WORK. USA+45 SOCIETY CONTROL ROUTINE DRIVE SKILL...PSY SOC STAT OBS METH/COMP PERS/COMP 20. PAGE 44 F0862 — AUTOMAT WORKER INDUS PERSON

B61
STROUD G.S.,LABOR HISTORY IN THE UNITED STATES: A GENERAL BIBLIOGRAPHY. USA+45 USA-45 STRATA VOL/ASSN — BIBLIOG WORKER

AUTOMAT GP/REL INGP/REL ATTIT HEALTH 18/20. PAGE 127 F2504 — LABOR

B62
CHRISTENSON C.L.,ECONOMIC REDEVELOPMENT IN BITUMINOUS COAL: THE SPECIAL CASE OF TECHNOLOGICAL ADVANCE IN US COAL MINES 1930-1960. USA+45 USA-45 ECO/TAC AUTOMAT INCOME PRODUC...CHARTS 20. PAGE 24 F0471 — EXTR/IND LABOR TEC/DEV ECO/DEV

B62
LITWACK L.,THE AMERICAN LABOR MOVEMENT. USA-45 NAT/G CREATE TEC/DEV CAP/ISM ECO/TAC ADJUD AUTOMAT SKILL...TREND ANTHOL 19/20. PAGE 81 F1588 — INDUS LABOR GP/REL METH/COMP

B63
MCDONOUGH A.M.,INFORMATION ECONOMICS AND MANAGEMENT SYSTEMS. ECO/DEV OP/RES AUTOMAT EFFICIENCY 20. PAGE 88 F1726 — COMPUT/IR MGT CONCPT COMPUTER

B64
BARKSDALE H.C.,MARKETING: CHANGE AND EXCHANGE. USA+45 FINAN ACADEM TEC/DEV PRICE AUTOMAT WEALTH ...CHARTS 20. PAGE 10 F0187 — MARKET ECO/DEV DEMAND TREND

B64
BRIGHT J.R.,RESEARCH, DEVELOPMENT AND TECHNOLOGICAL INNOVATION. CULTURE R+D CREATE PLAN PROB/SOLV AUTOMAT RISK PERSON...DECISION CONCPT PREDICT BIBLIOG. PAGE 18 F0352 — TEC/DEV NEW/IDEA INDUS MGT

B64
LANG A.S.,URBAN RAIL TRANSIT. OP/RES PLAN PROB/SOLV TEC/DEV AUTOMAT COST...TECHNIC MATH CON/ANAL CHARTS METH/COMP SIMUL MUNICH 20 RAILROAD PUB/TRANS. PAGE 75 F1474 — DIST/IND ECOMETRIC

B64
LITVAK I.A.,MARKETING: CANADA. CANADA STRATA PROC/MFG LEGIS TEC/DEV DIPLOM INT/TRADE PRICE AUTOMAT ATTIT WEALTH...ANTHOL 20. PAGE 81 F1587 — ECO/TAC MARKET ECO/DEV EFFICIENCY

B64
WERNETTE J.P.,GOVERNMENT AND BUSINESS. LABOR CAP/ISM ECO/TAC INT/TRADE TAX ADMIN AUTOMAT NUC/PWR CIVMIL/REL DEMAND...MGT 20 MONOPOLY. PAGE 145 F2859 — NAT/G FINAN ECO/DEV CONTROL

B65
LYONS G.M.,AMERICA: PURPOSE AND POWER. UK USA+45 FINAN INDUS MARKET WORKER TEC/DEV DIPLOM AUTOMAT NUC/PWR WAR RACE/REL ORD/FREE 20 EEC CONGRESS SUPREME/CT CIV/RIGHTS. PAGE 82 F1617 — PWR PROB/SOLV ECO/DEV TASK

B65
PEARL A.,NEW CAREERS FOR THE POOR: THE NON-PROFESSIONAL IN HUMAN SERVICE. USA+45 SERV/IND NAT/G NEIGH WORKER EDU/PROP AUTOMAT SKILL...WELF/ST NEW/IDEA BIBLIOG SOC/INTEG 20. PAGE 104 F2044 — SOC/WK WEALTH STRATA POLICY

B65
SMERK G.M.,URBAN TRANSPORTATION; THE FEDERAL ROLE. FUT USA+45 FINAN PROB/SOLV TEC/DEV AUTOMAT GOV/REL COST...STAT BIBLIOG MUNICH 20 PUB/TRANS. PAGE 123 F2426 — PLAN DIST/IND NAT/G

S65
VAN DER HORST S.T.,"THE ECONOMICS OF DECENTRALISATION OF INDUSTRY." SOUTH/AFR ECO/DEV LG/CO AUTOMAT DISCRIM...POLICY MUNICH 20. PAGE 140 F2761 — PLAN INDUS CENTRAL TEC/DEV

B66
BOWEN H.R.,AUTOMATION AND ECONOMIC PROGRESS. EUR+WWI USA+45 ECO/DEV INCOME ORD/FREE WEALTH ...POLICY ANTHOL 20. PAGE 17 F0327 — AUTOMAT TEC/DEV WORKER LEISURE

B66
LANDERS D.S.,RISE OF CAPITALISM. LABOR AUTOMAT GP/REL CENTRAL COST PROFIT...SOC CONCPT ANTHOL 19/20. PAGE 75 F1469 — CAP/ISM INDUS AGRI

B66
LEONTIEF W.,ESSAYS IN ECONOMICS. ECO/UNDEV INDUS NAT/G CAP/ISM FOR/AID AUTOMAT MARXISM...ECOMETRIC CHARTS ANTHOL METH 20 KEYNES/JM. PAGE 78 F1528 — CONCPT METH/CNCPT METH/COMP

B66
LILLEY S.,MEN, MACHINES AND HISTORY: THE STORY OF TOOLS AND MACHINES IN RELATION TO SOCIAL PROGRESS. PREHIST SPACE STRUCT COMPUTER AUTOMAT NUC/PWR ...POLICY SOC. PAGE 80 F1564 — AGRI TEC/DEV SOCIETY

B66
SHULTZ G.P.,STRATEGIES FOR THE DISPLACED WORKER. USA+45 COMPUTER TEC/DEV BARGAIN RECEIVE EDU/PROP CONFER GP/REL...MGT METH/COMP 20. PAGE 121 F2391 — ECO/DEV WORKER PLAN AUTOMAT

B66
US DEPARTMENT OF LABOR,PRODUCTIVITY: A BIBLIOGRAPHY. ECO/DEV INDUS MARKET OP/RES AUTOMAT COST...STAT 20. PAGE 135 F2668 — BIBLIOG/A PRODUC LABOR PLAN

B66
US DEPARTMENT OF LABOR,TECHNOLOGICAL TRENDS IN MAJOR AMERICAN INDUSTRIES. USA+45 R+D LABOR GP/REL PRODUC...MGT BIBLIOG 20. PAGE 135 F2669 — TEC/DEV INDUS TREND AUTOMAT

B66
US SENATE COMM GOVT OPERATIONS,INTERGOVERNMENTAL PERSONNEL ACT OF 1966. USA+45 NAT/G CONSULT DELIB/GP WORKER TEC/DEV PAY AUTOMAT UTIL 20 CONGRESS. PAGE 139 F2730 — ADMIN LEGIS EFFICIENCY EDU/PROP

B67
BARANSON J.,TECHNOLOGY FOR UNDERDEVELOPED AREAS: AN ANNOTATED BIBLIOGRAPHY. FUT WOR+45 CULTURE INDUS INT/ORG CREATE PROB/SOLV INT/TRADE EDU/PROP AUTOMAT ...CONCPT METH. PAGE 10 F0181 — BIBLIOG/A ECO/UNDEV TEC/DEV R+D

B67
ELSNER H.,THE TECHNOCRATS, PROPHETS OF AUTOMATION. SOCIETY INDUS VOL/ASSN COST INCOME ATTIT 20. PAGE 37 F0726 — AUTOMAT TECHRACY PRODUC HIST/WRIT

B67
KRANZBERG M.,TECHNOLOGY IN WESTERN CIVILIZATION VOLUME ONE. UNIV INDUS SKILL. PAGE 73 F1431 — TEC/DEV ACT/RES AUTOMAT POLICY

S67
MORTON J.A.,"A SYSTEMS APPROACH TO THE INNOVATION PROCESS: ITS USE IN THE BELL SYSTEM." USA+45 INTELL INDUS LG/CO CONSULT WORKER COMPUTER AUTOMAT DEMAND ...MGT CHARTS 20. PAGE 94 F1841 — TEC/DEV GEN/METH R+D COM/IND

S67
MYERS S.,"TECHNOLOGY AND URBAN TRANSIT: THE ENORMOUS POTENTIAL OF BUS AND RAIL SYSTEMS." USA+45 FINAN LOC/G WORKER PLAN PROB/SOLV PRICE AUTOMAT MUNICH 20. PAGE 96 F1877 — R+D TEC/DEV DIST/IND ACT/RES

AUTOMOBILE....AUTOMOBILE

B64
CHANDLER A.D. JR.,GIANT ENTERPRISE: FORD, GENERAL MOTORS, AND THE AUTOMOBILE INDUSTRY; SOURCES AND READINGS. USA+45 USA-45 FINAN MARKET CREATE ADMIN ...TIME/SEQ ANTHOL 20 AUTOMOBILE. PAGE 23 F0447 — LG/CO DIST/IND LABOR MGT

AVERAGE....MEAN, AVERAGE BEHAVIORS

AVERY R.S. F0989

AVRAMOVIC D. F0143

AVTORKHANOV A. F0144

AYAL E.B. F0145

AYRES C.E. F0146

AZERBAIJAN....AZERBAIJAN, IRAN

B

BA/MBUTI....BA MBUTI - THE FOREST PEOPLE (CONGO)

BABIES....SEE AGE/C

BACHARACH M.O. F1648

BACKMAN J. F0147

BACKUS/I....ISAAC BACKUS

BACON/F....FRANCIS BACON

BADEN....BADEN

BADGLEY R.F. F0148

BAERRESEN D.W. F0149

BAERWALD F. F0150,F0151

BAGDKIAN B.H. F0152

BAGHDAD....BAGHDAD, IRAQ

BAHAWALPUR....BAHAWALPUR, PAKISTAN

BAHIA....BAHIA

BAIL....BAIL

BAILEY/JM....JOHN MORAN BAILEY

BAILEY/S....S. BAILEY

BAILEY/T....THOMAS BAILEY

BAILKEY N.M. F2809

BAILY S.L. F0153,F0154

BAKKE E.W. F0155

BAL/PAY....BALANCE OF PAYMENTS

N
PEN I.,PRIMER ON INTERNATIONAL TRADE. WOR+45 WOR-45 ECO/DEV DIPLOM EFFICIENCY 16/20 EEC. PAGE 104 F2055
INT/TRADE BAL/PAY ECO/TAC EQUILIB

N19
BOS H.C.,A DISCUSSION ON METHODS OF MONETARY ANALYSIS AND NORMS FOR MONETARY POLICY (PAMPHLET). BAL/PAY COST INCOME...METH/COMP 20. PAGE 17 F0319
FINAN POLICY EQUILIB SIMUL

N19
CONGRESSIONAL QUARTERLY SERV,FEDERAL ECONOMIC POLICY 1945-1965 (PAMPHLET). USA+45 FINAN OP/RES BAL/PWR ECO/TAC TAX BAL/PAY CENTRAL COST WEALTH ...CHARTS 20. PAGE 27 F0525
NAT/G ECO/DEV BUDGET POLICY

N19
GROSECLOSE E.,THE DECAY OF MONEY; A SURVEY OF WESTERN CURRENCIES 1912-1962 (PAMPHLET). AFR FRANCE GERMANY UK LAW INT/TRADE BAL/PAY COST EQUILIB ...POLICY 20 DEPRESSION. PAGE 51 F1004
FINAN NAT/G ECO/DEV ECO/TAC

N19
HABERLER G.,INFLATION; ITS CAUSES AND CURES (PAMPHLET). AFR USA+45 FINAN BUDGET PAY PRICE COST DEMAND 20. PAGE 52 F1021
ECO/DEV BAL/PAY POLICY NAT/G

N19
HABERLER G.,A SURVEY OF INTERNATIONAL TRADE THEORY (PAMPHLET). FINAN NAT/G COST INCOME 18/20 MONEY HUME/D MARSHALL/A. PAGE 52 F1022
INT/TRADE BAL/PAY GEN/LAWS POLICY

N19
HANSEN B.,INFLATION PROBLEMS IN SMALL COUNTRIES (PAMPHLET). AFR UNIV FOR/AID CONTROL BAL/PAY DEMAND PRODUC 20. PAGE 54 F1066
PRICE FINAN ECO/UNDEV ECO/TAC

N19
KINDLEBERGER C.P.,BALANCE-OF-PAYMENTS DEFICITS AND THE INTERNATIONAL MARKET FOR LIQUIDITY (PAMPHLET). ECO/DEV NAT/G PLAN DIPLOM ECO/TAC PRODUC...POLICY STAT CHARTS. PAGE 71 F1389
BAL/PAY INT/TRADE MARKET FINAN

N19
LUTZ F.A.,THE PROBLEM OF INTERNATIONAL LIQUIDITY AND THE MULTIPLECURRENCY STANDARD (PAMPHLET). WOR+45 MARKET INT/ORG PRICE BAL/PAY...NEW/IDEA METH/COMP BIBLIOG 20 IMF. PAGE 82 F1609
PROB/SOLV FINAN DIPLOM ECO/TAC

N19
PATRICK H.T.,CYCLICAL INSTABILITY AND FISCAL-MONETARY POLICY IN POST-WAR JAPAN (PAMPHLET). INDUS MARKET DIPLOM TAX PRICE BAL/PAY...TREND CHARTS EQULIB 20 CHINJAP. PAGE 104 F2036
ECO/DEV PRODUC STAT

B20
MALTHUS T.R.,PRINCIPLES OF POLITICAL ECONOMY. UK AGRI INDUS MARKET NAT/G DIPLOM PRICE CONTROL BAL/PAY COST OWN PWR LAISSEZ 18/19. PAGE 84 F1650
GEN/LAWS DEMAND WEALTH

B28
CASSEL G.,FOREIGN INVESTMENTS. GERMANY UK USA-45 WOR-45 ECO/DEV NAT/G VOL/ASSN CAP/ISM REPAR ATTIT WEALTH...METH/CNCPT STAT SIMUL STERTYP ANTHOL FOR/TRADE TOT/POP VAL/FREE 20. PAGE 22 F0426
FINAN ECO/TAC BAL/PAY

B47
ENKE S.,INTERNATIONAL ECONOMICS. UK USA+45 USSR INT/ORG BAL/PWR BARGAIN CAP/ISM BAL/PAY...NAT/COMP 20 TREATY. PAGE 38 F0735
INT/TRADE FINAN TARIFFS ECO/TAC

B48
GRAHAM F.D.,THE THEORY OF INTERNATIONAL VALUES. FUT WOR+45 WOR-45 ECO/DEV FINAN INT/ORG PLAN TEC/DEV CAP/ISM DIPLOM ECO/TAC TARIFFS ROUTINE BAL/PAY DRIVE PWR WEALTH SOCISM...POLICY STAT HYPO/EXP GEN/LAWS 20. PAGE 50 F0971
NEW/IDEA INT/TRADE

B48
HART A.G.,MONEY, DEBT, AND ECONOMIC ACTIVITY. AFR WORKER DIPLOM PRICE CONTROL BAL/PAY COST OWN PRODUC ...METH/COMP 20 FED/RESERV. PAGE 56 F1097
FINAN WEALTH ECO/TAC NAT/G

B48
ROBERTSON D.H.,MONEY. AFR ECO/DEV NAT/G DIPLOM INT/TRADE BAL/PAY INCOME WEALTH...TIME/SEQ 20 DEPRESSION. PAGE 112 F2212
FINAN MARKET COST PRICE

B49
DE JOUVENEL B.,PROBLEMS OF SOCIALIST ENGLAND. AFR UK USSR BAL/PWR ECO/TAC INT/TRADE PRICE WAR BAL/PAY PEACE 20. PAGE 31 F0601
SOCISM NEW/LIB PROB/SOLV PLAN

B49
HANSEN A.H.,MONETARY THEORY AND FISCAL POLICY. CONSULT PLAN INT/TRADE BAL/PAY OPTIMAL...TREND CHARTS METH/COMP BIBLIOG T 19/20 MONEY. PAGE 54 F1063
FINAN GEN/LAWS POLICY ECO/TAC

B50
HARTLAND P.C.,BALANCE OF INTERREGIONAL PAYMENTS OF NEW ENGLAND. USA+45 TEC/DEV ECO/TAC LEGIT ROUTINE BAL/PAY PROFIT 20 NEW/ENGLND FED/RESERV. PAGE 56 F1102
ECO/DEV FINAN REGION PLAN

C50
ELLSWORTH P.T.,"INTERNATIONAL ECONOMY." ECO/DEV ECO/UNDEV FINAN LABOR DIPLOM FOR/AID TARIFFS BAL/PAY EQUILIB NAT/LISM OPTIMAL...INT/LAW 20 ILO GATT. PAGE 37 F0724
BIBLIOG INT/TRADE ECO/TAC INT/ORG

C52
HUME D.,"OF THE BALANCE OF TRADE" IN D. HUME, POLITICAL DISCOURSES (1752)" UK FINAN NAT/G TARIFFS PRICE PWR LAISSEZ...POLICY GEN/LAWS 18. PAGE 63 F1237
BAL/PAY INT/TRADE DIPLOM WEALTH

B53
HARROD R.,THE DOLLAR. AFR USA+45 USA-45 ECO/DEV OPTIMAL WEALTH 18/20 FED/RESERV. PAGE 56 F1093
FINAN DIPLOM BAL/PAY

B53
NEISSER H.,NATIONAL INCOMES AND INTERNATIONAL TRADE. FRANCE GERMANY SWEDEN UK USA-45 EXTR/IND FINAN INDUS TEC/DEV PRICE BAL/PAY EQUILIB INCOME WEALTH...CHARTS METH 19 CHINJAP. PAGE 97 F1908
INT/TRADE PRODUC MARKET CON/ANAL

B53
WILLIAMS J.H.,ECONOMIC STABILITY IN A CHANGING WORLD. FRANCE USA+45 USSR AGRI WORKER BUDGET INT/TRADE TAX WAR BAL/PAY COST EFFICIENCY ALL/IDEOS EQULIB 20 KEYNES/JM. PAGE 147 F2892
POLICY FINAN ECO/TAC WEALTH

S53
BLOUGH R.,"THE ROLE OF THE ECONOMIST IN FEDERAL POLICY MAKING." USA+45 ELITES INTELL ECO/DEV NAT/G CONSULT EX/STRUC ACT/RES PLAN INT/TRADE BAL/PAY WEALTH...POLICY METH/GP CONGRESS 20. PAGE 16 F0301
DELIB/GP ECO/TAC

B54
O.E.E.C.,PRIVATE UNITED STATES INVESTMENT IN EUROPE AND THE OVERSEAS TERRITORIES. EUR+WWI WOR+45 ECO/DEV ECO/UNDEV INT/ORG NAT/G VOL/ASSN ECO/TAC ATTIT WEALTH...GEOG STAT SYS/QU CHARTS VAL/FREE 20. PAGE 99 F1950
USA+45 FINAN BAL/PAY FOR/AID

B54
TINBERGEN J.,INTERNATIONAL ECONOMIC INTEGRATION. WOR+45 WOR-45 ECO/UNDEV NAT/G ECO/TAC BAL/PAY ...METH/CNCPT STAT TIME/SEQ GEN/METH OEEC 20. PAGE 130 F2574
INT/ORG ECO/DEV INT/TRADE

B56
KINDLEBERGER C.P.,THE TERMS OF TRADE: A EUROPEAN CASE-STUDY. EUR+WWI MOD/EUR ECO/DEV ECO/UNDEV AGRI INDUS BAL/PAY...METH/CNCPT STAT CONT/OBS CON/ANAL SOC/EXP SIMUL FOR/TRADE 20. PAGE 71 F1390
PLAN ECO/TAC

B56
MYRDAL G.,AN INTERNATIONAL ECONOMY. EUR+WWI USA+45 WOR+45 WOR-45 NAT/G DIPLOM ECO/TAC BAL/PAY...PSY CONCPT OEEC TOT/POP 20. PAGE 96 F1879
VOL/ASSN AFR

B57
BEHRMAN J.N.,INTERNATIONAL ECONOMICS: THEORY, PRACTICE, POLICY. AGRI INDUS NAT/G TARIFFS CONTROL BAL/PAY...POLICY METH/CNCPT T 19/20. PAGE 12 F0230
INT/TRADE FINAN DIPLOM FOR/AID

B57
DAY A.C.L.,OUTLINE OF MONETARY ECONOMICS. AFR WOR-45 INT/ORG WORKER DIPLOM BAL/PAY COST INCOME WEALTH...TIME/SEQ SIMUL 20. PAGE 31 F0594
FINAN NAT/G EQUILIB PRICE

B57
GOLD N.L.,REGIONAL ECONOMIC DEVELOPMENT AND NUCLEAR POWER IN INDIA. FUT INDIA FINAN FOR/AID INT/TRADE BAL/PAY EFFICIENCY OPTIMAL PRODUC WEALTH...PREDICT 20. PAGE 48 F0934
ECO/UNDEV TEC/DEV NUC/PWR INDUS

B57
HARRIS S.E.,INTERNATIONAL AND INTERREGIONAL ECONOMICS. AFR WOR+45 WOR-45 NAT/G TARIFFS BAL/PAY EQUILIB...POLICY CONCPT STAT CHARTS IDEA/COMP 19/20. PAGE 55 F1088
INT/TRADE ECO/DEV MARKET FINAN

B57
LUNDBERG E.,BUSINESS CYCLES AND ECONOMIC POLICY (TRANS. BY J. POTTER). SWEDEN ECO/DEV FINAN DELIB/GP PLAN PRICE CONTROL BAL/PAY 20 INTRVN/ECO. PAGE 82 F1607
ECO/TAC INDUS INT/TRADE BUDGET

B57
MEIER G.M.,ECONOMIC DEVELOPMENT: THEORY, HISTORY, AND POLICY. WOR+45 WOR-45 ECO/DEV ECO/UNDEV PLAN CAP/ISM BAL/PAY ATTIT PWR WEALTH SOCISM...CHARTS TOT/POP FOR/TRADE 20. PAGE 89 F1748
ECO/TAC GEN/LAWS

B57
SINGH D.B.,INFLATIONARY PRICE TRENDS IN INDIA SINCE 1939. AFR INDIA ECO/TAC RATION CONTROL WAR GOV/REL BAL/PAY DEMAND INCOME PEACE PRODUC...POLICY CHARTS 20. PAGE 122 F2413
BUDGET ECO/UNDEV PRICE FINAN

B57
THOMAS R.G.,OUR MODERN BANKING AND MONETARY SYSTEM (3RD ED.). AFR USA+45 USA-45 ACT/RES PLAN PROB/SOLV INT/TRADE PRICE WAR BAL/PAY INCOME...POLICY METH/CNCPT 20 DEPRESSION. PAGE 130 F2563
FINAN SERV/IND ECO/TAC

B57
TRIFFIN R.,EUROPE AND THE MONEY MUDDLE. USA+45
EUR+WWI

INT/ORG NAT/G CONSULT PLAN ECO/TAC EXEC ROUTINE BAL/PAY WEALTH...METH/CNCPT OBS TREND CHARTS STERTYP GEN/METH EEC TERR/GP VAL/FREE ECSC. PAGE 131 F2587 ECO/DEV REGION

B58
AVRAMOVIC D.,POSTWAR GROWTH IN INTERNATIONAL INDEBTEDNESS. AFR WOR+45 AGRI INDUS CAP/ISM PRICE INCOME...NAT/COMP 20 SILVER. PAGE 8 F0143 INT/TRADE FINAN COST BAL/PAY

B58
BARRERE A.,POLITIQUE FINANCIERE. FRANCE BUDGET ECO/TAC TAX BAL/PAY INCOME PRODUC...MGT BIBLIOG T 20. PAGE 10 F0193 FINAN NAT/G PLAN

B58
CHANG C.,THE INFLATIONARY SPIRAL: THE EXPERIENCE IN CHINA 1939-50. CHINA/COM BUDGET INT/TRADE PRICE ADMIN CONTROL WAR DEMAND...POLICY CHARTS 20. PAGE 23 F0451 FINAN ECO/TAC BAL/PAY GOV/REL

B58
ELLSWORTH P.T.,THE INTERNATIONAL ECONOMY. EUR+WWI MOD/EUR INT/ORG CAP/ISM FOR/AID BAL/PAY LAISSEZ 16/20. PAGE 37 F0725 INT/TRADE TARIFFS ECO/DEV

B58
HENNING C.N.,INTERNATIONAL FINANCING. WOR+45 ECO/DEV INT/ORG EX/STRUC INSPECT CAP/ISM BAL/PAY COST PROFIT...MGT CHARTS T 20. PAGE 58 F1150 FINAN DIPLOM INT/TRADE

B58
HIRSCHMAN A.O.,STRATEGY OF ECONOMIC DEVELOPMENT. WOR+45 WOR-45 CULTURE ECO/DEV NAT/G PLAN TEC/DEV INT/TRADE BAL/PAY ATTIT DRIVE RIGID/FLEX WEALTH ...CONCPT METH/CNCPT OBS CHARTS SIMUL GEN/LAWS TOT/POP VAL/FREE. PAGE 60 F1176 ECO/UNDEV ECO/TAC CAP/ISM

B58
JOHNSON H.G.,INTERNATIONAL TRADE AND ECONOMIC GROWTH. WOR+45 BUDGET CAP/ISM ECO/TAC TARIFFS BAL/PAY 20. PAGE 67 F1323 INT/TRADE BAL/PWR BARGAIN DIPLOM

B58
MIKESELL R.F.,FINANCING FREE WORLD TRADE WITH THE SINO-SOVIET BLOC. CHINA/COM COM USSR WOR+45 ECO/DEV AGRI DIST/IND EXTR/IND FINAN INDUS MARKET PROC/MFG NAT/G PLAN TEC/DEV ECO/TAC...CHARTS METH/GP EEC FOR/TRADE 20. PAGE 91 F1780 STAT BAL/PAY

B58
SCITOUSKY T.,ECONOMIC THEORY AND WESTERN EUROPEAN INTEGRATION. EUR+WWI INT/ORG ACT/RES INT/TRADE REGION BAL/PAY WEALTH...METH/CNCPT STAT CHARTS GEN/METH ECSC TOT/POP EEC OEEC 20. PAGE 118 F2328 ECO/TAC

N58
EUROPEAN COMM ECO-SOC PROG,EUROPEAN BUSINESS CYCLE POLICY (PAMPHLET). AFR EUR+WWI MARKET WORKER DIPLOM PRICE BAL/PAY 20 EUROPE. PAGE 39 F0754 ECO/DEV FINAN ECO/TAC PROB/SOLV

B59
AITKEN H.G.,THE AMERICAN ECONOMIC IMPACT ON CANADA. CANADA USA+45 AGRI FINAN INDUS LABOR INT/TRADE BAL/PAY...INT/LAW TREND 20. PAGE 3 F0055 DIPLOM ECO/TAC POLICY NAT/G

B59
ALLEN W.R.,FOREIGN TRADE AND FINANCE. ECO/DEV DIPLOM BAL/PAY...POLICY CONCPT ANTHOL 20. PAGE 4 F0073 INT/TRADE EQUILIB FINAN

B59
GUDIN E.,INFLACAO (2ND ED.). INDUS NAT/G PLAN ECO/TAC CONTROL COST 20. PAGE 52 F1012 ECO/UNDEV INT/TRADE BAL/PAY FINAN

B59
OGBURN C.,ECONOMIC PLAN AND ACTION. USA+45 FINAN LABOR DIPLOM ECO/TAC FOR/AID 20. PAGE 101 F1981 ECO/DEV INT/TRADE PLAN BAL/PAY

B59
ROPKE W.,INTERNATIONAL ORDER AND ECONOMIC INTEGRATION. ECO/DEV ECO/UNDEV AGRI FINAN INDUS INT/ORG WAR PEACE ORD/FREE...SOC METH/COMP 20 EEC. PAGE 114 F2238 INT/TRADE DIPLOM BAL/PAY ALL/IDEOS

B59
SHACKLE G.L.S.,ECONOMICS FOR PLEASURE. FINAN MARKET NAT/G WORKER PLAN INT/TRADE TARIFFS PAY BAL/PAY COST PRODUC 20. PAGE 120 F2361 METH/CNCPT WEALTH INCOME

B59
SILCOCK T.H.,THE COMMONWEALTH ECONOMY IN SOUTHEAST ASIA. AFR INDIA MALAYSIA S/ASIA ECO/DEV AGRI LOC/G PLAN TARIFFS COLONIAL BAL/PAY DEMAND...BIBLIOG/A 20 GATT. PAGE 122 F2401 ECO/TAC INT/TRADE RACE/REL DIPLOM

B59
STOVEL J.A.,CANADA IN THE WORLD ECONOMY. CANADA PRICE DEMAND...STAT CHARTS BIBLIOG 20 VINER/J. PAGE 127 F2499 INT/TRADE BAL/PAY FINAN ECO/TAC

B60
BATOR F.M.,QUESTION OF GOVERNMENT SPENDING. USA+45 DIST/IND FINAN BAL/PAY...STAT CENSUS CHARTS CONGRESS 20. PAGE 11 F0210 ECO/DEV

B60
BELLAN R.C.,PRINCIPLES OF ECONOMICS AND THE CANADIAN ECONOMY (2ND ED.). CANADA UK USA+45 LABOR WORKER CAP/ISM INT/TRADE RISK BAL/PAY EQUILIB ALL/IDEOS 20. PAGE 12 F0236 ECO/DEV PRODUC WEALTH FINAN

B60
COMMITTEE ECONOMIC DEVELOPMENT,NATIONAL OBJECTIVES AND THE BALANCE OF PAYMENTS PROBLEM: A STATEMENT ON NATIONAL POLICY. USA+45 WOR+45 DIST/IND FINAN INDUS LABOR NAT/G DELIB/GP ACT/RES FOR/AID INT/TRADE ...STAT CHARTS FOR/TRADE 20. PAGE 27 F0516 ECO/DEV ECO/TAC BAL/PAY

B60
DALE W.B.,THE FOREIGN DEFICIT OF THE UNITED STATES. ECO/TAC TARIFFS PAY PRICE CONTROL COST WEALTH POLICY. PAGE 30 F0573 BAL/PAY DIPLOM FINAN INT/TRADE

B60
KENEN P.B.,GIANT AMONG NATIONS: PROBLEMS IN UNITED STATES FOREIGN ECONOMIC POLICY. AFR USA+45 FINAN DIPLOM TARIFFS BAL/PAY WEALTH 20. PAGE 70 F1376 FOR/AID ECO/UNDEV INT/TRADE PLAN

B60
KENEN P.B.,BRITISH MONETARY POLICY AND THE BALANCE OF PAYMENTS 1951-57. UK PLAN BUDGET ECO/TAC INT/TRADE PAY PRICE COST ATTIT 20. PAGE 70 F1377 BAL/PAY PROB/SOLV FINAN NAT/G

B60
KILLOUGH H.B.,INTERNATIONAL ECONOMICS. PLAN PROB/SOLV FOR/AID TARIFFS CONTROL BAL/PAY...POLICY CHARTS T 20. PAGE 71 F1388 CONCPT ECO/UNDEV INT/ORG INT/TRADE

B60
THEOBALD R.,THE RICH AND THE POOR: A STUDY OF THE ECONOMICS OF RISING EXPECTATIONS. WOR+45 CONSTN ECO/DEV ECO/UNDEV INT/ORG NAT/G PLAN FOR/AID ROUTINE BAL/PAY ORD/FREE PWR WEALTH...GEOG TREND WORK FOR/TRADE 20. PAGE 129 F2553 ECO/TAC INT/TRADE

B60
THORBECKE E.,THE TENDENCY TOWARDS REGIONALIZATION IN INTERNATIONAL TRADE, 1928-1956. WOR+45 WOR-45 ECO/DEV FINAN ECO/TAC WEALTH...GEOG CHARTS TOT/POP FOR/TRADE 20. PAGE 130 F2569 STAT BAL/PAY REGION

S60
MARTIN E.M.,"NEW TRENDS IN UNITED STATES ECONOMIC FOREIGN POLICY." USA+45 INTELL DELIB/GP FOR/AID INT/TRADE ROUTINE BAL/PAY...RELATIV TRUE/GP 20. PAGE 86 F1682 NAT/G PLAN DIPLOM

B61
BENHAM F.,ECONOMIC AID TO UNDERDEVELOPED COUNTRIES. WOR+45 INDUS BAL/PAY ALL/VALS 20. PAGE 13 F0244 ECO/UNDEV FOR/AID INT/TRADE FINAN

B61
EINZIG P.,A DYNAMIC THEORY OF FORWARD EXCHANGE. FUT WOR+45 WOR-45 INT/TRADE BAL/PAY WEALTH...OLD/LIB NEW/IDEA OBS TREND FOR/TRADE 20. PAGE 37 F0713 FINAN ECO/TAC

B61
ELLIS H.S.,ECONOMIC DEVELOPMENT FOR LATIN AMERICA. L/A+17C AGRI FINAN INDUS FOR/AID GP/REL BAL/PAY DEMAND...ANTHOL 20 INTL/ECON. PAGE 37 F0723 ECO/UNDEV ECO/TAC PLAN INT/TRADE

B61
ESTEBAN J.C.,IMPERIALISMO Y DESARROLLO ECONOMICO. L/A+17C FINAN INDUS NAT/G ECO/TAC CONTROL ROLE. PAGE 38 F0747 ECO/UNDEV NAT/LISM DIPLOM BAL/PAY

B61
GREY A.L.,ECONOMIC ISSUES AND POLICIES; READINGS IN INTRODUCTORY ECONOMICS (2ND ED.). WOR+45 ECO/UNDEV FINAN MARKET LABOR LG/CO INT/TRADE BAL/PAY WEALTH ...ANTHOL T. PAGE 51 F0996 ECO/TAC PROB/SOLV METH/COMP

B61
GURTOO D.H.N.,INDIA'S BALANCE OF PAYMENTS (1920-1960). INDIA FINAN DIPLOM FOR/AID INT/TRADE PRICE COLONIAL...CHARTS BIBLIOG 20. PAGE 52 F1014 BAL/PAY STAT ECO/TAC ECO/UNDEV

B61
HARRIS S.E.,THE DOLLAR IN CRISIS. AFR USA+45 MARKET INT/ORG ECO/TAC PRICE CONTROL WEALTH...METH/COMP ANTHOL 20. PAGE 55 F1089 BAL/PAY DIPLOM FINAN INT/TRADE

B61
OECD,STATISTICS OF BALANCE OF PAYMENTS 1950-61. WOR+45 FINAN ECO/TAC INT/TRADE DEMAND WEALTH...STAT NAT/COMP 20 OEEC OECD. PAGE 100 F1965 BAL/PAY ECO/DEV INT/ORG CHARTS

B61
SCAMMEL W.M.,INTERNATIONAL MONETARY POLICY. WOR+45 WOR-45 ACT/RES ECO/TAC LEGIT WEALTH...GEN/METH UN 20. PAGE 116 F2286 INT/ORG FINAN BAL/PAY

B61
TRIFFIN R.,GOLD AND THE DOLLAR CRISIS: THE FUTURE OF CONVERTIBILITY. AFR USA+45 USA-45 INT/ORG PROB/SOLV BUDGET INT/TRADE PRICE...STAT CHARTS 19/20. PAGE 131 F2588 FINAN ECO/DEV ECO/TAC BAL/PAY

B61
US CONGRESS JOINT ECO COMM,INTERNATIONAL PAYMENTS IMBALANCES AND NEED FOR STRENGTHENING INTERNATIONAL FINANCIAL ARRANGEMENTS. USA+45 WOR+45 DELIB/GP DIPLOM INT/TRADE...CHARTS 20 CONGRESS OEEC. PAGE 134 F2651 BAL/PAY INT/ORG FINAN PROB/SOLV

B61
WAGLE S.S.,TECHNIQUE OF PLANNING FOR ACCELERATED ECONOMIC GROWTH OF UNDERDEVELOPED COUNTRIES. WOR+45 ACT/RES PROB/SOLV RATION BAL/PAY DEMAND INCOME 20. PAGE 142 F2798 ECO/UNDEV PLAN INDUS ECO/TAC

S61
DELLA PORT G.,"PROBLEMI E PROSPETTIVE DI COESISTENZA FRA ORIENTE ED OCCIDENTE, (PART 3)." COM FUT WOR+45 NAT/G BAL/PWR FOR/AID BAL/PAY PWR WEALTH...SOC CONCPT GEN/LAWS 20. PAGE 32 F0616 AFR INT/TRADE

S61
NYANZI S.,"THE EAST AFRICAN MARKET: FOR BETTER OF FOR WORSE." AFR TANZANIA UGANDA PROB/SOLV TARIFFS TAX BAL/PAY. PAGE 99 F1947 ECO/TAC ECO/UNDEV INT/ORG INT/TRADE

S61
VINER J.,"ECONOMIC FOREIGN POLICY ON THE NEW FRONTIER." USA+45 ECO/UNDEV AGRI FINAN INDUS MARKET INT/ORG NAT/G FOR/AID INT/TRADE ADMIN ATTIT PWR 20 KENNEDY/JF. PAGE 141 F2786 TOP/EX ECO/TAC BAL/PAY TARIFFS

B62
ROUND TABLE ON EUROPE'S ROLE IN LATIN AMERICAN DEVELOPMENT. EUR+WWI L/A+17C PLAN BAL/PAY UTIL ROLE WEALTH...CHARTS ANTHOL 20 UN INT/AM/DEV. PAGE 1 F0017 ECO/UNDEV FINAN TEC/DEV FOR/AID

B62
FORD A.G.,THE GOLD STANDARD 1880-1914: BRITAIN AND ARGENTINA. AFR UK ECO/UNDEV INT/TRADE ADMIN GOV/REL DEMAND EFFICIENCY...STAT CHARTS 19/20 ARGEN. PAGE 42 F0823 FINAN ECO/TAC BUDGET BAL/PAY

B62
HOLMAN A.G.,SOME MEASURES AND INTERPRETATIONS OF EFFECTS OF US FOREIGN ENTERPRISES ON US BALANCE OF PAYMENTS. USA+45 COST INCOME WEALTH...MATH CHARTS 20. PAGE 61 F1199 BAL/PAY INT/TRADE FINAN ECO/TAC

B62
HOOVER C.B.,ECONOMIC SYSTEMS OF THE COMMONWEALTH. AFR CANADA INDIA UK ECO/DEV ECO/UNDEV AGRI INDUS TEC/DEV TARIFFS PRICE BAL/PAY DEMAND...SIMUL 20 AUSTRAL. PAGE 61 F1208 CAP/ISM SOCISM ECO/TAC PLAN

B62
HUMPHREY D.D.,THE UNITED STATES AND THE COMMON MARKET. USA+45 INDUS MARKET INT/ORG PLAN EDU/PROP BAL/PAY DRIVE PWR WEALTH...TREND STERTYP FOR/TRADE EEC 20. PAGE 63 F1241 ATTIT ECO/TAC

B62
JOHNSON H.G.,MONEY, TRADE AND ECONOMIC GROWTH. ECO/DEV ECO/UNDEV FINAN COST WEALTH...POLICY SOC IDEA/COMP 20 KEYNES/JM MONEY. PAGE 67 F1324 PLAN BAL/PAY INT/TRADE ECO/TAC

B62
KINDLEBERGER C.P.,FOREIGN TRADE AND THE NATIONAL ECONOMY. WOR+45 ECO/DEV ECO/UNDEV ECO/TAC COST DEMAND 20. PAGE 71 F1393 INT/TRADE GOV/COMP BAL/PAY POLICY

B62
LUTZ F.A.,THE PROBLEM OF INTERNATIONAL ECONOMIC EQUILIBRIUM. FINAN PRODUC WEALTH 20 MONEY. PAGE 82 F1611 DIPLOM EQUILIB BAL/PAY PROB/SOLV

B62
MCCRONE G.,THE ECONOMICS OF SUBSIDING AGRICULTURE. UK ECO/DEV MARKET PLAN TARIFFS PROFIT 20 EEC. PAGE 88 F1725 AGRI BAL/PAY INT/TRADE LABOR

B62
MEYER F.V.,THE TERMS OF TRADE. WOR+45 AGRI MARKET PROC/MFG DIPLOM PRICE DEMAND PRODUC 20. PAGE 90 F1769 INT/TRADE BAL/PAY SIMUL EQUILIB

B62
ROBINSON M.A.,AN INTRODUCTION TO ECONOMIC REASONING. FINAN MARKET LABOR DIPLOM INT/TRADE BAL/PAY INCOME PRODUC WEALTH...POLICY MGT 20. PAGE 113 F2223 ECO/TAC METH/CNCPT NAT/G

B62
SHANNON I.,THE ECONOMIC FUNCTIONS OF GOLD. AFR FUT WOR+45 WOR-45 INT/ORG BUDGET INT/TRADE BAL/PAY DEMAND PEACE 20 MONEY. PAGE 120 F2366 FINAN PRICE ECO/DEV ECO/TAC

B62
THEOBALD R.,NATIONAL DEVELOPMENT EFFORTS (PAMPHLET). WOR+45 AGRI BUDGET FOR/AID INT/TRADE TAX 20. PAGE 129 F2555 ECO/UNDEV PLAN BAL/PAY WEALTH

B62
URQUIDI V.L.,FREE TRADE AND ECONOMIC INTEGRATION IN LATIN AMERICA: THE EVOLUTION OF A COMMON MARKET POLICY. ECO/UNDEV MARKET DIPLOM BAL/PAY FEDERAL ...POLICY CHARTS 20 LAFTA. PAGE 133 F2627 INT/TRADE REGION INT/ORG L/A+17C

B62
US CONGRESS JOINT ECO COMM,FACTORS AFFECTING THE UNITED STATES BALANCE OF PAYMENTS. USA+45 DELIB/GP PLAN DIPLOM FOR/AID PRODUC WEALTH...CHARTS 20 CONGRESS OEEC. PAGE 134 F2653 BAL/PAY INT/TRADE ECO/TAC FINAN

B62
VANEK J.,INTERNATIONAL TRADE - THEORY AND ECONOMIC POLICY. LABOR BAL/PWR ECO/TAC TARIFFS PRICE BAL/PAY COST DEMAND 20. PAGE 140 F2765 INT/TRADE DIPLOM BARGAIN MARKET

B62
VANEK J.,THE BALANCE OF PAYMENTS, LEVEL OF ECONOMIC ACTIVITY AND THE VALUE OF CURRENCY: THEORY AND SOME RECENT EXPERIENCES. UNIV PRICE INCOME...MATH 20 KEYNES/JM. PAGE 140 F2766 BAL/PAY ECO/TAC FINAN GEN/LAWS

B62
ZOOK P.D.,FOREIGN TRADE AND HUMAN CAPITAL. L/A+17C USA+45 FINAN DIPLOM ECO/TAC PRODUC...POLICY 20. PAGE 151 F2970 INT/TRADE ECO/UNDEV FOR/AID BAL/PAY

L62
MACHLUP F.,"PLANS FOR REFORM OF THE INTERNATIONAL MONETARY SYSTEM. PRINCETON: U. PR., 1962, 70 PP., $0.25." WOR+45 INT/ORG ECO/TAC BAL/PAY HEALTH ORD/FREE WEALTH MID/EX TERR/GP VAL/FREE APPLIC 20. PAGE 83 F1631 ECO/DEV STAT

S62
MEAD W.,"SOME POLITICAL-ECONOMIC ISSUES DETERMINING USA TARIFF POLICY." USA+45 USA-45 ECO/DEV NAT/G TARIFFS ATTIT...TIME/SEQ TREND CHARTS 19/20. PAGE 89 F1736 ECO/TAC METH/CNCPT BAL/PAY

N62
BANK INTERNATIONAL SETTLEMENTS,AUSTRIA: MONETARY AND ECONOMIC SITUATION 1952-61 (PAMPHLET). AUSTRIA WORKER BUDGET INT/TRADE PRICE BAL/PAY DEMAND EFFICIENCY INCOME PRODUC...STAT 20 SILVER. PAGE 9 F0174 FINAN ECO/DEV CHARTS WEALTH

B63
BANERJI A.K.,INDIA'S BALANCE OF PAYMENTS. INDIA NAT/G PRICE BAL/PAY COST INCOME 20. PAGE 9 F0171 INT/TRADE DIPLOM FINAN BUDGET

B63
BENOIT E.,DISARMAMENT AND THE ECONOMY. USA+45 NAT/G ACT/RES ECO/TAC BAL/PAY...STAT CON/ANAL GEN/LAWS 20. PAGE 13 F0252 ECO/DEV ARMS/CONT

B63
BERGSON A.,ECONOMIC TRENDS IN THE SOVIET UNION. USSR ECO/UNDEV AGRI NAT/G FORCES PLAN TEC/DEV INT/TRADE BAL/PAY...POLICY ANTHOL 20. PAGE 14 F0259 ECO/DEV NAT/COMP INDUS LABOR

B63
CHATTERJEE I.K.,ECONOMIC DEVELOPMENT PAYMENTS DEFICIT AND PAYMENT RESTRICTION. INDIA WOR+45 FINAN INT/TRADE CONTROL BAL/PAY WEALTH...POLICY CONCPT STAT CHARTS IDEA/COMP BIBLIOG 20. PAGE 23 F0456 ECO/DEV ECO/TAC PAY GOV/REL

B63
FATEMI N.S.,THE DOLLAR CRISIS. USA+45 INDUS NAT/G LEGIS BUDGET TAX COST...CHARTS METH/COMP 20 EEC. PAGE 39 F0766 PROB/SOLV BAL/PAY FOR/AID PLAN

B63
GRUBEL H.G.,WORLD MONETARY REFORM: PLANS AND ISSUES. FUT WOR+45 ECO/DEV ECO/UNDEV R+D DELIB/GP CREATE ECO/TAC ATTIT RIGID/FLEX WEALTH...STAT ANTHOL VAL/FREE 20. PAGE 52 F1009 FINAN INT/ORG BAL/PAY INT/TRADE

B63
HAHN L.A.,DIE AMERIKANISCHE KONJUNKTURPOLITIK DER DOLLAR UND DIE DMARK. GERMANY/W USA+45 DIPLOM PRICE BAL/PAY COST...POLICY MONEY. PAGE 53 F1038 FINAN BUDGET ECO/TAC LABOR

B63
HARROD R.F.,INTERNATIONAL TRADE THEORY IN A DEVELOPING WORLD. COM WOR+45 FOR/AID REGION COST DEMAND WEALTH...POLICY 20 INTL/ECON. PAGE 56 F1095 INT/TRADE BAL/PAY ECO/UNDEV METH/COMP

B63
HOLLAND E.P.,EXPERIMENTS ON A SIMULATED UNDERDEVELOPED ECONOMY: DEVELOPMENT PLANS AND BALANCE-OF-PAYMENTS POLICIES. WOR+45 ECO/UNDEV FINAN PLAN ECO/TAC...MATH STAT CHARTS SIMUL VAL/FREE. PAGE 61 F1196 AFR BAL/PAY

B63
INTERNATIONAL MONETARY FUND,COMPENSATORY FINANCING OF EXPORT FLUCTUATIONS (PAMPHLET). WOR+45 ECO/DEV ECO/UNDEV INT/ORG WEALTH...TREND 20 IMF MONEY. PAGE 65 F1281 BAL/PAY FINAN BUDGET INT/TRADE

B63
LARY M.B.,PROBLEMS OF THE UNITED STATES AS WORLD TRADER AND BANKER. USA+45 NAT/G PLAN DIPLOM FOR/AID ...TREND CHARTS. PAGE 76 F1482 ECO/DEV FINAN BAL/PAY INT/TRADE

B63
MEIER G.,INTERNATIONAL TRADE AND DEVELOPMENT. FINAN BAL/PAY COST DEMAND DISCRIM EQUILIB WEALTH...POLICY ECOMETRIC MATH STAT BIBLIOG/A 20. PAGE 89 F1747 ECO/UNDEV ECO/TAC INT/TRADE

IDEA/COMP

B63
MYRDAL G.,CHALLENGE TO AFFLUENCE. USA+45 WOR+45 FINAN INT/ORG NAT/G PLAN ECO/TAC INT/TRADE BAL/PAY ORD/FREE 20 EUROPE/W. PAGE 96 F1882
ECO/DEV WEALTH DIPLOM PRODUC

B63
ROBBINS L.,POLITICS AND ECONOMICS. ECO/DEV FINAN BUDGET DIPLOM BAL/PAY ORD/FREE 20. PAGE 112 F2204
NAT/G ATTIT

B63
ROPKE W.,ECONOMICS OF THE FREE SOCIETY. FINAN INT/TRADE BAL/PAY COST DEMAND EFFICIENCY ORD/FREE WEALTH...CON/ANAL METH/COMP T 20 KEYNES/JM. PAGE 114 F2240
SOCIETY BUDGET ECO/DEV ECO/TAC

B63
SALANT W.S.,THE UNITED STATES BALANCE OF PAYMENTS IN 1968. USA+45 ECO/DEV ECO/UNDEV INT/ORG DELIB/GP ECO/TAC...POLICY STAT SIMUL 20. PAGE 115 F2273
FUT FINAN BAL/PAY

B63
SALENT W.S.,THE UNITED STATES BALANCE OF PAYMENTS IN 1968. EUR+WWI UK USA+45 AGRI R+D LABOR FORCES PRODUC...GEOG CONCPT CHARTS 20 CHINJAP EEC. PAGE 115 F2274
BAL/PAY DEMAND FINAN INT/TRADE

B63
SCHOECK H.,THE NEW ARGUMENT IN ECONOMICS. UK USA+45 INDUS MARKET LABOR NAT/G ECO/TAC ADMIN ROUTINE BAL/PAY PWR...POLICY BOLIV. PAGE 117 F2309
WELF/ST FOR/AID ECO/DEV ALL/IDEOS

B63
US CONGRESS JOINT ECO COMM,THE UNITED STATES BALANCE OF PAYMENTS. AFR USA+45 DELIB/GP BUDGET PRICE PRODUC 20 CONGRESS MONEY. PAGE 135 F2655
BAL/PAY INT/TRADE FINAN ECO/TAC

B63
US CONGRESS JOINT ECO COMM,THE UNITED STATES BALANCE OF PAYMENTS. USA+45 DELIB/GP CONFER...MATH PREDICT CHARTS 20 CONGRESS. PAGE 135 F2656
BAL/PAY ECO/TAC INT/TRADE CONSULT

B63
US CONGRESS JOINT ECO COMM,OUTLOOK FOR UNITED STATES BALANCE OF PAYMENTS. AFR USA+45 ECO/DEV NAT/G FORCES DIPLOM FOR/AID COST EFFICIENCY ...POLICY CONGRESS EEC. PAGE 135 F2657
BAL/PAY FINAN INT/TRADE PROB/SOLV

B63
US HOUSE COMM BANKING-CURR,RECENT CHANGES IN MONETARY POLICY AND BALANCE OF PAYMENTS PROBLEMS. USA+45 DELIB/GP PLAN DIPLOM...CHARTS 20 CONGRESS. PAGE 136 F2688
BAL/PAY FINAN ECO/TAC POLICY

S63
CARTER A.G.T.,"THE BALANCE OF PAYMENTS OF EAST AFRICA" AFR ECO/TAC FOR/AID RATION TARIFFS TAX ADMIN...STAT 20 AFRICA/E. PAGE 22 F0423
BUDGET ECO/UNDEV BAL/PAY INT/TRADE

S63
MASON E.S.,"INTERESTS, IDEOLOGIES AND THE PROBLEM OF STABILITY AND GROWTH." EUR+WWI USA+45 DELIB/GP CREATE PLAN EXEC ROUTINE BAL/PAY ATTIT PWR...MGT CONCPT OEEC 20. PAGE 87 F1698
NAT/G ECO/DEV

S63
MIKESELL R.F.,"COMMODITY AGREEMENTS AND AID TO DEVELOPING COUNTRIES." WOR+45 WOR-45 INT/ORG ECO/TAC ATTIT WEALTH WORK FOR/TRADE 20. PAGE 91 F1782
FINAN ECO/UNDEV BAL/PAY FOR/AID

S63
NADLER E.B.,"SOME ECONOMIC DISADVANTAGES OF THE ARMS RACE." AFR USA+45 INDUS R+D FORCES PLAN TEC/DEV ECO/TAC FOR/AID EDU/PROP PWR WEALTH...TREND FOR/TRADE 20. PAGE 96 F1886
ECO/DEV MGT BAL/PAY

S63
POLYANOV N.,"THE DOLLAR'S VENTURES IN EUROPE." EUR+WWI FRANCE USA+45 ECO/DEV MARKET POL/PAR TEC/DEV ECO/TAC EDU/PROP DRIVE PWR WEALTH...MARXIST MYTH STAT TREND EEC 20. PAGE 107 F2100
FINAN PLAN BAL/PAY CAP/ISM

S63
REDDAWAY W.B.,"THE ECONOMICS OF UNDERDEVELOPED COUNTRIES." S/ASIA WOR+45 WOR-45 STRATA AGRI COM/IND DIST/IND MARKET PROC/MFG PLAN TEC/DEV FOR/AID BAL/PAY ATTIT DRIVE SKILL WORK FOR/TRADE 20. PAGE 110 F2165
ECO/TAC ECO/UNDEV INDIA

N63
LEDERER W.,THE BALANCE ON FOREIGN TRANSACTIONS: PROBLEMS OF DEFINITION AND MEASUREMENT (PAMPHLET). USA+45 BUDGET DIPLOM ECO/TAC PRICE GOV/REL...POLICY STAT NAT/COMP METH 20. PAGE 77 F1502
FINAN BAL/PAY INT/TRADE ECO/DEV

N63
US AGENCY INTERNATIONAL DEV,PRINCIPLES OF FOREIGN ECONOMIC ASSISTANCE (PAMPHLET). USA+45 FINAN GP/REL BAL/PAY EFFICIENCY 20 AID. PAGE 134 F2638
FOR/AID PLAN ECO/UNDEV ATTIT

B64
AUBREY H.G.,THE DOLLAR IN WORLD AFFAIRS. FUT USA+45 WOR+45 ECO/DEV CAP/ISM INT/TRADE BAL/PAY...CHARTS 20. PAGE 7 F0140
FINAN ECO/TAC DIPLOM POLICY

B64
BALASSA B.,CHANGING PATTERNS IN FOREIGN TRADE AND PAYMENTS. AFR USA+45 USA-45 ECO/DEV NAT/G PLAN BAL/PWR...POLICY ANTHOL BIBLIOG 20. PAGE 8 F0159
ECO/TAC INT/TRADE BAL/PAY WEALTH

B64
BALL R.J.,INFLATION AND THE THEORY OF MONEY. MARKET TAX PAY PRICE TASK ADJUST BAL/PAY COST INCOME PRODUC WEALTH...METH/COMP 20 KEYNES/JM MONEY. PAGE 9 F0167
EQUILIB DEMAND POLICY

B64
BOARMAN P.M.,GERMANY'S ECONOMIC DILEMMA - INFLATION AND THE BALANCE OF PAYMENTS. AFR GERMANY/W LABOR CAP/ISM PRICE BAL/PAY COST INCOME 20. PAGE 16 F0302
ECO/DEV FINAN INT/TRADE BUDGET

B64
BROWN E.H.P.,A COURSE IN APPLIED ECONOMICS (2ND ED.). ECO/DEV FINAN MARKET WORKER INT/TRADE RATION RENT PAY PRICE BAL/PAY...DECISION T RESOURCE/N. PAGE 19 F0368
POLICY ECO/TAC PROB/SOLV

B64
CENTRO ESTUDIOS MONETARIOS LAT,PROBLEMAS DE PAGOS EN AMERICA LATINA. L/A+17C MARKET BUDGET ECO/TAC EFFICIENCY WEALTH 20 CENTRAL/AM. PAGE 22 F0434
FINAN INT/TRADE BAL/PAY ECO/UNDEV

B64
CLAIRBORN E.L.,FORECASTING THE BALANCE OF PAYMENTS: AN EVALUATION. AFR FUT UK USA+45 WOR+45 FINAN PLAN BUDGET PAY CONTROL...STAT CHARTS BIBLIOG 20. PAGE 24 F0474
PREDICT BAL/PAY ECO/DEV ECO/TAC

B64
EINZIG P.,MONETARY POLICY: ENDS AND MEANS. AFR UK INDUS WORKER PLAN DIPLOM PRICE BAL/PAY COST WEALTH ...DECISION TIME/SEQ 20. PAGE 37 F0715
FINAN POLICY ECO/TAC BUDGET

B64
GEORGIADIS H.G.,BALANCE OF PAYMENTS EQUILIBRIUM. COST DEMAND...CONCPT MATH GEN/LAWS 20 KEYNES/JM. PAGE 47 F0916
BAL/PAY EQUILIB SIMUL INT/TRADE

B64
GOWDA K.V.,INTERNATIONAL CURRENCY PLANS AND EXPANSION OF WORLD TRADE. INT/ORG CREATE BUDGET CONTROL BAL/PAY WEALTH 20 KEYNES/JM. PAGE 50 F0969
INT/TRADE FINAN METH/COMP

B64
HANSEN B.,INTERNATIONAL LIQUIDITY. USA+45 INT/ORG ECO/TAC PRICE CONTROL WEALTH...POLICY 20. PAGE 54 F1068
BAL/PAY INT/TRADE DIPLOM FINAN

B64
KALDOR N.,ESSAYS ON ECONOMIC POLICY (VOL. II). CHILE GERMANY INDIA FINAN...GOV/COMP METH/COMP 20 KEYNES/JM. PAGE 69 F1348
BAL/PAY INT/TRADE METH/CNCPT ECO/UNDEV

B64
KUZNETS S.,POSTWAR ECONOMIC GROWTH: FOUR LECTURES. WOR+45 INDUS NAT/G WORKER TEC/DEV ECO/TAC RATION TARIFFS PRICE BAL/PAY COST DEMAND 20. PAGE 74 F1455
ECO/DEV ECO/UNDEV TREND FINAN

B64
LAURSEN K.,THE GERMAN INFLATION, 1918-23. EUR+WWI GERMANY/E GERMANY/W WOR-45 BUDGET TAX GOV/REL BAL/PAY DEMAND PEACE...POLICY CHARTS 20 WEIMAR/REP. PAGE 76 F1489
ECO/DEV FINAN REPAR ECO/TAC

B64
MAGALHAES S.,PRATICA DA EMANCIPACAO NACIONAL. L/A+17C INDUS PLAN ECO/TAC CONTROL NAT/LISM ORD/FREE. PAGE 84 F1640
BAL/PAY ECO/UNDEV DIPLOM WEALTH

B64
MAZA ZAVALA D.F.,VENEZUELA; UNA ECONOMIA DEPENDIENTE. L/A+17C VENEZUELA FINAN INDUS ...ECOMETRIC STAT TREND 20. PAGE 87 F1710
ECO/UNDEV BAL/PAY INT/TRADE PRICE

B64
MORRISSENS L.,ECONOMIC POLICY IN OUR TIME: COUNTRY STUDIES. BELGIUM EUR+WWI FRANCE GERMANY/W ITALY NETHERLAND INDUS BARGAIN BUDGET GOV/REL BAL/PAY PRODUC...CON/ANAL CHARTS COSTS 20. PAGE 94 F1839
ECO/DEV ECO/TAC METH/COMP PLAN

B64
ORGANIZATION AMERICAN STATES,ECONOMIC SURVEY OF LATIN AMERICA, 1962. L/A+17C AGRI DIST/IND INDUS MARKET PROC/MFG R+D PLAN TEC/DEV ECO/TAC REGION BAL/PAY ALL/VALS...CON/ANAL ORG/CHARTS GEN/METH OAS ALL/PROG 20 ALL/PROG. PAGE 102 F1998
ECO/UNDEV CHARTS

B64
PIERSON J.H.,INSURING FULL EMPLOYMENT. USA+45 LABOR DIPLOM ECO/TAC PAY BAL/PAY 20. PAGE 106 F2084
ECO/DEV INT/TRADE POLICY WORKER

B64
REUSS H.S.,THE CRITICAL DECADE - AN ECONOMIC POLICY FOR AMERICA AND THE FREE WORLD. AFR USA+45 FINAN POL/PAR WORKER PLAN DIPLOM ECO/TAC TARIFFS BAL/PAY ...POLICY 20 CONGRESS. PAGE 111 F2181
FOR/AID INT/TRADE LABOR LEGIS

B64
RIVKIN A.,AFRICA AND THE EUROPEAN COMMON MARKET (PAMPHLET). AFR MOD/EUR WOR+45 TEC/DEV FOR/AID
INT/ORG INT/TRADE

TARIFFS BAL/PAY...POLICY 20 EEC. PAGE 111 F2196
ECO/TAC ECO/UNDEV

B64
ROBINSON R.D.,INTERNATIONAL BUSINESS POLICY. AFR INDIA L/A+17C USA+45 ELITES AGRI FOR/AID COERCE BAL/PAY...DECISION INT/LAW MGT 20. PAGE 113 F2224
ECO/TAC DIST/IND COLONIAL FINAN

B64
SHANNON I.,INTERNATIONAL LIQUIDITY. AFR FUT USA+45 WOR+45 ECO/TAC PRICE DEMAND WEALTH...CONCPT 20. PAGE 120 F2367
FINAN DIPLOM BAL/PAY ECO/DEV

B64
US HOUSE COMM BANKING-CURR,INTERNATIONAL DEVELOPMENT ASSOCIATION ACT AMENDMENT. CHINA/COM USA+45 USSR FINAN FORCES LEGIS DIPLOM CONFER EFFICIENCY...CHARTS GOV/COMP 20 PRESIDENT CONGRESS INTL/DEV. PAGE 136 F2689
BAL/PAY FOR/AID RECORD ECO/TAC

B64
WILLIAMSON J.G.,AMERICAN GROWTH AND THE BALANCE OF PAYMENTS, 1820-1913: A STUDY OF THE LONG SWING. EUR+WWI MOD/EUR USA+45 USA-45 ECO/DEV NAT/G ECO/TAC ROUTINE ORD/FREE WEALTH...MATH STAT TIME/SEQ CHARTS SIMUL GEN/LAWS TRUE/GP METH/GP VAL/FREE 19/20. PAGE 147 F2896
FINAN BAL/PAY

L64
CARNEGIE ENDOWMENT INT. PEACE,"ECONOMIC AND SOCIAL QUESTION (ISSUES BEFORE THE NINETEENTH GENERAL ASSEMBLY)." WOR+45 ECO/DEV ECO/UNDEV INDUS R+D DELIB/GP CREATE PLAN TEC/DEV ECO/TAC FOR/AID BAL/PAY...RECORD UN 20. PAGE 21 F0414
INT/ORG INT/TRADE

L64
KORBONSKI A.,"COMECON." ASIA ECO/DEV ECO/UNDEV ECO/TAC BAL/PAY NAT/LISM FOR/TRADE 20 COMECON. PAGE 73 F1425
COM INT/ORG INT/TRADE

S64
HUELIN D.,"ECONOMIC INTEGRATION IN LATIN AMERICAN: PROGRESS AND PROBLEMS." L/A+17C ECO/DEV AGRI DIST/IND FINAN INDUS NAT/G VOL/ASSN CONSULT DELIB/GP EX/STRUC ACT/RES PLAN TEC/DEV ECO/TAC ROUTINE BAL/PAY WEALTH FOR/TRADE WORK TERR/GP 20. PAGE 63 F1232
MARKET ECO/UNDEV INT/TRADE

S64
NEISSER H.,"THE EXTERNAL EQUILIBRIUM OF THE UNITED STATES ECONOMY." FUT USA+45 NAT/G ACT/RES PLAN ECO/TAC ATTIT WEALTH...METH/CNCPT GEN/METH VAL/FREE FOR/TRADE 20. PAGE 97 F1910
FINAN ECO/DEV BAL/PAY INT/TRADE

S64
SCHMITT H.D.,"POLITICAL CONDITIONS FOR INTERNATIONAL CURRENCY REFORM." WOR+45 SOCIETY ECO/DEV PLAN ECO/TAC BAL/PAY ATTIT ORD/FREE WEALTH ...SOC CONCPT OBS TREND EEC VAL/FREE ECSC 20. PAGE 117 F2301
FINAN VOL/ASSN REGION

B65
ARTEL R.,THE STRUCTURE OF THE STOCKHOLM ECONOMY. SWEDEN DIST/IND LABOR LOC/G TEC/DEV DEMAND MUNICH LOUISIANA 20. PAGE 7 F0125
ECO/DEV METH/COMP BAL/PAY

B65
BALDWIN D.A.,SOFT LOANS AND AMERICAN FOREIGN POLICY: 1943-1962 (THESIS). USA+45 WOR+45 FINAN NAT/G FOR/AID BAL/PAY ATTIT...POLICY METH/COMP 20 UN CONGRESS. PAGE 9 F0161
DIPLOM ECO/TAC ECO/UNDEV

B65
CASSELL F.,GOLD OR CREDIT? THE ECONOMICS AND POLITICS OF INTERNATIONAL MONEY. AFR WOR+45 PLAN PROB/SOLV BAL/PAY SOVEREIGN WEALTH 20 OEEC. PAGE 22 F0428
FINAN INT/ORG DIPLOM ECO/TAC

B65
DEMAS W.G.,THE ECONOMICS OF DEVELOPMENT IN SMALL COUNTRIES WITH SPECIAL REFERENCE TO THE CARIBBEAN. WOR+45 BAL/PAY DEMAND EFFICIENCY PRODUC...GEOG CARIBBEAN. PAGE 32 F0618
ECO/UNDEV PLAN WEALTH INT/TRADE

B65
EDELMAN M.,THE POLITICS OF WAGE-PRICE DECISIONS. GERMANY ITALY NETHERLAND UK INDUS LABOR POL/PAR PROB/SOLV BARGAIN PRICE ROUTINE BAL/PAY COST DEMAND 20. PAGE 36 F0699
GOV/COMP CONTROL ECO/TAC PLAN

B65
HABERLER G.,A SURVEY OF INTERNATIONAL TRADE THEORY. CANADA FRANCE GERMANY ECO/TAC TARIFFS AGREE COST DEMAND WEALTH...ECOMETRIC 19/20 MONOPOLY TREATY. PAGE 52 F1024
INT/TRADE BAL/PAY DIPLOM POLICY

B65
HONDURAS CONSEJO NAC DE ECO,PLAN NACIONAL DE DESARROLLO ECONOMICO Y SOCIAL DE HONDURAS 1965-69. HONDURAS AGRI INDUS BAL/PAY INCOME 20. PAGE 61 F1203
ECO/UNDEV NAT/G PLAN POLICY

B65
KLEIN J.J.,MONEY AND THE ECONOMY. USA+45 NAT/G DIPLOM CONTROL...POLICY T 20 FED/RESERV. PAGE 72 F1406
FINAN PLAN WEALTH BAL/PAY

B65
LITTLE I.M.D.,INTERNATIONAL AID. UK WOR+45 AGRI INDUS GIVE RECEIVE COLONIAL BAL/PAY WEALTH...POLICY GOV/COMP METH/COMP 20. PAGE 81 F1584
FOR/AID DIPLOM ECO/UNDEV NAT/G

B65
MARK S.M.,ECONOMICS IN ACTION (3RD ED.). USA+45 ECO/UNDEV AGRI INDUS FOR/AID INT/TRADE BAL/PAY COST ORD/FREE...ANTHOL 20 RESOURCE/N. PAGE 85 F1670
POLICY ECO/TAC EFFICIENCY PRICE

B65
MCCOLL G.D.,THE AUSTRALIAN BALANCE OF PAYMENTS. UK USA+45 AGRI WORKER DIPLOM EQUILIB PRODUC...STAT TREND CHARTS BIBLIOG/A 20 AUSTRAL. PAGE 88 F1719
ECO/DEV BAL/PAY INT/TRADE COST

B65
PROCHNOW H.V.,WORLD ECONOMIC PROBLEMS AND POLICIES. INDIA ISRAEL WOR+45 AGRI LABOR PROB/SOLV FOR/AID TARIFFS CONTROL BAL/PAY NAT/LISM WEALTH...TREND CHARTS 20 CHINJAP EEC. PAGE 108 F2124
MARKET ECO/TAC PRODUC IDEA/COMP

B65
ROLFE S.E.,GOLD AND WORLD POWER. AFR UK USA+45 WOR-45 INDUS WORKER INT/TRADE DEMAND...MGT CHARTS 20. PAGE 113 F2234
BAL/PAY EQUILIB ECO/TAC DIPLOM

B65
ROOSA R.V.,MONETARY REFORM FOR THE WORLD ECONOMY. AFR EUR+WWI USA+45 WOR+45 CREATE BUDGET DIPLOM FOR/AID EQUILIB WEALTH IMF. PAGE 114 F2237
FINAN INT/ORG INT/TRADE BAL/PAY

B65
RUEFF J.,THE ROLE AND THE RULE OF GOLD: AN ARGUMENT (PAMPHLET). AFR FRANCE USA+45 WOR+45 MARKET NAT/G PLAN DIPLOM ATTIT...POLICY INT 20 DEGAULLE/C. PAGE 115 F2258
FINAN ECO/DEV INT/TRADE BAL/PAY

B65
SCITOVSKY T.,REQUIREMENTS OF AN INTERNATIONAL RESERVE SYSTEM. AFR ECO/TAC...PREDICT 20 SILVER MONEY. PAGE 118 F2330
BAL/PAY FINAN EQUILIB INT/TRADE

B65
SHARIF A.,THE BALANCE OF PAYMENTS OF PAKISTAN, 1948-1958 (THESIS, UNIVERSITY OF TORONTO). PAKISTAN FINAN INDUS FOR/AID PRICE WEALTH...TREND CHARTS 20. PAGE 120 F2368
BAL/PAY BUDGET INT/TRADE ECO/UNDEV

B65
TEW B.,WEALTH AND INCOME. UK BUDGET INT/TRADE PRICE BAL/PAY DEMAND...CHARTS GOV/COMP 20 AUSTRAL. PAGE 129 F2546
FINAN ECO/DEV WEALTH INCOME

B65
US BUREAU OF THE BUDGET,THE BALANCE OF PAYMENTS STATISTICS OF THE UNITED STATES: A REVIEW AND APPRAISAL. USA+45 FINAN NAT/G PROB/SOLV DIPLOM. PAGE 134 F2644
BAL/PAY STAT METH/COMP BUDGET

B65
US CONGRESS JOINT ECO COMM,GUIDELINES FOR INTERNATIONAL MONETARY REFORM. USA+45 WOR+45 DELIB/GP BAL/PAY 20 CONGRESS IMF MONEY. PAGE 135 F2659
DIPLOM FINAN PLAN INT/ORG

B65
US HOUSE COMM BANKING-CURR,INTERNATIONAL TRAVEL IN RELATION TO THE BALANCE OF PAYMENTS DEFICIT. USA+45 DELIB/GP...CHARTS 20 CONGRESS TRAVEL. PAGE 136 F2690
BAL/PAY ECO/TAC SERV/IND PROB/SOLV

B65
US SENATE COMM ON JUDICIARY,ANTITRUST EXEMPTIONS FOR AGREEMENTS RELATING TO BALANCE OF PAYMENTS. FINAN ECO/TAC CONTROL WEALTH...POLICY 20 CONGRESS. PAGE 140 F2750
BAL/PAY ADJUD MARKET INT/TRADE

B65
WARD R.J.,INTERNATIONAL FINANCE. INT/ORG DIPLOM DEMAND INCOME...POLICY METH/COMP 20. PAGE 143 F2819
INT/TRADE ECO/TAC FINAN BAL/PAY

B65
WASSERMAN M.J.,THE BALANCE OF PAYMENTS: HISTORY, METHODOLOGY, THEORY. UK USA+45 USA-45 CAP/ISM DIPLOM EFFICIENCY...DECISION METH/CNCPT BIBLIOG 18/20 LEAGUE/NAT. PAGE 144 F2828
BAL/PAY ECO/TAC GEN/LAWS EQUILIB

L65
DAANE J.D.,"THE EVOLVING INTERNATIONAL MONETARY MECHANISM." VOL/ASSN CREATE PLAN FOR/AID INT/TRADE CONFER BAL/PAY...RECORD PREDICT IMF. PAGE 29 F0569
INT/ORG ECO/TAC TREND GP/COMP

S65
RUSINOW D.I.,"YUGOSLAV DEVELOPMENT BETWEEN EAST AND WEST." AGRI VOL/ASSN PLAN CAP/ISM ECO/TAC FOR/AID INT/TRADE BAL/PAY...MARXIST EEC COMECON. PAGE 115 F2262
YUGOSLAVIA ECO/UNDEV STAT

B66
CONAN A.R.,THE PROBLEM OF STERLING. UK WOR+45 BUDGET ECO/TAC...POLICY STAT CHARTS 20 SILVER. PAGE 27 F0521
FINAN ECO/DEV BAL/PAY DIPLOM

B66
FELLNER W.,MAINTAINING AND RESTORING BALANCE IN INTERNATIONAL PAYMENTS. ECO/UNDEV MARKET ECO/TAC PRICE INCOME WEALTH...POLICY METH/COMP 20 MONEY. PAGE 40 F0781
BAL/PAY DIPLOM FINAN INT/TRADE

B66
FRIEDMANN W.G.,INTERNATIONAL FINANCIAL AID. USA+45 INT/ORG
ECO/DEV ECO/UNDEV NAT/G VOL/ASSN EX/STRUC PLAN RENT FOR/AID
GIVE BAL/PAY PWR...GEOG INT/LAW STAT TREND UN EEC TEC/DEV
COMECON. PAGE 44 F0866 ECO/TAC

B66
HACKETT J.,L'ECONOMIE BRITANNIQUE: PROBLEMES ET ECO/DEV
PERSPECTIVES. FRANCE UK LABOR NAT/G EX/STRUC FINAN
PROB/SOLV BAL/PAY INCOME RIGID/FLEX...MGT PHIL/SCI ECO/TAC
CHARTS MUNICH 20. PAGE 53 F1027 PLAN

B66
INGRAM J.C.,INTERNATIONAL ECONOMIC PROBLEMS. INT/TRADE
ECO/DEV ECO/UNDEV INDUS MARKET TEC/DEV TARIFFS INT/ORG
BAL/PAY CENTRAL...POLICY 20 EEC. PAGE 64 F1265 FINAN

B66
INTERNATIONAL ECO POLICY ASSN,THE UNITED STATES BAL/PAY
BALANCE OF PAYMENTS. INT/ORG NAT/G PROB/SOLV BUDGET ECO/TAC
DIPLOM INT/TRADE WEALTH 20. PAGE 65 F1274 POLICY
FINAN

B66
INTERNATIONAL ECONOMIC ASSN,STABILITY AND PROGRESS INT/TRADE
IN THE WORLD ECONOMY: THE FIRST CONGRESS OF THE
INTERNATIONAL ECONOMIC ASSOCIATION. WOR+45 ECO/DEV
ECO/UNDEV DELIB/GP FOR/AID BAL/PAY...TREND CMN/WLTH
20. PAGE 65 F1276

B66
JENSEN F.B.,READINGS IN INTERNATIONAL ECONOMIC BAL/PAY
RELATIONS. COM ECO/UNDEV MARKET NAT/G FOR/AID INT/TRADE
...ANTHOL 20. PAGE 67 F1317 FINAN

B66
KINDLEBERGER C.P.,EUROPE AND THE DOLLAR. AFR BAL/PAY
EUR+WWI FRANCE GERMANY/W USA+45 CONSTN INT/ORG BUDGET
DIPLOM INT/TRADE...ANTHOL 20. PAGE 71 F1395 FINAN
ECO/DEV

B66
KOMIYA R.,POSTWAR ECONOMIC GROWTH IN JAPAN. ELITES ECO/DEV
NAT/G EX/STRUC TEC/DEV BUDGET DIPLOM CONTROL POLICY
BAL/PAY PRODUC...BIBLIOG 20 CHINJAP. PAGE 73 F1424 PLAN
ADJUST

B66
LEAGUE OF WOMEN VOTERS OF US,FOREIGN AID AT THE FOR/AID
CROSSROADS. USA+45 WOR+45 DELIB/GP PROB/SOLV DIPLOM GIVE
INT/TRADE RECEIVE BAL/PAY...CHARTS 20 UN ALL/PROG. ECO/UNDEV
PAGE 76 F1498 PLAN

B66
MEERHAEGHE M.,INTERNATIONAL ECONOMIC INSTITUTIONS. ECO/TAC
EUR+WWI FINAN INDUS MARKET PLAN TARIFFS BAL/PAY ECO/DEV
EQUILIB...POLICY BIBLIOG/A 20 GATT OEEC EEC IBRD INT/TRADE
EURCOALSTL. PAGE 89 F1745 INT/ORG

B66
NATIONAL INDUSTRIAL CONF BOARD,GOLD AND WORLD FINAN
MONETARY PROBLEMS. AFR FUT WOR+45 PROB/SOLV BUDGET ECO/TAC
INT/TRADE PAY GOV/REL...POLICY ANTHOL 20. PAGE 97 PRICE
F1902 BAL/PAY

B66
PIQUET H.S.,THE US BALANCE OF PAYMENTS AND BAL/PAY
INTERNATIONAL MONETARY RESERVES. AFR USA+45 DIPLOM
PROB/SOLV INT/TRADE GOV/REL EQUILIB...POLICY STAT FINAN
CHARTS 20. PAGE 106 F2090 ECO/TAC

B66
POLK J.,U S PRODUCTION ABROAD AND THE BALANCE OF BAL/PAY
PAYMENTS* A SURVEY OF CORPORATE INVESTMENT FINAN
EXPERIENCE. USA+45 SERV/IND NAT/G OP/RES COST INT/TRADE
PROFIT ATTIT...ECOMETRIC STAT INT QU GEN/METH. INDUS
PAGE 107 F2096

B66
ROBERTSON D.J.,THE BRITISH BALANCE OF PAYMENTS. UK FINAN
WOR+45 INDUS BUDGET TAX ADJUST...CHARTS ANTHOL 20. BAL/PAY
PAGE 112 F2213 ECO/DEV
INT/TRADE

B66
SHULTZ G.P.,GUIDELINES, INFORMAL CONTROLS, AND THE ECO/TAC
MARKET PLACE: POLICY CHOICES IN A FULL EMPLOYMENT CONTROL
ECONOMY. UK ECO/DEV LABOR INT/TRADE CONFER GOV/REL FINAN
BAL/PAY DEMAND INCOME...POLICY ANTHOL 20 PRESIDENT. RATION
PAGE 121 F2392

B66
TRIFFIN R.,THE WORLD MONEY MAZE. AFR INT/ORG BAL/PAY
ECO/TAC PRICE OPTIMAL WEALTH...METH/COMP 20 EEC FINAN
OEEC SILVER. PAGE 131 F2589 INT/TRADE
DIPLOM

B66
TRIFFIN R.,THE BALANCE OF PAYMENTS AND THE FOREIGN BAL/PAY
INVESTMENT POSITION OF THE UNITED STATES. AFR DIPLOM
USA+45 INT/ORG INT/TRADE PRICE CONTROL...POLICY 20. FINAN
PAGE 131 F2590 ECO/TAC

B66
US CONGRESS JOINT ECO COMM,NEW APPROACH TO UNITED DIPLOM
STATES INTERNATIONAL ECONOMIC POLICY. USA+45 WOR+45 ECO/TAC
CHIEF DELIB/GP CONFER...CHARTS 20 CONGRESS MONEY. BAL/PAY
PAGE 135 F2660 FINAN

B66
US PRES COMM ECO IMPACT DEFENS,REPORT* JULY 1965. ACT/RES
USA+45 ECO/DEV INDUS DELIB/GP FORCES OP/RES STAT
ARMS/CONT NUC/PWR WEAPON BAL/PAY...PREDICT SIMUL. WAR
PAGE 138 F2726 BUDGET

B66
YEAGER L.B.,INTERNATIONAL MONETARY RELATIONS: FINAN
THEORY, HISTORY, AND POLICY. WOR+45 WOR-45 DIPLOM
INT/TRADE BAL/PAY...NAT/COMP 18/20 MONEY. PAGE 150 ECO/TAC
F2947 IDEA/COMP

S66
ANGELL J.W.,"THE LONGER RUN PROSPECTS FOR THE US BAL/PAY
BALANCE OF PAYMENTS." USA+45 DIPLOM FOR/AID RATION ECO/TAC
ORD/FREE WEALTH...IDEA/COMP GATT. PAGE 6 F0104 INT/TRADE
FINAN

S66
LAURENS H.,"LES PAYS OCCIDENTAUX ET LE MARCHE ASIA
CHINOIS." EUR+WWI FUT S/ASIA AGRI INDUS VOL/ASSN INT/TRADE
ECO/TAC BAL/PAY...RECORD PREDICT TREATY. PAGE 76 TREND
F1488 STAT

S66
NEWLYN W.T.,"MONEY MARKETS IN EAST AFRICA." AFR FINAN
TANZANIA UGANDA UK DIPLOM CENTRAL 20. PAGE 98 F1923 WEALTH
BAL/PAY
ECO/UNDEV

N66
BRITISH DEVELOPMENT POLICIES: 1966 (PAMPHLET). UK WEALTH
AGRI TARIFFS BAL/PAY...TREND CHARTS 20 OVRSEA/DEV. DIPLOM
PAGE 1 F0023 INT/TRADE
FOR/AID

N66
EOMMITTEE ECONOMIC DEVELOPMENT,THE DOLLAR AND THE FINAN
WORLD MONETARY SYSTEM: A STATEMENT ON NATIONAL BAL/PAY
POLICY (PAMPHLET). AFR USA+45 NAT/G PLAN PROB/SOLV DIPLOM
BUDGET ECO/TAC FOR/AID INCOME...POLICY 20 EUROPE. ECO/DEV
PAGE 38 F0740

N66
OECD,THE BALANCE OF PAYMENTS ADJUSTMENT PROCESS BAL/PAY
(PAMPHLET). EUR+WWI ECO/DEV FINAN CONSULT PLAN ECO/TAC
PROB/SOLV BUDGET CAP/ISM INT/TRADE PRICE CONTROL DIPLOM
EQUILIB 20. PAGE 101 F1975 INT/ORG

B67
BALDWIN G.B.,PLANNING AND DEVELOPMENT IN IRAN. IRAN PLAN
AGRI INDUS CONSULT WORKER EDU/PROP BAL/PAY...CHARTS ECO/UNDEV
20. PAGE 9 F0164 ADMIN
PROB/SOLV

B67
BRIEFS H.W.,REGAINING BALANCE IN A HIGH EMPLOYMENT ECO/DEV
ECONOMY: UNRESOLVED ISSUES FOR 1967 AND BEYOND. FINAN
USA+45 NAT/G PLAN PROB/SOLV FOR/AID...CHARTS 20. BAL/PAY
PAGE 18 F0350 BUDGET

B67
CLEMENT M.O.,THEORETICAL ISSUES IN INTERNATIONAL INT/TRADE
ECONOMICS. WOR+45 PLAN PROB/SOLV TEC/DEV FINAN
...ECOMETRIC METH/CNCPT MATH BIBLIOG T MONEY. CREATE
PAGE 25 F0489 BAL/PAY

B67
ENKE S.,DEFENSE MANAGEMENT. USA+45 R+D FORCES DECISION
WORKER PLAN ECO/TAC ADMIN NUC/PWR BAL/PAY UTIL DELIB/GP
WEALTH...MGT DEPT/DEFEN. PAGE 38 F0738 EFFICIENCY
BUDGET

B67
HOGAN J.,THE US BALANCE OF PAYMENTS AND CAPITAL BAL/PAY
FLOWS. MARKET INT/ORG ECO/TAC PRICE CONTROL WEALTH FINAN
...METH/COMP 20 EEC. PAGE 61 F1192 DIPLOM
INT/TRADE

B67
KAPLAN J.J.,CHALLENGE OF FOREIGN AID. USA+45 FOR/AID
CONTROL BAL/PAY COST ATTIT ALL/VALS...METH/COMP 20. PLAN
PAGE 69 F1352 GIVE
POLICY

B67
KARDOUCHE G.K.,THE UAR IN DEVELOPMENT. UAR ECO/TAC FINAN
INT/TRADE BAL/PAY...STAT CHARTS BIBLIOG 20. PAGE 69 MGT
F1355 CAP/ISM
ECO/UNDEV

B67
KEWEN P.B.,INTERNATIONAL ECONOMICS (2ND ED.). INT/TRADE
USA+45 WOR+45 MARKET TARIFFS...BIBLIOG T 20. BAL/PAY
PAGE 70 F1384 FINAN
EQUILIB

B67
KREININ M.E.,ALTERNATIVE COMMERCIAL POLICIES - INT/TRADE
THEIR EFFECT ON THE AMERICAN ECONOMY. USA+45 LAW BAL/PAY
ECO/DEV MARKET INT/ORG DIPLOM ECO/TAC TARIFFS PRICE NAT/G
DEMAND WEALTH...QUANT EEC AFTA. PAGE 73 F1437 POLICY

B67
ROBINSON E.A.G.,ECONOMIC PLANNING IN THE UNITED ECO/DEV
KINGDOM. UK WORKER PLAN PROB/SOLV BAL/PAY 20. INDUS
PAGE 113 F2220 PRODUC
BUDGET

B67
RUEFF J.,BALANCE OF PAYMENTS: PROPOSALS FOR BAL/PAY
RESOLVING THE CRITICAL WORLD ECONOMIC PROBLEM OF INT/TRADE
OUR TIME. USA+45 INDUS FOR/AID REPAR DEMAND OPTIMAL FINAN
...ECOMETRIC CHARTS METH/COMP 20. PAGE 115 F2259 NEW/IDEA

B67
THOMAN R.S.,GEOGRAPHY OF INTERNATIONAL TRADE. INT/TRADE
WOR+45 ECO/DEV ECO/UNDEV INT/ORG LG/CO PLAN BAL/PAY GEOG
...STAT CHARTS NAT/COMP 20. PAGE 130 F2559 ECO/TAC
DIPLOM

B67
US AGENCY INTERNATIONAL DEV,PROPOSED FOREIGN AID PROGRAM FOR 1968: SUMMARY PRESENTATION TO THE CONGRESS. AFR S/ASIA USA+45 AGRI TEC/DEV DIPLOM ECO/TAC BAL/PAY COST HEALTH KNOWL SKILL 20 AID CONGRESS ALL/PROG. PAGE 134 F2640
ECO/UNDEV BUDGET FOR/AID STAT

B67
US CONGRESS JOINT ECO COMM,AN ECONOMIC PROFILE OF MAINLAND CHINA, VOLUMES I AND II. CHINA/COM AGRI DIST/IND FINAN INDUS LABOR FORCES ACT/RES PLAN INT/TRADE INGP/REL BAL/PAY 20 CONGRESS. PAGE 135 F2664
ECO/UNDEV WEALTH ECO/TAC DELIB/GP

B67
US CONGRESS SENATE,SURVEY OF THE ALLIANCE FOR PROGRESS; INFLATION IN LATIN AMERICA (PAMPHLET). USA+45 MARKET INT/ORG DIPLOM INT/TRADE BAL/PAY SENATE ALL/PROG. PAGE 135 F2666
L/A+17C FINAN POLICY FOR/AID

B67
US SENATE COMM ON FOREIGN REL,INTER-AMERICAN DEVELOPMENT BANK ACT AMENDMENT. L/A+17C USA+45 DELIB/GP DIPLOM FOR/AID BAL/PAY...CHARTS SENATE. PAGE 139 F2741
LAW FINAN INT/ORG ECO/UNDEV

B67
US SENATE COMM ON FOREIGN REL,FOREIGN ASSISTANCE ACT OF 1967. VIETNAM WOR+45 DELIB/GP CONFER CONTROL WAR WEAPON BAL/PAY...CENSUS CHARTS SENATE. PAGE 139 F2744
FOR/AID LAW DIPLOM POLICY

S67
AUBERT DE LA RUE P.,"PERSPECTIVES ECONOMIQUES ENTRE LES ETATS-UNIS ET L'EUROPE." FUT INDUS R+D INT/ORG ACT/RES ECO/TAC AGREE BAL/PAY PRODUC...CHARTS 20 EEC GATT WORLD/BANK. PAGE 7 F0138
INT/TRADE ECO/DEV FINAN TARIFFS

S67
BARTLETT J.L.,"AMERICAN BOND ISSUES IN THE EUROPEAN ECONOMIC COMMUNITY." EUR+WWI LUXEMBOURG USA+45 DIPLOM CONTROL BAL/PAY EEC. PAGE 11 F0201
LAW ECO/TAC FINAN TAX

BAL/PWR....BALANCE OF POWER

B14
DE BLOCH J.,THE FUTURE OF WAR IN ITS TECHNICAL, ECONOMIC, AND POLITICAL RELATIONS (1899). MOD/EUR TEC/DEV BUDGET INT/TRADE DETER GUERRILLA WEAPON COST PEACE 20. PAGE 31 F0596
WAR BAL/PWR PREDICT FORCES

B15
VEBLEN T.,IMPERIAL GERMANY AND THE INDUSTRIAL REVOLUTION. GERMANY MOD/EUR UK USA-45 NAT/G TEC/DEV CAP/ISM...MAJORIT NAT/COMP 19/20 CHINJAP. PAGE 141 F2769
ECO/DEV INDUS TECHNIC BAL/PWR

N19
CASSELL F.,INTERNATIONAL MONETARY PROBLEMS (PAMPHLET). AFR BAL/PWR CONTROL EFFICIENCY WEALTH 20 EEC. PAGE 22 F0427
INT/TRADE FINAN DIPLOM TREND

N19
CONGRESSIONAL QUARTERLY SERV,FEDERAL ECONOMIC POLICY 1945-1965 (PAMPHLET). USA+45 FINAN OP/RES BAL/PWR ECO/TAC TAX BAL/PAY CENTRAL COST WEALTH ...CHARTS 20. PAGE 27 F0525
NAT/G ECO/DEV BUDGET POLICY

N19
DEANE H.,THE WAR IN VIETNAM (PAMPHLET). AFR CHINA/COM VIETNAM BAL/PWR DIPLOM ECO/TAC SOCISM INTERVENT INTERVENT. PAGE 31 F0610
WAR SOCIALIST MORAL CAP/ISM

B38
HOBSON J.A.,IMPERIALISM. MOD/EUR UK WOR-45 CULTURE ECO/UNDEV NAT/G VOL/ASSN PLAN EDU/PROP LEGIT REGION COERCE ATTIT PWR...POLICY PLURIST TIME/SEQ GEN/LAWS TERR/GP 19/20. PAGE 60 F1187
DOMIN ECO/TAC BAL/PWR COLONIAL

S41
BRITT S.H.,"CONFORMITY OF LABOR NEWSPAPERS WITH RESPECT TO THE AFL-CIO CONFLICT." BAL/PWR CONSEN ATTIT. PAGE 18 F0355
LABOR PRESS DOMIN GP/REL

B47
ENKE S.,INTERNATIONAL ECONOMICS. UK USA+45 USSR INT/ORG BAL/PWR BARGAIN CAP/ISM BAL/PAY...NAT/COMP 20 TREATY. PAGE 38 F0735
INT/TRADE FINAN TARIFFS ECO/TAC

B49
DE JOUVENEL B.,PROBLEMS OF SOCIALIST ENGLAND. AFR UK USSR BAL/PWR ECO/TAC INT/TRADE PRICE WAR BAL/PAY PEACE 20. PAGE 31 F0601
SOCISM NEW/LIB PROB/SOLV PLAN

B50
SURANYI-UNGER T.,PRIVATE ENTERPRISE AND GOVERNMENTAL PLANNING. STRUCT FINAN BAL/PWR HAPPINESS DRIVE NEW/LIB PLURISM...MATH QUANT STAT TREND BIBLIOG. PAGE 127 F2516
PLAN NAT/G LAISSEZ POLICY

B51
HARBISON F.H.,GOALS AND STRATEGY IN COLLECTIVE BARGAINING. WORKER BAL/PWR PARTIC DRIVE...POLICY MGT. PAGE 55 F1074
LABOR BARGAIN GP/REL ADMIN

B51
US HOUSE COMM APPROPRIATIONS,MUTUAL SECURITY PROGRAM APPROPRIATIONS FOR 1952: HEARINGS BEFORE A SUBCOMMITTEE OF THE COMMITTEE ON APPROPRIATIONS. AFR KOREA L/A+17C ECO/DEV ECO/UNDEV INT/ORG INSPECT BAL/PWR DIPLOM DEBATE WAR...POLICY STAT ASIA/S 20 CONGRESS NATO MID/EAST. PAGE 136 F2686
LEGIS FORCES BUDGET FOR/AID

B53
MENDE T.,WORLD POWER IN THE BALANCE. FUT USA+45 USSR WOR-45 ECO/DEV ECO/TAC INT/TRADE EDU/PROP UTOPIA ATTIT...HUM CONCPT TREND TOT/POP 20. PAGE 90 F1756
WOR+45 PWR BAL/PWR AFR

S53
DRUCKER P.F.,"THE EMPLOYEE SOCIETY." STRUCT BAL/PWR PARTIC REPRESENT PWR...DECISION CONCPT. PAGE 34 F0666
LABOR MGT WORKER CULTURE

S53
LINCOLN G.,"FACTORS DETERMINING ARMS AID." COM FUT USA+45 USSR WOR+45 ECO/DEV NAT/G CONSULT PLAN TEC/DEV DIPLOM DOMIN EDU/PROP PERCEPT PWR ...DECISION CONCPT TREND MARX/KARL 20. PAGE 80 F1566
FORCES POLICY BAL/PWR FOR/AID

B55
HELANDER S.,DAS AUTARKIEPROBLEM IN DER WELTWIRTSCHAFT. PROB/SOLV BAL/PWR BARGAIN CAP/ISM ECO/TAC SOVEREIGN FOR/TRADE 20. PAGE 58 F1144
NAT/COMP COLONIAL DIPLOM

B55
PALAMOUNTAIN JC J.R.,THE POLITICS OF DISTRIBUTION. USA+45 LG/CO SML/CO BAL/PWR CONTROL EQUILIB 20. PAGE 103 F2019
DIST/IND ECO/TAC CAP/ISM GP/REL

B55
US OFFICE OF THE PRESIDENT,REPORT TO CONGRESS ON THE MUTUAL SECURITY PROGRAM FOR THE SIX MONTHS ENDED JUNE 30, 1955. ECO/DEV INT/ORG NAT/G CREATE TEC/DEV BAL/PWR ECO/TAC AGREE DETER COST ORD/FREE 20 DEPT/STATE DEPT/DEFEN. PAGE 138 F2722
DIPLOM FORCES PLAN FOR/AID

B56
US OFFICE OF THE PRESIDENT,REPORT TO CONGRESS ON THE MUTUAL SECURITY PROGRAM FOR THE SIX MONTHS ENDED DECEMBER 31, 1955. ASIA USSR ECO/DEV ECO/UNDEV INT/ORG CREATE TEC/DEV BAL/PWR ECO/TAC AGREE DETER COST ORD/FREE 20 DEPT/STATE DEPT/DEFEN EISNHWR/DD. PAGE 138 F2723
DIPLOM FORCES PLAN FOR/AID

B58
BERLINER J.S.,SOVIET ECONOMIC AID: THE AID AND TRADE POLICY IN UNDERDEVELOPED COUNTRIES. AFR COM ISLAM L/A+17C S/ASIA USSR ECO/DEV DIST/IND FINAN MARKET INT/ORG ACT/RES PLAN BAL/PWR WEAPON PWR WEALTH...CHARTS FOR/TRADE 20. PAGE 14 F0263
ECO/UNDEV ECO/TAC FOR/AID

B58
JOHNSON H.G.,INTERNATIONAL TRADE AND ECONOMIC GROWTH. WOR+45 BUDGET CAP/ISM ECO/TAC TARIFFS BAL/PAY 20. PAGE 67 F1323
INT/TRADE BAL/PWR BARGAIN DIPLOM

B58
KINDLEBERGER C.P.,INTERNATIONAL ECONOMICS. WOR+45 WOR-45 ECO/DEV ECO/UNDEV FINAN VOL/ASSN ACT/RES DIPLOM ECO/TAC LEGIT REGION ATTIT DRIVE ORD/FREE WEALTH...POLICY STAT TREND GEN/LAWS EEC ECSC OEEC 20. PAGE 71 F1391
INT/ORG BAL/PWR TARIFFS

B59
BARNETT A.D.,COMMUNIST ECONOMIC STRATEGY: THE RISE OF MAINLAND CHINA. CHINA/COM USSR WOR+45 AGRI INDUS FOR/AID INGP/REL ATTIT. PAGE 10 F0188
ECO/UNDEV INT/TRADE TOTALISM BAL/PWR

B60
FORM W.H.,INDUSTRY, LABOR, AND COMMUNITY. STRUCT NEIGH SECT BAL/PWR EDU/PROP PARTIC ATTIT ROLE PWR WEALTH...METH/CNCPT CHARTS. PAGE 42 F0828
LABOR MGT GP/REL CONTROL

B60
KRISTENSEN T.,THE ECONOMIC WORLD BALANCE. FUT WOR+45 CULTURE ECO/DEV BAL/PWR INT/TRADE REGION PWR WEALTH...STAT TREND CHARTS 20. PAGE 73 F1442
ECO/UNDEV ECO/TAC FOR/AID

B60
STOLPER W.F.,GERMANY BETWEEN EAST AND WEST: THE ECONOMICS OF COMPETITIVE COEXISTENCE. AFR FUT GERMANY/E GERMANY/W WOR+45 FINAN POL/PAR BUDGET ECO/TAC FOR/AID INT/TRADE...STAT CHARTS METH/COMP 20. PAGE 126 F2495
ECO/DEV DIPLOM GOV/COMP BAL/PWR

S60
MIKESELL R.F.,"AMERICA'S ECONOMIC RESPONSIBILITY AS A GREAT POWER." COM FUT USA+45 USSR WOR+45 INT/ORG PLAN ECO/TAC FOR/AID EDU/PROP CHOOSE WEALTH ...POLICY 20. PAGE 91 F1781
ECO/UNDEV BAL/PWR CAP/ISM

S60
NICHOLS J.P.,"HAZARDS OF AMERICAN PRIVATE INVESTMENT IN UNDERDEVELOPED COUNTRIES." FUT L/A+17C USA+45 USA-45 EXTR/IND CONSULT BAL/PWR ECO/TAC DOMIN ADJUD ATTIT SOVEREIGN WEALTH ...HIST/WRIT TIME/SEQ TREND TERR/GP VAL/FREE 20. PAGE 98 F1924
FINAN ECO/UNDEV CAP/ISM NAT/LISM

B61
AUBREY H.G.,COEXISTENCE: ECONOMIC CHALLENGE AND
POLICY

RESPONSE. AFR USSR WOR+45 ACT/RES BAL/PWR CAP/ISM DIPLOM ECO/TAC FOR/AID INT/TRADE PEACE SOCISM ...METH/COMP NAT/COMP. PAGE 7 F0139
ECO/UNDEV PLAN COM

B61
MORLEY L.,THE PATCHWORK HISTORY OF FOREIGN AID. AFR KOREA/S USA+45 USSR LAW FINAN INT/ORG TEC/DEV BAL/PWR GIVE 20 NATO. PAGE 93 F1834
FOR/AID ECO/UNDEV FORCES DIPLOM

S61
DELLA PORT G.,"PROBLEMI E PROSPETTIVE DI COESISTENZA FRA ORIENTE ED OCCIDENTE, (PART 3)." COM FUT WOR+45 NAT/G BAL/PWR FOR/AID BAL/PAY PWR WEALTH...SOC CONCPT GEN/LAWS 20. PAGE 32 F0616
AFR INT/TRADE

S61
VALLET R.,"IRAN: KEY TO THE MIDDLE EAST." COM IRAQ ISLAM KUWAIT LEBANON SAUDI/ARAB TURKEY ELITES SOCIETY INDUS PROC/MFG POL/PAR TOP/EX PLAN BAL/PWR DIPLOM ECO/TAC ALL/VALS...TREND FOR/TRADE CENTO 20. PAGE 140 F2760
NAT/G ECO/UNDEV IRAN

B62
SCHILLING W.R.,STRATEGY, POLITICS, AND DEFENSE BUDGETS. AFR USA+45 CHIEF LEGIS PLAN TEC/DEV BAL/PWR BUDGET NUC/PWR WAR CIVMIL/REL GOV/REL PWR 20 EISNHWR/DD. PAGE 117 F2297
NAT/G POLICY FORCES DETER

B62
VANEK J.,INTERNATIONAL TRADE - THEORY AND ECONOMIC POLICY. LABOR BAL/PWR ECO/TAC TARIFFS PRICE BAL/PAY COST DEMAND 20. PAGE 140 F2765
INT/TRADE DIPLOM BARGAIN MARKET

B63
ABSHIRE D.M.,NATIONAL SECURITY: POLITICAL, MILITARY, AND ECONOMIC STRATEGIES IN THE DECADE AHEAD. ASIA COM USA+45 WOR+45 ECO/DEV ECO/UNDEV INT/ORG DELIB/GP FORCES ECO/TAC COERCE ATTIT RIGID/FLEX HEALTH ORD/FREE PWR WEALTH...POLICY STAT CHARTS ANTHOL COLD/WAR VAL/FREE APP/SCI. PAGE 2 F0032
FUT ACT/RES BAL/PWR

B63
LEWIN J.,POLITICS AND LAW IN SOUTH AFRICA. SOUTH/AFR UK POL/PAR BAL/PWR ECO/TAC COLONIAL CONTROL GP/REL DISCRIM PWR 20 NEGRO. PAGE 79 F1545
NAT/LISM POLICY LAW RACE/REL

B63
MENEZES A.J.,SUBDESENVOLVIMENTO E POLITICA INTERNACIONAL. BRAZIL WOR+45 PLAN CONTROL LEAD NAT/LISM ORD/FREE 20 THIRD/WRLD. PAGE 90 F1759
ECO/UNDEV DIPLOM POLICY BAL/PWR

S63
EMERSON R.,"THE ATLANTIC COMMUNITY AND THE EMERGING COUNTRIES." FUT WOR+45 ECO/DEV ECO/UNDEV R+D NAT/G DELIB/GP BAL/PWR ECO/TAC EDU/PROP ROUTINE ORD/FREE PWR WEALTH...POLICY CONCPT TREND GEN/METH EEC 20 NATO. PAGE 37 F0729
ATTIT INT/TRADE

S63
SHWADRAN B.,"MIDDLE EAST OIL, 1962." ISLAM USSR ECO/DEV DIST/IND INDUS PLAN BAL/PWR DISPL DRIVE ...POLICY STAT TREND GEN/LAWS TERR/GP METH/GP EEC OEEC 20 OIL. PAGE 121 F2394
MARKET ECO/TAC INT/TRADE

S63
TENNYSON L.B.,"THE USA IN ATLANTIC COMMUNITY." EUR+WWI FRANCE UK USA+45 ECO/UNDEV VOL/ASSN DELIB/GP TOP/EX DIPLOM DOMIN PWR...POLICY CONCPT TREND GEN/LAWS EEC 20. PAGE 129 F2545
ATTIT ECO/TAC BAL/PWR

S63
VINER J.,"REPORT OF THE CLAY COMMITTEE ON FOREIGN AID: A SYMPOSIUM." USA+45 WOR+45 NAT/G CONSULT PLAN BAL/PWR ATTIT WEALTH...MGT CONCPT TOT/POP 20. PAGE 142 F2788
ACT/RES ECO/TAC FOR/AID

N63
US COMM STRENG SEC FREE WORLD,THE SCOPE AND DISTRIBUTION OF UNITED STATES MILITARY AND ECONOMIC ASSISTANCE PROGRAMS (PAMPHLET). USA+45 PLAN BAL/PWR BUDGET DIPLOM CONTROL CIVMIL/REL ATTIT. PAGE 134 F2648
DELIB/GP POLICY FOR/AID ORD/FREE

B64
BALASSA B.,CHANGING PATTERNS IN FOREIGN TRADE AND PAYMENTS. AFR USA+45 USA-45 ECO/DEV NAT/G PLAN BAL/PWR...POLICY ANTHOL BIBLIOG 20. PAGE 8 F0159
ECO/TAC INT/TRADE BAL/PAY WEALTH

B64
HACKER A.,THE CORPORATION TAKE-OVER. CONSTN LABOR PLAN BAL/PWR CONTROL EXEC LOBBY REPRESENT GP/REL ROLE ORD/FREE POLICY. PAGE 52 F1025
LG/CO STRUCT PWR

B64
HEKHUIS D.J.,INTERNATIONAL STABILITY: MILITARY, ECONOMIC AND POLITICAL DIMENSIONS. FUT WOR+45 LAW ECO/UNDEV INT/ORG NAT/G VOL/ASSN FORCES ACT/RES BAL/PWR PWR WEALTH...STAT UN 20. PAGE 58 F1143
TEC/DEV DETER REGION

B64
LISKA G.,EUROPE ASCENDANT. EUR+WWI ECO/DEV FORCES INT/TRADE MARXISM 20 EEC. PAGE 81 F1579
DIPLOM BAL/PWR TARIFFS CENTRAL

B64
MEZERIK A.G.,TRADE, AID AND ECONOMIC DEVELOPMENT. WOR+45 FINAN INDUS MARKET PLAN BAL/PWR BARGAIN FOR/AID TARIFFS EDU/PROP WEALTH...GP/COMP 20 UN GATT IMF IBRD. PAGE 91 F1777
ECO/TAC ECO/DEV INT/ORG INT/TRADE

B64
WHEARE K.C.,FEDERAL GOVERNMENT (4TH ED.). WOR+45 WOR-45 POL/PAR LEGIS BAL/PWR CT/SYS...POLICY JURID CONCPT GOV/COMP 17/20. PAGE 145 F2866
FEDERAL CONSTN EX/STRUC NAT/COMP

S64
PADELFORD N.J.,"THE ORGANIZATION OF AFRICAN UNITY." ECO/UNDEV INT/ORG PLAN BAL/PWR DIPLOM ECO/TAC NAT/LISM ORD/FREE PWR WEALTH...CONCPT TREND STERTYP TERR/GP VAL/FREE 20. PAGE 102 F2013
AFR VOL/ASSN REGION

B65
PEACE RESEARCH ABSTRACTS. FUT WOR+45 R+D INT/ORG NAT/G PLAN TEC/DEV BAL/PWR DIPLOM FOR/AID NUC/PWR HEALTH. PAGE 1 F0022
BIBLIOG/A PEACE ARMS/CONT WAR

B65
CAMPBELL J.C.,AMERICAN POLICY TOWARDS COMMUNIST EASTERN EUROPE* THE CHOICES AHEAD. AFR USA+45 ECO/DEV BAL/PWR MARXISM TREND. PAGE 21 F0406
POLAND YUGOSLAVIA DIPLOM COM

B65
CRABB C.V. JR.,THE ELEPHANTS AND THE GRASS* A STUDY OF NONALIGNMENT. ASIA INDIA S/ASIA USA+45 USSR BAL/PWR NEUTRAL ATTIT...TREND NAT/COMP. PAGE 28 F0549
ECO/UNDEV AFR DIPLOM CONCPT

B65
SHONFIELD A.,MODERN CAPITALISM: THE CHANGING BALANCE OF PUBLIC AND PRIVATE POWER. FRANCE GERMANY/W UK USA+45 WOR+45 ECO/DEV INT/ORG NAT/G CONSULT INT/TRADE PRODUC...POLICY CONCPT METH/COMP 20. PAGE 121 F2386
CAP/ISM CONTROL BAL/PWR CREATE

S65
GOLDMAN M.I.,"A BALANCE SHEET OF SOVIET FOREIGN AID." USA+45 ECO/UNDEV BAL/PWR ECO/TAC RENT GIVE EDU/PROP CONTROL COST PROFIT GEN/METH. PAGE 48 F0939
USSR FOR/AID NAT/COMP EFFICIENCY

B66
HEVESY P.D.,THE UNIFICATION OF THE WORLD. FUT USA+45 WOR+45 ECO/DEV ECO/UNDEV LEGIS PROB/SOLV BAL/PWR ECO/TAC INT/TRADE PEACE. PAGE 59 F1160
DIPLOM FINAN INT/ORG

B66
HOROWITZ I.L.,THREE WORLDS OF DEVELOPMENT. COM USA+45 STRUCT ECO/DEV PLAN PROB/SOLV TEC/DEV CIVMIL/REL...PHIL/SCI IDEA/COMP 20. PAGE 62 F1216
ECO/UNDEV BAL/PWR POL/PAR REV

B66
KUENNE R.E.,THE POLARIS MISSILE STRIKE* A GENERAL ECONOMIC SYSTEMS ANALYSIS. USA+45 USSR NAT/G BAL/PWR ARMS/CONT WAR...MATH PROBABIL COMPUT/IR CHARTS HYPO/EXP SIMUL. PAGE 74 F1446
NUC/PWR FORCES DETER DIPLOM

B66
UREN P.E.,EAST - WEST TRADE* A SYMPOSIUM. COM AGRI INT/ORG PRICE HABITAT RIGID/FLEX...GEOG INT/LAW ANTHOL NATO. PAGE 133 F2625
INT/TRADE BAL/PWR AFR CANADA

B67
BEATON L.,THE STRUGGLE FOR PEACE. INT/ORG FORCES NUC/PWR COST PWR...POLICY TREND 20. PAGE 12 F0225
PEACE BAL/PWR DIPLOM WAR

B67
DAVIS F.M.,COME AS A CONQUEROR: THE UNITED STATES ARMY'S OCCUPATION OF GERMANY: 1945-1949. EUR+WWI GERMANY USA+45 SOCIETY PLAN BAL/PWR DIPLOM FOR/AID PERS/REL DEMAND PEACE ORD/FREE 20. PAGE 30 F0588
FORCES CIVMIL/REL ECO/TAC CONTROL

B67
HALLE L.J.,THE COLD WAR AS HISTORY. AFR USSR WOR+45 ECO/TAC FOR/AID NUC/PWR WAR PEACE ORD/FREE ...MAJORIT TREND 20 KENNEDY/JF KHRUSH/N BERLIN/BLO. PAGE 54 F1048
DIPLOM BAL/PWR

B67
OGLESBY C.,CONTAINMENT AND CHANGE. AFR COM USA+45 ECO/UNDEV TEC/DEV ECO/TAC FOR/AID INT/TRADE DOMIN GUERRILLA REV PEACE 20 STALIN/J. PAGE 101 F1983
DIPLOM BAL/PWR MARXISM CULTURE

B67
US SENATE COMM ON FOREIGN REL,ARMS SALES TO NEAR EAST AND SOUTH ASIAN COUNTRIES. INDIA IRAN PAKISTAN WOR+45 PROC/MFG BAL/PWR DIPLOM...DECISION SENATE. PAGE 139 F2742
WEAPON FOR/AID FORCES POLICY

B67
WOLF C. JR.,UNITED STATES POLICY AND THE THIRD WORLD. USA+45 WOR+45 FORCES ACT/RES BAL/PWR ECO/TAC FOR/AID DETER GUERRILLA NUC/PWR REV...CHARTS 20. PAGE 148 F2916
DIPLOM ECO/UNDEV POLICY NAT/G

L67
MCALLISTER J.T. JR.,"THE POSSIBILITIES FOR DIPLOMACY IN SOUTHEAST ASIA." LAOS VIETNAM INT/ORG NAT/G PROVS BAL/PWR DOMIN AGREE COLONIAL WAR PWR 17/20 TREATY. PAGE 88 F1716
DIPLOM S/ASIA

S67
APEL H.,"LES NOUVEAUX ASPECTS DE LA POLITIQUE ETRANGERE ALLEMANDE." AFR EUR+WWI GERMANY POL/PAR BAL/PWR ECO/TAC INT/TRADE NUC/PWR NAT/LISM PEACE
DIPLOM INT/ORG FEDERAL

...POLICY 20 EEC. PAGE 6 F0107

S67
COSGROVE C.A.,"AGRICULTURE, FINANCE AND POLITICS IN THE EUROPEAN COMMUNITY." EUR+WWI DIST/IND MARKET INT/ORG VOL/ASSN DELIB/GP TEC/DEV BAL/PWR BARGAIN ECO/TAC RATION CONFER 20 EEC. PAGE 28 F0538 — ECO/DEV DIPLOM AGRI INT/TRADE

S67
CROKER F.P.U.,"ECONOMIC PEACEKEEPING." UK PLAN PROB/SOLV TEC/DEV BAL/PWR DIPLOM COERCE PEACE ...POLICY DECISION 20. PAGE 28 F0553 — FORCES WEAPON COST WAR

S67
GORMAN W.,"ELLUL - A PROPHETIC VOICE." WOR+45 ELITES SOCIETY ACT/RES PLAN BAL/PWR DOMIN CONTROL PARTIC TOTALISM PWR 20. PAGE 49 F0963 — CREATE ORD/FREE EX/STRUC UTOPIA

S67
ISELIN J.J.,"THE TRUMAN DOCTRINE: ITS PASSAGE THROUGH CONGRESS AND THE AFTERMATH." USA+45 ECO/UNDEV R+D INT/ORG DELIB/GP BAL/PWR REV PEACE ...POLICY UN. PAGE 66 F1291 — DIPLOM COM FOR/AID AFR

S67
WARNER G.,"FRANCE, BRITAIN AND THE EEC." FRANCE UK INT/ORG DELIB/GP ECO/TAC CONTROL 20 EEC. PAGE 143 F2822 — INT/TRADE BAL/PWR DIPLOM

BALANCE OF PAYMENTS....SEE BAL/PAY

BALANCE OF POWER....SEE BAL/PWR

BALASSA B. F0157,F0158,F0159

BALDWIN D.A. F0160,F0161,F0162,F0163

BALDWIN G.B. F0164

BALDWIN H.W. F0165

BALDWIN R. F1748

BALDWIN R.E. F0166

BALDWIN/J....JAMES BALDWIN

BALKANS....BALKANS

B56
WOLFF R.L.,THE BALKANS IN OUR TIME. ALBANIA FUT MOD/EUR USSR YUGOSLAVIA CULTURE INT/ORG SECT DIPLOM EDU/PROP COERCE WAR ORD/FREE...CHARTS 4/20 BALKANS COMINFORM. PAGE 148 F2919 — GEOG COM

BALL R.J. F0167

BALLAINE W.C. F2260

BALOGH T. F0168,F0169

BALTIMORE....BALTIMORE, MD.

BANCROFT G. F0170

BANDA/HK....H.K. BANDA, PRIME MINISTER OF MALAWI

BANERJI A.K. F0171

BANFIELD E.C. F0172,F0173

BANK INTERNATIONAL SETTLEMENTS F0174

BANK/ENGL....THE BANK OF ENGLAND

BANKING....SEE FINAN

BANKRUPTCY....BANKRUPTCY

BANOVETZ J.M. F0175

BANTU....BANTU NATION AND CULTURE

BANTUSTANS....BANTUSTANS, REPUBLIC OF SOUTH AFRICA

BAO/DAI....BAO DAI

BARALL M. F0176

BARAN P. F0177

BARAN P.A. F0178,F0179

BARANSON J. F0180,F0181

BARBARIAN....BARBARIAN

BARBASH J. F0182,F0183,F0184

BARBOUR V. F0185

BARDENS D. F0186

BARGAIN....BARGAINING; SEE ALSO ECO/TAC, MARKET, DIPLOM

N
US SUPERINTENDENT OF DOCUMENTS,LABOR (PRICE LIST 33). USA+45 LAW AGRI CONSTRUC INDUS NAT/G BARGAIN PRICE ADMIN AUTOMAT PRODUC MGT. PAGE 140 F2753 — BIBLIOG/A WORKER LABOR LEGIS

B04
MARX K.,A CONTRIBUTION TO THE CRITIQUE OF POLITICAL ECONOMY (TRANS. FROM 2ND ED. BY N.I. STONE). UK STRATA ECO/DEV FINAN MARKET PLAN BARGAIN CAP/ISM ECO/TAC ATTIT WEALTH...METH/CNCPT BIOG 19. PAGE 86 F1687 — MARXIST NEW/IDEA MARXISM

N19
CARPER E.T.,LOBBYING AND THE NATURAL GAS BILL (PAMPHLET). USA+45 SERV/IND BARGAIN PAY DRIVE ROLE WEALTH 20 CONGRESS SENATE EISNHWR/DD. PAGE 22 F0418 — LOBBY ADJUD TRIBUTE NAT/G

B31
CROOK W.H.,THE GENERAL STRIKE: A STUDY OF LABOR'S TRAGIC WEAPON IN THEORY AND PRACTICE. BELGIUM FRANCE SWEDEN UK WOR-45 PROB/SOLV ECO/TAC DOMIN PWR ...POLICY TIME/SEQ NAT/COMP GEN/LAWS 19/20 STRIKE. PAGE 29 F0555 — LABOR WORKER LG/CO BARGAIN

B35
SCHATTSCHNEIDER E.E.,POLITICS, PRESSURES AND THE TARIFF: A STUDY OF FREE PRIVATE ENTERPRISE IN PRESSURE POLITICS IN TARIFF REVISION 1929-1930. NAT/G BARGAIN ECO/TAC ROUTINE REPRESENT GOV/REL GP/REL PWR POLICY. PAGE 116 F2290 — LOBBY LEGIS TARIFFS

B38
LAWLEY F.E.,THE GROWTH OF COLLECTIVE ECONOMY VOL. 1: NATIONAL. EUR+WWI AGRI INDUS NAT/G BARGAIN CAP/ISM ECO/TAC WAR OPTIMAL WEALTH...GOV/COMP METH/COMP 19/20 MONOPOLY. PAGE 76 F1492 — SOCISM PRICE CONTROL OWN

B38
REICH N.,LABOR RELATIONS IN REPUBLICAN GERMANY. GERMANY CONSTN ECO/DEV INDUS NAT/G ADMIN CONTROL GP/REL FASCISM POPULISM 20 WEIMAR/REP. PAGE 110 F2176 — WORKER MGT LABOR BARGAIN

B40
WUNDERLICH F.,LABOR UNDER GERMAN DEMOCRACY, ARBITRATION 1918-1933. GERMANY NAT/G PAY REPAR ADJUD CT/SYS GP/REL...MAJORIT 20. PAGE 149 F2941 — LABOR WORKER INDUS BARGAIN

B41
LESTER R.A.,ECONOMICS OF LABOR. UK USA-45 TEC/DEV BARGAIN PAY INGP/REL INCOME...MGT 19/20. PAGE 78 F1532 — LABOR ECO/DEV INDUS WORKER

B41
SLICHTER S.H.,UNION POLICIES AND INDUSTRIAL MANAGEMENT. USA-45 INDUS TEC/DEV PAY GP/REL INGP/REL COST EFFICIENCY PRODUC...POLICY 20. PAGE 123 F2420 — BARGAIN LABOR MGT WORKER

B42
ROBBINS J.J.,THE GOVERNMENT OF LABOR RELATIONS IN SWEDEN. SWEDEN LAW CONSTN ADJUD CT/SYS GP/REL ...JURID 20. PAGE 112 F2200 — NAT/G BARGAIN LABOR INDUS

B47
ENKE S.,INTERNATIONAL ECONOMICS. UK USA+45 USSR INT/ORG BAL/PWR BARGAIN CAP/ISM BAL/PAY...NAT/COMP 20 TREATY. PAGE 38 F0735 — INT/TRADE FINAN TARIFFS ECO/TAC

S47
DAHL R.A.,"WORKERS' CONTROL OF INDUSTRY AND THE BRITISH LABOUR PARTY." UK STRATA STRUCT DELIB/GP BARGAIN CAP/ISM DEBATE CONTROL CHOOSE GP/REL ATTIT ROLE PWR 19/20 PARLIAMENT LABOR/PAR FABIAN. PAGE 29 F0570 — INDUS LABOR WORKER SOCISM

B49
SHISTER J.,ECONOMICS OF THE LABOR MARKET. LOC/G NAT/G WORKER TEC/DEV BARGAIN PAY PRICE EXEC GP/REL INCOME...MGT T 20. PAGE 121 F2381 — MARKET LABOR INDUS

B51
DIMOCK M.E.,FREE ENTERPRISE AND THE ADMINISTRATIVE STATE. FINAN LG/CO BARGAIN BUDGET DOMIN CONTROL INGP/REL EFFICIENCY 20. PAGE 33 F0640 — CAP/ISM ADMIN MGT MARKET

B51
HARBISON F.H.,GOALS AND STRATEGY IN COLLECTIVE BARGAINING. WORKER BAL/PWR PARTIC DRIVE...POLICY MGT. PAGE 55 F1074 — LABOR BARGAIN GP/REL ADMIN

B51
PETERSON F.,SURVEY OF LABOR ECONOMICS (REV. ED.). STRATA ECO/DEV LABOR INSPECT BARGAIN PAY PRICE EXEC ROUTINE GP/REL ALL/VALS ORD/FREE 20 AFL/CIO DEPT/LABOR. PAGE 105 F2069 — WORKER DEMAND IDEA/COMP T

B51
PRINCETON U INDUSTRIAL REL SEC,COMPULSORY — BARGAIN

ARBITRATION OF UTILITY DISPUTES IN NEW JERSEY AND PENNSYLVANIA. USA+45 LEGIS WORKER ADJUD ORD/FREE ...POLICY MGT METH/COMP 20 NEW/JERSEY PENNSYLVAN. PAGE 108 F2118 PROVS INDUS LABOR

B53
DAHL R.A.,POLITICS, ECONOMICS, AND WELFARE. TEC/DEV BARGAIN ECO/TAC RECEIVE PRICE CONTROL LEAD INGP/REL ...POLICY GEN/LAWS. PAGE 29 F0572 SOCIETY GIVE

B54
BERNSTEIN I.,ARBITRATION OF WAGES. USA+45 CONSULT PAY COST PRODUC WEALTH...CHARTS 20. PAGE 14 F0266 DELIB/GP BARGAIN WORKER PRICE

B54
RICHTER R.,DAS KONKURRENZ PROBLEM IM OLIGOPOL. LG/CO BARGAIN PRICE COST...CONCPT 20 MONOPOLY. PAGE 111 F2188 CONTROL GAME ECO/TAC GP/REL

B55
BRAUN K.,LABOR DISPUTES AND THEIR SETTLEMENT. ECO/TAC ROUTINE TASK GP/REL...DECISION GEN/LAWS. PAGE 18 F0342 INDUS LABOR BARGAIN ADJUD

B55
HELANDER S.,DAS AUTARKIEPROBLEM IN DER WELTWIRTSCHAFT. PROB/SOLV BAL/PWR BARGAIN CAP/ISM ECO/TAC SOVEREIGN FOR/TRADE 20. PAGE 58 F1144 NAT/COMP COLONIAL DIPLOM

L56
SCHELLING T.C.,"AN ESSAY ON BARGAINING" (BMR)" OP/RES PROB/SOLV PRICE CHOOSE PWR...DECISION MODELS 20. PAGE 116 F2294 BARGAIN MARKET ECO/TAC GAME

B57
DUNLOP J.T.,THE THEORY OF WAGE DETERMINATION; PROCEEDINGS OF CONFERENCE HELD BY INTERNATIONAL ECONOMIC ASSOCIATION. AFR ECO/DEV LABOR BARGAIN PAY CONFER...CHARTS ANTHOL 20. PAGE 35 F0679 PRICE WORKER GEN/LAWS INCOME

S57
DUBIN R.,"POWER AND UNION-MANAGEMENT RELATIONS." PROB/SOLV ADJUD ROUTINE ATTIT ORD/FREE...MGT STERTYP. PAGE 34 F0668 PWR LABOR BARGAIN GP/REL

B58
CHAMBERLIN E.H.,LABOR UNIONS AND PUBLIC POLICY. PLAN BARGAIN SANCTION INGP/REL JURID. PAGE 23 F0444 LABOR WEALTH PWR NAT/G

B58
CUNNINGHAM W.B.,COMPULSORY CONCILIATION AND COLLECTIVE BARGAINING. CANADA NAT/G LEGIS ADJUD CT/SYS GP/REL...MGT 20 NEW/BRUNS STRIKE CASEBOOK. PAGE 29 F0563 POLICY BARGAIN LABOR INDUS

B58
JOHNSON H.G.,INTERNATIONAL TRADE AND ECONOMIC GROWTH. WOR+45 BUDGET CAP/ISM ECO/TAC TARIFFS BAL/PAY 20. PAGE 67 F1323 INT/TRADE BAL/PWR BARGAIN DIPLOM

B58
LESTER R.A.,AS UNIONS MATURE. POL/PAR BARGAIN LEAD PARTIC GP/REL CENTRAL...MAJORIT TIME/SEQ METH/COMP. PAGE 78 F1533 LABOR INDUS POLICY MGT

B58
WARNER A.W.,CONCEPTS AND CASES IN ECONOMIC ANALYSIS. PROB/SOLV BARGAIN CONTROL INCOME PRODUC ...ECOMETRIC MGT CONCPT CLASSIF CHARTS 20 KEYNES/JM. PAGE 143 F2820 ECO/TAC DEMAND EQUILIB COST

B58
WOODS H.D.,PATTERNS OF INDUSTRIAL DISPUTE SETTLEMENT IN FIVE CANADIAN INDUSTRIES. CANADA USA+45 CONSULT ADJUD GP/REL...JURID GOV/COMP METH/COMP ANTHOL 20. PAGE 148 F2923 BARGAIN INDUS LABOR NAT/G

L59
SIMON H.A.,"THEORIES OF DECISION-MAKING IN ECONOMICS AND BEHAVIORAL SCIENCE" (BMR)" MARKET BARGAIN UTIL DRIVE...DECISION MGT PROBABIL HYPO/EXP SIMUL 20 BEHAVIORSM. PAGE 122 F2409 PSY GEN/LAWS PROB/SOLV

B60
ELKOURI F.,HOW ARBITRATION WORKS (REV. ED.). LAW INDUS BARGAIN 20. PAGE 37 F0720 MGT LABOR ADJUD GP/REL

B60
GARBARINO J.W.,HEALTH PLANS AND COLLECTIVE BARGAINING. USA+45 LABOR BARGAIN GP/REL WEALTH ...WELF/ST CHARTS 20 DEPT/HEW SAN/FRAN. PAGE 46 F0900 HEAL PLAN FINAN SERV/IND

B60
SIEGEL S.,BARGAINING AND GROUP DECISION-MAKING: EXPERIMENTS IN BILATERAL MONOPOLY. EFFICIENCY...PSY CHARTS. PAGE 122 F2397 DECISION PERS/REL PROB/SOLV BARGAIN

B61
BARRASH J.,LABOR'S GRASS ROOTS; A STUDY OF THE LOCAL UNION. STRATA BARGAIN LEAD REPRESENT DEMAND ATTIT PWR. PAGE 10 F0192 LABOR USA+45 INGP/REL EXEC

B61
CARROTHERS A.W.R.,LABOR ARBITRATION IN CANADA. CANADA LAW NAT/G CONSULT LEGIS WORKER ADJUD ADMIN CT/SYS 20. PAGE 22 F0422 LABOR MGT GP/REL BARGAIN

B61
MACMAHON A.W.,DELEGATION AND AUTONOMY. INDIA STRUCT LEGIS BARGAIN BUDGET ECO/TAC LEGIT EXEC REPRESENT GOV/REL CENTRAL DEMAND EFFICIENCY PRODUC. PAGE 84 F1637 ADMIN PLAN FEDERAL

B61
MCCRACKEN H.L.,KEYNESIAN ECONOMICS IN THE STREAM OF ECONOMIC THOUGHT. FINAN MARKET BARGAIN EFFICIENCY OPTIMAL...PHIL/SCI CONCPT IDEA/COMP BIBLIOG 18/20 KEYNES/JM. PAGE 88 F1724 ECO/TAC DEMAND ECOMETRIC

B62
DOUGLAS A.,INDUSTRIAL PEACEMAKING. CONSULT ACT/RES ...MGT PSY METH 20. PAGE 34 F0656 BARGAIN INDUS LABOR GP/REL

B62
GALENSON W.,LABOR IN DEVELOPING COUNTRIES. BRAZIL INDONESIA ISRAEL PAKISTAN TURKEY AGRI INDUS WORKER PAY PRICE GP/REL WEALTH...MGT CHARTS METH/COMP NAT/COMP 20. PAGE 45 F0888 LABOR ECO/UNDEV BARGAIN POL/PAR

B62
HAGUE D.C.,INFLATION. AFR ECO/DEV ECO/UNDEV LABOR BUDGET CAP/ISM INT/TRADE TARIFFS SOCISM 20. PAGE 53 F1036 FINAN NAT/COMP BARGAIN ECO/TAC

B62
REES A.,THE ECONOMICS OF TRADE UNIONS. FUT ECO/DEV INDUS BARGAIN CAP/ISM PRICE SENIOR CONTROL GP/REL COST...TREND 20 AFL/CIO. PAGE 110 F2172 LABOR WORKER ECO/TAC

B62
SRIVASTAVA G.L.,COLLECTIVE BARGAINING AND LABOR-MANAGEMENT RELATIONS IN INDIA. INDIA UK USA+45 INDUS LEGIS WORKER ADJUD EFFICIENCY PRODUC ...METH/COMP 20. PAGE 125 F2462 LABOR MGT BARGAIN GP/REL

B62
VANEK J.,INTERNATIONAL TRADE - THEORY AND ECONOMIC POLICY. LABOR BAL/PWR ECO/TAC TARIFFS PRICE BAL/PAY COST DEMAND 20. PAGE 140 F2765 INT/TRADE DIPLOM BARGAIN MARKET

B62
WOODS H.D.,LABOUR POLICY AND LABOUR ECONOMICS IN CANADA. CANADA FUT NAT/G VOL/ASSN WORKER BARGAIN ECO/TAC PAY CONFER GP/REL 20. PAGE 148 F2924 LABOR POLICY INDUS ECO/DEV

B63
BURTT E.J. JR.,LABOR MARKETS, UNIONS, AND GOVERNMENT POLICIES. USA+45 MARKET NAT/G DELIB/GP CREATE BARGAIN GP/REL ORD/FREE PWR...POLICY CHARTS 20 AFL/CIO. PAGE 20 F0393 LABOR ECO/DEV CONTROL WORKER

B63
JACOBS P.,STATE OF UNIONS. USA+45 STRATA TOP/EX GP/REL RACE/REL DEMAND DISCRIM ATTIT PWR 20 CONGRESS NEGRO HOFFA/J. PAGE 66 F1296 LABOR ECO/TAC BARGAIN DECISION

S63
GREEN P.E.,"BAYESIAN DECISION THEORY IN PRICING STRATEGY."...STAT CHARTS. PAGE 51 F0988 OP/RES PROB/SOLV BARGAIN PRICE

S63
REES A.,"THE EFFECTS OF UNIONS ON RESOURCE ALLOCATION." USA+45 WORKER PRICE CONTROL GP/REL ...MGT METH/COMP 20. PAGE 110 F2173 LABOR BARGAIN RATION INCOME

B64
MEZERIK A.G.,TRADE, AID AND ECONOMIC DEVELOPMENT. WOR+45 FINAN INDUS MARKET PLAN BAL/PWR BARGAIN FOR/AID TARIFFS EDU/PROP WEALTH...GP/COMP 20 UN GATT IMF IBRD. PAGE 91 F1777 ECO/TAC ECO/DEV INT/ORG INT/TRADE

B64
MORGAN H.W.,AMERICAN SOCIALISM 1900-1960. AFR USA+45 USA-45 INTELL AGRI LABOR WORKER BARGAIN ECO/TAC GP/REL RACE/REL 20 NEGRO MIGRATION. PAGE 93 F1830 SOCISM POL/PAR ECO/DEV STRATA

B64
MORRISSENS L.,ECONOMIC POLICY IN OUR TIME: COUNTRY STUDIES. BELGIUM EUR+WWI FRANCE GERMANY/W ITALY NETHERLAND INDUS BARGAIN BUDGET GOV/REL BAL/PAY PRODUC...CON/ANAL CHARTS COSTS 20. PAGE 94 F1839 ECO/DEV ECO/TAC METH/COMP PLAN

B64
RUSTAMJI R.F.,THE LAW OF INDUSTRIAL DISPUTES IN INDIA. INDIA LEGIS WORKER CONTROL GP/REL...JURID MGT TIME/SEQ 20. PAGE 115 F2264 INDUS ADJUD BARGAIN LABOR

B65
ALEXANDER R.J.,ORGANIZED LABOR IN LATIN AMERICA. L/A+17C INT/ORG LEGIS WORKER TEC/DEV BARGAIN INT/TRADE REV...NAT/COMP BIBLIOG 20. PAGE 3 F0059 LABOR POL/PAR ECO/UNDEV POLICY

B65
EDELMAN M.,THE POLITICS OF WAGE-PRICE DECISIONS. GOV/COMP
GERMANY ITALY NETHERLAND UK INDUS LABOR POL/PAR CONTROL
PROB/SOLV BARGAIN PRICE ROUTINE BAL/PAY COST DEMAND ECO/TAC
20. PAGE 36 F0699 PLAN

B65
FLEMING R.W.,THE LABOR ARBITRATION PROCESS. USA+45 GP/REL
LAW BARGAIN ADJUD ROUTINE SANCTION COST...PREDICT LABOR
CHARTS TIME 20. PAGE 41 F0809 CONSULT
DELIB/GP

B65
PAYNE J.L.,LABOR AND POLITICS IN PERU; THE SYSTEM LABOR
OF POLITICAL BARGAINING. PERU CONSTN VOL/ASSN POL/PAR
EX/STRUC LEAD PWR...CHARTS 20. PAGE 104 F2042 BARGAIN
GP/REL

B65
ROSS P.,THE GOVERNMENT AS A SOURCE OF UNION POWER. LABOR
USA+45 LAW ECO/DEV PROB/SOLV ECO/TAC LEAD GP/REL BARGAIN
...MGT 20. PAGE 114 F2245 POLICY
NAT/G

B65
WALTON R.E.,A BEHAVIORAL THEORY OF LABOR SOC
NEGOTIATIONS: AN ANALYSIS OF A SOCIAL INTERACTION LABOR
SYSTEM. USA+45 FINAN PROB/SOLV ECO/TAC GP/REL BARGAIN
INGP/REL...DECISION BIBLIOG. PAGE 143 F2812 ADMIN

S65
KAUN D.E.,"THE FAIR LABOUR STANDARDS ACT: AN ECO/TAC
EVALUATION IN TERMS OF ITS STATED GOALS." SOUTH/AFR PRICE
LAW LABOR BARGAIN PAY INGP/REL WEALTH 20. PAGE 69 WORKER
F1364 LEGIS

S65
STEENKAMP W.F.J.,"THE PROBLEM OF WAGE REGULATION." ECO/TAC
SOUTH/AFR LAW ECO/DEV ECO/UNDEV LABOR NAT/G BARGAIN PRICE
PAY INGP/REL DISCRIM WEALTH...METH/COMP 20. WORKER
PAGE 125 F2473 RATION

B66
BAKKE E.W.,MUTUAL SURVIVAL; THE GOAL OF UNION AND MGT
MANAGEMENT (2ND ED.). USA+45 ELITES ECO/DEV ECO/TAC LABOR
CONFER ADMIN REPRESENT GP/REL INGP/REL ATTIT BARGAIN
...GP/COMP 20. PAGE 8 F0155 INDUS

B66
COOK P.W. JR.,PROBLEMS OF CORPORATE POWER. WOR+45 ADMIN
FINAN INDUS BARGAIN GP/REL...MGT ANTHOL. PAGE 27 LG/CO
F0530 PWR
ECO/TAC

B66
HAYS P.R.,LABOR ARBITRATION: A DISSENTING VIEW. GP/REL
USA+45 LAW DELIB/GP BARGAIN ADJUD...PREDICT 20. LABOR
PAGE 57 F1126 CONSULT
CT/SYS

B66
MOSKOW M.H.,TEACHERS AND UNIONS. SCHOOL WORKER EDU/PROP
ADJUD LOBBY ATTIT ORD/FREE 20. PAGE 94 F1844 PROF/ORG
LABOR
BARGAIN

B66
ROSS A.M.,INDUSTRIAL RELATIONS AND ECONOMIC ECO/UNDEV
DEVELOPMENT. POL/PAR LEGIS WORKER BARGAIN PRICE LABOR
EXEC LOBBY INCOME PWR...DECISION ANTHOL BIBLIOG 20. NAT/G
PAGE 114 F2243 GP/REL

B66
SHULTZ G.P.,STRATEGIES FOR THE DISPLACED WORKER. ECO/DEV
USA+45 COMPUTER TEC/DEV BARGAIN RECEIVE EDU/PROP WORKER
CONFER GP/REL...MGT METH/COMP 20. PAGE 121 F2391 PLAN
AUTOMAT

B66
ZISCHKA A.,WAR ES EIN WUNDER? GERMANY/W ECO/DEV ECO/TAC
FINAN LG/CO BARGAIN CAP/ISM FOR/AID RATION 20 INT/TRADE
MARSHL/PLN. PAGE 150 F2965 INDUS
WAR

N66
PRINCETON U INDUSTRIAL REL SEC,RECENT MATERIAL ON BIBLIOG/A
COLLECTIVE BARGAINING IN GOVERNMENT (PAMPHLET NO. BARGAIN
130). USA+45 ECO/DEV LABOR WORKER ECO/TAC GOV/REL NAT/G
...MGT 20. PAGE 108 F2120 GP/REL

B67
ADLER J.H.,CAPITAL MOVEMENTS AND ECONOMIC DIPLOM
DEVELOPMENT. WOR+45 FINAN NAT/G BARGAIN ECO/TAC ECO/DEV
FOR/AID INT/TRADE ANTHOL. PAGE 2 F0042 ECO/UNDEV

B67
BADGLEY R.F.,DOCTORS' STRIKE; MEDICAL CARE AND HEALTH
CONFLICT IN SASKATCHEWAN. CANADA NAT/G PROF/ORG PLAN
GP/REL ADJUST ATTIT...HEAL SOC 20. PAGE 8 F0148 LABOR
BARGAIN

B67
BEAL E.F.,THE PRACTICE OF COLLECTIVE BARGAINING BARGAIN
(3RD ED.). USA+45 WOR+45 ECO/DEV INDUS LG/CO MGT
PROF/ORG WORKER ECO/TAC GP/REL WEALTH...JURID LABOR
METH/CNCPT. PAGE 12 F0221 ADJUD

B67
EGGERT G.G.,RAILROAD LABOR DISPUTES. USA+45 USA-45 GP/REL
ELITES DIST/IND DELIB/GP FORCES JUDGE WORKER NAT/G
PROB/SOLV DOMIN PWR...POLICY 20. PAGE 36 F0707 LABOR
BARGAIN

B67
ROBERTS B.C.,COLLECTIVE BARGAINING IN AFRICAN LABOR
COUNTRIES. AFR LAW ECO/UNDEV BARGAIN GP/REL MGT
...DECISION METH/COMP 20. PAGE 112 F2206 PLAN
ECO/TAC

B67
ULMAN L.,CHALLENGES TO COLLECTIVE BARGAINING. LABOR
ECO/TAC DISCRIM EQUILIB ATTIT...JURID SOC/WK. BARGAIN
PAGE 132 F2599 ADJUD
POLICY

L67
GOULD W.B.,"THE STATUS OF UNAUTHORIZED AND ECO/DEV
'WILDCAT' STRIKES UNDER THE NATIONAL LABOR INDUS
RELATIONS ACT." USA+45 ACT/RES BARGAIN ECO/TAC LABOR
LEGIT ADJUD ADMIN GP/REL MGT. PAGE 50 F0968 POLICY

L67
MACDONALD R.M.,"COLLECTIVE BARGAINING IN THE LABOR
POSTWAR PERIOD." WORKER PROB/SOLV ECO/TAC PARTIC INDUS
RISK CENTRAL EFFICIENCY DRIVE WEALTH...TREND 20. BARGAIN
PAGE 83 F1624 CAP/ISM

S67
ASCH P.,"CONGLOMERATE MERGERS AND PUBLIC POLICY." INDUS
USA+45 ECO/DEV LG/CO NAT/G ECO/TAC ADJUD CENTRAL CAP/ISM
20. PAGE 7 F0126 BARGAIN

S67
CHAMBERLAIN N.W.,"STRIKES IN CONTEMPORARY CONTEXT." LABOR
LAW INDUS NAT/G CHIEF CONFER COST ATTIT ORD/FREE BARGAIN
...POLICY MGT 20. PAGE 23 F0442 EFFICIENCY
PROB/SOLV

S67
COSGROVE C.A.,"AGRICULTURE, FINANCE AND POLITICS IN ECO/DEV
THE EUROPEAN COMMUNITY." EUR+WWI DIST/IND MARKET DIPLOM
INT/ORG VOL/ASSN DELIB/GP TEC/DEV BAL/PWR BARGAIN AGRI
ECO/TAC RATION CONFER 20 EEC. PAGE 28 F0538 INT/TRADE

S67
CURTIN W.J.,"NATIONAL EMERGENCY DISPUTES JURID
LEGISLATION* ITS NEED AND ITS PROSPECTS IN THE LABOR
TRANSPORTATION INDUSTRIES." USA+45 ECO/DEV INDUS ADJUD
NAT/G LEGIS ACT/RES BARGAIN POLICY. PAGE 29 F0565 DIST/IND

S67
FOX R.G.,"FAMILY, CASTE, AND COMMERCE IN A NORTH CULTURE
INDIAN MARKET TOWN." INDIA STRATA AGRI FACE/GP FAM GP/REL
NEIGH OP/RES BARGAIN ADMIN ROUTINE WEALTH...SOC ECO/UNDEV
CHARTS 20. PAGE 43 F0838 DIST/IND

S67
HALL B.,"THE COALITION AGAINST DISHWASHERS." USA+45 LABOR
POL/PAR PROB/SOLV BARGAIN LEAD CHOOSE REPRESENT ADMIN
GP/REL ORD/FREE PWR...POLICY 20. PAGE 53 F1044 DOMIN
WORKER

S67
KENDALL R.J.,"CHANGED CONDITIONS AS CONTROL
MISREPRESENTATION IN GOVERNMENT CONSTRUCTION CONSTRUC
CONTRACTS." USA+45 BARGAIN ADJUD COST. PAGE 70 NAT/G
F1375 LAW

S67
PRASOW P.,"THE DEVELOPMENT OF JUDICIAL ARBITRATION LABOR
IN LABOR-MANAGEMENT DISPUTES." LAW INDUS WORKER BARGAIN
GP/REL ROLE...HIST/WRIT 20. PAGE 107 F2113 ADJUD
TREND

S67
SCHELLING T.C.,"ECONOMICS AND CRIMINAL ENTERPRISE." CRIME
LAW FORCES BARGAIN ECO/TAC CONTROL GAMBLE ROUTINE PROB/SOLV
ADJUST DEMAND INCOME PROFIT CRIMLGY. PAGE 116 F2295 CONCPT

S67
WARNER K.O.,"FINANCIAL IMPLICATION OF EMPLOYEE BARGAIN
BARGAINING IN THE PUBLIC SERVICE." CANADA USA+45 LABOR
FINAN ADMIN...MGT 20. PAGE 143 F2823 COST
LOC/G

S67
ZACK A.M.,"ARE STRIKES OF PUBLIC EMPLOYEES LABOR
NECESSARY?" USA+45 DELIB/GP PROB/SOLV REPRESENT NAT/G
GP/REL MGT. PAGE 150 F2956 WORKER
BARGAIN

S67
ZOETEWEIJ B.,"INCOME POLICIES ABROAD: AN INTERIM METH/COMP
REPORT." NAT/G PROB/SOLV BARGAIN BUDGET PRICE RISK INCOME
CENTRAL EFFICIENCY EQUILIB...MGT NAT/COMP 20. POLICY
PAGE 150 F2967 LABOR

N67
US CONGRESS JT COMM ECO GOVT,BACKGROUND MATERIAL ON BUDGET
ECONOMY IN GOVERNMENT 1967 (PAMPHLET). WOR+45 COST
ECO/DEV BARGAIN PRICE DEMAND OPTIMAL...STAT MGT
DEPT/DEFEN. PAGE 135 F2665 NAT/G

S86
SMITH R.M.,"THE NATIONAL BUREAU OF LABOR AND LABOR
INDUSTRIAL DEPRESSIONS" USA-45 DELIB/GP BARGAIN INDUS
CONTROL COST INCOME WEALTH...STAT 19 DEPRESSION. FINAN
PAGE 123 F2433 GOV/REL

BARKSDALE H.C. F0187

BARNETT A.D. F0188,F0189

BARNETT H.J. F0190,F0191

BARNETT/R....ROSS BARNETT

BAROTSE....BAROTSE TRIBE OF RHODESIA

BARRASH J. F0192

BARRERE A. F0193,F0194

BARRO S. F0195

BARRON J.A. F0196

BARROW T.C. F0197

BARRY E.E. F0198

BARTELS R. F0199

BARTHELEMY G. F0200

BARTLETT J.L. F0201

BARZANSKI S. F0202

BASCH A. F0203

BASHILELE....BASHILELE TRIBE

BASOV V. F0204

BASSIE V.L. F0205

BASTIAT F. F0206,F0207

BATAK....BATAK TRIBE, PHILIPPINES

BATCHELOR B. F0208

BATES J.L. F0209

BATISTA/J....JUAN BATISTA

BATOR F.M. F0210

BATTEN T.R. F0211

BAUCHET P. F0212

BAUER P.T. F0213,F0214,F0215,F0216

BAUER R.A. F0217

BAUM M. F0218

BAUMOL W.J. F0219

BAVARIA....BAVARIA

BAWONGO....BAWONGO TRIBE

BAYER H. F0220

BAYESIAN INFLUENCE....SEE SIMUL

BEAL E.F. F0221

BEARD C.A. F0222

BEARD/CA....CHARLES A. BEARD

B56
BROWN R.E.,CHARLES BEARD AND THE CONSTITUTION. USA-45 NAT/G ORD/FREE WEALTH...HUM TIME/SEQ METH/COMP 20 BEARD/CA. PAGE 19 F0372 — CONSTN ELITES HIST/WRIT

BEARDSLEY R.K. F0223

BEASLEY K.E. F0224

BEATON L. F0225

BEAUFRE A. F0226

BECCARIA/C....CAESARE BONESARA BECCARIA

BECKER A.S. F0227

BECKER/E....ERNEST BECKER

BEGUIN B. F0228

BEGUIN H. F0229

BEHAV/SCI....BEHAVIORAL SCIENCES

BEHAVIOR TESTS....SEE PERS/TEST

BEHAVIORSM....BEHAVIORISM

L59
SIMON H.A.,"THEORIES OF DECISION-MAKING IN ECONOMICS AND BEHAVIORAL SCIENCE" (BMR)" MARKET BARGAIN UTIL DRIVE...DECISION MGT PROBABIL HYPO/EXP SIMUL 20 BEHAVIORSM. PAGE 122 F2409 — PSY GEN/LAWS PROB/SOLV

BEHRMAN J.N. F0230

BEHRMAN N.J. F1780

BEIM D. F0231

BELASSA B. F0232

BELGIUM....BELGIUM

B31
CROOK W.H.,THE GENERAL STRIKE: A STUDY OF LABOR'S TRAGIC WEAPON IN THEORY AND PRACTICE. BELGIUM FRANCE SWEDEN UK WOR-45 PROB/SOLV ECO/TAC DOMIN PWR ...POLICY TIME/SEQ NAT/COMP GEN/LAWS 19/20 STRIKE. PAGE 29 F0555 — LABOR WORKER LG/CO BARGAIN

B60
ASPREMONT-LYNDEN H.,RAPPORT SUR L'ADMINISTRATION BELGE DU RUANDA-URUNDI PENDANT L'ANNEE 1959. BELGIUM RWANDA AGRI INDUS DIPLOM ECO/TAC INT/TRADE DOMIN ADMIN RACE/REL...GEOG CENSUS 20 UN. PAGE 7 F0132 — AFR COLONIAL ECO/UNDEV INT/ORG

B61
LAMFALUSSY A.,INVESTMENT AND GROWTH IN MATURE ECONOMIES. BELGIUM EUR+WWI LABOR PRICE PRODUC PROFIT...STAT CONT/OBS CHARTS 20. PAGE 75 F1464 — FINAN INDUS ECO/DEV CAP/ISM

B62
GRANICK D.,THE EUROPEAN EXECUTIVE. BELGIUM FRANCE GERMANY/W UK INDUS LABOR LG/CO SML/CO EX/STRUC PLAN TEC/DEV CAP/ISM COST DEMAND...POLICY CHARTS 20. PAGE 50 F0977 — MGT ECO/DEV ECO/TAC EXEC

B62
MEADE J.E.,CASE STUDIES IN EUROPEAN ECONOMIC UNION. BELGIUM EUR+WWI LUXEMBOURG NAT/G INT/TRADE REGION ROUTINE WEALTH...METH/CNCPT STAT CHARTS ECSC TOT/POP OEEC EEC FOR/TRADE 20. PAGE 89 F1738 — INT/ORG ECO/TAC

B64
MORRISSENS L.,ECONOMIC POLICY IN OUR TIME: COUNTRY STUDIES. BELGIUM EUR+WWI FRANCE GERMANY/W ITALY NETHERLAND INDUS BARGAIN BUDGET GOV/REL BAL/PAY PRODUC...CON/ANAL CHARTS COSTS 20. PAGE 94 F1839 — ECO/DEV ECO/TAC METH/COMP PLAN

B65
WEIL G.L.,A HANDBOOK ON THE EUROPEAN ECONOMIC COMMUNITY. BELGIUM EUR+WWI FRANCE GERMANY/W ITALY CONSTN ECO/DEV CREATE PARTIC GP/REL...DECISION MGT CHARTS 20 EEC. PAGE 144 F2846 — INT/TRADE INT/ORG TEC/DEV INT/LAW

BELIEF....SEE SECT, ATTIT

BELISLE J. F0233

BELL D.E. F0234

BELL P.W. F0235

BELLAN R.C. F0236

BELLAS/HES....NATIONAL BELLAS HESS

BELLOC H. F0237,F0238

BELOFF M. F0239,F0240

BELSHAW D.G.R. F0242

BEN/BELLA....AHMED BEN BELLA

BENDIX R. F0243

BENESE....BENES

BENGAL....BENGAL + BENGALIS

BENHAM F. F0244

BENIN....BENIN - DISTRICT IN NIGERIA

BEN-PORATH Y. F0245

BENN W. F0246

BENNETT J.T. F0247

BENNION E.G. F0248

BENOIT E. F0249,F0250,F0251,F0252

BENOIT J. F0253

BENTHAM J. F0254,F0255

BENTHAM/J....JEREMY BENTHAM

BENTLEY/AF....ARTHUR F. BENTLEY

BENVENISTE G. F0743

BEQIRAJ M. F0256

BERG E.J. F0257

BERGMANN D. F0258

BERGSON A. F0259

BERGSON/H....HENRI BERGSON

BERGSON/WJ....W. JAMES BERGSON

BERKELEY....BERKELEY, CALIFORNIA

BERLE A.A. F0260,F0261,F0262,F1076

BERLIN....BERLIN

BERLIN/BLO....BERLIN BLOCKADE

B67
HALLE L.J.,THE COLD WAR AS HISTORY. AFR USSR WOR+45 ECO/TAC FOR/AID NUC/PWR WAR PEACE ORD/FREE ...MAJORIT TREND 20 KENNEDY/JF KHRUSH/N BERLIN/BLO. PAGE 54 F1048
DIPLOM
BAL/PWR

BERLINER J.S. F0263

BERNAYS E.L. F0264

BERNAYS/EL....EDWARD L. BERNAYS

BERNHARD R.C. F0265

BERNSTEIN I. F0266

BERNSTEIN M.H. F0267,F0268

BERNSTEIN P.L. F0269

BERREBY J.J. F0270

BERRILL K. F0271

BESSARABIA....BESSARABIA; SEE ALSO USSR

BESTERS H. F1839

BEUGEL E.V.D. F0272

BEVAN A. F0273

BEVERIDGE W.H. F0274

BEY A.S. F1774

BEYER G.H. F0275

BHAGWATI J. F0276

BHAMBHRI C.P. F0277

BHUMIBOL/A....BHUMIBOL ADULYADEJ

BHUTAN....SEE ALSO ASIA

BIAFRA....BIAFRA

BIBBY J. F0278

BIBLE....BIBLE: OLD AND NEW TESTAMENTS

BIBLIOG....BIBLIOGRAPHY OVER 50 ITEMS

N
INTERNATIONAL BIBLIOGRAPHY OF ECONOMICS. WOR+45 FINAN MARKET ADMIN DEMAND INCOME PRODUC...POLICY IDEA/COMP METH. PAGE 1 F0002
BIBLIOG
ECO/DEV
ECO/UNDEV
INT/TRADE

N
TEXTBOOKS IN PRINT. WOR+45 WOR-45 LAW DIPLOM ALL/VALS ALL/IDEOS...SOC T 19/20. PAGE 1 F0003
BIBLIOG
SCHOOL
KNOWL

N
LONDON TIMES OFFICIAL INDEX. UK LAW ECO/DEV NAT/G DIPLOM LEAD ATTIT 20. PAGE 1 F0006
BIBLIOG
INDEX
PRESS
WRITING

N
THE MIDDLE EAST. CULTURE...BIOG BIBLIOG. PAGE 1 F0010
ISLAM
INDUS
FINAN

N
DEUTSCHE BUCHEREI,DEUTSCHES BUCHERVERZEICHNIS. GERMANY LAW CULTURE POL/PAR ADMIN LEAD ATTIT PERSON ...SOC 20. PAGE 32 F0626
BIBLIOG
NAT/G
DIPLOM
ECO/DEV

N
MINISTRY OF OVERSEAS DEVELOPME,TECHNICAL CO-OPERATION -- A BIBLIOGRAPHY. UK LAW SOCIETY DIPLOM ECO/TAC FOR/AID...STAT 20 CMN/WLTH. PAGE 92 F1803
BIBLIOG
TEC/DEV
ECO/DEV
NAT/G

N
RAND SCHOOL OF SOCIAL SCIENCE,INDEX TO LABOR ARTICLES. ECO/DEV INT/ORG LEGIS DIPLOM GP/REL ...NAT/COMP 20. PAGE 109 F2143
BIBLIOG
LABOR
MGT
ADJUD

N
UNESCO,INTERNATIONAL BIBLIOGRAPHY OF ECONOMICS (VOLUMES 1-8). WOR+45 AGRI INDUS LABOR PLAN TEC/DEV 20. PAGE 132 F2607
BIBLIOG
ECO/DEV
ECO/UNDEV

N
UNIVERSITY OF FLORIDA,CARIBBEAN ACQUISITIONS: MATERIALS ACQUIRED BY THE UNIVERSITY OF FLORIDA 1957-1960. L/A+17C...ART/METH GEOG MGT 20. PAGE 133 F2620
BIBLIOG
ECO/UNDEV
EDU/PROP
JURID

N
US LIBRARY OF CONGRESS,EAST EUROPEAN ACCESSIONS INDEX. NAT/G ISOLAT ATTIT KNOWL...POLICY 20. PAGE 138 F2711
BIBLIOG
COM
MARXIST
DIPLOM

B03
GRIFFIN A.P.C.,LISTS PUBLISHED 1902-03: GOVERNMENT OWNERSHIP OF RAILROADS (PAMPHLET). USA-45 LAW NAT/G RATION GOV/REL CENTRAL SOCISM...POLICY 19/20. PAGE 51 F0998
BIBLIOG
DIST/IND
CONTROL
ADJUD

B14
LEVINE L.,SYNDICALISM IN FRANCE (2ND ED.). FRANCE LAW SOCIETY ECO/DEV NAT/G ECO/TAC LEAD ATTIT ...POLICY CONCPT STAT BIBLIOG 18/20 REFORMERS. PAGE 79 F1542
LABOR
INDUS
SOCISM
REV

N19
FAHRNKOPF N.,STATE AND LOCAL GOVERNMENT IN ILLINOIS (PAMPHLET). CONSTN ADMIN PARTIC CHOOSE REPRESENT GOV/REL...JURID MGT 20 ILLINOIS. PAGE 39 F0759
BIBLIOG
LOC/G
LEGIS
CT/SYS

N19
HAGEN E.E.,AN ANALYTICAL MODEL OF THE TRANSITION TO ECONOMIC GROWTH (PAMPHLET). WOR+45 WOR-45 SOCIETY STRATA FINAN NAT/G CONTROL PARTIC PRODUC...PHIL/SCI BIBLIOG 17/20. PAGE 53 F1033
SIMUL
ECO/DEV
METH
TEC/DEV

N19
LUTZ F.A.,THE PROBLEM OF INTERNATIONAL LIQUIDITY AND THE MULTIPLECURRENCY STANDARD (PAMPHLET). WOR+45 MARKET INT/ORG PRICE BAL/PAY...NEW/IDEA METH/COMP BIBLIOG 20 IMF. PAGE 82 F1609
PROB/SOLV
FINAN
DIPLOM
ECO/TAC

N19
MORGENSTERN O.,A NEW LOOK AT ECONOMIC TIMES SERIES ANALYSIS (PAMPHLET). WEALTH...BIBLIOG 20 NSF NAVAL/RES. PAGE 93 F1831
TREND
IDEA/COMP
EFFICIENCY

B28
TRUE A.C.,A HISTORY OF AGRICULTURAL EXTENSION WORK IN THE UNITED STATES, 1785-1923. USA-45 LAW SCHOOL WAR ADJUST...CHARTS BIBLIOG 18/20 SMITH/LEVR COUNTY/AGT. PAGE 131 F2591
EDU/PROP
AGRI
VOL/ASSN
PLAN

B30
GREEN F.M.,CONSTITUTIONAL DEVELOPMENT IN THE SOUTH ATLANTIC STATES, 1776-1860; A STUDY IN THE EVOLUTION OF DEMOCRACY. USA-45 ELITES SOCIETY STRATA ECO/DEV AGRI POL/PAR EX/STRUC LEGIS CT/SYS REGION...BIBLIOG 18/19 MARYLAND VIRGINIA GEORGIA NORTH/CAR SOUTH/CAR. PAGE 50 F0984
CONSTN
PROVS
PLURISM
REPRESENT

B31
JEVONS W.S.,THE THEORY OF POLITICAL ECONOMY (4TH ED.; 1ST ED. 1871). WOR-45 FINAN MARKET RENT WEALTH ...LOG MATH QUANT CON/ANAL IDEA/COMP BIBLIOG METH 17/19. PAGE 67 F1318
GEN/LAWS
UTIL
LABOR

B37
MACKENZIE F.,PLANNED SOCIETY: YESTERDAY, TODAY, AND TOMORROW. ECO/DEV ECO/UNDEV AGRI FINAN INDUS PLAN INSPECT CONTROL ALL/IDEOS...TREND METH/COMP BIBLIOG 20 RESOURCE/N. PAGE 83 F1635
SOC
CONCPT
ANTHOL

B39
THOMAS J.A.,THE HOUSE OF COMMONS, 1832-1901; A STUDY OF ITS ECONOMIC AND FUNCTIONAL CHARACTER. UK LAW STRATA FINAN DIPLOM CONTROL LEAD LOBBY REPRESENT WEALTH...POLICY STAT BIBLIOG 19/20 PARLIAMENT. PAGE 130 F2561
PARL/PROC
LEGIS
POL/PAR
ECO/DEV

B40
SIKES E.R.,CONTEMPORARY ECONOMIC SYSTEMS: THEIR ANALYSIS AND SOCIAL BACKGROUND. GERMANY ITALY USSR AGRI INDUS PLAN CAP/ISM ROUTINE TOTALISM FASCISM ...POLICY CON/ANAL BIBLIOG 20. PAGE 122 F2400
COM
SOCISM
CONCPT

B41
HAYEK F.A.,THE PURE THEORY OF CAPITAL. UNIV ECO/DEV ECO/TAC COST EQUILIB PROFIT WEALTH...SIMUL GEN/LAWS BIBLIOG INDEX TIME 20. PAGE 57 F1120 CAP/ISM METH/CNCPT PRODUC FINAN

B42
JACKSON M.V.,EUROPEAN POWERS AND SOUTH-EAST AFRICA: A STUDY OF INTERNATIONAL RELATIONS ON SOUTH-EAST COAST OF AFRICA, 1796-1856. AFR FRANCE PORTUGAL SOUTH/AFR UK USA-45 FORCES INT/TRADE PWR...CHARTS BIBLIOG 18/19 TREATY. PAGE 66 F1294 DOMIN POLICY ORD/FREE DIPLOM

B42
SWEEZY P.M.,THE THEORY OF CAPITALIST DEVELOPMENT. FUT NAT/G COST FASCISM BIBLIOG. PAGE 128 F2519 ECO/DEV CAP/ISM MARXISM COLONIAL

B42
WRIGHT D.M.,THE CREATION OF PURCHASING POWER. USA-45 NAT/G PRICE ADMIN WAR INCOME PRODUC...POLICY CONCPT IDEA/COMP BIBLIOG 20 MONEY. PAGE 149 F2930 FINAN ECO/TAC ECO/DEV CREATE

B46
ERNST M.L.,THE FIRST FREEDOM. USA-45 CONSTN PRESS PRIVIL...CHARTS IDEA/COMP BIBLIOG 20 AMEND/I. PAGE 38 F0746 EDU/PROP COM/IND ORD/FREE CONTROL

B46
HARRISON S.M.,AMERICAN FOUNDATIONS FOR SOCIAL WELFARE. OP/RES CONTROL...POLICY MGT METH/CNCPT STAT TREND BIBLIOG. PAGE 56 F1092 GIVE FINAN CLASSIF ADMIN

B47
BAERWALD F.,FUNDAMENTALS OF LABOR ECONOMICS. LAW INDUS LABOR LG/CO CONTROL GP/REL INCOME TOTALISM ...MGT CHARTS GEN/LAWS BIBLIOG 20. PAGE 8 F0150 ECO/DEV WORKER MARKET

B47
BALDWIN H.W.,THE PRICE OF POWER. USA+45 FORCES PLAN NUC/PWR ADJUST COST ORD/FREE...POLICY PSY BIBLIOG 20. PAGE 9 F0165 PROB/SOLV PWR POPULISM PRICE

B48
CLYDE P.H.,THE FAR EAST: A HISTORY OF THE IMPACT OF THE WEST ON EASTERN ASIA. CHINA/COM CULTURE INT/TRADE DOMIN COLONIAL WAR PWR...CHARTS BIBLIOG 19/20 CHINJAP. PAGE 25 F0494 DIPLOM ASIA

B48
LAUTERBACH A.,ECONOMIC SECURITY AND INDIVIDUAL FREEDOM: CAN WE HAVE BOTH? COM EUR+WWI MOD/EUR UNIV WOR+45 CAP/ISM TOTALISM ALL/VALS...GOV/COMP BIBLIOG 20. PAGE 76 F1490 ORD/FREE ECO/DEV DECISION INGP/REL

B48
NOYES C.R.,ECONOMIC MAN IN RELATION TO HIS NATURAL ENVIRONMENT (2 VOLS.). UNIV COST DEMAND EFFICIENCY HAPPINESS INCOME PRODUC PROFIT HEREDITY...CHARTS BIBLIOG. PAGE 99 F1944 HABITAT METH/CNCPT GEN/METH

B48
OSBORN F.,OUR PLUNDERED PLANET. UNIV DEATH WAR ...BIBLIOG RESOURCE/N. PAGE 102 F2001 HABITAT GEOG ADJUST AGRI

B48
TAYLOR P.E.,THE ECONOMICS OF PUBLIC FINANCE. USA+45 USA-45 ECO/DEV WORKER PLAN BUDGET WAR INCOME WEALTH ...CONCPT STAT BIBLIOG 20. PAGE 129 F2540 FINAN POLICY NAT/G TAX

B48
WINSLOW E.M.,THE PATTERN OF IMPERIALISM; A STUDY IN THE THEORIES OF POWER. DOMIN WAR PWR MARXISM ...IDEA/COMP METH/COMP BIBLIOG 20. PAGE 147 F2906 SOCISM CAP/ISM COLONIAL ECO/TAC

B49
HANSEN A.H.,MONETARY THEORY AND FISCAL POLICY. CONSULT PLAN INT/TRADE BAL/PAY OPTIMAL...TREND CHARTS METH/COMP BIBLIOG T 19/20 MONEY. PAGE 54 F1063 FINAN GEN/LAWS POLICY ECO/TAC

B49
MACGREGOR D.H.,ECONOMIC THOUGHT AND POLICY. WOR-45 WORKER WAR DEMAND EFFICIENCY WEALTH LAISSEZ SOCISM ...MAJORIT BIBLIOG 19/20. PAGE 83 F1629 CONCPT POLICY ECO/TAC

B49
PELZER K.J.,SELECTED BIBLIOGRAPHY ON THE GEOGRAPHY OF SOUTHEAST ASIA (3 VOLS., 1949-1956). PHILIPPINE CULTURE...SOC 20 MALAYA. PAGE 104 F2053 BIBLIOG S/ASIA GEOG

B50
SURANYI-UNGER T.,PRIVATE ENTERPRISE AND GOVERNMENTAL PLANNING. STRUCT FINAN BAL/PWR HAPPINESS DRIVE NEW/LIB PLURISM...MATH QUANT STAT TREND BIBLIOG. PAGE 127 F2516 PLAN NAT/G LAISSEZ POLICY

C50
ELLSWORTH P.T.,"INTERNATIONAL ECONOMY." ECO/DEV ECO/UNDEV FINAN LABOR DIPLOM FOR/AID TARIFFS BAL/PAY EQUILIB NAT/LISM OPTIMAL...INT/LAW 20 ILO GATT. PAGE 37 F0724 BIBLIOG INT/TRADE ECO/TAC INT/ORG

B51
CHANDLER L.V.,INFLATION IN THE UNITED STATES 1940-1948. AFR NAT/G BUDGET PAY PRICE CONTROL WAR INCOME PRODUC...POLICY BIBLIOG 20. PAGE 23 F0448 ECO/TAC FINAN PROB/SOLV WEALTH

B51
LEONARD L.L.,INTERNATIONAL ORGANIZATION. WOR+45 WOR-45 EX/STRUC FORCES LEGIS ECO/TAC INT/TRADE COLONIAL ARMS/CONT...SOC/WK GOV/COMP BIBLIOG. PAGE 78 F1527 NAT/G DIPLOM INT/ORG DELIB/GP

B52
GOLDSTEIN J.,THE GOVERNMENT OF BRITISH TRADE UNIONS. UK ECO/DEV EX/STRUC INGP/REL...BIBLIOG 20. PAGE 48 F0940 LABOR PARTIC

B52
SURANYI-UNGER T.,COMPARATIVE ECONOMIC SYSTEMS. FINAN MARKET DIPLOM PRICE WEALTH...GEOG SOC BIBLIOG METH T 20. PAGE 128 F2517 LAISSEZ PLAN ECO/DEV IDEA/COMP

B53
BOWEN H.R.,SOCIAL RESPONSIBILITIES OF THE BUSINESSMAN (FIRST EDITION). LAW FINAN ACT/RES CAP/ISM ROUTINE DRIVE PWR LAISSEZ...DECISION BIBLIOG. PAGE 17 F0326 MGT PERSON SUPEGO MORAL

B53
MIT CENTER INTERNATIONAL STU,BIBLIOGRAPHY OF THE ECONOMIC AND POLITICAL DEVELOPMENT OF INDONESIA. INDONESIA STRUCT NAT/G COLONIAL LEAD...STAT 20. PAGE 92 F1805 BIBLIOG ECO/UNDEV TEC/DEV S/ASIA

B53
PURCELL T.V.,THE WORKER SPEAKS HIS MIND ON COMPANY AND UNION. WORKER ADJUD LEAD RACE/REL ATTIT DRIVE MARXISM...MGT CLASSIF STAT OBS INT SAMP BIBLIOG. PAGE 108 F2131 LABOR PARTIC INGP/REL HAPPINESS

B53
SCHLEIFFER H.,INDEX TO ECONOMIC HISTORY ESSAYS IN FESTSCHRIFTEN (PAMPHLET). WOR+45 WOR-45...CONCPT IDEA/COMP ANTHOL. PAGE 117 F2299 BIBLIOG NAT/G

B54
CHILDS M.W.,ETHICS IN A BUSINESS SOCIETY. PROF/ORG LEAD WAR GP/REL ATTIT DRIVE PERSON KNOWL MORAL PWR ...WELF/ST BIBLIOG. PAGE 24 F0466 MGT SOCIETY

B54
INTERNATIONAL LABOUR OFF LIB,BIBLIOGRAPHY ON THE INTERNATIONAL LABOUR ORGANISATION. WORKER 20. PAGE 65 F1277 BIBLIOG LABOR INT/ORG CONFER

B55
JONES T.B.,A BIBLIOGRAPHY ON SOUTH AMERICAN ECONOMIC AFFAIRS: ARTICLES IN NINETEENTH CENTURY PERIODICALS (PAMPHLET). AGRI COM/IND DIST/IND EXTR/IND FINAN INDUS LABOR NAT/G 19. PAGE 68 F1340 BIBLIOG ECO/UNDEV L/A+17C TEC/DEV

B55
WOYTINSKY W.S.,WORLD COMMERCE AND GOVERNMENTS: TRENDS AND OUTLOOK. WOR+45 FINAN POL/PAR DIPLOM ECO/TAC FOR/AID DOMIN WAR CHOOSE...CHARTS BIBLIOG 20 LEAGUE/NAT UN ILO. PAGE 149 F2929 INT/TRADE DIST/IND NAT/COMP NAT/G

B56
BARBASH J.,THE PRACTICE OF UNIONISM. ECO/TAC LEAD LOBBY GP/REL INGP/REL DRIVE MARXISM BIBLIOG. PAGE 10 F0182 LABOR REPRESENT CONTROL ADMIN

B56
FELLNER W.,TRENDS AND CYCLES IN ECONOMIC ACTIVITY: AN INTRODUCTION TO PROBLEMS OF ECONOMIC GROWTH. USA+45 INDUS ACT/RES CAP/ISM EQUILIB...MODAL METH/COMP BIBLIOG 20. PAGE 40 F0779 ECO/TAC TREND FINAN ECO/DEV

B56
GREENHUT M.L.,PLANT LOCATION IN THEORY AND PRACTICE; THE ECONOMICS OF SPACE. WOR+45 WOR-45 MARKET WORKER COST DEMAND...CONCPT STAT CHARTS HYPO/EXP BIBLIOG 19/20. PAGE 51 F0991 SML/CO ECO/DEV CAP/ISM IDEA/COMP

B56
JUAN T.L.,ECONOMIC AND SOCIAL DEVELOPMENT OF MODERN CHINA: A BIBLIOGRAPHICAL GUIDE. ASIA AGRI COM/IND DIST/IND FINAN INDUS DIPLOM...STAT 20. PAGE 68 F1342 BIBLIOG SOC

B56
UN HEADQUARTERS LIBRARY,BIBLIOGRAPHY OF INDUSTRIALIZATION IN UNDERDEVELOPED COUNTRIES (BIBLIOGRAPHICAL SERIES NO. 6). WOR+45 R+D ACADEM INT/ORG NAT/G. PAGE 132 F2602 BIBLIOG ECO/UNDEV TEC/DEV

B56
UNITED NATIONS,BIBLIOGRAPHY ON INDUSTRIALIZATION IN UNDER-DEVELOPED COUNTRIES. WOR+45 R+D INT/ORG NAT/G FOR/AID ADMIN LEAD 20 UN. PAGE 132 F2612 BIBLIOG ECO/UNDEV INDUS TEC/DEV

B56
US DEPARTMENT OF STATE,ECONOMIC PROBLEMS OF UNDERDEVELOPED AREAS (PAMPHLET). AFR ASIA ISLAM L/A+17C AGRI FINAN INDUS INT/ORG LABOR INT/TRADE ...PSY SOC 20. PAGE 136 F2673 BIBLIOG ECO/UNDEV TEC/DEV R+D

B56
YABUKI K.,JAPAN BIBLIOGRAPHIC ANNUAL, 1956: THE LATEST LIST OF OLD AND NEW BOOKS ON JAPAN IN ENGLISH. EDU/PROP...LING 20 CHINJAP. PAGE 149 F2945 BIBLIOG SOC

B56
YUAN TUNG-LI,ECONOMIC AND SOCIAL DEVELOPMENT OF MODERN CHINA: A BIBLIOGRAPHIC GUIDE. COM/IND FINAN BIBLIOG ASIA

FAM LABOR SECT CRIME INCOME...STAT SAMP CON/ANAL. PAGE 150 F2954
ECO/UNDEV SOC

L56
TAGLIACOZZO D.L.,"TRADE-UNION GOVERNMENT, ITS NATURE AND ITS PROBLEMS: A BIBLIOGRAPHICAL REVIEW, 1945-1955." STRUCT LEAD PARTIC CHOOSE ATTIT ...MAJORIT METH/CNCPT BIBLIOG. PAGE 128 F2526
CLASSIF LABOR INGP/REL GP/REL

B57
ASSN U BUREAUS BUS-ECO RES,INDEX OF PUBLICATIONS OF BUREAUS OF BUSINESS AND ECONOMIC RESEARCH 1950-56 AND YEARLY SUPPLEMENTS THROUGH 1967. FINAN OP/RES PLAN GOV/REL INCOME AGE...POLICY 20. PAGE 7 F0133
BIBLIOG ECO/DEV ECO/TAC LG/CO

B57
HALD M.,A SELECTED BIBLIOGRAPHY ON ECONOMIC DEVELOPMENT AND FOREIGN AID. INT/ORG PROB/SOLV ...SOC 20. PAGE 53 F1040
BIBLIOG ECO/UNDEV TEC/DEV FOR/AID

B57
LOUCKS W.N.,COMPARATIVE ECONOMIC SYSTEMS (5TH ED.). COM UK USSR INDUS POL/PAR PLAN CAP/ISM TOTALISM MARXISM...PHIL/SCI BIBLIOG 19/20. PAGE 82 F1603
NAT/COMP IDEA/COMP SOCISM

B57
NAUMANN R.,THEORIE UND PRAXIS DES NEOLIBERALISMUS; DAS MAERCHEN VON DER FREIEN ODER SOZIALEN MARKTWIRTSCHAFT. GERMANY/W FORCES PLAN EDU/PROP SOCISM...POLICY MARXIST IDEA/COMP BIBLIOG 18/20 ADENAUER/K. PAGE 97 F1903
MARXISM NEW/LIB ECO/TAC CAP/ISM

B57
OLIVER H.M. JR.,ECONOMIC OPINION AND POLICY IN CEYLON. CEYLON FINAN POL/PAR WORKER INT/TRADE INCOME WEALTH...GEOG UNPLAN/INT BIBLIOG 20 CMN/WLTH. PAGE 101 F1987
ECO/UNDEV NAT/LISM POLICY COLONIAL

B57
ROBERTSON H.M.,SOUTH AFRICA, ECONOMIC AND POLITICAL ASPECTS. SOUTH/AFR CONSTN CULTURE POL/PAR LEGIS DIPLOM DOMIN COLONIAL...SOC BIBLIOG 19/20. PAGE 112 F2214
RACE/REL ECO/UNDEV ECO/TAC DISCRIM

B57
SCHNEIDER E.V.,INDUSTRIAL SOCIOLOGY: THE SOCIAL RELATIONS OF INDUSTRY AND COMMUNITY. STRATA INDUS NAT/G NEIGH CREATE ADMIN PARTIC GP/REL RACE/REL ROLE PWR...POLICY BIBLIOG. PAGE 117 F2308
LABOR MGT INGP/REL STRUCT

B57
UDY S.H. JR.,THE ORGANIZATION OF PRODUCTION IN NONINDUSTRIAL CULTURE. VOL/ASSN DELIB/GP TEC/DEV ...CHARTS BIBLIOG. PAGE 132 F2598
METH/COMP ECO/UNDEV PRODUC ADMIN

B58
BARRERE A.,POLITIQUE FINANCIERE. FRANCE BUDGET ECO/TAC TAX BAL/PAY INCOME PRODUC...MGT BIBLIOG T 20. PAGE 10 F0193
FINAN NAT/G PLAN

B58
BUGEDA LANZAS J.,A STATEMENT OF THE LAWS OF CUBA IN MATTERS AFFECTING BUSINESS (2ND ED. REV., ENLARGED). CUBA L/A+17C LAW FINAN FAM LEGIS ACT/RES ADMIN GP/REL...BIBLIOG 20 OAS. PAGE 20 F0382
JURID NAT/G INDUS WORKER

B58
CLAIRMONTE F.,LE LIBERALISME ECONOMIQUE ET LES PAYS SOUS-DEVELOPPES: ETUDES SUR L'EVOLUTION D'UNE IDEE. ASIA INDIA UK FINAN INDUS PLAN CAP/ISM ECO/TAC COLONIAL NEW/LIB...BIBLIOG 20 THIRD/WRLD. PAGE 24 F0475
LAISSEZ ECO/UNDEV

B58
COLE G.D.H.,COMMUNISM AND SOCIAL DEMOCRACY (VOL. IV OF "HISTORY OF SOCIAL THOUGHT"). COM GERMANY ITALY UK AGRI INT/ORG WORKER DIPLOM COLONIAL NAT/LISM ALL/IDEOS...BIBLIOG 20 LEAGUE/NAT AUST/HUNG. PAGE 26 F0502
MARXISM REV POL/PAR SOCISM

B58
DUBIN R.,WORKING UNION-MANAGEMENT RELATIONS. LAW PLAN ECO/TAC CHOOSE REPRESENT INGP/REL PWR...POLICY SOC BIBLIOG. PAGE 34 F0669
LABOR MGT AUTHORIT GP/REL

B58
HANCE W.A.,AFRICAN ECONOMIC DEVELOPMENT. AGRI DIST/IND INDUS R+D ACT/RES PLAN CAP/ISM FOR/AID ...GOV/COMP BIBLIOG 20. PAGE 54 F1058
AFR ECO/UNDEV PROB/SOLV TEC/DEV

B58
MCIVOR R.C.,CANADIAN MONETARY, BANKING, AND FISCAL DEVELOPMENT. CANADA INDUS LG/CO NAT/G SML/CO CONTROL WAR...GEN/LAWS BIBLIOG 17/20. PAGE 88 F1729
ECO/TAC FINAN ECO/DEV WEALTH

B58
PALYI M.,MANAGED MONEY AT THE CROSSROADS: THE EUROPEAN EXPERIENCE. AFR WOR+45 WOR-45 TEC/DEV DIPLOM INT/TRADE DEMAND WEALTH...CHARTS BIBLIOG 19/20 EUROPE SILVER. PAGE 103 F2022
FINAN ECO/TAC ECO/DEV PRODUC

B58
PAN AMERICAN UNION,REPERTORIO DE PUBLICACIONES PERIODICAS ACTUALES LATINO-AMERICANAS. CULTURE ECO/UNDEV ADMIN LEAD GOV/REL 20 OAS. PAGE 103 F2023
BIBLIOG L/A+17C NAT/G DIPLOM

B58
SHAW S.J.,THE FINANCIAL AND ADMINISTRATIVE ORGANIZATION AND DEVELOPMENT OF OTTOMAN EGYPT 1517-1798. UAR LOC/G FORCES BUDGET INT/TRADE TAX EATING INCOME WEALTH...CHARTS BIBLIOG 16/18 OTTOMAN NAPOLEON/B. PAGE 120 F2371
FINAN ADMIN GOV/REL CULTURE

B58
TANNENBAUM A.S.,PARTICIPATION IN UNION LOCALS. SOCIETY FINAN CONTROL LEAD GP/REL...BIBLIOG 20. PAGE 128 F2531
LABOR MGT PARTIC INGP/REL

B58
UNIVERSITY OF LONDON,THE FAR EAST AND SOUTH-EAST ASIA: A CUMULATED LIST OF PERIODICAL ARTICLES, MAY 1956-APRIL 1957. ASIA S/ASIA LAW ADMIN...LING 20. PAGE 133 F2621
BIBLIOG SOC

S58
THOMAS D.S.,"AGE AND ECONOMIC DIFFERENTIALS IN INTERSTATE MIGRATION." SEX...GEOG SAMP/SIZ TREND CON/ANAL CHARTS BIBLIOG. PAGE 130 F2560
AGE WEALTH HABITAT CENSUS

B59
BLACK J.D.,ECONOMICS FOR AGRICULTURE. USA+45 EXTR/IND FAM WORKER ACT/RES PLAN PRICE EATING INCOME...CENSUS BIBLIOG 20. PAGE 15 F0291
AGRI ECO/TAC MARKET POLICY

B59
CHECCHI V.,HONDURAS: A PROBLEM IN ECONOMIC DEVELOPMENT. HONDURAS AGRI FINAN INDUS LABOR WORKER INT/TRADE EDU/PROP PRICE HEALTH...GEOG CHARTS BIBLIOG 20. PAGE 24 F0458
ECO/UNDEV ECO/TAC PROB/SOLV PLAN

B59
CUCCORESE H.J.,HISTORIA DE LA CONVERSION DEL PAPEL MONEDA EN BUENOS AIRES, 1861-1867. AFR LAW LOC/G NAT/G ATTIT...POLICY BIBLIOG 19 ARGEN BUENOS/AIR. PAGE 29 F0560
FINAN PLAN LEGIS

B59
HAX K.,DIE HOCHSCHULLEHRER DER WIRTSCHAFTSWISSENSCHAFTEN IN DER BUNDESREPUBLIK DEUTSCHLAND EINSCHL. WESTBERLIN, OSTERREICH. AUSTRIA GERMANY/W SWITZERLND FINAN MARKET PROF/ORG BUDGET ECO/TAC INT/TRADE PRICE COST 20. PAGE 57 F1119
BIBLIOG ACADEM INTELL

B59
LEWIS J.P.,BUSINESS CONDITIONS ANALYSIS. USA+45 MARKET LABOR BUDGET TAX AUTOMAT WAR DEMAND PRODUC ...ECOMETRIC CHARTS BIBLIOG 19/20. PAGE 79 F1549
FINAN PRICE TREND

B59
LINK R.G.,ENGLISH THEORIES OF ECONOMIC FLUCTUATIONS: 1815-1848. FRANCE UK AGRI WORKER DIPLOM PRICE TASK WAR DEMAND PRODUC...POLICY BIBLIOG 18 MALTHUS MILL/JS WILSON/J. PAGE 80 F1574
IDEA/COMP ECO/DEV WEALTH EQUILIB

B59
MARTIN D.D.,MERGERS AND THE CLAYTON ACT. FINAN LEGIS GP/REL...DECISION METH/COMP BIBLIOG 20. PAGE 86 F1681
OWN ECO/TAC LG/CO POLICY

B59
STOVEL J.A.,CANADA IN THE WORLD ECONOMY. CANADA PRICE DEMAND...STAT CHARTS BIBLIOG 20 VINER/J. PAGE 127 F2499
INT/TRADE BAL/PAY FINAN ECO/TAC

C59
FAINSOD M.,"GOVERNMENT AND THE AMERICAN ECONOMY." USA+45 USA-45 INDUS LABOR OP/RES PROB/SOLV ECO/TAC CONTROL...CHARTS BIBLIOG T 20. PAGE 39 F0760
CONSTN ECO/DEV CAP/ISM NAT/G

C59
KURIHARA K.K.,"THE KEYNESIAN THEORY OF ECONOMIC DEVELOPMENT." WOR+45 WOR-45 PLAN OPTIMAL PRODUC ...CONCPT BIBLIOG 20. PAGE 74 F1451
ECO/DEV ECO/UNDEV OP/RES TEC/DEV

C59
MINTZ S.W.,"INTERNAL MARKET SYS AS MECHANISMS OF SOCIAL ARTIC," IN V.F. RAY, INTERMED SOCIETIES, SOCIAL MOBILITY, AND COMMUNIC (BMR). UNIV STRATA GP/REL INGP/REL...GEOG SOC BIBLIOG. PAGE 92 F1804
MARKET SOCIETY ECO/UNDEV STRUCT

B60
ANGERS F.A.,ESSAI SUR LA CENTRALISATION: ANALYSE DES PRINCIPES ET PERSPECTIVES CANADIENNES. CANADA ECO/TAC CONTROL...SOC IDEA/COMP BIBLIOG 20. PAGE 6 F0105
CENTRAL ADMIN

B60
AUSTRUY J.,STRUCTURE ECONOMIQUE ET CIVILISATION: L'EGYPTE ET LE DESTIN ECONOMIQUE DE L'ISLAM. ISLAM UAR CREATE OP/RES ECO/TAC...SOC BIBLIOG 20 MUSLIM. PAGE 8 F0142
ECO/UNDEV CULTURE STRUCT

B60
HALL C.A. JR.,FISCAL POLICY FOR STABLE GROWTH. USA+45 FINAN TEC/DEV TAX COST DEMAND INCOME ...BIBLIOG 20. PAGE 53 F1045
ECO/TAC BUDGET NAT/G POLICY

B60
HEYSE T.,PROBLEMS FONCIERS ET REGIME DES TERRES (ASPECTS ECONOMIQUES, JURIDIQUES ET SOCIAUX). AFR CONGO/BRAZ INT/ORG DIPLOM SOVEREIGN...GEOG TREATY 20. PAGE 59 F1161
BIBLIOG AGRI ECO/UNDEV LEGIS

B60
MC CLELLAN G.S.,INDIA. AFR CHINA/COM INDIA CONSTN
DIPLOM

ELITES STRATA AGRI POL/PAR FOR/AID ARMS/CONT REV MARXISM...CENSUS BIBLIOG 20 GANDHI/M NEHRU/J. PAGE 87 F1712
NAT/G SOCIETY ECO/UNDEV

B60
MORRIS W.T.,ENGINEERING ECONOMY. AUTOMAT RISK RATIONAL...PROBABIL STAT CHARTS GAME SIMUL BIBLIOG T 20. PAGE 94 F1838
OP/RES DECISION MGT PROB/SOLV

B60
RAY D.D.,ACCOUNTING AND BUSINESS FLUCTUATIONS. LG/CO SML/CO FEEDBACK DEMAND...CHARTS IDEA/COMP BIBLIOG 20. PAGE 109 F2154
FINAN AFR CONTROL

B60
SLOTKIN J.S.,FROM FIELD TO FACTORY; NEW INDUSTRIAL EMPLOYEES. HABITAT...MGT NEW/IDEA NAT/COMP BIBLIOG SOC/INTEG 20. PAGE 123 F2423
INDUS LABOR CULTURE WORKER

B60
SMET G.,BIBLIOGRAPHIE DE LA CONTRIBUTION A L'ETUDE DE LA PROGRESSION ECONOMIQUE DE L'AFRIQUE. AFR DIST/IND EXTR/IND TEC/DEV 20. PAGE 123 F2427
BIBLIOG ECO/UNDEV INDUS AGRI

S60
SPINRAD W.,"CORRELATES OF TRADE UNION PARTICIPATION: A SUMMARY OF LITERATURE." ACT/RES PERS/REL HAPPINESS HABITAT...BIBLIOG WORK. PAGE 125 F2456
LABOR PARTIC CORREL ROLE

N60
ERDMAN P.E.,COMMON MARKETS AND FREE TRADE AREAS (PAMPHLET). USA+45 MARKET INT/ORG TEC/DEV DIPLOM UTIL...CON/ANAL CHARTS BIBLIOG 20 EEC OEEC. PAGE 38 F0743
TREND PROB/SOLV INT/TRADE ECO/DEV

B61
AGARWAL R.C.,STATE ENTERPRISE IN INDIA. FUT INDIA UK FINAN INDUS ADMIN CONTROL OWN...POLICY CHARTS BIBLIOG 20 RAILROAD. PAGE 3 F0048
ECO/UNDEV SOCISM GOV/REL LG/CO

B61
BARBASH J.,LABOR'S GRASS ROOTS. CONSTN NAT/G EX/STRUC LEGIS WORKER LEAD...MAJORIT BIBLIOG. PAGE 10 F0184
LABOR INGP/REL GP/REL LAW

B61
CARNEY D.E.,GOVERNMENT AND ECONOMY IN BRITISH WEST AFRICA. GAMBIA GHANA NIGERIA SIER/LEONE DOMIN ADMIN GOV/REL SOVEREIGN WEALTH LAISSEZ...BIBLIOG 20 CMN/WLTH. PAGE 21 F0417
METH/COMP COLONIAL ECO/TAC ECO/UNDEV

B61
DE GRAZIA A.,AMERICAN WELFARE. CLIENT FINAN LABOR LOC/G NAT/G NEIGH EDU/PROP GP/REL...CLASSIF CON/ANAL CHARTS BIBLIOG. PAGE 31 F0598
GIVE WEALTH SECT VOL/ASSN

B61
DIMOCK M.E.,BUSINESS AND GOVERNMENT (4TH ED.). AGRI FINAN OP/RES PLAN BUDGET DIPLOM LOBBY NUC/PWR NEW/LIB SOCISM...POLICY BIBLIOG 20. PAGE 33 F0641
NAT/G INDUS LABOR ECO/TAC

B61
DOIG J.W.,THE POLITICS OF METROPOLITAN TRANSPORTATION. DELIB/GP WORKER DIPLOM TASK EFFICIENCY UTIL...CHARTS BIBLIOG MUNICH 20 NEW/YORK NEW/JERSEY PUB/TRANS RAILROAD. PAGE 34 F0652
PROB/SOLV STRATA DIST/IND

B61
GURTOO D.H.N.,INDIA'S BALANCE OF PAYMENTS (1920-1960). INDIA FINAN DIPLOM FOR/AID INT/TRADE PRICE COLONIAL...CHARTS BIBLIOG 20. PAGE 52 F1014
BAL/PAY STAT ECO/TAC ECO/UNDEV

B61
HOLMANS A.E.,UNITED STATES FISCAL POLICY 1945-1959. AFR USA+45 USA-45 ECO/DEV TAX PRICE WAR...BIBLIOG 20 DEMOCRAT REPUBLICAN. PAGE 61 F1200
POLICY BUDGET NAT/G ECO/TAC

B61
HUBBARD P.J.,ORIGINS OF THE TVA: THE MUSCLE SHOALS CONTROVERSY, 1920-1932. USA-45 DELIB/GP LEGIS LEAD LOBBY GOV/REL GP/REL INGP/REL OWN PERSON...BIBLIOG 20 TVA CONGRESS WATER. PAGE 62 F1229
SEA CONTROL NAT/G INDUS

B61
INTL UNION LOCAL AUTHORITIES,METROPOLIS. WOR+45 DIST/IND FINAN GIVE EDU/PROP CRIME COST HEALTH WEALTH MUNICH 20. PAGE 65 F1286
GOV/COMP LOC/G BIBLIOG

B61
LANDSKROY W.A.,OFFICIAL SERIAL PUBLICATIONS RELATING TO ECONOMIC DEVELOPMENT IN AFRICA SOUTH OF THE SAHARA (PAMPHLET). AFR UK R+D ACT/RES 20 UN. PAGE 75 F1471
BIBLIOG ECO/UNDEV COLONIAL INT/ORG

B61
MCCRACKEN H.L.,KEYNESIAN ECONOMICS IN THE STREAM OF ECONOMIC THOUGHT. FINAN MARKET BARGAIN EFFICIENCY OPTIMAL...PHIL/SCI CONCPT IDEA/COMP BIBLIOG 18/20 KEYNES/JM. PAGE 88 F1724
ECO/TAC DEMAND ECOMETRIC

B61
MIT CENTER INTERNATIONAL STU,OFFICIAL SERIAL PUBLICATIONS RELATING TO ECONOMIC DEVELOPMENT IN AFRICA SOUTH OF THE SAHARA. AFR SOCIETY AGRI FINAN INDUS LG/CO ADMIN 20. PAGE 92 F1806
BIBLIOG ECO/UNDEV ECO/TAC NAT/G

B61
MOORE G.H.,BUSINESS CYCLE INDICATORS (TWO VOLS.). LABOR DIPLOM PRICE RISK TASK WAR PRODUC...CHARTS BIBLIOG 20. PAGE 93 F1822
MARKET FINAN WEALTH

B61
NOVE A.,THE SOVIET ECONOMY. USSR ECO/DEV FINAN NAT/G ECO/TAC PRICE ADMIN EFFICIENCY MARXISM ...TREND BIBLIOG 20. PAGE 99 F1943
PLAN PRODUC POLICY

B61
PAUNIO J.J.,A STUDY IN THE THEORY OF OPEN INFLATION. AFR FINAN CAP/ISM PRICE DEMAND INCOME ...CHARTS BIBLIOG 20. PAGE 104 F2040
ACT/RES ECO/DEV ECO/TAC COST

B61
SACKS S.,FINANCING GOVERNMENT IN A METROPOLITAN GOVERNMENT. USA+45 ECO/DEV R+D LOC/G GOV/REL ...BIBLIOG MUNICH 20 CLEVELAND. PAGE 115 F2269
FINAN PLAN BUDGET

B61
SCHNAPPER B.,LA POLITIQUE ET LE COMMERCE FRANCAIS DANS LE GOLFE DE GUINEE DE 1838 A 1871. FRANCE GUINEA UK SEA EXTR/IND NAT/G DELIB/GP LEGIS ADMIN ORD/FREE...POLICY GEOG CENSUS CHARTS BIBLIOG 19. PAGE 117 F2303
COLONIAL INT/TRADE DOMIN AFR

B61
SEPULVEDA C.,A STATEMENT OF THE LAWS OF MEXICO IN MATTERS AFFECTING BUSINESS (3RD ED.). AGRI DIST/IND EXTR/IND FINAN INDUS WORKER TAX MARRIAGE OWN ORD/FREE...BIBLIOG 20 MEXIC/AMER TREATY MIGRATION MONOPOLY. PAGE 119 F2356
CONSTN NAT/G JURID LEGIS

B61
STANLEY C.J.,LATE CH'ING FINANCE: HU KUANG-YUNG AS AN INNOVATOR. ASIA NAT/G FORCES BUDGET TAX WAR GOV/REL COST...POLICY BIOG CHARTS BIBLIOG 19. PAGE 125 F2469
FINAN ECO/TAC CIVMIL/REL ADMIN

B61
STARK H.,SOCIAL AND ECONOMIC FRONTIERS IN LATIN AMERICA (2ND ED.). CUBA FUT CULTURE AGRI INDUS ECO/TAC PRODUC ATTIT MARXISM...NAT/COMP BIBLIOG T 20. PAGE 125 F2470
L/A+17C SOCIETY DIPLOM ECO/UNDEV

B61
STROUD G.S.,LABOR HISTORY IN THE UNITED STATES: A GENERAL BIBLIOGRAPHY. USA+45 USA-45 STRATA VOL/ASSN AUTOMAT GP/REL INGP/REL ATTIT HEALTH 18/20. PAGE 127 F2504
BIBLIOG WORKER LABOR

L61
CHENERY H.B.,"COMPARATIVE ADVANTAGE AND DEVELOPMENT POLICY." FINAN INT/TRADE RATION OPTIMAL...CHARTS METH/COMP GEN/LAWS BIBLIOG 20 RESOURCE/N. PAGE 24 F0463
ECO/UNDEV ECO/TAC PLAN EFFICIENCY

L61
JOHNSTON B.F.,"THE ROLE OF AGRICULTURE IN ECONOMIC DEVELOPMENT." FINAN PRODUC ROLE BIBLIOG. PAGE 68 F1332
AGRI ECO/UNDEV PLAN INDUS

S61
DALTON G.,"ECONOMIC THEORY AND PRIMITIVE SOCIETY" (BMR)" UNIV AGRI KIN TEC/DEV ECO/TAC REGION HABITAT SKILL...METH/COMP BIBLIOG. PAGE 30 F0574
ECO/UNDEV METH PHIL/SCI SOC

C61
FILLOL T.R.,"SOCIAL FACTORS IN ECONOMIC DEVELOPMENT: THE ARGENTINE CASE" INDUS LABOR CREATE TEC/DEV PERS/REL EFFICIENCY PRODUC DRIVE ...METH/CNCPT METH/COMP 20 ARGEN. PAGE 41 F0794
BIBLIOG ECO/UNDEV MGT TREND

B62
FATOUROS A.A.,GOVERNMENT GUARANTEES TO FOREIGN INVESTORS. WOR+45 ECO/UNDEV INDUS WORKER ADJUD ...NAT/COMP BIBLIOG TREATY. PAGE 39 F0767
NAT/G FINAN INT/TRADE ECO/DEV

B62
GREEN L.P.,DEVELOPMENT IN AFRICA. AFR CENTRL/AFR GHANA RHODESIA SOUTH/AFR AGRI PROC/MFG INT/TRADE DEMAND NAT/LISM PRODUC WEALTH...GEOG METH/CNCPT CHARTS BIBLIOG 20. PAGE 50 F0987
CULTURE ECO/UNDEV GOV/REL TREND

B62
GROVE J.W.,GOVERNMENT AND INDUSTRY IN BRITAIN. UK FINAN LOC/G CONSULT DELIB/GP INT/TRADE ADMIN CONTROL...BIBLIOG 20. PAGE 52 F1008
ECO/TAC INDUS NAT/G GP/REL

B62
HENDERSON W.O.,THE GENESIS OF THE COMMON MARKET. EUR+WWI FRANCE MOD/EUR UK SEA COM/IND EXTR/IND COLONIAL DISCRIM...TIME/SEQ CHARTS BIBLIOG 18/20 EEC TREATY. PAGE 58 F1149
ECO/DEV INT/TRADE DIPLOM

B62
JORDAN A.A. JR.,FOREIGN AID AND THE DEFENSE OF SOUTHEAST ASIA. PAKISTAN VIETNAM/S FINAN PLAN BUDGET ECO/TAC DETER WAR ORD/FREE...POLICY DECISION CENSUS CHARTS BIBLIOG 20. PAGE 68 F1341
FOR/AID S/ASIA FORCES ECO/UNDEV

B62
KOLKO G.,WEALTH AND POWER IN AMERICA. USA+45 SOCIETY STRATA LG/CO ECO/TAC TAX PWR...SOC BIBLIOG 20 DEPRESSION. PAGE 72 F1420
STRUCT INCOME ECO/DEV WEALTH

B62
LEVENSTEIN A.,WHY PEOPLE WORK; CHANGING INCENTIVES
DRIVE

IN A TROUBLED WORLD. USA+45 SOCIETY PROB/SOLV TEC/DEV EDU/PROP ADJUST...CENSUS BIBLIOG 20. PAGE 79 F1538 — WORKER ECO/DEV ANOMIE

B62
PHELPS E.S.,THE GOAL OF ECONOMIC GROWTH: SOURCES, COSTS, BENEFITS. USA+45 USSR FINAN TAX CONTROL DEMAND WEALTH...POLICY NAT/COMP ANTHOL BIBLIOG 20. PAGE 106 F2079 — ECO/TAC ECO/DEV NAT/G FUT

B62
SCHNEIDER E.,MONEY, INCOME AND EMPLOYMENT. TAX PAY DEMAND...CHARTS BIBLIOG 20. PAGE 117 F2305 — ECO/DEV FINAN INCOME

B62
SIRUGO F.,L'ECONOMIA DEGLI STAT' ITALIANI PRIMA DELL' UNIFICAZIONE (10 VOLS.). ITALY...TIME/SEQ 18/19. PAGE 122 F2417 — BIBLIOG PROVS NAT/G

B62
UNECA LIBRARY,BOOKS ON AFRICA IN THE UNECA LIBRARY. WOR+45 AGRI INT/ORG NAT/G PLAN WRITING REGION...SOC STAT UN. PAGE 132 F2605 — BIBLIOG AFR ECO/UNDEV TEC/DEV

B62
UNECA LIBRARY,NEW ACQUISITIONS IN THE UNECA LIBRARY. LAW NAT/G PLAN PROB/SOLV TEC/DEV ADMIN REGION...GEOG SOC 20 UN. PAGE 132 F2606 — BIBLIOG AFR ECO/UNDEV INT/ORG

B62
US LIBRARY OF CONGRESS,A LIST OF AMERICAN DOCTORAL DISSERTATIONS ON AFRICA. SOCIETY SECT DIPLOM EDU/PROP ADMIN...GEOG 19/20. PAGE 138 F2717 — BIBLIOG AFR ACADEM CULTURE

B62
VACCARO J.R.,A STATEMENT OF THE LAWS OF CHILE IN MATTERS AFFECTING BUSINESS (3RD ED.). CHILE AGRI FINAN FAM LABOR ECO/TAC FOR/AID TAX ADJUD CONTROL MARRIAGE STRANGE...BIBLIOG 20. PAGE 140 F2756 — CONSTN LAW INDUS MGT

C62
GREEN L.P.,"DEVELOPMENT IN AFRICA." RHODESIA SOUTH/AFR UGANDA MARKET PROC/MFG PRODUC WEALTH ...GEOG 20. PAGE 50 F0986 — BIBLIOG ECO/UNDEV AFR AGRI

C62
JOINT ECONOMIC COMMITTEE,"DIMENSIONS OF SOVIET ECONOMIC POWER." USSR R+D FORCES ACT/RES OP/RES TEC/DEV...GEOG STAT BIBLIOG 20. PAGE 68 F1337 — ECO/DEV PLAN PRODUC LABOR

B63
ALPERT P.,ECONOMIC DEVELOPMENT. WOR+45 FINAN TEC/DEV ECO/TAC PRICE GOV/REL HABITAT...GEOG BIBLIOG T 20 THIRD/WRLD. PAGE 4 F0079 — ECO/DEV ECO/UNDEV INT/TRADE FOR/AID

B63
BARBOUR V.,CAPITALISM IN AMSTERDAM IN THE 17TH CENTURY. NETHERLAND FINAN ECO/TAC...METH/COMP BIBLIOG MUNICH 16. PAGE 10 F0185 — CAP/ISM INT/TRADE MARKET WEALTH

B63
BATES J.L.,THE ORIGINS OF TEAPOT DOME: PROGRESSIVES, PARTIES, AND PETROLEUM, 1909-1921. USA-45 INDUS LG/CO POL/PAR DELIB/GP CONTROL GOV/REL CONSERVE...BIBLIOG 20 NAVY. PAGE 11 F0209 — EXTR/IND CRIME NAT/G

B63
BONINI C.P.,SIMULATION OF INFORMATION AND DECISION SYSTEMS IN THE FIRM. MARKET BUDGET DOMIN EDU/PROP ADMIN COST ATTIT HABITAT PERCEPT PWR...CONCPT PROBABIL QUANT PREDICT HYPO/EXP BIBLIOG. PAGE 16 F0313 — INDUS SIMUL DECISION MGT

B63
CHAMPION J.M.,CRITICAL INCIDENTS IN MANAGEMENT. MARKET LG/CO SML/CO OP/RES ADMIN CONTROL LEAD GP/REL PERS/REL COST ATTIT SUPEGO ALL/VALS...PSY PERS/TEST BIBLIOG. PAGE 23 F0445 — MGT DECISION EX/STRUC INDUS

B63
CHATTERJEE I.K.,ECONOMIC DEVELOPMENT PAYMENTS DEFICIT AND PAYMENT RESTRICTION. INDIA WOR+45 FINAN INT/TRADE CONTROL BAL/PAY WEALTH...POLICY CONCPT STAT CHARTS IDEA/COMP BIBLIOG 20. PAGE 23 F0456 — ECO/DEV ECO/TAC PAY GOV/REL

B63
CHEN N.-.R.,THE ECONOMY OF MAINLAND CHINA, 1949-1963: A BIBLIOGRAPHY OF MATERIALS IN ENGLISH. CHINA/COM ECO/UNDEV PRESS 20. PAGE 24 F0461 — BIBLIOG MARXISM NAT/G ASIA

B63
CHOJNACKI S.,REGISTER ON CURRENT RESEARCH ON ETHIOPIA AND THE HORN OF AFRICA. ETHIOPIA LAW CULTURE AGRI SECT EDU/PROP ADMIN...GEOG HEAL LING 20. PAGE 24 F0470 — BIBLIOG ACT/RES INTELL ACADEM

B63
CLARK J.J.,BUSINESS FLUCTUATIONS, GROWTH, AND ECONOMIC STABILIZATION. USA+45 FINAN INT/TRADE OPTIMAL...METH/CNCPT ANTHOL BIBLIOG 20. PAGE 25 F0479 — CAP/ISM ECO/TAC EQUILIB POLICY

B63
COSSA L.,SAGGI BIBLIOGRAFICI DI ECONOMIA POLITICA. MOD/EUR LABOR PRICE COST INCOME 18/19. PAGE 28 F0539 — BIBLIOG FINAN WEALTH

B63
ENKE S.,ECONOMICS FOR DEVELOPMENT. AGRI TEC/DEV CAP/ISM DIPLOM ECO/TAC TAX ATTIT DRIVE HABITAT WEALTH...GOV/COMP BIBLIOG 20. PAGE 38 F0737 — ECO/UNDEV PHIL/SCI CON/ANAL

B63
FRIEDRICH C.J.,MAN AND HIS GOVERNMENT: AN EMPIRICAL THEORY OF POLITICS. UNIV LOC/G NAT/G ADJUD REV INGP/REL DISCRIM PWR BIBLIOG. PAGE 44 F0867 — PERSON ORD/FREE PARTIC CONTROL

B63
GANGULY D.S.,PUBLIC CORPORATIONS IN A NATIONAL ECONOMY. INDIA WOR+45 FINAN INDUS TOP/EX PRICE EFFICIENCY...MGT STAT CHARTS BIBLIOG 20. PAGE 46 F0897 — ECO/UNDEV LG/CO SOCISM GOV/REL

B63
GODWIN F.W.,THE HIDDEN FORCE. PUERT/RICO WOR+45 STRUCT VOL/ASSN PROB/SOLV DIPLOM CONFER...BIBLIOG 20 PEACE/CORP. PAGE 48 F0931 — ECO/UNDEV WORKER SKILL ECO/TAC

B63
GOLDMAN M.I.,SOVIET MARKETING. USSR DIST/IND FINAN RATION OWN WEALTH...SOC BIBLIOG 20. PAGE 48 F0937 — MARKET ECO/TAC CONTROL MARXISM

B63
GRIGSBY W.G.,HOUSING MARKETS AND PUBLIC POLICY. USA+45 FAM NEIGH PRICE DEMAND WEALTH...POLICY CHARTS BIBLIOG METH MUNICH 20. PAGE 51 F1002 — MARKET RENT HABITAT PLAN

B63
LAFEBER W.,THE NEW EMPIRE: AN INTERPRETATION OF AMERICAN EXPANSION, 1860-1898. USA-45 CONSTN NAT/LISM SOVEREIGN...TREND BIBLIOG 19/20. PAGE 74 F1457 — INDUS NAT/G DIPLOM CAP/ISM

B63
MACHLUP F.,ESSAYS ON ECONOMIC SEMANTICS. UNIV ECO/DEV FINAN COST DEMAND PRODUC...POLICY STAT CHARTS BIBLIOG. PAGE 83 F1632 — LING CONCPT METH

B63
RAFUSE R.W. JR.,STATE AND LOCAL FISCAL BEHAVIOR OVER THE POSTWAR CYCLES (DISSERTATION). USA+45 TAX PRICE ATTIT...POLICY TIME/SEQ TREND CHARTS BIBLIOG 20. PAGE 109 F2135 — BUDGET LOC/G ECO/TAC PROVS

B63
STIFEL L.D.,THE TEXTILE INDUSTRY - A CASE STUDY OF INDUSTRIAL DEVELOPMENT IN THE PHILIPPINES (PAPER). PHILIPPINE WORKER CAP/ISM INT/TRADE TARIFFS RECEIVE PRICE ADMIN COST EFFICIENCY WEALTH...BIBLIOG 20. PAGE 126 F2486 — S/ASIA ECO/UNDEV PROC/MFG NAT/G

B63
STUCKI C.W.,AMERICAN DOCTORAL DISSERTATIONS ON ASIA 1933-62 (A PAPER). PREHIST INDUS NAT/G GOV/REL ALL/IDEOS...ART/METH GEOG SOC LING 20. PAGE 127 F2506 — BIBLIOG ASIA SOCIETY S/ASIA

B63
WALINSKY L.J.,PLANNING AND EXECUTION OF ECONOMIC DEVELOPMENT. PROB/SOLV TEC/DEV BUDGET COST WEALTH ...CHARTS BIBLIOG 20. PAGE 142 F2802 — PLAN ECO/UNDEV ECO/TAC OPTIMAL

L63
MEYER J.R.,"REGIONAL ECONOMICS: A SURVEY." INTELL ACADEM CREATE...IDEA/COMP BIBLIOG. PAGE 90 F1770 — REGION ECO/TAC GEN/LAWS PROB/SOLV

N63
NORTH CAROLINA U INST GOVT,COSTING URBAN DEVELOPMENT AND REDEVELOPMENT (PAMPHLET). USA+45 USA-45 NEIGH PLAN TEC/DEV TAX OWN...GEOG MUNICH 20. PAGE 98 F1934 — BIBLIOG COST FINAN

B64
AHMAD M.,THE CIVIL SERVANT IN PAKISTAN. PAKISTAN ECO/UNDEV COLONIAL INGP/REL...SOC CHARTS BIBLIOG 20 CIVIL/SERV. PAGE 3 F0051 — WELF/ST ADMIN ATTIT STRATA

B64
ASH W.,MARXISM AND MORAL CONCEPTS. CAP/ISM GP/REL ORD/FREE...BIBLIOG 20. PAGE 7 F0128 — MARXISM CONCPT MORAL SOCIETY

B64
BALASSA B.,CHANGING PATTERNS IN FOREIGN TRADE AND PAYMENTS. AFR USA+45 USA-45 ECO/DEV NAT/G PLAN BAL/PWR...POLICY ANTHOL BIBLIOG 20. PAGE 8 F0159 — ECO/TAC INT/TRADE BAL/PAY WEALTH

B64
BRIGHT J.R.,RESEARCH, DEVELOPMENT AND TECHNOLOGICAL INNOVATION. CULTURE R+D CREATE PLAN PROB/SOLV AUTOMAT RISK PERSON...DECISION CONCPT PREDICT BIBLIOG. PAGE 18 F0352 — TEC/DEV NEW/IDEA INDUS MGT

B64
CLAIRBORN E.L.,FORECASTING THE BALANCE OF PAYMENTS: AN EVALUATION. AFR FUT UK USA+45 WOR+45 FINAN PLAN BUDGET PAY CONTROL...STAT CHARTS BIBLIOG 20. PAGE 24 F0474 — PREDICT BAL/PAY ECO/DEV ECO/TAC

B64
FLORENCE P.S.,ECONOMICS AND SOCIOLOGY OF INDUSTRY; — INDUS

A REALISTIC ANALYSIS OF DEVELOPMENT. ECO/UNDEV LG/CO NAT/G PLAN...GEOG MGT BIBLIOG 20. PAGE 42 F0814
SOC
ADMIN

B64
FREYMOND J.,WESTERN EUROPE SINCE THE WAR. COM EUR+WWI USA+45 DIPLOM...BIBLIOG 20 NATO UN EEC. PAGE 44 F0854
INT/ORG
POLICY
ECO/DEV
ECO/TAC

B64
FRIEDMANN J.,REGIONAL DEVELOPMENT AND PLANNING: A READER. AGRI MARKET NAT/G ECO/TAC INCOME...GEOG STAT CENSUS CHARTS ANTHOL BIBLIOG MUNICH 20 OPEN/SPACE. PAGE 44 F0863
PLAN
REGION
INDUS
ECO/DEV

B64
GUTMANN P.M.,ECONOMIC GROWTH: AN AMERICAN PROBLEM. USA+45 FINAN R+D...POLICY NAT/COMP ANTHOL BIBLIOG 20. PAGE 52 F1016
WEALTH
ECO/DEV
CAP/ISM
ORD/FREE

B64
HAMBRIDGE G.,DYNAMICS OF DEVELOPMENT. AGRI FINAN INDUS LABOR INT/TRADE EDU/PROP ADMIN LEAD OWN HEALTH...ANTHOL BIBLIOG 20. PAGE 54 F1054
ECO/UNDEV
ECO/TAC
OP/RES
ACT/RES

B64
LAFONT P.B.,BIBLIOGRAPHIE DU LAOS. LAOS S/ASIA EDU/PROP...GEOG 20. PAGE 74 F1458
BIBLIOG
LAW
SOC

B64
LANGHOFF P.,MODELS, MEASUREMENT AND MARKETING. ACT/RES COMPUTER OP/RES PLAN BUDGET...MGT PHIL/SCI METH/CNCPT STAT PROG/TEAC BIBLIOG. PAGE 75 F1478
DECISION
SIMUL
MARKET
R+D

B64
LETICHE J.M.,A HISTORY OF RUSSIAN ECONOMIC THOUGHT: NINTH THROUGH EIGHTEENTH CENTURIES. RUSSIA FINAN SECT CAP/ISM DOMIN DEMAND EFFICIENCY OWN MARXISM ...TECHNIC ANTHOL BIBLIOG 9/18. PAGE 78 F1536
ECO/TAC
TIME/SEQ
IDEA/COMP
ECO/UNDEV

B64
MARRIS R.,THE ECONOMIC THEORY OF "MANAGERIAL" CAPITALISM. USA+45 ECO/DEV LG/CO ECO/TAC DEMAND ...CHARTS BIBLIOG 20. PAGE 86 F1675
CAP/ISM
MGT
CONTROL
OP/RES

B64
MCNULTY J.E.,SOME ECONOMIC ASPECTS OF BUSINESS ORGANIZATION. ECO/DEV UTIL...MGT CHARTS BIBLIOG METH 20. PAGE 88 F1734
ADMIN
LG/CO
GEN/LAWS

B64
NEUFIELD M.F.,A REPRESENTATIVE BIBLIOGRAPHY OF AMERICAN LABOR HISTORY. USA+45 USA-45 20. PAGE 97 F1914
BIBLIOG
LABOR
WORKER
INDUS

B64
NEWCOMER H.A.,INTERNATIONAL AIDS TO OVERSEAS INVESTMENTS AND TRADE. ECO/UNDEV TARIFFS PROFIT ...BIBLIOG 20 GATT UN. PAGE 98 F1921
INT/TRADE
FINAN
DIPLOM
FOR/AID

B64
STEWART C.F.,A BIBLIOGRAPHY OF INTERNATIONAL BUSINESS. WOR+45 FINAN LG/CO NAT/G PLAN ECO/TAC TARIFFS...DECISION MGT GP/COMP NAT/COMP 20 EEC. PAGE 126 F2484
BIBLIOG
INT/ORG
OP/RES
INT/TRADE

B64
TELLADO A.,A STATEMENT OF THE LAWS OF THE DOMINICAN REPUBLIC IN MATTERS AFFECTING BUSINESS (3RD ED.). DOMIN/REP AGRI DIST/IND EXTR/IND FINAN FAM WORKER ECO/TAC TAX CT/SYS MARRIAGE OWN...BIBLIOG 20 MIGRATION. PAGE 129 F2542
CONSTN
LEGIS
NAT/G
INDUS

B64
WILLIAMSON O.E.,THE ECONOMICS OF DISCRETIONARY BEHAVIOR: MANAGERIAL OBJECTIVES IN A THEORY OF THE FIRM. MARKET BUDGET CAP/ISM PRODUC DRIVE PERSON ...STAT CHARTS BIBLIOG METH 20. PAGE 147 F2897
EFFICIENCY
MGT
ECO/TAC
CHOOSE

S64
FYFE J.,"LIST OF CURRENT ACQUISITIONS OF PERIODICALS AND NEWSPAPERS DEALING WITH THE SOVIET UNION AND EAST EUROPEAN COUNTRIES." USSR WRITING GP/REL INGP/REL MARXISM 20. PAGE 45 F0879
BIBLIOG
COM
EDU/PROP
PRESS

S64
STONE P.A.,"DECISION TECHNIQUES FOR TOWN DEVELOPMENT." PLAN COST PROFIT...DECISION MGT CON/ANAL CHARTS METH/COMP BIBLIOG MUNICH 20. PAGE 127 F2497
OP/RES
ADMIN
PROB/SOLV

C64
GOLDMAN M.I.,"COMPARATIVE ECONOMIC SYSTEMS: A READER." COM ECO/UNDEV NAT/G BUDGET CAP/ISM ADMIN TOTALISM MARXISM SOCISM...MGT ANTHOL BIBLIOG 19/20. PAGE 48 F0938
NAT/COMP
CONTROL
IDEA/COMP

C64
LANDAUER C.,"CONTEMPORARY ECONOMIC SYSTEMS." COM WOR+45 ECO/UNDEV PLAN GP/REL...BIBLIOG 20. PAGE 75 F1466
CAP/ISM
SOCISM
MARXISM
IDEA/COMP

C64
LOUFTY A.,"LA PLANIFICATION DE L'ECONOMIE." FRANCE USSR FINAN INDUS BUDGET INCOME PRODUC...BIBLIOG 20. PAGE 82 F1604
PLAN
ECO/UNDEV
ECO/DEV

C64
NORGREN P.H.,"TOWARD FAIR EMPLOYMENT." USA+45 LAW STRATA LABOR NAT/G FORCES ACT/RES ADMIN ATTIT ...POLICY BIBLIOG 20 NEGRO. PAGE 98 F1932
RACE/REL
DISCRIM
WORKER
MGT

N64
US BOARD GOVERNORS FEDL RESRV,SELECTED BIBLIOGRAPHY ON MONETARY POLICY AND MANAGEMENT OF THE PUBLIC DEBT 1947-1960 AND 1961-1963 SUPPLEMENT (PAMPH.). USA+45 PLAN...POLICY MGT OWE 20. PAGE 134 F2642
BIBLIOG
FINAN
NAT/G

B65
ALEXANDER R.J.,ORGANIZED LABOR IN LATIN AMERICA. L/A+17C INT/ORG LEGIS WORKER TEC/DEV BARGAIN INT/TRADE REV...NAT/COMP BIBLIOG 20. PAGE 3 F0059
LABOR
POL/PAR
ECO/UNDEV
POLICY

B65
AMERICAN ECONOMIC ASSOCIATION,INDEX OF ECONOMIC JOURNALS 1886-1965 (7 VOLS.). UK USA+45 USA-45 AGRI FINAN PLAN ECO/TAC INT/TRADE ADMIN...STAT CENSUS 19/20. PAGE 5 F0087
BIBLIOG
WRITING
INDUS

B65
BARRERE A.,ECONOMIE ET INSTITUTIONS FINANCIERES (VOL. I). AFR FRANCE PLAN...BIBLIOG T 20. PAGE 10 F0194
ECO/DEV
BUDGET
NAT/G
FINAN

B65
BEYER G.H.,HOUSING AND SOCIETY. USA+45 ECO/DEV FAM NAT/G PLAN RENT...CHARTS BIBLIOG MUNICH 20. PAGE 14 F0275
HABITAT
AGE/O
CONSTRUC

B65
BLAIR T.L.V.,AFRICA: A MARKET PROFILE. AFR COM/IND DIST/IND FINAN UTIL...DECISION CHARTS BIBLIOG 20. PAGE 15 F0295
MARKET
OP/RES
ECO/UNDEV
INDUS

B65
CHAO K.,THE RATE AND PATTERN OF INDUSTRIAL GROWTH IN COMMUNIST CHINA. CHINA/COM ECO/UNDEV TEC/DEV PRICE...NAT/COMP BIBLIOG 20. PAGE 23 F0452
INDUS
INDEX
STAT
PRODUC

B65
COLLINS H.,KARL MARX AND THE BRITISH LABOUR MOVEMENT; YEARS OF THE FIRST INTERNATIONAL. FRANCE SWITZERLND UK CAP/ISM WAR...MARXIST IDEA/COMP BIBLIOG 19. PAGE 26 F0506
MARXISM
LABOR
INT/ORG
REV

B65
FERMAN L.A.,POVERTY IN AMERICA: A BOOK OF READINGS. USA+45 CULTURE ECO/DEV PROB/SOLV ALL/VALS...POLICY ANTHOL BIBLIOG 20 POVRTY/WAR. PAGE 40 F0785
WEALTH
TEC/DEV
CONCPT
RECEIVE

B65
GRAMPP W.D.,ECONOMIC LIBERALISM; THE BEGINNINGS (VOL. I). USA-45 WOR-45 MARKET LABOR ATTIT WEALTH ...POLICY CONCPT BIBLIOG GREECE/ANC MERCANTLST REPUBLICAN FEDERALIST. PAGE 50 F0974
ECO/DEV
CAP/ISM
IDEA/COMP
ECO/TAC

B65
GRAMPP W.D.,ECONOMIC LIBERALISM; THE CLASSICAL VIEW (VOL. II). MOD/EUR SOCIETY MARKET INT/TRADE NAT/LISM WEALTH LAISSEZ...POLICY PSY CONCPT BIBLIOG 19 SMITH/ADAM HUME/D MILL/JS. PAGE 50 F0975
ECO/DEV
CAP/ISM
IDEA/COMP
ECO/TAC

B65
HOLLER J.E.,POPULATION TRENDS AND ECONOMIC DEVELOPMENT IN THE FAR EAST (PAMPHLET). KOREA S/ASIA AGRI INDUS DELIB/GP PROB/SOLV RATIONAL ...POLICY CHARTS BIBLIOG 20 OUTER/MONG CHINJAP HONG/KONG. PAGE 61 F1197
CENSUS
TREND
ECO/UNDEV
ASIA

B65
JOHNSTONE A.,UNITED STATES DIRECT INVESTMENT IN FRANCE: AN INVESTIGATION OF THE FRENCH CHARGES. FRANCE USA+45 ECO/DEV INDUS LG/CO NAT/G ECO/TAC CONTROL WEALTH...BIBLIOG 20 INTERVENT. PAGE 68 F1335
FINAN
DIPLOM
POLICY
SOVEREIGN

B65
MACAVOY P.W.,THE ECONOMIC EFFECTS OF REGULATION: THE TRUNK-LINE RAILROAD CARTELS AND THE INTERSTATE COMMERCE COMMISSION BEFORE 1900. USA-45 PRICE PROFIT...STAT CHARTS BIBLIOG 19 RAILROAD. PAGE 83 F1620
ECO/TAC
DIST/IND
PROF/ORG
RATION

B65
MACDONALD R.W.,THE LEAGUE OF ARAB STATES: A STUDY IN THE DYNAMICS OF REGIONAL ORGANIZATION. ISRAEL UAR USSR FINAN INT/ORG DELIB/GP ECO/TAC AGREE NEUTRAL ORD/FREE PWR...DECISION BIBLIOG 20 TREATY UN. PAGE 83 F1626
ISLAM
REGION
DIPLOM
ADMIN

B65
MARCUS E.,INTERNATIONAL TRADE AND FINANCE. EFFICIENCY EQUILIB...CHARTS METH/COMP BIBLIOG METH T 20. PAGE 85 F1664
INT/TRADE
FINAN
MARKET
WEALTH

B65
NATIONAL CENTRAL LIBRARY,LATIN AMERICAN ECONOMIC AND SOCIAL SERIALS. UK SOCIETY NAT/G PLAN PROB/SOLV ...SOC 20. PAGE 97 F1897
BIBLIOG
INT/TRADE
ECO/UNDEV
L/A+17C

B65
OECD,TECHNIQUES OF ECONOMIC FORECASTING. CANADA FRANCE NETHERLAND SWEDEN UK USA+45 PROB/SOLV
PREDICT
METH/COMP

ROUTINE...CONCPT MATH CHARTS BIBLIOG METH 20. PAGE 100 F1974 PLAN

B65
ONUOHA B.,THE ELEMENTS OF AFRICAN SOCIALISM. AFR FINAN SECT TEC/DEV FOR/AID GP/REL OWN LAISSEZ MARXISM...CONCPT BIBLIOG 20. PAGE 101 F1992
SOCISM ECO/UNDEV NAT/G EX/STRUC

B65
PEARL A.,NEW CAREERS FOR THE POOR: THE NON-PROFESSIONAL IN HUMAN SERVICE. USA+45 SERV/IND NAT/G NEIGH WORKER EDU/PROP AUTOMAT SKILL...WELF/ST NEW/IDEA BIBLIOG SOC/INTEG 20. PAGE 104 F2044
SOC/WK WEALTH STRATA POLICY

B65
REDFORD E.S.,AMERICAN GOVERNMENT AND THE ECONOMY. FUT USA+45 USA-45 INDUS PROB/SOLV GOV/REL...POLICY DECISION METH/COMP BIBLIOG T 18/20. PAGE 110 F2168
CONSTN NAT/G

B65
SCHULER E.A.,THE PAKISTAN ACADEMIES FOR RURAL DEVELOPMENT COMILLA AND PESHAWAR 1959-1964. PAKISTAN S/ASIA SOCIETY STRUCT AGRI NAT/G TEC/DEV EDU/PROP 20. PAGE 117 F2314
BIBLIOG PLAN ECO/TAC ECO/UNDEV

B65
SCOTT A.M.,THE REVOLUTION IN STATECRAFT: INFORMAL PENETRATION. WOR+45 WOR-45 CULTURE INT/ORG FORCES ECO/TAC ROUTINE...BIBLIOG 20. PAGE 118 F2331
DIPLOM EDU/PROP FOR/AID

B65
SHEPHERD W.G.,ECONOMIC PERFORMANCE UNDER PUBLIC OWNERSHIP: BRITISH FUEL AND POWER. UK BUDGET GP/REL ...METH/CNCPT CHARTS BIBLIOG 20. PAGE 120 F2375
PROC/MFG NAT/G OWN FINAN

B65
SHOSTAK A.B.,NEW PERSPECTIVES ON POVERTY. USA+45 SCHOOL WORKER INGP/REL RACE/REL AGE/C AGE/Y ATTIT HEALTH...ANTHOL BIBLIOG 20 JOHNSON/LB POVRTY/WAR. PAGE 121 F2388
WEALTH NAT/G RECEIVE INCOME

B65
SIMON B.,EDUCATION AND THE LABOR MOVEMENT, 1870-1920. UK SOCIETY STRATA LABOR POL/PAR SCHOOL CONTROL PARTIC SOCISM...BIBLIOG 19/20. PAGE 122 F2406
EDU/PROP WORKER ADJUST LAW

B65
SMERK G.M.,URBAN TRANSPORTATION; THE FEDERAL ROLE. FUT USA+45 FINAN PROB/SOLV TEC/DEV AUTOMAT GOV/REL COST...STAT BIBLIOG MUNICH 20 PUB/TRANS. PAGE 123 F2426
PLAN DIST/IND NAT/G

B65
THAYER F.C. JR.,AIR TRANSPORT POLICY AND NATIONAL SECURITY: A POLITICAL, ECONOMIC, AND MILITARY ANALYSIS. DIST/IND OP/RES PLAN TEC/DEV DIPLOM DETER WAR COST EFFICIENCY...POLICY BIBLIOG 20 DEPT/DEFEN FAA CAB. PAGE 129 F2548
AIR FORCES CIVMIL/REL ORD/FREE

B65
US OFFICE ECONOMIC OPPORTUNITY,CATALOG OF FEDERAL PROGRAMS FOR INDIVIDUAL AND COMMUNITY IMPROVEMENT. USA+45 GIVE RECEIVE ADMIN HEALTH KNOWL SKILL WEALTH ...CHARTS MUNICH. PAGE 138 F2721
BIBLIOG CLIENT ECO/TAC

B65
VON RENESSE E.A.,UNVOLLENDETE DEMOKRATIEN. AFR ISLAM S/ASIA SOCIETY ACT/RES COLONIAL...JURID CHARTS BIBLIOG METH 13/20. PAGE 142 F2795
ECO/UNDEV NAT/COMP SOVEREIGN

B65
WALTON R.E.,A BEHAVIORAL THEORY OF LABOR NEGOTIATIONS: AN ANALYSIS OF A SOCIAL INTERACTION SYSTEM. USA+45 FINAN PROB/SOLV ECO/TAC GP/REL INGP/REL...DECISION BIBLIOG. PAGE 143 F2812
SOC LABOR BARGAIN ADMIN

B65
WASSERMAN M.J.,THE BALANCE OF PAYMENTS: HISTORY, METHODOLOGY, THEORY. UK USA+45 USA-45 CAP/ISM DIPLOM EFFICIENCY...DECISION METH/CNCPT BIBLIOG 18/20 LEAGUE/NAT. PAGE 144 F2828
BAL/PAY ECO/TAC GEN/LAWS EQUILIB

B65
WATERSTON A.,DEVELOPMENT PLANNING* LESSONS OF EXPERIENCE. ECO/TAC CENTRAL...MGT QUANT BIBLIOG. PAGE 144 F2830
ECO/UNDEV CREATE PLAN ADMIN

B65
WEAVER J.N.,THE INTERNATIONAL DEVELOPMENT ASSOCIATION: A NEW APPROACH TO FOREIGN AID. USA+45 NAT/G OP/RES PLAN PROB/SOLV WEALTH...CHARTS BIBLIOG 20 UN. PAGE 144 F2836
FOR/AID INT/ORG ECO/UNDEV FINAN

B65
WISCONSIN HISTORICAL SOCIETY,LABOR PAPERS ON MICROFILM: A COMBINED LIST. USA+45 USA-45 WORKER 20. PAGE 148 F2910
BIBLIOG LABOR PRESS

L65
LOFTUS M.L.,"INTERNATIONAL MONETARY FUND, 1962-1965: A SELECTED BIBLIOGRAPHY." WOR+45 PLAN BUDGET INCOME PROFIT WEALTH. PAGE 81 F1596
BIBLIOG FINAN INT/TRADE INT/ORG

C65
PEGRUM D.E.,"PUBLIC REGULATION OF BUSINESS (REV ED)" LAW CONSTN DIST/IND SERV/IND LG/CO LEGIS OWN LAISSEZ SOCISM...POLICY DECISION BIBLIOG 20. PAGE 104 F2048
INDUS PLAN NEW/LIB PRICE

C65
WUORINEN J.H.,"SCANDINAVIA." DENMARK FINLAND ICELAND NORWAY SWEDEN SOCIETY AGRI POL/PAR DELIB/GP DIPLOM INT/TRADE NEUTRAL WAR...CHARTS IND TREATY 20. PAGE 149 F2942
BIBLIOG NAT/G POLICY

B66
ALEXANDER Y.,INTERNATIONAL TECHNICAL ASSISTANCE EXPERTS: A CASE STUDY OF THE U.N. EXPERIENCE. USA+45 WOR+45 WORKER CREATE PLAN PROB/SOLV ECO/TAC FOR/AID GIVE EDU/PROP...CHARTS BIBLIOG 20 UN. PAGE 3 F0062
SKILL INT/ORG TEC/DEV CONSULT

B66
BIRMINGHAM W.,A STUDY OF CONTEMPORARY GHANA VOL I: THE ECONOMY OF GHANA. AFR GHANA PLAN...POLICY STAT CHARTS ANTHOL BIBLIOG 20. PAGE 15 F0286
ECO/UNDEV ECO/TAC NAT/G PRODUC

B66
BOLTON R.E.,DEFENSE AND DISARMAMENT: THE ECONOMICS OF TRANSITION. USA+45 R+D FORCES PLAN LOBBY DETER WAR COST PEACE...ANTHOL BIBLIOG 20. PAGE 16 F0310
ARMS/CONT POLICY INDUS

B66
BRODERSEN A.,THE SOVIET WORKER: LABOR AND GOVERNMENT IN SOVIET SOCIETY. USSR STRUCT INDUS LABOR PLAN PAY INGP/REL PRODUC...POLICY GEN/LAWS BIBLIOG 20 STALIN/J LENIN/VI BOLSHEVISM KHRUSH/N. PAGE 19 F0357
WORKER ROLE NAT/G MARXISM

B66
BROWN J.F.,THE NEW EASTERN EUROPE. ALBANIA BULGARIA HUNGARY POLAND ROMANIA CULTURE AGRI POL/PAR WAR NAT/LISM MARXISM...CHARTS BIBLIOG 20. PAGE 19 F0369
DIPLOM COM NAT/G ECO/UNDEV

B66
CANNING HOUSE LIBRARY,AUTHOR AND SUBJECT CATALOGUES OF THE CANNING HOUSE LIBRARY (5 VOLS.). UK CULTURE LEAD...SOC 19/20. PAGE 21 F0411
BIBLIOG L/A+17C NAT/G DIPLOM

B66
CROWDER M.,A SHORT HISTORY OF NIGERIA. AFR NIGERIA UK ECO/UNDEV CHIEF INT/TRADE RACE/REL NAT/LISM ORD/FREE...GEOG SOC CHARTS BIBLIOG 14/20. PAGE 29 F0558
COLONIAL NAT/G CULTURE

B66
DEBENKO E.,RESEARCH SOURCES FOR SOUTH ASIAN STUDIES IN ECONOMIC DEVELOPMENT: A SELECT BIBLIOGRAPHY OF SERIAL PUBLICATIONS. CEYLON INDIA NEPAL PAKISTAN PROB/SOLV ADMIN...POLICY 20. PAGE 32 F0611
BIBLIOG ECO/UNDEV S/ASIA PLAN

B66
DILLEY M.R.,BRITISH POLICY IN KENYA COLONY (2ND ED.). AFR INDIA UK LABOR BUDGET TAX ADMIN PARL/PROC GP/REL...BIBLIOG 20 PARLIAMENT. PAGE 33 F0639
COLONIAL REPRESENT SOVEREIGN

B66
HAINES W.W.,MONEY PRICES AND POLICY. WOR+45 ECO/DEV BUDGET CONTROL INCOME...POLICY STAT CHARTS BIBLIOG T 20. PAGE 53 F1039
PRICE FINAN ECO/TAC GOV/REL

B66
HASTINGS P.G.,THE MANAGEMENT OF BUSINESS FINANCE. ECO/DEV PLAN BUDGET CONTROL COST...DECISION CHARTS BIBLIOG T 20. PAGE 56 F1109
FINAN MGT INDUS ECO/TAC

B66
HO YHI-MIN,AGRICULTURAL DEVELOPMENT OF TAIWAN: 1903-1960. FINAN WORKER EDU/PROP...STAT CHARTS BIBLIOG 20. PAGE 60 F1181
ECO/UNDEV AGRI PRODUC PLAN

B66
HOLT R.T.,THE POLITICAL BASIS OF ECONOMIC DEVELOPMENT. STRATA STRUCT NAT/G DIPLOM ADMIN...SOC NAT/COMP BIBLIOG 20. PAGE 61 F1201
ECO/TAC GOV/COMP CONSTN EX/STRUC

B66
HOWE R.W.,BLACK AFRICA: FROM PRE-HISTORY TO THE EVE OF THE COLONIAL ERA. ECO/UNDEV KIN PROVS SECT INT/TRADE EDU/PROP COLONIAL...BIBLIOG WORSHIP. PAGE 62 F1226
AFR CULTURE SOC

B66
KAESTNER K.,GESAMTWIRTSCHAFTLICHE PLANUNG IN EINER GEMISCHTEN WIRTSCHAFTSORDNUNG (WIRTSCHAFTSPOLITISCHE STUDIEN 5). GERMANY/W WOR+45 WOR-45 INDUS MARKET NAT/G ACT/RES GP/REL INGP/REL PRODUC...ECOMETRIC MGT BIBLIOG 20. PAGE 68 F1346
ECO/TAC PLAN POLICY PREDICT

B66
KOMIYA R.,POSTWAR ECONOMIC GROWTH IN JAPAN. ELITES NAT/G EX/STRUC TEC/DEV BUDGET DIPLOM CONTROL BAL/PAY PRODUC...BIBLIOG 20 CHINJAP. PAGE 73 F1424
ECO/DEV POLICY PLAN ADJUST

B66
MACBEAN A.I.,EXPORT INSTABILITY AND ECONOMIC DEVELOPMENT. CHILE PAKISTAN PUERT/RICO TANZANIA UGANDA WOR+45 MARKET ECO/TAC...POLICY REGRESS CHARTS BIBLIOG TIME 20. PAGE 83 F1622
INT/TRADE ECO/UNDEV ECOMETRIC INSPECT

B66
MIKESELL R.F.,PUBLIC INTERNATIONAL LENDING FOR DEVELOPMENT. WOR+45 WOR-45 DELIB/GP...TIME/SEQ CHARTS BIBLIOG 20. PAGE 91 F1783
INT/ORG FOR/AID ECO/UNDEV FINAN

B66
OHLIN G.,FOREIGN AID POLICIES RECONSIDERED. ECO/DEV FOR/AID

ECO/UNDEV VOL/ASSN CONSULT PLAN CONTROL ATTIT ...CONCPT CHARTS BIBLIOG 20. PAGE 101 F1985
DIPLOM GIVE

B66
PERSALL E.S.,AN ECONOMETRIC STUDY OF FINANCIAL MARKETS. COMPUTER PROB/SOLV TEC/DEV...MATH STAT CHARTS METH/COMP BIBLIOG 20. PAGE 105 F2066
ECOMETRIC FINAN MARKET METH

B66
RAO Y.V.L.,COMMUNICATION AND DEVELOPMENT. INDIA S/ASIA SOCIETY ACT/RES EDU/PROP PARTIC ATTIT...SOC GP/COMP BIBLIOG MUNICH MUNICH 20. PAGE 109 F2149
COM/IND ECO/UNDEV OBS

B66
ROSS A.M.,INDUSTRIAL RELATIONS AND ECONOMIC DEVELOPMENT. POL/PAR LEGIS WORKER BARGAIN PRICE EXEC LOBBY INCOME PWR...DECISION ANTHOL BIBLIOG 20. PAGE 114 F2243
ECO/UNDEV LABOR NAT/G GP/REL

B66
SINGH L.P.,THE POLITICS OF ECONOMIC COOPERATION IN ASIA; A STUDY OF ASIAN INTERNATIONAL ORGANIZATIONS. ASIA INT/ORG ACT/RES PLAN GP/REL...POLICY GP/COMP BIBLIOG 20 UN SEATO. PAGE 122 F2414
ECO/UNDEV ECO/TAC REGION DIPLOM

B66
SMITH H.E.,READINGS IN ECONOMIC DEVELOPMENT AND ADMINISTRATION IN TANZANIA. TANZANIA FINAN INDUS LABOR NAT/G PLAN PROB/SOLV INT/TRADE COLONIAL REGION...ANTHOL BIBLIOG 20 AFRICA/E. PAGE 123 F2431
TEC/DEV ADMIN GOV/REL

B66
SOCIAL SCIENCE RESEARCH COUN,BIBLIOGRAPHY OF RESEARCH IN THE SOCIAL SCIENCES IN AUSTRALIA 1957-1960. LAW R+D DIPLOM 20 AUSTRAL. PAGE 124 F2437
BIBLIOG SOC PSY

B66
US DEPARTMENT OF LABOR,TECHNOLOGICAL TRENDS IN MAJOR AMERICAN INDUSTRIES. USA+45 R+D LABOR GP/REL PRODUC...MGT BIBLIOG 20. PAGE 135 F2669
TEC/DEV INDUS TREND AUTOMAT

L66
AFRICAN BIBLIOGRAPHIC CENTER,"AFRICAN ECONOMIC AFFAIRS: A SELECT BIBLIOGRAPHICAL SURVEY, 1965-1966." AFR FINAN INDUS INT/ORG LABOR PLAN BUDGET DIPLOM INT/TRADE ADMIN EFFICIENCY WEALTH 20. PAGE 3 F0046
BIBLIOG ECO/UNDEV TEC/DEV FOR/AID

C66
WINT G.,"ASIA: A HANDBOOK." ASIA S/ASIA INDUS LABOR SECT PRESS RACE/REL MARXISM...STAT CHARTS BIBLIOG 20. PAGE 148 F2908
ECO/UNDEV DIPLOM NAT/G SOCIETY

B67
ALNASRAWI A.,FINANCING ECONOMIC DEVELOPMENT IN IRAQ. IRAQ INDUS CAP/ISM COST PRODUC...STAT CHARTS BIBLIOG 20. PAGE 4 F0076
ECO/UNDEV EXTR/IND TEC/DEV INT/TRADE

B67
ANDERSON S.V.,THE NORDIC COUNCIL: A STUDY OF SCANDINAVIAN REGIONALISM. DENMARK FINLAND ICELAND NORWAY SWEDEN MARKET NAT/G VOL/ASSN CONSULT PARL/PROC ATTIT...TIME/SEQ BIBLIOG 20. PAGE 5 F0098
INT/ORG REGION DIPLOM LEGIS

B67
ANDERSON T.,RUSSIAN POLITICAL THOUGHT; AN INTRODUCTION. USSR NAT/G POL/PAR CHIEF MARXISM ...TIME/SEQ BIBLIOG 9/20. PAGE 5 F0099
TREND CONSTN ATTIT

B67
BIBBY J.,ON CAPITOL HILL. POL/PAR LOBBY PARL/PROC GOV/REL PERS/REL...JURID PHIL/SCI OBS INT BIBLIOG 20 CONGRESS PRESIDENT. PAGE 15 F0278
CONFER LEGIS CREATE LEAD

B67
BROMKE A.,POLAND'S POLITICS: IDEALISM VS. REALISM. COM GERMANY POLAND RUSSIA USSR POL/PAR CATHISM ...BIBLIOG 19/20. PAGE 19 F0360
NAT/G DIPLOM MARXISM

B67
BUSEY J.L.,NOTES ON COSTA RICAN DEMOCRACY. COSTA/RICA L/A+17C NAT/G POL/PAR LEGIS CHOOSE OWN ATTIT...BIBLIOG 20. PAGE 20 F0394
CONSTN MAJORIT SOCIETY ECO/UNDEV

B67
CAMPBELL A.K.,METROPOLITAN AMERICA* FISCAL PATTERNS AND GOVERNMENTAL SYSTEMS. PROVS PLAN COST...POLICY DECISION GOV/COMP METH/COMP BIBLIOG. PAGE 21 F0405
USA+45 NAT/G LOC/G BUDGET

B67
CASTILLO C.M.,GROWTH AND INTEGRATION IN CENTRAL AMERICA. L/A+17C CREATE PROB/SOLV ECO/TAC REGION PRODUC...OBS BIBLIOG 20. PAGE 22 F0429
ECO/UNDEV INT/TRADE NAT/COMP

B67
CHANDRASEKHAR S.,PROBLEMS OF ECONOMIC DEVELOPMENT. AFR INDIA PHILIPPINE UAR WOR+45 INDUS...GEOG SOC ANTHOL BIBLIOG 20 CHINJAP. PAGE 23 F0450
ECO/UNDEV PLAN AGRI PROB/SOLV

B67
CHAPIN F.S. JR.,SELECTED REFERENCES ON URBAN PLANNING METHODS AND TECHNIQUES. USA+45 LAW ECO/DEV LOC/G NAT/G SCHOOL CONSULT CREATE PROB/SOLV TEC/DEV ...SOC/WK MUNICH. PAGE 23 F0454
BIBLIOG NEIGH PLAN

B67
CHILCOTE R.H.,PORTUGUESE AFRICA. PORTUGAL CULTURE SOCIETY ECO/UNDEV DOMIN NAT/LISM...TREND IDEA/COMP NAT/COMP BIBLIOG 15/20. PAGE 24 F0465
AFR COLONIAL ORD/FREE PROB/SOLV

B67
CHO S.S.,KOREA IN WORLD POLITICS 1940-1950; AN EVALUATION OF AMERICAN RESPONSIBILITY. KOREA USA+45 USSR CONSTN INT/ORG NAT/G FORCES FOR/AID ANOMIE SUPEGO MARXISM...DECISION BIBLIOG 20. PAGE 24 F0469
POLICY DIPLOM PROB/SOLV WAR

B67
CLEMENT M.O.,THEORETICAL ISSUES IN INTERNATIONAL ECONOMICS. WOR+45 PLAN PROB/SOLV TEC/DEV ...ECOMETRIC METH/CNCPT MATH BIBLIOG T MONEY. PAGE 25 F0489
INT/TRADE FINAN CREATE BAL/PAY

B67
COWLING M.,1867 DISRAELI, GLADSTONE, AND REVOLUTION; THE PASSING OF THE SECOND REFORM BILL. UK LEGIS LEAD LOBBY GP/REL INGP/REL...DECISION BIBLIOG 19 REFORMERS. PAGE 28 F0545
PARL/PROC POL/PAR ATTIT LAW

B67
DE JOUVENAL B.,THE ART OF CONJECTURE. WOR+45 EFFICIENCY PERCEPT KNOWL...DECISION PHIL/SCI CONCPT METH/COMP BIBLIOG 20. PAGE 31 F0600
FUT PREDICT SIMUL METH

B67
EVANS R.H.,COEXISTENCE: COMMUNISM AND ITS PRACTICE IN BOLOGNA, 1945-1965. ITALY CAP/ISM ADMIN CHOOSE PEACE ORD/FREE...SOC STAT DEEP/INT SAMP CHARTS BIBLIOG MUNICH 20. PAGE 39 F0756
MARXISM CULTURE POL/PAR

B67
GARAUDY R.,KARL MARX: THE EVOLUTION OF HIS THOUGHT. SOCIETY...BIBLIOG 20 MARX/KARL STALIN/J. PAGE 46 F0899
MARXIST GEN/LAWS CONCPT TIME/SEQ

B67
GREEN C.,NEGATIVE TAXES AND THE POVERTY PROBLEM. COST EFFICIENCY INCOME NEW/LIB...METH/CNCPT CHARTS METH/COMP BIBLIOG 20. PAGE 50 F0983
TAX RECEIVE WEALTH PLAN

B67
GUTKIND E.A.,URBAN DEVELOPMENT IN SOUTHERN EUROPE* SPAIN AND PORTUGAL. CHRIST-17C EUR+WWI MOD/EUR PORTUGAL SPAIN CULTURE AGRI...SOC SAMP/SIZ BIBLIOG MUNICH. PAGE 52 F1015
TEC/DEV ECO/DEV

B67
INTERNATIONAL LABOUR OFFICE,SUBJECT GUIDE TO PUBLICATIONS OF THE INTERNATIONAL LABOUR OFFICE, 1919-1964. DIPLOM 20. PAGE 65 F1280
BIBLIOG LABOR INT/ORG WORKER

B67
JHANGIANI M.A.,JANA SANGH AND SWATANTRA: A PROFILE OF THE RIGHTIST PARTIES IN INDIA. INDIA ADMIN CHOOSE MARXISM SOCISM...INT CHARTS BIBLIOG 20. PAGE 67 F1320
POL/PAR LAISSEZ NAT/LISM ATTIT

B67
KARDOUCHE G.K.,THE UAR IN DEVELOPMENT. UAR ECO/TAC INT/TRADE BAL/PAY...STAT CHARTS BIBLIOG 20. PAGE 69 F1355
FINAN MGT CAP/ISM ECO/UNDEV

B67
KEWEN P.B.,INTERNATIONAL ECONOMICS (2ND ED.). USA+45 WOR+45 MARKET TARIFFS...BIBLIOG T 20. PAGE 70 F1384
INT/TRADE BAL/PAY FINAN EQUILIB

B67
KULSKI J.E.,LAND OF URBAN PROMISE* CONTINUING THE GREAT TRADITION* A SEARCH FOR SIGNIFICANT URBAN SPACE IN URBANIZED NORTHEAST. USA+45 DIST/IND PUB/INST CONSULT CREATE TEC/DEV...SOC NEW/IDEA CHARTS BIBLIOG MUNICH. PAGE 74 F1448
PLAN PROB/SOLV ECO/DEV

B67
LANDEN R.G.,OMAN SINCE 1856: DISRUPTIVE MODERNIZATION IN A TRADITIONAL ARAB SOCIETY. UK DIST/IND EXTR/IND SECT DIPLOM INT/TRADE...SOC LING CHARTS BIBLIOG 19/20. PAGE 75 F1468
ISLAM CULTURE ECO/UNDEV NAT/G

B67
LINDER S.B.,TRADE AND TRADE POLICY FOR DEVELOPMENT. OP/RES DIPLOM TARIFFS UTIL WEALTH...BIBLIOG 20. PAGE 80 F1569
ECO/UNDEV ECO/TAC TEC/DEV INT/TRADE

B67
MARCUS S.,COMPETITION AND THE LAW. USA+45 INDUS LG/CO NAT/G CONSERVE LAISSEZ...BIBLIOG 20 FTC SUPREME/CT. PAGE 85 F1665
LAW ECO/DEV FINAN JURID

B67
NARVER J.C.,CONGLOMERATE MERGERS AND MARKET COMPETITION. USA+45 LAW STRUCT ADMIN LEAD RISK COST PROFIT WEALTH...POLICY CHARTS BIBLIOG. PAGE 96 F1892
DEMAND LG/CO MARKET MGT

B67
NELSON R.R.,TECHNOLOGY, ECONOMIC GROWTH, AND PUBLIC POLICY. USA+45 PLAN GP/REL UTIL KNOWL...POLICY PHIL/SCI CHARTS BIBLIOG 20. PAGE 97 F1912
R+D CONSULT CREATE ACT/RES

B67
NYOMARKAY J.,CHARISMA AND FACTIONALISM IN THE NAZI
FASCISM

PARTY. GERMANY POL/PAR LEGIT LEAD MARXISM INGP/REL
...NEW/IDEA METH/COMP GEN/LAWS BIBLIOG 20 HITLER/A. CHIEF
PAGE 99 F1949 PWR

B67
PIKE F.B.,FREEDOM AND REFORM IN LATIN AMERICA. L/A+17C
BRAZIL URUGUAY CONSTN CULTURE SECT DIPLOM EDU/PROP ORD/FREE
PARTIC DRIVE ALL/VALS CATHISM...GEOG ANTHOL BIBLIOG ECO/UNDEV
REFORMERS BOLIV. PAGE 106 F2086 REV

B67
POLLACK N.,THE POPULIST MIND. USA-45 STRATA AGRI POPULISM
NAT/G POL/PAR LEGIS WORKER RACE/REL WEALTH...ANTHOL HIST/WRIT
BIBLIOG 19 NEGRO. PAGE 107 F2097 ATTIT
INGP/REL

B67
PORWIT K.,CENTRAL PLANNING: EVALUATION OF VARIANTS. PLAN
PRICE OPTIMAL PRODUC...DECISION MATH CHARTS SIMUL MGT
BIBLIOG MODELS 20. PAGE 107 F2106 ECOMETRIC

B67
SACKS B.,SOUTH AFRICA: AN IMPERIAL DILEMMA. COLONIAL
SOUTH/AFR UK ECO/UNDEV KIN DOMIN DEBATE CONTROL REV RACE/REL
DISCRIM ISOLAT...POLICY STAT BIBLIOG 20. PAGE 115 DIPLOM
F2268 ORD/FREE

B67
SCHECTER J.,THE NEW FACE OF BUDDHA: BUDDHISM AND SECT
POLITICAL POWER IN SOUTHEAST ASIA. S/ASIA NAT/G POLICY
POL/PAR NAT/LISM ATTIT MARXISM...BIBLIOG 20. PWR
PAGE 116 F2292 LEAD

B67
STEARNS P.N.,EUROPEAN SOCIETY IN UPHEAVAL* SOCIAL REGION
HISTORY SINCE 1800. EUR+WWI MOD/EUR STRATA SECT ECO/DEV
WORKER TEC/DEV WAR...WELF/ST SOC TREND BIBLIOG SOCIETY
19/20. PAGE 125 F2472 INDUS

B67
SYMONS L.,AGRICULTURAL GEOGRAPHY. OP/RES SKILL AGRI
...CONCPT CHARTS BIBLIOG T 20. PAGE 128 F2520 GEOG
METH/COMP
OBS

B67
TANSKY L.,US AND USSR AID TO DEVELOPING COUNTRIES. ECO/UNDEV
INDIA TURKEY USA+45 USSR INDUS PLAN CAP/ISM WAR PWR FOR/AID
WEALTH MARXISM...CHARTS NAT/COMP BIBLIOG 20. DIPLOM
PAGE 128 F2534 ECO/TAC

B67
WALLBANK T.W.,CIVILIZATION PAST AND PRESENT (3RD CULTURE
ED.). FUT WOR+45 WOR-45 SOCIETY...SOC CONCPT STRUCT
TIME/SEQ CHARTS BIBLIOG T. PAGE 143 F2809 TREND

B67
WEINBERG M.,SCHOOL INTEGRATION: A COMPREHENSIVE BIBLIOG
CLASSIFIED BIBLIOGRAPHY OF 3,100 REFERENCES. USA+45 SCHOOL
LAW NAT/G NEIGH SECT PLAN ROUTINE AGE/C WEALTH DISCRIM
SOC/INTEG INDIAN/AM. PAGE 145 F2849 RACE/REL

B67
WESSON R.G.,THE IMPERIAL ORDER. WOR-45 STRUCT SECT PWR
DOMIN ADMIN COLONIAL LEAD CONSERVE...CONCPT BIBLIOG CHIEF
20. PAGE 145 F2861 CONTROL
SOCIETY

B67
WILLIAMS E.J.,LATIN AMERICAN CHRISTIAN DEMOCRATIC POL/PAR
PARTIES. L/A+17C FAM LABOR FORCES...CATH TREND GP/COMP
BIBLIOG 20. PAGE 147 F2890 CATHISM
ALL/VALS

B67
WILLS A.J.,AN INTRODUCTION TO THE HISTORY OF AFR
CENTRAL AFRICA. RHODESIA ZAMBIA CULTURE SOCIETY COLONIAL
ECO/UNDEV TEC/DEV DOMIN WAR ALL/VALS...POLICY TREND ORD/FREE
BIBLIOG T 14/20 NYASALAND. PAGE 147 F2899

B67
ZONDAG C.H.,THE BOLIVIAN ECONOMY 1952-65. L/A+17C ECO/UNDEV
TEC/DEV FOR/AID ADMIN...OBS TREND CHARTS BIBLIOG 20 INDUS
BOLIV. PAGE 151 F2969 PRODUC

L67
ZEIDBERG L.D.,"THE NASHVILLE AIR POLLUTION STUDY" DEATH
(PARTS V-VII)" USA+45 PLAN AGE HEALTH...GEOG STAT HABITAT
CENSUS SAMP/SIZ CHARTS BIBLIOG MUNICH. PAGE 150 AIR
F2962 BIO/SOC

BIBLIOG/A....BIBLIOGRAPHY OVER 50 ITEMS ANNOTATED

B
BRITISH COMMONWEALTH BUR AGRI,WORLD AGRICULTURAL BIBLIOG/A
ECONOMICS AND RURAL SOCIOLOGY ABSTRACTS. NAT/G AGRI
OP/RES PLAN TEC/DEV LEAD PRODUC...GEOG MGT NAT/COMP SOC
20. PAGE 18 F0354 WORKER

N
AMERICAN ECONOMIC REVIEW. FINAN INDUS LABOR OP/RES BIBLIOG/A
CAP/ISM INT/TRADE TAX WEALTH...CON/ANAL CHARTS 20. USA+45
PAGE 1 F0001 ECO/DEV
NAT/G

N
DOCUMENTATION ECONOMIQUE: REVUE BIBLIOGRAPHIQUE DE BIBLIOG/A
SYNTHESE. WOR+45 COM/IND FINAN BUDGET DIPLOM...GEOG SOC
20. PAGE 1 F0004

N
ECONOMIC ABSTRACTS. WOR+45 FINAN INDUS MARKET LABOR BIBLIOG/A
ACT/RES INT/TRADE WRITING GP/REL...MGT 20. PAGE 1 EDU/PROP
F0005

N
ECONOMIC LIBRARY SELECTIONS. AGRI INDUS MARKET BIBLIOG/A
ADMIN...STAT NAT/COMP 20. PAGE 1 F0007 WRITING
FINAN

N
SOUTH AFRICAN JOURNAL OF ECONOMICS. SOUTH/AFR FINAN ECO/UNDEV
MARKET ACT/RES OP/RES...PHIL/SCI STAT CON/ANAL ACADEM
METH/COMP BIBLIOG/A 20. PAGE 1 F0009 INTELL
R+D

N
AMERICAN ECONOMIC ASSOCIATION,THE JOURNAL OF BIBLIOG/A
ECONOMIC ABSTRACTS. ECO/UNDEV MARKET LABOR DIPLOM R+D
...MGT CONCPT METH 20. PAGE 5 F0086 FINAN

N
SCIENTIFIC COUNCIL FOR AFRICA,INVENTORY OF ECONOMIC BIBLIOG/A
STUDIES CONCERNING AFRICA SOUTH OF THE SAHARA. AFR GEOG
...PHIL/SCI 20. PAGE 118 F2327 ECO/UNDEV

N
UNESCO,SOUTH ASIA SOCIAL SCIENCES ABSTRACTS. BURMA BIBLIOG/A
CEYLON INDIA S/ASIA PRESS...PSY 20. PAGE 132 F2608 SOC

N
US LIBRARY OF CONGRESS,SELECTED AND ANNOTATED BIBLIOG/A
BIBLIOGRAPHY ON AGRICULTURAL PROBLEMS AND POLICIES WAR
IN A WARTIME ECONOMY (PAMPHLET). R+D WORKER PRODUC AGRI
20. PAGE 137 F2706 EXTR/IND

N
US LIBRARY OF CONGRESS,SELECTED AND ANNOTATED BIBLIOG/A
BIBLIOGRAPHY ON INDUSTRIAL PROBLEMS AND POLICIES IN ECO/DEV
WARTIME (PAMPHLET). WOR-45 CONSTRUC NAT/G PROB/SOLV INDUS
COST DEMAND PRODUC 20. PAGE 137 F2707 WAR

N
US LIBRARY OF CONGRESS,SELECTED AND ANNOTATED BIBLIOG/A
BIBLIOGRAPHY ON LABOR PROBLEMS AND POLICIES IN A WAR
WARTIME ECONOMY (PAMPHLET). USA-45 INDUS LEGIS LABOR
GP/REL DISCRIM PRODUC...SOC 20. PAGE 137 F2708 WORKER

N
US LIBRARY OF CONGRESS,SELECTED AND ANNOTATED BIBLIOG/A
BIBLIOGRAPHY ON RAW MATERIALS IN A WARTIME ECONOMY ECO/DEV
(PAMPHLET). WOR-45 NAT/G DEMAND PRODUC 20. PAGE 137 EXTR/IND
F2709 WAR

N
US LIBRARY OF CONGRESS,SOUTHERN ASIA ACCESSIONS BIBLIOG/A
LIST. BURMA CEYLON INDIA NEPAL PAKISTAN S/ASIA SOCIETY
THAILAND AGRI INDUS SCHOOL WORKER...ART/METH GEOG CULTURE
HEAL PHIL/SCI LING 20. PAGE 137 F2710 ECO/UNDEV

N
US SUPERINTENDENT OF DOCUMENTS,CENSUS PUBLICATIONS BIBLIOG/A
(PRICE LIST 70). AGRI CONSTRUC DIST/IND FINAN LOC/G CENSUS
NAT/G PROVS INT/TRADE APPORT INCOME. PAGE 140 F2751 STAT
USA+45

N
US SUPERINTENDENT OF DOCUMENTS,INTERSTATE COMMERCE BIBLIOG/A
(PRICE LIST 59). USA+45 LAW LOC/G NAT/G LEGIS DIST/IND
TARIFFS TAX ADMIN CONTROL HEALTH DECISION. PAGE 140 GOV/REL
F2752 PROVS

N
US SUPERINTENDENT OF DOCUMENTS,LABOR (PRICE LIST BIBLIOG/A
33). USA+45 LAW AGRI CONSTRUC INDUS NAT/G BARGAIN WORKER
PRICE ADMIN AUTOMAT PRODUC MGT. PAGE 140 F2753 LABOR
LEGIS

N
US SUPERINTENDENT OF DOCUMENTS,TARIFF AND TAXATION BIBLIOG/A
(PRICE LIST 37). USA+45 LAW INT/TRADE ADJUD ADMIN TAX
CT/SYS INCOME OWN...DECISION GATT. PAGE 140 F2754 TARIFFS
NAT/G

B02
WEBB S.,THE HISTORY OF TRADE UNIONISM. UK PARTIC LABOR
...OBS CHARTS BIBLIOG/A 15/19 CASEBOOK. PAGE 144 VOL/ASSN
F2837 GP/REL

B26
SUFRIN S.C.,A BRIEF ANNOTATED BIBLIOGRAPHY ON LABOR BIBLIOG/A
IN EMERGING SOCIETIES. WOR+45 CULTURE SOCIETY INDUS LABOR
EDU/PROP GP/REL INGP/REL. PAGE 127 F2510 ECO/UNDEV
WORKER

B35
O'CONNOR H.,REVOLUTION IN SEATTLE. USA-45 STRATA REV
WORKER GP/REL ATTIT SOCISM...OBS BIBLIOG/A 20 EDU/PROP
SEATTLE STRIKE COM/PARTY. PAGE 99 F1954 LABOR
MARXISM

B40
FULLER G.H.,LIST OF REFERENCES ON PRIORITIES BIBLIOG/A
(MIMEOGRAPHED PAPER). WOR-45 NAT/G RATION 20. WAR
PAGE 45 F0874 ECO/TAC
PLAN

B40
HELLMAN F.S.,THE NEW DEAL: SELECTED LIST OF BIBLIOG/A
REFERENCES. USA-45 FINAN LABOR EX/STRUC CREATE ECO/TAC
INT/TRADE ADMIN CT/SYS 20 SUPREME/CT. PAGE 58 F1145 PLAN
POLICY

B42
US LIBRARY OF CONGRESS,ECONOMICS OF WAR (APRIL BIBLIOG/A
1941-MARCH 1942). WOR-45 FINAN INDUS LOC/G NAT/G INT/TRADE
PLAN BUDGET RATION COST DEMAND...POLICY 20. ECO/TAC
PAGE 138 F2712 WAR

B42
US LIBRARY OF CONGRESS,THE WAR PRODUCTION PROGRAM: BIBLIOG/A

SELECTED DOCUMENTATION ON THE ECONOMICS OF WAR (PAMPHLET). USA-45 ECO/DEV AGRI FINAN NAT/G ECO/TAC RATION PRICE EFFICIENCY 20. PAGE 138 F2713 — WAR PRODUC INDUS

B47
US LIBRARY OF CONGRESS,POSTWAR PLANNING AND RECONSTRUCTION: JANUARY-MARCH 1943. WOR+45 SOCIETY INT/ORG DIPLOM...SOC PREDICT 20. PAGE 138 F2714 — BIBLIOG/A WAR PEACE PLAN

B49
US DEPARTMENT OF STATE,SOVIET BIBLIOGRAPHY (PAMPHLET). CHINA/COM COM USSR LAW AGRI INT/ORG ECO/TAC EDU/PROP...POLICY GEOG IND 20. PAGE 135 F2670 — BIBLIOG/A MARXISM CULTURE DIPLOM

B50
HUTCHISON K.,THE DECLINE AND FALL OF BRITISH CAPITALISM. UK ELITES STRATA ECO/DEV LABOR WORKER CONTROL WAR PWR...BIBLIOG/A 19/20. PAGE 63 F1249 — CAP/ISM SOCISM LAISSEZ DOMIN

B51
US DEPARTMENT OF STATE,POINT FOUR, NEAR EAST AND AFRICA, A SELECTED BIBLIOGRAPHY OF STUDIES ON ECONOMICALLY UNDERDEVELOPED COUNTRIES. AGRI COM/IND FINAN INDUS PLAN INT/TRADE...SOC TREND 20. PAGE 135 F2672 — BIBLIOG/A AFR S/ASIA ISLAM

B51
US LIBRARY OF CONGRESS,EAST EUROPEAN ACCESSIONS LIST (VOL. I). POL/PAR DIPLOM ADMIN LEAD 20. PAGE 138 F2715 — BIBLIOG/A COM SOCIETY NAT/G

B52
AYRES C.E.,THE INDUSTRIAL ECONOMY. USA+45 FINAN MARKET NAT/G PUB/INST PLAN ECO/TAC TAX DEMAND INCOME...BIBLIOG/A 20. PAGE 8 F0146 — ECO/DEV INDUS FUT PROB/SOLV

C54
BERLE A.A. JR.,"THE 20TH CENTURY CAPITALIST REVOLUTION." ECO/DEV NAT/G DIPLOM PRICE CONTROL ATTIT...BIBLIOG/A 20. PAGE 14 F0260 — LG/CO CAP/ISM MGT PWR

B55
FOGARTY M.P.,ECONOMIC CONTROL. FUT UK ECO/DEV FINAN CONSULT INT/TRADE...CHARTS BIBLIOG/A 20. PAGE 42 F0819 — ECO/TAC NAT/G CONTROL PROB/SOLV

B55
O'CONNOR H.,THE EMPIRE OF OIL. USA+45 DIST/IND FINAN MARKET CAP/ISM TAX CONTROL...POLICY MARXIST BIBLIOG/A 20. PAGE 100 F1955 — EXTR/IND INT/TRADE CENTRAL NAT/G

C55
ADAMS G.P. JR.,"COMPETITIVE ECONOMIC SYSTEMS." WOR+45 WOR-45 PWR...BIBLIOG/A 20. PAGE 2 F0038 — METH/COMP ECO/TAC TEC/DEV DIPLOM

B56
HISTORICAL ABSTRACTS. NAT/G CREATE DIPLOM ATTIT ...SOC DICTIONARY INDEX 18/20. PAGE 1 F0011 — WOR-45 COMPUT/IR BIBLIOG/A

B56
PARSONS T.,ECONOMY AND SOCIETY: A STUDY IN THE INTEGRATION OF ECONOMIC AND SOCIAL THEORY. UNIV ACT/RES...SOC CHARTS IDEA/COMP BIBLIOG/A. PAGE 103 F2031 — STRUCT METH/CNCPT UTIL PHIL/SCI

B56
UNIVERSITY OF CHICAGO,BIBLIOGRAPHY OF UKRAINE (PAMPHLET). USSR...SOC 20. PAGE 133 F2619 — BIBLIOG/A COM

B56
US LIBRARY OF CONGRESS,UNITED STATES DIRECT ECONOMIC AID TO FOREIGN COUNTRIES: A COLLECTION OF EXCERPTS AND A BIBLIOGRAPHY (PAMPHLET). USA+45 PRESS DEBATE...ANTHOL BIBLIOG/A CONGRESS. PAGE 138 F2716 — FOR/AID POLICY DIPLOM ECO/UNDEV

B57
BAUER P.T.,ECONOMIC ANALYSIS AND POLICY IN UNDERDEVELOPED COUNTRIES. AFR WOR+45 AGRI INT/TRADE TAX PRICE...GEN/METH BIBLIOG/A 20. PAGE 11 F0214 — ECO/UNDEV METH/COMP POLICY

B57
PATAI R.,JORDAN, LEBANON AND SYRIA: AN ANNOTATED BIBLIOGRAPHY. ISLAM JORDAN LEBANON SYRIA...GEOG 20. PAGE 103 F2034 — BIBLIOG/A SOC

B58
CHEEK G.,ECONOMIC AND SOCIAL IMPLICATIONS OF AUTOMATION: A BIBLIOGRAPHIC REVIEW (PAMPHLET). USA+45 LG/CO WORKER CREATE PLAN CONTROL ROUTINE PERS/REL EFFICIENCY PRODUC...METH/COMP 20. PAGE 24 F0459 — BIBLIOG/A SOCIETY INDUS AUTOMAT

B58
HAMEROW T.S.,RESTORATION, REVOLUTION, REACTION: ECONOMICS AND POLITICS IN GERMANY, 1815-1871. CAP/ISM ADJUST ATTIT PWR...BIBLIOG/A 19 GER/CONFED FRANK/PARL. PAGE 54 F1055 — REV ORD/FREE ECO/DEV

B58
MASON J.B.,THAILAND BIBLIOGRAPHY. S/ASIA THAILAND CULTURE EDU/PROP ADMIN...GEOG SOC LING 20. PAGE 87 F1701 — BIBLIOG/A ECO/UNDEV DIPLOM NAT/G

B58
SCOTT D.J.R.,RUSSIAN POLITICAL INSTITUTIONS. RUSSIA USSR CONSTN AGRI DELIB/GP PLAN EDU/PROP CONTROL CHOOSE EFFICIENCY ATTIT MARXISM...BIBLIOG/A IND 13/20. PAGE 118 F2332 — NAT/G POL/PAR ADMIN DECISION

L58
TRAGER F.N.,"A SELECTED AND ANNOTATED BIBLIOGRAPHY ON ECONOMIC DEVELOPMENT, 1953-1957." WOR+45 AGRI FINAN INDUS MARKET LABOR WORKER PLAN INT/TRADE PRODUC...CENSUS MUNICH. PAGE 131 F2583 — BIBLIOG/A ECO/UNDEV ECO/DEV

B59
HAZLEWOOD A.,THE ECONOMICS OF "UNDER-DEVELOPED" AREAS. WOR+45 DIST/IND EXTR/IND FINAN INDUS MARKET PLAN FOR/AID...GEOG 20. PAGE 57 F1129 — BIBLIOG/A ECO/UNDEV AGRI INT/TRADE

B59
SILCOCK T.H.,THE COMMONWEALTH ECONOMY IN SOUTHEAST ASIA. AFR INDIA MALAYSIA S/ASIA ECO/DEV AGRI LOC/G PLAN TARIFFS COLONIAL BAL/PAY DEMAND...BIBLIOG/A 20 GATT. PAGE 122 F2401 — ECO/TAC INT/TRADE RACE/REL DIPLOM

B60
AHMED J.,NATURAL RESOURCES IN LOW INCOME COUNTRIES: AN ANALYTICAL SURVEY OF SOCIO-ECONOMIC RESEARCH (PAMPHLET). WOR+45 20. PAGE 3 F0052 — BIBLIOG/A ECO/UNDEV INDUS AGRI

B60
AMERICAN U BEIRUT ECO RES INST,A SELECTED AND ANNOTATED BIBLIOGRAPHY OF ECONOMIC LITERATURE ON THE ARABIC SPEAKING COUNTRIES OF THE MIDDLE EAST. ISLAM AGRI COM/IND DIST/IND FINAN INDUS LABOR ...GEOG 20. PAGE 5 F0091 — BIBLIOG/A ECO/UNDEV STAT

B60
FINKLE J.L.,THE PRESIDENT MAKES A DECISION: A STUDY OF DIXON-YATES. OP/RES PROB/SOLV BUDGET ADMIN GOV/REL...POLICY BIBLIOG/A 20 PRESIDENT. PAGE 41 F0799 — DECISION CHIEF PWR POL/PAR

B60
PITCHER G.M.,BIBLIOGRAPHY OF GHANA. AFR GHANA NAT/G 20. PAGE 106 F2091 — BIBLIOG/A SOC

B60
UNESCO,SOUTHERN ASIA SOCIAL SCIENCE BIBLIOGRAPHY (WITH ANNOTATIONS AND ABSTRACTS), 1959 (PAMPHLET). S/ASIA...SOC 20. PAGE 132 F2609 — BIBLIOG/A ECO/UNDEV TEC/DEV INDUS

C60
FAULKNER H.U.,"AMERICAN ECONOMIC HISTORY (8TH ED.)" USA+45 USA-45 FINAN...CHARTS BIBLIOG/A T 17/20. PAGE 39 F0769 — AGRI INDUS ECO/DEV CAP/ISM

B61
DETHINE P.,BIBLIOGRAPHIE DES ASPECTS ECONOMIQUES ET SOCIAUX DE L'INDUSTRIALISATION EN AFRIQUE. AFR FINAN LABOR FOR/AID...SOC 20. PAGE 32 F0623 — BIBLIOG/A ECO/UNDEV INDUS TEC/DEV

B61
FILLOL T.R.,SOCIAL FACTORS IN ECONOMIC DEVELOPMENT: THE ARGENTINE CASE. STRUCT INDUS LABOR CREATE TEC/DEV EFFICIENCY PRODUC DRIVE...METH/CNCPT METH/COMP BIBLIOG/A 20 ARGEN. PAGE 41 F0795 — ECO/UNDEV MGT PERS/REL TREND

B61
HEMPSTONE S.,THE NEW AFRICA. AGRI INDUS KIN NAT/G COLONIAL MARXISM...SOC INT TREND NAT/COMP BIBLIOG/A 20. PAGE 58 F1146 — AFR ORD/FREE PERSON CULTURE

B61
LEE R.R.,ENGINEERING-ECONOMIC PLANNING MISCELLANEOUS SUBJECTS: A SELECTED BIBLIOGRAPHY (MIMEOGRAPHED). FINAN LOC/G NEIGH ADMIN CONTROL INGP/REL HABITAT...GEOG MGT SOC/WK MUNICH 20 RESOURCE/N. PAGE 77 F1509 — BIBLIOG/A PLAN REGION

B61
LEHMAN R.L.,AFRICA SOUTH OF THE SAHARA (PAMPHLET). DIPLOM COLONIAL NAT/LISM. PAGE 77 F1512 — BIBLIOG/A AFR CULTURE NAT/G

B61
THEOBALD R.,THE CHALLENGE OF ABUNDANCE. USA+45 WOR+45 MARKET DIPLOM FOR/AID REV PRODUC UTOPIA SUPEGO...POLICY TREND BIBLIOG/A 20. PAGE 129 F2554 — WELF/ST ECO/UNDEV PROB/SOLV ECO/TAC

B61
WRIGHT H.M.,THE "NEW IMPERIALISM": ANALYSIS OF LATE NINETEENTH-CENTURY EXPANSION. MOD/EUR WOR-45 SOCIETY FINAN ECO/TAC INT/TRADE NAT/LISM...ANTHOL BIBLIOG/A 19. PAGE 149 F2933 — HIST/WRIT IDEA/COMP COLONIAL DOMIN

B62
BOGARDUS J.,OUTLINE FOR THE COURSE IN BUSINESS AND ECONOMICS LITERATURE (REV. ED; PAMPHLET). USA+45 FINAN INDUS NAT/G VOL/ASSN PRESS WRITING INDEX. PAGE 16 F0305 — BIBLIOG/A STAT

B62
KIRPICEVA I.K.,HANDBUCH DER RUSSISCHEN UND SOWJETISCHEN BIBLIOGRAPHIEN (5 VOLS.). USSR STRUCT ECO/DEV DIPLOM LEAD ATTIT 18/20. PAGE 71 F1400 — BIBLIOG/A NAT/G MARXISM COM

B62
VIET J.,INTERNATIONAL COOPERATION AND PROGRAMMES OF ECONOMIC AND SOCIAL DEVELOPMENT. TEC/DEV FOR/AID DOMIN COLONIAL PEACE WEALTH 20 UNESCO. PAGE 141 F2784
BIBLIOG/A INT/ORG DIPLOM ECO/UNDEV

L62
"BIBLIOGRAPHY ON EDUCATION AND ECONOMIC AND SOCIAL DEVELOPMENT (AMERICAN SOURCES)" L/A+17C ECO/UNDEV PROB/SOLV...SOC 20. PAGE 1 F0015
BIBLIOG/A ACADEM EDU/PROP INTELL

L62
"HIGHER EDUCATION AND ECONOMIC AND SOCIAL DEVELOPMENT IN LATIN AMERICA: A BIBLIOGRAPHY." L/A+17C SOCIETY ECO/UNDEV PROF/ORG DIPLOM CONFER ...SOC 20. PAGE 1 F0016
BIBLIOG/A ACADEM INTELL EDU/PROP

B63
BURNS T.G.,DEVELOPMENT BANKING BIBLIOGRAPHY (PAPER). WOR+45 SML/CO VOL/ASSN PLAN BUDGET. PAGE 20 F0391
BIBLIOG/A ECO/DEV FINAN ECO/UNDEV

B63
FREITAG R.S.,AGRICULTURAL DEVELOPMENT SCHEMES IN SUB-SAHARAN AFRICA. AFR EDU/PROP 20. PAGE 44 F0852
BIBLIOG/A AGRI TEC/DEV KNOWL

B63
KATZ S.M.,A SELECTED LIST OF US READINGS ON DEVELOPMENT. AGRI COM/IND DIST/IND INDUS LABOR PLAN FOR/AID EDU/PROP HEALTH...POLICY SOC/WK 20. PAGE 69 F1361
BIBLIOG/A ECO/UNDEV TEC/DEV ACT/RES

B63
MEIER G.,INTERNATIONAL TRADE AND DEVELOPMENT. FINAN BAL/PAY COST DEMAND DISCRIM EQUILIB WEALTH...POLICY ECOMETRIC MATH STAT BIBLIOG/A 20. PAGE 89 F1747
ECO/UNDEV ECO/TAC INT/TRADE IDEA/COMP

B63
UN FAO,BIBLIOGRAPHY ON THE ANALYSIS AND PROJECTION OF DEMAND AND PRODUCTION, 1963. WOR+45 ECO/DEV ECO/UNDEV...PREDICT TREND 20. PAGE 132 F2601
BIBLIOG/A AGRI INDUS

B64
DUSCHA J.,ARMS, MONEY, AND POLITICS. USA+45 INDUS POL/PAR ECO/TAC TAX DETER NUC/PWR WAR WEAPON GOV/REL ATTIT...BIBLIOG/A 20 CONGRESS MONEY DEPT/DEFEN. PAGE 35 F0687
NAT/G FORCES POLICY BUDGET

B64
HAZLEWOOD A.,THE ECONOMICS OF DEVELOPMENT: AN ANNOTATED LIST OF BOOKS AND ARTICLES PUBLISHED 1958-1962. AGRI FINAN INDUS LABOR NAT/G DIPLOM INT/TRADE INCOME...MGT 20. PAGE 58 F1130
BIBLIOG/A ECO/UNDEV TEC/DEV

B64
KNIGHT R.,BIBLIOGRAPHY ON INCOME AND WEALTH, 1957-1960 (VOL VIII). WOR+45 ECO/DEV FINAN INT/TRADE...GOV/COMP METH/COMP. PAGE 72 F1412
BIBLIOG/A ECO/UNDEV WEALTH INCOME

B64
RESOURCES FOR THE FUTURE,URBAN AND REGIONAL STUDIES AT US UNIVERSITIES; A REPORT BASED ON A 1963 SURVEY OF URBAN AND REGIONAL RESEARCH. USA+45 SOCIETY CONSTRUC DIST/IND ACADEM NAT/G ACT/RES ECO/TAC ...CENSUS IDEA/COMP MUNICH. PAGE 111 F2179
BIBLIOG/A REGION PLAN

B64
US LIBRARY OF CONGRESS,SOUTHEAST ASIA. CULTURE ...SOC STAT 20. PAGE 138 F2718
BIBLIOG/A S/ASIA ECO/UNDEV NAT/G

B64
WITHERELL J.W.,OFFICIAL PUBLICATIONS OF FRENCH EQUATORIAL AFRICA, FRENCH CAMEROONS, AND TOGO, 1946-1958 (PAMPHLET). CAMEROON CHAD FRANCE GABON TOGO LAW ECO/UNDEV EXTR/IND INT/TRADE...GEOG HEAL 20. PAGE 148 F2913
BIBLIOG/A AFR NAT/G ADMIN

S64
HORECKY P.L.,"LIBRARY OF CONGRESS PUBLICATIONS IN AID OF USSR AND EAST EUROPEAN RESEARCH." BULGARIA CZECHOSLVK POLAND USSR YUGOSLAVIA NAT/G POL/PAR DIPLOM ADMIN GOV/REL...CLASSIF 20. PAGE 62 F1214
BIBLIOG/A COM MARXISM

B65
PEACE RESEARCH ABSTRACTS. FUT WOR+45 R+D INT/ORG NAT/G PLAN TEC/DEV BAL/PWR DIPLOM FOR/AID NUC/PWR HEALTH. PAGE 1 F0022
BIBLIOG/A PEACE ARMS/CONT WAR

B65
HERRICK B.H.,URBAN MIGRATION AND ECONOMIC DEVELOPMENT IN CHILE. CHILE AGRI INDUS LABOR NAT/G CENTRAL PRODUC...STAT SAMP CHARTS BIBLIOG/A MUNICH 20 MIGRATION. PAGE 59 F1156
HABITAT GEOG ECO/UNDEV

B65
MCCOLL G.D.,THE AUSTRALIAN BALANCE OF PAYMENTS. UK USA+45 AGRI WORKER DIPLOM EQUILIB PRODUC...STAT TREND CHARTS BIBLIOG/A 20 AUSTRAL. PAGE 88 F1719
ECO/DEV BAL/PAY INT/TRADE COST

B65
SABLE M.H.,PERIODICALS FOR LATIN AMERICAN ECONOMIC DEVELOPMENT, TRADE, AND FINANCE: AN ANNOTATED BIBLIOGRAPHY (A PAMPHLET). ECO/TAC PRODUC PROFIT ...STAT NAT/COMP 20 OAS. PAGE 115 F2266
BIBLIOG/A L/A+17C ECO/UNDEV INT/TRADE

B65
SIMMS R.P.,URBANIZATION IN WEST AFRICA; A REVIEW OF CURRENT LITERATURE. AFR PLAN TEC/DEV...SOC OBS NAT/COMP MUNICH 20. PAGE 122 F2405
BIBLIOG/A ECO/DEV ECO/UNDEV

B65
WISH J.R.,ECONOMIC DEVELOPMENT IN LATIN AMERICA: AN ANNOTATED BIBLIOGRAPHY. L/A+17C COM/IND MARKET R+D CREATE CAP/ISM ATTIT...STAT METH 20. PAGE 148 F2912
BIBLIOG/A ECO/UNDEV TEC/DEV AGRI

B66
ALI S.,PLANNING, DEVELOPMENT AND CHANGE: AN ANNOTATED BIBLIOGRAPHY ON DEVELOPMENTAL ADMINISTRATION. PAKISTAN SOCIETY ORD/FREE 20. PAGE 4 F0066
BIBLIOG/A ADMIN ECO/UNDEV PLAN

B66
CANNON M.,THE LAND BOOMERS....BIBLIOG/A 19 AUSTRAL. PAGE 21 F0412
FINAN HABITAT LAISSEZ ECO/UNDEV

B66
ECONOMIC RESEARCH SERVICE,RESEARCH DATA ON MINORITY GROUPS: AN ANNOTATED BIBLIOGRAPHY OF ECONOMIC RESEARCH SERVICE REPORTS: 1955-1965 (PAMPHLET). USA+45 STRATA ECO/DEV AGRI SCHOOL WORKER EDU/PROP HEALTH NEW/LIB SOC. PAGE 36 F0697
BIBLIOG/A DISCRIM WEALTH RACE/REL

B66
GITTINGER J.P.,THE LITERATURE OF AGRICULTURAL PLANNING. UNIV INT/ORG CONSULT WORKER TEC/DEV ECO/TAC OPTIMAL...POLICY METH/COMP BIBLIOG/A 20. PAGE 47 F0927
ECO/UNDEV AGRI PLAN WRITING

B66
HALLET R.,PEOPLE AND PROGRESS IN WEST AFRICA: AN INTRODUCTION TO THE PROBLEMS OF DEVELOPMENT. COM/IND INDUS KIN DIPLOM FOR/AID INT/TRADE HEALTH ...GEOG TREND CHARTS BIBLIOG/A 20 AFRICA/W. PAGE 54 F1050
AFR SOCIETY ECO/UNDEV ECO/TAC

B66
MEERHAEGHE M.,INTERNATIONAL ECONOMIC INSTITUTIONS. EUR+WWI FINAN INDUS MARKET PLAN TARIFFS BAL/PAY EQUILIB...POLICY BIBLIOG/A 20 GATT OEEC EEC IBRD EURCOALSTL. PAGE 89 F1745
ECO/TAC ECO/DEV INT/TRADE INT/ORG

B66
SPULBER N.,THE STATE AND ECONOMIC DEVELOPMENT IN EASTERN EUROPE. BULGARIA COM CZECHOSLVK HUNGARY POLAND YUGOSLAVIA CULTURE PLAN CAP/ISM INT/TRADE CONTROL...POLICY CHARTS METH/COMP BIBLIOG/A 19/20. PAGE 125 F2460
ECO/DEV ECO/UNDEV NAT/G TOTALISM

B66
US DEPARTMENT OF LABOR,PRODUCTIVITY: A BIBLIOGRAPHY. ECO/DEV INDUS MARKET OP/RES AUTOMAT COST...STAT 20. PAGE 135 F2668
BIBLIOG/A PRODUC LABOR PLAN

B66
US DEPARTMENT OF STATE,RESEARCH ON THE USSR AND EASTERN EUROPE (EXTERNAL RESEARCH LIST NO 1-25). USSR LAW CULTURE SOCIETY NAT/G TEC/DEV DIPLOM EDU/PROP REGION...GEOG LING. PAGE 136 F2675
BIBLIOG/A EUR+WWI COM MARXISM

B66
US DEPARTMENT OF STATE,RESEARCH ON WESTERN EUROPE, GREAT BRITAIN, AND CANADA (EXTERNAL RESEARCH LIST NO 3-25). CANADA GERMANY/W UK LAW CULTURE NAT/G POL/PAR FORCES EDU/PROP REGION MARXISM...GEOG SOC WORSHIP 20 CMN/WLTH. PAGE 136 F2676
BIBLIOG/A EUR+WWI DIPLOM

L66
AFRICAN BIBLIOGRAPHIC CENTER,"AFRICAN ECONOMIC AFFAIRS: A SELECT BIBLIOGRAPHICAL SURVEY, 1965-1966; SUPPLEMENTS NUMBERS 1-3." AFR FINAN INDUS LABOR PLAN BUDGET CAP/ISM DIPLOM INT/TRADE ADMIN...GEOG 20. PAGE 3 F0047
BIBLIOG/A ECO/UNDEV FOR/AID TEC/DEV

L66
AMERICAN ECONOMIC REVIEW,"SIXTY-THIRD LIST OF DOCTORAL DISSERTATIONS IN POLITICAL ECONOMY IN AMERICAN UNIVERSITIES AND COLLEGES." ECO/DEV AGRI FINAN LABOR WORKER PLAN BUDGET INT/TRADE ADMIN DEMAND...MGT STAT 20. PAGE 5 F0088
BIBLIOG/A CONCPT ACADEM

S66
ERB GF,"THE UNITED NATIONS CONFERENCE ON TRADE AND DEVELOPMENT (UNCTAD): A SELECTED CURRENT READING LIST." FINAN FOR/AID CONFER 20 UN. PAGE 38 F0742
BIBLIOG/A INT/TRADE ECO/UNDEV INT/ORG

N66
PRINCETON U INDUSTRIAL REL SEC,PUBLIC PROGRAMS TO CREATE JOBS (PAMPHLET NO. 125). USA+45 ECO/DEV INDUS PLAN ECO/TAC AGE/Y 20. PAGE 108 F2119
BIBLIOG/A NAT/G POLICY WORKER

N66
PRINCETON U INDUSTRIAL REL SEC,RECENT MATERIAL ON COLLECTIVE BARGAINING IN GOVERNMENT (PAMPHLET NO. 130). USA+45 ECO/DEV LABOR WORKER ECO/TAC GOV/REL ...MGT 20. PAGE 108 F2120
BIBLIOG/A BARGAIN NAT/G GP/REL

N66
PRINCETON U INDUSTRIAL REL SEC,THE ROLE OF THE PUBLIC EMPLOYMENT SERVICE (PAMPHLET NO. 129). USA+45 ECO/DEV PLAN ECO/TAC GOV/REL 20. PAGE 108 F2121
BIBLIOG/A NAT/G POLICY LABOR

N66
US ADVISORY COMN INTERGOV REL,CATALOGS AND OTHER INFORMATION SOURCES ON FEDERAL AND STATE AID PROGRAMS: A SECTED BIBLIOGRAPHY (PAPER). USA+45 LAW LOC/G NAT/G PROVS VOL/ASSN TEC/DEV ADMIN HEALTH ...WELF/ST SOC/WK MUNICH. PAGE 134 F2635 BIBLIOG/A GOV/REL FINAN ECO/DEV

B67
BAILY S.L.,LABOR, NATIONALISM, AND POLITICS IN ARGENTINA. POL/PAR TOP/EX GP/REL...BIBLIOG/A 19/20 MIGRATION PERON/JUAN ARGEN. PAGE 8 F0154 LABOR NAT/LISM

B67
BARANSON J.,TECHNOLOGY FOR UNDERDEVELOPED AREAS: AN ANNOTATED BIBLIOGRAPHY. FUT WOR+45 CULTURE INDUS INT/ORG CREATE PROB/SOLV INT/TRADE EDU/PROP AUTOMAT ...CONCPT METH. PAGE 10 F0181 BIBLIOG/A ECO/UNDEV TEC/DEV R+D

B67
BLAUG M.,ECONOMICS OF EDUCATION: A SELECTED ANNOTATED BIBLIOGRAPHY. EUR+WWI INTELL ECO/DEV ECO/UNDEV ACADEM INT/ORG NAT/G CREATE ADMIN EFFICIENCY ROLE PREDICT. PAGE 16 F0298 BIBLIOG/A EDU/PROP FINAN PLAN

B67
CLEGERN W.M.,BRITISH HONDURAS: COLONIAL DEAD END, 1859-1900. HONDURAS AGRI FINAN PROB/SOLV INT/TRADE PWR WEALTH...BIBLIOG/A 19. PAGE 25 F0487 COLONIAL POLICY ECO/UNDEV DOMIN

B67
GRIPP R.C.,PATTERNS OF SOVIET POLITICS (REV. ED.). USSR LAW ELITES LOC/G PLAN CONTROL CT/SYS CHOOSE ...POLICY BIBLIOG/A DICTIONARY 9/20. PAGE 51 F1003 COM ADJUD POL/PAR

B67
MONTGOMERY J.D.,FOREIGN AID IN INTERNATIONAL POLITICS. USA+45 USA-45 WOR+45 ECO/TAC EFFICIENCY ...SOC TREND CHARTS BIBLIOG/A 20 AID. PAGE 93 F1818 DIPLOM FOR/AID

B67
SHAFFER H.G.,THE COMMUNIST WORLD: MARXIST AND NON-MARXIST VIEWS. WOR+45 SOCIETY DIPLOM ECO/TAC CONTROL SOCISM...MARXIST ANTHOL BIBLIOG/A 20. PAGE 120 F2363 MARXISM NAT/COMP IDEA/COMP COM

B67
SPECTOR S.D.,CHECKLIST OF ITEMS IN THE NDEA INSTITUTE LIBRARY (PAMPHLET). USA+45 NAT/G SECT EDU/PROP ATTIT ALL/IDEOS...SOC BIOG. PAGE 124 F2448 BIBLIOG/A COM MARXISM

B67
UNIVERSAL REFERENCE SYSTEM,BIBLIOGRAPHY OF BIBLIOGRAPHIES IN POLITICAL SCIENCE, GOVERNMENT, AND PUBLIC POLICY (VOLUME III). WOR+45 WOR-45 LAW ADMIN...SOC CON/ANAL COMPUT/IR GEN/METH. PAGE 133 F2615 BIBLIOG/A NAT/G DIPLOM POLICY

B67
UNIVERSAL REFERENCE SYSTEM,ADMINISTRATIVE MANAGEMENT: PUBLIC AND PRIVATE BUREAUCRACY (VOLUME IV). WOR+45 WOR-45 ECO/DEV LG/CO LOC/G PUB/INST VOL/ASSN GOV/REL...COMPUT/IR GEN/METH. PAGE 133 F2616 BIBLIOG/A MGT ADMIN NAT/G

B67
UNIVERSAL REFERENCE SYSTEM,ECONOMIC REGULATION, BUSINESS, AND GOVERNMENT (VOLUME VIII). WOR+45 WOR-45 ECO/DEV ECO/UNDEV FINAN LABOR TEC/DEV ECO/TAC INT/TRADE GOV/REL...POLICY COMPUT/IR. PAGE 133 F2617 BIBLIOG/A CONTROL NAT/G

B67
UNIVERSAL REFERENCE SYSTEM,PUBLIC POLICY AND THE MANAGEMENT OF SCIENCE (VOLUME IX). FUT SPACE WOR+45 LAW NAT/G TEC/DEV CONTROL NUC/PWR GOV/REL ...COMPUT/IR GEN/METH. PAGE 133 F2618 BIBLIOG/A POLICY MGT PHIL/SCI

B67
YOUNG J.M.,THE BRAZILIAN REVOLUTION OF 1930 AND THE AFTERMATH. BRAZIL COLONIAL PWR...BIBLIOG/A 16/20. PAGE 150 F2951 PLAN CHIEF FORCES REV

S67
MALKIN A.,"BUSINESS BOOKS OF 1966." INDUS LABOR OP/RES TEC/DEV CAP/ISM ECO/TAC INCOME WEALTH 20. PAGE 84 F1649 BIBLIOG/A FINAN MARKET

BICAMERALISM....SEE LEGIS, CONGRESS, HOUSE/REP, SENATE

BIDWELL P.W. F0279

BIEL G. F0280

BIENSTOCK G. F0281

BIERKAEMPER C. F2795

BIERMAN H. F0282,F0283

BIGELOW K.W. F0532

BIGLER/W....WILLIAM BIGLER

BILL J.A. F0284

BILL/RIGHT....BILL OF RIGHTS

BILLERBECK K. F0285

BINNS/JJ....JOSEPH J. BINNS

BIO/SOC....BIO-SOCIAL PROCESSES, DRUGS, SEXUALITY

N19
PALAMOUNTAIN JC J.R.,THE DOLCIN CASE AND THE FEDERAL TRADE COMMISSION (PAMPHLET). USA+45 LAW MARKET SERV/IND LG/CO NAT/G BIO/SOC 20 FTC. PAGE 103 F2018 ADJUD PROB/SOLV EDU/PROP HEALTH

B22
VON ENGELIN O.D.,INHERITING THE EARTH, THE GEOGRAPHICAL FACTOR IN NATIONAL DEVELOPMENT. WOR-45 CULTURE DIPLOM BIO/SOC HABITAT PERSON...PSY SOC CONCPT IDEA/COMP. PAGE 142 F2791 INGP/REL GEOG SOCIETY ROLE

B30
THOMPSON W.R.,POPULATION PROBLEMS. FUT UNIV WOR-45 STRUCT DIST/IND ACT/RES ECO/TAC BIO/SOC...CONCPT OBS TIME/SEQ TOT/POP 20. PAGE 130 F2567 ECO/UNDEV GEOG

B50
CLARK J.M.,ALTERNATIVE TO SERFDOM. SOCIETY STRATA INDUS MARKET WORKER PRICE GP/REL PROFIT BIO/SOC PWR WEALTH...GEN/LAWS 20 KEYNES/JM. PAGE 25 F0481 ORD/FREE POPULISM ECO/TAC REPRESENT

S53
HANSER P.M.,"EXPLODING POPULATIONS: INTERNATIONAL AND REGIONAL ASPECTS." AFR S/ASIA ECO/TAC WEAPON BIO/SOC LOVE ORD/FREE...NEW/IDEA CENSUS TOT/POP 20. PAGE 55 F1069 ECO/UNDEV GEOG

S59
THOMPSON W.S.,"POPULATION AND PROGRESS IN THE FAR EAST." ASIA S/ASIA DIST/IND CREATE ECO/TAC WAR LOVE SKILL WEALTH...CONT/OBS TOT/POP 20. PAGE 130 F2568 ECO/UNDEV BIO/SOC GEOG

S60
JAFFEE A.J.,"POPULATION TRENDS AND CONTROLS IN UNDERDEVELOPED COUNTRIES." AFR FUT ISLAM L/A+17C S/ASIA CULTURE R+D FAM ACT/RES PLAN EDU/PROP BIO/SOC RIGID/FLEX HEALTH...SOC STAT OBS CHARTS 20. PAGE 66 F1303 ECO/UNDEV GEOG

S60
MILLER A.S.,"SOME OBSERVATIONS ON THE POLITICAL ECONOMY OF POPULATION GROWTH." FUT USA+45 ECO/DEV R+D CONSULT PLAN TEC/DEV ECO/TAC ROUTINE BIO/SOC WEALTH...POLICY OBS. PAGE 91 F1790 SOCIETY GEOG

B65
LUGO-MARENCO J.J.,A STATEMENT OF THE LAWS OF NICARAGUA IN MATTERS AFFECTING BUSINESS. NICARAGUA AGRI DIST/IND EXTR/IND FINAN INDUS FAM WORKER INT/TRADE TAX MARRIAGE OWN BIO/SOC 20 TREATY RESOURCE/N MIGRATION. PAGE 82 F1606 CONSTN NAT/G LEGIS JURID

B67
HEADLEY J.C.,PESTICIDE PROBLEM: AN ECONOMIC APPROACH TO PUBLIC POLICY. AGRI TEC/DEV GOV/REL COST ATTIT CHARTS. PAGE 58 F1131 HABITAT POLICY BIO/SOC CONTROL

B67
SPURRIER R.B.,THE OVERPOPULATED SOCIETY. WORKER EATING PERS/REL DEMAND EQUILIB ILLEGIT INCOME HABITAT 20. PAGE 125 F2461 BIO/SOC FOR/AID DRIVE RECEIVE

L67
SEABERG G.P.,"THE DRUG ABUSE PROBLEMS AND SOME PROPOSALS." UK USA+45 MARKET SANCTION CRIME ...POLICY NEW/IDEA. PAGE 119 F2339 BIO/SOC LAW ADJUD PROB/SOLV

L67
ZEIDBERG L.D.,"THE NASHVILLE AIR POLLUTION STUDY" (PARTS V-VII)" USA+45 PLAN AGE HEALTH...GEOG STAT CENSUS SAMP/SIZ CHARTS BIBLIOG MUNICH. PAGE 150 F2962 DEATH HABITAT AIR BIO/SOC

BIOG....BIOGRAPHY (INCLUDES PSYCHOANALYSIS)

N
THE MIDDLE EAST. CULTURE...BIOG BIBLIOG. PAGE 1 F0010 ISLAM INDUS FINAN

B04
MARX K.,A CONTRIBUTION TO THE CRITIQUE OF POLITICAL ECONOMY (TRANS. FROM 2ND ED. BY N.I. STONE). UK STRATA ECO/DEV FINAN MARKET PLAN BARGAIN CAP/ISM ECO/TAC ATTIT WEALTH...METH/CNCPT BIOG 19. PAGE 86 F1687 MARXIST NEW/IDEA MARXISM

B13
BEARD C.A.,AN ECONOMIC INTERPRETATION OF THE CONSTITUTION OF THE UNITED STATES. USA-45 AGRI INT/TRADE SUFF OWN ATTIT...CONCPT MYTH BIOG HIST/WRIT 18. PAGE 12 F0222 CONSTN ECO/TAC CHOOSE

B47
WEBER M.,THE THEORY OF SOCIAL AND ECONOMIC ORGANIZATION. STRUCT LABOR POL/PAR ECO/TAC LEGIT PRODUC BIOG. PAGE 144 F2840 ECO/DEV SOC PHIL/SCI LEAD

B51
HARROD R.F.,THE LIFE OF JOHN MAYNARD KEYNES. UK INTELL FAM CAP/ISM DIPLOM ECO/TAC WAR ATTIT PERSON ROLE 20 KEYNES/JM WWI. PAGE 56 F1094 BIOG FINAN GEN/LAWS

B61
STANLEY C.J.,LATE CH'ING FINANCE: HU KUANG-YUNG AS AN INNOVATOR. ASIA NAT/G FORCES BUDGET TAX WAR GOV/REL COST...POLICY BIOG CHARTS BIBLIOG 19. PAGE 125 F2469 FINAN ECO/TAC CIVMIL/REL ADMIN

S63
MATHUR P.N.,"GAINS IN ECONOMIC GROWTH FROM INTERNATIONAL TRADE." USA-45 ECO/DEV FINAN INDUS ATTIT WEALTH...MATH QUANT STAT BIOG TREND GEN/LAWS WORK 20. PAGE 87 F1704 MARKET ECO/TAC CAP/ISM INT/TRADE

B64
SULLIVAN G.,THE STORY OF THE PEACE CORPS. USA+45 WOR+45 INTELL FACE/GP NAT/G SCHOOL VOL/ASSN CONSULT EX/STRUC PLAN EDU/PROP ADMIN ATTIT DRIVE ALL/VALS ...POLICY HEAL SOC CONCPT INT QU BIOG TREND SOC/EXP WORK. PAGE 127 F2511 INT/ORG ECO/UNDEV FOR/AID PEACE

S64
WOOD N.,"THE FAMILY FIRM - BASE OF JAPAN'S GROWING ECONOMY." ECO/DEV ECO/UNDEV ECO/TAC WEALTH...POLICY TRADIT BIOG TREND 20 CHINJAP. PAGE 148 F2921 ASIA SML/CO FAM

B65
ACHTERBERG E.,BERLINER HOCHFINANZ - KAISER, FURSTEN, MILLIONARE UM 1900. GERMANY NAT/G EDU/PROP PERSON...MGT MUNICH 19/20. PAGE 2 F0033 FINAN BIOG ECO/TAC

B66
EBONY,THE NEGRO HANDBOOK. ACADEM LABOR LOC/G SECT FORCES WORKER CT/SYS CRIME DISCRIM ORD/FREE...BIOG SOC/INTEG 19/20 NEGRO CIV/RIGHTS. PAGE 36 F0692 RACE/REL EDU/PROP LAW STAT

B66
FRANKEL P.H.,MATTEI; OIL AND POWER POLITICS. ITALY EXTR/IND MARKET GP/REL NAT/LISM SOCISM...POLICY MGT BIOG 20 MATTEI/E. PAGE 43 F0844 LEAD NAT/G CONTROL LG/CO

B66
WECHSBERG J.,THE MERCHANT BANKERS. EUR+WWI MOD/EUR CONTROL...BIOG GP/COMP PERS/COMP 16/20. PAGE 144 F2842 FINAN PWR WEALTH FAM

B67
MENDEL A.P.,POLITICAL MEMOIRS 1905-1917 BY PAUL MILIUKOV (TRANS. BY CARL GOLDBERG). USSR AGRI DIPLOM ECO/TAC POPULISM...MAJORIT 20. PAGE 90 F1757 BIOG LEAD NAT/G CONSTN

B67
SPECTOR S.D.,CHECKLIST OF ITEMS IN THE NDEA INSTITUTE LIBRARY (PAMPHLET). USA+45 NAT/G SECT EDU/PROP ATTIT ALL/IDEOS...SOC BIOG. PAGE 124 F2448 BIBLIOG/A COM MARXISM

S67
GOSALVEZ R.B.,"PERFIL DEL GENERAL VINCENTE ROJO." SPAIN DIPLOM CIVMIL/REL EFFICIENCY PERSON SKILL 20 BOLIV. PAGE 49 F0966 WAR FORCES ELITES BIOG

L86
OSGOOD H.L.,"SCIENTIFIC SOCIALISM: RODBERTUS" GERMANY CAP/ISM COST WEALTH...MAJORIT BIOG IDEA/COMP 19 RODBRTUS/C. PAGE 102 F2002 SOCISM MARXISM ECO/DEV ECO/TAC

BIRCH/SOC....JOHN BIRCH SOCIETY

BIRD R.M. F0030

BIRMINGHAM W. F0286,F0287

BIRNBAUM N. F0288

BIRTH/CON....BIRTH CONTROL POLICIES AND TECHNIQUES

S41
MUKERJEE R.,"POPULATION THEORY AND POLITICS (BMR)" WOR-45 NAT/G PLAN PROB/SOLV ECO/TAC INT/TRADE CONTROL WAR PEACE...CENSUS 20 BIRTH/CON RESOURCE/N. PAGE 94 F1854 GEOG OPTIMAL CONCPT

B66
US SENATE COMM GOVT OPERATIONS,HEARINGS BEFORE SUBCOMMITTEE ON FOREIGN AID EXPENDITURES: POPULATION CRISIS VOLUMES 1-5 JUNE-SEPT 1965. STRATA ECO/UNDEV PLAN TEC/DEV EDU/PROP ATTIT HEALTH ...GEOG CHARTS 20 CONGRESS BIRTH/CON CASEBOOK. PAGE 138 F2729 ECO/DEV CENSUS FAM CONTROL

BISMARCK/O....OTTO VON BISMARCK

BISSON A. F0289

BLACK E.R. F0290

BLACK J.D. F0291

BLACK R.L. F0537

BLACK/EUG....EUGENE BLACK

B66
US SENATE COMM ON FOREIGN REL,ASIAN DEVELOPMENT BANK ACT. USA+45 LAW DIPLOM...CHARTS 20 BLACK/EUG S/EASTASIA. PAGE 139 F2736 FOR/AID FINAN ECO/UNDEV S/ASIA

BLACK/HL....HUGO L. BLACK

BLACK/MUS....BLACK MUSLIMS

BLACK/PWR....BLACK POWER; SEE ALSO NEGRO

BLACK/ZION....BLACK ZIONISM

BLACKSTN/W....SIR WILLIAM BLACKSTONE

BLACKSTOCK P.W. F0292

BLAIR G.S. F0293

BLAIR P.W. F0294

BLAIR T.L.V. F0295

BLAISDELL D.C. F0296

BLAKE R.R. F0297

BLAUG M. F0298

BLOCH/E....ERNEST BLOCH

BLOCK H.D. F0124

BLOMSTROM R.L. F0591

BLOOM G.F. F0299

BLOOMFIELD A. F0300

BLOUGH R. F0301

BLUEPRINTS....SEE ORG/CHARTS

BMA....BRITISH MEDICAL ASSOCIATION

BOARD....SEE DELIB/GP

BOARD/MDCN....BOARD ON MEDICINE

BOARMAN P.M. F0302

BOAS/FRANZ....FRANZ BOAS

BOB....BUREAU OF THE BUDGET

S56
MERRIAM R.E.,"THE BUREAU OF THE BUDGET AS PART OF THE PRESIDENT'S STAFF." 20 BUR/BUDGET 20 BOB. PAGE 90 F1763 CHIEF CONTROL LEAD EXEC

BOCK E. F0303

BODIN/JEAN....JEAN BODIN

BOEKE J.H. F0304

BOER/WAR....BOER WAR

BOGARDUS J. F0305

BOGARDUS....BOGARDUS SCALE

BOGEN J.I. F0306

BOHM F. F0307

BOHME/H....HELMUT BOHME

BOKOR-SZEGO H. F0308

BOLIVIA....SEE ALSO L/A+17C

B62
URQUIDI C.W.,A STATEMENT OF THE LAWS OF BOLIVIA IN MATTERS AFFECTING BUSINESS (3RD ED. REV., ENLARGED). L/A+17C LAW FINAN FAM WORKER ACT/RES DIPLOM ADJUD ADMIN GP/REL 20 BOLIV OAS. PAGE 133 F2626 JURID INDUS NAT/G LEGIT

B63
SCHOECK H.,THE NEW ARGUMENT IN ECONOMICS. UK USA+45 INDUS MARKET LABOR NAT/G ECO/TAC ADMIN ROUTINE BAL/PAY PWR...POLICY BOLIV. PAGE 117 F2309 WELF/ST FOR/AID ECO/DEV ALL/IDEOS

S64
KLEIN H.,"AMERICAN OIL COMPANIES IN LATIN AMERICA: THE BOLIVIAN EXPERIENCE." L/A+17C USA+45 USA-45 EXTR/IND LG/CO NAT/G ECO/TAC WEALTH...POLICY GEN/LAWS BOLIV TOT/POP 20 OIL. PAGE 72 F1405
MARKET ECO/UNDEV NAT/LISM

B67
PIKE F.B.,FREEDOM AND REFORM IN LATIN AMERICA. BRAZIL URUGUAY CONSTN CULTURE SECT DIPLOM EDU/PROP PARTIC DRIVE ALL/VALS CATHISM...GEOG ANTHOL BIBLIOG REFORMERS BOLIV. PAGE 106 F2086
L/A+17C ORD/FREE ECO/UNDEV REV

B67
ZONDAG C.H.,THE BOLIVIAN ECONOMY 1952-65. L/A+17C TEC/DEV FOR/AID ADMIN...OBS TREND CHARTS BIBLIOG 20 BOLIV. PAGE 151 F2969
ECO/UNDEV INDUS PRODUC

S67
GOSALVEZ R.B.,"PERFIL DEL GENERAL VINCENTE ROJO." SPAIN DIPLOM CIVMIL/REL EFFICIENCY PERSON SKILL 20 BOLIV. PAGE 49 F0966
WAR FORCES ELITES BIOG

S67
HEATH D.B.,"BOLIVIA UNDER BARRIENTOS." L/A+17C NAT/G CHIEF DIPLOM ECO/TAC...POLICY 20 BOLIV. PAGE 58 F1132
ECO/UNDEV POL/PAR REV CONSTN

BOLIVAR/S....SIMON BOLIVAR

N19
LANGE O.R.,"DISARMAMENT ECONOMIC GROWTH AND INTERNATIONAL CO-OPERATION" (PAMPHLET). WOR+45 DIST/IND PLAN INT/TRADE GIVE TASK DETER WEALTH SOCISM 18/19 BOLIVAR/S. PAGE 75 F1477
ARMS/CONT DIPLOM ECO/DEV ECO/UNDEV

BOLLENS J.C. F0309

BOLSHEVISM....BOLSHEVISM AND BOLSHEVIKS

B59
HENDEL S.,THE SOVIET CRUCIBLE. USSR LEAD COERCE NAT/LISM UTOPIA PWR...POLICY CONCPT ANTHOL 20 STALIN/J LENIN/VI MARX/KARL BOLSHEVIK. PAGE 58 F1147
COM MARXISM REV TOTALISM

B66
BRODERSEN A.,THE SOVIET WORKER: LABOR AND GOVERNMENT IN SOVIET SOCIETY. USSR STRUCT INDUS LABOR PLAN PAY INGP/REL PRODUC...POLICY GEN/LAWS BIBLIOG 20 STALIN/J LENIN/VI BOLSHEVISM KHRUSH/N. PAGE 19 F0357
WORKER ROLE NAT/G MARXISM

BOLTON R.E. F0310

BONAPART/L....LOUIS BONAPARTE (KING OF HOLLAND)

BONFIELD A.E. F0311

BONILLA F. F0312

BONINI C.P. F0313

BONNEFOUS M. F0314

BONNET R. F0911

BONNETT C.E. F0315,F0316,F0317

BONTOC....BONTOC, A MOUNTAIN TRIBE OF LUZON, PHILIPPINES

BOONE A. F0318

BOONE/DANL....DANIEL BOONE

BORDEN/R....SIR ROBER BORDEN

BORK R.H. F0331

BORNEO....SEE ALSO S/A A

BOS H.C. F0319

BOSCH/JUAN....JUAN BOSC

BOSHER J.F. F0320

BOSSISM....BOSSISM; MONOPOLY OF POLITICAL POWER (U.S.)

BOSTON....BOSTON, MASSACHUSETTS

B60
CARPER E.T.,THE DEFENSE APPROPRIATIONS RIDER (PAMPHLET). USA+45 CONSTN CHIEF DELIB/GP LEGIS BUDGET LOBBY CIVMIL/REL...POLICY 20 CONGRESS EISNHWR/DD DEPT/DEFEN PRESIDENT BOSTON. PAGE 22 F0419
GOV/REL ADJUD LAW CONTROL

B65
GREER S.,URBAN RENEWAL AND AMERICAN CITIES: THE DILEMMA OF DEMOCRATIC INTERVENTION. USA+45 R+D LOC/G VOL/ASSN ACT/RES BUDGET ADMIN GOV/REL...SOC INT SAMP MUNICH 20 BOSTON CHICAGO LOS/ANG MIAMI URBAN/RNWL. PAGE 51 F0992
PROB/SOLV PLAN NAT/G

BOTSWANA....BOTSWANA

BOULDER....BOULDER, COLORADO

BOULDING K.E. F0252,F0321,F0322,F0323

BOURASSA/H....HENRI BOURASSA

BOURGOIGNIE G.E. F0324

BOUSTEDT O. F0325

BOWEN H.R. F0326,F0327

BOWEN R.H. F0328

BOWEN W.G. F0329,F0330

BOWIE R.R. F0331

BOWMAN M.J. F0092

BOXER/REBL....BOXER REBELLION

BOYD H.W. F0332

BRADLEY J.F. F0333

BRADLEY P.H. F0444

BRADLEY/FH....FRANCIS HERBERT BRADLEY

BRADY R.A. F0334

BRAFF A.J. F0335

BRAHMANAND P.R. F2759

BRAHMIN....BRAHMIN CASTE

BRAIBANTI R.J.D. F0336,F0337

BRAINWASHING....SEE EDU/PROP

BRANCH M.C. F0338

BRANCO R. F0339

BRANDEIS/L....LOUIS BRANDEIS

BRANDENBURG F. F0340

BRANNAN/C....CHARLES BRANNAN (SECRETARY OF AGRICULTURE)

BRAUCHER R. F0341

BRAUN K. F0342

BRAY J.J. F1496

BRAYBROOKE D. F0343

BRAZIL....SEE ALSO L/A+17C

B38
CARVALHO C.M.,GEOGRAPHIA HUMANA; POLITICA E ECONOMICA (3RD ED.). BRAZIL CULTURE AGRI INDUS DIPLOM COLONIAL GP/REL RACE/REL...LING 20 RESOURCE/N. PAGE 22 F0424
GEOG HABITAT

B55
GOMES F.A.,OPERACAO MUNICIPIO. BRAZIL L/A+17C SERV/IND LOC/G BUDGET ECO/TAC COST DEMAND...POLICY MUNICH 20. PAGE 48 F0944
ECO/UNDEV FEDERAL GOV/REL

B59
ROCHE J.,LA COLONISATION ALLEMANDE ET LE RIO GRANDE DO SUL. BRAZIL L/A+17C NAT/G PROVS INGP/REL RACE/REL DISCRIM HABITAT...GEOG SOC/INTEG 19/20 MIGRATION. PAGE 113 F2228
ECO/UNDEV GP/REL ATTIT

B60
FERNANDES F.,MUDANCAS SOCIAIS NO BRASIL. BRAZIL L/A+17C SOCIETY AGRI PROVS LEAD GP/REL RACE/REL ORD/FREE...SOC SOC/INTEG 20 SAO/PAULO. PAGE 40 F0786
ECO/UNDEV STRATA INDUS

B61
LUZ N.V.,A LUTA PELA INDUSTRIALIZACAO DO BRAZIL. BRAZIL L/A+17C AGRI NAT/G TEC/DEV COLONIAL 19/20. PAGE 82 F1615
ECO/UNDEV INDUS NAT/LISM POLICY

B62
GALENSON W.,LABOR IN DEVELOPING COUNTRIES. BRAZIL INDONESIA ISRAEL PAKISTAN TURKEY AGRI INDUS WORKER PAY PRICE GP/REL WEALTH...MGT CHARTS METH/COMP NAT/COMP 20. PAGE 45 F0888
LABOR ECO/UNDEV BARGAIN POL/PAR

B62
LEVY H.V.,LIBERDADE E JUSTICA SOCIAL (2ND ED.). BRAZIL COM L/A+17C USSR INT/ORG PARTIC GP/REL WEALTH 20 UN COM/PARTY. PAGE 79 F1544
ORD/FREE MARXISM CAP/ISM LAW

B63
HIRSCHMAN A.O.,JOURNEYS TOWARD PROGRESS: STUDIES OF ECONOMIC POLICYMAKING IN LATIN AMERICA. CHILE FUT ECO/UNDEV AGRI FINAN INDUS CONSULT DELIB/GP PLAN ATTIT HEALTH ORD/FREE WEALTH...POLICY STAT VAL/FREE COLOMB 20. PAGE 60 F1177
L/A+17C ECO/TAC BRAZIL

B63
IANNI O.,INDUSTRIALIZACAO E DESENVOLVIMENTO SOCIAL NO BRASIL. BRAZIL L/A+17C STRATA STRUCT ECO/UNDEV EDU/PROP LEAD LOBBY NAT/LISM 20. PAGE 64 F1257
WORKER GP/REL INDUS PARTIC

B63
MENEZES A.J.,SUBDESENVOLVIMENTO E POLITICA INTERNACIONAL. BRAZIL WOR+45 PLAN CONTROL LEAD NAT/LISM ORD/FREE 20 THIRD/WRLD. PAGE 90 F1759
ECO/UNDEV DIPLOM POLICY BAL/PWR

B63
RANGEL I.,A INFLACAO BRASILEIRA (2ND ED.). AFR BRAZIL AGRI INDUS MARKET INT/TRADE DEMAND EQUILIB ATTIT 20. PAGE 109 F2144
ECO/UNDEV FINAN PRICE TAX

B63
WAGLEY C.,INTRODUCTION TO BRAZIL. BRAZIL L/A+17C FAM KIN SCHOOL SECT ATTIT WEALTH...GEOG SOC. PAGE 142 F2799
ECO/UNDEV ELITES HABITAT STRATA

S63
POPPINO R.E.,"IMBALANCE IN BRAZIL." L/A+17C NAT/G TOP/EX PLAN DIPLOM LEGIT DRIVE WEALTH...CON/ANAL FOR/TRADE LAFTA 20. PAGE 107 F2105
POL/PAR ECO/TAC BRAZIL

B64
COMPOS R.O.,A MOEDA, O GOVERNO E O TEMPO. AFR BRAZIL WOR+45 FINAN TEC/DEV FOR/AID REGION DEMAND ...ANTHOL 20. PAGE 27 F0520
ECO/UNDEV PLAN DIPLOM INT/TRADE

B64
ODEH H.S.,THE IMPACT OF INFLATION ON THE LEVEL OF ECONOMIC ACTIVITY. AFR BRAZIL CHILE BUDGET GOV/REL COST DEMAND INCOME WEALTH...STAT METH 20 MONEY. PAGE 100 F1963
ECOMETRIC ECO/TAC ECO/UNDEV FINAN

B64
SINGER H.W.,INTERNATIONAL DEVELOPMENT: GROWTH AND CHANGE. AFR BRAZIL L/A+17C WOR+45 CULTURE AGRI INDUS NAT/G ACT/RES ECO/TAC EDU/PROP WEALTH...GEOG CONCPT METH/CNCPT STAT HYPO/EXP WORK TOT/POP 20. PAGE 122 F2412
FINAN ECO/UNDEV FOR/AID INT/TRADE

B64
WITHERS W.,THE ECONOMIC CRISIS IN LATIN AMERICA. BRAZIL CHILE STRATA AGRI DIPLOM FOR/AID PWR SOCISM ...POLICY 20 MEXIC/AMER ARGEN ALL/PROG. PAGE 148 F2914
L/A+17C ECO/UNDEV CAP/ISM ALL/IDEOS

S65
BRANDENBURG F.,"THE RELEVANCE OF MEXICAN EXPERIENCE TO LATIN AMERICAN DEVELOPMENT." BRAZIL CHILE VENEZUELA STRUCT ECO/UNDEV AGRI CREATE ECO/TAC ...STAT RECORD MEXIC/AMER ARGEN COLOMB. PAGE 18 F0340
L/A+17C GOV/COMP

S65
TENDLER J.D.,"TECHNOLOGY AND ECONOMIC DEVELOPMENT* THE CASE OF HYDRO VS THERMAL POWER." CONSTRUC DIST/IND CREATE TEC/DEV INT/TRADE CENTRAL PWR SKILL WEALTH...MGT NAT/COMP ARGEN. PAGE 129 F2544
BRAZIL INDUS ECO/UNDEV

B66
BAKLANOFF E.N.,NEW PERSPECTIVES ON BRAZIL. BRAZIL SOCIETY INDUS DOMIN LEAD REV CIVMIL/REL...GEOG PSY LING ANTHOL 20. PAGE 8 F0156
ECO/UNDEV TEC/DEV DIPLOM ORD/FREE

B66
BOYD H.W.,MARKETING MANAGEMENT: CASES FROM EMERGING COUNTRIES. BRAZIL GHANA ISRAEL WOR+45 ADMIN PERS/REL ATTIT HABITAT WEALTH...ANTHOL 20 ARGEN CASEBOOK. PAGE 17 F0332
MGT ECO/UNDEV PROB/SOLV MARKET

B67
PIKE F.B.,FREEDOM AND REFORM IN LATIN AMERICA. BRAZIL URUGUAY CONSTN CULTURE SECT DIPLOM EDU/PROP PARTIC DRIVE ALL/VALS CATHISM...GEOG ANTHOL BIBLIOG REFORMERS BOLIV. PAGE 106 F2086
L/A+17C ORD/FREE ECO/UNDEV REV

B67
YOUNG J.M.,THE BRAZILIAN REVOLUTION OF 1930 AND THE AFTERMATH. BRAZIL COLONIAL PWR...BIBLIOG/A 16/20. PAGE 150 F2951
PLAN CHIEF FORCES REV

S67
ALVES V.,"FOREIGN CAPITAL IN BRAZIL." BRAZIL USA+45 CAP/ISM DIPLOM ECO/TAC INT/TRADE CONTROL PWR ...POLICY 20. PAGE 4 F0081
ECO/UNDEV FINAN SOCIALIST SOCISM

S67
GRAHAM R.,"BRAZIL'S DILEMMA." BRAZIL FUT L/A+17C NAT/G CHIEF PROB/SOLV ECO/TAC PWR 20. PAGE 50 F0972
ECO/UNDEV CONSTN POL/PAR POLICY

BREAK G.F. F0344,F0345

BREHON....BREHON LAW (ANCIENT CELTIC)

BRENNAN M.J. F0346

BRESCIANI-TURRONI C F0347

BREWIS T.N. F0348

BRIAND/A....ARISTIDE BRIAND

BRIDGEPORT....BRIDGEPORT, CONNECTICUT

BRIDGES F.J. F0445

BRIEFS H.W. F0349,F0350,F0438

BRIGHAM E.F. F0351

BRIGHT J.R. F0352

BRIMMER A.F. F0353

BRIT/COLUM....BRITISH COLUMBIA, CANADA

BRITISH COLUMBIA, CANADA....SEE BRIT/COLUM

BRITISH COMMONWEALTH OF NATIONS....SEE COMMONWLTH

BRITISH GUIANA....SEE GUIANA/BR

BRITISH COMMONWEALTH BUR AGRI F0354

BRITT S.H. F0355

BROCKWAY A.F. F0356

BRODERSEN A. F0357

BRODIE H. F2845

BROEKMEIJER M.W.J. F0358

BROGAN D.W. F0359

BROMKE A. F0360

BROMWICH L. F0361

BROOK/EDGR....EDGAR H. BROOKES

BROOKINGS INSTITUTION F0362,F0363,F2549

BROOKINGS....BROOKINGS INSTITUTION, THE

BROOKS R.R. F0364

BROUDE H.W. F0365

BROWN B. F0366

BROWN C.V. F0367

BROWN E.H.P. F0368

BROWN J.F. F0369

BROWN J.S. F0370,F2326

BROWN M. F1732

BROWN M.B. F0371

BROWN R.E. F0372

BROWN R.T. F0373

BROWN S.D. F0374

BROWN W.A. F0129

BROWN W.M. F0375,F0376

BROWN/JOHN....JOHN BROWN

BROWNELL/H....HERBERT BROWNELL

BRUGADA R.S. F2033

BRUMBERG A. F0377

BRYAN/WJ....WILLIAM JENNINGS BRYAN

BRYCE M.D. F0378,F0379

BRYCE/J....JAMES BRYCE

BRZEZNSK/Z....ZBIGNIEW K. BRZEZINSKI

BUCHANAN N.S. F0380

BUCHANAN/J....PRESIDENT JAMES BUCHANAN

BUCK S.J. F0381

BUCKLEY/WF....WILLIAM F. BUCKLEY

BUDDHISM....BUDDHISM

BUDGET....BUDGETING, BUDGETS, FISCAL PLANNING

N
DOCUMENTATION ECONOMIQUE: REVUE BIBLIOGRAPHIQUE DE SYNTHESE. WOR+45 COM/IND FINAN BUDGET DIPLOM...GEOG 20. PAGE 1 F0004
BIBLIOG/A SOC

B14
DE BLOCH J.,THE FUTURE OF WAR IN ITS TECHNICAL, ECONOMIC, AND POLITICAL RELATIONS (1899). MOD/EUR TEC/DEV BUDGET INT/TRADE DETER GUERRILLA WEAPON COST PEACE 20. PAGE 31 F0596
WAR BAL/PWR PREDICT FORCES

N19
CHATTERS C.H.,NEW MUNICIPAL REVENUES FOR NEW MUNICIPAL EXPENDITURES (PAMPHLET). PLAN PRICE UTIL HABITAT...IDEA/COMP MUNICH 20. PAGE 23 F0457
LOC/G BUDGET TAX

N19
CONGRESSIONAL QUARTERLY SERV,FEDERAL ECONOMIC POLICY 1945-1965 (PAMPHLET). USA+45 FINAN OP/RES BAL/PWR ECO/TAC TAX BAL/PAY CENTRAL COST WEALTH ...CHARTS 20. PAGE 27 F0525
NAT/G ECO/DEV BUDGET POLICY

N19
DWYER J.W.,YARDSTICKS FOR PERFORMANCE (PAMPHLET). USA+45 FINAN CONTROL...CONCPT METH/COMP MUNICH. PAGE 35 F0688
BUDGET LOC/G EFFICIENCY

N19
FIKS M.,PUBLIC ADMINISTRATION IN ISRAEL (PAMPHLET). ISRAEL SCHOOL EX/STRUC BUDGET PAY INGP/REL ...DECISION 20 CIVIL/SERV. PAGE 41 F0792
EDU/PROP NAT/G ADMIN WORKER

N19
HABERLER G.,INFLATION; ITS CAUSES AND CURES (PAMPHLET). AFR USA+45 FINAN BUDGET PAY PRICE COST DEMAND 20. PAGE 52 F1021
ECO/DEV BAL/PAY POLICY NAT/G

N19
HERZBERG D.G.,A BUDGET FOR NEW YORK STATE, 1956-1957 (PAMPHLET). USA+45 ADMIN GOV/REL 20 NEW/YORK HARRIMAN/A. PAGE 59 F1159
POL/PAR PROVS BUDGET LEGIS

N19
KRESSBACH T.W.,HE MICHIGAN CITY MANAGER IN BUDGETARY PROCEEDINGS (PAMPHLET). USA+45 PROVS DELIB/GP GP/REL SUPEGO...POLICY MUNICH. PAGE 73 F1438
LOC/G BUDGET FINAN

N19
MARSH J.F. JR.,THE FBI RETIREMENT BILL (PAMPHLET). USA+45 EX/STRUC WORKER PLAN PROB/SOLV BUDGET LEAD LOBBY PARL/PROC PERS/REL RIGID/FLEX...POLICY 20 FBI PRESIDENT BUR/BUDGET. PAGE 86 F1677
ADMIN NAT/G SENIOR GOV/REL

N19
MASON E.S.,THE DIPLOMACY OF ECONOMIC ASSISTANCE (PAMPHLET). INDIA PAKISTAN USA+45 ECO/UNDEV NAT/G BUDGET ATTIT...POLICY 20. PAGE 87 F1695
FOR/AID DIPLOM FINAN

N19
MUSHKIN S.J.,LOCAL SCHOOL EXPENDITURES: 1970 PROJECTIONS (PAMPHLET). FUT USA+45 CONSTRUC FINAN PROVS EDU/PROP COST...GEOG CENSUS PREDICT CHARTS SIMUL 20. PAGE 95 F1871
LOC/G SCHOOL BUDGET

N19
ROBERTSON D.,GROWTH, WAGES, MONEY (PAMPHLET). UNIV WORKER BUDGET PRICE DEMAND PRODUC WEALTH...CONCPT MATH MONEY. PAGE 112 F2210
FINAN ECO/DEV ECO/TAC PAY

N19
US MARITIME ADMINISTRATION,CONTRIBUTION OF FEDERAL AID PROGRAMS TO THE OCEANBORNE FOREIGN TRADE OF THE UNITED STATES: 1959-62 (PAMPHLET). USA+45 SEA FINAN NAT/G BUDGET...POLICY 20. PAGE 138 F2719
INT/TRADE ECO/TAC DIST/IND GIVE

B25
WILLIAMS B.,THE SELBORNE MEMORANDUM. AFR FUT SOUTH/AFR UK NAT/G BUDGET DIPLOM REGION GOV/REL SOVEREIGN...POLICY CHARTS 20 UNIFICA SELBORNE/W. PAGE 147 F2888
COLONIAL PROVS

S30
CRAWFORD F.G.,"THE EXECUTIVE BUDGET DECISION IN NEW YORK." LEGIS EXEC PWR NEW/YORK. PAGE 28 F0552
LEAD BUDGET PROVS PROB/SOLV

B37
UNION OF SOUTH AFRICA,REPORT CONCERNING ADMINISTRATION OF SOUTH WEST AFRICA (6 VOLS.). SOUTH/AFR INDUS PUB/INST FORCES LEGIS BUDGET DIPLOM EDU/PROP ADJUD CT/SYS...GEOG CHARTS 20 AFRICA/SW LEAGUE/NAT. PAGE 132 F2610
NAT/G ADMIN COLONIAL CONSTN

B39
JENNINGS W.I.,PARLIAMENT. UK POL/PAR OP/RES BUDGET LEAD CHOOSE GP/REL...MGT 20 PARLIAMENT HOUSE/LORD HOUSE/CMNS. PAGE 67 F1315
PARL/PROC LEGIS CONSTN NAT/G

S39
COLE G.D.H.,"NAZI ECONOMICS: HOW DO THEY MANAGE IT?" GERMANY FORCES WORKER BUDGET INT/TRADE ROUTINE COERCE WAR 20 HITLER/A NAZI. PAGE 26 F0500
FASCISM ECO/TAC ATTIT PLAN

B41
ESTEY J.A.,BUSINESS CYCLES; THEIR NATURE, CAUSE, AND CONTROL. NAT/G BUDGET CAP/ISM TAX PRICE CONTROL INCOME...MODAL TIME/SEQ GEN/METH T 18/20 KEYNES/JM MONEY. PAGE 38 F0749
INDUS FINAN ECO/TAC POLICY

B41
MACMAHON A.W.,THE ADMINISTRATION OF FEDERAL WORK RELIEF. USA-45 EX/STRUC WORKER BUDGET EFFICIENCY ...CONT/OBS CHARTS 20 WPA. PAGE 84 F1636
ADMIN NAT/G MGT GIVE

B42
US LIBRARY OF CONGRESS,ECONOMICS OF WAR (APRIL 1941-MARCH 1942). WOR-45 FINAN INDUS LOC/G NAT/G PLAN BUDGET RATION COST DEMAND...POLICY 20. PAGE 138 F2712
BIBLIOG/A INT/TRADE ECO/TAC WAR

B43
WILMERDING L. JR.,THE SPENDING POWER: A HISTORY OF THE EFFORTS OF CONGRESS TO CONTROL EXPENDITURES. USA-45 POL/PAR DELIB/GP EX/STRUC TOP/EX TARIFFS ADMIN GOV/REL...TIME/SEQ SENATE HOUSE/REP. PAGE 147 F2900
LEGIS BUDGET CONTROL

S43
HUZAR E.,"CONGRESS AND THE ARMY: APPROPRIATIONS." USA-45 CONFER CONTROL ATTIT SUPEGO SKILL CONGRESS. PAGE 64 F1255
LEGIS FORCES BUDGET DELIB/GP

B44
FABIAN SOCIETY,CAN PLANNING BE DEMOCRATIC? UK CULTURE INDUS NAT/G BUDGET ORD/FREE...GEN/LAWS ANTHOL 20. PAGE 39 F0757
PLAN MAJORIT SOCIALIST ECO/DEV

B48
TAYLOR P.E.,THE ECONOMICS OF PUBLIC FINANCE. USA+45 USA-45 ECO/DEV WORKER PLAN BUDGET WAR INCOME WEALTH ...CONCPT STAT BIBLIOG 20. PAGE 129 F2540
FINAN POLICY NAT/G TAX

S48
HARDIN L.M.,"REFLECTIONS ON AGRICULTURAL POLICY FORMATION IN THE UNITED STATES." LEGIS PLAN BUDGET ECO/TAC LEAD CENTRAL...MGT SOC NEW/IDEA STAT FAO. PAGE 55 F1078
AGRI POLICY ADMIN NEW/LIB

S49
BANFIELD E.C.,"CONGRESS AND THE BUDGET: A PLANNER'S CRITICISM" USA+45 NAT/G PLAN LOBBY. PAGE 9 F0172
LEGIS BUDGET EXEC POLICY

B51
CHANDLER L.V.,INFLATION IN THE UNITED STATES 1940-1948. AFR NAT/G BUDGET PAY PRICE CONTROL WAR INCOME PRODUC...POLICY BIBLIOG 20. PAGE 23 F0448
ECO/TAC FINAN PROB/SOLV WEALTH

B51
DIMOCK M.E.,FREE ENTERPRISE AND THE ADMINISTRATIVE STATE. FINAN LG/CO BARGAIN BUDGET DOMIN CONTROL INGP/REL EFFICIENCY 20. PAGE 33 F0640
CAP/ISM ADMIN MGT MARKET

B51
US HOUSE COMM APPROPRIATIONS,MUTUAL SECURITY PROGRAM APPROPRIATIONS FOR 1952: HEARINGS BEFORE A SUBCOMMITTEE OF THE COMMITTEE ON APPROPRIATIONS. AFR KOREA L/A+17C ECO/DEV ECO/UNDEV INT/ORG INSPECT BAL/PWR DIPLOM DEBATE WAR...POLICY STAT ASIA/S 20 CONGRESS NATO MID/EAST. PAGE 136 F2686
LEGIS FORCES BUDGET FOR/AID

S51
HAWLEY A.H.,"METROPOLITAN POPULATION AND MUNICIPAL GOVERNMENT EXPENDITURES IN CENTRAL CITIES" (BMR)" USA+45 FINAN TAX...STAT CON/ANAL CHARTS MUNICH 20. PAGE 57 F1117
GEOG LOC/G COST BUDGET

S52
LEWIS V.B.,"TOWARD A THEORY OF BUDGETING" (BMR)"
BUDGET

USA+45 NAT/G PLAN PROB/SOLV...IDEA/COMP METH 20 SUPREME/CT. PAGE 79 F1551
CONCPT CREATE

B53
MILLIKAN M.F.,INCOME STABILIZATION FOR A DEVELOPING DEMOCRACY. USA+45 ECO/DEV LABOR BUDGET ECO/TAC TAX ADMIN ADJUST PRODUC WEALTH...POLICY TREND 20. PAGE 91 F1794
ANTHOL MARKET EQUILIB EFFICIENCY

B53
WILLIAMS J.H.,ECONOMIC STABILITY IN A CHANGING WORLD. FRANCE USA+45 USSR AGRI WORKER BUDGET INT/TRADE TAX WAR BAL/PAY COST EFFICIENCY ALL/IDEOS EQULIB 20 KEYNES/JM. PAGE 147 F2892
POLICY FINAN ECO/TAC WEALTH

S53
LAWTON F.J.,"LEGISLATIVE-EXECUTIVE RELATIONS IN BUDGETING AS VIEWED BY THE EXECUTIVE." NAT/G LEGIS ADMIN REPRESENT EFFICIENCY 20. PAGE 76 F1495
BUDGET EX/STRUC EXEC CONTROL

B54
HOBBS E.H.,BEHIND THE PRESIDENT - A STUDY OF EXECUTIVE OFFICE AGENCIES. USA+45 NAT/G PLAN BUDGET ECO/TAC EXEC ORD/FREE 20 BUR/BUDGET. PAGE 60 F1183
EX/STRUC DELIB/GP CONFER CONSULT

B54
MEYER F.V.,INFLATION AND CAPITAL. AFR UK WOR+45 BUDGET GOV/REL INCOME PRODUC PROFIT WEALTH...CONCPT CHARTS 20. PAGE 90 F1768
ECO/DEV FINAN ECO/TAC DEMAND

B55
GOMES F.A.,OPERACAO MUNICIPIO. BRAZIL L/A+17C SERV/IND LOC/G BUDGET ECO/TAC COST DEMAND...POLICY MUNICH 20. PAGE 48 F0944
ECO/UNDEV FEDERAL GOV/REL

B55
OECD,MARSHALL PLAN IN TURKEY. TURKEY USA+45 COM/IND CONSTRUC SERV/IND FORCES BUDGET...STAT 20 MARSHL/PLN. PAGE 100 F1964
FOR/AID ECO/UNDEV AGRI INDUS

B55
SMITHIES A.,THE BUDGETARY PROCESS IN THE UNITED STATES. AFR ECO/DEV AGRI EX/STRUC FORCES LEGIS PROB/SOLV TAX ROUTINE EFFICIENCY...MGT CONGRESS PRESIDENT. PAGE 124 F2436
NAT/G ADMIN BUDGET GOV/REL

S55
KELLY W.E.,"HOW SALES EXECUTIVES USE FACTORING TO BOOST SALES AND PROFITS TODAY." FINAN LG/CO BUDGET EFFICIENCY PROFIT...MGT PRODUCT. PAGE 70 F1372
INDUS ECO/DEV CONSULT MARKET

B56
BURKHEAD J.,GOVERNMENT BUDGETING. ECO/DEV PROB/SOLV ECO/TAC ADMIN ROUTINE GOV/REL EFFICIENCY...DECISION MGT. PAGE 20 F0388
BUDGET NAT/G PROVS EX/STRUC

B56
KOHLER E.L.,ACCOUNTING IN THE FEDERAL GOVERNMENT. USA+45 LOC/G PLAN TAX CONTROL COST 20. PAGE 72 F1416
BUDGET AFR NAT/G FINAN

B56
POOLE K.E.,PUBLIC FINANCE AND ECONOMIC WELFARE. STRUCT ECO/DEV LOC/G NAT/G BUDGET PAY ROUTINE COST EQUILIB WEALTH...SOC/WK METH/COMP 20. PAGE 107 F2103
FINAN TAX ORD/FREE

B56
VAKIL C.N.,PLANNING FOR AN EXPANDING ECONOMY. INDIA TAX COST 20. PAGE 140 F2759
TEC/DEV LABOR BUDGET CAP/ISM

S56
KNAPP D.C.,"CONGRESSIONAL CONTROL OF AGRICULTURAL CONSERVATION POLICY: A CASE STUDY OF THE APPROPRIATIONS PROCESS." DELIB/GP PLAN PROB/SOLV CONFER PARL/PROC...POLICY INT CONGRESS. PAGE 72 F1411
LEGIS AGRI BUDGET CONTROL

S56
MARGOLIS J.,"ON MUNICIPAL LAND POLICY FOR FISCAL GAINS." USA+45 PLAN TAX COST EFFICIENCY HABITAT KNOWL...MGT MUNICH 20. PAGE 85 F1667
BUDGET POLICY GEOG LOC/G

S56
MILNE R.S.,"CONTROL OF GOVERNMENT CORPORATIONS IN THE UNITED STATES." USA+45 NAT/G CHIEF LEGIS BUDGET 20 GENACCOUNT. PAGE 92 F1800
CONTROL EX/STRUC GOV/REL PWR

B57
LUNDBERG E.,BUSINESS CYCLES AND ECONOMIC POLICY (TRANS. BY J. POTTER). SWEDEN ECO/DEV FINAN DELIB/GP PLAN PRICE CONTROL BAL/PAY 20 INTRVN/ECO. PAGE 82 F1607
ECO/TAC INDUS INT/TRADE BUDGET

B57
MURDESHWAR A.K.,ADMINISTRATIVE PROBLEMS RELATING TO NATIONALISATION: WITH SPECIAL REFERENCE TO INDIAN STATE ENTERPRISES. CZECHOSLVK FRANCE INDIA UK USA+45 LEGIS WORKER PROB/SOLV BUDGET PRICE CONTROL ...MGT GEN/LAWS 20 PARLIAMENT. PAGE 95 F1863
NAT/G OWN INDUS ADMIN

B57
SINGH D.B.,INFLATIONARY PRICE TRENDS IN INDIA SINCE 1939. AFR INDIA ECO/TAC RATION CONTROL WAR GOV/REL BAL/PAY DEMAND INCOME PEACE PRODUC...POLICY CHARTS 20. PAGE 122 F2413
BUDGET ECO/UNDEV PRICE FINAN

B58
BARRERE A.,POLITIQUE FINANCIERE. FRANCE BUDGET ECO/TAC TAX BAL/PAY INCOME PRODUC...MGT BIBLIOG T 20. PAGE 10 F0193
FINAN NAT/G PLAN

B58
CHANG C.,THE INFLATIONARY SPIRAL: THE EXPERIENCE IN CHINA 1939-50. CHINA/COM BUDGET INT/TRADE PRICE ADMIN CONTROL WAR DEMAND...POLICY CHARTS 20. PAGE 23 F0451
FINAN ECO/TAC BAL/PAY GOV/REL

B58
EHRHARD J.,LE DESTIN DU COLONIALISME. AFR FRANCE ECO/UNDEV AGRI FINAN MARKET CREATE PLAN TEC/DEV BUDGET DIPLOM PRICE 20. PAGE 36 F0710
COLONIAL FOR/AID INT/TRADE INDUS

B58
HOOD W.C.,FINANCING OF ECONOMIC ACTIVITY IN CANADA. CANADA FUT VOL/ASSN WORKER ECO/TAC ADJUD ADMIN ...CHARTS 20. PAGE 61 F1204
BUDGET FINAN GP/REL ECO/DEV

B58
INDIAN INST OF PUBLIC ADMIN,IMPROVING CITY GOVERNMENT. INDIA ECO/UNDEV PLAN BUDGET PARTIC GP/REL MUNICH 20. PAGE 64 F1263
LOC/G PROB/SOLV ADMIN

B58
JOHNSON H.G.,INTERNATIONAL TRADE AND ECONOMIC GROWTH. WOR+45 BUDGET CAP/ISM ECO/TAC TARIFFS BAL/PAY 20. PAGE 67 F1323
INT/TRADE BAL/PWR BARGAIN DIPLOM

B58
SHAW S.J.,THE FINANCIAL AND ADMINISTRATIVE ORGANIZATION AND DEVELOPMENT OF OTTOMAN EGYPT 1517-1798. UAR LOC/G FORCES BUDGET INT/TRADE TAX EATING INCOME WEALTH...CHARTS BIBLIOG 16/18 OTTOMAN NAPOLEON/B. PAGE 120 F2371
FINAN ADMIN GOV/REL CULTURE

B58
US OPERATIONS MISSION TO VIET,BUILDING ECONOMIC STRENGTH (PAMPHLET). USA+45 VIETNAM/S INDUS TEC/DEV BUDGET ADMIN EATING HEALTH...STAT 20. PAGE 138 F2725
FOR/AID ECO/UNDEV AGRI EDU/PROP

B59
BAUER P.T.,UNITED STATES AID AND INDIAN ECONOMIC DEVELOPMENT. INDIA STRATA FINAN PLAN BUDGET DIPLOM INGP/REL EFFICIENCY SOCISM 20 AID. PAGE 11 F0215
FOR/AID ECO/UNDEV ECO/TAC POLICY

B59
HAX K.,DIE HOCHSCHULLEHRER DER WIRTSCHAFTSWISSENSCHAFTEN IN DER BUNDESREPUBLIK DEUTSCHLAND EINSCHL. WESTBERLIN, OSTERREICH. AUSTRIA GERMANY/W SWITZERLND FINAN MARKET PROF/ORG BUDGET ECO/TAC INT/TRADE PRICE COST 20. PAGE 57 F1119
BIBLIOG ACADEM INTELL

B59
LEWIS J.P.,BUSINESS CONDITIONS ANALYSIS. USA+45 MARKET LABOR BUDGET TAX AUTOMAT WAR DEMAND PRODUC ...ECOMETRIC CHARTS BIBLIOG 19/20. PAGE 79 F1549
FINAN PRICE TREND

B59
NORTON P.L.,URBAN PROBLEMS AND TECHNIQUES. AIR AGRI INDUS MARKET TEC/DEV BUDGET LEISURE ALL/VALS ...ANTHOL MUNICH 20 URBAN/RNWL. PAGE 99 F1936
PLAN LOC/G HABITAT

B59
STANFORD U, BOARD OF TRUSTEES,THE ALLOCATION OF ECONOMIC RESOURCES. WORKER PLAN BUDGET ECO/TAC TAX RECEIVE COST PRODUC...POLICY IDEA/COMP SIMUL ANTHOL 20. PAGE 125 F2468
INCOME PRICE FINAN

B59
US DEPARTMENT OF STATE,THE UNITED STATES ECONOMY AND THE MUTUAL SECURITY PROGRAM. USA+45 ECO/UNDEV FINAN INDUS DIPLOM INT/TRADE DETER 20. PAGE 136 F2674
ECO/DEV FORCES BUDGET FOR/AID

B59
WENTHOLT W.,SOME COMMENTS ON THE LIQUIDATION OF THE EUROPEAN PAYMENT UNION AND RELATED PROBLEMS (PAMPHLET). AFR WOR+45 PLAN BUDGET PRICE CONTROL 20 EEC. PAGE 145 F2857
FINAN ECO/DEV INT/ORG ECO/TAC

S59
WALLACE R.A.,"CONGRESSIONAL CONTROL OF THE BUDGET." USA+45 NAT/G CHIEF GP/REL FEDERAL OBJECTIVE...MGT CONGRESS. PAGE 143 F2807
LEGIS EX/STRUC BUDGET CONSTN

B60
BIERMAN H.,THE CAPITAL BUDGETING DECISION. AFR ECO/DEV MARKET TAX PRICE RISK COST INCOME TIME 20. PAGE 15 F0282
FINAN OPTIMAL BUDGET PROFIT

B60
BISSON A.,INSTITUTIONS FINANCIERES ET ECONOMIQUES EN FRANCE. FRANCE INDUS OP/RES TAX COST PRODUC ...CHARTS 20. PAGE 15 F0289
FINAN BUDGET PLAN

B60
CARPER E.T.,THE DEFENSE APPROPRIATIONS RIDER (PAMPHLET). USA+45 CONSTN CHIEF DELIB/GP LEGIS BUDGET LOBBY CIVMIL/REL...POLICY 20 CONGRESS EISNHWR/DD DEPT/DEFEN PRESIDENT BOSTON. PAGE 22 F0419
GOV/REL ADJUD LAW CONTROL

B60
FINKLE J.L.,THE PRESIDENT MAKES A DECISION: A STUDY OF DIXON-YATES. OP/RES PROB/SOLV BUDGET ADMIN GOV/REL...POLICY BIBLIOG/A 20 PRESIDENT. PAGE 41 F0799
DECISION CHIEF PWR POL/PAR

B60
FIRESTONE J.M.,FEDERAL RECEIPTS AND EXPENDITURES DURING BUSINESS CYCLES, 1879-1958. USA+45 USA-45 INDUS PLAN ECO/TAC TAX WAR COST...CHARTS 19/20. PAGE 41 F0801
FINAN INCOME BUDGET NAT/G

B60
FRYE R.J.,GOVERNMENT AND LABOR: THE ALABAMA PROGRAM. USA+45 INDUS R+D LABOR WORKER BUDGET EFFICIENCY AGE/Y HEALTH...CHARTS 20 ALABAMA. PAGE 45 F0870
ADMIN LEGIS LOC/G PROVS

B60
HALL C.A. JR.,FISCAL POLICY FOR STABLE GROWTH. USA+45 FINAN TEC/DEV TAX COST DEMAND INCOME ...BIBLIOG 20. PAGE 53 F1045
ECO/TAC BUDGET NAT/G POLICY

B60
KENEN P.B.,BRITISH MONETARY POLICY AND THE BALANCE OF PAYMENTS 1951-57. UK PLAN BUDGET ECO/TAC INT/TRADE PAY PRICE COST ATTIT 20. PAGE 70 F1377
BAL/PAY PROB/SOLV FINAN NAT/G

B60
MARSHALL A.H.,FINANCIAL ADMINISTRATION IN LOCAL GOVERNMENT. UK DELIB/GP CONFER COST INCOME PERSON ...JURID 20. PAGE 86 F1679
FINAN LOC/G BUDGET ADMIN

B60
PENNSYLVANIA ECONOMY LEAGUE,URBAN RENEWAL IMPACT STUDY: ADMINISTRATIVE-LEGAL-FISCAL. USA+45 FINAN LOC/G NEIGH ADMIN EFFICIENCY...CENSUS CHARTS MUNICH 20 PENNSYLVAN. PAGE 105 F2059
PLAN BUDGET ADJUD

B60
ROBINSON R.I.,FINANCIAL INSTITUTIONS. USA+45 PRICE GOV/REL DEMAND WEALTH...CHARTS T 20 MONEY. PAGE 113 F2226
FINAN ECO/TAC ECO/DEV BUDGET

B60
STOLPER W.F.,GERMANY BETWEEN EAST AND WEST: THE ECONOMICS OF COMPETITIVE COEXISTENCE. AFR FUT GERMANY/E GERMANY/W WOR+45 FINAN POL/PAR BUDGET ECO/TAC FOR/AID INT/TRADE...STAT CHARTS METH/COMP 20. PAGE 126 F2495
ECO/DEV DIPLOM GOV/COMP BAL/PWR

B60
US HOUSE COMM GOVT OPERATIONS,OPERATIONS OF THE DEVELOPMENT LOAN FUND: HEARINGS (COMMITTEE ON GOVERNMENT OPERATIONS). USA+45 PLAN BUDGET DIPLOM GOV/REL COST...CHARTS 20 CONGRESS DEPT/STATE AID. PAGE 137 F2698
FINAN FOR/AID ECO/TAC EFFICIENCY

B60
US OPERATIONS MISSION - TURKEY,SOME POSSIBILITIES FOR ACCELERATING TURKEY'S ECONOMIC GROWTH. TURKEY USA+45 AGRI FINAN INDUS NAT/G ACT/RES BUDGET COST ...CHARTS 20. PAGE 138 F2724
ECO/UNDEV ECO/TAC FOR/AID PRODUC

B60
WALLACE R.A.,CONGRESSIONAL CONTROL OF FEDERAL SPENDING. USA+45 CONSTN NAT/G OP/RES CONFER DEBATE PERS/REL UTIL RIGID/FLEX PWR OBJECTIVE...OBS CHARTS. PAGE 143 F2808
LEGIS DELIB/GP BUDGET

B60
WATSON D.S.,ECONOMIC POLICY: BUSINESS AND GOVERNMENT. USA+45 FINAN LABOR PLAN BUDGET INT/TRADE GP/REL WEALTH LAISSEZ...CHARTS T. PAGE 144 F2832
ECO/TAC NAT/G POLICY ECO/DEV

B61
ASCHHEIM J.,TECHNIQUES OF MONETARY CONTROL. UK USA+45 CONTROL WAR DEMAND INCOME WEALTH...TREND CHARTS 20 MONEY. PAGE 7 F0127
FINAN MARKET BUDGET CENTRAL

B61
ASHER R.E.,GRANTS, LOANS, AND LOCAL CURRENCIES; THEIR ROLE IN FOREIGN AID. AFR USA+45 ECO/UNDEV INT/ORG ACT/RES PLAN ECO/TAC GIVE CONTROL WEALTH 20. PAGE 7 F0130
FOR/AID FINAN NAT/G BUDGET

B61
BAUER P.T.,INDIAN ECONOMIC POLICY AND DEVELOPMENT. INDIA STRATA AGRI FINAN POL/PAR BUDGET FOR/AID GOV/REL EFFICIENCY...CENSUS 20. PAGE 11 F0216
ECO/UNDEV ECO/TAC POLICY PLAN

B61
BEASLEY K.E.,STATE SUPERVISION OF MUNICIPAL DEBT IN KANSAS - A CASE STUDY. USA+45 USA-45 FINAN PROVS BUDGET TAX ADJUD ADMIN CONTROL SUPEGO MUNICH. PAGE 12 F0224
LOC/G LEGIS JURID

B61
BREWIS T.N.,CANADIAN ECONOMIC POLICY. AFR CANADA BUDGET CAP/ISM INT/TRADE RATION TARIFFS TAX PRICE CONTROL ROUTINE FEDERAL INCOME PRODUC 20. PAGE 18 F0348
ECO/DEV ECO/TAC NAT/G PLAN

B61
DIMOCK M.E.,BUSINESS AND GOVERNMENT (4TH ED.). AGRI FINAN OP/RES PLAN BUDGET DIPLOM LOBBY NUC/PWR NEW/LIB SOCISM...POLICY BIBLIOG 20. PAGE 33 F0641
NAT/G INDUS LABOR

ECO/TAC

B61
ESTEVEZ A.,ASPECTOS ECONOMICO-FINANCIEROS DE LA CAMPANA SANMARITANA. L/A+17C SPAIN FINAN COLONIAL LEAD ROLE ORD/FREE WEALTH 19 SOUTH/AMER SAN/MARTIN. PAGE 38 F0748
ECO/UNDEV REV BUDGET NAT/G

B61
FELLNER W.,THE PROBLEM OF RISING PRICES. AGRI INDUS WORKER BUDGET CAP/ISM ECO/TAC INT/TRADE PAY DEMAND ...POLICY 20 EEC. PAGE 40 F0780
PRICE MARKET ECO/DEV COST

B61
HAUSER M.,DIE URSACHEN DER FRANZOSISCHEN INFLATION IN DEN JAHREN 1946-1952. AFR FRANCE INDUS NAT/G BUDGET DIPLOM ECO/TAC FOR/AID COST MONEY 20. PAGE 57 F1114
ECO/DEV FINAN PRICE

B61
HICKS U.K.,FEDERALISM AND ECONOMIC GROWTH IN UNDERDEVELOPED COUNTRIES. WOR+45 WOR-45 FINAN NAT/G PLAN BUDGET DIPLOM INT/TRADE DEMAND WEALTH...ANTHOL 20. PAGE 59 F1167
ECO/UNDEV ECO/TAC FEDERAL CONSTN

B61
HOLMANS A.E.,UNITED STATES FISCAL POLICY 1945-1959. AFR USA+45 USA-45 ECO/DEV TAX PRICE WAR...BIBLIOG 20 DEMOCRAT REPUBLICAN. PAGE 61 F1200
POLICY BUDGET NAT/G ECO/TAC

B61
INTL BANKING SUMMER SCHOOL,TRENDS IN BANK CREDIT AND FINANCE. EUR+WWI NETHERLAND ECO/DEV PROF/ORG PLAN BUDGET 20 EEC. PAGE 65 F1283
FINAN ECO/TAC NAT/G LG/CO

B61
MACMAHON A.W.,DELEGATION AND AUTONOMY. INDIA STRUCT LEGIS BARGAIN BUDGET ECO/TAC LEGIT EXEC REPRESENT GOV/REL CENTRAL DEMAND EFFICIENCY PRODUC. PAGE 84 F1637
ADMIN PLAN FEDERAL

B61
MORRIS B.R.,PROBLEMS OF AMERICAN ECONOMIC GROWTH. USA+45 LABOR WORKER BUDGET ECO/TAC INT/TRADE EQUILIB 20. PAGE 94 F1836
ECO/DEV POLICY TEC/DEV DEMAND

B61
NEW JERSEY LEGISLATURE-SENATE,PUBLIC HEARINGS BEFORE COMMITTEE ON REVISION AND AMENDMENT OF LAWS ON SENATE BILL NO. 8. USA+45 FINAN PROVS WORKER ACT/RES PLAN BUDGET TAX CRIME...IDEA/COMP MUNICH 20 NEW/JERSEY URBAN/RNWL. PAGE 98 F1919
LEGIS INDUS PROB/SOLV

B61
QURESHI S.,INCENTIVES IN AMERICAN EMPLOYMENT (THESIS, UNIVERSITY OF PENNSYLVANIA). DELIB/GP TOP/EX BUDGET ROUTINE SANCTION COST TECHRACY MGT. PAGE 108 F2134
SERV/IND ADMIN PAY EX/STRUC

B61
SACKS S.,FINANCING GOVERNMENT IN A METROPOLITAN GOVERNMENT. USA+45 ECO/DEV R+D LOC/G GOV/REL ...BIBLIOG MUNICH 20 CLEVELAND. PAGE 115 F2269
FINAN PLAN BUDGET

B61
SHONFIELD A.,ECONOMIC GROWTH AND INFLATION; A STUDY OF INDIAN PLANNING. AFR INDIA AGRI INDUS TEC/DEV CONTROL DEMAND UTIL 20. PAGE 121 F2384
ECO/UNDEV PRICE PLAN BUDGET

B61
STANLEY C.J.,LATE CH'ING FINANCE: HU KUANG-YUNG AS AN INNOVATOR. ASIA NAT/G FORCES BUDGET TAX WAR GOV/REL COST...POLICY BIOG CHARTS BIBLIOG 19. PAGE 125 F2469
FINAN ECO/TAC CIVMIL/REL ADMIN

B61
TRIFFIN R.,GOLD AND THE DOLLAR CRISIS: THE FUTURE OF CONVERTIBILITY. AFR USA+45 USA-45 INT/ORG PROB/SOLV BUDGET INT/TRADE PRICE...STAT CHARTS 19/20. PAGE 131 F2588
FINAN ECO/DEV ECO/TAC BAL/PAY

B61
UNIVS-NATL BUR COMM ECO RES,PUBLIC FINANCES: NEEDS, SOURCES, AND UTILIZATION. USA+45 FORCES PLAN TAX CONFER PRICE FEDERAL UTIL...ANTHOL MUNICH 20. PAGE 133 F2623
NAT/G FINAN DECISION BUDGET

S61
WILDAVSKY A.,"POLITICAL IMPLICATIONS OF BUDGETARY REFORM." AFR NAT/G POL/PAR DELIB/GP EX/STRUC ATTIT PWR CONGRESS. PAGE 146 F2881
BUDGET PLAN LEGIS

B62
CONGRES ECONOMISTES LANG FRAN,MONNAIE ET EXPANSION. AFR FRANCE PROB/SOLV BUDGET CENTRAL COST OPTIMAL PRODUC WEALTH 20. PAGE 27 F0524
FINAN PLAN EUR+WWI

B62
FORD A.G.,THE GOLD STANDARD 1880-1914: BRITAIN AND ARGENTINA. AFR UK ECO/UNDEV INT/TRADE ADMIN GOV/REL DEMAND EFFICIENCY...STAT CHARTS 19/20 ARGEN. PAGE 42 F0823
FINAN ECO/TAC BUDGET BAL/PAY

B62
GWYN W.B.,DEMOCRACY AND THE COST OF POLITICS IN BRITAIN. UK BUDGET CRIME CHOOSE ORD/FREE WEALTH ...TIME/SEQ 18/20. PAGE 52 F1017
COST POL/PAR POPULISM PAY

B62
HAGUE D.C.,INFLATION. AFR ECO/DEV ECO/UNDEV LABOR
FINAN

BUDGET CAP/ISM INT/TRADE TARIFFS SOCISM 20. PAGE 53 F1036
NAT/COMP BARGAIN ECO/TAC

B62
HARRIS S.E.,THE ECONOMICS OF THE POLITICAL PARTIES. USA+45 FINAN CHIEF ACT/RES PLAN BUDGET GP/REL INGP/REL NEW/LIB...IDEA/COMP PERS/COMP 20 EISNHWR/DD KENNEDY/JF. PAGE 56 F1090
POLICY ECO/DEV NAT/G POL/PAR

B62
JORDAN A.A. JR.,FOREIGN AID AND THE DEFENSE OF SOUTHEAST ASIA. PAKISTAN VIETNAM/S FINAN PLAN BUDGET ECO/TAC DETER WAR ORD/FREE...POLICY DECISION CENSUS CHARTS BIBLIOG 20. PAGE 68 F1341
FOR/AID S/ASIA FORCES ECO/UNDEV

B62
LICHFIELD N.,COST-BENEFIT ANALYSIS IN URBAN REDEVELOPMENT. CONSTRUC LOC/G NEIGH ACT/RES PROB/SOLV TEC/DEV BUDGET TAX...DECISION STAT CHARTS SOC/EXP MUNICH 20. PAGE 80 F1558
PLAN COST GOV/REL

B62
LUTZ F.A.,GELD UND WAHRUNG. AFR MARKET LABOR BUDGET 20 EUROPE. PAGE 82 F1610
ECO/TAC FINAN DIPLOM POLICY

B62
ROTHBARD M.N.,THE PANIC OF 1819; REACTIONS AND POLICIES. AFR USA-45 LAW FINAN BUDGET TARIFFS DEMAND 19 DEPRESSION. PAGE 114 F2247
ECO/UNDEV POLICY ATTIT ECO/TAC

B62
SCHALLER H.G.,PUBLIC EXPENDITURE DECISIONS IN THE URBAN COMMUNITY: PREPARED FOR RESOURCES FOR THE FUTURE, INC. INDUS SERV/IND LOC/G PUB/INST PLAN PROB/SOLV BUDGET DEMAND PRODUC...CHARTS MUNICH. PAGE 116 F2289
FINAN DECISION

B62
SCHILLING W.R.,STRATEGY, POLITICS, AND DEFENSE BUDGETS. AFR USA+45 CHIEF LEGIS PLAN TEC/DEV BAL/PWR BUDGET NUC/PWR WAR CIVMIL/REL GOV/REL PWR 20 EISNHWR/DD. PAGE 117 F2297
NAT/G POLICY FORCES DETER

B62
SHANNON I.,THE ECONOMIC FUNCTIONS OF GOLD. AFR FUT WOR+45 WOR-45 INT/ORG BUDGET INT/TRADE BAL/PAY DEMAND PEACE 20 MONEY. PAGE 120 F2366
FINAN PRICE ECO/DEV ECO/TAC

B62
THEOBALD R.,NATIONAL DEVELOPMENT EFFORTS (PAMPHLET). WOR+45 AGRI BUDGET FOR/AID INT/TRADE TAX 20. PAGE 129 F2555
ECO/UNDEV PLAN BAL/PAY WEALTH

B62
US AGENCY INTERNATIONAL DEV,OPERATIONS REPORT - 1962 (PAMPHLET). AFR ASIA L/A+17C USA+45 ECO/UNDEV FINAN INT/ORG NAT/G 20 MICHIGAN. PAGE 134 F2636
FOR/AID CHARTS STAT BUDGET

S62
KRISHNA K.G.V.,"PLANNING AND ECONOMIC DEVELOPMENT" AFR UGANDA AGRI INDUS R+D BUDGET RATION TAX COLONIAL 20. PAGE 73 F1441
ECO/UNDEV ECO/TAC NAT/LISM PLAN

N62
BANK INTERNATIONAL SETTLEMENTS,AUSTRIA: MONETARY AND ECONOMIC SITUATION 1952-61 (PAMPHLET). AUSTRIA WORKER BUDGET INT/TRADE PRICE BAL/PAY DEMAND EFFICIENCY INCOME PRODUC...STAT 20 SILVER. PAGE 9 F0174
FINAN ECO/DEV CHARTS WEALTH

B63
BANERJI A.K.,INDIA'S BALANCE OF PAYMENTS. INDIA NAT/G PRICE BAL/PAY COST INCOME 20. PAGE 9 F0171
INT/TRADE DIPLOM FINAN BUDGET

B63
BONINI C.P.,SIMULATION OF INFORMATION AND DECISION SYSTEMS IN THE FIRM. MARKET BUDGET DOMIN EDU/PROP ADMIN COST ATTIT HABITAT PERCEPT PWR...CONCPT PROBABIL QUANT PREDICT HYPO/EXP BIBLIOG. PAGE 16 F0313
INDUS SIMUL DECISION MGT

B63
BURNS T.G.,DEVELOPMENT BANKING BIBLIOGRAPHY (PAPER). WOR+45 SML/CO VOL/ASSN PLAN BUDGET. PAGE 20 F0391
BIBLIOG/A ECO/DEV FINAN ECO/UNDEV

B63
DUE J.F.,STATE SALES TAX ADMINISTRATION. OP/RES BUDGET PAY ADMIN EXEC ROUTINE COST EFFICIENCY PROFIT...CHARTS METH/COMP 20. PAGE 34 F0671
PROVS TAX STAT GOV/COMP

B63
FATEMI N.S.,THE DOLLAR CRISIS. USA+45 INDUS NAT/G LEGIS BUDGET TAX COST...CHARTS METH/COMP 20 EEC. PAGE 39 F0766
PROB/SOLV BAL/PAY FOR/AID PLAN

B63
FOX S.,ECONOMIC CONTROL AND FREE ENTERPRISE. PLAN BUDGET INT/TRADE TAX...TREND 20. PAGE 43 F0839
CONTROL FINAN ECO/TAC

B63
GANGULI B.N.,ECONOMIC CONSEQUENCES OF DISARMAMENT. EUR+WWI ECO/DEV ECO/UNDEV FORCES ACT/RES BUDGET DIPLOM INT/TRADE...STAT CHARTS NAT/COMP. PAGE 46 F0896
ECOMETRIC ARMS/CONT COST HYPO/EXP

B63
HAHN L.A.,DIE AMERIKANISCHE KONJUNKTURPOLITIK DER DOLLAR UND DIE DMARK. GERMANY/W USA+45 DIPLOM PRICE BAL/PAY COST...POLICY MONEY. PAGE 53 F1038
FINAN BUDGET ECO/TAC LABOR

B63
INTERNATIONAL ASSOCIATION RES,AFRICAN STUDIES IN INCOME AND WEALTH. AFR NAT/G PROB/SOLV DEMAND INCOME...ECOMETRIC METH/COMP 20. PAGE 64 F1270
WEALTH PLAN ECO/UNDEV BUDGET

B63
INTERNATIONAL MONETARY FUND,COMPENSATORY FINANCING OF EXPORT FLUCTUATIONS (PAMPHLET). WOR+45 ECO/DEV ECO/UNDEV INT/ORG WEALTH...TREND 20 IMF MONEY. PAGE 65 F1281
BAL/PAY FINAN BUDGET INT/TRADE

B63
RAFUSE R.W. JR.,STATE AND LOCAL FISCAL BEHAVIOR OVER THE POSTWAR CYCLES (DISSERTATION). USA+45 TAX PRICE ATTIT...POLICY TIME/SEQ TREND CHARTS BIBLIOG 20. PAGE 109 F2135
BUDGET LOC/G ECO/TAC PROVS

B63
REAGAN M.D.,THE MANAGED ECONOMY. USA+45 INDUS LG/CO BUDGET GP/REL ORD/FREE PWR WEALTH 20. PAGE 110 F2161
PLAN ECO/DEV NAT/G ROLE

B63
ROBBINS L.,POLITICS AND ECONOMICS. ECO/DEV FINAN BUDGET DIPLOM BAL/PAY ORD/FREE 20. PAGE 112 F2204
NAT/G ATTIT

B63
ROPKE W.,ECONOMICS OF THE FREE SOCIETY. FINAN INT/TRADE BAL/PAY COST DEMAND EFFICIENCY ORD/FREE WEALTH...CON/ANAL METH/COMP T 20 KEYNES/JM. PAGE 114 F2240
SOCIETY BUDGET ECO/DEV ECO/TAC

B63
TREVES G.,GOVERNMENT ORGANIZATION FOR ECONOMIC DEVELOPMENT (PAMPHLET). WOR+45 LAW BUDGET ECO/TAC GOV/REL...DECISION 20. PAGE 131 F2585
ECO/DEV ECO/UNDEV PLAN POLICY

B63
UN SECRETARY GENERAL,PLANNING FOR ECONOMIC DEVELOPMENT. ECO/UNDEV FINAN BUDGET INT/TRADE TARIFFS TAX ADMIN 20 UN. PAGE 132 F2603
PLAN ECO/TAC MGT NAT/COMP

B63
US AGENCY INTERNATIONAL DEV,OPERATIONS REPORT 1963. AFR ASIA L/A+17C USA+45 ECO/UNDEV FINAN INT/ORG NAT/G. PAGE 134 F2637
FOR/AID CHARTS STAT BUDGET

B63
US BD GOVERNORS FEDL RESRV,THE FEDERAL RESERVE AND THE TREASURY. USA+45 WORKER PROB/SOLV PRICE COST DEMAND WEALTH...STAT INT CHARTS 20 FED/RESERV DEPT/TREAS. PAGE 134 F2641
FINAN GOV/REL CONTROL BUDGET

B63
US CONGRESS JOINT ECO COMM,THE UNITED STATES BALANCE OF PAYMENTS. AFR USA+45 DELIB/GP BUDGET PRICE PRODUC 20 CONGRESS MONEY. PAGE 135 F2655
BAL/PAY INT/TRADE FINAN ECO/TAC

B63
US DEPARTMENT OF LABOR,THE ANVIL AND THE PLOW. KOREA USA+45 USA-45 INDUS WORKER BUDGET WAR ...POLICY AUD/VIS CHARTS 20 DEPT/LABOR. PAGE 135 F2667
ECO/DEV LABOR ECO/TAC NAT/G

B63
US HOUSE,URBAN RENEWAL: HOUSE COMMITTEE ON BANKING AND CURRENCY. USA+45 FINAN LOC/G NAT/G NEIGH DELIB/GP TEC/DEV BUDGET GOV/REL COST...CHARTS MUNICH 20 CONGRESS URBAN/RNWL. PAGE 136 F2684
PLAN PROB/SOLV LEGIS

B63
US SENATE COMM GOVT OPERATIONS,REPORT OF A STUDY OF US FOREIGN AID IN TEN MIDDLE EASTERN AND AFRICAN COUNTRIES. AFR ISLAM USA+45 FORCES PLAN BUDGET DIPLOM TAX DETER WEALTH...STAT CHARTS 20 CONGRESS AID MID/EAST. PAGE 138 F2728
FOR/AID EFFICIENCY ECO/TAC FINAN

B63
WALINSKY L.J.,PLANNING AND EXECUTION OF ECONOMIC DEVELOPMENT. PROB/SOLV TEC/DEV BUDGET COST WEALTH ...CHARTS BIBLIOG 20. PAGE 142 F2802
PLAN ECO/UNDEV ECO/TAC OPTIMAL

L63
PADELFORD N.J.,"FINANCIAL CRISIS AND THE UNITED NATIONS." FUT USSR WOR+45 LAW CONSTN FINAN INT/ORG DELIB/GP FORCES PLAN BUDGET DIPLOM COST WEALTH ...STAT CHARTS UN CONGO 20. PAGE 102 F2012
CREATE ECO/TAC

S63
CARTER A.G.T.,"THE BALANCE OF PAYMENTS OF EAST AFRICA" AFR ECO/TAC FOR/AID RATION TARIFFS TAX ADMIN...STAT 20 AFRICA/E. PAGE 22 F0423
BUDGET ECO/UNDEV BAL/PAY INT/TRADE

S63
ENTHOVEN A.C.,"ECONOMIC ANALYSIS IN THE DEPARTMENT
PLAN

OF DEFENSE." USA+45 NAT/G DELIB/GP PROB/SOLV RATION BUDGET
NUC/PWR WEAPON COST...DECISION 20 DEPT/DEFEN ECO/TAC
RESOURCE/N. PAGE 38 F0739 FORCES

N63
COMMITTEE ECONOMIC DEVELOPMENT,TAXES AND TRADE: 20 FINAN
YEARS OF CED POLICY (PAMPHLET). USA+45 ECO/DEV PLAN ECO/TAC
BUDGET LEAD...POLICY KENNEDY/JF PRESIDENT. PAGE 27 NAT/G
F0518 DELIB/GP

N63
LEDERER W.,THE BALANCE ON FOREIGN TRANSACTIONS: FINAN
PROBLEMS OF DEFINITION AND MEASUREMENT (PAMPHLET). BAL/PAY
USA+45 BUDGET DIPLOM ECO/TAC PRICE GOV/REL...POLICY INT/TRADE
STAT NAT/COMP METH 20. PAGE 77 F1502 ECO/DEV

N63
US COMM STRENG SEC FREE WORLD,THE SCOPE AND DELIB/GP
DISTRIBUTION OF UNITED STATES MILITARY AND ECONOMIC POLICY
ASSISTANCE PROGRAMS (PAMPHLET). USA+45 PLAN BAL/PWR FOR/AID
BUDGET DIPLOM CONTROL CIVMIL/REL ATTIT. PAGE 134 ORD/FREE
F2648

B64
BASTIAT F.,ECONOMIC HARMONIES (1850). STRATA STRUCT ECO/TAC
ECO/DEV BUDGET TAX PRICE LOBBY COST. PAGE 11 F0206 PLAN
INT/TRADE
LAISSEZ

B64
BOARMAN P.M.,GERMANY'S ECONOMIC DILEMMA - INFLATION ECO/DEV
AND THE BALANCE OF PAYMENTS. AFR GERMANY/W LABOR FINAN
CAP/ISM PRICE BAL/PAY COST INCOME 20. PAGE 16 F0302 INT/TRADE
BUDGET

B64
CENTRO ESTUDIOS MONETARIOS LAT,PROBLEMAS DE PAGOS FINAN
EN AMERICA LATINA. L/A+17C MARKET BUDGET ECO/TAC INT/TRADE
EFFICIENCY WEALTH 20 CENTRAL/AM. PAGE 22 F0434 BAL/PAY
ECO/UNDEV

B64
CHINITZ B.,CITY AND SUBURB: THE ECONOMICS OF TEC/DEV
METROPOLITAN GROWTH. DIST/IND BUDGET GOV/REL DEMAND PLAN
ATTIT HABITAT MUNICH PHILADELPH. PAGE 24 F0467

B64
CLAIRBORN E.L.,FORECASTING THE BALANCE OF PAYMENTS: PREDICT
AN EVALUATION. AFR FUT UK USA+45 WOR+45 FINAN PLAN BAL/PAY
BUDGET PAY CONTROL...STAT CHARTS BIBLIOG 20. ECO/DEV
PAGE 24 F0474 ECO/TAC

B64
DUSCHA J.,ARMS, MONEY, AND POLITICS. USA+45 INDUS NAT/G
POL/PAR ECO/TAC TAX DETER NUC/PWR WAR WEAPON FORCES
GOV/REL ATTIT...BIBLIOG/A 20 CONGRESS MONEY POLICY
DEPT/DEFEN. PAGE 35 F0687 BUDGET

B64
EDWARDS E.O.,THE NATION'S ECONOMIC OBJECTIVES. NAT/G
INDUS WORKER BUDGET DIPLOM CONTROL ORD/FREE ECO/TAC
...POLICY SOC METH/CNCPT ANTHOL 20. PAGE 36 F0704

B64
EINZIG P.,MONETARY POLICY: ENDS AND MEANS. AFR UK FINAN
INDUS WORKER PLAN DIPLOM PRICE BAL/PAY COST WEALTH POLICY
...DECISION TIME/SEQ 20. PAGE 37 F0715 ECO/TAC
BUDGET

B64
FATOUROS A.A.,CANADA'S OVERSEAS AID. CANADA WOR+45 FOR/AID
ECO/DEV FINAN NAT/G BUDGET ECO/TAC CONFER ADMIN 20. DIPLOM
PAGE 39 F0768 ECO/UNDEV
POLICY

B64
FRIEDEN B.J.,THE FUTURE OF OLD NEIGHBORHOODS: NEIGH
REBUILDING FOR A CHANGING POPULATION. CONSTRUC PROB/SOLV
LOC/G NAT/G ACT/RES ECO/TAC REGION ATTIT...INT SAMP PLAN
MUNICH 20 NEWYORK/C LOS/ANG HARTFORD URBAN/RNWL. BUDGET
PAGE 44 F0855

B64
GOWDA K.V.,INTERNATIONAL CURRENCY PLANS AND INT/TRADE
EXPANSION OF WORLD TRADE. INT/ORG CREATE BUDGET FINAN
CONTROL BAL/PAY WEALTH 20 KEYNES/JM. PAGE 50 F0969 METH/COMP

B64
HAAR C.M.,LAW AND LAND: ANGLO-AMERICAN PLANNING LAW
PRACTICE. UK USA+45 NAT/G TEC/DEV BUDGET CT/SYS PLAN
INGP/REL EFFICIENCY OWN...JURID MUNICH 20. PAGE 52 NAT/COMP
F1019

B64
HARRIS S.E.,ECONOMICS OF THE KENNEDY YEARS AND A ECO/TAC
LOOK AHEAD. USA+45 PLAN BUDGET NEW/LIB...STAT CHIEF
RECORD IDEA/COMP PERS/COMP INDEX 20 KENNEDY/JF POLICY
EISNHWR/DD JOHNSON/LB. PAGE 56 F1091 NAT/G

B64
HOLLEY I.B. JR.,US ARMY IN WORLD WAR II: SPECIAL FORCES
STUDIES: BUYING AIRCRAFT: MATERIEL PROCUREMENT FOR COST
THE ARMY AIR FORCES. USA+45 USA-45 BUDGET WEAPON DIST/IND
GOV/REL PRODUC 20. PAGE 61 F1198 CIVMIL/REL

B64
LANGHOFF P.,MODELS, MEASUREMENT AND MARKETING. DECISION
ACT/RES COMPUTER OP/RES PLAN BUDGET...MGT PHIL/SCI SIMUL
METH/CNCPT STAT PROG/TEAC BIBLIOG. PAGE 75 F1478 MARKET
R+D

B64
LAURSEN K.,THE GERMAN INFLATION, 1918-23. EUR+WWI ECO/DEV
GERMANY/E GERMANY/W WOR-45 BUDGET TAX GOV/REL FINAN
BAL/PAY DEMAND PEACE...POLICY CHARTS 20 WEIMAR/REP. REPAR
PAGE 76 F1489 ECO/TAC

B64
MOAK L.L.,A MANUAL OF SUGGESTED PRACTICE FOR THE LOC/G
PREPARATION AND ADOPTION OF CAPITAL PROGRAMS AND BUDGET
CAPITAL BUDGETS BY LOCAL GOVERN. USA+45 DELIB/GP LEGIS
PLAN TAX GP/REL COST DECISION. PAGE 92 F1812 PROB/SOLV

B64
MORRISSENS L.,ECONOMIC POLICY IN OUR TIME: COUNTRY ECO/DEV
STUDIES. BELGIUM EUR+WWI FRANCE GERMANY/W ITALY ECO/TAC
NETHERLAND INDUS BARGAIN BUDGET GOV/REL BAL/PAY METH/COMP
PRODUC...CON/ANAL CHARTS COSTS 20. PAGE 94 F1839 PLAN

B64
ODEH H.S.,THE IMPACT OF INFLATION ON THE LEVEL OF ECOMETRIC
ECONOMIC ACTIVITY. AFR BRAZIL CHILE BUDGET GOV/REL ECO/TAC
COST DEMAND INCOME WEALTH...STAT METH 20 MONEY. ECO/UNDEV
PAGE 100 F1963 FINAN

B64
OECD,DEVELOPMENT ASSISTANCE EFFORTS - POLICIES OF INT/ORG
THE MEMBERS. AGRI INDUS BUDGET...GEOG NAT/COMP 20 FOR/AID
OECD. PAGE 100 F1967 ECO/UNDEV
TEC/DEV

B64
OECD,THE FLOW OF FINANCIAL RESOURCES TO LESS FOR/AID
DEVELOPED COUNTRIES 1956-1963. WOR+45 FINAN CAP/ISM BUDGET
...POLICY STAT 20. PAGE 100 F1968 INT/ORG
ECO/UNDEV

B64
ROBINSON E.A.G.,ECONOMIC DEVELOPMENT FOR AFRICA ECO/UNDEV
SOUTH OF THE SAHARA. AFR AGRI INDUS LABOR BUDGET ECO/TAC
INT/TRADE PRICE...POLICY GEOG ANTHOL 20. PAGE 113 ACT/RES
F2219 PLAN

B64
THAILAND NATIONAL ECO DEV,THE NATIONAL ECONOMIC ECO/UNDEV
DEVELOPMENT PLAN: 1961-66: SECOND PHASE 1964-66. ECO/TAC
THAILAND AGRI FINAN BUDGET EFFICIENCY INCOME...STAT PLAN
CHARTS 20. PAGE 129 F2547 NAT/G

B64
US HOUSE COMM GOVT OPERATIONS,US OWNED FOREIGN FINAN
CURRENCIES: HEARINGS (COMMITTEE ON GOVERNMENT ECO/TAC
OPERATIONS). INDIA ECO/DEV PLAN BUDGET TAX DEMAND FOR/AID
EFFICIENCY 20 AID CONGRESS. PAGE 137 F2699 OWN

B64
WEIDENBAUM M.L.,CONGRESS AND THE FEDERAL BUDGET: LEGIS
FEDERAL BUDGETING AND THE RESPONSIBLE USE OF POWER. EX/STRUC
LOC/G PLAN TAX CONGRESS. PAGE 144 F2843 BUDGET
ADMIN

B64
WELLISZ S.,THE ECONOMICS OF THE SOVIET BLOC. COM EFFICIENCY
USSR INDUS WORKER PLAN BUDGET INT/TRADE TAX PRICE ADMIN
PRODUC WEALTH MARXISM...METH/COMP 20. PAGE 145 MARKET
F2854

B64
WILLIAMSON O.E.,THE ECONOMICS OF DISCRETIONARY EFFICIENCY
BEHAVIOR: MANAGERIAL OBJECTIVES IN A THEORY OF THE MGT
FIRM. MARKET BUDGET CAP/ISM PRODUC DRIVE PERSON ECO/TAC
...STAT CHARTS BIBLIOG METH 20. PAGE 147 F2897 CHOOSE

B64
WILSON T.,POLICIES FOR REGIONAL DEVELOPMENT. CANADA REGION
UK FINAN INDUS NAT/G BUDGET TAX GIVE COST PLAN
...NAT/COMP 20. PAGE 147 F2904 ECO/DEV
ECO/TAC

B64
ZOBER M.,MARKETING MANAGEMENT. FINAN BUDGET ECO/DEV
EDU/PROP PRICE PRODUC ATTIT...POLICY TREND CHARTS MGT
METH/COMP EQULIB 20. PAGE 150 F2966 CONTROL
MARKET

L64
KOLODZIEJ E.A.,"RATIONAL CONSENT AND DEFENSE DECISION
BUDGETS: THE ROLE OF CONGRESS, 1945-1962." LEGIS PLAN
DIPLOM CONTROL PARL/PROC 20 CONGRESS. PAGE 72 F1423 CIVMIL/REL
BUDGET

S64
CARNEGIE ENDOWMENT INT. PEACE,"ADMINISTRATION AND INT/ORG
BUDGET (ISSUES BEFORE THE NINETEENTH GENERAL ADMIN
ASSEMBLY)." WOR+45 FINAN BUDGET ECO/TAC ROUTINE
COST...STAT RECORD UN. PAGE 21 F0415

S64
NEWLYN W.T.,"MONETARY SYSTEMS AND INTEGRATION" AFR ECO/UNDEV
BUDGET ADMIN FEDERAL PRODUC PROFIT UTIL...CHARTS 20 REGION
AFRICA/E. PAGE 98 F1922 METH/COMP
FINAN

S64
TOBIN J.,"ECONOMIC GROWTH AS AN OBJECTIVE OF ECO/DEV
GOVERNMENT POLICY." FUT WOR+45 FINAN WORKER BUDGET POLICY
INCOME...SOC 20. PAGE 131 F2579 ECO/TAC
IDEA/COMP

C64
GOLDMAN M.I.,"COMPARATIVE ECONOMIC SYSTEMS: A NAT/COMP
READER." COM ECO/UNDEV NAT/G BUDGET CAP/ISM ADMIN CONTROL
TOTALISM MARXISM SOCISM...MGT ANTHOL BIBLIOG 19/20. IDEA/COMP
PAGE 48 F0938

C64
LOUFTY A.,"LA PLANIFICATION DE L'ECONOMIE." FRANCE PLAN
USSR FINAN INDUS BUDGET INCOME PRODUC...BIBLIOG 20. ECO/UNDEV
PAGE 82 F1604 ECO/DEV

B65
ANALYSIS AND ASSESSMENT OF THE ECONOMIC EFFECTS: PUBLIC LAW 480 TITLE I PROGRAM TURKEY. INDIA TURKEY USA+45 AGRI NAT/G PLAN BUDGET DIPLOM COST EFFICIENCY...CHARTS 20. PAGE 1 F0021
ECO/TAC FOR/AID FINAN ECO/UNDEV

B65
BARRERE A.,ECONOMIE ET INSTITUTIONS FINANCIERES (VOL. I). AFR FRANCE PLAN...BIBLIOG T 20. PAGE 10 F0194
ECO/DEV BUDGET NAT/G FINAN

B65
BAUMOL W.J.,ECONOMIC THEORY AND OPERATIONS ANALYSIS (2ND ED.). MARKET LG/CO BUDGET PRICE COST EQUILIB PRODUC...DECISION MATH CHARTS GAME 20. PAGE 12 F0219
OP/RES ECO/DEV METH/COMP STAT

B65
BREAK G.F.,FEDERAL LENDING AND ECONOMIC STABILITY. USA+45 ECO/DEV LG/CO SML/CO EQUILIB...CHARTS 20. PAGE 18 F0344
BUDGET FINAN NAT/G ECO/TAC

B65
DUGGAR G.S.,RENEWAL OF TOWN AND VILLAGE I: A WORLD-WIDE SURVEY OF LOCAL GOVERNMENT EXPERIENCE. WOR+45 CONSTRUC INDUS CREATE BUDGET REGION GOV/REL...QU NAT/COMP MUNICH 20 URBAN/RNWL. PAGE 35 F0673
NEIGH PLAN ADMIN

B65
FRYE R.J.,HOUSING AND URBAN RENEWAL IN ALABAMA. USA+45 NEIGH LEGIS BUDGET ADJUD ADMIN PARTIC...MGT MUNICH 20 ALABAMA URBAN/RNWL. PAGE 45 F0871
PROB/SOLV PLAN GOV/REL

B65
GOODSELL C.T.,ADMINISTRATION OF A REVOLUTION. PUERT/RICO ECO/UNDEV FINAN POL/PAR PROVS LEGIS PLAN BUDGET RECEIVE ADMIN COLONIAL LEAD MUNICH 20 ROOSEVLT/F. PAGE 49 F0951
EXEC SOC

B65
GREER S.,URBAN RENEWAL AND AMERICAN CITIES: THE DILEMMA OF DEMOCRATIC INTERVENTION. USA+45 R+D LOC/G VOL/ASSN ACT/RES BUDGET ADMIN GOV/REL...SOC INT SAMP MUNICH 20 BOSTON CHICAGO LOS/ANG MIAMI URBAN/RNWL. PAGE 51 F0992
PROB/SOLV PLAN NAT/G

B65
MAO J.C.T.,EFFICIENCY IN PUBLIC URBAN RENEWAL EXPENDITURES THROUGH CAPITAL BUDGETING. USA+45 FINAN LOC/G NAT/G NEIGH REGION UTIL...GEOG METH/CNCPT STAT SIMUL GEN/LAWS MUNICH 20 URBAN/RNWL. PAGE 85 F1662
TEC/DEV BUDGET PROB/SOLV

B65
MELMANS S.,OUR DEPLETED SOCIETY. AFR SPACE USA+45 ECO/DEV FORCES BUDGET ECO/TAC ADMIN WEAPON EFFICIENCY 20. PAGE 89 F1753
CIVMIL/REL INDUS EDU/PROP CONTROL

B65
MUND V.A.,GOVERNMENT AND BUSINESS (4TH ED.). USA+45 INDUS LG/CO SML/CO LEGIS INT/TRADE LICENSE PRICE ADJUD. PAGE 95 F1860
NAT/G ECO/TAC BUDGET CONTROL

B65
PHELPS E.S.,FISCAL NEUTRALITY TOWARD ECONOMIC GROWTH. FINAN NAT/G BUDGET CAP/ISM CONTROL INCOME 20. PAGE 106 F2080
ECO/DEV POLICY ECO/TAC TAX

B65
PINCUS J.A.,ECONOMIC AID AND INTERNATIONAL COST SHARING* A RAND CORPORATION RESEARCH STUDY. INT/ORG BUDGET CENTRAL...ECOMETRIC MATH QUANT STAT SIMUL. PAGE 106 F2088
ECO/UNDEV COST FOR/AID INT/TRADE

B65
ROOSA R.V.,MONETARY REFORM FOR THE WORLD ECONOMY. AFR EUR+WWI USA+45 WOR+45 CREATE BUDGET DIPLOM FOR/AID EQUILIB WEALTH IMF. PAGE 114 F2237
FINAN INT/ORG INT/TRADE BAL/PAY

B65
SHARIF A.,THE BALANCE OF PAYMENTS OF PAKISTAN, 1948-1958 (THESIS, UNIVERSITY OF TORONTO). PAKISTAN FINAN INDUS FOR/AID PRICE WEALTH...TREND CHARTS 20. PAGE 120 F2368
BAL/PAY BUDGET INT/TRADE ECO/UNDEV

B65
SHEPHERD W.G.,ECONOMIC PERFORMANCE UNDER PUBLIC OWNERSHIP: BRITISH FUEL AND POWER. UK BUDGET GP/REL ...METH/CNCPT CHARTS BIBLIOG 20. PAGE 120 F2375
PROC/MFG NAT/G OWN FINAN

B65
TEW B.,WEALTH AND INCOME. UK BUDGET INT/TRADE PRICE BAL/PAY DEMAND...CHARTS GOV/COMP 20 AUSTRAL. PAGE 129 F2546
FINAN ECO/DEV WEALTH INCOME

B65
US BUREAU OF THE BUDGET,THE BALANCE OF PAYMENTS STATISTICS OF THE UNITED STATES: A REVIEW AND APPRAISAL. USA+45 FINAN NAT/G PROB/SOLV DIPLOM. PAGE 134 F2644
BAL/PAY STAT METH/COMP BUDGET

B65
US SENATE COMM ON FOREIGN REL,HEARINGS ON THE FOREIGN ASSISTANCE PROGRAM. AFR ASIA L/A+17C USA+45 WOR+45 FORCES TEC/DEV BUDGET CONTROL WEAPON ORD/FREE 20 UN CONGRESS SEC/STATE. PAGE 139 F2734
FOR/AID DIPLOM INT/ORG ECO/UNDEV

B65
WARNER A.W.,THE IMPACT OF SCIENCE ON TECHNOLOGY. UNIV INTELL SOCIETY NAT/G ACT/RES PLAN PROB/SOLV BUDGET OPTIMAL GEN/METH. PAGE 143 F2821
DECISION TEC/DEV CREATE POLICY

B65
WEIDENBAUM M.L.,CONGRESS AND THE FEDERAL BUDGET. FINAN ACT/RES DOMIN CONFER EXEC UTIL PWR NEW/LIB ...CHARTS CONGRESS. PAGE 144 F2844
BUDGET LEGIS PLAN DECISION

B65
YOUNG A.N.,CHINA'S WARTIME FINANCE AND INFLATION. ASIA AGRI INDUS NAT/G ECO/TAC CONFER PRICE WAR COST 20. PAGE 150 F2949
FINAN FOR/AID TAX BUDGET

L65
HAMMOND A.,"COMPREHENSIVE VERSUS INCREMENTAL BUDGETING IN THE DEPARTMENT OF AGRICULTURE" USA+45 GP/REL ATTIT...PSY INT 20 DEPT/AGRI. PAGE 54 F1057
TOP/EX EX/STRUC AGRI BUDGET

L65
LOFTUS M.L.,"INTERNATIONAL MONETARY FUND, 1962-1965: A SELECTED BIBLIOGRAPHY." WOR+45 PLAN BUDGET INCOME PROFIT WEALTH. PAGE 81 F1596
BIBLIOG FINAN INT/TRADE INT/ORG

S65
HUTT W.H.,"KEYNESIAN REVISIONS" SOUTH/AFR ECO/DEV FINAN NAT/G WORKER BUDGET TAX PRICE EQUILIB WEALTH 20 KEYNES/JM. PAGE 64 F1252
ECO/TAC GEN/LAWS LOG

S65
KEE W.S.,"CENTRAL CITY EXPENDITURES AND METROPOLITAN AREAS." PLAN BUDGET ECO/TAC TAX GP/REL WEALTH...CHARTS MUNICH 20. PAGE 70 F1366
LOC/G GOV/COMP NEIGH

C65
MANSFIELD H.C.,"THE CONGRESS AND ECONOMIC POLICY" IN C. TRUMAN ED., THE CONGRESS AND AMERICA'S FUTURE." USA+45 USA-45 CONSTN NAT/G BUDGET ADMIN CONTROL EXEC LOBBY. PAGE 85 F1661
POLICY ECO/TAC PWR LEGIS

N65
STUDY GP CREATE RESERVE ASSETS,REPORT TO DEPUTIES (PAMPHLET). AFR FUT PLAN CONTROL DEMAND WEALTH ...ANTHOL METH 20. PAGE 127 F2507
INT/ORG INT/TRADE FINAN BUDGET

B66
AGGARWALA R.N.,FINANCIAL COMMITTEES OF THE INDIAN PARLIAMENT: A STUDY IN PARLIAMENTARY CONTROL OVER PUBLIC EXPENDITURE. INDIA FINAN NAT/G ROLE...CHARTS METH/COMP METH 20 PARLIAMENT. PAGE 3 F0049
PARL/PROC BUDGET CONTROL DELIB/GP

B66
CHASE S.B. JR.,PROBLEMS IN PUBLIC EXPENDITURE ANALYSIS. DIST/IND INDUS OP/RES PLAN BUDGET RECEIVE PRICE RISK COST INCOME...CHARTS ANTHOL 20. PAGE 23 F0455
ECO/DEV FINAN NAT/G INSPECT

B66
CONAN A.R.,THE PROBLEM OF STERLING. UK WOR+45 BUDGET ECO/TAC...POLICY STAT CHARTS 20 SILVER. PAGE 27 F0521
FINAN ECO/DEV BAL/PAY DIPLOM

B66
CONGRESSIONAL QUARTERLY SERV,FEDERAL ECONOMIC POLICY 1945-1965. USA+45 FINAN NAT/G CHIEF CONSULT TAX...CHARTS 20 PRESIDENT DEBT. PAGE 27 F0526
ECO/TAC BUDGET LEGIS

B66
DILLEY M.R.,BRITISH POLICY IN KENYA COLONY (2ND ED.). AFR INDIA UK LABOR BUDGET TAX ADMIN PARL/PROC GP/REL...BIBLIOG 20 PARLIAMENT. PAGE 33 F0639
COLONIAL REPRESENT SOVEREIGN

B66
GOODWIN C.D.W.,ECONOMIC INQUIRY IN AUSTRALIA. ECO/DEV ECO/UNDEV ACADEM INT/TRADE RENT TARIFFS TAX PRESS GOV/REL SOCISM 18/20 AUSTRAL. PAGE 49 F0953
ECO/TAC IDEA/COMP BUDGET COLONIAL

B66
GREENE L.E.,GOVERNMENT IN TENNESSEE (2ND ED.). USA+45 DIST/IND INDUS POL/PAR EX/STRUC LEGIS PLAN BUDGET GIVE CT/SYS...MGT T 20 TENNESSEE. PAGE 51 F0989
PROVS LOC/G CONSTN ADMIN

B66
HAINES W.W.,MONEY PRICES AND POLICY. WOR+45 ECO/DEV BUDGET CONTROL INCOME...POLICY STAT CHARTS BIBLIOG T 20. PAGE 53 F1039
PRICE FINAN ECO/TAC GOV/REL

B66
HASTINGS P.G.,THE MANAGEMENT OF BUSINESS FINANCE. ECO/DEV PLAN BUDGET CONTROL COST...DECISION CHARTS BIBLIOG T 20. PAGE 56 F1109
FINAN MGT INDUS ECO/TAC

B66
HAYER T.,FRENCH AID. AFR FRANCE AGRI FINAN BUDGET ADMIN WAR PRODUC...CHARTS 18/20 THIRD/WRLD OVRSEA/DEV. PAGE 57 F1125
TEC/DEV COLONIAL FOR/AID ECO/UNDEV

B66
INARRITU A.L.,EL PATRON CAMBIO-ORO Y SUS REFORMAS. AFR L/A+17C WOR+45 PLAN PROB/SOLV BUDGET ECO/TAC INT/TRADE EFFICIENCY ORD/FREE 20 MEXIC/AMER. PAGE 64 F1262
ECO/UNDEV FINAN DIPLOM POLICY

B66
INTERNATIONAL ECO POLICY ASSN,THE UNITED STATES BALANCE OF PAYMENTS. INT/ORG NAT/G PROB/SOLV BUDGET DIPLOM INT/TRADE WEALTH 20. PAGE 65 F1274
BAL/PAY ECO/TAC POLICY FINAN

B66
KINDLEBERGER C.P.,EUROPE AND THE DOLLAR. AFR EUR+WWI FRANCE GERMANY/W USA+45 CONSTN INT/ORG DIPLOM INT/TRADE...ANTHOL 20. PAGE 71 F1395
BAL/PAY BUDGET FINAN ECO/DEV

B66
KOMIYA R.,POSTWAR ECONOMIC GROWTH IN JAPAN. ELITES NAT/G EX/STRUC TEC/DEV BUDGET DIPLOM CONTROL BAL/PAY PRODUC...BIBLIOG 20 CHINJAP. PAGE 73 F1424
ECO/DEV POLICY PLAN ADJUST

B66
LECHT L.,GOAL, PRIORITIES, AND DOLLARS: THE NEXT DECADE. SPACE USA+45 SOCIETY AGRI BUDGET FOR/AID ...HEAL SOC/WK STAT CHARTS 20 URBAN/RNWL PUB/TRANS. PAGE 76 F1499
IDEA/COMP POLICY CONSEN PLAN

B66
LEE M.W.,TOWARD ECONOMIC STABILITY. USA+45 BUDGET TAX PRICE EQUILIB INCOME. PAGE 77 F1506
ECO/TAC CONTROL POLICY NAT/G

B66
MANGONE G.J.,UN ADMINISTRATION OF ECONOMIC AND AOCIAL PROGRAMS. CONSULT BUDGET INT/TRADE REGION 20 UN. PAGE 84 F1653
ADMIN MGT ECO/TAC DELIB/GP

B66
MASON E.S.,ECONOMIC DEVELOPMENT IN INDIA AND PAKISTAN. INDIA PAKISTAN AGRI FINAN PLAN BUDGET INT/TRADE WEALTH...POLICY STAT TREND CHARTS 20. PAGE 87 F1700
NAT/COMP ECO/UNDEV ECO/TAC FOR/AID

B66
NATIONAL INDUSTRIAL CONF BOARD,GOLD AND WORLD MONETARY PROBLEMS. AFR FUT WOR+45 PROB/SOLV BUDGET INT/TRADE PAY GOV/REL...POLICY ANTHOL 20. PAGE 97 F1902
FINAN ECO/TAC PRICE BAL/PAY

B66
ROBERTSON D.J.,THE BRITISH BALANCE OF PAYMENTS. UK WOR+45 INDUS BUDGET TAX ADJUST...CHARTS ANTHOL 20. PAGE 112 F2213
FINAN BAL/PAY ECO/DEV INT/TRADE

B66
SASTRI K.V.S.,FEDERAL-STATE FISCAL RELATIONS IN INDIA: A STUDY OF THE FINANCE COMMISSION AND TECHNIQUES OF FINANCIAL ADJUSTMENT. INDIA PROVS DELIB/GP GOV/REL FEDERAL...MATH CHARTS 20. PAGE 116 F2283
TAX BUDGET FINAN NAT/G

B66
US PRES COMM ECO IMPACT DEFENS,REPORT* JULY 1965. USA+45 ECO/DEV INDUS DELIB/GP FORCES OP/RES ARMS/CONT NUC/PWR WEAPON BAL/PAY...PREDICT SIMUL. PAGE 138 F2726
ACT/RES STAT WAR BUDGET

B66
US SENATE COMM APPROPRIATIONS,FOREIGN ASSISTANCE AND RELATED AGENCIES APPROPRIATIONS FOR FISCAL YEAR 1967: HEARINGS... ON H. R. 17788. ECO/UNDEV INT/ORG FORCES INSPECT ECO/TAC GIVE DEBATE WEAPON CIVMIL/REL WEALTH...INT 20 CONGRESS DEPT/DEFEN DEPT/STATE DEPT/HEW AID. PAGE 138 F2727
BUDGET FOR/AID DIPLOM COST

B66
US SENATE COMM ON FOREIGN REL,HEARINGS ON S 2859 AND S 2861. USA+45 WOR+45 FORCES BUDGET CAP/ISM ADMIN DETER WEAPON TOTALISM...NAT/COMP 20 UN CONGRESS. PAGE 139 F2735
FOR/AID DIPLOM ORD/FREE ECO/UNDEV

L66
AFRICAN BIBLIOGRAPHIC CENTER,"AFRICAN ECONOMIC AFFAIRS: A SELECT BIBLIOGRAPHICAL SURVEY, 1965-1966." AFR FINAN INDUS INT/ORG LABOR PLAN BUDGET DIPLOM INT/TRADE ADMIN EFFICIENCY WEALTH 20. PAGE 3 F0046
BIBLIOG ECO/UNDEV TEC/DEV FOR/AID

L66
AFRICAN BIBLIOGRAPHIC CENTER,"AFRICAN ECONOMIC AFFAIRS: A SELECT BIBLIOGRAPHICAL SURVEY, 1965-1966; SUPPLEMENTS NUMBERS 1-3." AFR FINAN INDUS LABOR PLAN BUDGET CAP/ISM DIPLOM INT/TRADE ADMIN...GEOG 20. PAGE 3 F0047
BIBLIOG/A ECO/UNDEV FOR/AID TEC/DEV

L66
AMERICAN ECONOMIC REVIEW,"SIXTY-THIRD LIST OF DOCTORAL DISSERTATIONS IN POLITICAL ECONOMY IN AMERICAN UNIVERSITIES AND COLLEGES." ECO/DEV AGRI FINAN LABOR WORKER PLAN BUDGET INT/TRADE ADMIN DEMAND...MGT STAT 20. PAGE 5 F0088
BIBLIOG/A CONCPT ACADEM

S66
BENOIT J.,"WORLD DEFENSE EXPENDITURES." WOR+45 WEAPON COST PRODUC. PAGE 13 F0253
FORCES STAT NAT/COMP BUDGET

S66
DAVIS O.A.,"A THEORY OF THE BUDGETARY PROCESS." ECO/DEV FINAN LEGIS PROB/SOLV GOV/REL...ECOMETRIC METH/CNCPT STAT CONT/OBS TREND METH/COMP SIMUL 20 CONGRESS. PAGE 30 F0592
DECISION NAT/G BUDGET EFFICIENCY

S66
VENTRE F.T.,"LOCAL INITIATIVES IN URBAN INDUSTRIAL DEVELOPMENT." FINAN SERV/IND TOP/EX PLAN BUDGET RENT TAX...GP/COMP MUNICH 20. PAGE 141 F2777
ECO/TAC LOC/G INDUS

N66
EOMMITTEE ECONOMIC DEVELOPMENT,THE DOLLAR AND THE WORLD MONETARY SYSTEM: A STATEMENT ON NATIONAL POLICY (PAMPHLET). AFR USA+45 NAT/G PLAN PROB/SOLV BUDGET ECO/TAC FOR/AID INCOME...POLICY 20 EUROPE. PAGE 38 F0740
FINAN BAL/PAY DIPLOM ECO/DEV

N66
OECD,THE BALANCE OF PAYMENTS ADJUSTMENT PROCESS (PAMPHLET). EUR+WWI ECO/DEV FINAN CONSULT PLAN PROB/SOLV BUDGET CAP/ISM INT/TRADE PRICE CONTROL EQUILIB 20. PAGE 101 F1975
BAL/PAY ECO/TAC DIPLOM INT/ORG

B67
BREAK G.F.,INTERGOVERNMENTAL FISCAL RELATIONS IN THE UNITED STATES. USA+45 USA-45 DELIB/GP PLAN BUDGET TAX GOV/REL CENTRAL...TREND CHARTS MUNICH. PAGE 18 F0345
LOC/G NAT/G PROVS FINAN

B67
BRIEFS H.W.,REGAINING BALANCE IN A HIGH EMPLOYMENT ECONOMY: UNRESOLVED ISSUES FOR 1967 AND BEYOND. USA+45 NAT/G PLAN PROB/SOLV FOR/AID...CHARTS 20. PAGE 18 F0350
ECO/DEV FINAN BAL/PAY BUDGET

B67
CAMPBELL A.K.,METROPOLITAN AMERICA* FISCAL PATTERNS AND GOVERNMENTAL SYSTEMS. PROVS PLAN COST...POLICY DECISION GOV/COMP METH/COMP BIBLIOG. PAGE 21 F0405
USA+45 NAT/G LOC/G BUDGET

B67
DE TORRES J.,FINANCING LOCAL GOVERNMENT. USA+45 USA-45 NAT/G PROVS GIVE ADJUST PWR...TIME/SEQ CHARTS MUNICH 20. PAGE 31 F0606
LOC/G BUDGET TAX TREND

B67
ENKE S.,DEFENSE MANAGEMENT. USA+45 R+D FORCES WORKER PLAN ECO/TAC ADMIN NUC/PWR BAL/PAY UTIL WEALTH...MGT DEPT/DEFEN. PAGE 38 F0738
DECISION DELIB/GP EFFICIENCY BUDGET

B67
GITTELL M.,PARTICIPANTS AND PARTICIPATION: A STUDY OF SCHOOL POLICY IN NEW YORK. USA+45 EX/STRUC BUDGET PAY ATTIT...POLICY MUNICH 20 NEWYORK/C. PAGE 47 F0926
SCHOOL DECISION PARTIC ADMIN

B67
O'LEARY M.K.,THE POLITICS OF AMERICAN FOREIGN AID. USA+45 POL/PAR CHIEF BUDGET EDU/PROP LOBBY CONGRESS. PAGE 100 F1958
FOR/AID DIPLOM PARL/PROC ATTIT

B67
ROBINSON E.A.G.,ECONOMIC PLANNING IN THE UNITED KINGDOM. UK WORKER PLAN PROB/SOLV BAL/PAY 20. PAGE 113 F2220
ECO/DEV INDUS PRODUC BUDGET

B67
THOMAS M.J.,PRESIDENTIAL STATEMENTS ON EDUCATION: EXCERPTS FROM INAUGURAL AND STATE OF THE UNION MESSAGES 1789-1967. USA+45 USA-45 NAT/G BUDGET ...IDEA/COMP 18/20 PRESIDENT. PAGE 130 F2562
EDU/PROP TOP/EX LEGIS SCHOOL

B67
US AGENCY INTERNATIONAL DEV,PROPOSED FOREIGN AID PROGRAM FOR 1968: SUMMARY PRESENTATION TO THE CONGRESS. AFR S/ASIA USA+45 AGRI TEC/DEV DIPLOM ECO/TAC BAL/PAY COST HEALTH KNOWL SKILL 20 AID CONGRESS ALL/PROG. PAGE 134 F2640
ECO/UNDEV BUDGET FOR/AID STAT

B67
US CONGRESS JOINT ECO COMM,REPORT ON JANUARY 1967 ECONOMIC REPORT OF THE PRESIDENT. FINAN LABOR NAT/G LEGIS BUDGET INT/TRADE COST DEMAND INCOME PRODUC ...POLICY IDEA/COMP 20 CONGRESS. PAGE 135 F2663
CHIEF ECO/TAC PLAN DELIB/GP

B67
US SENATE COMM ON FOREIGN REL,LATIN AMERICAN SUMMIT CONFERENCE. L/A+17C USA+45 FINAN PLAN SENATE ALL/PROG. PAGE 139 F2740
FOR/AID BUDGET DIPLOM INT/ORG

L67
LENT G.E.,"TAX INCENTIVES FOR INVESTMENT IN DEVELOPING COUNTRIES" WOR+45 LAW INDUS PLAN BUDGET TARIFFS ADMIN...METH/COMP 20. PAGE 78 F1526
ECO/UNDEV TAX FINAN ECO/TAC

L67
TANDON Y.,"CONSENSUS AND AUTHORITY BEHIND UNITED NATIONS PEACEKEEPING OPERATIONS." FINAN VOL/ASSN BUDGET DIPLOM PAY DOMIN...CHARTS 20 UN. PAGE 128 F2528
CONSEN INT/ORG PWR PEACE

L67
WILKINSON J.H. JR.,"THE NET OPERATING LOSS DEDUCTION AND RELATED INCOME TAX DEVICES." PROB/SOLV BUDGET PAY GOV/REL ORD/FREE...MATH CHARTS METH 20. PAGE 146 F2886
TAX FINAN LAW ADJUD

S67
BASOV V.,"THE DEVELOPMENT OF PUBLIC EDUCATION AND THE BUDGET." USSR NAT/G CONTROL REV COST AGE...STAT 20. PAGE 11 F0204
BUDGET GIVE EDU/PROP SCHOOL

S67
BRANCO R.,"LAND REFORM* THE ANSWER TO LATIN AMERICA'S AGRICULTURAL DEVELOPMENT?" L/A+17C NAT/G PLAN TEC/DEV BUDGET RENT EFFICIENCY 20. PAGE 18 F0339
ECO/UNDEV AGRI TAX OWN

S67
FERGUSON D.E.,"DETERMINING CAPACITY FOR CAPITAL EXPENDITURES." USA+45 LOC/G BUDGET TAX ADMIN CONTROL...TREND MUNICH 20. PAGE 40 F0784
FINAN PAY COST

S67
FRANKEL T.,"ECONOMIC REFORM* A TENTATIVE APPRAISAL." COM USSR OP/RES BUDGET CONFER EFFICIENCY PRODUC MARXISM SOCISM...MGT 20. PAGE 43 F0847
ECO/DEV INDUS PLAN WEALTH

S67
GREEN C.,"SCHEMES FOR TRANSFERRING INCOME TO THE POOR." BUDGET GIVE RECEIVE DEBATE COST INCOME ...SOC/WK METH/COMP. PAGE 50 F0982
TAX WEALTH PLAN ACT/RES

S67
HILDEBRAND G.H.,"SECOND THOUGHTS ON THE NEGATIVE INCOME TAX." PLAN BUDGET ECO/TAC GIVE RECEIVE DEBATE EFFICIENCY INCOME...METH/COMP COSTS. PAGE 59 F1169
TAX WEALTH SOC/WK ACT/RES

S67
HILTON G.W.,"FEDERAL PARTICIPATION IN THE SUPERSONIC TRANSPORT PROGRAM." USA+45 LEGIS PROB/SOLV BUDGET ATTIT 20. PAGE 60 F1172
DIST/IND TEC/DEV FINAN NAT/G

S67
JAVITS J.K.,"THE USE OF AMERICAN PLURALISM." USA+45 ECO/DEV BUDGET ADMIN ALL/IDEOS...DECISION TREND. PAGE 67 F1309
CENTRAL ATTIT POLICY NAT/G

S67
KOTLER P.,"OPERATIONS RESEARCH IN MARKETING." USA+45 DIST/IND INDUS LG/CO CONSULT BUDGET TASK DEMAND EFFICIENCY PROFIT WEALTH DECISION. PAGE 73 F1429
ECOMETRIC OP/RES MARKET PLAN

S67
LINEBERRY R.L.,"REFORMISM AND PUBLIC POLICIES IN AMERICAN CITIES." USA+45 POL/PAR EX/STRUC LEGIS BUDGET TAX GP/REL...STAT CHARTS MUNICH. PAGE 80 F1573
DECISION POLICY LOC/G

S67
MERON T.,"THE UN'S 'COMMON SYSTEM' OF SALARY, ALLOWANCE, AND BENEFITS: CRITICAL APPR'SAL OF COORD IN PERSONNEL MATTERS." VOL/ASSN PAY EFFICIENCY ...CHARTS 20 UN. PAGE 90 F1761
ADMIN EX/STRUC INT/ORG BUDGET

S67
NOURSE E.G.,"EARLY FLOWERING OF THE EMPLOYMENT ACT" USA+45 LABOR CONSULT DELIB/GP LEGIS BUDGET GOV/REL PRODUC WEALTH 20 INTRVN/ECO. PAGE 99 F1939
NAT/G WORKER ECO/TAC CONTROL

S67
PAI G.A.,"TAXATION AND PLANNING IN INDIA: A BIRDS-EYE VIEW." INDIA ELITES NAT/G LEGIS BUDGET CONTROL LOBBY INCOME...STAT CHARTS 20. PAGE 102 F2015
TAX PLAN WEALTH STRATA

S67
SIDDIQ M.M.,"LOCAL GOVERNMENT IN PAKISTAN." PAKISTAN PROB/SOLV TAX COLONIAL GOV/REL MUNICH 20. PAGE 121 F2395
ADMIN LOC/G DELIB/GP BUDGET

S67
STILL J.F.,"THE FUTURE OF METROPOLITAN GOVERNMENT ORGANIZATION." USA+45 LOC/G BUDGET COST ATTIT MUNICH 20. PAGE 126 F2488
ADMIN FINAN CONTROL

S67
WASSERMAN M.,"BEYOND TOKENISM: REVERSE INTEGRATION IN ALBANY, GEORGIA." USA+45 PLAN BUDGET EDU/PROP LEAD AGE/C AGE/Y GEORGIA NEGRO. PAGE 144 F2827
REGION RACE/REL DISCRIM SCHOOL

S67
WOLFSON M.,"GOVERNMENT'S ROLE IN TOURISM DEVELOPMENT." WOR+45 ECO/DEV ECO/UNDEV FINAN BUDGET DIPLOM EDU/PROP. PAGE 148 F2920
SERV/IND NAT/G CONTROL PLAN

S67
ZOETEWEIJ B.,"INCOME POLICIES ABROAD: AN INTERIM REPORT." NAT/G PROB/SOLV BARGAIN BUDGET PRICE RISK CENTRAL EFFICIENCY EQUILIB...MGT NAT/COMP 20. PAGE 150 F2967
METH/COMP INCOME POLICY LABOR

N67
NATIONAL COMN COMMUNITY HEALTH,ACTION - PLANNING FOR COMMUNITY HEALTH SERVICES (PAMPHLET). USA+45 PROF/ORG DELIB/GP BUDGET ROUTINE GP/REL ATTIT ...HEAL SOC SOC/WK CHARTS MUNICH TIME 20. PAGE 97 F1898
PLAN HEALTH ADJUST

N67
US CONGRESS JOINT ECO COMM,ECONOMY IN GOVERNMENT (PAMPHLET). USA+45 ECO/DEV FINAN NAT/G PLAN BUDGET SENATE. PAGE 135 F2662
ECO/TAC COST EFFICIENCY MGT

N67
US CONGRESS JT COMM ECO GOVT,BACKGROUND MATERIAL ON ECONOMY IN GOVERNMENT 1967 (PAMPHLET). WOR+45 ECO/DEV BARGAIN PRICE DEMAND OPTIMAL...STAT DEPT/DEFEN. PAGE 135 F2665
BUDGET COST MGT NAT/G

N67
US HOUSE,MESSAGE FROM THE PRESIDENT OF THE UNITED STATES: URBAN AND RURAL POVERTY (PAMPHLET). USA+45 ACT/RES PLAN BUDGET RENT MUNICH 20 PRESIDENT. PAGE 136 F2685
NAT/G POLICY CREATE RECEIVE

N67
US HOUSE COMM GOVT OPERATIONS,FEDERALLY FINANCED SOCIAL RESEARCH, EXPENDITURES, STATUS, AND OBJECTIVES (PAMPHLET). WOR+45 CREATE LEAD GP/REL ATTIT...GEOG PSY SOC. PAGE 137 F2700
ACT/RES NAT/G GIVE BUDGET

N67
US HOUSE COMM ON COMMERCE,PARTNERSHIP FOR HEALTH AMENDMENTS FOR 1967 (PAMPHLET). PUB/INST DELIB/GP PROB/SOLV BUDGET EFFICIENCY 20 CONGRESS. PAGE 137 F2701
HEAL PLAN NAT/G JURID

N67
US HOUSE COMM SCI ASTRONAUT,AUTHORIZING APPROPRIATIONS TO THE NATIONAL AERONAUTICS AND SPACE ADMINISTRATION (PAMPHLET). USA+45 NAT/G OP/RES TEC/DEV BUDGET NASA HOUSE/REP. PAGE 137 F2704
SPACE R+D PHIL/SCI NUC/PWR

N67
US SENATE COMM ON FOREIGN REL,THE UNITED NATIONS AT TWENTY-ONE (PAMPHLET). WOR+45 BUDGET ADMIN SENATE UN. PAGE 139 F2738
INT/ORG DIPLOM PEACE

BUENOS/AIR....BUENOS AIRES, ARGENTINA

B59
CUCCORESE H.J.,HISTORIA DE LA CONVERSION DEL PAPEL MONEDA EN BUENOS AIRES, 1861-1867. AFR LAW LOC/G NAT/G ATTIT...POLICY BIBLIOG 19 ARGEN BUENOS/AIR. PAGE 29 F0560
FINAN PLAN LEGIS

BUGANDA....BUGANDA, UGANDA

BUGEDA LANZAS J. F0382

BUKHARIN/N....NIKOLAI BUKHARIN

BULGARIA....BULGARIA; SEE ALSO COM

B59
ETSCHMANN R.,DIE WAHRUNGS- UND DEVISENPOLITIK DES OSTBLOCKS UND IHRE AUSWIRKUNGEN AUF DIE WIRTSCHAFTSBEZIEHUNGEN ZWISCHEN OST U WEST. BULGARIA CZECHOSLVK HUNGARY POLAND USSR MARKET NAT/G PLAN DIPLOM...NAT/COMP 20. PAGE 39 F0753
ECO/TAC FINAN POLICY INT/TRADE

S64
HORECKY P.L.,"LIBRARY OF CONGRESS PUBLICATIONS IN AID OF USSR AND EAST EUROPEAN RESEARCH." BULGARIA CZECHOSLVK POLAND USSR YUGOSLAVIA NAT/G POL/PAR DIPLOM ADMIN GOV/REL...CLASSIF 20. PAGE 62 F1214
BIBLIOG/A COM MARXISM

B66
BROWN J.F.,THE NEW EASTERN EUROPE. ALBANIA BULGARIA HUNGARY POLAND ROMANIA CULTURE AGRI POL/PAR WAR NAT/LISM MARXISM...CHARTS BIBLIOG 20. PAGE 19 F0369
DIPLOM COM NAT/G ECO/UNDEV

B66
JACKSON G.D.,COMINTERN AND PEASANT IN EAST EUROPE 1919-1930. BULGARIA COM CZECHOSLVK EUR+WWI POLAND ROMANIA YUGOSLAVIA STRATA AGRI VOL/ASSN DIPLOM CONTROL CROWD WEALTH...POLICY NAT/COMP 20. PAGE 66 F1293
MARXISM ECO/UNDEV WORKER INT/ORG

B66
SPULBER N.,THE STATE AND ECONOMIC DEVELOPMENT IN EASTERN EUROPE. BULGARIA COM CZECHOSLVK HUNGARY POLAND YUGOSLAVIA CULTURE PLAN CAP/ISM INT/TRADE CONTROL...POLICY CHARTS METH/COMP BIBLIOG/A 19/20. PAGE 125 F2460
ECO/DEV ECO/UNDEV NAT/G TOTALISM

BULLITT/WC....WILLIAM C. BULLITT

BUNCHE/R....RALPH BUNCHE

BUNDY/M....MCGEORGE BUNDY

BUNZEL J.H. F0383

BUR/BUDGET....BUREAU OF THE BUDGET

N19
DOTSON A.,PRODUCTION PLANNING IN THE PATENT OFFICE (PAMPHLET). USA+45 DIST/IND PROB/SOLV PRODUC...MGT PHIL/SCI 20 BUR/BUDGET PATENT/OFF. PAGE 34 F0655
EFFICIENCY PLAN NAT/G ADMIN

N19
MARSH J.F. JR.,THE FBI RETIREMENT BILL (PAMPHLET). USA+45 EX/STRUC WORKER PLAN PROB/SOLV BUDGET LEAD LOBBY PARL/PROC PERS/REL RIGID/FLEX...POLICY 20 FBI PRESIDENT BUR/BUDGET. PAGE 86 F1677
ADMIN NAT/G SENIOR GOV/REL

B54
HOBBS E.H.,BEHIND THE PRESIDENT - A STUDY OF EXECUTIVE OFFICE AGENCIES. USA+45 NAT/G PLAN BUDGET ECO/TAC EXEC ORD/FREE 20 BUR/BUDGET. PAGE 60 F1183 — EX/STRUC DELIB/GP CONFER CONSULT

S56
MERRIAM R.E.,"THE BUREAU OF THE BUDGET AS PART OF THE PRESIDENT'S STAFF." 20 BUR/BUDGET 20 BOB. PAGE 90 F1763 — CHIEF CONTROL LEAD EXEC

BUR/STNDRD....BUREAU OF STANDARDS

N19
LAWRENCE S.A.,THE BATTERY ADDITIVE CONTROVERSY (PAMPHLET). USA+45 LAW MARKET PROC/MFG R+D CAP/ISM CT/SYS GOV/REL OWN FTC CONGRESS BUR/STNDRD RITCHIE/JM. PAGE 76 F1494 — PHIL/SCI LOBBY INSPECT

BURAGR/ECO....BUREAU OF AGRICULTURAL ECONOMICS

B66
KIRKENDALL R.S.,SOCIAL SCIENTISTS AND FARM POLITICS IN THE AGE OF ROOSEVELT. ACADEM PLAN ECO/TAC GIVE ADMIN CONTROL PRODUC...SOC 20 NEW/DEAL ROOSEVLT/F BURAGR/ECO. PAGE 71 F1399 — AGRI INTELL POLICY NAT/G

BURDEN H.T. F0384

BUREAU OF AGRICULTURAL ECONOMICS....SEE BURAGR/ECO

BUREAU OF STANDARDS....SEE BUR/STNDRD

BUREAU OF THE BUDGET....SEE BUR/BUDGET

BUREAU NATIONAL AFFAIRS F0385

BUREAU OF NATIONAL AFFAIRS F0386

BUREAUCRCY....BUREAUCRACY; SEE ALSO ADMIN

B54
WASHBURNE N.F.,INTERPRETING SOCIAL CHANGE IN AMERICA. USA+45 STRATA FAM NAT/G SECT OP/RES ECO/TAC EDU/PROP HABITAT...SOC TIME/SEQ TREND 20 BUREAUCRCY. PAGE 143 F2826 — CULTURE STRUCT CREATE TEC/DEV

BURKE E. F0387

BURKE/EDM....EDMUND BURKE

BURKHEAD J. F0388

BURMA....BURMA

N
UNESCO,SOUTH ASIA SOCIAL SCIENCES ABSTRACTS. BURMA CEYLON INDIA S/ASIA PRESS...PSY 20. PAGE 132 F2608 — BIBLIOG/A SOC

N
US LIBRARY OF CONGRESS,SOUTHERN ASIA ACCESSIONS LIST. BURMA CEYLON INDIA NEPAL PAKISTAN S/ASIA THAILAND AGRI INDUS SCHOOL WORKER...ART/METH GEOG HEAL PHIL/SCI LING 20. PAGE 137 F2710 — BIBLIOG/A SOCIETY CULTURE ECO/UNDEV

B61
SAKAI R.K.,STUDIES ON ASIA, 1961. ASIA BURMA INDIA S/ASIA FINAN ECO/TAC NAT/LISM SOCISM...POLICY ANTHOL 19/20 CHINJAP. PAGE 115 F2271 — ECO/UNDEV SECT

B62
BROWN S.D.,STUDIES ON ASIA, 1962. ASIA BURMA INDIA ISLAM ISRAEL S/ASIA ECO/UNDEV POL/PAR SECT ECO/TAC ...ANTHOL 20 CHINJAP. PAGE 19 F0374 — PWR PARL/PROC

S63
GORDON B.,"ECONOMIC IMPEDIMENTS TO REGIONALISM IN SOUTH EAST ASIA." BURMA FUT S/ASIA THAILAND USA+45 AGRI INDUS R+D NAT/G PLAN ECO/TAC WEALTH...STAT CONT/OBS 20. PAGE 49 F0954 — VOL/ASSN ECO/UNDEV INT/TRADE REGION

B65
ONSLOW C.,ASIAN ECONOMIC DEVELOPMENT. BURMA CEYLON INDIA MALAYSIA PAKISTAN S/ASIA AGRI INDUS MARKET PROB/SOLV CAP/ISM FOR/AID INT/TRADE DEMAND WEALTH ...POLICY ANTHOL 20. PAGE 101 F1991 — ECO/UNDEV ECO/TAC PLAN NAT/G

S66
VERSLUYS J.D.N.,"SOME NOTES ON THE SOCIAL AND ECONOMIC EFFECTS OF RURAL ELECTRIFICATION IN BURMA" BURMA EDU/PROP PRODUC ORD/FREE...SOC QU MUNICH TIME 20. PAGE 141 F2782 — TEC/DEV SOCIETY CREATE

B67
ANDERSON C.W.,ISSUES OF POLITICAL DEVELOPMENT. BURMA WOR+45 CULTURE TOP/EX ECO/TAC MARXISM ...CHARTS NAT/COMP 20 COLOMB CONGO/LEOP. PAGE 5 F0094 — NAT/LISM COERCE ECO/UNDEV SOCISM

BURNS A.E. F0389

BURNS A.L. F1143

BURNS A.R. F0390

BURNS J.M. F2052

BURNS T.G. F0391

BURR/AARON....AARON BURR

BURRUS B.R. F0392

BURTT E.J. F0393

BURUNDI....SEE ALSO AFR

BUSEY J.L. F0394

BUSINESS CYCLE....SEE ECO, FINAN

BUSINESS MANAGEMENT....SEE MGT

C56
MCKEE J.B.,"THE POWER TO DECIDE" IN M. WEINBERG AND O. SHABET, SOCIETY AND MAN." ELITES STRATA REPRESENT GP/REL ATTIT PWR MUNICH BUSINESS. PAGE 88 F1731 — LABOR DECISION LEAD

BUSINESS ECONOMISTS' GROUP F0395

BUSSCHAU W.J. F0396

BUTLER W.F. F0397

BUTT R. F0398

BUTTRICK J.A. F2895

BYZANTINE....BYZANTINE EMPIRE

C

CAB....CIVIL AERONAUTICS BOARD

B64
FISK W.M.,ADMINISTRATIVE PROCEDURE IN A REGULATORY AGENCY: THE CAB AND THE NEW YORK-CHICAGO CASE (PAMPHLET). USA+45 DIST/IND ADMIN CONTROL LOBBY GP/REL ROLE ORD/FREE NEWYORK/C CHICAGO CAB. PAGE 41 F0805 — SERV/IND ECO/DEV AIR JURID

B65
THAYER F.C. JR.,AIR TRANSPORT POLICY AND NATIONAL SECURITY: A POLITICAL, ECONOMIC, AND MILITARY ANALYSIS. DIST/IND OP/RES PLAN TEC/DEV DIPLOM DETER WAR COST EFFICIENCY...POLICY BIBLIOG 20 DEPT/DEFEN FAA CAB. PAGE 129 F2548 — AIR FORCES CIVMIL/REL ORD/FREE

CABINET....SEE ALSO EX/STRUC, DELIB/GP, CONSULT

B65
SCHECHTER A.,THE BUSINESSMAN IN GOVERNMENT (THESIS, COLUMBIA UNIVERSITY). USA+45 CONFER GP/REL PERSON ...QU 20 PRESIDENT TRUMAN/HS CABINET. PAGE 116 F2291 — INDUS NAT/G EX/STRUC DELIB/GP

CAESAR/JUL....JULIUS CAESAR

CAIRNCROSS A.K. F0399

CAIRO....CAIRO, EGYPT

CALCUTTA....CALCUTTA, INDIA

CALDER R. F0400

CALDERWOOD J.D. F2223

CALHOUN/JC....JOHN C. CALHOUN

CALIFORNIA....CALIFORNIA

B61
STARNER F.L.,GENERAL OBLIGATION BOND FINANCING BY LOCAL GOVERNMENTS: A SURVEY OF STATE CONTROLS. CANADA UK USA+45 CONSTN PROVS...POLICY JURID METH/COMP 20 EUROPE CALIFORNIA. PAGE 125 F2471 — FINAN LOC/G GOV/REL ADJUD

B67
BLAIR G.S.,LEGISLATIVE BODIES IN CALIFORNIA. USA+45 LAW POL/PAR LOBBY APPORT CHOOSE REPRESENT GP/REL ...T CALIFORNIA. PAGE 15 F0293 — LEGIS PROVS LOC/G ADJUD

CALKINS R.D. F0401

CALVIN/J....JOHN CALVIN

CAMB/SOMER....CAMBRIDGE-SOMERVILLE YOUTH STUDY

CAMBODIA....SEE ALSO S/ASIA

S63
DELWERT J.,"L'ECONOMIE CAMBODGIENNE ET SON EVOLUTION ACTUELLE." FUT S/ASIA ECO/UNDEV ACT/RES PLAN WEALTH...CONCPT OBS TIME/SEQ TREND 20. PAGE 32 F0617 — FINAN ATTIT CAMBODIA

CAMELOT....PROJECT CAMELOT (CHILE)

CAMERON W.J. F0402

CAMEROON....SEE ALSO AFR

B64
WITHERELL J.W.,OFFICIAL PUBLICATIONS OF FRENCH EQUATORIAL AFRICA, FRENCH CAMEROONS, AND TOGO, 1946-1958 (PAMPHLET). CAMEROON CHAD FRANCE GABON TOGO LAW ECO/UNDEV EXTR/IND INT/TRADE...GEOG HEAL 20. PAGE 148 F2913 — BIBLIOG/A AFR NAT/G ADMIN

CAMMETT J.M. F0403

CAMPAIGNE J.G. F0404

CAMPBELL A.K. F0405

CAMPBELL J.C. F0406,F0407

CAMPBELL P. F0408

CAMPBELL R.W. F0409

CAMPBELL T.M. F0590

CAMPOLONGO A. F0410

CAND/CRWN....CANADIAN CROWN CORPORATIONS

CANADA....SEE ALSO COMMONWLTH

N19
WILSON T.,FINANCIAL ASSISTANCE WITH REGIONAL DEVELOPMENT (PAMPHLET). CANADA INDUS NAT/G PLAN TAX CONTROL COST EFFICIENCY...POLICY CHARTS 20. PAGE 147 F2902 — FINAN ECO/TAC REGION GOV/REL

S49
HART C.W.M.,"INDUSTRIAL RELATIONS RESEARCH AND SOCIAL THEORY." CANADA VOL/ASSN WORKER LEAD EFFICIENCY...MGT SOC METH/CNCPT METH/COMP MUNICH 20. PAGE 56 F1099 — GEN/LAWS LABOR GP/REL

B50
LIPSET S.M.,AGRARIAN SOCIALISM. CANADA POL/PAR OP/RES ECO/TAC ADMIN ATTIT...TIME/SEQ NAT/COMP SOC/EXP 20 SASKATCH. PAGE 80 F1576 — SOCISM AGRI METH/COMP STRUCT

B55
WRONG D.H.,AMERICAN AND CANADIAN VIEWPOINTS. CANADA USA+45 CONSTN STRATA FAM SECT WORKER ECO/TAC EDU/PROP ADJUD MARRIAGE...IDEA/COMP 20. PAGE 149 F2936 — DIPLOM ATTIT NAT/COMP CULTURE

B58
CUNNINGHAM W.B.,COMPULSORY CONCILIATION AND COLLECTIVE BARGAINING. CANADA NAT/G LEGIS ADJUD CT/SYS GP/REL...MGT 20 NEW/BRUNS STRIKE CASEBOOK. PAGE 29 F0563 — POLICY BARGAIN LABOR INDUS

B58
HOOD W.C.,FINANCING OF ECONOMIC ACTIVITY IN CANADA. CANADA FUT VOL/ASSN WORKER ECO/TAC ADJUD ADMIN ...CHARTS 20. PAGE 61 F1204 — BUDGET FINAN GP/REL ECO/DEV

B58
MCIVOR R.C.,CANADIAN MONETARY, BANKING, AND FISCAL DEVELOPMENT. CANADA INDUS LG/CO NAT/G SML/CO CONTROL WAR...GEN/LAWS BIBLIOG 17/20. PAGE 88 F1729 — ECO/TAC FINAN ECO/DEV WEALTH

B58
WOODS H.D.,PATTERNS OF INDUSTRIAL DISPUTE SETTLEMENT IN FIVE CANADIAN INDUSTRIES. CANADA USA+45 CONSULT ADJUD GP/REL...JURID GOV/COMP METH/COMP ANTHOL 20. PAGE 148 F2923 — BARGAIN INDUS LABOR NAT/G

B59
AITKEN H.G.,THE AMERICAN ECONOMIC IMPACT ON CANADA. CANADA USA+45 AGRI FINAN INDUS LABOR INT/TRADE BAL/PAY...INT/LAW TREND 20. PAGE 3 F0055 — DIPLOM ECO/TAC POLICY NAT/G

B59
MUSOLF L.D.,PUBLIC OWNERSHIP AND ACCOUNTABILITY: THE CANADIAN EXPERIENCE. CANADA REPRESENT PWR 20. PAGE 95 F1873 — MGT CONTROL INDUS

B59
STOVEL J.A.,CANADA IN THE WORLD ECONOMY. CANADA PRICE DEMAND...STAT CHARTS BIBLIOG 20 VINER/J. PAGE 127 F2499 — INT/TRADE BAL/PAY FINAN ECO/TAC

B60
ANGERS F.A.,ESSAI SUR LA CENTRALISATION: ANALYSE DES PRINCIPES ET PERSPECTIVES CANADIENNES. CANADA ECO/TAC CONTROL...SOC IDEA/COMP BIBLIOG 20. PAGE 6 F0105 — CENTRAL ADMIN

B60
BELLAN R.C.,PRINCIPLES OF ECONOMICS AND THE CANADIAN ECONOMY (2ND ED.). CANADA UK USA+45 LABOR WORKER CAP/ISM INT/TRADE RISK BAL/PAY EQUILIB ALL/IDEOS 20. PAGE 12 F0236 — ECO/DEV PRODUC WEALTH FINAN

B61
BREWIS T.N.,CANADIAN ECONOMIC POLICY. AFR CANADA BUDGET CAP/ISM INT/TRADE RATION TARIFFS TAX PRICE CONTROL ROUTINE FEDERAL INCOME PRODUC 20. PAGE 18 F0348 — ECO/DEV ECO/TAC NAT/G PLAN

B61
CARROTHERS A.W.R.,LABOR ARBITRATION IN CANADA. CANADA LAW NAT/G CONSULT LEGIS WORKER ADJUD ADMIN CT/SYS 20. PAGE 22 F0422 — LABOR MGT GP/REL BARGAIN

B61
GOODWIN C.D.W.,CANADIAN ECONOMIC THOUGHT. CANADA STRATA TEC/DEV CAP/ISM TARIFFS TAX COST EFFICIENCY WEALTH...METH/CNCPT TREND 20 MARITIME ONTARIO. PAGE 49 F0952 — INT/TRADE ECO/DEV FINAN DEMAND

B61
STARNER F.L.,GENERAL OBLIGATION BOND FINANCING BY LOCAL GOVERNMENTS: A SURVEY OF STATE CONTROLS. CANADA UK USA+45 CONSTN PROVS...POLICY JURID METH/COMP 20 EUROPE CALIFORNIA. PAGE 125 F2471 — FINAN LOC/G GOV/REL ADJUD

B62
HOOVER C.B.,ECONOMIC SYSTEMS OF THE COMMONWEALTH. AFR CANADA INDIA UK ECO/DEV ECO/UNDEV AGRI INDUS TEC/DEV TARIFFS PRICE BAL/PAY DEMAND...SIMUL 20 AUSTRAL. PAGE 61 F1208 — CAP/ISM SOCISM ECO/TAC PLAN

B62
WOODS H.D.,LABOUR POLICY AND LABOUR ECONOMICS IN CANADA. CANADA FUT NAT/G VOL/ASSN WORKER BARGAIN ECO/TAC PAY CONFER GP/REL 20. PAGE 148 F2924 — LABOR POLICY INDUS ECO/DEV

B64
THE SPECIAL COMMONWEALTH AFRICAN ASSISTANCE PLAN. AFR CANADA INDIA NIGERIA UK FINAN SCHOOL...CHARTS 20 COMMONWLTH. PAGE 1 F0019 — ECO/UNDEV TREND FOR/AID ADMIN

B64
BROWN W.M.,THE EXTERNAL LIQUIDITY OF AN ADVANCED COUNTRY. CANADA FRANCE GERMANY/W SWEDEN UK USA+45 ECO/DEV DIPLOM PRICE...CONCPT STAT NAT/COMP 20. PAGE 20 F0376 — FINAN INT/TRADE COST INCOME

B64
FATOUROS A.A.,CANADA'S OVERSEAS AID. CANADA WOR+45 ECO/DEV FINAN NAT/G BUDGET ECO/TAC CONFER ADMIN 20. PAGE 39 F0768 — FOR/AID DIPLOM ECO/UNDEV POLICY

B64
LITVAK I.A.,MARKETING: CANADA. CANADA STRATA PROC/MFG LEGIS TEC/DEV DIPLOM INT/TRADE PRICE AUTOMAT ATTIT WEALTH...ANTHOL 20. PAGE 81 F1587 — ECO/TAC MARKET ECO/DEV EFFICIENCY

B64
MEISEL J.,PAPERS ON THE 1962 ELECTION. CANADA PROVS SECT GP/REL CONSEN EFFICIENCY...MAJORIT 20. PAGE 89 F1751 — POL/PAR RECORD CHOOSE STRATA

B64
WILSON T.,POLICIES FOR REGIONAL DEVELOPMENT. CANADA UK FINAN INDUS NAT/G BUDGET TAX GIVE COST ...NAT/COMP 20. PAGE 147 F2904 — REGION PLAN ECO/DEV ECO/TAC

B65
HABERLER G.,A SURVEY OF INTERNATIONAL TRADE THEORY. CANADA FRANCE GERMANY ECO/TAC TARIFFS AGREE COST DEMAND WEALTH...ECOMETRIC 19/20 MONOPOLY TREATY. PAGE 52 F1024 — INT/TRADE BAL/PAY DIPLOM POLICY

B65
OECD,TECHNIQUES OF ECONOMIC FORECASTING. CANADA FRANCE NETHERLAND SWEDEN UK USA+45 PROB/SOLV ROUTINE...CONCPT MATH CHARTS BIBLIOG METH 20. PAGE 100 F1974 — PREDICT METH/COMP PLAN

B66
SPICER K.,A SAMARITAN STATE? AFR CANADA INDIA PAKISTAN UK USA+45 FINAN INDUS PRODUC...CHARTS 20 NATO. PAGE 124 F2455 — DIPLOM FOR/AID ECO/DEV ADMIN

B66
UREN P.E.,EAST - WEST TRADE* A SYMPOSIUM. COM AGRI INT/ORG PRICE HABITAT RIGID/FLEX...GEOG INT/LAW ANTHOL NATO. PAGE 133 F2625 — INT/TRADE BAL/PWR AFR CANADA

B66
US DEPARTMENT OF STATE,RESEARCH ON WESTERN EUROPE, GREAT BRITAIN, AND CANADA (EXTERNAL RESEARCH LIST NO 3-25). CANADA GERMANY/W UK LAW CULTURE NAT/G POL/PAR FORCES EDU/PROP REGION MARXISM...GEOG SOC WORSHIP 20 CMN/WLTH. PAGE 136 F2676 — BIBLIOG/A EUR+WWI DIPLOM

B67
BADGLEY R.F.,DOCTORS' STRIKE; MEDICAL CARE AND CONFLICT IN SASKATCHEWAN. CANADA NAT/G PROF/ORG GP/REL ADJUST ATTIT...HEAL SOC 20. PAGE 8 F0148
HEALTH PLAN LABOR BARGAIN

B67
JOHNSON H.G.,ECONOMIC NATIONALISM IN OLD AND NEW STATES. CANADA CHINA/COM MALI UK DIPLOM...SIMUL GEN/LAWS 19/20 MEXIC/AMER. PAGE 68 F1328
NAT/LISM ECO/UNDEV ECO/DEV NAT/COMP

B67
MARTIN P.,CANADA AND THE QUEST FOR PEACE. CANADA VIETNAM ECO/UNDEV PLAN FOR/AID WAR 20 UN. PAGE 86 F1684
DIPLOM PEACE INT/ORG POLICY

S67
BOSHER J.F.,"GOVERNMENT AND PRIVATE INTERESTS IN NEW FRANCE." CANADA FRANCE INDUS LG/CO SML/CO CAP/ISM INT/TRADE COLONIAL GP/REL...HIST/WRIT 17/18. PAGE 17 F0320
NAT/G FINAN ADMIN CONTROL

S67
DEWHURST A.,"THE WAGE MOVEMENT IN CANADA." CANADA AGRI NAT/G PARTIC COST PRODUC PROFIT 20. PAGE 32 F0627
WORKER MARXIST INDUS LABOR

S67
RONNING C.,"NANKING: 1950." ASIA CANADA CHINA/COM NAT/G PLAN ECO/TAC REV ADJUST 20. PAGE 113 F2235
DIPLOM ROLE PEACE

S67
WARNER K.O.,"FINANCIAL IMPLICATION OF EMPLOYEE BARGAINING IN THE PUBLIC SERVICE." CANADA USA+45 FINAN ADMIN...MGT 20. PAGE 143 F2823
BARGAIN LABOR COST LOC/G

S67
WHITE W.L.,"THE TREASURY BOARD AND PARLIAMENT." CANADA CONSTN CONSULT LEGIS LEAD PARL/PROC GP/REL ...DECISION 20. PAGE 146 F2871
FINAN DELIB/GP NAT/G ADMIN

CANADIAN MEDICAL ASSOCIATION....SEE CMA

CANAL/ZONE....CANAL ZONE

CANNING HOUSE LIBRARY F0411

CANNON M. F0412

CANNON/JG....JOSEPH G. CANNON

CANON/LAW....CANON LAW

B24
HOLDSWORTH W.S.,A HISTORY OF ENGLISH LAW; THE COMMON LAW AND ITS RIVALS (VOL. IV). UK SEA AGRI CHIEF ADJUD CONTROL CRIME GOV/REL...INT/LAW JURID NAT/COMP 16/17 PARLIAMENT COMMON/LAW CANON/LAW ENGLSH/LAW. PAGE 61 F1195
LAW LEGIS CT/SYS CONSTN

CANTERBERY E.R. F0413

CANTRIL/H....HADLEY CANTRIL

CAP/ISM....CAPITALISM

B61
CLARK J.M.,COMPETITION AS A DYNAMIC PROCESS. ECO/DEV EXTR/IND INDUS LG/CO TEC/DEV ECO/TAC PRICE EQUILIB PRODUC...NEW/IDEA CAP 20. PAGE 25 F0483
WEALTH GP/REL FINAN PROFIT

N
BROCKWAY A.F.,AFRICAN SOCIALISM. EUR+WWI GHANA ISLAM UAR ECO/UNDEV CAP/ISM INT/TRADE COLONIAL COERCE GOV/REL DISCRIM 20 NEGRO NKRUMAH/K NASSER/G. PAGE 19 F0356
AFR SOCISM MARXISM

N
AMERICAN ECONOMIC REVIEW. FINAN INDUS LABOR OP/RES CAP/ISM INT/TRADE TAX WEALTH...CON/ANAL CHARTS 20. PAGE 1 F0001
BIBLIOG/A USA+45 ECO/DEV NAT/G

B04
MARX K.,A CONTRIBUTION TO THE CRITIQUE OF POLITICAL ECONOMY (TRANS. FROM 2ND ED. BY N.I. STONE). UK STRATA ECO/DEV FINAN MARKET PLAN BARGAIN CAP/ISM ECO/TAC ATTIT WEALTH...METH/CNCPT BIOG 19. PAGE 86 F1687
MARXIST NEW/IDEA MARXISM

B12
HOBSON J.A.,THE EVOLUTION OF MODERN CAPITALISM. MOD/EUR UK STRATA ECO/DEV INDUS INCOME UTIL WEALTH ...SOC GEN/LAWS 7/20. PAGE 60 F1184
CAP/ISM WORKER TEC/DEV TIME/SEQ

B13
DAVENPORT H.J.,THE ECONOMICS OF ENTERPRISE. UNIV FINAN SML/CO RENT COST WEALTH GEN/LAWS. PAGE 30 F0582
CAP/ISM PRICE ECO/TAC LG/CO

B15
VEBLEN T.,IMPERIAL GERMANY AND THE INDUSTRIAL REVOLUTION. GERMANY MOD/EUR UK USA-45 NAT/G TEC/DEV CAP/ISM...MAJORIT NAT/COMP 19/20 CHINJAP. PAGE 141 F2769
ECO/DEV INDUS TECHNIC BAL/PWR

B18
MARX K.,CAPITAL. FUT MOD/EUR STRATA DIST/IND PROC/MFG TEC/DEV WEALTH...MARXIST WORK 19. PAGE 86 F1688
ECO/DEV CAP/ISM SOCISM

B19
SUMNER W.G.,WAR AND OTHER ESSAYS. USA-45 DELIB/GP DIPLOM TARIFFS COLONIAL PEACE SOVEREIGN 20. PAGE 127 F2514
INT/TRADE ORD/FREE CAP/ISM ECO/TAC

B19
VEBLEN T.B.,THE VESTED INTERESTS AND THE STATE OF THE INDUSTRIAL ARTS. USA-45 LAW FINAN WORKER PAY DOMIN PRICE COST SOCISM...MARXIST 19/20. PAGE 141 F2771
INDUS CAP/ISM METH/COMP WEALTH

N19
DEANE H.,THE WAR IN VIETNAM (PAMPHLET). AFR CHINA/COM VIETNAM BAL/PWR DIPLOM ECO/TAC SOCISM INTERVENT INTERVENT. PAGE 31 F0610
WAR SOCIALIST MORAL CAP/ISM

N19
HALL G.,MAIN STREET TO WALL STREET: END THE COLD WAR (PAMPHLET). AFR USA+45 LAW STRUCT POL/PAR WORKER INT/TRADE DOMIN INCOME...POLICY 20 COM/PARTY. PAGE 53 F1046
MARXIST CAP/ISM DIPLOM NAT/G

N19
HAYEK FA V.O.N.,FREEDOM AND THE ECONOMIC SYSTEM. GERMANY USSR PLAN REPRESENT TOTALISM FASCISM POPULISM...MAJORIT METH/COMP GEN/LAWS 20. PAGE 57 F1123
ORD/FREE ECO/TAC CAP/ISM SOCISM

N19
HUBERMAN L.,SOCIALISM IS THE ONLY ANSWER (PAMPHLET). CREATE ECO/TAC EDU/PROP CONTROL ...SOCIALIST GEN/LAWS ANTHOL 20. PAGE 62 F1230
SOCISM ECO/DEV CAP/ISM PLAN

N19
LAWRENCE S.A.,THE BATTERY ADDITIVE CONTROVERSY (PAMPHLET). USA+45 LAW MARKET PROC/MFG R+D CAP/ISM CT/SYS GOV/REL OWN FTC CONGRESS BUR/STNDRD RITCHIE/JM. PAGE 76 F1494
PHIL/SCI LOBBY INSPECT

N19
MARCUS W.,US PRIVATE INVESTMENT AND ECONOMIC AID IN UNDERDEVELOPED COUNTRIES (PAMPHLET). USA+45 LG/CO NAT/G CAP/ISM EDU/PROP 20. PAGE 85 F1666
FOR/AID ECO/UNDEV FINAN PLAN

N19
YLVISAKER P.N.,THE NATURAL CEMENT ISSUE (PAMPHLET). USA+45 USA-45 CONSTRUC PROVS CAP/ISM ADMIN LOBBY PERS/REL OWN RIGID/FLEX ROLE 20 MINNESOTA. PAGE 150 F2948
POLICY NAT/G PLAN GOV/REL

B20
MOREL E.D.,THE BLACK MAN'S BURDEN. AFR MOD/EUR AGRI EXTR/IND PROB/SOLV INT/TRADE ADMIN CONTROL COERCE DISCRIM...POLICY 19/20 NEGRO LEAGUE/NAT. PAGE 93 F1828
ORD/FREE CAP/ISM RACE/REL DOMIN

B20
TAWNEY R.H.,THE ACQUISITIVE SOCIETY. STRATA WORKER PROB/SOLV CAP/ISM ECO/TAC CONTROL GP/REL OWN PRIVIL ATTIT ORD/FREE WEALTH 20. PAGE 128 F2536
INDUS SOCIETY PRODUC MORAL

B25
EDGEWORTH F.Y.,PAPERS RELATING TO POLITICAL ECONOMY. MOD/EUR SOCIETY STRATA DIST/IND INDUS MARKET NAT/G ACT/RES ECO/TAC EXEC WEALTH ...METH/CNCPT MATH TREND HYPO/EXP SIMUL GEN/METH FOR/TRADE VAL/FREE LOG/LING. PAGE 36 F0702
ECO/DEV CAP/ISM

B26
TAWNEY R.H.,RELIGION AND THE RISE OF CAPITALISM. UK CULTURE NAT/G TEC/DEV OWN LAISSEZ...POLICY SOC TIME/SEQ 16/19. PAGE 129 F2537
SECT WEALTH INDUS CAP/ISM

B27
BELLOC H.,THE SERVILE STATE (1912) (3RD ED.). PRUSSIA UK CULTURE STRATA INDUS NAT/G ECO/TAC CONTROL LEAD SUFF DISCRIM EQUILIB ORD/FREE WEALTH 20. PAGE 12 F0237
WORKER CAP/ISM DOMIN CATH

B27
WEBER M.,GENERAL ECONOMIC HISTORY. CHRIST-17C MOD/EUR STRUCT AGRI EXTR/IND FINAN INDUS MARKET FAM NAT/G PROF/ORG SECT ECO/TAC MUNICH 8/20. PAGE 144 F2839
ECO/DEV CAP/ISM

B28
CASSEL G.,FOREIGN INVESTMENTS. GERMANY UK USA-45 WOR-45 ECO/DEV NAT/G VOL/ASSN CAP/ISM REPAR ATTIT WEALTH...METH/CNCPT STAT SIMUL STERTYP ANTHOL FOR/TRADE TOT/POP VAL/FREE 20. PAGE 22 F0426
FINAN ECO/TAC BAL/PAY

S32
DODD E.M. JR.,"FOR WHOM ARE CORPORATE MANAGERS TRUSTEES'." SERV/IND CAP/ISM GIVE LEAD REPRESENT ORD/FREE WEALTH. PAGE 33 F0648
LG/CO ROLE NAT/G PLAN

B34
GRAHAM F.D.,PROTECTIVE TARIFFS. FUT USA+45 WOR-45 INDUS MARKET VOL/ASSN PLAN CAP/ISM ECO/TAC PEACE ATTIT DRIVE HEALTH ORD/FREE...OBS TREND GEN/LAWS FOR/TRADE 20. PAGE 50 F0970
INT/ORG TARIFFS

B35
LASKI H.J.,THE STATE IN THEORY AND PRACTICE. ELITES ECO/TAC REPRESENT ORD/FREE PWR WEALTH POPULISM ...GOV/COMP GEN/LAWS 19/20. PAGE 76 F1483
CAP/ISM COERCE NAT/G FASCISM

B35
STALEY E.,WAR AND THE PRIVATE INVESTOR. UNIV WOR-45 INTELL SOCIETY INT/ORG NAT/G TOP/EX CAP/ISM ECO/TAC WAR ATTIT ALL/VALS...INT TIME/SEQ TREND CON/ANAL WORK TOT/POP 20. PAGE 125 F2464
FINAN INT/TRADE DIPLOM

B36
BELLOC H.,THE RESTORATION OF PROPERTY. UK STRATA NAT/G PROF/ORG DELIB/GP WORKER CREATE PROB/SOLV ECO/TAC PARTIC UTOPIA ORD/FREE SOCISM 20. PAGE 13 F0238
CONTROL MAJORIT CAP/ISM OWN

B36
HUBERMAN L.,MAN'S WORLDLY GOODS: THE STORY OF THE WEALTH OF NATIONS. CHRIST-17C EUR+WWI MOD/EUR SOCIETY DOMIN REV ORD/FREE...TIME/SEQ METH/COMP. PAGE 63 F1231
WEALTH CAP/ISM MARXISM CREATE

B38
DAVIES E.,"NATIONAL" CAPITALISM: THE GOVERNMENT'S RECORD AS PROTECTOR OF PRIVATE MONOPOLY. UK ELITES SOCIETY STRATA POL/PAR WORKER PROB/SOLV CONTROL SOCISM 20 MONOPOLY LABOR/PAR CHAMBRLN/N. PAGE 30 F0583
CAP/ISM NAT/G INDUS POLICY

B38
HEIMANN E.,COMMUNISM, FASCISM, OR DEMOCRACY? WOR-45 CONSTN SOCIETY STRATA AGRI CAP/ISM MORAL ORD/FREE ...MAJORIT METH/COMP NAT/COMP 19/20. PAGE 58 F1141
SOCISM MARXISM FASCISM PLURISM

B38
LAWLEY F.E.,THE GROWTH OF COLLECTIVE ECONOMY VOL. 1: NATIONAL. EUR+WWI AGRI INDUS NAT/G BARGAIN CAP/ISM ECO/TAC WAR OPTIMAL WEALTH...GOV/COMP METH/COMP 19/20 MONOPOLY. PAGE 76 F1492
SOCISM PRICE CONTROL OWN

S38
HALL R.C.,"REPRESENTATION OF BIG BUSINESS IN THE HOUSE OF COMMONS." UK ECO/DEV INDUS PROF/ORG LEGIS CAP/ISM ECO/TAC LAISSEZ...POLICY OLD/LIB PLURIST MGT 20 HOUSE/CMNS. PAGE 53 F1047
LOBBY NAT/G

B39
CLARK J.M.,SOCIAL CONTROL OF BUSINESS (2ND ED.). ECO/DEV FINAN LG/CO PLAN ECO/TAC PRICE SUPEGO...T 20. PAGE 25 F0480
CAP/ISM CONTROL LAISSEZ METH/COMP

B39
FIRTH R.,PRIMITIVE POLYNESIAN ECONOMY. SOCIETY DIST/IND SECT CHIEF CAP/ISM PRODUC WEALTH...SOC OBS METH WORSHIP 20 POLYNESIA. PAGE 41 F0802
ECO/UNDEV CULTURE AGRI ECO/TAC

B40
BATCHELOR B.,THE NEW OUTLOOK IN BUSINESS. LAW WORKER TAX LEAD ORD/FREE...POLICY TREND. PAGE 11 F0208
LG/CO GP/REL CAP/ISM LABOR

B40
CAMPBELL P.,CONSUMER REPRESENTATION IN THE NEW DEAL. AGRI INDUS MARKET EX/STRUC PLAN CAP/ISM CONTROL GP/REL DEMAND POLICY. PAGE 21 F0408
CLIENT REPRESENT NAT/G

B40
SIKES E.R.,CONTEMPORARY ECONOMIC SYSTEMS: THEIR ANALYSIS AND SOCIAL BACKGROUND. GERMANY ITALY USSR AGRI INDUS PLAN CAP/ISM ROUTINE TOTALISM FASCISM ...POLICY CON/ANAL BIBLIOG 20. PAGE 122 F2400
COM SOCISM CONCPT

B41
ESTEY J.A.,BUSINESS CYCLES; THEIR NATURE, CAUSE, AND CONTROL. NAT/G BUDGET CAP/ISM TAX PRICE CONTROL INCOME...MODAL TIME/SEQ GEN/METH T 18/20 KEYNES/JM MONEY. PAGE 38 F0749
INDUS FINAN ECO/TAC POLICY

B41
HAYEK F.A.,THE PURE THEORY OF CAPITAL. UNIV ECO/DEV ECO/TAC COST EQUILIB PROFIT WEALTH...SIMUL GEN/LAWS BIBLIOG INDEX TIME 20. PAGE 57 F1120
CAP/ISM METH/CNCPT PRODUC FINAN

B42
SWEEZY P.M.,THE THEORY OF CAPITALIST DEVELOPMENT. FUT NAT/G COST FASCISM BIBLIOG. PAGE 128 F2519
ECO/DEV CAP/ISM MARXISM COLONIAL

B46
CLOUGH S.B.,ECONOMIC HISTORY OF EUROPE. CHRIST-17C EUR+WWI MOD/EUR WOR-45 SOCIETY EXEC ATTIT WEALTH ...CONCPT GEN/LAWS WORK TOT/POP VAL/FREE 7/20. PAGE 25 F0493
ECO/TAC CAP/ISM

B47
ENKE S.,INTERNATIONAL ECONOMICS. UK USA+45 USSR INT/ORG BAL/PWR BARGAIN CAP/ISM BAL/PAY...NAT/COMP 20 TREATY. PAGE 38 F0735
INT/TRADE FINAN TARIFFS ECO/TAC

S47
DAHL R.A.,"WORKERS' CONTROL OF INDUSTRY AND THE BRITISH LABOUR PARTY." UK STRATA STRUCT DELIB/GP BARGAIN CAP/ISM DEBATE CONTROL CHOOSE GP/REL ATTIT ROLE PWR 19/20 PARLIAMENT LABOR/PAR FABIAN. PAGE 29 F0570
INDUS LABOR WORKER SOCISM

B48
GRAHAM F.D.,THE THEORY OF INTERNATIONAL VALUES. FUT WOR+45 WOR-45 ECO/DEV FINAN INT/ORG PLAN TEC/DEV CAP/ISM DIPLOM ECO/TAC TARIFFS ROUTINE BAL/PAY DRIVE PWR WEALTH SOCISM...POLICY STAT HYPO/EXP GEN/LAWS 20. PAGE 50 F0971
NEW/IDEA INT/TRADE

B48
LAUTERBACH A.,ECONOMIC SECURITY AND INDIVIDUAL FREEDOM: CAN WE HAVE BOTH? COM EUR+WWI MOD/EUR UNIV WOR+45 CAP/ISM TOTALISM ALL/VALS...GOV/COMP BIBLIOG 20. PAGE 76 F1490
ORD/FREE ECO/DEV DECISION INGP/REL

B48
MCCABE D.A.,LABOR AND SOCIAL ORGANIZATION. LEGIS WORKER CAP/ISM ECO/TAC PAY MARXISM SOCISM SOC/INTEG 20 INTRVN/ECO. PAGE 88 F1717
LABOR STRATA NEW/LIB

B48
VON HAYEK F.A.,INDIVIDUALISM AND ECONOMIC ORDER. GERMANY USA-45 USSR FINAN MARKET INT/ORG ECO/TAC INT/TRADE PRICE REPRESENT ORD/FREE...PLURIST GEN/LAWS 20. PAGE 142 F2793
SOCISM CAP/ISM POPULISM FEDERAL

B48
WINSLOW E.M.,THE PATTERN OF IMPERIALISM; A STUDY IN THE THEORIES OF POWER. DOMIN WAR PWR MARXISM ...IDEA/COMP METH/COMP BIBLIOG 20. PAGE 147 F2906
SOCISM CAP/ISM COLONIAL ECO/TAC

B50
HOOVER G.,TWENTIETH CENTURY ECONOMIC THOUGHT. USA+45 ECO/DEV AGRI FINAN INDUS MARKET SERV/IND LABOR NAT/G...STAT 20. PAGE 62 F1213
ECO/TAC CAP/ISM INT/TRADE

B50
HUTCHISON K.,THE DECLINE AND FALL OF BRITISH CAPITALISM. UK ELITES STRATA ECO/DEV LABOR WORKER CONTROL WAR PWR...BIBLIOG/A 19/20. PAGE 63 F1249
CAP/ISM SOCISM LAISSEZ DOMIN

B50
MARX H.L.,THE WELFARE STATE. USA+45 USA-45 CHIEF CAP/ISM CENTRAL ORD/FREE LAISSEZ...SOC ANTHOL 20. PAGE 86 F1686
ECO/DEV INDUS WEALTH WELF/ST

B50
SCHUMPETER J.A.,CAPITALISM, SOCIALISM, AND DEMOCRACY (3RD ED.). USA-45 USSR WOR+45 WOR-45 INTELL ECO/DEV ECO/UNDEV ECO/TAC WAR PRODUC ORD/FREE...MGT SOC 20 MARX/KARL. PAGE 118 F2321
SOCIALIST CAP/ISM MARXISM IDEA/COMP

B51
CLARK C.,THE CONDITIONS OF ECONOMIC PROGRESS. EUR+WWI WOR+45 WOR-45 ECO/DEV INDUS CAP/ISM MORAL ...WELF/ST METH/CNCPT STAT TOT/POP VAL/FREE 20. PAGE 25 F0477
MARKET WEALTH

B51
COOKE C.A.,CORPORATION TRUST AND COMPANY: AN ESSAY IN LEGAL HISTORY. UK STRUCT LEGIS CAP/ISM GP/REL PROFIT 13/20 COMPNY/ACT. PAGE 27 F0531
LG/CO FINAN ECO/TAC JURID

B51
DIMOCK M.E.,FREE ENTERPRISE AND THE ADMINISTRATIVE STATE. FINAN LG/CO BARGAIN BUDGET DOMIN CONTROL INGP/REL EFFICIENCY 20. PAGE 33 F0640
CAP/ISM ADMIN MGT MARKET

B51
HARROD R.F.,THE LIFE OF JOHN MAYNARD KEYNES. UK INTELL FAM CAP/ISM DIPLOM ECO/TAC WAR ATTIT PERSON ROLE 20 KEYNES/JM WWI. PAGE 56 F1094
BIOG FINAN GEN/LAWS

B51
LUXEMBORG R.,THE ACCUMULATION OF CAPITAL (TRANS. BY AGNES SCHWARZSCHILD). ECO/TAC DOMIN COLONIAL ATTIT LAISSEZ 19 MONEY. PAGE 82 F1614
MARXIST INT/TRADE CAP/ISM FINAN

B52
EGLE W.P.,ECONOMIC STABILIZATION. USA+45 SOCIETY FINAN MARKET PLAN ECO/TAC DOMIN EDU/PROP LEGIT EXEC WEALTH...CONCPT METH/CNCPT TREND HYPO/EXP GEN/METH TOT/POP VAL/FREE 20. PAGE 36 F0708
NAT/G ECO/DEV CAP/ISM

B52
EGLE W.P.,ECONOMIC STABILIZATION: OBJECTIVES, RULES, AND MECHANISMS. UNIV FINAN PROB/SOLV CAP/ISM ECO/TAC CONTROL...IDEA/COMP 20. PAGE 36 F0709
EQUILIB PLAN NAT/G ECO/DEV

B52
GALBRAITH J.K.,AMERICAN CAPITALISM: THE CONCEPT OF COUNTERVAILING POWER. AFR FUT USA+45 FINAN PRICE CENTRAL INCOME PEACE WEALTH...POLICY DECISION 20. PAGE 45 F0881
ECO/TAC CAP/ISM TREND NAT/G

B52
MACHLUP F.,THE POLITICAL ECONOMY OF MONOPOLY:
ECO/TAC

BUSINESS, LABOR AND GOVERNMENT POLICIES. USA+45 USA-45 ECO/DEV LABOR NAT/G CAP/ISM PWR...POLICY CHARTS T 20. PAGE 83 F1630
DOMIN LG/CO CONTROL

B53
BOEKE J.H.,ECONOMICS AND ECONOMIC POLICY OF DUAL SOCIETIES AS EXEMPLIFIED BY INDONESIA. INDIA INDONESIA SOCIETY CAP/ISM INT/TRADE GIVE PRICE GP/REL WEALTH SOCISM...POLICY NAT/COMP GEN/LAWS 20. PAGE 16 F0304
ECO/TAC ECO/UNDEV NAT/G CONTROL

B53
BOWEN H.R.,SOCIAL RESPONSIBILITIES OF THE BUSINESSMAN (FIRST EDITION). LAW FINAN ACT/RES CAP/ISM ROUTINE DRIVE PWR LAISSEZ...DECISION BIBLIOG. PAGE 17 F0326
MGT PERSON SUPEGO MORAL

B53
FLORENCE P.S.,THE LOGIC OF BRITISH AND AMERICAN INDUSTRY; A REALISTIC ANALYSIS OF ECONOMIC STRUCTURE AND GOVERNMENT. UK USA+45 USA-45 FINAN LABOR CAP/ISM INGP/REL EFFICIENCY...MGT CONCPT STAT CHARTS METH 20. PAGE 42 F0813
INDUS ECO/DEV NAT/G NAT/COMP

S53
BIRNBAUM N.,"CONFLICTING INTERPRETATIONS OF THE RISE OF CAPITALISM: MARX AND WEBER" (BMR)" WOR-45 INTELL SOCIETY STRUCT INDUS WORKER...PHIL/SCI SOC PERS/COMP 19/20 MARX/KARL WEBER/MAX. PAGE 15 F0288
CAP/ISM IDEA/COMP ECO/DEV MARXISM

B54
HAYEK FA V.O.N.,CAPITALISM AND THE HISTORIANS. MOD/EUR TEC/DEV GP/REL WEALTH...HIST/WRIT ANTHOL 19. PAGE 57 F1124
CAP/ISM LABOR STRATA ECO/TAC

B54
LENIN V.I.,SELECTED WORKS (12 VOLS.). USSR INTELL SOCIETY STRATA STRUCT NAT/G POL/PAR WORKER CAP/ISM REV WAR...MARXIST PHIL/SCI 20 MARX/KARL LENIN/VI. PAGE 78 F1520
COM MARXISM

B54
MEYER A.G.,MARXISM. INTELL ECO/DEV WORKER CAP/ISM LEAD WAR ATTIT ALL/IDEOS...SOC 19/20 MARX/KARL. PAGE 90 F1766
MARXISM CONCPT ECO/TAC STRUCT

B54
MOSK S.A.,INDUSTRIAL REVOLUTION IN MEXICO. MARKET LABOR CREATE CAP/ISM ADMIN ATTIT SOCISM...POLICY 20 MEXIC/AMER. PAGE 94 F1843
INDUS TEC/DEV ECO/UNDEV NAT/G

B54
RECK D.,GOVERNMENT PURCHASING AND COMPETITION. USA+45 LEGIS CAP/ISM ECO/TAC GOV/REL CENTRAL ...POLICY 20 CONGRESS. PAGE 110 F2164
NAT/G FINAN MGT COST

B54
STALEY E.,THE FUTURE OF UNDERDEVELOPED COUNTRIES: POLITICAL IMPLICATIONS OF ECONOMIC DEVELOPMENT. AFR COM FUT USA+45 SOCIETY ECO/UNDEV CREATE PLAN CAP/ISM ATTIT DRIVE MARXISM SOCISM...POLICY CONCPT CHARTS 20. PAGE 125 F2466
EDU/PROP ECO/TAC FOR/AID

C54
BERLE A.A. JR.,"THE 20TH CENTURY CAPITALIST REVOLUTION." ECO/DEV NAT/G DIPLOM PRICE CONTROL ATTIT...BIBLIOG/A 20. PAGE 14 F0260
LG/CO CAP/ISM MGT PWR

B55
BLOOM G.F.,ECONOMICS OF LABOR RELATIONS. USA+45 LAW CONSULT WORKER CAP/ISM PAY ADJUD CONTROL EFFICIENCY ORD/FREE...CHARTS 19/20 AFL/CIO NLRB DEPT/LABOR. PAGE 16 F0299
ECO/DEV ECO/TAC LABOR GOV/REL

B55
BOULDING K.E.,ECONOMIC ANALYSIS (3RD ED.). USA+45 PLAN ECO/TAC COST DEMAND INCOME...POLICY STAT CHARTS SIMUL T. PAGE 17 F0322
PHIL/SCI ECO/DEV CAP/ISM

B55
GEORGE H.,PROGRESS AND POVERTY (1880). STRATA STRUCT INDUS TEC/DEV CAP/ISM EQUILIB INCOME OWN UTOPIA...WELF/ST CONCPT NEW/IDEA 19. PAGE 47 F0915
ECO/DEV ECO/TAC TAX WEALTH

B55
HELANDER S.,DAS AUTARKIEPROBLEM IN DER WELTWIRTSCHAFT. PROB/SOLV BAL/PWR BARGAIN CAP/ISM ECO/TAC SOVEREIGN FOR/TRADE 20. PAGE 58 F1144
NAT/COMP COLONIAL DIPLOM

B55
MAYO H.B.,DEMOCRACY AND MARXISM. COM USSR STRATA NAT/G WORKER ECO/TAC REV MORAL...PHIL/SCI HIST/WRIT IDEA/COMP WORSHIP 20 MARX/KARL LENIN/VI STALIN/J TROTSKY/L. PAGE 87 F1708
MARXISM CAP/ISM

B55
O'CONNOR H.,THE EMPIRE OF OIL. USA+45 DIST/IND FINAN MARKET CAP/ISM TAX CONTROL...POLICY MARXIST BIBLIOG/A 20. PAGE 100 F1955
EXTR/IND INT/TRADE CENTRAL NAT/G

B55
PALAMOUNTAIN JC J.R.,THE POLITICS OF DISTRIBUTION. USA+45 LG/CO SML/CO BAL/PWR CONTROL EQUILIB 20. PAGE 103 F2019
DIST/IND ECO/TAC CAP/ISM GP/REL

B55
UYEHARA C.H.,COMPARATIVE PLATFORMS OF JAPAN'S MAJOR PARTIES... USA+45 AGRI LEGIS WORKER CAP/ISM ORD/FREE MARXISM SOCISM...IDEA/COMP 20 CHINJAP. PAGE 140 F2755
POLICY POL/PAR DIPLOM NAT/G

B56
FELLNER W.,TRENDS AND CYCLES IN ECONOMIC ACTIVITY: AN INTRODUCTION TO PROBLEMS OF ECONOMIC GROWTH. USA+45 INDUS ACT/RES CAP/ISM EQUILIB...MODAL METH/COMP BIBLIOG 20. PAGE 40 F0779
ECO/TAC TREND FINAN ECO/DEV

B56
GILBERT L.D.,DIVIDENDS AND DEMOCRACY. DELIB/GP LEGIS CAP/ISM ADJUD LOBBY OWN PWR LAISSEZ MAJORIT. PAGE 47 F0922
LG/CO INGP/REL CONTROL PARTIC

B56
GREENHUT M.L.,PLANT LOCATION IN THEORY AND PRACTICE; THE ECONOMICS OF SPACE. WOR+45 WOR-45 MARKET WORKER COST DEMAND...CONCPT STAT CHARTS HYPO/EXP BIBLIOG 19/20. PAGE 51 F0991
SML/CO ECO/DEV CAP/ISM IDEA/COMP

B56
KNORR K.E.,RUBLE DIPLOMACY: CHALLENGE TO AMERICAN FOREIGN AID(PAMPHLET). AFR CHINA/COM USA+45 USSR PLAN TEC/DEV CAP/ISM INT/TRADE DOMIN EDU/PROP CONTROL LEAD 20. PAGE 72 F1413
ECO/UNDEV COM DIPLOM FOR/AID

B56
VAKIL C.N.,PLANNING FOR AN EXPANDING ECONOMY. INDIA TAX COST 20. PAGE 140 F2759
TEC/DEV LABOR BUDGET CAP/ISM

B57
BARAN P.A.,THE POLITICAL ECONOMY OF GROWTH. MOD/EUR USA+45 USA-45 TEC/DEV TAX SOCISM...MGT CONCPT GOV/COMP. PAGE 9 F0178
CAP/ISM CONTROL ECO/UNDEV FINAN

B57
BAUER P.T.,THE ECONOMICS OF UNDERDEVELOPED COUNTRIES. WOR+45 AGRI FINAN INDUS PROC/MFG WORKER CAP/ISM PAY PRICE INCOME MARXISM...METH/COMP 20 RESOURCE/N. PAGE 11 F0213
ECO/UNDEV ECO/TAC PROB/SOLV NAT/G

B57
BERLE A.A. JR.,ECONOMIC POWER AND FREE SOCIETY (PAMPHLET). CLIENT CONSTN EX/STRUC ECO/TAC CONTROL PARTIC PWR WEALTH MAJORIT. PAGE 14 F0261
LG/CO CAP/ISM INGP/REL LEGIT

B57
CLARK J.M.,ECONOMIC INSTITUTIONS AND HUMAN WELFARE. USA+45 SOCIETY ECO/DEV NAT/G WORKER PLAN PROB/SOLV CAP/ISM CONTROL...POLICY 20. PAGE 25 F0482
ECO/TAC ORD/FREE WEALTH

B57
INTL BANKING SUMMER SCHOOL,RELATIONS BETWEEN THE CENTRAL BANKS AND COMMERCIAL BANKS. EUR+WWI FRANCE GERMANY/W ITALY UK USA+45 USSR INDUS INT/ORG CAP/ISM CONTROL MONEY. PAGE 65 F1282
FINAN NAT/G GP/REL LG/CO

B57
LEIBENSTEIN H.,ECONOMIC BACKWARDNESS AND ECONOMIC GROWTH. WOR+45 SOCIETY AGRI INDUS TEC/DEV CAP/ISM FOR/AID COST DEMAND WEALTH...CHARTS IDEA/COMP 20. PAGE 77 F1513
ECO/UNDEV ECO/TAC PRODUC POLICY

B57
LENIN V.I.,THE DEVELOPMENT OF CAPITALISM IN RUSSIA. MOD/EUR USSR AGRI MARKET POL/PAR TEC/DEV...CONCPT 19/20. PAGE 78 F1521
COM INDUS CAP/ISM

B57
LOUCKS W.N.,COMPARATIVE ECONOMIC SYSTEMS (5TH ED.). COM UK USSR INDUS POL/PAR PLAN CAP/ISM TOTALISM MARXISM...PHIL/SCI BIBLIOG 19/20. PAGE 82 F1603
NAT/COMP IDEA/COMP SOCISM

B57
MEIER G.M.,ECONOMIC DEVELOPMENT: THEORY, HISTORY, AND POLICY. WOR+45 WOR-45 ECO/DEV ECO/UNDEV PLAN CAP/ISM BAL/PAY ATTIT PWR WEALTH SOCISM...CHARTS TOT/POP FOR/TRADE 20. PAGE 89 F1748
ECO/TAC GEN/LAWS

B57
NAUMANN R.,THEORIE UND PRAXIS DES NEOLIBERALISMUS; DAS MAERCHEN VON DER FREIEN ODER SOZIALEN MARKTWIRTSCHAFT. GERMANY/W FORCES PLAN EDU/PROP SOCISM...POLICY MARXIST IDEA/COMP BIBLIOG 18/20 ADENAUER/K. PAGE 97 F1903
MARXISM NEW/LIB ECO/TAC CAP/ISM

B58
AVRAMOVIC D.,POSTWAR GROWTH IN INTERNATIONAL INDEBTEDNESS. AFR WOR+45 AGRI INDUS CAP/ISM PRICE INCOME...NAT/COMP 20 SILVER. PAGE 8 F0143
INT/TRADE FINAN COST BAL/PAY

B58
CLAIRMONTE F.,LE LIBERALISME ECONOMIQUE ET LES PAYS SOUS-DEVELOPPES: ETUDES SUR L'EVOLUTION D'UNE IDEE. ASIA INDIA UK FINAN INDUS PLAN CAP/ISM ECO/TAC COLONIAL NEW/LIB...BIBLIOG 20 THIRD/WRLD. PAGE 24 F0475
LAISSEZ ECO/UNDEV

B58
COLM G.,THE ECONOMY OF THE AMERICAN PEOPLE: PROGRESS, PROBLEMS, PROSPECTS. USA+45 INDUS MARKET LABOR TEC/DEV INCOME 20. PAGE 26 F0509
WEALTH PRODUC CAP/ISM MGT

B58
ELLSWORTH P.T.,THE INTERNATIONAL ECONOMY. EUR+WWI MOD/EUR INT/ORG CAP/ISM FOR/AID BAL/PAY LAISSEZ 16/20. PAGE 37 F0725
INT/TRADE TARIFFS ECO/DEV

B58
GALBRAITH J.K.,THE AFFLUENT SOCIETY. EUR+WWI FUT USA+45 USSR CULTURE SERV/IND PEACE WEALTH SOCISM ...NEW/IDEA TREND VAL/FREE 20. PAGE 45 F0882
ATTIT ECO/TAC CAP/ISM

B58
HAMEROW T.S.,RESTORATION, REVOLUTION, REACTION: ECONOMICS AND POLITICS IN GERMANY, 1815-1871. CAP/ISM ADJUST ATTIT PWR...BIBLIOG/A 19 GER/CONFED FRANK/PARL. PAGE 54 F1055
REV ORD/FREE ECO/DEV

B58
HANCE W.A.,AFRICAN ECONOMIC DEVELOPMENT. AGRI DIST/IND INDUS R+D ACT/RES PLAN CAP/ISM FOR/AID ...GOV/COMP BIBLIOG 20. PAGE 54 F1058
AFR ECO/UNDEV PROB/SOLV TEC/DEV

B58
HENNING C.N.,INTERNATIONAL FINANCING. WOR+45 ECO/DEV INT/ORG EX/STRUC INSPECT CAP/ISM BAL/PAY COST PROFIT...MGT CHARTS T 20. PAGE 58 F1150
FINAN DIPLOM INT/TRADE

B58
HIRSCHMAN A.O.,STRATEGY OF ECONOMIC DEVELOPMENT. WOR+45 WOR-45 CULTURE ECO/DEV NAT/G PLAN TEC/DEV INT/TRADE BAL/PAY ATTIT DRIVE RIGID/FLEX WEALTH ...CONCPT METH/CNCPT OBS CHARTS SIMUL GEN/LAWS TOT/POP VAL/FREE. PAGE 60 F1176
ECO/UNDEV ECO/TAC CAP/ISM

B58
JOHNSON H.G.,INTERNATIONAL TRADE AND ECONOMIC GROWTH. WOR+45 BUDGET CAP/ISM ECO/TAC TARIFFS BAL/PAY 20. PAGE 67 F1323
INT/TRADE BAL/PWR BARGAIN DIPLOM

B58
MOULTON H.G.,CAN INFLATION BE CONTROLLED? ECO/DEV INDUS CAP/ISM RATION GOV/REL COST INCOME PEACE WEALTH...CHARTS TIME 20 KEYNES/JM MONEY. PAGE 94 F1847
ECO/TAC CONTROL DEMAND FINAN

B58
MUSGRAVE R.A.,CLASSICS IN THE THEORY OF PUBLIC FINANCE. UNIV MARKET LG/CO NAT/G CAP/ISM PRICE OPTIMAL...IDEA/COMP ANTHOL 19/20 SAY/EMIL EDGEWORTH LINDAHL/E RITSCHL/H. PAGE 95 F1870
TAX FINAN ECO/TAC GP/REL

B58
POLLOCK F.,AUTOMATION: A STUDY OF ITS ECONOMIC AND SOCIAL CONSEQUENCES. FUT USA+45 USA-45 SOCIETY ECO/DEV LABOR ACT/RES PLAN ECO/TAC AUTOMAT ROUTINE ALL/VALS...STAT TREND COMPUT/IR CHARTS SOC/EXP WORK 20. PAGE 107 F2099
TEC/DEV SOC CAP/ISM

B58
THEIL H.,ECONOMIC FORECASTS AND POLICY. UNIV CAP/ISM PRICE EFFICIENCY...DECISION CONCPT STAT 20. PAGE 129 F2551
SIMUL MATH ECOMETRIC PREDICT

B59
BARBASH J.,UNIONS AND UNION LEADERSHIP. NAT/G WORKER TEC/DEV ECO/TAC PARTIC GP/REL RACE/REL ORD/FREE CLASSIF. PAGE 10 F0183
LABOR VOL/ASSN CAP/ISM LEAD

B59
FELS R.,AMERICAN BUSINESS CYCLES 1865-1897. USA+45 ECO/DEV LG/CO SML/CO PROB/SOLV TEC/DEV CAP/ISM INT/TRADE DEMAND...POLICY CHARTS METH 19 DEPRESSION. PAGE 40 F0782
FINAN INDUS TREND ECO/TAC

B59
HOOVER C.B.,THE ECONOMY, LIBERTY AND THE STATE. COM EUR+WWI USA+45 USA-45 USSR CAP/ISM EDU/PROP COERCE TOTALISM ORD/FREE...POLICY OBS INT TREND NAZI 20. PAGE 61 F1206
ECO/DEV ECO/TAC

B59
KRIPALANI J.B.,CLASS STRUGGLE. INDIA WOR+45 ECO/UNDEV LABOR CAP/ISM EDU/PROP INGP/REL ...SOCIALIST IDEA/COMP 17/20. PAGE 73 F1440
MARXISM STRATA COERCE ECO/TAC

B59
MADHOK B.,POLITICAL TRENDS IN INDIA. INDIA PAKISTAN UK STRATA ECO/UNDEV POL/PAR LEGIS CAP/ISM DIPLOM COLONIAL CHOOSE MARXISM...SOC TREND 20 GANDHI/M NEHRU/J. PAGE 84 F1639
GEOG NAT/G

B59
NOVE A.,COMMUNIST ECONOMIC STRATEGY: SOVIET GROWTH AND CAPABILITIES. USSR AGRI LABOR PLAN TEC/DEV CAP/ISM INT/TRADE EFFICIENCY MARXISM 20 THIRD/WRLD. PAGE 99 F1941
FOR/AID ECO/TAC DIPLOM INDUS

B59
VERNEY D.V.,PUBLIC ENTERPRISE IN SWEDEN. FUT SWEDEN UK INDUS POL/PAR LEGIS PROB/SOLV CAP/ISM INT/TRADE CONTROL SOCISM...MGT CONCPT NAT/COMP 20 SOCDEM/PAR CIVIL/SERV. PAGE 141 F2778
ECO/DEV POLICY LG/CO NAT/G

S59
SOLDATI A.,"EOCNOMIC DISINTEGRATION IN EUROPE." EUR+WWI FUT WOR+45 INDUS INT/ORG NAT/G CAP/ISM WEALTH...NEW/IDEA OBS TREND CHARTS EEC 20. PAGE 124 F2438
FINAN ECO/TAC

S59
STREETEN P.,"UNBALANCED GROWTH" UK ECO/DEV AGRI MARKET TEC/DEV CAP/ISM ECO/TAC FOR/AID INT/TRADE DEMAND ORD/FREE...CONCPT 20. PAGE 127 F2502
IDEA/COMP FINAN PRODUC EQUILIB

S59
TEITSWORTH C.S.,"GROWING ROLE OF THE COMPANY ECONOMIST." USA+45 PLAN PROB/SOLV CAP/ISM ECO/TAC ADMIN ATTIT MGT. PAGE 129 F2541
INDUS CONSULT UTIL DECISION

C59
FAINSOD M.,"GOVERNMENT AND THE AMERICAN ECONOMY." USA+45 USA-45 INDUS LABOR OP/RES PROB/SOLV ECO/TAC CONTROL...CHARTS BIBLIOG T 20. PAGE 39 F0760
CONSTN ECO/DEV CAP/ISM NAT/G

B60
APTHEKER H.,DISARMAMENT AND THE AMERICAN ECONOMY: A SYMPOSIUM. FUT USA+45 ECO/DEV DIST/IND FINAN INDUS PROC/MFG LABOR NAT/G POL/PAR CONSULT PLAN CAP/ISM INT/TRADE PEACE ATTIT MORAL WEALTH...TREND GEN/LAWS TOT/POP 20. PAGE 6 F0110
MARXIST ARMS/CONT

B60
ARON R.,COLLOQUES DE RHEINFELDEN. AFR USA+45 USSR WOR+45 WOR-45 CULTURE ECO/UNDEV NAT/G POL/PAR DIPLOM NAT/LISM TOTALISM ATTIT DRIVE ALL/VALS ...PLURIST CONCPT STERTYP GEN/LAWS TOT/POP 20. PAGE 6 F0120
ECO/DEV SOCIETY CAP/ISM SOCISM

B60
BAYER H.,WIRTSCHAFTSPROGNOSE UND WIRTSCHAFTSGESTALTUNG. GERMANY NETHERLAND MARKET PLAN CAP/ISM DEBATE...NAT/COMP 20. PAGE 12 F0220
ECO/DEV ECO/UNDEV FINAN POLICY

B60
BELLAN R.C.,PRINCIPLES OF ECONOMICS AND THE CANADIAN ECONOMY (2ND ED.). CANADA UK USA+45 LABOR WORKER CAP/ISM INT/TRADE RISK BAL/PAY EQUILIB ALL/IDEOS 20. PAGE 12 F0236
ECO/DEV PRODUC WEALTH FINAN

B60
CAMPBELL R.W.,SOVIET ECONOMIC POWER. COM USA+45 DIST/IND MARKET TOP/EX ACT/RES CAP/ISM ECO/TAC DOMIN EDU/PROP ADMIN ROUTINE DRIVE...MATH TIME/SEQ CHARTS WORK 20. PAGE 21 F0409
ECO/DEV PLAN SOCISM USSR

B60
CROSSER P.K.,STATE CAPITALISM IN THE ECONOMY OF THE UNITED STATES. USA+45 USA-45 AGRI FINAN INDUS LABOR WORKER RATION CONTROL GOV/REL DEMAND...NEW/IDEA 20. PAGE 29 F0557
CAP/ISM ECO/DEV ECO/TAC NAT/G

B60
HOFFMANN P.G.,ONE HUNDRED COUNTRIES, ONE AND ONE QUARTER BILLION PEOPLE. MARKET INT/ORG TEC/DEV CAP/ISM...GEOG CHARTS METH/COMP 20 UN. PAGE 61 F1191
FOR/AID ECO/TAC ECO/UNDEV INT/TRADE

B60
HOSELITZ B.F.,SOCIOLOGICAL ASPECTS OF ECONOMIC GROWTH. WOR+45 WOR-45 ECO/UNDEV CAP/ISM RIGID/FLEX WEALTH...MATH CHARTS. PAGE 62 F1221
ECO/DEV SOC

B60
HUGHES J.,NATIONALISED INDUSTRIES IN THE MIXED ECONOMY (PAMPHLET). FINAN PROB/SOLV CAP/ISM OWN ...SOCIALIST STAT METH/COMP 20. PAGE 63 F1233
SOCISM LG/CO GOV/REL ECO/DEV

B60
LERNER A.P.,THE ECONOMICS OF CONTROL. USA+45 ECO/UNDEV INT/ORG ACT/RES PLAN CAP/ISM INT/TRADE ATTIT WEALTH...SOC MATH STAT GEN/LAWS INDEX 20. PAGE 78 F1530
ECO/DEV ROUTINE ECO/TAC SOCISM

B60
MYRDAL G.,BEYOND THE WELFARE STATE: ECONOMIC PLANNING AND ITS IMPLICATIONS. EUR+WWI FUT USA+45 USSR ECO/DEV ECO/UNDEV TEC/DEV SKILL WEALTH...PSY TREND FOR/TRADE 20. PAGE 96 F1881
PLAN ECO/TAC CAP/ISM

B60
OEEC,STATISTICS OF SOURCES AND USES OF FINANCE. NAT/G CAP/ISM TAX PRICE COST 20 OEEC. PAGE 101 F1978
FINAN PRODUC INCOME NAT/COMP

B60
RICHARDSON G.B.,INFORMATION AND INVESTMENT. PLAN PROB/SOLV CAP/ISM ECO/TAC KNOWL...CONCPT 20 MONEY. PAGE 111 F2184
ECO/DEV EQUILIB FINAN PHIL/SCI

B60
ROBINSON J.,AN ESSAY ON MARXIAN ECONOMICS. USA+45 STRATA INDUS MARKET CAP/ISM...METH/COMP 19/20 MARX/KARL. PAGE 113 F2222
IDEA/COMP MARXISM ACADEM

B60
ROEPKE W.,A HUMANE ECONOMY: THE SOCIAL FRAMEWORK OF THE FREE MARKET. FUT USSR WOR+45 CULTURE SOCIETY ECO/DEV PLAN ECO/TAC ADMIN ATTIT PERSON RIGID/FLEX SUPEGO MORAL WEALTH SOCISM...POLICY OLD/LIB CONCPT TREND GEN/LAWS 20. PAGE 113 F2232
DRIVE EDU/PROP CAP/ISM

B60
ROSTOW W.W.,THE STAGES OF ECONOMIC GROWTH. UK USA+45 USSR WOR+45 WOR-45 ECO/DEV PERSON MARXISM ...METH/CNCPT TIME/SEQ GEN/LAWS GEN/METH 20. PAGE 114 F2246
ECO/UNDEV NEW/IDEA CAP/ISM

B60
SILK L.S.,THE RESEARCH REVOLUTION. USA+45 FINAN CAP/ISM ECO/TAC PRICE EQUILIB PRODUC...STAT TREND CHARTS. PAGE 122 F2402
ECO/DEV R+D TEC/DEV PROB/SOLV

B60
WALLICH H.C.,THE COST OF FREEDOM: A NEW LOOK AT CAPITALISM. USA+45 SOCIETY ECO/DEV INGP/REL CONSEN LAISSEZ SOCISM...OLD/LIB IDEA/COMP. PAGE 143 F2810
CAP/ISM ORD/FREE POLICY ECO/TAC

B60
WENTHOLT W.,INFLATION OR SECURITY? EUR+WWI USA+45 INDUS CONSULT TEC/DEV CAP/ISM DIPLOM FOR/AID INT/TRADE MARXISM 20 EEC. PAGE 145 F2858
ECO/DEV ECO/TAC FINAN ORD/FREE

L60
SPENGLER J.J.,"ECONOMIC DEVELOPMENT: POLITICAL PRECONDITIONS AND POLITICAL CONSEQUENCE." WOR+45 STRUCT ECO/UNDEV NAT/G PLAN ECO/TAC EDU/PROP ATTIT ORD/FREE WEALTH SOCISM...SOC CONCPT TREND SIMUL GEN/METH WORK 20. PAGE 124 F2452
TEC/DEV METH/CNCPT CAP/ISM

S60
BAUM M.,"THE CASE FOR BUSINESS CIVILIZATION." R+D CAP/ISM GIVE EDU/PROP HAPPINESS...SOC TREND. PAGE 12 F0218
MGT CULTURE WEALTH

S60
FRANKEL S.H.,"ECONOMIC ASPECTS OF POLITICAL INDEPENDENCE IN AFRICA." AFR FUT SOCIETY ECO/UNDEV COM/IND FINAN LEGIS PLAN TEC/DEV CAP/ISM ECO/TAC INT/TRADE ADMIN ATTIT DRIVE RIGID/FLEX PWR WEALTH ...MGT NEW/IDEA MATH TIME/SEQ VAL/FREE 20. PAGE 43 F0846
NAT/G FOR/AID

S60
MIKESELL R.F.,"AMERICA'S ECONOMIC RESPONSIBILITY AS A GREAT POWER." COM FUT USA+45 USSR WOR+45 INT/ORG PLAN ECO/TAC FOR/AID EDU/PROP CHOOSE WEALTH ...POLICY 20. PAGE 91 F1781
ECO/DEV BAL/PWR CAP/ISM

S60
NEISSER H.,"ECONOMIC IMPERALISM RECONSIDERED." WOR+45 WOR-45 ECO/DEV ECO/UNDEV DIST/IND LEGIT COLONIAL PWR WEALTH SOCISM...MYTH MATH TIME/SEQ 20. PAGE 97 F1909
ACT/RES ECO/TAC CAP/ISM INT/TRADE

S60
NICHOLS J.P.,"HAZARDS OF AMERICAN PRIVATE INVESTMENT IN UNDERDEVELOPED COUNTRIES." FUT L/A+17C USA+45 USA-45 EXTR/IND CONSULT BAL/PWR ECO/TAC DOMIN ADJUD ATTIT SOVEREIGN WEALTH ...HIST/WRIT TIME/SEQ TREND TERR/GP VAL/FREE 20. PAGE 98 F1924
FINAN ECO/UNDEV CAP/ISM NAT/LISM

C60
FAULKNER H.U.,"AMERICAN ECONOMIC HISTORY (8TH ED.)" USA+45 USA-45 FINAN...CHARTS BIBLIOG/A T 17/20. PAGE 39 F0769
AGRI INDUS ECO/DEV CAP/ISM

B61
AUBREY H.G.,COEXISTENCE: ECONOMIC CHALLENGE AND RESPONSE. AFR USSR WOR+45 ACT/RES BAL/PWR CAP/ISM DIPLOM ECO/TAC FOR/AID INT/TRADE PEACE SOCISM ...METH/COMP NAT/COMP. PAGE 7 F0139
POLICY ECO/UNDEV PLAN COM

B61
BALASSA B.,THE THEORY OF ECONOMIC INTEGRATION. EUR+WWI L/A+17C MOD/EUR WOR+45 ECO/UNDEV MARKET INT/ORG NAT/G VOL/ASSN DELIB/GP PLAN CAP/ISM ECO/TAC...MAJORIT FOR/TRADE OEEC 20. PAGE 8 F0157
ECO/DEV ACT/RES INT/TRADE

B61
BONNEFOUS M.,EUROPE ET TIERS MONDE. EUR+WWI SOCIETY INT/ORG NAT/G VOL/ASSN ACT/RES TEC/DEV CAP/ISM ECO/TAC ATTIT ORD/FREE SOVEREIGN...POLICY CONCPT TREND TERR/GP COMMUN 20. PAGE 16 F0314
AFR ECO/UNDEV FOR/AID INT/TRADE

B61
BREWIS T.N.,CANADIAN ECONOMIC POLICY. AFR CANADA BUDGET CAP/ISM INT/TRADE RATION TARIFFS TAX PRICE CONTROL ROUTINE FEDERAL INCOME PRODUC 20. PAGE 18 F0348
ECO/DEV ECO/TAC NAT/G PLAN

B61
FELLNER W.,THE PROBLEM OF RISING PRICES. AGRI INDUS WORKER BUDGET CAP/ISM ECO/TAC INT/TRADE PAY DEMAND ...POLICY 20 EEC. PAGE 40 F0780
PRICE MARKET ECO/DEV COST

B61
FERTIG L.,PROSPERITY THROUGH FREEDOM. COM INDUS LABOR CAP/ISM ECO/TAC PRODUC PROFIT ORD/FREE WEALTH SOCISM...METH/CNCPT 20. PAGE 40 F0788
NAT/G CONTROL POLICY

B61
GANGULI B.N.,ECONOMIC INTEGRATION. FINAN LABOR CAP/ISM DIPLOM WEALTH...NAT/COMP 20. PAGE 46 F0895
ECO/TAC METH/CNCPT EQUILIB ECO/UNDEV

B61
GOODWIN C.D.W.,CANADIAN ECONOMIC THOUGHT. CANADA STRATA TEC/DEV CAP/ISM TARIFFS TAX COST EFFICIENCY WEALTH...METH/CNCPT TREND 20 MARITIME ONTARIO. PAGE 49 F0952
INT/TRADE ECO/DEV FINAN DEMAND

B61
HENDERSON W.O.,THE INDUSTRIAL REVOLUTION IN EUROPE. FRANCE GERMANY MOD/EUR RUSSIA WORKER PROFIT PWR MARXISM SOCISM...SOC HIST/WRIT 19 INDUS/REV. PAGE 58 F1148
INDUS REV CAP/ISM TEC/DEV

B61
HORVATH B.,THE CHARACTERISTICS OF YUGOSLAV ECONOMIC DEVELOPMENT. COM ECO/UNDEV AGRI INDUS PLAN CAP/ISM ECO/TAC ROUTINE WEALTH...SOCIALIST STAT CHARTS STERTYP WORK 20. PAGE 62 F1217
ACT/RES YUGOSLAVIA

B61
KELSO L.O.,THE NEW CAPITALISTS: A PROPOSAL TO FREE ECONOMIC GROWTH FROM THE SLAVERY OF SAVINGS. UNIV USA+45 ECO/DEV CAP/ISM PRODUC WEALTH SOCISM ...NEW/IDEA 20. PAGE 70 F1373
ECO/TAC WORKER FINAN GEN/LAWS

B61
LAMFALUSSY A.,INVESTMENT AND GROWTH IN MATURE ECONOMIES. BELGIUM EUR+WWI LABOR PRICE PRODUC PROFIT...STAT CONT/OBS CHARTS 20. PAGE 75 F1464
FINAN INDUS ECO/DEV CAP/ISM

B61
LENIN V.I.,WHAT IS TO BE DONE? (1902). RUSSIA LABOR NAT/G POL/PAR WORKER CAP/ISM ECO/TAC ADMIN PARTIC ...MARXIST IDEA/COMP GEN/LAWS 19/20. PAGE 78 F1522
EDU/PROP PRESS MARXISM METH/COMP

B61
LHOSTE-LACHAUME P.,OU GIT LE DESACCORD ENTRE LIBERAUX ET SOCIALISTES. EUR+WWI USA+45 USA-45 USSR CAP/ISM EDU/PROP MARXISM...MAJORIT IDEA/COMP 20 KEYNES/JM NEW/DEAL DEPRESSION. PAGE 79 F1555
LAISSEZ SOCISM FINAN

B61
LICHTHEIM G.,MARXISM. GERMANY SOCIETY WORKER CAP/ISM ECO/TAC NAT/LISM POPULISM...TIME/SEQ GOV/COMP NAT/COMP 18/20 COM/PARTY. PAGE 80 F1559
MARXISM SOCISM IDEA/COMP CULTURE

B61
MARX K.,THE COMMUNIST MANIFESTO. IN (MENDEL A. ESSENTIAL WORKS OF MARXISM, NEW YORK: BANTAM. FUT MOD/EUR CULTURE ECO/DEV ECO/UNDEV AGRI FINAN INDUS MARKET PROC/MFG LABOR POL/PAR CONSULT FORCES CREATE PLAN ADMIN ATTIT DRIVE RIGID/FLEX ORD/FREE PWR RESPECT MARX/KARL MUNICH WORK. PAGE 86 F1691
COM NEW/IDEA CAP/ISM REV

B61
NORTH D.C.,THE ECONOMIC GROWTH OF THE UNITED STATES 1790-1860. USA-45 INDUS TEC/DEV CAP/ISM ECO/TAC PRICE COST DEMAND LAISSEZ...ECOMETRIC STAT TREND 19. PAGE 98 F1933
AGRI ECO/UNDEV

B61
PAUNIO J.J.,A STUDY IN THE THEORY OF OPEN INFLATION. AFR FINAN CAP/ISM PRICE DEMAND INCOME ...CHARTS BIBLIOG 20. PAGE 104 F2040
ACT/RES ECO/DEV ECO/TAC COST

B61
PERLO V.,EL IMPERIALISMO NORTHEAMERICANO. USA+45 USA-45 FINAN CAP/ISM DIPLOM DOMIN CONTROL DISCRIM 19/20. PAGE 105 F2063
SOCIALIST ECO/DEV INT/TRADE ECO/TAC

B61
SLICHTER S.H.,ECONOMIC GROWTH IN THE UNITED STATES. FUT USA+45 USA-45 LABOR PAY INCOME PRODUC...MGT 19/20. PAGE 123 F2422
ECO/DEV TEC/DEV CAP/ISM DEMAND

B61
VEIT O.,GRUNDRISS DER WAHRUNGSPOLITIK. AFR FRANCE GERMANY USSR DIPLOM INT/TRADE...NAT/COMP 19/20 SILVER. PAGE 141 F2773
FINAN POLICY ECO/TAC CAP/ISM

B61
WILSON T.,INFLATION. FINAN PLAN CAP/ISM PRICE CONTROL...CHARTS 20. PAGE 147 F2903
ECO/DEV ECO/TAC POLICY COST

S61
GORDON L.,"ECONOMIC REGIONALISM RECONSIDERED." FUT USA+45 WOR+45 INDUS NAT/G TEC/DEV DIPLOM ROUTINE PERCEPT WEALTH...WELF/ST METH/CNCPT WORK 20. PAGE 49 F0957
ECO/DEV ATTIT CAP/ISM REGION

B62
ARNOLD T.W.,THE FOLKLORE OF CAPITALISM. USA+45 USA-45 SOCIETY LG/CO SML/CO EX/STRUC ECO/TAC EDU/PROP ADJUST INCOME...MYTH CHARTS 20. PAGE 6 F0116
CAP/ISM ATTIT STERTYP ECO/DEV

B62
COPPOCK J.D.,INTERNATIONAL ECONOMIC INSTABILITY: THE EXPERIENCE AFTER WORLD WAR II. WOR+45 FINAN CAP/ISM CONTROL EFFICIENCY...CHARTS 20. PAGE 28 F0536
ECO/TAC ECOMETRIC INT/TRADE STAT

B62
COX O.C.,CAPITALISM AND AMERICAN LEADERSHIP. WOR+45 WOR-45 STRATA INDUS SECT INT/TRADE EXEC INGP/REL RACE/REL RATIONAL PWR WEALTH. PAGE 28 F0548
CAP/ISM LEAD ECO/DEV SOCIETY

B62
DENISON E.F.,THE SOURCES OF ECONOMIC GROWTH IN THE UNITED STATES AND THE ALTERNATIVES BEFORE US. AGRI INDUS SCHOOL TEC/DEV CAP/ISM ECO/TAC PRICE COST WEALTH...STAT TREND CHARTS 20. PAGE 32 F0620
ECO/DEV WORKER PRODUC

B62
DOBB M.,CAPITALISM YESTERDAY AND TODAY. UK WORKER WAR PRODUC PROFIT 18/20 MONOPOLY. PAGE 33 F0646
CAP/ISM TIME/SEQ CONCPT ECO/TAC

B62
FRIEDMAN M.,CAPITALISM AND FREEDOM. USA+45 FINAN
CAP/ISM

LG/CO WORKER INT/TRADE RECEIVE EDU/PROP CONTROL DISCRIM INCOME WEALTH POLICY. PAGE 44 F0859
ORD/FREE NAT/G ECO/DEV

B62

FRIEDMANN W.,METHODS AND POLICIES OF PRINCIPAL DONOR COUNTRIES IN PUBLIC INTERNATIONAL DEVELOPMENT FINANCING: PRELIMINARY APPRAISAL. FRANCE GERMANY/W UK USA+45 USSR WOR+45 FINAN TEC/DEV CAP/ISM DIPLOM ECO/TAC ATTIT 20 EEC. PAGE 44 F0864
INT/ORG FOR/AID NAT/COMP ADMIN

B62

GRANICK D.,THE EUROPEAN EXECUTIVE. BELGIUM FRANCE GERMANY/W UK INDUS LABOR LG/CO SML/CO EX/STRUC PLAN TEC/DEV CAP/ISM COST DEMAND...POLICY CHARTS 20. PAGE 50 F0977
MGT ECO/DEV ECO/TAC EXEC

B62

HAGUE D.C.,INFLATION. AFR ECO/DEV ECO/UNDEV LABOR BUDGET CAP/ISM INT/TRADE TARIFFS SOCISM 20. PAGE 53 F1036
FINAN NAT/COMP BARGAIN ECO/TAC

B62

HEILBRONER R.L.,THE MAKING OF ECONOMIC SOCIETY. FUT WOR-45 SOCIETY STRATA ECO/DEV ECO/UNDEV ECO/TAC LEGIT ROUTINE...SOC RECORD REC/INT KNO/TEST CENSUS STERTYP GEN/LAWS. PAGE 58 F1136
CAP/ISM SOCISM

B62

HOOVER C.B.,ECONOMIC SYSTEMS OF THE COMMONWEALTH. AFR CANADA INDIA UK ECO/DEV ECO/UNDEV AGRI INDUS TEC/DEV TARIFFS PRICE BAL/PAY DEMAND...SIMUL 20 AUSTRAL. PAGE 61 F1208
CAP/ISM SOCISM ECO/TAC PLAN

B62

KAUTSKY J.H.,POLITICAL CHANGE IN UNDERDEVELOPED COUNTRIES: NATIONALISM AND COMMUNISM. WOR+45 AGRI TEC/DEV EDU/PROP ATTIT...POLICY METH/CNCPT STYLE INT QU CENSUS TREND SOC/EXP GEN/LAWS 20. PAGE 69 F1365
ECO/UNDEV SOCIETY CAP/ISM REV

B62

LEVY H.V.,LIBERDADE E JUSTICA SOCIAL (2ND ED.). BRAZIL COM L/A+17C USSR INT/ORG PARTIC GP/REL WEALTH 20 UN COM/PARTY. PAGE 79 F1544
ORD/FREE MARXISM CAP/ISM LAW

B62

LITWACK L.,THE AMERICAN LABOR MOVEMENT. USA-45 NAT/G CREATE TEC/DEV CAP/ISM ECO/TAC ADJUD AUTOMAT SKILL...TREND ANTHOL 19/20. PAGE 81 F1588
INDUS LABOR GP/REL METH/COMP

B62

MEANS G.C.,THE CORPORATE REVOLUTION IN AMERICA: ECONOMIC REALITY VS. ECONOMIC THEORY. USA+45 USA-45 INDUS WORKER PLAN CAP/ISM ADMIN...IDEA/COMP 20. PAGE 89 F1742
LG/CO MARKET CONTROL PRICE

B62

MORGAN C.A.,LABOR ECONOMICS. LAW INDUS MARKET WORKER PLAN PROB/SOLV GOV/REL INCOME ROLE...T 20 DEPT/LABOR NLRB. PAGE 93 F1829
LABOR ECO/TAC ECO/DEV CAP/ISM

B62

MOUSSA P.,THE UNDERPRIVILEGED NATIONS. FINAN INT/ORG PLAN PROB/SOLV CAP/ISM GIVE TASK WEALTH ...POLICY SOC IND 20. PAGE 94 F1850
ECO/UNDEV NAT/G DIPLOM FOR/AID

B62

PERROUX F.,L'ECONOMIE DES JEUNES NATIONS. EUR+WWI SOUTH/AFR FINAN MARKET TEC/DEV CAP/ISM FOR/AID INT/TRADE 20. PAGE 105 F2065
INDUS ECO/UNDEV ECO/TAC DIPLOM

B62

REES A.,THE ECONOMICS OF TRADE UNIONS. FUT ECO/DEV INDUS BARGAIN CAP/ISM PRICE SENIOR CONTROL GP/REL COST...TREND 20 AFL/CIO. PAGE 110 F2172
LABOR WORKER ECO/TAC

B62

SEN S.R.,THE STRATEGY FOR AGRICULTURAL DEVELOPMENT AND OTHER ESSAYS ON ECONOMIC POLICY AND PLANNING. INDIA FINAN ACT/RES TEC/DEV CAP/ISM PRICE...STAT 20. PAGE 119 F2354
ECO/UNDEV PLAN AGRI POLICY

B62

SHINOHARA M.,GROWTH AND CYCLES IN THE JAPANESE ECONOMY. INDUS LABOR TEC/DEV CAP/ISM INT/TRADE PAY COST EFFICIENCY INCOME WEALTH...METH/COMP 20 CHINJAP. PAGE 121 F2380
PRODUC ECO/DEV EQUILIB ECOMETRIC

B62

WARD B.,THE RICH NATIONS AND THE POOR NATIONS. FUT WOR+45 CULTURE ECO/DEV ECO/UNDEV PLAN CAP/ISM EDU/PROP REV NAT/LISM ATTIT DRIVE SOCISM...POLICY CONCPT TIME/SEQ 20. PAGE 143 F2816
ECO/TAC GEN/LAWS

L62

DURAND-REVILLE L.,"LE REGIME DES INVESTISSEMENTS DANS LES ETATS AFRICAINS D'EXPRESSION FRANCAISE ET A MADAGASCAR." MADAGASCAR ECO/UNDEV CAP/ISM ECO/TAC WEALTH...SOC TREND CHARTS 20. PAGE 35 F0683
AFR FINAN

L62

GALBRAITH J.K.,"ECONOMIC DEVELOPMENT IN PERSPECTIVE." CAP/ISM ECO/TAC ROUTINE ATTIT WEALTH ...TREND CHARTS SOC/EXP WORK TERR/GP 20. PAGE 45 F0884
ECO/UNDEV PLAN

S62

IOVTCHOUK M.T.,"ON SOME THEORETICAL PRINCIPLES AND METHODS OF SOCIOLOGICAL INVESTIGATIONS (IN RUSSIAN)." FUT USA+45 STRATA R+D NAT/G POL/PAR TOP/EX ACT/RES PLAN ECO/TAC EDU/PROP ROUTINE ATTIT RIGID/FLEX MARXISM SOCISM...MARXIST METH/CNCPT OBS TREND NAT/COMP GEN/LAWS 20. PAGE 65 F1288
COM ECO/DEV CAP/ISM USSR

B63

AHN L.A.,FUNFZIG JAHRE ZWISCHEN INFLATION UND DEFLATION. AFR GERMANY DIPLOM PRICE...CONCPT 20. PAGE 3 F0053
FINAN CAP/ISM NAT/COMP ECO/TAC

B63

BARBOUR V.,CAPITALISM IN AMSTERDAM IN THE 17TH CENTURY. NETHERLAND FINAN ECO/TAC...METH/COMP BIBLIOG MUNICH 16. PAGE 10 F0185
CAP/ISM INT/TRADE MARKET WEALTH

B63

BERLE A.A. JR.,THE AMERICAN ECONOMIC REPUBLIC. STRUCT FINAN MARKET LABOR NAT/G PLAN...POLICY WELF/ST DECISION. PAGE 14 F0262
CAP/ISM ECO/TAC TREND CONCPT

B63

CLARK J.J.,BUSINESS FLUCTUATIONS, GROWTH, AND ECONOMIC STABILIZATION. USA+45 FINAN INT/TRADE OPTIMAL...METH/CNCPT ANTHOL BIBLIOG 20. PAGE 25 F0479
CAP/ISM ECO/TAC EQUILIB POLICY

B63

ENKE S.,ECONOMICS FOR DEVELOPMENT. AGRI TEC/DEV CAP/ISM DIPLOM ECO/TAC TAX ATTIT DRIVE HABITAT WEALTH...GOV/COMP BIBLIOG 20. PAGE 38 F0737
ECO/UNDEV PHIL/SCI CON/ANAL

B63

HYDE D.,THE PEACEFUL ASSAULT. COM UAR USSR ECO/DEV ECO/UNDEV NAT/G POL/PAR CAP/ISM PWR 20. PAGE 64 F1256
MARXISM CONTROL ECO/TAC DIPLOM

B63

KAPP W.K.,SOCIAL COSTS OF BUSINESS ENTERPRISE. WOR+45 LABOR TEC/DEV CAP/ISM HABITAT...PHIL/SCI NEW/IDEA CON/ANAL 20. PAGE 69 F1354
COST SOCIETY INDUS RIGID/FLEX

B63

KOLKO G.,THE TRIUMPH OF CONSERVATISM. USA-45 INDUS LG/CO NAT/G PWR 20 PRESIDENT CONGRESS MONOPOLY PROGRSV/M. PAGE 72 F1421
CONSERVE CAP/ISM FINAN MARKET

B63

LAFEBER W.,THE NEW EMPIRE: AN INTERPRETATION OF AMERICAN EXPANSION, 1860-1898. USA-45 CONSTN NAT/LISM SOVEREIGN...TREND BIBLIOG 19/20. PAGE 74 F1457
INDUS NAT/G DIPLOM CAP/ISM

B63

LANGE O.,ECONOMIC DEVELOPMENT, PLANNING, AND INTERNATIONAL COOPERATION. UAR WOR+45 FINAN CAP/ISM PERS/REL 20. PAGE 75 F1476
ECO/UNDEV DIPLOM INT/TRADE PLAN

B63

LUTZ F.A.,DAS PROBLEM DES INTERNATIONALEN WIRTSCHAFTLICHEN GLEICHGEWICHTS. DIPLOM INT/TRADE COST INCOME 20. PAGE 82 F1612
FINAN CAP/ISM ECO/TAC PRODUC

B63

MEEK R.L.,THE ECONOMICS OF PHYSIOCRACY. FRANCE UK AGRI FINAN WORKER CAP/ISM TAX DEMAND EQUILIB INCOME HABITAT...CHARTS ANTHOL 17. PAGE 89 F1744
PRODUC WEALTH MARKET

B63

PATTON R.,THE DEVELOPMENT OF THE AMERICAN ECONOMY: REVISED. USA+45 USA-45 INDUS LABOR NAT/G CAP/ISM DIPLOM INT/TRADE WAR WEALTH 16/20. PAGE 104 F2038
ECO/TAC ECO/DEV DEMAND

B63

ROTHBARD M.N.,AMERICA'S GREAT DEPRESSION. USA-45 NAT/G ECO/TAC LAISSEZ...POLICY IDEA/COMP 20. PAGE 114 F2248
FINAN CAP/ISM MARKET GEN/LAWS

B63

STIFEL L.D.,THE TEXTILE INDUSTRY - A CASE STUDY OF INDUSTRIAL DEVELOPMENT IN THE PHILIPPINES (PAPER). PHILIPPINE WORKER CAP/ISM INT/TRADE TARIFFS RECEIVE PRICE ADMIN COST EFFICIENCY WEALTH...BIBLIOG 20. PAGE 126 F2486
S/ASIA ECO/UNDEV PROC/MFG NAT/G

B63

THEOBALD R.,FREE MEN AND FREE MARKETS. USA+45 USA-45 ECO/DEV NAT/G TEC/DEV DIPLOM INT/TRADE INCOME ORD/FREE WEALTH...TREND 19/20 KEYNES/JM. PAGE 130 F2556
CONCPT ECO/TAC CAP/ISM MARKET

B63

VON BECKERATH E.,PROBLEME DER NORMATIVEN OKONOMIK UND DER WIRTSCHAFTSPOLITISCHEN BERATUNG. GERMANY UK ELITES CAP/ISM EFFICIENCY...CONCPT GOV/COMP IDEA/COMP 20. PAGE 142 F2789
ECO/TAC DELIB/GP ECO/DEV CONSULT

S63

AYAL E.B.,"VALUE SYSTEM AND ECONOMIC DEVELOPMENT IN JAPAN AND THAILAND." ASIA S/ASIA THAILAND CULTURE ECO/DEV CAP/ISM DOMIN NAT/LISM DRIVE RIGID/FLEX SOCISM...WELF/ST OBS TREND CON/ANAL GEN/LAWS TERR/GP 20 CHINJAP. PAGE 8 F0145
ECO/UNDEV ALL/VALS

S63

HOOVER C.B.,"ECONOMIC REFORM VERSUS ECONOMIC GROWTH
ECO/DEV

IN UNDERDEVELOPED COUNTRIES." FUT WOR+45 ELITES STRATA ECO/UNDEV DIST/IND INDUS TEC/DEV CAP/ISM FOR/AID INT/TRADE ATTIT WEALTH...MYTH TREND STERTYP GEN/LAWS WORK 20. PAGE 61 F1209 — ECO/TAC

S63
MATHUR P.N.,"GAINS IN ECONOMIC GROWTH FROM INTERNATIONAL TRADE." USA-45 ECO/DEV FINAN INDUS ATTIT WEALTH...MATH QUANT STAT BIOG TREND GEN/LAWS WORK 20. PAGE 87 F1704 — MARKET ECO/TAC CAP/ISM INT/TRADE

S63
POLYANOV N.,"THE DOLLAR'S VENTURES IN EUROPE." EUR+WWI FRANCE USA+45 ECO/DEV MARKET POL/PAR TEC/DEV ECO/TAC EDU/PROP DRIVE PWR WEALTH...MARXIST MYTH STAT TREND EEC 20. PAGE 107 F2100 — FINAN PLAN BAL/PAY CAP/ISM

S63
WILES P.J.D.,"WILL CAPITALISM AND COMMUNISM SPONTANEOUSLY CONVERGE." COM FUT USA+45 ECO/DEV DIST/IND MARKET CAP/ISM ECO/TAC RIGID/FLEX WEALTH MARXISM SOCISM...MATH STAT TREND COMPUT/IR 20. PAGE 146 F2885 — PLAN TEC/DEV USSR

B64
ASH W.,MARXISM AND MORAL CONCEPTS. CAP/ISM GP/REL ORD/FREE...BIBLIOG 20. PAGE 7 F0128 — MARXISM CONCPT MORAL SOCIETY

B64
AUBREY H.G.,THE DOLLAR IN WORLD AFFAIRS. FUT USA+45 WOR+45 ECO/DEV CAP/ISM INT/TRADE BAL/PAY...CHARTS 20. PAGE 7 F0140 — FINAN ECO/TAC DIPLOM POLICY

B64
BASTIAT F.,ECONOMIC SOPHISMS (1845). FINAN MARKET INT/TRADE TAX EDU/PROP LAISSEZ. PAGE 11 F0207 — TARIFFS INDUS ECO/TAC CAP/ISM

B64
BAUCHET P.,ECONOMIC PLANNING. FRANCE STRATA LG/CO CAP/ISM ADMIN PARL/PROC DEMAND OPTIMAL ATTIT PWR SOCISM...POLICY CHARTS 20. PAGE 11 F0212 — ECO/DEV NAT/G PLAN ECO/TAC

B64
BERRILL K.,ECONOMIC DEVELOPMENT WITH SPECIAL REFERENCE TO EAST ASIA. ASIA INDIA S/ASIA AGRI INDUS LABOR DELIB/GP PLAN INT/TRADE COST PRODUC 20 CHINJAP. PAGE 14 F0271 — FINAN ECO/UNDEV INT/ORG CAP/ISM

B64
BOARMAN P.M.,GERMANY'S ECONOMIC DILEMMA - INFLATION AND THE BALANCE OF PAYMENTS. AFR GERMANY/W LABOR CAP/ISM PRICE BAL/PAY COST INCOME 20. PAGE 16 F0302 — ECO/DEV FINAN INT/TRADE BUDGET

B64
CHEIT E.F.,THE BUSINESS ESTABLISHMENT. FRANCE WOR+45 PROF/ORG TOP/EX PROB/SOLV CAP/ISM ADMIN SUPEGO MORAL PWR...METH/CNCPT MYTH NEW/IDEA 20. PAGE 24 F0460 — PERSON EX/STRUC MGT INDUS

B64
GUTMANN P.M.,ECONOMIC GROWTH: AN AMERICAN PROBLEM. USA+45 FINAN R+D...POLICY NAT/COMP ANTHOL BIBLIOG 20. PAGE 52 F1016 — WEALTH ECO/DEV CAP/ISM ORD/FREE

B64
LETICHE J.M.,A HISTORY OF RUSSIAN ECONOMIC THOUGHT: NINTH THROUGH EIGHTEENTH CENTURIES. RUSSIA FINAN SECT CAP/ISM DOMIN DEMAND EFFICIENCY OWN MARXISM ...TECHNIC ANTHOL BIBLIOG 9/18. PAGE 78 F1536 — ECO/TAC TIME/SEQ IDEA/COMP ECO/UNDEV

B64
MANSFIELD E.,MONOPOLY POWER AND ECONOMIC PERFORMANCE: AN INTRODUCTION TO A CURRENT ISSUE OF PUBLIC POLICY. ECO/DEV INDUS NAT/G PLAN CAP/ISM PRICE CONTROL LOBBY EFFICIENCY PRODUC...POLICY 20 CONGRESS KENNEDY/JF MONOPOLY. PAGE 85 F1659 — LG/CO PWR ECO/TAC MARKET

B64
MARRIS R.,THE ECONOMIC THEORY OF "MANAGERIAL" CAPITALISM. USA+45 ECO/DEV LG/CO ECO/TAC DEMAND ...CHARTS BIBLIOG 20. PAGE 86 F1675 — CAP/ISM MGT CONTROL OP/RES

B64
MILIBAND R.,THE SOCIALIST REGISTER: 1964. GERMANY/W ITALY UK LABOR POL/PAR ECO/TAC FOR/AID NUC/PWR ...POLICY SOCIALIST IDEA/COMP 20 MAO NASSER/G. PAGE 91 F1784 — MARXISM SOCISM CAP/ISM PROB/SOLV

B64
NEHEMKIS P.,LATIN AMERICA: MYTH AND REALITY. INDUS INT/ORG PROB/SOLV CAP/ISM DIPLOM REV...SOC MUNICH 20. PAGE 97 F1907 — REGION MYTH L/A+17C ECO/UNDEV

B64
OECD,THE FLOW OF FINANCIAL RESOURCES TO LESS DEVELOPED COUNTRIES 1956-1963. WOR+45 FINAN CAP/ISM ...POLICY STAT 20. PAGE 100 F1968 — FOR/AID BUDGET INT/ORG ECO/UNDEV

B64
RANIS G.,THE UNITED STATES AND THE DEVELOPING ECONOMIES. COM USA+45 AGRI FINAN TEC/DEV CAP/ISM ECO/TAC INT/TRADE...POLICY METH/COMP ANTHOL 20 AID. PAGE 109 F2145 — ECO/UNDEV DIPLOM FOR/AID

B64
WERNETTE J.P.,GOVERNMENT AND BUSINESS. LABOR CAP/ISM ECO/TAC INT/TRADE TAX ADMIN AUTOMAT NUC/PWR CIVMIL/REL DEMAND...MGT 20 MONOPOLY. PAGE 145 F2859 — NAT/G FINAN ECO/DEV CONTROL

B64
WILLIAMSON O.E.,THE ECONOMICS OF DISCRETIONARY BEHAVIOR: MANAGERIAL OBJECTIVES IN A THEORY OF THE FIRM. MARKET BUDGET CAP/ISM PRODUC DRIVE PERSON ...STAT CHARTS BIBLIOG METH 20. PAGE 147 F2897 — EFFICIENCY MGT ECO/TAC CHOOSE

B64
WITHERS W.,THE ECONOMIC CRISIS IN LATIN AMERICA. BRAZIL CHILE STRATA AGRI DIPLOM FOR/AID PWR SOCISM ...POLICY 20 MEXIC/AMER ARGEN ALL/PROG. PAGE 148 F2914 — L/A+17C ECO/UNDEV CAP/ISM ALL/IDEOS

L64
ARMENGALD A.,"ECONOMIE ET COEXISTENCE." COM EUR+WWI FUT USA+45 WOR+45 ECO/DEV ECO/UNDEV FINAN INT/ORG NAT/G EXEC CHOOSE ATTIT ALL/VALS...POLICY RELATIV DECISION TREND SOC/EXP WORK 20. PAGE 6 F0113 — MARKET ECO/TAC AFR CAP/ISM

S64
HERMAN L.M.,"THE ECONOMIC CONTENT OF SOVIET TRADE WITH THE WEST." WOR+45 ECO/DEV ECO/UNDEV AGRI COM/IND INDUS CAP/ISM ECO/TAC ATTIT RIGID/FLEX WEALTH...OBS TREND VAL/FREE MARX/KARL 20. PAGE 59 F1152 — COM MARKET INT/TRADE USSR

S64
SALVADORI M.,"EL CAPITALISMO EN LA EUROPA DE LA POSGUERRA." AFR INT/ORG NAT/G POL/PAR PLAN ECO/TAC ATTIT ORD/FREE WEALTH...HIST/WRIT EEC 20. PAGE 115 F2275 — EUR+WWI ECO/DEV CAP/ISM

C64
GOLDMAN M.I.,"COMPARATIVE ECONOMIC SYSTEMS: A READER." COM ECO/UNDEV NAT/G BUDGET CAP/ISM ADMIN TOTALISM MARXISM SOCISM...MGT ANTHOL BIBLIOG 19/20. PAGE 48 F0938 — NAT/COMP CONTROL IDEA/COMP

C64
LANDAUER C.,"CONTEMPORARY ECONOMIC SYSTEMS." COM WOR+45 ECO/UNDEV PLAN GP/REL...BIBLIOG 20. PAGE 75 F1466 — CAP/ISM SOCISM MARXISM IDEA/COMP

B65
ALDERSON W.,DYNAMIC MARKETING BEHAVIOR. USA+45 FINAN CREATE TEC/DEV EDU/PROP PRICE COST 20. PAGE 3 F0057 — MGT MARKET ATTIT CAP/ISM

B65
BRENNAN M.J.,PATTERNS OF MARKET BEHAVIOR. AFR USA+45 OP/RES CAP/ISM ECO/TAC INT/TRADE...CHARTS METH/COMP ANTHOL TIME 20. PAGE 18 F0346 — MARKET LABOR FINAN ECOMETRIC

B65
BROOKINGS INSTITUTION,BROOKINGS PAPERS ON PUBLIC POLICY. USA+45 ECO/UNDEV LEGIS CAP/ISM ECO/TAC TAX EDU/PROP CONTROL APPORT 20. PAGE 19 F0363 — DIPLOM FOR/AID POLICY FINAN

B65
COLBERG M.R.,HUMAN CAPITAL IN SOUTHERN DEVELOPMENT. USA+45 AGRI ACADEM LABOR SCHOOL WORKER CAP/ISM DISCRIM. PAGE 26 F0498 — PROVS RACE/REL GP/REL

B65
COLLINS H.,KARL MARX AND THE BRITISH LABOUR MOVEMENT; YEARS OF THE FIRST INTERNATIONAL. FRANCE SWITZERLND UK CAP/ISM WAR...MARXIST IDEA/COMP BIBLIOG 19. PAGE 26 F0506 — MARXISM LABOR INT/ORG REV

B65
COPELAND M.A.,OUR FREE ENTERPRISE ECONOMY. USA+45 INDUS LABOR ADMIN CONTROL GP/REL MGT. PAGE 27 F0533 — CAP/ISM PLAN FINAN ECO/DEV

B65
FARER T.J.,FINANCING AFRICAN DEVELOPMENT. AFR ECO/TAC FOR/AID SOCISM 20. PAGE 39 F0764 — ECO/UNDEV FINAN CAP/ISM PLAN

B65
GRAMPP W.D.,ECONOMIC LIBERALISM; THE BEGINNINGS (VOL. I). USA-45 WOR-45 MARKET LABOR ATTIT WEALTH ...POLICY CONCPT BIBLIOG GREECE/ANC MERCANTLST REPUBLICAN FEDERALIST. PAGE 50 F0974 — ECO/DEV CAP/ISM IDEA/COMP ECO/TAC

B65
GRAMPP W.D.,ECONOMIC LIBERALISM; THE CLASSICAL VIEW (VOL. II). MOD/EUR SOCIETY MARKET INT/TRADE NAT/LISM WEALTH LAISSEZ...POLICY PSY CONCPT BIBLIOG 19 SMITH/ADAM HUME/D MILL/JS. PAGE 50 F0975 — ECO/DEV CAP/ISM IDEA/COMP ECO/TAC

B65
GRIFFIN C.E.,THE FREE SOCIETY. CONSTN SOCIETY MARKET FEDERAL RATIONAL WEALTH...MAJORIT 20 CIVIL/LIB. PAGE 51 F0999 — CONCPT ORD/FREE CAP/ISM POPULISM

B65
JAIN S.C.,THE STATE AND AGRICULTURE. INDIA S/ASIA ECO/UNDEV PROB/SOLV CAP/ISM MARXISM SOCISM 20. PAGE 66 F1304 — NAT/G POLICY AGRI ECO/TAC

B65
KLASSEN L.H.,AREA ECONOMIC AND SOCIAL REDEVELOPMENT. ECO/UNDEV INDUS NAT/G PLAN CAP/ISM TAX...ECOMETRIC SIMUL 20. PAGE 72 F1404
OPTIMAL WORKER METH ECO/TAC

B65
THE STATE AND ECONOMIC ENTERPRISE IN JAPAN; ESSAYS IN THE POLITICAL ECONOMY OF GROWTH. AGRI INDUS DRIVE POPULISM...CHARTS NAT/COMP ANTHOL 19/20 CHINJAP. PAGE 81 F1594
ECO/UNDEV ECO/DEV CAP/ISM ECO/TAC

B65
MORRIS M.D.,THE EMERGENCE OF AN INDUSTRIAL LABOR FORCE IN INDIA: A STUDY OF THE BOMBAY COTTON MILLS, 1854-1947. INDIA WORKER OP/RES ADMIN 19/20. PAGE 94 F1837
INDUS LABOR ECO/UNDEV CAP/ISM

B65
MUSOLF L.D.,PROMOTING THE GENERAL WELFARE: GOVERNMENT AND THE ECONOMY. USA+45 ECO/DEV CAP/ISM DEMAND OPTIMAL 20. PAGE 95 F1874
ECO/TAC NAT/G EX/STRUC NEW/LIB

B65
NARASIMHAN V.K.,DEMOCRACY AND MIXED ECONOMY. INDIA CONTROL...CENSUS IDEA/COMP 20. PAGE 96 F1891
CAP/ISM MARXISM ORD/FREE NEW/LIB

B65
ONSLOW C.,ASIAN ECONOMIC DEVELOPMENT. BURMA CEYLON INDIA MALAYSIA PAKISTAN S/ASIA AGRI INDUS MARKET PROB/SOLV CAP/ISM FOR/AID INT/TRADE DEMAND WEALTH ...POLICY ANTHOL 20. PAGE 101 F1991
ECO/UNDEV ECO/TAC PLAN NAT/G

B65
OXENFELDT A.R.,ECONOMIC SYSTEMS IN ACTION. FRANCE USA+45 USSR CULTURE PLAN PROB/SOLV TEC/DEV INCOME PRODUC WEALTH...METH/COMP 20. PAGE 102 F2007
ECO/DEV CAP/ISM MARXISM ECO/TAC

B65
PHELPS E.S.,FISCAL NEUTRALITY TOWARD ECONOMIC GROWTH. FINAN NAT/G BUDGET CAP/ISM CONTROL INCOME 20. PAGE 106 F2080
ECO/DEV POLICY ECO/TAC TAX

B65
PHELPS E.S.,PRIVATE WANTS AND PUBLIC NEEDS - AN INTRODUCTION TO A CURRENT ISSUE OF PUBLIC POLICY (REV. ED.). USA+45 PLAN CAP/ISM INGP/REL ROLE ...DECISION TIME/SEQ 20. PAGE 106 F2081
NAT/G POLICY DEMAND

B65
ROWE J.W.,PRIMARY COMMODITIES IN INTERNATIONAL TRADE. MARKET CAP/ISM ECO/TAC DEMAND...NAT/COMP 20. PAGE 114 F2253
INT/TRADE AGRI RATION PRICE

B65
SCHULTZ T.W.,ECONOMIC CRISES IN WORLD AGRICULTURE. ASIA INDIA USSR ECO/DEV ECO/UNDEV INDUS VOL/ASSN CAP/ISM RATION COLONIAL 20. PAGE 117 F2317
AGRI ECO/TAC INCOME WORKER

B65
SHONFIELD A.,MODERN CAPITALISM: THE CHANGING BALANCE OF PUBLIC AND PRIVATE POWER. FRANCE GERMANY/W UK USA+45 WOR+45 ECO/DEV INT/ORG NAT/G CONSULT INT/TRADE PRODUC...POLICY CONCPT METH/COMP 20. PAGE 121 F2386
CAP/ISM CONTROL BAL/PWR CREATE

B65
STEINER G.A.,THE CREATIVE ORGANIZATION. ELITES LG/CO PLAN PROB/SOLV TEC/DEV INSPECT CAP/ISM CONTROL EXEC PERSON...METH/COMP HYPO/EXP 20. PAGE 126 F2476
CREATE MGT ADMIN SOC

B65
WASSERMAN M.J.,THE BALANCE OF PAYMENTS: HISTORY, METHODOLOGY, THEORY. UK USA+45 USA-45 CAP/ISM DIPLOM EFFICIENCY...DECISION METH/CNCPT BIBLIOG 18/20 LEAGUE/NAT. PAGE 144 F2828
BAL/PAY ECO/TAC GEN/LAWS EQUILIB

B65
WILKINSON T.O.,THE URBANIZATION OF JAPANESE LABOR, 1868-1955. AGRI PROC/MFG CAP/ISM PRODUC PROFIT ...SOC CLASSIF CENSUS CHARTS MUNICH 19/20 CHINJAP. PAGE 146 F2887
LABOR INDUS GEOG

B65
WISH J.R.,ECONOMIC DEVELOPMENT IN LATIN AMERICA: AN ANNOTATED BIBLIOGRAPHY. L/A+17C COM/IND MARKET R+D CREATE CAP/ISM ATTIT...STAT METH 20. PAGE 148 F2912
BIBLIOG/A ECO/UNDEV TEC/DEV AGRI

B65
WURFEL S.W.,FOREIGN ENTERPRISE IN COLOMBIA. FINAN LABOR NAT/G ECO/TAC TAX REGION 20 COLOMB. PAGE 149 F2944
ECO/UNDEV INT/TRADE JURID CAP/ISM

B65
ZAWADZKI K.K.F.,THE ECONOMICS OF INFLATIONARY PROCESSES. FINAN INT/TRADE PRICE CONTROL DEMAND EQUILIB PROFIT 20. PAGE 150 F2960
ECO/DEV COST ECO/TAC CAP/ISM

L65
WILLIAMS S.,"NEGOTIATING INVESTMENT IN EMERGING COUNTRIES." USA+45 WOR+45 INDUS MARKET NAT/G TOP/EX TEC/DEV CAP/ISM ECO/TAC ADMIN SKILL WEALTH...POLICY RELATIV MGT WORK 20. PAGE 147 F2894
FINAN ECO/UNDEV

S65
MULLER A.L.,"THE ECONOMIC POSITION OF THE ASIANS IN AFRICA." AFR SOUTH/AFR ECO/UNDEV MARKET ECO/TAC GP/REL INCOME...CHARTS IND 20 MONOPOLY ASIANS. PAGE 95 F1856
WORKER RACE/REL CAP/ISM DISCRIM

S65
RUSINOW D.I.,"YUGOSLAV DEVELOPMENT BETWEEN EAST AND WEST." AGRI VOL/ASSN PLAN CAP/ISM ECO/TAC FOR/AID INT/TRADE BAL/PAY...MARXIST EEC COMECON. PAGE 115 F2262
YUGOSLAVIA ECO/UNDEV STAT

S65
WHITE J.,"WEST GERMAN AID TO DEVELOPING COUNTRIES." AFR INT/ORG OP/RES GIVE CENTRAL ATTIT DRIVE...STAT NAT/COMP. PAGE 146 F2869
GERMANY FOR/AID ECO/UNDEV CAP/ISM

B66
BALDWIN R.E.,ECONOMIC DEVELOPMENT AND EXPORT GROWTH: A STUDY OF NORTHERN RHODESIA, 1920-1960. AFR RHODESIA AGRI EXTR/IND FINAN MARKET LABOR WORKER ECO/TAC...CONCPT NEW/IDEA MUNICH 20. PAGE 9 F0166
ECO/UNDEV TEC/DEV INT/TRADE CAP/ISM

B66
BARAN P.A.,MONOPOLY CAPITAL; AN ESSAY ON THE AMERICAN ECONOMIC AND SOCIAL ORDER. USA+45 USA-45 ECO/UNDEV FINAN MARKET PLAN DIPLOM COLONIAL RACE/REL DEMAND MARXISM...CHARTS 20. PAGE 9 F0179
LG/CO CAP/ISM PRICE CONTROL

B66
BEN-PORATH Y.,THE ARAB LABOR FORCE IN ISRAEL. ISLAM ISRAEL AGRI INDUS SCHOOL CAP/ISM PAY DEMAND...GEOG REGRESS STAT CHARTS 20 ARABS. PAGE 13 F0245
WORKER CENSUS GP/REL STRUCT

B66
DAVIS K.,BUSINESS AND ITS ENVIRONMENT. LAW ECO/DEV INDUS OP/RES ADMIN CONTROL ROUTINE GP/REL PROFIT POLICY. PAGE 30 F0591
EX/STRUC PROB/SOLV CAP/ISM EXEC

B66
EDWARDS C.D.,TRADE REGULATIONS OVERSEAS. IRELAND NEW/ZEALND SOUTH/AFR NAT/G CAP/ISM TARIFFS CONTROL ...POLICY JURID 20 EEC CHINJAP. PAGE 36 F0703
INT/TRADE DIPLOM INT/LAW ECO/TAC

B66
FUSFELD D.R.,THE AGE OF THE ECONOMIST. ECO/TAC WEALTH LAISSEZ MARXISM...EPIST 18/20 KEYNES/JM. PAGE 45 F0878
PHIL/SCI CAP/ISM POLICY

B66
KROOSS H.E.,AMERICAN ECONOMIC DEVELOPMENT (2ND ED.). USA+45 USA-45 AGRI INDUS LABOR WORKER INT/TRADE TAX WAR...CHARTS 18/20. PAGE 73 F1443
ECO/TAC NAT/G CAP/ISM ECO/DEV

B66
LANDERS D.S.,RISE OF CAPITALISM. LABOR AUTOMAT GP/REL CENTRAL COST PROFIT...SOC CONCPT ANTHOL 19/20. PAGE 75 F1469
CAP/ISM INDUS AGRI

B66
LEONTIEF W.,ESSAYS IN ECONOMICS. ECO/UNDEV INDUS NAT/G CAP/ISM FOR/AID AUTOMAT MARXISM...ECOMETRIC CHARTS ANTHOL METH 20 KEYNES/JM. PAGE 78 F1528
CONCPT METH/CNCPT METH/COMP

B66
LICHTMAN R.,TOWARD COMMUNITY (PAPER). PLAN PROB/SOLV WEALTH MARXISM...HEAL CONCPT 20. PAGE 80 F1561
NEW/LIB EFFICIENCY CAP/ISM ADJUST

B66
MADAN G.R.,ECONOMIC THINKING IN INDIA. INDIA ECO/UNDEV AGRI FINAN INDUS LABOR PLAN CAP/ISM INT/TRADE MARXISM SOCISM...POLICY 1/20. PAGE 84 F1638
ECO/TAC PHIL/SCI NAT/G POL/PAR

B66
NAMBOODIRIPAD E.M.,ECONOMICS AND POLITICS OF INDIA'S SOCIALIST PATTERN. INDIA STRATA AGRI INDUS NAT/G PRICE ORD/FREE SOVEREIGN 20. PAGE 96 F1888
ECO/UNDEV PLAN SOCISM CAP/ISM

B66
PASSIN H.,THE UNITED STATES AND JAPAN. USA+45 INDUS CAP/ISM...TREND 20 CHINJAP TREATY. PAGE 103 F2032
DIPLOM INT/TRADE ECO/DEV ECO/TAC

B66
REDFORD E.S.,THE ROLE OF GOVERNMENT IN THE AMERICAN ECONOMY. USA+45 USA-45 FINAN INDUS LG/CO PROB/SOLV ADMIN INGP/REL INCOME PRODUC 18/20. PAGE 110 F2169
NAT/G ECO/DEV CAP/ISM ECO/TAC

B66
SPULBER N.,THE STATE AND ECONOMIC DEVELOPMENT IN EASTERN EUROPE. BULGARIA COM CZECHOSLVK HUNGARY POLAND YUGOSLAVIA CULTURE PLAN CAP/ISM INT/TRADE CONTROL...POLICY CHARTS METH/COMP BIBLIOG/A 19/20. PAGE 125 F2460
ECO/DEV ECO/UNDEV NAT/G TOTALISM

B66
US SENATE COMM ON FOREIGN REL,HEARINGS ON S 2859 AND S 2861. USA+45 WOR+45 FORCES BUDGET CAP/ISM ADMIN DETER WEAPON TOTALISM...NAT/COMP 20 UN CONGRESS. PAGE 139 F2735
FOR/AID DIPLOM ORD/FREE ECO/UNDEV

B66
WETTER G.A.,SOVIET IDEOLOGY TODAY. USSR ECO/UNDEV
ALL/IDEOS

SECT WORKER CAP/ISM CONTROL TASK EFFICIENCY TOTALISM DRIVE WEALTH...TREND 18/20. PAGE 145 F2864 MARXISM REV

B66
WILCOX C.,ECONOMIES OF THE WORLD TODAY: THEIR ORGANIZATION, DEVELOPMENT, AND PERFORMANCE (2ND ED.). CHINA/COM COM INDIA NIGERIA UK WOR+45 WOR-45 INDUS MARKET PLAN ECO/TAC SOCISM...CHARTS METH/COMP 20. PAGE 146 F2878 ECO/DEV ECO/UNDEV MARXISM CAP/ISM

B66
ZISCHKA A.,WAR ES EIN WUNDER? GERMANY/W ECO/DEV FINAN LG/CO BARGAIN CAP/ISM FOR/AID RATION 20 MARSHL/PLN. PAGE 150 F2965 ECO/TAC INT/TRADE INDUS WAR

L66
AFRICAN BIBLIOGRAPHIC CENTER,"AFRICAN ECONOMIC AFFAIRS: A SELECT BIBLIOGRAPHICAL SURVEY, 1965-1966; SUPPLEMENTS NUMBERS 1-3." AFR FINAN INDUS LABOR PLAN BUDGET CAP/ISM DIPLOM INT/TRADE ADMIN...GEOG 20. PAGE 3 F0047 BIBLIOG/A ECO/UNDEV FOR/AID TEC/DEV

S66
DUROSELLE J.B.,"THE FUTURE OF THE ATLANTIC COMMUNITY." EUR+WWI USA+45 USSR NAT/G CAP/ISM REGION DETER NUC/PWR ATTIT MARXISM...INT/LAW 20 NATO. PAGE 35 F0686 FUT DIPLOM MYTH POLICY

S66
JACOBS P.,"RE-RADICALIZING THE DE-RADICALIZED." USA+45 SOCIETY STRUCT FINAN PLAN PROB/SOLV CAP/ISM WEALTH CONSERVE NEW/LIB 20. PAGE 66 F1297 NAT/G POLICY MARXIST ADMIN

N66
OECD,THE BALANCE OF PAYMENTS ADJUSTMENT PROCESS (PAMPHLET). EUR+WWI ECO/DEV FINAN CONSULT PLAN PROB/SOLV BUDGET CAP/ISM INT/TRADE PRICE CONTROL EQUILIB 20. PAGE 101 F1975 BAL/PAY ECO/TAC DIPLOM INT/ORG

B67
ALNASRAWI A.,FINANCING ECONOMIC DEVELOPMENT IN IRAQ. IRAQ INDUS CAP/ISM COST PRODUC...STAT CHARTS BIBLIOG 20. PAGE 4 F0076 ECO/UNDEV EXTR/IND TEC/DEV INT/TRADE

B67
EBENSTEIN W.,TODAY'S ISMS: COMMUNISM, FASCISM, CAPITALISM, SOCIALISM (5TH ED.). COM WOR+45 PERCEPT PWR...SOC TREND IDEA/COMP NAT/COMP 20. PAGE 35 F0691 FASCISM MARXISM SOCISM CAP/ISM

B67
EVANS R.H.,COEXISTENCE: COMMUNISM AND ITS PRACTICE IN BOLOGNA, 1945-1965. ITALY CAP/ISM ADMIN CHOOSE PEACE ORD/FREE...SOC STAT DEEP/INT SAMP CHARTS BIBLIOG MUNICH 20. PAGE 39 F0756 MARXISM CULTURE POL/PAR

B67
FILENE P.G.,AMERICANS AND THE SOVIET EXPERIMENT, 1917-1933. USA-45 USSR INTELL NAT/G CAP/ISM DIPLOM EDU/PROP PRESS REV SOCISM...PSY 20. PAGE 41 F0793 ATTIT RIGID/FLEX MARXISM SOCIETY

B67
HAGUE D.C.,PRICE FORMATION IN VARIOUS ECONOMIES; PROCEEDINGS OF A CONFERENCE HELD BY THE INTERNATIONAL ECONOMIC ASSOCIATION. WOR+45 FINAN MARKET PLAN CONFER COST...DECISION MATH PREDICT CHARTS SIMUL 20 INTL/ECON. PAGE 53 F1037 PRICE CAP/ISM SOCISM METH/COMP

B67
HEILBRONER R.L.,THE LIMITS OF AMERICAN CAPITALISM. FUT ECO/DEV INDUS LG/CO EX/STRUC LEAD PWR TECHRACY 20. PAGE 58 F1137 ELITES CREATE TEC/DEV CAP/ISM

B67
JACOBY N.H.,US AID TO TAIWAN. CAP/ISM DIPLOM FEEDBACK COST PRODUC...OBS INT CHARTS 20. PAGE 66 F1301 FOR/AID OP/RES ECO/TAC ECO/UNDEV

B67
JOHNSON H.G.,ECONOMIC POLICY TOWARD LESS DEVELOPED COUNTRIES. USA+45 ECO/DEV INT/ORG PLAN CAP/ISM FOR/AID TARIFFS GIVE WEALTH...NEW/IDEA CHARTS 20 UN GATT. PAGE 67 F1327 ECO/UNDEV ECO/TAC METH/COMP

B67
KARDOUCHE G.K.,THE UAR IN DEVELOPMENT. UAR ECO/TAC INT/TRADE BAL/PAY...STAT CHARTS BIBLIOG 20. PAGE 69 F1355 FINAN MGT CAP/ISM ECO/UNDEV

B67
SCOTT J.C.,ANTITRUST AND TRADE REGULATION TODAY: 1967. USA+45 MARKET LG/CO DELIB/GP LEGIS CAP/ISM INT/TRADE TAX PRICE INGP/REL WEALTH 20 SUPREME/CT. PAGE 118 F2334 NAT/G INDUS CONTROL JURID

B67
TANSKY L.,US AND USSR AID TO DEVELOPING COUNTRIES. INDIA TURKEY USA+45 USSR INDUS PLAN CAP/ISM WAR PWR WEALTH MARXISM...CHARTS NAT/COMP BIBLIOG 20. PAGE 128 F2534 ECO/UNDEV FOR/AID DIPLOM ECO/TAC

B67
TANSKY L.,US AND USSR AID TO DEVELOPING COUNTRIES. INDIA TURKEY UAR USA+45 USSR FINAN PLAN TEC/DEV ADMIN WEALTH...TREND METH/COMP 20. PAGE 128 F2535 FOR/AID ECO/UNDEV MARXISM CAP/ISM

L67
DOERFER G.L.,"THE LIMITS ON TRADE SECRET LAW IMPOSED BY FEDERAL PATENT & ANTITRUST SUPREMACY." USA+45 LAW R+D CAP/ISM LICENSE CONTROL SANCTION ORD/FREE. PAGE 33 F0651 JURID GOV/REL POLICY LEGIT

L67
HOSHII I.,"JAPAN'S STAKE IN ASIA." ASIA S/ASIA CAP/ISM ECO/TAC ROLE...GEOG 20 CHINJAP. PAGE 62 F1224 DIPLOM REGION NAT/G INT/ORG

L67
MACDONALD R.M.,"COLLECTIVE BARGAINING IN THE POSTWAR PERIOD." WORKER PROB/SOLV ECO/TAC PARTIC RISK CENTRAL EFFICIENCY DRIVE WEALTH...TREND 20. PAGE 83 F1624 LABOR INDUS BARGAIN CAP/ISM

L67
MANNE H.G.,"OUR TWO CORPORATION SYSTEMS* LAW AND ECONOMICS." LAW CONTROL SANCTION GP/REL...JURID 20. PAGE 85 F1657 INDUS ELITES CAP/ISM ADMIN

L67
STRUVE G.M.,"THE LESS-RESTRICTIVE-ALTERNATIVE PRINCIPLE AND ECONOMIC DUE PROCESS." USA+45 ECO/DEV LABOR NAT/G CONSULT DELIB/GP OP/RES PLAN WEALTH. PAGE 127 F2505 JURID JUDGE SANCTION CAP/ISM

L67
WHITNEY S.N.,"MERGERS, CONGLOMERATES, AND OLIGOPOLIES* A WIDENING OF ANTI TRUST TARGETS." LAW NAT/G TEC/DEV CAP/ISM GP/REL PWR...OLD/LIB 20. PAGE 146 F2873 ECO/TAC INDUS JURID

S67
ALVES V.,"FOREIGN CAPITAL IN BRAZIL." BRAZIL USA+45 CAP/ISM DIPLOM ECO/TAC INT/TRADE CONTROL PWR ...POLICY 20. PAGE 4 F0081 ECO/UNDEV FINAN SOCIALIST SOCISM

S67
ASCH P.,"CONGLOMERATE MERGERS AND PUBLIC POLICY." USA+45 ECO/DEV LG/CO NAT/G ECO/TAC ADJUD CENTRAL 20. PAGE 7 F0126 INDUS CAP/ISM BARGAIN

S67
BOSHER J.F.,"GOVERNMENT AND PRIVATE INTERESTS IN NEW FRANCE." CANADA FRANCE INDUS LG/CO SML/CO CAP/ISM INT/TRADE COLONIAL GP/REL...HIST/WRIT 17/18. PAGE 17 F0320 NAT/G FINAN ADMIN CONTROL

S67
FADDEYEV N.,"CMEA CO-OPERATION OF EQUAL NATIONS." COM R+D PLAN CAP/ISM DIPLOM FOR/AID WEALTH...POLICY MARXIST. PAGE 39 F0758 MARXISM ECO/TAC INT/ORG ECO/UNDEV

S67
FRIEDENBERG D.M.,"THE US IN LATIN AMERICA; A RECKONING OF SHAME." L/A+17C USA+45 USA-45 INT/ORG CAP/ISM FOR/AID 17/20 OAS. PAGE 44 F0857 DIPLOM POLICY DOMIN COLONIAL

S67
GAMARNIKOW M.,"THE NEW ROLE OF PRIVATE ENTERPRISE." ECO/DEV INDUS NAT/G SML/CO CREATE PROB/SOLV MARXISM ...POLICY TREND IDEA/COMP 20. PAGE 46 F0890 ECO/TAC ATTIT CAP/ISM COM

S67
HADDOCK G.B.,"CORPORATE GROWTH AS AFFECTED BY THE FEDERAL ANTITRUST LAWS" ECO/DEV NAT/G PLAN TEC/DEV CAP/ISM ECO/TAC 20. PAGE 53 F1029 INDUS JURID ADJUD

S67
KINGSLEY R.E.,"THE US BUSINESS IMAGE IN LATIN AMERICA." L/A+17C USA+45 NAT/G TEC/DEV CAP/ISM FOR/AID DOMIN EDU/PROP...CONCPT LING IDEA/COMP 20. PAGE 71 F1396 ATTIT LOVE DIPLOM ECO/UNDEV

S67
LEONTYEV L.,"THE LENINIST PRINCIPLES OF SOCIALIST ECONOMIC MANAGEMENT." USA+45 USSR POL/PAR WORKER PLAN ECO/TAC EFFICIENCY PRODUC MARXISM...POLICY SOCIALIST MGT TREND 20 LENIN/VI MARX/KARL. PAGE 78 F1529 SOCISM CAP/ISM IDEA/COMP ECO/DEV

S67
LIFLAND W.T.,"BANKING PRACTICE AND THE ANTITRUST LAWS." NAT/G GP/REL...CONCPT IDEA/COMP 20. PAGE 80 F1563 FINAN CAP/ISM JURID

S67
MALKIN A.,"BUSINESS BOOKS OF 1966." INDUS LABOR OP/RES TEC/DEV CAP/ISM ECO/TAC INCOME WEALTH 20. PAGE 84 F1649 BIBLIOG/A FINAN MARKET

S67
MANGLAPUS R.S.,"ASIAN REVOLUTION AND AMERICAN IDEOLOGY." USA+45 SOCIETY CAP/ISM DIPLOM ADJUST CENTRAL...NAT/COMP 20. PAGE 84 F1652 REV POPULISM ATTIT ASIA

S67
MYRDAL G.,"ECONOMIC DEVELOPMENT IN THE BACKWARD COUNTRIES." INT/ORG TEC/DEV CAP/ISM DIPLOM INT/TRADE PRODUC WEALTH 20. PAGE 96 F1883 ECO/UNDEV INDUS NAT/G ECO/TAC

S67
ORAZEM F.,"THE NEW SOVIET PLAN FOR AGRICULTURE (1960-1970)" USSR WORKER CAP/ISM ECO/TAC PRICE OWN HABITAT MARXISM...CHARTS 20. PAGE 101 F1994 AGRI PLAN COM

ECO/DEV

S67
RICHMAN B.M.,"CAPITALISTS & MANAGERS IN COMMUNIST CHINA." ASIA CHINA/COM ECO/UNDEV NAT/G CONSULT EX/STRUC PLAN EFFICIENCY PRODUC WEALTH MARXISM ...MGT CHARTS 20. PAGE 111 F2185
CAP/ISM INDUS

S67
RONY V.,"HEARTBREAK IN TENNESSEE* POOR WHITES AND THE UNIONS." LAW STRUCT CAP/ISM ADJUD GP/REL. PAGE 113 F2236
LABOR LOC/G WORKER PWR

S67
SCOVILLE W.J.,"GOVERNMENT REGULATION AND GROWTH IN THE FRENCH PAPER INDUSTRY DURING THE EIGHTEENTH CENTURY." FRANCE MOD/EUR FINAN CAP/ISM TAX ADMIN CONTROL PRIVIL LAISSEZ...POLICY 18. PAGE 118 F2337
NAT/G PROC/MFG ECO/DEV INGP/REL

S67
SOLT L.F.,"PURITANISM, CAPITALISM, DEMOCRACY, AND THE NEW SCIENCE." NAT/G GP/REL CONSERVE...IDEA/COMP GEN/LAWS. PAGE 124 F2440
SECT CAP/ISM RATIONAL POPULISM

S67
WALZER M.,"THE CONDITION OF GREECE; TWENTY YEARS AFTER THE TRUMAN DOCTRINE." AFR GREECE FORCES CAP/ISM 20 TRUMAN/HS. PAGE 143 F2814
DIPLOM POLICY FOR/AID TOTALISM

S67
WEISSKOPF W.A.,"THE DIALECTICS OF ABUNDANCE." UNIV CAP/ISM ATTIT MARXISM...CONCPT 20. PAGE 145 F2853
INDUS SOCIETY IDEA/COMP ALL/VALS

S67
WILLMANN J.,"LA COMMUNAUTE EUROPEENNE ET LA GRANDE-BRETAGNE." UK PROB/SOLV TEC/DEV CAP/ISM DIPLOM CONFER FEDERAL...POLICY 20 EEC. PAGE 147 F2898
INT/ORG DRIVE NAT/LISM INT/TRADE

B76
PROUDHON P.J.,WHAT IS PROPERTY? (TRANS. BY B.R. TUCKER). SOCIETY AGRI CAP/ISM CRIME GP/REL PERSON MORAL ORD/FREE WEALTH. PAGE 108 F2127
OWN WORKER PRODUC ANARCH

B82
CUNNINGHAM W.,THE GROWTH OF ENGLISH INDUSTRY AND COMMERCE. FUT UK FINAN NAT/G CAP/ISM...POLICY 20 MERCANTLST CHRISTIAN POPE. PAGE 29 F0562
INDUS INT/TRADE SML/CO CONSERVE

L86
OSGOOD H.L.,"SCIENTIFIC SOCIALISM: RODBERTUS" GERMANY CAP/ISM COST WEALTH...MAJORIT BIOG IDEA/COMP 19 RODBRTUS/C. PAGE 102 F2002
SOCISM MARXISM ECO/DEV ECO/TAC

B92
ENGELS F.,THE CONDITION OF THE WORKING-CLASS IN ENGLAND (1848). UK INDUS LABOR PRICE CONTROL COST INCOME HEALTH MARXISM MUNICH 19. PAGE 38 F0733
WORKER WEALTH MARXIST CAP/ISM

CAPE/HOPE....CAPE OF GOOD HOPE

CAPITAL....SEE FINAN

CAPITALISM....SEE CAP/ISM

CAPODIST/J....JOHN CAPODISTRIAS

CAPONE/AL....AL CAPONE

CARDOZA/JN....JACOB N. CARDOZA

CARIBBEAN....CARIBBEAN

B64
FIRTH R.,CAPITAL, SAVING AND CREDIT IN PEASANT SOCIETIES. WOR+45 WOR-45 FAM ACT/RES ECO/TAC HEALTH ...SOC CONCPT STAT CHARTS ANTHOL CARIBBEAN VAL/FREE 20. PAGE 41 F0803
AGRI FINAN

B65
DEMAS W.G.,THE ECONOMICS OF DEVELOPMENT IN SMALL COUNTRIES WITH SPECIAL REFERENCE TO THE CARIBBEAN. WOR+45 BAL/PAY DEMAND EFFICIENCY PRODUC...GEOG CARIBBEAN. PAGE 32 F0618
ECO/UNDEV PLAN WEALTH INT/TRADE

CARLETON W.T. F1531

CARNEG/COM....CARNEGIE COMMISSION

CARNEGIE ENDOWMENT INT. PEACE F0414,F0415

CARNELL F.G. F1167

CARNEY D. F0416

CARNEY D.E. F0417

CARNOY M. F0149

CARPER E.T. F0418,F0419,F0420

CARRANZA/V....VENUSTIANZO CARRANZA

CARRINGTON C.E. F0421

CARROTHERS A.W.R. F0422

CARTER A.G.T. F0423

CARVALHO C.M. F0424

CASE STUDIES....CARRIED UNDER THE SPECIAL TECHNIQUES USED, OR TOPICS COVERED

CASEBOOK....CASEBOOK, SUCH AS LEGAL OR SOCIOLOGICAL CASEBOOK

B02
WEBB S.,THE HISTORY OF TRADE UNIONISM. UK PARTIC ...OBS CHARTS BIBLIOG/A 15/19 CASEBOOK. PAGE 144 F2837
LABOR VOL/ASSN GP/REL

B58
COOK P.L.,EFFECTS OF MERGERS: SIX STUDIES. USA+45 ECO/DEV LABOR LG/CO SML/CO VOL/ASSN ADMIN EFFICIENCY 20 CASEBOOK. PAGE 27 F0529
INDUS FINAN EX/STRUC GP/REL

B58
CUNNINGHAM W.B.,COMPULSORY CONCILIATION AND COLLECTIVE BARGAINING. CANADA NAT/G LEGIS ADJUD CT/SYS GP/REL...MGT 20 NEW/BRUNS STRIKE CASEBOOK. PAGE 29 F0563
POLICY BARGAIN LABOR INDUS

B64
MITAU G.T.,INSOLUBLE PROBLEMS: CASE PROBLEMS ON THE FUNCTIONS OF STATE AND LOCAL GOVERNMENT. USA+45 AIR FINAN LABOR POL/PAR PROB/SOLV TAX RECEIVE CONTROL GP/REL 20 CASEBOOK ZONING. PAGE 92 F1807
ADJUD LOC/G PROVS

B66
BOYD H.W.,MARKETING MANAGEMENT: CASES FROM EMERGING COUNTRIES. BRAZIL GHANA ISRAEL WOR+45 ADMIN PERS/REL ATTIT HABITAT WEALTH...ANTHOL 20 ARGEN CASEBOOK. PAGE 17 F0332
MGT ECO/UNDEV PROB/SOLV MARKET

B66
US SENATE COMM GOVT OPERATIONS,HEARINGS BEFORE SUBCOMMITTEE ON FOREIGN AID EXPENDITURES: POPULATION CRISIS VOLUMES 1-5 JUNE-SEPT 1965. STRATA ECO/UNDEV PLAN TEC/DEV EDU/PROP ATTIT HEALTH ...GEOG CHARTS 20 CONGRESS BIRTH/CON CASEBOOK. PAGE 138 F2729
ECO/DEV CENSUS FAM CONTROL

CASEY R.G. F0425

CASSEL G. F0426

CASSELL F. F0427,F0428

CASTE....SEE INDIA + STRATA

CASTILLO C.M. F0429

CASTRO/F....FIDEL CASTRO

B59
NUNEZ JIMENEZ A.,LA LIBERACION DE LAS ISLAS. CUBA L/A+17C USA+45 LAW CHIEF PLAN DIPLOM FOR/AID OWN WEALTH 20 CASTRO/F. PAGE 99 F1945
AGRI REV ECO/UNDEV NAT/G

S67
ALEXANDER R.J.,"'THIRD FORCE' IN WORLD COMMUNISM?" CHINA/COM CUBA USSR INT/ORG DIPLOM TASK INGP/REL ATTIT PWR 20 CASTRO/F. PAGE 3 F0060
CHIEF MARXISM LEAD REV

S67
GONZALEZ M.P.,"CUBA, UNA REVOLUCION EN MARCHA." CUBA L/A+17C USA+45 VIETNAM ECO/UNDEV FORCES DIPLOM DOMIN...POLICY MARXIST NAT/COMP CASTRO/F. PAGE 48 F0946
REV NAT/G COLONIAL SOVEREIGN

CATER D. F0466

CATH....ROMAN CATHOLIC

B27
BELLOC H.,THE SERVILE STATE (1912) (3RD ED.). PRUSSIA UK CULTURE STRATA INDUS NAT/G ECO/TAC CONTROL LEAD SUFF DISCRIM EQUILIB ORD/FREE WEALTH 20. PAGE 12 F0237
WORKER CAP/ISM DOMIN CATH

B64
CEPEDE M.,POPULATION AND FOOD. USA+45 STRUCT ECO/UNDEV FAM PLAN TEC/DEV FOR/AID CONTROL...CATH SOC TREND 19/20. PAGE 22 F0436
FUT GEOG AGRI CENSUS

B67
WILLIAMS E.J.,LATIN AMERICAN CHRISTIAN DEMOCRATIC PARTIES. L/A+17C FAM LABOR FORCES...CATH TREND BIBLIOG 20. PAGE 147 F2890
POL/PAR GP/COMP CATHISM ALL/VALS

CATHISM....ROMAN CATHOLICISM

B47
BOWEN R.H.,GERMAN THEORIES OF THE CORPORATIVE STATE, WITH SPECIAL REFERENCES TO THE PERIOD 1870-1919. GERMANY INDUS LG/CO CATHISM SOCISM...SOC 18/20. PAGE 17 F0328
IDEA/COMP CENTRAL NAT/G POLICY

B58
PAYNO M.,LA REFORMA SOCIAL EN ESPANA Y MEXICO. SPAIN ECO/TAC TAX LOBBY COERCE REV OWN CATHISM 19/20 MEXIC/AMER. PAGE 104 F2043
SECT NAT/G LAW ELITES

B61
LENSKI G.,THE RELIGIOUS FACTOR: A SOCIOLOGICAL STUDY OF RELIGION'S IMPACT ON POLITICS, ECONOMICS, AND FAMILY LIFE. FAM PROF/ORG EDU/PROP ROLE CATHISM ...INT SAMP MUNICH. PAGE 78 F1524
SECT GP/REL

B63
LEWIS G.K.,PUERTO RICO: FREEDOM AND POWER IN THE CARIBBEAN. PUERT/RICO USA+45 CULTURE STRUCT INDUS POL/PAR WORKER EDU/PROP CATHISM 20. PAGE 79 F1548
ECO/UNDEV COLONIAL NAT/LISM GEOG

B66
FORD P.,CARDINAL MORAN AND THE A. L. P. NAT/G POL/PAR SECT DELIB/GP LOBBY REV CHOOSE ORD/FREE MARXISM 19/20 AUSTRAL PROTESTANT LABOR/PAR. PAGE 42 F0825
CATHISM SOCISM LABOR SOCIETY

B66
MUNBY D.,ECONOMIC GROWTH IN WORLD PERSPECTIVE. AFR WOR+45 SOCIETY INDUS PLAN TEC/DEV ECO/TAC FOR/AID INT/TRADE COST CATHISM...ANTHOL 20 EUROPE/W CHURCH/STA. PAGE 95 F1859
SECT ECO/UNDEV ECO/DEV

B67
BROMKE A.,POLAND'S POLITICS: IDEALISM VS. REALISM. COM GERMANY POLAND RUSSIA USSR POL/PAR CATHISM ...BIBLIOG 19/20. PAGE 19 F0360
NAT/G DIPLOM MARXISM

B67
PIKE F.B.,FREEDOM AND REFORM IN LATIN AMERICA. BRAZIL URUGUAY CONSTN CULTURE SECT DIPLOM EDU/PROP PARTIC DRIVE ALL/VALS CATHISM...GEOG ANTHOL BIBLIOG REFORMERS BOLIV. PAGE 106 F2086
L/A+17C ORD/FREE ECO/UNDEV REV

B67
WILLIAMS E.J.,LATIN AMERICAN CHRISTIAN DEMOCRATIC PARTIES. L/A+17C FAM LABOR FORCES...CATH TREND BIBLIOG 20. PAGE 147 F2890
POL/PAR GP/COMP CATHISM ALL/VALS

S67
RAMA C.M.,"PASADO Y PRESENTE DE LA RELIGION EN AMERICA LATINA." L/A+17C ELITES SOCIETY STRATA MARXISM...STAT WORSHIP PROTESTANT. PAGE 109 F2139
SECT CATHISM STRUCT NAT/COMP

S67
STYCOS J.M.,"POLITICS AND POPULATION CONTROL IN LATIN AMERICA." USA+45 FAM NAT/G GP/REL AGE/C ATTIT CATHISM MARXISM...POLICY UN WHO. PAGE 127 F2509
PLAN CENSUS CONTROL L/A+17C

B86
O'CONNOR T.P.,THE PARNELL MOVEMENT: WITH A SKETCH OF IRISH PARTIES FROM 1843. IRELAND UK USA-45 LEGIS WORKER ECO/TAC COERCE CRIME REV CHOOSE ORD/FREE CATHISM LAISSEZ...SOC 19/20 PARLIAMENT PARNELL/CS LAND/LEAG. PAGE 100 F1957
LEAD DOMIN POL/PAR POLICY

CATHOLICISM....SEE CATH, CATHISM

CATTELL D.T. F0430

CAUCUS....SEE PARL/PROC

CAUGHEY R.R. F1060

CAWELTI J.G. F1772

CECIL C.O. F0431

CED....COMMITTEE FOR ECONOMIC DEVELOPMENT

CEFKIN J.L. F0432

CENSORSHIP....SEE EDU/PROP

CENSUS....POPULATION ENUMERATION

N
US SUPERINTENDENT OF DOCUMENTS,CENSUS PUBLICATIONS (PRICE LIST 70). AGRI CONSTRUC DIST/IND FINAN LOC/G NAT/G PROVS INT/TRADE APPORT INCOME. PAGE 140 F2751
BIBLIOG/A CENSUS STAT USA+45

N19
MEZERIK A.G.,ECONOMIC AID FOR UNDERDEVELOPED COUNTRIES (PAMPHLET). AFR USSR WOR+45 FINAN LG/CO DELIB/GP NUC/PWR...GEOG CENSUS CHARTS 20 UN THIRD/WRLD. PAGE 90 F1775
FOR/AID ECO/UNDEV DIPLOM POLICY

N19
MUSHKIN S.J.,LOCAL SCHOOL EXPENDITURES: 1970 PROJECTIONS (PAMPHLET). FUT USA+45 CONSTRUC FINAN PROVS EDU/PROP COST...GEOG CENSUS PREDICT CHARTS SIMUL 20. PAGE 95 F1871
LOC/G SCHOOL BUDGET

B20
BUCK S.J.,THE AGRARIAN CRUSADE: A CHRONICLE OF THE FARMER IN POLITICS. USA-45 INDUS PROB/SOLV PWR WEALTH...GEOG CENSUS 19/20 GREENBACK GRANGE SILVER. PAGE 20 F0381
AGRI POPULISM VOL/ASSN POL/PAR

S41
MUKERJEE R.,"POPULATION THEORY AND POLITICS (BMR)" WOR-45 NAT/G PLAN PROB/SOLV ECO/TAC INT/TRADE CONTROL WAR PEACE...CENSUS 20 BIRTH/CON RESOURCE/N. PAGE 94 F1854
GEOG OPTIMAL CONCPT

S53
HANSER P.M.,"EXPLODING POPULATIONS: INTERNATIONAL AND REGIONAL ASPECTS." AFR S/ASIA ECO/TAC WEAPON BIO/SOC LOVE ORD/FREE...NEW/IDEA CENSUS TOT/POP 20. PAGE 55 F1069
ECO/UNDEV GEOG

B54
WILLIAMSON H.F.,ECONOMIC DEVELOPMENT - PRINCIPLES AND PATTERNS. INDIA KOREA CULTURE ECO/DEV ECO/UNDEV TEC/DEV...CENSUS NAT/COMP FOR/TRADE 20 CHINJAP MEXIC/AMER RESOURCE/N. PAGE 147 F2895
ECO/TAC GEOG LABOR

S56
SPENGLER J.J.,"POPULATION THREATENS PROSPERITY" (BMR)" WOR+45 SOCIETY FINAN RATION COST INCOME ...SOC CHARTS 20 RESOURCE/N. PAGE 124 F2451
CENSUS GEOG WEALTH TREND

B57
DRUCKER P.F.,AMERICA'S NEXT TWENTY YEARS. USA+45 DIST/IND ACADEM SCHOOL DIPLOM ECO/TAC AUTOMAT HABITAT HEALTH...SOC/WK TREND MUNICH 20 URBAN/RNWL PUB/TRANS. PAGE 34 F0667
WORKER FOR/AID CENSUS GEOG

S57
VERNON R.,"PRODUCTION AND DISTRIBUTION IN THE LARGE METROPOLIS" (BMR)" USA+45 PROC/MFG ECO/TAC HABITAT ...CENSUS TREND MUNICH 20. PAGE 141 F2779
PRODUC DIST/IND PROB/SOLV

B58
BANCROFT G.,THE AMERICAN LABOR FORCE: ITS GROWTH AND CHANGING COMPOSITION. FUT USA+45 USA-45 ECO/DEV INDUS WORKER...GEOG CHARTS 19/20. PAGE 9 F0170
LABOR STAT TREND CENSUS

B58
BROWN B.,INCOME TRENDS IN THE UNITED STATES THROUGH 1975. USA+45 NAT/G WEALTH...GEOG CENSUS PREDICT CHARTS METH 20. PAGE 19 F0366
STAT INCOME TREND TAX

B58
CLAUNCH J.M.,THE PROBLEM OF GOVERNMENT IN METROPOLITAN AREAS. CULTURE INDUS POL/PAR PLAN REGION GP/REL...CENSUS ANTHOL MUNICH 20. PAGE 25 F0486
PROB/SOLV SOC

B58
COALE A.J.,POPULATION GROWTH AND ECONOMIC DEVELOPMENT IN LOW-INCOME COUNTRIES: A CASE STUDY OF INDIA'S PROSPECTS. INDIA AGRI WORKER INCOME AGE WEALTH...CHARTS 20 MEXIC/AMER. PAGE 25 F0495
ECO/UNDEV GEOG CENSUS SEX

B58
INTERNATIONAL ECONOMIC ASSN,ECONOMICS OF INTERNATIONAL MIGRATION. WOR+45 WOR-45 ECO/UNDEV FINAN NAT/G REGION...NAT/COMP METH 20. PAGE 65 F1275
CENSUS GEOG DIPLOM ECO/TAC

L58
TRAGER F.N.,"A SELECTED AND ANNOTATED BIBLIOGRAPHY ON ECONOMIC DEVELOPMENT, 1953-1957." WOR+45 AGRI FINAN INDUS MARKET LABOR WORKER PLAN INT/TRADE PRODUC...CENSUS MUNICH. PAGE 131 F2583
BIBLIOG/A ECO/UNDEV ECO/DEV

S58
SCHULZE R.O.,"THE ROLE OF ECONOMIC DOMINANTS IN COMMUNITY POWER STRUCTURE." ECO/TAC ROUTINE ATTIT OBJECTIVE...SOC RECORD CENSUS. PAGE 118 F2319
SOCIETY STRUCT PROB/SOLV

S58
THOMAS D.S.,"AGE AND ECONOMIC DIFFERENTIALS IN INTERSTATE MIGRATION." SEX...GEOG SAMP/SIZ TREND CON/ANAL CHARTS BIBLIOG. PAGE 130 F2560
AGE WEALTH HABITAT CENSUS

B59
BLACK J.D.,ECONOMICS FOR AGRICULTURE. USA+45 EXTR/IND FAM WORKER ACT/RES PLAN PRICE EATING INCOME...CENSUS BIBLIOG 20. PAGE 15 F0291
AGRI ECO/TAC MARKET POLICY

B59
MAYER H.M.,READINGS IN URBAN GEOGRAPHY. WOR+45 SOCIETY DIST/IND INDUS MARKET HABITAT...CLASSIF CENSUS CHARTS ANTHOL MUNICH 20 WATER. PAGE 87 F1706
GEOG STRUCT

B60
ASPREMONT-LYNDEN H.,RAPPORT SUR L'ADMINISTRATION BELGE DU RUANDA-URUNDI PENDANT L'ANNEE 1959. BELGIUM RWANDA AGRI INDUS DIPLOM ECO/TAC INT/TRADE DOMIN ADMIN RACE/REL...GEOG CENSUS 20 UN. PAGE 7 F0132
AFR COLONIAL ECO/UNDEV INT/ORG

B60
BATOR F.M.,QUESTION OF GOVERNMENT SPENDING. USA+45 DIST/IND FINAN BAL/PAY...STAT CENSUS CHARTS CONGRESS 20. PAGE 11 F0210 — ECO/DEV

B60
GONZALEZ NAVARRO M.,LA COLONIZACION EN MEXICO, 1877-1910. AGRI NAT/G PLAN PROB/SOLV INCOME ...POLICY JURID CENSUS 19/20 MEXIC/AMER MIGRATION. PAGE 48 F0947 — ECO/UNDEV GEOG HABITAT COLONIAL

B60
MC CLELLAN G.S.,INDIA. AFR CHINA/COM INDIA CONSTN ELITES STRATA AGRI POL/PAR FOR/AID ARMS/CONT REV MARXISM...CENSUS BIBLIOG 20 GANDHI/M NEHRU/J. PAGE 87 F1712 — DIPLOM NAT/G SOCIETY ECO/UNDEV

B60
PENNSYLVANIA ECONOMY LEAGUE,URBAN RENEWAL IMPACT STUDY: ADMINISTRATIVE-LEGAL-FISCAL. USA+45 FINAN LOC/G NEIGH ADMIN EFFICIENCY...CENSUS CHARTS MUNICH 20 PENNSYLVAN. PAGE 105 F2059 — PLAN BUDGET ADJUD

B60
THE ECONOMIST (LONDON),THE COMMONWEALTH AND EUROPE. EUR+WWI WOR+45 AGRI FINAN INCOME...STAT CENSUS CHARTS CMN/WLTH EEC. PAGE 129 F2550 — INT/TRADE INDUS INT/ORG NAT/COMP

B61
BAUER P.T.,INDIAN ECONOMIC POLICY AND DEVELOPMENT. INDIA STRATA AGRI FINAN POL/PAR BUDGET FOR/AID GOV/REL EFFICIENCY...CENSUS 20. PAGE 11 F0216 — ECO/UNDEV ECO/TAC POLICY PLAN

B61
FLINN M.W.,AN ECONOMIC AND SOCIAL HISTORY OF BRITAIN, 1066-1939. UK LAW STRATA STRUCT AGRI DIST/IND INDUS WORKER INT/TRADE WAR...CENSUS 11/20. PAGE 42 F0811 — SOCIETY SOC

B61
SCHNAPPER B.,LA POLITIQUE ET LE COMMERCE FRANCAIS DANS LE GOLFE DE GUINEE DE 1838 A 1871. FRANCE GUINEA UK SEA EXTR/IND NAT/G DELIB/GP LEGIS ADMIN ORD/FREE...POLICY GEOG CENSUS CHARTS BIBLIOG 19. PAGE 117 F2303 — COLONIAL INT/TRADE DOMIN AFR

B62
HEILBRONER R.L.,THE MAKING OF ECONOMIC SOCIETY. FUT WOR-45 SOCIETY STRATA ECO/DEV ECO/UNDEV ECO/TAC LEGIT ROUTINE...SOC RECORD REC/INT KNO/TEST CENSUS STERTYP GEN/LAWS. PAGE 58 F1136 — CAP/ISM SOCISM

B62
JORDAN A.A. JR.,FOREIGN AID AND THE DEFENSE OF SOUTHEAST ASIA. PAKISTAN VIETNAM/S FINAN PLAN BUDGET ECO/TAC DETER WAR ORD/FREE...POLICY DECISION CENSUS CHARTS BIBLIOG 20. PAGE 68 F1341 — FOR/AID S/ASIA FORCES ECO/UNDEV

B62
KAUTSKY J.H.,POLITICAL CHANGE IN UNDERDEVELOPED COUNTRIES: NATIONALISM AND COMMUNISM. WOR+45 AGRI TEC/DEV EDU/PROP ATTIT...POLICY METH/CNCPT STYLE INT QU CENSUS TREND SOC/EXP GEN/LAWS 20. PAGE 69 F1365 — ECO/UNDEV SOCIETY CAP/ISM REV

B62
LEVENSTEIN A.,WHY PEOPLE WORK; CHANGING INCENTIVES IN A TROUBLED WORLD. USA+45 SOCIETY PROB/SOLV TEC/DEV EDU/PROP ADJUST...CENSUS BIBLIOG 20. PAGE 79 F1538 — DRIVE WORKER ECO/DEV ANOMIE

S62
ADISESHIAN M.,"EDUCATION AND DEVELOPMENT." FUT WOR+45 SOCIETY ACT/RES INT/TRADE EDU/PROP KNOWL SKILL WEALTH...POLICY CONCPT CONT/OBS CENSUS CHARTS TOT/POP VAL/FREE APPLIC FAO FOR/TRADE 20. PAGE 2 F0041 — SCHOOL ECO/UNDEV

B63
BARNETT H.J.,SCARCITY AND GROWTH: THE ECONOMICS OF NATURAL RESOURCE AVAILABILITY. FUT WOR+45 AGRI INDUS PROB/SOLV TEC/DEV CONTROL PRODUC...SOC/WK IDEA/COMP METH/COMP SIMUL 20 RESOURCE/N MALTHUS RICARDO/D MILL/JS DARWIN/C. PAGE 10 F0191 — DEMAND HABITAT CENSUS GEOG

B63
BRAYBROOKE D.,A STRATEGY OF DECISION: POLICY EVALUATION AS A SOCIAL PROCESS. UNIV ELITES OP/RES DOMIN CONFER FEEDBACK CONSEN PLURISM...CONCPT CENSUS. PAGE 18 F0343 — DECISION POLICY CONTROL

B63
GEERTZ C.,PEDDLERS AND PRINCES: SOCIAL DEVELOPMENT AND ECONOMIC CHANGE IN TWO INDONESIAN TOWNS. S/ASIA CULTURE SOCIETY STRATA FACE/GP CREATE TEC/DEV ECO/TAC ORD/FREE WEALTH...OBS INT CENSUS CHARTS WORK TOT/POP METH/GP TERR/GP VAL/FREE 20 MUNICH. PAGE 47 F0913 — ECO/UNDEV SOC ELITES INDONESIA

B64
CEPEDE M.,POPULATION AND FOOD. USA+45 STRUCT ECO/UNDEV FAM PLAN TEC/DEV FOR/AID CONTROL...CATH SOC TREND 19/20. PAGE 22 F0436 — FUT GEOG AGRI CENSUS

B64
FRIEDMANN J.,REGIONAL DEVELOPMENT AND PLANNING: A READER. AGRI MARKET NAT/G ECO/TAC INCOME...GEOG STAT CENSUS CHARTS ANTHOL BIBLIOG MUNICH 20 OPEN/SPACE. PAGE 44 F0863 — PLAN REGION INDUS ECO/DEV

B64
RESOURCES FOR THE FUTURE,URBAN AND REGIONAL STUDIES AT US UNIVERSITIES: A REPORT BASED ON A 1963 SURVEY OF URBAN AND REGIONAL RESEARCH. USA+45 SOCIETY CONSTRUC DIST/IND ACADEM NAT/G ACT/RES ECO/TAC ...CENSUS IDEA/COMP MUNICH. PAGE 111 F2179 — BIBLIOG/A REGION PLAN

B64
TAEUBER I.B.,POPULATION TRENDS IN THE UNITED STATES: 1900 TO 1960. USA+45 USA-45 PROVS INCOME AGE...SOC TIME/SEQ TREND CHARTS MUNICH TIME 20 NEGRO. PAGE 128 F2522 — CENSUS GEOG STRATA STRUCT

B64
WRIGHT G.,RURAL REVOLUTION IN FRANCE: THE PEASANTRY IN THE TWENTIETH CENTURY. EUR+WWI MOD/EUR LAW CULTURE AGRI POL/PAR DELIB/GP LEGIS ECO/TAC EDU/PROP COERCE CHOOSE ATTIT RIGID/FLEX HEALTH ...STAT CENSUS CHARTS VAL/FREE 20. PAGE 149 F2932 — PWR STRATA FRANCE REV

B65
AMERICAN ECONOMIC ASSOCIATION,INDEX OF ECONOMIC JOURNALS 1886-1965 (7 VOLS.). UK USA+45 USA-45 AGRI FINAN PLAN ECO/TAC INT/TRADE ADMIN...STAT CENSUS 19/20. PAGE 5 F0087 — BIBLIOG WRITING INDUS

B65
BOLLENS J.C.,THE METROPOLIS: ITS PEOPLE, POLITICS, AND ECONOMIC LIFE. USA+45 PLAN PROB/SOLV PERS/REL PWR...DECISION GEOG CENSUS TREND CON/ANAL MUNICH 20 NEWYORK/C LOS/ANG SAN/FRAN CHICAGO PHILADELPH. PAGE 16 F0309 — HABITAT SOC LOC/G

B65
FRIEDLANDER S.L.,LABOR MIGRATION AND ECONOMIC GROWTH: A CASE STUDY OF PUERTO RICO. PUERT/RICO AGRI WORKER PLAN PROB/SOLV...ECOMETRIC STAT PREDICT CHARTS HYPO/EXP SIMUL 20. PAGE 44 F0858 — CENSUS GEOG ECO/UNDEV WEALTH

B65
HLA MYINT U.,THE ECONOMICS OF THE DEVELOPING COUNTRIES. USA+45 WOR+45 AGRI FINAN NAT/G INT/TRADE ...CLASSIF CENSUS TREND NAT/COMP SIMUL GEN/LAWS. PAGE 60 F1180 — ECO/UNDEV FOR/AID GEOG

B65
HOLLER J.E.,POPULATION TRENDS AND ECONOMIC DEVELOPMENT IN THE FAR EAST (PAMPHLET). KOREA S/ASIA AGRI INDUS DELIB/GP PROB/SOLV RATIONAL ...POLICY CHARTS BIBLIOG 20 OUTER/MONG CHINJAP HONG/KONG. PAGE 61 F1197 — CENSUS TREND ECO/UNDEV ASIA

B65
MUSHKIN S.J.,PROPERTY TAXES: THE 1970 OUTLOOK (PAMPHLET). FUT USA+45 ECO/DEV MARKET PROVS PLAN ...PROBABIL STAT CENSUS PREDICT CHARTS METH 20. PAGE 95 F1872 — TAX OWN FINAN LOC/G

B65
NARASIMHAN V.K.,DEMOCRACY AND MIXED ECONOMY. INDIA CONTROL...CENSUS IDEA/COMP 20. PAGE 96 F1891 — CAP/ISM MARXISM ORD/FREE NEW/LIB

B65
WILKINSON T.O.,THE URBANIZATION OF JAPANESE LABOR, 1868-1955. AGRI PROC/MFG CAP/ISM PRODUC PROFIT ...SOC CLASSIF CENSUS CHARTS MUNICH 19/20 CHINJAP. PAGE 146 F2887 — LABOR INDUS GEOG

B65
WINT G.,ASIA: A HANDBOOK. ASIA COM INDIA USSR CULTURE INTELL NAT/G...GEOG STAT CENSUS NAT/COMP WORSHIP 20 TREATY CHINJAP. PAGE 148 F2907 — DIPLOM SOC

S65
SCHROEDER G.,"LABOR PLANNING IN THE USSR." COM USSR ECO/DEV INDUS SCHOOL PRODUC WEALTH...PREDICT TIME/SEQ TREND TIME 20. PAGE 117 F2313 — WORKER PLAN CENSUS

B66
BEN-PORATH Y.,THE ARAB LABOR FORCE IN ISRAEL. ISLAM ISRAEL AGRI INDUS SCHOOL CAP/ISM PAY DEMAND...GEOG REGRESS STAT CHARTS 20 ARABS. PAGE 13 F0245 — WORKER CENSUS GP/REL STRUCT

B66
ODEGARD P.H.,POLITICAL POWER AND SOCIAL CHANGE. UNIV NAT/G CREATE ALL/IDEOS...POLICY GEOG SOC CENSUS TREND. PAGE 100 F1962 — PWR TEC/DEV IDEA/COMP

B66
THOMPSON J.H.,MODERNIZATION OF THE ARAB WORLD. FUT ISRAEL STRUCT ECO/UNDEV DIPLOM INGP/REL ATTIT ...CENSUS ANTHOL 20 ARABS. PAGE 130 F2565 — ADJUST ISLAM PROB/SOLV NAT/COMP

B66
US SENATE COMM GOVT OPERATIONS,HEARINGS BEFORE SUBCOMMITTEE ON FOREIGN AID EXPENDITURES: POPULATION CRISIS VOLUMES 1-5 JUNE-SEPT 1965. STRATA ECO/UNDEV PLAN TEC/DEV EDU/PROP ATTIT HEALTH ...GEOG CHARTS 20 CONGRESS BIRTH/CON CASEBOOK. PAGE 138 F2729 — ECO/DEV CENSUS FAM CONTROL

B67
BIRMINGHAM W.,A STUDY OF CONTEMPORARY GHANA VOL. I: SOME ASPECTS OF SOCIAL STRUCTURE. AFR GHANA AGRI FAM SECT PLAN EDU/PROP MARRIAGE OWN...POLICY STAT CHARTS MUNICH 20. PAGE 15 F0287 — SOCIETY STRUCT CENSUS ECO/UNDEV

B67
BLAIR P.W.,THE MINISTATE DILEMMA. WOR+45 AGREE COLONIAL ORD/FREE...GEOG CHARTS MUNICH LEAGUE/NAT — INT/ORG NAT/G

UN. PAGE 15 F0294 — CENSUS

B67
US SENATE COMM ON FOREIGN REL,FOREIGN ASSISTANCE ACT OF 1967. VIETNAM WOR+45 DELIB/GP CONFER CONTROL WAR WEAPON BAL/PAY...CENSUS CHARTS SENATE. PAGE 139 F2744 — FOR/AID LAW DIPLOM POLICY

L67
MIXON J.,"JANE JACOBS AND THE LAW - ZONING FOR DIVERSITY EXAMINED." FUT USA+45 CONSTN NEIGH PROB/SOLV CONTROL CT/SYS PARTIC ATTIT...POLICY CENSUS METH/COMP MUNICH. PAGE 92 F1810 — IDEA/COMP PLAN LAW

L67
ZEIDBERG L.D.,"THE NASHVILLE AIR POLLUTION STUDY" (PARTS V-VII)" USA+45 PLAN AGE HEALTH...GEOG STAT CENSUS SAMP/SIZ CHARTS BIBLIOG MUNICH. PAGE 150 F2962 — DEATH HABITAT AIR BIO/SOC

S67
MENCHER S.,"THE PROBLEM OF MEASURING POVERTY." UNIV USA+45 STRATA PROB/SOLV...NEW/IDEA METH/COMP 20. PAGE 89 F1755 — WEALTH CENSUS STAT GEN/LAWS

S67
STYCOS J.M.,"POLITICS AND POPULATION CONTROL IN LATIN AMERICA." USA+45 FAM NAT/G GP/REL AGE/C ATTIT CATHISM MARXISM...POLICY UN WHO. PAGE 127 F2509 — PLAN CENSUS CONTROL L/A+17C

S67
WALLACE H.M.,"AVAILABILITY AND USEFULNESS OF SELECTED HEALTH AND SOCIOECONOMIC DATA FOR COMMUNITY PLANNING." NEIGH EFFICIENCY...CORREL STAT CENSUS CHARTS. PAGE 142 F2806 — HEALTH PLAN SOC/WK HEAL

CENTER/PAR....CENTER PARTY (ALL NATIONS)

CENTO....CENTRAL TREATY ORGANIZATION

S61
VALLET R.,"IRAN: KEY TO THE MIDDLE EAST." COM IRAQ ISLAM KUWAIT LEBANON SAUDI/ARAB TURKEY ELITES SOCIETY INDUS PROC/MFG POL/PAR TOP/EX PLAN BAL/PWR DIPLOM ECO/TAC ALL/VALS...TREND FOR/TRADE CENTO 20. PAGE 140 F2760 — NAT/G ECO/UNDEV IRAN

B67
MACCLOSKEY M.,PACTS FOR PEACE: UN, NATO, SEATO, CENTO, OAS. WOR+45 PLAN DIPLOM CONTROL PEACE ORD/FREE...ORG/CHARTS UN NATO SEATO OAS CENTO. PAGE 83 F1623 — FORCES INT/ORG LEAD POLICY

CENTRAL AFRICAN REPUBLIC....SEE CENTRL/AFR

CENTRAL INTELLIGENCE AGENCY....SEE CIA

CENTRAL TREATY ORGANIZATION....SEE CENTO

CENTRAL....CENTRALIZATION

N
NEW JERSEY STATE OF,SECOND REPORT TO GOVERNOR, SENATE, ASSEMBLY BY UNIFORM COMMERCIAL CODE STUDY COMMISSION. USA+45 INDUS LOC/G NAT/G PROF/ORG CONSULT ACT/RES LEGIT CT/SYS ATTIT NEW/JERSEY. PAGE 98 F1920 — LAW FINAN CENTRAL PROVS

B03
GRIFFIN A.P.C.,LISTS PUBLISHED 1902-03: GOVERNMENT OWNERSHIP OF RAILROADS (PAMPHLET). USA-45 LAW NAT/G RATION GOV/REL CENTRAL SOCISM...POLICY 19/20. PAGE 51 F0998 — BIBLIOG DIST/IND CONTROL ADJUD

N19
ANDERSON J.,THE ORGANIZATION OF ECONOMIC STUDIES IN RELATION TO THE PROBLEMS OF GOVERNMENT (PAMPHLET). UK FINAN INDUS DELIB/GP PLAN PROB/SOLV ADMIN 20. PAGE 5 F0095 — ECO/TAC ACT/RES NAT/G CENTRAL

N19
CONGRESSIONAL QUARTERLY SERV,FEDERAL ECONOMIC POLICY 1945-1965 (PAMPHLET). USA+45 FINAN OP/RES BAL/PWR ECO/TAC TAX BAL/PAY CENTRAL COST WEALTH ...CHARTS 20. PAGE 27 F0525 — NAT/G ECO/DEV BUDGET POLICY

B42
DRUCKER P.F.,THE FUTURE OF INDUSTRIAL MAN; A CONSERVATIVE APPROACH. USA-45 LOC/G PLAN WAR CENTRAL RATIONAL TOTALISM ORD/FREE LAISSEZ ...PLURIST IDEA/COMP 19/20 HITLER/A. PAGE 34 F0664 — INDUS SOCIETY REGION PROB/SOLV

B46
DRUCKER P.F.,CONCEPT OF CORPORATION. LAW LABOR WORKER PRICE CONTROL LEAD GP/REL POLICY. PAGE 34 F0665 — LG/CO CENTRAL INGP/REL

B47
BOWEN R.H.,GERMAN THEORIES OF THE CORPORATIVE STATE, WITH SPECIAL REFERENCES TO THE PERIOD 1870-1919. GERMANY INDUS LG/CO CATHISM SOCISM...SOC 18/20. PAGE 17 F0328 — IDEA/COMP CENTRAL NAT/G POLICY

S48
HARDIN L.M.,"REFLECTIONS ON AGRICULTURAL POLICY FORMATION IN THE UNITED STATES." LEGIS PLAN BUDGET ECO/TAC LEAD CENTRAL...MGT SOC NEW/IDEA STAT FAO. PAGE 55 F1078 — AGRI POLICY ADMIN NEW/LIB

S49
SHEPHARD H.A.,"DEMOCRATIC CONTROL IN A LABOR UNION." FUT CONSTN STRUCT TEC/DEV LEAD PARTIC RACE/REL CENTRAL DRIVE HABITAT RECORD. PAGE 120 F2374 — LABOR MAJORIT CONTROL PWR

B50
MARX H.L.,THE WELFARE STATE. USA+45 USA-45 CHIEF CAP/ISM CENTRAL ORD/FREE LAISSEZ...SOC ANTHOL 20. PAGE 86 F1686 — ECO/DEV INDUS WEALTH WELF/ST

B52
GALBRAITH J.K.,AMERICAN CAPITALISM: THE CONCEPT OF COUNTERVAILING POWER. AFR FUT USA+45 FINAN PRICE CENTRAL INCOME PEACE WEALTH...POLICY DECISION 20. PAGE 45 F0881 — ECO/TAC CAP/ISM TREND NAT/G

B54
FRIEDMAN W.,THE PUBLIC CORPORATION: A COMPARATIVE SYMPOSIUM (UNIVERSITY OF TORONTO SCHOOL OF LAW COMPARATIVE LAW SERIES, VOL. I). AFR SWEDEN USA+45 INDUS INT/ORG NAT/G REGION CENTRAL FEDERAL...POLICY JURID IDEA/COMP NAT/COMP ANTHOL 20 MONOPOLY EUROPE. PAGE 44 F0861 — LAW SOCISM LG/CO OWN

B54
RECK D.,GOVERNMENT PURCHASING AND COMPETITION. USA+45 LEGIS CAP/ISM ECO/TAC GOV/REL CENTRAL ...POLICY 20 CONGRESS. PAGE 110 F2164 — NAT/G FINAN MGT COST

B55
O'CONNOR H.,THE EMPIRE OF OIL. USA+45 DIST/IND FINAN MARKET CAP/ISM TAX CONTROL...POLICY MARXIST BIBLIOG/A 20. PAGE 100 F1955 — EXTR/IND INT/TRADE CENTRAL NAT/G

S57
LEWIS E.G.,"PARLIAMENTARY CONTROL OF NATIONALIZED INDUSTRY IN FRANCE." FRANCE NAT/G DELIB/GP ACT/RES PLAN PROB/SOLV ECO/TAC DOMIN CENTRAL. PAGE 79 F1547 — PWR LEGIS INDUS CONTROL

B58
LESTER R.A.,AS UNIONS MATURE. POL/PAR BARGAIN LEAD PARTIC GP/REL CENTRAL...MAJORIT TIME/SEQ METH/COMP. PAGE 78 F1533 — LABOR INDUS POLICY MGT

B58
TAFT P.,CORRUPTION AND RACKETEERING IN THE LABOR MOVEMENT (PAMPHLET). ADMIN SANCTION CENTRAL ROLE WEALTH...POLICY CLASSIF. PAGE 128 F2525 — LABOR INGP/REL GP/REL CRIME

B59
HARTOG F.,EUROPEAN TRADE CYCLE POLICY. WORKER TAX PRICE WAR CENTRAL DEMAND...TREND CHARTS 20 UN. PAGE 56 F1103 — EQUILIB EUR+WWI INT/TRADE

B59
RAMANADHAM V.V.,PROBLEMS OF PUBLIC ENTERPRISE: THOUGHTS ON BRITISH EXPERIENCE. UK FINAN INDUS PLAN PRICE CENTRAL...POLICY 20. PAGE 109 F2140 — SOCISM LG/CO ECO/DEV GOV/REL

B60
ANGERS F.A.,ESSAI SUR LA CENTRALISATION: ANALYSE DES PRINCIPES ET PERSPECTIVES CANADIENNES. CANADA ECO/TAC CONTROL...SOC IDEA/COMP BIBLIOG 20. PAGE 6 F0105 — CENTRAL ADMIN

B60
ROPKE W.,A HUMANE ECONOMY. CULTURE ECO/DEV FINAN INDUS GP/REL CENTRAL WEALTH...GEOG SOC IDEA/COMP 20 EEC. PAGE 114 F2239 — ECO/TAC INT/ORG DIPLOM ORD/FREE

S60
POLLARD J.A.,"EMERGING PATTERNS OF CORPORATE GIVING." FINAN DELIB/GP PLAN EDU/PROP CENTRAL TREND. PAGE 107 F2098 — GIVE LG/CO ADMIN MGT

B61
ASCHHEIM J.,TECHNIQUES OF MONETARY CONTROL. UK USA+45 CONTROL WAR DEMAND INCOME WEALTH...TREND CHARTS 20 MONEY. PAGE 7 F0127 — FINAN MARKET BUDGET CENTRAL

B61
MACMAHON A.W.,DELEGATION AND AUTONOMY. INDIA STRUCT LEGIS BARGAIN BUDGET ECO/TAC LEGIT EXEC REPRESENT GOV/REL CENTRAL DEMAND EFFICIENCY PRODUC. PAGE 84 F1637 — ADMIN PLAN FEDERAL

B61
WESTON J.F.,THE ROLE OF MERGERS IN THE GROWTH OF LARGE FIRMS. USA+45 USA-45 LEGIS CONTROL...CONCPT STAT CHARTS 19/20. PAGE 145 F2862 — LG/CO CENTRAL INDUS FINAN

B62
CONGRES ECONOMISTES LANG FRAN,MONNAIE ET EXPANSION. AFR FRANCE PROB/SOLV BUDGET CENTRAL COST OPTIMAL PRODUC WEALTH 20. PAGE 27 F0524 — FINAN PLAN EUR+WWI

B62
DIMOCK M.E.,THE NEW AMERICAN POLITICAL ECONOMY: A SYNTHESIS OF POLITICS AND ECONOMICS. USA+45 FINAN LG/CO PLAN ADMIN REGION GP/REL CENTRAL MORAL 20. — FEDERAL ECO/TAC NAT/G

PAGE 33 F0642 — PARTIC

B62
HARRINGTON M.,THE RETAIL CLERKS. ECO/TAC LEAD PARTIC CHOOSE GP/REL INGP/REL CENTRAL POLICY. PAGE 55 F1087 — LABOR SERV/IND STRUCT DELIB/GP

L62
BELSHAW D.G.R.,"PUBLIC INVESTMENT IN AGRICULTURE AND ECONOMIC DEVELOPMENT OF UGANDA" UGANDA AGRI INDUS R+D ECO/TAC RATION TAX PAY COLONIAL 20 WORLD/BANK. PAGE 13 F0242 — ECO/UNDEV PLAN ADMIN CENTRAL

B64
LISKA G.,EUROPE ASCENDANT. EUR+WWI ECO/DEV FORCES INT/TRADE MARXISM 20 EEC. PAGE 81 F1579 — DIPLOM BAL/PWR TARIFFS CENTRAL

B64
TINBERGEN J.,CENTRAL PLANNING. COM INTELL ECO/DEV ECO/UNDEV FINAN INT/ORG PROB/SOLV ECO/TAC CONTROL EXEC ROUTINE DECISION. PAGE 130 F2576 — PLAN INDUS MGT CENTRAL

S64
DOE J.F.,"TROPICAL AFRICAN CONTRIBUTIONS TO FEDERAL FINANCE." AFR NAT/G PROVS CENTRAL RIGID/FLEX PWR WEALTH...STAT VAL/FREE 20 CMN/WLTH. PAGE 33 F0650 — FINAN ECO/TAC

B65
CERNY K.H.,NATO IN QUEST OF COHESION* A CONFRONTATION OF VIEWPOINTS. COM EUR+WWI USA+45 FORCES LEAD REGION DETER...ANTHOL NATO. PAGE 22 F0438 — CENTRAL NUC/PWR VOL/ASSN

B65
HERRICK B.H.,URBAN MIGRATION AND ECONOMIC DEVELOPMENT IN CHILE. CHILE AGRI INDUS LABOR NAT/G CENTRAL PRODUC...STAT SAMP CHARTS BIBLIOG/A MUNICH 20 MIGRATION. PAGE 59 F1156 — HABITAT GEOG ECO/UNDEV

B65
KASER M.,COMECON* INTEGRATION PROBLEMS OF THE PLANNED ECONOMIES. INT/ORG TEC/DEV INT/TRADE PRICE ADMIN ADJUST CENTRAL...STAT TIME/SEQ ORG/CHARTS COMECON. PAGE 69 F1359 — PLAN ECO/DEV COM REGION

B65
PARRIS H.W.,GOVERNMENT AND THE RAILWAYS IN NINETEENTH-CENTURY BRITAIN. UK DELIB/GP CONTROL LEAD CENTRAL 19 RAILROAD. PAGE 103 F2029 — DIST/IND NAT/G PLAN GP/REL

B65
PINCUS J.A.,ECONOMIC AID AND INTERNATIONAL COST SHARING* A RAND CORPORATION RESEARCH STUDY. INT/ORG BUDGET CENTRAL...ECOMETRIC MATH QUANT STAT SIMUL. PAGE 106 F2088 — ECO/UNDEV COST FOR/AID INT/TRADE

B65
RATNAM K.J.,COMMUNALISM AND THE POLITICAL PROCESS IN MALAYA. MALAYSIA WOR+45 ECO/UNDEV PARTIC CHOOSE REPRESENT GP/REL CENTRAL ATTIT...CHARTS WORSHIP 20. PAGE 109 F2152 — CONSTN GOV/REL REGION

B65
WATERSTON A.,DEVELOPMENT PLANNING* LESSONS OF EXPERIENCE. ECO/TAC CENTRAL...MGT QUANT BIBLIOG. PAGE 144 F2830 — ECO/UNDEV CREATE PLAN ADMIN

S65
HADDAD W.F.,"MR. SHRIVER AND THE SAVAGE POLITICS OF POVERTY" USA+45 LAW NAT/G DELIB/GP LEGIS GIVE LEAD CENTRAL PWR...SOC/WK CHARTS 20 CONGRESS POVRTY/WAR SHRIVER/S OEO. PAGE 53 F1028 — WEALTH GOV/REL CONTROL TOP/EX

S65
HAYTER T.,"FRENCH AID TO AFRICA* ITS SCOPE AND ACHIEVEMENTS." CULTURE ECO/TAC INT/TRADE ADMIN REGION CENTRAL FEDERAL LOVE PWR SOVEREIGN EEC. PAGE 57 F1127 — AFR FRANCE FOR/AID COLONIAL

S65
SOPER T.,"THE EEC AND AID TO AFRICA." FRANCE UK ECO/UNDEV INT/TRADE TARIFFS REGION ROUTINE CENTRAL DISCRIM...DECISION RECORD EEC. PAGE 124 F2443 — AFR FOR/AID COLONIAL

S65
TENDLER J.D.,"TECHNOLOGY AND ECONOMIC DEVELOPMENT* THE CASE OF HYDRO VS THERMAL POWER." CONSTRUC DIST/IND CREATE TEC/DEV INT/TRADE CENTRAL PWR SKILL WEALTH...MGT NAT/COMP ARGEN. PAGE 129 F2544 — BRAZIL INDUS ECO/UNDEV

S65
VAN DER HORST S.T.,"THE ECONOMICS OF DECENTRALISATION OF INDUSTRY." SOUTH/AFR ECO/DEV LG/CO AUTOMAT DISCRIM...POLICY MUNICH 20. PAGE 140 F2761 — PLAN INDUS CENTRAL TEC/DEV

S65
WHITE J.,"WEST GERMAN AID TO DEVELOPING COUNTRIES." AFR INT/ORG OP/RES GIVE CENTRAL ATTIT DRIVE...STAT NAT/COMP. PAGE 146 F2869 — GERMANY FOR/AID ECO/UNDEV CAP/ISM

B66
INGRAM J.C.,INTERNATIONAL ECONOMIC PROBLEMS. ECO/DEV ECO/UNDEV INDUS MARKET TEC/DEV TARIFFS BAL/PAY CENTRAL...POLICY 20 EEC. PAGE 64 F1265 — INT/TRADE INT/ORG FINAN

B66
LANDERS D.S.,RISE OF CAPITALISM. LABOR AUTOMAT GP/REL CENTRAL COST PROFIT...SOC CONCPT ANTHOL 19/20. PAGE 75 F1469 — CAP/ISM INDUS AGRI

B66
LONDON K.,EASTERN EUROPE IN TRANSITION. CHINA/COM USSR DOMIN COLONIAL CENTRAL RIGID/FLEX PWR...SOC ANTHOL 20. PAGE 82 F1597 — SOVEREIGN COM NAT/LISM DIPLOM

B66
RUBIN S.J.,THE CONSCIENCE OF THE RICH NATIONS: THE DEVELOPMENT ASSISTANCE COMMITTEE AND THE COMMON AID EFFORT. EUR+WWI USA+45 ECO/UNDEV INT/ORG NAT/G VOL/ASSN ECO/TAC INT/TRADE...OBS UN AID DEV/ASSIST IBRD OECD. PAGE 114 F2256 — FOR/AID ECO/DEV CONFER CENTRAL

S66
FELD W.,"EXTERNAL RELATIONS OF THE COMMON MARKET AND GROUP LEADERSHIP ATTITUDES IN THE MEMBER STATES." COM USA+45 ELITES AGRI NAT/G ATTIT...OBS EEC GATT. PAGE 40 F0776 — DIPLOM CENTRAL TARIFFS INT/TRADE

S66
FELD W.,"NATIONAL ECONOMIC INTEREST GROUPS AND POLICY FORMATION IN THE EEC." NAT/G POL/PAR REGION CENTRAL SOVEREIGN...INT NET/THEORY EEC. PAGE 40 F0777 — LOBBY ELITES DECISION

S66
NEWLYN W.T.,"MONEY MARKETS IN EAST AFRICA." AFR TANZANIA UGANDA UK DIPLOM CENTRAL 20. PAGE 98 F1923 — FINAN WEALTH BAL/PAY ECO/UNDEV

S66
POSEN G.S.,"RECENT TRENDS IN SOVIET ECONOMIC THOUGHT." USSR ECO/DEV PLAN CONTROL CENTRAL 20. PAGE 107 F2107 — ECO/TAC MARXISM INDUS PROFIT

B67
BREAK G.F.,INTERGOVERNMENTAL FISCAL RELATIONS IN THE UNITED STATES. USA+45 USA-45 DELIB/GP PLAN BUDGET TAX GOV/REL CENTRAL...TREND CHARTS MUNICH. PAGE 18 F0345 — LOC/G NAT/G PROVS FINAN

B67
ZALESKI E.,PLANNING REFORMS IN THE SOVIET UNION 1962-1966. COM USSR NAT/G CONFER CONTROL EFFICIENCY MARXISM...POLICY DECISION 20. PAGE 150 F2957 — ECO/DEV PLAN ADMIN CENTRAL

L67
MACDONALD R.M.,"COLLECTIVE BARGAINING IN THE POSTWAR PERIOD." WORKER PROB/SOLV ECO/TAC PARTIC RISK CENTRAL EFFICIENCY DRIVE WEALTH...TREND 20. PAGE 83 F1624 — LABOR INDUS BARGAIN CAP/ISM

S67
ANDERSON S.S.,"SOVIET RUSSIA AND THE TWO EUROPES." AFR USSR PROB/SOLV CENTRAL SOVEREIGN 20. PAGE 5 F0097 — DIPLOM POLICY MARXISM

S67
ASCH P.,"CONGLOMERATE MERGERS AND PUBLIC POLICY." USA+45 ECO/DEV LG/CO NAT/G ECO/TAC ADJUD CENTRAL 20. PAGE 7 F0126 — INDUS CAP/ISM BARGAIN

S67
GAUSE M.E.,"ELEMENTS OF FINANCE DEPARTMENT ORGANIZATION FOR SMALL GOVERNMENTAL UNITS." USA+45 PROB/SOLV CONTROL CENTRAL...METH MUNICH. PAGE 47 F0910 — ADMIN LOC/G FINAN

S67
JAVITS J.K.,"THE USE OF AMERICAN PLURALISM." USA+45 ECO/DEV BUDGET ADMIN ALL/IDEOS...DECISION TREND. PAGE 67 F1309 — CENTRAL ATTIT POLICY NAT/G

S67
LASLETT J.H.M.,"SOCIALISM AND THE AMERICAN LABOR MOVEMENT* SOME NEW REFLECTIONS." USA-45 VOL/ASSN LOBBY PARTIC CENTRAL ALL/VALS SOCISM...GP/COMP 20. PAGE 76 F1484 — LABOR ROUTINE ATTIT GP/REL

S67
MAJSTRENKO I.W.,"PROBLEMS CONFRONTING SOVIET AGRICULTURE." COM USSR ECO/DEV ECO/TAC EFFICIENCY OPTIMAL WEALTH MARXISM 20. PAGE 84 F1643 — AGRI PROB/SOLV CENTRAL TEC/DEV

S67
MANGLAPUS R.S.,"ASIAN REVOLUTION AND AMERICAN IDEOLOGY." USA+45 SOCIETY CAP/ISM DIPLOM ADJUST CENTRAL...NAT/COMP 20. PAGE 84 F1652 — REV POPULISM ATTIT ASIA

S67
RICHMAN B.M.,"SOVIET MANAGEMENT IN TRANSITION." USSR FINAN MARKET EX/STRUC PLAN PROB/SOLV TEC/DEV CONTROL LEAD CENTRAL EFFICIENCY...METH/COMP 20 REFORMERS. PAGE 111 F2186 — MGT MARXISM POLICY AUTHORIT

S67
SHISTER J.,"THE DIRECTION OF UNIONISM 1947-1967: THRUST OF DRIFT?" INDUS CENTRAL EFFICIENCY INCOME ATTIT SOCISM...POLICY TREND 20 AFL/CIO. PAGE 121 F2382 — LABOR PROF/ORG LEAD LAW

S67
TELLER A.,"AIR-POLLUTION ABATEMENT: ECONOMIC RATIONALITY AND REALITY." NAT/G DELIB/GP ECO/TAC GOV/REL CENTRAL EFFICIENCY HEALTH...CHARTS METH MUNICH. PAGE 129 F2543 — PROB/SOLV CONTROL COST AIR

S67
WEIL G.L.,"THE MERGER OF THE INSTITUTIONS OF THE EUROPEAN COMMUNITIES" EUR+WWI ECO/DEV INT/TRADE CONSEN PLURISM...DECISION MGT 20 EEC EURATOM ECSC TREATY. PAGE 145 F2847 ECO/TAC INT/ORG CENTRAL INT/LAW

S67
WILLIAMS C.,"REGIONAL MANAGEMENT OVERSEAS." USA+45 WOR+45 DIST/IND LG/CO EX/STRUC INT/TRADE TARIFFS ADMIN TASK CENTRAL. PAGE 147 F2889 MGT EUR+WWI ECO/DEV PLAN

S67
ZOETEWEIJ B.,"INCOME POLICIES ABROAD: AN INTERIM REPORT." NAT/G PROB/SOLV BARGAIN BUDGET PRICE RISK CENTRAL EFFICIENCY EQUILIB...MGT NAT/COMP 20. PAGE 150 F2967 METH/COMP INCOME POLICY LABOR

CENTRAL/AM....CENTRAL AMERICA

B64
CENTRO ESTUDIOS MONETARIOS LAT,PROBLEMAS DE PAGOS EN AMERICA LATINA. L/A+17C MARKET BUDGET ECO/TAC EFFICIENCY WEALTH 20 CENTRAL/AM. PAGE 22 F0434 FINAN INT/TRADE BAL/PAY ECO/UNDEV

CENTRL/AFR....CENTRAL AFRICAN REPUBLIC

B62
GREEN L.P.,DEVELOPMENT IN AFRICA. AFR CENTRL/AFR GHANA RHODESIA SOUTH/AFR AGRI PROC/MFG INT/TRADE DEMAND NAT/LISM PRODUC WEALTH...GEOG METH/CNCPT CHARTS BIBLIOG 20. PAGE 50 F0987 CULTURE ECO/UNDEV GOV/REL TREND

CENTRO ESTUDIOS MONETARIOS LAT F0433,F0434

CENTRO PARA EL DESARROLLO F0435

CEPEDE M. F0436

CERAMI C.A. F0437

CERMAK/AJ....ANTON J. CERMAK

CERNY K.H. F0438

CEWA....CEWA (AFRICAN TRIBE)

CEYLON....CEYLON

N
UNESCO,SOUTH ASIA SOCIAL SCIENCES ABSTRACTS. BURMA CEYLON INDIA S/ASIA PRESS...PSY 20. PAGE 132 F2608 BIBLIOG/A SOC

N
US LIBRARY OF CONGRESS,SOUTHERN ASIA ACCESSIONS LIST. BURMA CEYLON INDIA NEPAL PAKISTAN S/ASIA THAILAND AGRI INDUS SCHOOL WORKER...ART/METH GEOG HEAL PHIL/SCI LING 20. PAGE 137 F2710 BIBLIOG/A SOCIETY CULTURE ECO/UNDEV

B55
UN ECONOMIC COMN ASIA & FAR E,ECONOMIC SURVEY OF ASIA AND THE FAR EAST, 1954. AFGHANISTN CEYLON INDIA PHILIPPINE S/ASIA ECO/DEV FINAN INDUS INT/TRADE PRODUC WEALTH...STAT CHARTS 20 CHINJAP. PAGE 132 F2600 ECO/UNDEV PRICE NAT/COMP ASIA

B57
OLIVER H.M. JR.,ECONOMIC OPINION AND POLICY IN CEYLON. CEYLON FINAN POL/PAR WORKER INT/TRADE INCOME WEALTH...GEOG UNPLAN/INT BIBLIOG 20 CMN/WLTH. PAGE 101 F1987 ECO/UNDEV NAT/LISM POLICY COLONIAL

B58
JENNINGS I.,PROBLEMS OF THE NEW COMMONWEALTH. AFR CEYLON INDIA PAKISTAN S/ASIA ECO/UNDEV INT/ORG LOC/G DIPLOM ECO/TAC INT/TRADE COLONIAL RACE/REL DISCRIM 20 PARLIAMENT. PAGE 67 F1314 NAT/LISM NEUTRAL FOR/AID POL/PAR

B59
HICKS J.R.,ESSAYS IN WORLD ECONOMICS. AFR CEYLON NIGERIA WOR+45 SOCIETY ECO/DEV ORD/FREE WEALTH ...GEN/LAWS TOT/POP 20. PAGE 59 F1166 ECO/UNDEV ECO/TAC UK

B65
ONSLOW C.,ASIAN ECONOMIC DEVELOPMENT. BURMA CEYLON INDIA MALAYSIA PAKISTAN S/ASIA AGRI INDUS MARKET PROB/SOLV CAP/ISM FOR/AID INT/TRADE DEMAND WEALTH ...POLICY ANTHOL 20. PAGE 101 F1991 ECO/UNDEV ECO/TAC PLAN NAT/G

B66
DEBENKO E.,RESEARCH SOURCES FOR SOUTH ASIAN STUDIES IN ECONOMIC DEVELOPMENT: A SELECT BIBLIOGRAPHY OF SERIAL PUBLICATIONS. CEYLON INDIA NEPAL PAKISTAN PROB/SOLV ADMIN...POLICY 20. PAGE 32 F0611 BIBLIOG ECO/UNDEV S/ASIA PLAN

CHACO/WAR....CHACO WAR

CHAD....SEE ALSO AFR

B64
WITHERELL J.W.,OFFICIAL PUBLICATIONS OF FRENCH EQUATORIAL AFRICA, FRENCH CAMEROONS, AND TOGO, 1946-1958 (PAMPHLET). CAMEROON CHAD FRANCE GABON TOGO LAW ECO/UNDEV EXTR/IND INT/TRADE...GEOG HEAL 20. PAGE 148 F2913 BIBLIOG/A AFR NAT/G ADMIN

CHADWELL J.T. F0439

CHALMERS W.E. F0621

CHAMBER OF COMMERCE OF USA F0440

CHAMBERLAIN N.W. F0442

CHAMBERLIN E.H. F0441,F0443,F0444

CHAMBERS/J....JORDAN CHAMBERS

CHAMBR/DEP....CHAMBER OF DEPUTIES (FRANCE)

CHAMBRLN/J....JOSEPH CHAMBERLAIN

CHAMBRLN/N....NEVILLE CHAMBERLAIN

B38
DAVIES E.,"NATIONAL" CAPITALISM: THE GOVERNMENT'S RECORD AS PROTECTOR OF PRIVATE MONOPOLY. UK ELITES SOCIETY STRATA POL/PAR WORKER PROB/SOLV CONTROL SOCISM 20 MONOPOLY LABOR/PAR CHAMBRLN/N. PAGE 30 F0583 CAP/ISM NAT/G INDUS POLICY

CHAMPION J.M. F0445

CHANDLER A.D. F0446,F0447

CHANDLER L.V. F0448

CHANDRASEKHAR S. F0449,F0450

CHANG C. F0451

CHANGE (AS GOAL)....SEE ORD/FREE

CHANGE (AS INNOVATION)....SEE CREATE

CHANGE (SOCIAL MOBILITY)....SEE GEOG, STRATA

CHAO K. F0452

CHAPIN F.S. F0453,F0454

CHARACTER....SEE PERSON

CHARISMA....CHARISMA

CHARLES/I....CHARLES I OF ENGLAND

CHARTISM....CHARTISM

CHARTS....GRAPHS, CHARTS, DIAGRAMS, MAPS

CHASE H.W. F1807

CHASE S.B. F0455

CHASE/S....STUART CHASE

CHATEAUB/F....VICOMTE FRANCOIS RENE DE CHATEAUBRIAND

CHATTANOOG....CHATTANOOGA, TENNESSEE

CHATTERJEE I.K. F0456

CHATTERS C.H. F0457

CHECCHI V. F0458

CHECKS AND BALANCES SYSTEM....SEE BAL/PWR

CHEEK G. F0459

CHEIT E.F. F0460

CHEN N.-R. F0461

CHEN/YUN....CH'EN YUN

CHENERY H.B. F0462,F0463,F0464

CHIANG....CHIANG KAI-SHEK

CHICAGO....CHICAGO, ILLINOIS

B64
FISK W.M.,ADMINISTRATIVE PROCEDURE IN A REGULATORY AGENCY: THE CAB AND THE NEW YORK-CHICAGO CASE SERV/IND ECO/DEV

(PAMPHLET). USA+45 DIST/IND ADMIN CONTROL LOBBY GP/REL ROLE ORD/FREE NEWYORK/C CHICAGO CAB. PAGE 41 F0805
AIR JURID

B64
FITCH L.C.,URBAN TRANSPORTATION AND PUBLIC POLICY. FINAN NAT/G LEGIS PROB/SOLV TEC/DEV PRICE COST EFFICIENCY...DECISION STAT CHARTS METH/COMP MUNICH 20 NEWYORK/C PHILADELPH LOS/ANG CHICAGO WASHING/DC. PAGE 41 F0806
DIST/IND PLAN LOC/G

B65
BOLLENS J.C.,THE METROPOLIS: ITS PEOPLE, POLITICS, AND ECONOMIC LIFE. USA+45 PLAN PROB/SOLV PERS/REL PWR...DECISION GEOG CENSUS TREND CON/ANAL MUNICH 20 NEWYORK/C LOS/ANG SAN/FRAN CHICAGO PHILADELPH. PAGE 16 F0309
HABITAT SOC LOC/G

B65
GREER S.,URBAN RENEWAL AND AMERICAN CITIES: THE DILEMMA OF DEMOCRATIC INTERVENTION. USA+45 R+D LOC/G VOL/ASSN ACT/RES BUDGET ADMIN GOV/REL...SOC INT SAMP MUNICH 20 BOSTON CHICAGO LOS/ANG MIAMI URBAN/RNWL. PAGE 51 F0992
PROB/SOLV PLAN NAT/G

CHIEF....PRESIDENT, MONARCH, PRESIDENCY, PREMIER, CHIEF OFFICER OF ANY GOVERNMENT

B02
MOREL E.D.,AFFAIRS OF WEST AFRICA. UK FINAN INDUS FAM KIN SECT CHIEF WORKER DIPLOM RACE/REL LITERACY HEALTH...CHARTS 18/20 AFRICA/W NEGRO. PAGE 93 F1826
COLONIAL ADMIN AFR

S21
MALINOWSKI B.,"THE PRIMITIVE ECONOMICS OF THE TROBRIAND ISLANDERS" (BMR)" CULTURE SOCIETY NAT/G CHIEF LEAD OWN...SOC MYTH WORSHIP 20 NEW/GUINEA TROBRIAND RESOURCE/N. PAGE 84 F1647
ECO/UNDEV AGRI PRODUC STRUCT

B24
HOLDSWORTH W.S.,A HISTORY OF ENGLISH LAW; THE COMMON LAW AND ITS RIVALS (VOL. VI). AFR UK STRATA EX/STRUC ADJUD ADMIN CONTROL CT/SYS...JURID CONCPT GEN/LAWS 17 PARLIAMENT ENGLSH/LAW COMMON/LAW. PAGE 61 F1194
LAW CONSTN LEGIS CHIEF

B24
HOLDSWORTH W.S.,A HISTORY OF ENGLISH LAW; THE COMMON LAW AND ITS RIVALS (VOL. IV). UK SEA AGRI CHIEF ADJUD CONTROL CRIME GOV/REL...INT/LAW JURID NAT/COMP 16/17 PARLIAMENT COMMON/LAW CANON/LAW ENGLSH/LAW. PAGE 61 F1195
LAW LEGIS CT/SYS CONSTN

B25
MATHEWS J.M.,AMERICAN STATE GOVERNMENT. USA-45 LOC/G CHIEF EX/STRUC LEGIS ADJUD CONTROL CT/SYS ROUTINE GOV/REL PWR 20 GOVERNOR. PAGE 87 F1703
PROVS ADMIN FEDERAL CONSTN

B39
FIRTH R.,PRIMITIVE POLYNESIAN ECONOMY. SOCIETY DIST/IND SECT CHIEF CAP/ISM PRODUC WEALTH...SOC OBS METH WORSHIP 20 POLYNESIA. PAGE 41 F0802
ECO/UNDEV CULTURE AGRI ECO/TAC

B48
KEIR D.L.,CASES IN CONSTITUTIONAL LAW. UK CHIEF LEGIS DIPLOM TAX PARL/PROC CRIME GOV/REL...INT/LAW JURID 17/20. PAGE 70 F1368
CONSTN LAW ADJUD CT/SYS

S48
NOURSE E.G.,"THE ROLE OF THE COUNCIL OF ECONOMIC ADVISERS." USA+45 DELIB/GP...DECISION PRESIDENT. PAGE 99 F1938
EX/STRUC CHIEF PROB/SOLV

B50
MARX H.L.,THE WELFARE STATE. USA+45 USA-45 CHIEF CAP/ISM CENTRAL ORD/FREE LAISSEZ...SOC ANTHOL 20. PAGE 86 F1686
ECO/DEV INDUS WEALTH WELF/ST

B52
JENNINGS W.I.,CONSTITUTIONAL LAWS OF THE COMMONWEALTH. AFR UK LAW CHIEF LEGIS TAX CT/SYS PARL/PROC GOV/REL...INT/LAW 18/20 ENGLSH/LAW COMMON/LAW. PAGE 67 F1316
CONSTN JURID ADJUD COLONIAL

B55
BERNSTEIN M.H.,REGULATING BUSINESS BY INDEPENDENT COMMISSION. USA+45 USA-45 LG/CO CHIEF LEGIS PROB/SOLV ADJUD SANCTION GP/REL ATTIT...TIME/SEQ 19/20 MONOPOLY PRESIDENT CONGRESS. PAGE 14 F0268
DELIB/GP CONTROL CONSULT

B56
ABELS J.,THE TRUMAN SCANDALS. USA+45 USA-45 POL/PAR TAX LEGIT CT/SYS CHOOSE PRIVIL MORAL WEALTH 20 TRUMAN/HS PRESIDENT CONGRESS. PAGE 2 F0031
CRIME ADMIN CHIEF TRIBUTE

S56
BONILLA F.,"WHEN IS PETITION 'PRESSURE?'" (BMR)" USA+45 ELITES INDUS LABOR CHIEF EDU/PROP LEGIT ATTIT...INT CHARTS 20 CONGRESS PRESIDENT EISNHWR/DD. PAGE 16 F0312
LEGIS EX/STRUC INT/TRADE TARIFFS

S56
MERRIAM R.E.,"THE BUREAU OF THE BUDGET AS PART OF THE PRESIDENT'S STAFF." 20 BUR/BUDGET 20 BOB. PAGE 90 F1763
CHIEF CONTROL LEAD EXEC

S56
MILNE R.S.,"CONTROL OF GOVERNMENT CORPORATIONS IN THE UNITED STATES." USA+45 NAT/G CHIEF LEGIS BUDGET 20 GENACCOUNT. PAGE 92 F1800
CONTROL EX/STRUC GOV/REL PWR

S56
TYLER G.,"THE PRESIDENCY AND LABOR." USA+45 USA-45 NAT/G LOBBY GOV/REL PWR 20 PRESIDENT. PAGE 131 F2595
LABOR REPRESENT CHIEF

B58
PALMER E.E.,THE ECONOMY AND THE DEMOCRATIC IDEAL. USA+45 USA-45 STRATA CHIEF CT/SYS ORD/FREE SOCISM ...MAJORIT CONCPT ANTHOL 18/20 PRESIDENT. PAGE 103 F2021
ECO/DEV POPULISM METH/COMP ECO/TAC

B59
NUNEZ JIMENEZ A.,LA LIBERACION DE LAS ISLAS. CUBA L/A+17C USA+45 LAW CHIEF PLAN DIPLOM FOR/AID OWN WEALTH 20 CASTRO/F. PAGE 99 F1945
AGRI REV ECO/UNDEV NAT/G

S59
WALLACE R.A.,"CONGRESSIONAL CONTROL OF THE BUDGET." USA+45 NAT/G CHIEF GP/REL FEDERAL OBJECTIVE...MGT CONGRESS. PAGE 143 F2807
LEGIS EX/STRUC BUDGET CONSTN

B60
CARPER E.T.,THE DEFENSE APPROPRIATIONS RIDER (PAMPHLET). USA+45 CONSTN CHIEF DELIB/GP LEGIS BUDGET LOBBY CIVMIL/REL...POLICY 20 CONGRESS EISNHWR/DD DEPT/DEFEN PRESIDENT BOSTON. PAGE 22 F0419
GOV/REL ADJUD LAW CONTROL

B60
FINKLE J.L.,THE PRESIDENT MAKES A DECISION: A STUDY OF DIXON-YATES. OP/RES PROB/SOLV BUDGET ADMIN GOV/REL...POLICY BIBLIOG/A 20 PRESIDENT. PAGE 41 F0799
DECISION CHIEF PWR POL/PAR

S60
MANN S.Z.,"POLICY FORMULATION IN THE EXECUTIVE BRANCH: THE TAFT-HARTLEY EXPERIENCE." USA+45 LABOR CHIEF INGP/REL 20 NLRB. PAGE 85 F1656
EXEC GOV/REL EX/STRUC PROB/SOLV

B61
CANTERBERY E.R.,THE PRESIDENT'S COUNCIL OF ECONOMIC ADVISERS. AFR USA+45 FINAN LABOR NAT/G PLAN ADMIN OPTIMAL WEALTH 20 EISNHWR/DD PRESIDENT TRUMAN/HS KEYNES/JM. PAGE 21 F0413
ECO/TAC OP/RES EXEC CHIEF

S61
SCHER S.,"REGULATORY AGENCY CONTROL THROUGH APPOINTMENT: THE CASE OF THE EISENHOWER ADMINISTRATION AND THE NLRB." USA+45 EX/STRUC GOV/REL 20 NLRB. PAGE 116 F2296
CHIEF LOBBY CONTROL TOP/EX

B62
BRUMBERG A.,RUSSIA UNDER KHRUSHCHEV. FUT USSR SOCIETY ECO/DEV AGRI PERF/ART WORKER PWR...SOC ANTHOL 20 KHRUSH/N. PAGE 20 F0377
COM MARXISM NAT/G CHIEF

B62
HARRIS S.E.,THE ECONOMICS OF THE POLITICAL PARTIES. USA+45 FINAN CHIEF ACT/RES PLAN BUDGET GP/REL INGP/REL NEW/LIB...IDEA/COMP PERS/COMP 20 EISNHWR/DD KENNEDY/JF. PAGE 56 F1090
POLICY ECO/DEV NAT/G POL/PAR

B62
SCHILLING W.R.,STRATEGY, POLITICS, AND DEFENSE BUDGETS. AFR USA+45 CHIEF LEGIS PLAN TEC/DEV BAL/PWR BUDGET NUC/PWR WAR CIVMIL/REL GOV/REL PWR 20 EISNHWR/DD. PAGE 117 F2297
NAT/G POLICY FORCES DETER

B63
ERHARD L.,THE ECONOMICS OF SUCCESS. GERMANY/W WOR+45 LABOR CHIEF TAX REGION COST DEMAND ANTHOL. PAGE 38 F0745
ECO/DEV INT/TRADE PLAN DIPLOM

B63
HOOPES R.,THE STEEL CRISIS. USA+45 INDUS ECO/TAC EDU/PROP PRICE CONTROL ATTIT...POLICY 20 KENNEDY/JF. PAGE 61 F1205
PROC/MFG NAT/G RATION CHIEF

B63
MCCONNELL G.,STEEL AND THE PRESIDENCY, 1962. USA+45 INDUS PROB/SOLV CONFER ROLE...POLICY 20 PRESIDENT. PAGE 88 F1722
PWR CHIEF REPRESENT DOMIN

B64
HARRIS S.E.,ECONOMICS OF THE KENNEDY YEARS AND A LOOK AHEAD. USA+45 PLAN BUDGET NEW/LIB...STAT RECORD IDEA/COMP PERS/COMP INDEX 20 KENNEDY/JF EISNHWR/DD JOHNSON/LB. PAGE 56 F1091
ECO/TAC CHIEF POLICY NAT/G

B64
IMAZ J.L.,LOS QUE MANDAN. INDUS LABOR NAT/G POL/PAR PROVS SECT CHIEF TOP/EX CONTROL 20 ARGEN. PAGE 64 F1261
LEAD FORCES ELITES ATTIT

B65
FLASH E.S. JR.,ECONOMIC ADVICE AND PRESIDENTIAL LEADERSHIP: THE COUNCIL OF ECONOMIC ADVISORS. USA+45 NAT/G EX/STRUC LEGIS TOP/EX ACT/RES ADMIN PRESIDENT CONGRESS. PAGE 41 F0808
PLAN CONSULT CHIEF

B66
CONGRESSIONAL QUARTERLY SERV,FEDERAL ECONOMIC POLICY 1945-1965. USA+45 FINAN NAT/G CHIEF CONSULT TAX...CHARTS 20 PRESIDENT DEBT. PAGE 27 F0526
ECO/TAC BUDGET LEGIS

B66
CROWDER M.,A SHORT HISTORY OF NIGERIA. AFR NIGERIA UK ECO/UNDEV CHIEF INT/TRADE RACE/REL NAT/LISM ORD/FREE...GEOG SOC CHARTS BIBLIOG 14/20. PAGE 29 F0558
COLONIAL NAT/G CULTURE

B66
GYORGY A.,ISSUES OF WORLD COMMUNISM. ALBANIA CHINA/COM COM USSR YUGOSLAVIA STRATA AGRI INT/ORG CHIEF FORCES WORKER WAR ALL/IDEOS...GEOG 20 MAO. PAGE 52 F1018
ECO/UNDEV REV MARXISM CON/ANAL

B66
MACFARQUHAR R.,CHINA UNDER MAO: POLITICS TAKES COMMAND. CHINA/COM COM AGRI INDUS CHIEF FORCES DIPLOM INT/TRADE EDU/PROP TASK REV ADJUST...ANTHOL 20 MAO. PAGE 83 F1628
ECO/UNDEV TEC/DEV ECO/TAC ADMIN

B66
US CONGRESS JOINT ECO COMM,NEW APPROACH TO UNITED STATES INTERNATIONAL ECONOMIC POLICY. USA+45 WOR+45 CHIEF DELIB/GP CONFER...CHARTS 20 CONGRESS MONEY. PAGE 135 F2660
DIPLOM ECO/TAC BAL/PAY FINAN

B66
WILLIAMS G.,MERTHYR POLITICS: THE MAKING OF A WORKING-CLASS TRADITION. UK CHIEF WORKER LEAD SOCISM...ANTHOL MUNICH 19/20 MERTHYR RICHARD/H. PAGE 147 F2891
LOC/G POL/PAR INDUS

B67
ANDERSON T.,RUSSIAN POLITICAL THOUGHT; AN INTRODUCTION. USSR NAT/G POL/PAR CHIEF MARXISM ...TIME/SEQ BIBLIOG 9/20. PAGE 5 F0099
TREND CONSTN ATTIT

B67
GRIFFITH W.E.,SINO-SOVIET RELATIONS, 1964-1965. CHINA/COM COM USSR CHIEF 20. PAGE 51 F1001
DIPLOM PWR DOMIN MARXISM

B67
MAZOUR A.G.,SOVIET ECONOMIC DEVELOPMENT: OPERATION OUTSTRIP: 1921-1965. USSR ECO/UNDEV FINAN CHIEF WORKER PROB/SOLV CONTROL PRODUC MARXISM...CHARTS ORG/CHARTS 20 STALIN/J. PAGE 87 F1711
ECO/TAC AGRI INDUS PLAN

B67
NYOMARKAY J.,CHARISMA AND FACTIONALISM IN THE NAZI PARTY. GERMANY POL/PAR LEGIT LEAD MARXISM ...NEW/IDEA METH/COMP GEN/LAWS BIBLIOG 20 HITLER/A. PAGE 99 F1949
FASCISM INGP/REL CHIEF PWR

B67
O'LEARY M.K.,THE POLITICS OF AMERICAN FOREIGN AID. USA+45 POL/PAR CHIEF BUDGET EDU/PROP LOBBY CONGRESS. PAGE 100 F1958
FOR/AID DIPLOM PARL/PROC ATTIT

B67
US CONGRESS JOINT ECO COMM,REPORT ON JANUARY 1967 ECONOMIC REPORT OF THE PRESIDENT. FINAN LABOR NAT/G LEGIS BUDGET INT/TRADE COST DEMAND INCOME PRODUC ...POLICY IDEA/COMP 20 CONGRESS. PAGE 135 F2663
CHIEF ECO/TAC PLAN DELIB/GP

B67
WESSON R.G.,THE IMPERIAL ORDER. WOR-45 STRUCT SECT DOMIN ADMIN COLONIAL LEAD CONSERVE...CONCPT BIBLIOG 20. PAGE 145 F2861
PWR CHIEF CONTROL SOCIETY

B67
YOUNG J.M.,THE BRAZILIAN REVOLUTION OF 1930 AND THE AFTERMATH. BRAZIL COLONIAL PWR...BIBLIOG/A 16/20. PAGE 150 F2951
PLAN CHIEF FORCES REV

L67
SCALAPINO R.A.,"A SURVEY OF ASIA IN 1966." ASIA S/ASIA CONSTN SOCIETY POL/PAR CHIEF WAR...ANTHOL 20. PAGE 116 F2285
DIPLOM

S67
AGUILAR M.A.,"?UNA OEA MAS FUERTE O UNA AMERICA LATINA MAS DEBIL?" L/A+17C USA+45 USA-45 ECO/UNDEV INDUS CHIEF DELIB/GP FORCES CONTROL PWR 20 OAS KENNEDY/JF JOHNSON/LB. PAGE 3 F0050
INT/ORG DIPLOM POLICY COLONIAL

S67
ALEXANDER R.J.,"'THIRD FORCE' IN WORLD COMMUNISM?" CHINA/COM CUBA USSR INT/ORG DIPLOM TASK INGP/REL ATTIT PWR 20 CASTRO/F. PAGE 3 F0060
CHIEF MARXISM LEAD REV

S67
BUTT R.,"THE COMMON MARKET AND CONSERVATIVE POLITICS, 1961-2." UK CHIEF DIPLOM ECO/TAC INT/TRADE CONFER DEBATE REGION ATTIT...POLICY 20 EEC. PAGE 21 F0398
EUR+WWI INT/ORG POL/PAR

S67
CATTELL D.T.,"THE FIFTIETH ANNIVERSARY: A SOVIET WATERSHED?" USSR CONSTN ECO/DEV NAT/G LEAD TOTALISM 20 KHRUSH/N. PAGE 22 F0430
MARXISM CHIEF POLICY ADJUST

S67
CHAMBERLAIN N.W.,"STRIKES IN CONTEMPORARY CONTEXT." LAW INDUS NAT/G CHIEF CONFER COST ATTIT ORD/FREE ...POLICY MGT 20. PAGE 23 F0442
LABOR BARGAIN EFFICIENCY

PROB/SOLV

S67
CRAIG A.,"ARGENTINA: THE LATEST REVOLUTION." ELITES NAT/G CHIEF FORCES ECO/TAC CIVMIL/REL GOV/REL EQUILIB PRIVIL 20 ARGEN. PAGE 28 F0550
ECO/UNDEV FINAN ATTIT REV

S67
GRAHAM R.,"BRAZIL'S DILEMMA." BRAZIL FUT L/A+17C NAT/G CHIEF PROB/SOLV ECO/TAC PWR 20. PAGE 50 F0972
ECO/UNDEV CONSTN POL/PAR POLICY

S67
HALL B.,"THE PAINTER'S UNION: A PARTIAL VICTORY." USA+45 PROB/SOLV LEGIT ADMIN REPRESENT 20. PAGE 53 F1043
LABOR CHIEF CHOOSE CRIME

S67
HEATH D.B.,"BOLIVIA UNDER BARRIENTOS." L/A+17C NAT/G CHIEF DIPLOM ECO/TAC...POLICY 20 BOLIV. PAGE 58 F1132
ECO/UNDEV POL/PAR REV CONSTN

S67
KRAUS J.,"A MARXIST IN GHANA." GHANA ELITES CHIEF PROB/SOLV TEC/DEV DIPLOM ECO/TAC COLONIAL PARTIC PWR 20 NKRUMAH/K. PAGE 73 F1432
MARXISM PLAN ATTIT CREATE

N67
US CONGRESS JOINT ECO COMM,MAINLAND CHINA IN THE WORLD ECONOMY (PAMPHLET). CHINA/COM USA+45 AGRI CHIEF MARXISM CONGRESS. PAGE 135 F2661
ECO/UNDEV POLICY ECO/TAC INT/TRADE

N67
US SENATE COMM ON FOREIGN REL,WAR OR PEACE IN THE MIDDLE EAST (PAMPHLET). GREECE ISLAM ISRAEL JORDAN UAR CHIEF PROB/SOLV FOR/AID WAR PWR 20 SENATE. PAGE 139 F2739
DIPLOM FORCES PLAN

CHIKIN V.V. F1011

CHILCOTE R.H. F0465

CHILDREN....SEE AGE/C

CHILDS M.W. F0466

CHILDS/RS....RICHARD SPENCER CHILDS

CHILE....SEE ALSO L/A+17C

B62
VACCARO J.R.,A STATEMENT OF THE LAWS OF CHILE IN MATTERS AFFECTING BUSINESS (3RD ED.). CHILE AGRI FINAN FAM LABOR ECO/TAC FOR/AID TAX ADJUD CONTROL MARRIAGE STRANGE...BIBLIOG 20. PAGE 140 F2756
CONSTN LAW INDUS MGT

B63
HIRSCHMAN A.O.,JOURNEYS TOWARD PROGRESS: STUDIES OF ECONOMIC POLICYMAKING IN LATIN AMERICA. CHILE FUT ECO/UNDEV AGRI FINAN INDUS CONSULT DELIB/GP PLAN ATTIT HEALTH ORD/FREE WEALTH...POLICY STAT VAL/FREE COLOMB 20. PAGE 60 F1177
L/A+17C ECO/TAC BRAZIL

B64
KALDOR N.,ESSAYS ON ECONOMIC POLICY (VOL. II). CHILE GERMANY INDIA FINAN...GOV/COMP METH/COMP 20 KEYNES/JM. PAGE 69 F1348
BAL/PAY INT/TRADE METH/CNCPT ECO/UNDEV

B64
ODEH H.S.,THE IMPACT OF INFLATION ON THE LEVEL OF ECONOMIC ACTIVITY. AFR BRAZIL CHILE BUDGET GOV/REL COST DEMAND INCOME WEALTH...STAT METH 20 MONEY. PAGE 100 F1963
ECOMETRIC ECO/TAC ECO/UNDEV FINAN

B64
WITHERS W.,THE ECONOMIC CRISIS IN LATIN AMERICA. BRAZIL CHILE STRATA AGRI DIPLOM FOR/AID PWR SOCISM ...POLICY 20 MEXIC/AMER ARGEN ALL/PROG. PAGE 148 F2914
L/A+17C ECO/UNDEV CAP/ISM ALL/IDEOS

B65
HERRICK B.H.,URBAN MIGRATION AND ECONOMIC DEVELOPMENT IN CHILE. CHILE AGRI INDUS LABOR NAT/G CENTRAL PRODUC...STAT SAMP CHARTS BIBLIOG/A MUNICH 20 MIGRATION. PAGE 59 F1156
HABITAT GEOG ECO/UNDEV

S65
BRANDENBURG F.,"THE RELEVANCE OF MEXICAN EXPERIENCE TO LATIN AMERICAN DEVELOPMENT." BRAZIL CHILE VENEZUELA STRUCT ECO/UNDEV AGRI CREATE ECO/TAC ...STAT RECORD MEXIC/AMER ARGEN COLOMB. PAGE 18 F0340
L/A+17C GOV/COMP

B66
MACBEAN A.I.,EXPORT INSTABILITY AND ECONOMIC DEVELOPMENT. CHILE PAKISTAN PUERT/RICO TANZANIA UGANDA WOR+45 MARKET ECO/TAC...POLICY REGRESS CHARTS BIBLIOG TIME 20. PAGE 83 F1622
INT/TRADE ECO/UNDEV ECOMETRIC INSPECT

B66
MOUNTJOY A.B.,INDUSTRIALIZATION AND UNDER-DEVELOPED COUNTRIES (2ND REV. ED.). CHILE GHANA INDIA NIGERIA WOR+45 SOCIETY PROB/SOLV ECO/TAC...SOC CHARTS 20 INDUS/REV. PAGE 94 F1848
ECO/UNDEV INDUS GEOG HABITAT

B66
THIESENHUSEN W.C.,CHILE'S EXPERIMENTS IN AGRARIAN REFORM. CHILE STRUCT NAT/G ACT/RES ECO/TAC GOV/REL COST SOCISM...TREND CHARTS SOC/EXP 20. PAGE 130 F2558
AGRI ECO/UNDEV SOC TEC/DEV

S67
PETRAS J.,"MINERS AND AGRARIAN RADICALISM." CHILE AGRI EXTR/IND WORKER CHOOSE ATTIT SOCISM MUNICH 20. PAGE 105 F2073
PARTIC EDU/PROP LABOR

CHIN R. F1893

CHINA....PEOPLE'S REPUBLIC OF CHINA: SEE CHINA/COM
REPUBLIC OF CHINA: SEE TAIWAN

CHINA/COM....COMMUNIST CHINA

N19
DEANE H.,THE WAR IN VIETNAM (PAMPHLET). AFR CHINA/COM VIETNAM BAL/PWR DIPLOM ECO/TAC SOCISM INTERVENT INTERVENT. PAGE 31 F0610
WAR SOCIALIST MORAL CAP/ISM

N19
SAPIR H.M.,JAPAN, CHINA, AND THE WEST (PAMPHLET). AFR ASIA CHINA/COM PROB/SOLV GOV/REL 20 CHINJAP. PAGE 116 F2282
ECO/UNDEV INT/TRADE DECISION PLAN

B48
CLYDE P.H.,THE FAR EAST: A HISTORY OF THE IMPACT OF THE WEST ON EASTERN ASIA. CHINA/COM CULTURE INT/TRADE DOMIN COLONIAL WAR PWR...CHARTS BIBLIOG 19/20 CHINJAP. PAGE 25 F0494
DIPLOM ASIA

B49
US DEPARTMENT OF STATE,SOVIET BIBLIOGRAPHY (PAMPHLET). CHINA/COM COM USSR LAW AGRI INT/ORG ECO/TAC EDU/PROP...POLICY GEOG IND 20. PAGE 135 F2670
BIBLIOG/A MARXISM CULTURE DIPLOM

B56
KNORR K.E.,RUBLE DIPLOMACY: CHALLENGE TO AMERICAN FOREIGN AID(PAMPHLET). AFR CHINA/COM USA+45 USSR PLAN TEC/DEV CAP/ISM INT/TRADE DOMIN EDU/PROP CONTROL LEAD 20. PAGE 72 F1413
ECO/UNDEV COM DIPLOM FOR/AID

B58
CHANG C.,THE INFLATIONARY SPIRAL: THE EXPERIENCE IN CHINA 1939-50. CHINA/COM BUDGET INT/TRADE PRICE ADMIN CONTROL WAR DEMAND...POLICY CHARTS 20. PAGE 23 F0451
FINAN ECO/TAC BAL/PAY GOV/REL

B58
MIKESELL R.F.,FINANCING FREE WORLD TRADE WITH THE SINO-SOVIET BLOC. CHINA/COM COM USSR WOR+45 ECO/DEV AGRI DIST/IND EXTR/IND FINAN INDUS MARKET PROC/MFG NAT/G PLAN TEC/DEV ECO/TAC...CHARTS METH/GP EEC FOR/TRADE 20. PAGE 91 F1780
STAT BAL/PAY

B59
BARNETT A.D.,COMMUNIST ECONOMIC STRATEGY: THE RISE OF MAINLAND CHINA. CHINA/COM USSR WOR+45 AGRI INDUS FOR/AID INGP/REL ATTIT. PAGE 10 F0188
ECO/UNDEV INT/TRADE TOTALISM BAL/PWR

B59
LI CHOH-MING,ECONOMIC DEVELOPMENT OF COMMUNIST CHINA. ASIA CHINA/COM AGRI FINAN TAX INCOME MARXISM ...MGT 20. PAGE 80 F1557
ECO/UNDEV INDUS ORD/FREE TEC/DEV

B60
HUGHES R.,THE CHINESE COMMUNES; A BACKGROUND BOOK. CHINA/COM SOCIETY CONTROL ROUTINE ADJUST EFFICIENCY PRODUC 20. PAGE 63 F1234
AGRI INDUS STRUCT MARXISM

B60
MC CLELLAN G.S.,INDIA. AFR CHINA/COM INDIA CONSTN ELITES STRATA AGRI POL/PAR FOR/AID ARMS/CONT REV MARXISM...CENSUS BIBLIOG 20 GANDHI/M NEHRU/J. PAGE 87 F1712
DIPLOM NAT/G SOCIETY ECO/UNDEV

B60
SAKAI R.K.,STUDIES ON ASIA, 1960. ASIA CHINA/COM S/ASIA COM/IND ECO/TAC...ANTHOL 17/20 MALAYA. PAGE 115 F2270
ECO/UNDEV SOC

B61
LETHBRIDGE H.J.,CHINA'S URBAN COMMUNES. CHINA/COM FUT ECO/UNDEV DIPLOM EDU/PROP DEMAND INCOME MARXISM ...POLICY MUNICH 20. PAGE 78 F1534
CONTROL ECO/TAC NAT/G

B62
FRIEDRICH-EBERT-STIFTUNG,THE SOVIET BLOC AND DEVELOPING COUNTRIES. CHINA/COM COM GERMANY/E USSR WOR+45 ECO/UNDEV INT/ORG NAT/G TEC/DEV NEUTRAL PWR ...POLICY 20. PAGE 44 F0868
MARXISM DIPLOM ECO/TAC FOR/AID

B62
WALSTON H.,AGRICULTURE UNDER COMMUNISM. CHINA/COM COM PROB/SOLV HAPPINESS RIGID/FLEX...POLICY METH/COMP 20. PAGE 143 F2811
AGRI MARXISM PLAN CREATE

S62
ZAUBERMAN A.,"SOVIET AND CHINESE STRATEGY FOR ECONOMIC GROWTH." ASIA CHINA/COM COM USSR STRATA VOL/ASSN PLAN ATTIT PWR...METH/CNCPT GEN/LAWS WORK TERR/GP 20. PAGE 150 F2959
ECO/DEV EDU/PROP

B63
CHEN N.-R.,THE ECONOMY OF MAINLAND CHINA, 1949-1963: A BIBLIOGRAPHY OF MATERIALS IN ENGLISH. CHINA/COM ECO/UNDEV PRESS 20. PAGE 24 F0461
BIBLIOG MARXISM NAT/G ASIA

B63
LETHBRIDGE H.J.,THE PEASANT AND THE COMMUNES. CHINA/COM COM USSR NEIGH PROB/SOLV ADJUST EFFICIENCY...POLICY METH/COMP NAT/COMP 20. PAGE 78 F1535
MARXISM ECO/TAC AGRI WORKER

S63
SCHURMANN F.,"ECONOMIC POLICY AND POLITICAL POWER IN COMMUNIST CHINA." ASIA CHINA/COM USSR SOCIETY ECO/UNDEV AGRI INDUS CREATE ADMIN ROUTINE ATTIT DRIVE RIGID/FLEX PWR WEALTH...HIST/WRIT TREND CHARTS WORK 20. PAGE 118 F2323
PLAN ECO/TAC

B64
LI C.M.,INDUSTRIAL DEVELOPMENT IN COMMUNIST CHINA. CHINA/COM ECO/DEV ECO/UNDEV AGRI FINAN INDUS MARKET LABOR NAT/G ECO/TAC INT/TRADE EXEC ALL/VALS ...POLICY RELATIV TREND WORK TOT/POP VAL/FREE 20. PAGE 79 F1556
ASIA TEC/DEV

B64
SAKAI R.K.,STUDIES ON ASIA, 1964. ASIA CHINA/COM ISRAEL MALAYSIA S/ASIA USA+45 USSR ECO/UNDEV FAM POL/PAR SECT CONSULT NAT/LISM...POLICY SOC 20 CHINJAP. PAGE 115 F2272
PWR DIPLOM

B64
STRONG A.L.,THE RISE OF THE CHINESE PEOPLE'S COMMUNES - AND SIX YEARS AFTER (2ND ED.). CHINA/COM AGRI INDUS FORCES WORKER PROB/SOLV EDU/PROP EFFICIENCY ISOLAT 20. PAGE 127 F2503
NEIGH ECO/TAC MARXISM METH/COMP

B64
US HOUSE COMM BANKING-CURR,INTERNATIONAL DEVELOPMENT ASSOCIATION ACT AMENDMENT. CHINA/COM USA+45 USSR FINAN FORCES LEGIS DIPLOM CONFER EFFICIENCY...CHARTS GOV/COMP 20 PRESIDENT CONGRESS INTL/DEV. PAGE 136 F2689
BAL/PAY FOR/AID RECORD ECO/TAC

B64
ZEBOT C.A.,THE ECONOMICS OF COMPETITIVE COEXISTENCE. CHINA/COM USSR WOR+45 FINAN MARKET FOR/AID PRICE DEMAND EQUILIB WEALTH ALL/IDEOS 20. PAGE 150 F2961
TEC/DEV DIPLOM METH/COMP

S64
POLARIS J.,"THE SINO-SOVIET DISPUTE: ITS ECONOMIC IMPACT ON CHINA." ASIA CHINA/COM COM WOR+45 NAT/G ATTIT PWR WEALTH...STAT TREND FOR/TRADE 20. PAGE 107 F2095
ECO/UNDEV ECO/TAC

S64
WU Y.,"CHINA'S ECONOMY AND ITS PROSPECTS." ASIA CHINA/COM FUT USSR AGRI INDUS PLAN ECO/TAC LEGIT WEALTH...STAT CON/ANAL CHARTS GEN/LAWS FOR/TRADE 20. PAGE 149 F2938
ECO/DEV

B65
CHANDRASEKHAR S.,AMERICAN AID AND INDIA'S ECONOMIC DEVELOPMENT. AFR CHINA/COM INDIA USA+45 GIVE EDU/PROP EATING HEALTH ORD/FREE 20 AID. PAGE 23 F0449
FOR/AID PEACE DIPLOM ECO/UNDEV

B65
CHAO K.,THE RATE AND PATTERN OF INDUSTRIAL GROWTH IN COMMUNIST CHINA. CHINA/COM ECO/UNDEV TEC/DEV PRICE...NAT/COMP BIBLIOG 20. PAGE 23 F0452
INDUS INDEX STAT PRODUC

B65
HARBISON F.,MANPOWER AND EDUCATION. AFR CHINA/COM IRAN L/A+17C S/ASIA TEC/DEV ADJUST OPTIMAL SKILL ...ANTHOL 20. PAGE 55 F1073
ECO/UNDEV EDU/PROP WORKER NAT/COMP

B65
WU YUAN-LI,THE ECONOMY OF COMMUNIST CHINA. CHINA/COM USSR AGRI FINAN INDUS POL/PAR WORKER PROB/SOLV INT/TRADE PRICE EATING INCOME OWN WEALTH 20. PAGE 149 F2939
ECO/TAC MARXISM PLAN EFFICIENCY

B66
GYORGY A.,ISSUES OF WORLD COMMUNISM. ALBANIA CHINA/COM COM USSR YUGOSLAVIA STRATA AGRI INT/ORG CHIEF FORCES WORKER WAR ALL/IDEOS...GEOG 20 MAO. PAGE 52 F1018
ECO/UNDEV REV MARXISM CON/ANAL

B66
LONDON K.,EASTERN EUROPE IN TRANSITION. CHINA/COM USSR DOMIN COLONIAL CENTRAL RIGID/FLEX PWR...SOC ANTHOL 20. PAGE 82 F1597
SOVEREIGN COM NAT/LISM DIPLOM

B66
MACFARQUHAR R.,CHINA UNDER MAO: POLITICS TAKES COMMAND. CHINA/COM COM AGRI INDUS CHIEF FORCES DIPLOM INT/TRADE EDU/PROP TASK REV ADJUST...ANTHOL 20 MAO. PAGE 83 F1628
ECO/UNDEV TEC/DEV ECO/TAC ADMIN

B66
WILCOX C.,ECONOMIES OF THE WORLD TODAY: THEIR ORGANIZATION, DEVELOPMENT, AND PERFORMANCE (2ND ED.). CHINA/COM COM INDIA NIGERIA UK WOR+45 WOR-45 INDUS MARKET PLAN ECO/TAC SOCISM...CHARTS METH/COMP 20. PAGE 146 F2878
ECO/DEV ECO/UNDEV MARXISM CAP/ISM

B67
BARNETT A.D.,CHINA AFTER MAO. ASIA CHINA/COM
POL/PAR

CULTURE ECO/UNDEV ECO/TAC CONTROL EFFICIENCY NAT/LISM MARXISM 20. PAGE 10 F0189 — NAT/G TEC/DEV GP/REL

B67
GRIFFITH W.E.,SINO-SOVIET RELATIONS, 1964-1965. CHINA/COM COM USSR CHIEF 20. PAGE 51 F1001 — DIPLOM PWR DOMIN MARXISM

B67
JOHNSON H.G.,ECONOMIC NATIONALISM IN OLD AND NEW STATES. CANADA CHINA/COM MALI UK DIPLOM...SIMUL GEN/LAWS 19/20 MEXIC/AMER. PAGE 68 F1328 — NAT/LISM ECO/UNDEV ECO/DEV NAT/COMP

B67
US CONGRESS JOINT ECO COMM,AN ECONOMIC PROFILE OF MAINLAND CHINA, VOLUMES I AND II. CHINA/COM AGRI DIST/IND FINAN INDUS LABOR FORCES ACT/RES PLAN INT/TRADE INGP/REL BAL/PAY 20 CONGRESS. PAGE 135 F2664 — ECO/UNDEV WEALTH ECO/TAC DELIB/GP

B67
US SENATE COMM ON FOREIGN REL,HARRISON E. SALISBURY'S TRIP TO NORTH VIETNAM. CHINA/COM USA+45 VIETNAM/N PRESS TASK GUERRILLA CONSEN EFFICIENCY PEACE DRIVE...OBS SENATE. PAGE 139 F2743 — DIPLOM WAR FORCES ATTIT

B67
VAN SLYKE L.P.,ENEMIES AND FRIENDS; THE UNITED FRONT IN CHINESE COMMUNIST HISTORY. CHINA/COM SOCIETY FORCES PLAN ADJUST 20 MAO. PAGE 140 F2764 — INGP/REL MARXISM ATTIT GP/REL

B67
WILCOX W.A.,ASIA AND UNITED STATES POLICY. CHINA/COM USA+45. PAGE 146 F2879 — ASIA S/ASIA DIPLOM POLICY

B67
WILLIAMS M.,THE EAST IS RED: THE VIEW INSIDE CHINA. CHINA/COM CONSTN COERCE AGE/Y ATTIT PERSON...OBS 20 MAO. PAGE 147 F2893 — REV MARXIST GP/REL DIPLOM

S67
ALEXANDER R.J.,"'THIRD FORCE' IN WORLD COMMUNISM?" CHINA/COM CUBA USSR INT/ORG DIPLOM TASK INGP/REL ATTIT PWR 20 CASTRO/F. PAGE 3 F0060 — CHIEF MARXISM LEAD REV

S67
LEE R.L.,"THE PARADOX OF EQUALITY: A THREAT TO INDIVIDUAL AND SYSTEM FUNCTIONING." CHINA/COM ECO/UNDEV WORKER...SIMUL GEN/LAWS 20. PAGE 77 F1508 — SOCIETY STRATA MARXISM IDEA/COMP

S67
PERKINS D.H.,"ECONOMIC GROWTH IN CHINA AND THE CULTURAL REVOLUTION(1960APRIL 1967)" CHINA/COM FUT AGRI INDUS PLAN LEAD MARXISM...CHARTS 20 MAO. PAGE 105 F2062 — ECO/TAC CULTURE REV ECO/UNDEV

S67
RICHMAN B.M.,"CAPITALISTS & MANAGERS IN COMMUNIST CHINA." ASIA CHINA/COM ECO/UNDEV NAT/G CONSULT EX/STRUC PLAN EFFICIENCY PRODUC WEALTH MARXISM ...MGT CHARTS 20. PAGE 111 F2185 — CAP/ISM INDUS

S67
RONNING C.,"NANKING: 1950." ASIA CANADA CHINA/COM NAT/G PLAN ECO/TAC REV ADJUST 20. PAGE 113 F2235 — DIPLOM ROLE PEACE

S67
WALKER R.L.,"THE WEST AND THE 'NEW ASIA'." CHINA/COM ECO/UNDEV DIPLOM...PREDICT 20. PAGE 142 F2805 — ASIA INT/TRADE COLONIAL REGION

N67
US CONGRESS JOINT ECO COMM,MAINLAND CHINA IN THE WORLD ECONOMY (PAMPHLET). CHINA/COM USA+45 AGRI CHIEF MARXISM CONGRESS. PAGE 135 F2661 — ECO/UNDEV POLICY ECO/TAC INT/TRADE

CHINESE/AM....CHINESE IMMIGRANTS TO US AND THEIR DESCENDANTS

CHINITZ B. F0467

CHINOY E. F0468

CHITTAGONG....CHITTAGONG HILL TRIBES

CHO S.S. F0469

CHOICE (IN DECISION-MAKING)....SEE PROB/SOLV

CHOJNACKI S. F0470

CHOOSE....CHOICE, ELECTION

B08
LLOYD H.D.,THE SWISS DEMOCRACY. SWITZERLND INDUS NAT/G WORKER CHOOSE OWN ORD/FREE SOCISM...PLURIST 19/20 MONOPOLY. PAGE 81 F1590 — NAT/COMP GOV/COMP REPRESENT POPULISM

B13
BEARD C.A.,AN ECONOMIC INTERPRETATION OF THE CONSTITUTION OF THE UNITED STATES. USA-45 AGRI INT/TRADE SUFF OWN ATTIT...CONCPT MYTH BIOG HIST/WRIT 18. PAGE 12 F0222 — CONSTN ECO/TAC CHOOSE

N19
FAHRNKOPF N.,STATE AND LOCAL GOVERNMENT IN ILLINOIS (PAMPHLET). CONSTN ADMIN PARTIC CHOOSE REPRESENT GOV/REL...JURID MGT 20 ILLINOIS. PAGE 39 F0759 — BIBLIOG LOC/G LEGIS CT/SYS

B39
JENNINGS W.I.,PARLIAMENT. UK POL/PAR OP/RES BUDGET LEAD CHOOSE GP/REL...MGT 20 PARLIAMENT HOUSE/LORD HOUSE/CMNS. PAGE 67 F1315 — PARL/PROC LEGIS CONSTN NAT/G

S47
DAHL R.A.,"WORKERS' CONTROL OF INDUSTRY AND THE BRITISH LABOUR PARTY." UK STRATA STRUCT DELIB/GP BARGAIN CAP/ISM DEBATE CONTROL CHOOSE GP/REL ATTIT ROLE PWR 19/20 PARLIAMENT LABOR/PAR FABIAN. PAGE 29 F0570 — INDUS LABOR WORKER SOCISM

S52
HEBERLE R.,"ON POLITICAL ECOLOGY" (BMR)" INCOME ATTIT WEALTH...GEOG METH SOC/INTEG 20. PAGE 58 F1133 — HABITAT STRATA CHOOSE

S52
KLUMB S.,"EMPLOYEE DETERMINATION OF MANAGERIAL FUNCTIONS AND CHARACTERISTICS." DELIB/GP WORKER PARTIC ROUTINE INGP/REL...CLASSIF OBS QU. PAGE 72 F1410 — MGT INDUS EX/STRUC CHOOSE

S52
KORNHAUSER W.,"THE NEGRO UNION OFFICIAL: A STUDY OF SPONSORSHIP AND CONTROL" (BMR)" USA+45 CONTROL DISCRIM ROLE SUPEGO...OBS 20 NEGRO. PAGE 73 F1428 — LABOR LEAD RACE/REL CHOOSE

B53
SAYLES L.R.,THE LOCAL UNION. CONSTN CULTURE DELIB/GP PARTIC CHOOSE GP/REL INGP/REL ATTIT ROLE ...MAJORIT DECISION MGT. PAGE 116 F2284 — LABOR LEAD ADJUD ROUTINE

B55
WOYTINSKY W.S.,WORLD COMMERCE AND GOVERNMENTS: TRENDS AND OUTLOOK. WOR+45 FINAN POL/PAR DIPLOM ECO/TAC FOR/AID DOMIN WAR CHOOSE...CHARTS BIBLIOG 20 LEAGUE/NAT UN ILO. PAGE 149 F2929 — INT/TRADE DIST/IND NAT/COMP NAT/G

B56
ABELS J.,THE TRUMAN SCANDALS. USA+45 USA-45 POL/PAR TAX LEGIT CT/SYS CHOOSE PRIVIL MORAL WEALTH 20 TRUMAN/HS PRESIDENT CONGRESS. PAGE 2 F0031 — CRIME ADMIN CHIEF TRIBUTE

L56
PENNOCK J.R.,"PARTY AND CONSTITUENCY IN POSTWAR AGRICULTURAL PRICE SUPPORT LEGISLATION." USA+45 LEGIS DEBATE LOBBY RIGID/FLEX. PAGE 105 F2057 — POL/PAR REPRESENT AGRI CHOOSE

L56
SCHELLING T.C.,"AN ESSAY ON BARGAINING" (BMR)" OP/RES PROB/SOLV PRICE CHOOSE PWR...DECISION MODELS 20. PAGE 116 F2294 — BARGAIN MARKET ECO/TAC GAME

L56
TAGLIACOZZO D.L.,"TRADE-UNION GOVERNMENT, ITS NATURE AND ITS PROBLEMS: A BIBLIOGRAPHICAL REVIEW, 1945-1955." STRUCT LEAD PARTIC CHOOSE ATTIT ...MAJORIT METH/CNCPT BIBLIOG. PAGE 128 F2526 — CLASSIF LABOR INGP/REL GP/REL

S56
BROWN J.S.,"UNION SIZE AS A FUNCTION OF INTRA-UNION CONFLICT." CLIENT CONTROL CHOOSE EFFICIENCY ATTIT TREND. PAGE 19 F0370 — LABOR INGP/REL CONSEN DRIVE

B57
DOWNS A.,AN ECONOMIC THEORY OF DEMOCRACY. NAT/G EDU/PROP RISK CHOOSE PERS/REL EQUILIB...SOC METH/CNCPT LOG STYLE. PAGE 34 F0659 — DECISION RATIONAL

S57
CUNNINGHAM E.M.,"THE BUSINESS MAN AND HIS LAWYER." USA+45 LG/CO SML/CO TOP/EX CHOOSE SKILL...JURID MGT 20. PAGE 29 F0561 — CONSULT LAW DECISION SERV/IND

S57
KAHN R.L.,"UNION PRACTICES AND MEMBER PARTICIPATION." PARTIC CHOOSE REPRESENT PERS/REL PERSON SKILL...DECISION METH/CNCPT QU. PAGE 69 F1347 — INGP/REL LABOR ATTIT LEAD

B58
DUBIN R.,WORKING UNION-MANAGEMENT RELATIONS. LAW PLAN ECO/TAC CHOOSE REPRESENT INGP/REL PWR...POLICY SOC BIBLIOG. PAGE 34 F0669 — LABOR MGT AUTHORIT GP/REL

B58
OGDEN F.D.,THE POLL TAX IN THE SOUTH. USA+45 USA-45 CONSTN ADJUD ADMIN PARTIC CRIME...TIME/SEQ GOV/COMP METH/COMP 18/20 SOUTH/US. PAGE 101 F1982 — TAX CHOOSE RACE/REL DISCRIM

B58
SCOTT D.J.R.,RUSSIAN POLITICAL INSTITUTIONS. RUSSIA — NAT/G

USSR CONSTN AGRI DELIB/GP PLAN EDU/PROP CONTROL POL/PAR
CHOOSE EFFICIENCY ATTIT MARXISM...BIBLIOG/A IND ADMIN
13/20. PAGE 118 F2332 DECISION

S58
LANE F.C.,"ECONOMIC CONSEQUENCES OF ORGANIZED WEALTH
VIOLENCE." FUT WOR+45 WOR-45 ECO/DEV DIST/IND COERCE
SERV/IND NAT/G PROVS EX/STRUC CHOOSE ORD/FREE PWR
...TIME/SEQ GEN/LAWS MUNICH 20. PAGE 75 F1472

S58
LATTIN N.D.,"MINORITY AND DISSENTING SHAREHOLDERS' MAJORIT
RIGHTS IN FUNDAMENTAL CHANGES." FINAN LEGIS ADJUD LG/CO
PARTIC ROUTINE CHOOSE REPRESENT INGP/REL TREND. LAW
PAGE 76 F1487 CREATE

S58
O'NEAL F.H.,"RECENT LEGISLATION AFFECTING CLOSE LG/CO
CORPORATIONS." LAW EX/STRUC ECO/TAC ROUTINE CHOOSE LEGIS
RIGID/FLEX...MAJORIT MGT TREND. PAGE 100 F1959 REPRESENT
PARTIC

B59
BROMWICH L.,UNION CONSTITUTIONS. CONSTN EX/STRUC LABOR
PRESS ADJUD CONTROL CHOOSE REPRESENT PWR SAMP. ROUTINE
PAGE 19 F0361 INGP/REL
RACE/REL

B59
MADHOK B.,POLITICAL TRENDS IN INDIA. INDIA PAKISTAN GEOG
UK STRATA ECO/UNDEV POL/PAR LEGIS CAP/ISM DIPLOM NAT/G
COLONIAL CHOOSE MARXISM...SOC TREND 20 GANDHI/M
NEHRU/J. PAGE 84 F1639

B59
VINCENT W.S.,ROLES OF THE CITIZENS: PRINCIPLES AND INGP/REL
PRACTICES. LOC/G POL/PAR VOL/ASSN CHOOSE ROLE EDU/PROP
ORD/FREE PWR...POLICY 20. PAGE 141 F2785 CREATE
LOBBY

B59
WAHLKE J.C.,LEGISLATIVE BEHAVIOR: A READER IN LEGIS
THEORY AND RESEARCH. USA+45 CONSTN ELITES POL/PAR CHOOSE
LOBBY REPRESENT PERS/REL PERSON ROLE...IDEA/COMP INGP/REL
METH/COMP SIMUL. PAGE 142 F2800 ATTIT

B59
WORTHY J.C.,BIG BUSINESS AND FREE MEN. LG/CO ELITES
EX/STRUC EDU/PROP LEAD CHOOSE GP/REL ATTIT DRIVE LOC/G
ROLE ORD/FREE...MAJORIT 20. PAGE 149 F2927 TOP/EX
PARTIC

B59
WUERTHNER J.J.,THE BUSINESSMAN'S GUIDE TO PRACTICAL LOBBY
POLITICS. USA+45 PWR 20. PAGE 149 F2940 CHOOSE
REPRESENT

S59
GILPATRICK T.V.,"PRICE SUPPORT POLICY AND THE POL/PAR
MIDWEST FARM VOTE" (BMR)" NAT/G PRICE CONTROL AGRI
REGION...POLICY CHARTS 440 20 MIDWEST/US CONGRESS ATTIT
REPUBLICAN EISNHWR/DD 20. PAGE 47 F0925 CHOOSE

S59
SHEPPARD H.L.,"THE POLITICAL ATTITUDES AND LABOR
PREFERENCES OF UNION MEMBERS: THE CASE OF THE ATTIT
DETROIT AUTO WORKERS." LOBBY CHOOSE ROLE...CLASSIF WORKER
QU SAMP TREND. PAGE 120 F2376

S59
ZAUBERMAN A.,"SOVIET BLOC ECONOMIC INTEGRATION." MARKET
COM CULTURE INTELL ECO/DEV INDUS TOP/EX ACT/RES INT/ORG
PLAN ECO/TAC INT/TRADE ROUTINE CHOOSE ATTIT USSR
...TIME/SEQ 20. PAGE 150 F2958 TOTALISM

S60
MIKESELL R.F.,"AMERICA'S ECONOMIC RESPONSIBILITY AS ECO/UNDEV
A GREAT POWER." COM FUT USA+45 USSR WOR+45 INT/ORG BAL/PWR
PLAN ECO/TAC FOR/AID EDU/PROP CHOOSE WEALTH CAP/ISM
...POLICY 20. PAGE 91 F1781

B61
BENOIT E.,EUROPE AT SIXES AND SEVENS: THE COMMON FINAN
MARKET, THE FREE TRADE ASSOCIATION AND THE UNITED ECO/DEV
STATES. EUR+WWI FUT USA+45 INDUS CONSULT DELIB/GP VOL/ASSN
EX/STRUC TOP/EX ACT/RES ECO/TAC EDU/PROP ROUTINE
CHOOSE PERCEPT WEALTH...MGT TREND EEC FOR/TRADE
TOT/POP 20 EFTA. PAGE 13 F0249

N61
US ADVISORY COMN INTERGOV REL,STATE CONSTITUTIONAL TAX
AND STATUTORY RESTRICTIONS ON LOCAL GOVERNMENT DEBT PROVS
(PAMPHLET). LAW CONSTN CHOOSE PWR...DECISION GOV/REL
MUNICH. PAGE 133 F2631

B62
GWYN W.B.,DEMOCRACY AND THE COST OF POLITICS IN COST
BRITAIN. UK BUDGET CRIME CHOOSE ORD/FREE WEALTH POL/PAR
...TIME/SEQ 18/20. PAGE 52 F1017 POPULISM
PAY

B62
HARRINGTON M.,THE RETAIL CLERKS. ECO/TAC LEAD LABOR
PARTIC CHOOSE GP/REL INGP/REL CENTRAL POLICY. SERV/IND
PAGE 55 F1087 STRUCT
DELIB/GP

B62
VAN RENSBURG P.,GUILTY LAND: THE HISTORY OF RACE/REL
APARTHEID. SOUTH/AFR NAT/G POL/PAR DOMIN CHOOSE DISCRIM
...SOC 19/20 NEGRO. PAGE 140 F2763 NAT/LISM
POLICY

B63
BAUER R.A.,AMERICAN BUSINESS AND PUBLIC POLICY: THE ECO/DEV
POLITICS OF FOREIGN TRADE. USA+45 COM/IND LG/CO ATTIT
NAT/G PROF/ORG SML/CO VOL/ASSN LEGIS TOP/EX ECO/TAC
EDU/PROP CHOOSE HEALTH PWR WEALTH...CONCPT
METH/CNCPT OBS INT QU SAMP FOR/TRADE TRUE/GP
VAL/FREE HI. PAGE 11 F0217

B64
MEISEL J.,PAPERS ON THE 1962 ELECTION. CANADA PROVS POL/PAR
SECT GP/REL CONSEN EFFICIENCY...MAJORIT 20. PAGE 89 RECORD
F1751 CHOOSE
STRATA

B64
US DEPT LABOR OFF SOLICITOR,LEGISLATIVE HISTORY OF LABOR
THE LABOR-MANAGEMENT AND DISCLOSURE ACT OF 1959. LEGIS
DELIB/GP WORKER ADMIN LOBBY PARL/PROC SANCTION DEBATE
CHOOSE GOV/REL 20 CONGRESS PRESIDENT. PAGE 136 POLICY
F2677

B64
WILLIAMSON O.E.,THE ECONOMICS OF DISCRETIONARY EFFICIENCY
BEHAVIOR: MANAGERIAL OBJECTIVES IN A THEORY OF THE MGT
FIRM. MARKET BUDGET CAP/ISM PRODUC DRIVE PERSON ECO/TAC
...STAT CHARTS BIBLIOG METH 20. PAGE 147 F2897 CHOOSE

B64
WRIGHT G.,RURAL REVOLUTION IN FRANCE: THE PEASANTRY PWR
IN THE TWENTIETH CENTURY. EUR+WWI MOD/EUR LAW STRATA
CULTURE AGRI POL/PAR DELIB/GP LEGIS ECO/TAC FRANCE
EDU/PROP COERCE CHOOSE ATTIT RIGID/FLEX HEALTH REV
...STAT CENSUS CHARTS VAL/FREE 20. PAGE 149 F2932

L64
ARMENGALD A.,"ECONOMIE ET COEXISTENCE." COM EUR+WWI MARKET
FUT USA+45 WOR+45 ECO/DEV ECO/UNDEV FINAN INT/ORG ECO/TAC
NAT/G EXEC CHOOSE ATTIT ALL/VALS...POLICY RELATIV AFR
DECISION TREND SOC/EXP WORK 20. PAGE 6 F0113 CAP/ISM

B65
HADWIGER D.F.,PRESSURES AND PROTEST. NAT/G LEGIS AGRI
PLAN LEAD PARTIC ROUTINE ATTIT POLICY. PAGE 53 GP/REL
F1030 LOBBY
CHOOSE

B65
MARGOLIS J.,THE PUBLIC ECONOMY OF URBAN LOC/G
COMMUNITIES. USA+45 LEGIS PROB/SOLV TAX LOBBY DECISION
CHOOSE ATTIT MUNICH. PAGE 85 F1668 FINAN

B65
RATNAM K.J.,COMMUNALISM AND THE POLITICAL PROCESS CONSTN
IN MALAYA. MALAYSIA WOR+45 ECO/UNDEV PARTIC CHOOSE GOV/REL
REPRESENT GP/REL CENTRAL ATTIT...CHARTS WORSHIP 20. REGION
PAGE 109 F2152

B65
SHAFFER H.G.,THE SOVIET SYSTEM IN THEORY AND MARXISM
PRACTICE: SELECTED WESTERN AND SOVIET VIEWS. USSR SOCISM
LAW SOCIETY CREATE FOR/AID EDU/PROP PRESS CHOOSE IDEA/COMP
PEACE ORD/FREE...ANTHOL 20 STALIN/J. PAGE 120 F2362

S65
SELLERS C.,"THE EQUILIBRIUM CYCLE IN TWO-PARTY CHOOSE
POLITICS." USA+45 USA-45 CULTURE R+D GP/REL TREND
MAJORITY DECISION. PAGE 119 F2351 POL/PAR

B66
COLE A.B.,SOCIALIST PARTIES IN POSTWAR JAPAN. POL/PAR
STRATA AGRI LABOR PLAN DIPLOM ECO/TAC AGREE LEAD POLICY
CHOOSE ATTIT...CHARTS 20 CHINJAP SOC/DEMPAR. SOCISM
PAGE 26 F0499 NAT/G

B66
DAVIES JC I.I.I.,NEIGHBORHOOD GROUPS AND URBAN NEIGH
RENEWAL. USA+45 PLAN LOBBY PARTIC CHOOSE RACE/REL CREATE
...POLICY DECISION SOC INT MUNICH SOC/INTEG 20 PROB/SOLV
NEWYORK/C. PAGE 30 F0586

B66
FORD P.,CARDINAL MORAN AND THE A. L. P. NAT/G CATHISM
POL/PAR SECT DELIB/GP LOBBY REV CHOOSE ORD/FREE SOCISM
MARXISM 19/20 AUSTRAL PROTESTANT LABOR/PAR. PAGE 42 LABOR
F0825 SOCIETY

B67
BLAIR G.S.,LEGISLATIVE BODIES IN CALIFORNIA. USA+45 LEGIS
LAW POL/PAR LOBBY APPORT CHOOSE REPRESENT GP/REL PROVS
...T CALIFORNIA. PAGE 15 F0293 LOC/G
ADJUD

B67
BUSEY J.L.,NOTES ON COSTA RICAN DEMOCRACY. CONSTN
COSTA/RICA L/A+17C NAT/G POL/PAR LEGIS CHOOSE OWN MAJORIT
ATTIT...BIBLIOG 20. PAGE 20 F0394 SOCIETY
ECO/UNDEV

B67
EVANS R.H.,COEXISTENCE: COMMUNISM AND ITS PRACTICE MARXISM
IN BOLOGNA, 1945-1965. ITALY CAP/ISM ADMIN CHOOSE CULTURE
PEACE ORD/FREE...SOC STAT DEEP/INT SAMP CHARTS POL/PAR
BIBLIOG MUNICH 20. PAGE 39 F0756

B67
GRIPP R.C.,PATTERNS OF SOVIET POLITICS (REV. ED.). COM
USSR LAW ELITES LOC/G PLAN CONTROL CT/SYS CHOOSE ADJUD
...POLICY BIBLIOG/A DICTIONARY 9/20. PAGE 51 F1003 POL/PAR

B67
JHANGIANI M.A.,JANA SANGH AND SWATANTRA: A PROFILE POL/PAR
OF THE RIGHTIST PARTIES IN INDIA. INDIA ADMIN LAISSEZ
CHOOSE MARXISM SOCISM...INT CHARTS BIBLIOG 20. NAT/LISM
PAGE 67 F1320 ATTIT

B67
MORRIS A.J.A.,PARLIAMENTARY DEMOCRACY IN THE TIME/SEQ

NINETEENTH CENTURY. UK INDUS LOC/G NAT/G POL/PAR CONSULT LEGIS INT/TRADE ADMIN CHOOSE SUFF SOVEREIGN 19 PARLIAMENT. PAGE 93 F1835 — CONSTN PARL/PROC POPULISM

B67
PRINCE C.E.,NEW JERSEY'S JEFFERSONIAN REPUBLICANS; THE GENESIS OF AN EARLY PARTY MACHINE (1789-1817). USA-45 LOC/G EDU/PROP PRESS CONTROL CHOOSE...CHARTS 18/19 NEW/JERSEY REPUBLICAN. PAGE 108 F2117 — POL/PAR CONSTN ADMIN PROVS

B67
TOMA P.A.,THE POLITICS OF FOOD FOR PEACE; EXECUTIVE-LEGISLATIVE INTERACTION. USA+45 ECO/UNDEV POL/PAR DEBATE EXEC LOBBY CHOOSE PEACE...DECISION CHARTS. PAGE 131 F2580 — FOR/AID POLICY LEGIS AGRI

L67
LAMBERT J.D.,"CORPORATE POLITICAL SPENDING AND CAMPAIGN FINANCE." LAW CONSTN FINAN LABOR LG/CO LOC/G NAT/G VOL/ASSN TEC/DEV ADJUD ADMIN PARTIC. PAGE 75 F1463 — USA+45 POL/PAR CHOOSE COST

S67
HALL B.,"THE PAINTER'S UNION: A PARTIAL VICTORY." USA+45 PROB/SOLV LEGIT ADMIN REPRESENT 20. PAGE 53 F1043 — LABOR CHIEF CHOOSE CRIME

S67
HALL B.,"THE COALITION AGAINST DISHWASHERS." USA+45 POL/PAR PROB/SOLV BARGAIN LEAD CHOOSE REPRESENT GP/REL ORD/FREE PWR...POLICY 20. PAGE 53 F1044 — LABOR ADMIN DOMIN WORKER

S67
NEALE R.S.,"WORKING CLASS WOMEN AND WOMEN'S SUFFRAGE." UK LAW CONSTN LABOR NAT/G DELIB/GP LEGIS WORKER PAY PARTIC CHOOSE 19 FEMALE/SEX. PAGE 97 F1906 — STRATA SEX SUFF DISCRIM

S67
PETRAS J.,"MINERS AND AGRARIAN RADICALISM." CHILE AGRI EXTR/IND WORKER CHOOSE ATTIT SOCISM MUNICH 20. PAGE 105 F2073 — PARTIC EDU/PROP LABOR

S67
PLOTT C.R.,"A NOTION OF EQUILIBRIUM AND ITS POSSIBILITY UNDER MAJORITY RULE." CREATE...DECISION STAT CHARTS 20. PAGE 106 F2094 — SIMUL EQUILIB CHOOSE MAJORITY

S67
SIPPEL D.,"INDIENS UNSICHERE ZUKUNFT." INDIA CULTURE ACADEM POL/PAR LEGIS COLONIAL CHOOSE SOVEREIGN...JURID 20. PAGE 122 F2416 — SOCIETY STRUCT ECO/UNDEV NAT/G

B86
O'CONNOR T.P.,THE PARNELL MOVEMENT: WITH A SKETCH OF IRISH PARTIES FROM 1843. IRELAND UK USA-45 LEGIS WORKER ECO/TAC COERCE CRIME REV CHOOSE ORD/FREE CATHISM LAISSEZ...SOC 19/20 PARLIAMENT PARNELL/CS LAND/LEAG. PAGE 100 F1957 — LEAD DOMIN POL/PAR POLICY

CHOU/ENLAI....CHOU EN-LAI

CHRIS/DEM....CHRISTIAN DEMOCRATIC PARTY (ALL NATIONS)

CHRISTENSEN C.R. F2430

CHRISTENSON C.L. F0471

CHRISTIAN....CHRISTIAN BELIEFS OR CHURCHES

B61
DE VRIES E.,MAN IN RAPID SOCIAL CHANGE. WOR+45 SOCIETY ECO/DEV ECO/UNDEV AGRI INDUS FAM SECT TEC/DEV ATTIT...RECORD 20 CHRISTIAN. PAGE 31 F0607 — CULTURE ALL/VALS SOC TASK

B66
PFEFFER K.H.,WELT IM UMBRUCH. SOCIETY STRUCT INDUS PROF/ORG SECT TEC/DEV PARTIC SUPEGO WORSHIP 20 CHRISTIAN. PAGE 106 F2076 — ORD/FREE STRATA CREATE

B66
RIZK C.,LE REGIME POLITIQUE LIBANAIS. ISLAM LEBANON STRUCT POL/PAR SECT LOBBY GP/REL 20 ARABS MUSLIM CHRISTIAN. PAGE 112 F2198 — ECO/UNDEV NAT/G CULTURE

B82
CUNNINGHAM W.,THE GROWTH OF ENGLISH INDUSTRY AND COMMERCE. FUT UK FINAN NAT/G CAP/ISM...POLICY 20 MERCANTLST CHRISTIAN POPE. PAGE 29 F0562 — INDUS INT/TRADE SML/CO CONSERVE

CHRIST-17C.... CHRISTENDOM TO 1700

B27
WEBER M.,GENERAL ECONOMIC HISTORY. CHRIST-17C MOD/EUR STRUCT AGRI EXTR/IND FINAN INDUS MARKET FAM NAT/G PROF/ORG SECT ECO/TAC MUNICH 8/20. PAGE 144 F2839 — ECO/DEV CAP/ISM

B36
HUBERMAN L.,MAN'S WORLDLY GOODS: THE STORY OF THE WEALTH OF NATIONS. CHRIST-17C EUR+WWI MOD/EUR SOCIETY DOMIN REV ORD/FREE...TIME/SEQ METH/COMP. PAGE 63 F1231 — WEALTH CAP/ISM MARXISM CREATE

L42
GRANT J.A.C.,"THE GUILD RETURNS TO AMERICA." CHRIST-17C USA-45 LEGIS LICENSE ADJUD CONTROL GP/REL. PAGE 50 F0978 — PROF/ORG JURID LABOR PWR

B46
CLOUGH S.B.,ECONOMIC HISTORY OF EUROPE. CHRIST-17C EUR+WWI MOD/EUR WOR-45 SOCIETY EXEC ATTIT WEALTH ...CONCPT GEN/LAWS WORK TOT/POP VAL/FREE 7/20. PAGE 25 F0493 — ECO/TAC CAP/ISM

B62
EINZIG P.,THE HISTORY OF FOREIGN EXCHANGE. CHRIST-17C ISLAM MEDIT-7 PRE/AMER WOR+45 ECO/DEV FINAN PLAN ECO/TAC ATTIT KNOWL WEALTH...SIMUL GEN/LAWS. PAGE 37 F0714 — MARKET TIME/SEQ INT/TRADE

B64
REDLICH F.,THE GERMAN MILITARY ENTERPRISER AND HIS WORK FORCE. CHRIST-17C GERMANY ELITES SOCIETY FINAN ECO/TAC CIVMIL/REL GP/REL INGP/REL...HIST/WRIT METH/COMP 14/17. PAGE 110 F2170 — EX/STRUC FORCES PROFIT WORKER

B67
GUTKIND E.A.,URBAN DEVELOPMENT IN SOUTHERN EUROPE* SPAIN AND PORTUGAL. CHRIST-17C EUR+WWI MOD/EUR PORTUGAL SPAIN CULTURE AGRI...SOC SAMP/SIZ BIBLIOG MUNICH. PAGE 52 F1015 — TEC/DEV ECO/DEV

S67
DEYRUP F.J.,"SOCIAL MOBILITY AS A MAJOR FACTOR IN ECONOMIC DEVELOPMENT." CHRIST-17C EUR+WWI MOD/EUR ECO/UNDEV DEMAND 20. PAGE 32 F0630 — STRATA ECO/DEV INDUS WORKER

S67
WAITS C.R.,"CRAFT GILDS AS AN INSTITUTIONAL BARRIER TO THE INDUSTRIAL REVOLUTION." CHRIST-17C MOD/EUR ECO/UNDEV CONTROL GP/REL ATTIT 16/19. PAGE 142 F2801 — TEC/DEV INDUS REV PROF/ORG

CHRONOLOGY....SEE TIME/SEQ

CHU K. F0472

CHURCH....SEE SECT

CHURCH/STA....CHURCH-STATE RELATIONS (ALL NATIONS)

B63
PRITCHETT C.H.,THE THIRD BRANCH OF GOVERNMENT. USA+45 USA-45 CONSTN SOCIETY INDUS SECT LEGIS JUDGE PROB/SOLV GOV/REL 20 SUPREME/CT CHURCH/STA. PAGE 108 F2122 — JURID NAT/G ADJUD CT/SYS

B66
MUNBY D.,ECONOMIC GROWTH IN WORLD PERSPECTIVE. AFR WOR+45 SOCIETY INDUS PLAN TEC/DEV ECO/TAC FOR/AID INT/TRADE COST CATHISM...ANTHOL 20 EUROPE/W CHURCH/STA. PAGE 95 F1859 — SECT ECO/UNDEV ECO/DEV

CHURCHLL/W....SIR WINSTON CHURCHILL

B67
BARDENS D.,CHURCHILL IN PARLIAMENT. UK DIPLOM ADJUD CONTROL AUTHORIT PERSON ORD/FREE 20 CHURCHLL/W PARLIAMENT. PAGE 10 F0186 — TOP/EX LEGIS GOV/REL

CIA....CENTRAL INTELLIGENCE AGENCY

B64
BLACKSTOCK P.W.,THE STRATEGY OF SUBVERSION. USA+45 FORCES EDU/PROP ADMIN COERCE GOV/REL...DECISION MGT 20 DEPT/DEFEN CIA DEPT/STATE. PAGE 15 F0292 — ORD/FREE DIPLOM CONTROL

S66
LANGLEY D.,"POSTSCRIPT ON THE COLONIZATION OF THE INTERNATIONAL TRADE UNION MOVEMENT" USA+45 ELITES FINAN DOMIN LEGIT ADMIN PWR...SOCIALIST 20 AFL/CIO CIA LOVESTN/J. PAGE 75 F1479 — INT/TRADE LABOR NAT/G CONTROL

B67
COTTAM R.W.,COMPETITIVE INTERFERENCE AND TWENTIETH CENTURY DIPLOMACY. IRAN ACT/RES CREATE PLAN ECO/TAC EFFICIENCY ATTIT...DECISION NEW/IDEA TREND 20 CIA. PAGE 28 F0541 — DIPLOM DOMIN GAME

CICERO....CICERO

CINCINNATI....CINCINNATI, OHIO

CINEMA....SEE FILM

CITIES....SEE MUNIC

CITIZENSHIP....SEE CITIZENSHP

CITIZENSHP....CITIZENSHIP

CITY/MGT....CITY MANAGEMENT, CITY MANAGERS; SEE ALSO MUNIC, ADMIN, MGT, LOC/G

CIV/DEFENS....CIVIL DEFENSE (SYSTEMS, PLANNING, AND

B55
US ADVISORY COMN INTERGOV REL,THE COMMISSION ON INTERGOVERNMENTAL RELATIONS; A REPORT TO THE PRESIDENT FOR TRANSMITTAL TO THE CONGRESS. USA+45 ECO/DEV AGRI COM/IND FINAN FORCES PLAN EDU/PROP HEALTH WEALTH...STAT MUNICH 20 CIV/DEFENS. PAGE 133 F2630
GOV/REL NAT/G LOC/G PROVS

CIV/DISOBD....CIVIL DISOBEDIENCE

CIV/RIGHTS....CIVIL RIGHTS: CONTEMPORARY CIVIL RIGHTS MOVEMENTS; SEE ALSO RACE/REL, CONSTN + LAW

B58
MOSKOWITZ M.,HUMAN RIGHTS AND WORLD ORDER. INT/ORG PLAN GP/REL NAT/LISM SOVEREIGN...CONCPT 20 UN TREATY CIV/RIGHTS. PAGE 94 F1845
DIPLOM INT/LAW ORD/FREE

B65
LYONS G.M.,AMERICA: PURPOSE AND POWER. UK USA+45 FINAN INDUS MARKET WORKER TEC/DEV DIPLOM AUTOMAT NUC/PWR WAR RACE/REL ORD/FREE 20 EEC CONGRESS SUPREME/CT CIV/RIGHTS. PAGE 82 F1617
PWR PROB/SOLV ECO/DEV TASK

B66
EBONY,THE NEGRO HANDBOOK. ACADEM LABOR LOC/G SECT FORCES WORKER CT/SYS CRIME DISCRIM ORD/FREE...BIOG SOC/INTEG 19/20 NEGRO CIV/RIGHTS. PAGE 36 F0692
RACE/REL EDU/PROP LAW STAT

B66
SOVERN M.I.,LEGAL RESTRAINTS ON RACIAL DISCRIMINATION IN EMPLOYMENT. USA+45 LAW INDUS LG/CO SML/CO DELIB/GP LEGIS SANCTION 20 NLRB PRESIDENT NEGRO CIV/RIGHTS RAILROAD. PAGE 124 F2446
DISCRIM RACE/REL WORKER JURID

S67
EDGEWORTH A.B. JR.,"CIVIL RIGHTS PLUS THREE YEARS: BANKS AND THE ANTI-DISCRIMINATION LAW" USA+45 SOCIETY DELIB/GP RACE/REL EFFICIENCY 20 NEGRO CIV/RIGHTS. PAGE 36 F0701
WORKER DISCRIM FINAN LAW

CIVIL AERONAUTICS BOARD....SEE CAB

CIVIL DEFENSE....SEE CIV/DEFENS

CIVIL RIGHTS....SEE CIV/RIGHTS

CIVIL SERVICE....SEE ADMIN

CIVIL/CODE....CIVIL CODE (FRANCE)

CIVIL/LAW....CIVIL LAW

CIVIL/LIB....CIVIL LIBERTIES; SEE ALSO CONSTN + LAW

B62
HIRSCHFIELD R.S.,THE CONSTITUTION AND THE COURT. AFR SCHOOL WAR RACE/REL EQUILIB ORD/FREE...POLICY MAJORIT DECISION JURID 18/20 PRESIDENT CIVIL/LIB SUPREME/CT CONGRESS. PAGE 60 F1175
ADJUD PWR CONSTN LAW

B65
GRIFFIN C.E.,THE FREE SOCIETY. CONSTN SOCIETY MARKET FEDERAL RATIONAL WEALTH...MAJORIT 20 CIVIL/LIB. PAGE 51 F0999
CONCPT ORD/FREE CAP/ISM POPULISM

CIVIL/SERV....CIVIL SERVICE; SEE ALSO ADMIN

N19
FIKS M.,PUBLIC ADMINISTRATION IN ISRAEL (PAMPHLET). ISRAEL SCHOOL EX/STRUC BUDGET PAY INGP/REL ...DECISION 20 CIVIL/SERV. PAGE 41 F0792
EDU/PROP NAT/G ADMIN WORKER

B58
US HOUSE COMM POST OFFICE,MANPOWER UTILIZATION IN THE FEDERAL GOVERNMENT. USA+45 DIST/IND EX/STRUC LEGIS CONFER EFFICIENCY 20 CONGRESS CIVIL/SERV. PAGE 137 F2702
ADMIN WORKER DELIB/GP NAT/G

B58
US HOUSE COMM POST OFFICE,MANPOWER UTILIZATION IN THE FEDERAL GOVERNMENT. USA+45 DIST/IND EX/STRUC LEGIS CONFER EFFICIENCY 20 CONGRESS CIVIL/SERV. PAGE 137 F2703
ADMIN WORKER DELIB/GP NAT/G

B59
VERNEY D.V.,PUBLIC ENTERPRISE IN SWEDEN. FUT SWEDEN UK INDUS POL/PAR LEGIS PROB/SOLV CAP/ISM INT/TRADE CONTROL SOCISM...MGT CONCPT NAT/COMP 20 SOCDEM/PAR CIVIL/SERV. PAGE 141 F2778
ECO/DEV POLICY LG/CO NAT/G

B64
AHMAD M.,THE CIVIL SERVANT IN PAKISTAN. PAKISTAN ECO/UNDEV COLONIAL INGP/REL...SOC CHARTS BIBLIOG 20 CIVIL/SERV. PAGE 3 F0051
WELF/ST ADMIN ATTIT STRATA

B66
ZINKIN T.,CHALLENGES IN INDIA. INDIA PAKISTAN LAW AGRI FINAN INDUS TOP/EX TEC/DEV CONTROL ROUTINE ORD/FREE PWR 20 NEHRU/J SHASTRI/LB CIVIL/SERV.
NAT/G ECO/TAC POLICY

PAGE 150 F2964
ADMIN

CIVIL/WAR....CIVIL WAR

CIVIL-MILITARY RELATIONS....SEE CIVMIL/REL

CIVMIL/REL....CIVIL-MILITARY RELATIONS

S41
LASSWELL H.D.,"THE GARRISON STATE" (BMR)" FUT WOR+45 ELITES INTELL FORCES ECO/TAC DOMIN EDU/PROP COERCE INGP/REL 20. PAGE 76 F1485
NAT/G DIPLOM PWR CIVMIL/REL

B50
KOENIG L.W.,THE SALE OF THE TANKERS. USA+45 SEA DIST/IND POL/PAR DIPLOM ADMIN CIVMIL/REL ATTIT ...DECISION 20 PRESIDENT DEPT/STATE. PAGE 72 F1414
NAT/G POLICY PLAN GOV/REL

B59
STERNBERG F.,THE MILITARY AND INDUSTRIAL REVOLUTION OF OUR TIME. USA+45 USSR WOR+45 WORKER COMPUTER PLAN TEC/DEV NUC/PWR GP/REL...POLICY NAT/COMP 20. PAGE 126 F2481
DIPLOM FORCES INDUS CIVMIL/REL

B60
CARPER E.T.,THE DEFENSE APPROPRIATIONS RIDER (PAMPHLET). USA+45 CONSTN CHIEF DELIB/GP LEGIS BUDGET LOBBY CIVMIL/REL...POLICY 20 CONGRESS EISNHWR/DD DEPT/DEFEN PRESIDENT BOSTON. PAGE 22 F0419
GOV/REL ADJUD LAW CONTROL

B61
STANLEY C.J.,LATE CH'ING FINANCE: HU KUANG-YUNG AS AN INNOVATOR. ASIA NAT/G FORCES BUDGET TAX WAR GOV/REL COST...POLICY BIOG CHARTS BIBLIOG 19. PAGE 125 F2469
FINAN ECO/TAC CIVMIL/REL ADMIN

B61
US SENATE COMM ON FOREIGN RELS,INTERNATIONAL DEVELOPMENT AND SECURITY: HEARINGS ON BILL (2 VOLS.). ECO/UNDEV FINAN FORCES REV COST WEALTH ...CHARTS 20 AID PRESIDENT. PAGE 139 F2747
FOR/AID CIVMIL/REL ORD/FREE ECO/TAC

B62
CARPER E.T.,ILLINOIS GOES TO CONGRESS FOR ARMY LAND. USA+45 LAW EXTR/IND PROVS REGION CIVMIL/REL GOV/REL FEDERAL ATTIT 20 ILLINOIS SENATE CONGRESS DIRKSEN/E DOUGLAS/P. PAGE 22 F0420
ADMIN LOBBY GEOG LEGIS

B62
DUPRE J.S.,SCIENCE AND THE NATION: POLICY AND POLITICS. USA+45 LAW ACADEM FORCES ADMIN CIVMIL/REL GOV/REL EFFICIENCY PEACE...TREND 20 SCI/ADVSRY. PAGE 35 F0682
R+D INDUS TEC/DEV NUC/PWR

B62
SCHILLING W.R.,STRATEGY, POLITICS, AND DEFENSE BUDGETS. AFR USA+45 CHIEF LEGIS PLAN TEC/DEV BAL/PWR BUDGET NUC/PWR WAR CIVMIL/REL GOV/REL PWR 20 EISNHWR/DD. PAGE 117 F2297
NAT/G POLICY FORCES DETER

B63
PERLO V.,MILITARISM AND INDUSTRY. USA+45 INT/TRADE EDU/PROP DETER KNOWL...CHARTS MAPS 20. PAGE 105 F2064
CIVMIL/REL INDUS LOBBY ARMS/CONT

N63
US COMM STRENG SEC FREE WORLD,THE SCOPE AND DISTRIBUTION OF UNITED STATES MILITARY AND ECONOMIC ASSISTANCE PROGRAMS (PAMPHLET). USA+45 PLAN BAL/PWR BUDGET DIPLOM CONTROL CIVMIL/REL ATTIT. PAGE 134 F2648
DELIB/GP POLICY FOR/AID ORD/FREE

B64
FIESER M.E.,ECONOMIC POLICY AND WAR POTENTIAL. AFR WOR+45 ECO/DEV INDUS NAT/G FORCES TEC/DEV NUC/PWR CIVMIL/REL ORD/FREE 20. PAGE 40 F0791
INT/TRADE POLICY ECO/TAC DETER

B64
HOLLEY I.B. JR.,US ARMY IN WORLD WAR II: SPECIAL STUDIES: BUYING AIRCRAFT: MATERIEL PROCUREMENT FOR THE ARMY AIR FORCES. USA+45 USA-45 BUDGET WEAPON GOV/REL PRODUC 20. PAGE 61 F1198
FORCES COST DIST/IND CIVMIL/REL

B64
REDLICH F.,THE GERMAN MILITARY ENTERPRISER AND HIS WORK FORCE. CHRIST-17C GERMANY ELITES SOCIETY FINAN ECO/TAC CIVMIL/REL GP/REL INGP/REL...HIST/WRIT METH/COMP 14/17. PAGE 110 F2170
EX/STRUC FORCES PROFIT WORKER

B64
WERNETTE J.P.,GOVERNMENT AND BUSINESS. LABOR CAP/ISM ECO/TAC INT/TRADE TAX ADMIN AUTOMAT NUC/PWR CIVMIL/REL DEMAND...MGT 20 MONOPOLY. PAGE 145 F2859
NAT/G FINAN ECO/DEV CONTROL

L64
KOLODZIEJ E.A.,"RATIONAL CONSENT AND DEFENSE BUDGETS: THE ROLE OF CONGRESS, 1945-1962." LEGIS DIPLOM CONTROL PARL/PROC 20 CONGRESS. PAGE 72 F1423
DECISION PLAN CIVMIL/REL BUDGET

B65
BEAUFRE A.,AN INTRODUCTION TO STRATEGY, WITH PARTICULAR REFERENCE TO PROBLEMS OF DEFENSE, POLITICS, ECONOMICS IN THE NUCLEAR AGE. WOR+45 FORCES DIPLOM DETER CIVMIL/REL GP/REL...NEW/IDEA IDEA/COMP 20. PAGE 12 F0226
PLAN NUC/PWR WEAPON DECISION

B65
MELMANS S.,OUR DEPLETED SOCIETY. AFR SPACE USA+45 ECO/DEV FORCES BUDGET ECO/TAC ADMIN WEAPON EFFICIENCY 20. PAGE 89 F1753
CIVMIL/REL INDUS EDU/PROP CONTROL

B65
THAYER F.C. JR.,AIR TRANSPORT POLICY AND NATIONAL SECURITY: A POLITICAL, ECONOMIC, AND MILITARY ANALYSIS. DIST/IND OP/RES PLAN TEC/DEV DIPLOM DETER WAR COST EFFICIENCY...POLICY BIBLIOG 20 DEPT/DEFEN FAA CAB. PAGE 129 F2548
AIR FORCES CIVMIL/REL ORD/FREE

B65
WARD R.,BACKGROUND MATERIAL ON ECONOMIC IMPACT OF FEDERAL PROCUREMENT - 1965: FOR JOINT ECONOMIC COMMITTEE US CONGRESS. FINAN ROUTINE WEAPON CIVMIL/REL EFFICIENCY...STAT CHARTS 20 CONGRESS. PAGE 143 F2818
ECO/DEV NAT/G OWN GOV/REL

B66
BAKLANOFF E.N.,NEW PERSPECTIVES ON BRAZIL. BRAZIL SOCIETY INDUS DOMIN LEAD REV CIVMIL/REL...GEOG PSY LING ANTHOL 20. PAGE 8 F0156
ECO/UNDEV TEC/DEV DIPLOM ORD/FREE

B66
HOROWITZ I.L.,THREE WORLDS OF DEVELOPMENT. COM USA+45 STRUCT ECO/DEV PLAN PROB/SOLV TEC/DEV CIVMIL/REL...PHIL/SCI IDEA/COMP 20. PAGE 62 F1216
ECO/UNDEV BAL/PWR POL/PAR REV

B66
RUPPENTHAL K.M.,TRANSPORTATION AND TOMORROW. FUT SPACE USA+45 SEA AIR FORCES TEC/DEV INT/TRADE ...ANTHOL 20 RAILROAD. PAGE 115 F2261
DIST/IND PLAN CIVMIL/REL PREDICT

B66
US SENATE COMM APPROPRIATIONS,FOREIGN ASSISTANCE AND RELATED AGENCIES APPROPRIATIONS FOR FISCAL YEAR 1967: HEARINGS... ON H. R. 17788. ECO/UNDEV INT/ORG FORCES INSPECT ECO/TAC GIVE DEBATE WEAPON CIVMIL/REL WEALTH...INT 20 CONGRESS DEPT/DEFEN DEPT/STATE DEPT/HEW AID. PAGE 138 F2727
BUDGET FOR/AID DIPLOM COST

S66
COHEN A.,"THE TECHNOLOGY/ELITE APPROACH TO THE DEVELOPMENTAL PROCESS* PERUVIAN CASE STUDY." L/A+17C STRUCT CREATE ECO/TAC FOR/AID CIVMIL/REL MARXISM TECHRACY HYPO/EXP. PAGE 26 F0496
ECO/UNDEV ELITES PERU

B67
DAVIS F.M.,COME AS A CONQUEROR: THE UNITED STATES ARMY'S OCCUPATION OF GERMANY: 1945-1949. EUR+WWI GERMANY USA+45 SOCIETY PLAN BAL/PWR DIPLOM FOR/AID PERS/REL DEMAND PEACE ORD/FREE 20. PAGE 30 F0588
FORCES CIVMIL/REL ECO/TAC CONTROL

B67
PELTASON J.W.,FUNCTIONS AND POLICIES OF AMERICAN GOVERNMENT (3RD ED.). USA+45 FINAN INDUS EDU/PROP CIVMIL/REL RACE/REL ORD/FREE...ANTHOL T 20 JOHNSON/LB. PAGE 104 F2052
NAT/G GOV/REL POLICY PLAN

S67
CRAIG A.,"ARGENTINA: THE LATEST REVOLUTION." ELITES NAT/G CHIEF FORCES ECO/TAC CIVMIL/REL GOV/REL EQUILIB PRIVIL 20 ARGEN. PAGE 28 F0550
ECO/UNDEV FINAN ATTIT REV

S67
FLACKS R.,"CONSCRIPTION IN A DEMOCRATIC SOCIETY." USA+45 WORKER CONTROL SUFF SUPEGO. PAGE 41 F0807
POLICY FORCES ORD/FREE CIVMIL/REL

S67
GOSALVEZ R.B.,"PERFIL DEL GENERAL VINCENTE ROJO." SPAIN DIPLOM CIVMIL/REL EFFICIENCY PERSON SKILL 20 BOLIV. PAGE 49 F0966
WAR FORCES ELITES BIOG

S67
MOLTMANN G.,"ZUR FORMULIERUNG DER AMERIKANISCHEN BESATZUNGSPOLITIK IN DEUTSCHLAND AM ENDE DES ZWEITEN WELTKRIEGES" GERMANY ECO/TAC ADMIN WAR CIVMIL/REL ORD/FREE FASCISM 20. PAGE 92 F1815
FORCES CONTROL POLICY INDUS

S67
WOLFE T.W.,"SOVIET MILITARY POLICY AT THE FIFTY YEAR MARK." USSR VIETNAM WOR+45 RATION AGREE WAR WEAPON CIVMIL/REL TREATY. PAGE 148 F2917
FORCES POLICY TIME/SEQ PLAN

N67
US SENATE COMM ON FOREIGN REL,SURVEY OF THE ALLIANCE FOR PROGRESS: THE LATIN AMERICAN MILITARY (PAMPHLET). USA+45 INT/ORG POL/PAR DIPLOM AGREE GP/REL ROLE ORD/FREE 20. PAGE 139 F2746
L/A+17C FORCES CIVMIL/REL POLICY

CLABAULT J.M. F0473

CLAIRBORN E.L. F0474

CLAIRMONTE F. F0475

CLAN....SEE KIN

CLAPHAN J.H. F0476

CLARK C. F0477

CLARK J.B. F0478

CLARK J.J. F0479

CLARK J.M. F0480,F0481,F0482,F0483

CLARK P.G. F0484

CLARK T.D. F0485

CLARK/JB....JOHN BATES CLARK

B35
HICKS J.R.,THE THEORY OF WAGES. INDUS NAT/G PAY PRICE CONTROL COST EFFICIENCY WEALTH 19/20 MARSHALL/A CLARK/JB. PAGE 59 F1164
INCOME WORKER LABOR PRODUC

CLASS DIVISION....SEE STRATA

CLASS, SOCIAL....SEE STRATA

CLASSIF....CLASSIFICATION, TYPOLOGY, SET THEORY

B31
LORWIN L.L.,ADVISORY ECONOMIC COUNCILS. EUR+WWI FRANCE GERMANY PROB/SOLV INGP/REL...CLASSIF GP/COMP. PAGE 82 F1601
CONSULT DELIB/GP ECO/TAC NAT/G

B38
MEADE J.E.,AN INTRODUCTION TO ECONOMIC ANALYSIS AND POLICY (AMERICAN EDITION EDITED BY C.J. HITCH). FINAN INDUS MARKET LABOR INT/TRADE CONTROL COST DEMAND INCOME...CLASSIF CHARTS T 20 KEYNES/JM MONOPOLY. PAGE 89 F1737
CONCPT PROFIT PRODUC

B46
HARRISON S.M.,AMERICAN FOUNDATIONS FOR SOCIAL WELFARE. OP/RES CONTROL...POLICY MGT METH/CNCPT STAT TREND BIBLIOG. PAGE 56 F1092
GIVE FINAN CLASSIF ADMIN

S52
KLUMB S.,"EMPLOYEE DETERMINATION OF MANAGERIAL FUNCTIONS AND CHARACTERISTICS." DELIB/GP WORKER PARTIC ROUTINE INGP/REL...CLASSIF OBS QU. PAGE 72 F1410
MGT INDUS EX/STRUC CHOOSE

B53
PURCELL T.V.,THE WORKER SPEAKS HIS MIND ON COMPANY AND UNION. WORKER ADJUD LEAD RACE/REL ATTIT DRIVE MARXISM...MGT CLASSIF STAT OBS INT SAMP BIBLIOG. PAGE 108 F2131
LABOR PARTIC INGP/REL HAPPINESS

B55
COLE G.D.H.,STUDIES IN CLASS STRUCTURE. UK NAT/G WORKER TEC/DEV EDU/PROP...CLASSIF CHARTS 20. PAGE 26 F0501
STRUCT STRATA ELITES CONCPT

L56
TAGLIACOZZO D.L.,"TRADE-UNION GOVERNMENT, ITS NATURE AND ITS PROBLEMS: A BIBLIOGRAPHICAL REVIEW, 1945-1955." STRUCT LEAD PARTIC CHOOSE ATTIT ...MAJORIT METH/CNCPT BIBLIOG. PAGE 128 F2526
CLASSIF LABOR INGP/REL GP/REL

S57
TANNENBAUM A.S.,"ORGANIZATIONAL CONTROL STRUCTURE: A GENERAL DESCRIPTIVE TECHNIQUE AS APPLIED TO FOUR LOCAL UNIONS." LABOR PWR...METH/CNCPT CLASSIF QU CHARTS. PAGE 128 F2530
WORKER PARTIC STRUCT CONTROL

B58
TAFT P.,CORRUPTION AND RACKETEERING IN THE LABOR MOVEMENT (PAMPHLET). ADMIN SANCTION CENTRAL ROLE WEALTH...POLICY CLASSIF. PAGE 128 F2525
LABOR INGP/REL GP/REL CRIME

B58
WARNER A.W.,CONCEPTS AND CASES IN ECONOMIC ANALYSIS. PROB/SOLV BARGAIN CONTROL INCOME PRODUC ...ECOMETRIC MGT CONCPT CLASSIF CHARTS 20 KEYNES/JM. PAGE 143 F2820
ECO/TAC DEMAND EQUILIB COST

B59
BARBASH J.,UNIONS AND UNION LEADERSHIP. NAT/G WORKER TEC/DEV ECO/TAC PARTIC GP/REL RACE/REL ORD/FREE CLASSIF. PAGE 10 F0183
LABOR VOL/ASSN CAP/ISM LEAD

B59
MAYER H.M.,READINGS IN URBAN GEOGRAPHY. WOR+45 SOCIETY DIST/IND INDUS MARKET HABITAT...CLASSIF CENSUS CHARTS ANTHOL MUNICH 20 WATER. PAGE 87 F1706
GEOG STRUCT

S59
DUNNING J.H.,"NON-PECUNIARY ELEMENTS AND BUSINESS BEHAVIOUR." PLAN PROB/SOLV COST...METH/CNCPT CLASSIF QUANT STAT. PAGE 35 F0681
DECISION DRIVE PRODUC PRICE

S59
SHEPPARD H.L.,"THE POLITICAL ATTITUDES AND PREFERENCES OF UNION MEMBERS: THE CASE OF THE DETROIT AUTO WORKERS." LOBBY CHOOSE ROLE...CLASSIF QU SAMP TREND. PAGE 120 F2376
LABOR ATTIT WORKER

S59
STINCHCOMBE A.L.,"BUREAUCRATIC AND CRAFT
CONSTRUC

ADMINISTRATION OF PRODUCTION: A COMPARATIVE STUDY" (BMR)" USA+45 STRUCT EX/STRUC ECO/TAC GP/REL ...CLASSIF GP/COMP IDEA/COMP GEN/LAWS 20 WEBER/MAX. PAGE 126 F2490 — PROC/MFG ADMIN PLAN

B61
DE GRAZIA A.,AMERICAN WELFARE. CLIENT FINAN LABOR LOC/G NAT/G NEIGH EDU/PROP GP/REL...CLASSIF CON/ANAL CHARTS BIBLIOG. PAGE 31 F0598 — GIVE WEALTH SECT VOL/ASSN

B62
GORT M.,DIVERSIFICATION AND INTEGRATION IN AMERICAN INDUSTRY. CLIENT DIST/IND PROC/MFG SERV/IND LG/CO CONTROL DEMAND PWR...METH/CNCPT STAT TREND CON/ANAL GP/COMP. PAGE 49 F0964 — CONCPT GP/REL CLASSIF

B63
RILEY J.W. JR.,THE CORPORATION AND ITS PUBLICS. ESSAYS ON THE CORPORATE IMAGE. CLIENT ISOLAT AGE ATTIT...POLICY SOC METH/CNCPT INT. PAGE 111 F2193 — LG/CO CLASSIF GP/REL NEIGH

L63
LIVERNASH E.R.,"THE RELATION OF POWER TO THE STRUCTURE AND PROCESS OF COLLECTIVE BARGAINING." ADJUD ORD/FREE...POLICY MGT CLASSIF GP/COMP. PAGE 81 F1589 — LABOR GP/REL PWR ECO/TAC

B64
BALASSA B.,TRADE PROSPECTS FOR DEVELOPING COUNTRIES. WOR+45 ECO/DEV AGRI EXTR/IND INDUS CREATE PLAN PRICE...ECOMETRIC CLASSIF TIME/SEQ GEN/METH. PAGE 8 F0158 — INT/TRADE ECO/UNDEV TREND STAT

S64
HORECKY P.L.,"LIBRARY OF CONGRESS PUBLICATIONS IN AID OF USSR AND EAST EUROPEAN RESEARCH." BULGARIA CZECHOSLVK POLAND USSR YUGOSLAVIA NAT/G POL/PAR DIPLOM ADMIN GOV/REL...CLASSIF 20. PAGE 62 F1214 — BIBLIOG/A COM MARXISM

B65
HLA MYINT U.,THE ECONOMICS OF THE DEVELOPING COUNTRIES. USA+45 WOR+45 AGRI FINAN NAT/G INT/TRADE ...CLASSIF CENSUS TREND NAT/COMP SIMUL GEN/LAWS. PAGE 60 F1180 — ECO/UNDEV FOR/AID GEOG

B65
WILKINSON T.O.,THE URBANIZATION OF JAPANESE LABOR, 1868-1955. AGRI PROC/MFG CAP/ISM PRODUC PROFIT ...SOC CLASSIF CENSUS CHARTS MUNICH 19/20 CHINJAP. PAGE 146 F2887 — LABOR INDUS GEOG

B67
TUMIN M.M.,SOCIAL STRATIFICATION; THE FORMS AND FUNCTIONS OF INEQUALITY. SENIOR SANCTION WEALTH ...SOC CLASSIF METH 20. PAGE 131 F2592 — STRATA DISCRIM CONCPT SOCIETY

S67
ADAMS D.W.,"MINIFUNDIA IN AGRARIAN REFORM: A COLOMBIAN EXAMPLE."...SOC CLASSIF 20 COLOMB. PAGE 2 F0035 — AGRI METH/COMP OWN PRODUC

S67
MERIKOSKI V.,"BASIC PROBLEMS OF UNIVERSITY ADMINISTRATION." PROVS SECT CONTROL...CLASSIF 20. PAGE 90 F1760 — ACADEM ADMIN SOVEREIGN METH/COMP

S67
SANDMEYER R.L.,"METHODOLOGICAL ISSUES IN THE STUDY OF LABOR FORCE PARTICIPATION RATES." WOR+45 ...CLASSIF REGRESS CHARTS SIMUL. PAGE 116 F2278 — METH CON/ANAL PARTIC WORKER

S67
SCHWARZWELLER H.K.,"SOCIAL CLASS ORIGINS, RURAL-URBAN MIGRATION, AND ECONOMIC LIFE CHANGES." USA+45 SOCIETY STRUCT FAM NEIGH INCOME...SOC RECORD CHARTS MUNICH. PAGE 118 F2326 — CLASSIF WEALTH AGRI

CLAUNCH J.M. F0486

CLAUSWTZ/K....KARL VON CLAUSEWITZ

CLEGERN W.M. F0487

CLELLAND D.A. F0488

CLEMENCE/G....GEORGES CLEMENCEAU

CLEMENCEAU, GEORGES....SEE CLEMENCE/G

CLEMENT M.O. F0489

CLEMHOUT S. F0490

CLEMSON....CLEMSON UNIVERSITY

CLEVELAND A.S. F0491

CLEVELAND....CLEVELAND, OHIO

B61
SACKS S.,FINANCING GOVERNMENT IN A METROPOLITAN GOVERNMENT. USA+45 ECO/DEV R+D LOC/G GOV/REL ...BIBLIOG MUNICH 20 CLEVELAND. PAGE 115 F2269 — FINAN PLAN BUDGET

CLEVELND/G....PRESIDENT GROVER CLEVELAND

CLIENT....CLIENTS, CLIENTELE (BUT NOT CUSTOMERS)

B40
CAMPBELL P.,CONSUMER REPRESENTATION IN THE NEW DEAL. AGRI INDUS MARKET EX/STRUC PLAN CAP/ISM CONTROL GP/REL DEMAND POLICY. PAGE 21 F0408 — CLIENT REPRESENT NAT/G

B47
SLICHTER S.H.,THE CHALLENGE OF INDUSTRIAL RELATIONS: TRADE UNIONS, MANAGEMENT AND THE PUBLIC INTEREST. PLAN ECO/TAC ADJUD CONTROL LEAD SANCTION GP/REL INGP/REL INCOME. PAGE 123 F2421 — LABOR MGT CLIENT POLICY

B48
WHYTE W.F.,HUMAN RELATIONS IN THE RESTAURANT INDUSTRY (1ST ED). CLIENT WORKER WAR ATTIT...MGT OBS INT. PAGE 146 F2874 — INGP/REL GP/REL SERV/IND LABOR

S48
CLEVELAND A.S.,"NAM: SPOKESMAN FOR INDUSTRY?" LEGIS PLAN LEAD LOBBY PARTIC CONSEN INCOME ATTIT ROLE ORD/FREE POLICY. PAGE 25 F0491 — VOL/ASSN CLIENT REPRESENT INDUS

B56
REDFORD E.S.,PUBLIC ADMINISTRATION AND POLICY FORMATION: STUDIES IN OIL, GAS, BANKING, RIVER DEVELOPMENT AND CORPORATE INVESTIGATIONS. USA+45 CLIENT NAT/G ADMIN LOBBY REPRESENT GOV/REL INGP/REL 20. PAGE 110 F2167 — EX/STRUC PROB/SOLV CONTROL EXEC

B56
WILCOX W.W.,SOCIAL RESPONSIBILITY IN FARM LEADERSHIP. CLIENT LEGIS EXEC LOBBY GP/REL ATTIT WEALTH. PAGE 146 F2880 — AGRI LEAD VOL/ASSN WORKER

S56
BROWN J.S.,"UNION SIZE AS A FUNCTION OF INTRA-UNION CONFLICT." CLIENT CONTROL CHOOSE EFFICIENCY ATTIT TREND. PAGE 19 F0370 — LABOR INGP/REL CONSEN DRIVE

S56
LANDAUER J.D.,"PROFESSIONAL CONSULTANTS: A NEW FACTOR IN REAL ESTATE." USA+45 PROB/SOLV ECO/TAC PERS/REL DEMAND EFFICIENCY DECISION. PAGE 75 F1467 — CONSULT CONSTRUC CLIENT

B57
BERLE A.A. JR.,ECONOMIC POWER AND FREE SOCIETY (PAMPHLET). CLIENT CONSTN EX/STRUC ECO/TAC CONTROL PARTIC PWR WEALTH MAJORIT. PAGE 14 F0261 — LG/CO CAP/ISM INGP/REL LEGIT

S58
EMERSON F.D.,"THE ROLES OF MANAGEMENT AND SHAREHOLDERS IN CORPORATE GOVERNMENT." CLIENT DELIB/GP CREATE ADMIN EXEC PARTIC PERS/REL PWR. PAGE 37 F0728 — LG/CO LAW INGP/REL REPRESENT

B59
FERRY W.H.,THE CORPORATION AND THE ECONOMY. CLIENT LAW CONSTN LABOR NAT/G PLAN INT/TRADE PARTIC CONSEN ORD/FREE PWR POLICY. PAGE 40 F0787 — LG/CO CONTROL REPRESENT

B60
FORBUSH D.R.,PROBLEMS OF CORPORATE POWER. CLIENT LAW ELITES ADJUD...DECISION MGT. PAGE 42 F0822 — LG/CO PWR CONTROL GP/REL

B60
THOMPSON V.A.,THE REGULATORY PROCESS IN OPA RATIONING. USA-45 CLIENT PROB/SOLV ADMIN LOBBY REPRESENT 20. PAGE 130 F2566 — EX/STRUC GOV/REL INGP/REL

B61
DE GRAZIA A.,AMERICAN WELFARE. CLIENT FINAN LABOR LOC/G NAT/G NEIGH EDU/PROP GP/REL...CLASSIF CON/ANAL CHARTS BIBLIOG. PAGE 31 F0598 — GIVE WEALTH SECT VOL/ASSN

B61
ENGLER R.,THE POLITICS OF OIL. USA+45 CLIENT ELITES DOMIN EDU/PROP EXEC PWR 20. PAGE 38 F0734 — LOBBY REPRESENT POLICY

B62
GORT M.,DIVERSIFICATION AND INTEGRATION IN AMERICAN INDUSTRY. CLIENT DIST/IND PROC/MFG SERV/IND LG/CO CONTROL DEMAND PWR...METH/CNCPT STAT TREND CON/ANAL GP/COMP. PAGE 49 F0964 — CONCPT GP/REL CLASSIF

B62
HATTERY L.H.,INFORMATION RETRIEVAL MANAGEMENT. CLIENT INDUS TOP/EX COMPUTER OP/RES TEC/DEV ROUTINE COST EFFICIENCY RIGID/FLEX...METH/COMP ANTHOL 20. PAGE 57 F1113 — R+D COMPUT/IR MGT CREATE

B63
RILEY J.W. JR.,THE CORPORATION AND ITS PUBLICS. ESSAYS ON THE CORPORATE IMAGE. CLIENT ISOLAT AGE ATTIT...POLICY SOC METH/CNCPT INT. PAGE 111 F2193 — LG/CO CLASSIF GP/REL NEIGH

S64
LEFF N.H.,"ECONOMIC DEVELOPMENT THROUGH BUREAUCRATIC CORRUPTION." ELITES NAT/G ROUTINE REPRESENT GP/REL PERS/REL. PAGE 77 F1511 — ECO/UNDEV CLIENT EX/STRUC

B65
US OFFICE ECONOMIC OPPORTUNITY,CATALOG OF FEDERAL — BIBLIOG

PROGRAMS FOR INDIVIDUAL AND COMMUNITY IMPROVEMENT. CLIENT
USA+45 GIVE RECEIVE ADMIN HEALTH KNOWL SKILL WEALTH ECO/TAC
...CHARTS MUNICH. PAGE 138 F2721

S65
WILDAVSKY A.,"TVA AND POWER POLITICS." USA+45 PWR
CLIENT PROB/SOLV EXEC GOV/REL 20. PAGE 146 F2882 EX/STRUC
LOBBY

L67
ROBERTS E.F.,"THE CASE OF THE UNWARY HOME BUYER: ADJUD
THE HOUSING MERCHANT DID IT." USA+45 CLIENT CONSTRUC
DIST/IND MARKET LG/CO SML/CO PROB/SOLV LEGIT COST OWN
PROFIT. PAGE 112 F2207 LAW

S67
BRAUCHER R.,"RECLAMATION OF GOODS FROM A FRAUDULENT LAW
BUYER." USA+45 CLIENT FINAN CT/SYS PERS/REL COST ADJUD
WEALTH. PAGE 18 F0341 GOV/REL
INT/TRADE

S67
ROY E.V.,"AN INTERPRETATION OF NORTHERN THAI STRUCT
PEASANT ECONOMY." THAILAND CLIENT CULTURE AGRI STRATA
PROC/MFG FACE/GP DEMAND INCOME 20. PAGE 114 F2254 ECO/UNDEV
INGP/REL

CLIFFORD J.M. F1584

CLIFFORD/C....CLARK CLIFFORD

CLIQUES....SEE FACE/GP

CLONER A. F0492

CLOUGH S.B. F0493

CLUBS....SEE VOL/ASSN, FACE/GP

CLYDE P.H. F0494

CMA....CANADIAN MEDICAL ASSOCIATION

CMN/WLTH....BRITISH COMMONWEALTH OF NATIONS; SEE
ALSO VOL/ASSN, APPROPRIATE NATIONS, COMMONWLTH

N
MINISTRY OF OVERSEAS DEVELOPME,TECHNICAL CO- BIBLIOG
OPERATION -- A BIBLIOGRAPHY. UK LAW SOCIETY DIPLOM TEC/DEV
ECO/TAC FOR/AID...STAT 20 CMN/WLTH. PAGE 92 F1803 ECO/DEV
NAT/G

L52
HUTH A.G.,"COMMUNICATION AND ECONOMIC DEVELOPMENT." ECO/UNDEV
FUT WOR+45 CULTURE SOCIETY INT/ORG PLAN TEC/DEV
EDU/PROP DRIVE KNOWL WEALTH...POLICY CONCPT RECORD
STERTYP GEN/LAWS COMMUN TOT/POP UNESCO 20 UN
CMN/WLTH. PAGE 64 F1250

L53
NELSON J.R.,"UNITED STATES FOREIGN ECONOMIC POLICY FINAN
AND THE STERLING AREA." USA-45 WOR+45 WOR-45 NAT/G DIPLOM
ECO/TAC WEALTH...STAT TIME/SEQ TREND CHARTS METH/GP UK
TERR/GP CMN/WLTH 20. PAGE 97 F1911

S55
HALLETT D.,"THE HISTORY AND STRUCTURE OF OEEC." VOL/ASSN
EUR+WWI USA+45 CONSTN INDUS INT/ORG NAT/G DELIB/GP ECO/DEV
ACT/RES PLAN ORD/FREE WEALTH...CONCPT OEEC 20
CMN/WLTH. PAGE 54 F1051

B57
OLIVER H.M. JR.,ECONOMIC OPINION AND POLICY IN ECO/UNDEV
CEYLON. CEYLON FINAN POL/PAR WORKER INT/TRADE NAT/LISM
INCOME WEALTH...GEOG UNPLAN/INT BIBLIOG 20 POLICY
CMN/WLTH. PAGE 101 F1987 COLONIAL

B60
THE ECONOMIST (LONDON),THE COMMONWEALTH AND EUROPE. INT/TRADE
EUR+WWI WOR+45 AGRI FINAN INCOME...STAT CENSUS INDUS
CHARTS CMN/WLTH EEC. PAGE 129 F2550 INT/ORG
NAT/COMP

B60
WHEARE K.C.,THE CONSTITUTIONAL STRUCTURE OF THE CONSTN
COMMONWEALTH. UK EX/STRUC DIPLOM DOMIN ADMIN INT/ORG
COLONIAL CONTROL LEAD INGP/REL SUPEGO 20 CMN/WLTH. VOL/ASSN
PAGE 145 F2865 SOVEREIGN

B61
CARNEY D.E.,GOVERNMENT AND ECONOMY IN BRITISH WEST METH/COMP
AFRICA. GAMBIA GHANA NIGERIA SIER/LEONE DOMIN ADMIN COLONIAL
GOV/REL SOVEREIGN WEALTH LAISSEZ...BIBLIOG 20 ECO/TAC
CMN/WLTH. PAGE 21 F0417 ECO/UNDEV

S61
RAY J.,"THE EUROPEAN FREE-TRADE ASSOCIATION AND ITS ECO/DEV
IMPACT ON INDIA'S TRADE." EUR+WWI FRANCE GERMANY ECO/TAC
INDIA S/ASIA UK NAT/G VOL/ASSN PLAN INT/TRADE
ROUTINE WEALTH...STAT CHARTS TERR/GP CMN/WLTH EEC
FOR/TRADE OEEC 20 EFTA. PAGE 109 F2155

B62
PAKISTAN MINISTRY OF FINANCE,FOREIGN ECONOMIC AID: FOR/AID
A REVIEW OF FOREIGN ECONOMIC AID TO PAKISTAN. RECEIVE
EUR+WWI PAKISTAN UK USA+45 USSR ECO/UNDEV INT/ORG WEALTH
DELIB/GP DIPLOM ECO/TAC...CHARTS CMN/WLTH CHINJAP. FINAN
PAGE 103 F2016

S62
SCOTT J.B.,"ANGLO-SOVIET TRADE AND ITS EFFECTS ON NAT/G
THE COMMONWEALTH." COM FUT UK USSR WOR+45 ECO/DEV ECO/TAC
MARKET INT/ORG CONSULT WEALTH...POLICY TREND
CMN/WLTH FOR/TRADE 20. PAGE 118 F2333

S63
BELOFF M.,"BRITAIN, EUROPE AND THE ATLANTIC INT/ORG
COMMUNITY." EUR+WWI ELITES NAT/G VOL/ASSN TOP/EX ECO/DEV
ATTIT ORD/FREE PWR SOVEREIGN WEALTH EEC TOT/POP UK
VAL/FREE CMN/WLTH 20. PAGE 13 F0240

S63
MONROE A.D.,"BRITAIN AND THE EUROPEAN COMMUNITY." VOL/ASSN
EUR+WWI FRANCE NAT/G DELIB/GP TOP/EX ECO/TAC DOMIN ATTIT
PWR...POLICY RECORD GEN/LAWS EEC EFTA 20 EFTA UK
CMN/WLTH. PAGE 93 F1817

S63
SHONFIELD A.,"AFTER BRUSSELS." EUR+WWI FRANCE PLAN
GERMANY UK ECO/DEV DIST/IND MARKET VOL/ASSN ECO/TAC
DELIB/GP CREATE INT/TRADE ATTIT RIGID/FLEX...RECORD
TREND GEN/LAWS EEC COMMUN CMN/WLTH 20. PAGE 121
F2385

B64
ESTHUS R.A.,FROM ENMITY TO ALLIANCE: US AUSTRALIAN DIPLOM
RELATIONS. S/ASIA DIST/IND VOL/ASSN FORCES ATTIT 20 WAR
AUSTRAL TREATY CMN/WLTH. PAGE 39 F0751 INT/TRADE
FOR/AID

S64
DOE J.F.,"TROPICAL AFRICAN CONTRIBUTIONS TO FEDERAL FINAN
FINANCE." AFR NAT/G PROVS CENTRAL RIGID/FLEX PWR ECO/TAC
WEALTH...STAT VAL/FREE 20 CMN/WLTH. PAGE 33 F0650

B65
CAMERON W.J.,NEW ZEALAND. NEW/ZEALND S/ASIA DIPLOM SOCIETY
INT/TRADE WRITING COLONIAL PARL/PROC...GEOG GP/REL
CMN/WLTH. PAGE 21 F0402 STRUCT

B66
INTERNATIONAL ECONOMIC ASSN,STABILITY AND PROGRESS INT/TRADE
IN THE WORLD ECONOMY: THE FIRST CONGRESS OF THE
INTERNATIONAL ECONOMIC ASSOCIATION. WOR+45 ECO/DEV
ECO/UNDEV DELIB/GP FOR/AID BAL/PAY...TREND CMN/WLTH
20. PAGE 65 F1276

B66
US DEPARTMENT OF STATE,RESEARCH ON WESTERN EUROPE, BIBLIOG/A
GREAT BRITAIN, AND CANADA (EXTERNAL RESEARCH LIST EUR+WWI
NO 3-25). CANADA GERMANY/W UK LAW CULTURE NAT/G DIPLOM
POL/PAR FORCES EDU/PROP REGION MARXISM...GEOG SOC
WORSHIP 20 CMN/WLTH. PAGE 136 F2676

B67
WISEMAN H.V.,BRITAIN AND THE COMMONWEALTH. EUR+WWI INT/ORG
FUT UK ECO/DEV POL/PAR TEC/DEV INT/TRADE LEAD ROLE DIPLOM
SOVEREIGN...SOC TREND 20 CMN/WLTH. PAGE 148 F2911 NAT/G
NAT/COMP

S67
LEIFER M.,"ASTRIDE THE STRAITS OF JAHORE: THE DIPLOM
BRITISH PRESENCE AND COMMONWEALTH RIVALRY IN NAT/LISM
SOUTHEAST ASIA." MALAYSIA UK FORCES PLAN ECO/TAC COLONIAL
...DECISION 20 CMN/WLTH. PAGE 77 F1515

S67
ROCKE J.R.M.,"THE BRITISH EXPORT BATTLE FOR THE INT/TRADE
CARIBBEAN" GP/REL...POLICY 20 CMN/WLTH. PAGE 113 DIPLOM
F2229 MARKET
ECO/TAC

COALE A.J. F0495

COALITIONS....SEE VOL/ASSN

COASTGUARD....COAST GUARD

COBB/HOWLL....HOWELL COBB

COERCE....COERCION, VIOLENCE; SEE ALSO FORCES,
PROCESSES AND PRACTICES INDEX, PART G, P. XIII

N
BROCKWAY A.F.,AFRICAN SOCIALISM. EUR+WWI GHANA AFR
ISLAM UAR ECO/UNDEV CAP/ISM INT/TRADE COLONIAL SOCISM
COERCE GOV/REL DISCRIM 20 NEGRO NKRUMAH/K NASSER/G. MARXISM
PAGE 19 F0356

B03
MOREL E.D.,THE BRITISH CASE IN FRENCH CONGO. DIPLOM
CONGO/BRAZ FRANCE UK COERCE MORAL WEALTH...POLICY INT/TRADE
INT/LAW 20 CONGO/LEOP. PAGE 93 F1827 COLONIAL
AFR

N19
FREEMAN H.A.,COERCION OF STATES IN FEDERAL UNIONS FEDERAL
(PAMPHLET). WOR-45 DIPLOM CONTROL COERCE PEACE WAR
ORD/FREE...GOV/COMP METH/COMP NAT/COMP PACIFIST 20. INT/ORG
PAGE 43 F0850 PACIFISM

B20
MOREL E.D.,THE BLACK MAN'S BURDEN. AFR MOD/EUR AGRI ORD/FREE
EXTR/IND PROB/SOLV INT/TRADE ADMIN CONTROL COERCE CAP/ISM
DISCRIM...POLICY 19/20 NEGRO LEAGUE/NAT. PAGE 93 RACE/REL
F1828 DOMIN

B30
HAWTREY R.G.,ECONOMIC ASPECTS OF SOVEREIGNTY. UNIV FORCES
WOR+45 WOR-45 ECO/DEV ECO/UNDEV AGRI COM/IND INDUS PWR

MARKET NAT/G TEC/DEV ECO/TAC EDU/PROP COERCE ATTIT KNOWL WEALTH...CONCPT CON/ANAL GEN/LAWS 20. PAGE 57 F1118 SOVEREIGN WAR

B35
LASKI H.J.,THE STATE IN THEORY AND PRACTICE. ELITES ECO/TAC REPRESENT ORD/FREE PWR WEALTH POPULISM ...GOV/COMP GEN/LAWS 19/20. PAGE 76 F1483 CAP/ISM COERCE NAT/G FASCISM

B38
HOBSON J.A.,IMPERIALISM. MOD/EUR UK WOR-45 CULTURE ECO/UNDEV NAT/G VOL/ASSN PLAN EDU/PROP LEGIT REGION COERCE ATTIT PWR...POLICY PLURIST TIME/SEQ GEN/LAWS TERR/GP 19/20. PAGE 60 F1187 DOMIN ECO/TAC BAL/PWR COLONIAL

B39
ROBBINS L.,ECONOMIC CAUSES OF WAR. WOR-45 ECO/DEV ECO/UNDEV INT/ORG NAT/G TEC/DEV DIPLOM DOMIN COLONIAL ATTIT DRIVE PWR WEALTH...POLICY CONCPT OBS SAMP TREND CON/ANAL GEN/LAWS MARX/KARL 20. PAGE 112 F2203 COERCE ECO/TAC WAR

S39
COLE G.D.H.,"NAZI ECONOMICS: HOW DO THEY MANAGE IT?" GERMANY FORCES WORKER BUDGET INT/TRADE ROUTINE COERCE WAR 20 HITLER/A NAZI. PAGE 26 F0500 FASCISM ECO/TAC ATTIT PLAN

B40
HUNTER R.,REVOLUTION: WHY, HOW, WHEN? NAT/G ECO/TAC EDU/PROP COERCE ORD/FREE FASCISM POPULISM SOCISM 18/20 HITLER/A LENIN/VI. PAGE 63 F1246 REV METH/COMP LEAD CONSTN

B40
SPENCER H.,THE MAN VS. THE STATE (1892). UK POL/PAR LEGIS TARIFFS COERCE CRIME REPRESENT PWR SOCISM ...POLICY GEN/LAWS 19/20. PAGE 124 F2450 FASCISM POPULISM LAISSEZ ORD/FREE

S41
LASSWELL H.D.,"THE GARRISON STATE" (BMR)" FUT WOR+45 ELITES INTELL FORCES ECO/TAC DOMIN EDU/PROP COERCE INGP/REL 20. PAGE 76 F1485 NAT/G DIPLOM PWR CIVMIL/REL

B48
DURBIN E.F.M.,THE POLITICS OF DEMOCRATIC SOCIALISM; AN ESSAY ON SOCIAL POLICY. STRATA POL/PAR PLAN COERCE DRIVE PERSON PWR MARXISM...CHARTS METH/COMP. PAGE 35 F0684 SOCIALIST POPULISM POLICY SOCIETY

B50
LINCOLN G.,ECONOMICS OF NATIONAL SECURITY. USA+45 ELITES COM/IND DIST/IND INDUS NAT/G VOL/ASSN DELIB/GP EX/STRUC FOR/AID EDU/PROP COERCE NUC/PWR WAR ATTIT KNOWL ORD/FREE PWR TOT/POP VAL/FREE 20. PAGE 80 F1565 FORCES ECO/TAC AFR

B50
SOREL G.,REFLECTIONS ON VIOLENCE (1908) (TRANS. BY T.E. HULME AND J. ROTH). UNIV SOCIETY LABOR UTOPIA MORAL SOCISM...ANARCH SOCIALIST CONCPT 20. PAGE 124 F2445 COERCE REV WORKER MYTH

B54
KARTUN D.,AFRICA, AFRICA: A CONTINENT RISES TO ITS FEET. AFR SOUTH/AFR UK ELITES AGRI LABOR LOC/G POL/PAR EDU/PROP CONTROL COERCE DISCRIM AGE/Y NEGRO THIRD/WRLD GOLD/COAST. PAGE 69 F1358 COLONIAL ORD/FREE PROFIT EXTR/IND

B56
WOLFF R.L.,THE BALKANS IN OUR TIME. ALBANIA FUT MOD/EUR USSR YUGOSLAVIA CULTURE INT/ORG SECT DIPLOM EDU/PROP COERCE WAR ORD/FREE...CHARTS 4/20 BALKANS COMINFORM. PAGE 148 F2919 GEOG COM

S57
HOAG M.W.,"ECONOMIC PROBLEMS OF ALLIANCE." AFR COM EUR+WWI WOR+45 ECO/DEV ECO/UNDEV NAT/G VOL/ASSN FORCES PLAN TEC/DEV DIPLOM COERCE ORD/FREE PWR WEALTH...DECISION GEN/LAWS NATO TERR/GP. PAGE 60 F1182 INT/ORG ECO/TAC

B58
PAYNO M.,LA REFORMA SOCIAL EN ESPANA Y MEXICO. SPAIN ECO/TAC TAX LOBBY COERCE REV OWN CATHISM 19/20 MEXIC/AMER. PAGE 104 F2043 SECT NAT/G LAW ELITES

S58
LANE F.C.,"ECONOMIC CONSEQUENCES OF ORGANIZED VIOLENCE." FUT WOR+45 WOR-45 ECO/DEV DIST/IND SERV/IND NAT/G PROVS EX/STRUC CHOOSE ORD/FREE PWR ...TIME/SEQ GEN/LAWS MUNICH 20. PAGE 75 F1472 WEALTH COERCE

B59
HENDEL S.,THE SOVIET CRUCIBLE. USSR LEAD COERCE NAT/LISM UTOPIA PWR...POLICY CONCPT ANTHOL 20 STALIN/J LENIN/VI MARX/KARL BOLSHEVIK. PAGE 58 F1147 COM MARXISM REV TOTALISM

B59
HOOVER C.B.,THE ECONOMY, LIBERTY AND THE STATE. COM EUR+WWI USA+45 USA-45 USSR CAP/ISM EDU/PROP COERCE TOTALISM ORD/FREE...POLICY OBS INT TREND NAZI 20. PAGE 61 F1206 ECO/DEV ECO/TAC

B59
KRIPALANI J.B.,CLASS STRUGGLE. INDIA WOR+45 ECO/UNDEV LABOR CAP/ISM EDU/PROP INGP/REL ...SOCIALIST IDEA/COMP 17/20. PAGE 73 F1440 MARXISM STRATA COERCE ECO/TAC

L59
OBERER W.E.,"VOLUNTARY IMPARTIAL REVIEW OF LABOR: SOME REFLECTIONS." DELIB/GP LEGIS PROB/SOLV ADJUD CONTROL COERCE PWR PLURISM POLICY. PAGE 100 F1960 LABOR LAW PARTIC INGP/REL

B60
GRAMPP W.D.,THE MANCHESTER SCHOOL OF ECONOMICS. UK LAW ECO/DEV COERCE ATTIT ORD/FREE LAISSEZ ...PHIL/SCI IDEA/COMP 19/20 MANCHESTER CORN/LAWS. PAGE 50 F0973 ECO/TAC VOL/ASSN LOBBY NAT/G

B60
LENCZOWSKI G.,OIL AND STATE IN THE MIDDLE EAST. FUT IRAN LAW ECO/UNDEV EXTR/IND NAT/G TOP/EX PLAN TEC/DEV ECO/TAC LEGIT ADMIN COERCE ATTIT ALL/VALS PWR...CHARTS 20. PAGE 78 F1519 ISLAM INDUS NAT/LISM

S60
HERZ J.H.,"EAST GERMANY: PROGRESS AND PROSPECTS." COM AGRI FINAN INDUS LOC/G NAT/G FORCES PLAN TEC/DEV DOMIN ADMIN COERCE DRIVE PERCEPT RIGID/FLEX MORAL ORD/FREE PWR...MARXIST PSY SOC RECORD STERTYP WORK. PAGE 59 F1158 POL/PAR STRUCT GERMANY

B61
CAMPAIGNE J.G.,CHECK-OFF: LABOR BOSSES AND WORKING MEN. LEGIS WORKER EDU/PROP DEBATE COERCE REPRESENT GP/REL ORD/FREE CONSERVE. PAGE 21 F0404 LABOR ELITES PWR CONTROL

B61
DUKE UNIVERSITY,EXPULSION OR OPPRESSION OF BUSINESS ASSOCIATES: "SQUEEZE-OUTS" IN SMALL ENTERPRISES. LAW CONTROL PARTIC COERCE INGP/REL...POLICY RECORD INT. PAGE 35 F0674 PWR MGT SML/CO ECO/TAC

B62
MCCLELLAN J.L.,CRIME WITHOUT PUNISHMENT. USA+45 LAW SOCIETY DELIB/GP TRIBUTE CONTROL LOBBY COERCE GP/REL ANOMIE MORAL...CRIMLGY 20 CONGRESS HOFFA/J. PAGE 88 F1718 CRIME ACT/RES LABOR PWR

B63
ABSHIRE D.M.,NATIONAL SECURITY: POLITICAL, MILITARY, AND ECONOMIC STRATEGIES IN THE DECADE AHEAD. ASIA COM USA+45 WOR+45 ECO/DEV ECO/UNDEV INT/ORG DELIB/GP FORCES ECO/TAC COERCE ATTIT RIGID/FLEX HEALTH ORD/FREE PWR WEALTH...POLICY STAT CHARTS ANTHOL COLD/WAR VAL/FREE APP/SCI. PAGE 2 F0032 FUT ACT/RES BAL/PWR

B63
CHAMBERLAIN E.H.,THE ECONOMIC ANALYSIS OF LABOR UNION POWER (PAMPHLET). WORKER ECO/TAC DOMIN COERCE GP/REL DRIVE WEALTH POLICY. PAGE 23 F0441 LABOR PWR CONTROL

B63
DEUTSCH K.W.,THE POLITICAL ROLE OF LABOR IN DEVELOPING COUNTRIES. AFR ASIA S/ASIA USA+45 WOR+45 ECO/UNDEV POL/PAR ECO/TAC EDU/PROP LEGIT COERCE ORD/FREE PWR WEALTH...OBS INT TREND VAL/FREE 20. PAGE 32 F0625 LABOR NAT/LISM

B63
FLORES E.,LAND REFORM AND THE ALLIANCE FOR PROGRESS (PAMPHLET). L/A+17C USA+45 STRUCT ECO/UNDEV NAT/G WORKER CREATE PLAN ECO/TAC COERCE REV 20 ALL/PROG. PAGE 42 F0815 AGRI INT/ORG DIPLOM POLICY

L63
ADERBIGDE A.,"SYMPOSIUM ON WEST AFRICA INTEGRATION." AFR EUR+WWI FUT CULTURE SOCIETY STRATA DIST/IND INDUS MARKET SERV/IND DELIB/GP PLAN TEC/DEV DOMIN EDU/PROP LEGIT COERCE ATTIT ALL/VALS ...POLICY STAT TREND CHARTS VAL/FREE. PAGE 2 F0040 FINAN ECO/TAC REGION

L63
NASH M.,"PSYCHO-CULTURAL FACTORS IN ASIAN ECONOMIC GROWTH." ASIA ISLAM S/ASIA CULTURE ECO/UNDEV DELIB/GP EDU/PROP COERCE ATTIT PERSON HEALTH KNOWL ORD/FREE...PSY SOC STAT TREND ANTHOL VAL/FREE 20. PAGE 96 F1893 SOCIETY ECO/TAC

S63
BILL J.A.,"THE SOCIAL AND ECONOMIC FOUNDATIONS OF POWER IN CONTEMPORARY IRAN." ISLAM CULTURE NAT/G ECO/TAC DOMIN COERCE ATTIT PWR WEALTH...TREND VAL/FREE 20. PAGE 15 F0284 SOCIETY STRATA IRAN

S63
GRUSHIN B.A.,"PROBLEMS OF THE MOVEMENT OF COMMUNIST LABOR IN THE USSR." COM SOCIETY LABOR ECO/TAC EDU/PROP COERCE RIGID/FLEX ORD/FREE...POLICY MARXIST STAT QU WORK 20. PAGE 52 F1011 ATTIT USSR

B64
BLACKSTOCK P.W.,THE STRATEGY OF SUBVERSION. USA+45 FORCES EDU/PROP ADMIN COERCE GOV/REL...DECISION MGT 20 DEPT/DEFEN CIA DEPT/STATE. PAGE 15 F0292 ORD/FREE DIPLOM CONTROL

B64
ROBINSON R.D.,INTERNATIONAL BUSINESS POLICY. AFR INDIA L/A+17C USA+45 ELITES AGRI FOR/AID COERCE BAL/PAY...DECISION INT/LAW MGT 20. PAGE 113 F2224 ECO/TAC DIST/IND COLONIAL FINAN

B64
SEERS D.,CUBA: THE ECONOMIC AND SOCIAL REVOLUTION. L/A+17C USSR YUGOSLAVIA STRATA AGRI INDUS SCHOOL DELIB/GP PLAN ECO/TAC DOMIN EDU/PROP ATTIT RIGID/FLEX ALL/VALS...STAT OBS TIME/SEQ WORK VAL/FREE 20. PAGE 119 F2341 ACT/RES COERCE CUBA REV

B64
TONG T.,UNITED STATES DIPLOMACY IN CHINA, 1844-1860. ASIA USA-45 ECO/UNDEV ECO/TAC COERCE GP/REL...INT/LAW 19 TREATY. PAGE 131 F2581
DIPLOM INT/TRADE COLONIAL

B64
WRIGHT G.,RURAL REVOLUTION IN FRANCE: THE PEASANTRY IN THE TWENTIETH CENTURY. EUR+WWI MOD/EUR LAW CULTURE AGRI POL/PAR DELIB/GP LEGIS ECO/TAC EDU/PROP COERCE CHOOSE ATTIT RIGID/FLEX HEALTH ...STAT CENSUS CHARTS VAL/FREE 20. PAGE 149 F2932
PWR STRATA FRANCE REV

S64
FINLEY D.D.,"A POLITICAL PERSPECTIVE OF ECONOMIC RELATIONS IN THE COMMUNIST CAMP." COM USSR FACE/GP NAT/G ACT/RES PLAN DOMIN COERCE ATTIT ORD/FREE WEALTH...TIME/SEQ 20. PAGE 41 F0800
VOL/ASSN ECO/TAC DIPLOM REGION

S64
RUSSETT B.M.,"INEQUALITY AND INSTABILITY: THE RELATION OF LAND TENURE TO POLITICS." WOR+45 ECO/DEV ECO/UNDEV AGRI NAT/G COERCE PWR...MATH STAT CHARTS GEN/LAWS TERR/GP TRUE/GP METH/GP VAL/FREE 20. PAGE 115 F2263
WEALTH GEOG ECO/TAC ORD/FREE

B65
RANSOM H.H.,AN AMERICAN FOREIGN POLICY READER. USA+45 FORCES EDU/PROP COERCE NUC/PWR WAR PEACE ...DECISION 20. PAGE 109 F2146
NAT/G DIPLOM POLICY

S65
WHITAKER A.P.,"ARGENTINA: STRUGGLE FOR RECOVERY." L/A+17C USA+45 NAT/G TOP/EX PLAN LEGIT COERCE REV RIGID/FLEX PWR WEALTH...RECORD ALL/PROG ARGEN FOR/TRADE 20. PAGE 146 F2867
POL/PAR ECO/TAC NAT/LISM

B67
ANDERSON C.W.,ISSUES OF POLITICAL DEVELOPMENT. BURMA WOR+45 CULTURE TOP/EX ECO/TAC MARXISM ...CHARTS NAT/COMP 20 COLOMB CONGO/LEOP. PAGE 5 F0094
NAT/LISM COERCE ECO/UNDEV SOCISM

B67
APTHEKER H.,THE NATURE OF DEMOCRACY, FREEDOM AND REVOLUTION. WOR+45 PROB/SOLV COERCE COST...CONCPT TIME/SEQ METH/COMP. PAGE 6 F0111
REV POPULISM MARXIST ORD/FREE

B67
DINERSTEIN H.S.,INTERVENTION AGAINST COMMUNISM (STUDIES IN INTERNATIONAL AFFAIRS NO. 1). CUBA DOMIN/REP GREECE USA+45 USSR VIETNAM OP/RES COERCE WAR 20. PAGE 33 F0643
MARXISM DIPLOM NAT/LISM

B67
FALL B.B.,HO CHI MINH ON REVOLUTION: SELECTED WRITINGS, 1920-66. COM VIETNAM ELITES NAT/G COERCE GUERRILLA RACE/REL MARXISM...MARXIST ANTHOL 20. PAGE 39 F0761
REV COLONIAL ECO/UNDEV S/ASIA

B67
LISS S.B.,THE CANAL, ASPECTS OF UNITED STATES-PANAMANIAN RELATIONS. AFR FUT PANAMA DOMIN COERCE ATTIT SOVEREIGN MARXISM 20 JOHNSON/LB KENNEDY/JF. PAGE 81 F1580
DIPLOM POLICY

B67
PETRO S.,THE KINGSPORT STRIKE. USA+45 PROC/MFG NAT/G JUDGE PRESS PARTIC PERS/REL...OLD/LIB OBS INT 20 NLRB. PAGE 105 F2074
LABOR COERCE SANCTION ALL/VALS

B67
WILLIAMS M.,THE EAST IS RED: THE VIEW INSIDE CHINA. CHINA/COM CONSTN COERCE AGE/Y ATTIT PERSON...OBS 20 MAO. PAGE 147 F2893
REV MARXIST GP/REL DIPLOM

L67
MACDONALD R.S.J.,"THE RESORT TO ECONOMIC COERCION BY INTERNATIONAL POLITICAL ORGANIZATIONS." CUBA ETHIOPIA RHODESIA SOUTH/AFR NAT/G FOR/AID INT/TRADE DOMIN CONTROL SANCTION...DECISION LEAGUE/NAT UN OAS 20. PAGE 83 F1625
INT/ORG COERCE ECO/TAC DIPLOM

S67
CROKER F.P.U.,"ECONOMIC PEACEKEEPING." UK PLAN PROB/SOLV TEC/DEV BAL/PWR DIPLOM COERCE PEACE ...POLICY DECISION 20. PAGE 28 F0553
FORCES WEAPON COST WAR

S67
JEDLICKI W.,"THE FREE SPEECH MOVEMENT IN WARSAW." POLAND FORCES EDU/PROP LEAD ATTIT MARXISM ...IDEA/COMP 20. PAGE 67 F1310
COERCE CROWD ORD/FREE ACADEM

S67
KENNY L.M.,"THE AFTERMATH OF DEFEAT IN EGYPT." ISLAM ISRAEL UAR UK USA+45 USSR INDUS FORCES ECO/TAC PRICE COERCE WEAPON COST ATTIT. PAGE 70 F1378
WAR ECO/UNDEV DIPLOM POLICY

S67
RAZA M.A.,"EMERGING TRENDS IN PUBLIC LABOR POLICIES AND UNION - GOVERN MENT RELATIONS IN ASIA AND AFRICA." LAW NAT/G POL/PAR COLONIAL COERCE GP/REL ATTIT 20. PAGE 110 F2157
LABOR CONTROL TREND

N67
US HOUSE COMM FOREIGN AFFAIRS,COMMUNIST ACTIVITIES IN LATIN AMERICA 1967 (PAMPHLET). CUBA USA+45 DIPLOM INT/TRADE EDU/PROP COERCE GUERRILLA HOUSE/REP OAS. PAGE 137 F2696
L/A+17C MARXISM ORD/FREE ECO/TAC

B86
O'CONNOR T.P.,THE PARNELL MOVEMENT: WITH A SKETCH OF IRISH PARTIES FROM 1843. IRELAND UK USA-45 LEGIS WORKER ECO/TAC COERCE CRIME REV CHOOSE ORD/FREE CATHISM LAISSEZ...SOC 19/20 PARLIAMENT PARNELL/CS LAND/LEAG. PAGE 100 F1957
LEAD DOMIN POL/PAR POLICY

B96
SMITH A.,LECTURES ON JUSTICE, POLICE, REVENUE AND ARMS (1763). UK LAW FAM FORCES TARIFFS AGREE COERCE INCOME OWN WEALTH LAISSEZ...GEN/LAWS 17/18. PAGE 123 F2429
DIPLOM JURID OLD/LIB TAX

COERCION....SEE COERCE

COEXIST....COEXISTENCE; SEE ALSO COLD/WAR, PEACE

COEXISTENCE....SEE COLD/WAR, PEACE

COFFIN/WS....WILLIAM SLOANE COFFIN, JR.

COGNITION....SEE PERCEPT

COGNITIVE DISSONANCE....SEE PERCEPT, ROLE

COHEN A. F0496

COHEN M.R. F0497

COHESION....SEE CONSEN

COL....COLORADO

N
JOHNSON R.B.,FINANCING A SUBURBAN CITY. USA+45 TAX COST...SAMP/SIZ MUNICH 20 COL. PAGE 68 F1331
FINAN PAY PROB/SOLV

COLBERG M.R. F0498

COLD/WAR....COLD WAR

B63
ABSHIRE D.M.,NATIONAL SECURITY: POLITICAL, MILITARY, AND ECONOMIC STRATEGIES IN THE DECADE AHEAD. ASIA COM USA+45 WOR+45 ECO/DEV ECO/UNDEV INT/ORG DELIB/GP FORCES ECO/TAC COERCE ATTIT RIGID/FLEX HEALTH ORD/FREE PWR WEALTH...POLICY STAT CHARTS ANTHOL COLD/WAR VAL/FREE APP/SCI. PAGE 2 F0032
FUT ACT/RES BAL/PWR

COLE A.B. F0499

COLE C.W. F0493

COLE G.D.H. F0500,F0501,F0502

COLE W.E. F0503

COLE/GEO....GEORGE COLE

COLEMAM J.R. F1074

COLEMAN J.S. F1577

COLLECTIVE BARGAINING....SEE BARGAIN+LABOR+GP/REL

COLLECTIVE SECURITY....SEE INT/ORG+FORCES

COLLEGES....SEE ACADEM

COLLERY A. F0504

COLLIER A.T. F0505

COLLINS H. F0506,F0507

COLLOQUE SUR LA PLANIFICATION F0508

COLM G. F0509

COLOMBIA....SEE ALSO L/A&17C

B61
RUEDA B.,A STATEMENT OF THE LAWS OF COLOMBIA IN MATTERS AFFECTING BUSINESS (3RD ED.). INDUS FAM LABOR LG/CO NAT/G LEGIS TAX CONTROL MARRIAGE 20 COLOMB. PAGE 115 F2257
FINAN ECO/UNDEV LAW CONSTN

B63
HIRSCHMAN A.O.,JOURNEYS TOWARD PROGRESS: STUDIES OF ECONOMIC POLICYMAKING IN LATIN AMERICA. CHILE FUT ECO/UNDEV AGRI FINAN INDUS CONSULT DELIB/GP PLAN ATTIT HEALTH ORD/FREE WEALTH...POLICY STAT VAL/FREE COLOMB 20. PAGE 60 F1177
L/A+17C ECO/TAC BRAZIL

B63
VELEZ GARCIA J.,DEVALUACION 1962; HISTORIA DOCUMENTAL DE UN PROCESO ECONOMICO. AFR L/A+17C
ECO/UNDEV ECO/TAC

USA+45 FINAN FOR/AID PRODUC WEALTH...POLICY STAT CHARTS ANTHOL 20 COLOMB. PAGE 141 F2774
PLAN NAT/G

B65
WURFEL S.W.,FOREIGN ENTERPRISE IN COLOMBIA. FINAN LABOR NAT/G ECO/TAC TAX REGION 20 COLOMB. PAGE 149 F2944
ECO/UNDEV INT/TRADE JURID CAP/ISM

S65
BRANDENBURG F.,"THE RELEVANCE OF MEXICAN EXPERIENCE TO LATIN AMERICAN DEVELOPMENT." BRAZIL CHILE VENEZUELA STRUCT ECO/UNDEV AGRI CREATE ECO/TAC ...STAT RECORD MEXIC/AMER ARGEN COLOMB. PAGE 18 F0340
L/A+17C GOV/COMP

B67
ANDERSON C.W.,ISSUES OF POLITICAL DEVELOPMENT. BURMA WOR+45 CULTURE TOP/EX ECO/TAC MARXISM ...CHARTS NAT/COMP 20 COLOMB CONGO/LEOP. PAGE 5 F0094
NAT/LISM COERCE ECO/UNDEV SOCISM

B67
SMITH T.L.,THE PROCESS OF RURAL DEVELOPMENT IN LATIN AMERICA (A MONOGRAPH). L/A+17C STRATA INDUS PLAN GP/REL PERS/REL RIGID/FLEX WEALTH...OBS CHARTS ORG/CHARTS ANTHOL 20 COLOMB. PAGE 123 F2434
IDEA/COMP SOC AGRI ECO/UNDEV

S67
ADAMS D.W.,"MINIFUNDIA IN AGRARIAN REFORM: A COLOMBIAN EXAMPLE."...SOC CLASSIF 20 COLOMB. PAGE 2 F0035
AGRI METH/COMP OWN PRODUC

S67
PETRAS J.,"GUERRILLA MOVEMENTS IN LATIN AMERICA - I." GUATEMALA PERU VENEZUELA NAT/G COLONIAL LEAD ATTIT PWR...TIME/SEQ METH/COMP 20 COLOMB. PAGE 105 F2072
GUERRILLA REV L/A+17C MARXISM

COLOMBIA....SEE ALSO L/A+17C

B66
CURRIE L.,ACCELERATING DEVELOPMENT: THE NECESSITY AND MEANS. COLOMBIA USA+45 INDUS DIPLOM EFFICIENCY WEALTH...METH/CNCPT NEW/IDEA 20. PAGE 29 F0564
PLAN ECO/UNDEV FOR/AID TEC/DEV

COLONIAL AMERICA....SEE PRE/US/AM, PRE/AMER

COLONIAL....COLONIALISM; SEE ALSO DOMIN

N
BROCKWAY A.F.,AFRICAN SOCIALISM. EUR+WWI GHANA ISLAM UAR ECO/UNDEV CAP/ISM INT/TRADE COLONIAL COERCE GOV/REL DISCRIM 20 NEGRO NKRUMAH/K NASSER/G. PAGE 19 F0356
AFR SOCISM MARXISM

NCO
CARRINGTON C.E.,THE COMMONWEALTH IN AFRICA (PAMPHLET). UK STRUCT NAT/G COLONIAL REPRESENT GOV/REL RACE/REL NAT/LISM...MAJORIT 20 EEC NEGRO. PAGE 22 F0421
ECO/UNDEV AFR DIPLOM PLAN

B02
MOREL E.D.,AFFAIRS OF WEST AFRICA. UK FINAN INDUS FAM KIN SECT CHIEF WORKER DIPLOM RACE/REL LITERACY HEALTH...CHARTS 18/20 AFRICA/W NEGRO. PAGE 93 F1826
COLONIAL ADMIN AFR

B03
MOREL E.D.,THE BRITISH CASE IN FRENCH CONGO. CONGO/BRAZ FRANCE UK COERCE MORAL WEALTH...POLICY INT/LAW 20 CONGO/LEOP. PAGE 93 F1827
DIPLOM INT/TRADE COLONIAL AFR

B19
SUMNER W.G.,WAR AND OTHER ESSAYS. USA-45 DELIB/GP DIPLOM TARIFFS COLONIAL PEACE SOVEREIGN 20. PAGE 127 F2514
INT/TRADE ORD/FREE CAP/ISM ECO/TAC

N19
VELYAMINOV G.,AFRICA AND THE COMMON MARKET (PAMPHLET). AFR MARKET VOL/ASSN ECO/TAC COLONIAL ORD/FREE...SOCIALIST 20 THIRD/WRLD. PAGE 141 F2775
INT/ORG INT/TRADE SOVEREIGN ECO/UNDEV

B25
WILLIAMS B.,THE SELBORNE MEMORANDUM. AFR FUT SOUTH/AFR UK NAT/G BUDGET DIPLOM REGION GOV/REL SOVEREIGN...POLICY CHARTS 20 UNIFICA SELBORNE/W. PAGE 147 F2888
COLONIAL PROVS

B26
MCPHEE A.,THE ECONOMIC REVOLUTION IN BRITISH WEST AFRICA. AFR UK CULTURE DIST/IND FINAN INDUS PLAN GP/REL RACE/REL 20 AFRICA/W. PAGE 88 F1735
ECO/UNDEV INT/TRADE COLONIAL GEOG

B28
CROS L.,AFRIQUE FRANCAISE POUR TOUS. EUR+WWI FRANCE PLAN TEC/DEV ATTIT 20. PAGE 29 F0556
COLONIAL DOMIN ECO/TAC AFR

B33
TANNENBAUM F.,PEACE BY REVOLUTION. ECO/UNDEV AGRI SECT WORKER DIPLOM EDU/PROP DISCRIM OWN WEALTH POPULISM 17/20 MEXIC/AMER INDIAN/AM. PAGE 128 F2532
CULTURE COLONIAL RACE/REL REV

B37
UNION OF SOUTH AFRICA,REPORT CONCERNING ADMINISTRATION OF SOUTH WEST AFRICA (6 VOLS.). SOUTH/AFR INDUS PUB/INST FORCES LEGIS BUDGET DIPLOM EDU/PROP ADJUD CT/SYS...GEOG CHARTS 20 AFRICA/SW LEAGUE/NAT. PAGE 132 F2610
NAT/G ADMIN COLONIAL CONSTN

B38
CARVALHO C.M.,GEOGRAPHIA HUMANA; POLITICA E ECONOMICA (3RD ED.). BRAZIL CULTURE AGRI INDUS DIPLOM COLONIAL GP/REL RACE/REL...LING 20 RESOURCE/N. PAGE 22 F0424
GEOG HABITAT

B38
HOBSON J.A.,IMPERIALISM. MOD/EUR UK WOR-45 CULTURE ECO/UNDEV NAT/G VOL/ASSN PLAN EDU/PROP LEGIT REGION COERCE ATTIT PWR...POLICY PLURIST TIME/SEQ GEN/LAWS TERR/GP 19/20. PAGE 60 F1187
DOMIN ECO/TAC BAL/PWR COLONIAL

B39
FURNIVALL J.S.,NETHERLANDS INDIA. INDIA NETHERLAND CULTURE INDUS NAT/G DIPLOM ADMIN WEALTH...POLICY CHARTS 17/20. PAGE 45 F0876
COLONIAL ECO/UNDEV SOVEREIGN PLURISM

B39
ROBBINS L.,ECONOMIC CAUSES OF WAR. WOR-45 ECO/DEV ECO/UNDEV INT/ORG NAT/G TEC/DEV DIPLOM DOMIN COLONIAL ATTIT DRIVE PWR WEALTH...POLICY CONCPT OBS SAMP TREND CON/ANAL GEN/LAWS MARX/KARL 20. PAGE 112 F2203
COERCE ECO/TAC WAR

B40
MEEK C.K.,EUROPE AND WEST AFRICA. AFR EUR+WWI EXTR/IND DIPLOM INT/TRADE EDU/PROP GP/REL...SOC 20. PAGE 89 F1743
CULTURE TEC/DEV ECO/UNDEV COLONIAL

B42
SWEEZY P.M.,THE THEORY OF CAPITALIST DEVELOPMENT. FUT NAT/G COST FASCISM BIBLIOG. PAGE 128 F2519
ECO/DEV CAP/ISM MARXISM COLONIAL

B45
DAVIS J.,AFRICA ADVANCING. AFR CONGO/BRAZ LIBERIA NIGER INT/ORG SCHOOL DIPLOM GIVE KNOWL SKILL 20. PAGE 30 F0590
SECT COLONIAL AGRI ECO/UNDEV

B47
ISAAC J.,ECONOMICS OF MIGRATION. MOD/EUR CULTURE STRATA STRUCT NAT/G COLONIAL WEALTH...OLD/LIB TREND TIME 19/20 EUROPE/W MIGRATION. PAGE 65 F1289
HABITAT SOC GEOG

B48
CLYDE P.H.,THE FAR EAST: A HISTORY OF THE IMPACT OF THE WEST ON EASTERN ASIA. CHINA/COM CULTURE INT/TRADE DOMIN COLONIAL WAR PWR...CHARTS BIBLIOG 19/20 CHINJAP. PAGE 25 F0494
DIPLOM ASIA

B48
WINSLOW E.M.,THE PATTERN OF IMPERIALISM; A STUDY IN THE THEORIES OF POWER. DOMIN WAR PWR MARXISM ...IDEA/COMP METH/COMP BIBLIOG 20. PAGE 147 F2906
SOCISM CAP/ISM COLONIAL ECO/TAC

S49
STEINMETZ H.,"THE PROBLEMS OF THE LANDRAT: A STUDY OF COUNTY GOVERNMENT IN THE US ZONE OF GERMANY." GERMANY/W USA+45 INDUS PLAN DIPLOM EDU/PROP CONTROL WAR GOV/REL FEDERAL WEALTH PLURISM...GOV/COMP 20 LANDRAT. PAGE 126 F2478
LOC/G COLONIAL MGT TOP/EX

B51
BROGAN D.W.,THE PRICE OF REVOLUTION. FRANCE USA+45 USA-45 USSR CONSTN NAT/G DIPLOM COLONIAL NAT/LISM ORD/FREE POPULISM...CONCPT 18/20 PRE/US/AM. PAGE 19 F0359
REV METH/COMP COST MARXISM

B51
HALEVY E.,IMPERIALISM AND THE RISE OF LABOR (2ND ED.). UK NAT/G POL/PAR TOP/EX ATTIT ORD/FREE PWR 19/20 PARLIAMENT LABOR/PAR. PAGE 53 F1042
COLONIAL LABOR POLICY WAR

B51
LEONARD L.L.,INTERNATIONAL ORGANIZATION. WOR+45 WOR-45 EX/STRUC FORCES LEGIS ECO/TAC INT/TRADE COLONIAL ARMS/CONT...SOC/WK GOV/COMP BIBLIOG. PAGE 78 F1527
NAT/G DIPLOM INT/ORG DELIB/GP

B51
LUXEMBORG R.,THE ACCUMULATION OF CAPITAL (TRANS. BY AGNES SCHWARZSCHILD). ECO/TAC DOMIN COLONIAL ATTIT LAISSEZ 19 MONEY. PAGE 82 F1614
MARXIST INT/TRADE CAP/ISM FINAN

B52
JENNINGS W.I.,CONSTITUTIONAL LAWS OF THE COMMONWEALTH. AFR UK LAW CHIEF LEGIS TAX CT/SYS PARL/PROC GOV/REL...INT/LAW 18/20 ENGLSH/LAW COMMON/LAW. PAGE 67 F1316
CONSTN JURID ADJUD COLONIAL

B53
FRANKEL S.H.,THE ECONOMIC IMPACT ON UNDERDEVELOPED SOCIETIES: ESSAYS ON INTERNATIONAL INVESTMENT AND SOCIAL CHANGE. AFR WOR+45 ECO/DEV FINAN INDUS NAT/G ACT/RES TEC/DEV COLONIAL ATTIT...CONCPT OBS TREND 20. PAGE 43 F0845
ECO/UNDEV FOR/AID INT/TRADE

B53
MIT CENTER INTERNATIONAL STU,BIBLIOGRAPHY OF THE ECONOMIC AND POLITICAL DEVELOPMENT OF INDONESIA.
BIBLIOG ECO/UNDEV

INDONESIA STRUCT NAT/G COLONIAL LEAD...STAT 20. PAGE 92 F1805 TEC/DEV S/ASIA

B54
KARTUN D., AFRICA, AFRICA: A CONTINENT RISES TO ITS FEET. AFR SOUTH/AFR UK ELITES AGRI LABOR LOC/G POL/PAR EDU/PROP CONTROL COERCE DISCRIM AGE/Y NEGRO THIRD/WRLD GOLD/COAST. PAGE 69 F1358 COLONIAL ORD/FREE PROFIT EXTR/IND

B55
HELANDER S., DAS AUTARKIEPROBLEM IN DER WELTWIRTSCHAFT. PROB/SOLV BAL/PWR BARGAIN CAP/ISM ECO/TAC SOVEREIGN FOR/TRADE 20. PAGE 58 F1144 NAT/COMP COLONIAL DIPLOM

B55
PANT Y.P., PLANNING IN UNDERDEVELOPED ECONOMIES. INDIA NEPAL INT/TRADE COLONIAL SOVEREIGN ALL/IDEOS ...TIME/SEQ METH/COMP 20. PAGE 103 F2026 ECO/UNDEV PLAN ECO/TAC DIPLOM

B55
STILLMAN C.W., AFRICA IN THE MODERN WORLD. AFR USA+45 WOR+45 INT/TRADE COLONIAL PARTIC REGION GOV/REL RACE/REL 20. PAGE 126 F2489 ECO/UNDEV DIPLOM POLICY STRUCT

N56
US HOUSE COMM FOREIGN AFFAIRS, REPORT OF THE SPECIAL STUDY MISSION TO AFRICA, SOUTH AND EAST OF THE SAHARA (PAMPHLET). AFR SOUTH/AFR USA+45 STRUCT INT/TRADE PARL/PROC NAT/LISM ATTIT ALL/VALS HEALTH ...POLICY 20 CONGRESS. PAGE 136 F2691 FOR/AID COLONIAL ECO/UNDEV DIPLOM

B57
NEUMARK S.D., ECONOMIC INFLUENCES ON THE SOUTH AFRICAN FRONTIER, 1652-1836. SOUTH/AFR SEA AGRI NAT/G FORCES WORKER DIPLOM INT/TRADE PRICE DEMAND PRODUC...STAT CHARTS 17/19 FRONTIER. PAGE 97 F1915 COLONIAL ECO/UNDEV ECO/TAC MARKET

B57
OLIVER H.M. JR., ECONOMIC OPINION AND POLICY IN CEYLON. CEYLON FINAN POL/PAR WORKER INT/TRADE INCOME WEALTH...GEOG UNPLAN/INT BIBLIOG 20 CMN/WLTH. PAGE 101 F1987 ECO/UNDEV NAT/LISM POLICY COLONIAL

B57
ROBERTSON H.M., SOUTH AFRICA, ECONOMIC AND POLITICAL ASPECTS. SOUTH/AFR CONSTN CULTURE POL/PAR LEGIS DIPLOM DOMIN COLONIAL...SOC BIBLIOG 19/20. PAGE 112 F2214 RACE/REL ECO/UNDEV ECO/TAC DISCRIM

B57
WATSON G., THE UNSERVILE STATE: ESSAYS IN LIBERTY AND WELFARE. UK LEGIS RECEIVE EDU/PROP COLONIAL ...WELF/ST 20 LIB/PARTY. PAGE 144 F2833 POL/PAR ORD/FREE CONTROL NEW/LIB

B57
WEIGERT H.W., PRINCIPLES OF POLITICAL GEOGRAPHY. WOR+45 ECO/DEV ECO/UNDEV SECT ECO/TAC COLONIAL HABITAT...CHARTS T 20. PAGE 144 F2845 GEOG CULTURE

B58
CLAIRMONTE F., LE LIBERALISME ECONOMIQUE ET LES PAYS SOUS-DEVELOPPES: ETUDES SUR L'EVOLUTION D'UNE IDEE. ASIA INDIA UK FINAN INDUS PLAN CAP/ISM ECO/TAC COLONIAL NEW/LIB...BIBLIOG 20 THIRD/WRLD. PAGE 24 F0475 LAISSEZ ECO/UNDEV

B58
COLE G.D.H., COMMUNISM AND SOCIAL DEMOCRACY (VOL. IV OF "HISTORY OF SOCIAL THOUGHT"). COM GERMANY ITALY UK AGRI INT/ORG WORKER DIPLOM COLONIAL NAT/LISM ALL/IDEOS...BIBLIOG 20 LEAGUE/NAT AUST/HUNG. PAGE 26 F0502 MARXISM REV POL/PAR SOCISM

B58
EHRHARD J., LE DESTIN DU COLONIALISME. AFR FRANCE ECO/UNDEV AGRI FINAN MARKET CREATE PLAN TEC/DEV BUDGET DIPLOM PRICE 20. PAGE 36 F0710 COLONIAL FOR/AID INT/TRADE INDUS

B58
JENNINGS I., PROBLEMS OF THE NEW COMMONWEALTH. AFR CEYLON INDIA PAKISTAN S/ASIA ECO/UNDEV INT/ORG LOC/G DIPLOM ECO/TAC INT/TRADE COLONIAL RACE/REL DISCRIM 20 PARLIAMENT. PAGE 67 F1314 NAT/LISM NEUTRAL FOR/AID POL/PAR

B58
NICULESCU B., COLONIAL PLANNING: A COMPARATIVE STUDY. AFR AGRI LOC/G NAT/G DELIB/GP COLONIAL MUNICH 20. PAGE 98 F1927 PLAN ECO/UNDEV TEC/DEV NAT/COMP

B58
TILLION G., ALGERIA: THE REALITIES. ALGERIA FRANCE ISLAM CULTURE STRATA PROB/SOLV DOMIN REV NAT/LISM WEALTH MARXISM...GEOG 20. PAGE 130 F2573 ECO/UNDEV SOC COLONIAL DIPLOM

B59
ARON R., IMPERIALISM AND COLONIALISM (PAMPHLET). WOR+45 WOR-45 ECO/TAC CONTROL REV ORD/FREE 19/20. PAGE 6 F0119 COLONIAL DOMIN ECO/UNDEV DIPLOM

B59
MADHOK B., POLITICAL TRENDS IN INDIA. INDIA PAKISTAN UK STRATA ECO/UNDEV POL/PAR LEGIS CAP/ISM DIPLOM COLONIAL CHOOSE MARXISM...SOC TREND 20 GANDHI/M NEHRU/J. PAGE 84 F1639 GEOG NAT/G

B59
MARTIN K., WAR, HISTORY, AND HUMAN NATURE. FRANCE GERMANY INDIA UK UNIV POL/PAR COLONIAL DETER REV MARXISM PACIFISM...PSY CONCPT PREDICT LENIN/VI GANDHI/M. PAGE 86 F1683 PERSON WAR ATTIT IDEA/COMP

B59
PANIKKAR K.M., THE AFRO-ASIAN STATES AND THEIR PROBLEMS. COM CULTURE KIN POL/PAR SECT DIPLOM EDU/PROP COLONIAL SOVEREIGN...TECHNIC GOV/COMP 20. PAGE 103 F2025 AFR S/ASIA ECO/UNDEV

B59
SILCOCK T.H., THE COMMONWEALTH ECONOMY IN SOUTHEAST ASIA. AFR INDIA MALAYSIA S/ASIA ECO/DEV AGRI LOC/G PLAN TARIFFS COLONIAL BAL/PAY DEMAND...BIBLIOG/A 20 GATT. PAGE 122 F2401 ECO/TAC INT/TRADE RACE/REL DIPLOM

B59
WARD B., 5 IDEAS THAT CHANGE THE WORLD. WOR+45 WOR-45 SOCIETY STRUCT AGRI INDUS INT/ORG NAT/G FORCES ACT/RES ARMS/CONT TOTALISM ATTIT DRIVE GEN/LAWS. PAGE 143 F2815 ECO/UNDEV ALL/VALS NAT/LISM COLONIAL

B60
ASPREMONT-LYNDEN H., RAPPORT SUR L'ADMINISTRATION BELGE DU RUANDA-URUNDI PENDANT L'ANNEE 1959. BELGIUM RWANDA AGRI INDUS DIPLOM ECO/TAC INT/TRADE DOMIN ADMIN RACE/REL...GEOG CENSUS 20 UN. PAGE 7 F0132 AFR COLONIAL ECO/UNDEV INT/ORG

B60
GONZALEZ NAVARRO M., LA COLONIZACION EN MEXICO, 1877-1910. AGRI NAT/G PLAN PROB/SOLV INCOME ...POLICY JURID CENSUS 19/20 MEXIC/AMER MIGRATION. PAGE 48 F0947 ECO/UNDEV GEOG HABITAT COLONIAL

B60
LATIFI D., INDIA AND UNITED STATES AID. ASIA INDIA UK USA+45 AGRI FINAN INDUS COLONIAL ORD/FREE SOVEREIGN WEALTH...METH/COMP 20. PAGE 76 F1486 FOR/AID DIPLOM ECO/UNDEV

B60
WHEARE K.C., THE CONSTITUTIONAL STRUCTURE OF THE COMMONWEALTH. UK EX/STRUC DIPLOM DOMIN ADMIN COLONIAL CONTROL LEAD INGP/REL SUPEGO 20 CMN/WLTH. PAGE 145 F2865 CONSTN INT/ORG VOL/ASSN SOVEREIGN

B60
WODDIS J., AFRICA: THE ROOTS OF REVOLT. SOUTH/AFR WORKER INT/TRADE RACE/REL DISCRIM ORD/FREE 20. PAGE 148 F2915 COLONIAL SOVEREIGN WAR ECO/UNDEV

S60
BERG E.J., "ECONOMIC BASIS OF POLITICAL CHOICE IN FRENCH WEST AFRICA." FRANCE ECO/UNDEV AGRI INDUS NAT/G PLAN LEGIT COLONIAL REGION ATTIT PWR WEALTH ...CONCPT FOR/TRADE 20. PAGE 13 F0257 AFR ECO/TAC

S60
NEISSER H., "ECONOMIC IMPERALISM RECONSIDERED." WOR+45 WOR-45 ECO/DEV ECO/UNDEV DIST/IND LEGIT COLONIAL PWR WEALTH SOCISM...MYTH MATH TIME/SEQ 20. PAGE 97 F1909 ACT/RES ECO/TAC CAP/ISM INT/TRADE

B61
CARNEY D.E., GOVERNMENT AND ECONOMY IN BRITISH WEST AFRICA. GAMBIA GHANA NIGERIA SIER/LEONE DOMIN ADMIN GOV/REL SOVEREIGN WEALTH LAISSEZ...BIBLIOG 20 CMN/WLTH. PAGE 21 F0417 METH/COMP COLONIAL ECO/TAC ECO/UNDEV

B61
ESTEVEZ A., ASPECTOS ECONOMICO-FINANCIEROS DE LA CAMPANA SANMARITANA. L/A+17C SPAIN FINAN COLONIAL LEAD ROLE ORD/FREE WEALTH 19 SOUTH/AMER SAN/MARTIN. PAGE 38 F0748 ECO/UNDEV REV BUDGET NAT/G

B61
FEARN H., AN AFRICAN ECONOMY. AFR EUR+WWI PLAN COLONIAL WEALTH...CONT/OBS TREND EEC VAL/FREE 20. PAGE 39 F0770 ECO/UNDEV

B61
GURTOO D.H.N., INDIA'S BALANCE OF PAYMENTS (1920-1960). INDIA FINAN DIPLOM FOR/AID INT/TRADE PRICE COLONIAL...CHARTS BIBLIOG 20. PAGE 52 F1014 BAL/PAY STAT ECO/TAC ECO/UNDEV

B61
HEMPSTONE S., THE NEW AFRICA. AGRI INDUS KIN NAT/G COLONIAL MARXISM...SOC INT TREND NAT/COMP BIBLIOG/A 20. PAGE 58 F1146 AFR ORD/FREE PERSON CULTURE

B61
INDUSTRIAL COUN SOC-ECO STU, THE SWEDISH ECONOMY AND THE UNDERDEVELOPED COUNTRIES. SWEDEN INDUS DELIB/GP TEC/DEV INT/TRADE EDU/PROP COLONIAL DRIVE...CHARTS 20. PAGE 64 F1264 FOR/AID ECO/UNDEV PLAN FINAN

B61
LANDSKROY W.A., OFFICIAL SERIAL PUBLICATIONS RELATING TO ECONOMIC DEVELOPMENT IN AFRICA SOUTH OF THE SAHARA (PAMPHLET). AFR UK R+D ACT/RES 20 UN. PAGE 75 F1471 BIBLIOG ECO/UNDEV COLONIAL INT/ORG

B61
LEHMAN R.L., AFRICA SOUTH OF THE SAHARA (PAMPHLET). DIPLOM COLONIAL NAT/LISM. PAGE 77 F1512 BIBLIOG/A AFR CULTURE NAT/G

B61
LUZ N.V., A LUTA PELA INDUSTRIALIZACAO DO BRAZIL. BRAZIL L/A+17C AGRI NAT/G TEC/DEV COLONIAL 19/20. PAGE 82 F1615 ECO/UNDEV INDUS NAT/LISM POLICY

B61
PERKINS D.,THE UNITED STATES AND LATIN AMERICAN. L/A+17C USA+45 USA-45 STRUCT COLONIAL REV ORD/FREE 19/20. PAGE 105 F2061 — DIPLOM INT/TRADE NAT/G

B61
SCHNAPPER B.,LA POLITIQUE ET LE COMMERCE FRANCAIS DANS LE GOLFE DE GUINEE DE 1838 A 1871. FRANCE GUINEA UK SEA EXTR/IND NAT/G DELIB/GP LEGIS ADMIN ORD/FREE...POLICY GEOG CENSUS CHARTS BIBLIOG 19. PAGE 117 F2303 — COLONIAL INT/TRADE DOMIN AFR

B61
WARD B.J.,INDIA AND THE WEST. INDIA UK USA+45 INT/TRADE GIVE COLONIAL ATTIT MARXISM 19/20. PAGE 143 F2817 — PLAN ECO/UNDEV ECO/TAC FOR/AID

B61
WRIGHT H.M.,THE "NEW IMPERIALISM": ANALYSIS OF LATE NINETEENTH-CENTURY EXPANSION. MOD/EUR WOR-45 SOCIETY FINAN ECO/TAC INT/TRADE NAT/LISM...ANTHOL BIBLIOG/A 19. PAGE 149 F2933 — HIST/WRIT IDEA/COMP COLONIAL DOMIN

B62
HENDERSON W.O.,THE GENESIS OF THE COMMON MARKET. EUR+WWI FRANCE MOD/EUR UK SEA COM/IND EXTR/IND COLONIAL DISCRIM...TIME/SEQ CHARTS BIBLIOG 18/20 EEC TREATY. PAGE 58 F1149 — ECO/DEV INT/TRADE DIPLOM

B62
KENT R.K.,FROM MADAGASCAR TO THE MALAGASY REPUBLIC. FRANCE MADAGASCAR DIPLOM NAT/LISM ORD/FREE...MGT 18/20. PAGE 70 F1379 — COLONIAL SOVEREIGN REV POL/PAR

B62
PONCET J.,LA COLONISATION ET L'AGRICULTURE EUROPEENNES EN TUNISIE DEPUIS 1881. FRANCE WORKER TEC/DEV ECO/TAC CONTROL EFFICIENCY ROLE WEALTH 19/20 TUNIS. PAGE 107 F2101 — ECO/UNDEV AGRI COLONIAL FINAN

B62
RIMALOV V.V.,ECONOMIC COOPERATION BETWEEN USSR AND UNDERDEVELOPED COUNTRIES. USSR FINAN TEC/DEV INT/TRADE DOMIN EDU/PROP COLONIAL NAT/LISM DRIVE SOVEREIGN...AUD/VIS 20. PAGE 111 F2194 — FOR/AID PLAN ECO/UNDEV DIPLOM

B62
SELOSOEMARDJAN O.,SOCIAL CHANGES IN JOGJAKARTA. INDONESIA NETHERLAND ELITES STRATA STRUCT FAM POL/PAR CREATE DIPLOM INT/TRADE EDU/PROP ADMIN GOV/REL...SOC 20 JAVA CHINJAP. PAGE 119 F2352 — ECO/UNDEV CULTURE REV COLONIAL

B62
VIET J.,INTERNATIONAL COOPERATION AND PROGRAMMES OF ECONOMIC AND SOCIAL DEVELOPMENT. TEC/DEV FOR/AID DOMIN COLONIAL PEACE WEALTH 20 UNESCO. PAGE 141 F2784 — BIBLIOG/A INT/ORG DIPLOM ECO/UNDEV

L62
BELSHAW D.G.R.,"PUBLIC INVESTMENT IN AGRICULTURE AND ECONOMIC DEVELOPMENT OF UGANDA" UGANDA AGRI INDUS R+D ECO/TAC RATION TAX PAY COLONIAL 20 WORLD/BANK. PAGE 13 F0242 — ECO/UNDEV PLAN ADMIN CENTRAL

S62
ALPERT P.,"ECONOMIC POLICIES AND PLANNING IN NEWLY INDEPENDENT AFRICA." PLAN ATTIT PWR WEALTH ...STERTYP GEN/LAWS VAL/FREE 20. PAGE 4 F0078 — AFR ECO/DEV NAT/LISM COLONIAL

S62
GILL P.J.,"FUTURE TAXATION POLICY IN AN INDEPENDENT EAST AFRICA" UGANDA LOC/G ECO/TAC ADMIN EFFICIENCY INCOME PRODUC...CHARTS 20. PAGE 47 F0923 — ECO/UNDEV TAX AFR COLONIAL

S62
KRISHNA K.G.V.,"PLANNING AND ECONOMIC DEVELOPMENT" AFR UGANDA AGRI INDUS R+D BUDGET RATION TAX COLONIAL 20. PAGE 73 F1441 — ECO/UNDEV ECO/TAC NAT/LISM PLAN

B63
BRITISH AID. UK AGRI DIST/IND INDUS SCHOOL TEC/DEV INT/TRADE COLONIAL DEMAND...TREND CHARTS 20. PAGE 1 F0018 — FOR/AID ECO/UNDEV NAT/G FINAN

B63
FURTADO C.,THE ECONOMIC GROWTH OF BRAZIL: A SURVEY FROM COLONIAL TO MODERN TIMES. L/A+17C AGRI DIST/IND EXTR/IND INDUS WORKER COLONIAL RACE/REL OWN GOV/COMP. PAGE 45 F0877 — ECO/UNDEV TEC/DEV LABOR DOMIN

B63
LEWIN J.,POLITICS AND LAW IN SOUTH AFRICA. SOUTH/AFR UK POL/PAR BAL/PWR ECO/TAC COLONIAL CONTROL GP/REL DISCRIM PWR 20 NEGRO. PAGE 79 F1545 — NAT/LISM POLICY LAW RACE/REL

B63
LEWIS G.K.,PUERTO RICO: FREEDOM AND POWER IN THE CARIBBEAN. PUERT/RICO USA+45 CULTURE STRUCT INDUS POL/PAR WORKER EDU/PROP CATHISM 20. PAGE 79 F1548 — ECO/UNDEV COLONIAL NAT/LISM GEOG

B63
OTERO L.M.,HONDURAS. HONDURAS SPAIN STRUCT SECT COLONIAL REV WAR ATTIT PWR...GEOG WORSHIP 16/20. PAGE 102 F2003 — NAT/G SOCIETY NAT/LISM ECO/UNDEV

B64
AHMAD M.,THE CIVIL SERVANT IN PAKISTAN. PAKISTAN ECO/UNDEV COLONIAL INGP/REL...SOC CHARTS BIBLIOG 20 CIVIL/SERV. PAGE 3 F0051 — WELF/ST ADMIN ATTIT STRATA

B64
BALOGH T.,THE ECONOMIC IMPACT OF MONETARY AND COMMERCIAL INSTITUTIONS OF A EUROPEAN ORIGIN IN AFRICA. AFR UAR INDUS FOR/AID COLONIAL CONTROL ...NAT/COMP 20. PAGE 9 F0169 — TEC/DEV FINAN ECO/UNDEV ECO/TAC

B64
CASEY R.G.,THE FUTURE OF THE COMMONWEALTH. INDIA PAKISTAN UK ECO/UNDEV INT/ORG TEC/DEV COLONIAL SUPEGO 20 EEC AUSTRAL. PAGE 22 F0425 — DIPLOM SOVEREIGN NAT/LISM FOR/AID

B64
LUTHULI A.,AFRICA'S FREEDOM. KIN LABOR POL/PAR SCHOOL DIPLOM NEUTRAL REGION REV NAT/LISM PWR WEALTH SOCISM SOC/INTEG 20. PAGE 82 F1608 — AFR ECO/UNDEV COLONIAL

B64
PENNOCK J.R.,SELF-GOVERNMENT IN MODERNIZING NATIONS. AFR COM USA+45 ECO/DEV POL/PAR PROB/SOLV DIPLOM ECO/TAC COLONIAL REV POPULISM SOCISM 20. PAGE 105 F2058 — ECO/UNDEV POLICY SOVEREIGN NAT/G

B64
RENO P.,THE ORDEAL OF BRITISH GUIANA. L/A+17C USA+45 STRUCT AGRI EXTR/IND INDUS NAT/G FOR/AID ORD/FREE...GEOG 20 GUIANA/BR INTRVN/ECO. PAGE 111 F2178 — COLONIAL ECO/UNDEV SOCISM PWR

B64
ROBINSON R.D.,INTERNATIONAL BUSINESS POLICY. AFR INDIA L/A+17C USA+45 ELITES AGRI FOR/AID COERCE BAL/PAY...DECISION INT/LAW MGT 20. PAGE 113 F2224 — ECO/TAC DIST/IND COLONIAL FINAN

B64
TONG T.,UNITED STATES DIPLOMACY IN CHINA, 1844-1860. ASIA USA-45 ECO/UNDEV ECO/TAC COERCE GP/REL...INT/LAW 19 TREATY. PAGE 131 F2581 — DIPLOM INT/TRADE COLONIAL

N64
KENYA MINISTRY ECO PLAN DEV,AFRICAN SOCIALISM AND ITS APPLICATION TO PLANNING IN KENYA (PAMPHLET). AFR AGRI INDUS WORKER TAX COLONIAL WEALTH 20. PAGE 70 F1380 — NAT/G SOCISM PLAN ECO/UNDEV

B65
APTER D.E.,THE POLITICS OF MODERNIZATION. AFR L/A+17C CULTURE NAT/G POL/PAR ADMIN COLONIAL NAT/LISM ATTIT RIGID/FLEX PWR...SOC CONCPT. PAGE 6 F0109 — ECO/UNDEV GEN/LAWS STRATA CREATE

B65
CAMERON W.J.,NEW ZEALAND. NEW/ZEALND S/ASIA DIPLOM INT/TRADE WRITING COLONIAL PARL/PROC...GEOG CMN/WLTH. PAGE 21 F0402 — SOCIETY GP/REL STRUCT

B65
GOODSELL C.T.,ADMINISTRATION OF A REVOLUTION. PUERT/RICO ECO/UNDEV FINAN POL/PAR PROVS LEGIS PLAN BUDGET RECEIVE ADMIN COLONIAL LEAD MUNICH 20 ROOSEVLT/F. PAGE 49 F0951 — EXEC SOC

B65
HAPGOOD D.,AFRICA: FROM INDEPENDENCE TO TOMARROW. AFR GUINEA SENEGAL CULTURE ELITES ECO/UNDEV AGRI SCHOOL FOR/AID COLONIAL MARXISM...TREND 20. PAGE 55 F1070 — ECO/TAC SOCIETY NAT/G

B65
LITTLE I.M.D.,INTERNATIONAL AID. UK WOR+45 AGRI INDUS GIVE RECEIVE COLONIAL BAL/PAY WEALTH...POLICY GOV/COMP METH/COMP 20. PAGE 81 F1584 — FOR/AID DIPLOM ECO/UNDEV NAT/G

B65
NKRUMAH K.,NEO-COLONIALISM: THE LAST STAGE OF IMPERIALISM. AFR INT/ORG WORKER FOR/AID INT/TRADE EDU/PROP GOV/REL NAT/LISM SOVEREIGN POPULISM SOCISM ...SOCIALIST 20 THIRD/WRLD INTRVN/ECO. PAGE 98 F1929 — COLONIAL DIPLOM ECO/UNDEV ECO/TAC

B65
SCHULTZ T.W.,ECONOMIC CRISES IN WORLD AGRICULTURE. ASIA INDIA USSR ECO/DEV ECO/UNDEV INDUS VOL/ASSN CAP/ISM RATION COLONIAL 20. PAGE 117 F2317 — AGRI ECO/TAC INCOME WORKER

B65
SPENCE J.E.,REPUBLIC UNDER PRESSURE: A STUDY OF SOUTH AFRICAN FOREIGN POLICY. SOUTH/AFR ADMIN COLONIAL GOV/REL RACE/REL DISCRIM NAT/LISM ATTIT ROLE...TREND 20 NEGRO. PAGE 124 F2449 — DIPLOM POLICY AFR

B65
THORNTON A.P.,DOCTRINES OF IMPERIALISM. WOR+45 WOR-45 DOMIN NAT/LISM PROFIT ATTIT PERSON PWR RESPECT SOVEREIGN...CONCPT STERTYP. PAGE 130 F2571 — IDEA/COMP COLONIAL DRIVE

B65
VON RENESSE E.A.,UNVOLLENDETE DEMOKRATIEN. AFR ISLAM S/ASIA SOCIETY ACT/RES COLONIAL...JURID CHARTS BIBLIOG METH 13/20. PAGE 142 F2795 — ECO/UNDEV NAT/COMP SOVEREIGN

S65
BERREBY J.J.,"IMPERATIFS STRATEGIQUES DU PETROLE." ECO/UNDEV VOL/ASSN ECO/TAC COLONIAL NUC/PWR WAR. PAGE 14 F0270 — ISLAM EXTR/IND STAT OBS

S65
HAYTER T.,"FRENCH AID TO AFRICA* ITS SCOPE AND ACHIEVEMENTS." CULTURE ECO/TAC INT/TRADE ADMIN REGION CENTRAL FEDERAL LOVE PWR SOVEREIGN EEC. PAGE 57 F1127
AFR FRANCE FOR/AID COLONIAL

S65
SOPER T.,"THE EEC AND AID TO AFRICA." FRANCE UK ECO/UNDEV INT/TRADE TARIFFS REGION ROUTINE CENTRAL DISCRIM...DECISION RECORD EEC. PAGE 124 F2443
AFR FOR/AID COLONIAL

B66
AMERICAN ASSEMBLY COLUMBIA U,THE UNITED STATES AND THE PHILIPPINES. PHILIPPINE S/ASIA USA+45 USA-45 SOCIETY FORCES INT/TRADE...POLICY 20. PAGE 5 F0085
COLONIAL DIPLOM NAT/LISM

B66
BARAN P.A.,MONOPOLY CAPITAL; AN ESSAY ON THE AMERICAN ECONOMIC AND SOCIAL ORDER. USA+45 USA-45 ECO/UNDEV FINAN MARKET PLAN DIPLOM COLONIAL RACE/REL DEMAND MARXISM...CHARTS 20. PAGE 9 F0179
LG/CO CAP/ISM PRICE CONTROL

B66
CROWDER M.,A SHORT HISTORY OF NIGERIA. AFR NIGERIA UK ECO/UNDEV CHIEF INT/TRADE RACE/REL NAT/LISM ORD/FREE...GEOG SOC CHARTS BIBLIOG 14/20. PAGE 29 F0558
COLONIAL NAT/G CULTURE

B66
DAVIES I.,AFRICAN TRADE UNIONS. AFR ECO/UNDEV INT/ORG GP/REL ORD/FREE SOVEREIGN SOCISM 20. PAGE 30 F0585
LABOR COLONIAL PWR INDUS

B66
DILLEY M.R.,BRITISH POLICY IN KENYA COLONY (2ND ED.). AFR INDIA UK LABOR BUDGET TAX ADMIN PARL/PROC GP/REL...BIBLIOG 20 PARLIAMENT. PAGE 33 F0639
COLONIAL REPRESENT SOVEREIGN

B66
GOODWIN C.D.W.,ECONOMIC INQUIRY IN AUSTRALIA. ECO/DEV ECO/UNDEV ACADEM INT/TRADE RENT TARIFFS TAX PRESS GOV/REL SOCISM 18/20 AUSTRAL. PAGE 49 F0953
ECO/TAC IDEA/COMP BUDGET COLONIAL

B66
HAYER T.,FRENCH AID. AFR FRANCE AGRI FINAN BUDGET ADMIN WAR PRODUC...CHARTS 18/20 THIRD/WRLD OVRSEA/DEV. PAGE 57 F1125
TEC/DEV COLONIAL FOR/AID ECO/UNDEV

B66
HOWE R.W.,BLACK AFRICA: FROM PRE-HISTORY TO THE EVE OF THE COLONIAL ERA. ECO/UNDEV KIN PROVS SECT INT/TRADE EDU/PROP COLONIAL...BIBLIOG WORSHIP. PAGE 62 F1226
AFR CULTURE SOC

B66
HUTTENBACH R.A.,BRITISH IMPERIAL EXPERIENCE. AFR S/ASIA UK WOR-45 INT/ORG TEC/DEV...CHARTS 16/20 MERCANTLST. PAGE 64 F1253
COLONIAL TIME/SEQ INT/TRADE

B66
LONDON K.,EASTERN EUROPE IN TRANSITION. CHINA/COM USSR DOMIN COLONIAL CENTRAL RIGID/FLEX PWR...SOC ANTHOL 20. PAGE 82 F1597
SOVEREIGN COM NAT/LISM DIPLOM

B66
O'CONNER A.M.,AN ECONOMIC GEOGRAPHY OF EAST AFRICA. AFR TANZANIA UGANDA AGRI WORKER INT/TRADE COLONIAL GOV/REL...CHARTS METH/COMP 20 AFRICA/E. PAGE 99 F1953
ECO/UNDEV EXTR/IND GEOG HABITAT

B66
RAYBACK J.G.,A HISTORY OF AMERICAN LABOR. USA+45 USA-45 ECO/DEV LEGIS COLONIAL WAR INGP/REL PWR WEALTH 17/20. PAGE 110 F2156
LABOR LOBBY ECO/UNDEV NAT/G

B66
SMITH H.E.,READINGS IN ECONOMIC DEVELOPMENT AND ADMINISTRATION IN TANZANIA. TANZANIA FINAN INDUS LABOR NAT/G PLAN PROB/SOLV INT/TRADE COLONIAL REGION...ANTHOL BIBLIOG 20 AFRICA/E. PAGE 123 F2431
TEC/DEV ADMIN GOV/REL

S66
FLEMING W.G.,"AUTHORITY, EFFICIENCY, AND ROLE STRESS: PROBLEMS IN THE DEVELOPMENT OF EAST AFRICAN BUREAUCRACIES." AFR UGANDA STRUCT PROB/SOLV ROUTINE INGP/REL ROLE...MGT SOC GP/COMP GOV/COMP 20 TANGANYIKA AFRICA/E. PAGE 41 F0810
DOMIN EFFICIENCY COLONIAL ADMIN

S66
ROTHCHILD D.,"THE LIMITS OF FEDERALISM: AN EXAMINATION OF POLITICAL INSTITUTIONAL TRANSFER IN AFRICA." AFR CONSTN CULTURE ELITES ECO/UNDEV KIN PROB/SOLV ADMIN ORD/FREE PWR...POLICY 20. PAGE 114 F2250
FEDERAL NAT/G NAT/LISM COLONIAL

B67
BARROW T.C.,TRADE AND EMPIRE: THE BRITISH CUSTOMS SERVICE IN COLONIAL AMERICA, 1660-1775. UK USA-45 ECO/UNDEV NAT/G ECO/TAC DOMIN REV 17/18. PAGE 10 F0197
COLONIAL TARIFFS ADMIN EX/STRUC

B67
BLAIR P.W.,THE MINISTATE DILEMMA. WOR+45 AGREE COLONIAL ORD/FREE...GEOG CHARTS MUNICH LEAGUE/NAT UN. PAGE 15 F0294
INT/ORG NAT/G CENSUS

B67
CHILCOTE R.H.,PORTUGUESE AFRICA. PORTUGAL CULTURE SOCIETY ECO/UNDEV DOMIN NAT/LISM...TREND IDEA/COMP NAT/COMP BIBLIOG 15/20. PAGE 24 F0465
AFR COLONIAL ORD/FREE

PROB/SOLV

B67
CLEGERN W.M.,BRITISH HONDURAS: COLONIAL DEAD END, 1859-1900. HONDURAS AGRI FINAN PROB/SOLV INT/TRADE PWR WEALTH...BIBLIOG/A 19. PAGE 25 F0487
COLONIAL POLICY ECO/UNDEV DOMIN

B67
FALL B.B.,HO CHI MINH ON REVOLUTION: SELECTED WRITINGS, 1920-66. COM VIETNAM ELITES NAT/G COERCE GUERRILLA RACE/REL MARXISM...MARXIST ANTHOL 20. PAGE 39 F0761
REV COLONIAL ECO/UNDEV S/ASIA

B67
FANON F.,TOWARD THE AFRICAN REVOLUTION. AFR FRANCE CULTURE ELITES LEAD REV GP/REL ORD/FREE SOVEREIGN 20. PAGE 39 F0762
COLONIAL DOMIN ECO/UNDEV RACE/REL

B67
MCNELLY T.,SOURCES IN MODERN EAST ASIAN HISTORY AND POLITICS. KOREA VIETNAM CULTURE DIPLOM COLONIAL REV WAR PWR ALL/IDEOS MARXISM...ANTHOL 20 CHINJAP. PAGE 88 F1733
NAT/COMP ASIA S/ASIA SOCIETY

B67
MEYERS M.,SOURCES OF THE AMERICAN REPUBLIC; A DOCUMENTARY HISTORY OF POLITICS, SOCIETY, AND THOUGHT (VOL. I, REV. ED.). USA-45 CULTURE STRUCT NAT/G LEGIS LEAD ATTIT...JURID SOC ANTHOL 17/19 PRESIDENT. PAGE 90 F1772
COLONIAL REV WAR

B67
MEYNAUD J.,TRADE UNIONISM IN AFRICA; A STUDY OF ITS GROWTH AND ORIENTATION (TRANS. BY ANGELA BRENCH). INT/ORG PROB/SOLV COLONIAL PWR...TIME/SEQ TREND ILO. PAGE 90 F1774
LABOR AFR NAT/LISM ORD/FREE

B67
MUHAMMAD A.C.,THE EMERGENCE OF PAKISTAN. PAKISTAN S/ASIA CONSTN ECO/UNDEV NAT/G CONTROL NAT/LISM 20. PAGE 94 F1853
DIPLOM COLONIAL SECT PROB/SOLV

B67
RAVKIN A.,THE NEW STATES OF AFRICA (HEADLINE SERIES, NO. 183((PAMPHLET). CULTURE STRUCT INDUS COLONIAL NAT/LISM...SOC 20. PAGE 109 F2153
AFR ECO/UNDEV SOCIETY ADMIN

B67
ROACH J.R.,THE UNITED STATES AND THE ATLANTIC COMMUNITY; ISSUES AND PROSPECTS. AFR WOR+45 TEC/DEV ECO/TAC COLONIAL REGION PEACE ROLE...ANTHOL NATO EEC. PAGE 112 F2199
INT/ORG POLICY ADJUST DIPLOM

B67
SACKS B.,SOUTH AFRICA: AN IMPERIAL DILEMMA. SOUTH/AFR UK ECO/UNDEV KIN DOMIN DEBATE CONTROL REV DISCRIM ISOLAT...POLICY STAT BIBLIOG 20. PAGE 115 F2268
COLONIAL RACE/REL DIPLOM ORD/FREE

B67
VENKATESWARAN R.J.,CABINET GOVERNMENT IN INDIA. INDIA UK SOCIETY OP/RES COLONIAL LEAD EFFICIENCY ORD/FREE 20. PAGE 141 F2776
DELIB/GP ADMIN CONSTN NAT/G

B67
WESSON R.G.,THE IMPERIAL ORDER. WOR-45 STRUCT SECT DOMIN ADMIN COLONIAL LEAD CONSERVE...CONCPT BIBLIOG 20. PAGE 145 F2861
PWR CHIEF CONTROL SOCIETY

B67
WILLS A.J.,AN INTRODUCTION TO THE HISTORY OF CENTRAL AFRICA. RHODESIA ZAMBIA CULTURE SOCIETY ECO/UNDEV TEC/DEV DOMIN WAR ALL/VALS...POLICY TREND BIBLIOG T 14/20 NYASALAND. PAGE 147 F2899
AFR COLONIAL ORD/FREE

B67
YOUNG J.M.,THE BRAZILIAN REVOLUTION OF 1930 AND THE AFTERMATH. BRAZIL COLONIAL PWR...BIBLIOG/A 16/20. PAGE 150 F2951
PLAN CHIEF FORCES REV

L67
AUSTIN D.A.,"POLITICAL CONFLICT IN AFRICA." CONSTN NAT/G CREATE ADMIN COLONIAL ORD/FREE MARXISM POPULISM SOCISM...NAT/COMP ANTHOL 20. PAGE 8 F0141
ANOMIE AFR POL/PAR

L67
MCALLISTER J.T. JR.,"THE POSSIBILITIES FOR DIPLOMACY IN SOUTHEAST ASIA." LAOS VIETNAM INT/ORG NAT/G PROVS BAL/PWR DOMIN AGREE COLONIAL WAR PWR 17/20 TREATY. PAGE 88 F1716
DIPLOM S/ASIA

S67
"PROTEST AGAINST SOVIET INDUSTRIALIZATION ILLS IN LITHUANIA* A MEMORANDUM." USSR LITHUANIA NAT/G PROVS COST GEOG. PAGE 1 F0024
INDUS COLONIAL NAT/LISM PLAN

S67
AGUILAR M.A.,"?UNA OEA MAS FUERTE O UNA AMERICA LATINA MAS DEBIL?" L/A+17C USA+45 USA-45 ECO/UNDEV INDUS CHIEF DELIB/GP FORCES CONTROL PWR 20 OAS KENNEDY/JF JOHNSON/LB. PAGE 3 F0050
INT/ORG DIPLOM POLICY COLONIAL

S67
BOSHER J.F.,"GOVERNMENT AND PRIVATE INTERESTS IN NEW FRANCE." CANADA FRANCE INDUS LG/CO SML/CO CAP/ISM INT/TRADE COLONIAL GP/REL...HIST/WRIT 17/18. PAGE 17 F0320
NAT/G FINAN ADMIN CONTROL

S67
CAMMETT J.M.,"COMMUNIST THEORIES OF FASCISM, 1920-35." ITALY POL/PAR PROF/ORG VOL/ASSN WORKER COLONIAL TOTALISM...SOCIALIST 20. PAGE 21 F0403
MARXISM FASCISM ATTIT

S67
FRIEDENBERG D.M.,"THE US IN LATIN AMERICA; A RECKONING OF SHAME." L/A+17C USA+45 USA-45 INT/ORG CAP/ISM FOR/AID 17/20 OAS. PAGE 44 F0857
DIPLOM POLICY DOMIN COLONIAL

S67
GONZALEZ M.P.,"CUBA, UNA REVOLUCION EN MARCHA." CUBA L/A+17C USA+45 VIETNAM ECO/UNDEV FORCES DIPLOM DOMIN...POLICY MARXIST NAT/COMP CASTRO/F. PAGE 48 F0946
REV NAT/G COLONIAL SOVEREIGN

S67
IBARRA J.,"EL EXPERIMENTO CUBANO." COM CUBA L/A+17C USA+45 ECO/UNDEV LEGIS INT/TRADE CONTROL REV NAT/LISM PWR 19/20 TREATY. PAGE 64 F1259
COLONIAL DIPLOM NAT/G POLICY

S67
KRAUS J.,"A MARXIST IN GHANA." GHANA ELITES CHIEF PROB/SOLV TEC/DEV DIPLOM ECO/TAC COLONIAL PARTIC PWR 20 NKRUMAH/K. PAGE 73 F1432
MARXISM PLAN ATTIT CREATE

S67
LEIFER M.,"ASTRIDE THE STRAITS OF JAHORE: THE BRITISH PRESENCE AND COMMONWEALTH RIVALRY IN SOUTHEAST ASIA." MALAYSIA UK FORCES PLAN ECO/TAC ...DECISION 20 CMN/WLTH. PAGE 77 F1515
DIPLOM NAT/LISM COLONIAL

S67
PETRAS J.,"GUERRILLA MOVEMENTS IN LATIN AMERICA - I." GUATEMALA PERU VENEZUELA NAT/G COLONIAL LEAD ATTIT PWR...TIME/SEQ METH/COMP 20 COLOMB. PAGE 105 F2072
GUERRILLA REV L/A+17C MARXISM

S67
PFEFFERMANN G.,"TRADE UNIONS AND POLITICS IN FRENCH WEST AFRICA DURING THE FOURTH REPUBLIC." AFR INDUS POL/PAR COLONIAL ATTIT PWR 20. PAGE 106 F2077
PARTIC DRIVE INT/TRADE LABOR

S67
RAZA M.A.,"EMERGING TRENDS IN PUBLIC LABOR POLICIES AND UNION - GOVERN MENT RELATIONS IN ASIA AND AFRICA." LAW NAT/G POL/PAR COLONIAL COERCE GP/REL ATTIT 20. PAGE 110 F2157
LABOR CONTROL TREND

S67
SIDDIQ M.M.,"LOCAL GOVERNMENT IN PAKISTAN." PAKISTAN PROB/SOLV TAX COLONIAL GOV/REL MUNICH 20. PAGE 121 F2395
ADMIN LOC/G DELIB/GP BUDGET

S67
SIPPEL D.,"INDIENS UNSICHERE ZUKUNFT." INDIA CULTURE ACADEM POL/PAR LEGIS COLONIAL CHOOSE SOVEREIGN...JURID 20. PAGE 122 F2416
SOCIETY STRUCT ECO/UNDEV NAT/G

S67
TABORSKY E.,"THE CLASS STRUGGLE, THE PROLETARIAT, AND THE DEVELOPING NATIONS." USSR LABOR POL/PAR FOR/AID COLONIAL GP/REL 20. PAGE 128 F2521
DIPLOM MARXISM ECO/UNDEV WORKER

S67
WALKER R.L.,"THE WEST AND THE 'NEW ASIA'." CHINA/COM ECO/UNDEV DIPLOM...PREDICT 20. PAGE 142 F2805
ASIA INT/TRADE COLONIAL REGION

S67
WILSON C.E.,"AMERICAN INVESTMENT IN PORTUGUESE AFRICA: A PROBLEM OF "DEMOCRATIC" COLONIALISM." AFR ECO/UNDEV DIPLOM MORAL...IDEA/COMP 20 ANGOLA MOZAMBIQUE. PAGE 147 F2901
COLONIAL DOMIN ORD/FREE POLICY

C83
BURKE E.,"RESOLUTIONS FOR CONCILIATION WITH AMERICA" (1775), IN E. BURKE, COLLECTED WORKS, VOL. 2." UK USA-45 FORCES INT/TRADE TARIFFS TAX SANCTION PEACE...POLICY 18 PRE/US/AM. PAGE 20 F0387
COLONIAL WAR SOVEREIGN ECO/TAC

COLORADO....COLORADO

COLSTON RESEARCH SOCIETY F0510

COLUMBIA U SCHOOL OF LAW F0511,F0512

COLUMBIA/U....COLUMBIA UNIVERSITY

COM....COMMUNIST COUNTRIES, EXCEPT CHINA; SEE ALSO APPROPRIATE NATIONS, MARXISM

N
US LIBRARY OF CONGRESS,EAST EUROPEAN ACCESSIONS INDEX. NAT/G ISOLAT ATTIT KNOWL...POLICY 20. PAGE 138 F2711
BIBLIOG COM MARXIST DIPLOM

B38
HARPER S.N.,THE GOVERNMENT OF THE SOVIET UNION. COM USSR LAW CONSTN ECO/DEV PLAN TEC/DEV DIPLOM INT/TRADE ADMIN REV NAT/LISM...POLICY 20. PAGE 55 F1085
MARXISM NAT/G LEAD POL/PAR

B40
SIKES E.R.,CONTEMPORARY ECONOMIC SYSTEMS: THEIR ANALYSIS AND SOCIAL BACKGROUND. GERMANY ITALY USSR AGRI INDUS PLAN CAP/ISM ROUTINE TOTALISM FASCISM ...POLICY CON/ANAL BIBLIOG 20. PAGE 122 F2400
COM SOCISM CONCPT

B48
LAUTERBACH A.,ECONOMIC SECURITY AND INDIVIDUAL FREEDOM: CAN WE HAVE BOTH? COM EUR+WWI MOD/EUR UNIV WOR+45 CAP/ISM TOTALISM ALL/VALS...GOV/COMP BIBLIOG 20. PAGE 76 F1490
ORD/FREE ECO/DEV DECISION INGP/REL

B49
US DEPARTMENT OF STATE,SOVIET BIBLIOGRAPHY (PAMPHLET). CHINA/COM COM USSR LAW AGRI INT/ORG ECO/TAC EDU/PROP...POLICY GEOG IND 20. PAGE 135 F2670
BIBLIOG/A MARXISM CULTURE DIPLOM

B51
US LIBRARY OF CONGRESS,EAST EUROPEAN ACCESSIONS LIST (VOL. I). POL/PAR DIPLOM ADMIN LEAD 20. PAGE 138 F2715
BIBLIOG/A COM SOCIETY NAT/G

B52
MACARTHUR D.,REVITALIZING A NATION. ASIA COM FUT KOREA WOR+45 NAT/G FOR/AID TAX GIVE WAR ATTIT SOCISM 20 CHINJAP EUROPE. PAGE 83 F1619
LEAD FORCES TOP/EX POLICY

S53
LINCOLN G.,"FACTORS DETERMINING ARMS AID." COM FUT USA+45 USSR WOR+45 ECO/DEV NAT/G CONSULT PLAN TEC/DEV DIPLOM DOMIN EDU/PROP PERCEPT PWR ...DECISION CONCPT TREND MARX/KARL 20. PAGE 80 F1566
FORCES POLICY BAL/PWR FOR/AID

B54
LENIN V.I.,SELECTED WORKS (12 VOLS.). USSR INTELL SOCIETY STRATA STRUCT NAT/G POL/PAR WORKER CAP/ISM REV WAR...MARXIST PHIL/SCI 20 MARX/KARL LENIN/VI. PAGE 78 F1520
COM MARXISM

B54
STALEY E.,THE FUTURE OF UNDERDEVELOPED COUNTRIES: POLITICAL IMPLICATIONS OF ECONOMIC DEVELOPMENT. AFR COM FUT USA+45 SOCIETY ECO/UNDEV CREATE PLAN CAP/ISM ATTIT DRIVE MARXISM SOCISM...POLICY CONCPT CHARTS 20. PAGE 125 F2466
EDU/PROP ECO/TAC FOR/AID

B55
MAYO H.B.,DEMOCRACY AND MARXISM. COM USSR STRATA NAT/G WORKER ECO/TAC REV MORAL...PHIL/SCI HIST/WRIT IDEA/COMP WORSHIP 20 MARX/KARL LENIN/VI STALIN/J TROTSKY/L. PAGE 87 F1708
MARXISM CAP/ISM

B56
KNORR K.E.,RUBLE DIPLOMACY: CHALLENGE TO AMERICAN FOREIGN AID(PAMPHLET). AFR CHINA/COM COM USA+45 USSR PLAN TEC/DEV CAP/ISM INT/TRADE DOMIN EDU/PROP CONTROL LEAD 20. PAGE 72 F1413
ECO/UNDEV COM DIPLOM FOR/AID

B56
UNIVERSITY OF CHICAGO,BIBLIOGRAPHY OF UKRAINE (PAMPHLET). USSR...SOC 20. PAGE 133 F2619
BIBLIOG/A COM

B56
WATT D.C.,BRITAIN AND THE SUEZ CANAL. COM UAR UK ...INT/LAW 20 SUEZ TREATY. PAGE 144 F2835
DIPLOM INT/TRADE DIST/IND NAT/G

B56
WOLFF R.L.,THE BALKANS IN OUR TIME. ALBANIA FUT MOD/EUR USSR YUGOSLAVIA CULTURE INT/ORG SECT DIPLOM EDU/PROP COERCE WAR ORD/FREE...CHARTS 4/20 BALKANS COMINFORM. PAGE 148 F2919
GEOG COM

B57
LENIN V.I.,THE DEVELOPMENT OF CAPITALISM IN RUSSIA. MOD/EUR USSR AGRI MARKET POL/PAR TEC/DEV...CONCPT 19/20. PAGE 78 F1521
COM INDUS CAP/ISM

B57
LOUCKS W.N.,COMPARATIVE ECONOMIC SYSTEMS (5TH ED.). COM UK USSR INDUS POL/PAR PLAN CAP/ISM TOTALISM MARXISM...PHIL/SCI BIBLIOG 19/20. PAGE 82 F1603
NAT/COMP IDEA/COMP SOCISM

L57
MASS. INST. TECH.,"THE CENTER FOR INTERNATIONAL STUDIES." AFR ASIA COM EUR+WWI ISLAM L/A+17C S/ASIA USA+45 USA-45 DIST/IND CONSULT FORCES ACT/RES TEC/DEV DIPLOM REV ATTIT WEALTH...CONCPT FOR/TRADE 20. PAGE 87 F1702
R+D ECO/UNDEV

S57
HOAG M.W.,"ECONOMIC PROBLEMS OF ALLIANCE." AFR COM EUR+WWI WOR+45 ECO/DEV ECO/UNDEV NAT/G VOL/ASSN FORCES PLAN TEC/DEV DIPLOM COERCE ORD/FREE PWR WEALTH...DECISION GEN/LAWS NATO TERR/GP. PAGE 60 F1182
INT/ORG ECO/TAC

B58
BERLINER J.S.,SOVIET ECONOMIC AID: THE AID AND TRADE POLICY IN UNDERDEVELOPED COUNTRIES. AFR COM ISLAM L/A+17C S/ASIA USSR ECO/DEV DIST/IND FINAN MARKET INT/ORG ACT/RES PLAN BAL/PWR WEAPON PWR WEALTH...CHARTS FOR/TRADE 20. PAGE 14 F0263
ECO/UNDEV ECO/TAC FOR/AID

B58
COLE G.D.H.,COMMUNISM AND SOCIAL DEMOCRACY (VOL. IV OF "HISTORY OF SOCIAL THOUGHT"). COM GERMANY ITALY UK AGRI INT/ORG WORKER DIPLOM COLONIAL NAT/LISM ALL/IDEOS...BIBLIOG 20 LEAGUE/NAT AUST/HUNG.
MARXISM REV POL/PAR SOCISM

PAGE 26 F0502

B58
MIKESELL R.F.,FINANCING FREE WORLD TRADE WITH THE SINO-SOVIET BLOC. CHINA/COM COM USSR WOR+45 ECO/DEV AGRI DIST/IND EXTR/IND FINAN INDUS MARKET PROC/MFG NAT/G PLAN TEC/DEV ECO/TAC...CHARTS METH/GP EEC FOR/TRADE 20. PAGE 91 F1780
STAT BAL/PAY

B59
AITKEN H.,THE STATE AND ECONOMIC GROWTH. COM EUR+WWI MOD/EUR S/ASIA USA+45 FINAN NAT/G DELIB/GP PLAN PWR WEALTH 20. PAGE 3 F0054
DIST/IND ECO/DEV

B59
HENDEL S.,THE SOVIET CRUCIBLE. USSR LEAD COERCE NAT/LISM UTOPIA PWR...POLICY CONCPT ANTHOL 20 STALIN/J LENIN/VI MARX/KARL BOLSHEVIK. PAGE 58 F1147
COM MARXISM REV TOTALISM

B59
HOOVER C.B.,THE ECONOMY, LIBERTY AND THE STATE. COM EUR+WWI USA+45 USA-45 USSR CAP/ISM EDU/PROP COERCE TOTALISM ORD/FREE...POLICY OBS INT TREND NAZI 20. PAGE 61 F1206
ECO/DEV ECO/TAC

B59
PANIKKAR K.M.,THE AFRO-ASIAN STATES AND THEIR PROBLEMS. COM CULTURE KIN POL/PAR SECT DIPLOM EDU/PROP COLONIAL SOVEREIGN...TECHNIC GOV/COMP 20. PAGE 103 F2025
AFR S/ASIA ECO/UNDEV

S59
ALKHIMOV V.S.,"SOVIET FOREIGN TRADE CHANNELS." COM FUT USA+45 USSR ECO/DEV MARKET CONSULT PLAN WEALTH ...MARXIST OBS CON/ANAL FOR/TRADE 20. PAGE 4 F0068
FINAN ECO/TAC DIPLOM

S59
ZAUBERMAN A.,"SOVIET BLOC ECONOMIC INTEGRATION." COM CULTURE INTELL ECO/DEV INDUS TOP/EX ACT/RES PLAN ECO/TAC INT/TRADE ROUTINE CHOOSE ATTIT ...TIME/SEQ 20. PAGE 150 F2958
MARKET INT/ORG USSR TOTALISM

B60
ALLEN R.L.,SOVIET ECONOMIC WARFARE. USSR FINAN INDUS NAT/G PLAN TEC/DEV FOR/AID DETER WEALTH ...TREND GEN/LAWS FOR/TRADE 20. PAGE 4 F0072
COM ECO/TAC

B60
BILLERBECK K.,SOVIET BLOC FOREIGN AID TO UNDERDEVELOPED COUNTRIES. COM FUT USSR FINAN FORCES TEC/DEV DIPLOM INT/TRADE EDU/PROP NUC/PWR...TREND 20. PAGE 15 F0285
FOR/AID ECO/UNDEV ECO/TAC MARXISM

B60
CAMPBELL R.W.,SOVIET ECONOMIC POWER. COM USA+45 DIST/IND MARKET TOP/EX ACT/RES CAP/ISM ECO/TAC DOMIN EDU/PROP ADMIN ROUTINE DRIVE...MATH TIME/SEQ CHARTS WORK 20. PAGE 21 F0409
ECO/DEV PLAN SOCISM USSR

B60
GRANICK D.,THE RED EXECUTIVE. COM USA+45 SOCIETY ECO/DEV INDUS NAT/G POL/PAR EX/STRUC PLAN ECO/TAC EDU/PROP ADMIN EXEC ATTIT DRIVE...GP/COMP 20. PAGE 50 F0976
PWR STRATA USSR ELITES

S60
BECKER A.S.,"COMPARISIONS OF UNITED STATES AND USSR NATIONAL OUTPUT: SOME RULES OF THE GAME." COM USA+45 ECO/DEV AGRI DIST/IND INDUS R+D CONSULT PLAN ECO/TAC RIGID/FLEX KNOWL...METH/CNCPT CHARTS 20. PAGE 12 F0227
STAT USSR

S60
GROSSMAN G.,"SOVIET GROWTH: ROUTINE, INERTIA, AND PRESSURE." COM STRATA NAT/G DELIB/GP PLAN TEC/DEV ECO/TAC EDU/PROP ADMIN ROUTINE DRIVE WEALTH 20. PAGE 52 F1007
POL/PAR ECO/DEV AFR USSR

S60
HERZ J.H.,"EAST GERMANY: PROGRESS AND PROSPECTS." COM AGRI FINAN INDUS LOC/G NAT/G FORCES PLAN TEC/DEV DOMIN ADMIN COERCE DRIVE PERCEPT RIGID/FLEX MORAL ORD/FREE PWR...MARXIST PSY SOC RECORD STERTYP WORK. PAGE 59 F1158
POL/PAR STRUCT GERMANY

S60
HOOVER C.B.,"NATIONAL POLICY AND RATES OF ECONOMIC GROWTH: THE US SOVIET RUSSIA AND WESTERN EUROPE." COM EUR+WWI USA+45 USSR NAT/G PLAN ECO/TAC PWR WEALTH...MATH STAT GEN/LAWS 20. PAGE 61 F1207
ECO/DEV ACT/RES

S60
JACOBSON H.K.,"THE USSR AND ILO." AFR COM STRUCT ECO/DEV ECO/UNDEV CONSULT DELIB/GP ECO/TAC ILO WORK 20. PAGE 66 F1298
INT/ORG LABOR USSR

S60
MIKESELL R.F.,"AMERICA'S ECONOMIC RESPONSIBILITY AS A GREAT POWER." COM FUT USA+45 USSR WOR+45 INT/ORG PLAN ECO/TAC FOR/AID EDU/PROP CHOOSE WEALTH ...POLICY 20. PAGE 91 F1781
ECO/UNDEV BAL/PWR CAP/ISM

S60
OWEN C.F.,"US AND SOVIET RELATIONS WITH UNDERDEVELOPED COUNTRIES: LATIN AMERICA-A CASE STUDY." AFR COM L/A+17C USA+45 USSR EXTR/IND MARKET TEC/DEV DIPLOM ECO/TAC NAT/LISM ORD/FREE PWR ...TREND WORK 20. PAGE 102 F2005
ECO/UNDEV DRIVE INT/TRADE

S60
PYE L.W.,"SOVIET AND AMERICAN STYLES IN FOREIGN AID." COM USA+45 USSR WOR+45 NAT/G PLAN ECO/TAC ROUTINE RIGID/FLEX...POLICY CONCPT TREND GEN/LAWS TOT/POP 20. PAGE 108 F2132
ECO/UNDEV ATTIT FOR/AID

B61
AUBREY H.G.,COEXISTENCE: ECONOMIC CHALLENGE AND RESPONSE. AFR USSR WOR+45 ACT/RES BAL/PWR CAP/ISM DIPLOM ECO/TAC FOR/AID INT/TRADE PEACE SOCISM ...METH/COMP NAT/COMP. PAGE 7 F0139
POLICY ECO/UNDEV PLAN COM

B61
FERTIG L.,PROSPERITY THROUGH FREEDOM. COM INDUS LABOR CAP/ISM ECO/TAC PRODUC PROFIT ORD/FREE WEALTH SOCISM...METH/CNCPT 20. PAGE 40 F0788
NAT/G CONTROL POLICY

B61
HORVATH B.,THE CHARACTERISTICS OF YUGOSLAV ECONOMIC DEVELOPMENT. COM ECO/UNDEV AGRI INDUS PLAN CAP/ISM ECO/TAC ROUTINE WEALTH...SOCIALIST STAT CHARTS STERTYP WORK 20. PAGE 62 F1217
ACT/RES YUGOSLAVIA

B61
KATKOFF U.,SOVIET ECONOMY 1940-1965. COM WOR+45 WOR-45 INTELL NAT/G POL/PAR TOP/EX ATTIT PWR ...POLICY TIME/SEQ VAL/FREE 20. PAGE 69 F1360
AGRI PERSON TOTALISM USSR

B61
KOVNER M.,THE CHALLENGE OF COEXISTENCE: A STUDY OF SOVIET ECONOMIC DIPLOMACY. COM FUT ECO/DEV ECO/UNDEV PLAN EDU/PROP DETER SKILL...OBS VAL/FREE 20. PAGE 73 F1430
PWR DIPLOM USSR AFR

B61
MARX K.,THE COMMUNIST MANIFESTO. IN (MENDEL A. ESSENTIAL WORKS OF MARXISM, NEW YORK: BANTAM. FUT MOD/EUR CULTURE ECO/DEV ECO/UNDEV AGRI FINAN INDUS MARKET PROC/MFG LABOR POL/PAR CONSULT FORCES CREATE PLAN ADMIN ATTIT DRIVE RIGID/FLEX ORD/FREE PWR RESPECT MARX/KARL MUNICH WORK. PAGE 86 F1691
COM NEW/IDEA CAP/ISM REV

S61
DELLA PORT G.,"PROBLEMI E PROSPETTIVE DI COESISTENZA FRA ORIENTE ED OCCIDENTE, (PART 3)." COM FUT WOR+45 NAT/G BAL/PWR FOR/AID BAL/PAY PWR WEALTH...SOC CONCPT GEN/LAWS 20. PAGE 32 F0616
AFR INT/TRADE

S61
HAYTES W.,"THREE VIEWS ON THE SOVIET ECONOMIC THREAT." AFR COM USA+45 USA-45 USSR WOR+45 WOR-45 INDUS TEC/DEV ECO/TAC DOMIN ATTIT PERCEPT PWR FOR/TRADE 20. PAGE 57 F1128
ECO/DEV PLAN TOTALISM

S61
NEAL A.C.,"NEW ECONOMIC POLICIES FOR THE WEST." COM EUR+WWI FUT USA+45 WOR+45 ECO/DEV ECO/UNDEV INDUS MARKET ROUTINE HEALTH ORD/FREE PWR...OLD/LIB METH/CNCPT 20. PAGE 97 F1904
PLAN ECO/TAC

S61
NOVE A.,"THE SOVIET MODEL AND UNDERDEVELOPED COUNTRIES." COM FUT USSR WOR+45 CULTURE ECO/DEV POL/PAR FOR/AID EDU/PROP ADMIN MORAL WEALTH ...POLICY RECORD HIST/WRIT 20. PAGE 99 F1942
ECO/UNDEV PLAN

S61
VALLET R.,"IRAN: KEY TO THE MIDDLE EAST." COM IRAQ ISLAM KUWAIT LEBANON SAUDI/ARAB TURKEY ELITES SOCIETY INDUS PROC/MFG POL/PAR TOP/EX PLAN BAL/PWR DIPLOM ECO/TAC ALL/VALS...TREND FOR/TRADE CENTO 20. PAGE 140 F2760
NAT/G ECO/UNDEV IRAN

S61
VERNON R.,"A TRADE POLICY FOR THE 1960'S." COM FUT USA+45 WOR+45 ECO/DEV ECO/UNDEV FINAN TOP/EX ACT/RES...WELF/ST METH/CNCPT CONT/OBS TOT/POP 20. PAGE 141 F2781
PLAN INT/TRADE

B62
ARNOLD H.J.P.,AID FOR DEVELOPING COUNTRIES. COM EUR+WWI USA+45 USSR WOR+45 EDU/PROP ATTIT DRIVE PWR WEALTH...TREND CHARTS STERTYP NAT/ 20. PAGE 6 F0115
ECO/UNDEV ECO/TAC FOR/AID

B62
BRUMBERG A.,RUSSIA UNDER KHRUSHCHEV. FUT USSR SOCIETY ECO/DEV AGRI PERF/ART WORKER PWR...SOC ANTHOL 20 KHRUSH/N. PAGE 20 F0377
COM MARXISM NAT/G CHIEF

B62
ELLIOTT J.R.,THE APPEAL OF COMMUNISM IN THE UNDERDEVELOPED NATIONS. AFR USSR WOR+45 INT/ORG NAT/G DIPLOM DOMIN EDU/PROP ROUTINE ATTIT RIGID/FLEX ORD/FREE PWR WEALTH MARXISM...POLICY SOC METH/CNCPT MYTH TOT/POP METH/GP 20. PAGE 37 F0722
COM ECO/UNDEV

B62
FRIEDRICH-EBERT-STIFTUNG,THE SOVIET BLOC AND DEVELOPING COUNTRIES. CHINA/COM COM GERMANY/E USSR WOR+45 ECO/UNDEV INT/ORG NAT/G TEC/DEV NEUTRAL PWR ...POLICY 20. PAGE 44 F0868
MARXISM DIPLOM ECO/TAC FOR/AID

B62
KIRPICEVA I.K.,HANDBUCH DER RUSSISCHEN UND SOWJETISCHEN BIBLIOGRAPHIEN (5 VOLS.). USSR STRUCT ECO/DEV DIPLOM LEAD ATTIT 18/20. PAGE 71 F1400
BIBLIOG/A NAT/G MARXISM COM

B62
LEVY H.V.,LIBERDADE E JUSTICA SOCIAL (2ND ED.). BRAZIL COM L/A+17C USSR INT/ORG PARTIC GP/REL WEALTH 20 UN COM/PARTY. PAGE 79 F1544
ORD/FREE MARXISM CAP/ISM LAW

B62
WALSTON H.,AGRICULTURE UNDER COMMUNISM. CHINA/COM COM PROB/SOLV HAPPINESS RIGID/FLEX...POLICY METH/COMP 20. PAGE 143 F2811
AGRI MARXISM PLAN

CREATE

L62
PRYOR F.L.,"FOREIGN TRADE IN THE COMMUNIST BLOC." COM ECO/DEV VOL/ASSN...METH/CNCPT GEN/LAWS FOR/TRADE TERR/GP 20. PAGE 108 F2129
ECO/TAC STERTYP USSR

S62
BOKOR-SZEGO H.,"LA CONVENTION DE BELGRADE ET LE REGIME DU DANUBE." COM EUR+WWI WOR+45 STRUCT POL/PAR VOL/ASSN PLAN EDU/PROP WEALTH...TIME/SEQ METH/GP COMMUN 20. PAGE 16 F0308
INT/ORG TOTALISM YUGOSLAVIA

S62
IOVTCHOUK M.T.,"ON SOME THEORETICAL PRINCIPLES AND METHODS OF SOCIOLOGICAL INVESTIGATIONS (IN RUSSIAN)." FUT USA+45 STRATA R+D NAT/G POL/PAR TOP/EX ACT/RES PLAN ECO/TAC EDU/PROP ROUTINE ATTIT RIGID/FLEX MARXISM SOCISM...MARXIST METH/CNCPT OBS TREND NAT/COMP GEN/LAWS 20. PAGE 65 F1288
COM ECO/DEV CAP/ISM USSR

S62
SCOTT J.B.,"ANGLO-SOVIET TRADE AND ITS EFFECTS ON THE COMMONWEALTH." COM FUT UK USSR WOR+45 ECO/DEV MARKET INT/ORG CONSULT WEALTH...POLICY TREND CMN/WLTH FOR/TRADE 20. PAGE 118 F2333
NAT/G ECO/TAC

S62
ZAUBERMAN A.,"SOVIET AND CHINESE STRATEGY FOR ECONOMIC GROWTH." ASIA CHINA/COM COM USSR STRATA VOL/ASSN PLAN ATTIT PWR...METH/CNCPT GEN/LAWS WORK TERR/GP 20. PAGE 150 F2959
ECO/DEV EDU/PROP

B63
ABSHIRE D.M.,NATIONAL SECURITY: POLITICAL, MILITARY, AND ECONOMIC STRATEGIES IN THE DECADE AHEAD. ASIA COM USA+45 WOR+45 ECO/DEV ECO/UNDEV INT/ORG DELIB/GP FORCES ECO/TAC COERCE ATTIT RIGID/FLEX HEALTH ORD/FREE PWR WEALTH...POLICY STAT CHARTS ANTHOL COLD/WAR VAL/FREE APP/SCI. PAGE 2 F0032
FUT ACT/RES BAL/PWR

B63
DELL S.,TRADE BLOCS AND COMMON MARKETS. COM WOR+45 ECO/DEV ECO/UNDEV GP/COMP. PAGE 32 F0615
DIPLOM ECO/TAC INT/TRADE FEDERAL

B63
HARROD R.F.,INTERNATIONAL TRADE THEORY IN A DEVELOPING WORLD. COM WOR+45 FOR/AID REGION COST DEMAND WEALTH...POLICY 20 INTL/ECON. PAGE 56 F1095
INT/TRADE BAL/PAY ECO/UNDEV METH/COMP

B63
HYDE D.,THE PEACEFUL ASSAULT. COM UAR USSR ECO/DEV ECO/UNDEV NAT/G POL/PAR CAP/ISM PWR 20. PAGE 64 F1256
MARXISM CONTROL ECO/TAC DIPLOM

B63
LAIRD R.D.,SOVIET AGRICULTURAL AND PEASANT AFFAIRS. FUT STRATA LOC/G DELIB/GP ACT/RES TEC/DEV ECO/TAC EDU/PROP ATTIT RIGID/FLEX ORD/FREE SKILL WEALTH ...STAT CON/ANAL ANTHOL MUNICH WORK VAL/FREE 20. PAGE 74 F1461
COM AGRI POLICY

B63
LETHBRIDGE H.J.,THE PEASANT AND THE COMMUNES. CHINA/COM COM USSR NEIGH PROB/SOLV ADJUST EFFICIENCY...POLICY METH/COMP NAT/COMP 20. PAGE 78 F1535
MARXISM ECO/TAC AGRI WORKER

B63
PRYOR F.L.,THE COMMUNIST FOREIGN TRADE SYSTEM. COM CZECHOSLVK GERMANY YUGOSLAVIA LAW ECO/DEV DIST/IND POL/PAR PLAN DOMIN TOTALISM DRIVE RIGID/FLEX WEALTH ...STAT STAND/INT CHARTS FOR/TRADE 20. PAGE 108 F2130
ATTIT ECO/TAC

L63
MOUSKHELY M.,"LE BLOC COMMUNISTE ET LA COMMUNAUTE ECONOMIQUE EUROPEENNE." AFR COM EUR+WWI FUT USSR WOR+45 INTELL ECO/UNDEV LABOR POL/PAR NUC/PWR RIGID/FLEX...TIME/SEQ ORG/CHARTS EEC TOT/POP 20. PAGE 94 F1849
INT/ORG ECO/DEV

S63
FLOREA I.,"CU PRIVIRE LA OBIECTUL MATERIALISMULUI ISTORIC SI AL COMUNISMULUI STIINTIFIC SI LA RAPORTUL DINTRE ELE." EUR+WWI WOR+45 WOR-45 INTELL NAT/G POL/PAR WORKER EDU/PROP PERCEPT MARXISM ...MARXIST PHIL/SCI CONCPT TOT/POP 20. PAGE 42 F0812
COM ATTIT TOTALISM

S63
GRUSHIN B.A.,"PROBLEMS OF THE MOVEMENT OF COMMUNIST LABOR IN THE USSR." COM SOCIETY LABOR ECO/TAC EDU/PROP COERCE RIGID/FLEX ORD/FREE...POLICY MARXIST STAT QU WORK 20. PAGE 52 F1011
ATTIT USSR

S63
PRYBYLA J.,"THE QUEST FOR ECONOMIC RATIONALITY IN THE SOVIET BLOC." COM FUT WOR+45 WOR-45 DIST/IND MARKET PLAN ECO/TAC ATTIT...METH/CNCPT TOT/POP 20. PAGE 108 F2128
ECO/DEV TREND USSR

S63
RAMERIE L.,"TENSION AU SEIN DU COMECON: LE CAS ROUMAIN." COM EUR+WWI USSR WOR+45 ECO/DEV DIST/IND NAT/G POL/PAR VOL/ASSN EDU/PROP TOTALISM ATTIT WEALTH...TIME/SEQ 20 COMECON. PAGE 109 F2142
INT/ORG ECO/TAC INT/TRADE ROMANIA

S63
WILES P.J.D.,"WILL CAPITALISM AND COMMUNISM SPONTANEOUSLY CONVERGE." COM FUT USA+45 ECO/DEV DIST/IND MARKET CAP/ISM ECO/TAC RIGID/FLEX WEALTH MARXISM SOCISM...MATH STAT TREND COMPUT/IR 20. PAGE 146 F2885
PLAN TEC/DEV USSR

B64
FREYMOND J.,WESTERN EUROPE SINCE THE WAR. COM EUR+WWI USA+45 DIPLOM...BIBLIOG 20 NATO UN EEC. PAGE 44 F0854
INT/ORG POLICY ECO/DEV ECO/TAC

B64
GRIFFITH W.E.,COMMUNISM IN EUROPE (2 VOLS.). CZECHOSLVK USSR WOR+45 WOR-45 YUGOSLAVIA INGP/REL MARXISM SOCISM...ANTHOL 20 EUROPE/E. PAGE 51 F1000
COM POL/PAR DIPLOM GOV/COMP

B64
PENNOCK J.R.,SELF-GOVERNMENT IN MODERNIZING NATIONS. AFR COM USA+45 ECO/DEV POL/PAR PROB/SOLV DIPLOM ECO/TAC COLONIAL REV POPULISM SOCISM 20. PAGE 105 F2058
ECO/UNDEV POLICY SOVEREIGN NAT/G

B64
RANIS G.,THE UNITED STATES AND THE DEVELOPING ECONOMIES. COM USA+45 AGRI FINAN TEC/DEV CAP/ISM ECO/TAC INT/TRADE...POLICY METH/COMP ANTHOL 20 AID. PAGE 109 F2145
ECO/UNDEV DIPLOM FOR/AID

B64
TINBERGEN J.,CENTRAL PLANNING. COM INTELL ECO/DEV ECO/UNDEV FINAN INT/ORG PROB/SOLV ECO/TAC CONTROL EXEC ROUTINE DECISION. PAGE 130 F2576
PLAN INDUS MGT CENTRAL

B64
WELLISZ S.,THE ECONOMICS OF THE SOVIET BLOC. COM USSR INDUS WORKER PLAN BUDGET INT/TRADE TAX PRICE PRODUC WEALTH MARXISM...METH/COMP 20. PAGE 145 F2854
EFFICIENCY ADMIN MARKET

L64
ARMENGALD A.,"ECONOMIE ET COEXISTENCE." COM EUR+WWI FUT USA+45 WOR+45 ECO/DEV ECO/UNDEV FINAN INT/ORG NAT/G EXEC CHOOSE ATTIT ALL/VALS...POLICY RELATIV DECISION TREND SOC/EXP WORK 20. PAGE 6 F0113
MARKET ECO/TAC AFR CAP/ISM

L64
KORBONSKI A.,"COMECON." ASIA ECO/DEV ECO/UNDEV ECO/TAC BAL/PAY NAT/LISM FOR/TRADE 20 COMECON. PAGE 73 F1425
COM INT/ORG INT/TRADE

S64
BEIM D.,"THE COMMUNIST BLOC AND THE FOREIGN-AID GAME." AFR WOR+45 NAT/G PLAN ROUTINE ATTIT KNOWL ORD/FREE...DECISION QUANT CONT/OBS TIME/SEQ CHARTS GAME SIMUL LOG/LING 20. PAGE 12 F0231
COM ECO/UNDEV ECO/TAC FOR/AID

S64
FINLEY D.D.,"A POLITICAL PERSPECTIVE OF ECONOMIC RELATIONS IN THE COMMUNIST CAMP." COM USSR FACE/GP NAT/G ACT/RES PLAN DOMIN COERCE ATTIT ORD/FREE WEALTH...TIME/SEQ 20. PAGE 41 F0800
VOL/ASSN ECO/TAC DIPLOM REGION

S64
FLORINSKY M.T.,"TRENDS IN THE SOVIET ECONOMY." COM USA+45 USSR INDUS LABOR NAT/G PLAN TEC/DEV ECO/TAC ALL/VALS SOCISM...MGT METH/CNCPT STYLE CON/ANAL GEN/METH WORK 20. PAGE 42 F0817
ECO/DEV AGRI

S64
FYFE J.,"LIST OF CURRENT ACQUISITIONS OF PERIODICALS AND NEWSPAPERS DEALING WITH THE SOVIET UNION AND EAST EUROPEAN COUNTRIES." USSR WRITING GP/REL INGP/REL MARXISM 20. PAGE 45 F0879
BIBLIOG COM EDU/PROP PRESS

S64
HERMAN L.M.,"THE ECONOMIC CONTENT OF SOVIET TRADE WITH THE WEST." WOR+45 ECO/DEV ECO/UNDEV AGRI COM/IND INDUS CAP/ISM ECO/TAC ATTIT RIGID/FLEX WEALTH...OBS TREND VAL/FREE MARX/KARL 20. PAGE 59 F1152
COM MARKET INT/TRADE USSR

S64
HORECKY P.L.,"LIBRARY OF CONGRESS PUBLICATIONS IN AID OF USSR AND EAST EUROPEAN RESEARCH." BULGARIA CZECHOSLVK POLAND USSR YUGOSLAVIA NAT/G POL/PAR DIPLOM ADMIN GOV/REL...CLASSIF 20. PAGE 62 F1214
BIBLIOG/A COM MARXISM

S64
PESELT B.M.,"COMMUNIST ECONOMIC OFFENSIVE." WOR+45 SOCIETY INT/ORG PLAN ECO/TAC DOMIN EDU/PROP ATTIT PERSON PWR WEALTH...TREND CHARTS METH/GP 20. PAGE 105 F2067
COM ECO/UNDEV FOR/AID USSR

S64
POLARIS J.,"THE SINO-SOVIET DISPUTE: ITS ECONOMIC IMPACT ON CHINA." ASIA CHINA/COM COM WOR+45 NAT/G ATTIT PWR WEALTH...STAT TREND FOR/TRADE 20. PAGE 107 F2095
ECO/UNDEV ECO/TAC

C64
GOLDMAN M.I.,"COMPARATIVE ECONOMIC SYSTEMS: A READER." COM ECO/UNDEV NAT/G BUDGET CAP/ISM ADMIN TOTALISM MARXISM SOCISM...MGT ANTHOL BIBLIOG 19/20. PAGE 48 F0938
NAT/COMP CONTROL IDEA/COMP

C64
LANDAUER C.,"CONTEMPORARY ECONOMIC SYSTEMS." COM WOR+45 ECO/UNDEV PLAN GP/REL...BIBLIOG 20. PAGE 75 F1466
CAP/ISM SOCISM MARXISM IDEA/COMP

B65
CAMPBELL J.C.,AMERICAN POLICY TOWARDS COMMUNIST EASTERN EUROPE* THE CHOICES AHEAD. AFR USA+45 ECO/DEV BAL/PWR MARXISM TREND. PAGE 21 F0406 — POLAND YUGOSLAVIA DIPLOM COM

B65
CERNY K.H.,NATO IN QUEST OF COHESION* A CONFRONTATION OF VIEWPOINTS. COM EUR+WWI USA+45 FORCES LEAD REGION DETER...ANTHOL NATO. PAGE 22 F0438 — CENTRAL NUC/PWR VOL/ASSN

B65
JOHNSON H.G.,THE WORLD ECONOMY AT THE CROSSROADS. COM WOR-45 ECO/DEV AGRI INDUS INT/TRADE REGION NAT/LISM 20. PAGE 67 F1326 — FINAN DIPLOM INT/ORG ECO/UNDEV

B65
KASER M.,COMECON* INTEGRATION PROBLEMS OF THE PLANNED ECONOMIES. INT/ORG TEC/DEV INT/TRADE PRICE ADMIN ADJUST CENTRAL...STAT TIME/SEQ ORG/CHARTS COMECON. PAGE 69 F1359 — PLAN ECO/DEV COM REGION

B65
O'BRIEN F.,CRISIS IN WORLD COMMUNISM* MARXISM IN SEARCH OF EFFICIENCY. AFR COM ECO/DEV PLAN INT/TRADE WAR ADJUST PEACE...STAT TIME/SEQ GOV/COMP NAT/COMP. PAGE 99 F1951 — MARXISM USSR DRIVE EFFICIENCY

B65
WINT G.,ASIA: A HANDBOOK. ASIA COM INDIA USSR CULTURE INTELL NAT/G...GEOG STAT CENSUS NAT/COMP WORSHIP 20 TREATY CHINJAP. PAGE 148 F2907 — DIPLOM SOC

S65
KORBONSKI A.,"USA POLICY IN EAST EUROPE." COM EUR+WWI GERMANY USA+45 CULTURE ECO/UNDEV EDU/PROP RIGID/FLEX WEALTH FOR/TRADE 20. PAGE 73 F1426 — ACT/RES ECO/TAC FOR/AID

S65
SCHROEDER G.,"LABOR PLANNING IN THE USSR." COM USSR ECO/DEV INDUS SCHOOL PRODUC WEALTH...PREDICT TIME/SEQ TREND TIME 20. PAGE 117 F2313 — WORKER PLAN CENSUS

B66
BROWN J.F.,THE NEW EASTERN EUROPE. ALBANIA BULGARIA HUNGARY POLAND ROMANIA CULTURE AGRI POL/PAR WAR NAT/LISM MARXISM...CHARTS BIBLIOG 20. PAGE 19 F0369 — DIPLOM COM NAT/G ECO/UNDEV

B66
ECKSTEIN A.,COMMUNIST CHINA'S ECONOMIC GROWTH AND FOREIGN TRADE* IMPLICATIONS FOR US POLICY. COM USA+45 USSR STRUCT INDUS MARKET DIPLOM ECO/TAC FOR/AID INT/TRADE...STAT CHARTS. PAGE 36 F0696 — ASIA ECO/UNDEV CREATE PWR

B66
GYORGY A.,ISSUES OF WORLD COMMUNISM. ALBANIA CHINA/COM COM USSR YUGOSLAVIA STRATA AGRI INT/ORG CHIEF FORCES WORKER WAR ALL/IDEOS...GEOG 20 MAO. PAGE 52 F1018 — ECO/UNDEV REV MARXISM CON/ANAL

B66
HOROWITZ I.L.,THREE WORLDS OF DEVELOPMENT. COM USA+45 STRUCT ECO/DEV PLAN PROB/SOLV TEC/DEV CIVMIL/REL...PHIL/SCI IDEA/COMP 20. PAGE 62 F1216 — ECO/UNDEV BAL/PWR POL/PAR REV

B66
JACKSON G.D.,COMINTERN AND PEASANT IN EAST EUROPE 1919-1930. BULGARIA COM CZECHOSLVK EUR+WWI POLAND ROMANIA YUGOSLAVIA STRATA AGRI VOL/ASSN DIPLOM CONTROL CROWD WEALTH...POLICY NAT/COMP 20. PAGE 66 F1293 — MARXISM ECO/UNDEV WORKER INT/ORG

B66
JENSEN F.B.,READINGS IN INTERNATIONAL ECONOMIC RELATIONS. COM ECO/UNDEV MARKET NAT/G FOR/AID ...ANTHOL 20. PAGE 67 F1317 — BAL/PAY INT/TRADE FINAN

B66
LONDON K.,EASTERN EUROPE IN TRANSITION. CHINA/COM USSR DOMIN COLONIAL CENTRAL RIGID/FLEX PWR...SOC ANTHOL 20. PAGE 82 F1597 — SOVEREIGN COM NAT/LISM DIPLOM

B66
MACFARQUHAR R.,CHINA UNDER MAO: POLITICS TAKES COMMAND. CHINA/COM COM AGRI INDUS CHIEF FORCES DIPLOM INT/TRADE EDU/PROP TASK REV ADJUST...ANTHOL 20 MAO. PAGE 83 F1628 — ECO/UNDEV TEC/DEV ECO/TAC ADMIN

B66
SPULBER N.,THE STATE AND ECONOMIC DEVELOPMENT IN EASTERN EUROPE. BULGARIA COM CZECHOSLVK HUNGARY POLAND YUGOSLAVIA CULTURE PLAN CAP/ISM INT/TRADE CONTROL...POLICY CHARTS METH/COMP BIBLIOG/A 19/20. PAGE 125 F2460 — ECO/DEV ECO/UNDEV NAT/G TOTALISM

B66
UREN P.E.,EAST - WEST TRADE* A SYMPOSIUM. COM AGRI INT/ORG PRICE HABITAT RIGID/FLEX...GEOG INT/LAW ANTHOL NATO. PAGE 133 F2625 — INT/TRADE BAL/PWR AFR CANADA

B66
US DEPARTMENT OF STATE,RESEARCH ON THE USSR AND EASTERN EUROPE (EXTERNAL RESEARCH LIST NO 1-25). USSR LAW CULTURE SOCIETY NAT/G TEC/DEV DIPLOM EDU/PROP REGION...GEOG LING. PAGE 136 F2675 — BIBLIOG/A EUR+WWI COM MARXISM

B66
WILCOX C.,ECONOMIES OF THE WORLD TODAY: THEIR ORGANIZATION, DEVELOPMENT, AND PERFORMANCE (2ND ED.). CHINA/COM COM INDIA NIGERIA UK WOR+45 WOR-45 INDUS MARKET PLAN ECO/TAC SOCISM...CHARTS METH/COMP 20. PAGE 146 F2878 — ECO/DEV ECO/UNDEV MARXISM CAP/ISM

S66
FELD W.,"EXTERNAL RELATIONS OF THE COMMON MARKET AND GROUP LEADERSHIP ATTITUDES IN THE MEMBER STATES." COM USA+45 ELITES AGRI NAT/G ATTIT...OBS EEC GATT. PAGE 40 F0776 — DIPLOM CENTRAL TARIFFS INT/TRADE

S66
MARKSHAK J.,"ECONOMIC PLANNING AND THE COST OF THINKING." COM MARKET EX/STRUC...DECISION GEN/LAWS. PAGE 85 F1672 — ECO/UNDEV ECO/TAC PLAN ECO/DEV

B67
BROMKE A.,POLAND'S POLITICS: IDEALISM VS. REALISM. COM GERMANY POLAND RUSSIA USSR POL/PAR CATHISM ...BIBLIOG 19/20. PAGE 19 F0360 — NAT/G DIPLOM MARXISM

B67
EBENSTEIN W.,TODAY'S ISMS: COMMUNISM, FASCISM, CAPITALISM, SOCIALISM (5TH ED.). COM WOR+45 PERCEPT PWR...SOC TREND IDEA/COMP NAT/COMP 20. PAGE 35 F0691 — FASCISM MARXISM SOCISM CAP/ISM

B67
FALL B.B.,HO CHI MINH ON REVOLUTION: SELECTED WRITINGS, 1920-66. COM VIETNAM ELITES NAT/G COERCE GUERRILLA RACE/REL MARXISM...MARXIST ANTHOL 20. PAGE 39 F0761 — REV COLONIAL ECO/UNDEV S/ASIA

B67
GRIFFITH W.E.,SINO-SOVIET RELATIONS, 1964-1965. CHINA/COM COM USSR CHIEF 20. PAGE 51 F1001 — DIPLOM PWR DOMIN MARXISM

B67
GRIPP R.C.,PATTERNS OF SOVIET POLITICS (REV. ED.). USSR LAW ELITES LOC/G PLAN CONTROL CT/SYS CHOOSE ...POLICY BIBLIOG/A DICTIONARY 9/20. PAGE 51 F1003 — COM ADJUD POL/PAR

B67
HARDT J.P.,MATHEMATICS AND COMPUTERS IN SOVIET ECONOMIC PLANNING. COM USSR OP/RES PROB/SOLV OPTIMAL...MODAL SIMUL 20. PAGE 55 F1082 — PLAN TEC/DEV MATH COMPUT/IR

B67
OGLESBY C.,CONTAINMENT AND CHANGE. AFR COM USA+45 ECO/UNDEV TEC/DEV ECO/TAC FOR/AID INT/TRADE DOMIN GUERRILLA REV PEACE 20 STALIN/J. PAGE 101 F1983 — DIPLOM BAL/PWR MARXISM CULTURE

B67
SHAFFER H.G.,THE COMMUNIST WORLD: MARXIST AND NON-MARXIST VIEWS. WOR+45 SOCIETY DIPLOM ECO/TAC CONTROL SOCISM...MARXIST ANTHOL BIBLIOG/A 20. PAGE 120 F2363 — MARXISM NAT/COMP IDEA/COMP COM

B67
SPECTOR S.D.,CHECKLIST OF ITEMS IN THE NDEA INSTITUTE LIBRARY (PAMPHLET). USA+45 NAT/G SECT EDU/PROP ATTIT ALL/IDEOS...SOC BIOG. PAGE 124 F2448 — BIBLIOG/A COM MARXISM

B67
ZALESKI E.,PLANNING REFORMS IN THE SOVIET UNION 1962-1966. COM USSR NAT/G CONFER CONTROL EFFICIENCY MARXISM...POLICY DECISION 20. PAGE 150 F2957 — ECO/DEV PLAN ADMIN CENTRAL

S67
AVTORKHANOV A.,"A NEW AGRARIAN REVOLUTION." COM USSR ECO/DEV PLAN TEC/DEV ADMIN CONTROL OPTIMAL WEALTH SOCISM 20 KHRUSH/N STALIN/J. PAGE 8 F0144 — AGRI METH/COMP MARXISM OWN

S67
FADDEYEV N.,"CMEA CO-OPERATION OF EQUAL NATIONS." COM R+D PLAN CAP/ISM DIPLOM FOR/AID WEALTH...POLICY MARXIST. PAGE 39 F0758 — MARXISM ECO/TAC INT/ORG ECO/UNDEV

S67
FRANKEL T.,"ECONOMIC REFORM* A TENTATIVE APPRAISAL." COM USSR OP/RES BUDGET CONFER EFFICIENCY PRODUC MARXISM SOCISM...MGT 20. PAGE 43 F0847 — ECO/DEV INDUS PLAN WEALTH

S67
GAMARNIKOW M.,"THE NEW ROLE OF PRIVATE ENTERPRISE." ECO/DEV INDUS NAT/G SML/CO CREATE PROB/SOLV MARXISM ...POLICY TREND IDEA/COMP 20. PAGE 46 F0890 — ECO/TAC ATTIT CAP/ISM COM

S67
GUPTA S.,"FOREIGN POLICY IN THE 1967 MANIFESTOS." ASIA COM INDIA USA+45 FORCES FOR/AID TAX ATTIT ...DECISION 20. PAGE 52 F1013 — IDEA/COMP POL/PAR POLICY DIPLOM

S67
IBARRA J.,"EL EXPERIMENTO CUBANO." COM CUBA L/A+17C USA+45 ECO/UNDEV LEGIS INT/TRADE CONTROL REV NAT/LISM PWR 19/20 TREATY. PAGE 64 F1259 — COLONIAL DIPLOM NAT/G POLICY

S67
ISELIN J.J.,"THE TRUMAN DOCTRINE: ITS PASSAGE THROUGH CONGRESS AND THE AFTERMATH." USA+45 ECO/UNDEV R+D INT/ORG DELIB/GP BAL/PWR REV PEACE ...POLICY UN. PAGE 66 F1291 — DIPLOM COM FOR/AID AFR

S67
MAJSTRENKO I.W.,"PROBLEMS CONFRONTING SOVIET AGRICULTURE." COM USSR ECO/DEV ECO/TAC EFFICIENCY OPTIMAL WEALTH MARXISM 20. PAGE 84 F1643 — AGRI PROB/SOLV CENTRAL TEC/DEV

S67
MOSELY P.E.,"EASTERN EUROPE IN WORLD POWER POLITICS: WHERE DE-STALINIZATION HAS LED." ECO/UNDEV NAT/LISM 20. PAGE 94 F1842 — COM NAT/G DIPLOM MARXISM

S67
ORAZEM F.,"THE NEW SOVIET PLAN FOR AGRICULTURE (1960-1970)" USSR WORKER CAP/ISM ECO/TAC PRICE OWN HABITAT MARXISM...CHARTS 20. PAGE 101 F1994 — AGRI PLAN COM ECO/DEV

S67
PETROVICH M.B.,"UNITED STATES POLICY IN EAST EUROPE." ECO/DEV ECO/TAC IDEA/COMP. PAGE 105 F2075 — COM INT/TRADE USA+45 DIPLOM

S67
SPITTMANN I.,"EAST GERMANY: THE SWINGING PENDULUM." COM GERMANY/E NAT/G EFFICIENCY MARXISM 20. PAGE 125 F2458 — PRODUC POL/PAR WEALTH ATTIT

S67
STOLTE S.C.,"THREE PROBLEMS FACING THE SOVIET BLOC." ASIA COM USA+45 USSR FORCES MARXISM ...IDEA/COMP METH/COMP 20 NATO WARSAW/P. PAGE 127 F2496 — ECO/TAC DIPLOM INT/ORG POLICY

S67
WILES P.J.,"THE POLITICAL AND SOCIAL PREREQUISITES FOR A SOVIET-TYPE ECONOMY." COM USSR LAW CULTURE CREATE ADMIN FEEDBACK ROUTINE COST OPTIMAL TOTALISM MARXISM 20. PAGE 146 F2883 — ECO/DEV PLAN EX/STRUC EFFICIENCY

B68
NENAROKOV A.P.,RUSSIA IN THE 20TH CENTURY: THE OFFICIAL SOVIET HISTORY. USSR SOCIETY REV...AUD/VIS 20. PAGE 97 F1913 — COM ADJUST MARXISM

COM/IND....COMMUNICATIONS INDUSTRY

N
DOCUMENTATION ECONOMIQUE: REVUE BIBLIOGRAPHIQUE DE SYNTHESE. WOR+45 COM/IND FINAN BUDGET DIPLOM...GEOG 20. PAGE 1 F0004 — BIBLIOG/A SOC

B21
CLAPHAN J.H.,THE ECONOMIC DEVELOPMENT OF FRANCE AND GERMANY 1815-1914. FRANCE GERMANY MOD/EUR COM/IND DIST/IND FINAN INT/TRADE EDU/PROP 19/20. PAGE 24 F0476 — ECO/UNDEV ECO/DEV AGRI INDUS

B30
HAWTREY R.G.,ECONOMIC ASPECTS OF SOVEREIGNTY. UNIV WOR+45 WOR-45 ECO/DEV ECO/UNDEV AGRI COM/IND INDUS MARKET NAT/G TEC/DEV ECO/TAC EDU/PROP COERCE ATTIT KNOWL WEALTH...CONCPT CON/ANAL GEN/LAWS 20. PAGE 57 F1118 — FORCES PWR SOVEREIGN WAR

B46
ERNST M.L.,THE FIRST FREEDOM. USA-45 CONSTN PRESS PRIVIL...CHARTS IDEA/COMP BIBLIOG 20 AMEND/I. PAGE 38 F0746 — EDU/PROP COM/IND ORD/FREE CONTROL

B47
LEVER E.A.,ADVERTISING AND ECONOMIC THEORY. FINAN ECO/TAC DEMAND EFFICIENCY ATTIT...MGT PSY SAMP/SIZ CHARTS 20. PAGE 79 F1539 — EDU/PROP MARKET COM/IND ECO/DEV

B50
LINCOLN G.,ECONOMICS OF NATIONAL SECURITY. USA+45 ELITES COM/IND DIST/IND INDUS NAT/G VOL/ASSN DELIB/GP EX/STRUC FOR/AID EDU/PROP COERCE NUC/PWR WAR ATTIT KNOWL ORD/FREE PWR TOT/POP VAL/FREE 20. PAGE 80 F1565 — FORCES ECO/TAC AFR

B51
US DEPARTMENT OF STATE,POINT FOUR, NEAR EAST AND AFRICA, A SELECTED BIBLIOGRAPHY OF STUDIES ON ECONOMICALLY UNDERDEVELOPED COUNTRIES. AGRI COM/IND FINAN INDUS PLAN INT/TRADE...SOC TREND 20. PAGE 135 F2672 — BIBLIOG/A AFR S/ASIA ISLAM

B55
JONES T.B.,A BIBLIOGRAPHY ON SOUTH AMERICAN ECONOMIC AFFAIRS: ARTICLES IN NINETEENTH CENTURY PERIODICALS (PAMPHLET). AGRI COM/IND DIST/IND EXTR/IND FINAN INDUS LABOR NAT/G 19. PAGE 68 F1340 — BIBLIOG ECO/UNDEV L/A+17C TEC/DEV

B55
OECD,MARSHALL PLAN IN TURKEY. TURKEY USA+45 COM/IND CONSTRUC SERV/IND FORCES BUDGET...STAT 20 MARSHL/PLN. PAGE 100 F1964 — FOR/AID ECO/UNDEV AGRI INDUS

B55
US ADVISORY COMN INTERGOV REL,THE COMMISSION ON INTERGOVERNMENTAL RELATIONS; A REPORT TO THE PRESIDENT FOR TRANSMITTAL TO THE CONGRESS. USA+45 ECO/DEV AGRI COM/IND FINAN FORCES PLAN EDU/PROP HEALTH WEALTH...STAT MUNICH 20 CIV/DEFENS. PAGE 133 F2630 — GOV/REL NAT/G LOC/G PROVS

B56
JUAN T.L.,ECONOMIC AND SOCIAL DEVELOPMENT OF MODERN CHINA: A BIBLIOGRAPHICAL GUIDE. ASIA AGRI COM/IND DIST/IND FINAN INDUS DIPLOM...STAT 20. PAGE 68 F1342 — BIBLIOG SOC

B56
YUAN TUNG-LI,ECONOMIC AND SOCIAL DEVELOPMENT OF MODERN CHINA: A BIBLIOGRAPHIC GUIDE. COM/IND FINAN FAM LABOR SECT CRIME INCOME...STAT SAMP CON/ANAL. PAGE 150 F2954 — BIBLIOG ASIA ECO/UNDEV SOC

B57
ASHER R.E.,THE UNITED NATIONS AND ECONOMIC AND SOCIAL COOPERATION. ECO/UNDEV COM/IND DIST/IND FINAN PLAN PROB/SOLV INT/TRADE TASK WEALTH...SOC 20 UN. PAGE 7 F0129 — INT/ORG DIPLOM FOR/AID

B58
RUBIN B.,PUBLIC RELATIONS AND THE STATE, A CASE STUDY OF NEW YORK STATE ADMINISTRATION, 1943-54. USA+45 USA-45 COM/IND EDU/PROP GOV/REL...CHARTS 20 NEW/YORK DEWEY/THOM. PAGE 114 F2255 — INGP/REL PRESS PROVS GP/REL

B60
AMERICAN U BEIRUT ECO RES INST,A SELECTED AND ANNOTATED BIBLIOGRAPHY OF ECONOMIC LITERATURE ON THE ARABIC SPEAKING COUNTRIES OF THE MIDDLE EAST. ISLAM AGRI COM/IND DIST/IND FINAN INDUS LABOR ...GEOG 20. PAGE 5 F0091 — BIBLIOG/A ECO/UNDEV STAT

B60
SAKAI R.K.,STUDIES ON ASIA, 1960. ASIA CHINA/COM S/ASIA COM/IND ECO/TAC...ANTHOL 17/20 MALAYA. PAGE 115 F2270 — ECO/UNDEV SOC

S60
FRANKEL S.H.,"ECONOMIC ASPECTS OF POLITICAL INDEPENDENCE IN AFRICA." AFR FUT SOCIETY ECO/UNDEV COM/IND FINAN LEGIS PLAN TEC/DEV CAP/ISM ECO/TAC INT/TRADE ADMIN ATTIT DRIVE RIGID/FLEX PWR WEALTH ...MGT NEW/IDEA MATH TIME/SEQ VAL/FREE 20. PAGE 43 F0846 — NAT/G FOR/AID

S60
RIVKIN A.,"AFRICAN ECONOMIC DEVELOPMENT: ADVANCED TECHNOLOGY AND THE STAGES OF GROWTH." CULTURE ECO/UNDEV AGRI COM/IND EXTR/IND PLAN ECO/TAC ATTIT DRIVE RIGID/FLEX SKILL WEALTH...MGT SOC GEN/LAWS FOR/TRADE WORK TOT/POP 20. PAGE 111 F2195 — AFR TEC/DEV FOR/AID

B61
INTERNATIONAL BANK RECONST DEV,THE WORLD BANK IN AFRICA: SUMMARY OF ACTIVITIES. AGRI COM/IND DIST/IND EXTR/IND INDUS TAX COST...CHARTS 20. PAGE 65 F1271 — FINAN ECO/UNDEV INT/ORG AFR

B62
HENDERSON W.O.,THE GENESIS OF THE COMMON MARKET. EUR+WWI FRANCE MOD/EUR UK SEA COM/IND EXTR/IND COLONIAL DISCRIM...TIME/SEQ CHARTS BIBLIOG 18/20 EEC TREATY. PAGE 58 F1149 — ECO/DEV INT/TRADE DIPLOM

B62
INTERNATIONAL BANK RECONST DEV,THE WORLD BANK AND IDA IN ASIA. ASIA S/ASIA COM/IND DIST/IND...CHARTS 20. PAGE 65 F1272 — FINAN ECO/UNDEV AGRI INDUS

B62
MOWITZ R.J.,PROFILE OF A METROPOLIS: A CASE BOOK. COM/IND CONSTRUC INDUS PUB/INST PLAN TEC/DEV LEAD GP/REL...POLICY TECHNIC WELF/ST MUNICH. PAGE 94 F1851 — DECISION ADMIN

B63
BAUER R.A.,AMERICAN BUSINESS AND PUBLIC POLICY: THE POLITICS OF FOREIGN TRADE. USA+45 COM/IND LG/CO NAT/G PROF/ORG SML/CO VOL/ASSN LEGIS TOP/EX ECO/TAC EDU/PROP CHOOSE HEALTH PWR WEALTH...CONCPT METH/CNCPT OBS INT QU SAMP FOR/TRADE TRUE/GP VAL/FREE HI. PAGE 11 F0217 — ECO/DEV ATTIT

B63
KATZ S.M.,A SELECTED LIST OF US READINGS ON DEVELOPMENT. AGRI COM/IND DIST/IND INDUS LABOR PLAN FOR/AID EDU/PROP HEALTH...POLICY SOC/WK 20. PAGE 69 F1361 — BIBLIOG/A ECO/UNDEV TEC/DEV ACT/RES

B63
NEUMARK S.D.,FOREIGN TRADE AND ECONOMIC DEVELOPMENT IN AFRICA: A HISTORICAL PERSPECTIVE. EUR+WWI MOD/EUR ECO/UNDEV AGRI COM/IND EXTR/IND PROC/MFG SKILL WEALTH...CONCPT TIME/SEQ TREND SIMUL FOR/TRADE WORK TOT/POP TERR/GP VAL/FREE 19/20. PAGE 98 F1916 — AFR

S63
DUCROS B.,"MOBILISATION DES RESSOURCES PRODUCTIVES ET DEVELOPPEMENT." FUT INTELL SOCIETY COM/IND DIST/IND EXTR/IND FINAN INDUS ROUTINE WEALTH ...METH/CNCPT OBS 20. PAGE 34 F0670 — ECO/UNDEV TEC/DEV

S63
REDDAWAY W.B.,"THE ECONOMICS OF UNDERDEVELOPED COUNTRIES." S/ASIA WOR+45 WOR-45 STRATA AGRI COM/IND DIST/IND MARKET PROC/MFG PLAN TEC/DEV FOR/AID BAL/PAY ATTIT DRIVE SKILL WORK FOR/TRADE 20. PAGE 110 F2165 — ECO/TAC ECO/UNDEV INDIA

B64
PAWERA J.C.,ALGERIA'S INFRASTRUCTURE. ALGERIA PLAN WEALTH...METH/CNCPT 20. PAGE 104 F2041 — ECO/UNDEV INDUS

TEC/DEV
COM/IND

S64
HERMAN L.M.,"THE ECONOMIC CONTENT OF SOVIET TRADE WITH THE WEST." WOR+45 ECO/DEV ECO/UNDEV AGRI COM/IND INDUS CAP/ISM ECO/TAC ATTIT RIGID/FLEX WEALTH...OBS TREND VAL/FREE MARX/KARL 20. PAGE 59 F1152 — COM MARKET INT/TRADE USSR

B65
BLAIR T.L.V.,AFRICA: A MARKET PROFILE. AFR COM/IND DIST/IND FINAN UTIL...DECISION CHARTS BIBLIOG 20. PAGE 15 F0295 — MARKET OP/RES ECO/UNDEV INDUS

B65
WISH J.R.,ECONOMIC DEVELOPMENT IN LATIN AMERICA: AN ANNOTATED BIBLIOGRAPHY. L/A+17C COM/IND MARKET R+D CREATE CAP/ISM ATTIT...STAT METH 20. PAGE 148 F2912 — BIBLIOG/A ECO/UNDEV TEC/DEV AGRI

B66
HALLET R.,PEOPLE AND PROGRESS IN WEST AFRICA: AN INTRODUCTION TO THE PROBLEMS OF DEVELOPMENT. COM/IND INDUS KIN DIPLOM FOR/AID INT/TRADE HEALTH ...GEOG TREND CHARTS BIBLIOG/A 20 AFRICA/W. PAGE 54 F1050 — AFR SOCIETY ECO/UNDEV ECO/TAC

B66
RAO Y.V.L.,COMMUNICATION AND DEVELOPMENT. INDIA S/ASIA SOCIETY ACT/RES EDU/PROP PARTIC ATTIT...SOC GP/COMP BIBLIOG MUNICH MUNICH 20. PAGE 109 F2149 — COM/IND ECO/UNDEV OBS

B67
MURTY B.S.,PROPAGANDA AND WORLD PUBLIC ORDER. FUT WOR+45 COM/IND INT/ORG PROB/SOLV ATTIT KNOWL ORD/FREE...POLICY UN. PAGE 95 F1868 — EDU/PROP DIPLOM CONTROL JURID

L67
BARRON J.A.,"ACCESS TO THE PRESS." USA+45 TEC/DEV PRESS TV ADJUD AUD/VIS. PAGE 10 F0196 — ORD/FREE COM/IND EDU/PROP LAW

S67
BAGDKIAN B.H.,"NEWS AS A BYPRODUCT: WHAT HAPPENS WHEN JOURNALISM IS HITCHED TO GREAT, DIVERSIFIED CORPORATIONS?" USA+45 INDUS EDU/PROP PARTIC PROFIT ATTIT. PAGE 8 F0152 — COM/IND PRESS CONTROL LG/CO

S67
DAVIS O.A.,"ON THE DISTINCTION BETWEEN PUBLIC AND PRIVATE GOODS." USA+45 COM/IND LG/CO NAT/G TV DEBATE PRICE ADMIN ROLE...MATH IDEA/COMP. PAGE 31 F0593 — MARKET OWN CONCPT

S67
KELLY F.K.,"A PROPOSAL FOR AN ANNUAL REPORT ON THE STATE OF MANKIND." FUT INTELL COM/IND INT/ORG CREATE PROB/SOLV PERS/REL...CONCPT 20 UN. PAGE 70 F1371 — SOCIETY UNIV ATTIT NEW/IDEA

S67
MORTON J.A.,"A SYSTEMS APPROACH TO THE INNOVATION PROCESS: ITS USE IN THE BELL SYSTEM." USA+45 INTELL INDUS LG/CO CONSULT WORKER COMPUTER AUTOMAT DEMAND ...MGT CHARTS 20. PAGE 94 F1841 — TEC/DEV GEN/METH R+D COM/IND

S67
STEMPEL GH I.I.I.,"A NEW ANALYSIS OF MONOPOLY AND COMPETITION." USA+45 INDUS TV ATTIT MUNICH. PAGE 126 F2479 — PRESS COM/IND GP/REL

COM/PARTY....COMMUNIST PARTY (ALL NATIONS)

N19
HALL G.,MAIN STREET TO WALL STREET: END THE COLD WAR (PAMPHLET). AFR USA+45 LAW STRUCT POL/PAR WORKER INT/TRADE DOMIN INCOME...POLICY 20 COM/PARTY. PAGE 53 F1046 — MARXIST CAP/ISM DIPLOM NAT/G

B35
O'CONNOR H.,REVOLUTION IN SEATTLE. USA-45 STRATA WORKER GP/REL ATTIT SOCISM...OBS BIBLIOG/A 20 SEATTLE STRIKE COM/PARTY. PAGE 99 F1954 — REV EDU/PROP LABOR MARXISM

B61
LICHTHEIM G.,MARXISM. GERMANY SOCIETY WORKER CAP/ISM ECO/TAC NAT/LISM POPULISM...TIME/SEQ GOV/COMP NAT/COMP 18/20 COM/PARTY. PAGE 80 F1559 — MARXISM SOCISM IDEA/COMP CULTURE

B62
LEVY H.V.,LIBERDADE E JUSTICA SOCIAL (2ND ED.). BRAZIL COM L/A+17C USSR INT/ORG PARTIC GP/REL WEALTH 20 UN COM/PARTY. PAGE 79 F1544 — ORD/FREE MARXISM CAP/ISM LAW

COM/SCITEC....COMMITTEE ON SCIENCE AND TECHNOLOGY (OF

COMECON....COMMUNIST ECONOMIC ORGANIZATION EAST EUROPE

S63
RAMERIE L.,"TENSION AU SEIN DU COMECON: LE CAS ROUMAIN." COM EUR+WWI USSR WOR+45 ECO/DEV DIST/IND NAT/G POL/PAR VOL/ASSN EDU/PROP TOTALISM ATTIT WEALTH...TIME/SEQ 20 COMECON. PAGE 109 F2142 — INT/ORG ECO/TAC INT/TRADE ROMANIA

L64
KORBONSKI A.,"COMECON." ASIA ECO/DEV ECO/UNDEV ECO/TAC BAL/PAY NAT/LISM FOR/TRADE 20 COMECON. PAGE 73 F1425 — COM INT/ORG INT/TRADE

B65
KASER M.,COMECON* INTEGRATION PROBLEMS OF THE PLANNED ECONOMIES. INT/ORG TEC/DEV INT/TRADE PRICE ADMIN ADJUST CENTRAL...STAT TIME/SEQ ORG/CHARTS COMECON. PAGE 69 F1359 — PLAN ECO/DEV COM REGION

S65
RUSINOW D.I.,"YUGOSLAV DEVELOPMENT BETWEEN EAST AND WEST." AGRI VOL/ASSN PLAN CAP/ISM ECO/TAC FOR/AID INT/TRADE BAL/PAY...MARXIST EEC COMECON. PAGE 115 F2262 — YUGOSLAVIA ECO/UNDEV STAT

B66
FRIEDMANN W.G.,INTERNATIONAL FINANCIAL AID. USA+45 ECO/DEV ECO/UNDEV NAT/G VOL/ASSN EX/STRUC PLAN RENT GIVE BAL/PAY PWR...GEOG INT/LAW STAT TREND UN EEC COMECON. PAGE 44 F0866 — INT/ORG FOR/AID TEC/DEV ECO/TAC

S67
LEVI M.,"LES RELATIONS ECONOMIQUES ENTRE L'EST ET L'OUEST EN EUROPE" INDUS...STAT CHARTS 20 OECD COMECON. PAGE 79 F1540 — INT/TRADE INT/ORG FINAN PRODUC

COMINFORM....COMMUNIST INFORMATION BUREAU

B56
WOLFF R.L.,THE BALKANS IN OUR TIME. ALBANIA FUT MOD/EUR USSR YUGOSLAVIA CULTURE INT/ORG SECT DIPLOM EDU/PROP COERCE WAR ORD/FREE...CHARTS 4/20 BALKANS COMINFORM. PAGE 148 F2919 — GEOG COM

COMINTERN....COMMUNIST THIRD INTERNATIONAL

COMM ON FEDERAL TAX POLICY F0513

COMM/SPACE....COMMITTEE ON SPACE RESEARCH

COMMANDS....SEE LEAD, DOMIN

COMMISSION ON MONEY AND CREDIT F0514

COMMISSIONS....SEE CONFER, DELIB/GP

COMMITTEE ECONOMIC DEVELOPMENT F0515,F0516,F0517,F0518,F0519,F0740

COMMITTEE FOR ECONOMIC DEVELOPMENT....SEE CED

COMMITTEE ON SCIENCE AND TECHNOLOGY (OF THE BRITISH PARLIAMENT)....SEE COM/SCITEC

COMMITTEES....SEE CONFER, DELIB/GP

COMMON/LAW....COMMON LAW

B24
HOLDSWORTH W.S.,A HISTORY OF ENGLISH LAW; THE COMMON LAW AND ITS RIVALS (VOL. VI). AFR UK STRATA EX/STRUC ADJUD ADMIN CONTROL CT/SYS...JURID CONCPT GEN/LAWS 17 PARLIAMENT ENGLSH/LAW COMMON/LAW. PAGE 61 F1194 — LAW CONSTN LEGIS CHIEF

B24
HOLDSWORTH W.S.,A HISTORY OF ENGLISH LAW; THE COMMON LAW AND ITS RIVALS (VOL. IV). UK SEA AGRI CHIEF ADJUD CONTROL CRIME GOV/REL...INT/LAW JURID NAT/COMP 16/17 PARLIAMENT COMMON/LAW CANON/LAW ENGLSH/LAW. PAGE 61 F1195 — LAW LEGIS CT/SYS CONSTN

B52
JENNINGS W.I.,CONSTITUTIONAL LAWS OF THE COMMONWEALTH. AFR UK LAW CHIEF LEGIS TAX CT/SYS PARL/PROC GOV/REL...INT/LAW 18/20 ENGLSH/LAW COMMON/LAW. PAGE 67 F1316 — CONSTN JURID ADJUD COLONIAL

COMMONWEALTH....SEE COMMONWLTH

COMMONWLTH....BRITISH COMMONWEALTH OF NATIONS; SEE ALSO VOL/ASSN, APPROPRIATE NATIONS, CMN/WLTH

B64
THE SPECIAL COMMONWEALTH AFRICAN ASSISTANCE PLAN. AFR CANADA INDIA NIGERIA UK FINAN SCHOOL...CHARTS 20 COMMONWLTH. PAGE 1 F0019 — ECO/UNDEV TREND FOR/AID ADMIN

COMMUN....INTERPERSONAL COMMUNICATION; SEE ALSO PERS/REL

L52
HUTH A.G.,"COMMUNICATION AND ECONOMIC DEVELOPMENT." FUT WOR+45 CULTURE SOCIETY INT/ORG PLAN TEC/DEV EDU/PROP DRIVE KNOWL WEALTH...POLICY CONCPT RECORD STERTYP GEN/LAWS COMMUN TOT/POP UNESCO 20 UN CMN/WLTH. PAGE 64 F1250 — ECO/UNDEV

B55
BUCHANAN N.S.,APPROACHES TO ECONOMIC DEVELOPMENT. FUT USA+45 WOR+45 STRATA ECO/DEV INT/ORG NAT/G — ECO/UNDEV ECO/TAC

TEC/DEV DIPLOM FOR/AID ATTIT KNOWL PWR WEALTH ...RELATIV METH/CNCPT SELF/OBS TREND CON/ANAL STERTYP GEN/LAWS FOR/TRADE COMMUN 20. PAGE 20 F0380
INT/TRADE

L55

KISER M.,"ORGANIZATION OF AMERICAN STATES." L/A+17C USA+45 ECO/UNDEV INT/ORG NAT/G PLAN TEC/DEV DIPLOM ECO/TAC INT/TRADE EDU/PROP ADMIN ALL/VALS...POLICY MGT RECORD ORG/CHARTS OAS COMMUN 20. PAGE 71 F1401
VOL/ASSN ECO/DEV REGION

B61

BONNEFOUS M.,EUROPE ET TIERS MONDE. EUR+WWI SOCIETY INT/ORG NAT/G VOL/ASSN ACT/RES TEC/DEV CAP/ISM ECO/TAC ATTIT ORD/FREE SOVEREIGN...POLICY CONCPT TREND TERR/GP COMMUN 20. PAGE 16 F0314
AFR ECO/UNDEV FOR/AID INT/TRADE

B62

ROBINSON A.D.,DUTCH ORGANIZED AGRICULTURE IN INTERNATIONAL POLITICS, 1945-1960. EUR+WWI NETHERLAND STRUCT ECO/DEV NAT/G VOL/ASSN CONSULT DELIB/GP PLAN TEC/DEV INT/TRADE EDU/PROP ATTIT RIGID/FLEX ALL/VALS...NEW/IDEA TREND EEC COMMUN 20. PAGE 112 F2215
AGRI INT/ORG

S62

BOKOR-SZEGO H.,"LA CONVENTION DE BELGRADE ET LE REGIME DU DANUBE." COM EUR+WWI WOR+45 STRUCT POL/PAR VOL/ASSN PLAN EDU/PROP WEALTH...TIME/SEQ METH/GP COMMUN 20. PAGE 16 F0308
INT/ORG TOTALISM YUGOSLAVIA

S63

SHONFIELD A.,"AFTER BRUSSELS." EUR+WWI FRANCE GERMANY UK ECO/DEV DIST/IND MARKET VOL/ASSN DELIB/GP CREATE INT/TRADE ATTIT RIGID/FLEX...RECORD TREND GEN/LAWS EEC COMMUN CMN/WLTH 20. PAGE 121 F2385
PLAN ECO/TAC

COMMUN/DEV....COMMUNITY DEVELOPMENT MOVEMENT IN INDIA

COMMUNES....COMMUNES

COMMUNICATION, MASS....SEE EDU/PROP

COMMUNICATION, PERSONAL....SEE PERS/REL

COMMUNICATION, POLITICAL....SEE EDU/PROP

COMMUNICATIONS INDUSTRY....SEE COM/IND

COMMUNISM....SEE MARXISM

COMMUNIST CHINA....SEE CHINA/COM

COMMUNIST COUNTRIES (EXCEPT CHINA)....SEE COM

COMMUNIST ECONOMIC ORGANIZATION....SEE COMECON

COMMUNIST INFORMATION BUREAU....SEE COMINFORM

COMMUNITY....SEE NEIGH

COMPANY, LARGE....SEE LG/CO

COMPANY, SMALL....SEE SML/CO

COMPARATIVE....SEE APPROPRIATE COMPARATIVE ANALYSIS INDEX

COMPETITION....SEE APPROPRIATE RELATIONS AND VALUES INDEXES

COMPNY/ACT....COMPANIES ACT (U.K., 1882)

B51

COOKE C.A.,CORPORATION TRUST AND COMPANY: AN ESSAY IN LEGAL HISTORY. UK STRUCT LEGIS CAP/ISM GP/REL PROFIT 13/20 COMPNY/ACT. PAGE 27 F0531
LG/CO FINAN ECO/TAC JURID

COMPOS R.O. F0520

COMPUT/IR....INFORMATION RETRIEVAL

B56

HISTORICAL ABSTRACTS. NAT/G CREATE DIPLOM ATTIT ...SOC DICTIONARY INDEX 18/20. PAGE 1 F0011
WOR-45 COMPUT/IR BIBLIOG/A

B58

POLLOCK F.,AUTOMATION: A STUDY OF ITS ECONOMIC AND SOCIAL CONSEQUENCES. FUT USA+45 USA-45 SOCIETY ECO/DEV LABOR ACT/RES PLAN ECO/TAC AUTOMAT ROUTINE ALL/VALS...STAT TREND COMPUT/IR CHARTS SOC/EXP WORK 20. PAGE 107 F2099
TEC/DEV SOC CAP/ISM

B60

STEIN E.,AMERICAN ENTERPRISE IN THE EUROPEAN COMMON MARKET: A LEGAL PROFILE. EUR+WWI FUT USA+45 SOCIETY STRUCT ECO/DEV NAT/G VOL/ASSN CONSULT PLAN TEC/DEV ECO/TAC INT/TRADE ADMIN ATTIT RIGID/FLEX PWR...MGT NEW/IDEA STAT TREND COMPUT/IR SIMUL EEC 20. PAGE 125 F2475
MARKET ADJUD INT/LAW

B61

KLEIN L.R.,AN ECONOMETRIC MODEL OF THE UNITED KINGDOM. UK PRICE COST...MATH PREDICT TREND CHARTS SIMUL METH 20. PAGE 72 F1407
ECOMETRIC COMPUTER STAT COMPUT/IR

B62

HATTERY L.H.,INFORMATION RETRIEVAL MANAGEMENT. CLIENT INDUS TOP/EX COMPUTER OP/RES TEC/DEV ROUTINE COST EFFICIENCY RIGID/FLEX...METH/COMP ANTHOL 20. PAGE 57 F1113
R+D COMPUT/IR MGT CREATE

B63

MCDONOUGH A.M.,INFORMATION ECONOMICS AND MANAGEMENT SYSTEMS. ECO/DEV OP/RES AUTOMAT EFFICIENCY 20. PAGE 88 F1726
COMPUT/IR MGT CONCPT COMPUTER

S63

WILES P.J.D.,"WILL CAPITALISM AND COMMUNISM SPONTANEOUSLY CONVERGE." COM FUT USA+45 ECO/DEV DIST/IND MARKET CAP/ISM ECO/TAC RIGID/FLEX WEALTH MARXISM SOCISM...MATH STAT TREND COMPUT/IR 20. PAGE 146 F2885
PLAN TEC/DEV USSR

B66

KUENNE R.E.,THE POLARIS MISSILE STRIKE* A GENERAL ECONOMIC SYSTEMS ANALYSIS. USA+45 USSR NAT/G BAL/PWR ARMS/CONT WAR...MATH PROBABIL COMPUT/IR CHARTS HYPO/EXP SIMUL. PAGE 74 F1446
NUC/PWR FORCES DETER DIPLOM

B67

HARDT J.P.,MATHEMATICS AND COMPUTERS IN SOVIET ECONOMIC PLANNING. COM USSR OP/RES PROB/SOLV OPTIMAL...MODAL SIMUL 20. PAGE 55 F1082
PLAN TEC/DEV MATH COMPUT/IR

B67

UNIVERSAL REFERENCE SYSTEM,BIBLIOGRAPHY OF BIBLIOGRAPHIES IN POLITICAL SCIENCE, GOVERNMENT, AND PUBLIC POLICY (VOLUME III). WOR+45 WOR-45 LAW ADMIN...SOC CON/ANAL COMPUT/IR GEN/METH. PAGE 133 F2615
BIBLIOG/A NAT/G DIPLOM POLICY

B67

UNIVERSAL REFERENCE SYSTEM,ADMINISTRATIVE MANAGEMENT: PUBLIC AND PRIVATE BUREAUCRACY (VOLUME IV). WOR+45 WOR-45 ECO/DEV LG/CO LOC/G PUB/INST VOL/ASSN GOV/REL...COMPUT/IR GEN/METH. PAGE 133 F2616
BIBLIOG/A MGT ADMIN NAT/G

B67

UNIVERSAL REFERENCE SYSTEM,ECONOMIC REGULATION, BUSINESS, AND GOVERNMENT (VOLUME VIII). WOR+45 WOR-45 ECO/DEV ECO/UNDEV FINAN LABOR TEC/DEV ECO/TAC INT/TRADE GOV/REL...POLICY COMPUT/IR. PAGE 133 F2617
BIBLIOG/A CONTROL NAT/G

B67

UNIVERSAL REFERENCE SYSTEM,PUBLIC POLICY AND THE MANAGEMENT OF SCIENCE (VOLUME IX). FUT SPACE WOR+45 LAW NAT/G TEC/DEV CONTROL NUC/PWR GOV/REL ...COMPUT/IR GEN/METH. PAGE 133 F2618
BIBLIOG/A POLICY MGT PHIL/SCI

COMPUTER....COMPUTER TECHNIQUES AND TECHNOLOGY

N19

MASCHLER M.,STABLE PAYOFF CONFIGURATIONS FOR QUOTA GAMES (PAMPHLET). PLAN PERS/REL 20. PAGE 87 F1694
ECOMETRIC GAME COMPUTER DECISION

L58

FORRESTER J.W.,"INDUSTRIAL DYNAMICS* A MAJOR BREAKTHROUGH FOR DECISION MAKERS." COMPUTER OP/RES ...DECISION CONCPT NEW/IDEA. PAGE 42 F0830
INDUS ACT/RES MGT PROB/SOLV

B59

KARLIN S.,MATHEMATICAL METHODS AND THEORY IN GAMES, PROGRAMMING, AND ECONOMICS. COMPUTER PLAN CONTROL TASK...MATH 20. PAGE 69 F1357
GAME METH/COMP ACT/RES DECISION

B59

SELIGSOHN I.J.,"USING COMPUTER SERVICES IN SMALL BUSINESS" MANAGEMENT AIDS FOR SMALL MANUFACTURERS 109 (PAMPHLET). DIST/IND MARKET PROC/MFG COST EFFICIENCY PRODUC...DECISION IDEA/COMP. PAGE 119 F2350
SML/CO COMPUTER MGT PROB/SOLV

B59

STERNBERG F.,THE MILITARY AND INDUSTRIAL REVOLUTION OF OUR TIME. USA+45 USSR WOR+45 WORKER COMPUTER PLAN TEC/DEV NUC/PWR GP/REL...POLICY NAT/COMP 20. PAGE 126 F2481
DIPLOM FORCES INDUS CIVMIL/REL

B60

BAERWALD F.,ECONOMIC SYSTEM ANALYSIS: CONCEPTS AND PERSPECTIVES. USA+45 ECO/DEV NAT/G COMPUTER EQUILIB INCOME ATTIT...DECISION CONCPT IDEA/COMP. PAGE 8 F0151
ACT/RES ECO/TAC ROUTINE FINAN

B60

BOULDING K.E.,LINEAR PROGRAMMING AND THE THEORY OF THE FIRM. ACT/RES PLAN...MGT MATH. PAGE 17 F0323
LG/CO NEW/IDEA COMPUTER

B61

KLEIN L.R.,AN ECONOMETRIC MODEL OF THE UNITED KINGDOM. UK PRICE COST...MATH PREDICT TREND CHARTS
ECOMETRIC COMPUTER

SIMUL METH 20. PAGE 72 F1407 — STAT COMPUT/IR

S61
BENNION E.G.,"ECONOMETRICS FOR MANAGEMENT." USA+45 INDUS EX/STRUC ACT/RES COMPUTER UTIL...MATH STAT PREDICT METH/COMP HYPO/EXP. PAGE 13 F0248 — ECOMETRIC MGT SIMUL DECISION

S61
SHUBIK M.,"APPROACHES TO THE STUDY OF DECISION-MAKING RELEVANT TO THE FIRM." INDUS COMPUTER OP/RES ...PROBABIL STAT 20. PAGE 121 F2390 — GAME DECISION MGT SIMUL

B62
HATTERY L.H.,INFORMATION RETRIEVAL MANAGEMENT. CLIENT INDUS TOP/EX COMPUTER OP/RES TEC/DEV ROUTINE COST EFFICIENCY RIGID/FLEX...METH/COMP ANTHOL 20. PAGE 57 F1113 — R+D COMPUT/IR MGT CREATE

B63
MCDONOUGH A.M.,INFORMATION ECONOMICS AND MANAGEMENT SYSTEMS. ECO/DEV OP/RES AUTOMAT EFFICIENCY 20. PAGE 88 F1726 — COMPUT/IR MGT CONCPT COMPUTER

B63
RUMMEL J.F.,RESEARCH METHODOLOGY IN BUSINESS. COMPUTER CREATE PROB/SOLV...CONT/OBS REC/INT QU/SEMANT SYS/QU SAMP CHARTS METH/COMP T 20. PAGE 115 F2260 — OP/RES METH/CNCPT METH STAT

B64
LANGHOFF P.,MODELS, MEASUREMENT AND MARKETING. ACT/RES COMPUTER OP/RES PLAN BUDGET...MGT PHIL/SCI METH/CNCPT STAT PROG/TEAC BIBLIOG. PAGE 75 F1478 — DECISION SIMUL MARKET R+D

B65
RIGBY P.H.,CONCEPTUAL FOUNDATIONS OF BUSINESS RESEARCH. COMPUTER PROB/SOLV OPTIMAL...MGT CONCPT MATH STAT TESTS SIMUL GEN/METH. PAGE 111 F2192 — PROFIT R+D INDUS DECISION

S65
CHU K.,"A DYNAMIC MODEL OF THE FIRM." OP/RES PROB/SOLV...DECISION ECOMETRIC NEW/IDEA STAT GAME ORG/CHARTS SIMUL. PAGE 24 F0472 — INDUS COMPUTER TEC/DEV

B66
LILLEY S.,MEN, MACHINES AND HISTORY: THE STORY OF TOOLS AND MACHINES IN RELATION TO SOCIAL PROGRESS. PREHIST SPACE STRUCT COMPUTER AUTOMAT NUC/PWR ...POLICY SOC. PAGE 80 F1564 — AGRI TEC/DEV SOCIETY

B66
MANSFIELD E.,MANAGERIAL ECONOMICS AND OPERATIONS RESEARCH; A NONMATHEMATICAL INTRODUCTION. USA+45 ELITES ECO/DEV CONSULT EX/STRUC PROB/SOLV ROUTINE EFFICIENCY OPTIMAL...GAME T 20. PAGE 85 F1660 — ECO/TAC OP/RES MGT COMPUTER

B66
PERSALL E.S.,AN ECONOMETRIC STUDY OF FINANCIAL MARKETS. COMPUTER PROB/SOLV TEC/DEV...MATH STAT CHARTS METH/COMP BIBLIOG 20. PAGE 105 F2066 — ECOMETRIC FINAN MARKET METH

B66
SHULTZ G.P.,STRATEGIES FOR THE DISPLACED WORKER. USA+45 COMPUTER TEC/DEV BARGAIN RECEIVE EDU/PROP CONFER GP/REL...MGT METH/COMP 20. PAGE 121 F2391 — ECO/DEV WORKER PLAN AUTOMAT

B67
ELDREDGE H.W.,TAMING MEGALOPOLIS; HOW TO MANAGE AN URBANIZED WORLD. WOR+45 SOCIETY ECO/DEV ECO/UNDEV NAT/G COMPUTER CREATE PARTIC EFFICIENCY WEALTH ...MGT ANTHOL MUNICH. PAGE 37 F0716 — TEC/DEV PLAN PROB/SOLV

B67
MALINVAUD E.,ACTIVITY ANALYSIS IN THE THEORY OF GROWTH AND PLANNING. UNIV AGRI COMPUTER OP/RES REGION...CHARTS ANTHOL METH. PAGE 84 F1648 — MATH GAME SIMUL

B67
SAPARINA Y.,CYBERNETICS WITHIN US. WOR+45 EDU/PROP FEEDBACK PERCEPT HEALTH...DECISION METH/CNCPT NEW/IDEA 20. PAGE 116 F2281 — COMPUTER METH/COMP CONTROL SIMUL

S67
ALBAUM G.,"INFORMATION FLOW AND DECENTRALIZED DECISION MAKING IN MARKETING." EX/STRUC COMPUTER OP/RES PROB/SOLV EFFICIENCY OPTIMAL...METH/COMP ORG/CHARTS 20. PAGE 3 F0056 — LG/CO ROUTINE KNOWL MARKET

S67
BARAN P.,"THE FUTURE COMPUTER UTILITY." USA+45 NAT/G PLAN CONTROL COST...POLICY 20. PAGE 9 F0177 — COMPUTER UTIL FUT TEC/DEV

S67
MORTON J.A.,"A SYSTEMS APPROACH TO THE INNOVATION PROCESS: ITS USE IN THE BELL SYSTEM." USA+45 INTELL INDUS LG/CO CONSULT WORKER COMPUTER AUTOMAT DEMAND ...MGT CHARTS 20. PAGE 94 F1841 — TEC/DEV GEN/METH R+D COM/IND

COMTE/A....AUGUST COMTE

CON/ANAL....QUANTITATIVE CONTENT ANALYSIS

N
AMERICAN ECONOMIC REVIEW. FINAN INDUS LABOR OP/RES CAP/ISM INT/TRADE TAX WEALTH...CON/ANAL CHARTS 20. PAGE 1 F0001 — BIBLIOG/A USA+45 ECO/DEV NAT/G

N
SOUTH AFRICAN JOURNAL OF ECONOMICS. SOUTH/AFR FINAN MARKET ACT/RES OP/RES...PHIL/SCI STAT CON/ANAL METH/COMP BIBLIOG/A 20. PAGE 1 F0009 — ECO/UNDEV ACADEM INTELL R+D

C01
LOWELL A.L.,"THE INFLUENCE OF PARTY UPON LEGISLATION IN ENGLAND AND AMERICA" IN ANNUAL REPORT OF AMER HISTORICAL ASSN." LEGIS CONTROL ...CON/ANAL CHARTS 19/20 CONGRESS PARLIAMENT. PAGE 82 F1605 — PARL/PROC POL/PAR DECISION OP/RES

N19
HATANAKA M.,A SPECTRAL ANALYSIS OF BUSINESS CYCLE INDICATORS: LEAD-LAG IN TERMS OF ALL TIME POINTS (PAMPHLET). UNIV WORKER EFFICIENCY...REGRESS STAT CHARTS TIME 20. PAGE 56 F1110 — ECOMETRIC ADJUST PRODUC CON/ANAL

B30
HAWTREY R.G.,ECONOMIC ASPECTS OF SOVEREIGNTY. UNIV WOR+45 WOR-45 ECO/DEV ECO/UNDEV AGRI COM/IND INDUS MARKET NAT/G TEC/DEV ECO/TAC EDU/PROP COERCE ATTIT KNOWL WEALTH...CONCPT CON/ANAL GEN/LAWS 20. PAGE 57 F1118 — FORCES PWR SOVEREIGN WAR

B31
JEVONS W.S.,THE THEORY OF POLITICAL ECONOMY (4TH ED.; 1ST ED. 1871). WOR-45 FINAN MARKET RENT WEALTH ...LOG MATH QUANT CON/ANAL IDEA/COMP BIBLIOG METH 17/19. PAGE 67 F1318 — GEN/LAWS UTIL LABOR

B35
STALEY E.,WAR AND THE PRIVATE INVESTOR. UNIV WOR-45 INTELL SOCIETY INT/ORG NAT/G TOP/EX CAP/ISM ECO/TAC WAR ATTIT ALL/VALS...INT TIME/SEQ TREND CON/ANAL WORK TOT/POP 20. PAGE 125 F2464 — FINAN INT/TRADE DIPLOM

B39
ROBBINS L.,ECONOMIC CAUSES OF WAR. WOR-45 ECO/DEV ECO/UNDEV INT/ORG NAT/G TEC/DEV DIPLOM DOMIN COLONIAL ATTIT DRIVE PWR WEALTH...POLICY CONCPT OBS SAMP TREND CON/ANAL GEN/LAWS MARX/KARL 20. PAGE 112 F2203 — COERCE ECO/TAC WAR

B40
SIKES E.R.,CONTEMPORARY ECONOMIC SYSTEMS: THEIR ANALYSIS AND SOCIAL BACKGROUND. GERMANY ITALY USSR AGRI INDUS PLAN CAP/ISM ROUTINE TOTALISM FASCISM ...POLICY CON/ANAL BIBLIOG 20. PAGE 122 F2400 — COM SOCISM CONCPT

S45
MILLS C.W.,"THE TRADE UNION LEADER: A COLLECTIVE PORTRAIT." EX/STRUC TOP/EX INGP/REL...QU CON/ANAL CHARTS. PAGE 92 F1798 — LABOR LEAD STAT STRATA

B51
ROEPKE W.,THE PROBLEM OF ECONOMIC ORDER. WOR+45 SOCIETY PROB/SOLV CONTROL EFFICIENCY...CON/ANAL IDEA/COMP GEN/METH 20. PAGE 113 F2231 — ECO/TAC ORD/FREE MARKET PROC/MFG

S51
HAWLEY A.H.,"METROPOLITAN POPULATION AND MUNICIPAL GOVERNMENT EXPENDITURES IN CENTRAL CITIES" (BMR)" USA+45 FINAN TAX...STAT CON/ANAL CHARTS MUNICH 20. PAGE 57 F1117 — GEOG LOC/G COST BUDGET

B53
NEISSER H.,NATIONAL INCOMES AND INTERNATIONAL TRADE. FRANCE GERMANY SWEDEN UK USA-45 EXTR/IND FINAN INDUS TEC/DEV PRICE BAL/PAY EQUILIB INCOME WEALTH...CHARTS METH 19 CHINJAP. PAGE 97 F1908 — INT/TRADE PRODUC MARKET CON/ANAL

B55
BUCHANAN N.S.,APPROACHES TO ECONOMIC DEVELOPMENT. FUT USA+45 WOR+45 STRATA ECO/DEV INT/ORG NAT/G TEC/DEV DIPLOM FOR/AID ATTIT KNOWL PWR WEALTH ...RELATIV METH/CNCPT SELF/OBS TREND CON/ANAL STERTYP GEN/LAWS FOR/TRADE COMMUN 20. PAGE 20 F0380 — ECO/UNDEV ECO/TAC INT/TRADE

B56
KINDLEBERGER C.P.,THE TERMS OF TRADE: A EUROPEAN CASE-STUDY. EUR+WWI MOD/EUR ECO/DEV ECO/UNDEV AGRI INDUS BAL/PAY...METH/CNCPT STAT CONT/OBS CON/ANAL SOC/EXP SIMUL FOR/TRADE 20. PAGE 71 F1390 — PLAN ECO/TAC

B56
YUAN TUNG-LI,ECONOMIC AND SOCIAL DEVELOPMENT OF MODERN CHINA: A BIBLIOGRAPHIC GUIDE. COM/IND FINAN FAM LABOR SECT CRIME INCOME...STAT SAMP CON/ANAL. PAGE 150 F2954 — BIBLIOG ASIA ECO/UNDEV SOC

S56
HARSANYI J.C.,"APPROACHES TO THE BARGAINING PROBLEM BEFORE AND AFTER THE THEORY OF GAMES."...DECISION CON/ANAL SIMUL GEN/LAWS. PAGE 56 F1096 — NEW/IDEA GAME IDEA/COMP

S58
THOMAS D.S.,"AGE AND ECONOMIC DIFFERENTIALS IN INTERSTATE MIGRATION." SEX...GEOG SAMP/SIZ TREND CON/ANAL CHARTS BIBLIOG. PAGE 130 F2560 — AGE WEALTH HABITAT CENSUS

B59
ENGELS F.,SOCIALISM: UTOPIAN AND SCIENTIFIC (2ND ED.). SOCISM...CONCPT CON/ANAL GEN/LAWS 19 — MARXISM PHIL/SCI

DUHRING/E. PAGE 38 F0732 UTOPIA IDEA/COMP
B59

MORGENSTERN O.,INTERNATIONAL FINANCIAL TRANSACTIONS AND BUSINESS CYCLES. FRANCE GERMANY UK USA+45 USA-45 WOR+45 WOR-45 ECO/DEV ECO/TAC WEALTH ...CONCPT STAT CON/ANAL CHARTS 19/20. PAGE 93 F1832 FINAN TIME/SEQ INT/TRADE
S59

ALKHIMOV V.S.,"SOVIET FOREIGN TRADE CHANNELS." COM FUT USA+45 USSR ECO/DEV MARKET CONSULT PLAN WEALTH ...MARXIST OBS CON/ANAL FOR/TRADE 20. PAGE 4 F0068 FINAN ECO/TAC DIPLOM
S59

KINDLEBERGER C.P.,"UNITED STATES ECONOMIC FOREIGN POLICY: RESEARCH REQUIREMENTS FOR 1965." FUT USA+45 WOR+45 DIST/IND MARKET INT/ORG ECO/TAC INT/TRADE WEALTH...OBS TREND CON/ANAL GEN/LAWS FOR/TRADE VAL/FREE 20. PAGE 71 F1392 FINAN ECO/DEV FOR/AID
B60

HARBERGER A.C.,THE DEMAND FOR DURABLE GOODS. AGRI FINAN COST EQUILIB...MATH STAT TIME/SEQ TREND CON/ANAL CHARTS SIMUL ANTHOL 20. PAGE 55 F1072 ECOMETRIC DEMAND PRICE
B60

HITCH C.J.,THE ECONOMICS OF DEFENSE IN THE NUCLEAR AGE. USA+45 WOR+45 CREATE PLAN NUC/PWR ATTIT ...CON/ANAL CHARTS HYPO/EXP NATO 20. PAGE 60 F1179 R+D FORCES
L60

CHENERY H.B.,"PATTERNS OF INDUSTRIAL GROWTH." INT/TRADE DEMAND PRODUC...MATH REGRESS CHARTS SIMUL METH 20. PAGE 24 F0462 ECO/TAC ECO/DEV GP/COMP CON/ANAL
S60

NANES A.,"THE EUROPEAN COMMUNITY AND THE UNITED STATES: EVOLVING RELATIONS." EUR+WWI USA+45 WOR+45 ECO/UNDEV MARKET NAT/G DELIB/GP PLAN LEGIT ATTIT PWR WEALTH...CONCPT STAT TIME/SEQ CON/ANAL EEC METH/GP OEEC 20 EURATOM. PAGE 96 F1889 INT/ORG REGION
N60

ERDMAN P.E.,COMMON MARKETS AND FREE TRADE AREAS (PAMPHLET). USA+45 MARKET INT/ORG TEC/DEV DIPLOM UTIL...CON/ANAL CHARTS BIBLIOG 20 EEC OEEC. PAGE 38 F0743 TREND PROB/SOLV INT/TRADE ECO/DEV
B61

DE GRAZIA A.,AMERICAN WELFARE. CLIENT FINAN LABOR LOC/G NAT/G NEIGH EDU/PROP GP/REL...CLASSIF CON/ANAL CHARTS BIBLIOG. PAGE 31 F0598 GIVE WEALTH SECT VOL/ASSN
B62

GORT M.,DIVERSIFICATION AND INTEGRATION IN AMERICAN INDUSTRY. CLIENT DIST/IND PROC/MFG SERV/IND LG/CO CONTROL DEMAND PWR...METH/CNCPT STAT TREND CON/ANAL GP/COMP. PAGE 49 F0964 CONCPT GP/REL CLASSIF
S62

MILLIKEN M.,"NEW AND OLD CRITERIA FOR AID." WOR+45 ECO/DEV ECO/UNDEV ACT/RES PLAN ATTIT KNOWL...TREND CON/ANAL SIMUL GEN/METH TERR/GP 20. PAGE 92 F1796 USA+45 ECO/TAC FOR/AID
B63

BENOIT E.,DISARMAMENT AND THE ECONOMY. USA+45 NAT/G ACT/RES ECO/TAC BAL/PAY...STAT CON/ANAL GEN/LAWS 20. PAGE 13 F0252 ECO/DEV ARMS/CONT
B63

ENKE S.,ECONOMICS FOR DEVELOPMENT. AGRI TEC/DEV CAP/ISM DIPLOM ECO/TAC TAX ATTIT DRIVE HABITAT WEALTH...GOV/COMP BIBLIOG 20. PAGE 38 F0737 ECO/UNDEV PHIL/SCI CON/ANAL
B63

KAPP W.K.,SOCIAL COSTS OF BUSINESS ENTERPRISE. WOR+45 LABOR TEC/DEV CAP/ISM HABITAT...PHIL/SCI NEW/IDEA CON/ANAL 20. PAGE 69 F1354 COST SOCIETY INDUS RIGID/FLEX
B63

LAIRD R.D.,SOVIET AGRICULTURAL AND PEASANT AFFAIRS. FUT STRATA LOC/G DELIB/GP ACT/RES TEC/DEV ECO/TAC EDU/PROP ATTIT RIGID/FLEX ORD/FREE SKILL WEALTH ...STAT CON/ANAL ANTHOL MUNICH WORK VAL/FREE 20. PAGE 74 F1461 COM AGRI POLICY
B63

ROPKE W.,ECONOMICS OF THE FREE SOCIETY. FINAN INT/TRADE BAL/PAY COST DEMAND EFFICIENCY ORD/FREE WEALTH...CON/ANAL METH/COMP T 20 KEYNES/JM. PAGE 114 F2240 SOCIETY BUDGET ECO/DEV ECO/TAC
S63

AYAL E.B.,"VALUE SYSTEM AND ECONOMIC DEVELOPMENT IN JAPAN AND THAILAND." ASIA S/ASIA THAILAND CULTURE ECO/DEV CAP/ISM DOMIN NAT/LISM DRIVE RIGID/FLEX SOCISM...WELF/ST OBS TREND CON/ANAL GEN/LAWS TERR/GP 20 CHINJAP. PAGE 8 F0145 ECO/UNDEV ALL/VALS
S63

CLEMHOUT S.,"PRODUCTION FUNCTION ANALYSIS APPLIED TO THE LEONTIEF SCARCE-FACTOR PARADOX OF INTERNATIONAL TRADE." EUR+WWI USA+45 DIST/IND NAT/G PLAN TEC/DEV DIPLOM PWR WEALTH...MGT METH/CNCPT CONT/OBS CON/ANAL CHARTS SIMUL GEN/LAWS FOR/TRADE 20. PAGE 25 F0490 ECO/DEV ECO/TAC
S63

GANDOLFI A.,"LES ACCORDS DE COOPERATION EN MATIERE DE POLITIQUE ETRANGERE ENTRE LA FRANCE ET LES NOUVEAUX ETATS AFRICAINS ET." AFR ISLAM MADAGASCAR WOR+45 ECO/DEV INT/ORG NAT/G DELIB/GP ECO/TAC ALL/VALS...CON/ANAL 20. PAGE 46 F0894 VOL/ASSN ECO/UNDEV DIPLOM FRANCE
S63

POPPINO R.E.,"IMBALANCE IN BRAZIL." L/A+17C NAT/G TOP/EX PLAN DIPLOM LEGIT DRIVE WEALTH...CON/ANAL FOR/TRADE LAFTA 20. PAGE 107 F2105 POL/PAR ECO/TAC BRAZIL
B64

JUSTER F.T.,ANTICIPATIONS AND PURCHASES; AN ANALYSIS OF CONSUMER BEHAVIOR. PROB/SOLV RISK COST PRODUC DRIVE...STAT STYLE SAMP CON/ANAL CHARTS HYPO/EXP GAME SIMUL. PAGE 68 F1345 PROBABIL DECISION PREDICT DEMAND
B64

KEMP M.C.,THE PURE THEORY OF INTERNATIONAL TRADE. WOR+45 WOR-45 ECO/DEV ECO/UNDEV DIST/IND ECO/TAC ...MATH CON/ANAL CHARTS VAL/FREE. PAGE 70 F1374 FINAN CREATE INT/TRADE
B64

LANG A.S.,URBAN RAIL TRANSIT. OP/RES PLAN PROB/SOLV TEC/DEV AUTOMAT COST...TECHNIC MATH CON/ANAL CHARTS METH/COMP SIMUL MUNICH 20 RAILROAD PUB/TRANS. PAGE 75 F1474 DIST/IND ECOMETRIC
B64

MORRISSENS L.,ECONOMIC POLICY IN OUR TIME: COUNTRY STUDIES. BELGIUM EUR+WWI FRANCE GERMANY/W ITALY NETHERLAND INDUS BARGAIN BUDGET GOV/REL BAL/PAY PRODUC...CON/ANAL CHARTS COSTS 20. PAGE 94 F1839 ECO/DEV ECO/TAC METH/COMP PLAN
B64

ORGANIZATION AMERICAN STATES,ECONOMIC SURVEY OF LATIN AMERICA, 1962. L/A+17C AGRI DIST/IND INDUS MARKET PROC/MFG R+D PLAN TEC/DEV ECO/TAC REGION BAL/PAY ALL/VALS...CON/ANAL ORG/CHARTS GEN/METH OAS ALL/PROG 20 ALL/PROG. PAGE 102 F1998 ECO/UNDEV CHARTS
S64

FLORINSKY M.T.,"TRENDS IN THE SOVIET ECONOMY." COM USA+45 USSR INDUS LABOR NAT/G PLAN TEC/DEV ECO/TAC ALL/VALS SOCISM...MGT METH/CNCPT STYLE CON/ANAL GEN/METH WORK 20. PAGE 42 F0817 ECO/DEV AGRI
S64

KOJIMA K.,"THE PATTERN OF INTERNATIONAL TRADE AMONG ADVANCED COUNTRIES." EUR+WWI UK USA+45 WOR+45 MARKET NAT/G ECO/TAC WEALTH...MATH STAT CON/ANAL CHARTS METH/GP EEC CHINJAP 20 CHINJAP. PAGE 72 F1419 ECO/DEV TREND INT/TRADE
S64

STONE P.A.,"DECISION TECHNIQUES FOR TOWN DEVELOPMENT." PLAN COST PROFIT...DECISION MGT CON/ANAL CHARTS METH/COMP BIBLIOG MUNICH 20. PAGE 127 F2497 OP/RES ADMIN PROB/SOLV
S64

WU Y.,"CHINA'S ECONOMY AND ITS PROSPECTS." ASIA CHINA/COM FUT USSR AGRI INDUS PLAN ECO/TAC LEGIT WEALTH...STAT CON/ANAL CHARTS GEN/LAWS FOR/TRADE 20. PAGE 149 F2938 ECO/DEV
B65

BOLLENS J.C.,THE METROPOLIS: ITS PEOPLE, POLITICS, AND ECONOMIC LIFE. USA+45 PLAN PROB/SOLV PERS/REL PWR...DECISION GEOG CENSUS TREND CON/ANAL MUNICH 20 NEWYORK/C LOS/ANG SAN/FRAN CHICAGO PHILADELPH. PAGE 16 F0309 HABITAT SOC LOC/G
B65

INT. BANK RECONSTR. DEVELOP.,ECONOMIC DEVELOPMENT OF KUWAIT. ISLAM KUWAIT AGRI FINAN MARKET EX/STRUC TEC/DEV ECO/TAC ADMIN WEALTH...OBS CON/ANAL CHARTS 20. PAGE 64 F1266 INDUS NAT/G
L65

LETICHE J.M.,"EUROPEAN INTEGRATION: AN AMERICAN VIEW." EUR+WWI FRANCE WOR+45 ECO/DEV DIST/IND EXTR/IND NAT/G DELIB/GP TOP/EX PLAN ECO/TAC ATTIT ...STAT CON/ANAL CHARTS EEC 20. PAGE 78 F1537 INDUS AGRI
B66

GYORGY A.,ISSUES OF WORLD COMMUNISM. ALBANIA CHINA/COM COM USSR YUGOSLAVIA STRATA AGRI INT/ORG CHIEF FORCES WORKER WAR ALL/IDEOS...GEOG 20 MAO. PAGE 52 F1018 ECO/UNDEV REV MARXISM CON/ANAL
S66

SHORTE F.C.,"THE APPLICATION OF DEVELOPMENT HYPOTHESES IN MIDDLE EASTERN STUDIES." STRUCT AGRI CREATE DEMAND...GEOG STAT CON/ANAL CHARTS. PAGE 121 F2387 ECO/UNDEV ISLAM SOC HYPO/EXP
B67

MCDOUGAL M.S.,THE INTERPRETATION OF AGREEMENTS AND WORLD PUBLIC ORDER: PRINCIPLES OF CONTENT AND PROCEDURE. WOR+45 CONSTN PROB/SOLV TEC/DEV ...CON/ANAL TREATY. PAGE 88 F1727 INT/LAW STRUCT ECO/UNDEV DIPLOM
B67

UNIVERSAL REFERENCE SYSTEM,BIBLIOGRAPHY OF BIBLIOGRAPHIES IN POLITICAL SCIENCE, GOVERNMENT, AND PUBLIC POLICY (VOLUME III). WOR+45 WOR-45 LAW ADMIN...SOC CON/ANAL COMPUT/IR GEN/METH. PAGE 133 F2615 BIBLIOG/A NAT/G DIPLOM POLICY
S67

OLIVIER G.,"ASPECTS JURIDIQUES DE L'ADOPTION DU TRAITE CECA A LA CRISE CHARBONNIERE (SUITE ET FIN)" LAW DIST/IND PLAN DIPLOM RATION PRICE ADMIN COST DEMAND...POLICY CON/ANAL ECSC TREATY. PAGE 101 F1988 INT/TRADE INT/ORG EXTR/IND CONSTN

S67
SANDMEYER R.L.,"METHODOLOGICAL ISSUES IN THE STUDY OF LABOR FORCE PARTICIPATION RATES." WOR+45 ...CLASSIF REGRESS CHARTS SIMUL. PAGE 116 F2278
METH CON/ANAL PARTIC WORKER

CON/INTERP....CONSTITUTIONAL INTERPRETATION

CONAN A.R. F0521

CONCEN/CMP....CONCENTRATION CAMPS

CONCPT....SUBJECT-MATTER CONCEPTS

CONDEMNATN....CONDEMNATION OF LAND OR PROPERTY

CONDOTTIER....CONDOTTIERI - HIRED MILITIA

CONF ON FUTURE OF COMMONWEALTH F0522

CONFER....CONFERENCES; SEE ALSO DELIB/GP

N
UNITED NATIONS,OFFICIAL RECORDS OF THE ECONOMIC AND SOCIAL COUNCIL OF THE UNITED NATIONS. WOR+45 DIPLOM INT/TRADE CONFER...SOC SOC/WK 20 UN UNESCO. PAGE 132 F2611
INT/ORG DELIB/GP WRITING

S43
HUZAR E.,"CONGRESS AND THE ARMY: APPROPRIATIONS." USA-45 CONFER CONTROL ATTIT SUPEGO SKILL CONGRESS. PAGE 64 F1255
LEGIS FORCES BUDGET DELIB/GP

B48
SPERO S.D.,GOVERNMENT AS EMPLOYER. USA+45 NAT/G EX/STRUC ADMIN CONTROL EXEC 20. PAGE 124 F2453
SOVEREIGN INGP/REL REPRESENT CONFER

B49
SELZNICK P.,TVA AND THE GRASS ROOTS: A STUDY IN THE SOCIOLOGY OF FORMAL ORGANIZATION. USA-45 EX/STRUC PROB/SOLV CONFER PARTIC ROUTINE PWR 20 TVA. PAGE 119 F2353
REPRESENT LOBBY CONSULT

B54
HOBBS E.H.,BEHIND THE PRESIDENT - A STUDY OF EXECUTIVE OFFICE AGENCIES. USA+45 NAT/G PLAN BUDGET ECO/TAC EXEC ORD/FREE 20 BUR/BUDGET. PAGE 60 F1183
EX/STRUC DELIB/GP CONFER CONSULT

B54
INTERNATIONAL LABOUR OFF LIB,BIBLIOGRAPHY ON THE INTERNATIONAL LABOUR ORGANISATION. WORKER 20. PAGE 65 F1277
BIBLIOG LABOR INT/ORG CONFER

B56
ATOMIC INDUSTRIAL FORUM,PUBLIC RELATIONS FOR THE ATOMIC INDUSTRY. WOR+45 PLAN PROB/SOLV EDU/PROP PRESS CONFER...AUD/VIS ANTHOL 20. PAGE 7 F0135
NUC/PWR INDUS GP/REL ATTIT

S56
KNAPP D.C.,"CONGRESSIONAL CONTROL OF AGRICULTURAL CONSERVATION POLICY: A CASE STUDY OF THE APPROPRIATIONS PROCESS." DELIB/GP PLAN PROB/SOLV CONFER PARL/PROC...POLICY INT CONGRESS. PAGE 72 F1411
LEGIS AGRI BUDGET CONTROL

B57
COMMITTEE ECONOMIC DEVELOPMENT,ECONOMIC DEVELOPMENT ASSISTANCE. USA+45 WOR+45 AGRI CONFER ORD/FREE ...MGT CHARTS 20. PAGE 27 F0515
FOR/AID ECO/UNDEV FINAN PLAN

B57
DUNLOP J.T.,THE THEORY OF WAGE DETERMINATION; PROCEEDINGS OF CONFERENCE HELD BY INTERNATIONAL ECONOMIC ASSOCIATION. AFR ECO/DEV LABOR BARGAIN PAY CONFER...CHARTS ANTHOL 20. PAGE 35 F0679
PRICE WORKER GEN/LAWS INCOME

S57
ANSHEN M.,"BUSINESS, LAWYERS, AND ECONOMISTS." PROB/SOLV ECO/TAC CONFER PROFIT RIGID/FLEX OBJECTIVE...MGT GP/COMP. PAGE 6 F0106
INDUS CONSULT ROUTINE EFFICIENCY

B58
ATOMIC INDUSTRIAL FORUM,MANAGEMENT AND ATOMIC ENERGY. WOR+45 SEA LAW MARKET NAT/G TEC/DEV INSPECT INT/TRADE CONFER PEACE HEALTH...ANTHOL 20. PAGE 7 F0136
NUC/PWR INDUS MGT ECO/TAC

B58
OEEC,THE INDUSTRIAL CHALLENGE OF NUCLEAR ENERGY. EUR+WWI ECO/DEV INDUS OP/RES CONFER RISK PWR ...AUD/VIS CHARTS ANTHOL 20 OEEC. PAGE 101 F1977
NUC/PWR ACT/RES ECO/TAC INT/ORG

B58
US HOUSE COMM POST OFFICE,MANPOWER UTILIZATION IN THE FEDERAL GOVERNMENT. USA+45 DIST/IND EX/STRUC LEGIS CONFER EFFICIENCY 20 CONGRESS CIVIL/SERV. PAGE 137 F2702
ADMIN WORKER DELIB/GP NAT/G

B58
US HOUSE COMM POST OFFICE,MANPOWER UTILIZATION IN THE FEDERAL GOVERNMENT. USA+45 DIST/IND EX/STRUC LEGIS CONFER EFFICIENCY 20 CONGRESS CIVIL/SERV. PAGE 137 F2703
ADMIN WORKER DELIB/GP NAT/G

B60
MARSHALL A.H.,FINANCIAL ADMINISTRATION IN LOCAL GOVERNMENT. UK DELIB/GP CONFER COST INCOME PERSON ...JURID 20. PAGE 86 F1679
FINAN LOC/G BUDGET ADMIN

B60
WALLACE R.A.,CONGRESSIONAL CONTROL OF FEDERAL SPENDING. USA+45 CONSTN NAT/G OP/RES CONFER DEBATE PERS/REL UTIL RIGID/FLEX PWR OBJECTIVE...OBS CHARTS. PAGE 143 F2808
LEGIS DELIB/GP BUDGET

B61
UNIVS-NATL BUR COMM ECO RES,PUBLIC FINANCES: NEEDS, SOURCES, AND UTILIZATION. USA+45 FORCES PLAN TAX CONFER PRICE FEDERAL UTIL...ANTHOL MUNICH 20. PAGE 133 F2623
NAT/G FINAN DECISION BUDGET

B62
SCHMITT H.A.,THE PATH TO EUROPEAN UNITY. EUR+WWI USA+45 PLAN TEC/DEV DIPLOM FOR/AID CONFER...INT/LAW 20 EEC EURCOALSTL MARSHL/PLN UNIFICA. PAGE 117 F2300
INT/ORG INT/TRADE REGION ECO/DEV

B62
WOODS H.D.,LABOUR POLICY AND LABOUR ECONOMICS IN CANADA. CANADA FUT NAT/G VOL/ASSN WORKER BARGAIN ECO/TAC PAY CONFER GP/REL 20. PAGE 148 F2924
LABOR POLICY INDUS ECO/DEV

L62
"HIGHER EDUCATION AND ECONOMIC AND SOCIAL DEVELOPMENT IN LATIN AMERICA: A BIBLIOGRAPHY." L/A+17C SOCIETY ECO/UNDEV PROF/ORG DIPLOM CONFER ...SOC 20. PAGE 1 F0016
BIBLIOG/A ACADEM INTELL EDU/PROP

L62
SCHULTZ T.W.,"INVESTMENT IN HUMAN BEINGS." ECO/DEV ECO/TAC CONFER COST INCOME PRODUC HEALTH...GEOG ANTHOL. PAGE 117 F2315
FINAN WORKER EDU/PROP SKILL

N62
US SENATE COMM ON JUDICIARY,LEGISLATION TO STRENGTHEN PENALTIES UNDER THE ANTITRUST LAWS (PAMPHLET). USA+45 LG/CO CONFER CONTROL SANCTION ORD/FREE 20 SENATE MONOPOLY. PAGE 139 F2748
LEAD ADJUD INDUS ECO/TAC

B63
BRAYBROOKE D.,A STRATEGY OF DECISION: POLICY EVALUATION AS A SOCIAL PROCESS. UNIV ELITES OP/RES DOMIN CONFER FEEDBACK CONSEN PLURISM...CONCPT CENSUS. PAGE 18 F0343
DECISION POLICY CONTROL

B63
GODWIN F.W.,THE HIDDEN FORCE. PUERT/RICO WOR+45 STRUCT VOL/ASSN PROB/SOLV DIPLOM CONFER...BIBLIOG 20 PEACE/CORP. PAGE 48 F0931
ECO/UNDEV WORKER SKILL ECO/TAC

B63
HARVEY O.L.,THE ANVIL AND THE PLOW: A HISTORY OF THE UNITED STATES DEPARTMENT OF LABOR: 1913-1963. USA+45 USA-45 NAT/G CONFER NEW/LIB 20 DEPT/LABOR. PAGE 56 F1106
EX/STRUC REPRESENT GP/REL LABOR

B63
MCCONNELL G.,STEEL AND THE PRESIDENCY, 1962. USA+45 INDUS PROB/SOLV CONFER ROLE...POLICY 20 PRESIDENT. PAGE 88 F1722
PWR CHIEF REPRESENT DOMIN

B63
US CONGRESS JOINT ECO COMM,THE UNITED STATES BALANCE OF PAYMENTS. USA+45 DELIB/GP CONFER...MATH PREDICT CHARTS 20 CONGRESS. PAGE 135 F2656
BAL/PAY ECO/TAC INT/TRADE CONSULT

B64
FATOUROS A.A.,CANADA'S OVERSEAS AID. CANADA WOR+45 ECO/DEV FINAN NAT/G BUDGET ECO/TAC CONFER ADMIN 20. PAGE 39 F0768
FOR/AID DIPLOM ECO/UNDEV POLICY

B64
US HOUSE COMM BANKING-CURR,INTERNATIONAL DEVELOPMENT ASSOCIATION ACT AMENDMENT. CHINA/COM USA+45 USSR FINAN FORCES LEGIS DIPLOM CONFER EFFICIENCY...CHARTS GOV/COMP 20 PRESIDENT CONGRESS INTL/DEV. PAGE 136 F2689
BAL/PAY FOR/AID RECORD ECO/TAC

S64
HOWE M.,"THE TRANSPORT ACT, 1962, AND THE CONSUMERS' CONSULTATIVE COMMITTEES." UK CONFER EXEC PWR 20. PAGE 62 F1225
PARTIC REPRESENT DELIB/GP DIST/IND

B65
LEYS C.T.,FEDERATION IN EAST AFRICA. LAW AGRI DIST/IND FINAN INT/ORG LABOR INT/TRADE CONFER ADMIN CONTROL GP/REL...ANTHOL 20 AFRICA/E. PAGE 79 F1554
FEDERAL REGION ECO/UNDEV PLAN

B65
SCHECHTER A.,THE BUSINESSMAN IN GOVERNMENT (THESIS, COLUMBIA UNIVERSITY). USA+45 CONFER GP/REL PERSON ...QU 20 PRESIDENT TRUMAN/HS CABINET. PAGE 116
INDUS NAT/G EX/STRUC

F2291 DELIB/GP

B65
WEIDENBAUM M.L.,CONGRESS AND THE FEDERAL BUDGET. FINAN ACT/RES DOMIN CONFER EXEC UTIL PWR NEW/LIB ...CHARTS CONGRESS. PAGE 144 F2844
BUDGET LEGIS PLAN DECISION

B65
WEILER J.,L'ECONOMIE INTERNATIONALE DEPUIS 1950. WOR+45 DIPLOM TARIFFS CONFER...POLICY TREATY. PAGE 145 F2848
FINAN INT/TRADE REGION FOR/AID

B65
YOUNG A.N.,CHINA'S WARTIME FINANCE AND INFLATION. ASIA AGRI INDUS NAT/G ECO/TAC CONFER PRICE WAR COST 20. PAGE 150 F2949
FINAN FOR/AID TAX BUDGET

L65
DAANE J.D.,"THE EVOLVING INTERNATIONAL MONETARY MECHANISM." VOL/ASSN CREATE PLAN FOR/AID INT/TRADE CONFER BAL/PAY...RECORD PREDICT IMF. PAGE 29 F0569
INT/ORG ECO/TAC TREND GP/COMP

B66
BAKKE E.W.,MUTUAL SURVIVAL; THE GOAL OF UNION AND MANAGEMENT (2ND ED.). USA+45 ELITES ECO/DEV ECO/TAC CONFER ADMIN REPRESENT GP/REL INGP/REL ATTIT ...GP/COMP 20. PAGE 8 F0155
MGT LABOR BARGAIN INDUS

B66
KAREFA-SMART J.,AFRICA: PROGRESS THROUGH COOPERATION. AFR FINAN TEC/DEV DIPLOM FOR/AID EDU/PROP CONFER REGION GP/REL WEALTH...HEAL SOC/INTEG 20. PAGE 69 F1356
ORD/FREE ECO/UNDEV VOL/ASSN PLAN

B66
ROBINSON E.A.,THE ECONOMICS OF EDUCATION. WOR+45 CULTURE ECO/UNDEV FINAN SCHOOL DIPLOM PRICE COST DEMAND...CHARTS METH/COMP 20. PAGE 112 F2216
EDU/PROP ADJUST CONFER

B66
RUBIN S.J.,THE CONSCIENCE OF THE RICH NATIONS: THE DEVELOPMENT ASSISTANCE COMMITTEE AND THE COMMON AID EFFORT. EUR+WWI USA+45 ECO/UNDEV INT/ORG NAT/G VOL/ASSN ECO/TAC INT/TRADE...OBS UN AID DEV/ASSIST IBRD OECD. PAGE 114 F2256
FOR/AID ECO/DEV CONFER CENTRAL

B66
SHULTZ G.P.,STRATEGIES FOR THE DISPLACED WORKER. USA+45 COMPUTER TEC/DEV BARGAIN RECEIVE EDU/PROP CONFER GP/REL...MGT METH/COMP 20. PAGE 121 F2391
ECO/DEV WORKER PLAN AUTOMAT

B66
SHULTZ G.P.,GUIDELINES, INFORMAL CONTROLS, AND THE MARKET PLACE: POLICY CHOICES IN A FULL EMPLOYMENT ECONOMY. UK ECO/DEV LABOR INT/TRADE CONFER GOV/REL BAL/PAY DEMAND INCOME...POLICY ANTHOL 20 PRESIDENT. PAGE 121 F2392
ECO/TAC CONTROL FINAN RATION

B66
US CONGRESS JOINT ECO COMM,NEW APPROACH TO UNITED STATES INTERNATIONAL ECONOMIC POLICY. USA+45 WOR+45 CHIEF DELIB/GP CONFER...CHARTS 20 CONGRESS MONEY. PAGE 135 F2660
DIPLOM ECO/TAC BAL/PAY FINAN

S66
ERB GF,"THE UNITED NATIONS CONFERENCE ON TRADE AND DEVELOPMENT (UNCTAD): A SELECTED CURRENT READING LIST." FINAN FOR/AID CONFER 20 UN. PAGE 38 F0742
BIBLIOG/A INT/TRADE ECO/UNDEV INT/ORG

B67
BIBBY J.,ON CAPITOL HILL. POL/PAR LOBBY PARL/PROC GOV/REL PERS/REL...JURID PHIL/SCI OBS INT BIBLIOG 20 CONGRESS PRESIDENT. PAGE 15 F0278
CONFER LEGIS CREATE LEAD

B67
HAGUE D.C.,PRICE FORMATION IN VARIOUS ECONOMIES; PROCEEDINGS OF A CONFERENCE HELD BY THE INTERNATIONAL ECONOMIC ASSOCIATION. WOR+45 FINAN MARKET PLAN CONFER COST...DECISION MATH PREDICT CHARTS SIMUL 20 INTL/ECON. PAGE 53 F1037
PRICE CAP/ISM SOCISM METH/COMP

B67
US SENATE COMM ON FOREIGN REL,FOREIGN ASSISTANCE ACT OF 1967. VIETNAM WOR+45 DELIB/GP CONFER CONTROL WAR WEAPON BAL/PAY...CENSUS CHARTS SENATE. PAGE 139 F2744
FOR/AID LAW DIPLOM POLICY

B67
ZALESKI E.,PLANNING REFORMS IN THE SOVIET UNION 1962-1966. COM USSR NAT/G CONFER CONTROL EFFICIENCY MARXISM...POLICY DECISION 20. PAGE 150 F2957
ECO/DEV PLAN ADMIN CENTRAL

L67
MEIER G.M.,"UNCTAD PROPOSALS FOR INTERNATIONAL ECONOMIC REFORM." WOR+45 MARKET INT/ORG TARIFFS CONFER UN GATT IMF. PAGE 89 F1749
INT/TRADE FINAN INT/LAW ECO/UNDEV

S67
BUTT R.,"THE COMMON MARKET AND CONSERVATIVE POLITICS, 1961-2." UK CHIEF DIPLOM ECO/TAC INT/TRADE CONFER DEBATE REGION ATTIT...POLICY 20 EEC. PAGE 21 F0398
EUR+WWI INT/ORG POL/PAR

S67
CHAMBERLAIN N.W.,"STRIKES IN CONTEMPORARY CONTEXT." LAW INDUS NAT/G CHIEF CONFER COST ATTIT ORD/FREE ...POLICY MGT 20. PAGE 23 F0442
LABOR BARGAIN EFFICIENCY PROB/SOLV

S67
COSGROVE C.A.,"AGRICULTURE, FINANCE AND POLITICS IN THE EUROPEAN COMMUNITY." EUR+WWI DIST/IND MARKET INT/ORG VOL/ASSN DELIB/GP TEC/DEV BAL/PWR BARGAIN ECO/TAC RATION CONFER 20 EEC. PAGE 28 F0538
ECO/DEV DIPLOM AGRI INT/TRADE

S67
DRAPER A.P.,"UNIONS AND THE WAR IN VIETNAM." USA+45 CONFER ADMIN LEAD WAR ORD/FREE PACIFIST 20. PAGE 34 F0660
LABOR PACIFISM ATTIT ELITES

S67
FRANKEL T.,"ECONOMIC REFORM* A TENTATIVE APPRAISAL." COM USSR OP/RES BUDGET CONFER EFFICIENCY PRODUC MARXISM SOCISM...MGT 20. PAGE 43 F0847
ECO/DEV INDUS PLAN WEALTH

S67
MELTZER B.D.,"RUMINATIONS ABOUT IDEOLOGY, LAW, AND LABOR ARBITRATION." USA+45 ECO/DEV PROB/SOLV CONFER MGT. PAGE 89 F1754
JURID ADJUD LABOR CONSULT

S67
PEMBERTON J., JR.,"CONSTITUTIONAL PROBLEMS IN RESTRAINT ON THE MEDIA." CONSTN PROB/SOLV EDU/PROP CONFER CONTROL JURID. PAGE 104 F2054
LAW PRESS ORD/FREE

S67
SMALL A.H.,"THE EFFECT OF TARIFF REDUCTIONS ON US IMPORT VOLUME." USA+45 INT/ORG NAT/G DIPLOM CONFER DEMAND...POLICY INT/LAW STAT CHARTS GATT EEC. PAGE 123 F2424
TARIFFS INT/TRADE PRICE ECO/TAC

S67
WILLMANN J.,"LA COMMUNAUTE EUROPEENNE ET LA GRANDE-BRETAGNE." UK PROB/SOLV TEC/DEV CAP/ISM DIPLOM CONFER FEDERAL...POLICY 20 EEC. PAGE 147 F2898
INT/ORG DRIVE NAT/LISM INT/TRADE

N67
US HOUSE COMM SCI ASTRONAUT,GOVERNMENT, SCIENCE, AND INTERNATIONAL POLICY (PAMPHLET). INDIA NETHERLAND ECO/DEV ECO/UNDEV R+D ACADEM PLAN DIPLOM FOR/AID CONFER...PREDICT 20 CHINJAP. PAGE 137 F2705
NAT/G POLICY CREATE TEC/DEV

CONFERENCE REGIONAL ACCOUNTS F0523

CONFERENCES....SEE CONFER, DELIB/GP

CONFIDENCE, PERSONAL....SEE SUPEGO

CONFLICT, MILITARY....SEE WAR, FORCES+COERCE

CONFLICT, PERSONAL....SEE PERS/REL, ROLE

CONFLICT....CONFLICT THEORY

CONFORMITY....SEE CONSEN, DOMIN

CONFRONTATION....SEE CONFRONTN

CONFRONTN....CONFRONTATION

CONFUCIUS....CONFUCIUS

CONGO....CONGO, PRE-INDEPENDENCE OR GENERAL

L63
PADELFORD N.J.,"FINANCIAL CRISIS AND THE UNITED NATIONS." FUT USSR WOR+45 LAW CONSTN FINAN INT/ORG DELIB/GP FORCES PLAN BUDGET DIPLOM COST WEALTH ...STAT CHARTS UN CONGO 20. PAGE 102 F2012
CREATE ECO/TAC

B65
HAEFELE E.T.,GOVERNMENT CONTROLS ON TRANSPORT. AFR RHODESIA TANZANIA DIPLOM ECO/TAC TARIFFS PRICE ADJUD CONTROL REGION EFFICIENCY...POLICY 20 CONGO. PAGE 53 F1031
ECO/UNDEV DIST/IND FINAN NAT/G

CONGO/BRAZ....CONGO, BRAZZAVILLE; SEE ALSO AFR

B03
MOREL E.D.,THE BRITISH CASE IN FRENCH CONGO. CONGO/BRAZ FRANCE UK COERCE MORAL WEALTH...POLICY INT/LAW 20 CONGO/LEOP. PAGE 93 F1827
DIPLOM INT/TRADE COLONIAL AFR

B45
DAVIS J.,AFRICA ADVANCING. AFR CONGO/BRAZ LIBERIA NIGER INT/ORG SCHOOL DIPLOM GIVE KNOWL SKILL 20. PAGE 30 F0590
SECT COLONIAL AGRI ECO/UNDEV

B60
HEYSE T.,PROBLEMS FONCIERS ET REGIME DES TERRES (ASPECTS ECONOMIQUES, JURIDIQUES ET SOCIAUX). AFR CONGO/BRAZ INT/ORG DIPLOM SOVEREIGN...GEOG TREATY 20. PAGE 59 F1161
BIBLIOG AGRI ECO/UNDEV LEGIS

B61
PETCH G.A.,ECONOMIC DEVELOPMENT AND MODERN WEST AFRICA. AFR CONGO/BRAZ GHANA NIGER SIER/LEONE AGRI MARKET LABOR FOR/AID TAX COST EFFICIENCY EQUILIB
ECO/UNDEV TEC/DEV EXTR/IND

PRODUC...GEOG TREND 20. PAGE 105 F2068 ECO/TAC

B62
FAO,FOOD AND AGRICULTURE ORGANIZATION AFRICAN SURVEY. AFR CONGO/BRAZ GHANA STRATA AGRI INT/ORG TEC/DEV FOR/AID INT/TRADE RACE/REL DEMAND EFFICIENCY PRODUC...GEOG 20 UN CONGO/LEOP. PAGE 39 F0763 ECO/TAC WEALTH EXTR/IND ECO/UNDEV

CONGO/KINS....CONGO, KINSHASA; SEE ALSO AFR

B03
MOREL E.D.,THE BRITISH CASE IN FRENCH CONGO. CONGO/BRAZ FRANCE UK COERCE MORAL WEALTH...POLICY INT/LAW 20 CONGO/LEOP. PAGE 93 F1827 DIPLOM INT/TRADE COLONIAL AFR

B62
FAO,FOOD AND AGRICULTURE ORGANIZATION AFRICAN SURVEY. AFR CONGO/BRAZ GHANA STRATA AGRI INT/ORG TEC/DEV FOR/AID INT/TRADE RACE/REL DEMAND EFFICIENCY PRODUC...GEOG 20 UN CONGO/LEOP. PAGE 39 F0763 ECO/TAC WEALTH EXTR/IND ECO/UNDEV

B67
ANDERSON C.W.,ISSUES OF POLITICAL DEVELOPMENT. BURMA WOR+45 CULTURE TOP/EX ECO/TAC MARXISM ...CHARTS NAT/COMP 20 COLOMB CONGO/LEOP. PAGE 5 F0094 NAT/LISM COERCE ECO/UNDEV SOCISM

B67
NKRUMAH K.,CHALLENGE OF THE CONGO. FORCES ECO/TAC FOR/AID REGION MURDER REPRESENT 20 CONGO/LEOP UN. PAGE 98 F1930 REV ECO/UNDEV ORD/FREE DIPLOM

CONGRES ECONOMISTES LANG FRAN F0524

CONGRESS....CONGRESS (ALL NATIONS); SEE ALSO LEGIS, HOUSE/REP, SENATE, DELIB/GP

C01
LOWELL A.L.,"THE INFLUENCE OF PARTY UPON LEGISLATION IN ENGLAND AND AMERICA" IN ANNUAL REPORT OF AMER HISTORICAL ASSN." LEGIS CONTROL ...CON/ANAL CHARTS 19/20 CONGRESS PARLIAMENT. PAGE 82 F1605 PARL/PROC POL/PAR DECISION OP/RES

N19
ATOMIC INDUSTRIAL FORUM,COMMENTARY ON LEGISLATION TO PERMIT PRIVATE OWNERSHIP OF SPECIAL NUCLEAR MATERIAL (PAMPHLET). USA+45 DELIB/GP LEGIS PLAN OWN ...POLICY 20 AEC CONGRESS. PAGE 7 F0134 NUC/PWR MARKET INDUS LAW

N19
CARPER E.T.,LOBBYING AND THE NATURAL GAS BILL (PAMPHLET). USA+45 SERV/IND BARGAIN PAY DRIVE ROLE WEALTH 20 CONGRESS SENATE EISNHWR/DD. PAGE 22 F0418 LOBBY ADJUD TRIBUTE NAT/G

N19
LAWRENCE S.A.,THE BATTERY ADDITIVE CONTROVERSY (PAMPHLET). USA+45 LAW MARKET PROC/MFG R+D CAP/ISM CT/SYS GOV/REL OWN FTC CONGRESS BUR/STNDRD RITCHIE/JM. PAGE 76 F1494 PHIL/SCI LOBBY INSPECT

N19
MCCONNELL G.,THE STEEL SEIZURE OF 1952 (PAMPHLET). USA+45 FINAN INDUS PROC/MFG LG/CO EX/STRUC ADJUD CONTROL GP/REL ORD/FREE PWR 20 TRUMAN/HS PRESIDENT CONGRESS. PAGE 88 F1721 DELIB/GP LABOR PROB/SOLV NAT/G

N19
SILVERMAN C.,THE PRESIDENT'S ECONOMIC ADVISERS (PAMPHLET). USA+45 LAW ELITES ECO/DEV EX/STRUC ADMIN LEAD GOV/REL PERS/REL ROLE...POLICY DECISION 20 PRESIDENT CONGRESS EISNHWR/DD. PAGE 122 F2404 CONSULT PROB/SOLV NAT/G PLAN

N19
US BUREAU OF THE CENSUS,THE PROPORTION OF THE SHIPMENTS (OR EMPLOYEES) OF EACH INDUSTRY... (PAMPHLET). USA+45 ECO/DEV EXTR/IND INDUS CONTROL PROFIT...STAT 20 CONGRESS MONOPOLY. PAGE 134 F2645 PROC/MFG PRODUC MARKET CHARTS

B28
FRANKFURTER F.,THE BUSINESS OF THE SUPREME COURT; A STUDY IN THE FEDERAL JUDICIAL SYSTEM. USA-45 CONSTN EX/STRUC PROB/SOLV GP/REL ATTIT PWR...POLICY JURID 18/20 SUPREME/CT CONGRESS. PAGE 43 F0848 CT/SYS ADJUD LAW FEDERAL

S43
HUZAR E.,"CONGRESS AND THE ARMY: APPROPRIATIONS." USA-45 CONFER CONTROL ATTIT SUPEGO SKILL CONGRESS. PAGE 64 F1255 LEGIS FORCES BUDGET DELIB/GP

B50
US DEPARTMENT OF STATE,POINT FOUR: COOPERATIVE PROGRAM FOR AID IN THE DEVELOPMENT OF ECONOMICALLY UNDERDEVELOPED AREAS. WOR+45 AGRI INDUS INT/ORG PLAN TEC/DEV DIPLOM EDU/PROP ADMIN PEACE PRODUC WEALTH 20 CONGRESS UN. PAGE 135 F2671 ECO/UNDEV FOR/AID FINAN INT/TRADE

B51
US HOUSE COMM APPROPRIATIONS,MUTUAL SECURITY PROGRAM APPROPRIATIONS FOR 1952: HEARINGS BEFORE A SUBCOMMITTEE OF THE COMMITTEE ON APPROPRIATIONS. AFR KOREA L/A+17C ECO/DEV ECO/UNDEV INT/ORG INSPECT BAL/PWR DIPLOM DEBATE WAR...POLICY STAT ASIA/S 20 CONGRESS NATO MID/EAST. PAGE 136 F2686 LEGIS FORCES BUDGET FOR/AID

S52
PHILLIPS C.,"THE HIGH COST OF OUR LOW-PAID CONGRESS" (NYT MAG. 2/24/52)" USA+45 FINAN WRITING TASK TIME CONGRESS. PAGE 106 F2082 LEGIS INCOME COST EFFICIENCY

S53
BLOUGH R.,"THE ROLE OF THE ECONOMIST IN FEDERAL POLICY MAKING." USA+45 ELITES INTELL ECO/DEV NAT/G CONSULT EX/STRUC ACT/RES PLAN INT/TRADE BAL/PAY WEALTH...POLICY METH/GP CONGRESS 20. PAGE 16 F0301 DELIB/GP ECO/TAC

S53
GABLE R.W.,"NAM: INFLUENTIAL LOBBY OR KISS OF DEATH?" (BMR)" USA+45 LAW INSPECT EDU/PROP ADMIN CONTROL INGP/REL EFFICIENCY PWR 20 CONGRESS NAM TAFT/HART. PAGE 45 F0880 LOBBY LEGIS INDUS LG/CO

B54
RECK D.,GOVERNMENT PURCHASING AND COMPETITION. USA+45 LEGIS CAP/ISM ECO/TAC GOV/REL CENTRAL ...POLICY 20 CONGRESS. PAGE 110 F2164 NAT/G FINAN MGT COST

B55
BERNSTEIN M.H.,REGULATING BUSINESS BY INDEPENDENT COMMISSION. USA+45 USA-45 LG/CO CHIEF LEGIS PROB/SOLV ADJUD SANCTION GP/REL ATTIT...TIME/SEQ 19/20 MONOPOLY PRESIDENT CONGRESS. PAGE 14 F0268 DELIB/GP CONTROL CONSULT

B55
SMITHIES A.,THE BUDGETARY PROCESS IN THE UNITED STATES. AFR ECO/DEV AGRI EX/STRUC FORCES LEGIS PROB/SOLV TAX ROUTINE EFFICIENCY...MGT CONGRESS PRESIDENT. PAGE 124 F2436 NAT/G ADMIN BUDGET GOV/REL

B56
ABELS J.,THE TRUMAN SCANDALS. USA+45 USA-45 POL/PAR TAX LEGIT CT/SYS CHOOSE PRIVIL MORAL WEALTH 20 TRUMAN/HS PRESIDENT CONGRESS. PAGE 2 F0031 CRIME ADMIN CHIEF TRIBUTE

B56
US LIBRARY OF CONGRESS,UNITED STATES DIRECT ECONOMIC AID TO FOREIGN COUNTRIES: A COLLECTION OF EXCERPTS AND A BIBLIOGRAPHY (PAMPHLET). USA+45 PRESS DEBATE...ANTHOL BIBLIOG/A CONGRESS. PAGE 138 F2716 FOR/AID POLICY DIPLOM ECO/UNDEV

S56
BONILLA F.,"WHEN IS PETITION 'PRESSURE?'" (BMR)" USA+45 ELITES INDUS LABOR CHIEF EDU/PROP LEGIT ATTIT...INT CHARTS 20 CONGRESS PRESIDENT EISNHWR/DD. PAGE 16 F0312 LEGIS EX/STRUC INT/TRADE TARIFFS

S56
KNAPP D.C.,"CONGRESSIONAL CONTROL OF AGRICULTURAL CONSERVATION POLICY: A CASE STUDY OF THE APPROPRIATIONS PROCESS." DELIB/GP PLAN PROB/SOLV CONFER PARL/PROC...POLICY INT CONGRESS. PAGE 72 F1411 LEGIS AGRI BUDGET CONTROL

N56
US HOUSE COMM FOREIGN AFFAIRS,REPORT OF THE SPECIAL STUDY MISSION TO AFRICA, SOUTH AND EAST OF THE SAHARA (PAMPHLET). AFR SOUTH/AFR USA+45 STRUCT INT/TRADE PARL/PROC NAT/LISM ATTIT ALL/VALS HEALTH ...POLICY 20 CONGRESS. PAGE 136 F2691 FOR/AID COLONIAL ECO/UNDEV DIPLOM

L57
SURREY S.S.,"THE CONGRESS AND THE TAX LOBBYIST - HOW SPECIAL TAX PROVISIONS GET ENACTED." LOBBY REPRESENT PRIVIL CONGRESS. PAGE 128 F2518 LEGIS TAX EX/STRUC ROLE

S57
ROURKE F.E.,"THE POLITICS OF ADMINISTRATIVE ORGANIZATION: A CASE HISTORY." USA+45 LABOR WORKER PLAN ADMIN TASK EFFICIENCY 20 DEPT/LABOR CONGRESS. PAGE 114 F2251 POLICY ATTIT MGT GP/COMP

B58
BIDWELL P.W.,RAW MATERIALS: A STUDY OF AMERICAN POLICY. USA+45 USA-45 ECO/UNDEV AGRI INDUS KIN CREATE PLAN ECO/TAC WAR PEACE ATTIT DRIVE WEALTH ...STAT CHARTS CONGRESS FOR/TRADE VAL/FREE. PAGE 15 F0279 EXTR/IND ECO/DEV

B58
US CONGRESS JOINT ECO COMM,THE RELATIONSHIP OF PRICES TO ECONOMIC STABILITY AND GROWTH. USA+45 MARKET TAX ADJUST COST DEMAND INCOME PRODUC ...POLICY TREND CHARTS ANTHOL 20 CONGRESS. PAGE 134 F2650 ECO/DEV PLAN EQUILIB PRICE

B58
US HOUSE COMM POST OFFICE,MANPOWER UTILIZATION IN THE FEDERAL GOVERNMENT. USA+45 DIST/IND EX/STRUC LEGIS CONFER EFFICIENCY 20 CONGRESS CIVIL/SERV. PAGE 137 F2702 ADMIN WORKER DELIB/GP NAT/G

B58
US HOUSE COMM POST OFFICE,MANPOWER UTILIZATION IN THE FEDERAL GOVERNMENT. USA+45 DIST/IND EX/STRUC LEGIS CONFER EFFICIENCY 20 CONGRESS CIVIL/SERV. PAGE 137 F2703 ADMIN WORKER DELIB/GP NAT/G

B59
US GENERAL ACCOUNTING OFFICE,EXAM OF ECONOMIC AND FOR/AID

TECHNICAL ASSISTANCE PROGRAM FOR INDIA INT'NAT'L COOP ADMIN REPORT TO CONGRESS 1955-1958. INDIA USA+45 ECO/UNDEV FINAN PLAN DIPLOM COST UTIL WEALTH ...CHARTS 20 CONGRESS AID. PAGE 136 F2679
EFFICIENCY ECO/TAC TEC/DEV

S59
GILPATRICK T.V.,"PRICE SUPPORT POLICY AND THE MIDWEST FARM VOTE" (BMR)" NAT/G PRICE CONTROL REGION...POLICY CHARTS 440 20 MIDWEST/US CONGRESS REPUBLICAN EISNHWR/DD 20. PAGE 47 F0925
POL/PAR AGRI ATTIT CHOOSE

S59
WALLACE R.A.,"CONGRESSIONAL CONTROL OF THE BUDGET." USA+45 NAT/G CHIEF GP/REL FEDERAL OBJECTIVE...MGT CONGRESS. PAGE 143 F2807
LEGIS EX/STRUC BUDGET CONSTN

N59
CHAMBER OF COMMERCE OF USA,ECONOMIC LESSONS OF POSTWAR RECESSIONS (PAMPHLET). AFR USA+45 LAW LEGIS WORKER TAX...CHARTS 20 CONGRESS FED/RESERV. PAGE 23 F0440
ECO/DEV PROB/SOLV FINAN ECO/TAC

B60
BATOR F.M.,QUESTION OF GOVERNMENT SPENDING. USA+45 DIST/IND FINAN BAL/PAY...STAT CENSUS CHARTS CONGRESS 20. PAGE 11 F0210
ECO/DEV

B60
CARPER E.T.,THE DEFENSE APPROPRIATIONS RIDER (PAMPHLET). USA+45 CONSTN CHIEF DELIB/GP LEGIS BUDGET LOBBY CIVMIL/REL...POLICY 20 CONGRESS EISNHWR/DD DEPT/DEFEN PRESIDENT BOSTON. PAGE 22 F0419
GOV/REL ADJUD LAW CONTROL

B60
SHANNON D.A.,THE GREAT DEPRESSION. USA-45 FINAN LG/CO SCHOOL SML/CO DELIB/GP RECEIVE REV EATING INCOME...ANTHOL MUNICH 20 ROOSEVLT/F CONGRESS. PAGE 120 F2365
WEALTH NAT/G AGRI INDUS

B60
US HOUSE COMM GOVT OPERATIONS,OPERATIONS OF THE DEVELOPMENT LOAN FUND: HEARINGS (COMMITTEE ON GOVERNMENT OPERATIONS). USA+45 PLAN BUDGET DIPLOM GOV/REL COST...CHARTS 20 CONGRESS DEPT/STATE AID. PAGE 137 F2698
FINAN FOR/AID ECO/TAC EFFICIENCY

B61
HUBBARD P.J.,ORIGINS OF THE TVA: THE MUSCLE SHOALS CONTROVERSY, 1920-1932. USA-45 DELIB/GP LEGIS LEAD LOBBY GOV/REL GP/REL INGP/REL OWN PERSON...BIBLIOG 20 TVA CONGRESS WATER. PAGE 62 F1229
SEA CONTROL NAT/G INDUS

B61
US CONGRESS JOINT ECO COMM,INTERNATIONAL PAYMENTS IMBALANCES AND NEED FOR STRENGTHENING INTERNATIONAL FINANCIAL ARRANGEMENTS. USA+45 WOR+45 DELIB/GP DIPLOM INT/TRADE...CHARTS 20 CONGRESS OEEC. PAGE 134 F2651
BAL/PAY INT/ORG FINAN PROB/SOLV

S61
WILDAVSKY A.,"POLITICAL IMPLICATIONS OF BUDGETARY REFORM." AFR NAT/G POL/PAR DELIB/GP EX/STRUC ATTIT PWR CONGRESS. PAGE 146 F2881
BUDGET PLAN LEGIS

B62
BUREAU OF NATIONAL AFFAIRS,FEDERAL-STATE REGULATION OF WELFARE FUNDS (REV. ED.). USA+45 LAW LEGIS DEBATE AGE/O 20 CONGRESS. PAGE 20 F0386
WELF/ST WEALTH PLAN SOC/WK

B62
CARPER E.T.,ILLINOIS GOES TO CONGRESS FOR ARMY LAND. USA+45 LAW EXTR/IND PROVS REGION CIVMIL/REL GOV/REL FEDERAL ATTIT 20 ILLINOIS SENATE CONGRESS DIRKSEN/E DOUGLAS/P. PAGE 22 F0420
ADMIN LOBBY GEOG LEGIS

B62
HIRSCHFIELD R.S.,THE CONSTITUTION AND THE COURT. AFR SCHOOL WAR RACE/REL EQUILIB ORD/FREE...POLICY MAJORIT DECISION JURID 18/20 PRESIDENT CIVIL/LIB SUPREME/CT CONGRESS. PAGE 60 F1175
ADJUD PWR CONSTN LAW

B62
MCCLELLAN J.L.,CRIME WITHOUT PUNISHMENT. USA+45 LAW SOCIETY DELIB/GP TRIBUTE CONTROL LOBBY COERCE GP/REL ANOMIE MORAL...CRIMLGY 20 CONGRESS HOFFA/J. PAGE 88 F1718
CRIME ACT/RES LABOR PWR

B62
US BUREAU OF THE CENSUS,REPORT FOR SUBCOMMITTEE ON ANTITRUST AND MONOPOLY: CONCENTRATION RATIOS IN MANUFACTURING INDUSTRY 1958. USA+45 ECO/DEV CONTROL GOV/REL OWN PRODUC PROFIT...STAT 20 CONGRESS MONOPOLY. PAGE 134 F2646
CHARTS PROC/MFG MARKET LG/CO

B62
US CONGRESS,LEGISLATIVE HISTORY OF UNITED STATES TAX CONVENTIONS(VOL. 1). USA+45 USA-45 DELIB/GP WEALTH...CHARTS 20 CONGRESS. PAGE 134 F2649
TAX LEGIS LAW DIPLOM

B62
US CONGRESS JOINT ECO COMM,INVENTORY FLUCTUATIONS AND ECONOMIC STABILIZATION. USA+45 LG/CO...MATH CHARTS CONGRESS. PAGE 134 F2652
ECO/TAC FINAN INDUS PROB/SOLV

B62
US CONGRESS JOINT ECO COMM,FACTORS AFFECTING THE UNITED STATES BALANCE OF PAYMENTS. USA+45 DELIB/GP PLAN DIPLOM FOR/AID PRODUC WEALTH...CHARTS 20 CONGRESS OEEC. PAGE 134 F2653
BAL/PAY INT/TRADE ECO/TAC FINAN

B62
US CONGRESS JOINT ECO COMM,ECONOMIC DEVELOPMENTS IN SOUTH AMERICA. USA+45 SOCIETY FINAN NAT/G PROB/SOLV TEC/DEV INT/TRADE TAX EFFICIENCY PRODUC ATTIT ...POLICY 20 ALL/PROG CONGRESS SOUTH/AMER. PAGE 135 F2654
L/A+17C ECO/UNDEV FOR/AID DIPLOM

B63
JACOBS P.,STATE OF UNIONS. USA+45 STRATA TOP/EX GP/REL RACE/REL DEMAND DISCRIM ATTIT PWR 20 CONGRESS NEGRO HOFFA/J. PAGE 66 F1296
LABOR ECO/TAC BARGAIN DECISION

B63
KOLKO G.,THE TRIUMPH OF CONSERVATISM. USA-45 INDUS LG/CO NAT/G PWR 20 PRESIDENT CONGRESS MONOPOLY PROGRSV/M. PAGE 72 F1421
CONSERVE CAP/ISM FINAN MARKET

B63
US CONGRESS JOINT ECO COMM,THE UNITED STATES BALANCE OF PAYMENTS. AFR USA+45 DELIB/GP BUDGET PRICE PRODUC 20 CONGRESS MONEY. PAGE 135 F2655
BAL/PAY INT/TRADE FINAN ECO/TAC

B63
US CONGRESS JOINT ECO COMM,THE UNITED STATES BALANCE OF PAYMENTS. USA+45 DELIB/GP CONFER...MATH PREDICT CHARTS 20 CONGRESS. PAGE 135 F2656
BAL/PAY ECO/TAC INT/TRADE CONSULT

B63
US CONGRESS JOINT ECO COMM,OUTLOOK FOR UNITED STATES BALANCE OF PAYMENTS. AFR USA+45 ECO/DEV NAT/G FORCES DIPLOM FOR/AID COST EFFICIENCY ...POLICY CONGRESS EEC. PAGE 135 F2657
BAL/PAY FINAN INT/TRADE PROB/SOLV

B63
US HOUSE,URBAN RENEWAL: HOUSE COMMITTEE ON BANKING AND CURRENCY. USA+45 FINAN LOC/G NAT/G NEIGH DELIB/GP TEC/DEV BUDGET GOV/REL COST...CHARTS MUNICH 20 CONGRESS URBAN/RNWL. PAGE 136 F2684
PLAN PROB/SOLV LEGIS

B63
US HOUSE COMM BANKING-CURR,RECENT CHANGES IN MONETARY POLICY AND BALANCE OF PAYMENTS PROBLEMS. USA+45 DELIB/GP PLAN DIPLOM...CHARTS 20 CONGRESS. PAGE 136 F2688
BAL/PAY FINAN ECO/TAC POLICY

B63
US SENATE COMM GOVT OPERATIONS,REPORT OF A STUDY OF US FOREIGN AID IN TEN MIDDLE EASTERN AND AFRICAN COUNTRIES. AFR ISLAM USA+45 FORCES PLAN BUDGET DIPLOM TAX DETER WEALTH...STAT CHARTS 20 CONGRESS AID MID/EAST. PAGE 138 F2728
FOR/AID EFFICIENCY ECO/TAC FINAN

B63
WILTZ J.E.,IN SEARCH OF PEACE: THE SENATE MUNITIONS INQUIRY, 1934-36. EUR+WWI USA-45 ELITES INDUS LG/CO LEGIS INT/TRADE LOBBY NEUTRAL ARMS/CONT...POLICY CONGRESS 20 LEAGUE/NAT PRESIDENT SENATE CONSCRIPTN. PAGE 147 F2905
DELIB/GP PROFIT WAR WEAPON

B64
DUSCHA J.,ARMS, MONEY, AND POLITICS. USA+45 INDUS POL/PAR ECO/TAC TAX DETER NUC/PWR WAR WEAPON GOV/REL ATTIT...BIBLIOG/A 20 CONGRESS MONEY DEPT/DEFEN. PAGE 35 F0687
NAT/G FORCES POLICY BUDGET

B64
MANSFIELD E.,MONOPOLY POWER AND ECONOMIC PERFORMANCE: AN INTRODUCTION TO A CURRENT ISSUE OF PUBLIC POLICY. ECO/DEV INDUS NAT/G PLAN CAP/ISM PRICE CONTROL LOBBY EFFICIENCY PRODUC...POLICY 20 CONGRESS KENNEDY/JF MONOPOLY. PAGE 85 F1659
LG/CO PWR ECO/TAC MARKET

B64
MASON E.S.,FOREIGN AID AND FOREIGN POLICY. USA+45 AGRI INDUS NAT/G EX/STRUC ACT/RES RIGID/FLEX ALL/VALS...POLICY GEN/LAWS MARSHL/PLN ALL/PROG CONGRESS 20. PAGE 87 F1699
ECO/UNDEV ECO/TAC FOR/AID DIPLOM

B64
REUSS H.S.,THE CRITICAL DECADE - AN ECONOMIC POLICY FOR AMERICA AND THE FREE WORLD. AFR USA+45 FINAN POL/PAR WORKER PLAN DIPLOM ECO/TAC TARIFFS BAL/PAY ...POLICY 20 CONGRESS. PAGE 111 F2181
FOR/AID INT/TRADE LABOR LEGIS

B64
US CONGRESS JOINT ECO COMM,PRIVATE INVESTMENT IN LATIN AMERICA. L/A+17C USA+45 INT/ORG PROB/SOLV ECO/TAC ATTIT...INT 20 CONGRESS. PAGE 135 F2658
FINAN ECO/UNDEV PARL/PROC LEGIS

B64
US DEPT LABOR OFF SOLICITOR,LEGISLATIVE HISTORY OF THE LABOR-MANAGEMENT AND DISCLOSURE ACT OF 1959. DELIB/GP WORKER ADMIN LOBBY PARL/PROC SANCTION CHOOSE GOV/REL 20 CONGRESS PRESIDENT. PAGE 136 F2677
LABOR LEGIS DEBATE POLICY

B64
US HOUSE COMM BANKING-CURR,INTERNATIONAL DEVELOPMENT ASSOCIATION ACT AMENDMENT. CHINA/COM USA+45 USSR FINAN FORCES LEGIS DIPLOM CONFER EFFICIENCY...CHARTS GOV/COMP 20 PRESIDENT CONGRESS INTL/DEV. PAGE 136 F2689
BAL/PAY FOR/AID RECORD ECO/TAC

B64
US HOUSE COMM GOVT OPERATIONS,US OWNED FOREIGN CURRENCIES: HEARINGS (COMMITTEE ON GOVERNMENT OPERATIONS). INDIA ECO/DEV PLAN BUDGET TAX DEMAND EFFICIENCY 20 AID CONGRESS. PAGE 137 F2699
FINAN ECO/TAC FOR/AID OWN

B64
US SENATE COMM ON FOREIGN REL,HEARING ON BILLS RELATING TO FOREIGN ASSISTANCE. USA+45 WOR+45 ECO/UNDEV FINAN INDUS 20 UN CONGRESS. PAGE 139 F2733
FOR/AID DIPLOM TEC/DEV INT/ORG

B64
US SENATE COMM ON JUDICIARY,HEARINGS BEFORE SUBCOMMITTEE ON ANTITRUST AND MONOPOLY: ECONOMIC CONCENTRATION VOLUMES 1-5 JULY 1964-SEPT 1966. USA+45 LAW FINAN ECO/TAC ADJUD COST EFFICIENCY PRODUC...STAT CHARTS 20 CONGRESS MONOPOLY. PAGE 140 F2749
ECO/DEV CONTROL MARKET LG/CO

B64
WEIDENBAUM M.L.,CONGRESS AND THE FEDERAL BUDGET: FEDERAL BUDGETING AND THE RESPONSIBLE USE OF POWER. LOC/G PLAN TAX CONGRESS. PAGE 144 F2843
LEGIS EX/STRUC BUDGET ADMIN

L64
KOLODZIEJ E.A.,"RATIONAL CONSENT AND DEFENSE BUDGETS: THE ROLE OF CONGRESS, 1945-1962." LEGIS DIPLOM CONTROL PARL/PROC 20 CONGRESS. PAGE 72 F1423
DECISION PLAN CIVMIL/REL BUDGET

B65
BALDWIN D.A.,SOFT LOANS AND AMERICAN FOREIGN POLICY: 1943-1962 (THESIS). USA+45 WOR+45 FINAN NAT/G FOR/AID BAL/PAY ATTIT...POLICY METH/COMP 20 UN CONGRESS. PAGE 9 F0161
DIPLOM ECO/TAC ECO/UNDEV

B65
BOCK E.,GOVERNMENT REGULATION OF BUSINESS. USA+45 LAW EX/STRUC LEGIS EXEC ORD/FREE PWR...ANTHOL CONGRESS. PAGE 16 F0303
MGT ADMIN NAT/G CONTROL

B65
FLASH E.S. JR.,ECONOMIC ADVICE AND PRESIDENTIAL LEADERSHIP: THE COUNCIL OF ECONOMIC ADVISORS. USA+45 NAT/G EX/STRUC LEGIS TOP/EX ACT/RES ADMIN PRESIDENT CONGRESS. PAGE 41 F0808
PLAN CONSULT CHIEF

B65
LYONS G.M.,AMERICA: PURPOSE AND POWER. UK USA+45 FINAN INDUS MARKET WORKER TEC/DEV DIPLOM AUTOMAT NUC/PWR WAR RACE/REL ORD/FREE 20 EEC CONGRESS SUPREME/CT CIV/RIGHTS. PAGE 82 F1617
PWR PROB/SOLV ECO/DEV TASK

B65
US CONGRESS JOINT ECO COMM,GUIDELINES FOR INTERNATIONAL MONETARY REFORM. USA+45 WOR+45 DELIB/GP BAL/PAY 20 CONGRESS IMF MONEY. PAGE 135 F2659
DIPLOM FINAN PLAN INT/ORG

B65
US HOUSE COMM BANKING-CURR,INTERNATIONAL TRAVEL IN RELATION TO THE BALANCE OF PAYMENTS DEFICIT. USA+45 DELIB/GP...CHARTS 20 CONGRESS TRAVEL. PAGE 136 F2690
BAL/PAY ECO/TAC SERV/IND PROB/SOLV

B65
US SENATE COMM ON FOREIGN REL,HEARINGS ON THE FOREIGN ASSISTANCE PROGRAM. AFR ASIA L/A+17C USA+45 WOR+45 FORCES TEC/DEV BUDGET CONTROL WEAPON ORD/FREE 20 UN CONGRESS SEC/STATE. PAGE 139 F2734
FOR/AID DIPLOM INT/ORG ECO/UNDEV

B65
US SENATE COMM ON JUDICIARY,ANTITRUST EXEMPTIONS FOR AGREEMENTS RELATING TO BALANCE OF PAYMENTS. FINAN ECO/TAC CONTROL WEALTH...POLICY 20 CONGRESS. PAGE 140 F2750
BAL/PAY ADJUD MARKET INT/TRADE

B65
WARD R.,BACKGROUND MATERIAL ON ECONOMIC IMPACT OF FEDERAL PROCUREMENT - 1965: FOR JOINT ECONOMIC COMMITTEE US CONGRESS. FINAN ROUTINE WEAPON CIVMIL/REL EFFICIENCY...STAT CHARTS 20 CONGRESS. PAGE 143 F2818
ECO/DEV NAT/G OWN GOV/REL

B65
WEIDENBAUM M.L.,CONGRESS AND THE FEDERAL BUDGET. FINAN ACT/RES DOMIN CONFER EXEC UTIL PWR NEW/LIB ...CHARTS CONGRESS. PAGE 144 F2844
BUDGET LEGIS PLAN DECISION

S65
HADDAD W.F.,"MR. SHRIVER AND THE SAVAGE POLITICS OF POVERTY" USA+45 LAW NAT/G DELIB/GP LEGIS GIVE LEAD CENTRAL PWR...SOC/WK CHARTS 20 CONGRESS POVRTY/WAR SHRIVER/S OEO. PAGE 53 F1028
WEALTH GOV/REL CONTROL TOP/EX

B66
LEE R.A.,TRUMAN AND TAFT-HARTLEY: A QUESTION OF MANDATE. USA+45 LAW CONSTN LG/CO CONTROL LOBBY GOV/REL PEACE NEW/LIB 20 TRUMAN/HS CONGRESS. PAGE 77 F1507
LEGIS TOP/EX ADJUD LABOR

B66
US CONGRESS JOINT ECO COMM,NEW APPROACH TO UNITED STATES INTERNATIONAL ECONOMIC POLICY. USA+45 WOR+45 CHIEF DELIB/GP CONFER...CHARTS 20 CONGRESS MONEY. PAGE 135 F2660
DIPLOM ECO/TAC BAL/PAY FINAN

B66
US HOUSE COMM BANKING CURRENCY,HEARINGS BEFORE HOUSE COMMITTEE ON BANKING AND CURRENCY: SALE OF SBA LOAN POOL PARTICIPATIONS. USA+45 LAW LEGIS ECO/TAC RATION 20 CONGRESS. PAGE 136 F2687
FINAN SML/CO ADJUD GOV/REL

B66
US HOUSE COMM FOREIGN AFFAIRS,HEARINGS ON HR 12449 A BILL TO AMEND FURTHER THE FOREIGN ASSISTANCE ACT OF 1961. AFR ASIA L/A+17C USA+45 VIETNAM INT/ORG TEC/DEV INT/TRADE ATTIT ORD/FREE 20 UN NATO CONGRESS AID. PAGE 137 F2692
FOR/AID ECO/TAC ECO/UNDEV DIPLOM

B66
US SENATE COMM APPROPRIATIONS,FOREIGN ASSISTANCE AND RELATED AGENCIES APPROPRIATIONS FOR FISCAL YEAR 1967: HEARINGS... ON H. R. 17788. ECO/UNDEV INT/ORG FORCES INSPECT ECO/TAC GIVE DEBATE WEAPON CIVMIL/REL WEALTH...INT 20 CONGRESS DEPT/DEFEN DEPT/STATE DEPT/HEW AID. PAGE 138 F2727
BUDGET FOR/AID DIPLOM COST

B66
US SENATE COMM GOVT OPERATIONS,HEARINGS BEFORE SUBCOMMITTEE ON FOREIGN AID EXPENDITURES: POPULATION CRISIS VOLUMES 1-5 JUNE-SEPT 1965. STRATA ECO/UNDEV PLAN TEC/DEV EDU/PROP ATTIT HEALTH ...GEOG CHARTS 20 CONGRESS BIRTH/CON CASEBOOK. PAGE 138 F2729
ECO/DEV CENSUS FAM CONTROL

B66
US SENATE COMM GOVT OPERATIONS,INTERGOVERNMENTAL PERSONNEL ACT OF 1966. USA+45 NAT/G CONSULT DELIB/GP WORKER TEC/DEV PAY AUTOMAT UTIL 20 CONGRESS. PAGE 139 F2730
ADMIN LEGIS EFFICIENCY EDU/PROP

B66
US SENATE COMM LABOR-PUB WELF,AMEND THE RAILWAY LABOR ACT. USA+45 CONSTN CONSULT DELIB/GP ADJUD CONGRESS RAILROAD. PAGE 139 F2731
GP/REL LABOR DIST/IND LAW

B66
US SENATE COMM ON FOREIGN REL,HEARINGS ON S 2859 AND S 2861. USA+45 WOR+45 FORCES BUDGET CAP/ISM ADMIN DETER WEAPON TOTALISM...NAT/COMP 20 UN CONGRESS. PAGE 139 F2735
FOR/AID DIPLOM ORD/FREE ECO/UNDEV

S66
DAVIS O.A.,"A THEORY OF THE BUDGETARY PROCESS." ECO/DEV FINAN LEGIS PROB/SOLV GOV/REL...ECOMETRIC METH/CNCPT STAT CONT/OBS TREND METH/COMP SIMUL 20 CONGRESS. PAGE 30 F0592
DECISION NAT/G BUDGET EFFICIENCY

B67
BIBBY J.,ON CAPITOL HILL. POL/PAR LOBBY PARL/PROC GOV/REL PERS/REL...JURID PHIL/SCI OBS INT BIBLIOG 20 CONGRESS PRESIDENT. PAGE 15 F0278
CONFER LEGIS CREATE LEAD

B67
NORTON H.S.,NATIONAL TRANSPORTATION POLICY: FORMATION AND IMPLEMENTATION. USA+45 USA-45 DELIB/GP LEAD...DECISION TIME/SEQ 19/20 PRESIDENT CONGRESS. PAGE 98 F1935
POLICY DIST/IND NAT/G PROB/SOLV

B67
O'LEARY M.K.,THE POLITICS OF AMERICAN FOREIGN AID. USA+45 POL/PAR CHIEF BUDGET EDU/PROP LOBBY CONGRESS. PAGE 100 F1958
FOR/AID DIPLOM PARL/PROC ATTIT

B67
US AGENCY INTERNATIONAL DEV,PROPOSED FOREIGN AID PROGRAM FOR 1968: SUMMARY PRESENTATION TO THE CONGRESS. AFR S/ASIA USA+45 AGRI TEC/DEV DIPLOM ECO/TAC BAL/PAY COST HEALTH KNOWL SKILL 20 AID CONGRESS ALL/PROG. PAGE 134 F2640
ECO/UNDEV BUDGET FOR/AID STAT

B67
US CONGRESS JOINT ECO COMM,REPORT ON JANUARY 1967 ECONOMIC REPORT OF THE PRESIDENT. FINAN LABOR NAT/G LEGIS BUDGET INT/TRADE COST DEMAND INCOME PRODUC ...POLICY IDEA/COMP 20 CONGRESS. PAGE 135 F2663
CHIEF ECO/TAC PLAN DELIB/GP

B67
US CONGRESS JOINT ECO COMM,AN ECONOMIC PROFILE OF MAINLAND CHINA. VOLUMES I AND II. CHINA/COM AGRI DIST/IND FINAN INDUS LABOR FORCES ACT/RES PLAN INT/TRADE INGP/REL BAL/PAY 20 CONGRESS. PAGE 135 F2664
ECO/UNDEV WEALTH ECO/TAC DELIB/GP

B67
US GOVERNMENT,SECTION-BY-SECTION ANALYSIS OF THE PROPOSED FOREIGN ASSISTANCE ACT OF 1967 (PAMPHLET). USA+45 ECO/UNDEV NAT/G CONGRESS. PAGE 136 F2683
FOR/AID POLICY FORCES INT/TRADE

L67
JACOBY S.B.,"THE 89TH CONGRESS AND GOVERNMENT LITIGATION." USA+45 ADMIN COST...JURID 20 CONGRESS. PAGE 66 F1302
LAW NAT/G ADJUD SANCTION

L67
TRAVERS H. JR.,"AN EXAMINATION OF THE CAB'S MERGER POLICY." USA+45 USA-45 LAW NAT/G LEGIS PLAN ADMIN ...DECISION 20 CONGRESS. PAGE 131 F2584
ADJUD LG/CO POLICY DIST/IND

S67
"THE FEDERAL AGRICULTURAL STABILIZATION PROGRAM AND THE NEGRO." LAW CONSTN PLAN REPRESENT DISCRIM ORD/FREE 20 NEGRO CONGRESS. PAGE 2 F0025
AGRI CONTROL NAT/G RACE/REL

N67
US CONGRESS JOINT ECO COMM,MAINLAND CHINA IN THE WORLD ECONOMY (PAMPHLET). CHINA/COM USA+45 AGRI CHIEF MARXISM CONGRESS. PAGE 135 F2661
ECO/UNDEV POLICY ECO/TAC INT/TRADE

N67
US HOUSE COMM FOREIGN AFFAIRS,THE FOREIGN POLICY
POLICY

ASPECTS OF THE KENNEDY ROUND (PAMPHLET). USA+45 INDUS KENNEDY/JF CONGRESS HOUSE/REP EEC. PAGE 137 F2693 INT/TRADE FOR/AID ECO/DEV

N67
US HOUSE COMM FOREIGN AFFAIRS,FOREIGN ASSISTANCE ACT OF 1967 (PAMPHLET). USA+45 WOR+45 FINAN CONGRESS HOUSE/REP UN. PAGE 137 F2695 FOR/AID POLICY INT/ORG ECO/UNDEV

N67
US HOUSE COMM ON COMMERCE,PARTNERSHIP FOR HEALTH AMENDMENTS FOR 1967 (PAMPHLET). PUB/INST DELIB/GP PROB/SOLV BUDGET EFFICIENCY 20 CONGRESS. PAGE 137 F2701 HEAL PLAN NAT/G JURID

CONGRESS/P....CONGRESS PARTY (ALL NATIONS)

CONGRESSIONAL QUARTERLY SERV F0525,F0526

CONKLING E.C. F2559

CONLEY R.W. F0527

CONNECTICT....CONNECTICUT

N19
STUTZ R.L.,COLLECTIVE DEALING BY UNITS OF LOCAL GOVERNMENT IN CONNECTICUT (PAMPHLET). USA+45 LOC/G PROVS...STAT MUNICH 20 CONNECTICT. PAGE 127 F2508 VOL/ASSN LABOR WORKER

CONRAD/JOS....JOSEPH CONRAD

CONSCIENCE....SEE SUPEGO

CONSCN/OBJ....CONSCIENTIOUS OBJECTION TO WAR AND KILLING

CONSCRIPTN....CONSCRIPTION

B63
WILTZ J.E.,IN SEARCH OF PEACE: THE SENATE MUNITIONS INQUIRY, 1934-36. EUR+WWI USA-45 ELITES INDUS LG/CO LEGIS INT/TRADE LOBBY NEUTRAL ARMS/CONT...POLICY CONGRESS 20 LEAGUE/NAT PRESIDENT SENATE CONSCRIPTN. PAGE 147 F2905 DELIB/GP PROFIT WAR WEAPON

CONSEN....CONSENSUS

N19
ADMINISTRATIVE STAFF COLLEGE,THE ACCOUNTABILITY OF GOVERNMENT DEPARTMENTS (PAMPHLET) (REV. ED.). UK CONSTN FINAN NAT/G CONSULT ADMIN INGP/REL CONSEN PRIVIL 20 PARLIAMENT. PAGE 2 F0043 PARL/PROC ELITES SANCTION PROB/SOLV

S41
BRITT S.H.,"CONFORMITY OF LABOR NEWSPAPERS WITH RESPECT TO THE AFL-CIO CONFLICT." BAL/PWR CONSEN ATTIT. PAGE 18 F0355 LABOR PRESS DOMIN GP/REL

S48
CLEVELAND A.S.,"NAM: SPOKESMAN FOR INDUSTRY?" LEGIS PLAN LEAD LOBBY PARTIC CONSEN INCOME ATTIT ROLE ORD/FREE POLICY. PAGE 25 F0491 VOL/ASSN CLIENT REPRESENT INDUS

C50
ROUSSEAU J.J.,"A DISCOURSE ON POLITICAL ECONOMY" (1755) IN THE SOCIAL CONTRACT AND DISCOURSES." UNIV SOCIETY STRATA STRUCT CONSEN EQUILIB HAPPINESS UTOPIA HEALTH WEALTH...POLICY WELF/ST. PAGE 114 F2252 NAT/G ECO/TAC TAX GEN/LAWS

B56
WHYTE W.H. JR.,THE ORGANIZATION MAN. CULTURE FINAN VOL/ASSN DOMIN EDU/PROP EXEC DISPL HABITAT ROLE ...PERS/TEST STERTYP. PAGE 146 F2875 ADMIN LG/CO PERSON CONSEN

S56
BROWN J.S.,"UNION SIZE AS A FUNCTION OF INTRA-UNION CONFLICT." CLIENT CONTROL CHOOSE EFFICIENCY ATTIT TREND. PAGE 19 F0370 LABOR INGP/REL CONSEN DRIVE

S56
TANNENBAUM A.S.,"CONTROL OF STRUCTURE AND UNION FUNCTIONS." PARTIC GP/REL INGP/REL CONSEN ATTIT PWR ...QU SAMP. PAGE 128 F2529 LABOR STRUCT CONTROL LEAD

B59
FERRY W.H.,THE CORPORATION AND THE ECONOMY. CLIENT LAW CONSTN LABOR NAT/G PLAN INT/TRADE PARTIC CONSEN ORD/FREE PWR POLICY. PAGE 40 F0787 LG/CO CONTROL REPRESENT

B60
WALLICH H.C.,THE COST OF FREEDOM: A NEW LOOK AT CAPITALISM. USA+45 SOCIETY ECO/DEV INGP/REL CONSEN LAISSEZ SOCISM...OLD/LIB IDEA/COMP. PAGE 143 F2810 CAP/ISM ORD/FREE POLICY ECO/TAC

B63
BRAYBROOKE D.,A STRATEGY OF DECISION: POLICY EVALUATION AS A SOCIAL PROCESS. UNIV ELITES OP/RES DOMIN CONFER FEEDBACK CONSEN PLURISM...CONCPT CENSUS. PAGE 18 F0343 DECISION POLICY CONTROL

B64
MEISEL J.,PAPERS ON THE 1962 ELECTION. CANADA PROVS SECT GP/REL CONSEN EFFICIENCY...MAJORIT 20. PAGE 89 F1751 POL/PAR RECORD CHOOSE STRATA

B64
PRESTHUS R.,MEN AT THE TOP; A STUDY IN COMMUNITY POWER. USA+45 STRUCT ACT/RES REPRESENT CONSEN ALL/VALS ORD/FREE...SAMP/SIZ 20. PAGE 108 F2116 PLURISM LG/CO PWR ADMIN

B65
LAZARUS S.,RESOLVING BUSINESS DISPUTES: THE POTENTIAL OF COMMERCIAL ARBITRATION. USA+45 INDUS LG/CO ACT/RES PROB/SOLV EDU/PROP CONSEN UTIL ...TREND 20. PAGE 76 F1496 FINAN DELIB/GP CONSULT ADJUD

S65
SPAAK P.H.,"THE SEARCH FOR CONSENSUS: A NEW EFFORT TO BUILD EUROPE." FRANCE GERMANY ECO/DEV NAT/G CONSULT FORCES PLAN EDU/PROP REGION CONSEN ATTIT ...SOC METH/CNCPT OBS TREND EEC NATO WORK TERR/GP METH/GP 20. PAGE 124 F2447 EUR+WWI INT/ORG

B66
LECHT L.,GOAL, PRIORITIES, AND DOLLARS: THE NEXT DECADE. SPACE USA+45 SOCIETY AGRI BUDGET FOR/AID ...HEAL SOC/WK STAT CHARTS 20 URBAN/RNWL PUB/TRANS. PAGE 76 F1499 IDEA/COMP POLICY CONSEN PLAN

B67
HANRIEDER W.F.,WEST GERMAN FOREIGN POLICY 1949-1963: INTERNATIONAL PRESSURE AND DOMESTIC RESPONSE. EUR+WWI GERMANY/W POL/PAR LOBBY CONSEN 20. PAGE 54 F1061 DIPLOM POLICY NAT/G ATTIT

B67
US SENATE COMM ON FOREIGN REL,HARRISON E. SALISBURY'S TRIP TO NORTH VIETNAM. CHINA/COM USA+45 VIETNAM/N PRESS TASK GUERRILLA CONSEN EFFICIENCY PEACE DRIVE...OBS SENATE. PAGE 139 F2743 DIPLOM WAR FORCES ATTIT

L67
GLAZER N.,"HOUSING PROBLEMS AND HOUSING POLICIES." USA+45 PLAN RENT ADJUST CONSEN DEMAND DISCRIM AGE ATTIT HEALTH WEALTH MUNICH NEGRO. PAGE 48 F0929 POLICY CONSTRUC CREATE HABITAT

L67
TANDON Y.,"CONSENSUS AND AUTHORITY BEHIND UNITED NATIONS PEACEKEEPING OPERATIONS." FINAN VOL/ASSN BUDGET DIPLOM PAY DOMIN...CHARTS 20 UN. PAGE 128 F2528 CONSEN INT/ORG PWR PEACE

S67
FINER S.E.,"THE ONE-PARTY REGIMES IN AFRICA: RECONSIDERATIONS." AFR DOMIN CONSEN ORD/FREE 20. PAGE 41 F0798 ELITES POL/PAR CONSTN ECO/UNDEV

S67
GATELL F.O.,"MONEY AND PARTY IN JACKSONIAN AMERICA* A QUANTITATIVE LOOK AT NEW YORK CITY'S MEN OF QUALITY." USA-45 STRATA SECT SUFF CONSEN MAJORITY ATTIT...CHARTS HYPO/EXP 19. PAGE 46 F0908 WEALTH POL/PAR PERSON IDEA/COMP

S67
WEIL G.L.,"THE MERGER OF THE INSTITUTIONS OF THE EUROPEAN COMMUNITIES" EUR+WWI ECO/DEV INT/TRADE CONSEN PLURISM...DECISION MGT 20 EEC EURATOM ECSC TREATY. PAGE 145 F2847 ECO/TAC INT/ORG CENTRAL INT/LAW

CONSENSUS....SEE CONSEN

CONSERVATISM....SEE CONSERVE

CONSERVE....TRADITIONALISM

B34
MARX K.,THE CLASS STRUGGLES IN FRANCE. FRANCE INDUS WORKER CONSERVE...TREND GEN/LAWS 19. PAGE 86 F1689 MARXIST STRATA REV INT/TRADE

B61
BRAIBANTI R.,TRADITION, VALUES AND SOCIO-ECONOMIC DEVELOPMENT. WOR+45 ACT/RES TEC/DEV ATTIT ORD/FREE CONSERVE...POLICY SOC ANTHOL. PAGE 17 F0336 ALL/VALS ECO/UNDEV CONCPT METH/CNCPT

B61
CAMPAIGNE J.G.,CHECK-OFF: LABOR BOSSES AND WORKING MEN. LEGIS WORKER EDU/PROP DEBATE COERCE REPRESENT GP/REL ORD/FREE CONSERVE. PAGE 21 F0404 LABOR ELITES PWR CONTROL

B63
BATES J.L.,THE ORIGINS OF TEAPOT DOME: PROGRESSIVES, PARTIES, AND PETROLEUM, 1909-1921. USA-45 INDUS LG/CO POL/PAR DELIB/GP CONTROL GOV/REL CONSERVE...BIBLIOG 20 NAVY. PAGE 11 F0209 EXTR/IND CRIME NAT/G

B63
KOLKO G.,THE TRIUMPH OF CONSERVATISM. USA-45 INDUS LG/CO NAT/G PWR 20 PRESIDENT CONGRESS MONOPOLY PROGRSV/M. PAGE 72 F1421 CONSERVE CAP/ISM FINAN MARKET

B64
RAISON T.,WHY CONSERVATIVE? UK FORCES DIPLOM ECO/TAC GIVE EDU/PROP ORD/FREE WEALTH LAISSEZ PLURISM CONSERVE

...GOV/COMP 20 TORY/PARTY CONSRV/PAR. PAGE 109 F2137 — POL/PAR NAT/G

B65

BARRY E.E.,NATIONALISATION IN BRITISH POLITICS: THE HISTORICAL BACKGROUND. UK AGRI DIST/IND EXTR/IND LABOR LG/CO ATTIT CONSERVE SOCISM 19/20 LABOR/PAR. PAGE 10 F0198 — NAT/G OWN INDUS POL/PAR

S65

CECIL C.O.,"THE DETERMINANTS OF LIBYAN FOREIGN POLICY." AFR INTELL ECO/UNDEV EXTR/IND POL/PAR CREATE REGION SOVEREIGN CONSERVE MAGHREB NASSER/G. PAGE 22 F0431 — LIBYA DIPLOM WEALTH ISLAM

S66

JACOBS P.,"RE-RADICALIZING THE DE-RADICALIZED." USA+45 SOCIETY STRUCT FINAN PLAN PROB/SOLV CAP/ISM WEALTH CONSERVE NEW/LIB 20. PAGE 66 F1297 — NAT/G POLICY MARXIST ADMIN

S66

MALENBAUM W.,"GOVERNMENT, ENTREPRENEURSHIP, AND ECONOMIC GROWTH IN POOR LANDS." ELITES ECO/UNDEV INDUS CREATE DRIVE. PAGE 84 F1645 — ECO/TAC PLAN CONSERVE NAT/G

B67

MARCUS S.,COMPETITION AND THE LAW. USA+45 INDUS LG/CO NAT/G CONSERVE LAISSEZ...BIBLIOG 20 FTC SUPREME/CT. PAGE 85 F1665 — LAW ECO/DEV FINAN JURID

B67

SPIRO H.S.,PATTERNS OF AFRICAN DEVLOPMENT: FIVE COMPARISONS. STRUCT ECO/UNDEV NAT/G CONSERVE SOCISM ...PREDICT NAT/COMP 20 CHINJAP. PAGE 125 F2457 — AFR CONSTN NAT/LISM TREND

B67

WESSON R.G.,THE IMPERIAL ORDER. WOR-45 STRUCT SECT DOMIN ADMIN COLONIAL LEAD CONSERVE...CONCPT BIBLIOG 20. PAGE 145 F2861 — PWR CHIEF CONTROL SOCIETY

S67

DEMUTH J.,"GE: PROFILE OF A CORPORATION." USA+45 USA-45 LABOR ACT/RES RATION EDU/PROP ADJUD CT/SYS FASCISM 20. PAGE 32 F0619 — LG/CO CONSERVE PRICE

S67

KOHN W.S.G.,"THE SOVEREIGNTY OF LIECHTENSTEIN." LIECHTENST SWITZERLND USSR CONSTN DEBATE WAR CONSERVE 18/20 UN. PAGE 72 F1417 — SOVEREIGN NAT/G PWR DIPLOM

S67

SOLT L.F.,"PURITANISM, CAPITALISM, DEMOCRACY, AND THE NEW SCIENCE." NAT/G GP/REL CONSERVE...IDEA/COMP GEN/LAWS. PAGE 124 F2440 — SECT CAP/ISM RATIONAL POPULISM

B76

TAINE H.A.,THE ANCIENT REGIME. FRANCE STRATA FORCES PARTIC EQUILIB WEALTH CONSERVE POPULISM...GOV/COMP SOC/INTEG 18/19. PAGE 128 F2527 — NAT/G GOV/REL TAX REV

B82

CUNNINGHAM W.,THE GROWTH OF ENGLISH INDUSTRY AND COMMERCE. FUT UK FINAN NAT/G CAP/ISM...POLICY 20 MERCANTLST CHRISTIAN POPE. PAGE 29 F0562 — INDUS INT/TRADE SML/CO CONSERVE

CONSRV/PAR....CONSERVATIVE PARTY (ALL NATIONS)

B64

RAISON T.,WHY CONSERVATIVE? UK FORCES DIPLOM ECO/TAC GIVE EDU/PROP ORD/FREE WEALTH LAISSEZ ...GOV/COMP 20 TORY/PARTY CONSRV/PAR. PAGE 109 F2137 — PLURISM CONSERVE POL/PAR NAT/G

CONSTITUTION....SEE CONSTN

CONSTN....CONSTITUTIONS

B13

BEARD C.A.,AN ECONOMIC INTERPRETATION OF THE CONSTITUTION OF THE UNITED STATES. USA-45 AGRI INT/TRADE SUFF OWN ATTIT...CONCPT MYTH BIOG HIST/WRIT 18. PAGE 12 F0222 — CONSTN ECO/TAC CHOOSE

N19

ADMINISTRATIVE STAFF COLLEGE,THE ACCOUNTABILITY OF GOVERNMENT DEPARTMENTS (PAMPHLET) (REV. ED.). UK CONSTN FINAN NAT/G CONSULT ADMIN INGP/REL CONSEN PRIVIL 20 PARLIAMENT. PAGE 2 F0043 — PARL/PROC ELITES SANCTION PROB/SOLV

N19

FAHRNKOPF N.,STATE AND LOCAL GOVERNMENT IN ILLINOIS (PAMPHLET). CONSTN ADMIN PARTIC CHOOSE REPRESENT GOV/REL...JURID MGT 20 ILLINOIS. PAGE 39 F0759 — BIBLIOG LOC/G LEGIS CT/SYS

B23

FINER H.,REPRESENTATIVE GOVERNMENT AND A PARLIAMENT OF INDUSTRY. A STUDY OF THE GERMAN FEDERAL ECONOMIC COUNCIL. GERMANY UK CONSTN INDUS PARL/PROC ...NAT/COMP 20. PAGE 41 F0796 — DELIB/GP ECO/TAC WAR REV

B24

HOLDSWORTH W.S.,A HISTORY OF ENGLISH LAW; THE COMMON LAW AND ITS RIVALS (VOL. VI). AFR UK STRATA EX/STRUC ADJUD ADMIN CONTROL CT/SYS...JURID CONCPT GEN/LAWS 17 PARLIAMENT ENGLSH/LAW COMMON/LAW. PAGE 61 F1194 — LAW CONSTN LEGIS CHIEF

B24

HOLDSWORTH W.S.,A HISTORY OF ENGLISH LAW; THE COMMON LAW AND ITS RIVALS (VOL. IV). UK SEA AGRI CHIEF ADJUD CONTROL CRIME GOV/REL...INT/LAW JURID NAT/COMP 16/17 PARLIAMENT COMMON/LAW CANON/LAW ENGLSH/LAW. PAGE 61 F1195 — LAW LEGIS CT/SYS CONSTN

B25

MATHEWS J.M.,AMERICAN STATE GOVERNMENT. USA-45 LOC/G CHIEF EX/STRUC LEGIS ADJUD CONTROL CT/SYS ROUTINE GOV/REL PWR 20 GOVERNOR. PAGE 87 F1703 — PROVS ADMIN FEDERAL CONSTN

B28

FRANKFURTER F.,THE BUSINESS OF THE SUPREME COURT; A STUDY IN THE FEDERAL JUDICIAL SYSTEM. USA-45 CONSTN EX/STRUC PROB/SOLV GP/REL ATTIT PWR...POLICY JURID 18/20 SUPREME/CT CONGRESS. PAGE 43 F0848 — CT/SYS ADJUD LAW FEDERAL

B30

GREEN F.M.,CONSTITUTIONAL DEVELOPMENT IN THE SOUTH ATLANTIC STATES, 1776-1860; A STUDY IN THE EVOLUTION OF DEMOCRACY. USA-45 ELITES SOCIETY STRATA ECO/DEV AGRI POL/PAR EX/STRUC LEGIS CT/SYS REGION...BIBLIOG 18/19 MARYLAND VIRGINIA GEORGIA NORTH/CAR SOUTH/CAR. PAGE 50 F0984 — CONSTN PROVS PLURISM REPRESENT

B35

WADE J.,HISTORY OF THE MIDDLE AND WORKING CLASSES; WITH A POPULAR EXPOSITION OF THE ECONOMICAL AND POLITICAL PRINCIPLES.... FRANCE UK CONSTN FINAN INDUS LABOR INCOME PROFIT KNOWL MORAL ORD/FREE WEALTH...CHARTS 14/19. PAGE 142 F2797 — WORKER STRATA CONCPT

B37

HAMILTON W.H.,THE POWER TO GOVERN. ECO/DEV FINAN INDUS ECO/TAC INT/TRADE TARIFFS TAX CONTROL CT/SYS WAR COST PWR 18/20 SUPREME/CT. PAGE 54 F1056 — LING CONSTN NAT/G POLICY

B37

UNION OF SOUTH AFRICA,REPORT CONCERNING ADMINISTRATION OF SOUTH WEST AFRICA (6 VOLS.). SOUTH/AFR INDUS PUB/INST FORCES LEGIS BUDGET DIPLOM EDU/PROP ADJUD CT/SYS...GEOG CHARTS 20 AFRICA/SW LEAGUE/NAT. PAGE 132 F2610 — NAT/G ADMIN COLONIAL CONSTN

B38

HARPER S.N.,THE GOVERNMENT OF THE SOVIET UNION. COM USSR LAW CONSTN ECO/DEV PLAN TEC/DEV DIPLOM INT/TRADE ADMIN REV NAT/LISM...POLICY 20. PAGE 55 F1085 — MARXISM NAT/G LEAD POL/PAR

B38

HEIMANN E.,COMMUNISM, FASCISM, OR DEMOCRACY? WOR-45 CONSTN SOCIETY STRATA AGRI CAP/ISM MORAL ORD/FREE ...MAJORIT METH/COMP NAT/COMP 19/20. PAGE 58 F1141 — SOCISM MARXISM FASCISM PLURISM

B38

REICH N.,LABOR RELATIONS IN REPUBLICAN GERMANY. GERMANY CONSTN ECO/DEV INDUS NAT/G ADMIN CONTROL GP/REL FASCISM POPULISM 20 WEIMAR/REP. PAGE 110 F2176 — WORKER MGT LABOR BARGAIN

B39

JENNINGS W.I.,PARLIAMENT. UK POL/PAR OP/RES BUDGET LEAD CHOOSE GP/REL...MGT 20 PARLIAMENT HOUSE/LORD HOUSE/CMNS. PAGE 67 F1315 — PARL/PROC LEGIS CONSTN NAT/G

B40

HUNTER R.,REVOLUTION: WHY, HOW, WHEN? NAT/G ECO/TAC EDU/PROP COERCE ORD/FREE FASCISM POPULISM SOCISM 18/20 HITLER/A LENIN/VI. PAGE 63 F1246 — REV METH/COMP LEAD CONSTN

B42

ROBBINS J.J.,THE GOVERNMENT OF LABOR RELATIONS IN SWEDEN. SWEDEN LAW CONSTN ADJUD CT/SYS GP/REL ...JURID 20. PAGE 112 F2200 — NAT/G BARGAIN LABOR INDUS

S43

HERBERG W.,"BUREAUCRACY AND DEMOCRACY IN LABOR UNIONS." LAW CONSTN STRUCT WORKER ADMIN CONTROL PARTIC RIGID/FLEX PWR TREND. PAGE 59 F1151 — LABOR REPRESENT ROUTINE INGP/REL

B46

ERNST M.L.,THE FIRST FREEDOM. USA-45 CONSTN PRESS PRIVIL...CHARTS IDEA/COMP BIBLIOG 20 AMEND/I. PAGE 38 F0746 — EDU/PROP COM/IND ORD/FREE CONTROL

B48

KEIR D.L.,CASES IN CONSTITUTIONAL LAW. UK CHIEF LEGIS DIPLOM TAX PARL/PROC CRIME GOV/REL...INT/LAW JURID 17/20. PAGE 70 F1368 — CONSTN LAW ADJUD CT/SYS

S49

SHEPHARD H.A.,"DEMOCRATIC CONTROL IN A LABOR UNION." FUT CONSTN STRUCT TEC/DEV LEAD PARTIC RACE/REL CENTRAL DRIVE HABITAT RECORD. PAGE 120 F2374 — LABOR MAJORIT CONTROL PWR

B51

BROGAN D.W.,THE PRICE OF REVOLUTION. FRANCE USA+45 — REV

USA-45 USSR CONSTN NAT/G DIPLOM COLONIAL NAT/LISM ORD/FREE POPULISM...CONCPT 18/20 PRE/US/AM. PAGE 19 F0359
METH/COMP COST MARXISM

L51
SUMMERS C.W.,"UNION POWERS AND WORKERS RIGHTS." WORKER PROB/SOLV ECO/TAC PARTIC INGP/REL PWR. PAGE 127 F2513
LABOR CONSTN LAW REPRESENT

B52
JENNINGS W.I.,CONSTITUTIONAL LAWS OF THE COMMONWEALTH. AFR UK LAW CHIEF LEGIS TAX CT/SYS PARL/PROC GOV/REL...INT/LAW 18/20 ENGLSH/LAW COMMON/LAW. PAGE 67 F1316
CONSTN JURID ADJUD COLONIAL

B53
SAYLES L.R.,THE LOCAL UNION. CONSTN CULTURE DELIB/GP PARTIC CHOOSE GP/REL INGP/REL ATTIT ROLE ...MAJORIT DECISION MGT. PAGE 116 F2284
LABOR LEAD ADJUD ROUTINE

B55
SERRANO MOSCOSO E.,A STATEMENT OF THE LAWS OF ECUADOR IN MATTERS AFFECTING BUSINESS (2ND ED.). ECUADOR INDUS LABOR LG/CO NAT/G LEGIS TAX CONTROL MARRIAGE 20. PAGE 120 F2359
FINAN ECO/UNDEV LAW CONSTN

B55
WRONG D.H.,AMERICAN AND CANADIAN VIEWPOINTS. CANADA USA+45 CONSTN STRATA FAM SECT WORKER ECO/TAC EDU/PROP ADJUD MARRIAGE...IDEA/COMP 20. PAGE 149 F2936
DIPLOM ATTIT NAT/COMP CULTURE

S55
HALLETT D.,"THE HISTORY AND STRUCTURE OF OEEC." EUR+WWI USA+45 CONSTN INDUS INT/ORG NAT/G DELIB/GP ACT/RES PLAN ORD/FREE WEALTH...CONCPT OEEC 20 CMN/WLTH. PAGE 54 F1051
VOL/ASSN ECO/DEV

B56
BROWN R.E.,CHARLES BEARD AND THE CONSTITUTION. USA-45 NAT/G ORD/FREE WEALTH...HUM TIME/SEQ METH/COMP 20 BEARD/CA. PAGE 19 F0372
CONSTN ELITES HIST/WRIT

B57
BERLE A.A. JR.,ECONOMIC POWER AND FREE SOCIETY (PAMPHLET). CLIENT CONSTN EX/STRUC ECO/TAC CONTROL PARTIC PWR WEALTH MAJORIT. PAGE 14 F0261
LG/CO CAP/ISM INGP/REL LEGIT

B57
ROBERTSON H.M.,SOUTH AFRICA, ECONOMIC AND POLITICAL ASPECTS. SOUTH/AFR CONSTN CULTURE POL/PAR LEGIS DIPLOM DOMIN COLONIAL...SOC BIBLIOG 19/20. PAGE 112 F2214
RACE/REL ECO/UNDEV ECO/TAC DISCRIM

B58
OGDEN F.D.,THE POLL TAX IN THE SOUTH. USA+45 USA-45 CONSTN ADJUD ADMIN PARTIC CRIME...TIME/SEQ GOV/COMP METH/COMP 18/20 SOUTH/US. PAGE 101 F1982
TAX CHOOSE RACE/REL DISCRIM

B58
SCOTT D.J.R.,RUSSIAN POLITICAL INSTITUTIONS. RUSSIA USSR CONSTN AGRI DELIB/GP PLAN EDU/PROP CONTROL CHOOSE EFFICIENCY ATTIT MARXISM...BIBLIOG/A IND 13/20. PAGE 118 F2332
NAT/G POL/PAR ADMIN DECISION

B58
SEIDMAN J.I.,DEMOCRACY IN THE LABOR MOVEMENT (PAMPHLET). LAW CONSTN STRUCT DELIB/GP WORKER ADJUD PARTIC SANCTION POLICY. PAGE 119 F2345
LABOR INGP/REL PWR MAJORIT

S58
ELKIN A.B.,"OEEC-ITS STRUCTURE AND POWERS." EUR+WWI CONSTN INDUS INT/ORG NAT/G VOL/ASSN DELIB/GP ACT/RES PLAN ORD/FREE WEALTH...CHARTS ORG/CHARTS OEEC 20. PAGE 37 F0719
ECO/DEV EX/STRUC

B59
BROMWICH L.,UNION CONSTITUTIONS. CONSTN EX/STRUC PRESS ADJUD CONTROL CHOOSE REPRESENT PWR SAMP. PAGE 19 F0361
LABOR ROUTINE INGP/REL RACE/REL

B59
FERRY W.H.,THE CORPORATION AND THE ECONOMY. CLIENT LAW CONSTN LABOR NAT/G PLAN INT/TRADE PARTIC CONSEN ORD/FREE PWR POLICY. PAGE 40 F0787
LG/CO CONTROL REPRESENT

B59
LEISERSON W.,AMERICAN TRADE UNION DEMOCRACY. CONSTN STRUCT ADJUD EXEC REPRESENT GP/REL INGP/REL MAJORITY ATTIT PWR. PAGE 77 F1516
LABOR LEAD PARTIC DELIB/GP

B59
LOPEZ VILLAMIL H.,A STATEMENT OF THE LAWS OF THE HONDURAS IN MATTERS AFFECTING BUSINESS (2ND ED.). HONDURAS DIST/IND EXTR/IND FINAN WORKER TAX DEATH MARRIAGE OWN MARITIME 20 MIGRATION. PAGE 82 F1600
CONSTN INDUS LEGIS NAT/G

B59
VOSE C.E.,CAUCASIANS ONLY: THE SUPREME COURT, THE NAACP, AND THE RESTRICTIVE COVENANT CASES. USA+45 LAW CONSTN LOBBY...SOC 20 NAACP SUPREME/CT NEGRO. PAGE 142 F2796
CT/SYS RACE/REL DISCRIM

B59
WAHLKE J.C.,LEGISLATIVE BEHAVIOR: A READER IN THEORY AND RESEARCH. USA+45 CONSTN ELITES POL/PAR LOBBY REPRESENT PERS/REL PERSON ROLE...IDEA/COMP METH/COMP SIMUL. PAGE 142 F2800
LEGIS CHOOSE INGP/REL ATTIT

L59
BEGUIN B.,"ILO AND THE TRIPARTITE SYSTEM." EUR+WWI WOR+45 WOR-45 CONSTN ECO/DEV ECO/UNDEV INDUS INT/ORG NAT/G VOL/ASSN DELIB/GP PLAN TEC/DEV LEGIT ORD/FREE WEALTH...CONCPT TIME/SEQ WORK ILO 20. PAGE 12 F0228
LABOR

S59
MILLER A.S.,"CONSTITUTIONALIZING THE CORPORATION." LABOR NAT/G WORKER PWR...POLICY MGT. PAGE 91 F1789
CONSTN INGP/REL LG/CO CONTROL

S59
WALLACE R.A.,"CONGRESSIONAL CONTROL OF THE BUDGET." USA+45 NAT/G CHIEF GP/REL FEDERAL OBJECTIVE...MGT CONGRESS. PAGE 143 F2807
LEGIS EX/STRUC BUDGET CONSTN

C59
FAINSOD M.,"GOVERNMENT AND THE AMERICAN ECONOMY." USA+45 USA-45 INDUS LABOR OP/RES PROB/SOLV ECO/TAC CONTROL...CHARTS BIBLIOG T 20. PAGE 39 F0760
CONSTN ECO/DEV CAP/ISM NAT/G

B60
CARPER E.T.,THE DEFENSE APPROPRIATIONS RIDER (PAMPHLET). USA+45 CONSTN CHIEF DELIB/GP LEGIS BUDGET LOBBY CIVMIL/REL...POLICY 20 CONGRESS EISNHWR/DD DEPT/DEFEN PRESIDENT BOSTON. PAGE 22 F0419
GOV/REL ADJUD LAW CONTROL

B60
MC CLELLAN G.S.,INDIA. AFR CHINA/COM INDIA CONSTN ELITES STRATA AGRI POL/PAR FOR/AID ARMS/CONT REV MARXISM...CENSUS BIBLIOG 20 GANDHI/M NEHRU/J. PAGE 87 F1712
DIPLOM NAT/G SOCIETY ECO/UNDEV

B60
MENDELSON W.,CAPITALISM, DEMOCRACY, AND THE SUPREME COURT. USA+45 USA-45 CONSTN DIPLOM GOV/REL ATTIT ORD/FREE LAISSEZ...POLICY CHARTS PERS/COMP 18/20 SUPREME/CT MARSHALL/J HOLMES/OW TANEY/RB FIELD/JJ. PAGE 90 F1758
JUDGE CT/SYS JURID NAT/G

B60
SANTHANAM K.,UNION-STATE RELATIONS IN INDIA. INDIA FINAN PROVS PLAN ECO/TAC...LING 20. PAGE 116 F2280
FEDERAL GOV/REL CONSTN POLICY

B60
THEOBALD R.,THE RICH AND THE POOR: A STUDY OF THE ECONOMICS OF RISING EXPECTATIONS. WOR+45 CONSTN ECO/DEV ECO/UNDEV INT/ORG NAT/G PLAN FOR/AID ROUTINE BAL/PAY ORD/FREE PWR WEALTH...GEOG TREND WORK FOR/TRADE 20. PAGE 129 F2553
ECO/TAC INT/TRADE

B60
WALLACE R.A.,CONGRESSIONAL CONTROL OF FEDERAL SPENDING. USA+45 CONSTN NAT/G OP/RES CONFER DEBATE PERS/REL UTIL RIGID/FLEX PWR OBJECTIVE...OBS CHARTS. PAGE 143 F2808
LEGIS DELIB/GP BUDGET

B60
WHEARE K.C.,THE CONSTITUTIONAL STRUCTURE OF THE COMMONWEALTH. UK EX/STRUC DIPLOM DOMIN ADMIN COLONIAL CONTROL LEAD INGP/REL SUPEGO 20 CMN/WLTH. PAGE 145 F2865
CONSTN INT/ORG VOL/ASSN SOVEREIGN

B61
BARBASH J.,LABOR'S GRASS ROOTS. CONSTN NAT/G EX/STRUC LEGIS WORKER LEAD...MAJORIT BIBLIOG. PAGE 10 F0184
LABOR INGP/REL GP/REL LAW

B61
HICKS U.K.,FEDERALISM AND ECONOMIC GROWTH IN UNDERDEVELOPED COUNTRIES. WOR+45 WOR-45 FINAN NAT/G PLAN BUDGET DIPLOM INT/TRADE DEMAND WEALTH...ANTHOL 20. PAGE 59 F1167
ECO/UNDEV ECO/TAC FEDERAL CONSTN

B61
RUEDA B.,A STATEMENT OF THE LAWS OF COLOMBIA IN MATTERS AFFECTING BUSINESS (3RD ED.). INDUS FAM LABOR LG/CO NAT/G LEGIS TAX CONTROL MARRIAGE 20 COLOMB. PAGE 115 F2257
FINAN ECO/UNDEV LAW CONSTN

B61
SEPULVEDA C.,A STATEMENT OF THE LAWS OF MEXICO IN MATTERS AFFECTING BUSINESS (3RD ED.). AGRI DIST/IND EXTR/IND FINAN INDUS WORKER TAX MARRIAGE OWN ORD/FREE...BIBLIOG 20 MEXIC/AMER TREATY MIGRATION MONOPOLY. PAGE 119 F2356
CONSTN NAT/G JURID LEGIS

B61
SHARP W.R.,FIELD ADMINISTRATION IN THE UNITED NATION SYSTEM: THE CONDUCT OF INTERNATIONAL ECONOMIC AND SOCIAL PROGRAMS. FUT WOR+45 CONSTN SOCIETY ECO/UNDEV R+D DELIB/GP ACT/RES PLAN TEC/DEV EDU/PROP EXEC ROUTINE HEALTH WEALTH...HUM CONCPT CHARTS METH ILO UNESCO GP VAL/FREE UN 20. PAGE 120 F2369
INT/ORG CONSULT

B61
STARNER F.L.,GENERAL OBLIGATION BOND FINANCING BY LOCAL GOVERNMENTS: A SURVEY OF STATE CONTROLS. CANADA UK USA+45 CONSTN PROVS...POLICY JURID METH/COMP 20 EUROPE CALIFORNIA. PAGE 125 F2471
FINAN LOC/G GOV/REL ADJUD

L61
GERWIG R.,"PUBLIC AUTHORITIES IN THE UNITED STATES." LAW CONSTN PROVS TAX ADMIN FEDERAL MUNICH.
LOC/G GOV/REL

PAGE 47 F0920 PWR

N61

US ADVISORY COMN INTERGOV REL,STATE CONSTITUTIONAL AND STATUTORY RESTRICTIONS ON LOCAL GOVERNMENT DEBT (PAMPHLET). LAW CONSTN CHOOSE PWR...DECISION MUNICH. PAGE 133 F2631 TAX PROVS GOV/REL

B62

DE LAVALLE H.,A STATEMENT OF THE LAWS OF PERU IN MATTERS AFFECTING BUSINESS (3RD ED.). PERU WORKER INT/TRADE INCOME ORD/FREE...INT/LAW 20. PAGE 31 F0603 CONSTN JURID FINAN TAX

B62

GALENSON W.,TRADE UNIONS MONOGRAPH SERIES (A SERIES OF NINE TEXTS). DELIB/GP LEAD PARTIC...DECISION ORG/CHARTS. PAGE 45 F0887 LABOR INGP/REL CONSTN REPRESENT

B62

HIRSCHFIELD R.S.,THE CONSTITUTION AND THE COURT. AFR SCHOOL WAR RACE/REL EQUILIB ORD/FREE...POLICY MAJORIT DECISION JURID 18/20 PRESIDENT CIVIL/LIB SUPREME/CT CONGRESS. PAGE 60 F1175 ADJUD PWR CONSTN LAW

B62

PASTOR R.S.,A STATEMENT OF THE LAWS OF PARAGUAY IN MATTERS AFFECTING BUSINESS (2ND ED.). PARAGUAY INDUS FAM LABOR LG/CO NAT/G LEGIS TAX CONTROL MARRIAGE 20. PAGE 103 F2033 FINAN ECO/UNDEV LAW CONSTN

B62

US ADVISORY COMN INTERGOV REL,STATE CONSTITUTIONAL AND STATUTORY RESTRICTIONS ON LOCAL TAXING POWERS. USA+45 USA-45 LAW CONSTN ACT/RES CONTROL WEALTH ...JURID CHARTS 20. PAGE 133 F2632 LOC/G PROVS GOV/REL TAX

B62

VACCARO J.R.,A STATEMENT OF THE LAWS OF CHILE IN MATTERS AFFECTING BUSINESS (3RD ED.). CHILE AGRI FINAN FAM LABOR ECO/TAC FOR/AID TAX ADJUD CONTROL MARRIAGE STRANGE...BIBLIOG 20. PAGE 140 F2756 CONSTN LAW INDUS MGT

B63

BURRUS B.R.,ADMINSTRATIVE LAW AND LOCAL GOVERNMENT. USA+45 PROVS LEGIS LICENSE ADJUD ORD/FREE 20. PAGE 20 F0392 EX/STRUC LOC/G JURID CONSTN

B63

CORLEY R.N.,THE LEGAL ENVIRONMENT OF BUSINESS. CONSTN LEGIS TAX ADMIN CT/SYS DISCRIM ATTIT PWR ...TREND 18/20. PAGE 28 F0537 NAT/G INDUS JURID DECISION

B63

LAFEBER W.,THE NEW EMPIRE: AN INTERPRETATION OF AMERICAN EXPANSION, 1860-1898. USA-45 CONSTN NAT/LISM SOVEREIGN...TREND BIBLIOG 19/20. PAGE 74 F1457 INDUS NAT/G DIPLOM CAP/ISM

B63

PRITCHETT C.H.,THE THIRD BRANCH OF GOVERNMENT. USA+45 USA-45 CONSTN SOCIETY INDUS SECT LEGIS JUDGE PROB/SOLV GOV/REL 20 SUPREME/CT CHURCH/STA. PAGE 108 F2122 JURID NAT/G ADJUD CT/SYS

L63

PADELFORD N.J.,"FINANCIAL CRISIS AND THE UNITED NATIONS." FUT USSR WOR+45 LAW CONSTN FINAN INT/ORG DELIB/GP FORCES PLAN BUDGET DIPLOM COST WEALTH ...STAT CHARTS UN CONGO 20. PAGE 102 F2012 CREATE ECO/TAC

L63

RIDAH A.,"LE NEO-DESTOUR DEPUIS L'INDEPENDANCE." FUT ISLAM WOR+45 ECO/UNDEV INT/ORG SCHOOL DELIB/GP TOP/EX ACT/RES EDU/PROP LEGIT ATTIT ALL/VALS 20 TUNIS. PAGE 111 F2189 NAT/G CONSTN

B64

HACKER A.,THE CORPORATION TAKE-OVER. CONSTN LABOR PLAN BAL/PWR CONTROL EXEC LOBBY REPRESENT GP/REL ROLE ORD/FREE POLICY. PAGE 52 F1025 LG/CO STRUCT PWR

B64

HALLOWELL J.H.,DEVELOPMENT: FOR WHAT. WOR+45 POL/PAR SECT FOR/AID INT/TRADE CT/SYS PARTIC PRODUC PLURISM. PAGE 54 F1052 ECO/UNDEV CONSTN NAT/LISM ECO/TAC

B64

MANN B.,STATE CONSTITUTIONAL RESTRICTIONS ON LOCAL BORROWING AND PROPERTY TAXING POWERS. USA+45 CONSTN PROVS CT/SYS GOV/REL PWR...DECISION JURID CHARTS 20. PAGE 84 F1654 LOC/G TAX FINAN LAW

B64

MARSH D.C.,THE FUTURE OF THE WELFARE STATE. UK CONSTN NAT/G POL/PAR...POLICY WELF/ST 20. PAGE 86 F1676 NEW/LIB ADMIN CONCPT INSPECT

B64

STOESSINGER J.G.,FINANCING THE UNITED NATIONS SYSTEM. FUT WOR+45 CONSTN NAT/G VOL/ASSN DELIB/GP EX/STRUC ECO/TAC LEGIT CT/SYS PWR WEALTH...STAT TIME/SEQ TREND CHARTS TRUE/GP METH/GP TERR/GP VAL/FREE. PAGE 126 F2493 FINAN INT/ORG

B64

TELLADO A.,A STATEMENT OF THE LAWS OF THE DOMINICAN REPUBLIC IN MATTERS AFFECTING BUSINESS (3RD ED.). DOMIN/REP AGRI DIST/IND EXTR/IND FINAN FAM WORKER ECO/TAC TAX CT/SYS MARRIAGE OWN...BIBLIOG 20 MIGRATION. PAGE 129 F2542 CONSTN LEGIS NAT/G INDUS

B64

VON DER MEHDEN F.R.,POLITICS OF THE DEVELOPING NATIONS. WOR+45 CONSTN PROB/SOLV ORD/FREE WEALTH OBJECTIVE. PAGE 142 F2790 ECO/UNDEV SOCIETY STRUCT

B64

WHEARE K.C.,FEDERAL GOVERNMENT (4TH ED.). WOR+45 WOR-45 POL/PAR LEGIS BAL/PWR CT/SYS...POLICY JURID CONCPT GOV/COMP 17/20. PAGE 145 F2866 FEDERAL CONSTN EX/STRUC NAT/COMP

B65

GRIFFIN C.E.,THE FREE SOCIETY. CONSTN SOCIETY MARKET FEDERAL RATIONAL WEALTH...MAJORIT 20 CIVIL/LIB. PAGE 51 F0999 CONCPT ORD/FREE CAP/ISM POPULISM

B65

LUGO-MARENCO J.J.,A STATEMENT OF THE LAWS OF NICARAGUA IN MATTERS AFFECTING BUSINESS. NICARAGUA AGRI DIST/IND EXTR/IND FINAN INDUS FAM WORKER INT/TRADE TAX MARRIAGE OWN BIO/SOC 20 TREATY RESOURCE/N MIGRATION. PAGE 82 F1606 CONSTN NAT/G LEGIS JURID

B65

NATIONAL CONF SOCIAL WELFARE,THE SOCIAL WELFARE FORUM, 1965. LAW CULTURE VOL/ASSN CONTROL PERS/REL ADJUST POLICY. PAGE 97 F1899 CONSTN WEALTH ORD/FREE NEIGH

B65

PAYNE J.L.,LABOR AND POLITICS IN PERU; THE SYSTEM OF POLITICAL BARGAINING. PERU CONSTN VOL/ASSN EX/STRUC LEAD PWR...CHARTS 20. PAGE 104 F2042 LABOR POL/PAR BARGAIN GP/REL

B65

RATNAM K.J.,COMMUNALISM AND THE POLITICAL PROCESS IN MALAYA. MALAYSIA WOR+45 ECO/UNDEV PARTIC CHOOSE REPRESENT GP/REL CENTRAL ATTIT...CHARTS WORSHIP 20. PAGE 109 F2152 CONSTN GOV/REL REGION

B65

REDFORD E.S.,AMERICAN GOVERNMENT AND THE ECONOMY. FUT USA+45 USA-45 INDUS PROB/SOLV GOV/REL...POLICY DECISION METH/COMP BIBLIOG T 18/20. PAGE 110 F2168 CONSTN NAT/G

B65

WEIL G.L.,A HANDBOOK ON THE EUROPEAN ECONOMIC COMMUNITY. BELGIUM EUR+WWI FRANCE GERMANY/W ITALY CONSTN ECO/DEV CREATE PARTIC GP/REL...DECISION MGT CHARTS 20 EEC. PAGE 144 F2846 INT/TRADE INT/ORG TEC/DEV INT/LAW

C65

MANSFIELD H.C.,"THE CONGRESS AND ECONOMIC POLICY" IN C. TRUMAN ED., THE CONGRESS AND AMERICA'S FUTURE." USA+45 USA-45 CONSTN NAT/G BUDGET ADMIN CONTROL EXEC LOBBY. PAGE 85 F1661 POLICY ECO/TAC PWR LEGIS

C65

PEGRUM D.E.,"PUBLIC REGULATION OF BUSINESS (REV ED)" LAW CONSTN DIST/IND SERV/IND LG/CO LEGIS OWN LAISSEZ SOCISM...POLICY DECISION BIBLIOG 20. PAGE 104 F2048 INDUS PLAN NEW/LIB PRICE

B66

GREENE L.E.,GOVERNMENT IN TENNESSEE (2ND ED.). USA+45 DIST/IND INDUS POL/PAR EX/STRUC LEGIS PLAN BUDGET GIVE CT/SYS...MGT T 20 TENNESSEE. PAGE 51 F0989 PROVS LOC/G CONSTN ADMIN

B66

HOLT R.T.,THE POLITICAL BASIS OF ECONOMIC DEVELOPMENT. STRATA STRUCT NAT/G DIPLOM ADMIN...SOC NAT/COMP BIBLIOG 20. PAGE 61 F1201 ECO/TAC GOV/COMP CONSTN EX/STRUC

B66

KINDLEBERGER C.P.,EUROPE AND THE DOLLAR. AFR EUR+WWI FRANCE GERMANY/W USA+45 CONSTN INT/ORG DIPLOM INT/TRADE...ANTHOL 20. PAGE 71 F1395 BAL/PAY BUDGET FINAN ECO/DEV

B66

LEE R.A.,TRUMAN AND TAFT-HARTLEY: A QUESTION OF MANDATE. USA+45 LAW CONSTN LG/CO CONTROL LOBBY GOV/REL PEACE NEW/LIB 20 TRUMAN/HS CONGRESS. PAGE 77 F1507 LEGIS TOP/EX ADJUD LABOR

B66

RAPHAEL J.S.,GOVERNMENTAL REGULATION OF BUSINESS. USA+45 LAW CONSTN TAX ADJUD ADMIN EFFICIENCY PWR 20. PAGE 109 F2150 LG/CO GOV/REL CONTROL ECO/DEV

B66

US SENATE COMM LABOR-PUB WELF,AMEND THE RAILWAY LABOR ACT. USA+45 CONSTN CONSULT DELIB/GP ADJUD CONGRESS RAILROAD. PAGE 139 F2731 GP/REL LABOR DIST/IND LAW

B66

WALTON S.D.,AMERICAN BUSINESS AND ITS ENVIRONMENT. USA+45 LAW CONSTN FINAN MARKET LOC/G EX/STRUC CT/SYS COST PRODUC...STAT 20. PAGE 143 F2813 PRICE PROFIT

S66

ROTHCHILD D.,"THE LIMITS OF FEDERALISM: AN EXAMINATION OF POLITICAL INSTITUTIONAL TRANSFER IN AFRICA." AFR CONSTN CULTURE ELITES ECO/UNDEV KIN PROB/SOLV ADMIN ORD/FREE PWR...POLICY 20. PAGE 114 F2250 FEDERAL NAT/G NAT/LISM COLONIAL

B67
ANDERSON T.,RUSSIAN POLITICAL THOUGHT; AN INTRODUCTION. USSR NAT/G POL/PAR CHIEF MARXISM ...TIME/SEQ BIBLIOG 9/20. PAGE 5 F0099
TREND CONSTN ATTIT

B67
BUREAU NATIONAL AFFAIRS,LABOR RELATIONS REFERENCE MANUAL VOL. 63. USA+45 CONSTN ECO/DEV PROVS WORKER DEBATE INGP/REL...DECISION 20. PAGE 20 F0385
LABOR ADJUD CT/SYS NAT/G

B67
BUSEY J.L.,NOTES ON COSTA RICAN DEMOCRACY. COSTA/RICA L/A+17C NAT/G POL/PAR LEGIS CHOOSE OWN ATTIT...BIBLIOG 20. PAGE 20 F0394
CONSTN MAJORIT SOCIETY ECO/UNDEV

B67
CHO S.S.,KOREA IN WORLD POLITICS 1940-1950; AN EVALUATION OF AMERICAN RESPONSIBILITY. KOREA USA+45 USSR CONSTN INT/ORG NAT/G FORCES FOR/AID ANOMIE SUPEGO MARXISM...DECISION BIBLIOG 20. PAGE 24 F0469
POLICY DIPLOM PROB/SOLV WAR

B67
MCDOUGAL M.S.,THE INTERPRETATION OF AGREEMENTS AND WORLD PUBLIC ORDER: PRINCIPLES OF CONTENT AND PROCEDURE. WOR+45 CONSTN PROB/SOLV TEC/DEV ...CON/ANAL TREATY. PAGE 88 F1727
INT/LAW STRUCT ECO/UNDEV DIPLOM

B67
MENDEL A.P.,POLITICAL MEMOIRS 1905-1917 BY PAUL MILIUKOV (TRANS. BY CARL GOLDBERG). USSR AGRI DIPLOM ECO/TAC POPULISM...MAJORIT 20. PAGE 90 F1757
BIOG LEAD NAT/G CONSTN

B67
MORRIS A.J.A.,PARLIAMENTARY DEMOCRACY IN THE NINETEENTH CENTURY. UK INDUS LOC/G NAT/G POL/PAR CONSULT LEGIS INT/TRADE ADMIN CHOOSE SUFF SOVEREIGN 19 PARLIAMENT. PAGE 93 F1835
TIME/SEQ CONSTN PARL/PROC POPULISM

B67
MUHAMMAD A.C.,THE EMERGENCE OF PAKISTAN. PAKISTAN S/ASIA CONSTN ECO/UNDEV NAT/G CONTROL NAT/LISM 20. PAGE 94 F1853
DIPLOM COLONIAL SECT PROB/SOLV

B67
PIKE F.B.,FREEDOM AND REFORM IN LATIN AMERICA. BRAZIL URUGUAY CONSTN CULTURE SECT DIPLOM EDU/PROP PARTIC DRIVE ALL/VALS CATHISM...GEOG ANTHOL BIBLIOG REFORMERS BOLIV. PAGE 106 F2086
L/A+17C ORD/FREE ECO/UNDEV REV

B67
PRINCE C.E.,NEW JERSEY'S JEFFERSONIAN REPUBLICANS; THE GENESIS OF AN EARLY PARTY MACHINE (1789-1817). USA-45 LOC/G EDU/PROP PRESS CONTROL CHOOSE...CHARTS 18/19 NEW/JERSEY REPUBLICAN. PAGE 108 F2117
POL/PAR CONSTN ADMIN PROVS

B67
SCHAEFER W.V.,THE SUSPECT AND SOCIETY: CRIMINAL PROCEDURE AND CONVERGING CONSTITUTIONAL DOCTRINES. USA+45 TEC/DEV LOBBY ROUTINE SANCTION...INT 20. PAGE 116 F2288
CRIME FORCES CONSTN JURID

B67
SPICER G.W.,THE SUPREME COURT AND FUNDAMENTAL FREEDOMS (2ND ED.). USA+45 CONSTN SOCIETY ATTIT 20 SUPREME/CT. PAGE 124 F2454
CT/SYS JURID CONTROL ORD/FREE

B67
SPIRO H.S.,PATTERNS OF AFRICAN DEVLOPMENT: FIVE COMPARISONS. STRUCT ECO/UNDEV NAT/G CONSERVE SOCISM ...PREDICT NAT/COMP 20 CHINJAP. PAGE 125 F2457
AFR CONSTN NAT/LISM TREND

B67
VENKATESWARAN R.J.,CABINET GOVERNMENT IN INDIA. INDIA UK SOCIETY OP/RES COLONIAL LEAD EFFICIENCY ORD/FREE 20. PAGE 141 F2776
DELIB/GP ADMIN CONSTN NAT/G

B67
WILLIAMS M.,THE EAST IS RED: THE VIEW INSIDE CHINA. CHINA/COM CONSTN COERCE AGE/Y ATTIT PERSON...OBS 20 MAO. PAGE 147 F2893
REV MARXIST GP/REL DIPLOM

L67
"GOVERNMENT CONTROL OF LAND: PROTECTING THE I-KNOW-IT-WHENI-SEE-IT INTEREST." USA+45 LAW CONSTN DELIB/GP CT/SYS HABITAT ILLINOIS. PAGE 2 F0026
PLAN LOC/G CONTROL ADJUD

L67
AUSTIN D.A.,"POLITICAL CONFLICT IN AFRICA." CONSTN NAT/G CREATE ADMIN COLONIAL ORD/FREE MARXISM POPULISM SOCISM...NAT/COMP ANTHOL 20. PAGE 8 F0141
ANOMIE AFR POL/PAR

L67
GOLD J.,"INTERPRETATION BY THE INTERNATIONAL MONETARY FUND OF ITS ARTICLES OF AGREEMENT." INT/TRADE ADJUD ATTIT...POLICY JURID. PAGE 48 F0933
CONSTN INT/ORG LAW DIPLOM

L67
LAMBERT J.D.,"CORPORATE POLITICAL SPENDING AND CAMPAIGN FINANCE." LAW CONSTN FINAN LABOR LG/CO LOC/G NAT/G VOL/ASSN TEC/DEV ADJUD ADMIN PARTIC. PAGE 75 F1463
USA+45 POL/PAR CHOOSE COST

L67
MIXON J.,"JANE JACOBS AND THE LAW - ZONING FOR DIVERSITY EXAMINED." FUT USA+45 CONSTN NEIGH PROB/SOLV CONTROL CT/SYS PARTIC ATTIT...POLICY CENSUS METH/COMP MUNICH. PAGE 92 F1810
IDEA/COMP PLAN LAW

L67
SCALAPINO R.A.,"A SURVEY OF ASIA IN 1966." ASIA S/ASIA CONSTN SOCIETY POL/PAR CHIEF WAR...ANTHOL 20. PAGE 116 F2285
DIPLOM

S67
"THE FEDERAL AGRICULTURAL STABILIZATION PROGRAM AND THE NEGRO." LAW CONSTN PLAN REPRESENT DISCRIM ORD/FREE 20 NEGRO CONGRESS. PAGE 2 F0025
AGRI CONTROL NAT/G RACE/REL

S67
"IMPORT-EXPORT CLAUSE: A BLANKET PROHIBITION MISAPPLIED." USA+45 INT/TRADE ADJUD INCOME PWR 20. PAGE 2 F0029
CONSTN TAX PROVS LAW

S67
CATTELL D.T.,"THE FIFTIETH ANNIVERSARY: A SOVIET WATERSHED?" USSR CONSTN ECO/DEV NAT/G LEAD TOTALISM 20 KHRUSH/N. PAGE 22 F0430
MARXISM CHIEF POLICY ADJUST

S67
FINER S.E.,"THE ONE-PARTY REGIMES IN AFRICA: RECONSIDERATIONS." AFR DOMIN CONSEN ORD/FREE 20. PAGE 41 F0798
ELITES POL/PAR CONSTN ECO/UNDEV

S67
GRAHAM R.,"BRAZIL'S DILEMMA." BRAZIL FUT L/A+17C NAT/G CHIEF PROB/SOLV ECO/TAC PWR 20. PAGE 50 F0972
ECO/UNDEV CONSTN POL/PAR POLICY

S67
GREGORY R.,"THE MINISTER'S LINE: OR, THE M4 COMES TO BERKSHIRE. PART I." UK CONSTN DIST/IND LEGIS TOP/EX PLAN ADJUD...GEOG 20. PAGE 51 F0994
DECISION CONSTRUC NAT/G DELIB/GP

S67
HEATH D.B.,"BOLIVIA UNDER BARRIENTOS." L/A+17C NAT/G CHIEF DIPLOM ECO/TAC...POLICY 20 BOLIV. PAGE 58 F1132
ECO/UNDEV POL/PAR REV CONSTN

S67
KOHN W.S.G.,"THE SOVEREIGNTY OF LIECHTENSTEIN." LIECHTENST SWITZERLND USSR CONSTN DEBATE WAR CONSERVE 18/20 UN. PAGE 72 F1417
SOVEREIGN NAT/G PWR DIPLOM

S67
MITCHELL J.D.B.,"THE CONSTITUTIONAL IMPLICATIONS OF JUDICIAL CONTROL OF THE ADMINISTRATION IN THE UNITED KINGDOM." UK LAW ADJUD ADMIN GOV/REL ROLE ...GP/COMP 20. PAGE 92 F1808
CONSTN CT/SYS CONTROL EX/STRUC

S67
NEALE R.S.,"WORKING CLASS WOMEN AND WOMEN'S SUFFRAGE." UK LAW CONSTN LABOR NAT/G DELIB/GP LEGIS WORKER PAY PARTIC CHOOSE 19 FEMALE/SEX. PAGE 97 F1906
STRATA SEX SUFF DISCRIM

S67
NILES J.G.,"CIVIL ACTIONS FOR DAMAGES UNDER THE FEDERAL CIVIL RIGHTS STATUTES." CONSTN FINAN ADJUD CT/SYS GOV/REL RACE/REL 20. PAGE 98 F1928
DISCRIM LAW CONTROL ORD/FREE

S67
OLIVIER G.,"ASPECTS JURIDIQUES DE L'ADOPTION DU TRAITE CECA A LA CRISE CHARBONNIERE (SUITE ET FIN)" LAW DIST/IND PLAN DIPLOM RATION PRICE ADMIN COST DEMAND...POLICY CON/ANAL ECSC TREATY. PAGE 101 F1988
INT/TRADE INT/ORG EXTR/IND CONSTN

S67
PEMBERTON J., JR.,"CONSTITUTIONAL PROBLEMS IN RESTRAINT ON THE MEDIA." CONSTN PROB/SOLV EDU/PROP CONFER CONTROL JURID. PAGE 104 F2054
LAW PRESS ORD/FREE

S67
THEROUX P.,"HATING THE ASIANS." TANZANIA UGANDA CONSTN INDUS NAT/G POL/PAR WORKER ECO/TAC HABITAT LOVE...POLICY GEOG 20 MIGRATION. PAGE 130 F2557
AFR RACE/REL SOVEREIGN ATTIT

S67
WHITE W.L.,"THE TREASURY BOARD AND PARLIAMENT." CANADA CONSTN CONSULT LEGIS LEAD PARL/PROC GP/REL ...DECISION 20. PAGE 146 F2871
FINAN DELIB/GP NAT/G ADMIN

B96
MARX K.,REVOLUTION AND COUNTER-REVOLUTION. GERMANY CONSTN ELITES INDUS NAT/G DIPLOM ECO/TAC WEALTH. PAGE 86 F1693
MARXIST REV PWR STRATA

CONSTN/CNV....CONSTITUTIONAL CONVENTION

CONSTRUC....CONSTRUCTION INDUSTRY

N
US LIBRARY OF CONGRESS,SELECTED AND ANNOTATED BIBLIOGRAPHY ON INDUSTRIAL PROBLEMS AND POLICIES IN WARTIME (PAMPHLET). WOR-45 CONSTRUC NAT/G PROB/SOLV COST DEMAND PRODUC 20. PAGE 137 F2707
BIBLIOG/A ECO/DEV INDUS WAR

N
US SUPERINTENDENT OF DOCUMENTS,CENSUS PUBLICATIONS (PRICE LIST 70). AGRI CONSTRUC DIST/IND FINAN LOC/G NAT/G PROVS INT/TRADE APPORT INCOME. PAGE 140 F2751
BIBLIOG/A CENSUS STAT USA+45

N
US SUPERINTENDENT OF DOCUMENTS,LABOR (PRICE LIST 33). USA+45 LAW AGRI CONSTRUC INDUS NAT/G BARGAIN PRICE ADMIN AUTOMAT PRODUC MGT. PAGE 140 F2753
BIBLIOG/A WORKER LABOR LEGIS

N19
EAST KENTUCKY REGIONAL PLAN,PROGRAM 60: A DECADE OF ACTION FOR PROGRESS IN EASTERN KENTUCKY (PAMPHLET). USA+45 AGRI CONSTRUC INDUS CONSULT ACT/RES PROB/SOLV EDU/PROP GOV/REL HEALTH KENTUCKY. PAGE 35 F0689
REGION ADMIN PLAN ECO/UNDEV

N19
EAST KENTUCKY REGIONAL PLAN,PROGRAM 60 REPORT: ACTION FOR PORGRESS IN EASTERN KENTUCKY (PAMPHLET). USA+45 CONSTRUC INDUS ACT/RES PROB/SOLV EDU/PROP ADMIN GOV/REL KENTUCKY. PAGE 35 F0690
REGION PLAN ECO/UNDEV CONSULT

N19
MUSHKIN S.J.,LOCAL SCHOOL EXPENDITURES: 1970 PROJECTIONS (PAMPHLET). FUT USA+45 CONSTRUC FINAN PROVS EDU/PROP COST...GEOG CENSUS PREDICT CHARTS SIMUL 20. PAGE 95 F1871
LOC/G SCHOOL BUDGET

N19
YLVISAKER P.N.,THE NATURAL CEMENT ISSUE (PAMPHLET). USA+45 USA-45 CONSTRUC PROVS CAP/ISM ADMIN LOBBY PERS/REL OWN RIGID/FLEX ROLE 20 MINNESOTA. PAGE 150 F2948
POLICY NAT/G PLAN GOV/REL

B55
OECD,MARSHALL PLAN IN TURKEY. TURKEY USA+45 COM/IND CONSTRUC SERV/IND FORCES BUDGET...STAT 20 MARSHL/PLN. PAGE 100 F1964
FOR/AID ECO/UNDEV AGRI INDUS

S56
LANDAUER J.D.,"PROFESSIONAL CONSULTANTS: A NEW FACTOR IN REAL ESTATE." USA+45 PROB/SOLV ECO/TAC PERS/REL DEMAND EFFICIENCY DECISION. PAGE 75 F1467
CONSULT CONSTRUC CLIENT

S59
STINCHCOMBE A.L.,"BUREAUCRATIC AND CRAFT ADMINISTRATION OF PRODUCTION: A COMPARATIVE STUDY" (BMR)" USA+45 STRUCT EX/STRUC ECO/TAC GP/REL ...CLASSIF GP/COMP IDEA/COMP GEN/LAWS 20 WEBER/MAX. PAGE 126 F2490
CONSTRUC PROC/MFG ADMIN PLAN

B60
GRIER E.,PRIVATELY DEVELOPED INTERRACIAL HOUSING: AN ANALYSIS OF EXPERIENCE. FINAN MARKET COST DISCRIM PROFIT SOC/INTEG 20. PAGE 51 F0997
RACE/REL CONSTRUC HABITAT

B62
LICHFIELD N.,COST-BENEFIT ANALYSIS IN URBAN REDEVELOPMENT. CONSTRUC LOC/G NEIGH ACT/RES PROB/SOLV TEC/DEV BUDGET TAX...DECISION STAT CHARTS SOC/EXP MUNICH 20. PAGE 80 F1558
PLAN COST GOV/REL

B62
MOWITZ R.J.,PROFILE OF A METROPOLIS: A CASE BOOK. COM/IND CONSTRUC INDUS PUB/INST PLAN TEC/DEV LEAD GP/REL...POLICY TECHNIC WELF/ST MUNICH. PAGE 94 F1851
DECISION ADMIN

B64
FRIEDEN B.J.,THE FUTURE OF OLD NEIGHBORHOODS: REBUILDING FOR A CHANGING POPULATION. CONSTRUC LOC/G NAT/G ACT/RES ECO/TAC REGION ATTIT...INT SAMP MUNICH 20 NEWYORK/C LOS/ANG HARTFORD URBAN/RNWL. PAGE 44 F0855
NEIGH PROB/SOLV PLAN BUDGET

B64
GREBLER L.,URBAN RENEWAL IN EUROPEAN COUNTRIES: ITS EMERGENCE AND POTENTIALS. EUR+WWI UK ECO/DEV LOC/G NEIGH CREATE ADMIN ATTIT...TREND NAT/COMP MUNICH 20 URBAN/RNWL. PAGE 50 F0981
PLAN CONSTRUC NAT/G

B64
RESOURCES FOR THE FUTURE,URBAN AND REGIONAL STUDIES AT US UNIVERSITIES; A REPORT BASED ON A 1963 SURVEY OF URBAN AND REGIONAL RESEARCH. USA+45 SOCIETY CONSTRUC DIST/IND ACADEM NAT/G ACT/RES ECO/TAC ...CENSUS IDEA/COMP MUNICH. PAGE 111 F2179
BIBLIOG/A REGION PLAN

B65
BEYER G.H.,HOUSING AND SOCIETY. USA+45 ECO/DEV FAM NAT/G PLAN RENT...CHARTS BIBLIOG MUNICH 20. PAGE 14 F0275
HABITAT AGE/O CONSTRUC

B65
DUGGAR G.S.,RENEWAL OF TOWN AND VILLAGE I: A WORLD-WIDE SURVEY OF LOCAL GOVERNMENT EXPERIENCE. WOR+45 CONSTRUC INDUS CREATE BUDGET REGION GOV/REL...QU NAT/COMP MUNICH 20 URBAN/RNWL. PAGE 35 F0673
NEIGH PLAN ADMIN

S65
TENDLER J.D.,"TECHNOLOGY AND ECONOMIC DEVELOPMENT* THE CASE OF HYDRO VS THERMAL POWER." CONSTRUC DIST/IND CREATE TEC/DEV INT/TRADE CENTRAL PWR SKILL WEALTH...MGT NAT/COMP ARGEN. PAGE 129 F2544
BRAZIL INDUS ECO/UNDEV

L67
GLAZER N.,"HOUSING PROBLEMS AND HOUSING POLICIES." USA+45 PLAN RENT ADJUST CONSEN DEMAND DISCRIM AGE ATTIT HEALTH WEALTH MUNICH NEGRO. PAGE 48 F0929
POLICY CONSTRUC CREATE HABITAT

L67
ROBERTS E.F.,"THE CASE OF THE UNWARY HOME BUYER: THE HOUSING MERCHANT DID IT." USA+45 CLIENT DIST/IND MARKET LG/CO SML/CO PROB/SOLV LEGIT COST PROFIT. PAGE 112 F2207
ADJUD CONSTRUC OWN LAW

S67
GRAYSON D.K.,"RISK ALLOCATIONS UNDER THE PERMITS AND RESPONSIBILITIES CLAUSE OF THE STANDARD GOVERNMENT CONSTRUCTION CONTRACT." USA+45 LAW WORKER. PAGE 50 F0979
CONSTRUC CONTROL RISK NAT/G

S67
GREGORY R.,"THE MINISTER'S LINE: OR, THE M4 COMES TO BERKSHIRE. PART I." UK CONSTN DIST/IND LEGIS TOP/EX PLAN ADJUD...GEOG 20. PAGE 51 F0994
DECISION CONSTRUC NAT/G DELIB/GP

S67
HANCOCK J.L.,"PLANNERS IN THE CHANGING AMERICAN CITY, 1900-1940." USA-45 CONSTRUC NAT/G POL/PAR ...SOC/WK TREND MUNICH 20. PAGE 54 F1059
PLAN CONSULT LOC/G

S67
KENDALL R.J.,"CHANGED CONDITIONS AS MISREPRESENTATION IN GOVERNMENT CONSTRUCTION CONTRACTS." USA+45 BARGAIN ADJUD COST. PAGE 70 F1375
CONTROL CONSTRUC NAT/G LAW

S67
LEFCOE G.,"CONSTRUCTION LENDING AND THE EQUITABLE LIEN." LICENSE CT/SYS OWN...STAT 20. PAGE 77 F1510
CONSTRUC RENT ADJUD

CONSTRUCTION INDUSTRY....SEE CONSTRUC

CONSULT....CONSULTANTS

N
NEW JERSEY STATE OF,SECOND REPORT TO GOVERNOR, SENATE, ASSEMBLY BY UNIFORM COMMERCIAL CODE STUDY COMMISSION. USA+45 INDUS LOC/G NAT/G PROF/ORG CONSULT ACT/RES LEGIT CT/SYS ATTIT NEW/JERSEY. PAGE 98 F1920
LAW FINAN CENTRAL PROVS

N19
ADMINISTRATIVE STAFF COLLEGE,THE ACCOUNTABILITY OF GOVERNMENT DEPARTMENTS (PAMPHLET) (REV. ED.). UK CONSTN FINAN NAT/G CONSULT ADMIN INGP/REL CONSEN PRIVIL 20 PARLIAMENT. PAGE 2 F0043
PARL/PROC ELITES SANCTION PROB/SOLV

N19
EAST KENTUCKY REGIONAL PLAN,PROGRAM 60: A DECADE OF ACTION FOR PROGRESS IN EASTERN KENTUCKY (PAMPHLET). USA+45 AGRI CONSTRUC INDUS CONSULT ACT/RES PROB/SOLV EDU/PROP GOV/REL HEALTH KENTUCKY. PAGE 35 F0689
REGION ADMIN PLAN ECO/UNDEV

N19
EAST KENTUCKY REGIONAL PLAN,PROGRAM 60 REPORT: ACTION FOR PORGRESS IN EASTERN KENTUCKY (PAMPHLET). USA+45 CONSTRUC INDUS ACT/RES PROB/SOLV EDU/PROP ADMIN GOV/REL KENTUCKY. PAGE 35 F0690
REGION PLAN ECO/UNDEV CONSULT

N19
SILVERMAN C.,THE PRESIDENT'S ECONOMIC ADVISERS (PAMPHLET). USA+45 LAW ELITES ECO/DEV EX/STRUC ADMIN LEAD GOV/REL PERS/REL ROLE...POLICY DECISION 20 PRESIDENT CONGRESS EISNHWR/DD. PAGE 122 F2404
CONSULT PROB/SOLV NAT/G PLAN

N19
STALEY E.,SCIENTIFIC RESEARCH AND PROGRESS IN NEWLY DEVELOPING COUNTRIES (PAMPHLET). AFR ASIA L/A+17C CONSULT DIPLOM...METH/COMP 20. PAGE 125 F2463
ECO/UNDEV ACT/RES FOR/AID TEC/DEV

B31
LORWIN L.L.,ADVISORY ECONOMIC COUNCILS. EUR+WWI FRANCE GERMANY PROB/SOLV INGP/REL...CLASSIF GP/COMP. PAGE 82 F1601
CONSULT DELIB/GP ECO/TAC NAT/G

B32
WRIGHT Q.,GOLD AND MONETARY STABILIZATION. FUT USA-45 WOR-45 INTELL ECO/DEV INT/ORG NAT/G CONSULT PLAN ECO/TAC ADMIN ATTIT WEALTH...CONCPT TREND 20. PAGE 149 F2935
FINAN POLICY

B44
BIENSTOCK G.,MANAGEMENT IN RUSSIAN INDUSTRY AND AGRICULTURE. USSR CONSULT WORKER LEAD COST PROFIT ATTIT DRIVE PWR...MGT METH/COMP DICTIONARY ACCT 20. PAGE 15 F0281
ADMIN MARXISM SML/CO AGRI

B47
GORDON D.L.,THE HIDDEN WEAPON: THE STORY OF ECONOMIC WARFARE. EUR+WWI USA-45 LAW FINAN INDUS NAT/G CONSULT FORCES PLAN DOMIN PWR WEALTH ...INT/LAW CONCPT OBS TOT/POP NAZI 20. PAGE 49 F0955
INT/ORG ECO/TAC INT/TRADE WAR

B47
MILLETT J.D.,THE PROCESS AND ORGANIZATION OF GOVERNMENT PLANNING. USA+45 DELIB/GP ACT/RES LEAD LOBBY TASK...POLICY GEOG TIME 20 RESOURCE/N. PAGE 91 F1793
ADMIN NAT/G PLAN CONSULT

B49
HANSEN A.H.,MONETARY THEORY AND FISCAL POLICY. CONSULT PLAN INT/TRADE BAL/PAY OPTIMAL...TREND CHARTS METH/COMP BIBLIOG T 19/20 MONEY. PAGE 54 F1063
FINAN GEN/LAWS POLICY ECO/TAC

B49
SELZNICK P.,TVA AND THE GRASS ROOTS: A STUDY IN THE SOCIOLOGY OF FORMAL ORGANIZATION. USA-45 EX/STRUC PROB/SOLV CONFER PARTIC ROUTINE PWR 20 TVA. PAGE 119 F2353
REPRESENT LOBBY CONSULT

S50
DREYFUS S.,"THE INDUSTRIAL DESIGNER AND THE BUSINESSMAN." SERV/IND PROB/SOLV ECO/TAC COST EFFICIENCY PROFIT RATIONAL...DECISION MGT. PAGE 34 F0662
CONSULT INDUS PRODUC UTIL

B52
SECRETARIAT COUNCIL OF EUROPE,THE STRASBOURG PLAN. EUR+WWI CONSULT PLAN ECO/TAC TARIFFS DEBATE REGION 20 COUNCL/EUR STRASBOURG. PAGE 119 F2340
INT/ORG ECO/DEV INT/TRADE DIPLOM

S53
BLOUGH R.,"THE ROLE OF THE ECONOMIST IN FEDERAL POLICY MAKING." USA+45 ELITES INTELL ECO/DEV NAT/G CONSULT EX/STRUC ACT/RES PLAN INT/TRADE BAL/PAY WEALTH...POLICY METH/GP CONGRESS 20. PAGE 16 F0301
DELIB/GP ECO/TAC

S53
LINCOLN G.,"FACTORS DETERMINING ARMS AID." COM FUT USA+45 USSR WOR+45 ECO/DEV NAT/G CONSULT PLAN TEC/DEV DIPLOM DOMIN EDU/PROP PERCEPT PWR ...DECISION CONCPT TREND MARX/KARL 20. PAGE 80 F1566
FORCES POLICY BAL/PWR FOR/AID

B54
BERNSTEIN I.,ARBITRATION OF WAGES. USA+45 CONSULT PAY COST PRODUC WEALTH...CHARTS 20. PAGE 14 F0266
DELIB/GP BARGAIN WORKER PRICE

B54
HOBBS E.H.,BEHIND THE PRESIDENT - A STUDY OF EXECUTIVE OFFICE AGENCIES. USA+45 NAT/G PLAN BUDGET ECO/TAC EXEC ORD/FREE 20 BUR/BUDGET. PAGE 60 F1183
EX/STRUC DELIB/GP CONFER CONSULT

L54
OPLER M.E.,"SOCIAL ASPECTS OF TECHNICAL ASSISTANCE IN OPERATION." WOR+45 VOL/ASSN CREATE PLAN TEC/DEV EDU/PROP ALL/VALS...METH/CNCPT OBS RECORD TREND UN 20. PAGE 101 F1993
INT/ORG CONSULT FOR/AID

B55
BERNSTEIN M.H.,REGULATING BUSINESS BY INDEPENDENT COMMISSION. USA+45 USA-45 LG/CO CHIEF LEGIS PROB/SOLV ADJUD SANCTION GP/REL ATTIT...TIME/SEQ 19/20 MONOPOLY PRESIDENT CONGRESS. PAGE 14 F0268
DELIB/GP CONTROL CONSULT

B55
BLOOM G.F.,ECONOMICS OF LABOR RELATIONS. USA+45 LAW CONSULT WORKER CAP/ISM PAY ADJUD CONTROL EFFICIENCY ORD/FREE...CHARTS 19/20 AFL/CIO NLRB DEPT/LABOR. PAGE 16 F0299
ECO/DEV ECO/TAC LABOR GOV/REL

B55
FOGARTY M.P.,ECONOMIC CONTROL. FUT UK ECO/DEV FINAN CONSULT INT/TRADE...CHARTS BIBLIOG/A 20. PAGE 42 F0819
ECO/TAC NAT/G CONTROL PROB/SOLV

B55
JOHR W.A.,THE ROLE OF THE ECONOMIST AS OFFICIAL ADVISER. WOR+45 INTELL ECO/DEV NAT/G PLAN GP/REL ROLE...DECISION PREDICT IDEA/COMP. PAGE 68 F1336
CONSULT ECO/TAC POLICY INGP/REL

S55
KELLY W.E.,"HOW SALES EXECUTIVES USE FACTORING TO BOOST SALES AND PROFITS TODAY." FINAN LG/CO BUDGET EFFICIENCY PROFIT...MGT PRODUCT. PAGE 70 F1372
INDUS ECO/DEV CONSULT MARKET

S56
GORDON L.,"THE ORGANIZATION FOR EUROPEAN ECONOMIC COOPERATION." EUR+WWI INDUS INT/ORG NAT/G CONSULT DELIB/GP ACT/RES CREATE PLAN TEC/DEV EDU/PROP LEGIT WEALTH OEEC 20. PAGE 49 F0956
VOL/ASSN ECO/DEV

S56
LANDAUER J.D.,"PROFESSIONAL CONSULTANTS: A NEW FACTOR IN REAL ESTATE." USA+45 PROB/SOLV ECO/TAC PERS/REL DEMAND EFFICIENCY DECISION. PAGE 75 F1467
CONSULT CONSTRUC CLIENT

S56
MYERS C.A.,"LINE AND STAFF IN INDUSTRIAL RELATIONS." INDUS LABOR GP/REL PWR...MGT INT. PAGE 96 F1876
ROLE PROB/SOLV ADMIN CONSULT

B57
LAVES W.H.C.,UNESCO. FUT WOR+45 NAT/G CONSULT DELIB/GP TEC/DEV ECO/TAC EDU/PROP PEACE ORD/FREE ...CONCPT TIME/SEQ TREND UNESCO VAL/FREE 20. PAGE 76 F1491
INT/ORG KNOWL

B57
TRIFFIN R.,EUROPE AND THE MONEY MUDDLE. USA+45 INT/ORG NAT/G CONSULT PLAN ECO/TAC EXEC ROUTINE BAL/PAY WEALTH...METH/CNCPT OBS TREND CHARTS STERTYP GEN/METH EEC TERR/GP VAL/FREE ECSC. PAGE 131 F2587
EUR+WWI ECO/DEV REGION

L57
MASS. INST. TECH.,"THE CENTER FOR INTERNATIONAL STUDIES." AFR ASIA COM EUR+WWI ISLAM L/A+17C S/ASIA USA+45 USA-45 DIST/IND CONSULT FORCES ACT/RES TEC/DEV DIPLOM REV ATTIT WEALTH...CONCPT FOR/TRADE 20. PAGE 87 F1702
R+D ECO/UNDEV

S57
ANSHEN M.,"BUSINESS, LAWYERS, AND ECONOMISTS." PROB/SOLV ECO/TAC CONFER PROFIT RIGID/FLEX OBJECTIVE...MGT GP/COMP. PAGE 6 F0106
INDUS CONSULT ROUTINE EFFICIENCY

S57
CUNNINGHAM E.M.,"THE BUSINESS MAN AND HIS LAWYER." USA+45 LG/CO SML/CO TOP/EX CHOOSE SKILL...JURID MGT 20. PAGE 29 F0561
CONSULT LAW DECISION SERV/IND

B58
CROWE S.,THE LANDSCAPE OF POWER. UK CULTURE SERV/IND NAT/G CONSULT PARTIC NUC/PWR LEISURE...SOC EXHIBIT 20. PAGE 29 F0559
HABITAT TEC/DEV PLAN CONTROL

B58
WOODS H.D.,PATTERNS OF INDUSTRIAL DISPUTE SETTLEMENT IN FIVE CANADIAN INDUSTRIES. CANADA USA+45 CONSULT ADJUD GP/REL...JURID GOV/COMP METH/COMP ANTHOL 20. PAGE 148 F2923
BARGAIN INDUS LABOR NAT/G

B59
DIEBOLD W. JR.,THE SCHUMAN PLAN: A STUDY IN ECONOMIC COOPERATION, 1950-1959. EUR+WWI FRANCE GERMANY USA+45 EXTR/IND CONSULT DELIB/GP PLAN DIPLOM ECO/TAC INT/TRADE ROUTINE ORD/FREE WEALTH ...METH/CNCPT STAT CONT/OBS INT TIME/SEQ ECSC 20. PAGE 33 F0635
INT/ORG REGION

L59
GARDNER R.N.,"NEW DIRECTIONS IN UNITED STATES FOREIGN ECONOMIC POLICY." AFR USA+45 CONSULT ...GEN/LAWS GEN/METH FOR/TRADE 20. PAGE 46 F0903
ECO/UNDEV ECO/TAC FOR/AID DIPLOM

S59
ALKHIMOV V.S.,"SOVIET FOREIGN TRADE CHANNELS." COM FUT USA+45 USSR ECO/DEV MARKET CONSULT PLAN WEALTH ...MARXIST OBS CON/ANAL FOR/TRADE 20. PAGE 4 F0068
FINAN ECO/TAC DIPLOM

S59
HOFFMAN P.,"OPERATION BREAKTHROUGH." AFR S/ASIA STRUCT INDUS CONSULT TEC/DEV ATTIT RIGID/FLEX SKILL WEALTH...TECHNIC CONCPT STYLE RECORD CHARTS ORG/CHARTS GEN/METH VAL/FREE 20. PAGE 61 F1190
ECO/UNDEV EDU/PROP FOR/AID

S59
REUBENS E.D.,"THE BASIS FOR REORIENATION OF AMERICAN FOREIGN AID POLICY." USA+45 USSR STRUCT INT/ORG CONSULT ECO/TAC ADMIN DRIVE MORAL ORD/FREE PWR WEALTH...RELATIV MATH STAT TREND GEN/LAWS VAL/FREE 20. PAGE 111 F2180
ECO/UNDEV PLAN FOR/AID DIPLOM

S59
TEITSWORTH C.S.,"GROWING ROLE OF THE COMPANY ECONOMIST." USA+45 PLAN PROB/SOLV CAP/ISM ECO/TAC ADMIN ATTIT MGT. PAGE 129 F2541
INDUS CONSULT UTIL DECISION

B60
APTHEKER H.,DISARMAMENT AND THE AMERICAN ECONOMY: A SYMPOSIUM. FUT USA+45 ECO/DEV DIST/IND FINAN INDUS PROC/MFG LABOR NAT/G POL/PAR CONSULT PLAN CAP/ISM INT/TRADE PEACE ATTIT MORAL WEALTH...TREND GEN/LAWS TOT/POP 20. PAGE 6 F0110
MARXIST ARMS/CONT

B60
BLACK E.R.,THE DIPLOMACY OF ECONOMIC DEVELOPMENT. WOR+45 CONSULT PLAN TEC/DEV DIPLOM ECO/TAC FOR/AID ...CONCPT TREND 20. PAGE 15 F0290
ECO/UNDEV ACT/RES

B60
ROOLEY B.J.,THE EVOLUTION OF BRITISH PLANNING LEGISLATION. UK ECO/DEV LOC/G CONSULT DELIB/GP ADMIN MUNICH 20 URBAN/RNWL. PAGE 107 F2104
PLAN LEGIS PROB/SOLV

B60
STEIN E.,AMERICAN ENTERPRISE IN THE EUROPEAN COMMON MARKET: A LEGAL PROFILE. EUR+WWI FUT USA+45 SOCIETY STRUCT ECO/DEV NAT/G VOL/ASSN CONSULT PLAN TEC/DEV ECO/TAC INT/TRADE ADMIN ATTIT RIGID/FLEX PWR...MGT NEW/IDEA STAT TREND COMPUT/IR SIMUL EEC 20. PAGE 125 F2475
MARKET ADJUD INT/LAW

B60
WENTHOLT W.,INFLATION OR SECURITY? EUR+WWI USA+45 INDUS CONSULT TEC/DEV CAP/ISM DIPLOM FOR/AID INT/TRADE MARXISM 20 EEC. PAGE 145 F2858
ECO/DEV ECO/TAC FINAN ORD/FREE

S60
BECKER A.S.,"COMPARISIONS OF UNITED STATES AND USSR NATIONAL OUTPUT: SOME RULES OF THE GAME." COM USA+45 ECO/DEV AGRI DIST/IND INDUS R+D CONSULT PLAN ECO/TAC RIGID/FLEX KNOWL...METH/CNCPT CHARTS 20. PAGE 12 F0227
STAT USSR

S60
ENKE S.,"THE ECONOMIES OF GOVERNMENT PAYMENTS TO LIMIT POPULATION." FUT INDIA WOR+45 CULTURE FINAN NAT/G CONSULT PLAN LEGIT CONTROL COST ATTIT RIGID/FLEX HEALTH WEALTH...STAT OBS CHARTS TOT/POP VAL/FREE 20. PAGE 38 F0736
FAM ACT/RES

S60
HERRERA F.,"THE INTER-AMERICAN DEVELOPMENT BANK." USA+45 ECO/UNDEV INT/ORG CONSULT DELIB/GP PLAN ECO/TAC INT/TRADE ROUTINE WEALTH...STAT TERR/GP 20. PAGE 59 F1153
L/A+17C FINAN FOR/AID REGION

S60
JACOBSON H.K.,"THE USSR AND ILO." AFR COM STRUCT ECO/DEV ECO/UNDEV CONSULT DELIB/GP ECO/TAC ILO WORK 20. PAGE 66 F1298
INT/ORG LABOR USSR

S60
MILLER A.S.,"SOME OBSERVATIONS ON THE POLITICAL ECONOMY OF POPULATION GROWTH." FUT USA+45 ECO/DEV R+D CONSULT PLAN TEC/DEV ECO/TAC ROUTINE BIO/SOC WEALTH...POLICY OBS. PAGE 91 F1790
SOCIETY GEOG

S60
NICHOLS J.P.,"HAZARDS OF AMERICAN PRIVATE INVESTMENT IN UNDERDEVELOPED COUNTRIES." FUT L/A+17C USA+45 USA-45 EXTR/IND CONSULT BAL/PWR ECO/TAC DOMIN ADJUD ATTIT SOVEREIGN WEALTH ...HIST/WRIT TIME/SEQ TREND TERR/GP VAL/FREE 20. PAGE 98 F1924
FINAN ECO/UNDEV CAP/ISM NAT/LISM

B61
BENOIT E.,EUROPE AT SIXES AND SEVENS: THE COMMON MARKET, THE FREE TRADE ASSOCIATION AND THE UNITED STATES. EUR+WWI FUT USA+45 INDUS CONSULT DELIB/GP EX/STRUC TOP/EX ACT/RES ECO/TAC EDU/PROP ROUTINE CHOOSE PERCEPT WEALTH...MGT TREND EEC FOR/TRADE TOT/POP 20 EFTA. PAGE 13 F0249
FINAN ECO/DEV VOL/ASSN

B61
CARROTHERS A.W.R.,LABOR ARBITRATION IN CANADA. CANADA LAW NAT/G CONSULT LEGIS WORKER ADJUD ADMIN CT/SYS 20. PAGE 22 F0422
LABOR MGT GP/REL BARGAIN

B61
FRIEDMANN W.G.,JOINT INTERNATIONAL BUSINESS VENTURES. ASIA ISLAM L/A+17C ECO/DEV DIST/IND FINAN PROC/MFG FACE/GP LG/CO NAT/G VOL/ASSN CONSULT EX/STRUC PLAN ADMIN ROUTINE WEALTH...OLD/LIB FOR/TRADE WORK 20. PAGE 44 F0865
ECO/UNDEV INT/TRADE

B61
LAHAYE R.,LES ENTREPRISES PUBLIQUES AU MAROC. FRANCE MOROCCO LAW DIST/IND EXTR/IND FINAN CONSULT PLAN TEC/DEV ADMIN AGREE CONTROL OWN...POLICY 20. PAGE 74 F1460
NAT/G INDUS ECO/UNDEV ECO/TAC

B61
MARX K.,THE COMMUNIST MANIFESTO. IN (MENDEL A. ESSENTIAL WORKS OF MARXISM, NEW YORK: BANTAM. FUT MOD/EUR CULTURE ECO/DEV ECO/UNDEV AGRI FINAN INDUS MARKET PROC/MFG LABOR POL/PAR CONSULT FORCES CREATE PLAN ADMIN ATTIT DRIVE RIGID/FLEX ORD/FREE PWR RESPECT MARX/KARL MUNICH WORK. PAGE 86 F1691
COM NEW/IDEA CAP/ISM REV

B61
SHARP W.R.,FIELD ADMINISTRATION IN THE UNITED NATION SYSTEM: THE CONDUCT OF INTERNATIONAL ECONOMIC AND SOCIAL PROGRAMS. FUT WOR+45 CONSTN SOCIETY ECO/UNDEV R+D DELIB/GP ACT/RES PLAN TEC/DEV EDU/PROP EXEC ROUTINE HEALTH WEALTH...HUM CONCPT CHARTS METH ILO UNESCO GP VAL/FREE UN 20. PAGE 120 F2369
INT/ORG CONSULT

B61
STOCKING G.W.,WORKABLE COMPETITION AND ANTITRUST POLICY. USA+45 NAT/G CONSULT PLAN PRICE GOV/REL COST DEMAND PROFIT...POLICY 20. PAGE 126 F2491
LG/CO INDUS ECO/TAC CONTROL

S61
GALBRAITH J.K.,"A POSITIVE APPROACH TO ECONOMIC AID." FUT USA+45 INTELL NAT/G CONSULT ACT/RES DIPLOM ECO/TAC EDU/PROP ATTIT KNOWL PWR WEALTH ...SOC STERTYP MID/EX METH/GP 20. PAGE 45 F0883
ECO/UNDEV ROUTINE FOR/AID

B62
ALEXANDROWICZ C.H.,WORLD ECONOMIC AGENCIES: LAW AND PRACTICE. WOR+45 DIST/IND FINAN LABOR CONSULT INT/TRADE TARIFFS REPRESENT HEALTH...JURID 20 UN GATT EEC OAS ECSC. PAGE 4 F0064
INT/LAW INT/ORG DIPLOM ADJUD

B62
DOUGLAS A.,INDUSTRIAL PEACEMAKING. CONSULT ACT/RES ...MGT PSY METH 20. PAGE 34 F0656
BARGAIN INDUS LABOR GP/REL

B62
FERBER R.,RESEARCH METHODS IN ECONOMICS AND BUSINESS. AFR ECO/DEV FINAN MARKET LG/CO SML/CO CONSULT CONTROL COST...STAT METH/COMP 20. PAGE 40 F0783
ACT/RES PROB/SOLV ECO/TAC MGT

B62
GROVE J.W.,GOVERNMENT AND INDUSTRY IN BRITAIN. UK FINAN LOC/G CONSULT DELIB/GP INT/TRADE ADMIN CONTROL...BIBLIOG 20. PAGE 52 F1008
ECO/TAC INDUS NAT/G GP/REL

B62
INTERNAT CONGRESS OF JURISTS,EXECUTIVE ACTION AND THE RULE OF RULE: REPORTION PROCEEDINGS OF INT'T CONGRESS OF JURISTS,-RIO DE JANEIRO, BRAZIL. WOR+45 ACADEM CONSULT JUDGE EDU/PROP ADJUD CT/SYS INGP/REL PERSON DEPT/DEFEN. PAGE 64 F1269
JURID EXEC ORD/FREE CONTROL

B62
ROBINSON A.D.,DUTCH ORGANIZED AGRICULTURE IN INTERNATIONAL POLITICS, 1945-1960. EUR+WWI NETHERLAND STRUCT ECO/DEV NAT/G VOL/ASSN CONSULT DELIB/GP PLAN TEC/DEV INT/TRADE EDU/PROP ATTIT RIGID/FLEX ALL/VALS...NEW/IDEA TREND EEC COMMUN 20. PAGE 112 F2215
AGRI INT/ORG

S62
SCOTT J.B.,"ANGLO-SOVIET TRADE AND ITS EFFECTS ON THE COMMONWEALTH." COM FUT UK USSR WOR+45 ECO/DEV MARKET INT/ORG CONSULT WEALTH...POLICY TREND CMN/WLTH FOR/TRADE 20. PAGE 118 F2333
NAT/G ECO/TAC

B63
CALKINS R.D.,ECONOMICS AS AN AID TO POLICY (PAMPHLET). USA+45 NAT/G LEAD 20. PAGE 21 F0401
CONSULT DECISION EFFICIENCY

B63
HIRSCHMAN A.O.,JOURNEYS TOWARD PROGRESS: STUDIES OF ECONOMIC POLICYMAKING IN LATIN AMERICA. CHILE FUT ECO/UNDEV AGRI FINAN INDUS CONSULT DELIB/GP PLAN ATTIT HEALTH ORD/FREE WEALTH...POLICY STAT VAL/FREE COLOMB 20. PAGE 60 F1177
L/A+17C ECO/TAC BRAZIL

B63
US CONGRESS JOINT ECO COMM,THE UNITED STATES BALANCE OF PAYMENTS. USA+45 DELIB/GP CONFER...MATH PREDICT CHARTS 20 CONGRESS. PAGE 135 F2656
BAL/PAY ECO/TAC INT/TRADE CONSULT

B63
VON BECKERATH E.,PROBLEME DER NORMATIVEN OKONOMIK UND DER WIRTSCHAFTSPOLITISCHEN BERATUNG. GERMANY UK ELITES CAP/ISM EFFICIENCY...CONCPT GOV/COMP IDEA/COMP 20. PAGE 142 F2789
ECO/TAC DELIB/GP ECO/DEV CONSULT

S63
ADAMS F.G.,"ECONOMIC CONSIDERATIONS OF AN ATLANTIC ENERGY POLICY." EUR+WWI FUT USA+45 DIST/IND EXTR/IND MARKET CONSULT LEGIS ECO/TAC WEALTH ...POLICY EEC FOR/TRADE OEEC 20. PAGE 2 F0037
ECO/DEV TEC/DEV NUC/PWR

S63
BARZANSKI S.,"REGIONAL UNDERDEVELOPMENT IN THE EUROPEAN ECONOMIC COMMUNITY." EUR+WWI ELITES DIST/IND MARKET VOL/ASSN CONSULT EX/STRUC ECO/TAC RIGID/FLEX WEALTH EEC OEEC 20. PAGE 11 F0202
ECO/UNDEV PLAN

S63
SCHOFLING J.A.,"EFTA: THE OTHER EUROPE." ECO/DEV MARKET CONSULT ECO/TAC WEALTH...TIME/SEQ EEC OEEC 20 EFTA. PAGE 117 F2310
EUR+WWI INT/ORG REGION

S63
VINER J.,"REPORT OF THE CLAY COMMITTEE ON FOREIGN AID: A SYMPOSIUM." USA+45 WOR+45 NAT/G CONSULT PLAN BAL/PWR ATTIT WEALTH...MGT CONCPT TOT/POP 20. PAGE 142 F2788
ACT/RES ECO/TAC FOR/AID

S63
WALKER H.,"THE INTERNATIONAL LAW OF COMMODITY AGREEMENTS." FUT WOR+45 ECO/DEV ECO/UNDEV FINAN INT/ORG NAT/G CONSULT CREATE PLAN ECO/TAC ATTIT PERCEPT...CONCPT GEN/LAWS TOT/POP GATT 20. PAGE 142 F2804
MARKET VOL/ASSN INT/LAW INT/TRADE

B64
LINDHOLM R.W.,ECONOMIC DEVELOPMENT POLICY WITH EMPHASIS ON VIET-NAM. KOREA/S PAKISTAN VIETNAM/S AGRI INDUS CONSULT DELIB/GP FOR/AID...METH 20. PAGE 80 F1571
ECO/UNDEV TAX FINAN ECO/TAC

B64
SAKAI R.K.,STUDIES ON ASIA, 1964. ASIA CHINA/COM ISRAEL MALAYSIA S/ASIA USA+45 USSR ECO/UNDEV FAM POL/PAR SECT CONSULT NAT/LISM...POLICY SOC 20 CHINJAP. PAGE 115 F2272
PWR DIPLOM

B64
SULLIVAN G.,THE STORY OF THE PEACE CORPS. USA+45 WOR+45 INTELL FACE/GP NAT/G SCHOOL VOL/ASSN CONSULT EX/STRUC PLAN EDU/PROP ADMIN ATTIT DRIVE ALL/VALS ...POLICY HEAL SOC CONCPT INT QU BIOG TREND SOC/EXP WORK. PAGE 127 F2511
INT/ORG ECO/UNDEV FOR/AID PEACE

S64
HUELIN D.,"ECONOMIC INTEGRATION IN LATIN AMERICAN: PROGRESS AND PROBLEMS." L/A+17C ECO/DEV AGRI DIST/IND FINAN INDUS NAT/G VOL/ASSN CONSULT DELIB/GP EX/STRUC ACT/RES PLAN TEC/DEV ECO/TAC ROUTINE BAL/PAY WEALTH FOR/TRADE WORK TERR/GP 20. PAGE 63 F1232
MARKET ECO/UNDEV INT/TRADE

S64
MC WILLIAM M.,"THE WORLD BANK AND THE TRANSFER OF POWER IN KENYA." AFR ECO/UNDEV CONSULT ACT/RES TEC/DEV PERCEPT PWR SKILL WEALTH...CONCPT OBS TREND 20. PAGE 88 F1715
NAT/G ECO/TAC

S64
PATEL S.J.,"THE ECONOMIC DISTANCE BETWEEN NATIONS: ITS ORIGIN, MEASUREMENT AND OUTLOOK." WOR+45 ECO/DEV AGRI FINAN INDUS MARKET LABOR NAT/G CONSULT TEC/DEV ECO/TAC WEALTH...POLICY RELATIV MGT TREND WORK 20. PAGE 103 F2035
ECO/UNDEV PLAN

B65
BRADLEY J.F.,THE ROLE OF TRADE ASSOCIATIONS AND PROFESSIONAL BUSINESS SOCIETIES IN AMERICA. USA+45 USA-45 STRUCT CONSULT DELIB/GP CREATE LOBBY GP/REL 20. PAGE 17 F0333
ECO/DEV PROF/ORG VOL/ASSN SOCIETY

B65
BRYCE M.D.,POLICIES AND METHODS FOR INDUSTRIAL DEVELOPMENT. WOR+45 FINAN MARKET CONSULT TARIFFS TAX COST. PAGE 20 F0379
INDUS PLAN ECO/DEV TEC/DEV

B65
FLASH E.S. JR.,ECONOMIC ADVICE AND PRESIDENTIAL LEADERSHIP: THE COUNCIL OF ECONOMIC ADVISORS. USA+45 NAT/G EX/STRUC LEGIS TOP/EX ACT/RES ADMIN PRESIDENT CONGRESS. PAGE 41 F0808
PLAN CONSULT CHIEF

B65
FLEMING R.W.,THE LABOR ARBITRATION PROCESS. USA+45 LAW BARGAIN ADJUD ROUTINE SANCTION COST...PREDICT CHARTS TIME 20. PAGE 41 F0809
GP/REL LABOR CONSULT DELIB/GP

B65
LAZARUS S.,RESOLVING BUSINESS DISPUTES: THE POTENTIAL OF COMMERCIAL ARBITRATION. USA+45 INDUS LG/CO ACT/RES PROB/SOLV EDU/PROP CONSEN UTIL ...TREND 20. PAGE 76 F1496
FINAN DELIB/GP CONSULT ADJUD

B65
SHONFIELD A.,MODERN CAPITALISM: THE CHANGING BALANCE OF PUBLIC AND PRIVATE POWER. FRANCE GERMANY/W UK USA+45 WOR+45 ECO/DEV INT/ORG NAT/G CONSULT INT/TRADE PRODUC...POLICY CONCPT METH/COMP 20. PAGE 121 F2386
CAP/ISM CONTROL BAL/PWR CREATE

S65
SPAAK P.H.,"THE SEARCH FOR CONSENSUS: A NEW EFFORT TO BUILD EUROPE." FRANCE GERMANY ECO/DEV NAT/G CONSULT FORCES PLAN EDU/PROP REGION CONSEN ATTIT ...SOC METH/CNCPT OBS TREND EEC NATO WORK TERR/GP METH/GP 20. PAGE 124 F2447
EUR+WWI INT/ORG

B66
ALEXANDER Y.,INTERNATIONAL TECHNICAL ASSISTANCE EXPERTS* A CASE STUDY OF THE U.N. EXPERIENCE. ECO/UNDEV CONSULT EX/STRUC CREATE PLAN DIPLOM FOR/AID TASK EFFICIENCY...ORG/CHARTS UN. PAGE 3 F0061
ECO/TAC INT/ORG ADMIN MGT

B66
ALEXANDER Y.,INTERNATIONAL TECHNICAL ASSISTANCE EXPERTS: A CASE STUDY OF THE U.N. EXPERIENCE. USA+45 WOR+45 WORKER CREATE PLAN PROB/SOLV ECO/TAC FOR/AID GIVE EDU/PROP...CHARTS BIBLIOG 20 UN. PAGE 3 F0062
SKILL INT/ORG TEC/DEV CONSULT

B66
CONGRESSIONAL QUARTERLY SERV,FEDERAL ECONOMIC POLICY 1945-1965. USA+45 FINAN NAT/G CHIEF CONSULT TAX...CHARTS 20 PRESIDENT DEBT. PAGE 27 F0526
ECO/TAC BUDGET LEGIS

B66
GITTINGER J.P.,THE LITERATURE OF AGRICULTURAL PLANNING. UNIV INT/ORG CONSULT WORKER TEC/DEV ECO/TAC OPTIMAL...POLICY METH/COMP BIBLIOG/A 20. PAGE 47 F0927
ECO/UNDEV AGRI PLAN WRITING

B66
HAYS P.R.,LABOR ARBITRATION: A DISSENTING VIEW. USA+45 LAW DELIB/GP BARGAIN ADJUD...PREDICT 20. PAGE 57 F1126
GP/REL LABOR CONSULT CT/SYS

B66
MALASSIS L.,ECONOMIC DEVELOPMENT AND THE PROGRAMMING OF RURAL EDUCATION. CONSULT PROB/SOLV LITERACY KNOWL...CHARTS GEN/METH 20. PAGE 84 F1644
AGRI ECO/UNDEV SCHOOL PLAN

B66
MANGONE G.J.,UN ADMINISTRATION OF ECONOMIC AND AOCIAL PROGRAMS. CONSULT BUDGET INT/TRADE REGION 20 UN. PAGE 84 F1653
ADMIN MGT ECO/TAC DELIB/GP

B66
MANSFIELD E.,MANAGERIAL ECONOMICS AND OPERATIONS RESEARCH; A NONMATHEMATICAL INTRODUCTION. USA+45 ELITES ECO/DEV CONSULT EX/STRUC PROB/SOLV ROUTINE EFFICIENCY OPTIMAL...GAME T 20. PAGE 85 F1660
ECO/TAC OP/RES MGT COMPUTER

B66
NICOSIA F.N.,CONSUMER DECISION PROCESSES* MARKETING AND ADVERTISING IMPLICATIONS. DIST/IND INDUS CONSULT EDU/PROP ATTIT. PAGE 98 F1925
MARKET PROB/SOLV SERV/IND

B66
OHLIN G.,FOREIGN AID POLICIES RECONSIDERED. ECO/DEV ECO/UNDEV VOL/ASSN CONSULT PLAN CONTROL ATTIT ...CONCPT CHARTS BIBLIOG 20. PAGE 101 F1985
FOR/AID DIPLOM GIVE

B66
THEIL H.,APPLIED ECONOMIC FORECASTING. UNIV USA+45 ELITES INTELL CONSULT PRODUC...DECISION MGT PREDICT CHARTS METH/COMP SIMUL 20. PAGE 129 F2552
FUT OP/RES PLAN

B66
US SENATE COMM GOVT OPERATIONS,INTERGOVERNMENTAL PERSONNEL ACT OF 1966. USA+45 NAT/G CONSULT DELIB/GP WORKER TEC/DEV PAY AUTOMAT UTIL 20 CONGRESS. PAGE 139 F2730
ADMIN LEGIS EFFICIENCY EDU/PROP

B66
US SENATE COMM LABOR-PUB WELF,AMEND THE RAILWAY LABOR ACT. USA+45 CONSTN CONSULT DELIB/GP ADJUD CONGRESS RAILROAD. PAGE 139 F2731
GP/REL LABOR DIST/IND LAW

N66
OECD,THE BALANCE OF PAYMENTS ADJUSTMENT PROCESS (PAMPHLET). EUR+WWI ECO/DEV FINAN CONSULT PLAN PROB/SOLV BUDGET CAP/ISM INT/TRADE PRICE CONTROL EQUILIB 20. PAGE 101 F1975
BAL/PAY ECO/TAC DIPLOM INT/ORG

B67
ANDERSON S.V.,THE NORDIC COUNCIL: A STUDY OF SCANDINAVIAN REGIONALISM. DENMARK FINLAND ICELAND NORWAY SWEDEN MARKET NAT/G VOL/ASSN CONSULT PARL/PROC ATTIT...TIME/SEQ BIBLIOG 20. PAGE 5 F0098
INT/ORG REGION DIPLOM LEGIS

B67
BALDWIN G.B.,PLANNING AND DEVELOPMENT IN IRAN. IRAN AGRI INDUS CONSULT WORKER EDU/PROP BAL/PAY...CHARTS 20. PAGE 9 F0164
PLAN ECO/UNDEV ADMIN PROB/SOLV

B67
CHAPIN F.S. JR.,SELECTED REFERENCES ON URBAN PLANNING METHODS AND TECHNIQUES. USA+45 LAW ECO/DEV LOC/G NAT/G SCHOOL CONSULT CREATE PROB/SOLV TEC/DEV ...SOC/WK MUNICH. PAGE 23 F0454
BIBLIOG NEIGH PLAN

B67
COHEN M.R.,LAW AND THE SOCIAL ORDER: ESSAYS IN LEGAL PHILOSOPHY. USA-45 CONSULT WORKER ECO/TAC ATTIT WEALTH...POLICY WELF/ST SOC 20 NEW/DEAL DEPRESSION. PAGE 26 F0497
JURID LABOR IDEA/COMP

B67
KULSKI J.E.,LAND OF URBAN PROMISE* CONTINUING THE GREAT TRADITION* A SEARCH FOR SIGNIFICANT URBAN SPACE IN URBANIZED NORTHEAST. USA+45 DIST/IND PUB/INST CONSULT CREATE TEC/DEV...SOC NEW/IDEA CHARTS BIBLIOG MUNICH. PAGE 74 F1448
PLAN PROB/SOLV ECO/DEV

B67
MORRIS A.J.A.,PARLIAMENTARY DEMOCRACY IN THE NINETEENTH CENTURY. UK INDUS LOC/G NAT/G POL/PAR CONSULT LEGIS INT/TRADE ADMIN CHOOSE SUFF SOVEREIGN 19 PARLIAMENT. PAGE 93 F1835
TIME/SEQ CONSTN PARL/PROC POPULISM

B67
NELSON R.R.,TECHNOLOGY, ECONOMIC GROWTH, AND PUBLIC POLICY. USA+45 PLAN GP/REL UTIL KNOWL...POLICY PHIL/SCI CHARTS BIBLIOG 20. PAGE 97 F1912
R+D CONSULT CREATE ACT/RES

L67
STRUVE G.M.,"THE LESS-RESTRICTIVE-ALTERNATIVE PRINCIPLE AND ECONOMIC DUE PROCESS." USA+45 ECO/DEV LABOR NAT/G CONSULT DELIB/GP OP/RES PLAN WEALTH. PAGE 127 F2505
JURID JUDGE SANCTION CAP/ISM

S67
ADAMS R.N.,"ETHICS AND THE SOCIAL ANTHROPOLOGIST IN LATIN AMERICA." USA+45 INTELL PROB/SOLV ECO/TAC LEAD...DECISION SOC NAT/COMP PERS/COMP. PAGE 2 F0039
L/A+17C POLICY ECO/UNDEV CONSULT

S67
BARRO S.,"ECONOMIC IMPACT OF SPACE EXPENDITURES: SOME BROAD ISSUES DEALING WITH COSTS AND BENEFITS." USA+45 PROC/MFG R+D LG/CO CONSULT COST PRODUC 20. PAGE 10 F0195
SPACE FINAN ECO/TAC NAT/G

S67
BENN W.,"TECHNOLOGY HAS AN INEXORABLE EFFECT." FUT UK ECO/DEV INT/ORG CONSULT PLAN EDU/PROP ADMIN LEAD GP/REL PRODUC...INT 20 EEC. PAGE 13 F0246
R+D LG/CO TEC/DEV INDUS

S67
FLOYD D.,"FIFTH AMENDMENT RIGHT TO COUNSEL IN FEDERAL INCOME TAX INVESTIGATIONS." USA+45 LAW OP/RES INGP/REL. PAGE 42 F0818
JURID CT/SYS TAX CONSULT

S67
HANCOCK J.L.,"PLANNERS IN THE CHANGING AMERICAN CITY, 1900-1940." USA-45 CONSTRUC NAT/G POL/PAR ...SOC/WK TREND MUNICH 20. PAGE 54 F1059
PLAN CONSULT LOC/G

S67
KOTLER P.,"OPERATIONS RESEARCH IN MARKETING." USA+45 DIST/IND INDUS LG/CO CONSULT BUDGET TASK DEMAND EFFICIENCY PROFIT WEALTH DECISION. PAGE 73 F1429
ECOMETRIC OP/RES MARKET PLAN

S67
MELTZER B.D.,"RUMINATIONS ABOUT IDEOLOGY, LAW, AND LABOR ARBITRATION." USA+45 ECO/DEV PROB/SOLV CONFER MGT. PAGE 89 F1754
JURID ADJUD LABOR CONSULT

S67
MORTON J.A.,"A SYSTEMS APPROACH TO THE INNOVATION PROCESS: ITS USE IN THE BELL SYSTEM." USA+45 INTELL INDUS LG/CO CONSULT WORKER COMPUTER AUTOMAT DEMAND ...MGT CHARTS 20. PAGE 94 F1841
TEC/DEV GEN/METH R+D COM/IND

S67
MUNDHEIM R.H.,"SOME THOUGHTS ON THE DUTIES AND RESPONSIBILITIES OF UNAFFILIATED DIRECTORS OF MUTUAL FUNDS." USA+45 LG/CO SML/CO CONSULT LEAD PARTIC. PAGE 95 F1861
FINAN WEALTH ECO/TAC ADMIN

S67
NOURSE E.G.,"EARLY FLOWERING OF THE EMPLOYMENT ACT" USA+45 LABOR CONSULT DELIB/GP LEGIS BUDGET GOV/REL PRODUC WEALTH 20 INTRVN/ECO. PAGE 99 F1939
NAT/G WORKER ECO/TAC CONTROL

S67
RICHMAN B.M.,"CAPITALISTS & MANAGERS IN COMMUNIST CHINA." ASIA CHINA/COM ECO/UNDEV NAT/G CONSULT EX/STRUC PLAN EFFICIENCY PRODUC WEALTH MARXISM ...MGT CHARTS 20. PAGE 111 F2185
CAP/ISM INDUS

S67
SKOLNICK J.H.,"SOCIAL CONTROL IN THE ADVERSARY SYSTEM." USA+45 CONSULT OP/RES ADMIN CONTROL. PAGE 123 F2419 PROB/SOLV PERS/REL ADJUD CT/SYS

S67
WHITE W.L.,"THE TREASURY BOARD AND PARLIAMENT." CANADA CONSTN CONSULT LEGIS LEAD PARL/PROC GP/REL ...DECISION 20. PAGE 146 F2871 FINAN DELIB/GP NAT/G ADMIN

CONSULTANTS....SEE CONSULT

CONSUMER....SEE MARKET,

CONT/OBS....CONTROLLED DIRECT OBSERVATION

B41
MACMAHON A.W.,THE ADMINISTRATION OF FEDERAL WORK RELIEF. USA-45 EX/STRUC WORKER BUDGET EFFICIENCY ...CONT/OBS CHARTS 20 WPA. PAGE 84 F1636 ADMIN NAT/G MGT GIVE

B56
KINDLEBERGER C.P.,THE TERMS OF TRADE: A EUROPEAN CASE-STUDY. EUR+WWI MOD/EUR ECO/DEV ECO/UNDEV AGRI INDUS BAL/PAY...METH/CNCPT STAT CONT/OBS CON/ANAL SOC/EXP SIMUL FOR/TRADE 20. PAGE 71 F1390 PLAN ECO/TAC

B59
DIEBOLD W. JR.,THE SCHUMAN PLAN: A STUDY IN ECONOMIC COOPERATION, 1950-1959. EUR+WWI FRANCE GERMANY USA+45 EXTR/IND CONSULT DELIB/GP PLAN DIPLOM ECO/TAC INT/TRADE ROUTINE ORD/FREE WEALTH ...METH/CNCPT STAT CONT/OBS INT TIME/SEQ ECSC 20. PAGE 33 F0635 INT/ORG REGION

S59
THOMPSON W.S.,"POPULATION AND PROGRESS IN THE FAR EAST." ASIA S/ASIA DIST/IND CREATE ECO/TAC WAR LOVE SKILL WEALTH...CONT/OBS TOT/POP 20. PAGE 130 F2568 ECO/UNDEV BIO/SOC GEOG

B60
SHONFIELD A.,THE ATTACK ON WORLD POVERTY. WOR+45 ECO/DEV ECO/UNDEV FINAN VOL/ASSN PLAN EDU/PROP DRIVE KNOWL WEALTH...CONT/OBS STAND/INT ORG/CHARTS TOT/POP UNESCO 20. PAGE 121 F2383 INT/ORG ECO/TAC FOR/AID INT/TRADE

S60
MORALES C.J.,"TRADE AND ECONOMIC INTEGRATION IN LATIN AMERICA." FUT L/A+17C LAW STRATA ECO/UNDEV DIST/IND INDUS LABOR NAT/G LEGIS ECO/TAC ADMIN RIGID/FLEX WEALTH...CONCPT NEW/IDEA CONT/OBS TIME/SEQ WORK 20. PAGE 93 F1825 FINAN INT/TRADE REGION

B61
FEARN H.,AN AFRICAN ECONOMY. AFR EUR+WWI PLAN COLONIAL WEALTH...CONT/OBS TREND EEC VAL/FREE 20. PAGE 39 F0770 ECO/UNDEV

B61
LAMFALUSSY A.,INVESTMENT AND GROWTH IN MATURE ECONOMIES. BELGIUM EUR+WWI LABOR PRICE PRODUC PROFIT...STAT CONT/OBS CHARTS 20. PAGE 75 F1464 FINAN INDUS ECO/DEV CAP/ISM

S61
VERNON R.,"A TRADE POLICY FOR THE 1960'S." COM FUT USA+45 WOR+45 ECO/DEV ECO/UNDEV FINAN TOP/EX ACT/RES...WELF/ST METH/CNCPT CONT/OBS TOT/POP 20. PAGE 141 F2781 PLAN INT/TRADE

S62
ADISESHIAN M.,"EDUCATION AND DEVELOPMENT." FUT WOR+45 SOCIETY ACT/RES INT/TRADE EDU/PROP KNOWL SKILL WEALTH...POLICY CONCPT CONT/OBS CENSUS CHARTS TOT/POP VAL/FREE APPLIC FAO FOR/TRADE 20. PAGE 2 F0041 SCHOOL ECO/UNDEV

S62
LIPSON H.A.,"FORMAL REASONING AND MARKETING STRATEGY." ECO/DEV PROB/SOLV PRICE ALL/VALS CONT/OBS. PAGE 81 F1578 MARKET DECISION GAME ECO/TAC

B63
RUMMEL J.F.,RESEARCH METHODOLOGY IN BUSINESS. COMPUTER CREATE PROB/SOLV...CONT/OBS REC/INT QU/SEMANT SYS/QU SAMP CHARTS METH/COMP T 20. PAGE 115 F2260 OP/RES METH/CNCPT METH STAT

S63
CLEMHOUT S.,"PRODUCTION FUNCTION ANALYSIS APPLIED TO THE LEONTIEF SCARCE-FACTOR PARADOX OF INTERNATIONAL TRADE." EUR+WWI USA+45 DIST/IND NAT/G PLAN TEC/DEV DIPLOM PWR WEALTH...MGT METH/CNCPT CONT/OBS CON/ANAL CHARTS SIMUL GEN/LAWS FOR/TRADE 20. PAGE 25 F0490 ECO/DEV ECO/TAC

S63
GORDON B.,"ECONOMIC IMPEDIMENTS TO REGIONALISM IN SOUTH EAST ASIA." BURMA FUT S/ASIA THAILAND USA+45 AGRI INDUS R+D NAT/G PLAN ECO/TAC WEALTH...STAT CONT/OBS 20. PAGE 49 F0954 VOL/ASSN ECO/UNDEV INT/TRADE REGION

S63
SHWADRAN B.,"MIDDLE EAST OIL, 1962." ISLAM DIST/IND INDUS PLAN ATTIT DRIVE WEALTH...POLICY STAT CONT/OBS TREND CHARTS GEN/LAWS TERR/GP METH/GP 20 OIL. PAGE 121 F2393 PROC/MFG ECO/TAC ELITES REGION

S64
BEIM D.,"THE COMMUNIST BLOC AND THE FOREIGN-AID GAME." AFR WOR+45 NAT/G PLAN ROUTINE ATTIT KNOWL ORD/FREE...DECISION QUANT CONT/OBS TIME/SEQ CHARTS GAME SIMUL LOG/LING 20. PAGE 12 F0231 COM ECO/UNDEV ECO/TAC FOR/AID

S66
DAVIS O.A.,"A THEORY OF THE BUDGETARY PROCESS." ECO/DEV FINAN LEGIS PROB/SOLV GOV/REL...ECOMETRIC METH/CNCPT STAT CONT/OBS TREND METH/COMP SIMUL 20 CONGRESS. PAGE 30 F0592 DECISION NAT/G BUDGET EFFICIENCY

CONTEMPT....SEE RESPECT

CONTENT ANALYSIS....SEE CON/ANAL

CONTROL....CONTROL OF HUMAN GROUP OPERATIONS

N
US SUPERINTENDENT OF DOCUMENTS,INTERSTATE COMMERCE (PRICE LIST 59). USA+45 LAW LOC/G NAT/G LEGIS TARIFFS TAX ADMIN CONTROL HEALTH DECISION. PAGE 140 F2752 BIBLIOG/A DIST/IND GOV/REL PROVS

C01
LOWELL A.L.,"THE INFLUENCE OF PARTY UPON LEGISLATION IN ENGLAND AND AMERICA" IN ANNUAL REPORT OF AMER HISTORICAL ASSN." LEGIS CONTROL ...CON/ANAL CHARTS 19/20 CONGRESS PARLIAMENT. PAGE 82 F1605 PARL/PROC POL/PAR DECISION OP/RES

B03
GRIFFIN A.P.C.,LISTS PUBLISHED 1902-03: GOVERNMENT OWNERSHIP OF RAILROADS (PAMPHLET). USA-45 LAW NAT/G RATION GOV/REL CENTRAL SOCISM...POLICY 19/20. PAGE 51 F0998 BIBLIOG DIST/IND CONTROL ADJUD

B12
FOUAD M.,LE REGIME DE LA PRESSE EN EGYPTE: THESE POUR LE DOCTORAT. UAR LICENSE EDU/PROP ADMIN SANCTION CRIME SUPEGO PWR...ART/METH JURID 19/20. PAGE 43 F0832 ORD/FREE LEGIS CONTROL PRESS

N19
BLOOMFIELD A.,MONETARY POLICY UNDER THE INTERNATIONAL GOLD STANDARD: 18801914 (PAMPHLET). AFR USA-45 DIPLOM CONTROL...POLICY 19. PAGE 16 F0300 FINAN ROLE EFFICIENCY

N19
CASSELL F.,INTERNATIONAL MONETARY PROBLEMS (PAMPHLET). AFR BAL/PWR CONTROL EFFICIENCY WEALTH 20 EEC. PAGE 22 F0427 INT/TRADE FINAN DIPLOM TREND

N19
DWYER J.W.,YARDSTICKS FOR PERFORMANCE (PAMPHLET). USA+45 FINAN CONTROL...CONCPT METH/COMP MUNICH. PAGE 35 F0688 BUDGET LOC/G EFFICIENCY

N19
FRANCK P.G.,AFGHANISTAN BETWEEN EAST AND WEST: THE ECONOMICS OF COMPETITIVE COEXISTENCE (PAMPHLET). AFGHANISTN USA+45 USA-45 USSR INDUS ECO/TAC INT/TRADE CONTROL NEUTRAL ORD/FREE MARXISM...GEOG 20 UN. PAGE 43 F0842 FOR/AID PLAN DIPLOM ECO/UNDEV

N19
FREEMAN H.A.,COERCION OF STATES IN FEDERAL UNIONS (PAMPHLET). WOR-45 DIPLOM CONTROL COERCE PEACE ORD/FREE...GOV/COMP METH/COMP NAT/COMP PACIFIST 20. PAGE 43 F0850 FEDERAL WAR INT/ORG PACIFISM

N19
HACKETT J.,ECONOMIC PLANNING IN FRANCE; ITS RELATION TO THE POLICIES OF THE DEVELOPED COUNTRIES OF WESTERN EUROPE (PAMPHLET). EUR+WWI FRANCE ECO/DEV PROB/SOLV CONTROL...POLICY 20 EUROPE/W. PAGE 52 F1026 ECO/TAC NAT/G PLAN INSPECT

N19
HAGEN E.E.,AN ANALYTICAL MODEL OF THE TRANSITION TO ECONOMIC GROWTH (PAMPHLET). WOR+45 WOR-45 SOCIETY STRATA FINAN NAT/G CONTROL PARTIC PRODUC...PHIL/SCI BIBLIOG 17/20. PAGE 53 F1033 SIMUL ECO/DEV METH TEC/DEV

N19
HANSEN B.,INFLATION PROBLEMS IN SMALL COUNTRIES (PAMPHLET). AFR UNIV FOR/AID CONTROL BAL/PAY DEMAND PRODUC 20. PAGE 54 F1066 PRICE FINAN ECO/UNDEV ECO/TAC

N19
HUBERMAN L.,SOCIALISM IS THE ONLY ANSWER (PAMPHLET). CREATE ECO/TAC EDU/PROP CONTROL ...SOCIALIST GEN/LAWS ANTHOL 20. PAGE 62 F1230 SOCISM ECO/DEV CAP/ISM PLAN

N19
JACKSON R.G.A.,THE CASE FOR AN INTERNATIONAL DEVELOPMENT AUTHORITY (PAMPHLET). WOR+45 ECO/DEV DIPLOM GIVE CONTROL GP/REL EFFICIENCY NAT/LISM SOVEREIGN 20. PAGE 66 F1295 FOR/AID INT/ORG ECO/UNDEV ADMIN

N19
MCCONNELL G.,THE STEEL SEIZURE OF 1952 (PAMPHLET). USA+45 FINAN INDUS PROC/MFG LG/CO EX/STRUC ADJUD CONTROL GP/REL ORD/FREE PWR 20 TRUMAN/HS PRESIDENT CONGRESS. PAGE 88 F1721 DELIB/GP LABOR PROB/SOLV NAT/G

N19
US BUREAU OF THE CENSUS,THE PROPORTION OF THE PROC/MFG

SHIPMENTS (OR EMPLOYEES) OF EACH INDUSTRY... (PAMPHLET). USA+45 ECO/DEV EXTR/IND INDUS CONTROL PROFIT...STAT 20 CONGRESS MONOPOLY. PAGE 134 F2645 PRODUC MARKET CHARTS N19

US CHAMBER OF COMMERCE,THE SIGNIFICANCE OF CONCENTRATION RATIOS (PAMPHLET). USA+45 FINAN INDUS ADMIN...METH/CNCPT SAMP CHARTS 20. PAGE 134 F2647 MARKET PREDICT LG/CO CONTROL N19

WILSON T.,FINANCIAL ASSISTANCE WITH REGIONAL DEVELOPMENT (PAMPHLET). CANADA INDUS NAT/G PLAN TAX CONTROL COST EFFICIENCY...POLICY CHARTS 20. PAGE 147 F2902 FINAN ECO/TAC REGION GOV/REL B20

MALTHUS T.R.,PRINCIPLES OF POLITICAL ECONOMY. UK AGRI INDUS MARKET NAT/G DIPLOM PRICE CONTROL BAL/PAY COST OWN PWR LAISSEZ 18/19. PAGE 84 F1650 GEN/LAWS DEMAND WEALTH B20

MOREL E.D.,THE BLACK MAN'S BURDEN. AFR MOD/EUR AGRI EXTR/IND PROB/SOLV INT/TRADE ADMIN CONTROL COERCE DISCRIM...POLICY 19/20 NEGRO LEAGUE/NAT. PAGE 93 F1828 ORD/FREE CAP/ISM RACE/REL DOMIN B20

PIGOU A.C.,THE ECONOMICS OF WELFARE. UNIV INDUS WORKER ACT/RES RECEIVE INCOME NEW/LIB...MAJORIT SOC/WK. PAGE 106 F2085 ECO/TAC WEALTH FINAN CONTROL B20

TAWNEY R.H.,THE ACQUISITIVE SOCIETY. STRATA WORKER PROB/SOLV CAP/ISM ECO/TAC CONTROL GP/REL OWN PRIVIL ATTIT ORD/FREE WEALTH 20. PAGE 128 F2536 INDUS SOCIETY PRODUC MORAL B24

HOLDSWORTH W.S.,A HISTORY OF ENGLISH LAW; THE COMMON LAW AND ITS RIVALS (VOL. VI). AFR UK STRATA EX/STRUC ADJUD ADMIN CONTROL CT/SYS...JURID CONCPT GEN/LAWS 17 PARLIAMENT ENGLSH/LAW COMMON/LAW. PAGE 61 F1194 LAW CONSTN LEGIS CHIEF B24

HOLDSWORTH W.S.,A HISTORY OF ENGLISH LAW; THE COMMON LAW AND ITS RIVALS (VOL. IV). UK SEA AGRI CHIEF ADJUD CONTROL CRIME GOV/REL...INT/LAW JURID NAT/COMP 16/17 PARLIAMENT COMMON/LAW CANON/LAW ENGLSH/LAW. PAGE 61 F1195 LAW LEGIS CT/SYS CONSTN B25

MATHEWS J.M.,AMERICAN STATE GOVERNMENT. USA-45 LOC/G CHIEF EX/STRUC LEGIS ADJUD CONTROL CT/SYS ROUTINE GOV/REL PWR 20 GOVERNOR. PAGE 87 F1703 PROVS ADMIN FEDERAL CONSTN B27

BELLOC H.,THE SERVILE STATE (1912) (3RD ED.). PRUSSIA UK CULTURE STRATA INDUS NAT/G ECO/TAC CONTROL LEAD SUFF DISCRIM EQUILIB ORD/FREE WEALTH 20. PAGE 12 F0237 WORKER CAP/ISM DOMIN CATH B29

JONES M.M.,CORPORATION CONTRIBUTIONS TO COMMUNITY WELFARE AGENCIES (PAMPHLET). DELIB/GP TAX CONTROL PARTIC RATIONAL POLICY. PAGE 68 F1339 LG/CO GIVE NEIGH SOC/WK B30

KEYNES J.M.,A TREATISE ON MONEY (2 VOLS.). UK USA-45 INDUS MARKET WORKER PRICE CONTROL COST OPTIMAL PROFIT WEALTH...POLICY 19/20 KEYNES/JM. PAGE 70 F1385 EQUILIB ECO/TAC FINAN GEN/LAWS B32

THOMPSON C.D.,CONFESSIONS OF THE POWER TRUST. MARKET ACT/RES EDU/PROP CONTROL GOV/REL INCOME OWN ...MGT 20 FTC MONOPOLY. PAGE 130 F2564 LG/CO SERV/IND PWR FINAN B35

HICKS J.R.,THE THEORY OF WAGES. INDUS NAT/G PAY PRICE CONTROL COST EFFICIENCY WEALTH 19/20 MARSHALL/A CLARK/JB. PAGE 59 F1164 INCOME WORKER LABOR PRODUC B36

BELLOC H.,THE RESTORATION OF PROPERTY. UK STRATA NAT/G PROF/ORG DELIB/GP WORKER CREATE PROB/SOLV ECO/TAC PARTIC UTOPIA ORD/FREE SOCISM 20. PAGE 13 F0238 CONTROL MAJORIT CAP/ISM OWN B36

BURNS A.R.,THE DECLINE OF COMPETITION. LAW LG/CO NAT/G SML/CO LEGIS PRICE AGREE CONTROL GP/REL INCOME PRODUC...POLICY 19/20 NRA. PAGE 20 F0390 MARKET GEN/LAWS INDUS B37

DALTON J.E.,SUGAR: A CASE STUDY OF GOVERNMENT CONTROL. USA-45 AGRI PROC/MFG LG/CO LEGIS PROB/SOLV ECO/TAC GP/REL...CHARTS 19/20. PAGE 30 F0575 CONTROL NAT/G INDUS POLICY B37

HAMILTON W.H.,THE POWER TO GOVERN. ECO/DEV FINAN INDUS ECO/TAC INT/TRADE TARIFFS TAX CONTROL CT/SYS WAR COST PWR 18/20 SUPREME/CT. PAGE 54 F1056 LING CONSTN NAT/G POLICY B37

MACKENZIE F.,PLANNED SOCIETY: YESTERDAY, TODAY, AND TOMORROW. ECO/DEV ECO/UNDEV AGRI FINAN INDUS PLAN INSPECT CONTROL ALL/IDEOS...TREND METH/COMP BIBLIOG 20 RESOURCE/N. PAGE 83 F1635 SOC CONCPT ANTHOL B38

DAVIES E.,"NATIONAL" CAPITALISM: THE GOVERNMENT'S RECORD AS PROTECTOR OF PRIVATE MONOPOLY. UK ELITES SOCIETY STRATA POL/PAR WORKER PROB/SOLV CONTROL SOCISM 20 MONOPOLY LABOR/PAR CHAMBRLN/N. PAGE 30 F0583 CAP/ISM NAT/G INDUS POLICY B38

LAWLEY F.E.,THE GROWTH OF COLLECTIVE ECONOMY VOL. 1: NATIONAL. EUR+WWI AGRI INDUS NAT/G BARGAIN CAP/ISM ECO/TAC WAR OPTIMAL WEALTH...GOV/COMP METH/COMP 19/20 MONOPOLY. PAGE 76 F1492 SOCISM PRICE CONTROL OWN B38

LAWLEY F.E.,THE GROWTH OF COLLECTIVE ECONOMY VOL. 2: INTERNATIONAL. WOR-45 AGRI INDUS EQUILIB OPTIMAL OWN WEALTH...NAT/COMP 19/20 NAZI NEW/DEAL MONOPOLY. PAGE 76 F1493 ECO/TAC SOCISM NAT/LISM CONTROL B38

MEADE J.E.,AN INTRODUCTION TO ECONOMIC ANALYSIS AND POLICY (AMERICAN EDITION EDITED BY C.J. HITCH). FINAN INDUS MARKET LABOR INT/TRADE CONTROL COST DEMAND INCOME...CLASSIF CHARTS T 20 KEYNES/JM MONOPOLY. PAGE 89 F1737 CONCPT PROFIT PRODUC B38

REICH N.,LABOR RELATIONS IN REPUBLICAN GERMANY. GERMANY CONSTN ECO/DEV INDUS NAT/G ADMIN CONTROL GP/REL FASCISM POPULISM 20 WEIMAR/REP. PAGE 110 F2176 WORKER MGT LABOR BARGAIN B39

CLARK J.M.,SOCIAL CONTROL OF BUSINESS (2ND ED.). ECO/DEV FINAN LG/CO PLAN ECO/TAC PRICE SUPEGO...T 20. PAGE 25 F0480 CAP/ISM CONTROL LAISSEZ METH/COMP B39

THOMAS J.A.,THE HOUSE OF COMMONS, 1832-1901; A STUDY OF ITS ECONOMIC AND FUNCTIONAL CHARACTER. UK LAW STRATA FINAN DIPLOM CONTROL LEAD LOBBY REPRESENT WEALTH...POLICY STAT BIBLIOG 19/20 PARLIAMENT. PAGE 130 F2561 PARL/PROC LEGIS POL/PAR ECO/DEV B40

CAMPBELL P.,CONSUMER REPRESENTATION IN THE NEW DEAL. AGRI INDUS MARKET EX/STRUC PLAN CAP/ISM CONTROL GP/REL DEMAND POLICY. PAGE 21 F0408 CLIENT REPRESENT NAT/G B41

ESTEY J.A.,BUSINESS CYCLES; THEIR NATURE, CAUSE, AND CONTROL. NAT/G BUDGET CAP/ISM TAX PRICE CONTROL INCOME...MODAL TIME/SEQ GEN/METH T 18/20 KEYNES/JM MONEY. PAGE 38 F0749 INDUS FINAN ECO/TAC POLICY S41

MUKERJEE R.,"POPULATION THEORY AND POLITICS (BMR)" WOR-45 NAT/G PLAN PROB/SOLV ECO/TAC INT/TRADE CONTROL WAR PEACE...CENSUS 20 BIRTH/CON RESOURCE/N. PAGE 94 F1854 GEOG OPTIMAL CONCPT L42

GRANT J.A.C.,"THE GUILD RETURNS TO AMERICA." CHRIST-17C USA-45 LEGIS LICENSE ADJUD CONTROL GP/REL. PAGE 50 F0978 PROF/ORG JURID LABOR PWR B43

BRADY R.A.,BUSINESS AS A SYSTEM OF POWER. EX/STRUC PLAN ECO/TAC CONTROL GP/REL PWR...TREND GP/COMP. PAGE 17 F0334 VOL/ASSN LOBBY POLICY B43

WILMERDING L. JR.,THE SPENDING POWER: A HISTORY OF THE EFFORTS OF CONGRESS TO CONTROL EXPENDITURES. USA-45 POL/PAR DELIB/GP EX/STRUC TOP/EX TARIFFS ADMIN GOV/REL...TIME/SEQ SENATE HOUSE/REP. PAGE 147 F2900 LEGIS BUDGET CONTROL S43

HERBERG W.,"BUREAUCRACY AND DEMOCRACY IN LABOR UNIONS." LAW CONSTN STRUCT WORKER ADMIN CONTROL PARTIC RIGID/FLEX PWR TREND. PAGE 59 F1151 LABOR REPRESENT ROUTINE INGP/REL S43

HUZAR E.,"CONGRESS AND THE ARMY: APPROPRIATIONS." USA-45 CONFER CONTROL ATTIT SUPEGO SKILL CONGRESS. PAGE 64 F1255 LEGIS FORCES BUDGET DELIB/GP B44

LANDAUER C.,THEORY OF NATIONAL ECONOMIC PLANNING. USA-45 INDUS MARKET WORKER PROB/SOLV DIPLOM RATION PRICE CONTROL WAR COST 20. PAGE 75 F1465 ECO/TAC PLAN NAT/G ECO/DEV B44

LOCKE J.,FURTHER CONSIDERATIONS CONCERNING RAISING THE VALUE OF MONEY. AFR UK NAT/G ECO/TAC INCOME WEALTH...METH/COMP GEN/LAWS 17 SILVER. PAGE 81 F1591 COST FINAN PRICE CONTROL B44

MCFADYEAN A.,GOVERNMENT AND INDUSTRY (PAMPHLET). UK INDUS CONTROL REPRESENT 20. PAGE 88 F1728 POL/PAR SOCISM B45

MILLIS H.A.,ORGANIZED LABOR (FIRST ED.). LAW STRUCT DELIB/GP WORKER ECO/TAC ADJUD CONTROL REPRESENT INGP/REL INCOME MGT. PAGE 92 F1797 LABOR POLICY ROUTINE

GP/REL

B45
WOOTTON B.,FREEDOM UNDER PLANNING. UNIV ROUTINE ATTIT AUTHORIT DECISION. PAGE 148 F2926
PLAN ORD/FREE ECO/TAC CONTROL

B46
DAVIES E.,NATIONAL ENTERPRISE: THE DEVELOPMENT OF THE PUBLIC CORPORATION. UK LG/CO EX/STRUC WORKER PROB/SOLV COST ATTIT SOCISM 20. PAGE 30 F0584
ADMIN NAT/G CONTROL INDUS

B46
DRUCKER P.F.,CONCEPT OF CORPORATION. LAW LABOR WORKER PRICE CONTROL LEAD GP/REL POLICY. PAGE 34 F0665
LG/CO CENTRAL INGP/REL

B46
ERNST M.L.,THE FIRST FREEDOM. USA-45 CONSTN PRESS PRIVIL...CHARTS IDEA/COMP BIBLIOG 20 AMEND/I. PAGE 38 F0746
EDU/PROP COM/IND ORD/FREE CONTROL

B46
HARRISON S.M.,AMERICAN FOUNDATIONS FOR SOCIAL WELFARE. OP/RES CONTROL...POLICY MGT METH/CNCPT STAT TREND BIBLIOG. PAGE 56 F1092
GIVE FINAN CLASSIF ADMIN

B47
BAERWALD F.,FUNDAMENTALS OF LABOR ECONOMICS. LAW INDUS LABOR LG/CO CONTROL GP/REL INCOME TOTALISM ...MGT CHARTS GEN/LAWS BIBLIOG 20. PAGE 8 F0150
ECO/DEV WORKER MARKET

B47
SLICHTER S.H.,THE CHALLENGE OF INDUSTRIAL RELATIONS: TRADE UNIONS, MANAGEMENT AND THE PUBLIC INTEREST. PLAN ECO/TAC ADJUD CONTROL LEAD SANCTION GP/REL INGP/REL INCOME. PAGE 123 F2421
LABOR MGT CLIENT POLICY

S47
DAHL R.A.,"WORKERS' CONTROL OF INDUSTRY AND THE BRITISH LABOUR PARTY." UK STRATA STRUCT DELIB/GP BARGAIN CAP/ISM DEBATE CONTROL CHOOSE GP/REL ATTIT ROLE PWR 19/20 PARLIAMENT LABOR/PAR FABIAN. PAGE 29 F0570
INDUS LABOR WORKER SOCISM

B48
HART A.G.,MONEY, DEBT, AND ECONOMIC ACTIVITY. AFR WORKER DIPLOM PRICE CONTROL BAL/PAY COST OWN PRODUC ...METH/COMP 20 FED/RESERV. PAGE 56 F1097
FINAN WEALTH ECO/TAC NAT/G

B48
SPERO S.D.,GOVERNMENT AS EMPLOYER. USA+45 NAT/G EX/STRUC ADMIN CONTROL EXEC 20. PAGE 124 F2453
SOVEREIGN INGP/REL REPRESENT CONFER

S49
SHEPHARD H.A.,"DEMOCRATIC CONTROL IN A LABOR UNION." FUT CONSTN STRUCT TEC/DEV LEAD PARTIC RACE/REL CENTRAL DRIVE HABITAT RECORD. PAGE 120 F2374
LABOR MAJORIT CONTROL PWR

S49
STEINMETZ H.,"THE PROBLEMS OF THE LANDRAT: A STUDY OF COUNTY GOVERNMENT IN THE US ZONE OF GERMANY." GERMANY/W USA+45 INDUS PLAN DIPLOM EDU/PROP CONTROL WAR GOV/REL FEDERAL WEALTH PLURISM...GOV/COMP 20 LANDRAT. PAGE 126 F2478
LOC/G COLONIAL MGT TOP/EX

B50
HUTCHISON K.,THE DECLINE AND FALL OF BRITISH CAPITALISM. UK ELITES STRATA ECO/DEV LABOR WORKER CONTROL WAR PWR...BIBLIOG/A 19/20. PAGE 63 F1249
CAP/ISM SOCISM LAISSEZ DOMIN

B50
ORTON W.A.,THE ECONOMIC ROLE OF THE STATE. INTELL ECO/UNDEV PLAN CONTROL PWR SOVEREIGN...POLICY 17/20. PAGE 102 F2000
ECO/DEV NAT/G ECO/TAC ORD/FREE

B50
SHAW E.S.,MONEY, INCOME, AND MONETARY POLICY. AFR USA-45 NAT/G DIPLOM PAY CONTROL COST INCOME PRODUC WEALTH...T 20 FED/RESERV DEPT/TREAS. PAGE 120 F2370
FINAN ECO/TAC ECO/DEV PRICE

B51
CHANDLER L.V.,INFLATION IN THE UNITED STATES 1940-1948. AFR NAT/G BUDGET PAY PRICE CONTROL WAR INCOME PRODUC...POLICY BIBLIOG 20. PAGE 23 F0448
ECO/TAC FINAN PROB/SOLV WEALTH

B51
DIMOCK M.E.,FREE ENTERPRISE AND THE ADMINISTRATIVE STATE. FINAN LG/CO BARGAIN BUDGET DOMIN CONTROL INGP/REL EFFICIENCY 20. PAGE 33 F0640
CAP/ISM ADMIN MGT MARKET

B51
HART A.G.,DEFENSE WITHOUT INFLATION. AFR KOREA FINAN INDUS NAT/G WORKER DIPLOM RATION TAX PRICE COST OPTIMAL 20 RESOURCE/N. PAGE 56 F1098
ECO/TAC CONTROL WAR PLAN

B51
OWENS R.N.,BUSINESS, ORGANIZATION, AND COMBINATION. USA+45 USA-45 LAW NAT/G LEGIS ECO/TAC CONTROL INGP/REL...JURID GP/COMP 20 NEW/DEAL. PAGE 102 F2006
SML/CO LG/CO STRUCT GP/REL

B51
ROEPKE W.,THE PROBLEM OF ECONOMIC ORDER. WOR+45 SOCIETY PROB/SOLV CONTROL EFFICIENCY...CON/ANAL IDEA/COMP GEN/METH 20. PAGE 113 F2231
ECO/TAC ORD/FREE MARKET PROC/MFG

B52
EGLE W.P.,ECONOMIC STABILIZATION: OBJECTIVES, RULES, AND MECHANISMS. UNIV FINAN PROB/SOLV CAP/ISM ECO/TAC CONTROL...IDEA/COMP 20. PAGE 36 F0709
EQUILIB PLAN NAT/G ECO/DEV

B52
MACHLUP F.,THE POLITICAL ECONOMY OF MONOPOLY: BUSINESS, LABOR AND GOVERNMENT POLICIES. USA+45 USA-45 ECO/DEV LABOR NAT/G LG/CO CAP/ISM PWR...POLICY CHARTS T 20. PAGE 83 F1630
ECO/TAC DOMIN LG/CO CONTROL

B52
REDFORD E.S.,ADMINISTRATION OF NATIONAL ECONOMIC CONTROL. ECO/DEV DELIB/GP ADJUD CONTROL EQUILIB 20. PAGE 110 F2166
ADMIN ROUTINE GOV/REL LOBBY

B52
WU Y.,ECONOMIC WARFARE. MARKET PLAN PROB/SOLV FOR/AID CONTROL EFFICIENCY WEALTH...METH/COMP 20. PAGE 149 F2937
ECO/TAC WAR INT/TRADE DIPLOM

S52
KORNHAUSER W.,"THE NEGRO UNION OFFICIAL: A STUDY OF SPONSORSHIP AND CONTROL" (BMR)" USA+45 CONTROL DISCRIM ROLE SUPEGO...OBS 20 NEGRO. PAGE 73 F1428
LABOR LEAD RACE/REL CHOOSE

B53
BOEKE J.H.,ECONOMICS AND ECONOMIC POLICY OF DUAL SOCIETIES AS EXEMPLIFIED BY INDONESIA. INDIA INDONESIA SOCIETY CAP/ISM INT/TRADE GIVE PRICE GP/REL WEALTH SOCISM...POLICY NAT/COMP GEN/LAWS 20. PAGE 16 F0304
ECO/TAC ECO/UNDEV NAT/G CONTROL

B53
DAHL R.A.,POLITICS, ECONOMICS, AND WELFARE. TEC/DEV BARGAIN ECO/TAC RECEIVE PRICE CONTROL LEAD INGP/REL ...POLICY GEN/LAWS. PAGE 29 F0572
SOCIETY GIVE

S53
GABLE R.W.,"NAM: INFLUENTIAL LOBBY OR KISS OF DEATH?" (BMR)" USA+45 LAW INSPECT EDU/PROP ADMIN CONTROL INGP/REL EFFICIENCY PWR 20 CONGRESS NAM TAFT/HART. PAGE 45 F0880
LOBBY LEGIS INDUS LG/CO

S53
LAWTON F.J.,"LEGISLATIVE-EXECUTIVE RELATIONS IN BUDGETING AS VIEWED BY THE EXECUTIVE." NAT/G LEGIS ADMIN REPRESENT EFFICIENCY 20. PAGE 76 F1495
BUDGET EX/STRUC EXEC CONTROL

B54
EMERSON F.D.,SHAREHOLDER DEMOCRACY: A BROADER OUTLOOK FOR CORPORATIONS. DELIB/GP EX/STRUC LEGIS ADJUD CONTROL REPRESENT INGP/REL OWN PWR...POLICY STAT RECORD. PAGE 37 F0727
LG/CO PARTIC MAJORIT TREND

B54
KARTUN D.,AFRICA, AFRICA: A CONTINENT RISES TO ITS FEET. AFR SOUTH/AFR UK ELITES AGRI LABOR LOC/G POL/PAR EDU/PROP CONTROL COERCE DISCRIM AGE/Y NEGRO THIRD/WRLD GOLD/COAST. PAGE 69 F1358
COLONIAL ORD/FREE PROFIT EXTR/IND

B54
LOCKLIN D.P.,ECONOMICS OF TRANSPORTATION (4TH ED.). USA+45 USA-45 SEA AIR LAW FINAN LG/CO EX/STRUC ADMIN CONTROL...STAT CHARTS 19/20 RAILROAD PUB/TRANS. PAGE 81 F1592
ECO/DEV DIST/IND ECO/TAC TEC/DEV

B54
RICHTER R.,DAS KONKURRENZ PROBLEM IM OLIGOPOL. LG/CO BARGAIN PRICE COST...CONCPT 20 MONOPOLY. PAGE 111 F2188
CONTROL GAME ECO/TAC GP/REL

C54
BERLE A.A. JR.,"THE 20TH CENTURY CAPITALIST REVOLUTION." ECO/DEV NAT/G DIPLOM PRICE CONTROL ATTIT...BIBLIOG/A 20. PAGE 14 F0260
LG/CO CAP/ISM MGT PWR

B55
BERNSTEIN M.H.,REGULATING BUSINESS BY INDEPENDENT COMMISSION. USA+45 USA-45 LG/CO CHIEF LEGIS PROB/SOLV ADJUD SANCTION GP/REL ATTIT...TIME/SEQ 19/20 MONOPOLY PRESIDENT CONGRESS. PAGE 14 F0268
DELIB/GP CONTROL CONSULT

B55
BLOOM G.F.,ECONOMICS OF LABOR RELATIONS. USA+45 LAW CONSULT WORKER CAP/ISM PAY ADJUD CONTROL EFFICIENCY ORD/FREE...CHARTS 19/20 AFL/CIO NLRB DEPT/LABOR. PAGE 16 F0299
ECO/DEV ECO/TAC LABOR GOV/REL

B55
FOGARTY M.P.,ECONOMIC CONTROL. FUT UK ECO/DEV FINAN CONSULT INT/TRADE...CHARTS BIBLIOG/A 20. PAGE 42 F0819
ECO/TAC NAT/G CONTROL PROB/SOLV

B55
O'CONNOR H.,THE EMPIRE OF OIL. USA+45 DIST/IND FINAN MARKET CAP/ISM TAX CONTROL...POLICY MARXIST BIBLIOG/A 20. PAGE 100 F1955
EXTR/IND INT/TRADE CENTRAL NAT/G

B55
PALAMOUNTAIN JC J.R.,THE POLITICS OF DISTRIBUTION. USA+45 LG/CO SML/CO BAL/PWR CONTROL EQUILIB 20. PAGE 103 F2019 DIST/IND ECO/TAC CAP/ISM GP/REL

B55
SERRANO MOSCOSO E.,A STATEMENT OF THE LAWS OF ECUADOR IN MATTERS AFFECTING BUSINESS (2ND ED.). ECUADOR INDUS LABOR LG/CO NAT/G LEGIS TAX CONTROL MARRIAGE 20. PAGE 120 F2359 FINAN ECO/UNDEV LAW CONSTN

B56
BARBASH J.,THE PRACTICE OF UNIONISM. ECO/TAC LEAD LOBBY GP/REL INGP/REL DRIVE MARXISM BIBLIOG. PAGE 10 F0182 LABOR REPRESENT CONTROL ADMIN

B56
GILBERT L.D.,DIVIDENDS AND DEMOCRACY. DELIB/GP LEGIS CAP/ISM ADJUD LOBBY OWN PWR LAISSEZ MAJORIT. PAGE 47 F0922 LG/CO INGP/REL CONTROL PARTIC

B56
HICKMAN C.A.,INDIVIDUALS, GROUPS, AND ECONOMIC BEHAVIOR. WORKER PAY CONTROL EXEC GP/REL INGP/REL PERSON ROLE...PSY SOC PERS/COMP METH 20. PAGE 59 F1163 MGT ADMIN ECO/TAC PLAN

B56
KNORR K.E.,RUBLE DIPLOMACY: CHALLENGE TO AMERICAN FOREIGN AID(PAMPHLET). AFR CHINA/COM USA+45 USSR PLAN TEC/DEV CAP/ISM INT/TRADE DOMIN EDU/PROP CONTROL LEAD 20. PAGE 72 F1413 ECO/UNDEV COM DIPLOM FOR/AID

B56
KOHLER E.L.,ACCOUNTING IN THE FEDERAL GOVERNMENT. USA+45 LOC/G PLAN TAX CONTROL COST 20. PAGE 72 F1416 BUDGET AFR NAT/G FINAN

B56
LIPSET S.M.,UNION DEMOCRACY. STRUCT INDUS FACE/GP WORKER CONTROL LEAD PARTIC GP/REL ATTIT LAISSEZ ...INT QU CHARTS. PAGE 80 F1577 LABOR INGP/REL MAJORIT

B56
REDFORD E.S.,PUBLIC ADMINISTRATION AND POLICY FORMATION: STUDIES IN OIL, GAS, BANKING, RIVER DEVELOPMENT AND CORPORATE INVESTIGATIONS. USA+45 CLIENT NAT/G ADMIN LOBBY REPRESENT GOV/REL INGP/REL 20. PAGE 110 F2167 EX/STRUC PROB/SOLV CONTROL EXEC

S56
BROWN J.S.,"UNION SIZE AS A FUNCTION OF INTRA-UNION CONFLICT." CLIENT CONTROL CHOOSE EFFICIENCY ATTIT TREND. PAGE 19 F0370 LABOR INGP/REL CONSEN DRIVE

S56
KNAPP D.C.,"CONGRESSIONAL CONTROL OF AGRICULTURAL CONSERVATION POLICY: A CASE STUDY OF THE APPROPRIATIONS PROCESS." DELIB/GP PLAN PROB/SOLV CONFER PARL/PROC...POLICY INT CONGRESS. PAGE 72 F1411 LEGIS AGRI BUDGET CONTROL

S56
MERRIAM R.E.,"THE BUREAU OF THE BUDGET AS PART OF THE PRESIDENT'S STAFF." 20 BUR/BUDGET 20 BOB. PAGE 90 F1763 CHIEF CONTROL LEAD EXEC

S56
MILNE R.S.,"CONTROL OF GOVERNMENT CORPORATIONS IN THE UNITED STATES." USA+45 NAT/G CHIEF LEGIS BUDGET 20 GENACCOUNT. PAGE 92 F1800 CONTROL EX/STRUC GOV/REL PWR

S56
TANNENBAUM A.S.,"CONTROL OF STRUCTURE AND UNION FUNCTIONS." PARTIC GP/REL INGP/REL CONSEN ATTIT PWR ...QU SAMP. PAGE 128 F2529 LABOR STRUCT CONTROL LEAD

B57
BARAN P.A.,THE POLITICAL ECONOMY OF GROWTH. MOD/EUR USA+45 USA-45 TEC/DEV TAX SOCISM...MGT CONCPT GOV/COMP. PAGE 9 F0178 CAP/ISM CONTROL ECO/UNDEV FINAN

B57
BEHRMAN J.N.,INTERNATIONAL ECONOMICS: THEORY, PRACTICE, POLICY. AGRI INDUS NAT/G TARIFFS CONTROL BAL/PAY...POLICY METH/CNCPT T 19/20. PAGE 12 F0230 INT/TRADE FINAN DIPLOM FOR/AID

B57
BERLE A.A. JR.,ECONOMIC POWER AND FREE SOCIETY (PAMPHLET). CLIENT CONSTN EX/STRUC ECO/TAC CONTROL PARTIC PWR WEALTH MAJORIT. PAGE 14 F0261 LG/CO CAP/ISM INGP/REL LEGIT

B57
CLARK J.M.,ECONOMIC INSTITUTIONS AND HUMAN WELFARE. USA+45 SOCIETY ECO/DEV NAT/G WORKER PLAN PROB/SOLV CAP/ISM CONTROL...POLICY 20. PAGE 25 F0482 ECO/TAC ORD/FREE WEALTH

B57
FOUSEK P.G.,FOREIGN CENTRAL BANKING: THE INSTRUMENTS OF MONETARY POLICY. WOR+45 CONTROL ...TREND CHARTS 20 MONEY. PAGE 43 F0836 FINAN ECO/TAC ECO/DEV MARKET

B57
HARWOOD E.C.,CAUSE AND CONTROL OF THE BUSINESS CYCLE (5TH ED.). AFR USA-45 PRICE CONTROL WAR DEMAND INCOME WEALTH...TREND CHARTS 19. PAGE 56 F1107 PRODUC MARKET FINAN

B57
INTL BANKING SUMMER SCHOOL,RELATIONS BETWEEN THE CENTRAL BANKS AND COMMERCIAL BANKS. EUR+WWI FRANCE GERMANY/W ITALY UK USA+45 USSR INDUS INT/ORG CAP/ISM CONTROL MONEY. PAGE 65 F1282 FINAN NAT/G GP/REL LG/CO

B57
LUNDBERG E.,BUSINESS CYCLES AND ECONOMIC POLICY (TRANS. BY J. POTTER). SWEDEN ECO/DEV FINAN DELIB/GP PLAN PRICE CONTROL BAL/PAY 20 INTRVN/ECO. PAGE 82 F1607 ECO/TAC INDUS INT/TRADE BUDGET

B57
MASON E.S.,ECONOMIC CONCENTRATION AND THE MONOPOLY PROBLEM. USA+45 USA-45 LAW ELITES ECO/DEV LABOR RATION PRICE PWR WEALTH...CHARTS 20 MONOPOLY. PAGE 87 F1696 GP/REL LG/CO CONTROL MARKET

B57
MURDESHWAR A.K.,ADMINISTRATIVE PROBLEMS RELATING TO NATIONALISATION: WITH SPECIAL REFERENCE TO INDIAN STATE ENTERPRISES. CZECHOSLVK FRANCE INDIA UK USA+45 LEGIS WORKER PROB/SOLV BUDGET PRICE CONTROL ...MGT GEN/LAWS 20 PARLIAMENT. PAGE 95 F1863 NAT/G OWN INDUS ADMIN

B57
PALACIOS A.L.,PETROLEO, MONOPOLIOS, Y LATIFUNDIOS. L/A+17C EXTR/IND NAT/G TEC/DEV ECO/TAC CONTROL PRODUC 20 ARGEN MONOPOLY RESOURCE/N. PAGE 103 F2017 ECO/UNDEV NAT/LISM INDUS AGRI

B57
SINGH D.B.,INFLATIONARY PRICE TRENDS IN INDIA SINCE 1939. AFR INDIA ECO/TAC RATION CONTROL WAR GOV/REL BAL/PAY DEMAND INCOME PEACE PRODUC...POLICY CHARTS 20. PAGE 122 F2413 BUDGET ECO/UNDEV PRICE FINAN

B57
WATSON G.,THE UNSERVILE STATE: ESSAYS IN LIBERTY AND WELFARE. UK LEGIS RECEIVE EDU/PROP COLONIAL ...WELF/ST 20 LIB/PARTY. PAGE 144 F2833 POL/PAR ORD/FREE CONTROL NEW/LIB

S57
LEWIS E.G.,"PARLIAMENTARY CONTROL OF NATIONALIZED INDUSTRY IN FRANCE." FRANCE NAT/G DELIB/GP ACT/RES PLAN PROB/SOLV ECO/TAC DOMIN CENTRAL. PAGE 79 F1547 PWR LEGIS INDUS CONTROL

S57
TANNENBAUM A.S.,"ORGANIZATIONAL CONTROL STRUCTURE: A GENERAL DESCRIPTIVE TECHNIQUE AS APPLIED TO FOUR LOCAL UNIONS." LABOR PWR...METH/CNCPT CLASSIF QU CHARTS. PAGE 128 F2530 WORKER PARTIC STRUCT CONTROL

B58
CHANG C.,THE INFLATIONARY SPIRAL: THE EXPERIENCE IN CHINA 1939-50. CHINA/COM BUDGET INT/TRADE PRICE ADMIN CONTROL WAR DEMAND...POLICY CHARTS 20. PAGE 23 F0451 FINAN ECO/TAC BAL/PAY GOV/REL

B58
CHEEK G.,ECONOMIC AND SOCIAL IMPLICATIONS OF AUTOMATION: A BIBLIOGRAPHIC REVIEW (PAMPHLET). USA+45 LG/CO WORKER CREATE PLAN CONTROL ROUTINE PERS/REL EFFICIENCY PRODUC...METH/COMP 20. PAGE 24 F0459 BIBLIOG/A SOCIETY INDUS AUTOMAT

B58
CROWE S.,THE LANDSCAPE OF POWER. UK CULTURE SERV/IND NAT/G CONSULT PARTIC NUC/PWR LEISURE...SOC EXHIBIT 20. PAGE 29 F0559 HABITAT TEC/DEV PLAN CONTROL

B58
FINER S.E.,PRIVATE INDUSTRY AND POLITICAL POWER (PAMPHLET). UK INDUS CONTROL LOBBY PWR. PAGE 41 F0797 PLURISM REPRESENT EX/STRUC

B58
MCIVOR R.C.,CANADIAN MONETARY, BANKING, AND FISCAL DEVELOPMENT. CANADA INDUS LG/CO NAT/G SML/CO CONTROL WAR...GEN/LAWS BIBLIOG 17/20. PAGE 88 F1729 ECO/TAC FINAN ECO/DEV WEALTH

B58
MOULTON H.G.,CAN INFLATION BE CONTROLLED? ECO/DEV INDUS CAP/ISM RATION GOV/REL COST INCOME PEACE WEALTH...CHARTS TIME 20 KEYNES/JM MONEY. PAGE 94 F1847 ECO/TAC CONTROL DEMAND FINAN

B58
SCOTT D.J.R.,RUSSIAN POLITICAL INSTITUTIONS. RUSSIA USSR CONSTN AGRI DELIB/GP PLAN EDU/PROP CONTROL CHOOSE EFFICIENCY ATTIT MARXISM...BIBLIOG/A IND 13/20. PAGE 118 F2332 NAT/G POL/PAR ADMIN DECISION

B58
TANNENBAUM A.S.,PARTICIPATION IN UNION LOCALS. SOCIETY FINAN CONTROL LEAD GP/REL...BIBLIOG 20. PAGE 128 F2531 LABOR MGT PARTIC INGP/REL

B58
WARNER A.W.,CONCEPTS AND CASES IN ECONOMIC ANALYSIS. PROB/SOLV BARGAIN CONTROL INCOME PRODUC ...ECOMETRIC MGT CONCPT CLASSIF CHARTS 20 KEYNES/JM. PAGE 143 F2820 ECO/TAC DEMAND EQUILIB COST

S58
LOCKWOOD W.W.,"THE SOCIALISTIC SOCIETY: INDIA AND JAPAN." INDIA ECO/DEV ECO/UNDEV INDUS NAT/G CONTROL LEAD PRODUC WEALTH 20 CHINJAP. PAGE 81 F1593
ECO/TAC NAT/COMP FINAN SOCISM

B59
ARON R.,IMPERIALISM AND COLONIALISM (PAMPHLET). WOR+45 WOR-45 ECO/TAC CONTROL REV ORD/FREE 19/20. PAGE 6 F0119
COLONIAL DOMIN ECO/UNDEV DIPLOM

B59
BROMWICH L.,UNION CONSTITUTIONS. CONSTN EX/STRUC PRESS ADJUD CONTROL CHOOSE REPRESENT PWR SAMP. PAGE 19 F0361
LABOR ROUTINE INGP/REL RACE/REL

B59
FERRY W.H.,THE CORPORATION AND THE ECONOMY. CLIENT LAW CONSTN LABOR NAT/G PLAN INT/TRADE PARTIC CONSEN ORD/FREE PWR POLICY. PAGE 40 F0787
LG/CO CONTROL REPRESENT

B59
GUDIN E.,INFLACAO (2ND ED.). INDUS NAT/G PLAN ECO/TAC CONTROL COST 20. PAGE 52 F1012
ECO/UNDEV INT/TRADE BAL/PAY FINAN

B59
HARVARD UNIVERSITY LAW SCHOOL,INTERNATIONAL PROBLEMS OF FINANCIAL PROTECTION AGAINST NUCLEAR RISK. WOR+45 NAT/G DELIB/GP PROB/SOLV DIPLOM CONTROL ATTIT...POLICY INT/LAW MATH 20. PAGE 56 F1105
NUC/PWR ADJUD INDUS FINAN

B59
JENKINS C.,POWER AT THE TOP: A CRITICAL SURVEY OF THE NATIONALIZED INDUSTRIES. UK POL/PAR CONTROL ...WELF/ST CHARTS 20 LABOR/PAR. PAGE 67 F1313
NAT/G OWN INDUS NEW/LIB

B59
KARLIN S.,MATHEMATICAL METHODS AND THEORY IN GAMES, PROGRAMMING, AND ECONOMICS. COMPUTER PLAN CONTROL TASK...MATH 20. PAGE 69 F1357
GAME METH/COMP ACT/RES DECISION

B59
MUSOLF L.D.,PUBLIC OWNERSHIP AND ACCOUNTABILITY: THE CANADIAN EXPERIENCE. CANADA REPRESENT PWR 20. PAGE 95 F1873
MGT CONTROL INDUS

B59
U OF MICHIGAN LAW SCHOOL,ATOMS AND THE LAW. USA+45 PROVS WORKER PROB/SOLV DIPLOM ADMIN GOV/REL ANTHOL. PAGE 132 F2596
NUC/PWR NAT/G CONTROL LAW

B59
VERNEY D.V.,PUBLIC ENTERPRISE IN SWEDEN. FUT SWEDEN UK INDUS POL/PAR LEGIS PROB/SOLV CAP/ISM INT/TRADE CONTROL SOCISM...MGT CONCPT NAT/COMP 20 SOCDEM/PAR CIVIL/SERV. PAGE 141 F2778
ECO/DEV POLICY LG/CO NAT/G

B59
WENTHOLT W.,SOME COMMENTS ON THE LIQUIDATION OF THE EUROPEAN PAYMENT UNION AND RELATED PROBLEMS (PAMPHLET). AFR WOR+45 PLAN BUDGET PRICE CONTROL 20 EEC. PAGE 145 F2857
FINAN ECO/DEV INT/ORG ECO/TAC

L59
OBERER W.E.,"VOLUNTARY IMPARTIAL REVIEW OF LABOR: SOME REFLECTIONS." DELIB/GP LEGIS PROB/SOLV ADJUD CONTROL COERCE PWR PLURISM POLICY. PAGE 100 F1960
LABOR LAW PARTIC INGP/REL

S59
GILPATRICK T.V.,"PRICE SUPPORT POLICY AND THE MIDWEST FARM VOTE" (BMR)" NAT/G PRICE CONTROL REGION...POLICY CHARTS 440 20 MIDWEST/US CONGRESS REPUBLICAN EISNHWR/DD 20. PAGE 47 F0925
POL/PAR AGRI ATTIT CHOOSE

S59
MILLER A.S.,"CONSTITUTIONALIZING THE CORPORATION." LABOR NAT/G WORKER PWR...POLICY MGT. PAGE 91 F1789
CONSTN INGP/REL LG/CO CONTROL

S59
REES A.,"DO UNIONS CAUSE INFLATION?" CONTROL 20. PAGE 110 F2171
LABOR ECO/TAC PRICE WORKER

S59
SCHEEHAN D.,"PUBLIC AND PRIVATE GROUPS AS IDENTIFIED IN THE FIELD OF TRADE REGULATIONS." USA+45 ADMIN REPRESENT GOV/REL. PAGE 116 F2293
LAW CONTROL ADJUD LOBBY

S59
SEIDMAN H.,"THE GOVERNMENT CORPORATION IN THE UNITED STATES." USA+45 LEGIS ADMIN PLURISM 20. PAGE 119 F2344
CONTROL GOV/REL EX/STRUC EXEC

S59
SHEENAN D.,"PUBLIC CORPORATIONS AND PUBLIC ACTION." UK ADMIN CONTROL REPRESENT SOCISM 20. PAGE 120 F2372
ECO/DEV EFFICIENCY EX/STRUC EXEC

C59
FAINSOD M.,"GOVERNMENT AND THE AMERICAN ECONOMY." USA+45 USA-45 INDUS LABOR OP/RES PROB/SOLV ECO/TAC CONTROL...CHARTS BIBLIOG T 20. PAGE 39 F0760
CONSTN ECO/DEV CAP/ISM NAT/G

B60
ANGERS F.A.,ESSAI SUR LA CENTRALISATION: ANALYSE DES PRINCIPES ET PERSPECTIVES CANADIENNES. CANADA ECO/TAC CONTROL...SOC IDEA/COMP BIBLIOG 20. PAGE 6 F0105
CENTRAL ADMIN

B60
BHAMBHRI C.P.,PARLIAMENTARY CONTROL OVER STATE ENTERPRISE IN INDIA. INDIA DELIB/GP ADMIN CONTROL INGP/REL EFFICIENCY 20 PARLIAMENT. PAGE 14 F0277
NAT/G OWN INDUS PARL/PROC

B60
CARPER E.T.,THE DEFENSE APPROPRIATIONS RIDER (PAMPHLET). USA+45 CONSTN CHIEF DELIB/GP LEGIS BUDGET LOBBY CIVMIL/REL...POLICY 20 CONGRESS EISNHWR/DD DEPT/DEFEN PRESIDENT BOSTON. PAGE 22 F0419
GOV/REL ADJUD LAW CONTROL

B60
CROSSER P.K.,STATE CAPITALISM IN THE ECONOMY OF THE UNITED STATES. USA+45 USA-45 AGRI FINAN INDUS LABOR WORKER RATION CONTROL GOV/REL DEMAND...NEW/IDEA 20. PAGE 29 F0557
CAP/ISM ECO/DEV ECO/TAC NAT/G

B60
DALE W.B.,THE FOREIGN DEFICIT OF THE UNITED STATES. ECO/TAC TARIFFS PAY PRICE CONTROL COST WEALTH POLICY. PAGE 30 F0573
BAL/PAY DIPLOM FINAN INT/TRADE

B60
FORBUSH D.R.,PROBLEMS OF CORPORATE POWER. CLIENT LAW ELITES ADJUD...DECISION MGT. PAGE 42 F0822
LG/CO PWR CONTROL GP/REL

B60
FORM W.H.,INDUSTRY, LABOR, AND COMMUNITY. STRUCT NEIGH SECT BAL/PWR EDU/PROP PARTIC ATTIT ROLE PWR WEALTH...METH/CNCPT CHARTS. PAGE 42 F0828
LABOR MGT GP/REL CONTROL

B60
HARBRECHT P.P.,TOWARD THE PARAPROPRIETAL SOCIETY. REPRESENT INCOME OWN PROFIT AGE/O. PAGE 55 F1076
PWR ADMIN ELITES CONTROL

B60
HUGHES R.,THE CHINESE COMMUNES; A BACKGROUND BOOK. CHINA/COM SOCIETY CONTROL ROUTINE ADJUST EFFICIENCY PRODUC 20. PAGE 63 F1234
AGRI INDUS STRUCT MARXISM

B60
KILLOUGH H.B.,INTERNATIONAL ECONOMICS. PLAN PROB/SOLV FOR/AID TARIFFS CONTROL BAL/PAY...POLICY CHARTS T 20. PAGE 71 F1388
CONCPT ECO/UNDEV INT/ORG INT/TRADE

B60
RAY D.D.,ACCOUNTING AND BUSINESS FLUCTUATIONS. LG/CO SML/CO FEEDBACK DEMAND...CHARTS IDEA/COMP BIBLIOG 20. PAGE 109 F2154
FINAN AFR CONTROL

B60
ROBERTSON D.,THE CONTROL OF INDUSTRY. UK MARKET LABOR WORKER PRICE CONTROL GP/REL COST DEMAND ORD/FREE WEALTH NEW/LIB SOCISM 20. PAGE 112 F2211
INDUS FINAN NAT/G ECO/DEV

B60
WEINER H.E.,BRITISH LABOR AND PUBLIC OWNERSHIP. UK SERV/IND LG/CO WORKER CONTROL OWN 20. PAGE 145 F2850
LABOR NAT/G INDUS ATTIT

B60
WHEARE K.C.,THE CONSTITUTIONAL STRUCTURE OF THE COMMONWEALTH. UK EX/STRUC DIPLOM DOMIN ADMIN COLONIAL CONTROL LEAD INGP/REL SUPEGO 20 CMN/WLTH. PAGE 145 F2865
CONSTN INT/ORG VOL/ASSN SOVEREIGN

[illegible]0
ENKE S.,"THE ECONOMIES OF GOVERNMENT PAYMENTS TO LIMIT POPULATION." FUT INDIA WOR+45 CULTURE FINAN NAT/G CONSULT PLAN LEGIT CONTROL COST ATTIT RIGID/FLEX HEALTH WEALTH...STAT OBS CHARTS TOT/POP VAL/FREE 20. PAGE 38 F0736
FAM ACT/RES

S60
FORM W.H.,"ORGANIZED LABOR'S IMAGE OF COMMUNITY POWER STRUCTURE." LABOR LG/CO CONTROL LEAD REPRESENT...DECISION METH/CNCPT INT QU SAMP. PAGE 42 F0829
NEIGH PARTIC PWR GP/REL

B61
AGARWAL R.C.,STATE ENTERPRISE IN INDIA. FUT INDIA UK FINAN INDUS ADMIN CONTROL OWN...POLICY CHARTS BIBLIOG 20 RAILROAD. PAGE 3 F0048
ECO/UNDEV SOCISM GOV/REL LG/CO

B61
ALFRED H.,PUBLIC OWNERSHIP IN THE USA: GOALS AND PRIORITIES. LAW INDUS INT/TRADE ADJUD GOV/REL EFFICIENCY PEACE SOCISM...POLICY ANTHOL 20 TVA. PAGE 4 F0065
CONTROL OWN ECO/DEV ECO/TAC

B61
AMERICAN MANAGEMENT ASSN,SUPERIOR-SUBORDINATE
MGT

COMMUNICATION IN MANAGEMENT. STRATA FINAN INDUS SML/CO WORKER CONTROL EXEC ATTIT 20. PAGE 5 F0090
ACT/RES PERS/REL LG/CO

B61
ASCHHEIM J.,TECHNIQUES OF MONETARY CONTROL. UK USA+45 CONTROL WAR DEMAND INCOME WEALTH...TREND CHARTS 20 MONEY. PAGE 7 F0127
FINAN MARKET BUDGET CENTRAL

B61
ASHER R.E.,GRANTS, LOANS, AND LOCAL CURRENCIES; THEIR ROLE IN FOREIGN AID. AFR USA+45 ECO/UNDEV INT/ORG ACT/RES PLAN ECO/TAC GIVE CONTROL WEALTH 20. PAGE 7 F0130
FOR/AID FINAN NAT/G BUDGET

B61
BEASLEY K.E.,STATE SUPERVISION OF MUNICIPAL DEBT IN KANSAS - A CASE STUDY. USA+45 USA-45 FINAN PROVS BUDGET TAX ADJUD ADMIN CONTROL SUPEGO MUNICH. PAGE 12 F0224
LOC/G LEGIS JURID

B61
BREWIS T.N.,CANADIAN ECONOMIC POLICY. AFR CANADA BUDGET CAP/ISM INT/TRADE RATION TARIFFS TAX PRICE CONTROL ROUTINE FEDERAL INCOME PRODUC 20. PAGE 18 F0348
ECO/DEV ECO/TAC NAT/G PLAN

B61
CAMPAIGNE J.G.,CHECK-OFF: LABOR BOSSES AND WORKING MEN. LEGIS WORKER EDU/PROP DEBATE COERCE REPRESENT GP/REL ORD/FREE CONSERVE. PAGE 21 F0404
LABOR ELITES PWR CONTROL

B61
DUKE UNIVERSITY,EXPULSION OR OPPRESSION OF BUSINESS ASSOCIATES: "SQUEEZE-OUTS" IN SMALL ENTERPRISES. LAW CONTROL PARTIC COERCE INGP/REL...POLICY RECORD INT. PAGE 35 F0674
PWR MGT SML/CO ECO/TAC

B61
ESTEBAN J.C.,IMPERIALISMO Y DESARROLLO ECONOMICO. L/A+17C FINAN INDUS NAT/G ECO/TAC CONTROL ROLE. PAGE 38 F0747
ECO/UNDEV NAT/LISM DIPLOM BAL/PAY

B61
FERTIG L.,PROSPERITY THROUGH FREEDOM. COM INDUS LABOR CAP/ISM ECO/TAC PRODUC PROFIT ORD/FREE WEALTH SOCISM...METH/CNCPT 20. PAGE 40 F0788
NAT/G CONTROL POLICY

B61
FRIEDMANN G.,THE ANATOMY OF WORK. USA+45 SOCIETY CONTROL ROUTINE DRIVE SKILL...PSY SOC STAT OBS METH/COMP PERS/COMP 20. PAGE 44 F0862
AUTOMAT WORKER INDUS PERSON

B61
GORDON R.A.,BUSINESS LEADERSHIP IN THE LARGE CORPORATION. USA+45 SOCIETY EX/STRUC ADMIN CONTROL ROUTINE GP/REL PWR...MGT 20. PAGE 49 F0960
LG/CO LEAD DECISION LOBBY

B61
HARRIS S.E.,THE DOLLAR IN CRISIS. AFR USA+45 MARKET INT/ORG ECO/TAC PRICE CONTROL WEALTH...METH/COMP ANTHOL 20. PAGE 55 F1089
BAL/PAY DIPLOM FINAN INT/TRADE

B61
HUBBARD P.J.,ORIGINS OF THE TVA: THE MUSCLE SHOALS CONTROVERSY, 1920-1932. USA-45 DELIB/GP LEGIS LEAD LOBBY GOV/REL GP/REL INGP/REL OWN PERSON...BIBLIOG 20 TVA CONGRESS WATER. PAGE 62 F1229
SEA CONTROL NAT/G INDUS

B61
LAHAYE R.,LES ENTREPRISES PUBLIQUES AU MAROC. FRANCE MOROCCO LAW DIST/IND EXTR/IND FINAN CONSULT PLAN TEC/DEV ADMIN AGREE CONTROL OWN...POLICY 20. PAGE 74 F1460
NAT/G INDUS ECO/UNDEV ECO/TAC

B61
LEE R.R.,ENGINEERING-ECONOMIC PLANNING MISCELLANEOUS SUBJECTS: A SELECTED BIBLIOGRAPHY (MIMEOGRAPHED). FINAN LOC/G NEIGH ADMIN CONTROL INGP/REL HABITAT...GEOG MGT SOC/WK MUNICH 20 RESOURCE/N. PAGE 77 F1509
BIBLIOG/A PLAN REGION

B61
LETHBRIDGE H.J.,CHINA'S URBAN COMMUNES. CHINA/COM FUT ECO/UNDEV DIPLOM EDU/PROP DEMAND INCOME MARXISM ...POLICY MUNICH 20. PAGE 78 F1534
CONTROL ECO/TAC NAT/G

B61
PERLO V.,EL IMPERIALISMO NORTHEAMERICANO. USA+45 USA-45 FINAN CAP/ISM DIPLOM DOMIN CONTROL DISCRIM 19/20. PAGE 105 F2063
SOCIALIST ECO/DEV INT/TRADE ECO/TAC

B61
RUEDA B.,A STATEMENT OF THE LAWS OF COLOMBIA IN MATTERS AFFECTING BUSINESS (3RD ED.). INDUS FAM LABOR LG/CO NAT/G LEGIS TAX CONTROL MARRIAGE 20 COLOMB. PAGE 115 F2257
FINAN ECO/UNDEV LAW CONSTN

B61
SHONFIELD A.,ECONOMIC GROWTH AND INFLATION; A STUDY OF INDIAN PLANNING. AFR INDIA AGRI INDUS TEC/DEV CONTROL DEMAND UTIL 20. PAGE 121 F2384
ECO/UNDEV PRICE PLAN BUDGET

B61
STOCKING G.W.,WORKABLE COMPETITION AND ANTITRUST POLICY. USA+45 NAT/G CONSULT PLAN PRICE GOV/REL COST DEMAND PROFIT...POLICY 20. PAGE 126 F2491
LG/CO INDUS ECO/TAC

CONTROL

B61
US GENERAL ACCOUNTING OFFICE,EXAMINATION OF ECONOMIC AND TECHNICAL ASSISTANCE PROGRAM FOR IRAN. IRAN USA+45 AGRI INDUS DIPLOM CONTROL COST 20. PAGE 136 F2681
FOR/AID ADMIN TEC/DEV ECO/UNDEV

B61
WESTON J.F.,THE ROLE OF MERGERS IN THE GROWTH OF LARGE FIRMS. USA+45 USA-45 LEGIS CONTROL...CONCPT STAT CHARTS 19/20. PAGE 145 F2862
LG/CO CENTRAL INDUS FINAN

B61
WILSON T.,INFLATION. FINAN PLAN CAP/ISM PRICE CONTROL...CHARTS 20. PAGE 147 F2903
ECO/DEV ECO/TAC POLICY COST

S61
SCHER S.,"REGULATORY AGENCY CONTROL THROUGH APPOINTMENT: THE CASE OF THE EISENHOWER ADMINISTRATION AND THE NLRB." USA+45 EX/STRUC GOV/REL 20 NLRB. PAGE 116 F2296
CHIEF LOBBY CONTROL TOP/EX

N61
US ADVISORY COMM INTERGOV REL,STATE AND LOCAL TAXATION ON PRIVATELY OWNED PROPERTY LOCATED ON FEDERAL AREAS: PROPOSED AMENDMENT OF BUCK ACT (PAMPHLET). USA+45 ACT/RES PLAN CONTROL GOV/REL INGP/REL OWN...POLICY JURID CHARTS GP/COMP 20. PAGE 133 F2629
PROVS LOC/G NAT/G TAX

B62
ALTMAN G.T.,INVISIBLE BARRIER: THE OPTIMUM GROWTH CURVE. USA+45 USA-45 ECO/DEV PLAN PAY CONTROL DEMAND OPTIMAL PRODUC WEALTH...STAT CHARTS 20. PAGE 4 F0080
INDUS FINAN ECO/TAC TAX

B62
BERNSTEIN P.L.,THE PRICE OF PROSPERITY. USA+45 TAX CONTROL OPTIMAL WEALTH...PREDICT 20. PAGE 14 F0269
ECO/DEV ECO/TAC NAT/G DEMAND

B62
BRANCH M.C.,THE CORPORATE PLANNING PROCESS. FINAN EX/STRUC EDU/PROP CONTROL LEAD GP/REL PERS/REL RATIONAL PERCEPT...MGT MATH PROBABIL STAT GAME. PAGE 18 F0338
PROF/ORG PLAN DECISION PERSON

B62
BRIEFS H.W.,PRICING POWER AND "ADMINISTRATIVE" INFLATION (PAMPHLET). AFR USA+45 PROC/MFG CONTROL EFFICIENCY MONEY. PAGE 18 F0349
ECO/DEV PRICE POLICY EXEC

B62
COPPOCK J.D.,INTERNATIONAL ECONOMIC INSTABILITY: THE EXPERIENCE AFTER WORLD WAR II. WOR+45 FINAN CAP/ISM CONTROL EFFICIENCY...CHARTS 20. PAGE 28 F0536
ECO/TAC ECOMETRIC INT/TRADE STAT

B62
FERBER R.,RESEARCH METHODS IN ECONOMICS AND BUSINESS. AFR ECO/DEV FINAN MARKET LG/CO SML/CO CONSULT CONTROL COST...STAT METH/COMP 20. PAGE 40 F0783
ACT/RES PROB/SOLV ECO/TAC MGT

B62
FRIEDMAN M.,CAPITALISM AND FREEDOM. USA+45 FINAN LG/CO WORKER INT/TRADE RECEIVE EDU/PROP CONTROL DISCRIM INCOME WEALTH POLICY. PAGE 44 F0859
CAP/ISM ORD/FREE NAT/G ECO/DEV

B62
GORT M.,DIVERSIFICATION AND INTEGRATION IN AMERICAN INDUSTRY. CLIENT DIST/IND PROC/MFG SERV/IND LG/CO CONTROL DEMAND PWR...METH/CNCPT STAT TREND CON/ANAL GP/COMP. PAGE 49 F0964
CONCPT GP/REL CLASSIF

B62
GROVE J.W.,GOVERNMENT AND INDUSTRY IN BRITAIN. UK FINAN LOC/G CONSULT DELIB/GP INT/TRADE ADMIN CONTROL...BIBLIOG 20. PAGE 52 F1008
ECO/TAC INDUS NAT/G GP/REL

B62
INTERNAT CONGRESS OF JURISTS,EXECUTIVE ACTION AND THE RULE OF RULE: REPORTION PROCEEDINGS OF INT'T CONGRESS OF JURISTS,-RIO DE JANEIRO, BRAZIL. WOR+45 ACADEM CONSULT JUDGE EDU/PROP ADJUD CT/SYS INGP/REL PERSON DEPT/DEFEN. PAGE 64 F1269
JURID EXEC ORD/FREE CONTROL

B62
INTNTL COTTON ADVISORY COMMITT,GOVERNMENT REGULATIONS ON COTTON, 1962 (PAMPHLET). WOR+45 RATION PRODUC...CHARTS 20. PAGE 65 F1287
ECO/TAC LAW CONTROL AGRI

B62
LITTLEFIELD N.,METROPOLITAN AREA PROBLEMS AND MUNICIPAL HOME RULE. USA+45 PROVS ADMIN CONTROL GP/REL PWR. PAGE 81 F1586
LOC/G SOVEREIGN JURID LEGIS

B62
MCCLELLAN J.L.,CRIME WITHOUT PUNISHMENT. USA+45 LAW SOCIETY DELIB/GP TRIBUTE CONTROL LOBBY COERCE GP/REL ANOMIE MORAL...CRIMLGY 20 CONGRESS HOFFA/J. PAGE 88 F1718
CRIME ACT/RES LABOR PWR

B62
MEANS G.C.,THE CORPORATE REVOLUTION IN AMERICA:
LG/CO

ECONOMIC REALITY VS. ECONOMIC THEORY. USA+45 USA-45 INDUS WORKER PLAN CAP/ISM ADMIN...IDEA/COMP 20. PAGE 89 F1742
MARKET CONTROL PRICE

B62
PASTOR R.S.,A STATEMENT OF THE LAWS OF PARAGUAY IN MATTERS AFFECTING BUSINESS (2ND ED.). PARAGUAY INDUS FAM LABOR LG/CO NAT/G LEGIS TAX CONTROL MARRIAGE 20. PAGE 103 F2033
FINAN ECO/UNDEV LAW CONSTN

B62
PHELPS E.S.,THE GOAL OF ECONOMIC GROWTH: SOURCES, COSTS, BENEFITS. USA+45 USSR FINAN TAX CONTROL DEMAND WEALTH...POLICY NAT/COMP ANTHOL BIBLIOG 20. PAGE 106 F2079
ECO/TAC ECO/DEV NAT/G FUT

B62
PONCET J.,LA COLONISATION ET L'AGRICULTURE EUROPEENNES EN TUNISIE DEPUIS 1881. FRANCE WORKER TEC/DEV ECO/TAC CONTROL EFFICIENCY ROLE WEALTH 19/20 TUNIS. PAGE 107 F2101
ECO/UNDEV AGRI COLONIAL FINAN

B62
REES A.,THE ECONOMICS OF TRADE UNIONS. FUT ECO/DEV INDUS BARGAIN CAP/ISM PRICE SENIOR CONTROL GP/REL COST...TREND 20 AFL/CIO. PAGE 110 F2172
LABOR WORKER ECO/TAC

B62
SIEVERS A.M.,REVOLUTION, EVOLUTION AND THE ECONOMIC ORDER. INDUS LABOR TAX CONTROL REV WAR DEMAND PRODUC WEALTH...IDEA/COMP 19/20 KEYNES/JM. PAGE 122 F2399
EFFICIENCY ALL/IDEOS ECO/DEV WELF/ST

B62
SMITH G.A. JR.,POLICY FORMULATION AND ADMINISTRATION: A CASEBOOK OF TOPMANAGEMENT PROBLEMS IN BUSINESS. EX/STRUC PLAN PROB/SOLV ADMIN CONTROL EXEC LEAD ROUTINE EFFICIENCY ATTIT MGT. PAGE 123 F2430
INDUS SOC/EXP TOP/EX DECISION

B62
US ADVISORY COMN INTERGOV REL,STATE CONSTITUTIONAL AND STATUTORY RESTRICTIONS ON LOCAL TAXING POWERS. USA+45 USA-45 LAW CONSTN ACT/RES CONTROL WEALTH ...JURID CHARTS 20. PAGE 133 F2632
LOC/G PROVS GOV/REL TAX

B62
US BUREAU OF THE CENSUS,REPORT FOR SUBCOMMITTEE ON ANTITRUST AND MONOPOLY: CONCENTRATION RATIOS IN MANUFACTURING INDUSTRY 1958. USA+45 ECO/DEV CONTROL GOV/REL OWN PRODUC PROFIT...STAT 20 CONGRESS MONOPOLY. PAGE 134 F2646
CHARTS PROC/MFG MARKET LG/CO

B62
VACCARO J.R.,A STATEMENT OF THE LAWS OF CHILE IN MATTERS AFFECTING BUSINESS (3RD ED.). CHILE AGRI FINAN FAM LABOR ECO/TAC FOR/AID TAX ADJUD CONTROL MARRIAGE STRANGE...BIBLIOG 20. PAGE 140 F2756
CONSTN LAW INDUS MGT

B62
WRIGHT D.M.,THE KEYNESIAN SYSTEM. WOR+45 WOR-45 LABOR NAT/G CONTROL COST DEMAND EFFICIENCY...POLICY CONCPT CHARTS SIMUL 20 KEYNES/JM. PAGE 149 F2931
INCOME ECO/DEV FINAN ECO/TAC

L62
N,"UNION INVESTMENT IN BUSINESS: A SOURCE OF UNION CONFLICT OF INTEREST." LAW NAT/G LEGIS CONTROL GP/REL INGP/REL DECISION. PAGE 96 F1884
LABOR POLICY FINAN LG/CO

N62
US SENATE COMM ON JUDICIARY,LEGISLATION TO STRENGTHEN PENALTIES UNDER THE ANTITRUST LAWS (PAMPHLET). USA+45 LG/CO CONFER CONTROL SANCTION ORD/FREE 20 SENATE MONOPOLY. PAGE 139 F2748
LEAD ADJUD INDUS ECO/TAC

B63
BARNETT H.J.,SCARCITY AND GROWTH: THE ECONOMICS OF NATURAL RESOURCE AVAILABILITY. FUT WOR+45 AGRI INDUS PROB/SOLV TEC/DEV CONTROL PRODUC...SOC/WK IDEA/COMP METH/COMP SIMUL 20 RESOURCE/N MALTHUS RICARDO/D MILL/JS DARWIN/C. PAGE 10 F0191
DEMAND HABITAT CENSUS GEOG

B63
BATES J.L.,THE ORIGINS OF TEAPOT DOME: PROGRESSIVES, PARTIES, AND PETROLEUM, 1909-1921. USA-45 INDUS LG/CO POL/PAR DELIB/GP CONTROL GOV/REL CONSERVE...BIBLOG 20 NAVY. PAGE 11 F0209
EXTR/IND CRIME NAT/G

B63
BOWIE R.R.,GOVERNMENT REGULATION OF BUSINESS: CASES FROM THE NATIONAL REPORTER SYSTEM. USA+45 USA-45 NAT/G ECO/TAC ADJUD...ANTHOL 19/20 SUPREME/CT FTC FAIR/LABOR MONOPOLY. PAGE 17 F0331
LAW CONTROL INDUS CT/SYS

B63
BRAYBROOKE D.,A STRATEGY OF DECISION: POLICY EVALUATION AS A SOCIAL PROCESS. UNIV ELITES OP/RES DOMIN CONFER FEEDBACK CONSEN PLURISM...CONCPT CENSUS. PAGE 18 F0343
DECISION POLICY CONTROL

B63
BROUDE H.W.,STEEL DECISIONS AND THE NATIONAL ECONOMY. USA+45 LG/CO PLAN ADMIN COST DECISION. PAGE 19 F0365
PROC/MFG NAT/G CONTROL ECO/TAC

B63
BURTT E.J. JR.,LABOR MARKETS, UNIONS, AND GOVERNMENT POLICIES. USA+45 MARKET NAT/G DELIB/GP CREATE BARGAIN GP/REL ORD/FREE PWR...POLICY CHARTS 20 AFL/CIO. PAGE 20 F0393
LABOR ECO/DEV CONTROL WORKER

B63
CENTRO ESTUDIOS MONETARIOS LAT,COOPERACION FINANCIERA EN AMERICA LATINA. L/A+17C PLAN PROB/SOLV CONTROL REGION DEMAND...POLICY ANTHOL 20. PAGE 22 F0433
ECO/UNDEV INT/TRADE MARKET FINAN

B63
CHAMBERLAIN E.H.,THE ECONOMIC ANALYSIS OF LABOR UNION POWER (PAMPHLET). WORKER ECO/TAC DOMIN COERCE GP/REL DRIVE WEALTH POLICY. PAGE 23 F0441
LABOR PWR CONTROL

B63
CHAMPION J.M.,CRITICAL INCIDENTS IN MANAGEMENT. MARKET LG/CO SML/CO OP/RES ADMIN CONTROL LEAD GP/REL PERS/REL COST ATTIT SUPEGO ALL/VALS...PSY PERS/TEST BIBLIOG. PAGE 23 F0445
MGT DECISION EX/STRUC INDUS

B63
CHATTERJEE I.K.,ECONOMIC DEVELOPMENT PAYMENTS DEFICIT AND PAYMENT RESTRICTION. INDIA WOR+45 FINAN INT/TRADE CONTROL BAL/PAY WEALTH...POLICY CONCPT STAT CHARTS IDEA/COMP BIBLIOG 20. PAGE 23 F0456
ECO/DEV ECO/TAC PAY GOV/REL

B63
COURNOT A.A.,RESEARCHES INTO THE MATHEMATICAL PRINCIPLES OF THE THEORY OF WEALTH (1838). UNIV ECO/DEV ECO/UNDEV AGRI INDUS MARKET PAY CONTROL COST INCOME 19. PAGE 28 F0544
ECOMETRIC GEN/LAWS WEALTH

B63
FOX S.,ECONOMIC CONTROL AND FREE ENTERPRISE. PLAN BUDGET INT/TRADE TAX...TREND 20. PAGE 43 F0839
CONTROL FINAN ECO/TAC

B63
FRIEDRICH C.J.,MAN AND HIS GOVERNMENT: AN EMPIRICAL THEORY OF POLITICS. UNIV LOC/G NAT/G ADJUD REV INGP/REL DISCRIM PWR BIBLIOG. PAGE 44 F0867
PERSON ORD/FREE PARTIC CONTROL

B63
GOLDMAN M.I.,SOVIET MARKETING. USSR DIST/IND FINAN RATION OWN WEALTH...SOC BIBLIOG 20. PAGE 48 F0937
MARKET ECO/TAC CONTROL MARXISM

B63
HAQ M.,THE STRATEGY OF ECONOMIC PLANNING. PAKISTAN AGRI FINAN INDUS NAT/G FOR/AID TAX CONTROL REGION PRODUC...POLICY CHARTS 20. PAGE 55 F1071
ECO/TAC ECO/UNDEV PLAN PROB/SOLV

B63
HOOPES R.,THE STEEL CRISIS. USA+45 INDUS ECO/TAC EDU/PROP PRICE CONTROL ATTIT...POLICY 20 KENNEDY/JF. PAGE 61 F1205
PROC/MFG NAT/G RATION CHIEF

B63
HYDE D.,THE PEACEFUL ASSAULT. COM UAR USSR ECO/DEV ECO/UNDEV NAT/G POL/PAR CAP/ISM PWR 20. PAGE 64 F1256
MARXISM CONTROL ECO/TAC DIPLOM

B63
LEWIN J.,POLITICS AND LAW IN SOUTH AFRICA. SOUTH/AFR UK POL/PAR BAL/PWR ECO/TAC COLONIAL CONTROL GP/REL DISCRIM PWR 20 NEGRO. PAGE 79 F1545
NAT/LISM POLICY LAW RACE/REL

B63
MARITANO N.,AN ALLIANCE FOR PROGRESS. FUT L/A+17C USA+45 CULTURE ECO/UNDEV NAT/G PLAN CONTROL ...POLICY ALL/PROG. PAGE 85 F1669
DIPLOM INT/ORG ECO/TAC FOR/AID

B63
MENEZES A.J.,SUBDESENVOLVIMENTO E POLITICA INTERNACIONAL. BRAZIL WOR+45 PLAN CONTROL LEAD NAT/LISM ORD/FREE 20 THIRD/WRLD. PAGE 90 F1759
ECO/UNDEV DIPLOM POLICY BAL/PWR

B63
MINGAY G.E.,ENGLISH LANDED SOCIETY IN THE EIGHTEENTH CENTURY. UK ELITES STRUCT AGRI INDUS CONTROL WEALTH 18. PAGE 92 F1802
OWN STRATA PWR

B63
RAO V.K.R.,FOREIGN AID AND INDIA'S ECONOMIC DEVELOPMENT. INDIA INT/ORG PROB/SOLV TEC/DEV ECO/TAC CONTROL WEALTH...TREND 20. PAGE 109 F2148
FOR/AID ECO/UNDEV RECEIVE DIPLOM

B63
SELF P.,THE STATE AND THE FARMER. UK ECO/DEV MARKET WORKER PRICE CONTROL GP/REL...WELF/ST 20 DEPT/AGRI. PAGE 119 F2346
AGRI NAT/G ADMIN VOL/ASSN

B63
SMITH R.A.,CORPORATIONS IN CRISIS. USA+45 LG/CO EX/STRUC ECO/TAC CONTROL LEAD PERS/REL...MGT 20. PAGE 123 F2432
ELITES INDUS PROB/SOLV METH/COMP

B63
US BD GOVERNORS FEDL RESRV,THE FEDERAL RESERVE AND THE TREASURY. USA+45 WORKER PROB/SOLV PRICE COST DEMAND WEALTH...STAT INT CHARTS 20 FED/RESERV DEPT/TREAS. PAGE 134 F2641
FINAN GOV/REL CONTROL BUDGET

S63
REES A.,"THE EFFECTS OF UNIONS ON RESOURCE ALLOCATION." USA+45 WORKER PRICE CONTROL GP/REL ...MGT METH/COMP 20. PAGE 110 F2173
LABOR BARGAIN RATION

INCOME

N63

US COMM STRENG SEC FREE WORLD,THE SCOPE AND DISTRIBUTION OF UNITED STATES MILITARY AND ECONOMIC ASSISTANCE PROGRAMS (PAMPHLET). USA+45 PLAN BAL/PWR BUDGET DIPLOM CONTROL CIVMIL/REL ATTIT. PAGE 134 F2648

DELIB/GP POLICY FOR/AID ORD/FREE

B64

BALOGH T.,THE ECONOMIC IMPACT OF MONETARY AND COMMERCIAL INSTITUTIONS OF A EUROPEAN ORIGIN IN AFRICA. AFR UAR INDUS FOR/AID COLONIAL CONTROL ...NAT/COMP 20. PAGE 9 F0169

TEC/DEV FINAN ECO/UNDEV ECO/TAC

B64

BLACKSTOCK P.W.,THE STRATEGY OF SUBVERSION. USA+45 FORCES EDU/PROP ADMIN COERCE GOV/REL...DECISION MGT 20 DEPT/DEFEN CIA DEPT/STATE. PAGE 15 F0292

ORD/FREE DIPLOM CONTROL

B64

CEPEDE M.,POPULATION AND FOOD. USA+45 STRUCT ECO/UNDEV FAM PLAN TEC/DEV FOR/AID CONTROL...CATH SOC TREND 19/20. PAGE 22 F0436

FUT GEOG AGRI CENSUS

B64

CLAIRBORN E.L.,FORECASTING THE BALANCE OF PAYMENTS: AN EVALUATION. AFR FUT UK USA+45 WOR+45 FINAN PLAN BUDGET PAY CONTROL...STAT CHARTS BIBLIOG 20. PAGE 24 F0474

PREDICT BAL/PAY ECO/DEV ECO/TAC

B64

EDWARDS E.O.,THE NATION'S ECONOMIC OBJECTIVES. INDUS WORKER BUDGET DIPLOM CONTROL ORD/FREE ...POLICY SOC METH/CNCPT ANTHOL 20. PAGE 36 F0704

NAT/G ECO/TAC

B64

FISK W.M.,ADMINISTRATIVE PROCEDURE IN A REGULATORY AGENCY: THE CAB AND THE NEW YORK-CHICAGO CASE (PAMPHLET). USA+45 DIST/IND ADMIN CONTROL LOBBY GP/REL ROLE ORD/FREE NEWYORK/C CHICAGO CAB. PAGE 41 F0805

SERV/IND ECO/DEV AIR JURID

B64

GOWDA K.V.,INTERNATIONAL CURRENCY PLANS AND EXPANSION OF WORLD TRADE. INT/ORG CREATE BUDGET CONTROL BAL/PAY WEALTH 20 KEYNES/JM. PAGE 50 F0969

INT/TRADE FINAN METH/COMP

B64

HACKER A.,THE CORPORATION TAKE-OVER. CONSTN LABOR PLAN BAL/PWR CONTROL EXEC LOBBY REPRESENT GP/REL ROLE ORD/FREE POLICY. PAGE 52 F1025

LG/CO STRUCT PWR

B64

HANSEN B.,INTERNATIONAL LIQUIDITY. USA+45 INT/ORG ECO/TAC PRICE CONTROL WEALTH...POLICY 20. PAGE 54 F1068

BAL/PAY INT/TRADE DIPLOM FINAN

B64

IMAZ J.L.,LOS QUE MANDAN. INDUS LABOR NAT/G POL/PAR PROVS SECT CHIEF TOP/EX CONTROL 20 ARGEN. PAGE 64 F1261

LEAD FORCES ELITES ATTIT

B64

INTERNATIONAL LABOUR OFFICE,EMPLOYMENT AND ECONOMIC GROWTH. ECO/DEV ECO/UNDEV NAT/G PLAN DIPLOM INT/TRADE CONTROL INCOME PRODUC WEALTH...STAT NAT/COMP 20 ILO. PAGE 65 F1279

WORKER METH/COMP ECO/TAC OPTIMAL

B64

KAPLAN A.D.H.,BIG ENTERPRISE IN A COMPETITIVE SYSTEM (REV. ED.). USA+45 INDUS MARKET WORKER TEC/DEV ECO/TAC PRICE ADJUD ADMIN CONTROL...MGT CHARTS 20 MONOPOLY. PAGE 69 F1351

FINAN GP/REL NAT/G LG/CO

B64

MAGALHAES S.,PRATICA DA EMANCIPACAO NACIONAL. L/A+17C INDUS PLAN ECO/TAC CONTROL NAT/LISM ORD/FREE. PAGE 84 F1640

BAL/PAY ECO/UNDEV DIPLOM WEALTH

B64

MANSFIELD E.,MONOPOLY POWER AND ECONOMIC PERFORMANCE: AN INTRODUCTION TO A CURRENT ISSUE OF PUBLIC POLICY. ECO/DEV INDUS NAT/G PLAN CAP/ISM PRICE CONTROL PRODUC...POLICY 20 CONGRESS KENNEDY/JF MONOPOLY. PAGE 85 F1659

LG/CO PWR ECO/TAC MARKET

B64

MARRIS R.,THE ECONOMIC THEORY OF "MANAGERIAL" CAPITALISM. USA+45 ECO/DEV LG/CO ECO/TAC DEMAND ...CHARTS BIBLIOG 20. PAGE 86 F1675

CAP/ISM MGT CONTROL OP/RES

B64

MITAU G.T.,INSOLUBLE PROBLEMS: CASE PROBLEMS ON THE FUNCTIONS OF STATE AND LOCAL GOVERNMENT. USA+45 AIR FINAN LABOR POL/PAR PROB/SOLV TAX RECEIVE CONTROL GP/REL 20 CASEBOOK ZONING. PAGE 92 F1807

ADJUD LOC/G PROVS

B64

NOVACK D.E.,DEVELOPMENT AND SOCIETY; THE DYNAMICS OF ECONOMIC CHANGE. WOR+45 STRATA STRUCT ECO/TAC CONTROL CROWD REV GP/REL ADJUST PRODUC WEALTH PSY. PAGE 99 F1940

SOCIETY CULTURE SOC ECO/UNDEV

B64

RUSTAMJI R.F.,THE LAW OF INDUSTRIAL DISPUTES IN INDIA. INDIA LEGIS WORKER CONTROL GP/REL...JURID MGT TIME/SEQ 20. PAGE 115 F2264

INDUS ADJUD BARGAIN LABOR

B64

SULTAN P.E.,THE DISENCHANTED UNIONIST. NAT/G ADJUD CONTROL SANCTION RACE/REL ANOMIE ATTIT ROLE ...METH/CNCPT INT. PAGE 127 F2512

LABOR INGP/REL CHARTS MAJORIT

B64

TINBERGEN J.,CENTRAL PLANNING. COM INTELL ECO/DEV ECO/UNDEV FINAN INT/ORG PROB/SOLV ECO/TAC CONTROL EXEC ROUTINE DECISION. PAGE 130 F2576

PLAN INDUS MGT CENTRAL

B64

US SENATE COMM ON JUDICIARY,HEARINGS BEFORE SUBCOMMITTEE ON ANTITRUST AND MONOPOLY: ECONOMIC CONCENTRATION VOLUMES 1-5 JULY 1964-SEPT 1966. USA+45 LAW FINAN ECO/TAC ADJUD COST EFFICIENCY PRODUC...STAT CHARTS 20 CONGRESS MONOPOLY. PAGE 140 F2749

ECO/DEV CONTROL MARKET LG/CO

B64

WERNETTE J.P.,GOVERNMENT AND BUSINESS. LABOR CAP/ISM ECO/TAC INT/TRADE TAX ADMIN AUTOMAT NUC/PWR CIVMIL/REL DEMAND...MGT 20 MONOPOLY. PAGE 145 F2859

NAT/G FINAN ECO/DEV CONTROL

B64

ZOBER M.,MARKETING MANAGEMENT. FINAN BUDGET EDU/PROP PRICE PRODUC ATTIT...POLICY TREND CHARTS METH/COMP EQULIB 20. PAGE 150 F2966

ECO/DEV MGT CONTROL MARKET

L64

KOLODZIEJ E.A.,"RATIONAL CONSENT AND DEFENSE BUDGETS: THE ROLE OF CONGRESS, 1945-1962." LEGIS DIPLOM CONTROL PARL/PROC 20 CONGRESS. PAGE 72 F1423

DECISION PLAN CIVMIL/REL BUDGET

C64

GOLDMAN M.I.,"COMPARATIVE ECONOMIC SYSTEMS: A READER." COM ECO/UNDEV NAT/G BUDGET CAP/ISM ADMIN TOTALISM MARXISM SOCISM...MGT ANTHOL BIBLIOG 19/20. PAGE 48 F0938

NAT/COMP CONTROL IDEA/COMP

B65

BOCK E.,GOVERNMENT REGULATION OF BUSINESS. USA+45 LAW EX/STRUC LEGIS EXEC ORD/FREE PWR...ANTHOL CONGRESS. PAGE 16 F0303

MGT ADMIN NAT/G CONTROL

B65

BROOKINGS INSTITUTION,BROOKINGS PAPERS ON PUBLIC POLICY. USA+45 ECO/UNDEV LEGIS CAP/ISM ECO/TAC TAX EDU/PROP CONTROL APPORT 20. PAGE 19 F0363

DIPLOM FOR/AID POLICY FINAN

B65

COPELAND M.A.,OUR FREE ENTERPRISE ECONOMY. USA+45 INDUS LABOR ADMIN CONTROL GP/REL MGT. PAGE 27 F0533

CAP/ISM PLAN FINAN ECO/DEV

B65

EDELMAN M.,THE POLITICS OF WAGE-PRICE DECISIONS. GERMANY ITALY NETHERLAND UK INDUS LABOR POL/PAR PROB/SOLV BARGAIN PRICE ROUTINE BAL/PAY COST DEMAND 20. PAGE 36 F0699

GOV/COMP CONTROL ECO/TAC PLAN

B65

GREENFIELD K.R.,ECONOMICS AND LIBERALISM IN THE RISORGIMENTO (REV. ED.). ITALY AGRI FINAN PROC/MFG PLAN INT/TRADE CONTROL PWR 19. PAGE 51 F0990

NAT/LISM PRESS POLICY

B65

HAEFELE E.T.,GOVERNMENT CONTROLS ON TRANSPORT. AFR RHODESIA TANZANIA DIPLOM ECO/TAC TARIFFS PRICE ADJUD CONTROL REGION EFFICIENCY...POLICY 20 CONGO. PAGE 53 F1031

ECO/UNDEV DIST/IND FINAN NAT/G

B65

INTERAMERICAN ECO AND SOC COUN,THE ALLIANCE FOR PROGRESS: ITS THIRD YEAR 1963-1964. FUT L/A+17C WOR+45 ECO/DEV INT/ORG PLAN CONTROL ADJUST...STAT ANTHOL SOC/INTEG 20 ALL/PROG. PAGE 64 F1268

ECO/UNDEV ECO/TAC FINAN FOR/AID

B65

JOHNSTONE A.,UNITED STATES DIRECT INVESTMENT IN FRANCE: AN INVESTIGATION OF THE FRENCH CHARGES. FRANCE USA+45 ECO/DEV INDUS LG/CO NAT/G ECO/TAC CONTROL WEALTH...BIBLIOG 20 INTERVENT. PAGE 68 F1335

FINAN DIPLOM POLICY SOVEREIGN

B65

KANTOROVICH L.V.,THE BEST USE OF ECONOMIC RESOURCES. USSR SOCIETY FINAN ACT/RES TEC/DEV ECO/TAC PRICE CONTROL COST DEMAND EFFICIENCY OPTIMAL...MGT STAT. PAGE 69 F1350

PLAN MATH DECISION

B65

KLEIN J.J.,MONEY AND THE ECONOMY. USA+45 NAT/G DIPLOM CONTROL...POLICY T 20 FED/RESERV. PAGE 72 F1406

FINAN PLAN WEALTH BAL/PAY

B65

LEYS C.T.,FEDERATION IN EAST AFRICA. LAW AGRI DIST/IND FINAN INT/ORG LABOR INT/TRADE CONFER ADMIN CONTROL GP/REL...ANTHOL 20 AFRICA/E. PAGE 79 F1554

FEDERAL REGION ECO/UNDEV PLAN

B65

MELMANS S.,OUR DEPLETED SOCIETY. AFR SPACE USA+45 ECO/DEV FORCES BUDGET ECO/TAC ADMIN WEAPON EFFICIENCY 20. PAGE 89 F1753

CIVMIL/REL INDUS EDU/PROP

CONTROL

B65
MUND V.A.,GOVERNMENT AND BUSINESS (4TH ED.). USA+45 INDUS LG/CO SML/CO LEGIS INT/TRADE LICENSE PRICE ADJUD. PAGE 95 F1860 — NAT/G ECO/TAC BUDGET CONTROL

B65
NARASIMHAN V.K.,DEMOCRACY AND MIXED ECONOMY. INDIA CONTROL...CENSUS IDEA/COMP 20. PAGE 96 F1891 — CAP/ISM MARXISM ORD/FREE NEW/LIB

B65
NATIONAL CONF SOCIAL WELFARE,THE SOCIAL WELFARE FORUM, 1965. LAW CULTURE VOL/ASSN CONTROL PERS/REL ADJUST POLICY. PAGE 97 F1899 — CONSTN WEALTH ORD/FREE NEIGH

B65
PARRIS H.W.,GOVERNMENT AND THE RAILWAYS IN NINETEENTH-CENTURY BRITAIN. UK DELIB/GP CONTROL LEAD CENTRAL 19 RAILROAD. PAGE 103 F2029 — DIST/IND NAT/G PLAN GP/REL

B65
PHELPS E.S.,FISCAL NEUTRALITY TOWARD ECONOMIC GROWTH. FINAN NAT/G BUDGET CAP/ISM CONTROL INCOME 20. PAGE 106 F2080 — ECO/DEV POLICY ECO/TAC TAX

B65
PROCHNOW H.V.,WORLD ECONOMIC PROBLEMS AND POLICIES. INDIA ISRAEL WOR+45 AGRI LABOR PROB/SOLV FOR/AID TARIFFS CONTROL BAL/PAY NAT/LISM WEALTH...TREND CHARTS 20 CHINJAP EEC. PAGE 108 F2124 — MARKET ECO/TAC PRODUC IDEA/COMP

B65
SCHWARTZ G.,SCIENCE IN MARKETING. OP/RES PROB/SOLV INT/TRADE PRICE CONTROL ADJUST PRODUC...CONCPT 20. PAGE 118 F2324 — PHIL/SCI TREND ECO/DEV MARKET

B65
SHONFIELD A.,MODERN CAPITALISM: THE CHANGING BALANCE OF PUBLIC AND PRIVATE POWER. FRANCE GERMANY/W UK USA+45 WOR+45 ECO/DEV INT/ORG NAT/G CONSULT INT/TRADE PRODUC...POLICY CONCPT METH/COMP 20. PAGE 121 F2386 — CAP/ISM CONTROL BAL/PWR CREATE

B65
SIMON B.,EDUCATION AND THE LABOR MOVEMENT, 1870-1920. UK SOCIETY STRATA LABOR POL/PAR SCHOOL CONTROL PARTIC SOCISM...BIBLIOG 19/20. PAGE 122 F2406 — EDU/PROP WORKER ADJUST LAW

B65
SINHA M.R.,THE ECONOMICS OF MANPOWER PLANNING. FUT HUNGARY NAT/G CONTROL...POLICY GEOG ANTHOL 20 CHINJAP. PAGE 122 F2415 — ECO/UNDEV PLAN WORKER ECO/TAC

B65
STEINER G.A.,THE CREATIVE ORGANIZATION. ELITES LG/CO PLAN PROB/SOLV TEC/DEV INSPECT CAP/ISM CONTROL EXEC PERSON...METH/COMP HYPO/EXP 20. PAGE 126 F2476 — CREATE MGT ADMIN SOC

B65
STEWART I.G.,AFRICAN PRIMARY PRODUCTS AND INTERNATIONAL TRADE. ECO/UNDEV AGRI FINAN DIPLOM CONTROL 20. PAGE 126 F2485 — AFR INT/TRADE INT/ORG

B65
US SENATE COMM ON FOREIGN REL,HEARINGS ON THE FOREIGN ASSISTANCE PROGRAM. AFR ASIA L/A+17C USA+45 WOR+45 FORCES TEC/DEV BUDGET CONTROL WEAPON ORD/FREE 20 UN CONGRESS SEC/STATE. PAGE 139 F2734 — FOR/AID DIPLOM INT/ORG ECO/UNDEV

B65
US SENATE COMM ON JUDICIARY,ANTITRUST EXEMPTIONS FOR AGREEMENTS RELATING TO BALANCE OF PAYMENTS. FINAN ECO/TAC CONTROL WEALTH...POLICY 20 CONGRESS. PAGE 140 F2750 — BAL/PAY ADJUD MARKET INT/TRADE

B65
VAID K.N.,STATE AND LABOR IN INDIA. INDIA INDUS WORKER PAY PRICE ADJUD CONTROL PARL/PROC GP/REL ORD/FREE 20. PAGE 140 F2757 — LAW LABOR MGT NEW/LIB

B65
ZAWADZKI K.K.F.,THE ECONOMICS OF INFLATIONARY PROCESSES. FINAN INT/TRADE PRICE CONTROL DEMAND EQUILIB PROFIT 20. PAGE 150 F2960 — ECO/DEV COST ECO/TAC CAP/ISM

L65
FORTE W.E.,"THE FOOD AND DRUG ADMINISTRATION, THE FEDERAL TRADE COMMISSION AND THE DECEPTIVE PACKAGING." ROUTINE...JURID 20 FTC. PAGE 43 F0831 — CONTROL HEALTH ADJUD INDUS

S65
GOLDMAN M.I.,"A BALANCE SHEET OF SOVIET FOREIGN AID." USA+45 ECO/UNDEV BAL/PWR ECO/TAC RENT GIVE EDU/PROP CONTROL COST PROFIT GEN/METH. PAGE 48 F0939 — USSR FOR/AID NAT/COMP EFFICIENCY

S65
HADDAD W.F.,"MR. SHRIVER AND THE SAVAGE POLITICS OF POVERTY" USA+45 LAW NAT/G DELIB/GP LEGIS GIVE LEAD CENTRAL PWR...SOC/WK CHARTS 20 CONGRESS POVRTY/WAR SHRIVER/S OEO. PAGE 53 F1028 — WEALTH GOV/REL CONTROL TOP/EX

C65
MANSFIELD H.C.,"THE CONGRESS AND ECONOMIC POLICY" IN C. TRUMAN ED., THE CONGRESS AND AMERICA'S FUTURE." USA+45 USA-45 CONSTN NAT/G BUDGET ADMIN CONTROL EXEC LOBBY. PAGE 85 F1661 — POLICY ECO/TAC PWR LEGIS

N65
STUDY GP CREATE RESERVE ASSETS,REPORT TO DEPUTIES (PAMPHLET). AFR FUT PLAN CONTROL DEMAND WEALTH ...ANTHOL METH 20. PAGE 127 F2507 — INT/ORG INT/TRADE FINAN BUDGET

B66
AGGARWALA R.N.,FINANCIAL COMMITTEES OF THE INDIAN PARLIAMENT: A STUDY IN PARLIAMENTARY CONTROL OVER PUBLIC EXPENDITURE. INDIA FINAN NAT/G ROLE...CHARTS METH/COMP METH 20 PARLIAMENT. PAGE 3 F0049 — PARL/PROC BUDGET CONTROL DELIB/GP

B66
ANDERSON J.E.,POLITICS AND THE ECONOMY. NAT/G LOBBY PWR 20. PAGE 5 F0096 — REPRESENT EX/STRUC CONTROL

B66
BARAN P.A.,MONOPOLY CAPITAL; AN ESSAY ON THE AMERICAN ECONOMIC AND SOCIAL ORDER. USA+45 USA-45 ECO/UNDEV FINAN MARKET PLAN DIPLOM COLONIAL RACE/REL DEMAND MARXISM...CHARTS 20. PAGE 9 F0179 — LG/CO CAP/ISM PRICE CONTROL

B66
CONFERENCE REGIONAL ACCOUNTS,REGIONAL ACCOUNTS FOR POLICY DECISIONS. PROB/SOLV CONTROL RATIONAL KNOWL ORD/FREE...POLICY DECISION MATH STAT ANTHOL 20. PAGE 27 F0523 — GOV/REL REGION PLAN ECO/TAC

B66
DAVIS K.,BUSINESS AND ITS ENVIRONMENT. LAW ECO/DEV INDUS OP/RES ADMIN CONTROL ROUTINE GP/REL PROFIT POLICY. PAGE 30 F0591 — EX/STRUC PROB/SOLV CAP/ISM EXEC

B66
EDWARDS C.D.,TRADE REGULATIONS OVERSEAS. IRELAND NEW/ZEALND SOUTH/AFR NAT/G CAP/ISM TARIFFS CONTROL ...POLICY JURID 20 EEC CHINJAP. PAGE 36 F0703 — INT/TRADE DIPLOM INT/LAW ECO/TAC

B66
FRANCK L.R.,LA POLITIQUE ECONOMIQUE DES ETATS-UNIS. USA+45 USA-45 FINAN INDUS CONTROL CROWD GOV/REL GP/REL...POLICY SOC CHARTS 18/20. PAGE 43 F0841 — NAT/G INT/TRADE GEOG

B66
FRANKEL P.H.,MATTEI; OIL AND POWER POLITICS. ITALY EXTR/IND MARKET GP/REL NAT/LISM SOCISM...POLICY MGT BIOG 20 MATTEI/E. PAGE 43 F0844 — LEAD NAT/G CONTROL LG/CO

B66
FREIDEL F.,AMERICAN ISSUES IN THE TWENTIETH CENTURY. SOCIETY FINAN ECO/TAC FOR/AID CONTROL NUC/PWR WAR RACE/REL PEACE ATTIT...ANTHOL T 20 WILSON/W ROOSEVLT/F KENNEDY/JF TRUMAN/HS. PAGE 44 F0851 — DIPLOM POLICY NAT/G ORD/FREE

B66
HAINES W.W.,MONEY PRICES AND POLICY. WOR+45 ECO/DEV BUDGET CONTROL INCOME...POLICY STAT CHARTS BIBLIOG T 20. PAGE 53 F1039 — PRICE FINAN ECO/TAC GOV/REL

B66
HASTINGS P.G.,THE MANAGEMENT OF BUSINESS FINANCE. ECO/DEV PLAN BUDGET CONTROL COST...DECISION CHARTS BIBLIOG T 20. PAGE 56 F1109 — FINAN MGT INDUS ECO/TAC

B66
JACKSON G.D.,COMINTERN AND PEASANT IN EAST EUROPE 1919-1930. BULGARIA COM CZECHOSLVK EUR+WWI POLAND ROMANIA YUGOSLAVIA STRATA AGRI VOL/ASSN DIPLOM CONTROL CROWD WEALTH...POLICY NAT/COMP 20. PAGE 66 F1293 — MARXISM ECO/UNDEV WORKER INT/ORG

B66
KIRKENDALL R.S.,SOCIAL SCIENTISTS AND FARM POLITICS IN THE AGE OF ROOSEVELT. ACADEM PLAN ECO/TAC GIVE ADMIN CONTROL PRODUC...SOC 20 NEW/DEAL ROOSEVLT/F BURAGR/ECO. PAGE 71 F1399 — AGRI INTELL POLICY NAT/G

B66
KOMIYA R.,POSTWAR ECONOMIC GROWTH IN JAPAN. ELITES NAT/G EX/STRUC TEC/DEV BUDGET DIPLOM CONTROL BAL/PAY PRODUC...BIBLIOG 20 CHINJAP. PAGE 73 F1424 — ECO/DEV POLICY PLAN ADJUST

B66
LEE M.W.,TOWARD ECONOMIC STABILITY. USA+45 BUDGET TAX PRICE EQUILIB INCOME. PAGE 77 F1506 — ECO/TAC CONTROL POLICY NAT/G

B66
LEE R.A.,TRUMAN AND TAFT-HARTLEY: A QUESTION OF MANDATE. USA+45 LAW CONSTN LG/CO CONTROL LOBBY GOV/REL PEACE NEW/LIB 20 TRUMAN/HS CONGRESS. PAGE 77 F1507 — LEGIS TOP/EX ADJUD LABOR

B66
NEVITT A.A.,HOUSING, TAXATION AND SUBSIDIES; A STUDY OF HOUSING IN THE UNITED KINGDOM. UK FINAN GIVE CONTROL COST INCOME...CHARTS 20. PAGE 98 F1918 — PLAN TAX HABITAT RENT

B66
OHLIN G.,FOREIGN AID POLICIES RECONSIDERED. ECO/DEV ECO/UNDEV VOL/ASSN CONSULT PLAN CONTROL ATTIT ...CONCPT CHARTS BIBLIOG 20. PAGE 101 F1985
FOR/AID DIPLOM GIVE

B66
RAPHAEL J.S.,GOVERNMENTAL REGULATION OF BUSINESS. USA+45 LAW CONSTN TAX ADJUD ADMIN EFFICIENCY PWR 20. PAGE 109 F2150
LG/CO GOV/REL CONTROL ECO/DEV

B66
SHULTZ G.P.,GUIDELINES, INFORMAL CONTROLS, AND THE MARKET PLACE: POLICY CHOICES IN A FULL EMPLOYMENT ECONOMY. UK ECO/DEV LABOR INT/TRADE CONFER GOV/REL BAL/PAY DEMAND INCOME...POLICY ANTHOL 20 PRESIDENT. PAGE 121 F2392
ECO/TAC CONTROL FINAN RATION

B66
SPULBER N.,THE STATE AND ECONOMIC DEVELOPMENT IN EASTERN EUROPE. BULGARIA COM CZECHOSLVK HUNGARY POLAND YUGOSLAVIA CULTURE PLAN CAP/ISM INT/TRADE CONTROL...POLICY CHARTS METH/COMP BIBLIOG/A 19/20. PAGE 125 F2460
ECO/DEV ECO/UNDEV NAT/G TOTALISM

B66
TIVEY L.J.,NATIONALISATION IN BRITISH INDUSTRY. UK LEGIS PARL/PROC GP/REL OWN ATTIT SOCISM 20. PAGE 131 F2578
NAT/G INDUS CONTROL LG/CO

B66
TRIFFIN R.,THE BALANCE OF PAYMENTS AND THE FOREIGN INVESTMENT POSITION OF THE UNITED STATES. AFR USA+45 INT/ORG INT/TRADE PRICE CONTROL...POLICY 20. PAGE 131 F2590
BAL/PAY DIPLOM FINAN ECO/TAC

B66
TURNER H.A.,PRICES, WAGES, AND INCOME POLICIES IN INDUSTRIALIZED MARKET ECONOMIES. AFR WOR+45 ECO/DEV INDUS PROB/SOLV ECO/TAC CONTROL WEALTH...CHARTS 20 INTRVN/ECO. PAGE 131 F2593
PRICE PAY MARKET INCOME

B66
US SENATE COMM GOVT OPERATIONS,HEARINGS BEFORE SUBCOMMITTEE ON FOREIGN AID EXPENDITURES: POPULATION CRISIS VOLUMES 1-5 JUNE-SEPT 1965. STRATA ECO/UNDEV PLAN TEC/DEV EDU/PROP ATTIT HEALTH ...GEOG CHARTS 20 CONGRESS BIRTH/CON CASEBOOK. PAGE 138 F2729
ECO/DEV CENSUS FAM CONTROL

B66
WECHSBERG J.,THE MERCHANT BANKERS. EUR+WWI MOD/EUR CONTROL...BIOG GP/COMP PERS/COMP 16/20. PAGE 144 F2842
FINAN PWR WEALTH FAM

B66
WESTON J.F.,THE SCOPE AND METHODOLOGY OF FINANCE. PLAN TEC/DEV CONTROL EFFICIENCY INCOME UTIL...MGT CONCPT MATH STAT TREND METH 20. PAGE 145 F2863
FINAN ECO/DEV POLICY PRICE

B66
WETTER G.A.,SOVIET IDEOLOGY TODAY. USSR ECO/UNDEV SECT WORKER CAP/ISM CONTROL TASK EFFICIENCY TOTALISM DRIVE WEALTH...TREND 18/20. PAGE 145 F2864
ALL/IDEOS MARXISM REV

B66
YOUNG S.,MANAGEMENT: A SYSTEMS ANALYSIS. DELIB/GP EX/STRUC ECO/TAC CONTROL EFFICIENCY...NET/THEORY 20. PAGE 150 F2952
PROB/SOLV MGT DECISION SIMUL

B66
ZINKIN T.,CHALLENGES IN INDIA. INDIA PAKISTAN LAW AGRI FINAN INDUS TOP/EX TEC/DEV CONTROL ROUTINE ORD/FREE PWR 20 NEHRU/J SHASTRI/LB CIVIL/SERV. PAGE 150 F2964
NAT/G ECO/TAC POLICY ADMIN

S66
LANGLEY D.,"POSTSCRIPT ON THE COLONIZATION OF THE INTERNATIONAL TRADE UNION MOVEMENT" USA+45 ELITES FINAN DOMIN LEGIT ADMIN PWR...SOCIALIST 20 AFL/CIO CIA LOVESTN/J. PAGE 75 F1479
INT/TRADE LABOR NAT/G CONTROL

S66
POSEN G.S.,"RECENT TRENDS IN SOVIET ECONOMIC THOUGHT." USSR ECO/DEV PLAN CONTROL CENTRAL 20. PAGE 107 F2107
ECO/TAC MARXISM INDUS PROFIT

N66
OECD,THE BALANCE OF PAYMENTS ADJUSTMENT PROCESS (PAMPHLET). EUR+WWI ECO/DEV FINAN CONSULT PLAN PROB/SOLV BUDGET CAP/ISM INT/TRADE PRICE CONTROL EQUILIB 20. PAGE 101 F1975
BAL/PAY ECO/TAC DIPLOM INT/ORG

B67
ALEXANDER G.J.,HONESTY AND COMPETITION: FALSE-ADVERTISING LAW AND POLICY UNDER FTC ADMINISTRATION. USA+45 INDUS NAT/G PRICE GP/REL 20 FTC. PAGE 3 F0058
EDU/PROP SERV/IND CONTROL DELIB/GP

B67
BARDENS D.,CHURCHILL IN PARLIAMENT. UK DIPLOM ADJUD CONTROL AUTHORIT PERSON ORD/FREE 20 CHURCHLL/W PARLIAMENT. PAGE 10 F0186
TOP/EX LEGIS GOV/REL

B67
BARNETT A.D.,CHINA AFTER MAO. ASIA CHINA/COM CULTURE ECO/UNDEV ECO/TAC CONTROL EFFICIENCY NAT/LISM MARXISM 20. PAGE 10 F0189
POL/PAR NAT/G TEC/DEV GP/REL

B67
BURDEN H.T.,THE NUREMBERG PARTY RALLIES 1923-39. GERMANY POL/PAR SECT CREATE DOMIN WAR ATTIT ...AUD/VIS FILM 20. PAGE 20 F0384
EDU/PROP CONTROL CROWD TOTALISM

B67
DAVIS F.M.,COME AS A CONQUEROR: THE UNITED STATES ARMY'S OCCUPATION OF GERMANY: 1945-1949. EUR+WWI GERMANY USA+45 SOCIETY PLAN BAL/PWR DIPLOM FOR/AID PERS/REL DEMAND PEACE ORD/FREE 20. PAGE 30 F0588
FORCES CIVMIL/REL ECO/TAC CONTROL

B67
DONALD A.G.,MANAGEMENT, INFORMATION, AND SYSTEMS. WOR+45 LG/CO PROB/SOLV CONTROL FEEDBACK KNOWL MGT. PAGE 34 F0653
ROUTINE TEC/DEV CONCPT ADMIN

B67
ESTEY M.,THE UNIONS: STRUCTURE, DEVELOPMENT, AND MANAGEMENT. FUT USA+45 ADJUD CONTROL INGP/REL DRIVE ...DECISION T 20 AFL/CIO. PAGE 38 F0750
LABOR EX/STRUC ADMIN GOV/REL

B67
FARRIS M.T.,MODERN TRANSPORTATION: SELECTED READINGS. UNIV CONTROL...POLICY ANTHOL T 20. PAGE 39 F0765
DIST/IND MGT COST

B67
GOLDMAN M.,CONTROLLING POLLUTION: THE ECONOMICS OF A CLEANER AMERICA. USA+45 SOCIETY PROB/SOLV CONTROL COST ANTHOL. PAGE 48 F0936
HEALTH ECO/DEV NAT/G FINAN

B67
GOLEMBIEWSKI R.T.,ORGANIZING MEN AND POWER: PATTERNS OF BEHAVIOR AND LINESTAFF MODELS. WOR+45 EX/STRUC ACT/RES DOMIN PERS/REL...NEW/IDEA 20. PAGE 48 F0943
ADMIN CONTROL SIMUL MGT

B67
GRIPP R.C.,PATTERNS OF SOVIET POLITICS (REV. ED.). USSR LAW ELITES LOC/G PLAN CONTROL CT/SYS CHOOSE ...POLICY BIBLIOG/A DICTIONARY 9/20. PAGE 51 F1003
COM ADJUD POL/PAR

B67
HEADLEY J.C.,PESTICIDE PROBLEM: AN ECONOMIC APPROACH TO PUBLIC POLICY. AGRI TEC/DEV GOV/REL COST ATTIT CHARTS. PAGE 58 F1131
HABITAT POLICY BIO/SOC CONTROL

B67
HOGAN J.,THE US BALANCE OF PAYMENTS AND CAPITAL FLOWS. MARKET INT/ORG ECO/TAC PRICE CONTROL WEALTH ...METH/COMP 20 EEC. PAGE 61 F1192
BAL/PAY FINAN DIPLOM INT/TRADE

B67
KAPLAN J.J.,CHALLENGE OF FOREIGN AID. USA+45 CONTROL BAL/PAY COST ATTIT ALL/VALS...METH/COMP 20. PAGE 69 F1352
FOR/AID PLAN GIVE POLICY

B67
MACAVOY P.W.,REGULATION OF TRANSPORT INNOVATION. ACT/RES ADJUD COST DEMAND...POLICY CHARTS 20. PAGE 83 F1621
DIST/IND CONTROL PRICE PROFIT

B67
MACCLOSKEY M.,PACTS FOR PEACE: UN, NATO, SEATO, CENTO, OAS. WOR+45 PLAN DIPLOM CONTROL PEACE ORD/FREE...ORG/CHARTS UN NATO SEATO OAS CENTO. PAGE 83 F1623
FORCES INT/ORG LEAD POLICY

B67
MAZOUR A.G.,SOVIET ECONOMIC DEVELOPMENT: OPERATION OUTSTRIP: 1921-1965. USSR ECO/UNDEV FINAN CHIEF WORKER PROB/SOLV CONTROL PRODUC MARXISM...CHARTS ORG/CHARTS 20 STALIN/J. PAGE 87 F1711
ECO/TAC AGRI INDUS PLAN

B67
MOSS F.M.,THE WATER CRISIS. PROB/SOLV CONTROL ...POLICY NEW/IDEA. PAGE 94 F1846
GEOG ACT/RES PRODUC WEALTH

B67
MUHAMMAD A.C.,THE EMERGENCE OF PAKISTAN. PAKISTAN S/ASIA CONSTN ECO/UNDEV NAT/G CONTROL NAT/LISM 20. PAGE 94 F1853
DIPLOM COLONIAL SECT PROB/SOLV

B67
MURTY B.S.,PROPAGANDA AND WORLD PUBLIC ORDER. FUT WOR+45 COM/IND INT/ORG PROB/SOLV ATTIT KNOWL ORD/FREE...POLICY UN. PAGE 95 F1868
EDU/PROP DIPLOM CONTROL JURID

B67
ORLANS H.,CONTRACTING FOR ATOMS. AFR USA+45 LAW INTELL ACADEM LG/CO NAT/G PLAN TEC/DEV CONTROL DETER...TREND 20. PAGE 102 F1999
NUC/PWR R+D PRODUC PEACE

B67
PRINCE C.E.,NEW JERSEY'S JEFFERSONIAN REPUBLICANS; THE GENESIS OF AN EARLY PARTY MACHINE (1789-1817). USA-45 LOC/G EDU/PROP PRESS CONTROL CHOOSE...CHARTS 18/19 NEW/JERSEY REPUBLICAN. PAGE 108 F2117
POL/PAR CONSTN ADMIN PROVS

B67
ROBINSON R.D.,INTERNATIONAL MANAGEMENT. LAW MARKET LABOR PRICE CONTROL COST DEMAND OWN PRODUC WEALTH
T OP/RES

20. PAGE 113 F2225 MGT DIPLOM

B67
SACKS B.,SOUTH AFRICA: AN IMPERIAL DILEMMA. SOUTH/AFR UK ECO/UNDEV KIN DOMIN DEBATE CONTROL REV DISCRIM ISOLAT...POLICY STAT BIBLIOG 20. PAGE 115 F2268 COLONIAL RACE/REL DIPLOM ORD/FREE

B67
SAPARINA Y.,CYBERNETICS WITHIN US. WOR+45 EDU/PROP FEEDBACK PERCEPT HEALTH...DECISION METH/CNCPT NEW/IDEA 20. PAGE 116 F2281 COMPUTER METH/COMP CONTROL SIMUL

B67
SCHON D.A.,TECHNOLOGY AND CHANGE* THE NEW HERACLITUS. TEC/DEV CONTROL COST DEMAND EFFICIENCY RIGID/FLEX...MYTH 20. PAGE 117 F2311 INDUS PROB/SOLV R+D CREATE

B67
SCOTT J.C.,ANTITRUST AND TRADE REGULATION TODAY: 1967. USA+45 MARKET LG/CO DELIB/GP LEGIS CAP/ISM INT/TRADE TAX PRICE INGP/REL WEALTH 20 SUPREME/CT. PAGE 118 F2334 NAT/G INDUS CONTROL JURID

B67
SHAFFER H.G.,THE COMMUNIST WORLD: MARXIST AND NON-MARXIST VIEWS. WOR+45 SOCIETY DIPLOM ECO/TAC CONTROL SOCISM...MARXIST ANTHOL BIBLIOG/A 20. PAGE 120 F2363 MARXISM NAT/COMP IDEA/COMP COM

B67
SPICER G.W.,THE SUPREME COURT AND FUNDAMENTAL FREEDOMS (2ND ED.). USA+45 CONSTN SOCIETY ATTIT 20 SUPREME/CT. PAGE 124 F2454 CT/SYS JURID CONTROL ORD/FREE

B67
UNIVERSAL REFERENCE SYSTEM,ECONOMIC REGULATION, BUSINESS, AND GOVERNMENT (VOLUME VIII). WOR+45 WOR-45 ECO/DEV ECO/UNDEV FINAN LABOR TEC/DEV ECO/TAC INT/TRADE GOV/REL...POLICY COMPUT/IR. PAGE 133 F2617 BIBLIOG/A CONTROL NAT/G

B67
UNIVERSAL REFERENCE SYSTEM,PUBLIC POLICY AND THE MANAGEMENT OF SCIENCE (VOLUME IX). FUT SPACE WOR+45 LAW NAT/G TEC/DEV CONTROL NUC/PWR GOV/REL ...COMPUT/IR GEN/METH. PAGE 133 F2618 BIBLIOG/A POLICY MGT PHIL/SCI

B67
US SENATE COMM ON FOREIGN REL,FOREIGN ASSISTANCE ACT OF 1967. VIETNAM WOR+45 DELIB/GP CONFER CONTROL WAR WEAPON BAL/PAY...CENSUS CHARTS SENATE. PAGE 139 F2744 FOR/AID LAW DIPLOM POLICY

B67
WESSON R.G.,THE IMPERIAL ORDER. WOR-45 STRUCT SECT DOMIN ADMIN COLONIAL LEAD CONSERVE...CONCPT BIBLIOG 20. PAGE 145 F2861 PWR CHIEF CONTROL SOCIETY

B67
ZALESKI E.,PLANNING REFORMS IN THE SOVIET UNION 1962-1966. COM USSR NAT/G CONFER CONTROL EFFICIENCY MARXISM...POLICY DECISION 20. PAGE 150 F2957 ECO/DEV PLAN ADMIN CENTRAL

L67
"GOVERNMENT CONTROL OF LAND: PROTECTING THE I-KNOW-IT-WHENI-SEE-IT INTEREST." USA+45 LAW CONSTN DELIB/GP CT/SYS HABITAT ILLINOIS. PAGE 2 F0026 PLAN LOC/G CONTROL ADJUD

L67
AFFELDT R.J.,"THE INDEPENDENT LABOR UNION AND THE GOOD LIFE." USA+45 ADJUD CONTROL SANCTION GP/REL ORD/FREE JURID. PAGE 3 F0045 LABOR CT/SYS PWR SOVEREIGN

L67
BERNHARD R.C.,"COMPETITION IN LAW AND ECONOMICS." LAW PLAN PRICE CONTROL PRODUC PROFIT...METH/CNCPT IDEA/COMP GEN/LAWS 20. PAGE 14 F0265 MARKET POLICY NAT/G CT/SYS

L67
COSTANZA J.F.,"WHOLESOME NEUTRALITY: LAW AND EDUCATION." USA+45 GIVE EDU/PROP ADJUD CONTROL GP/REL...DECISION JURID. PAGE 28 F0540 SECT PROVS ACADEM

L67
DEALEY S.,"MONETARY RECOVERY UNDER FEDERAL TRANSPORTATION STATUTES." USA+45 SEA WORKER TAX PAY ADJUD DEATH GOV/REL OWN HEALTH ORD/FREE 20. PAGE 31 F0609 DIST/IND LAW CONTROL FINAN

L67
DOERFER G.L.,"THE LIMITS ON TRADE SECRET LAW IMPOSED BY FEDERAL PATENT & ANTITRUST SUPREMACY." USA+45 LAW R+D CAP/ISM LICENSE CONTROL SANCTION ORD/FREE. PAGE 33 F0651 JURID GOV/REL POLICY LEGIT

L67
HUBBARD P.H.,"MONETARY RECOVERY UNDER THE COPYRIGHT, PATENT, AND TRADEMARK ACTS." PROC/MFG TAX PAY LEGIT ADJUD GOV/REL OWN ORD/FREE 20. PAGE 62 F1228 CREATE LAW CONTROL FINAN

L67
JOHNSTON J.D. JR.,"CONSTITUTION OF SUBDIVISION CONTROL EXACTIONS: THE QUEST FOR A RATIONALE." USA+45 PROVS PUB/INST ADJUD CT/SYS GP/REL MUNICH. PAGE 68 F1334 PLAN CONTROL LOC/G FORCES

L67
MACDONALD R.S.J.,"THE RESORT TO ECONOMIC COERCION BY INTERNATIONAL POLITICAL ORGANIZATIONS." CUBA ETHIOPIA RHODESIA SOUTH/AFR NAT/G FOR/AID INT/TRADE DOMIN CONTROL SANCTION...DECISION LEAGUE/NAT UN OAS 20. PAGE 83 F1625 INT/ORG COERCE ECO/TAC DIPLOM

L67
MANNE H.G.,"OUR TWO CORPORATION SYSTEMS* LAW AND ECONOMICS." LAW CONTROL SANCTION GP/REL...JURID 20. PAGE 85 F1657 INDUS ELITES CAP/ISM ADMIN

L67
MESTMACKER E.J.,"STATE TRADING MONOPOLIES IN THE EUROPEAN ECONOMIC COMMUNITY. DIPLOM ECO/TAC ADJUD CONTROL DISCRIM 20 EEC. PAGE 90 F1764 INT/TRADE INT/ORG LAW TARIFFS

L67
MIXON J.,"JANE JACOBS AND THE LAW - ZONING FOR DIVERSITY EXAMINED." FUT USA+45 CONSTN NEIGH PROB/SOLV CONTROL CT/SYS PARTIC ATTIT...POLICY CENSUS METH/COMP MUNICH. PAGE 92 F1810 IDEA/COMP PLAN LAW

L67
PARKER G.P. JR.,"MONETARY RECOVERY UNDER THE FEDERAL LABOR STATUTES." USA+45 USA-45 INDUS ADJUD CT/SYS GOV/REL HEALTH ORD/FREE 20 DEPT/LABOR NLRB. PAGE 103 F2027 LABOR CONTROL LAW FINAN

L67
SCHNEIDER C.W.,"REFORM OF THE FEDERAL SECURITIES LAWS." FUT USA+45 LAW FINAN INDUS DELIB/GP ACT/RES PROB/SOLV GP/REL. PAGE 117 F2304 NAT/G LG/CO ADMIN CONTROL

L67
STILL C.H.,"MONETARY RECOVERY UNDER THE FAIR LABOR STANDARDS ACT." USA+45 USA-45 WORKER PAY ADJUD GOV/REL HEALTH ORD/FREE...MATH 20 NLRB. PAGE 126 F2487 LABOR CONTROL LAW FINAN

L67
VIA J.W. JR.,"ANTITRUST AND THE AMENDED BANK MERGER AND HOLDING COMPANY ACTS: THE SEARCH FOR STANDARDS." USA+45 CONTROL GP/REL WEALTH SUPREME/CT. PAGE 141 F2783 FINAN CT/SYS LAW EX/STRUC

L67
WATKINS J.B.,"MONETARY RECOVERY UNDER FEDERAL ANTITRUST STATUTES." USA+45 PROB/SOLV ADJUD CT/SYS GOV/REL ORD/FREE 20. PAGE 144 F2831 LG/CO CONTROL LAW FINAN

S67
"THE FEDERAL AGRICULTURAL STABILIZATION PROGRAM AND THE NEGRO." LAW CONSTN PLAN REPRESENT DISCRIM ORD/FREE 20 NEGRO CONGRESS. PAGE 2 F0025 AGRI CONTROL NAT/G RACE/REL

S67
"ANTITRUST VENUE: TRANSACTING BUSINESS UNDER THE CLAYTON ACT." USA+45 DIST/IND PROB/SOLV ECO/TAC ADJUD CT/SYS 20. PAGE 2 F0028 LAW LG/CO CONTROL NAT/G

S67
AGUILAR M.A.,"?UNA OEA MAS FUERTE O UNA AMERICA LATINA MAS DEBIL?" L/A+17C USA+45 USA-45 ECO/UNDEV INDUS CHIEF DELIB/GP FORCES CONTROL PWR 20 OAS KENNEDY/JF JOHNSON/LB. PAGE 3 F0050 INT/ORG DIPLOM POLICY COLONIAL

S67
ALVES V.,"FOREIGN CAPITAL IN BRAZIL." BRAZIL USA+45 CAP/ISM DIPLOM ECO/TAC INT/TRADE CONTROL PWR ...POLICY 20. PAGE 4 F0081 ECO/UNDEV FINAN SOCIALIST SOCISM

S67
AMERASINGHE C.F.,"SOME LEGAL PROBLEMS OF STATE TRADING IN SOUTHEAST ASIA." PROB/SOLV ADJUD CONTROL CT/SYS GP/REL 20. PAGE 5 F0084 INT/TRADE NAT/G INT/LAW PRIVIL

S67
AVTORKHANOV A.,"A NEW AGRARIAN REVOLUTION." COM USSR ECO/DEV PLAN TEC/DEV ADMIN CONTROL OPTIMAL WEALTH SOCISM 20 KHRUSH/N STALIN/J. PAGE 8 F0144 AGRI METH/COMP MARXISM OWN

S67
BAGDKIAN B.H.,"NEWS AS A BYPRODUCT: WHAT HAPPENS WHEN JOURNALISM IS HITCHED TO GREAT, DIVERSIFIED CORPORATIONS?" USA+45 INDUS EDU/PROP PARTIC PROFIT ATTIT. PAGE 8 F0152 COM/IND PRESS CONTROL LG/CO

S67
BARAN P.,"THE FUTURE COMPUTER UTILITY." USA+45 NAT/G PLAN CONTROL COST...POLICY 20. PAGE 9 F0177 COMPUTER UTIL FUT TEC/DEV

S67
BARTLETT J.L.,"AMERICAN BOND ISSUES IN THE EUROPEAN ECONOMIC COMMUNITY." EUR+WWI LUXEMBOURG USA+45 DIPLOM CONTROL BAL/PAY EEC. PAGE 11 F0201 LAW ECO/TAC FINAN TAX

S67
BASOV V.,"THE DEVELOPMENT OF PUBLIC EDUCATION AND THE BUDGET." USSR NAT/G CONTROL REV COST AGE...STAT 20. PAGE 11 F0204 BUDGET GIVE EDU/PROP

SCHOOL

S67
BELISLE J.,"FOREIGN RESTRAINTS ON US BANKS ABROAD" WOR+45 LAW. PAGE 12 F0233
DIPLOM FINAN CONTROL LICENSE

S67
BOSHER J.F.,"GOVERNMENT AND PRIVATE INTERESTS IN NEW FRANCE." CANADA FRANCE INDUS LG/CO SML/CO CAP/ISM INT/TRADE COLONIAL GP/REL...HIST/WRIT 17/18. PAGE 17 F0320
NAT/G FINAN ADMIN CONTROL

S67
CHADWELL J.T.,"ANTITRUST ASPECTS OF DEALER LICENSING AND FRANCHISING." ACT/RES LICENSE ADJUD CONTROL OWN. PAGE 23 F0439
LAW PRIVIL INDUS

S67
DANIEL C.,"THE REGULATION OF PRIVATE ENTERPRISES AS PUBLIC UTILITIES." WOR+45 LAW LICENSE POLICY. PAGE 30 F0577
LOC/G NAT/G CONTROL SERV/IND

S67
DURIEZ P.,"THE IMPACT OF EX PARTE 230 (PIGGYBACKING) ON RAIL-MOTOR COMPETITION." USA+45 USA-45 LG/CO COST EFFICIENCY...CHARTS 20. PAGE 35 F0685
DIST/IND LAW CONTROL AGREE

S67
EDWARDS N.,"EDUCATION IN THE FEDERAL-STATE STRUCTURE OF GOVERNMENT." USA+45 SECT CONTROL GOV/REL RACE/REL DISCRIM FEDERAL ROLE PWR SOVEREIGN. PAGE 36 F0705
EDU/PROP NAT/G PROVS POLICY

S67
FERGUSON D.E.,"DETERMINING CAPACITY FOR CAPITAL EXPENDITURES." USA+45 LOC/G BUDGET TAX ADMIN CONTROL...TREND MUNICH 20. PAGE 40 F0784
FINAN PAY COST

S67
FLACKS R.,"CONSCRIPTION IN A DEMOCRATIC SOCIETY." USA+45 WORKER CONTROL SUFF SUPEGO. PAGE 41 F0807
POLICY FORCES ORD/FREE CIVMIL/REL

S67
GANZ G.,"THE CONTROL OF INDUSTRY BY ADMINISTRATIVE PROCESS." UK DELIB/GP WORKER 20. PAGE 46 F0898
INDUS LAW ADMIN CONTROL

S67
GAUSE M.E.,"ELEMENTS OF FINANCE DEPARTMENT ORGANIZATION FOR SMALL GOVERNMENTAL UNITS." USA+45 PROB/SOLV CONTROL CENTRAL...METH MUNICH. PAGE 47 F0910
ADMIN LOC/G FINAN

S67
GOLDSTEIN W.,"THE SCIENCE ESTABLISHMENT AND ITS POLITICAL CONTROL." WOR+45 SOCIETY GP/REL RATIONAL ORD/FREE. PAGE 48 F0941
CREATE ADJUST CONTROL

S67
GORMAN W.,"ELLUL - A PROPHETIC VOICE." WOR+45 ELITES SOCIETY ACT/RES PLAN BAL/PWR DOMIN CONTROL PARTIC TOTALISM PWR 20. PAGE 49 F0963
CREATE ORD/FREE EX/STRUC UTOPIA

S67
GRAYSON D.K.,"RISK ALLOCATIONS UNDER THE PERMITS AND RESPONSIBILITIES CLAUSE OF THE STANDARD GOVERNMENT CONSTRUCTION CONTRACT." USA+45 LAW WORKER. PAGE 50 F0979
CONSTRUC CONTROL RISK NAT/G

S67
HALE G.E.,"EXPANDING ENTERPRISE: GEOGRAPHICAL CURBS ON MERGERS." USA+45 MARKET LG/CO ADJUD CONTROL GP/REL 20. PAGE 53 F1041
LAW HABITAT INDUS EX/STRUC

S67
IBARRA J.,"EL EXPERIMENTO CUBANO." COM CUBA L/A+17C USA+45 ECO/UNDEV LEGIS INT/TRADE CONTROL REV NAT/LISM PWR 19/20 TREATY. PAGE 64 F1259
COLONIAL DIPLOM NAT/G POLICY

S67
JENCKS C.E.,"SOCIAL STATUS OF COAL MINERS IN BRITAIN SINCE NATIONALIZATION." UK STRATA STRUCT LABOR RECEIVE GP/REL INCOME OWN ATTIT HABITAT...MGT T 20. PAGE 67 F1312
EXTR/IND WORKER CONTROL NAT/G

S67
KENDALL R.J.,"CHANGED CONDITIONS AS MISREPRESENTATION IN GOVERNMENT CONSTRUCTION CONTRACTS." USA+45 BARGAIN ADJUD COST. PAGE 70 F1375
CONTROL CONSTRUC NAT/G LAW

S67
LEMIEUX V.,"LA DIMENSION POLITIQUE DE L'ACTION RATIONNELLE." CONTROL GP/REL PERS/REL...DECISION NEW/IDEA GAME 20. PAGE 77 F1518
GEN/LAWS RATIONAL PWR

S67
LOSMAN D.L.,"FOREIGN AID, SOCIALISM AND THE EMERGING COUNTRIES" WOR+45 ADMIN CONTROL PWR 20. PAGE 82 F1602
ECO/UNDEV FOR/AID SOC

S67
MCCOLL R.W.,"A POLITICAL GEOGRAPHY OF REVOLUTION: CHINA, VIETNAM, AND THAILAND." ASIA THAILAND VIETNAM FORCES CONTROL 20. PAGE 88 F1720
REV GEOG PLAN DECISION

S67
MERIKOSKI V.,"BASIC PROBLEMS OF UNIVERSITY ADMINISTRATION." PROVS SECT CONTROL...CLASSIF 20. PAGE 90 F1760
ACADEM ADMIN SOVEREIGN METH/COMP

S67
MITCHELL J.D.B.,"THE CONSTITUTIONAL IMPLICATIONS OF JUDICIAL CONTROL OF THE ADMINISTRATION IN THE UNITED KINGDOM." UK LAW ADJUD ADMIN GOV/REL ROLE ...GP/COMP 20. PAGE 92 F1808
CONSTN CT/SYS CONTROL EX/STRUC

S67
MODESITT L.E.,"THE MUTUAL FUND - A CORPORATE ANOMALY." USA+45 CONTROL...MGT 20. PAGE 92 F1813
SERV/IND FINAN ADMIN LAW

S67
MOLTMANN G.,"ZUR FORMULIERUNG DER AMERIKANISCHEN BESATZUNGSPOLITIK IN DEUTSCHLAND AM ENDE DES ZWEITEN WELTKRIEGES" GERMANY ECO/TAC ADMIN WAR CIVMIL/REL ORD/FREE FASCISM 20. PAGE 92 F1815
FORCES CONTROL POLICY INDUS

S67
NILES J.G.,"CIVIL ACTIONS FOR DAMAGES UNDER THE FEDERAL CIVIL RIGHTS STATUTES." CONSTN FINAN ADJUD CT/SYS GOV/REL RACE/REL 20. PAGE 98 F1928
DISCRIM LAW CONTROL ORD/FREE

S67
NOURSE E.G.,"EARLY FLOWERING OF THE EMPLOYMENT ACT" USA+45 LABOR CONSULT DELIB/GP LEGIS BUDGET GOV/REL PRODUC WEALTH 20 INTRVN/ECO. PAGE 99 F1939
NAT/G WORKER ECO/TAC CONTROL

S67
PAI G.A.,"TAXATION AND PLANNING IN INDIA: A BIRDS-EYE VIEW." INDIA ELITES NAT/G LEGIS BUDGET CONTROL LOBBY INCOME...STAT CHARTS 20. PAGE 102 F2015
TAX PLAN WEALTH STRATA

S67
PEMBERTON J., JR.,"CONSTITUTIONAL PROBLEMS IN RESTRAINT ON THE MEDIA." CONSTN PROB/SOLV EDU/PROP CONFER CONTROL JURID. PAGE 104 F2054
LAW PRESS ORD/FREE

S67
POWELL D.,"THE EFFECTIVENESS OF SOVIET ANTI-RELIGIOUS PROPAGANDA." USSR NAT/G DOMIN LEGIT NAT/LISM 20. PAGE 107 F2109
EDU/PROP ATTIT SECT CONTROL

S67
PRATT R.C.,"THE ADMINISTRATION OF ECONOMIC PLANNING IN A NEWLY INDEPEND ENT STATE* THE TANZANIAN EXPERIENCE 1963-1966." AFR TANZANIA ECO/UNDEV PLAN CONTROL ROUTINE TASK EFFICIENCY 20. PAGE 107 F2114
NAT/G DELIB/GP ADMIN TEC/DEV

S67
RAGAN S.,"THE ABA RECOMMENDATIONS: A NEWSPAPERMAN'S CRITIQUE." EDU/PROP CONTROL GP/REL...JURID ABA. PAGE 109 F2136
LAW PRESS ADJUD ORD/FREE

S67
RAZA M.A.,"EMERGING TRENDS IN PUBLIC LABOR POLICIES AND UNION - GOVERN MENT RELATIONS IN ASIA AND AFRICA." LAW NAT/G POL/PAR COLONIAL COERCE GP/REL ATTIT 20. PAGE 110 F2157
LABOR CONTROL TREND

S67
REILLY T.J.,"FREEZING AND CONFISCATION OF CUBAN PROPERTY." CUBA USA+45 LAW DIPLOM LEGIT ADJUD CONTROL. PAGE 111 F2177
STRANGE OWN ECO/TAC

S67
RICHMAN B.M.,"SOVIET MANAGEMENT IN TRANSITION." USSR FINAN MARKET EX/STRUC PLAN PROB/SOLV TEC/DEV CONTROL LEAD CENTRAL EFFICIENCY...METH/COMP 20 REFORMERS. PAGE 111 F2186
MGT MARXISM POLICY AUTHORIT

S67
SCHACHTER G.,"REGIONAL DEVELOPMENT IN THE ITALIAN DUAL ECONOMY" ITALY AGRI INDUS MARKET WORKER ECO/TAC CONTROL INCOME PRODUC 20. PAGE 116 F2287
REGION ECO/UNDEV NAT/G PROB/SOLV

S67
SCHELLING T.C.,"ECONOMICS AND CRIMINAL ENTERPRISE." LAW FORCES BARGAIN ECO/TAC CONTROL GAMBLE ROUTINE ADJUST DEMAND INCOME PROFIT CRIMLGY. PAGE 116 F2295
CRIME PROB/SOLV CONCPT

S67
SCOVILLE W.J.,"GOVERNMENT REGULATION AND GROWTH IN THE FRENCH PAPER INDUSTRY DURING THE EIGHTEENTH CENTURY." FRANCE MOD/EUR FINAN CAP/ISM TAX ADMIN CONTROL PRIVIL LAISSEZ...POLICY 18. PAGE 118 F2337
NAT/G PROC/MFG ECO/DEV INGP/REL

S67
SCRIPP J.,"CONTROLLING PREJUDICIAL PUBLICITY BY THE CONTEMPT POWER: THE BRITISH PRACTICE AND ITS PROSPECT IN AMERICAN LAW." UK USA+45 EDU/PROP CONTROL GP/REL ORD/FREE JURID. PAGE 119 F2338
METH/COMP LAW PRESS ADJUD

S67
SKOLNICK J.H.,"SOCIAL CONTROL IN THE ADVERSARY SYSTEM." USA+45 CONSULT OP/RES ADMIN CONTROL. PAGE 123 F2419
PROB/SOLV PERS/REL ADJUD CT/SYS

S67
SMITH W.H.T.,"THE IMPLICATIONS OF THE AMERICAN BAR ASSOCIATION ADVISORY COMMITTEE RECOMMENDATIONS FOR POLICE ADMINISTRATION." AFR ADMIN...JURID 20.
EDU/PROP CONTROL GP/REL

PAGE 123 F2435 ORD/FREE

S67
STILL J.F.,"THE FUTURE OF METROPOLITAN GOVERNMENT ORGANIZATION." USA+45 LOC/G BUDGET COST ATTIT MUNICH 20. PAGE 126 F2488 ADMIN FINAN CONTROL

S67
STYCOS J.M.,"POLITICS AND POPULATION CONTROL IN LATIN AMERICA." USA+45 FAM NAT/G GP/REL AGE/C ATTIT CATHISM MARXISM...POLICY UN WHO. PAGE 127 F2509 PLAN CENSUS CONTROL L/A+17C

S67
TELLER A.,"AIR-POLLUTION ABATEMENT: ECONOMIC RATIONALITY AND REALITY." NAT/G DELIB/GP ECO/TAC GOV/REL CENTRAL EFFICIENCY HEALTH...CHARTS METH MUNICH. PAGE 129 F2543 PROB/SOLV CONTROL COST AIR

S67
WAITS C.R.,"CRAFT GILDS AS AN INSTITUTIONAL BARRIER TO THE INDUSTRIAL REVOLUTION." CHRIST-17C MOD/EUR ECO/UNDEV CONTROL GP/REL ATTIT 16/19. PAGE 142 F2801 TEC/DEV INDUS REV PROF/ORG

S67
WARNER G.,"FRANCE, BRITAIN AND THE EEC." FRANCE UK INT/ORG DELIB/GP ECO/TAC CONTROL 20 EEC. PAGE 143 F2822 INT/TRADE BAL/PWR DIPLOM

S67
WOLFSON M.,"GOVERNMENT'S ROLE IN TOURISM DEVELOPMENT." WOR+45 ECO/DEV ECO/UNDEV FINAN BUDGET DIPLOM EDU/PROP. PAGE 148 F2920 SERV/IND NAT/G CONTROL PLAN

N67
US SENATE COMM ON FOREIGN REL,ARMS SALES AND FOREIGN POLICY (PAMPHLET). FINAN FOR/AID CONTROL 20. PAGE 139 F2737 ARMS/CONT ADMIN OP/RES DIPLOM

S86
SMITH R.M.,"THE NATIONAL BUREAU OF LABOR AND INDUSTRIAL DEPRESSIONS" USA-45 DELIB/GP BARGAIN CONTROL COST INCOME WEALTH...STAT 19 DEPRESSION. PAGE 123 F2433 LABOR INDUS FINAN GOV/REL

B88
BENTHAM J.,DEFENCE OF USURY (1787). UK LAW NAT/G TEC/DEV ECO/TAC CONTROL ATTIT...CONCPT IDEA/COMP 18 SMITH/ADAM. PAGE 13 F0255 TAX FINAN ECO/DEV POLICY

B92
ENGELS F.,THE CONDITION OF THE WORKING-CLASS IN ENGLAND (1848). UK INDUS LABOR PRICE CONTROL COST INCOME HEALTH MARXISM MUNICH 19. PAGE 38 F0733 WORKER WEALTH MARXIST CAP/ISM

B95
SELIGMAN E.R.A.,ESSAYS IN TAXATION. NEW/ZEALND PRUSSIA UK USA-45 MARKET LOC/G CREATE PRICE CONTROL INCOME OWN WEALTH...GOV/COMP METH/COMP 19. PAGE 119 F2349 TAX TARIFFS INDUS NAT/G

CONTROLLED DIRECT OBSERVATION....SEE CONT/OBS

CONTY J.M. F0528

CONV/LEASE....CONVICT LEASE SYSTEM IN SOUTH

CONVNTL....CONVENTIONAL

COOK P.L. F0529

COOK P.W. F0530

COOKE C.A. F0531

COOLIDGE/C....CALVIN COOLIDGE

COOMBS P.H. F0532

COOPERATION....SEE AGREE

COOPERATIVE....SEE VOL/ASSN

COORDINATION....SEE CENTRAL

COPELAND M.A. F0533

COPLAND D. F0534

COPPOCK J. F0535

COPPOCK J.D. F0536

COPYRIGHT....COPYRIGHT

CORE....CONGRESS OF RACIAL EQUALITY

CORLEY R.N. F0537

CORN/LAWS....CORN LAWS (U.K.)

B60
GRAMPP W.D.,THE MANCHESTER SCHOOL OF ECONOMICS. UK LAW ECO/DEV COERCE ATTIT ORD/FREE LAISSEZ ...PHIL/SCI IDEA/COMP 19/20 MANCHESTER CORN/LAWS. PAGE 50 F0973 ECO/TAC VOL/ASSN LOBBY NAT/G

CORNELL/U....CORNELL UNIVERSITY

CORPORATION....SEE CORPORATN

CORPORATN....CORPORATION

CORRECTIONAL INSTITUTION....SEE PUB/INST

CORREL....STATISTICAL CORRELATIONS

S60
SPINRAD W.,"CORRELATES OF TRADE UNION PARTICIPATION: A SUMMARY OF LITERATURE." ACT/RES PERS/REL HAPPINESS HABITAT...BIBLIOG WORK. PAGE 125 F2456 LABOR PARTIC CORREL ROLE

S62
READ W.H.,"UPWARD COMMUNICATION IN INDUSTRIAL HIERARCHIES." LG/CO TOP/EX PROB/SOLV DOMIN EXEC PERS/REL ATTIT DRIVE PERCEPT...CORREL STAT CHARTS 20. PAGE 110 F2159 ADMIN INGP/REL PSY MGT

L63
MCKERSIE R.B.,"NONPROFESSIONAL HOSPITAL WORKERS AND A UNION ORGANIZING DRIVE." PLAN GP/REL RACE/REL ATTIT DRIVE...CORREL STAT INT GP/COMP. PAGE 88 F1732 VOL/ASSN HEALTH INGP/REL LABOR

S67
WALLACE H.M.,"AVAILABILITY AND USEFULNESS OF SELECTED HEALTH AND SOCIOECONOMIC DATA FOR COMMUNITY PLANNING." NEIGH EFFICIENCY...CORREL STAT CENSUS CHARTS. PAGE 142 F2806 HEALTH PLAN SOC/WK HEAL

COSGROVE C.A. F0538

COSSA L. F0539

COST....ECONOMIC VALUE; SEE ALSO PROFIT, COSTS

N
JOHNSON R.B.,FINANCING A SUBURBAN CITY. USA+45 TAX COST...SAMP/SIZ MUNICH 20 COL. PAGE 68 F1331 FINAN PAY PROB/SOLV

N
US LIBRARY OF CONGRESS,SELECTED AND ANNOTATED BIBLIOGRAPHY ON INDUSTRIAL PROBLEMS AND POLICIES IN WARTIME (PAMPHLET). WOR-45 CONSTRUC NAT/G PROB/SOLV COST DEMAND PRODUC 20. PAGE 137 F2707 BIBLIOG/A ECO/DEV INDUS WAR

LCA
GODFREY E.M.,"THE ECONOMICS OF AN AFRICAN UNIVERSITY." AFR SCHOOL PRICE EFFICIENCY INCOME WEALTH...ECOMETRIC CHARTS 20. PAGE 48 F0930 ACADEM ECO/TAC COST EDU/PROP

B04
VEBLEN T.B.,THE THEORY OF BUSINESS ENTERPRISE. USA-45 FINAN WORKER ECO/TAC PRICE GP/REL COST ...POLICY 19/20. PAGE 141 F2770 TEC/DEV GEN/LAWS SOCIETY WEALTH

B13
DAVENPORT H.J.,THE ECONOMICS OF ENTERPRISE. UNIV FINAN SML/CO RENT COST WEALTH GEN/LAWS. PAGE 30 F0582 CAP/ISM PRICE ECO/TAC LG/CO

B14
DE BLOCH J.,THE FUTURE OF WAR IN ITS TECHNICAL, ECONOMIC, AND POLITICAL RELATIONS (1899). MOD/EUR TEC/DEV BUDGET INT/TRADE DETER GUERRILLA WEAPON COST PEACE 20. PAGE 31 F0596 WAR BAL/PWR PREDICT FORCES

B14
HOBSON J.A.,WORK AND WEALTH. CULTURE FINAN INDUS WORKER TEC/DEV ECO/TAC GIVE PAY PRICE COST PRODUC UTIL. PAGE 60 F1185 WEALTH INCOME GEN/LAWS

B19
VEBLEN T.B.,THE VESTED INTERESTS AND THE STATE OF THE INDUSTRIAL ARTS. USA-45 LAW FINAN WORKER PAY DOMIN PRICE COST SOCISM...MARXIST 19/20. PAGE 141 F2771 INDUS CAP/ISM METH/COMP WEALTH

N19
ARNDT H.W.,AUSTRALIAN FOREIGN AID POLICY (PAMPHLET). ECO/UNDEV DIPLOM GIVE GOV/REL COST UTIL PWR...CHARTS 20 AUSTRAL PAPUA NEW/GUINEA. PAGE 6 F0114 FOR/AID POLICY ECO/TAC EFFICIENCY

N19
BOS H.C.,A DISCUSSION ON METHODS OF MONETARY ANALYSIS AND NORMS FOR MONETARY POLICY (PAMPHLET). BAL/PAY COST INCOME...METH/COMP 20. PAGE 17 F0319 FINAN POLICY EQUILIB SIMUL

N19
BROWN W.M.,THE DESIGN AND PERFORMANCE OF "OPTIMUM" BLAST SHELTER PROGRAMS (PAMPHLET). USA+45 ACT/RES HABITAT NUC/PWR

PLAN DEATH COST EFFICIENCY OPTIMAL...POLICY CHARTS 20. PAGE 19 F0375
WAR HEALTH

N19
BUSINESS ECONOMISTS' GROUP,INCOME POLICIES (PAMPHLET). UK INDUS LABOR TOP/EX PAY COST PRODUC ...ECOMETRIC GOV/COMP SIMUL ANTHOL 20. PAGE 20 F0395
INCOME WORKER WEALTH POLICY

N19
CONGRESSIONAL QUARTERLY SERV,FEDERAL ECONOMIC POLICY 1945-1965 (PAMPHLET). USA+45 FINAN OP/RES BAL/PWR ECO/TAC TAX BAL/PAY CENTRAL COST WEALTH ...CHARTS 20. PAGE 27 F0525
NAT/G ECO/DEV BUDGET POLICY

N19
GROSECLOSE E.,THE DECAY OF MONEY; A SURVEY OF WESTERN CURRENCIES 1912-1962 (PAMPHLET). AFR FRANCE GERMANY UK LAW INT/TRADE BAL/PAY COST EQUILIB ...POLICY 20 DEPRESSION. PAGE 51 F1004
FINAN NAT/G ECO/DEV ECO/TAC

N19
HABERLER G.,INFLATION; ITS CAUSES AND CURES (PAMPHLET). AFR USA+45 FINAN BUDGET PAY PRICE COST DEMAND 20. PAGE 52 F1021
ECO/DEV BAL/PAY POLICY NAT/G

N19
HABERLER G.,A SURVEY OF INTERNATIONAL TRADE THEORY (PAMPHLET). FINAN NAT/G COST INCOME 18/20 MONEY HUME/D MARSHALL/A. PAGE 52 F1022
INT/TRADE BAL/PAY GEN/LAWS POLICY

N19
MIYASAWA K.,AN ECONOMIC SURVIVAL GAME (PAMPHLET). COST DEMAND EQUILIB INCOME PROFIT 20. PAGE 92 F1811
ECOMETRIC GAME ECO/TAC DECISION

N19
MUSHKIN S.J.,LOCAL SCHOOL EXPENDITURES: 1970 PROJECTIONS (PAMPHLET). FUT USA+45 CONSTRUC FINAN PROVS EDU/PROP COST...GEOG CENSUS PREDICT CHARTS SIMUL 20. PAGE 95 F1871
LOC/G SCHOOL BUDGET

N19
WILSON T.,FINANCIAL ASSISTANCE WITH REGIONAL DEVELOPMENT (PAMPHLET). CANADA INDUS NAT/G PLAN TAX CONTROL COST EFFICIENCY...POLICY CHARTS 20. PAGE 147 F2902
FINAN ECO/TAC REGION GOV/REL

B20
MALTHUS T.R.,PRINCIPLES OF POLITICAL ECONOMY. UK AGRI INDUS MARKET NAT/G DIPLOM PRICE CONTROL BAL/PAY COST OWN PWR LAISSEZ 18/19. PAGE 84 F1650
GEN/LAWS DEMAND WEALTH

B23
HOBSON J.A.,INCENTIVES IN THE NEW INDUSTRIAL ORDER. USA-45 NAT/G PAY COST EFFICIENCY PRODUC WEALTH ...MAJORIT PSY SOC/WK 20. PAGE 60 F1186
INDUS LABOR INCOME OPTIMAL

B30
BIEL G.,TREATISE ON THE POWER AND UTILITY OF MONEY (1484). INDUS MARKET LOC/G NAT/G SECT ECO/TAC PRODUC WEALTH 15. PAGE 15 F0280
FINAN COST PRICE GEN/LAWS

B30
KEYNES J.M.,A TREATISE ON MONEY (2 VOLS.). UK USA-45 INDUS MARKET WORKER PRICE CONTROL COST OPTIMAL PROFIT WEALTH...POLICY 19/20 KEYNES/JM. PAGE 70 F1385
EQUILIB ECO/TAC FINAN GEN/LAWS

B34
ROBINSON J.,THE ECONOMICS OF IMPERFECT COMPETITION. FINAN ECO/TAC PRICE COST DEMAND EQUILIB OPTIMAL WEALTH...METH MONOPOLY. PAGE 113 F2221
MARKET WORKER INDUS

B35
HICKS J.R.,THE THEORY OF WAGES. INDUS NAT/G PAY PRICE CONTROL COST EFFICIENCY WEALTH 19/20 MARSHALL/A CLARK/JB. PAGE 59 F1164
INCOME WORKER LABOR PRODUC

B35
MARX K.,WAGE-LABOR AND CAPITAL -- VALUE, PRICE AND PROFIT. LABOR PAY PRICE COST INCOME OWN PROFIT WEALTH 19. PAGE 86 F1690
STRATA WORKER MARXIST MARXISM

B37
HAMILTON W.H.,THE POWER TO GOVERN. ECO/DEV FINAN INDUS ECO/TAC INT/TRADE TARIFFS TAX CONTROL CT/SYS WAR COST PWR 18/20 SUPREME/CT. PAGE 54 F1056
LING CONSTN NAT/G POLICY

B38
MEADE J.E.,AN INTRODUCTION TO ECONOMIC ANALYSIS AND POLICY (AMERICAN EDITION EDITED BY C.J. HITCH). FINAN INDUS MARKET LABOR INT/TRADE CONTROL COST DEMAND INCOME...CLASSIF CHARTS T 20 KEYNES/JM MONOPOLY. PAGE 89 F1737
CONCPT PROFIT PRODUC

B40
TRIFFIN R.,MONOPOLISTIC COMPETITION AND GENERAL EQUILIBRIUM THEORY. DIST/IND PLAN TASK EQUILIB OPTIMAL...IDEA/COMP 20 MONOPOLY. PAGE 131 F2586
INT/TRADE INDUS COST

B41
HAYEK F.A.,THE PURE THEORY OF CAPITAL. UNIV ECO/DEV ECO/TAC COST EQUILIB PROFIT WEALTH...SIMUL GEN/LAWS BIBLIOG INDEX TIME 20. PAGE 57 F1120
CAP/ISM METH/CNCPT PRODUC FINAN

B41
SLICHTER S.H.,UNION POLICIES AND INDUSTRIAL MANAGEMENT. USA-45 INDUS TEC/DEV PAY GP/REL INGP/REL COST EFFICIENCY PRODUC...POLICY 20. PAGE 123 F2420
BARGAIN LABOR MGT WORKER

B42
SWEEZY P.M.,THE THEORY OF CAPITALIST DEVELOPMENT. FUT NAT/G COST FASCISM BIBLIOG. PAGE 128 F2519
ECO/DEV CAP/ISM MARXISM COLONIAL

B42
US LIBRARY OF CONGRESS,ECONOMICS OF WAR (APRIL 1941-MARCH 1942). WOR-45 FINAN INDUS LOC/G NAT/G PLAN BUDGET RATION COST DEMAND...POLICY 20. PAGE 138 F2712
BIBLIOG/A INT/TRADE ECO/TAC WAR

B44
BIENSTOCK G.,MANAGEMENT IN RUSSIAN INDUSTRY AND AGRICULTURE. USSR CONSULT WORKER LEAD COST PROFIT ATTIT DRIVE PWR...MGT METH/COMP DICTIONARY ACCT 20. PAGE 15 F0281
ADMIN MARXISM SML/CO AGRI

B44
LANDAUER C.,THEORY OF NATIONAL ECONOMIC PLANNING. USA-45 INDUS MARKET WORKER PROB/SOLV DIPLOM RATION PRICE CONTROL WAR COST 20. PAGE 75 F1465
ECO/TAC PLAN NAT/G ECO/DEV

B44
LOCKE J.,FURTHER CONSIDERATIONS CONCERNING RAISING THE VALUE OF MONEY. AFR UK NAT/G ECO/TAC INCOME WEALTH...METH/COMP GEN/LAWS 17 SILVER. PAGE 81 F1591
COST FINAN PRICE CONTROL

B46
DAVIES E.,NATIONAL ENTERPRISE: THE DEVELOPMENT OF THE PUBLIC CORPORATION. UK LG/CO EX/STRUC WORKER PROB/SOLV COST ATTIT SOCISM 20. PAGE 30 F0584
ADMIN NAT/G CONTROL INDUS

B47
BALDWIN H.W.,THE PRICE OF POWER. USA+45 FORCES PLAN NUC/PWR ADJUST COST ORD/FREE...POLICY PSY BIBLIOG 20. PAGE 9 F0165
PROB/SOLV PWR POPULISM PRICE

B48
HART A.G.,MONEY, DEBT, AND ECONOMIC ACTIVITY. AFR WORKER DIPLOM PRICE CONTROL BAL/PAY COST OWN PRODUC ...METH/COMP 20 FED/RESERV. PAGE 56 F1097
FINAN WEALTH ECO/TAC NAT/G

B48
HOOVER E.M.,THE LOCATION OF ECONOMIC ACTIVITY. WOR+45 MARKET WORKER PROB/SOLV INT/TRADE ADMIN COST ...POLICY CHARTS T MUNICH 20. PAGE 62 F1211
HABITAT INDUS ECO/TAC GEOG

B48
METZLER L.A.,INCOME, EMPLOYMENT, AND PUBLIC POLICY. FINAN INDUS LOC/G NAT/G TAX GIVE PAY COST PRODUC ...MGT TIME/SEQ 20. PAGE 90 F1765
INCOME WEALTH POLICY ECO/TAC

B48
NOYES C.R.,ECONOMIC MAN IN RELATION TO HIS NATURAL ENVIRONMENT (2 VOLS.). UNIV COST DEMAND EFFICIENCY HAPPINESS INCOME PRODUC PROFIT HEREDITY...CHARTS BIBLIOG. PAGE 99 F1944
HABITAT METH/CNCPT GEN/METH

B48
ROBERTSON D.H.,MONEY. AFR ECO/DEV NAT/G DIPLOM INT/TRADE BAL/PAY INCOME WEALTH...TIME/SEQ 20 DEPRESSION. PAGE 112 F2212
FINAN MARKET COST PRICE

B50
CHAMBERLIN E.,THE THEORY OF MONOPOLISTIC COMPETITION (1933). INDUS PAY GP/REL COST DEMAND EFFICIENCY OPTIMAL PRODUC WEALTH...GEN/LAWS 20. PAGE 23 F0443
MARKET PRICE ECO/TAC EQUILIB

B50
SHAW E.S.,MONEY, INCOME, AND MONETARY POLICY. AFR USA-45 NAT/G DIPLOM PAY CONTROL COST INCOME PRODUC WEALTH...T 20 FED/RESERV DEPT/TREAS. PAGE 120 F2370
FINAN ECO/TAC ECO/DEV PRICE

S50
DREYFUS S.,"THE INDUSTRIAL DESIGNER AND THE BUSINESSMAN." SERV/IND PROB/SOLV ECO/TAC COST EFFICIENCY PROFIT RATIONAL...DECISION MGT. PAGE 34 F0662
CONSULT INDUS PRODUC UTIL

B51
BROGAN D.W.,THE PRICE OF REVOLUTION. FRANCE USA+45 USA-45 USSR CONSTN NAT/G DIPLOM COLONIAL NAT/LISM ORD/FREE POPULISM...CONCPT 18/20 PRE/US/AM. PAGE 19 F0359
REV METH/COMP COST MARXISM

B51
HART A.G.,DEFENSE WITHOUT INFLATION. AFR KOREA FINAN INDUS NAT/G WORKER DIPLOM RATION TAX PRICE COST OPTIMAL 20 RESOURCE/N. PAGE 56 F1098
ECO/TAC CONTROL WAR PLAN

B51
POOLE K.,FISCAL POLICIES AND THE AMERICAN ECONOMY. AFR ECO/DEV FINAN INDUS WORKER OP/RES INT/TRADE TAX COST INCOME PROFIT WEALTH...GP/COMP 20. PAGE 107 F2102
NAT/G POLICY ANTHOL

S51
HAWLEY A.H.,"METROPOLITAN POPULATION AND MUNICIPAL GOVERNMENT EXPENDITURES IN CENTRAL CITIES" (BMR)" USA+45 FINAN TAX...STAT CON/ANAL CHARTS MUNICH 20. PAGE 57 F1117
GEOG LOC/G COST BUDGET

S52
PHILLIPS C.,"THE HIGH COST OF OUR LOW-PAID CONGRESS" (NYT MAG. 2/24/52)" USA+45 FINAN WRITING TASK TIME CONGRESS. PAGE 106 F2082
LEGIS INCOME COST EFFICIENCY

C52
HUME D.,"OF TAXES" IN D. HUME, POLITICAL DISCOURSES (1752)" UK NAT/G COST INCOME LAISSEZ...GEN/LAWS 18. PAGE 63 F1236
TAX FINAN WEALTH POLICY

C52
HUME D.,"OF INTEREST" IN D. HUME, POLITICAL DISCOURSES (1752)" UK INDUS WORKER DIPLOM PAY DEMAND INCOME WEALTH...GEN/LAWS 18 MONEY. PAGE 63 F1239
PRICE COST FINAN INT/TRADE

C52
HUME D.,"OF MONEY" IN D. HUME, POLITICAL DISCOURSES (1752)" UK INDUS DIPLOM INT/TRADE...GEN/LAWS 18 MONEY. PAGE 63 F1240
FINAN COST PRICE WEALTH

B53
WILLIAMS J.H.,ECONOMIC STABILITY IN A CHANGING WORLD. FRANCE USA+45 USSR AGRI WORKER BUDGET INT/TRADE TAX WAR BAL/PAY COST EFFICIENCY ALL/IDEOS EQULIB 20 KEYNES/JM. PAGE 147 F2892
POLICY FINAN ECO/TAC WEALTH

B54
BERNSTEIN I.,ARBITRATION OF WAGES. USA+45 CONSULT PAY COST PRODUC WEALTH...CHARTS 20. PAGE 14 F0266
DELIB/GP BARGAIN WORKER PRICE

B54
MITCHELL W.G.,BUSINESS CYCLES. FINAN MARKET PRICE COST EQUILIB OPTIMAL PRODUC PROFIT...IDEA/COMP GEN/LAWS 19/20. PAGE 92 F1809
INDUS TIME/SEQ METH/COMP STAT

B54
RECK D.,GOVERNMENT PURCHASING AND COMPETITION. USA+45 LEGIS CAP/ISM ECO/TAC GOV/REL CENTRAL ...POLICY 20 CONGRESS. PAGE 110 F2164
NAT/G FINAN MGT COST

B54
RICHTER R.,DAS KONKURRENZ PROBLEM IM OLIGOPOL. LG/CO BARGAIN PRICE COST...CONCPT 20 MONOPOLY. PAGE 111 F2188
CONTROL GAME ECO/TAC GP/REL

B55
BOULDING K.E.,ECONOMIC ANALYSIS (3RD ED.). USA+45 PLAN ECO/TAC COST DEMAND INCOME...POLICY STAT CHARTS SIMUL T. PAGE 17 F0322
PHIL/SCI ECO/DEV CAP/ISM

B55
GOMES F.A.,OPERACAO MUNICIPIO. BRAZIL L/A+17C SERV/IND LOC/G BUDGET ECO/TAC COST DEMAND...POLICY MUNICH 20. PAGE 48 F0944
ECO/UNDEV FEDERAL GOV/REL

B55
US OFFICE OF THE PRESIDENT,REPORT TO CONGRESS ON THE MUTUAL SECURITY PROGRAM FOR THE SIX MONTHS ENDED JUNE 30, 1955. ECO/DEV INT/ORG NAT/G CREATE TEC/DEV BAL/PWR ECO/TAC AGREE DETER COST ORD/FREE 20 DEPT/STATE DEPT/DEFEN. PAGE 138 F2722
DIPLOM FORCES PLAN FOR/AID

B56
GREENHUT M.L.,PLANT LOCATION IN THEORY AND PRACTICE; THE ECONOMICS OF SPACE. WOR+45 WOR-45 MARKET WORKER COST DEMAND...CONCPT STAT CHARTS HYPO/EXP BIBLIOG 19/20. PAGE 51 F0991
SML/CO ECO/DEV CAP/ISM IDEA/COMP

B56
KOHLER E.L.,ACCOUNTING IN THE FEDERAL GOVERNMENT. USA+45 LOC/G PLAN TAX CONTROL COST 20. PAGE 72 F1416
BUDGET AFR NAT/G FINAN

B56
POOLE K.E.,PUBLIC FINANCE AND ECONOMIC WELFARE. STRUCT ECO/DEV LOC/G NAT/G BUDGET PAY ROUTINE COST EQUILIB WEALTH...SOC/WK METH/COMP 20. PAGE 107 F2103
FINAN TAX ORD/FREE

B56
US OFFICE OF THE PRESIDENT,REPORT TO CONGRESS ON THE MUTUAL SECURITY PROGRAM FOR THE SIX MONTHS ENDED DECEMBER 31, 1955. ASIA USSR ECO/DEV ECO/UNDEV INT/ORG CREATE TEC/DEV BAL/PWR ECO/TAC AGREE DETER COST ORD/FREE 20 DEPT/STATE DEPT/DEFEN EISNHWR/DD. PAGE 138 F2723
DIPLOM FORCES PLAN FOR/AID

B56
VAKIL C.N.,PLANNING FOR AN EXPANDING ECONOMY. INDIA TAX COST 20. PAGE 140 F2759
TEC/DEV LABOR BUDGET CAP/ISM

S56
MARGOLIS J.,"ON MUNICIPAL LAND POLICY FOR FISCAL GAINS." USA+45 PLAN TAX COST EFFICIENCY HABITAT KNOWL...MGT MUNICH 20. PAGE 85 F1667
BUDGET POLICY GEOG LOC/G

S56
SPENGLER J.J.,"POPULATION THREATENS PROSPERITY" (BMR)" WOR+45 SOCIETY FINAN RATION COST INCOME ...SOC CHARTS 20 RESOURCE/N. PAGE 124 F2451
CENSUS GEOG WEALTH TREND

B57
DAY A.C.L.,OUTLINE OF MONETARY ECONOMICS. AFR WOR-45 INT/ORG WORKER DIPLOM BAL/PAY COST INCOME WEALTH...TIME/SEQ SIMUL 20. PAGE 31 F0594
FINAN NAT/G EQUILIB PRICE

B57
HUTTON D.G.,INFLATION AND SOCIETY. AFR FINAN PLAN COST DEMAND EQUILIB...CONCPT 20. PAGE 64 F1254
ECO/DEV POLICY NAT/G ECO/TAC

B57
LEIBENSTEIN H.,ECONOMIC BACKWARDNESS AND ECONOMIC GROWTH. WOR+45 SOCIETY AGRI INDUS TEC/DEV CAP/ISM FOR/AID COST DEMAND WEALTH...CHARTS IDEA/COMP 20. PAGE 77 F1513
ECO/UNDEV ECO/TAC PRODUC POLICY

B58
AVRAMOVIC D.,POSTWAR GROWTH IN INTERNATIONAL INDEBTEDNESS. AFR WOR+45 AGRI INDUS CAP/ISM PRICE INCOME...NAT/COMP 20 SILVER. PAGE 8 F0143
INT/TRADE FINAN COST BAL/PAY

B58
HENNING C.N.,INTERNATIONAL FINANCING. WOR+45 ECO/DEV INT/ORG EX/STRUC INSPECT CAP/ISM BAL/PAY COST PROFIT...MGT CHARTS T 20. PAGE 58 F1150
FINAN DIPLOM INT/TRADE

B58
JUCKER-FLEETWOOD E.,ECONOMIC THEORY AND POLICY IN FINLAND 1914-1925. FINLAND INT/TRADE PRICE COST 20 MONEY. PAGE 68 F1343
FINAN GEN/LAWS ECO/TAC PLAN

B58
MOULTON H.G.,CAN INFLATION BE CONTROLLED? ECO/DEV INDUS CAP/ISM RATION GOV/REL COST INCOME PEACE WEALTH...CHARTS TIME 20 KEYNES/JM MONEY. PAGE 94 F1847
ECO/TAC CONTROL DEMAND FINAN

B58
US CONGRESS JOINT ECO COMM,THE RELATIONSHIP OF PRICES TO ECONOMIC STABILITY AND GROWTH. USA+45 MARKET TAX ADJUST COST DEMAND INCOME PRODUC ...POLICY TREND CHARTS ANTHOL 20 CONGRESS. PAGE 134 F2650
ECO/DEV PLAN EQUILIB PRICE

B58
WARNER A.W.,CONCEPTS AND CASES IN ECONOMIC ANALYSIS. PROB/SOLV BARGAIN CONTROL INCOME PRODUC ...ECOMETRIC MGT CONCPT CLASSIF CHARTS 20 KEYNES/JM. PAGE 143 F2820
ECO/TAC DEMAND EQUILIB COST

S58
MANSFIELD E.,"A STUDY OF DECISION-MAKING WITHIN THE FIRM." LG/CO WORKER INGP/REL COST EFFICIENCY PRODUC ...CHARTS 20. PAGE 85 F1658
OP/RES PROB/SOLV AUTOMAT ROUTINE

B59
GUDIN E.,INFLACAO (2ND ED.). INDUS NAT/G PLAN ECO/TAC CONTROL COST 20. PAGE 52 F1012
ECO/UNDEV INT/TRADE BAL/PAY FINAN

B59
HAX K.,DIE HOCHSCHULLEHRER DER WIRTSCHAFTSWISSENSCHAFTEN IN DER BUNDESREPUBLIK DEUTSCHLAND EINSCHL. WESTBERLIN, OSTERREICH. AUSTRIA GERMANY/W SWITZERLND FINAN MARKET PROF/ORG BUDGET ECO/TAC INT/TRADE PRICE COST 20. PAGE 57 F1119
BIBLIOG ACADEM INTELL

B59
SELIGSOHN I.J.,"USING COMPUTER SERVICES IN SMALL BUSINESS" MANAGEMENT AIDS FOR SMALL MANUFACTURERS 109 (PAMPHLET). DIST/IND MARKET PROC/MFG COST EFFICIENCY PRODUC...DECISION IDEA/COMP. PAGE 119 F2350
SML/CO COMPUTER MGT PROB/SOLV

B59
SHACKLE G.L.S.,ECONOMICS FOR PLEASURE. FINAN MARKET NAT/G WORKER PLAN INT/TRADE TARIFFS PAY BAL/PAY COST PRODUC 20. PAGE 120 F2361
METH/CNCPT WEALTH INCOME

B59
STANFORD U, BOARD OF TRUSTEES,THE ALLOCATION OF ECONOMIC RESOURCES. WORKER PLAN BUDGET ECO/TAC TAX RECEIVE COST PRODUC...POLICY IDEA/COMP SIMUL ANTHOL 20. PAGE 125 F2468
INCOME PRICE FINAN

B59
US GENERAL ACCOUNTING OFFICE,EXAM OF ECONOMIC AND TECHNICAL ASSISTANCE PROGRAM FOR INDIA INT'NAT'L COOP ADMIN REPORT TO CONGRESS 1955-1958. INDIA USA+45 ECO/UNDEV FINAN PLAN DIPLOM COST UTIL WEALTH ...CHARTS 20 CONGRESS AID. PAGE 136 F2679
FOR/AID EFFICIENCY ECO/TAC TEC/DEV

B59
WIBBERLEY G.P.,AGRICULTURE AND URBAN GROWTH. UK USA+45 ECO/DEV FINAN PROB/SOLV INT/TRADE COST ...GEOG STAT CHARTS METH/COMP HYPO/EXP METH MUNICH 20. PAGE 146 F2876
AGRI PLAN

S59
DUNNING J.H.,"NON-PECUNIARY ELEMENTS AND BUSINESS BEHAVIOUR." PLAN PROB/SOLV COST...METH/CNCPT
DECISION DRIVE

CLASSIF QUANT STAT. PAGE 35 F0681
PRODUC PRICE

B60
ATOMIC INDUSTRIAL FORUM,ATOMS FOR INDUSTRY: WORLD FORUM. WOR+45 FINAN COST UTIL...JURID ANTHOL 20. PAGE 7 F0137
NUC/PWR INDUS PLAN PROB/SOLV

B60
BIERMAN H.,THE CAPITAL BUDGETING DECISION. AFR ECO/DEV MARKET TAX PRICE RISK COST INCOME TIME 20. PAGE 15 F0282
FINAN OPTIMAL BUDGET PROFIT

B60
BISSON A.,INSTITUTIONS FINANCIERES ET ECONOMIQUES EN FRANCE. FRANCE INDUS OP/RES TAX COST PRODUC ...CHARTS 20. PAGE 15 F0289
FINAN BUDGET PLAN

B60
BRYCE M.D.,INDUSTRIAL DEVELOPMENT: A GUIDE FOR ACCELERATING ECONOMIC GROWTH. WOR+45 FINAN MARKET COST EFFICIENCY PRODUC. PAGE 20 F0378
INDUS PLAN ECO/UNDEV TEC/DEV

B60
DALE W.B.,THE FOREIGN DEFICIT OF THE UNITED STATES. ECO/TAC TARIFFS PAY PRICE CONTROL COST WEALTH POLICY. PAGE 30 F0573
BAL/PAY DIPLOM FINAN INT/TRADE

B60
FIRESTONE J.M.,FEDERAL RECEIPTS AND EXPENDITURES DURING BUSINESS CYCLES, 1879-1958. USA+45 USA-45 INDUS PLAN ECO/TAC TAX WAR COST...CHARTS 19/20. PAGE 41 F0801
FINAN INCOME BUDGET NAT/G

B60
GRIER E.,PRIVATELY DEVELOPED INTERRACIAL HOUSING: AN ANALYSIS OF EXPERIENCE. FINAN MARKET COST DISCRIM PROFIT SOC/INTEG 20. PAGE 51 F0997
RACE/REL CONSTRUC HABITAT

B60
HALL C.A. JR.,FISCAL POLICY FOR STABLE GROWTH. USA+45 FINAN TEC/DEV TAX COST DEMAND INCOME ...BIBLIOG 20. PAGE 53 F1045
ECO/TAC BUDGET NAT/G POLICY

B60
HARBERGER A.C.,THE DEMAND FOR DURABLE GOODS. AGRI FINAN COST EQUILIB...MATH STAT TIME/SEQ TREND CON/ANAL CHARTS SIMUL ANTHOL 20. PAGE 55 F1072
ECOMETRIC DEMAND PRICE

B60
KENEN P.B.,BRITISH MONETARY POLICY AND THE BALANCE OF PAYMENTS 1951-57. UK PLAN BUDGET ECO/TAC INT/TRADE PAY PRICE COST ATTIT 20. PAGE 70 F1377
BAL/PAY PROB/SOLV FINAN NAT/G

B60
MARSHALL A.H.,FINANCIAL ADMINISTRATION IN LOCAL GOVERNMENT. UK DELIB/GP CONFER COST INCOME PERSON ...JURID 20. PAGE 86 F1679
FINAN LOC/G BUDGET ADMIN

B60
OEEC,STATISTICS OF SOURCES AND USES OF FINANCE. NAT/G CAP/ISM TAX PRICE COST 20 OEEC. PAGE 101 F1978
FINAN PRODUC INCOME NAT/COMP

B60
RAPKIN C.,THE DEMAND FOR HOUSING IN RACIALLY MIXED AREAS: A STUDY OF THE NATURE OF NEIGHBORHOOD CHANGE. USA+45 FINAN PRICE COST DRIVE...GEOG 20. PAGE 109 F2151
RACE/REL NEIGH DISCRIM MARKET

B60
ROBERTSON D.,THE CONTROL OF INDUSTRY. UK MARKET LABOR WORKER PRICE CONTROL GP/REL COST DEMAND ORD/FREE WEALTH NEW/LIB SOCISM 20. PAGE 112 F2211
INDUS FINAN NAT/G ECO/DEV

B60
US HOUSE COMM GOVT OPERATIONS,OPERATIONS OF THE DEVELOPMENT LOAN FUND: HEARINGS (COMMITTEE ON GOVERNMENT OPERATIONS). USA+45 PLAN BUDGET DIPLOM GOV/REL COST...CHARTS 20 CONGRESS DEPT/STATE AID. PAGE 137 F2698
FINAN FOR/AID ECO/TAC EFFICIENCY

B60
US OPERATIONS MISSION - TURKEY,SOME POSSIBILITIES FOR ACCELERATING TURKEY'S ECONOMIC GROWTH. TURKEY USA+45 AGRI FINAN INDUS NAT/G ACT/RES BUDGET COST ...CHARTS 20. PAGE 138 F2724
ECO/UNDEV ECO/TAC FOR/AID PRODUC

S60
ENKE S.,"THE ECONOMIES OF GOVERNMENT PAYMENTS TO LIMIT POPULATION." FUT INDIA WOR+45 CULTURE FINAN NAT/G CONSULT PLAN LEGIT CONTROL COST ATTIT RIGID/FLEX HEALTH WEALTH...STAT OBS CHARTS TOT/POP VAL/FREE 20. PAGE 38 F0736
FAM ACT/RES

B61
ACKLEY G.,MACROECONOMIC THEORY. AFR FINAN WORKER ECO/TAC PRICE COST INCOME PRODUC...MATH TREND CHARTS IDEA/COMP T KEYNES/JM. PAGE 2 F0034
SIMUL ECOMETRIC WEALTH

B61
FELLNER W.,THE PROBLEM OF RISING PRICES. AGRI INDUS WORKER BUDGET CAP/ISM ECO/TAC INT/TRADE PAY DEMAND ...POLICY 20 EEC. PAGE 40 F0780
PRICE MARKET ECO/DEV COST

B61
GOODWIN C.D.W.,CANADIAN ECONOMIC THOUGHT. CANADA STRATA TEC/DEV CAP/ISM TARIFFS TAX COST EFFICIENCY WEALTH...METH/CNCPT TREND 20 MARITIME ONTARIO. PAGE 49 F0952
INT/TRADE ECO/DEV FINAN DEMAND

B61
HAUSER M.,DIE URSACHEN DER FRANZOSISCHEN INFLATION IN DEN JAHREN 1946-1952. AFR FRANCE INDUS NAT/G BUDGET DIPLOM ECO/TAC FOR/AID COST MONEY 20. PAGE 57 F1114
ECO/DEV FINAN PRICE

B61
INTERNATIONAL BANK RECONST DEV,THE WORLD BANK IN AFRICA: SUMMARY OF ACTIVITIES. AGRI COM/IND DIST/IND EXTR/IND INDUS TAX COST...CHARTS 20. PAGE 65 F1271
FINAN ECO/UNDEV INT/ORG AFR

B61
INTL UNION LOCAL AUTHORITIES,METROPOLIS. WOR+45 DIST/IND FINAN GIVE EDU/PROP CRIME COST HEALTH WEALTH MUNICH 20. PAGE 65 F1286
GOV/COMP LOC/G BIBLIOG

B61
KLEIN L.R.,AN ECONOMETRIC MODEL OF THE UNITED KINGDOM. UK PRICE COST...MATH PREDICT TREND CHARTS SIMUL METH 20. PAGE 72 F1407
ECOMETRIC COMPUTER STAT COMPUT/IR

B61
LIEFMANN-KEIL E.,OKONOMISCHE THEORIE DER SOZIALPOLITIK. INT/ORG LABOR WORKER COST INCOME NEW/LIB...CONCPT SOC/INTEG 20. PAGE 80 F1562
ECO/DEV INDUS NAT/G SOC/WK

B61
NORTH D.C.,THE ECONOMIC GROWTH OF THE UNITED STATES 1790-1860. USA-45 INDUS TEC/DEV CAP/ISM ECO/TAC PRICE COST DEMAND LAISSEZ...ECOMETRIC STAT TREND 19. PAGE 98 F1933
AGRI ECO/UNDEV

B61
PAUNIO J.J.,A STUDY IN THE THEORY OF OPEN INFLATION. AFR FINAN CAP/ISM PRICE DEMAND INCOME ...CHARTS BIBLIOG 20. PAGE 104 F2040
ACT/RES ECO/DEV ECO/TAC COST

B61
PETCH G.A.,ECONOMIC DEVELOPMENT AND MODERN WEST AFRICA. AFR CONGO/BRAZ GHANA NIGER SIER/LEONE AGRI MARKET LABOR FOR/AID TAX COST EFFICIENCY EQUILIB PRODUC...GEOG TREND 20. PAGE 105 F2068
ECO/UNDEV TEC/DEV EXTR/IND ECO/TAC

B61
QURESHI S.,INCENTIVES IN AMERICAN EMPLOYMENT (THESIS, UNIVERSITY OF PENNSYLVANIA). DELIB/GP TOP/EX BUDGET ROUTINE SANCTION COST TECHRACY MGT. PAGE 108 F2134
SERV/IND ADMIN PAY EX/STRUC

B61
STANLEY C.J.,LATE CH'ING FINANCE: HU KUANG-YUNG AS AN INNOVATOR. ASIA NAT/G FORCES BUDGET TAX WAR GOV/REL COST...POLICY BIOG CHARTS BIBLIOG 19. PAGE 125 F2469
FINAN ECO/TAC CIVMIL/REL ADMIN

B61
STOCKING G.W.,WORKABLE COMPETITION AND ANTITRUST POLICY. USA+45 NAT/G CONSULT PLAN PRICE GOV/REL COST DEMAND PROFIT...POLICY 20. PAGE 126 F2491
LG/CO INDUS ECO/TAC CONTROL

B61
US GENERAL ACCOUNTING OFFICE,EXAMINATION OF ECONOMIC AND TECHNICAL ASSISTANCE PROGRAM FOR IRAN. IRAN USA+45 AGRI INDUS DIPLOM CONTROL COST 20. PAGE 130 F2081
FOR/AID ADMIN TEC/DEV ECO/UNDEV

B61
US SENATE COMM ON FOREIGN RELS,INTERNATIONAL DEVELOPMENT AND SECURITY: HEARINGS ON BILL (2 VOLS.). ECO/UNDEV FINAN FORCES REV COST WEALTH ...CHARTS 20 AID PRESIDENT. PAGE 139 F2747
FOR/AID CIVMIL/REL ORD/FREE ECO/TAC

B61
WILSON T.,INFLATION. FINAN PLAN CAP/ISM PRICE CONTROL...CHARTS 20. PAGE 147 F2903
ECO/DEV ECO/TAC POLICY COST

B62
BACKMAN J.,THE ECONOMICS OF THE ELECTRICAL MACHINERY INDUSTRY. USA+45 PROC/MFG LABOR WORKER INT/TRADE TV PRICE COST...CHARTS 19/20. PAGE 8 F0147
PRODUC TEC/DEV TREND

B62
CONGRES ECONOMISTES LANG FRAN,MONNAIE ET EXPANSION. AFR FRANCE PROB/SOLV BUDGET CENTRAL COST OPTIMAL PRODUC WEALTH 20. PAGE 27 F0524
FINAN PLAN EUR+WWI

B62
DENISON E.F.,THE SOURCES OF ECONOMIC GROWTH IN THE UNITED STATES AND THE ALTERNATIVES BEFORE US. AGRI INDUS SCHOOL TEC/DEV CAP/ISM ECO/TAC PRICE COST WEALTH...STAT TREND CHARTS 20. PAGE 32 F0620
ECO/DEV WORKER PRODUC

B62
FERBER R.,RESEARCH METHODS IN ECONOMICS AND BUSINESS. AFR ECO/DEV FINAN MARKET LG/CO SML/CO CONSULT CONTROL COST...STAT METH/COMP 20. PAGE 40 F0783
ACT/RES PROB/SOLV ECO/TAC MGT

B62
GRANICK D.,THE EUROPEAN EXECUTIVE. BELGIUM FRANCE GERMANY/W UK INDUS LABOR LG/CO SML/CO EX/STRUC PLAN
MGT ECO/DEV

TEC/DEV CAP/ISM COST DEMAND...POLICY CHARTS 20. PAGE 50 F0977
ECO/TAC EXEC

B62
GWYN W.B.,DEMOCRACY AND THE COST OF POLITICS IN BRITAIN. UK BUDGET CRIME CHOOSE ORD/FREE WEALTH ...TIME/SEQ 18/20. PAGE 52 F1017
COST POL/PAR POPULISM PAY

B62
HATTERY L.H.,INFORMATION RETRIEVAL MANAGEMENT. CLIENT INDUS TOP/EX COMPUTER OP/RES TEC/DEV ROUTINE COST EFFICIENCY RIGID/FLEX...METH/COMP ANTHOL 20. PAGE 57 F1113
R+D COMPUT/IR MGT CREATE

B62
HOLMAN A.G.,SOME MEASURES AND INTERPRETATIONS OF EFFECTS OF US FOREIGN ENTERPRISES ON US BALANCE OF PAYMENTS. USA+45 COST INCOME WEALTH...MATH CHARTS 20. PAGE 61 F1199
BAL/PAY INT/TRADE FINAN ECO/TAC

B62
HOOVER E.M.,ANATOMY OF A METROPOLIS. FUT USA+45 SOCIETY ECO/DEV DIST/IND INDUS WORKER ECO/TAC TAX GP/REL COST WEALTH MUNICH 20 NEWYORK/C. PAGE 62 F1212
ROUTINE TREND INCOME

B62
JOHNSON H.G.,MONEY, TRADE AND ECONOMIC GROWTH. ECO/DEV ECO/UNDEV FINAN COST WEALTH...POLICY SOC IDEA/COMP 20 KEYNES/JM MONEY. PAGE 67 F1324
PLAN BAL/PAY INT/TRADE ECO/TAC

B62
KINDLEBERGER C.P.,FOREIGN TRADE AND THE NATIONAL ECONOMY. WOR+45 ECO/DEV ECO/UNDEV ECO/TAC COST DEMAND 20. PAGE 71 F1393
INT/TRADE GOV/COMP BAL/PAY POLICY

B62
LICHFIELD N.,COST-BENEFIT ANALYSIS IN URBAN REDEVELOPMENT. CONSTRUC LOC/G NEIGH ACT/RES PROB/SOLV TEC/DEV BUDGET TAX...DECISION STAT CHARTS SOC/EXP MUNICH 20. PAGE 80 F1558
PLAN COST GOV/REL

B62
MEANS G.C.,PRICING POWER AND THE PUBLIC INTEREST. PLAN PROB/SOLV COST EFFICIENCY PROFIT RIGID/FLEX WEALTH. PAGE 89 F1741
LG/CO EX/STRUC PRICE ECO/TAC

B62
REES A.,THE ECONOMICS OF TRADE UNIONS. FUT ECO/DEV INDUS BARGAIN CAP/ISM PRICE SENIOR CONTROL GP/REL COST...TREND 20 AFL/CIO. PAGE 110 F2172
LABOR WORKER ECO/TAC

B62
SHINOHARA M.,GROWTH AND CYCLES IN THE JAPANESE ECONOMY. INDUS LABOR TEC/DEV CAP/ISM INT/TRADE PAY COST EFFICIENCY INCOME WEALTH...METH/COMP 20 CHINJAP. PAGE 121 F2380
PRODUC ECO/DEV EQUILIB ECOMETRIC

B62
VAIZEY J.,THE ECONOMICS OF EDUCATION. INTELL ECO/TAC PAY COST PRODUC 20. PAGE 140 F2758
ECO/DEV SCHOOL ACADEM PROFIT

B62
VANEK J.,INTERNATIONAL TRADE - THEORY AND ECONOMIC POLICY. LABOR BAL/PWR ECO/TAC TARIFFS PRICE BAL/PAY COST DEMAND 20. PAGE 140 F2765
INT/TRADE DIPLOM BARGAIN MARKET

B62
WRIGHT D.M.,THE KEYNESIAN SYSTEM. WOR+45 WOR-45 LABOR NAT/G CONTROL COST DEMAND EFFICIENCY...POLICY CONCPT CHARTS SIMUL 20 KEYNES/JM. PAGE 149 F2931
INCOME ECO/DEV FINAN ECO/TAC

L62
SCHULTZ T.W.,"INVESTMENT IN HUMAN BEINGS." ECO/DEV ECO/TAC CONFER COST INCOME PRODUC HEALTH...GEOG ANTHOL. PAGE 117 F2315
FINAN WORKER EDU/PROP SKILL

B63
BANERJI A.K.,INDIA'S BALANCE OF PAYMENTS. INDIA NAT/G PRICE BAL/PAY COST INCOME 20. PAGE 9 F0171
INT/TRADE DIPLOM FINAN BUDGET

B63
BONINI C.P.,SIMULATION OF INFORMATION AND DECISION SYSTEMS IN THE FIRM. MARKET BUDGET DOMIN EDU/PROP ADMIN COST ATTIT HABITAT PERCEPT PWR...CONCPT PROBABIL QUANT PREDICT HYPO/EXP BIBLIOG. PAGE 16 F0313
INDUS SIMUL DECISION MGT

B63
BROUDE H.W.,STEEL DECISIONS AND THE NATIONAL ECONOMY. USA+45 LG/CO PLAN ADMIN COST DECISION. PAGE 19 F0365
PROC/MFG NAT/G CONTROL ECO/TAC

B63
CHAMPION J.M.,CRITICAL INCIDENTS IN MANAGEMENT. MARKET LG/CO SML/CO OP/RES ADMIN CONTROL LEAD GP/REL PERS/REL COST ATTIT SUPEGO ALL/VALS...PSY PERS/TEST BIBLIOG. PAGE 23 F0445
MGT DECISION EX/STRUC INDUS

B63
COSSA L.,SAGGI BIBLIOGRAFICI DI ECONOMIA POLITICA. MOD/EUR LABOR PRICE COST INCOME 18/19. PAGE 28 F0539
BIBLIOG FINAN WEALTH

B63
COURNOT A.A.,RESEARCHES INTO THE MATHEMATICAL PRINCIPLES OF THE THEORY OF WEALTH (1838). UNIV ECO/DEV ECO/UNDEV AGRI INDUS MARKET PAY CONTROL COST INCOME 19. PAGE 28 F0544
ECOMETRIC GEN/LAWS WEALTH

B63
DUE J.F.,STATE SALES TAX ADMINISTRATION. OP/RES BUDGET PAY ADMIN EXEC ROUTINE COST EFFICIENCY PROFIT...CHARTS METH/COMP 20. PAGE 34 F0671
PROVS TAX STAT GOV/COMP

B63
ERHARD L.,THE ECONOMICS OF SUCCESS. GERMANY/W WOR+45 LABOR CHIEF TAX REGION COST DEMAND ANTHOL. PAGE 38 F0745
ECO/DEV INT/TRADE PLAN DIPLOM

B63
FATEMI N.S.,THE DOLLAR CRISIS. USA+45 INDUS NAT/G LEGIS BUDGET TAX COST...CHARTS METH/COMP 20 EEC. PAGE 39 F0766
PROB/SOLV BAL/PAY FOR/AID PLAN

B63
GANGULI B.N.,ECONOMIC CONSEQUENCES OF DISARMAMENT. EUR+WWI ECO/DEV ECO/UNDEV FORCES ACT/RES BUDGET DIPLOM INT/TRADE...STAT CHARTS NAT/COMP. PAGE 46 F0896
ECOMETRIC ARMS/CONT COST HYPO/EXP

B63
HAHN L.A.,DIE AMERIKANISCHE KONJUNKTURPOLITIK DER DOLLAR UND DIE DMARK. GERMANY/W USA+45 DIPLOM PRICE BAL/PAY COST...POLICY MONEY. PAGE 53 F1038
FINAN BUDGET ECO/TAC LABOR

B63
HARROD R.F.,INTERNATIONAL TRADE THEORY IN A DEVELOPING WORLD. COM WOR+45 FOR/AID REGION COST DEMAND WEALTH...POLICY 20 INTL/ECON. PAGE 56 F1095
INT/TRADE BAL/PAY ECO/UNDEV METH/COMP

B63
KAPP W.K.,SOCIAL COSTS OF BUSINESS ENTERPRISE. WOR+45 LABOR TEC/DEV CAP/ISM HABITAT...PHIL/SCI NEW/IDEA CON/ANAL 20. PAGE 69 F1354
COST SOCIETY INDUS RIGID/FLEX

B63
LUTZ F.A.,DAS PROBLEM DES INTERNATIONALEN WIRTSCHAFTLICHEN GLEICHGEWICHTS. DIPLOM INT/TRADE COST INCOME 20. PAGE 82 F1612
FINAN CAP/ISM ECO/TAC PRODUC

B63
MACHLUP F.,ESSAYS ON ECONOMIC SEMANTICS. UNIV ECO/DEV FINAN COST DEMAND PRODUC...POLICY STAT CHARTS BIBLIOG. PAGE 83 F1632
LING CONCPT METH

B63
MANN D.E.,THE POLITICS OF WATER IN ARIZONA. AGRI EXTR/IND PROVS ACT/RES CREATE PLAN GOV/REL COST HABITAT...MGT CHARTS 20 ARIZONA WATER. PAGE 84 F1655
POLICY ECO/TAC TEC/DEV

B63
MEIER G.,INTERNATIONAL TRADE AND DEVELOPMENT. FINAN BAL/PAY COST DEMAND DISCRIM EQUILIB WEALTH...POLICY ECOMETRIC MATH STAT BIBLIOG/A 20. PAGE 89 F1747
ECO/UNDEV ECO/TAC INT/TRADE IDEA/COMP

B63
MILLER W.,REVENUE-COST RATIOS OF RURAL TOWNSHIPS WITH CHANGING LAND USES. USA+45 INDUS SERV/IND PROVS GP/REL HABITAT...CHARTS GP/COMP MUNICH 20 NEW/JERSEY. PAGE 91 F1792
TAX COST AGRI

B63
MINER J.,SOCIAL AND ECONOMIC FACTORS IN SPENDING FOR PUBLIC EDUCATION. USA+45 FINAN SCHOOL OPTIMAL ...POLICY DECISION REGRESS PREDICT CHARTS SIMUL 20. PAGE 92 F1801
EDU/PROP NAT/G COST ACT/RES

B63
RICARDO D.,THE PRINCIPLES OF POLITICAL ECONOMY AND TAXATION (1817). UK INDUS MARKET ECO/TAC INT/TRADE TARIFFS PRICE COST DEMAND OPTIMAL WEALTH...CONCPT 19 INTRVN/ECO. PAGE 111 F2183
GEN/LAWS TAX LAISSEZ

B63
ROPKE W.,ECONOMICS OF THE FREE SOCIETY. FINAN INT/TRADE BAL/PAY COST DEMAND EFFICIENCY ORD/FREE WEALTH...CON/ANAL METH/COMP T 20 KEYNES/JM. PAGE 114 F2240
SOCIETY BUDGET ECO/DEV ECO/TAC

B63
STIFEL L.D.,THE TEXTILE INDUSTRY - A CASE STUDY OF INDUSTRIAL DEVELOPMENT IN THE PHILIPPINES (PAPER). PHILIPPINE WORKER CAP/ISM INT/TRADE TARIFFS RECEIVE PRICE ADMIN COST EFFICIENCY WEALTH...BIBLIOG 20. PAGE 126 F2486
S/ASIA ECO/UNDEV PROC/MFG NAT/G

B63
UNITED NATIONS,THE GROWTH OF WORLD INDUSTRY, 1938-1961: NATIONAL TABLES. WOR+45 STRUCT ECO/DEV ECO/UNDEV NAT/G COST...CHARTS UN. PAGE 132 F2613
STAT INDUS PRODUC ORD/FREE

B63
US BD GOVERNORS FEDL RESRV,THE FEDERAL RESERVE AND THE TREASURY. USA+45 WORKER PROB/SOLV PRICE COST DEMAND WEALTH...STAT INT CHARTS 20 FED/RESERV DEPT/TREAS. PAGE 134 F2641
FINAN GOV/REL CONTROL BUDGET

B63
US CONGRESS JOINT ECO COMM,OUTLOOK FOR UNITED STATES BALANCE OF PAYMENTS. AFR USA+45 ECO/DEV NAT/G FORCES DIPLOM FOR/AID COST EFFICIENCY ...POLICY CONGRESS EEC. PAGE 135 F2657
BAL/PAY FINAN INT/TRADE PROB/SOLV

B63
US HOUSE,URBAN RENEWAL: HOUSE COMMITTEE ON BANKING AND CURRENCY. USA+45 FINAN LOC/G NAT/G NEIGH DELIB/GP TEC/DEV BUDGET GOV/REL COST...CHARTS MUNICH 20 CONGRESS URBAN/RNWL. PAGE 136 F2684
PLAN PROB/SOLV LEGIS

B63
WALINSKY L.J.,PLANNING AND EXECUTION OF ECONOMIC DEVELOPMENT. PROB/SOLV TEC/DEV BUDGET COST WEALTH ...CHARTS BIBLIOG 20. PAGE 142 F2802
PLAN ECO/UNDEV ECO/TAC OPTIMAL

L63
PADELFORD N.J.,"FINANCIAL CRISIS AND THE UNITED NATIONS." FUT USSR WOR+45 LAW CONSTN FINAN INT/ORG DELIB/GP FORCES PLAN BUDGET DIPLOM COST WEALTH ...STAT CHARTS UN CONGO 20. PAGE 102 F2012
CREATE ECO/TAC

S63
ENTHOVEN A.C.,"ECONOMIC ANALYSIS IN THE DEPARTMENT OF DEFENSE." USA+45 NAT/G DELIB/GP PROB/SOLV RATION NUC/PWR WEAPON COST...DECISION 20 DEPT/DEFEN RESOURCE/N. PAGE 38 F0739
PLAN BUDGET ECO/TAC FORCES

S63
NYE J.,"TANGANYIKA'S SELF-HELP." TANZANIA NAT/G GIVE COST EFFICIENCY NAT/LISM 20. PAGE 99 F1948
ECO/TAC POL/PAR ECO/UNDEV WORKER

N63
NORTH CAROLINA U INST GOVT,COSTING URBAN DEVELOPMENT AND REDEVELOPMENT (PAMPHLET). USA+45 USA-45 NEIGH PLAN TEC/DEV TAX OWN...GEOG MUNICH 20. PAGE 98 F1934
BIBLIOG COST FINAN

B64
INTERNATIONAL MONETARY ARRANGEMENTS: THE PROBLEM OF CHOICE. PLAN PROB/SOLV INT/TRADE ADJUST COST EQUILIB 20. PAGE 1 F0020
POLICY DIPLOM FINAN ECO/DEV

B64
BALL R.J.,INFLATION AND THE THEORY OF MONEY. MARKET TAX PAY PRICE TASK ADJUST BAL/PAY COST INCOME PRODUC WEALTH...METH/COMP 20 KEYNES/JM MONEY. PAGE 9 F0167
EQUILIB DEMAND POLICY

B64
BASTIAT F.,ECONOMIC HARMONIES (1850). STRATA STRUCT ECO/DEV BUDGET TAX PRICE LOBBY COST. PAGE 11 F0206
ECO/TAC PLAN INT/TRADE LAISSEZ

B64
BERRILL K.,ECONOMIC DEVELOPMENT WITH SPECIAL REFERENCE TO EAST ASIA. ASIA INDIA S/ASIA AGRI INDUS LABOR DELIB/GP PLAN INT/TRADE COST PRODUC 20 CHINJAP. PAGE 14 F0271
FINAN ECO/UNDEV INT/ORG CAP/ISM

B64
BOARMAN P.M.,GERMANY'S ECONOMIC DILEMMA - INFLATION AND THE BALANCE OF PAYMENTS. AFR GERMANY/W LABOR CAP/ISM PRICE BAL/PAY COST INCOME 20. PAGE 16 F0302
ECO/DEV FINAN INT/TRADE BUDGET

B64
BROWN W.M.,THE EXTERNAL LIQUIDITY OF AN ADVANCED COUNTRY. CANADA FRANCE GERMANY/W SWEDEN UK USA+45 ECO/DEV DIPLOM PRICE...CONCPT STAT NAT/COMP 20. PAGE 20 F0376
FINAN INT/TRADE COST INCOME

B64
EINZIG P.,MONETARY POLICY: ENDS AND MEANS. AFR UK INDUS WORKER PLAN DIPLOM PRICE BAL/PAY COST WEALTH ...DECISION TIME/SEQ 20. PAGE 37 F0715
FINAN POLICY ECO/TAC BUDGET

B64
FITCH L.C.,URBAN TRANSPORTATION AND PUBLIC POLICY. FINAN NAT/G LEGIS PROB/SOLV TEC/DEV PRICE COST EFFICIENCY...DECISION STAT CHARTS METH/COMP MUNICH 20 NEWYORK/C PHILADELPH LOS/ANG CHICAGO WASHING/DC. PAGE 41 F0806
DIST/IND PLAN LOC/G

B64
GARFIELD PJ LOVEJOY WF,PUBLIC UTILITY ECONOMICS. DIST/IND FINAN MARKET ADMIN COST DEMAND ...TECHNIC JURID MUNICH 20 MONOPOLY. PAGE 46 F0906
T ECO/TAC OWN SERV/IND

B64
GEORGIADIS H.G.,BALANCE OF PAYMENTS EQUILIBRIUM. COST DEMAND...CONCPT MATH GEN/LAWS 20 KEYNES/JM. PAGE 47 F0916
BAL/PAY EQUILIB SIMUL INT/TRADE

B64
HAGGER A.J.,THE THEORY OF INFLATION. AFR PLAN PROB/SOLV PAY COST INCOME 20. PAGE 53 F1035
DEMAND TEC/DEV FINAN

B64
HANSEN A.H.,BUSINESS CYCLES AND NATIONAL INCOME. USA+45 FINAN ECO/TAC COST OPTIMAL...POLICY METH 20 KEYNES/JM. PAGE 54 F1065
INCOME WEALTH PRODUC INDUS

B64
HOLLEY I.B. JR.,US ARMY IN WORLD WAR II: SPECIAL STUDIES: BUYING AIRCRAFT: MATERIEL PROCUREMENT FOR THE ARMY AIR FORCES. USA+45 USA-45 BUDGET WEAPON GOV/REL PRODUC 20. PAGE 61 F1198
FORCES COST DIST/IND CIVMIL/REL

B64
JUSTER F.T.,ANTICIPATIONS AND PURCHASES; AN ANALYSIS OF CONSUMER BEHAVIOR. PROB/SOLV RISK COST PRODUC DRIVE...STAT STYLE SAMP CON/ANAL CHARTS HYPO/EXP GAME SIMUL. PAGE 68 F1345
PROBABIL DECISION PREDICT DEMAND

B64
KUZNETS S.,POSTWAR ECONOMIC GROWTH: FOUR LECTURES. WOR+45 INDUS NAT/G WORKER TEC/DEV ECO/TAC RATION TARIFFS PRICE BAL/PAY COST DEMAND 20. PAGE 74 F1455
ECO/DEV ECO/UNDEV TREND FINAN

B64
LANG A.S.,URBAN RAIL TRANSIT. OP/RES PLAN PROB/SOLV TEC/DEV AUTOMAT COST...TECHNIC MATH CON/ANAL CHARTS METH/COMP SIMUL MUNICH 20 RAILROAD PUB/TRANS. PAGE 75 F1474
DIST/IND ECOMETRIC

B64
MOAK L.L.,A MANUAL OF SUGGESTED PRACTICE FOR THE PREPARATION AND ADOPTION OF CAPITAL PROGRAMS AND CAPITAL BUDGETS BY LOCAL GOVERN. USA+45 DELIB/GP PLAN TAX GP/REL COST DECISION. PAGE 92 F1812
LOC/G BUDGET LEGIS PROB/SOLV

B64
MYINT H.,THE ECONOMICS OF THE DEVELOPING COUNTRIES. WOR+45 AGRI PLAN COST...POLICY GEOG 20 MONEY. PAGE 96 F1878
ECO/UNDEV INT/TRADE EXTR/IND FINAN

B64
ODEH H.S.,THE IMPACT OF INFLATION ON THE LEVEL OF ECONOMIC ACTIVITY. AFR BRAZIL CHILE BUDGET GOV/REL COST DEMAND INCOME WEALTH...STAT METH 20 MONEY. PAGE 100 F1963
ECOMETRIC ECO/TAC ECO/UNDEV FINAN

B64
TAX S.,EL CAPITALISMO DEL CENTAVO; UNA ECONOMIA INDIGENA DE GUATEMALA (2 VOLS.). GUATEMALA L/A+17C SOCIETY GP/REL DEMAND INCOME HABITAT...SOC MUNICH 20 INDIAN/AM. PAGE 129 F2539
ECO/UNDEV AGRI WEALTH COST

B64
US AGENCY INTERNATIONAL DEV,A.I.D. PROJECTS IN FISCAL YEAR 1963: BY COUNTRY AND FIELD OF ACTIVITY. USA+45 ECO/UNDEV ECO/TAC EDU/PROP GOV/REL...CHARTS 20 AID. PAGE 134 F2639
FINAN FOR/AID COST STAT

B64
US SENATE COMM ON JUDICIARY,HEARINGS BEFORE SUBCOMMITTEE ON ANTITRUST AND MONOPOLY: ECONOMIC CONCENTRATION VOLUMES 1-5 JULY 1964-SEPT 1966. USA+45 LAW FINAN ECO/TAC ADJUD COST EFFICIENCY PRODUC...STAT CHARTS 20 CONGRESS MONOPOLY. PAGE 140 F2749
ECO/DEV CONTROL MARKET LG/CO

B64
WILSON T.,POLICIES FOR REGIONAL DEVELOPMENT. CANADA UK FINAN INDUS NAT/G BUDGET TAX GIVE COST ...NAT/COMP 20. PAGE 147 F2904
REGION PLAN ECO/DEV ECO/TAC

S64
CARNEGIE ENDOWMENT INT. PEACE,"ADMINISTRATION AND BUDGET (ISSUES BEFORE THE NINETEENTH GENERAL ASSEMBLY)." WOR+45 FINAN BUDGET ECO/TAC ROUTINE COST...STAT RECORD UN. PAGE 21 F0415
INT/ORG ADMIN

S64
STONE P.A.,"DECISION TECHNIQUES FOR TOWN DEVELOPMENT." PLAN COST PROFIT...DECISION MGT CON/ANAL CHARTS METH/COMP BIBLIOG MUNICH 20. PAGE 127 F2497
OP/RES ADMIN PROB/SOLV

B65
ANALYSIS AND ASSESSMENT OF THE ECONOMIC EFFECTS: PUBLIC LAW 480 TITLE I PROGRAM TURKEY. INDIA TURKEY USA+45 AGRI NAT/G PLAN BUDGET DIPLOM COST EFFICIENCY...CHARTS 20. PAGE 1 F0021
ECO/TAC FOR/AID FINAN ECO/UNDEV

B65
ALDERSON W.,DYNAMIC MARKETING BEHAVIOR. USA+45 FINAN CREATE TEC/DEV EDU/PROP PRICE COST 20. PAGE 3 F0057
MGT MARKET ATTIT CAP/ISM

B65
BAUMOL W.J.,ECONOMIC THEORY AND OPERATIONS ANALYSIS (2ND ED.). MARKET LG/CO BUDGET PRICE COST EQUILIB PRODUC...DECISION MATH CHARTS GAME 20. PAGE 12 F0219
OP/RES ECO/DEV METH/COMP STAT

B65
BELASSA B.,ECONOMIC DEVELOPMENT AND INTEGRATION. LG/CO PROB/SOLV TEC/DEV INT/TRADE TARIFFS COST WEALTH...POLICY METH/COMP 20. PAGE 12 F0232
ECO/UNDEV ECO/TAC INT/ORG INDUS

B65
BRYCE M.D.,POLICIES AND METHODS FOR INDUSTRIAL DEVELOPMENT. WOR+45 FINAN MARKET CONSULT TARIFFS TAX COST. PAGE 20 F0379
INDUS PLAN ECO/DEV TEC/DEV

B65
CONLEY R.W.,THE ECONOMICS OF VOCATIONAL REHABILITATION. USA+45 VOL/ASSN CREATE EDU/PROP COST EFFICIENCY SOC/INTEG 20. PAGE 27 F0527
PUB/INST HEALTH GIVE

GP/REL

B65
DODDY F.S.,INTRODUCTION TO THE USE OF ECONOMIC INDICATORS. FINAN LABOR PLAN COST...ECOMETRIC INDICATOR MATH PREDICT CHARTS METH 20. PAGE 33 F0649 TEC/DEV STAT PRODUC PRICE

B65
EDELMAN M.,THE POLITICS OF WAGE-PRICE DECISIONS. GERMANY ITALY NETHERLAND UK INDUS LABOR POL/PAR PROB/SOLV BARGAIN PRICE ROUTINE BAL/PAY COST DEMAND 20. PAGE 36 F0699 GOV/COMP CONTROL ECO/TAC PLAN

B65
FLEMING R.W.,THE LABOR ARBITRATION PROCESS. USA+45 LAW BARGAIN ADJUD ROUTINE SANCTION COST...PREDICT CHARTS TIME 20. PAGE 41 F0809 GP/REL LABOR CONSULT DELIB/GP

B65
HABERLER G.,A SURVEY OF INTERNATIONAL TRADE THEORY. CANADA FRANCE GERMANY ECO/TAC TARIFFS AGREE COST DEMAND WEALTH...ECOMETRIC 19/20 MONOPOLY TREATY. PAGE 52 F1024 INT/TRADE BAL/PAY DIPLOM POLICY

B65
HASSON J.A.,THE ECONOMICS OF NUCLEAR POWER. INDIA UK USA+45 WOR+45 INT/ORG TEC/DEV COST...SOC STAT CHARTS 20 EURATOM. PAGE 56 F1108 NUC/PWR INDUS ECO/DEV METH

B65
KANTOROVICH L.V.,THE BEST USE OF ECONOMIC RESOURCES. USSR SOCIETY FINAN ACT/RES TEC/DEV ECO/TAC PRICE CONTROL COST DEMAND EFFICIENCY OPTIMAL...MGT STAT. PAGE 69 F1350 PLAN MATH DECISION

B65
MACESICH G.,COMMERCIAL BANKING AND REGIONAL DEVELOPMENT IN THE US, 1950-1960. USA+45 NAT/G PLAN ECO/TAC DEMAND...MGT 20 FED/RESERV SOUTH/US. PAGE 83 F1627 FINAN ECO/DEV INCOME COST

B65
MARK S.M.,ECONOMICS IN ACTION (3RD ED.). USA+45 ECO/UNDEV AGRI INDUS FOR/AID INT/TRADE BAL/PAY COST ORD/FREE...ANTHOL 20 RESOURCE/N. PAGE 85 F1670 POLICY ECO/TAC EFFICIENCY PRICE

B65
MCCOLL G.D.,THE AUSTRALIAN BALANCE OF PAYMENTS. UK USA+45 AGRI WORKER DIPLOM EQUILIB PRODUC...STAT TREND CHARTS BIBLIOG/A 20 AUSTRAL. PAGE 88 F1719 ECO/DEV BAL/PAY INT/TRADE COST

B65
OECD,MEDITERRANEAN REGIONAL PROJECT: TURKEY; EDUCATION AND DEVELOPMENT. FUT TURKEY SOCIETY STRATA FINAN NAT/G PROF/ORG PLAN PROB/SOLV ADMIN COST...STAT CHARTS 20 OECD. PAGE 100 F1969 EDU/PROP ACADEM SCHOOL ECO/UNDEV

B65
OECD,THE MEDITERRANEAN REGIONAL PROJECT: SPAIN; EDUCATION AND DEVELOPMENT. FUT SPAIN STRATA FINAN NAT/G WORKER PLAN PROB/SOLV ADMIN COST...POLICY STAT CHARTS 20 OECD. PAGE 100 F1973 ECO/UNDEV EDU/PROP ACADEM SCHOOL

B65
ORG FOR ECO COOP AND DEVEL,THE MEDITERRANEAN REGIONAL PROJECT: AN EXPERIMENT IN PLANNING BY SIX COUNTRIES. FUT GREECE SPAIN TURKEY YUGOSLAVIA SOCIETY FINAN NAT/G PROF/ORG EDU/PROP ADMIN REGION COST...POLICY STAT CHARTS 20 OECD. PAGE 102 F1995 PLAN ECO/UNDEV ACADEM SCHOOL

B65
ORG FOR ECO COOP AND DEVEL,THE MEDITERRANEAN REGIONAL PROJECT: YUGOSLAVIA; EDUCATION AND DEVELOPMENT. YUGOSLAVIA SOCIETY FINAN PROF/ORG PLAN ADMIN COST DEMAND MARXISM...STAT TREND CHARTS METH 20 OECD. PAGE 102 F1996 EDU/PROP ACADEM SCHOOL ECO/UNDEV

B65
PINCUS J.A.,ECONOMIC AID AND INTERNATIONAL COST SHARING* A RAND CORPORATION RESEARCH STUDY. INT/ORG BUDGET CENTRAL...ECOMETRIC MATH QUANT STAT SIMUL. PAGE 106 F2088 ECO/UNDEV COST FOR/AID INT/TRADE

B65
SMERK G.M.,URBAN TRANSPORTATION; THE FEDERAL ROLE. FUT USA+45 FINAN PROB/SOLV TEC/DEV AUTOMAT GOV/REL COST...STAT BIBLIOG MUNICH 20 PUB/TRANS. PAGE 123 F2426 PLAN DIST/IND NAT/G

B65
THAYER F.C. JR.,AIR TRANSPORT POLICY AND NATIONAL SECURITY: A POLITICAL, ECONOMIC, AND MILITARY ANALYSIS. DIST/IND OP/RES PLAN TEC/DEV DIPLOM DETER WAR COST EFFICIENCY...POLICY BIBLIOG 20 DEPT/DEFEN FAA CAB. PAGE 129 F2548 AIR FORCES CIVMIL/REL ORD/FREE

B65
YOUNG A.N.,CHINA'S WARTIME FINANCE AND INFLATION. ASIA AGRI INDUS NAT/G ECO/TAC CONFER PRICE WAR COST 20. PAGE 150 F2949 FINAN FOR/AID TAX BUDGET

B65
ZAWADZKI K.K.F.,THE ECONOMICS OF INFLATIONARY PROCESSES. FINAN INT/TRADE PRICE CONTROL DEMAND EQUILIB PROFIT 20. PAGE 150 F2960 ECO/DEV COST ECO/TAC CAP/ISM

S65
BALDWIN D.A.,"THE INTERNATIONAL BANK IN POLITICAL PERSPECTIVE" USA+45 TEC/DEV FOR/AID RENT GIVE COST ...IDEA/COMP GAME IBRD. PAGE 9 F0160 FINAN INT/ORG

S65
BRIGHAM E.F.,"THE DETERMINANTS OF RESIDENTIAL LAND VALUES." USA+45 ECO/DEV PROB/SOLV RENT PRICE ...REGRESS STAT CHARTS GEN/METH MUNICH 20 LOS/ANG. PAGE 18 F0351 COST INDICATOR SIMUL ECOMETRIC

S65
GOLDMAN M.I.,"A BALANCE SHEET OF SOVIET FOREIGN AID." USA+45 ECO/UNDEV BAL/PWR ECO/TAC RENT GIVE EDU/PROP CONTROL COST PROFIT GEN/METH. PAGE 48 F0939 USSR FOR/AID NAT/COMP EFFICIENCY

S65
JOHNSON H.G.,"A THEORETICAL MODEL OF ECONOMIC NATIONALISM IN NEW AND DEVELOPING STATES." ELITES INDUS INT/TRADE EDU/PROP COST OPTIMAL RATIONAL PWR WEALTH SOCISM STERTYP. PAGE 67 F1325 NAT/LISM ECO/UNDEV GEN/LAWS

B66
ALIBER R.Z.,THE FUTURE OF THE DOLLAR AS AN INTERNATIONAL CURRENCY. AFR USA+45 USA-45 ECO/DEV PRICE COST INCOME...POLICY 20. PAGE 4 F0067 FINAN DIPLOM INT/ORG INT/TRADE

B66
AMER ENTERPRISE INST FOR PUBL,INTERNATIONAL PAYMENTS PROBLEM. MARKET DIPLOM DEBATE PRICE COST INCOME 20. PAGE 4 F0082 FINAN INT/TRADE POLICY

B66
BOLTON R.E.,DEFENSE AND DISARMAMENT: THE ECONOMICS OF TRANSITION. USA+45 R+D FORCES PLAN LOBBY DETER WAR COST PEACE...ANTHOL BIBLIOG 20. PAGE 16 F0310 ARMS/CONT POLICY INDUS

B66
CHASE S.B. JR.,PROBLEMS IN PUBLIC EXPENDITURE ANALYSIS. DIST/IND INDUS OP/RES PLAN BUDGET RECEIVE PRICE RISK COST INCOME...CHARTS ANTHOL 20. PAGE 23 F0455 ECO/DEV FINAN NAT/G INSPECT

B66
GROSS H.,MAKE OR BUY. AFR USA+45 FINAN INDUS CREATE PRICE PRODUC 20. PAGE 51 F1006 ECO/TAC PLAN MGT COST

B66
HALLER H.,DAS PROBLEM DER GELDWERTSTABILITAT. MARKET LABOR INCOME PRODUC...POLICY 20. PAGE 54 F1049 PRICE COST FINAN ECO/TAC

B66
HASTINGS P.G.,THE MANAGEMENT OF BUSINESS FINANCE. ECO/DEV PLAN BUDGET CONTROL COST...DECISION CHARTS BIBLIOG T 20. PAGE 56 F1109 FINAN MGT INDUS ECO/TAC

B66
KURAKOV I.G.,SCIENCE, TECHNOLOGY AND COMMUNISM; SOME QUESTIONS OF DEVELOPMENT (TRANS. BY CARIN DEDIJER). USSR INDUS PLAN PROB/SOLV COST PRODUC ...MGT MATH CHARTS METH 20. PAGE 74 F1450 CREATE TEC/DEV MARXISM ECO/TAC

B66
LANDERS D.S.,RISE OF CAPITALISM. LABOR AUTOMAT GP/REL CENTRAL COST PROFIT...SOC CONCPT ANTHOL 19/20. PAGE 75 F1469 CAP/ISM INDUS AGRI

B66
LANSING J.B.,TRANSPORTATION AND ECONOMIC POLICY. USA+45 COST DEMAND...ECOMETRIC TREND CHARTS IDEA/COMP T 20. PAGE 76 F1481 DIST/IND OP/RES ECO/DEV UTIL

B66
LERNER E.M.,A THEORY OF FINANCIAL ANALYSIS. UNIV LG/CO COST DEMAND INCOME PROFIT...MATH STAT CHARTS SIMUL T 20. PAGE 78 F1531 CONCPT FINAN ECO/DEV OPTIMAL

B66
MUNBY D.,ECONOMIC GROWTH IN WORLD PERSPECTIVE. AFR WOR+45 SOCIETY INDUS PLAN TEC/DEV ECO/TAC FOR/AID INT/TRADE COST CATHISM...ANTHOL 20 EUROPE/W CHURCH/STA. PAGE 95 F1859 SECT ECO/UNDEV ECO/DEV

B66
MURPHY G.G.,SOVIET MONGOLIA: A STUDY OF THE OLDEST POLITICAL SATELLITE. USSR STRATA STRUCT COST INCOME ATTIT SOCISM 20. PAGE 95 F1865 DIPLOM ECO/TAC PLAN DOMIN

B66
NEVITT A.A.,HOUSING, TAXATION AND SUBSIDIES; A STUDY OF HOUSING IN THE UNITED KINGDOM. UK FINAN GIVE CONTROL COST INCOME...CHARTS 20. PAGE 98 F1918 PLAN TAX HABITAT RENT

B66
POLK J.,U S PRODUCTION ABROAD AND THE BALANCE OF PAYMENTS* A SURVEY OF CORPORATE INVESTMENT EXPERIENCE. USA+45 SERV/IND NAT/G OP/RES COST PROFIT ATTIT...ECOMETRIC STAT INT QU GEN/METH. PAGE 107 F2096 BAL/PAY FINAN INT/TRADE INDUS

B66
ROBINSON E.A.,THE ECONOMICS OF EDUCATION. WOR+45 CULTURE ECO/UNDEV FINAN SCHOOL DIPLOM PRICE COST DEMAND...CHARTS METH/COMP 20. PAGE 112 F2216 EDU/PROP ADJUST CONFER

B66
SCHNEIDER E.,WIRTSCHAFTSKREISLAUF UND ECO/TAC

WIRTSCHAFTSWACHSTUM. ECO/DEV MARKET...CONCPT 20 MONEY. PAGE 117 F2306
FINAN INCOME COST
B66

THIESENHUSEN W.C.,CHILE'S EXPERIMENTS IN AGRARIAN REFORM. CHILE STRUCT NAT/G ACT/RES ECO/TAC GOV/REL COST SOCISM...TREND CHARTS SOC/EXP 20. PAGE 130 F2558
AGRI ECO/UNDEV SOC TEC/DEV
B66

US DEPARTMENT OF LABOR,PRODUCTIVITY: A BIBLIOGRAPHY. ECO/DEV INDUS MARKET OP/RES AUTOMAT COST...STAT 20. PAGE 135 F2668
BIBLIOG/A PRODUC LABOR PLAN
B66

US SENATE COMM APPROPRIATIONS,FOREIGN ASSISTANCE AND RELATED AGENCIES APPROPRIATIONS FOR FISCAL YEAR 1967: HEARINGS... ON H. R. 17788. ECO/UNDEV INT/ORG FORCES INSPECT ECO/TAC GIVE DEBATE WEAPON CIVMIL/REL WEALTH...INT 20 CONGRESS DEPT/DEFEN DEPT/STATE DEPT/HEW AID. PAGE 138 F2727
BUDGET FOR/AID DIPLOM COST
B66

WALTON S.D.,AMERICAN BUSINESS AND ITS ENVIRONMENT. USA+45 LAW CONSTN FINAN MARKET LOC/G EX/STRUC CT/SYS COST PRODUC...STAT 20. PAGE 143 F2813
PRICE PROFIT
S66

BENOIT J.,"WORLD DEFENSE EXPENDITURES." WOR+45 WEAPON COST PRODUC. PAGE 13 F0253
FORCES STAT NAT/COMP BUDGET
B67

ALNASRAWI A.,FINANCING ECONOMIC DEVELOPMENT IN IRAQ. IRAQ INDUS CAP/ISM COST PRODUC...STAT CHARTS BIBLIOG 20. PAGE 4 F0076
ECO/UNDEV EXTR/IND TEC/DEV INT/TRADE
B67

APTHEKER H.,THE NATURE OF DEMOCRACY, FREEDOM AND REVOLUTION. WOR+45 PROB/SOLV COERCE COST...CONCPT TIME/SEQ METH/COMP. PAGE 6 F0111
REV POPULISM MARXIST ORD/FREE
B67

BEATON L.,THE STRUGGLE FOR PEACE. INT/ORG FORCES NUC/PWR COST PWR...POLICY TREND 20. PAGE 12 F0225
PEACE BAL/PWR DIPLOM WAR
B67

CAMPBELL A.K.,METROPOLITAN AMERICA* FISCAL PATTERNS AND GOVERNMENTAL SYSTEMS. PROVS PLAN COST...POLICY DECISION GOV/COMP METH/COMP BIBLIOG. PAGE 21 F0405
USA+45 NAT/G LOC/G BUDGET
B67

ELSNER H.,THE TECHNOCRATS, PROPHETS OF AUTOMATION. SOCIETY INDUS VOL/ASSN COST INCOME ATTIT 20. PAGE 37 F0726
AUTOMAT TECHRACY PRODUC HIST/WRIT
B67

FARRIS M.T.,MODERN TRANSPORTATION: SELECTED READINGS. UNIV CONTROL...POLICY ANTHOL T 20. PAGE 39 F0765
DIST/IND MGT COST
B67

GOLDMAN M.,CONTROLLING POLLUTION: THE ECONOMICS OF A CLEANER AMERICA. USA+45 SOCIETY PROB/SOLV CONTROL COST ANTHOL. PAGE 48 F0936
HEALTH ECO/DEV NAT/G FINAN
B67

GREEN C.,NEGATIVE TAXES AND THE POVERTY PROBLEM. COST EFFICIENCY INCOME NEW/LIB...METH/CNCPT CHARTS METH/COMP BIBLIOG 20. PAGE 50 F0983
TAX RECEIVE WEALTH PLAN
B67

HAGUE D.C.,PRICE FORMATION IN VARIOUS ECONOMIES; PROCEEDINGS OF A CONFERENCE HELD BY THE INTERNATIONAL ECONOMIC ASSOCIATION. WOR+45 FINAN MARKET PLAN CONFER COST...DECISION MATH PREDICT CHARTS SIMUL 20 INTL/ECON. PAGE 53 F1037
PRICE CAP/ISM SOCISM METH/COMP
B67

HEADLEY J.C.,PESTICIDE PROBLEM: AN ECONOMIC APPROACH TO PUBLIC POLICY. AGRI TEC/DEV GOV/REL COST ATTIT CHARTS. PAGE 58 F1131
HABITAT POLICY BIO/SOC CONTROL
B67

JACOBY N.H.,US AID TO TAIWAN. CAP/ISM DIPLOM FEEDBACK COST PRODUC...OBS INT CHARTS 20. PAGE 66 F1301
FOR/AID OP/RES ECO/TAC ECO/UNDEV
B67

KAPLAN J.J.,CHALLENGE OF FOREIGN AID. USA+45 CONTROL BAL/PAY COST ATTIT ALL/VALS...METH/COMP 20. PAGE 69 F1352
FOR/AID PLAN GIVE POLICY
B67

LITTLE AD, INC.,COMMUNITY RENEWAL PROGRAMMING. CULTURE LOC/G ACT/RES TASK COST ATTIT...SOC/WK MODAL STAT STAND/INT CHARTS 20 SAN/FRAN. PAGE 81 F1585
STRATA NEIGH PLAN CREATE
B67

MACAVOY P.W.,REGULATION OF TRANSPORT INNOVATION.
DIST/IND

ACT/RES ADJUD COST DEMAND...POLICY CHARTS 20. PAGE 83 F1621
CONTROL PRICE PROFIT
B67

MARRIS P.,DILEMMAS OF SOCIAL REFORM: POVERTY AND COMMUNITY ACTION IN THE UNITED STATES. USA+45 NAT/G OP/RES ADMIN PARTIC EFFICIENCY WEALTH...SOC METH/COMP T MUNICH 20 REFORMERS. PAGE 85 F1674
STRUCT PROB/SOLV COST
B67

NARVER J.C.,CONGLOMERATE MERGERS AND MARKET COMPETITION. USA+45 LAW STRUCT ADMIN LEAD RISK COST PROFIT WEALTH...POLICY CHARTS BIBLIOG. PAGE 96 F1892
DEMAND LG/CO MARKET MGT
B67

ROBINSON R.D.,INTERNATIONAL MANAGEMENT. LAW MARKET LABOR PRICE CONTROL COST DEMAND OWN PRODUC WEALTH 20. PAGE 113 F2225
T OP/RES MGT DIPLOM
B67

SCHON D.A.,TECHNOLOGY AND CHANGE* THE NEW HERACLITUS. TEC/DEV CONTROL COST DEMAND EFFICIENCY RIGID/FLEX...MYTH 20. PAGE 117 F2311
INDUS PROB/SOLV R+D CREATE
B67

US AGENCY INTERNATIONAL DEV,PROPOSED FOREIGN AID PROGRAM FOR 1968: SUMMARY PRESENTATION TO THE CONGRESS. AFR S/ASIA USA+45 AGRI TEC/DEV DIPLOM ECO/TAC BAL/PAY COST HEALTH KNOWL SKILL 20 AID CONGRESS ALL/PROG. PAGE 134 F2640
ECO/UNDEV BUDGET FOR/AID STAT
B67

US CONGRESS JOINT ECO COMM,REPORT ON JANUARY 1967 ECONOMIC REPORT OF THE PRESIDENT. FINAN LABOR NAT/G LEGIS BUDGET INT/TRADE COST DEMAND INCOME PRODUC ...POLICY IDEA/COMP 20 CONGRESS. PAGE 135 F2663
CHIEF ECO/TAC PLAN DELIB/GP
L67

JACOBY S.B.,"THE 89TH CONGRESS AND GOVERNMENT LITIGATION." USA+45 ADMIN COST...JURID 20 CONGRESS. PAGE 66 F1302
LAW NAT/G ADJUD SANCTION
L67

LAMBERT J.D.,"CORPORATE POLITICAL SPENDING AND CAMPAIGN FINANCE." LAW CONSTN FINAN LABOR LG/CO LOC/G NAT/G VOL/ASSN TEC/DEV ADJUD ADMIN PARTIC. PAGE 75 F1463
USA+45 POL/PAR CHOOSE COST
L67

ROBERTS E.F.,"THE CASE OF THE UNWARY HOME BUYER: THE HOUSING MERCHANT DID IT." USA+45 CLIENT DIST/IND MARKET LG/CO SML/CO PROB/SOLV LEGIT COST PROFIT. PAGE 112 F2207
ADJUD CONSTRUC OWN LAW
S67

"PROTEST AGAINST SOVIET INDUSTRIALIZATION ILLS IN LITHUANIA* A MEMORANDUM." USSR LITHUANIA NAT/G PROVS COST GEOG. PAGE 1 F0024
INDUS COLONIAL NAT/LISM PLAN
S67

BARAN P.,"THE FUTURE COMPUTER UTILITY." USA+45 NAT/G PLAN CONTROL COST...POLICY 20. PAGE 9 F0177
COMPUTER UTIL FUT TEC/DEV
S67

BARRO S.,"ECONOMIC IMPACT OF SPACE EXPENDITURES: SOME BROAD ISSUES DEALING WITH COSTS AND BENEFITS." USA+45 PROC/MFG R+D LG/CO CONSULT COST PRODUC 20. PAGE 10 F0195
SPACE FINAN ECO/TAC NAT/G
S67

BASOV V.,"THE DEVELOPMENT OF PUBLIC EDUCATION AND THE BUDGET." USSR NAT/G CONTROL REV COST AGE...STAT 20. PAGE 11 F0204
BUDGET GIVE EDU/PROP SCHOOL
S67

BRAUCHER R.,"RECLAMATION OF GOODS FROM A FRAUDULENT BUYER." USA+45 CLIENT FINAN CT/SYS PERS/REL COST WEALTH. PAGE 18 F0341
LAW ADJUD GOV/REL INT/TRADE
S67

CHAMBERLAIN N.W.,"STRIKES IN CONTEMPORARY CONTEXT." LAW INDUS NAT/G CHIEF CONFER COST ATTIT ORD/FREE ...POLICY MGT 20. PAGE 23 F0442
LABOR BARGAIN EFFICIENCY PROB/SOLV
S67

CROKER F.P.U.,"ECONOMIC PEACEKEEPING." UK PLAN PROB/SOLV TEC/DEV BAL/PWR DIPLOM COERCE PEACE ...POLICY DECISION 20. PAGE 28 F0553
FORCES WEAPON COST WAR
S67

DEWHURST A.,"THE WAGE MOVEMENT IN CANADA." CANADA AGRI NAT/G PARTIC COST PRODUC PROFIT 20. PAGE 32 F0627
WORKER MARXIST INDUS LABOR
S67

DURIEZ P.,"THE IMPACT OF EX PARTE 230 (PIGGYBACKING) ON RAIL-MOTOR COMPETITION." USA+45 USA-45 LG/CO COST EFFICIENCY...CHARTS 20. PAGE 35 F0685
DIST/IND LAW CONTROL AGREE
S67

FERGUSON D.E.,"DETERMINING CAPACITY FOR CAPITAL
FINAN

EXPENDITURES." USA+45 LOC/G BUDGET TAX ADMIN CONTROL...TREND MUNICH 20. PAGE 40 F0784 — PAY COST

S67
FUCHS V.R.,"REDEFINING POVERTY AND REDISTRIBUTING INCOME." USA+45 NAT/G ECO/TAC GIVE COST...NEW/IDEA CHARTS. PAGE 45 F0873 — WEALTH INCOME STRATA PROB/SOLV

S67
GREEN C.,"SCHEMES FOR TRANSFERRING INCOME TO THE POOR." BUDGET GIVE RECEIVE DEBATE COST INCOME ...SOC/WK METH/COMP. PAGE 50 F0982 — TAX WEALTH PLAN ACT/RES

S67
KENDALL R.J.,"CHANGED CONDITIONS AS MISREPRESENTATION IN GOVERNMENT CONSTRUCTION CONTRACTS." USA+45 BARGAIN ADJUD COST. PAGE 70 F1375 — CONTROL CONSTRUC NAT/G LAW

S67
KENNY L.M.,"THE AFTERMATH OF DEFEAT IN EGYPT." ISLAM ISRAEL UAR UK USA+45 USSR INDUS FORCES ECO/TAC PRICE COERCE WEAPON COST ATTIT. PAGE 70 F1378 — WAR ECO/UNDEV DIPLOM POLICY

S67
LEDEBUR L.C.,"THE PROBLEM OF SOCIAL COST." STRUCT PROB/SOLV...CHARTS GEN/LAWS. PAGE 77 F1501 — COST INCOME SOCIETY ECO/TAC

S67
OLIVIER G.,"ASPECTS JURIDIQUES DE L'ADOPTION DU TRAITE CECA A LA CRISE CHARBONNIERE (SUITE ET FIN)" LAW DIST/IND PLAN DIPLOM RATION PRICE ADMIN COST DEMAND...POLICY CON/ANAL ECSC TREATY. PAGE 101 F1988 — INT/TRADE INT/ORG EXTR/IND CONSTN

S67
PAULY M.V.,"MIXED PUBLIC AND PRIVATE FINANCING OF EDUCATION." STRATA PAY RECEIVE COST INCOME OPTIMAL METH/COMP. PAGE 104 F2039 — SCHOOL PLAN TAX EFFICIENCY

S67
PENNEY N.,"BANK STATEMENTS, CANCELLED CHECKS, AND ARTICLE FOUR IN THE ELECTRONIC AGE." USA+45 TEC/DEV COST EFFICIENCY WEALTH. PAGE 104 F2056 — CREATE LAW ADJUD FINAN

S67
SIMONE A.J.,"SCIENTIFIC PUBLIC POLICY, MARKET PERFORMANCE, AND SIZE OF FIRM." GP/REL COST EFFICIENCY OPTIMAL PRODUC PWR. PAGE 122 F2410 — LAW INDUS NAT/G PROB/SOLV

S67
SKILTON R.M.,"PROTECTION OF THE INSTALLMENT BUYER OF GOODS UNDER THE UNIFORM COMMERCIAL CODE." USA+45 NAT/G COST. PAGE 123 F2418 — LAW ADJUD LEGIT FINAN

S67
STILL J.F.,"THE FUTURE OF METROPOLITAN GOVERNMENT ORGANIZATION." USA+45 LOC/G BUDGET COST ATTIT MUNICH 20. PAGE 126 F2488 — ADMIN FINAN CONTROL

S67
TELLER A.,"AIR-POLLUTION ABATEMENT: ECONOMIC RATIONALITY AND REALITY." NAT/G DELIB/GP ECO/TAC GOV/REL CENTRAL EFFICIENCY HEALTH...CHARTS METH MUNICH. PAGE 129 F2543 — PROB/SOLV CONTROL COST AIR

S67
THORKELSON H.,"FOOD STAMPS AND HUNGER IN AMERICA." USA+45 LAW DELIB/GP ADMIN COST DEMAND POLICY. PAGE 130 F2570 — WEALTH RECEIVE EATING PLAN

S67
WARNER K.O.,"FINANCIAL IMPLICATION OF EMPLOYEE BARGAINING IN THE PUBLIC SERVICE." CANADA USA+45 FINAN ADMIN...MGT 20. PAGE 143 F2823 — BARGAIN LABOR COST LOC/G

S67
WILES P.J.,"THE POLITICAL AND SOCIAL PREREQUISITES FOR A SOVIET-TYPE ECONOMY." COM USSR LAW CULTURE CREATE ADMIN FEEDBACK ROUTINE COST OPTIMAL TOTALISM MARXISM 20. PAGE 146 F2883 — ECO/DEV PLAN EX/STRUC EFFICIENCY

N67
US CONGRESS JOINT ECO COMM,ECONOMY IN GOVERNMENT (PAMPHLET). USA+45 ECO/DEV FINAN NAT/G PLAN BUDGET SENATE. PAGE 135 F2662 — ECO/TAC COST EFFICIENCY MGT

N67
US CONGRESS JT COMM ECO GOVT,BACKGROUND MATERIAL ON ECONOMY IN GOVERNMENT 1967 (PAMPHLET). WOR+45 ECO/DEV BARGAIN PRICE DEMAND OPTIMAL...STAT DEPT/DEFEN. PAGE 135 F2665 — BUDGET COST MGT NAT/G

B75
JEVONS W.S.,MONEY AND THE MECHANISM OF EXCHANGE. INDUS MARKET DIPLOM COST EQUILIB WEALTH LAISSEZ ...GEN/LAWS 19 MONEY. PAGE 67 F1319 — PRICE FINAN ECO/TAC POLICY

L86
OSGOOD H.L.,"SCIENTIFIC SOCIALISM: RODBERTUS" GERMANY CAP/ISM COST WEALTH...MAJORIT BIOG IDEA/COMP 19 RODBRTUS/C. PAGE 102 F2002 — SOCISM MARXISM ECO/DEV ECO/TAC

S86
SMITH R.M.,"THE NATIONAL BUREAU OF LABOR AND INDUSTRIAL DEPRESSIONS" USA-45 DELIB/GP BARGAIN CONTROL COST INCOME WEALTH...STAT 19 DEPRESSION. PAGE 123 F2433 — LABOR INDUS FINAN GOV/REL

B92
ENGELS F.,THE CONDITION OF THE WORKING-CLASS IN ENGLAND (1848). UK INDUS LABOR PRICE CONTROL COST INCOME HEALTH MARXISM MUNICH 19. PAGE 38 F0733 — WORKER WEALTH MARXIST CAP/ISM

B98
MARSHALL A.,PRINCIPLES OF ECONOMICS. INDUS WORKER PRICE COST EQUILIB INCOME OPTIMAL PRODUC...TIME/SEQ METH RICARDO/D. PAGE 86 F1678 — WEALTH GEN/LAWS MARKET

COSTA/RICA....SEE ALSO L/A+17C

B67
BUSEY J.L.,NOTES ON COSTA RICAN DEMOCRACY. COSTA/RICA L/A+17C NAT/G POL/PAR LEGIS CHOOSE OWN ATTIT...BIBLIOG 20. PAGE 20 F0394 — CONSTN MAJORIT SOCIETY ECO/UNDEV

COSTANZA J.F. F0540

COSTS....SEE ALSO COST

B61
WEISBROD B.A.,ECONOMICS OF PUBLIC HEALTH. USA+45 INGP/REL HABITAT...POLICY STAT COSTS 20. PAGE 145 F2851 — SOCIETY HEALTH NEW/IDEA ECO/DEV

B64
MORRISSENS L.,ECONOMIC POLICY IN OUR TIME: COUNTRY STUDIES. BELGIUM EUR+WWI FRANCE GERMANY/W ITALY NETHERLAND INDUS BARGAIN BUDGET GOV/REL BAL/PAY PRODUC...CON/ANAL CHARTS COSTS 20. PAGE 94 F1839 — ECO/DEV ECO/TAC METH/COMP PLAN

S67
HILDEBRAND G.H.,"SECOND THOUGHTS ON THE NEGATIVE INCOME TAX." PLAN BUDGET ECO/TAC GIVE RECEIVE DEBATE EFFICIENCY INCOME...METH/COMP COSTS. PAGE 59 F1169 — TAX WEALTH SOC/WK ACT/RES

COTTAM R.W. F0541

COUGHLIN B.J. F0542

COUGHLIN/C....CHARLES EDWARD COUGHLIN

COULANGES F D.E. F0543

COUNCIL OF EUROPE, SECRETARIAT F2340

COUNCL/EUR....COUNCIL OF EUROPE

B52
SECRETARIAT COUNCIL OF EUROPE,THE STRASBOURG PLAN. EUR+WWI CONSULT PLAN ECO/TAC TARIFFS DEBATE REGION 20 COUNCL/EUR STRASBOURG. PAGE 119 F2340 — INT/ORG ECO/DEV INT/TRADE DIPLOM

B64
ECONOMIDES C.P.,LE POUVOIR DE DECISION DES ORGANISATIONS INTERNATIONALES EUROPEENNES. DIPLOM DOMIN INGP/REL EFFICIENCY...INT/LAW JURID 20 NATO OEEC EEC COUNCL/EUR EURATOM. PAGE 36 F0698 — INT/ORG PWR DECISION GP/COMP

COUNCL/MGR....COUNCIL-MANAGER SYSTEM OF LOCAL GOVERNMENT

COUNTIES....SEE LOC/G

COUNTY AGRICULTURAL AGENT....SEE COUNTY/AGT

COUNTY/AGT....COUNTY AGRICULTURAL AGENT

B28
TRUE A.C.,A HISTORY OF AGRICULTURAL EXTENSION WORK IN THE UNITED STATES, 1785-1923. USA-45 LAW SCHOOL WAR ADJUST...CHARTS BIBLIOG 18/20 SMITH/LEVR COUNTY/AGT. PAGE 131 F2591 — EDU/PROP AGRI VOL/ASSN PLAN

COURAGE....SEE DRIVE

COURNOT A.A. F0544

COURT OF APPEALS....SEE CT/APPEALS

COURT SYSTEMS....SEE CT/SYS

COURT/DIST....DISTRICT COURTS

COURTHEOUX J.P. F0833

COURTS OF WESTMINSTER HALL....SEE CTS/WESTM

COWLING M. F0545

COWPER/W....WILLIAM COWPER

COX D.W. F0546

COX H. F0547

COX O.C. F0548

CRABB C.V. F0549

CRAIG A. F0550

CRANDALL R. F2299

CRANE E. F0551

CRAWFORD F.G. F0552

CREATE....CREATIVE PROCESSES

B14
VEBLEN T.,THE INSTINCT OF WORKMANSHIP. UNIV SOCIETY ECO/DEV ECO/UNDEV CREATE TEC/DEV ECO/TAC EDU/PROP ROUTINE PERSON...HUM CONCPT TIME/SEQ GEN/LAWS. PAGE 140 F2768
DRIVE SKILL

N19
HUBERMAN L.,SOCIALISM IS THE ONLY ANSWER (PAMPHLET). CREATE ECO/TAC EDU/PROP CONTROL ...SOCIALIST GEN/LAWS ANTHOL 20. PAGE 62 F1230
SOCISM ECO/DEV CAP/ISM PLAN

B36
BELLOC H.,THE RESTORATION OF PROPERTY. UK STRATA NAT/G PROF/ORG DELIB/GP WORKER CREATE PROB/SOLV ECO/TAC PARTIC UTOPIA ORD/FREE SOCISM 20. PAGE 13 F0238
CONTROL MAJORIT CAP/ISM OWN

B36
HUBERMAN L.,MAN'S WORLDLY GOODS: THE STORY OF THE WEALTH OF NATIONS. CHRIST-17C EUR+WWI MOD/EUR SOCIETY DOMIN REV ORD/FREE...TIME/SEQ METH/COMP. PAGE 63 F1231
WEALTH CAP/ISM MARXISM CREATE

B38
LEVINSON E.,LABOR ON THE MARCH. WORKER CREATE ECO/TAC ADJUD LEAD PARL/PROC PARTIC INGP/REL SKILL POLICY. PAGE 79 F1543
LABOR INCOME NAT/G PLAN

B40
HELLMAN F.S.,THE NEW DEAL: SELECTED LIST OF REFERENCES. USA-45 FINAN LABOR EX/STRUC CREATE INT/TRADE ADMIN CT/SYS 20 SUPREME/CT. PAGE 58 F1145
BIBLIOG/A ECO/TAC PLAN POLICY

B42
VEBLEN T.B.,THE THEORY OF THE LEISURE CLASS. USA-45 SOCIETY STRATA STRUCT NAT/G SECT WORKER CREATE EDU/PROP ATTIT...SOC GEN/LAWS 19. PAGE 141 F2772
WEALTH ELITES LEISURE PRODUC

B42
WRIGHT D.M.,THE CREATION OF PURCHASING POWER. USA-45 NAT/G PRICE ADMIN WAR INCOME PRODUC...POLICY CONCPT IDEA/COMP BIBLIOG 20 MONEY. PAGE 149 F2930
FINAN ECO/TAC ECO/DEV CREATE

C43
BENTHAM J.,"THE RATIONALE OF REWARD" IN J. BOWRING, ED., THE WORKS OF JEREMY BENTHAM (VOL. 2)" LAW WORKER CREATE INSPECT PAY ROUTINE HAPPINESS PRODUC SUPEGO WEALTH METH/CNCPT. PAGE 13 F0254
SANCTION ECO/TAC INCOME PWR

B44
HAYEK F.A.,THE ROAD TO SERFDOM. NAT/G POL/PAR CREATE EDU/PROP ATTIT WEALTH LAISSEZ...OLD/LIB CONCPT TREND 20. PAGE 57 F1121
FUT PLAN ECO/TAC SOCISM

B52
TANNENBAUM F.,A PHILOSOPHY OF LABOR. SOCIETY STRATA INDUS LG/CO AGREE ADJUST OWN ORD/FREE PWR...CONCPT 20. PAGE 128 F2533
LABOR PHIL/SCI WORKER CREATE

S52
LEWIS V.B.,"TOWARD A THEORY OF BUDGETING" (BMR)" USA+45 NAT/G PLAN PROB/SOLV...IDEA/COMP METH 20 SUPREME/CT. PAGE 79 F1551
BUDGET CONCPT CREATE

B53
DAHL R.A.,POLITICS, ECONOMICS AND WELFARE: PLANNING AND POLITICOECONOMIC SYSTEMS RESOLVED INTO BASIC SOCIAL PROCESSES. WOR+45 WOR-45 ECO/DEV ECO/UNDEV R+D CREATE PLAN TEC/DEV EDU/PROP HEALTH WEALTH ...SOC SELF/OBS TREND CHARTS GEN/METH 20. PAGE 29 F0571
ECO/TAC PHIL/SCI

B54
MOSK S.A.,INDUSTRIAL REVOLUTION IN MEXICO. MARKET LABOR CREATE CAP/ISM ADMIN ATTIT SOCISM...POLICY 20 MEXIC/AMER. PAGE 94 F1843
INDUS TEC/DEV ECO/UNDEV NAT/G

B54
STALEY E.,THE FUTURE OF UNDERDEVELOPED COUNTRIES: POLITICAL IMPLICATIONS OF ECONOMIC DEVELOPMENT. AFR COM FUT USA+45 SOCIETY ECO/UNDEV CREATE PLAN CAP/ISM ATTIT DRIVE MARXISM SOCISM...POLICY CONCPT CHARTS 20. PAGE 125 F2466
EDU/PROP ECO/TAC FOR/AID

B54
WASHBURNE N.F.,INTERPRETING SOCIAL CHANGE IN AMERICA. USA+45 STRATA FAM NAT/G SECT OP/RES ECO/TAC EDU/PROP HABITAT...SOC TIME/SEQ TREND 20 BUREAUCRCY. PAGE 143 F2826
CULTURE STRUCT CREATE TEC/DEV

L54
OPLER M.E.,"SOCIAL ASPECTS OF TECHNICAL ASSISTANCE IN OPERATION." WOR+45 VOL/ASSN CREATE PLAN TEC/DEV EDU/PROP ALL/VALS...METH/CNCPT OBS RECORD TREND UN 20. PAGE 101 F1993
INT/ORG CONSULT FOR/AID

B55
US OFFICE OF THE PRESIDENT,REPORT TO CONGRESS ON THE MUTUAL SECURITY PROGRAM FOR THE SIX MONTHS ENDED JUNE 30, 1955. ECO/DEV INT/ORG NAT/G CREATE TEC/DEV BAL/PWR ECO/TAC AGREE DETER COST ORD/FREE 20 DEPT/STATE DEPT/DEFEN. PAGE 138 F2722
DIPLOM FORCES PLAN FOR/AID

B56
HISTORICAL ABSTRACTS. NAT/G CREATE DIPLOM ATTIT ...SOC DICTIONARY INDEX 18/20. PAGE 1 F0011
WOR-45 COMPUT/IR BIBLIOG/A

B56
US OFFICE OF THE PRESIDENT,REPORT TO CONGRESS ON THE MUTUAL SECURITY PROGRAM FOR THE SIX MONTHS ENDED DECEMBER 31, 1955. ASIA USSR ECO/DEV ECO/UNDEV INT/ORG NAT/G CREATE TEC/DEV BAL/PWR ECO/TAC AGREE DETER COST ORD/FREE 20 DEPT/STATE DEPT/DEFEN EISNHWR/DD. PAGE 138 F2723
DIPLOM FORCES PLAN FOR/AID

S56
GORDON L.,"THE ORGANIZATION FOR EUROPEAN ECONOMIC COOPERATION." EUR+WWI INDUS INT/ORG NAT/G CONSULT DELIB/GP ACT/RES CREATE PLAN TEC/DEV EDU/PROP LEGIT WEALTH OEEC 20. PAGE 49 F0956
VOL/ASSN ECO/DEV

B57
SCHNEIDER E.V.,INDUSTRIAL SOCIOLOGY: THE SOCIAL RELATIONS OF INDUSTRY AND COMMUNITY. STRATA INDUS NAT/G NEIGH CREATE ADMIN PARTIC GP/REL RACE/REL ROLE PWR...POLICY BIBLIOG. PAGE 117 F2308
LABOR MGT INGP/REL STRUCT

B58
BIDWELL P.W.,RAW MATERIALS: A STUDY OF AMERICAN POLICY. USA+45 USA-45 ECO/UNDEV AGRI INDUS KIN CREATE PLAN ECO/TAC WAR PEACE ATTIT DRIVE WEALTH ...STAT CHARTS CONGRESS FOR/TRADE VAL/FREE. PAGE 15 F0279
EXTR/IND ECO/DEV

B58
CHEEK G.,ECONOMIC AND SOCIAL IMPLICATIONS OF AUTOMATION: A BIBLIOGRAPHIC REVIEW (PAMPHLET). USA+45 LG/CO WORKER CREATE PLAN CONTROL ROUTINE PERS/REL EFFICIENCY PRODUC...METH/COMP 20. PAGE 24 F0459
BIBLIOG/A SOCIETY INDUS AUTOMAT

B58
EHRHARD J.,LE DESTIN DU COLONIALISME. AFR FRANCE ECO/UNDEV AGRI FINAN MARKET CREATE PLAN TEC/DEV BUDGET DIPLOM PRICE 20. PAGE 36 F0710
COLONIAL FOR/AID INT/TRADE INDUS

B58
ROBERTS B.C.,NATIONAL WAGES POLICY IN WAR AND PEACE. EUR+WWI GERMANY S/ASIA SWEDEN UK USA+45 USA-45 STRATA ECO/DEV LABOR NAT/G DELIB/GP PLAN INT/TRADE WEALTH...STAT TREND CHARTS 20. PAGE 112 F2205
CREATE ECO/TAC

S58
ARROW K.J.,"UTILITIES, ATTITUDES, CHOICES: A REVIEW NOTE." USA+45 PLAN...METH/CNCPT MATH STAT CHARTS HYPO/EXP. PAGE 6 F0121
DECISION DIST/IND MARKET CREATE

S58
EMERSON F.D.,"THE ROLES OF MANAGEMENT AND SHAREHOLDERS IN CORPORATE GOVERNMENT." CLIENT DELIB/GP CREATE ADMIN EXEC PARTIC PERS/REL PWR. PAGE 37 F0728
LG/CO LAW INGP/REL REPRESENT

S58
LATTIN N.D.,"MINORITY AND DISSENTING SHAREHOLDERS' RIGHTS IN FUNDAMENTAL CHANGES." FINAN LEGIS ADJUD PARTIC ROUTINE CHOOSE REPRESENT INGP/REL TREND. PAGE 76 F1487
MAJORIT LG/CO LAW CREATE

B59
THE BROOKINGS INSTITUTION,ECONOMICS AND THE POLICY MAKER. USA+45 CREATE...ANTHOL 20. PAGE 129 F2549
ELITES ECO/TAC PROB/SOLV ECO/DEV

B59
VINCENT W.S.,ROLES OF THE CITIZENS: PRINCIPLES AND PRACTICES. LOC/G POL/PAR VOL/ASSN CHOOSE ROLE ORD/FREE PWR...POLICY 20. PAGE 141 F2785
INGP/REL EDU/PROP CREATE LOBBY

S59
THOMPSON W.S.,"POPULATION AND PROGRESS IN THE FAR EAST." ASIA S/ASIA DIST/IND CREATE ECO/TAC WAR LOVE SKILL WEALTH...CONT/OBS TOT/POP 20. PAGE 130 F2568
ECO/UNDEV BIO/SOC GEOG

B60
AUSTRUY J.,STRUCTURE ECONOMIQUE ET CIVILISATION: L'EGYPTE ET LE DESTIN ECONOMIQUE DE L'ISLAM. ISLAM UAR CREATE OP/RES ECO/TAC...SOC BIBLIOG 20 MUSLIM.
ECO/UNDEV CULTURE STRUCT

PAGE 8 F0142

B60
DIA M.,REFLEXIONS SUR L'ECONOMIE DE L'AFRIQUE NOIRE (REV. ED.). CULTURE ECO/UNDEV CREATE TEC/DEV DIPLOM INT/TRADE OPTIMAL ATTIT...POLICY 20. PAGE 32 F0631
AFR ECO/TAC SOCISM PLAN

B60
GILMORE D.R.,DEVELOPING THE "LITTLE" ECONOMIES. USA+45 FINAN LG/CO PROF/ORG VOL/ASSN CREATE ADMIN. PAGE 47 F0924
ECO/TAC LOC/G PROVS PLAN

B60
HITCH C.J.,THE ECONOMICS OF DEFENSE IN THE NUCLEAR AGE. USA+45 WOR+45 CREATE PLAN NUC/PWR ATTIT ...CON/ANAL CHARTS HYPO/EXP NATO 20. PAGE 60 F1179
R+D FORCES

B60
SIMOONS F.J.,NORTHWEST ETHIOPIA; PEOPLES AND ECONOMY. ETHIOPIA MARKET CREATE 20. PAGE 122 F2411
SOCIETY STRUCT AGRI INDUS

B60
US SENATE COMM ON COMMERCE,URBAN MASS TRANSPORTATION. FUT USA+45 AIR ECO/DEV FINAN LOC/G LEGIS CREATE PROB/SOLV TEC/DEV MUNICH 20 PUB/TRANS. PAGE 139 F2732
DIST/IND PLAN NAT/G LAW

S60
BARNETT H.J.,"RESEARCH AND DEVELOPMENT, ECONOMIC GROWTH, AND NATIONAL SECURITY." AFR USA+45 R+D CREATE ECO/TAC ATTIT DRIVE PWR...POLICY SOC METH/CNCPT QUANT STAT TIME/SEQ ORG/CHARTS LOG/LING 20. PAGE 10 F0190
ACT/RES PLAN

B61
FILLOL T.R.,SOCIAL FACTORS IN ECONOMIC DEVELOPMENT: THE ARGENTINE CASE. STRUCT INDUS LABOR CREATE TEC/DEV EFFICIENCY PRODUC DRIVE...METH/CNCPT METH/COMP BIBLIOG/A 20 ARGEN. PAGE 41 F0795
ECO/UNDEV MGT PERS/REL TREND

B61
MARX K.,THE COMMUNIST MANIFESTO. IN (MENDEL A. ESSENTIAL WORKS OF MARXISM, NEW YORK: BANTAM. FUT MOD/EUR CULTURE ECO/DEV ECO/UNDEV AGRI FINAN INDUS MARKET PROC/MFG LABOR POL/PAR CONSULT FORCES CREATE PLAN ADMIN ATTIT DRIVE RIGID/FLEX ORD/FREE PWR RESPECT MARX/KARL MUNICH WORK. PAGE 86 F1691
COM NEW/IDEA CAP/ISM REV

B61
MAYNE A.,DESIGNING AND ADMINISTERING A REGIONAL ECONOMIC DEVELOPMENT PLAN WITH SPECIFIC REFERENCE TO PUERTO RICO (PAMPHLET). PUERT/RICO SOCIETY NAT/G DELIB/GP REGION...DECISION 20. PAGE 87 F1707
ECO/UNDEV PLAN CREATE ADMIN

S61
BARALL M.,"THE UNITED STATES GOVERNMENT RESPONDS." L/A+17C USA+45 SOCIETY NAT/G CREATE PLAN DIPLOM ECO/TAC ATTIT DRIVE RIGID/FLEX KNOWL SKILL WEALTH ...METH/CNCPT TIME/SEQ GEN/METH 20. PAGE 9 F0176
ECO/UNDEV ACT/RES FOR/AID

C61
FILLOL T.R.,"SOCIAL FACTORS IN ECONOMIC DEVELOPMENT: THE ARGENTINE CASE" INDUS LABOR CREATE TEC/DEV PERS/REL EFFICIENCY PRODUC DRIVE ...METH/CNCPT METH/COMP 20 ARGEN. PAGE 41 F0794
BIBLIOG ECO/UNDEV MGT TREND

B62
HARRINGTON M.,THE OTHER AMERICA: POVERTY IN THE UNITED STATES. WORKER CREATE REPRESENT RACE/REL AGE/O DRIVE POLICY. PAGE 55 F1086
WEALTH WELF/ST INCOME CULTURE

B62
HATTERY L.H.,INFORMATION RETRIEVAL MANAGEMENT. CLIENT INDUS TOP/EX COMPUTER OP/RES TEC/DEV ROUTINE COST EFFICIENCY RIGID/FLEX...METH/COMP ANTHOL 20. PAGE 57 F1113
R+D COMPUT/IR MGT CREATE

B62
LITWACK L.,THE AMERICAN LABOR MOVEMENT. USA-45 NAT/G CREATE TEC/DEV CAP/ISM ECO/TAC ADJUD AUTOMAT SKILL...TREND ANTHOL 19/20. PAGE 81 F1588
INDUS LABOR GP/REL METH/COMP

B62
NATIONAL BUREAU ECONOMIC RES,THE RATE AND DIRECTION OF INVENTIVE ACTIVITY: ECONOMIC AND SOCIAL FACTORS. STRUCT INDUS MARKET R+D CREATE OP/RES TEC/DEV EFFICIENCY PRODUC RATIONAL UTIL...WELF/ST PHIL/SCI METH/CNCPT TIME. PAGE 97 F1895
DECISION PROB/SOLV MGT

B62
SELOSOEMARDJAN O.,SOCIAL CHANGES IN JOGJAKARTA. INDONESIA NETHERLAND ELITES STRATA STRUCT FAM POL/PAR CREATE DIPLOM INT/TRADE EDU/PROP ADMIN GOV/REL...SOC 20 JAVA CHINJAP. PAGE 119 F2352
ECO/UNDEV CULTURE REV COLONIAL

B62
WALSTON H.,AGRICULTURE UNDER COMMUNISM. CHINA/COM COM PROB/SOLV HAPPINESS RIGID/FLEX...POLICY METH/COMP 20. PAGE 143 F2811
AGRI MARXISM PLAN CREATE

B63
BURTT E.J. JR.,LABOR MARKETS, UNIONS, AND GOVERNMENT POLICIES. USA+45 MARKET NAT/G DELIB/GP CREATE BARGAIN GP/REL ORD/FREE PWR...POLICY CHARTS 20 AFL/CIO. PAGE 20 F0393
LABOR ECO/DEV CONTROL WORKER

B63
FLORES E.,LAND REFORM AND THE ALLIANCE FOR PROGRESS (PAMPHLET). L/A+17C USA+45 STRUCT ECO/UNDEV NAT/G WORKER CREATE PLAN ECO/TAC COERCE REV 20 ALL/PROG. PAGE 42 F0815
AGRI INT/ORG DIPLOM POLICY

B63
GEERTZ C.,PEDDLERS AND PRINCES: SOCIAL DEVELOPMENT AND ECONOMIC CHANGE IN TWO INDONESIAN TOWNS. S/ASIA CULTURE SOCIETY STRATA FACE/GP CREATE TEC/DEV ECO/TAC ORD/FREE WEALTH...OBS INT CENSUS CHARTS WORK TOT/POP METH/GP TERR/GP VAL/FREE 20 MUNICH. PAGE 47 F0913
ECO/UNDEV SOC ELITES INDONESIA

B63
GRUBEL H.G.,WORLD MONETARY REFORM: PLANS AND ISSUES. FUT WOR+45 ECO/DEV ECO/UNDEV R+D DELIB/GP CREATE ECO/TAC ATTIT RIGID/FLEX WEALTH...STAT ANTHOL VAL/FREE 20. PAGE 52 F1009
FINAN INT/ORG BAL/PAY INT/TRADE

B63
MANN D.E.,THE POLITICS OF WATER IN ARIZONA. AGRI EXTR/IND PROVS ACT/RES CREATE PLAN GOV/REL COST HABITAT...MGT CHARTS 20 ARIZONA WATER. PAGE 84 F1655
POLICY ECO/TAC TEC/DEV

B63
RUMMEL J.F.,RESEARCH METHODOLOGY IN BUSINESS. COMPUTER CREATE PROB/SOLV...CONT/OBS REC/INT QU/SEMANT SYS/QU SAMP CHARTS METH/COMP T 20. PAGE 115 F2260
OP/RES METH/CNCPT METH STAT

B63
WIGHTMAN D.,TOWARD ECONOMIC CO-OPERATION IN ASIA. ASIA S/ASIA VOL/ASSN ACT/RES PLAN TEC/DEV ECO/TAC EDU/PROP RIGID/FLEX SKILL...POLICY METH/CNCPT OBS INT GEN/LAWS UN 20 ECAFE. PAGE 146 F2877
ECO/UNDEV CREATE

L63
MEYER J.R.,"REGIONAL ECONOMICS: A SURVEY." INTELL ACADEM CREATE...IDEA/COMP BIBLIOG. PAGE 90 F1770
REGION ECO/TAC GEN/LAWS PROB/SOLV

L63
OLSON M. JR.,"RAPID ECONOMIC GROWTH AS A DESTABILIZING FORCE." WOR+45 WOR-45 STRATA ECO/UNDEV FAM KIN CREATE TEC/DEV DIPLOM PEACE ATTIT PERSON RIGID/FLEX PWR RESPECT WEALTH...SOC 20. PAGE 101 F1989
SOCIETY FOR/AID

L63
PADELFORD N.J.,"FINANCIAL CRISIS AND THE UNITED NATIONS." FUT USSR WOR+45 LAW CONSTN FINAN INT/ORG DELIB/GP FORCES PLAN BUDGET DIPLOM COST WEALTH ...STAT CHARTS UN CONGO 20. PAGE 102 F2012
CREATE ECO/TAC

S63
DE FOREST J.D.,"LOW LEVELS OF TECHNOLOGY AND ECONOMIC DEVELOPMENT PROSPECTS." WOR+45 WOR-45 CULTURE ACT/RES CREATE PLAN ECO/TAC ROUTINE PERCEPT WEALTH...METH/CNCPT GEN/LAWS 20. PAGE 31 F0597
ECO/UNDEV TEC/DEV

S63
MASON E.S.,"INTERESTS, IDEOLOGIES AND THE PROBLEM OF STABILITY AND GROWTH." EUR+WWI USA+45 DELIB/GP CREATE PLAN EXEC ROUTINE BAL/PAY ATTIT PWR...MGT CONCPT OEEC 20. PAGE 87 F1698
NAT/G ECO/DEV

S63
PINCUS J.,"THE COST OF FOREIGN AID." WOR+45 ECO/DEV FINAN NAT/G VOL/ASSN CREATE ECO/TAC EDU/PROP WEALTH ...METH/CNCPT STAT CHARTS HYPO/EXP TOT/POP VAL/FREE 20. PAGE 106 F2087
USA+45 ECO/UNDEV FOR/AID

S63
SCHURMANN F.,"ECONOMIC POLICY AND POLITICAL POWER IN COMMUNIST CHINA." ASIA CHINA/COM USSR SOCIETY ECO/UNDEV AGRI INDUS CREATE ADMIN ROUTINE ATTIT DRIVE RIGID/FLEX PWR WEALTH...HIST/WRIT TREND CHARTS WORK 20. PAGE 118 F2323
PLAN ECO/TAC

S63
SHONFIELD A.,"AFTER BRUSSELS." EUR+WWI FRANCE GERMANY UK ECO/DEV DIST/IND MARKET VOL/ASSN DELIB/GP CREATE INT/TRADE ATTIT RIGID/FLEX...RECORD TREND GEN/LAWS EEC COMMUN CMN/WLTH 20. PAGE 121 F2385
PLAN ECO/TAC

S63
WALKER H.,"THE INTERNATIONAL LAW OF COMMODITY AGREEMENTS." FUT WOR+45 ECO/DEV ECO/UNDEV FINAN INT/ORG NAT/G CONSULT CREATE PLAN ECO/TAC ATTIT PERCEPT...CONCPT GEN/LAWS TOT/POP GATT 20. PAGE 142 F2804
MARKET VOL/ASSN INT/LAW INT/TRADE

S63
WOLFERS A.,"INTEGRATION IN THE WEST: THE CONFLICT OF PERSPECTIVES." AFR EUR+WWI USA+45 ECO/DEV INT/ORG DELIB/GP CREATE TEC/DEV DIPLOM ATTIT PWR ...CONCPT HIST/WRIT TREND GEN/LAWS EEC 20. PAGE 148 F2918
RIGID/FLEX ECO/TAC

B64
BALASSA B.,TRADE PROSPECTS FOR DEVELOPING COUNTRIES. WOR+45 ECO/DEV AGRI EXTR/IND INDUS CREATE PLAN PRICE...ECOMETRIC CLASSIF TIME/SEQ GEN/METH. PAGE 8 F0158
INT/TRADE ECO/UNDEV TREND STAT

B64
BLAKE R.R.,MANAGING INTERGROUP CONFLICT IN INDUSTRY. INDUS DELIB/GP EX/STRUC GP/REL PERS/REL GAME. PAGE 16 F0297
CREATE PROB/SOLV OP/RES ADJUD

B64
BOURGOIGNIE G.E.,JEUNE AFRIQUE MOBILISABLE; LES PROBLEMES DE LA JEUNESSE DESOEUVREE EN AFRIQUE NOIRE. INT/ORG VOL/ASSN ECO/TAC ROUTINE UTIL ATTIT 20. PAGE 17 F0324
AGE/Y AFR CREATE ECO/UNDEV

B64
BRIGHT J.R.,RESEARCH, DEVELOPMENT AND TECHNOLOGICAL INNOVATION. CULTURE R+D CREATE PLAN PROB/SOLV AUTOMAT RISK PERSON...DECISION CONCPT PREDICT BIBLIOG. PAGE 18 F0352
TEC/DEV NEW/IDEA INDUS MGT

B64
CHANDLER A.D. JR.,GIANT ENTERPRISE: FORD, GENERAL MOTORS, AND THE AUTOMOBILE INDUSTRY; SOURCES AND READINGS. USA+45 USA-45 FINAN MARKET CREATE ADMIN ...TIME/SEQ ANTHOL 20 AUTOMOBILE. PAGE 23 F0447
LG/CO DIST/IND LABOR MGT

B64
COMMITTEE ECONOMIC DEVELOPMENT,COMMUNITY ECONOMIC DEVELOPMENT PROGRAMS. USA+45 FINAN INDUS LG/CO PROF/ORG CREATE GP/REL MUNICH NEW/YORK VERMONT PENNSYLVAN IN ARKANSAS. PAGE 27 F0519
LOC/G LABOR PLAN

B64
GOWDA K.V.,INTERNATIONAL CURRENCY PLANS AND EXPANSION OF WORLD TRADE. INT/ORG CREATE BUDGET CONTROL BAL/PAY WEALTH 20 KEYNES/JM. PAGE 50 F0969
INT/TRADE FINAN METH/COMP

B64
GREBLER L.,URBAN RENEWAL IN EUROPEAN COUNTRIES: ITS EMERGENCE AND POTENTIALS. EUR+WWI UK ECO/DEV LOC/G NEIGH CREATE ADMIN ATTIT...TREND NAT/COMP MUNICH 20 URBAN/RNWL. PAGE 50 F0981
PLAN CONSTRUC NAT/G

B64
KEMP M.C.,THE PURE THEORY OF INTERNATIONAL TRADE. WOR+45 WOR-45 ECO/DEV ECO/UNDEV DIST/IND ECO/TAC ...MATH CON/ANAL CHARTS VAL/FREE. PAGE 70 F1374
FINAN CREATE INT/TRADE

B64
LEWIN P.,THE FOREIGN TRADE OF COMMUNIST CHINA* ITS IMPACT ON THE FREE WORLD. AFR EUR+WWI L/A+17C S/ASIA ECO/UNDEV CREATE FOR/AID...STAT NET/THEORY TREND CHARTS. PAGE 79 F1546
ASIA INT/TRADE NAT/COMP USSR

L64
CARNEGIE ENDOWMENT INT. PEACE,"ECONOMIC AND SOCIAL QUESTION (ISSUES BEFORE THE NINETEENTH GENERAL ASSEMBLY)." WOR+45 ECO/DEV ECO/UNDEV INDUS R+D DELIB/GP CREATE PLAN TEC/DEV ECO/TAC FOR/AID BAL/PAY...RECORD UN 20. PAGE 21 F0414
INT/ORG INT/TRADE

L64
HAAS E.B.,"ECONOMICS AND DIFFERENTIAL PATTERNS OF POLITICAL INTEGRATION: PROJECTIONS ABOUT UNITY IN LATIN AMERICA." SOCIETY NAT/G DELIB/GP ACT/RES CREATE PLAN ECO/TAC REGION ROUTINE ATTIT DRIVE PWR WEALTH...CONCPT TREND CHARTS LAFTA TERR/GP 20. PAGE 52 F1020
L/A+17C INT/ORG MARKET

S64
GALBRAITH V.,"JAPAN'S POSITION IN WORLD TRADE." ASIA AGRI INDUS CREATE ECO/TAC LEGIT DRIVE WEALTH ...TREND EEC GATT FOR/TRADE 20 CHINJAP. PAGE 45 F0885
ECO/DEV DELIB/GP

B65
ALDERSON W.,DYNAMIC MARKETING BEHAVIOR. USA+45 FINAN CREATE TEC/DEV EDU/PROP PRICE COST 20. PAGE 3 F0057
MGT MARKET ATTIT CAP/ISM

B65
APTER D.E.,THE POLITICS OF MODERNIZATION. AFR L/A+17C CULTURE NAT/G POL/PAR ADMIN COLONIAL NAT/LISM ATTIT RIGID/FLEX PWR...SOC CONCPT. PAGE 6 F0109
ECO/UNDEV GEN/LAWS STRATA CREATE

B65
BAERRESEN D.W.,LATIN AMERICAN TRADE PATTERNS. L/A+17C ECO/UNDEV AGRI INDUS MARKET CREATE ...NET/THEORY CHARTS LAFTA. PAGE 8 F0149
INT/TRADE STAT REGION

B65
BRADLEY J.F.,THE ROLE OF TRADE ASSOCIATIONS AND PROFESSIONAL BUSINESS SOCIETIES IN AMERICA. USA+45 USA-45 STRUCT CONSULT DELIB/GP CREATE LOBBY GP/REL 20. PAGE 17 F0333
ECO/DEV PROF/ORG VOL/ASSN SOCIETY

B65
CONLEY R.W.,THE ECONOMICS OF VOCATIONAL REHABILITATION. USA+45 VOL/ASSN CREATE EDU/PROP COST EFFICIENCY SOC/INTEG 20. PAGE 27 F0527
PUB/INST HEALTH GIVE GP/REL

B65
COX D.W.,THE PERILS OF PEACE* CONVERSION TO WHAT? FUT USA+45 ECO/DEV NAT/G ACT/RES CREATE PLAN NUC/PWR WAR DEMAND MGT. PAGE 28 F0546
PEACE WORKER FORCES MARKET

B65
DUGGAR G.S.,RENEWAL OF TOWN AND VILLAGE I: A WORLD-WIDE SURVEY OF LOCAL GOVERNMENT EXPERIENCE. WOR+45 CONSTRUC INDUS CREATE BUDGET REGION GOV/REL...QU NAT/COMP MUNICH 20 URBAN/RNWL. PAGE 35 F0673
NEIGH PLAN ADMIN

B65
HOSELITZ B.F.,ECONOMICS AND THE IDEA OF MANKIND. UNIV ECO/DEV ECO/UNDEV DIST/IND INDUS INT/ORG NAT/G ACT/RES ECO/TAC WEALTH...CONCPT STAT. PAGE 62 F1223
CREATE INT/TRADE

B65
ROOSA R.V.,MONETARY REFORM FOR THE WORLD ECONOMY. AFR EUR+WWI USA+45 WOR+45 CREATE BUDGET DIPLOM FOR/AID EQUILIB WEALTH IMF. PAGE 114 F2237
FINAN INT/ORG INT/TRADE BAL/PAY

B65
SHAFFER H.G.,THE SOVIET SYSTEM IN THEORY AND PRACTICE: SELECTED WESTERN AND SOVIET VIEWS. USSR LAW SOCIETY CREATE FOR/AID EDU/PROP PRESS CHOOSE PEACE ORD/FREE...ANTHOL 20 STALIN/J. PAGE 120 F2362
MARXISM SOCISM IDEA/COMP

B65
SHONFIELD A.,MODERN CAPITALISM: THE CHANGING BALANCE OF PUBLIC AND PRIVATE POWER. FRANCE GERMANY/W UK USA+45 WOR+45 ECO/DEV INT/ORG NAT/G CONSULT INT/TRADE PRODUC...POLICY CONCPT METH/COMP 20. PAGE 121 F2386
CAP/ISM CONTROL BAL/PWR CREATE

B65
STEINER G.A.,THE CREATIVE ORGANIZATION. ELITES LG/CO PLAN PROB/SOLV TEC/DEV INSPECT CAP/ISM CONTROL EXEC PERSON...METH/COMP HYPO/EXP 20. PAGE 126 F2476
CREATE MGT ADMIN SOC

B65
WARNER A.W.,THE IMPACT OF SCIENCE ON TECHNOLOGY. UNIV INTELL SOCIETY NAT/G ACT/RES PLAN PROB/SOLV BUDGET OPTIMAL GEN/METH. PAGE 143 F2821
DECISION TEC/DEV CREATE POLICY

B65
WATERSTON A.,DEVELOPMENT PLANNING* LESSONS OF EXPERIENCE. ECO/TAC CENTRAL...MGT QUANT BIBLIOG. PAGE 144 F2830
ECO/UNDEV CREATE PLAN ADMIN

B65
WEIL G.L.,A HANDBOOK ON THE EUROPEAN ECONOMIC COMMUNITY. BELGIUM EUR+WWI FRANCE GERMANY/W ITALY CONSTN ECO/DEV CREATE PARTIC GP/REL...DECISION MGT CHARTS 20 EEC. PAGE 144 F2846
INT/TRADE INT/ORG TEC/DEV INT/LAW

B65
WISH J.R.,ECONOMIC DEVELOPMENT IN LATIN AMERICA: AN ANNOTATED BIBLIOGRAPHY. L/A+17C COM/IND MARKET R+D CREATE CAP/ISM ATTIT...STAT METH 20. PAGE 148 F2912
BIBLIOG/A ECO/UNDEV TEC/DEV AGRI

L65
DAANE J.D.,"THE EVOLVING INTERNATIONAL MONETARY MECHANISM." VOL/ASSN CREATE PLAN FOR/AID INT/TRADE CONFER BAL/PAY...RECORD PREDICT IMF. PAGE 29 F0569
INT/ORG ECO/TAC TREND GP/COMP

S65
BRANDENBURG F.,"THE RELEVANCE OF MEXICAN EXPERIENCE TO LATIN AMERICAN DEVELOPMENT." BRAZIL CHILE VENEZUELA STRUCT ECO/UNDEV AGRI CREATE ECO/TAC ...STAT RECORD MEXIC/AMER ARGEN COLOMB. PAGE 18 F0340
L/A+17C GOV/COMP

S65
CECIL C.O.,"THE DETERMINANTS OF LIBYAN FOREIGN POLICY." AFR INTELL ECO/UNDEV EXTR/IND POL/PAR CREATE REGION SOVEREIGN CONSERVE MAGHREB NASSER/G. PAGE 22 F0431
LIBYA DIPLOM WEALTH ISLAM

S65
KUNKEL J.H.,"VALUES AND BEHAVIOR IN ECONOMIC DEVELOPMENT." INDIA PERU CULTURE STRUCT CREATE PERS/REL ATTIT PERSON...CHARTS HYPO/EXP ARGEN. PAGE 74 F1449
SIMUL ECO/UNDEV PSY STERTYP

S65
LECLERCQ H.,"ECONOMIC RESEARCH AND DEVELOPMENT IN TROPICAL AFRICA." ECO/UNDEV INT/ORG CREATE PLAN UN. PAGE 77 F1500
AFR R+D ACADEM ECO/TAC

S65
TENDLER J.D.,"TECHNOLOGY AND ECONOMIC DEVELOPMENT* THE CASE OF HYDRO VS THERMAL POWER." CONSTRUC DIST/IND CREATE TEC/DEV INT/TRADE CENTRAL PWR SKILL WEALTH...MGT NAT/COMP ARGEN. PAGE 129 F2544
BRAZIL INDUS ECO/UNDEV

B66
ALEXANDER Y.,INTERNATIONAL TECHNICAL ASSISTANCE EXPERTS* A CASE STUDY OF THE U.N. EXPERIENCE. ECO/UNDEV CONSULT EX/STRUC CREATE PLAN DIPLOM FOR/AID TASK EFFICIENCY...ORG/CHARTS UN. PAGE 3 F0061
ECO/TAC INT/ORG ADMIN MGT

B66
ALEXANDER Y.,INTERNATIONAL TECHNICAL ASSISTANCE EXPERTS: A CASE STUDY OF THE U.N. EXPERIENCE. USA+45 WOR+45 WORKER CREATE PLAN PROB/SOLV ECO/TAC FOR/AID GIVE EDU/PROP...CHARTS BIBLIOG 20 UN. PAGE 3 F0062
SKILL INT/ORG TEC/DEV CONSULT

B66
DAVIES JC I.I.I.,NEIGHBORHOOD GROUPS AND URBAN RENEWAL. USA+45 PLAN LOBBY PARTIC CHOOSE RACE/REL ...POLICY DECISION SOC INT MUNICH SOC/INTEG 20 NEWYORK/C. PAGE 30 F0586
NEIGH CREATE PROB/SOLV

B66
ECKSTEIN A.,COMMUNIST CHINA'S ECONOMIC GROWTH AND FOREIGN TRADE* IMPLICATIONS FOR US POLICY. COM USA+45 USSR STRUCT INDUS MARKET DIPLOM ECO/TAC FOR/AID INT/TRADE...STAT CHARTS. PAGE 36 F0696
ASIA ECO/UNDEV CREATE PWR

B66
GROSS H.,MAKE OR BUY. AFR USA+45 FINAN INDUS CREATE PRICE PRODUC 20. PAGE 51 F1006
ECO/TAC PLAN MGT

COST

B66

KURAKOV I.G.,SCIENCE, TECHNOLOGY AND COMMUNISM; SOME QUESTIONS OF DEVELOPMENT (TRANS. BY CARIN DEDIJER). USSR INDUS PLAN PROB/SOLV COST PRODUC ...MGT MATH CHARTS METH 20. PAGE 74 F1450
CREATE TEC/DEV MARXISM ECO/TAC

B66

LEWIS W.A.,DEVELOPMENT PLANNING; THE ESSENTIALS OF ECONOMIC POLICY. USA+45 FINAN INDUS NAT/G WORKER FOR/AID INT/TRADE ADMIN ROUTINE WEALTH...CONCPT STAT. PAGE 79 F1552
PLAN ECO/DEV POLICY CREATE

B66

NICOSIA M.N.,CONSUMER DECISION PROCESSES: MARKETING AND ADVERTISING IMPLICATIONS. ECO/TAC ATTIT PERSON ...DECISION MGT SOC. PAGE 98 F1926
MARKET SOCIETY CREATE ACT/RES

B66

ODEGARD P.H.,POLITICAL POWER AND SOCIAL CHANGE. UNIV NAT/G CREATE ALL/IDEOS...POLICY GEOG SOC CENSUS TREND. PAGE 100 F1962
PWR TEC/DEV IDEA/COMP

B66

PFEFFER K.H.,WELT IM UMBRUCH. SOCIETY STRUCT INDUS PROF/ORG SECT TEC/DEV PARTIC SUPEGO WORSHIP 20 CHRISTIAN. PAGE 106 F2076
ORD/FREE STRATA CREATE

L66

PACKENHAM R.A.,"POLITICAL-DEVELOPMENT DOCTRINES IN THE AMERICAN FOREIGN AID PROGRAM." STRUCT R+D CREATE DIPLOM AID. PAGE 102 F2011
FOR/AID ECO/UNDEV GEN/LAWS

S66

COHEN A.,"THE TECHNOLOGY/ELITE APPROACH TO THE DEVELOPMENTAL PROCESS* PERUVIAN CASE STUDY." L/A+17C STRUCT CREATE ECO/TAC FOR/AID CIVMIL/REL MARXISM TECHRACY HYPO/EXP. PAGE 26 F0496
ECO/UNDEV ELITES PERU

S66

MALENBAUM W.,"GOVERNMENT, ENTREPRENEURSHIP, AND ECONOMIC GROWTH IN POOR LANDS." ELITES ECO/UNDEV INDUS CREATE DRIVE. PAGE 84 F1645
ECO/TAC PLAN CONSERVE NAT/G

S66

SHORTE F.C.,"THE APPLICATION OF DEVELOPMENT HYPOTHESES IN MIDDLE EASTERN STUDIES." STRUCT AGRI CREATE DEMAND...GEOG STAT CON/ANAL CHARTS. PAGE 121 F2387
ECO/UNDEV ISLAM SOC HYPO/EXP

S66

VERSLUYS J.D.N.,"SOME NOTES ON THE SOCIAL AND ECONOMIC EFFECTS OF RURAL ELECTRIFICATION IN BURMA" BURMA EDU/PROP PRODUC ORD/FREE...SOC QU MUNICH TIME 20. PAGE 141 F2782
TEC/DEV SOCIETY CREATE

B67

AARON H.J.,FINANCING URBAN DEVELOPMENT IN MEXICO CITY: A CASE STUDY OF PROPERTY TAX, LAND USE, HOUSING, AND URBAN PLANNING. LOC/G CREATE EFFICIENCY WEALTH...CHARTS MUNICH 20 MEXIC/AMER. PAGE 2 F0030
PLAN TAX PROB/SOLV

B67

BARANSON J.,TECHNOLOGY FOR UNDERDEVELOPED AREAS: AN ANNOTATED BIBLIOGRAPHY. FUT WOR+45 CULTURE INDUS INT/ORG CREATE PROB/SOLV INT/TRADE EDU/PROP AUTOMAT ...CONCPT METH. PAGE 10 F0181
BIBLIOG/A ECO/UNDEV TEC/DEV R+D

B67

BIBBY J.,ON CAPITOL HILL. POL/PAR LOBBY PARL/PROC GOV/REL PERS/REL...JURID PHIL/SCI OBS INT BIBLIOG 20 CONGRESS PRESIDENT. PAGE 15 F0278
CONFER LEGIS CREATE LEAD

B67

BLAUG M.,ECONOMICS OF EDUCATION: A SELECTED ANNOTATED BIBLIOGRAPHY. EUR+WWI INTELL ECO/DEV ECO/UNDEV ACADEM INT/ORG NAT/G CREATE ADMIN EFFICIENCY ROLE PREDICT. PAGE 16 F0298
BIBLIOG/A EDU/PROP FINAN PLAN

B67

BURDEN H.T.,THE NUREMBERG PARTY RALLIES 1923-39. GERMANY POL/PAR SECT CREATE DOMIN WAR ATTIT ...AUD/VIS FILM 20. PAGE 20 F0384
EDU/PROP CONTROL CROWD TOTALISM

B67

CASTILLO C.M.,GROWTH AND INTEGRATION IN CENTRAL AMERICA. L/A+17C CREATE PROB/SOLV ECO/TAC REGION PRODUC...OBS BIBLIOG 20. PAGE 22 F0429
ECO/UNDEV INT/TRADE NAT/COMP

B67

CHAPIN F.S. JR.,SELECTED REFERENCES ON URBAN PLANNING METHODS AND TECHNIQUES. USA+45 LAW ECO/DEV LOC/G NAT/G SCHOOL CONSULT CREATE PROB/SOLV TEC/DEV ...SOC/WK MUNICH. PAGE 23 F0454
BIBLIOG NEIGH PLAN

B67

CLEMENT M.O.,THEORETICAL ISSUES IN INTERNATIONAL ECONOMICS. WOR+45 PLAN PROB/SOLV TEC/DEV ...ECOMETRIC METH/CNCPT MATH BIBLIOG T MONEY. PAGE 25 F0489
INT/TRADE FINAN CREATE BAL/PAY

B67

COTTAM R.W.,COMPETITIVE INTERFERENCE AND TWENTIETH CENTURY DIPLOMACY. IRAN ACT/RES CREATE PLAN ECO/TAC EFFICIENCY ATTIT...DECISION NEW/IDEA TREND 20 CIA. PAGE 28 F0541
DIPLOM DOMIN GAME

B67

ELDREDGE H.W.,TAMING MEGALOPOLIS; HOW TO MANAGE AN URBANIZED WORLD. WOR+45 SOCIETY ECO/DEV ECO/UNDEV
TEC/DEV PLAN

NAT/G COMPUTER CREATE PARTIC EFFICIENCY WEALTH ...MGT ANTHOL MUNICH. PAGE 37 F0716
PROB/SOLV

B67

HANNAH H.W.,THE LEGAL BASE FOR UNIVERSITIES IN DEVELOPING COUNTRIES. AFR ASIA L/A+17C S/ASIA USA+45 FINAN CREATE EDU/PROP TASK EFFICIENCY ...JURID METH/COMP 20. PAGE 54 F1060
ADMIN LAW ACADEM LEGIS

B67

HEILBRONER R.L.,THE LIMITS OF AMERICAN CAPITALISM. FUT ECO/DEV INDUS LG/CO EX/STRUC LEAD PWR TECHRACY 20. PAGE 58 F1137
ELITES CREATE TEC/DEV CAP/ISM

B67

KULSKI J.E.,LAND OF URBAN PROMISE* CONTINUING THE GREAT TRADITION* A SEARCH FOR SIGNIFICANT URBAN SPACE IN URBANIZED NORTHEAST. USA+45 DIST/IND PUB/INST CONSULT CREATE TEC/DEV...SOC NEW/IDEA CHARTS BIBLIOG MUNICH. PAGE 74 F1448
PLAN PROB/SOLV ECO/DEV

B67

LITTLE AD, INC.,COMMUNITY RENEWAL PROGRAMMING. CULTURE LOC/G ACT/RES TASK COST ATTIT...SOC/WK MODAL STAT STAND/INT CHARTS 20 SAN/FRAN. PAGE 81 F1585
STRATA NEIGH PLAN CREATE

B67

NELSON R.R.,TECHNOLOGY, ECONOMIC GROWTH, AND PUBLIC POLICY. USA+45 PLAN GP/REL UTIL KNOWL...POLICY PHIL/SCI CHARTS BIBLIOG 20. PAGE 97 F1912
R+D CONSULT CREATE ACT/RES

B67

SCHON D.A.,TECHNOLOGY AND CHANGE* THE NEW HERACLITUS. TEC/DEV CONTROL COST DEMAND EFFICIENCY RIGID/FLEX...MYTH 20. PAGE 117 F2311
INDUS PROB/SOLV R+D CREATE

L67

AUSTIN D.A.,"POLITICAL CONFLICT IN AFRICA." CONSTN NAT/G CREATE ADMIN COLONIAL ORD/FREE MARXISM POPULISM SOCISM...NAT/COMP ANTHOL 20. PAGE 8 F0141
ANOMIE AFR POL/PAR

L67

GLAZER N.,"HOUSING PROBLEMS AND HOUSING POLICIES." USA+45 PLAN RENT ADJUST CONSEN DEMAND DISCRIM AGE ATTIT HEALTH WEALTH MUNICH NEGRO. PAGE 48 F0929
POLICY CONSTRUC CREATE HABITAT

L67

HUBBARD P.H.,"MONETARY RECOVERY UNDER THE COPYRIGHT, PATENT, AND TRADEMARK ACTS." PROC/MFG TAX PAY LEGIT ADJUD GOV/REL OWN ORD/FREE 20. PAGE 62 F1228
CREATE LAW CONTROL FINAN

S67

GAMARNIKOW M.,"THE NEW ROLE OF PRIVATE ENTERPRISE." ECO/DEV INDUS NAT/G SML/CO CREATE PROB/SOLV MARXISM ...POLICY TREND IDEA/COMP 20. PAGE 46 F0890
ECO/TAC ATTIT CAP/ISM COM

S67

GOLDSTEIN W.,"THE SCIENCE ESTABLISHMENT AND ITS POLITICAL CONTROL." WOR+45 SOCIETY GP/REL RATIONAL ORD/FREE. PAGE 48 F0941
CREATE ADJUST CONTROL

S67

GORMAN W.,"ELLUL - A PROPHETIC VOICE." WOR+45 ELITES SOCIETY ACT/RES PLAN BAL/PWR DOMIN CONTROL PARTIC TOTALISM PWR 20. PAGE 49 F0963
CREATE ORD/FREE EX/STRUC UTOPIA

S67

KELLY F.K.,"A PROPOSAL FOR AN ANNUAL REPORT ON THE STATE OF MANKIND." FUT INTELL COM/IND INT/ORG CREATE PROB/SOLV PERS/REL...CONCPT 20 UN. PAGE 70 F1371
SOCIETY UNIV ATTIT NEW/IDEA

S67

KRAUS J.,"A MARXIST IN GHANA." GHANA ELITES CHIEF PROB/SOLV TEC/DEV DIPLOM ECO/TAC COLONIAL PARTIC PWR 20 NKRUMAH/K. PAGE 73 F1432
MARXISM PLAN ATTIT CREATE

S67

LAZUTKIN Y.,"SOCIALISM AND SPARE TIME." ECO/DEV WORKER CREATE TEC/DEV ROUTINE TIME. PAGE 76 F1497
LEISURE PRODUC SOCISM SOCIALIST

S67

MEHTA A.,"INDIA* POVERTY AND CHANGE." STRATA INDUS CREATE ECO/TAC FOR/AID NEUTRAL GP/REL ADJUST INCOME ...NEW/IDEA 20. PAGE 89 F1746
INDIA SOCIETY ECO/UNDEV TEC/DEV

S67

PENNEY N.,"BANK STATEMENTS, CANCELLED CHECKS, AND ARTICLE FOUR IN THE ELECTRONIC AGE." USA+45 TEC/DEV COST EFFICIENCY WEALTH. PAGE 104 F2056
CREATE LAW ADJUD FINAN

S67

PLOTT C.R.,"A NOTION OF EQUILIBRIUM AND ITS POSSIBILITY UNDER MAJORITY RULE." CREATE...DECISION STAT CHARTS 20. PAGE 106 F2094
SIMUL EQUILIB CHOOSE MAJORITY

S67

WILES P.J.,"THE POLITICAL AND SOCIAL PREREQUISITES FOR A SOVIET-TYPE ECONOMY." COM USSR LAW CULTURE CREATE ADMIN FEEDBACK ROUTINE COST OPTIMAL TOTALISM MARXISM 20. PAGE 146 F2883
ECO/DEV PLAN EX/STRUC EFFICIENCY

N67
US HOUSE,MESSAGE FROM THE PRESIDENT OF THE UNITED STATES: URBAN AND RURAL POVERTY (PAMPHLET). USA+45 ACT/RES PLAN BUDGET RENT MUNICH 20 PRESIDENT. PAGE 136 F2685 — NAT/G POLICY CREATE RECEIVE

N67
US HOUSE COMM GOVT OPERATIONS,FEDERALLY FINANCED SOCIAL RESEARCH, EXPENDITURES, STATUS, AND OBJECTIVES (PAMPHLET). WOR+45 CREATE LEAD GP/REL ATTIT...GEOG PSY SOC. PAGE 137 F2700 — ACT/RES NAT/G GIVE BUDGET

N67
US HOUSE COMM SCI ASTRONAUT,GOVERNMENT, SCIENCE, AND INTERNATIONAL POLICY (PAMPHLET). INDIA NETHERLAND ECO/DEV ECO/UNDEV R+D ACADEM PLAN DIPLOM FOR/AID CONFER...PREDICT 20 CHINJAP. PAGE 137 F2705 — NAT/G POLICY CREATE TEC/DEV

B95
SELIGMAN E.R.A.,ESSAYS IN TAXATION. NEW/ZEALND PRUSSIA UK USA-45 MARKET LOC/G CREATE PRICE CONTROL INCOME OWN WEALTH...GOV/COMP METH/COMP 19. PAGE 119 F2349 — TAX TARIFFS INDUS NAT/G

CREDIT....CREDIT

CRIME....SEE ALSO ANOMIE

B12
FOUAD M.,LE REGIME DE LA PRESSE EN EGYPTE: THESE POUR LE DOCTORAT. UAR LICENSE EDU/PROP ADMIN SANCTION CRIME SUPEGO PWR...ART/METH JURID 19/20. PAGE 43 F0832 — ORD/FREE LEGIS CONTROL PRESS

B24
HOLDSWORTH W.S.,A HISTORY OF ENGLISH LAW; THE COMMON LAW AND ITS RIVALS (VOL. IV). UK SEA AGRI CHIEF ADJUD CONTROL CRIME GOV/REL...INT/LAW JURID NAT/COMP 16/17 PARLIAMENT COMMON/LAW CANON/LAW ENGLSH/LAW. PAGE 61 F1195 — LAW LEGIS CT/SYS CONSTN

B37
COLE W.E.,RECENT TRENDS IN RURAL PLANNING. USA-45 LAW ECO/DEV LOC/G SECT EDU/PROP CRIME LEISURE AGE/Y HABITAT...SOC/WK MUNICH 20. PAGE 26 F0503 — AGRI NEIGH PLAN ACT/RES

B40
SPENCER H.,THE MAN VS. THE STATE (1892). UK POL/PAR LEGIS TARIFFS COERCE CRIME REPRESENT PWR SOCISM ...POLICY GEN/LAWS 19/20. PAGE 124 F2450 — FASCISM POPULISM LAISSEZ ORD/FREE

B48
KEIR D.L.,CASES IN CONSTITUTIONAL LAW. UK CHIEF LEGIS DIPLOM TAX PARL/PROC CRIME GOV/REL...INT/LAW JURID 17/20. PAGE 70 F1368 — CONSTN LAW ADJUD CT/SYS

B49
LEE A.M.,SOCIAL PROBLEMS IN AMERICA: A SOURCE BOOK. STRATA STRUCT KIN NEIGH VOL/ASSN ACT/RES LEAD CRIME AGE SEX 20. PAGE 77 F1504 — SOC SOCIETY PERSON EDU/PROP

B56
ABELS J.,THE TRUMAN SCANDALS. USA+45 USA-45 POL/PAR TAX LEGIT CT/SYS CHOOSE PRIVIL MORAL WEALTH 20 TRUMAN/HS PRESIDENT CONGRESS. PAGE 2 F0031 — CRIME ADMIN CHIEF TRIBUTE

B56
YUAN TUNG-LI,ECONOMIC AND SOCIAL DEVELOPMENT OF MODERN CHINA: A BIBLIOGRAPHIC GUIDE. COM/IND FINAN FAM LABOR SECT CRIME INCOME...STAT SAMP CON/ANAL. PAGE 150 F2954 — BIBLIOG ASIA ECO/UNDEV SOC

B58
OGDEN F.D.,THE POLL TAX IN THE SOUTH. USA+45 USA-45 CONSTN ADJUD ADMIN PARTIC CRIME...TIME/SEQ GOV/COMP METH/COMP 18/20 SOUTH/US. PAGE 101 F1982 — TAX CHOOSE RACE/REL DISCRIM

B58
TAFT P.,CORRUPTION AND RACKETEERING IN THE LABOR MOVEMENT (PAMPHLET). ADMIN SANCTION CENTRAL ROLE WEALTH...POLICY CLASSIF. PAGE 128 F2525 — LABOR INGP/REL GP/REL CRIME

B60
BOHM F.,REDEN UND SCHRIFTEN UBER DIE ORDNUNG EINER FREIEN GESELLSCHAFT, EINER FREIEN WIRTSCHAFT, UND UBER DIE WIEDERGUTMACH. DIPLOM CRIME ORD/FREE RESPECT FASCISM 20 NAZI. PAGE 16 F0307 — ECO/TAC NEW/LIB SUPEGO REPAR

B61
INTL UNION LOCAL AUTHORITIES,METROPOLIS. WOR+45 DIST/IND FINAN GIVE EDU/PROP CRIME COST HEALTH WEALTH MUNICH 20. PAGE 65 F1286 — GOV/COMP LOC/G BIBLIOG

B61
NEW JERSEY LEGISLATURE-SENATE,PUBLIC HEARINGS BEFORE COMMITTEE ON REVISION AND AMENDMENT OF LAWS ON SENATE BILL NO. 8. USA+45 FINAN PROVS WORKER ACT/RES PLAN BUDGET TAX CRIME...IDEA/COMP MUNICH 20 NEW/JERSEY URBAN/RNWL. PAGE 98 F1919 — LEGIS INDUS PROB/SOLV

B62
GWYN W.B.,DEMOCRACY AND THE COST OF POLITICS IN BRITAIN. UK BUDGET CRIME CHOOSE ORD/FREE WEALTH ...TIME/SEQ 18/20. PAGE 52 F1017 — COST POL/PAR POPULISM PAY

B62
MCCLELLAN J.L.,CRIME WITHOUT PUNISHMENT. USA+45 LAW SOCIETY DELIB/GP TRIBUTE CONTROL LOBBY COERCE GP/REL ANOMIE MORAL...CRIMLGY 20 CONGRESS HOFFA/J. PAGE 88 F1718 — CRIME ACT/RES LABOR PWR

B63
BATES J.L.,THE ORIGINS OF TEAPOT DOME: PROGRESSIVES, PARTIES, AND PETROLEUM, 1909-1921. USA-45 INDUS LG/CO POL/PAR DELIB/GP CONTROL GOV/REL CONSERVE...BIBLIOG 20 NAVY. PAGE 11 F0209 — EXTR/IND CRIME NAT/G

B66
EBONY,THE NEGRO HANDBOOK. ACADEM LABOR LOC/G SECT FORCES WORKER CT/SYS CRIME DISCRIM ORD/FREE...BIOG SOC/INTEG 19/20 NEGRO CIV/RIGHTS. PAGE 36 F0692 — RACE/REL EDU/PROP LAW STAT

B66
MC CONNELL J.P.,LAW AND BUSINESS: PATTERNS AND ISSUES IN COMMERCIAL LAW. USA+45 USA-45 LOC/G WORKER LICENSE CRIME REPRESENT GP/REL 20. PAGE 87 F1713 — ECO/DEV JURID ADJUD MGT

B67
SCHAEFER W.V.,THE SUSPECT AND SOCIETY: CRIMINAL PROCEDURE AND CONVERGING CONSTITUTIONAL DOCTRINES. USA+45 TEC/DEV LOBBY ROUTINE SANCTION...INT 20. PAGE 116 F2288 — CRIME FORCES CONSTN JURID

L67
SEABERG G.P.,"THE DRUG ABUSE PROBLEMS AND SOME PROPOSALS." UK USA+45 MARKET SANCTION CRIME ...POLICY NEW/IDEA. PAGE 119 F2339 — BIO/SOC LAW ADJUD PROB/SOLV

S67
HALL B.,"THE PAINTER'S UNION: A PARTIAL VICTORY." USA+45 PROB/SOLV LEGIT ADMIN REPRESENT 20. PAGE 53 F1043 — LABOR CHIEF CHOOSE CRIME

S67
SCHELLING T.C.,"ECONOMICS AND CRIMINAL ENTERPRISE." LAW FORCES BARGAIN ECO/TAC CONTROL GAMBLE ROUTINE ADJUST DEMAND INCOME PROFIT CRIMLGY. PAGE 116 F2295 — CRIME PROB/SOLV CONCPT

B76
PROUDHON P.J.,WHAT IS PROPERTY? (TRANS. BY B.R. TUCKER). SOCIETY AGRI CAP/ISM CRIME GP/REL PERSON MORAL ORD/FREE WEALTH. PAGE 108 F2127 — OWN WORKER PRODUC ANARCH

B86
O'CONNOR T.P.,THE PARNELL MOVEMENT: WITH A SKETCH OF IRISH PARTIES FROM 1843. IRELAND UK USA-45 LEGIS WORKER ECO/TAC COERCE CRIME REV CHOOSE ORD/FREE CATHISM LAISSEZ...SOC 19/20 PARLIAMENT PARNELL/CS LAND/LEAG. PAGE 100 F1957 — LEAD DOMIN POL/PAR POLICY

CRIMINOLOGY....SEE CRIMLGY

CRIMLGY....CRIMINOLOGY

B62
MCCLELLAN J.L.,CRIME WITHOUT PUNISHMENT. USA+45 LAW SOCIETY DELIB/GP TRIBUTE CONTROL LOBBY COERCE GP/REL ANOMIE MORAL...CRIMLGY 20 CONGRESS HOFFA/J. PAGE 88 F1718 — CRIME ACT/RES LABOR PWR

S67
SCHELLING T.C.,"ECONOMICS AND CRIMINAL ENTERPRISE." LAW FORCES BARGAIN ECO/TAC CONTROL GAMBLE ROUTINE ADJUST DEMAND INCOME PROFIT CRIMLGY. PAGE 116 F2295 — CRIME PROB/SOLV CONCPT

CRIMNL/LAW....CRIMINAL LAW

CROKER F.P.U. F0553

CROMER EARL OF F0554

CROMWELL/O....OLIVER CROMWELL

CROOK W.H. F0555

CROS L. F0556

CROSSER P.K. F0557

CROSS-PRESSURES .... SEE ROLE

CROWD....MOB BEHAVIOR, MASS BEHAVIOR

B64
NOVACK D.E.,DEVELOPMENT AND SOCIETY; THE DYNAMICS OF ECONOMIC CHANGE. WOR+45 STRATA STRUCT ECO/TAC CONTROL CROWD REV GP/REL ADJUST PRODUC WEALTH PSY. PAGE 99 F1940 — SOCIETY CULTURE SOC ECO/UNDEV

B65
CRANE E.,MARKETING COMMUNICATION: A BEHAVIORAL APPROACH TO MEN, MESSAGES, AND MEDIA. STRATA R+D VOL/ASSN CROWD DRIVE PERSON SKILL WEALTH. PAGE 28 F0551 — EDU/PROP MARKET PERCEPT ATTIT

B66
FRANCK L.R.,LA POLITIQUE ECONOMIQUE DES ETATS-UNIS. USA+45 USA-45 FINAN INDUS CONTROL CROWD GOV/REL — NAT/G INT/TRADE

GP/REL...POLICY SOC CHARTS 18/20. PAGE 43 F0841 — GEOG

B66
JACKSON G.D.,COMINTERN AND PEASANT IN EAST EUROPE 1919-1930. BULGARIA COM CZECHOSLVK EUR+WWI POLAND ROMANIA YUGOSLAVIA STRATA AGRI VOL/ASSN DIPLOM CONTROL CROWD WEALTH...POLICY NAT/COMP 20. PAGE 66 F1293 — MARXISM ECO/UNDEV WORKER INT/ORG

B67
BURDEN H.T.,THE NUREMBERG PARTY RALLIES 1923-39. GERMANY POL/PAR SECT CREATE DOMIN WAR ATTIT ...AUD/VIS FILM 20. PAGE 20 F0384 — EDU/PROP CONTROL CROWD TOTALISM

S67
JEDLICKI W.,"THE FREE SPEECH MOVEMENT IN WARSAW." POLAND FORCES EDU/PROP LEAD ATTIT MARXISM ...IDEA/COMP 20. PAGE 67 F1310 — COERCE CROWD ORD/FREE ACADEM

S67
LANGLEY L.D.,"THE DEMOCRATIC TRADITION AND MILITARY REFORM, 1878-1885." USA-45 SECT EDU/PROP CROWD EFFICIENCY NAT/LISM 19 INDIAN/AM. PAGE 75 F1480 — ATTIT FORCES POPULISM

CROWDER M. F0558

CROWE H.P. F0503

CROWE S. F0559

CRUMP/ED....EDWARD H. CRUMP

CRUSADES....CRUSADES, CRUSADERS OF HOLY WARS;

CT/APPEALS....COURT OF APPEALS AND APPELLATE COURT SYSTEM

CT/SYS....COURT SYSTEMS

N
NEW JERSEY STATE OF,SECOND REPORT TO GOVERNOR, SENATE, ASSEMBLY BY UNIFORM COMMERCIAL CODE STUDY COMMISSION. USA+45 INDUS LOC/G NAT/G PROF/ORG CONSULT ACT/RES LEGIT CT/SYS ATTIT NEW/JERSEY. PAGE 98 F1920 — LAW FINAN CENTRAL PROVS

N
US SUPERINTENDENT OF DOCUMENTS,TARIFF AND TAXATION (PRICE LIST 37). USA+45 LAW INT/TRADE ADJUD ADMIN CT/SYS INCOME OWN...DECISION GATT. PAGE 140 F2754 — BIBLIOG/A TAX TARIFFS NAT/G

N19
FAHRNKOPF N.,STATE AND LOCAL GOVERNMENT IN ILLINOIS (PAMPHLET). CONSTN ADMIN PARTIC CHOOSE REPRESENT GOV/REL...JURID MGT 20 ILLINOIS. PAGE 39 F0759 — BIBLIOG LOC/G LEGIS CT/SYS

N19
LAWRENCE S.A.,THE BATTERY ADDITIVE CONTROVERSY (PAMPHLET). USA+45 LAW MARKET PROC/MFG R+D CAP/ISM CT/SYS GOV/REL OWN FTC CONGRESS BUR/STNDRD RITCHIE/JM. PAGE 76 F1494 — PHIL/SCI LOBBY INSPECT

B24
HOLDSWORTH W.S.,A HISTORY OF ENGLISH LAW; THE COMMON LAW AND ITS RIVALS (VOL. VI). AFR UK STRATA EX/STRUC ADJUD ADMIN CONTROL CT/SYS...JURID CONCPT GEN/LAWS 17 PARLIAMENT ENGLSH/LAW COMMON/LAW. PAGE 61 F1194 — LAW CONSTN LEGIS CHIEF

B24
HOLDSWORTH W.S.,A HISTORY OF ENGLISH LAW; THE COMMON LAW AND ITS RIVALS (VOL. IV). UK SEA AGRI CHIEF ADJUD CONTROL CRIME GOV/REL...INT/LAW JURID NAT/COMP 16/17 PARLIAMENT COMMON/LAW CANON/LAW ENGLSH/LAW. PAGE 61 F1195 — LAW LEGIS CT/SYS CONSTN

B25
MATHEWS J.M.,AMERICAN STATE GOVERNMENT. USA-45 LOC/G CHIEF EX/STRUC LEGIS ADJUD CONTROL CT/SYS ROUTINE GOV/REL PWR 20 GOVERNOR. PAGE 87 F1703 — PROVS ADMIN FEDERAL CONSTN

B28
FRANKFURTER F.,THE BUSINESS OF THE SUPREME COURT; A STUDY IN THE FEDERAL JUDICIAL SYSTEM. USA-45 CONSTN EX/STRUC PROB/SOLV GP/REL ATTIT PWR...POLICY JURID 18/20 SUPREME/CT CONGRESS. PAGE 43 F0848 — CT/SYS ADJUD LAW FEDERAL

B30
GREEN F.M.,CONSTITUTIONAL DEVELOPMENT IN THE SOUTH ATLANTIC STATES, 1776-1860; A STUDY IN THE EVOLUTION OF DEMOCRACY. USA-45 ELITES SOCIETY STRATA ECO/DEV AGRI POL/PAR EX/STRUC LEGIS CT/SYS REGION...BIBLIOG 18/19 MARYLAND VIRGINIA GEORGIA NORTH/CAR SOUTH/CAR. PAGE 50 F0984 — CONSTN PROVS PLURISM REPRESENT

B37
HAMILTON W.H.,THE POWER TO GOVERN. ECO/DEV FINAN INDUS ECO/TAC INT/TRADE TARIFFS TAX CONTROL CT/SYS WAR COST PWR 18/20 SUPREME/CT. PAGE 54 F1056 — LING CONSTN NAT/G POLICY

B37
UNION OF SOUTH AFRICA,REPORT CONCERNING ADMINISTRATION OF SOUTH WEST AFRICA (6 VOLS.). SOUTH/AFR INDUS PUB/INST FORCES LEGIS BUDGET DIPLOM EDU/PROP ADJUD CT/SYS...GEOG CHARTS 20 AFRICA/SW LEAGUE/NAT. PAGE 132 F2610 — NAT/G ADMIN COLONIAL CONSTN

B40
HELLMAN F.S.,THE NEW DEAL: SELECTED LIST OF REFERENCES. USA-45 FINAN LABOR EX/STRUC CREATE INT/TRADE ADMIN CT/SYS 20 SUPREME/CT. PAGE 58 F1145 — BIBLIOG/A ECO/TAC PLAN POLICY

B40
WUNDERLICH F.,LABOR UNDER GERMAN DEMOCRACY, ARBITRATION 1918-1933. GERMANY NAT/G PAY REPAR ADJUD CT/SYS GP/REL...MAJORIT 20. PAGE 149 F2941 — LABOR WORKER INDUS BARGAIN

B42
ROBBINS J.J.,THE GOVERNMENT OF LABOR RELATIONS IN SWEDEN. SWEDEN LAW CONSTN ADJUD CT/SYS GP/REL ...JURID 20. PAGE 112 F2200 — NAT/G BARGAIN LABOR INDUS

B48
KEIR D.L.,CASES IN CONSTITUTIONAL LAW. UK CHIEF LEGIS DIPLOM TAX PARL/PROC CRIME GOV/REL...INT/LAW JURID 17/20. PAGE 70 F1368 — CONSTN LAW ADJUD CT/SYS

B52
JENNINGS W.I.,CONSTITUTIONAL LAWS OF THE COMMONWEALTH. AFR UK LAW CHIEF LEGIS TAX CT/SYS PARL/PROC GOV/REL...INT/LAW 18/20 ENGLSH/LAW COMMON/LAW. PAGE 67 F1316 — CONSTN JURID ADJUD COLONIAL

B56
ABELS J.,THE TRUMAN SCANDALS. USA+45 USA-45 POL/PAR TAX LEGIT CT/SYS CHOOSE PRIVIL MORAL WEALTH 20 TRUMAN/HS PRESIDENT CONGRESS. PAGE 2 F0031 — CRIME ADMIN CHIEF TRIBUTE

B58
CUNNINGHAM W.B.,COMPULSORY CONCILIATION AND COLLECTIVE BARGAINING. CANADA NAT/G LEGIS ADJUD CT/SYS GP/REL...MGT 20 NEW/BRUNS STRIKE CASEBOOK. PAGE 29 F0563 — POLICY BARGAIN LABOR INDUS

B58
PALMER E.E.,THE ECONOMY AND THE DEMOCRATIC IDEAL. USA+45 USA-45 STRATA CHIEF CT/SYS ORD/FREE SOCISM ...MAJORIT CONCPT ANTHOL 18/20 PRESIDENT. PAGE 103 F2021 — ECO/DEV POPULISM METH/COMP ECO/TAC

B59
VOSE C.E.,CAUCASIANS ONLY: THE SUPREME COURT, THE NAACP, AND THE RESTRICTIVE COVENANT CASES. USA+45 LAW CONSTN LOBBY...SOC 20 NAACP SUPREME/CT NEGRO. PAGE 142 F2796 — CT/SYS RACE/REL DISCRIM

B60
MENDELSON W.,CAPITALISM, DEMOCRACY, AND THE SUPREME COURT. USA+45 USA-45 CONSTN DIPLOM GOV/REL ATTIT ORD/FREE LAISSEZ...POLICY CHARTS PERS/COMP 18/20 SUPREME/CT MARSHALL/J HOLMES/OW TANEY/RB FIELD/JJ. PAGE 90 F1758 — JUDGE CT/SYS JURID NAT/G

B61
CARROTHERS A.W.R.,LABOR ARBITRATION IN CANADA. CANADA LAW NAT/G CONSULT LEGIS WORKER ADJUD ADMIN CT/SYS 20. PAGE 22 F0422 — LABOR MGT GP/REL BARGAIN

B62
INTERNAT CONGRESS OF JURISTS,EXECUTIVE ACTION AND THE RULE OF RULE: REPORTION PROCEEDINGS OF INT'T CONGRESS OF JURISTS,-RIO DE JANEIRO, BRAZIL. WOR+45 ACADEM CONSULT JUDGE EDU/PROP ADJUD CT/SYS INGP/REL PERSON DEPT/DEFEN. PAGE 64 F1269 — JURID EXEC ORD/FREE CONTROL

B63
BOWIE R.R.,GOVERNMENT REGULATION OF BUSINESS: CASES FROM THE NATIONAL REPORTER SYSTEM. USA+45 USA-45 NAT/G ECO/TAC ADJUD...ANTHOL 19/20 SUPREME/CT FTC FAIR/LABOR MONOPOLY. PAGE 17 F0331 — LAW CONTROL INDUS CT/SYS

B63
CORLEY R.N.,THE LEGAL ENVIRONMENT OF BUSINESS. CONSTN LEGIS TAX ADMIN CT/SYS DISCRIM ATTIT PWR ...TREND 18/20. PAGE 28 F0537 — NAT/G INDUS JURID DECISION

B63
PRITCHETT C.H.,THE THIRD BRANCH OF GOVERNMENT. USA+45 USA-45 CONSTN SOCIETY INDUS SECT LEGIS JUDGE PROB/SOLV GOV/REL 20 SUPREME/CT CHURCH/STA. PAGE 108 F2122 — JURID NAT/G ADJUD CT/SYS

B64
HAAR C.M.,LAW AND LAND: ANGLO-AMERICAN PLANNING PRACTICE. UK USA+45 NAT/G TEC/DEV BUDGET CT/SYS INGP/REL EFFICIENCY OWN...JURID MUNICH 20. PAGE 52 F1019 — LAW PLAN NAT/COMP

B64
HALLOWELL J.H.,DEVELOPMENT: FOR WHAT. WOR+45 POL/PAR SECT FOR/AID INT/TRADE CT/SYS PARTIC PRODUC PLURISM. PAGE 54 F1052 — ECO/UNDEV CONSTN NAT/LISM ECO/TAC

B64
MANN B.,STATE CONSTITUTIONAL RESTRICTIONS ON LOCAL BORROWING AND PROPERTY TAXING POWERS. USA+45 CONSTN PROVS CT/SYS GOV/REL PWR...DECISION JURID CHARTS 20. PAGE 84 F1654 — LOC/G TAX FINAN LAW

B64
STOESSINGER J.G.,FINANCING THE UNITED NATIONS SYSTEM. FUT WOR+45 CONSTN NAT/G VOL/ASSN DELIB/GP — FINAN INT/ORG

EX/STRUC ECO/TAC LEGIT CT/SYS PWR WEALTH...STAT TIME/SEQ TREND CHARTS TRUE/GP METH/GP TERR/GP VAL/FREE. PAGE 126 F2493

B64
TELLADO A.,A STATEMENT OF THE LAWS OF THE DOMINICAN REPUBLIC IN MATTERS AFFECTING BUSINESS (3RD ED.). DOMIN/REP AGRI DIST/IND EXTR/IND FINAN FAM WORKER ECO/TAC TAX CT/SYS MARRIAGE OWN...BIBLIOG 20 MIGRATION. PAGE 129 F2542
CONSTN LEGIS NAT/G INDUS

B64
WHEARE K.C.,FEDERAL GOVERNMENT (4TH ED.). WOR+45 WOR-45 POL/PAR LEGIS BAL/PWR CT/SYS...POLICY JURID CONCPT GOV/COMP 17/20. PAGE 145 F2866
FEDERAL CONSTN EX/STRUC NAT/COMP

B65
O'CONNELL D.P.,INTERNATIONAL LAW (2 VOLS.). WOR+45 WOR-45 ECO/DEV ECO/UNDEV INT/ORG NAT/G AGREE ...POLICY JURID CONCPT NAT/COMP 20 TREATY. PAGE 99 F1952
INT/LAW DIPLOM CT/SYS

B66
DUNCOMBE H.S.,COUNTY GOVERNMENT IN AMERICA. USA+45 FINAN ADMIN ROUTINE GOV/REL...GOV/COMP MUNICH 20. PAGE 35 F0678
LOC/G PROVS CT/SYS TOP/EX

B66
EBONY,THE NEGRO HANDBOOK. ACADEM LABOR LOC/G SECT FORCES WORKER CT/SYS CRIME DISCRIM ORD/FREE...BIOG SOC/INTEG 19/20 NEGRO CIV/RIGHTS. PAGE 36 F0692
RACE/REL EDU/PROP LAW STAT

B66
GREENE L.E.,GOVERNMENT IN TENNESSEE (2ND ED.). USA+45 DIST/IND INDUS POL/PAR EX/STRUC LEGIS PLAN BUDGET GIVE CT/SYS...MGT T 20 TENNESSEE. PAGE 51 F0989
PROVS LOC/G CONSTN ADMIN

B66
HAYS P.R.,LABOR ARBITRATION: A DISSENTING VIEW. USA+45 LAW DELIB/GP BARGAIN ADJUD...PREDICT 20. PAGE 57 F1126
GP/REL LABOR CONSULT CT/SYS

B66
WALTON S.D.,AMERICAN BUSINESS AND ITS ENVIRONMENT. USA+45 LAW CONSTN FINAN MARKET LOC/G EX/STRUC CT/SYS COST PRODUC...STAT 20. PAGE 143 F2813
PRICE PROFIT

B67
BUREAU NATIONAL AFFAIRS,LABOR RELATIONS REFERENCE MANUAL VOL. 63. USA+45 CONSTN ECO/DEV PROVS WORKER DEBATE INGP/REL...DECISION 20. PAGE 20 F0385
LABOR ADJUD CT/SYS NAT/G

B67
GRIPP R.C.,PATTERNS OF SOVIET POLITICS (REV. ED.). USSR LAW ELITES LOC/G PLAN CONTROL CT/SYS CHOOSE ...POLICY BIBLIOG/A DICTIONARY 9/20. PAGE 51 F1003
COM ADJUD POL/PAR

B67
LYTLE C.M.,THE WARREN COURT AND ITS CRITICS. USA+45 NAT/G PROVS FORCES LOBBY RACE/REL DISCRIM SOVEREIGN 20 SUPREME/CT WARRN/EARL. PAGE 83 F1618
CT/SYS ADJUD PROB/SOLV ATTIT

B67
SPICER G.W.,THE SUPREME COURT AND FUNDAMENTAL FREEDOMS (2ND ED.). USA+45 CONSTN SOCIETY ATTIT 20 SUPREME/CT. PAGE 124 F2454
CT/SYS JURID CONTROL ORD/FREE

L67
"GOVERNMENT CONTROL OF LAND: PROTECTING THE I-KNOW-IT-WHENI-SEE-IT INTEREST." USA+45 LAW CONSTN DELIB/GP CT/SYS HABITAT ILLINOIS. PAGE 2 F0026
PLAN LOC/G CONTROL ADJUD

L67
AFFELDT R.J.,"THE INDEPENDENT LABOR UNION AND THE GOOD LIFE." USA+45 ADJUD CONTROL SANCTION GP/REL ORD/FREE JURID. PAGE 3 F0045
LABOR CT/SYS PWR SOVEREIGN

L67
BERNHARD R.C.,"COMPETITION IN LAW AND ECONOMICS." LAW PLAN PRICE CONTROL PRODUC PROFIT...METH/CNCPT IDEA/COMP GEN/LAWS 20. PAGE 14 F0265
MARKET POLICY NAT/G CT/SYS

L67
JOHNSTON J.D. JR.,"CONSTITUTION OF SUBDIVISION CONTROL EXACTIONS: THE QUEST FOR A RATIONALE." USA+45 PROVS PUB/INST ADJUD CT/SYS GP/REL MUNICH. PAGE 68 F1334
PLAN CONTROL LOC/G FORCES

L67
MIXON J.,"JANE JACOBS AND THE LAW - ZONING FOR DIVERSITY EXAMINED." FUT USA+45 CONSTN NEIGH PROB/SOLV CONTROL CT/SYS PARTIC ATTIT...POLICY CENSUS METH/COMP MUNICH. PAGE 92 F1810
IDEA/COMP PLAN LAW

L67
PARKER G.P. JR.,"MONETARY RECOVERY UNDER THE FEDERAL LABOR STATUTES." USA+45 USA-45 INDUS ADJUD CT/SYS GOV/REL HEALTH ORD/FREE 20 DEPT/LABOR NLRB. PAGE 103 F2027
LABOR CONTROL LAW FINAN

L67
VIA J.W. JR.,"ANTITRUST AND THE AMENDED BANK MERGER AND HOLDING COMPANY ACTS: THE SEARCH FOR STANDARDS." USA+45 CONTROL GP/REL WEALTH SUPREME/CT. PAGE 141 F2783
FINAN CT/SYS LAW EX/STRUC

L67
WATKINS J.B.,"MONETARY RECOVERY UNDER FEDERAL ANTITRUST STATUTES." USA+45 PROB/SOLV ADJUD CT/SYS GOV/REL ORD/FREE 20. PAGE 144 F2831
LG/CO CONTROL LAW FINAN

S67
"ANTITRUST VENUE: TRANSACTING BUSINESS UNDER THE CLAYTON ACT." USA+45 DIST/IND PROB/SOLV ECO/TAC ADJUD CT/SYS 20. PAGE 2 F0028
LAW LG/CO CONTROL NAT/G

S67
AMERASINGHE C.F.,"SOME LEGAL PROBLEMS OF STATE TRADING IN SOUTHEAST ASIA." PROB/SOLV ADJUD CONTROL CT/SYS GP/REL 20. PAGE 5 F0084
INT/TRADE NAT/G INT/LAW PRIVIL

S67
BRAUCHER R.,"RECLAMATION OF GOODS FROM A FRAUDULENT BUYER." USA+45 CLIENT FINAN CT/SYS PERS/REL COST WEALTH. PAGE 18 F0341
LAW ADJUD GOV/REL INT/TRADE

S67
DEMUTH J.,"GE: PROFILE OF A CORPORATION." USA+45 USA-45 LABOR ACT/RES RATION EDU/PROP ADJUD CT/SYS FASCISM 20. PAGE 32 F0619
LG/CO CONSERVE PRICE

S67
FLOYD D.,"FIFTH AMENDMENT RIGHT TO COUNSEL IN FEDERAL INCOME TAX INVESTIGATIONS." USA+45 LAW OP/RES INGP/REL. PAGE 42 F0818
JURID CT/SYS TAX CONSULT

S67
KESTENBAUM L.,"PRIMARY JURISDICTION TO DECIDE ANTITRUST JURISDICTION* A PRACTICAL APPROACH TO THE ALLOCATION OF FUNCTIONS." USA+45 ECO/DEV INDUS VOL/ASSN ECO/TAC. PAGE 70 F1383
JURID CT/SYS LABOR ADJUD

S67
LEFCOE G.,"CONSTRUCTION LENDING AND THE EQUITABLE LIEN." LICENSE CT/SYS OWN...STAT 20. PAGE 77 F1510
CONSTRUC RENT ADJUD

S67
MITCHELL J.D.B.,"THE CONSTITUTIONAL IMPLICATIONS OF JUDICIAL CONTROL OF THE ADMINISTRATION IN THE UNITED KINGDOM." UK LAW ADJUD ADMIN GOV/REL ROLE ...GP/COMP 20. PAGE 92 F1808
CONSTN CT/SYS CONTROL EX/STRUC

S67
NILES J.G.,"CIVIL ACTIONS FOR DAMAGES UNDER THE FEDERAL CIVIL RIGHTS STATUTES." CONSTN FINAN ADJUD CT/SYS GOV/REL RACE/REL 20. PAGE 98 F1928
DISCRIM LAW CONTROL ORD/FREE

S67
PIERPONT J.R.,"NEW STAGE IN THE LONGSHORE STRUGGLE." USA+45 SENIOR ADJUD RACE/REL...JURID 20 NEGRO. PAGE 106 F2083
LABOR DISCRIM WORKER CT/SYS

S67
SEIDLER G.L.,"MARXIST LEGAL THOUGHT IN POLAND." POLAND SOCIETY R+D LOC/G NAT/G ACT/RES ADJUD CT/SYS SUPEGO PWR...SOC TREND 20 MARX/KARL. PAGE 119 F2343
MARXISM LAW CONCPT EFFICIENCY

S67
SKOLNICK J.H.,"SOCIAL CONTROL IN THE ADVERSARY SYSTEM." USA+45 CONSULT OP/RES ADMIN CONTROL. PAGE 123 F2419
PROB/SOLV PERS/REL ADJUD CT/SYS

CTS/WESTM....COURTS OF WESTMINSTER HALL

CUBA....SEE ALSO L/A+17C

B58
BUGEDA LANZAS J.,A STATEMENT OF THE LAWS OF CUBA IN MATTERS AFFECTING BUSINESS (2ND ED. REV., ENLARGED). CUBA L/A+17C LAW FINAN FAM LEGIS ACT/RES ADMIN GP/REL...BIBLIOG 20 OAS. PAGE 20 F0382
JURID NAT/G INDUS WORKER

B59
NUNEZ JIMENEZ A.,LA LIBERACION DE LAS ISLAS. CUBA L/A+17C USA+45 LAW CHIEF PLAN DIPLOM FOR/AID OWN WEALTH 20 CASTRO/F. PAGE 99 F1945
AGRI REV ECO/UNDEV NAT/G

B61
STARK H.,SOCIAL AND ECONOMIC FRONTIERS IN LATIN AMERICA (2ND ED.). CUBA FUT CULTURE AGRI INDUS ECO/TAC PRODUC ATTIT MARXISM...NAT/COMP BIBLIOG T 20. PAGE 125 F2470
L/A+17C SOCIETY DIPLOM ECO/UNDEV

B64
SEERS D.,CUBA: THE ECONOMIC AND SOCIAL REVOLUTION. L/A+17C USSR YUGOSLAVIA STRATA AGRI INDUS SCHOOL DELIB/GP PLAN ECO/TAC DOMIN EDU/PROP ATTIT RIGID/FLEX ALL/VALS...STAT OBS TIME/SEQ WORK VAL/FREE 20. PAGE 119 F2341
ACT/RES COERCE CUBA REV

S65
JOHNSON L.L.,"US BUSINESS INTERESTS IN CUBA AND THE RISE OF CASTRO." L/A+17C USA+45 ECO/UNDEV INDUS NAT/G VOL/ASSN ATTIT ORD/FREE PWR WEALTH ALL/PROG. PAGE 68 F1330
DIPLOM CUBA ECO/TAC INT/TRADE

B67
DINERSTEIN H.S.,INTERVENTION AGAINST COMMUNISM (STUDIES IN INTERNATIONAL AFFAIRS NO. 1). CUBA DOMIN/REP GREECE USA+45 USSR VIETNAM OP/RES COERCE WAR 20. PAGE 33 F0643 MARXISM DIPLOM NAT/LISM

L67
MACDONALD R.S.J.,"THE RESORT TO ECONOMIC COERCION BY INTERNATIONAL POLITICAL ORGANIZATIONS." CUBA ETHIOPIA RHODESIA SOUTH/AFR NAT/G FOR/AID INT/TRADE DOMIN CONTROL SANCTION...DECISION LEAGUE/NAT UN OAS 20. PAGE 83 F1625 INT/ORG COERCE ECO/TAC DIPLOM

S67
ALEXANDER R.J.,"'THIRD FORCE' IN WORLD COMMUNISM?" CHINA/COM CUBA USSR INT/ORG DIPLOM TASK INGP/REL ATTIT PWR 20 CASTRO/F. PAGE 3 F0060 CHIEF MARXISM LEAD REV

S67
GONZALEZ M.P.,"CUBA, UNA REVOLUCION EN MARCHA." CUBA L/A+17C USA+45 VIETNAM ECO/UNDEV FORCES DIPLOM DOMIN...POLICY MARXIST NAT/COMP CASTRO/F. PAGE 48 F0946 REV NAT/G COLONIAL SOVEREIGN

S67
IBARRA J.,"EL EXPERIMENTO CUBANO." COM CUBA L/A+17C USA+45 ECO/UNDEV LEGIS INT/TRADE CONTROL REV NAT/LISM PWR 19/20 TREATY. PAGE 64 F1259 COLONIAL DIPLOM NAT/G POLICY

S67
REILLY T.J.,"FREEZING AND CONFISCATION OF CUBAN PROPERTY." CUBA USA+45 LAW DIPLOM LEGIT ADJUD CONTROL. PAGE 111 F2177 STRANGE OWN ECO/TAC

N67
US HOUSE COMM FOREIGN AFFAIRS,COMMUNIST ACTIVITIES IN LATIN AMERICA 1967 (PAMPHLET). CUBA USA+45 DIPLOM INT/TRADE EDU/PROP COERCE GUERRILLA HOUSE/REP OAS. PAGE 137 F2696 L/A+17C MARXISM ORD/FREE ECO/TAC

CUBAN CRISIS....SEE INT/REL+APPROPRIATE NATIONS+COLD WAR

CUCCORESE H.J. F0560

CULTS....SEE SECT

CULTUR/REV....CULTURAL REVOLUTION IN CHINA

CULTURE....CULTURAL PATTERNS

N
THE MIDDLE EAST AND NORTH AFRICA. AFR ISLAM CULTURE ECO/UNDEV AGRI NAT/G TEC/DEV FOR/AID INT/TRADE EDU/PROP...CHARTS 20. PAGE 1 F0008 INDEX INDUS FINAN STAT

N
THE MIDDLE EAST. CULTURE...BIOG BIBLIOG. PAGE 1 F0010 ISLAM INDUS FINAN

N
DEUTSCHE BUCHEREI,DEUTSCHES BUCHERVERZEICHNIS. GERMANY LAW CULTURE POL/PAR ADMIN LEAD ATTIT PERSON ...SOC 20. PAGE 32 F0626 BIBLIOG NAT/G DIPLOM ECO/DEV

N
US LIBRARY OF CONGRESS,SOUTHERN ASIA ACCESSIONS LIST. BURMA CEYLON INDIA NEPAL PAKISTAN S/ASIA THAILAND AGRI INDUS SCHOOL WORKER...ART/METH GEOG HEAL PHIL/SCI LING 20. PAGE 137 F2710 BIBLIOG/A SOCIETY CULTURE ECO/UNDEV

NCO
STOLPER W.,"SOCIAL FACTORS IN ECONOMIC PLANNING, WITH SPECIAL REFERENCE TO NIGERIA" AFR NIGER CULTURE FAM SECT RECEIVE ETIQUET ADMIN DEMAND 20. PAGE 126 F2494 ECO/UNDEV PLAN ADJUST RISK

B00
MILL J.S.,PRINCIPLES OF POLITICAL ECONOMY. WOR-45 CULTURE SOCIETY STRATA ECO/DEV AGRI EXTR/IND FINAN INDUS DELIB/GP ECO/TAC WEALTH...CONCPT MATH TREND 20. PAGE 91 F1786 MARKET INT/ORG INT/TRADE

B14
HOBSON J.A.,WORK AND WEALTH. CULTURE FINAN INDUS WORKER TEC/DEV ECO/TAC GIVE PAY PRICE COST PRODUC UTIL. PAGE 60 F1185 WEALTH INCOME GEN/LAWS

S21
MALINOWSKI B.,"THE PRIMITIVE ECONOMICS OF THE TROBRIAND ISLANDERS" (BMR)" CULTURE SOCIETY NAT/G CHIEF LEAD OWN...SOC MYTH WORSHIP 20 NEW/GUINEA TROBRIAND RESOURCE/N. PAGE 84 F1647 ECO/UNDEV AGRI PRODUC STRUCT

B22
VON ENGELIN O.D.,INHERITING THE EARTH, THE GEOGRAPHICAL FACTOR IN NATIONAL DEVELOPMENT. WOR-45 CULTURE DIPLOM BIO/SOC HABITAT PERSON...PSY SOC CONCPT IDEA/COMP. PAGE 142 F2791 INGP/REL GEOG SOCIETY ROLE

B26
MCPHEE A.,THE ECONOMIC REVOLUTION IN BRITISH WEST AFRICA. AFR UK CULTURE DIST/IND FINAN INDUS PLAN GP/REL RACE/REL 20 AFRICA/W. PAGE 88 F1735 ECO/UNDEV INT/TRADE COLONIAL GEOG

B26
SUFRIN S.C.,A BRIEF ANNOTATED BIBLIOGRAPHY ON LABOR IN EMERGING SOCIETIES. WOR+45 CULTURE SOCIETY INDUS EDU/PROP GP/REL INGP/REL. PAGE 127 F2510 BIBLIOG/A LABOR ECO/UNDEV WORKER

B26
TAWNEY R.H.,RELIGION AND THE RISE OF CAPITALISM. UK CULTURE NAT/G TEC/DEV OWN LAISSEZ...POLICY SOC TIME/SEQ 16/19. PAGE 129 F2537 SECT WEALTH INDUS CAP/ISM

B27
BELLOC H.,THE SERVILE STATE (1912) (3RD ED.). PRUSSIA UK CULTURE STRATA INDUS NAT/G ECO/TAC CONTROL LEAD SUFF DISCRIM EQUILIB ORD/FREE WEALTH 20. PAGE 12 F0237 WORKER CAP/ISM DOMIN CATH

B27
SIEGFRIED A.,AMERICA COMES OF AGE: A FRENCH ANALYSIS (TRANS. BY H.H. HEMMING AND DORIS HEMMING). FRANCE UK POL/PAR WORKER TEC/DEV DIPLOM REGION RACE/REL ADJUST PRODUC HEREDITY...TIME/SEQ GP/COMP SOC/INTEG 20 DEMOCRAT REPUBLICAN KKK. PAGE 122 F2398 USA-45 CULTURE ECO/DEV SOC

B33
TANNENBAUM F.,PEACE BY REVOLUTION. ECO/UNDEV AGRI SECT WORKER DIPLOM EDU/PROP DISCRIM OWN WEALTH POPULISM 17/20 MEXIC/AMER INDIAN/AM. PAGE 128 F2532 CULTURE COLONIAL RACE/REL REV

B38
CARVALHO C.M.,GEOGRAPHIA HUMANA; POLITICA E ECONOMICA (3RD ED.). BRAZIL CULTURE AGRI INDUS DIPLOM COLONIAL GP/REL RACE/REL...LING 20 RESOURCE/N. PAGE 22 F0424 GEOG HABITAT

B38
HOBSON J.A.,IMPERIALISM. MOD/EUR UK WOR-45 CULTURE ECO/UNDEV NAT/G VOL/ASSN PLAN EDU/PROP LEGIT REGION COERCE ATTIT PWR...POLICY PLURIST TIME/SEQ GEN/LAWS TERR/GP 19/20. PAGE 60 F1187 DOMIN ECO/TAC BAL/PWR COLONIAL

B39
ENGELS F.,HERRN EUGEN DUHRING'S REVOLUTION IN SCIENCE (1878). CULTURE STRATA STRUCT FAM SECT ECO/TAC REV WAR SOCISM...MARXIST 19. PAGE 37 F0731 PWR SOCIETY WEALTH GEN/LAWS

B39
FIRTH R.,PRIMITIVE POLYNESIAN ECONOMY. SOCIETY DIST/IND SECT CHIEF CAP/ISM PRODUC WEALTH...SOC OBS METH WORSHIP 20 POLYNESIA. PAGE 41 F0802 ECO/UNDEV CULTURE AGRI ECO/TAC

B39
FURNIVALL J.S.,NETHERLANDS INDIA. INDIA NETHERLAND CULTURE INDUS NAT/G DIPLOM ADMIN WEALTH...POLICY CHARTS 17/20. PAGE 45 F0876 COLONIAL ECO/UNDEV SOVEREIGN PLURISM

B40
MEEK C.K.,EUROPE AND WEST AFRICA. AFR EUR+WWI EXTR/IND DIPLOM INT/TRADE EDU/PROP GP/REL...SOC 20. PAGE 89 F1743 CULTURE TEC/DEV ECO/UNDEV COLONIAL

B44
FABIAN SOCIETY,CAN PLANNING BE DEMOCRATIC? UK CULTURE INDUS NAT/G BUDGET ORD/FREE...GEN/LAWS ANTHOL 20. PAGE 39 F0757 PLAN MAJORIT SOCIALIST ECO/DEV

B47
HEILPERIN M.A.,THE TRADE OF NATIONS. USA+45 USA-45 WOR+45 WOR-45 CULTURE ECO/DEV NAT/G DELIB/GP EDU/PROP ATTIT DISPL ORD/FREE PWR WEALTH TOT/POP 20. PAGE 58 F1139 MARKET INT/ORG INT/TRADE PEACE

B47
ISAAC J.,ECONOMICS OF MIGRATION. MOD/EUR CULTURE STRATA STRUCT NAT/G COLONIAL WEALTH...OLD/LIB TREND TIME 19/20 EUROPE/W MIGRATION. PAGE 65 F1289 HABITAT SOC GEOG

B48
CLYDE P.H.,THE FAR EAST: A HISTORY OF THE IMPACT OF THE WEST ON EASTERN ASIA. CHINA/COM CULTURE INT/TRADE DOMIN COLONIAL WAR PWR...CHARTS BIBLIOG 19/20 CHINJAP. PAGE 25 F0494 DIPLOM ASIA

B48
WHITE C.L.,HUMAN GEOGRAPHY: AN ECOLOGICAL STUDY OF GEOGRAPHY. UNIV SEA CULTURE AGRI EXTR/IND RACE/REL PRODUC...CHARTS HYPO/EXP SIMUL GEN/LAWS T. PAGE 146 F2868 SOC HABITAT GEOG SOCIETY

B49
PELZER K.J.,SELECTED BIBLIOGRAPHY ON THE GEOGRAPHY OF SOUTHEAST ASIA (3 VOLS., 1949-1956). PHILIPPINE CULTURE...SOC 20 MALAYA. PAGE 104 F2053 BIBLIOG S/ASIA GEOG

B49
US DEPARTMENT OF STATE,SOVIET BIBLIOGRAPHY (PAMPHLET). CHINA/COM COM USSR LAW AGRI INT/ORG ECO/TAC EDU/PROP...POLICY GEOG IND 20. PAGE 135 F2670 BIBLIOG/A MARXISM CULTURE DIPLOM

L52
HUTH A.G.,"COMMUNICATION AND ECONOMIC DEVELOPMENT." FUT WOR+45 CULTURE SOCIETY INT/ORG PLAN TEC/DEV EDU/PROP DRIVE KNOWL WEALTH...POLICY CONCPT RECORD STERTYP GEN/LAWS COMMUN TOT/POP UNESCO 20 UN CMN/WLTH. PAGE 64 F1250 ECO/UNDEV

B53
BOULDING K.E.,THE ORGANIZATIONAL REVOLUTION. FUT CULTURE ECO/DEV LABOR PROF/ORG ECO/TAC MORAL...SOC CONCPT RECORD INT SOC/EXP 20. PAGE 17 F0321 SOCIETY TREND

B53
SAYLES L.R.,THE LOCAL UNION. CONSTN CULTURE DELIB/GP PARTIC CHOOSE GP/REL INGP/REL ATTIT ROLE ...MAJORIT DECISION MGT. PAGE 116 F2284 LABOR LEAD ADJUD ROUTINE

B53
WOYTINSKY W.S.,WORLD POPULATION AND PRODUCTION: TRENDS AND OUTLOOK. FUT WOR+45 WOR-45 CULTURE SOCIETY ECO/DEV AGRI INDUS TEC/DEV EDU/PROP SKILL WEALTH...SOC TREND. PAGE 149 F2928 ECO/UNDEV METH/CNCPT GEOG PERSON

S53
DRUCKER P.F.,"THE EMPLOYEE SOCIETY." STRUCT BAL/PWR PARTIC REPRESENT PWR...DECISION CONCPT. PAGE 34 F0666 LABOR MGT WORKER CULTURE

B54
POTTER D.M.,PEOPLE OF PLENTY: ECONOMIC ABUNDANCE AND THE AMERICAN CHARACTER. USA+45 USA-45 ECO/DEV ATTIT PERSON...PSY SOC CONCPT TREND GEN/METH TOT/POP 20. PAGE 107 F2108 CULTURE WEALTH

B54
WASHBURNE N.F.,INTERPRETING SOCIAL CHANGE IN AMERICA. USA+45 STRATA FAM NAT/G SECT OP/RES ECO/TAC EDU/PROP HABITAT...SOC TIME/SEQ TREND 20 BUREAUCRCY. PAGE 143 F2826 CULTURE STRUCT CREATE TEC/DEV

B54
WILLIAMSON H.F.,ECONOMIC DEVELOPMENT - PRINCIPLES AND PATTERNS. INDIA KOREA CULTURE ECO/DEV ECO/UNDEV TEC/DEV...CENSUS NAT/COMP FOR/TRADE 20 CHINJAP MEXIC/AMER RESOURCE/N. PAGE 147 F2895 ECO/TAC GEOG LABOR

S54
MACK R.W.,"ECOLOGICAL PATTERNS IN AN INDUSTRIAL SHOP" (BMR)" USA+45 CULTURE SOCIETY STRATA STRUCT LABOR NEIGH GP/REL ADJUST HABITAT...SOC SOC/INTEG 20. PAGE 83 F1634 INDUS DISCRIM WORKER

B55
WRONG D.H.,AMERICAN AND CANADIAN VIEWPOINTS. CANADA USA+45 CONSTN STRATA FAM SECT WORKER ECO/TAC EDU/PROP ADJUD MARRIAGE...IDEA/COMP 20. PAGE 149 F2936 DIPLOM ATTIT NAT/COMP CULTURE

B56
WHYTE W.H. JR.,THE ORGANIZATION MAN. CULTURE FINAN VOL/ASSN DOMIN EDU/PROP EXEC DISPL HABITAT ROLE ...PERS/TEST STERTYP. PAGE 146 F2875 ADMIN LG/CO PERSON CONSEN

B56
WOLFF R.L.,THE BALKANS IN OUR TIME. ALBANIA FUT MOD/EUR USSR YUGOSLAVIA CULTURE INT/ORG SECT DIPLOM EDU/PROP COERCE WAR ORD/FREE...CHARTS 4/20 BALKANS COMINFORM. PAGE 148 F2919 GEOG COM

B57
ROBERTSON H.M.,SOUTH AFRICA, ECONOMIC AND POLITICAL ASPECTS. SOUTH/AFR CONSTN CULTURE POL/PAR LEGIS DIPLOM DOMIN COLONIAL...SOC BIBLIOG 19/20. PAGE 112 F2214 RACE/REL ECO/UNDEV ECO/TAC DISCRIM

B57
WEIGERT H.W.,PRINCIPLES OF POLITICAL GEOGRAPHY. WOR+45 ECO/DEV ECO/UNDEV SECT ECO/TAC COLONIAL HABITAT...CHARTS T 20. PAGE 144 F2845 GEOG CULTURE

B58
CLAUNCH J.M.,THE PROBLEM OF GOVERNMENT IN METROPOLITAN AREAS. CULTURE INDUS POL/PAR PLAN REGION GP/REL...CENSUS ANTHOL MUNICH 20. PAGE 25 F0486 PROB/SOLV SOC

B58
CROWE S.,THE LANDSCAPE OF POWER. UK CULTURE SERV/IND NAT/G CONSULT PARTIC NUC/PWR LEISURE...SOC EXHIBIT 20. PAGE 29 F0559 HABITAT TEC/DEV PLAN CONTROL

B58
GALBRAITH J.K.,THE AFFLUENT SOCIETY. EUR+WWI FUT USA+45 USSR CULTURE SERV/IND PEACE WEALTH SOCISM ...NEW/IDEA TREND VAL/FREE 20. PAGE 45 F0882 ATTIT ECO/TAC CAP/ISM

B58
HIRSCHMAN A.O.,STRATEGY OF ECONOMIC DEVELOPMENT. WOR+45 WOR-45 CULTURE ECO/DEV NAT/G PLAN TEC/DEV INT/TRADE BAL/PAY ATTIT DRIVE RIGID/FLEX WEALTH ...CONCPT METH/CNCPT OBS CHARTS SIMUL GEN/LAWS TOT/POP VAL/FREE. PAGE 60 F1176 ECO/UNDEV ECO/TAC CAP/ISM

B58
MASON J.B.,THAILAND BIBLIOGRAPHY. S/ASIA THAILAND CULTURE EDU/PROP ADMIN...GEOG SOC LING 20. PAGE 87 F1701 BIBLIOG/A ECO/UNDEV DIPLOM NAT/G

B58
PALMER E.E.,INDUSTRIAL MAN. USA+45 PERSON ORD/FREE POPULISM...PREDICT TREND ANTHOL 20. PAGE 103 F2020 INDUS ECO/UNDEV CULTURE WEALTH

B58
PAN AMERICAN UNION,REPERTORIO DE PUBLICACIONES PERIODICAS ACTUALES LATINO-AMERICANAS. CULTURE ECO/UNDEV ADMIN LEAD GOV/REL 20 OAS. PAGE 103 F2023 BIBLIOG L/A+17C NAT/G DIPLOM

B58
SHAW S.J.,THE FINANCIAL AND ADMINISTRATIVE ORGANIZATION AND DEVELOPMENT OF OTTOMAN EGYPT 1517-1798. UAR LOC/G FORCES BUDGET INT/TRADE TAX EATING INCOME WEALTH...CHARTS BIBLIOG 16/18 OTTOMAN NAPOLEON/B. PAGE 120 F2371 FINAN ADMIN GOV/REL CULTURE

B58
TILLION G.,ALGERIA: THE REALITIES. ALGERIA FRANCE ISLAM CULTURE STRATA PROB/SOLV DOMIN REV NAT/LISM WEALTH MARXISM...GEOG 20. PAGE 130 F2573 ECO/UNDEV SOC COLONIAL DIPLOM

B59
MEYER A.J.,MIDDLE EASTERN CAPITALISM: NINE ESSAYS. ISLAM CULTURE ECO/UNDEV INDUS MARKET NAT/G PLAN ATTIT RIGID/FLEX...STAT OBS TREND GEN/LAWS. PAGE 90 F1767 TEC/DEV ECO/TAC ANTHOL

B59
PANIKKAR K.M.,THE AFRO-ASIAN STATES AND THEIR PROBLEMS. COM CULTURE KIN POL/PAR SECT DIPLOM EDU/PROP COLONIAL SOVEREIGN...TECHNIC GOV/COMP 20. PAGE 103 F2025 AFR S/ASIA ECO/UNDEV

S59
PLAZA G.,"FOR A REGIONAL MARKET IN LATIN AMERICA." FUT L/A+17C CULTURE INDUS NAT/G ECO/TAC INT/TRADE ATTIT WEALTH...NEW/IDEA TREND OAS 20. PAGE 106 F2092 MARKET INT/ORG REGION

S59
ZAUBERMAN A.,"SOVIET BLOC ECONOMIC INTEGRATION." COM CULTURE INTELL ECO/DEV INDUS TOP/EX ACT/RES PLAN ECO/TAC INT/TRADE ROUTINE CHOOSE ATTIT ...TIME/SEQ 20. PAGE 150 F2958 MARKET INT/ORG USSR TOTALISM

B60
ARON R.,COLLOQUES DE RHEINFELDEN. AFR USA+45 USSR WOR+45 WOR-45 CULTURE ECO/UNDEV NAT/G POL/PAR DIPLOM NAT/LISM TOTALISM ATTIT DRIVE ALL/VALS ...PLURIST CONCPT STERTYP GEN/LAWS TOT/POP 20. PAGE 6 F0120 ECO/DEV SOCIETY CAP/ISM SOCISM

B60
AUSTRUY J.,STRUCTURE ECONOMIQUE ET CIVILISATION: L'EGYPTE ET LE DESTIN ECONOMIQUE DE L'ISLAM. ISLAM UAR CREATE OP/RES ECO/TAC...SOC BIBLIOG 20 MUSLIM. PAGE 8 F0142 ECO/UNDEV CULTURE STRUCT

B60
DIA M.,REFLEXIONS SUR L'ECONOMIE DE L'AFRIQUE NOIRE (REV. ED.). CULTURE ECO/UNDEV CREATE TEC/DEV DIPLOM INT/TRADE OPTIMAL ATTIT...POLICY 20. PAGE 32 F0631 AFR ECO/TAC SOCISM PLAN

B60
KERR C.,INDUSTRIALISM AND INDUSTRIAL MAN. CULTURE SOCIETY ECO/UNDEV NAT/G ADMIN PRODUC WEALTH ...PREDICT TREND NAT/COMP 19/20. PAGE 70 F1381 WORKER MGT ECO/DEV INDUS

B60
KRISTENSEN T.,THE ECONOMIC WORLD BALANCE. FUT WOR+45 CULTURE ECO/DEV BAL/PWR INT/TRADE REGION PWR WEALTH...STAT TREND CHARTS 20. PAGE 73 F1442 ECO/UNDEV ECO/TAC FOR/AID

B60
ROEPKE W.,A HUMANE ECONOMY: THE SOCIAL FRAMEWORK OF THE FREE MARKET. FUT USSR WOR+45 CULTURE SOCIETY ECO/DEV PLAN ECO/TAC ADMIN ATTIT PERSON RIGID/FLEX SUPEGO MORAL WEALTH SOCISM...POLICY OLD/LIB CONCPT TREND GEN/LAWS 20. PAGE 113 F2232 DRIVE EDU/PROP CAP/ISM

B60
ROPKE W.,A HUMANE ECONOMY. CULTURE ECO/DEV FINAN INDUS GP/REL CENTRAL WEALTH...GEOG SOC IDEA/COMP 20 EEC. PAGE 114 F2239 ECO/TAC INT/ORG DIPLOM ORD/FREE

B60
SLOTKIN J.S.,FROM FIELD TO FACTORY; NEW INDUSTRIAL EMPLOYEES. HABITAT...MGT NEW/IDEA NAT/COMP BIBLIOG SOC/INTEG 20. PAGE 123 F2423 INDUS LABOR CULTURE WORKER

S60
BAUM M.,"THE CASE FOR BUSINESS CIVILIZATION." R+D CAP/ISM GIVE EDU/PROP HAPPINESS...SOC TREND. PAGE 12 F0218 MGT CULTURE WEALTH

S60
ENKE S.,"THE ECONOMIES OF GOVERNMENT PAYMENTS TO LIMIT POPULATION." FUT INDIA WOR+45 CULTURE FINAN NAT/G CONSULT PLAN LEGIT CONTROL COST ATTIT RIGID/FLEX HEALTH WEALTH...STAT OBS CHARTS TOT/POP VAL/FREE 20. PAGE 38 F0736 FAM ACT/RES

S60
GARNICK D.H.,"ON THE ECONOMIC FEASIBILITY OF A MIDDLE EASTERN COMMON MARKET." AFR ISLAM CULTURE INDUS NAT/G PLAN TEC/DEV ECO/TAC ADMIN ATTIT DRIVE RIGID/FLEX...PLURIST STAT TREND GEN/LAWS 20. PAGE 46 F0907 MARKET INT/TRADE

S60
JAFFEE A.J.,"POPULATION TRENDS AND CONTROLS IN UNDERDEVELOPED COUNTRIES." AFR FUT ISLAM L/A+17C S/ASIA CULTURE R+D FAM ACT/RES PLAN EDU/PROP BIO/SOC RIGID/FLEX HEALTH...SOC STAT OBS CHARTS 20. PAGE 66 F1303 ECO/UNDEV GEOG

S60
MURPHEY R.,"ECONOMIC CONFLICTS IN SOUTH ASIA." ASIA CULTURE INTELL ECO/TAC REGION ATTIT DRIVE KNOWL ...METH/CNCPT TIME/SEQ STERTYP TOT/POP METH/GP VAL/FREE 20. PAGE 95 F1864 S/ASIA ECO/UNDEV

S60
RIVKIN A.,"AFRICAN ECONOMIC DEVELOPMENT: ADVANCED TECHNOLOGY AND THE STAGES OF GROWTH." CULTURE ECO/UNDEV AGRI COM/IND EXTR/IND PLAN ECO/TAC ATTIT DRIVE RIGID/FLEX SKILL WEALTH...MGT SOC GEN/LAWS FOR/TRADE WORK TOT/POP 20. PAGE 111 F2195 AFR TEC/DEV FOR/AID

C60
HOSELITZ B.,"THE ROLE OF CITIES IN THE ECONOMIC GROWTH OF UNDERDEVELOPED COUNTRIES" IN "SOCIOLOGICAL ASPECTS OF ECONOMIC GROWTH"(BMR). CULTURE LOC/G ACT/RES...SOC IDEA/COMP METH/COMP METH MUNICH IND 14/20 REDFIELD/R. PAGE 62 F1218 METH/CNCPT TEC/DEV ECO/UNDEV

B61
DE VRIES E.,MAN IN RAPID SOCIAL CHANGE. WOR+45 SOCIETY ECO/DEV ECO/UNDEV AGRI INDUS FAM SECT TEC/DEV ATTIT...RECORD 20 CHRISTIAN. PAGE 31 F0607 CULTURE ALL/VALS SOC TASK

B61
DELEFORTRIE-SOU N.,LES DIRIGEANTS DE L'INDUSTRIE FRANCAISE. FRANCE CULTURE ELITES PROB/SOLV ...DECISION STAT CHARTS 20. PAGE 32 F0613 INDUS STRATA TOP/EX LEAD

B61
ERASMUS C.J.,MAN TAKES CONTROL: CULTURAL DEVELOPMENT AND AMERICAN AID. STRUCT OWN DRIVE PERCEPT...SOC 20 MEXIC/AMER. PAGE 38 F0741 ORD/FREE CULTURE ECO/UNDEV TEC/DEV

B61
HEMPSTONE S.,THE NEW AFRICA. AGRI INDUS KIN NAT/G COLONIAL MARXISM...SOC INT TREND NAT/COMP BIBLIOG/A 20. PAGE 58 F1146 AFR ORD/FREE PERSON CULTURE

B61
LEHMAN R.L.,AFRICA SOUTH OF THE SAHARA (PAMPHLET). DIPLOM COLONIAL NAT/LISM. PAGE 77 F1512 BIBLIOG/A AFR CULTURE NAT/G

B61
LICHTHEIM G.,MARXISM. GERMANY SOCIETY WORKER CAP/ISM ECO/TAC NAT/LISM POPULISM...TIME/SEQ GOV/COMP NAT/COMP 18/20 COM/PARTY. PAGE 80 F1559 MARXISM SOCISM IDEA/COMP CULTURE

B61
MARX K.,THE COMMUNIST MANIFESTO. IN (MENDEL A. ESSENTIAL WORKS OF MARXISM, NEW YORK: BANTAM. FUT MOD/EUR CULTURE ECO/DEV ECO/UNDEV AGRI FINAN INDUS MARKET PROC/MFG LABOR POL/PAR CONSULT FORCES CREATE PLAN ADMIN ATTIT DRIVE RIGID/FLEX ORD/FREE PWR RESPECT MARX/KARL MUNICH WORK. PAGE 86 F1691 COM NEW/IDEA CAP/ISM REV

B61
STARK H.,SOCIAL AND ECONOMIC FRONTIERS IN LATIN AMERICA (2ND ED.). CUBA FUT CULTURE AGRI INDUS ECO/TAC PRODUC ATTIT MARXISM...NAT/COMP BIBLIOG T 20. PAGE 125 F2470 L/A+17C SOCIETY DIPLOM ECO/UNDEV

S61
NOVE A.,"THE SOVIET MODEL AND UNDERDEVELOPED COUNTRIES." COM FUT USSR WOR+45 CULTURE ECO/DEV POL/PAR FOR/AID EDU/PROP ADMIN MORAL WEALTH ...POLICY RECORD HIST/WRIT 20. PAGE 99 F1942 ECO/UNDEV PLAN

B62
DE GRAZIA S.,OF TIME, WORK, AND LEISURE. USA+45 ECO/DEV WORKER HAPPINESS UTOPIA ALL/VALS...SOC NEW/IDEA TIME. PAGE 31 F0599 CULTURE LEISURE CONCPT

B62
DREIER J.C.,THE ALLIANCE FOR PROGRESS. L/A+17C USA+45 CULTURE ECO/DEV ECO/UNDEV NAT/G PLAN DIPLOM PWR 20 OAS ALL/PROG. PAGE 34 F0661 FOR/AID INT/ORG ECO/TAC POLICY

B62
GREEN L.P.,DEVELOPMENT IN AFRICA. AFR CENTRL/AFR GHANA RHODESIA SOUTH/AFR AGRI PROC/MFG INT/TRADE DEMAND NAT/LISM PRODUC WEALTH...GEOG METH/CNCPT CHARTS BIBLIOG 20. PAGE 50 F0987 CULTURE ECO/UNDEV GOV/REL TREND

B62
HARRINGTON M.,THE OTHER AMERICA: POVERTY IN THE UNITED STATES. WORKER CREATE REPRESENT RACE/REL AGE/O DRIVE POLICY. PAGE 55 F1086 WEALTH WELF/ST INCOME CULTURE

B62
SELOSOEMARDJAN O.,SOCIAL CHANGES IN JOGJAKARTA. INDONESIA NETHERLAND ELITES STRATA STRUCT FAM POL/PAR CREATE DIPLOM INT/TRADE EDU/PROP ADMIN GOV/REL...SOC 20 JAVA CHINJAP. PAGE 119 F2352 ECO/UNDEV CULTURE REV COLONIAL

B62
SHERIF M.,INTERGROUP RELATIONS AND LEADERSHIP: APPROACHES AND RESEARCH IN INDUSTRIAL, ETHNIC, CULTURAL AND POLITICAL AREAS. CULTURE R+D LABOR DIPLOM GP/REL RACE/REL PERCEPT...PSY CONCPT. PAGE 121 F2377 LEAD REPRESENT PWR INGP/REL

B62
US LIBRARY OF CONGRESS,A LIST OF AMERICAN DOCTORAL DISSERTATIONS ON AFRICA. SOCIETY SECT DIPLOM EDU/PROP ADMIN...GEOG 19/20. PAGE 138 F2717 BIBLIOG AFR ACADEM CULTURE

B62
WARD B.,THE RICH NATIONS AND THE POOR NATIONS. FUT WOR+45 CULTURE ECO/DEV ECO/UNDEV PLAN CAP/ISM EDU/PROP REV NAT/LISM ATTIT DRIVE SOCISM...POLICY CONCPT TIME/SEQ 20. PAGE 143 F2816 ECO/TAC GEN/LAWS

B63
CHOJNACKI S.,REGISTER ON CURRENT RESEARCH ON ETHIOPIA AND THE HORN OF AFRICA. ETHIOPIA LAW CULTURE AGRI SECT EDU/PROP ADMIN...GEOG HEAL LING 20. PAGE 24 F0470 BIBLIOG ACT/RES INTELL ACADEM

B63
DE VRIES E.,SOCIAL ASPECTS OF ECONOMIC DEVELOPMENT IN LATIN AMERICA. CULTURE SOCIETY STRATA FINAN INDUS INT/ORG DELIB/GP ACT/RES ECO/TAC EDU/PROP ADMIN ATTIT SUPEGO HEALTH KNOWL ORD/FREE...SOC STAT TREND ANTHOL TOT/POP VAL/FREE. PAGE 31 F0608 L/A+17C ECO/UNDEV

B63
GAMBLE S.D.,NORTH CHINA VILLAGES: SOCIAL, POLITICAL, AND ECONOMIC ACTIVITIES BEFORE 1933. ASIA CULTURE STRUCT FAM DOMIN EDU/PROP MUNICH WORSHIP 20. PAGE 46 F0891 AGRI LEAD FINAN

B63
GEERTZ C.,PEDDLERS AND PRINCES: SOCIAL DEVELOPMENT AND ECONOMIC CHANGE IN TWO INDONESIAN TOWNS. S/ASIA CULTURE SOCIETY STRATA FACE/GP CREATE TEC/DEV ECO/TAC ORD/FREE WEALTH...OBS INT CENSUS CHARTS WORK TOT/POP METH/GP TERR/GP VAL/FREE 20 MUNICH. PAGE 47 F0913 ECO/UNDEV SOC ELITES INDONESIA

B63
GLADE W.P. JR.,THE POLITICAL ECONOMY OF MEXICO. FUT L/A+17C CULTURE SOCIETY AGRI INDUS DELIB/GP ACT/RES ECO/TAC ATTIT HEALTH ORD/FREE...STAT TIME/SEQ TREND MEXIC/AMER TOT/POP VAL/FREE 20. PAGE 48 F0928 FINAN ECO/UNDEV

B63
GORDON L.,A NEW DEAL FOR LATIN AMERICA. L/A+17C USA+45 CULTURE NAT/G TEC/DEV DIPLOM FOR/AID REGION TASK...POLICY 20 ALL/PROG DEPT/STATE. PAGE 49 F0958 ECO/UNDEV ECO/TAC INT/ORG PLAN

B63
KAPP W.K.,HINDU CULTURE: ECONOMIC DEVELOPMENT AND ECONOMIC PLANNING IN INDIA. INDIA S/ASIA CULTURE ECO/TAC EDU/PROP ADMIN ALL/VALS...POLICY MGT TIME/SEQ TRUE/GP VAL/FREE 20. PAGE 69 F1353 SECT ECO/UNDEV

B63
LEWIS G.K.,PUERTO RICO: FREEDOM AND POWER IN THE CARIBBEAN. PUERT/RICO USA+45 CULTURE STRUCT INDUS POL/PAR WORKER EDU/PROP CATHISM 20. PAGE 79 F1548 ECO/UNDEV COLONIAL NAT/LISM GEOG

B63
MANGER W.,THE ALLIANCE FOR PROGRESS: A CRITICAL APPRAISAL. FUT L/A+17C USA+45 CULTURE ECO/UNDEV ACADEM NAT/G SCHOOL PLAN FOR/AID...POLICY OAS ALL/PROG. PAGE 84 F1651 DIPLOM INT/ORG ECO/TAC REGION

B63
MARITANO N.,AN ALLIANCE FOR PROGRESS. FUT L/A+17C USA+45 CULTURE ECO/UNDEV NAT/G PLAN CONTROL ...POLICY ALL/PROG. PAGE 85 F1669 DIPLOM INT/ORG ECO/TAC FOR/AID

B63
SMELSER N.J.,THE SOCIOLOGY OF ECONOMIC LIFE. UNIV CULTURE PERCEPT...PSY T 18/20. PAGE 123 F2425 SOC METH/COMP IDEA/COMP

L63
ADERBIGDE A.,"SYMPOSIUM ON WEST AFRICA INTEGRATION." AFR EUR+WWI FUT CULTURE SOCIETY STRATA DIST/IND INDUS MARKET SERV/IND DELIB/GP PLAN TEC/DEV DOMIN EDU/PROP LEGIT COERCE ATTIT ALL/VALS ...POLICY STAT TREND CHARTS VAL/FREE. PAGE 2 F0040 FINAN ECO/TAC REGION

L63
NASH M.,"PSYCHO-CULTURAL FACTORS IN ASIAN ECONOMIC GROWTH." ASIA ISLAM S/ASIA CULTURE ECO/UNDEV DELIB/GP EDU/PROP COERCE ATTIT PERSON HEALTH KNOWL ORD/FREE...PSY SOC STAT TREND ANTHOL VAL/FREE 20. PAGE 96 F1893 SOCIETY ECO/TAC

S63
AYAL E.B.,"VALUE SYSTEM AND ECONOMIC DEVELOPMENT IN JAPAN AND THAILAND." ASIA S/ASIA THAILAND CULTURE ECO/DEV CAP/ISM DOMIN NAT/LISM DRIVE RIGID/FLEX SOCISM...WELF/ST OBS TREND CON/ANAL GEN/LAWS TERR/GP 20 CHINJAP. PAGE 8 F0145 ECO/UNDEV ALL/VALS

S63
BILL J.A.,"THE SOCIAL AND ECONOMIC FOUNDATIONS OF POWER IN CONTEMPORARY IRAN." ISLAM CULTURE NAT/G ECO/TAC DOMIN COERCE ATTIT PWR WEALTH...TREND VAL/FREE 20. PAGE 15 F0284 SOCIETY STRATA IRAN

S63
DE FOREST J.D.,"LOW LEVELS OF TECHNOLOGY AND ECONOMIC DEVELOPMENT PROSPECTS." WOR+45 WOR-45 CULTURE ACT/RES CREATE PLAN ECO/TAC ROUTINE PERCEPT WEALTH...METH/CNCPT GEN/LAWS 20. PAGE 31 F0597 ECO/UNDEV TEC/DEV

S63
FOURASTIE J.,"LES SCIENCES ECONOMIQUES ET SOCIALES EN EUROPE." EUR+WWI FUT MOD/EUR WOR+45 WOR-45 ACT/RES CULTURE

INTELL SOCIETY R+D PLAN ROUTINE ATTIT RIGID/FLEX KNOWL...OBS TREND. PAGE 43 F0833

B64
BRIGHT J.R.,RESEARCH, DEVELOPMENT AND TECHNOLOGICAL INNOVATION. CULTURE R+D CREATE PLAN PROB/SOLV AUTOMAT RISK PERSON...DECISION CONCPT PREDICT BIBLIOG. PAGE 18 F0352 TEC/DEV NEW/IDEA INDUS MGT

B64
DE BARY W.T.,APPROACHES TO ASIAN CIVILIZATIONS. INDIA ISLAM USA+45 CULTURE ACADEM...SOC ANTHOL 20 CHINJAP ARABS. PAGE 31 F0595 ASIA EDU/PROP SOCIETY

B64
NOVACK D.E.,DEVELOPMENT AND SOCIETY; THE DYNAMICS OF ECONOMIC CHANGE. WOR+45 STRATA STRUCT ECO/TAC CONTROL CROWD REV GP/REL ADJUST PRODUC WEALTH PSY. PAGE 99 F1940 SOCIETY CULTURE SOC ECO/UNDEV

B64
SCHULTZ T.W.,TRANSFORMING TRADITIONAL AGRICULTURE. WOR+45 WOR-45 CULTURE STRATA FINAN ACT/RES ECO/TAC ATTIT KNOWL SKILL...MATH STAT TIME/SEQ GEN/LAWS VAL/FREE. PAGE 117 F2316 AGRI ECO/UNDEV

B64
SINGER H.W.,INTERNATIONAL DEVELOPMENT: GROWTH AND CHANGE. AFR BRAZIL L/A+17C WOR+45 CULTURE AGRI INDUS NAT/G ACT/RES ECO/TAC EDU/PROP WEALTH...GEOG CONCPT METH/CNCPT STAT HYPO/EXP WORK TOT/POP 20. PAGE 122 F2412 FINAN ECO/UNDEV FOR/AID INT/TRADE

B64
TAWNEY R.H.,EQUALITY. UK CULTURE STRATA ECO/TAC EDU/PROP REPRESENT OWN NEW/LIB...MAJORIT WELF/ST SOC 20. PAGE 129 F2538 WEALTH STRUCT ELITES POPULISM

B64
US LIBRARY OF CONGRESS,SOUTHEAST ASIA. CULTURE ...SOC STAT 20. PAGE 138 F2718 BIBLIOG/A S/ASIA ECO/UNDEV NAT/G

B64
WERTHEIM W.F.,EAST-WEST PARALLELS. INDONESIA S/ASIA NAT/G SECT...TIME/SEQ METH REFORMERS S/EASTASIA. PAGE 145 F2860 SOC ECO/UNDEV CULTURE NAT/LISM

B64
WRIGHT G.,RURAL REVOLUTION IN FRANCE: THE PEASANTRY IN THE TWENTIETH CENTURY. EUR+WWI MOD/EUR LAW CULTURE AGRI POL/PAR DELIB/GP LEGIS ECO/TAC EDU/PROP COERCE CHOOSE ATTIT RIGID/FLEX HEALTH ...STAT CENSUS CHARTS VAL/FREE 20. PAGE 149 F2932 PWR STRATA FRANCE REV

B64
ZOLLSCHAN G.K.,EXPLORATIONS IN SOCIAL CHANGE. SOCIETY STRATA STRUCT ECO/UNDEV EX/STRUC...PSY ANTHOL 20. PAGE 151 F2968 ORD/FREE SIMUL CONCPT CULTURE

S64
NASH M.,"SOCIAL PREREQUISITES TO ECONOMIC GROWTH IN LATIN AMERICA AND SOUTHEAST ASIA." L/A+17C S/ASIA CULTURE SOCIETY ECO/UNDEV AGRI INDUS NAT/G PLAN TEC/DEV EDU/PROP ROUTINE ALL/VALS...POLICY RELATIV SOC NAT/COMP WORK TOT/POP 20. PAGE 96 F1894 ECO/DEV PERCEPT

B65
APTER D.E.,THE POLITICS OF MODERNIZATION. AFR L/A+17C CULTURE NAT/G POL/PAR ADMIN COLONIAL NAT/LISM ATTIT RIGID/FLEX PWR...SOC CONCPT. PAGE 6 F0109 ECO/UNDEV GEN/LAWS STRATA CREATE

B65
COUGHLIN B.J.,CHURCH AND STATE IN SOCIAL WELFARE. USA+45 RECEIVE GP/REL ORD/FREE WEALTH NEW/LIB. PAGE 28 F0542 CULTURE SECT VOL/ASSN GIVE

B65
FERMAN L.A.,POVERTY IN AMERICA: A BOOK OF READINGS. USA+45 CULTURE ECO/DEV PROB/SOLV ALL/VALS...POLICY ANTHOL BIBLIOG 20 POVRTY/WAR. PAGE 40 F0785 WEALTH TEC/DEV CONCPT RECEIVE

B65
HAPGOOD D.,AFRICA: FROM INDEPENDENCE TO TOMARROW. AFR GUINEA SENEGAL CULTURE ELITES ECO/UNDEV AGRI SCHOOL FOR/AID COLONIAL MARXISM...TREND 20. PAGE 55 F1070 ECO/TAC SOCIETY NAT/G

B65
HAUSER P.M.,THE STUDY OF URBANIZATION. S/ASIA ECO/DEV ECO/UNDEV NEIGH ACT/RES...GEOG MUNICH. PAGE 57 F1115 CULTURE SOC

B65
MOORE W.E.,THE IMPACT OF INDUSTRY. CULTURE STRUCT ORD/FREE...TREND 20. PAGE 93 F1824 INDUS MGT TEC/DEV ECO/UNDEV

B65
NATIONAL CONF SOCIAL WELFARE,THE SOCIAL WELFARE FORUM, 1965. LAW CULTURE VOL/ASSN CONTROL PERS/REL ADJUST POLICY. PAGE 97 F1899 CONSTN WEALTH ORD/FREE NEIGH

B65
OXENFELDT A.R.,ECONOMIC SYSTEMS IN ACTION. FRANCE USA+45 USSR CULTURE PLAN PROB/SOLV TEC/DEV INCOME PRODUC WEALTH...METH/COMP 20. PAGE 102 F2007 ECO/DEV CAP/ISM MARXISM ECO/TAC

B65
SCOTT A.M.,THE REVOLUTION IN STATECRAFT: INFORMAL PENETRATION. WOR+45 WOR-45 CULTURE INT/ORG FORCES ECO/TAC ROUTINE...BIBLIOG 20. PAGE 118 F2331 DIPLOM EDU/PROP FOR/AID

B65
US ADVISORY COMN INTERGOV REL,METROPOLITAN SOCIAL AND ECONOMIC DISPARITIES: IMPLICATIONS FOR INTERGOVERNMENTAL RELATIONS IN CENT'L CITIES AND SUBURBS. CULTURE STRATA DIST/IND LOC/G PLAN GP/REL DISCRIM HABITAT MUNICH. PAGE 134 F2634 GOV/REL GEOG

B65
US BUREAU EDUC CULTURAL AFF,RESOURCES SURVEY FOR LATIN AMERICAN COUNTRIES. L/A+17C USA+45 CULTURE INDUS INT/ORG SECT PLAN EDU/PROP POLICY. PAGE 134 F2643 NAT/G ECO/UNDEV FOR/AID DIPLOM

B65
WINT G.,ASIA: A HANDBOOK. ASIA COM INDIA USSR CULTURE INTELL NAT/G...GEOG STAT CENSUS NAT/COMP WORSHIP 20 TREATY CHINJAP. PAGE 148 F2907 DIPLOM SOC

S65
HAYTER T.,"FRENCH AID TO AFRICA* ITS SCOPE AND ACHIEVEMENTS." CULTURE ECO/TAC INT/TRADE ADMIN REGION CENTRAL FEDERAL LOVE PWR SOVEREIGN EEC. PAGE 57 F1127 AFR FRANCE FOR/AID COLONIAL

S65
KORBONSKI A.,"USA POLICY IN EAST EUROPE." COM EUR+WWI GERMANY USA+45 CULTURE ECO/UNDEV EDU/PROP RIGID/FLEX WEALTH FOR/TRADE 20. PAGE 73 F1426 ACT/RES ECO/TAC FOR/AID

S65
KUNKEL J.H.,"VALUES AND BEHAVIOR IN ECONOMIC DEVELOPMENT." INDIA PERU CULTURE STRUCT CREATE PERS/REL ATTIT PERSON...CHARTS HYPO/EXP ARGEN. PAGE 74 F1449 SIMUL ECO/UNDEV PSY STERTYP

S65
SELLERS C.,"THE EQUILIBRIUM CYCLE IN TWO-PARTY POLITICS." USA+45 USA-45 CULTURE R+D GP/REL MAJORITY DECISION. PAGE 119 F2351 CHOOSE TREND POL/PAR

B66
ANDRESKI S.,PARASITISM AND SUBVERSION* THE CASE OF LATIN AMERICA. CULTURE ECO/UNDEV LABOR NAT/G SECT PROB/SOLV RACE/REL TOTALISM ATTIT WEALTH ALL/IDEOS. PAGE 5 F0100 L/A+17C GOV/COMP STRATA REV

B66
BROWN J.F.,THE NEW EASTERN EUROPE. ALBANIA BULGARIA HUNGARY POLAND ROMANIA CULTURE AGRI POL/PAR WAR NAT/LISM MARXISM...CHARTS BIBLIOG 20. PAGE 19 F0369 DIPLOM COM NAT/G ECO/UNDEV

B66
CANNING HOUSE LIBRARY,AUTHOR AND SUBJECT CATALOGUES OF THE CANNING HOUSE LIBRARY (5 VOLS.). UK CULTURE LEAD...SOC 19/20. PAGE 21 F0411 BIBLIOG L/A+17C NAT/G DIPLOM

B66
CROWDER M.,A SHORT HISTORY OF NIGERIA. AFR NIGERIA UK ECO/UNDEV CHIEF INT/TRADE RACE/REL NAT/LISM ORD/FREE...GEOG SOC CHARTS BIBLIOG 14/20. PAGE 29 F0558 COLONIAL NAT/G CULTURE

B66
HOWE R.W.,BLACK AFRICA: FROM PRE-HISTORY TO THE EVE OF THE COLONIAL ERA. ECO/UNDEV KIN PROVS SECT INT/TRADE EDU/PROP COLONIAL...BIBLIOG WORSHIP. PAGE 62 F1226 AFR CULTURE SOC

B66
LENSKI G.E.,POWER AND PRIVILEGE: A THEORY OF SOCIAL STRATIFICATION. SWEDEN UK UNIV USSR CULTURE ECO/UNDEV PRIVIL PWR...PHIL/SCI CONCPT CHARTS IDEA/COMP HYPO/EXP METH MARX/KARL. PAGE 78 F1525 SOC STRATA STRUCT SOCIETY

B66
RIZK C.,LE REGIME POLITIQUE LIBANAIS. ISLAM LEBANON STRUCT POL/PAR SECT LOBBY GP/REL 20 ARABS MUSLIM CHRISTIAN. PAGE 112 F2198 ECO/UNDEV NAT/G CULTURE

B66
ROBINSON E.A.,THE ECONOMICS OF EDUCATION. WOR+45 CULTURE ECO/UNDEV FINAN SCHOOL DIPLOM PRICE COST DEMAND...CHARTS METH/COMP 20. PAGE 112 F2216 EDU/PROP ADJUST CONFER

B66
SPULBER N.,THE STATE AND ECONOMIC DEVELOPMENT IN EASTERN EUROPE. BULGARIA COM CZECHOSLVK HUNGARY POLAND YUGOSLAVIA CULTURE PLAN CAP/ISM INT/TRADE CONTROL...POLICY CHARTS METH/COMP BIBLIOG/A 19/20. PAGE 125 F2460 ECO/DEV ECO/UNDEV NAT/G TOTALISM

B66
US DEPARTMENT OF STATE,RESEARCH ON THE USSR AND EASTERN EUROPE (EXTERNAL RESEARCH LIST NO 1-25). USSR LAW CULTURE SOCIETY NAT/G TEC/DEV DIPLOM EDU/PROP REGION...GEOG LING. PAGE 136 F2675 BIBLIOG/A EUR+WWI COM MARXISM

B66
US DEPARTMENT OF STATE,RESEARCH ON WESTERN EUROPE, GREAT BRITAIN, AND CANADA (EXTERNAL RESEARCH LIST NO 3-25). CANADA GERMANY/W UK LAW CULTURE NAT/G POL/PAR FORCES EDU/PROP REGION MARXISM...GEOG SOC WORSHIP 20 CMN/WLTH. PAGE 136 F2676 BIBLIOG/A EUR+WWI DIPLOM

B66
WOODMAN H.D.,SLAVERY AND THE SOUTHERN ECONOMY: ECO/DEV

SOURCES AND READINGS. USA-45 CULTURE STRUCT AGRI ECO/TAC LEAD RACE/REL DISCRIM EFFICIENCY...CHARTS ANTHOL MUNICH 18/19 NEGRO SOUTH/US. PAGE 148 F2922
STRATA WORKER UTIL

S66
ROTHCHILD D.,"THE LIMITS OF FEDERALISM: AN EXAMINATION OF POLITICAL INSTITUTIONAL TRANSFER IN AFRICA." AFR CONSTN CULTURE ELITES ECO/UNDEV KIN PROB/SOLV ADMIN ORD/FREE PWR...POLICY 20. PAGE 114 F2250
FEDERAL NAT/G NAT/LISM COLONIAL

B67
ANDERSON C.W.,ISSUES OF POLITICAL DEVELOPMENT. BURMA WOR+45 CULTURE TOP/EX ECO/TAC MARXISM ...CHARTS NAT/COMP 20 COLOMB CONGO/LEOP. PAGE 5 F0094
NAT/LISM COERCE ECO/UNDEV SOCISM

B67
BARANSON J.,TECHNOLOGY FOR UNDERDEVELOPED AREAS: AN ANNOTATED BIBLIOGRAPHY. FUT WOR+45 CULTURE INDUS INT/ORG CREATE PROB/SOLV INT/TRADE EDU/PROP AUTOMAT ...CONCPT METH. PAGE 10 F0181
BIBLIOG/A ECO/UNDEV TEC/DEV R+D

B67
BARNETT A.D.,CHINA AFTER MAO. ASIA CHINA/COM CULTURE ECO/UNDEV ECO/TAC CONTROL EFFICIENCY NAT/LISM MARXISM 20. PAGE 10 F0189
POL/PAR NAT/G TEC/DEV GP/REL

B67
CHILCOTE R.H.,PORTUGUESE AFRICA. PORTUGAL CULTURE SOCIETY ECO/UNDEV DOMIN NAT/LISM...TREND IDEA/COMP NAT/COMP BIBLIOG 15/20. PAGE 24 F0465
AFR COLONIAL ORD/FREE PROB/SOLV

B67
DUN J.L.,THE ESSENCE OF CHINESE CIVILIZATION. ASIA FAM NAT/G TEC/DEV ADMIN SANCTION WAR HABITAT ...ANTHOL WORSHIP. PAGE 35 F0676
CULTURE SOCIETY

B67
EVANS R.H.,COEXISTENCE: COMMUNISM AND ITS PRACTICE IN BOLOGNA, 1945-1965. ITALY CAP/ISM ADMIN CHOOSE PEACE ORD/FREE...SOC STAT DEEP/INT SAMP CHARTS BIBLIOG MUNICH 20. PAGE 39 F0756
MARXISM CULTURE POL/PAR

B67
FANON F.,TOWARD THE AFRICAN REVOLUTION. AFR FRANCE CULTURE ELITES LEAD REV GP/REL ORD/FREE SOVEREIGN 20. PAGE 39 F0762
COLONIAL DOMIN ECO/UNDEV RACE/REL

B67
FORDE D.,WEST AFRICAN KINGDOMS IN THE NINETEENTH CENTURY. ECO/UNDEV AGRI KIN...SOC CHARTS NAT/COMP 19. PAGE 42 F0826
AFR REGION CULTURE

B67
GUTKIND E.A.,URBAN DEVELOPMENT IN SOUTHERN EUROPE* SPAIN AND PORTUGAL. CHRIST-17C EUR+WWI MOD/EUR PORTUGAL SPAIN CULTURE AGRI...SOC SAMP/SIZ BIBLIOG MUNICH. PAGE 52 F1015
TEC/DEV ECO/DEV

B67
LANDEN R.G.,OMAN SINCE 1856: DISRUPTIVE MODERNIZATION IN A TRADITIONAL ARAB SOCIETY. UK DIST/IND EXTR/IND SECT DIPLOM INT/TRADE...SOC LING CHARTS BIBLIOG 19/20. PAGE 75 F1468
ISLAM CULTURE ECO/UNDEV NAT/G

B67
LITTLE AD, INC.,COMMUNITY RENEWAL PROGRAMMING. CULTURE LOC/G ACT/RES TASK COST ATTIT...SOC/WK MODAL STAT STAND/INT CHARTS 20 SAN/FRAN. PAGE 81 F1585
STRATA NEIGH PLAN CREATE

B67
MCNELLY T.,SOURCES IN MODERN EAST ASIAN HISTORY AND POLITICS. KOREA VIETNAM CULTURE DIPLOM COLONIAL REV WAR PWR ALL/IDEOS MARXISM...ANTHOL 20 CHINJAP. PAGE 88 F1733
NAT/COMP ASIA S/ASIA SOCIETY

B67
MEYERS M.,SOURCES OF THE AMERICAN REPUBLIC; A DOCUMENTARY HISTORY OF POLITICS, SOCIETY, AND THOUGHT (VOL. I, REV. ED.). USA-45 CULTURE STRUCT NAT/G LEGIS LEAD ATTIT...JURID SOC ANTHOL 17/19 PRESIDENT. PAGE 90 F1772
COLONIAL REV WAR

B67
OGLESBY C.,CONTAINMENT AND CHANGE. AFR COM USA+45 ECO/UNDEV TEC/DEV ECO/TAC FOR/AID INT/TRADE DOMIN GUERRILLA REV PEACE 20 STALIN/J. PAGE 101 F1983
DIPLOM BAL/PWR MARXISM CULTURE

B67
PIKE F.B.,FREEDOM AND REFORM IN LATIN AMERICA. BRAZIL URUGUAY CONSTN CULTURE SECT DIPLOM EDU/PROP PARTIC DRIVE ALL/VALS CATHISM...GEOG ANTHOL BIBLIOG REFORMERS BOLIV. PAGE 106 F2086
L/A+17C ORD/FREE ECO/UNDEV REV

B67
RAVKIN A.,THE NEW STATES OF AFRICA (HEADLINE SERIES, NO. 183((PAMPHLET). CULTURE STRUCT INDUS COLONIAL NAT/LISM...SOC 20. PAGE 109 F2153
AFR ECO/UNDEV SOCIETY ADMIN

B67
WALLBANK T.W.,CIVILIZATION PAST AND PRESENT (3RD ED.). FUT WOR+45 WOR-45 SOCIETY...SOC CONCPT TIME/SEQ CHARTS BIBLIOG T. PAGE 143 F2809
CULTURE STRUCT TREND

B67
WILLS A.J.,AN INTRODUCTION TO THE HISTORY OF CENTRAL AFRICA. RHODESIA ZAMBIA CULTURE SOCIETY ECO/UNDEV TEC/DEV DOMIN WAR ALL/VALS...POLICY TREND BIBLIOG T 14/20 NYASALAND. PAGE 147 F2899
AFR COLONIAL ORD/FREE

S67
FOX R.G.,"FAMILY, CASTE, AND COMMERCE IN A NORTH INDIAN MARKET TOWN." INDIA STRATA AGRI FACE/GP FAM NEIGH OP/RES BARGAIN ADMIN ROUTINE WEALTH...SOC CHARTS 20. PAGE 43 F0838
CULTURE GP/REL ECO/UNDEV DIST/IND

S67
PERKINS D.H.,"ECONOMIC GROWTH IN CHINA AND THE CULTURAL REVOLUTION(1960APRIL 1967)" CHINA/COM FUT AGRI INDUS PLAN LEAD MARXISM...CHARTS 20 MAO. PAGE 105 F2062
ECO/TAC CULTURE REV ECO/UNDEV

S67
ROY E.V.,"AN INTERPRETATION OF NORTHERN THAI PEASANT ECONOMY." THAILAND CLIENT CULTURE AGRI PROC/MFG FACE/GP DEMAND INCOME 20. PAGE 114 F2254
STRUCT STRATA ECO/UNDEV INGP/REL

S67
SIPPEL D.,"INDIENS UNSICHERE ZUKUNFT." INDIA CULTURE ACADEM POL/PAR LEGIS COLONIAL CHOOSE SOVEREIGN...JURID 20. PAGE 122 F2416
SOCIETY STRUCT ECO/UNDEV NAT/G

S67
WILES P.J.,"THE POLITICAL AND SOCIAL PREREQUISITES FOR A SOVIET-TYPE ECONOMY." COM USSR LAW CULTURE CREATE ADMIN FEEDBACK ROUTINE COST OPTIMAL TOTALISM MARXISM 20. PAGE 146 F2883
ECO/DEV PLAN EX/STRUC EFFICIENCY

B96
SCHMOLLER G.,THE MERCANTILE SYSTEM AND ITS HISTORICAL SIGNIFICANCE: ILLUSTRATED CHIEFLY FROM PRUSSIAN HISTORY (TRANS.). PRUSSIA CULTURE INDUS KIN NAT/G PROVS OP/RES ECO/TAC INT/TRADE SUPEGO PWR WEALTH MUNICH 19 MERCANTLST. PAGE 117 F2302
GEN/METH INGP/REL CONCPT

CUNNINGHAM E.M. F0561

CUNNINGHAM W. F0562

CUNNINGHAM W.B. F0563

CURLEY/JM....JAMES M. CURLEY

CURRIE L. F0564

CURTIN W.J. F0565

CURZON/GN....GEORGE NATHANIEL CURZON

CYBERNETICS....SEE FEEDBACK, SIMUL, CONTROL

CYCLES....SEE TIME/SEQ

CYERT R.M. F0566,F0567,F0568

CYPRUS....SEE ALSO APPROPRIATE TIME/SPACE/CULTURE INDEX

CZECHOSLVK....CZECHOSLOVAKIA; SEE ALSO COM

B54
REYNOLDS P.A.,BRITISH FOREIGN POLICY IN THE INTER-WAR YEARS. CZECHOSLVK GERMANY POLAND UK USA-45 POL/PAR FORCES ECO/TAC ARMS/CONT WAR ATTIT 20. PAGE 111 F2182
DIPLOM POLICY NAT/G

B57
MURDESHWAR A.K.,ADMINISTRATIVE PROBLEMS RELATING TO NATIONALISATION: WITH SPECIAL REFERENCE TO INDIAN STATE ENTERPRISES. CZECHOSLVK FRANCE INDIA UK USA+45 LEGIS WORKER PROB/SOLV BUDGET PRICE CONTROL ...MGT GEN/LAWS 20 PARLIAMENT. PAGE 95 F1863
NAT/G OWN INDUS ADMIN

B59
ETSCHMANN R.,DIE WAHRUNGS- UND DEVISENPOLITIK DES OSTBLOCKS UND IHRE AUSWIRKUNGEN AUF DIE WIRTSCHAFTSBEZIEHUNGEN ZWISCHEN OST U WEST. BULGARIA CZECHOSLVK HUNGARY POLAND USSR MARKET NAT/G PLAN DIPLOM...NAT/COMP 20. PAGE 39 F0753
ECO/TAC FINAN POLICY INT/TRADE

B63
PRYOR F.L.,THE COMMUNIST FOREIGN TRADE SYSTEM. COM CZECHOSLVK GERMANY YUGOSLAVIA LAW ECO/DEV DIST/IND POL/PAR PLAN DOMIN TOTALISM DRIVE RIGID/FLEX WEALTH ...STAT STAND/INT CHARTS FOR/TRADE 20. PAGE 108 F2130
ATTIT ECO/TAC

B64
GRIFFITH W.E.,COMMUNISM IN EUROPE (2 VOLS.). CZECHOSLVK USSR WOR+45 WOR-45 YUGOSLAVIA INGP/REL MARXISM SOCISM...ANTHOL 20 EUROPE/E. PAGE 51 F1000
COM POL/PAR DIPLOM GOV/COMP

S64
HORECKY P.L.,"LIBRARY OF CONGRESS PUBLICATIONS IN AID OF USSR AND EAST EUROPEAN RESEARCH." BULGARIA CZECHOSLVK POLAND USSR YUGOSLAVIA NAT/G POL/PAR DIPLOM ADMIN GOV/REL...CLASSIF 20. PAGE 62 F1214
BIBLIOG/A COM MARXISM

B66
JACKSON G.D.,COMINTERN AND PEASANT IN EAST EUROPE 1919-1930. BULGARIA COM CZECHOSLVK EUR+WWI POLAND ROMANIA YUGOSLAVIA STRATA AGRI VOL/ASSN DIPLOM
MARXISM ECO/UNDEV WORKER

CONTROL CROWD WEALTH...POLICY NAT/COMP 20. PAGE 66 F1293 INT/ORG

B66
LAMBERG R.F.,PRAG UND DIE DRITTE WELT. AFR ASIA CZECHOSLVK L/A+17C MARKET TEC/DEV ECO/TAC REV ATTIT 20 TREATY. PAGE 75 F1462 DIPLOM ECO/UNDEV INT/TRADE FOR/AID

B66
SPULBER N.,THE STATE AND ECONOMIC DEVELOPMENT IN EASTERN EUROPE. BULGARIA COM CZECHOSLVK HUNGARY POLAND YUGOSLAVIA CULTURE PLAN CAP/ISM INT/TRADE CONTROL...POLICY CHARTS METH/COMP BIBLIOG/A 19/20. PAGE 125 F2460 ECO/DEV ECO/UNDEV NAT/G TOTALISM

D

DAANE J.D. F0569

DAC....DEVELOPMENT ASSISTANCE COMMITTEE (PART OF OECD)

DAHL R.A. F0570,F0571,F0572

DAHOMEY....SEE ALSO AFR

DAKAR....DAKAR, SENEGAL

DALE E.L. F1821

DALE W.B. F0573

DALTON G. F0574

DALTON J.E. F0575

DALTON M. F0576

DANGERFIELD R. F0955

DANIEL C. F0577,F0578

DANIEL/Y....YULI DANIEL

DANIELS R.V. F0579

DANIELSON M.N. F0580

DANTE....DANTE ALIGHIERI

DARWIN/C....CHARLES DARWIN

B63
BARNETT H.J.,SCARCITY AND GROWTH: THE ECONOMICS OF NATURAL RESOURCE AVAILABILITY. FUT WOR+45 AGRI INDUS PROB/SOLV TEC/DEV CONTROL PRODUC...SOC/WK IDEA/COMP METH/COMP SIMUL 20 RESOURCE/N MALTHUS RICARDO/D MILL/JS DARWIN/C. PAGE 10 F0191 DEMAND HABITAT CENSUS GEOG

DATA ANALYSIS....SEE CON/ANAL, STAT, MATH, COMPUTER

DAUGHERTY C.R. F0581

DAVENPORT H.J. F0582

DAVIDSON R. F0278

DAVIES E. F0583,F0584

DAVIES I. F0585

DAVIES J.C. F0586

DAVIS E.H. F0587

DAVIS F.M. F0588

DAVIS H.B. F0589

DAVIS J. F0590

DAVIS K. F0591

DAVIS O.A. F0592,F0593

DAVIS/JEFF....JEFFERSON DAVIS

DAVIS/W....WARREN DAVIS

DAY A.C.L. F0594

DE BARY W.T. F0595

DE BELLECOMBE L.G. F2206

DE BLOCH J. F0596

DE FOREST J.D. F0597

DE GRAZIA A. F0598

DE GRAZIA S. F0599

DE JOUVENAL B. F0600

DE JOUVENEL B. F0601,F0602

DE LAVALLE H. F0603

DE MAN H. F0604,F0605

DE TORRES J. F0606

DE VRIES E. F0607,F0608

DEALEY S. F0609

DEANE H. F0610

DEATH....DEATH

N19
BROWN W.M.,THE DESIGN AND PERFORMANCE OF "OPTIMUM" BLAST SHELTER PROGRAMS (PAMPHLET). USA+45 ACT/RES PLAN DEATH COST EFFICIENCY OPTIMAL...POLICY CHARTS 20. PAGE 19 F0375 HABITAT NUC/PWR WAR HEALTH

B48
OSBORN F.,OUR PLUNDERED PLANET. UNIV DEATH WAR ...BIBLIOG RESOURCE/N. PAGE 102 F2001 HABITAT GEOG ADJUST AGRI

B59
LOPEZ VILLAMIL H.,A STATEMENT OF THE LAWS OF THE HONDURAS IN MATTERS AFFECTING BUSINESS (2ND ED.). HONDURAS DIST/IND EXTR/IND FINAN WORKER TAX DEATH MARRIAGE OWN MARITIME 20 MIGRATION. PAGE 82 F1600 CONSTN INDUS LEGIS NAT/G

L67
DEALEY S.,"MONETARY RECOVERY UNDER FEDERAL TRANSPORTATION STATUTES." USA+45 SEA WORKER TAX PAY ADJUD DEATH GOV/REL OWN HEALTH ORD/FREE 20. PAGE 31 F0609 DIST/IND LAW CONTROL FINAN

L67
ZEIDBERG L.D.,"THE NASHVILLE AIR POLLUTION STUDY" (PARTS V-VII)" USA+45 PLAN AGE HEALTH...GEOG STAT CENSUS SAMP/SIZ CHARTS BIBLIOG MUNICH. PAGE 150 F2962 DEATH HABITAT AIR BIO/SOC

DEBATE....ORGANIZED COLLECTIVE ARGUMENT

S47
DAHL R.A.,"WORKERS' CONTROL OF INDUSTRY AND THE BRITISH LABOUR PARTY." UK STRATA STRUCT DELIB/GP BARGAIN CAP/ISM DEBATE CONTROL CHOOSE GP/REL ATTIT ROLE PWR 19/20 PARLIAMENT LABOR/PAR FABIAN. PAGE 29 F0570 INDUS LABOR WORKER SOCISM

B51
US HOUSE COMM APPROPRIATIONS,MUTUAL SECURITY PROGRAM APPROPRIATIONS FOR 1952: HEARINGS BEFORE A SUBCOMMITTEE OF THE COMMITTEE ON APPROPRIATIONS. AFR KOREA L/A+17C ECO/DEV ECO/UNDEV INT/ORG INSPECT BAL/PWR DIPLOM DEBATE WAR...POLICY STAT ASIA/S 20 CONGRESS NATO MID/EAST. PAGE 136 F2686 LEGIS FORCES BUDGET FOR/AID

B52
SECRETARIAT COUNCIL OF EUROPE,THE STRASBOURG PLAN. EUR+WWI CONSULT PLAN ECO/TAC TARIFFS DEBATE REGION 20 COUNCL/EUR STRASBOURG. PAGE 119 F2340 INT/ORG ECO/DEV INT/TRADE DIPLOM

B56
US LIBRARY OF CONGRESS,UNITED STATES DIRECT ECONOMIC AID TO FOREIGN COUNTRIES: A COLLECTION OF EXCERPTS AND A BIBLIOGRAPHY (PAMPHLET). USA+45 PRESS DEBATE...ANTHOL BIBLIOG/A CONGRESS. PAGE 138 F2716 FOR/AID POLICY DIPLOM ECO/UNDEV

L56
PENNOCK J.R.,"PARTY AND CONSTITUENCY IN POSTWAR AGRICULTURAL PRICE SUPPORT LEGISLATION." USA+45 LEGIS DEBATE LOBBY RIGID/FLEX. PAGE 105 F2057 POL/PAR REPRESENT AGRI CHOOSE

B60
BAYER H.,WIRTSCHAFTSPROGNOSE UND WIRTSCHAFTSGESTALTUNG. GERMANY NETHERLAND MARKET PLAN CAP/ISM DEBATE...NAT/COMP 20. PAGE 12 F0220 ECO/DEV ECO/UNDEV FINAN POLICY

B60
WALLACE R.A.,CONGRESSIONAL CONTROL OF FEDERAL SPENDING. USA+45 CONSTN NAT/G OP/RES CONFER DEBATE PERS/REL UTIL RIGID/FLEX PWR OBJECTIVE...OBS CHARTS. PAGE 143 F2808 LEGIS DELIB/GP BUDGET

B61
CAMPAIGNE J.G.,CHECK-OFF: LABOR BOSSES AND WORKING MEN. LEGIS WORKER EDU/PROP DEBATE COERCE REPRESENT GP/REL ORD/FREE CONSERVE. PAGE 21 F0404 LABOR ELITES PWR CONTROL

B62
BUREAU OF NATIONAL AFFAIRS,FEDERAL-STATE REGULATION OF WELFARE FUNDS (REV. ED.). USA+45 LAW LEGIS DEBATE AGE/O 20 CONGRESS. PAGE 20 F0386 WELF/ST WEALTH PLAN

SOC/WK

B62
COLLIER A.T.,MANAGEMENT, MEN, AND VALUES. INDUS FACE/GP EX/STRUC PLAN PROB/SOLV DEBATE SENIOR ADMIN PROFIT PERSON...PSY SOC 20. PAGE 26 F0505 MGT ATTIT PERS/REL DECISION

B64
US DEPT LABOR OFF SOLICITOR,LEGISLATIVE HISTORY OF THE LABOR-MANAGEMENT AND DISCLOSURE ACT OF 1959. DELIB/GP WORKER ADMIN LOBBY PARL/PROC SANCTION CHOOSE GOV/REL 20 CONGRESS PRESIDENT. PAGE 136 F2677 LABOR LEGIS DEBATE POLICY

B66
AMER ENTERPRISE INST FOR PUBL,INTERNATIONAL PAYMENTS PROBLEM. MARKET DIPLOM DEBATE PRICE COST INCOME 20. PAGE 4 F0082 FINAN INT/TRADE POLICY

B66
US SENATE COMM APPROPRIATIONS,FOREIGN ASSISTANCE AND RELATED AGENCIES APPROPRIATIONS FOR FISCAL YEAR 1967: HEARINGS... ON H. R. 17788. ECO/UNDEV INT/ORG FORCES INSPECT ECO/TAC GIVE DEBATE WEAPON CIVMIL/REL WEALTH...INT 20 CONGRESS DEPT/DEFEN DEPT/STATE DEPT/HEW AID. PAGE 138 F2727 BUDGET FOR/AID DIPLOM COST

B67
BUREAU NATIONAL AFFAIRS,LABOR RELATIONS REFERENCE MANUAL VOL. 63. USA+45 CONSTN ECO/DEV PROVS WORKER DEBATE INGP/REL...DECISION 20. PAGE 20 F0385 LABOR ADJUD CT/SYS NAT/G

B67
SACKS B.,SOUTH AFRICA: AN IMPERIAL DILEMMA. SOUTH/AFR UK ECO/UNDEV KIN DOMIN DEBATE CONTROL REV DISCRIM ISOLAT...POLICY STAT BIBLIOG 20. PAGE 115 F2268 COLONIAL RACE/REL DIPLOM ORD/FREE

B67
TOMA P.A.,THE POLITICS OF FOOD FOR PEACE; EXECUTIVE-LEGISLATIVE INTERACTION. USA+45 ECO/UNDEV POL/PAR DEBATE EXEC LOBBY CHOOSE PEACE...DECISION CHARTS. PAGE 131 F2580 FOR/AID POLICY LEGIS AGRI

S67
BUTT R.,"THE COMMON MARKET AND CONSERVATIVE POLITICS, 1961-2." UK CHIEF DIPLOM ECO/TAC INT/TRADE CONFER DEBATE REGION ATTIT...POLICY 20 EEC. PAGE 21 F0398 EUR+WWI INT/ORG POL/PAR

S67
DAVIS O.A.,"ON THE DISTINCTION BETWEEN PUBLIC AND PRIVATE GOODS." USA+45 COM/IND LG/CO NAT/G TV DEBATE PRICE ADMIN ROLE...MATH IDEA/COMP. PAGE 31 F0593 MARKET OWN CONCPT

S67
GREEN C.,"SCHEMES FOR TRANSFERRING INCOME TO THE POOR." BUDGET GIVE RECEIVE DEBATE COST INCOME ...SOC/WK METH/COMP. PAGE 50 F0982 TAX WEALTH PLAN ACT/RES

S67
HILDEBRAND G.H.,"SECOND THOUGHTS ON THE NEGATIVE INCOME TAX." PLAN BUDGET ECO/TAC GIVE RECEIVE DEBATE EFFICIENCY INCOME...METH/COMP COSTS. PAGE 59 F1169 TAX WEALTH SOC/WK ACT/RES

S67
KOHN W.S.G.,"THE SOVEREIGNTY OF LIECHTENSTEIN." LIECHTENST SWITZERLND USSR CONSTN DEBATE WAR CONSERVE 18/20 UN. PAGE 72 F1417 SOVEREIGN NAT/G PWR DIPLOM

DEBENKO E. F0611

DEBS/E....EUGENE DEBS

DEBT....PUBLIC DEBT, INCLUDING NATIONAL DEBT;

B66
CONGRESSIONAL QUARTERLY SERV,FEDERAL ECONOMIC POLICY 1945-1965. USA+45 FINAN NAT/G CHIEF CONSULT TAX...CHARTS 20 PRESIDENT DEBT. PAGE 27 F0526 ECO/TAC BUDGET LEGIS

DEBUYST F. F0612

DECISION....DECISION-MAKING AND GAME THEORY; SEE ALSO GAME

N
US SUPERINTENDENT OF DOCUMENTS,INTERSTATE COMMERCE (PRICE LIST 59). USA+45 LAW LOC/G NAT/G LEGIS TARIFFS TAX ADMIN CONTROL HEALTH DECISION. PAGE 140 F2752 BIBLIOG/A DIST/IND GOV/REL PROVS

N
US SUPERINTENDENT OF DOCUMENTS,TARIFF AND TAXATION (PRICE LIST 37). USA+45 LAW INT/TRADE ADJUD ADMIN CT/SYS INCOME OWN...DECISION GATT. PAGE 140 F2754 BIBLIOG/A TAX TARIFFS NAT/G

C01
LOWELL A.L.,"THE INFLUENCE OF PARTY UPON LEGISLATION IN ENGLAND AND AMERICA" IN ANNUAL REPORT OF AMER HISTORICAL ASSN." LEGIS CONTROL ...CON/ANAL CHARTS 19/20 CONGRESS PARLIAMENT. PAGE 82 F1605 PARL/PROC POL/PAR DECISION OP/RES

N19
BASSIE V.L.,UNCERTAINTY IN FORECASTING AND POLICY FORMATION (PAMPHLET). UNIV MARKET ECO/TAC PRODUC ...POLICY DECISION MGT MATH CHARTS 20. PAGE 11 F0205 ECO/DEV FINAN PREDICT PROB/SOLV

N19
FIKS M.,PUBLIC ADMINISTRATION IN ISRAEL (PAMPHLET). ISRAEL SCHOOL EX/STRUC BUDGET PAY INGP/REL ...DECISION 20 CIVIL/SERV. PAGE 41 F0792 EDU/PROP NAT/G ADMIN WORKER

N19
KRIESBERG M.,CANCELLATION OF THE RATION STAMPS (PAMPHLET). USA+45 USA-45 MARKET PROB/SOLV PRICE GOV/REL RIGID/FLEX 20 OPA. PAGE 73 F1439 RATION DECISION ADMIN NAT/G

N19
MASCHLER M.,STABLE PAYOFF CONFIGURATIONS FOR QUOTA GAMES (PAMPHLET). PLAN PERS/REL 20. PAGE 87 F1694 ECOMETRIC GAME COMPUTER DECISION

N19
MIYASAWA K.,AN ECONOMIC SURVIVAL GAME (PAMPHLET). COST DEMAND EQUILIB INCOME PROFIT 20. PAGE 92 F1811 ECOMETRIC GAME ECO/TAC DECISION

N19
SAPIR H.M.,JAPAN, CHINA, AND THE WEST (PAMPHLET). AFR ASIA CHINA/COM PROB/SOLV GOV/REL 20 CHINJAP. PAGE 116 F2282 ECO/UNDEV INT/TRADE DECISION PLAN

N19
SILVERMAN C.,THE PRESIDENT'S ECONOMIC ADVISERS (PAMPHLET). USA+45 USA-45 ECO/DEV EX/STRUC ADMIN LEAD GOV/REL PERS/REL ROLE...POLICY DECISION 20 PRESIDENT CONGRESS EISNHWR/DD. PAGE 122 F2404 CONSULT PROB/SOLV NAT/G PLAN

B45
WOOTTON B.,FREEDOM UNDER PLANNING. UNIV ROUTINE ATTIT AUTHORIT DECISION. PAGE 148 F2926 PLAN ORD/FREE ECO/TAC CONTROL

B48
HAYEK F.A.,INDIVIDUALISM AND ECONOMIC ORDER. FINAN PLAN MORAL LAISSEZ SOCISM...POLICY DECISION PHIL/SCI HIST/WRIT. PAGE 57 F1122 RATIONAL KNOWL PERSON

B48
LAUTERBACH A.,ECONOMIC SECURITY AND INDIVIDUAL FREEDOM: CAN WE HAVE BOTH? COM EUR+WWI MOD/EUR UNIV WOR+45 CAP/ISM TOTALISM ALL/VALS...GOV/COMP BIBLIOG 20. PAGE 76 F1490 ORD/FREE ECO/DEV DECISION INGP/REL

S48
NOURSE E.G.,"THE ROLE OF THE COUNCIL OF ECONOMIC ADVISERS." USA+45 DELIB/GP...DECISION PRESIDENT. PAGE 99 F1938 EX/STRUC CHIEF PROB/SOLV

B50
KOENIG L.W.,THE SALE OF THE TANKERS. USA+45 SEA DIST/IND POL/PAR DIPLOM ADMIN CIVMIL/REL ATTIT ...DECISION 20 PRESIDENT DEPT/STATE. PAGE 72 F1414 NAT/G POLICY PLAN GOV/REL

S50
DREYFUS S.,"THE INDUSTRIAL DESIGNER AND THE BUSINESSMAN." SERV/IND PROB/SOLV ECO/TAC COST EFFICIENCY PROFIT RATIONAL...DECISION MGT. PAGE 34 F0662 CONSULT INDUS PRODUC UTIL

B52
GALBRAITH J.K.,AMERICAN CAPITALISM: THE CONCEPT OF COUNTERVAILING POWER. AFR FUT USA+45 FINAN PRICE CENTRAL INCOME PEACE WEALTH...POLICY DECISION 20. PAGE 45 F0881 ECO/TAC CAP/ISM TREND NAT/G

B53
BOWEN H.R.,SOCIAL RESPONSIBILITIES OF THE BUSINESSMAN (FIRST EDITION). LAW FINAN ACT/RES CAP/ISM ROUTINE DRIVE PWR LAISSEZ...DECISION BIBLIOG. PAGE 17 F0326 MGT PERSON SUPEGO MORAL

B53
SAYLES L.R.,THE LOCAL UNION. CONSTN CULTURE DELIB/GP PARTIC CHOOSE GP/REL INGP/REL ATTIT ROLE ...MAJORIT DECISION MGT. PAGE 116 F2284 LABOR LEAD ADJUD ROUTINE

S53
DRUCKER P.F.,"THE EMPLOYEE SOCIETY." STRUCT BAL/PWR PARTIC REPRESENT PWR...DECISION CONCPT. PAGE 34 F0666 LABOR MGT WORKER CULTURE

S53
LINCOLN G.,"FACTORS DETERMINING ARMS AID." COM FUT USA+45 USSR WOR+45 ECO/DEV NAT/G CONSULT PLAN TEC/DEV DIPLOM DOMIN EDU/PROP PERCEPT PWR ...DECISION CONCPT TREND MARX/KARL 20. PAGE 80 F1566 FORCES POLICY BAL/PWR FOR/AID

B55
BRAUN K.,LABOR DISPUTES AND THEIR SETTLEMENT. ECO/TAC ROUTINE TASK GP/REL...DECISION GEN/LAWS. PAGE 18 F0342 INDUS LABOR BARGAIN ADJUD

B55
JOHR W.A.,THE ROLE OF THE ECONOMIST AS OFFICIAL CONSULT

ADVISER. WOR+45 INTELL ECO/DEV NAT/G PLAN GP/REL ROLE...DECISION PREDICT IDEA/COMP. PAGE 68 F1336
ECO/TAC POLICY INGP/REL

S55
DIESING P.,"NONECONOMIC DECISION-MAKING" (BMR)" PROB/SOLV GP/REL ORD/FREE...STAT METH/COMP SIMUL 20. PAGE 33 F0638
DECISION METH EFFICIENCY SOC

B56
BURKHEAD J.,GOVERNMENT BUDGETING. ECO/DEV PROB/SOLV ECO/TAC ADMIN ROUTINE GOV/REL EFFICIENCY...DECISION MGT. PAGE 20 F0388
BUDGET NAT/G PROVS EX/STRUC

L56
SCHELLING T.C.,"AN ESSAY ON BARGAINING" (BMR)" OP/RES PROB/SOLV PRICE CHOOSE PWR...DECISION MODELS 20. PAGE 116 F2294
BARGAIN MARKET ECO/TAC GAME

S56
HARSANYI J.C.,"APPROACHES TO THE BARGAINING PROBLEM BEFORE AND AFTER THE THEORY OF GAMES."...DECISION CON/ANAL SIMUL GEN/LAWS. PAGE 56 F1096
NEW/IDEA GAME IDEA/COMP

S56
LANDAUER J.D.,"PROFESSIONAL CONSULTANTS: A NEW FACTOR IN REAL ESTATE." USA+45 PROB/SOLV ECO/TAC PERS/REL DEMAND EFFICIENCY DECISION. PAGE 75 F1467
CONSULT CONSTRUC CLIENT

C56
MCKEE J.B.,"THE POWER TO DECIDE" IN M. WEINBERG AND O. SHABET, SOCIETY AND MAN." ELITES STRATA REPRESENT GP/REL ATTIT PWR MUNICH BUSINESS. PAGE 88 F1731
LABOR DECISION LEAD

B57
DOWNS A.,AN ECONOMIC THEORY OF DEMOCRACY. NAT/G EDU/PROP RISK CHOOSE PERS/REL EQUILIB...SOC METH/CNCPT LOG STYLE. PAGE 34 F0659
DECISION RATIONAL

S57
CUNNINGHAM E.M.,"THE BUSINESS MAN AND HIS LAWYER." USA+45 LG/CO SML/CO TOP/EX CHOOSE SKILL...JURID MGT 20. PAGE 29 F0561
CONSULT LAW DECISION SERV/IND

S57
DETAMBEL M.H.,"PROBABILITY AND WORK AS DETERMINERS OF MULTICHOICE BEHAVIOR." PLAN TASK EFFICIENCY ...DECISION GAME. PAGE 32 F0622
HYPO/EXP PROB/SOLV GEN/LAWS PROBABIL

S57
HOAG M.W.,"ECONOMIC PROBLEMS OF ALLIANCE." AFR COM EUR+WWI WOR+45 ECO/DEV ECO/UNDEV NAT/G VOL/ASSN FORCES PLAN TEC/DEV DIPLOM COERCE ORD/FREE PWR WEALTH...DECISION GEN/LAWS NATO TERR/GP. PAGE 60 F1182
INT/ORG ECO/TAC

S57
KAHN R.L.,"UNION PRACTICES AND MEMBER PARTICIPATION." PARTIC CHOOSE REPRESENT PERS/REL PERSON SKILL...DECISION METH/CNCPT QU. PAGE 69 F1347
INGP/REL LABOR ATTIT LEAD

N57
U WISCONSIN BUREAU OF GOVT,SERVICE SALES OF THE CITY OF MADISON TO METROPOLITAN COMMUNITIES AND NONRESIDENTS (PAMPHLET). DIST/IND LOC/G ADMIN ...DECISION GOV/COMP MUNICH. PAGE 132 F2597
REGION ECO/TAC PLAN

B58
SCOTT D.J.R.,RUSSIAN POLITICAL INSTITUTIONS. RUSSIA USSR CONSTN AGRI DELIB/GP PLAN EDU/PROP CONTROL CHOOSE EFFICIENCY ATTIT MARXISM...BIBLIOG/A IND 13/20. PAGE 118 F2332
NAT/G POL/PAR ADMIN DECISION

B58
THEIL H.,ECONOMIC FORECASTS AND POLICY. UNIV CAP/ISM PRICE EFFICIENCY...DECISION CONCPT STAT 20. PAGE 129 F2551
SIMUL MATH ECOMETRIC PREDICT

L58
ARROW K.J.,"ON THE STABILITY OF THE COMPETITIVE EQUILIBRIUM: I." WOR+45...METH/CNCPT MATH STAT CHARTS SIMUL. PAGE 6 F0122
DECISION MARKET ECO/DEV ECO/TAC

L58
CYERT R.M.,"THE ROLE OF EXPECTATIONS IN BUSINESS DECISION-MAKING." PROB/SOLV PRICE RIGID/FLEX. PAGE 29 F0566
LG/CO DECISION ROUTINE EXEC

L58
FORRESTER J.W.,"INDUSTRIAL DYNAMICS* A MAJOR BREAKTHROUGH FOR DECISION MAKERS." COMPUTER OP/RES ...DECISION CONCPT NEW/IDEA. PAGE 42 F0830
INDUS ACT/RES MGT PROB/SOLV

S58
ARROW K.J.,"UTILITIES, ATTITUDES, CHOICES: A REVIEW NOTE." USA+45 PLAN...METH/CNCPT MATH STAT CHARTS HYPO/EXP. PAGE 6 F0121
DECISION DIST/IND MARKET CREATE

S58
ARROW K.J.,"A NOTE ON EXPECTATIONS AND STABILITY." WOR+45...METH/CNCPT MATH STAT CHARTS HYPO/EXP. PAGE 7 F0123
DECISION MARKET ECO/DEV ECO/TAC

S58
FOLDES L.,"UNCERTAINTY, PROBABILITY AND POTENTIAL SURPRISE." MARKET PROB/SOLV RISK PERSON...DECISION MGT HYPO/EXP GAME. PAGE 42 F0820
PROBABIL ADMIN ROUTINE

B59
CONTY J.M.,PSYCHOLOGIE DE LA DECISION....PSY GAME 20. PAGE 27 F0528
DECISION PROB/SOLV OP/RES METH/COMP

B59
KARLIN S.,MATHEMATICAL METHODS AND THEORY IN GAMES, PROGRAMMING, AND ECONOMICS. COMPUTER PLAN CONTROL TASK...MATH 20. PAGE 69 F1357
GAME METH/COMP ACT/RES DECISION

B59
MARTIN D.D.,MERGERS AND THE CLAYTON ACT. FINAN LEGIS GP/REL...DECISION METH/COMP BIBLIOG 20. PAGE 86 F1681
OWN ECO/TAC LG/CO POLICY

B59
SELIGSOHN I.J.,"USING COMPUTER SERVICES IN SMALL BUSINESS" MANAGEMENT AIDS FOR SMALL MANUFACTURERS 109 (PAMPHLET). DIST/IND MARKET PROC/MFG COST EFFICIENCY PRODUC...DECISION IDEA/COMP. PAGE 119 F2350
SML/CO COMPUTER MGT PROB/SOLV

B59
SERAPHIM H.J.,PROBLEME DER WILLENSBILDUNG UND DER WIRTSCHAFTSPOLITISCHEN FUEHRUNG. WOR+45 MARKET ACT/RES OP/RES PLAN EDU/PROP INGP/REL HABITAT PLURISM...MGT PERS/COMP METH 20. PAGE 119 F2357
POLICY DECISION PSY

B59
SHUBIK M.,STRATEGY AND MARKET STRUCTURE: COMPETITION, OLIGOPOLY, AND THE THEORY OF GAMES. ELITES STRUCT MARKET OP/RES EXEC EFFICIENCY INCOME ...MGT MATH STAT CHARTS 20. PAGE 121 F2389
ECO/DEV ECO/TAC DECISION GAME

L59
ARROW K.J.,"ON THE STABILITY OF THE COMPETITIVE EQUILIBRIUM: II." WOR+45...METH/CNCPT MATH STAT CHARTS HYPO/EXP. PAGE 7 F0124
DECISION MARKET ECO/DEV ECO/TAC

L59
SIMON H.A.,"THEORIES OF DECISION-MAKING IN ECONOMICS AND BEHAVIORAL SCIENCE" (BMR)" MARKET BARGAIN UTIL DRIVE...DECISION MGT PROBABIL HYPO/EXP SIMUL 20 BEHAVIORSM. PAGE 122 F2409
PSY GEN/LAWS PROB/SOLV

S59
CYERT R.M.,"MODELS IN A BEHAVIORAL THEORY OF THE FIRM." ROUTINE...DECISION MGT METH/CNCPT MATH. PAGE 29 F0567
SIMUL GAME PREDICT INDUS

S59
DUNNING J.H.,"NON-PECUNIARY ELEMENTS AND BUSINESS BEHAVIOUR." PLAN PROB/SOLV COST...METH/CNCPT CLASSIF QUANT STAT. PAGE 35 F0681
DECISION DRIVE PRODUC PRICE

S59
HARING J.E.,"UTILITY THEORY, DECISION THEORY, AND PROFIT MAXIMIZATION." PROB/SOLV GAMBLE UTIL ...DECISION CHARTS IDEA/COMP HYPO/EXP SIMUL GEN/METH. PAGE 55 F1083
PROBABIL RISK GAME

S59
TEITSWORTH C.S.,"GROWING ROLE OF THE COMPANY ECONOMIST." USA+45 PLAN PROB/SOLV CAP/ISM ECO/TAC ADMIN ATTIT MGT. PAGE 129 F2541
INDUS CONSULT UTIL DECISION

B60
BAERWALD F.,ECONOMIC SYSTEM ANALYSIS: CONCEPTS AND PERSPECTIVES. USA+45 ECO/DEV NAT/G COMPUTER EQUILIB INCOME ATTIT...DECISION CONCPT IDEA/COMP. PAGE 8 F0151
ACT/RES ECO/TAC ROUTINE FINAN

B60
EELLS R.S.F.,THE MEANING OF MODERN BUSINESS. LOC/G NAT/G NEIGH EX/STRUC PARTIC GP/REL INGP/REL DECISION. PAGE 36 F0706
LG/CO REPRESENT POLICY PLAN

B60
FINKLE J.L.,THE PRESIDENT MAKES A DECISION: A STUDY OF DIXON-YATES. OP/RES PROB/SOLV BUDGET ADMIN GOV/REL...POLICY BIBLIOG/A 20 PRESIDENT. PAGE 41 F0799
DECISION CHIEF PWR POL/PAR

B60
FORBUSH D.R.,PROBLEMS OF CORPORATE POWER. CLIENT LAW ELITES ADJUD...DECISION MGT. PAGE 42 F0822
LG/CO PWR CONTROL GP/REL

B60
FRANCIS R.G.,THE PREDICTIVE PROCESS. PLAN MARXISM ...DECISION SOC CONCPT NAT/COMP 19/20. PAGE 43 F0840
PREDICT PHIL/SCI TREND

B60
MORRIS W.T.,ENGINEERING ECONOMY. AUTOMAT RISK RATIONAL...PROBABIL STAT CHARTS GAME SIMUL BIBLIOG T 20. PAGE 94 F1838
OP/RES DECISION MGT PROB/SOLV

B60
SIEGEL S.,BARGAINING AND GROUP DECISION-MAKING:
DECISION

EXPERIMENTS IN BILATERAL MONOPOLY. EFFICIENCY...PSY CHARTS. PAGE 122 F2397 PERS/REL PROB/SOLV BARGAIN
B60

VERNON R.,METROPOLIS 1985. LOC/G PLAN TAX LEAD PWR MUNICH. PAGE 141 F2780 REGION ECO/TAC DECISION
S60

FORM W.H.,"ORGANIZED LABOR'S IMAGE OF COMMUNITY POWER STRUCTURE." LABOR LG/CO CONTROL LEAD REPRESENT...DECISION METH/CNCPT INT QU SAMP. PAGE 42 F0829 NEIGH PARTIC PWR GP/REL
S60

FRENCH J.R.P. JR.,"AN EXPERIMENT ON PARTICIPATION IN A NORWEGIAN FACTORY:INTERPERSONAL DIMENSIONS OF DECISION-MAKING." LABOR LEAD PERS/REL EFFICIENCY PRODUC...DECISION SOC CHARTS SOC/EXP. PAGE 44 F0853 INDUS PLAN RIGID/FLEX GP/REL
B61

DELEFORTRIE-SOU N.,LES DIRIGEANTS DE L'INDUSTRIE FRANCAISE. FRANCE CULTURE ELITES PROB/SOLV ...DECISION STAT CHARTS 20. PAGE 32 F0613 INDUS STRATA TOP/EX LEAD
B61

GORDON R.A.,BUSINESS LEADERSHIP IN THE LARGE CORPORATION. USA+45 SOCIETY EX/STRUC ADMIN CONTROL ROUTINE GP/REL PWR...MGT 20. PAGE 49 F0960 LG/CO LEAD DECISION LOBBY
B61

MAYNE A.,DESIGNING AND ADMINISTERING A REGIONAL ECONOMIC DEVELOPMENT PLAN WITH SPECIFIC REFERENCE TO PUERTO RICO (PAMPHLET). PUERT/RICO SOCIETY NAT/G DELIB/GP REGION...DECISION 20. PAGE 87 F1707 ECO/UNDEV PLAN CREATE ADMIN
B61

UNIVS-NATL BUR COMM ECO RES,PUBLIC FINANCES: NEEDS, SOURCES, AND UTILIZATION. USA+45 FORCES PLAN TAX CONFER PRICE FEDERAL UTIL...ANTHOL MUNICH 20. PAGE 133 F2623 NAT/G FINAN DECISION BUDGET
S61

BENNION E.G.,"ECONOMETRICS FOR MANAGEMENT." USA+45 INDUS EX/STRUC ACT/RES COMPUTER UTIL...MATH STAT PREDICT METH/COMP HYPO/EXP. PAGE 13 F0248 ECOMETRIC MGT SIMUL DECISION
S61

CYERT R.M.,"TWO EXPERIMENTS ON BIAS AND CONFLICT IN ORGANIZATIONAL ESTIMATION." WORKER PROB/SOLV EFFICIENCY...MGT PSY STAT CHARTS. PAGE 29 F0568 LAB/EXP ROUTINE ADMIN DECISION
S61

HIRSHLEIFER J.,"THE BAYESIAN APPROACH TO STATISTICAL DECISION: AN EXPOSITION." OP/RES PROB/SOLV UTIL...PROBABIL CHARTS IDEA/COMP HYPO/EXP 20. PAGE 60 F1178 DECISION GAME SIMUL STAT
S61

SHUBIK M.,"APPROACHES TO THE STUDY OF DECISION-MAKING RELEVANT TO THE FIRM." INDUS COMPUTER OP/RES ...PROBABIL STAT 20. PAGE 121 F2390 GAME DECISION MGT SIMUL
N61

US ADVISORY COMN INTERGOV REL,STATE CONSTITUTIONAL AND STATUTORY RESTRICTIONS ON LOCAL GOVERNMENT DEBT (PAMPHLET). LAW CONSTN CHOOSE PWR...DECISION MUNICH. PAGE 133 F2631 TAX PROVS GOV/REL
B62

BRANCH M.C.,THE CORPORATE PLANNING PROCESS. FINAN EX/STRUC EDU/PROP CONTROL LEAD GP/REL PERS/REL RATIONAL PERCEPT...MGT MATH PROBABIL STAT GAME. PAGE 18 F0338 PROF/ORG PLAN DECISION PERSON
B62

CHANDLER A.D.,STRATEGY AND STRUCTURE: CHAPTERS IN THE HISTORY OF THE INDUSTRIAL ENTERPRISE. USA+45 USA-45 ECO/DEV EX/STRUC ECO/TAC EXEC...DECISION 20. PAGE 23 F0446 LG/CO PLAN ADMIN FINAN
B62

COLLIER A.T.,MANAGEMENT, MEN, AND VALUES. INDUS FACE/GP EX/STRUC PLAN PROB/SOLV DEBATE SENIOR ADMIN PROFIT PERSON...PSY SOC 20. PAGE 26 F0505 MGT ATTIT PERS/REL DECISION
B62

GALENSON W.,TRADE UNIONS MONOGRAPH SERIES (A SERIES OF NINE TEXTS). DELIB/GP LEAD PARTIC...DECISION ORG/CHARTS. PAGE 45 F0887 LABOR INGP/REL CONSTN REPRESENT
B62

GERSCHENKRON A.,ECONOMIC BACKWARDNESS IN HISTORICAL PERSPECTIVE. WOR+45 WOR-45 ECO/DEV ECO/UNDEV INDUS NAT/G LEGIT DRIVE...WELF/ST DECISION QUANT TREND CHARTS 20. PAGE 47 F0919 TEC/DEV USSR
B62

HIRSCHFIELD R.S.,THE CONSTITUTION AND THE COURT. AFR SCHOOL WAR RACE/REL EQUILIB ORD/FREE...POLICY MAJORIT DECISION JURID 18/20 PRESIDENT CIVIL/LIB SUPREME/CT CONGRESS. PAGE 60 F1175 ADJUD PWR CONSTN LAW
B62

JORDAN A.A. JR.,FOREIGN AID AND THE DEFENSE OF SOUTHEAST ASIA. PAKISTAN VIETNAM/S FINAN PLAN BUDGET ECO/TAC DETER WAR ORD/FREE...POLICY DECISION CENSUS CHARTS BIBLIOG 20. PAGE 68 F1341 FOR/AID S/ASIA FORCES ECO/UNDEV
B62

LICHFIELD N.,COST-BENEFIT ANALYSIS IN URBAN REDEVELOPMENT. CONSTRUC LOC/G NEIGH ACT/RES PROB/SOLV TEC/DEV BUDGET TAX...DECISION STAT CHARTS SOC/EXP MUNICH 20. PAGE 80 F1558 PLAN COST GOV/REL
B62

MOWITZ R.J.,PROFILE OF A METROPOLIS: A CASE BOOK. COM/IND CONSTRUC INDUS PUB/INST PLAN TEC/DEV LEAD GP/REL...POLICY TECHNIC WELF/ST MUNICH. PAGE 94 F1851 DECISION ADMIN
B62

NATIONAL BUREAU ECONOMIC RES,THE RATE AND DIRECTION OF INVENTIVE ACTIVITY: ECONOMIC AND SOCIAL FACTORS. STRUCT INDUS MARKET R+D CREATE OP/RES TEC/DEV EFFICIENCY PRODUC RATIONAL UTIL...WELF/ST PHIL/SCI METH/CNCPT TIME. PAGE 97 F1895 DECISION PROB/SOLV MGT
B62

SCHALLER H.G.,PUBLIC EXPENDITURE DECISIONS IN THE URBAN COMMUNITY: PREPARED FOR RESOURCES FOR THE FUTURE, INC. INDUS SERV/IND LOC/G PUB/INST PLAN PROB/SOLV BUDGET DEMAND PRODUC...CHARTS MUNICH. PAGE 116 F2289 FINAN DECISION
B62

SMITH G.A. JR.,POLICY FORMULATION AND ADMINISTRATION: A CASEBOOK OF TOPMANAGEMENT PROBLEMS IN BUSINESS. EX/STRUC PLAN PROB/SOLV ADMIN CONTROL EXEC LEAD ROUTINE EFFICIENCY ATTIT MGT. PAGE 123 F2430 INDUS SOC/EXP TOP/EX DECISION
L62

ERDMANN H.H.,"ADMINISTRATIVE LAW AND FARM ECONOMICS." USA+45 LOC/G NAT/G PLAN PROB/SOLV LOBBY ...DECISION ANTHOL 20. PAGE 38 F0744 AGRI ADMIN ADJUD POLICY
L62

N,"UNION INVESTMENT IN BUSINESS: A SOURCE OF UNION CONFLICT OF INTEREST." LAW NAT/G LEGIS CONTROL GP/REL INGP/REL DECISION. PAGE 96 F1884 LABOR POLICY FINAN LG/CO
S62

BIERMAN H.,"PROBABILITY, STATISTICAL DECISION THEORY, AND ACCOUNTING." ACADEM TASK EFFICIENCY ...METH/CNCPT GEN/METH 20. PAGE 15 F0283 FINAN QUANT DECISION STAT
S62

LIPSON H.A.,"FORMAL REASONING AND MARKETING STRATEGY." ECO/DEV PROB/SOLV PRICE ALL/VALS CONT/OBS. PAGE 81 F1578 MARKET DECISION GAME ECO/TAC
S62

MUELLER E.,"LOCATION DECISIONS OF MANUFACTURERS." USA+45 MARKET ATTIT...POLICY STAT INT CHARTS 20. PAGE 94 F1852 DECISION PROC/MFG GEOG TOP/EX
B63

BERLE A.A. JR.,THE AMERICAN ECONOMIC REPUBLIC. STRUCT FINAN MARKET LABOR NAT/G PLAN...POLICY WELF/ST DECISION. PAGE 14 F0262 CAP/ISM ECO/TAC TREND CONCPT
B63

BONINI C.P.,SIMULATION OF INFORMATION AND DECISION SYSTEMS IN THE FIRM. MARKET BUDGET DOMIN EDU/PROP ADMIN COST ATTIT HABITAT PERCEPT PWR...CONCPT PROBABIL QUANT PREDICT HYPO/EXP BIBLIOG. PAGE 16 F0313 INDUS SIMUL DECISION MGT
B63

BRAYBROOKE D.,A STRATEGY OF DECISION: POLICY EVALUATION AS A SOCIAL PROCESS. UNIV ELITES OP/RES DOMIN CONFER FEEDBACK CONSEN PLURISM...CONCPT CENSUS. PAGE 18 F0343 DECISION POLICY CONTROL
B63

BROUDE H.W.,STEEL DECISIONS AND THE NATIONAL ECONOMY. USA+45 LG/CO PLAN ADMIN COST DECISION. PAGE 19 F0365 PROC/MFG NAT/G CONTROL ECO/TAC
B63

CALKINS R.D.,ECONOMICS AS AN AID TO POLICY (PAMPHLET). USA+45 NAT/G LEAD 20. PAGE 21 F0401 CONSULT DECISION EFFICIENCY
B63

CHAMPION J.M.,CRITICAL INCIDENTS IN MANAGEMENT. MARKET LG/CO SML/CO OP/RES ADMIN CONTROL LEAD GP/REL PERS/REL COST ATTIT SUPEGO ALL/VALS...PSY PERS/TEST BIBLIOG. PAGE 23 F0445 MGT DECISION EX/STRUC INDUS
B63

CORLEY R.N.,THE LEGAL ENVIRONMENT OF BUSINESS. CONSTN LEGIS TAX ADMIN CT/SYS DISCRIM ATTIT PWR ...TREND 18/20. PAGE 28 F0537 NAT/G INDUS JURID DECISION
B63

JACOBS P.,STATE OF UNIONS. USA+45 STRATA TOP/EX GP/REL RACE/REL DEMAND DISCRIM ATTIT PWR 20 CONGRESS NEGRO HOFFA/J. PAGE 66 F1296 LABOR ECO/TAC BARGAIN DECISION
B63

LINDBERG L.,POLITICAL DYNAMICS OF EUROPEAN ECONOMIC MARKET

INTEGRATION. EUR+WWI ECO/DEV INT/ORG VOL/ASSN DELIB/GP ADMIN WEALTH...DECISION EEC TERR/GP 20. PAGE 80 F1567
ECO/TAC

B63
MEYNAUD J.,PLANIFICATION ET POLITIQUE. FRANCE ITALY FINAN LABOR DELIB/GP LEGIS ADMIN EFFICIENCY ...MAJORIT DECISION 20. PAGE 90 F1773
PLAN ECO/TAC PROB/SOLV

B63
MINER J.,SOCIAL AND ECONOMIC FACTORS IN SPENDING FOR PUBLIC EDUCATION. USA+45 FINAN SCHOOL OPTIMAL ...POLICY DECISION REGRESS PREDICT CHARTS SIMUL 20. PAGE 92 F1801
EDU/PROP NAT/G COST ACT/RES

B63
TREVES G.,GOVERNMENT ORGANIZATION FOR ECONOMIC DEVELOPMENT (PAMPHLET). WOR+45 LAW BUDGET ECO/TAC GOV/REL...DECISION 20. PAGE 131 F2585
ECO/DEV ECO/UNDEV PLAN POLICY

B63
US ADVISORY COMN INTERGOV REL,PERFORMANCE OF URBAN FUNCTIONS: LOCAL AND AREAWIDE. TEC/DEV PARTIC REPRESENT PWR...DECISION GOV/COMP MUNICH. PAGE 133 F2633
REGION LOC/G ECO/TAC

S63
ENTHOVEN A.C.,"ECONOMIC ANALYSIS IN THE DEPARTMENT OF DEFENSE." USA+45 NAT/G DELIB/GP PROB/SOLV RATION NUC/PWR WEAPON COST...DECISION 20 DEPT/DEFEN RESOURCE/N. PAGE 38 F0739
PLAN BUDGET ECO/TAC FORCES

B64
BLACKSTOCK P.W.,THE STRATEGY OF SUBVERSION. USA+45 FORCES EDU/PROP ADMIN COERCE GOV/REL...DECISION MGT 20 DEPT/DEFEN CIA DEPT/STATE. PAGE 15 F0292
ORD/FREE DIPLOM CONTROL

B64
BRIGHT J.R.,RESEARCH, DEVELOPMENT AND TECHNOLOGICAL INNOVATION. CULTURE R+D CREATE PLAN PROB/SOLV AUTOMAT RISK PERSON...DECISION CONCPT PREDICT BIBLIOG. PAGE 18 F0352
TEC/DEV NEW/IDEA INDUS MGT

B64
BROWN E.H.P.,A COURSE IN APPLIED ECONOMICS (2ND ED.). ECO/DEV FINAN MARKET WORKER INT/TRADE RATION RENT PAY PRICE BAL/PAY...DECISION T RESOURCE/N. PAGE 19 F0368
POLICY ECO/TAC PROB/SOLV

B64
DANIELS R.V.,RUSSIA. RUSSIA USSR STRUCT NAT/LISM TOTALISM ORD/FREE WEALTH...POLICY DECISION TREND. PAGE 30 F0579
MARXISM REV ECO/DEV DIPLOM

B64
ECONOMIDES C.P.,LE POUVOIR DE DECISION DES ORGANISATIONS INTERNATIONALES EUROPEENNES. DIPLOM DOMIN INGP/REL EFFICIENCY...INT/LAW JURID 20 NATO OEEC EEC COUNCL/EUR EURATOM. PAGE 36 F0698
INT/ORG PWR DECISION GP/COMP

B64
EINZIG P.,MONETARY POLICY: ENDS AND MEANS. AFR UK INDUS WORKER PLAN DIPLOM PRICE BAL/PAY COST WEALTH ...DECISION TIME/SEQ 20. PAGE 37 F0715
FINAN POLICY ECO/TAC BUDGET

B64
FITCH L.C.,URBAN TRANSPORTATION AND PUBLIC POLICY. FINAN NAT/G LEGIS PROB/SOLV TEC/DEV PRICE COST EFFICIENCY...DECISION STAT CHARTS METH/COMP MUNICH 20 NEWYORK/C PHILADELPH LOS/ANG CHICAGO WASHING/DC. PAGE 41 F0806
DIST/IND PLAN LOC/G

B64
JUSTER F.T.,ANTICIPATIONS AND PURCHASES; AN ANALYSIS OF CONSUMER BEHAVIOR. PROB/SOLV RISK COST PRODUC DRIVE...STAT STYLE SAMP CON/ANAL CHARTS HYPO/EXP GAME SIMUL. PAGE 68 F1345
PROBABIL DECISION PREDICT DEMAND

B64
LANGHOFF P.,MODELS, MEASUREMENT AND MARKETING. ACT/RES COMPUTER OP/RES PLAN BUDGET...MGT PHIL/SCI METH/CNCPT STAT PROG/TEAC BIBLIOG. PAGE 75 F1478
DECISION SIMUL MARKET R+D

B64
MANN B.,STATE CONSTITUTIONAL RESTRICTIONS ON LOCAL BORROWING AND PROPERTY TAXING POWERS. USA+45 CONSTN PROVS CT/SYS GOV/REL PWR...DECISION JURID CHARTS 20. PAGE 84 F1654
LOC/G TAX FINAN LAW

B64
MEYER J.R.,INVESTMENT DECISIONS, ECONOMIC FORECASTING, AND PUBLIC POLICY. ECO/DEV ECO/TAC ...DECISION REGRESS TIME/SEQ CHARTS GP/COMP SIMUL 20. PAGE 90 F1771
FINAN PROB/SOLV PREDICT LG/CO

B64
MOAK L.L.,A MANUAL OF SUGGESTED PRACTICE FOR THE PREPARATION AND ADOPTION OF CAPITAL PROGRAMS AND CAPITAL BUDGETS BY LOCAL GOVERN. USA+45 DELIB/GP PLAN TAX GP/REL COST DECISION. PAGE 92 F1812
LOC/G BUDGET LEGIS PROB/SOLV

B64
ROBINSON R.D.,INTERNATIONAL BUSINESS POLICY. AFR INDIA L/A+17C USA+45 ELITES AGRI FOR/AID COERCE BAL/PAY...DECISION INT/LAW MGT 20. PAGE 113 F2224
ECO/TAC DIST/IND COLONIAL FINAN

B64
STEWART C.F.,A BIBLIOGRAPHY OF INTERNATIONAL BUSINESS. WOR+45 FINAN LG/CO NAT/G PLAN ECO/TAC TARIFFS...DECISION MGT GP/COMP NAT/COMP 20 EEC. PAGE 126 F2484
BIBLIOG INT/ORG OP/RES INT/TRADE

B64
TINBERGEN J.,CENTRAL PLANNING. COM INTELL ECO/DEV ECO/UNDEV FINAN INT/ORG PROB/SOLV ECO/TAC CONTROL EXEC ROUTINE DECISION. PAGE 130 F2576
PLAN INDUS MGT CENTRAL

L64
ARMENGALD A.,"ECONOMIE ET COEXISTENCE." COM EUR+WWI FUT USA+45 WOR+45 ECO/DEV ECO/UNDEV FINAN INT/ORG NAT/G EXEC CHOOSE ATTIT ALL/VALS...POLICY RELATIV DECISION TREND SOC/EXP WORK 20. PAGE 6 F0113
MARKET ECO/TAC AFR CAP/ISM

L64
KOLODZIEJ E.A.,"RATIONAL CONSENT AND DEFENSE BUDGETS: THE ROLE OF CONGRESS, 1945-1962." LEGIS DIPLOM CONTROL PARL/PROC 20 CONGRESS. PAGE 72 F1423
DECISION PLAN CIVMIL/REL BUDGET

S64
BEIM D.,"THE COMMUNIST BLOC AND THE FOREIGN-AID GAME." AFR WOR+45 NAT/G PLAN ROUTINE ATTIT KNOWL ORD/FREE...DECISION QUANT CONT/OBS TIME/SEQ CHARTS GAME SIMUL LOG/LING 20. PAGE 12 F0231
COM ECO/UNDEV ECO/TAC FOR/AID

S64
CLELLAND D.A.,"ECONOMIC DOMINANTS AND COMMUNITY POWER: A COMPARATIVE ANALYSIS." ELITES ADJUST ATTIT WEALTH...DECISION MUNICH. PAGE 25 F0488
LEAD MGT PWR

S64
GARDNER R.N.,"GATT AND THE UNITED NATIONS CONFERENCE ON TRADE AND DEVELOPMENT." USA+45 WOR+45 SOCIETY ECO/UNDEV MARKET NAT/G DELIB/GP ACT/RES PLAN ECO/TAC TARIFFS EDU/PROP ROUTINE DRIVE RIGID/FLEX WEALTH...DECISION MGT TREND UN TOT/POP 20 GATT. PAGE 46 F0905
INT/ORG INT/TRADE

S64
STONE P.A.,"DECISION TECHNIQUES FOR TOWN DEVELOPMENT." PLAN COST PROFIT...DECISION MGT CON/ANAL CHARTS METH/COMP BIBLIOG MUNICH 20. PAGE 127 F2497
OP/RES ADMIN PROB/SOLV

B65
BAUMOL W.J.,ECONOMIC THEORY AND OPERATIONS ANALYSIS (2ND ED.). MARKET LG/CO BUDGET PRICE COST EQUILIB PRODUC...DECISION MATH CHARTS GAME 20. PAGE 12 F0219
OP/RES ECO/DEV METH/COMP STAT

B65
BEAUFRE A.,AN INTRODUCTION TO STRATEGY, WITH PARTICULAR REFERENCE TO PROBLEMS OF DEFENSE, POLITICS, ECONOMICS IN THE NUCLEAR AGE. WOR+45 FORCES DIPLOM DETER CIVMIL/REL GP/REL...NEW/IDEA IDEA/COMP 20. PAGE 12 F0226
PLAN NUC/PWR WEAPON DECISION

B65
BLAIR T.L.V.,AFRICA: A MARKET PROFILE. AFR COM/IND DIST/IND FINAN UTIL...DECISION CHARTS BIBLIOG 20. PAGE 15 F0295
MARKET OP/RES ECO/UNDEV INDUS

B65
BOLLENS J.C.,THE METROPOLIS: ITS PEOPLE, POLITICS, AND ECONOMIC LIFE. USA+45 PLAN PROB/SOLV PERS/REL PWR...DECISION GEOG CENSUS TREND CON/ANAL MUNICH 20 NEWYORK/C LOS/ANG SAN/FRAN CHICAGO PHILADELPH. PAGE 16 F0309
HABITAT SOC LOC/G

B65
DANIELSON M.N.,FEDERAL-METROPOLITAN POLITICS AND THE COMMUTER CRISIS. PROVS LEGIS EXEC LEAD PWR ...DECISION MUNICH. PAGE 30 F0580
FEDERAL GOV/REL DIST/IND

B65
DERBER M.,PLANT UNION-MANAGEMENT RELATIONS: FROM PRACTICE TO THEORY. PROC/MFG NEIGH PROB/SOLV ORD/FREE...DECISION MGT OBS QU SAMP. PAGE 32 F0621
LG/CO LABOR GP/REL ATTIT

B65
HICKMAN B.G.,QUANTITATIVE PLANNING OF ECONOMIC POLICY. FRANCE NETHERLAND OP/RES PRICE ROUTINE UTIL ...POLICY DECISION ECOMETRIC METH/CNCPT STAT STYLE CHINJAP. PAGE 59 F1162
PROB/SOLV PLAN QUANT

B65
KANTOROVICH L.V.,THE BEST USE OF ECONOMIC RESOURCES. USSR SOCIETY FINAN ACT/RES TEC/DEV ECO/TAC PRICE CONTROL COST DEMAND EFFICIENCY OPTIMAL...MGT STAT. PAGE 69 F1350
PLAN MATH DECISION

B65
MACDONALD R.W.,THE LEAGUE OF ARAB STATES: A STUDY IN THE DYNAMICS OF REGIONAL ORGANIZATION. ISRAEL UAR USSR FINAN INT/ORG DELIB/GP ECO/TAC AGREE NEUTRAL ORD/FREE PWR...DECISION BIBLIOG 20 TREATY UN. PAGE 83 F1626
ISLAM REGION DIPLOM ADMIN

B65
MARGOLIS J.,THE PUBLIC ECONOMY OF URBAN COMMUNITIES. USA+45 LEGIS PROB/SOLV TAX LOBBY CHOOSE ATTIT MUNICH. PAGE 85 F1668
LOC/G DECISION FINAN

B65
PHELPS E.S.,PRIVATE WANTS AND PUBLIC NEEDS - AN INTRODUCTION TO A CURRENT ISSUE OF PUBLIC POLICY (REV. ED.). USA+45 PLAN CAP/ISM INGP/REL ROLE ...DECISION TIME/SEQ 20. PAGE 106 F2081
NAT/G POLICY DEMAND

B65
PLOSS S.I.,CONFLICT AND DECISION-MAKING IN SOVIET RUSSIA - A CASE STUDY OF AGRICULTURAL POLICY -
AGRI DECISION

1953-1963. USSR DELIB/GP INGP/REL PWR MARXISM. PAGE 106 F2093 — ATTIT

B65
RANSOM H.H.,AN AMERICAN FOREIGN POLICY READER. USA+45 FORCES EDU/PROP COERCE NUC/PWR WAR PEACE ...DECISION 20. PAGE 109 F2146 — NAT/G DIPLOM POLICY

B65
REDFORD E.S.,AMERICAN GOVERNMENT AND THE ECONOMY. FUT USA+45 USA-45 INDUS PROB/SOLV GOV/REL...POLICY DECISION METH/COMP BIBLIOG T 18/20. PAGE 110 F2168 — CONSTN NAT/G

B65
RIGBY P.H.,CONCEPTUAL FOUNDATIONS OF BUSINESS RESEARCH. COMPUTER PROB/SOLV OPTIMAL...MGT CONCPT MATH STAT TESTS SIMUL GEN/METH. PAGE 111 F2192 — PROFIT R+D INDUS DECISION

B65
TYBOUT R.A.,ECONOMICS OF RESEARCH AND DEVELOPMENT. ECO/DEV ECO/UNDEV INDUS PROFIT DECISION. PAGE 131 F2594 — R+D FORCES ADMIN DIPLOM

B65
WALTON R.E.,A BEHAVIORAL THEORY OF LABOR NEGOTIATIONS: AN ANALYSIS OF A SOCIAL INTERACTION SYSTEM. USA+45 FINAN PROB/SOLV ECO/TAC GP/REL INGP/REL...DECISION BIBLIOG. PAGE 143 F2812 — SOC LABOR BARGAIN ADMIN

B65
WARNER A.W.,THE IMPACT OF SCIENCE ON TECHNOLOGY. UNIV INTELL SOCIETY NAT/G ACT/RES PLAN PROB/SOLV BUDGET OPTIMAL GEN/METH. PAGE 143 F2821 — DECISION TEC/DEV CREATE POLICY

B65
WASSERMAN M.J.,THE BALANCE OF PAYMENTS: HISTORY, METHODOLOGY, THEORY. UK USA+45 USA-45 CAP/ISM DIPLOM EFFICIENCY...DECISION METH/CNCPT BIBLIOG 18/20 LEAGUE/NAT. PAGE 144 F2828 — BAL/PAY ECO/TAC GEN/LAWS EQUILIB

B65
WEIDENBAUM M.L.,CONGRESS AND THE FEDERAL BUDGET. FINAN ACT/RES DOMIN CONFER EXEC UTIL PWR NEW/LIB ...CHARTS CONGRESS. PAGE 144 F2844 — BUDGET LEGIS PLAN DECISION

B65
WEIL G.L.,A HANDBOOK ON THE EUROPEAN ECONOMIC COMMUNITY. BELGIUM EUR+WWI FRANCE GERMANY/W ITALY CONSTN ECO/DEV CREATE PARTIC GP/REL...DECISION MGT CHARTS 20 EEC. PAGE 144 F2846 — INT/TRADE INT/ORG TEC/DEV INT/LAW

S65
CHU K.,"A DYNAMIC MODEL OF THE FIRM." OP/RES PROB/SOLV...DECISION ECOMETRIC NEW/IDEA STAT GAME ORG/CHARTS SIMUL. PAGE 24 F0472 — INDUS COMPUTER TEC/DEV

S65
GRENIEWSKI H.,"INTENTION AND PERFORMANCE: A PRIMER OF CYBERNETICS OF PLANNING." EFFICIENCY OPTIMAL KNOWL SKILL...DECISION MGT EQULIB. PAGE 51 F0995 — SIMUL GAME GEN/METH PLAN

S65
SELLERS C.,"THE EQUILIBRIUM CYCLE IN TWO-PARTY POLITICS." USA+45 USA-45 CULTURE R+D GP/REL MAJORITY DECISION. PAGE 119 F2351 — CHOOSE TREND POL/PAR

S65
SOPER T.,"THE EEC AND AID TO AFRICA." FRANCE UK ECO/UNDEV INT/TRADE TARIFFS REGION ROUTINE CENTRAL DISCRIM...DECISION RECORD EEC. PAGE 124 F2443 — AFR FOR/AID COLONIAL

C65
PEGRUM D.E.,"PUBLIC REGULATION OF BUSINESS (REV ED)" LAW CONSTN DIST/IND SERV/IND LG/CO LEGIS OWN LAISSEZ SOCISM...POLICY DECISION BIBLIOG 20. PAGE 104 F2048 — INDUS PLAN NEW/LIB PRICE

B66
AMER ENTERPRISE INST PUB POL,SIGNIFICANT ISSUES IN ECONOMIC AID TO DEVELOPING COUNTRIES. FINAN INT/ORG NAT/G PLAN PROB/SOLV GIVE TASK WEALTH...DECISION 20. PAGE 4 F0083 — ECO/UNDEV FOR/AID DIPLOM POLICY

B66
CONFERENCE REGIONAL ACCOUNTS,REGIONAL ACCOUNTS FOR POLICY DECISIONS. PROB/SOLV CONTROL RATIONAL KNOWL ORD/FREE...POLICY DECISION MATH STAT ANTHOL 20. PAGE 27 F0523 — GOV/REL REGION PLAN ECO/TAC

B66
DAVIES JC I.I.I.,NEIGHBORHOOD GROUPS AND URBAN RENEWAL. USA+45 PLAN LOBBY PARTIC CHOOSE RACE/REL ...POLICY DECISION SOC INT MUNICH SOC/INTEG 20 NEWYORK/C. PAGE 30 F0586 — NEIGH CREATE PROB/SOLV

B66
FOX K.A.,THE THEORY OF QUANTITATIVE ECONOMIC POLICY WITH APPLICATIONS TO ECONOMIC GROWTH AND STABILIZATION. ECO/DEV AGRI NAT/G PLAN ADMIN RISK ...DECISION IDEA/COMP SIMUL T. PAGE 43 F0837 — ECO/TAC ECOMETRIC EQUILIB GEN/LAWS

B66
GORDON R.A.,PROSPERITY AND UNEMPLOYMENT. USA+45 PLAN ECO/TAC ADJUST DEMAND ALL/VALS...POLICY DECISION TREND CHARTS ANTHOL 20. PAGE 49 F0961 — WORKER INDUS ECO/DEV WEALTH

B66
GOULD J.M.,THE TECHNICAL ELITE. INDUS LABOR TECHRACY...POLICY DECISION STAT CHARTS 20. PAGE 49 F0967 — ECO/DEV TEC/DEV ELITES

TECHNIC

B66
HASTINGS P.G.,THE MANAGEMENT OF BUSINESS FINANCE. ECO/DEV PLAN BUDGET CONTROL COST...DECISION CHARTS BIBLIOG T 20. PAGE 56 F1109 — FINAN MGT INDUS ECO/TAC

B66
HEISS K.P.,GAME THEORY AND HUMAN CONFLICTS (RESEARCH MEMORANDUM). UNIV ACT/RES...DECISION SOC MATH PROBABIL SIMUL 20 DEFINETT/B. PAGE 58 F1142 — GAME ECOMETRIC PLAN PROB/SOLV

B66
NICOSIA M.N.,CONSUMER DECISION PROCESSES: MARKETING AND ADVERTISING IMPLICATIONS. ECO/TAC ATTIT PERSON ...DECISION MGT SOC. PAGE 98 F1926 — MARKET SOCIETY CREATE ACT/RES

B66
ROSS A.M.,INDUSTRIAL RELATIONS AND ECONOMIC DEVELOPMENT. POL/PAR LEGIS WORKER BARGAIN PRICE EXEC LOBBY INCOME PWR...DECISION ANTHOL BIBLIOG 20. PAGE 114 F2243 — ECO/UNDEV LABOR NAT/G GP/REL

B66
THEIL H.,APPLIED ECONOMIC FORECASTING. UNIV USA+45 ELITES INTELL CONSULT PRODUC...DECISION MGT PREDICT CHARTS METH/COMP SIMUL 20. PAGE 129 F2552 — FUT OP/RES PLAN

B66
YOUNG S.,MANAGEMENT: A SYSTEMS ANALYSIS. DELIB/GP EX/STRUC ECO/TAC CONTROL EFFICIENCY...NET/THEORY 20. PAGE 150 F2952 — PROB/SOLV MGT DECISION SIMUL

S66
DAVIS O.A.,"A THEORY OF THE BUDGETARY PROCESS." ECO/DEV FINAN LEGIS PROB/SOLV GOV/REL...ECOMETRIC METH/CNCPT STAT CONT/OBS TREND METH/COMP SIMUL 20 CONGRESS. PAGE 30 F0592 — DECISION NAT/G BUDGET EFFICIENCY

S66
FELD W.,"NATIONAL ECONOMIC INTEREST GROUPS AND POLICY FORMATION IN THE EEC." NAT/G POL/PAR REGION CENTRAL SOVEREIGN...INT NET/THEORY EEC. PAGE 40 F0777 — LOBBY ELITES DECISION

S66
MARKSHAK J.,"ECONOMIC PLANNING AND THE COST OF THINKING." COM MARKET EX/STRUC...DECISION GEN/LAWS. PAGE 85 F1672 — ECO/UNDEV ECO/TAC PLAN ECO/DEV

B67
BUREAU NATIONAL AFFAIRS,LABOR RELATIONS REFERENCE MANUAL VOL. 63. USA+45 CONSTN ECO/DEV PROVS WORKER DEBATE INGP/REL...DECISION 20. PAGE 20 F0385 — LABOR ADJUD CT/SYS NAT/G

B67
CAMPBELL A.K.,METROPOLITAN AMERICA* FISCAL PATTERNS AND GOVERNMENTAL SYSTEMS. PROVS PLAN COST...POLICY DECISION GOV/COMP METH/COMP BIBLIOG. PAGE 21 F0405 — USA+45 NAT/G LOC/G BUDGET

B67
CHO S.S.,KOREA IN WORLD POLITICS 1940-1950; AN EVALUATION OF AMERICAN RESPONSIBILITY. KOREA USA+45 USSR CONSTN INT/ORG NAT/G FORCES FOR/AID ANOMIE SUPEGO MARXISM...DECISION BIBLIOG 20. PAGE 24 F0469 — POLICY DIPLOM PROB/SOLV WAR

B67
COTTAM R.W.,COMPETITIVE INTERFERENCE AND TWENTIETH CENTURY DIPLOMACY. IRAN ACT/RES CREATE PLAN ECO/TAC EFFICIENCY ATTIT...DECISION NEW/IDEA TREND 20 CIA. PAGE 28 F0541 — DIPLOM DOMIN GAME

B67
COWLING M.,1867 DISRAELI, GLADSTONE, AND REVOLUTION; THE PASSING OF THE SECOND REFORM BILL. UK LEGIS LEAD LOBBY GP/REL INGP/REL...DECISION BIBLIOG 19 REFORMERS. PAGE 28 F0545 — PARL/PROC POL/PAR ATTIT LAW

B67
DE JOUVENAL B.,THE ART OF CONJECTURE. WOR+45 EFFICIENCY PERCEPT KNOWL...DECISION PHIL/SCI CONCPT METH/COMP BIBLIOG 20. PAGE 31 F0600 — FUT PREDICT SIMUL METH

B67
ENKE S.,DEFENSE MANAGEMENT. USA+45 R+D FORCES WORKER PLAN ECO/TAC ADMIN NUC/PWR BAL/PAY UTIL WEALTH...MGT DEPT/DEFEN. PAGE 38 F0738 — DECISION DELIB/GP EFFICIENCY BUDGET

B67
ESTEY M.,THE UNIONS: STRUCTURE, DEVELOPMENT, AND MANAGEMENT. FUT USA+45 ADJUD CONTROL INGP/REL DRIVE ...DECISION T 20 AFL/CIO. PAGE 38 F0750 — LABOR EX/STRUC ADMIN GOV/REL

B67
GITTELL M.,PARTICIPANTS AND PARTICIPATION: A STUDY OF SCHOOL POLICY IN NEW YORK. USA+45 EX/STRUC BUDGET PAY ATTIT...POLICY MUNICH 20 NEWYORK/C. PAGE 47 F0926 — SCHOOL DECISION PARTIC ADMIN

B67
GROSS B.M.,ACTION UNDER PLANNING: THE GUIDANCE OF ECONOMIC DEVELOPMENT. STRUCT R+D NAT/G ACT/RES HABITAT...DECISION 20. PAGE 51 F1005 — ECO/UNDEV PLAN ADMIN MGT

B67
HAGUE D.C.,PRICE FORMATION IN VARIOUS ECONOMIES; PROCEEDINGS OF A CONFERENCE HELD BY THE INTERNATIONAL ECONOMIC ASSOCIATION. WOR+45 FINAN MARKET PLAN CONFER COST...DECISION MATH PREDICT CHARTS SIMUL 20 INTL/ECON. PAGE 53 F1037
PRICE CAP/ISM SOCISM METH/COMP

B67
NORTON H.S.,NATIONAL TRANSPORTATION POLICY: FORMATION AND IMPLEMENTATION. USA+45 USA-45 DELIB/GP LEAD...DECISION TIME/SEQ 19/20 PRESIDENT CONGRESS. PAGE 98 F1935
POLICY DIST/IND NAT/G PROB/SOLV

B67
PORWIT K.,CENTRAL PLANNING: EVALUATION OF VARIANTS. PRICE OPTIMAL PRODUC...DECISION MATH CHARTS SIMUL BIBLIOG MODELS 20. PAGE 107 F2106
PLAN MGT ECOMETRIC

B67
ROBERTS B.C.,COLLECTIVE BARGAINING IN AFRICAN COUNTRIES. AFR LAW ECO/UNDEV BARGAIN GP/REL ...DECISION METH/COMP 20. PAGE 112 F2206
LABOR MGT PLAN ECO/TAC

B67
SAPARINA Y.,CYBERNETICS WITHIN US. WOR+45 EDU/PROP FEEDBACK PERCEPT HEALTH...DECISION METH/CNCPT NEW/IDEA 20. PAGE 116 F2281
COMPUTER METH/COMP CONTROL SIMUL

B67
TOMA P.A.,THE POLITICS OF FOOD FOR PEACE; EXECUTIVE-LEGISLATIVE INTERACTION. USA+45 ECO/UNDEV POL/PAR DEBATE EXEC LOBBY CHOOSE PEACE...DECISION CHARTS. PAGE 131 F2580
FOR/AID POLICY LEGIS AGRI

B67
US SENATE COMM ON FOREIGN REL,ARMS SALES TO NEAR EAST AND SOUTH ASIAN COUNTRIES. INDIA IRAN PAKISTAN WOR+45 PROC/MFG BAL/PWR DIPLOM...DECISION SENATE. PAGE 139 F2742
WEAPON FOR/AID FORCES POLICY

B67
ZALESKI E.,PLANNING REFORMS IN THE SOVIET UNION 1962-1966. COM USSR NAT/G CONFER CONTROL EFFICIENCY MARXISM...POLICY DECISION 20. PAGE 150 F2957
ECO/DEV PLAN ADMIN CENTRAL

L67
COSTANZA J.F.,"WHOLESOME NEUTRALITY: LAW AND EDUCATION." USA+45 GIVE EDU/PROP ADJUD CONTROL GP/REL...DECISION JURID. PAGE 28 F0540
SECT PROVS ACADEM

L67
MACDONALD R.S.J.,"THE RESORT TO ECONOMIC COERCION BY INTERNATIONAL POLITICAL ORGANIZATIONS." CUBA ETHIOPIA RHODESIA SOUTH/AFR NAT/G FOR/AID INT/TRADE DOMIN CONTROL SANCTION...DECISION LEAGUE/NAT UN OAS 20. PAGE 83 F1625
INT/ORG COERCE ECO/TAC DIPLOM

L67
TRAVERS H. JR.,"AN EXAMINATION OF THE CAB'S MERGER POLICY." USA+45 USA-45 LAW NAT/G LEGIS PLAN ADMIN ...DECISION 20 CONGRESS. PAGE 131 F2584
ADJUD LG/CO POLICY DIST/IND

S67
ADAMS R.N.,"ETHICS AND THE SOCIAL ANTHROPOLOGIST IN LATIN AMERICA." USA+45 INTELL PROB/SOLV ECO/TAC LEAD...DECISION SOC NAT/COMP PERS/COMP. PAGE 2 F0039
L/A+17C POLICY ECO/UNDEV CONSULT

S67
CROKER F.P.U.,"ECONOMIC PEACEKEEPING." UK PLAN PROB/SOLV TEC/DEV BAL/PWR DIPLOM COERCE PEACE ...POLICY DECISION 20. PAGE 28 F0553
FORCES WEAPON COST WAR

S67
EHRLICH S.,"INTERNATIONAL PRESSURE GROUPS: A CONTRIBUTION TO THE SOCIOLOGY OF INTERNATIONAL RELATIONS IN THE CAPITALIST WORLD." GP/REL...METH 20. PAGE 36 F0711
INT/ORG LOBBY DIPLOM DECISION

S67
GREGORY R.,"THE MINISTER'S LINE: OR, THE M4 COMES TO BERKSHIRE. PART I." UK CONSTN DIST/IND LEGIS TOP/EX PLAN ADJUD...GEOG 20. PAGE 51 F0994
DECISION CONSTRUC NAT/G DELIB/GP

S67
GUPTA S.,"FOREIGN POLICY IN THE 1967 MANIFESTOS." ASIA COM INDIA USA+45 FORCES FOR/AID TAX ATTIT ...DECISION 20. PAGE 52 F1013
IDEA/COMP POL/PAR POLICY DIPLOM

S67
JAVITS J.K.,"THE USE OF AMERICAN PLURALISM." USA+45 ECO/DEV BUDGET ADMIN ALL/IDEOS...DECISION TREND. PAGE 67 F1309
CENTRAL ATTIT POLICY NAT/G

S67
KOTLER P.,"OPERATIONS RESEARCH IN MARKETING." USA+45 DIST/IND INDUS LG/CO CONSULT BUDGET TASK DEMAND EFFICIENCY PROFIT WEALTH DECISION. PAGE 73 F1429
ECOMETRIC OP/RES MARKET PLAN

S67
LEIFER M.,"ASTRIDE THE STRAITS OF JAHORE: THE BRITISH PRESENCE AND COMMONWEALTH RIVALRY IN SOUTHEAST ASIA." MALAYSIA UK FORCES PLAN ECO/TAC ...DECISION 20 CMN/WLTH. PAGE 77 F1515
DIPLOM NAT/LISM COLONIAL

S67
LEMIEUX V.,"LA DIMENSION POLITIQUE DE L'ACTION RATIONNELLE." CONTROL GP/REL PERS/REL...DECISION NEW/IDEA GAME 20. PAGE 77 F1518
GEN/LAWS RATIONAL PWR

S67
LINEBERRY R.L.,"REFORMISM AND PUBLIC POLICIES IN AMERICAN CITIES." USA+45 POL/PAR EX/STRUC LEGIS BUDGET TAX GP/REL...STAT CHARTS MUNICH. PAGE 80 F1573
DECISION POLICY LOC/G

S67
MCCOLL R.W.,"A POLITICAL GEOGRAPHY OF REVOLUTION: CHINA, VIETNAM, AND THAILAND." ASIA THAILAND VIETNAM FORCES CONTROL 20. PAGE 88 F1720
REV GEOG PLAN DECISION

S67
PLOTT C.R.,"A NOTION OF EQUILIBRIUM AND ITS POSSIBILITY UNDER MAJORITY RULE." CREATE...DECISION STAT CHARTS 20. PAGE 106 F2094
SIMUL EQUILIB CHOOSE MAJORITY

S67
WEIL G.L.,"THE MERGER OF THE INSTITUTIONS OF THE EUROPEAN COMMUNITIES" EUR+WWI ECO/DEV INT/TRADE CONSEN PLURISM...DECISION MGT 20 EEC EURATOM ECSC TREATY. PAGE 145 F2847
ECO/TAC INT/ORG CENTRAL INT/LAW

S67
WHITE W.L.,"THE TREASURY BOARD AND PARLIAMENT." CANADA CONSTN CONSULT LEGIS LEAD PARL/PROC GP/REL ...DECISION 20. PAGE 146 F2871
FINAN DELIB/GP NAT/G ADMIN

DECISION-MAKING, DISIPLINE....SEE DECISION

DECISION-MAKING, INDIVIDUAL....SEE PROB/SOLV, PWR

DECISION-MAKING, PROCEDURAL....SEE PROB/SOLV

DECISION-MAKING, THEORY....SEE GAME

DECLAR/IND....DECLARATION OF INDEPENDENCE (U.S.)

DEEP/INT....DEPTH INTERVIEWS

L59
FURASH E.A.,"PROBLEMS IN REVIEW: INDUSTRIAL ESPIONAGE." WORKER ECO/TAC PERS/REL OPTIMAL AGE ATTIT KNOWL...MGT DEEP/INT DEEP/QU GP/COMP IDEA/COMP. PAGE 45 F0875
INDUS TOP/EX MAJORITY

B67
EVANS R.H.,COEXISTENCE: COMMUNISM AND ITS PRACTICE IN BOLOGNA, 1945-1965. ITALY CAP/ISM ADMIN CHOOSE PEACE ORD/FREE...SOC STAT DEEP/INT SAMP CHARTS BIBLIOG MUNICH 20. PAGE 39 F0756
MARXISM CULTURE POL/PAR

DEEP/QU....DEPTH QUESTIONNAIRES

L59
FURASH E.A.,"PROBLEMS IN REVIEW: INDUSTRIAL ESPIONAGE." WORKER ECO/TAC PERS/REL OPTIMAL AGE ATTIT KNOWL...MGT DEEP/INT DEEP/QU GP/COMP IDEA/COMP. PAGE 45 F0875
INDUS TOP/EX MAJORITY

DEFENSE....SEE DETER, PLAN, FORCES, WAR, COERCE

DEFENSE DEPARTMENT....SEE DEPT/DEFEN

DEFINETT/B....BRUNO DEFINETTI

B66
HEISS K.P.,GAME THEORY AND HUMAN CONFLICTS (RESEARCH MEMORANDUM). UNIV ACT/RES...DECISION SOC MATH PROBABIL SIMUL 20 DEFINETT/B. PAGE 58 F1142
GAME ECOMETRIC PLAN PROB/SOLV

DEFLATION....DEFLATION

DEGAULLE/C....CHARLES DE GAULLE

B65
RUEFF J.,THE ROLE AND THE RULE OF GOLD: AN ARGUMENT (PAMPHLET). AFR FRANCE USA+45 WOR+45 MARKET NAT/G PLAN DIPLOM ATTIT...POLICY INT 20 DEGAULLE/C. PAGE 115 F2258
FINAN ECO/DEV INT/TRADE BAL/PAY

DEITY....DEITY: GOD AND GODS

DE-STALINIZATION....SEE DESTALIN

DELAWARE....DELAWARE

DELEFORTRIE-SOU N. F0613

DELEGATION OF POWER....SEE EX/STRUC

DELHI INSTITUTE OF ECO GROWTH F0614

DELIB/GP....CONFERENCES, COMMITTEES, BOARDS, CABINETS

N
UNITED NATIONS,OFFICIAL RECORDS OF THE ECONOMIC AND SOCIAL COUNCIL OF THE UNITED NATIONS. WOR+45 DIPLOM INT/TRADE CONFER...SOC SOC/WK 20 UN UNESCO. PAGE 132 F2611
INT/ORG DELIB/GP WRITING

B00
MILL J.S.,PRINCIPLES OF POLITICAL ECONOMY. WOR-45 CULTURE SOCIETY STRATA ECO/DEV AGRI EXTR/IND FINAN INDUS DELIB/GP ECO/TAC WEALTH...CONCPT MATH TREND 20. PAGE 91 F1786
MARKET INT/ORG INT/TRADE

B19
SUMNER W.G.,WAR AND OTHER ESSAYS. USA-45 DELIB/GP DIPLOM TARIFFS COLONIAL PEACE SOVEREIGN 20. PAGE 127 F2514
INT/TRADE ORD/FREE CAP/ISM ECO/TAC

N19
ANDERSON J.,THE ORGANIZATION OF ECONOMIC STUDIES IN RELATION TO THE PROBLEMS OF GOVERNMENT (PAMPHLET). UK FINAN INDUS DELIB/GP PLAN PROB/SOLV ADMIN 20. PAGE 5 F0095
ECO/TAC ACT/RES NAT/G CENTRAL

N19
ATOMIC INDUSTRIAL FORUM,COMMENTARY ON LEGISLATION TO PERMIT PRIVATE OWNERSHIP OF SPECIAL NUCLEAR MATERIAL (PAMPHLET). USA+45 DELIB/GP LEGIS PLAN OWN ...POLICY 20 AEC CONGRESS. PAGE 7 F0134
NUC/PWR MARKET INDUS LAW

N19
KRESSBACH T.W.,HE MICHIGAN CITY MANAGER IN BUDGETARY PROCEEDINGS (PAMPHLET). USA+45 PROVS DELIB/GP GP/REL SUPEGO...POLICY MUNICH. PAGE 73 F1438
LOC/G BUDGET FINAN

N19
KUWAIT FUND ARAB ECO DEVELOPMT,ANNUAL REPORTS 1962-65 (PAMPHLET). KUWAIT ECO/UNDEV DIPLOM ...POLICY 20 ARABS. PAGE 74 F1453
FOR/AID DELIB/GP FINAN ISLAM

N19
MCCONNELL G.,THE STEEL SEIZURE OF 1952 (PAMPHLET). USA+45 FINAN INDUS PROC/MFG LG/CO EX/STRUC ADJUD CONTROL GP/REL ORD/FREE PWR 20 TRUMAN/HS PRESIDENT CONGRESS. PAGE 88 F1721
DELIB/GP LABOR PROB/SOLV NAT/G

N19
MEZERIK A.G.,ECONOMIC AID FOR UNDERDEVELOPED COUNTRIES (PAMPHLET). AFR USSR WOR+45 FINAN LG/CO DELIB/GP NUC/PWR...GEOG CENSUS CHARTS 20 UN THIRD/WRLD. PAGE 90 F1775
FOR/AID ECO/UNDEV DIPLOM POLICY

B23
FINER H.,REPRESENTATIVE GOVERNMENT AND A PARLIAMENT OF INDUSTRY. A STUDY OF THE GERMAN FEDERAL ECONOMIC COUNCIL. GERMANY UK CONSTN INDUS PARL/PROC ...NAT/COMP 20. PAGE 41 F0796
DELIB/GP ECO/TAC WAR REV

B29
JONES M.M.,CORPORATION CONTRIBUTIONS TO COMMUNITY WELFARE AGENCIES (PAMPHLET). DELIB/GP TAX CONTROL PARTIC RATIONAL POLICY. PAGE 68 F1339
LG/CO GIVE NEIGH SOC/WK

B30
BEVERIDGE W.H.,UNEMPLOYMENT: A PROBLEM OF INDUSTRY (1909-1930). USA-45 LAW ECO/DEV MARKET DELIB/GP WAR DEMAND INCOME...POLICY STAT CHARTS 20. PAGE 14 F0274
WORKER ECO/TAC GEN/LAWS

B31
LORWIN L.L.,ADVISORY ECONOMIC COUNCILS. EUR+WWI FRANCE GERMANY PROB/SOLV INGP/REL...CLASSIF GP/COMP. PAGE 82 F1601
CONSULT DELIB/GP ECO/TAC NAT/G

B36
BELLOC H.,THE RESTORATION OF PROPERTY. UK STRATA NAT/G PROF/ORG DELIB/GP WORKER CREATE PROB/SOLV ECO/TAC PARTIC UTOPIA ORD/FREE SOCISM 20. PAGE 13 F0238
CONTROL MAJORIT CAP/ISM OWN

B40
BLAISDELL D.C.,GOVERNMENT AND AGRICULTURE; THE GROWTH OF FEDERAL FARM AID. USA-45 MARKET PLAN PROB/SOLV TEC/DEV ECO/TAC GOV/REL ADJUST ATTIT ...CHARTS 20 DEPT/AGRI. PAGE 15 F0296
NAT/G GIVE AGRI DELIB/GP

B40
GAUS J.M.,PUBLIC ADMINISTRATION AND THE UNITED STATES DEPARTMENT OF AGRICULTURE. USA-45 STRUCT DIST/IND FINAN MARKET EX/STRUC PROB/SOLV GIVE PRODUC...POLICY GEOG CHARTS 20 DEPT/AGRI. PAGE 47 F0909
ADMIN AGRI DELIB/GP OP/RES

B43
WILMERDING L. JR.,THE SPENDING POWER: A HISTORY OF THE EFFORTS OF CONGRESS TO CONTROL EXPENDITURES. USA-45 POL/PAR DELIB/GP EX/STRUC TOP/EX TARIFFS ADMIN GOV/REL...TIME/SEQ SENATE HOUSE/REP. PAGE 147 F2900
LEGIS BUDGET CONTROL

S43
GOLDEN C.S.,"NEW PATTERNS OF DEMOCRACY." NEIGH DELIB/GP EDU/PROP EXEC PARTIC...MGT METH/CNCPT OBS TREND. PAGE 48 F0935
LABOR REPRESENT LG/CO GP/REL

S43
HUZAR E.,"CONGRESS AND THE ARMY: APPROPRIATIONS." USA-45 CONFER CONTROL ATTIT SUPEGO SKILL CONGRESS. PAGE 64 F1255
LEGIS FORCES BUDGET

DELIB/GP

B45
MILLIS H.A.,ORGANIZED LABOR (FIRST ED.). LAW STRUCT DELIB/GP WORKER ECO/TAC ADJUD CONTROL REPRESENT INGP/REL INCOME MGT. PAGE 92 F1797
LABOR POLICY ROUTINE GP/REL

B47
HEILPERIN M.A.,THE TRADE OF NATIONS. USA+45 USA-45 WOR+45 WOR-45 CULTURE ECO/DEV NAT/G DELIB/GP EDU/PROP ATTIT DISPL ORD/FREE PWR WEALTH TOT/POP 20. PAGE 58 F1139
MARKET INT/ORG INT/TRADE PEACE

B47
MILLETT J.D.,THE PROCESS AND ORGANIZATION OF GOVERNMENT PLANNING. USA+45 DELIB/GP ACT/RES LEAD LOBBY TASK...POLICY GEOG TIME 20 RESOURCE/N. PAGE 91 F1793
ADMIN NAT/G PLAN CONSULT

S47
DAHL R.A.,"WORKERS' CONTROL OF INDUSTRY AND THE BRITISH LABOUR PARTY." UK STRATA STRUCT DELIB/GP BARGAIN CAP/ISM DEBATE CONTROL CHOOSE GP/REL ATTIT ROLE PWR 19/20 PARLIAMENT LABOR/PAR FABIAN. PAGE 29 F0570
INDUS LABOR WORKER SOCISM

S48
NOURSE E.G.,"THE ROLE OF THE COUNCIL OF ECONOMIC ADVISERS." USA+45 DELIB/GP...DECISION PRESIDENT. PAGE 99 F1938
EX/STRUC CHIEF PROB/SOLV

B50
LINCOLN G.,ECONOMICS OF NATIONAL SECURITY. USA+45 ELITES COM/IND DIST/IND INDUS NAT/G VOL/ASSN DELIB/GP EX/STRUC FOR/AID EDU/PROP COERCE NUC/PWR WAR ATTIT KNOWL ORD/FREE PWR TOT/POP VAL/FREE 20. PAGE 80 F1565
FORCES ECO/TAC AFR

B51
LEONARD L.L.,INTERNATIONAL ORGANIZATION. WOR+45 WOR-45 EX/STRUC FORCES LEGIS ECO/TAC INT/TRADE COLONIAL ARMS/CONT...SOC/WK GOV/COMP BIBLIOG. PAGE 78 F1527
NAT/G DIPLOM INT/ORG DELIB/GP

B52
REDFORD E.S.,ADMINISTRATION OF NATIONAL ECONOMIC CONTROL. ECO/DEV DELIB/GP ADJUD CONTROL EQUILIB 20. PAGE 110 F2166
ADMIN ROUTINE GOV/REL LOBBY

S52
KLUMB S.,"EMPLOYEE DETERMINATION OF MANAGERIAL FUNCTIONS AND CHARACTERISTICS." DELIB/GP WORKER PARTIC ROUTINE INGP/REL...CLASSIF OBS QU. PAGE 72 F1410
MGT INDUS EX/STRUC CHOOSE

B53
SAYLES L.R.,THE LOCAL UNION. CONSTN CULTURE DELIB/GP PARTIC CHOOSE GP/REL INGP/REL ATTIT ROLE ...MAJORIT DECISION MGT. PAGE 116 F2284
LABOR LEAD ADJUD ROUTINE

S53
BLOUGH R.,"THE ROLE OF THE ECONOMIST IN FEDERAL POLICY MAKING." USA+45 ELITES INTELL ECO/DEV NAT/G CONSULT EX/STRUC ACT/RES PLAN INT/TRADE BAL/PAY WEALTH...POLICY METH/GP CONGRESS 20. PAGE 16 F0301
DELIB/GP ECO/TAC

B54
BERNSTEIN I.,ARBITRATION OF WAGES. USA+45 CONSULT PAY COST PRODUC WEALTH...CHARTS 20. PAGE 14 F0266
DELIB/GP BARGAIN WORKER PRICE

B54
EMERSON F.D.,SHAREHOLDER DEMOCRACY: A BROADER OUTLOOK FOR CORPORATIONS. DELIB/GP EX/STRUC LEGIS ADJUD CONTROL REPRESENT INGP/REL OWN PWR...POLICY STAT RECORD. PAGE 37 F0727
LG/CO PARTIC MAJORIT TREND

B54
HOBBS E.H.,BEHIND THE PRESIDENT - A STUDY OF EXECUTIVE OFFICE AGENCIES. USA+45 NAT/G PLAN BUDGET ECO/TAC EXEC ORD/FREE 20 BUR/BUDGET. PAGE 60 F1183
EX/STRUC DELIB/GP CONFER CONSULT

B55
BERNSTEIN M.H.,REGULATING BUSINESS BY INDEPENDENT COMMISSION. USA+45 USA-45 LG/CO CHIEF LEGIS PROB/SOLV ADJUD SANCTION GP/REL ATTIT...TIME/SEQ 19/20 MONOPOLY PRESIDENT CONGRESS. PAGE 14 F0268
DELIB/GP CONTROL CONSULT

S55
HALLETT D.,"THE HISTORY AND STRUCTURE OF OEEC." EUR+WWI USA+45 CONSTN INDUS INT/ORG NAT/G DELIB/GP ACT/RES PLAN ORD/FREE WEALTH...CONCPT OEEC 20 CMN/WLTH. PAGE 54 F1051
VOL/ASSN ECO/DEV

B56
GILBERT L.D.,DIVIDENDS AND DEMOCRACY. DELIB/GP LEGIS CAP/ISM ADJUD LOBBY OWN PWR LAISSEZ MAJORIT. PAGE 47 F0922
LG/CO INGP/REL CONTROL PARTIC

S56
GORDON L.,"THE ORGANIZATION FOR EUROPEAN ECONOMIC COOPERATION." EUR+WWI INDUS INT/ORG NAT/G CONSULT DELIB/GP ACT/RES CREATE PLAN TEC/DEV EDU/PROP LEGIT WEALTH OEEC 20. PAGE 49 F0956
VOL/ASSN ECO/DEV

S56
KNAPP D.C.,"CONGRESSIONAL CONTROL OF AGRICULTURAL CONSERVATION POLICY: A CASE STUDY OF THE APPROPRIATIONS PROCESS." DELIB/GP PLAN PROB/SOLV
LEGIS AGRI BUDGET

CONFER PARL/PROC...POLICY INT CONGRESS. PAGE 72 F1411 — CONTROL

B57
LAVES W.H.C.,UNESCO. FUT WOR+45 NAT/G CONSULT DELIB/GP TEC/DEV ECO/TAC EDU/PROP PEACE ORD/FREE ...CONCPT TIME/SEQ TREND UNESCO VAL/FREE 20. PAGE 76 F1491 — INT/ORG KNOWL

B57
LUNDBERG E.,BUSINESS CYCLES AND ECONOMIC POLICY (TRANS. BY J. POTTER). SWEDEN ECO/DEV FINAN DELIB/GP PLAN PRICE CONTROL BAL/PAY 20 INTRVN/ECO. PAGE 82 F1607 — ECO/TAC INDUS INT/TRADE BUDGET

B57
MILLIKAN M.F.,A PROPOSAL: KEY TO AN EFFECTIVE FOREIGN POLICY. USA+45 AGRI FINAN DELIB/GP DIPLOM REPRESENT MAJORITY...NEW/IDEA CHARTS. PAGE 91 F1795 — FOR/AID GIVE ECO/UNDEV PLAN

B57
UDY S.H. JR.,THE ORGANIZATION OF PRODUCTION IN NONINDUSTRIAL CULTURE. VOL/ASSN DELIB/GP TEC/DEV ...CHARTS BIBLIOG. PAGE 132 F2598 — METH/COMP ECO/UNDEV PRODUC ADMIN

S57
LEWIS E.G.,"PARLIAMENTARY CONTROL OF NATIONALIZED INDUSTRY IN FRANCE." FRANCE NAT/G DELIB/GP ACT/RES PLAN PROB/SOLV ECO/TAC DOMIN CENTRAL. PAGE 79 F1547 — PWR LEGIS INDUS CONTROL

B58
NICULESCU B.,COLONIAL PLANNING: A COMPARATIVE STUDY. AFR AGRI LOC/G NAT/G DELIB/GP COLONIAL MUNICH 20. PAGE 98 F1927 — PLAN ECO/UNDEV TEC/DEV NAT/COMP

B58
ROBERTS B.C.,NATIONAL WAGES POLICY IN WAR AND PEACE. EUR+WWI GERMANY S/ASIA SWEDEN UK USA+45 USA-45 STRATA ECO/DEV LABOR NAT/G DELIB/GP PLAN INT/TRADE WEALTH...STAT TREND CHARTS 20. PAGE 112 F2205 — CREATE ECO/TAC

B58
SCOTT D.J.R.,RUSSIAN POLITICAL INSTITUTIONS. RUSSIA USSR CONSTN AGRI DELIB/GP PLAN EDU/PROP CONTROL CHOOSE EFFICIENCY ATTIT MARXISM...BIBLIOG/A IND 13/20. PAGE 118 F2332 — NAT/G POL/PAR ADMIN DECISION

B58
SEIDMAN J.I.,DEMOCRACY IN THE LABOR MOVEMENT (PAMPHLET). LAW CONSTN STRUCT DELIB/GP WORKER ADJUD PARTIC SANCTION POLICY. PAGE 119 F2345 — LABOR INGP/REL PWR MAJORIT

B58
US HOUSE COMM POST OFFICE,MANPOWER UTILIZATION IN THE FEDERAL GOVERNMENT. USA+45 DIST/IND EX/STRUC LEGIS CONFER EFFICIENCY 20 CONGRESS CIVIL/SERV. PAGE 137 F2702 — ADMIN WORKER DELIB/GP NAT/G

B58
US HOUSE COMM POST OFFICE,MANPOWER UTILIZATION IN THE FEDERAL GOVERNMENT. USA+45 DIST/IND EX/STRUC LEGIS CONFER EFFICIENCY 20 CONGRESS CIVIL/SERV. PAGE 137 F2703 — ADMIN WORKER DELIB/GP NAT/G

S58
ELKIN A.B.,"OEEC-ITS STRUCTURE AND POWERS." EUR+WWI CONSTN INDUS INT/ORG NAT/G VOL/ASSN DELIB/GP ACT/RES PLAN ORD/FREE WEALTH...CHARTS ORG/CHARTS OEEC 20. PAGE 37 F0719 — ECO/DEV EX/STRUC

S58
EMERSON F.D.,"THE ROLES OF MANAGEMENT AND SHAREHOLDERS IN CORPORATE GOVERNMENT." CLIENT DELIB/GP CREATE ADMIN EXEC PARTIC PERS/REL PWR. PAGE 37 F0728 — LG/CO LAW INGP/REL REPRESENT

S58
SCHUMM S.,"INTEREST REPRESENTATION IN FRANCE AND GERMANY." EUR+WWI FRANCE GERMANY INSPECT PARL/PROC REPRESENT 20 WEIMAR/REP. PAGE 118 F2320 — LOBBY DELIB/GP NAT/G

B59
AITKEN H.,THE STATE AND ECONOMIC GROWTH. COM EUR+WWI MOD/EUR S/ASIA USA+45 FINAN NAT/G DELIB/GP PLAN PWR WEALTH 20. PAGE 3 F0054 — DIST/IND ECO/DEV

B59
DIEBOLD W. JR.,THE SCHUMAN PLAN: A STUDY IN ECONOMIC COOPERATION, 1950-1959. EUR+WWI FRANCE GERMANY USA+45 EXTR/IND CONSULT DELIB/GP PLAN DIPLOM ECO/TAC INT/TRADE ROUTINE ORD/FREE WEALTH ...METH/CNCPT STAT CONT/OBS INT TIME/SEQ ECSC 20. PAGE 33 F0635 — INT/ORG REGION

B59
HARVARD UNIVERSITY LAW SCHOOL,INTERNATIONAL PROBLEMS OF FINANCIAL PROTECTION AGAINST NUCLEAR RISK. WOR+45 NAT/G DELIB/GP PROB/SOLV DIPLOM CONTROL ATTIT...POLICY INT/LAW MATH 20. PAGE 56 F1105 — NUC/PWR ADJUD INDUS FINAN

B59
LEISERSON W.,AMERICAN TRADE UNION DEMOCRACY. CONSTN STRUCT ADJUD EXEC REPRESENT GP/REL INGP/REL MAJORITY ATTIT PWR. PAGE 77 F1516 — LABOR LEAD PARTIC DELIB/GP

L59
BEGUIN B.,"ILO AND THE TRIPARTITE SYSTEM." EUR+WWI WOR+45 WOR-45 CONSTN ECO/DEV ECO/UNDEV INDUS INT/ORG NAT/G VOL/ASSN DELIB/GP PLAN TEC/DEV LEGIT ORD/FREE WEALTH...CONCPT TIME/SEQ WORK ILO 20. PAGE 12 F0228 — LABOR

L59
OBERER W.E.,"VOLUNTARY IMPARTIAL REVIEW OF LABOR: SOME REFLECTIONS." DELIB/GP LEGIS PROB/SOLV ADJUD CONTROL COERCE PWR PLURISM POLICY. PAGE 100 F1960 — LABOR LAW PARTIC INGP/REL

S59
ALLEN G.,"NATIONAL FARMERS UNION AS A PRESSURE GROUP: II." UK ECO/DEV MARKET POL/PAR DELIB/GP PROB/SOLV ECO/TAC LOBBY INCOME...POLICY METH/COMP 19/20 NAT/FARMER. PAGE 4 F0069 — DIST/IND AGRI PROF/ORG TREND

B60
BHAMBHRI C.P.,PARLIAMENTARY CONTROL OVER STATE ENTERPRISE IN INDIA. INDIA DELIB/GP ADMIN CONTROL INGP/REL EFFICIENCY 20 PARLIAMENT. PAGE 14 F0277 — NAT/G OWN INDUS PARL/PROC

B60
CARPER E.T.,THE DEFENSE APPROPRIATIONS RIDER (PAMPHLET). USA+45 CONSTN CHIEF DELIB/GP LEGIS BUDGET LOBBY CIVMIL/REL...POLICY 20 CONGRESS EISNHWR/DD DEPT/DEFEN PRESIDENT BOSTON. PAGE 22 F0419 — GOV/REL ADJUD LAW CONTROL

B60
COMMITTEE ECONOMIC DEVELOPMENT,NATIONAL OBJECTIVES AND THE BALANCE OF PAYMENTS PROBLEM: A STATEMENT ON NATIONAL POLICY. USA+45 WOR+45 DIST/IND FINAN INDUS LABOR NAT/G DELIB/GP ACT/RES FOR/AID INT/TRADE ...STAT CHARTS FOR/TRADE 20. PAGE 27 F0516 — ECO/DEV ECO/TAC BAL/PAY

B60
ILLINOIS U BUR COMMUNITY PLAN,PROCEEDINGS OF ILLINOIS STATEWIDE PLANNING CONFERENCE 1960. USA+45 FINAN LOC/G ACT/RES LEAD GOV/REL GP/REL WEALTH MUNICH 20 ILLINOIS. PAGE 64 F1260 — PLAN DELIB/GP VOL/ASSN

B60
LISTER L.,EUROPE'S COAL AND STEEL COMMUNITY. FRANCE GERMANY STRUCT ECO/DEV EXTR/IND INDUS MARKET NAT/G DELIB/GP ECO/TAC INT/TRADE EDU/PROP ATTIT RIGID/FLEX ORD/FREE PWR WEALTH...CONCPT STAT TIME/SEQ CHARTS ECSC TERR/GP 20. PAGE 81 F1582 — EUR+WWI INT/ORG REGION

B60
MARSHALL A.H.,FINANCIAL ADMINISTRATION IN LOCAL GOVERNMENT. UK DELIB/GP CONFER COST INCOME PERSON ...JURID 20. PAGE 86 F1679 — FINAN LOC/G BUDGET ADMIN

B60
POOLEY B.J.,THE EVOLUTION OF BRITISH PLANNING LEGISLATION. UK ECO/DEV LOC/G CONSULT DELIB/GP ADMIN MUNICH 20 URBAN/RNWL. PAGE 107 F2104 — PLAN LEGIS PROB/SOLV

B60
ROBINSON E.A.G.,ECONOMIC CONSEQUENCES OF THE SIZE OF NATIONS. AGRI INDUS DELIB/GP FOR/AID ADMIN EFFICIENCY...METH/COMP 20. PAGE 113 F2218 — CONCPT INT/ORG NAT/COMP

B60
SERAPHIM H.J.,ZUR GRUNDLEGUNG WIRTSCHAFTSPOLITISCHER KONZEPTIONEN (SCHRIFTEN DES VEREINS FUR SOZIALPOLITIK, N.F. BAND 18). GERMANY/W WOR+45 ECO/DEV DELIB/GP ACT/RES ECO/TAC INGP/REL ORD/FREE...CONCPT IDEA/COMP GEN/LAWS 20. PAGE 120 F2358 — POLICY PHIL/SCI PLAN

B60
SHANNON D.A.,THE GREAT DEPRESSION. USA-45 FINAN LG/CO SCHOOL SML/CO DELIB/GP RECEIVE REV EATING INCOME...ANTHOL MUNICH 20 ROOSEVLT/F CONGRESS. PAGE 120 F2365 — WEALTH NAT/G AGRI INDUS

B60
WALLACE R.A.,CONGRESSIONAL CONTROL OF FEDERAL SPENDING. USA+45 CONSTN NAT/G OP/RES CONFER DEBATE PERS/REL UTIL RIGID/FLEX PWR OBJECTIVE...OBS CHARTS. PAGE 143 F2808 — LEGIS DELIB/GP BUDGET

S60
GROSSMAN G.,"SOVIET GROWTH: ROUTINE, INERTIA, AND PRESSURE." COM STRATA NAT/G DELIB/GP PLAN TEC/DEV ECO/TAC EDU/PROP ADMIN ROUTINE DRIVE WEALTH 20. PAGE 52 F1007 — POL/PAR ECO/DEV AFR USSR

S60
HERRERA F.,"THE INTER-AMERICAN DEVELOPMENT BANK." USA+45 ECO/UNDEV INT/ORG CONSULT DELIB/GP PLAN ECO/TAC INT/TRADE ROUTINE WEALTH...STAT TERR/GP 20. PAGE 59 F1153 — L/A+17C FINAN FOR/AID REGION

S60
JACOBSON H.K.,"THE USSR AND ILO." AFR COM STRUCT ECO/DEV ECO/UNDEV CONSULT DELIB/GP ECO/TAC ILO WORK 20. PAGE 66 F1298 — INT/ORG LABOR USSR

S60
MARTIN E.M.,"NEW TRENDS IN UNITED STATES ECONOMIC FOREIGN POLICY." USA+45 INTELL DELIB/GP FOR/AID INT/TRADE ROUTINE BAL/PAY...RELATIV TRUE/GP 20. PAGE 86 F1682 — NAT/G PLAN DIPLOM

S60
NANES A.,"THE EUROPEAN COMMUNITY AND THE UNITED STATES: EVOLVING RELATIONS." EUR+WWI USA+45 WOR+45 ECO/UNDEV MARKET NAT/G DELIB/GP PLAN LEGIT ATTIT PWR WEALTH...CONCPT STAT TIME/SEQ CON/ANAL EEC — INT/ORG REGION

METH/GP OEEC 20 EURATOM. PAGE 96 F1889

S60

POLLARD J.A.,"EMERGING PATTERNS OF CORPORATE GIVING." FINAN DELIB/GP PLAN EDU/PROP CENTRAL TREND. PAGE 107 F2098
GIVE LG/CO ADMIN MGT

B61

BALASSA B.,THE THEORY OF ECONOMIC INTEGRATION. EUR+WWI L/A+17C MOD/EUR WOR+45 ECO/UNDEV MARKET INT/ORG NAT/G VOL/ASSN DELIB/GP PLAN CAP/ISM ECO/TAC...MAJORIT FOR/TRADE OEEC 20. PAGE 8 F0157
ECO/DEV ACT/RES INT/TRADE

B61

BENOIT E.,EUROPE AT SIXES AND SEVENS: THE COMMON MARKET, THE FREE TRADE ASSOCIATION AND THE UNITED STATES. EUR+WWI FUT USA+45 INDUS CONSULT DELIB/GP EX/STRUC TOP/EX ACT/RES ECO/TAC EDU/PROP ROUTINE CHOOSE PERCEPT WEALTH...MGT TREND EEC FOR/TRADE TOT/POP 20 EFTA. PAGE 13 F0249
FINAN ECO/DEV VOL/ASSN

B61

DOIG J.W.,THE POLITICS OF METROPOLITAN TRANSPORTATION. DELIB/GP WORKER DIPLOM TASK EFFICIENCY UTIL...CHARTS BIBLIOG MUNICH 20 NEW/YORK NEW/JERSEY PUB/TRANS RAILROAD. PAGE 34 F0652
PROB/SOLV STRATA DIST/IND

B61

HUBBARD P.J.,ORIGINS OF THE TVA: THE MUSCLE SHOALS CONTROVERSY, 1920-1932. USA-45 DELIB/GP LEGIS LEAD LOBBY GOV/REL GP/REL INGP/REL OWN PERSON...BIBLIOG 20 TVA CONGRESS WATER. PAGE 62 F1229
SEA CONTROL NAT/G INDUS

B61

INDUSTRIAL COUN SOC-ECO STU,THE SWEDISH ECONOMY AND THE UNDERDEVELOPED COUNTRIES. SWEDEN INDUS DELIB/GP TEC/DEV INT/TRADE EDU/PROP COLONIAL DRIVE...CHARTS 20. PAGE 64 F1264
FOR/AID ECO/UNDEV PLAN FINAN

B61

MAYNE A.,DESIGNING AND ADMINISTERING A REGIONAL ECONOMIC DEVELOPMENT PLAN WITH SPECIFIC REFERENCE TO PUERTO RICO (PAMPHLET). PUERT/RICO SOCIETY NAT/G DELIB/GP REGION...DECISION 20. PAGE 87 F1707
ECO/UNDEV PLAN CREATE ADMIN

B61

QURESHI S.,INCENTIVES IN AMERICAN EMPLOYMENT (THESIS, UNIVERSITY OF PENNSYLVANIA). DELIB/GP TOP/EX BUDGET ROUTINE SANCTION COST TECHRACY MGT. PAGE 108 F2134
SERV/IND ADMIN PAY EX/STRUC

B61

SCHNAPPER B.,LA POLITIQUE ET LE COMMERCE FRANCAIS DANS LE GOLFE DE GUINEE DE 1838 A 1871. FRANCE GUINEA UK SEA EXTR/IND NAT/G DELIB/GP LEGIS ADMIN ORD/FREE...POLICY GEOG CENSUS CHARTS BIBLIOG 19. PAGE 117 F2303
COLONIAL INT/TRADE DOMIN AFR

B61

SHARP W.R.,FIELD ADMINISTRATION IN THE UNITED NATION SYSTEM: THE CONDUCT OF INTERNATIONAL ECONOMIC AND SOCIAL PROGRAMS. FUT WOR+45 CONSTN SOCIETY ECO/UNDEV R+D DELIB/GP ACT/RES PLAN TEC/DEV EDU/PROP EXEC ROUTINE HEALTH WEALTH...HUM CONCPT CHARTS METH ILO UNESCO GP VAL/FREE UN 20. PAGE 120 F2369
INT/ORG CONSULT

B61

US CONGRESS JOINT ECO COMM,INTERNATIONAL PAYMENTS IMBALANCES AND NEED FOR STRENGTHENING INTERNATIONAL FINANCIAL ARRANGEMENTS. USA+45 WOR+45 DELIB/GP DIPLOM INT/TRADE...CHARTS 20 CONGRESS OEEC. PAGE 134 F2651
BAL/PAY INT/ORG FINAN PROB/SOLV

S61

LANFALUSSY A.,"EUROPE'S PROGRESS: DUE TO COMMON MARKET." EUR+WWI ECO/DEV DELIB/GP PLAN ECO/TAC ROUTINE WEALTH...GEOG TREND EEC TERR/GP 20. PAGE 75 F1473
INT/ORG MARKET

S61

WILDAVSKY A.,"POLITICAL IMPLICATIONS OF BUDGETARY REFORM." AFR NAT/G POL/PAR DELIB/GP EX/STRUC ATTIT PWR CONGRESS. PAGE 146 F2881
BUDGET PLAN LEGIS

B62

GALENSON W.,TRADE UNIONS MONOGRAPH SERIES (A SERIES OF NINE TEXTS). DELIB/GP LEAD PARTIC...DECISION ORG/CHARTS. PAGE 45 F0887
LABOR INGP/REL CONSTN REPRESENT

B62

GROVE J.W.,GOVERNMENT AND INDUSTRY IN BRITAIN. UK FINAN LOC/G CONSULT DELIB/GP INT/TRADE ADMIN CONTROL...BIBLIOG 20. PAGE 52 F1008
ECO/TAC INDUS NAT/G GP/REL

B62

HARRINGTON M.,THE RETAIL CLERKS. ECO/TAC LEAD PARTIC CHOOSE GP/REL INGP/REL CENTRAL POLICY. PAGE 55 F1087
LABOR SERV/IND STRUCT DELIB/GP

B62

MCCLELLAN J.L.,CRIME WITHOUT PUNISHMENT. USA+45 LAW SOCIETY DELIB/GP TRIBUTE CONTROL LOBBY COERCE GP/REL ANOMIE MORAL...CRIMLGY 20 CONGRESS HOFFA/J. PAGE 88 F1718
CRIME ACT/RES LABOR PWR

B62

PAKISTAN MINISTRY OF FINANCE,FOREIGN ECONOMIC AID: A REVIEW OF FOREIGN ECONOMIC AID TO PAKISTAN. EUR+WWI PAKISTAN UK USA+45 USSR ECO/UNDEV INT/ORG DELIB/GP DIPLOM ECO/TAC...CHARTS CMN/WLTH CHINJAP. PAGE 103 F2016
FOR/AID RECEIVE WEALTH FINAN

B62

ROBINSON A.D.,DUTCH ORGANIZED AGRICULTURE IN INTERNATIONAL POLITICS, 1945-1960. EUR+WWI NETHERLAND STRUCT ECO/DEV NAT/G VOL/ASSN CONSULT DELIB/GP PLAN TEC/DEV INT/TRADE EDU/PROP ATTIT RIGID/FLEX ALL/VALS...NEW/IDEA TREND EEC COMMUN 20. PAGE 112 F2215
AGRI INT/ORG

B62

US CONGRESS,LEGISLATIVE HISTORY OF UNITED STATES TAX CONVENTIONS(VOL. 1). USA+45 USA-45 DELIB/GP WEALTH...CHARTS 20 CONGRESS. PAGE 134 F2649
TAX LEGIS LAW DIPLOM

B62

US CONGRESS JOINT ECO COMM,FACTORS AFFECTING THE UNITED STATES BALANCE OF PAYMENTS. USA+45 DELIB/GP PLAN DIPLOM FOR/AID PRODUC WEALTH...CHARTS 20 CONGRESS OEEC. PAGE 134 F2653
BAL/PAY INT/TRADE ECO/TAC FINAN

S62

MORGENTHAU H.J.,"A POLITICAL THEORY OF FOREIGN AID." ECO/UNDEV NAT/G DELIB/GP PLAN ECO/TAC EDU/PROP EXEC ORD/FREE RESPECT WEALTH...METH/CNCPT TREND 20. PAGE 93 F1833
USA+45 PHIL/SCI FOR/AID

B63

ABSHIRE D.M.,NATIONAL SECURITY: POLITICAL, MILITARY, AND ECONOMIC STRATEGIES IN THE DECADE AHEAD. ASIA COM USA+45 WOR+45 ECO/DEV ECO/UNDEV INT/ORG DELIB/GP FORCES ECO/TAC COERCE ATTIT RIGID/FLEX HEALTH ORD/FREE PWR WEALTH...POLICY STAT CHARTS ANTHOL COLD/WAR VAL/FREE APP/SCI. PAGE 2 F0032
FUT ACT/RES BAL/PWR

B63

BATES J.L.,THE ORIGINS OF TEAPOT DOME: PROGRESSIVES, PARTIES, AND PETROLEUM, 1909-1921. USA-45 INDUS LG/CO POL/PAR DELIB/GP CONTROL GOV/REL CONSERVE...BIBLIOG 20 NAVY. PAGE 11 F0209
EXTR/IND CRIME NAT/G

B63

BURTT E.J. JR.,LABOR MARKETS, UNIONS, AND GOVERNMENT POLICIES. USA+45 MARKET NAT/G DELIB/GP CREATE BARGAIN GP/REL ORD/FREE PWR...POLICY CHARTS 20 AFL/CIO. PAGE 20 F0393
LABOR ECO/DEV CONTROL WORKER

B63

COLUMBIA U SCHOOL OF LAW,PUBLIC INTERNATIONAL DEVELOPMENT FINANCING IN SENEGAL. SENEGAL FINAN DELIB/GP GIVE EFFICIENCY...CHARTS GOV/COMP ANTHOL 20. PAGE 26 F0511
FOR/AID PLAN RECEIVE ECO/UNDEV

B63

DE VRIES E.,SOCIAL ASPECTS OF ECONOMIC DEVELOPMENT IN LATIN AMERICA. CULTURE SOCIETY STRATA FINAN INDUS INT/ORG DELIB/GP ACT/RES ECO/TAC EDU/PROP ADMIN ATTIT SUPEGO HEALTH KNOWL ORD/FREE...SOC STAT TREND ANTHOL TOT/POP VAL/FREE. PAGE 31 F0608
L/A+17C ECO/UNDEV

B63

GLADE W.P. JR.,THE POLITICAL ECONOMY OF MEXICO. FUT L/A+17C CULTURE SOCIETY AGRI INDUS DELIB/GP ACT/RES ECO/TAC ATTIT HEALTH ORD/FREE...STAT TIME/SEQ TREND MEXIC/AMER TOT/POP VAL/FREE 20. PAGE 48 F0928
FINAN ECO/UNDEV

B63

GRUBEL H.G.,WORLD MONETARY REFORM: PLANS AND ISSUES. FUT WOR+45 ECO/DEV ECO/UNDEV R+D DELIB/GP CREATE ECO/TAC ATTIT RIGID/FLEX WEALTH...STAT ANTHOL VAL/FREE 20. PAGE 52 F1009
FINAN INT/ORG BAL/PAY INT/TRADE

B63

HIRSCHMAN A.O.,JOURNEYS TOWARD PROGRESS: STUDIES OF ECONOMIC POLICYMAKING IN LATIN AMERICA. CHILE FUT ECO/UNDEV AGRI FINAN INDUS CONSULT DELIB/GP PLAN ATTIT HEALTH ORD/FREE WEALTH...POLICY STAT VAL/FREE COLOMB 20. PAGE 60 F1177
L/A+17C ECO/TAC BRAZIL

B63

KRAVIS I.B.,DOMESTIC INTERESTS AND INTERNATIONAL OBLIGATIONS: SAFEGUARDS IN INTERNATIONAL TRADE ORGANIZATIONS. EUR+WWI USA+45 WOR+45 FINAN DELIB/GP ATTIT RIGID/FLEX HEALTH...STAT EEC VAL/FREE OEEC ECSC 20. PAGE 73 F1435
INT/ORG ECO/TAC INT/TRADE

B63

LAIRD R.D.,SOVIET AGRICULTURAL AND PEASANT AFFAIRS. FUT STRATA LOC/G DELIB/GP ACT/RES TEC/DEV ECO/TAC EDU/PROP ATTIT RIGID/FLEX ORD/FREE SKILL WEALTH ...STAT CON/ANAL ANTHOL MUNICH WORK VAL/FREE 20. PAGE 74 F1461
COM AGRI POLICY

B63

LINDBERG L.,POLITICAL DYNAMICS OF EUROPEAN ECONOMIC INTEGRATION. EUR+WWI ECO/DEV INT/ORG VOL/ASSN DELIB/GP ADMIN WEALTH...DECISION EEC TERR/GP 20. PAGE 80 F1567
MARKET ECO/TAC

B63

MEYNAUD J.,PLANIFICATION ET POLITIQUE. FRANCE ITALY FINAN LABOR DELIB/GP LEGIS ADMIN EFFICIENCY ...MAJORIT DECISION 20. PAGE 90 F1773
PLAN ECO/TAC PROB/SOLV

B63

MULLENBACH P.,CIVILIAN NUCLEAR POWER: ECONOMIC ISSUES AND POLICY FORMATION. AFR FINAN INT/ORG DELIB/GP ACT/RES ECO/TAC ATTIT SUPEGO HEALTH ORD/FREE PWR...POLICY CONCPT MATH STAT CHARTS VAL/FREE 20. PAGE 94 F1855
USA+45 ECO/DEV NUC/PWR

B63
SALANT W.S.,THE UNITED STATES BALANCE OF PAYMENTS IN 1968. USA+45 ECO/DEV ECO/UNDEV INT/ORG DELIB/GP ECO/TAC...POLICY STAT SIMUL 20. PAGE 115 F2273 — FUT FINAN BAL/PAY

B63
US CONGRESS JOINT ECO COMM,THE UNITED STATES BALANCE OF PAYMENTS. AFR USA+45 DELIB/GP BUDGET PRICE PRODUC 20 CONGRESS MONEY. PAGE 135 F2655 — BAL/PAY INT/TRADE FINAN ECO/TAC

B63
US CONGRESS JOINT ECO COMM,THE UNITED STATES BALANCE OF PAYMENTS. USA+45 DELIB/GP CONFER...MATH PREDICT CHARTS 20 CONGRESS. PAGE 135 F2656 — BAL/PAY ECO/TAC INT/TRADE CONSULT

B63
US HOUSE,URBAN RENEWAL: HOUSE COMMITTEE ON BANKING AND CURRENCY. USA+45 FINAN LOC/G NAT/G NEIGH DELIB/GP TEC/DEV BUDGET GOV/REL COST...CHARTS MUNICH 20 CONGRESS URBAN/RNWL. PAGE 136 F2684 — PLAN PROB/SOLV LEGIS

B63
US HOUSE COMM BANKING-CURR,RECENT CHANGES IN MONETARY POLICY AND BALANCE OF PAYMENTS PROBLEMS. USA+45 DELIB/GP PLAN DIPLOM...CHARTS 20 CONGRESS. PAGE 136 F2688 — BAL/PAY FINAN ECO/TAC POLICY

B63
VON BECKERATH E.,PROBLEME DER NORMATIVEN OKONOMIK UND DER WIRTSCHAFTSPOLITISCHEN BERATUNG. GERMANY UK ELITES CAP/ISM EFFICIENCY...CONCPT GOV/COMP IDEA/COMP 20. PAGE 142 F2789 — ECO/TAC DELIB/GP ECO/DEV CONSULT

B63
WILTZ J.E.,IN SEARCH OF PEACE: THE SENATE MUNITIONS INQUIRY, 1934-36. EUR+WWI USA-45 ELITES INDUS LG/CO LEGIS INT/TRADE LOBBY NEUTRAL ARMS/CONT...POLICY CONGRESS 20 LEAGUE/NAT PRESIDENT SENATE CONSCRIPTN. PAGE 147 F2905 — DELIB/GP PROFIT WAR WEAPON

L63
ADERBIGDE A.,"SYMPOSIUM ON WEST AFRICA INTEGRATION." AFR EUR+WWI FUT CULTURE SOCIETY STRATA DIST/IND INDUS MARKET SERV/IND DELIB/GP PLAN TEC/DEV DOMIN EDU/PROP LEGIT COERCE ATTIT ALL/VALS ...POLICY STAT TREND CHARTS VAL/FREE. PAGE 2 F0040 — FINAN ECO/TAC REGION

L63
NASH M.,"PSYCHO-CULTURAL FACTORS IN ASIAN ECONOMIC GROWTH." ASIA ISLAM S/ASIA CULTURE ECO/UNDEV DELIB/GP EDU/PROP COERCE ATTIT PERSON HEALTH KNOWL ORD/FREE...PSY SOC STAT TREND ANTHOL VAL/FREE 20. PAGE 96 F1893 — SOCIETY ECO/TAC

L63
PADELFORD N.J.,"FINANCIAL CRISIS AND THE UNITED NATIONS." FUT USSR WOR+45 LAW CONSTN FINAN INT/ORG DELIB/GP FORCES PLAN BUDGET DIPLOM COST WEALTH ...STAT CHARTS UN CONGO 20. PAGE 102 F2012 — CREATE ECO/TAC

L63
RIDAH A.,"LE NEO-DESTOUR DEPUIS L'INDEPENDANCE." FUT ISLAM WOR+45 ECO/UNDEV INT/ORG SCHOOL DELIB/GP TOP/EX ACT/RES EDU/PROP LEGIT ATTIT ALL/VALS 20 TUNIS. PAGE 111 F2189 — NAT/G CONSTN

S63
ARDANT G.,"A PLAN FOR FULL EMPLOYMENT IN THE DEVELOPING COUNTRIES." AFR FUT WOR+45 DELIB/GP ACT/RES PLAN ECO/TAC ATTIT ALL/VALS...POLICY STAT CHARTS TUNIS VAL/FREE 20. PAGE 6 F0112 — ECO/UNDEV SOCIETY MOROCCO

S63
EMERSON R.,"THE ATLANTIC COMMUNITY AND THE EMERGING COUNTRIES." FUT WOR+45 ECO/DEV ECO/UNDEV R+D NAT/G DELIB/GP BAL/PWR ECO/TAC EDU/PROP ROUTINE ORD/FREE PWR WEALTH...POLICY CONCPT TREND GEN/METH EEC 20 NATO. PAGE 37 F0729 — ATTIT INT/TRADE

S63
ENTHOVEN A.C.,"ECONOMIC ANALYSIS IN THE DEPARTMENT OF DEFENSE." USA+45 NAT/G DELIB/GP PROB/SOLV RATION NUC/PWR WEAPON COST...DECISION 20 DEPT/DEFEN RESOURCE/N. PAGE 38 F0739 — PLAN BUDGET ECO/TAC FORCES

S63
GANDOLFI A.,"LES ACCORDS DE COOPERATION EN MATIERE DE POLITIQUE ETRANGERE ENTRE LA FRANCE ET LES NOUVEAUX ETATS AFRICAINS ET." AFR ISLAM MADAGASCAR WOR+45 ECO/DEV INT/ORG NAT/G DELIB/GP ECO/TAC ALL/VALS...CON/ANAL 20. PAGE 46 F0894 — VOL/ASSN ECO/UNDEV DIPLOM FRANCE

S63
HALLSTEIN W.,"THE EUROPEAN COMMUNITY AND ATLANTIC PARTNERSHIP." EUR+WWI USA+45 MARKET NAT/G VOL/ASSN DELIB/GP ARMS/CONT NUC/PWR ATTIT PWR...CONCPT STAT TIME/SEQ TREND OEEC 20 EEC. PAGE 54 F1053 — INT/ORG ECO/TAC UK

S63
MASON E.S.,"INTERESTS, IDEOLOGIES AND THE PROBLEM OF STABILITY AND GROWTH." EUR+WWI USA+45 DELIB/GP CREATE PLAN EXEC ROUTINE BAL/PAY ATTIT PWR...MGT CONCPT OEEC 20. PAGE 87 F1698 — NAT/G ECO/DEV

S63
MONROE A.D.,"BRITAIN AND THE EUROPEAN COMMUNITY." EUR+WWI FRANCE NAT/G DELIB/GP TOP/EX ECO/TAC DOMIN PWR...POLICY RECORD GEN/LAWS EEC EFTA 20 EFTA CMN/WLTH. PAGE 93 F1817 — VOL/ASSN ATTIT UK

S63
SHONFIELD A.,"AFTER BRUSSELS." EUR+WWI FRANCE GERMANY UK ECO/DEV DIST/IND MARKET VOL/ASSN DELIB/GP CREATE INT/TRADE ATTIT RIGID/FLEX...RECORD TREND GEN/LAWS EEC COMMUN CMN/WLTH 20. PAGE 121 F2385 — PLAN ECO/TAC

S63
TENNYSON L.B.,"THE USA IN ATLANTIC COMMUNITY." EUR+WWI FRANCE UK USA+45 ECO/UNDEV VOL/ASSN DELIB/GP TOP/EX DIPLOM DOMIN PWR...POLICY CONCPT TREND GEN/LAWS EEC 20. PAGE 129 F2545 — ATTIT ECO/TAC BAL/PWR

S63
WOLFERS A.,"INTEGRATION IN THE WEST: THE CONFLICT OF PERSPECTIVES." AFR EUR+WWI USA+45 ECO/DEV INT/ORG DELIB/GP CREATE TEC/DEV DIPLOM ATTIT PWR ...CONCPT HIST/WRIT TREND GEN/LAWS EEC 20. PAGE 148 F2918 — RIGID/FLEX ECO/TAC

N63
COMM ON FEDERAL TAX POLICY,FINANCING AMERICA'S FUTURE: TAXES, ECONOMIC STABILITY AND GROWTH (PAMPHLET). USA+45 LG/CO SML/CO DELIB/GP INCOME ...CHARTS 20. PAGE 26 F0513 — TAX NAT/G EQUILIB PLAN

N63
COMMITTEE ECONOMIC DEVELOPMENT,TAXES AND TRADE: 20 YEARS OF CED POLICY (PAMPHLET). USA+45 ECO/DEV PLAN BUDGET LEAD...POLICY KENNEDY/JF PRESIDENT. PAGE 27 F0518 — FINAN ECO/TAC NAT/G DELIB/GP

N63
US COMM STRENG SEC FREE WORLD,THE SCOPE AND DISTRIBUTION OF UNITED STATES MILITARY AND ECONOMIC ASSISTANCE PROGRAMS (PAMPHLET). USA+45 PLAN BAL/PWR BUDGET DIPLOM CONTROL CIVMIL/REL ATTIT. PAGE 134 F2648 — DELIB/GP POLICY FOR/AID ORD/FREE

B64
BERRILL K.,ECONOMIC DEVELOPMENT WITH SPECIAL REFERENCE TO EAST ASIA. ASIA INDIA S/ASIA AGRI INDUS LABOR DELIB/GP PLAN INT/TRADE COST PRODUC 20 CHINJAP. PAGE 14 F0271 — FINAN ECO/UNDEV INT/ORG CAP/ISM

B64
BLAKE R.R.,MANAGING INTERGROUP CONFLICT IN INDUSTRY. INDUS DELIB/GP EX/STRUC GP/REL PERS/REL GAME. PAGE 16 F0297 — CREATE PROB/SOLV OP/RES ADJUD

B64
COLSTON RESEARCH SOCIETY,ECONOMETRIC ANALYSIS FOR NATIONAL ECONOMIC PLANNING (PROCEEDINGS OF SIXTEENTH SYMPOSIUM OF COLSTON RESEARCH SOCIETY). UK USA+45 FINAN FAM LABOR NAT/G PLAN PRICE ...METH/CNCPT TREND CHARTS TIME 20. PAGE 26 F0510 — ECOMETRIC DELIB/GP ECO/TAC PROB/SOLV

B64
LINDHOLM R.W.,ECONOMIC DEVELOPMENT POLICY WITH EMPHASIS ON VIET-NAM. KOREA/S PAKISTAN VIETNAM/S AGRI INDUS CONSULT DELIB/GP FOR/AID...METH 20. PAGE 80 F1571 — ECO/UNDEV TAX FINAN ECO/TAC

B64
MARKHAM J.W.,THE COMMON MARKET: FRIEND OR COMPETITOR. AFR EUR+WWI FUT USA+45 INT/ORG LG/CO NAT/G VOL/ASSN DELIB/GP EX/STRUC PLAN TARIFFS ORD/FREE PWR WEALTH...POLICY STAT TREND EEC VAL/FREE 20. PAGE 85 F1671 — ECO/DEV ECO/TAC

B64
MELADY T.,FACES OF AFRICA. AFR FUT ISLAM NAT/G POL/PAR SCHOOL DELIB/GP PLAN ECO/TAC EDU/PROP ATTIT ALL/VALS...CHARTS TOT/POP TERR/GP VAL/FREE 20. PAGE 89 F1752 — ECO/UNDEV TREND NAT/LISM

B64
MOAK L.L.,A MANUAL OF SUGGESTED PRACTICE FOR THE PREPARATION AND ADOPTION OF CAPITAL PROGRAMS AND CAPITAL BUDGETS BY LOCAL GOVERN. USA+45 DELIB/GP PLAN TAX GP/REL COST DECISION. PAGE 92 F1812 — LOC/G BUDGET LEGIS PROB/SOLV

B64
SEERS D.,CUBA: THE ECONOMIC AND SOCIAL REVOLUTION. L/A+17C USSR YUGOSLAVIA STRATA AGRI INDUS SCHOOL DELIB/GP PLAN ECO/TAC DOMIN EDU/PROP ATTIT RIGID/FLEX ALL/VALS...STAT OBS TIME/SEQ WORK VAL/FREE 20. PAGE 119 F2341 — ACT/RES COERCE CUBA REV

B64
STOESSINGER J.G.,FINANCING THE UNITED NATIONS SYSTEM. FUT WOR+45 CONSTN NAT/G VOL/ASSN DELIB/GP EX/STRUC ECO/TAC LEGIT CT/SYS PWR WEALTH...STAT TIME/SEQ TREND CHARTS TRUE/GP METH/GP TERR/GP VAL/FREE. PAGE 126 F2493 — FINAN INT/ORG

B64
US DEPT LABOR OFF SOLICITOR,LEGISLATIVE HISTORY OF THE LABOR-MANAGEMENT AND DISCLOSURE ACT OF 1959. DELIB/GP WORKER ADMIN LOBBY PARL/PROC SANCTION CHOOSE GOV/REL 20 CONGRESS PRESIDENT. PAGE 136 F2677 — LABOR LEGIS DEBATE POLICY

B64
WRIGHT G.,RURAL REVOLUTION IN FRANCE: THE PEASANTRY IN THE TWENTIETH CENTURY. EUR+WWI MOD/EUR LAW CULTURE AGRI POL/PAR DELIB/GP LEGIS ECO/TAC EDU/PROP COERCE CHOOSE ATTIT RIGID/FLEX HEALTH ...STAT CENSUS CHARTS VAL/FREE 20. PAGE 149 F2932 — PWR STRATA FRANCE REV

L64
CARNEGIE ENDOWMENT INT. PEACE,"ECONOMIC AND SOCIAL QUESTION (ISSUES BEFORE THE NINETEENTH GENERAL ASSEMBLY)." WOR+45 ECO/DEV ECO/UNDEV INDUS R+D — INT/ORG INT/TRADE

DELIB/GP CREATE PLAN TEC/DEV ECO/TAC FOR/AID BAL/PAY...RECORD UN 20. PAGE 21 F0414

L64
HAAS E.B.,"ECONOMICS AND DIFFERENTIAL PATTERNS OF POLITICAL INTEGRATION: PROJECTIONS ABOUT UNITY IN LATIN AMERICA." SOCIETY NAT/G DELIB/GP ACT/RES CREATE PLAN ECO/TAC REGION ROUTINE ATTIT DRIVE PWR WEALTH...CONCPT TREND CHARTS LAFTA TERR/GP 20. PAGE 52 F1020 — L/A+17C INT/ORG MARKET

L64
STERN R.M.,"POLICIES FOR TRADE AND DEVELOPMENT." AFR FUT WOR+45 DIST/IND FINAN NAT/G DELIB/GP PLAN ECO/TAC ORD/FREE WEALTH...POLICY STAT TIME/SEQ CHARTS METH/GP 20. PAGE 126 F2480 — MARKET ECO/UNDEV INT/TRADE

S64
GALBRAITH V.,"JAPAN'S POSITION IN WORLD TRADE." ASIA AGRI INDUS CREATE ECO/TAC LEGIT DRIVE WEALTH ...TREND EEC GATT FOR/TRADE 20 CHINJAP. PAGE 45 F0885 — ECO/DEV DELIB/GP

S64
GARDNER R.N.,"GATT AND THE UNITED NATIONS CONFERENCE ON TRADE AND DEVELOPMENT." USA+45 WOR+45 SOCIETY ECO/UNDEV MARKET NAT/G DELIB/GP ACT/RES PLAN ECO/TAC TARIFFS EDU/PROP ROUTINE DRIVE RIGID/FLEX WEALTH...DECISION MGT TREND UN TOT/POP 20 GATT. PAGE 46 F0905 — INT/ORG INT/TRADE

S64
HOWE M.,"THE TRANSPORT ACT, 1962, AND THE CONSUMERS' CONSULTATIVE COMMITTEES." UK CONFER EXEC PWR 20. PAGE 62 F1225 — PARTIC REPRESENT DELIB/GP DIST/IND

S64
HUELIN D.,"ECONOMIC INTEGRATION IN LATIN AMERICAN: PROGRESS AND PROBLEMS." L/A+17C ECO/DEV AGRI DIST/IND FINAN INDUS NAT/G VOL/ASSN CONSULT DELIB/GP EX/STRUC ACT/RES PLAN TEC/DEV ECO/TAC ROUTINE BAL/PAY WEALTH FOR/TRADE WORK TERR/GP 20. PAGE 63 F1232 — MARKET ECO/UNDEV INT/TRADE

B65
BRADLEY J.F.,THE ROLE OF TRADE ASSOCIATIONS AND PROFESSIONAL BUSINESS SOCIETIES IN AMERICA. USA+45 USA-45 STRUCT CONSULT DELIB/GP CREATE LOBBY GP/REL 20. PAGE 17 F0333 — ECO/DEV PROF/ORG VOL/ASSN SOCIETY

B65
DELHI INSTITUTE OF ECO GROWTH,A STUDY IN THE WORKING OF THE INTENSIVE AREA SCHEME OF THE KHADI AND VILLAGE INDUSTRIES COMMISSION. INDIA AGRI FINAN DELIB/GP ECO/TAC EFFICIENCY...QU CHARTS MUNICH 20. PAGE 32 F0614 — PLAN INDUS ECO/UNDEV

B65
FLEMING R.W.,THE LABOR ARBITRATION PROCESS. USA+45 LAW BARGAIN ADJUD ROUTINE SANCTION COST...PREDICT CHARTS TIME 20. PAGE 41 F0809 — GP/REL LABOR CONSULT DELIB/GP

B65
HOLLER J.E.,POPULATION TRENDS AND ECONOMIC DEVELOPMENT IN THE FAR EAST (PAMPHLET). KOREA S/ASIA AGRI INDUS DELIB/GP PROB/SOLV RATIONAL ...POLICY CHARTS BIBLIOG 20 OUTER/MONG CHINJAP HONG/KONG. PAGE 61 F1197 — CENSUS TREND ECO/UNDEV ASIA

B65
LAZARUS S.,RESOLVING BUSINESS DISPUTES: THE POTENTIAL OF COMMERCIAL ARBITRATION. USA+45 INDUS LG/CO ACT/RES PROB/SOLV EDU/PROP CONSEN UTIL ...TREND 20. PAGE 76 F1496 — FINAN DELIB/GP CONSULT ADJUD

B65
MACDONALD R.W.,THE LEAGUE OF ARAB STATES: A STUDY IN THE DYNAMICS OF REGIONAL ORGANIZATION. ISRAEL UAR USSR FINAN INT/ORG DELIB/GP ECO/TAC AGREE NEUTRAL ORD/FREE PWR...DECISION BIBLIOG 20 TREATY UN. PAGE 83 F1626 — ISLAM REGION DIPLOM ADMIN

B65
MEAGHER R.F.,PUBLIC INTERNATIONAL DEVELOPMENT FINANCING IN SUDAN. SUDAN FINAN DELIB/GP GIVE ...CHARTS GOV/COMP 20. PAGE 89 F1740 — FOR/AID PLAN RECEIVE ECO/UNDEV

B65
PARRIS H.W.,GOVERNMENT AND THE RAILWAYS IN NINETEENTH-CENTURY BRITAIN. UK DELIB/GP CONTROL LEAD CENTRAL 19 RAILROAD. PAGE 103 F2029 — DIST/IND NAT/G PLAN GP/REL

B65
PLOSS S.I.,CONFLICT AND DECISION-MAKING IN SOVIET RUSSIA - A CASE STUDY OF AGRICULTURAL POLICY - 1953-1963. USSR DELIB/GP INGP/REL PWR MARXISM. PAGE 106 F2093 — AGRI DECISION ATTIT

B65
SCHECHTER A.,THE BUSINESSMAN IN GOVERNMENT (THESIS, COLUMBIA UNIVERSITY). USA+45 CONFER GP/REL PERSON ...QU 20 PRESIDENT TRUMAN/HS CABINET. PAGE 116 F2291 — INDUS NAT/G EX/STRUC DELIB/GP

B65
US CONGRESS JOINT ECO COMM,GUIDELINES FOR INTERNATIONAL MONETARY REFORM. USA+45 WOR+45 DELIB/GP BAL/PAY 20 CONGRESS IMF MONEY. PAGE 135 F2659 — DIPLOM FINAN PLAN INT/ORG

B65
US HOUSE COMM BANKING-CURR,INTERNATIONAL TRAVEL IN RELATION TO THE BALANCE OF PAYMENTS DEFICIT. USA+45 DELIB/GP...CHARTS 20 CONGRESS TRAVEL. PAGE 136 F2690 — BAL/PAY ECO/TAC SERV/IND PROB/SOLV

L65
LETICHE J.M.,"EUROPEAN INTEGRATION: AN AMERICAN VIEW." EUR+WWI FRANCE WOR+45 ECO/DEV DIST/IND EXTR/IND NAT/G DELIB/GP TOP/EX PLAN ECO/TAC ATTIT ...STAT CON/ANAL CHARTS EEC 20. PAGE 78 F1537 — INDUS AGRI

S65
HADDAD W.F.,"MR. SHRIVER AND THE SAVAGE POLITICS OF POVERTY" USA+45 LAW NAT/G DELIB/GP LEGIS GIVE LEAD CENTRAL PWR...SOC/WK CHARTS 20 CONGRESS POVRTY/WAR SHRIVER/S OEO. PAGE 53 F1028 — WEALTH GOV/REL CONTROL TOP/EX

C65
WUORINEN J.H.,"SCANDINAVIA." DENMARK FINLAND ICELAND NORWAY SWEDEN SOCIETY AGRI POL/PAR DELIB/GP DIPLOM INT/TRADE NEUTRAL WAR...CHARTS IND TREATY 20. PAGE 149 F2942 — BIBLIOG NAT/G POLICY

B66
AGGARWALA R.N.,FINANCIAL COMMITTEES OF THE INDIAN PARLIAMENT: A STUDY IN PARLIAMENTARY CONTROL OVER PUBLIC EXPENDITURE. INDIA FINAN NAT/G ROLE...CHARTS METH/COMP METH 20 PARLIAMENT. PAGE 3 F0049 — PARL/PROC BUDGET CONTROL DELIB/GP

B66
FORD P.,CARDINAL MORAN AND THE A. L. P. NAT/G POL/PAR SECT DELIB/GP LOBBY REV CHOOSE ORD/FREE MARXISM 19/20 AUSTRAL PROTESTANT LABOR/PAR. PAGE 42 F0825 — CATHISM SOCISM LABOR SOCIETY

B66
HAYS P.R.,LABOR ARBITRATION: A DISSENTING VIEW. USA+45 LAW DELIB/GP BARGAIN ADJUD...PREDICT 20. PAGE 57 F1126 — GP/REL LABOR CONSULT CT/SYS

B66
INTERNATIONAL ECONOMIC ASSN,STABILITY AND PROGRESS IN THE WORLD ECONOMY: THE FIRST CONGRESS OF THE INTERNATIONAL ECONOMIC ASSOCIATION. WOR+45 ECO/DEV ECO/UNDEV DELIB/GP FOR/AID BAL/PAY...TREND CMN/WLTH 20. PAGE 65 F1276 — INT/TRADE

B66
LEAGUE OF WOMEN VOTERS OF US,FOREIGN AID AT THE CROSSROADS. USA+45 WOR+45 DELIB/GP PROB/SOLV DIPLOM INT/TRADE RECEIVE BAL/PAY...CHARTS 20 UN ALL/PROG. PAGE 76 F1498 — FOR/AID GIVE ECO/UNDEV PLAN

B66
MANGONE G.J.,UN ADMINISTRATION OF ECONOMIC AND AOCIAL PROGRAMS. CONSULT BUDGET INT/TRADE REGION 20 UN. PAGE 84 F1653 — ADMIN MGT ECO/TAC DELIB/GP

B66
MIKESELL R.F.,PUBLIC INTERNATIONAL LENDING FOR DEVELOPMENT. WOR+45 WOR-45 DELIB/GP...TIME/SEQ CHARTS BIBLIOG 20. PAGE 91 F1783 — INT/ORG FOR/AID ECO/UNDEV FINAN

B66
NEVITT A.A.,THE ECONOMIC PROBLEMS OF HOUSING. WOR+45 ECO/DEV ECO/UNDEV ACT/RES PROB/SOLV ECO/TAC RENT...OBS CHARTS 20. PAGE 98 F1917 — HABITAT PROC/MFG DELIB/GP NAT/COMP

B66
SASTRI K.V.S.,FEDERAL-STATE FISCAL RELATIONS IN INDIA: A STUDY OF THE FINANCE COMMISSION AND TECHNIQUES OF FINANCIAL ADJUSTMENT. INDIA PROVS DELIB/GP GOV/REL FEDERAL...MATH CHARTS 20. PAGE 116 F2283 — TAX BUDGET FINAN NAT/G

B66
SOVERN M.I.,LEGAL RESTRAINTS ON RACIAL DISCRIMINATION IN EMPLOYMENT. USA+45 LAW INDUS LG/CO SML/CO DELIB/GP LEGIS SANCTION 20 NLRB PRESIDENT NEGRO CIV/RIGHTS RAILROAD. PAGE 124 F2446 — DISCRIM RACE/REL WORKER JURID

B66
US CONGRESS JOINT ECO COMM,NEW APPROACH TO UNITED STATES INTERNATIONAL ECONOMIC POLICY. USA+45 WOR+45 CHIEF DELIB/GP CONFER...CHARTS 20 CONGRESS MONEY. PAGE 135 F2660 — DIPLOM ECO/TAC BAL/PAY FINAN

B66
US PRES COMM ECO IMPACT DEFENS,REPORT* JULY 1965. USA+45 ECO/DEV INDUS DELIB/GP FORCES OP/RES ARMS/CONT NUC/PWR WEAPON BAL/PAY...PREDICT SIMUL. PAGE 138 F2726 — ACT/RES STAT WAR BUDGET

B66
US SENATE COMM GOVT OPERATIONS,INTERGOVERNMENTAL PERSONNEL ACT OF 1966. USA+45 NAT/G CONSULT DELIB/GP WORKER TEC/DEV PAY AUTOMAT UTIL 20 CONGRESS. PAGE 139 F2730 — ADMIN LEGIS EFFICIENCY EDU/PROP

B66
US SENATE COMM LABOR-PUB WELF,AMEND THE RAILWAY LABOR ACT. USA+45 CONSTN CONSULT DELIB/GP ADJUD CONGRESS RAILROAD. PAGE 139 F2731 — GP/REL LABOR DIST/IND LAW

B66
YOUNG S.,MANAGEMENT: A SYSTEMS ANALYSIS. DELIB/GP EX/STRUC ECO/TAC CONTROL EFFICIENCY...NET/THEORY 20. PAGE 150 F2952 — PROB/SOLV MGT DECISION

SIMUL

B67
ALEXANDER G.J.,HONESTY AND COMPETITION: FALSE-ADVERTISING LAW AND POLICY UNDER FTC ADMINISTRATION. USA+45 INDUS NAT/G PRICE GP/REL 20 FTC. PAGE 3 F0058
EDU/PROP SERV/IND CONTROL DELIB/GP

B67
BREAK G.F.,INTERGOVERNMENTAL FISCAL RELATIONS IN THE UNITED STATES. USA+45 USA-45 DELIB/GP PLAN BUDGET TAX GOV/REL CENTRAL...TREND CHARTS MUNICH. PAGE 18 F0345
LOC/G NAT/G PROVS FINAN

B67
EGGERT G.G.,RAILROAD LABOR DISPUTES. USA+45 USA-45 ELITES DIST/IND DELIB/GP FORCES JUDGE WORKER PROB/SOLV DOMIN PWR...POLICY 20. PAGE 36 F0707
GP/REL NAT/G LABOR BARGAIN

B67
ENKE S.,DEFENSE MANAGEMENT. USA+45 R+D FORCES WORKER PLAN ECO/TAC ADMIN NUC/PWR BAL/PAY UTIL WEALTH...MGT DEPT/DEFEN. PAGE 38 F0738
DECISION DELIB/GP EFFICIENCY BUDGET

B67
LEIBY J.,CHARITY AND CORRECTION IN JERSEY; A HISTORY OF STATE WELFARE INSTITUTIONS. DELIB/GP EX/STRUC PROB/SOLV INSPECT LEAD ADJUST HEALTH ...POLICY PSY NEW/JERSEY. PAGE 77 F1514
PROVS PUB/INST ADMIN

B67
NORTON H.S.,NATIONAL TRANSPORTATION POLICY: FORMATION AND IMPLEMENTATION. USA+45 USA-45 DELIB/GP LEAD...DECISION TIME/SEQ 19/20 PRESIDENT CONGRESS. PAGE 98 F1935
POLICY DIST/IND NAT/G PROB/SOLV

B67
SCOTT J.C.,ANTITRUST AND TRADE REGULATION TODAY: 1967. USA+45 MARKET LG/CO DELIB/GP LEGIS CAP/ISM INT/TRADE TAX PRICE INGP/REL WEALTH 20 SUPREME/CT. PAGE 118 F2334
NAT/G INDUS CONTROL JURID

B67
US CONGRESS JOINT ECO COMM,REPORT ON JANUARY 1967 ECONOMIC REPORT OF THE PRESIDENT. FINAN LABOR NAT/G LEGIS BUDGET INT/TRADE COST DEMAND INCOME PRODUC ...POLICY IDEA/COMP 20 CONGRESS. PAGE 135 F2663
CHIEF ECO/TAC PLAN DELIB/GP

B67
US CONGRESS JOINT ECO COMM,AN ECONOMIC PROFILE OF MAINLAND CHINA, VOLUMES I AND II. CHINA/COM AGRI DIST/IND FINAN INDUS LABOR FORCES ACT/RES PLAN INT/TRADE INGP/REL BAL/PAY 20 CONGRESS. PAGE 135 F2664
ECO/UNDEV WEALTH ECO/TAC DELIB/GP

B67
US SENATE COMM ON FOREIGN REL,INTER-AMERICAN DEVELOPMENT BANK ACT AMENDMENT. L/A+17C USA+45 DELIB/GP DIPLOM FOR/AID BAL/PAY...CHARTS SENATE. PAGE 139 F2741
LAW FINAN INT/ORG ECO/UNDEV

B67
US SENATE COMM ON FOREIGN REL,FOREIGN ASSISTANCE ACT OF 1967. VIETNAM WOR+45 DELIB/GP CONFER CONTROL WAR WEAPON BAL/PAY...CENSUS CHARTS SENATE. PAGE 139 F2744
FOR/AID LAW DIPLOM POLICY

B67
VENKATESWARAN R.J.,CABINET GOVERNMENT IN INDIA. INDIA UK SOCIETY OP/RES COLONIAL LEAD EFFICIENCY ORD/FREE 20. PAGE 141 F2776
DELIB/GP ADMIN CONSTN NAT/G

L67
"GOVERNMENT CONTROL OF LAND: PROTECTING THE I-KNOW-IT-WHENI-SEE-IT INTEREST." USA+45 LAW CONSTN DELIB/GP CT/SYS HABITAT ILLINOIS. PAGE 2 F0026
PLAN LOC/G CONTROL ADJUD

L67
SCHNEIDER C.W.,"REFORM OF THE FEDERAL SECURITIES LAWS." FUT USA+45 LAW FINAN INDUS DELIB/GP ACT/RES PROB/SOLV GP/REL. PAGE 117 F2304
NAT/G LG/CO ADMIN CONTROL

L67
STRUVE G.M.,"THE LESS-RESTRICTIVE-ALTERNATIVE PRINCIPLE AND ECONOMIC DUE PROCESS." USA+45 ECO/DEV LABOR NAT/G CONSULT DELIB/GP OP/RES PLAN WEALTH. PAGE 127 F2505
JURID JUDGE SANCTION CAP/ISM

S67
AGUILAR M.A.,"?UNA OEA MAS FUERTE O UNA AMERICA LATINA MAS DEBIL?" L/A+17C USA+45 USA-45 ECO/UNDEV INDUS CHIEF DELIB/GP FORCES CONTROL PWR 20 OAS KENNEDY/JF JOHNSON/LB. PAGE 3 F0050
INT/ORG DIPLOM POLICY COLONIAL

S67
COSGROVE C.A.,"AGRICULTURE, FINANCE AND POLITICS IN THE EUROPEAN COMMUNITY." EUR+WWI DIST/IND MARKET INT/ORG VOL/ASSN DELIB/GP TEC/DEV BAL/PWR BARGAIN ECO/TAC RATION CONFER 20 EEC. PAGE 28 F0538
ECO/DEV DIPLOM AGRI INT/TRADE

S67
EDGEWORTH A.B. JR.,"CIVIL RIGHTS PLUS THREE YEARS: BANKS AND THE ANTI-DISCRIMINATION LAW" USA+45 SOCIETY DELIB/GP RACE/REL EFFICIENCY 20 NEGRO CIV/RIGHTS. PAGE 36 F0701
WORKER DISCRIM FINAN LAW

S67
GANZ G.,"THE CONTROL OF INDUSTRY BY ADMINISTRATIVE PROCESS." UK DELIB/GP WORKER 20. PAGE 46 F0898
INDUS LAW ADMIN

CONTROL

S67
GREGORY R.,"THE MINISTER'S LINE: OR, THE M4 COMES TO BERKSHIRE. PART I." UK CONSTN DIST/IND LEGIS TOP/EX PLAN ADJUD...GEOG 20. PAGE 51 F0994
DECISION CONSTRUC NAT/G DELIB/GP

S67
ISELIN J.J.,"THE TRUMAN DOCTRINE: ITS PASSAGE THROUGH CONGRESS AND THE AFTERMATH." USA+45 ECO/UNDEV R+D INT/ORG DELIB/GP BAL/PWR REV PEACE ...POLICY UN. PAGE 66 F1291
DIPLOM COM FOR/AID AFR

S67
NEALE R.S.,"WORKING CLASS WOMEN AND WOMEN'S SUFFRAGE." UK LAW CONSTN LABOR NAT/G DELIB/GP LEGIS WORKER PAY PARTIC CHOOSE 19 FEMALE/SEX. PAGE 97 F1906
STRATA SEX SUFF DISCRIM

S67
NOURSE E.G.,"EARLY FLOWERING OF THE EMPLOYMENT ACT" USA+45 LABOR CONSULT DELIB/GP LEGIS BUDGET GOV/REL PRODUC WEALTH 20 INTRVN/ECO. PAGE 99 F1939
NAT/G WORKER ECO/TAC CONTROL

S67
PRATT R.C.,"THE ADMINISTRATION OF ECONOMIC PLANNING IN A NEWLY INDEPEND ENT STATE* THE TANZANIAN EXPERIENCE 1963-1966." AFR TANZANIA ECO/UNDEV PLAN CONTROL ROUTINE TASK EFFICIENCY 20. PAGE 107 F2114
NAT/G DELIB/GP ADMIN TEC/DEV

S67
SIDDIQ M.M.,"LOCAL GOVERNMENT IN PAKISTAN." PAKISTAN PROB/SOLV TAX COLONIAL GOV/REL MUNICH 20. PAGE 121 F2395
ADMIN LOC/G DELIB/GP BUDGET

S67
TELLER A.,"AIR-POLLUTION ABATEMENT: ECONOMIC RATIONALITY AND REALITY." NAT/G DELIB/GP ECO/TAC GOV/REL CENTRAL EFFICIENCY HEALTH...CHARTS METH MUNICH. PAGE 129 F2543
PROB/SOLV CONTROL COST AIR

S67
THORKELSON H.,"FOOD STAMPS AND HUNGER IN AMERICA." USA+45 LAW DELIB/GP ADMIN COST DEMAND POLICY. PAGE 130 F2570
WEALTH RECEIVE EATING PLAN

S67
WARNER G.,"FRANCE, BRITAIN AND THE EEC." FRANCE UK INT/ORG DELIB/GP ECO/TAC CONTROL 20 EEC. PAGE 143 F2822
INT/TRADE BAL/PWR DIPLOM

S67
WHITE W.L.,"THE TREASURY BOARD AND PARLIAMENT." CANADA CONSTN CONSULT LEGIS LEAD PARL/PROC GP/REL ...DECISION 20. PAGE 146 F2871
FINAN DELIB/GP NAT/G ADMIN

S67
ZACK A.M.,"ARE STRIKES OF PUBLIC EMPLOYEES NECESSARY?" USA+45 DELIB/GP PROB/SOLV REPRESENT GP/REL MGT. PAGE 150 F2956
LABOR NAT/G WORKER BARGAIN

N67
NATIONAL COMN COMMUNITY HEALTH,ACTION - PLANNING FOR COMMUNITY HEALTH SERVICES (PAMPHLET). USA+45 PROF/ORG DELIB/GP BUDGET ROUTINE GP/REL ATTIT ...HEAL SOC SOC/WK CHARTS MUNICH TIME 20. PAGE 97 F1898
PLAN HEALTH ADJUST

N67
US HOUSE COMM ON COMMERCE,PARTNERSHIP FOR HEALTH AMENDMENTS FOR 1967 (PAMPHLET). PUB/INST DELIB/GP PROB/SOLV BUDGET EFFICIENCY 20 CONGRESS. PAGE 137 F2701
HEAL PLAN NAT/G JURID

S86
SMITH R.M.,"THE NATIONAL BUREAU OF LABOR AND INDUSTRIAL DEPRESSIONS" USA-45 DELIB/GP BARGAIN CONTROL COST INCOME WEALTH...STAT 19 DEPRESSION. PAGE 123 F2433
LABOR INDUS FINAN GOV/REL

DELL S. F0615

DELLA PORT G. F0616

DELWERT J. F0617

DEMAND....ECONOMIC DEMAND

N
INTERNATIONAL BIBLIOGRAPHY OF ECONOMICS. WOR+45 FINAN MARKET ADMIN DEMAND INCOME PRODUC...POLICY IDEA/COMP METH. PAGE 1 F0002
BIBLIOG ECO/DEV ECO/UNDEV INT/TRADE

N
US LIBRARY OF CONGRESS,SELECTED AND ANNOTATED BIBLIOGRAPHY ON INDUSTRIAL PROBLEMS AND POLICIES IN WARTIME (PAMPHLET). WOR-45 CONSTRUC NAT/G PROB/SOLV COST DEMAND PRODUC 20. PAGE 137 F2707
BIBLIOG/A ECO/DEV INDUS WAR

N
US LIBRARY OF CONGRESS,SELECTED AND ANNOTATED BIBLIOGRAPHY ON RAW MATERIALS IN A WARTIME ECONOMY (PAMPHLET). WOR-45 NAT/G DEMAND PRODUC 20. PAGE 137 F2709
BIBLIOG/A ECO/DEV EXTR/IND WAR

NCO
STOLPER W.,"SOCIAL FACTORS IN ECONOMIC PLANNING, WITH SPECIAL REFERENCE TO NIGERIA" AFR NIGER CULTURE FAM SECT RECEIVE ETIQUET ADMIN DEMAND 20. PAGE 126 F2494 — ECO/UNDEV PLAN ADJUST RISK

B11
SCOTT W.D.,INFLUENCING MEN IN BUSINESS: THE PSYCHOLOGY OF ARGUMENT AND SUGGESTION. WOR-45 WORKER EDU/PROP DEMAND ATTIT PERSON 20. PAGE 118 F2336 — PSY MARKET SML/CO TOP/EX

N19
HABERLER G.,INFLATION; ITS CAUSES AND CURES (PAMPHLET). AFR USA+45 FINAN BUDGET PAY PRICE COST DEMAND 20. PAGE 52 F1021 — ECO/DEV BAL/PAY POLICY NAT/G

N19
HANSEN B.,INFLATION PROBLEMS IN SMALL COUNTRIES (PAMPHLET). AFR UNIV FOR/AID CONTROL BAL/PAY DEMAND PRODUC 20. PAGE 54 F1066 — PRICE FINAN ECO/UNDEV ECO/TAC

N19
MIYASAWA K.,AN ECONOMIC SURVIVAL GAME (PAMPHLET). COST DEMAND EQUILIB INCOME PROFIT 20. PAGE 92 F1811 — ECOMETRIC GAME ECO/TAC DECISION

N19
ROBERTSON D.,GROWTH, WAGES, MONEY (PAMPHLET). UNIV WORKER BUDGET PRICE DEMAND PRODUC WEALTH...CONCPT MATH MONEY. PAGE 112 F2210 — FINAN ECO/DEV ECO/TAC PAY

B20
MALTHUS T.R.,PRINCIPLES OF POLITICAL ECONOMY. UK AGRI INDUS MARKET NAT/G DIPLOM PRICE CONTROL BAL/PAY COST OWN PWR LAISSEZ 18/19. PAGE 84 F1650 — GEN/LAWS DEMAND WEALTH

B30
BEVERIDGE W.H.,UNEMPLOYMENT: A PROBLEM OF INDUSTRY (1909-1930). USA-45 LAW ECO/DEV MARKET DELIB/GP WAR DEMAND INCOME...POLICY STAT CHARTS 20. PAGE 14 F0274 — WORKER ECO/TAC GEN/LAWS

B32
ROBBINS L.,AN ESSAY ON THE NATURE AND SIGNIFICANCE OF ECONOMIC SCIENCE. DEMAND EQUILIB PRODUC UTIL ...ECOMETRIC 20. PAGE 112 F2201 — GEN/LAWS METH/COMP ECO/DEV

B34
ROBINSON J.,THE ECONOMICS OF IMPERFECT COMPETITION. FINAN ECO/TAC PRICE COST DEMAND EQUILIB OPTIMAL WEALTH...METH MONOPOLY. PAGE 113 F2221 — MARKET WORKER INDUS

B35
KEYNES J.M.,THE GENERAL THEORY OF EMPLOYMENT, INTEREST, AND MONEY. AGRI INDUS WORKER ECO/TAC DEMAND EQUILIB INCOME PRODUC PROFIT ATTIT WEALTH 20. PAGE 71 F1386 — FINAN GEN/LAWS MARKET PRICE

B38
MEADE J.E.,AN INTRODUCTION TO ECONOMIC ANALYSIS AND POLICY (AMERICAN EDITION EDITED BY C.J. HITCH). FINAN INDUS MARKET LABOR INT/TRADE CONTROL COST DEMAND INCOME...CLASSIF CHARTS T 20 KEYNES/JM MONOPOLY. PAGE 89 F1737 — CONCPT PROFIT PRODUC

B40
CAMPBELL P.,CONSUMER REPRESENTATION IN THE NEW DEAL. AGRI INDUS MARKET EX/STRUC PLAN CAP/ISM CONTROL GP/REL DEMAND POLICY. PAGE 21 F0408 — CLIENT REPRESENT NAT/G

B42
US LIBRARY OF CONGRESS,ECONOMICS OF WAR (APRIL 1941-MARCH 1942). WOR-45 FINAN INDUS LOC/G NAT/G PLAN BUDGET RATION COST DEMAND...POLICY 20. PAGE 138 F2712 — BIBLIOG/A INT/TRADE ECO/TAC WAR

B47
LEVER E.A.,ADVERTISING AND ECONOMIC THEORY. FINAN ECO/TAC DEMAND EFFICIENCY ATTIT...MGT PSY SAMP/SIZ CHARTS 20. PAGE 79 F1539 — EDU/PROP MARKET COM/IND ECO/DEV

B48
HICKS J.R.,VALUE AND CAPITAL. FINAN PRICE EQUILIB INCOME PRODUC WEALTH...TIME/SEQ 20 MARSHALL/A PARETO/V SAMUELSN/P. PAGE 59 F1165 — ECOMETRIC MATH DEMAND PROB/SOLV

B48
NOYES C.R.,ECONOMIC MAN IN RELATION TO HIS NATURAL ENVIRONMENT (2 VOLS.). UNIV COST DEMAND EFFICIENCY HAPPINESS INCOME PRODUC PROFIT HEREDITY...CHARTS BIBLIOG. PAGE 99 F1944 — HABITAT METH/CNCPT GEN/METH

B48
SAMUELSON P.A.,FOUNDATIONS OF ECONOMIC ANALYSIS. MARKET RATION DEMAND UTIL...MATH METH T 20. PAGE 115 F2276 — EQUILIB GEN/LAWS ECO/DEV

B49
MACGREGOR D.H.,ECONOMIC THOUGHT AND POLICY. WOR-45 WORKER WAR DEMAND EFFICIENCY WEALTH LAISSEZ SOCISM ...MAJORIT BIBLIOG 19/20. PAGE 83 F1629 — CONCPT POLICY ECO/TAC

B50
CHAMBERLIN E.,THE THEORY OF MONOPOLISTIC COMPETITION (1933). INDUS PAY GP/REL COST DEMAND EFFICIENCY OPTIMAL PRODUC WEALTH...GEN/LAWS 20. PAGE 23 F0443 — MARKET PRICE ECO/TAC EQUILIB

B51
HANSEN B.,A STUDY IN THE THEORY OF INFLATION. WOR-45 FINAN WAR DEMAND...CHARTS 20. PAGE 54 F1067 — PRICE ECO/TAC EQUILIB PRODUC

B51
PETERSON F.,SURVEY OF LABOR ECONOMICS (REV. ED.). STRATA ECO/DEV LABOR INSPECT BARGAIN PAY PRICE EXEC ROUTINE GP/REL ALL/VALS ORD/FREE 20 AFL/CIO DEPT/LABOR. PAGE 105 F2069 — WORKER DEMAND IDEA/COMP T

B52
AYRES C.E.,THE INDUSTRIAL ECONOMY. USA+45 FINAN MARKET NAT/G PUB/INST PLAN ECO/TAC TAX DEMAND INCOME...BIBLIOG/A 20. PAGE 8 F0146 — ECO/DEV INDUS FUT PROB/SOLV

C52
HUME D.,"OF INTEREST" IN D. HUME, POLITICAL DISCOURSES (1752)" UK INDUS WORKER DIPLOM PAY DEMAND INCOME WEALTH...GEN/LAWS 18 MONEY. PAGE 63 F1239 — PRICE COST FINAN INT/TRADE

B54
MEYER F.V.,INFLATION AND CAPITAL. AFR UK WOR+45 BUDGET GOV/REL INCOME PRODUC PROFIT WEALTH...CONCPT CHARTS 20. PAGE 90 F1768 — ECO/DEV FINAN ECO/TAC DEMAND

B55
BOULDING K.E.,ECONOMIC ANALYSIS (3RD ED.). USA+45 PLAN ECO/TAC COST DEMAND INCOME...POLICY STAT CHARTS SIMUL T. PAGE 17 F0322 — PHIL/SCI ECO/DEV CAP/ISM

B55
GOMES F.A.,OPERACAO MUNICIPIO. BRAZIL L/A+17C SERV/IND LOC/G BUDGET ECO/TAC COST DEMAND...POLICY MUNICH 20. PAGE 48 F0944 — ECO/UNDEV FEDERAL GOV/REL

B55
PEDLER F.J.,ECONOMIC GEOGRAPHY OF WEST AFRICA. GAMBIA NIGER SIER/LEONE STRATA EXTR/IND MARKET LABOR INT/TRADE DEMAND HABITAT WEALTH...CHARTS 20. PAGE 104 F2046 — ECO/UNDEV GEOG PRODUC EFFICIENCY

B56
GREENHUT M.L.,PLANT LOCATION IN THEORY AND PRACTICE; THE ECONOMICS OF SPACE. WOR+45 WOR-45 MARKET WORKER COST DEMAND...CONCPT STAT CHARTS HYPO/EXP BIBLIOG 19/20. PAGE 51 F0991 — SML/CO ECO/DEV CAP/ISM IDEA/COMP

S56
LANDAUER J.D.,"PROFESSIONAL CONSULTANTS: A NEW FACTOR IN REAL ESTATE." USA+45 PROB/SOLV ECO/TAC PERS/REL DEMAND EFFICIENCY DECISION. PAGE 75 F1467 — CONSULT CONSTRUC CLIENT

B57
HARWOOD E.C.,CAUSE AND CONTROL OF THE BUSINESS CYCLE (5TH ED.). AFR USA-45 PRICE CONTROL WAR DEMAND INCOME WEALTH...TREND CHARTS 19. PAGE 56 F1107 — PRODUC MARKET FINAN

B57
HUTTON D.G.,INFLATION AND SOCIETY. AFR FINAN PLAN COST DEMAND EQUILIB...CONCPT 20. PAGE 64 F1254 — ECO/DEV POLICY NAT/G ECO/TAC

B57
LEIBENSTEIN H.,ECONOMIC BACKWARDNESS AND ECONOMIC GROWTH. WOR+45 SOCIETY AGRI INDUS TEC/DEV CAP/ISM FOR/AID COST DEMAND WEALTH...CHARTS IDEA/COMP 20. PAGE 77 F1513 — ECO/UNDEV ECO/TAC PRODUC POLICY

B57
NANIWADA H.,STAAT UND WIRTSCHAFT; GRUNDLEGUNG DER NATIONALOEKONOMIE ALS DER LOGIK DER BURGERLICHEN GESELLSCHAFT. WOR+45 WOR-45 STRATA MARKET WORKER INGP/REL DEMAND EQUILIB WEALTH...POLICY IDEA/COMP GEN/LAWS 17/20 MARX/KARL KEYNES/JM LENIN/VI. PAGE 96 F1890 — ALL/IDEOS ECO/TAC SOCIETY NAT/G

B57
NEUMARK S.D.,ECONOMIC INFLUENCES ON THE SOUTH AFRICAN FRONTIER, 1652-1836. SOUTH/AFR SEA AGRI NAT/G FORCES WORKER DIPLOM INT/TRADE PRICE DEMAND PRODUC...STAT CHARTS 17/19 FRONTIER. PAGE 97 F1915 — COLONIAL ECO/UNDEV ECO/TAC MARKET

B57
SINGH D.B.,INFLATIONARY PRICE TRENDS IN INDIA SINCE 1939. AFR INDIA ECO/TAC RATION CONTROL WAR GOV/REL BAL/PAY DEMAND INCOME PEACE PRODUC...POLICY CHARTS 20. PAGE 122 F2413 — BUDGET ECO/UNDEV PRICE FINAN

B58
DEFENSE AGAINST INFLATION. USA+45 LEGIS WORKER TAX PRICE DEMAND INCOME PRODUC...POLICY TREND METH/COMP 20 GOLD/STAND. PAGE 1 F0012 — ECO/TAC EQUILIB WEALTH PROB/SOLV

B58
CHANG C.,THE INFLATIONARY SPIRAL: THE EXPERIENCE IN CHINA 1939-50. CHINA/COM BUDGET INT/TRADE PRICE ADMIN CONTROL WAR DEMAND...POLICY CHARTS 20. PAGE 23 F0451 — FINAN ECO/TAC BAL/PAY GOV/REL

B58
MOULTON H.G.,CAN INFLATION BE CONTROLLED? ECO/DEV INDUS CAP/ISM RATION GOV/REL COST INCOME PEACE WEALTH...CHARTS TIME 20 KEYNES/JM MONEY. PAGE 94 F1847 — ECO/TAC CONTROL DEMAND FINAN

B58
PALYI M.,MANAGED MONEY AT THE CROSSROADS: THE — FINAN

EUROPEAN EXPERIENCE. AFR WOR+45 WOR-45 TEC/DEV DIPLOM INT/TRADE DEMAND WEALTH...CHARTS BIBLIOG 19/20 EUROPE SILVER. PAGE 103 F2022 ECO/TAC ECO/DEV PRODUC B58

US CONGRESS JOINT ECO COMM,THE RELATIONSHIP OF PRICES TO ECONOMIC STABILITY AND GROWTH. USA+45 MARKET TAX ADJUST COST DEMAND INCOME PRODUC ...POLICY TREND CHARTS ANTHOL 20 CONGRESS. PAGE 134 F2650 ECO/DEV PLAN EQUILIB PRICE B58

WARNER A.W.,CONCEPTS AND CASES IN ECONOMIC ANALYSIS. PROB/SOLV BARGAIN CONTROL INCOME PRODUC ...ECOMETRIC MGT CONCPT CLASSIF CHARTS 20 KEYNES/JM. PAGE 143 F2820 ECO/TAC DEMAND EQUILIB COST B59

FELS R.,AMERICAN BUSINESS CYCLES 1865-1897. USA+45 ECO/DEV LG/CO SML/CO PROB/SOLV TEC/DEV CAP/ISM INT/TRADE DEMAND...POLICY CHARTS METH 19 DEPRESSION. PAGE 40 F0782 FINAN INDUS TREND ECO/TAC B59

HARTOG F.,EUROPEAN TRADE CYCLE POLICY. WORKER TAX PRICE WAR CENTRAL DEMAND...TREND CHARTS 20 UN. PAGE 56 F1103 EQUILIB EUR+WWI INT/TRADE B59

LEWIS J.P.,BUSINESS CONDITIONS ANALYSIS. USA+45 MARKET LABOR BUDGET TAX AUTOMAT WAR DEMAND PRODUC ...ECOMETRIC CHARTS BIBLIOG 19/20. PAGE 79 F1549 FINAN PRICE TREND B59

LINK R.G.,ENGLISH THEORIES OF ECONOMIC FLUCTUATIONS: 1815-1848. FRANCE UK AGRI WORKER DIPLOM PRICE TASK WAR DEMAND PRODUC...POLICY BIBLIOG 18 MALTHUS MILL/JS WILSON/J. PAGE 80 F1574 IDEA/COMP ECO/DEV WEALTH EQUILIB B59

MATTHEWS R.C.O.,THE BUSINESS CYCLE. AFR LABOR INT/TRADE TAX PRICE RISK ADJUST WEALTH...POLICY ECOMETRIC CHARTS SIMUL TIME 20. PAGE 87 F1705 FINAN DEMAND TASK B59

SILCOCK T.H.,THE COMMONWEALTH ECONOMY IN SOUTHEAST ASIA. AFR INDIA MALAYSIA S/ASIA ECO/DEV AGRI LOC/G PLAN TARIFFS COLONIAL BAL/PAY DEMAND...BIBLIOG/A 20 GATT. PAGE 122 F2401 ECO/TAC INT/TRADE RACE/REL DIPLOM B59

STOVEL J.A.,CANADA IN THE WORLD ECONOMY. CANADA PRICE DEMAND...STAT CHARTS BIBLIOG 20 VINER/J. PAGE 127 F2499 INT/TRADE BAL/PAY FINAN ECO/TAC S59

STREETEN P.,"UNBALANCED GROWTH" UK ECO/DEV AGRI MARKET TEC/DEV CAP/ISM ECO/TAC FOR/AID INT/TRADE DEMAND ORD/FREE...CONCPT 20. PAGE 127 F2502 IDEA/COMP FINAN PRODUC EQUILIB B60

CROSSER P.K.,STATE CAPITALISM IN THE ECONOMY OF THE UNITED STATES. USA+45 USA-45 AGRI FINAN INDUS LABOR WORKER RATION CONTROL GOV/REL DEMAND...NEW/IDEA 20. PAGE 29 F0557 CAP/ISM ECO/DEV ECO/TAC NAT/G B60

HALL C.A. JR.,FISCAL POLICY FOR STABLE GROWTH. USA+45 FINAN TEC/DEV TAX COST DEMAND INCOME ...BIBLIOG 20. PAGE 53 F1045 ECO/TAC BUDGET NAT/G POLICY B60

HARBERGER A.C.,THE DEMAND FOR DURABLE GOODS. AGRI FINAN COST EQUILIB...MATH STAT TIME/SEQ TREND CON/ANAL CHARTS SIMUL ANTHOL 20. PAGE 55 F1072 ECOMETRIC DEMAND PRICE B60

RAY D.D.,ACCOUNTING AND BUSINESS FLUCTUATIONS. LG/CO SML/CO FEEDBACK DEMAND...CHARTS IDEA/COMP BIBLIOG 20. PAGE 109 F2154 FINAN AFR CONTROL B60

ROBERTSON D.,THE CONTROL OF INDUSTRY. UK MARKET LABOR WORKER PRICE CONTROL GP/REL COST DEMAND ORD/FREE WEALTH NEW/LIB SOCISM 20. PAGE 112 F2211 INDUS FINAN NAT/G ECO/DEV B60

ROBINSON R.I.,FINANCIAL INSTITUTIONS. USA+45 PRICE GOV/REL DEMAND WEALTH...CHARTS T 20 MONEY. PAGE 113 F2226 FINAN ECO/TAC ECO/DEV BUDGET B60

SIEGEL B.N.,AGGREGATE ECONOMICS AND PUBLIC POLICY. ECO/DEV TEC/DEV ECO/TAC TASK DEMAND EQUILIB INCOME ...CHARTS 20. PAGE 121 F2396 ECOMETRIC WEALTH PRODUC MARKET L60

CHENERY H.B.,"PATTERNS OF INDUSTRIAL GROWTH." INT/TRADE DEMAND PRODUC...MATH REGRESS CHARTS SIMUL METH 20. PAGE 24 F0462 ECO/TAC ECO/DEV GP/COMP CON/ANAL B61

ASCHHEIM J.,TECHNIQUES OF MONETARY CONTROL. UK USA+45 CONTROL WAR DEMAND INCOME WEALTH...TREND CHARTS 20 MONEY. PAGE 7 F0127 FINAN MARKET BUDGET CENTRAL B61

BARRASH J.,LABOR'S GRASS ROOTS; A STUDY OF THE LOCAL UNION. STRATA BARGAIN LEAD REPRESENT DEMAND ATTIT PWR. PAGE 10 F0192 LABOR USA+45 INGP/REL EXEC B61

ELLIS H.S.,ECONOMIC DEVELOPMENT FOR LATIN AMERICA. L/A+17C AGRI FINAN INDUS FOR/AID GP/REL BAL/PAY DEMAND...ANTHOL 20 INTL/ECON. PAGE 37 F0723 ECO/UNDEV ECO/TAC PLAN INT/TRADE B61

FELLNER W.,THE PROBLEM OF RISING PRICES. AGRI INDUS WORKER BUDGET CAP/ISM ECO/TAC INT/TRADE PAY DEMAND ...POLICY 20 EEC. PAGE 40 F0780 PRICE MARKET ECO/DEV COST B61

GOODWIN C.D.W.,CANADIAN ECONOMIC THOUGHT. CANADA STRATA TEC/DEV CAP/ISM TARIFFS TAX COST EFFICIENCY WEALTH...METH/CNCPT TREND 20 MARITIME ONTARIO. PAGE 49 F0952 INT/TRADE ECO/DEV FINAN DEMAND B61

HICKS U.K.,FEDERALISM AND ECONOMIC GROWTH IN UNDERDEVELOPED COUNTRIES. WOR+45 WOR-45 FINAN NAT/G PLAN BUDGET DIPLOM INT/TRADE DEMAND WEALTH...ANTHOL 20. PAGE 59 F1167 ECO/UNDEV ECO/TAC FEDERAL CONSTN B61

LETHBRIDGE H.J.,CHINA'S URBAN COMMUNES. CHINA/COM FUT ECO/UNDEV DIPLOM EDU/PROP DEMAND INCOME MARXISM ...POLICY MUNICH 20. PAGE 78 F1534 CONTROL ECO/TAC NAT/G B61

MACMAHON A.W.,DELEGATION AND AUTONOMY. INDIA STRUCT LEGIS BARGAIN BUDGET ECO/TAC LEGIT EXEC REPRESENT GOV/REL CENTRAL DEMAND EFFICIENCY PRODUC. PAGE 84 F1637 ADMIN PLAN FEDERAL B61

MCCRACKEN H.L.,KEYNESIAN ECONOMICS IN THE STREAM OF ECONOMIC THOUGHT. FINAN MARKET BARGAIN EFFICIENCY OPTIMAL...PHIL/SCI CONCPT IDEA/COMP BIBLIOG 18/20 KEYNES/JM. PAGE 88 F1724 ECO/TAC DEMAND ECOMETRIC B61

MORRIS B.R.,PROBLEMS OF AMERICAN ECONOMIC GROWTH. USA+45 LABOR WORKER BUDGET ECO/TAC INT/TRADE EQUILIB 20. PAGE 94 F1836 ECO/DEV POLICY TEC/DEV DEMAND B61

NORTH D.C.,THE ECONOMIC GROWTH OF THE UNITED STATES 1790-1860. USA-45 INDUS TEC/DEV CAP/ISM ECO/TAC PRICE COST DEMAND LAISSEZ...ECOMETRIC STAT TREND 19. PAGE 98 F1933 AGRI ECO/UNDEV B61

OECD,STATISTICS OF BALANCE OF PAYMENTS 1950-61. WOR+45 FINAN ECO/TAC INT/TRADE DEMAND WEALTH...STAT NAT/COMP 20 OEEC OECD. PAGE 100 F1965 BAL/PAY ECO/DEV INT/ORG CHARTS B61

PAUNIO J.J.,A STUDY IN THE THEORY OF OPEN INFLATION. AFR FINAN CAP/ISM PRICE DEMAND INCOME ...CHARTS BIBLIOG 20. PAGE 104 F2040 ACT/RES ECO/DEV ECO/TAC COST B61

SHONFIELD A.,ECONOMIC GROWTH AND INFLATION; A STUDY OF INDIAN PLANNING. AFR INDIA AGRI INDUS TEC/DEV CONTROL DEMAND UTIL 20. PAGE 121 F2384 ECO/UNDEV PRICE PLAN BUDGET B61

SLICHTER S.H.,ECONOMIC GROWTH IN THE UNITED STATES. FUT USA+45 USA-45 LABOR PAY INCOME PRODUC...MGT 19/20. PAGE 123 F2422 ECO/DEV TEC/DEV CAP/ISM DEMAND B61

STOCKING G.W.,WORKABLE COMPETITION AND ANTITRUST POLICY. USA+45 NAT/G CONSULT PLAN PRICE GOV/REL COST DEMAND PROFIT...POLICY 20. PAGE 126 F2491 LG/CO INDUS ECO/TAC CONTROL B61

WAGLE S.S.,TECHNIQUE OF PLANNING FOR ACCELERATED ECONOMIC GROWTH OF UNDERDEVELOPED COUNTRIES. WOR+45 ACT/RES PROB/SOLV RATION BAL/PAY DEMAND INCOME 20. PAGE 142 F2798 ECO/UNDEV PLAN INDUS ECO/TAC S61

DICKS-MIREAUX L.A.,"THE INTERRELATIONSHIP BETWEEN COST AND PRICE CHANGES 19461959: A STUDY OF INFLATION IN POST-WAR BRITAIN" AFR UK ECO/DEV INDUS WORKER ECO/TAC ORD/FREE WEALTH...ECOMETRIC REGRESS STAT TREND CHARTS 20. PAGE 33 F0634 PRICE PAY DEMAND B62

ALTMAN G.T.,INVISIBLE BARRIER: THE OPTIMUM GROWTH CURVE. USA+45 USA-45 ECO/DEV PLAN PAY CONTROL DEMAND OPTIMAL PRODUC WEALTH...STAT CHARTS 20. PAGE 4 F0080 INDUS FINAN ECO/TAC TAX B62

BERNSTEIN P.L.,THE PRICE OF PROSPERITY. USA+45 TAX CONTROL OPTIMAL WEALTH...PREDICT 20. PAGE 14 F0269 ECO/DEV ECO/TAC NAT/G DEMAND B62

FAO,FOOD AND AGRICULTURE ORGANIZATION AFRICAN SURVEY. AFR CONGO/BRAZ GHANA STRATA AGRI INT/ORG ECO/TAC WEALTH

TEC/DEV FOR/AID INT/TRADE RACE/REL DEMAND EFFICIENCY PRODUC...GEOG 20 UN CONGO/LEOP. PAGE 39 F0763 — EXTR/IND ECO/UNDEV

B62
FORD A.G.,THE GOLD STANDARD 1880-1914: BRITAIN AND ARGENTINA. AFR UK ECO/UNDEV INT/TRADE ADMIN GOV/REL DEMAND EFFICIENCY...STAT CHARTS 19/20 ARGEN. PAGE 42 F0823 — FINAN ECO/TAC BUDGET BAL/PAY

B62
GEARY R.C.,EUROPE'S FUTURE IN FIGURES. FUT GOV/REL DEMAND PRODUC...STAT CHARTS METH/COMP ANTHOL METH 20 EUROPE. PAGE 47 F0912 — FINAN ECO/DEV PREDICT WEALTH

B62
GORT M.,DIVERSIFICATION AND INTEGRATION IN AMERICAN INDUSTRY. CLIENT DIST/IND PROC/MFG SERV/IND LG/CO CONTROL DEMAND PWR...METH/CNCPT STAT TREND CON/ANAL GP/COMP. PAGE 49 F0964 — CONCPT GP/REL CLASSIF

B62
GRANICK D.,THE EUROPEAN EXECUTIVE. BELGIUM FRANCE GERMANY/W UK INDUS LABOR LG/CO SML/CO EX/STRUC PLAN TEC/DEV CAP/ISM COST DEMAND...POLICY CHARTS 20. PAGE 50 F0977 — MGT ECO/DEV ECO/TAC EXEC

B62
GREEN L.P.,DEVELOPMENT IN AFRICA. AFR CENTRL/AFR GHANA RHODESIA SOUTH/AFR AGRI PROC/MFG INT/TRADE DEMAND NAT/LISM PRODUC WEALTH...GEOG METH/CNCPT CHARTS BIBLIOG 20. PAGE 50 F0987 — CULTURE ECO/UNDEV GOV/REL TREND

B62
HOOVER C.B.,ECONOMIC SYSTEMS OF THE COMMONWEALTH. AFR CANADA INDIA UK ECO/DEV ECO/UNDEV AGRI INDUS TEC/DEV TARIFFS PRICE BAL/PAY DEMAND...SIMUL 20 AUSTRAL. PAGE 61 F1208 — CAP/ISM SOCISM ECO/TAC PLAN

B62
KINDLEBERGER C.P.,FOREIGN TRADE AND THE NATIONAL ECONOMY. WOR+45 ECO/DEV ECO/UNDEV ECO/TAC COST DEMAND 20. PAGE 71 F1393 — INT/TRADE GOV/COMP BAL/PAY POLICY

B62
KLEIN L.R.,AN INTRODUCTION TO ECONOMETRICS. DIST/IND DEMAND PRODUC WEALTH...MATH TIME/SEQ T 20. PAGE 72 F1408 — ECOMETRIC SIMUL PREDICT STAT

B62
MARTINS A.F.,REVOLUCAO BRANCA NO CAMPO. L/A+17C SERV/IND DEMAND EFFICIENCY PRODUC...POLICY METH/COMP. PAGE 86 F1685 — AGRI ECO/UNDEV TEC/DEV NAT/COMP

B62
MEYER F.V.,THE TERMS OF TRADE. WOR+45 AGRI MARKET PROC/MFG DIPLOM PRICE DEMAND PRODUC 20. PAGE 90 F1769 — INT/TRADE BAL/PAY SIMUL EQUILIB

B62
PHELPS E.S.,THE GOAL OF ECONOMIC GROWTH: SOURCES, COSTS, BENEFITS. USA+45 USSR FINAN TAX CONTROL DEMAND WEALTH...POLICY NAT/COMP ANTHOL BIBLIOG 20. PAGE 106 F2079 — ECO/TAC ECO/DEV NAT/G FUT

B62
ROTHBARD M.N.,THE PANIC OF 1819; REACTIONS AND POLICIES. AFR USA-45 LAW FINAN BUDGET TARIFFS DEMAND 19 DEPRESSION. PAGE 114 F2247 — ECO/UNDEV POLICY ATTIT ECO/TAC

B62
SCHALLER H.G.,PUBLIC EXPENDITURE DECISIONS IN THE URBAN COMMUNITY: PREPARED FOR RESOURCES FOR THE FUTURE, INC. INDUS SERV/IND LOC/G PUB/INST PLAN PROB/SOLV BUDGET DEMAND PRODUC...CHARTS MUNICH. PAGE 116 F2289 — FINAN DECISION

B62
SCHNEIDER E.,MONEY, INCOME AND EMPLOYMENT. TAX PAY DEMAND...CHARTS BIBLIOG 20. PAGE 117 F2305 — ECO/DEV FINAN INCOME

B62
SHANNON I.,THE ECONOMIC FUNCTIONS OF GOLD. AFR FUT WOR+45 WOR-45 INT/ORG BUDGET INT/TRADE BAL/PAY DEMAND PEACE 20 MONEY. PAGE 120 F2366 — FINAN PRICE ECO/DEV ECO/TAC

B62
SIEVERS A.M.,REVOLUTION, EVOLUTION AND THE ECONOMIC ORDER. INDUS LABOR TAX CONTROL REV WAR DEMAND PRODUC WEALTH...IDEA/COMP 19/20 KEYNES/JM. PAGE 122 F2399 — EFFICIENCY ALL/IDEOS ECO/DEV WELF/ST

B62
TIEBOUT C.M.,THE COMMUNITY ECONOMIC BASE STUDY (PAMPHLET). USA+45 ECO/TAC LEAD DEMAND HABITAT 20. PAGE 130 F2572 — NEIGH INCOME ACT/RES

B62
VANEK J.,INTERNATIONAL TRADE - THEORY AND ECONOMIC POLICY. LABOR BAL/PWR ECO/TAC TARIFFS PRICE BAL/PAY COST DEMAND 20. PAGE 140 F2765 — INT/TRADE DIPLOM BARGAIN MARKET

B62
WRIGHT D.M.,THE KEYNESIAN SYSTEM. WOR+45 WOR-45 LABOR NAT/G CONTROL COST DEMAND EFFICIENCY...POLICY CONCPT CHARTS SIMUL 20 KEYNES/JM. PAGE 149 F2931 — INCOME ECO/DEV FINAN

ECO/TAC

N62
BANK INTERNATIONAL SETTLEMENTS,AUSTRIA: MONETARY AND ECONOMIC SITUATION 1952-61 (PAMPHLET). AUSTRIA WORKER BUDGET INT/TRADE PRICE BAL/PAY DEMAND EFFICIENCY INCOME PRODUC...STAT 20 SILVER. PAGE 9 F0174 — FINAN ECO/DEV CHARTS WEALTH

B63
BRITISH AID. UK AGRI DIST/IND INDUS SCHOOL TEC/DEV INT/TRADE COLONIAL DEMAND...TREND CHARTS 20. PAGE 1 F0018 — FOR/AID ECO/UNDEV NAT/G FINAN

B63
BARNETT H.J.,SCARCITY AND GROWTH: THE ECONOMICS OF NATURAL RESOURCE AVAILABILITY. FUT WOR+45 AGRI INDUS PROB/SOLV TEC/DEV CONTROL PRODUC...SOC/WK IDEA/COMP METH/COMP SIMUL 20 RESOURCE/N MALTHUS RICARDO/D MILL/JS DARWIN/C. PAGE 10 F0191 — DEMAND HABITAT CENSUS GEOG

B63
CENTRO ESTUDIOS MONETARIOS LAT,COOPERACION FINANCIERA EN AMERICA LATINA. L/A+17C PLAN PROB/SOLV CONTROL REGION DEMAND...POLICY ANTHOL 20. PAGE 22 F0433 — ECO/UNDEV INT/TRADE MARKET FINAN

B63
EL-NAGGAR S.,FOREIGN AID TO UNITED ARAB REPUBLIC. UAR USA+45 USSR AGRI FINAN INDUS FORCES EATING DEMAND...CHARTS METH/COMP 20 RESOURCE/N AID. PAGE 37 F0718 — FOR/AID ECO/UNDEV RECEIVE PLAN

B63
ERHARD L.,THE ECONOMICS OF SUCCESS. GERMANY/W WOR+45 LABOR CHIEF TAX REGION COST DEMAND ANTHOL. PAGE 38 F0745 — ECO/DEV INT/TRADE PLAN DIPLOM

B63
FRIEDMAN M.,INFLATION: CAUSES AND CURES. AFR INDIA ECO/DEV ECO/TAC INT/TRADE RATION PRICE DEMAND ...POLICY 20. PAGE 44 F0860 — ECO/UNDEV PLAN FINAN EQUILIB

B63
GRIGSBY W.G.,HOUSING MARKETS AND PUBLIC POLICY. USA+45 FAM NEIGH PRICE DEMAND WEALTH...POLICY CHARTS BIBLIOG METH MUNICH 20. PAGE 51 F1002 — MARKET RENT HABITAT PLAN

B63
HARROD R.F.,INTERNATIONAL TRADE THEORY IN A DEVELOPING WORLD. COM WOR+45 FOR/AID REGION COST DEMAND WEALTH...POLICY 20 INTL/ECON. PAGE 56 F1095 — INT/TRADE BAL/PAY ECO/UNDEV METH/COMP

B63
INTERNATIONAL ASSOCIATION RES,AFRICAN STUDIES IN INCOME AND WEALTH. AFR NAT/G PROB/SOLV DEMAND INCOME...ECOMETRIC METH/COMP 20. PAGE 64 F1270 — WEALTH PLAN ECO/UNDEV BUDGET

B63
JACOBS P.,STATE OF UNIONS. USA+45 STRATA TOP/EX GP/REL RACE/REL DEMAND DISCRIM ATTIT PWR 20 CONGRESS NEGRO HOFFA/J. PAGE 66 F1296 — LABOR ECO/TAC BARGAIN DECISION

B63
MACHLUP F.,ESSAYS ON ECONOMIC SEMANTICS. UNIV ECO/DEV FINAN COST DEMAND PRODUC...POLICY STAT CHARTS BIBLIOG. PAGE 83 F1632 — LING CONCPT METH

B63
MEEK R.L.,THE ECONOMICS OF PHYSIOCRACY. FRANCE UK AGRI FINAN WORKER CAP/ISM TAX DEMAND EQUILIB INCOME HABITAT...CHARTS ANTHOL 17. PAGE 89 F1744 — PRODUC WEALTH MARKET

B63
MEIER G.,INTERNATIONAL TRADE AND DEVELOPMENT. FINAN BAL/PAY COST DEMAND DISCRIM EQUILIB WEALTH...POLICY ECOMETRIC MATH STAT BIBLIOG/A 20. PAGE 89 F1747 — ECO/UNDEV ECO/TAC INT/TRADE IDEA/COMP

B63
OLSON M. JR.,THE ECONOMICS OF WARTIME SHORTAGE. FRANCE GERMANY MOD/EUR UK AGRI PROB/SOLV ADMIN DEMAND WEALTH...POLICY OLD/LIB FOR/TRADE 17/20. PAGE 101 F1990 — WAR ADJUST ECO/TAC NAT/COMP

B63
PAENSON I.,SYSTEMATIC GLOSSARY ENGLISH, FRENCH, SPANISH, RUSSIAN OF SELECTED ECONOMIC AND SOCIAL TERMS. WOR+45 FINAN LABOR INT/TRADE DEMAND PRODUC 20. PAGE 102 F2014 — DICTIONARY SOC LING

B63
PATTON R.,THE DEVELOPMENT OF THE AMERICAN ECONOMY: REVISED. USA+45 USA-45 INDUS LABOR NAT/G CAP/ISM DIPLOM INT/TRADE WAR WEALTH 16/20. PAGE 104 F2038 — ECO/TAC ECO/DEV DEMAND

B63
RANGEL I.,A INFLACAO BRASILEIRA (2ND ED.). AFR BRAZIL AGRI INDUS MARKET INT/TRADE DEMAND EQUILIB ATTIT 20. PAGE 109 F2144 — ECO/UNDEV FINAN PRICE TAX

B63
RICARDO D.,THE PRINCIPLES OF POLITICAL ECONOMY AND TAXATION (1817). UK INDUS MARKET ECO/TAC INT/TRADE TARIFFS PRICE COST DEMAND OPTIMAL WEALTH...CONCPT 19 INTRVN/ECO. PAGE 111 F2183 — GEN/LAWS TAX LAISSEZ

B63
ROPKE W.,ECONOMICS OF THE FREE SOCIETY. FINAN INT/TRADE BAL/PAY COST DEMAND EFFICIENCY ORD/FREE WEALTH...CON/ANAL METH/COMP T 20 KEYNES/JM. PAGE 114 F2240
SOCIETY BUDGET ECO/DEV ECO/TAC

B63
SALENT W.S.,THE UNITED STATES BALANCE OF PAYMENTS IN 1968. EUR+WWI UK USA+45 AGRI R+D LABOR FORCES PRODUC...GEOG CONCPT CHARTS 20 CHINJAP EEC. PAGE 115 F2274
BAL/PAY DEMAND FINAN INT/TRADE

B63
US BD GOVERNORS FEDL RESRV,THE FEDERAL RESERVE AND THE TREASURY. USA+45 WORKER PROB/SOLV PRICE COST DEMAND WEALTH...STAT INT CHARTS 20 FED/RESERV DEPT/TREAS. PAGE 134 F2641
FINAN GOV/REL CONTROL BUDGET

B63
VON MISES L.,HUMAN ACTION: A TREATISE ON ECONOMICS (2ND ED.). SOCIETY MARKET TAX PAY PRICE DEMAND EQUILIB RATIONAL...PSY 20. PAGE 142 F2794
PLAN DRIVE ATTIT

B63
WALKER F.V.,GROWTH, EMPLOYMENT, AND THE PRICE LEVEL. USA+45 NAT/G PLAN ECO/TAC DEMAND EFFICIENCY CHARTS. PAGE 142 F2803
ECO/DEV FINAN PRICE WORKER

B64
BALL R.J.,INFLATION AND THE THEORY OF MONEY. MARKET TAX PAY PRICE TASK ADJUST BAL/PAY COST INCOME PRODUC WEALTH...METH/COMP 20 KEYNES/JM MONEY. PAGE 9 F0167
EQUILIB DEMAND POLICY

B64
BARKSDALE H.C.,MARKETING: CHANGE AND EXCHANGE. USA+45 FINAN ACADEM TEC/DEV PRICE AUTOMAT WEALTH ...CHARTS 20. PAGE 10 F0187
MARKET ECO/DEV DEMAND TREND

B64
BAUCHET P.,ECONOMIC PLANNING. FRANCE STRATA LG/CO CAP/ISM ADMIN PARL/PROC DEMAND OPTIMAL ATTIT PWR SOCISM...POLICY CHARTS 20. PAGE 11 F0212
ECO/DEV NAT/G PLAN ECO/TAC

B64
CHINITZ B.,CITY AND SUBURB: THE ECONOMICS OF METROPOLITAN GROWTH. DIST/IND BUDGET GOV/REL DEMAND ATTIT HABITAT MUNICH PHILADELPH. PAGE 24 F0467
TEC/DEV PLAN

B64
COMPOS R.O.,A MOEDA, O GOVERNO E O TEMPO. AFR BRAZIL WOR+45 FINAN TEC/DEV FOR/AID REGION DEMAND ...ANTHOL 20. PAGE 27 F0520
ECO/UNDEV PLAN DIPLOM INT/TRADE

B64
GARFIELD PJ LOVEJOY WF,PUBLIC UTILITY ECONOMICS. DIST/IND FINAN MARKET ADMIN COST DEMAND ...TECHNIC JURID MUNICH 20 MONOPOLY. PAGE 46 F0906
T ECO/TAC OWN SERV/IND

B64
GEORGIADIS H.G.,BALANCE OF PAYMENTS EQUILIBRIUM. COST DEMAND...CONCPT MATH GEN/LAWS 20 KEYNES/JM. PAGE 47 F0916
BAL/PAY EQUILIB SIMUL INT/TRADE

B64
HAGGER A.J.,THE THEORY OF INFLATION. AFR PLAN PROB/SOLV PAY COST INCOME 20. PAGE 53 F1035
DEMAND TEC/DEV FINAN

B64
HATHAWAY D.E.,PROBLEMS OF PROGRESS IN THE AGRICULTURAL ECONOMY. USA+45 USA-45 ECO/DEV NAT/G INT/TRADE PRICE DEMAND EFFICIENCY OPTIMAL 20. PAGE 57 F1112
AGRI ECO/TAC MARKET PLAN

B64
JUSTER F.T.,ANTICIPATIONS AND PURCHASES; AN ANALYSIS OF CONSUMER BEHAVIOR. PROB/SOLV RISK COST PRODUC DRIVE...STAT STYLE SAMP CON/ANAL CHARTS HYPO/EXP GAME SIMUL. PAGE 68 F1345
PROBABIL DECISION PREDICT DEMAND

B64
KUZNETS S.,POSTWAR ECONOMIC GROWTH: FOUR LECTURES. WOR+45 INDUS NAT/G WORKER TEC/DEV ECO/TAC RATION TARIFFS PRICE BAL/PAY COST DEMAND 20. PAGE 74 F1455
ECO/DEV ECO/UNDEV TREND FINAN

B64
LAURSEN K.,THE GERMAN INFLATION, 1918-23. EUR+WWI GERMANY/E GERMANY/W WOR-45 BUDGET TAX GOV/REL BAL/PAY DEMAND PEACE...POLICY CHARTS 20 WEIMAR/REP. PAGE 76 F1489
ECO/DEV FINAN REPAR ECO/TAC

B64
LETICHE J.M.,A HISTORY OF RUSSIAN ECONOMIC THOUGHT: NINTH THROUGH EIGHTEENTH CENTURIES. RUSSIA FINAN SECT CAP/ISM DOMIN DEMAND EFFICIENCY OWN MARXISM ...TECHNIC ANTHOL BIBLIOG 9/18. PAGE 78 F1536
ECO/TAC TIME/SEQ IDEA/COMP ECO/UNDEV

B64
MARRIS R.,THE ECONOMIC THEORY OF "MANAGERIAL" CAPITALISM. USA+45 ECO/DEV LG/CO ECO/TAC DEMAND ...CHARTS BIBLIOG 20. PAGE 86 F1675
CAP/ISM MGT CONTROL OP/RES

B64
MC GOVERN G.S.,WAR AGAINST WANT. USA+45 AGRI DIPLOM INT/TRADE GIVE RECEIVE DEMAND HEALTH 20 KENNEDY/JF FOOD/PEACE. PAGE 87 F1714
FOR/AID ECO/DEV POLICY

EATING

B64
ODEH H.S.,THE IMPACT OF INFLATION ON THE LEVEL OF ECONOMIC ACTIVITY. AFR BRAZIL CHILE BUDGET GOV/REL COST DEMAND INCOME WEALTH...STAT METH 20 MONEY. PAGE 100 F1963
ECOMETRIC ECO/TAC ECO/UNDEV FINAN

B64
SHANNON I.,INTERNATIONAL LIQUIDITY. AFR FUT USA+45 WOR+45 ECO/TAC PRICE DEMAND WEALTH...CONCPT 20. PAGE 120 F2367
FINAN DIPLOM BAL/PAY ECO/DEV

B64
TAX S.,EL CAPITALISMO DEL CENTAVO; UNA ECONOMIA INDIGENA DE GUATEMALA (2 VOLS.). GUATEMALA L/A+17C SOCIETY GP/REL DEMAND INCOME HABITAT...SOC MUNICH 20 INDIAN/AM. PAGE 129 F2539
ECO/UNDEV AGRI WEALTH COST

B64
US HOUSE COMM GOVT OPERATIONS,US OWNED FOREIGN CURRENCIES: HEARINGS (COMMITTEE ON GOVERNMENT OPERATIONS). INDIA ECO/DEV PLAN BUDGET TAX DEMAND EFFICIENCY 20 AID CONGRESS. PAGE 137 F2699
FINAN ECO/TAC FOR/AID OWN

B64
WERNETTE J.P.,GOVERNMENT AND BUSINESS. LABOR CAP/ISM ECO/TAC INT/TRADE TAX ADMIN AUTOMAT NUC/PWR CIVMIL/REL DEMAND...MGT 20 MONOPOLY. PAGE 145 F2859
NAT/G FINAN ECO/DEV CONTROL

B64
ZEBOT C.A.,THE ECONOMICS OF COMPETITIVE COEXISTENCE. CHINA/COM USSR WOR+45 FINAN MARKET FOR/AID PRICE DEMAND EQUILIB WEALTH ALL/IDEOS 20. PAGE 150 F2961
TEC/DEV DIPLOM METH/COMP

B65
ALLEN W.R.,INTERNATIONAL TRADE THEORY: HUME TO OHLIN. FINAN LABOR TARIFFS TAX PRICE DEMAND PRODUC PROFIT...ANTHOL 18/20. PAGE 4 F0074
INT/TRADE WEALTH METH/CNCPT

B65
ARTEL R.,THE STRUCTURE OF THE STOCKHOLM ECONOMY. SWEDEN DIST/IND LABOR LOC/G TEC/DEV DEMAND MUNICH LOUISIANA 20. PAGE 7 F0125
ECO/DEV METH/COMP BAL/PAY

B65
BOWEN W.G.,UNEMPLOYMENT IN A PROSPEROUS ECONOMY. USA+45 ECO/DEV NAT/G ACT/RES PLAN PAY EDU/PROP DEMAND...POLICY IDEA/COMP ANTHOL 20. PAGE 17 F0330
WORKER ECO/TAC WEALTH PROB/SOLV

B65
COX D.W.,THE PERILS OF PEACE* CONVERSION TO WHAT? FUT USA+45 ECO/DEV NAT/G ACT/RES CREATE PLAN NUC/PWR WAR DEMAND MGT. PAGE 28 F0546
PEACE WORKER FORCES MARKET

B65
DEMAS W.G.,THE ECONOMICS OF DEVELOPMENT IN SMALL COUNTRIES WITH SPECIAL REFERENCE TO THE CARIBBEAN. WOR+45 BAL/PAY DEMAND EFFICIENCY PRODUC...GEOG CARIBBEAN. PAGE 32 F0618
ECO/UNDEV PLAN WEALTH INT/TRADE

B65
EDELMAN M.,THE POLITICS OF WAGE-PRICE DECISIONS. GERMANY ITALY NETHERLAND UK INDUS LABOR POL/PAR PROB/SOLV BARGAIN PRICE ROUTINE BAL/PAY COST DEMAND 20. PAGE 36 F0699
GOV/COMP CONTROL ECO/TAC PLAN

B65
FORD J.L.,THE OHLIN-HECKSCHER THEORY OF THE BASIS AND EFFECTS OF COMMODITY TRADE. WOR+45 ECO/TAC DEMAND INCOME...CONCPT GEN/METH 20 OHLIN/HECK. PAGE 42 F0824
ECOMETRIC INT/TRADE NEW/IDEA SIMUL

B65
HABERLER G.,A SURVEY OF INTERNATIONAL TRADE THEORY. CANADA FRANCE GERMANY ECO/TAC TARIFFS AGREE COST DEMAND WEALTH...ECOMETRIC 19/20 MONOPOLY TREATY. PAGE 52 F1024
INT/TRADE BAL/PAY DIPLOM POLICY

B65
KANTOROVICH L.V.,THE BEST USE OF ECONOMIC RESOURCES. USSR SOCIETY FINAN ACT/RES TEC/DEV ECO/TAC PRICE CONTROL COST DEMAND EFFICIENCY OPTIMAL...MGT STAT. PAGE 69 F1350
PLAN MATH DECISION

B65
MACESICH G.,COMMERCIAL BANKING AND REGIONAL DEVELOPMENT IN THE US, 1950-1960. USA+45 NAT/G PLAN ECO/TAC DEMAND...MGT 20 FED/RESERV SOUTH/US. PAGE 83 F1627
FINAN ECO/DEV INCOME COST

B65
MURUMBI J.,PROBLEMS OF ECONOMIC DEVELOPMENT IN EAST AFRICA. FINAN INDUS WORKER TEC/DEV INT/TRADE TAX DEMAND EFFICIENCY PRODUC SOCISM...TREND CHARTS 20 AFRICA/E. PAGE 95 F1869
AGRI ECO/TAC ECO/UNDEV PROC/MFG

B65
MUSOLF L.D.,PROMOTING THE GENERAL WELFARE: GOVERNMENT AND THE ECONOMY. USA+45 ECO/DEV CAP/ISM DEMAND OPTIMAL 20. PAGE 95 F1874
ECO/TAC NAT/G EX/STRUC NEW/LIB

B65
OECD,THE MEDITERRANEAN REGIONAL PROJECT: GREECE; EDUCATION AND DEVELOPMENT. FUT GREECE SOCIETY AGRI FINAN NAT/G PROF/ORG WORKER PLAN PROB/SOLV ADMIN DEMAND ATTIT 20 OECD. PAGE 100 F1972
EDU/PROP SCHOOL ACADEM ECO/UNDEV

B65
ONSLOW C.,ASIAN ECONOMIC DEVELOPMENT. BURMA CEYLON
ECO/UNDEV

INDIA MALAYSIA PAKISTAN S/ASIA AGRI INDUS MARKET PROB/SOLV CAP/ISM FOR/AID INT/TRADE DEMAND WEALTH ...POLICY ANTHOL 20. PAGE 101 F1991
ECO/TAC PLAN NAT/G

B65
ORG FOR ECO COOP AND DEVEL,THE MEDITERRANEAN REGIONAL PROJECT: YUGOSLAVIA; EDUCATION AND DEVELOPMENT. YUGOSLAVIA SOCIETY FINAN PROF/ORG PLAN ADMIN COST DEMAND MARXISM...STAT TREND CHARTS METH 20 OECD. PAGE 102 F1996
EDU/PROP ACADEM SCHOOL ECO/UNDEV

B65
PHELPS E.S.,PRIVATE WANTS AND PUBLIC NEEDS - AN INTRODUCTION TO A CURRENT ISSUE OF PUBLIC POLICY (REV. ED.). USA+45 PLAN CAP/ISM INGP/REL ROLE ...DECISION TIME/SEQ 20. PAGE 106 F2081
NAT/G POLICY DEMAND

B65
ROLFE S.E.,GOLD AND WORLD POWER. AFR UK USA+45 WOR-45 INDUS WORKER INT/TRADE DEMAND...MGT CHARTS 20. PAGE 113 F2234
BAL/PAY EQUILIB ECO/TAC DIPLOM

B65
ROSS A.M.,EMPLOYMENT POLICY AND THE LABOR MARKET. USA+45 MARKET LABOR NAT/G PROB/SOLV PAY EDU/PROP PARTIC UTIL...POLICY 20. PAGE 114 F2242
ECO/DEV WORKER WEALTH DEMAND

B65
ROWE J.W.,PRIMARY COMMODITIES IN INTERNATIONAL TRADE. MARKET CAP/ISM ECO/TAC DEMAND...NAT/COMP 20. PAGE 114 F2253
INT/TRADE AGRI RATION PRICE

B65
TEW B.,WEALTH AND INCOME. UK BUDGET INT/TRADE PRICE BAL/PAY DEMAND...CHARTS GOV/COMP 20 AUSTRAL. PAGE 129 F2546
FINAN ECO/DEV WEALTH INCOME

B65
WARD R.J.,INTERNATIONAL FINANCE. INT/ORG DIPLOM DEMAND INCOME...POLICY METH/COMP 20. PAGE 143 F2819
INT/TRADE ECO/TAC FINAN BAL/PAY

B65
ZAWADZKI K.K.F.,THE ECONOMICS OF INFLATIONARY PROCESSES. FINAN INT/TRADE PRICE CONTROL DEMAND EQUILIB PROFIT 20. PAGE 150 F2960
ECO/DEV COST ECO/TAC CAP/ISM

N65
STUDY GP CREATE RESERVE ASSETS,REPORT TO DEPUTIES (PAMPHLET). AFR FUT PLAN CONTROL DEMAND WEALTH ...ANTHOL METH 20. PAGE 127 F2507
INT/ORG INT/TRADE FINAN BUDGET

B66
BARAN P.A.,MONOPOLY CAPITAL; AN ESSAY ON THE AMERICAN ECONOMIC AND SOCIAL ORDER. USA+45 USA-45 ECO/UNDEV FINAN MARKET PLAN DIPLOM COLONIAL RACE/REL DEMAND MARXISM...CHARTS 20. PAGE 9 F0179
LG/CO CAP/ISM PRICE CONTROL

B66
BEN-PORATH Y.,THE ARAB LABOR FORCE IN ISRAEL. ISLAM ISRAEL AGRI INDUS SCHOOL CAP/ISM PAY DEMAND...GEOG REGRESS STAT CHARTS 20 ARABS. PAGE 13 F0245
WORKER CENSUS GP/REL STRUCT

B66
GORDON R.A.,PROSPERITY AND UNEMPLOYMENT. USA+45 PLAN ECO/TAC ADJUST DEMAND ALL/VALS...POLICY DECISION TREND CHARTS ANTHOL 20. PAGE 49 F0961
WORKER INDUS ECO/DEV WEALTH

B66
KEENLEYSIDE H.L.,INTERNATIONAL AID: A SUMMARY. AFR INDIA S/ASIA UK STRATA EXTR/IND TEC/DEV ADMIN RACE/REL DEMAND NAT/LISM WEALTH...TREND CHINJAP. PAGE 70 F1367
ECO/UNDEV FOR/AID DIPLOM TASK

B66
LANSING J.B.,TRANSPORTATION AND ECONOMIC POLICY. USA+45 COST DEMAND...ECOMETRIC TREND CHARTS IDEA/COMP T 20. PAGE 76 F1481
DIST/IND OP/RES ECO/DEV UTIL

B66
LERNER E.M.,A THEORY OF FINANCIAL ANALYSIS. UNIV LG/CO COST DEMAND INCOME PROFIT...MATH STAT CHARTS SIMUL T 20. PAGE 78 F1531
CONCPT FINAN ECO/DEV OPTIMAL

B66
ROBINSON E.A.,THE ECONOMICS OF EDUCATION. WOR+45 CULTURE ECO/UNDEV FINAN SCHOOL DIPLOM PRICE COST DEMAND...CHARTS METH/COMP 20. PAGE 112 F2216
EDU/PROP ADJUST CONFER

B66
SHULTZ G.P.,GUIDELINES, INFORMAL CONTROLS, AND THE MARKET PLACE: POLICY CHOICES IN A FULL EMPLOYMENT ECONOMY. UK ECO/DEV LABOR INT/TRADE CONFER GOV/REL BAL/PAY DEMAND INCOME...POLICY ANTHOL 20 PRESIDENT. PAGE 121 F2392
ECO/TAC CONTROL FINAN RATION

L66
AMERICAN ECONOMIC REVIEW,"SIXTY-THIRD LIST OF DOCTORAL DISSERTATIONS IN POLITICAL ECONOMY IN AMERICAN UNIVERSITIES AND COLLEGES." ECO/DEV AGRI FINAN LABOR WORKER PLAN BUDGET INT/TRADE ADMIN DEMAND...MGT STAT 20. PAGE 5 F0088
BIBLIOG/A CONCPT ACADEM

S66
SHORTE F.C.,"THE APPLICATION OF DEVELOPMENT HYPOTHESES IN MIDDLE EASTERN STUDIES." STRUCT AGRI CREATE DEMAND...GEOG STAT CON/ANAL CHARTS. PAGE 121 F2387
ECO/UNDEV ISLAM SOC HYPO/EXP

B67
ANDERSON C.W.,POLITICS AND ECONOMIC CHANGE IN LATIN AMERICA. L/A+17C INDUS NAT/G OP/RES ADMIN DEMAND ...POLICY STAT CHARTS NAT/COMP 20. PAGE 5 F0093
ECO/UNDEV PROB/SOLV PLAN ECO/TAC

B67
BERGMANN D KAUN B.,STRUCTURAL UNEMPLOYMENT IN THE UNITED STATES. USA+45 ECO/DEV PRICE ADMIN INGP/REL DEMAND EQUILIB WEALTH...MATH REGRESS STAT 20 NEGRO. PAGE 13 F0258
ECOMETRIC METH WORKER ECO/TAC

B67
DAVIS F.M.,COME AS A CONQUEROR: THE UNITED STATES ARMY'S OCCUPATION OF GERMANY: 1945-1949. EUR+WWI GERMANY USA+45 SOCIETY PLAN BAL/PWR DIPLOM FOR/AID PERS/REL DEMAND PEACE ORD/FREE 20. PAGE 30 F0588
FORCES CIVMIL/REL ECO/TAC CONTROL

B67
KREININ M.E.,ALTERNATIVE COMMERCIAL POLICIES - THEIR EFFECT ON THE AMERICAN ECONOMY. USA+45 LAW ECO/DEV MARKET INT/ORG DIPLOM ECO/TAC TARIFFS PRICE DEMAND WEALTH...QUANT EEC AFTA. PAGE 73 F1437
INT/TRADE BAL/PAY NAT/G POLICY

B67
MACAVOY P.W.,REGULATION OF TRANSPORT INNOVATION. ACT/RES ADJUD COST DEMAND...POLICY CHARTS 20. PAGE 83 F1621
DIST/IND CONTROL PRICE PROFIT

B67
NARVER J.C.,CONGLOMERATE MERGERS AND MARKET COMPETITION. USA+45 LAW STRUCT ADMIN LEAD RISK COST PROFIT WEALTH...POLICY CHARTS BIBLIOG. PAGE 96 F1892
DEMAND LG/CO MARKET MGT

B67
ROBINSON R.D.,INTERNATIONAL MANAGEMENT. LAW MARKET LABOR PRICE CONTROL COST DEMAND OWN PRODUC WEALTH 20. PAGE 113 F2225
T OP/RES MGT DIPLOM

B67
RUEFF J.,BALANCE OF PAYMENTS: PROPOSALS FOR RESOLVING THE CRITICAL WORLD ECONOMIC PROBLEM OF OUR TIME. USA+45 INDUS FOR/AID REPAR DEMAND OPTIMAL ...ECOMETRIC CHARTS METH/COMP 20. PAGE 115 F2259
BAL/PAY INT/TRADE FINAN NEW/IDEA

B67
SCHON D.A.,TECHNOLOGY AND CHANGE* THE NEW HERACLITUS. TEC/DEV CONTROL COST DEMAND EFFICIENCY RIGID/FLEX...MYTH 20. PAGE 117 F2311
INDUS PROB/SOLV R+D CREATE

B67
SPURRIER R.B.,THE OVERPOPULATED SOCIETY. WORKER EATING PERS/REL DEMAND EQUILIB ILLEGIT INCOME HABITAT 20. PAGE 125 F2461
BIO/SOC FOR/AID DRIVE RECEIVE

B67
US CONGRESS JOINT ECO COMM,REPORT ON JANUARY 1967 ECONOMIC REPORT OF THE PRESIDENT. FINAN LABOR NAT/G LEGIS BUDGET INT/TRADE COST DEMAND INCOME PRODUC ...POLICY IDEA/COMP 20 CONGRESS. PAGE 135 F2663
CHIEF ECO/TAC PLAN DELIB/GP

L67
GLAZER N.,"HOUSING PROBLEMS AND HOUSING POLICIES." USA+45 PLAN RENT ADJUST CONSEN DEMAND DISCRIM AGE ATTIT HEALTH WEALTH MUNICH NEGRO. PAGE 48 F0929
POLICY CONSTRUC CREATE HABITAT

S67
DEYRUP F.J.,"SOCIAL MOBILITY AS A MAJOR FACTOR IN ECONOMIC DEVELOPMENT." CHRIST-17C EUR+WWI MOD/EUR ECO/UNDEV DEMAND 20. PAGE 32 F0630
STRATA ECO/DEV INDUS WORKER

S67
FRANKLIN N.N.,"THE CONCEPT AND MEASUREMENT OF 'MINIMUM LIVING STANDARDS'." UNIV OP/RES PAY INGP/REL DEMAND INCOME DRIVE WEALTH...SOC CHARTS METH/COMP. PAGE 43 F0849
CONCPT PHIL/SCI ALL/VALS HAPPINESS

S67
JOHNSON L.B.,"BULLETS DO NOT DISCRIMINATE-LANDLORDS DO." PROB/SOLV EXEC LOBBY DEMAND...REALPOL SOC 20. PAGE 68 F1329
NAT/G DISCRIM POLICY

S67
KOTLER P.,"OPERATIONS RESEARCH IN MARKETING." USA+45 DIST/IND INDUS LG/CO CONSULT BUDGET TASK DEMAND EFFICIENCY PROFIT WEALTH DECISION. PAGE 73 F1429
ECOMETRIC OP/RES MARKET PLAN

S67
MORTON J.A.,"A SYSTEMS APPROACH TO THE INNOVATION PROCESS: ITS USE IN THE BELL SYSTEM." USA+45 INTELL INDUS LG/CO CONSULT WORKER COMPUTER AUTOMAT DEMAND ...MGT CHARTS 20. PAGE 94 F1841
TEC/DEV GEN/METH R+D COM/IND

S67
OLIVIER G.,"ASPECTS JURIDIQUES DE L'ADOPTION DU TRAITE CECA A LA CRISE CHARBONNIERE (SUITE ET FIN)" LAW DIST/IND PLAN DIPLOM RATION PRICE ADMIN COST DEMAND...POLICY CON/ANAL ECSC TREATY. PAGE 101 F1988
INT/TRADE INT/ORG EXTR/IND CONSTN

S67
ROY E.V.,"AN INTERPRETATION OF NORTHERN THAI PEASANT ECONOMY." THAILAND CLIENT CULTURE AGRI PROC/MFG FACE/GP DEMAND INCOME 20. PAGE 114 F2254
STRUCT STRATA ECO/UNDEV INGP/REL

S67
SCHELLING T.C.,"ECONOMICS AND CRIMINAL ENTERPRISE." LAW FORCES BARGAIN ECO/TAC CONTROL GAMBLE ROUTINE ADJUST DEMAND INCOME PROFIT CRIMLGY. PAGE 116 F2295
CRIME PROB/SOLV CONCPT

S67
SMALL A.H.,"THE EFFECT OF TARIFF REDUCTIONS ON US IMPORT VOLUME." USA+45 INT/ORG NAT/G DIPLOM CONFER DEMAND...POLICY INT/LAW STAT CHARTS GATT EEC. PAGE 123 F2424
TARIFFS INT/TRADE PRICE ECO/TAC

S67
THORKELSON H.,"FOOD STAMPS AND HUNGER IN AMERICA." USA+45 LAW DELIB/GP ADMIN COST DEMAND POLICY. PAGE 130 F2570
WEALTH RECEIVE EATING PLAN

S67
VAN KLAVEREN J.,"DIE WIRTSCHAFTLICHEN AUSWIRKUNGEN DES SCHWARZEN TODES" GERMANY PRICE DEMAND PRODUC MUNICH 14/15 DEPRESSION. PAGE 140 F2762
HEALTH AGRI GEOG

N67
US CONGRESS JT COMM ECO GOVT,BACKGROUND MATERIAL ON ECONOMY IN GOVERNMENT 1967 (PAMPHLET). WOR+45 ECO/DEV BARGAIN PRICE DEMAND OPTIMAL...STAT DEPT/DEFEN. PAGE 135 F2665
BUDGET COST MGT NAT/G

DEMAS W.G. F0618

DEMOCRACY....SEE MAJORIT, REPRESENT, CHOOSE, PWR POPULISM, NEW/LIB, ET AL.

DEMOCRAT....DEMOCRATIC PARTY (ALL NATIONS)

B27
SIEGFRIED A.,AMERICA COMES OF AGE: A FRENCH ANALYSIS (TRANS. BY H.H. HEMMING AND DORIS HEMMING). FRANCE UK POL/PAR WORKER TEC/DEV DIPLOM REGION RACE/REL ADJUST PRODUC HEREDITY...TIME/SEQ GP/COMP SOC/INTEG 20 DEMOCRAT REPUBLICAN KKK. PAGE 122 F2398
USA-45 CULTURE ECO/DEV SOC

B61
HOLMANS A.E.,UNITED STATES FISCAL POLICY 1945-1959. AFR USA+45 USA-45 ECO/DEV TAX PRICE WAR...BIBLIOG 20 DEMOCRAT REPUBLICAN. PAGE 61 F1200
POLICY BUDGET NAT/G ECO/TAC

B67
GOODMAN J.S.,THE DEMOCRATS AND LABOR IN RHODE ISLAND 9152-1962; CHANGES IN THE OLD ALLIANCE. USA+45 EDU/PROP LEAD GP/REL ROLE RHODE/ISL DEMOCRAT. PAGE 49 F0948
LABOR LOBBY POL/PAR LEGIS

DEMOGRAPHY....SEE GEOG

DEMPSTER M.A.H. F0592

DEMUTH J. F0619

DENISON E.F. F0620

DENMARK....SEE ALSO APPROPRIATE TIME/SPACE/CULTURE INDEX

C65
WUORINEN J.H.,"SCANDINAVIA." DENMARK FINLAND ICELAND NORWAY SWEDEN SOCIETY AGRI POL/PAR DELIB/GP DIPLOM INT/TRADE NEUTRAL WAR...CHARTS IND TREATY 20. PAGE 149 F2942
BIBLIOG NAT/G POLICY

B67
ANDERSON S.V.,THE NORDIC COUNCIL: A STUDY OF SCANDINAVIAN REGIONALISM. DENMARK FINLAND ICELAND NORWAY SWEDEN MARKET NAT/G VOL/ASSN CONSULT PARL/PROC ATTIT...TIME/SEQ BIBLIOG 20. PAGE 5 F0098
INT/ORG REGION DIPLOM LEGIS

B67
DIXON W.,SOCIETY, SCHOOLS AND PROGRESS IN SCANDINAVIA. DENMARK NORWAY SWEDEN 20. PAGE 33 F0644
EDU/PROP SOCIETY ADJUST PLAN

DENNISON S. F2211

DENVER....DENVER, COLORADO

DEPARTMENT HEADS...SEE EX/STRUC, TOP/EX

DEPORT....DEPORTATION

DEPRESSION....ECONOMIC DEPRESSION;

N19
GROSECLOSE E.,THE DECAY OF MONEY; A SURVEY OF WESTERN CURRENCIES 1912-1962 (PAMPHLET). AFR FRANCE GERMANY UK LAW INT/TRADE BAL/PAY COST EQUILIB ...POLICY 20 DEPRESSION. PAGE 51 F1004
FINAN NAT/G ECO/DEV ECO/TAC

B48
ROBERTSON D.H.,MONEY. AFR ECO/DEV NAT/G DIPLOM INT/TRADE BAL/PAY INCOME WEALTH...TIME/SEQ 20 DEPRESSION. PAGE 112 F2212
FINAN MARKET COST PRICE

B57
THOMAS R.G.,OUR MODERN BANKING AND MONETARY SYSTEM (3RD ED.). AFR USA+45 USA-45 ACT/RES PLAN PROB/SOLV INT/TRADE PRICE WAR BAL/PAY INCOME...POLICY METH/CNCPT 20 DEPRESSION. PAGE 130 F2563
FINAN SERV/IND ECO/TAC

B58
DUESENBERRY J.S.,BUSINESS CYCLES AND ECONOMIC GROWTH. USA+45 PROB/SOLV PAY PRICE...CONCPT MATH CHARTS IDEA/COMP 20 DEPRESSION KEYNES/JM. PAGE 34 F0672
FINAN ECO/DEV ECO/TAC INCOME

B59
FELS R.,AMERICAN BUSINESS CYCLES 1865-1897. USA+45 ECO/DEV LG/CO SML/CO PROB/SOLV TEC/DEV CAP/ISM INT/TRADE DEMAND...POLICY CHARTS METH 19 DEPRESSION. PAGE 40 F0782
FINAN INDUS TREND ECO/TAC

B61
LHOSTE-LACHAUME P.,OU GIT LE DESACCORD ENTRE LIBERAUX ET SOCIALISTES. EUR+WWI USA+45 USA-45 USSR CAP/ISM EDU/PROP MARXISM...MAJORIT IDEA/COMP 20 KEYNES/JM NEW/DEAL DEPRESSION. PAGE 79 F1555
LAISSEZ SOCISM FINAN

B62
KOLKO G.,WEALTH AND POWER IN AMERICA. USA+45 SOCIETY STRATA LG/CO ECO/TAC TAX PWR...SOC BIBLIOG 20 DEPRESSION. PAGE 72 F1420
STRUCT INCOME ECO/DEV WEALTH

B62
ROTHBARD M.N.,THE PANIC OF 1819; REACTIONS AND POLICIES. AFR USA-45 LAW FINAN BUDGET TARIFFS DEMAND 19 DEPRESSION. PAGE 114 F2247
ECO/UNDEV POLICY ATTIT ECO/TAC

B63
MARCHAL J.,EXPANSION ET RECESSION. FRANCE OP/RES PROB/SOLV ROLE ORD/FREE...TREND SIMUL 20 DEPRESSION. PAGE 85 F1663
FINAN PLAN ECO/DEV

B67
COHEN M.R.,LAW AND THE SOCIAL ORDER: ESSAYS IN LEGAL PHILOSOPHY. USA-45 CONSULT WORKER ECO/TAC ATTIT WEALTH...POLICY WELF/ST SOC 20 NEW/DEAL DEPRESSION. PAGE 26 F0497
JURID LABOR IDEA/COMP

S67
VAN KLAVEREN J.,"DIE WIRTSCHAFTLICHEN AUSWIRKUNGEN DES SCHWARZEN TODES" GERMANY PRICE DEMAND PRODUC MUNICH 14/15 DEPRESSION. PAGE 140 F2762
HEALTH AGRI GEOG

S86
SMITH R.M.,"THE NATIONAL BUREAU OF LABOR AND INDUSTRIAL DEPRESSIONS" USA-45 DELIB/GP BARGAIN CONTROL COST INCOME WEALTH...STAT 19 DEPRESSION. PAGE 123 F2433
LABOR INDUS FINAN GOV/REL

DEPT/AGRI....U.S. DEPARTMENT OF AGRICULTURE

B40
BLAISDELL D.C.,GOVERNMENT AND AGRICULTURE; THE GROWTH OF FEDERAL FARM AID. USA-45 MARKET PLAN PROB/SOLV TEC/DEV ECO/TAC GOV/REL ADJUST ATTIT ...CHARTS 20 DEPT/AGRI. PAGE 15 F0296
NAT/G GIVE AGRI DELIB/GP

B40
GAUS J.M.,PUBLIC ADMINISTRATION AND THE UNITED STATES DEPARTMENT OF AGRICULTURE. USA-45 STRUCT DIST/IND FINAN MARKET EX/STRUC PROB/SOLV GIVE PRODUC...POLICY GEOG CHARTS 20 DEPT/AGRI. PAGE 47 F0909
ADMIN AGRI DELIB/GP OP/RES

B52
HARDIN C.M.,THE POLITICS OF AGRICULTURE. USA+45 NAT/G PROF/ORG LEGIS LOBBY 20 DEPT/AGRI. PAGE 55 F1077
AGRI POLICY ECO/TAC GOV/REL

B63
SELF P.,THE STATE AND THE FARMER. UK ECO/DEV MARKET WORKER PRICE CONTROL GP/REL...WELF/ST 20 DEPT/AGRI. PAGE 119 F2346
AGRI NAT/G ADMIN VOL/ASSN

L65
HAMMOND A.,"COMPREHENSIVE VERSUS INCREMENTAL BUDGETING IN THE DEPARTMENT OF AGRICULTURE" USA+45 GP/REL ATTIT...PSY INT 20 DEPT/AGRI. PAGE 54 F1057
TOP/EX EX/STRUC AGRI BUDGET

DEPT/COM....U.S. DEPARTMENT OF COMMERCE

DEPT/DEFEN....U.S. DEPARTMENT OF DEFENSE

B55
US OFFICE OF THE PRESIDENT,REPORT TO CONGRESS ON THE MUTUAL SECURITY PROGRAM FOR THE SIX MONTHS ENDED JUNE 30, 1955. ECO/DEV INT/ORG NAT/G CREATE TEC/DEV BAL/PWR ECO/TAC AGREE DETER COST ORD/FREE 20 DEPT/STATE DEPT/DEFEN. PAGE 138 F2722
DIPLOM FORCES PLAN FOR/AID

B56
US OFFICE OF THE PRESIDENT,REPORT TO CONGRESS ON THE MUTUAL SECURITY PROGRAM FOR THE SIX MONTHS
DIPLOM FORCES

ENDED DECEMBER 31, 1955. ASIA USSR ECO/DEV ECO/UNDEV INT/ORG CREATE TEC/DEV BAL/PWR ECO/TAC AGREE DETER COST ORD/FREE 20 DEPT/STATE DEPT/DEFEN EISNHWR/DD. PAGE 138 F2723 — PLAN FOR/AID

B60
CARPER E.T.,THE DEFENSE APPROPRIATIONS RIDER (PAMPHLET). USA+45 CONSTN CHIEF DELIB/GP LEGIS BUDGET LOBBY CIVMIL/REL...POLICY 20 CONGRESS EISNHWR/DD DEPT/DEFEN PRESIDENT BOSTON. PAGE 22 F0419 — GOV/REL ADJUD LAW CONTROL

B62
INTERNAT CONGRESS OF JURISTS,EXECUTIVE ACTION AND THE RULE OF RULE: REPORTION PROCEEDINGS OF INT'T CONGRESS OF JURISTS,-RIO DE JANEIRO, BRAZIL. WOR+45 ACADEM CONSULT JUDGE EDU/PROP ADJUD CT/SYS INGP/REL PERSON DEPT/DEFEN. PAGE 64 F1269 — JURID EXEC ORD/FREE CONTROL

S63
ENTHOVEN A.C.,"ECONOMIC ANALYSIS IN THE DEPARTMENT OF DEFENSE." USA+45 NAT/G DELIB/GP PROB/SOLV RATION NUC/PWR WEAPON COST...DECISION 20 DEPT/DEFEN RESOURCE/N. PAGE 38 F0739 — PLAN BUDGET ECO/TAC FORCES

B64
BLACKSTOCK P.W.,THE STRATEGY OF SUBVERSION. USA+45 FORCES EDU/PROP ADMIN COERCE GOV/REL...DECISION MGT 20 DEPT/DEFEN CIA DEPT/STATE. PAGE 15 F0292 — ORD/FREE DIPLOM CONTROL

B64
DUSCHA J.,ARMS, MONEY, AND POLITICS. USA+45 INDUS POL/PAR ECO/TAC TAX DETER NUC/PWR WAR WEAPON GOV/REL ATTIT...BIBLIOG/A 20 CONGRESS MONEY DEPT/DEFEN. PAGE 35 F0687 — NAT/G FORCES POLICY BUDGET

B65
THAYER F.C. JR.,AIR TRANSPORT POLICY AND NATIONAL SECURITY: A POLITICAL, ECONOMIC, AND MILITARY ANALYSIS. DIST/IND OP/RES PLAN TEC/DEV DIPLOM DETER WAR COST EFFICIENCY...POLICY BIBLIOG 20 DEPT/DEFEN FAA CAB. PAGE 129 F2548 — AIR FORCES CIVMIL/REL ORD/FREE

B66
US SENATE COMM APPROPRIATIONS,FOREIGN ASSISTANCE AND RELATED AGENCIES APPROPRIATIONS FOR FISCAL YEAR 1967: HEARINGS... ON H. R. 17788. ECO/UNDEV INT/ORG FORCES INSPECT ECO/TAC GIVE DEBATE WEAPON CIVMIL/REL WEALTH...INT 20 CONGRESS DEPT/DEFEN DEPT/STATE DEPT/HEW AID. PAGE 138 F2727 — BUDGET FOR/AID DIPLOM COST

B67
ENKE S.,DEFENSE MANAGEMENT. USA+45 R+D FORCES WORKER PLAN ECO/TAC ADMIN NUC/PWR BAL/PAY UTIL WEALTH...MGT DEPT/DEFEN. PAGE 38 F0738 — DECISION DELIB/GP EFFICIENCY BUDGET

N67
US CONGRESS JT COMM ECO GOVT,BACKGROUND MATERIAL ON ECONOMY IN GOVERNMENT 1967 (PAMPHLET). WOR+45 ECO/DEV BARGAIN PRICE DEMAND OPTIMAL...STAT DEPT/DEFEN. PAGE 135 F2665 — BUDGET COST MGT NAT/G

DEPT/HEW....U.S. DEPARTMENT OF HEALTH, EDUCATION, AND WELFARE

B60
GARBARINO J.W.,HEALTH PLANS AND COLLECTIVE BARGAINING. USA+45 LABOR BARGAIN GP/REL WEALTH ...WELF/ST CHARTS 20 DEPT/HEW SAN/FRAN. PAGE 46 F0900 — HEAL PLAN FINAN SERV/IND

B66
US SENATE COMM APPROPRIATIONS,FOREIGN ASSISTANCE AND RELATED AGENCIES APPROPRIATIONS FOR FISCAL YEAR 1967: HEARINGS... ON H. R. 17788. ECO/UNDEV INT/ORG FORCES INSPECT ECO/TAC GIVE DEBATE WEAPON CIVMIL/REL WEALTH...INT 20 CONGRESS DEPT/DEFEN DEPT/STATE DEPT/HEW AID. PAGE 138 F2727 — BUDGET FOR/AID DIPLOM COST

DEPT/HUD....U.S. DEPARTMENT OF HOUSING AND URBAN DEVELOPMENT

DEPT/INTER....U.S. DEPARTMENT OF THE INTERIOR

DEPT/JUST....U.S. DEPARTMENT OF JUSTICE

DEPT/LABOR....U.S. DEPARTMENT OF LABOR AND INDUSTRY

B51
PETERSON F.,SURVEY OF LABOR ECONOMICS (REV. ED.). STRATA ECO/DEV LABOR INSPECT BARGAIN PAY PRICE EXEC ROUTINE GP/REL ALL/VALS ORD/FREE 20 AFL/CIO DEPT/LABOR. PAGE 105 F2069 — WORKER DEMAND IDEA/COMP T

B55
BLOOM G.F.,ECONOMICS OF LABOR RELATIONS. USA+45 LAW CONSULT WORKER CAP/ISM PAY ADJUD CONTROL EFFICIENCY ORD/FREE...CHARTS 19/20 AFL/CIO NLRB DEPT/LABOR. PAGE 16 F0299 — ECO/DEV ECO/TAC LABOR GOV/REL

S57
ROURKE F.E.,"THE POLITICS OF ADMINISTRATIVE ORGANIZATION: A CASE HISTORY." USA+45 LABOR WORKER PLAN ADMIN TASK EFFICIENCY 20 DEPT/LABOR CONGRESS. PAGE 114 F2251 — POLICY ATTIT MGT GP/COMP

B62
MORGAN C.A.,LABOR ECONOMICS. LAW INDUS MARKET WORKER PLAN PROB/SOLV GOV/REL INCOME ROLE...T 20 DEPT/LABOR NLRB. PAGE 93 F1829 — LABOR ECO/TAC ECO/DEV CAP/ISM

B63
HARVEY O.L.,THE ANVIL AND THE PLOW: A HISTORY OF THE UNITED STATES DEPARTMENT OF LABOR: 1913-1963. USA+45 USA-45 NAT/G CONFER NEW/LIB 20 DEPT/LABOR. PAGE 56 F1106 — EX/STRUC REPRESENT GP/REL LABOR

B63
US DEPARTMENT OF LABOR,THE ANVIL AND THE PLOW. KOREA USA+45 USA-45 INDUS WORKER BUDGET WAR ...POLICY AUD/VIS CHARTS 20 DEPT/LABOR. PAGE 135 F2667 — ECO/DEV LABOR ECO/TAC NAT/G

L67
PARKER G.P. JR.,"MONETARY RECOVERY UNDER THE FEDERAL LABOR STATUTES." USA+45 USA-45 INDUS ADJUD CT/SYS GOV/REL HEALTH ORD/FREE 20 DEPT/LABOR NLRB. PAGE 103 F2027 — LABOR CONTROL LAW FINAN

DEPT/STATE....U.S. DEPARTMENT OF STATE

B50
KOENIG L.W.,THE SALE OF THE TANKERS. USA+45 SEA DIST/IND POL/PAR DIPLOM ADMIN CIVMIL/REL ATTIT ...DECISION 20 PRESIDENT DEPT/STATE. PAGE 72 F1414 — NAT/G POLICY PLAN GOV/REL

B55
US OFFICE OF THE PRESIDENT,REPORT TO CONGRESS ON THE MUTUAL SECURITY PROGRAM FOR THE SIX MONTHS ENDED JUNE 30, 1955. ECO/DEV INT/ORG NAT/G CREATE TEC/DEV BAL/PWR ECO/TAC AGREE DETER COST ORD/FREE 20 DEPT/STATE DEPT/DEFEN. PAGE 138 F2722 — DIPLOM FORCES PLAN FOR/AID

B56
US OFFICE OF THE PRESIDENT,REPORT TO CONGRESS ON THE MUTUAL SECURITY PROGRAM FOR THE SIX MONTHS ENDED DECEMBER 31, 1955. ASIA USSR ECO/DEV ECO/UNDEV INT/ORG CREATE TEC/DEV BAL/PWR ECO/TAC AGREE DETER COST ORD/FREE 20 DEPT/STATE DEPT/DEFEN EISNHWR/DD. PAGE 138 F2723 — DIPLOM FORCES PLAN FOR/AID

B60
US GENERAL ACCOUNTING OFFICE,EXAMINATION OF ECONOMIC AND TECHNICAL ASSISTANCE PROGRAM FOR GUATEMALA. GUATEMALA L/A+17C USA+45 FINAN INDUS PLAN...POLICY STAT CHARTS 20 DEPT/STATE. PAGE 136 F2680 — FOR/AID ECO/UNDEV TEC/DEV NAT/G

B60
US HOUSE COMM GOVT OPERATIONS,OPERATIONS OF THE DEVELOPMENT LOAN FUND: HEARINGS (COMMITTEE ON GOVERNMENT OPERATIONS). USA+45 PLAN BUDGET DIPLOM GOV/REL COST...CHARTS 20 CONGRESS DEPT/STATE AID. PAGE 137 F2698 — FINAN FOR/AID ECO/TAC EFFICIENCY

B63
GORDON L.,A NEW DEAL FOR LATIN AMERICA. L/A+17C USA+45 CULTURE NAT/G TEC/DEV DIPLOM FOR/AID REGION TASK...POLICY 20 ALL/PROG DEPT/STATE. PAGE 49 F0958 — ECO/UNDEV ECO/TAC INT/ORG PLAN

B64
BLACKSTOCK P.W.,THE STRATEGY OF SUBVERSION. USA+45 FORCES EDU/PROP ADMIN COERCE GOV/REL...DECISION MGT 20 DEPT/DEFEN CIA DEPT/STATE. PAGE 15 F0292 — ORD/FREE DIPLOM CONTROL

B66
US SENATE COMM APPROPRIATIONS,FOREIGN ASSISTANCE AND RELATED AGENCIES APPROPRIATIONS FOR FISCAL YEAR 1967: HEARINGS... ON H. R. 17788. ECO/UNDEV INT/ORG FORCES INSPECT ECO/TAC GIVE DEBATE WEAPON CIVMIL/REL WEALTH...INT 20 CONGRESS DEPT/DEFEN DEPT/STATE DEPT/HEW AID. PAGE 138 F2727 — BUDGET FOR/AID DIPLOM COST

S67
PROBERT J.R.,"STREAMLINING THE FOREIGN POLICY MACHINE." USA+45 EFFICIENCY DEPT/STATE. PAGE 108 F2123 — DIPLOM ADMIN EXEC GOV/REL

DEPT/TREAS....U.S. DEPARTMENT OF THE TREASURY

N19
ARNOW K.,SELF-INSURANCE IN THE TREASURY (PAMPHLET). USA+45 LAW RIGID/FLEX...POLICY METH/COMP 20 DEPT/TREAS. PAGE 6 F0117 — ADMIN PLAN EFFICIENCY NAT/G

B50
SHAW E.S.,MONEY, INCOME, AND MONETARY POLICY. AFR USA-45 NAT/G DIPLOM PAY CONTROL COST INCOME PRODUC WEALTH...T 20 FED/RESERV DEPT/TREAS. PAGE 120 F2370 — FINAN ECO/TAC ECO/DEV PRICE

B63
US BD GOVERNORS FEDL RESRV,THE FEDERAL RESERVE AND THE TREASURY. USA+45 WORKER PROB/SOLV PRICE COST DEMAND WEALTH...STAT INT CHARTS 20 FED/RESERV DEPT/TREAS. PAGE 134 F2641 — FINAN GOV/REL CONTROL BUDGET

DERBER M. F0621

DESCARTE/R....RENE DESCARTES

DESEGREGATION....SEE NEGRO, SOUTH/US, RACE/REL, SOC/INTEG, CIV/RIGHTS, DISCRIM, MISCEGEN, ISOLAT, SCHOOL, STRANGE

DESSALIN/J....JEAN-JACQUES DESSALINES

DESTALIN....DE-STALINIZATION

DETAMBEL M.H. F0622

DETER....DETERRENCE; SEE ALSO PWR, PLAN

B14
DE BLOCH J.,THE FUTURE OF WAR IN ITS TECHNICAL, ECONOMIC, AND POLITICAL RELATIONS (1899). MOD/EUR TEC/DEV BUDGET INT/TRADE DETER GUERRILLA WEAPON COST PEACE 20. PAGE 31 F0596
WAR BAL/PWR PREDICT FORCES

N19
LANGE O.R.,"DISARMAMENT ECONOMIC GROWTH AND INTERNATIONAL CO-OPERATION" (PAMPHLET). WOR+45 DIST/IND PLAN INT/TRADE GIVE TASK DETER WEALTH SOCISM 18/19 BOLIVAR/S. PAGE 75 F1477
ARMS/CONT DIPLOM ECO/DEV ECO/UNDEV

B55
US OFFICE OF THE PRESIDENT,REPORT TO CONGRESS ON THE MUTUAL SECURITY PROGRAM FOR THE SIX MONTHS ENDED JUNE 30, 1955. ECO/DEV INT/ORG NAT/G CREATE TEC/DEV BAL/PWR ECO/TAC AGREE DETER COST ORD/FREE 20 DEPT/STATE DEPT/DEFEN. PAGE 138 F2722
DIPLOM FORCES PLAN FOR/AID

B56
BONNETT C.E.,HISTORY OF EMPLOYERS' ASSOCIATIONS IN THE UNITED STATES (1ST ED.). MARKET DETER GP/REL ADJUST. PAGE 16 F0316
LABOR VOL/ASSN LG/CO

B56
US OFFICE OF THE PRESIDENT,REPORT TO CONGRESS ON THE MUTUAL SECURITY PROGRAM FOR THE SIX MONTHS ENDED DECEMBER 31, 1955. ASIA USSR ECO/DEV ECO/UNDEV INT/ORG CREATE TEC/DEV BAL/PWR ECO/TAC AGREE DETER COST ORD/FREE 20 DEPT/STATE DEPT/DEFEN EISNHWR/DD. PAGE 138 F2723
DIPLOM FORCES PLAN FOR/AID

B59
MARTIN K.,WAR, HISTORY, AND HUMAN NATURE. FRANCE GERMANY INDIA UK UNIV POL/PAR COLONIAL DETER REV MARXISM PACIFISM...PSY CONCPT PREDICT LENIN/VI GANDHI/M. PAGE 86 F1683
PERSON WAR ATTIT IDEA/COMP

B59
US DEPARTMENT OF STATE,THE UNITED STATES ECONOMY AND THE MUTUAL SECURITY PROGRAM. USA+45 ECO/UNDEV FINAN INDUS DIPLOM INT/TRADE DETER 20. PAGE 136 F2674
ECO/DEV FORCES BUDGET FOR/AID

B60
ALLEN R.L.,SOVIET ECONOMIC WARFARE. USSR FINAN INDUS NAT/G PLAN TEC/DEV FOR/AID DETER WEALTH ...TREND GEN/LAWS FOR/TRADE 20. PAGE 4 F0072
COM ECO/TAC

B61
KOVNER M.,THE CHALLENGE OF COEXISTENCE: A STUDY OF SOVIET ECONOMIC DIPLOMACY. COM FUT ECO/DEV ECO/UNDEV PLAN EDU/PROP DETER SKILL...OBS VAL/FREE 20. PAGE 73 F1430
PWR DIPLOM USSR AFR

B62
JORDAN A.A. JR.,FOREIGN AID AND THE DEFENSE OF SOUTHEAST ASIA. PAKISTAN VIETNAM/S FINAN PLAN BUDGET ECO/TAC DETER WAR ORD/FREE...POLICY DECISION CENSUS CHARTS BIBLIOG 20. PAGE 68 F1341
FOR/AID S/ASIA FORCES ECO/UNDEV

B62
SCHILLING W.R.,STRATEGY, POLITICS, AND DEFENSE BUDGETS. AFR USA+45 CHIEF LEGIS PLAN TEC/DEV BAL/PWR BUDGET NUC/PWR WAR CIVMIL/REL GOV/REL PWR 20 EISNHWR/DD. PAGE 117 F2297
NAT/G POLICY FORCES DETER

B63
PERLO V.,MILITARISM AND INDUSTRY. USA+45 INT/TRADE EDU/PROP DETER KNOWL...CHARTS MAPS 20. PAGE 105 F2064
CIVMIL/REL INDUS LOBBY ARMS/CONT

B63
US SENATE COMM GOVT OPERATIONS,REPORT OF A STUDY OF US FOREIGN AID IN TEN MIDDLE EASTERN AND AFRICAN COUNTRIES. AFR ISLAM USA+45 FORCES PLAN BUDGET DIPLOM TAX DETER WEALTH...STAT CHARTS 20 CONGRESS AID MID/EAST. PAGE 138 F2728
FOR/AID EFFICIENCY ECO/TAC FINAN

B64
DUSCHA J.,ARMS, MONEY, AND POLITICS. USA+45 INDUS POL/PAR ECO/TAC TAX DETER NUC/PWR WAR WEAPON GOV/REL ATTIT...BIBLIOG/A 20 CONGRESS MONEY DEPT/DEFEN. PAGE 35 F0687
NAT/G FORCES POLICY BUDGET

B64
FIESER M.E.,ECONOMIC POLICY AND WAR POTENTIAL. AFR WOR+45 ECO/DEV INDUS NAT/G FORCES TEC/DEV NUC/PWR CIVMIL/REL ORD/FREE 20. PAGE 40 F0791
INT/TRADE POLICY ECO/TAC DETER

B64
HEKHUIS D.J.,INTERNATIONAL STABILITY: MILITARY, ECONOMIC AND POLITICAL DIMENSIONS. FUT WOR+45 LAW ECO/UNDEV INT/ORG NAT/G VOL/ASSN FORCES ACT/RES BAL/PWR PWR WEALTH...STAT UN 20. PAGE 58 F1143
TEC/DEV DETER REGION

B65
BEAUFRE A.,AN INTRODUCTION TO STRATEGY, WITH PARTICULAR REFERENCE TO PROBLEMS OF DEFENSE, POLITICS, ECONOMICS IN THE NUCLEAR AGE. WOR+45 FORCES DIPLOM DETER CIVMIL/REL GP/REL...NEW/IDEA IDEA/COMP 20. PAGE 12 F0226
PLAN NUC/PWR WEAPON DECISION

B65
CERNY K.H.,NATO IN QUEST OF COHESION* A CONFRONTATION OF VIEWPOINTS. COM EUR+WWI USA+45 FORCES LEAD REGION DETER...ANTHOL NATO. PAGE 22 F0438
CENTRAL NUC/PWR VOL/ASSN

B65
THAYER F.C. JR.,AIR TRANSPORT POLICY AND NATIONAL SECURITY: A POLITICAL, ECONOMIC, AND MILITARY ANALYSIS. DIST/IND OP/RES PLAN TEC/DEV DIPLOM DETER WAR COST EFFICIENCY...POLICY BIBLIOG 20 DEPT/DEFEN FAA CAB. PAGE 129 F2548
AIR FORCES CIVMIL/REL ORD/FREE

B66
BOLTON R.E.,DEFENSE AND DISARMAMENT: THE ECONOMICS OF TRANSITION. USA+45 R+D FORCES PLAN LOBBY DETER WAR COST PEACE...ANTHOL BIBLIOG 20. PAGE 16 F0310
ARMS/CONT POLICY INDUS

B66
KUENNE R.E.,THE POLARIS MISSILE STRIKE* A GENERAL ECONOMIC SYSTEMS ANALYSIS. USA+45 USSR NAT/G BAL/PWR ARMS/CONT WAR...MATH PROBABIL COMPUT/IR CHARTS HYPO/EXP SIMUL. PAGE 74 F1446
NUC/PWR FORCES DETER DIPLOM

B66
US SENATE COMM ON FOREIGN REL,HEARINGS ON S 2859 AND S 2861. USA+45 WOR+45 FORCES BUDGET CAP/ISM ADMIN DETER WEAPON TOTALISM...NAT/COMP 20 UN CONGRESS. PAGE 139 F2735
FOR/AID DIPLOM ORD/FREE ECO/UNDEV

S66
DUROSELLE J.B.,"THE FUTURE OF THE ATLANTIC COMMUNITY." EUR+WWI USA+45 USSR NAT/G CAP/ISM REGION DETER NUC/PWR ATTIT MARXISM...INT/LAW 20 NATO. PAGE 35 F0686
FUT DIPLOM MYTH POLICY

B67
ORLANS H.,CONTRACTING FOR ATOMS. AFR USA+45 LAW INTELL ACADEM LG/CO NAT/G PLAN TEC/DEV CONTROL DETER...TREND 20. PAGE 102 F1999
NUC/PWR R+D PRODUC PEACE

B67
WOLF C. JR.,UNITED STATES POLICY AND THE THIRD WORLD. USA+45 WOR+45 FORCES ACT/RES BAL/PWR ECO/TAC FOR/AID DETER GUERRILLA NUC/PWR REV...CHARTS 20. PAGE 148 F2916
DIPLOM ECO/UNDEV POLICY NAT/G

DETERRENCE....SEE DETER

DETHINE P. F0623

DETROIT....DETROIT, MICHIGAN

DEUTSCH J.J. F0055

DEUTSCH K.W. F0624,F0625

DEUTSCHE BUCHEREI F0626

DEV/ASSIST....DEVELOPMENT AND ASSISTANCE COMMITTEE

B66
RUBIN S.J.,THE CONSCIENCE OF THE RICH NATIONS: THE DEVELOPMENT ASSISTANCE COMMITTEE AND THE COMMON AID EFFORT. EUR+WWI USA+45 ECO/UNDEV INT/ORG NAT/G VOL/ASSN ECO/TAC INT/TRADE...OBS UN AID DEV/ASSIST IBRD OECD. PAGE 114 F2256
FOR/AID ECO/DEV CONFER CENTRAL

DEVELOPMENT....SEE CREATE+ECO/UNDEV

DEVELOPMENT AND ASSISTANCE COMMITTEE....SEE DEV/ASSIST

DEVELOPMNT....HUMAN DEVELOPMENTAL CHANGE, PSYCHOLOGICAL AND PHYSIOLOGICAL

DEVIANT BEHAVIOR....SEE ANOMIE, CRIME

DEWEY/JOHN....JOHN DEWEY

DEWEY/THOM....THOMAS DEWEY

B58
RUBIN B.,PUBLIC RELATIONS AND THE STATE, A CASE STUDY OF NEW YORK STATE ADMINISTRATION, 1943-54. USA+45 USA-45 COM/IND EDU/PROP GOV/REL...CHARTS 20 NEW/YORK DEWEY/THOM. PAGE 114 F2255
INGP/REL PRESS PROVS GP/REL

DEWHURST A. F0627

DEWITT N. F0629

DEXTER L.A. F0217

DEYRUP F.J. F0630

DIA M. F0631

DIAZ/P....PORFIRIO DIAZ

DICKINSON H.D. F0632

DICKMAN A.B. F0633

DICKS-MIREAUX L.A. F0634

DICTIONARY....DICTIONARY

B44
BIENSTOCK G.,MANAGEMENT IN RUSSIAN INDUSTRY AND AGRICULTURE. USSR CONSULT WORKER LEAD COST PROFIT ATTIT DRIVE PWR...MGT METH/COMP DICTIONARY ACCT 20. PAGE 15 F0281 — ADMIN MARXISM SML/CO AGRI

B44
INTL CHAMBER OF COMMERCE,TERMS COMMONLY USED IN DISTRIBUTION AND ADVERTISING. PORTUGAL SPAIN UK WOR-45 SERV/IND 20. PAGE 65 F1284 — DICTIONARY EDU/PROP DIST/IND INT/TRADE

B56
HISTORICAL ABSTRACTS. NAT/G CREATE DIPLOM ATTIT ...SOC DICTIONARY INDEX 18/20. PAGE 1 F0011 — WOR-45 COMPUT/IR BIBLIOG/A

B63
PAENSON I.,SYSTEMATIC GLOSSARY ENGLISH, FRENCH, SPANISH, RUSSIAN OF SELECTED ECONOMIC AND SOCIAL TERMS. WOR+45 FINAN LABOR INT/TRADE DEMAND PRODUC 20. PAGE 102 F2014 — DICTIONARY SOC LING

B64
BOGEN J.I.,FINANCIAL HANDBOOK (4TH ED.). UNIV LAW PLAN TAX RISK 20. PAGE 16 F0306 — FINAN DICTIONARY

B67
GRIPP R.C.,PATTERNS OF SOVIET POLITICS (REV. ED.). USSR LAW ELITES LOC/G PLAN CONTROL CT/SYS CHOOSE ...POLICY BIBLIOG/A DICTIONARY 9/20. PAGE 51 F1003 — COM ADJUD POL/PAR

DIDEROT/D....DENIS DIDEROT

DIEBOLD W. F0635,F0636

DIEGUES M. F0637

DIEM....NGO DINH DIEM

DIESING P. F0638

DILL W.R. F0566

DILLEY M.R. F0639

DIMOCK M.E. F0640,F0641,F0642

DINERSTEIN H.S. F0643

DIPLOM....DIPLOMACY

N
PEN I.,PRIMER ON INTERNATIONAL TRADE. WOR+45 WOR-45 ECO/DEV DIPLOM EFFICIENCY 16/20 EEC. PAGE 104 F2055 — INT/TRADE BAL/PAY ECO/TAC EQUILIB

N
TEXTBOOKS IN PRINT. WOR+45 WOR-45 LAW DIPLOM ALL/VALS ALL/IDEOS...SOC T 19/20. PAGE 1 F0003 — BIBLIOG SCHOOL KNOWL

N
DOCUMENTATION ECONOMIQUE: REVUE BIBLIOGRAPHIQUE DE SYNTHESE. WOR+45 COM/IND FINAN BUDGET DIPLOM...GEOG 20. PAGE 1 F0004 — BIBLIOG/A SOC

N
LONDON TIMES OFFICIAL INDEX. UK LAW ECO/DEV NAT/G DIPLOM LEAD ATTIT 20. PAGE 1 F0006 — BIBLIOG INDEX PRESS WRITING

N
AMERICAN ECONOMIC ASSOCIATION,THE JOURNAL OF ECONOMIC ABSTRACTS. ECO/UNDEV MARKET LABOR DIPLOM ...MGT CONCPT METH 20. PAGE 5 F0086 — BIBLIOG/A R+D FINAN

N
DEUTSCHE BUCHEREI,DEUTSCHES BUCHERVERZEICHNIS. GERMANY LAW CULTURE POL/PAR ADMIN LEAD ATTIT PERSON ...SOC 20. PAGE 32 F0626 — BIBLIOG NAT/G DIPLOM ECO/DEV

N
MINISTRY OF OVERSEAS DEVELOPME,TECHNICAL CO-OPERATION -- A BIBLIOGRAPHY. UK LAW SOCIETY DIPLOM ECO/TAC FOR/AID...STAT 20 CMN/WLTH. PAGE 92 F1803 — BIBLIOG TEC/DEV ECO/DEV NAT/G

N
RAND SCHOOL OF SOCIAL SCIENCE,INDEX TO LABOR ARTICLES. ECO/DEV INT/ORG LEGIS DIPLOM GP/REL ...NAT/COMP 20. PAGE 109 F2143 — BIBLIOG LABOR MGT ADJUD

N
UNITED NATIONS,OFFICIAL RECORDS OF THE ECONOMIC AND SOCIAL COUNCIL OF THE UNITED NATIONS. WOR+45 DIPLOM INT/TRADE CONFER...SOC SOC/WK 20 UN UNESCO. PAGE 132 F2611 — INT/ORG DELIB/GP WRITING

N
US LIBRARY OF CONGRESS,EAST EUROPEAN ACCESSIONS INDEX. NAT/G ISOLAT ATTIT KNOWL...POLICY 20. PAGE 138 F2711 — BIBLIOG COM MARXIST DIPLOM

NCO
CARRINGTON C.E.,THE COMMONWEALTH IN AFRICA (PAMPHLET). UK STRUCT NAT/G COLONIAL REPRESENT GOV/REL RACE/REL NAT/LISM...MAJORIT 20 EEC NEGRO. PAGE 22 F0421 — ECO/UNDEV AFR DIPLOM PLAN

B02
MOREL E.D.,AFFAIRS OF WEST AFRICA. UK FINAN INDUS FAM KIN SECT CHIEF WORKER DIPLOM RACE/REL LITERACY HEALTH...CHARTS 18/20 AFRICA/W NEGRO. PAGE 93 F1826 — COLONIAL ADMIN AFR

B03
MOREL E.D.,THE BRITISH CASE IN FRENCH CONGO. CONGO/BRAZ FRANCE UK COERCE MORAL WEALTH...POLICY INT/LAW 20 CONGO/LEOP. PAGE 93 F1827 — DIPLOM INT/TRADE COLONIAL AFR

B19
SUMNER W.G.,WAR AND OTHER ESSAYS. USA-45 DELIB/GP DIPLOM TARIFFS COLONIAL PEACE SOVEREIGN 20. PAGE 127 F2514 — INT/TRADE ORD/FREE CAP/ISM ECO/TAC

N19
ARNDT H.W.,AUSTRALIAN FOREIGN AID POLICY (PAMPHLET). ECO/UNDEV DIPLOM GIVE GOV/REL COST UTIL PWR...CHARTS 20 AUSTRAL PAPUA NEW/GUINEA. PAGE 6 F0114 — FOR/AID POLICY ECO/TAC EFFICIENCY

N19
BASCH A.,THE FUTURE OF FOREIGN LENDING FOR DEVELOPMENT (PAMPHLET). WOR+45 ECO/UNDEV FINAN INT/ORG ECO/TAC ATTIT...PREDICT 20. PAGE 11 F0203 — FOR/AID ECO/DEV DIPLOM GIVE

N19
BLOOMFIELD A.,MONETARY POLICY UNDER THE INTERNATIONAL GOLD STANDARD: 18801914 (PAMPHLET). AFR USA-45 DIPLOM CONTROL...POLICY 19. PAGE 16 F0300 — FINAN ROLE EFFICIENCY

N19
CASSELL F.,INTERNATIONAL MONETARY PROBLEMS (PAMPHLET). AFR BAL/PWR CONTROL EFFICIENCY WEALTH 20 EEC. PAGE 22 F0427 — INT/TRADE FINAN DIPLOM TREND

N19
DEANE H.,THE WAR IN VIETNAM (PAMPHLET). AFR CHINA/COM VIETNAM BAL/PWR DIPLOM ECO/TAC SOCISM INTERVENT INTERVENT. PAGE 31 F0610 — WAR SOCIALIST MORAL CAP/ISM

N19
FRANCK P.G.,AFGHANISTAN BETWEEN EAST AND WEST: THE ECONOMICS OF COMPETITIVE COEXISTENCE (PAMPHLET). AFGHANISTN USA+45 USA-45 USSR INDUS ECO/TAC INT/TRADE CONTROL NEUTRAL ORD/FREE MARXISM...GEOG 20 UN. PAGE 43 F0842 — FOR/AID PLAN DIPLOM ECO/UNDEV

N19
FREEMAN H.A.,COERCION OF STATES IN FEDERAL UNIONS (PAMPHLET). WOR-45 DIPLOM CONTROL COERCE PEACE ORD/FREE...GOV/COMP METH/COMP NAT/COMP PACIFIST 20. PAGE 43 F0850 — FEDERAL WAR INT/ORG PACIFISM

N19
HALL G.,MAIN STREET TO WALL STREET: END THE COLD WAR (PAMPHLET). AFR USA+45 LAW STRUCT POL/PAR WORKER INT/TRADE DOMIN INCOME...POLICY 20 COM/PARTY. PAGE 53 F1046 — MARXIST CAP/ISM DIPLOM NAT/G

N19
JACKSON R.G.A.,THE CASE FOR AN INTERNATIONAL DEVELOPMENT AUTHORITY (PAMPHLET). WOR+45 ECO/DEV DIPLOM GIVE CONTROL GP/REL EFFICIENCY NAT/LISM SOVEREIGN 20. PAGE 66 F1295 — FOR/AID INT/ORG ECO/UNDEV ADMIN

N19
KINDLEBERGER C.P.,BALANCE-OF-PAYMENTS DEFICITS AND THE INTERNATIONAL MARKET FOR LIQUIDITY (PAMPHLET). ECO/DEV NAT/G PLAN DIPLOM ECO/TAC PRODUC...POLICY STAT CHARTS. PAGE 71 F1389 — BAL/PAY INT/TRADE MARKET FINAN

N19
KUWAIT ARABIA,KUWAIT FUND FOR ARAB ECONOMIC DEVELOPMENT (PAMPHLET). ISLAM KUWAIT UAR ECO/UNDEV LEGIS ECO/TAC WEALTH 20. PAGE 74 F1452 — FOR/AID DIPLOM FINAN ADMIN

N19
KUWAIT FUND ARAB ECO DEVELOPMT,ANNUAL REPORTS 1962-65 (PAMPHLET). KUWAIT ECO/UNDEV DIPLOM ...POLICY 20 ARABS. PAGE 74 F1453 — FOR/AID DELIB/GP FINAN ISLAM

N19
LANGE O.R.,"DISARMAMENT ECONOMIC GROWTH AND INTERNATIONAL CO-OPERATION" (PAMPHLET). WOR+45 DIST/IND PLAN INT/TRADE GIVE TASK DETER WEALTH SOCISM 18/19 BOLIVAR/S. PAGE 75 F1477 — ARMS/CONT DIPLOM ECO/DEV ECO/UNDEV

N19
LUTZ F.A.,THE PROBLEM OF INTERNATIONAL LIQUIDITY AND THE MULTIPLECURRENCY STANDARD (PAMPHLET). WOR+45 MARKET INT/ORG PRICE BAL/PAY...NEW/IDEA METH/COMP BIBLIOG 20 IMF. PAGE 82 F1609 — PROB/SOLV FINAN DIPLOM ECO/TAC

N19
MASON E.S.,THE DIPLOMACY OF ECONOMIC ASSISTANCE (PAMPHLET). INDIA PAKISTAN USA+45 ECO/UNDEV NAT/G BUDGET ATTIT...POLICY 20. PAGE 87 F1695 FOR/AID DIPLOM FINAN

N19
MEZERIK A.G.,ECONOMIC AID FOR UNDERDEVELOPED COUNTRIES (PAMPHLET). AFR USSR WOR+45 FINAN LG/CO DELIB/GP NUC/PWR...GEOG CENSUS CHARTS 20 UN THIRD/WRLD. PAGE 90 F1775 FOR/AID ECO/UNDEV DIPLOM POLICY

N19
PATRICK H.T.,CYCLICAL INSTABILITY AND FISCAL-MONETARY POLICY IN POST-WAR JAPAN (PAMPHLET). INDUS MARKET DIPLOM TAX PRICE BAL/PAY...TREND CHARTS EQULIB 20 CHINJAP. PAGE 104 F2036 ECO/DEV PRODUC STAT

N19
SENGHOR L.S.,AFRICAN SOCIALISM (PAMPHLET). AFR FRANCE MALI USSR ELITES ECO/UNDEV NAT/G DIPLOM DOMIN EDU/PROP ATTIT 20 NEGRO. PAGE 119 F2355 SOCISM MARXISM ORD/FREE NAT/LISM

N19
STALEY E.,SCIENTIFIC RESEARCH AND PROGRESS IN NEWLY DEVELOPING COUNTRIES (PAMPHLET). AFR ASIA L/A+17C CONSULT DIPLOM...METH/COMP 20. PAGE 125 F2463 ECO/UNDEV ACT/RES FOR/AID TEC/DEV

N19
STEUBER F.A.,THE CONTRIBUTION OF SWITZERLAND TO THE ECONOMIC AND SOCIAL DEVELOPMENT OF LOW-INCOME COUNTRIES (PAMPHLET). SWITZERLND FINAN NAT/G VOL/ASSN INT/TRADE DRIVE...CHARTS 20. PAGE 126 F2482 FOR/AID ECO/UNDEV PLAN DIPLOM

B20
MALTHUS T.R.,PRINCIPLES OF POLITICAL ECONOMY. UK AGRI INDUS MARKET NAT/G DIPLOM PRICE CONTROL BAL/PAY COST OWN PWR LAISSEZ 18/19. PAGE 84 F1650 GEN/LAWS DEMAND WEALTH

B22
VON ENGELIN O.D.,INHERITING THE EARTH, THE GEOGRAPHICAL FACTOR IN NATIONAL DEVELOPMENT. WOR-45 CULTURE DIPLOM BIO/SOC HABITAT PERSON...PSY SOC CONCPT IDEA/COMP. PAGE 142 F2791 INGP/REL GEOG SOCIETY ROLE

B25
WILLIAMS B.,THE SELBORNE MEMORANDUM. AFR FUT SOUTH/AFR UK NAT/G BUDGET DIPLOM REGION GOV/REL SOVEREIGN...POLICY CHARTS 20 UNIFICA SELBORNE/W. PAGE 147 F2888 COLONIAL PROVS

B27
SIEGFRIED A.,AMERICA COMES OF AGE: A FRENCH ANALYSIS (TRANS. BY H.H. HEMMING AND DORIS HEMMING). FRANCE UK POL/PAR WORKER TEC/DEV DIPLOM REGION RACE/REL ADJUST PRODUC HEREDITY...TIME/SEQ GP/COMP SOC/INTEG 20 DEMOCRAT REPUBLICAN KKK. PAGE 122 F2398 USA-45 CULTURE ECO/DEV SOC

B30
FEIS H.,EUROPE, THE WORLD'S BANKER, 1871-1914. FRANCE GERMANY MOD/EUR UK WOR-45 NAT/G PLAN ECO/TAC EXEC ATTIT PWR WEALTH...CONCPT HIST/WRIT GEN/LAWS VAL/FREE 19/20. PAGE 40 F0773 FINAN DIPLOM INT/TRADE

B33
TANNENBAUM F.,PEACE BY REVOLUTION. ECO/UNDEV AGRI SECT WORKER DIPLOM EDU/PROP DISCRIM OWN WEALTH POPULISM 17/20 MEXIC/AMER INDIAN/AM. PAGE 128 F2532 CULTURE COLONIAL RACE/REL REV

B35
STALEY E.,WAR AND THE PRIVATE INVESTOR. UNIV WOR-45 INTELL SOCIETY INT/ORG NAT/G TOP/EX CAP/ISM ECO/TAC WAR ATTIT ALL/VALS...INT TIME/SEQ TREND CON/ANAL WORK TOT/POP 20. PAGE 125 F2464 FINAN INT/TRADE DIPLOM

B37
UNION OF SOUTH AFRICA,REPORT CONCERNING ADMINISTRATION OF SOUTH WEST AFRICA (6 VOLS.). SOUTH/AFR INDUS PUB/INST FORCES LEGIS BUDGET DIPLOM EDU/PROP ADJUD CT/SYS...GEOG CHARTS 20 AFRICA/SW LEAGUE/NAT. PAGE 132 F2610 NAT/G ADMIN COLONIAL CONSTN

B37
VON HAYEK F.A.,MONETARY NATIONALISM AND INTERNATIONAL STABILITY. WOR-45 ECO/DEV NAT/G PROB/SOLV INT/TRADE...POLICY CONCPT METH/COMP NAT/COMP 20. PAGE 142 F2792 ECO/TAC FINAN DIPLOM NAT/LISM

B38
CARVALHO C.M.,GEOGRAPHIA HUMANA; POLITICA E ECONOMICA (3RD ED.). BRAZIL CULTURE AGRI INDUS DIPLOM COLONIAL GP/REL RACE/REL...LING 20 RESOURCE/N. PAGE 22 F0424 GEOG HABITAT

B38
HARPER S.N.,THE GOVERNMENT OF THE SOVIET UNION. COM USSR LAW CONSTN ECO/DEV PLAN TEC/DEV DIPLOM INT/TRADE ADMIN REV NAT/LISM...POLICY 20. PAGE 55 F1085 MARXISM NAT/G LEAD POL/PAR

B39
FURNIVALL J.S.,NETHERLANDS INDIA. INDIA NETHERLAND CULTURE INDUS NAT/G DIPLOM ADMIN WEALTH...POLICY CHARTS 17/20. PAGE 45 F0876 COLONIAL ECO/UNDEV SOVEREIGN PLURISM

B39
ROBBINS L.,ECONOMIC CAUSES OF WAR. WOR-45 ECO/DEV ECO/UNDEV INT/ORG NAT/G TEC/DEV DIPLOM DOMIN COLONIAL ATTIT DRIVE PWR WEALTH...POLICY CONCPT OBS SAMP TREND CON/ANAL GEN/LAWS MARX/KARL 20. PAGE 112 F2203 COERCE ECO/TAC WAR

B39
THOMAS J.A.,THE HOUSE OF COMMONS, 1832-1901; A STUDY OF ITS ECONOMIC AND FUNCTIONAL CHARACTER. UK LAW STRATA FINAN DIPLOM CONTROL LEAD LOBBY REPRESENT WEALTH...POLICY STAT BIBLIOG 19/20 PARLIAMENT. PAGE 130 F2561 PARL/PROC LEGIS POL/PAR ECO/DEV

B40
MEEK C.K.,EUROPE AND WEST AFRICA. AFR EUR+WWI EXTR/IND DIPLOM INT/TRADE EDU/PROP GP/REL...SOC 20. PAGE 89 F1743 CULTURE TEC/DEV ECO/UNDEV COLONIAL

B41
HANSEN A.H.,FISCAL POLICY AND BUSINESS CYCLES. UK INDUS PROB/SOLV DIPLOM INT/TRADE OPTIMAL...POLICY TIME/SEQ CHARTS 19/20. PAGE 54 F1062 FINAN PLAN ECO/TAC GOV/REL

S41
LASSWELL H.D.,"THE GARRISON STATE" (BMR)" FUT WOR+45 ELITES INTELL FORCES ECO/TAC DOMIN EDU/PROP COERCE INGP/REL 20. PAGE 76 F1485 NAT/G DIPLOM PWR CIVMIL/REL

B42
JACKSON M.V.,EUROPEAN POWERS AND SOUTH-EAST AFRICA: A STUDY OF INTERNATIONAL RELATIONS ON SOUTH-EAST COAST OF AFRICA, 1796-1856. AFR FRANCE PORTUGAL SOUTH/AFR UK USA-45 FORCES INT/TRADE PWR...CHARTS BIBLIOG 18/19 TREATY. PAGE 66 F1294 DOMIN POLICY ORD/FREE DIPLOM

B44
LANDAUER C.,THEORY OF NATIONAL ECONOMIC PLANNING. USA-45 INDUS MARKET WORKER PROB/SOLV DIPLOM RATION PRICE CONTROL WAR COST 20. PAGE 75 F1465 ECO/TAC PLAN NAT/G ECO/DEV

B45
DAVIS J.,AFRICA ADVANCING. AFR CONGO/BRAZ LIBERIA NIGER INT/ORG SCHOOL DIPLOM GIVE KNOWL SKILL 20. PAGE 30 F0590 SECT COLONIAL AGRI ECO/UNDEV

B47
US LIBRARY OF CONGRESS,POSTWAR PLANNING AND RECONSTRUCTION: JANUARY-MARCH 1943. WOR+45 SOCIETY INT/ORG DIPLOM...SOC PREDICT 20. PAGE 138 F2714 BIBLIOG/A WAR PEACE PLAN

B48
CLYDE P.H.,THE FAR EAST: A HISTORY OF THE IMPACT OF THE WEST ON EASTERN ASIA. CHINA/COM CULTURE INT/TRADE DOMIN COLONIAL WAR PWR...CHARTS BIBLIOG 19/20 CHINJAP. PAGE 25 F0494 DIPLOM ASIA

B48
GRAHAM F.D.,THE THEORY OF INTERNATIONAL VALUES. FUT WOR+45 WOR-45 ECO/DEV FINAN INT/ORG PLAN TEC/DEV CAP/ISM DIPLOM ECO/TAC TARIFFS ROUTINE BAL/PAY DRIVE PWR WEALTH SOCISM...POLICY STAT HYPO/EXP GEN/LAWS 20. PAGE 50 F0971 NEW/IDEA INT/TRADE

B48
HART A.G.,MONEY, DEBT, AND ECONOMIC ACTIVITY. AFR WORKER DIPLOM PRICE CONTROL BAL/PAY COST OWN PRODUC ...METH/COMP 20 FED/RESERV. PAGE 56 F1097 FINAN WEALTH ECO/TAC NAT/G

B48
KEIR D.L.,CASES IN CONSTITUTIONAL LAW. UK CHIEF LEGIS DIPLOM TAX PARL/PROC CRIME GOV/REL...INT/LAW JURID 17/20. PAGE 70 F1368 CONSTN LAW ADJUD CT/SYS

B48
ROBERTSON D.H.,MONEY. AFR ECO/DEV NAT/G DIPLOM INT/TRADE BAL/PAY INCOME WEALTH...TIME/SEQ 20 DEPRESSION. PAGE 112 F2212 FINAN MARKET COST PRICE

B49
US DEPARTMENT OF STATE,SOVIET BIBLIOGRAPHY (PAMPHLET). CHINA/COM COM USSR LAW AGRI INT/ORG ECO/TAC EDU/PROP...POLICY GEOG IND 20. PAGE 135 F2670 BIBLIOG/A MARXISM CULTURE DIPLOM

S49
STEINMETZ H.,"THE PROBLEMS OF THE LANDRAT: A STUDY OF COUNTY GOVERNMENT IN THE US ZONE OF GERMANY." GERMANY/W USA+45 INDUS PLAN DIPLOM EDU/PROP CONTROL WAR GOV/REL FEDERAL WEALTH PLURISM...GOV/COMP 20 LANDRAT. PAGE 126 F2478 LOC/G COLONIAL MGT TOP/EX

B50
FEIS H.,THE DIPLOMACY OF THE DOLLAR: FIRST ERA 1919-32. EUR+WWI USA-45 FOR/AID REPAR ATTIT ...POLICY 20. PAGE 40 F0774 FINAN NAT/G DIPLOM ECO/TAC

B50
KOENIG L.W.,THE SALE OF THE TANKERS. USA+45 SEA DIST/IND POL/PAR DIPLOM ADMIN CIVMIL/REL ATTIT ...DECISION 20 PRESIDENT DEPT/STATE. PAGE 72 F1414 NAT/G POLICY PLAN GOV/REL

B50
SHAW E.S.,MONEY, INCOME, AND MONETARY POLICY. AFR USA-45 NAT/G DIPLOM PAY CONTROL COST INCOME PRODUC WEALTH...T 20 FED/RESERV DEPT/TREAS. PAGE 120 F2370 FINAN ECO/TAC ECO/DEV PRICE

B50
US DEPARTMENT OF STATE,POINT FOUR: COOPERATIVE PROGRAM FOR AID IN THE DEVELOPMENT OF ECONOMICALLY UNDERDEVELOPED AREAS. WOR+45 AGRI INDUS INT/ORG PLAN TEC/DEV DIPLOM EDU/PROP ADMIN PEACE PRODUC WEALTH 20 CONGRESS UN. PAGE 135 F2671
ECO/UNDEV FOR/AID FINAN INT/TRADE

C50
ELLSWORTH P.T.,"INTERNATIONAL ECONOMY." ECO/DEV ECO/UNDEV FINAN LABOR DIPLOM FOR/AID TARIFFS BAL/PAY EQUILIB NAT/LISM OPTIMAL...INT/LAW 20 ILO GATT. PAGE 37 F0724
BIBLIOG INT/TRADE ECO/TAC INT/ORG

B51
BROGAN D.W.,THE PRICE OF REVOLUTION. FRANCE USA+45 USA-45 USSR CONSTN NAT/G DIPLOM COLONIAL NAT/LISM ORD/FREE POPULISM...CONCPT 18/20 PRE/US/AM. PAGE 19 F0359
REV METH/COMP COST MARXISM

B51
HARROD R.F.,THE LIFE OF JOHN MAYNARD KEYNES. UK INTELL FAM CAP/ISM DIPLOM ECO/TAC WAR ATTIT PERSON ROLE 20 KEYNES/JM WWI. PAGE 56 F1094
BIOG FINAN GEN/LAWS

B51
HART A.G.,DEFENSE WITHOUT INFLATION. AFR KOREA FINAN INDUS NAT/G WORKER DIPLOM RATION TAX PRICE COST OPTIMAL 20 RESOURCE/N. PAGE 56 F1098
ECO/TAC CONTROL WAR PLAN

B51
LEONARD L.L.,INTERNATIONAL ORGANIZATION. WOR+45 WOR-45 EX/STRUC FORCES LEGIS ECO/TAC INT/TRADE COLONIAL ARMS/CONT...SOC/WK GOV/COMP BIBLIOG. PAGE 78 F1527
NAT/G DIPLOM INT/ORG DELIB/GP

B51
US HOUSE COMM APPROPRIATIONS,MUTUAL SECURITY PROGRAM APPROPRIATIONS FOR 1952: HEARINGS BEFORE A SUBCOMMITTEE OF THE COMMITTEE ON APPROPRIATIONS. AFR KOREA L/A+17C ECO/DEV ECO/UNDEV INT/ORG INSPECT BAL/PWR DIPLOM DEBATE WAR...POLICY STAT ASIA/S 20 CONGRESS NATO MID/EAST. PAGE 136 F2686
LEGIS FORCES BUDGET FOR/AID

B51
US LIBRARY OF CONGRESS,EAST EUROPEAN ACCESSIONS LIST (VOL. I). POL/PAR DIPLOM ADMIN LEAD 20. PAGE 138 F2715
BIBLIOG/A COM SOCIETY NAT/G

B52
SECRETARIAT COUNCIL OF EUROPE,THE STRASBOURG PLAN. EUR+WWI CONSULT PLAN ECO/TAC TARIFFS DEBATE REGION 20 COUNCL/EUR STRASBOURG. PAGE 119 F2340
INT/ORG ECO/DEV INT/TRADE DIPLOM

B52
SURANYI-UNGER T.,COMPARATIVE ECONOMIC SYSTEMS. FINAN MARKET DIPLOM PRICE WEALTH...GEOG SOC BIBLIOG METH T 20. PAGE 128 F2517
LAISSEZ PLAN ECO/DEV IDEA/COMP

B52
WU Y.,ECONOMIC WARFARE. MARKET PLAN PROB/SOLV FOR/AID CONTROL EFFICIENCY WEALTH...METH/COMP 20. PAGE 149 F2937
ECO/TAC WAR INT/TRADE DIPLOM

C52
HUME D.,"OF THE BALANCE OF TRADE" IN D. HUME, POLITICAL DISCOURSES (1752)" UK FINAN NAT/G TARIFFS PRICE PWR LAISSEZ...POLICY GEN/LAWS 18. PAGE 63 F1237
BAL/PAY INT/TRADE DIPLOM WEALTH

C52
HUME D.,"OF COMMERCE" IN D. HUME, POLITICAL DISCOURSES (1752)" UK FINAN DIPLOM WEALTH ...GEN/LAWS 18 MONEY. PAGE 63 F1238
INDUS INT/TRADE PWR AGRI

C52
HUME D.,"OF INTEREST" IN D. HUME, POLITICAL DISCOURSES (1752)" UK INDUS WORKER DIPLOM PAY DEMAND INCOME WEALTH...GEN/LAWS 18 MONEY. PAGE 63 F1239
PRICE COST FINAN INT/TRADE

C52
HUME D.,"OF MONEY" IN D. HUME, POLITICAL DISCOURSES (1752)" UK INDUS DIPLOM INT/TRADE...GEN/LAWS 18 MONEY. PAGE 63 F1240
FINAN COST PRICE WEALTH

B53
HARROD R.,THE DOLLAR. AFR USA+45 USA-45 ECO/DEV OPTIMAL WEALTH 18/20 FED/RESERV. PAGE 56 F1093
FINAN DIPLOM BAL/PAY

B53
ROBINSON E.A.G.,THE STRUCTURE OF COMPETITIVE INDUSTRY. UK ECO/DEV DIST/IND MARKET TEC/DEV DIPLOM EDU/PROP ADMIN EFFICIENCY WEALTH...MGT 19/20. PAGE 113 F2217
INDUS PRODUC WORKER OPTIMAL

L53
NELSON J.R.,"UNITED STATES FOREIGN ECONOMIC POLICY AND THE STERLING AREA." USA-45 WOR+45 WOR-45 NAT/G ECO/TAC WEALTH...STAT TIME/SEQ TREND CHARTS METH/GP TERR/GP CMN/WLTH 20. PAGE 97 F1911
FINAN DIPLOM UK

S53
LINCOLN G.,"FACTORS DETERMINING ARMS AID." COM FUT USA+45 USSR WOR+45 ECO/DEV NAT/G CONSULT PLAN TEC/DEV DIPLOM DOMIN EDU/PROP PERCEPT PWR ...DECISION CONCPT TREND MARX/KARL 20. PAGE 80 F1566
FORCES POLICY BAL/PWR FOR/AID

B54
REYNOLDS P.A.,BRITISH FOREIGN POLICY IN THE INTER-WAR YEARS. CZECHOSLVK GERMANY POLAND UK USA-45 POL/PAR FORCES ECO/TAC ARMS/CONT WAR ATTIT 20. PAGE 111 F2182
DIPLOM POLICY NAT/G

C54
BERLE A.A. JR.,"THE 20TH CENTURY CAPITALIST REVOLUTION." ECO/DEV NAT/G DIPLOM PRICE CONTROL ATTIT...BIBLIOG/A 20. PAGE 14 F0260
LG/CO CAP/ISM MGT PWR

B55
BUCHANAN N.S.,APPROACHES TO ECONOMIC DEVELOPMENT. FUT USA+45 WOR+45 STRATA ECO/DEV INT/ORG NAT/G TEC/DEV DIPLOM FOR/AID ATTIT KNOWL PWR WEALTH ...RELATIV METH/CNCPT SELF/OBS TREND CON/ANAL STERTYP GEN/LAWS FOR/TRADE COMMUN 20. PAGE 20 F0380
ECO/UNDEV ECO/TAC INT/TRADE

B55
HELANDER S.,DAS AUTARKIEPROBLEM IN DER WELTWIRTSCHAFT. PROB/SOLV BAL/PWR BARGAIN CAP/ISM ECO/TAC SOVEREIGN FOR/TRADE 20. PAGE 58 F1144
NAT/COMP COLONIAL DIPLOM

B55
PANT Y.P.,PLANNING IN UNDERDEVELOPED ECONOMIES. INDIA NEPAL INT/TRADE COLONIAL SOVEREIGN ALL/IDEOS ...TIME/SEQ METH/COMP 20. PAGE 103 F2026
ECO/UNDEV PLAN ECO/TAC DIPLOM

B55
STILLMAN C.W.,AFRICA IN THE MODERN WORLD. AFR USA+45 WOR+45 INT/TRADE COLONIAL PARTIC REGION GOV/REL RACE/REL 20. PAGE 126 F2489
ECO/UNDEV DIPLOM POLICY STRUCT

B55
US OFFICE OF THE PRESIDENT,REPORT TO CONGRESS ON THE MUTUAL SECURITY PROGRAM FOR THE SIX MONTHS ENDED JUNE 30, 1955. ECO/DEV INT/ORG NAT/G CREATE TEC/DEV BAL/PWR ECO/TAC AGREE DETER COST ORD/FREE 20 DEPT/STATE DEPT/DEFEN. PAGE 138 F2722
DIPLOM FORCES PLAN FOR/AID

B55
UYEHARA C.H.,COMPARATIVE PLATFORMS OF JAPAN'S MAJOR PARTIES... USA+45 AGRI LEGIS WORKER CAP/ISM ORD/FREE MARXISM SOCISM...IDEA/COMP 20 CHINJAP. PAGE 140 F2755
POLICY POL/PAR DIPLOM NAT/G

B55
WOYTINSKY W.S.,WORLD COMMERCE AND GOVERNMENTS: TRENDS AND OUTLOOK. WOR+45 FINAN POL/PAR DIPLOM ECO/TAC FOR/AID DOMIN WAR CHOOSE...CHARTS BIBLIOG 20 LEAGUE/NAT UN ILO. PAGE 149 F2929
INT/TRADE DIST/IND NAT/COMP NAT/G

B55
WRONG D.H.,AMERICAN AND CANADIAN VIEWPOINTS. CANADA USA+45 CONSTN STRATA FAM SECT WORKER ECO/TAC EDU/PROP ADJUD MARRIAGE...IDEA/COMP 20. PAGE 149 F2936
DIPLOM ATTIT NAT/COMP CULTURE

L55
KISER M.,"ORGANIZATION OF AMERICAN STATES." L/A+17C USA+45 ECO/UNDEV INT/ORG NAT/G PLAN TEC/DEV DIPLOM ECO/TAC INT/TRADE EDU/PROP ADMIN ALL/VALS...POLICY MGT RECORD ORG/CHARTS OAS COMMUN 20. PAGE 71 F1401
VOL/ASSN ECO/DEV REGION

C55
ADAMS G.P. JR.,"COMPETITIVE ECONOMIC SYSTEMS." WOR+45 WOR-45 PWR...BIBLIOG/A 20. PAGE 2 F0038
METH/COMP ECO/TAC TEC/DEV DIPLOM

B56
HISTORICAL ABSTRACTS. NAT/G CREATE DIPLOM ATTIT ...SOC DICTIONARY INDEX 18/20. PAGE 1 F0011
WOR-45 COMPUT/IR BIBLIOG/A

B56
BELL P.W.,THE STERLING AREA IN THE POSTWAR WORLD. EUR+WWI FUT S/ASIA UK ECO/DEV PLAN DIPLOM WEALTH ...STAT RECORD CHARTS GEN/LAWS FOR/TRADE TOT/POP 20. PAGE 12 F0235
FINAN ECO/TAC

B56
FIELD G.C.,POLITICAL THEORY. POL/PAR REPRESENT MORAL SOVEREIGN...JURID IDEA/COMP. PAGE 40 F0789
CONCPT NAT/G ORD/FREE DIPLOM

B56
GARDNER R.N.,STERLING-DOLLAR DIPLOMACY. EUR+WWI USA+45 INT/ORG NAT/G PLAN INT/TRADE EDU/PROP ADMIN KNOWL PWR WEALTH...POLICY SOC METH/CNCPT STAT CHARTS SIMUL GEN/LAWS 20. PAGE 46 F0902
ECO/DEV DIPLOM

B56
JUAN T.L.,ECONOMIC AND SOCIAL DEVELOPMENT OF MODERN CHINA: A BIBLIOGRAPHICAL GUIDE. ASIA AGRI COM/IND DIST/IND FINAN INDUS DIPLOM...STAT 20. PAGE 68 F1342
BIBLIOG SOC

B56
KNORR K.E.,RUBLE DIPLOMACY: CHALLENGE TO AMERICAN FOREIGN AID(PAMPHLET). AFR CHINA/COM USA+45 USSR PLAN TEC/DEV CAP/ISM INT/TRADE DOMIN EDU/PROP CONTROL LEAD 20. PAGE 72 F1413
ECO/UNDEV COM DIPLOM FOR/AID

B56
MYRDAL G.,AN INTERNATIONAL ECONOMY. EUR+WWI USA+45 WOR+45 WOR-45 NAT/G DIPLOM ECO/TAC BAL/PAY...PSY CONCPT OEEC TOT/POP 20. PAGE 96 F1879
VOL/ASSN AFR

B56
US LIBRARY OF CONGRESS,UNITED STATES DIRECT ECONOMIC AID TO FOREIGN COUNTRIES: A COLLECTION OF EXCERPTS AND A BIBLIOGRAPHY (PAMPHLET). USA+45 PRESS DEBATE...ANTHOL BIBLIOG/A CONGRESS. PAGE 138 F2716
FOR/AID POLICY DIPLOM ECO/UNDEV

B56
US OFFICE OF THE PRESIDENT,REPORT TO CONGRESS ON THE MUTUAL SECURITY PROGRAM FOR THE SIX MONTHS ENDED DECEMBER 31, 1955. ASIA USSR ECO/DEV ECO/UNDEV INT/ORG CREATE TEC/DEV BAL/PWR ECO/TAC AGREE DETER COST ORD/FREE 20 DEPT/STATE DEPT/DEFEN EISNHWR/DD. PAGE 138 F2723
DIPLOM FORCES PLAN FOR/AID

B56
WATT D.C.,BRITAIN AND THE SUEZ CANAL. COM UAR UK ...INT/LAW 20 SUEZ TREATY. PAGE 144 F2835
DIPLOM INT/TRADE DIST/IND NAT/G

B56
WOLFF R.L.,THE BALKANS IN OUR TIME. ALBANIA FUT MOD/EUR USSR YUGOSLAVIA CULTURE INT/ORG SECT DIPLOM EDU/PROP COERCE WAR ORD/FREE...CHARTS 4/20 BALKANS COMINFORM. PAGE 148 F2919
GEOG COM

N56
US HOUSE COMM FOREIGN AFFAIRS,REPORT OF THE SPECIAL STUDY MISSION TO AFRICA, SOUTH AND EAST OF THE SAHARA (PAMPHLET). AFR SOUTH/AFR USA+45 STRUCT INT/TRADE PARL/PROC NAT/LISM ATTIT ALL/VALS HEALTH ...POLICY 20 CONGRESS. PAGE 136 F2691
FOR/AID COLONIAL ECO/UNDEV DIPLOM

B57
ASHER R.E.,THE UNITED NATIONS AND ECONOMIC AND SOCIAL COOPERATION. ECO/UNDEV COM/IND DIST/IND FINAN PLAN PROB/SOLV INT/TRADE TASK WEALTH...SOC 20 UN. PAGE 7 F0129
INT/ORG DIPLOM FOR/AID

B57
BEHRMAN J.N.,INTERNATIONAL ECONOMICS: THEORY, PRACTICE, POLICY. AGRI INDUS NAT/G TARIFFS CONTROL BAL/PAY...POLICY METH/CNCPT T 19/20. PAGE 12 F0230
INT/TRADE FINAN DIPLOM FOR/AID

B57
DAY A.C.L.,OUTLINE OF MONETARY ECONOMICS. AFR WOR-45 INT/ORG WORKER DIPLOM BAL/PAY COST INCOME WEALTH...TIME/SEQ SIMUL 20. PAGE 31 F0594
FINAN NAT/G EQUILIB PRICE

B57
DRUCKER P.F.,AMERICA'S NEXT TWENTY YEARS. USA+45 DIST/IND ACADEM SCHOOL DIPLOM ECO/TAC AUTOMAT HABITAT HEALTH...SOC/WK TREND MUNICH 20 URBAN/RNWL PUB/TRANS. PAGE 34 F0667
WORKER FOR/AID CENSUS GEOG

B57
MILLIKAN M.F.,A PROPOSAL: KEY TO AN EFFECTIVE FOREIGN POLICY. USA+45 AGRI FINAN DELIB/GP DIPLOM REPRESENT MAJORITY...NEW/IDEA CHARTS. PAGE 91 F1795
FOR/AID GIVE ECO/UNDEV PLAN

B57
NEUMARK S.D.,ECONOMIC INFLUENCES ON THE SOUTH AFRICAN FRONTIER, 1652-1836. SOUTH/AFR SEA AGRI NAT/G FORCES WORKER DIPLOM INT/TRADE PRICE DEMAND PRODUC...STAT CHARTS 17/19 FRONTIER. PAGE 97 F1915
COLONIAL ECO/UNDEV ECO/TAC MARKET

B57
ROBERTSON H.M.,SOUTH AFRICA, ECONOMIC AND POLITICAL ASPECTS. SOUTH/AFR CONSTN CULTURE POL/PAR LEGIS DIPLOM DOMIN COLONIAL...SOC BIBLIOG 19/20. PAGE 112 F2214
RACE/REL ECO/UNDEV ECO/TAC DISCRIM

L57
MASS. INST. TECH.,"THE CENTER FOR INTERNATIONAL STUDIES." AFR ASIA COM EUR+WWI ISLAM L/A+17C S/ASIA USA+45 USA-45 DIST/IND CONSULT FORCES ACT/RES TEC/DEV DIPLOM REV ATTIT WEALTH...CONCPT FOR/TRADE 20. PAGE 87 F1702
R+D ECO/UNDEV

S57
HOAG M.W.,"ECONOMIC PROBLEMS OF ALLIANCE." AFR COM EUR+WWI WOR+45 ECO/DEV ECO/UNDEV NAT/G VOL/ASSN FORCES PLAN TEC/DEV DIPLOM COERCE ORD/FREE PWR WEALTH...DECISION GEN/LAWS NATO TERR/GP. PAGE 60 F1182
INT/ORG ECO/TAC

B58
COLE G.D.H.,COMMUNISM AND SOCIAL DEMOCRACY (VOL. IV OF "HISTORY OF SOCIAL THOUGHT"). COM GERMANY ITALY UK AGRI INT/ORG WORKER DIPLOM COLONIAL NAT/LISM ALL/IDEOS...BIBLIOG 20 LEAGUE/NAT AUST/HUNG. PAGE 26 F0502
MARXISM REV POL/PAR SOCISM

B58
EHRHARD J.,LE DESTIN DU COLONIALISME. AFR FRANCE ECO/UNDEV AGRI FINAN MARKET CREATE PLAN TEC/DEV BUDGET DIPLOM PRICE 20. PAGE 36 F0710
COLONIAL FOR/AID INT/TRADE INDUS

B58
HENNING C.N.,INTERNATIONAL FINANCING. WOR+45 ECO/DEV INT/ORG EX/STRUC INSPECT CAP/ISM BAL/PAY COST PROFIT...MGT CHARTS T 20. PAGE 58 F1150
FINAN DIPLOM INT/TRADE

B58
INTERNATIONAL ECONOMIC ASSN,ECONOMICS OF INTERNATIONAL MIGRATION. WOR+45 WOR-45 ECO/UNDEV FINAN NAT/G REGION...NAT/COMP METH 20. PAGE 65 F1275
CENSUS GEOG DIPLOM ECO/TAC

B58
JACOBSSON P.,SOME MONETARY PROBLEMS, INTERNATIONAL AND NATIONAL. WOR+45 WOR-45 ECO/DEV FORCES WORKER PROB/SOLV DIPLOM INT/TRADE...ANTHOL 20. PAGE 66 F1299
FINAN PLAN ECO/TAC NAT/COMP

B58
JENNINGS I.,PROBLEMS OF THE NEW COMMONWEALTH. AFR CEYLON INDIA PAKISTAN S/ASIA ECO/UNDEV INT/ORG LOC/G DIPLOM ECO/TAC INT/TRADE COLONIAL RACE/REL DISCRIM 20 PARLIAMENT. PAGE 67 F1314
NAT/LISM NEUTRAL FOR/AID POL/PAR

B58
JOHNSON H.G.,INTERNATIONAL TRADE AND ECONOMIC GROWTH. WOR+45 BUDGET CAP/ISM ECO/TAC TARIFFS BAL/PAY 20. PAGE 67 F1323
INT/TRADE BAL/PWR BARGAIN DIPLOM

B58
KINDLEBERGER C.P.,INTERNATIONAL ECONOMICS. WOR+45 WOR-45 ECO/DEV ECO/UNDEV FINAN VOL/ASSN ACT/RES DIPLOM ECO/TAC LEGIT REGION ATTIT DRIVE ORD/FREE WEALTH...POLICY STAT TREND GEN/LAWS EEC ECSC OEEC 20. PAGE 71 F1391
INT/ORG BAL/PWR TARIFFS

B58
MASON J.B.,THAILAND BIBLIOGRAPHY. S/ASIA THAILAND CULTURE EDU/PROP ADMIN...GEOG SOC LING 20. PAGE 87 F1701
BIBLIOG/A ECO/UNDEV DIPLOM NAT/G

B58
MOSKOWITZ M.,HUMAN RIGHTS AND WORLD ORDER. INT/ORG PLAN GP/REL NAT/LISM SOVEREIGN...CONCPT 20 UN TREATY CIV/RIGHTS. PAGE 94 F1845
DIPLOM INT/LAW ORD/FREE

B58
PALYI M.,MANAGED MONEY AT THE CROSSROADS: THE EUROPEAN EXPERIENCE. AFR WOR+45 WOR-45 TEC/DEV DIPLOM INT/TRADE DEMAND WEALTH...CHARTS BIBLIOG 19/20 EUROPE SILVER. PAGE 103 F2022
FINAN ECO/TAC ECO/DEV PRODUC

B58
PAN AMERICAN UNION,REPERTORIO DE PUBLICACIONES PERIODICAS ACTUALES LATINO-AMERICANAS. CULTURE ECO/UNDEV ADMIN LEAD GOV/REL 20 OAS. PAGE 103 F2023
BIBLIOG L/A+17C NAT/G DIPLOM

B58
TILLION G.,ALGERIA: THE REALITIES. ALGERIA FRANCE ISLAM CULTURE STRATA PROB/SOLV DOMIN REV NAT/LISM WEALTH MARXISM...GEOG 20. PAGE 130 F2573
ECO/UNDEV SOC COLONIAL DIPLOM

N58
EUROPEAN COMM ECO-SOC PROG,EUROPEAN BUSINESS CYCLE POLICY (PAMPHLET). AFR EUR+WWI MARKET WORKER DIPLOM PRICE BAL/PAY 20 EUROPE. PAGE 39 F0754
ECO/DEV FINAN ECO/TAC PROB/SOLV

B59
AITKEN H.G.,THE AMERICAN ECONOMIC IMPACT ON CANADA. CANADA USA+45 AGRI FINAN INDUS LABOR INT/TRADE BAL/PAY...INT/LAW TREND 20. PAGE 3 F0055
DIPLOM ECO/TAC POLICY NAT/G

B59
ALLEN W.R.,FOREIGN TRADE AND FINANCE. ECO/DEV DIPLOM BAL/PAY...POLICY CONCPT ANTHOL 20. PAGE 4 F0073
INT/TRADE EQUILIB FINAN

B59
ARON R.,IMPERIALISM AND COLONIALISM (PAMPHLET). WOR+45 WOR-45 ECO/TAC CONTROL REV ORD/FREE 19/20. PAGE 6 F0119
COLONIAL DOMIN ECO/UNDEV DIPLOM

B59
BAUER P.T.,UNITED STATES AID AND INDIAN ECONOMIC DEVELOPMENT. INDIA STRATA FINAN PLAN BUDGET DIPLOM INGP/REL EFFICIENCY SOCISM 20 AID. PAGE 11 F0215
FOR/AID ECO/UNDEV ECO/TAC POLICY

B59
DIEBOLD W. JR.,THE SCHUMAN PLAN: A STUDY IN ECONOMIC COOPERATION, 1950-1959. EUR+WWI FRANCE GERMANY USA+45 EXTR/IND CONSULT DELIB/GP PLAN DIPLOM ECO/TAC INT/TRADE ROUTINE ORD/FREE WEALTH ...METH/CNCPT STAT CONT/OBS INT TIME/SEQ ECSC 20. PAGE 33 F0635
INT/ORG REGION

B59
ETSCHMANN R.,DIE WAHRUNGS- UND DEVISENPOLITIK DES OSTBLOCKS UND IHRE AUSWIRKUNGEN AUF DIE WIRTSCHAFTSBEZIEHUNGEN ZWISCHEN OST U WEST. BULGARIA CZECHOSLVK HUNGARY POLAND USSR MARKET NAT/G PLAN DIPLOM...NAT/COMP 20. PAGE 39 F0753
ECO/TAC FINAN POLICY INT/TRADE

B59
GOMEZ ROBLES J.,A STATEMENT OF THE LAWS OF GUATEMALA IN MATTERS AFFECTING BUSINESS (2ND ED. REV., ENLARGED). GUATEMALA L/A+17C LAW FINAN FAM WORKER ACT/RES DIPLOM ADJUD ADMIN GP/REL 20 OAS. PAGE 48 F0945
JURID NAT/G INDUS LEGIT

B59
HARVARD UNIVERSITY LAW SCHOOL,INTERNATIONAL PROBLEMS OF FINANCIAL PROTECTION AGAINST NUCLEAR RISK. WOR+45 NAT/G DELIB/GP PROB/SOLV DIPLOM CONTROL ATTIT...POLICY INT/LAW MATH 20. PAGE 56 F1105
NUC/PWR ADJUD INDUS FINAN

B59
KOREAN MINISTRY RECONSTRUCTION,KOREAN ECONOMY AND
FOR/AID

ITS REQUIREMENTS. KOREA USA+45 ECO/TAC EQUILIB INCOME WEALTH...CHARTS 20. PAGE 73 F1427
WAR FINAN DIPLOM

B59
LINK R.G.,ENGLISH THEORIES OF ECONOMIC FLUCTUATIONS: 1815-1848. FRANCE UK AGRI WORKER DIPLOM PRICE TASK WAR DEMAND PRODUC...POLICY BIBLIOG 18 MALTHUS MILL/JS WILSON/J. PAGE 80 F1574
IDEA/COMP ECO/DEV WEALTH EQUILIB

B59
MADHOK B.,POLITICAL TRENDS IN INDIA. INDIA PAKISTAN UK STRATA ECO/UNDEV POL/PAR LEGIS CAP/ISM DIPLOM COLONIAL CHOOSE MARXISM...SOC TREND 20 GANDHI/M NEHRU/J. PAGE 84 F1639
GEOG NAT/G

B59
MEZERK A.G.,FINANCIAL ASSISTANCE FOR ECONOMIC DEVELOPMENT. WOR+45 INDUS DIPLOM INT/TRADE...CHARTS GOV/COMP UN. PAGE 91 F1778
FOR/AID FINAN ECO/TAC ECO/UNDEV

B59
NOVE A.,COMMUNIST ECONOMIC STRATEGY: SOVIET GROWTH AND CAPABILITIES. USSR AGRI LABOR PLAN TEC/DEV CAP/ISM INT/TRADE EFFICIENCY MARXISM 20 THIRD/WRLD. PAGE 99 F1941
FOR/AID ECO/TAC DIPLOM INDUS

B59
NUNEZ JIMENEZ A.,LA LIBERACION DE LAS ISLAS. CUBA L/A+17C USA+45 LAW CHIEF PLAN DIPLOM FOR/AID OWN WEALTH 20 CASTRO/F. PAGE 99 F1945
AGRI REV ECO/UNDEV NAT/G

B59
OGBURN C.,ECONOMIC PLAN AND ACTION. USA+45 FINAN LABOR DIPLOM ECO/TAC FOR/AID 20. PAGE 101 F1981
ECO/DEV INT/TRADE PLAN BAL/PAY

B59
PANIKKAR K.M.,THE AFRO-ASIAN STATES AND THEIR PROBLEMS. COM CULTURE KIN POL/PAR SECT DIPLOM EDU/PROP COLONIAL SOVEREIGN...TECHNIC GOV/COMP 20. PAGE 103 F2025
AFR S/ASIA ECO/UNDEV

B59
ROBERTSON A.H.,EUROPEAN INSTITUTIONS: COOPERATION, INTEGRATION, UNIFICATION. EUR+WWI FINAN INT/ORG FORCES INT/TRADE TARIFFS 20 EEC EURATOM ECSC NATO TREATY. PAGE 112 F2208
ECO/DEV DIPLOM INDUS ECO/TAC

B59
ROPKE W.,INTERNATIONAL ORDER AND ECONOMIC INTEGRATION. ECO/DEV ECO/UNDEV AGRI FINAN INDUS INT/ORG WAR PEACE ORD/FREE...SOC METH/COMP 20 EEC. PAGE 114 F2238
INT/TRADE DIPLOM BAL/PAY ALL/IDEOS

B59
SILCOCK T.H.,THE COMMONWEALTH ECONOMY IN SOUTHEAST ASIA. AFR INDIA MALAYSIA S/ASIA ECO/DEV AGRI LOC/G PLAN TARIFFS COLONIAL BAL/PAY DEMAND...BIBLIOG/A 20 GATT. PAGE 122 F2401
ECO/TAC INT/TRADE RACE/REL DIPLOM

B59
STERNBERG F.,THE MILITARY AND INDUSTRIAL REVOLUTION OF OUR TIME. USA+45 USSR WOR+45 WORKER COMPUTER PLAN TEC/DEV NUC/PWR GP/REL...POLICY NAT/COMP 20. PAGE 126 F2481
DIPLOM FORCES INDUS CIVMIL/REL

B59
U OF MICHIGAN LAW SCHOOL,ATOMS AND THE LAW. USA+45 PROVS WORKER PROB/SOLV DIPLOM ADMIN GOV/REL ANTHOL. PAGE 132 F2596
NUC/PWR NAT/G CONTROL LAW

B59
US DEPARTMENT OF STATE,THE UNITED STATES ECONOMY AND THE MUTUAL SECURITY PROGRAM. USA+45 ECO/UNDEV FINAN INDUS DIPLOM INT/TRADE DETER 20. PAGE 136 F2674
ECO/DEV FORCES BUDGET FOR/AID

B59
US GENERAL ACCOUNTING OFFICE,EXAM OF ECONOMIC AND TECHNICAL ASSISTANCE PROGRAM FOR INDIA INT'NAT'L COOP ADMIN REPORT TO CONGRESS 1955-1958. INDIA USA+45 ECO/UNDEV FINAN PLAN DIPLOM COST UTIL WEALTH ...CHARTS 20 CONGRESS AID. PAGE 136 F2679
FOR/AID EFFICIENCY ECO/TAC TEC/DEV

B59
WELTON H.,THE THIRD WORLD WAR; TRADE AND INDUSTRY, THE NEW BATTLEGROUND. AFR WOR+45 ECO/DEV INDUS MARKET TASK...MGT IDEA/COMP. PAGE 145 F2855
INT/TRADE PLAN DIPLOM

B59
YRARRAZAVAL E.,AMERICA LATINE EN LA GUERRA FRIA. AFR EUR+WWI L/A+17C USA+45 USSR WOR+45 INDUS INT/ORG NAT/LISM POLICY. PAGE 150 F2953
REGION DIPLOM ECO/UNDEV INT/TRADE

L59
GARDNER R.N.,"NEW DIRECTIONS IN UNITED STATES FOREIGN ECONOMIC POLICY." AFR USA+45 CONSULT ...GEN/LAWS GEN/METH FOR/TRADE 20. PAGE 46 F0903
ECO/UNDEV ECO/TAC FOR/AID DIPLOM

L59
WURFEL D.,"FOREIGN AID AND SOCIAL REFORM IN POLITICAL DEVELOPMENT" (BMR)" PHILIPPINE USA+45 WOR+45 SOCIETY POL/PAR ACT/RES TEC/DEV DIPLOM 20. PAGE 149 F2943
FOR/AID PROB/SOLV ECO/TAC ECO/UNDEV

S59
ALKHIMOV V.S.,"SOVIET FOREIGN TRADE CHANNELS." COM FUT USA+45 USSR ECO/DEV MARKET CONSULT PLAN WEALTH ...MARXIST OBS CON/ANAL FOR/TRADE 20. PAGE 4 F0068
FINAN ECO/TAC DIPLOM

S59
REUBENS E.D.,"THE BASIS FOR REORIENATION OF AMERICAN FOREIGN AID POLICY." USA+45 USSR STRUCT INT/ORG CONSULT ECO/TAC ADMIN DRIVE MORAL ORD/FREE PWR WEALTH...RELATIV MATH STAT TREND GEN/LAWS VAL/FREE 20. PAGE 111 F2180
ECO/UNDEV PLAN FOR/AID DIPLOM

B60
ARON R.,COLLOQUES DE RHEINFELDEN. AFR USA+45 USSR WOR+45 WOR-45 CULTURE ECO/UNDEV NAT/G POL/PAR DIPLOM NAT/LISM TOTALISM ATTIT DRIVE ALL/VALS ...PLURIST CONCPT STERTYP GEN/LAWS TOT/POP 20. PAGE 6 F0120
ECO/DEV SOCIETY CAP/ISM SOCISM

B60
ASPREMONT-LYNDEN H.,RAPPORT SUR L'ADMINISTRATION BELGE DU RUANDA-URUNDI PENDANT L'ANNEE 1959. BELGIUM RWANDA AGRI INDUS DIPLOM ECO/TAC INT/TRADE DOMIN ADMIN RACE/REL...GEOG CENSUS 20 UN. PAGE 7 F0132
AFR COLONIAL ECO/UNDEV INT/ORG

B60
BILLERBECK K.,SOVIET BLOC FOREIGN AID TO UNDERDEVELOPED COUNTRIES. COM FUT USSR FINAN FORCES TEC/DEV DIPLOM INT/TRADE EDU/PROP NUC/PWR...TREND 20. PAGE 15 F0285
FOR/AID ECO/UNDEV ECO/TAC MARXISM

B60
BLACK E.R.,THE DIPLOMACY OF ECONOMIC DEVELOPMENT. WOR+45 CONSULT PLAN TEC/DEV DIPLOM ECO/TAC FOR/AID ...CONCPT TREND 20. PAGE 15 F0290
ECO/UNDEV ACT/RES

B60
BOHM F.,REDEN UND SCHRIFTEN UBER DIE ORDNUNG EINER FREIEN GESELLSCHAFT, EINER FREIEN WIRTSCHAFT, UND UBER DIE WIEDERGUTMACH. DIPLOM CRIME ORD/FREE RESPECT FASCISM 20 NAZI. PAGE 16 F0307
ECO/TAC NEW/LIB SUPEGO REPAR

B60
DALE W.B.,THE FOREIGN DEFICIT OF THE UNITED STATES. ECO/TAC TARIFFS PAY PRICE CONTROL COST WEALTH POLICY. PAGE 30 F0573
BAL/PAY DIPLOM FINAN INT/TRADE

B60
DIA M.,REFLEXIONS SUR L'ECONOMIE DE L'AFRIQUE NOIRE (REV. ED.). CULTURE ECO/UNDEV CREATE TEC/DEV DIPLOM INT/TRADE OPTIMAL ATTIT...POLICY 20. PAGE 32 F0631
AFR ECO/TAC SOCISM PLAN

B60
HEYSE T.,PROBLEMS FONCIERS ET REGIME DES TERRES (ASPECTS ECONOMIQUES, JURIDIQUES ET SOCIAUX). AFR CONGO/BRAZ INT/ORG DIPLOM SOVEREIGN...GEOG TREATY 20. PAGE 59 F1161
BIBLIOG AGRI ECO/UNDEV LEGIS

B60
KENEN P.B.,GIANT AMONG NATIONS: PROBLEMS IN UNITED STATES FOREIGN ECONOMIC POLICY. AFR USA+45 FINAN DIPLOM TARIFFS BAL/PAY WEALTH 20. PAGE 70 F1376
FOR/AID ECO/UNDEV INT/TRADE PLAN

B60
LATIFI D.,INDIA AND UNITED STATES AID. ASIA INDIA UK USA+45 AGRI FINAN INDUS COLONIAL ORD/FREE SOVEREIGN WEALTH...METH/COMP 20. PAGE 76 F1486
FOR/AID DIPLOM ECO/UNDEV

B60
MC CLELLAN G.S.,INDIA. AFR CHINA/COM INDIA CONSTN ELITES STRATA AGRI POL/PAR FOR/AID ARMS/CONT REV MARXISM...CENSUS BIBLIOG 20 GANDHI/M NEHRU/J. PAGE 87 F1712
DIPLOM NAT/G SOCIETY ECO/UNDEV

B60
MENDELSON W.,CAPITALISM, DEMOCRACY, AND THE SUPREME COURT. USA+45 USA-45 CONSTN DIPLOM GOV/REL ATTIT ORD/FREE LAISSEZ...POLICY CHARTS PERS/COMP 18/20 SUPREME/CT MARSHALL/J HOLMES/OW TANEY/RB FIELD/JJ. PAGE 90 F1758
JUDGE CT/SYS JURID NAT/G

B60
NEALE A.D.,THE FLOW OF RESOURCES FROM RICH TO POOR. WOR+45 ECO/DEV ECO/UNDEV FINAN INDUS NAT/G PLAN EFFICIENCY WEALTH...POLICY NAT/COMP 20 RESOURCE/N. PAGE 97 F1905
FOR/AID DIPLOM METH/CNCPT

B60
PENTONY D.E.,UNITED STATES FOREIGN AID. INDIA LAOS USA+45 ECO/UNDEV INT/TRADE ADMIN PEACE ATTIT ...POLICY METH/COMP ANTHOL 20. PAGE 105 F2060
FOR/AID DIPLOM ECO/TAC

B60
RAO V.K.R.,INTERNATIONAL AID FOR ECONOMIC DEVELOPMENT - POSSIBILITIES AND LIMITATIONS. FINAN PLAN TEC/DEV ADMIN TASK EFFICIENCY...POLICY SOC METH/CNCPT CHARTS 20 UN. PAGE 109 F2147
FOR/AID DIPLOM INT/ORG ECO/UNDEV

B60
ROPKE W.,A HUMANE ECONOMY. CULTURE ECO/DEV FINAN INDUS GP/REL CENTRAL WEALTH...GEOG SOC IDEA/COMP 20 EEC. PAGE 114 F2239
ECO/TAC INT/ORG DIPLOM ORD/FREE

B60
STANFORD RESEARCH INSTITUTE,AFRICAN DEVELOPMENT: A TEST FOR INTERNATIONAL COOPERATION. AFR USA+45 WOR+45 FINAN INT/ORG PLAN PROB/SOLV ECO/TAC INT/TRADE ADMIN...CHARTS 20. PAGE 125 F2467
FOR/AID ECO/UNDEV ATTIT DIPLOM

B60
STEVENSON A.E.,PUTTING FIRST THINGS FIRST. USA+45 INT/ORG NEIGH FOR/AID DISCRIM...ANTHOL 20. PAGE 126 F2483
DIPLOM ECO/UNDEV ORD/FREE

EDU/PROP

B60
STOLPER W.F.,GERMANY BETWEEN EAST AND WEST: THE ECONOMICS OF COMPETITIVE COEXISTENCE. AFR FUT GERMANY/E GERMANY/W WOR+45 FINAN POL/PAR BUDGET ECO/TAC FOR/AID INT/TRADE...STAT CHARTS METH/COMP 20. PAGE 126 F2495
ECO/DEV DIPLOM GOV/COMP BAL/PWR

B60
US HOUSE COMM GOVT OPERATIONS,OPERATIONS OF THE DEVELOPMENT LOAN FUND: HEARINGS (COMMITTEE ON GOVERNMENT OPERATIONS). USA+45 PLAN BUDGET DIPLOM GOV/REL COST...CHARTS 20 CONGRESS DEPT/STATE AID. PAGE 137 F2698
FINAN FOR/AID ECO/TAC EFFICIENCY

B60
WENTHOLT W.,INFLATION OR SECURITY? EUR+WWI USA+45 INDUS CONSULT TEC/DEV CAP/ISM DIPLOM FOR/AID INT/TRADE MARXISM 20 EEC. PAGE 145 F2858
ECO/DEV ECO/TAC FINAN ORD/FREE

B60
WHEARE K.C.,THE CONSTITUTIONAL STRUCTURE OF THE COMMONWEALTH. UK EX/STRUC DIPLOM DOMIN ADMIN COLONIAL CONTROL LEAD INGP/REL SUPEGO 20 CMN/WLTH. PAGE 145 F2865
CONSTN INT/ORG VOL/ASSN SOVEREIGN

S60
MARTIN E.M.,"NEW TRENDS IN UNITED STATES ECONOMIC FOREIGN POLICY." USA+45 INTELL DELIB/GP FOR/AID INT/TRADE ROUTINE BAL/PAY...RELATIV TRUE/GP 20. PAGE 86 F1682
NAT/G PLAN DIPLOM

S60
OWEN C.F.,"US AND SOVIET RELATIONS WITH UNDERDEVELOPED COUNTRIES: LATIN AMERICA-A CASE STUDY." AFR COM L/A+17C USA+45 USSR EXTR/IND MARKET TEC/DEV DIPLOM ECO/TAC NAT/LISM ORD/FREE PWR ...TREND WORK 20. PAGE 102 F2005
ECO/UNDEV DRIVE INT/TRADE

N60
ERDMAN P.E.,COMMON MARKETS AND FREE TRADE AREAS (PAMPHLET). USA+45 MARKET INT/ORG TEC/DEV DIPLOM UTIL...CON/ANAL CHARTS BIBLIOG 20 EEC OEEC. PAGE 38 F0743
TREND PROB/SOLV INT/TRADE ECO/DEV

B61
AUBREY H.G.,COEXISTENCE: ECONOMIC CHALLENGE AND RESPONSE. AFR USSR WOR+45 ACT/RES BAL/PWR CAP/ISM DIPLOM ECO/TAC FOR/AID INT/TRADE PEACE SOCISM ...METH/COMP NAT/COMP. PAGE 7 F0139
POLICY ECO/UNDEV PLAN COM

B61
BUSSCHAU W.J.,GOLD AND INTERNATIONAL LIQUIDITY. AFR WOR+45 PRICE EQUILIB WEALTH...CHARTS 20. PAGE 20 F0396
FINAN DIPLOM PROB/SOLV

B61
DIMOCK M.E.,BUSINESS AND GOVERNMENT (4TH ED.). AGRI FINAN OP/RES PLAN BUDGET DIPLOM LOBBY NUC/PWR NEW/LIB SOCISM...POLICY BIBLIOG 20. PAGE 33 F0641
NAT/G INDUS LABOR ECO/TAC

B61
DOIG J.W.,THE POLITICS OF METROPOLITAN TRANSPORTATION. DELIB/GP WORKER DIPLOM TASK EFFICIENCY UTIL...CHARTS BIBLIOG MUNICH 20 NEW/YORK NEW/JERSEY PUB/TRANS RAILROAD. PAGE 34 F0652
PROB/SOLV STRATA DIST/IND

B61
ESTEBAN J.C.,IMPERIALISMO Y DESARROLLO ECONOMICO. L/A+17C FINAN INDUS NAT/G ECO/TAC CONTROL ROLE. PAGE 38 F0747
ECO/UNDEV NAT/LISM DIPLOM BAL/PAY

B61
GANGULI B.N.,ECONOMIC INTEGRATION. FINAN LABOR CAP/ISM DIPLOM WEALTH...NAT/COMP 20. PAGE 46 F0895
ECO/TAC METH/CNCPT EQUILIB ECO/UNDEV

B61
GURTOO D.H.N.,INDIA'S BALANCE OF PAYMENTS (1920-1960). INDIA FINAN DIPLOM FOR/AID INT/TRADE PRICE COLONIAL...CHARTS BIBLIOG 20. PAGE 52 F1014
BAL/PAY STAT ECO/TAC ECO/UNDEV

B61
HARDT J.P.,THE COLD WAR ECONOMIC GAP. AFR USA+45 USSR ECO/DEV FORCES INT/TRADE NUC/PWR PWR 20. PAGE 55 F1081
DIPLOM ECO/TAC NAT/COMP POLICY

B61
HARRIS S.E.,THE DOLLAR IN CRISIS. AFR USA+45 MARKET INT/ORG ECO/TAC PRICE CONTROL WEALTH...METH/COMP ANTHOL 20. PAGE 55 F1089
BAL/PAY DIPLOM FINAN INT/TRADE

B61
HAUSER M.,DIE URSACHEN DER FRANZOSISCHEN INFLATION IN DEN JAHREN 1946-1952. AFR FRANCE INDUS NAT/G BUDGET DIPLOM ECO/TAC FOR/AID COST MONEY 20. PAGE 57 F1114
ECO/DEV FINAN PRICE

B61
HICKS U.K.,FEDERALISM AND ECONOMIC GROWTH IN UNDERDEVELOPED COUNTRIES. WOR+45 WOR-45 FINAN NAT/G PLAN BUDGET DIPLOM INT/TRADE DEMAND WEALTH...ANTHOL 20. PAGE 59 F1167
ECO/UNDEV ECO/TAC FEDERAL CONSTN

B61
JAVITS B.A.,THE PEACE BY INVESTMENT CORPORATION. WOR+45 NAT/G LEGIS PROB/SOLV PERS/REL WEALTH ...POLICY 20. PAGE 66 F1307
ECO/UNDEV DIPLOM FOR/AID PEACE

B61
KOVNER M.,THE CHALLENGE OF COEXISTENCE: A STUDY OF SOVIET ECONOMIC DIPLOMACY. COM FUT ECO/DEV ECO/UNDEV PLAN EDU/PROP DETER SKILL...OBS VAL/FREE 20. PAGE 73 F1430
PWR DIPLOM USSR AFR

B61
LEHMAN R.L.,AFRICA SOUTH OF THE SAHARA (PAMPHLET). DIPLOM COLONIAL NAT/LISM. PAGE 77 F1512
BIBLIOG/A AFR CULTURE NAT/G

B61
LETHBRIDGE H.J.,CHINA'S URBAN COMMUNES. CHINA/COM FUT ECO/UNDEV DIPLOM EDU/PROP DEMAND INCOME MARXISM ...POLICY MUNICH 20. PAGE 78 F1534
CONTROL ECO/TAC NAT/G

B61
MEZERIK A.G.,ECONOMIC DEVELOPMENT AIDS FOR UNDERDEVELOPED COUNTRIES. WOR+45 FINAN LEGIS PROB/SOLV TEC/DEV DIPLOM FOR/AID GIVE TASK WAR 20 UN. PAGE 91 F1776
ECO/UNDEV INT/ORG WEALTH PLAN

B61
MOORE G.H.,BUSINESS CYCLE INDICATORS (TWO VOLS.). LABOR DIPLOM PRICE RISK TASK WAR PRODUC...CHARTS BIBLIOG 20. PAGE 93 F1822
MARKET FINAN WEALTH

B61
MORLEY L.,THE PATCHWORK HISTORY OF FOREIGN AID. AFR KOREA/S USA+45 USSR LAW FINAN INT/ORG TEC/DEV BAL/PWR GIVE 20 NATO. PAGE 93 F1834
FOR/AID ECO/UNDEV FORCES DIPLOM

B61
PERKINS D.,THE UNITED STATES AND LATIN AMERICAN. L/A+17C USA+45 USA-45 STRUCT COLONIAL REV ORD/FREE 19/20. PAGE 105 F2061
DIPLOM INT/TRADE NAT/G

B61
PERLO V.,EL IMPERIALISMO NORTHEAMERICANO. USA+45 USA-45 FINAN CAP/ISM DIPLOM DOMIN CONTROL DISCRIM 19/20. PAGE 105 F2063
SOCIALIST ECO/DEV INT/TRADE ECO/TAC

B61
SCHWARTZ H.,THE RED PHOENIX: RUSSIA SINCE WORLD WAR II. USA+45 WOR+45 ELITES POL/PAR TEC/DEV ECO/TAC MARXISM. PAGE 118 F2325
DIPLOM NAT/G ECO/DEV

B61
STARK H.,SOCIAL AND ECONOMIC FRONTIERS IN LATIN AMERICA (2ND ED.). CUBA FUT CULTURE AGRI INDUS ECO/TAC PRODUC ATTIT MARXISM...NAT/COMP BIBLIOG T 20. PAGE 125 F2470
L/A+17C SOCIETY DIPLOM ECO/UNDEV

B61
THEOBALD R.,THE CHALLENGE OF ABUNDANCE. USA+45 WOR+45 MARKET DIPLOM FOR/AID REV PRODUC UTOPIA SUPEGO...POLICY TREND BIBLIOG/A 20. PAGE 129 F2554
WELF/ST ECO/UNDEV PROB/SOLV ECO/TAC

B61
US CONGRESS JOINT ECO COMM,INTERNATIONAL PAYMENTS IMBALANCES AND NEED FOR STRENGTHENING INTERNATIONAL FINANCIAL ARRANGEMENTS. USA+45 WOR+45 DELIB/GP DIPLOM INT/TRADE...CHARTS 20 CONGRESS OEEC. PAGE 134 F2651
BAL/PAY INT/ORG FINAN PROB/SOLV

B61
US GENERAL ACCOUNTING OFFICE,EXAMINATION OF ECONOMIC AND TECHNICAL ASSISTANCE PROGRAM FOR IRAN. IRAN USA+45 AGRI INDUS DIPLOM CONTROL COST 20. PAGE 136 F2681
FOR/AID ADMIN TEC/DEV ECO/UNDEV

B61
VEIT O.,GRUNDRISS DER WAHRUNGSPOLITIK. AFR FRANCE GERMANY USSR DIPLOM INT/TRADE...NAT/COMP 19/20 SILVER. PAGE 141 F2773
FINAN POLICY ECO/TAC CAP/ISM

S61
BARALL M.,"THE UNITED STATES GOVERNMENT RESPONDS." L/A+17C USA+45 SOCIETY NAT/G CREATE PLAN DIPLOM ECO/TAC ATTIT DRIVE RIGID/FLEX KNOWL SKILL WEALTH ...METH/CNCPT TIME/SEQ GEN/METH 20. PAGE 9 F0176
ECO/UNDEV ACT/RES FOR/AID

S61
GALBRAITH J.K.,"A POSITIVE APPROACH TO ECONOMIC AID." FUT USA+45 INTELL NAT/G CONSULT ACT/RES DIPLOM ECO/TAC EDU/PROP ATTIT KNOWL PWR WEALTH ...SOC STERTYP MID/EX METH/GP 20. PAGE 45 F0883
ECO/UNDEV ROUTINE FOR/AID

S61
GORDON L.,"ECONOMIC REGIONALISM RECONSIDERED." FUT USA+45 WOR+45 INDUS NAT/G TEC/DEV DIPLOM ROUTINE PERCEPT WEALTH...WELF/ST METH/CNCPT WORK 20. PAGE 49 F0957
ECO/DEV ATTIT CAP/ISM REGION

S61
LINDSAY F.A.,"PLANNING IN FOREIGN AFFAIRS: THE MISSING ELEMENT." FUT USA+45 ROUTINE SKILL...MGT TOT/POP 20. PAGE 80 F1572
ECO/DEV PLAN DIPLOM

S61
OCHENG D.,"ECONOMIC FORCES AND UGANDA'S FOREIGN POLICY." AFR UGANDA INT/TRADE TARIFFS INCOME SOVEREIGN WEALTH 20 EACM EEC TANGANYIKA. PAGE 100 F1961
ECO/TAC DIPLOM ECO/UNDEV INT/ORG

S61
VALLET R.,"IRAN: KEY TO THE MIDDLE EAST." COM IRAQ ISLAM KUWAIT LEBANON SAUDI/ARAB TURKEY ELITES
NAT/G ECO/UNDEV

SOCIETY INDUS PROC/MFG POL/PAR TOP/EX PLAN BAL/PWR DIPLOM ECO/TAC ALL/VALS...TREND FOR/TRADE CENTO 20. PAGE 140 F2760
IRAN

B62
ALEXANDROWICZ C.H.,WORLD ECONOMIC AGENCIES: LAW AND PRACTICE. WOR+45 DIST/IND FINAN LABOR CONSULT INT/TRADE TARIFFS REPRESENT HEALTH...JURID 20 UN GATT EEC OAS ECSC. PAGE 4 F0064
INT/LAW INT/ORG DIPLOM ADJUD

B62
DREIER J.C.,THE ALLIANCE FOR PROGRESS. L/A+17C USA+45 CULTURE ECO/DEV ECO/UNDEV NAT/G PLAN DIPLOM PWR 20 OAS ALL/PROG. PAGE 34 F0661
FOR/AID INT/ORG ECO/TAC POLICY

B62
ELLIOTT J.R.,THE APPEAL OF COMMUNISM IN THE UNDERDEVELOPED NATIONS. AFR USSR WOR+45 INT/ORG NAT/G DIPLOM DOMIN EDU/PROP ROUTINE ATTIT RIGID/FLEX ORD/FREE PWR WEALTH MARXISM...POLICY SOC METH/CNCPT MYTH TOT/POP METH/GP 20. PAGE 37 F0722
COM ECO/UNDEV

B62
FRIEDMANN W.,METHODS AND POLICIES OF PRINCIPAL DONOR COUNTRIES IN PUBLIC INTERNATIONAL DEVELOPMENT FINANCING: PRELIMINARY APPRAISAL. FRANCE GERMANY/W UK USA+45 USSR WOR+45 FINAN TEC/DEV CAP/ISM DIPLOM ECO/TAC ATTIT 20 EEC. PAGE 44 F0864
INT/ORG FOR/AID NAT/COMP ADMIN

B62
FRIEDRICH-EBERT-STIFTUNG,THE SOVIET BLOC AND DEVELOPING COUNTRIES. CHINA/COM COM GERMANY/E USSR WOR+45 ECO/UNDEV INT/ORG NAT/G TEC/DEV NEUTRAL PWR ...POLICY 20. PAGE 44 F0868
MARXISM DIPLOM ECO/TAC FOR/AID

B62
GOLDWIN R.A.,WHY FOREIGN AID? - TWO MESSAGES BY PRESIDENT KENNEDY AND ESSAYS. S/ASIA USA+45 ECO/UNDEV 20 KENNEDY/JF THIRD/WRLD. PAGE 48 F0942
DIPLOM FOR/AID POLICY

B62
HENDERSON W.O.,THE GENESIS OF THE COMMON MARKET. EUR+WWI FRANCE MOD/EUR UK SEA COM/IND EXTR/IND COLONIAL DISCRIM...TIME/SEQ CHARTS BIBLIOG 18/20 EEC TREATY. PAGE 58 F1149
ECO/DEV INT/TRADE DIPLOM

B62
HIGGANS B.,UNITED NATIONS AND U.S. FOREIGN ECONOMIC POLICY. FUT USA+45 WOR+45 ECO/DEV ECO/UNDEV NAT/G ECO/TAC WEALTH...TIME/SEQ TOT/POP UN 20. PAGE 59 F1168
INT/ORG ACT/RES FOR/AID DIPLOM

B62
KENT R.K.,FROM MADAGASCAR TO THE MALAGASY REPUBLIC. FRANCE MADAGASCAR DIPLOM NAT/LISM ORD/FREE...MGT 18/20. PAGE 70 F1379
COLONIAL SOVEREIGN REV POL/PAR

B62
KIRPICEVA I.K.,HANDBUCH DER RUSSISCHEN UND SOWJETISCHEN BIBLIOGRAPHIEN (5 VOLS.). USSR STRUCT ECO/DEV DIPLOM LEAD ATTIT 18/20. PAGE 71 F1400
BIBLIOG/A NAT/G MARXISM COM

B62
LIPPMANN W.,WESTERN UNITY AND THE COMMON MARKET. EUR+WWI FRANCE GERMANY/W UK USA+45 ECO/DEV AGRI FINAN MARKET INT/ORG NAT/G FOR/AID AGREE WEALTH 20 EEC. PAGE 80 F1575
DIPLOM INT/TRADE VOL/ASSN

B62
LUTZ F.A.,GELD UND WAHRUNG. AFR MARKET LABOR BUDGET 20 EUROPE. PAGE 82 F1610
ECO/TAC FINAN DIPLOM POLICY

B62
LUTZ F.A.,THE PROBLEM OF INTERNATIONAL ECONOMIC EQUILIBRIUM. FINAN PRODUC WEALTH 20 MONEY. PAGE 82 F1611
DIPLOM EQUILIB BAL/PAY PROB/SOLV

B62
MEYER F.V.,THE TERMS OF TRADE. WOR+45 AGRI MARKET PROC/MFG DIPLOM PRICE DEMAND PRODUC 20. PAGE 90 F1769
INT/TRADE BAL/PAY SIMUL EQUILIB

B62
MOUSSA P.,THE UNDERPRIVILEGED NATIONS. FINAN INT/ORG PLAN PROB/SOLV CAP/ISM GIVE TASK WEALTH ...POLICY SOC IND 20. PAGE 94 F1850
ECO/UNDEV NAT/G DIPLOM FOR/AID

B62
O'CONNOR H.,WORLD CRISES IN OIL (BMR). ISLAM L/A+17C INDUS LG/CO INT/TRADE 20. PAGE 100 F1956
EXTR/IND DIPLOM ECO/UNDEV SOCISM

B62
PAKISTAN MINISTRY OF FINANCE,FOREIGN ECONOMIC AID: A REVIEW OF FOREIGN ECONOMIC AID TO PAKISTAN. EUR+WWI PAKISTAN UK USA+45 USSR ECO/UNDEV INT/ORG DELIB/GP DIPLOM ECO/TAC...CHARTS CMN/WLTH CHINJAP. PAGE 103 F2016
FOR/AID RECEIVE WEALTH FINAN

B62
PERROUX F.,L'ECONOMIE DES JEUNES NATIONS. EUR+WWI SOUTH/AFR FINAN MARKET TEC/DEV CAP/ISM FOR/AID INT/TRADE 20. PAGE 105 F2065
INDUS ECO/UNDEV ECO/TAC DIPLOM

B62
RIMALOV V.V.,ECONOMIC COOPERATION BETWEEN USSR AND UNDERDEVELOPED COUNTRIES. USSR FINAN TEC/DEV INT/TRADE DOMIN EDU/PROP COLONIAL NAT/LISM DRIVE SOVEREIGN...AUD/VIS 20. PAGE 111 F2194
FOR/AID PLAN ECO/UNDEV DIPLOM

B62
ROBINSON M.A.,AN INTRODUCTION TO ECONOMIC REASONING. FINAN MARKET LABOR DIPLOM INT/TRADE BAL/PAY INCOME PRODUC WEALTH...POLICY MGT 20. PAGE 113 F2223
ECO/TAC METH/CNCPT NAT/G

B62
SCHMITT H.A.,THE PATH TO EUROPEAN UNITY. EUR+WWI USA+45 PLAN TEC/DEV DIPLOM FOR/AID CONFER...INT/LAW 20 EEC EURCOALSTL MARSHL/PLN UNIFICA. PAGE 117 F2300
INT/ORG INT/TRADE REGION ECO/DEV

B62
SELOSOEMARDJAN O.,SOCIAL CHANGES IN JOGJAKARTA. INDONESIA NETHERLAND ELITES STRATA STRUCT FAM POL/PAR CREATE DIPLOM INT/TRADE EDU/PROP ADMIN GOV/REL...SOC 20 JAVA CHINJAP. PAGE 119 F2352
ECO/UNDEV CULTURE REV COLONIAL

B62
SHERIF M.,INTERGROUP RELATIONS AND LEADERSHIP: APPROACHES AND RESEARCH IN INDUSTRIAL, ETHNIC, CULTURAL AND POLITICAL AREAS. CULTURE R+D LABOR DIPLOM GP/REL RACE/REL PERCEPT...PSY CONCPT. PAGE 121 F2377
LEAD REPRESENT PWR INGP/REL

B62
UNIVERSITY OF TENNESSEE,GOVERNMENT AND WORLD CRISIS. USA+45 FOR/AID ORD/FREE...ANTHOL 20 UN ALL/PROG. PAGE 133 F2622
ECO/DEV DIPLOM NAT/G INT/ORG

B62
URQUIDI C.W.,A STATEMENT OF THE LAWS OF BOLIVIA IN MATTERS AFFECTING BUSINESS (3RD ED. REV., ENLARGED). L/A+17C LAW FINAN FAM WORKER ACT/RES DIPLOM ADJUD ADMIN GP/REL 20 BOLIV OAS. PAGE 133 F2626
JURID INDUS NAT/G LEGIT

B62
URQUIDI V.L.,FREE TRADE AND ECONOMIC INTEGRATION IN LATIN AMERICA: THE EVOLUTION OF A COMMON MARKET POLICY. ECO/UNDEV MARKET DIPLOM BAL/PAY FEDERAL ...POLICY CHARTS 20 LAFTA. PAGE 133 F2627
INT/TRADE REGION INT/ORG L/A+17C

B62
US CONGRESS,LEGISLATIVE HISTORY OF UNITED STATES TAX CONVENTIONS(VOL. 1). USA+45 USA-45 DELIB/GP WEALTH...CHARTS 20 CONGRESS. PAGE 134 F2649
TAX LEGIS LAW DIPLOM

B62
US CONGRESS JOINT ECO COMM,FACTORS AFFECTING THE UNITED STATES BALANCE OF PAYMENTS. USA+45 DELIB/GP PLAN DIPLOM FOR/AID PRODUC WEALTH...CHARTS 20 CONGRESS OEEC. PAGE 134 F2653
BAL/PAY INT/TRADE ECO/TAC FINAN

B62
US CONGRESS JOINT ECO COMM,ECONOMIC DEVELOPMENTS IN SOUTH AMERICA. USA+45 SOCIETY FINAN NAT/G PROB/SOLV TEC/DEV INT/TRADE TAX EFFICIENCY PRODUC ATTIT ...POLICY 20 ALL/PROG CONGRESS SOUTH/AMER. PAGE 135 F2654
L/A+17C ECO/UNDEV FOR/AID DIPLOM

B62
US LIBRARY OF CONGRESS,A LIST OF AMERICAN DOCTORAL DISSERTATIONS ON AFRICA. SOCIETY SECT DIPLOM EDU/PROP ADMIN...GEOG 19/20. PAGE 138 F2717
BIBLIOG AFR ACADEM CULTURE

B62
VANEK J.,INTERNATIONAL TRADE - THEORY AND ECONOMIC POLICY. LABOR BAL/PWR ECO/TAC TARIFFS PRICE BAL/PAY COST DEMAND 20. PAGE 140 F2765
INT/TRADE DIPLOM BARGAIN MARKET

B62
VIET J.,INTERNATIONAL COOPERATION AND PROGRAMMES OF ECONOMIC AND SOCIAL DEVELOPMENT. TEC/DEV FOR/AID DOMIN COLONIAL PEACE WEALTH 20 UNESCO. PAGE 141 F2784
BIBLIOG/A INT/ORG DIPLOM ECO/UNDEV

B62
ZOOK P.D.,FOREIGN TRADE AND HUMAN CAPITAL. L/A+17C USA+45 FINAN DIPLOM ECO/TAC PRODUC...POLICY 20. PAGE 151 F2970
INT/TRADE ECO/UNDEV FOR/AID BAL/PAY

L62
"HIGHER EDUCATION AND ECONOMIC AND SOCIAL DEVELOPMENT IN LATIN AMERICA: A BIBLIOGRAPHY." L/A+17C SOCIETY ECO/UNDEV PROF/ORG DIPLOM CONFER ...SOC 20. PAGE 1 F0016
BIBLIOG/A ACADEM INTELL EDU/PROP

S62
PYE L.W.,"THE POLITICAL IMPULSES AND FANTASIES BEHIND FOREIGN AID." FUT USA+45 ECO/UNDEV DIPLOM ECO/TAC ROUTINE DRIVE KNOWL...SOC METH/CNCPT NEW/IDEA TREND HYPO/EXP STERTYP GEN/METH 20. PAGE 108 F2133
ACT/RES ATTIT FOR/AID

B63
AHN L.A.,FUNFZIG JAHRE ZWISCHEN INFLATION UND DEFLATION. AFR GERMANY DIPLOM PRICE...CONCPT 20. PAGE 3 F0053
FINAN CAP/ISM NAT/COMP ECO/TAC

B63
BANERJI A.K.,INDIA'S BALANCE OF PAYMENTS. INDIA
INT/TRADE

NAT/G PRICE BAL/PAY COST INCOME 20. PAGE 9 F0171 DIPLOM FINAN BUDGET

B63
BELOFF M.,THE UNITED STATES AND THE UNITY OF EUROPE. EUR+WWI UK USA+45 WOR+45 VOL/ASSN DIPLOM REGION ATTIT PWR...CONCPT EEC OEEC 20 NATO. PAGE 13 F0239 ECO/DEV INT/ORG

B63
CENTRO PARA EL DESARROLLO,LA ALIANZA PARA EL PROGRESO Y EL DESARROLLO SOCIAL DE AMERICA LATINA. L/A+17C INT/ORG DIPLOM ECO/TAC INT/TRADE ATTIT 20 ALL/PROG. PAGE 22 F0435 ECO/UNDEV FOR/AID PLAN REGION

B63
CERAMI C.A.,ALLIANCE BORN OF DANGER. EUR+WWI USA+45 USSR ECO/DEV INDUS VOL/ASSN ECO/TAC REGION ATTIT MARXISM ATLAN/ALL 20 NATO EEC. PAGE 22 F0437 DIPLOM INT/ORG NAT/G POLICY

B63
CONF ON FUTURE OF COMMONWEALTH,THE FUTURE OF THE COMMONWEALTH. AFR UK ECO/UNDEV AGRI EDU/PROP ADMIN SOC/INTEG 20. PAGE 27 F0522 DIPLOM RACE/REL ORD/FREE TEC/DEV

B63
DELL S.,TRADE BLOCS AND COMMON MARKETS. COM WOR+45 ECO/DEV ECO/UNDEV GP/COMP. PAGE 32 F0615 DIPLOM ECO/TAC INT/TRADE FEDERAL

B63
ELLENDER A.J.,A REPORT ON UNITED STATES FOREIGN OPERATIONS IN AFRICA. SOUTH/AFR USA+45 STRATA EXTR/IND FORCES RACE/REL ISOLAT SOVEREIGN...CHARTS 20 NEGRO. PAGE 37 F0721 FOR/AID DIPLOM WEALTH ECO/UNDEV

B63
ENKE S.,ECONOMICS FOR DEVELOPMENT. AGRI TEC/DEV CAP/ISM DIPLOM ECO/TAC TAX ATTIT DRIVE HABITAT WEALTH...GOV/COMP BIBLIOG 20. PAGE 38 F0737 ECO/UNDEV PHIL/SCI CON/ANAL

B63
ERHARD L.,THE ECONOMICS OF SUCCESS. GERMANY/W WOR+45 LABOR CHIEF TAX REGION COST DEMAND ANTHOL. PAGE 38 F0745 ECO/DEV INT/TRADE PLAN DIPLOM

B63
FLORES E.,LAND REFORM AND THE ALLIANCE FOR PROGRESS (PAMPHLET). L/A+17C USA+45 STRUCT ECO/UNDEV NAT/G WORKER CREATE PLAN ECO/TAC COERCE REV 20 ALL/PROG. PAGE 42 F0815 AGRI INT/ORG DIPLOM POLICY

B63
GANGULI B.N.,ECONOMIC CONSEQUENCES OF DISARMAMENT. EUR+WWI ECO/DEV ECO/UNDEV FORCES ACT/RES BUDGET DIPLOM INT/TRADE...STAT CHARTS NAT/COMP. PAGE 46 F0896 ECOMETRIC ARMS/CONT COST HYPO/EXP

B63
GODWIN F.W.,THE HIDDEN FORCE. PUERT/RICO WOR+45 STRUCT VOL/ASSN PROB/SOLV DIPLOM CONFER...BIBLIOG 20 PEACE/CORP. PAGE 48 F0931 ECO/UNDEV WORKER SKILL ECO/TAC

B63
GORDON L.,A NEW DEAL FOR LATIN AMERICA. L/A+17C USA+45 CULTURE NAT/G TEC/DEV DIPLOM FOR/AID REGION TASK...POLICY 20 ALL/PROG DEPT/STATE. PAGE 49 F0958 ECO/UNDEV ECO/TAC INT/ORG PLAN

B63
HAHN L.A.,DIE AMERIKANISCHE KONJUNKTURPOLITIK DER DOLLAR UND DIE DMARK. GERMANY/W USA+45 DIPLOM PRICE BAL/PAY COST...POLICY MONEY. PAGE 53 F1038 FINAN BUDGET ECO/TAC LABOR

B63
HYDE D.,THE PEACEFUL ASSAULT. COM UAR USSR ECO/DEV ECO/UNDEV NAT/G POL/PAR CAP/ISM PWR 20. PAGE 64 F1256 MARXISM CONTROL ECO/TAC DIPLOM

B63
INTERNATIONAL BANK RECONST DEV,THE WORLD BANK GROUP IN ASIA. ASIA S/ASIA INDUS TEC/DEV ECO/TAC...RECORD 20 IBRD WORLD/BANK. PAGE 65 F1273 INT/ORG DIPLOM ECO/UNDEV FINAN

B63
LAFEBER W.,THE NEW EMPIRE: AN INTERPRETATION OF AMERICAN EXPANSION, 1860-1898. USA-45 CONSTN NAT/LISM SOVEREIGN...TREND BIBLIOG 19/20. PAGE 74 F1457 INDUS NAT/G DIPLOM CAP/ISM

B63
LANGE O.,ECONOMIC DEVELOPMENT, PLANNING, AND INTERNATIONAL COOPERATION. UAR WOR+45 FINAN CAP/ISM PERS/REL 20. PAGE 75 F1476 ECO/UNDEV DIPLOM INT/TRADE PLAN

B63
LARY M.B.,PROBLEMS OF THE UNITED STATES AS WORLD TRADER AND BANKER. USA+45 NAT/G PLAN DIPLOM FOR/AID ...TREND CHARTS. PAGE 76 F1482 ECO/DEV FINAN BAL/PAY INT/TRADE

B63
LICHTHEIM G.,THE NEW EUROPE: TODAY AND TOMORROW. EUR+WWI FINAN 20 EEC EUROPE/W. PAGE 80 F1560 DIPLOM ECO/DEV INT/ORG

INT/TRADE

B63
LUTZ F.A.,DAS PROBLEM DES INTERNATIONALEN WIRTSCHAFTLICHEN GLEICHGEWICHTS. DIPLOM INT/TRADE COST INCOME 20. PAGE 82 F1612 FINAN CAP/ISM ECO/TAC PRODUC

B63
MANGER W.,THE ALLIANCE FOR PROGRESS: A CRITICAL APPRAISAL. FUT L/A+17C USA+45 CULTURE ECO/UNDEV ACADEM NAT/G SCHOOL PLAN FOR/AID...POLICY OAS ALL/PROG. PAGE 84 F1651 DIPLOM INT/ORG ECO/TAC REGION

B63
MARITANO N.,AN ALLIANCE FOR PROGRESS. FUT L/A+17C USA+45 CULTURE ECO/UNDEV NAT/G PLAN CONTROL ...POLICY ALL/PROG. PAGE 85 F1669 DIPLOM INT/ORG ECO/TAC FOR/AID

B63
MENEZES A.J.,SUBDESENVOLVIMENTO E POLITICA INTERNACIONAL. BRAZIL WOR+45 PLAN CONTROL LEAD NAT/LISM ORD/FREE 20 THIRD/WRLD. PAGE 90 F1759 ECO/UNDEV DIPLOM POLICY BAL/PWR

B63
MYRDAL G.,CHALLENGE TO AFFLUENCE. USA+45 WOR+45 FINAN INT/ORG NAT/G PLAN ECO/TAC INT/TRADE BAL/PAY ORD/FREE 20 EUROPE/W. PAGE 96 F1882 ECO/DEV WEALTH DIPLOM PRODUC

B63
OECD,FOOD AID: ITS ROLE IN ECONOMIC DEVELOPMENT. FINAN NAT/G PLAN DIPLOM GIVE TASK WEALTH ...METH/COMP METH 20. PAGE 100 F1966 ECO/UNDEV FOR/AID INT/ORG POLICY

B63
PATTON R.,THE DEVELOPMENT OF THE AMERICAN ECONOMY: REVISED. USA+45 USA-45 INDUS LABOR NAT/G CAP/ISM DIPLOM INT/TRADE WAR WEALTH 16/20. PAGE 104 F2038 ECO/TAC ECO/DEV DEMAND

B63
RAO V.K.R.,FOREIGN AID AND INDIA'S ECONOMIC DEVELOPMENT. INDIA INT/ORG PROB/SOLV TEC/DEV ECO/TAC CONTROL WEALTH...TREND 20. PAGE 109 F2148 FOR/AID ECO/UNDEV RECEIVE DIPLOM

B63
ROBBINS L.,POLITICS AND ECONOMICS. ECO/DEV FINAN BUDGET DIPLOM BAL/PAY ORD/FREE 20. PAGE 112 F2204 NAT/G ATTIT

B63
THEOBALD R.,FREE MEN AND FREE MARKETS. USA+45 USA-45 ECO/DEV NAT/G TEC/DEV DIPLOM INT/TRADE INCOME ORD/FREE WEALTH...TREND 19/20 KEYNES/JM. PAGE 130 F2556 CONCPT ECO/TAC CAP/ISM MARKET

B63
US CONGRESS JOINT ECO COMM,OUTLOOK FOR UNITED STATES BALANCE OF PAYMENTS. AFR USA+45 ECO/DEV NAT/G FORCES DIPLOM FOR/AID COST EFFICIENCY ...POLICY CONGRESS EEC. PAGE 135 F2657 BAL/PAY FINAN INT/TRADE PROB/SOLV

B63
US ECON SURVEY TEAM INDONESIA,INDONESIA - PERSPECTIVE AND PROPOSALS FOR UNITED STATES ECONOMIC AID. INDONESIA AGRI MARKET TEC/DEV DIPLOM INT/TRADE EDU/PROP 20. PAGE 136 F2678 FOR/AID ECO/UNDEV PLAN INDUS

B63
US GOVERNMENT,REPORT TO INTER-AMERICAN ECONOMIC AND SOCIAL COUNCIL AT SECOND ANNUAL MEETING. L/A+17C USA+45 VOL/ASSN TEC/DEV DIPLOM TAX EATING EFFICIENCY HEALTH...STAT CHARTS 20 AID. PAGE 136 F2682 ECO/TAC FOR/AID FINAN PLAN

B63
US HOUSE COMM BANKING-CURR,RECENT CHANGES IN MONETARY POLICY AND BALANCE OF PAYMENTS PROBLEMS. USA+45 DELIB/GP PLAN DIPLOM...CHARTS 20 CONGRESS. PAGE 136 F2688 BAL/PAY FINAN ECO/TAC POLICY

B63
US SENATE COMM GOVT OPERATIONS,REPORT OF A STUDY OF US FOREIGN AID IN TEN MIDDLE EASTERN AND AFRICAN COUNTRIES. AFR ISLAM USA+45 FORCES PLAN BUDGET DIPLOM TAX DETER WEALTH...STAT CHARTS 20 CONGRESS AID MID/EAST. PAGE 138 F2728 FOR/AID EFFICIENCY ECO/TAC FINAN

L63
OLSON M. JR.,"RAPID ECONOMIC GROWTH AS A DESTABILIZING FORCE." WOR+45 WOR-45 STRATA ECO/UNDEV FAM KIN CREATE TEC/DEV DIPLOM PEACE ATTIT PERSON RIGID/FLEX PWR RESPECT WEALTH...SOC 20. PAGE 101 F1989 SOCIETY FOR/AID

L63
PADELFORD N.J.,"FINANCIAL CRISIS AND THE UNITED NATIONS." FUT USSR WOR+45 LAW CONSTN FINAN INT/ORG DELIB/GP FORCES PLAN BUDGET DIPLOM COST WEALTH ...STAT CHARTS UN CONGO 20. PAGE 102 F2012 CREATE ECO/TAC

S63
CLEMHOUT S.,"PRODUCTION FUNCTION ANALYSIS APPLIED TO THE LEONTIEF SCARCE-FACTOR PARADOX OF INTERNATIONAL TRADE." EUR+WWI USA+45 DIST/IND NAT/G PLAN TEC/DEV DIPLOM PWR WEALTH...MGT METH/CNCPT CONT/OBS CON/ANAL CHARTS SIMUL GEN/LAWS FOR/TRADE 20. PAGE 25 F0490 ECO/DEV ECO/TAC

S63
GANDOLFI A.,"LES ACCORDS DE COOPERATION EN MATIERE DE POLITIQUE ETRANGERE ENTRE LA FRANCE ET LES VOL/ASSN ECO/UNDEV

NOUVEAUX ETATS AFRICAINS ET." AFR ISLAM MADAGASCAR WOR+45 ECO/DEV INT/ORG NAT/G DELIB/GP ECO/TAC ALL/VALS...CON/ANAL 20. PAGE 46 F0894 DIPLOM FRANCE

POPPINO R.E.,"IMBALANCE IN BRAZIL." L/A+17C NAT/G TOP/EX PLAN DIPLOM LEGIT DRIVE WEALTH...CON/ANAL FOR/TRADE LAFTA 20. PAGE 107 F2105 S63 POL/PAR ECO/TAC BRAZIL

TENNYSON L.B.,"THE USA IN ATLANTIC COMMUNITY." EUR+WWI FRANCE UK USA+45 ECO/UNDEV VOL/ASSN DELIB/GP TOP/EX DIPLOM DOMIN PWR...POLICY CONCPT TREND GEN/LAWS EEC 20. PAGE 129 F2545 S63 ATTIT ECO/TAC BAL/PWR

WOLFERS A.,"INTEGRATION IN THE WEST: THE CONFLICT OF PERSPECTIVES." AFR EUR+WWI USA+45 ECO/DEV INT/ORG DELIB/GP CREATE TEC/DEV DIPLOM ATTIT PWR ...CONCPT HIST/WRIT TREND GEN/LAWS EEC 20. PAGE 148 F2918 S63 RIGID/FLEX ECO/TAC

LEDERER W.,THE BALANCE ON FOREIGN TRANSACTIONS: PROBLEMS OF DEFINITION AND MEASUREMENT (PAMPHLET). USA+45 BUDGET DIPLOM ECO/TAC PRICE GOV/REL...POLICY STAT NAT/COMP METH 20. PAGE 77 F1502 N63 FINAN BAL/PAY INT/TRADE ECO/DEV

US COMM STRENG SEC FREE WORLD,THE SCOPE AND DISTRIBUTION OF UNITED STATES MILITARY AND ECONOMIC ASSISTANCE PROGRAMS (PAMPHLET). USA+45 PLAN BAL/PWR BUDGET DIPLOM CONTROL CIVMIL/REL ATTIT. PAGE 134 F2648 N63 DELIB/GP POLICY FOR/AID ORD/FREE

INTERNATIONAL MONETARY ARRANGEMENTS: THE PROBLEM OF CHOICE. PLAN PROB/SOLV INT/TRADE ADJUST COST EQUILIB 20. PAGE 1 F0020 B64 POLICY DIPLOM FINAN ECO/DEV

AUBREY H.G.,THE DOLLAR IN WORLD AFFAIRS. FUT USA+45 WOR+45 ECO/DEV CAP/ISM INT/TRADE BAL/PAY...CHARTS 20. PAGE 7 F0140 B64 FINAN ECO/TAC DIPLOM POLICY

BLACKSTOCK P.W.,THE STRATEGY OF SUBVERSION. USA+45 FORCES EDU/PROP ADMIN COERCE GOV/REL...DECISION MGT 20 DEPT/DEFEN CIA DEPT/STATE. PAGE 15 F0292 B64 ORD/FREE DIPLOM CONTROL

BROWN W.M.,THE EXTERNAL LIQUIDITY OF AN ADVANCED COUNTRY. CANADA FRANCE GERMANY/W SWEDEN UK USA+45 ECO/DEV DIPLOM PRICE...CONCPT STAT NAT/COMP 20. PAGE 20 F0376 B64 FINAN INT/TRADE COST INCOME

CALDER R.,TWO-WAY PASSAGE. INT/ORG TEC/DEV WAR PERSON ORD/FREE 20. PAGE 21 F0400 B64 FOR/AID ECO/UNDEV ECO/TAC DIPLOM

CASEY R.G.,THE FUTURE OF THE COMMONWEALTH. INDIA PAKISTAN UK ECO/UNDEV INT/ORG TEC/DEV COLONIAL SUPEGO 20 EEC AUSTRAL. PAGE 22 F0425 B64 DIPLOM SOVEREIGN NAT/LISM FOR/AID

COLUMBIA U SCHOOL OF LAW,PUBLIC INTERNATIONAL DEVELOPMENT FINANCING IN INDIA. GERMANY/W INDIA UK USA+45 INDUS PLAN TEC/DEV DIPLOM ECO/TAC GIVE ADMIN UTIL ATTIT 20. PAGE 26 F0512 B64 ECO/UNDEV FINAN FOR/AID INT/ORG

COMPOS R.O.,A MOEDA, O GOVERNO E O TEMPO. AFR BRAZIL WOR+45 FINAN TEC/DEV FOR/AID REGION DEMAND ...ANTHOL 20. PAGE 27 F0520 B64 ECO/UNDEV PLAN DIPLOM INT/TRADE

DANIELS R.V.,RUSSIA. RUSSIA USSR STRUCT NAT/LISM TOTALISM ORD/FREE WEALTH...POLICY DECISION TREND. PAGE 30 F0579 B64 MARXISM REV ECO/DEV DIPLOM

ECONOMIDES C.P.,LE POUVOIR DE DECISION DES ORGANISATIONS INTERNATIONALES EUROPEENNES. DIPLOM DOMIN INGP/REL EFFICIENCY...INT/LAW JURID 20 NATO OEEC EEC COUNCL/EUR EURATOM. PAGE 36 F0698 B64 INT/ORG PWR DECISION GP/COMP

EDWARDS E.O.,THE NATION'S ECONOMIC OBJECTIVES. INDUS WORKER BUDGET DIPLOM CONTROL ORD/FREE ...POLICY SOC METH/CNCPT ANTHOL 20. PAGE 36 F0704 B64 NAT/G ECO/TAC

EINZIG P.,MONETARY POLICY: ENDS AND MEANS. AFR UK INDUS WORKER PLAN DIPLOM PRICE BAL/PAY COST WEALTH ...DECISION TIME/SEQ 20. PAGE 37 F0715 B64 FINAN POLICY ECO/TAC BUDGET

ESTHUS R.A.,FROM ENMITY TO ALLIANCE: US AUSTRALIAN RELATIONS. S/ASIA DIST/IND VOL/ASSN FORCES ATTIT 20 AUSTRAL TREATY CMN/WLTH. PAGE 39 F0751 B64 DIPLOM WAR INT/TRADE FOR/AID

FATOUROS A.A.,CANADA'S OVERSEAS AID. CANADA WOR+45 ECO/DEV FINAN NAT/G BUDGET ECO/TAC CONFER ADMIN 20. PAGE 39 F0768 B64 FOR/AID DIPLOM ECO/UNDEV

POLICY

FEIS H.,FOREIGN AID AND FOREIGN POLICY. USA+45 WOR+45 NAT/G VOL/ASSN ACT/RES TEC/DEV ATTIT HEALTH WEALTH...SOC GEN/LAWS 20. PAGE 40 F0775 B64 ECO/UNDEV ECO/TAC FOR/AID DIPLOM

FREYMOND J.,WESTERN EUROPE SINCE THE WAR. COM EUR+WWI USA+45 DIPLOM...BIBLIOG 20 NATO UN EEC. PAGE 44 F0854 B64 INT/ORG POLICY ECO/DEV ECO/TAC

GARDNER L.C.,ECONOMIC ASPECTS OF NEW DEAL DIPLOMACY. USA-45 WOR-45 LAW ECO/DEV INT/ORG NAT/G VOL/ASSN LEGIS TOP/EX EDU/PROP ORD/FREE PWR WEALTH ...POLICY TIME/SEQ VAL/FREE 20 ROOSEVLT/F. PAGE 46 F0901 B64 ECO/TAC DIPLOM

GRIFFITH W.E.,COMMUNISM IN EUROPE (2 VOLS.). CZECHOSLVK USSR WOR+45 WOR-45 YUGOSLAVIA INGP/REL MARXISM SOCISM...ANTHOL 20 EUROPE/E. PAGE 51 F1000 B64 COM POL/PAR DIPLOM GOV/COMP

HANSEN B.,INTERNATIONAL LIQUIDITY. USA+45 INT/ORG ECO/TAC PRICE CONTROL WEALTH...POLICY 20. PAGE 54 F1068 B64 BAL/PAY INT/TRADE DIPLOM FINAN

HAZLEWOOD A.,THE ECONOMICS OF DEVELOPMENT: AN ANNOTATED LIST OF BOOKS AND ARTICLES PUBLISHED 1958-1962. AGRI FINAN INDUS LABOR NAT/G DIPLOM INT/TRADE INCOME...MGT 20. PAGE 58 F1130 B64 BIBLIOG/A ECO/UNDEV TEC/DEV

INTERNATIONAL LABOUR OFFICE,EMPLOYMENT AND ECONOMIC GROWTH. ECO/DEV ECO/UNDEV NAT/G PLAN DIPLOM INT/TRADE CONTROL INCOME PRODUC WEALTH...STAT NAT/COMP 20 ILO. PAGE 65 F1279 B64 WORKER METH/COMP ECO/TAC OPTIMAL

INTL INF CTR LOCAL CREDIT,GOVERNMENT MEASURES FOR THE PROMOTION OF REGIONAL ECONOMIC DEVELOPMENT. WOR+45 ECO/UNDEV FINAN INT/ORG DIPLOM ORD/FREE ...POLICY GEOG 20. PAGE 65 F1285 B64 FOR/AID PLAN ECO/TAC REGION

KOHNSTAMM M.,THE EUROPEAN COMMUNITY AND ITS ROLE IN THE WORLD. FUT MOD/EUR UK USA+45 ECO/DEV 20. PAGE 72 F1418 B64 INT/ORG NAT/G REGION DIPLOM

KRAUSE L.B.,THE COMMON MARKET: PROGRESS AND CONTROVERSY. EUR+WWI UK ECO/DEV REGION...ANTHOL NATO EEC. PAGE 73 F1433 B64 DIPLOM MARKET INT/TRADE INT/ORG

LISKA G.,EUROPE ASCENDANT. EUR+WWI ECO/DEV FORCES INT/TRADE MARXISM 20 EEC. PAGE 81 F1579 B64 DIPLOM BAL/PWR TARIFFS CENTRAL

LITTLE I.M.D.,AID TO AFRICA. AFR UK TEC/DEV DIPLOM ECO/TAC INCOME WEALTH 20. PAGE 81 F1583 B64 FOR/AID ECO/UNDEV ADMIN POLICY

LITVAK I.A.,MARKETING: CANADA. CANADA STRATA PROC/MFG LEGIS TEC/DEV DIPLOM INT/TRADE PRICE AUTOMAT ATTIT WEALTH...ANTHOL 20. PAGE 81 F1587 B64 ECO/TAC MARKET ECO/DEV EFFICIENCY

LUTHULI A.,AFRICA'S FREEDOM. KIN LABOR POL/PAR SCHOOL DIPLOM NEUTRAL REGION REV NAT/LISM PWR WEALTH SOCISM SOC/INTEG 20. PAGE 82 F1608 B64 AFR ECO/UNDEV COLONIAL

MAGALHAES S.,PRATICA DA EMANCIPACAO NACIONAL. L/A+17C INDUS PLAN ECO/TAC CONTROL NAT/LISM ORD/FREE. PAGE 84 F1640 B64 BAL/PAY ECO/UNDEV DIPLOM WEALTH

MASON E.S.,FOREIGN AID AND FOREIGN POLICY. USA+45 AGRI INDUS NAT/G EX/STRUC ACT/RES RIGID/FLEX ALL/VALS...POLICY GEN/LAWS MARSHL/PLN ALL/PROG CONGRESS 20. PAGE 87 F1699 B64 ECO/UNDEV ECO/TAC FOR/AID DIPLOM

MC GOVERN G.S.,WAR AGAINST WANT. USA+45 AGRI DIPLOM INT/TRADE GIVE RECEIVE DEMAND HEALTH 20 KENNEDY/JF FOOD/PEACE. PAGE 87 F1714 B64 FOR/AID ECO/DEV POLICY EATING

NEHEMKIS P.,LATIN AMERICA: MYTH AND REALITY. INDUS INT/ORG PROB/SOLV CAP/ISM DIPLOM REV...SOC MUNICH 20. PAGE 97 F1907 B64 REGION MYTH L/A+17C ECO/UNDEV

NEWCOMER H.A.,INTERNATIONAL AIDS TO OVERSEAS INVESTMENTS AND TRADE. ECO/UNDEV TARIFFS PROFIT ...BIBLIOG 20 GATT UN. PAGE 98 F1921 B64 INT/TRADE FINAN DIPLOM FOR/AID

B64
PENNOCK J.R.,SELF-GOVERNMENT IN MODERNIZING NATIONS. AFR COM USA+45 ECO/DEV POL/PAR PROB/SOLV DIPLOM ECO/TAC COLONIAL REV POPULISM SOCISM 20. PAGE 105 F2058
ECO/UNDEV POLICY SOVEREIGN NAT/G

B64
PIERSON J.H.,INSURING FULL EMPLOYMENT. USA+45 LABOR DIPLOM ECO/TAC PAY BAL/PAY 20. PAGE 106 F2084
ECO/DEV INT/TRADE POLICY WORKER

B64
POWELSON J.P.,LATIN AMERICA: TODAY'S ECONOMIC AND SOCIAL REVOLUTION. L/A+17C INTELL SOCIETY STRUCT AGRI INDUS NAT/G DIPLOM ECO/TAC REV...POLICY 20. PAGE 107 F2110
ECO/UNDEV WEALTH ADJUST PLAN

B64
RAISON T.,WHY CONSERVATIVE? UK FORCES DIPLOM ECO/TAC GIVE EDU/PROP ORD/FREE WEALTH LAISSEZ ...GOV/COMP 20 TORY/PARTY CONSRV/PAR. PAGE 109 F2137
PLURISM CONSERVE POL/PAR NAT/G

B64
RANIS G.,THE UNITED STATES AND THE DEVELOPING ECONOMIES. COM USA+45 AGRI FINAN TEC/DEV CAP/ISM ECO/TAC INT/TRADE...POLICY METH/COMP ANTHOL 20 AID. PAGE 109 F2145
ECO/UNDEV DIPLOM FOR/AID

B64
REUSS H.S.,THE CRITICAL DECADE - AN ECONOMIC POLICY FOR AMERICA AND THE FREE WORLD. AFR USA+45 FINAN POL/PAR WORKER PLAN DIPLOM ECO/TAC TARIFFS BAL/PAY ...POLICY 20 CONGRESS. PAGE 111 F2181
FOR/AID INT/TRADE LABOR LEGIS

B64
SAKAI R.K.,STUDIES ON ASIA, 1964. ASIA CHINA/COM ISRAEL MALAYSIA S/ASIA USA+45 USSR ECO/UNDEV FAM POL/PAR SECT CONSULT NAT/LISM...POLICY SOC 20 CHINJAP. PAGE 115 F2272
PWR DIPLOM

B64
SHANNON I.,INTERNATIONAL LIQUIDITY. AFR FUT USA+45 WOR+45 ECO/TAC PRICE DEMAND WEALTH...CONCPT 20. PAGE 120 F2367
FINAN DIPLOM BAL/PAY ECO/DEV

B64
TONG T.,UNITED STATES DIPLOMACY IN CHINA, 1844-1860. ASIA USA-45 ECO/UNDEV ECO/TAC COERCE GP/REL...INT/LAW 19 TREATY. PAGE 131 F2581
DIPLOM INT/TRADE COLONIAL

B64
URQUIDI V.L.,THE CHALLENGE OF DEVELOPMENT IN LATIN AMERICA. L/A+17C FINAN INT/ORG TEC/DEV DIPLOM INT/TRADE PRICE REGION PRODUC...CHARTS 20 ALL/PROG. PAGE 133 F2628
ECO/UNDEV ECO/TAC NAT/G TREND

B64
US HOUSE COMM BANKING-CURR,INTERNATIONAL DEVELOPMENT ASSOCIATION ACT AMENDMENT. CHINA/COM USA+45 USSR FINAN FORCES LEGIS DIPLOM CONFER EFFICIENCY...CHARTS GOV/COMP 20 PRESIDENT CONGRESS INTL/DEV. PAGE 136 F2689
BAL/PAY FOR/AID RECORD ECO/TAC

B64
US SENATE COMM ON FOREIGN REL,HEARING ON BILLS RELATING TO FOREIGN ASSISTANCE. USA+45 WOR+45 ECO/UNDEV FINAN INDUS 20 UN CONGRESS. PAGE 139 F2733
FOR/AID DIPLOM TEC/DEV INT/ORG

B64
WITHERS W.,THE ECONOMIC CRISIS IN LATIN AMERICA. BRAZIL CHILE STRATA AGRI DIPLOM FOR/AID PWR SOCISM ...POLICY 20 MEXIC/AMER ARGEN ALL/PROG. PAGE 148 F2914
L/A+17C ECO/UNDEV CAP/ISM ALL/IDEOS

B64
ZEBOT C.A.,THE ECONOMICS OF COMPETITIVE COEXISTENCE. CHINA/COM USSR WOR+45 FINAN MARKET FOR/AID PRICE DEMAND EQUILIB WEALTH ALL/IDEOS 20. PAGE 150 F2961
TEC/DEV DIPLOM METH/COMP

L64
KOLODZIEJ E.A.,"RATIONAL CONSENT AND DEFENSE BUDGETS: THE ROLE OF CONGRESS, 1945-1962." LEGIS DIPLOM CONTROL PARL/PROC 20 CONGRESS. PAGE 72 F1423
DECISION PLAN CIVMIL/REL BUDGET

S64
FINLEY D.D.,"A POLITICAL PERSPECTIVE OF ECONOMIC RELATIONS IN THE COMMUNIST CAMP." COM USSR FACE/GP NAT/G ACT/RES PLAN DOMIN COERCE ATTIT ORD/FREE WEALTH...TIME/SEQ 20. PAGE 41 F0800
VOL/ASSN ECO/TAC DIPLOM REGION

S64
HORECKY P.L.,"LIBRARY OF CONGRESS PUBLICATIONS IN AID OF USSR AND EAST EUROPEAN RESEARCH." BULGARIA CZECHOSLVK POLAND USSR YUGOSLAVIA NAT/G POL/PAR DIPLOM ADMIN GOV/REL...CLASSIF 20. PAGE 62 F1214
BIBLIOG/A COM MARXISM

S64
PADELFORD N.J.,"THE ORGANIZATION OF AFRICAN UNITY." ECO/UNDEV INT/ORG PLAN BAL/PWR DIPLOM ECO/TAC NAT/LISM ORD/FREE PWR WEALTH...CONCPT TREND STERTYP TERR/GP VAL/FREE 20. PAGE 102 F2013
AFR VOL/ASSN REGION

S64
ROTHCHILD D.,"EAST AFRICAN FEDERATION." AFR TANZANIA UGANDA INDUS REGION 20. PAGE 114 F2249
INT/ORG DIPLOM ECO/UNDEV ECO/TAC

B65
ANALYSIS AND ASSESSMENT OF THE ECONOMIC EFFECTS: PUBLIC LAW 480 TITLE I PROGRAM TURKEY. INDIA TURKEY USA+45 AGRI NAT/G PLAN BUDGET DIPLOM COST EFFICIENCY...CHARTS 20. PAGE 1 F0021
ECO/TAC FOR/AID FINAN ECO/UNDEV

B65
PEACE RESEARCH ABSTRACTS. FUT WOR+45 R+D INT/ORG NAT/G PLAN TEC/DEV BAL/PWR DIPLOM FOR/AID NUC/PWR HEALTH. PAGE 1 F0022
BIBLIOG/A PEACE ARMS/CONT WAR

B65
BALDWIN D.A.,SOFT LOANS AND AMERICAN FOREIGN POLICY: 1943-1962 (THESIS). USA+45 WOR+45 FINAN NAT/G FOR/AID BAL/PAY ATTIT...POLICY METH/COMP 20 UN CONGRESS. PAGE 9 F0161
DIPLOM ECO/TAC ECO/UNDEV

B65
BEAUFRE A.,AN INTRODUCTION TO STRATEGY, WITH PARTICULAR REFERENCE TO PROBLEMS OF DEFENSE, POLITICS, ECONOMICS IN THE NUCLEAR AGE. WOR+45 FORCES DIPLOM DETER CIVMIL/REL GP/REL...NEW/IDEA IDEA/COMP 20. PAGE 12 F0226
PLAN NUC/PWR WEAPON DECISION

B65
BROOKINGS INSTITUTION,BROOKINGS PAPERS ON PUBLIC POLICY. USA+45 ECO/UNDEV LEGIS CAP/ISM ECO/TAC TAX EDU/PROP CONTROL APPORT 20. PAGE 19 F0363
DIPLOM FOR/AID POLICY FINAN

B65
CAMERON W.J.,NEW ZEALAND. NEW/ZEALND S/ASIA DIPLOM INT/TRADE WRITING COLONIAL PARL/PROC...GEOG CMN/WLTH. PAGE 21 F0402
SOCIETY GP/REL STRUCT

B65
CAMPBELL J.C.,AMERICAN POLICY TOWARDS COMMUNIST EASTERN EUROPE* THE CHOICES AHEAD. AFR USA+45 ECO/DEV BAL/PWR MARXISM TREND. PAGE 21 F0406
POLAND YUGOSLAVIA DIPLOM COM

B65
CASSELL F.,GOLD OR CREDIT? THE ECONOMICS AND POLITICS OF INTERNATIONAL MONEY. AFR WOR+45 PLAN PROB/SOLV BAL/PAY SOVEREIGN WEALTH 20 OEEC. PAGE 22 F0428
FINAN INT/ORG DIPLOM ECO/TAC

B65
CHANDRASEKHAR S.,AMERICAN AID AND INDIA'S ECONOMIC DEVELOPMENT. AFR CHINA/COM INDIA USA+45 GIVE EDU/PROP EATING HEALTH ORD/FREE 20 AID. PAGE 23 F0449
FOR/AID PEACE DIPLOM ECO/UNDEV

B65
COOMBS P.H.,EDUCATION AND FOREIGN AID. AFR USA+45 DIPLOM EFFICIENCY KNOWL ORD/FREE...ANTHOL 20 AID. PAGE 27 F0532
EDU/PROP FOR/AID SCHOOL ECO/UNDEV

B65
CRABB C.V. JR.,THE ELEPHANTS AND THE GRASS* A STUDY OF NONALIGNMENT. ASIA INDIA S/ASIA USA+45 USSR BAL/PWR NEUTRAL ATTIT...TREND NAT/COMP. PAGE 28 F0549
ECO/UNDEV AFR DIPLOM CONCPT

B65
DOWD L.P.,PRINCIPLES OF WORLD BUSINESS. SERV/IND NAT/G DIPLOM ECO/TAC TARIFFS...INT/LAW JURID 20. PAGE 34 F0657
INT/TRADE MGT FINAN MARKET

B65
HABERLER G.,A SURVEY OF INTERNATIONAL TRADE THEORY. CANADA FRANCE GERMANY ECO/TAC TARIFFS AGREE COST DEMAND WEALTH...ECOMETRIC 19/20 MONOPOLY TREATY. PAGE 52 F1024
INT/TRADE BAL/PAY DIPLOM POLICY

B65
HAEFELE E.T.,GOVERNMENT CONTROLS ON TRANSPORT. AFR RHODESIA TANZANIA DIPLOM ECO/TAC TARIFFS PRICE ADJUD CONTROL REGION EFFICIENCY...POLICY 20 CONGO. PAGE 53 F1031
ECO/UNDEV DIST/IND FINAN NAT/G

B65
JOHNSON H.G.,THE WORLD ECONOMY AT THE CROSSROADS. COM WOR-45 ECO/DEV AGRI INDUS INT/TRADE REGION NAT/LISM 20. PAGE 67 F1326
FINAN DIPLOM INT/ORG ECO/UNDEV

B65
JOHNSTONE A.,UNITED STATES DIRECT INVESTMENT IN FRANCE: AN INVESTIGATION OF THE FRENCH CHARGES. FRANCE USA+45 ECO/DEV INDUS LG/CO NAT/G ECO/TAC CONTROL WEALTH...BIBLIOG 20 INTERVENT. PAGE 68 F1335
FINAN DIPLOM POLICY SOVEREIGN

B65
KISSINGER H.A.,THE TROUBLED PARTNERSHIP* RE-APPRAISAL OF THE WESTERN ALLIANCE. EUR+WWI USA+45 INT/ORG NAT/G VOL/ASSN TOP/EX DIPLOM ORD/FREE PWR NATO. PAGE 71 F1402
FRANCE NUC/PWR ECO/DEV

B65
KLEIN J.J.,MONEY AND THE ECONOMY. USA+45 NAT/G DIPLOM CONTROL...POLICY T 20 FED/RESERV. PAGE 72 F1406
FINAN PLAN WEALTH BAL/PAY

B65
LITTLE I.M.D.,INTERNATIONAL AID. UK WOR+45 AGRI INDUS GIVE RECEIVE COLONIAL BAL/PAY WEALTH...POLICY GOV/COMP METH/COMP 20. PAGE 81 F1584
FOR/AID DIPLOM ECO/UNDEV NAT/G

B65
LYONS G.M.,AMERICA: PURPOSE AND POWER. UK USA+45 FINAN INDUS MARKET WORKER TEC/DEV DIPLOM AUTOMAT NUC/PWR WAR RACE/REL ORD/FREE 20 EEC CONGRESS SUPREME/CT CIV/RIGHTS. PAGE 82 F1617 PWR PROB/SOLV ECO/DEV TASK

B65
MACDONALD R.W.,THE LEAGUE OF ARAB STATES: A STUDY IN THE DYNAMICS OF REGIONAL ORGANIZATION. ISRAEL UAR USSR FINAN INT/ORG DELIB/GP ECO/TAC AGREE NEUTRAL ORD/FREE PWR...DECISION BIBLIOG 20 TREATY UN. PAGE 83 F1626 ISLAM REGION DIPLOM ADMIN

B65
MCCOLL G.D.,THE AUSTRALIAN BALANCE OF PAYMENTS. UK USA+45 AGRI WORKER DIPLOM EQUILIB PRODUC...STAT TREND CHARTS BIBLIOG/A 20 AUSTRAL. PAGE 88 F1719 ECO/DEV BAL/PAY INT/TRADE COST

B65
NKRUMAH K.,NEO-COLONIALISM: THE LAST STAGE OF IMPERIALISM. AFR INT/ORG WORKER FOR/AID INT/TRADE EDU/PROP GOV/REL NAT/LISM SOVEREIGN POPULISM SOCISM ...SOCIALIST 20 THIRD/WRLD INTRVN/ECO. PAGE 98 F1929 COLONIAL DIPLOM ECO/UNDEV ECO/TAC

B65
O'CONNELL D.P.,INTERNATIONAL LAW (2 VOLS.). WOR+45 WOR-45 ECO/DEV ECO/UNDEV INT/ORG NAT/G AGREE ...POLICY JURID CONCPT NAT/COMP 20 TREATY. PAGE 99 F1952 INT/LAW DIPLOM CT/SYS

B65
RANSOM H.H.,AN AMERICAN FOREIGN POLICY READER. USA+45 FORCES EDU/PROP COERCE NUC/PWR WAR PEACE ...DECISION 20. PAGE 109 F2146 NAT/G DIPLOM POLICY

B65
ROLFE S.E.,GOLD AND WORLD POWER. AFR UK USA+45 WOR-45 INDUS WORKER INT/TRADE DEMAND...MGT CHARTS 20. PAGE 113 F2234 BAL/PAY EQUILIB ECO/TAC DIPLOM

B65
ROOSA R.V.,MONETARY REFORM FOR THE WORLD ECONOMY. AFR EUR+WWI USA+45 WOR+45 CREATE BUDGET DIPLOM FOR/AID EQUILIB WEALTH IMF. PAGE 114 F2237 FINAN INT/ORG INT/TRADE BAL/PAY

B65
RUEFF J.,THE ROLE AND THE RULE OF GOLD: AN ARGUMENT (PAMPHLET). AFR FRANCE USA+45 WOR+45 MARKET NAT/G PLAN DIPLOM ATTIT...POLICY INT 20 DEGAULLE/C. PAGE 115 F2258 FINAN ECO/DEV INT/TRADE BAL/PAY

B65
SCOTT A.M.,THE REVOLUTION IN STATECRAFT: INFORMAL PENETRATION. WOR+45 WOR-45 CULTURE INT/ORG FORCES ECO/TAC ROUTINE...BIBLIOG 20. PAGE 118 F2331 DIPLOM EDU/PROP FOR/AID

B65
SPENCE J.E.,REPUBLIC UNDER PRESSURE: A STUDY OF SOUTH AFRICAN FOREIGN POLICY. SOUTH/AFR ADMIN COLONIAL GOV/REL RACE/REL DISCRIM NAT/LISM ATTIT ROLE...TREND 20 NEGRO. PAGE 124 F2449 DIPLOM POLICY AFR

B65
STEWART I.G.,AFRICAN PRIMARY PRODUCTS AND INTERNATIONAL TRADE. ECO/UNDEV AGRI FINAN DIPLOM CONTROL 20. PAGE 126 F2485 AFR INT/TRADE INT/ORG

B65
THAYER F.C. JR.,AIR TRANSPORT POLICY AND NATIONAL SECURITY: A POLITICAL, ECONOMIC, AND MILITARY ANALYSIS. DIST/IND OP/RES PLAN TEC/DEV DIPLOM DETER WAR COST EFFICIENCY...POLICY BIBLIOG 20 DEPT/DEFEN FAA CAB. PAGE 129 F2548 AIR FORCES CIVMIL/REL ORD/FREE

B65
TYBOUT R.A.,ECONOMICS OF RESEARCH AND DEVELOPMENT. ECO/DEV ECO/UNDEV INDUS PROFIT DECISION. PAGE 131 F2594 R+D FORCES ADMIN DIPLOM

B65
US BUREAU EDUC CULTURAL AFF,RESOURCES SURVEY FOR LATIN AMERICAN COUNTRIES. L/A+17C USA+45 CULTURE INDUS INT/ORG SECT PLAN EDU/PROP POLICY. PAGE 134 F2643 NAT/G ECO/UNDEV FOR/AID DIPLOM

B65
US BUREAU OF THE BUDGET,THE BALANCE OF PAYMENTS STATISTICS OF THE UNITED STATES: A REVIEW AND APPRAISAL. USA+45 FINAN NAT/G PROB/SOLV DIPLOM. PAGE 134 F2644 BAL/PAY STAT METH/COMP BUDGET

B65
US CONGRESS JOINT ECO COMM,GUIDELINES FOR INTERNATIONAL MONETARY REFORM. USA+45 WOR+45 DELIB/GP BAL/PAY 20 CONGRESS IMF MONEY. PAGE 135 F2659 DIPLOM FINAN PLAN INT/ORG

B65
US SENATE COMM ON FOREIGN REL,HEARINGS ON THE FOREIGN ASSISTANCE PROGRAM. AFR ASIA L/A+17C USA+45 WOR+45 FORCES TEC/DEV BUDGET CONTROL WEAPON ORD/FREE 20 UN CONGRESS SEC/STATE. PAGE 139 F2734 FOR/AID DIPLOM INT/ORG ECO/UNDEV

B65
WARD R.J.,INTERNATIONAL FINANCE. INT/ORG DIPLOM DEMAND INCOME...POLICY METH/COMP 20. PAGE 143 F2819 INT/TRADE ECO/TAC FINAN BAL/PAY

B65
WASSERMAN M.J.,THE BALANCE OF PAYMENTS: HISTORY, METHODOLOGY, THEORY. UK USA+45 USA-45 CAP/ISM DIPLOM EFFICIENCY...DECISION METH/CNCPT BIBLIOG 18/20 LEAGUE/NAT. PAGE 144 F2828 BAL/PAY ECO/TAC GEN/LAWS EQUILIB

B65
WEILER J.,L'ECONOMIE INTERNATIONALE DEPUIS 1950. WOR+45 DIPLOM TARIFFS CONFER...POLICY TREATY. PAGE 145 F2848 FINAN INT/TRADE REGION FOR/AID

B65
WHITE J.,GERMAN AID. GERMANY/W FINAN PLAN TEC/DEV INT/TRADE ADMIN ATTIT...POLICY 20. PAGE 146 F2870 FOR/AID ECO/UNDEV DIPLOM ECO/TAC

B65
WINT G.,ASIA: A HANDBOOK. ASIA COM INDIA USSR CULTURE INTELL NAT/G...GEOG STAT CENSUS NAT/COMP WORSHIP 20 TREATY CHINJAP. PAGE 148 F2907 DIPLOM SOC

S65
CAMPOLONGO A.,"EUROPEAN INVESTMENT BANK* ACTIVITY AND PROSPECTS." FUT ECO/UNDEV FINAN PLAN DIPLOM ...STAT EEC LOAN EIB. PAGE 21 F0410 ECO/TAC PREDICT

S65
CECIL C.O.,"THE DETERMINANTS OF LIBYAN FOREIGN POLICY." AFR INTELL ECO/UNDEV EXTR/IND POL/PAR CREATE REGION SOVEREIGN CONSERVE MAGHREB NASSER/G. PAGE 22 F0431 LIBYA DIPLOM WEALTH ISLAM

S65
JOHNSON L.L.,"US BUSINESS INTERESTS IN CUBA AND THE RISE OF CASTRO." L/A+17C USA+45 ECO/UNDEV INDUS NAT/G VOL/ASSN ATTIT ORD/FREE PWR WEALTH ALL/PROG. PAGE 68 F1330 DIPLOM CUBA ECO/TAC INT/TRADE

C65
WUORINEN J.H.,"SCANDINAVIA." DENMARK FINLAND ICELAND NORWAY SWEDEN SOCIETY AGRI POL/PAR DELIB/GP DIPLOM INT/TRADE NEUTRAL WAR...CHARTS IND TREATY 20. PAGE 149 F2942 BIBLIOG NAT/G POLICY

B66
ALEXANDER Y.,INTERNATIONAL TECHNICAL ASSISTANCE EXPERTS* A CASE STUDY OF THE U.N. EXPERIENCE. ECO/UNDEV CONSULT EX/STRUC CREATE PLAN DIPLOM FOR/AID TASK EFFICIENCY...ORG/CHARTS UN. PAGE 3 F0061 ECO/TAC INT/ORG ADMIN MGT

B66
ALIBER R.Z.,THE FUTURE OF THE DOLLAR AS AN INTERNATIONAL CURRENCY. AFR USA+45 USA-45 ECO/DEV PRICE COST INCOME...POLICY 20. PAGE 4 F0067 FINAN DIPLOM INT/ORG INT/TRADE

B66
AMER ENTERPRISE INST FOR PUBL,INTERNATIONAL PAYMENTS PROBLEM. MARKET DIPLOM DEBATE PRICE COST INCOME 20. PAGE 4 F0082 FINAN INT/TRADE POLICY

B66
AMER ENTERPRISE INST PUB POL,SIGNIFICANT ISSUES IN ECONOMIC AID TO DEVELOPING COUNTRIES. FINAN INT/ORG NAT/G PLAN PROB/SOLV GIVE TASK WEALTH...DECISION 20. PAGE 4 F0083 ECO/UNDEV FOR/AID DIPLOM POLICY

B66
AMERICAN ASSEMBLY COLUMBIA U,THE UNITED STATES AND THE PHILIPPINES. PHILIPPINE S/ASIA USA+45 USA-45 SOCIETY FORCES INT/TRADE...POLICY 20. PAGE 5 F0085 COLONIAL DIPLOM NAT/LISM

B66
BAKLANOFF E.N.,NEW PERSPECTIVES ON BRAZIL. BRAZIL SOCIETY INDUS DOMIN LEAD REV CIVMIL/REL...GEOG PSY LING ANTHOL 20. PAGE 8 F0156 ECO/UNDEV TEC/DEV DIPLOM ORD/FREE

B66
BALDWIN D.A.,FOREIGN AID AND AMERICAN FOREIGN POLICY; A DOCUMENTARY ANALYSIS. USA+45 ECO/UNDEV ADMIN...ECOMETRIC STAT STYLE CHARTS PROG/TEAC GEN/LAWS ANTHOL. PAGE 9 F0162 FOR/AID DIPLOM IDEA/COMP

B66
BALDWIN D.A.,ECONOMIC DEVELOPMENT AND AMERICAN FOREIGN POLICY. USA+45 FINAN LG/CO LEGIS DIPLOM GIVE 20. PAGE 9 F0163 ECO/TAC FOR/AID ECO/UNDEV POLICY

B66
BARAN P.A.,MONOPOLY CAPITAL; AN ESSAY ON THE AMERICAN ECONOMIC AND SOCIAL ORDER. USA+45 USA-45 ECO/UNDEV FINAN MARKET PLAN DIPLOM COLONIAL RACE/REL DEMAND MARXISM...CHARTS 20. PAGE 9 F0179 LG/CO CAP/ISM PRICE CONTROL

B66
BEUGEL E.V.D.,FROM MARSHALL AID TO ATLANTIC PARTNERSHIP* EUROPEAN INTEGRATION AS A CONCERN OF AMERICAN FOREIGN POLICY. USA+45 INT/ORG FORCES PERSON EEC NATO. PAGE 14 F0272 REGION DIPLOM EUR+WWI VOL/ASSN

B66
BROEKMEIJER M.W.J.,FICTION AND TRUTH ABOUT THE "DECADE OF DEVELOPMENT" WOR+45 AGRI FINAN INDUS NAT/G TEC/DEV DIPLOM EDU/PROP LEAD SKILL 20 THIRD/WRLD. PAGE 19 F0358 FOR/AID POLICY ECO/UNDEV PLAN

B66
BROWN J.F.,THE NEW EASTERN EUROPE. ALBANIA BULGARIA HUNGARY POLAND ROMANIA CULTURE AGRI POL/PAR WAR NAT/LISM MARXISM...CHARTS BIBLIOG 20. PAGE 19 F0369 DIPLOM COM NAT/G

ECO/UNDEV

B66

BROWN R.T.,TRANSPORT AND THE ECONOMIC INTEGRATION OF SOUTH AMERICA. L/A+17C ECO/UNDEV NAT/G OP/RES DIPLOM INT/TRADE REGION WEALTH...ECOMETRIC GEOG STAT LAFTA TIME. PAGE 19 F0373
MARKET DIST/IND SIMUL

B66

CANNING HOUSE LIBRARY,AUTHOR AND SUBJECT CATALOGUES OF THE CANNING HOUSE LIBRARY (5 VOLS.). UK CULTURE LEAD...SOC 19/20. PAGE 21 F0411
BIBLIOG L/A+17C NAT/G DIPLOM

B66

COLE A.B.,SOCIALIST PARTIES IN POSTWAR JAPAN. STRATA AGRI LABOR PLAN DIPLOM ECO/TAC AGREE LEAD CHOOSE ATTIT...CHARTS 20 CHINJAP SOC/DEMPAR. PAGE 26 F0499
POL/PAR POLICY SOCISM NAT/G

B66

CONAN A.R.,THE PROBLEM OF STERLING. UK WOR+45 BUDGET ECO/TAC...POLICY STAT CHARTS 20 SILVER. PAGE 27 F0521
FINAN ECO/DEV BAL/PAY DIPLOM

B66

CURRIE L.,ACCELERATING DEVELOPMENT: THE NECESSITY AND MEANS. COLOMBIA USA+45 INDUS DIPLOM EFFICIENCY WEALTH...METH/CNCPT NEW/IDEA 20. PAGE 29 F0564
PLAN ECO/UNDEV FOR/AID TEC/DEV

B66

ECKSTEIN A.,COMMUNIST CHINA'S ECONOMIC GROWTH AND FOREIGN TRADE* IMPLICATIONS FOR US POLICY. COM USA+45 USSR STRUCT INDUS MARKET DIPLOM ECO/TAC FOR/AID INT/TRADE...STAT CHARTS. PAGE 36 F0696
ASIA ECO/UNDEV CREATE PWR

B66

EDWARDS C.D.,TRADE REGULATIONS OVERSEAS. IRELAND NEW/ZEALND SOUTH/AFR NAT/G CAP/ISM TARIFFS CONTROL ...POLICY JURID 20 EEC CHINJAP. PAGE 36 F0703
INT/TRADE DIPLOM INT/LAW ECO/TAC

B66

FELLNER W.,MAINTAINING AND RESTORING BALANCE IN INTERNATIONAL PAYMENTS. ECO/UNDEV MARKET ECO/TAC PRICE INCOME WEALTH...POLICY METH/COMP 20 MONEY. PAGE 40 F0781
BAL/PAY DIPLOM FINAN INT/TRADE

B66

FREIDEL F.,AMERICAN ISSUES IN THE TWENTIETH CENTURY. SOCIETY FINAN ECO/TAC FOR/AID CONTROL NUC/PWR WAR RACE/REL PEACE ATTIT...ANTHOL T 20 WILSON/W ROOSEVLT/F KENNEDY/JF TRUMAN/HS. PAGE 44 F0851
DIPLOM POLICY NAT/G ORD/FREE

B66

HALLET R.,PEOPLE AND PROGRESS IN WEST AFRICA: AN INTRODUCTION TO THE PROBLEMS OF DEVELOPMENT. COM/IND INDUS KIN DIPLOM FOR/AID INT/TRADE HEALTH ...GEOG TREND CHARTS BIBLIOG/A 20 AFRICA/W. PAGE 54 F1050
AFR SOCIETY ECO/UNDEV ECO/TAC

B66

HEVESY P.D.,THE UNIFICATION OF THE WORLD. FUT USA+45 WOR+45 ECO/DEV ECO/UNDEV LEGIS PROB/SOLV BAL/PWR ECO/TAC INT/TRADE PEACE. PAGE 59 F1160
DIPLOM FINAN INT/ORG

B66

HOLT R.T.,THE POLITICAL BASIS OF ECONOMIC DEVELOPMENT. STRATA STRUCT NAT/G DIPLOM ADMIN...SOC NAT/COMP BIBLIOG 20. PAGE 61 F1201
ECO/TAC GOV/COMP CONSTN EX/STRUC

B66

HOROWITZ D.,HEMISPHERES NORTH AND SOUTH: ECONOMIC DISPARITY AMONG NATIONS. WOR+45 ECO/DEV ECO/UNDEV INT/ORG PLAN DIPLOM INT/TRADE GIVE PARTIC GP/REL ...WELF/ST 20. PAGE 62 F1215
ECO/TAC FOR/AID STRATA WEALTH

B66

INARRITU A.L.,EL PATRON CAMBIO-ORO Y SUS REFORMAS. AFR L/A+17C WOR+45 PLAN PROB/SOLV BUDGET ECO/TAC INT/TRADE EFFICIENCY ORD/FREE 20 MEXIC/AMER. PAGE 64 F1262
ECO/UNDEV FINAN DIPLOM POLICY

B66

INTERNATIONAL ECO POLICY ASSN,THE UNITED STATES BALANCE OF PAYMENTS. INT/ORG NAT/G PROB/SOLV BUDGET DIPLOM INT/TRADE WEALTH 20. PAGE 65 F1274
BAL/PAY ECO/TAC POLICY FINAN

B66

JACKSON G.D.,COMINTERN AND PEASANT IN EAST EUROPE 1919-1930. BULGARIA COM CZECHOSLVK EUR+WWI POLAND ROMANIA YUGOSLAVIA STRATA AGRI VOL/ASSN DIPLOM CONTROL CROWD WEALTH...POLICY NAT/COMP 20. PAGE 66 F1293
MARXISM ECO/UNDEV WORKER INT/ORG

B66

KAREFA-SMART J.,AFRICA: PROGRESS THROUGH COOPERATION. AFR FINAN TEC/DEV DIPLOM FOR/AID EDU/PROP CONFER REGION GP/REL WEALTH...HEAL SOC/INTEG 20. PAGE 69 F1356
ORD/FREE ECO/UNDEV VOL/ASSN PLAN

B66

KEENLEYSIDE H.L.,INTERNATIONAL AID: A SUMMARY. AFR INDIA S/ASIA UK STRATA EXTR/IND TEC/DEV ADMIN RACE/REL DEMAND NAT/LISM WEALTH...TREND CHINJAP. PAGE 70 F1367
ECO/UNDEV FOR/AID DIPLOM TASK

B66

KINDLEBERGER C.P.,EUROPE AND THE DOLLAR. AFR EUR+WWI FRANCE GERMANY/W USA+45 CONSTN INT/ORG
BAL/PAY BUDGET

DIPLOM INT/TRADE...ANTHOL 20. PAGE 71 F1395
FINAN ECO/DEV

B66

KOMIYA R.,POSTWAR ECONOMIC GROWTH IN JAPAN. ELITES NAT/G EX/STRUC TEC/DEV BUDGET DIPLOM CONTROL BAL/PAY PRODUC...BIBLIOG 20 CHINJAP. PAGE 73 F1424
ECO/DEV POLICY PLAN ADJUST

B66

KUENNE R.E.,THE POLARIS MISSILE STRIKE* A GENERAL ECONOMIC SYSTEMS ANALYSIS. USA+45 USSR NAT/G BAL/PWR ARMS/CONT WAR...MATH PROBABIL COMPUT/IR CHARTS HYPO/EXP SIMUL. PAGE 74 F1446
NUC/PWR FORCES DETER DIPLOM

B66

LAMBERG R.F.,PRAG UND DIE DRITTE WELT. AFR ASIA CZECHOSLVK L/A+17C MARKET TEC/DEV ECO/TAC REV ATTIT 20 TREATY. PAGE 75 F1462
DIPLOM ECO/UNDEV INT/TRADE FOR/AID

B66

LEAGUE OF WOMEN VOTERS OF US,FOREIGN AID AT THE CROSSROADS. USA+45 WOR+45 DELIB/GP PROB/SOLV DIPLOM INT/TRADE RECEIVE BAL/PAY...CHARTS 20 UN ALL/PROG. PAGE 76 F1498
FOR/AID GIVE ECO/UNDEV PLAN

B66

LONDON K.,EASTERN EUROPE IN TRANSITION. CHINA/COM USSR DOMIN COLONIAL CENTRAL RIGID/FLEX PWR...SOC ANTHOL 20. PAGE 82 F1597
SOVEREIGN COM NAT/LISM DIPLOM

B66

MACFARQUHAR R.,CHINA UNDER MAO: POLITICS TAKES COMMAND. CHINA/COM COM AGRI INDUS CHIEF FORCES DIPLOM INT/TRADE EDU/PROP TASK REV ADJUST...ANTHOL 20 MAO. PAGE 83 F1628
ECO/UNDEV TEC/DEV ECO/TAC ADMIN

B66

MURPHY G.G.,SOVIET MONGOLIA: A STUDY OF THE OLDEST POLITICAL SATELLITE. USSR STRATA STRUCT COST INCOME ATTIT SOCISM 20. PAGE 95 F1865
DIPLOM ECO/TAC PLAN DOMIN

B66

OHLIN G.,AID AND INDEBTEDNESS. AUSTRIA FINAN INT/ORG PLAN DIPLOM GIVE...POLICY MATH CHARTS 20. PAGE 101 F1984
FOR/AID ECO/UNDEV ADMIN WEALTH

B66

OHLIN G.,FOREIGN AID POLICIES RECONSIDERED. ECO/DEV ECO/UNDEV VOL/ASSN CONSULT PLAN CONTROL ATTIT ...CONCPT CHARTS BIBLIOG 20. PAGE 101 F1985
FOR/AID DIPLOM GIVE

B66

ORG FOR ECO COOP AND DEVEL,GEOGRAPHICAL DISTRIBUTION OF FINANCIAL FLOWS TO LESS DEVELOPED COUNTRIES. WOR+45 DIPLOM INT/TRADE GIVE RECEIVE REPAR REGION WEALTH...GEOG STAT CHARTS 20 OECD. PAGE 102 F1997
FINAN ECO/UNDEV INT/ORG FOR/AID

B66

PASSIN H.,THE UNITED STATES AND JAPAN. USA+45 INDUS CAP/ISM...TREND 20 CHINJAP TREATY. PAGE 103 F2032
DIPLOM INT/TRADE ECO/DEV ECO/TAC

B66

PIQUET H.S.,THE US BALANCE OF PAYMENTS AND INTERNATIONAL MONETARY RESERVES. AFR USA+45 PROB/SOLV INT/TRADE GOV/REL EQUILIB...POLICY STAT CHARTS 20. PAGE 106 F2090
BAL/PAY DIPLOM FINAN ECO/TAC

B66

ROBINSON E.A.,THE ECONOMICS OF EDUCATION. WOR+45 CULTURE ECO/UNDEV FINAN SCHOOL DIPLOM PRICE COST DEMAND...CHARTS METH/COMP 20. PAGE 112 F2216
EDU/PROP ADJUST CONFER

B66

SEWELL J.P.,FUNCTIONALISM AND WORLD POLITICS* A STUDY BASED ON UNITED NATIONS PROGRAMS FINANCING ECONOMICAL DEVELOPMENT. ECO/UNDEV FINAN PROB/SOLV DIPLOM ECO/TAC FEEDBACK REGION ADJUST ATTIT UN IBRD INTL/FINAN INTL/DEV UNSF. PAGE 120 F2360
TASK INT/ORG IDEA/COMP GEN/LAWS

B66

SINGH L.P.,THE POLITICS OF ECONOMIC COOPERATION IN ASIA; A STUDY OF ASIAN INTERNATIONAL ORGANIZATIONS. ASIA INT/ORG ACT/RES PLAN GP/REL...POLICY GP/COMP BIBLIOG 20 UN SEATO. PAGE 122 F2414
ECO/UNDEV ECO/TAC REGION DIPLOM

B66

SOCIAL SCIENCE RESEARCH COUN,BIBLIOGRAPHY OF RESEARCH IN THE SOCIAL SCIENCES IN AUSTRALIA 1957-1960. LAW R+D DIPLOM 20 AUSTRAL. PAGE 124 F2437
BIBLIOG SOC PSY

B66

SPICER K.,A SAMARITAN STATE? AFR CANADA INDIA PAKISTAN UK USA+45 FINAN INDUS PRODUC...CHARTS 20 NATO. PAGE 124 F2455
DIPLOM FOR/AID ECO/DEV ADMIN

B66

THOMPSON J.H.,MODERNIZATION OF THE ARAB WORLD. FUT ISRAEL STRUCT ECO/UNDEV DIPLOM INGP/REL ATTIT ...CENSUS ANTHOL 20 ARABS. PAGE 130 F2565
ADJUST ISLAM PROB/SOLV NAT/COMP

B66

TRIFFIN R.,THE WORLD MONEY MAZE. AFR INT/ORG ECO/TAC PRICE OPTIMAL WEALTH...METH/COMP 20 EEC OEEC SILVER. PAGE 131 F2589
BAL/PAY FINAN INT/TRADE

DIPLOM

B66
TRIFFIN R.,THE BALANCE OF PAYMENTS AND THE FOREIGN INVESTMENT POSITION OF THE UNITED STATES. AFR USA+45 INT/ORG INT/TRADE PRICE CONTROL...POLICY 20. PAGE 131 F2590
BAL/PAY DIPLOM FINAN ECO/TAC

B66
UNITED NATIONS,YEARBOOK OF INTERNATIONAL TRADE STATISTICS, 1964 (15TH ISSUE). WOR+45 ECO/DEV ECO/UNDEV UN. PAGE 132 F2614
STAT INT/TRADE DIPLOM CHARTS

B66
US CONGRESS JOINT ECO COMM,NEW APPROACH TO UNITED STATES INTERNATIONAL ECONOMIC POLICY. USA+45 WOR+45 CHIEF DELIB/GP CONFER...CHARTS 20 CONGRESS MONEY. PAGE 135 F2660
DIPLOM ECO/TAC BAL/PAY FINAN

B66
US DEPARTMENT OF STATE,RESEARCH ON THE USSR AND EASTERN EUROPE (EXTERNAL RESEARCH LIST NO 1-25). USSR LAW CULTURE SOCIETY NAT/G TEC/DEV DIPLOM EDU/PROP REGION...GEOG LING. PAGE 136 F2675
BIBLIOG/A EUR+WWI COM MARXISM

B66
US DEPARTMENT OF STATE,RESEARCH ON WESTERN EUROPE, GREAT BRITAIN, AND CANADA (EXTERNAL RESEARCH LIST NO 3-25). CANADA GERMANY/W UK LAW CULTURE NAT/G POL/PAR FORCES EDU/PROP REGION MARXISM...GEOG SOC WORSHIP 20 CMN/WLTH. PAGE 136 F2676
BIBLIOG/A EUR+WWI DIPLOM

B66
US HOUSE COMM FOREIGN AFFAIRS,HEARINGS ON HR 12449 A BILL TO AMEND FURTHER THE FOREIGN ASSISTANCE ACT OF 1961. AFR ASIA L/A+17C USA+45 VIETNAM INT/ORG TEC/DEV INT/TRADE ATTIT ORD/FREE 20 UN NATO CONGRESS AID. PAGE 137 F2692
FOR/AID ECO/TAC ECO/UNDEV DIPLOM

B66
US SENATE COMM APPROPRIATIONS,FOREIGN ASSISTANCE AND RELATED AGENCIES APPROPRIATIONS FOR FISCAL YEAR 1967: HEARINGS... ON H. R. 17788. ECO/UNDEV INT/ORG FORCES INSPECT ECO/TAC GIVE DEBATE WEAPON CIVMIL/REL WEALTH...INT 20 CONGRESS DEPT/DEFEN DEPT/STATE DEPT/HEW AID. PAGE 138 F2727
BUDGET FOR/AID DIPLOM COST

B66
US SENATE COMM ON FOREIGN REL,HEARINGS ON S 2859 AND S 2861. USA+45 WOR+45 FORCES BUDGET CAP/ISM ADMIN DETER WEAPON TOTALISM...NAT/COMP 20 UN CONGRESS. PAGE 139 F2735
FOR/AID DIPLOM ORD/FREE ECO/UNDEV

B66
US SENATE COMM ON FOREIGN REL,ASIAN DEVELOPMENT BANK ACT. USA+45 LAW DIPLOM...CHARTS 20 BLACK/EUG S/EASTASIA. PAGE 139 F2736
FOR/AID FINAN ECO/UNDEV S/ASIA

B66
YEAGER L.B.,INTERNATIONAL MONETARY RELATIONS: THEORY, HISTORY, AND POLICY. WOR+45 WOR-45 INT/TRADE BAL/PAY...NAT/COMP 18/20 MONEY. PAGE 150 F2947
FINAN DIPLOM ECO/TAC IDEA/COMP

L66
AFRICAN BIBLIOGRAPHIC CENTER,"AFRICAN ECONOMIC AFFAIRS: A SELECT BIBLIOGRAPHICAL SURVEY, 1965-1966." AFR FINAN INDUS INT/ORG LABOR PLAN BUDGET DIPLOM INT/TRADE ADMIN EFFICIENCY WEALTH 20. PAGE 3 F0046
BIBLIOG ECO/UNDEV TEC/DEV FOR/AID

L66
AFRICAN BIBLIOGRAPHIC CENTER,"AFRICAN ECONOMIC AFFAIRS: A SELECT BIBLIOGRAPHICAL SURVEY, 1965-1966; SUPPLEMENTS NUMBERS 1-3." AFR FINAN INDUS LABOR PLAN BUDGET CAP/ISM DIPLOM INT/TRADE ADMIN...GEOG 20. PAGE 3 F0047
BIBLIOG/A ECO/UNDEV FOR/AID TEC/DEV

L66
CHENERY H.B.,"FOREIGN ASSISTANCE AND ECONOMIC DEVELOPMENT" FUT WOR+45 NAT/G DIPLOM GIVE PRODUC ...METH/CNCPT CHARTS 20. PAGE 24 F0464
FOR/AID EFFICIENCY ECO/UNDEV TEC/DEV

L66
PACKENHAM R.A.,"POLITICAL-DEVELOPMENT DOCTRINES IN THE AMERICAN FOREIGN AID PROGRAM." STRUCT R+D CREATE DIPLOM AID. PAGE 102 F2011
FOR/AID ECO/UNDEV GEN/LAWS

S66
ANGELL J.W.,"THE LONGER RUN PROSPECTS FOR THE US BALANCE OF PAYMENTS." USA+45 DIPLOM FOR/AID RATION ORD/FREE WEALTH...IDEA/COMP GATT. PAGE 6 F0104
BAL/PAY ECO/TAC INT/TRADE FINAN

S66
DUROSELLE J.B.,"THE FUTURE OF THE ATLANTIC COMMUNITY." EUR+WWI USA+45 USSR NAT/G CAP/ISM REGION DETER NUC/PWR ATTIT MARXISM...INT/LAW 20 NATO. PAGE 35 F0686
FUT DIPLOM MYTH POLICY

S66
FELD W.,"EXTERNAL RELATIONS OF THE COMMON MARKET AND GROUP LEADERSHIP ATTITUDES IN THE MEMBER STATES." COM USA+45 ELITES AGRI NAT/G ATTIT...OBS EEC GATT. PAGE 40 F0776
DIPLOM CENTRAL TARIFFS INT/TRADE

S66
KLEIN S.,"A SURVEY OF SINO-JAPANESE TRADE, 1950-1966" TAIWAN EDU/PROP 20 CHINJAP. PAGE 72 F1409
INT/TRADE DIPLOM MARXISM

S66
NEWLYN W.T.,"MONEY MARKETS IN EAST AFRICA." AFR TANZANIA UGANDA UK DIPLOM CENTRAL 20. PAGE 98 F1923
FINAN WEALTH BAL/PAY ECO/UNDEV

C66
WINT G.,"ASIA: A HANDBOOK." ASIA S/ASIA INDUS LABOR SECT PRESS RACE/REL MARXISM...STAT CHARTS BIBLIOG 20. PAGE 148 F2908
ECO/UNDEV DIPLOM NAT/G SOCIETY

N66
BRITISH DEVELOPMENT POLICIES: 1966 (PAMPHLET). UK AGRI TARIFFS BAL/PAY...TREND CHARTS 20 OVRSEA/DEV. PAGE 1 F0023
WEALTH DIPLOM INT/TRADE FOR/AID

N66
EOMMITTEE ECONOMIC DEVELOPMENT,THE DOLLAR AND THE WORLD MONETARY SYSTEM: A STATEMENT ON NATIONAL POLICY (PAMPHLET). AFR USA+45 NAT/G PLAN PROB/SOLV BUDGET ECO/TAC FOR/AID INCOME...POLICY 20 EUROPE. PAGE 38 F0740
FINAN BAL/PAY DIPLOM ECO/DEV

N66
OECD,THE BALANCE OF PAYMENTS ADJUSTMENT PROCESS (PAMPHLET). EUR+WWI ECO/DEV FINAN CONSULT PLAN PROB/SOLV BUDGET CAP/ISM INT/TRADE PRICE CONTROL EQUILIB 20. PAGE 101 F1975
BAL/PAY ECO/TAC DIPLOM INT/ORG

B67
ADLER J.H.,CAPITAL MOVEMENTS AND ECONOMIC DEVELOPMENT. WOR+45 FINAN NAT/G BARGAIN ECO/TAC FOR/AID INT/TRADE ANTHOL. PAGE 2 F0042
DIPLOM ECO/DEV ECO/UNDEV

B67
ANDERSON S.V.,THE NORDIC COUNCIL: A STUDY OF SCANDINAVIAN REGIONALISM. DENMARK FINLAND ICELAND NORWAY SWEDEN MARKET NAT/G VOL/ASSN CONSULT PARL/PROC ATTIT...TIME/SEQ BIBLIOG 20. PAGE 5 F0098
INT/ORG REGION DIPLOM LEGIS

B67
BARDENS D.,CHURCHILL IN PARLIAMENT. UK DIPLOM ADJUD CONTROL AUTHORIT PERSON ORD/FREE 20 CHURCHLL/W PARLIAMENT. PAGE 10 F0186
TOP/EX LEGIS GOV/REL

B67
BEATON L.,THE STRUGGLE FOR PEACE. INT/ORG FORCES NUC/PWR COST PWR...POLICY TREND 20. PAGE 12 F0225
PEACE BAL/PWR DIPLOM WAR

B67
BROMKE A.,POLAND'S POLITICS: IDEALISM VS. REALISM. COM GERMANY POLAND RUSSIA USSR POL/PAR CATHISM ...BIBLIOG 19/20. PAGE 19 F0360
NAT/G DIPLOM MARXISM

B67
CEFKIN J.L.,THE BACKGROUND OF CURRENT WORLD PROBLEMS. AFR NAT/G MARXISM...T 20 UN. PAGE 22 F0432
DIPLOM NAT/LISM ECO/UNDEV

B67
CHO S.S.,KOREA IN WORLD POLITICS 1940-1950; AN EVALUATION OF AMERICAN RESPONSIBILITY. KOREA USA+45 USSR CONSTN INT/ORG NAT/G FORCES FOR/AID ANOMIE SUPEGO MARXISM...DECISION BIBLIOG 20. PAGE 24 F0469
POLICY DIPLOM PROB/SOLV WAR

B67
COTTAM R.W.,COMPETITIVE INTERFERENCE AND TWENTIETH CENTURY DIPLOMACY. IRAN ACT/RES CREATE PLAN ECO/TAC EFFICIENCY ATTIT...DECISION NEW/IDEA TREND 20 CIA. PAGE 28 F0541
DIPLOM DOMIN GAME

B67
DAVIS F.M.,COME AS A CONQUEROR: THE UNITED STATES ARMY'S OCCUPATION OF GERMANY: 1945-1949. EUR+WWI GERMANY USA+45 SOCIETY PLAN BAL/PWR DIPLOM FOR/AID PERS/REL DEMAND PEACE ORD/FREE 20. PAGE 30 F0588
FORCES CIVMIL/REL ECO/TAC CONTROL

B67
DINERSTEIN H.S.,INTERVENTION AGAINST COMMUNISM (STUDIES IN INTERNATIONAL AFFAIRS NO. 1). CUBA DOMIN/REP GREECE USA+45 USSR VIETNAM OP/RES COERCE WAR 20. PAGE 33 F0643
MARXISM DIPLOM NAT/LISM

B67
FILENE P.G.,AMERICANS AND THE SOVIET EXPERIMENT, 1917-1933. USA-45 USSR INTELL NAT/G CAP/ISM DIPLOM EDU/PROP PRESS REV SOCISM...PSY 20. PAGE 41 F0793
ATTIT RIGID/FLEX MARXISM SOCIETY

B67
FONER P.S.,THE BOLSHEVIK REVOLUTION. USA-45 POL/PAR WORKER DIPLOM EDU/PROP MARXISM...STERTYP 20. PAGE 42 F0821
LABOR INTELL REV PRESS

B67
GRIFFITH W.E.,SINO-SOVIET RELATIONS, 1964-1965. CHINA/COM COM USSR CHIEF 20. PAGE 51 F1001
DIPLOM PWR DOMIN MARXISM

B67
HALLE L.J.,THE COLD WAR AS HISTORY. AFR USSR WOR+45 ECO/TAC FOR/AID NUC/PWR WAR PEACE ORD/FREE ...MAJORIT TREND 20 KENNEDY/JF KHRUSH/N BERLIN/BLO. PAGE 54 F1048
DIPLOM BAL/PWR

B67
HANRIEDER W.F.,WEST GERMAN FOREIGN POLICY 1949-1963: INTERNATIONAL PRESSURE AND DOMESTIC RESPONSE. EUR+WWI GERMANY/W POL/PAR LOBBY CONSEN
DIPLOM POLICY NAT/G

20. PAGE 54 F1061 ATTIT

B67
HOGAN J.,THE US BALANCE OF PAYMENTS AND CAPITAL FLOWS. MARKET INT/ORG ECO/TAC PRICE CONTROL WEALTH ...METH/COMP 20 EEC. PAGE 61 F1192
BAL/PAY FINAN DIPLOM INT/TRADE

B67
HUMPHREY R.A.,UNIVERSITIES...AND DEVELOPMENT ASSISTANCE ABROAD. USA+45 OP/RES ECO/TAC FOR/AID ...ANTHOL 20. PAGE 63 F1242
ACADEM DIPLOM KNOWL ECO/UNDEV

B67
INTERNATIONAL LABOUR OFFICE,SUBJECT GUIDE TO PUBLICATIONS OF THE INTERNATIONAL LABOUR OFFICE, 1919-1964. DIPLOM 20. PAGE 65 F1280
BIBLIOG LABOR INT/ORG WORKER

B67
JACOBY N.H.,US AID TO TAIWAN. CAP/ISM DIPLOM FEEDBACK COST PRODUC...OBS INT CHARTS 20. PAGE 66 F1301
FOR/AID OP/RES ECO/TAC ECO/UNDEV

B67
JOHNSON H.G.,ECONOMIC NATIONALISM IN OLD AND NEW STATES. CANADA CHINA/COM MALI UK DIPLOM...SIMUL GEN/LAWS 19/20 MEXIC/AMER. PAGE 68 F1328
NAT/LISM ECO/UNDEV ECO/DEV NAT/COMP

B67
KIRK R.,THE POLITICAL PRINCIPLES OF ROBERT A. TAFT. USA+45 LABOR DIPLOM ADJUD ADJUST ORD/FREE TAFT/RA. PAGE 71 F1398
POL/PAR LEAD LEGIS ATTIT

B67
KREININ M.E.,ALTERNATIVE COMMERCIAL POLICIES - THEIR EFFECT ON THE AMERICAN ECONOMY. USA+45 LAW ECO/DEV MARKET INT/ORG DIPLOM ECO/TAC TARIFFS PRICE DEMAND WEALTH...QUANT EEC AFTA. PAGE 73 F1437
INT/TRADE BAL/PAY NAT/G POLICY

B67
LANDEN R.G.,OMAN SINCE 1856: DISRUPTIVE MODERNIZATION IN A TRADITIONAL ARAB SOCIETY. UK DIST/IND EXTR/IND SECT DIPLOM INT/TRADE...SOC LING CHARTS BIBLIOG 19/20. PAGE 75 F1468
ISLAM CULTURE ECO/UNDEV NAT/G

B67
LINDER S.B.,TRADE AND TRADE POLICY FOR DEVELOPMENT. OP/RES DIPLOM TARIFFS UTIL WEALTH...BIBLIOG 20. PAGE 80 F1569
ECO/UNDEV ECO/TAC TEC/DEV INT/TRADE

B67
LISS S.B.,THE CANAL, ASPECTS OF UNITED STATES-PANAMANIAN RELATIONS. AFR FUT PANAMA DOMIN COERCE ATTIT SOVEREIGN MARXISM 20 JOHNSON/LB KENNEDY/JF. PAGE 81 F1580
DIPLOM POLICY

B67
MACCLOSKEY M.,PACTS FOR PEACE: UN, NATO, SEATO, CENTO, OAS. WOR+45 PLAN DIPLOM CONTROL PEACE ORD/FREE...ORG/CHARTS UN NATO SEATO OAS CENTO. PAGE 83 F1623
FORCES INT/ORG LEAD POLICY

B67
MARTIN P.,CANADA AND THE QUEST FOR PEACE. CANADA VIETNAM ECO/UNDEV PLAN FOR/AID WAR 20 UN. PAGE 86 F1684
DIPLOM PEACE INT/ORG POLICY

B67
MCDOUGAL M.S.,THE INTERPRETATION OF AGREEMENTS AND WORLD PUBLIC ORDER: PRINCIPLES OF CONTENT AND PROCEDURE. WOR+45 CONSTN PROB/SOLV TEC/DEV ...CON/ANAL TREATY. PAGE 88 F1727
INT/LAW STRUCT ECO/UNDEV DIPLOM

B67
MCNELLY T.,SOURCES IN MODERN EAST ASIAN HISTORY AND POLITICS. KOREA VIETNAM CULTURE DIPLOM COLONIAL REV WAR PWR ALL/IDEOS MARXISM...ANTHOL 20 CHINJAP. PAGE 88 F1733
NAT/COMP ASIA S/ASIA SOCIETY

B67
MENDEL A.P.,POLITICAL MEMOIRS 1905-1917 BY PAUL MILIUKOV (TRANS. BY CARL GOLDBERG). USSR AGRI DIPLOM ECO/TAC POPULISM...MAJORIT 20. PAGE 90 F1757
BIOG LEAD NAT/G CONSTN

B67
MONTGOMERY J.D.,FOREIGN AID IN INTERNATIONAL POLITICS. USA+45 USA-45 WOR+45 ECO/TAC EFFICIENCY ...SOC TREND CHARTS BIBLIOG/A 20 AID. PAGE 93 F1818
DIPLOM FOR/AID

B67
MUHAMMAD A.C.,THE EMERGENCE OF PAKISTAN. PAKISTAN S/ASIA CONSTN ECO/UNDEV NAT/G CONTROL NAT/LISM 20. PAGE 94 F1853
DIPLOM COLONIAL SECT PROB/SOLV

B67
MURTY B.S.,PROPAGANDA AND WORLD PUBLIC ORDER. FUT WOR+45 COM/IND INT/ORG PROB/SOLV ATTIT KNOWL ORD/FREE...POLICY UN. PAGE 95 F1868
EDU/PROP DIPLOM CONTROL JURID

B67
NKRUMAH K.,CHALLENGE OF THE CONGO. FORCES ECO/TAC FOR/AID REGION MURDER REPRESENT 20 CONGO/LEOP UN. PAGE 98 F1930
REV ECO/UNDEV ORD/FREE DIPLOM

B67
O'LEARY M.K.,THE POLITICS OF AMERICAN FOREIGN AID. USA+45 POL/PAR CHIEF BUDGET EDU/PROP LOBBY CONGRESS. PAGE 100 F1958
FOR/AID DIPLOM PARL/PROC ATTIT

B67
OFER G.,THE SERVICE INDUSTRIES IN A DEVELOPING ECONOMY: ISRAEL AS A CASE STUDY. ISRAEL ECO/TAC INT/TRADE PRODUC WEALTH SOCISM...TIME/SEQ TREND CHARTS 20. PAGE 101 F1979
DIPLOM ECO/DEV SERV/IND

B67
OGLESBY C.,CONTAINMENT AND CHANGE. AFR COM USA+45 ECO/UNDEV TEC/DEV ECO/TAC FOR/AID INT/TRADE DOMIN GUERRILLA REV PEACE 20 STALIN/J. PAGE 101 F1983
DIPLOM BAL/PWR MARXISM CULTURE

B67
OVERSEAS DEVELOPMENT INSTIT,EFFECTIVE AID. WOR+45 INT/ORG TEC/DEV DIPLOM INT/TRADE ADMIN. PAGE 102 F2004
FOR/AID ECO/UNDEV ECO/TAC NAT/COMP

B67
PIKE F.B.,FREEDOM AND REFORM IN LATIN AMERICA. BRAZIL URUGUAY CONSTN CULTURE SECT DIPLOM EDU/PROP PARTIC DRIVE ALL/VALS CATHISM...GEOG ANTHOL BIBLIOG REFORMERS BOLIV. PAGE 106 F2086
L/A+17C ORD/FREE ECO/UNDEV REV

B67
ROACH J.R.,THE UNITED STATES AND THE ATLANTIC COMMUNITY; ISSUES AND PROSPECTS. AFR WOR+45 TEC/DEV ECO/TAC COLONIAL REGION PEACE ROLE...ANTHOL NATO EEC. PAGE 112 F2199
INT/ORG POLICY ADJUST DIPLOM

B67
ROBINSON R.D.,INTERNATIONAL MANAGEMENT. LAW MARKET LABOR PRICE CONTROL COST DEMAND OWN PRODUC WEALTH 20. PAGE 113 F2225
T OP/RES MGT DIPLOM

B67
ROELOFS H.M.,THE LANGUAGE OF MODERN POLITICS: AN INTRODUCTION TO THE STUDY OF GOVERNMENT. DIPLOM ADMIN MARXISM NEW/LIB...JURID CONCPT METH/COMP T 20. PAGE 113 F2230
LEAD NAT/COMP PERS/REL NAT/G

B67
SACKS B.,SOUTH AFRICA: AN IMPERIAL DILEMMA. SOUTH/AFR UK ECO/UNDEV KIN DOMIN DEBATE CONTROL REV DISCRIM ISOLAT...POLICY STAT BIBLIOG 20. PAGE 115 F2268
COLONIAL RACE/REL DIPLOM ORD/FREE

B67
SHAFFER H.G.,THE COMMUNIST WORLD: MARXIST AND NON-MARXIST VIEWS. WOR+45 SOCIETY DIPLOM ECO/TAC CONTROL SOCISM...MARXIST ANTHOL BIBLIOG/A 20. PAGE 120 F2363
MARXISM NAT/COMP IDEA/COMP COM

B67
TANSKY L.,US AND USSR AID TO DEVELOPING COUNTRIES. INDIA TURKEY USA+45 USSR INDUS PLAN CAP/ISM WAR PWR WEALTH MARXISM...CHARTS NAT/COMP BIBLIOG 20. PAGE 128 F2534
ECO/UNDEV FOR/AID DIPLOM ECO/TAC

B67
THOMAN R.S.,GEOGRAPHY OF INTERNATIONAL TRADE. WOR+45 ECO/DEV ECO/UNDEV INT/ORG LG/CO PLAN BAL/PAY ...STAT CHARTS NAT/COMP 20. PAGE 130 F2559
INT/TRADE GEOG ECO/TAC DIPLOM

B67
UNIVERSAL REFERENCE SYSTEM,BIBLIOGRAPHY OF BIBLIOGRAPHIES IN POLITICAL SCIENCE, GOVERNMENT, AND PUBLIC POLICY (VOLUME III). WOR+45 WOR-45 LAW ADMIN...SOC CON/ANAL COMPUT/IR GEN/METH. PAGE 133 F2615
BIBLIOG/A NAT/G DIPLOM POLICY

B67
US AGENCY INTERNATIONAL DEV,PROPOSED FOREIGN AID PROGRAM FOR 1968: SUMMARY PRESENTATION TO THE CONGRESS. AFR S/ASIA USA+45 AGRI TEC/DEV DIPLOM ECO/TAC BAL/PAY COST HEALTH KNOWL SKILL 20 AID CONGRESS ALL/PROG. PAGE 134 F2640
ECO/UNDEV BUDGET FOR/AID STAT

B67
US CONGRESS SENATE,SURVEY OF THE ALLIANCE FOR PROGRESS; INFLATION IN LATIN AMERICA (PAMPHLET). USA+45 MARKET INT/ORG DIPLOM INT/TRADE BAL/PAY SENATE ALL/PROG. PAGE 135 F2666
L/A+17C FINAN POLICY FOR/AID

B67
US SENATE COMM ON FOREIGN REL,LATIN AMERICAN SUMMIT CONFERENCE. L/A+17C USA+45 FINAN PLAN SENATE ALL/PROG. PAGE 139 F2740
FOR/AID BUDGET DIPLOM INT/ORG

B67
US SENATE COMM ON FOREIGN REL,INTER-AMERICAN DEVELOPMENT BANK ACT AMENDMENT. L/A+17C USA+45 DELIB/GP DIPLOM FOR/AID BAL/PAY...CHARTS SENATE. PAGE 139 F2741
LAW FINAN INT/ORG ECO/UNDEV

B67
US SENATE COMM ON FOREIGN REL,ARMS SALES TO NEAR EAST AND SOUTH ASIAN COUNTRIES. INDIA IRAN PAKISTAN WOR+45 PROC/MFG BAL/PWR DIPLOM...DECISION SENATE. PAGE 139 F2742
WEAPON FOR/AID FORCES POLICY

B67
US SENATE COMM ON FOREIGN REL,HARRISON E. SALISBURY'S TRIP TO NORTH VIETNAM. CHINA/COM USA+45 VIETNAM/N PRESS TASK GUERRILLA CONSEN EFFICIENCY
DIPLOM WAR FORCES

PEACE DRIVE...OBS SENATE. PAGE 139 F2743 — ATTIT

B67
US SENATE COMM ON FOREIGN REL,FOREIGN ASSISTANCE ACT OF 1967. VIETNAM WOR+45 DELIB/GP CONFER CONTROL WAR WEAPON BAL/PAY...CENSUS CHARTS SENATE. PAGE 139 F2744 — FOR/AID LAW DIPLOM POLICY

B67
WATT A.,THE EVOLUTION OF AUSTRALIAN FOREIGN POLICY 1938-65. ASIA S/ASIA USA+45 USA-45 INT/ORG NAT/G FORCES FOR/AID TREATY 20 AUSTRAL. PAGE 144 F2834 — DIPLOM WAR

B67
WILCOX W.A.,ASIA AND UNITED STATES POLICY. CHINA/COM USA+45. PAGE 146 F2879 — ASIA S/ASIA DIPLOM POLICY

B67
WILLIAMS M.,THE EAST IS RED: THE VIEW INSIDE CHINA. CHINA/COM CONSTN COERCE AGE/Y ATTIT PERSON...OBS 20 MAO. PAGE 147 F2893 — REV MARXIST GP/REL DIPLOM

B67
WISEMAN H.V.,BRITAIN AND THE COMMONWEALTH. EUR+WWI FUT UK ECO/DEV POL/PAR TEC/DEV INT/TRADE LEAD ROLE SOVEREIGN...SOC TREND 20 CMN/WLTH. PAGE 148 F2911 — INT/ORG DIPLOM NAT/G NAT/COMP

B67
WOLF C. JR.,UNITED STATES POLICY AND THE THIRD WORLD. USA+45 WOR+45 FORCES ACT/RES BAL/PWR ECO/TAC FOR/AID DETER GUERRILLA NUC/PWR REV...CHARTS 20. PAGE 148 F2916 — DIPLOM ECO/UNDEV POLICY NAT/G

B67
YAMAMURA K.,ECONOMIC POLICY IN POSTWAR JAPAN. ASIA FINAN POL/PAR DIPLOM LEAD NAT/LISM ATTIT NEW/LIB POPULISM 20 CHINJAP. PAGE 149 F2946 — ECO/DEV POLICY NAT/G TEC/DEV

B67
ZUPNICK E.,UNDERSTANDING THE INTERNATIONAL MONEY SYSTEM (HEADLINE SERIES, NO. 182) (PAMPHLET). ECO/DEV NAT/G DIPLOM INT/TRADE...METH/COMP 20 IMF. PAGE 151 F2971 — FINAN PLAN INT/ORG PROB/SOLV

L67
DROBNIG U.,"CONFLICT OF LAWS AND THE EUROPEAN ECONOMIC COMMUNITY." EUR+WWI PROB/SOLV DIPLOM ...JURID EEC. PAGE 34 F0663 — INT/LAW ADJUD INT/ORG MARKET

L67
GOLD J.,"INTERPRETATION BY THE INTERNATIONAL MONETARY FUND OF ITS ARTICLES OF AGREEMENT." INT/TRADE ADJUD ATTIT...POLICY JURID. PAGE 48 F0933 — CONSTN INT/ORG LAW DIPLOM

L67
HOSHII I.,"JAPAN'S STAKE IN ASIA." ASIA S/ASIA CAP/ISM ECO/TAC ROLE...GEOG 20 CHINJAP. PAGE 62 F1224 — DIPLOM REGION NAT/G INT/ORG

L67
MACDONALD R.S.J.,"THE RESORT TO ECONOMIC COERCION BY INTERNATIONAL POLITICAL ORGANIZATIONS." CUBA ETHIOPIA RHODESIA SOUTH/AFR NAT/G FOR/AID INT/TRADE DOMIN CONTROL SANCTION...DECISION LEAGUE/NAT UN OAS 20. PAGE 83 F1625 — INT/ORG COERCE ECO/TAC DIPLOM

L67
MCALLISTER J.T. JR.,"THE POSSIBILITIES FOR DIPLOMACY IN SOUTHEAST ASIA." LAOS VIETNAM INT/ORG NAT/G PROVS BAL/PWR DOMIN AGREE COLONIAL WAR PWR 17/20 TREATY. PAGE 88 F1716 — DIPLOM S/ASIA

L67
MESTMACKER E.J.,"STATE TRADING MONOPOLIES IN THE EUROPEAN ECONOMIC COMMUNITY. DIPLOM ECO/TAC ADJUD CONTROL DISCRIM 20 EEC. PAGE 90 F1764 — INT/TRADE INT/ORG LAW TARIFFS

L67
SCALAPINO R.A.,"A SURVEY OF ASIA IN 1966." ASIA S/ASIA CONSTN SOCIETY POL/PAR CHIEF WAR...ANTHOL 20. PAGE 116 F2285 — DIPLOM

L67
TANDON Y.,"CONSENSUS AND AUTHORITY BEHIND UNITED NATIONS PEACEKEEPING OPERATIONS." FINAN VOL/ASSN BUDGET DIPLOM PAY DOMIN...CHARTS 20 UN. PAGE 128 F2528 — CONSEN INT/ORG PWR PEACE

S67
AGUILAR M.A.,"?UNA OEA MAS FUERTE O UNA AMERICA LATINA MAS DEBIL?" L/A+17C USA+45 USA-45 ECO/UNDEV INDUS CHIEF DELIB/GP FORCES CONTROL PWR 20 OAS KENNEDY/JF JOHNSON/LB. PAGE 3 F0050 — INT/ORG DIPLOM POLICY COLONIAL

S67
ALEXANDER R.J.,"'THIRD FORCE' IN WORLD COMMUNISM?" CHINA/COM CUBA USSR INT/ORG DIPLOM TASK INGP/REL ATTIT PWR 20 CASTRO/F. PAGE 3 F0060 — CHIEF MARXISM LEAD REV

S67
ALVES V.,"FOREIGN CAPITAL IN BRAZIL." BRAZIL USA+45 CAP/ISM DIPLOM ECO/TAC INT/TRADE CONTROL PWR ...POLICY 20. PAGE 4 F0081 — ECO/UNDEV FINAN SOCIALIST SOCISM

S67
ANDERSON S.S.,"SOVIET RUSSIA AND THE TWO EUROPES." AFR USSR PROB/SOLV CENTRAL SOVEREIGN 20. PAGE 5 F0097 — DIPLOM POLICY MARXISM

S67
APEL H.,"LES NOUVEAUX ASPECTS DE LA POLITIQUE ETRANGERE ALLEMANDE." AFR EUR+WWI GERMANY POL/PAR BAL/PWR ECO/TAC INT/TRADE NUC/PWR NAT/LISM PEACE ...POLICY 20 EEC. PAGE 6 F0107 — DIPLOM INT/ORG FEDERAL

S67
BARTLETT J.L.,"AMERICAN BOND ISSUES IN THE EUROPEAN ECONOMIC COMMUNITY." EUR+WWI LUXEMBOURG USA+45 DIPLOM CONTROL BAL/PAY EEC. PAGE 11 F0201 — LAW ECO/TAC FINAN TAX

S67
BELISLE J.,"FOREIGN RESTRAINTS ON US BANKS ABROAD" WOR+45 LAW. PAGE 12 F0233 — DIPLOM FINAN CONTROL LICENSE

S67
BELL D.E.,"THE QUALITY OF AID." USA+45 R+D DIPLOM GP/REL. PAGE 12 F0234 — POLICY FOR/AID PROB/SOLV INSPECT

S67
BUTT R.,"THE COMMON MARKET AND CONSERVATIVE POLITICS, 1961-2." UK CHIEF DIPLOM ECO/TAC INT/TRADE CONFER DEBATE REGION ATTIT...POLICY 20 EEC. PAGE 21 F0398 — EUR+WWI INT/ORG POL/PAR

S67
CAMPBELL J.C.,"SOVIET-AMERICAN RELATIONS: CONFLICT AND COOPERATION." AFR USA+45 USSR AGREE WAR PEACE 20 KHRUSH/N KENNEDY/JF. PAGE 21 F0407 — DIPLOM POLICY

S67
COSGROVE C.A.,"AGRICULTURE, FINANCE AND POLITICS IN THE EUROPEAN COMMUNITY." EUR+WWI DIST/IND MARKET INT/ORG VOL/ASSN DELIB/GP TEC/DEV BAL/PWR BARGAIN ECO/TAC RATION CONFER 20 EEC. PAGE 28 F0538 — ECO/DEV DIPLOM AGRI INT/TRADE

S67
CROKER F.P.U.,"ECONOMIC PEACEKEEPING." UK PLAN PROB/SOLV TEC/DEV BAL/PWR DIPLOM COERCE PEACE ...POLICY DECISION 20. PAGE 28 F0553 — FORCES WEAPON COST WAR

S67
EHRLICH S.,"INTERNATIONAL PRESSURE GROUPS: A CONTRIBUTION TO THE SOCIOLOGY OF INTERNATIONAL RELATIONS IN THE CAPITALIST WORLD." GP/REL...METH 20. PAGE 36 F0711 — INT/ORG LOBBY DIPLOM DECISION

S67
FADDEYEV N.,"CMEA CO-OPERATION OF EQUAL NATIONS." COM R+D PLAN CAP/ISM DIPLOM FOR/AID WEALTH...POLICY MARXIST. PAGE 39 F0758 — MARXISM ECO/TAC INT/ORG ECO/UNDEV

S67
FRIEDENBERG D.M.,"THE US IN LATIN AMERICA; A RECKONING OF SHAME." L/A+17C USA+45 USA-45 INT/ORG CAP/ISM FOR/AID 17/20 OAS. PAGE 44 F0857 — DIPLOM POLICY DOMIN COLONIAL

S67
GEISS I.,"THE GERMANS AND THE MIDDLE EAST CRISIS." GERMANY/W ISLAM ISRAEL USSR POL/PAR RACE/REL MARXISM...GP/COMP 20 JEWS. PAGE 47 F0914 — ATTIT DIPLOM WAR POLICY

S67
GONZALEZ M.P.,"CUBA, UNA REVOLUCION EN MARCHA." CUBA L/A+17C USA+45 VIETNAM ECO/UNDEV FORCES DIPLOM DOMIN...POLICY MARXIST NAT/COMP CASTRO/F. PAGE 48 F0946 — REV NAT/G COLONIAL SOVEREIGN

S67
GOSALVEZ R.B.,"PERFIL DEL GENERAL VINCENTE ROJO." SPAIN DIPLOM CIVMIL/REL EFFICIENCY PERSON SKILL 20 BOLIV. PAGE 49 F0966 — WAR FORCES ELITES BIOG

S67
GUPTA S.,"FOREIGN POLICY IN THE 1967 MANIFESTOS." ASIA COM INDIA USA+45 FORCES FOR/AID TAX ATTIT ...DECISION 20. PAGE 52 F1013 — IDEA/COMP POL/PAR POLICY DIPLOM

S67
HEATH D.B.,"BOLIVIA UNDER BARRIENTOS." L/A+17C NAT/G CHIEF DIPLOM ECO/TAC...POLICY 20 BOLIV. PAGE 58 F1132 — ECO/UNDEV POL/PAR REV CONSTN

S67
HERRERA F.,"EUROPEAN PARTICIPATION IN THE LATIN AMERICAN REGIONAL INTEGRATION" EUR+WWI L/A+17C GP/REL INGP/REL 20. PAGE 59 F1154 — DIPLOM REGION INT/ORG FINAN

S67
HILDEBRAND J.R.,"THE CENTRAL AMERICAN COMMON MARKET: ECONOMIC AND POLITICAL INTEGRATION." L/A+17C USA+45 ECO/DEV ECO/UNDEV AGRI SOVEREIGN. PAGE 59 F1170 — DIPLOM ECO/TAC INT/TRADE INT/ORG

S67
IBARRA J.,"EL EXPERIMENTO CUBANO." COM CUBA L/A+17C USA+45 ECO/UNDEV LEGIS INT/TRADE CONTROL REV — COLONIAL DIPLOM

NAT/LISM PWR 19/20 TREATY. PAGE 64 F1259 NAT/G POLICY

S67
ISELIN J.J.,"THE TRUMAN DOCTRINE: ITS PASSAGE THROUGH CONGRESS AND THE AFTERMATH." USA+45 ECO/UNDEV R+D INT/ORG DELIB/GP BAL/PWR REV PEACE ...POLICY UN. PAGE 66 F1291 DIPLOM COM FOR/AID AFR

S67
KENNY L.M.,"THE AFTERMATH OF DEFEAT IN EGYPT." ISLAM ISRAEL UAR UK USA+45 USSR INDUS FORCES ECO/TAC PRICE COERCE WEAPON COST ATTIT. PAGE 70 F1378 WAR ECO/UNDEV DIPLOM POLICY

S67
KINGSLEY R.E.,"THE US BUSINESS IMAGE IN LATIN AMERICA." L/A+17C USA+45 NAT/G TEC/DEV CAP/ISM FOR/AID DOMIN EDU/PROP...CONCPT LING IDEA/COMP 20. PAGE 71 F1396 ATTIT LOVE DIPLOM ECO/UNDEV

S67
KOHN W.S.G.,"THE SOVEREIGNTY OF LIECHTENSTEIN." LIECHTENST SWITZERLND USSR CONSTN DEBATE WAR CONSERVE 18/20 UN. PAGE 72 F1417 SOVEREIGN NAT/G PWR DIPLOM

S67
KRAUS J.,"A MARXIST IN GHANA." GHANA ELITES CHIEF PROB/SOLV TEC/DEV DIPLOM ECO/TAC COLONIAL PARTIC PWR 20 NKRUMAH/K. PAGE 73 F1432 MARXISM PLAN ATTIT CREATE

S67
LEIFER M.,"ASTRIDE THE STRAITS OF JAHORE: THE BRITISH PRESENCE AND COMMONWEALTH RIVALRY IN SOUTHEAST ASIA." MALAYSIA UK FORCES PLAN ECO/TAC ...DECISION 20 CMN/WLTH. PAGE 77 F1515 DIPLOM NAT/LISM COLONIAL

S67
MANGLAPUS R.S.,"ASIAN REVOLUTION AND AMERICAN IDEOLOGY." USA+45 SOCIETY CAP/ISM DIPLOM ADJUST CENTRAL...NAT/COMP 20. PAGE 84 F1652 REV POPULISM ATTIT ASIA

S67
MEADE J.E.,"POPULATION EXPLOSION, THE STANDARD OF LIVING AND SOCIAL CONFLICT." DIPLOM FOR/AID OWN ...PREDICT TREND 20. PAGE 89 F1739 GEOG WEALTH PRODUC INCOME

S67
MILLER C.H.,"B. TRAVEN Y EL 'PROBLEMA PETROLERO'." USA-45 ECO/UNDEV INDUS TEC/DEV INT/TRADE ATTIT ORD/FREE SOVEREIGN 20 MEXIC/AMER. PAGE 91 F1791 EXTR/IND DIPLOM ECO/TAC DOMIN

S67
MOSELY P.E.,"EASTERN EUROPE IN WORLD POWER POLITICS: WHERE DE-STALINIZATION HAS LED." ECO/UNDEV NAT/LISM 20. PAGE 94 F1842 COM NAT/G DIPLOM MARXISM

S67
MYRDAL G.,"ECONOMIC DEVELOPMENT IN THE BACKWARD COUNTRIES." INT/ORG TEC/DEV CAP/ISM DIPLOM INT/TRADE PRODUC WEALTH 20. PAGE 96 F1883 ECO/UNDEV INDUS NAT/G ECO/TAC

S67
OLIVIER G.,"ASPECTS JURIDIQUES DE L'ADOPTION DU TRAITE CECA A LA CRISE CHARBONNIERE (SUITE ET FIN)" LAW DIST/IND PLAN DIPLOM RATION PRICE ADMIN COST DEMAND...POLICY CON/ANAL ECSC TREATY. PAGE 101 F1988 INT/TRADE INT/ORG EXTR/IND CONSTN

S67
PECCEI A.,"DEVELOPED-UNDERDEVELOPED AND EAST-WEST RELATIONS." ECO/UNDEV TEC/DEV DIPLOM LEAD EFFICIENCY GEOG. PAGE 104 F2045 FOR/AID TREND REGION ECO/DEV

S67
PETRAS J.,"U.S. HEGEMONY AND LATIN AMERICAN RULING CLASSES." L/A+17C USA+45 ECO/UNDEV FOR/AID REV SOC. PAGE 105 F2071 NAT/G ATTIT DIPLOM POLICY

S67
PETROVICH M.B.,"UNITED STATES POLICY IN EAST EUROPE." ECO/DEV ECO/TAC IDEA/COMP. PAGE 105 F2075 COM INT/TRADE USA+45 DIPLOM

S67
PROBERT J.R.,"STREAMLINING THE FOREIGN POLICY MACHINE." USA+45 EFFICIENCY DEPT/STATE. PAGE 108 F2123 DIPLOM ADMIN EXEC GOV/REL

S67
REILLY T.J.,"FREEZING AND CONFISCATION OF CUBAN PROPERTY." CUBA USA+45 LAW DIPLOM LEGIT ADJUD CONTROL. PAGE 111 F2177 STRANGE OWN ECO/TAC

S67
ROCKE J.R.M.,"THE BRITISH EXPORT BATTLE FOR THE CARIBBEAN" GP/REL...POLICY 20 CMN/WLTH. PAGE 113 F2229 INT/TRADE DIPLOM MARKET ECO/TAC

S67
RONNING C.,"NANKING: 1950." ASIA CANADA CHINA/COM NAT/G PLAN ECO/TAC REV ADJUST 20. PAGE 113 F2235 DIPLOM ROLE PEACE

S67
SCHNEIDER E.,"DIE ENTPOLITISIERUNG DES DEUTSCHEN OSTHANDELS." AFR MARKET TEC/DEV OBJECTIVE 20. PAGE 117 F2307 ATTIT INT/TRADE ECO/TAC DIPLOM

S67
SMALL A.H.,"THE EFFECT OF TARIFF REDUCTIONS ON US IMPORT VOLUME." USA+45 INT/ORG NAT/G DIPLOM CONFER DEMAND...POLICY INT/LAW STAT CHARTS GATT EEC. PAGE 123 F2424 TARIFFS INT/TRADE PRICE ECO/TAC

S67
STOLTE S.C.,"THREE PROBLEMS FACING THE SOVIET BLOC." ASIA COM USA+45 USSR FORCES MARXISM ...IDEA/COMP METH/COMP 20 NATO WARSAW/P. PAGE 127 F2496 ECO/TAC DIPLOM INT/ORG POLICY

S67
TABORSKY E.,"THE CLASS STRUGGLE, THE PROLETARIAT, AND THE DEVELOPING NATIONS." USSR LABOR POL/PAR FOR/AID COLONIAL GP/REL 20. PAGE 128 F2521 DIPLOM MARXISM ECO/UNDEV WORKER

S67
WALKER R.L.,"THE WEST AND THE 'NEW ASIA'." CHINA/COM ECO/UNDEV DIPLOM...PREDICT 20. PAGE 142 F2805 ASIA INT/TRADE COLONIAL REGION

S67
WALZER M.,"THE CONDITION OF GREECE; TWENTY YEARS AFTER THE TRUMAN DOCTRINE." AFR GREECE FORCES CAP/ISM 20 TRUMAN/HS. PAGE 143 F2814 DIPLOM POLICY FOR/AID TOTALISM

S67
WARNER G.,"FRANCE, BRITAIN AND THE EEC." FRANCE UK INT/ORG DELIB/GP ECO/TAC CONTROL 20 EEC. PAGE 143 F2822 INT/TRADE BAL/PWR DIPLOM

S67
WILLMANN J.,"LA COMMUNAUTE EUROPEENNE ET LA GRANDE-BRETAGNE." UK PROB/SOLV TEC/DEV CAP/ISM DIPLOM CONFER FEDERAL...POLICY 20 EEC. PAGE 147 F2898 INT/ORG DRIVE NAT/LISM INT/TRADE

S67
WILSON C.E.,"AMERICAN INVESTMENT IN PORTUGUESE AFRICA: A PROBLEM OF "DEMOCRATIC" COLONIALISM." AFR ECO/UNDEV DIPLOM MORAL...IDEA/COMP 20 ANGOLA MOZAMBIQUE. PAGE 147 F2901 COLONIAL DOMIN ORD/FREE POLICY

S67
WOLFSON M.,"GOVERNMENT'S ROLE IN TOURISM DEVELOPMENT." WOR+45 ECO/DEV ECO/UNDEV FINAN BUDGET DIPLOM EDU/PROP. PAGE 148 F2920 SERV/IND NAT/G CONTROL PLAN

N67
US HOUSE COMM FOREIGN AFFAIRS,REPORT OF SPECIAL STUDY MISSION TO THE NEAR EAST (PAMPHLET). ISRAEL USA+45 YEMEN ECO/UNDEV INT/ORG FOR/AID ARMS/CONT WAR WEAPON NAT/LISM PEACE...GEOG 20 UN HOUSE/REP. PAGE 137 F2694 ISLAM DIPLOM FORCES

N67
US HOUSE COMM FOREIGN AFFAIRS,COMMUNIST ACTIVITIES IN LATIN AMERICA 1967 (PAMPHLET). CUBA USA+45 DIPLOM INT/TRADE EDU/PROP COERCE GUERRILLA HOUSE/REP OAS. PAGE 137 F2696 L/A+17C MARXISM ORD/FREE ECO/TAC

N67
US HOUSE COMM SCI ASTRONAUT,GOVERNMENT, SCIENCE, AND INTERNATIONAL POLICY (PAMPHLET). INDIA NETHERLAND ECO/DEV ECO/UNDEV R+D ACADEM PLAN DIPLOM FOR/AID CONFER...PREDICT 20 CHINJAP. PAGE 137 F2705 NAT/G POLICY CREATE TEC/DEV

N67
US SENATE COMM ON FOREIGN REL,ARMS SALES AND FOREIGN POLICY (PAMPHLET). FINAN FOR/AID CONTROL 20. PAGE 139 F2737 ARMS/CONT ADMIN OP/RES DIPLOM

N67
US SENATE COMM ON FOREIGN REL,THE UNITED NATIONS AT TWENTY-ONE (PAMPHLET). WOR+45 BUDGET ADMIN SENATE UN. PAGE 139 F2738 INT/ORG DIPLOM PEACE

N67
US SENATE COMM ON FOREIGN REL,WAR OR PEACE IN THE MIDDLE EAST (PAMPHLET). GREECE ISLAM ISRAEL JORDAN UAR CHIEF PROB/SOLV FOR/AID WAR PWR 20 SENATE. PAGE 139 F2739 DIPLOM FORCES PLAN

N67
US SENATE COMM ON FOREIGN REL,SURVEY OF THE ALLIANCE FOR PROGRESS: THE LATIN AMERICAN MILITARY (PAMPHLET). USA+45 INT/ORG POL/PAR DIPLOM AGREE GP/REL ROLE ORD/FREE 20. PAGE 139 F2746 L/A+17C FORCES CIVMIL/REL POLICY

B75
JEVONS W.S.,MONEY AND THE MECHANISM OF EXCHANGE. INDUS MARKET DIPLOM COST EQUILIB WEALTH LAISSEZ ...GEN/LAWS 19 MONEY. PAGE 67 F1319 PRICE FINAN ECO/TAC POLICY

B76
SMITH A.,THE WEALTH OF NATIONS. UK STRUCT WORKER DIPLOM ECO/TAC OPTIMAL DRIVE PERSON ORD/FREE ...OLD/LIB GEN/LAWS 17/18. PAGE 123 F2428 WEALTH PRODUC INDUS LAISSEZ

B96
MARX K.,REVOLUTION AND COUNTER-REVOLUTION. GERMANY MARXIST

CONSTN ELITES INDUS NAT/G DIPLOM ECO/TAC WEALTH. PAGE 86 F1693 REV PWR STRATA

B96
SMITH A.,LECTURES ON JUSTICE, POLICE, REVENUE AND ARMS (1763). UK LAW FAM FORCES TARIFFS AGREE COERCE INCOME OWN WEALTH LAISSEZ...GEN/LAWS 17/18. PAGE 123 F2429 DIPLOM JURID OLD/LIB TAX

DIPLOMACY....SEE DIPLOM

DIRECT/NAT....DIRECTORY NATIONAL (IRELAND)

DIRKSEN/E....EVERETT DIRKSEN

B62
CARPER E.T.,ILLINOIS GOES TO CONGRESS FOR ARMY LAND. USA+45 LAW EXTR/IND PROVS REGION CIVMIL/REL GOV/REL FEDERAL ATTIT 20 ILLINOIS SENATE CONGRESS DIRKSEN/E DOUGLAS/P. PAGE 22 F0420 ADMIN LOBBY GEOG LEGIS

DISARMAMENT....SEE ARMS/CONT

DISCIPLINE....SEE EDU/PROP, CONTROL

DISCRIM....DISCRIMINATION; SEE ALSO GP/REL, RACE/REL, ISOLAT

N
BROCKWAY A.F.,AFRICAN SOCIALISM. EUR+WWI GHANA ISLAM UAR ECO/UNDEV CAP/ISM INT/TRADE COLONIAL COERCE GOV/REL DISCRIM 20 NEGRO NKRUMAH/K NASSER/G. PAGE 19 F0356 AFR SOCISM MARXISM

N
US LIBRARY OF CONGRESS,SELECTED AND ANNOTATED BIBLIOGRAPHY ON LABOR PROBLEMS AND POLICIES IN A WARTIME ECONOMY (PAMPHLET). USA-45 INDUS LEGIS GP/REL DISCRIM PRODUC...SOC 20. PAGE 137 F2708 BIBLIOG/A WAR LABOR WORKER

B20
MOREL E.D.,THE BLACK MAN'S BURDEN. AFR MOD/EUR AGRI EXTR/IND PROB/SOLV INT/TRADE ADMIN CONTROL COERCE DISCRIM...POLICY 19/20 NEGRO LEAGUE/NAT. PAGE 93 F1828 ORD/FREE CAP/ISM RACE/REL DOMIN

B27
BELLOC H.,THE SERVILE STATE (1912) (3RD ED.). PRUSSIA UK CULTURE STRATA INDUS NAT/G ECO/TAC CONTROL LEAD SUFF DISCRIM EQUILIB ORD/FREE WEALTH 20. PAGE 12 F0237 WORKER CAP/ISM DOMIN CATH

B33
TANNENBAUM F.,PEACE BY REVOLUTION. ECO/UNDEV AGRI SECT WORKER DIPLOM EDU/PROP DISCRIM OWN WEALTH POPULISM 17/20 MEXIC/AMER INDIAN/AM. PAGE 128 F2532 CULTURE COLONIAL RACE/REL REV

B48
KESSELMAN L.C.,THE SOCIAL POLITICS OF THE FEPC. INDUS WORKER EDU/PROP GP/REL RACE/REL 20 NEGRO JEWS FEPC. PAGE 70 F1382 POLICY NAT/G ADMIN DISCRIM

B50
ADORNO T.W.,THE AUTHORITARIAN PERSONALITY. STRATA SECT PROB/SOLV ECO/TAC DISCRIM ATTIT SEX...SOC INT CHARTS METH 20. PAGE 3 F0044 AUTHORIT PERSON ALL/IDEOS SOCIETY

B52
SACHS E.S.,THE CHOICE BEFORE SOUTH AFRICA. SOUTH/AFR AGRI EXTR/IND PROC/MFG PROB/SOLV ORD/FREE SOVEREIGN 20 NEGRO. PAGE 115 F2267 NAT/LISM DISCRIM RACE/REL LABOR

S52
KORNHAUSER W.,"THE NEGRO UNION OFFICIAL: A STUDY OF SPONSORSHIP AND CONTROL" (BMR)" USA+45 CONTROL DISCRIM ROLE SUPEGO...OBS 20 NEGRO. PAGE 73 F1428 LABOR LEAD RACE/REL CHOOSE

B54
KARTUN D.,AFRICA, AFRICA: A CONTINENT RISES TO ITS FEET. AFR SOUTH/AFR UK ELITES AGRI LABOR LOC/G POL/PAR EDU/PROP CONTROL COERCE DISCRIM AGE/Y NEGRO THIRD/WRLD GOLD/COAST. PAGE 69 F1358 COLONIAL ORD/FREE PROFIT EXTR/IND

S54
MACK R.W.,"ECOLOGICAL PATTERNS IN AN INDUSTRIAL SHOP" (BMR)" USA+45 CULTURE SOCIETY STRATA STRUCT LABOR NEIGH GP/REL ADJUST HABITAT...SOC SOC/INTEG 20. PAGE 83 F1634 INDUS DISCRIM WORKER

B57
ROBERTSON H.M.,SOUTH AFRICA, ECONOMIC AND POLITICAL ASPECTS. SOUTH/AFR CONSTN CULTURE POL/PAR LEGIS DIPLOM DOMIN COLONIAL...SOC BIBLIOG 19/20. PAGE 112 F2214 RACE/REL ECO/UNDEV ECO/TAC DISCRIM

B58
JENNINGS I.,PROBLEMS OF THE NEW COMMONWEALTH. AFR CEYLON INDIA PAKISTAN S/ASIA ECO/UNDEV INT/ORG LOC/G DIPLOM ECO/TAC INT/TRADE COLONIAL RACE/REL DISCRIM 20 PARLIAMENT. PAGE 67 F1314 NAT/LISM NEUTRAL FOR/AID POL/PAR

B58
OGDEN F.D.,THE POLL TAX IN THE SOUTH. USA+45 USA-45 CONSTN ADJUD ADMIN PARTIC CRIME...TIME/SEQ GOV/COMP METH/COMP 18/20 SOUTH/US. PAGE 101 F1982 TAX CHOOSE RACE/REL DISCRIM

B59
ROCHE J.,LA COLONISATION ALLEMANDE ET LE RIO GRANDE DO SUL. BRAZIL L/A+17C NAT/G PROVS INGP/REL RACE/REL DISCRIM HABITAT...GEOG SOC/INTEG 19/20 MIGRATION. PAGE 113 F2228 ECO/UNDEV GP/REL ATTIT

B59
VOSE C.E.,CAUCASIANS ONLY: THE SUPREME COURT, THE NAACP, AND THE RESTRICTIVE COVENANT CASES. USA+45 LAW CONSTN LOBBY...SOC 20 NAACP SUPREME/CT NEGRO. PAGE 142 F2796 CT/SYS RACE/REL DISCRIM

B60
GRIER E.,PRIVATELY DEVELOPED INTERRACIAL HOUSING: AN ANALYSIS OF EXPERIENCE. FINAN MARKET COST DISCRIM PROFIT SOC/INTEG 20. PAGE 51 F0997 RACE/REL CONSTRUC HABITAT

B60
RAPKIN C.,THE DEMAND FOR HOUSING IN RACIALLY MIXED AREAS: A STUDY OF THE NATURE OF NEIGHBORHOOD CHANGE. USA+45 FINAN PRICE COST DRIVE...GEOG 20. PAGE 109 F2151 RACE/REL NEIGH DISCRIM MARKET

B60
STEVENSON A.E.,PUTTING FIRST THINGS FIRST. USA+45 INT/ORG NEIGH FOR/AID DISCRIM...ANTHOL 20. PAGE 126 F2483 DIPLOM ECO/UNDEV ORD/FREE EDU/PROP

B60
WODDIS J.,AFRICA: THE ROOTS OF REVOLT. SOUTH/AFR WORKER INT/TRADE RACE/REL DISCRIM ORD/FREE 20. PAGE 148 F2915 COLONIAL SOVEREIGN WAR ECO/UNDEV

B61
PERLO V.,EL IMPERIALISMO NORTHEAMERICANO. USA+45 USA-45 FINAN CAP/ISM DIPLOM DOMIN CONTROL DISCRIM 19/20. PAGE 105 F2063 SOCIALIST ECO/DEV INT/TRADE ECO/TAC

B61
SPOONER F.P.,SOUTH AFRICAN PREDICAMENT. FUT SOUTH/AFR INDUS POL/PAR RACE/REL INCOME...CHARTS 20 NEGRO. PAGE 125 F2459 ECO/DEV DISCRIM ECO/TAC POLICY

B62
FRIEDMAN M.,CAPITALISM AND FREEDOM. USA+45 FINAN LG/CO WORKER INT/TRADE RECEIVE EDU/PROP CONTROL DISCRIM INCOME WEALTH POLICY. PAGE 44 F0859 CAP/ISM ORD/FREE NAT/G ECO/DEV

B62
HENDERSON W.O.,THE GENESIS OF THE COMMON MARKET. EUR+WWI FRANCE MOD/EUR UK SEA COM/IND EXTR/IND COLONIAL DISCRIM...TIME/SEQ CHARTS BIBLIOG 18/20 EEC TREATY. PAGE 58 F1149 ECO/DEV INT/TRADE DIPLOM

B62
VAN RENSBURG P.,GUILTY LAND: THE HISTORY OF APARTHEID. SOUTH/AFR NAT/G POL/PAR DOMIN CHOOSE ...SOC 19/20 NEGRO. PAGE 140 F2763 RACE/REL DISCRIM NAT/LISM POLICY

B63
CORLEY R.N.,THE LEGAL ENVIRONMENT OF BUSINESS. CONSTN LEGIS TAX ADMIN CT/SYS DISCRIM ATTIT PWR ...TREND 18/20. PAGE 28 F0537 NAT/G INDUS JURID DECISION

B63
FRIEDRICH C.J.,MAN AND HIS GOVERNMENT: AN EMPIRICAL THEORY OF POLITICS. UNIV LOC/G NAT/G ADJUD REV INGP/REL DISCRIM PWR BIBLIOG. PAGE 44 F0867 PERSON ORD/FREE PARTIC CONTROL

B63
GANDHI M.K.,THE WAY TO COMMUNAL HARMONY. INDIA MAJORITY RIGID/FLEX ROLE RESPECT 20 GANDHI/M. PAGE 46 F0892 RACE/REL DISCRIM ATTIT ADJUST

B63
JACOBS P.,STATE OF UNIONS. USA+45 STRATA TOP/EX GP/REL RACE/REL DEMAND DISCRIM ATTIT PWR 20 CONGRESS NEGRO HOFFA/J. PAGE 66 F1296 LABOR ECO/TAC BARGAIN DECISION

B63
LEWIN J.,POLITICS AND LAW IN SOUTH AFRICA. SOUTH/AFR UK POL/PAR BAL/PWR ECO/TAC COLONIAL CONTROL GP/REL DISCRIM PWR 20 NEGRO. PAGE 79 F1545 NAT/LISM POLICY LAW RACE/REL

B63
MEIER G.,INTERNATIONAL TRADE AND DEVELOPMENT. FINAN BAL/PAY COST DEMAND DISCRIM EQUILIB WEALTH...POLICY ECOMETRIC MATH STAT BIBLIOG/A 20. PAGE 89 F1747 ECO/UNDEV ECO/TAC INT/TRADE IDEA/COMP

B64
HUTT W.H.,THE ECONOMICS OF THE COLOUR BAR. SOUTH/AFR EXTR/IND LABOR ADJUD NEGRO. PAGE 64 F1251 INDUS DISCRIM RACE/REL ECO/UNDEV

B64
SEGAL R.,SANCTIONS AGAINST SOUTH AFRICA. AFR SANCTION

SOUTH/AFR NAT/G INT/TRADE RACE/REL PEACE PWR ...INT/LAW ANTHOL 20 UN. PAGE 119 F2342
DISCRIM ECO/TAC POLICY

C64
NORGREN P.H.,"TOWARD FAIR EMPLOYMENT." USA+45 LAW STRATA LABOR NAT/G FORCES ACT/RES ADMIN ATTIT ...POLICY BIBLIOG 20 NEGRO. PAGE 98 F1932
RACE/REL DISCRIM WORKER MGT

B65
COLBERG M.R.,HUMAN CAPITAL IN SOUTHERN DEVELOPMENT. USA+45 AGRI ACADEM LABOR SCHOOL WORKER CAP/ISM DISCRIM. PAGE 26 F0498
PROVS RACE/REL GP/REL

B65
SELIGMAN B.B.,POVERTY AS A PUBLIC ISSUE. USA+45 ECO/DEV NAT/G PAY RECEIVE PERS/REL INCOME NEW/LIB 20. PAGE 119 F2347
LEGIS ECO/TAC STRATA DISCRIM

B65
SPENCE J.E.,REPUBLIC UNDER PRESSURE: A STUDY OF SOUTH AFRICAN FOREIGN POLICY. SOUTH/AFR ADMIN COLONIAL GOV/REL RACE/REL DISCRIM NAT/LISM ATTIT ROLE...TREND 20 NEGRO. PAGE 124 F2449
DIPLOM POLICY AFR

B65
US ADVISORY COMN INTERGOV REL,METROPOLITAN SOCIAL AND ECONOMIC DISPARITIES: IMPLICATIONS FOR INTERGOVERNMENTAL RELATIONS IN CENT'L CITIES AND SUBURBS. CULTURE STRATA DIST/IND LOC/G PLAN GP/REL DISCRIM HABITAT MUNICH. PAGE 134 F2634
GOV/REL GEOG

B65
VANEK J.,GENERAL EQUILIBRIUM OF INTERNATIONAL DISCRIMINATION; THE CASE OF CUSTOMS UNIONS. LABOR PROB/SOLV ECO/TAC DISCRIM INCOME...MATH CHARTS METH 20. PAGE 140 F2767
INT/TRADE TARIFFS INT/ORG EQUILIB

B65
WEISBROD B.A.,THE ECONOMICS OF POVERTY: AN AMERICAN PARADOX. USA+45 NAT/G WORKER TASK INGP/REL DISCRIM POLICY. PAGE 145 F2852
ECO/DEV WEALTH RECEIVE STRATA

S65
BANOVETZ J.M.,"METROPOLITAN SUBSIDIES: AN APPRAISAL." LEAD GP/REL DISCRIM MUNICH. PAGE 9 F0175
REGION TAX GOV/REL

S65
MULLER A.L.,"THE ECONOMIC POSITION OF THE ASIANS IN AFRICA." AFR SOUTH/AFR ECO/UNDEV MARKET ECO/TAC GP/REL INCOME...CHARTS IND 20 MONOPOLY ASIANS. PAGE 95 F1856
WORKER RACE/REL CAP/ISM DISCRIM

S65
SOPER T.,"THE EEC AND AID TO AFRICA." FRANCE UK ECO/UNDEV INT/TRADE TARIFFS REGION ROUTINE CENTRAL DISCRIM...DECISION RECORD EEC. PAGE 124 F2443
AFR FOR/AID COLONIAL

S65
STEENKAMP W.F.J.,"THE PROBLEM OF WAGE REGULATION." SOUTH/AFR LAW ECO/DEV ECO/UNDEV LABOR NAT/G BARGAIN PAY INGP/REL DISCRIM WEALTH...METH/COMP 20. PAGE 125 F2473
ECO/TAC PRICE WORKER RATION

S65
VAN DER HORST S.T.,"THE ECONOMICS OF DECENTRALISATION OF INDUSTRY." SOUTH/AFR ECO/DEV LG/CO AUTOMAT DISCRIM...POLICY MUNICH 20. PAGE 140 F2761
PLAN INDUS CENTRAL TEC/DEV

B66
EBONY,THE NEGRO HANDBOOK. ACADEM LABOR LOC/G SECT FORCES WORKER CT/SYS CRIME DISCRIM ORD/FREE...BIOG SOC/INTEG 19/20 NEGRO CIV/RIGHTS. PAGE 36 F0692
RACE/REL EDU/PROP LAW STAT

B66
ECONOMIC RESEARCH SERVICE,RESEARCH DATA ON MINORITY GROUPS: AN ANNOTATED BIBLIOGRAPHY OF ECONOMIC RESEARCH SERVICE REPORTS: 1955-1965 (PAMPHLET). USA+45 STRATA ECO/DEV AGRI SCHOOL WORKER EDU/PROP HEALTH NEW/LIB SOC. PAGE 36 F0697
BIBLIOG/A DISCRIM WEALTH RACE/REL

B66
SOVERN M.I.,LEGAL RESTRAINTS ON RACIAL DISCRIMINATION IN EMPLOYMENT. USA+45 LAW INDUS LG/CO SML/CO DELIB/GP LEGIS SANCTION 20 NLRB PRESIDENT NEGRO CIV/RIGHTS RAILROAD. PAGE 124 F2446
DISCRIM RACE/REL WORKER JURID

B66
WOODMAN H.D.,SLAVERY AND THE SOUTHERN ECONOMY: SOURCES AND READINGS. USA-45 CULTURE STRUCT AGRI ECO/TAC LEAD RACE/REL DISCRIM EFFICIENCY...CHARTS ANTHOL MUNICH 18/19 NEGRO SOUTH/US. PAGE 148 F2922
ECO/DEV STRATA WORKER UTIL

B67
LYTLE C.M.,THE WARREN COURT AND ITS CRITICS. USA+45 NAT/G PROVS FORCES LOBBY RACE/REL DISCRIM SOVEREIGN 20 SUPREME/CT WARRN/EARL. PAGE 83 F1618
CT/SYS ADJUD PROB/SOLV ATTIT

B67
POWLEDGE F.,BLACK POWER WHITE RESISTANCE. USA+45 STRUCT PLAN GP/REL DISCRIM HABITAT ORD/FREE WEALTH ...METH/COMP SOC/INTEG NEGRO. PAGE 107 F2111
RACE/REL ATTIT PWR

B67
ROSS A.M.,EMPLOYMENT, RACE, AND POVERTY. USA+45 LAW STRATA MARKET LABOR EDU/PROP ISOLAT SKILL...MGT ANTHOL 20 NEGRO. PAGE 114 F2244
RACE/REL WORKER WEALTH DISCRIM

B67
SACKS B.,SOUTH AFRICA: AN IMPERIAL DILEMMA. SOUTH/AFR UK ECO/UNDEV KIN DOMIN DEBATE CONTROL REV DISCRIM ISOLAT...POLICY STAT BIBLIOG 20. PAGE 115 F2268
COLONIAL RACE/REL DIPLOM ORD/FREE

B67
TUMIN M.M.,SOCIAL STRATIFICATION; THE FORMS AND FUNCTIONS OF INEQUALITY. SENIOR SANCTION WEALTH ...SOC CLASSIF METH 20. PAGE 131 F2592
STRATA DISCRIM CONCPT SOCIETY

B67
ULMAN L.,CHALLENGES TO COLLECTIVE BARGAINING. ECO/TAC DISCRIM EQUILIB ATTIT...JURID SOC/WK. PAGE 132 F2599
LABOR BARGAIN ADJUD POLICY

B67
WEINBERG M.,SCHOOL INTEGRATION: A COMPREHENSIVE CLASSIFIED BIBLIOGRAPHY OF 3,100 REFERENCES. USA+45 LAW NAT/G NEIGH SECT PLAN ROUTINE AGE/C WEALTH SOC/INTEG INDIAN/AM. PAGE 145 F2849
BIBLIOG SCHOOL DISCRIM RACE/REL

L67
BONFIELD A.E.,"THE SUBSTANCE OF AMERICAN FAIR EMPLOYMENT PRACTICES LEGISLA TION II - EMPLOYMENT AGENCIES, LABOR ORGANIZATIONS, ETC." ACT/RES DISCRIM EFFICIENCY. PAGE 16 F0311
LAW WORKER LABOR SERV/IND

L67
GLAZER N.,"HOUSING PROBLEMS AND HOUSING POLICIES." USA+45 PLAN RENT ADJUST CONSEN DEMAND DISCRIM AGE ATTIT HEALTH WEALTH MUNICH NEGRO. PAGE 48 F0929
POLICY CONSTRUC CREATE HABITAT

L67
MESTMACKER E.J.,"STATE TRADING MONOPOLIES IN THE EUROPEAN ECONOMIC COMMUNITY. DIPLOM ECO/TAC ADJUD CONTROL DISCRIM 20 EEC. PAGE 90 F1764
INT/TRADE INT/ORG LAW TARIFFS

S67
"THE FEDERAL AGRICULTURAL STABILIZATION PROGRAM AND THE NEGRO." LAW CONSTN PLAN REPRESENT DISCRIM ORD/FREE 20 NEGRO CONGRESS. PAGE 2 F0025
AGRI CONTROL NAT/G RACE/REL

S67
BRIMMER A.F.,"EMPLOYMENT PATTERNS AND THE DILEMMA OF DESEGREGATION." USA+45 SOCIETY SKILL 20 NEGRO. PAGE 18 F0353
RACE/REL DISCRIM WORKER STRATA

S67
EDGEWORTH A.B. JR.,"CIVIL RIGHTS PLUS THREE YEARS: BANKS AND THE ANTI-DISCRIMINATION LAW" USA+45 SOCIETY DELIB/GP RACE/REL EFFICIENCY 20 NEGRO CIV/RIGHTS. PAGE 36 F0701
WORKER DISCRIM FINAN LAW

S67
EDWARDS N.,"EDUCATION IN THE FEDERAL-STATE STRUCTURE OF GOVERNMENT." USA+45 SECT CONTROL GOV/REL RACE/REL DISCRIM FEDERAL ROLE PWR SOVEREIGN. PAGE 36 F0705
EDU/PROP NAT/G PROVS POLICY

S67
GRUN C.,"DEUX ETUDES ALLEMANDES SUR LES PREJUGES NATIONAUX ET LES MOYENS DE LES COMBATTRE." FRANCE GERMANY DIST/IND PROB/SOLV GP/REL AGE/Y RIGID/FLEX ...PSY STAT INT SAMP. PAGE 52 F1010
ATTIT REGION DISCRIM STERTYP

S67
JOHNSON L.B.,"BULLETS DO NOT DISCRIMINATE-LANDLORDS DO." PROB/SOLV EXEC LOBBY DEMAND...REALPOL SOC 20. PAGE 68 F1329
NAT/G DISCRIM POLICY

S67
LANDES W.M.,"THE EFFECT OF STATE FAIR EMPLOYMENT LAWS ON THE ECONOMIC POSITION OF NONWHITES." USA+45 PROVS SECT LEGIS ADMIN GP/REL RACE/REL...JURID CONCPT CHARTS HYPO/EXP NEGRO. PAGE 75 F1470
DISCRIM LAW WORKER

S67
LENS S.,"WALTER REUTHER TRIES TO BUILD A FIRE." WORKER LEAD DISCRIM AGE ORD/FREE NEW/LIB SOC. PAGE 78 F1523
LABOR PARTIC NEIGH PLAN

S67
MOONEY J.D.,"URBAN POVERTY AND LABOR FORCE PARTICIPATION." FAM DISCRIM...SOC/WK STAT CHARTS MUNICH. PAGE 93 F1820
INCOME WORKER WEALTH

S67
NEALE R.S.,"WORKING CLASS WOMEN AND WOMEN'S SUFFRAGE." UK LAW CONSTN LABOR NAT/G DELIB/GP LEGIS WORKER PAY PARTIC CHOOSE 19 FEMALE/SEX. PAGE 97 F1906
STRATA SEX SUFF DISCRIM

S67
NILES J.G.,"CIVIL ACTIONS FOR DAMAGES UNDER THE FEDERAL CIVIL RIGHTS STATUTES." CONSTN FINAN ADJUD CT/SYS GOV/REL RACE/REL 20. PAGE 98 F1928
DISCRIM LAW CONTROL ORD/FREE

S67
PIERPONT J.R.,"NEW STAGE IN THE LONGSHORE STRUGGLE." USA+45 SENIOR ADJUD RACE/REL...JURID 20 NEGRO. PAGE 106 F2083
LABOR DISCRIM WORKER CT/SYS

S67
WASSERMAN M.,"BEYOND TOKENISM: REVERSE INTEGRATION IN ALBANY, GEORGIA." USA+45 PLAN BUDGET EDU/PROP
REGION RACE/REL

LEAD AGE/C AGE/Y GEORGIA NEGRO. PAGE 144 F2827 DISCRIM SCHOOL

DISCRIMINATION....SEE DISCRIM

DISEASE....SEE HEALTH

DISPL....DISPLACEMENT AND PROJECTION

B47
HEILPERIN M.A.,THE TRADE OF NATIONS. USA+45 USA-45 WOR+45 WOR-45 CULTURE ECO/DEV NAT/G DELIB/GP EDU/PROP ATTIT DISPL ORD/FREE PWR WEALTH TOT/POP 20. PAGE 58 F1139 MARKET INT/ORG INT/TRADE PEACE

B56
WHYTE W.H. JR.,THE ORGANIZATION MAN. CULTURE FINAN VOL/ASSN DOMIN EDU/PROP EXEC DISPL HABITAT ROLE ...PERS/TEST STERTYP. PAGE 146 F2875 ADMIN LG/CO PERSON CONSEN

S63
SHWADRAN B.,"MIDDLE EAST OIL, 1962." ISLAM USSR ECO/DEV DIST/IND INDUS PLAN BAL/PWR DISPL DRIVE ...POLICY STAT TREND GEN/LAWS TERR/GP METH/GP EEC OEEC 20 OIL. PAGE 121 F2394 MARKET ECO/TAC INT/TRADE

DISPLACEMENT....SEE DISPL

DISPUTE, RESOLUTION OF....SEE ADJUD

DISRAELI/B....BENJAMIN DISRAELI

DIST/IND....DISTRIBUTIVE SYSTEM

N
US SUPERINTENDENT OF DOCUMENTS,CENSUS PUBLICATIONS (PRICE LIST 70). AGRI CONSTRUC DIST/IND FINAN LOC/G NAT/G PROVS INT/TRADE APPORT INCOME. PAGE 140 F2751 BIBLIOG/A CENSUS STAT USA+45

N
US SUPERINTENDENT OF DOCUMENTS,INTERSTATE COMMERCE (PRICE LIST 59). USA+45 LAW LOC/G NAT/G LEGIS TARIFFS TAX ADMIN CONTROL HEALTH DECISION. PAGE 140 F2752 BIBLIOG/A DIST/IND GOV/REL PROVS

B03
GRIFFIN A.P.C.,LISTS PUBLISHED 1902-03: GOVERNMENT OWNERSHIP OF RAILROADS (PAMPHLET). USA-45 LAW NAT/G RATION GOV/REL CENTRAL SOCISM...POLICY 19/20. PAGE 51 F0998 BIBLIOG DIST/IND CONTROL ADJUD

B18
MARX K.,CAPITAL. FUT MOD/EUR STRATA DIST/IND PROC/MFG TEC/DEV WEALTH...MARXIST WORK 19. PAGE 86 F1688 ECO/DEV CAP/ISM SOCISM

N19
DOTSON A.,PRODUCTION PLANNING IN THE PATENT OFFICE (PAMPHLET). USA+45 DIST/IND PROB/SOLV PRODUC...MGT PHIL/SCI 20 BUR/BUDGET PATENT/OFF. PAGE 34 F0655 EFFICIENCY PLAN NAT/G ADMIN

N19
LANGE O.R.,"DISARMAMENT ECONOMIC GROWTH AND INTERNATIONAL CO-OPERATION" (PAMPHLET). WOR+45 DIST/IND PLAN INT/TRADE GIVE TASK DETER WEALTH SOCISM 18/19 BOLIVAR/S. PAGE 75 F1477 ARMS/CONT DIPLOM ECO/DEV ECO/UNDEV

N19
PEGRUM D.F.,URBAN TRANSPORT AND THE LOCATION OF INDUSTRY IN METROPOLITAN LOS ANGELES (PAMPHLET). USA+45 WORKER...GEOG CHARTS MUNICH. PAGE 104 F2049 DIST/IND REGION INDUS

N19
US MARITIME ADMINISTRATION,CONTRIBUTION OF FEDERAL AID PROGRAMS TO THE OCEANBORNE FOREIGN TRADE OF THE UNITED STATES: 1959-62 (PAMPHLET). USA+45 SEA FINAN NAT/G BUDGET...POLICY 20. PAGE 138 F2719 INT/TRADE ECO/TAC DIST/IND GIVE

B21
CLAPHAN J.H.,THE ECONOMIC DEVELOPMENT OF FRANCE AND GERMANY 1815-1914. FRANCE GERMANY MOD/EUR COM/IND DIST/IND FINAN INT/TRADE EDU/PROP 19/20. PAGE 24 F0476 ECO/UNDEV ECO/DEV AGRI INDUS

B25
EDGEWORTH F.Y.,PAPERS RELATING TO POLITICAL ECONOMY. MOD/EUR SOCIETY STRATA DIST/IND INDUS MARKET NAT/G ACT/RES ECO/TAC EXEC WEALTH ...METH/CNCPT MATH TREND HYPO/EXP SIMUL GEN/METH FOR/TRADE VAL/FREE LOG/LING. PAGE 36 F0702 ECO/DEV CAP/ISM

B26
MCPHEE A.,THE ECONOMIC REVOLUTION IN BRITISH WEST AFRICA. AFR UK CULTURE DIST/IND FINAN INDUS PLAN GP/REL RACE/REL 20 AFRICA/W. PAGE 88 F1735 ECO/UNDEV INT/TRADE COLONIAL GEOG

B30
THOMPSON W.R.,POPULATION PROBLEMS. FUT UNIV WOR-45 STRUCT DIST/IND ACT/RES ECO/TAC BIO/SOC...CONCPT OBS TIME/SEQ TOT/POP 20. PAGE 130 F2567 ECO/UNDEV GEOG

B39
FIRTH R.,PRIMITIVE POLYNESIAN ECONOMY. SOCIETY DIST/IND SECT CHIEF CAP/ISM PRODUC WEALTH...SOC OBS METH WORSHIP 20 POLYNESIA. PAGE 41 F0802 ECO/UNDEV CULTURE AGRI ECO/TAC

B40
GAUS J.M.,PUBLIC ADMINISTRATION AND THE UNITED STATES DEPARTMENT OF AGRICULTURE. USA-45 STRUCT DIST/IND FINAN MARKET EX/STRUC PROB/SOLV GIVE PRODUC...POLICY GEOG CHARTS 20 DEPT/AGRI. PAGE 47 F0909 ADMIN AGRI DELIB/GP OP/RES

B40
TRIFFIN R.,MONOPOLISTIC COMPETITION AND GENERAL EQUILIBRIUM THEORY. DIST/IND PLAN TASK EQUILIB OPTIMAL...IDEA/COMP 20 MONOPOLY. PAGE 131 F2586 INT/TRADE INDUS COST

B44
INTL CHAMBER OF COMMERCE,TERMS COMMONLY USED IN DISTRIBUTION AND ADVERTISING. PORTUGAL SPAIN UK WOR-45 SERV/IND 20. PAGE 65 F1284 DICTIONARY EDU/PROP DIST/IND INT/TRADE

B50
KOENIG L.W.,THE SALE OF THE TANKERS. USA+45 SEA DIST/IND POL/PAR DIPLOM ADMIN CIVMIL/REL ATTIT ...DECISION 20 PRESIDENT DEPT/STATE. PAGE 72 F1414 NAT/G POLICY PLAN GOV/REL

B50
LINCOLN G.,ECONOMICS OF NATIONAL SECURITY. USA+45 ELITES COM/IND DIST/IND INDUS NAT/G VOL/ASSN DELIB/GP EX/STRUC FOR/AID EDU/PROP COERCE NUC/PWR WAR ATTIT KNOWL ORD/FREE PWR TOT/POP VAL/FREE 20. PAGE 80 F1565 FORCES ECO/TAC AFR

B52
ALEXANDROWICZ C.H.,INTERNATIONAL ECONOMIC ORGANIZATION. WOR+45 ECO/DEV ECO/UNDEV DIST/IND FINAN MARKET PLAN ECO/TAC LEGIT DRIVE WEALTH ...POLICY CONCPT QUANT OBS TIME/SEQ GEN/LAWS WORK METH/GP EEC ILO OEEC UNESCO 20. PAGE 4 F0063 INT/ORG INT/TRADE

B53
ROBINSON E.A.G.,THE STRUCTURE OF COMPETITIVE INDUSTRY. UK ECO/DEV DIST/IND MARKET TEC/DEV DIPLOM EDU/PROP ADMIN EFFICIENCY WEALTH...MGT 19/20. PAGE 113 F2217 INDUS PRODUC WORKER OPTIMAL

B54
LOCKLIN D.P.,ECONOMICS OF TRANSPORTATION (4TH ED.). USA+45 USA-45 SEA AIR LAW FINAN LG/CO EX/STRUC ADMIN CONTROL...STAT CHARTS 19/20 RAILROAD PUB/TRANS. PAGE 81 F1592 ECO/DEV DIST/IND ECO/TAC TEC/DEV

B55
JONES T.B.,A BIBLIOGRAPHY ON SOUTH AMERICAN ECONOMIC AFFAIRS: ARTICLES IN NINETEENTH CENTURY PERIODICALS (PAMPHLET). AGRI COM/IND DIST/IND EXTR/IND FINAN INDUS LABOR NAT/G 19. PAGE 68 F1340 BIBLIOG ECO/UNDEV L/A+17C TEC/DEV

B55
O'CONNOR H.,THE EMPIRE OF OIL. USA+45 DIST/IND FINAN MARKET CAP/ISM TAX CONTROL...POLICY MARXIST BIBLIOG/A 20. PAGE 100 F1955 EXTR/IND INT/TRADE CENTRAL NAT/G

B55
PALAMOUNTAIN JC J.R.,THE POLITICS OF DISTRIBUTION. USA+45 LG/CO SML/CO BAL/PWR CONTROL EQUILIB 20. PAGE 103 F2019 DIST/IND ECO/TAC CAP/ISM GP/REL

B55
WOYTINSKY W.S.,WORLD COMMERCE AND GOVERNMENTS: TRENDS AND OUTLOOK. WOR+45 FINAN POL/PAR DIPLOM ECO/TAC FOR/AID DOMIN WAR CHOOSE...CHARTS BIBLIOG 20 LEAGUE/NAT UN ILO. PAGE 149 F2929 INT/TRADE DIST/IND NAT/COMP NAT/G

B56
ISARD W.,LOCATION AND SPACE-ECONOMY: GENERAL THEORY RELATING TO INDUSTRIAL LOCATION, MARKET AREAS, LAND USE, TRADE... UNIV DIST/IND MARKET LG/CO SML/CO TEC/DEV GP/REL EQUILIB HABITAT...NEW/IDEA MATH CHARTS 20. PAGE 66 F1290 GEN/LAWS GEOG INDUS REGION

B56
JUAN T.L.,ECONOMIC AND SOCIAL DEVELOPMENT OF MODERN CHINA: A BIBLIOGRAPHICAL GUIDE. ASIA AGRI COM/IND DIST/IND FINAN INDUS DIPLOM...STAT 20. PAGE 68 F1342 BIBLIOG SOC

B56
WATT D.C.,BRITAIN AND THE SUEZ CANAL. COM UAR UK ...INT/LAW 20 SUEZ TREATY. PAGE 144 F2835 DIPLOM INT/TRADE DIST/IND NAT/G

B57
ASHER R.E.,THE UNITED NATIONS AND ECONOMIC AND SOCIAL COOPERATION. ECO/UNDEV COM/IND DIST/IND FINAN PLAN PROB/SOLV INT/TRADE TASK WEALTH...SOC 20 UN. PAGE 7 F0129 INT/ORG DIPLOM FOR/AID

B57
DRUCKER P.F.,AMERICA'S NEXT TWENTY YEARS. USA+45 DIST/IND ACADEM SCHOOL DIPLOM ECO/TAC AUTOMAT HABITAT HEALTH...SOC/WK TREND MUNICH 20 URBAN/RNWL PUB/TRANS. PAGE 34 F0667 WORKER FOR/AID CENSUS GEOG

B57
WARRINER D.,LAND REFORM AND DEVELOPMENT IN THE MIDDLE EAST: A STUDY OF EGYPT, SYRIA AND IRAQ. IRAQ ISLAM SYRIA UAR AGRI DIST/IND PLAN TEC/DEV DOMIN REV ATTIT WEALTH...SOC METH/CNCPT STAT OBS RECORD HIST/WRIT TREND GEN/LAWS FAO 20. PAGE 143 F2825 ECO/UNDEV CONCPT

L57
MASS. INST. TECH.,"THE CENTER FOR INTERNATIONAL R+D

STUDIES." AFR ASIA COM EUR+WWI ISLAM L/A+17C S/ASIA USA+45 USA-45 DIST/IND CONSULT FORCES ACT/RES TEC/DEV DIPLOM REV ATTIT WEALTH...CONCPT FOR/TRADE 20. PAGE 87 F1702 ECO/UNDEV

S57
VERNON R.,"PRODUCTION AND DISTRIBUTION IN THE LARGE METROPOLIS" (BMR)" USA+45 PROC/MFG ECO/TAC HABITAT ...CENSUS TREND MUNICH 20. PAGE 141 F2779 PRODUC DIST/IND PROB/SOLV

N57
U WISCONSIN BUREAU OF GOVT,SERVICE SALES OF THE CITY OF MADISON TO METROPOLITAN COMMUNITIES AND NONRESIDENTS (PAMPHLET). DIST/IND LOC/G ADMIN ...DECISION GOV/COMP MUNICH. PAGE 132 F2597 REGION ECO/TAC PLAN

B58
BERLINER J.S.,SOVIET ECONOMIC AID: THE AID AND TRADE POLICY IN UNDERDEVELOPED COUNTRIES. AFR COM ISLAM L/A+17C S/ASIA USSR ECO/DEV DIST/IND FINAN MARKET INT/ORG ACT/RES PLAN BAL/PWR WEAPON PWR WEALTH...CHARTS FOR/TRADE 20. PAGE 14 F0263 ECO/UNDEV ECO/TAC FOR/AID

B58
HANCE W.A.,AFRICAN ECONOMIC DEVELOPMENT. AGRI DIST/IND INDUS R+D ACT/RES PLAN CAP/ISM FOR/AID ...GOV/COMP BIBLIOG 20. PAGE 54 F1058 AFR ECO/UNDEV PROB/SOLV TEC/DEV

B58
MIKESELL R.F.,FINANCING FREE WORLD TRADE WITH THE SINO-SOVIET BLOC. CHINA/COM COM USSR WOR+45 ECO/DEV AGRI DIST/IND EXTR/IND FINAN INDUS MARKET PROC/MFG NAT/G PLAN TEC/DEV ECO/TAC...CHARTS METH/GP EEC FOR/TRADE 20. PAGE 91 F1780 STAT BAL/PAY

B58
US HOUSE COMM POST OFFICE,MANPOWER UTILIZATION IN THE FEDERAL GOVERNMENT. USA+45 DIST/IND EX/STRUC LEGIS CONFER EFFICIENCY 20 CONGRESS CIVIL/SERV. PAGE 137 F2702 ADMIN WORKER DELIB/GP NAT/G

B58
US HOUSE COMM POST OFFICE,MANPOWER UTILIZATION IN THE FEDERAL GOVERNMENT. USA+45 DIST/IND EX/STRUC LEGIS CONFER EFFICIENCY 20 CONGRESS CIVIL/SERV. PAGE 137 F2703 ADMIN WORKER DELIB/GP NAT/G

S58
ARROW K.J.,"UTILITIES, ATTITUDES, CHOICES: A REVIEW NOTE." USA+45 PLAN...METH/CNCPT MATH STAT CHARTS HYPO/EXP. PAGE 6 F0121 DECISION DIST/IND MARKET CREATE

S58
LANE F.C.,"ECONOMIC CONSEQUENCES OF ORGANIZED VIOLENCE." FUT WOR+45 WOR-45 ECO/DEV DIST/IND SERV/IND NAT/G PROVS EX/STRUC CHOOSE ORD/FREE PWR ...TIME/SEQ GEN/LAWS MUNICH 20. PAGE 75 F1472 WEALTH COERCE

B59
AITKEN H.,THE STATE AND ECONOMIC GROWTH. COM EUR+WWI MOD/EUR S/ASIA USA+45 FINAN NAT/G DELIB/GP PLAN PWR WEALTH 20. PAGE 3 F0054 DIST/IND ECO/DEV

B59
HAZLEWOOD A.,THE ECONOMICS OF "UNDER-DEVELOPED" AREAS. WOR+45 DIST/IND EXTR/IND FINAN INDUS MARKET PLAN FOR/AID...GEOG 20. PAGE 57 F1129 BIBLIOG/A ECO/UNDEV AGRI INT/TRADE

B59
LOPEZ VILLAMIL H.,A STATEMENT OF THE LAWS OF THE HONDURAS IN MATTERS AFFECTING BUSINESS (2ND ED.). HONDURAS DIST/IND EXTR/IND FINAN WORKER TAX DEATH MARRIAGE OWN MARITIME 20 MIGRATION. PAGE 82 F1600 CONSTN INDUS LEGIS NAT/G

B59
MAYER H.M.,READINGS IN URBAN GEOGRAPHY. WOR+45 SOCIETY DIST/IND INDUS MARKET HABITAT...CLASSIF CENSUS CHARTS ANTHOL MUNICH 20 WATER. PAGE 87 F1706 GEOG STRUCT

B59
SELIGSOHN I.J.,"USING COMPUTER SERVICES IN SMALL BUSINESS" MANAGEMENT AIDS FOR SMALL MANUFACTURERS 109 (PAMPHLET). DIST/IND MARKET PROC/MFG COST EFFICIENCY PRODUC...DECISION IDEA/COMP. PAGE 119 F2350 SML/CO COMPUTER MGT PROB/SOLV

L59
MURPHY J.C.,"SOME IMPLICATIONS OF EUROPE'S COMMON MARKET. IN (COOK P, ECONOMIC DEVELOPMENT AND INTERNATIONAL TRADE.," EUR+WWI ECO/DEV DIST/IND INDUS NAT/G PLAN ECO/TAC INT/TRADE WEALTH...STAT TREND OEEC TOT/POP 20 EEC. PAGE 95 F1866 MARKET INT/ORG REGION

S59
ALLEN G.,"NATIONAL FARMERS UNION AS A PRESSURE GROUP: II." UK ECO/DEV MARKET POL/PAR DELIB/GP PROB/SOLV ECO/TAC LOBBY INCOME...POLICY METH/COMP 19/20 NAT/FARMER. PAGE 4 F0069 DIST/IND AGRI PROF/ORG TREND

S59
KINDLEBERGER C.P.,"UNITED STATES ECONOMIC FOREIGN POLICY: RESEARCH REQUIREMENTS FOR 1965." FUT USA+45 WOR+45 DIST/IND MARKET INT/ORG ECO/TAC INT/TRADE WEALTH...OBS TREND CON/ANAL GEN/LAWS FOR/TRADE VAL/FREE 20. PAGE 71 F1392 FINAN ECO/DEV FOR/AID

S59
THOMPSON W.S.,"POPULATION AND PROGRESS IN THE FAR EAST." ASIA S/ASIA DIST/IND CREATE ECO/TAC WAR LOVE SKILL WEALTH...CONT/OBS TOT/POP 20. PAGE 130 F2568 ECO/UNDEV BIO/SOC GEOG

B60
AMERICAN U BEIRUT ECO RES INST,A SELECTED AND ANNOTATED BIBLIOGRAPHY OF ECONOMIC LITERATURE ON THE ARABIC SPEAKING COUNTRIES OF THE MIDDLE EAST. ISLAM AGRI COM/IND DIST/IND FINAN INDUS LABOR ...GEOG 20. PAGE 5 F0091 BIBLIOG/A ECO/UNDEV STAT

B60
APTHEKER H.,DISARMAMENT AND THE AMERICAN ECONOMY: A SYMPOSIUM. FUT USA+45 ECO/DEV DIST/IND FINAN INDUS PROC/MFG LABOR NAT/G POL/PAR CONSULT PLAN CAP/ISM INT/TRADE PEACE ATTIT MORAL WEALTH...TREND GEN/LAWS TOT/POP 20. PAGE 6 F0110 MARXIST ARMS/CONT

B60
BATOR F.M.,QUESTION OF GOVERNMENT SPENDING. USA+45 DIST/IND FINAN BAL/PAY...STAT CENSUS CHARTS CONGRESS 20. PAGE 11 F0210 ECO/DEV

B60
CAMPBELL R.W.,SOVIET ECONOMIC POWER. COM USA+45 DIST/IND MARKET TOP/EX ACT/RES CAP/ISM ECO/TAC DOMIN EDU/PROP ADMIN ROUTINE DRIVE...MATH TIME/SEQ CHARTS WORK 20. PAGE 21 F0409 ECO/DEV PLAN SOCISM USSR

B60
COMMITTEE ECONOMIC DEVELOPMENT,NATIONAL OBJECTIVES AND THE BALANCE OF PAYMENTS PROBLEM: A STATEMENT ON NATIONAL POLICY. USA+45 WOR+45 DIST/IND FINAN INDUS LABOR NAT/G DELIB/GP ACT/RES FOR/AID INT/TRADE ...STAT CHARTS FOR/TRADE 20. PAGE 27 F0516 ECO/DEV ECO/TAC BAL/PAY

B60
COPLAND D.,THE ADVENTURE OF GROWTH: ESSAYS ON THE AUSTRALIAN ECONOMY AND ITS INTERNATIONAL SETTING. WOR+45 DIST/IND ACADEM EDU/PROP ADMIN INCOME 20 AUSTRAL. PAGE 27 F0534 ECO/DEV ECO/UNDEV ECO/TAC INT/TRADE

B60
SMET G.,BIBLIOGRAPHIE DE LA CONTRIBUTION A L'ETUDE DE LA PROGRESSION ECONOMIQUE DE L'AFRIQUE. AFR DIST/IND EXTR/IND TEC/DEV 20. PAGE 123 F2427 BIBLIOG ECO/UNDEV INDUS AGRI

B60
US SENATE COMM ON COMMERCE,URBAN MASS TRANSPORTATION. FUT USA+45 AIR ECO/DEV FINAN LOC/G LEGIS CREATE PROB/SOLV TEC/DEV MUNICH 20 PUB/TRANS. PAGE 139 F2732 DIST/IND PLAN NAT/G LAW

S60
"THE EMERGING COMMON MARKETS IN LATIN AMERICA." FUT L/A+17C STRATA DIST/IND INDUS LABOR NAT/G LEGIS ECO/TAC ADMIN RIGID/FLEX HEALTH...NEW/IDEA TIME/SEQ OAS 20. PAGE 1 F0013 FINAN ECO/UNDEV INT/TRADE

S60
BECKER A.S.,"COMPARISIONS OF UNITED STATES AND USSR NATIONAL OUTPUT: SOME RULES OF THE GAME." COM USA+45 ECO/DEV AGRI DIST/IND INDUS R+D CONSULT PLAN ECO/TAC RIGID/FLEX KNOWL...METH/CNCPT CHARTS 20. PAGE 12 F0227 STAT USSR

S60
KREININ M.E.,"THE 'OUTER-SEVEN' AND EUROPEAN INTEGRATION." EUR+WWI FRANCE GERMANY ITALY UK ECO/DEV DIST/IND INT/TRADE DRIVE WEALTH...MYTH CHARTS EEC OEEC 20. PAGE 73 F1436 ECO/TAC GEN/LAWS

S60
MORALES C.J.,"TRADE AND ECONOMIC INTEGRATION IN LATIN AMERICA." FUT L/A+17C LAW STRATA ECO/UNDEV DIST/IND INDUS LABOR NAT/G LEGIS ECO/TAC ADMIN RIGID/FLEX WEALTH...CONCPT NEW/IDEA CONT/OBS TIME/SEQ WORK 20. PAGE 93 F1825 FINAN INT/TRADE REGION

S60
NEISSER H.,"ECONOMIC IMPERIALISM RECONSIDERED." WOR+45 WOR-45 ECO/DEV ECO/UNDEV DIST/IND LEGIT COLONIAL PWR WEALTH SOCISM...MYTH MATH TIME/SEQ 20. PAGE 97 F1909 ACT/RES ECO/TAC CAP/ISM INT/TRADE

B61
DOIG J.W.,THE POLITICS OF METROPOLITAN TRANSPORTATION. DELIB/GP WORKER DIPLOM TASK EFFICIENCY UTIL...CHARTS BIBLIOG MUNICH 20 NEW/YORK NEW/JERSEY PUB/TRANS RAILROAD. PAGE 34 F0652 PROB/SOLV STRATA DIST/IND

B61
FLINN M.W.,AN ECONOMIC AND SOCIAL HISTORY OF BRITAIN, 1066-1939. UK LAW STRATA STRUCT AGRI DIST/IND INDUS WORKER INT/TRADE WAR...CENSUS 11/20. PAGE 42 F0811 SOCIETY SOC

B61
FRIEDMANN W.G.,JOINT INTERNATIONAL BUSINESS VENTURES. ASIA ISLAM L/A+17C ECO/DEV DIST/IND FINAN PROC/MFG FACE/GP LG/CO NAT/G VOL/ASSN CONSULT EX/STRUC PLAN ADMIN ROUTINE WEALTH...OLD/LIB FOR/TRADE WORK 20. PAGE 44 F0865 ECO/UNDEV INT/TRADE

B61
INTERNATIONAL BANK RECONST DEV,THE WORLD BANK IN AFRICA: SUMMARY OF ACTIVITIES. AGRI COM/IND DIST/IND EXTR/IND INDUS TAX COST...CHARTS 20. PAGE 65 F1271 FINAN ECO/UNDEV INT/ORG AFR

B61
INTL UNION LOCAL AUTHORITIES,METROPOLIS. WOR+45 DIST/IND FINAN GIVE EDU/PROP CRIME COST HEALTH WEALTH MUNICH 20. PAGE 65 F1286 GOV/COMP LOC/G BIBLIOG

B61
KITZINGER V.W.,THE CHALLENGE OF THE COMMON MARKET. MARKET

EUR+WWI ECO/DEV DIST/IND PLAN ECO/TAC INT/TRADE LEGIT ATTIT PWR WEALTH...TIME/SEQ TREND CHARTS EEC 20. PAGE 71 F1403 INT/ORG UK

B61
LAHAYE R.,LES ENTREPRISES PUBLIQUES AU MAROC. FRANCE MOROCCO LAW DIST/IND EXTR/IND FINAN CONSULT PLAN TEC/DEV ADMIN AGREE CONTROL OWN...POLICY 20. PAGE 74 F1460 NAT/G INDUS ECO/UNDEV ECO/TAC

B61
SEPULVEDA C.,A STATEMENT OF THE LAWS OF MEXICO IN MATTERS AFFECTING BUSINESS (3RD ED.). AGRI DIST/IND EXTR/IND FINAN INDUS WORKER TAX MARRIAGE OWN ORD/FREE...BIBLIOG 20 MEXIC/AMER TREATY MIGRATION MONOPOLY. PAGE 119 F2356 CONSTN NAT/G JURID LEGIS

S61
DEUTSCH K.W.,"NATIONAL INDUSTRIALIZATION AND THE DECLINING SHARE OF THE INTERNATIONAL ECONOMIC SECTOR." EUR+WWI FUT WOR+45 WOR-45 MARKET PLAN EDU/PROP WEALTH...WELF/ST OBS TESTS 20. PAGE 32 F0624 DIST/IND ECO/DEV INT/TRADE

B62
ALEXANDROWICZ C.H.,WORLD ECONOMIC AGENCIES: LAW AND PRACTICE. WOR+45 DIST/IND FINAN LABOR CONSULT INT/TRADE TARIFFS REPRESENT HEALTH...JURID 20 UN GATT EEC OAS ECSC. PAGE 4 F0064 INT/LAW INT/ORG DIPLOM ADJUD

B62
GORT M.,DIVERSIFICATION AND INTEGRATION IN AMERICAN INDUSTRY. CLIENT DIST/IND PROC/MFG SERV/IND LG/CO CONTROL DEMAND PWR...METH/CNCPT STAT TREND CON/ANAL GP/COMP. PAGE 49 F0964 CONCPT GP/REL CLASSIF

B62
HOOVER E.M.,ANATOMY OF A METROPOLIS. FUT USA+45 SOCIETY ECO/DEV DIST/IND INDUS WORKER ECO/TAC TAX GP/REL COST WEALTH MUNICH 20 NEWYORK/C. PAGE 62 F1212 ROUTINE TREND INCOME

B62
INTERNATIONAL BANK RECONST DEV,THE WORLD BANK AND IDA IN ASIA. ASIA S/ASIA COM/IND DIST/IND...CHARTS 20. PAGE 65 F1272 FINAN ECO/UNDEV AGRI INDUS

B62
KLEIN L.R.,AN INTRODUCTION TO ECONOMETRICS. DIST/IND DEMAND PRODUC WEALTH...MATH TIME/SEQ T 20. PAGE 72 F1408 ECOMETRIC SIMUL PREDICT STAT

L62
WATERSTON A.,"PLANNING IN MOROCCO, ORGANIZATION AND IMPLEMENTATION. BALTIMORE: HOPKINS ECON. DEVELOP. INT. BANK FOR." ISLAM ECO/DEV AGRI DIST/IND INDUS PROC/MFG SERV/IND LOC/G EX/STRUC ECO/TAC PWR WEALTH TOT/POP TRUE/GP METH/GP TERR/GP VAL/FREE 20. PAGE 144 F2829 NAT/G PLAN MOROCCO

B63
BRITISH AID. UK AGRI DIST/IND INDUS SCHOOL TEC/DEV INT/TRADE COLONIAL DEMAND...TREND CHARTS 20. PAGE 1 F0018 FOR/AID ECO/UNDEV NAT/G FINAN

B63
COPPOCK J.,NORTH ATLANTIC POLICY - THE AGRICULTURAL GAP. EUR+WWI ELITES ECO/DEV DIST/IND MARKET PLAN WEALTH...STAT TREND GEN/LAWS OEEC TOT/POP VAL/FREE FAO 20. PAGE 27 F0535 AGRI TEC/DEV INT/TRADE

B63
FURTADO C.,THE ECONOMIC GROWTH OF BRAZIL: A SURVEY FROM COLONIAL TO MODERN TIMES. L/A+17C AGRI DIST/IND EXTR/IND INDUS WORKER COLONIAL RACE/REL OWN GOV/COMP. PAGE 45 F0877 ECO/UNDEV TEC/DEV LABOR DOMIN

B63
GOLDMAN M.I.,SOVIET MARKETING. USSR DIST/IND FINAN RATION OWN WEALTH...SOC BIBLIOG 20. PAGE 48 F0937 MARKET ECO/TAC CONTROL MARXISM

B63
HUNTER A.,THE ECONOMICS OF AUSTRALIAN INDUSTRY. DIST/IND EXTR/IND FINAN PROC/MFG SERV/IND ACT/RES PLAN TARIFFS GP/REL INGP/REL 20 AUSTRAL. PAGE 63 F1245 INDUS ECO/DEV HABITAT GP/COMP

B63
KATZ S.M.,A SELECTED LIST OF US READINGS ON DEVELOPMENT. AGRI COM/IND DIST/IND INDUS LABOR PLAN FOR/AID EDU/PROP HEALTH...POLICY SOC/WK 20. PAGE 69 F1361 BIBLIOG/A ECO/UNDEV TEC/DEV ACT/RES

B63
PRYOR F.L.,THE COMMUNIST FOREIGN TRADE SYSTEM. COM CZECHOSLVK GERMANY YUGOSLAVIA LAW ECO/DEV DIST/IND POL/PAR PLAN DOMIN TOTALISM DRIVE RIGID/FLEX WEALTH ...STAT STAND/INT CHARTS FOR/TRADE 20. PAGE 108 F2130 ATTIT ECO/TAC

L63
ADERBIGDE A.,"SYMPOSIUM ON WEST AFRICA INTEGRATION." AFR EUR+WWI FUT CULTURE SOCIETY STRATA DIST/IND INDUS MARKET SERV/IND DELIB/GP PLAN TEC/DEV DOMIN EDU/PROP LEGIT COERCE ATTIT ALL/VALS ...POLICY STAT TREND CHARTS VAL/FREE. PAGE 2 F0040 FINAN ECO/TAC REGION

S63
ADAMS F.G.,"ECONOMIC CONSIDERATIONS OF AN ATLANTIC ENERGY POLICY." EUR+WWI FUT USA+45 DIST/IND EXTR/IND MARKET CONSULT LEGIS ECO/TAC WEALTH ...POLICY EEC FOR/TRADE OEEC 20. PAGE 2 F0037 ECO/DEV TEC/DEV NUC/PWR

S63
BARZANSKI S.,"REGIONAL UNDERDEVELOPMENT IN THE EUROPEAN ECONOMIC COMMUNITY." EUR+WWI ELITES DIST/IND MARKET VOL/ASSN CONSULT EX/STRUC ECO/TAC RIGID/FLEX WEALTH EEC OEEC 20. PAGE 11 F0202 ECO/UNDEV PLAN

S63
CLEMHOUT S.,"PRODUCTION FUNCTION ANALYSIS APPLIED TO THE LEONTIEF SCARCE-FACTOR PARADOX OF INTERNATIONAL TRADE." EUR+WWI USA+45 DIST/IND NAT/G PLAN TEC/DEV DIPLOM PWR WEALTH...MGT METH/CNCPT CONT/OBS CON/ANAL CHARTS SIMUL GEN/LAWS FOR/TRADE 20. PAGE 25 F0490 ECO/DEV ECO/TAC

S63
DIEBOLD W. JR.,"THE NEW SITUATION OF INTERNATIONAL TRADE POLICY." EUR+WWI FRANCE FUT UK USA+45 WOR+45 DIST/IND PLAN INT/TRADE EDU/PROP PWR WEALTH ...RECORD TREND GEN/LAWS EEC TRUE/GP VAL/FREE APPLIC 20. PAGE 33 F0636 MARKET ECO/TAC

S63
DUCROS B.,"MOBILISATION DES RESSOURCES PRODUCTIVES ET DEVELOPPEMENT." FUT INTELL SOCIETY COM/IND DIST/IND EXTR/IND FINAN INDUS ROUTINE WEALTH ...METH/CNCPT OBS 20. PAGE 34 F0670 ECO/UNDEV TEC/DEV

S63
GALENSON W.,"ECONOMIC DEVELOPMENT AND THE SECTORAL EXPANSION OF EMPLOYMENT, INT." FUT WOR+45 ECO/UNDEV DIST/IND PROC/MFG SERV/IND ACT/RES HEALTH SKILL WEALTH...STAT TIME/SEQ VAL/FREE 20. PAGE 46 F0889 INDUS ECO/TAC

S63
HOOVER C.B.,"ECONOMIC REFORM VERSUS ECONOMIC GROWTH IN UNDERDEVELOPED COUNTRIES." FUT WOR+45 ELITES STRATA ECO/UNDEV DIST/IND INDUS TEC/DEV CAP/ISM FOR/AID INT/TRADE ATTIT WEALTH...MYTH TREND STERTYP GEN/LAWS WORK 20. PAGE 61 F1209 ECO/DEV ECO/TAC

S63
PRYBYLA J.,"THE QUEST FOR ECONOMIC RATIONALITY IN THE SOVIET BLOC." COM FUT WOR+45 WOR-45 DIST/IND MARKET PLAN ECO/TAC ATTIT...METH/CNCPT TOT/POP 20. PAGE 108 F2128 ECO/DEV TREND USSR

S63
RAMERIE L.,"TENSION AU SEIN DU COMECON: LE CAS ROUMAIN." COM EUR+WWI USSR WOR+45 ECO/DEV DIST/IND NAT/G POL/PAR VOL/ASSN EDU/PROP TOTALISM ATTIT WEALTH...TIME/SEQ 20 COMECON. PAGE 109 F2142 INT/ORG ECO/TAC INT/TRADE ROMANIA

S63
REDDAWAY W.B.,"THE ECONOMICS OF UNDERDEVELOPED COUNTRIES." S/ASIA WOR+45 WOR-45 STRATA AGRI COM/IND DIST/IND MARKET PROC/MFG PLAN TEC/DEV FOR/AID BAL/PAY ATTIT DRIVE SKILL WORK FOR/TRADE 20. PAGE 110 F2165 ECO/TAC ECO/UNDEV INDIA

S63
SHONFIELD A.,"AFTER BRUSSELS." EUR+WWI FRANCE GERMANY UK ECO/DEV DIST/IND MARKET VOL/ASSN DELIB/GP CREATE INT/TRADE ATTIT RIGID/FLEX...RECORD TREND GEN/LAWS EEC COMMUN CMN/WLTH 20. PAGE 121 F2385 PLAN ECO/TAC

S63
SHWADRAN B.,"MIDDLE EAST OIL, 1962." ISLAM DIST/IND INDUS PLAN ATTIT DRIVE WEALTH...POLICY STAT CONT/OBS TREND CHARTS GEN/LAWS TERR/GP METH/GP 20 OIL. PAGE 121 F2393 PROC/MFG ECO/TAC ELITES REGION

S63
SHWADRAN B.,"MIDDLE EAST OIL, 1962." ISLAM USSR ECO/DEV DIST/IND INDUS PLAN BAL/PWR DISPL DRIVE ...POLICY STAT TREND GEN/LAWS TERR/GP METH/GP EEC OEEC 20 OIL. PAGE 121 F2394 MARKET ECO/TAC INT/TRADE

S63
WILES P.J.D.,"WILL CAPITALISM AND COMMUNISM SPONTANEOUSLY CONVERGE." COM FUT USA+45 ECO/DEV DIST/IND MARKET CAP/ISM ECO/TAC RIGID/FLEX WEALTH MARXISM SOCISM...MATH STAT TREND COMPUT/IR 20. PAGE 146 F2885 PLAN TEC/DEV USSR

B64
CHANDLER A.D. JR.,GIANT ENTERPRISE: FORD, GENERAL MOTORS, AND THE AUTOMOBILE INDUSTRY; SOURCES AND READINGS. USA+45 USA-45 FINAN MARKET CREATE ADMIN ...TIME/SEQ ANTHOL 20 AUTOMOBILE. PAGE 23 F0447 LG/CO DIST/IND LABOR MGT

B64
CHINITZ B.,CITY AND SUBURB: THE ECONOMICS OF METROPOLITAN GROWTH. DIST/IND BUDGET GOV/REL DEMAND ATTIT HABITAT MUNICH PHILADELPH. PAGE 24 F0467 TEC/DEV PLAN

B64
ESTHUS R.A.,FROM ENMITY TO ALLIANCE: US AUSTRALIAN RELATIONS. S/ASIA DIST/IND VOL/ASSN FORCES ATTIT 20 AUSTRAL TREATY CMN/WLTH. PAGE 39 F0751 DIPLOM WAR INT/TRADE FOR/AID

B64
FISK W.M.,ADMINISTRATIVE PROCEDURE IN A REGULATORY AGENCY: THE CAB AND THE NEW YORK-CHICAGO CASE (PAMPHLET). USA+45 DIST/IND ADMIN CONTROL LOBBY GP/REL ROLE ORD/FREE NEWYORK/C CHICAGO CAB. PAGE 41 F0805 SERV/IND ECO/DEV AIR JURID

B64
FITCH L.C.,URBAN TRANSPORTATION AND PUBLIC POLICY. FINAN NAT/G LEGIS PROB/SOLV TEC/DEV PRICE COST EFFICIENCY...DECISION STAT CHARTS METH/COMP MUNICH 20 NEWYORK/C PHILADELPH LOS/ANG CHICAGO WASHING/DC. PAGE 41 F0806
DIST/IND PLAN LOC/G

B64
GARFIELD PJ LOVEJOY WF,PUBLIC UTILITY ECONOMICS. DIST/IND FINAN MARKET ADMIN COST DEMAND ...TECHNIC JURID MUNICH 20 MONOPOLY. PAGE 46 F0906
T ECO/TAC OWN SERV/IND

B64
HOLLEY I.B. JR.,US ARMY IN WORLD WAR II: SPECIAL STUDIES: BUYING AIRCRAFT: MATERIEL PROCUREMENT FOR THE ARMY AIR FORCES. USA+45 USA-45 BUDGET WEAPON GOV/REL PRODUC 20. PAGE 61 F1198
FORCES COST DIST/IND CIVMIL/REL

B64
KEMP M.C.,THE PURE THEORY OF INTERNATIONAL TRADE. WOR+45 WOR-45 ECO/DEV ECO/UNDEV DIST/IND ECO/TAC ...MATH CON/ANAL CHARTS VAL/FREE. PAGE 70 F1374
FINAN CREATE INT/TRADE

B64
LANG A.S.,URBAN RAIL TRANSIT. OP/RES PLAN PROB/SOLV TEC/DEV AUTOMAT COST...TECHNIC MATH CON/ANAL CHARTS METH/COMP SIMUL MUNICH 20 RAILROAD PUB/TRANS. PAGE 75 F1474
DIST/IND ECOMETRIC

B64
NATIONAL COUN APPLIED ECO RES,A STRATEGY FOR THE FOURTH PLAN. INDIA DIST/IND EXTR/IND SERV/IND ECO/TAC RATION EDU/PROP EATING HEALTH...CHARTS 20. PAGE 97 F1900
ECO/UNDEV PLAN AGRI WORKER

B64
ORGANIZATION AMERICAN STATES,ECONOMIC SURVEY OF LATIN AMERICA, 1962. L/A+17C AGRI DIST/IND INDUS MARKET PROC/MFG R+D PLAN TEC/DEV ECO/TAC REGION BAL/PAY ALL/VALS...CON/ANAL ORG/CHARTS GEN/METH OAS ALL/PROG 20 ALL/PROG. PAGE 102 F1998
ECO/UNDEV CHARTS

B64
RESOURCES FOR THE FUTURE,URBAN AND REGIONAL STUDIES AT US UNIVERSITIES; A REPORT BASED ON A 1963 SURVEY OF URBAN AND REGIONAL RESEARCH. USA+45 SOCIETY CONSTRUC DIST/IND ACADEM NAT/G ACT/RES ECO/TAC ...CENSUS IDEA/COMP MUNICH. PAGE 111 F2179
BIBLIOG/A REGION PLAN

B64
ROBINSON R.D.,INTERNATIONAL BUSINESS POLICY. AFR INDIA L/A+17C USA+45 ELITES AGRI FOR/AID COERCE BAL/PAY...DECISION INT/LAW MGT 20. PAGE 113 F2224
ECO/TAC DIST/IND COLONIAL FINAN

B64
TELLADO A.,A STATEMENT OF THE LAWS OF THE DOMINICAN REPUBLIC IN MATTERS AFFECTING BUSINESS (3RD ED.). DOMIN/REP AGRI DIST/IND EXTR/IND FINAN FAM WORKER ECO/TAC TAX CT/SYS MARRIAGE OWN...BIBLIOG 20 MIGRATION. PAGE 129 F2542
CONSTN LEGIS NAT/G INDUS

L64
STERN R.M.,"POLICIES FOR TRADE AND DEVELOPMENT." AFR FUT WOR+45 DIST/IND FINAN NAT/G DELIB/GP PLAN ECO/TAC ORD/FREE WEALTH...POLICY STAT TIME/SEQ CHARTS METH/GP 20. PAGE 126 F2480
MARKET ECO/UNDEV INT/TRADE

S64
HOWE M.,"THE TRANSPORT ACT, 1962, AND THE CONSUMERS' CONSULTATIVE COMMITTEES." UK CONFER EXEC PWR 20. PAGE 62 F1225
PARTIC REPRESENT DELIB/GP DIST/IND

S64
HUELIN D.,"ECONOMIC INTEGRATION IN LATIN AMERICAN: PROGRESS AND PROBLEMS." L/A+17C ECO/DEV AGRI DIST/IND FINAN INDUS NAT/G VOL/ASSN CONSULT DELIB/GP EX/STRUC ACT/RES PLAN TEC/DEV ECO/TAC ROUTINE BAL/PAY WEALTH FOR/TRADE WORK TERR/GP 20. PAGE 63 F1232
MARKET ECO/UNDEV INT/TRADE

B65
ARTEL R.,THE STRUCTURE OF THE STOCKHOLM ECONOMY. SWEDEN DIST/IND LABOR LOC/G TEC/DEV DEMAND MUNICH LOUISIANA 20. PAGE 7 F0125
ECO/DEV METH/COMP BAL/PAY

B65
BARRY E.E.,NATIONALISATION IN BRITISH POLITICS: THE HISTORICAL BACKGROUND. UK AGRI DIST/IND EXTR/IND LABOR LG/CO ATTIT CONSERVE SOCISM 19/20 LABOR/PAR. PAGE 10 F0198
NAT/G OWN INDUS POL/PAR

B65
BLAIR T.L.V.,AFRICA: A MARKET PROFILE. AFR COM/IND DIST/IND FINAN UTIL...DECISION CHARTS BIBLIOG 20. PAGE 15 F0295
MARKET OP/RES ECO/UNDEV INDUS

B65
DANIELSON M.N.,FEDERAL-METROPOLITAN POLITICS AND THE COMMUTER CRISIS. PROVS LEGIS EXEC LEAD PWR ...DECISION MUNICH. PAGE 30 F0580
FEDERAL GOV/REL DIST/IND

B65
HAEFELE E.T.,GOVERNMENT CONTROLS ON TRANSPORT. AFR RHODESIA TANZANIA DIPLOM ECO/TAC TARIFFS PRICE ADJUD CONTROL REGION EFFICIENCY...POLICY 20 CONGO. PAGE 53 F1031
ECO/UNDEV DIST/IND FINAN NAT/G

B65
HOSELITZ B.F.,ECONOMICS AND THE IDEA OF MANKIND. UNIV ECO/DEV ECO/UNDEV DIST/IND INDUS INT/ORG NAT/G ACT/RES ECO/TAC WEALTH...CONCPT STAT. PAGE 62 F1223
CREATE INT/TRADE

B65
LEYS C.T.,FEDERATION IN EAST AFRICA. LAW AGRI DIST/IND FINAN INT/ORG LABOR INT/TRADE CONFER ADMIN CONTROL GP/REL...ANTHOL 20 AFRICA/E. PAGE 79 F1554
FEDERAL REGION ECO/UNDEV PLAN

B65
LUGO-MARENCO J.J.,A STATEMENT OF THE LAWS OF NICARAGUA IN MATTERS AFFECTING BUSINESS. NICARAGUA AGRI DIST/IND EXTR/IND FINAN INDUS FAM WORKER INT/TRADE TAX MARRIAGE OWN BIO/SOC 20 TREATY RESOURCE/N MIGRATION. PAGE 82 F1606
CONSTN NAT/G LEGIS JURID

B65
MACAVOY P.W.,THE ECONOMIC EFFECTS OF REGULATION: THE TRUNK-LINE RAILROAD CARTELS AND THE INTERSTATE COMMERCE COMMISSION BEFORE 1900. USA-45 PRICE PROFIT...STAT CHARTS BIBLIOG 19 RAILROAD. PAGE 83 F1620
ECO/TAC DIST/IND PROF/ORG RATION

B65
PARRIS H.W.,GOVERNMENT AND THE RAILWAYS IN NINETEENTH-CENTURY BRITAIN. UK DELIB/GP CONTROL LEAD CENTRAL 19 RAILROAD. PAGE 103 F2029
DIST/IND NAT/G PLAN GP/REL

B65
SMERK G.M.,URBAN TRANSPORTATION; THE FEDERAL ROLE. FUT USA+45 FINAN PROB/SOLV TEC/DEV AUTOMAT GOV/REL COST...STAT BIBLIOG MUNICH 20 PUB/TRANS. PAGE 123 F2426
PLAN DIST/IND NAT/G

B65
THAYER F.C. JR.,AIR TRANSPORT POLICY AND NATIONAL SECURITY: A POLITICAL, ECONOMIC, AND MILITARY ANALYSIS. DIST/IND OP/RES PLAN TEC/DEV DIPLOM DETER WAR COST EFFICIENCY...POLICY BIBLIOG 20 DEPT/DEFEN FAA CAB. PAGE 129 F2548
AIR FORCES CIVMIL/REL ORD/FREE

B65
US ADVISORY COMN INTERGOV REL,METROPOLITAN SOCIAL AND ECONOMIC DISPARITIES: IMPLICATIONS FOR INTERGOVERNMENTAL RELATIONS IN CENT'L CITIES AND SUBURBS. CULTURE STRATA DIST/IND LOC/G PLAN GP/REL DISCRIM HABITAT MUNICH. PAGE 134 F2634
GOV/REL GEOG

L65
LETICHE J.M.,"EUROPEAN INTEGRATION: AN AMERICAN VIEW." EUR+WWI FRANCE WOR+45 ECO/DEV DIST/IND EXTR/IND NAT/G DELIB/GP TOP/EX PLAN ECO/TAC ATTIT ...STAT CON/ANAL CHARTS EEC 20. PAGE 78 F1537
INDUS AGRI

L65
WIONCZEK M.,"LATIN AMERICA FREE TRADE ASSOCIATION." AGRI DIST/IND FINAN INDUS INT/ORG LABOR NAT/G TEC/DEV ECO/TAC HEALTH SKILL WEALTH...POLICY RELATIV MGT LAFTA 20. PAGE 148 F2909
L/A+17C MARKET REGION

S65
TENDLER J.D.,"TECHNOLOGY AND ECONOMIC DEVELOPMENT* THE CASE OF HYDRO VS THERMAL POWER." CONSTRUC DIST/IND CREATE TEC/DEV INT/TRADE CENTRAL PWR SKILL WEALTH...MGT NAT/COMP ARGEN. PAGE 129 F2544
BRAZIL INDUS ECO/UNDEV

C65
PEGRUM D.E.,"PUBLIC REGULATION OF BUSINESS (REV ED)" LAW CONSTN DIST/IND SERV/IND LG/CO LEGIS OWN LAISSEZ SOCISM...POLICY DECISION BIBLIOG 20. PAGE 104 F2048
INDUS PLAN NEW/LIB PRICE

B66
BROWN R.T.,TRANSPORT AND THE ECONOMIC INTEGRATION OF SOUTH AMERICA. L/A+17C ECO/UNDEV NAT/G OP/RES DIPLOM INT/TRADE REGION WEALTH...ECOMETRIC GEOG STAT LAFTA TIME. PAGE 19 F0373
MARKET DIST/IND SIMUL

B66
CHASE S.B. JR.,PROBLEMS IN PUBLIC EXPENDITURE ANALYSIS. DIST/IND INDUS OP/RES PLAN BUDGET RECEIVE PRICE RISK COST INCOME...CHARTS ANTHOL 20. PAGE 23 F0455
ECO/DEV FINAN NAT/G INSPECT

B66
GREENE L.E.,GOVERNMENT IN TENNESSEE (2ND ED.). USA+45 DIST/IND INDUS POL/PAR EX/STRUC LEGIS PLAN BUDGET GIVE CT/SYS...MGT T 20 TENNESSEE. PAGE 51 F0989
PROVS LOC/G CONSTN ADMIN

B66
LANSING J.B.,TRANSPORTATION AND ECONOMIC POLICY. USA+45 COST DEMAND...ECOMETRIC TREND CHARTS IDEA/COMP T 20. PAGE 76 F1481
DIST/IND OP/RES ECO/DEV UTIL

B66
NICOSIA F.N.,CONSUMER DECISION PROCESSES* MARKETING AND ADVERTISING IMPLICATIONS. DIST/IND INDUS CONSULT EDU/PROP ATTIT. PAGE 98 F1925
MARKET PROB/SOLV SERV/IND

B66
RUPPENTHAL K.M.,TRANSPORTATION AND TOMORROW. FUT SPACE USA+45 SEA AIR FORCES TEC/DEV INT/TRADE ...ANTHOL 20 RAILROAD. PAGE 115 F2261
DIST/IND PLAN CIVMIL/REL PREDICT

B66
US SENATE COMM LABOR-PUB WELF,AMEND THE RAILWAY LABOR ACT. USA+45 CONSTN CONSULT DELIB/GP ADJUD CONGRESS RAILROAD. PAGE 139 F2731
GP/REL LABOR DIST/IND LAW

B67
EGGERT G.G.,RAILROAD LABOR DISPUTES. USA+45 USA-45
GP/REL

ELITES DIST/IND DELIB/GP FORCES JUDGE WORKER PROB/SOLV DOMIN PWR...POLICY 20. PAGE 36 F0707 NAT/G LABOR BARGAIN

B67
FARRIS M.T.,MODERN TRANSPORTATION: SELECTED READINGS. UNIV CONTROL...POLICY ANTHOL T 20. PAGE 39 F0765 DIST/IND MGT COST

B67
KULSKI J.E.,LAND OF URBAN PROMISE* CONTINUING THE GREAT TRADITION* A SEARCH FOR SIGNIFICANT URBAN SPACE IN URBANIZED NORTHEAST. USA+45 DIST/IND PUB/INST CONSULT CREATE TEC/DEV...SOC NEW/IDEA CHARTS BIBLIOG MUNICH. PAGE 74 F1448 PLAN PROB/SOLV ECO/DEV

B67
LANDEN R.G.,OMAN SINCE 1856: DISRUPTIVE MODERNIZATION IN A TRADITIONAL ARAB SOCIETY. UK DIST/IND EXTR/IND SECT DIPLOM INT/TRADE...SOC LING CHARTS BIBLIOG 19/20. PAGE 75 F1468 ISLAM CULTURE ECO/UNDEV NAT/G

B67
MACAVOY P.W.,REGULATION OF TRANSPORT INNOVATION. ACT/RES ADJUD COST DEMAND...POLICY CHARTS 20. PAGE 83 F1621 DIST/IND CONTROL PRICE PROFIT

B67
NORTON H.S.,NATIONAL TRANSPORTATION POLICY: FORMATION AND IMPLEMENTATION. USA+45 USA-45 DELIB/GP LEAD...DECISION TIME/SEQ 19/20 PRESIDENT CONGRESS. PAGE 98 F1935 POLICY DIST/IND NAT/G PROB/SOLV

B67
US CONGRESS JOINT ECO COMM,AN ECONOMIC PROFILE OF MAINLAND CHINA, VOLUMES I AND II. CHINA/COM AGRI DIST/IND FINAN INDUS LABOR FORCES ACT/RES PLAN INT/TRADE INGP/REL BAL/PAY 20 CONGRESS. PAGE 135 F2664 ECO/UNDEV WEALTH ECO/TAC DELIB/GP

L67
DEALEY S.,"MONETARY RECOVERY UNDER FEDERAL TRANSPORTATION STATUTES." USA+45 SEA WORKER TAX PAY ADJUD DEATH GOV/REL OWN HEALTH ORD/FREE 20. PAGE 31 F0609 DIST/IND LAW CONTROL FINAN

L67
ROBERTS E.F.,"THE CASE OF THE UNWARY HOME BUYER: THE HOUSING MERCHANT DID IT." USA+45 CLIENT DIST/IND MARKET LG/CO SML/CO PROB/SOLV LEGIT COST PROFIT. PAGE 112 F2207 ADJUD CONSTRUC OWN LAW

L67
TRAVERS H. JR.,"AN EXAMINATION OF THE CAB'S MERGER POLICY." USA+45 USA-45 LAW NAT/G LEGIS PLAN ADMIN ...DECISION 20 CONGRESS. PAGE 131 F2584 ADJUD LG/CO POLICY DIST/IND

S67
"ANTITRUST VENUE: TRANSACTING BUSINESS UNDER THE CLAYTON ACT." USA+45 DIST/IND PROB/SOLV ECO/TAC ADJUD CT/SYS 20. PAGE 2 F0028 LAW LG/CO CONTROL NAT/G

S67
COSGROVE C.A.,"AGRICULTURE, FINANCE AND POLITICS IN THE EUROPEAN COMMUNITY." EUR+WWI DIST/IND MARKET INT/ORG VOL/ASSN DELIB/GP TEC/DEV BAL/PWR BARGAIN ECO/TAC RATION CONFER 20 EEC. PAGE 28 F0538 ECO/DEV DIPLOM AGRI INT/TRADE

S67
CURTIN W.J.,"NATIONAL EMERGENCY DISPUTES LEGISLATION* ITS NEED AND ITS PROSPECTS IN THE TRANSPORTATION INDUSTRIES." USA+45 ECO/DEV INDUS NAT/G LEGIS ACT/RES BARGAIN POLICY. PAGE 29 F0565 JURID LABOR ADJUD DIST/IND

S67
DURIEZ P.,"THE IMPACT OF EX PARTE 230 (PIGGYBACKING) ON RAIL-MOTOR COMPETITION." USA+45 USA-45 LG/CO COST EFFICIENCY...CHARTS 20. PAGE 35 F0685 DIST/IND LAW CONTROL AGREE

S67
FOX R.G.,"FAMILY, CASTE, AND COMMERCE IN A NORTH INDIAN MARKET TOWN." INDIA STRATA AGRI FACE/GP FAM NEIGH OP/RES BARGAIN ADMIN ROUTINE WEALTH...SOC CHARTS 20. PAGE 43 F0838 CULTURE GP/REL ECO/UNDEV DIST/IND

S67
GREGORY R.,"THE MINISTER'S LINE: OR, THE M4 COMES TO BERKSHIRE. PART I." UK CONSTN DIST/IND LEGIS TOP/EX PLAN ADJUD...GEOG 20. PAGE 51 F0994 DECISION CONSTRUC NAT/G DELIB/GP

S67
GRUN C.,"DEUX ETUDES ALLEMANDES SUR LES PREJUGES NATIONAUX ET LES MOYENS DE LES COMBATTRE." FRANCE GERMANY DIST/IND PROB/SOLV GP/REL AGE/Y RIGID/FLEX ...PSY STAT INT SAMP. PAGE 52 F1010 ATTIT REGION DISCRIM STERTYP

S67
HILTON G.W.,"FEDERAL PARTICIPATION IN THE SUPERSONIC TRANSPORT PROGRAM." USA+45 LEGIS PROB/SOLV BUDGET ATTIT 20. PAGE 60 F1172 DIST/IND TEC/DEV FINAN NAT/G

S67
KOTLER P.,"OPERATIONS RESEARCH IN MARKETING." USA+45 DIST/IND INDUS LG/CO CONSULT BUDGET TASK DEMAND EFFICIENCY PROFIT WEALTH DECISION. PAGE 73 F1429 ECOMETRIC OP/RES MARKET PLAN

S67
MYERS S.,"TECHNOLOGY AND URBAN TRANSIT: THE ENORMOUS POTENTIAL OF BUS AND RAIL SYSTEMS." USA+45 FINAN LOC/G WORKER PLAN PROB/SOLV PRICE AUTOMAT MUNICH 20. PAGE 96 F1877 R+D TEC/DEV DIST/IND ACT/RES

S67
OLIVIER G.,"ASPECTS JURIDIQUES DE L'ADOPTION DU TRAITE CECA A LA CRISE CHARBONNIERE (SUITE ET FIN)" LAW DIST/IND PLAN DIPLOM RATION PRICE ADMIN COST DEMAND...POLICY CON/ANAL ECSC TREATY. PAGE 101 F1988 INT/TRADE INT/ORG EXTR/IND CONSTN

S67
WILLIAMS C.,"REGIONAL MANAGEMENT OVERSEAS." USA+45 WOR+45 DIST/IND LG/CO EX/STRUC INT/TRADE TARIFFS ADMIN TASK CENTRAL. PAGE 147 F2889 MGT EUR+WWI ECO/DEV PLAN

DISTRIBUTIVE SYSTEM....SEE DIST/IND

DISTRICT OF COLUMBIA....SEE WASHING/DC

DISTRICTING...SEE APPORT

DIVORCE....DIVORCE

DIXON W. F0644

DIXON/YATE....DIXON-YATES BILL

DOBB M. F0646,F0647

DOC/ANAL....CONVENTIONAL CONTENT ANALYSIS

DODD E.M. F0648

DODD/TJ....SENATOR THOMAS J. DODD

DODDY F.S. F0649

DOE J.F. F0650

DOERFER G.L. F0651

DOIG J.W. F0652

DOMIN....DOMINATION THROUGH USE OF ESTABLISHED POWER

B19
VEBLEN T.B.,THE VESTED INTERESTS AND THE STATE OF THE INDUSTRIAL ARTS. USA-45 LAW FINAN WORKER PAY DOMIN PRICE COST SOCISM...MARXIST 19/20. PAGE 141 F2771 INDUS CAP/ISM METH/COMP WEALTH

N19
HALL G.,MAIN STREET TO WALL STREET: END THE COLD WAR (PAMPHLET). AFR USA+45 LAW STRUCT POL/PAR WORKER INT/TRADE DOMIN INCOME...POLICY 20 COM/PARTY. PAGE 53 F1046 MARXIST CAP/ISM DIPLOM NAT/G

N19
SENGHOR L.S.,AFRICAN SOCIALISM (PAMPHLET). AFR FRANCE MALI USSR ELITES ECO/UNDEV NAT/G DIPLOM DOMIN EDU/PROP ATTIT 20 NEGRO. PAGE 119 F2355 SOCISM MARXISM ORD/FREE NAT/LISM

B20
MOREL E.D.,THE BLACK MAN'S BURDEN. AFR MOD/EUR AGRI EXTR/IND PROB/SOLV INT/TRADE ADMIN CONTROL COERCE DISCRIM...POLICY 19/20 NEGRO LEAGUE/NAT. PAGE 93 F1828 ORD/FREE CAP/ISM RACE/REL DOMIN

B27
BELLOC H.,THE SERVILE STATE (1912) (3RD ED.). PRUSSIA UK CULTURE STRATA INDUS NAT/G ECO/TAC CONTROL LEAD SUFF DISCRIM EQUILIB ORD/FREE WEALTH 20. PAGE 12 F0237 WORKER CAP/ISM DOMIN CATH

B28
CROS L.,AFRIQUE FRANCAISE POUR TOUS. EUR+WWI FRANCE PLAN TEC/DEV ATTIT 20. PAGE 29 F0556 COLONIAL DOMIN ECO/TAC AFR

B28
HARDMAN J.B.,AMERICAN LABOR DYNAMICS. WORKER ECO/TAC DOMIN ADJUD LEAD LOBBY PWR...POLICY MGT. PAGE 55 F1079 LABOR INGP/REL ATTIT GP/REL

B31
CROOK W.H.,THE GENERAL STRIKE: A STUDY OF LABOR'S TRAGIC WEAPON IN THEORY AND PRACTICE. BELGIUM FRANCE SWEDEN UK WOR-45 PROB/SOLV ECO/TAC DOMIN PWR ...POLICY TIME/SEQ NAT/COMP GEN/LAWS 19/20 STRIKE. PAGE 29 F0555 LABOR WORKER LG/CO BARGAIN

B36
HUBERMAN L.,MAN'S WORLDLY GOODS: THE STORY OF THE WEALTH OF NATIONS. CHRIST-17C EUR+WWI MOD/EUR SOCIETY DOMIN REV ORD/FREE...TIME/SEQ METH/COMP. PAGE 63 F1231 WEALTH CAP/ISM MARXISM CREATE

B38
HOBSON J.A.,IMPERIALISM. MOD/EUR UK WOR-45 CULTURE ECO/UNDEV NAT/G VOL/ASSN PLAN EDU/PROP LEGIT REGION DOMIN ECO/TAC

COERCE ATTIT PWR...POLICY PLURIST TIME/SEQ GEN/LAWS TERR/GP 19/20. PAGE 60 F1187 BAL/PWR COLONIAL

B39
ROBBINS L.,ECONOMIC CAUSES OF WAR. WOR-45 ECO/DEV ECO/UNDEV INT/ORG NAT/G TEC/DEV DIPLOM DOMIN COLONIAL ATTIT DRIVE PWR WEALTH...POLICY CONCPT OBS SAMP TREND CON/ANAL GEN/LAWS MARX/KARL 20. PAGE 112 F2203 COERCE ECO/TAC WAR

S41
BRITT S.H.,"CONFORMITY OF LABOR NEWSPAPERS WITH RESPECT TO THE AFL-CIO CONFLICT." BAL/PWR CONSEN ATTIT. PAGE 18 F0355 LABOR PRESS DOMIN GP/REL

S41
LASSWELL H.D.,"THE GARRISON STATE" (BMR)" FUT WOR+45 ELITES INTELL FORCES ECO/TAC DOMIN EDU/PROP COERCE INGP/REL 20. PAGE 76 F1485 NAT/G DIPLOM PWR CIVMIL/REL

B42
JACKSON M.V.,EUROPEAN POWERS AND SOUTH-EAST AFRICA: A STUDY OF INTERNATIONAL RELATIONS ON SOUTH-EAST COAST OF AFRICA, 1796-1856. AFR FRANCE PORTUGAL SOUTH/AFR UK USA-45 FORCES INT/TRADE PWR...CHARTS BIBLIOG 18/19 TREATY. PAGE 66 F1294 DOMIN POLICY ORD/FREE DIPLOM

B47
GORDON D.L.,THE HIDDEN WEAPON: THE STORY OF ECONOMIC WARFARE. EUR+WWI USA-45 LAW FINAN INDUS NAT/G CONSULT FORCES PLAN DOMIN PWR WEALTH ...INT/LAW CONCPT OBS TOT/POP NAZI 20. PAGE 49 F0955 INT/ORG ECO/TAC INT/TRADE WAR

B48
CLYDE P.H.,THE FAR EAST: A HISTORY OF THE IMPACT OF THE WEST ON EASTERN ASIA. CHINA/COM CULTURE INT/TRADE DOMIN COLONIAL WAR PWR...CHARTS BIBLIOG 19/20 CHINJAP. PAGE 25 F0494 DIPLOM ASIA

B48
KILE O.M.,THE FARM BUREAU MOVEMENT: THE FARM BUREAU THROUGH THREE DECADES. NAT/G LEGIS LEAD LOBBY GP/REL INCOME POLICY. PAGE 71 F1387 AGRI STRUCT VOL/ASSN DOMIN

B48
WINSLOW E.M.,THE PATTERN OF IMPERIALISM; A STUDY IN THE THEORIES OF POWER. DOMIN WAR PWR MARXISM ...IDEA/COMP METH/COMP BIBLIOG 20. PAGE 147 F2906 SOCISM CAP/ISM COLONIAL ECO/TAC

B50
HUTCHISON K.,THE DECLINE AND FALL OF BRITISH CAPITALISM. UK ELITES STRATA ECO/DEV LABOR WORKER CONTROL WAR PWR...BIBLIOG/A 19/20. PAGE 63 F1249 CAP/ISM SOCISM LAISSEZ DOMIN

B51
DIMOCK M.E.,FREE ENTERPRISE AND THE ADMINISTRATIVE STATE. FINAN LG/CO BARGAIN BUDGET DOMIN CONTROL INGP/REL EFFICIENCY 20. PAGE 33 F0640 CAP/ISM ADMIN MGT MARKET

B51
LUXEMBORG R.,THE ACCUMULATION OF CAPITAL (TRANS. BY AGNES SCHWARZSCHILD). ECO/TAC DOMIN COLONIAL ATTIT LAISSEZ 19 MONEY. PAGE 82 F1614 MARXIST INT/TRADE CAP/ISM FINAN

B52
EGLE W.P.,ECONOMIC STABILIZATION. USA+45 SOCIETY FINAN MARKET PLAN ECO/TAC DOMIN EDU/PROP LEGIT EXEC WEALTH...CONCPT METH/CNCPT TREND HYPO/EXP GEN/METH TOT/POP VAL/FREE 20. PAGE 36 F0708 NAT/G ECO/DEV CAP/ISM

B52
MACHLUP F.,THE POLITICAL ECONOMY OF MONOPOLY: BUSINESS, LABOR AND GOVERNMENT POLICIES. USA+45 USA-45 ECO/DEV LABOR NAT/G CAP/ISM PWR...POLICY CHARTS T 20. PAGE 83 F1630 ECO/TAC DOMIN LG/CO CONTROL

S53
LINCOLN G.,"FACTORS DETERMINING ARMS AID." COM FUT USA+45 USSR WOR+45 ECO/DEV NAT/G CONSULT PLAN TEC/DEV DIPLOM DOMIN EDU/PROP PERCEPT PWR ...DECISION CONCPT TREND MARX/KARL 20. PAGE 80 F1566 FORCES POLICY BAL/PWR FOR/AID

B55
WOYTINSKY W.S.,WORLD COMMERCE AND GOVERNMENTS: TRENDS AND OUTLOOK. WOR+45 FINAN POL/PAR DIPLOM ECO/TAC FOR/AID DOMIN WAR CHOOSE...CHARTS BIBLIOG 20 LEAGUE/NAT UN ILO. PAGE 149 F2929 INT/TRADE DIST/IND NAT/COMP NAT/G

B56
KNORR K.E.,RUBLE DIPLOMACY: CHALLENGE TO AMERICAN FOREIGN AID(PAMPHLET). AFR CHINA/COM USA+45 USSR PLAN TEC/DEV CAP/ISM INT/TRADE DOMIN EDU/PROP CONTROL LEAD 20. PAGE 72 F1413 ECO/UNDEV COM DIPLOM FOR/AID

B56
WHYTE W.H. JR.,THE ORGANIZATION MAN. CULTURE FINAN VOL/ASSN DOMIN EDU/PROP EXEC DISPL HABITAT ROLE ...PERS/TEST STERTYP. PAGE 146 F2875 ADMIN LG/CO PERSON CONSEN

B57
ROBERTSON H.M.,SOUTH AFRICA, ECONOMIC AND POLITICAL ASPECTS. SOUTH/AFR CONSTN CULTURE POL/PAR LEGIS DIPLOM DOMIN COLONIAL...SOC BIBLIOG 19/20. PAGE 112 F2214 RACE/REL ECO/UNDEV ECO/TAC DISCRIM

B57
WARRINER D.,LAND REFORM AND DEVELOPMENT IN THE MIDDLE EAST: A STUDY OF EGYPT, SYRIA AND IRAQ. IRAQ ISLAM SYRIA UAR AGRI DIST/IND PLAN TEC/DEV DOMIN REV ATTIT WEALTH...SOC METH/CNCPT STAT OBS RECORD HIST/WRIT TREND GEN/LAWS FAO 20. PAGE 143 F2825 ECO/UNDEV CONCPT

S57
LEWIS E.G.,"PARLIAMENTARY CONTROL OF NATIONALIZED INDUSTRY IN FRANCE." FRANCE NAT/G DELIB/GP ACT/RES PLAN PROB/SOLV ECO/TAC DOMIN CENTRAL. PAGE 79 F1547 PWR LEGIS INDUS CONTROL

B58
TILLION G.,ALGERIA: THE REALITIES. ALGERIA FRANCE ISLAM CULTURE STRATA PROB/SOLV DOMIN REV NAT/LISM WEALTH MARXISM...GEOG 20. PAGE 130 F2573 ECO/UNDEV SOC COLONIAL DIPLOM

B59
ARON R.,IMPERIALISM AND COLONIALISM (PAMPHLET). WOR+45 WOR-45 ECO/TAC CONTROL REV ORD/FREE 19/20. PAGE 6 F0119 COLONIAL DOMIN ECO/UNDEV DIPLOM

B60
ASPREMONT-LYNDEN H.,RAPPORT SUR L'ADMINISTRATION BELGE DU RUANDA-URUNDI PENDANT L'ANNEE 1959. BELGIUM RWANDA AGRI INDUS DIPLOM ECO/TAC INT/TRADE DOMIN ADMIN RACE/REL...GEOG CENSUS 20 UN. PAGE 7 F0132 AFR COLONIAL ECO/UNDEV INT/ORG

B60
CAMPBELL R.W.,SOVIET ECONOMIC POWER. COM USA+45 DIST/IND MARKET TOP/EX ACT/RES CAP/ISM ECO/TAC DOMIN EDU/PROP ADMIN ROUTINE DRIVE...MATH TIME/SEQ CHARTS WORK 20. PAGE 21 F0409 ECO/DEV PLAN SOCISM USSR

B60
WHEARE K.C.,THE CONSTITUTIONAL STRUCTURE OF THE COMMONWEALTH. UK EX/STRUC DIPLOM DOMIN ADMIN COLONIAL CONTROL LEAD INGP/REL SUPEGO 20 CMN/WLTH. PAGE 145 F2865 CONSTN INT/ORG VOL/ASSN SOVEREIGN

S60
HERZ J.H.,"EAST GERMANY: PROGRESS AND PROSPECTS." COM AGRI FINAN INDUS LOC/G NAT/G FORCES PLAN TEC/DEV DOMIN ADMIN COERCE DRIVE PERCEPT RIGID/FLEX MORAL ORD/FREE PWR...MARXIST PSY SOC RECORD STERTYP WORK. PAGE 59 F1158 POL/PAR STRUCT GERMANY

S60
NICHOLS J.P.,"HAZARDS OF AMERICAN PRIVATE INVESTMENT IN UNDERDEVELOPED COUNTRIES." FUT L/A+17C USA+45 USA-45 EXTR/IND CONSULT BAL/PWR ECO/TAC DOMIN ADJUD ATTIT SOVEREIGN WEALTH ...HIST/WRIT TIME/SEQ TREND TERR/GP VAL/FREE 20. PAGE 98 F1924 FINAN ECO/UNDEV CAP/ISM NAT/LISM

B61
CARNEY D.E.,GOVERNMENT AND ECONOMY IN BRITISH WEST AFRICA. GAMBIA GHANA NIGERIA SIER/LEONE DOMIN ADMIN GOV/REL SOVEREIGN WEALTH LAISSEZ...BIBLIOG 20 CMN/WLTH. PAGE 21 F0417 METH/COMP COLONIAL ECO/TAC ECO/UNDEV

B61
ENGLER R.,THE POLITICS OF OIL. USA+45 CLIENT ELITES DOMIN EDU/PROP EXEC PWR 20. PAGE 38 F0734 LOBBY REPRESENT POLICY

B61
PERLO V.,EL IMPERIALISMO NORTHEAMERICANO. USA+45 USA-45 FINAN CAP/ISM DIPLOM DOMIN CONTROL DISCRIM 19/20. PAGE 105 F2063 SOCIALIST ECO/DEV INT/TRADE ECO/TAC

B61
SCHNAPPER B.,LA POLITIQUE ET LE COMMERCE FRANCAIS DANS LE GOLFE DE GUINEE DE 1838 A 1871. FRANCE GUINEA UK SEA EXTR/IND NAT/G DELIB/GP LEGIS ADMIN ORD/FREE...POLICY GEOG CENSUS CHARTS BIBLIOG 19. PAGE 117 F2303 COLONIAL INT/TRADE DOMIN AFR

B61
WRIGHT H.M.,THE "NEW IMPERIALISM": ANALYSIS OF LATE NINETEENTH-CENTURY EXPANSION. MOD/EUR WOR-45 SOCIETY FINAN ECO/TAC INT/TRADE NAT/LISM...ANTHOL BIBLIOG/A 19. PAGE 149 F2933 HIST/WRIT IDEA/COMP COLONIAL DOMIN

S61
HAYTES W.,"THREE VIEWS ON THE SOVIET ECONOMIC THREAT." AFR COM USA+45 USA-45 USSR WOR+45 WOR-45 INDUS TEC/DEV ECO/TAC DOMIN ATTIT PERCEPT PWR FOR/TRADE 20. PAGE 57 F1128 ECO/DEV PLAN TOTALISM

B62
ELLIOTT J.R.,THE APPEAL OF COMMUNISM IN THE UNDERDEVELOPED NATIONS. AFR USSR WOR+45 INT/ORG NAT/G DIPLOM DOMIN EDU/PROP ROUTINE ATTIT RIGID/FLEX ORD/FREE PWR WEALTH MARXISM...POLICY SOC METH/CNCPT MYTH TOT/POP METH/GP 20. PAGE 37 F0722 COM ECO/UNDEV

B62
RIMALOV V.V.,ECONOMIC COOPERATION BETWEEN USSR AND UNDERDEVELOPED COUNTRIES. USSR FINAN TEC/DEV INT/TRADE DOMIN EDU/PROP COLONIAL NAT/LISM DRIVE SOVEREIGN...AUD/VIS 20. PAGE 111 F2194 FOR/AID PLAN ECO/UNDEV DIPLOM

B62
VAN RENSBURG P.,GUILTY LAND: THE HISTORY OF APARTHEID. SOUTH/AFR NAT/G POL/PAR DOMIN CHOOSE ...SOC 19/20 NEGRO. PAGE 140 F2763 RACE/REL DISCRIM NAT/LISM POLICY

B62
VIET J.,INTERNATIONAL COOPERATION AND PROGRAMMES OF ECONOMIC AND SOCIAL DEVELOPMENT. TEC/DEV FOR/AID DOMIN COLONIAL PEACE WEALTH 20 UNESCO. PAGE 141 F2784 BIBLIOG/A INT/ORG DIPLOM ECO/UNDEV

S62
READ W.H.,"UPWARD COMMUNICATION IN INDUSTRIAL HIERARCHIES." LG/CO TOP/EX PROB/SOLV DOMIN EXEC PERS/REL ATTIT DRIVE PERCEPT...CORREL STAT CHARTS 20. PAGE 110 F2159 ADMIN INGP/REL PSY MGT

B63
BONINI C.P.,SIMULATION OF INFORMATION AND DECISION SYSTEMS IN THE FIRM. MARKET BUDGET DOMIN EDU/PROP ADMIN COST ATTIT HABITAT PERCEPT PWR...CONCPT PROBABIL QUANT PREDICT HYPO/EXP BIBLIOG. PAGE 16 F0313 INDUS SIMUL DECISION MGT

B63
BRAYBROOKE D.,A STRATEGY OF DECISION: POLICY EVALUATION AS A SOCIAL PROCESS. UNIV ELITES OP/RES DOMIN CONFER FEEDBACK CONSEN PLURISM...CONCPT CENSUS. PAGE 18 F0343 DECISION POLICY CONTROL

B63
CHAMBERLAIN E.H.,THE ECONOMIC ANALYSIS OF LABOR UNION POWER (PAMPHLET). WORKER ECO/TAC DOMIN COERCE GP/REL DRIVE WEALTH POLICY. PAGE 23 F0441 LABOR PWR CONTROL

B63
FURTADO C.,THE ECONOMIC GROWTH OF BRAZIL: A SURVEY FROM COLONIAL TO MODERN TIMES. L/A+17C AGRI DIST/IND EXTR/IND INDUS WORKER COLONIAL RACE/REL OWN GOV/COMP. PAGE 45 F0877 ECO/UNDEV TEC/DEV LABOR DOMIN

B63
GAMBLE S.D.,NORTH CHINA VILLAGES: SOCIAL, POLITICAL, AND ECONOMIC ACTIVITIES BEFORE 1933. ASIA CULTURE STRUCT FAM DOMIN EDU/PROP MUNICH WORSHIP 20. PAGE 46 F0891 AGRI LEAD FINAN

B63
MCCONNELL G.,STEEL AND THE PRESIDENCY, 1962. USA+45 INDUS PROB/SOLV CONFER ROLE...POLICY 20 PRESIDENT. PAGE 88 F1722 PWR CHIEF REPRESENT DOMIN

B63
PRYOR F.L.,THE COMMUNIST FOREIGN TRADE SYSTEM. COM CZECHOSLVK GERMANY YUGOSLAVIA LAW ECO/DEV DIST/IND POL/PAR PLAN DOMIN TOTALISM DRIVE RIGID/FLEX WEALTH ...STAT STAND/INT CHARTS FOR/TRADE 20. PAGE 108 F2130 ATTIT ECO/TAC

L63
ADERBIGDE A.,"SYMPOSIUM ON WEST AFRICA INTEGRATION." AFR EUR+WWI FUT CULTURE SOCIETY STRATA DIST/IND INDUS MARKET SERV/IND DELIB/GP PLAN TEC/DEV DOMIN EDU/PROP LEGIT COERCE ATTIT ALL/VALS ...POLICY STAT TREND CHARTS VAL/FREE. PAGE 2 F0040 FINAN ECO/TAC REGION

S63
AYAL E.B.,"VALUE SYSTEM AND ECONOMIC DEVELOPMENT IN JAPAN AND THAILAND." ASIA S/ASIA THAILAND CULTURE ECO/DEV CAP/ISM DOMIN NAT/LISM DRIVE RIGID/FLEX SOCISM...WELF/ST OBS TREND CON/ANAL GEN/LAWS TERR/GP 20 CHINJAP. PAGE 8 F0145 ECO/UNDEV ALL/VALS

S63
BILL J.A.,"THE SOCIAL AND ECONOMIC FOUNDATIONS OF POWER IN CONTEMPORARY IRAN." ISLAM CULTURE NAT/G ECO/TAC DOMIN COERCE ATTIT PWR WEALTH...TREND VAL/FREE 20. PAGE 15 F0284 SOCIETY STRATA IRAN

S63
MONROE A.D.,"BRITAIN AND THE EUROPEAN COMMUNITY." EUR+WWI FRANCE NAT/G DELIB/GP TOP/EX ECO/TAC DOMIN PWR...POLICY RECORD GEN/LAWS EEC EFTA 20 EFTA CMN/WLTH. PAGE 93 F1817 VOL/ASSN ATTIT UK

S63
TENNYSON L.B.,"THE USA IN ATLANTIC COMMUNITY." EUR+WWI FRANCE UK USA+45 ECO/UNDEV VOL/ASSN DELIB/GP TOP/EX DIPLOM DOMIN PWR...POLICY CONCPT TREND GEN/LAWS EEC 20. PAGE 129 F2545 ATTIT ECO/TAC BAL/PWR

B64
ECONOMIDES C.P.,LE POUVOIR DE DECISION DES ORGANISATIONS INTERNATIONALES EUROPEENNES. DIPLOM DOMIN INGP/REL EFFICIENCY...INT/LAW JURID 20 NATO OEEC EEC COUNCL/EUR EURATOM. PAGE 36 F0698 INT/ORG PWR DECISION GP/COMP

B64
LETICHE J.M.,A HISTORY OF RUSSIAN ECONOMIC THOUGHT: NINTH THROUGH EIGHTEENTH CENTURIES. RUSSIA FINAN SECT CAP/ISM DOMIN DEMAND EFFICIENCY OWN MARXISM ...TECHNIC ANTHOL BIBLIOG 9/18. PAGE 78 F1536 ECO/TAC TIME/SEQ IDEA/COMP ECO/UNDEV

B64
SEERS D.,CUBA: THE ECONOMIC AND SOCIAL REVOLUTION. L/A+17C USSR YUGOSLAVIA STRATA AGRI INDUS SCHOOL DELIB/GP PLAN ECO/TAC DOMIN EDU/PROP ATTIT RIGID/FLEX ALL/VALS...STAT OBS TIME/SEQ WORK VAL/FREE 20. PAGE 119 F2341 ACT/RES COERCE CUBA REV

S64
FINLEY D.D.,"A POLITICAL PERSPECTIVE OF ECONOMIC RELATIONS IN THE COMMUNIST CAMP." COM USSR FACE/GP NAT/G ACT/RES PLAN DOMIN COERCE ATTIT ORD/FREE WEALTH...TIME/SEQ 20. PAGE 41 F0800 VOL/ASSN ECO/TAC DIPLOM REGION

S64
HOOVER C.B.,"THE ROLE OF THE NATURAL AND DEVELOPED RESOURCES OF THE NATION STATES." FUT WOR+45 ECO/DEV ECO/UNDEV NAT/G PWR RESPECT SKILL WEALTH...POLICY GEOG TIME/SEQ TREND RESOURCE/N VAL/FREE 20. PAGE 62 F1210 EXTR/IND DOMIN

S64
PESELT B.M.,"COMMUNIST ECONOMIC OFFENSIVE." WOR+45 SOCIETY INT/ORG PLAN ECO/TAC DOMIN EDU/PROP ATTIT PERSON PWR WEALTH...TREND CHARTS METH/GP 20. PAGE 105 F2067 COM ECO/UNDEV FOR/AID USSR

B65
THORNTON A.P.,DOCTRINES OF IMPERIALISM. WOR+45 WOR-45 DOMIN NAT/LISM PROFIT ATTIT PERSON PWR RESPECT SOVEREIGN...CONCPT STERTYP. PAGE 130 F2571 IDEA/COMP COLONIAL DRIVE

B65
WEIDENBAUM M.L.,CONGRESS AND THE FEDERAL BUDGET. FINAN ACT/RES DOMIN CONFER EXEC UTIL PWR NEW/LIB ...CHARTS CONGRESS. PAGE 144 F2844 BUDGET LEGIS PLAN DECISION

B66
BAKLANOFF E.N.,NEW PERSPECTIVES ON BRAZIL. BRAZIL SOCIETY INDUS DOMIN LEAD REV CIVMIL/REL...GEOG PSY LING ANTHOL 20. PAGE 8 F0156 ECO/UNDEV TEC/DEV DIPLOM ORD/FREE

B66
LONDON K.,EASTERN EUROPE IN TRANSITION. CHINA/COM USSR DOMIN COLONIAL CENTRAL RIGID/FLEX PWR...SOC ANTHOL 20. PAGE 82 F1597 SOVEREIGN COM NAT/LISM DIPLOM

B66
MURPHY G.G.,SOVIET MONGOLIA: A STUDY OF THE OLDEST POLITICAL SATELLITE. USSR STRATA STRUCT COST INCOME ATTIT SOCISM 20. PAGE 95 F1865 DIPLOM ECO/TAC PLAN DOMIN

S66
FLEMING W.G.,"AUTHORITY, EFFICIENCY, AND ROLE STRESS: PROBLEMS IN THE DEVELOPMENT OF EAST AFRICAN BUREAUCRACIES." AFR UGANDA STRUCT PROB/SOLV ROUTINE INGP/REL ROLE...MGT SOC GP/COMP GOV/COMP 20 TANGANYIKA AFRICA/E. PAGE 41 F0810 DOMIN EFFICIENCY COLONIAL ADMIN

S66
LANGLEY D.,"POSTSCRIPT ON THE COLONIZATION OF THE INTERNATIONAL TRADE UNION MOVEMENT" USA+45 ELITES FINAN DOMIN LEGIT ADMIN PWR...SOCIALIST 20 AFL/CIO CIA LOVESTN/J. PAGE 75 F1479 INT/TRADE LABOR NAT/G CONTROL

B67
BARROW T.C.,TRADE AND EMPIRE: THE BRITISH CUSTOMS SERVICE IN COLONIAL AMERICA, 1660-1775. UK USA-45 ECO/UNDEV NAT/G ECO/TAC DOMIN REV 17/18. PAGE 10 F0197 COLONIAL TARIFFS ADMIN EX/STRUC

B67
BURDEN H.T.,THE NUREMBERG PARTY RALLIES 1923-39. GERMANY POL/PAR SECT CREATE DOMIN WAR ATTIT ...AUD/VIS FILM 20. PAGE 20 F0384 EDU/PROP CONTROL CROWD TOTALISM

B67
CHILCOTE R.H.,PORTUGUESE AFRICA. PORTUGAL CULTURE SOCIETY ECO/UNDEV DOMIN NAT/LISM...TREND IDEA/COMP NAT/COMP BIBLIOG 15/20. PAGE 24 F0465 AFR COLONIAL ORD/FREE PROB/SOLV

B67
CLEGERN W.M.,BRITISH HONDURAS: COLONIAL DEAD END, 1859-1900. HONDURAS AGRI FINAN PROB/SOLV INT/TRADE PWR WEALTH...BIBLIOG/A 19. PAGE 25 F0487 COLONIAL POLICY ECO/UNDEV DOMIN

B67
COTTAM R.W.,COMPETITIVE INTERFERENCE AND TWENTIETH CENTURY DIPLOMACY. IRAN ACT/RES CREATE PLAN ECO/TAC EFFICIENCY ATTIT...DECISION NEW/IDEA TREND 20 CIA. PAGE 28 F0541 DIPLOM DOMIN GAME

B67
EGGERT G.G.,RAILROAD LABOR DISPUTES. USA+45 USA-45 ELITES DIST/IND DELIB/GP FORCES JUDGE WORKER PROB/SOLV DOMIN PWR...POLICY 20. PAGE 36 F0707 GP/REL NAT/G LABOR BARGAIN

B67
FANON F.,TOWARD THE AFRICAN REVOLUTION. AFR FRANCE CULTURE ELITES LEAD REV GP/REL ORD/FREE SOVEREIGN 20. PAGE 39 F0762 COLONIAL DOMIN ECO/UNDEV RACE/REL

B67
GIAP V.N.,BIG VICTORY, GREAT TASK. VIETNAM WOR+45 FORCES PLAN DOMIN LEGIT RISK PEACE 20. PAGE 47 F0921 WAR LEAD ATTIT INSPECT

B67
GOLEMBIEWSKI R.T.,ORGANIZING MEN AND POWER: PATTERNS OF BEHAVIOR AND LINESTAFF MODELS. WOR+45 EX/STRUC ACT/RES DOMIN PERS/REL...NEW/IDEA 20. PAGE 48 F0943 ADMIN CONTROL SIMUL MGT

B67
GRIFFITH W.E.,SINO-SOVIET RELATIONS, 1964-1965. CHINA/COM COM USSR CHIEF 20. PAGE 51 F1001 DIPLOM PWR DOMIN MARXISM

B67
LISS S.B.,THE CANAL, ASPECTS OF UNITED STATES- DIPLOM

PANAMANIAN RELATIONS. AFR FUT PANAMA DOMIN COERCE POLICY
ATTIT SOVEREIGN MARXISM 20 JOHNSON/LB KENNEDY/JF.
PAGE 81 F1580

B67
OGLESBY C.,CONTAINMENT AND CHANGE. AFR COM USA+45 DIPLOM
ECO/UNDEV TEC/DEV ECO/TAC FOR/AID INT/TRADE DOMIN BAL/PWR
GUERRILLA REV PEACE 20 STALIN/J. PAGE 101 F1983 MARXISM
CULTURE

B67
SACKS B.,SOUTH AFRICA: AN IMPERIAL DILEMMA. COLONIAL
SOUTH/AFR UK ECO/UNDEV KIN DOMIN DEBATE CONTROL REV RACE/REL
DISCRIM ISOLAT...POLICY STAT BIBLIOG 20. PAGE 115 DIPLOM
F2268 ORD/FREE

B67
WESSON R.G.,THE IMPERIAL ORDER. WOR-45 STRUCT SECT PWR
DOMIN ADMIN COLONIAL LEAD CONSERVE...CONCPT BIBLIOG CHIEF
20. PAGE 145 F2861 CONTROL
SOCIETY

B67
WILLS A.J.,AN INTRODUCTION TO THE HISTORY OF AFR
CENTRAL AFRICA. RHODESIA ZAMBIA CULTURE SOCIETY COLONIAL
ECO/UNDEV TEC/DEV DOMIN WAR ALL/VALS...POLICY TREND ORD/FREE
BIBLIOG T 14/20 NYASALAND. PAGE 147 F2899

L67
MACDONALD R.S.J.,"THE RESORT TO ECONOMIC COERCION INT/ORG
BY INTERNATIONAL POLITICAL ORGANIZATIONS." CUBA COERCE
ETHIOPIA RHODESIA SOUTH/AFR NAT/G FOR/AID INT/TRADE ECO/TAC
DOMIN CONTROL SANCTION...DECISION LEAGUE/NAT UN OAS DIPLOM
20. PAGE 83 F1625

L67
MCALLISTER J.T. JR.,"THE POSSIBILITIES FOR DIPLOM
DIPLOMACY IN SOUTHEAST ASIA." LAOS VIETNAM INT/ORG S/ASIA
NAT/G PROVS BAL/PWR DOMIN AGREE COLONIAL WAR PWR
17/20 TREATY. PAGE 88 F1716

L67
TANDON Y.,"CONSENSUS AND AUTHORITY BEHIND UNITED CONSEN
NATIONS PEACEKEEPING OPERATIONS." FINAN VOL/ASSN INT/ORG
BUDGET DIPLOM PAY DOMIN...CHARTS 20 UN. PAGE 128 PWR
F2528 PEACE

S67
FINER S.E.,"THE ONE-PARTY REGIMES IN AFRICA: ELITES
RECONSIDERATIONS." AFR DOMIN CONSEN ORD/FREE 20. POL/PAR
PAGE 41 F0798 CONSTN
ECO/UNDEV

S67
FRIEDENBERG D.M.,"THE US IN LATIN AMERICA; A DIPLOM
RECKONING OF SHAME." L/A+17C USA+45 USA-45 INT/ORG POLICY
CAP/ISM FOR/AID 17/20 OAS. PAGE 44 F0857 DOMIN
COLONIAL

S67
GONZALEZ M.P.,"CUBA, UNA REVOLUCION EN MARCHA." REV
CUBA L/A+17C USA+45 VIETNAM ECO/UNDEV FORCES DIPLOM NAT/G
DOMIN...POLICY MARXIST NAT/COMP CASTRO/F. PAGE 48 COLONIAL
F0946 SOVEREIGN

S67
GORMAN W.,"ELLUL - A PROPHETIC VOICE." WOR+45 CREATE
ELITES SOCIETY ACT/RES PLAN BAL/PWR DOMIN CONTROL ORD/FREE
PARTIC TOTALISM PWR 20. PAGE 49 F0963 EX/STRUC
UTOPIA

S67
HALL B.,"THE COALITION AGAINST DISHWASHERS." USA+45 LABOR
POL/PAR PROB/SOLV BARGAIN LEAD CHOOSE REPRESENT ADMIN
GP/REL ORD/FREE PWR...POLICY 20. PAGE 53 F1044 DOMIN
WORKER

S67
KINGSLEY R.E.,"THE US BUSINESS IMAGE IN LATIN ATTIT
AMERICA." L/A+17C USA+45 NAT/G TEC/DEV CAP/ISM LOVE
FOR/AID DOMIN EDU/PROP...CONCPT LING IDEA/COMP 20. DIPLOM
PAGE 71 F1396 ECO/UNDEV

S67
MILLER C.H.,"B. TRAVEN Y EL 'PROBLEMA PETROLERO'." EXTR/IND
USA-45 ECO/UNDEV INDUS TEC/DEV INT/TRADE ATTIT DIPLOM
ORD/FREE SOVEREIGN 20 MEXIC/AMER. PAGE 91 F1791 ECO/TAC
DOMIN

S67
POWELL D.,"THE EFFECTIVENESS OF SOVIET ANTI- EDU/PROP
RELIGIOUS PROPAGANDA." USSR NAT/G DOMIN LEGIT ATTIT
NAT/LISM 20. PAGE 107 F2109 SECT
CONTROL

S67
WILSON C.E.,"AMERICAN INVESTMENT IN PORTUGUESE COLONIAL
AFRICA: A PROBLEM OF "DEMOCRATIC" COLONIALISM." AFR DOMIN
ECO/UNDEV DIPLOM MORAL...IDEA/COMP 20 ANGOLA ORD/FREE
MOZAMBIQUE. PAGE 147 F2901 POLICY

B86
O'CONNOR T.P.,THE PARNELL MOVEMENT: WITH A SKETCH LEAD
OF IRISH PARTIES FROM 1843. IRELAND UK USA-45 LEGIS DOMIN
WORKER ECO/TAC COERCE CRIME REV CHOOSE ORD/FREE POL/PAR
CATHISM LAISSEZ...SOC 19/20 PARLIAMENT PARNELL/CS POLICY
LAND/LEAG. PAGE 100 F1957

DOMIN/REP....DOMINICAN REPUBLIC; SEE ALSO L/A + 17C

B64
TELLADO A.,A STATEMENT OF THE LAWS OF THE DOMINICAN CONSTN
REPUBLIC IN MATTERS AFFECTING BUSINESS (3RD ED.). LEGIS
DOMIN/REP AGRI DIST/IND EXTR/IND FINAN FAM WORKER NAT/G
ECO/TAC TAX CT/SYS MARRIAGE OWN...BIBLIOG 20 INDUS
MIGRATION. PAGE 129 F2542

B67
DINERSTEIN H.S.,INTERVENTION AGAINST COMMUNISM MARXISM
(STUDIES IN INTERNATIONAL AFFAIRS NO. 1). CUBA DIPLOM
DOMIN/REP GREECE USA+45 USSR VIETNAM OP/RES COERCE NAT/LISM
WAR 20. PAGE 33 F0643

DOMINATION....SEE DOMIN

DOMINICAN REPUBLIC....SEE DOMIN/REP

DOMINO....THE DOMINO THEORY

DONALD A.G. F0653

DONNELLY/I....IGNATIUS DONNELLY

DOOLEY S. F2806

DOSSER D. F0654

DOSTOYEV/F....FYODOR DOSTOYEVSKY

DOTSON A. F0655

DOUGLAS A. F0656

DOUGLAS/P....PAUL DOUGLAS

B62
CARPER E.T.,ILLINOIS GOES TO CONGRESS FOR ARMY ADMIN
LAND. USA+45 LAW EXTR/IND PROVS REGION CIVMIL/REL LOBBY
GOV/REL FEDERAL ATTIT 20 ILLINOIS SENATE CONGRESS GEOG
DIRKSEN/E DOUGLAS/P. PAGE 22 F0420 LEGIS

DOUGLAS/WO....WILLIAM O. DOUGLAS

DOWD L.P. F0657

DOWNIE J. F0658

DOWNS A. F0659

DRAPER A.P. F0660

DRAPER/HAL....HAL DRAPER

DREAM....DREAMING

B64
NAGEL P.C.,ONE NATION INDIVISIBLE: THE UNION IN FEDERAL
AMERICAN THOUGHT 1776-1861. USA-45 INDUS TEC/DEV NAT/G
EDU/PROP DREAM...IDEA/COMP 18/19. PAGE 96 F1887 ATTIT
INGP/REL

DREIER J.C. F0661

DREYFUS S. F0662

DREYFUS/A....ALFRED DREYFUS OR DREYFUS AFFAIR

DRIVE....DRIVE AND MORALE

B14
VEBLEN T.,THE INSTINCT OF WORKMANSHIP. UNIV SOCIETY DRIVE
ECO/DEV ECO/UNDEV CREATE TEC/DEV ECO/TAC EDU/PROP SKILL
ROUTINE PERSON...HUM CONCPT TIME/SEQ GEN/LAWS.
PAGE 140 F2768

N19
CARPER E.T.,LOBBYING AND THE NATURAL GAS BILL LOBBY
(PAMPHLET). USA+45 SERV/IND BARGAIN PAY DRIVE ROLE ADJUD
WEALTH 20 CONGRESS SENATE EISNHWR/DD. PAGE 22 F0418 TRIBUTE
NAT/G

N19
STEUBER F.A.,THE CONTRIBUTION OF SWITZERLAND TO THE FOR/AID
ECONOMIC AND SOCIAL DEVELOPMENT OF LOW-INCOME ECO/UNDEV
COUNTRIES (PAMPHLET). SWITZERLND FINAN NAT/G PLAN
VOL/ASSN INT/TRADE DRIVE...CHARTS 20. PAGE 126 DIPLOM
F2482

B34
GRAHAM F.D.,PROTECTIVE TARIFFS. FUT USA+45 WOR-45 INT/ORG
INDUS MARKET VOL/ASSN PLAN CAP/ISM ECO/TAC PEACE TARIFFS
ATTIT DRIVE HEALTH ORD/FREE...OBS TREND GEN/LAWS
FOR/TRADE 20. PAGE 50 F0970

B39
ROBBINS L.,ECONOMIC CAUSES OF WAR. WOR-45 ECO/DEV COERCE
ECO/UNDEV INT/ORG NAT/G TEC/DEV DIPLOM DOMIN ECO/TAC
COLONIAL ATTIT DRIVE PWR WEALTH...POLICY CONCPT OBS WAR
SAMP TREND CON/ANAL GEN/LAWS MARX/KARL 20. PAGE 112
F2203

B44
BIENSTOCK G.,MANAGEMENT IN RUSSIAN INDUSTRY AND ADMIN
AGRICULTURE. USSR CONSULT WORKER LEAD COST PROFIT MARXISM
ATTIT DRIVE PWR...MGT METH/COMP DICTIONARY ACCT 20. SML/CO

PAGE 15 F0281

AGRI

B47

WHITEHEAD T.N.,LEADERSHIP IN A FREE SOCIETY; A STUDY IN HUMAN RELATIONS BASED ON AN ANALYSIS OF PRESENT-DAY INDUSTRIAL CIVILIZATION. WOR-45 STRUCT R+D LABOR LG/CO SML/CO WORKER PLAN PROB/SOLV TEC/DEV DRIVE...MGT 20. PAGE 146 F2872

INDUS
LEAD
ORD/FREE
SOCIETY

B48

DURBIN E.F.M.,THE POLITICS OF DEMOCRATIC SOCIALISM; AN ESSAY ON SOCIAL POLICY. STRATA POL/PAR PLAN COERCE DRIVE PERSON PWR MARXISM...CHARTS METH/COMP. PAGE 35 F0684

SOCIALIST
POPULISM
POLICY
SOCIETY

B48

GRAHAM F.D.,THE THEORY OF INTERNATIONAL VALUES. FUT WOR+45 WOR-45 ECO/DEV FINAN INT/ORG PLAN TEC/DEV CAP/ISM DIPLOM ECO/TAC TARIFFS ROUTINE BAL/PAY DRIVE PWR WEALTH SOCISM...POLICY STAT HYPO/EXP GEN/LAWS 20. PAGE 50 F0971

NEW/IDEA
INT/TRADE

S49

SHEPHARD H.A.,"DEMOCRATIC CONTROL IN A LABOR UNION." FUT CONSTN STRUCT TEC/DEV LEAD PARTIC RACE/REL CENTRAL DRIVE HABITAT RECORD. PAGE 120 F2374

LABOR
MAJORIT
CONTROL
PWR

B50

SURANYI-UNGER T.,PRIVATE ENTERPRISE AND GOVERNMENTAL PLANNING. STRUCT FINAN BAL/PWR HAPPINESS DRIVE NEW/LIB PLURISM...MATH QUANT STAT TREND BIBLIOG. PAGE 127 F2516

PLAN
NAT/G
LAISSEZ
POLICY

B51

HARBISON F.H.,GOALS AND STRATEGY IN COLLECTIVE BARGAINING. WORKER BAL/PWR PARTIC DRIVE...POLICY MGT. PAGE 55 F1074

LABOR
BARGAIN
GP/REL
ADMIN

B51

PARSONS T.,THE SOCIAL SYSTEM. UNIV INTELL SOCIETY ECO/DEV SECT PLAN PERCEPT...CONCPT METH/CNCPT. PAGE 103 F2030

DRIVE
SOC

C51

HOMANS G.C.,"THE WESTERN ELECTRIC RESEARCHES" IN S. HOSLETT, ED., HUMAN FACTORS IN MANAGEMENT (BMR)" ACT/RES GP/REL HAPPINESS PRODUC DRIVE...MGT OBS 20. PAGE 61 F1202

OP/RES
EFFICIENCY
SOC/EXP
WORKER

B52

ALEXANDROWICZ C.H.,INTERNATIONAL ECONOMIC ORGANIZATION. WOR+45 ECO/DEV ECO/UNDEV DIST/IND FINAN MARKET PLAN ECO/TAC LEGIT DRIVE WEALTH ...POLICY CONCPT QUANT OBS TIME/SEQ GEN/LAWS WORK METH/GP EEC ILO OEEC UNESCO 20. PAGE 4 F0063

INT/ORG
INT/TRADE

L52

HUTH A.G.,"COMMUNICATION AND ECONOMIC DEVELOPMENT." FUT WOR+45 CULTURE SOCIETY INT/ORG PLAN TEC/DEV EDU/PROP DRIVE KNOWL WEALTH...POLICY CONCPT RECORD STERTYP GEN/LAWS COMMUN TOT/POP UNESCO 20 UN CMN/WLTH. PAGE 64 F1250

ECO/UNDEV

S52

CHINOY E.,"THE TRADITION OF OPPORTUNITY AND THE ASPIRATIONS OF AUTOMOBILE WORKERS" (BMR)" STRATA ACT/RES ALL/VALS SKILL...INT 20. PAGE 24 F0468

WORKER
ECO/DEV
DRIVE
INDUS

B53

BOWEN H.R.,SOCIAL RESPONSIBILITIES OF THE BUSINESSMAN (FIRST EDITION). LAW FINAN ACT/RES CAP/ISM ROUTINE DRIVE PWR LAISSEZ...DECISION BIBLIOG. PAGE 17 F0326

MGT
PERSON
SUPEGO
MORAL

B53

PURCELL T.V.,THE WORKER SPEAKS HIS MIND ON COMPANY AND UNION. WORKER ADJUD LEAD RACE/REL ATTIT DRIVE MARXISM...MGT CLASSIF STAT OBS INT SAMP BIBLIOG. PAGE 108 F2131

LABOR
PARTIC
INGP/REL
HAPPINESS

B54

CHILDS M.W.,ETHICS IN A BUSINESS SOCIETY. PROF/ORG LEAD WAR GP/REL ATTIT DRIVE PERSON KNOWL MORAL PWR ...WELF/ST BIBLIOG. PAGE 24 F0466

MGT
SOCIETY

B54

STALEY E.,THE FUTURE OF UNDERDEVELOPED COUNTRIES: POLITICAL IMPLICATIONS OF ECONOMIC DEVELOPMENT. AFR COM FUT USA+45 SOCIETY ECO/UNDEV CREATE PLAN CAP/ISM ATTIT DRIVE MARXISM SOCISM...POLICY CONCPT CHARTS 20. PAGE 125 F2466

EDU/PROP
ECO/TAC
FOR/AID

B56

BARBASH J.,THE PRACTICE OF UNIONISM. ECO/TAC LEAD LOBBY GP/REL INGP/REL DRIVE MARXISM BIBLIOG. PAGE 10 F0182

LABOR
REPRESENT
CONTROL
ADMIN

B56

UPHOFF W.H.,UNDERSTANDING THE UNION MEMBER (PAMPHLET). STRATA R+D LEAD PARTIC...METH/CNCPT STAT QU. PAGE 133 F2624

LABOR
WORKER
ATTIT
DRIVE

S56

BROWN J.S.,"UNION SIZE AS A FUNCTION OF INTRA-UNION CONFLICT." CLIENT CONTROL CHOOSE EFFICIENCY ATTIT TREND. PAGE 19 F0370

LABOR
INGP/REL
CONSEN
DRIVE

B58

BIDWELL P.W.,RAW MATERIALS: A STUDY OF AMERICAN POLICY. USA+45 USA-45 ECO/UNDEV AGRI INDUS KIN CREATE PLAN ECO/TAC WAR PEACE ATTIT DRIVE WEALTH ...STAT CHARTS CONGRESS FOR/TRADE VAL/FREE. PAGE 15 F0279

EXTR/IND
ECO/DEV

B58

HIRSCHMAN A.O.,STRATEGY OF ECONOMIC DEVELOPMENT. WOR+45 WOR-45 CULTURE ECO/DEV NAT/G PLAN TEC/DEV INT/TRADE BAL/PAY ATTIT DRIVE RIGID/FLEX WEALTH ...CONCPT METH/CNCPT OBS CHARTS SIMUL GEN/LAWS TOT/POP VAL/FREE. PAGE 60 F1176

ECO/UNDEV
ECO/TAC
CAP/ISM

B58

KINDLEBERGER C.P.,INTERNATIONAL ECONOMICS. WOR+45 WOR-45 ECO/DEV ECO/UNDEV FINAN VOL/ASSN ACT/RES DIPLOM ECO/TAC LEGIT REGION ATTIT DRIVE ORD/FREE WEALTH...POLICY STAT TREND GEN/LAWS EEC ECSC OEEC 20. PAGE 71 F1391

INT/ORG
BAL/PWR
TARIFFS

B59

ALLEN R.L.,SOVIET INFLUENCE IN LATIN AMERICA. ECO/UNDEV FINAN PROC/MFG NAT/G TEC/DEV EDU/PROP EXEC ROUTINE ATTIT DRIVE PERSON ALL/VALS PWR...STAT CHARTS WORK FOR/TRADE 20. PAGE 4 F0071

L/A+17C
ECO/TAC
INT/TRADE
USSR

B59

WARD B.,5 IDEAS THAT CHANGE THE WORLD. WOR+45 WOR-45 SOCIETY STRUCT AGRI INDUS INT/ORG NAT/G FORCES ACT/RES ARMS/CONT TOTALISM ATTIT DRIVE GEN/LAWS. PAGE 143 F2815

ECO/UNDEV
ALL/VALS
NAT/LISM
COLONIAL

B59

WORTHY J.C.,BIG BUSINESS AND FREE MEN. LG/CO EX/STRUC EDU/PROP LEAD CHOOSE GP/REL ATTIT DRIVE ROLE ORD/FREE...MAJORIT 20. PAGE 149 F2927

ELITES
LOC/G
TOP/EX
PARTIC

L59

SIMON H.A.,"THEORIES OF DECISION-MAKING IN ECONOMICS AND BEHAVIORAL SCIENCE" (BMR)" MARKET BARGAIN UTIL DRIVE...DECISION MGT PROBABIL HYPO/EXP SIMUL 20 BEHAVIORSM. PAGE 122 F2409

PSY
GEN/LAWS
PROB/SOLV

S59

DUNNING J.H.,"NON-PECUNIARY ELEMENTS AND BUSINESS BEHAVIOUR." PLAN PROB/SOLV COST...METH/CNCPT CLASSIF QUANT STAT. PAGE 35 F0681

DECISION
DRIVE
PRODUC
PRICE

S59

REUBENS E.D.,"THE BASIS FOR REORIENATION OF AMERICAN FOREIGN AID POLICY." USA+45 USSR STRUCT INT/ORG CONSULT ECO/TAC ADMIN DRIVE MORAL ORD/FREE PWR WEALTH...RELATIV MATH STAT TREND GEN/LAWS VAL/FREE 20. PAGE 111 F2180

ECO/UNDEV
PLAN
FOR/AID
DIPLOM

B60

ARON R.,COLLOQUES DE RHEINFELDEN. AFR USA+45 USSR WOR+45 WOR-45 CULTURE ECO/UNDEV NAT/G POL/PAR DIPLOM NAT/LISM TOTALISM ATTIT DRIVE ALL/VALS ...PLURIST CONCPT STERTYP GEN/LAWS TOT/POP 20. PAGE 6 F0120

ECO/DEV
SOCIETY
CAP/ISM
SOCISM

B60

CAMPBELL R.W.,SOVIET ECONOMIC POWER. COM USA+45 DIST/IND MARKET TOP/EX ACT/RES CAP/ISM ECO/TAC DOMIN EDU/PROP ADMIN ROUTINE DRIVE...MATH TIME/SEQ CHARTS WORK 20. PAGE 21 F0409

ECO/DEV
PLAN
SOCISM
USSR

B60

GRANICK D.,THE RED EXECUTIVE. COM USA+45 SOCIETY ECO/DEV INDUS NAT/G POL/PAR EX/STRUC PLAN ECO/TAC EDU/PROP ADMIN EXEC ATTIT DRIVE...GP/COMP 20. PAGE 50 F0976

PWR
STRATA
USSR
ELITES

B60

RAPKIN C.,THE DEMAND FOR HOUSING IN RACIALLY MIXED AREAS: A STUDY OF THE NATURE OF NEIGHBORHOOD CHANGE. USA+45 FINAN PRICE COST DRIVE...GEOG 20. PAGE 109 F2151

RACE/REL
NEIGH
DISCRIM
MARKET

B60

ROEPKE W.,A HUMANE ECONOMY: THE SOCIAL FRAMEWORK OF THE FREE MARKET. FUT USSR WOR+45 CULTURE SOCIETY ECO/DEV PLAN ECO/TAC ADMIN ATTIT PERSON RIGID/FLEX SUPEGO MORAL WEALTH SOCISM...POLICY OLD/LIB CONCPT TREND GEN/LAWS 20. PAGE 113 F2232

DRIVE
EDU/PROP
CAP/ISM

B60

SHONFIELD A.,THE ATTACK ON WORLD POVERTY. WOR+45 ECO/DEV ECO/UNDEV FINAN VOL/ASSN PLAN EDU/PROP DRIVE KNOWL WEALTH...CONT/OBS STAND/INT ORG/CHARTS TOT/POP UNESCO 20. PAGE 121 F2383

INT/ORG
ECO/TAC
FOR/AID
INT/TRADE

S60

BARNETT H.J.,"RESEARCH AND DEVELOPMENT, ECONOMIC GROWTH, AND NATIONAL SECURITY." AFR USA+45 R+D CREATE ECO/TAC ATTIT DRIVE PWR...POLICY SOC METH/CNCPT QUANT STAT TIME/SEQ ORG/CHARTS LOG/LING 20. PAGE 10 F0190

ACT/RES
PLAN

S60

FRANKEL S.H.,"ECONOMIC ASPECTS OF POLITICAL INDEPENDENCE IN AFRICA." AFR FUT SOCIETY ECO/UNDEV COM/IND FINAN LEGIS PLAN TEC/DEV CAP/ISM ECO/TAC INT/TRADE ADMIN ATTIT DRIVE RIGID/FLEX PWR WEALTH ...MGT NEW/IDEA MATH TIME/SEQ VAL/FREE 20. PAGE 43 F0846

NAT/G
FOR/AID

S60

GARNICK D.H.,"ON THE ECONOMIC FEASIBILITY OF A MIDDLE EASTERN COMMON MARKET." AFR ISLAM CULTURE INDUS NAT/G PLAN TEC/DEV ECO/TAC ADMIN ATTIT DRIVE

MARKET
INT/TRADE

RIGID/FLEX...PLURIST STAT TREND GEN/LAWS 20. PAGE 46 F0907

S60
GROSSMAN G.,"SOVIET GROWTH: ROUTINE, INERTIA, AND PRESSURE." COM STRATA NAT/G DELIB/GP PLAN TEC/DEV ECO/TAC EDU/PROP ADMIN ROUTINE DRIVE WEALTH 20. PAGE 52 F1007
POL/PAR ECO/DEV AFR USSR

S60
HERZ J.H.,"EAST GERMANY: PROGRESS AND PROSPECTS." COM AGRI FINAN INDUS LOC/G NAT/G FORCES PLAN TEC/DEV DOMIN ADMIN COERCE DRIVE PERCEPT RIGID/FLEX MORAL ORD/FREE PWR...MARXIST PSY SOC RECORD STERTYP WORK. PAGE 59 F1158
POL/PAR STRUCT GERMANY

S60
KREININ M.E.,"THE 'OUTER-SEVEN' AND EUROPEAN INTEGRATION." EUR+WWI FRANCE GERMANY ITALY UK ECO/DEV DIST/IND INT/TRADE DRIVE WEALTH...MYTH CHARTS EEC OEEC 20. PAGE 73 F1436
ECO/TAC GEN/LAWS

S60
MAIR L.P.,"SOCIAL CHANGE IN SOUTH AFRICA." MOD/EUR SOUTH/AFR WOR+45 ECO/UNDEV EX/STRUC TEC/DEV ATTIT DRIVE PERCEPT ORD/FREE...MGT CONCPT TIME/SEQ IND 20. PAGE 84 F1641
AFR NAT/G REV SOVEREIGN

S60
MURPHEY R.,"ECONOMIC CONFLICTS IN SOUTH ASIA." ASIA CULTURE INTELL ECO/TAC REGION ATTIT DRIVE KNOWL ...METH/CNCPT TIME/SEQ STERTYP TOT/POP METH/GP VAL/FREE 20. PAGE 95 F1864
S/ASIA ECO/UNDEV

S60
OWEN C.F.,"US AND SOVIET RELATIONS WITH UNDERDEVELOPED COUNTRIES: LATIN AMERICA-A CASE STUDY." AFR COM L/A+17C USA+45 USSR EXTR/IND MARKET TEC/DEV DIPLOM ECO/TAC NAT/LISM ORD/FREE PWR ...TREND WORK 20. PAGE 102 F2005
ECO/UNDEV DRIVE INT/TRADE

S60
RIVKIN A.,"AFRICAN ECONOMIC DEVELOPMENT: ADVANCED TECHNOLOGY AND THE STAGES OF GROWTH." CULTURE ECO/UNDEV AGRI COM/IND EXTR/IND PLAN ECO/TAC ATTIT DRIVE RIGID/FLEX SKILL WEALTH...MGT SOC GEN/LAWS FOR/TRADE WORK TOT/POP 20. PAGE 111 F2195
AFR TEC/DEV FOR/AID

B61
ERASMUS C.J.,MAN TAKES CONTROL: CULTURAL DEVELOPMENT AND AMERICAN AID. STRUCT OWN DRIVE PERCEPT...SOC 20 MEXIC/AMER. PAGE 38 F0741
ORD/FREE CULTURE ECO/UNDEV TEC/DEV

B61
FILLOL T.R.,SOCIAL FACTORS IN ECONOMIC DEVELOPMENT: THE ARGENTINE CASE. STRUCT INDUS LABOR CREATE TEC/DEV EFFICIENCY PRODUC DRIVE...METH/CNCPT METH/COMP BIBLIOG/A 20 ARGEN. PAGE 41 F0795
ECO/UNDEV MGT PERS/REL TREND

B61
FRIEDMANN G.,THE ANATOMY OF WORK. USA+45 SOCIETY CONTROL ROUTINE DRIVE SKILL...PSY SOC STAT OBS METH/COMP PERS/COMP 20. PAGE 44 F0862
AUTOMAT WORKER INDUS PERSON

B61
INDUSTRIAL COUN SOC-ECO STU,THE SWEDISH ECONOMY AND THE UNDERDEVELOPED COUNTRIES. SWEDEN INDUS DELIB/GP TEC/DEV INT/TRADE EDU/PROP COLONIAL DRIVE...CHARTS 20. PAGE 64 F1264
FOR/AID ECO/UNDEV PLAN FINAN

B61
MARX K.,THE COMMUNIST MANIFESTO. IN (MENDEL A. ESSENTIAL WORKS OF MARXISM, NEW YORK: BANTAM. FUT MOD/EUR CULTURE ECO/DEV ECO/UNDEV AGRI FINAN INDUS MARKET PROC/MFG LABOR POL/PAR CONSULT FORCES CREATE PLAN ADMIN ATTIT DRIVE RIGID/FLEX ORD/FREE PWR RESPECT MARX/KARL MUNICH WORK. PAGE 86 F1691
COM NEW/IDEA CAP/ISM REV

S61
BARALL M.,"THE UNITED STATES GOVERNMENT RESPONDS." L/A+17C USA+45 SOCIETY NAT/G CREATE PLAN DIPLOM ECO/TAC ATTIT DRIVE RIGID/FLEX KNOWL SKILL WEALTH ...METH/CNCPT TIME/SEQ GEN/METH 20. PAGE 9 F0176
ECO/UNDEV ACT/RES FOR/AID

S61
HEILBRONER R.L.,"DYNAMICS OF FOREIGN AID: PROBLEMS OF UNDERDEVELOPED NATIONS PLAGUE ASSISTANCE PROGRAM." FUT USA+45 WOR+45 STRATA NAT/G PLAN TEC/DEV ATTIT DRIVE WEALTH WORK 20. PAGE 58 F1135
ECO/UNDEV ECO/TAC FOR/AID

C61
FILLOL T.R.,"SOCIAL FACTORS IN ECONOMIC DEVELOPMENT: THE ARGENTINE CASE" INDUS LABOR CREATE TEC/DEV PERS/REL EFFICIENCY PRODUC DRIVE ...METH/CNCPT METH/COMP 20 ARGEN. PAGE 41 F0794
BIBLIOG ECO/UNDEV MGT TREND

B62
ARNOLD H.J.P.,AID FOR DEVELOPING COUNTRIES. COM EUR+WWI USA+45 USSR WOR+45 EDU/PROP ATTIT DRIVE PWR WEALTH...TREND CHARTS STERTYP NAT/ 20. PAGE 6 F0115
ECO/UNDEV ECO/TAC FOR/AID

B62
GERSCHENKRON A.,ECONOMIC BACKWARDNESS IN HISTORICAL PERSPECTIVE. WOR+45 WOR-45 ECO/DEV ECO/UNDEV INDUS NAT/G LEGIT DRIVE...WELF/ST DECISION QUANT TREND CHARTS 20. PAGE 47 F0919
TEC/DEV USSR

B62
HARRINGTON M.,THE OTHER AMERICA: POVERTY IN THE UNITED STATES. WORKER CREATE REPRESENT RACE/REL AGE/O DRIVE POLICY. PAGE 55 F1086
WEALTH WELF/ST INCOME CULTURE

B62
HUMPHREY D.D.,THE UNITED STATES AND THE COMMON MARKET. USA+45 INDUS MARKET INT/ORG PLAN EDU/PROP BAL/PAY DRIVE PWR WEALTH...TREND STERTYP FOR/TRADE EEC 20. PAGE 63 F1241
ATTIT ECO/TAC

B62
LEVENSTEIN A.,WHY PEOPLE WORK; CHANGING INCENTIVES IN A TROUBLED WORLD. USA+45 SOCIETY PROB/SOLV TEC/DEV EDU/PROP ADJUST...CENSUS BIBLIOG 20. PAGE 79 F1538
DRIVE WORKER ECO/DEV ANOMIE

B62
RIMALOV V.V.,ECONOMIC COOPERATION BETWEEN USSR AND UNDERDEVELOPED COUNTRIES. USSR FINAN TEC/DEV INT/TRADE DOMIN EDU/PROP COLONIAL NAT/LISM DRIVE SOVEREIGN...AUD/VIS 20. PAGE 111 F2194
FOR/AID PLAN ECO/UNDEV DIPLOM

B62
WARD B.,THE RICH NATIONS AND THE POOR NATIONS. FUT WOR+45 CULTURE ECO/DEV ECO/UNDEV PLAN CAP/ISM EDU/PROP REV NAT/LISM ATTIT DRIVE SOCISM...POLICY CONCPT TIME/SEQ 20. PAGE 143 F2816
ECO/TAC GEN/LAWS

S62
PYE L.W.,"THE POLITICAL IMPULSES AND FANTASIES BEHIND FOREIGN AID." FUT USA+45 ECO/UNDEV DIPLOM ECO/TAC ROUTINE DRIVE KNOWL...SOC METH/CNCPT NEW/IDEA TREND HYPO/EXP STERTYP GEN/METH 20. PAGE 108 F2133
ACT/RES ATTIT FOR/AID

S62
READ W.H.,"UPWARD COMMUNICATION IN INDUSTRIAL HIERARCHIES." LG/CO TOP/EX PROB/SOLV DOMIN EXEC PERS/REL ATTIT DRIVE PERCEPT...CORREL STAT CHARTS 20. PAGE 110 F2159
ADMIN INGP/REL PSY MGT

B63
CHAMBERLAIN E.H.,THE ECONOMIC ANALYSIS OF LABOR UNION POWER (PAMPHLET). WORKER ECO/TAC DOMIN COERCE GP/REL DRIVE WEALTH POLICY. PAGE 23 F0441
LABOR PWR CONTROL

B63
ENKE S.,ECONOMICS FOR DEVELOPMENT. AGRI TEC/DEV CAP/ISM DIPLOM ECO/TAC TAX ATTIT DRIVE HABITAT WEALTH...GOV/COMP BIBLIOG 20. PAGE 38 F0737
ECO/UNDEV PHIL/SCI CON/ANAL

B63
PRYOR F.L.,THE COMMUNIST FOREIGN TRADE SYSTEM. COM CZECHOSLVK GERMANY YUGOSLAVIA LAW ECO/DEV DIST/IND POL/PAR PLAN DOMIN TOTALISM DRIVE RIGID/FLEX WEALTH ...STAT STAND/INT CHARTS FOR/TRADE 20. PAGE 108 F2130
ATTIT ECO/TAC

B63
VON MISES L.,HUMAN ACTION: A TREATISE ON ECONOMICS (2ND ED.). SOCIETY MARKET TAX PAY PRICE DEMAND EQUILIB RATIONAL...PSY 20. PAGE 142 F2794
PLAN DRIVE ATTIT

L63
MCKERSIE R.B.,"NONPROFESSIONAL HOSPITAL WORKERS AND A UNION ORGANIZING DRIVE." PLAN GP/REL RACE/REL ATTIT DRIVE...CORREL STAT INT GP/COMP. PAGE 88 F1732
VOL/ASSN HEALTH INGP/REL LABOR

S63
AYAL E.B.,"VALUE SYSTEM AND ECONOMIC DEVELOPMENT IN JAPAN AND THAILAND." ASIA S/ASIA THAILAND CULTURE ECO/DEV CAP/ISM DOMIN NAT/LISM DRIVE RIGID/FLEX SOCISM...WELF/ST OBS TREND CON/ANAL GEN/LAWS TERR/GP 20 CHINJAP. PAGE 8 F0145
ECO/UNDEV ALL/VALS

S63
POLYANOV N.,"THE DOLLAR'S VENTURES IN EUROPE." EUR+WWI FRANCE USA+45 ECO/DEV MARKET POL/PAR TEC/DEV ECO/TAC EDU/PROP DRIVE PWR WEALTH...MARXIST MYTH STAT TREND EEC 20. PAGE 107 F2100
FINAN PLAN BAL/PAY CAP/ISM

S63
POPPINO R.E.,"IMBALANCE IN BRAZIL." L/A+17C NAT/G TOP/EX PLAN DIPLOM LEGIT DRIVE WEALTH...CON/ANAL FOR/TRADE LAFTA 20. PAGE 107 F2105
POL/PAR ECO/TAC BRAZIL

S63
REDDAWAY W.B.,"THE ECONOMICS OF UNDERDEVELOPED COUNTRIES." S/ASIA WOR+45 WOR-45 STRATA AGRI COM/IND DIST/IND MARKET PROC/MFG PLAN TEC/DEV FOR/AID BAL/PAY ATTIT DRIVE SKILL WORK FOR/TRADE 20. PAGE 110 F2165
ECO/TAC ECO/UNDEV INDIA

S63
SCHURMANN F.,"ECONOMIC POLICY AND POLITICAL POWER IN COMMUNIST CHINA." ASIA CHINA/COM USSR SOCIETY ECO/UNDEV AGRI INDUS CREATE ADMIN ROUTINE ATTIT DRIVE RIGID/FLEX PWR WEALTH...HIST/WRIT TREND CHARTS WORK 20. PAGE 118 F2323
PLAN ECO/TAC

S63
SHWADRAN B.,"MIDDLE EAST OIL, 1962." ISLAM DIST/IND INDUS PLAN ATTIT DRIVE WEALTH...POLICY STAT CONT/OBS TREND CHARTS GEN/LAWS TERR/GP METH/GP 20 OIL. PAGE 121 F2393
PROC/MFG ECO/TAC ELITES REGION

S63
SHWADRAN B.,"MIDDLE EAST OIL, 1962." ISLAM USSR ECO/DEV DIST/IND INDUS PLAN BAL/PWR DISPL DRIVE ...POLICY STAT TREND GEN/LAWS TERR/GP METH/GP EEC OEEC 20 OIL. PAGE 121 F2394
MARKET ECO/TAC INT/TRADE

B64
JUSTER F.T.,ANTICIPATIONS AND PURCHASES; AN ANALYSIS OF CONSUMER BEHAVIOR. PROB/SOLV RISK COST PRODUC DRIVE...STAT STYLE SAMP CON/ANAL CHARTS HYPO/EXP GAME SIMUL. PAGE 68 F1345
PROBABIL DECISION PREDICT DEMAND

B64
RAMAZANI R.K.,THE MIDDLE EAST AND THE EUROPEAN COMMON MARKET. EUR+WWI ISLAM ECO/DEV EXTR/IND MARKET PROC/MFG INT/ORG NAT/G TEC/DEV ECO/TAC REGION DRIVE WEALTH...STAT CHARTS EEC TOT/POP 20. PAGE 109 F2141
ECO/UNDEV ATTIT INT/TRADE

B64
SULLIVAN G.,THE STORY OF THE PEACE CORPS. USA+45 WOR+45 INTELL FACE/GP NAT/G SCHOOL VOL/ASSN CONSULT EX/STRUC PLAN EDU/PROP ADMIN ATTIT DRIVE ALL/VALS ...POLICY HEAL SOC CONCPT INT QU BIOG TREND SOC/EXP WORK. PAGE 127 F2511
INT/ORG ECO/UNDEV FOR/AID PEACE

B64
WILLIAMSON O.E.,THE ECONOMICS OF DISCRETIONARY BEHAVIOR: MANAGERIAL OBJECTIVES IN A THEORY OF THE FIRM. MARKET BUDGET CAP/ISM PRODUC DRIVE PERSON ...STAT CHARTS BIBLIOG METH 20. PAGE 147 F2897
EFFICIENCY MGT ECO/TAC CHOOSE

L64
HAAS E.B.,"ECONOMICS AND DIFFERENTIAL PATTERNS OF POLITICAL INTEGRATION: PROJECTIONS ABOUT UNITY IN LATIN AMERICA." SOCIETY NAT/G DELIB/GP ACT/RES CREATE PLAN ECO/TAC REGION ROUTINE ATTIT DRIVE PWR WEALTH...CONCPT TREND CHARTS LAFTA TERR/GP 20. PAGE 52 F1020
L/A+17C INT/ORG MARKET

S64
GALBRAITH V.,"JAPAN'S POSITION IN WORLD TRADE." ASIA AGRI INDUS CREATE ECO/TAC LEGIT DRIVE WEALTH ...TREND EEC GATT FOR/TRADE 20 CHINJAP. PAGE 45 F0885
ECO/DEV DELIB/GP

S64
GARDNER R.N.,"GATT AND THE UNITED NATIONS CONFERENCE ON TRADE AND DEVELOPMENT." USA+45 WOR+45 SOCIETY ECO/UNDEV MARKET NAT/G DELIB/GP ACT/RES PLAN ECO/TAC TARIFFS EDU/PROP ROUTINE DRIVE RIGID/FLEX WEALTH...DECISION MGT TREND UN TOT/POP 20 GATT. PAGE 46 F0905
INT/ORG INT/TRADE

B65
CRANE E.,MARKETING COMMUNICATION: A BEHAVIORAL APPROACH TO MEN, MESSAGES, AND MEDIA. STRATA R+D VOL/ASSN CROWD DRIVE PERSON SKILL WEALTH. PAGE 28 F0551
EDU/PROP MARKET PERCEPT ATTIT

B65
THE STATE AND ECONOMIC ENTERPRISE IN JAPAN; ESSAYS IN THE POLITICAL ECONOMY OF GROWTH. AGRI INDUS DRIVE POPULISM...CHARTS NAT/COMP ANTHOL 19/20 CHINJAP. PAGE 81 F1594
ECO/UNDEV ECO/DEV CAP/ISM ECO/TAC

B65
O'BRIEN F.,CRISIS IN WORLD COMMUNISM* MARXISM IN SEARCH OF EFFICIENCY. AFR COM ECO/DEV PLAN INT/TRADE WAR ADJUST PEACE...STAT TIME/SEQ GOV/COMP NAT/COMP. PAGE 99 F1951
MARXISM USSR DRIVE EFFICIENCY

B65
THORNTON A.P.,DOCTRINES OF IMPERIALISM. WOR+45 WOR-45 DOMIN NAT/LISM PROFIT ATTIT PERSON PWR RESPECT SOVEREIGN...CONCPT STERTYP. PAGE 130 F2571
IDEA/COMP COLONIAL DRIVE

L65
HAGE J.,"AN AXIOMATIC THEORY OF ORGANIZATIONS" USA+45 STRUCT LABOR PRODUC DRIVE PERSON RIGID/FLEX 20 WEBER/MAX. PAGE 53 F1032
GP/REL EFFICIENCY PROF/ORG ATTIT

S65
WHITE J.,"WEST GERMAN AID TO DEVELOPING COUNTRIES." AFR INT/ORG OP/RES GIVE CENTRAL ATTIT DRIVE...STAT NAT/COMP. PAGE 146 F2869
GERMANY FOR/AID ECO/UNDEV CAP/ISM

B66
WETTER G.A.,SOVIET IDEOLOGY TODAY. USSR ECO/UNDEV SECT WORKER CAP/ISM CONTROL TASK EFFICIENCY TOTALISM DRIVE WEALTH...TREND 18/20. PAGE 145 F2864
ALL/IDEOS MARXISM REV

S66
MALENBAUM W.,"GOVERNMENT, ENTREPRENEURSHIP, AND ECONOMIC GROWTH IN POOR LANDS." ELITES ECO/UNDEV INDUS CREATE DRIVE. PAGE 84 F1645
ECO/TAC PLAN CONSERVE NAT/G

B67
ESTEY M.,THE UNIONS: STRUCTURE, DEVELOPMENT, AND MANAGEMENT. FUT USA+45 ADJUD CONTROL INGP/REL DRIVE ...DECISION T 20 AFL/CIO. PAGE 38 F0750
LABOR EX/STRUC ADMIN GOV/REL

B67
PIKE F.B.,FREEDOM AND REFORM IN LATIN AMERICA. BRAZIL URUGUAY CONSTN CULTURE SECT DIPLOM EDU/PROP PARTIC DRIVE ALL/VALS CATHISM...GEOG ANTHOL BIBLIOG REFORMERS BOLIV. PAGE 106 F2086
L/A+17C ORD/FREE ECO/UNDEV REV

B67
SPURRIER R.B.,THE OVERPOPULATED SOCIETY. WORKER EATING PERS/REL DEMAND EQUILIB ILLEGIT INCOME HABITAT 20. PAGE 125 F2461
BIO/SOC FOR/AID DRIVE RECEIVE

B67
US SENATE COMM ON FOREIGN REL,HARRISON E. SALISBURY'S TRIP TO NORTH VIETNAM. CHINA/COM USA+45 VIETNAM/N PRESS TASK GUERRILLA CONSEN EFFICIENCY PEACE DRIVE...OBS SENATE. PAGE 139 F2743
DIPLOM WAR FORCES ATTIT

B67
WOOTON G.,WORKERS, UNIONS, AND THE STATE. INDUS PROB/SOLV GP/REL DRIVE SUPEGO RESPECT...PSY SOC. PAGE 148 F2925
PARTIC WORKER NAT/G LABOR

L67
MACDONALD R.M.,"COLLECTIVE BARGAINING IN THE POSTWAR PERIOD." WORKER PROB/SOLV ECO/TAC PARTIC RISK CENTRAL EFFICIENCY DRIVE WEALTH...TREND 20. PAGE 83 F1624
LABOR INDUS BARGAIN CAP/ISM

S67
ALPANDER G.G.,"ENTREPRENEURS AND PRIVATE ENTERPRISE IN TURKEY." TURKEY INDUS PROC/MFG EDU/PROP ATTIT DRIVE WEALTH...GEOG MGT SOC STAT TREND CHARTS 20. PAGE 4 F0077
ECO/UNDEV LG/CO NAT/G POLICY

S67
FRANKLIN N.N.,"THE CONCEPT AND MEASUREMENT OF 'MINIMUM LIVING STANDARDS'." UNIV OP/RES PAY INGP/REL DEMAND INCOME DRIVE WEALTH...SOC CHARTS METH/COMP. PAGE 43 F0849
CONCPT PHIL/SCI ALL/VALS HAPPINESS

S67
LEVIN T.,"PSYCHOANALYSIS AND SOCIAL CHANGE." SOCIETY ANOMIE DRIVE PWR 20. PAGE 79 F1541
PSY PHIL/SCI ADJUST WEALTH

S67
PFEFFERMANN G.,"TRADE UNIONS AND POLITICS IN FRENCH WEST AFRICA DURING THE FOURTH REPUBLIC." AFR INDUS POL/PAR COLONIAL ATTIT PWR 20. PAGE 106 F2077
PARTIC DRIVE INT/TRADE LABOR

S67
WILLMANN J.,"LA COMMUNAUTE EUROPEENNE ET LA GRANDE-BRETAGNE." UK PROB/SOLV TEC/DEV CAP/ISM DIPLOM CONFER FEDERAL...POLICY 20 EEC. PAGE 147 F2898
INT/ORG DRIVE NAT/LISM INT/TRADE

B76
SMITH A.,THE WEALTH OF NATIONS. UK STRUCT WORKER DIPLOM ECO/TAC OPTIMAL DRIVE PERSON ORD/FREE ...OLD/LIB GEN/LAWS 17/18. PAGE 123 F2428
WEALTH PRODUC INDUS LAISSEZ

DROBNIG U. F0663

DRUCKER P.F. F0664,F0665,F0666,F0667

DRUG ADDICTION....SEE BIO/SOC, ANOMIE, CRIME

DUBCEK/A....ALEXANDER DUBCEK

DUBIN R. F0668,F0669

DUBOIS/J....JULES DUBOIS

DUBOIS/WEB....W.E.B. DUBOIS

DUCROS B. F0670

DUE J.F. F0671

DUESENBERRY J.S. F0672

DUGGAR G.S. F0673

DUGUIT/L....LEON DUGUIT

DUHRING/E....EUGEN DUHRING

B59
ENGELS F.,SOCIALISM: UTOPIAN AND SCIENTIFIC (2ND ED.). SOCISM...CONCPT CON/ANAL GEN/LAWS 19 DUHRING/E. PAGE 38 F0732
MARXISM PHIL/SCI UTOPIA IDEA/COMP

DUKE UNIVERSITY F0674

DULLES/JF....JOHN FOSTER DULLES

DUMONT R. F0675

DUN J.L. F0676

DUNCAN O. F0677

DUNCOMBE H.S. F0678

DUNETTE M.D. F2624

DUNLOP J.T. F0679

DUNN J.M. F0680

DUNNING J.H. F0681

DUPONT....DUPONT CORPORATION (E.I. DUPONT DE NEMOURS)

DUPRE J.S. F0682

DURAND-REVILLE L. F0683

DURBIN E.F.M. F0684

DURIEZ P. F0685

DURKHEIM/E....EMIL DURKHEIM

DUROSELLE J.B. F0686

DUSCHA J. F0687

DUTY....SEE SUPEGO

DUVERGER/M....MAURICE DUVERGER

DWYER J.W. F0688

E

EACM....EAST AFRICAN COMMON MARKET

S61
OCHENG D.,"ECONOMIC FORCES AND UGANDA'S FOREIGN POLICY." AFR UGANDA INT/TRADE TARIFFS INCOME SOVEREIGN WEALTH 20 EACM EEC TANGANYIKA. PAGE 100 F1961 — ECO/TAC DIPLOM ECO/UNDEV INT/ORG

EAST AFRICA....SEE AFRICA/E

EAST GERMANY....SEE GERMANY/E

EAST KENTUCKY REGIONAL PLAN F0689,F0690

EASTERN EUROPE....SEE EUROPE/E

EATING....EATING, CUISINE

B58
SHAW S.J.,THE FINANCIAL AND ADMINISTRATIVE ORGANIZATION AND DEVELOPMENT OF OTTOMAN EGYPT 1517-1798. UAR LOC/G FORCES BUDGET INT/TRADE TAX EATING INCOME WEALTH...CHARTS BIBLIOG 16/18 OTTOMAN NAPOLEON/B. PAGE 120 F2371 — FINAN ADMIN GOV/REL CULTURE

B58
US OPERATIONS MISSION TO VIET,BUILDING ECONOMIC STRENGTH (PAMPHLET). USA+45 VIETNAM/S INDUS TEC/DEV BUDGET ADMIN EATING HEALTH...STAT 20. PAGE 138 F2725 — FOR/AID ECO/UNDEV AGRI EDU/PROP

B59
BLACK J.D.,ECONOMICS FOR AGRICULTURE. USA+45 EXTR/IND FAM WORKER ACT/RES PLAN PRICE EATING INCOME...CENSUS BIBLIOG 20. PAGE 15 F0291 — AGRI ECO/TAC MARKET POLICY

B60
SHANNON D.A.,THE GREAT DEPRESSION. USA-45 FINAN LG/CO SCHOOL SML/CO DELIB/GP RECEIVE REV EATING INCOME...ANTHOL MUNICH 20 ROOSEVLT/F CONGRESS. PAGE 120 F2365 — WEALTH NAT/G AGRI INDUS

B63
EL-NAGGAR S.,FOREIGN AID TO UNITED ARAB REPUBLIC. UAR USA+45 USSR AGRI FINAN INDUS FORCES EATING DEMAND...CHARTS METH/COMP 20 RESOURCE/N AID. PAGE 37 F0718 — FOR/AID ECO/UNDEV RECEIVE PLAN

B63
US GOVERNMENT,REPORT TO INTER-AMERICAN ECONOMIC AND SOCIAL COUNCIL AT SECOND ANNUAL MEETING. L/A+17C USA+45 VOL/ASSN TEC/DEV DIPLOM TAX EATING EFFICIENCY HEALTH...STAT CHARTS 20 AID. PAGE 136 F2682 — ECO/TAC FOR/AID FINAN PLAN

B64
MC GOVERN G.S.,WAR AGAINST WANT. USA+45 AGRI DIPLOM INT/TRADE GIVE RECEIVE DEMAND HEALTH 20 KENNEDY/JF FOOD/PEACE. PAGE 87 F1714 — FOR/AID ECO/DEV POLICY EATING

B64
NATIONAL COUN APPLIED ECO RES,A STRATEGY FOR THE FOURTH PLAN. INDIA DIST/IND EXTR/IND SERV/IND ECO/TAC RATION EDU/PROP EATING HEALTH...CHARTS 20. PAGE 97 F1900 — ECO/UNDEV PLAN AGRI WORKER

B65
CHANDRASEKHAR S.,AMERICAN AID AND INDIA'S ECONOMIC DEVELOPMENT. AFR CHINA/COM INDIA USA+45 GIVE EDU/PROP EATING HEALTH ORD/FREE 20 AID. PAGE 23 F0449 — FOR/AID PEACE DIPLOM ECO/UNDEV

B65
WU YUAN-LI,THE ECONOMY OF COMMUNIST CHINA. CHINA/COM USSR AGRI FINAN INDUS POL/PAR WORKER PROB/SOLV INT/TRADE PRICE EATING INCOME OWN WEALTH 20. PAGE 149 F2939 — ECO/TAC MARXISM PLAN EFFICIENCY

B67
SPURRIER R.B.,THE OVERPOPULATED SOCIETY. WORKER EATING PERS/REL DEMAND EQUILIB ILLEGIT INCOME HABITAT 20. PAGE 125 F2461 — BIO/SOC FOR/AID DRIVE RECEIVE

S67
THORKELSON H.,"FOOD STAMPS AND HUNGER IN AMERICA." USA+45 LAW DELIB/GP ADMIN COST DEMAND POLICY. PAGE 130 F2570 — WEALTH RECEIVE EATING PLAN

EBENSTEIN W. F0691

EBONY F0692

EBY K. F0693

ECAFE....UN ECONOMIC COMMISSION FOR ASIA AND THE FAR EAST

B63
WIGHTMAN D.,TOWARD ECONOMIC CO-OPERATION IN ASIA. ASIA S/ASIA VOL/ASSN ACT/RES PLAN TEC/DEV ECO/TAC EDU/PROP RIGID/FLEX SKILL...POLICY METH/CNCPT OBS INT GEN/LAWS UN 20 ECAFE. PAGE 146 F2877 — ECO/UNDEV CREATE

ECHAVARRIA J.M. F0608

ECHR....EUROPEAN CONVENTION ON HUMAN RIGHTS

ECKLER A.R. F0694

ECKSTEIN A. F0624,F0696

ECO....ECONOMICS

ECO/DEV....ECONOMIC SYSTEM IN DEVELOPED COUNTRIES

ECO/TAC....ECONOMIC MEASURES

N
PEN I.,PRIMER ON INTERNATIONAL TRADE. WOR+45 WOR-45 ECO/DEV DIPLOM EFFICIENCY 16/20 EEC. PAGE 104 F2055 — INT/TRADE BAL/PAY ECO/TAC EQUILIB

N
MINISTRY OF OVERSEAS DEVELOPME,TECHNICAL CO-OPERATION -- A BIBLIOGRAPHY. UK LAW SOCIETY DIPLOM ECO/TAC FOR/AID...STAT 20 CMN/WLTH. PAGE 92 F1803 — BIBLIOG TEC/DEV ECO/DEV NAT/G

LCA
GODFREY E.M.,"THE ECONOMICS OF AN AFRICAN UNIVERSITY." AFR SCHOOL PRICE EFFICIENCY INCOME WEALTH...ECOMETRIC CHARTS 20. PAGE 48 F0930 — ACADEM ECO/TAC COST EDU/PROP

B00
LIST F.,NATIONAL SYSTEM OF POLITICAL ECONOMY. ECO/DEV AGRI EXTR/IND FINAN INDUS TEC/DEV ECO/TAC ATTIT WEALTH...TREND GEN/LAWS FOR/TRADE 19. PAGE 81 F1581 — MOD/EUR MARKET

B00
MILL J.S.,PRINCIPLES OF POLITICAL ECONOMY. WOR-45 CULTURE SOCIETY STRATA ECO/DEV AGRI EXTR/IND FINAN INDUS DELIB/GP ECO/TAC WEALTH...CONCPT MATH TREND 20. PAGE 91 F1786 — MARKET INT/ORG INT/TRADE

B02
SELIGMAN E.R.,THE ECONOMIC INTERPRETATION OF HISTORY. ECO/TAC MARXISM SOCISM...PHIL/SCI METH/CNCPT 18/20. PAGE 119 F2348 — IDEA/COMP HIST/WRIT GP/REL

B04
MARX K.,A CONTRIBUTION TO THE CRITIQUE OF POLITICAL ECONOMY (TRANS. FROM 2ND ED. BY N.I. STONE). UK STRATA ECO/DEV FINAN MARKET PLAN BARGAIN CAP/ISM ECO/TAC ATTIT WEALTH...METH/CNCPT BIOG 19. PAGE 86 F1687 — MARXIST NEW/IDEA MARXISM

B04
VEBLEN T.B.,THE THEORY OF BUSINESS ENTERPRISE. USA-45 FINAN WORKER ECO/TAC PRICE GP/REL COST ...POLICY 19/20. PAGE 141 F2770 — TEC/DEV GEN/LAWS SOCIETY WEALTH

B13
BEARD C.A.,AN ECONOMIC INTERPRETATION OF THE CONSTITUTION OF THE UNITED STATES. USA-45 AGRI INT/TRADE SUFF OWN ATTIT...CONCPT MYTH BIOG HIST/WRIT 18. PAGE 12 F0222 — CONSTN ECO/TAC CHOOSE

B13
DAVENPORT H.J.,THE ECONOMICS OF ENTERPRISE. UNIV FINAN SML/CO RENT COST WEALTH GEN/LAWS. PAGE 30 F0582 — CAP/ISM PRICE ECO/TAC LG/CO

B14
HOBSON J.A.,WORK AND WEALTH. CULTURE FINAN INDUS WORKER TEC/DEV ECO/TAC GIVE PAY PRICE COST PRODUC UTIL. PAGE 60 F1185 — WEALTH INCOME GEN/LAWS

B14
LEVINE L.,SYNDICALISM IN FRANCE (2ND ED.). FRANCE LAW SOCIETY ECO/DEV NAT/G ECO/TAC LEAD ATTIT ...POLICY CONCPT STAT BIBLIOG 18/20 REFORMERS. PAGE 79 F1542 — LABOR INDUS SOCISM REV

B14
VEBLEN T.,THE INSTINCT OF WORKMANSHIP. UNIV SOCIETY ECO/DEV ECO/UNDEV CREATE TEC/DEV ECO/TAC EDU/PROP ROUTINE PERSON...HUM CONCPT TIME/SEQ GEN/LAWS. PAGE 140 F2768 — DRIVE SKILL

B19
SUMNER W.G.,WAR AND OTHER ESSAYS. USA-45 DELIB/GP DIPLOM TARIFFS COLONIAL PEACE SOVEREIGN 20. PAGE 127 F2514 INT/TRADE ORD/FREE CAP/ISM ECO/TAC

N19
ANDERSON J.,THE ORGANIZATION OF ECONOMIC STUDIES IN RELATION TO THE PROBLEMS OF GOVERNMENT (PAMPHLET). UK FINAN INDUS DELIB/GP PLAN PROB/SOLV ADMIN 20. PAGE 5 F0095 ECO/TAC ACT/RES NAT/G CENTRAL

N19
ARNDT H.W.,AUSTRALIAN FOREIGN AID POLICY (PAMPHLET). ECO/UNDEV DIPLOM GIVE GOV/REL COST UTIL PWR...CHARTS 20 AUSTRAL PAPUA NEW/GUINEA. PAGE 6 F0114 FOR/AID POLICY ECO/TAC EFFICIENCY

N19
BASCH A.,THE FUTURE OF FOREIGN LENDING FOR DEVELOPMENT (PAMPHLET). WOR+45 ECO/UNDEV FINAN INT/ORG ECO/TAC ATTIT...PREDICT 20. PAGE 11 F0203 FOR/AID ECO/DEV DIPLOM GIVE

N19
BASSIE V.L.,UNCERTAINTY IN FORECASTING AND POLICY FORMATION (PAMPHLET). UNIV MARKET ECO/TAC PRODUC ...POLICY DECISION MGT MATH CHARTS 20. PAGE 11 F0205 ECO/DEV FINAN PREDICT PROB/SOLV

N19
CONGRESSIONAL QUARTERLY SERV,FEDERAL ECONOMIC POLICY 1945-1965 (PAMPHLET). USA+45 FINAN OP/RES BAL/PWR ECO/TAC TAX BAL/PAY CENTRAL COST WEALTH ...CHARTS 20. PAGE 27 F0525 NAT/G ECO/DEV BUDGET POLICY

N19
DEANE H.,THE WAR IN VIETNAM (PAMPHLET). AFR CHINA/COM VIETNAM BAL/PWR DIPLOM ECO/TAC SOCISM INTERVENT INTERVENT. PAGE 31 F0610 WAR SOCIALIST MORAL CAP/ISM

N19
ENGELS F.,THE BRITISH LABOUR MOVEMENT (PAMPHLET). FRANCE GERMANY MOD/EUR UK USA-45 POL/PAR WORKER PAY EDU/PROP PRICE REPRESENT GP/REL 19. PAGE 37 F0730 ECO/TAC MARXISM LABOR STRATA

N19
FRANCK P.G.,AFGHANISTAN BETWEEN EAST AND WEST: THE ECONOMICS OF COMPETITIVE COEXISTENCE (PAMPHLET). AFGHANISTN USA+45 USA-45 USSR INDUS ECO/TAC INT/TRADE CONTROL NEUTRAL ORD/FREE MARXISM...GEOG 20 UN. PAGE 43 F0842 FOR/AID PLAN DIPLOM ECO/UNDEV

N19
GROSECLOSE E.,THE DECAY OF MONEY; A SURVEY OF WESTERN CURRENCIES 1912-1962 (PAMPHLET). AFR FRANCE GERMANY UK LAW INT/TRADE BAL/PAY COST EQUILIB ...POLICY 20 DEPRESSION. PAGE 51 F1004 FINAN NAT/G ECO/DEV ECO/TAC

N19
HACKETT J.,ECONOMIC PLANNING IN FRANCE; ITS RELATION TO THE POLICIES OF THE DEVELOPED COUNTRIES OF WESTERN EUROPE (PAMPHLET). EUR+WWI FRANCE ECO/DEV PROB/SOLV CONTROL...POLICY 20 EUROPE/W. PAGE 52 F1026 ECO/TAC NAT/G PLAN INSPECT

N19
HANSEN B.,INFLATION PROBLEMS IN SMALL COUNTRIES (PAMPHLET). AFR UNIV FOR/AID CONTROL BAL/PAY DEMAND PRODUC 20. PAGE 54 F1066 PRICE FINAN ECO/UNDEV ECO/TAC

N19
HAYEK FA V.O.N.,FREEDOM AND THE ECONOMIC SYSTEM. GERMANY USSR PLAN REPRESENT TOTALISM FASCISM POPULISM...MAJORIT METH/COMP GEN/LAWS 20. PAGE 57 F1123 ORD/FREE ECO/TAC CAP/ISM SOCISM

N19
HUBERMAN L.,SOCIALISM IS THE ONLY ANSWER (PAMPHLET). CREATE ECO/TAC EDU/PROP CONTROL ...SOCIALIST GEN/LAWS ANTHOL 20. PAGE 62 F1230 SOCISM ECO/DEV CAP/ISM PLAN

N19
KINDLEBERGER C.P.,BALANCE-OF-PAYMENTS DEFICITS AND THE INTERNATIONAL MARKET FOR LIQUIDITY (PAMPHLET). ECO/DEV NAT/G PLAN DIPLOM ECO/TAC PRODUC...POLICY STAT CHARTS. PAGE 71 F1389 BAL/PAY INT/TRADE MARKET FINAN

N19
KUWAIT ARABIA,KUWAIT FUND FOR ARAB ECONOMIC DEVELOPMENT (PAMPHLET). ISLAM KUWAIT UAR ECO/UNDEV LEGIS ECO/TAC WEALTH 20. PAGE 74 F1452 FOR/AID DIPLOM FINAN ADMIN

N19
LUTZ F.A.,THE PROBLEM OF INTERNATIONAL LIQUIDITY AND THE MULTIPLECURRENCY STANDARD (PAMPHLET). WOR+45 MARKET INT/ORG PRICE BAL/PAY...NEW/IDEA METH/COMP BIBLIOG 20 IMF. PAGE 82 F1609 PROB/SOLV FINAN DIPLOM ECO/TAC

N19
MIYASAWA K.,AN ECONOMIC SURVIVAL GAME (PAMPHLET). COST DEMAND EQUILIB INCOME PROFIT 20. PAGE 92 F1811 ECOMETRIC GAME ECO/TAC DECISION

N19
ROBERTSON D.,GROWTH, WAGES, MONEY (PAMPHLET). UNIV WORKER BUDGET PRICE DEMAND PRODUC WEALTH...CONCPT MATH MONEY. PAGE 112 F2210 FINAN ECO/DEV ECO/TAC PAY

N19
US MARITIME ADMINISTRATION,CONTRIBUTION OF FEDERAL AID PROGRAMS TO THE OCEANBORNE FOREIGN TRADE OF THE UNITED STATES: 1959-62 (PAMPHLET). USA+45 SEA FINAN NAT/G BUDGET...POLICY 20. PAGE 138 F2719 INT/TRADE ECO/TAC DIST/IND GIVE

N19
VELYAMINOV G.,AFRICA AND THE COMMON MARKET (PAMPHLET). AFR MARKET VOL/ASSN ECO/TAC COLONIAL ORD/FREE...SOCIALIST 20 THIRD/WRLD. PAGE 141 F2775 INT/ORG INT/TRADE SOVEREIGN ECO/UNDEV

N19
WILSON T.,FINANCIAL ASSISTANCE WITH REGIONAL DEVELOPMENT (PAMPHLET). CANADA INDUS NAT/G PLAN TAX CONTROL COST EFFICIENCY...POLICY CHARTS 20. PAGE 147 F2902 FINAN ECO/TAC REGION GOV/REL

B20
COX H.,ECONOMIC LIBERTY. UNIV LAW INT/TRADE RATION TARIFFS RACE/REL SOCISM POLICY. PAGE 28 F0547 NAT/G ORD/FREE ECO/TAC PERSON

B20
PIGOU A.C.,THE ECONOMICS OF WELFARE. UNIV INDUS WORKER ACT/RES RECEIVE INCOME NEW/LIB...MAJORIT SOC/WK. PAGE 106 F2085 ECO/TAC WEALTH FINAN CONTROL

B20
TAWNEY R.H.,THE ACQUISITIVE SOCIETY. STRATA WORKER PROB/SOLV CAP/ISM ECO/TAC CONTROL GP/REL OWN PRIVIL ATTIT ORD/FREE WEALTH 20. PAGE 128 F2536 INDUS SOCIETY PRODUC MORAL

B22
FOURIER C.,TRAITE DE L'ASSOCIATION DOMESTIQUE-AGRICOLE (2 VOLS.). UNIV SOCIETY INDUS ECO/TAC PERSON MORAL ANARCH. PAGE 43 F0834 VOL/ASSN AGRI UTOPIA CONCPT

B23
FINER H.,REPRESENTATIVE GOVERNMENT AND A PARLIAMENT OF INDUSTRY. A STUDY OF THE GERMAN FEDERAL ECONOMIC COUNCIL. GERMANY UK CONSTN INDUS PARL/PROC ...NAT/COMP 20. PAGE 41 F0796 DELIB/GP ECO/TAC WAR REV

B24
CLARK J.B.,THE DISTRIBUTION OF WEALTH (1899). WORKER OWN PRODUC PROFIT WEALTH LAISSEZ...IDEA/COMP GEN/LAWS. PAGE 25 F0478 ECO/TAC INDUS LABOR INCOME

B25
EDGEWORTH F.Y.,PAPERS RELATING TO POLITICAL ECONOMY. MOD/EUR SOCIETY STRATA DIST/IND INDUS MARKET NAT/G ACT/RES ECO/TAC EXEC WEALTH ...METH/CNCPT MATH TREND HYPO/EXP SIMUL GEN/METH FOR/TRADE VAL/FREE LOG/LING. PAGE 36 F0702 ECO/DEV CAP/ISM

B27
BELLOC H.,THE SERVILE STATE (1912) (3RD ED.). PRUSSIA UK CULTURE STRATA INDUS NAT/G ECO/TAC CONTROL LEAD SUFF DISCRIM EQUILIB ORD/FREE WEALTH 20. PAGE 12 F0237 WORKER CAP/ISM DOMIN CATH

B27
WEBER M.,GENERAL ECONOMIC HISTORY. CHRIST-17C MOD/EUR STRUCT AGRI EXTR/IND FINAN INDUS MARKET FAM NAT/G PROF/ORG SECT ECO/TAC MUNICH 8/20. PAGE 144 F2839 ECO/DEV CAP/ISM

B28
CASSEL G.,FOREIGN INVESTMENTS. GERMANY UK USA-45 WOR-45 ECO/DEV NAT/G VOL/ASSN CAP/ISM REPAR ATTIT WEALTH...METH/CNCPT STAT SIMUL STERTYP ANTHOL FOR/TRADE TOT/POP VAL/FREE 20. PAGE 22 F0426 FINAN ECO/TAC BAL/PAY

B28
CROS L.,AFRIQUE FRANCAISE POUR TOUS. EUR+WWI FRANCE PLAN TEC/DEV ATTIT 20. PAGE 29 F0556 COLONIAL DOMIN ECO/TAC AFR

B28
HARDMAN J.B.,AMERICAN LABOR DYNAMICS. WORKER ECO/TAC DOMIN ADJUD LEAD LOBBY PWR...POLICY MGT. PAGE 55 F1079 LABOR INGP/REL ATTIT GP/REL

B29
DE MAN H.,JOY IN WORK. STRATA ECO/DEV ECO/TAC PRODUC ANOMIE ROLE SOCISM...IDEA/COMP 20. PAGE 31 F0605 SOC WORKER HAPPINESS RESPECT

B30
BEVERIDGE W.H.,UNEMPLOYMENT: A PROBLEM OF INDUSTRY (1909-1930). USA-45 LAW ECO/DEV MARKET DELIB/GP WAR DEMAND INCOME...POLICY STAT CHARTS 20. PAGE 14 F0274 WORKER ECO/TAC GEN/LAWS

B30
BIEL G.,TREATISE ON THE POWER AND UTILITY OF MONEY (1484). INDUS MARKET LOC/G NAT/G SECT ECO/TAC PRODUC WEALTH 15. PAGE 15 F0280 FINAN COST PRICE GEN/LAWS

B30
FEIS H.,EUROPE, THE WORLD'S BANKER, 1871-1914. FRANCE GERMANY MOD/EUR UK WOR-45 NAT/G PLAN ECO/TAC EXEC ATTIT PWR WEALTH...CONCPT HIST/WRIT GEN/LAWS FINAN DIPLOM INT/TRADE

VAL/FREE 19/20. PAGE 40 F0773

B30
HAWTREY R.G.,ECONOMIC ASPECTS OF SOVEREIGNTY. UNIV WOR+45 WOR-45 ECO/DEV ECO/UNDEV AGRI COM/IND INDUS MARKET NAT/G TEC/DEV ECO/TAC EDU/PROP COERCE ATTIT KNOWL WEALTH...CONCPT CON/ANAL GEN/LAWS 20. PAGE 57 F1118
FORCES PWR SOVEREIGN WAR

B30
KEYNES J.M.,A TREATISE ON MONEY (2 VOLS.). UK USA-45 INDUS MARKET WORKER PRICE CONTROL COST OPTIMAL PROFIT WEALTH...POLICY 19/20 KEYNES/JM. PAGE 70 F1385
EQUILIB ECO/TAC FINAN GEN/LAWS

B30
THOMPSON W.R.,POPULATION PROBLEMS. FUT UNIV WOR-45 STRUCT DIST/IND ACT/RES ECO/TAC BIO/SOC...CONCPT OBS TIME/SEQ TOT/POP 20. PAGE 130 F2567
ECO/UNDEV GEOG

B31
CROOK W.H.,THE GENERAL STRIKE: A STUDY OF LABOR'S TRAGIC WEAPON IN THEORY AND PRACTICE. BELGIUM FRANCE SWEDEN UK WOR-45 PROB/SOLV ECO/TAC DOMIN PWR ...POLICY TIME/SEQ NAT/COMP GEN/LAWS 19/20 STRIKE. PAGE 29 F0555
LABOR WORKER LG/CO BARGAIN

B31
LORWIN L.L.,ADVISORY ECONOMIC COUNCILS. EUR+WWI FRANCE GERMANY PROB/SOLV INGP/REL...CLASSIF GP/COMP. PAGE 82 F1601
CONSULT DELIB/GP ECO/TAC NAT/G

B32
WRIGHT Q.,GOLD AND MONETARY STABILIZATION. FUT USA-45 WOR-45 INTELL ECO/DEV INT/ORG NAT/G CONSULT PLAN ECO/TAC ADMIN ATTIT WEALTH...CONCPT TREND 20. PAGE 149 F2935
FINAN POLICY

B34
GRAHAM F.D.,PROTECTIVE TARIFFS. FUT USA+45 WOR-45 INDUS MARKET VOL/ASSN PLAN CAP/ISM ECO/TAC PEACE ATTIT DRIVE HEALTH ORD/FREE...OBS TREND GEN/LAWS FOR/TRADE 20. PAGE 50 F0970
INT/ORG TARIFFS

B34
ROBINSON J.,THE ECONOMICS OF IMPERFECT COMPETITION. FINAN ECO/TAC PRICE COST DEMAND EQUILIB OPTIMAL WEALTH...METH MONOPOLY. PAGE 113 F2221
MARKET WORKER INDUS

B35
KEYNES J.M.,THE GENERAL THEORY OF EMPLOYMENT, INTEREST, AND MONEY. AGRI INDUS WORKER ECO/TAC DEMAND EQUILIB INCOME PRODUC PROFIT ATTIT WEALTH 20. PAGE 71 F1386
FINAN GEN/LAWS MARKET PRICE

B35
LASKI H.J.,THE STATE IN THEORY AND PRACTICE. ELITES ECO/TAC REPRESENT ORD/FREE PWR WEALTH POPULISM ...GOV/COMP GEN/LAWS 19/20. PAGE 76 F1483
CAP/ISM COERCE NAT/G FASCISM

B35
SCHATTSCHNEIDER E.E.,POLITICS, PRESSURES AND THE TARIFF: A STUDY OF FREE PRIVATE ENTERPRISE IN PRESSURE POLITICS IN TARIFF REVISION 1929-1930. NAT/G BARGAIN ECO/TAC ROUTINE REPRESENT GOV/REL GP/REL PWR POLICY. PAGE 116 F2290
LOBBY LEGIS TARIFFS

B35
STALEY E.,WAR AND THE PRIVATE INVESTOR. UNIV WOR-45 INTELL SOCIETY INT/ORG NAT/G TOP/EX CAP/ISM ECO/TAC WAR ATTIT ALL/VALS...INT TIME/SEQ TREND CON/ANAL WORK TOT/POP 20. PAGE 125 F2464
FINAN INT/TRADE DIPLOM

S35
BONNETT C.E.,"THE EVOLUTION OF BUSINESS GROUPINGS." ECO/TAC EDU/PROP PRICE LOBBY ORD/FREE. PAGE 16 F0315
VOL/ASSN GP/REL PROB/SOLV

B36
BELLOC H.,THE RESTORATION OF PROPERTY. UK STRATA NAT/G PROF/ORG DELIB/GP WORKER CREATE PROB/SOLV ECO/TAC PARTIC UTOPIA ORD/FREE SOCISM 20. PAGE 13 F0238
CONTROL MAJORIT CAP/ISM OWN

B37
BRESCIANI-TURRONI C,THE ECONOMICS OF INFLATION: A STUDY OF CURRENCY DEPRECIATION IN POST-WAR GERMANY. AFR GERMANY FINAN INT/TRADE PRICE TOTALISM...POLICY TIME/SEQ CHARTS GEN/LAWS 20 HITLER/A. PAGE 18 F0347
ECO/TAC WEALTH SOCIETY

B37
DALTON J.E.,SUGAR: A CASE STUDY OF GOVERNMENT CONTROL. USA-45 AGRI PROC/MFG LG/CO LEGIS PROB/SOLV ECO/TAC GP/REL...CHARTS 19/20. PAGE 30 F0575
CONTROL NAT/G INDUS POLICY

B37
HAMILTON W.H.,THE POWER TO GOVERN. ECO/DEV FINAN INDUS ECO/TAC INT/TRADE TARIFFS TAX CONTROL CT/SYS WAR COST PWR 18/20 SUPREME/CT. PAGE 54 F1056
LING CONSTN NAT/G POLICY

B37
ROBBINS L.,ECONOMIC PLANNING AND INTERNATIONAL ORDER. WOR-45 SOCIETY FINAN INDUS NAT/G ECO/TAC ROUTINE WEALTH...SOC TIME/SEQ GEN/METH WORK 20 KEYNES/JM. PAGE 112 F2202
INT/ORG PLAN INT/TRADE

B37
VON HAYEK F.A.,MONETARY NATIONALISM AND INTERNATIONAL STABILITY. WOR-45 ECO/DEV NAT/G PROB/SOLV INT/TRADE...POLICY CONCPT METH/COMP NAT/COMP 20. PAGE 142 F2792
ECO/TAC FINAN DIPLOM NAT/LISM

B38
HOBSON J.A.,IMPERIALISM. MOD/EUR UK WOR-45 CULTURE ECO/UNDEV NAT/G VOL/ASSN PLAN EDU/PROP LEGIT REGION COERCE ATTIT PWR...POLICY PLURIST TIME/SEQ GEN/LAWS TERR/GP 19/20. PAGE 60 F1187
DOMIN ECO/TAC BAL/PWR COLONIAL

B38
LANGE O.,ON THE ECONOMIC THEORY OF SOCIALISM. UNIV ECO/DEV FINAN INDUS INT/ORG PUB/INST ROUTINE ATTIT ALL/VALS...SOC CONCPT STAT TREND 20. PAGE 75 F1475
MARKET ECO/TAC INT/TRADE SOCISM

B38
LAWLEY F.E.,THE GROWTH OF COLLECTIVE ECONOMY VOL. 1: NATIONAL. EUR+WWI AGRI INDUS NAT/G BARGAIN CAP/ISM ECO/TAC WAR OPTIMAL WEALTH...GOV/COMP METH/COMP 19/20 MONOPOLY. PAGE 76 F1492
SOCISM PRICE CONTROL OWN

B38
LAWLEY F.E.,THE GROWTH OF COLLECTIVE ECONOMY VOL. 2: INTERNATIONAL. WOR-45 AGRI INDUS EQUILIB OPTIMAL OWN WEALTH...NAT/COMP 19/20 NAZI NEW/DEAL MONOPOLY. PAGE 76 F1493
ECO/TAC SOCISM NAT/LISM CONTROL

B38
LEVINSON E.,LABOR ON THE MARCH. WORKER CREATE ECO/TAC ADJUD LEAD PARL/PROC PARTIC INGP/REL SKILL POLICY. PAGE 79 F1543
LABOR INCOME NAT/G PLAN

S38
HALL R.C.,"REPRESENTATION OF BIG BUSINESS IN THE HOUSE OF COMMONS." UK ECO/DEV INDUS PROF/ORG LEGIS CAP/ISM ECO/TAC LAISSEZ...POLICY OLD/LIB PLURIST MGT 20 HOUSE/CMNS. PAGE 53 F1047
LOBBY NAT/G

B39
CLARK J.M.,SOCIAL CONTROL OF BUSINESS (2ND ED.). ECO/DEV FINAN LG/CO PLAN ECO/TAC PRICE SUPEGO...T 20. PAGE 25 F0480
CAP/ISM CONTROL LAISSEZ METH/COMP

B39
ENGELS F.,HERRN EUGEN DUHRING'S REVOLUTION IN SCIENCE (1878). CULTURE STRATA STRUCT FAM SECT ECO/TAC REV WAR SOCISM...MARXIST 19. PAGE 37 F0731
PWR SOCIETY WEALTH GEN/LAWS

B39
FIRTH R.,PRIMITIVE POLYNESIAN ECONOMY. SOCIETY DIST/IND SECT CHIEF CAP/ISM PRODUC WEALTH...SOC OBS METH WORSHIP 20 POLYNESIA. PAGE 41 F0802
ECO/UNDEV CULTURE AGRI ECO/TAC

B39
ROBBINS L.,ECONOMIC CAUSES OF WAR. WOR-45 ECO/DEV ECO/UNDEV INT/ORG NAT/G TEC/DEV DIPLOM DOMIN COLONIAL ATTIT DRIVE PWR WEALTH...POLICY CONCPT OBS SAMP TREND CON/ANAL GEN/LAWS MARX/KARL 20. PAGE 112 F2203
COERCE ECO/TAC WAR

B39
STALEY E.,WORLD ECONOMY IN TRANSITION. WOR-45 SOCIETY INT/ORG PROF/ORG ECO/TAC ATTIT WEALTH ...METH/CNCPT TREND GEN/LAWS 20. PAGE 125 F2465
TEC/DEV INT/TRADE

S39
COLE G.D.H.,"NAZI ECONOMICS: HOW DO THEY MANAGE IT?" GERMANY FORCES WORKER BUDGET INT/TRADE ROUTINE COERCE WAR 20 HITLER/A NAZI. PAGE 26 F0500
FASCISM ECO/TAC ATTIT PLAN

B40
BLAISDELL D.C.,GOVERNMENT AND AGRICULTURE; THE GROWTH OF FEDERAL FARM AID. USA-45 MARKET PLAN PROB/SOLV TEC/DEV ECO/TAC GOV/REL ADJUST ATTIT ...CHARTS 20 DEPT/AGRI. PAGE 15 F0296
NAT/G GIVE AGRI DELIB/GP

B40
FULLER G.H.,LIST OF REFERENCES ON PRIORITIES (MIMEOGRAPHED PAPER). WOR-45 NAT/G RATION 20. PAGE 45 F0874
BIBLIOG/A WAR ECO/TAC PLAN

B40
HELLMAN F.S.,THE NEW DEAL: SELECTED LIST OF REFERENCES. USA-45 FINAN LABOR EX/STRUC CREATE INT/TRADE ADMIN CT/SYS 20 SUPREME/CT. PAGE 58 F1145
BIBLIOG/A ECO/TAC PLAN POLICY

B40
HUNTER R.,REVOLUTION: WHY, HOW, WHEN? NAT/G ECO/TAC EDU/PROP COERCE ORD/FREE FASCISM POPULISM SOCISM 18/20 HITLER/A LENIN/VI. PAGE 63 F1246
REV METH/COMP LEAD CONSTN

B41
DAUGHERTY C.R.,LABOR PROBLEMS IN AMERICAN INDUSTRY (5TH ED.). USA-45 SOCIETY OP/RES ECO/TAC...MGT PSY T 20. PAGE 30 F0581
LABOR INDUS GP/REL PROB/SOLV

B41
ESTEY J.A.,BUSINESS CYCLES; THEIR NATURE, CAUSE, AND CONTROL. NAT/G BUDGET CAP/ISM TAX PRICE CONTROL INCOME...MODAL TIME/SEQ GEN/METH T 18/20 KEYNES/JM MONEY. PAGE 38 F0749
INDUS FINAN ECO/TAC POLICY

B41
HANSEN A.H.,FISCAL POLICY AND BUSINESS CYCLES. UK INDUS PROB/SOLV DIPLOM INT/TRADE OPTIMAL...POLICY TIME/SEQ CHARTS 19/20. PAGE 54 F1062
FINAN PLAN ECO/TAC GOV/REL

B41
HAYEK F.A.,THE PURE THEORY OF CAPITAL. UNIV ECO/DEV ECO/TAC COST EQUILIB PROFIT WEALTH...SIMUL GEN/LAWS BIBLIOG INDEX TIME 20. PAGE 57 F1120
CAP/ISM METH/CNCPT PRODUC FINAN

S41
LASSWELL H.D.,"THE GARRISON STATE" (BMR)" FUT WOR+45 ELITES INTELL FORCES ECO/TAC DOMIN EDU/PROP COERCE INGP/REL 20. PAGE 76 F1485
NAT/G DIPLOM PWR CIVMIL/REL

S41
MUKERJEE R.,"POPULATION THEORY AND POLITICS (BMR)" WOR-45 NAT/G PLAN PROB/SOLV ECO/TAC INT/TRADE CONTROL WAR PEACE...CENSUS 20 BIRTH/CON RESOURCE/N. PAGE 94 F1854
GEOG OPTIMAL CONCPT

B42
US LIBRARY OF CONGRESS,ECONOMICS OF WAR (APRIL 1941-MARCH 1942). WOR-45 FINAN INDUS LOC/G NAT/G PLAN BUDGET RATION COST DEMAND...POLICY 20. PAGE 138 F2712
BIBLIOG/A INT/TRADE ECO/TAC WAR

B42
US LIBRARY OF CONGRESS,THE WAR PRODUCTION PROGRAM: SELECTED DOCUMENTATION ON THE ECONOMICS OF WAR (PAMPHLET). USA-45 ECO/DEV AGRI FINAN NAT/G ECO/TAC RATION PRICE EFFICIENCY 20. PAGE 138 F2713
BIBLIOG/A WAR PRODUC INDUS

B42
WRIGHT D.M.,THE CREATION OF PURCHASING POWER. USA-45 NAT/G PRICE ADMIN WAR INCOME PRODUC...POLICY CONCPT IDEA/COMP BIBLIOG 20 MONEY. PAGE 149 F2930
FINAN ECO/TAC ECO/DEV CREATE

B43
BRADY R.A.,BUSINESS AS A SYSTEM OF POWER. EX/STRUC PLAN ECO/TAC CONTROL GP/REL PWR...TREND GP/COMP. PAGE 17 F0334
VOL/ASSN LOBBY POLICY

C43
BENTHAM J.,"THE RATIONALE OF REWARD" IN J. BOWRING, ED., THE WORKS OF JEREMY BENTHAM (VOL. 2)" LAW WORKER CREATE INSPECT PAY ROUTINE HAPPINESS PRODUC SUPEGO WEALTH METH/CNCPT. PAGE 13 F0254
SANCTION ECO/TAC INCOME PWR

B44
HAYEK F.A.,THE ROAD TO SERFDOM. NAT/G POL/PAR CREATE EDU/PROP ATTIT WEALTH LAISSEZ...OLD/LIB CONCPT TREND 20. PAGE 57 F1121
FUT PLAN ECO/TAC SOCISM

B44
LANDAUER C.,THEORY OF NATIONAL ECONOMIC PLANNING. USA-45 INDUS MARKET WORKER PROB/SOLV DIPLOM RATION PRICE CONTROL WAR COST 20. PAGE 75 F1465
ECO/TAC PLAN NAT/G ECO/DEV

B44
LOCKE J.,FURTHER CONSIDERATIONS CONCERNING RAISING THE VALUE OF MONEY. AFR UK NAT/G ECO/TAC INCOME WEALTH...METH/COMP GEN/LAWS 17 SILVER. PAGE 81 F1591
COST FINAN PRICE CONTROL

B45
MILLIS H.A.,ORGANIZED LABOR (FIRST ED.). LAW STRUCT DELIB/GP WORKER ECO/TAC ADJUD CONTROL REPRESENT INGP/REL INCOME MGT. PAGE 92 F1797
LABOR POLICY ROUTINE GP/REL

B45
WOOTTON B.,FREEDOM UNDER PLANNING. UNIV ROUTINE ATTIT AUTHORIT DECISION. PAGE 148 F2926
PLAN ORD/FREE ECO/TAC CONTROL

B46
CLOUGH S.B.,ECONOMIC HISTORY OF EUROPE. CHRIST-17C EUR+WWI MOD/EUR WOR-45 SOCIETY EXEC ATTIT WEALTH ...CONCPT GEN/LAWS WORK TOT/POP VAL/FREE 7/20. PAGE 25 F0493
ECO/TAC CAP/ISM

B47
ENKE S.,INTERNATIONAL ECONOMICS. UK USA+45 USSR INT/ORG BAL/PWR BARGAIN CAP/ISM BAL/PAY...NAT/COMP 20 TREATY. PAGE 38 F0735
INT/TRADE FINAN TARIFFS ECO/TAC

B47
GORDON D.L.,THE HIDDEN WEAPON: THE STORY OF ECONOMIC WARFARE. EUR+WWI USA-45 LAW FINAN INDUS NAT/G CONSULT FORCES PLAN DOMIN PWR WEALTH ...INT/LAW CONCPT OBS TOT/POP NAZI 20. PAGE 49 F0955
INT/ORG ECO/TAC INT/TRADE WAR

B47
LEVER E.A.,ADVERTISING AND ECONOMIC THEORY. FINAN ECO/TAC DEMAND EFFICIENCY ATTIT...MGT PSY SAMP/SIZ CHARTS 20. PAGE 79 F1539
EDU/PROP MARKET COM/IND ECO/DEV

B47
SLICHTER S.H.,THE CHALLENGE OF INDUSTRIAL RELATIONS: TRADE UNIONS, MANAGEMENT AND THE PUBLIC INTEREST. PLAN ECO/TAC ADJUD CONTROL LEAD SANCTION GP/REL INGP/REL INCOME. PAGE 123 F2421
LABOR MGT CLIENT POLICY

B47
TOWLE L.W.,INTERNATIONAL TRADE AND COMMERCIAL POLICY. WOR+45 LAW ECO/DEV FINAN INDUS NAT/G ECO/TAC WEALTH...TIME/SEQ ILO 20. PAGE 131 F2582
MARKET INT/ORG INT/TRADE

B47
WARNER W.L.,THE SOCIAL SYSTEM OF THE MODERN FACTORY; THE STRIKE: AN ANALYSIS. USA-45 STRATA WORKER ECO/TAC GP/REL INGP/REL...MGT SOC CHARTS 20 YANKEE/C. PAGE 143 F2824
ROLE STRUCT LABOR PROC/MFG

B47
WEBER M.,THE THEORY OF SOCIAL AND ECONOMIC ORGANIZATION. STRUCT LABOR POL/PAR ECO/TAC LEGIT PRODUC BIOG. PAGE 144 F2840
ECO/DEV SOC PHIL/SCI LEAD

B48
GRAHAM F.D.,THE THEORY OF INTERNATIONAL VALUES. FUT WOR+45 WOR-45 ECO/DEV FINAN INT/ORG PLAN TEC/DEV CAP/ISM DIPLOM ECO/TAC TARIFFS ROUTINE BAL/PAY DRIVE PWR WEALTH SOCISM...POLICY STAT HYPO/EXP GEN/LAWS 20. PAGE 50 F0971
NEW/IDEA INT/TRADE

B48
HART A.G.,MONEY, DEBT, AND ECONOMIC ACTIVITY. AFR WORKER DIPLOM PRICE CONTROL BAL/PAY COST OWN PRODUC ...METH/COMP 20 FED/RESERV. PAGE 56 F1097
FINAN WEALTH ECO/TAC NAT/G

B48
HOOVER E.M.,THE LOCATION OF ECONOMIC ACTIVITY. WOR+45 MARKET WORKER PROB/SOLV INT/TRADE ADMIN COST ...POLICY CHARTS T MUNICH 20. PAGE 62 F1211
HABITAT INDUS ECO/TAC GEOG

B48
MCCABE D.A.,LABOR AND SOCIAL ORGANIZATION. LEGIS WORKER CAP/ISM ECO/TAC PAY MARXISM SOCISM SOC/INTEG 20 INTRVN/ECO. PAGE 88 F1717
LABOR STRATA NEW/LIB

B48
METZLER L.A.,INCOME, EMPLOYMENT, AND PUBLIC POLICY. FINAN INDUS LOC/G NAT/G TAX GIVE PAY COST PRODUC ...MGT TIME/SEQ 20. PAGE 90 F1765
INCOME WEALTH POLICY ECO/TAC

B48
VON HAYEK F.A.,INDIVIDUALISM AND ECONOMIC ORDER. GERMANY USA-45 USSR FINAN MARKET INT/ORG ECO/TAC INT/TRADE PRICE REPRESENT ORD/FREE...PLURIST GEN/LAWS 20. PAGE 142 F2793
SOCISM CAP/ISM POPULISM FEDERAL

B48
WINSLOW E.M.,THE PATTERN OF IMPERIALISM; A STUDY IN THE THEORIES OF POWER. DOMIN WAR PWR MARXISM ...IDEA/COMP METH/COMP BIBLIOG 20. PAGE 147 F2906
SOCISM CAP/ISM COLONIAL ECO/TAC

S48
HARDIN L.M.,"REFLECTIONS ON AGRICULTURAL POLICY FORMATION IN THE UNITED STATES." LEGIS PLAN BUDGET ECO/TAC LEAD CENTRAL...MGT SOC NEW/IDEA STAT FAO. PAGE 55 F1078
AGRI POLICY ADMIN NEW/LIB

B49
DE JOUVENEL B.,PROBLEMS OF SOCIALIST ENGLAND. AFR UK USSR BAL/PWR ECO/TAC INT/TRADE PRICE WAR BAL/PAY PEACE 20. PAGE 31 F0601
SOCISM NEW/LIB PROB/SOLV PLAN

B49
HANSEN A.H.,MONETARY THEORY AND FISCAL POLICY. CONSULT PLAN INT/TRADE BAL/PAY OPTIMAL...TREND CHARTS METH/COMP BIBLIOG T 19/20 MONEY. PAGE 54 F1063
FINAN GEN/LAWS POLICY ECO/TAC

B49
MACGREGOR D.H.,ECONOMIC THOUGHT AND POLICY. WOR-45 WORKER WAR DEMAND EFFICIENCY WEALTH LAISSEZ SOCISM ...MAJORIT BIBLIOG 19/20. PAGE 83 F1629
CONCPT POLICY ECO/TAC

B49
SCHULTZ W.J.,AMERICAN PUBLIC FINANCE. USA+45 ECO/TAC TAX ADMIN GOV/REL GP/REL INCOME 20. PAGE 117 F2318
FINAN POLICY ECO/DEV NAT/G

B49
US DEPARTMENT OF STATE,SOVIET BIBLIOGRAPHY (PAMPHLET). CHINA/COM COM USSR LAW AGRI INT/ORG ECO/TAC EDU/PROP...POLICY GEOG IND 20. PAGE 135 F2670
BIBLIOG/A MARXISM CULTURE DIPLOM

S49
ECKLER A.R.,"IMMIGRATION AND THE LABOR FORCE." USA+45 USA-45 EXTR/IND FINAN PROC/MFG AGE/Y SKILL ...CHARTS 19/20 MIGRATION. PAGE 36 F0694
WORKER STRANGE INDUS ECO/TAC

B50
ADORNO T.W.,THE AUTHORITARIAN PERSONALITY. STRATA SECT PROB/SOLV ECO/TAC DISCRIM ATTIT SEX...SOC INT CHARTS METH 20. PAGE 3 F0044
AUTHORIT PERSON ALL/IDEOS SOCIETY

B50
CHAMBERLIN E.,THE THEORY OF MONOPOLISTIC COMPETITION (1933). INDUS PAY GP/REL COST DEMAND EFFICIENCY OPTIMAL PRODUC WEALTH...GEN/LAWS 20. PAGE 23 F0443
MARKET PRICE ECO/TAC EQUILIB

B50
CLARK J.M.,ALTERNATIVE TO SERFDOM. SOCIETY STRATA INDUS MARKET WORKER PRICE GP/REL PROFIT BIO/SOC PWR WEALTH...GEN/LAWS 20 KEYNES/JM. PAGE 25 F0481
ORD/FREE POPULISM ECO/TAC REPRESENT

B50
FEIS H.,THE DIPLOMACY OF THE DOLLAR: FIRST ERA 1919-32. EUR+WWI USA-45 FOR/AID REPAR ATTIT ...POLICY 20. PAGE 40 F0774
FINAN NAT/G DIPLOM

ECO/TAC

B50
HARTLAND P.C.,BALANCE OF INTERREGIONAL PAYMENTS OF NEW ENGLAND. USA+45 TEC/DEV ECO/TAC LEGIT ROUTINE BAL/PAY PROFIT 20 NEW/ENGLND FED/RESERV. PAGE 56 F1102
ECO/DEV FINAN REGION PLAN

B50
HOOVER G.,TWENTIETH CENTURY ECONOMIC THOUGHT. USA+45 ECO/DEV AGRI FINAN INDUS MARKET SERV/IND LABOR NAT/G...STAT 20. PAGE 62 F1213
ECO/TAC CAP/ISM INT/TRADE

B50
LINCOLN G.,ECONOMICS OF NATIONAL SECURITY. USA+45 ELITES COM/IND DIST/IND INDUS NAT/G VOL/ASSN DELIB/GP EX/STRUC FOR/AID EDU/PROP COERCE NUC/PWR WAR ATTIT KNOWL ORD/FREE PWR TOT/POP VAL/FREE 20. PAGE 80 F1565
FORCES ECO/TAC AFR

B50
LIPSET S.M.,AGRARIAN SOCIALISM. CANADA POL/PAR OP/RES ECO/TAC ADMIN ATTIT...TIME/SEQ NAT/COMP SOC/EXP 20 SASKATCH. PAGE 80 F1576
SOCISM AGRI METH/COMP STRUCT

B50
ORTON W.A.,THE ECONOMIC ROLE OF THE STATE. INTELL ECO/UNDEV PLAN CONTROL PWR SOVEREIGN...POLICY 17/20. PAGE 102 F2000
ECO/DEV NAT/G ECO/TAC ORD/FREE

B50
SCHUMPETER J.A.,CAPITALISM, SOCIALISM, AND DEMOCRACY (3RD ED.). USA-45 USSR WOR+45 WOR-45 INTELL ECO/DEV ECO/UNDEV ECO/TAC WAR PRODUC ORD/FREE...MGT SOC 20 MARX/KARL. PAGE 118 F2321
SOCIALIST CAP/ISM MARXISM IDEA/COMP

B50
SHAW E.S.,MONEY, INCOME, AND MONETARY POLICY. AFR USA-45 NAT/G DIPLOM PAY CONTROL COST INCOME PRODUC WEALTH...T 20 FED/RESERV DEPT/TREAS. PAGE 120 F2370
FINAN ECO/TAC ECO/DEV PRICE

S50
DREYFUS S.,"THE INDUSTRIAL DESIGNER AND THE BUSINESSMAN." SERV/IND PROB/SOLV ECO/TAC COST EFFICIENCY PROFIT RATIONAL...DECISION MGT. PAGE 34 F0662
CONSULT INDUS PRODUC UTIL

C50
ELLSWORTH P.T.,"INTERNATIONAL ECONOMY." ECO/DEV ECO/UNDEV FINAN LABOR DIPLOM FOR/AID TARIFFS BAL/PAY EQUILIB NAT/LISM OPTIMAL...INT/LAW 20 ILO GATT. PAGE 37 F0724
BIBLIOG INT/TRADE ECO/TAC INT/ORG

C50
ROUSSEAU J.J.,"A DISCOURSE ON POLITICAL ECONOMY" (1755) IN THE SOCIAL CONTRACT AND DISCOURSES." UNIV SOCIETY STRATA STRUCT CONSEN EQUILIB HAPPINESS UTOPIA HEALTH WEALTH...POLICY WELF/ST. PAGE 114 F2252
NAT/G ECO/TAC TAX GEN/LAWS

B51
CHANDLER L.V.,INFLATION IN THE UNITED STATES 1940-1948. AFR NAT/G BUDGET PAY PRICE CONTROL WAR INCOME PRODUC...POLICY BIBLIOG 20. PAGE 23 F0448
ECO/TAC FINAN PROB/SOLV WEALTH

B51
COOKE C.A.,CORPORATION TRUST AND COMPANY: AN ESSAY IN LEGAL HISTORY. UK STRUCT LEGIS CAP/ISM GP/REL PROFIT 13/20 COMPNY/ACT. PAGE 27 F0531
LG/CO FINAN ECO/TAC JURID

B51
HANSEN B.,A STUDY IN THE THEORY OF INFLATION. WOR-45 FINAN WAR DEMAND...CHARTS 20. PAGE 54 F1067
PRICE ECO/TAC EQUILIB PRODUC

B51
HARROD R.F.,THE LIFE OF JOHN MAYNARD KEYNES. UK INTELL FAM CAP/ISM DIPLOM ECO/TAC WAR ATTIT PERSON ROLE 20 KEYNES/JM WWI. PAGE 56 F1094
BIOG FINAN GEN/LAWS

B51
HART A.G.,DEFENSE WITHOUT INFLATION. AFR KOREA FINAN INDUS NAT/G WORKER DIPLOM RATION TAX PRICE COST OPTIMAL 20 RESOURCE/N. PAGE 56 F1098
ECO/TAC CONTROL WAR PLAN

B51
LEONARD L.L.,INTERNATIONAL ORGANIZATION. WOR+45 WOR-45 EX/STRUC FORCES LEGIS ECO/TAC INT/TRADE COLONIAL ARMS/CONT...SOC/WK GOV/COMP BIBLIOG. PAGE 78 F1527
NAT/G DIPLOM INT/ORG DELIB/GP

B51
LUXEMBORG R.,THE ACCUMULATION OF CAPITAL (TRANS. BY AGNES SCHWARZSCHILD). ECO/TAC DOMIN COLONIAL ATTIT LAISSEZ 19 MONEY. PAGE 82 F1614
MARXIST INT/TRADE CAP/ISM FINAN

B51
OWENS R.N.,BUSINESS, ORGANIZATION, AND COMBINATION. USA+45 USA-45 LAW NAT/G LEGIS ECO/TAC CONTROL INGP/REL...JURID GP/COMP 20 NEW/DEAL. PAGE 102 F2006
SML/CO LG/CO STRUCT GP/REL

B51
ROEPKE W.,THE PROBLEM OF ECONOMIC ORDER. WOR+45 SOCIETY PROB/SOLV CONTROL EFFICIENCY...CON/ANAL IDEA/COMP GEN/METH 20. PAGE 113 F2231
ECO/TAC ORD/FREE MARKET PROC/MFG

L51
SUMMERS C.W.,"UNION POWERS AND WORKERS RIGHTS." WORKER PROB/SOLV ECO/TAC PARTIC INGP/REL PWR. PAGE 127 F2513
LABOR CONSTN LAW REPRESENT

B52
ALEXANDROWICZ C.H.,INTERNATIONAL ECONOMIC ORGANIZATION. WOR+45 ECO/DEV ECO/UNDEV DIST/IND FINAN MARKET PLAN ECO/TAC LEGIT DRIVE WEALTH ...POLICY CONCPT QUANT OBS TIME/SEQ GEN/LAWS WORK METH/GP EEC ILO OEEC UNESCO 20. PAGE 4 F0063
INT/ORG INT/TRADE

B52
ASHWORTH W.,A SHORT HISTORY OF THE INTERNATIONAL ECONOMY 1850-1950. WOR+45 WOR-45 AGRI FINAN INDUS MARKET LABOR ECO/TAC...CONCPT STAT HIST/WRIT FOR/TRADE ILO 19/20. PAGE 7 F0131
ECO/DEV TEC/DEV INT/TRADE

B52
AYRES C.E.,THE INDUSTRIAL ECONOMY. USA+45 FINAN MARKET NAT/G PUB/INST PLAN ECO/TAC TAX DEMAND INCOME...BIBLIOG/A 20. PAGE 8 F0146
ECO/DEV INDUS FUT PROB/SOLV

B52
EGLE W.P.,ECONOMIC STABILIZATION. USA+45 SOCIETY FINAN MARKET PLAN ECO/TAC DOMIN EDU/PROP LEGIT EXEC WEALTH...CONCPT METH/CNCPT TREND HYPO/EXP GEN/METH TOT/POP VAL/FREE 20. PAGE 36 F0708
NAT/G ECO/DEV CAP/ISM

B52
EGLE W.P.,ECONOMIC STABILIZATION: OBJECTIVES, RULES, AND MECHANISMS. UNIV FINAN PROB/SOLV CAP/ISM ECO/TAC CONTROL...IDEA/COMP 20. PAGE 36 F0709
EQUILIB PLAN NAT/G ECO/DEV

B52
GALBRAITH J.K.,AMERICAN CAPITALISM: THE CONCEPT OF COUNTERVAILING POWER. AFR FUT USA+45 FINAN PRICE CENTRAL INCOME PEACE WEALTH...POLICY DECISION 20. PAGE 45 F0881
ECO/TAC CAP/ISM TREND NAT/G

B52
HARDIN C.M.,THE POLITICS OF AGRICULTURE. USA+45 NAT/G PROF/ORG LEGIS LOBBY 20 DEPT/AGRI. PAGE 55 F1077
AGRI POLICY ECO/TAC GOV/REL

B52
HOSELITZ B.F.,THE PROGRESS OF UNDERDEVELOPED AREAS. AFR FUT WOR+45 WOR-45 ECO/DEV ECO/TAC INT/TRADE WEALTH...SOC TREND GEN/LAWS TOT/POP VAL/FREE FOR/TRADE 20. PAGE 62 F1219
ECO/UNDEV PLAN FOR/AID

B52
MACHLUP F.,THE POLITICAL ECONOMY OF MONOPOLY: BUSINESS, LABOR AND GOVERNMENT POLICIES. USA+45 USA-45 ECO/DEV LABOR NAT/G CAP/ISM PWR...POLICY CHARTS T 20. PAGE 83 F1630
ECO/TAC DOMIN LG/CO CONTROL

B52
SECRETARIAT COUNCIL OF EUROPE,THE STRASBOURG PLAN. EUR+WWI CONSULT PLAN ECO/TAC TARIFFS DEBATE REGION 20 COUNCL/EUR STRASBOURG. PAGE 119 F2340
INT/ORG ECO/DEV INT/TRADE DIPLOM

B52
WU Y.,ECONOMIC WARFARE. MARKET PLAN PROB/SOLV FOR/AID CONTROL EFFICIENCY WEALTH...METH/COMP 20. PAGE 149 F2937
ECO/TAC WAR INT/TRADE DIPLOM

B53
BOEKE J.H.,ECONOMICS AND ECONOMIC POLICY OF DUAL SOCIETIES AS EXEMPLIFIED BY INDONESIA. INDIA INDONESIA SOCIETY CAP/ISM INT/TRADE GIVE PRICE GP/REL WEALTH SOCISM...POLICY NAT/COMP GEN/LAWS 20. PAGE 16 F0304
ECO/TAC ECO/UNDEV NAT/G CONTROL

B53
BOULDING K.E.,THE ORGANIZATIONAL REVOLUTION. FUT CULTURE ECO/DEV LABOR PROF/ORG ECO/TAC MORAL...SOC CONCPT RECORD INT SOC/EXP 20. PAGE 17 F0321
SOCIETY TREND

B53
BURNS A.E.,MODERN ECONOMICS. UNIV ECO/DEV INT/TRADE PRICE INCOME WEALTH...POLICY CHARTS T 20 KEYNES/JM. PAGE 20 F0389
NAT/G ECO/TAC FINAN

B53
DAHL R.A.,POLITICS, ECONOMICS AND WELFARE: PLANNING AND POLITICOECONOMIC SYSTEMS RESOLVED INTO BASIC SOCIAL PROCESSES. WOR+45 WOR-45 ECO/DEV ECO/UNDEV R+D CREATE PLAN TEC/DEV EDU/PROP HEALTH WEALTH ...SOC SELF/OBS TREND CHARTS GEN/METH 20. PAGE 29 F0571
ECO/TAC PHIL/SCI

B53
DAHL R.A.,POLITICS, ECONOMICS, AND WELFARE. TEC/DEV BARGAIN ECO/TAC RECEIVE PRICE CONTROL LEAD INGP/REL ...POLICY GEN/LAWS. PAGE 29 F0572
SOCIETY GIVE

B53
MENDE T.,WORLD POWER IN THE BALANCE. FUT USA+45 USSR WOR-45 ECO/DEV ECO/TAC INT/TRADE EDU/PROP UTOPIA ATTIT...HUM CONCPT TREND TOT/POP 20. PAGE 90 F1756
WOR+45 PWR BAL/PWR AFR

B53
MILLIKAN M.F.,INCOME STABILIZATION FOR A DEVELOPING DEMOCRACY. USA+45 ECO/DEV LABOR BUDGET ECO/TAC TAX ADMIN ADJUST PRODUC WEALTH...POLICY TREND 20. PAGE 91 F1794
ANTHOL MARKET EQUILIB EFFICIENCY

B53
WILLIAMS J.H.,ECONOMIC STABILITY IN A CHANGING WORLD. FRANCE USA+45 USSR AGRI WORKER BUDGET INT/TRADE TAX WAR BAL/PAY COST EFFICIENCY ALL/IDEOS EQULIB 20 KEYNES/JM. PAGE 147 F2892
POLICY | FINAN | ECO/TAC | WEALTH

L53
NELSON J.R.,"UNITED STATES FOREIGN ECONOMIC POLICY AND THE STERLING AREA." USA-45 WOR+45 WOR-45 NAT/G ECO/TAC WEALTH...STAT TIME/SEQ TREND CHARTS METH/GP TERR/GP CMN/WLTH 20. PAGE 97 F1911
FINAN | DIPLOM | UK

S53
BLOUGH R.,"THE ROLE OF THE ECONOMIST IN FEDERAL POLICY MAKING." USA+45 ELITES INTELL ECO/DEV NAT/G CONSULT EX/STRUC ACT/RES PLAN INT/TRADE BAL/PAY WEALTH...POLICY METH/GP CONGRESS 20. PAGE 16 F0301
DELIB/GP | ECO/TAC

S53
HANSER P.M.,"EXPLODING POPULATIONS: INTERNATIONAL AND REGIONAL ASPECTS." AFR S/ASIA ECO/TAC WEAPON BIO/SOC LOVE ORD/FREE...NEW/IDEA CENSUS TOT/POP 20. PAGE 55 F1069
ECO/UNDEV | GEOG

B54
BATTEN T.R.,PROBLEMS OF AFRICAN DEVELOPMENT (2ND ED.). AFR LAW SOCIETY SCHOOL ECO/TAC TAX...GEOG HEAL SOC 20. PAGE 11 F0211
ECO/UNDEV | AGRI | LOC/G | PROB/SOLV

B54
HAYEK FA V.O.N.,CAPITALISM AND THE HISTORIANS. MOD/EUR TEC/DEV GP/REL WEALTH...HIST/WRIT ANTHOL 19. PAGE 57 F1124
CAP/ISM | LABOR | STRATA | ECO/TAC

B54
HOBBS E.H.,BEHIND THE PRESIDENT - A STUDY OF EXECUTIVE OFFICE AGENCIES. USA+45 NAT/G PLAN BUDGET ECO/TAC EXEC ORD/FREE 20 BUR/BUDGET. PAGE 60 F1183
EX/STRUC | DELIB/GP | CONFER | CONSULT

B54
LOCKLIN D.P.,ECONOMICS OF TRANSPORTATION (4TH ED.). USA+45 USA-45 SEA AIR LAW FINAN LG/CO EX/STRUC ADMIN CONTROL...STAT CHARTS 19/20 RAILROAD PUB/TRANS. PAGE 81 F1592
ECO/DEV | DIST/IND | ECO/TAC | TEC/DEV

B54
MEYER A.G.,MARXISM. INTELL ECO/DEV WORKER CAP/ISM LEAD WAR ATTIT ALL/IDEOS...SOC 19/20 MARX/KARL. PAGE 90 F1766
MARXISM | CONCPT | ECO/TAC | STRUCT

B54
MEYER F.V.,INFLATION AND CAPITAL. AFR UK WOR+45 BUDGET GOV/REL INCOME PRODUC PROFIT WEALTH...CONCPT CHARTS 20. PAGE 90 F1768
ECO/DEV | FINAN | ECO/TAC | DEMAND

B54
O.E.E.C.,PRIVATE UNITED STATES INVESTMENT IN EUROPE AND THE OVERSEAS TERRITORIES. EUR+WWI WOR+45 ECO/DEV ECO/UNDEV INT/ORG NAT/G VOL/ASSN ECO/TAC ATTIT WEALTH...GEOG STAT SYS/QU CHARTS VAL/FREE 20. PAGE 99 F1950
USA+45 | FINAN | BAL/PAY | FOR/AID

B54
RECK D.,GOVERNMENT PURCHASING AND COMPETITION. USA+45 LEGIS CAP/ISM ECO/TAC GOV/REL CENTRAL ...POLICY 20 CONGRESS. PAGE 110 F2164
NAT/G | FINAN | MGT | COST

B54
REYNOLDS P.A.,BRITISH FOREIGN POLICY IN THE INTER-WAR YEARS. CZECHOSLVK GERMANY POLAND UK USA-45 POL/PAR FORCES ECO/TAC ARMS/CONT WAR ATTIT 20. PAGE 111 F2182
DIPLOM | POLICY | NAT/G

B54
RICHTER R.,DAS KONKURRENZ PROBLEM IM OLIGOPOL. LG/CO BARGAIN PRICE COST...CONCPT 20 MONOPOLY. PAGE 111 F2188
CONTROL | GAME | ECO/TAC | GP/REL

B54
STALEY E.,THE FUTURE OF UNDERDEVELOPED COUNTRIES: POLITICAL IMPLICATIONS OF ECONOMIC DEVELOPMENT. AFR COM FUT USA+45 SOCIETY ECO/UNDEV CREATE PLAN CAP/ISM ATTIT DRIVE MARXISM SOCISM...POLICY CONCPT CHARTS 20. PAGE 125 F2466
EDU/PROP | ECO/TAC | FOR/AID

B54
TINBERGEN J.,INTERNATIONAL ECONOMIC INTEGRATION. WOR+45 WOR-45 ECO/UNDEV NAT/G ECO/TAC BAL/PAY ...METH/CNCPT STAT TIME/SEQ GEN/METH OEEC 20. PAGE 130 F2574
INT/ORG | ECO/DEV | INT/TRADE

B54
WASHBURNE N.F.,INTERPRETING SOCIAL CHANGE IN AMERICA. USA+45 STRATA FAM NAT/G SECT OP/RES ECO/TAC EDU/PROP HABITAT...SOC TIME/SEQ TREND 20 BUREAUCRCY. PAGE 143 F2826
CULTURE | STRUCT | CREATE | TEC/DEV

B54
WILLIAMSON H.F.,ECONOMIC DEVELOPMENT - PRINCIPLES AND PATTERNS. INDIA KOREA CULTURE ECO/DEV ECO/UNDEV TEC/DEV...CENSUS NAT/COMP FOR/TRADE 20 CHINJAP MEXIC/AMER RESOURCE/N. PAGE 147 F2895
ECO/TAC | GEOG | LABOR

B55
BLOOM G.F.,ECONOMICS OF LABOR RELATIONS. USA+45 LAW CONSULT WORKER CAP/ISM PAY ADJUD CONTROL EFFICIENCY ORD/FREE...CHARTS 19/20 AFL/CIO NLRB DEPT/LABOR. PAGE 16 F0299
ECO/DEV | ECO/TAC | LABOR | GOV/REL

B55
BOULDING K.E.,ECONOMIC ANALYSIS (3RD ED.). USA+45 PLAN ECO/TAC COST DEMAND INCOME...POLICY STAT CHARTS SIMUL T. PAGE 17 F0322
PHIL/SCI | ECO/DEV | CAP/ISM

B55
BRAUN K.,LABOR DISPUTES AND THEIR SETTLEMENT. ECO/TAC ROUTINE TASK GP/REL...DECISION GEN/LAWS. PAGE 18 F0342
INDUS | LABOR | BARGAIN | ADJUD

B55
BUCHANAN N.S.,APPROACHES TO ECONOMIC DEVELOPMENT. FUT USA+45 WOR+45 STRATA ECO/DEV INT/ORG NAT/G TEC/DEV DIPLOM FOR/AID ATTIT KNOWL PWR WEALTH ...RELATIV METH/CNCPT SELF/OBS TREND CON/ANAL STERTYP GEN/LAWS FOR/TRADE COMMUN 20. PAGE 20 F0380
ECO/UNDEV | ECO/TAC | INT/TRADE

B55
FLORINSKY M.T.,INTEGRATED EUROPE. EUR+WWI FRANCE ITALY NETHERLAND UK ECO/DEV INT/ORG FORCES LEGIT FEDERAL ATTIT PWR WEALTH...POLICY GEOG CONCPT GEN/LAWS TOT/POP EEC OEEC 20. PAGE 42 F0816
FUT | ECO/TAC | REGION

B55
FOGARTY M.P.,ECONOMIC CONTROL. FUT UK ECO/DEV FINAN CONSULT INT/TRADE...CHARTS BIBLIOG/A 20. PAGE 42 F0819
ECO/TAC | NAT/G | CONTROL | PROB/SOLV

B55
GEORGE H.,PROGRESS AND POVERTY (1880). STRATA STRUCT INDUS TEC/DEV CAP/ISM EQUILIB INCOME OWN UTOPIA...WELF/ST CONCPT NEW/IDEA 19. PAGE 47 F0915
ECO/DEV | ECO/TAC | TAX | WEALTH

B55
GOMES F.A.,OPERACAO MUNICIPIO. BRAZIL L/A+17C SERV/IND LOC/G BUDGET ECO/TAC COST DEMAND...POLICY MUNICH 20. PAGE 48 F0944
ECO/UNDEV | FEDERAL | GOV/REL

B55
HELANDER S.,DAS AUTARKIEPROBLEM IN DER WELTWIRTSCHAFT. PROB/SOLV BAL/PWR BARGAIN CAP/ISM ECO/TAC SOVEREIGN FOR/TRADE 20. PAGE 58 F1144
NAT/COMP | COLONIAL | DIPLOM

B55
JOHR W.A.,THE ROLE OF THE ECONOMIST AS OFFICIAL ADVISER. WOR+45 INTELL ECO/DEV NAT/G PLAN GP/REL ROLE...DECISION PREDICT IDEA/COMP. PAGE 68 F1336
CONSULT | ECO/TAC | POLICY | INGP/REL

B55
MAYO H.B.,DEMOCRACY AND MARXISM. COM USSR STRATA NAT/G WORKER ECO/TAC REV MORAL...PHIL/SCI HIST/WRIT IDEA/COMP WORSHIP 20 MARX/KARL LENIN/VI STALIN/J TROTSKY/L. PAGE 87 F1708
MARXISM | CAP/ISM

B55
PALAMOUNTAIN JC J.R.,THE POLITICS OF DISTRIBUTION. USA+45 LG/CO SML/CO BAL/PWR CONTROL EQUILIB 20. PAGE 103 F2019
DIST/IND | ECO/TAC | CAP/ISM | GP/REL

B55
PANT Y.P.,PLANNING IN UNDERDEVELOPED ECONOMIES. INDIA NEPAL INT/TRADE COLONIAL SOVEREIGN ALL/IDEOS ...TIME/SEQ METH/COMP 20. PAGE 103 F2026
ECO/UNDEV | PLAN | ECO/TAC | DIPLOM

B55
RUSTOW D.A.,THE POLITICS OF COMPROMISE. SWEDEN LABOR EX/STRUC LEGIS PLAN REPRESENT SOCISM...SOC 19/20. PAGE 115 F2265
POL/PAR | NAT/G | POLICY | ECO/TAC

B55
US OFFICE OF THE PRESIDENT,REPORT TO CONGRESS ON THE MUTUAL SECURITY PROGRAM FOR THE SIX MONTHS ENDED JUNE 30, 1955. ECO/DEV INT/ORG NAT/G CREATE TEC/DEV BAL/PWR ECO/TAC AGREE DETER COST ORD/FREE 20 DEPT/STATE DEPT/DEFEN. PAGE 138 F2722
DIPLOM | FORCES | PLAN | FOR/AID

B55
WOYTINSKY W.S.,WORLD COMMERCE AND GOVERNMENTS: TRENDS AND OUTLOOK. WOR+45 FINAN POL/PAR DIPLOM ECO/TAC FOR/AID DOMIN WAR CHOOSE...CHARTS BIBLIOG 20 LEAGUE/NAT UN ILO. PAGE 149 F2929
INT/TRADE | DIST/IND | NAT/COMP | NAT/G

B55
WRONG D.H.,AMERICAN AND CANADIAN VIEWPOINTS. CANADA USA+45 CONSTN STRATA FAM SECT WORKER ECO/TAC EDU/PROP ADJUD MARRIAGE...IDEA/COMP 20. PAGE 149 F2936
DIPLOM | ATTIT | NAT/COMP | CULTURE

L55
KISER M.,"ORGANIZATION OF AMERICAN STATES." L/A+17C USA+45 ECO/UNDEV INT/ORG NAT/G PLAN TEC/DEV DIPLOM ECO/TAC INT/TRADE EDU/PROP ADMIN ALL/VALS...POLICY MGT RECORD ORG/CHARTS OAS COMMUN 20. PAGE 71 F1401
VOL/ASSN | ECO/DEV | REGION

C55
ADAMS G.P. JR.,"COMPETITIVE ECONOMIC SYSTEMS." WOR+45 WOR-45 PWR...BIBLIOG/A 20. PAGE 2 F0038
METH/COMP | ECO/TAC | TEC/DEV | DIPLOM

B56
BARBASH J.,THE PRACTICE OF UNIONISM. ECO/TAC LEAD LOBBY GP/REL INGP/REL DRIVE MARXISM BIBLIOG. PAGE 10 F0182
LABOR | REPRESENT | CONTROL | ADMIN

B56
BELL P.W.,THE STERLING AREA IN THE POSTWAR WORLD. EUR+WWI FUT S/ASIA UK ECO/DEV PLAN DIPLOM WEALTH ...STAT RECORD CHARTS GEN/LAWS FOR/TRADE TOT/POP 20. PAGE 12 F0235
FINAN ECO/TAC

B56
BURKHEAD J.,GOVERNMENT BUDGETING. ECO/DEV PROB/SOLV ECO/TAC ADMIN ROUTINE GOV/REL EFFICIENCY...DECISION MGT. PAGE 20 F0388
BUDGET NAT/G PROVS EX/STRUC

B56
FELLNER W.,TRENDS AND CYCLES IN ECONOMIC ACTIVITY: AN INTRODUCTION TO PROBLEMS OF ECONOMIC GROWTH. USA+45 INDUS ACT/RES CAP/ISM EQUILIB...MODAL METH/COMP BIBLIOG 20. PAGE 40 F0779
ECO/TAC TREND FINAN ECO/DEV

B56
HICKMAN C.A.,INDIVIDUALS, GROUPS, AND ECONOMIC BEHAVIOR. WORKER PAY CONTROL EXEC GP/REL INGP/REL PERSON ROLE...PSY SOC PERS/COMP METH 20. PAGE 59 F1163
MGT ADMIN ECO/TAC PLAN

B56
KINDLEBERGER C.P.,THE TERMS OF TRADE: A EUROPEAN CASE-STUDY. EUR+WWI MOD/EUR ECO/DEV ECO/UNDEV AGRI INDUS BAL/PAY...METH/CNCPT STAT CONT/OBS CON/ANAL SOC/EXP SIMUL FOR/TRADE 20. PAGE 71 F1390
PLAN ECO/TAC

B56
MYRDAL G.,AN INTERNATIONAL ECONOMY. EUR+WWI USA+45 WOR+45 WOR-45 NAT/G DIPLOM ECO/TAC BAL/PAY...PSY CONCPT OEEC TOT/POP 20. PAGE 96 F1879
VOL/ASSN AFR

B56
US OFFICE OF THE PRESIDENT,REPORT TO CONGRESS ON THE MUTUAL SECURITY PROGRAM FOR THE SIX MONTHS ENDED DECEMBER 31, 1955. ASIA USSR ECO/DEV ECO/UNDEV INT/ORG CREATE TEC/DEV BAL/PWR ECO/TAC AGREE DETER COST ORD/FREE 20 DEPT/STATE DEPT/DEFEN EISNHWR/DD. PAGE 138 F2723
DIPLOM FORCES PLAN FOR/AID

L56
SCHELLING T.C.,"AN ESSAY ON BARGAINING" (BMR)" OP/RES PROB/SOLV PRICE CHOOSE PWR...DECISION MODELS 20. PAGE 116 F2294
BARGAIN MARKET ECO/TAC GAME

S56
LANDAUER J.D.,"PROFESSIONAL CONSULTANTS: A NEW FACTOR IN REAL ESTATE." USA+45 PROB/SOLV ECO/TAC PERS/REL DEMAND EFFICIENCY DECISION. PAGE 75 F1467
CONSULT CONSTRUC CLIENT

B57
ARON R.,L'UNIFICATION ECONOMIQUE DE L'EUROPE. EUR+WWI SWITZERLND UK INT/ORG NAT/G REGION NAT/LISM ORD/FREE PWR...CONCPT METH/CNCPT OBS TREND STERTYP GEN/LAWS EEC FOR/TRADE 20. PAGE 6 F0118
VOL/ASSN ECO/TAC

B57
ASSN U BUREAUS BUS-ECO RES,INDEX OF PUBLICATIONS OF BUREAUS OF BUSINESS AND ECONOMIC RESEARCH 1950-56 AND YEARLY SUPPLEMENTS THROUGH 1967. FINAN OP/RES PLAN GOV/REL INCOME AGE...POLICY 20. PAGE 7 F0133
BIBLIOG ECO/DEV ECO/TAC LG/CO

B57
BAUER P.T.,THE ECONOMICS OF UNDERDEVELOPED COUNTRIES. WOR+45 AGRI FINAN INDUS PROC/MFG WORKER CAP/ISM PAY PRICE INCOME MARXISM...METH/COMP 20 RESOURCE/N. PAGE 11 F0213
ECO/UNDEV ECO/TAC PROB/SOLV NAT/G

B57
BERLE A.A. JR.,ECONOMIC POWER AND FREE SOCIETY (PAMPHLET). CLIENT CONSTN EX/STRUC ECO/TAC CONTROL PARTIC PWR WEALTH MAJORIT. PAGE 14 F0261
LG/CO CAP/ISM INGP/REL LEGIT

B57
CLARK J.M.,ECONOMIC INSTITUTIONS AND HUMAN WELFARE. USA+45 SOCIETY ECO/DEV NAT/G WORKER PLAN PROB/SOLV CAP/ISM CONTROL...POLICY 20. PAGE 25 F0482
ECO/TAC ORD/FREE WEALTH

B57
DRUCKER P.F.,AMERICA'S NEXT TWENTY YEARS. USA+45 DIST/IND ACADEM SCHOOL DIPLOM ECO/TAC AUTOMAT HABITAT HEALTH...SOC/WK TREND MUNICH 20 URBAN/RNWL PUB/TRANS. PAGE 34 F0667
WORKER FOR/AID CENSUS GEOG

B57
EHRMANN H.W.,ORGANIZED BUSINESS IN FRANCE. EUR+WWI MOD/EUR ECO/DEV VOL/ASSN LEGIT ATTIT PERCEPT PWR RESPECT...PLURIST SOC INT TOT/POP 20. PAGE 36 F0712
PROF/ORG ECO/TAC FRANCE

B57
FOUSEK P.G.,FOREIGN CENTRAL BANKING: THE INSTRUMENTS OF MONETARY POLICY. WOR+45 CONTROL ...TREND CHARTS 20 MONEY. PAGE 43 F0836
FINAN ECO/TAC ECO/DEV MARKET

B57
HUTTON D.G.,INFLATION AND SOCIETY. AFR FINAN PLAN COST DEMAND EQUILIB...CONCPT 20. PAGE 64 F1254
ECO/DEV POLICY NAT/G ECO/TAC

B57
LAVES W.H.C.,UNESCO. FUT WOR+45 NAT/G CONSULT DELIB/GP TEC/DEV ECO/TAC EDU/PROP PEACE ORD/FREE ...CONCPT TIME/SEQ TREND UNESCO VAL/FREE 20. PAGE 76 F1491
INT/ORG KNOWL

B57
LEIBENSTEIN H.,ECONOMIC BACKWARDNESS AND ECONOMIC GROWTH. WOR+45 SOCIETY AGRI INDUS TEC/DEV CAP/ISM FOR/AID COST DEMAND WEALTH...CHARTS IDEA/COMP 20. PAGE 77 F1513
ECO/UNDEV ECO/TAC PRODUC POLICY

B57
LUNDBERG E.,BUSINESS CYCLES AND ECONOMIC POLICY (TRANS. BY J. POTTER). SWEDEN ECO/DEV FINAN DELIB/GP PLAN PRICE CONTROL BAL/PAY 20 INTRVN/ECO. PAGE 82 F1607
ECO/TAC INDUS INT/TRADE BUDGET

B57
MEIER G.M.,ECONOMIC DEVELOPMENT: THEORY, HISTORY, AND POLICY. WOR+45 WOR-45 ECO/DEV ECO/UNDEV PLAN CAP/ISM BAL/PAY ATTIT PWR WEALTH SOCISM...CHARTS TOT/POP FOR/TRADE 20. PAGE 89 F1748
ECO/TAC GEN/LAWS

B57
NANIWADA H.,STAAT UND WIRTSCHAFT; GRUNDLEGUNG DER NATIONALOEKONOMIE ALS DER LOGIK DER BURGERLICHEN GESELLSCHAFT. WOR+45 WOR-45 STRATA MARKET WORKER INGP/REL DEMAND EQUILIB WEALTH...POLICY IDEA/COMP GEN/LAWS 17/20 MARX/KARL KEYNES/JM LENIN/VI. PAGE 96 F1890
ALL/IDEOS ECO/TAC SOCIETY NAT/G

B57
NAUMANN R.,THEORIE UND PRAXIS DES NEOLIBERALISMUS; DAS MAERCHEN VON DER FREIEN ODER SOZIALEN MARKTWIRTSCHAFT. GERMANY/W FORCES PLAN EDU/PROP SOCISM...POLICY MARXIST IDEA/COMP BIBLIOG 18/20 ADENAUER/K. PAGE 97 F1903
MARXISM NEW/LIB ECO/TAC CAP/ISM

B57
NEUMARK S.D.,ECONOMIC INFLUENCES ON THE SOUTH AFRICAN FRONTIER, 1652-1836. SOUTH/AFR SEA AGRI NAT/G FORCES WORKER DIPLOM INT/TRADE PRICE DEMAND PRODUC...STAT CHARTS 17/19 FRONTIER. PAGE 97 F1915
COLONIAL ECO/UNDEV ECO/TAC MARKET

B57
OLIVECRONA K.,THE PROBLEM OF THE MONETARY UNIT. AFR UNIV PAY PRICE UTIL...MATH 20 MONEY SILVER. PAGE 101 F1986
FINAN ECO/TAC ECO/DEV CONCPT

B57
PALACIOS A.L.,PETROLEO, MONOPOLIOS, Y LATIFUNDIOS. L/A+17C EXTR/IND NAT/G TEC/DEV ECO/TAC CONTROL PRODUC 20 ARGEN MONOPOLY RESOURCE/N. PAGE 103 F2017
ECO/UNDEV NAT/LISM INDUS AGRI

B57
ROBERTSON H.M.,SOUTH AFRICA, ECONOMIC AND POLITICAL ASPECTS. SOUTH/AFR CONSTN CULTURE POL/PAR LEGIS DIPLOM DOMIN COLONIAL...SOC BIBLIOG 19/20. PAGE 112 F2214
RACE/REL ECO/UNDEV ECO/TAC DISCRIM

B57
SINGH D.B.,INFLATIONARY PRICE TRENDS IN INDIA SINCE 1939. AFR INDIA ECO/TAC RATION CONTROL WAR GOV/REL BAL/PAY DEMAND INCOME PEACE PRODUC...POLICY CHARTS 20. PAGE 122 F2413
BUDGET ECO/UNDEV PRICE FINAN

B57
THOMAS R.G.,OUR MODERN BANKING AND MONETARY SYSTEM (3RD ED.). AFR USA+45 USA-45 ACT/RES PLAN PROB/SOLV INT/TRADE PRICE WAR BAL/PAY INCOME...POLICY METH/CNCPT 20 DEPRESSION. PAGE 130 F2563
FINAN SERV/IND ECO/TAC

B57
TRIFFIN R.,EUROPE AND THE MONEY MUDDLE. USA+45 INT/ORG NAT/G CONSULT PLAN ECO/TAC EXEC ROUTINE BAL/PAY WEALTH...METH/CNCPT OBS TREND CHARTS STERTYP GEN/METH EEC TERR/GP VAL/FREE ECSC. PAGE 131 F2587
EUR+WWI ECO/DEV REGION

B57
WEIGERT H.W.,PRINCIPLES OF POLITICAL GEOGRAPHY. WOR+45 ECO/DEV ECO/UNDEV SECT ECO/TAC COLONIAL HABITAT...CHARTS T 20. PAGE 144 F2845
GEOG CULTURE

S57
ANSHEN M.,"BUSINESS, LAWYERS, AND ECONOMISTS." PROB/SOLV ECO/TAC CONFER PROFIT RIGID/FLEX OBJECTIVE...MGT GP/COMP. PAGE 6 F0106
INDUS CONSULT ROUTINE EFFICIENCY

S57
HOAG M.W.,"ECONOMIC PROBLEMS OF ALLIANCE." AFR COM EUR+WWI WOR+45 ECO/DEV ECO/UNDEV NAT/G VOL/ASSN FORCES PLAN TEC/DEV DIPLOM COERCE ORD/FREE PWR WEALTH...DECISION GEN/LAWS NATO TERR/GP. PAGE 60 F1182
INT/ORG ECO/TAC

S57
LEWIS E.G.,"PARLIAMENTARY CONTROL OF NATIONALIZED INDUSTRY IN FRANCE." FRANCE NAT/G DELIB/GP ACT/RES PLAN PROB/SOLV ECO/TAC DOMIN CENTRAL. PAGE 79 F1547
PWR LEGIS INDUS CONTROL

S57
VERNON R.,"PRODUCTION AND DISTRIBUTION IN THE LARGE METROPOLIS" (BMR)" USA+45 PROC/MFG ECO/TAC HABITAT ...CENSUS TREND MUNICH 20. PAGE 141 F2779
PRODUC DIST/IND PROB/SOLV

N57
U WISCONSIN BUREAU OF GOVT,SERVICE SALES OF THE CITY OF MADISON TO METROPOLITAN COMMUNITIES AND NONRESIDENTS (PAMPHLET). DIST/IND LOC/G ADMIN ...DECISION GOV/COMP MUNICH. PAGE 132 F2597
REGION ECO/TAC PLAN

B58
DEFENSE AGAINST INFLATION. USA+45 LEGIS WORKER TAX PRICE DEMAND INCOME PRODUC...POLICY TREND METH/COMP 20 GOLD/STAND. PAGE 1 F0012
ECO/TAC EQUILIB WEALTH PROB/SOLV

B58
ATOMIC INDUSTRIAL FORUM,MANAGEMENT AND ATOMIC ENERGY. WOR+45 SEA LAW MARKET NAT/G TEC/DEV INSPECT INT/TRADE CONFER PEACE HEALTH...ANTHOL 20. PAGE 7 F0136
NUC/PWR INDUS MGT ECO/TAC

B58
BARRERE A.,POLITIQUE FINANCIERE. FRANCE BUDGET ECO/TAC TAX BAL/PAY INCOME PRODUC...MGT BIBLIOG T 20. PAGE 10 F0193
FINAN NAT/G PLAN

B58
BERLINER J.S.,SOVIET ECONOMIC AID: THE AID AND TRADE POLICY IN UNDERDEVELOPED COUNTRIES. AFR COM ISLAM L/A+17C S/ASIA USSR ECO/DEV DIST/IND FINAN MARKET INT/ORG ACT/RES PLAN BAL/PWR WEAPON PWR WEALTH...CHARTS FOR/TRADE 20. PAGE 14 F0263
ECO/UNDEV ECO/TAC FOR/AID

B58
BIDWELL P.W.,RAW MATERIALS: A STUDY OF AMERICAN POLICY. USA+45 USA-45 ECO/UNDEV AGRI INDUS KIN CREATE PLAN ECO/TAC WAR PEACE ATTIT DRIVE WEALTH ...STAT CHARTS CONGRESS FOR/TRADE VAL/FREE. PAGE 15 F0279
EXTR/IND ECO/DEV

B58
CHANG C.,THE INFLATIONARY SPIRAL: THE EXPERIENCE IN CHINA 1939-50. CHINA/COM BUDGET INT/TRADE PRICE ADMIN CONTROL WAR DEMAND...POLICY CHARTS 20. PAGE 23 F0451
FINAN ECO/TAC BAL/PAY GOV/REL

B58
CLAIRMONTE F.,LE LIBERALISME ECONOMIQUE ET LES PAYS SOUS-DEVELOPPES: ETUDES SUR L'EVOLUTION D'UNE IDEE. ASIA INDIA UK FINAN INDUS PLAN CAP/ISM ECO/TAC COLONIAL NEW/LIB...BIBLIOG 20 THIRD/WRLD. PAGE 24 F0475
LAISSEZ ECO/UNDEV

B58
DOWNIE J.,THE COMPETITIVE PROCESS. ECO/TAC PRICE EFFICIENCY OPTIMAL PRODUC WEALTH...IDEA/COMP METH/COMP 20 MONOPOLY. PAGE 34 F0658
EQUILIB MARKET INDUS ECO/DEV

B58
DUBIN R.,WORKING UNION-MANAGEMENT RELATIONS. LAW PLAN ECO/TAC CHOOSE REPRESENT INGP/REL PWR...POLICY SOC BIBLIOG. PAGE 34 F0669
LABOR MGT AUTHORIT GP/REL

B58
DUESENBERRY J.S.,BUSINESS CYCLES AND ECONOMIC GROWTH. USA+45 PROB/SOLV PAY PRICE...CONCPT MATH CHARTS IDEA/COMP 20 DEPRESSION KEYNES/JM. PAGE 34 F0672
FINAN ECO/DEV ECO/TAC INCOME

B58
GALBRAITH J.K.,THE AFFLUENT SOCIETY. EUR+WWI FUT USA+45 USSR CULTURE SERV/IND PEACE WEALTH SOCISM ...NEW/IDEA TREND VAL/FREE 20. PAGE 45 F0882
ATTIT ECO/TAC CAP/ISM

B58
HIRSCHMAN A.O.,STRATEGY OF ECONOMIC DEVELOPMENT. WOR+45 WOR-45 CULTURE ECO/DEV NAT/G PLAN TEC/DEV INT/TRADE BAL/PAY ATTIT DRIVE RIGID/FLEX WEALTH ...CONCPT METH/CNCPT OBS CHARTS SIMUL GEN/LAWS TOT/POP VAL/FREE. PAGE 60 F1176
ECO/UNDEV ECO/TAC CAP/ISM

B58
HOOD W.C.,FINANCING OF ECONOMIC ACTIVITY IN CANADA. CANADA FUT VOL/ASSN WORKER ECO/TAC ADJUD ADMIN ...CHARTS 20. PAGE 61 F1204
BUDGET FINAN GP/REL ECO/DEV

B58
INTERNATIONAL ECONOMIC ASSN,ECONOMICS OF INTERNATIONAL MIGRATION. WOR+45 WOR-45 ECO/UNDEV FINAN NAT/G REGION...NAT/COMP METH 20. PAGE 65 F1275
CENSUS GEOG DIPLOM ECO/TAC

B58
JACOBSSON P.,SOME MONETARY PROBLEMS, INTERNATIONAL AND NATIONAL. WOR+45 WOR-45 ECO/DEV FORCES WORKER PROB/SOLV DIPLOM INT/TRADE...ANTHOL 20. PAGE 66 F1299
FINAN PLAN ECO/TAC NAT/COMP

B58
JENNINGS I.,PROBLEMS OF THE NEW COMMONWEALTH. AFR CEYLON INDIA PAKISTAN S/ASIA ECO/UNDEV INT/ORG LOC/G DIPLOM ECO/TAC INT/TRADE COLONIAL RACE/REL DISCRIM 20 PARLIAMENT. PAGE 67 F1314
NAT/LISM NEUTRAL FOR/AID POL/PAR

B58
JOHNSON H.G.,INTERNATIONAL TRADE AND ECONOMIC GROWTH. WOR+45 BUDGET CAP/ISM ECO/TAC TARIFFS BAL/PAY 20. PAGE 67 F1323
INT/TRADE BAL/PWR BARGAIN DIPLOM

B58
JUCKER-FLEETWOOD E.,ECONOMIC THEORY AND POLICY IN FINLAND 1914-1925. FINLAND INT/TRADE PRICE COST 20 MONEY. PAGE 68 F1343
FINAN GEN/LAWS ECO/TAC PLAN

B58
KINDLEBERGER C.P.,INTERNATIONAL ECONOMICS. WOR+45 WOR-45 ECO/DEV ECO/UNDEV FINAN VOL/ASSN ACT/RES DIPLOM ECO/TAC LEGIT REGION ATTIT DRIVE ORD/FREE WEALTH...POLICY STAT TREND GEN/LAWS EEC ECSC OEEC 20. PAGE 71 F1391
INT/ORG BAL/PWR TARIFFS

B58
MCIVOR R.C.,CANADIAN MONETARY, BANKING, AND FISCAL DEVELOPMENT. CANADA INDUS LG/CO NAT/G SML/CO CONTROL WAR...GEN/LAWS BIBLIOG 17/20. PAGE 88 F1729
ECO/TAC FINAN ECO/DEV WEALTH

B58
MIKESELL R.F.,FINANCING FREE WORLD TRADE WITH THE SINO-SOVIET BLOC. CHINA/COM COM USSR WOR+45 ECO/DEV AGRI DIST/IND EXTR/IND FINAN INDUS MARKET PROC/MFG NAT/G PLAN TEC/DEV ECO/TAC...CHARTS METH/GP EEC FOR/TRADE 20. PAGE 91 F1780
STAT BAL/PAY

B58
MOONEY R.E.,INFLATION AND RECESSION? AFR USA+45 LABOR LG/CO PRESS LEAD...IDEA/COMP ANTHOL 20. PAGE 93 F1821
PRICE ECO/TAC NAT/G PRODUC

B58
MOULTON H.G.,CAN INFLATION BE CONTROLLED? ECO/DEV INDUS CAP/ISM RATION GOV/REL COST INCOME PEACE WEALTH...CHARTS TIME 20 KEYNES/JM MONEY. PAGE 94 F1847
ECO/TAC CONTROL DEMAND FINAN

B58
MUSGRAVE R.A.,CLASSICS IN THE THEORY OF PUBLIC FINANCE. UNIV MARKET LG/CO NAT/G CAP/ISM PRICE OPTIMAL...IDEA/COMP ANTHOL 19/20 SAY/EMIL EDGEWORTH LINDAHL/E RITSCHL/H. PAGE 95 F1870
TAX FINAN ECO/TAC GP/REL

B58
MYRDAL G.,RICH LANDS AND POOR: THE ROAD TO WORLD PROSPERITY. FUT WOR+45 WOR-45 ECO/DEV ECO/UNDEV INT/ORG PLAN ECO/TAC REGION...GEOG TIME/SEQ GEN/LAWS TOT/POP 20. PAGE 96 F1880
WEALTH TREND FOR/AID INT/TRADE

B58
OEEC,THE INDUSTRIAL CHALLENGE OF NUCLEAR ENERGY. EUR+WWI ECO/DEV INDUS OP/RES CONFER RISK PWR ...AUD/VIS CHARTS ANTHOL 20 OEEC. PAGE 101 F1977
NUC/PWR ACT/RES ECO/TAC INT/ORG

B58
PALMER E.E.,THE ECONOMY AND THE DEMOCRATIC IDEAL. USA+45 USA-45 STRATA CHIEF CT/SYS ORD/FREE SOCISM ...MAJORIT CONCPT ANTHOL 18/20 PRESIDENT. PAGE 103 F2021
ECO/DEV POPULISM METH/COMP ECO/TAC

B58
PALYI M.,MANAGED MONEY AT THE CROSSROADS: THE EUROPEAN EXPERIENCE. AFR WOR+45 WOR-45 TEC/DEV DIPLOM INT/TRADE DEMAND WEALTH...CHARTS BIBLIOG 19/20 EUROPE SILVER. PAGE 103 F2022
FINAN ECO/TAC ECO/DEV PRODUC

B58
PAYNO M.,LA REFORMA SOCIAL EN ESPANA Y MEXICO. SPAIN ECO/TAC TAX LOBBY COERCE REV OWN CATHISM 19/20 MEXIC/AMER. PAGE 104 F2043
SECT NAT/G LAW ELITES

B58
POLLOCK F.,AUTOMATION: A STUDY OF ITS ECONOMIC AND SOCIAL CONSEQUENCES. FUT USA+45 USA-45 SOCIETY ECO/DEV LABOR ACT/RES PLAN ECO/TAC AUTOMAT ROUTINE ALL/VALS...STAT TREND COMPUT/IR CHARTS SOC/EXP WORK 20. PAGE 107 F2099
TEC/DEV SOC CAP/ISM

B58
ROBERTS B.C.,NATIONAL WAGES POLICY IN WAR AND PEACE. EUR+WWI GERMANY S/ASIA SWEDEN UK USA+45 USA-45 STRATA ECO/DEV LABOR NAT/G DELIB/GP PLAN INT/TRADE WEALTH...STAT TREND CHARTS 20. PAGE 112 F2205
CREATE ECO/TAC

B58
SCITOUSKY T.,ECONOMIC THEORY AND WESTERN EUROPEAN INTEGRATION. EUR+WWI INT/ORG ACT/RES INT/TRADE REGION BAL/PAY WEALTH...METH/CNCPT STAT CHARTS GEN/METH ECSC TOT/POP EEC OEEC 20. PAGE 118 F2328
ECO/TAC

B58
WARNER A.W.,CONCEPTS AND CASES IN ECONOMIC ANALYSIS. PROB/SOLV BARGAIN CONTROL INCOME PRODUC ...ECOMETRIC MGT CONCPT CLASSIF CHARTS 20 KEYNES/JM. PAGE 143 F2820
ECO/TAC DEMAND EQUILIB COST

L58
ARROW K.J.,"ON THE STABILITY OF THE COMPETITIVE EQUILIBRIUM: I." WOR+45...METH/CNCPT MATH STAT CHARTS SIMUL. PAGE 6 F0122
DECISION MARKET ECO/DEV ECO/TAC

S58
ARROW K.J.,"A NOTE ON EXPECTATIONS AND STABILITY." WOR+45...METH/CNCPT MATH STAT CHARTS HYPO/EXP. PAGE 7 F0123
DECISION MARKET ECO/DEV ECO/TAC

S58
JOHNSON D.G.,"GOVERNMENT AND AGRICULTURE: IS AGRICULTURE A SPECIAL CASE?" PLAN ECO/TAC LOBBY WEALTH POLICY. PAGE 67 F1321
INDUS GP/REL INCOME NAT/G

S58
LOCKWOOD W.W.,"THE SOCIALISTIC SOCIETY: INDIA AND JAPAN." INDIA ECO/DEV ECO/UNDEV INDUS NAT/G CONTROL LEAD PRODUC WEALTH 20 CHINJAP. PAGE 81 F1593
ECO/TAC NAT/COMP FINAN SOCISM

S58
O'NEAL F.H.,"RECENT LEGISLATION AFFECTING CLOSE CORPORATIONS." LAW EX/STRUC ECO/TAC ROUTINE CHOOSE RIGID/FLEX...MAJORIT MGT TREND. PAGE 100 F1959
LG/CO LEGIS REPRESENT PARTIC

S58
SCHULZE R.O.,"THE ROLE OF ECONOMIC DOMINANTS IN COMMUNITY POWER STRUCTURE." ECO/TAC ROUTINE ATTIT OBJECTIVE...SOC RECORD CENSUS. PAGE 118 F2319
SOCIETY STRUCT PROB/SOLV

N58
EUROPEAN COMM ECO-SOC PROG,EUROPEAN BUSINESS CYCLE POLICY (PAMPHLET). AFR EUR+WWI MARKET WORKER DIPLOM PRICE BAL/PAY 20 EUROPE. PAGE 39 F0754
ECO/DEV FINAN ECO/TAC PROB/SOLV

B59
AITKEN H.G.,THE AMERICAN ECONOMIC IMPACT ON CANADA. CANADA USA+45 AGRI FINAN INDUS LABOR INT/TRADE BAL/PAY...INT/LAW TREND 20. PAGE 3 F0055
DIPLOM ECO/TAC POLICY NAT/G

B59
ALLEN R.L.,SOVIET INFLUENCE IN LATIN AMERICA. ECO/UNDEV FINAN PROC/MFG NAT/G TEC/DEV EDU/PROP EXEC ROUTINE ATTIT DRIVE PERSON ALL/VALS PWR...STAT CHARTS WORK FOR/TRADE 20. PAGE 4 F0071
L/A+17C ECO/TAC INT/TRADE USSR

B59
ARON R.,IMPERIALISM AND COLONIALISM (PAMPHLET). WOR+45 WOR-45 ECO/TAC CONTROL REV ORD/FREE 19/20. PAGE 6 F0119
COLONIAL DOMIN ECO/UNDEV DIPLOM

B59
BARBASH J.,UNIONS AND UNION LEADERSHIP. NAT/G WORKER TEC/DEV ECO/TAC PARTIC GP/REL RACE/REL ORD/FREE CLASSIF. PAGE 10 F0183
LABOR VOL/ASSN CAP/ISM LEAD

B59
BAUER P.T.,UNITED STATES AID AND INDIAN ECONOMIC DEVELOPMENT. INDIA STRATA FINAN PLAN BUDGET DIPLOM INGP/REL EFFICIENCY SOCISM 20 AID. PAGE 11 F0215
FOR/AID ECO/UNDEV ECO/TAC POLICY

B59
BLACK J.D.,ECONOMICS FOR AGRICULTURE. USA+45 EXTR/IND FAM WORKER ACT/RES PLAN PRICE EATING INCOME...CENSUS BIBLIOG 20. PAGE 15 F0291
AGRI ECO/TAC MARKET POLICY

B59
CHECCHI V.,HONDURAS: A PROBLEM IN ECONOMIC DEVELOPMENT. HONDURAS AGRI FINAN INDUS LABOR WORKER INT/TRADE EDU/PROP PRICE HEALTH...GEOG CHARTS BIBLIOG 20. PAGE 24 F0458
ECO/UNDEV ECO/TAC PROB/SOLV PLAN

B59
DIEBOLD W. JR.,THE SCHUMAN PLAN: A STUDY IN ECONOMIC COOPERATION, 1950-1959. EUR+WWI FRANCE GERMANY USA+45 EXTR/IND CONSULT DELIB/GP PLAN DIPLOM ECO/TAC INT/TRADE ROUTINE ORD/FREE WEALTH ...METH/CNCPT STAT CONT/OBS INT TIME/SEQ ECSC 20. PAGE 33 F0635
INT/ORG REGION

B59
ETSCHMANN R.,DIE WAHRUNGS- UND DEVISENPOLITIK DES OSTBLOCKS UND IHRE AUSWIRKUNGEN AUF DIE WIRTSCHAFTSBEZIEHUNGEN ZWISCHEN OST U WEST. BULGARIA CZECHOSLVK HUNGARY POLAND USSR MARKET NAT/G PLAN DIPLOM...NAT/COMP 20. PAGE 39 F0753
ECO/TAC FINAN POLICY INT/TRADE

B59
FELS R.,AMERICAN BUSINESS CYCLES 1865-1897. USA+45 ECO/DEV LG/CO SML/CO PROB/SOLV TEC/DEV CAP/ISM INT/TRADE DEMAND...POLICY CHARTS METH 19 DEPRESSION. PAGE 40 F0782
FINAN INDUS TREND ECO/TAC

B59
GUDIN E.,INFLACAO (2ND ED.). INDUS NAT/G PLAN ECO/TAC CONTROL COST 20. PAGE 52 F1012
ECO/UNDEV INT/TRADE BAL/PAY FINAN

B59
HAX K.,DIE HOCHSCHULLEHRER DER WIRTSCHAFTSWISSENSCHAFTEN IN DER BUNDESREPUBLIK DEUTSCHLAND EINSCHL. WESTBERLIN, OSTERREICH. AUSTRIA GERMANY/W SWITZERLND FINAN MARKET PROF/ORG BUDGET ECO/TAC INT/TRADE PRICE COST 20. PAGE 57 F1119
BIBLIOG ACADEM INTELL

B59
HICKS J.R.,ESSAYS IN WORLD ECONOMICS. AFR CEYLON NIGERIA WOR+45 SOCIETY ECO/DEV ORD/FREE WEALTH ...GEN/LAWS TOT/POP 20. PAGE 59 F1166
ECO/UNDEV ECO/TAC UK

B59
HOOVER C.B.,THE ECONOMY, LIBERTY AND THE STATE. COM EUR+WWI USA+45 USA-45 USSR CAP/ISM EDU/PROP COERCE TOTALISM ORD/FREE...POLICY OBS INT TREND NAZI 20. PAGE 61 F1206
ECO/DEV ECO/TAC

B59
KELF-COHEN R.,NATIONALISATION IN BRITAIN: THE END OF DOGMA. EUR+WWI UK NAT/G POL/PAR WORKER ECO/TAC PARL/PROC WEALTH SOCISM...GOV/COMP 20. PAGE 70 F1369
NEW/LIB ECO/DEV INDUS OWN

B59
KOREAN MINISTRY RECONSTRUCTION,KOREAN ECONOMY AND ITS REQUIREMENTS. KOREA USA+45 ECO/TAC EQUILIB INCOME WEALTH...CHARTS 20. PAGE 73 F1427
FOR/AID WAR FINAN DIPLOM

B59
KRIPALANI J.B.,CLASS STRUGGLE. INDIA WOR+45 ECO/UNDEV LABOR CAP/ISM EDU/PROP INGP/REL ...SOCIALIST IDEA/COMP 17/20. PAGE 73 F1440
MARXISM STRATA COERCE ECO/TAC

B59
MARTIN D.D.,MERGERS AND THE CLAYTON ACT. FINAN LEGIS GP/REL...DECISION METH/COMP BIBLIOG 20. PAGE 86 F1681
OWN ECO/TAC LG/CO POLICY

B59
MEYER A.J.,MIDDLE EASTERN CAPITALISM: NINE ESSAYS. ISLAM CULTURE ECO/UNDEV INDUS MARKET NAT/G PLAN ATTIT RIGID/FLEX...STAT OBS TREND GEN/LAWS. PAGE 90 F1767
TEC/DEV ECO/TAC ANTHOL

B59
MEZERK A.G.,FINANCIAL ASSISTANCE FOR ECONOMIC DEVELOPMENT. WOR+45 INDUS DIPLOM INT/TRADE...CHARTS GOV/COMP UN. PAGE 91 F1778
FOR/AID FINAN ECO/TAC ECO/UNDEV

B59
MORGENSTERN O.,INTERNATIONAL FINANCIAL TRANSACTIONS AND BUSINESS CYCLES. FRANCE GERMANY UK USA+45 USA-45 WOR+45 WOR-45 ECO/DEV ECO/TAC WEALTH ...CONCPT STAT CON/ANAL CHARTS 19/20. PAGE 93 F1832
FINAN TIME/SEQ INT/TRADE

B59
NOVE A.,COMMUNIST ECONOMIC STRATEGY: SOVIET GROWTH AND CAPABILITIES. USSR AGRI LABOR PLAN TEC/DEV CAP/ISM INT/TRADE EFFICIENCY MARXISM 20 THIRD/WRLD. PAGE 99 F1941
FOR/AID ECO/TAC DIPLOM INDUS

B59
OGBURN C.,ECONOMIC PLAN AND ACTION. USA+45 FINAN LABOR DIPLOM ECO/TAC FOR/AID 20. PAGE 101 F1981
ECO/DEV INT/TRADE PLAN BAL/PAY

B59
ROBERTSON A.H.,EUROPEAN INSTITUTIONS: COOPERATION, INTEGRATION, UNIFICATION. EUR+WWI FINAN INT/ORG FORCES INT/TRADE TARIFFS 20 EEC EURATOM ECSC NATO TREATY. PAGE 112 F2208
ECO/DEV DIPLOM INDUS ECO/TAC

B59
SANNWALD R.E.,ECONOMIC INTEGRATION: THEORETICAL ASSUMPTIONS AND CONSEQUENCES OF EUROPEAN UNIFICATION. EUR+WWI FUT FINAN INDUS VOL/ASSN ACT/RES ECO/TAC...PLURIST EEC FOR/TRADE OEEC 20. PAGE 116 F2279
INT/ORG ECO/DEV INT/TRADE

B59
SHUBIK M.,STRATEGY AND MARKET STRUCTURE: COMPETITION, OLIGOPOLY, AND THE THEORY OF GAMES. ELITES STRUCT MARKET OP/RES EXEC EFFICIENCY INCOME ...MGT MATH STAT CHARTS 20. PAGE 121 F2389
ECO/DEV ECO/TAC DECISION GAME

B59
SILCOCK T.H.,THE COMMONWEALTH ECONOMY IN SOUTHEAST ASIA. AFR INDIA MALAYSIA S/ASIA ECO/DEV AGRI LOC/G PLAN TARIFFS COLONIAL BAL/PAY DEMAND...BIBLIOG/A 20 GATT. PAGE 122 F2401
ECO/TAC INT/TRADE RACE/REL DIPLOM

B59
STANFORD U, BOARD OF TRUSTEES,THE ALLOCATION OF ECONOMIC RESOURCES. WORKER PLAN BUDGET ECO/TAC TAX RECEIVE COST PRODUC...POLICY IDEA/COMP SIMUL ANTHOL 20. PAGE 125 F2468
INCOME PRICE FINAN

B59
STOVEL J.A.,CANADA IN THE WORLD ECONOMY. CANADA PRICE DEMAND...STAT CHARTS BIBLIOG 20 VINER/J. PAGE 127 F2499
INT/TRADE BAL/PAY FINAN ECO/TAC

B59
THE BROOKINGS INSTITUTION,ECONOMICS AND THE POLICY MAKER. USA+45 CREATE...ANTHOL 20. PAGE 129 F2549
ELITES ECO/TAC PROB/SOLV ECO/DEV

B59
US GENERAL ACCOUNTING OFFICE,EXAM OF ECONOMIC AND TECHNICAL ASSISTANCE PROGRAM FOR INDIA INT'NAT'L COOP ADMIN REPORT TO CONGRESS 1955-1958. INDIA USA+45 ECO/UNDEV FINAN PLAN DIPLOM COST UTIL WEALTH ...CHARTS 20 CONGRESS AID. PAGE 136 F2679
FOR/AID EFFICIENCY ECO/TAC TEC/DEV

B59
WENTHOLT W.,SOME COMMENTS ON THE LIQUIDATION OF THE EUROPEAN PAYMENT UNION AND RELATED PROBLEMS (PAMPHLET). AFR WOR+45 PLAN BUDGET PRICE CONTROL 20 EEC. PAGE 145 F2857
FINAN ECO/DEV INT/ORG ECO/TAC

L59
ARROW K.J.,"ON THE STABILITY OF THE COMPETITIVE EQUILIBRIUM: II." WOR+45...METH/CNCPT MATH STAT CHARTS HYPO/EXP. PAGE 7 F0124
DECISION MARKET ECO/DEV ECO/TAC

L59
FURASH E.A.,"PROBLEMS IN REVIEW: INDUSTRIAL ESPIONAGE." WORKER ECO/TAC PERS/REL OPTIMAL AGE ATTIT KNOWL...MGT DEEP/INT DEEP/QU GP/COMP IDEA/COMP. PAGE 45 F0875
INDUS TOP/EX MAJORITY

L59
GARDNER R.N.,"NEW DIRECTIONS IN UNITED STATES FOREIGN ECONOMIC POLICY." AFR USA+45 CONSULT ...GEN/LAWS GEN/METH FOR/TRADE 20. PAGE 46 F0903
ECO/UNDEV ECO/TAC FOR/AID DIPLOM

L59
MURPHY J.C.,"SOME IMPLICATIONS OF EUROPE'S COMMON
MARKET

MARKET. IN (COOK P, ECONOMIC DEVELOPMENT AND INTERNATIONAL TRADE..." EUR+WWI ECO/DEV DIST/IND INDUS NAT/G PLAN ECO/TAC INT/TRADE WEALTH...STAT TREND OEEC TOT/POP 20 EEC. PAGE 95 F1866
INT/ORG REGION

L59
WURFEL D.,"FOREIGN AID AND SOCIAL REFORM IN POLITICAL DEVELOPMENT" (BMR)" PHILIPPINE USA+45 WOR+45 SOCIETY POL/PAR ACT/RES TEC/DEV DIPLOM 20. PAGE 149 F2943
FOR/AID PROB/SOLV ECO/TAC ECO/UNDEV

S59
ALKHIMOV V.S.,"SOVIET FOREIGN TRADE CHANNELS." COM FUT USA+45 USSR ECO/DEV MARKET CONSULT PLAN WEALTH ...MARXIST OBS CON/ANAL FOR/TRADE 20. PAGE 4 F0068
FINAN ECO/TAC DIPLOM

S59
ALLEN G.,"NATIONAL FARMERS UNION AS A PRESSURE GROUP: II." UK ECO/DEV MARKET POL/PAR DELIB/GP PROB/SOLV ECO/TAC LOBBY INCOME...POLICY METH/COMP 19/20 NAT/FARMER. PAGE 4 F0069
DIST/IND AGRI PROF/ORG TREND

S59
KINDLEBERGER C.P.,"UNITED STATES ECONOMIC FOREIGN POLICY: RESEARCH REQUIREMENTS FOR 1965." FUT USA+45 WOR+45 DIST/IND MARKET INT/ORG ECO/TAC INT/TRADE WEALTH...OBS TREND CON/ANAL GEN/LAWS FOR/TRADE VAL/FREE 20. PAGE 71 F1392
FINAN ECO/DEV FOR/AID

S59
PLAZA G.,"FOR A REGIONAL MARKET IN LATIN AMERICA." FUT L/A+17C CULTURE INDUS NAT/G ECO/TAC INT/TRADE ATTIT WEALTH...NEW/IDEA TREND OAS 20. PAGE 106 F2092
MARKET INT/ORG REGION

S59
REES A.,"DO UNIONS CAUSE INFLATION?" CONTROL 20. PAGE 110 F2171
LABOR ECO/TAC PRICE WORKER

S59
REUBENS E.D.,"THE BASIS FOR REORIENATION OF AMERICAN FOREIGN AID POLICY." USA+45 USSR STRUCT INT/ORG CONSULT ECO/TAC ADMIN DRIVE MORAL ORD/FREE PWR WEALTH...RELATIV MATH STAT TREND GEN/LAWS VAL/FREE 20. PAGE 111 F2180
ECO/UNDEV PLAN FOR/AID DIPLOM

S59
SOLDATI A.,"EOCNOMIC DISINTEGRATION IN EUROPE." EUR+WWI FUT WOR+45 INDUS INT/ORG NAT/G CAP/ISM WEALTH...NEW/IDEA OBS TREND CHARTS EEC 20. PAGE 124 F2438
FINAN ECO/TAC

S59
STINCHCOMBE A.L.,"BUREAUCRATIC AND CRAFT ADMINISTRATION OF PRODUCTION: A COMPARATIVE STUDY" (BMR)" USA+45 STRUCT EX/STRUC ECO/TAC GP/REL ...CLASSIF GP/COMP IDEA/COMP GEN/LAWS 20 WEBER/MAX. PAGE 126 F2490
CONSTRUC PROC/MFG ADMIN PLAN

S59
STREETEN P.,"UNBALANCED GROWTH" UK ECO/DEV AGRI MARKET TEC/DEV CAP/ISM ECO/TAC FOR/AID INT/TRADE DEMAND ORD/FREE...CONCPT 20. PAGE 127 F2502
IDEA/COMP FINAN PRODUC EQUILIB

S59
TEITSWORTH C.S.,"GROWING ROLE OF THE COMPANY ECONOMIST." USA+45 PLAN PROB/SOLV CAP/ISM ECO/TAC ADMIN ATTIT MGT. PAGE 129 F2541
INDUS CONSULT UTIL DECISION

S59
THOMPSON W.S.,"POPULATION AND PROGRESS IN THE FAR EAST." ASIA S/ASIA DIST/IND CREATE ECO/TAC WAR LOVE SKILL WEALTH...CONT/OBS TOT/POP 20. PAGE 130 F2568
ECO/UNDEV BIO/SOC GEOG

S59
TIPTON J.B.,"PARTICIPATION OF THE UNITED STATES IN THE INTERNATIONAL LABOR ORGANIZATION." USA+45 LAW STRUCT ECO/DEV ECO/UNDEV INDUS TEC/DEV ECO/TAC ADMIN PERCEPT ORD/FREE SKILL...STAT HIST/WRIT GEN/METH ILO WORK 20. PAGE 131 F2577
LABOR INT/ORG

S59
ZAUBERMAN A.,"SOVIET BLOC ECONOMIC INTEGRATION." COM CULTURE INTELL ECO/DEV INDUS TOP/EX ACT/RES PLAN ECO/TAC INT/TRADE ROUTINE CHOOSE ATTIT ...TIME/SEQ 20. PAGE 150 F2958
MARKET INT/ORG USSR TOTALISM

C59
FAINSOD M.,"GOVERNMENT AND THE AMERICAN ECONOMY." USA+45 USA-45 INDUS LABOR OP/RES PROB/SOLV ECO/TAC CONTROL...CHARTS BIBLIOG T 20. PAGE 39 F0760
CONSTN ECO/DEV CAP/ISM NAT/G

N59
CHAMBER OF COMMERCE OF USA,ECONOMIC LESSONS OF POSTWAR RECESSIONS (PAMPHLET). AFR USA+45 LAW LEGIS WORKER TAX...CHARTS 20 CONGRESS FED/RESERV. PAGE 23 F0440
ECO/DEV PROB/SOLV FINAN ECO/TAC

B60
ALLEN R.L.,SOVIET ECONOMIC WARFARE. USSR FINAN INDUS NAT/G PLAN TEC/DEV FOR/AID DETER WEALTH ...TREND GEN/LAWS FOR/TRADE 20. PAGE 4 F0072
COM ECO/TAC

B60
ANGERS F.A.,ESSAI SUR LA CENTRALISATION: ANALYSE DES PRINCIPES ET PERSPECTIVES CANADIENNES. CANADA ECO/TAC CONTROL...SOC IDEA/COMP BIBLIOG 20. PAGE 6 F0105
CENTRAL ADMIN

B60
ASPREMONT-LYNDEN H.,RAPPORT SUR L'ADMINISTRATION BELGE DU RUANDA-URUNDI PENDANT L'ANNEE 1959. BELGIUM RWANDA AGRI INDUS DIPLOM ECO/TAC INT/TRADE DOMIN ADMIN RACE/REL...GEOG CENSUS 20 UN. PAGE 7 F0132
AFR COLONIAL ECO/UNDEV INT/ORG

B60
AUSTRUY J.,STRUCTURE ECONOMIQUE ET CIVILISATION: L'EGYPTE ET LE DESTIN ECONOMIQUE DE L'ISLAM. ISLAM UAR CREATE OP/RES ECO/TAC...SOC BIBLIOG 20 MUSLIM. PAGE 8 F0142
ECO/UNDEV CULTURE STRUCT

B60
BAERWALD F.,ECONOMIC SYSTEM ANALYSIS: CONCEPTS AND PERSPECTIVES. USA+45 ECO/DEV NAT/G COMPUTER EQUILIB INCOME ATTIT...DECISION CONCPT IDEA/COMP. PAGE 8 F0151
ACT/RES ECO/TAC ROUTINE FINAN

B60
BILLERBECK K.,SOVIET BLOC FOREIGN AID TO UNDERDEVELOPED COUNTRIES. COM FUT USSR FINAN FORCES TEC/DEV DIPLOM INT/TRADE EDU/PROP NUC/PWR...TREND 20. PAGE 15 F0285
FOR/AID ECO/UNDEV ECO/TAC MARXISM

B60
BLACK E.R.,THE DIPLOMACY OF ECONOMIC DEVELOPMENT. WOR+45 CONSULT PLAN TEC/DEV DIPLOM ECO/TAC FOR/AID ...CONCPT TREND 20. PAGE 15 F0290
ECO/UNDEV ACT/RES

B60
BOHM F.,REDEN UND SCHRIFTEN UBER DIE ORDNUNG EINER FREIEN GESELLSCHAFT, EINER FREIEN WIRTSCHAFT, UND UBER DIE WIEDERGUTMACH. DIPLOM CRIME ORD/FREE RESPECT FASCISM 20 NAZI. PAGE 16 F0307
ECO/TAC NEW/LIB SUPEGO REPAR

B60
CAMPBELL R.W.,SOVIET ECONOMIC POWER. COM USA+45 DIST/IND MARKET TOP/EX ACT/RES CAP/ISM ECO/TAC DOMIN EDU/PROP ADMIN ROUTINE DRIVE...MATH TIME/SEQ CHARTS WORK 20. PAGE 21 F0409
ECO/DEV PLAN SOCISM USSR

B60
COMMITTEE ECONOMIC DEVELOPMENT,NATIONAL OBJECTIVES AND THE BALANCE OF PAYMENTS PROBLEM: A STATEMENT ON NATIONAL POLICY. USA+45 WOR+45 DIST/IND FINAN INDUS LABOR NAT/G DELIB/GP ACT/RES FOR/AID INT/TRADE ...STAT CHARTS FOR/TRADE 20. PAGE 27 F0516
ECO/DEV ECO/TAC BAL/PAY

B60
COPLAND D.,THE ADVENTURE OF GROWTH: ESSAYS ON THE AUSTRALIAN ECONOMY AND ITS INTERNATIONAL SETTING. WOR+45 DIST/IND ACADEM EDU/PROP ADMIN INCOME 20 AUSTRAL. PAGE 27 F0534
ECO/DEV ECO/UNDEV ECO/TAC INT/TRADE

B60
CROSSER P.K.,STATE CAPITALISM IN THE ECONOMY OF THE UNITED STATES. USA+45 USA-45 AGRI FINAN INDUS LABOR WORKER RATION CONTROL GOV/REL DEMAND...NEW/IDEA 20. PAGE 29 F0557
CAP/ISM ECO/DEV ECO/TAC NAT/G

B60
DALE W.B.,THE FOREIGN DEFICIT OF THE UNITED STATES. ECO/TAC TARIFFS PAY PRICE CONTROL COST WEALTH POLICY. PAGE 30 F0573
BAL/PAY DIPLOM FINAN INT/TRADE

B60
DIA M.,REFLEXIONS SUR L'ECONOMIE DE L'AFRIQUE NOIRE (REV. ED.). CULTURE ECO/UNDEV CREATE TEC/DEV DIPLOM INT/TRADE OPTIMAL ATTIT...POLICY 20. PAGE 32 F0631
AFR ECO/TAC SOCISM PLAN

B60
FIRESTONE J.M.,FEDERAL RECEIPTS AND EXPENDITURES DURING BUSINESS CYCLES, 1879-1958. USA+45 USA-45 INDUS PLAN ECO/TAC TAX WAR COST...CHARTS 19/20. PAGE 41 F0801
FINAN INCOME BUDGET NAT/G

B60
FRANCK P.G.,AFGHANISTAN: BETWEEN EAST AND WEST. AFGHANISTN AFR USA+45 USSR ECO/UNDEV PLAN ADMIN ROUTINE ATTIT PWR...STAT OBS CHARTS TOT/POP FOR/TRADE 20. PAGE 43 F0843
ECO/TAC TREND FOR/AID

B60
GILMORE D.R.,DEVELOPING THE "LITTLE" ECONOMIES. USA+45 FINAN LG/CO PROF/ORG VOL/ASSN CREATE ADMIN. PAGE 47 F0924
ECO/TAC LOC/G PROVS PLAN

B60
GRAMPP W.D.,THE MANCHESTER SCHOOL OF ECONOMICS. UK LAW ECO/DEV COERCE ATTIT ORD/FREE LAISSEZ ...PHIL/SCI IDEA/COMP 19/20 MANCHESTER CORN/LAWS. PAGE 50 F0973
ECO/TAC VOL/ASSN LOBBY NAT/G

B60
GRANICK D.,THE RED EXECUTIVE. COM USA+45 SOCIETY ECO/DEV INDUS NAT/G POL/PAR EX/STRUC PLAN ECO/TAC EDU/PROP ADMIN EXEC ATTIT DRIVE...GP/COMP 20. PAGE 50 F0976
PWR STRATA USSR ELITES

B60
HALL C.A. JR.,FISCAL POLICY FOR STABLE GROWTH. USA+45 FINAN TEC/DEV TAX COST DEMAND INCOME ...BIBLIOG 20. PAGE 53 F1045
ECO/TAC BUDGET NAT/G POLICY

B60
HEILPERIN M.A.,STUDIES IN ECONOMIC NATIONALISM. EUR+WWI MOD/EUR USA+45 ECO/DEV PLAN INT/TRADE TARIFFS WAR PRODUC PROFIT 18/20 KEYNES/JM. PAGE 58 F1140
ECO/TAC NAT/G NAT/LISM POLICY

B60
HOFFMANN P.G.,ONE HUNDRED COUNTRIES, ONE AND ONE QUARTER BILLION PEOPLE. MARKET INT/ORG TEC/DEV CAP/ISM...GEOG CHARTS METH/COMP 20 UN. PAGE 61 F1191
FOR/AID ECO/TAC ECO/UNDEV INT/TRADE

B60
KENEN P.B.,BRITISH MONETARY POLICY AND THE BALANCE OF PAYMENTS 1951-57. UK PLAN BUDGET ECO/TAC INT/TRADE PAY PRICE COST ATTIT 20. PAGE 70 F1377
BAL/PAY PROB/SOLV FINAN NAT/G

B60
KRISTENSEN T.,THE ECONOMIC WORLD BALANCE. FUT WOR+45 CULTURE ECO/DEV BAL/PWR INT/TRADE REGION PWR WEALTH...STAT TREND CHARTS 20. PAGE 73 F1442
ECO/UNDEV ECO/TAC FOR/AID

B60
LENCZOWSKI G.,OIL AND STATE IN THE MIDDLE EAST. FUT IRAN LAW ECO/UNDEV EXTR/IND NAT/G TOP/EX PLAN TEC/DEV ECO/TAC LEGIT ADMIN COERCE ATTIT ALL/VALS PWR...CHARTS 20. PAGE 78 F1519
ISLAM INDUS NAT/LISM

B60
LERNER A.P.,THE ECONOMICS OF CONTROL. USA+45 ECO/UNDEV INT/ORG ACT/RES PLAN CAP/ISM INT/TRADE ATTIT WEALTH...SOC MATH STAT GEN/LAWS INDEX 20. PAGE 78 F1530
ECO/DEV ROUTINE ECO/TAC SOCISM

B60
LISTER L.,EUROPE'S COAL AND STEEL COMMUNITY. FRANCE GERMANY STRUCT ECO/DEV EXTR/IND INDUS MARKET NAT/G DELIB/GP ECO/TAC INT/TRADE EDU/PROP ATTIT RIGID/FLEX ORD/FREE PWR WEALTH...CONCPT STAT TIME/SEQ CHARTS ECSC TERR/GP 20. PAGE 81 F1582
EUR+WWI INT/ORG REGION

B60
MYRDAL G.,BEYOND THE WELFARE STATE: ECONOMIC PLANNING AND ITS IMPLICATIONS. EUR+WWI FUT USA+45 USSR ECO/DEV ECO/UNDEV TEC/DEV SKILL WEALTH...PSY TREND FOR/TRADE 20. PAGE 96 F1881
PLAN ECO/TAC CAP/ISM

B60
PENTONY D.E.,UNITED STATES FOREIGN AID. INDIA LAOS USA+45 ECO/UNDEV INT/TRADE ADMIN PEACE ATTIT ...POLICY METH/COMP ANTHOL 20. PAGE 105 F2060
FOR/AID DIPLOM ECO/TAC

B60
PETERSON W.C.,THE WELFARE STATE IN FRANCE. EUR+WWI FRANCE FUT STRATA PROB/SOLV TAX GIVE RECEIVE INCOME ORD/FREE PWR...CHARTS 20. PAGE 105 F2070
NEW/LIB ECO/TAC WEALTH NAT/G

B60
RICHARDSON G.B.,INFORMATION AND INVESTMENT. PLAN PROB/SOLV CAP/ISM ECO/TAC KNOWL...CONCPT 20 MONEY. PAGE 111 F2184
ECO/DEV EQUILIB FINAN PHIL/SCI

B60
ROBINSON R.I.,FINANCIAL INSTITUTIONS. USA+45 PRICE GOV/REL DEMAND WEALTH...CHARTS T 20 MONEY. PAGE 113 F2226
FINAN ECO/TAC ECO/DEV BUDGET

B60
ROEPKE W.,A HUMANE ECONOMY: THE SOCIAL FRAMEWORK OF THE FREE MARKET. FUT USSR WOR+45 CULTURE SOCIETY ECO/DEV PLAN ECO/TAC ADMIN ATTIT PERSON RIGID/FLEX SUPEGO MORAL WEALTH SOCISM...POLICY OLD/LIB CONCPT TREND GEN/LAWS 20. PAGE 113 F2232
DRIVE EDU/PROP CAP/ISM

B60
ROPKE W.,A HUMANE ECONOMY. CULTURE ECO/DEV FINAN INDUS GP/REL CENTRAL WEALTH...GEOG SOC IDEA/COMP 20 EEC. PAGE 114 F2239
ECO/TAC INT/ORG DIPLOM ORD/FREE

B60
SAKAI R.K.,STUDIES ON ASIA, 1960. ASIA CHINA/COM S/ASIA COM/IND ECO/TAC...ANTHOL 17/20 MALAYA. PAGE 115 F2270
ECO/UNDEV SOC

B60
SANTHANAM K.,UNION-STATE RELATIONS IN INDIA. INDIA FINAN PROVS PLAN ECO/TAC...LING 20. PAGE 116 F2280
FEDERAL GOV/REL CONSTN POLICY

B60
SERAPHIM H.J.,ZUR GRUNDLEGUNG WIRTSCHAFTSPOLITISCHER KONZEPTIONEN (SCHRIFTEN DES VEREINS FUR SOZIALPOLITIK, N.F. BAND 18). GERMANY/W WOR+45 ECO/DEV DELIB/GP ACT/RES ECO/TAC INGP/REL ORD/FREE...CONCPT IDEA/COMP GEN/LAWS 20. PAGE 120 F2358
POLICY PHIL/SCI PLAN

B60
SHONFIELD A.,THE ATTACK ON WORLD POVERTY. WOR+45 ECO/DEV ECO/UNDEV FINAN VOL/ASSN PLAN EDU/PROP DRIVE KNOWL WEALTH...CONT/OBS STAND/INT ORG/CHARTS TOT/POP UNESCO 20. PAGE 121 F2383
INT/ORG ECO/TAC FOR/AID INT/TRADE

B60
SIEGEL B.N.,AGGREGATE ECONOMICS AND PUBLIC POLICY. ECO/DEV TEC/DEV ECO/TAC TASK DEMAND EQUILIB INCOME ...CHARTS 20. PAGE 121 F2396
ECOMETRIC WEALTH PRODUC MARKET

B60
SILK L.S.,THE RESEARCH REVOLUTION. USA+45 FINAN CAP/ISM ECO/TAC PRICE EQUILIB PRODUC...STAT TREND CHARTS. PAGE 122 F2402
ECO/DEV R+D TEC/DEV PROB/SOLV

B60
STANFORD RESEARCH INSTITUTE,AFRICAN DEVELOPMENT: A TEST FOR INTERNATIONAL COOPERATION. AFR USA+45 WOR+45 FINAN INT/ORG PLAN PROB/SOLV ECO/TAC INT/TRADE ADMIN...CHARTS 20. PAGE 125 F2467
FOR/AID ECO/UNDEV ATTIT DIPLOM

B60
STEIN E.,AMERICAN ENTERPRISE IN THE EUROPEAN COMMON MARKET: A LEGAL PROFILE. EUR+WWI FUT USA+45 SOCIETY STRUCT ECO/DEV NAT/G VOL/ASSN CONSULT PLAN TEC/DEV ECO/TAC INT/TRADE ADMIN ATTIT RIGID/FLEX PWR...MGT NEW/IDEA STAT TREND COMPUT/IR SIMUL EEC 20. PAGE 125 F2475
MARKET ADJUD INT/LAW

B60
STOLPER W.F.,GERMANY BETWEEN EAST AND WEST: THE ECONOMICS OF COMPETITIVE COEXISTENCE. AFR FUT GERMANY/E GERMANY/W WOR+45 FINAN POL/PAR BUDGET ECO/TAC FOR/AID INT/TRADE...STAT CHARTS METH/COMP 20. PAGE 126 F2495
ECO/DEV DIPLOM GOV/COMP BAL/PWR

B60
THEOBALD R.,THE RICH AND THE POOR: A STUDY OF THE ECONOMICS OF RISING EXPECTATIONS. WOR+45 CONSTN ECO/DEV ECO/UNDEV INT/ORG NAT/G PLAN FOR/AID ROUTINE BAL/PAY ORD/FREE PWR WEALTH...GEOG TREND WORK FOR/TRADE 20. PAGE 129 F2553
ECO/TAC INT/TRADE

B60
THORBECKE E.,THE TENDENCY TOWARDS REGIONALIZATION IN INTERNATIONAL TRADE, 1928-1956. WOR+45 WOR-45 ECO/DEV FINAN ECO/TAC WEALTH...GEOG CHARTS TOT/POP FOR/TRADE 20. PAGE 130 F2569
STAT BAL/PAY REGION

B60
US HOUSE COMM GOVT OPERATIONS,OPERATIONS OF THE DEVELOPMENT LOAN FUND: HEARINGS (COMMITTEE ON GOVERNMENT OPERATIONS). USA+45 PLAN BUDGET DIPLOM GOV/REL COST...CHARTS 20 CONGRESS DEPT/STATE AID. PAGE 137 F2698
FINAN FOR/AID ECO/TAC EFFICIENCY

B60
US OPERATIONS MISSION - TURKEY,SOME POSSIBILITIES FOR ACCELERATING TURKEY'S ECONOMIC GROWTH. TURKEY USA+45 AGRI FINAN INDUS NAT/G ACT/RES BUDGET COST ...CHARTS 20. PAGE 138 F2724
ECO/UNDEV ECO/TAC FOR/AID PRODUC

B60
VERNON R.,METROPOLIS 1985. LOC/G PLAN TAX LEAD PWR MUNICH. PAGE 141 F2780
REGION ECO/TAC DECISION

B60
WALLICH H.C.,THE COST OF FREEDOM: A NEW LOOK AT CAPITALISM. USA+45 SOCIETY ECO/DEV INGP/REL CONSEN LAISSEZ SOCISM...OLD/LIB IDEA/COMP. PAGE 143 F2810
CAP/ISM ORD/FREE POLICY ECO/TAC

B60
WATSON D.S.,ECONOMIC POLICY: BUSINESS AND GOVERNMENT. USA+45 FINAN LABOR PLAN BUDGET INT/TRADE GP/REL WEALTH LAISSEZ...CHARTS T. PAGE 144 F2832
ECO/TAC NAT/G POLICY ECO/DEV

B60
WENTHOLT W.,INFLATION OR SECURITY? EUR+WWI USA+45 INDUS CONSULT TEC/DEV CAP/ISM DIPLOM FOR/AID INT/TRADE MARXISM 20 EEC. PAGE 145 F2858
ECO/DEV ECO/TAC FINAN ORD/FREE

L60
CHENERY H.B.,"PATTERNS OF INDUSTRIAL GROWTH." INT/TRADE DEMAND PRODUC...MATH REGRESS CHARTS SIMUL METH 20. PAGE 24 F0462
ECO/TAC ECO/DEV GP/COMP CON/ANAL

L60
SPENGLER J.J.,"ECONOMIC DEVELOPMENT: POLITICAL PRECONDITIONS AND POLITICAL CONSEQUENCE." WOR+45 STRUCT ECO/UNDEV NAT/G PLAN ECO/TAC EDU/PROP ATTIT ORD/FREE WEALTH SOCISM...SOC CONCPT TREND SIMUL GEN/METH WORK 20. PAGE 124 F2452
TEC/DEV METH/CNCPT CAP/ISM

S60
"THE EMERGING COMMON MARKETS IN LATIN AMERICA." FUT L/A+17C STRATA DIST/IND INDUS LABOR NAT/G LEGIS ECO/TAC ADMIN RIGID/FLEX HEALTH...NEW/IDEA TIME/SEQ OAS 20. PAGE 1 F0013
FINAN ECO/UNDEV INT/TRADE

S60
BARNETT H.J.,"RESEARCH AND DEVELOPMENT, ECONOMIC GROWTH, AND NATIONAL SECURITY." AFR USA+45 R+D CREATE ECO/TAC ATTIT DRIVE PWR...POLICY SOC METH/CNCPT QUANT STAT TIME/SEQ ORG/CHARTS LOG/LING 20. PAGE 10 F0190
ACT/RES PLAN

S60
BECKER A.S.,"COMPARISIONS OF UNITED STATES AND USSR NATIONAL OUTPUT: SOME RULES OF THE GAME." COM USA+45 ECO/DEV AGRI DIST/IND INDUS R+D CONSULT PLAN ECO/TAC RIGID/FLEX KNOWL...METH/CNCPT CHARTS 20. PAGE 12 F0227
STAT USSR

S60
BERG E.J.,"ECONOMIC BASIS OF POLITICAL CHOICE IN FRENCH WEST AFRICA." FRANCE ECO/UNDEV AGRI INDUS NAT/G PLAN LEGIT COLONIAL REGION ATTIT PWR WEALTH ...CONCPT FOR/TRADE 20. PAGE 13 F0257
AFR ECO/TAC

S60
BUTLER W.F.,"ECONOMIC PROGRESS IN LATIN AMERICA." L/A+17C USA+45 ECO/UNDEV AGRI FINAN NAT/G PLAN ECO/TAC FOR/AID ADMIN WEALTH...OLD/LIB TOT/POP 20.
INDUS ACT/RES

PAGE 21 F0397

S60

DUNN J.M.,"AMERICAN DEPENDENCE ON MATERIALS IMPORTS: THE WORLD-WIDE RESOURCE BASE." USA+45 WOR+45 NAT/G ATTIT WEALTH...RECORD TIME/SEQ CHARTS FOR/TRADE 20. PAGE 35 F0680 ACT/RES ECO/TAC

S60

FRANKEL S.H.,"ECONOMIC ASPECTS OF POLITICAL INDEPENDENCE IN AFRICA." AFR FUT SOCIETY ECO/UNDEV COM/IND FINAN LEGIS PLAN TEC/DEV CAP/ISM ECO/TAC INT/TRADE ADMIN ATTIT DRIVE RIGID/FLEX PWR WEALTH ...MGT NEW/IDEA MATH TIME/SEQ VAL/FREE 20. PAGE 43 F0846 NAT/G FOR/AID

S60

GARNICK D.H.,"ON THE ECONOMIC FEASIBILITY OF A MIDDLE EASTERN COMMON MARKET." AFR ISLAM CULTURE INDUS NAT/G PLAN TEC/DEV ECO/TAC ADMIN ATTIT DRIVE RIGID/FLEX...PLURIST STAT TREND GEN/LAWS 20. PAGE 46 F0907 MARKET INT/TRADE

S60

GROSSMAN G.,"SOVIET GROWTH: ROUTINE, INERTIA, AND PRESSURE." COM STRATA NAT/G DELIB/GP PLAN TEC/DEV ECO/TAC EDU/PROP ADMIN ROUTINE DRIVE WEALTH 20. PAGE 52 F1007 POL/PAR ECO/DEV AFR USSR

S60

HERRERA F.,"THE INTER-AMERICAN DEVELOPMENT BANK." USA+45 ECO/UNDEV INT/ORG CONSULT DELIB/GP PLAN ECO/TAC INT/TRADE ROUTINE WEALTH...STAT TERR/GP 20. PAGE 59 F1153 L/A+17C FINAN FOR/AID REGION

S60

HOOVER C.B.,"NATIONAL POLICY AND RATES OF ECONOMIC GROWTH: THE US SOVIET RUSSIA AND WESTERN EUROPE." COM EUR+WWI USA+45 USSR NAT/G PLAN ECO/TAC PWR WEALTH...MATH STAT GEN/LAWS 20. PAGE 61 F1207 ECO/DEV ACT/RES

S60

JACOBSON H.K.,"THE USSR AND ILO." AFR COM STRUCT ECO/DEV ECO/UNDEV CONSULT DELIB/GP ECO/TAC ILO WORK 20. PAGE 66 F1298 INT/ORG LABOR USSR

S60

KREININ M.E.,"THE 'OUTER-SEVEN' AND EUROPEAN INTEGRATION." EUR+WWI FRANCE GERMANY ITALY UK ECO/DEV DIST/IND INT/TRADE DRIVE WEALTH...MYTH CHARTS EEC OEEC 20. PAGE 73 F1436 ECO/TAC GEN/LAWS

S60

LINDHOLM R.W.,"ACCELERATED DEVELOPMENT WITH A MINIMUM OF FOREIGN AID AND ECONOMIC CONTROLS." SOCIETY INDUS ECO/TAC WEALTH...CONCPT 20. PAGE 80 F1570 ECO/DEV FINAN FOR/AID

S60

MIKESELL R.F.,"AMERICA'S ECONOMIC RESPONSIBILITY AS A GREAT POWER." COM FUT USA+45 USSR WOR+45 INT/ORG PLAN ECO/TAC FOR/AID EDU/PROP CHOOSE WEALTH ...POLICY 20. PAGE 91 F1781 ECO/UNDEV BAL/PWR CAP/ISM

S60

MILLER A.S.,"SOME OBSERVATIONS ON THE POLITICAL ECONOMY OF POPULATION GROWTH." FUT USA+45 ECO/DEV R+D CONSULT PLAN TEC/DEV ECO/TAC ROUTINE BIO/SOC WEALTH...POLICY OBS. PAGE 91 F1790 SOCIETY GEOG

S60

MORALES C.J.,"TRADE AND ECONOMIC INTEGRATION IN LATIN AMERICA." FUT L/A+17C LAW STRATA ECO/UNDEV DIST/IND INDUS LABOR NAT/G LEGIS ECO/TAC ADMIN RIGID/FLEX WEALTH...CONCPT NEW/IDEA CONT/OBS TIME/SEQ WORK 20. PAGE 93 F1825 FINAN INT/TRADE REGION

S60

MURPHEY R.,"ECONOMIC CONFLICTS IN SOUTH ASIA." ASIA CULTURE INTELL ECO/TAC REGION ATTIT DRIVE KNOWL ...METH/CNCPT TIME/SEQ STERTYP TOT/POP METH/GP VAL/FREE 20. PAGE 95 F1864 S/ASIA ECO/UNDEV

S60

NEISSER H.,"ECONOMIC IMPERIALISM RECONSIDERED." WOR+45 WOR-45 ECO/DEV ECO/UNDEV DIST/IND LEGIT COLONIAL PWR WEALTH SOCISM...MYTH MATH TIME/SEQ 20. PAGE 97 F1909 ACT/RES ECO/TAC CAP/ISM INT/TRADE

S60

NICHOLS J.P.,"HAZARDS OF AMERICAN PRIVATE INVESTMENT IN UNDERDEVELOPED COUNTRIES." FUT L/A+17C USA+45 USA-45 EXTR/IND CONSULT BAL/PWR ECO/TAC DOMIN ADJUD ATTIT SOVEREIGN WEALTH ...HIST/WRIT TIME/SEQ TREND TERR/GP VAL/FREE 20. PAGE 98 F1924 FINAN ECO/UNDEV CAP/ISM NAT/LISM

S60

OWEN C.F.,"US AND SOVIET RELATIONS WITH UNDERDEVELOPED COUNTRIES: LATIN AMERICA-A CASE STUDY." AFR COM L/A+17C USA+45 USSR EXTR/IND MARKET TEC/DEV DIPLOM ECO/TAC NAT/LISM ORD/FREE PWR ...TREND WORK 20. PAGE 102 F2005 ECO/UNDEV DRIVE INT/TRADE

S60

PYE L.W.,"SOVIET AND AMERICAN STYLES IN FOREIGN AID." COM USA+45 USSR WOR+45 NAT/G PLAN ECO/TAC ROUTINE RIGID/FLEX...POLICY CONCPT TREND GEN/LAWS TOT/POP 20. PAGE 108 F2132 ECO/UNDEV ATTIT FOR/AID

S60

RICHTER J.H.,"TOWARDS AN INTERNATIONAL POLICY ON AGRICULTURAL TRADE." EUR+WWI USA+45 ECO/DEV NAT/G PLAN ECO/TAC ATTIT PWR WEALTH...CONCPT GEN/LAWS 20. AGRI INT/ORG

PAGE 111 F2187

S60

RIVKIN A.,"AFRICAN ECONOMIC DEVELOPMENT: ADVANCED TECHNOLOGY AND THE STAGES OF GROWTH." CULTURE ECO/UNDEV AGRI COM/IND EXTR/IND PLAN ECO/TAC ATTIT DRIVE RIGID/FLEX SKILL WEALTH...MGT SOC GEN/LAWS FOR/TRADE WORK TOT/POP 20. PAGE 111 F2195 AFR TEC/DEV FOR/AID

S60

STOCKWELL E.G.,"THE MEASUREMENT OF ECONOMIC DEVELOPMENT." WOR+45 SOCIETY ECO/DEV ECO/UNDEV INDUS ECO/TAC HEALTH WEALTH...WELF/ST GEOG METH/CNCPT CHARTS METH METH/GP 20. PAGE 126 F2492 FAM STAT

B61

ACKLEY G.,MACROECONOMIC THEORY. AFR FINAN WORKER ECO/TAC PRICE COST INCOME PRODUC...MATH TREND CHARTS IDEA/COMP T KEYNES/JM. PAGE 2 F0034 SIMUL ECOMETRIC WEALTH

B61

ALFRED H.,PUBLIC OWNERSHIP IN THE USA: GOALS AND PRIORITIES. LAW INDUS INT/TRADE ADJUD GOV/REL EFFICIENCY PEACE SOCISM...POLICY ANTHOL 20 TVA. PAGE 4 F0065 CONTROL OWN ECO/DEV ECO/TAC

B61

ASHER R.E.,GRANTS, LOANS, AND LOCAL CURRENCIES; THEIR ROLE IN FOREIGN AID. AFR USA+45 ECO/UNDEV INT/ORG ACT/RES PLAN ECO/TAC GIVE CONTROL WEALTH 20. PAGE 7 F0130 FOR/AID FINAN NAT/G BUDGET

B61

AUBREY H.G.,COEXISTENCE: ECONOMIC CHALLENGE AND RESPONSE. AFR USSR WOR+45 ACT/RES BAL/PWR CAP/ISM DIPLOM ECO/TAC FOR/AID INT/TRADE PEACE SOCISM ...METH/COMP NAT/COMP. PAGE 7 F0139 POLICY ECO/UNDEV PLAN COM

B61

BALASSA B.,THE THEORY OF ECONOMIC INTEGRATION. EUR+WWI L/A+17C MOD/EUR WOR+45 ECO/UNDEV MARKET INT/ORG NAT/G VOL/ASSN DELIB/GP PLAN CAP/ISM ECO/TAC...MAJORIT FOR/TRADE OEEC 20. PAGE 8 F0157 ECO/DEV ACT/RES INT/TRADE

B61

BAUER P.T.,INDIAN ECONOMIC POLICY AND DEVELOPMENT. INDIA STRATA AGRI FINAN POL/PAR BUDGET FOR/AID GOV/REL EFFICIENCY...CENSUS 20. PAGE 11 F0216 ECO/UNDEV ECO/TAC POLICY PLAN

B61

BENOIT E.,EUROPE AT SIXES AND SEVENS: THE COMMON MARKET, THE FREE TRADE ASSOCIATION AND THE UNITED STATES. EUR+WWI FUT USA+45 INDUS CONSULT DELIB/GP EX/STRUC TOP/EX ACT/RES ECO/TAC EDU/PROP ROUTINE CHOOSE PERCEPT WEALTH...MGT TREND EEC FOR/TRADE TOT/POP 20 EFTA. PAGE 13 F0249 FINAN ECO/DEV VOL/ASSN

B61

BONNEFOUS M.,EUROPE ET TIERS MONDE. EUR+WWI SOCIETY INT/ORG NAT/G VOL/ASSN ACT/RES TEC/DEV CAP/ISM ECO/TAC ATTIT ORD/FREE SOVEREIGN...POLICY CONCPT TREND TERR/GP COMMUN 20. PAGE 16 F0314 AFR ECO/UNDEV FOR/AID INT/TRADE

B61

BREWIS T.N.,CANADIAN ECONOMIC POLICY. AFR CANADA BUDGET CAP/ISM INT/TRADE RATION TARIFFS TAX PRICE CONTROL ROUTINE FEDERAL INCOME PRODUC 20. PAGE 18 F0348 ECO/DEV ECO/TAC NAT/G PLAN

B61

CANTERBERY E.R.,THE PRESIDENT'S COUNCIL OF ECONOMIC ADVISERS. AFR USA+45 FINAN LABOR NAT/G PLAN ADMIN OPTIMAL WEALTH 20 EISNHWR/DD PRESIDENT TRUMAN/HS KEYNES/JM. PAGE 21 F0413 ECO/TAC OP/RES EXEC CHIEF

B61

CARNEY D.E.,GOVERNMENT AND ECONOMY IN BRITISH WEST AFRICA. GAMBIA GHANA NIGERIA SIER/LEONE DOMIN ADMIN GOV/REL SOVEREIGN WEALTH LAISSEZ...BIBLIOG 20 CMN/WLTH. PAGE 21 F0417 METH/COMP COLONIAL ECO/TAC ECO/UNDEV

B61

CLARK J.M.,COMPETITION AS A DYNAMIC PROCESS. ECO/DEV EXTR/IND INDUS LG/CO TEC/DEV ECO/TAC PRICE EQUILIB PRODUC...NEW/IDEA CAP 20. PAGE 25 F0483 WEALTH GP/REL FINAN PROFIT

B61

DIMOCK M.E.,BUSINESS AND GOVERNMENT (4TH ED.). AGRI FINAN OP/RES PLAN BUDGET DIPLOM LOBBY NUC/PWR NEW/LIB SOCISM...POLICY BIBLIOG 20. PAGE 33 F0641 NAT/G INDUS LABOR ECO/TAC

B61

DUKE UNIVERSITY,EXPULSION OR OPPRESSION OF BUSINESS ASSOCIATES: "SQUEEZE-OUTS" IN SMALL ENTERPRISES. LAW CONTROL PARTIC COERCE INGP/REL...POLICY RECORD INT. PAGE 35 F0674 PWR MGT SML/CO ECO/TAC

B61

EINZIG P.,A DYNAMIC THEORY OF FORWARD EXCHANGE. FUT WOR+45 INT/TRADE BAL/PAY WEALTH...OLD/LIB NEW/IDEA OBS TREND FOR/TRADE 20. PAGE 37 F0713 FINAN ECO/TAC

B61

ELLIS H.S.,ECONOMIC DEVELOPMENT FOR LATIN AMERICA. L/A+17C AGRI FINAN INDUS FOR/AID GP/REL BAL/PAY DEMAND...ANTHOL 20 INTL/ECON. PAGE 37 F0723 ECO/UNDEV ECO/TAC PLAN INT/TRADE

B61

ESTEBAN J.C.,IMPERIALISMO Y DESARROLLO ECONOMICO. L/A+17C FINAN INDUS NAT/G ECO/TAC CONTROL ROLE. PAGE 38 F0747 ECO/UNDEV NAT/LISM DIPLOM

BAL/PAY

B61
FELLNER W.,THE PROBLEM OF RISING PRICES. AGRI INDUS WORKER BUDGET CAP/ISM ECO/TAC INT/TRADE PAY DEMAND ...POLICY 20 EEC. PAGE 40 F0780
PRICE MARKET ECO/DEV COST

B61
FERTIG L.,PROSPERITY THROUGH FREEDOM. COM INDUS LABOR CAP/ISM ECO/TAC PRODUC PROFIT ORD/FREE WEALTH SOCISM...METH/CNCPT 20. PAGE 40 F0788
NAT/G CONTROL POLICY

B61
GALENSON W.,TRADE UNION DEMOCRACY IN WESTERN EUROPE. ECO/DEV INDUS PROF/ORG WORKER INCOME ...METH/COMP 20. PAGE 45 F0886
LABOR GP/REL ECO/TAC EUR+WWI

B61
GANGULI B.N.,ECONOMIC INTEGRATION. FINAN LABOR CAP/ISM DIPLOM WEALTH...NAT/COMP 20. PAGE 46 F0895
ECO/TAC METH/CNCPT EQUILIB ECO/UNDEV

B61
GREY A.L.,ECONOMIC ISSUES AND POLICIES; READINGS IN INTRODUCTORY ECONOMICS (2ND ED.). WOR+45 ECO/UNDEV FINAN MARKET LABOR LG/CO INT/TRADE BAL/PAY WEALTH ...ANTHOL T. PAGE 51 F0996
ECO/TAC PROB/SOLV METH/COMP

B61
GURTOO D.H.N.,INDIA'S BALANCE OF PAYMENTS (1920-1960). INDIA FINAN DIPLOM FOR/AID INT/TRADE PRICE COLONIAL...CHARTS BIBLIOG 20. PAGE 52 F1014
BAL/PAY STAT ECO/TAC ECO/UNDEV

B61
HARDT J.P.,THE COLD WAR ECONOMIC GAP. AFR USA+45 USSR ECO/DEV FORCES INT/TRADE NUC/PWR PWR 20. PAGE 55 F1081
DIPLOM ECO/TAC NAT/COMP POLICY

B61
HARRIS S.E.,THE DOLLAR IN CRISIS. AFR USA+45 MARKET INT/ORG ECO/TAC PRICE CONTROL WEALTH...METH/COMP ANTHOL 20. PAGE 55 F1089
BAL/PAY DIPLOM FINAN INT/TRADE

B61
HAUSER M.,DIE URSACHEN DER FRANZOSISCHEN INFLATION IN DEN JAHREN 1946-1952. AFR FRANCE INDUS NAT/G BUDGET DIPLOM ECO/TAC FOR/AID COST MONEY 20. PAGE 57 F1114
ECO/DEV FINAN PRICE

B61
HICKS U.K.,FEDERALISM AND ECONOMIC GROWTH IN UNDERDEVELOPED COUNTRIES. WOR+45 WOR-45 FINAN NAT/G PLAN BUDGET DIPLOM INT/TRADE DEMAND WEALTH...ANTHOL 20. PAGE 59 F1167
ECO/UNDEV ECO/TAC FEDERAL CONSTN

B61
HOLMANS A.E.,UNITED STATES FISCAL POLICY 1945-1959. AFR USA+45 USA-45 ECO/DEV TAX PRICE WAR...BIBLIOG 20 DEMOCRAT REPUBLICAN. PAGE 61 F1200
POLICY BUDGET NAT/G ECO/TAC

B61
HORVATH B.,THE CHARACTERISTICS OF YUGOSLAV ECONOMIC DEVELOPMENT. COM ECO/UNDEV AGRI INDUS PLAN CAP/ISM ECO/TAC ROUTINE WEALTH...SOCIALIST STAT CHARTS STERTYP WORK 20. PAGE 62 F1217
ACT/RES YUGOSLAVIA

B61
INTL BANKING SUMMER SCHOOL,TRENDS IN BANK CREDIT AND FINANCE. EUR+WWI NETHERLAND ECO/DEV PROF/ORG PLAN BUDGET 20 EEC. PAGE 65 F1283
FINAN ECO/TAC NAT/G LG/CO

B61
KELSO L.O.,THE NEW CAPITALISTS: A PROPOSAL TO FREE ECONOMIC GROWTH FROM THE SLAVERY OF SAVINGS. UNIV USA+45 ECO/DEV CAP/ISM PRODUC WEALTH SOCISM ...NEW/IDEA 20. PAGE 70 F1373
ECO/TAC WORKER FINAN GEN/LAWS

B61
KITZINGER V.W.,THE CHALLENGE OF THE COMMON MARKET. EUR+WWI ECO/DEV DIST/IND PLAN ECO/TAC INT/TRADE LEGIT ATTIT PWR WEALTH...TIME/SEQ TREND CHARTS EEC 20. PAGE 71 F1403
MARKET INT/ORG UK

B61
LAHAYE R.,LES ENTREPRISES PUBLIQUES AU MAROC. FRANCE MOROCCO LAW DIST/IND EXTR/IND FINAN CONSULT PLAN TEC/DEV ADMIN AGREE CONTROL OWN...POLICY 20. PAGE 74 F1460
NAT/G INDUS ECO/UNDEV ECO/TAC

B61
LENIN V.I.,WHAT IS TO BE DONE? (1902). RUSSIA LABOR NAT/G POL/PAR WORKER CAP/ISM ECO/TAC ADMIN PARTIC ...MARXIST IDEA/COMP GEN/LAWS 19/20. PAGE 78 F1522
EDU/PROP PRESS MARXISM METH/COMP

B61
LETHBRIDGE H.J.,CHINA'S URBAN COMMUNES. CHINA/COM FUT ECO/UNDEV DIPLOM EDU/PROP DEMAND INCOME MARXISM ...POLICY MUNICH 20. PAGE 78 F1534
CONTROL ECO/TAC NAT/G

B61
LICHTHEIM G.,MARXISM. GERMANY SOCIETY WORKER CAP/ISM ECO/TAC NAT/LISM POPULISM...TIME/SEQ GOV/COMP NAT/COMP 18/20 COM/PARTY. PAGE 80 F1559
MARXISM SOCISM IDEA/COMP CULTURE

B61
MACMAHON A.W.,DELEGATION AND AUTONOMY. INDIA STRUCT LEGIS BARGAIN BUDGET ECO/TAC LEGIT EXEC REPRESENT GOV/REL CENTRAL DEMAND EFFICIENCY PRODUC. PAGE 84 F1637
ADMIN PLAN FEDERAL

B61
MCCRACKEN H.L.,KEYNESIAN ECONOMICS IN THE STREAM OF ECONOMIC THOUGHT. FINAN MARKET BARGAIN EFFICIENCY OPTIMAL...PHIL/SCI CONCPT IDEA/COMP BIBLIOG 18/20 KEYNES/JM. PAGE 88 F1724
ECO/TAC DEMAND ECOMETRIC

B61
MIT CENTER INTERNATIONAL STU,OFFICIAL SERIAL PUBLICATIONS RELATING TO ECONOMIC DEVELOPMENT IN AFRICA SOUTH OF THE SAHARA. AFR SOCIETY AGRI FINAN INDUS LG/CO ADMIN 20. PAGE 92 F1806
BIBLIOG ECO/UNDEV ECO/TAC NAT/G

B61
MORRIS B.R.,PROBLEMS OF AMERICAN ECONOMIC GROWTH. USA+45 LABOR WORKER BUDGET ECO/TAC INT/TRADE EQUILIB 20. PAGE 94 F1836
ECO/DEV POLICY TEC/DEV DEMAND

B61
MYRDAL G.,THE POLITICAL ELEMENT IN THE DEVELOPMENT OF ECONOMIC THEORY. FINAN LOBBY ATTIT...WELF/ST CONCPT IDEA/COMP GEN/LAWS 20. PAGE 95 F1875
ECO/DEV ECO/TAC SOCIETY

B61
NORTH D.C.,THE ECONOMIC GROWTH OF THE UNITED STATES 1790-1860. USA-45 INDUS TEC/DEV CAP/ISM ECO/TAC PRICE COST DEMAND LAISSEZ...ECOMETRIC STAT TREND 19. PAGE 98 F1933
AGRI ECO/UNDEV

B61
NOVE A.,THE SOVIET ECONOMY. USSR ECO/DEV FINAN NAT/G ECO/TAC PRICE ADMIN EFFICIENCY MARXISM ...TREND BIBLIOG 20. PAGE 99 F1943
PLAN PRODUC POLICY

B61
OECD,STATISTICS OF BALANCE OF PAYMENTS 1950-61. WOR+45 FINAN ECO/TAC INT/TRADE DEMAND WEALTH...STAT NAT/COMP 20 OEEC OECD. PAGE 100 F1965
BAL/PAY ECO/DEV INT/ORG CHARTS

B61
PAUNIO J.J.,A STUDY IN THE THEORY OF OPEN INFLATION. AFR FINAN CAP/ISM PRICE DEMAND INCOME ...CHARTS BIBLIOG 20. PAGE 104 F2040
ACT/RES ECO/DEV ECO/TAC COST

B61
PERLO V.,EL IMPERIALISMO NORTHEAMERICANO. USA+45 USA-45 FINAN CAP/ISM DIPLOM DOMIN CONTROL DISCRIM 19/20. PAGE 105 F2063
SOCIALIST ECO/DEV INT/TRADE ECO/TAC

B61
PETCH G.A.,ECONOMIC DEVELOPMENT AND MODERN WEST AFRICA. AFR CONGO/BRAZ GHANA NIGER SIER/LEONE AGRI MARKET LABOR FOR/AID TAX COST EFFICIENCY EQUILIB PRODUC...GEOG TREND 20. PAGE 105 F2068
ECO/UNDEV TEC/DEV EXTR/IND ECO/TAC

B61
ROEPKE W.,JENSEITS VON ANGEBOT UND NACHFRAGE (DRITTE VERAENDERTE AUFLAGE). WOR+45 MARKET TEC/DEV ECO/TAC GP/REL INGP/REL NEW/LIB...POLICY SOC IDEA/COMP PERS/COMP 20. PAGE 113 F2233
SOCIETY STRANGE ECO/DEV STRUCT

B61
SAKAI R.K.,STUDIES ON ASIA, 1961. ASIA BURMA INDIA S/ASIA FINAN ECO/TAC NAT/LISM SOCISM...POLICY ANTHOL 19/20 CHINJAP. PAGE 115 F2271
ECO/UNDEV SECT

B61
SCAMMEL W.M.,INTERNATIONAL MONETARY POLICY. WOR+45 WOR-45 ACT/RES ECO/TAC LEGIT WEALTH...GEN/METH UN 20. PAGE 116 F2286
INT/ORG FINAN BAL/PAY

B61
SCHWARTZ H.,THE RED PHOENIX: RUSSIA SINCE WORLD WAR II. USA+45 WOR+45 ELITES POL/PAR TEC/DEV ECO/TAC MARXISM. PAGE 118 F2325
DIPLOM NAT/G ECO/DEV

B61
SPOONER F.P.,SOUTH AFRICAN PREDICAMENT. FUT SOUTH/AFR INDUS POL/PAR RACE/REL INCOME...CHARTS 20 NEGRO. PAGE 125 F2459
ECO/DEV DISCRIM ECO/TAC POLICY

B61
STANLEY C.J.,LATE CH'ING FINANCE: HU KUANG-YUNG AS AN INNOVATOR. ASIA NAT/G FORCES BUDGET TAX WAR GOV/REL COST...POLICY BIOG CHARTS BIBLIOG 19. PAGE 125 F2469
FINAN ECO/TAC CIVMIL/REL ADMIN

B61
STARK H.,SOCIAL AND ECONOMIC FRONTIERS IN LATIN AMERICA (2ND ED.). CUBA FUT CULTURE AGRI INDUS ECO/TAC PRODUC ATTIT MARXISM...NAT/COMP BIBLIOG T 20. PAGE 125 F2470
L/A+17C SOCIETY DIPLOM ECO/UNDEV

B61
STOCKING G.W.,WORKABLE COMPETITION AND ANTITRUST POLICY. USA+45 NAT/G CONSULT PLAN PRICE GOV/REL COST DEMAND PROFIT...POLICY 20. PAGE 126 F2491
LG/CO INDUS ECO/TAC CONTROL

B61
THEOBALD R.,THE CHALLENGE OF ABUNDANCE. USA+45 WOR+45 MARKET DIPLOM FOR/AID REV PRODUC UTOPIA SUPEGO...POLICY TREND BIBLIOG/A 20. PAGE 129 F2554
WELF/ST ECO/UNDEV PROB/SOLV ECO/TAC

B61
TRIFFIN R.,GOLD AND THE DOLLAR CRISIS: THE FUTURE OF CONVERTIBILITY. AFR USA+45 USA-45 INT/ORG
FINAN ECO/DEV

PROB/SOLV BUDGET INT/TRADE PRICE...STAT CHARTS 19/20. PAGE 131 F2588
ECO/TAC BAL/PAY

B61
US SENATE COMM ON FOREIGN RELS,INTERNATIONAL DEVELOPMENT AND SECURITY: HEARINGS ON BILL (2 VOLS.). ECO/UNDEV FINAN FORCES REV COST WEALTH ...CHARTS 20 AID PRESIDENT. PAGE 139 F2747
FOR/AID CIVMIL/REL ORD/FREE ECO/TAC

B61
VEIT O.,GRUNDRISS DER WAHRUNGSPOLITIK. AFR FRANCE GERMANY USSR DIPLOM INT/TRADE...NAT/COMP 19/20 SILVER. PAGE 141 F2773
FINAN POLICY ECO/TAC CAP/ISM

B61
WAGLE S.S.,TECHNIQUE OF PLANNING FOR ACCELERATED ECONOMIC GROWTH OF UNDERDEVELOPED COUNTRIES. WOR+45 ACT/RES PROB/SOLV RATION BAL/PAY DEMAND INCOME 20. PAGE 142 F2798
ECO/UNDEV PLAN INDUS ECO/TAC

B61
WARD B.J.,INDIA AND THE WEST. INDIA UK USA+45 INT/TRADE GIVE COLONIAL ATTIT MARXISM 19/20. PAGE 143 F2817
PLAN ECO/UNDEV ECO/TAC FOR/AID

B61
WILSON T.,INFLATION. FINAN PLAN CAP/ISM PRICE CONTROL...CHARTS 20. PAGE 147 F2903
ECO/DEV ECO/TAC POLICY COST

B61
WRIGHT H.M.,THE "NEW IMPERIALISM": ANALYSIS OF LATE NINETEENTH-CENTURY EXPANSION. MOD/EUR WOR-45 SOCIETY FINAN ECO/TAC INT/TRADE NAT/LISM...ANTHOL BIBLIOG/A 19. PAGE 149 F2933
HIST/WRIT IDEA/COMP COLONIAL DOMIN

L61
CHENERY H.B.,"COMPARATIVE ADVANTAGE AND DEVELOPMENT POLICY." FINAN INT/TRADE RATION OPTIMAL...CHARTS METH/COMP GEN/LAWS BIBLIOG 20 RESOURCE/N. PAGE 24 F0463
ECO/UNDEV ECO/TAC PLAN EFFICIENCY

S61
BARALL M.,"THE UNITED STATES GOVERNMENT RESPONDS." L/A+17C USA+45 SOCIETY NAT/G CREATE PLAN DIPLOM ECO/TAC ATTIT DRIVE RIGID/FLEX KNOWL SKILL WEALTH ...METH/CNCPT TIME/SEQ GEN/METH 20. PAGE 9 F0176
ECO/UNDEV ACT/RES FOR/AID

S61
BENOIT E.,"THE PROPENSITY TO REDUCE THE NATIONAL DEBT OUT OF DEFENSE SAVINGS." FUT USA+45 SOCIETY R+D PLAN...WELF/ST SOC REC/INT STERTYP TOT/POP 20. PAGE 13 F0250
WEALTH ECO/TAC

S61
DALTON G.,"ECONOMIC THEORY AND PRIMITIVE SOCIETY" (BMR)" UNIV AGRI KIN TEC/DEV ECO/TAC REGION HABITAT SKILL...METH/COMP BIBLIOG. PAGE 30 F0574
ECO/UNDEV METH PHIL/SCI SOC

S61
DICKS-MIREAUX L.A.,"THE INTERRELATIONSHIP BETWEEN COST AND PRICE CHANGES 19461959: A STUDY OF INFLATION IN POST-WAR BRITAIN" AFR UK ECO/DEV INDUS WORKER ECO/TAC ORD/FREE WEALTH...ECOMETRIC REGRESS STAT TREND CHARTS 20. PAGE 33 F0634
PRICE PAY DEMAND

S61
GALBRAITH J.K.,"A POSITIVE APPROACH TO ECONOMIC AID." FUT USA+45 INTELL NAT/G CONSULT ACT/RES DIPLOM ECO/TAC EDU/PROP ATTIT KNOWL PWR WEALTH ...SOC STERTYP MID/EX METH/GP 20. PAGE 45 F0883
ECO/UNDEV ROUTINE FOR/AID

S61
HAYTES W.,"THREE VIEWS ON THE SOVIET ECONOMIC THREAT." AFR COM USA+45 USA-45 USSR WOR+45 WOR-45 INDUS TEC/DEV ECO/TAC DOMIN ATTIT PERCEPT PWR FOR/TRADE 20. PAGE 57 F1128
ECO/DEV PLAN TOTALISM

S61
HEILBRONER R.L.,"DYNAMICS OF FOREIGN AID: PROBLEMS OF UNDERDEVELOPED NATIONS PLAGUE ASSISTANCE PROGRAM." FUT USA+45 WOR+45 STRATA NAT/G PLAN TEC/DEV ATTIT DRIVE WEALTH WORK 20. PAGE 58 F1135
ECO/UNDEV ECO/TAC FOR/AID

S61
LANFALUSSY A.,"EUROPE'S PROGRESS: DUE TO COMMON MARKET." EUR+WWI ECO/DEV DELIB/GP PLAN ECO/TAC ROUTINE WEALTH...GEOG TREND EEC TERR/GP 20. PAGE 75 F1473
INT/ORG MARKET

S61
NEAL A.C.,"NEW ECONOMIC POLICIES FOR THE WEST." COM EUR+WWI FUT USA+45 WOR+45 ECO/DEV ECO/UNDEV INDUS MARKET ROUTINE HEALTH ORD/FREE PWR...OLD/LIB METH/CNCPT 20. PAGE 97 F1904
PLAN ECO/TAC

S61
NYANZI S.,"THE EAST AFRICAN MARKET: FOR BETTER OF FOR WORSE." AFR TANZANIA UGANDA PROB/SOLV TARIFFS TAX BAL/PAY. PAGE 99 F1947
ECO/TAC ECO/UNDEV INT/ORG INT/TRADE

S61
OCHENG D.,"ECONOMIC FORCES AND UGANDA'S FOREIGN POLICY." AFR UGANDA INT/TRADE TARIFFS INCOME SOVEREIGN WEALTH 20 EACM EEC TANGANYIKA. PAGE 100 F1961
ECO/TAC DIPLOM ECO/UNDEV INT/ORG

S61
RAY J.,"THE EUROPEAN FREE-TRADE ASSOCIATION AND ITS IMPACT ON INDIA'S TRADE." EUR+WWI FRANCE GERMANY INDIA S/ASIA UK NAT/G VOL/ASSN PLAN INT/TRADE ROUTINE WEALTH...STAT CHARTS TERR/GP CMN/WLTH EEC FOR/TRADE OEEC 20 EFTA. PAGE 109 F2155
ECO/DEV ECO/TAC

S61
VALLET R.,"IRAN: KEY TO THE MIDDLE EAST." COM IRAQ ISLAM KUWAIT LEBANON SAUDI/ARAB TURKEY ELITES SOCIETY INDUS PROC/MFG POL/PAR TOP/EX PLAN BAL/PWR DIPLOM ECO/TAC ALL/VALS...TREND FOR/TRADE CENTO 20. PAGE 140 F2760
NAT/G ECO/UNDEV IRAN

S61
VINER J.,"ECONOMIC FOREIGN POLICY ON THE NEW FRONTIER." USA+45 ECO/UNDEV AGRI FINAN INDUS MARKET INT/ORG NAT/G FOR/AID INT/TRADE ADMIN ATTIT PWR 20 KENNEDY/JF. PAGE 141 F2786
TOP/EX ECO/TAC BAL/PAY TARIFFS

N61
VINER J.,THE INTELLECTUAL HISTORY OF LAISSEZ FAIRE (PAMPHLET). WOR+45 WOR-45 LAW INTELL...POLICY LING LOG 19/20. PAGE 141 F2787
ATTIT EDU/PROP LAISSEZ ECO/TAC

B62
ALTMAN G.T.,INVISIBLE BARRIER: THE OPTIMUM GROWTH CURVE. USA+45 USA-45 ECO/DEV PLAN PAY CONTROL DEMAND OPTIMAL PRODUC WEALTH...STAT CHARTS 20. PAGE 4 F0080
INDUS FINAN ECO/TAC TAX

B62
ARNOLD H.J.P.,AID FOR DEVELOPING COUNTRIES. COM EUR+WWI USA+45 USSR WOR+45 EDU/PROP ATTIT DRIVE PWR WEALTH...TREND CHARTS STERTYP NAT/ 20. PAGE 6 F0115
ECO/UNDEV ECO/TAC FOR/AID

B62
ARNOLD T.W.,THE FOLKLORE OF CAPITALISM. USA+45 USA-45 SOCIETY LG/CO SML/CO EX/STRUC ECO/TAC EDU/PROP ADJUST INCOME...MYTH CHARTS 20. PAGE 6 F0116
CAP/ISM ATTIT STERTYP ECO/DEV

B62
BARTELS R.,THE DEVELOPMENT OF MARKETING THOUGHT. USA+45 USA-45 FINAN ECO/TAC...CONCPT TREND. PAGE 11 F0199
ECO/DEV MARKET MGT EDU/PROP

B62
BERNSTEIN P.L.,THE PRICE OF PROSPERITY. USA+45 TAX CONTROL OPTIMAL WEALTH...PREDICT 20. PAGE 14 F0269
ECO/DEV ECO/TAC NAT/G DEMAND

B62
BROWN S.D.,STUDIES ON ASIA, 1962. ASIA BURMA INDIA ISLAM ISRAEL S/ASIA ECO/UNDEV POL/PAR SECT ECO/TAC ...ANTHOL 20 CHINJAP. PAGE 19 F0374
PWR PARL/PROC

B62
CAIRNCROSS A.K.,FACTORS IN ECONOMIC DEVELOPMENT. WOR+45 ECO/UNDEV INDUS R+D LG/CO NAT/G EX/STRUC PLAN TEC/DEV ECO/TAC ATTIT HEALTH KNOWL PWR WEALTH ...TIME/SEQ GEN/LAWS TOT/POP TRUE/GP VAL/FREE 20. PAGE 21 F0399
MARKET ECO/DEV

B62
CHANDLER A.D.,STRATEGY AND STRUCTURE: CHAPTERS IN THE HISTORY OF THE INDUSTRIAL ENTERPRISE. USA+45 USA-45 ECO/DEV EX/STRUC ECO/TAC EXEC...DECISION 20. PAGE 23 F0446
LG/CO PLAN ADMIN FINAN

B62
CHAPIN F.S.,URBAN GROWTH DYNAMICS IN A REGIONAL CLUSTER OF CITIES. TEC/DEV ECO/TAC HABITAT...GEOG SOC MUNICH. PAGE 23 F0453
REGION PLAN

B62
CHRISTENSON C.L.,ECONOMIC REDEVELOPMENT IN BITUMINOUS COAL: THE SPECIAL CASE OF TECHNOLOGICAL ADVANCE IN US COAL MINES 1930-1960. USA+45 USA-45 ECO/TAC AUTOMAT INCOME PRODUC...CHARTS 20. PAGE 24 F0471
EXTR/IND LABOR TEC/DEV ECO/DEV

B62
COPPOCK J.D.,INTERNATIONAL ECONOMIC INSTABILITY: THE EXPERIENCE AFTER WORLD WAR II. WOR+45 FINAN CAP/ISM CONTROL EFFICIENCY...CHARTS 20. PAGE 28 F0536
ECO/TAC ECOMETRIC INT/TRADE STAT

B62
DENISON E.F.,THE SOURCES OF ECONOMIC GROWTH IN THE UNITED STATES AND THE ALTERNATIVES BEFORE US. AGRI INDUS SCHOOL TEC/DEV CAP/ISM ECO/TAC PRICE COST WEALTH...STAT TREND CHARTS 20. PAGE 32 F0620
ECO/DEV WORKER PRODUC

B62
DIMOCK M.E.,THE NEW AMERICAN POLITICAL ECONOMY: A SYNTHESIS OF POLITICS AND ECONOMICS. USA+45 FINAN LG/CO PLAN ADMIN REGION GP/REL CENTRAL MORAL 20. PAGE 33 F0642
FEDERAL ECO/TAC NAT/G PARTIC

B62
DOBB M.,CAPITALISM YESTERDAY AND TODAY. UK WORKER WAR PRODUC PROFIT 18/20 MONOPOLY. PAGE 33 F0646
CAP/ISM TIME/SEQ CONCPT ECO/TAC

B62
DREIER J.C.,THE ALLIANCE FOR PROGRESS. L/A+17C USA+45 CULTURE ECO/DEV ECO/UNDEV NAT/G PLAN DIPLOM PWR 20 OAS ALL/PROG. PAGE 34 F0661
FOR/AID INT/ORG ECO/TAC POLICY

B62
EINZIG P.,THE HISTORY OF FOREIGN EXCHANGE. CHRIST-17C ISLAM MEDIT-7 PRE/AMER WOR+45 ECO/DEV
MARKET TIME/SEQ

FINAN PLAN ECO/TAC ATTIT KNOWL WEALTH...SIMUL GEN/LAWS. PAGE 37 F0714 — INT/TRADE

B62
FAO,FOOD AND AGRICULTURE ORGANIZATION AFRICAN SURVEY. AFR CONGO/BRAZ GHANA STRATA AGRI INT/ORG TEC/DEV FOR/AID INT/TRADE RACE/REL DEMAND EFFICIENCY PRODUC...GEOG 20 UN CONGO/LEOP. PAGE 39 F0763 — ECO/TAC WEALTH EXTR/IND ECO/UNDEV

B62
FERBER R.,RESEARCH METHODS IN ECONOMICS AND BUSINESS. AFR ECO/DEV FINAN MARKET LG/CO SML/CO CONSULT CONTROL COST...STAT METH/COMP 20. PAGE 40 F0783 — ACT/RES PROB/SOLV ECO/TAC MGT

B62
FORD A.G.,THE GOLD STANDARD 1880-1914: BRITAIN AND ARGENTINA. AFR UK ECO/UNDEV INT/TRADE ADMIN GOV/REL DEMAND EFFICIENCY...STAT CHARTS 19/20 ARGEN. PAGE 42 F0823 — FINAN ECO/TAC BUDGET BAL/PAY

B62
FRIEDMANN W.,METHODS AND POLICIES OF PRINCIPAL DONOR COUNTRIES IN PUBLIC INTERNATIONAL DEVELOPMENT FINANCING: PRELIMINARY APPRAISAL. FRANCE GERMANY/W UK USA+45 USSR WOR+45 FINAN TEC/DEV CAP/ISM DIPLOM ECO/TAC ATTIT 20 EEC. PAGE 44 F0864 — INT/ORG FOR/AID NAT/COMP ADMIN

B62
FRIEDRICH-EBERT-STIFTUNG,THE SOVIET BLOC AND DEVELOPING COUNTRIES. CHINA/COM COM GERMANY/E USSR WOR+45 ECO/UNDEV INT/ORG NAT/G TEC/DEV NEUTRAL PWR ...POLICY 20. PAGE 44 F0868 — MARXISM DIPLOM ECO/TAC FOR/AID

B62
GRANICK D.,THE EUROPEAN EXECUTIVE. BELGIUM FRANCE GERMANY/W UK INDUS LABOR LG/CO SML/CO EX/STRUC PLAN TEC/DEV CAP/ISM COST DEMAND...POLICY CHARTS 20. PAGE 50 F0977 — MGT ECO/DEV ECO/TAC EXEC

B62
GROVE J.W.,GOVERNMENT AND INDUSTRY IN BRITAIN. UK FINAN LOC/G CONSULT DELIB/GP INT/TRADE ADMIN CONTROL...BIBLIOG 20. PAGE 52 F1008 — ECO/TAC INDUS NAT/G GP/REL

B62
HAGUE D.C.,INFLATION. AFR ECO/DEV ECO/UNDEV LABOR BUDGET CAP/ISM INT/TRADE TARIFFS SOCISM 20. PAGE 53 F1036 — FINAN NAT/COMP BARGAIN ECO/TAC

B62
HARRINGTON M.,THE RETAIL CLERKS. ECO/TAC LEAD PARTIC CHOOSE GP/REL INGP/REL CENTRAL POLICY. PAGE 55 F1087 — LABOR SERV/IND STRUCT DELIB/GP

B62
HEILBRONER R.L.,THE MAKING OF ECONOMIC SOCIETY. FUT WOR-45 SOCIETY STRATA ECO/DEV ECO/UNDEV ECO/TAC LEGIT ROUTINE...SOC RECORD REC/INT KNO/TEST CENSUS STERTYP GEN/LAWS. PAGE 58 F1136 — CAP/ISM SOCISM

B62
HIGGANS B.,UNITED NATIONS AND U.S. FOREIGN ECONOMIC POLICY. FUT USA+45 WOR+45 ECO/DEV ECO/UNDEV NAT/G ECO/TAC WEALTH...TIME/SEQ TOT/POP UN 20. PAGE 59 F1168 — INT/ORG ACT/RES FOR/AID DIPLOM

B62
HOLMAN A.G.,SOME MEASURES AND INTERPRETATIONS OF EFFECTS OF US FOREIGN ENTERPRISES ON US BALANCE OF PAYMENTS. USA+45 COST INCOME WEALTH...MATH CHARTS 20. PAGE 61 F1199 — BAL/PAY INT/TRADE FINAN ECO/TAC

B62
HOOVER C.B.,ECONOMIC SYSTEMS OF THE COMMONWEALTH. AFR CANADA INDIA UK ECO/DEV ECO/UNDEV AGRI INDUS TEC/DEV TARIFFS PRICE BAL/PAY DEMAND...SIMUL 20 AUSTRAL. PAGE 61 F1208 — CAP/ISM SOCISM ECO/TAC PLAN

B62
HOOVER E.M.,ANATOMY OF A METROPOLIS. FUT USA+45 SOCIETY ECO/DEV DIST/IND INDUS WORKER ECO/TAC TAX GP/REL COST WEALTH MUNICH 20 NEWYORK/C. PAGE 62 F1212 — ROUTINE TREND INCOME

B62
HUMPHREY D.D.,THE UNITED STATES AND THE COMMON MARKET. USA+45 INDUS MARKET INT/ORG PLAN EDU/PROP BAL/PAY DRIVE PWR WEALTH...TREND STERTYP FOR/TRADE EEC 20. PAGE 63 F1241 — ATTIT ECO/TAC

B62
INTNTL COTTON ADVISORY COMMITT,GOVERNMENT REGULATIONS ON COTTON, 1962 (PAMPHLET). WOR+45 RATION PRODUC...CHARTS 20. PAGE 65 F1287 — ECO/TAC LAW CONTROL AGRI

B62
JOHNSON H.G.,MONEY, TRADE AND ECONOMIC GROWTH. ECO/DEV ECO/UNDEV FINAN COST WEALTH...POLICY SOC IDEA/COMP 20 KEYNES/JM MONEY. PAGE 67 F1324 — PLAN BAL/PAY INT/TRADE ECO/TAC

B62
JORDAN A.A. JR.,FOREIGN AID AND THE DEFENSE OF SOUTHEAST ASIA. PAKISTAN VIETNAM/S FINAN PLAN BUDGET ECO/TAC DETER WAR ORD/FREE...POLICY DECISION CENSUS CHARTS BIBLIOG 20. PAGE 68 F1341 — FOR/AID S/ASIA FORCES ECO/UNDEV

B62
KINDLEBERGER C.P.,FOREIGN TRADE AND THE NATIONAL ECONOMY. WOR+45 ECO/DEV ECO/UNDEV ECO/TAC COST DEMAND 20. PAGE 71 F1393 — INT/TRADE GOV/COMP BAL/PAY POLICY

B62
KOLKO G.,WEALTH AND POWER IN AMERICA. USA+45 SOCIETY STRATA LG/CO ECO/TAC TAX PWR...SOC BIBLIOG 20 DEPRESSION. PAGE 72 F1420 — STRUCT INCOME ECO/DEV WEALTH

B62
KUHN T.E.,PUBLIC ENTERPRISES, PROJECT PLANNING AND ECONOMIC DEVELOPMENT (PAMPHLET). ECO/UNDEV FINAN PLAN ADMIN EFFICIENCY OWN...MGT STAT CHARTS ANTHOL 20. PAGE 74 F1447 — ECO/DEV ECO/TAC LG/CO NAT/G

B62
LITWACK L.,THE AMERICAN LABOR MOVEMENT. USA-45 NAT/G CREATE TEC/DEV CAP/ISM ECO/TAC ADJUD AUTOMAT SKILL...TREND ANTHOL 19/20. PAGE 81 F1588 — INDUS LABOR GP/REL METH/COMP

B62
LUTZ F.A.,GELD UND WAHRUNG. AFR MARKET LABOR BUDGET 20 EUROPE. PAGE 82 F1610 — ECO/TAC FINAN DIPLOM POLICY

B62
MEADE J.E.,CASE STUDIES IN EUROPEAN ECONOMIC UNION. BELGIUM EUR+WWI LUXEMBOURG NAT/G INT/TRADE REGION ROUTINE WEALTH...METH/CNCPT STAT CHARTS ECSC TOT/POP OEEC EEC FOR/TRADE 20. PAGE 89 F1738 — INT/ORG ECO/TAC

B62
MEANS G.C.,PRICING POWER AND THE PUBLIC INTEREST. PLAN PROB/SOLV COST EFFICIENCY PROFIT RIGID/FLEX WEALTH. PAGE 89 F1741 — LG/CO EX/STRUC PRICE ECO/TAC

B62
MORGAN C.A.,LABOR ECONOMICS. LAW INDUS MARKET WORKER PLAN PROB/SOLV GOV/REL INCOME ROLE...T 20 DEPT/LABOR NLRB. PAGE 93 F1829 — LABOR ECO/TAC ECO/DEV CAP/ISM

B62
PAKISTAN MINISTRY OF FINANCE,FOREIGN ECONOMIC AID: A REVIEW OF FOREIGN ECONOMIC AID TO PAKISTAN. EUR+WWI PAKISTAN UK USA+45 USSR ECO/UNDEV INT/ORG DELIB/GP DIPLOM ECO/TAC...CHARTS CMN/WLTH CHINJAP. PAGE 103 F2016 — FOR/AID RECEIVE WEALTH FINAN

B62
PERROUX F.,L'ECONOMIE DES JEUNES NATIONS. EUR+WWI SOUTH/AFR FINAN MARKET TEC/DEV CAP/ISM FOR/AID INT/TRADE 20. PAGE 105 F2065 — INDUS ECO/UNDEV ECO/TAC DIPLOM

B62
PHELPS E.S.,THE GOAL OF ECONOMIC GROWTH: SOURCES, COSTS, BENEFITS. USA+45 USSR FINAN TAX CONTROL DEMAND WEALTH...POLICY NAT/COMP ANTHOL BIBLIOG 20. PAGE 106 F2079 — ECO/TAC ECO/DEV NAT/G FUT

B62
PONCET J.,LA COLONISATION ET L'AGRICULTURE EUROPEENNES EN TUNISIE DEPUIS 1881. FRANCE WORKER TEC/DEV ECO/TAC CONTROL EFFICIENCY ROLE WEALTH 19/20 TUNIS. PAGE 107 F2101 — ECO/UNDEV AGRI COLONIAL FINAN

B62
REES A.,THE ECONOMICS OF TRADE UNIONS. FUT ECO/DEV INDUS BARGAIN CAP/ISM PRICE SENIOR CONTROL GP/REL COST...TREND 20 AFL/CIO. PAGE 110 F2172 — LABOR WORKER ECO/TAC

B62
ROBERTSON B.C.,REGIONAL DEVELOPMENT IN THE EUROPEAN ECONOMIC COMMUNITY. EUR+WWI FRANCE FUT ITALY UK ECO/UNDEV WORKER ACT/RES PROB/SOLV TEC/DEV ECO/TAC INT/TRADE EEC. PAGE 112 F2209 — PLAN ECO/DEV INT/ORG REGION

B62
ROBINSON M.A.,AN INTRODUCTION TO ECONOMIC REASONING. FINAN MARKET LABOR DIPLOM INT/TRADE BAL/PAY INCOME PRODUC WEALTH...POLICY MGT 20. PAGE 113 F2223 — ECO/TAC METH/CNCPT NAT/G

B62
ROTHBARD M.N.,THE PANIC OF 1819; REACTIONS AND POLICIES. AFR USA-45 LAW FINAN BUDGET TARIFFS DEMAND 19 DEPRESSION. PAGE 114 F2247 — ECO/UNDEV POLICY ATTIT ECO/TAC

B62
SHANNON I.,THE ECONOMIC FUNCTIONS OF GOLD. AFR FUT WOR+45 WOR-45 INT/ORG BUDGET INT/TRADE BAL/PAY DEMAND PEACE 20 MONEY. PAGE 120 F2366 — FINAN PRICE ECO/DEV ECO/TAC

B62
TIEBOUT C.M.,THE COMMUNITY ECONOMIC BASE STUDY (PAMPHLET). USA+45 ECO/TAC LEAD DEMAND HABITAT 20. PAGE 130 F2572 — NEIGH INCOME ACT/RES

B62
US CONGRESS JOINT ECO COMM,INVENTORY FLUCTUATIONS AND ECONOMIC STABILIZATION. USA+45 LG/CO...MATH CHARTS CONGRESS. PAGE 134 F2652 — ECO/TAC FINAN INDUS PROB/SOLV

B62
US CONGRESS JOINT ECO COMM,FACTORS AFFECTING THE UNITED STATES BALANCE OF PAYMENTS. USA+45 DELIB/GP PLAN DIPLOM FOR/AID PRODUC WEALTH...CHARTS 20 — BAL/PAY INT/TRADE ECO/TAC

CONGRESS OEEC. PAGE 134 F2653 FINAN

B62
VACCARO J.R.,A STATEMENT OF THE LAWS OF CHILE IN MATTERS AFFECTING BUSINESS (3RD ED.). CHILE AGRI FINAN FAM LABOR ECO/TAC FOR/AID TAX ADJUD CONTROL MARRIAGE STRANGE...BIBLIOG 20. PAGE 140 F2756 CONSTN LAW INDUS MGT

B62
VAIZEY J.,THE ECONOMICS OF EDUCATION. INTELL ECO/TAC PAY COST PRODUC 20. PAGE 140 F2758 ECO/DEV SCHOOL ACADEM PROFIT

B62
VANEK J.,INTERNATIONAL TRADE - THEORY AND ECONOMIC POLICY. LABOR BAL/PWR ECO/TAC TARIFFS PRICE BAL/PAY COST DEMAND 20. PAGE 140 F2765 INT/TRADE DIPLOM BARGAIN MARKET

B62
VANEK J.,THE BALANCE OF PAYMENTS, LEVEL OF ECONOMIC ACTIVITY AND THE VALUE OF CURRENCY: THEORY AND SOME RECENT EXPERIENCES. UNIV PRICE INCOME...MATH 20 KEYNES/JM. PAGE 140 F2766 BAL/PAY ECO/TAC FINAN GEN/LAWS

B62
WARD B.,THE RICH NATIONS AND THE POOR NATIONS. FUT WOR+45 CULTURE ECO/DEV ECO/UNDEV PLAN CAP/ISM EDU/PROP REV NAT/LISM ATTIT DRIVE SOCISM...POLICY CONCPT TIME/SEQ 20. PAGE 143 F2816 ECO/TAC GEN/LAWS

B62
WOODS H.D.,LABOUR POLICY AND LABOUR ECONOMICS IN CANADA. CANADA FUT NAT/G VOL/ASSN WORKER BARGAIN ECO/TAC PAY CONFER GP/REL 20. PAGE 148 F2924 LABOR POLICY INDUS ECO/DEV

B62
WRIGHT D.M.,THE KEYNESIAN SYSTEM. WOR+45 WOR-45 LABOR NAT/G CONTROL COST DEMAND EFFICIENCY...POLICY CONCPT CHARTS SIMUL 20 KEYNES/JM. PAGE 149 F2931 INCOME ECO/DEV FINAN ECO/TAC

B62
ZOOK P.D.,FOREIGN TRADE AND HUMAN CAPITAL. L/A+17C USA+45 FINAN DIPLOM ECO/TAC PRODUC...POLICY 20. PAGE 151 F2970 INT/TRADE ECO/UNDEV FOR/AID BAL/PAY

L62
BELSHAW D.G.R.,"PUBLIC INVESTMENT IN AGRICULTURE AND ECONOMIC DEVELOPMENT OF UGANDA" UGANDA AGRI INDUS R+D ECO/TAC RATION TAX PAY COLONIAL 20 WORLD/BANK. PAGE 13 F0242 ECO/UNDEV PLAN ADMIN CENTRAL

L62
DURAND-REVILLE L.,"LE REGIME DES INVESTISSEMENTS DANS LES ETATS AFRICAINS D'EXPRESSION FRANCAISE ET A MADAGASCAR." MADAGASCAR ECO/UNDEV CAP/ISM ECO/TAC WEALTH...SOC TREND CHARTS 20. PAGE 35 F0683 AFR FINAN

L62
GALBRAITH J.K.,"ECONOMIC DEVELOPMENT IN PERSPECTIVE." CAP/ISM ECO/TAC ROUTINE ATTIT WEALTH ...TREND CHARTS SOC/EXP WORK TERR/GP 20. PAGE 45 F0884 ECO/UNDEV PLAN

L62
MACHLUP F.,"PLANS FOR REFORM OF THE INTERNATIONAL MONETARY SYSTEM. PRINCETON: U. PR., 1962, 70 PP., $0.25." WOR+45 INT/ORG ECO/TAC BAL/PAY HEALTH ORD/FREE WEALTH MID/EX TERR/GP VAL/FREE APPLIC 20. PAGE 83 F1631 ECO/DEV STAT

L62
PRYOR F.L.,"FOREIGN TRADE IN THE COMMUNIST BLOC." COM ECO/DEV VOL/ASSN...METH/CNCPT GEN/LAWS FOR/TRADE TERR/GP 20. PAGE 108 F2129 ECO/TAC STERTYP USSR

L62
SCHULTZ T.W.,"INVESTMENT IN HUMAN BEINGS." ECO/DEV ECO/TAC CONFER COST INCOME PRODUC HEALTH...GEOG ANTHOL. PAGE 117 F2315 FINAN WORKER EDU/PROP SKILL

L62
WATERSTON A.,"PLANNING IN MOROCCO, ORGANIZATION AND IMPLEMENTATION. BALTIMORE: HOPKINS ECON. DEVELOP. INT. BANK FOR." ISLAM ECO/DEV AGRI DIST/IND INDUS PROC/MFG SERV/IND LOC/G EX/STRUC ECO/TAC PWR WEALTH TOT/POP TRUE/GP METH/GP TERR/GP VAL/FREE 20. PAGE 144 F2829 NAT/G PLAN MOROCCO

S62
BOONE A.,"THE FOREIGN TRADE OF CHINA." AFR ECO/DEV ECO/UNDEV INDUS MARKET NAT/G TEC/DEV WEALTH ...POLICY STAT TREND CHARTS FOR/TRADE. PAGE 17 F0318 ASIA ECO/TAC

S62
GILL P.J.,"FUTURE TAXATION POLICY IN AN INDEPENDENT EAST AFRICA" UGANDA LOC/G ECO/TAC ADMIN EFFICIENCY INCOME PRODUC...CHARTS 20. PAGE 47 F0923 ECO/UNDEV TAX AFR COLONIAL

S62
IOVTCHOUK M.T.,"ON SOME THEORETICAL PRINCIPLES AND METHODS OF SOCIOLOGICAL INVESTIGATIONS (IN RUSSIAN)." FUT USA+45 STRATA R+D NAT/G POL/PAR TOP/EX ACT/RES PLAN ECO/TAC EDU/PROP ROUTINE ATTIT RIGID/FLEX MARXISM SOCISM...MARXIST METH/CNCPT OBS TREND NAT/COMP GEN/LAWS 20. PAGE 65 F1288 COM ECO/DEV CAP/ISM USSR

S62
KRISHNA K.G.V.,"PLANNING AND ECONOMIC DEVELOPMENT" AFR UGANDA AGRI INDUS R+D BUDGET RATION TAX COLONIAL 20. PAGE 73 F1441 ECO/UNDEV ECO/TAC NAT/LISM PLAN

S62
LIPSON H.A.,"FORMAL REASONING AND MARKETING STRATEGY." ECO/DEV PROB/SOLV PRICE ALL/VALS CONT/OBS. PAGE 81 F1578 MARKET DECISION GAME ECO/TAC

S62
MEAD W.,"SOME POLITICAL-ECONOMIC ISSUES DETERMINING USA TARIFF POLICY." USA+45 USA-45 ECO/DEV NAT/G TARIFFS ATTIT...TIME/SEQ TREND CHARTS 19/20. PAGE 89 F1736 ECO/TAC METH/CNCPT BAL/PAY

S62
MILLIKEN M.,"NEW AND OLD CRITERIA FOR AID." WOR+45 ECO/DEV ECO/UNDEV ACT/RES PLAN ATTIT KNOWL...TREND CON/ANAL SIMUL GEN/METH TERR/GP 20. PAGE 92 F1796 USA+45 ECO/TAC FOR/AID

S62
MORGENTHAU H.J.,"A POLITICAL THEORY OF FOREIGN AID." ECO/UNDEV NAT/G DELIB/GP PLAN ECO/TAC EDU/PROP EXEC ORD/FREE RESPECT WEALTH...METH/CNCPT TREND 20. PAGE 93 F1833 USA+45 PHIL/SCI FOR/AID

S62
PIQUEMAL M.,"LA COOPERATION FINANCIERE ENTRE LA FRANCE ET LES ETATS AFRICAINS ET MALGACHE." ISLAM INT/ORG TOP/EX ECO/TAC...JURID CHARTS 20. PAGE 106 F2089 AFR FINAN FRANCE MADAGASCAR

S62
PYE L.W.,"THE POLITICAL IMPULSES AND FANTASIES BEHIND FOREIGN AID." FUT USA+45 ECO/UNDEV DIPLOM ECO/TAC ROUTINE DRIVE KNOWL...SOC METH/CNCPT NEW/IDEA TREND HYPO/EXP STERTYP GEN/METH 20. PAGE 108 F2133 ACT/RES ATTIT FOR/AID

S62
RAZAFIMBAHINY J.,"L'ORGANISATION AFRICAINE ET MALGACHE DE COOPERATION ECONOMIQUE." AFR ISLAM MADAGASCAR NAT/G ACT/RES ECO/TAC ALL/VALS ...TIME/SEQ 20. PAGE 110 F2158 INT/ORG ECO/UNDEV

S62
SCOTT J.B.,"ANGLO-SOVIET TRADE AND ITS EFFECTS ON THE COMMONWEALTH." COM FUT UK USSR WOR+45 ECO/DEV MARKET INT/ORG CONSULT WEALTH...POLICY TREND CMN/WLTH FOR/TRADE 20. PAGE 118 F2333 NAT/G ECO/TAC

N62
US SENATE COMM ON JUDICIARY,LEGISLATION TO STRENGTHEN PENALTIES UNDER THE ANTITRUST LAWS (PAMPHLET). USA+45 LG/CO CONFER CONTROL SANCTION ORD/FREE 20 SENATE MONOPOLY. PAGE 139 F2748 LEAD ADJUD INDUS ECO/TAC

B63
ABSHIRE D.M.,NATIONAL SECURITY: POLITICAL, MILITARY, AND ECONOMIC STRATEGIES IN THE DECADE AHEAD. ASIA COM USA+45 WOR+45 ECO/DEV ECO/UNDEV INT/ORG DELIB/GP FORCES ECO/TAC COERCE ATTIT RIGID/FLEX HEALTH ORD/FREE PWR WEALTH...POLICY STAT CHARTS ANTHOL COLD/WAR VAL/FREE APP/SCI. PAGE 2 F0032 FUT ACT/RES BAL/PWR

B63
AHN L.A.,FUNFZIG JAHRE ZWISCHEN INFLATION UND DEFLATION. AFR GERMANY DIPLOM PRICE...CONCPT 20. PAGE 3 F0053 FINAN CAP/ISM NAT/COMP ECO/TAC

B63
ALPERT P.,ECONOMIC DEVELOPMENT. WOR+45 FINAN TEC/DEV ECO/TAC PRICE GOV/REL HABITAT...GEOG BIBLIOG T 20 THIRD/WRLD. PAGE 4 F0079 ECO/DEV ECO/UNDEV INT/TRADE FOR/AID

B63
BARBOUR V.,CAPITALISM IN AMSTERDAM IN THE 17TH CENTURY. NETHERLAND FINAN ECO/TAC...METH/COMP BIBLIOG MUNICH 16. PAGE 10 F0185 CAP/ISM INT/TRADE MARKET WEALTH

B63
BAUER R.A.,AMERICAN BUSINESS AND PUBLIC POLICY: THE POLITICS OF FOREIGN TRADE. USA+45 COM/IND LG/CO NAT/G PROF/ORG SML/CO VOL/ASSN LEGIS TOP/EX ECO/TAC EDU/PROP CHOOSE HEALTH PWR WEALTH...CONCPT METH/CNCPT OBS INT QU SAMP FOR/TRADE TRUE/GP VAL/FREE HI. PAGE 11 F0217 ECO/DEV ATTIT

B63
BENOIT E.,DISARMAMENT AND THE ECONOMY. USA+45 NAT/G ACT/RES ECO/TAC BAL/PAY...STAT CON/ANAL GEN/LAWS 20. PAGE 13 F0252 ECO/DEV ARMS/CONT

B63
BERLE A.A. JR.,THE AMERICAN ECONOMIC REPUBLIC. STRUCT FINAN MARKET LABOR NAT/G PLAN...POLICY WELF/ST DECISION. PAGE 14 F0262 CAP/ISM ECO/TAC TREND CONCPT

B63
BOWIE R.R.,GOVERNMENT REGULATION OF BUSINESS: CASES FROM THE NATIONAL REPORTER SYSTEM. USA+45 USA-45 NAT/G ECO/TAC ADJUD...ANTHOL 19/20 SUPREME/CT FTC FAIR/LABOR MONOPOLY. PAGE 17 F0331 LAW CONTROL INDUS CT/SYS

B63
BRAIBANTI R.J.D.,ADMINISTRATION AND ECONOMIC ECO/UNDEV

DEVELOPMENT IN INDIA. INDIA S/ASIA SOCIETY STRATA ECO/TAC PERSON WEALTH...MGT GEN/LAWS TOT/POP VAL/FREE 20. PAGE 18 F0337

ADMIN

B63

BROUDE H.W.,STEEL DECISIONS AND THE NATIONAL ECONOMY. USA+45 LG/CO PLAN ADMIN COST DECISION. PAGE 19 F0365

PROC/MFG
NAT/G
CONTROL
ECO/TAC

B63

CENTRO PARA EL DESARROLLO,LA ALIANZA PARA EL PROGRESO Y EL DESARROLLO SOCIAL DE AMERICA LATINA. L/A+17C INT/ORG DIPLOM ECO/TAC INT/TRADE ATTIT 20 ALL/PROG. PAGE 22 F0435

ECO/UNDEV
FOR/AID
PLAN
REGION

B63

CERAMI C.A.,ALLIANCE BORN OF DANGER. EUR+WWI USA+45 USSR ECO/DEV INDUS VOL/ASSN ECO/TAC REGION ATTIT MARXISM ATLAN/ALL 20 NATO EEC. PAGE 22 F0437

DIPLOM
INT/ORG
NAT/G
POLICY

B63

CHAMBERLAIN E.H.,THE ECONOMIC ANALYSIS OF LABOR UNION POWER (PAMPHLET). WORKER ECO/TAC DOMIN COERCE GP/REL DRIVE WEALTH POLICY. PAGE 23 F0441

LABOR
PWR
CONTROL

B63

CHATTERJEE I.K.,ECONOMIC DEVELOPMENT PAYMENTS DEFICIT AND PAYMENT RESTRICTION. INDIA WOR+45 FINAN INT/TRADE CONTROL BAL/PAY WEALTH...POLICY CONCPT STAT CHARTS IDEA/COMP BIBLIOG 20. PAGE 23 F0456

ECO/DEV
ECO/TAC
PAY
GOV/REL

B63

CLARK J.J.,BUSINESS FLUCTUATIONS, GROWTH, AND ECONOMIC STABILIZATION. USA+45 FINAN INT/TRADE OPTIMAL...METH/CNCPT ANTHOL BIBLIOG 20. PAGE 25 F0479

CAP/ISM
ECO/TAC
EQUILIB
POLICY

B63

DE VRIES E.,SOCIAL ASPECTS OF ECONOMIC DEVELOPMENT IN LATIN AMERICA. CULTURE SOCIETY STRATA FINAN INDUS INT/ORG DELIB/GP ACT/RES ECO/TAC EDU/PROP ADMIN ATTIT SUPEGO HEALTH KNOWL ORD/FREE...SOC STAT TREND ANTHOL TOT/POP VAL/FREE. PAGE 31 F0608

L/A+17C
ECO/UNDEV

B63

DELL S.,TRADE BLOCS AND COMMON MARKETS. COM WOR+45 ECO/DEV ECO/UNDEV GP/COMP. PAGE 32 F0615

DIPLOM
ECO/TAC
INT/TRADE
FEDERAL

B63

DEUTSCH K.W.,THE POLITICAL ROLE OF LABOR IN DEVELOPING COUNTRIES. AFR ASIA S/ASIA USA+45 WOR+45 ECO/UNDEV POL/PAR ECO/TAC EDU/PROP LEGIT COERCE ORD/FREE PWR WEALTH...OBS INT TREND VAL/FREE 20. PAGE 32 F0625

LABOR
NAT/LISM

B63

ENKE S.,ECONOMICS FOR DEVELOPMENT. AGRI TEC/DEV CAP/ISM DIPLOM ECO/TAC TAX ATTIT DRIVE HABITAT WEALTH...GOV/COMP BIBLIOG 20. PAGE 38 F0737

ECO/UNDEV
PHIL/SCI
CON/ANAL

B63

FLORES E.,LAND REFORM AND THE ALLIANCE FOR PROGRESS (PAMPHLET). L/A+17C USA+45 STRUCT ECO/UNDEV NAT/G WORKER CREATE PLAN ECO/TAC COERCE REV 20 ALL/PROG. PAGE 42 F0815

AGRI
INT/ORG
DIPLOM
POLICY

B63

FOX S.,ECONOMIC CONTROL AND FREE ENTERPRISE. PLAN BUDGET INT/TRADE TAX...TREND 20. PAGE 43 F0839

CONTROL
FINAN
ECO/TAC

B63

FRIEDMAN M.,INFLATION: CAUSES AND CURES. AFR INDIA ECO/DEV ECO/TAC INT/TRADE RATION PRICE DEMAND ...POLICY 20. PAGE 44 F0860

ECO/UNDEV
PLAN
FINAN
EQUILIB

B63

GEERTZ C.,PEDDLERS AND PRINCES: SOCIAL DEVELOPMENT AND ECONOMIC CHANGE IN TWO INDONESIAN TOWNS. S/ASIA CULTURE SOCIETY STRATA FACE/GP CREATE TEC/DEV ECO/TAC ORD/FREE WEALTH...OBS INT CENSUS CHARTS WORK TOT/POP METH/GP TERR/GP VAL/FREE 20 MUNICH. PAGE 47 F0913

ECO/UNDEV
SOC
ELITES
INDONESIA

B63

GLADE W.P. JR.,THE POLITICAL ECONOMY OF MEXICO. FUT L/A+17C CULTURE SOCIETY AGRI INDUS DELIB/GP ACT/RES ECO/TAC ATTIT HEALTH ORD/FREE...STAT TIME/SEQ TREND MEXIC/AMER TOT/POP VAL/FREE 20. PAGE 48 F0928

FINAN
ECO/UNDEV

B63

GODWIN F.W.,THE HIDDEN FORCE. PUERT/RICO WOR+45 STRUCT VOL/ASSN PROB/SOLV DIPLOM CONFER...BIBLIOG 20 PEACE/CORP. PAGE 48 F0931

ECO/UNDEV
WORKER
SKILL
ECO/TAC

B63

GOLDMAN M.I.,SOVIET MARKETING. USSR DIST/IND FINAN RATION OWN WEALTH...SOC BIBLIOG 20. PAGE 48 F0937

MARKET
ECO/TAC
CONTROL
MARXISM

B63

GORDON L.,A NEW DEAL FOR LATIN AMERICA. L/A+17C USA+45 CULTURE NAT/G TEC/DEV DIPLOM FOR/AID REGION TASK...POLICY 20 ALL/PROG DEPT/STATE. PAGE 49 F0958

ECO/UNDEV
ECO/TAC
INT/ORG
PLAN

B63

GORDON M.S.,THE ECONOMICS OF WELFARE POLICIES. INDUS LOC/G NAT/G LEGIS WORKER INCOME AGE/O SKILL WEALTH...METH/COMP NAT/COMP 20. PAGE 49 F0959

METH/CNCPT
ECO/TAC
POLICY

B63

GRUBEL H.G.,WORLD MONETARY REFORM: PLANS AND ISSUES. FUT WOR+45 ECO/DEV ECO/UNDEV R+D DELIB/GP CREATE ECO/TAC ATTIT RIGID/FLEX WEALTH...STAT ANTHOL VAL/FREE 20. PAGE 52 F1009

FINAN
INT/ORG
BAL/PAY
INT/TRADE

B63

HAHN L.A.,DIE AMERIKANISCHE KONJUNKTURPOLITIK DER DOLLAR UND DIE DMARK. GERMANY/W USA+45 DIPLOM PRICE BAL/PAY COST...POLICY MONEY. PAGE 53 F1038

FINAN
BUDGET
ECO/TAC
LABOR

B63

HAQ M.,THE STRATEGY OF ECONOMIC PLANNING. PAKISTAN AGRI FINAN INDUS NAT/G FOR/AID TAX CONTROL REGION PRODUC...POLICY CHARTS 20. PAGE 55 F1071

ECO/TAC
ECO/UNDEV
PLAN
PROB/SOLV

B63

HIRSCHMAN A.O.,JOURNEYS TOWARD PROGRESS: STUDIES OF ECONOMIC POLICYMAKING IN LATIN AMERICA. CHILE FUT ECO/UNDEV AGRI FINAN INDUS CONSULT DELIB/GP PLAN ATTIT HEALTH ORD/FREE WEALTH...POLICY STAT VAL/FREE COLOMB 20. PAGE 60 F1177

L/A+17C
ECO/TAC
BRAZIL

B63

HOLLAND E.P.,EXPERIMENTS ON A SIMULATED UNDERDEVELOPED ECONOMY: DEVELOPMENT PLANS AND BALANCE-OF-PAYMENTS POLICIES. WOR+45 ECO/UNDEV FINAN PLAN ECO/TAC...MATH STAT CHARTS SIMUL VAL/FREE. PAGE 61 F1196

AFR
BAL/PAY

B63

HOOPES R.,THE STEEL CRISIS. USA+45 INDUS ECO/TAC EDU/PROP PRICE CONTROL ATTIT...POLICY 20 KENNEDY/JF. PAGE 61 F1205

PROC/MFG
NAT/G
RATION
CHIEF

B63

HYDE D.,THE PEACEFUL ASSAULT. COM UAR USSR ECO/DEV ECO/UNDEV NAT/G POL/PAR CAP/ISM PWR 20. PAGE 64 F1256

MARXISM
CONTROL
ECO/TAC
DIPLOM

B63

INTERAMERICAN ECO AND SOC COUN,THE ALLIANCE FOR PROGRESS: ITS FIRST YEAR: 1961-1962. AGRI SCHOOL PLAN TEC/DEV INT/TRADE TAX GIVE ADMIN WEALTH...SOC 20 ALL/PROG SOUTH/AMER. PAGE 64 F1267

INT/ORG
PROB/SOLV
ECO/TAC
L/A+17C

B63

INTERNATIONAL BANK RECONST DEV,THE WORLD BANK GROUP IN ASIA. ASIA S/ASIA INDUS TEC/DEV ECO/TAC...RECORD 20 IBRD WORLD/BANK. PAGE 65 F1273

INT/ORG
DIPLOM
ECO/UNDEV
FINAN

B63

JACOBS P.,STATE OF UNIONS. USA+45 STRATA TOP/EX GP/REL RACE/REL DEMAND DISCRIM ATTIT PWR 20 CONGRESS NEGRO HOFFA/J. PAGE 66 F1296

LABOR
ECO/TAC
BARGAIN
DECISION

B63

KAPP W.K.,HINDU CULTURE: ECONOMIC DEVELOPMENT AND ECONOMIC PLANNING IN INDIA. INDIA S/ASIA CULTURE ECO/TAC EDU/PROP ADMIN ALL/VALS...POLICY MGT TIME/SEQ TRUE/GP VAL/FREE 20. PAGE 69 F1353

SECT
ECO/UNDEV

B63

KRAVIS I.B.,DOMESTIC INTERESTS AND INTERNATIONAL OBLIGATIONS: SAFEGUARDS IN INTERNATIONAL TRADE ORGANIZATIONS. EUR+WWI USA+45 WOR+45 FINAN DELIB/GP ATTIT RIGID/FLEX HEALTH...STAT EEC VAL/FREE OEEC ECSC 20. PAGE 73 F1435

INT/ORG
ECO/TAC
INT/TRADE

B63

LAGOS G.,INTERNATIONAL STRATIFICATION AND UNDERDEVELOPED COUNTRIES. L/A+17C WOR+45 PLAN ECO/TAC PWR RESPECT WEALTH...METH/CNCPT STAT CHARTS SIMUL GEN/LAWS TRUE/GP METH/GP VAL/FREE 20. PAGE 74 F1459

ECO/UNDEV
STRATA

B63

LAIRD R.D.,SOVIET AGRICULTURAL AND PEASANT AFFAIRS. FUT STRATA LOC/G DELIB/GP ACT/RES TEC/DEV ECO/TAC EDU/PROP ATTIT RIGID/FLEX ORD/FREE SKILL WEALTH ...STAT CON/ANAL ANTHOL MUNICH WORK VAL/FREE 20. PAGE 74 F1461

COM
AGRI
POLICY

B63

LETHBRIDGE H.J.,THE PEASANT AND THE COMMUNES. CHINA/COM COM USSR NEIGH PROB/SOLV ADJUST EFFICIENCY...POLICY METH/COMP NAT/COMP 20. PAGE 78 F1535

MARXISM
ECO/TAC
AGRI
WORKER

B63

LEWIN J.,POLITICS AND LAW IN SOUTH AFRICA. SOUTH/AFR UK POL/PAR BAL/PWR ECO/TAC COLONIAL CONTROL GP/REL DISCRIM PWR 20 NEGRO. PAGE 79 F1545

NAT/LISM
POLICY
LAW
RACE/REL

B63

LINDBERG L.,POLITICAL DYNAMICS OF EUROPEAN ECONOMIC INTEGRATION. EUR+WWI ECO/DEV INT/ORG VOL/ASSN DELIB/GP ADMIN WEALTH...DECISION EEC TERR/GP 20. PAGE 80 F1567

MARKET
ECO/TAC

B63

LUTZ F.A.,DAS PROBLEM DES INTERNATIONALEN WIRTSCHAFTLICHEN GLEICHGEWICHTS. DIPLOM INT/TRADE COST INCOME 20. PAGE 82 F1612

FINAN
CAP/ISM
ECO/TAC

PRODUC

B63

MAIZELS A.,INDUSTRIAL GROWTH AND WORLD TRADE. FUT WOR+45 ECO/DEV FINAN INT/ORG PLAN TEC/DEV ECO/TAC WEALTH...MATH STAT CHARTS VAL/FREE 19/20. PAGE 84 F1642
INDUS ECO/UNDEV INT/TRADE

B63

MANGER W.,THE ALLIANCE FOR PROGRESS: A CRITICAL APPRAISAL. FUT L/A+17C USA+45 CULTURE ECO/UNDEV ACADEM NAT/G SCHOOL PLAN FOR/AID...POLICY OAS ALL/PROG. PAGE 84 F1651
DIPLOM INT/ORG ECO/TAC REGION

B63

MANN D.E.,THE POLITICS OF WATER IN ARIZONA. AGRI EXTR/IND PROVS ACT/RES CREATE PLAN GOV/REL COST HABITAT...MGT CHARTS 20 ARIZONA WATER. PAGE 84 F1655
POLICY ECO/TAC TEC/DEV

B63

MARITANO N.,AN ALLIANCE FOR PROGRESS. FUT L/A+17C USA+45 CULTURE ECO/UNDEV NAT/G PLAN CONTROL ...POLICY ALL/PROG. PAGE 85 F1669
DIPLOM INT/ORG ECO/TAC FOR/AID

B63

MEIER G.,INTERNATIONAL TRADE AND DEVELOPMENT. FINAN BAL/PAY COST DEMAND DISCRIM EQUILIB WEALTH...POLICY ECOMETRIC MATH STAT BIBLIOG/A 20. PAGE 89 F1747
ECO/UNDEV ECO/TAC INT/TRADE IDEA/COMP

B63

MEYNAUD J.,PLANIFICATION ET POLITIQUE. FRANCE ITALY FINAN LABOR DELIB/GP LEGIS ADMIN EFFICIENCY ...MAJORIT DECISION 20. PAGE 90 F1773
PLAN ECO/TAC PROB/SOLV

B63

MULLENBACH P.,CIVILIAN NUCLEAR POWER: ECONOMIC ISSUES AND POLICY FORMATION. AFR FINAN INT/ORG DELIB/GP ACT/RES ECO/TAC ATTIT SUPEGO HEALTH ORD/FREE PWR...POLICY CONCPT MATH STAT CHARTS VAL/FREE 20. PAGE 94 F1855
USA+45 ECO/DEV NUC/PWR

B63

MYRDAL G.,CHALLENGE TO AFFLUENCE. USA+45 WOR+45 FINAN INT/ORG NAT/G PLAN ECO/TAC INT/TRADE BAL/PAY ORD/FREE 20 EUROPE/W. PAGE 96 F1882
ECO/DEV WEALTH DIPLOM PRODUC

B63

OLSON M. JR.,THE ECONOMICS OF WARTIME SHORTAGE. FRANCE GERMANY MOD/EUR UK AGRI PROB/SOLV ADMIN DEMAND WEALTH...POLICY OLD/LIB FOR/TRADE 17/20. PAGE 101 F1990
WAR ADJUST ECO/TAC NAT/COMP

B63

PATTON R.,THE DEVELOPMENT OF THE AMERICAN ECONOMY: REVISED. USA+45 USA-45 INDUS LABOR NAT/G CAP/ISM DIPLOM INT/TRADE WAR WEALTH 16/20. PAGE 104 F2038
ECO/TAC ECO/DEV DEMAND

B63

PREST A.R.,PUBLIC FINANCE IN UNDERDEVELOPED COUNTRIES. UK WOR+45 WOR-45 SOCIETY INT/ORG NAT/G LEGIS ACT/RES PLAN ECO/TAC ADMIN ROUTINE...CHARTS 20. PAGE 108 F2115
FINAN ECO/UNDEV NIGERIA

B63

PRYOR F.L.,THE COMMUNIST FOREIGN TRADE SYSTEM. COM CZECHOSLVK GERMANY YUGOSLAVIA LAW ECO/DEV DIST/IND POL/PAR PLAN DOMIN TOTALISM DRIVE RIGID/FLEX WEALTH ...STAT STAND/INT CHARTS FOR/TRADE 20. PAGE 108 F2130
ATTIT ECO/TAC

B63

RAFUSE R.W. JR.,STATE AND LOCAL FISCAL BEHAVIOR OVER THE POSTWAR CYCLES (DISSERTATION). USA+45 TAX PRICE ATTIT...POLICY TIME/SEQ TREND CHARTS BIBLIOG 20. PAGE 109 F2135
BUDGET LOC/G ECO/TAC PROVS

B63

RAO V.K.R.,FOREIGN AID AND INDIA'S ECONOMIC DEVELOPMENT. INDIA INT/ORG PROB/SOLV TEC/DEV ECO/TAC CONTROL WEALTH...TREND 20. PAGE 109 F2148
FOR/AID ECO/UNDEV RECEIVE DIPLOM

B63

RICARDO D.,THE PRINCIPLES OF POLITICAL ECONOMY AND TAXATION (1817). UK INDUS MARKET ECO/TAC INT/TRADE TARIFFS PRICE COST DEMAND OPTIMAL WEALTH...CONCPT 19 INTRVN/ECO. PAGE 111 F2183
GEN/LAWS TAX LAISSEZ

B63

ROPKE W.,ECONOMICS OF THE FREE SOCIETY. FINAN INT/TRADE BAL/PAY COST DEMAND EFFICIENCY ORD/FREE WEALTH...CON/ANAL METH/COMP T 20 KEYNES/JM. PAGE 114 F2240
SOCIETY BUDGET ECO/DEV ECO/TAC

B63

ROTHBARD M.N.,AMERICA'S GREAT DEPRESSION. USA-45 NAT/G ECO/TAC LAISSEZ...POLICY IDEA/COMP 20. PAGE 114 F2248
FINAN CAP/ISM MARKET GEN/LAWS

B63

SALANT W.S.,THE UNITED STATES BALANCE OF PAYMENTS IN 1968. USA+45 ECO/DEV ECO/UNDEV INT/ORG DELIB/GP ECO/TAC...POLICY STAT SIMUL 20. PAGE 115 F2273
FUT FINAN BAL/PAY

B63

SCHOECK H.,THE NEW ARGUMENT IN ECONOMICS. UK USA+45 INDUS MARKET LABOR NAT/G ECO/TAC ADMIN ROUTINE BAL/PAY PWR...POLICY BOLIV. PAGE 117 F2309
WELF/ST FOR/AID ECO/DEV ALL/IDEOS

B63

SHANKS M.,THE LESSONS OF PUBLIC ENTERPRISE. UK LEGIS WORKER ECO/TAC ADMIN PARL/PROC GOV/REL ATTIT ...POLICY MGT METH/COMP NAT/COMP ANTHOL 20 PARLIAMENT. PAGE 120 F2364
SOCISM OWN NAT/G INDUS

B63

SMITH R.A.,CORPORATIONS IN CRISIS. USA+45 LG/CO EX/STRUC ECO/TAC CONTROL LEAD PERS/REL...MGT 20. PAGE 123 F2432
ELITES INDUS PROB/SOLV METH/COMP

B63

THEOBALD R.,FREE MEN AND FREE MARKETS. USA+45 USA-45 ECO/DEV NAT/G TEC/DEV DIPLOM INT/TRADE INCOME ORD/FREE WEALTH...TREND 19/20 KEYNES/JM. PAGE 130 F2556
CONCPT ECO/TAC CAP/ISM MARKET

B63

TREVES G.,GOVERNMENT ORGANIZATION FOR ECONOMIC DEVELOPMENT (PAMPHLET). WOR+45 LAW BUDGET ECO/TAC GOV/REL...DECISION 20. PAGE 131 F2585
ECO/DEV ECO/UNDEV PLAN POLICY

B63

UN SECRETARY GENERAL,PLANNING FOR ECONOMIC DEVELOPMENT. ECO/UNDEV FINAN BUDGET INT/TRADE TARIFFS TAX ADMIN 20 UN. PAGE 132 F2603
PLAN ECO/TAC MGT NAT/COMP

B63

US ADVISORY COMN INTERGOV REL,PERFORMANCE OF URBAN FUNCTIONS: LOCAL AND AREAWIDE. TEC/DEV PARTIC REPRESENT PWR...DECISION GOV/COMP MUNICH. PAGE 133 F2633
REGION LOC/G ECO/TAC

B63

US CONGRESS JOINT ECO COMM,THE UNITED STATES BALANCE OF PAYMENTS. AFR USA+45 DELIB/GP BUDGET PRICE PRODUC 20 CONGRESS MONEY. PAGE 135 F2655
BAL/PAY INT/TRADE FINAN ECO/TAC

B63

US CONGRESS JOINT ECO COMM,THE UNITED STATES BALANCE OF PAYMENTS. USA+45 DELIB/GP CONFER...MATH PREDICT CHARTS 20 CONGRESS. PAGE 135 F2656
BAL/PAY ECO/TAC INT/TRADE CONSULT

B63

US DEPARTMENT OF LABOR,THE ANVIL AND THE PLOW. KOREA USA+45 USA-45 INDUS WORKER BUDGET WAR ...POLICY AUD/VIS CHARTS 20 DEPT/LABOR. PAGE 135 F2667
ECO/DEV LABOR ECO/TAC NAT/G

B63

US GOVERNMENT,REPORT TO INTER-AMERICAN ECONOMIC AND SOCIAL COUNCIL AT SECOND ANNUAL MEETING. L/A+17C USA+45 VOL/ASSN TEC/DEV DIPLOM TAX EATING EFFICIENCY HEALTH...STAT CHARTS 20 AID. PAGE 136 F2682
ECO/TAC FOR/AID FINAN PLAN

B63

US HOUSE COMM BANKING-CURR,RECENT CHANGES IN MONETARY POLICY AND BALANCE OF PAYMENTS PROBLEMS. USA+45 DELIB/GP PLAN DIPLOM...CHARTS 20 CONGRESS. PAGE 136 F2688
BAL/PAY FINAN ECO/TAC POLICY

B63

US SENATE COMM GOVT OPERATIONS,REPORT OF A STUDY OF US FOREIGN AID IN TEN MIDDLE EASTERN AND AFRICAN COUNTRIES. AFR ISLAM USA+45 FORCES PLAN BUDGET DIPLOM TAX DETER WEALTH...STAT CHARTS 20 CONGRESS AID MID/EAST. PAGE 138 F2728
FOR/AID EFFICIENCY ECO/TAC FINAN

B63

VELEZ GARCIA J.,DEVALUACION 1962; HISTORIA DOCUMENTAL DE UN PROCESO ECONOMICO. AFR L/A+17C USA+45 FINAN FOR/AID PRODUC WEALTH...POLICY STAT CHARTS ANTHOL 20 COLOMB. PAGE 141 F2774
ECO/UNDEV ECO/TAC PLAN NAT/G

B63

VON BECKERATH E.,PROBLEME DER NORMATIVEN OKONOMIK UND DER WIRTSCHAFTSPOLITISCHEN BERATUNG. GERMANY UK ELITES CAP/ISM EFFICIENCY...CONCPT GOV/COMP IDEA/COMP 20. PAGE 142 F2789
ECO/TAC DELIB/GP ECO/DEV CONSULT

B63

WALINSKY L.J.,PLANNING AND EXECUTION OF ECONOMIC DEVELOPMENT. PROB/SOLV TEC/DEV BUDGET COST WEALTH ...CHARTS BIBLIOG 20. PAGE 142 F2802
PLAN ECO/UNDEV ECO/TAC OPTIMAL

B63

WALKER F.V.,GROWTH, EMPLOYMENT, AND THE PRICE LEVEL. USA+45 NAT/G PLAN ECO/TAC DEMAND EFFICIENCY CHARTS. PAGE 142 F2803
ECO/DEV FINAN PRICE WORKER

B63

WIGHTMAN D.,TOWARD ECONOMIC CO-OPERATION IN ASIA. ASIA S/ASIA VOL/ASSN ACT/RES PLAN TEC/DEV ECO/TAC EDU/PROP RIGID/FLEX SKILL...POLICY METH/CNCPT OBS INT GEN/LAWS UN 20 ECAFE. PAGE 146 F2877
ECO/UNDEV CREATE

L63

ADERBIGDE A.,"SYMPOSIUM ON WEST AFRICA INTEGRATION." AFR EUR+WWI FUT CULTURE SOCIETY STRATA DIST/IND INDUS MARKET SERV/IND DELIB/GP PLAN TEC/DEV DOMIN EDU/PROP LEGIT COERCE ATTIT ALL/VALS ...POLICY STAT TREND CHARTS VAL/FREE. PAGE 2 F0040
FINAN ECO/TAC REGION

L63

KUZNETS S.,"QUANTITATIVE ASPECTS OF THE ECONOMIC GROWTH OF NATIONS: DISTRIBUTION OF INCOME BY SIZE."
WEALTH ECO/TAC

WOR+45 FINAN ACT/RES HEALTH...MATH STAT VAL/FREE 20. PAGE 74 F1454

L63
LIVERNASH E.R.,"THE RELATION OF POWER TO THE STRUCTURE AND PROCESS OF COLLECTIVE BARGAINING." ADJUD ORD/FREE...POLICY MGT CLASSIF GP/COMP. PAGE 81 F1589
LABOR GP/REL PWR ECO/TAC

L63
MEYER J.R.,"REGIONAL ECONOMICS: A SURVEY." INTELL ACADEM CREATE...IDEA/COMP BIBLIOG. PAGE 90 F1770
REGION ECO/TAC GEN/LAWS PROB/SOLV

L63
NASH M.,"PSYCHO-CULTURAL FACTORS IN ASIAN ECONOMIC GROWTH." ASIA ISLAM S/ASIA CULTURE ECO/UNDEV DELIB/GP EDU/PROP COERCE ATTIT PERSON HEALTH KNOWL ORD/FREE...PSY SOC STAT TREND ANTHOL VAL/FREE 20. PAGE 96 F1893
SOCIETY ECO/TAC

L63
PADELFORD N.J.,"FINANCIAL CRISIS AND THE UNITED NATIONS." FUT USSR WOR+45 LAW CONSTN FINAN INT/ORG DELIB/GP FORCES PLAN BUDGET DIPLOM COST WEALTH ...STAT CHARTS UN CONGO 20. PAGE 102 F2012
CREATE ECO/TAC

S63
ADAMS F.G.,"ECONOMIC CONSIDERATIONS OF AN ATLANTIC ENERGY POLICY." EUR+WWI FUT USA+45 DIST/IND EXTR/IND MARKET CONSULT LEGIS ECO/TAC WEALTH ...POLICY EEC FOR/TRADE OEEC 20. PAGE 2 F0037
ECO/DEV TEC/DEV NUC/PWR

S63
ANDREWS R.B.,"ECONOMIC PLANNING FOR SMALL AREAS: THE PLANNING PROCESS." INDUS PROC/MFG PROVS PROB/SOLV TAX EQUILIB...METH/COMP HYPO/EXP METH MUNICH 20. PAGE 5 F0103
ECO/TAC PLAN LOC/G

S63
ARDANT G.,"A PLAN FOR FULL EMPLOYMENT IN THE DEVELOPING COUNTRIES." AFR FUT WOR+45 DELIB/GP ACT/RES PLAN ECO/TAC ATTIT ALL/VALS...POLICY STAT CHARTS TUNIS VAL/FREE 20. PAGE 6 F0112
ECO/UNDEV SOCIETY MOROCCO

S63
BARZANSKI S.,"REGIONAL UNDERDEVELOPMENT IN THE EUROPEAN ECONOMIC COMMUNITY." EUR+WWI ELITES DIST/IND MARKET VOL/ASSN CONSULT EX/STRUC ECO/TAC RIGID/FLEX WEALTH EEC OEEC 20. PAGE 11 F0202
ECO/UNDEV PLAN

S63
BILL J.A.,"THE SOCIAL AND ECONOMIC FOUNDATIONS OF POWER IN CONTEMPORARY IRAN." ISLAM CULTURE NAT/G ECO/TAC DOMIN COERCE ATTIT PWR WEALTH...TREND VAL/FREE 20. PAGE 15 F0284
SOCIETY STRATA IRAN

S63
CARTER A.G.T.,"THE BALANCE OF PAYMENTS OF EAST AFRICA" AFR ECO/TAC FOR/AID RATION TARIFFS TAX ADMIN...STAT 20 AFRICA/E. PAGE 22 F0423
BUDGET ECO/UNDEV BAL/PAY INT/TRADE

S63
CLARK P.G.,"TOWARDS MORE COMPREHENSIVE PLANNING IN EAST AFRICA" AFR OP/RES ECO/TAC RATION TAX EFFICIENCY INCOME...MATH TREND CHARTS 20 AFRICA/E. PAGE 25 F0484
ECO/UNDEV PLAN STAT METH/COMP

S63
CLEMHOUT S.,"PRODUCTION FUNCTION ANALYSIS APPLIED TO THE LEONTIEF SCARCE-FACTOR PARADOX OF INTERNATIONAL TRADE." EUR+WWI USA+45 DIST/IND NAT/G PLAN TEC/DEV DIPLOM PWR WEALTH...MGT METH/CNCPT CONT/OBS CON/ANAL CHARTS SIMUL GEN/LAWS FOR/TRADE 20. PAGE 25 F0490
ECO/DEV ECO/TAC

S63
COLLERY A.,"A FULL EMPLOYMENT, KEYNESIAN THEORY OF INTERNATIONAL TRADE." WOR+45 ECO/DEV ACT/RES ECO/TAC ROUTINE ORD/FREE WEALTH...MATH CHARTS 20 KEYNES/JM. PAGE 26 F0504
SIMUL INT/TRADE

S63
DE FOREST J.D.,"LOW LEVELS OF TECHNOLOGY AND ECONOMIC DEVELOPMENT PROSPECTS." WOR+45 WOR-45 CULTURE ACT/RES CREATE PLAN ECO/TAC ROUTINE PERCEPT WEALTH...METH/CNCPT GEN/LAWS 20. PAGE 31 F0597
ECO/UNDEV TEC/DEV

S63
DIEBOLD W. JR.,"THE NEW SITUATION OF INTERNATIONAL TRADE POLICY." EUR+WWI FRANCE FUT UK USA+45 WOR+45 DIST/IND PLAN INT/TRADE EDU/PROP PWR WEALTH ...RECORD TREND GEN/LAWS EEC TRUE/GP VAL/FREE APPLIC 20. PAGE 33 F0636
MARKET ECO/TAC

S63
DOSSER D.,"TOWARD A THEORY OF INTERNATIONAL PUBLIC FINANCE." WOR+45 ECO/DEV PLAN ECO/TAC WEALTH ...WELF/ST TREND GEN/LAWS TRUE/GP METH/GP 20. PAGE 34 F0654
FINAN INT/ORG FOR/AID

S63
EMERSON R.,"THE ATLANTIC COMMUNITY AND THE EMERGING COUNTRIES." FUT WOR+45 ECO/DEV ECO/UNDEV R+D NAT/G DELIB/GP BAL/PWR ECO/TAC EDU/PROP ROUTINE ORD/FREE PWR WEALTH...POLICY CONCPT TREND GEN/METH EEC 20 NATO. PAGE 37 F0729
ATTIT INT/TRADE

S63
ENTHOVEN A.C.,"ECONOMIC ANALYSIS IN THE DEPARTMENT OF DEFENSE." USA+45 NAT/G DELIB/GP PROB/SOLV RATION NUC/PWR WEAPON COST...DECISION 20 DEPT/DEFEN RESOURCE/N. PAGE 38 F0739
PLAN BUDGET ECO/TAC FORCES

S63
ETHERINGTON D.M.,"LAND RESETTLEMENT IN KENYA; POLICY AND PRACTICE" AFR TEC/DEV ECO/TAC FOR/AID TAX PRODUC...CHARTS 20. PAGE 39 F0752
ECO/UNDEV AGRI WORKER PLAN

S63
GALENSON W.,"ECONOMIC DEVELOPMENT AND THE SECTORAL EXPANSION OF EMPLOYMENT, INT." FUT WOR+45 ECO/UNDEV DIST/IND PROC/MFG SERV/IND ACT/RES HEALTH SKILL WEALTH...STAT TIME/SEQ VAL/FREE 20. PAGE 46 F0889
INDUS ECO/TAC

S63
GANDOLFI A.,"LES ACCORDS DE COOPERATION EN MATIERE DE POLITIQUE ETRANGERE ENTRE LA FRANCE ET LES NOUVEAUX ETATS AFRICAINS ET." AFR ISLAM MADAGASCAR WOR+45 ECO/DEV INT/ORG NAT/G DELIB/GP ECO/TAC ALL/VALS...CON/ANAL 20. PAGE 46 F0894
VOL/ASSN ECO/UNDEV DIPLOM FRANCE

S63
GERHARD H.,"COMMODITY TRADE STABILIZATION THROUGH INTERNATIONAL AGREEMENTS." WOR+45 ECO/DEV ECO/UNDEV NAT/G ROUTINE ORD/FREE...INT/LAW OBS TREND GEN/METH TOT/POP 20. PAGE 47 F0918
PLAN ECO/TAC INT/TRADE

S63
GORDON B.,"ECONOMIC IMPEDIMENTS TO REGIONALISM IN SOUTH EAST ASIA." BURMA FUT S/ASIA THAILAND USA+45 AGRI INDUS R+D NAT/G PLAN ECO/TAC WEALTH...STAT CONT/OBS 20. PAGE 49 F0954
VOL/ASSN ECO/UNDEV INT/TRADE REGION

S63
GRUSHIN B.A.,"PROBLEMS OF THE MOVEMENT OF COMMUNIST LABOR IN THE USSR." COM SOCIETY LABOR ECO/TAC EDU/PROP COERCE RIGID/FLEX ORD/FREE...POLICY MARXIST STAT QU WORK 20. PAGE 52 F1011
ATTIT USSR

S63
HALLSTEIN W.,"THE EUROPEAN COMMUNITY AND ATLANTIC PARTNERSHIP." EUR+WWI USA+45 MARKET NAT/G VOL/ASSN DELIB/GP ARMS/CONT NUC/PWR ATTIT PWR...CONCPT STAT TIME/SEQ TREND OEEC 20 EEC. PAGE 54 F1053
INT/ORG ECO/TAC UK

S63
HINDLEY D.,"FOREIGN AID TO INDONESIA AND ITS POLITICAL IMPLICATIONS." INDONESIA POL/PAR ATTIT SOVEREIGN...CHARTS 20. PAGE 60 F1173
FOR/AID NAT/G WEALTH ECO/TAC

S63
HOOVER C.B.,"ECONOMIC REFORM VERSUS ECONOMIC GROWTH IN UNDERDEVELOPED COUNTRIES." FUT WOR+45 ELITES STRATA ECO/UNDEV DIST/IND INDUS TEC/DEV CAP/ISM FOR/AID INT/TRADE ATTIT WEALTH...MYTH TREND STERTYP GEN/LAWS WORK 20. PAGE 61 F1209
ECO/DEV ECO/TAC

S63
LEDUC G.,"L'AIDE INTERNATIONALE AU DEVELOPPEMENT." FUT WOR+45 ECO/DEV ECO/UNDEV R+D PROF/ORG TEC/DEV ECO/TAC ROUTINE ATTIT ALL/VALS...MGT TIME/SEQ FOR/TRADE TOT/POP 20. PAGE 77 F1503
FINAN PLAN FOR/AID

S63
MATHUR P.N.,"GAINS IN ECONOMIC GROWTH FROM INTERNATIONAL TRADE." USA-45 ECO/DEV FINAN INDUS ATTIT WEALTH...MATH QUANT STAT BIOG TREND GEN/LAWS WORK 20. PAGE 87 F1704
MARKET ECO/TAC CAP/ISM INT/TRADE

S63
MIKESELL R.F.,"COMMODITY AGREEMENTS AND AID TO DEVELOPING COUNTRIES." WOR+45 WOR-45 INT/ORG ECO/TAC ATTIT WEALTH WORK FOR/TRADE 20. PAGE 91 F1782
FINAN ECO/UNDEV BAL/PAY FOR/AID

S63
MILLEN B.H.,"INTERNATIONAL TRADE AND POLITICAL INDEPENDENCE." WOR+45 ECO/DEV WEALTH...STAT CHARTS FOR/TRADE METH/GP TERR/GP VAL/FREE 20. PAGE 91 F1788
ECO/UNDEV ECO/TAC INT/TRADE

S63
MONROE A.D.,"BRITAIN AND THE EUROPEAN COMMUNITY." EUR+WWI FRANCE NAT/G DELIB/GP TOP/EX ECO/TAC DOMIN PWR...POLICY RECORD GEN/LAWS EEC EFTA 20 EFTA CMN/WLTH. PAGE 93 F1817
VOL/ASSN ATTIT UK

S63
NADLER E.B.,"SOME ECONOMIC DISADVANTAGES OF THE ARMS RACE." AFR USA+45 INDUS R+D FORCES PLAN TEC/DEV ECO/TAC FOR/AID EDU/PROP PWR WEALTH...TREND FOR/TRADE 20. PAGE 96 F1886
ECO/DEV MGT BAL/PAY

S63
NYE J.,"TANGANYIKA'S SELF-HELP." TANZANIA NAT/G GIVE COST EFFICIENCY NAT/LISM 20. PAGE 99 F1948
ECO/TAC POL/PAR ECO/UNDEV WORKER

S63
PAAUW D.S.,"ECONOMIC PROGRESS IN SOUTHEAST ASIA." S/ASIA AGRI INDUS PROC/MFG ACT/RES ECO/TAC...CHARTS VAL/FREE 20. PAGE 102 F2010
ECO/UNDEV STAT

S63
PINCUS J.,"THE COST OF FOREIGN AID." WOR+45 ECO/DEV FINAN NAT/G VOL/ASSN CREATE ECO/TAC EDU/PROP WEALTH ...METH/CNCPT STAT CHARTS HYPO/EXP TOT/POP VAL/FREE 20. PAGE 106 F2087
USA+45 ECO/UNDEV FOR/AID

S63
POLYANOV N.,"THE DOLLAR'S VENTURES IN EUROPE." EUR+WWI FRANCE USA+45 ECO/DEV MARKET POL/PAR TEC/DEV ECO/TAC EDU/PROP DRIVE PWR WEALTH...MARXIST
FINAN PLAN BAL/PAY

MYTH STAT TREND EEC 20. PAGE 107 F2100 — CAP/ISM

S63
POPPINO R.E.,"IMBALANCE IN BRAZIL." L/A+17C NAT/G TOP/EX PLAN DIPLOM LEGIT DRIVE WEALTH...CON/ANAL FOR/TRADE LAFTA 20. PAGE 107 F2105 — POL/PAR ECO/TAC BRAZIL

S63
PRYBYLA J.,"THE QUEST FOR ECONOMIC RATIONALITY IN THE SOVIET BLOC." COM FUT WOR+45 WOR-45 DIST/IND MARKET PLAN ECO/TAC ATTIT...METH/CNCPT TOT/POP 20. PAGE 108 F2128 — ECO/DEV TREND USSR

S63
RAMERIE L.,"TENSION AU SEIN DU COMECON: LE CAS ROUMAIN." COM EUR+WWI USSR WOR+45 ECO/DEV DIST/IND NAT/G POL/PAR VOL/ASSN EDU/PROP TOTALISM ATTIT WEALTH...TIME/SEQ 20 COMECON. PAGE 109 F2142 — INT/ORG ECO/TAC INT/TRADE ROMANIA

S63
REDDAWAY W.B.,"THE ECONOMICS OF UNDERDEVELOPED COUNTRIES." S/ASIA WOR+45 WOR-45 STRATA AGRI COM/IND DIST/IND MARKET PROC/MFG PLAN TEC/DEV FOR/AID BAL/PAY ATTIT DRIVE SKILL WORK FOR/TRADE 20. PAGE 110 F2165 — ECO/TAC ECO/UNDEV INDIA

S63
SCHOFLING J.A.,"EFTA: THE OTHER EUROPE." ECO/DEV MARKET CONSULT ECO/TAC WEALTH...TIME/SEQ EEC OEEC 20 EFTA. PAGE 117 F2310 — EUR+WWI INT/ORG REGION

S63
SCHURMANN F.,"ECONOMIC POLICY AND POLITICAL POWER IN COMMUNIST CHINA." ASIA CHINA/COM USSR SOCIETY ECO/UNDEV AGRI INDUS CREATE ADMIN ROUTINE ATTIT DRIVE RIGID/FLEX PWR WEALTH...HIST/WRIT TREND CHARTS WORK 20. PAGE 118 F2323 — PLAN ECO/TAC

S63
SHONFIELD A.,"AFTER BRUSSELS." EUR+WWI FRANCE GERMANY UK ECO/DEV DIST/IND MARKET VOL/ASSN DELIB/GP CREATE INT/TRADE ATTIT RIGID/FLEX...RECORD TREND GEN/LAWS EEC COMMUN CMN/WLTH 20. PAGE 121 F2385 — PLAN ECO/TAC

S63
SHWADRAN B.,"MIDDLE EAST OIL, 1962." ISLAM DIST/IND INDUS PLAN ATTIT DRIVE WEALTH...POLICY STAT CONT/OBS TREND CHARTS GEN/LAWS TERR/GP METH/GP 20 OIL. PAGE 121 F2393 — PROC/MFG ECO/TAC ELITES REGION

S63
SHWADRAN B.,"MIDDLE EAST OIL, 1962." ISLAM USSR ECO/DEV DIST/IND INDUS PLAN BAL/PWR DISPL DRIVE ...POLICY STAT TREND GEN/LAWS TERR/GP METH/GP EEC OEEC 20 OIL. PAGE 121 F2394 — MARKET ECO/TAC INT/TRADE

S63
TENNYSON L.B.,"THE USA IN ATLANTIC COMMUNITY." EUR+WWI FRANCE UK USA+45 ECO/UNDEV VOL/ASSN DELIB/GP TOP/EX DIPLOM DOMIN PWR...POLICY CONCPT TREND GEN/LAWS EEC 20. PAGE 129 F2545 — ATTIT ECO/TAC BAL/PWR

S63
VINER J.,"REPORT OF THE CLAY COMMITTEE ON FOREIGN AID: A SYMPOSIUM." USA+45 WOR+45 NAT/G CONSULT PLAN BAL/PWR ATTIT WEALTH...MGT CONCPT TOT/POP 20. PAGE 142 F2788 — ACT/RES ECO/TAC FOR/AID

S63
WALKER H.,"THE INTERNATIONAL LAW OF COMMODITY AGREEMENTS." FUT WOR+45 ECO/DEV ECO/UNDEV FINAN INT/ORG NAT/G CONSULT CREATE PLAN ECO/TAC ATTIT PERCEPT...CONCPT GEN/LAWS TOT/POP GATT 20. PAGE 142 F2804 — MARKET VOL/ASSN INT/LAW INT/TRADE

S63
WILES P.J.D.,"WILL CAPITALISM AND COMMUNISM SPONTANEOUSLY CONVERGE." COM FUT USA+45 ECO/DEV DIST/IND MARKET CAP/ISM ECO/TAC RIGID/FLEX WEALTH MARXISM SOCISM...MATH STAT TREND COMPUT/IR 20. PAGE 146 F2885 — PLAN TEC/DEV USSR

S63
WOLFERS A.,"INTEGRATION IN THE WEST: THE CONFLICT OF PERSPECTIVES." AFR EUR+WWI USA+45 ECO/DEV INT/ORG DELIB/GP CREATE TEC/DEV DIPLOM ATTIT PWR ...CONCPT HIST/WRIT TREND GEN/LAWS EEC 20. PAGE 148 F2918 — RIGID/FLEX ECO/TAC

N63
COMMITTEE ECONOMIC DEVELOPMENT,TAXES AND TRADE: 20 YEARS OF CED POLICY (PAMPHLET). USA+45 ECO/DEV PLAN BUDGET LEAD...POLICY KENNEDY/JF PRESIDENT. PAGE 27 F0518 — FINAN ECO/TAC NAT/G DELIB/GP

N63
LEDERER W.,THE BALANCE ON FOREIGN TRANSACTIONS: PROBLEMS OF DEFINITION AND MEASUREMENT (PAMPHLET). USA+45 BUDGET DIPLOM ECO/TAC PRICE GOV/REL...POLICY STAT NAT/COMP METH 20. PAGE 77 F1502 — FINAN BAL/PAY INT/TRADE ECO/DEV

B64
AUBREY H.G.,THE DOLLAR IN WORLD AFFAIRS. FUT USA+45 WOR+45 ECO/DEV CAP/ISM INT/TRADE BAL/PAY...CHARTS 20. PAGE 7 F0140 — FINAN ECO/TAC DIPLOM POLICY

B64
BALASSA B.,CHANGING PATTERNS IN FOREIGN TRADE AND PAYMENTS. AFR USA+45 USA-45 ECO/DEV NAT/G PLAN BAL/PWR...POLICY ANTHOL BIBLIOG 20. PAGE 8 F0159 — ECO/TAC INT/TRADE BAL/PAY WEALTH

B64
BALOGH T.,THE ECONOMIC IMPACT OF MONETARY AND COMMERCIAL INSTITUTIONS OF A EUROPEAN ORIGIN IN AFRICA. AFR UAR INDUS FOR/AID COLONIAL CONTROL ...NAT/COMP 20. PAGE 9 F0169 — TEC/DEV FINAN ECO/UNDEV ECO/TAC

B64
BASTIAT F.,ECONOMIC HARMONIES (1850). STRATA STRUCT ECO/DEV BUDGET TAX PRICE LOBBY COST. PAGE 11 F0206 — ECO/TAC PLAN INT/TRADE LAISSEZ

B64
BASTIAT F.,ECONOMIC SOPHISMS (1845). FINAN MARKET INT/TRADE TAX EDU/PROP LAISSEZ. PAGE 11 F0207 — TARIFFS INDUS ECO/TAC CAP/ISM

B64
BAUCHET P.,ECONOMIC PLANNING. FRANCE STRATA LG/CO CAP/ISM ADMIN PARL/PROC DEMAND OPTIMAL ATTIT PWR SOCISM...POLICY CHARTS 20. PAGE 11 F0212 — ECO/DEV NAT/G PLAN ECO/TAC

B64
BOURGOIGNIE G.E.,JEUNE AFRIQUE MOBILISABLE; LES PROBLEMES DE LA JEUNESSE DESOEUVREE EN AFRIQUE NOIRE. INT/ORG VOL/ASSN ECO/TAC ROUTINE UTIL ATTIT 20. PAGE 17 F0324 — AGE/Y AFR CREATE ECO/UNDEV

B64
BROWN E.H.P.,A COURSE IN APPLIED ECONOMICS (2ND ED.). ECO/DEV FINAN MARKET WORKER INT/TRADE RATION RENT PAY PRICE BAL/PAY...DECISION T RESOURCE/N. PAGE 19 F0368 — POLICY ECO/TAC PROB/SOLV

B64
CALDER R.,TWO-WAY PASSAGE. INT/ORG TEC/DEV WAR PERSON ORD/FREE 20. PAGE 21 F0400 — FOR/AID ECO/UNDEV ECO/TAC DIPLOM

B64
CENTRO ESTUDIOS MONETARIOS LAT,PROBLEMAS DE PAGOS EN AMERICA LATINA. L/A+17C MARKET BUDGET ECO/TAC EFFICIENCY WEALTH 20 CENTRAL/AM. PAGE 22 F0434 — FINAN INT/TRADE BAL/PAY ECO/UNDEV

B64
CLAIRBORN E.L.,FORECASTING THE BALANCE OF PAYMENTS: AN EVALUATION. AFR FUT UK USA+45 WOR+45 FINAN PLAN BUDGET PAY CONTROL...STAT CHARTS BIBLIOG 20. PAGE 24 F0474 — PREDICT BAL/PAY ECO/DEV ECO/TAC

B64
COLSTON RESEARCH SOCIETY,ECONOMETRIC ANALYSIS FOR NATIONAL ECONOMIC PLANNING (PROCEEDINGS OF SIXTEENTH SYMPOSIUM OF COLSTON RESEARCH SOCIETY). UK USA+45 FINAN FAM LABOR NAT/G PLAN PRICE ...METH/CNCPT TREND CHARTS TIME 20. PAGE 26 F0510 — ECOMETRIC DELIB/GP ECO/TAC PROB/SOLV

B64
COLUMBIA U SCHOOL OF LAW,PUBLIC INTERNATIONAL DEVELOPMENT FINANCING IN INDIA. GERMANY/W INDIA UK USA+45 INDUS PLAN TEC/DEV DIPLOM ECO/TAC GIVE ADMIN UTIL ATTIT 20. PAGE 26 F0512 — ECO/UNDEV FINAN FOR/AID INT/ORG

B64
COMMISSION ON MONEY AND CREDIT,INFLATION, GROWTH, AND EMPLOYMENT. AFR USA+45 PLAN PROB/SOLV PAY PRICE EFFICIENCY PRODUC WEALTH 20. PAGE 26 F0514 — WORKER ECO/TAC OPTIMAL

B64
DUSCHA J.,ARMS, MONEY, AND POLITICS. USA+45 INDUS POL/PAR ECO/TAC TAX DETER NUC/PWR WAR WEAPON GOV/REL ATTIT...BIBLIOG/A 20 CONGRESS MONEY DEPT/DEFEN. PAGE 35 F0687 — NAT/G FORCES POLICY BUDGET

B64
EDWARDS E.O.,THE NATION'S ECONOMIC OBJECTIVES. INDUS WORKER BUDGET DIPLOM CONTROL ORD/FREE ...POLICY SOC METH/CNCPT ANTHOL 20. PAGE 36 F0704 — NAT/G ECO/TAC

B64
EINZIG P.,MONETARY POLICY: ENDS AND MEANS. AFR UK INDUS WORKER PLAN DIPLOM PRICE BAL/PAY COST WEALTH ...DECISION TIME/SEQ 20. PAGE 37 F0715 — FINAN POLICY ECO/TAC BUDGET

B64
FATOUROS A.A.,CANADA'S OVERSEAS AID. CANADA WOR+45 ECO/DEV FINAN NAT/G BUDGET ECO/TAC CONFER ADMIN 20. PAGE 39 F0768 — FOR/AID DIPLOM ECO/UNDEV POLICY

B64
FEI J.C.H.,DEVELOPMENT OF THE LABOR SURPLUS ECONOMY: THEORY AND POLICY. WOR+45 AGRI INDUS MARKET PROB/SOLV TEC/DEV...STAT CHARTS GEN/LAWS METH 20 THIRD/WRLD. PAGE 40 F0772 — ECO/TAC POLICY WORKER ECO/UNDEV

B64
FEIS H.,FOREIGN AID AND FOREIGN POLICY. USA+45 WOR+45 NAT/G VOL/ASSN ACT/RES TEC/DEV ATTIT HEALTH WEALTH...SOC GEN/LAWS 20. PAGE 40 F0775 — ECO/UNDEV ECO/TAC FOR/AID DIPLOM

B64
FIESER M.E.,ECONOMIC POLICY AND WAR POTENTIAL. AFR WOR+45 ECO/DEV INDUS NAT/G FORCES TEC/DEV NUC/PWR CIVMIL/REL ORD/FREE 20. PAGE 40 F0791 — INT/TRADE POLICY ECO/TAC DETER

B64
FIRTH R.,CAPITAL, SAVING AND CREDIT IN PEASANT — AGRI

SOCIETIES. WOR+45 WOR-45 FAM ACT/RES ECO/TAC HEALTH ...SOC CONCPT STAT CHARTS ANTHOL CARIBBEAN VAL/FREE 20. PAGE 41 F0803
FINAN

B64
FREYMOND J.,WESTERN EUROPE SINCE THE WAR. COM EUR+WWI USA+45 DIPLOM...BIBLIOG 20 NATO UN EEC. PAGE 44 F0854
INT/ORG POLICY ECO/DEV ECO/TAC

B64
FRIEDEN B.J.,THE FUTURE OF OLD NEIGHBORHOODS: REBUILDING FOR A CHANGING POPULATION. CONSTRUC LOC/G NAT/G ACT/RES ECO/TAC REGION ATTIT...INT SAMP MUNICH 20 NEWYORK/C LOS/ANG HARTFORD URBAN/RNWL. PAGE 44 F0855
NEIGH PROB/SOLV PLAN BUDGET

B64
FRIEDMANN J.,REGIONAL DEVELOPMENT AND PLANNING: A READER. AGRI MARKET NAT/G ECO/TAC INCOME...GEOG STAT CENSUS CHARTS ANTHOL BIBLIOG MUNICH 20 OPEN/SPACE. PAGE 44 F0863
PLAN REGION INDUS ECO/DEV

B64
GARDNER L.C.,ECONOMIC ASPECTS OF NEW DEAL DIPLOMACY. USA-45 WOR-45 LAW ECO/DEV INT/ORG NAT/G VOL/ASSN LEGIS TOP/EX EDU/PROP ORD/FREE PWR WEALTH ...POLICY TIME/SEQ VAL/FREE 20 ROOSEVLT/F. PAGE 46 F0901
ECO/TAC DIPLOM

B64
GARFIELD PJ LOVEJOY WF,PUBLIC UTILITY ECONOMICS. DIST/IND FINAN MARKET ADMIN COST DEMAND ...TECHNIC JURID MUNICH 20 MONOPOLY. PAGE 46 F0906
T ECO/TAC OWN SERV/IND

B64
HALLOWELL J.H.,DEVELOPMENT: FOR WHAT. WOR+45 POL/PAR SECT FOR/AID INT/TRADE CT/SYS PARTIC PRODUC PLURISM. PAGE 54 F1052
ECO/UNDEV CONSTN NAT/LISM ECO/TAC

B64
HAMBRIDGE G.,DYNAMICS OF DEVELOPMENT. AGRI FINAN INDUS LABOR INT/TRADE EDU/PROP ADMIN LEAD OWN HEALTH...ANTHOL BIBLIOG 20. PAGE 54 F1054
ECO/UNDEV ECO/TAC OP/RES ACT/RES

B64
HANSEN A.H.,BUSINESS CYCLES AND NATIONAL INCOME. USA+45 FINAN ECO/TAC COST OPTIMAL...POLICY METH 20 KEYNES/JM. PAGE 54 F1065
INCOME WEALTH PRODUC INDUS

B64
HANSEN B.,INTERNATIONAL LIQUIDITY. USA+45 INT/ORG ECO/TAC PRICE CONTROL WEALTH...POLICY 20. PAGE 54 F1068
BAL/PAY INT/TRADE DIPLOM FINAN

B64
HARRIS S.E.,ECONOMICS OF THE KENNEDY YEARS AND A LOOK AHEAD. USA+45 PLAN BUDGET NEW/LIB...STAT RECORD IDEA/COMP PERS/COMP INDEX 20 KENNEDY/JF EISNHWR/DD JOHNSON/LB. PAGE 56 F1091
ECO/TAC CHIEF POLICY NAT/G

B64
HATHAWAY D.E.,PROBLEMS OF PROGRESS IN THE AGRICULTURAL ECONOMY. USA+45 USA-45 ECO/DEV NAT/G INT/TRADE PRICE DEMAND EFFICIENCY OPTIMAL 20. PAGE 57 F1112
AGRI ECO/TAC MARKET PLAN

B64
HINSHAW R.,THE EUROPEAN COMMUNITY AND AMERICAN TRADE: A STUDY IN ATLANTIC ECONOMICS AND POLICY. EUR+WWI UK USA+45 ECO/DEV ECO/UNDEV AGRI INDUS INT/ORG NAT/G ECO/TAC TARIFFS REGION...STAT CHARTS EEC 20. PAGE 60 F1174
MARKET TREND INT/TRADE

B64
INTERNATIONAL LABOUR OFFICE,EMPLOYMENT AND ECONOMIC GROWTH. ECO/DEV ECO/UNDEV NAT/G PLAN DIPLOM INT/TRADE CONTROL INCOME PRODUC WEALTH...STAT NAT/COMP 20 ILO. PAGE 65 F1279
WORKER METH/COMP ECO/TAC OPTIMAL

B64
INTL INF CTR LOCAL CREDIT,GOVERNMENT MEASURES FOR THE PROMOTION OF REGIONAL ECONOMIC DEVELOPMENT. WOR+45 ECO/UNDEV FINAN INT/ORG DIPLOM ORD/FREE ...POLICY GEOG 20. PAGE 65 F1285
FOR/AID PLAN ECO/TAC REGION

B64
JACOBY N.H.,UNITED STATES MONETARY POLICY. UK USA+45 LAW NAT/G TEC/DEV TAX EQUILIB INCOME ...METH/COMP 20 FED/RESERV. PAGE 66 F1300
ECO/DEV POLICY ECO/TAC FINAN

B64
JUCKER-FLEETWOOD E.,MONEY AND FINANCE IN AFRICA. ISLAM ECO/UNDEV SERV/IND NAT/G EX/STRUC PLAN ECO/TAC ROUTINE WEALTH...MGT TOT/POP 20. PAGE 68 F1344
AFR FINAN

B64
KAPLAN A.D.H.,BIG ENTERPRISE IN A COMPETITIVE SYSTEM (REV. ED.). USA+45 INDUS MARKET WORKER TEC/DEV ECO/TAC PRICE ADJUD ADMIN CONTROL...MGT CHARTS 20 MONOPOLY. PAGE 69 F1351
FINAN GP/REL NAT/G LG/CO

B64
KEMP M.C.,THE PURE THEORY OF INTERNATIONAL TRADE. WOR+45 WOR-45 ECO/DEV ECO/UNDEV DIST/IND ECO/TAC ...MATH CON/ANAL CHARTS VAL/FREE. PAGE 70 F1374
FINAN CREATE INT/TRADE

B64
KUZNETS S.,POSTWAR ECONOMIC GROWTH: FOUR LECTURES. WOR+45 INDUS NAT/G WORKER TEC/DEV ECO/TAC RATION TARIFFS PRICE BAL/PAY COST DEMAND 20. PAGE 74 F1455
ECO/DEV ECO/UNDEV TREND FINAN

B64
LAURSEN K.,THE GERMAN INFLATION, 1918-23. EUR+WWI GERMANY/E GERMANY/W WOR-45 BUDGET TAX GOV/REL BAL/PAY DEMAND PEACE...POLICY CHARTS 20 WEIMAR/REP. PAGE 76 F1489
ECO/DEV FINAN REPAR ECO/TAC

B64
LETICHE J.M.,A HISTORY OF RUSSIAN ECONOMIC THOUGHT: NINTH THROUGH EIGHTEENTH CENTURIES. RUSSIA FINAN SECT CAP/ISM DOMIN DEMAND EFFICIENCY OWN MARXISM ...TECHNIC ANTHOL BIBLIOG 9/18. PAGE 78 F1536
ECO/TAC TIME/SEQ IDEA/COMP ECO/UNDEV

B64
LI C.M.,INDUSTRIAL DEVELOPMENT IN COMMUNIST CHINA. CHINA/COM ECO/DEV ECO/UNDEV AGRI FINAN INDUS MARKET LABOR NAT/G ECO/TAC INT/TRADE EXEC ALL/VALS ...POLICY RELATIV TREND WORK TOT/POP VAL/FREE 20. PAGE 79 F1556
ASIA TEC/DEV

B64
LINDHOLM R.W.,ECONOMIC DEVELOPMENT POLICY WITH EMPHASIS ON VIET-NAM. KOREA/S PAKISTAN VIETNAM/S AGRI INDUS CONSULT DELIB/GP FOR/AID...METH 20. PAGE 80 F1571
ECO/UNDEV TAX FINAN ECO/TAC

B64
LITTLE I.M.D.,AID TO AFRICA. AFR UK TEC/DEV DIPLOM ECO/TAC INCOME WEALTH 20. PAGE 81 F1583
FOR/AID ECO/UNDEV ADMIN POLICY

B64
LITVAK I.A.,MARKETING: CANADA. CANADA STRATA PROC/MFG LEGIS TEC/DEV DIPLOM INT/TRADE PRICE AUTOMAT ATTIT WEALTH...ANTHOL 20. PAGE 81 F1587
ECO/TAC MARKET ECO/DEV EFFICIENCY

B64
MAGALHAES S.,PRATICA DA EMANCIPACAO NACIONAL. L/A+17C INDUS PLAN ECO/TAC CONTROL NAT/LISM ORD/FREE. PAGE 84 F1640
BAL/PAY ECO/UNDEV DIPLOM WEALTH

B64
MANSFIELD E.,MONOPOLY POWER AND ECONOMIC PERFORMANCE: AN INTRODUCTION TO A CURRENT ISSUE OF PUBLIC POLICY. ECO/DEV INDUS NAT/G PLAN CAP/ISM PRICE CONTROL LOBBY EFFICIENCY PRODUC...POLICY 20 CONGRESS KENNEDY/JF MONOPOLY. PAGE 85 F1659
LG/CO PWR ECO/TAC MARKET

B64
MARKHAM J.W.,THE COMMON MARKET: FRIEND OR COMPETITOR. AFR EUR+WWI FUT USA+45 INT/ORG LG/CO NAT/G VOL/ASSN DELIB/GP EX/STRUC PLAN TARIFFS ORD/FREE PWR WEALTH...POLICY STAT TREND EEC VAL/FREE 20. PAGE 85 F1671
ECO/DEV ECO/TAC

B64
MARRIS R.,THE ECONOMIC THEORY OF "MANAGERIAL" CAPITALISM. USA+45 ECO/DEV LG/CO ECO/TAC DEMAND ...CHARTS BIBLIOG 20. PAGE 86 F1675
CAP/ISM MGT CONTROL OP/RES

B64
MASON E.S.,FOREIGN AID AND FOREIGN POLICY. USA+45 AGRI INDUS NAT/G EX/STRUC ACT/RES RIGID/FLEX ALL/VALS...POLICY GEN/LAWS MARSHL/PLN ALL/PROG CONGRESS 20. PAGE 87 F1699
ECO/UNDEV ECO/TAC FOR/AID DIPLOM

B64
MELADY T.,FACES OF AFRICA. AFR FUT ISLAM NAT/G POL/PAR SCHOOL DELIB/GP PLAN ECO/TAC EDU/PROP ATTIT ALL/VALS...CHARTS TOT/POP TERR/GP VAL/FREE 20. PAGE 89 F1752
ECO/UNDEV TREND NAT/LISM

B64
MEYER J.R.,INVESTMENT DECISIONS, ECONOMIC FORECASTING, AND PUBLIC POLICY. ECO/DEV ECO/TAC ...DECISION REGRESS TIME/SEQ CHARTS GP/COMP SIMUL 20. PAGE 90 F1771
FINAN PROB/SOLV PREDICT LG/CO

B64
MEZERIK A.G.,TRADE, AID AND ECONOMIC DEVELOPMENT. WOR+45 FINAN INDUS MARKET PLAN BAL/PWR BARGAIN FOR/AID TARIFFS EDU/PROP WEALTH...GP/COMP 20 UN GATT IMF IBRD. PAGE 91 F1777
ECO/TAC ECO/DEV INT/ORG INT/TRADE

B64
MILIBAND R.,THE SOCIALIST REGISTER: 1964. GERMANY/W ITALY UK LABOR POL/PAR ECO/TAC FOR/AID NUC/PWR ...POLICY SOCIALIST IDEA/COMP 20 MAO NASSER/G. PAGE 91 F1784
MARXISM SOCISM CAP/ISM PROB/SOLV

B64
MORGAN H.W.,AMERICAN SOCIALISM 1900-1960. AFR USA+45 USA-45 INTELL AGRI LABOR WORKER BARGAIN ECO/TAC GP/REL RACE/REL 20 NEGRO MIGRATION. PAGE 93 F1830
SOCISM POL/PAR ECO/DEV STRATA

B64
MORRISSENS L.,ECONOMIC POLICY IN OUR TIME: COUNTRY STUDIES. BELGIUM EUR+WWI FRANCE GERMANY/W ITALY NETHERLAND INDUS BARGAIN BUDGET GOV/REL BAL/PAY PRODUC...CON/ANAL CHARTS COSTS 20. PAGE 94 F1839
ECO/DEV ECO/TAC METH/COMP PLAN

B64
NATIONAL COUN APPLIED ECO RES,A STRATEGY FOR THE FOURTH PLAN. INDIA DIST/IND EXTR/IND SERV/IND
ECO/UNDEV PLAN

ECO/TAC RATION EDU/PROP EATING HEALTH...CHARTS 20. PAGE 97 F1900
AGRI WORKER

B64
NOSSITER B.D.,THE MYTHMAKERS: AN ESSAY ON POWER AND WEALTH. USA+45 LG/CO NAT/G TOP/EX PROB/SOLV ADMIN GP/REL ORD/FREE 20. PAGE 99 F1937
ECO/TAC WEALTH FINAN PLAN

B64
NOVACK D.E.,DEVELOPMENT AND SOCIETY; THE DYNAMICS OF ECONOMIC CHANGE. WOR+45 STRATA STRUCT ECO/TAC CONTROL CROWD REV GP/REL ADJUST PRODUC WEALTH PSY. PAGE 99 F1940
SOCIETY CULTURE SOC ECO/UNDEV

B64
ODEH H.S.,THE IMPACT OF INFLATION ON THE LEVEL OF ECONOMIC ACTIVITY. AFR BRAZIL CHILE BUDGET GOV/REL COST DEMAND INCOME WEALTH...STAT METH 20 MONEY. PAGE 100 F1963
ECOMETRIC ECO/TAC ECO/UNDEV FINAN

B64
ORGANIZATION AMERICAN STATES,ECONOMIC SURVEY OF LATIN AMERICA, 1962. L/A+17C AGRI DIST/IND INDUS MARKET PROC/MFG R+D PLAN TEC/DEV ECO/TAC REGION BAL/PAY ALL/VALS...CON/ANAL ORG/CHARTS GEN/METH OAS ALL/PROG 20 ALL/PROG. PAGE 102 F1998
ECO/UNDEV CHARTS

B64
PENNOCK J.R.,SELF-GOVERNMENT IN MODERNIZING NATIONS. AFR COM USA+45 ECO/DEV POL/PAR PROB/SOLV DIPLOM ECO/TAC COLONIAL REV POPULISM SOCISM 20. PAGE 105 F2058
ECO/UNDEV POLICY SOVEREIGN NAT/G

B64
PIERSON J.H.,INSURING FULL EMPLOYMENT. USA+45 LABOR DIPLOM ECO/TAC PAY BAL/PAY 20. PAGE 106 F2084
ECO/DEV INT/TRADE POLICY WORKER

B64
POWELSON J.P.,LATIN AMERICA: TODAY'S ECONOMIC AND SOCIAL REVOLUTION. L/A+17C INTELL SOCIETY STRUCT AGRI INDUS NAT/G DIPLOM ECO/TAC REV...POLICY 20. PAGE 107 F2110
ECO/UNDEV WEALTH ADJUST PLAN

B64
RAISON T.,WHY CONSERVATIVE? UK FORCES DIPLOM ECO/TAC GIVE EDU/PROP ORD/FREE WEALTH LAISSEZ ...GOV/COMP 20 TORY/PARTY CONSRV/PAR. PAGE 109 F2137
PLURISM CONSERVE POL/PAR NAT/G

B64
RAMAZANI R.K.,THE MIDDLE EAST AND THE EUROPEAN COMMON MARKET. EUR+WWI ISLAM ECO/DEV EXTR/IND MARKET PROC/MFG INT/ORG NAT/G TEC/DEV ECO/TAC REGION DRIVE WEALTH...STAT CHARTS EEC TOT/POP 20. PAGE 109 F2141
ECO/UNDEV ATTIT INT/TRADE

B64
RANIS G.,THE UNITED STATES AND THE DEVELOPING ECONOMIES. COM USA+45 AGRI FINAN TEC/DEV CAP/ISM ECO/TAC INT/TRADE...POLICY METH/COMP ANTHOL 20 AID. PAGE 109 F2145
ECO/UNDEV DIPLOM FOR/AID

B64
REDLICH F.,THE GERMAN MILITARY ENTERPRISER AND HIS WORK FORCE. CHRIST-17C GERMANY ELITES SOCIETY FINAN ECO/TAC CIVMIL/REL GP/REL INGP/REL...HIST/WRIT METH/COMP 14/17. PAGE 110 F2170
EX/STRUC FORCES PROFIT WORKER

B64
RESOURCES FOR THE FUTURE,URBAN AND REGIONAL STUDIES AT US UNIVERSITIES; A REPORT BASED ON A 1963 SURVEY OF URBAN AND REGIONAL RESEARCH. USA+45 SOCIETY CONSTRUC DIST/IND ACADEM NAT/G ACT/RES ECO/TAC ...CENSUS IDEA/COMP MUNICH. PAGE 111 F2179
BIBLIOG/A REGION PLAN

B64
REUSS H.S.,THE CRITICAL DECADE - AN ECONOMIC POLICY FOR AMERICA AND THE FREE WORLD. AFR USA+45 FINAN POL/PAR WORKER PLAN DIPLOM ECO/TAC TARIFFS BAL/PAY ...POLICY 20 CONGRESS. PAGE 111 F2181
FOR/AID INT/TRADE LABOR LEGIS

B64
RIVKIN A.,AFRICA AND THE EUROPEAN COMMON MARKET (PAMPHLET). AFR MOD/EUR WOR+45 TEC/DEV FOR/AID TARIFFS BAL/PAY...POLICY 20 EEC. PAGE 111 F2196
INT/ORG INT/TRADE ECO/TAC ECO/UNDEV

B64
ROBINSON E.A.G.,ECONOMIC DEVELOPMENT FOR AFRICA SOUTH OF THE SAHARA. AFR AGRI INDUS LABOR BUDGET INT/TRADE PRICE...POLICY GEOG ANTHOL 20. PAGE 113 F2219
ECO/UNDEV ECO/TAC ACT/RES PLAN

B64
ROBINSON R.D.,INTERNATIONAL BUSINESS POLICY. AFR INDIA L/A+17C USA+45 ELITES AGRI FOR/AID COERCE BAL/PAY...DECISION INT/LAW MGT 20. PAGE 113 F2224
ECO/TAC DIST/IND COLONIAL FINAN

B64
SCHULTZ T.W.,TRANSFORMING TRADITIONAL AGRICULTURE. WOR+45 WOR-45 CULTURE STRATA FINAN ACT/RES ECO/TAC ATTIT KNOWL SKILL...MATH STAT TIME/SEQ GEN/LAWS VAL/FREE. PAGE 117 F2316
AGRI ECO/UNDEV

B64
SEERS D.,CUBA: THE ECONOMIC AND SOCIAL REVOLUTION. L/A+17C USSR YUGOSLAVIA STRATA AGRI INDUS SCHOOL DELIB/GP PLAN ECO/TAC DOMIN EDU/PROP ATTIT RIGID/FLEX ALL/VALS...STAT OBS TIME/SEQ WORK VAL/FREE 20. PAGE 119 F2341
ACT/RES COERCE CUBA REV

B64
SEGAL R.,SANCTIONS AGAINST SOUTH AFRICA. AFR SOUTH/AFR NAT/G INT/TRADE RACE/REL PEACE PWR ...INT/LAW ANTHOL 20 UN. PAGE 119 F2342
SANCTION DISCRIM ECO/TAC POLICY

B64
SHANNON I.,INTERNATIONAL LIQUIDITY. AFR FUT USA+45 WOR+45 ECO/TAC PRICE DEMAND WEALTH...CONCPT 20. PAGE 120 F2367
FINAN DIPLOM BAL/PAY ECO/DEV

B64
SINGER H.W.,INTERNATIONAL DEVELOPMENT: GROWTH AND CHANGE. AFR BRAZIL L/A+17C WOR+45 CULTURE AGRI INDUS NAT/G ACT/RES ECO/TAC EDU/PROP WEALTH...GEOG CONCPT METH/CNCPT STAT HYPO/EXP WORK TOT/POP 20. PAGE 122 F2412
FINAN ECO/UNDEV FOR/AID INT/TRADE

B64
SOLOW R.M.,THE NATURE AND SOURCES OF UNEMPLOYMENT IN THE UNITED STATES (PAMPHLET). USA+45 INDUS LABOR TEC/DEV ECO/TAC SKILL WEALTH...TREND NAT/COMP 20. PAGE 124 F2439
ECO/DEV WORKER STAT PRODUC

B64
STEWART C.F.,A BIBLIOGRAPHY OF INTERNATIONAL BUSINESS. WOR+45 FINAN LG/CO NAT/G PLAN ECO/TAC TARIFFS...DECISION MGT GP/COMP NAT/COMP 20 EEC. PAGE 126 F2484
BIBLIOG INT/ORG OP/RES INT/TRADE

B64
STOESSINGER J.G.,FINANCING THE UNITED NATIONS SYSTEM. FUT WOR+45 CONSTN NAT/G VOL/ASSN DELIB/GP EX/STRUC ECO/TAC LEGIT CT/SYS PWR WEALTH...STAT TIME/SEQ TREND CHARTS TRUE/GP METH/GP TERR/GP VAL/FREE. PAGE 126 F2493
FINAN INT/ORG

B64
STRONG A.L.,THE RISE OF THE CHINESE PEOPLE'S COMMUNES - AND SIX YEARS AFTER (2ND ED.). CHINA/COM AGRI INDUS FORCES WORKER PROB/SOLV EDU/PROP EFFICIENCY ISOLAT 20. PAGE 127 F2503
NEIGH ECO/TAC MARXISM METH/COMP

B64
TAWNEY R.H.,EQUALITY. UK CULTURE STRATA ECO/TAC EDU/PROP REPRESENT OWN NEW/LIB...MAJORIT WELF/ST SOC 20. PAGE 129 F2538
WEALTH STRUCT ELITES POPULISM

B64
TELLADO A.,A STATEMENT OF THE LAWS OF THE DOMINICAN REPUBLIC IN MATTERS AFFECTING BUSINESS (3RD ED.). DOMIN/REP AGRI DIST/IND EXTR/IND FINAN FAM WORKER ECO/TAC TAX CT/SYS MARRIAGE OWN...BIBLIOG 20 MIGRATION. PAGE 129 F2542
CONSTN LEGIS NAT/G INDUS

B64
THAILAND NATIONAL ECO DEV,THE NATIONAL ECONOMIC DEVELOPMENT PLAN: 1961-66: SECOND PHASE 1964-66. THAILAND AGRI FINAN BUDGET EFFICIENCY INCOME...STAT CHARTS 20. PAGE 129 F2547
ECO/UNDEV ECO/TAC PLAN NAT/G

B64
TINBERGEN J.,CENTRAL PLANNING. COM INTELL ECO/DEV ECO/UNDEV FINAN INT/ORG PROB/SOLV ECO/TAC CONTROL EXEC ROUTINE DECISION. PAGE 130 F2576
PLAN INDUS MGT CENTRAL

B64
TONG T.,UNITED STATES DIPLOMACY IN CHINA, 1844-1860. ASIA USA-45 ECO/UNDEV ECO/TAC COERCE GP/REL...INT/LAW 19 TREATY. PAGE 131 F2581
DIPLOM INT/TRADE COLONIAL

B64
URQUIDI V.L.,THE CHALLENGE OF DEVELOPMENT IN LATIN AMERICA. L/A+17C FINAN INT/ORG TEC/DEV DIPLOM INT/TRADE PRICE REGION PRODUC...CHARTS 20 ALL/PROG. PAGE 133 F2628
ECO/UNDEV ECO/TAC NAT/G TREND

B64
US AGENCY INTERNATIONAL DEV,A.I.D. PROJECTS IN FISCAL YEAR 1963: BY COUNTRY AND FIELD OF ACTIVITY. USA+45 ECO/UNDEV ECO/TAC EDU/PROP GOV/REL...CHARTS 20 AID. PAGE 134 F2639
FINAN FOR/AID COST STAT

B64
US CONGRESS JOINT ECO COMM,PRIVATE INVESTMENT IN LATIN AMERICA. L/A+17C USA+45 INT/ORG PROB/SOLV ECO/TAC ATTIT...INT 20 CONGRESS. PAGE 135 F2658
FINAN ECO/UNDEV PARL/PROC LEGIS

B64
US HOUSE COMM BANKING-CURR,INTERNATIONAL DEVELOPMENT ASSOCIATION ACT AMENDMENT. CHINA/COM USA+45 USSR FINAN FORCES LEGIS DIPLOM CONFER EFFICIENCY...CHARTS GOV/COMP 20 PRESIDENT CONGRESS INTL/DEV. PAGE 136 F2689
BAL/PAY FOR/AID RECORD ECO/TAC

B64
US HOUSE COMM GOVT OPERATIONS,US OWNED FOREIGN CURRENCIES: HEARINGS (COMMITTEE ON GOVERNMENT OPERATIONS). INDIA ECO/DEV PLAN BUDGET TAX DEMAND EFFICIENCY 20 AID CONGRESS. PAGE 137 F2699
FINAN ECO/TAC FOR/AID OWN

B64
US SENATE COMM ON JUDICIARY,HEARINGS BEFORE SUBCOMMITTEE ON ANTITRUST AND MONOPOLY: ECONOMIC CONCENTRATION VOLUMES 1-5 JULY 1964-SEPT 1966. USA+45 LAW FINAN ECO/TAC ADJUD COST EFFICIENCY PRODUC...STAT CHARTS 20 CONGRESS MONOPOLY. PAGE 140 F2749
ECO/DEV CONTROL MARKET LG/CO

B64
WERNETTE J.P.,GOVERNMENT AND BUSINESS. LABOR CAP/ISM ECO/TAC INT/TRADE TAX ADMIN AUTOMAT NUC/PWR CIVMIL/REL DEMAND...MGT 20 MONOPOLY. PAGE 145 F2859 NAT/G FINAN ECO/DEV CONTROL

B64
WILLIAMSON J.G.,AMERICAN GROWTH AND THE BALANCE OF PAYMENTS, 1820-1913: A STUDY OF THE LONG SWING. EUR+WWI MOD/EUR USA+45 USA-45 ECO/DEV NAT/G ECO/TAC ROUTINE ORD/FREE WEALTH...MATH STAT TIME/SEQ CHARTS SIMUL GEN/LAWS TRUE/GP METH/GP VAL/FREE 19/20. PAGE 147 F2896 FINAN BAL/PAY

B64
WILLIAMSON O.E.,THE ECONOMICS OF DISCRETIONARY BEHAVIOR: MANAGERIAL OBJECTIVES IN A THEORY OF THE FIRM. MARKET BUDGET CAP/ISM PRODUC DRIVE PERSON ...STAT CHARTS BIBLIOG METH 20. PAGE 147 F2897 EFFICIENCY MGT ECO/TAC CHOOSE

B64
WILSON T.,POLICIES FOR REGIONAL DEVELOPMENT. CANADA UK FINAN INDUS NAT/G BUDGET TAX GIVE COST ...NAT/COMP 20. PAGE 147 F2904 REGION PLAN ECO/DEV ECO/TAC

B64
WRIGHT G.,RURAL REVOLUTION IN FRANCE: THE PEASANTRY IN THE TWENTIETH CENTURY. EUR+WWI MOD/EUR LAW CULTURE AGRI POL/PAR DELIB/GP LEGIS ECO/TAC EDU/PROP COERCE CHOOSE ATTIT RIGID/FLEX HEALTH ...STAT CENSUS CHARTS VAL/FREE 20. PAGE 149 F2932 PWR STRATA FRANCE REV

B64
YUDELMAN M.,AFRICANS ON THE LAND. RHODESIA MARKET LABOR OWN...ECOMETRIC TREND 20. PAGE 150 F2955 ECO/DEV AFR AGRI ECO/TAC

L64
ARMENGALD A.,"ECONOMIE ET COEXISTENCE." COM EUR+WWI FUT USA+45 WOR+45 ECO/DEV ECO/UNDEV FINAN INT/ORG NAT/G EXEC CHOOSE ATTIT ALL/VALS...POLICY RELATIV DECISION TREND SOC/EXP WORK 20. PAGE 6 F0113 MARKET ECO/TAC AFR CAP/ISM

L64
BHAGWATI J.,"THE PURE THEORY OF INTERNATIONAL TRADE: A SURVEY." WOR+45 ECO/DEV ECO/UNDEV FINAN MARKET PROC/MFG INT/ORG LABOR LG/CO NAT/G TEC/DEV ECO/TAC SKILL WEALTH...POLICY RELATIV MGT CONCPT NEW/IDEA MATH QUANT GEN/LAWS FOR/TRADE 20. PAGE 14 F0276 INDUS HYPO/EXP

L64
CARNEGIE ENDOWMENT INT. PEACE,"ECONOMIC AND SOCIAL QUESTION (ISSUES BEFORE THE NINETEENTH GENERAL ASSEMBLY)." WOR+45 ECO/DEV ECO/UNDEV INDUS R+D DELIB/GP CREATE PLAN TEC/DEV ECO/TAC FOR/AID BAL/PAY...RECORD UN 20. PAGE 21 F0414 INT/ORG INT/TRADE

L64
HAAS E.B.,"ECONOMICS AND DIFFERENTIAL PATTERNS OF POLITICAL INTEGRATION: PROJECTIONS ABOUT UNITY IN LATIN AMERICA." SOCIETY NAT/G DELIB/GP ACT/RES CREATE PLAN ECO/TAC REGION ROUTINE ATTIT DRIVE PWR WEALTH...CONCPT TREND CHARTS LAFTA TERR/GP 20. PAGE 52 F1020 L/A+17C INT/ORG MARKET

L64
KORBONSKI A.,"COMECON." ASIA ECO/DEV ECO/UNDEV ECO/TAC BAL/PAY NAT/LISM FOR/TRADE 20 COMECON. PAGE 73 F1425 COM INT/ORG INT/TRADE

L64
STERN R.M.,"POLICIES FOR TRADE AND DEVELOPMENT." AFR FUT WOR+45 DIST/IND FINAN NAT/G DELIB/GP PLAN ECO/TAC ORD/FREE WEALTH...POLICY STAT TIME/SEQ CHARTS METH/GP 20. PAGE 126 F2480 MARKET ECO/UNDEV INT/TRADE

S64
BEIM D.,"THE COMMUNIST BLOC AND THE FOREIGN-AID GAME." AFR WOR+45 NAT/G PLAN ROUTINE ATTIT KNOWL ORD/FREE...DECISION QUANT CONT/OBS TIME/SEQ CHARTS GAME SIMUL LOG/LING 20. PAGE 12 F0231 COM ECO/UNDEV ECO/TAC FOR/AID

S64
CARNEGIE ENDOWMENT INT. PEACE,"ADMINISTRATION AND BUDGET (ISSUES BEFORE THE NINETEENTH GENERAL ASSEMBLY)." WOR+45 FINAN BUDGET ECO/TAC ROUTINE COST...STAT RECORD UN. PAGE 21 F0415 INT/ORG ADMIN

S64
DOE J.F.,"TROPICAL AFRICAN CONTRIBUTIONS TO FEDERAL FINANCE." AFR NAT/G PROVS CENTRAL RIGID/FLEX PWR WEALTH...STAT VAL/FREE 20 CMN/WLTH. PAGE 33 F0650 FINAN ECO/TAC

S64
FINLEY D.D.,"A POLITICAL PERSPECTIVE OF ECONOMIC RELATIONS IN THE COMMUNIST CAMP." COM USSR FACE/GP NAT/G ACT/RES PLAN DOMIN COERCE ATTIT ORD/FREE WEALTH...TIME/SEQ 20. PAGE 41 F0800 VOL/ASSN ECO/TAC DIPLOM REGION

S64
FLORINSKY M.T.,"TRENDS IN THE SOVIET ECONOMY." COM USA+45 USSR INDUS LABOR NAT/G PLAN TEC/DEV ECO/TAC ALL/VALS SOCISM...MGT METH/CNCPT STYLE CON/ANAL GEN/METH WORK 20. PAGE 42 F0817 ECO/DEV AGRI

S64
GALBRAITH V.,"JAPAN'S POSITION IN WORLD TRADE." ASIA AGRI INDUS CREATE ECO/TAC LEGIT DRIVE WEALTH ...TREND EEC GATT FOR/TRADE 20 CHINJAP. PAGE 45 F0885 ECO/DEV DELIB/GP

S64
GARDNER R.N.,"GATT AND THE UNITED NATIONS CONFERENCE ON TRADE AND DEVELOPMENT." USA+45 WOR+45 SOCIETY ECO/UNDEV MARKET NAT/G DELIB/GP ACT/RES PLAN ECO/TAC TARIFFS EDU/PROP ROUTINE DRIVE RIGID/FLEX WEALTH...DECISION MGT TREND UN TOT/POP 20 GATT. PAGE 46 F0905 INT/ORG INT/TRADE

S64
HERMAN L.M.,"THE ECONOMIC CONTENT OF SOVIET TRADE WITH THE WEST." WOR+45 ECO/DEV ECO/UNDEV AGRI COM/IND INDUS CAP/ISM ECO/TAC ATTIT RIGID/FLEX WEALTH...OBS TREND VAL/FREE MARX/KARL 20. PAGE 59 F1152 COM MARKET INT/TRADE USSR

S64
HUELIN D.,"ECONOMIC INTEGRATION IN LATIN AMERICAN: PROGRESS AND PROBLEMS." L/A+17C ECO/DEV AGRI DIST/IND FINAN INDUS NAT/G VOL/ASSN CONSULT DELIB/GP EX/STRUC ACT/RES PLAN TEC/DEV ECO/TAC ROUTINE BAL/PAY WEALTH FOR/TRADE WORK TERR/GP 20. PAGE 63 F1232 MARKET ECO/UNDEV INT/TRADE

S64
HUTCHINSON E.C.,"AMERICAN AID TO AFRICA." FUT USA+45 MARKET INT/ORG LOC/G NAT/G PUB/INST PLAN ECO/TAC ATTIT RIGID/FLEX...POLICY CONCPT TREND TERR/GP 20. PAGE 63 F1248 AFR ECO/UNDEV FOR/AID

S64
KLEIN H.,"AMERICAN OIL COMPANIES IN LATIN AMERICA: THE BOLIVIAN EXPERIENCE." L/A+17C USA+45 USA-45 EXTR/IND LG/CO NAT/G ECO/TAC WEALTH...POLICY GEN/LAWS BOLIV TOT/POP 20 OIL. PAGE 72 F1405 MARKET ECO/UNDEV NAT/LISM

S64
KOJIMA K.,"THE PATTERN OF INTERNATIONAL TRADE AMONG ADVANCED COUNTRIES." EUR+WWI UK USA+45 WOR+45 MARKET NAT/G ECO/TAC WEALTH...MATH STAT CON/ANAL CHARTS METH/GP EEC CHINJAP 20 CHINJAP. PAGE 72 F1419 ECO/DEV TREND INT/TRADE

S64
MC WILLIAM M.,"THE WORLD BANK AND THE TRANSFER OF POWER IN KENYA." AFR ECO/UNDEV CONSULT ACT/RES TEC/DEV PERCEPT PWR SKILL WEALTH...CONCPT OBS TREND 20. PAGE 88 F1715 NAT/G ECO/TAC

S64
N,"QUASI-LEGISLATIVE ARBITRATION AGREEMENTS." LAW LG/CO ECO/TAC SANCTION ATTIT POLICY. PAGE 96 F1885 ADJUD ADJUST LABOR GP/REL

S64
NEISSER H.,"THE EXTERNAL EQUILIBRIUM OF THE UNITED STATES ECONOMY." FUT USA+45 NAT/G ACT/RES PLAN ECO/TAC ATTIT WEALTH...METH/CNCPT GEN/METH VAL/FREE FOR/TRADE 20. PAGE 97 F1910 FINAN ECO/DEV BAL/PAY INT/TRADE

S64
PADELFORD N.J.,"THE ORGANIZATION OF AFRICAN UNITY." ECO/UNDEV INT/ORG PLAN BAL/PWR DIPLOM ECO/TAC NAT/LISM ORD/FREE PWR WEALTH...CONCPT TREND STERTYP TERR/GP VAL/FREE 20. PAGE 102 F2013 AFR VOL/ASSN REGION

S64
PATEL S.J.,"THE ECONOMIC DISTANCE BETWEEN NATIONS: ITS ORIGIN, MEASUREMENT AND OUTLOOK." WOR+45 ECO/DEV AGRI FINAN INDUS MARKET LABOR NAT/G CONSULT TEC/DEV ECO/TAC WEALTH...POLICY RELATIV MGT TREND WORK 20. PAGE 103 F2035 ECO/UNDEV PLAN

S64
PESELT B.M.,"COMMUNIST ECONOMIC OFFENSIVE." WOR+45 SOCIETY INT/ORG PLAN ECO/TAC DOMIN EDU/PROP ATTIT PERSON PWR WEALTH...TREND CHARTS METH/GP 20. PAGE 105 F2067 COM ECO/UNDEV FOR/AID USSR

S64
POLARIS J.,"THE SINO-SOVIET DISPUTE: ITS ECONOMIC IMPACT ON CHINA." ASIA CHINA/COM COM WOR+45 NAT/G ATTIT PWR WEALTH...STAT TREND FOR/TRADE 20. PAGE 107 F2095 ECO/UNDEV ECO/TAC

S64
ROTHCHILD D.,"EAST AFRICAN FEDERATION." AFR TANZANIA UGANDA INDUS REGION 20. PAGE 114 F2249 INT/ORG DIPLOM ECO/UNDEV ECO/TAC

S64
RUSSETT B.M.,"INEQUALITY AND INSTABILITY: THE RELATION OF LAND TENURE TO POLITICS." WOR+45 ECO/DEV ECO/UNDEV AGRI NAT/G COERCE PWR...MATH STAT CHARTS GEN/LAWS TERR/GP TRUE/GP METH/GP VAL/FREE 20. PAGE 115 F2263 WEALTH GEOG ECO/TAC ORD/FREE

S64
SALVADORI M.,"EL CAPITALISMO EN LA EUROPA DE LA POSGUERRA." AFR INT/ORG NAT/G POL/PAR PLAN ECO/TAC ATTIT ORD/FREE WEALTH...HIST/WRIT EEC 20. PAGE 115 F2275 EUR+WWI ECO/DEV CAP/ISM

S64
SCHMITT H.D.,"POLITICAL CONDITIONS FOR INTERNATIONAL CURRENCY REFORM." WOR+45 SOCIETY ECO/DEV PLAN ECO/TAC BAL/PAY ATTIT ORD/FREE WEALTH ...SOC CONCPT OBS TREND EEC VAL/FREE ECSC 20. PAGE 117 F2301 FINAN VOL/ASSN REGION

S64
TOBIN J.,"ECONOMIC GROWTH AS AN OBJECTIVE OF ECO/DEV

GOVERNMENT POLICY." FUT WOR+45 FINAN WORKER BUDGET INCOME...SOC 20. PAGE 131 F2579
POLICY ECO/TAC IDEA/COMP

S64
WOOD N.,"THE FAMILY FIRM - BASE OF JAPAN'S GROWING ECONOMY." ECO/DEV ECO/UNDEV ECO/TAC WEALTH...POLICY TRADIT BIOG TREND 20 CHINJAP. PAGE 148 F2921
ASIA SML/CO FAM

S64
WU Y.,"CHINA'S ECONOMY AND ITS PROSPECTS." ASIA CHINA/COM FUT USSR AGRI INDUS PLAN ECO/TAC LEGIT WEALTH...STAT CON/ANAL CHARTS GEN/LAWS FOR/TRADE 20. PAGE 149 F2938
ECO/DEV

B65
ANALYSIS AND ASSESSMENT OF THE ECONOMIC EFFECTS: PUBLIC LAW 480 TITLE I PROGRAM TURKEY. INDIA TURKEY USA+45 AGRI NAT/G PLAN BUDGET DIPLOM COST EFFICIENCY...CHARTS 20. PAGE 1 F0021
ECO/TAC FOR/AID FINAN ECO/UNDEV

B65
ACHTERBERG E.,BERLINER HOCHFINANZ - KAISER, FURSTEN, MILLIONARE UM 1900. GERMANY NAT/G EDU/PROP PERSON...MGT MUNICH 19/20. PAGE 2 F0033
FINAN BIOG ECO/TAC

B65
AMERICAN ECONOMIC ASSOCIATION,INDEX OF ECONOMIC JOURNALS 1886-1965 (7 VOLS.). UK USA+45 USA-45 AGRI FINAN PLAN ECO/TAC INT/TRADE ADMIN...STAT CENSUS 19/20. PAGE 5 F0087
BIBLIOG WRITING INDUS

B65
AMERICAN FOREST PRODUCTS INDUS,GOVERNMENT LAND ACQUISITION: A SUMMARY OF LAND ACQUISITION BY FEDERAL, STATE, AND LOCAL GOVERNMENTS UP TO 1964. USA+45 USA-45 TAX...POLICY GEOG CHARTS 20. PAGE 5 F0089
NAT/G OWN ECO/TAC GOV/REL

B65
ANDERSON C.A.,EDUCATION AND ECONOMIC DEVELOPMENT. INDUS R+D SCHOOL TEC/DEV ECO/TAC EDU/PROP AGE HEREDITY PERCEPT SKILL 20. PAGE 5 F0092
ANTHOL ECO/DEV ECO/UNDEV WORKER

B65
BALDWIN D.A.,SOFT LOANS AND AMERICAN FOREIGN POLICY: 1943-1962 (THESIS). USA+45 WOR+45 FINAN NAT/G FOR/AID BAL/PAY ATTIT...POLICY METH/COMP 20 UN CONGRESS. PAGE 9 F0161
DIPLOM ECO/TAC ECO/UNDEV

B65
BELASSA B.,ECONOMIC DEVELOPMENT AND INTEGRATION. LG/CO PROB/SOLV TEC/DEV INT/TRADE TARIFFS COST WEALTH...POLICY METH/COMP 20. PAGE 12 F0232
ECO/UNDEV ECO/TAC INT/ORG INDUS

B65
BOWEN W.G.,UNEMPLOYMENT IN A PROSPEROUS ECONOMY. USA+45 ECO/DEV NAT/G ACT/RES PLAN PAY EDU/PROP DEMAND...POLICY IDEA/COMP ANTHOL 20. PAGE 17 F0330
WORKER ECO/TAC WEALTH PROB/SOLV

B65
BREAK G.F.,FEDERAL LENDING AND ECONOMIC STABILITY. USA+45 ECO/DEV LG/CO SML/CO EQUILIB...CHARTS 20. PAGE 18 F0344
BUDGET FINAN NAT/G ECO/TAC

B65
BRENNAN M.J.,PATTERNS OF MARKET BEHAVIOR. AFR USA+45 OP/RES CAP/ISM ECO/TAC INT/TRADE...CHARTS METH/COMP ANTHOL TIME 20. PAGE 18 F0346
MARKET LABOR FINAN ECOMETRIC

B65
BROOKINGS INSTITUTION,BROOKINGS PAPERS ON PUBLIC POLICY. USA+45 ECO/UNDEV LEGIS CAP/ISM ECO/TAC TAX EDU/PROP CONTROL APPORT 20. PAGE 19 F0363
DIPLOM FOR/AID POLICY FINAN

B65
CASSELL F.,GOLD OR CREDIT? THE ECONOMICS AND POLITICS OF INTERNATIONAL MONEY. AFR WOR+45 PLAN PROB/SOLV BAL/PAY SOVEREIGN WEALTH 20 OEEC. PAGE 22 F0428
FINAN INT/ORG DIPLOM ECO/TAC

B65
CLARK T.D.,THREE PATHS TO THE MODERN SOUTH: EDUCATION, AGRICULTURE, AND CONSERVATION. FUT USA-45 ECO/DEV ECO/TAC PEACE WEALTH...POLICY 20 SOUTH/US. PAGE 25 F0485
AGRI EDU/PROP GOV/REL REGION

B65
COLLOQUE SUR LA PLANIFICATION,LA PLANIFICATION COMME PROCESSUS DE DECISION. FRANCE SOCIETY MARKET LABOR LEGIS GP/REL EFFICIENCY INCOME ATTIT TECHRACY ...MYTH IDEA/COMP 20. PAGE 26 F0508
PLAN ECO/TAC PROB/SOLV

B65
DELHI INSTITUTE OF ECO GROWTH,A STUDY IN THE WORKING OF THE INTENSIVE AREA SCHEME OF THE KHADI AND VILLAGE INDUSTRIES COMMISSION. INDIA AGRI FINAN DELIB/GP ECO/TAC EFFICIENCY...QU CHARTS MUNICH 20. PAGE 32 F0614
PLAN INDUS ECO/UNDEV

B65
DOWD L.P.,PRINCIPLES OF WORLD BUSINESS. SERV/IND NAT/G DIPLOM ECO/TAC TARIFFS...INT/LAW JURID 20. PAGE 34 F0657
INT/TRADE MGT FINAN MARKET

B65
EDELMAN M.,THE POLITICS OF WAGE-PRICE DECISIONS. GERMANY ITALY NETHERLAND UK INDUS LABOR POL/PAR PROB/SOLV BARGAIN PRICE ROUTINE BAL/PAY COST DEMAND 20. PAGE 36 F0699
GOV/COMP CONTROL ECO/TAC PLAN

B65
FARER T.J.,FINANCING AFRICAN DEVELOPMENT. AFR ECO/TAC FOR/AID SOCISM 20. PAGE 39 F0764
ECO/UNDEV FINAN CAP/ISM PLAN

B65
FORD J.L.,THE OHLIN-HECKSCHER THEORY OF THE BASIS AND EFFECTS OF COMMODITY TRADE. WOR+45 ECO/TAC DEMAND INCOME...CONCPT GEN/METH 20 OHLIN/HECK. PAGE 42 F0824
ECOMETRIC INT/TRADE NEW/IDEA SIMUL

B65
GOETZ-GIREY R.,LE MOUVEMENT DES GREVES EN FRANCE. FRANCE FINAN OP/RES PROB/SOLV ECO/TAC INCOME HABITAT...STAT CHARTS 19/20. PAGE 48 F0932
LABOR WORKER GP/REL INDUS

B65
GRAMPP W.D.,ECONOMIC LIBERALISM; THE BEGINNINGS (VOL. I). USA-45 WOR-45 MARKET LABOR ATTIT WEALTH ...POLICY CONCPT BIBLIOG GREECE/ANC MERCANTLST REPUBLICAN FEDERALIST. PAGE 50 F0974
ECO/DEV CAP/ISM IDEA/COMP ECO/TAC

B65
GRAMPP W.D.,ECONOMIC LIBERALISM; THE CLASSICAL VIEW (VOL. II). MOD/EUR SOCIETY MARKET INT/TRADE NAT/LISM WEALTH LAISSEZ...POLICY PSY CONCPT BIBLIOG 19 SMITH/ADAM HUME/D MILL/JS. PAGE 50 F0975
ECO/DEV CAP/ISM IDEA/COMP ECO/TAC

B65
GREEN J.L.,METROPOLITAN ECONOMIC REPUBLICS. USA+45 ECO/TAC INCOME...GEOG SOC CONCPT SIMUL MUNICH 20 ATLANTA. PAGE 50 F0985
SOC/WK PLAN LABOR

B65
HABERLER G.,A SURVEY OF INTERNATIONAL TRADE THEORY. CANADA FRANCE GERMANY ECO/TAC TARIFFS AGREE COST DEMAND WEALTH...ECOMETRIC 19/20 MONOPOLY TREATY. PAGE 52 F1024
INT/TRADE BAL/PAY DIPLOM POLICY

B65
HAEFELE E.T.,GOVERNMENT CONTROLS ON TRANSPORT. AFR RHODESIA TANZANIA DIPLOM ECO/TAC TARIFFS PRICE ADJUD CONTROL REGION EFFICIENCY...POLICY 20 CONGO. PAGE 53 F1031
ECO/UNDEV DIST/IND FINAN NAT/G

B65
HAPGOOD D.,AFRICA: FROM INDEPENDENCE TO TOMARROW. AFR GUINEA SENEGAL CULTURE ELITES ECO/UNDEV AGRI SCHOOL FOR/AID COLONIAL MARXISM...TREND 20. PAGE 55 F1070
ECO/TAC SOCIETY NAT/G

B65
HOSELITZ B.F.,ECONOMICS AND THE IDEA OF MANKIND. UNIV ECO/DEV ECO/UNDEV DIST/IND INDUS INT/ORG NAT/G ACT/RES ECO/TAC WEALTH...CONCPT STAT. PAGE 62 F1223
CREATE INT/TRADE

B65
IANNI O.,ESTADO E CAPITALISMO. L/A+17C FINAN TEC/DEV ECO/TAC ORD/FREE WEALTH POLICY. PAGE 64 F1258
ECO/UNDEV STRUCT INDUS NAT/G

B65
INT. BANK RECONSTR. DEVELOP.,ECONOMIC DEVELOPMENT OF KUWAIT. ISLAM KUWAIT AGRI FINAN MARKET EX/STRUC TEC/DEV ECO/TAC ADMIN WEALTH...OBS CON/ANAL CHARTS 20. PAGE 64 F1266
INDUS NAT/G

B65
INTERAMERICAN ECO AND SOC COUN,THE ALLIANCE FOR PROGRESS: ITS THIRD YEAR 1963-1964. FUT L/A+17C WOR+45 ECO/DEV INT/ORG PLAN CONTROL ADJUST...STAT ANTHOL SOC/INTEG 20 ALL/PROG. PAGE 64 F1268
ECO/UNDEV ECO/TAC FINAN FOR/AID

B65
JAIN S.C.,THE STATE AND AGRICULTURE. INDIA S/ASIA ECO/UNDEV PROB/SOLV CAP/ISM MARXISM SOCISM 20. PAGE 66 F1304
NAT/G POLICY AGRI ECO/TAC

B65
JASNY H.,KHRUSHCHEV'S CROP POLICY. USSR ECO/DEV PLAN MARXISM...STAT 20 KHRUSH/N RESOURCE/N. PAGE 66 F1306
AGRI NAT/G POLICY ECO/TAC

B65
JOHNSTONE A.,UNITED STATES DIRECT INVESTMENT IN FRANCE: AN INVESTIGATION OF THE FRENCH CHARGES. FRANCE USA+45 ECO/DEV INDUS LG/CO NAT/G ECO/TAC CONTROL WEALTH...BIBLIOG 20 INTERVENT. PAGE 68 F1335
FINAN DIPLOM POLICY SOVEREIGN

B65
KANTOROVICH L.V.,THE BEST USE OF ECONOMIC RESOURCES. USSR SOCIETY FINAN ACT/RES TEC/DEV ECO/TAC PRICE CONTROL COST DEMAND EFFICIENCY OPTIMAL...MGT STAT. PAGE 69 F1350
PLAN MATH DECISION

B65
KLASSEN L.H.,AREA ECONOMIC AND SOCIAL REDEVELOPMENT. ECO/UNDEV INDUS NAT/G PLAN CAP/ISM TAX...ECOMETRIC SIMUL 20. PAGE 72 F1404
OPTIMAL WORKER METH ECO/TAC

B65
THE STATE AND ECONOMIC ENTERPRISE IN JAPAN; ESSAYS IN THE POLITICAL ECONOMY OF GROWTH. AGRI INDUS DRIVE POPULISM...CHARTS NAT/COMP ANTHOL 19/20 CHINJAP. PAGE 81 F1594
ECO/UNDEV ECO/DEV CAP/ISM ECO/TAC

MACAVOY P.W.,THE ECONOMIC EFFECTS OF REGULATION: THE TRUNK-LINE RAILROAD CARTELS AND THE INTERSTATE COMMERCE COMMISSION BEFORE 1900. USA-45 PRICE PROFIT...STAT CHARTS BIBLIOG 19 RAILROAD. PAGE 83 F1620 — B65 — ECO/TAC DIST/IND PROF/ORG RATION

MACDONALD R.W.,THE LEAGUE OF ARAB STATES: A STUDY IN THE DYNAMICS OF REGIONAL ORGANIZATION. ISRAEL UAR USSR FINAN INT/ORG DELIB/GP ECO/TAC AGREE NEUTRAL ORD/FREE PWR...DECISION BIBLIOG 20 TREATY UN. PAGE 83 F1626 — B65 — ISLAM REGION DIPLOM ADMIN

MACESICH G.,COMMERCIAL BANKING AND REGIONAL DEVELOPMENT IN THE US, 1950-1960. USA+45 NAT/G PLAN ECO/TAC DEMAND...MGT 20 FED/RESERV SOUTH/US. PAGE 83 F1627 — B65 — FINAN ECO/DEV INCOME COST

MARK S.M.,ECONOMICS IN ACTION (3RD ED.). USA+45 ECO/UNDEV AGRI INDUS FOR/AID INT/TRADE BAL/PAY COST ORD/FREE...ANTHOL 20 RESOURCE/N. PAGE 85 F1670 — B65 — POLICY ECO/TAC EFFICIENCY PRICE

MELMANS S.,OUR DEPLETED SOCIETY. AFR SPACE USA+45 ECO/DEV FORCES BUDGET ECO/TAC ADMIN WEAPON EFFICIENCY 20. PAGE 89 F1753 — B65 — CIVMIL/REL INDUS EDU/PROP CONTROL

MONCRIEFF A.,SECOND THOUGHTS ON AID. WOR+45 ECO/UNDEV AGRI FINAN VOL/ASSN PLAN TEC/DEV GIVE EDU/PROP ROLE WEALTH 20. PAGE 93 F1816 — B65 — FOR/AID ECO/TAC INT/ORG IDEA/COMP

MUND V.A.,GOVERNMENT AND BUSINESS (4TH ED.). USA+45 INDUS LG/CO SML/CO LEGIS INT/TRADE LICENSE PRICE ADJUD. PAGE 95 F1860 — B65 — NAT/G ECO/TAC BUDGET CONTROL

MURUMBI J.,PROBLEMS OF ECONOMIC DEVELOPMENT IN EAST AFRICA. FINAN INDUS WORKER TEC/DEV INT/TRADE TAX DEMAND EFFICIENCY PRODUC SOCISM...TREND CHARTS 20 AFRICA/E. PAGE 95 F1869 — B65 — AGRI ECO/TAC ECO/UNDEV PROC/MFG

MUSOLF L.D.,PROMOTING THE GENERAL WELFARE: GOVERNMENT AND THE ECONOMY. USA+45 ECO/DEV CAP/ISM DEMAND OPTIMAL 20. PAGE 95 F1874 — B65 — ECO/TAC NAT/G EX/STRUC NEW/LIB

NKRUMAH K.,NEO-COLONIALISM: THE LAST STAGE OF IMPERIALISM. AFR INT/ORG WORKER FOR/AID INT/TRADE EDU/PROP GOV/REL NAT/LISM SOVEREIGN POPULISM SOCISM ...SOCIALIST 20 THIRD/WRLD INTRVN/ECO. PAGE 98 F1929 — B65 — COLONIAL DIPLOM ECO/UNDEV ECO/TAC

ONSLOW C.,ASIAN ECONOMIC DEVELOPMENT. BURMA CEYLON INDIA MALAYSIA PAKISTAN S/ASIA AGRI INDUS MARKET PROB/SOLV CAP/ISM FOR/AID INT/TRADE DEMAND WEALTH ...POLICY ANTHOL 20. PAGE 101 F1991 — B65 — ECO/UNDEV ECO/TAC PLAN NAT/G

OXENFELDT A.R.,ECONOMIC SYSTEMS IN ACTION. FRANCE USA+45 USSR CULTURE PLAN PROB/SOLV TEC/DEV INCOME PRODUC WEALTH...METH/COMP 20. PAGE 102 F2007 — B65 — ECO/DEV CAP/ISM MARXISM ECO/TAC

PHELPS E.S.,FISCAL NEUTRALITY TOWARD ECONOMIC GROWTH. FINAN NAT/G BUDGET CAP/ISM CONTROL INCOME 20. PAGE 106 F2080 — B65 — ECO/DEV POLICY ECO/TAC TAX

PROCHNOW H.V.,WORLD ECONOMIC PROBLEMS AND POLICIES. INDIA ISRAEL WOR+45 AGRI LABOR PROB/SOLV FOR/AID TARIFFS CONTROL BAL/PAY NAT/LISM WEALTH...TREND CHARTS 20 CHINJAP EEC. PAGE 108 F2124 — B65 — MARKET ECO/TAC PRODUC IDEA/COMP

REAGAN M.D.,POLITICS, ECONOMICS, AND THE GENERAL WELFARE. USA+45 INDUS ECO/TAC TAX WEALTH...POLICY IDEA/COMP ANTHOL 20. PAGE 110 F2162 — B65 — NAT/G ECO/DEV R+D ACADEM

RIVKIN M.D.,AREA DEVELOPMENT FOR NATIONAL GROWTH; THE TURKISH PRECEDENT. ISLAM TURKEY ACT/RES INGP/REL...POLICY CHARTS GP/COMP MUNICH 20 ATATURK/MK INONU/I. PAGE 112 F2197 — B65 — ECO/UNDEV REGION ECO/TAC PLAN

ROLFE S.E.,GOLD AND WORLD POWER. AFR UK USA+45 WOR-45 INDUS WORKER INT/TRADE DEMAND...MGT CHARTS 20. PAGE 113 F2234 — B65 — BAL/PAY EQUILIB ECO/TAC DIPLOM

ROSS P.,THE GOVERNMENT AS A SOURCE OF UNION POWER. USA+45 LAW ECO/DEV PROB/SOLV ECO/TAC LEAD GP/REL ...MGT 20. PAGE 114 F2245 — B65 — LABOR BARGAIN POLICY NAT/G

ROWE J.W.,PRIMARY COMMODITIES IN INTERNATIONAL TRADE. MARKET CAP/ISM ECO/TAC DEMAND...NAT/COMP 20. PAGE 114 F2253 — B65 — INT/TRADE AGRI RATION PRICE

SABLE M.H.,PERIODICALS FOR LATIN AMERICAN ECONOMIC DEVELOPMENT, TRADE, AND FINANCE: AN ANNOTATED BIBLIOGRAPHY (A PAMPHLET). ECO/TAC PRODUC PROFIT ...STAT NAT/COMP 20 OAS. PAGE 115 F2266 — B65 — BIBLIOG/A L/A+17C ECO/UNDEV INT/TRADE

SCHULER E.A.,THE PAKISTAN ACADEMIES FOR RURAL DEVELOPMENT COMILLA AND PESHAWAR 1959-1964. PAKISTAN S/ASIA SOCIETY STRUCT AGRI NAT/G TEC/DEV EDU/PROP 20. PAGE 117 F2314 — B65 — BIBLIOG PLAN ECO/TAC ECO/UNDEV

SCHULTZ T.W.,ECONOMIC CRISES IN WORLD AGRICULTURE. ASIA INDIA USSR ECO/DEV ECO/UNDEV INDUS VOL/ASSN CAP/ISM RATION COLONIAL 20. PAGE 117 F2317 — B65 — AGRI ECO/TAC INCOME WORKER

SCITOVSKY T.,REQUIREMENTS OF AN INTERNATIONAL RESERVE SYSTEM. AFR ECO/TAC...PREDICT 20 SILVER MONEY. PAGE 118 F2330 — B65 — BAL/PAY FINAN EQUILIB INT/TRADE

SCOTT A.M.,THE REVOLUTION IN STATECRAFT: INFORMAL PENETRATION. WOR+45 WOR-45 CULTURE INT/ORG FORCES ECO/TAC ROUTINE...BIBLIOG 20. PAGE 118 F2331 — B65 — DIPLOM EDU/PROP FOR/AID

SELIGMAN B.B.,POVERTY AS A PUBLIC ISSUE. USA+45 ECO/DEV NAT/G PAY RECEIVE PERS/REL INCOME NEW/LIB 20. PAGE 119 F2347 — B65 — LEGIS ECO/TAC STRATA DISCRIM

SINHA M.R.,THE ECONOMICS OF MANPOWER PLANNING. FUT HUNGARY NAT/G CONTROL...POLICY GEOG ANTHOL 20 CHINJAP. PAGE 122 F2415 — B65 — ECO/UNDEV PLAN WORKER ECO/TAC

US HOUSE COMM BANKING-CURR,INTERNATIONAL TRAVEL IN RELATION TO THE BALANCE OF PAYMENTS DEFICIT. USA+45 DELIB/GP...CHARTS 20 CONGRESS TRAVEL. PAGE 136 F2690 — B65 — BAL/PAY ECO/TAC SERV/IND PROB/SOLV

US OFFICE ECONOMIC OPPORTUNITY,CATALOG OF FEDERAL PROGRAMS FOR INDIVIDUAL AND COMMUNITY IMPROVEMENT. USA+45 GIVE RECEIVE ADMIN HEALTH KNOWL SKILL WEALTH ...CHARTS MUNICH. PAGE 138 F2721 — B65 — BIBLIOG CLIENT ECO/TAC

US SENATE COMM ON JUDICIARY,ANTITRUST EXEMPTIONS FOR AGREEMENTS RELATING TO BALANCE OF PAYMENTS. FINAN ECO/TAC CONTROL WEALTH...POLICY 20 CONGRESS. PAGE 140 F2750 — B65 — BAL/PAY ADJUD MARKET INT/TRADE

VANEK J.,GENERAL EQUILIBRIUM OF INTERNATIONAL DISCRIMINATION; THE CASE OF CUSTOMS UNIONS. LABOR PROB/SOLV ECO/TAC DISCRIM INCOME...MATH CHARTS METH 20. PAGE 140 F2767 — B65 — INT/TRADE TARIFFS INT/ORG EQUILIB

WALTON R.E.,A BEHAVIORAL THEORY OF LABOR NEGOTIATIONS: AN ANALYSIS OF A SOCIAL INTERACTION SYSTEM. USA+45 FINAN PROB/SOLV ECO/TAC GP/REL INGP/REL...DECISION BIBLIOG. PAGE 143 F2812 — B65 — SOC LABOR BARGAIN ADMIN

WARD R.J.,INTERNATIONAL FINANCE. INT/ORG DIPLOM DEMAND INCOME...POLICY METH/COMP 20. PAGE 143 F2819 — B65 — INT/TRADE ECO/TAC FINAN BAL/PAY

WASSERMAN M.J.,THE BALANCE OF PAYMENTS: HISTORY, METHODOLOGY, THEORY. UK USA+45 USA-45 CAP/ISM DIPLOM EFFICIENCY...DECISION METH/CNCPT BIBLIOG 18/20 LEAGUE/NAT. PAGE 144 F2828 — B65 — BAL/PAY ECO/TAC GEN/LAWS EQUILIB

WATERSTON A.,DEVELOPMENT PLANNING* LESSONS OF EXPERIENCE. ECO/TAC CENTRAL...MGT QUANT BIBLIOG. PAGE 144 F2830 — B65 — ECO/UNDEV CREATE PLAN ADMIN

WHITE J.,GERMAN AID. GERMANY/W FINAN PLAN TEC/DEV INT/TRADE ADMIN ATTIT...POLICY 20. PAGE 146 F2870 — B65 — FOR/AID ECO/UNDEV DIPLOM ECO/TAC

WU YUAN-LI,THE ECONOMY OF COMMUNIST CHINA. CHINA/COM USSR AGRI FINAN INDUS POL/PAR WORKER PROB/SOLV INT/TRADE PRICE EATING INCOME OWN WEALTH 20. PAGE 149 F2939 — B65 — ECO/TAC MARXISM PLAN EFFICIENCY

WURFEL S.W.,FOREIGN ENTERPRISE IN COLOMBIA. FINAN LABOR NAT/G ECO/TAC TAX REGION 20 COLOMB. PAGE 149 F2944 — B65 — ECO/UNDEV INT/TRADE JURID CAP/ISM

YOUNG A.N.,CHINA'S WARTIME FINANCE AND INFLATION. ASIA AGRI INDUS NAT/G ECO/TAC CONFER PRICE WAR COST 20. PAGE 150 F2949 — B65 — FINAN FOR/AID TAX BUDGET

B65
ZAWADZKI K.K.F.,THE ECONOMICS OF INFLATIONARY PROCESSES. FINAN INT/TRADE PRICE CONTROL DEMAND EQUILIB PROFIT 20. PAGE 150 F2960
ECO/DEV COST ECO/TAC CAP/ISM

L65
DAANE J.D.,"THE EVOLVING INTERNATIONAL MONETARY MECHANISM." VOL/ASSN CREATE PLAN FOR/AID INT/TRADE CONFER BAL/PAY...RECORD PREDICT IMF. PAGE 29 F0569
INT/ORG ECO/TAC TREND GP/COMP

L65
LETICHE J.M.,"EUROPEAN INTEGRATION: AN AMERICAN VIEW." EUR+WWI FRANCE WOR+45 ECO/DEV DIST/IND EXTR/IND NAT/G DELIB/GP TOP/EX PLAN ECO/TAC ATTIT ...STAT CON/ANAL CHARTS EEC 20. PAGE 78 F1537
INDUS AGRI

L65
WILLIAMS S.,"NEGOTIATING INVESTMENT IN EMERGING COUNTRIES." USA+45 WOR+45 INDUS MARKET NAT/G TOP/EX TEC/DEV CAP/ISM ECO/TAC ADMIN SKILL WEALTH...POLICY RELATIV MGT WORK 20. PAGE 147 F2894
FINAN ECO/UNDEV

L65
WIONCZEK M.,"LATIN AMERICA FREE TRADE ASSOCIATION." AGRI DIST/IND FINAN INDUS INT/ORG LABOR NAT/G TEC/DEV ECO/TAC HEALTH SKILL WEALTH...POLICY RELATIV MGT LAFTA 20. PAGE 148 F2909
L/A+17C MARKET REGION

S65
BERREBY J.J.,"IMPERATIFS STRATEGIQUES DU PETROLE." ECO/UNDEV VOL/ASSN ECO/TAC COLONIAL NUC/PWR WAR. PAGE 14 F0270
ISLAM EXTR/IND STAT OBS

S65
BRANDENBURG F.,"THE RELEVANCE OF MEXICAN EXPERIENCE TO LATIN AMERICAN DEVELOPMENT." BRAZIL CHILE VENEZUELA STRUCT ECO/UNDEV AGRI CREATE ECO/TAC ...STAT RECORD MEXIC/AMER ARGEN COLOMB. PAGE 18 F0340
L/A+17C GOV/COMP

S65
CAMPOLONGO A.,"EUROPEAN INVESTMENT BANK* ACTIVITY AND PROSPECTS." FUT ECO/UNDEV FINAN PLAN DIPLOM ...STAT EEC LOAN EIB. PAGE 21 F0410
ECO/TAC PREDICT

S65
DUMONT R.,"SURPEUPLEMENT CHINOIS ET SES CONSEQUENCES." AFR ECO/UNDEV AGRI PLAN PROB/SOLV ECO/TAC FOR/AID NUC/PWR...OBS INT PREDICT. PAGE 35 F0675
GEOG ASIA STAT

S65
GOLDMAN M.I.,"A BALANCE SHEET OF SOVIET FOREIGN AID." USA+45 ECO/UNDEV BAL/PWR ECO/TAC RENT GIVE EDU/PROP CONTROL COST PROFIT GEN/METH. PAGE 48 F0939
USSR FOR/AID NAT/COMP EFFICIENCY

S65
HAYTER T.,"FRENCH AID TO AFRICA* ITS SCOPE AND ACHIEVEMENTS." CULTURE ECO/TAC INT/TRADE ADMIN REGION CENTRAL FEDERAL LOVE PWR SOVEREIGN EEC. PAGE 57 F1127
AFR FRANCE FOR/AID COLONIAL

S65
HUTT W.H.,"KEYNESIAN REVISIONS" SOUTH/AFR ECO/DEV FINAN NAT/G WORKER BUDGET TAX PRICE EQUILIB WEALTH 20 KEYNES/JM. PAGE 64 F1252
ECO/TAC GEN/LAWS LOG

S65
JOHNSON L.L.,"US BUSINESS INTERESTS IN CUBA AND THE RISE OF CASTRO." L/A+17C USA+45 ECO/UNDEV INDUS NAT/G VOL/ASSN ATTIT ORD/FREE PWR WEALTH ALL/PROG. PAGE 68 F1330
DIPLOM CUBA ECO/TAC INT/TRADE

S65
KAUN D.E.,"THE FAIR LABOUR STANDARDS ACT: AN EVALUATION IN TERMS OF ITS STATED GOALS." SOUTH/AFR LAW LABOR BARGAIN PAY INGP/REL WEALTH 20. PAGE 69 F1364
ECO/TAC PRICE WORKER LEGIS

S65
KEE W.S.,"CENTRAL CITY EXPENDITURES AND METROPOLITAN AREAS." PLAN BUDGET ECO/TAC TAX GP/REL WEALTH...CHARTS MUNICH 20. PAGE 70 F1366
LOC/G GOV/COMP NEIGH

S65
KORBONSKI A.,"USA POLICY IN EAST EUROPE." COM EUR+WWI GERMANY USA+45 CULTURE ECO/UNDEV EDU/PROP RIGID/FLEX WEALTH FOR/TRADE 20. PAGE 73 F1426
ACT/RES ECO/TAC FOR/AID

S65
LECLERCQ H.,"ECONOMIC RESEARCH AND DEVELOPMENT IN TROPICAL AFRICA." ECO/UNDEV INT/ORG CREATE PLAN UN. PAGE 77 F1500
AFR R+D ACADEM ECO/TAC

S65
MULLER A.L.,"THE ECONOMIC POSITION OF THE ASIANS IN AFRICA." AFR SOUTH/AFR ECO/UNDEV MARKET ECO/TAC GP/REL INCOME...CHARTS IND 20 MONOPOLY ASIANS. PAGE 95 F1856
WORKER RACE/REL CAP/ISM DISCRIM

S65
MUNZI U.,"THE EUROPEAN SOCIAL FUND IN THE DEVELOPMENT OF THE MEDITERRANEAN REGIONS OF THE EEC." FUT GREECE ITALY PORTUGAL SPAIN TURKEY WORKER TEC/DEV ECO/TAC REGION...STAT EEC. PAGE 95 F1862
ECO/UNDEV PREDICT RECORD

S65
RUSINOW D.I.,"YUGOSLAV DEVELOPMENT BETWEEN EAST AND WEST." AGRI VOL/ASSN PLAN CAP/ISM ECO/TAC FOR/AID INT/TRADE BAL/PAY...MARXIST EEC COMECON. PAGE 115 F2262
YUGOSLAVIA ECO/UNDEV STAT

S65
STEENKAMP W.F.J.,"THE PROBLEM OF WAGE REGULATION." SOUTH/AFR LAW ECO/DEV ECO/UNDEV LABOR NAT/G BARGAIN PAY INGP/REL DISCRIM WEALTH...METH/COMP 20. PAGE 125 F2473
ECO/TAC PRICE WORKER RATION

S65
WHITAKER A.P.,"ARGENTINA: STRUGGLE FOR RECOVERY." L/A+17C USA+45 NAT/G TOP/EX PLAN LEGIT COERCE REV RIGID/FLEX PWR WEALTH...RECORD ALL/PROG ARGEN FOR/TRADE 20. PAGE 146 F2867
POL/PAR ECO/TAC NAT/LISM

C65
MANSFIELD H.C.,"THE CONGRESS AND ECONOMIC POLICY" IN C. TRUMAN ED., THE CONGRESS AND AMERICA'S FUTURE." USA+45 USA-45 CONSTN NAT/G BUDGET ADMIN CONTROL EXEC LOBBY. PAGE 85 F1661
POLICY ECO/TAC PWR LEGIS

B66
ALEXANDER Y.,INTERNATIONAL TECHNICAL ASSISTANCE EXPERTS* A CASE STUDY OF THE U.N. EXPERIENCE. ECO/UNDEV CONSULT EX/STRUC CREATE PLAN DIPLOM FOR/AID TASK EFFICIENCY...ORG/CHARTS UN. PAGE 3 F0061
ECO/TAC INT/ORG ADMIN MGT

B66
ALEXANDER Y.,INTERNATIONAL TECHNICAL ASSISTANCE EXPERTS: A CASE STUDY OF THE U.N. EXPERIENCE. USA+45 WOR+45 WORKER CREATE PLAN PROB/SOLV ECO/TAC FOR/AID GIVE EDU/PROP...CHARTS BIBLIOG 20 UN. PAGE 3 F0062
SKILL INT/ORG TEC/DEV CONSULT

B66
BAKKE E.W.,MUTUAL SURVIVAL; THE GOAL OF UNION AND MANAGEMENT (2ND ED.). USA+45 ELITES ECO/DEV ECO/TAC CONFER ADMIN REPRESENT GP/REL INGP/REL ATTIT ...GP/COMP 20. PAGE 8 F0155
MGT LABOR BARGAIN INDUS

B66
BALDWIN D.A.,ECONOMIC DEVELOPMENT AND AMERICAN FOREIGN POLICY. USA+45 FINAN LG/CO LEGIS DIPLOM GIVE 20. PAGE 9 F0163
ECO/TAC FOR/AID ECO/UNDEV POLICY

B66
BALDWIN R.E.,ECONOMIC DEVELOPMENT AND EXPORT GROWTH: A STUDY OF NORTHERN RHODESIA, 1920-1960. AFR RHODESIA AGRI EXTR/IND FINAN MARKET LABOR WORKER ECO/TAC...CONCPT NEW/IDEA MUNICH 20. PAGE 9 F0166
ECO/UNDEV TEC/DEV INT/TRADE CAP/ISM

B66
BIRMINGHAM W.,A STUDY OF CONTEMPORARY GHANA VOL I: THE ECONOMY OF GHANA. AFR GHANA PLAN...POLICY STAT CHARTS ANTHOL BIBLIOG 20. PAGE 15 F0286
ECO/UNDEV ECO/TAC NAT/G PRODUC

B66
COLE A.B.,SOCIALIST PARTIES IN POSTWAR JAPAN. STRATA AGRI LABOR PLAN DIPLOM ECO/TAC AGREE LEAD CHOOSE ATTIT...CHARTS 20 CHINJAP SOC/DEMPAR. PAGE 26 F0499
POL/PAR POLICY SOCISM NAT/G

B66
CONAN A.R.,THE PROBLEM OF STERLING. UK WOR+45 BUDGET ECO/TAC...POLICY STAT CHARTS 20 SILVER. PAGE 27 F0521
FINAN ECO/DEV BAL/PAY DIPLOM

B66
CONFERENCE REGIONAL ACCOUNTS,REGIONAL ACCOUNTS FOR POLICY DECISIONS. PROB/SOLV CONTROL RATIONAL KNOWL ORD/FREE...POLICY DECISION MATH STAT ANTHOL 20. PAGE 27 F0523
GOV/REL REGION PLAN ECO/TAC

B66
CONGRESSIONAL QUARTERLY SERV,FEDERAL ECONOMIC POLICY 1945-1965. USA+45 FINAN NAT/G CHIEF CONSULT TAX...CHARTS 20 PRESIDENT DEBT. PAGE 27 F0526
ECO/TAC BUDGET LEGIS

B66
COOK P.W. JR.,PROBLEMS OF CORPORATE POWER. WOR+45 FINAN INDUS BARGAIN GP/REL...MGT ANTHOL. PAGE 27 F0530
ADMIN LG/CO PWR ECO/TAC

B66
DOBB M.,SOVIET ECONOMIC DEVELOPMENT SINCE 1917. USSR ECO/DEV ECO/UNDEV LABOR NAT/G TEC/DEV ECO/TAC ROUTINE PRODUC MARXISM 20. PAGE 33 F0647
PLAN INDUS WORKER

B66
DUNCAN O.,METROPOLIS AND REGION (PREPARED FOR RESOURCES FOR THE FUTURE INC., WASHINGTON, D.C.). FINAN INDUS ECO/TAC TAX...CHARTS GOV/COMP MUNICH. PAGE 35 F0677
REGION GEOG

B66
ECKSTEIN A.,COMMUNIST CHINA'S ECONOMIC GROWTH AND FOREIGN TRADE* IMPLICATIONS FOR US POLICY. COM USA+45 USSR STRUCT INDUS MARKET DIPLOM ECO/TAC FOR/AID INT/TRADE...STAT CHARTS. PAGE 36 F0696
ASIA ECO/UNDEV CREATE PWR

B66
EDWARDS C.D.,TRADE REGULATIONS OVERSEAS. IRELAND NEW/ZEALND SOUTH/AFR NAT/G CAP/ISM TARIFFS CONTROL ...POLICY JURID 20 EEC CHINJAP. PAGE 36 F0703
INT/TRADE DIPLOM INT/LAW ECO/TAC

B66
FELLNER W.,MAINTAINING AND RESTORING BALANCE IN INTERNATIONAL PAYMENTS. ECO/UNDEV MARKET ECO/TAC PRICE INCOME WEALTH...POLICY METH/COMP 20 MONEY.
BAL/PAY DIPLOM FINAN

PAGE 40 F0781 INT/TRADE

B66
FOX K.A.,THE THEORY OF QUANTITATIVE ECONOMIC POLICY WITH APPLICATIONS TO ECONOMIC GROWTH AND STABILIZATION. ECO/DEV AGRI NAT/G PLAN ADMIN RISK ...DECISION IDEA/COMP SIMUL T. PAGE 43 F0837
ECO/TAC ECOMETRIC EQUILIB GEN/LAWS

B66
FREIDEL F.,AMERICAN ISSUES IN THE TWENTIETH CENTURY. SOCIETY FINAN ECO/TAC FOR/AID CONTROL NUC/PWR WAR RACE/REL PEACE ATTIT...ANTHOL T 20 WILSON/W ROOSEVLT/F KENNEDY/JF TRUMAN/HS. PAGE 44 F0851
DIPLOM POLICY NAT/G ORD/FREE

B66
FRIEDMANN W.G.,INTERNATIONAL FINANCIAL AID. USA+45 ECO/DEV ECO/UNDEV NAT/G VOL/ASSN EX/STRUC PLAN RENT GIVE BAL/PAY PWR...GEOG INT/LAW STAT TREND UN EEC COMECON. PAGE 44 F0866
INT/ORG FOR/AID TEC/DEV ECO/TAC

B66
FUSFELD D.R.,THE AGE OF THE ECONOMIST. ECO/TAC WEALTH LAISSEZ MARXISM...EPIST 18/20 KEYNES/JM. PAGE 45 F0878
PHIL/SCI CAP/ISM POLICY

B66
GITTINGER J.P.,THE LITERATURE OF AGRICULTURAL PLANNING. UNIV INT/ORG CONSULT WORKER TEC/DEV ECO/TAC OPTIMAL...POLICY METH/COMP BIBLIOG/A 20. PAGE 47 F0927
ECO/UNDEV AGRI PLAN WRITING

B66
GOODMAN L.H.,ECONOMIC PROGRESS AND SOCIAL WELFARE. USA+45 STRATA STRUCT ECO/TAC EFFICIENCY...MGT 20. PAGE 49 F0949
SOC/WK RECEIVE GP/COMP POLICY

B66
GOODWIN C.D.W.,ECONOMIC INQUIRY IN AUSTRALIA. ECO/DEV ECO/UNDEV ACADEM INT/TRADE RENT TARIFFS TAX PRESS GOV/REL SOCISM 18/20 AUSTRAL. PAGE 49 F0953
ECO/TAC IDEA/COMP BUDGET COLONIAL

B66
GORDON R.A.,PROSPERITY AND UNEMPLOYMENT. USA+45 PLAN ECO/TAC ADJUST DEMAND ALL/VALS...POLICY DECISION TREND CHARTS ANTHOL 20. PAGE 49 F0961
WORKER INDUS ECO/DEV WEALTH

B66
GROSS H.,MAKE OR BUY. AFR USA+45 FINAN INDUS CREATE PRICE PRODUC 20. PAGE 51 F1006
ECO/TAC PLAN MGT COST

B66
HACKETT J.,L'ECONOMIE BRITANNIQUE: PROBLEMES ET PERSPECTIVES. FRANCE UK LABOR NAT/G EX/STRUC PROB/SOLV BAL/PAY INCOME RIGID/FLEX...MGT PHIL/SCI CHARTS MUNICH 20. PAGE 53 F1027
ECO/DEV FINAN ECO/TAC PLAN

B66
HAINES W.W.,MONEY PRICES AND POLICY. WOR+45 ECO/DEV BUDGET CONTROL INCOME...POLICY STAT CHARTS BIBLIOG T 20. PAGE 53 F1039
PRICE FINAN ECO/TAC GOV/REL

B66
HALLER H.,DAS PROBLEM DER GELDWERTSTABILITAT. MARKET LABOR INCOME PRODUC...POLICY 20. PAGE 54 F1049
PRICE COST FINAN ECO/TAC

B66
HALLET R.,PEOPLE AND PROGRESS IN WEST AFRICA: AN INTRODUCTION TO THE PROBLEMS OF DEVELOPMENT. COM/IND INDUS KIN DIPLOM FOR/AID INT/TRADE HEALTH ...GEOG TREND CHARTS BIBLIOG/A 20 AFRICA/W. PAGE 54 F1050
AFR SOCIETY ECO/UNDEV ECO/TAC

B66
HARLOW J.S.,FRENCH ECONOMIC PLANNING: A CHALLENGE TO REASON. EUR+WWI FRANCE PROB/SOLV 20 EUROPE. PAGE 55 F1084
ECO/TAC PLAN STRUCT

B66
HASTINGS P.G.,THE MANAGEMENT OF BUSINESS FINANCE. ECO/DEV PLAN BUDGET CONTROL COST...DECISION CHARTS BIBLIOG T 20. PAGE 56 F1109
FINAN MGT INDUS ECO/TAC

B66
HEVESY P.D.,THE UNIFICATION OF THE WORLD. FUT USA+45 WOR+45 ECO/DEV ECO/UNDEV LEGIS PROB/SOLV BAL/PWR ECO/TAC INT/TRADE PEACE. PAGE 59 F1160
DIPLOM FINAN INT/ORG

B66
HOLT R.T.,THE POLITICAL BASIS OF ECONOMIC DEVELOPMENT. STRATA STRUCT NAT/G DIPLOM ADMIN...SOC NAT/COMP BIBLIOG 20. PAGE 61 F1201
ECO/TAC GOV/COMP CONSTN EX/STRUC

B66
HOROWITZ D.,HEMISPHERES NORTH AND SOUTH: ECONOMIC DISPARITY AMONG NATIONS. WOR+45 ECO/DEV ECO/UNDEV INT/ORG PLAN DIPLOM INT/TRADE GIVE PARTIC GP/REL ...WELF/ST 20. PAGE 62 F1215
ECO/TAC FOR/AID STRATA WEALTH

B66
INARRITU A.L.,EL PATRON CAMBIO-ORO Y SUS REFORMAS. AFR L/A+17C WOR+45 PLAN PROB/SOLV BUDGET ECO/TAC INT/TRADE EFFICIENCY ORD/FREE 20 MEXIC/AMER. PAGE 64 F1262
ECO/UNDEV FINAN DIPLOM POLICY

B66
INTERNATIONAL ECO POLICY ASSN,THE UNITED STATES BALANCE OF PAYMENTS. INT/ORG NAT/G PROB/SOLV BUDGET DIPLOM INT/TRADE WEALTH 20. PAGE 65 F1274
BAL/PAY ECO/TAC POLICY FINAN

B66
KAESTNER K.,GESAMTWIRTSCHAFTLICHE PLANUNG IN EINER GEMISCHTEN WIRTSCHAFTSORDNUNG (WIRTSCHAFTSPOLITISCHE STUDIEN 5). GERMANY/W WOR+45 WOR-45 INDUS MARKET NAT/G ACT/RES GP/REL INGP/REL PRODUC...ECOMETRIC MGT BIBLIOG 20. PAGE 68 F1346
ECO/TAC PLAN POLICY PREDICT

B66
KIRKENDALL R.S.,SOCIAL SCIENTISTS AND FARM POLITICS IN THE AGE OF ROOSEVELT. ACADEM PLAN ECO/TAC GIVE ADMIN CONTROL PRODUC...SOC 20 NEW/DEAL ROOSEVLT/F BURAGR/ECO. PAGE 71 F1399
AGRI INTELL POLICY NAT/G

B66
KROOSS H.E.,AMERICAN ECONOMIC DEVELOPMENT (2ND ED.). USA+45 USA-45 AGRI INDUS LABOR WORKER INT/TRADE TAX WAR...CHARTS 18/20. PAGE 73 F1443
ECO/TAC NAT/G CAP/ISM ECO/DEV

B66
KURAKOV I.G.,SCIENCE, TECHNOLOGY AND COMMUNISM; SOME QUESTIONS OF DEVELOPMENT (TRANS. BY CARIN DEDIJER). USSR INDUS PLAN PROB/SOLV COST PRODUC ...MGT MATH CHARTS METH 20. PAGE 74 F1450
CREATE TEC/DEV MARXISM ECO/TAC

B66
LAMBERG R.F.,PRAG UND DIE DRITTE WELT. AFR ASIA CZECHOSLVK L/A+17C MARKET TEC/DEV ECO/TAC REV ATTIT 20 TREATY. PAGE 75 F1462
DIPLOM ECO/UNDEV INT/TRADE FOR/AID

B66
LEE M.W.,TOWARD ECONOMIC STABILITY. USA+45 BUDGET TAX PRICE EQUILIB INCOME. PAGE 77 F1506
ECO/TAC CONTROL POLICY NAT/G

B66
MACBEAN A.I.,EXPORT INSTABILITY AND ECONOMIC DEVELOPMENT. CHILE PAKISTAN PUERT/RICO TANZANIA UGANDA WOR+45 MARKET ECO/TAC...POLICY REGRESS CHARTS BIBLIOG TIME 20. PAGE 83 F1622
INT/TRADE ECO/UNDEV ECOMETRIC INSPECT

B66
MACFARQUHAR R.,CHINA UNDER MAO: POLITICS TAKES COMMAND. CHINA/COM COM AGRI INDUS CHIEF FORCES DIPLOM INT/TRADE EDU/PROP TASK REV ADJUST...ANTHOL 20 MAO. PAGE 83 F1628
ECO/UNDEV TEC/DEV ECO/TAC ADMIN

B66
MADAN G.R.,ECONOMIC THINKING IN INDIA. INDIA ECO/UNDEV AGRI FINAN INDUS LABOR PLAN CAP/ISM INT/TRADE MARXISM SOCISM...POLICY 1/20. PAGE 84 F1638
ECO/TAC PHIL/SCI NAT/G POL/PAR

B66
MANGONE G.J.,UN ADMINISTRATION OF ECONOMIC AND AOCIAL PROGRAMS. CONSULT BUDGET INT/TRADE REGION 20 UN. PAGE 84 F1653
ADMIN MGT ECO/TAC DELIB/GP

B66
MANSFIELD E.,MANAGERIAL ECONOMICS AND OPERATIONS RESEARCH; A NONMATHEMATICAL INTRODUCTION. USA+45 ELITES ECO/DEV CONSULT EX/STRUC PROB/SOLV ROUTINE EFFICIENCY OPTIMAL...GAME T 20. PAGE 85 F1660
ECO/TAC OP/RES MGT COMPUTER

B66
MASON E.S.,ECONOMIC DEVELOPMENT IN INDIA AND PAKISTAN. INDIA PAKISTAN AGRI FINAN PLAN BUDGET INT/TRADE WEALTH...POLICY STAT TREND CHARTS 20. PAGE 87 F1700
NAT/COMP ECO/UNDEV ECO/TAC FOR/AID

B66
MEERHAEGHE M.,INTERNATIONAL ECONOMIC INSTITUTIONS. EUR+WWI FINAN INDUS MARKET PLAN TARIFFS BAL/PAY EQUILIB...POLICY BIBLIOG/A 20 GATT OEEC EEC IBRD EURCOALSTL. PAGE 89 F1745
ECO/TAC ECO/DEV INT/TRADE INT/ORG

B66
MOUNTJOY A.B.,INDUSTRIALIZATION AND UNDER-DEVELOPED COUNTRIES (2ND REV. ED.). CHILE GHANA INDIA NIGERIA WOR+45 SOCIETY PROB/SOLV ECO/TAC...SOC CHARTS 20 INDUS/REV. PAGE 94 F1848
ECO/UNDEV INDUS GEOG HABITAT

B66
MUNBY D.,ECONOMIC GROWTH IN WORLD PERSPECTIVE. AFR WOR+45 SOCIETY INDUS PLAN TEC/DEV ECO/TAC FOR/AID INT/TRADE COST CATHISM...ANTHOL 20 EUROPE/W CHURCH/STA. PAGE 95 F1859
SECT ECO/UNDEV ECO/DEV

B66
MURPHY G.G.,SOVIET MONGOLIA: A STUDY OF THE OLDEST POLITICAL SATELLITE. USSR STRATA STRUCT COST INCOME ATTIT SOCISM 20. PAGE 95 F1865
DIPLOM ECO/TAC PLAN DOMIN

B66
NATIONAL INDUSTRIAL CONF BOARD,GOLD AND WORLD MONETARY PROBLEMS. AFR FUT WOR+45 PROB/SOLV BUDGET INT/TRADE PAY GOV/REL...POLICY ANTHOL 20. PAGE 97 F1902
FINAN ECO/TAC PRICE BAL/PAY

B66
NEVITT A.A.,THE ECONOMIC PROBLEMS OF HOUSING. WOR+45 ECO/DEV ECO/UNDEV ACT/RES PROB/SOLV ECO/TAC RENT...OBS CHARTS 20. PAGE 98 F1917
HABITAT PROC/MFG DELIB/GP NAT/COMP

B66
NICOSIA M.N.,CONSUMER DECISION PROCESSES: MARKETING AND ADVERTISING IMPLICATIONS. ECO/TAC ATTIT PERSON ...DECISION MGT SOC. PAGE 98 F1926
MARKET SOCIETY CREATE ACT/RES

B66
PASSIN H.,THE UNITED STATES AND JAPAN. USA+45 INDUS CAP/ISM...TREND 20 CHINJAP TREATY. PAGE 103 F2032
DIPLOM INT/TRADE ECO/DEV ECO/TAC

B66
PEIRCE W.S.,SELECTIVE MANPOWER POLICIES AND THE TRADE-OFF BETWEEN RISING PRICES AND UNEMPLOYMENT (DISSERTATION). ECO/DEV WORKER ACT/RES...PHIL/SCI 20. PAGE 104 F2050
PRICE LABOR POLICY ECO/TAC

B66
PIQUET H.S.,THE US BALANCE OF PAYMENTS AND INTERNATIONAL MONETARY RESERVES. AFR USA+45 PROB/SOLV INT/TRADE GOV/REL EQUILIB...POLICY STAT CHARTS 20. PAGE 106 F2090
BAL/PAY DIPLOM FINAN ECO/TAC

B66
REDFORD E.S.,THE ROLE OF GOVERNMENT IN THE AMERICAN ECONOMY. USA+45 USA-45 FINAN INDUS LG/CO PROB/SOLV ADMIN INGP/REL INCOME PRODUC 18/20. PAGE 110 F2169
NAT/G ECO/DEV CAP/ISM ECO/TAC

B66
RUBIN S.J.,THE CONSCIENCE OF THE RICH NATIONS: THE DEVELOPMENT ASSISTANCE COMMITTEE AND THE COMMON AID EFFORT. EUR+WWI USA+45 ECO/UNDEV INT/ORG NAT/G VOL/ASSN ECO/TAC INT/TRADE...OBS UN AID DEV/ASSIST IBRD OECD. PAGE 114 F2256
FOR/AID ECO/DEV CONFER CENTRAL

B66
SCHNEIDER E.,WIRTSCHAFTSKREISLAUF UND WIRTSCHAFTSWACHSTUM. ECO/DEV MARKET...CONCPT 20 MONEY. PAGE 117 F2306
ECO/TAC FINAN INCOME COST

B66
SEWELL J.P.,FUNCTIONALISM AND WORLD POLITICS* A STUDY BASED ON UNITED NATIONS PROGRAMS FINANCING ECONOMICAL DEVELOPMENT. ECO/UNDEV FINAN PROB/SOLV DIPLOM ECO/TAC FEEDBACK REGION ADJUST ATTIT UN IBRD INTL/FINAN INTL/DEV UNSF. PAGE 120 F2360
TASK INT/ORG IDEA/COMP GEN/LAWS

B66
SHULTZ G.P.,GUIDELINES, INFORMAL CONTROLS, AND THE MARKET PLACE: POLICY CHOICES IN A FULL EMPLOYMENT ECONOMY. UK ECO/DEV LABOR INT/TRADE CONFER GOV/REL BAL/PAY DEMAND INCOME...POLICY ANTHOL 20 PRESIDENT. PAGE 121 F2392
ECO/TAC CONTROL FINAN RATION

B66
SINGH L.P.,THE POLITICS OF ECONOMIC COOPERATION IN ASIA; A STUDY OF ASIAN INTERNATIONAL ORGANIZATIONS. ASIA INT/ORG ACT/RES PLAN GP/REL...POLICY GP/COMP BIBLIOG 20 UN SEATO. PAGE 122 F2414
ECO/UNDEV ECO/TAC REGION DIPLOM

B66
THIESENHUSEN W.C.,CHILE'S EXPERIMENTS IN AGRARIAN REFORM. CHILE STRUCT NAT/G ACT/RES ECO/TAC GOV/REL COST SOCISM...TREND CHARTS SOC/EXP 20. PAGE 130 F2558
AGRI ECO/UNDEV SOC TEC/DEV

B66
TRIFFIN R.,THE WORLD MONEY MAZE. AFR INT/ORG ECO/TAC PRICE OPTIMAL WEALTH...METH/COMP 20 EEC OEEC SILVER. PAGE 131 F2589
BAL/PAY FINAN INT/TRADE DIPLOM

B66
TRIFFIN R.,THE BALANCE OF PAYMENTS AND THE FOREIGN INVESTMENT POSITION OF THE UNITED STATES. AFR USA+45 INT/ORG INT/TRADE PRICE CONTROL...POLICY 20. PAGE 131 F2590
BAL/PAY DIPLOM FINAN ECO/TAC

B66
TURNER H.A.,PRICES, WAGES, AND INCOME POLICIES IN INDUSTRIALIZED MARKET ECONOMIES. AFR WOR+45 ECO/DEV INDUS PROB/SOLV ECO/TAC CONTROL WEALTH...CHARTS 20 INTRVN/ECO. PAGE 131 F2593
PRICE PAY MARKET INCOME

B66
US CONGRESS JOINT ECO COMM,NEW APPROACH TO UNITED STATES INTERNATIONAL ECONOMIC POLICY. USA+45 WOR+45 CHIEF DELIB/GP CONFER...CHARTS 20 CONGRESS MONEY. PAGE 135 F2660
DIPLOM ECO/TAC BAL/PAY FINAN

B66
US HOUSE COMM BANKING CURRENCY,HEARINGS BEFORE HOUSE COMMITTEE ON BANKING AND CURRENCY: SALE OF SBA LOAN POOL PARTICIPATIONS. USA+45 LAW LEGIS ECO/TAC RATION 20 CONGRESS. PAGE 136 F2687
FINAN SML/CO ADJUD GOV/REL

B66
US HOUSE COMM FOREIGN AFFAIRS,HEARINGS ON HR 12449 A BILL TO AMEND FURTHER THE FOREIGN ASSISTANCE ACT OF 1961. AFR ASIA L/A+17C USA+45 VIETNAM INT/ORG TEC/DEV INT/TRADE ATTIT ORD/FREE 20 UN NATO CONGRESS AID. PAGE 137 F2692
FOR/AID ECO/TAC ECO/UNDEV DIPLOM

B66
US SENATE COMM APPROPRIATIONS,FOREIGN ASSISTANCE AND RELATED AGENCIES APPROPRIATIONS FOR FISCAL YEAR 1967: HEARINGS... ON H. R. 17788. ECO/UNDEV INT/ORG FORCES INSPECT ECO/TAC GIVE DEBATE WEAPON CIVMIL/REL WEALTH...INT 20 CONGRESS DEPT/DEFEN DEPT/STATE DEPT/HEW AID. PAGE 138 F2727
BUDGET FOR/AID DIPLOM COST

B66
WILCOX C.,ECONOMIES OF THE WORLD TODAY: THEIR ORGANIZATION, DEVELOPMENT, AND PERFORMANCE (2ND ED.). CHINA/COM COM INDIA NIGERIA UK WOR+45 WOR-45 INDUS MARKET PLAN ECO/TAC SOCISM...CHARTS METH/COMP 20. PAGE 146 F2878
ECO/DEV ECO/UNDEV MARXISM CAP/ISM

B66
WOODMAN H.D.,SLAVERY AND THE SOUTHERN ECONOMY: SOURCES AND READINGS. USA-45 CULTURE STRUCT AGRI ECO/TAC LEAD RACE/REL DISCRIM EFFICIENCY...CHARTS ANTHOL MUNICH 18/19 NEGRO SOUTH/US. PAGE 148 F2922
ECO/DEV STRATA WORKER UTIL

B66
YEAGER L.B.,INTERNATIONAL MONETARY RELATIONS: THEORY, HISTORY, AND POLICY. WOR+45 WOR-45 INT/TRADE BAL/PAY...NAT/COMP 18/20 MONEY. PAGE 150 F2947
FINAN DIPLOM ECO/TAC IDEA/COMP

B66
YOUNG S.,MANAGEMENT: A SYSTEMS ANALYSIS. DELIB/GP EX/STRUC ECO/TAC CONTROL EFFICIENCY...NET/THEORY 20. PAGE 150 F2952
PROB/SOLV MGT DECISION SIMUL

B66
ZINKIN T.,CHALLENGES IN INDIA. INDIA PAKISTAN LAW AGRI FINAN INDUS TOP/EX TEC/DEV CONTROL ROUTINE ORD/FREE PWR 20 NEHRU/J SHASTRI/LB CIVIL/SERV. PAGE 150 F2964
NAT/G ECO/TAC POLICY ADMIN

B66
ZISCHKA A.,WAR ES EIN WUNDER? GERMANY/W ECO/DEV FINAN LG/CO BARGAIN CAP/ISM FOR/AID RATION 20 MARSHL/PLN. PAGE 150 F2965
ECO/TAC INT/TRADE INDUS WAR

S66
ANGELL J.W.,"THE LONGER RUN PROSPECTS FOR THE US BALANCE OF PAYMENTS." USA+45 DIPLOM FOR/AID RATION ORD/FREE WEALTH...IDEA/COMP GATT. PAGE 6 F0104
BAL/PAY ECO/TAC INT/TRADE FINAN

S66
COHEN A.,"THE TECHNOLOGY/ELITE APPROACH TO THE DEVELOPMENTAL PROCESS* PERUVIAN CASE STUDY." L/A+17C STRUCT CREATE ECO/TAC FOR/AID CIVMIL/REL MARXISM TECHRACY HYPO/EXP. PAGE 26 F0496
ECO/UNDEV ELITES PERU

S66
JAVITS J.K.,"POLITICAL ACTION VITAL FOR LATIN AMERICAN INTEGRATION." ECO/UNDEV INT/ORG POL/PAR VOL/ASSN PLAN PROB/SOLV INT/TRADE EFFICIENCY 20 OAS LAFTA ALL/PROG. PAGE 66 F1308
L/A+17C ECO/TAC REGION

S66
LAURENS H.,"LES PAYS OCCIDENTAUX ET LE MARCHE CHINOIS." EUR+WWI FUT S/ASIA AGRI INDUS VOL/ASSN ECO/TAC BAL/PAY...RECORD PREDICT TREATY. PAGE 76 F1488
ASIA INT/TRADE TREND STAT

S66
MALENBAUM W.,"GOVERNMENT, ENTREPRENEURSHIP, AND ECONOMIC GROWTH IN POOR LANDS." ELITES ECO/UNDEV INDUS CREATE DRIVE. PAGE 84 F1645
ECO/TAC PLAN CONSERVE NAT/G

S66
MARKSHAK J.,"ECONOMIC PLANNING AND THE COST OF THINKING." COM MARKET EX/STRUC...DECISION GEN/LAWS. PAGE 85 F1672
ECO/UNDEV ECO/TAC PLAN ECO/DEV

S66
POSEN G.S.,"RECENT TRENDS IN SOVIET ECONOMIC THOUGHT." USSR ECO/DEV PLAN CONTROL CENTRAL 20. PAGE 107 F2107
ECO/TAC MARXISM INDUS PROFIT

S66
VENTRE F.T.,"LOCAL INITIATIVES IN URBAN INDUSTRIAL DEVELOPMENT." FINAN SERV/IND TOP/EX PLAN BUDGET RENT TAX...GP/COMP MUNICH 20. PAGE 141 F2777
ECO/TAC LOC/G INDUS

N66
EOMMITTEE ECONOMIC DEVELOPMENT,THE DOLLAR AND THE WORLD MONETARY SYSTEM: A STATEMENT ON NATIONAL POLICY (PAMPHLET). AFR USA+45 NAT/G PLAN PROB/SOLV BUDGET ECO/TAC FOR/AID INCOME...POLICY 20 EUROPE. PAGE 38 F0740
FINAN BAL/PAY DIPLOM ECO/DEV

N66
OECD,THE BALANCE OF PAYMENTS ADJUSTMENT PROCESS (PAMPHLET). EUR+WWI ECO/DEV FINAN CONSULT PLAN PROB/SOLV BUDGET CAP/ISM INT/TRADE PRICE CONTROL EQUILIB 20. PAGE 101 F1975
BAL/PAY ECO/TAC DIPLOM INT/ORG

N66
PRINCETON U INDUSTRIAL REL SEC,PUBLIC PROGRAMS TO CREATE JOBS (PAMPHLET NO. 125). USA+45 ECO/DEV INDUS PLAN ECO/TAC AGE/Y 20. PAGE 108 F2119
BIBLIOG/A NAT/G POLICY WORKER

N66
PRINCETON U INDUSTRIAL REL SEC,RECENT MATERIAL ON COLLECTIVE BARGAINING IN GOVERNMENT (PAMPHLET NO. 130). USA+45 ECO/DEV LABOR WORKER ECO/TAC GOV/REL ...MGT 20. PAGE 108 F2120
BIBLIOG/A BARGAIN NAT/G GP/REL

N66
PRINCETON U INDUSTRIAL REL SEC,THE ROLE OF THE PUBLIC EMPLOYMENT SERVICE (PAMPHLET NO. 129). USA+45 ECO/DEV PLAN ECO/TAC GOV/REL 20. PAGE 108 F2121
BIBLIOG/A NAT/G POLICY LABOR

B67
ADLER J.H.,CAPITAL MOVEMENTS AND ECONOMIC DEVELOPMENT. WOR+45 FINAN NAT/G BARGAIN ECO/TAC FOR/AID INT/TRADE ANTHOL. PAGE 2 F0042
DIPLOM ECO/DEV ECO/UNDEV

B67
ANDERSON C.W.,POLITICS AND ECONOMIC CHANGE IN LATIN AMERICA. L/A+17C INDUS NAT/G OP/RES ADMIN DEMAND ...POLICY STAT CHARTS NAT/COMP 20. PAGE 5 F0093
ECO/UNDEV PROB/SOLV PLAN ECO/TAC

B67
ANDERSON C.W.,ISSUES OF POLITICAL DEVELOPMENT. BURMA WOR+45 CULTURE TOP/EX ECO/TAC MARXISM ...CHARTS NAT/COMP 20 COLOMB CONGO/LEOP. PAGE 5 F0094
NAT/LISM COERCE ECO/UNDEV SOCISM

B67
BARNETT A.D.,CHINA AFTER MAO. ASIA CHINA/COM CULTURE ECO/UNDEV ECO/TAC CONTROL EFFICIENCY NAT/LISM MARXISM 20. PAGE 10 F0189
POL/PAR NAT/G TEC/DEV GP/REL

B67
BARROW T.C.,TRADE AND EMPIRE: THE BRITISH CUSTOMS SERVICE IN COLONIAL AMERICA, 1660-1775. UK USA-45 ECO/UNDEV NAT/G ECO/TAC DOMIN REV 17/18. PAGE 10 F0197
COLONIAL TARIFFS ADMIN EX/STRUC

B67
BEAL E.F.,THE PRACTICE OF COLLECTIVE BARGAINING (3RD ED.). USA+45 WOR+45 ECO/DEV INDUS LG/CO PROF/ORG WORKER ECO/TAC GP/REL WEALTH...JURID METH/CNCPT. PAGE 12 F0221
BARGAIN MGT LABOR ADJUD

B67
BERGMANN D KAUN B.,STRUCTURAL UNEMPLOYMENT IN THE UNITED STATES. USA+45 ECO/DEV PRICE ADMIN INGP/REL DEMAND EQUILIB WEALTH...MATH REGRESS STAT 20 NEGRO. PAGE 13 F0258
ECOMETRIC METH WORKER ECO/TAC

B67
CASTILLO C.M.,GROWTH AND INTEGRATION IN CENTRAL AMERICA. L/A+17C CREATE PROB/SOLV ECO/TAC REGION PRODUC...OBS BIBLIOG 20. PAGE 22 F0429
ECO/UNDEV INT/TRADE NAT/COMP

B67
COHEN M.R.,LAW AND THE SOCIAL ORDER: ESSAYS IN LEGAL PHILOSOPHY. USA-45 CONSULT WORKER ECO/TAC ATTIT WEALTH...POLICY WELF/ST SOC 20 NEW/DEAL DEPRESSION. PAGE 26 F0497
JURID LABOR IDEA/COMP

B67
COTTAM R.W.,COMPETITIVE INTERFERENCE AND TWENTIETH CENTURY DIPLOMACY. IRAN ACT/RES CREATE PLAN ECO/TAC EFFICIENCY ATTIT...DECISION NEW/IDEA TREND 20 CIA. PAGE 28 F0541
DIPLOM DOMIN GAME

B67
DAVIS F.M.,COME AS A CONQUEROR: THE UNITED STATES ARMY'S OCCUPATION OF GERMANY: 1945-1949. EUR+WWI GERMANY USA+45 SOCIETY PLAN BAL/PWR DIPLOM FOR/AID PERS/REL DEMAND PEACE ORD/FREE 20. PAGE 30 F0588
FORCES CIVMIL/REL ECO/TAC CONTROL

B67
ENKE S.,DEFENSE MANAGEMENT. USA+45 R+D FORCES WORKER PLAN ECO/TAC ADMIN NUC/PWR BAL/PAY UTIL WEALTH...MGT DEPT/DEFEN. PAGE 38 F0738
DECISION DELIB/GP EFFICIENCY BUDGET

B67
GORZ A.,STRATEGY FOR LABOR: A RADICAL PROPOSAL (TRANS. BY MARTIN NICOLAUS AND VICTORIA ORTIZ). EUR+WWI FRANCE ITALY ECO/DEV POL/PAR OP/RES PLAN GP/REL ALL/IDEOS...SOC 20 EEC. PAGE 49 F0965
LABOR PWR STRUCT ECO/TAC

B67
HALLE L.J.,THE COLD WAR AS HISTORY. AFR USSR WOR+45 ECO/TAC FOR/AID NUC/PWR WAR PEACE ORD/FREE ...MAJORIT TREND 20 KENNEDY/JF KHRUSH/N BERLIN/BLO. PAGE 54 F1048
DIPLOM BAL/PWR

B67
HOGAN J.,THE US BALANCE OF PAYMENTS AND CAPITAL FLOWS. MARKET INT/ORG ECO/TAC PRICE CONTROL WEALTH ...METH/COMP 20 EEC. PAGE 61 F1192
BAL/PAY FINAN DIPLOM INT/TRADE

B67
HUMPHREY R.A.,UNIVERSITIES...AND DEVELOPMENT ASSISTANCE ABROAD. USA+45 OP/RES ECO/TAC FOR/AID ...ANTHOL 20. PAGE 63 F1242
ACADEM DIPLOM KNOWL ECO/UNDEV

B67
JACOBY N.H.,US AID TO TAIWAN. CAP/ISM DIPLOM FEEDBACK COST PRODUC...OBS INT CHARTS 20. PAGE 66 F1301
FOR/AID OP/RES ECO/TAC ECO/UNDEV

B67
JOHNSON H.G.,ECONOMIC POLICY TOWARD LESS DEVELOPED COUNTRIES. USA+45 ECO/DEV INT/ORG PLAN CAP/ISM FOR/AID TARIFFS GIVE WEALTH...NEW/IDEA CHARTS 20 UN GATT. PAGE 67 F1327
ECO/UNDEV ECO/TAC METH/COMP

B67
KANNER L.,THE NEW YORK TIMES WORLD ECONOMIC REVIEW AND FORECAST: 1967. WOR+45 ECO/DEV ECO/UNDEV TEC/DEV...STAT PREDICT CHARTS 20. PAGE 69 F1349
INDUS FINAN TREND ECO/TAC

B67
KARDOUCHE G.K.,THE UAR IN DEVELOPMENT. UAR ECO/TAC INT/TRADE BAL/PAY...STAT CHARTS BIBLIOG 20. PAGE 69 F1355
FINAN MGT CAP/ISM ECO/UNDEV

B67
KREININ M.E.,ALTERNATIVE COMMERCIAL POLICIES - THEIR EFFECT ON THE AMERICAN ECONOMY. USA+45 LAW ECO/DEV MARKET INT/ORG DIPLOM ECO/TAC TARIFFS PRICE DEMAND WEALTH...QUANT EEC AFTA. PAGE 73 F1437
INT/TRADE BAL/PAY NAT/G POLICY

B67
LEWIS L.J.,SOCIETY, SCHOOLS AND PROGRESS IN NIGERIA. NIGERIA WORKER ECO/TAC ADJUST 20. PAGE 79 F1550
EDU/PROP ECO/UNDEV SKILL SOCIETY

B67
LINDER S.B.,TRADE AND TRADE POLICY FOR DEVELOPMENT. OP/RES DIPLOM TARIFFS UTIL WEALTH...BIBLIOG 20. PAGE 80 F1569
ECO/UNDEV ECO/TAC TEC/DEV INT/TRADE

B67
LYND S.,RECONSTRUCTION. USA-45 PROB/SOLV RACE/REL ...IDEA/COMP ANTHOL 19. PAGE 82 F1616
SUFF ECO/TAC ADJUST

B67
MAZOUR A.G.,SOVIET ECONOMIC DEVELOPMENT: OPERATION OUTSTRIP: 1921-1965. USSR ECO/UNDEV FINAN CHIEF WORKER PROB/SOLV CONTROL PRODUC MARXISM...CHARTS ORG/CHARTS 20 STALIN/J. PAGE 87 F1711
ECO/TAC AGRI INDUS PLAN

B67
MENDEL A.P.,POLITICAL MEMOIRS 1905-1917 BY PAUL MILIUKOV (TRANS. BY CARL GOLDBERG). USSR AGRI DIPLOM ECO/TAC POPULISM...MAJORIT 20. PAGE 90 F1757
BIOG LEAD NAT/G CONSTN

B67
MONTGOMERY J.D.,FOREIGN AID IN INTERNATIONAL POLITICS. USA+45 USA-45 WOR+45 ECO/TAC EFFICIENCY ...SOC TREND CHARTS BIBLIOG/A 20 AID. PAGE 93 F1818
DIPLOM FOR/AID

B67
NKRUMAH K.,CHALLENGE OF THE CONGO. FORCES ECO/TAC FOR/AID REGION MURDER REPRESENT 20 CONGO/LEOP UN. PAGE 98 F1930
REV ECO/UNDEV ORD/FREE DIPLOM

B67
OFER G.,THE SERVICE INDUSTRIES IN A DEVELOPING ECONOMY: ISRAEL AS A CASE STUDY. ISRAEL ECO/TAC INT/TRADE PRODUC WEALTH SOCISM...TIME/SEQ TREND CHARTS 20. PAGE 101 F1979
DIPLOM ECO/DEV SERV/IND

B67
OGLESBY C.,CONTAINMENT AND CHANGE. AFR COM USA+45 ECO/UNDEV TEC/DEV ECO/TAC FOR/AID INT/TRADE DOMIN GUERRILLA REV PEACE 20 STALIN/J. PAGE 101 F1983
DIPLOM BAL/PWR MARXISM CULTURE

B67
OVERSEAS DEVELOPMENT INSTIT,EFFECTIVE AID. WOR+45 INT/ORG TEC/DEV DIPLOM INT/TRADE ADMIN. PAGE 102 F2004
FOR/AID ECO/UNDEV ECO/TAC NAT/COMP

B67
ROACH J.R.,THE UNITED STATES AND THE ATLANTIC COMMUNITY; ISSUES AND PROSPECTS. AFR WOR+45 TEC/DEV ECO/TAC COLONIAL REGION PEACE ROLE...ANTHOL NATO EEC. PAGE 112 F2199
INT/ORG POLICY ADJUST DIPLOM

B67
ROBERTS B.C.,COLLECTIVE BARGAINING IN AFRICAN COUNTRIES. AFR LAW ECO/UNDEV BARGAIN GP/REL ...DECISION METH/COMP 20. PAGE 112 F2206
LABOR MGT PLAN ECO/TAC

B67
SHAFFER H.G.,THE COMMUNIST WORLD: MARXIST AND NON-MARXIST VIEWS. WOR+45 SOCIETY DIPLOM ECO/TAC CONTROL SOCISM...MARXIST ANTHOL BIBLIOG/A 20. PAGE 120 F2363
MARXISM NAT/COMP IDEA/COMP COM

B67
TANSKY L.,US AND USSR AID TO DEVELOPING COUNTRIES. INDIA TURKEY USA+45 USSR INDUS PLAN CAP/ISM WAR PWR WEALTH MARXISM...CHARTS NAT/COMP BIBLIOG 20. PAGE 128 F2534
ECO/UNDEV FOR/AID DIPLOM ECO/TAC

B67
THOMAN R.S.,GEOGRAPHY OF INTERNATIONAL TRADE. WOR+45 ECO/DEV ECO/UNDEV INT/ORG LG/CO PLAN BAL/PAY ...STAT CHARTS NAT/COMP 20. PAGE 130 F2559
INT/TRADE GEOG ECO/TAC DIPLOM

B67
ULMAN L.,CHALLENGES TO COLLECTIVE BARGAINING. ECO/TAC DISCRIM EQUILIB ATTIT...JURID SOC/WK. PAGE 132 F2599
LABOR BARGAIN ADJUD POLICY

B67
UNIVERSAL REFERENCE SYSTEM,ECONOMIC REGULATION, BUSINESS, AND GOVERNMENT (VOLUME VIII). WOR+45 WOR-45 ECO/DEV ECO/UNDEV FINAN LABOR TEC/DEV ECO/TAC INT/TRADE GOV/REL...POLICY COMPUT/IR. PAGE 133 F2617
BIBLIOG/A CONTROL NAT/G

B67
US AGENCY INTERNATIONAL DEV,PROPOSED FOREIGN AID PROGRAM FOR 1968: SUMMARY PRESENTATION TO THE CONGRESS. AFR S/ASIA USA+45 AGRI TEC/DEV DIPLOM ECO/TAC BAL/PAY COST HEALTH KNOWL SKILL 20 AID
ECO/UNDEV BUDGET FOR/AID STAT

CONGRESS ALL/PROG. PAGE 134 F2640

B67

US CONGRESS JOINT ECO COMM,REPORT ON JANUARY 1967 ECONOMIC REPORT OF THE PRESIDENT. FINAN LABOR NAT/G LEGIS BUDGET INT/TRADE COST DEMAND INCOME PRODUC ...POLICY IDEA/COMP 20 CONGRESS. PAGE 135 F2663
CHIEF ECO/TAC PLAN DELIB/GP

B67

US CONGRESS JOINT ECO COMM,AN ECONOMIC PROFILE OF MAINLAND CHINA, VOLUMES I AND II. CHINA/COM AGRI DIST/IND FINAN INDUS LABOR FORCES ACT/RES PLAN INT/TRADE INGP/REL BAL/PAY 20 CONGRESS. PAGE 135 F2664
ECO/UNDEV WEALTH ECO/TAC DELIB/GP

B67

WOLF C. JR.,UNITED STATES POLICY AND THE THIRD WORLD. USA+45 WOR+45 FORCES ACT/RES BAL/PWR ECO/TAC FOR/AID DETER GUERRILLA NUC/PWR REV...CHARTS 20. PAGE 148 F2916
DIPLOM ECO/UNDEV POLICY NAT/G

L67

GOULD W.B.,"THE STATUS OF UNAUTHORIZED AND 'WILDCAT' STRIKES UNDER THE NATIONAL LABOR RELATIONS ACT." USA+45 ACT/RES BARGAIN ECO/TAC LEGIT ADJUD ADMIN GP/REL MGT. PAGE 50 F0968
ECO/DEV INDUS LABOR POLICY

L67

HOSHII I.,"JAPAN'S STAKE IN ASIA." ASIA S/ASIA CAP/ISM ECO/TAC ROLE...GEOG 20 CHINJAP. PAGE 62 F1224
DIPLOM REGION NAT/G INT/ORG

L67

LENT G.E.,"TAX INCENTIVES FOR INVESTMENT IN DEVELOPING COUNTRIES" WOR+45 LAW INDUS PLAN BUDGET TARIFFS ADMIN...METH/COMP 20. PAGE 78 F1526
ECO/UNDEV TAX FINAN ECO/TAC

L67

MACDONALD R.M.,"COLLECTIVE BARGAINING IN THE POSTWAR PERIOD." WORKER PROB/SOLV ECO/TAC PARTIC RISK CENTRAL EFFICIENCY DRIVE WEALTH...TREND 20. PAGE 83 F1624
LABOR INDUS BARGAIN CAP/ISM

L67

MACDONALD R.S.J.,"THE RESORT TO ECONOMIC COERCION BY INTERNATIONAL POLITICAL ORGANIZATIONS." CUBA ETHIOPIA RHODESIA SOUTH/AFR NAT/G FOR/AID INT/TRADE DOMIN CONTROL SANCTION...DECISION LEAGUE/NAT UN OAS 20. PAGE 83 F1625
INT/ORG COERCE ECO/TAC DIPLOM

L67

MESTMACKER E.J.,"STATE TRADING MONOPOLIES IN THE EUROPEAN ECONOMIC COMMUNITY. DIPLOM ECO/TAC ADJUD CONTROL DISCRIM 20 EEC. PAGE 90 F1764
INT/TRADE INT/ORG LAW TARIFFS

L67

WHITNEY S.N.,"MERGERS, CONGLOMERATES, AND OLIGOPOLIES* A WIDENING OF ANTI TRUST TARGETS." LAW NAT/G TEC/DEV CAP/ISM GP/REL PWR...OLD/LIB 20. PAGE 146 F2873
ECO/TAC INDUS JURID

S67

"ANTITRUST VENUE: TRANSACTING BUSINESS UNDER THE CLAYTON ACT." USA+45 DIST/IND PROB/SOLV ECO/TAC ADJUD CT/SYS 20. PAGE 2 F0028
LAW LG/CO CONTROL NAT/G

S67

ADAMS R.N.,"ETHICS AND THE SOCIAL ANTHROPOLOGIST IN LATIN AMERICA." USA+45 INTELL PROB/SOLV ECO/TAC LEAD...DECISION SOC NAT/COMP PERS/COMP. PAGE 2 F0039
L/A+17C POLICY ECO/UNDEV CONSULT

S67

ALVES V.,"FOREIGN CAPITAL IN BRAZIL." BRAZIL USA+45 CAP/ISM DIPLOM ECO/TAC INT/TRADE CONTROL PWR ...POLICY 20. PAGE 4 F0081
ECO/UNDEV FINAN SOCIALIST SOCISM

S67

APEL H.,"LES NOUVEAUX ASPECTS DE LA POLITIQUE ETRANGERE ALLEMANDE." AFR EUR+WWI GERMANY POL/PAR BAL/PWR ECO/TAC INT/TRADE NUC/PWR NAT/LISM PEACE ...POLICY 20 EEC. PAGE 6 F0107
DIPLOM INT/ORG FEDERAL

S67

ASCH P.,"CONGLOMERATE MERGERS AND PUBLIC POLICY." USA+45 ECO/DEV LG/CO NAT/G ECO/TAC ADJUD CENTRAL 20. PAGE 7 F0126
INDUS CAP/ISM BARGAIN

S67

AUBERT DE LA RUE P.,"PERSPECTIVES ECONOMIQUES ENTRE LES ETATS-UNIS ET L'EUROPE." FUT INDUS R+D INT/ORG ACT/RES ECO/TAC AGREE BAL/PAY PRODUC...CHARTS 20 EEC GATT WORLD/BANK. PAGE 7 F0138
INT/TRADE ECO/DEV FINAN TARIFFS

S67

BARRO S.,"ECONOMIC IMPACT OF SPACE EXPENDITURES: SOME BROAD ISSUES DEALING WITH COSTS AND BENEFITS." USA+45 PROC/MFG R+D LG/CO CONSULT COST PRODUC 20. PAGE 10 F0195
SPACE FINAN ECO/TAC NAT/G

S67

BARTLETT J.L.,"AMERICAN BOND ISSUES IN THE EUROPEAN ECONOMIC COMMUNITY." EUR+WWI LUXEMBOURG USA+45 DIPLOM CONTROL BAL/PAY EEC. PAGE 11 F0201
LAW ECO/TAC FINAN TAX

S67

BUTT R.,"THE COMMON MARKET AND CONSERVATIVE POLITICS, 1961-2." UK CHIEF DIPLOM ECO/TAC INT/TRADE CONFER DEBATE REGION ATTIT...POLICY 20 EEC. PAGE 21 F0398
EUR+WWI INT/ORG POL/PAR

S67

COSGROVE C.A.,"AGRICULTURE, FINANCE AND POLITICS IN THE EUROPEAN COMMUNITY." EUR+WWI DIST/IND MARKET INT/ORG VOL/ASSN DELIB/GP TEC/DEV BAL/PWR BARGAIN ECO/TAC RATION CONFER 20 EEC. PAGE 28 F0538
ECO/DEV DIPLOM AGRI INT/TRADE

S67

CRAIG A.,"ARGENTINA: THE LATEST REVOLUTION." ELITES NAT/G CHIEF FORCES ECO/TAC CIVMIL/REL GOV/REL EQUILIB PRIVIL 20 ARGEN. PAGE 28 F0550
ECO/UNDEV FINAN ATTIT REV

S67

CROMER EARL OF,"STERLING AND THE COMMON MARKET." UK ECO/DEV INT/ORG 20 EEC. PAGE 29 F0554
ECO/TAC FINAN CHARTS INT/TRADE

S67

DANIEL C.,"FREEDOM, EQUITY, AND THE WAR ON POVERTY." USA+45 WORKER ECO/TAC JURID. PAGE 30 F0578
WEALTH INCOME SOCIETY ORD/FREE

S67

FADDEYEV N.,"CMEA CO-OPERATION OF EQUAL NATIONS." COM R+D PLAN CAP/ISM DIPLOM FOR/AID WEALTH...POLICY MARXIST. PAGE 39 F0758
MARXISM ECO/TAC INT/ORG ECO/UNDEV

S67

FUCHS V.R.,"REDEFINING POVERTY AND REDISTRIBUTING INCOME." USA+45 NAT/G ECO/TAC GIVE COST...NEW/IDEA CHARTS. PAGE 45 F0873
WEALTH INCOME STRATA PROB/SOLV

S67

GAMARNIKOW M.,"THE NEW ROLE OF PRIVATE ENTERPRISE." ECO/DEV INDUS NAT/G SML/CO CREATE PROB/SOLV MARXISM ...POLICY TREND IDEA/COMP 20. PAGE 46 F0890
ECO/TAC ATTIT CAP/ISM COM

S67

GRAHAM R.,"BRAZIL'S DILEMMA." BRAZIL FUT L/A+17C NAT/G CHIEF PROB/SOLV ECO/TAC PWR 20. PAGE 50 F0972
ECO/UNDEV CONSTN POL/PAR POLICY

S67

HADDOCK G.B.,"CORPORATE GROWTH AS AFFECTED BY THE FEDERAL ANTITRUST LAWS" ECO/DEV NAT/G PLAN TEC/DEV CAP/ISM ECO/TAC 20. PAGE 53 F1029
INDUS JURID ADJUD

S67

HEATH D.B.,"BOLIVIA UNDER BARRIENTOS." L/A+17C NAT/G CHIEF DIPLOM ECO/TAC...POLICY 20 BOLIV. PAGE 58 F1132
ECO/UNDEV POL/PAR REV CONSTN

S67

HILDEBRAND G.H.,"SECOND THOUGHTS ON THE NEGATIVE INCOME TAX." PLAN BUDGET ECO/TAC GIVE RECEIVE DEBATE EFFICIENCY INCOME...METH/COMP COSTS. PAGE 59 F1169
TAX WEALTH SOC/WK ACT/RES

S67

HILDEBRAND J.R.,"THE CENTRAL AMERICAN COMMON MARKET: ECONOMIC AND POLITICAL INTEGRATION." L/A+17C USA+45 ECO/DEV ECO/UNDEV AGRI SOVEREIGN. PAGE 59 F1170
DIPLOM ECO/TAC INT/TRADE INT/ORG

S67

HUTCHINGS R.,"THE ENDING OF UNEMPLOYMENT IN THE USSR" USSR PLAN ECO/TAC PRICE INGP/REL...GEOG STAT CHARTS 20 MIGRATION. PAGE 63 F1247
WORKER AGRI INDUS MARXISM

S67

KENNY L.M.,"THE AFTERMATH OF DEFEAT IN EGYPT." ISLAM ISRAEL UAR UK USA+45 USSR INDUS FORCES ECO/TAC PRICE COERCE WEAPON COST ATTIT. PAGE 70 F1378
WAR ECO/UNDEV DIPLOM POLICY

S67

KESTENBAUM L.,"PRIMARY JURISDICTION TO DECIDE ANTITRUST JURISDICTION* A PRACTICAL APPROACH TO THE ALLOCATION OF FUNCTIONS." USA+45 ECO/DEV INDUS VOL/ASSN ECO/TAC. PAGE 70 F1383
JURID CT/SYS LABOR ADJUD

S67

KRAUS J.,"A MARXIST IN GHANA." GHANA ELITES CHIEF PROB/SOLV TEC/DEV DIPLOM ECO/TAC COLONIAL PARTIC PWR 20 NKRUMAH/K. PAGE 73 F1432
MARXISM PLAN ATTIT CREATE

S67

LEDEBUR L.C.,"THE PROBLEM OF SOCIAL COST." STRUCT PROB/SOLV...CHARTS GEN/LAWS. PAGE 77 F1501
COST INCOME SOCIETY ECO/TAC

S67

LEIFER M.,"ASTRIDE THE STRAITS OF JAHORE: THE BRITISH PRESENCE AND COMMONWEALTH RIVALRY IN SOUTHEAST ASIA." MALAYSIA UK FORCES PLAN ECO/TAC ...DECISION 20 CMN/WLTH. PAGE 77 F1515
DIPLOM NAT/LISM COLONIAL

S67

LEONTYEV L.,"THE LENINIST PRINCIPLES OF SOCIALIST ECONOMIC MANAGEMENT." USA+45 USSR POL/PAR WORKER PLAN ECO/TAC EFFICIENCY PRODUC MARXISM...POLICY SOCIALIST MGT TREND 20 LENIN/VI MARX/KARL. PAGE 78 F1529
SOCISM CAP/ISM IDEA/COMP ECO/DEV

S67
MAJSTRENKO I.W.,"PROBLEMS CONFRONTING SOVIET AGRICULTURE." COM USSR ECO/DEV ECO/TAC EFFICIENCY OPTIMAL WEALTH MARXISM 20. PAGE 84 F1643
AGRI PROB/SOLV CENTRAL TEC/DEV

S67
MALKIN A.,"BUSINESS BOOKS OF 1966." INDUS LABOR OP/RES TEC/DEV CAP/ISM ECO/TAC INCOME WEALTH 20. PAGE 84 F1649
BIBLIOG/A FINAN MARKET

S67
MEHTA A.,"INDIA* POVERTY AND CHANGE." STRATA INDUS CREATE ECO/TAC FOR/AID NEUTRAL GP/REL ADJUST INCOME ...NEW/IDEA 20. PAGE 89 F1746
INDIA SOCIETY ECO/UNDEV TEC/DEV

S67
MILLER C.H.,"B. TRAVEN Y EL 'PROBLEMA PETROLERO'." USA-45 ECO/UNDEV INDUS TEC/DEV INT/TRADE ATTIT ORD/FREE SOVEREIGN 20 MEXIC/AMER. PAGE 91 F1791
EXTR/IND DIPLOM ECO/TAC DOMIN

S67
MOLTMANN G.,"ZUR FORMULIERUNG DER AMERIKANISCHEN BESATZUNGSPOLITIK IN DEUTSCHLAND AM ENDE DES ZWEITEN WELTKRIEGES" GERMANY ECO/TAC ADMIN WAR CIVMIL/REL ORD/FREE FASCISM 20. PAGE 92 F1815
FORCES CONTROL POLICY INDUS

S67
MUNDHEIM R.H.,"SOME THOUGHTS ON THE DUTIES AND RESPONSIBILITIES OF UNAFFILIATED DIRECTORS OF MUTUAL FUNDS." USA+45 LG/CO SML/CO CONSULT LEAD PARTIC. PAGE 95 F1861
FINAN WEALTH ECO/TAC ADMIN

S67
MYRDAL G.,"ECONOMIC DEVELOPMENT IN THE BACKWARD COUNTRIES." INT/ORG TEC/DEV CAP/ISM DIPLOM INT/TRADE PRODUC WEALTH 20. PAGE 96 F1883
ECO/UNDEV INDUS NAT/G ECO/TAC

S67
NOURSE E.G.,"EARLY FLOWERING OF THE EMPLOYMENT ACT" USA+45 LABOR CONSULT DELIB/GP LEGIS BUDGET GOV/REL PRODUC WEALTH 20 INTRVN/ECO. PAGE 99 F1939
NAT/G WORKER ECO/TAC CONTROL

S67
ORAZEM F.,"THE NEW SOVIET PLAN FOR AGRICULTURE (1960-1970)" USSR WORKER CAP/ISM ECO/TAC PRICE OWN HABITAT MARXISM...CHARTS 20. PAGE 101 F1994
AGRI PLAN COM ECO/DEV

S67
PERKINS D.H.,"ECONOMIC GROWTH IN CHINA AND THE CULTURAL REVOLUTION(1960APRIL 1967)" CHINA/COM FUT AGRI INDUS PLAN LEAD MARXISM...CHARTS 20 MAO. PAGE 105 F2062
ECO/TAC CULTURE REV ECO/UNDEV

S67
PETROVICH M.B.,"UNITED STATES POLICY IN EAST EUROPE." ECO/DEV ECO/TAC IDEA/COMP. PAGE 105 F2075
COM INT/TRADE USA+45 DIPLOM

S67
REILLY T.J.,"FREEZING AND CONFISCATION OF CUBAN PROPERTY." CUBA USA+45 LAW DIPLOM LEGIT ADJUD CONTROL. PAGE 111 F2177
STRANGE OWN ECO/TAC

S67
ROCKE J.R.M.,"THE BRITISH EXPORT BATTLE FOR THE CARIBBEAN" GP/REL...POLICY 20 CMN/WLTH. PAGE 113 F2229
INT/TRADE DIPLOM MARKET ECO/TAC

S67
RONNING C.,"NANKING: 1950." ASIA CANADA CHINA/COM NAT/G PLAN ECO/TAC REV ADJUST 20. PAGE 113 F2235
DIPLOM ROLE PEACE

S67
SCHACHTER G.,"REGIONAL DEVELOPMENT IN THE ITALIAN DUAL ECONOMY" ITALY AGRI INDUS MARKET WORKER ECO/TAC CONTROL INCOME PRODUC 20. PAGE 116 F2287
REGION ECO/UNDEV NAT/G PROB/SOLV

S67
SCHELLING T.C.,"ECONOMICS AND CRIMINAL ENTERPRISE." LAW FORCES BARGAIN ECO/TAC CONTROL GAMBLE ROUTINE ADJUST DEMAND INCOME PROFIT CRIMLGY. PAGE 116 F2295
CRIME PROB/SOLV CONCPT

S67
SCHNEIDER E.,"DIE ENTPOLITISIERUNG DES DEUTSCHEN OSTHANDELS." AFR MARKET TEC/DEV OBJECTIVE 20. PAGE 117 F2307
ATTIT INT/TRADE ECO/TAC DIPLOM

S67
SCOTT R.,"TRADE UNIONS IN AFRICA." AFR UGANDA USA-45 ECO/UNDEV INDUS INT/ORG POL/PAR ECO/TAC WEALTH...GP/COMP 20 NKRUMAH/K. PAGE 118 F2335
LABOR WORKER NAT/G

S67
SMALL A.H.,"THE EFFECT OF TARIFF REDUCTIONS ON US IMPORT VOLUME." USA+45 INT/ORG NAT/G DIPLOM CONFER DEMAND...POLICY INT/LAW STAT CHARTS GATT EEC. PAGE 123 F2424
TARIFFS INT/TRADE PRICE ECO/TAC

S67
STOLTE S.C.,"THREE PROBLEMS FACING THE SOVIET BLOC." ASIA COM USA+45 USSR FORCES MARXISM ...IDEA/COMP METH/COMP 20 NATO WARSAW/P. PAGE 127 F2496
ECO/TAC DIPLOM INT/ORG POLICY

S67
TELLER A.,"AIR-POLLUTION ABATEMENT: ECONOMIC RATIONALITY AND REALITY." NAT/G DELIB/GP ECO/TAC GOV/REL CENTRAL EFFICIENCY HEALTH...CHARTS METH MUNICH. PAGE 129 F2543
PROB/SOLV CONTROL COST AIR

S67
THEROUX P.,"HATING THE ASIANS." TANZANIA UGANDA CONSTN INDUS NAT/G POL/PAR WORKER ECO/TAC HABITAT LOVE...POLICY GEOG 20 MIGRATION. PAGE 130 F2557
AFR RACE/REL SOVEREIGN ATTIT

S67
WARNER G.,"FRANCE, BRITAIN AND THE EEC." FRANCE UK INT/ORG DELIB/GP ECO/TAC CONTROL 20 EEC. PAGE 143 F2822
INT/TRADE BAL/PWR DIPLOM

S67
WEIL G.L.,"THE MERGER OF THE INSTITUTIONS OF THE EUROPEAN COMMUNITIES" EUR+WWI ECO/DEV INT/TRADE CONSEN PLURISM...DECISION MGT 20 EEC EURATOM ECSC TREATY. PAGE 145 F2847
ECO/TAC INT/ORG CENTRAL INT/LAW

N67
US CONGRESS JOINT ECO COMM,MAINLAND CHINA IN THE WORLD ECONOMY (PAMPHLET). CHINA/COM USA+45 AGRI CHIEF MARXISM CONGRESS. PAGE 135 F2661
ECO/UNDEV POLICY ECO/TAC INT/TRADE

N67
US CONGRESS JOINT ECO COMM,ECONOMY IN GOVERNMENT (PAMPHLET). USA+45 ECO/DEV FINAN NAT/G PLAN BUDGET SENATE. PAGE 135 F2662
ECO/TAC COST EFFICIENCY MGT

N67
US HOUSE COMM FOREIGN AFFAIRS,COMMUNIST ACTIVITIES IN LATIN AMERICA 1967 (PAMPHLET). CUBA USA+45 DIPLOM INT/TRADE EDU/PROP COERCE GUERRILLA HOUSE/REP OAS. PAGE 137 F2696
L/A+17C MARXISM ORD/FREE ECO/TAC

B75
JEVONS W.S.,MONEY AND THE MECHANISM OF EXCHANGE. INDUS MARKET DIPLOM COST EQUILIB WEALTH LAISSEZ ...GEN/LAWS 19 MONEY. PAGE 67 F1319
PRICE FINAN ECO/TAC POLICY

B76
SMITH A.,THE WEALTH OF NATIONS. UK STRUCT WORKER DIPLOM ECO/TAC OPTIMAL DRIVE PERSON ORD/FREE ...OLD/LIB GEN/LAWS 17/18. PAGE 123 F2428
WEALTH PRODUC INDUS LAISSEZ

C83
BURKE E.,"RESOLUTIONS FOR CONCILIATION WITH AMERICA" (1775), IN E. BURKE, COLLECTED WORKS, VOL. 2." UK USA-45 FORCES INT/TRADE TARIFFS TAX SANCTION PEACE...POLICY 18 PRE/US/AM. PAGE 20 F0387
COLONIAL WAR SOVEREIGN ECO/TAC

B84
MILL J.,ELEMENTS OF POLITICAL ECONOMY. UK LAW ELITES FINAN WORKER ECO/TAC RENT OWN WEALTH ...POLICY GEN/LAWS 19. PAGE 91 F1785
TAX TARIFFS NAT/G INCOME

B86
O'CONNOR T.P.,THE PARNELL MOVEMENT: WITH A SKETCH OF IRISH PARTIES FROM 1843. IRELAND UK USA-45 LEGIS WORKER ECO/TAC COERCE CRIME REV CHOOSE ORD/FREE CATHISM LAISSEZ...SOC 19/20 PARLIAMENT PARNELL/CS LAND/LEAG. PAGE 100 F1957
LEAD DOMIN POL/PAR POLICY

L86
OSGOOD H.L.,"SCIENTIFIC SOCIALISM: RODBERTUS" GERMANY CAP/ISM COST WEALTH...MAJORIT BIOG IDEA/COMP 19 RODBRTUS/C. PAGE 102 F2002
SOCISM MARXISM ECO/DEV ECO/TAC

B88
BENTHAM J.,DEFENCE OF USURY (1787). UK LAW NAT/G TEC/DEV ECO/TAC CONTROL ATTIT...CONCPT IDEA/COMP 18 SMITH/ADAM. PAGE 13 F0255
TAX FINAN ECO/DEV POLICY

B91
MILL J.S.,SOCIALISM (1859). MOD/EUR AGRI INDUS NAT/G REV INCOME PRODUC ORD/FREE POPULISM SOCISM ...GOV/COMP METH/COMP 19. PAGE 91 F1787
WEALTH SOCIALIST ECO/TAC OWN

B96
MARX K.,REVOLUTION AND COUNTER-REVOLUTION. GERMANY CONSTN ELITES INDUS NAT/G DIPLOM ECO/TAC WEALTH. PAGE 86 F1693
MARXIST REV PWR STRATA

B96
SCHMOLLER G.,THE MERCANTILE SYSTEM AND ITS HISTORICAL SIGNIFICANCE: ILLUSTRATED CHIEFLY FROM PRUSSIAN HISTORY (TRANS.). PRUSSIA CULTURE INDUS KIN NAT/G PROVS OP/RES ECO/TAC INT/TRADE SUPEGO PWR WEALTH MUNICH 19 MERCANTLST. PAGE 117 F2302
GEN/METH INGP/REL CONCPT

B99
KROPOTKIN P.,FIELDS, FACTORIES, AND WORKSHOPS. UNIV INTELL ECO/DEV LG/CO SCHOOL SML/CO ECO/TAC PRODUC UTOPIA...NEW/IDEA MUNICH. PAGE 74 F1445
SOCIETY WORKER AGRI INDUS

ECO/UNDEV....ECONOMIC SYSTEM IN DEVELOPING COUNTRIES

N
BROCKWAY A.F.,AFRICAN SOCIALISM. EUR+WWI GHANA
AFR

ISLAM UAR ECO/UNDEV CAP/ISM INT/TRADE COLONIAL COERCE GOV/REL DISCRIM 20 NEGRO NKRUMAH/K NASSER/G. PAGE 19 F0356
SOCISM MARXISM

N

INTERNATIONAL BIBLIOGRAPHY OF ECONOMICS. WOR+45 FINAN MARKET ADMIN DEMAND INCOME PRODUC...POLICY IDEA/COMP METH. PAGE 1 F0002
BIBLIOG ECO/DEV ECO/UNDEV INT/TRADE

N

THE MIDDLE EAST AND NORTH AFRICA. AFR ISLAM CULTURE ECO/UNDEV AGRI NAT/G TEC/DEV FOR/AID INT/TRADE EDU/PROP...CHARTS 20. PAGE 1 F0008
INDEX INDUS FINAN STAT

N

SOUTH AFRICAN JOURNAL OF ECONOMICS. SOUTH/AFR FINAN MARKET ACT/RES OP/RES...PHIL/SCI STAT CON/ANAL METH/COMP BIBLIOG/A 20. PAGE 1 F0009
ECO/UNDEV ACADEM INTELL R+D

N

AMERICAN ECONOMIC ASSOCIATION,THE JOURNAL OF ECONOMIC ABSTRACTS. ECO/UNDEV MARKET LABOR DIPLOM ...MGT CONCPT METH 20. PAGE 5 F0086
BIBLIOG/A R+D FINAN

N

SCIENTIFIC COUNCIL FOR AFRICA,INVENTORY OF ECONOMIC STUDIES CONCERNING AFRICA SOUTH OF THE SAHARA. AFR ...PHIL/SCI 20. PAGE 118 F2327
BIBLIOG/A GEOG ECO/UNDEV

N

UNESCO,INTERNATIONAL BIBLIOGRAPHY OF ECONOMICS (VOLUMES 1-8). WOR+45 AGRI INDUS LABOR PLAN TEC/DEV 20. PAGE 132 F2607
BIBLIOG ECO/DEV ECO/UNDEV

N

UNIVERSITY OF FLORIDA,CARIBBEAN ACQUISITIONS: MATERIALS ACQUIRED BY THE UNIVERSITY OF FLORIDA 1957-1960. L/A+17C...ART/METH GEOG MGT 20. PAGE 133 F2620
BIBLIOG ECO/UNDEV EDU/PROP JURID

N

US LIBRARY OF CONGRESS,SOUTHERN ASIA ACCESSIONS LIST. BURMA CEYLON INDIA NEPAL PAKISTAN S/ASIA THAILAND AGRI INDUS SCHOOL WORKER...ART/METH GEOG HEAL PHIL/SCI LING 20. PAGE 137 F2710
BIBLIOG/A SOCIETY CULTURE ECO/UNDEV

NCO

CARRINGTON C.E.,THE COMMONWEALTH IN AFRICA (PAMPHLET). UK STRUCT NAT/G COLONIAL REPRESENT GOV/REL RACE/REL NAT/LISM...MAJORIT 20 EEC NEGRO. PAGE 22 F0421
ECO/UNDEV AFR DIPLOM PLAN

NCO

STOLPER W.,"SOCIAL FACTORS IN ECONOMIC PLANNING, WITH SPECIAL REFERENCE TO NIGERIA" AFR NIGER CULTURE FAM SECT RECEIVE ETIQUET ADMIN DEMAND 20. PAGE 126 F2494
ECO/UNDEV PLAN ADJUST RISK

B14

VEBLEN T.,THE INSTINCT OF WORKMANSHIP. UNIV SOCIETY ECO/DEV ECO/UNDEV CREATE TEC/DEV ECO/TAC EDU/PROP ROUTINE PERSON...HUM CONCPT TIME/SEQ GEN/LAWS. PAGE 140 F2768
DRIVE SKILL

N19

ARNDT H.W.,AUSTRALIAN FOREIGN AID POLICY (PAMPHLET). ECO/UNDEV DIPLOM GIVE GOV/REL COST UTIL PWR...CHARTS 20 AUSTRAL PAPUA NEW/GUINEA. PAGE 6 F0114
FOR/AID POLICY ECO/TAC EFFICIENCY

N19

BASCH A.,THE FUTURE OF FOREIGN LENDING FOR DEVELOPMENT (PAMPHLET). WOR+45 ECO/UNDEV FINAN INT/ORG ECO/TAC ATTIT...PREDICT 20. PAGE 11 F0203
FOR/AID ECO/DEV DIPLOM GIVE

N19

EAST KENTUCKY REGIONAL PLAN,PROGRAM 60: A DECADE OF ACTION FOR PROGRESS IN EASTERN KENTUCKY (PAMPHLET). USA+45 AGRI CONSTRUC INDUS CONSULT ACT/RES PROB/SOLV EDU/PROP GOV/REL HEALTH KENTUCKY. PAGE 35 F0689
REGION ADMIN PLAN ECO/UNDEV

N19

EAST KENTUCKY REGIONAL PLAN,PROGRAM 60 REPORT: ACTION FOR PORGRESS IN EASTERN KENTUCKY (PAMPHLET). USA+45 CONSTRUC INDUS ACT/RES PROB/SOLV EDU/PROP ADMIN GOV/REL KENTUCKY. PAGE 35 F0690
REGION PLAN ECO/UNDEV CONSULT

N19

FRANCK P.G.,AFGHANISTAN BETWEEN EAST AND WEST: THE ECONOMICS OF COMPETITIVE COEXISTENCE (PAMPHLET). AFGHANISTN USA+45 USA-45 USSR INDUS ECO/TAC INT/TRADE CONTROL NEUTRAL ORD/FREE MARXISM...GEOG 20 UN. PAGE 43 F0842
FOR/AID PLAN DIPLOM ECO/UNDEV

N19

HANSEN B.,INFLATION PROBLEMS IN SMALL COUNTRIES (PAMPHLET). AFR UNIV FOR/AID CONTROL BAL/PAY DEMAND PRODUC 20. PAGE 54 F1066
PRICE FINAN ECO/UNDEV ECO/TAC

N19

JACKSON R.G.A.,THE CASE FOR AN INTERNATIONAL DEVELOPMENT AUTHORITY (PAMPHLET). WOR+45 ECO/DEV DIPLOM GIVE CONTROL GP/REL EFFICIENCY NAT/LISM SOVEREIGN 20. PAGE 66 F1295
FOR/AID INT/ORG ECO/UNDEV ADMIN

N19

KUWAIT ARABIA,KUWAIT FUND FOR ARAB ECONOMIC DEVELOPMENT (PAMPHLET). ISLAM KUWAIT UAR ECO/UNDEV LEGIS ECO/TAC WEALTH 20. PAGE 74 F1452
FOR/AID DIPLOM FINAN ADMIN

N19

KUWAIT FUND ARAB ECO DEVELOPMT,ANNUAL REPORTS 1962-65 (PAMPHLET). KUWAIT ECO/UNDEV DIPLOM ...POLICY 20 ARABS. PAGE 74 F1453
FOR/AID DELIB/GP FINAN ISLAM

N19

LANGE O.R.,"DISARMAMENT ECONOMIC GROWTH AND INTERNATIONAL CO-OPERATION" (PAMPHLET). WOR+45 DIST/IND PLAN INT/TRADE GIVE TASK DETER WEALTH SOCISM 18/19 BOLIVAR/S. PAGE 75 F1477
ARMS/CONT DIPLOM ECO/DEV ECO/UNDEV

N19

MARCUS W.,US PRIVATE INVESTMENT AND ECONOMIC AID IN UNDERDEVELOPED COUNTRIES (PAMPHLET). USA+45 LG/CO NAT/G CAP/ISM EDU/PROP 20. PAGE 85 F1666
FOR/AID ECO/UNDEV FINAN PLAN

N19

MASON E.S.,THE DIPLOMACY OF ECONOMIC ASSISTANCE (PAMPHLET). INDIA PAKISTAN USA+45 ECO/UNDEV NAT/G BUDGET ATTIT...POLICY 20. PAGE 87 F1695
FOR/AID DIPLOM FINAN

N19

MEZERIK A.G.,ECONOMIC AID FOR UNDERDEVELOPED COUNTRIES (PAMPHLET). AFR USSR WOR+45 FINAN LG/CO DELIB/GP NUC/PWR...GEOG CENSUS CHARTS 20 UN THIRD/WRLD. PAGE 90 F1775
FOR/AID ECO/UNDEV DIPLOM POLICY

N19

SAPIR H.M.,JAPAN, CHINA, AND THE WEST (PAMPHLET). AFR ASIA CHINA/COM PROB/SOLV GOV/REL 20 CHINJAP. PAGE 116 F2282
ECO/UNDEV INT/TRADE DECISION PLAN

N19

SENGHOR L.S.,AFRICAN SOCIALISM (PAMPHLET). AFR FRANCE MALI USSR ELITES ECO/UNDEV NAT/G DIPLOM DOMIN EDU/PROP ATTIT 20 NEGRO. PAGE 119 F2355
SOCISM MARXISM ORD/FREE NAT/LISM

N19

STALEY E.,SCIENTIFIC RESEARCH AND PROGRESS IN NEWLY DEVELOPING COUNTRIES (PAMPHLET). AFR ASIA L/A+17C CONSULT DIPLOM...METH/COMP 20. PAGE 125 F2463
ECO/UNDEV ACT/RES FOR/AID TEC/DEV

N19

STEUBER F.A.,THE CONTRIBUTION OF SWITZERLAND TO THE ECONOMIC AND SOCIAL DEVELOPMENT OF LOW-INCOME COUNTRIES (PAMPHLET). SWITZERLND FINAN NAT/G VOL/ASSN INT/TRADE DRIVE...CHARTS 20. PAGE 126 F2482
FOR/AID ECO/UNDEV PLAN DIPLOM

N19

VELYAMINOV G.,AFRICA AND THE COMMON MARKET (PAMPHLET). AFR MARKET VOL/ASSN ECO/TAC COLONIAL ORD/FREE...SOCIALIST 20 THIRD/WRLD. PAGE 141 F2775
INT/ORG INT/TRADE SOVEREIGN ECO/UNDEV

B21

CLAPHAN J.H.,THE ECONOMIC DEVELOPMENT OF FRANCE AND GERMANY 1815-1914. FRANCE GERMANY MOD/EUR COM/IND DIST/IND FINAN INT/TRADE EDU/PROP 19/20. PAGE 24 F0476
ECO/UNDEV ECO/DEV AGRI INDUS

S21

MALINOWSKI B.,"THE PRIMITIVE ECONOMICS OF THE TROBRIAND ISLANDERS" (BMR)" CULTURE SOCIETY NAT/G CHIEF LEAD OWN...SOC MYTH WORSHIP 20 NEW/GUINEA TROBRIAND RESOURCE/N. PAGE 84 F1647
ECO/UNDEV AGRI PRODUC STRUCT

B26

MCPHEE A.,THE ECONOMIC REVOLUTION IN BRITISH WEST AFRICA. AFR UK CULTURE DIST/IND FINAN INDUS PLAN GP/REL RACE/REL 20 AFRICA/W. PAGE 88 F1735
ECO/UNDEV INT/TRADE COLONIAL GEOG

B26

SUFRIN S.C.,A BRIEF ANNOTATED BIBLIOGRAPHY ON LABOR IN EMERGING SOCIETIES. WOR+45 CULTURE SOCIETY INDUS EDU/PROP GP/REL INGP/REL. PAGE 127 F2510
BIBLIOG/A LABOR ECO/UNDEV WORKER

B30

HAWTREY R.G.,ECONOMIC ASPECTS OF SOVEREIGNTY. UNIV WOR+45 WOR-45 ECO/DEV ECO/UNDEV AGRI COM/IND INDUS MARKET NAT/G TEC/DEV ECO/TAC EDU/PROP COERCE ATTIT KNOWL WEALTH...CONCPT CON/ANAL GEN/LAWS 20. PAGE 57 F1118
FORCES PWR SOVEREIGN WAR

B30

THOMPSON W.R.,POPULATION PROBLEMS. FUT UNIV WOR-45 STRUCT DIST/IND ACT/RES ECO/TAC BIO/SOC...CONCPT OBS TIME/SEQ TOT/POP 20. PAGE 130 F2567
ECO/UNDEV GEOG

B33

TANNENBAUM F.,PEACE BY REVOLUTION. ECO/UNDEV AGRI SECT WORKER DIPLOM EDU/PROP DISCRIM OWN WEALTH POPULISM 17/20 MEXIC/AMER INDIAN/AM. PAGE 128 F2532
CULTURE COLONIAL RACE/REL REV

B37

MACKENZIE F.,PLANNED SOCIETY: YESTERDAY, TODAY, AND TOMORROW. ECO/DEV ECO/UNDEV AGRI FINAN INDUS PLAN INSPECT CONTROL ALL/IDEOS...TREND METH/COMP BIBLIOG 20 RESOURCE/N. PAGE 83 F1635
SOC CONCPT ANTHOL

B38

HOBSON J.A.,IMPERIALISM. MOD/EUR UK WOR-45 CULTURE ECO/UNDEV NAT/G VOL/ASSN PLAN EDU/PROP LEGIT REGION COERCE ATTIT PWR...POLICY PLURIST TIME/SEQ GEN/LAWS TERR/GP 19/20. PAGE 60 F1187
DOMIN ECO/TAC BAL/PWR COLONIAL

B39
FIRTH R.,PRIMITIVE POLYNESIAN ECONOMY. SOCIETY DIST/IND SECT CHIEF CAP/ISM PRODUC WEALTH...SOC OBS METH WORSHIP 20 POLYNESIA. PAGE 41 F0802
ECO/UNDEV CULTURE AGRI ECO/TAC

B39
FURNIVALL J.S.,NETHERLANDS INDIA. INDIA NETHERLAND CULTURE INDUS NAT/G DIPLOM ADMIN WEALTH...POLICY CHARTS 17/20. PAGE 45 F0876
COLONIAL ECO/UNDEV SOVEREIGN PLURISM

B39
ROBBINS L.,ECONOMIC CAUSES OF WAR. WOR-45 ECO/DEV ECO/UNDEV INT/ORG NAT/G TEC/DEV DIPLOM DOMIN COLONIAL ATTIT DRIVE PWR WEALTH...POLICY CONCPT OBS SAMP TREND CON/ANAL GEN/LAWS MARX/KARL 20. PAGE 112 F2203
COERCE ECO/TAC WAR

B40
MEEK C.K.,EUROPE AND WEST AFRICA. AFR EUR+WWI EXTR/IND DIPLOM INT/TRADE EDU/PROP GP/REL...SOC 20. PAGE 89 F1743
CULTURE TEC/DEV ECO/UNDEV COLONIAL

B45
DAVIS J.,AFRICA ADVANCING. AFR CONGO/BRAZ LIBERIA NIGER INT/ORG SCHOOL DIPLOM GIVE KNOWL SKILL 20. PAGE 30 F0590
SECT COLONIAL AGRI ECO/UNDEV

B50
ORTON W.A.,THE ECONOMIC ROLE OF THE STATE. INTELL ECO/UNDEV PLAN CONTROL PWR SOVEREIGN...POLICY 17/20. PAGE 102 F2000
ECO/DEV NAT/G ECO/TAC ORD/FREE

B50
SCHUMPETER J.A.,CAPITALISM, SOCIALISM, AND DEMOCRACY (3RD ED.). USA-45 USSR WOR+45 WOR-45 INTELL ECO/DEV ECO/UNDEV ECO/TAC WAR PRODUC ORD/FREE...MGT SOC 20 MARX/KARL. PAGE 118 F2321
SOCIALIST CAP/ISM MARXISM IDEA/COMP

B50
US DEPARTMENT OF STATE,POINT FOUR: COOPERATIVE PROGRAM FOR AID IN THE DEVELOPMENT OF ECONOMICALLY UNDERDEVELOPED AREAS. WOR+45 AGRI INDUS INT/ORG PLAN TEC/DEV DIPLOM EDU/PROP ADMIN PEACE PRODUC WEALTH 20 CONGRESS UN. PAGE 135 F2671
ECO/UNDEV FOR/AID FINAN INT/TRADE

C50
ELLSWORTH P.T.,"INTERNATIONAL ECONOMY." ECO/DEV ECO/UNDEV FINAN LABOR DIPLOM FOR/AID TARIFFS BAL/PAY EQUILIB NAT/LISM OPTIMAL...INT/LAW 20 ILO GATT. PAGE 37 F0724
BIBLIOG INT/TRADE ECO/TAC INT/ORG

B51
US HOUSE COMM APPROPRIATIONS,MUTUAL SECURITY PROGRAM APPROPRIATIONS FOR 1952: HEARINGS BEFORE A SUBCOMMITTEE OF THE COMMITTEE ON APPROPRIATIONS. AFR KOREA L/A+17C ECO/DEV ECO/UNDEV INT/ORG INSPECT BAL/PWR DIPLOM DEBATE WAR...POLICY STAT ASIA/S 20 CONGRESS NATO MID/EAST. PAGE 136 F2686
LEGIS FORCES BUDGET FOR/AID

B52
ALEXANDROWICZ C.H.,INTERNATIONAL ECONOMIC ORGANIZATION. WOR+45 ECO/DEV ECO/UNDEV DIST/IND FINAN MARKET PLAN ECO/TAC LEGIT DRIVE WEALTH ...POLICY CONCPT QUANT OBS TIME/SEQ GEN/LAWS WORK METH/GP EEC ILO OEEC UNESCO 20. PAGE 4 F0063
INT/ORG INT/TRADE

B52
HOSELITZ B.F.,THE PROGRESS OF UNDERDEVELOPED AREAS. AFR FUT WOR+45 WOR-45 ECO/DEV ECO/TAC INT/TRADE WEALTH...SOC TREND GEN/LAWS TOT/POP VAL/FREE FOR/TRADE 20. PAGE 62 F1219
ECO/UNDEV PLAN FOR/AID

L52
HUTH A.G.,"COMMUNICATION AND ECONOMIC DEVELOPMENT." FUT WOR+45 CULTURE SOCIETY INT/ORG PLAN TEC/DEV EDU/PROP DRIVE KNOWL WEALTH...POLICY CONCPT RECORD STERTYP GEN/LAWS COMMUN TOT/POP UNESCO 20 UN CMN/WLTH. PAGE 64 F1250
ECO/UNDEV

B53
BOEKE J.H.,ECONOMICS AND ECONOMIC POLICY OF DUAL SOCIETIES AS EXEMPLIFIED BY INDONESIA. INDIA INDONESIA SOCIETY CAP/ISM INT/TRADE GIVE PRICE GP/REL WEALTH SOCISM...POLICY NAT/COMP GEN/LAWS 20. PAGE 16 F0304
ECO/TAC ECO/UNDEV NAT/G CONTROL

B53
DAHL R.A.,POLITICS, ECONOMICS AND WELFARE: PLANNING AND POLITICOECONOMIC SYSTEMS RESOLVED INTO BASIC SOCIAL PROCESSES. WOR+45 WOR-45 ECO/DEV ECO/UNDEV R+D CREATE PLAN TEC/DEV EDU/PROP HEALTH WEALTH ...SOC SELF/OBS TREND CHARTS GEN/METH 20. PAGE 29 F0571
ECO/TAC PHIL/SCI

B53
FRANKEL S.H.,THE ECONOMIC IMPACT ON UNDERDEVELOPED SOCIETIES: ESSAYS ON INTERNATIONAL INVESTMENT AND SOCIAL CHANGE. AFR WOR+45 ECO/DEV FINAN INDUS NAT/G ACT/RES TEC/DEV COLONIAL ATTIT...CONCPT OBS TREND 20. PAGE 43 F0845
ECO/UNDEV FOR/AID INT/TRADE

B53
MIT CENTER INTERNATIONAL STU,BIBLIOGRAPHY OF THE ECONOMIC AND POLITICAL DEVELOPMENT OF INDONESIA. INDONESIA STRUCT NAT/G COLONIAL LEAD...STAT 20. PAGE 92 F1805
BIBLIOG ECO/UNDEV TEC/DEV S/ASIA

B53
WOYTINSKY W.S.,WORLD POPULATION AND PRODUCTION: TRENDS AND OUTLOOK. FUT WOR+45 WOR-45 CULTURE SOCIETY ECO/DEV AGRI INDUS TEC/DEV EDU/PROP SKILL WEALTH...SOC TREND. PAGE 149 F2928
ECO/UNDEV METH/CNCPT GEOG PERSON

S53
HANSER P.M.,"EXPLODING POPULATIONS: INTERNATIONAL AND REGIONAL ASPECTS." AFR S/ASIA ECO/TAC WEAPON BIO/SOC LOVE ORD/FREE...NEW/IDEA CENSUS TOT/POP 20. PAGE 55 F1069
ECO/UNDEV GEOG

B54
BATTEN T.R.,PROBLEMS OF AFRICAN DEVELOPMENT (2ND ED.). AFR LAW SOCIETY SCHOOL ECO/TAC TAX...GEOG HEAL SOC 20. PAGE 11 F0211
ECO/UNDEV AGRI LOC/G PROB/SOLV

B54
MOSK S.A.,INDUSTRIAL REVOLUTION IN MEXICO. MARKET LABOR CREATE CAP/ISM ADMIN ATTIT SOCISM...POLICY 20 MEXIC/AMER. PAGE 94 F1843
INDUS TEC/DEV ECO/UNDEV NAT/G

B54
O.E.E.C.,PRIVATE UNITED STATES INVESTMENT IN EUROPE AND THE OVERSEAS TERRITORIES. EUR+WWI WOR+45 ECO/DEV ECO/UNDEV INT/ORG NAT/G VOL/ASSN ECO/TAC ATTIT WEALTH...GEOG STAT SYS/QU CHARTS VAL/FREE 20. PAGE 99 F1950
USA+45 FINAN BAL/PAY FOR/AID

B54
STALEY E.,THE FUTURE OF UNDERDEVELOPED COUNTRIES: POLITICAL IMPLICATIONS OF ECONOMIC DEVELOPMENT. AFR COM FUT USA+45 SOCIETY ECO/UNDEV CREATE PLAN CAP/ISM ATTIT DRIVE MARXISM SOCISM...POLICY CONCPT CHARTS 20. PAGE 125 F2466
EDU/PROP ECO/TAC FOR/AID

B54
TINBERGEN J.,INTERNATIONAL ECONOMIC INTEGRATION. WOR+45 WOR-45 ECO/UNDEV NAT/G ECO/TAC BAL/PAY ...METH/CNCPT STAT TIME/SEQ GEN/METH OEEC 20. PAGE 130 F2574
INT/ORG ECO/DEV INT/TRADE

B54
WILLIAMSON H.F.,ECONOMIC DEVELOPMENT - PRINCIPLES AND PATTERNS. INDIA KOREA CULTURE ECO/DEV ECO/UNDEV TEC/DEV...CENSUS NAT/COMP FOR/TRADE 20 CHINJAP MEXIC/AMER RESOURCE/N. PAGE 147 F2895
ECO/TAC GEOG LABOR

B55
BUCHANAN N.S.,APPROACHES TO ECONOMIC DEVELOPMENT. FUT USA+45 WOR+45 STRATA ECO/DEV INT/ORG NAT/G TEC/DEV DIPLOM FOR/AID ATTIT KNOWL PWR WEALTH ...RELATIV METH/CNCPT SELF/OBS TREND CON/ANAL STERTYP GEN/LAWS FOR/TRADE COMMUN 20. PAGE 20 F0380
ECO/UNDEV ECO/TAC INT/TRADE

B55
GOMES F.A.,OPERACAO MUNICIPIO. BRAZIL L/A+17C SERV/IND LOC/G BUDGET ECO/TAC COST DEMAND...POLICY MUNICH 20. PAGE 48 F0944
ECO/UNDEV FEDERAL GOV/REL

B55
JONES T.B.,A BIBLIOGRAPHY ON SOUTH AMERICAN ECONOMIC AFFAIRS: ARTICLES IN NINETEENTH CENTURY PERIODICALS (PAMPHLET). AGRI COM/IND DIST/IND EXTR/IND FINAN INDUS LABOR NAT/G 19. PAGE 68 F1340
BIBLIOG ECO/UNDEV L/A+17C TEC/DEV

B55
OECD,MARSHALL PLAN IN TURKEY. TURKEY USA+45 COM/IND CONSTRUC SERV/IND FORCES BUDGET...STAT 20 MARSHL/PLN. PAGE 100 F1964
FOR/AID ECO/UNDEV AGRI INDUS

B55
PANT Y.P.,PLANNING IN UNDERDEVELOPED ECONOMIES. INDIA NEPAL INT/TRADE COLONIAL SOVEREIGN ALL/IDEOS ...TIME/SEQ METH/COMP 20. PAGE 103 F2026
ECO/UNDEV PLAN ECO/TAC DIPLOM

B55
PEDLER F.J.,ECONOMIC GEOGRAPHY OF WEST AFRICA. GAMBIA NIGER SIER/LEONE STRATA EXTR/IND MARKET LABOR INT/TRADE DEMAND HABITAT WEALTH...CHARTS 20. PAGE 104 F2046
ECO/UNDEV GEOG PRODUC EFFICIENCY

B55
SERRANO MOSCOSO E.,A STATEMENT OF THE LAWS OF ECUADOR IN MATTERS AFFECTING BUSINESS (2ND ED.). ECUADOR INDUS LABOR LG/CO NAT/G LEGIS TAX CONTROL MARRIAGE 20. PAGE 120 F2359
FINAN ECO/UNDEV LAW CONSTN

B55
STILLMAN C.W.,AFRICA IN THE MODERN WORLD. AFR USA+45 WOR+45 INT/TRADE COLONIAL PARTIC REGION GOV/REL RACE/REL 20. PAGE 126 F2489
ECO/UNDEV DIPLOM POLICY STRUCT

B55
UN ECONOMIC COMN ASIA & FAR E,ECONOMIC SURVEY OF ASIA AND THE FAR EAST, 1954. AFGHANISTN CEYLON INDIA PHILIPPINE S/ASIA ECO/DEV FINAN INDUS INT/TRADE PRODUC WEALTH...STAT CHARTS 20 CHINJAP. PAGE 132 F2600
ECO/UNDEV PRICE NAT/COMP ASIA

L55
KISER M.,"ORGANIZATION OF AMERICAN STATES." L/A+17C USA+45 ECO/UNDEV INT/ORG NAT/G PLAN TEC/DEV DIPLOM ECO/TAC INT/TRADE EDU/PROP ADMIN ALL/VALS...POLICY MGT RECORD ORG/CHARTS OAS COMMUN 20. PAGE 71 F1401
VOL/ASSN ECO/DEV REGION

B56
KINDLEBERGER C.P.,THE TERMS OF TRADE: A EUROPEAN CASE-STUDY. EUR+WWI MOD/EUR ECO/DEV ECO/UNDEV AGRI
PLAN ECO/TAC

INDUS BAL/PAY...METH/CNCPT STAT CONT/OBS CON/ANAL SOC/EXP SIMUL FOR/TRADE 20. PAGE 71 F1390

B56
KNORR K.E.,RUBLE DIPLOMACY: CHALLENGE TO AMERICAN FOREIGN AID(PAMPHLET). AFR CHINA/COM USA+45 USSR PLAN TEC/DEV CAP/ISM INT/TRADE DOMIN EDU/PROP CONTROL LEAD 20. PAGE 72 F1413 ECO/UNDEV COM DIPLOM FOR/AID

B56
UN HEADQUARTERS LIBRARY,BIBLIOGRAPHY OF INDUSTRIALIZATION IN UNDERDEVELOPED COUNTRIES (BIBLIOGRAPHICAL SERIES NO. 6). WOR+45 R+D ACADEM INT/ORG NAT/G. PAGE 132 F2602 BIBLIOG ECO/UNDEV TEC/DEV

B56
UNITED NATIONS,BIBLIOGRAPHY ON INDUSTRIALIZATION IN UNDER-DEVELOPED COUNTRIES. WOR+45 R+D INT/ORG NAT/G FOR/AID ADMIN LEAD 20 UN. PAGE 132 F2612 BIBLIOG ECO/UNDEV INDUS TEC/DEV

B56
US DEPARTMENT OF STATE,ECONOMIC PROBLEMS OF UNDERDEVELOPED AREAS (PAMPHLET). AFR ASIA ISLAM L/A+17C AGRI FINAN INDUS INT/ORG LABOR INT/TRADE ...PSY SOC 20. PAGE 136 F2673 BIBLIOG ECO/UNDEV TEC/DEV R+D

B56
US LIBRARY OF CONGRESS,UNITED STATES DIRECT ECONOMIC AID TO FOREIGN COUNTRIES: A COLLECTION OF EXCERPTS AND A BIBLIOGRAPHY (PAMPHLET). USA+45 PRESS DEBATE...ANTHOL BIBLIOG/A CONGRESS. PAGE 138 F2716 FOR/AID POLICY DIPLOM ECO/UNDEV

B56
US OFFICE OF THE PRESIDENT,REPORT TO CONGRESS ON THE MUTUAL SECURITY PROGRAM FOR THE SIX MONTHS ENDED DECEMBER 31, 1955. ASIA USSR ECO/DEV ECO/UNDEV INT/ORG CREATE TEC/DEV BAL/PWR ECO/TAC AGREE DETER COST ORD/FREE 20 DEPT/STATE DEPT/DEFEN EISNHWR/DD. PAGE 138 F2723 DIPLOM FORCES PLAN FOR/AID

B56
YUAN TUNG-LI,ECONOMIC AND SOCIAL DEVELOPMENT OF MODERN CHINA: A BIBLIOGRAPHIC GUIDE. COM/IND FINAN FAM LABOR SECT CRIME INCOME...STAT SAMP CON/ANAL. PAGE 150 F2954 BIBLIOG ASIA ECO/UNDEV SOC

N56
US HOUSE COMM FOREIGN AFFAIRS,REPORT OF THE SPECIAL STUDY MISSION TO AFRICA, SOUTH AND EAST OF THE SAHARA (PAMPHLET). AFR SOUTH/AFR USA+45 STRUCT INT/TRADE PARL/PROC NAT/LISM ATTIT ALL/VALS HEALTH ...POLICY 20 CONGRESS. PAGE 136 F2691 FOR/AID COLONIAL ECO/UNDEV DIPLOM

B57
ASHER R.E.,THE UNITED NATIONS AND ECONOMIC AND SOCIAL COOPERATION. ECO/UNDEV COM/IND DIST/IND FINAN PLAN PROB/SOLV INT/TRADE TASK WEALTH...SOC 20 UN. PAGE 7 F0129 INT/ORG DIPLOM FOR/AID

B57
BARAN P.A.,THE POLITICAL ECONOMY OF GROWTH. MOD/EUR USA+45 USA-45 TEC/DEV TAX SOCISM...MGT CONCPT GOV/COMP. PAGE 9 F0178 CAP/ISM CONTROL ECO/UNDEV FINAN

B57
BAUER P.T.,THE ECONOMICS OF UNDERDEVELOPED COUNTRIES. WOR+45 AGRI FINAN INDUS PROC/MFG WORKER CAP/ISM PAY PRICE INCOME MARXISM...METH/COMP 20 RESOURCE/N. PAGE 11 F0213 ECO/UNDEV ECO/TAC PROB/SOLV NAT/G

B57
BAUER P.T.,ECONOMIC ANALYSIS AND POLICY IN UNDERDEVELOPED COUNTRIES. AFR WOR+45 AGRI INT/TRADE TAX PRICE...GEN/METH BIBLIOG/A 20. PAGE 11 F0214 ECO/UNDEV METH/COMP POLICY

B57
COMMITTEE ECONOMIC DEVELOPMENT,ECONOMIC DEVELOPMENT ASSISTANCE. USA+45 WOR+45 AGRI CONFER ORD/FREE ...MGT CHARTS 20. PAGE 27 F0515 FOR/AID ECO/UNDEV FINAN PLAN

B57
GOLD N.L.,REGIONAL ECONOMIC DEVELOPMENT AND NUCLEAR POWER IN INDIA. FUT INDIA FINAN FOR/AID INT/TRADE BAL/PAY EFFICIENCY OPTIMAL PRODUC WEALTH...PREDICT 20. PAGE 48 F0934 ECO/UNDEV TEC/DEV NUC/PWR INDUS

B57
HALD M.,A SELECTED BIBLIOGRAPHY ON ECONOMIC DEVELOPMENT AND FOREIGN AID. INT/ORG PROB/SOLV ...SOC 20. PAGE 53 F1040 BIBLIOG ECO/UNDEV TEC/DEV FOR/AID

B57
LEIBENSTEIN H.,ECONOMIC BACKWARDNESS AND ECONOMIC GROWTH. WOR+45 SOCIETY AGRI INDUS TEC/DEV CAP/ISM FOR/AID COST DEMAND WEALTH...CHARTS IDEA/COMP 20. PAGE 77 F1513 ECO/UNDEV ECO/TAC PRODUC POLICY

B57
MEIER G.M.,ECONOMIC DEVELOPMENT: THEORY, HISTORY, AND POLICY. WOR+45 WOR-45 ECO/DEV ECO/UNDEV PLAN CAP/ISM BAL/PAY ATTIT PWR WEALTH SOCISM...CHARTS TOT/POP FOR/TRADE 20. PAGE 89 F1748 ECO/TAC GEN/LAWS

B57
MILLIKAN M.F.,A PROPOSAL: KEY TO AN EFFECTIVE FOREIGN POLICY. USA+45 AGRI FINAN DELIB/GP DIPLOM REPRESENT MAJORITY...NEW/IDEA CHARTS. PAGE 91 F1795 FOR/AID GIVE ECO/UNDEV PLAN

B57
NEUMARK S.D.,ECONOMIC INFLUENCES ON THE SOUTH AFRICAN FRONTIER, 1652-1836. SOUTH/AFR SEA AGRI NAT/G FORCES WORKER DIPLOM INT/TRADE PRICE DEMAND PRODUC...STAT CHARTS 17/19 FRONTIER. PAGE 97 F1915 COLONIAL ECO/UNDEV ECO/TAC MARKET

B57
OLIVER H.M. JR.,ECONOMIC OPINION AND POLICY IN CEYLON. CEYLON FINAN POL/PAR WORKER INT/TRADE INCOME WEALTH...GEOG UNPLAN/INT BIBLIOG 20 CMN/WLTH. PAGE 101 F1987 ECO/UNDEV NAT/LISM POLICY COLONIAL

B57
PALACIOS A.L.,PETROLEO, MONOPOLIOS, Y LATIFUNDIOS. L/A+17C EXTR/IND NAT/G TEC/DEV ECO/TAC CONTROL PRODUC 20 ARGEN MONOPOLY RESOURCE/N. PAGE 103 F2017 ECO/UNDEV NAT/LISM INDUS AGRI

B57
ROBERTSON H.M.,SOUTH AFRICA, ECONOMIC AND POLITICAL ASPECTS. SOUTH/AFR CONSTN CULTURE POL/PAR LEGIS DIPLOM DOMIN COLONIAL...SOC BIBLIOG 19/20. PAGE 112 F2214 RACE/REL ECO/UNDEV ECO/TAC DISCRIM

B57
SINGH D.B.,INFLATIONARY PRICE TRENDS IN INDIA SINCE 1939. AFR INDIA ECO/TAC RATION CONTROL WAR GOV/REL BAL/PAY DEMAND INCOME PEACE PRODUC...POLICY CHARTS 20. PAGE 122 F2413 BUDGET ECO/UNDEV PRICE FINAN

B57
UDY S.H. JR.,THE ORGANIZATION OF PRODUCTION IN NONINDUSTRIAL CULTURE. VOL/ASSN DELIB/GP TEC/DEV ...CHARTS BIBLIOG. PAGE 132 F2598 METH/COMP ECO/UNDEV PRODUC ADMIN

B57
WARRINER D.,LAND REFORM AND DEVELOPMENT IN THE MIDDLE EAST: A STUDY OF EGYPT, SYRIA AND IRAQ. IRAQ ISLAM SYRIA UAR AGRI DIST/IND PLAN TEC/DEV DOMIN REV ATTIT WEALTH...SOC METH/CNCPT STAT OBS RECORD HIST/WRIT TREND GEN/LAWS FAO 20. PAGE 143 F2825 ECO/UNDEV CONCPT

B57
WEIGERT H.W.,PRINCIPLES OF POLITICAL GEOGRAPHY. WOR+45 ECO/DEV ECO/UNDEV SECT ECO/TAC COLONIAL HABITAT...CHARTS T 20. PAGE 144 F2845 GEOG CULTURE

L57
MASS. INST. TECH.,"THE CENTER FOR INTERNATIONAL STUDIES." AFR ASIA COM EUR+WWI ISLAM L/A+17C S/ASIA USA+45 USA-45 DIST/IND CONSULT FORCES ACT/RES TEC/DEV DIPLOM REV ATTIT WEALTH...CONCPT FOR/TRADE 20. PAGE 87 F1702 R+D ECO/UNDEV

S57
HOAG M.W.,"ECONOMIC PROBLEMS OF ALLIANCE." AFR COM EUR+WWI WOR+45 ECO/DEV ECO/UNDEV NAT/G VOL/ASSN FORCES PLAN TEC/DEV DIPLOM COERCE ORD/FREE PWR WEALTH...DECISION GEN/LAWS NATO TERR/GP. PAGE 60 F1182 INT/ORG ECO/TAC

B58
BERLINER J.S.,SOVIET ECONOMIC AID: THE AID AND TRADE POLICY IN UNDERDEVELOPED COUNTRIES. AFR COM ISLAM L/A+17C S/ASIA USSR ECO/DEV DIST/IND FINAN MARKET INT/ORG ACT/RES PLAN BAL/PWR WEAPON PWR WEALTH...CHARTS FOR/TRADE 20. PAGE 14 F0263 ECO/UNDEV ECO/TAC FOR/AID

B58
BIDWELL P.W.,RAW MATERIALS: A STUDY OF AMERICAN POLICY. USA+45 USA-45 ECO/UNDEV AGRI INDUS KIN CREATE PLAN ECO/TAC WAR PEACE ATTIT DRIVE WEALTH ...STAT CHARTS CONGRESS FOR/TRADE VAL/FREE. PAGE 15 F0279 EXTR/IND ECO/DEV

B58
CLAIRMONTE F.,LE LIBERALISME ECONOMIQUE ET LES PAYS SOUS-DEVELOPPES: ETUDES SUR L'EVOLUTION D'UNE IDEE. ASIA INDIA UK FINAN INDUS PLAN CAP/ISM ECO/TAC COLONIAL NEW/LIB...BIBLIOG 20 THIRD/WRLD. PAGE 24 F0475 LAISSEZ ECO/UNDEV

B58
COALE A.J.,POPULATION GROWTH AND ECONOMIC DEVELOPMENT IN LOW-INCOME COUNTRIES: A CASE STUDY OF INDIA'S PROSPECTS. INDIA AGRI WORKER INCOME AGE WEALTH...CHARTS 20 MEXIC/AMER. PAGE 25 F0495 ECO/UNDEV GEOG CENSUS SEX

B58
EHRHARD J.,LE DESTIN DU COLONIALISME. AFR FRANCE ECO/UNDEV AGRI FINAN MARKET CREATE PLAN TEC/DEV BUDGET DIPLOM PRICE 20. PAGE 36 F0710 COLONIAL FOR/AID INT/TRADE INDUS

B58
HANCE W.A.,AFRICAN ECONOMIC DEVELOPMENT. AGRI DIST/IND INDUS R+D ACT/RES PLAN CAP/ISM FOR/AID ...GOV/COMP BIBLIOG 20. PAGE 54 F1058 AFR ECO/UNDEV PROB/SOLV TEC/DEV

B58
HIRSCHMAN A.O.,STRATEGY OF ECONOMIC DEVELOPMENT. WOR+45 WOR-45 CULTURE ECO/DEV NAT/G PLAN TEC/DEV INT/TRADE BAL/PAY ATTIT DRIVE RIGID/FLEX WEALTH ...CONCPT METH/CNCPT OBS CHARTS SIMUL GEN/LAWS TOT/POP VAL/FREE. PAGE 60 F1176 ECO/UNDEV ECO/TAC CAP/ISM

B58
INDIAN INST OF PUBLIC ADMIN,IMPROVING CITY GOVERNMENT. INDIA ECO/UNDEV PLAN BUDGET PARTIC GP/REL MUNICH 20. PAGE 64 F1263 LOC/G PROB/SOLV ADMIN

B58
INTERNATIONAL ECONOMIC ASSN,ECONOMICS OF INTERNATIONAL MIGRATION. WOR+45 WOR-45 ECO/UNDEV FINAN NAT/G REGION...NAT/COMP METH 20. PAGE 65 F1275
CENSUS GEOG DIPLOM ECO/TAC

B58
JENNINGS I.,PROBLEMS OF THE NEW COMMONWEALTH. AFR CEYLON INDIA PAKISTAN S/ASIA ECO/UNDEV INT/ORG LOC/G DIPLOM ECO/TAC INT/TRADE COLONIAL RACE/REL DISCRIM 20 PARLIAMENT. PAGE 67 F1314
NAT/LISM NEUTRAL FOR/AID POL/PAR

B58
KINDLEBERGER C.P.,INTERNATIONAL ECONOMICS. WOR+45 WOR-45 ECO/DEV ECO/UNDEV FINAN VOL/ASSN ACT/RES DIPLOM ECO/TAC LEGIT REGION ATTIT DRIVE ORD/FREE WEALTH...POLICY STAT TREND GEN/LAWS EEC ECSC OEEC 20. PAGE 71 F1391
INT/ORG BAL/PWR TARIFFS

B58
MASON J.B.,THAILAND BIBLIOGRAPHY. S/ASIA THAILAND CULTURE EDU/PROP ADMIN...GEOG SOC LING 20. PAGE 87 F1701
BIBLIOG/A ECO/UNDEV DIPLOM NAT/G

B58
MYRDAL G.,RICH LANDS AND POOR: THE ROAD TO WORLD PROSPERITY. FUT WOR+45 WOR-45 ECO/DEV ECO/UNDEV INT/ORG PLAN ECO/TAC REGION...GEOG TIME/SEQ GEN/LAWS TOT/POP 20. PAGE 96 F1880
WEALTH TREND FOR/AID INT/TRADE

B58
NICULESCU B.,COLONIAL PLANNING: A COMPARATIVE STUDY. AFR AGRI LOC/G NAT/G DELIB/GP COLONIAL MUNICH 20. PAGE 98 F1927
PLAN ECO/UNDEV TEC/DEV NAT/COMP

B58
PALMER E.E.,INDUSTRIAL MAN. USA+45 PERSON ORD/FREE POPULISM...PREDICT TREND ANTHOL 20. PAGE 103 F2020
INDUS ECO/UNDEV CULTURE WEALTH

B58
PAN AMERICAN UNION,REPERTORIO DE PUBLICACIONES PERIODICAS ACTUALES LATINO-AMERICANAS. CULTURE ECO/UNDEV ADMIN LEAD GOV/REL 20 OAS. PAGE 103 F2023
BIBLIOG L/A+17C NAT/G DIPLOM

B58
SILOW R.A.,THE POTENTIAL CONTRIBUTION OF ATOMIC ENERGY TO DEVELOPMENT IN AGRICULTURE AND RELATED INDUSTRIES (PAMPHLET). WOR+45 R+D TEC/DEV EFFICIENCY 20 UN. PAGE 122 F2403
NUC/PWR ECO/UNDEV AGRI

B58
TILLION G.,ALGERIA: THE REALITIES. ALGERIA FRANCE ISLAM CULTURE STRATA PROB/SOLV DOMIN REV NAT/LISM WEALTH MARXISM...GEOG 20. PAGE 130 F2573
ECO/UNDEV SOC COLONIAL DIPLOM

B58
US OPERATIONS MISSION TO VIET,BUILDING ECONOMIC STRENGTH (PAMPHLET). USA+45 VIETNAM/S INDUS TEC/DEV BUDGET ADMIN EATING HEALTH...STAT 20. PAGE 138 F2725
FOR/AID ECO/UNDEV AGRI EDU/PROP

L58
MASON E.S.,"ECONOMIC PLANNING IN UNDERDEVELOPED AREAS." FUT WOR+45 PLAN TEC/DEV EDU/PROP ATTIT RIGID/FLEX KNOWL...SOC CONCPT GEN/LAWS TOT/POP 20. PAGE 87 F1697
NAT/G ECO/UNDEV

L58
TRAGER F.N.,"A SELECTED AND ANNOTATED BIBLIOGRAPHY ON ECONOMIC DEVELOPMENT, 1953-1957." WOR+45 AGRI FINAN INDUS MARKET LABOR WORKER PLAN INT/TRADE PRODUC...CENSUS MUNICH. PAGE 131 F2583
BIBLIOG/A ECO/UNDEV ECO/DEV

S58
LOCKWOOD W.W.,"THE SOCIALISTIC SOCIETY: INDIA AND JAPAN." INDIA ECO/DEV ECO/UNDEV INDUS NAT/G CONTROL LEAD PRODUC WEALTH 20 CHINJAP. PAGE 81 F1593
ECO/TAC NAT/COMP FINAN SOCISM

B59
ALLEN R.L.,SOVIET INFLUENCE IN LATIN AMERICA. ECO/UNDEV FINAN PROC/MFG NAT/G TEC/DEV EDU/PROP EXEC ROUTINE ATTIT DRIVE PERSON ALL/VALS PWR...STAT CHARTS WORK FOR/TRADE 20. PAGE 4 F0071
L/A+17C ECO/TAC INT/TRADE USSR

B59
ARON R.,IMPERIALISM AND COLONIALISM (PAMPHLET). WOR+45 WOR-45 ECO/TAC CONTROL REV ORD/FREE 19/20. PAGE 6 F0119
COLONIAL DOMIN ECO/UNDEV DIPLOM

B59
BARNETT A.D.,COMMUNIST ECONOMIC STRATEGY: THE RISE OF MAINLAND CHINA. CHINA/COM USSR WOR+45 AGRI INDUS FOR/AID INGP/REL ATTIT. PAGE 10 F0188
ECO/UNDEV INT/TRADE TOTALISM BAL/PWR

B59
BAUER P.T.,UNITED STATES AID AND INDIAN ECONOMIC DEVELOPMENT. INDIA STRATA FINAN PLAN BUDGET DIPLOM INGP/REL EFFICIENCY SOCISM 20 AID. PAGE 11 F0215
FOR/AID ECO/UNDEV ECO/TAC POLICY

B59
CHECCHI V.,HONDURAS: A PROBLEM IN ECONOMIC DEVELOPMENT. HONDURAS AGRI FINAN INDUS LABOR WORKER INT/TRADE EDU/PROP PRICE HEALTH...GEOG CHARTS BIBLIOG 20. PAGE 24 F0458
ECO/UNDEV ECO/TAC PROB/SOLV PLAN

B59
GUDIN E.,INFLACAO (2ND ED.). INDUS NAT/G PLAN ECO/TAC CONTROL COST 20. PAGE 52 F1012
ECO/UNDEV INT/TRADE BAL/PAY FINAN

B59
HAZLEWOOD A.,THE ECONOMICS OF "UNDER-DEVELOPED" AREAS. WOR+45 DIST/IND EXTR/IND FINAN INDUS MARKET PLAN FOR/AID...GEOG 20. PAGE 57 F1129
BIBLIOG/A ECO/UNDEV AGRI INT/TRADE

B59
HICKS J.R.,ESSAYS IN WORLD ECONOMICS. AFR CEYLON NIGERIA WOR+45 SOCIETY ECO/DEV ORD/FREE WEALTH ...GEN/LAWS TOT/POP 20. PAGE 59 F1166
ECO/UNDEV ECO/TAC UK

B59
KRIPALANI J.B.,CLASS STRUGGLE. INDIA WOR+45 ECO/UNDEV LABOR CAP/ISM EDU/PROP INGP/REL ...SOCIALIST IDEA/COMP 17/20. PAGE 73 F1440
MARXISM STRATA COERCE ECO/TAC

B59
LI CHOH-MING,ECONOMIC DEVELOPMENT OF COMMUNIST CHINA. ASIA CHINA/COM AGRI FINAN TAX INCOME MARXISM ...MGT 20. PAGE 80 F1557
ECO/UNDEV INDUS ORD/FREE TEC/DEV

B59
MADHOK B.,POLITICAL TRENDS IN INDIA. INDIA PAKISTAN UK STRATA ECO/UNDEV POL/PAR LEGIS CAP/ISM DIPLOM COLONIAL CHOOSE MARXISM...SOC TREND 20 GANDHI/M NEHRU/J. PAGE 84 F1639
GEOG NAT/G

B59
MEYER A.J.,MIDDLE EASTERN CAPITALISM: NINE ESSAYS. ISLAM CULTURE ECO/UNDEV INDUS MARKET NAT/G PLAN ATTIT RIGID/FLEX...STAT OBS TREND GEN/LAWS. PAGE 90 F1767
TEC/DEV ECO/TAC ANTHOL

B59
MEZERK A.G.,FINANCIAL ASSISTANCE FOR ECONOMIC DEVELOPMENT. WOR+45 INDUS DIPLOM INT/TRADE...CHARTS GOV/COMP UN. PAGE 91 F1778
FOR/AID FINAN ECO/TAC ECO/UNDEV

B59
NUNEZ JIMENEZ A.,LA LIBERACION DE LAS ISLAS. CUBA L/A+17C USA+45 LAW CHIEF PLAN DIPLOM FOR/AID OWN WEALTH 20 CASTRO/F. PAGE 99 F1945
AGRI REV ECO/UNDEV NAT/G

B59
PANIKKAR K.M.,THE AFRO-ASIAN STATES AND THEIR PROBLEMS. COM CULTURE KIN POL/PAR SECT DIPLOM EDU/PROP COLONIAL SOVEREIGN...TECHNIC GOV/COMP 20. PAGE 103 F2025
AFR S/ASIA ECO/UNDEV

B59
ROCHE J.,LA COLONISATION ALLEMANDE ET LE RIO GRANDE DO SUL. BRAZIL L/A+17C NAT/G PROVS INGP/REL RACE/REL DISCRIM HABITAT...GEOG SOC/INTEG 19/20 MIGRATION. PAGE 113 F2228
ECO/UNDEV GP/REL ATTIT

B59
ROPKE W.,INTERNATIONAL ORDER AND ECONOMIC INTEGRATION. ECO/DEV ECO/UNDEV AGRI FINAN INDUS INT/ORG WAR PEACE ORD/FREE...SOC METH/COMP 20 EEC. PAGE 114 F2238
INT/TRADE DIPLOM BAL/PAY ALL/IDEOS

B59
US DEPARTMENT OF STATE,THE UNITED STATES ECONOMY AND THE MUTUAL SECURITY PROGRAM. USA+45 ECO/UNDEV FINAN INDUS DIPLOM INT/TRADE DETER 20. PAGE 136 F2674
ECO/DEV FORCES BUDGET FOR/AID

B59
US GENERAL ACCOUNTING OFFICE,EXAM OF ECONOMIC AND TECHNICAL ASSISTANCE PROGRAM FOR INDIA INT'NAT'L COOP ADMIN REPORT TO CONGRESS 1955-1958. INDIA USA+45 ECO/UNDEV FINAN PLAN DIPLOM COST UTIL WEALTH ...CHARTS 20 CONGRESS AID. PAGE 136 F2679
FOR/AID EFFICIENCY ECO/TAC TEC/DEV

B59
US HOUSE COMM GOVT OPERATIONS,UNITED STATES AID OPERATIONS IN LAOS. LAOS USA+45 PLAN INSPECT HOUSE/REP. PAGE 137 F2697
FOR/AID ADMIN FORCES ECO/UNDEV

B59
WARD B.,5 IDEAS THAT CHANGE THE WORLD. WOR+45 WOR-45 SOCIETY STRUCT AGRI INDUS INT/ORG NAT/G FORCES ACT/RES ARMS/CONT TOTALISM ATTIT DRIVE GEN/LAWS. PAGE 143 F2815
ECO/UNDEV ALL/VALS NAT/LISM COLONIAL

B59
YRARRAZAVAL E.,AMERICA LATINE EN LA GUERRA FRIA. AFR EUR+WWI L/A+17C USA+45 USSR WOR+45 INDUS INT/ORG NAT/LISM POLICY. PAGE 150 F2953
REGION DIPLOM ECO/UNDEV INT/TRADE

L59
BEGUIN B.,"ILO AND THE TRIPARTITE SYSTEM." EUR+WWI WOR+45 WOR-45 CONSTN ECO/DEV ECO/UNDEV INDUS INT/ORG NAT/G VOL/ASSN DELIB/GP PLAN TEC/DEV LEGIT ORD/FREE WEALTH...CONCPT TIME/SEQ WORK ILO 20. PAGE 12 F0228
LABOR

L59
GARDNER R.N.,"NEW DIRECTIONS IN UNITED STATES FOREIGN ECONOMIC POLICY." AFR USA+45 CONSULT ...GEN/LAWS GEN/METH FOR/TRADE 20. PAGE 46 F0903
ECO/UNDEV ECO/TAC FOR/AID DIPLOM

L59
WURFEL D.,"FOREIGN AID AND SOCIAL REFORM IN POLITICAL DEVELOPMENT" (BMR)" PHILIPPINE USA+45 WOR+45 SOCIETY POL/PAR ACT/RES TEC/DEV DIPLOM 20. PAGE 149 F2943 — FOR/AID PROB/SOLV ECO/TAC ECO/UNDEV

S59
HOFFMAN P.,"OPERATION BREAKTHROUGH." AFR S/ASIA STRUCT INDUS CONSULT TEC/DEV ATTIT RIGID/FLEX SKILL WEALTH...TECHNIC CONCPT STYLE RECORD CHARTS ORG/CHARTS GEN/METH VAL/FREE 20. PAGE 61 F1190 — ECO/UNDEV EDU/PROP FOR/AID

S59
REUBENS E.D.,"THE BASIS FOR REORIENATION OF AMERICAN FOREIGN AID POLICY." USA+45 USSR STRUCT INT/ORG CONSULT ECO/TAC ADMIN DRIVE MORAL ORD/FREE PWR WEALTH...RELATIV MATH STAT TREND GEN/LAWS VAL/FREE 20. PAGE 111 F2180 — ECO/UNDEV PLAN FOR/AID DIPLOM

S59
THOMPSON W.S.,"POPULATION AND PROGRESS IN THE FAR EAST." ASIA S/ASIA DIST/IND CREATE ECO/TAC WAR LOVE SKILL WEALTH...CONT/OBS TOT/POP 20. PAGE 130 F2568 — ECO/UNDEV BIO/SOC GEOG

S59
TIPTON J.B.,"PARTICIPATION OF THE UNITED STATES IN THE INTERNATIONAL LABOR ORGANIZATION." USA+45 LAW STRUCT ECO/DEV ECO/UNDEV INDUS TEC/DEV ECO/TAC ADMIN PERCEPT ORD/FREE SKILL...STAT HIST/WRIT GEN/METH ILO WORK 20. PAGE 131 F2577 — LABOR INT/ORG

C59
KURIHARA K.L.,"THE KEYNESIAN THEORY OF ECONOMIC DEVELOPMENT." WOR+45 WOR-45 PLAN OPTIMAL PRODUC ...CONCPT BIBLIOG 20. PAGE 74 F1451 — ECO/DEV ECO/UNDEV OP/RES TEC/DEV

C59
MINTZ S.W.,"INTERNAL MARKET SYS AS MECHANISMS OF SOCIAL ARTIC," IN V.F. RAY, INTERMED SOCIETIES, SOCIAL MOBILITY, AND COMMUNIC (BMR). UNIV STRATA GP/REL INGP/REL...GEOG SOC BIBLIOG. PAGE 92 F1804 — MARKET SOCIETY ECO/UNDEV STRUCT

B60
AHMED J.,NATURAL RESOURCES IN LOW INCOME COUNTRIES: AN ANALYTICAL SURVEY OF SOCIO-ECONOMIC RESEARCH (PAMPHLET). WOR+45 20. PAGE 3 F0052 — BIBLIOG/A ECO/UNDEV INDUS AGRI

B60
AMERICAN U BEIRUT ECO RES INST,A SELECTED AND ANNOTATED BIBLIOGRAPHY OF ECONOMIC LITERATURE ON THE ARABIC SPEAKING COUNTRIES OF THE MIDDLE EAST. ISLAM AGRI COM/IND DIST/IND FINAN INDUS LABOR ...GEOG 20. PAGE 5 F0091 — BIBLIOG/A ECO/UNDEV STAT

B60
ARON R.,COLLOQUES DE RHEINFELDEN. AFR USA+45 USSR WOR+45 WOR-45 CULTURE ECO/UNDEV NAT/G POL/PAR DIPLOM NAT/LISM TOTALISM ATTIT DRIVE ALL/VALS ...PLURIST CONCPT STERTYP GEN/LAWS TOT/POP 20. PAGE 6 F0120 — ECO/DEV SOCIETY CAP/ISM SOCISM

B60
ASPREMONT-LYNDEN H.,RAPPORT SUR L'ADMINISTRATION BELGE DU RUANDA-URUNDI PENDANT L'ANNEE 1959. BELGIUM RWANDA AGRI INDUS DIPLOM ECO/TAC INT/TRADE DOMIN ADMIN RACE/REL...GEOG CENSUS 20 UN. PAGE 7 F0132 — AFR COLONIAL ECO/UNDEV INT/ORG

B60
AUSTRUY J.,STRUCTURE ECONOMIQUE ET CIVILISATION: L'EGYPTE ET LE DESTIN ECONOMIQUE DE L'ISLAM. ISLAM UAR CREATE OP/RES ECO/TAC...SOC BIBLIOG 20 MUSLIM. PAGE 8 F0142 — ECO/UNDEV CULTURE STRUCT

B60
BAYER H.,WIRTSCHAFTSPROGNOSE UND WIRTSCHAFTSGESTALTUNG. GERMANY NETHERLAND MARKET PLAN CAP/ISM DEBATE...NAT/COMP 20. PAGE 12 F0220 — ECO/DEV ECO/UNDEV FINAN POLICY

B60
BILLERBECK K.,SOVIET BLOC FOREIGN AID TO UNDERDEVELOPED COUNTRIES. COM FUT USSR FINAN FORCES TEC/DEV DIPLOM INT/TRADE EDU/PROP NUC/PWR...TREND 20. PAGE 15 F0285 — FOR/AID ECO/UNDEV ECO/TAC MARXISM

B60
BLACK E.R.,THE DIPLOMACY OF ECONOMIC DEVELOPMENT. WOR+45 CONSULT PLAN TEC/DEV DIPLOM ECO/TAC FOR/AID ...CONCPT TREND 20. PAGE 15 F0290 — ECO/UNDEV ACT/RES

B60
BRYCE M.D.,INDUSTRIAL DEVELOPMENT: A GUIDE FOR ACCELERATING ECONOMIC GROWTH. WOR+45 FINAN MARKET COST EFFICIENCY PRODUC. PAGE 20 F0378 — INDUS PLAN ECO/UNDEV TEC/DEV

B60
COPLAND D.,THE ADVENTURE OF GROWTH: ESSAYS ON THE AUSTRALIAN ECONOMY AND ITS INTERNATIONAL SETTING. WOR+45 DIST/IND ACADEM EDU/PROP ADMIN INCOME 20 AUSTRAL. PAGE 27 F0534 — ECO/DEV ECO/UNDEV ECO/TAC INT/TRADE

B60
DIA M.,REFLEXIONS SUR L'ECONOMIE DE L'AFRIQUE NOIRE (REV. ED.). CULTURE ECO/UNDEV CREATE TEC/DEV DIPLOM INT/TRADE OPTIMAL ATTIT...POLICY 20. PAGE 32 F0631 — AFR ECO/TAC SOCISM PLAN

B60
FERNANDES F.,MUDANCAS SOCIAIS NO BRASIL. BRAZIL L/A+17C SOCIETY AGRI PROVS LEAD GP/REL RACE/REL ORD/FREE...SOC SOC/INTEG 20 SAO/PAULO. PAGE 40 F0786 — ECO/UNDEV STRATA INDUS

B60
FRANCK P.G.,AFGHANISTAN: BETWEEN EAST AND WEST. AFGHANISTN AFR USA+45 USSR ECO/UNDEV PLAN ADMIN ROUTINE ATTIT PWR...STAT OBS CHARTS TOT/POP FOR/TRADE 20. PAGE 43 F0843 — ECO/TAC TREND FOR/AID

B60
GONZALEZ NAVARRO M.,LA COLONIZACION EN MEXICO, 1877-1910. AGRI NAT/G PLAN PROB/SOLV INCOME ...POLICY JURID CENSUS 19/20 MEXIC/AMER MIGRATION. PAGE 48 F0947 — ECO/UNDEV GEOG HABITAT COLONIAL

B60
HEYSE T.,PROBLEMS FONCIERS ET REGIME DES TERRES (ASPECTS ECONOMIQUES, JURIDIQUES ET SOCIAUX). AFR CONGO/BRAZ INT/ORG DIPLOM SOVEREIGN...GEOG TREATY 20. PAGE 59 F1161 — BIBLIOG AGRI ECO/UNDEV LEGIS

B60
HOFFMANN P.G.,ONE HUNDRED COUNTRIES, ONE AND ONE QUARTER BILLION PEOPLE. MARKET INT/ORG TEC/DEV CAP/ISM...GEOG CHARTS METH/COMP 20 UN. PAGE 61 F1191 — FOR/AID ECO/TAC ECO/UNDEV INT/TRADE

B60
HOSELITZ B.F.,THEORIES OF ECONOMIC GROWTH. UK WOR+45 WOR-45 ECO/UNDEV PLAN INT/TRADE KNOWL ...CONCPT METH/CNCPT TIME/SEQ GEN/LAWS TOT/POP. PAGE 62 F1220 — ECO/DEV INTELL

B60
HOSELITZ B.F.,SOCIOLOGICAL ASPECTS OF ECONOMIC GROWTH. WOR+45 WOR-45 ECO/UNDEV CAP/ISM RIGID/FLEX WEALTH...MATH CHARTS. PAGE 62 F1221 — ECO/DEV SOC

B60
KENEN P.B.,GIANT AMONG NATIONS: PROBLEMS IN UNITED STATES FOREIGN ECONOMIC POLICY. AFR USA+45 FINAN DIPLOM TARIFFS BAL/PAY WEALTH 20. PAGE 70 F1376 — FOR/AID ECO/UNDEV INT/TRADE PLAN

B60
KERR C.,INDUSTRIALISM AND INDUSTRIAL MAN. CULTURE SOCIETY ECO/UNDEV NAT/G ADMIN PRODUC WEALTH ...PREDICT TREND NAT/COMP 19/20. PAGE 70 F1381 — WORKER MGT ECO/DEV INDUS

B60
KILLOUGH H.B.,INTERNATIONAL ECONOMICS. PLAN PROB/SOLV FOR/AID TARIFFS CONTROL BAL/PAY...POLICY CHARTS T 20. PAGE 71 F1388 — CONCPT ECO/UNDEV INT/ORG INT/TRADE

B60
KRISTENSEN T.,THE ECONOMIC WORLD BALANCE. FUT WOR+45 CULTURE ECO/DEV BAL/PWR INT/TRADE REGION PWR WEALTH...STAT TREND CHARTS 20. PAGE 73 F1442 — ECO/UNDEV ECO/TAC FOR/AID

B60
LATIFI D.,INDIA AND UNITED STATES AID. ASIA INDIA UK USA+45 AGRI FINAN INDUS COLONIAL ORD/FREE SOVEREIGN WEALTH...METH/COMP 20. PAGE 76 F1486 — FOR/AID DIPLOM ECO/UNDEV

B60
LENCZOWSKI G.,OIL AND STATE IN THE MIDDLE EAST. FUT IRAN LAW ECO/UNDEV EXTR/IND NAT/G TOP/EX PLAN TEC/DEV ECO/TAC LEGIT ADMIN COERCE ATTIT ALL/VALS PWR...CHARTS 20. PAGE 78 F1519 — ISLAM INDUS NAT/LISM

B60
LERNER A.P.,THE ECONOMICS OF CONTROL. USA+45 ECO/UNDEV INT/ORG ACT/RES PLAN CAP/ISM INT/TRADE ATTIT WEALTH...SOC MATH STAT GEN/LAWS INDEX 20. PAGE 78 F1530 — ECO/DEV ROUTINE ECO/TAC SOCISM

B60
MC CLELLAN G.S.,INDIA. AFR CHINA/COM INDIA CONSTN ELITES STRATA AGRI POL/PAR FOR/AID ARMS/CONT REV MARXISM...CENSUS BIBLIOG 20 GANDHI/M NEHRU/J. PAGE 87 F1712 — DIPLOM NAT/G SOCIETY ECO/UNDEV

B60
MOORE W.E.,LABOR COMMITMENT AND SOCIAL CHANGE IN DEVELOPING AREAS. SOCIETY STRATA ECO/UNDEV MARKET VOL/ASSN WORKER AUTHORIT SKILL...MGT NAT/COMP SOC/INTEG 20. PAGE 93 F1823 — LABOR ORD/FREE ATTIT INDUS

B60
MYRDAL G.,BEYOND THE WELFARE STATE: ECONOMIC PLANNING AND ITS IMPLICATIONS. EUR+WWI FUT USA+45 USSR ECO/DEV ECO/UNDEV TEC/DEV SKILL WEALTH...PSY TREND FOR/TRADE 20. PAGE 96 F1881 — PLAN ECO/TAC CAP/ISM

B60
NEALE A.D.,THE FLOW OF RESOURCES FROM RICH TO POOR. WOR+45 ECO/DEV ECO/UNDEV FINAN INDUS NAT/G PLAN EFFICIENCY WEALTH...POLICY NAT/COMP 20 RESOURCE/N. PAGE 97 F1905 — FOR/AID DIPLOM METH/CNCPT

B60
PENTONY D.E.,UNITED STATES FOREIGN AID. INDIA LAOS USA+45 ECO/UNDEV INT/TRADE ADMIN PEACE ATTIT ...POLICY METH/COMP ANTHOL 20. PAGE 105 F2060 — FOR/AID DIPLOM ECO/TAC

B60
RAMA C.M.,LAS CLASES SOCIALES EN EL URUGUAY. L/A+17C URUGUAY ELITES SOCIETY STRATA INDUS ATTIT HABITAT PWR...GEOG SOC/INTEG MUNICH 20. PAGE 109 F2138 — ECO/UNDEV STRUCT PARTIC

B60
RAO V.K.R.,INTERNATIONAL AID FOR ECONOMIC DEVELOPMENT - POSSIBILITIES AND LIMITATIONS. FINAN — FOR/AID DIPLOM

PLAN TEC/DEV ADMIN TASK EFFICIENCY...POLICY SOC METH/CNCPT CHARTS 20 UN. PAGE 109 F2147 — INT/ORG ECO/UNDEV

B60
ROSTOW W.W.,THE STAGES OF ECONOMIC GROWTH. UK USA+45 USSR WOR+45 WOR-45 ECO/DEV PERSON MARXISM ...METH/CNCPT TIME/SEQ GEN/LAWS GEN/METH 20. PAGE 114 F2246 — ECO/UNDEV NEW/IDEA CAP/ISM

B60
SAKAI R.K.,STUDIES ON ASIA, 1960. ASIA CHINA/COM S/ASIA COM/IND ECO/TAC...ANTHOL 17/20 MALAYA. PAGE 115 F2270 — ECO/UNDEV SOC

B60
SHONFIELD A.,THE ATTACK ON WORLD POVERTY. WOR+45 ECO/DEV ECO/UNDEV FINAN VOL/ASSN PLAN EDU/PROP DRIVE KNOWL WEALTH...CONT/OBS STAND/INT ORG/CHARTS TOT/POP UNESCO 20. PAGE 121 F2383 — INT/ORG ECO/TAC FOR/AID INT/TRADE

B60
SMET G.,BIBLIOGRAPHIE DE LA CONTRIBUTION A L'ETUDE DE LA PROGRESSION ECONOMIQUE DE L'AFRIQUE. AFR DIST/IND EXTR/IND TEC/DEV 20. PAGE 123 F2427 — BIBLIOG ECO/UNDEV INDUS AGRI

B60
STANFORD RESEARCH INSTITUTE,AFRICAN DEVELOPMENT: A TEST FOR INTERNATIONAL COOPERATION. AFR USA+45 WOR+45 FINAN INT/ORG PLAN PROB/SOLV ECO/TAC INT/TRADE ADMIN...CHARTS 20. PAGE 125 F2467 — FOR/AID ECO/UNDEV ATTIT DIPLOM

B60
STEVENSON A.E.,PUTTING FIRST THINGS FIRST. USA+45 INT/ORG NEIGH FOR/AID DISCRIM...ANTHOL 20. PAGE 126 F2483 — DIPLOM ECO/UNDEV ORD/FREE EDU/PROP

B60
THEOBALD R.,THE RICH AND THE POOR: A STUDY OF THE ECONOMICS OF RISING EXPECTATIONS. WOR+45 CONSTN ECO/DEV ECO/UNDEV INT/ORG NAT/G PLAN FOR/AID ROUTINE BAL/PAY ORD/FREE PWR WEALTH...GEOG TREND WORK FOR/TRADE 20. PAGE 129 F2553 — ECO/TAC INT/TRADE

B60
UNESCO,SOUTHERN ASIA SOCIAL SCIENCE BIBLIOGRAPHY (WITH ANNOTATIONS AND ABSTRACTS), 1959 (PAMPHLET). S/ASIA...SOC 20. PAGE 132 F2609 — BIBLIOG/A ECO/UNDEV TEC/DEV INDUS

B60
US GENERAL ACCOUNTING OFFICE,EXAMINATION OF ECONOMIC AND TECHNICAL ASSISTANCE PROGRAM FOR GUATEMALA. GUATEMALA L/A+17C USA+45 FINAN INDUS PLAN...POLICY STAT CHARTS 20 DEPT/STATE. PAGE 136 F2680 — FOR/AID ECO/UNDEV TEC/DEV NAT/G

B60
US OPERATIONS MISSION - TURKEY,SOME POSSIBILITIES FOR ACCELERATING TURKEY'S ECONOMIC GROWTH. TURKEY USA+45 AGRI FINAN INDUS NAT/G ACT/RES BUDGET COST ...CHARTS 20. PAGE 138 F2724 — ECO/UNDEV ECO/TAC FOR/AID PRODUC

B60
WODDIS J.,AFRICA: THE ROOTS OF REVOLT. SOUTH/AFR WORKER INT/TRADE RACE/REL DISCRIM ORD/FREE 20. PAGE 148 F2915 — COLONIAL SOVEREIGN WAR ECO/UNDEV

L60
SPENGLER J.J.,"ECONOMIC DEVELOPMENT: POLITICAL PRECONDITIONS AND POLITICAL CONSEQUENCE." WOR+45 STRUCT ECO/UNDEV NAT/G PLAN ECO/TAC EDU/PROP ATTIT ORD/FREE WEALTH SOCISM...SOC CONCPT TREND SIMUL GEN/METH WORK 20. PAGE 124 F2452 — TEC/DEV METH/CNCPT CAP/ISM

S60
"THE EMERGING COMMON MARKETS IN LATIN AMERICA." FUT L/A+17C STRATA DIST/IND INDUS LABOR NAT/G LEGIS ECO/TAC ADMIN RIGID/FLEX HEALTH...NEW/IDEA TIME/SEQ OAS 20. PAGE 1 F0013 — FINAN ECO/UNDEV INT/TRADE

S60
BERG E.J.,"ECONOMIC BASIS OF POLITICAL CHOICE IN FRENCH WEST AFRICA." FRANCE ECO/UNDEV AGRI INDUS NAT/G PLAN LEGIT COLONIAL REGION ATTIT PWR WEALTH ...CONCPT FOR/TRADE 20. PAGE 13 F0257 — AFR ECO/TAC

S60
BUTLER W.F.,"ECONOMIC PROGRESS IN LATIN AMERICA." L/A+17C USA+45 ECO/UNDEV AGRI FINAN NAT/G PLAN ECO/TAC FOR/AID ADMIN WEALTH...OLD/LIB TOT/POP 20. PAGE 21 F0397 — INDUS ACT/RES

S60
FRANKEL S.H.,"ECONOMIC ASPECTS OF POLITICAL INDEPENDENCE IN AFRICA." AFR FUT SOCIETY ECO/UNDEV COM/IND FINAN LEGIS PLAN TEC/DEV CAP/ISM ECO/TAC INT/TRADE ADMIN ATTIT DRIVE RIGID/FLEX PWR WEALTH ...MGT NEW/IDEA MATH TIME/SEQ VAL/FREE 20. PAGE 43 F0846 — NAT/G FOR/AID

S60
HERRERA F.,"THE INTER-AMERICAN DEVELOPMENT BANK." USA+45 ECO/UNDEV INT/ORG CONSULT DELIB/GP PLAN ECO/TAC INT/TRADE ROUTINE WEALTH...STAT TERR/GP 20. PAGE 59 F1153 — L/A+17C FINAN FOR/AID REGION

S60
JACOBSON H.K.,"THE USSR AND ILO." AFR COM STRUCT ECO/DEV ECO/UNDEV CONSULT DELIB/GP ECO/TAC ILO WORK 20. PAGE 66 F1298 — INT/ORG LABOR USSR

S60
JAFFEE A.J.,"POPULATION TRENDS AND CONTROLS IN UNDERDEVELOPED COUNTRIES." AFR FUT ISLAM L/A+17C S/ASIA CULTURE R+D FAM ACT/RES PLAN EDU/PROP BIO/SOC RIGID/FLEX HEALTH...SOC STAT OBS CHARTS 20. PAGE 66 F1303 — ECO/UNDEV GEOG

S60
KELLOGG C.E.,"TRANSFER OF BASIC SKILLS OF FOOD PRODUCTION." AFR FUT S/ASIA STRATA ECO/UNDEV LABOR VOL/ASSN RIGID/FLEX...OLD/LIB SOCIALIST NEW/IDEA STAT PROJ/TEST GEN/LAWS 20. PAGE 70 F1370 — AGRI PLAN

S60
MAIR L.P.,"SOCIAL CHANGE IN SOUTH AFRICA." MOD/EUR SOUTH/AFR WOR+45 ECO/UNDEV EX/STRUC TEC/DEV ATTIT DRIVE PERCEPT ORD/FREE...MGT CONCPT TIME/SEQ IND 20. PAGE 84 F1641 — AFR NAT/G REV SOVEREIGN

S60
MIKESELL R.F.,"AMERICA'S ECONOMIC RESPONSIBILITY AS A GREAT POWER." COM FUT USA+45 USSR WOR+45 INT/ORG PLAN ECO/TAC FOR/AID EDU/PROP CHOOSE WEALTH ...POLICY 20. PAGE 91 F1781 — ECO/UNDEV BAL/PWR CAP/ISM

S60
MORALES C.J.,"TRADE AND ECONOMIC INTEGRATION IN LATIN AMERICA." FUT L/A+17C LAW STRATA ECO/UNDEV DIST/IND INDUS LABOR NAT/G LEGIS ECO/TAC ADMIN RIGID/FLEX WEALTH...CONCPT NEW/IDEA CONT/OBS TIME/SEQ WORK 20. PAGE 93 F1825 — FINAN INT/TRADE REGION

S60
MURPHEY R.,"ECONOMIC CONFLICTS IN SOUTH ASIA." ASIA CULTURE INTELL ECO/TAC REGION ATTIT DRIVE KNOWL ...METH/CNCPT TIME/SEQ STERTYP TOT/POP METH/GP VAL/FREE 20. PAGE 95 F1864 — S/ASIA ECO/UNDEV

S60
MURPHY J.C.,"INTERNATIONAL INVESTMENT AND THE NATIONAL INTEREST." AFR WOR+45 WOR-45 ECO/DEV ECO/UNDEV NAT/G ACT/RES...CHARTS TOT/POP FOR/TRADE 20. PAGE 95 F1867 — FINAN WEALTH FOR/AID

S60
NANES A.,"THE EUROPEAN COMMUNITY AND THE UNITED STATES: EVOLVING RELATIONS." EUR+WWI USA+45 WOR+45 ECO/UNDEV MARKET NAT/G DELIB/GP PLAN LEGIT ATTIT PWR WEALTH...CONCPT STAT TIME/SEQ CON/ANAL EEC METH/GP OEEC 20 EURATOM. PAGE 96 F1889 — INT/ORG REGION

S60
NEISSER H.,"ECONOMIC IMPERIALISM RECONSIDERED." WOR+45 WOR-45 ECO/DEV ECO/UNDEV DIST/IND LEGIT COLONIAL PWR WEALTH SOCISM...MYTH MATH TIME/SEQ 20. PAGE 97 F1909 — ACT/RES ECO/TAC CAP/ISM INT/TRADE

S60
NICHOLS J.P.,"HAZARDS OF AMERICAN PRIVATE INVESTMENT IN UNDERDEVELOPED COUNTRIES." FUT L/A+17C USA+45 USA-45 EXTR/IND CONSULT BAL/PWR ECO/TAC DOMIN ADJUD ATTIT SOVEREIGN WEALTH ...HIST/WRIT TIME/SEQ TREND TERR/GP VAL/FREE 20. PAGE 98 F1924 — FINAN ECO/UNDEV CAP/ISM NAT/LISM

S60
OWEN C.F.,"US AND SOVIET RELATIONS WITH UNDERDEVELOPED COUNTRIES: LATIN AMERICA-A CASE STUDY." AFR COM L/A+17C USA+45 USSR EXTR/IND MARKET TEC/DEV DIPLOM ECO/TAC NAT/LISM ORD/FREE PWR ...TREND WORK 20. PAGE 102 F2005 — ECO/UNDEV DRIVE INT/TRADE

S60
PYE L.W.,"SOVIET AND AMERICAN STYLES IN FOREIGN AID." COM USA+45 USSR WOR+45 NAT/G PLAN ECO/TAC ROUTINE RIGID/FLEX...POLICY CONCPT TREND GEN/LAWS TOT/POP 20. PAGE 108 F2132 — ECO/UNDEV ATTIT FOR/AID

S60
RIVKIN A.,"AFRICAN ECONOMIC DEVELOPMENT: ADVANCED TECHNOLOGY AND THE STAGES OF GROWTH." CULTURE ECO/UNDEV AGRI COM/IND EXTR/IND PLAN ECO/TAC ATTIT DRIVE RIGID/FLEX SKILL WEALTH...MGT SOC GEN/LAWS FOR/TRADE WORK TOT/POP 20. PAGE 111 F2195 — AFR TEC/DEV FOR/AID

S60
STOCKWELL E.G.,"THE MEASUREMENT OF ECONOMIC DEVELOPMENT." WOR+45 SOCIETY ECO/DEV ECO/UNDEV INDUS ECO/TAC HEALTH WEALTH...WELF/ST GEOG METH/CNCPT CHARTS METH METH/GP 20. PAGE 126 F2492 — FAM STAT

C60
HOSELITZ B.,"THE ROLE OF CITIES IN THE ECONOMIC GROWTH OF UNDERDEVELOPED COUNTRIES" IN "SOCIOLOGICAL ASPECTS OF ECONOMIC GROWTH"(BMR). CULTURE LOC/G ACT/RES...SOC IDEA/COMP METH/COMP METH MUNICH IND 14/20 REDFIELD/R. PAGE 62 F1218 — METH/CNCPT TEC/DEV ECO/UNDEV

B61
MEXICO; CINCUENTA ANOS DE REVOLUCION VOL. II. L/A+17C SOCIETY LABOR RECEIVE GP/REL AGE/Y HEALTH ...SOC/WK ANTHOL MUNICH 20 MEXIC/AMER. PAGE 1 F0014 — ECO/UNDEV STRUCT INDUS POL/PAR

B61
AGARWAL R.C.,STATE ENTERPRISE IN INDIA. FUT INDIA UK FINAN INDUS ADMIN CONTROL OWN...POLICY CHARTS BIBLIOG 20 RAILROAD. PAGE 3 F0048 — ECO/UNDEV SOCISM GOV/REL LG/CO

B61
ASHER R.E.,GRANTS, LOANS, AND LOCAL CURRENCIES; THEIR ROLE IN FOREIGN AID. AFR USA+45 ECO/UNDEV — FOR/AID FINAN

INT/ORG ACT/RES PLAN ECO/TAC GIVE CONTROL WEALTH 20. PAGE 7 F0130 — NAT/G BUDGET

B61

AUBREY H.G.,COEXISTENCE: ECONOMIC CHALLENGE AND RESPONSE. AFR USSR WOR+45 ACT/RES BAL/PWR CAP/ISM DIPLOM ECO/TAC FOR/AID INT/TRADE PEACE SOCISM ...METH/COMP NAT/COMP. PAGE 7 F0139 — POLICY ECO/UNDEV PLAN COM

B61

BALASSA B.,THE THEORY OF ECONOMIC INTEGRATION. EUR+WWI L/A+17C MOD/EUR WOR+45 ECO/UNDEV MARKET INT/ORG NAT/G VOL/ASSN DELIB/GP PLAN CAP/ISM ECO/TAC...MAJORIT FOR/TRADE OEEC 20. PAGE 8 F0157 — ECO/DEV ACT/RES INT/TRADE

B61

BAUER P.T.,INDIAN ECONOMIC POLICY AND DEVELOPMENT. INDIA STRATA AGRI FINAN POL/PAR BUDGET FOR/AID GOV/REL EFFICIENCY...CENSUS 20. PAGE 11 F0216 — ECO/UNDEV ECO/TAC POLICY PLAN

B61

BENHAM F.,ECONOMIC AID TO UNDERDEVELOPED COUNTRIES. WOR+45 INDUS BAL/PAY ALL/VALS 20. PAGE 13 F0244 — ECO/UNDEV FOR/AID INT/TRADE FINAN

B61

BONNEFOUS M.,EUROPE ET TIERS MONDE. EUR+WWI SOCIETY INT/ORG NAT/G VOL/ASSN ACT/RES TEC/DEV CAP/ISM ECO/TAC ATTIT ORD/FREE SOVEREIGN...POLICY CONCPT TREND TERR/GP COMMUN 20. PAGE 16 F0314 — AFR ECO/UNDEV FOR/AID INT/TRADE

B61

BRAIBANTI R.,TRADITION, VALUES AND SOCIO-ECONOMIC DEVELOPMENT. WOR+45 ACT/RES TEC/DEV ATTIT ORD/FREE CONSERVE...POLICY SOC ANTHOL. PAGE 17 F0336 — ALL/VALS ECO/UNDEV CONCPT METH/CNCPT

B61

CARNEY D.E.,GOVERNMENT AND ECONOMY IN BRITISH WEST AFRICA. GAMBIA GHANA NIGERIA SIER/LEONE DOMIN ADMIN GOV/REL SOVEREIGN WEALTH LAISSEZ...BIBLIOG 20 CMN/WLTH. PAGE 21 F0417 — METH/COMP COLONIAL ECO/TAC ECO/UNDEV

B61

DE VRIES E.,MAN IN RAPID SOCIAL CHANGE. WOR+45 SOCIETY ECO/DEV ECO/UNDEV AGRI INDUS FAM SECT TEC/DEV ATTIT...RECORD 20 CHRISTIAN. PAGE 31 F0607 — CULTURE ALL/VALS SOC TASK

B61

DETHINE P.,BIBLIOGRAPHIE DES ASPECTS ECONOMIQUES ET SOCIAUX DE L'INDUSTRIALISATION EN AFRIQUE. AFR FINAN LABOR FOR/AID...SOC 20. PAGE 32 F0623 — BIBLIOG/A ECO/UNDEV INDUS TEC/DEV

B61

ELLIS H.S.,ECONOMIC DEVELOPMENT FOR LATIN AMERICA. L/A+17C AGRI FINAN INDUS FOR/AID GP/REL BAL/PAY DEMAND...ANTHOL 20 INTL/ECON. PAGE 37 F0723 — ECO/UNDEV ECO/TAC PLAN INT/TRADE

B61

ERASMUS C.J.,MAN TAKES CONTROL: CULTURAL DEVELOPMENT AND AMERICAN AID. STRUCT OWN DRIVE PERCEPT...SOC 20 MEXIC/AMER. PAGE 38 F0741 — ORD/FREE CULTURE ECO/UNDEV TEC/DEV

B61

ESTEBAN J.C.,IMPERIALISMO Y DESARROLLO ECONOMICO. L/A+17C FINAN INDUS NAT/G ECO/TAC CONTROL ROLE. PAGE 38 F0747 — ECO/UNDEV NAT/LISM DIPLOM BAL/PAY

B61

ESTEVEZ A.,ASPECTOS ECONOMICO-FINANCIEROS DE LA CAMPANA SANMARITANA. L/A+17C SPAIN FINAN COLONIAL LEAD ROLE ORD/FREE WEALTH 19 SOUTH/AMER SAN/MARTIN. PAGE 38 F0748 — ECO/UNDEV REV BUDGET NAT/G

B61

FEARN H.,AN AFRICAN ECONOMY. AFR EUR+WWI PLAN COLONIAL WEALTH...CONT/OBS TREND EEC VAL/FREE 20. PAGE 39 F0770 — ECO/UNDEV

B61

FILLOL T.R.,SOCIAL FACTORS IN ECONOMIC DEVELOPMENT: THE ARGENTINE CASE. STRUCT INDUS LABOR CREATE TEC/DEV EFFICIENCY PRODUC DRIVE...METH/CNCPT METH/COMP BIBLIOG/A 20 ARGEN. PAGE 41 F0795 — ECO/UNDEV MGT PERS/REL TREND

B61

FRIEDMANN W.G.,JOINT INTERNATIONAL BUSINESS VENTURES. ASIA ISLAM L/A+17C ECO/DEV DIST/IND FINAN PROC/MFG FACE/GP LG/CO NAT/G VOL/ASSN CONSULT EX/STRUC PLAN ADMIN ROUTINE WEALTH...OLD/LIB FOR/TRADE WORK 20. PAGE 44 F0865 — ECO/UNDEV INT/TRADE

B61

GANGULI B.N.,ECONOMIC INTEGRATION. FINAN LABOR CAP/ISM DIPLOM WEALTH...NAT/COMP 20. PAGE 46 F0895 — ECO/TAC METH/CNCPT EQUILIB ECO/UNDEV

B61

GREY A.L.,ECONOMIC ISSUES AND POLICIES; READINGS IN INTRODUCTORY ECONOMICS (2ND ED.). WOR+45 ECO/UNDEV FINAN MARKET LABOR LG/CO INT/TRADE BAL/PAY WEALTH ...ANTHOL T. PAGE 51 F0996 — ECO/TAC PROB/SOLV METH/COMP

B61

GURTOO D.H.N.,INDIA'S BALANCE OF PAYMENTS (1920-1960). INDIA FINAN DIPLOM FOR/AID INT/TRADE PRICE COLONIAL...CHARTS BIBLIOG 20. PAGE 52 F1014 — BAL/PAY STAT ECO/TAC ECO/UNDEV

B61

HICKS U.K.,FEDERALISM AND ECONOMIC GROWTH IN UNDERDEVELOPED COUNTRIES. WOR+45 WOR-45 FINAN NAT/G PLAN BUDGET DIPLOM INT/TRADE DEMAND WEALTH...ANTHOL 20. PAGE 59 F1167 — ECO/UNDEV ECO/TAC FEDERAL CONSTN

B61

HORVATH B.,THE CHARACTERISTICS OF YUGOSLAV ECONOMIC DEVELOPMENT. COM ECO/UNDEV AGRI INDUS PLAN CAP/ISM ECO/TAC ROUTINE WEALTH...SOCIALIST STAT CHARTS STERTYP WORK 20. PAGE 62 F1217 — ACT/RES YUGOSLAVIA

B61

INDUSTRIAL COUN SOC-ECO STU,THE SWEDISH ECONOMY AND THE UNDERDEVELOPED COUNTRIES. SWEDEN INDUS DELIB/GP TEC/DEV INT/TRADE EDU/PROP COLONIAL DRIVE...CHARTS 20. PAGE 64 F1264 — FOR/AID ECO/UNDEV PLAN FINAN

B61

INTERNATIONAL BANK RECONST DEV,THE WORLD BANK IN AFRICA: SUMMARY OF ACTIVITIES. AGRI COM/IND DIST/IND EXTR/IND INDUS TAX COST...CHARTS 20. PAGE 65 F1271 — FINAN ECO/UNDEV INT/ORG AFR

B61

JAVITS B.A.,THE PEACE BY INVESTMENT CORPORATION. WOR+45 NAT/G LEGIS PROB/SOLV PERS/REL WEALTH ...POLICY 20. PAGE 66 F1307 — ECO/UNDEV DIPLOM FOR/AID PEACE

B61

KOVNER M.,THE CHALLENGE OF COEXISTENCE: A STUDY OF SOVIET ECONOMIC DIPLOMACY. COM FUT ECO/DEV ECO/UNDEV PLAN EDU/PROP DETER SKILL...OBS VAL/FREE 20. PAGE 73 F1430 — PWR DIPLOM USSR AFR

B61

LAHAYE R.,LES ENTREPRISES PUBLIQUES AU MAROC. FRANCE MOROCCO LAW DIST/IND EXTR/IND FINAN CONSULT PLAN TEC/DEV ADMIN AGREE CONTROL OWN...POLICY 20. PAGE 74 F1460 — NAT/G INDUS ECO/UNDEV ECO/TAC

B61

LANDSKROY W.A.,OFFICIAL SERIAL PUBLICATIONS RELATING TO ECONOMIC DEVELOPMENT IN AFRICA SOUTH OF THE SAHARA (PAMPHLET). AFR UK R+D ACT/RES 20 UN. PAGE 75 F1471 — BIBLIOG ECO/UNDEV COLONIAL INT/ORG

B61

LETHBRIDGE H.J.,CHINA'S URBAN COMMUNES. CHINA/COM FUT ECO/UNDEV DIPLOM EDU/PROP DEMAND INCOME MARXISM ...POLICY MUNICH 20. PAGE 78 F1534 — CONTROL ECO/TAC NAT/G

B61

LONGRIGG S.H.,OIL IN THE MIDDLE EAST: ITS DISCOVERY AND DEVELOPMENT. ECO/UNDEV LG/CO LOC/G TEC/DEV WEALTH...STAT TIME/SEQ 20 OIL. PAGE 82 F1599 — ISLAM EXTR/IND

B61

LUZ N.V.,A LUTA PELA INDUSTRIALIZACAO DO BRAZIL. BRAZIL L/A+17C AGRI NAT/G TEC/DEV COLONIAL 19/20. PAGE 82 F1615 — ECO/UNDEV INDUS NAT/LISM POLICY

B61

MARX K.,THE COMMUNIST MANIFESTO. IN (MENDEL A. ESSENTIAL WORKS OF MARXISM, NEW YORK: BANTAM. FUT MOD/EUR CULTURE ECO/DEV ECO/UNDEV AGRI FINAN INDUS MARKET PROC/MFG LABOR POL/PAR CONSULT FORCES CREATE PLAN ADMIN ATTIT DRIVE RIGID/FLEX ORD/FREE PWR RESPECT MARX/KARL MUNICH WORK. PAGE 86 F1691 — COM NEW/IDEA CAP/ISM REV

B61

MAYNE A.,DESIGNING AND ADMINISTERING A REGIONAL ECONOMIC DEVELOPMENT PLAN WITH SPECIFIC REFERENCE TO PUERTO RICO (PAMPHLET). PUERT/RICO SOCIETY NAT/G DELIB/GP REGION...DECISION 20. PAGE 87 F1707 — ECO/UNDEV PLAN CREATE ADMIN

B61

MEZERIK A.G.,ECONOMIC DEVELOPMENT AIDS FOR UNDERDEVELOPED COUNTRIES. WOR+45 FINAN LEGIS PROB/SOLV TEC/DEV DIPLOM FOR/AID GIVE TASK WAR 20 UN. PAGE 91 F1776 — ECO/UNDEV INT/ORG WEALTH PLAN

B61

MIT CENTER INTERNATIONAL STU,OFFICIAL SERIAL PUBLICATIONS RELATING TO ECONOMIC DEVELOPMENT IN AFRICA SOUTH OF THE SAHARA. AFR SOCIETY AGRI FINAN INDUS LG/CO ADMIN 20. PAGE 92 F1806 — BIBLIOG ECO/UNDEV ECO/TAC NAT/G

B61

MORLEY L.,THE PATCHWORK HISTORY OF FOREIGN AID. AFR KOREA/S USA+45 USSR LAW FINAN INT/ORG TEC/DEV BAL/PWR GIVE 20 NATO. PAGE 93 F1834 — FOR/AID ECO/UNDEV FORCES DIPLOM

B61

NORTH D.C.,THE ECONOMIC GROWTH OF THE UNITED STATES 1790-1860. USA-45 INDUS TEC/DEV CAP/ISM ECO/TAC PRICE COST DEMAND LAISSEZ...ECOMETRIC STAT TREND 19. PAGE 98 F1933 — AGRI ECO/UNDEV

B61

PETCH G.A.,ECONOMIC DEVELOPMENT AND MODERN WEST AFRICA. AFR CONGO/BRAZ GHANA NIGER SIER/LEONE AGRI MARKET LABOR FOR/AID TAX COST EFFICIENCY EQUILIB PRODUC...GEOG TREND 20. PAGE 105 F2068 — ECO/UNDEV TEC/DEV EXTR/IND ECO/TAC

B61

RUEDA B.,A STATEMENT OF THE LAWS OF COLOMBIA IN MATTERS AFFECTING BUSINESS (3RD ED.). INDUS FAM LABOR LG/CO NAT/G LEGIS TAX CONTROL MARRIAGE 20 COLOMB. PAGE 115 F2257 — FINAN ECO/UNDEV LAW CONSTN

B61
SAKAI R.K.,STUDIES ON ASIA, 1961. ASIA BURMA INDIA S/ASIA FINAN ECO/TAC NAT/LISM SOCISM...POLICY ANTHOL 19/20 CHINJAP. PAGE 115 F2271
ECO/UNDEV SECT

B61
SHARP W.R.,FIELD ADMINISTRATION IN THE UNITED NATION SYSTEM: THE CONDUCT OF INTERNATIONAL ECONOMIC AND SOCIAL PROGRAMS. FUT WOR+45 CONSTN SOCIETY ECO/UNDEV R+D DELIB/GP ACT/RES PLAN TEC/DEV EDU/PROP EXEC ROUTINE HEALTH WEALTH...HUM CONCPT CHARTS METH ILO UNESCO GP VAL/FREE UN 20. PAGE 120 F2369
INT/ORG CONSULT

B61
SHONFIELD A.,ECONOMIC GROWTH AND INFLATION; A STUDY OF INDIAN PLANNING. AFR INDIA AGRI INDUS TEC/DEV CONTROL DEMAND UTIL 20. PAGE 121 F2384
ECO/UNDEV PRICE PLAN BUDGET

B61
STARK H.,SOCIAL AND ECONOMIC FRONTIERS IN LATIN AMERICA (2ND ED.). CUBA FUT CULTURE AGRI INDUS ECO/TAC PRODUC ATTIT MARXISM...NAT/COMP BIBLIOG T 20. PAGE 125 F2470
L/A+17C SOCIETY DIPLOM ECO/UNDEV

B61
THEOBALD R.,THE CHALLENGE OF ABUNDANCE. USA+45 WOR+45 MARKET DIPLOM FOR/AID REV PRODUC UTOPIA SUPEGO...POLICY TREND BIBLIOG/A 20. PAGE 129 F2554
WELF/ST ECO/UNDEV PROB/SOLV ECO/TAC

B61
US GENERAL ACCOUNTING OFFICE,EXAMINATION OF ECONOMIC AND TECHNICAL ASSISTANCE PROGRAM FOR IRAN. IRAN USA+45 AGRI INDUS DIPLOM CONTROL COST 20. PAGE 136 F2681
FOR/AID ADMIN TEC/DEV ECO/UNDEV

B61
US SENATE COMM ON FOREIGN RELS,INTERNATIONAL DEVELOPMENT AND SECURITY: HEARINGS ON BILL (2 VOLS.). ECO/UNDEV FINAN FORCES REV COST WEALTH ...CHARTS 20 AID PRESIDENT. PAGE 139 F2747
FOR/AID CIVMIL/REL ORD/FREE ECO/TAC

B61
WAGLE S.S.,TECHNIQUE OF PLANNING FOR ACCELERATED ECONOMIC GROWTH OF UNDERDEVELOPED COUNTRIES. WOR+45 ACT/RES PROB/SOLV RATION BAL/PAY DEMAND INCOME 20. PAGE 142 F2798
ECO/UNDEV PLAN INDUS ECO/TAC

B61
WARD B.J.,INDIA AND THE WEST. INDIA UK USA+45 INT/TRADE GIVE COLONIAL ATTIT MARXISM 19/20. PAGE 143 F2817
PLAN ECO/UNDEV ECO/TAC FOR/AID

L61
CHENERY H.B.,"COMPARATIVE ADVANTAGE AND DEVELOPMENT POLICY." FINAN INT/TRADE RATION OPTIMAL...CHARTS METH/COMP GEN/LAWS BIBLIOG 20 RESOURCE/N. PAGE 24 F0463
ECO/UNDEV ECO/TAC PLAN EFFICIENCY

L61
JOHNSTON B.F.,"THE ROLE OF AGRICULTURE IN ECONOMIC DEVELOPMENT." FINAN PRODUC ROLE BIBLIOG. PAGE 68 F1332
AGRI ECO/UNDEV PLAN INDUS

S61
BARALL M.,"THE UNITED STATES GOVERNMENT RESPONDS." L/A+17C USA+45 SOCIETY NAT/G CREATE PLAN DIPLOM ECO/TAC ATTIT DRIVE RIGID/FLEX KNOWL SKILL WEALTH ...METH/CNCPT TIME/SEQ GEN/METH 20. PAGE 9 F0176
ECO/UNDEV ACT/RES FOR/AID

S61
DALTON G.,"ECONOMIC THEORY AND PRIMITIVE SOCIETY" (BMR)" UNIV AGRI KIN TEC/DEV ECO/TAC REGION HABITAT SKILL...METH/COMP BIBLIOG. PAGE 30 F0574
ECO/UNDEV METH PHIL/SCI SOC

S61
GALBRAITH J.K.,"A POSITIVE APPROACH TO ECONOMIC AID." FUT USA+45 INTELL NAT/G CONSULT ACT/RES DIPLOM ECO/TAC EDU/PROP ATTIT KNOWL PWR WEALTH ...SOC STERTYP MID/EX METH/GP 20. PAGE 45 F0883
ECO/UNDEV ROUTINE FOR/AID

S61
HEILBRONER R.L.,"DYNAMICS OF FOREIGN AID: PROBLEMS OF UNDERDEVELOPED NATIONS PLAGUE ASSISTANCE PROGRAM." FUT USA+45 WOR+45 STRATA NAT/G PLAN TEC/DEV ATTIT DRIVE WEALTH WORK 20. PAGE 58 F1135
ECO/UNDEV ECO/TAC FOR/AID

S61
HOSELITZ B.F.,"ECONOMIC DEVELOPMENT AND POLITICAL STABILITY IN INDIA" INDIA NAT/G GP/REL...POLICY 20. PAGE 62 F1222
ECO/UNDEV GEN/LAWS PROB/SOLV

S61
NEAL A.C.,"NEW ECONOMIC POLICIES FOR THE WEST." COM EUR+WWI FUT USA+45 WOR+45 ECO/DEV ECO/UNDEV INDUS MARKET ROUTINE HEALTH ORD/FREE PWR...OLD/LIB METH/CNCPT 20. PAGE 97 F1904
PLAN ECO/TAC

S61
NOVE A.,"THE SOVIET MODEL AND UNDERDEVELOPED COUNTRIES." COM FUT USSR WOR+45 CULTURE ECO/DEV POL/PAR FOR/AID EDU/PROP ADMIN MORAL WEALTH ...POLICY RECORD HIST/WRIT 20. PAGE 99 F1942
ECO/UNDEV PLAN

S61
NYANZI S.,"THE EAST AFRICAN MARKET: FOR BETTER OF FOR WORSE." AFR TANZANIA UGANDA PROB/SOLV TARIFFS TAX BAL/PAY. PAGE 99 F1947
ECO/TAC ECO/UNDEV INT/ORG INT/TRADE

S61
OCHENG D.,"ECONOMIC FORCES AND UGANDA'S FOREIGN POLICY." AFR UGANDA INT/TRADE TARIFFS INCOME SOVEREIGN WEALTH 20 EACM EEC TANGANYIKA. PAGE 100 F1961
ECO/TAC DIPLOM ECO/UNDEV INT/ORG

S61
VALLET R.,"IRAN: KEY TO THE MIDDLE EAST." COM IRAQ ISLAM KUWAIT LEBANON SAUDI/ARAB TURKEY ELITES SOCIETY INDUS PROC/MFG POL/PAR TOP/EX PLAN BAL/PWR DIPLOM ECO/TAC ALL/VALS...TREND FOR/TRADE CENTO 20. PAGE 140 F2760
NAT/G ECO/UNDEV IRAN

S61
VERNON R.,"A TRADE POLICY FOR THE 1960'S." COM FUT USA+45 WOR+45 ECO/DEV ECO/UNDEV FINAN TOP/EX ACT/RES...WELF/ST METH/CNCPT CONT/OBS TOT/POP 20. PAGE 141 F2781
PLAN INT/TRADE

S61
VINER J.,"ECONOMIC FOREIGN POLICY ON THE NEW FRONTIER." USA+45 ECO/UNDEV AGRI FINAN INDUS MARKET INT/ORG NAT/G FOR/AID INT/TRADE ADMIN ATTIT PWR 20 KENNEDY/JF. PAGE 141 F2786
TOP/EX ECO/TAC BAL/PAY TARIFFS

C61
FILLOL T.R.,"SOCIAL FACTORS IN ECONOMIC DEVELOPMENT: THE ARGENTINE CASE" INDUS LABOR CREATE TEC/DEV PERS/REL EFFICIENCY PRODUC DRIVE ...METH/CNCPT METH/COMP 20 ARGEN. PAGE 41 F0794
BIBLIOG ECO/UNDEV MGT TREND

B62
ROUND TABLE ON EUROPE'S ROLE IN LATIN AMERICAN DEVELOPMENT. EUR+WWI L/A+17C PLAN BAL/PAY UTIL ROLE WEALTH...CHARTS ANTHOL 20 UN INT/AM/DEV. PAGE 1 F0017
ECO/UNDEV FINAN TEC/DEV FOR/AID

B62
ARNOLD H.J.P.,AID FOR DEVELOPING COUNTRIES. COM EUR+WWI USA+45 USSR WOR+45 EDU/PROP ATTIT DRIVE PWR WEALTH...TREND CHARTS STERTYP NAT/ 20. PAGE 6 F0115
ECO/UNDEV ECO/TAC FOR/AID

B62
BROOKINGS INSTITUTION,DEVELOPMENT OF THE EMERGING COUNTRIES; AN AGENDA FOR RESEARCH. WOR+45 AGRI TEC/DEV FOR/AID EDU/PROP ADJUST HABITAT KNOWL...PSY SOC ANTHOL 20 THIRD/WRLD. PAGE 19 F0362
ECO/UNDEV R+D SOCIETY PROB/SOLV

B62
BROWN S.D.,STUDIES ON ASIA, 1962. ASIA BURMA INDIA ISLAM ISRAEL S/ASIA ECO/UNDEV POL/PAR SECT ECO/TAC ...ANTHOL 20 CHINJAP. PAGE 19 F0374
PWR PARL/PROC

B62
CAIRNCROSS A.K.,FACTORS IN ECONOMIC DEVELOPMENT. WOR+45 ECO/UNDEV INDUS R+D LG/CO NAT/G EX/STRUC PLAN TEC/DEV ECO/TAC ATTIT HEALTH KNOWL PWR WEALTH ...TIME/SEQ GEN/LAWS TOT/POP TRUE/GP VAL/FREE 20. PAGE 21 F0399
MARKET ECO/DEV

B62
DREIER J.C.,THE ALLIANCE FOR PROGRESS. L/A+17C USA+45 CULTURE ECO/DEV ECO/UNDEV NAT/G PLAN DIPLOM PWR 20 OAS ALL/PROG. PAGE 34 F0661
FOR/AID INT/ORG ECO/TAC POLICY

B62
ELLIOTT J.R.,THE APPEAL OF COMMUNISM IN THE UNDERDEVELOPED NATIONS. AFR USSR WOR+45 INT/ORG NAT/G DIPLOM DOMIN EDU/PROP ROUTINE ATTIT RIGID/FLEX ORD/FREE PWR WEALTH MARXISM...POLICY SOC METH/CNCPT MYTH TOT/POP METH/GP 20. PAGE 37 F0722
COM ECO/UNDEV

B62
FAO,FOOD AND AGRICULTURE ORGANIZATION AFRICAN SURVEY. AFR CONGO/BRAZ GHANA STRATA AGRI INT/ORG TEC/DEV FOR/AID INT/TRADE RACE/REL DEMAND EFFICIENCY PRODUC...GEOG 20 UN CONGO/LEOP. PAGE 39 F0763
ECO/TAC WEALTH EXTR/IND ECO/UNDEV

B62
FATOUROS A.A.,GOVERNMENT GUARANTEES TO FOREIGN INVESTORS. WOR+45 ECO/UNDEV INDUS WORKER ADJUD ...NAT/COMP BIBLIOG TREATY. PAGE 39 F0767
NAT/G FINAN INT/TRADE ECO/DEV

B62
FORD A.G.,THE GOLD STANDARD 1880-1914: BRITAIN AND ARGENTINA. AFR UK ECO/UNDEV INT/TRADE ADMIN GOV/REL DEMAND EFFICIENCY...STAT CHARTS 19/20 ARGEN. PAGE 42 F0823
FINAN ECO/TAC BUDGET BAL/PAY

B62
FRIEDRICH-EBERT-STIFTUNG,THE SOVIET BLOC AND DEVELOPING COUNTRIES. CHINA/COM COM GERMANY/E USSR WOR+45 ECO/UNDEV INT/ORG NAT/G TEC/DEV NEUTRAL PWR ...POLICY 20. PAGE 44 F0868
MARXISM DIPLOM ECO/TAC FOR/AID

B62
GALENSON W.,LABOR IN DEVELOPING COUNTRIES. BRAZIL INDONESIA ISRAEL PAKISTAN TURKEY AGRI INDUS WORKER PAY PRICE GP/REL WEALTH...MGT CHARTS METH/COMP NAT/COMP 20. PAGE 45 F0888
LABOR ECO/UNDEV BARGAIN POL/PAR

B62
GERSCHENKRON A.,ECONOMIC BACKWARDNESS IN HISTORICAL PERSPECTIVE. WOR+45 WOR-45 ECO/DEV ECO/UNDEV INDUS NAT/G LEGIT DRIVE...WELF/ST DECISION QUANT TREND CHARTS 20. PAGE 47 F0919
TEC/DEV USSR

B62
GOLDWIN R.A.,WHY FOREIGN AID? - TWO MESSAGES BY PRESIDENT KENNEDY AND ESSAYS. S/ASIA USA+45 ECO/UNDEV 20 KENNEDY/JF THIRD/WRLD. PAGE 48 F0942
DIPLOM FOR/AID POLICY

B62
GREEN L.P.,DEVELOPMENT IN AFRICA. AFR CENTRL/AFR GHANA RHODESIA SOUTH/AFR AGRI PROC/MFG INT/TRADE DEMAND NAT/LISM PRODUC WEALTH...GEOG METH/CNCPT CHARTS BIBLIOG 20. PAGE 50 F0987
CULTURE ECO/UNDEV GOV/REL TREND

B62
HAGUE D.C.,INFLATION. AFR ECO/DEV ECO/UNDEV LABOR BUDGET CAP/ISM INT/TRADE TARIFFS SOCISM 20. PAGE 53 F1036
FINAN NAT/COMP BARGAIN ECO/TAC

B62
HEILBRONER R.L.,THE MAKING OF ECONOMIC SOCIETY. FUT WOR-45 SOCIETY STRATA ECO/DEV ECO/UNDEV ECO/TAC LEGIT ROUTINE...SOC RECORD REC/INT KNO/TEST CENSUS STERTYP GEN/LAWS. PAGE 58 F1136
CAP/ISM SOCISM

B62
HIGGANS B.,UNITED NATIONS AND U.S. FOREIGN ECONOMIC POLICY. FUT USA+45 WOR+45 ECO/DEV ECO/UNDEV NAT/G ECO/TAC WEALTH...TIME/SEQ TOT/POP UN 20. PAGE 59 F1168
INT/ORG ACT/RES FOR/AID DIPLOM

B62
HOOVER C.B.,ECONOMIC SYSTEMS OF THE COMMONWEALTH. AFR CANADA INDIA UK ECO/DEV ECO/UNDEV AGRI INDUS TEC/DEV TARIFFS PRICE BAL/PAY DEMAND...SIMUL 20 AUSTRAL. PAGE 61 F1208
CAP/ISM SOCISM ECO/TAC PLAN

B62
HUHNE L.H.,FINANCING ECONOMIC DEVELOPMENT THROUGH NATIONAL AND INTERNATIONAL ORGANIZATIONS (THESIS; U OF WIS.). USA+45 INT/ORG PLAN GIVE GOV/REL WEALTH 20. PAGE 63 F1235
RATION FINAN FOR/AID ECO/UNDEV

B62
INTERNATIONAL BANK RECONST DEV,THE WORLD BANK AND IDA IN ASIA. ASIA S/ASIA COM/IND DIST/IND...CHARTS 20. PAGE 65 F1272
FINAN ECO/UNDEV AGRI INDUS

B62
JOHNSON H.G.,MONEY, TRADE AND ECONOMIC GROWTH. ECO/DEV ECO/UNDEV FINAN COST WEALTH...POLICY SOC IDEA/COMP 20 KEYNES/JM MONEY. PAGE 67 F1324
PLAN BAL/PAY INT/TRADE ECO/TAC

B62
JORDAN A.A. JR.,FOREIGN AID AND THE DEFENSE OF SOUTHEAST ASIA. PAKISTAN VIETNAM/S FINAN PLAN BUDGET ECO/TAC DETER WAR ORD/FREE...POLICY DECISION CENSUS CHARTS BIBLIOG 20. PAGE 68 F1341
FOR/AID S/ASIA FORCES ECO/UNDEV

B62
KAUTSKY J.H.,POLITICAL CHANGE IN UNDERDEVELOPED COUNTRIES: NATIONALISM AND COMMUNISM. WOR+45 AGRI TEC/DEV EDU/PROP ATTIT...POLICY METH/CNCPT STYLE INT QU CENSUS TREND SOC/EXP GEN/LAWS 20. PAGE 69 F1365
ECO/UNDEV SOCIETY CAP/ISM REV

B62
KINDLEBERGER C.P.,FOREIGN TRADE AND THE NATIONAL ECONOMY. WOR+45 ECO/DEV ECO/UNDEV ECO/TAC COST DEMAND 20. PAGE 71 F1393
INT/TRADE GOV/COMP BAL/PAY POLICY

B62
KUHN T.E.,PUBLIC ENTERPRISES, PROJECT PLANNING AND ECONOMIC DEVELOPMENT (PAMPHLET). ECO/UNDEV FINAN PLAN ADMIN EFFICIENCY OWN...MGT STAT CHARTS ANTHOL 20. PAGE 74 F1447
ECO/DEV ECO/TAC LG/CO NAT/G

B62
MARTINS A.F.,REVOLUCAO BRANCA NO CAMPO. L/A+17C SERV/IND DEMAND EFFICIENCY PRODUC...POLICY METH/COMP. PAGE 86 F1685
AGRI ECO/UNDEV TEC/DEV NAT/COMP

B62
MICHAELY M.,CONCENTRATION IN INTERNATIONAL TRADE. ECO/DEV ECO/UNDEV PRICE INCOME...CHARTS NAT/COMP 20. PAGE 91 F1779
INT/TRADE MARKET FINAN GEOG

B62
MOUSSA P.,THE UNDERPRIVILEGED NATIONS. FINAN INT/ORG PLAN PROB/SOLV CAP/ISM GIVE TASK WEALTH ...POLICY SOC IND 20. PAGE 94 F1850
ECO/UNDEV NAT/G DIPLOM FOR/AID

B62
O'CONNOR H.,WORLD CRISES IN OIL (BMR). ISLAM L/A+17C INDUS LG/CO INT/TRADE 20. PAGE 100 F1956
EXTR/IND DIPLOM ECO/UNDEV SOCISM

B62
PAKISTAN MINISTRY OF FINANCE,FOREIGN ECONOMIC AID: A REVIEW OF FOREIGN ECONOMIC AID TO PAKISTAN. EUR+WWI PAKISTAN UK USA+45 USSR ECO/UNDEV INT/ORG DELIB/GP DIPLOM ECO/TAC...CHARTS CMN/WLTH CHINJAP. PAGE 103 F2016
FOR/AID RECEIVE WEALTH FINAN

B62
PASTOR R.S.,A STATEMENT OF THE LAWS OF PARAGUAY IN MATTERS AFFECTING BUSINESS (2ND ED.). PARAGUAY INDUS FAM LABOR LG/CO NAT/G LEGIS TAX CONTROL MARRIAGE 20. PAGE 103 F2033
FINAN ECO/UNDEV LAW CONSTN

B62
PERROUX F.,L'ECONOMIE DES JEUNES NATIONS. EUR+WWI SOUTH/AFR FINAN MARKET TEC/DEV CAP/ISM FOR/AID INT/TRADE 20. PAGE 105 F2065
INDUS ECO/UNDEV ECO/TAC

DIPLOM

B62
PONCET J.,LA COLONISATION ET L'AGRICULTURE EUROPEENNES EN TUNISIE DEPUIS 1881. FRANCE WORKER TEC/DEV ECO/TAC CONTROL EFFICIENCY ROLE WEALTH 19/20 TUNIS. PAGE 107 F2101
ECO/UNDEV AGRI COLONIAL FINAN

B62
PRAKASH O.M.,THE THEORY AND WORKING OF STATE CORPORATIONS: WITH SPECIAL REFERENCE TO INDIA. INDIA UK USA+45 TOP/EX PRICE ADMIN EFFICIENCY...MGT METH/COMP 20 TVA. PAGE 107 F2112
LG/CO ECO/UNDEV GOV/REL SOCISM

B62
RIMALOV V.V.,ECONOMIC COOPERATION BETWEEN USSR AND UNDERDEVELOPED COUNTRIES. USSR FINAN TEC/DEV INT/TRADE DOMIN EDU/PROP COLONIAL NAT/LISM DRIVE SOVEREIGN...AUD/VIS 20. PAGE 111 F2194
FOR/AID PLAN ECO/UNDEV DIPLOM

B62
ROBERTSON B.C.,REGIONAL DEVELOPMENT IN THE EUROPEAN ECONOMIC COMMUNITY. EUR+WWI FRANCE FUT ITALY UK ECO/UNDEV WORKER ACT/RES PROB/SOLV TEC/DEV ECO/TAC INT/TRADE EEC. PAGE 112 F2209
PLAN ECO/DEV INT/ORG REGION

B62
ROTHBARD M.N.,THE PANIC OF 1819; REACTIONS AND POLICIES. AFR USA-45 LAW FINAN BUDGET TARIFFS DEMAND 19 DEPRESSION. PAGE 114 F2247
ECO/UNDEV POLICY ATTIT ECO/TAC

B62
SELOSOEMARDJAN O.,SOCIAL CHANGES IN JOGJAKARTA. INDONESIA NETHERLAND ELITES STRATA STRUCT FAM POL/PAR CREATE DIPLOM INT/TRADE EDU/PROP ADMIN GOV/REL...SOC 20 JAVA CHINJAP. PAGE 119 F2352
ECO/UNDEV CULTURE REV COLONIAL

B62
SEN S.R.,THE STRATEGY FOR AGRICULTURAL DEVELOPMENT AND OTHER ESSAYS ON ECONOMIC POLICY AND PLANNING. INDIA FINAN ACT/RES TEC/DEV CAP/ISM PRICE...STAT 20. PAGE 119 F2354
ECO/UNDEV PLAN AGRI POLICY

B62
THEOBALD R.,NATIONAL DEVELOPMENT EFFORTS (PAMPHLET). WOR+45 AGRI BUDGET FOR/AID INT/TRADE TAX 20. PAGE 129 F2555
ECO/UNDEV PLAN BAL/PAY WEALTH

B62
UNECA LIBRARY,BOOKS ON AFRICA IN THE UNECA LIBRARY. WOR+45 AGRI INT/ORG NAT/G PLAN WRITING REGION...SOC STAT UN. PAGE 132 F2605
BIBLIOG AFR ECO/UNDEV TEC/DEV

B62
UNECA LIBRARY,NEW ACQUISITIONS IN THE UNECA LIBRARY. LAW NAT/G PLAN PROB/SOLV TEC/DEV ADMIN REGION...GEOG SOC 20 UN. PAGE 132 F2606
BIBLIOG AFR ECO/UNDEV INT/ORG

B62
URQUIDI V.L.,FREE TRADE AND ECONOMIC INTEGRATION IN LATIN AMERICA: THE EVOLUTION OF A COMMON MARKET POLICY. ECO/UNDEV MARKET DIPLOM BAL/PAY FEDERAL ...POLICY CHARTS 20 LAFTA. PAGE 133 F2627
INT/TRADE REGION INT/ORG L/A+17C

B62
US AGENCY INTERNATIONAL DEV,OPERATIONS REPORT - 1962 (PAMPHLET). AFR ASIA L/A+17C USA+45 ECO/UNDEV FINAN INT/ORG NAT/G 20 MICHIGAN. PAGE 134 F2636
FOR/AID CHARTS STAT BUDGET

B62
US CONGRESS JOINT ECO COMM,ECONOMIC DEVELOPMENTS IN SOUTH AMERICA. USA+45 SOCIETY FINAN NAT/G PROB/SOLV TEC/DEV INT/TRADE TAX EFFICIENCY PRODUC ATTIT ...POLICY 20 ALL/PROG CONGRESS SOUTH/AMER. PAGE 135 F2654
L/A+17C ECO/UNDEV FOR/AID DIPLOM

B62
VIET J.,INTERNATIONAL COOPERATION AND PROGRAMMES OF ECONOMIC AND SOCIAL DEVELOPMENT. TEC/DEV FOR/AID DOMIN COLONIAL PEACE WEALTH 20 UNESCO. PAGE 141 F2784
BIBLIOG/A INT/ORG DIPLOM ECO/UNDEV

B62
WARD B.,THE RICH NATIONS AND THE POOR NATIONS. FUT WOR+45 CULTURE ECO/DEV ECO/UNDEV PLAN CAP/ISM EDU/PROP REV NAT/LISM ATTIT DRIVE SOCISM...POLICY CONCPT TIME/SEQ 20. PAGE 143 F2816
ECO/TAC GEN/LAWS

B62
ZOOK P.D.,FOREIGN TRADE AND HUMAN CAPITAL. L/A+17C USA+45 FINAN DIPLOM ECO/TAC PRODUC...POLICY 20. PAGE 151 F2970
INT/TRADE ECO/UNDEV FOR/AID BAL/PAY

L62
"BIBLIOGRAPHY ON EDUCATION AND ECONOMIC AND SOCIAL DEVELOPMENT (AMERICAN SOURCES)" L/A+17C ECO/UNDEV PROB/SOLV...SOC 20. PAGE 1 F0015
BIBLIOG/A ACADEM EDU/PROP INTELL

L62
"HIGHER EDUCATION AND ECONOMIC AND SOCIAL DEVELOPMENT IN LATIN AMERICA: A BIBLIOGRAPHY." L/A+17C SOCIETY ECO/UNDEV PROF/ORG DIPLOM CONFER ...SOC 20. PAGE 1 F0016
BIBLIOG/A ACADEM INTELL EDU/PROP

L62
BELSHAW D.G.R.,"PUBLIC INVESTMENT IN AGRICULTURE AND ECONOMIC DEVELOPMENT OF UGANDA" UGANDA AGRI INDUS R+D ECO/TAC RATION TAX PAY COLONIAL 20
ECO/UNDEV PLAN ADMIN

WORLD/BANK. PAGE 13 F0242 CENTRAL

L62
DURAND-REVILLE L.,"LE REGIME DES INVESTISSEMENTS DANS LES ETATS AFRICAINS D'EXPRESSION FRANCAISE ET A MADAGASCAR." MADAGASCAR ECO/UNDEV CAP/ISM ECO/TAC WEALTH...SOC TREND CHARTS 20. PAGE 35 F0683 AFR FINAN

L62
GALBRAITH J.K.,"ECONOMIC DEVELOPMENT IN PERSPECTIVE." CAP/ISM ECO/TAC ROUTINE ATTIT WEALTH ...TREND CHARTS SOC/EXP WORK TERR/GP 20. PAGE 45 F0884 ECO/UNDEV PLAN

S62
ADISESHIAN M.,"EDUCATION AND DEVELOPMENT." FUT WOR+45 SOCIETY ACT/RES INT/TRADE EDU/PROP KNOWL SKILL WEALTH...POLICY CONCPT CONT/OBS CENSUS CHARTS TOT/POP VAL/FREE APPLIC FAO FOR/TRADE 20. PAGE 2 F0041 SCHOOL ECO/UNDEV

S62
BOONE A.,"THE FOREIGN TRADE OF CHINA." AFR ECO/DEV ECO/UNDEV INDUS MARKET NAT/G TEC/DEV WEALTH ...POLICY STAT TREND CHARTS FOR/TRADE. PAGE 17 F0318 ASIA ECO/TAC

S62
GILL P.J.,"FUTURE TAXATION POLICY IN AN INDEPENDENT EAST AFRICA" UGANDA LOC/G ECO/TAC ADMIN EFFICIENCY INCOME PRODUC...CHARTS 20. PAGE 47 F0923 ECO/UNDEV TAX AFR COLONIAL

S62
KRISHNA K.G.V.,"PLANNING AND ECONOMIC DEVELOPMENT" AFR UGANDA AGRI INDUS R+D BUDGET RATION TAX COLONIAL 20. PAGE 73 F1441 ECO/UNDEV ECO/TAC NAT/LISM PLAN

S62
MILLIKEN M.,"NEW AND OLD CRITERIA FOR AID." WOR+45 ECO/DEV ECO/UNDEV ACT/RES PLAN ATTIT KNOWL...TREND CON/ANAL SIMUL GEN/METH TERR/GP 20. PAGE 92 F1796 USA+45 ECO/TAC FOR/AID

S62
MORGENTHAU H.J.,"A POLITICAL THEORY OF FOREIGN AID." ECO/UNDEV NAT/G DELIB/GP PLAN ECO/TAC EDU/PROP EXEC ORD/FREE RESPECT WEALTH...METH/CNCPT TREND 20. PAGE 93 F1833 USA+45 PHIL/SCI FOR/AID

S62
PYE L.W.,"THE POLITICAL IMPULSES AND FANTASIES BEHIND FOREIGN AID." FUT USA+45 ECO/UNDEV DIPLOM ECO/TAC ROUTINE DRIVE KNOWL...SOC METH/CNCPT NEW/IDEA TREND HYPO/EXP STERTYP GEN/METH 20. PAGE 108 F2133 ACT/RES ATTIT FOR/AID

S62
RAZAFIMBAHINY J.,"L'ORGANISATION AFRICAINE ET MALGACHE DE COOPERATION ECONOMIQUE." AFR ISLAM MADAGASCAR NAT/G ACT/RES ECO/TAC ALL/VALS ...TIME/SEQ 20. PAGE 110 F2158 INT/ORG ECO/UNDEV

C62
GREEN L.P.,"DEVELOPMENT IN AFRICA." RHODESIA SOUTH/AFR UGANDA MARKET PROC/MFG PRODUC WEALTH ...GEOG 20. PAGE 50 F0986 BIBLIOG ECO/UNDEV AFR AGRI

B63
BRITISH AID. UK AGRI DIST/IND INDUS SCHOOL TEC/DEV INT/TRADE COLONIAL DEMAND...TREND CHARTS 20. PAGE 1 F0018 FOR/AID ECO/UNDEV NAT/G FINAN

B63
ABSHIRE D.M.,NATIONAL SECURITY: POLITICAL, MILITARY, AND ECONOMIC STRATEGIES IN THE DECADE AHEAD. ASIA COM USA+45 WOR+45 ECO/DEV ECO/UNDEV INT/ORG DELIB/GP FORCES ECO/TAC COERCE ATTIT RIGID/FLEX HEALTH ORD/FREE PWR WEALTH...POLICY STAT CHARTS ANTHOL COLD/WAR VAL/FREE APP/SCI. PAGE 2 F0032 FUT ACT/RES BAL/PWR

B63
ALPERT P.,ECONOMIC DEVELOPMENT. WOR+45 FINAN TEC/DEV ECO/TAC PRICE GOV/REL HABITAT...GEOG BIBLIOG T 20 THIRD/WRLD. PAGE 4 F0079 ECO/DEV ECO/UNDEV INT/TRADE FOR/AID

B63
BERGSON A.,ECONOMIC TRENDS IN THE SOVIET UNION. USSR ECO/UNDEV AGRI NAT/G FORCES PLAN TEC/DEV INT/TRADE BAL/PAY...POLICY ANTHOL 20. PAGE 14 F0259 ECO/DEV NAT/COMP INDUS LABOR

B63
BRAIBANTI R.J.D.,ADMINISTRATION AND ECONOMIC DEVELOPMENT IN INDIA. INDIA S/ASIA SOCIETY STRATA ECO/TAC PERSON WEALTH...MGT GEN/LAWS TOT/POP VAL/FREE 20. PAGE 18 F0337 ECO/UNDEV ADMIN

B63
BURNS T.G.,DEVELOPMENT BANKING BIBLIOGRAPHY (PAPER). WOR+45 SML/CO VOL/ASSN PLAN BUDGET. PAGE 20 F0391 BIBLIOG/A ECO/DEV FINAN ECO/UNDEV

B63
CENTRO ESTUDIOS MONETARIOS LAT,COOPERACION FINANCIERA EN AMERICA LATINA. L/A+17C PLAN PROB/SOLV CONTROL REGION DEMAND...POLICY ANTHOL 20. PAGE 22 F0433 ECO/UNDEV INT/TRADE MARKET FINAN

B63
CENTRO PARA EL DESARROLLO,LA ALIANZA PARA EL PROGRESO Y EL DESARROLLO SOCIAL DE AMERICA LATINA. L/A+17C INT/ORG DIPLOM ECO/TAC INT/TRADE ATTIT 20 ALL/PROG. PAGE 22 F0435 ECO/UNDEV FOR/AID PLAN REGION

B63
CHEN N.-.R.,THE ECONOMY OF MAINLAND CHINA, 1949-1963: A BIBLIOGRAPHY OF MATERIALS IN ENGLISH. CHINA/COM ECO/UNDEV PRESS 20. PAGE 24 F0461 BIBLIOG MARXISM NAT/G ASIA

B63
COLUMBIA U SCHOOL OF LAW,PUBLIC INTERNATIONAL DEVELOPMENT FINANCING IN SENEGAL. SENEGAL FINAN DELIB/GP GIVE EFFICIENCY...CHARTS GOV/COMP ANTHOL 20. PAGE 26 F0511 FOR/AID PLAN RECEIVE ECO/UNDEV

B63
CONF ON FUTURE OF COMMONWEALTH,THE FUTURE OF THE COMMONWEALTH. AFR UK ECO/UNDEV AGRI EDU/PROP ADMIN SOC/INTEG 20. PAGE 27 F0522 DIPLOM RACE/REL ORD/FREE TEC/DEV

B63
COURNOT A.A.,RESEARCHES INTO THE MATHEMATICAL PRINCIPLES OF THE THEORY OF WEALTH (1838). UNIV ECO/DEV ECO/UNDEV AGRI INDUS MARKET PAY CONTROL COST INCOME 19. PAGE 28 F0544 ECOMETRIC GEN/LAWS WEALTH

B63
DE VRIES E.,SOCIAL ASPECTS OF ECONOMIC DEVELOPMENT IN LATIN AMERICA. CULTURE SOCIETY STRATA FINAN INDUS INT/ORG DELIB/GP ACT/RES ECO/TAC EDU/PROP ADMIN ATTIT SUPEGO HEALTH KNOWL ORD/FREE...SOC STAT TREND ANTHOL TOT/POP VAL/FREE. PAGE 31 F0608 L/A+17C ECO/UNDEV

B63
DELL S.,TRADE BLOCS AND COMMON MARKETS. COM WOR+45 ECO/DEV ECO/UNDEV GP/COMP. PAGE 32 F0615 DIPLOM ECO/TAC INT/TRADE FEDERAL

B63
DEUTSCH K.W.,THE POLITICAL ROLE OF LABOR IN DEVELOPING COUNTRIES. AFR ASIA S/ASIA USA+45 WOR+45 ECO/UNDEV POL/PAR ECO/TAC EDU/PROP LEGIT COERCE ORD/FREE PWR WEALTH...OBS INT TREND VAL/FREE 20. PAGE 32 F0625 LABOR NAT/LISM

B63
EL-NAGGAR S.,FOREIGN AID TO UNITED ARAB REPUBLIC. UAR USA+45 USSR AGRI FINAN INDUS FORCES EATING DEMAND...CHARTS METH/COMP 20 RESOURCE/N AID. PAGE 37 F0718 FOR/AID ECO/UNDEV RECEIVE PLAN

B63
ELLENDER A.J.,A REPORT ON UNITED STATES FOREIGN OPERATIONS IN AFRICA. SOUTH/AFR USA+45 STRATA EXTR/IND FORCES RACE/REL ISOLAT SOVEREIGN...CHARTS 20 NEGRO. PAGE 37 F0721 FOR/AID DIPLOM WEALTH ECO/UNDEV

B63
ENKE S.,ECONOMICS FOR DEVELOPMENT. AGRI TEC/DEV CAP/ISM DIPLOM ECO/TAC TAX ATTIT DRIVE HABITAT WEALTH...GOV/COMP BIBLIOG 20. PAGE 38 F0737 ECO/UNDEV PHIL/SCI CON/ANAL

B63
FLORES E.,LAND REFORM AND THE ALLIANCE FOR PROGRESS (PAMPHLET). L/A+17C USA+45 STRUCT ECO/UNDEV NAT/G WORKER CREATE PLAN ECO/TAC COERCE REV 20 ALL/PROG. PAGE 42 F0815 AGRI INT/ORG DIPLOM POLICY

B63
FRIEDMAN M.,INFLATION: CAUSES AND CURES. AFR INDIA ECO/DEV ECO/TAC INT/TRADE RATION PRICE DEMAND ...POLICY 20. PAGE 44 F0860 ECO/UNDEV PLAN FINAN EQUILIB

B63
FURTADO C.,THE ECONOMIC GROWTH OF BRAZIL: A SURVEY FROM COLONIAL TO MODERN TIMES. L/A+17C AGRI DIST/IND EXTR/IND INDUS WORKER COLONIAL RACE/REL OWN GOV/COMP. PAGE 45 F0877 ECO/UNDEV TEC/DEV LABOR DOMIN

B63
GANGULI B.N.,ECONOMIC CONSEQUENCES OF DISARMAMENT. EUR+WWI ECO/DEV ECO/UNDEV FORCES ACT/RES BUDGET DIPLOM INT/TRADE...STAT CHARTS NAT/COMP. PAGE 46 F0896 ECOMETRIC ARMS/CONT COST HYPO/EXP

B63
GANGULY D.S.,PUBLIC CORPORATIONS IN A NATIONAL ECONOMY. INDIA WOR+45 FINAN INDUS TOP/EX PRICE EFFICIENCY...MGT STAT CHARTS BIBLIOG 20. PAGE 46 F0897 ECO/UNDEV LG/CO SOCISM GOV/REL

B63
GEERTZ C.,PEDDLERS AND PRINCES: SOCIAL DEVELOPMENT AND ECONOMIC CHANGE IN TWO INDONESIAN TOWNS. S/ASIA CULTURE SOCIETY STRATA FACE/GP CREATE TEC/DEV ECO/TAC ORD/FREE WEALTH...OBS INT CENSUS CHARTS WORK TOT/POP METH/GP TERR/GP VAL/FREE 20 MUNICH. PAGE 47 F0913 ECO/UNDEV SOC ELITES INDONESIA

B63
GLADE W.P. JR.,THE POLITICAL ECONOMY OF MEXICO. FUT L/A+17C CULTURE SOCIETY AGRI INDUS DELIB/GP ACT/RES ECO/TAC ATTIT HEALTH ORD/FREE...STAT TIME/SEQ TREND MEXIC/AMER TOT/POP VAL/FREE 20. PAGE 48 F0928 FINAN ECO/UNDEV

B63
GODWIN F.W.,THE HIDDEN FORCE. PUERT/RICO WOR+45 STRUCT VOL/ASSN PROB/SOLV DIPLOM CONFER...BIBLIOG ECO/UNDEV WORKER

20 PEACE/CORP. PAGE 48 F0931 SKILL ECO/TAC

B63
GORDON L.,A NEW DEAL FOR LATIN AMERICA. L/A+17C USA+45 CULTURE NAT/G TEC/DEV DIPLOM FOR/AID REGION TASK...POLICY 20 ALL/PROG DEPT/STATE. PAGE 49 F0958 ECO/UNDEV ECO/TAC INT/ORG PLAN

B63
GRUBEL H.G.,WORLD MONETARY REFORM: PLANS AND ISSUES. FUT WOR+45 ECO/DEV ECO/UNDEV R+D DELIB/GP CREATE ECO/TAC ATTIT RIGID/FLEX WEALTH...STAT ANTHOL VAL/FREE 20. PAGE 52 F1009 FINAN INT/ORG BAL/PAY INT/TRADE

B63
HAQ M.,THE STRATEGY OF ECONOMIC PLANNING. PAKISTAN AGRI FINAN INDUS NAT/G FOR/AID TAX CONTROL REGION PRODUC...POLICY CHARTS 20. PAGE 55 F1071 ECO/TAC ECO/UNDEV PLAN PROB/SOLV

B63
HARROD R.F.,INTERNATIONAL TRADE THEORY IN A DEVELOPING WORLD. COM WOR+45 FOR/AID REGION COST DEMAND WEALTH...POLICY 20 INTL/ECON. PAGE 56 F1095 INT/TRADE BAL/PAY ECO/UNDEV METH/COMP

B63
HAUSMAN W.H.,MANAGING ECONOMIC DEVELOPMENT IN AFRICA. AFR USA+45 LAW FINAN WORKER TEC/DEV WEALTH ...ANTHOL 20. PAGE 57 F1116 ECO/UNDEV PLAN FOR/AID MGT

B63
HIRSCHMAN A.O.,JOURNEYS TOWARD PROGRESS: STUDIES OF ECONOMIC POLICYMAKING IN LATIN AMERICA. CHILE FUT ECO/UNDEV AGRI FINAN INDUS CONSULT DELIB/GP PLAN ATTIT HEALTH ORD/FREE WEALTH...POLICY STAT VAL/FREE COLOMB 20. PAGE 60 F1177 L/A+17C ECO/TAC BRAZIL

B63
HOLLAND E.P.,EXPERIMENTS ON A SIMULATED UNDERDEVELOPED ECONOMY: DEVELOPMENT PLANS AND BALANCE-OF-PAYMENTS POLICIES. WOR+45 ECO/UNDEV FINAN PLAN ECO/TAC...MATH STAT CHARTS SIMUL VAL/FREE. PAGE 61 F1196 AFR BAL/PAY

B63
HYDE D.,THE PEACEFUL ASSAULT. COM UAR USSR ECO/DEV ECO/UNDEV NAT/G POL/PAR CAP/ISM PWR 20. PAGE 64 F1256 MARXISM CONTROL ECO/TAC DIPLOM

B63
IANNI O.,INDUSTRIALIZACAO E DESENVOLVIMENTO SOCIAL NO BRASIL. BRAZIL L/A+17C STRATA STRUCT ECO/UNDEV EDU/PROP LEAD LOBBY NAT/LISM 20. PAGE 64 F1257 WORKER GP/REL INDUS PARTIC

B63
INTERNATIONAL ASSOCIATION RES,AFRICAN STUDIES IN INCOME AND WEALTH. AFR NAT/G PROB/SOLV DEMAND INCOME...ECOMETRIC METH/COMP 20. PAGE 64 F1270 WEALTH PLAN ECO/UNDEV BUDGET

B63
INTERNATIONAL BANK RECONST DEV,THE WORLD BANK GROUP IN ASIA. ASIA S/ASIA INDUS TEC/DEV ECO/TAC...RECORD 20 IBRD WORLD/BANK. PAGE 65 F1273 INT/ORG DIPLOM ECO/UNDEV FINAN

B63
INTERNATIONAL MONETARY FUND,COMPENSATORY FINANCING OF EXPORT FLUCTUATIONS (PAMPHLET). WOR+45 ECO/DEV ECO/UNDEV INT/ORG WEALTH...TREND 20 IMF MONEY. PAGE 65 F1281 BAL/PAY FINAN BUDGET INT/TRADE

B63
ISSAWI C.,EGYPT IN REVOLUTION: AN ECONOMIC ANALYSIS. ISLAM STRUCT ECO/UNDEV AGRI FINAN INDUS PLAN EXEC REV NAT/LISM ATTIT RIGID/FLEX WEALTH SOCISM...STAT FOR/TRADE WORK 20. PAGE 66 F1292 NAT/G UAR

B63
KAPP W.K.,HINDU CULTURE: ECONOMIC DEVELOPMENT AND ECONOMIC PLANNING IN INDIA. INDIA S/ASIA CULTURE ECO/TAC EDU/PROP ADMIN ALL/VALS...POLICY MGT TIME/SEQ TRUE/GP VAL/FREE 20. PAGE 69 F1353 SECT ECO/UNDEV

B63
KATZ S.M.,A SELECTED LIST OF US READINGS ON DEVELOPMENT. AGRI COM/IND DIST/IND INDUS LABOR PLAN FOR/AID EDU/PROP HEALTH...POLICY SOC/WK 20. PAGE 69 F1361 BIBLIOG/A ECO/UNDEV TEC/DEV ACT/RES

B63
LAGOS G.,INTERNATIONAL STRATIFICATION AND UNDERDEVELOPED COUNTRIES. L/A+17C WOR+45 PLAN ECO/TAC PWR RESPECT WEALTH...METH/CNCPT STAT CHARTS SIMUL GEN/LAWS TRUE/GP METH/GP VAL/FREE 20. PAGE 74 F1459 ECO/UNDEV STRATA

B63
LANGE O.,ECONOMIC DEVELOPMENT, PLANNING, AND INTERNATIONAL COOPERATION. UAR WOR+45 FINAN CAP/ISM PERS/REL 20. PAGE 75 F1476 ECO/UNDEV DIPLOM INT/TRADE PLAN

B63
LEWIS G.K.,PUERTO RICO: FREEDOM AND POWER IN THE CARIBBEAN. PUERT/RICO USA+45 CULTURE STRUCT INDUS POL/PAR WORKER EDU/PROP CATHISM 20. PAGE 79 F1548 ECO/UNDEV COLONIAL NAT/LISM GEOG

B63
MAIZELS A.,INDUSTRIAL GROWTH AND WORLD TRADE. FUT WOR+45 ECO/DEV FINAN INT/ORG PLAN TEC/DEV ECO/TAC WEALTH...MATH STAT CHARTS VAL/FREE 19/20. PAGE 84 F1642 INDUS ECO/UNDEV INT/TRADE

B63
MANGER W.,THE ALLIANCE FOR PROGRESS: A CRITICAL APPRAISAL. FUT L/A+17C USA+45 CULTURE ECO/UNDEV ACADEM NAT/G SCHOOL PLAN FOR/AID...POLICY OAS ALL/PROG. PAGE 84 F1651 DIPLOM INT/ORG ECO/TAC REGION

B63
MARITANO N.,AN ALLIANCE FOR PROGRESS. FUT L/A+17C USA+45 CULTURE ECO/UNDEV NAT/G PLAN CONTROL ...POLICY ALL/PROG. PAGE 85 F1669 DIPLOM INT/ORG ECO/TAC FOR/AID

B63
MEIER G.,INTERNATIONAL TRADE AND DEVELOPMENT. FINAN BAL/PAY COST DEMAND DISCRIM EQUILIB WEALTH...POLICY ECOMETRIC MATH STAT BIBLIOG/A 20. PAGE 89 F1747 ECO/UNDEV ECO/TAC INT/TRADE IDEA/COMP

B63
MENEZES A.J.,SUBDESENVOLVIMENTO E POLITICA INTERNACIONAL. BRAZIL WOR+45 PLAN CONTROL LEAD NAT/LISM ORD/FREE 20 THIRD/WRLD. PAGE 90 F1759 ECO/UNDEV DIPLOM POLICY BAL/PWR

B63
NEUMARK S.D.,FOREIGN TRADE AND ECONOMIC DEVELOPMENT IN AFRICA: A HISTORICAL PERSPECTIVE. EUR+WWI MOD/EUR ECO/UNDEV AGRI COM/IND EXTR/IND PROC/MFG SKILL WEALTH...CONCPT TIME/SEQ TREND SIMUL FOR/TRADE WORK TOT/POP TERR/GP VAL/FREE 19/20. PAGE 98 F1916 AFR

B63
OECD,FOOD AID: ITS ROLE IN ECONOMIC DEVELOPMENT. FINAN NAT/G PLAN DIPLOM GIVE TASK WEALTH ...METH/COMP METH 20. PAGE 100 F1966 ECO/UNDEV FOR/AID INT/ORG POLICY

B63
OTERO L.M.,HONDURAS. HONDURAS SPAIN STRUCT SECT COLONIAL REV WAR ATTIT PWR...GEOG WORSHIP 16/20. PAGE 102 F2003 NAT/G SOCIETY NAT/LISM ECO/UNDEV

B63
PAN AMERICAN UNION,THE EFFECTS OF THE EUROPEAN ECONOMIC COMMUNITY ON THE LATIN AMERICAN ECONOMIES (BMR). EUR+WWI L/A+17C ECO/UNDEV AGRI INDUS MARKET REGION 20 EEC TREATY. PAGE 103 F2024 INT/TRADE INT/ORG AGREE POLICY

B63
PREST A.R.,PUBLIC FINANCE IN UNDERDEVELOPED COUNTRIES. UK WOR+45 WOR-45 SOCIETY INT/ORG NAT/G LEGIS ACT/RES PLAN ECO/TAC ADMIN ROUTINE...CHARTS 20. PAGE 108 F2115 FINAN ECO/UNDEV NIGERIA

B63
RANGEL I.,A INFLACAO BRASILEIRA (2ND ED.). AFR BRAZIL AGRI INDUS MARKET INT/TRADE DEMAND EQUILIB ATTIT 20. PAGE 109 F2144 ECO/UNDEV FINAN PRICE TAX

B63
RAO V.K.R.,FOREIGN AID AND INDIA'S ECONOMIC DEVELOPMENT. INDIA INT/ORG PROB/SOLV TEC/DEV ECO/TAC CONTROL WEALTH...TREND 20. PAGE 109 F2148 FOR/AID ECO/UNDEV RECEIVE DIPLOM

B63
SALANT W.S.,THE UNITED STATES BALANCE OF PAYMENTS IN 1968. USA+45 ECO/DEV ECO/UNDEV INT/ORG DELIB/GP ECO/TAC...POLICY STAT SIMUL 20. PAGE 115 F2273 FUT FINAN BAL/PAY

B63
STIFEL L.D.,THE TEXTILE INDUSTRY - A CASE STUDY OF INDUSTRIAL DEVELOPMENT IN THE PHILIPPINES (PAPER). PHILIPPINE WORKER CAP/ISM INT/TRADE TARIFFS RECEIVE PRICE ADMIN COST EFFICIENCY WEALTH...BIBLIOG 20. PAGE 126 F2486 S/ASIA ECO/UNDEV PROC/MFG NAT/G

B63
TREVES G.,GOVERNMENT ORGANIZATION FOR ECONOMIC DEVELOPMENT (PAMPHLET). WOR+45 LAW BUDGET ECO/TAC GOV/REL...DECISION 20. PAGE 131 F2585 ECO/DEV ECO/UNDEV PLAN POLICY

B63
UN FAO,BIBLIOGRAPHY ON THE ANALYSIS AND PROJECTION OF DEMAND AND PRODUCTION, 1963. WOR+45 ECO/DEV ECO/UNDEV...PREDICT TREND 20. PAGE 132 F2601 BIBLIOG/A AGRI INDUS

B63
UN SECRETARY GENERAL,PLANNING FOR ECONOMIC DEVELOPMENT. ECO/UNDEV FINAN BUDGET INT/TRADE TARIFFS TAX ADMIN 20 UN. PAGE 132 F2603 PLAN ECO/TAC MGT NAT/COMP

B63
UNITED NATIONS,THE GROWTH OF WORLD INDUSTRY, 1938-1961: NATIONAL TABLES. WOR+45 STRUCT ECO/DEV ECO/UNDEV NAT/G COST...CHARTS UN. PAGE 132 F2613 STAT INDUS PRODUC ORD/FREE

B63
US AGENCY INTERNATIONAL DEV,OPERATIONS REPORT - 1963. AFR ASIA L/A+17C USA+45 ECO/UNDEV FINAN INT/ORG NAT/G. PAGE 134 F2637 FOR/AID CHARTS STAT BUDGET

B63
US ECON SURVEY TEAM INDONESIA,INDONESIA - PERSPECTIVE AND PROPOSALS FOR UNITED STATES ECONOMIC AID. INDONESIA AGRI MARKET TEC/DEV DIPLOM INT/TRADE EDU/PROP 20. PAGE 136 F2678
FOR/AID ECO/UNDEV PLAN INDUS

B63
VELEZ GARCIA J.,DEVALUACION 1962; HISTORIA DOCUMENTAL DE UN PROCESO ECONOMICO. AFR L/A+17C USA+45 FINAN FOR/AID PRODUC WEALTH...POLICY STAT CHARTS ANTHOL 20 COLOMB. PAGE 141 F2774
ECO/UNDEV ECO/TAC PLAN NAT/G

B63
WAGLEY C.,INTRODUCTION TO BRAZIL. BRAZIL L/A+17C FAM KIN SCHOOL SECT ATTIT WEALTH...GEOG SOC. PAGE 142 F2799
ECO/UNDEV ELITES HABITAT STRATA

B63
WALINSKY L.J.,PLANNING AND EXECUTION OF ECONOMIC DEVELOPMENT. PROB/SOLV TEC/DEV BUDGET COST WEALTH ...CHARTS BIBLIOG 20. PAGE 142 F2802
PLAN ECO/UNDEV ECO/TAC OPTIMAL

B63
WIGHTMAN D.,TOWARD ECONOMIC CO-OPERATION IN ASIA. ASIA S/ASIA VOL/ASSN ACT/RES PLAN TEC/DEV ECO/TAC EDU/PROP RIGID/FLEX SKILL...POLICY METH/CNCPT OBS INT GEN/LAWS UN 20 ECAFE. PAGE 146 F2877
ECO/UNDEV CREATE

L63
MOUSKHELY M.,"LE BLOC COMMUNISTE ET LA COMMUNAUTE ECONOMIQUE EUROPEENNE." AFR COM EUR+WWI FUT USSR WOR+45 INTELL ECO/UNDEV LABOR POL/PAR NUC/PWR RIGID/FLEX...TIME/SEQ ORG/CHARTS EEC TOT/POP 20. PAGE 94 F1849
INT/ORG ECO/DEV

L63
NASH M.,"PSYCHO-CULTURAL FACTORS IN ASIAN ECONOMIC GROWTH." ASIA ISLAM S/ASIA CULTURE ECO/UNDEV DELIB/GP EDU/PROP COERCE ATTIT PERSON HEALTH KNOWL ORD/FREE...PSY SOC STAT TREND ANTHOL VAL/FREE 20. PAGE 96 F1893
SOCIETY ECO/TAC

L63
OLSON M. JR.,"RAPID ECONOMIC GROWTH AS A DESTABILIZING FORCE." WOR+45 WOR-45 STRATA ECO/UNDEV FAM KIN CREATE TEC/DEV DIPLOM PEACE ATTIT PERSON RIGID/FLEX PWR RESPECT WEALTH...SOC 20. PAGE 101 F1989
SOCIETY FOR/AID

L63
RIDAH A.,"LE NEO-DESTOUR DEPUIS L'INDEPENDANCE." FUT ISLAM WOR+45 ECO/UNDEV INT/ORG SCHOOL DELIB/GP TOP/EX ACT/RES EDU/PROP LEGIT ATTIT ALL/VALS 20 TUNIS. PAGE 111 F2189
NAT/G CONSTN

S63
ARDANT G.,"A PLAN FOR FULL EMPLOYMENT IN THE DEVELOPING COUNTRIES." AFR FUT WOR+45 DELIB/GP ACT/RES PLAN ECO/TAC ATTIT ALL/VALS...POLICY STAT CHARTS TUNIS VAL/FREE 20. PAGE 6 F0112
ECO/UNDEV SOCIETY MOROCCO

S63
AYAL E.B.,"VALUE SYSTEM AND ECONOMIC DEVELOPMENT IN JAPAN AND THAILAND." ASIA S/ASIA THAILAND CULTURE ECO/DEV CAP/ISM DOMIN NAT/LISM DRIVE RIGID/FLEX SOCISM...WELF/ST OBS TREND CON/ANAL GEN/LAWS TERR/GP 20 CHINJAP. PAGE 8 F0145
ECO/UNDEV ALL/VALS

S63
BARANSON J.,"ECONOMIC AND SOCIAL CONSIDERATIONS IN ADAPTING TECHNOLOGIES FOR DEVELOPING COUNTRIES." WOR+45 PLAN WEALTH...TECHNIC SOC 20. PAGE 10 F0180
ECO/UNDEV TEC/DEV

S63
BARZANSKI S.,"REGIONAL UNDERDEVELOPMENT IN THE EUROPEAN ECONOMIC COMMUNITY." EUR+WWI ELITES DIST/IND MARKET VOL/ASSN CONSULT EX/STRUC ECO/TAC RIGID/FLEX WEALTH EEC OEEC 20. PAGE 11 F0202
ECO/UNDEV PLAN

S63
BEGUIN H.,"ASPECTS STRUCTURELS DU COMMERCE EXTERIEUR DES PAYS SOUS-DEVELOPPES." FUT WOR+45 STRUCT FINAN SERV/IND POL/PAR TEC/DEV PERCEPT WEALTH FOR/TRADE 20. PAGE 12 F0229
MARKET ECO/UNDEV FOR/AID

S63
CARTER A.G.T.,"THE BALANCE OF PAYMENTS OF EAST AFRICA" AFR ECO/TAC FOR/AID RATION TARIFFS TAX ADMIN...STAT 20 AFRICA/E. PAGE 22 F0423
BUDGET ECO/UNDEV BAL/PAY INT/TRADE

S63
CLARK P.G.,"TOWARDS MORE COMPREHENSIVE PLANNING IN EAST AFRICA" AFR OP/RES ECO/TAC RATION TAX EFFICIENCY INCOME...MATH TREND CHARTS 20 AFRICA/E. PAGE 25 F0484
ECO/UNDEV PLAN STAT METH/COMP

S63
DE FOREST J.D.,"LOW LEVELS OF TECHNOLOGY AND ECONOMIC DEVELOPMENT PROSPECTS." WOR+45 WOR-45 CULTURE ACT/RES CREATE PLAN ECO/TAC ROUTINE PERCEPT WEALTH...METH/CNCPT GEN/LAWS 20. PAGE 31 F0597
ECO/UNDEV TEC/DEV

S63
DELWERT J.,"L'ECONOMIE CAMBODGIENNE ET SON EVOLUTION ACTUELLE." FUT S/ASIA ECO/UNDEV ACT/RES PLAN WEALTH...CONCPT OBS TIME/SEQ TREND 20. PAGE 32 F0617
FINAN ATTIT CAMBODIA

S63
DUCROS B.,"MOBILISATION DES RESSOURCES PRODUCTIVES ET DEVELOPPEMENT." FUT INTELL SOCIETY COM/IND DIST/IND EXTR/IND FINAN INDUS ROUTINE WEALTH ...METH/CNCPT OBS 20. PAGE 34 F0670
ECO/UNDEV TEC/DEV

S63
EMERSON R.,"THE ATLANTIC COMMUNITY AND THE EMERGING COUNTRIES." FUT WOR+45 ECO/DEV ECO/UNDEV R+D NAT/G DELIB/GP BAL/PWR ECO/TAC EDU/PROP ROUTINE ORD/FREE PWR WEALTH...POLICY CONCPT TREND GEN/METH EEC 20 NATO. PAGE 37 F0729
ATTIT INT/TRADE

S63
ETHERINGTON D.M.,"LAND RESETTLEMENT IN KENYA; POLICY AND PRACTICE" AFR TEC/DEV ECO/TAC FOR/AID TAX PRODUC...CHARTS 20. PAGE 39 F0752
ECO/UNDEV AGRI WORKER PLAN

S63
GALENSON W.,"ECONOMIC DEVELOPMENT AND THE SECTORAL EXPANSION OF EMPLOYMENT, INT." FUT WOR+45 ECO/UNDEV DIST/IND PROC/MFG SERV/IND ACT/RES HEALTH SKILL WEALTH...STAT TIME/SEQ VAL/FREE 20. PAGE 46 F0889
INDUS ECO/TAC

S63
GANDILHON J.,"LA SCIENCE ET LA TECHNIQUE A L'AIDE DES REGIONS PEU DEVELOPPEES." FRANCE FUT WOR+45 ECO/DEV R+D PROF/ORG ACT/RES PLAN...MGT TOT/POP VAL/FREE 20 UN. PAGE 46 F0893
ECO/UNDEV TEC/DEV FOR/AID

S63
GANDOLFI A.,"LES ACCORDS DE COOPERATION EN MATIERE DE POLITIQUE ETRANGERE ENTRE LA FRANCE ET LES NOUVEAUX ETATS AFRICAINS ET." AFR ISLAM MADAGASCAR WOR+45 ECO/DEV INT/ORG NAT/G DELIB/GP ECO/TAC ALL/VALS...CON/ANAL 20. PAGE 46 F0894
VOL/ASSN ECO/UNDEV DIPLOM FRANCE

S63
GERHARD H.,"COMMODITY TRADE STABILIZATION THROUGH INTERNATIONAL AGREEMENTS." WOR+45 ECO/DEV ECO/UNDEV NAT/G ROUTINE ORD/FREE...INT/LAW OBS TREND GEN/METH TOT/POP 20. PAGE 47 F0918
PLAN ECO/TAC INT/TRADE

S63
GORDON B.,"ECONOMIC IMPEDIMENTS TO REGIONALISM IN SOUTH EAST ASIA." BURMA FUT S/ASIA THAILAND USA+45 AGRI INDUS R+D NAT/G PLAN ECO/TAC WEALTH...STAT CONT/OBS 20. PAGE 49 F0954
VOL/ASSN ECO/UNDEV INT/TRADE REGION

S63
HOOVER C.B.,"ECONOMIC REFORM VERSUS ECONOMIC GROWTH IN UNDERDEVELOPED COUNTRIES." FUT WOR+45 ELITES STRATA ECO/UNDEV DIST/IND INDUS TEC/DEV CAP/ISM FOR/AID INT/TRADE ATTIT WEALTH...MYTH TREND STERTYP GEN/LAWS WORK 20. PAGE 61 F1209
ECO/DEV ECO/TAC

S63
LEDUC G.,"L'AIDE INTERNATIONALE AU DEVELOPPEMENT." FUT WOR+45 ECO/DEV ECO/UNDEV R+D PROF/ORG TEC/DEV ECO/TAC ROUTINE ATTIT ALL/VALS...MGT TIME/SEQ FOR/TRADE TOT/POP 20. PAGE 77 F1503
FINAN PLAN FOR/AID

S63
MIKESELL R.F.,"COMMODITY AGREEMENTS AND AID TO DEVELOPING COUNTRIES." WOR+45 WOR-45 INT/ORG ECO/TAC ATTIT WEALTH WORK FOR/TRADE 20. PAGE 91 F1782
FINAN ECO/UNDEV BAL/PAY FOR/AID

S63
MILLEN B.H.,"INTERNATIONAL TRADE AND POLITICAL INDEPENDENCE." WOR+45 ECO/DEV WEALTH...STAT CHARTS FOR/TRADE METH/GP TERR/GP VAL/FREE 20. PAGE 91 F1788
ECO/UNDEV ECO/TAC INT/TRADE

S63
NYE J.,"TANGANYIKA'S SELF-HELP." TANZANIA NAT/G GIVE COST EFFICIENCY NAT/LISM 20. PAGE 99 F1948
ECO/TAC POL/PAR ECO/UNDEV WORKER

S63
PAAUW D.S.,"ECONOMIC PROGRESS IN SOUTHEAST ASIA." S/ASIA AGRI INDUS PROC/MFG ACT/RES ECO/TAC...CHARTS VAL/FREE 20. PAGE 102 F2010
ECO/UNDEV STAT

S63
PINCUS J.,"THE COST OF FOREIGN AID." WOR+45 ECO/DEV FINAN NAT/G VOL/ASSN CREATE ECO/TAC EDU/PROP WEALTH ...METH/CNCPT STAT CHARTS HYPO/EXP TOT/POP VAL/FREE 20. PAGE 106 F2087
USA+45 ECO/UNDEV FOR/AID

S63
REDDAWAY W.B.,"THE ECONOMICS OF UNDERDEVELOPED COUNTRIES." S/ASIA WOR+45 WOR-45 STRATA AGRI COM/IND DIST/IND MARKET PROC/MFG PLAN TEC/DEV FOR/AID BAL/PAY ATTIT DRIVE SKILL WORK FOR/TRADE 20. PAGE 110 F2165
ECO/TAC ECO/UNDEV INDIA

S63
SCHURMANN F.,"ECONOMIC POLICY AND POLITICAL POWER IN COMMUNIST CHINA." ASIA CHINA/COM USSR SOCIETY ECO/UNDEV AGRI INDUS CREATE ADMIN ROUTINE ATTIT DRIVE RIGID/FLEX PWR WEALTH...HIST/WRIT TREND CHARTS WORK 20. PAGE 118 F2323
PLAN ECO/TAC

S63
TENNYSON L.B.,"THE USA IN ATLANTIC COMMUNITY." EUR+WWI FRANCE UK USA+45 ECO/UNDEV VOL/ASSN DELIB/GP TOP/EX DIPLOM DOMIN PWR...POLICY CONCPT TREND GEN/LAWS EEC 20. PAGE 129 F2545
ATTIT ECO/TAC BAL/PWR

S63
WALKER H.,"THE INTERNATIONAL LAW OF COMMODITY AGREEMENTS." FUT WOR+45 ECO/DEV ECO/UNDEV FINAN INT/ORG NAT/G CONSULT CREATE PLAN ECO/TAC ATTIT PERCEPT...CONCPT GEN/LAWS TOT/POP GATT 20. PAGE 142
MARKET VOL/ASSN INT/LAW INT/TRADE

F2804

N63
US AGENCY INTERNATIONAL DEV,PRINCIPLES OF FOREIGN ECONOMIC ASSISTANCE (PAMPHLET). USA+45 FINAN GP/REL BAL/PAY EFFICIENCY 20 AID. PAGE 134 F2638 FOR/AID PLAN ECO/UNDEV ATTIT

B64
THE SPECIAL COMMONWEALTH AFRICAN ASSISTANCE PLAN. AFR CANADA INDIA NIGERIA UK FINAN SCHOOL...CHARTS 20 COMMONWLTH. PAGE 1 F0019 ECO/UNDEV TREND FOR/AID ADMIN

B64
AHMAD M.,THE CIVIL SERVANT IN PAKISTAN. PAKISTAN ECO/UNDEV COLONIAL INGP/REL...SOC CHARTS BIBLIOG 20 CIVIL/SERV. PAGE 3 F0051 WELF/ST ADMIN ATTIT STRATA

B64
BALASSA B.,TRADE PROSPECTS FOR DEVELOPING COUNTRIES. WOR+45 ECO/DEV AGRI EXTR/IND INDUS CREATE PLAN PRICE...ECOMETRIC CLASSIF TIME/SEQ GEN/METH. PAGE 8 F0158 INT/TRADE ECO/UNDEV TREND STAT

B64
BALOGH T.,THE ECONOMIC IMPACT OF MONETARY AND COMMERCIAL INSTITUTIONS OF A EUROPEAN ORIGIN IN AFRICA. AFR UAR INDUS FOR/AID COLONIAL CONTROL ...NAT/COMP 20. PAGE 9 F0169 TEC/DEV FINAN ECO/UNDEV ECO/TAC

B64
BERRILL K.,ECONOMIC DEVELOPMENT WITH SPECIAL REFERENCE TO EAST ASIA. ASIA INDIA S/ASIA AGRI INDUS LABOR DELIB/GP PLAN INT/TRADE COST PRODUC 20 CHINJAP. PAGE 14 F0271 FINAN ECO/UNDEV INT/ORG CAP/ISM

B64
BOURGOIGNIE G.E.,JEUNE AFRIQUE MOBILISABLE; LES PROBLEMES DE LA JEUNESSE DESOEUVREE EN AFRIQUE NOIRE. INT/ORG VOL/ASSN ECO/TAC ROUTINE UTIL ATTIT 20. PAGE 17 F0324 AGE/Y AFR CREATE ECO/UNDEV

B64
BROWN C.V.,GOVERNMENT AND BANKING IN WESTERN NIGERIA. AFR NIGERIA GOV/REL GP/REL...POLICY 20. PAGE 19 F0367 ADMIN ECO/UNDEV FINAN NAT/G

B64
CALDER R.,TWO-WAY PASSAGE. INT/ORG TEC/DEV WAR PERSON ORD/FREE 20. PAGE 21 F0400 FOR/AID ECO/UNDEV ECO/TAC DIPLOM

B64
CASEY R.G.,THE FUTURE OF THE COMMONWEALTH. INDIA PAKISTAN UK ECO/UNDEV INT/ORG TEC/DEV COLONIAL SUPEGO 20 EEC AUSTRAL. PAGE 22 F0425 DIPLOM SOVEREIGN NAT/LISM FOR/AID

B64
CENTRO ESTUDIOS MONETARIOS LAT,PROBLEMAS DE PAGOS EN AMERICA LATINA. L/A+17C MARKET BUDGET ECO/TAC EFFICIENCY WEALTH 20 CENTRAL/AM. PAGE 22 F0434 FINAN INT/TRADE BAL/PAY ECO/UNDEV

B64
CEPEDE M.,POPULATION AND FOOD. USA+45 STRUCT ECO/UNDEV FAM PLAN TEC/DEV FOR/AID CONTROL...CATH SOC TREND 19/20. PAGE 22 F0436 FUT GEOG AGRI CENSUS

B64
COLUMBIA U SCHOOL OF LAW,PUBLIC INTERNATIONAL DEVELOPMENT FINANCING IN INDIA. GERMANY/W INDIA UK USA+45 INDUS PLAN TEC/DEV DIPLOM ECO/TAC GIVE ADMIN UTIL ATTIT 20. PAGE 26 F0512 ECO/UNDEV FINAN FOR/AID INT/ORG

B64
COMPOS R.O.,A MOEDA, O GOVERNO E O TEMPO. AFR BRAZIL WOR+45 FINAN TEC/DEV FOR/AID REGION DEMAND ...ANTHOL 20. PAGE 27 F0520 ECO/UNDEV PLAN DIPLOM INT/TRADE

B64
FATOUROS A.A.,CANADA'S OVERSEAS AID. CANADA WOR+45 ECO/DEV FINAN NAT/G BUDGET ECO/TAC CONFER ADMIN 20. PAGE 39 F0768 FOR/AID DIPLOM ECO/UNDEV POLICY

B64
FEI J.C.H.,DEVELOPMENT OF THE LABOR SURPLUS ECONOMY: THEORY AND POLICY. WOR+45 AGRI INDUS MARKET PROB/SOLV TEC/DEV...STAT CHARTS GEN/LAWS METH 20 THIRD/WRLD. PAGE 40 F0772 ECO/TAC POLICY WORKER ECO/UNDEV

B64
FEIS H.,FOREIGN AID AND FOREIGN POLICY. USA+45 WOR+45 NAT/G VOL/ASSN ACT/RES TEC/DEV ATTIT HEALTH WEALTH...SOC GEN/LAWS 20. PAGE 40 F0775 ECO/UNDEV ECO/TAC FOR/AID DIPLOM

B64
FLORENCE P.S.,ECONOMICS AND SOCIOLOGY OF INDUSTRY; A REALISTIC ANALYSIS OF DEVELOPMENT. ECO/UNDEV LG/CO NAT/G PLAN...GEOG MGT BIBLIOG 20. PAGE 42 F0814 INDUS SOC ADMIN

B64
HALLOWELL J.H.,DEVELOPMENT: FOR WHAT. WOR+45 POL/PAR SECT FOR/AID INT/TRADE CT/SYS PARTIC PRODUC PLURISM. PAGE 54 F1052 ECO/UNDEV CONSTN NAT/LISM ECO/TAC

B64
HAMBRIDGE G.,DYNAMICS OF DEVELOPMENT. AGRI FINAN INDUS LABOR INT/TRADE EDU/PROP ADMIN LEAD OWN HEALTH...ANTHOL BIBLIOG 20. PAGE 54 F1054 ECO/UNDEV ECO/TAC OP/RES ACT/RES

B64
HARBISON F.H.,EDUCATION, MANPOWER, AND ECONOMIC GROWTH. WOR+45 ECO/DEV ECO/UNDEV ACADEM LABOR SCHOOL WORKER UTIL...IDEA/COMP NAT/COMP. PAGE 55 F1075 PLAN TEC/DEV EDU/PROP SKILL

B64
HAZLEWOOD A.,THE ECONOMICS OF DEVELOPMENT: AN ANNOTATED LIST OF BOOKS AND ARTICLES PUBLISHED 1958-1962. AGRI FINAN INDUS LABOR NAT/G DIPLOM INT/TRADE INCOME...MGT 20. PAGE 58 F1130 BIBLIOG/A ECO/UNDEV TEC/DEV

B64
HEKHUIS D.J.,INTERNATIONAL STABILITY: MILITARY, ECONOMIC AND POLITICAL DIMENSIONS. FUT WOR+45 LAW ECO/UNDEV INT/ORG NAT/G VOL/ASSN FORCES ACT/RES BAL/PWR PWR WEALTH...STAT UN 20. PAGE 58 F1143 TEC/DEV DETER REGION

B64
HERSKOVITS M.J.,ECONOMIC TRANSITION IN AFRICA. FUT INT/ORG NAT/G WORKER PROB/SOLV TEC/DEV INT/TRADE EQUILIB INCOME...ANTHOL 20. PAGE 59 F1157 AFR ECO/UNDEV PLAN ADMIN

B64
HINSHAW R.,THE EUROPEAN COMMUNITY AND AMERICAN TRADE: A STUDY IN ATLANTIC ECONOMICS AND POLICY. EUR+WWI UK USA+45 ECO/DEV ECO/UNDEV AGRI INDUS INT/ORG NAT/G ECO/TAC TARIFFS REGION...STAT CHARTS EEC 20. PAGE 60 F1174 MARKET TREND INT/TRADE

B64
HUTT W.H.,THE ECONOMICS OF THE COLOUR BAR. SOUTH/AFR EXTR/IND LABOR ADJUD NEGRO. PAGE 64 F1251 INDUS DISCRIM RACE/REL ECO/UNDEV

B64
INTERNATIONAL LABOUR OFFICE,EMPLOYMENT AND ECONOMIC GROWTH. ECO/DEV ECO/UNDEV NAT/G PLAN DIPLOM INT/TRADE CONTROL INCOME PRODUC WEALTH...STAT NAT/COMP 20 ILO. PAGE 65 F1279 WORKER METH/COMP ECO/TAC OPTIMAL

B64
INTL INF CTR LOCAL CREDIT,GOVERNMENT MEASURES FOR THE PROMOTION OF REGIONAL ECONOMIC DEVELOPMENT. WOR+45 ECO/UNDEV FINAN INT/ORG DIPLOM ORD/FREE ...POLICY GEOG 20. PAGE 65 F1285 FOR/AID PLAN ECO/TAC REGION

B64
JUCKER-FLEETWOOD E.,MONEY AND FINANCE IN AFRICA. ISLAM ECO/UNDEV SERV/IND NAT/G EX/STRUC PLAN ECO/TAC ROUTINE WEALTH...MGT TOT/POP 20. PAGE 68 F1344 AFR FINAN

B64
KALDOR N.,ESSAYS ON ECONOMIC POLICY (VOL. II). CHILE GERMANY INDIA FINAN...GOV/COMP METH/COMP 20 KEYNES/JM. PAGE 69 F1348 BAL/PAY INT/TRADE METH/CNCPT ECO/UNDEV

B64
KEMP M.C.,THE PURE THEORY OF INTERNATIONAL TRADE. WOR+45 WOR-45 ECO/DEV ECO/UNDEV DIST/IND ECO/TAC ...MATH CON/ANAL CHARTS VAL/FREE. PAGE 70 F1374 FINAN CREATE INT/TRADE

B64
KNIGHT R.,BIBLIOGRAPHY ON INCOME AND WEALTH, 1957-1960 (VOL VIII). WOR+45 ECO/DEV FINAN INT/TRADE...GOV/COMP METH/COMP. PAGE 72 F1412 BIBLIOG/A ECO/UNDEV WEALTH INCOME

B64
KUZNETS S.,POSTWAR ECONOMIC GROWTH: FOUR LECTURES. WOR+45 INDUS NAT/G WORKER TEC/DEV ECO/TAC RATION TARIFFS PRICE BAL/PAY COST DEMAND 20. PAGE 74 F1455 ECO/DEV ECO/UNDEV TREND FINAN

B64
LETICHE J.M.,A HISTORY OF RUSSIAN ECONOMIC THOUGHT: NINTH THROUGH EIGHTEENTH CENTURIES. RUSSIA FINAN SECT CAP/ISM DOMIN DEMAND EFFICIENCY OWN MARXISM ...TECHNIC ANTHOL BIBLIOG 9/18. PAGE 78 F1536 ECO/TAC TIME/SEQ IDEA/COMP ECO/UNDEV

B64
LEWIN P.,THE FOREIGN TRADE OF COMMUNIST CHINA* ITS IMPACT ON THE FREE WORLD. AFR EUR+WWI L/A+17C S/ASIA ECO/UNDEV CREATE FOR/AID...STAT NET/THEORY TREND CHARTS. PAGE 79 F1546 ASIA INT/TRADE NAT/COMP USSR

B64
LI C.M.,INDUSTRIAL DEVELOPMENT IN COMMUNIST CHINA. CHINA/COM ECO/DEV ECO/UNDEV AGRI FINAN INDUS MARKET LABOR NAT/G ECO/TAC INT/TRADE EXEC ALL/VALS ...POLICY RELATIV TREND WORK TOT/POP VAL/FREE 20. PAGE 79 F1556 ASIA TEC/DEV

B64
LINDHOLM R.W.,ECONOMIC DEVELOPMENT POLICY WITH EMPHASIS ON VIET-NAM. KOREA/S PAKISTAN VIETNAM/S AGRI INDUS CONSULT DELIB/GP FOR/AID...METH 20. PAGE 80 F1571 ECO/UNDEV TAX FINAN ECO/TAC

B64
LITTLE I.M.D.,AID TO AFRICA. AFR UK TEC/DEV DIPLOM ECO/TAC INCOME WEALTH 20. PAGE 81 F1583 FOR/AID ECO/UNDEV ADMIN POLICY

B64
LUTHULI A.,AFRICA'S FREEDOM. KIN LABOR POL/PAR SCHOOL DIPLOM NEUTRAL REGION REV NAT/LISM PWR WEALTH SOCISM SOC/INTEG 20. PAGE 82 F1608
AFR ECO/UNDEV COLONIAL

B64
MAGALHAES S.,PRATICA DA EMANCIPACAO NACIONAL. L/A+17C INDUS PLAN ECO/TAC CONTROL NAT/LISM ORD/FREE. PAGE 84 F1640
BAL/PAY ECO/UNDEV DIPLOM WEALTH

B64
MASON E.S.,FOREIGN AID AND FOREIGN POLICY. USA+45 AGRI INDUS NAT/G EX/STRUC ACT/RES RIGID/FLEX ALL/VALS...POLICY GEN/LAWS MARSHL/PLN ALL/PROG CONGRESS 20. PAGE 87 F1699
ECO/UNDEV ECO/TAC FOR/AID DIPLOM

B64
MAZA ZAVALA D.F.,VENEZUELA; UNA ECONOMIA DEPENDIENTE. L/A+17C VENEZUELA FINAN INDUS ...ECOMETRIC STAT TREND 20. PAGE 87 F1710
ECO/UNDEV BAL/PAY INT/TRADE PRICE

B64
MELADY T.,FACES OF AFRICA. AFR FUT ISLAM NAT/G POL/PAR SCHOOL DELIB/GP PLAN ECO/TAC EDU/PROP ATTIT ALL/VALS...CHARTS TOT/POP TERR/GP VAL/FREE 20. PAGE 89 F1752
ECO/UNDEV TREND NAT/LISM

B64
MYINT H.,THE ECONOMICS OF THE DEVELOPING COUNTRIES. WOR+45 AGRI PLAN COST...POLICY GEOG 20 MONEY. PAGE 96 F1878
ECO/UNDEV INT/TRADE EXTR/IND FINAN

B64
NATIONAL COUN APPLIED ECO RES,A STRATEGY FOR THE FOURTH PLAN. INDIA DIST/IND EXTR/IND SERV/IND ECO/TAC RATION EDU/PROP EATING HEALTH...CHARTS 20. PAGE 97 F1900
ECO/UNDEV PLAN AGRI WORKER

B64
NEHEMKIS P.,LATIN AMERICA: MYTH AND REALITY. INDUS INT/ORG PROB/SOLV CAP/ISM DIPLOM REV...SOC MUNICH 20. PAGE 97 F1907
REGION MYTH L/A+17C ECO/UNDEV

B64
NEWCOMER H.A.,INTERNATIONAL AIDS TO OVERSEAS INVESTMENTS AND TRADE. ECO/UNDEV TARIFFS PROFIT ...BIBLIOG 20 GATT UN. PAGE 98 F1921
INT/TRADE FINAN DIPLOM FOR/AID

B64
NOVACK D.E.,DEVELOPMENT AND SOCIETY; THE DYNAMICS OF ECONOMIC CHANGE. WOR+45 STRATA STRUCT ECO/TAC CONTROL CROWD REV GP/REL ADJUST PRODUC WEALTH PSY. PAGE 99 F1940
SOCIETY CULTURE SOC ECO/UNDEV

B64
ODEH H.S.,THE IMPACT OF INFLATION ON THE LEVEL OF ECONOMIC ACTIVITY. AFR BRAZIL CHILE BUDGET GOV/REL COST DEMAND INCOME WEALTH...STAT METH 20 MONEY. PAGE 100 F1963
ECOMETRIC ECO/TAC ECO/UNDEV FINAN

B64
OECD,DEVELOPMENT ASSISTANCE EFFORTS - POLICIES OF THE MEMBERS. AGRI INDUS BUDGET...GEOG NAT/COMP 20 OECD. PAGE 100 F1967
INT/ORG FOR/AID ECO/UNDEV TEC/DEV

B64
OECD,THE FLOW OF FINANCIAL RESOURCES TO LESS DEVELOPED COUNTRIES 1956-1963. WOR+45 FINAN CAP/ISM ...POLICY STAT 20. PAGE 100 F1968
FOR/AID BUDGET INT/ORG ECO/UNDEV

B64
ORGANIZATION AMERICAN STATES,ECONOMIC SURVEY OF LATIN AMERICA, 1962. L/A+17C AGRI DIST/IND INDUS MARKET PROC/MFG R+D PLAN TEC/DEV ECO/TAC REGION BAL/PAY ALL/VALS...CON/ANAL ORG/CHARTS GEN/METH OAS ALL/PROG 20 ALL/PROG. PAGE 102 F1998
ECO/UNDEV CHARTS

B64
PAWERA J.C.,ALGERIA'S INFRASTRUCTURE. ALGERIA PLAN WEALTH...METH/CNCPT 20. PAGE 104 F2041
ECO/UNDEV INDUS TEC/DEV COM/IND

B64
PENNOCK J.R.,SELF-GOVERNMENT IN MODERNIZING NATIONS. AFR COM USA+45 ECO/DEV POL/PAR PROB/SOLV DIPLOM ECO/TAC COLONIAL REV POPULISM SOCISM 20. PAGE 105 F2058
ECO/UNDEV POLICY SOVEREIGN NAT/G

B64
POWELSON J.P.,LATIN AMERICA: TODAY'S ECONOMIC AND SOCIAL REVOLUTION. L/A+17C INTELL SOCIETY STRUCT AGRI INDUS NAT/G DIPLOM ECO/TAC REV...POLICY 20. PAGE 107 F2110
ECO/UNDEV WEALTH ADJUST PLAN

B64
RAMAZANI R.K.,THE MIDDLE EAST AND THE EUROPEAN COMMON MARKET. EUR+WWI ISLAM ECO/DEV EXTR/IND MARKET PROC/MFG INT/ORG NAT/G TEC/DEV ECO/TAC REGION DRIVE WEALTH...STAT CHARTS EEC TOT/POP 20. PAGE 109 F2141
ECO/UNDEV ATTIT INT/TRADE

B64
RANIS G.,THE UNITED STATES AND THE DEVELOPING ECONOMIES. COM USA+45 AGRI FINAN TEC/DEV CAP/ISM ECO/TAC INT/TRADE...POLICY METH/COMP ANTHOL 20 AID. PAGE 109 F2145
ECO/UNDEV DIPLOM FOR/AID

B64
RENO P.,THE ORDEAL OF BRITISH GUIANA. L/A+17C USA+45 STRUCT AGRI EXTR/IND INDUS NAT/G FOR/AID ORD/FREE...GEOG 20 GUIANA/BR INTRVN/ECO. PAGE 111 F2178
COLONIAL ECO/UNDEV SOCISM PWR

B64
RIVKIN A.,AFRICA AND THE EUROPEAN COMMON MARKET (PAMPHLET). AFR MOD/EUR WOR+45 TEC/DEV FOR/AID TARIFFS BAL/PAY...POLICY 20 EEC. PAGE 111 F2196
INT/ORG INT/TRADE ECO/TAC ECO/UNDEV

B64
ROBINSON E.A.G.,ECONOMIC DEVELOPMENT FOR AFRICA SOUTH OF THE SAHARA. AFR AGRI INDUS LABOR BUDGET INT/TRADE PRICE...POLICY GEOG ANTHOL 20. PAGE 113 F2219
ECO/UNDEV ECO/TAC ACT/RES PLAN

B64
SAKAI R.K.,STUDIES ON ASIA, 1964. ASIA CHINA/COM ISRAEL MALAYSIA S/ASIA USA+45 USSR ECO/UNDEV FAM POL/PAR SECT CONSULT NAT/LISM...POLICY SOC 20 CHINJAP. PAGE 115 F2272
PWR DIPLOM

B64
SCHULTZ T.W.,TRANSFORMING TRADITIONAL AGRICULTURE. WOR+45 WOR-45 CULTURE STRATA FINAN ACT/RES ECO/TAC ATTIT KNOWL SKILL...MATH STAT TIME/SEQ GEN/LAWS VAL/FREE. PAGE 117 F2316
AGRI ECO/UNDEV

B64
SINGER H.W.,INTERNATIONAL DEVELOPMENT: GROWTH AND CHANGE. AFR BRAZIL L/A+17C WOR+45 CULTURE AGRI INDUS NAT/G ACT/RES ECO/TAC EDU/PROP WEALTH...GEOG CONCPT METH/CNCPT STAT HYPO/EXP WORK TOT/POP 20. PAGE 122 F2412
FINAN ECO/UNDEV FOR/AID INT/TRADE

B64
SULLIVAN G.,THE STORY OF THE PEACE CORPS. USA+45 WOR+45 INTELL FACE/GP NAT/G SCHOOL VOL/ASSN CONSULT EX/STRUC PLAN EDU/PROP ADMIN ATTIT DRIVE ALL/VALS ...POLICY HEAL SOC CONCPT INT QU BIOG TREND SOC/EXP WORK. PAGE 127 F2511
INT/ORG ECO/UNDEV FOR/AID PEACE

B64
TAX S.,EL CAPITALISMO DEL CENTAVO; UNA ECONOMIA INDIGENA DE GUATEMALA (2 VOLS.). GUATEMALA L/A+17C SOCIETY GP/REL DEMAND INCOME HABITAT...SOC MUNICH 20 INDIAN/AM. PAGE 129 F2539
ECO/UNDEV AGRI WEALTH COST

B64
THAILAND NATIONAL ECO DEV,THE NATIONAL ECONOMIC DEVELOPMENT PLAN: 1961-66: SECOND PHASE 1964-66. THAILAND AGRI FINAN BUDGET EFFICIENCY INCOME...STAT CHARTS 20. PAGE 129 F2547
ECO/UNDEV ECO/TAC PLAN NAT/G

B64
TINBERGEN J.,CENTRAL PLANNING. COM INTELL ECO/DEV ECO/UNDEV FINAN INT/ORG PROB/SOLV ECO/TAC CONTROL EXEC ROUTINE DECISION. PAGE 130 F2576
PLAN INDUS MGT CENTRAL

B64
TONG T.,UNITED STATES DIPLOMACY IN CHINA, 1844-1860. ASIA USA-45 ECO/UNDEV ECO/TAC COERCE GP/REL...INT/LAW 19 TREATY. PAGE 131 F2581
DIPLOM INT/TRADE COLONIAL

B64
URQUIDI V.L.,THE CHALLENGE OF DEVELOPMENT IN LATIN AMERICA. L/A+17C FINAN INT/ORG TEC/DEV DIPLOM INT/TRADE PRICE REGION PRODUC...CHARTS 20 ALL/PROG. PAGE 133 F2628
ECO/UNDEV ECO/TAC NAT/G TREND

B64
US AGENCY INTERNATIONAL DEV,A.I.D. PROJECTS IN FISCAL YEAR 1963: BY COUNTRY AND FIELD OF ACTIVITY. USA+45 ECO/UNDEV ECO/TAC EDU/PROP GOV/REL...CHARTS 20 AID. PAGE 134 F2639
FINAN FOR/AID COST STAT

B64
US CONGRESS JOINT ECO COMM,PRIVATE INVESTMENT IN LATIN AMERICA. L/A+17C USA+45 INT/ORG PROB/SOLV ECO/TAC ATTIT...INT 20 CONGRESS. PAGE 135 F2658
FINAN ECO/UNDEV PARL/PROC LEGIS

B64
US LIBRARY OF CONGRESS,SOUTHEAST ASIA. CULTURE ...SOC STAT 20. PAGE 138 F2718
BIBLIOG/A S/ASIA ECO/UNDEV NAT/G

B64
US SENATE COMM ON FOREIGN REL,HEARING ON BILLS RELATING TO FOREIGN ASSISTANCE. USA+45 WOR+45 ECO/UNDEV FINAN INDUS 20 UN CONGRESS. PAGE 139 F2733
FOR/AID DIPLOM TEC/DEV INT/ORG

B64
VON DER MEHDEN F.R.,POLITICS OF THE DEVELOPING NATIONS. WOR+45 CONSTN PROB/SOLV ORD/FREE WEALTH OBJECTIVE. PAGE 142 F2790
ECO/UNDEV SOCIETY STRUCT

B64
WERTHEIM W.F.,EAST-WEST PARALLELS. INDONESIA S/ASIA NAT/G SECT...TIME/SEQ METH REFORMERS S/EASTASIA. PAGE 145 F2860
SOC ECO/UNDEV CULTURE NAT/LISM

B64
WITHERELL J.W.,OFFICIAL PUBLICATIONS OF FRENCH EQUATORIAL AFRICA, FRENCH CAMEROONS, AND TOGO, 1946-1958 (PAMPHLET). CAMEROON CHAD FRANCE GABON TOGO LAW ECO/UNDEV EXTR/IND INT/TRADE...GEOG HEAL 20. PAGE 148 F2913
BIBLIOG/A AFR NAT/G ADMIN

B64
WITHERS W.,THE ECONOMIC CRISIS IN LATIN AMERICA. BRAZIL CHILE STRATA AGRI DIPLOM FOR/AID PWR SOCISM ...POLICY 20 MEXIC/AMER ARGEN ALL/PROG. PAGE 148 F2914
L/A+17C ECO/UNDEV CAP/ISM ALL/IDEOS

B64
ZOLLSCHAN G.K.,EXPLORATIONS IN SOCIAL CHANGE. SOCIETY STRATA STRUCT ECO/UNDEV EX/STRUC...PSY ANTHOL 20. PAGE 151 F2968
ORD/FREE SIMUL CONCPT CULTURE

L64
ARMENGALD A.,"ECONOMIE ET COEXISTENCE." COM EUR+WWI FUT USA+45 WOR+45 ECO/DEV ECO/UNDEV FINAN INT/ORG NAT/G EXEC CHOOSE ATTIT ALL/VALS...POLICY RELATIV DECISION TREND SOC/EXP WORK 20. PAGE 6 F0113
MARKET ECO/TAC AFR CAP/ISM

L64
BHAGWATI J.,"THE PURE THEORY OF INTERNATIONAL TRADE: A SURVEY." WOR+45 ECO/DEV ECO/UNDEV FINAN MARKET PROC/MFG INT/ORG LABOR LG/CO NAT/G TEC/DEV ECO/TAC SKILL WEALTH...POLICY RELATIV MGT CONCPT NEW/IDEA MATH QUANT GEN/LAWS FOR/TRADE 20. PAGE 14 F0276
INDUS HYPO/EXP

L64
CARNEGIE ENDOWMENT INT. PEACE,"ECONOMIC AND SOCIAL QUESTION (ISSUES BEFORE THE NINETEENTH GENERAL ASSEMBLY)." WOR+45 ECO/DEV ECO/UNDEV INDUS R+D DELIB/GP CREATE PLAN TEC/DEV ECO/TAC FOR/AID BAL/PAY...RECORD UN 20. PAGE 21 F0414
INT/ORG INT/TRADE

L64
KORBONSKI A.,"COMECON." ASIA ECO/DEV ECO/UNDEV ECO/TAC BAL/PAY NAT/LISM FOR/TRADE 20 COMECON. PAGE 73 F1425
COM INT/ORG INT/TRADE

L64
STERN R.M.,"POLICIES FOR TRADE AND DEVELOPMENT." AFR FUT WOR+45 DIST/IND FINAN NAT/G DELIB/GP PLAN ECO/TAC ORD/FREE WEALTH...POLICY STAT TIME/SEQ CHARTS METH/GP 20. PAGE 126 F2480
MARKET ECO/UNDEV INT/TRADE

S64
BEIM D.,"THE COMMUNIST BLOC AND THE FOREIGN-AID GAME." AFR WOR+45 NAT/G PLAN ROUTINE ATTIT KNOWL ORD/FREE...DECISION QUANT CONT/OBS TIME/SEQ CHARTS GAME SIMUL LOG/LING 20. PAGE 12 F0231
COM ECO/UNDEV ECO/TAC FOR/AID

S64
GARDNER R.N.,"GATT AND THE UNITED NATIONS CONFERENCE ON TRADE AND DEVELOPMENT." USA+45 WOR+45 SOCIETY ECO/UNDEV MARKET NAT/G DELIB/GP ACT/RES PLAN ECO/TAC TARIFFS EDU/PROP ROUTINE DRIVE RIGID/FLEX WEALTH...DECISION MGT TREND UN TOT/POP 20 GATT. PAGE 46 F0905
INT/ORG INT/TRADE

S64
HABERLER G.,"INTEGRATION AND GROWTH OF THE WORLD ECONOMY IN HISTORICAL PERSPECTIVE." FUT WOR+45 WOR-45 ECO/DEV ECO/UNDEV...TIME/SEQ TREND VAL/FREE 20. PAGE 52 F1023
WEALTH INT/TRADE

S64
HERMAN L.M.,"THE ECONOMIC CONTENT OF SOVIET TRADE WITH THE WEST." WOR+45 ECO/DEV ECO/UNDEV AGRI COM/IND INDUS CAP/ISM ECO/TAC ATTIT RIGID/FLEX WEALTH...OBS TREND VAL/FREE MARX/KARL 20. PAGE 59 F1152
COM MARKET INT/TRADE USSR

S64
HOOVER C.B.,"THE ROLE OF THE NATURAL AND DEVELOPED RESOURCES OF THE NATION STATES." FUT WOR+45 ECO/DEV ECO/UNDEV NAT/G PWR RESPECT SKILL WEALTH...POLICY GEOG TIME/SEQ TREND RESOURCE/N VAL/FREE 20. PAGE 62 F1210
EXTR/IND DOMIN

S64
HUELIN D.,"ECONOMIC INTEGRATION IN LATIN AMERICAN: PROGRESS AND PROBLEMS." L/A+17C ECO/DEV AGRI DIST/IND FINAN INDUS NAT/G VOL/ASSN CONSULT DELIB/GP EX/STRUC ACT/RES PLAN TEC/DEV ECO/TAC ROUTINE BAL/PAY WEALTH FOR/TRADE WORK TERR/GP 20. PAGE 63 F1232
MARKET ECO/UNDEV INT/TRADE

S64
HUTCHINSON E.C.,"AMERICAN AID TO AFRICA." FUT USA+45 MARKET INT/ORG LOC/G NAT/G PUB/INST PLAN ECO/TAC ATTIT RIGID/FLEX...POLICY CONCPT TREND TERR/GP 20. PAGE 63 F1248
AFR ECO/UNDEV FOR/AID

S64
KLEIN H.,"AMERICAN OIL COMPANIES IN LATIN AMERICA: THE BOLIVIAN EXPERIENCE." L/A+17C USA+45 USA-45 EXTR/IND LG/CO NAT/G ECO/TAC WEALTH...POLICY GEN/LAWS BOLIV TOT/POP 20 OIL. PAGE 72 F1405
MARKET ECO/UNDEV NAT/LISM

S64
LEFF N.H.,"ECONOMIC DEVELOPMENT THROUGH BUREAUCRATIC CORRUPTION." ELITES NAT/G ROUTINE REPRESENT GP/REL PERS/REL. PAGE 77 F1511
ECO/UNDEV CLIENT EX/STRUC

S64
MC WILLIAM M.,"THE WORLD BANK AND THE TRANSFER OF POWER IN KENYA." AFR ECO/UNDEV CONSULT ACT/RES TEC/DEV PERCEPT PWR SKILL WEALTH...CONCPT OBS TREND 20. PAGE 88 F1715
NAT/G ECO/TAC

S64
NASH M.,"SOCIAL PREREQUISITES TO ECONOMIC GROWTH IN LATIN AMERICA AND SOUTHEAST ASIA." L/A+17C S/ASIA CULTURE SOCIETY ECO/UNDEV AGRI INDUS NAT/G PLAN TEC/DEV EDU/PROP ROUTINE ALL/VALS...POLICY RELATIV SOC NAT/COMP WORK TOT/POP 20. PAGE 96 F1894
ECO/DEV PERCEPT

S64
NEWLYN W.T.,"MONETARY SYSTEMS AND INTEGRATION" AFR BUDGET ADMIN FEDERAL PRODUC PROFIT UTIL...CHARTS 20 AFRICA/E. PAGE 98 F1922
ECO/UNDEV REGION METH/COMP FINAN

S64
PADELFORD N.J.,"THE ORGANIZATION OF AFRICAN UNITY." ECO/UNDEV INT/ORG PLAN BAL/PWR DIPLOM ECO/TAC NAT/LISM ORD/FREE PWR WEALTH...CONCPT TREND STERTYP TERR/GP VAL/FREE 20. PAGE 102 F2013
AFR VOL/ASSN REGION

S64
PATEL S.J.,"THE ECONOMIC DISTANCE BETWEEN NATIONS: ITS ORIGIN, MEASUREMENT AND OUTLOOK." WOR+45 ECO/DEV AGRI FINAN INDUS MARKET LABOR NAT/G CONSULT TEC/DEV ECO/TAC WEALTH...POLICY RELATIV MGT TREND WORK 20. PAGE 103 F2035
ECO/UNDEV PLAN

S64
PESELT B.M.,"COMMUNIST ECONOMIC OFFENSIVE." WOR+45 SOCIETY INT/ORG PLAN ECO/TAC DOMIN EDU/PROP ATTIT PERSON PWR WEALTH...TREND CHARTS METH/GP 20. PAGE 105 F2067
COM ECO/UNDEV FOR/AID USSR

S64
POLARIS J.,"THE SINO-SOVIET DISPUTE: ITS ECONOMIC IMPACT ON CHINA." ASIA CHINA/COM COM WOR+45 NAT/G ATTIT PWR WEALTH...STAT TREND FOR/TRADE 20. PAGE 107 F2095
ECO/UNDEV ECO/TAC

S64
READER D.H.,"A SURVEY OF CATEGORIES OF ECONOMIC ACTIVITIES AMONG THE PEOPLES OF AFRICA." AGRI INDUS MARKET KIN HEALTH SKILL WEALTH...GEOG METH/CNCPT CHARTS TERR/GP WORK TOT/POP VAL/FREE 20. PAGE 110 F2160
TEC/DEV ECO/UNDEV AFR

S64
ROTHCHILD D.,"EAST AFRICAN FEDERATION." AFR TANZANIA UGANDA INDUS REGION 20. PAGE 114 F2249
INT/ORG DIPLOM ECO/UNDEV ECO/TAC

S64
RUSSETT B.M.,"INEQUALITY AND INSTABILITY: THE RELATION OF LAND TENURE TO POLITICS." WOR+45 ECO/DEV ECO/UNDEV AGRI NAT/G COERCE PWR...MATH STAT CHARTS GEN/LAWS TERR/GP TRUE/GP METH/GP VAL/FREE 20. PAGE 115 F2263
WEALTH GEOG ECO/TAC ORD/FREE

S64
WOOD N.,"THE FAMILY FIRM - BASE OF JAPAN'S GROWING ECONOMY." ECO/DEV ECO/UNDEV ECO/TAC WEALTH...POLICY TRADIT BIOG TREND 20 CHINJAP. PAGE 148 F2921
ASIA SML/CO FAM

C64
GOLDMAN M.I.,"COMPARATIVE ECONOMIC SYSTEMS: A READER." COM ECO/UNDEV NAT/G BUDGET CAP/ISM ADMIN TOTALISM MARXISM SOCISM...MGT ANTHOL BIBLIOG 19/20. PAGE 48 F0938
NAT/COMP CONTROL IDEA/COMP

C64
LANDAUER C.,"CONTEMPORARY ECONOMIC SYSTEMS." COM WOR+45 ECO/UNDEV PLAN GP/REL...BIBLIOG 20. PAGE 75 F1466
CAP/ISM SOCISM MARXISM IDEA/COMP

C64
LOUFTY A.,"LA PLANIFICATION DE L'ECONOMIE." FRANCE USSR FINAN INDUS BUDGET INCOME PRODUC...BIBLIOG 20. PAGE 82 F1604
PLAN ECO/UNDEV ECO/DEV

N64
GREAT BRITAIN CENTRAL OFF INF,THE COLOMBO PLAN (PAMPHLET). AFR ASIA S/ASIA USA+45 VOL/ASSN ...CHARTS 20 RESOURCE/N. PAGE 50 F0980
FOR/AID PLAN INT/ORG ECO/UNDEV

N64
KENYA MINISTRY ECO PLAN DEV,AFRICAN SOCIALISM AND ITS APPLICATION TO PLANNING IN KENYA (PAMPHLET). AFR AGRI INDUS WORKER TAX COLONIAL WEALTH 20. PAGE 70 F1380
NAT/G SOCISM PLAN ECO/UNDEV

B65
ANALYSIS AND ASSESSMENT OF THE ECONOMIC EFFECTS: PUBLIC LAW 480 TITLE I PROGRAM TURKEY. INDIA TURKEY USA+45 AGRI NAT/G PLAN BUDGET DIPLOM COST EFFICIENCY...CHARTS 20. PAGE 1 F0021
ECO/TAC FOR/AID FINAN ECO/UNDEV

B65
ALEXANDER R.J.,ORGANIZED LABOR IN LATIN AMERICA. L/A+17C INT/ORG LEGIS WORKER TEC/DEV BARGAIN INT/TRADE REV...NAT/COMP BIBLIOG 20. PAGE 3 F0059
LABOR POL/PAR ECO/UNDEV POLICY

B65
ANDERSON C.A.,EDUCATION AND ECONOMIC DEVELOPMENT. INDUS R+D SCHOOL TEC/DEV ECO/TAC EDU/PROP AGE HEREDITY PERCEPT SKILL 20. PAGE 5 F0092
ANTHOL ECO/DEV ECO/UNDEV WORKER

B65
APTER D.E.,THE POLITICS OF MODERNIZATION. AFR L/A+17C CULTURE NAT/G POL/PAR ADMIN COLONIAL NAT/LISM ATTIT RIGID/FLEX PWR...SOC CONCPT. PAGE 6 F0109
ECO/UNDEV GEN/LAWS STRATA CREATE

B65
BAERRESEN D.W.,LATIN AMERICAN TRADE PATTERNS. L/A+17C ECO/UNDEV AGRI INDUS MARKET CREATE
INT/TRADE STAT

...NET/THEORY CHARTS LAFTA. PAGE 8 F0149 REGION

B65
BALDWIN D.A.,SOFT LOANS AND AMERICAN FOREIGN POLICY: 1943-1962 (THESIS). USA+45 WOR+45 FINAN NAT/G FOR/AID BAL/PAY ATTIT...POLICY METH/COMP 20 UN CONGRESS. PAGE 9 F0161 DIPLOM ECO/TAC ECO/UNDEV

B65
BELASSA B.,ECONOMIC DEVELOPMENT AND INTEGRATION. LG/CO PROB/SOLV TEC/DEV INT/TRADE TARIFFS COST WEALTH...POLICY METH/COMP 20. PAGE 12 F0232 ECO/UNDEV ECO/TAC INT/ORG INDUS

B65
BLAIR T.L.V.,AFRICA: A MARKET PROFILE. AFR COM/IND DIST/IND FINAN UTIL...DECISION CHARTS BIBLIOG 20. PAGE 15 F0295 MARKET OP/RES ECO/UNDEV INDUS

B65
BROOKINGS INSTITUTION,BROOKINGS PAPERS ON PUBLIC POLICY. USA+45 ECO/UNDEV LEGIS CAP/ISM ECO/TAC TAX EDU/PROP CONTROL APPORT 20. PAGE 19 F0363 DIPLOM FOR/AID POLICY FINAN

B65
CHANDRASEKHAR S.,AMERICAN AID AND INDIA'S ECONOMIC DEVELOPMENT. AFR CHINA/COM INDIA USA+45 GIVE EDU/PROP EATING HEALTH ORD/FREE 20 AID. PAGE 23 F0449 FOR/AID PEACE DIPLOM ECO/UNDEV

B65
CHAO K.,THE RATE AND PATTERN OF INDUSTRIAL GROWTH IN COMMUNIST CHINA. CHINA/COM ECO/UNDEV TEC/DEV PRICE...NAT/COMP BIBLIOG 20. PAGE 23 F0452 INDUS INDEX STAT PRODUC

B65
COOMBS P.H.,EDUCATION AND FOREIGN AID. AFR USA+45 DIPLOM EFFICIENCY KNOWL ORD/FREE...ANTHOL 20 AID. PAGE 27 F0532 EDU/PROP FOR/AID SCHOOL ECO/UNDEV

B65
CRABB C.V. JR.,THE ELEPHANTS AND THE GRASS* A STUDY OF NONALIGNMENT. ASIA INDIA S/ASIA USA+45 USSR BAL/PWR NEUTRAL ATTIT...TREND NAT/COMP. PAGE 28 F0549 ECO/UNDEV AFR DIPLOM CONCPT

B65
DELHI INSTITUTE OF ECO GROWTH,A STUDY IN THE WORKING OF THE INTENSIVE AREA SCHEME OF THE KHADI AND VILLAGE INDUSTRIES COMMISSION. INDIA AGRI FINAN DELIB/GP ECO/TAC EFFICIENCY...QU CHARTS MUNICH 20. PAGE 32 F0614 PLAN INDUS ECO/UNDEV

B65
DEMAS W.G.,THE ECONOMICS OF DEVELOPMENT IN SMALL COUNTRIES WITH SPECIAL REFERENCE TO THE CARIBBEAN. WOR+45 BAL/PAY DEMAND EFFICIENCY PRODUC...GEOG CARIBBEAN. PAGE 32 F0618 ECO/UNDEV PLAN WEALTH INT/TRADE

B65
EUROPEAN FREE TRADE ASSN,REGIONAL DEVELOPMENT POLICIES IN EFTA. ECO/UNDEV INT/ORG PLAN REGION ...POLICY GEOG EFTA. PAGE 39 F0755 EUR+WWI ECO/DEV NAT/COMP INT/TRADE

B65
FARER T.J.,FINANCING AFRICAN DEVELOPMENT. AFR ECO/TAC FOR/AID SOCISM 20. PAGE 39 F0764 ECO/UNDEV FINAN CAP/ISM PLAN

B65
FRIEDLANDER S.L.,LABOR MIGRATION AND ECONOMIC GROWTH: A CASE STUDY OF PUERTO RICO. PUERT/RICO AGRI WORKER PLAN PROB/SOLV...ECOMETRIC STAT PREDICT CHARTS HYPO/EXP SIMUL 20. PAGE 44 F0858 CENSUS GEOG ECO/UNDEV WEALTH

B65
GOODSELL C.T.,ADMINISTRATION OF A REVOLUTION. PUERT/RICO ECO/UNDEV FINAN POL/PAR PROVS LEGIS PLAN BUDGET RECEIVE ADMIN COLONIAL LEAD MUNICH 20 ROOSEVLT/F. PAGE 49 F0951 EXEC SOC

B65
GORDON W.,THE POLITICAL ECONOMY OF LATIN AMERICA. L/A+17C FINAN MARKET PROB/SOLV TEC/DEV RECEIVE ADMIN WEALTH 20. PAGE 49 F0962 ECO/UNDEV INT/TRADE REGION POLICY

B65
HAEFELE E.T.,GOVERNMENT CONTROLS ON TRANSPORT. AFR RHODESIA TANZANIA DIPLOM ECO/TAC TARIFFS PRICE ADJUD CONTROL REGION EFFICIENCY...POLICY 20 CONGO. PAGE 53 F1031 ECO/UNDEV DIST/IND FINAN NAT/G

B65
HAPGOOD D.,AFRICA: FROM INDEPENDENCE TO TOMARROW. AFR GUINEA SENEGAL CULTURE ELITES ECO/UNDEV AGRI SCHOOL FOR/AID COLONIAL MARXISM...TREND 20. PAGE 55 F1070 ECO/TAC SOCIETY NAT/G

B65
HARBISON F.,MANPOWER AND EDUCATION. AFR CHINA/COM IRAN L/A+17C S/ASIA TEC/DEV ADJUST OPTIMAL SKILL ...ANTHOL 20. PAGE 55 F1073 ECO/UNDEV EDU/PROP WORKER NAT/COMP

B65
HAUSER P.M.,THE STUDY OF URBANIZATION. S/ASIA ECO/DEV ECO/UNDEV NEIGH ACT/RES...GEOG MUNICH. PAGE 57 F1115 CULTURE SOC

B65
HERRICK B.H.,URBAN MIGRATION AND ECONOMIC DEVELOPMENT IN CHILE. CHILE AGRI INDUS LABOR NAT/G CENTRAL PRODUC...STAT SAMP CHARTS BIBLIOG/A MUNICH 20 MIGRATION. PAGE 59 F1156 HABITAT GEOG ECO/UNDEV

B65
HLA MYINT U.,THE ECONOMICS OF THE DEVELOPING COUNTRIES. USA+45 WOR+45 AGRI FINAN NAT/G INT/TRADE ...CLASSIF CENSUS TREND NAT/COMP SIMUL GEN/LAWS. PAGE 60 F1180 ECO/UNDEV FOR/AID GEOG

B65
HOLLER J.E.,POPULATION TRENDS AND ECONOMIC DEVELOPMENT IN THE FAR EAST (PAMPHLET). KOREA S/ASIA AGRI INDUS DELIB/GP PROB/SOLV RATIONAL ...POLICY CHARTS BIBLIOG 20 OUTER/MONG CHINJAP HONG/KONG. PAGE 61 F1197 CENSUS TREND ECO/UNDEV ASIA

B65
HONDURAS CONSEJO NAC DE ECO,PLAN NACIONAL DE DESARROLLO ECONOMICO Y SOCIAL DE HONDURAS 1965-69. HONDURAS AGRI INDUS BAL/PAY INCOME 20. PAGE 61 F1203 ECO/UNDEV NAT/G PLAN POLICY

B65
HOSELITZ B.F.,ECONOMICS AND THE IDEA OF MANKIND. UNIV ECO/DEV ECO/UNDEV DIST/IND INDUS INT/ORG NAT/G ACT/RES ECO/TAC WEALTH...CONCPT STAT. PAGE 62 F1223 CREATE INT/TRADE

B65
IANNI O.,ESTADO E CAPITALISMO. L/A+17C FINAN TEC/DEV ECO/TAC ORD/FREE WEALTH POLICY. PAGE 64 F1258 ECO/UNDEV STRUCT INDUS NAT/G

B65
INTERAMERICAN ECO AND SOC COUN,THE ALLIANCE FOR PROGRESS: ITS THIRD YEAR 1963-1964. FUT L/A+17C WOR+45 ECO/DEV INT/ORG PLAN CONTROL ADJUST...STAT ANTHOL SOC/INTEG 20 ALL/PROG. PAGE 64 F1268 ECO/UNDEV ECO/TAC FINAN FOR/AID

B65
JAIN S.C.,THE STATE AND AGRICULTURE. INDIA S/ASIA ECO/UNDEV PROB/SOLV CAP/ISM MARXISM SOCISM 20. PAGE 66 F1304 NAT/G POLICY AGRI ECO/TAC

B65
JOHNSON H.G.,THE WORLD ECONOMY AT THE CROSSROADS. COM WOR-45 ECO/DEV AGRI INDUS INT/TRADE REGION NAT/LISM 20. PAGE 67 F1326 FINAN DIPLOM INT/ORG ECO/UNDEV

B65
KLASSEN L.H.,AREA ECONOMIC AND SOCIAL REDEVELOPMENT. ECO/UNDEV INDUS NAT/G PLAN CAP/ISM TAX...ECOMETRIC SIMUL 20. PAGE 72 F1404 OPTIMAL WORKER METH ECO/TAC

B65
KRAUSE W.,ECONOMIC DEVELOPMENT: THE UNDERDEVELOPED WORLD AND THE AMERICAN INTEREST. USA+45 AGRI PLAN MARXISM...CHARTS 20. PAGE 73 F1434 FOR/AID ECO/UNDEV FINAN PROB/SOLV

B65
LEYS C.T.,FEDERATION IN EAST AFRICA. LAW AGRI DIST/IND FINAN INT/ORG LABOR INT/TRADE CONFER ADMIN CONTROL GP/REL...ANTHOL 20 AFRICA/E. PAGE 79 F1554 FEDERAL REGION ECO/UNDEV PLAN

B65
LITTLE I.M.D.,INTERNATIONAL AID. UK WOR+45 AGRI INDUS GIVE RECEIVE COLONIAL BAL/PAY WEALTH...POLICY GOV/COMP METH/COMP 20. PAGE 81 F1584 FOR/AID DIPLOM ECO/UNDEV NAT/G

B65
THE STATE AND ECONOMIC ENTERPRISE IN JAPAN; ESSAYS IN THE POLITICAL ECONOMY OF GROWTH. AGRI INDUS DRIVE POPULISM...CHARTS NAT/COMP ANTHOL 19/20 CHINJAP. PAGE 81 F1594 ECO/UNDEV ECO/DEV CAP/ISM ECO/TAC

B65
MARK S.M.,ECONOMICS IN ACTION (3RD ED.). USA+45 ECO/UNDEV AGRI INDUS FOR/AID INT/TRADE BAL/PAY COST ORD/FREE...ANTHOL 20 RESOURCE/N. PAGE 85 F1670 POLICY ECO/TAC EFFICIENCY PRICE

B65
MEAGHER R.F.,PUBLIC INTERNATIONAL DEVELOPMENT FINANCING IN SUDAN. SUDAN FINAN DELIB/GP GIVE ...CHARTS GOV/COMP 20. PAGE 89 F1740 FOR/AID PLAN RECEIVE ECO/UNDEV

B65
MONCRIEFF A.,SECOND THOUGHTS ON AID. WOR+45 ECO/UNDEV AGRI FINAN VOL/ASSN PLAN TEC/DEV GIVE EDU/PROP ROLE WEALTH 20. PAGE 93 F1816 FOR/AID ECO/TAC INT/ORG IDEA/COMP

B65
MOORE W.E.,THE IMPACT OF INDUSTRY. CULTURE STRUCT ORD/FREE...TREND 20. PAGE 93 F1824 INDUS MGT TEC/DEV ECO/UNDEV

B65
MORRIS M.D.,THE EMERGENCE OF AN INDUSTRIAL LABOR FORCE IN INDIA: A STUDY OF THE BOMBAY COTTON MILLS, 1854-1947. INDIA WORKER OP/RES ADMIN 19/20. PAGE 94 F1837 INDUS LABOR ECO/UNDEV CAP/ISM

B65
MURUMBI J.,PROBLEMS OF ECONOMIC DEVELOPMENT IN EAST AFRICA. FINAN INDUS WORKER TEC/DEV INT/TRADE TAX DEMAND EFFICIENCY PRODUC SOCISM...TREND CHARTS 20 AFRICA/E. PAGE 95 F1869 AGRI ECO/TAC ECO/UNDEV PROC/MFG

B65
NATIONAL CENTRAL LIBRARY,LATIN AMERICAN ECONOMIC AND SOCIAL SERIALS. UK SOCIETY NAT/G PLAN PROB/SOLV ...SOC 20. PAGE 97 F1897 BIBLIOG INT/TRADE ECO/UNDEV L/A+17C

B65
NKRUMAH K.,NEO-COLONIALISM: THE LAST STAGE OF IMPERIALISM. AFR INT/ORG WORKER FOR/AID INT/TRADE EDU/PROP GOV/REL NAT/LISM SOVEREIGN POPULISM SOCISM ...SOCIALIST 20 THIRD/WRLD INTRVN/ECO. PAGE 98 F1929 COLONIAL DIPLOM ECO/UNDEV ECO/TAC

B65
O'CONNELL D.P.,INTERNATIONAL LAW (2 VOLS.). WOR+45 WOR-45 ECO/DEV ECO/UNDEV INT/ORG NAT/G AGREE ...POLICY JURID CONCPT NAT/COMP 20 TREATY. PAGE 99 F1952 INT/LAW DIPLOM CT/SYS

B65
OECD,MEDITERRANEAN REGIONAL PROJECT: TURKEY; EDUCATION AND DEVELOPMENT. FUT TURKEY SOCIETY STRATA FINAN NAT/G PROF/ORG PLAN PROB/SOLV ADMIN COST...STAT CHARTS 20 OECD. PAGE 100 F1969 EDU/PROP ACADEM SCHOOL ECO/UNDEV

B65
OECD,THE MEDITERRANEAN REGIONAL PROJECT: PORTUGAL; EDUCATION AND DEVELOPMENT. PORTUGAL SOCIETY STRATA FINAN PROF/ORG WORKER PLAN PROB/SOLV ADMIN...POLICY STAT CHARTS METH 20 OECD. PAGE 100 F1970 EDU/PROP SCHOOL ACADEM ECO/UNDEV

B65
OECD,THE MEDITERRANEAN REGIONAL PROJECT: ITALY; EDUCATION AND DEVELOPMENT. ITALY SOCIETY STRATA FINAN NAT/G PROF/ORG WORKER PLAN PROB/SOLV ADMIN ...STAT CHARTS METH 20 OECD. PAGE 100 F1971 SCHOOL EDU/PROP ECO/UNDEV ACADEM

B65
OECD,THE MEDITERRANEAN REGIONAL PROJECT: GREECE; EDUCATION AND DEVELOPMENT. FUT GREECE SOCIETY AGRI FINAN NAT/G PROF/ORG WORKER PLAN PROB/SOLV ADMIN DEMAND ATTIT 20 OECD. PAGE 100 F1972 EDU/PROP SCHOOL ACADEM ECO/UNDEV

B65
OECD,THE MEDITERRANEAN REGIONAL PROJECT: SPAIN; EDUCATION AND DEVELOPMENT. FUT SPAIN STRATA FINAN NAT/G WORKER PLAN PROB/SOLV ADMIN COST...POLICY STAT CHARTS 20 OECD. PAGE 100 F1973 ECO/UNDEV EDU/PROP ACADEM SCHOOL

B65
OFFICE OF ECONOMIC OPPORTUNITY,CATALOG OF FEDERAL PROGRAMS FOR INDIVIDUAL AND COMMUNITY IMPROVEMENT. USA+45 WEALTH NEW/LIB 20. PAGE 101 F1980 INDEX ECO/UNDEV RECEIVE NAT/G

B65
ONSLOW C.,ASIAN ECONOMIC DEVELOPMENT. BURMA CEYLON INDIA MALAYSIA PAKISTAN S/ASIA AGRI INDUS MARKET PROB/SOLV CAP/ISM FOR/AID INT/TRADE DEMAND WEALTH ...POLICY ANTHOL 20. PAGE 101 F1991 ECO/UNDEV ECO/TAC PLAN NAT/G

B65
ONUOHA B.,THE ELEMENTS OF AFRICAN SOCIALISM. AFR FINAN SECT TEC/DEV FOR/AID GP/REL OWN LAISSEZ MARXISM...CONCPT BIBLIOG 20. PAGE 101 F1992 SOCISM ECO/UNDEV NAT/G EX/STRUC

B65
ORG FOR ECO COOP AND DEVEL,THE MEDITERRANEAN REGIONAL PROJECT: AN EXPERIMENT IN PLANNING BY SIX COUNTRIES. FUT GREECE SPAIN TURKEY YUGOSLAVIA SOCIETY FINAN NAT/G PROF/ORG EDU/PROP ADMIN REGION COST...POLICY STAT CHARTS 20 OECD. PAGE 102 F1995 PLAN ECO/UNDEV ACADEM SCHOOL

B65
ORG FOR ECO COOP AND DEVEL,THE MEDITERRANEAN REGIONAL PROJECT: YUGOSLAVIA; EDUCATION AND DEVELOPMENT. YUGOSLAVIA SOCIETY FINAN PROF/ORG PLAN ADMIN COST DEMAND MARXISM...STAT TREND CHARTS METH 20 OECD. PAGE 102 F1996 EDU/PROP ACADEM SCHOOL ECO/UNDEV

B65
PINCUS J.A.,ECONOMIC AID AND INTERNATIONAL COST SHARING* A RAND CORPORATION RESEARCH STUDY. INT/ORG BUDGET CENTRAL...ECOMETRIC MATH QUANT STAT SIMUL. PAGE 106 F2088 ECO/UNDEV COST FOR/AID INT/TRADE

B65
RATNAM K.J.,COMMUNALISM AND THE POLITICAL PROCESS IN MALAYA. MALAYSIA WOR+45 ECO/UNDEV PARTIC CHOOSE REPRESENT GP/REL CENTRAL ATTIT...CHARTS WORSHIP 20. PAGE 109 F2152 CONSTN GOV/REL REGION

B65
RIVKIN M.D.,AREA DEVELOPMENT FOR NATIONAL GROWTH; THE TURKISH PRECEDENT. ISLAM TURKEY ACT/RES INGP/REL...POLICY CHARTS GP/COMP MUNICH 20 ATATURK/MK INONU/I. PAGE 112 F2197 ECO/UNDEV REGION ECO/TAC PLAN

B65
SABLE M.H.,PERIODICALS FOR LATIN AMERICAN ECONOMIC DEVELOPMENT, TRADE, AND FINANCE: AN ANNOTATED BIBLIOGRAPHY (A PAMPHLET). ECO/TAC PRODUC PROFIT ...STAT NAT/COMP 20 OAS. PAGE 115 F2266 BIBLIOG/A L/A+17C ECO/UNDEV INT/TRADE

B65
SCHULER E.A.,THE PAKISTAN ACADEMIES FOR RURAL DEVELOPMENT COMILLA AND PESHAWAR 1959-1964. PAKISTAN S/ASIA SOCIETY STRUCT AGRI NAT/G TEC/DEV EDU/PROP 20. PAGE 117 F2314 BIBLIOG PLAN ECO/TAC ECO/UNDEV

B65
SCHULTZ T.W.,ECONOMIC CRISES IN WORLD AGRICULTURE. ASIA INDIA USSR ECO/DEV ECO/UNDEV INDUS VOL/ASSN CAP/ISM RATION COLONIAL 20. PAGE 117 F2317 AGRI ECO/TAC INCOME WORKER

B65
SHARIF A.,THE BALANCE OF PAYMENTS OF PAKISTAN, 1948-1958 (THESIS, UNIVERSITY OF TORONTO). PAKISTAN FINAN INDUS FOR/AID PRICE WEALTH...TREND CHARTS 20. PAGE 120 F2368 BAL/PAY BUDGET INT/TRADE ECO/UNDEV

B65
SIMMS R.P.,URBANIZATION IN WEST AFRICA; A REVIEW OF CURRENT LITERATURE. AFR PLAN TEC/DEV...SOC OBS NAT/COMP MUNICH 20. PAGE 122 F2405 BIBLIOG/A ECO/DEV ECO/UNDEV

B65
SINHA M.R.,THE ECONOMICS OF MANPOWER PLANNING. FUT HUNGARY NAT/G CONTROL...POLICY GEOG ANTHOL 20 CHINJAP. PAGE 122 F2415 ECO/UNDEV PLAN WORKER ECO/TAC

B65
STEWART I.G.,AFRICAN PRIMARY PRODUCTS AND INTERNATIONAL TRADE. ECO/UNDEV AGRI FINAN DIPLOM CONTROL 20. PAGE 126 F2485 AFR INT/TRADE INT/ORG

B65
TYBOUT R.A.,ECONOMICS OF RESEARCH AND DEVELOPMENT. ECO/DEV ECO/UNDEV INDUS PROFIT DECISION. PAGE 131 F2594 R+D FORCES ADMIN DIPLOM

B65
US BUREAU EDUC CULTURAL AFF,RESOURCES SURVEY FOR LATIN AMERICAN COUNTRIES. L/A+17C USA+45 CULTURE INDUS INT/ORG SECT PLAN EDU/PROP POLICY. PAGE 134 F2643 NAT/G ECO/UNDEV FOR/AID DIPLOM

B65
US SENATE COMM ON FOREIGN REL,HEARINGS ON THE FOREIGN ASSISTANCE PROGRAM. AFR ASIA L/A+17C USA+45 WOR+45 FORCES TEC/DEV BUDGET CONTROL WEAPON ORD/FREE 20 UN CONGRESS SEC/STATE. PAGE 139 F2734 FOR/AID DIPLOM INT/ORG ECO/UNDEV

B65
VON RENESSE E.A.,UNVOLLENDETE DEMOKRATIEN. AFR ISLAM S/ASIA SOCIETY ACT/RES COLONIAL...JURID CHARTS BIBLIOG METH 13/20. PAGE 142 F2795 ECO/UNDEV NAT/COMP SOVEREIGN

B65
WATERSTON A.,DEVELOPMENT PLANNING* LESSONS OF EXPERIENCE. ECO/TAC CENTRAL...MGT QUANT BIBLIOG. PAGE 144 F2830 ECO/UNDEV CREATE PLAN ADMIN

B65
WEAVER J.N.,THE INTERNATIONAL DEVELOPMENT ASSOCIATION: A NEW APPROACH TO FOREIGN AID. USA+45 NAT/G OP/RES PLAN PROB/SOLV WEALTH...CHARTS BIBLIOG 20 UN. PAGE 144 F2836 FOR/AID INT/ORG ECO/UNDEV FINAN

B65
WHITE J.,GERMAN AID. GERMANY/W FINAN PLAN TEC/DEV INT/TRADE ADMIN ATTIT...POLICY 20. PAGE 146 F2870 FOR/AID ECO/UNDEV DIPLOM ECO/TAC

B65
WISH J.R.,ECONOMIC DEVELOPMENT IN LATIN AMERICA: AN ANNOTATED BIBLIOGRAPHY. L/A+17C COM/IND MARKET R+D CREATE CAP/ISM ATTIT...STAT METH 20. PAGE 148 F2912 BIBLIOG/A ECO/UNDEV TEC/DEV AGRI

B65
WRIGHT L.B.,THE DREAM OF PROSPERITY IN COLONIAL AMERICA. USA-45 ECO/UNDEV AGRI EXTR/IND PARLIAMENT 17/18. PAGE 149 F2934 PROVS WEALTH MOD/EUR

B65
WURFEL S.W.,FOREIGN ENTERPRISE IN COLOMBIA. FINAN LABOR NAT/G ECO/TAC TAX REGION 20 COLOMB. PAGE 149 F2944 ECO/UNDEV INT/TRADE JURID CAP/ISM

L65
WILLIAMS S.,"NEGOTIATING INVESTMENT IN EMERGING COUNTRIES." USA+45 WOR+45 INDUS MARKET NAT/G TOP/EX TEC/DEV CAP/ISM ECO/TAC ADMIN SKILL WEALTH...POLICY RELATIV MGT WORK 20. PAGE 147 F2894 FINAN ECO/UNDEV

S65
BERREBY J.J.,"IMPERATIFS STRATEGIQUES DU PETROLE." ECO/UNDEV VOL/ASSN ECO/TAC COLONIAL NUC/PWR WAR. PAGE 14 F0270 ISLAM EXTR/IND STAT OBS

S65
BRANDENBURG F.,"THE RELEVANCE OF MEXICAN EXPERIENCE TO LATIN AMERICAN DEVELOPMENT." BRAZIL CHILE VENEZUELA STRUCT ECO/UNDEV AGRI CREATE ECO/TAC ...STAT RECORD MEXIC/AMER ARGEN COLOMB. PAGE 18 F0340 L/A+17C GOV/COMP

S65
CAMPOLONGO A.,"EUROPEAN INVESTMENT BANK* ACTIVITY AND PROSPECTS." FUT ECO/UNDEV FINAN PLAN DIPLOM ...STAT EEC LOAN EIB. PAGE 21 F0410 ECO/TAC PREDICT

S65
CECIL C.O.,"THE DETERMINANTS OF LIBYAN FOREIGN POLICY." AFR INTELL ECO/UNDEV EXTR/IND POL/PAR LIBYA DIPLOM

CREATE REGION SOVEREIGN CONSERVE MAGHREB NASSER/G. PAGE 22 F0431
WEALTH ISLAM

S65
DUMONT R.,"SURPEUPLEMENT CHINOIS ET SES CONSEQUENCES." AFR ECO/UNDEV AGRI PLAN PROB/SOLV ECO/TAC FOR/AID NUC/PWR...OBS INT PREDICT. PAGE 35 F0675
GEOG ASIA STAT

S65
GOLDMAN M.I.,"A BALANCE SHEET OF SOVIET FOREIGN AID." USA+45 ECO/UNDEV BAL/PWR ECO/TAC RENT GIVE EDU/PROP CONTROL COST PROFIT GEN/METH. PAGE 48 F0939
USSR FOR/AID NAT/COMP EFFICIENCY

S65
JOHNSON H.G.,"A THEORETICAL MODEL OF ECONOMIC NATIONALISM IN NEW AND DEVELOPING STATES." ELITES INDUS INT/TRADE EDU/PROP COST OPTIMAL RATIONAL PWR WEALTH SOCISM STERTYP. PAGE 67 F1325
NAT/LISM ECO/UNDEV GEN/LAWS

S65
JOHNSON L.L.,"US BUSINESS INTERESTS IN CUBA AND THE RISE OF CASTRO." L/A+17C USA+45 ECO/UNDEV INDUS NAT/G VOL/ASSN ATTIT ORD/FREE PWR WEALTH ALL/PROG. PAGE 68 F1330
DIPLOM CUBA ECO/TAC INT/TRADE

S65
KINDLEBERGER C.P.,"MASS MIGRATION, THEN AND NOW." LAW ECO/DEV ECO/UNDEV INDUS LABOR INT/TRADE FEEDBACK REGION RIGID/FLEX...SOC NAT/COMP EEC. PAGE 71 F1394
EUR+WWI USA-45 WORKER IDEA/COMP

S65
KORBONSKI A.,"USA POLICY IN EAST EUROPE." COM EUR+WWI GERMANY USA+45 CULTURE ECO/UNDEV EDU/PROP RIGID/FLEX WEALTH FOR/TRADE 20. PAGE 73 F1426
ACT/RES ECO/TAC FOR/AID

S65
KUNKEL J.H.,"VALUES AND BEHAVIOR IN ECONOMIC DEVELOPMENT." INDIA PERU CULTURE STRUCT CREATE PERS/REL ATTIT PERSON...CHARTS HYPO/EXP ARGEN. PAGE 74 F1449
SIMUL ECO/UNDEV PSY STERTYP

S65
LECLERCQ H.,"ECONOMIC RESEARCH AND DEVELOPMENT IN TROPICAL AFRICA." ECO/UNDEV INT/ORG CREATE PLAN UN. PAGE 77 F1500
AFR R+D ACADEM ECO/TAC

S65
MULLER A.L.,"THE ECONOMIC POSITION OF THE ASIANS IN AFRICA." AFR SOUTH/AFR ECO/UNDEV MARKET ECO/TAC GP/REL INCOME...CHARTS IND 20 MONOPOLY ASIANS. PAGE 95 F1856
WORKER RACE/REL CAP/ISM DISCRIM

S65
MUNZI U.,"THE EUROPEAN SOCIAL FUND IN THE DEVELOPMENT OF THE MEDITERRANEAN REGIONS OF THE EEC." FUT GREECE ITALY PORTUGAL SPAIN TURKEY WORKER TEC/DEV ECO/TAC REGION...STAT EEC. PAGE 95 F1862
ECO/UNDEV PREDICT RECORD

S65
RUSINOW D.I.,"YUGOSLAV DEVELOPMENT BETWEEN EAST AND WEST." AGRI VOL/ASSN PLAN CAP/ISM ECO/TAC FOR/AID INT/TRADE BAL/PAY...MARXIST EEC COMECON. PAGE 115 F2262
YUGOSLAVIA ECO/UNDEV STAT

S65
SOPER T.,"THE EEC AND AID TO AFRICA." FRANCE UK ECO/UNDEV INT/TRADE TARIFFS REGION ROUTINE CENTRAL DISCRIM...DECISION RECORD EEC. PAGE 124 F2443
AFR FOR/AID COLONIAL

S65
STEENKAMP W.F.J.,"THE PROBLEM OF WAGE REGULATION." SOUTH/AFR LAW ECO/DEV ECO/UNDEV LABOR NAT/G BARGAIN PAY INGP/REL DISCRIM WEALTH...METH/COMP 20. PAGE 125 F2473
ECO/TAC PRICE WORKER RATION

S65
TENDLER J.D.,"TECHNOLOGY AND ECONOMIC DEVELOPMENT* THE CASE OF HYDRO VS THERMAL POWER." CONSTRUC DIST/IND CREATE TEC/DEV INT/TRADE CENTRAL PWR SKILL WEALTH...MGT NAT/COMP ARGEN. PAGE 129 F2544
BRAZIL INDUS ECO/UNDEV

S65
WHITE J.,"WEST GERMAN AID TO DEVELOPING COUNTRIES." AFR INT/ORG OP/RES GIVE CENTRAL ATTIT DRIVE...STAT NAT/COMP. PAGE 146 F2869
GERMANY FOR/AID ECO/UNDEV CAP/ISM

B66
ALEXANDER Y.,INTERNATIONAL TECHNICAL ASSISTANCE EXPERTS* A CASE STUDY OF THE U.N. EXPERIENCE. ECO/UNDEV CONSULT EX/STRUC CREATE PLAN DIPLOM FOR/AID TASK EFFICIENCY...ORG/CHARTS UN. PAGE 3 F0061
ECO/TAC INT/ORG ADMIN MGT

B66
ALI S.,PLANNING, DEVELOPMENT AND CHANGE: AN ANNOTATED BIBLIOGRAPHY ON DEVELOPMENTAL ADMINISTRATION. PAKISTAN SOCIETY ORD/FREE 20. PAGE 4 F0066
BIBLIOG/A ADMIN ECO/UNDEV PLAN

B66
AMER ENTERPRISE INST PUB POL,SIGNIFICANT ISSUES IN ECONOMIC AID TO DEVELOPING COUNTRIES. FINAN INT/ORG NAT/G PLAN PROB/SOLV GIVE TASK WEALTH...DECISION 20. PAGE 4 F0083
ECO/UNDEV FOR/AID DIPLOM POLICY

B66
ANDRESKI S.,PARASITISM AND SUBVERSION* THE CASE OF LATIN AMERICA. CULTURE ECO/UNDEV LABOR NAT/G SECT PROB/SOLV RACE/REL TOTALISM ATTIT WEALTH ALL/IDEOS. PAGE 5 F0100
L/A+17C GOV/COMP STRATA REV

B66
BAKLANOFF E.N.,NEW PERSPECTIVES ON BRAZIL. BRAZIL SOCIETY INDUS DOMIN LEAD REV CIVMIL/REL...GEOG PSY LING ANTHOL 20. PAGE 8 F0156
ECO/UNDEV TEC/DEV DIPLOM ORD/FREE

B66
BALDWIN D.A.,FOREIGN AID AND AMERICAN FOREIGN POLICY; A DOCUMENTARY ANALYSIS. USA+45 ECO/UNDEV ADMIN...ECOMETRIC STAT STYLE CHARTS PROG/TEAC GEN/LAWS ANTHOL. PAGE 9 F0162
FOR/AID DIPLOM IDEA/COMP

B66
BALDWIN D.A.,ECONOMIC DEVELOPMENT AND AMERICAN FOREIGN POLICY. USA+45 FINAN LG/CO LEGIS DIPLOM GIVE 20. PAGE 9 F0163
ECO/TAC FOR/AID ECO/UNDEV POLICY

B66
BALDWIN R.E.,ECONOMIC DEVELOPMENT AND EXPORT GROWTH: A STUDY OF NORTHERN RHODESIA, 1920-1960. AFR RHODESIA AGRI EXTR/IND FINAN MARKET LABOR WORKER ECO/TAC...CONCPT NEW/IDEA MUNICH 20. PAGE 9 F0166
ECO/UNDEV TEC/DEV INT/TRADE CAP/ISM

B66
BARAN P.A.,MONOPOLY CAPITAL; AN ESSAY ON THE AMERICAN ECONOMIC AND SOCIAL ORDER. USA+45 USA-45 ECO/UNDEV FINAN MARKET PLAN DIPLOM COLONIAL RACE/REL DEMAND MARXISM...CHARTS 20. PAGE 9 F0179
LG/CO CAP/ISM PRICE CONTROL

B66
BEQIRAJ M.,PEASANTRY IN REVOLUTION. STRATA ECO/UNDEV AGRI ROUTINE REV HABITAT RIGID/FLEX ...EPIST GEOG NEW/IDEA TREND MUNICH 20. PAGE 13 F0256
WORKER KNOWL NAT/LISM SOC

B66
BIRMINGHAM W.,A STUDY OF CONTEMPORARY GHANA VOL I: THE ECONOMY OF GHANA. AFR GHANA PLAN...POLICY STAT CHARTS ANTHOL BIBLIOG 20. PAGE 15 F0286
ECO/UNDEV ECO/TAC NAT/G PRODUC

B66
BOYD H.W.,MARKETING MANAGEMENT: CASES FROM EMERGING COUNTRIES. BRAZIL GHANA ISRAEL WOR+45 ADMIN PERS/REL ATTIT HABITAT WEALTH...ANTHOL 20 ARGEN CASEBOOK. PAGE 17 F0332
MGT ECO/UNDEV PROB/SOLV MARKET

B66
BROEKMEIJER M.W.J.,FICTION AND TRUTH ABOUT THE "DECADE OF DEVELOPMENT" WOR+45 AGRI FINAN INDUS NAT/G TEC/DEV DIPLOM EDU/PROP LEAD SKILL 20 THIRD/WRLD. PAGE 19 F0358
FOR/AID POLICY ECO/UNDEV PLAN

B66
BROWN J.F.,THE NEW EASTERN EUROPE. ALBANIA BULGARIA HUNGARY POLAND ROMANIA CULTURE AGRI POL/PAR WAR NAT/LISM MARXISM...CHARTS BIBLIOG 20. PAGE 19 F0369
DIPLOM COM NAT/G ECO/UNDEV

B66
BROWN R.T.,TRANSPORT AND THE ECONOMIC INTEGRATION OF SOUTH AMERICA. L/A+17C ECO/UNDEV NAT/G OP/RES DIPLOM INT/TRADE REGION WEALTH...ECOMETRIC GEOG STAT LAFTA TIME. PAGE 19 F0373
MARKET DIST/IND SIMUL

B66
CANNON M.,THE LAND BOOMERS....BIBLIOG/A 19 AUSTRAL. PAGE 21 F0412
FINAN HABITAT LAISSEZ ECO/UNDEV

B66
CROWDER M.,A SHORT HISTORY OF NIGERIA. AFR NIGERIA UK ECO/UNDEV CHIEF INT/TRADE RACE/REL NAT/LISM ORD/FREE...GEOG SOC CHARTS BIBLIOG 14/20. PAGE 29 F0558
COLONIAL NAT/G CULTURE

B66
CURRIE L.,ACCELERATING DEVELOPMENT: THE NECESSITY AND MEANS. COLOMBIA USA+45 INDUS DIPLOM EFFICIENCY WEALTH...METH/CNCPT NEW/IDEA 20. PAGE 29 F0564
PLAN ECO/UNDEV FOR/AID TEC/DEV

B66
DAVIES I.,AFRICAN TRADE UNIONS. AFR ECO/UNDEV INT/ORG GP/REL ORD/FREE SOVEREIGN SOCISM 20. PAGE 30 F0585
LABOR COLONIAL PWR INDUS

B66
DEBENKO E.,RESEARCH SOURCES FOR SOUTH ASIAN STUDIES IN ECONOMIC DEVELOPMENT: A SELECT BIBLIOGRAPHY OF SERIAL PUBLICATIONS. CEYLON INDIA NEPAL PAKISTAN PROB/SOLV ADMIN...POLICY 20. PAGE 32 F0611
BIBLIOG ECO/UNDEV S/ASIA PLAN

B66
DOBB M.,SOVIET ECONOMIC DEVELOPMENT SINCE 1917. USSR ECO/DEV ECO/UNDEV LABOR NAT/G TEC/DEV ECO/TAC ROUTINE PRODUC MARXISM 20. PAGE 33 F0647
PLAN INDUS WORKER

B66
ECKSTEIN A.,COMMUNIST CHINA'S ECONOMIC GROWTH AND FOREIGN TRADE* IMPLICATIONS FOR US POLICY. COM USA+45 USSR STRUCT INDUS MARKET DIPLOM ECO/TAC FOR/AID INT/TRADE...STAT CHARTS. PAGE 36 F0696
ASIA ECO/UNDEV CREATE PWR

B66
FELLNER W.,MAINTAINING AND RESTORING BALANCE IN INTERNATIONAL PAYMENTS. ECO/UNDEV MARKET ECO/TAC PRICE INCOME WEALTH...POLICY METH/COMP 20 MONEY. PAGE 40 F0781
BAL/PAY DIPLOM FINAN INT/TRADE

B66
FISK E.K.,NEW GUINEA ON THE THRESHOLD; ASPECTS OF SOCIAL, POLITICAL, AND ECONOMIC DEVELOPMENT. AGRI NAT/G INT/TRADE ADMIN ADJUST LITERACY ROLE...CHARTS ANTHOL 20 NEW/GUINEA. PAGE 41 F0804
ECO/UNDEV SOCIETY

B66
FRIEDMANN W.G.,INTERNATIONAL FINANCIAL AID. USA+45 ECO/DEV ECO/UNDEV NAT/G VOL/ASSN EX/STRUC PLAN RENT GIVE BAL/PAY PWR...GEOG INT/LAW STAT TREND UN EEC COMECON. PAGE 44 F0866
INT/ORG FOR/AID TEC/DEV ECO/TAC

B66
GITTINGER J.P.,THE LITERATURE OF AGRICULTURAL PLANNING. UNIV INT/ORG CONSULT WORKER TEC/DEV ECO/TAC OPTIMAL...POLICY METH/COMP BIBLIOG/A 20. PAGE 47 F0927
ECO/UNDEV AGRI PLAN WRITING

B66
GOODWIN C.D.W.,ECONOMIC INQUIRY IN AUSTRALIA. ECO/DEV ECO/UNDEV ACADEM INT/TRADE RENT TARIFFS TAX PRESS GOV/REL SOCISM 18/20 AUSTRAL. PAGE 49 F0953
ECO/TAC IDEA/COMP BUDGET COLONIAL

B66
GYORGY A.,ISSUES OF WORLD COMMUNISM. ALBANIA CHINA/COM COM USSR YUGOSLAVIA STRATA AGRI INT/ORG CHIEF FORCES WORKER WAR ALL/IDEOS...GEOG 20 MAO. PAGE 52 F1018
ECO/UNDEV REV MARXISM CON/ANAL

B66
HALLET R.,PEOPLE AND PROGRESS IN WEST AFRICA: AN INTRODUCTION TO THE PROBLEMS OF DEVELOPMENT. COM/IND INDUS KIN DIPLOM FOR/AID INT/TRADE HEALTH ...GEOG TREND CHARTS BIBLIOG/A 20 AFRICA/W. PAGE 54 F1050
AFR SOCIETY ECO/UNDEV ECO/TAC

B66
HAYER T.,FRENCH AID. AFR FRANCE AGRI FINAN BUDGET ADMIN WAR PRODUC...CHARTS 18/20 THIRD/WRLD OVRSEA/DEV. PAGE 57 F1125
TEC/DEV COLONIAL FOR/AID ECO/UNDEV

B66
HEVESY P.D.,THE UNIFICATION OF THE WORLD. FUT USA+45 WOR+45 ECO/DEV ECO/UNDEV LEGIS PROB/SOLV BAL/PWR ECO/TAC INT/TRADE PEACE. PAGE 59 F1160
DIPLOM FINAN INT/ORG

B66
HO YHI-MIN,AGRICULTURAL DEVELOPMENT OF TAIWAN: 1903-1960. FINAN WORKER EDU/PROP...STAT CHARTS BIBLIOG 20. PAGE 60 F1181
ECO/UNDEV AGRI PRODUC PLAN

B66
HOROWITZ D.,HEMISPHERES NORTH AND SOUTH: ECONOMIC DISPARITY AMONG NATIONS. WOR+45 ECO/DEV ECO/UNDEV INT/ORG PLAN DIPLOM INT/TRADE GIVE PARTIC GP/REL ...WELF/ST 20. PAGE 62 F1215
ECO/TAC FOR/AID STRATA WEALTH

B66
HOROWITZ I.L.,THREE WORLDS OF DEVELOPMENT. COM USA+45 STRUCT ECO/DEV PLAN PROB/SOLV TEC/DEV CIVMIL/REL...PHIL/SCI IDEA/COMP 20. PAGE 62 F1216
ECO/UNDEV BAL/PWR POL/PAR REV

B66
HOWE R.W.,BLACK AFRICA: FROM PRE-HISTORY TO THE EVE OF THE COLONIAL ERA. ECO/UNDEV KIN PROVS SECT INT/TRADE EDU/PROP COLONIAL...BIBLIOG WORSHIP. PAGE 62 F1226
AFR CULTURE SOC

B66
HUNT C.L.,SOCIAL ASPECTS OF ECONOMIC DEVELOPMENT. S/ASIA AGRI FAM TEC/DEV RECEIVE EDU/PROP OWN...GEOG MUNICH 20. PAGE 63 F1243
SOC STRATA ATTIT ECO/UNDEV

B66
INARRITU A.L.,EL PATRON CAMBIO-ORO Y SUS REFORMAS. AFR L/A+17C WOR+45 PLAN PROB/SOLV BUDGET ECO/TAC INT/TRADE EFFICIENCY ORD/FREE 20 MEXIC/AMER. PAGE 64 F1262
ECO/UNDEV FINAN DIPLOM POLICY

B66
INGRAM J.C.,INTERNATIONAL ECONOMIC PROBLEMS. ECO/DEV ECO/UNDEV INDUS MARKET TEC/DEV TARIFFS BAL/PAY CENTRAL...POLICY 20 EEC. PAGE 64 F1265
INT/TRADE INT/ORG FINAN

B66
INTERNATIONAL ECONOMIC ASSN,STABILITY AND PROGRESS IN THE WORLD ECONOMY: THE FIRST CONGRESS OF THE INTERNATIONAL ECONOMIC ASSOCIATION. WOR&45 ECO/DEV ECO/UNDEV DELIB/GP FOR/AID BAL/PAY...TREND CMN/WLTH 20. PAGE 65 F1276
INT/TRADE

B66
JACKSON G.D.,COMINTERN AND PEASANT IN EAST EUROPE 1919-1930. BULGARIA COM CZECHOSLVK EUR+WWI POLAND ROMANIA YUGOSLAVIA STRATA AGRI VOL/ASSN DIPLOM CONTROL CROWD WEALTH...POLICY NAT/COMP 20. PAGE 66 F1293
MARXISM ECO/UNDEV WORKER INT/ORG

B66
JENSEN F.B.,READINGS IN INTERNATIONAL ECONOMIC RELATIONS. COM ECO/UNDEV MARKET NAT/G FOR/AID ...ANTHOL 20. PAGE 67 F1317
BAL/PAY INT/TRADE FINAN

B66
KAREFA-SMART J.,AFRICA: PROGRESS THROUGH COOPERATION. AFR FINAN TEC/DEV DIPLOM FOR/AID EDU/PROP CONFER REGION GP/REL WEALTH...HEAL SOC/INTEG 20. PAGE 69 F1356
ORD/FREE ECO/UNDEV VOL/ASSN PLAN

B66
KEENLEYSIDE H.L.,INTERNATIONAL AID: A SUMMARY. AFR INDIA S/ASIA UK STRATA EXTR/IND TEC/DEV ADMIN RACE/REL DEMAND NAT/LISM WEALTH...TREND CHINJAP. PAGE 70 F1367
ECO/UNDEV FOR/AID DIPLOM TASK

B66
KIRDAR U.,THE STRUCTURE OF UNITED NATIONS ECONOMIC AID TO UNDERDEVELOPED COUNTRIES. AGRI FINAN INDUS NAT/G EX/STRUC PLAN GIVE TASK...POLICY 20 UN. PAGE 71 F1397
INT/ORG FOR/AID ECO/UNDEV ADMIN

B66
KOH S.J.,STAGES OF INDUSTRIAL DEVELOPMENT IN ASIA. ASIA INDIA KOREA STRATA STRUCT NAT/G INT/TRADE ...CHARTS 19/20 CHINJAP. PAGE 72 F1415
INDUS ECO/UNDEV ECO/DEV LABOR

B66
KUZNETS S.,MODERN ECONOMIC GROWTH. WOR+45 WOR-45 ECO/DEV ECO/UNDEV AGRI FINAN INDUS TEC/DEV EFFICIENCY INCOME...NAT/COMP 19/20. PAGE 74 F1456
TIME/SEQ WEALTH PRODUC

B66
LAMBERG R.F.,PRAG UND DIE DRITTE WELT. AFR ASIA CZECHOSLVK L/A+17C MARKET TEC/DEV ECO/TAC REV ATTIT 20 TREATY. PAGE 75 F1462
DIPLOM ECO/UNDEV INT/TRADE FOR/AID

B66
LEAGUE OF WOMEN VOTERS OF US,FOREIGN AID AT THE CROSSROADS. USA+45 WOR+45 DELIB/GP PROB/SOLV DIPLOM INT/TRADE RECEIVE BAL/PAY...CHARTS 20 UN ALL/PROG. PAGE 76 F1498
FOR/AID GIVE ECO/UNDEV PLAN

B66
LENSKI G.E.,POWER AND PRIVILEGE: A THEORY OF SOCIAL STRATIFICATION. SWEDEN UK UNIV USSR CULTURE ECO/UNDEV PRIVIL PWR...PHIL/SCI CONCPT CHARTS IDEA/COMP HYPO/EXP METH MARX/KARL. PAGE 78 F1525
SOC STRATA STRUCT SOCIETY

B66
LEONTIEF W.,ESSAYS IN ECONOMICS. ECO/UNDEV INDUS NAT/G CAP/ISM FOR/AID AUTOMAT MARXISM...ECOMETRIC CHARTS ANTHOL METH 20 KEYNES/JM. PAGE 78 F1528
CONCPT METH/CNCPT METH/COMP

B66
MACBEAN A.I.,EXPORT INSTABILITY AND ECONOMIC DEVELOPMENT. CHILE PAKISTAN PUERT/RICO TANZANIA UGANDA WOR+45 MARKET ECO/TAC...POLICY REGRESS CHARTS BIBLIOG TIME 20. PAGE 83 F1622
INT/TRADE ECO/UNDEV ECOMETRIC INSPECT

B66
MACFARQUHAR R.,CHINA UNDER MAO: POLITICS TAKES COMMAND. CHINA/COM COM AGRI INDUS CHIEF FORCES DIPLOM INT/TRADE EDU/PROP TASK REV ADJUST...ANTHOL 20 MAO. PAGE 83 F1628
ECO/UNDEV TEC/DEV ECO/TAC ADMIN

B66
MADAN G.R.,ECONOMIC THINKING IN INDIA. INDIA ECO/UNDEV AGRI FINAN INDUS LABOR PLAN CAP/ISM INT/TRADE MARXISM SOCISM...POLICY 1/20. PAGE 84 F1638
ECO/TAC PHIL/SCI NAT/G POL/PAR

B66
MALASSIS L.,ECONOMIC DEVELOPMENT AND THE PROGRAMMING OF RURAL EDUCATION. CONSULT PROB/SOLV LITERACY KNOWL...CHARTS GEN/METH 20. PAGE 84 F1644
AGRI ECO/UNDEV SCHOOL PLAN

B66
MASON E.S.,ECONOMIC DEVELOPMENT IN INDIA AND PAKISTAN. INDIA PAKISTAN AGRI FINAN PLAN BUDGET INT/TRADE WEALTH...POLICY STAT TREND CHARTS 20. PAGE 87 F1700
NAT/COMP ECO/UNDEV ECO/TAC FOR/AID

B66
MIKESELL R.F.,PUBLIC INTERNATIONAL LENDING FOR DEVELOPMENT. WOR+45 WOR-45 DELIB/GP...TIME/SEQ CHARTS BIBLIOG 20. PAGE 91 F1783
INT/ORG FOR/AID ECO/UNDEV FINAN

B66
MOUNTJOY A.B.,INDUSTRIALIZATION AND UNDER-DEVELOPED COUNTRIES (2ND REV. ED.). CHILE GHANA INDIA NIGERIA WOR+45 SOCIETY PROB/SOLV ECO/TAC...SOC CHARTS 20 INDUS/REV. PAGE 94 F1848
ECO/UNDEV INDUS GEOG HABITAT

B66
MUNBY D.,ECONOMIC GROWTH IN WORLD PERSPECTIVE. AFR WOR+45 SOCIETY INDUS PLAN TEC/DEV ECO/TAC FOR/AID INT/TRADE COST CATHISM...ANTHOL 20 EUROPE/W CHURCH/STA. PAGE 95 F1859
SECT ECO/UNDEV ECO/DEV

B66
NAMBOODIRIPAD E.M.,ECONOMICS AND POLITICS OF INDIA'S SOCIALIST PATTERN. INDIA STRATA AGRI INDUS NAT/G PRICE ORD/FREE SOVEREIGN 20. PAGE 96 F1888
ECO/UNDEV PLAN SOCISM CAP/ISM

B66
NATIONAL COUN APPLIED ECO RES,DEVELOPMENT WITHOUT AID. INDIA FINAN TEC/DEV EFFICIENCY...ANTHOL 20. PAGE 97 F1901
FOR/AID PLAN SOVEREIGN ECO/UNDEV

B66
NEVITT A.A.,THE ECONOMIC PROBLEMS OF HOUSING. WOR+45 ECO/DEV ECO/UNDEV ACT/RES PROB/SOLV ECO/TAC RENT...OBS CHARTS 20. PAGE 98 F1917
HABITAT PROC/MFG DELIB/GP NAT/COMP

B66
O'CONNER A.M.,AN ECONOMIC GEOGRAPHY OF EAST AFRICA. AFR TANZANIA UGANDA AGRI WORKER INT/TRADE COLONIAL
ECO/UNDEV EXTR/IND

GOV/REL...CHARTS METH/COMP 20 AFRICA/E. PAGE 99 F1953
GEOG HABITAT

B66

OECD DEVELOPMENT CENTRE,CATALOGUE OF SOCIAL AND ECONOMIC DEVELOPMENT INSTITUTES AND PROGRAMMES* RESEARCH. ACT/RES PLAN TEC/DEV EDU/PROP...SOC GP/COMP NAT/COMP. PAGE 101 F1976
ECO/UNDEV ECO/DEV R+D ACADEM

B66

OHLIN G.,AID AND INDEBTEDNESS. AUSTRIA FINAN INT/ORG PLAN DIPLOM GIVE...POLICY MATH CHARTS 20. PAGE 101 F1984
FOR/AID ECO/UNDEV ADMIN WEALTH

B66

OHLIN G.,FOREIGN AID POLICIES RECONSIDERED. ECO/DEV ECO/UNDEV VOL/ASSN CONSULT PLAN CONTROL ATTIT ...CONCPT CHARTS BIBLIOG 20. PAGE 101 F1985
FOR/AID DIPLOM GIVE

B66

ORG FOR ECO COOP AND DEVEL,GEOGRAPHICAL DISTRIBUTION OF FINANCIAL FLOWS TO LESS DEVELOPED COUNTRIES. WOR+45 DIPLOM INT/TRADE GIVE RECEIVE REPAR REGION WEALTH...GEOG STAT CHARTS 20 OECD. PAGE 102 F1997
FINAN ECO/UNDEV INT/ORG FOR/AID

B66

RAO Y.V.L.,COMMUNICATION AND DEVELOPMENT. INDIA S/ASIA SOCIETY ACT/RES EDU/PROP PARTIC ATTIT...SOC GP/COMP BIBLIOG MUNICH MUNICH 20. PAGE 109 F2149
COM/IND ECO/UNDEV OBS

B66

RAYBACK J.G.,A HISTORY OF AMERICAN LABOR. USA+45 USA-45 ECO/DEV LEGIS COLONIAL WAR INGP/REL PWR WEALTH 17/20. PAGE 110 F2156
LABOR LOBBY ECO/UNDEV NAT/G

B66

RIZK C.,LE REGIME POLITIQUE LIBANAIS. ISLAM LEBANON STRUCT POL/PAR SECT LOBBY GP/REL 20 ARABS MUSLIM CHRISTIAN. PAGE 112 F2198
ECO/UNDEV NAT/G CULTURE

B66

ROBINSON E.A.,THE ECONOMICS OF EDUCATION. WOR+45 CULTURE ECO/UNDEV FINAN SCHOOL DIPLOM PRICE COST DEMAND...CHARTS METH/COMP 20. PAGE 112 F2216
EDU/PROP ADJUST CONFER

B66

ROSS A.M.,INDUSTRIAL RELATIONS AND ECONOMIC DEVELOPMENT. POL/PAR LEGIS WORKER BARGAIN PRICE EXEC LOBBY INCOME PWR...DECISION ANTHOL BIBLIOG 20. PAGE 114 F2243
ECO/UNDEV LABOR NAT/G GP/REL

B66

RUBIN S.J.,THE CONSCIENCE OF THE RICH NATIONS: THE DEVELOPMENT ASSISTANCE COMMITTEE AND THE COMMON AID EFFORT. EUR+WWI USA+45 ECO/UNDEV INT/ORG NAT/G VOL/ASSN ECO/TAC INT/TRADE...OBS UN AID DEV/ASSIST IBRD OECD. PAGE 114 F2256
FOR/AID ECO/DEV CONFER CENTRAL

B66

SEWELL J.P.,FUNCTIONALISM AND WORLD POLITICS* A STUDY BASED ON UNITED NATIONS PROGRAMS FINANCING ECONOMICAL DEVELOPMENT. ECO/UNDEV FINAN PROB/SOLV DIPLOM ECO/TAC FEEDBACK REGION ADJUST ATTIT UN IBRD INTL/FINAN INTL/DEV UNSF. PAGE 120 F2360
TASK INT/ORG IDEA/COMP GEN/LAWS

B66

SINGH L.P.,THE POLITICS OF ECONOMIC COOPERATION IN ASIA; A STUDY OF ASIAN INTERNATIONAL ORGANIZATIONS. ASIA INT/ORG ACT/RES PLAN GP/REL...POLICY GP/COMP BIBLIOG 20 UN SEATO. PAGE 122 F2414
ECO/UNDEV ECO/TAC REGION DIPLOM

B66

SOMMERFELD R.M.,TAX REFORM AND THE ALLIANCE FOR PROGRESS. USA+45 ECO/DEV ECO/UNDEV FINAN NAT/G INCOME ORD/FREE WEALTH...STAT CHARTS 20 ALL/PROG. PAGE 124 F2442
TAX INT/ORG L/A+17C FOR/AID

B66

SPULBER N.,THE STATE AND ECONOMIC DEVELOPMENT IN EASTERN EUROPE. BULGARIA COM CZECHOSLVK HUNGARY POLAND YUGOSLAVIA CULTURE PLAN CAP/ISM INT/TRADE CONTROL...POLICY CHARTS METH/COMP BIBLIOG/A 19/20. PAGE 125 F2460
ECO/DEV ECO/UNDEV NAT/G TOTALISM

B66

THIESENHUSEN W.C.,CHILE'S EXPERIMENTS IN AGRARIAN REFORM. CHILE STRUCT NAT/G ACT/RES ECO/TAC GOV/REL COST SOCISM...TREND CHARTS SOC/EXP 20. PAGE 130 F2558
AGRI ECO/UNDEV SOC TEC/DEV

B66

THOMPSON J.H.,MODERNIZATION OF THE ARAB WORLD. FUT ISRAEL STRUCT ECO/UNDEV DIPLOM INGP/REL ATTIT ...CENSUS ANTHOL 20 ARABS. PAGE 130 F2565
ADJUST ISLAM PROB/SOLV NAT/COMP

B66

UNITED NATIONS,YEARBOOK OF INTERNATIONAL TRADE STATISTICS, 1964 (15TH ISSUE). WOR+45 ECO/DEV ECO/UNDEV UN. PAGE 132 F2614
STAT INT/TRADE DIPLOM CHARTS

B66

US HOUSE COMM FOREIGN AFFAIRS,HEARINGS ON HR 12449 A BILL TO AMEND FURTHER THE FOREIGN ASSISTANCE ACT OF 1961. AFR ASIA L/A+17C USA+45 VIETNAM INT/ORG TEC/DEV INT/TRADE ATTIT ORD/FREE 20 UN NATO CONGRESS AID. PAGE 137 F2692
FOR/AID ECO/TAC ECO/UNDEV DIPLOM

B66

US SENATE COMM APPROPRIATIONS,FOREIGN ASSISTANCE AND RELATED AGENCIES APPROPRIATIONS FOR FISCAL YEAR 1967: HEARINGS... ON H. R. 17788. ECO/UNDEV INT/ORG FORCES INSPECT ECO/TAC GIVE DEBATE WEAPON CIVMIL/REL WEALTH...INT 20 CONGRESS DEPT/DEFEN DEPT/STATE DEPT/HEW AID. PAGE 138 F2727
BUDGET FOR/AID DIPLOM COST

B66

US SENATE COMM GOVT OPERATIONS,HEARINGS BEFORE SUBCOMMITTEE ON FOREIGN AID EXPENDITURES: POPULATION CRISIS VOLUMES 1-5 JUNE-SEPT 1965. STRATA ECO/UNDEV PLAN TEC/DEV EDU/PROP ATTIT HEALTH ...GEOG CHARTS 20 CONGRESS BIRTH/CON CASEBOOK. PAGE 138 F2729
ECO/DEV CENSUS FAM CONTROL

B66

US SENATE COMM ON FOREIGN REL,HEARINGS ON S 2859 AND S 2861. USA+45 WOR+45 FORCES BUDGET CAP/ISM ADMIN DETER WEAPON TOTALISM...NAT/COMP 20 UN CONGRESS. PAGE 139 F2735
FOR/AID DIPLOM ORD/FREE ECO/UNDEV

B66

US SENATE COMM ON FOREIGN REL,ASIAN DEVELOPMENT BANK ACT. USA+45 LAW DIPLOM...CHARTS 20 BLACK/EUG S/EASTASIA. PAGE 139 F2736
FOR/AID FINAN ECO/UNDEV S/ASIA

B66

WETTER G.A.,SOVIET IDEOLOGY TODAY. USSR ECO/UNDEV SECT WORKER CAP/ISM CONTROL TASK EFFICIENCY TOTALISM DRIVE WEALTH...TREND 18/20. PAGE 145 F2864
ALL/IDEOS MARXISM REV

B66

WILCOX C.,ECONOMIES OF THE WORLD TODAY: THEIR ORGANIZATION, DEVELOPMENT, AND PERFORMANCE (2ND ED.). CHINA/COM COM INDIA NIGERIA UK WOR+45 WOR-45 INDUS MARKET PLAN ECO/TAC SOCISM...CHARTS METH/COMP 20. PAGE 146 F2878
ECO/DEV ECO/UNDEV MARXISM CAP/ISM

L66

AFRICAN BIBLIOGRAPHIC CENTER,"AFRICAN ECONOMIC AFFAIRS: A SELECT BIBLIOGRAPHICAL SURVEY, 1965-1966." AFR FINAN INDUS INT/ORG LABOR PLAN BUDGET DIPLOM INT/TRADE ADMIN EFFICIENCY WEALTH 20. PAGE 3 F0046
BIBLIOG ECO/UNDEV TEC/DEV FOR/AID

L66

AFRICAN BIBLIOGRAPHIC CENTER,"AFRICAN ECONOMIC AFFAIRS: A SELECT BIBLIOGRAPHICAL SURVEY, 1965-1966; SUPPLEMENTS NUMBERS 1-3." AFR FINAN INDUS LABOR PLAN BUDGET CAP/ISM DIPLOM INT/TRADE ADMIN...GEOG 20. PAGE 3 F0047
BIBLIOG/A ECO/UNDEV FOR/AID TEC/DEV

L66

CHENERY H.B.,"FOREIGN ASSISTANCE AND ECONOMIC DEVELOPMENT" FUT WOR+45 NAT/G DIPLOM GIVE PRODUC ...METH/CNCPT CHARTS 20. PAGE 24 F0464
FOR/AID EFFICIENCY ECO/UNDEV TEC/DEV

L66

PACKENHAM R.A.,"POLITICAL-DEVELOPMENT DOCTRINES IN THE AMERICAN FOREIGN AID PROGRAM." STRUCT R+D CREATE DIPLOM AID. PAGE 102 F2011
FOR/AID ECO/UNDEV GEN/LAWS

S66

COHEN A.,"THE TECHNOLOGY/ELITE APPROACH TO THE DEVELOPMENTAL PROCESS* PERUVIAN CASE STUDY." L/A+17C STRUCT CREATE ECO/TAC FOR/AID CIVMIL/REL MARXISM TECHRACY HYPO/EXP. PAGE 26 F0496
ECO/UNDEV ELITES PERU

S66

ERB GF,"THE UNITED NATIONS CONFERENCE ON TRADE AND DEVELOPMENT (UNCTAD): A SELECTED CURRENT READING LIST." FINAN FOR/AID CONFER 20 UN. PAGE 38 F0742
BIBLIOG/A INT/TRADE ECO/UNDEV INT/ORG

S66

JAVITS J.K.,"POLITICAL ACTION VITAL FOR LATIN AMERICAN INTEGRATION." ECO/UNDEV INT/ORG POL/PAR VOL/ASSN PLAN PROB/SOLV INT/TRADE EFFICIENCY 20 OAS LAFTA ALL/PROG. PAGE 66 F1308
L/A+17C ECO/TAC REGION

S66

LINDBLOOM C.E.,"HAS INDIA AN ECONOMIC FUTURE?" FUT INDIA NAT/G PROB/SOLV...POLICY 20. PAGE 80 F1568
AGRI PRODUC PLAN ECO/UNDEV

S66

MALENBAUM W.,"GOVERNMENT, ENTREPRENEURSHIP, AND ECONOMIC GROWTH IN POOR LANDS." ELITES ECO/UNDEV INDUS CREATE DRIVE. PAGE 84 F1645
ECO/TAC PLAN CONSERVE NAT/G

S66

MARKSHAK J.,"ECONOMIC PLANNING AND THE COST OF THINKING." COM MARKET EX/STRUC...DECISION GEN/LAWS. PAGE 85 F1672
ECO/UNDEV ECO/TAC PLAN ECO/DEV

S66

NEWLYN W.T.,"MONEY MARKETS IN EAST AFRICA." AFR TANZANIA UGANDA UK DIPLOM CENTRAL 20. PAGE 98 F1923
FINAN WEALTH BAL/PAY ECO/UNDEV

S66

ROTHCHILD D.,"THE LIMITS OF FEDERALISM: AN EXAMINATION OF POLITICAL INSTITUTIONAL TRANSFER IN AFRICA." AFR CONSTN CULTURE ELITES ECO/UNDEV KIN PROB/SOLV ADMIN ORD/FREE PWR...POLICY 20. PAGE 114 F2250
FEDERAL NAT/G NAT/LISM COLONIAL

S66

SHORTE F.C.,"THE APPLICATION OF DEVELOPMENT HYPOTHESES IN MIDDLE EASTERN STUDIES." STRUCT AGRI
ECO/UNDEV ISLAM

CREATE DEMAND...GEOG STAT CON/ANAL CHARTS. PAGE 121 F2387
SOC HYPO/EXP
C66

WINT G.,"ASIA: A HANDBOOK." ASIA S/ASIA INDUS LABOR SECT PRESS RACE/REL MARXISM...STAT CHARTS BIBLIOG 20. PAGE 148 F2908
ECO/UNDEV DIPLOM NAT/G SOCIETY
B67

ADLER J.H.,CAPITAL MOVEMENTS AND ECONOMIC DEVELOPMENT. WOR+45 FINAN NAT/G BARGAIN ECO/TAC FOR/AID INT/TRADE ANTHOL. PAGE 2 F0042
DIPLOM ECO/DEV ECO/UNDEV
B67

ALNASRAWI A.,FINANCING ECONOMIC DEVELOPMENT IN IRAQ. IRAQ INDUS CAP/ISM COST PRODUC...STAT CHARTS BIBLIOG 20. PAGE 4 F0076
ECO/UNDEV EXTR/IND TEC/DEV INT/TRADE
B67

ANDERSON C.W.,POLITICS AND ECONOMIC CHANGE IN LATIN AMERICA. L/A+17C INDUS NAT/G OP/RES ADMIN DEMAND ...POLICY STAT CHARTS NAT/COMP 20. PAGE 5 F0093
ECO/UNDEV PROB/SOLV PLAN ECO/TAC
B67

ANDERSON C.W.,ISSUES OF POLITICAL DEVELOPMENT. BURMA WOR+45 CULTURE TOP/EX ECO/TAC MARXISM ...CHARTS NAT/COMP 20 COLOMB CONGO/LEOP. PAGE 5 F0094
NAT/LISM COERCE ECO/UNDEV SOCISM
B67

BALDWIN G.B.,PLANNING AND DEVELOPMENT IN IRAN. IRAN AGRI INDUS CONSULT WORKER EDU/PROP BAL/PAY...CHARTS 20. PAGE 9 F0164
PLAN ECO/UNDEV ADMIN PROB/SOLV
B67

BARANSON J.,TECHNOLOGY FOR UNDERDEVELOPED AREAS: AN ANNOTATED BIBLIOGRAPHY. FUT WOR+45 CULTURE INDUS INT/ORG CREATE PROB/SOLV INT/TRADE EDU/PROP AUTOMAT ...CONCPT METH. PAGE 10 F0181
BIBLIOG/A ECO/UNDEV TEC/DEV R+D
B67

BARNETT A.D.,CHINA AFTER MAO. ASIA CHINA/COM CULTURE ECO/UNDEV ECO/TAC CONTROL EFFICIENCY NAT/LISM MARXISM 20. PAGE 10 F0189
POL/PAR NAT/G TEC/DEV GP/REL
B67

BARROW T.C.,TRADE AND EMPIRE: THE BRITISH CUSTOMS SERVICE IN COLONIAL AMERICA, 1660-1775. UK USA-45 ECO/UNDEV NAT/G ECO/TAC DOMIN REV 17/18. PAGE 10 F0197
COLONIAL TARIFFS ADMIN EX/STRUC
B67

BIRMINGHAM W.,A STUDY OF CONTEMPORARY GHANA VOL. I: SOME ASPECTS OF SOCIAL STRUCTURE. AFR GHANA AGRI FAM SECT PLAN EDU/PROP MARRIAGE OWN...POLICY STAT CHARTS MUNICH 20. PAGE 15 F0287
SOCIETY STRUCT CENSUS ECO/UNDEV
B67

BLAUG M.,ECONOMICS OF EDUCATION: A SELECTED ANNOTATED BIBLIOGRAPHY. EUR+WWI INTELL ECO/DEV ECO/UNDEV ACADEM INT/ORG NAT/G CREATE ADMIN EFFICIENCY ROLE PREDICT. PAGE 16 F0298
BIBLIOG/A EDU/PROP FINAN PLAN
B67

BUSEY J.L.,NOTES ON COSTA RICAN DEMOCRACY. COSTA/RICA L/A+17C NAT/G POL/PAR LEGIS CHOOSE OWN ATTIT...BIBLIOG 20. PAGE 20 F0394
CONSTN MAJORIT SOCIETY ECO/UNDEV
B67

CASTILLO C.M.,GROWTH AND INTEGRATION IN CENTRAL AMERICA. L/A+17C CREATE PROB/SOLV ECO/TAC REGION PRODUC...OBS BIBLIOG 20. PAGE 22 F0429
ECO/UNDEV INT/TRADE NAT/COMP
B67

CEFKIN J.L.,THE BACKGROUND OF CURRENT WORLD PROBLEMS. AFR NAT/G MARXISM...T 20 UN. PAGE 22 F0432
DIPLOM NAT/LISM ECO/UNDEV
B67

CHANDRASEKHAR S.,PROBLEMS OF ECONOMIC DEVELOPMENT. AFR INDIA PHILIPPINE UAR WOR+45 INDUS...GEOG SOC ANTHOL BIBLIOG 20 CHINJAP. PAGE 23 F0450
ECO/UNDEV PLAN AGRI PROB/SOLV
B67

CHILCOTE R.H.,PORTUGUESE AFRICA. PORTUGAL CULTURE SOCIETY ECO/UNDEV DOMIN NAT/LISM...TREND IDEA/COMP NAT/COMP BIBLIOG 15/20. PAGE 24 F0465
AFR COLONIAL ORD/FREE PROB/SOLV
B67

CLEGERN W.M.,BRITISH HONDURAS: COLONIAL DEAD END, 1859-1900. HONDURAS AGRI FINAN PROB/SOLV INT/TRADE PWR WEALTH...BIBLIOG/A 19. PAGE 25 F0487
COLONIAL POLICY ECO/UNDEV DOMIN
B67

ELDREDGE H.W.,TAMING MEGALOPOLIS; HOW TO MANAGE AN URBANIZED WORLD. WOR+45 SOCIETY ECO/DEV ECO/UNDEV NAT/G COMPUTER CREATE PARTIC EFFICIENCY WEALTH ...MGT ANTHOL MUNICH. PAGE 37 F0716
TEC/DEV PLAN PROB/SOLV
B67

FALL B.B.,HO CHI MINH ON REVOLUTION: SELECTED WRITINGS, 1920-66. COM VIETNAM ELITES NAT/G COERCE GUERRILLA RACE/REL MARXISM...MARXIST ANTHOL 20. PAGE 39 F0761
REV COLONIAL ECO/UNDEV S/ASIA
B67

FANON F.,TOWARD THE AFRICAN REVOLUTION. AFR FRANCE CULTURE ELITES LEAD REV GP/REL ORD/FREE SOVEREIGN 20. PAGE 39 F0762
COLONIAL DOMIN ECO/UNDEV RACE/REL
B67

FORDE D.,WEST AFRICAN KINGDOMS IN THE NINETEENTH CENTURY. ECO/UNDEV AGRI KIN...SOC CHARTS NAT/COMP 19. PAGE 42 F0826
AFR REGION CULTURE
B67

GROSS B.M.,ACTION UNDER PLANNING: THE GUIDANCE OF ECONOMIC DEVELOPMENT. STRUCT R+D NAT/G ACT/RES HABITAT...DECISION 20. PAGE 51 F1005
ECO/UNDEV PLAN ADMIN MGT
B67

HUMPHREY R.A.,UNIVERSITIES...AND DEVELOPMENT ASSISTANCE ABROAD. USA+45 OP/RES ECO/TAC FOR/AID ...ANTHOL 20. PAGE 63 F1242
ACADEM DIPLOM KNOWL ECO/UNDEV
B67

JACOBY N.H.,US AID TO TAIWAN. CAP/ISM DIPLOM FEEDBACK COST PRODUC...OBS INT CHARTS 20. PAGE 66 F1301
FOR/AID OP/RES ECO/TAC ECO/UNDEV
B67

JOHNSON D.G.,THE STRUGGLE AGAINST WORLD HUNGER (HEADLINE SERIES, NO. 184) (PAMPHLET). PLAN TEC/DEV FOR/AID...CHARTS 20 FAO MEXIC/AMER. PAGE 67 F1322
AGRI PROB/SOLV ECO/UNDEV HEALTH
B67

JOHNSON H.G.,ECONOMIC POLICY TOWARD LESS DEVELOPED COUNTRIES. USA+45 ECO/DEV INT/ORG PLAN CAP/ISM FOR/AID TARIFFS GIVE WEALTH...NEW/IDEA CHARTS 20 UN GATT. PAGE 67 F1327
ECO/UNDEV ECO/TAC METH/COMP
B67

JOHNSON H.G.,ECONOMIC NATIONALISM IN OLD AND NEW STATES. CANADA CHINA/COM MALI UK DIPLOM...SIMUL GEN/LAWS 19/20 MEXIC/AMER. PAGE 68 F1328
NAT/LISM ECO/UNDEV ECO/DEV NAT/COMP
B67

KANNER L.,THE NEW YORK TIMES WORLD ECONOMIC REVIEW AND FORECAST: 1967. WOR+45 ECO/DEV ECO/UNDEV TEC/DEV...STAT PREDICT CHARTS 20. PAGE 69 F1349
INDUS FINAN TREND ECO/TAC
B67

KARDOUCHE G.K.,THE UAR IN DEVELOPMENT. UAR ECO/TAC INT/TRADE BAL/PAY...STAT CHARTS BIBLIOG 20. PAGE 69 F1355
FINAN MGT CAP/ISM ECO/UNDEV
B67

LANDEN R.G.,OMAN SINCE 1856: DISRUPTIVE MODERNIZATION IN A TRADITIONAL ARAB SOCIETY. UK DIST/IND EXTR/IND SECT DIPLOM INT/TRADE...SOC LING CHARTS BIBLIOG 19/20. PAGE 75 F1468
ISLAM CULTURE ECO/UNDEV NAT/G
B67

LEWIS L.J.,SOCIETY, SCHOOLS AND PROGRESS IN NIGERIA. NIGERIA WORKER ECO/TAC ADJUST 20. PAGE 79 F1550
EDU/PROP ECO/UNDEV SKILL SOCIETY
B67

LINDER S.B.,TRADE AND TRADE POLICY FOR DEVELOPMENT. OP/RES DIPLOM TARIFFS UTIL WEALTH...BIBLIOG 20. PAGE 80 F1569
ECO/UNDEV ECO/TAC TEC/DEV INT/TRADE
B67

MARTIN P.,CANADA AND THE QUEST FOR PEACE. CANADA VIETNAM ECO/UNDEV PLAN FOR/AID WAR 20 UN. PAGE 86 F1684
DIPLOM PEACE INT/ORG POLICY
B67

MAZOUR A.G.,SOVIET ECONOMIC DEVELOPMENT: OPERATION OUTSTRIP: 1921-1965. USSR ECO/UNDEV FINAN CHIEF WORKER PROB/SOLV CONTROL PRODUC MARXISM...CHARTS ORG/CHARTS 20 STALIN/J. PAGE 87 F1711
ECO/TAC AGRI INDUS PLAN
B67

MCDOUGAL M.S.,THE INTERPRETATION OF AGREEMENTS AND WORLD PUBLIC ORDER: PRINCIPLES OF CONTENT AND PROCEDURE. WOR+45 CONSTN PROB/SOLV TEC/DEV ...CON/ANAL TREATY. PAGE 88 F1727
INT/LAW STRUCT ECO/UNDEV DIPLOM
B67

MUHAMMAD A.C.,THE EMERGENCE OF PAKISTAN. PAKISTAN S/ASIA CONSTN ECO/UNDEV NAT/G CONTROL NAT/LISM 20. PAGE 94 F1853
DIPLOM COLONIAL SECT PROB/SOLV
B67

NKRUMAH K.,CHALLENGE OF THE CONGO. FORCES ECO/TAC FOR/AID REGION MURDER REPRESENT 20 CONGO/LEOP UN. PAGE 98 F1930
REV ECO/UNDEV ORD/FREE DIPLOM
B67

OGLESBY C.,CONTAINMENT AND CHANGE. AFR COM USA+45 ECO/UNDEV TEC/DEV ECO/TAC FOR/AID INT/TRADE DOMIN GUERRILLA REV PEACE 20 STALIN/J. PAGE 101 F1983
DIPLOM BAL/PWR MARXISM CULTURE
B67

OVERSEAS DEVELOPMENT INSTIT,EFFECTIVE AID. WOR+45 INT/ORG TEC/DEV DIPLOM INT/TRADE ADMIN. PAGE 102 F2004
FOR/AID ECO/UNDEV ECO/TAC

NAT/COMP

B67
PIKE F.B.,FREEDOM AND REFORM IN LATIN AMERICA. L/A+17C
BRAZIL URUGUAY CONSTN CULTURE SECT DIPLOM EDU/PROP ORD/FREE
PARTIC DRIVE ALL/VALS CATHISM...GEOG ANTHOL BIBLIOG ECO/UNDEV
REFORMERS BOLIV. PAGE 106 F2086 REV

B67
RAVKIN A.,THE NEW STATES OF AFRICA (HEADLINE AFR
SERIES, NO. 183((PAMPHLET). CULTURE STRUCT INDUS ECO/UNDEV
COLONIAL NAT/LISM...SOC 20. PAGE 109 F2153 SOCIETY
ADMIN

B67
ROBERTS B.C.,COLLECTIVE BARGAINING IN AFRICAN LABOR
COUNTRIES. AFR LAW ECO/UNDEV BARGAIN GP/REL MGT
...DECISION METH/COMP 20. PAGE 112 F2206 PLAN
ECO/TAC

B67
SACKS B.,SOUTH AFRICA: AN IMPERIAL DILEMMA. COLONIAL
SOUTH/AFR UK ECO/UNDEV KIN DOMIN DEBATE CONTROL REV RACE/REL
DISCRIM ISOLAT...POLICY STAT BIBLIOG 20. PAGE 115 DIPLOM
F2268 ORD/FREE

B67
SMITH T.L.,THE PROCESS OF RURAL DEVELOPMENT IN IDEA/COMP
LATIN AMERICA (A MONOGRAPH). L/A+17C STRATA INDUS SOC
PLAN GP/REL PERS/REL RIGID/FLEX WEALTH...OBS CHARTS AGRI
ORG/CHARTS ANTHOL 20 COLOMB. PAGE 123 F2434 ECO/UNDEV

B67
SPIRO H.S.,PATTERNS OF AFRICAN DEVLOPMENT: FIVE AFR
COMPARISONS. STRUCT ECO/UNDEV NAT/G CONSERVE SOCISM CONSTN
...PREDICT NAT/COMP 20 CHINJAP. PAGE 125 F2457 NAT/LISM
TREND

B67
TANSKY L.,US AND USSR AID TO DEVELOPING COUNTRIES. ECO/UNDEV
INDIA TURKEY USA+45 USSR INDUS PLAN CAP/ISM WAR PWR FOR/AID
WEALTH MARXISM...CHARTS NAT/COMP BIBLIOG 20. DIPLOM
PAGE 128 F2534 ECO/TAC

B67
TANSKY L.,US AND USSR AID TO DEVELOPING COUNTRIES. FOR/AID
INDIA TURKEY UAR USA+45 USSR FINAN PLAN TEC/DEV ECO/UNDEV
ADMIN WEALTH...TREND METH/COMP 20. PAGE 128 F2535 MARXISM
CAP/ISM

B67
THOMAN R.S.,GEOGRAPHY OF INTERNATIONAL TRADE. INT/TRADE
WOR+45 ECO/DEV ECO/UNDEV INT/ORG LG/CO PLAN BAL/PAY GEOG
...STAT CHARTS NAT/COMP 20. PAGE 130 F2559 ECO/TAC
DIPLOM

B67
TOMA P.A.,THE POLITICS OF FOOD FOR PEACE; FOR/AID
EXECUTIVE-LEGISLATIVE INTERACTION. USA+45 ECO/UNDEV POLICY
POL/PAR DEBATE EXEC LOBBY CHOOSE PEACE...DECISION LEGIS
CHARTS. PAGE 131 F2580 AGRI

B67
UNIVERSAL REFERENCE SYSTEM,ECONOMIC REGULATION, BIBLIOG/A
BUSINESS, AND GOVERNMENT (VOLUME VIII). WOR+45 CONTROL
WOR-45 ECO/DEV ECO/UNDEV FINAN LABOR TEC/DEV NAT/G
ECO/TAC INT/TRADE GOV/REL...POLICY COMPUT/IR.
PAGE 133 F2617

B67
US AGENCY INTERNATIONAL DEV,PROPOSED FOREIGN AID ECO/UNDEV
PROGRAM FOR 1968: SUMMARY PRESENTATION TO THE BUDGET
CONGRESS. AFR S/ASIA USA+45 AGRI TEC/DEV DIPLOM FOR/AID
ECO/TAC BAL/PAY COST HEALTH KNOWL SKILL 20 AID STAT
CONGRESS ALL/PROG. PAGE 134 F2640

B67
US CONGRESS JOINT ECO COMM,AN ECONOMIC PROFILE OF ECO/UNDEV
MAINLAND CHINA, VOLUMES I AND II. CHINA/COM AGRI WEALTH
DIST/IND FINAN INDUS LABOR FORCES ACT/RES PLAN ECO/TAC
INT/TRADE INGP/REL BAL/PAY 20 CONGRESS. PAGE 135 DELIB/GP
F2664

B67
US GOVERNMENT,SECTION-BY-SECTION ANALYSIS OF THE FOR/AID
PROPOSED FOREIGN ASSISTANCE ACT OF 1967 (PAMPHLET). POLICY
USA+45 ECO/UNDEV NAT/G CONGRESS. PAGE 136 F2683 FORCES
INT/TRADE

B67
US SENATE COMM ON FOREIGN REL,INTER-AMERICAN LAW
DEVELOPMENT BANK ACT AMENDMENT. L/A+17C USA+45 FINAN
DELIB/GP DIPLOM FOR/AID BAL/PAY...CHARTS SENATE. INT/ORG
PAGE 139 F2741 ECO/UNDEV

B67
WILLS A.J.,AN INTRODUCTION TO THE HISTORY OF AFR
CENTRAL AFRICA. RHODESIA ZAMBIA CULTURE SOCIETY COLONIAL
ECO/UNDEV TEC/DEV DOMIN WAR ALL/VALS...POLICY TREND ORD/FREE
BIBLIOG T 14/20 NYASALAND. PAGE 147 F2899

B67
WOLF C. JR.,UNITED STATES POLICY AND THE THIRD DIPLOM
WORLD. USA+45 WOR+45 FORCES ACT/RES BAL/PWR ECO/TAC ECO/UNDEV
FOR/AID DETER GUERRILLA NUC/PWR REV...CHARTS 20. POLICY
PAGE 148 F2916 NAT/G

B67
ZONDAG C.H.,THE BOLIVIAN ECONOMY 1952-65. L/A+17C ECO/UNDEV
TEC/DEV FOR/AID ADMIN...OBS TREND CHARTS BIBLIOG 20 INDUS
BOLIV. PAGE 151 F2969 PRODUC

L67
LENT G.E.,"TAX INCENTIVES FOR INVESTMENT IN ECO/UNDEV
DEVELOPING COUNTRIES" WOR+45 LAW INDUS PLAN BUDGET TAX
TARIFFS ADMIN...METH/COMP 20. PAGE 78 F1526 FINAN
ECO/TAC

L67
MEIER G.M.,"UNCTAD PROPOSALS FOR INTERNATIONAL INT/TRADE
ECONOMIC REFORM." WOR+45 MARKET INT/ORG TARIFFS FINAN
CONFER UN GATT IMF. PAGE 89 F1749 INT/LAW
ECO/UNDEV

S67
ADAMS R.N.,"ETHICS AND THE SOCIAL ANTHROPOLOGIST IN L/A+17C
LATIN AMERICA." USA+45 INTELL PROB/SOLV ECO/TAC POLICY
LEAD...DECISION SOC NAT/COMP PERS/COMP. PAGE 2 ECO/UNDEV
F0039 CONSULT

S67
AGUILAR M.A.,"?UNA OEA MAS FUERTE O UNA AMERICA INT/ORG
LATINA MAS DEBIL?" L/A+17C USA+45 USA-45 ECO/UNDEV DIPLOM
INDUS CHIEF DELIB/GP FORCES CONTROL PWR 20 OAS POLICY
KENNEDY/JF JOHNSON/LB. PAGE 3 F0050 COLONIAL

S67
ALPANDER G.G.,"ENTREPRENEURS AND PRIVATE ENTERPRISE ECO/UNDEV
IN TURKEY." TURKEY INDUS PROC/MFG EDU/PROP ATTIT LG/CO
DRIVE WEALTH...GEOG MGT SOC STAT TREND CHARTS 20. NAT/G
PAGE 4 F0077 POLICY

S67
ALVES V.,"FOREIGN CAPITAL IN BRAZIL." BRAZIL USA+45 ECO/UNDEV
CAP/ISM DIPLOM ECO/TAC INT/TRADE CONTROL PWR FINAN
...POLICY 20. PAGE 4 F0081 SOCIALIST
SOCISM

S67
BENNETT J.T.,"POLITICAL IMPLICATIONS OF ECONOMIC ECO/UNDEV
CHANGE: SOUTH VIETNAM." VIETNAM/S INGP/REL INCOME INDUS
ATTIT 20 AID. PAGE 13 F0247 AGRI
PRODUC

S67
BRANCO R.,"LAND REFORM* THE ANSWER TO LATIN ECO/UNDEV
AMERICA'S AGRICULTURAL DEVELOPMENT?" L/A+17C NAT/G AGRI
PLAN TEC/DEV BUDGET RENT EFFICIENCY 20. PAGE 18 TAX
F0339 OWN

S67
CRAIG A.,"ARGENTINA: THE LATEST REVOLUTION." ELITES ECO/UNDEV
NAT/G CHIEF FORCES ECO/TAC CIVMIL/REL GOV/REL FINAN
EQUILIB PRIVIL 20 ARGEN. PAGE 28 F0550 ATTIT
REV

S67
DEYRUP F.J.,"SOCIAL MOBILITY AS A MAJOR FACTOR IN STRATA
ECONOMIC DEVELOPMENT." CHRIST-17C EUR+WWI MOD/EUR ECO/DEV
ECO/UNDEV DEMAND 20. PAGE 32 F0630 INDUS
WORKER

S67
FADDEYEV N.,"CMEA CO-OPERATION OF EQUAL NATIONS." MARXISM
COM R+D PLAN CAP/ISM DIPLOM FOR/AID WEALTH...POLICY ECO/TAC
MARXIST. PAGE 39 F0758 INT/ORG
ECO/UNDEV

S67
FINER S.E.,"THE ONE-PARTY REGIMES IN AFRICA: ELITES
RECONSIDERATIONS." AFR DOMIN CONSEN ORD/FREE 20. POL/PAR
PAGE 41 F0798 CONSTN
ECO/UNDEV

S67
FOX R.G.,"FAMILY, CASTE, AND COMMERCE IN A NORTH CULTURE
INDIAN MARKET TOWN." INDIA STRATA AGRI FACE/GP FAM GP/REL
NEIGH OP/RES BARGAIN ADMIN ROUTINE WEALTH...SOC ECO/UNDEV
CHARTS 20. PAGE 43 F0838 DIST/IND

S67
GONZALEZ M.P.,"CUBA, UNA REVOLUCION EN MARCHA." REV
CUBA L/A+17C USA+45 VIETNAM ECO/UNDEV FORCES DIPLOM NAT/G
DOMIN...POLICY MARXIST NAT/COMP CASTRO/F. PAGE 48 COLONIAL
F0946 SOVEREIGN

S67
GRAHAM R.,"BRAZIL'S DILEMMA." BRAZIL FUT L/A+17C ECO/UNDEV
NAT/G CHIEF PROB/SOLV ECO/TAC PWR 20. PAGE 50 F0972 CONSTN
POL/PAR
POLICY

S67
HEATH D.B.,"BOLIVIA UNDER BARRIENTOS." L/A+17C ECO/UNDEV
NAT/G CHIEF DIPLOM ECO/TAC...POLICY 20 BOLIV. POL/PAR
PAGE 58 F1132 REV
CONSTN

S67
HEILBRONER R.L.,"BUILDING NEW NATIONS." AFR STRUCT PROB/SOLV
PLAN TEC/DEV ADJUST MARXISM...POLICY 20. PAGE 58 REV
F1138 NAT/LISM
ECO/UNDEV

S67
HILDEBRAND J.R.,"THE CENTRAL AMERICAN COMMON DIPLOM
MARKET: ECONOMIC AND POLITICAL INTEGRATION." ECO/TAC
L/A+17C USA+45 ECO/DEV ECO/UNDEV AGRI SOVEREIGN. INT/TRADE
PAGE 59 F1170 INT/ORG

S67
IBARRA J.,"EL EXPERIMENTO CUBANO." COM CUBA L/A+17C COLONIAL
USA+45 ECO/UNDEV LEGIS INT/TRADE CONTROL REV DIPLOM
NAT/LISM PWR 19/20 TREATY. PAGE 64 F1259 NAT/G
POLICY

S67
ISELIN J.J.,"THE TRUMAN DOCTRINE: ITS PASSAGE DIPLOM
THROUGH CONGRESS AND THE AFTERMATH." USA+45 COM
ECO/UNDEV R+D INT/ORG DELIB/GP BAL/PWR REV PEACE FOR/AID

...POLICY UN. PAGE 66 F1291 — AFR

S67
KENNY L.M.,"THE AFTERMATH OF DEFEAT IN EGYPT." ISLAM ISRAEL UAR UK USA+45 USSR INDUS FORCES ECO/TAC PRICE COERCE WEAPON COST ATTIT. PAGE 70 F1378 — WAR ECO/UNDEV DIPLOM POLICY

S67
KINGSLEY R.E.,"THE US BUSINESS IMAGE IN LATIN AMERICA." L/A+17C USA+45 NAT/G TEC/DEV CAP/ISM FOR/AID DOMIN EDU/PROP...CONCPT LING IDEA/COMP 20. PAGE 71 F1396 — ATTIT LOVE DIPLOM ECO/UNDEV

S67
LEE R.L.,"THE PARADOX OF EQUALITY: A THREAT TO INDIVIDUAL AND SYSTEM FUNCTIONING." CHINA/COM ECO/UNDEV WORKER...SIMUL GEN/LAWS 20. PAGE 77 F1508 — SOCIETY STRATA MARXISM IDEA/COMP

S67
LOSMAN D.L.,"FOREIGN AID, SOCIALISM AND THE EMERGING COUNTRIES" WOR+45 ADMIN CONTROL PWR 20. PAGE 82 F1602 — ECO/UNDEV FOR/AID SOC

S67
MCCORD W.,"ARMIES AND POLITICS; A PROBLEM IN THE THIRD WORLD." AFR ISLAM USA+45 ECO/UNDEV TOTALISM 20. PAGE 88 F1723 — FOR/AID POLICY NAT/G FORCES

S67
MEHTA A.,"INDIA* POVERTY AND CHANGE." STRATA INDUS CREATE ECO/TAC FOR/AID NEUTRAL GP/REL ADJUST INCOME ...NEW/IDEA 20. PAGE 89 F1746 — INDIA SOCIETY ECO/UNDEV TEC/DEV

S67
MILLER C.H.,"B. TRAVEN Y EL 'PROBLEMA PETROLERO'." USA-45 ECO/UNDEV INDUS TEC/DEV INT/TRADE ATTIT ORD/FREE SOVEREIGN 20 MEXIC/AMER. PAGE 91 F1791 — EXTR/IND DIPLOM ECO/TAC DOMIN

S67
MOSELY P.E.,"EASTERN EUROPE IN WORLD POWER POLITICS: WHERE DE-STALINIZATION HAS LED." ECO/UNDEV NAT/LISM 20. PAGE 94 F1842 — COM NAT/G DIPLOM MARXISM

S67
MYRDAL G.,"ECONOMIC DEVELOPMENT IN THE BACKWARD COUNTRIES." INT/ORG TEC/DEV CAP/ISM DIPLOM INT/TRADE PRODUC WEALTH 20. PAGE 96 F1883 — ECO/UNDEV INDUS NAT/G ECO/TAC

S67
PECCEI A.,"DEVELOPED-UNDERDEVELOPED AND EAST-WEST RELATIONS." ECO/UNDEV TEC/DEV DIPLOM LEAD EFFICIENCY GEOG. PAGE 104 F2045 — FOR/AID TREND REGION ECO/DEV

S67
PERKINS D.H.,"ECONOMIC GROWTH IN CHINA AND THE CULTURAL REVOLUTION(1960APRIL 1967)" CHINA/COM FUT AGRI INDUS PLAN LEAD MARXISM...CHARTS 20 MAO. PAGE 105 F2062 — ECO/TAC CULTURE REV ECO/UNDEV

S67
PETRAS J.,"U.S. HEGEMONY AND LATIN AMERICAN RULING CLASSES." L/A+17C USA+45 ECO/UNDEV FOR/AID REV SOC. PAGE 105 F2071 — NAT/G ATTIT DIPLOM POLICY

S67
PRATT R.C.,"THE ADMINISTRATION OF ECONOMIC PLANNING IN A NEWLY INDEPEND ENT STATE* THE TANZANIAN EXPERIENCE 1963-1966." AFR TANZANIA ECO/UNDEV PLAN CONTROL ROUTINE TASK EFFICIENCY 20. PAGE 107 F2114 — NAT/G DELIB/GP ADMIN TEC/DEV

S67
RICHMAN B.M.,"CAPITALISTS & MANAGERS IN COMMUNIST CHINA." ASIA CHINA/COM ECO/UNDEV NAT/G CONSULT EX/STRUC PLAN EFFICIENCY PRODUC WEALTH MARXISM ...MGT CHARTS 20. PAGE 111 F2185 — CAP/ISM INDUS

S67
ROY E.V.,"AN INTERPRETATION OF NORTHERN THAI PEASANT ECONOMY." THAILAND CLIENT CULTURE AGRI PROC/MFG FACE/GP DEMAND INCOME 20. PAGE 114 F2254 — STRUCT STRATA ECO/UNDEV INGP/REL

S67
SCHACHTER G.,"REGIONAL DEVELOPMENT IN THE ITALIAN DUAL ECONOMY" ITALY AGRI INDUS MARKET WORKER ECO/TAC CONTROL INCOME PRODUC 20. PAGE 116 F2287 — REGION ECO/UNDEV NAT/G PROB/SOLV

S67
SCOTT R.,"TRADE UNIONS IN AFRICA." AFR UGANDA USA-45 ECO/UNDEV INDUS INT/ORG POL/PAR ECO/TAC WEALTH...GP/COMP 20 NKRUMAH/K. PAGE 118 F2335 — LABOR WORKER NAT/G

S67
SHERWOOD W.B.,"THE RISE OF THE JUSTICE PARTY IN TURKEY." FUT TURKEY LEAD ATTIT 20. PAGE 121 F2378 — POL/PAR ECO/UNDEV STRUCT SOCIETY

S67
SIPPEL D.,"INDIENS UNSICHERE ZUKUNFT." INDIA CULTURE ACADEM POL/PAR LEGIS COLONIAL CHOOSE SOVEREIGN...JURID 20. PAGE 122 F2416 — SOCIETY STRUCT ECO/UNDEV NAT/G

S67
STRANGE S.,"DEBTS, DEFAULTERS AND DEVELOPMENT." WOR+45 PROB/SOLV FOR/AID INT/TRADE. PAGE 127 F2500 — NAT/G FINAN ECO/UNDEV

S67
TABORSKY E.,"THE CLASS STRUGGLE, THE PROLETARIAT, AND THE DEVELOPING NATIONS." USSR LABOR POL/PAR FOR/AID COLONIAL GP/REL 20. PAGE 128 F2521 — DIPLOM MARXISM ECO/UNDEV WORKER

S67
WAITS C.R.,"CRAFT GILDS AS AN INSTITUTIONAL BARRIER TO THE INDUSTRIAL REVOLUTION." CHRIST-17C MOD/EUR ECO/UNDEV CONTROL GP/REL ATTIT 16/19. PAGE 142 F2801 — TEC/DEV INDUS REV PROF/ORG

S67
WALKER R.L.,"THE WEST AND THE 'NEW ASIA'." CHINA/COM ECO/UNDEV DIPLOM...PREDICT 20. PAGE 142 F2805 — ASIA INT/TRADE COLONIAL REGION

S67
WILSON C.E.,"AMERICAN INVESTMENT IN PORTUGUESE AFRICA: A PROBLEM OF "DEMOCRATIC" COLONIALISM." AFR ECO/UNDEV DIPLOM MORAL...IDEA/COMP 20 ANGOLA MOZAMBIQUE. PAGE 147 F2901 — COLONIAL DOMIN ORD/FREE POLICY

S67
WOLFSON M.,"GOVERNMENT'S ROLE IN TOURISM DEVELOPMENT." WOR+45 ECO/DEV ECO/UNDEV FINAN BUDGET DIPLOM EDU/PROP. PAGE 148 F2920 — SERV/IND NAT/G CONTROL PLAN

N67
US CONGRESS JOINT ECO COMM,MAINLAND CHINA IN THE WORLD ECONOMY (PAMPHLET). CHINA/COM USA+45 AGRI CHIEF MARXISM CONGRESS. PAGE 135 F2661 — ECO/UNDEV POLICY ECO/TAC INT/TRADE

N67
US HOUSE COMM FOREIGN AFFAIRS,REPORT OF SPECIAL STUDY MISSION TO THE NEAR EAST (PAMPHLET). ISRAEL USA+45 YEMEN ECO/UNDEV INT/ORG FOR/AID ARMS/CONT WAR WEAPON NAT/LISM PEACE...GEOG 20 UN HOUSE/REP. PAGE 137 F2694 — ISLAM DIPLOM FORCES

N67
US HOUSE COMM FOREIGN AFFAIRS,FOREIGN ASSISTANCE ACT OF 1967 (PAMPHLET). USA+45 WOR+45 FINAN CONGRESS HOUSE/REP UN. PAGE 137 F2695 — FOR/AID POLICY INT/ORG ECO/UNDEV

N67
US HOUSE COMM SCI ASTRONAUT,GOVERNMENT, SCIENCE, AND INTERNATIONAL POLICY (PAMPHLET). INDIA NETHERLAND ECO/DEV ECO/UNDEV R+D ACADEM PLAN DIPLOM FOR/AID CONFER...PREDICT 20 CHINJAP. PAGE 137 F2705 — NAT/G POLICY CREATE TEC/DEV

ECOLOGY....SEE HABITAT

ECOMETRIC....MATHEMATICAL ECONOMICS, ECONOMETRICS

LCA
GODFREY E.M.,"THE ECONOMICS OF AN AFRICAN UNIVERSITY." AFR SCHOOL PRICE EFFICIENCY INCOME WEALTH...ECOMETRIC CHARTS 20. PAGE 48 F0930 — ACADEM ECO/TAC COST EDU/PROP

N19
BUSINESS ECONOMISTS' GROUP,INCOME POLICIES (PAMPHLET). UK INDUS LABOR TOP/EX PAY COST PRODUC ...ECOMETRIC GOV/COMP SIMUL ANTHOL 20. PAGE 20 F0395 — INCOME WORKER WEALTH POLICY

N19
HATANAKA M.,A SPECTRAL ANALYSIS OF BUSINESS CYCLE INDICATORS: LEAD-LAG IN TERMS OF ALL TIME POINTS (PAMPHLET). UNIV WORKER EFFICIENCY...REGRESS STAT CHARTS TIME 20. PAGE 56 F1110 — ECOMETRIC ADJUST PRODUC CON/ANAL

N19
MASCHLER M.,STABLE PAYOFF CONFIGURATIONS FOR QUOTA GAMES (PAMPHLET). PLAN PERS/REL 20. PAGE 87 F1694 — ECOMETRIC GAME COMPUTER DECISION

N19
MIYASAWA K.,AN ECONOMIC SURVIVAL GAME (PAMPHLET). COST DEMAND EQUILIB INCOME PROFIT 20. PAGE 92 F1811 — ECOMETRIC GAME ECO/TAC DECISION

B32
ROBBINS L.,AN ESSAY ON THE NATURE AND SIGNIFICANCE OF ECONOMIC SCIENCE. DEMAND EQUILIB PRODUC UTIL ...ECOMETRIC 20. PAGE 112 F2201 — GEN/LAWS METH/COMP ECO/DEV

B48
HICKS J.R.,VALUE AND CAPITAL. FINAN PRICE EQUILIB INCOME PRODUC WEALTH...TIME/SEQ 20 MARSHALL/A PARETO/V SAMUELSN/P. PAGE 59 F1165 — ECOMETRIC MATH DEMAND PROB/SOLV

B58
THEIL H.,ECONOMIC FORECASTS AND POLICY. UNIV CAP/ISM PRICE EFFICIENCY...DECISION CONCPT STAT 20. PAGE 129 F2551 — SIMUL MATH ECOMETRIC PREDICT

B58
WARNER A.W.,CONCEPTS AND CASES IN ECONOMIC ANALYSIS. PROB/SOLV BARGAIN CONTROL INCOME PRODUC ...ECOMETRIC MGT CONCPT CLASSIF CHARTS 20 — ECO/TAC DEMAND EQUILIB

KEYNES/JM. PAGE 143 F2820 COST
B59

LEWIS J.P.,BUSINESS CONDITIONS ANALYSIS. USA+45 MARKET LABOR BUDGET TAX AUTOMAT WAR DEMAND PRODUC ...ECOMETRIC CHARTS BIBLIOG 19/20. PAGE 79 F1549 FINAN PRICE TREND
B59

MATTHEWS R.C.O.,THE BUSINESS CYCLE. AFR LABOR INT/TRADE TAX PRICE RISK ADJUST WEALTH...POLICY ECOMETRIC CHARTS SIMUL TIME 20. PAGE 87 F1705 FINAN DEMAND TASK
B60

HARBERGER A.C.,THE DEMAND FOR DURABLE GOODS. AGRI FINAN COST EQUILIB...MATH STAT TIME/SEQ TREND CON/ANAL CHARTS SIMUL ANTHOL 20. PAGE 55 F1072 ECOMETRIC DEMAND PRICE
B60

PFOUTS R.W.,THE TECHNIQUES OF URBAN ECONOMIC ANALYSIS. USA+45...ECOMETRIC CONCPT CHARTS IDEA/COMP ANTHOL MUNICH 20. PAGE 106 F2078 METH ECO/DEV METH/COMP
B60

SIEGEL B.N.,AGGREGATE ECONOMICS AND PUBLIC POLICY. ECO/DEV TEC/DEV ECO/TAC TASK DEMAND EQUILIB INCOME ...CHARTS 20. PAGE 121 F2396 ECOMETRIC WEALTH PRODUC MARKET
B61

ACKLEY G.,MACROECONOMIC THEORY. AFR FINAN WORKER ECO/TAC PRICE COST INCOME PRODUC...MATH TREND CHARTS IDEA/COMP T KEYNES/JM. PAGE 2 F0034 SIMUL ECOMETRIC WEALTH
B61

KLEIN L.R.,AN ECONOMETRIC MODEL OF THE UNITED KINGDOM. UK PRICE COST...MATH PREDICT TREND CHARTS SIMUL METH 20. PAGE 72 F1407 ECOMETRIC COMPUTER STAT COMPUT/IR
B61

MCCRACKEN H.L.,KEYNESIAN ECONOMICS IN THE STREAM OF ECONOMIC THOUGHT. FINAN MARKET BARGAIN EFFICIENCY OPTIMAL...PHIL/SCI CONCPT IDEA/COMP BIBLIOG 18/20 KEYNES/JM. PAGE 88 F1724 ECO/TAC DEMAND ECOMETRIC
B61

NORTH D.C.,THE ECONOMIC GROWTH OF THE UNITED STATES 1790-1860. USA-45 INDUS TEC/DEV CAP/ISM ECO/TAC PRICE COST DEMAND LAISSEZ...ECOMETRIC STAT TREND 19. PAGE 98 F1933 AGRI ECO/UNDEV
S61

ANDREWS R.B.,"URBAN ECONOMICS: AN APPRAISAL OF PROGRESS." LOC/G PROB/SOLV TEC/DEV...CONCPT OBS/ENVIR METH/COMP HYPO/EXP SOC/EXP SIMUL GEN/METH METH MUNICH 20. PAGE 5 F0102 PHIL/SCI ECOMETRIC
S61

BENNION E.G.,"ECONOMETRICS FOR MANAGEMENT." USA+45 INDUS EX/STRUC ACT/RES COMPUTER UTIL...MATH STAT PREDICT METH/COMP HYPO/EXP. PAGE 13 F0248 ECOMETRIC MGT SIMUL DECISION
S61

DICKS-MIREAUX L.A.,"THE INTERRELATIONSHIP BETWEEN COST AND PRICE CHANGES 19461959: A STUDY OF INFLATION IN POST-WAR BRITAIN" AFR UK ECO/DEV INDUS WORKER ECO/TAC ORD/FREE WEALTH...ECOMETRIC REGRESS STAT TREND CHARTS 20. PAGE 33 F0634 PRICE PAY DEMAND
B62

COPPOCK J.D.,INTERNATIONAL ECONOMIC INSTABILITY: THE EXPERIENCE AFTER WORLD WAR II. WOR+45 FINAN CAP/ISM CONTROL EFFICIENCY...CHARTS 20. PAGE 28 F0536 ECO/TAC ECOMETRIC INT/TRADE STAT
B62

KLEIN L.R.,AN INTRODUCTION TO ECONOMETRICS. DIST/IND DEMAND PRODUC WEALTH...MATH TIME/SEQ T 20. PAGE 72 F1408 ECOMETRIC SIMUL PREDICT STAT
B62

SHINOHARA M.,GROWTH AND CYCLES IN THE JAPANESE ECONOMY. INDUS LABOR TEC/DEV CAP/ISM INT/TRADE PAY COST EFFICIENCY INCOME WEALTH...METH/COMP 20 CHINJAP. PAGE 121 F2380 PRODUC ECO/DEV EQUILIB ECOMETRIC
B63

COURNOT A.A.,RESEARCHES INTO THE MATHEMATICAL PRINCIPLES OF THE THEORY OF WEALTH (1838). UNIV ECO/DEV ECO/UNDEV AGRI INDUS MARKET PAY CONTROL COST INCOME 19. PAGE 28 F0544 ECOMETRIC GEN/LAWS WEALTH
B63

GANGULI B.N.,ECONOMIC CONSEQUENCES OF DISARMAMENT. EUR+WWI ECO/DEV ECO/UNDEV FORCES ACT/RES BUDGET DIPLOM INT/TRADE...STAT CHARTS NAT/COMP. PAGE 46 F0896 ECOMETRIC ARMS/CONT COST HYPO/EXP
B63

INTERNATIONAL ASSOCIATION RES,AFRICAN STUDIES IN INCOME AND WEALTH. AFR NAT/G PROB/SOLV DEMAND INCOME...ECOMETRIC METH/COMP 20. PAGE 64 F1270 WEALTH PLAN ECO/UNDEV BUDGET
B63

JOHNSTON J.,ECONOMETRIC METHODS. PROB/SOLV WRITING ...REGRESS CHARTS T. PAGE 68 F1333 ECOMETRIC PHIL/SCI OP/RES STAT
B63

LEE M.W.,MACROECONOMICS: FLUCTUATIONS, GROWTH AND STABILITY (3RD ED.). MARKET LABOR TEC/DEV INT/TRADE TAX PRICE WAR PRODUC...POLICY ECOMETRIC CHARTS 19/20. PAGE 77 F1505 EQUILIB TREND WEALTH
B63

MEIER G.,INTERNATIONAL TRADE AND DEVELOPMENT. FINAN BAL/PAY COST DEMAND DISCRIM EQUILIB WEALTH...POLICY ECOMETRIC MATH STAT BIBLIOG/A 20. PAGE 89 F1747 ECO/UNDEV ECO/TAC INT/TRADE IDEA/COMP
B64

BALASSA B.,TRADE PROSPECTS FOR DEVELOPING COUNTRIES. WOR+45 ECO/DEV AGRI EXTR/IND INDUS CREATE PLAN PRICE...ECOMETRIC CLASSIF TIME/SEQ GEN/METH. PAGE 8 F0158 INT/TRADE ECO/UNDEV TREND STAT
B64

COLSTON RESEARCH SOCIETY,ECONOMETRIC ANALYSIS FOR NATIONAL ECONOMIC PLANNING (PROCEEDINGS OF SIXTEENTH SYMPOSIUM OF COLSTON RESEARCH SOCIETY). UK USA+45 FINAN FAM LABOR NAT/G PLAN PRICE ...METH/CNCPT TREND CHARTS TIME 20. PAGE 26 F0510 ECOMETRIC DELIB/GP ECO/TAC PROB/SOLV
B64

HART P.E.,ECONOMETRIC ANALYSIS FOR NATIONAL ECONOMIC PLANNING. INDUS OP/RES PRICE PRODUC ...SIMUL ANTHOL MODELS 20. PAGE 56 F1100 PLAN ECOMETRIC STAT
B64

LANG A.S.,URBAN RAIL TRANSIT. OP/RES PLAN PROB/SOLV TEC/DEV AUTOMAT COST...TECHNIC MATH CON/ANAL CHARTS METH/COMP SIMUL MUNICH 20 RAILROAD PUB/TRANS. PAGE 75 F1474 DIST/IND ECOMETRIC
B64

MAZA ZAVALA D.F.,VENEZUELA; UNA ECONOMIA DEPENDIENTE. L/A+17C VENEZUELA FINAN INDUS ...ECOMETRIC STAT TREND 20. PAGE 87 F1710 ECO/UNDEV BAL/PAY INT/TRADE PRICE
B64

ODEH H.S.,THE IMPACT OF INFLATION ON THE LEVEL OF ECONOMIC ACTIVITY. AFR BRAZIL CHILE BUDGET GOV/REL COST DEMAND INCOME WEALTH...STAT METH 20 MONEY. PAGE 100 F1963 ECOMETRIC ECO/TAC ECO/UNDEV FINAN
B64

YUDELMAN M.,AFRICANS ON THE LAND. RHODESIA MARKET LABOR OWN...ECOMETRIC TREND 20. PAGE 150 F2955 ECO/DEV AFR AGRI ECO/TAC
B65

BRENNAN M.J.,PATTERNS OF MARKET BEHAVIOR. AFR USA+45 OP/RES CAP/ISM ECO/TAC INT/TRADE...CHARTS METH/COMP ANTHOL TIME 20. PAGE 18 F0346 MARKET LABOR FINAN ECOMETRIC
B65

DODDY F.S.,INTRODUCTION TO THE USE OF ECONOMIC INDICATORS. FINAN LABOR PLAN COST...ECOMETRIC INDICATOR MATH PREDICT CHARTS METH 20. PAGE 33 F0649 TEC/DEV STAT PRODUC PRICE
B65

FORD J.L.,THE OHLIN-HECKSCHER THEORY OF THE BASIS AND EFFECTS OF COMMODITY TRADE. WOR+45 ECO/TAC DEMAND INCOME...CONCPT GEN/METH 20 OHLIN/HECK. PAGE 42 F0824 ECOMETRIC INT/TRADE NEW/IDEA SIMUL
B65

FRIEDLANDER S.L.,LABOR MIGRATION AND ECONOMIC GROWTH: A CASE STUDY OF PUERTO RICO. PUERT/RICO AGRI WORKER PLAN PROB/SOLV...ECOMETRIC STAT PREDICT CHARTS HYPO/EXP SIMUL 20. PAGE 44 F0858 CENSUS GEOG ECO/UNDEV WEALTH
B65

HABERLER G.,A SURVEY OF INTERNATIONAL TRADE THEORY. CANADA FRANCE GERMANY ECO/TAC TARIFFS AGREE COST DEMAND WEALTH...ECOMETRIC 19/20 MONOPOLY TREATY. PAGE 52 F1024 INT/TRADE BAL/PAY DIPLOM POLICY
B65

HICKMAN B.G.,QUANTITATIVE PLANNING OF ECONOMIC POLICY. FRANCE NETHERLAND OP/RES PRICE ROUTINE UTIL ...POLICY DECISION ECOMETRIC METH/CNCPT STAT STYLE CHINJAP. PAGE 59 F1162 PROB/SOLV PLAN QUANT
B65

KLASSEN L.H.,AREA ECONOMIC AND SOCIAL REDEVELOPMENT. ECO/UNDEV INDUS NAT/G PLAN CAP/ISM TAX...ECOMETRIC SIMUL 20. PAGE 72 F1404 OPTIMAL WORKER METH ECO/TAC
B65

OZGA S.A.,EXPECTATIONS IN ECONOMIC THEORY. MORAL ...ECOMETRIC MATH STAT IDEA/COMP 20. PAGE 102 F2008 RISK GAME CONCPT PREDICT
B65

PINCUS J.A.,ECONOMIC AID AND INTERNATIONAL COST SHARING* A RAND CORPORATION RESEARCH STUDY. INT/ORG BUDGET CENTRAL...ECOMETRIC MATH QUANT STAT SIMUL. PAGE 106 F2088 ECO/UNDEV COST FOR/AID INT/TRADE
S65

BRIGHAM E.F.,"THE DETERMINANTS OF RESIDENTIAL LAND VALUES." USA+45 ECO/DEV PROB/SOLV RENT PRICE ...REGRESS STAT CHARTS GEN/METH MUNICH 20 LOS/ANG. PAGE 18 F0351 COST INDICATOR SIMUL ECOMETRIC
S65

CHU K.,"A DYNAMIC MODEL OF THE FIRM." OP/RES PROB/SOLV...DECISION ECOMETRIC NEW/IDEA STAT GAME ORG/CHARTS SIMUL. PAGE 24 F0472 INDUS COMPUTER TEC/DEV

B66
BALDWIN D.A.,FOREIGN AID AND AMERICAN FOREIGN POLICY; A DOCUMENTARY ANALYSIS. USA+45 ECO/UNDEV ADMIN...ECOMETRIC STAT STYLE CHARTS PROG/TEAC GEN/LAWS ANTHOL. PAGE 9 F0162
FOR/AID DIPLOM IDEA/COMP

B66
BROWN R.T.,TRANSPORT AND THE ECONOMIC INTEGRATION OF SOUTH AMERICA. L/A+17C ECO/UNDEV NAT/G OP/RES DIPLOM INT/TRADE REGION WEALTH...ECOMETRIC GEOG STAT LAFTA TIME. PAGE 19 F0373
MARKET DIST/IND SIMUL

B66
FOX K.A.,THE THEORY OF QUANTITATIVE ECONOMIC POLICY WITH APPLICATIONS TO ECONOMIC GROWTH AND STABILIZATION. ECO/DEV AGRI NAT/G PLAN ADMIN RISK ...DECISION IDEA/COMP SIMUL T. PAGE 43 F0837
ECO/TAC ECOMETRIC EQUILIB GEN/LAWS

B66
HEISS K.P.,GAME THEORY AND HUMAN CONFLICTS (RESEARCH MEMORANDUM). UNIV ACT/RES...DECISION SOC MATH PROBABIL SIMUL 20 DEFINETT/B. PAGE 58 F1142
GAME ECOMETRIC PLAN PROB/SOLV

B66
KAESTNER K.,GESAMTWIRTSCHAFTLICHE PLANUNG IN EINER GEMISCHTEN WIRTSCHAFTSORDNUNG (WIRTSCHAFTSPOLITISCHE STUDIEN 5). GERMANY/W WOR+45 WOR-45 INDUS MARKET NAT/G ACT/RES GP/REL INGP/REL PRODUC...ECOMETRIC MGT BIBLIOG 20. PAGE 68 F1346
ECO/TAC PLAN POLICY PREDICT

B66
LANSING J.B.,TRANSPORTATION AND ECONOMIC POLICY. USA+45 COST DEMAND...ECOMETRIC TREND CHARTS IDEA/COMP T 20. PAGE 76 F1481
DIST/IND OP/RES ECO/DEV UTIL

B66
LEONTIEF W.,ESSAYS IN ECONOMICS. ECO/UNDEV INDUS NAT/G CAP/ISM FOR/AID AUTOMAT MARXISM...ECOMETRIC CHARTS ANTHOL METH 20 KEYNES/JM. PAGE 78 F1528
CONCPT METH/CNCPT METH/COMP

B66
MACBEAN A.I.,EXPORT INSTABILITY AND ECONOMIC DEVELOPMENT. CHILE PAKISTAN PUERT/RICO TANZANIA UGANDA WOR+45 MARKET ECO/TAC...POLICY REGRESS CHARTS BIBLIOG TIME 20. PAGE 83 F1622
INT/TRADE ECO/UNDEV ECOMETRIC INSPECT

B66
PERSALL E.S.,AN ECONOMETRIC STUDY OF FINANCIAL MARKETS. COMPUTER PROB/SOLV TEC/DEV...MATH STAT CHARTS METH/COMP BIBLIOG 20. PAGE 105 F2066
ECOMETRIC FINAN MARKET METH

B66
POLK J.,U S PRODUCTION ABROAD AND THE BALANCE OF PAYMENTS* A SURVEY OF CORPORATE INVESTMENT EXPERIENCE. USA+45 SERV/IND NAT/G OP/RES COST PROFIT ATTIT...ECOMETRIC STAT INT QU GEN/METH. PAGE 107 F2096
BAL/PAY FINAN INT/TRADE INDUS

S66
DAVIS O.A.,"A THEORY OF THE BUDGETARY PROCESS." ECO/DEV FINAN LEGIS PROB/SOLV GOV/REL...ECOMETRIC METH/CNCPT STAT CONT/OBS TREND METH/COMP SIMUL 20 CONGRESS. PAGE 30 F0592
DECISION NAT/G BUDGET EFFICIENCY

S66
FROMM G.,"RECENT MONETARY POLICY: AN ECONOMETRIC VIEW" USA+45 ECO/DEV INDUS PAY PRICE PRODUC ORD/FREE WEALTH...STAT 20 FED/RESERV. PAGE 45 F0869
ECOMETRIC FINAN POLICY SIMUL

B67
ALLEN R.G.,MACRO-ECONOMIC THEORY: A MATHEMATICAL TREATMENT. UNIV...SIMUL T. PAGE 4 F0070
ECOMETRIC MATH EQUILIB GAME

B67
BERGMANN D KAUN B.,STRUCTURAL UNEMPLOYMENT IN THE UNITED STATES. USA+45 ECO/DEV PRICE ADMIN INGP/REL DEMAND EQUILIB WEALTH...MATH REGRESS STAT 20 NEGRO. PAGE 13 F0258
ECOMETRIC METH WORKER ECO/TAC

B67
CLEMENT M.O.,THEORETICAL ISSUES IN INTERNATIONAL ECONOMICS. WOR+45 PLAN PROB/SOLV TEC/DEV ...ECOMETRIC METH/CNCPT MATH BIBLIOG T MONEY. PAGE 25 F0489
INT/TRADE FINAN CREATE BAL/PAY

B67
PORWIT K.,CENTRAL PLANNING: EVALUATION OF VARIANTS. PRICE OPTIMAL PRODUC...DECISION MATH CHARTS SIMUL BIBLIOG MODELS 20. PAGE 107 F2106
PLAN MGT ECOMETRIC

B67
RUEFF J.,BALANCE OF PAYMENTS: PROPOSALS FOR RESOLVING THE CRITICAL WORLD ECONOMIC PROBLEM OF OUR TIME. USA+45 INDUS FOR/AID REPAR DEMAND OPTIMAL ...ECOMETRIC CHARTS METH/COMP 20. PAGE 115 F2259
BAL/PAY INT/TRADE FINAN NEW/IDEA

S67
KOTLER P.,"OPERATIONS RESEARCH IN MARKETING." USA+45 DIST/IND INDUS LG/CO CONSULT BUDGET TASK DEMAND EFFICIENCY PROFIT WEALTH DECISION. PAGE 73 F1429
ECOMETRIC OP/RES MARKET PLAN

ECONOMIC DETERMINISM....SEE GEN/LAWS

ECONOMIC WARFARE....SEE ECO/TAC

ECONOMIC RESEARCH SERVICE F0697

ECONOMIDES C.P. F0698

ECOSOC....UNITED NATIONS ECONOMIC AND SOCIAL COUNCIL

ECSC....EUROPEAN COAL AND STEEL COMMUNITY, SEE ALSO VOL/ASSN, INT/ORG

B57
TRIFFIN R.,EUROPE AND THE MONEY MUDDLE. USA+45 INT/ORG NAT/G CONSULT PLAN ECO/TAC EXEC ROUTINE BAL/PAY WEALTH...METH/CNCPT OBS TREND CHARTS STERTYP GEN/METH EEC TERR/GP VAL/FREE ECSC. PAGE 131 F2587
EUR+WWI ECO/DEV REGION

B58
KINDLEBERGER C.P.,INTERNATIONAL ECONOMICS. WOR+45 WOR-45 ECO/DEV ECO/UNDEV FINAN VOL/ASSN ACT/RES DIPLOM ECO/TAC LEGIT REGION ATTIT DRIVE ORD/FREE WEALTH...POLICY STAT TREND GEN/LAWS EEC ECSC OEEC 20. PAGE 71 F1391
INT/ORG BAL/PWR TARIFFS

B58
SCITOUSKY T.,ECONOMIC THEORY AND WESTERN EUROPEAN INTEGRATION. EUR+WWI INT/ORG ACT/RES INT/TRADE REGION BAL/PAY WEALTH...METH/CNCPT STAT CHARTS GEN/METH ECSC TOT/POP EEC OEEC 20. PAGE 118 F2328
ECO/TAC

B59
DIEBOLD W. JR.,THE SCHUMAN PLAN: A STUDY IN ECONOMIC COOPERATION, 1950-1959. EUR+WWI FRANCE GERMANY USA+45 EXTR/IND CONSULT DELIB/GP PLAN DIPLOM ECO/TAC INT/TRADE ROUTINE ORD/FREE WEALTH ...METH/CNCPT STAT CONT/OBS INT TIME/SEQ ECSC 20. PAGE 33 F0635
INT/ORG REGION

B59
ROBERTSON A.H.,EUROPEAN INSTITUTIONS: COOPERATION, INTEGRATION, UNIFICATION. EUR+WWI FINAN INT/ORG FORCES INT/TRADE TARIFFS 20 EEC EURATOM ECSC NATO TREATY. PAGE 112 F2208
ECO/DEV DIPLOM INDUS ECO/TAC

B60
LISTER L.,EUROPE'S COAL AND STEEL COMMUNITY. FRANCE GERMANY STRUCT ECO/DEV EXTR/IND INDUS MARKET NAT/G DELIB/GP ECO/TAC INT/TRADE EDU/PROP ATTIT RIGID/FLEX ORD/FREE PWR WEALTH...CONCPT STAT TIME/SEQ CHARTS ECSC TERR/GP 20. PAGE 81 F1582
EUR+WWI INT/ORG REGION

B62
ALEXANDROWICZ C.H.,WORLD ECONOMIC AGENCIES: LAW AND PRACTICE. WOR+45 DIST/IND FINAN LABOR CONSULT INT/TRADE TARIFFS REPRESENT HEALTH...JURID 20 UN GATT EEC OAS ECSC. PAGE 4 F0064
INT/LAW INT/ORG DIPLOM ADJUD

B62
MEADE J.E.,CASE STUDIES IN EUROPEAN ECONOMIC UNION. BELGIUM EUR+WWI LUXEMBOURG NAT/G INT/TRADE REGION ROUTINE WEALTH...METH/CNCPT STAT CHARTS ECSC TOT/POP OEEC EEC FOR/TRADE 20. PAGE 89 F1738
INT/ORG ECO/TAC

B63
KRAVIS I.B.,DOMESTIC INTERESTS AND INTERNATIONAL OBLIGATIONS: SAFEGUARDS IN INTERNATIONAL TRADE ORGANIZATIONS. EUR+WWI USA+45 WOR+45 FINAN DELIB/GP ATTIT RIGID/FLEX HEALTH...STAT EEC VAL/FREE OEEC ECSC 20. PAGE 73 F1435
INT/ORG ECO/TAC INT/TRADE

S64
SCHMITT H.D.,"POLITICAL CONDITIONS FOR INTERNATIONAL CURRENCY REFORM." WOR+45 SOCIETY ECO/DEV PLAN ECO/TAC BAL/PAY ATTIT ORD/FREE WEALTH ...SOC CONCPT OBS TREND EEC VAL/FREE ECSC 20. PAGE 117 F2301
FINAN VOL/ASSN REGION

S67
OLIVIER G.,"ASPECTS JURIDIQUES DE L'ADOPTION DU TRAITE CECA A LA CRISE CHARBONNIERE (SUITE ET FIN)" LAW DIST/IND PLAN DIPLOM RATION PRICE ADMIN COST DEMAND...POLICY CON/ANAL ECSC TREATY. PAGE 101 F1988
INT/TRADE INT/ORG EXTR/IND CONSTN

S67
WEIL G.L.,"THE MERGER OF THE INSTITUTIONS OF THE EUROPEAN COMMUNITIES" EUR+WWI ECO/DEV INT/TRADE CONSEN PLURISM...DECISION MGT 20 EEC EURATOM ECSC TREATY. PAGE 145 F2847
ECO/TAC INT/ORG CENTRAL INT/LAW

ECUADOR....SEE ALSO L/A+17C

B55
SERRANO MOSCOSO E.,A STATEMENT OF THE LAWS OF ECUADOR IN MATTERS AFFECTING BUSINESS (2ND ED.). ECUADOR INDUS LABOR LG/CO NAT/G LEGIS TAX CONTROL MARRIAGE 20. PAGE 120 F2359
FINAN ECO/UNDEV LAW CONSTN

ECUMENIC....ECUMENICAL MOVEMENT OF CHURCHES

EDELMAN M. F0699

EDELMAN M.J. F0700

EDEN/A....ANTHONY EDEN

EDGEWORTH A.B. F0701

EDGEWORTH F.Y. F0702

EDGEWORTH

B58
MUSGRAVE R.A.,CLASSICS IN THE THEORY OF PUBLIC FINANCE. UNIV MARKET LG/CO NAT/G CAP/ISM PRICE OPTIMAL...IDEA/COMP ANTHOL 19/20 SAY/EMIL EDGEWORTH LINDAHL/E RITSCHL/H. PAGE 95 F1870 — TAX FINAN ECO/TAC GP/REL

EDSEL....EDSEL (AUTOMOBILE)

EDU/PROP....EDUCATION, PROPAGANDA, PERSUASION

N
ECONOMIC ABSTRACTS. WOR+45 FINAN INDUS MARKET LABOR ACT/RES INT/TRADE WRITING GP/REL...MGT 20. PAGE 1 F0005 — BIBLIOG/A EDU/PROP

N
THE MIDDLE EAST AND NORTH AFRICA. AFR ISLAM CULTURE ECO/UNDEV AGRI NAT/G TEC/DEV FOR/AID INT/TRADE EDU/PROP...CHARTS 20. PAGE 1 F0008 — INDEX INDUS FINAN STAT

N
UNIVERSITY OF FLORIDA,CARIBBEAN ACQUISITIONS: MATERIALS ACQUIRED BY THE UNIVERSITY OF FLORIDA 1957-1960. L/A+17C...ART/METH GEOG MGT 20. PAGE 133 F2620 — BIBLIOG ECO/UNDEV EDU/PROP JURID

LCA
GODFREY E.M.,"THE ECONOMICS OF AN AFRICAN UNIVERSITY." AFR SCHOOL PRICE EFFICIENCY INCOME WEALTH...ECOMETRIC CHARTS 20. PAGE 48 F0930 — ACADEM ECO/TAC COST EDU/PROP

B11
SCOTT W.D.,INFLUENCING MEN IN BUSINESS: THE PSYCHOLOGY OF ARGUMENT AND SUGGESTION. WOR-45 WORKER EDU/PROP DEMAND ATTIT PERSON 20. PAGE 118 F2336 — PSY MARKET SML/CO TOP/EX

B12
FOUAD M.,LE REGIME DE LA PRESSE EN EGYPTE: THESE POUR LE DOCTORAT. UAR LICENSE EDU/PROP ADMIN SANCTION CRIME SUPEGO PWR...ART/METH JURID 19/20. PAGE 43 F0832 — ORD/FREE LEGIS CONTROL PRESS

B14
VEBLEN T.,THE INSTINCT OF WORKMANSHIP. UNIV SOCIETY ECO/DEV ECO/UNDEV CREATE TEC/DEV ECO/TAC EDU/PROP ROUTINE PERSON...HUM CONCPT TIME/SEQ GEN/LAWS. PAGE 140 F2768 — DRIVE SKILL

N19
EAST KENTUCKY REGIONAL PLAN,PROGRAM 60: A DECADE OF ACTION FOR PROGRESS IN EASTERN KENTUCKY (PAMPHLET). USA+45 AGRI CONSTRUC INDUS CONSULT ACT/RES PROB/SOLV EDU/PROP GOV/REL HEALTH KENTUCKY. PAGE 35 F0689 — REGION ADMIN PLAN ECO/UNDEV

N19
EAST KENTUCKY REGIONAL PLAN,PROGRAM 60 REPORT: ACTION FOR PORGRESS IN EASTERN KENTUCKY (PAMPHLET). USA+45 CONSTRUC INDUS ACT/RES PROB/SOLV EDU/PROP ADMIN GOV/REL KENTUCKY. PAGE 35 F0690 — REGION PLAN ECO/UNDEV CONSULT

N19
ENGELS F.,THE BRITISH LABOUR MOVEMENT (PAMPHLET). FRANCE GERMANY MOD/EUR UK USA-45 POL/PAR WORKER PAY EDU/PROP PRICE REPRESENT GP/REL 19. PAGE 37 F0730 — ECO/TAC MARXISM LABOR STRATA

N19
FIKS M.,PUBLIC ADMINISTRATION IN ISRAEL (PAMPHLET). ISRAEL SCHOOL EX/STRUC BUDGET PAY INGP/REL ...DECISION 20 CIVIL/SERV. PAGE 41 F0792 — EDU/PROP NAT/G ADMIN WORKER

N19
HUBERMAN L.,SOCIALISM IS THE ONLY ANSWER (PAMPHLET). CREATE ECO/TAC EDU/PROP CONTROL ...SOCIALIST GEN/LAWS ANTHOL 20. PAGE 62 F1230 — SOCISM ECO/DEV CAP/ISM PLAN

N19
MARCUS W.,US PRIVATE INVESTMENT AND ECONOMIC AID IN UNDERDEVELOPED COUNTRIES (PAMPHLET). USA+45 LG/CO NAT/G CAP/ISM EDU/PROP 20. PAGE 85 F1666 — FOR/AID ECO/UNDEV FINAN PLAN

N19
MUSHKIN S.J.,LOCAL SCHOOL EXPENDITURES: 1970 PROJECTIONS (PAMPHLET). FUT USA+45 CONSTRUC FINAN PROVS EDU/PROP COST...GEOG CENSUS PREDICT CHARTS SIMUL 20. PAGE 95 F1871 — LOC/G SCHOOL BUDGET

N19
PALAMOUNTAIN JC J.R.,THE DOLCIN CASE AND THE FEDERAL TRADE COMMISSION (PAMPHLET). USA+45 LAW MARKET SERV/IND LG/CO NAT/G BIO/SOC 20 FTC. PAGE 103 F2018 — ADJUD PROB/SOLV EDU/PROP HEALTH

N19
SENGHOR L.S.,AFRICAN SOCIALISM (PAMPHLET). AFR FRANCE MALI USSR ELITES ECO/UNDEV NAT/G DIPLOM DOMIN EDU/PROP ATTIT 20 NEGRO. PAGE 119 F2355 — SOCISM MARXISM ORD/FREE NAT/LISM

B21
CLAPHAN J.H.,THE ECONOMIC DEVELOPMENT OF FRANCE AND GERMANY 1815-1914. FRANCE GERMANY MOD/EUR COM/IND DIST/IND FINAN INT/TRADE EDU/PROP 19/20. PAGE 24 F0476 — ECO/UNDEV ECO/DEV AGRI INDUS

B26
SUFRIN S.C.,A BRIEF ANNOTATED BIBLIOGRAPHY ON LABOR IN EMERGING SOCIETIES. WOR+45 CULTURE SOCIETY INDUS EDU/PROP GP/REL INGP/REL. PAGE 127 F2510 — BIBLIOG/A LABOR ECO/UNDEV WORKER

B28
TRUE A.C.,A HISTORY OF AGRICULTURAL EXTENSION WORK IN THE UNITED STATES, 1785-1923. USA-45 LAW SCHOOL WAR ADJUST...CHARTS BIBLIOG 18/20 SMITH/LEVR COUNTY/AGT. PAGE 131 F2591 — EDU/PROP AGRI VOL/ASSN PLAN

B30
HAWTREY R.G.,ECONOMIC ASPECTS OF SOVEREIGNTY. UNIV WOR+45 WOR-45 ECO/DEV ECO/UNDEV AGRI COM/IND INDUS MARKET NAT/G TEC/DEV ECO/TAC EDU/PROP COERCE ATTIT KNOWL WEALTH...CONCPT CON/ANAL GEN/LAWS 20. PAGE 57 F1118 — FORCES PWR SOVEREIGN WAR

B32
THOMPSON C.D.,CONFESSIONS OF THE POWER TRUST. MARKET ACT/RES EDU/PROP CONTROL GOV/REL INCOME OWN ...MGT 20 FTC MONOPOLY. PAGE 130 F2564 — LG/CO SERV/IND PWR FINAN

B33
TANNENBAUM F.,PEACE BY REVOLUTION. ECO/UNDEV AGRI SECT WORKER DIPLOM EDU/PROP DISCRIM OWN WEALTH POPULISM 17/20 MEXIC/AMER INDIAN/AM. PAGE 128 F2532 — CULTURE COLONIAL RACE/REL REV

B35
O'CONNOR H.,REVOLUTION IN SEATTLE. USA-45 STRATA WORKER GP/REL ATTIT SOCISM...OBS BIBLIOG/A 20 SEATTLE STRIKE COM/PARTY. PAGE 99 F1954 — REV EDU/PROP LABOR MARXISM

S35
BONNETT C.E.,"THE EVOLUTION OF BUSINESS GROUPINGS." ECO/TAC EDU/PROP PRICE LOBBY ORD/FREE. PAGE 16 F0315 — VOL/ASSN GP/REL PROB/SOLV

B37
BROOKS R.R.,WHEN LABOR ORGANIZES. FINAN EDU/PROP ADMIN LOBBY PARTIC REPRESENT WEALTH TREND. PAGE 19 F0364 — LABOR GP/REL POLICY

B37
COLE W.E.,RECENT TRENDS IN RURAL PLANNING. USA-45 LAW ECO/DEV LOC/G SECT EDU/PROP CRIME LEISURE AGE/Y HABITAT...SOC/WK MUNICH 20. PAGE 26 F0503 — AGRI NEIGH PLAN ACT/RES

B37
UNION OF SOUTH AFRICA,REPORT CONCERNING ADMINISTRATION OF SOUTH WEST AFRICA (6 VOLS.). SOUTH/AFR INDUS PUB/INST FORCES LEGIS BUDGET DIPLOM EDU/PROP ADJUD CT/SYS...GEOG CHARTS 20 AFRICA/SW LEAGUE/NAT. PAGE 132 F2610 — NAT/G ADMIN COLONIAL CONSTN

B38
HOBSON J.A.,IMPERIALISM. MOD/EUR UK WOR-45 CULTURE ECO/UNDEV NAT/G VOL/ASSN PLAN EDU/PROP LEGIT REGION COERCE ATTIT PWR...POLICY PLURIST TIME/SEQ GEN/LAWS TERR/GP 19/20. PAGE 60 F1187 — DOMIN ECO/TAC BAL/PWR COLONIAL

B40
HUNTER R.,REVOLUTION: WHY, HOW, WHEN? NAT/G ECO/TAC EDU/PROP COERCE ORD/FREE FASCISM POPULISM SOCISM 18/20 HITLER/A LENIN/VI. PAGE 63 F1246 — REV METH/COMP LEAD CONSTN

B40
MEEK C.K.,EUROPE AND WEST AFRICA. AFR EUR+WWI EXTR/IND DIPLOM INT/TRADE EDU/PROP GP/REL...SOC 20. PAGE 89 F1743 — CULTURE TEC/DEV ECO/UNDEV COLONIAL

S41
LASSWELL H.D.,"THE GARRISON STATE" (BMR)" FUT WOR+45 ELITES INTELL FORCES ECO/TAC DOMIN EDU/PROP COERCE INGP/REL 20. PAGE 76 F1485 — NAT/G DIPLOM PWR CIVMIL/REL

B42
VEBLEN T.B.,THE THEORY OF THE LEISURE CLASS. USA-45 SOCIETY STRATA STRUCT NAT/G SECT WORKER CREATE EDU/PROP ATTIT...SOC GEN/LAWS 19. PAGE 141 F2772 — WEALTH ELITES LEISURE PRODUC

S43
GOLDEN C.S.,"NEW PATTERNS OF DEMOCRACY." NEIGH DELIB/GP EDU/PROP EXEC PARTIC...MGT METH/CNCPT OBS TREND. PAGE 48 F0935 — LABOR REPRESENT LG/CO GP/REL

B44
HAYEK F.A.,THE ROAD TO SERFDOM. NAT/G POL/PAR CREATE EDU/PROP ATTIT WEALTH LAISSEZ...OLD/LIB CONCPT TREND 20. PAGE 57 F1121 — FUT PLAN ECO/TAC SOCISM

B44
INTL CHAMBER OF COMMERCE,TERMS COMMONLY USED IN DISTRIBUTION AND ADVERTISING. PORTUGAL SPAIN UK WOR-45 SERV/IND 20. PAGE 65 F1284 — DICTIONARY EDU/PROP DIST/IND INT/TRADE

B44
MERRIAM C.E.,PUBLIC AND PRIVATE GOVERNMENT. VOL/ASSN EDU/PROP ADMIN REPRESENT EFFICIENCY PWR PLURISM...MAJORIT CONCPT. PAGE 90 F1762
NAT/G NEIGH MGT POLICY

B46
ERNST M.L.,THE FIRST FREEDOM. USA-45 CONSTN PRESS PRIVIL...CHARTS IDEA/COMP BIBLIOG 20 AMEND/I. PAGE 38 F0746
EDU/PROP COM/IND ORD/FREE CONTROL

B47
HEILPERIN M.A.,THE TRADE OF NATIONS. USA+45 USA-45 WOR+45 WOR-45 CULTURE ECO/DEV NAT/G DELIB/GP EDU/PROP ATTIT DISPL ORD/FREE PWR WEALTH TOT/POP 20. PAGE 58 F1139
MARKET INT/ORG INT/TRADE PEACE

B47
LEVER E.A.,ADVERTISING AND ECONOMIC THEORY. FINAN ECO/TAC DEMAND EFFICIENCY ATTIT...MGT PSY SAMP/SIZ CHARTS 20. PAGE 79 F1539
EDU/PROP MARKET COM/IND ECO/DEV

B48
KESSELMAN L.C.,THE SOCIAL POLITICS OF THE FEPC. INDUS WORKER EDU/PROP GP/REL RACE/REL 20 NEGRO JEWS FEPC. PAGE 70 F1382
POLICY NAT/G ADMIN DISCRIM

B49
LEE A.M.,SOCIAL PROBLEMS IN AMERICA: A SOURCE BOOK. STRATA STRUCT KIN NEIGH VOL/ASSN ACT/RES LEAD CRIME AGE SEX 20. PAGE 77 F1504
SOC SOCIETY PERSON EDU/PROP

B49
US DEPARTMENT OF STATE,SOVIET BIBLIOGRAPHY (PAMPHLET). CHINA/COM COM USSR LAW AGRI INT/ORG ECO/TAC EDU/PROP...POLICY GEOG IND 20. PAGE 135 F2670
BIBLIOG/A MARXISM CULTURE DIPLOM

S49
STEINMETZ H.,"THE PROBLEMS OF THE LANDRAT: A STUDY OF COUNTY GOVERNMENT IN THE US ZONE OF GERMANY." GERMANY/W USA+45 INDUS PLAN DIPLOM EDU/PROP CONTROL WAR GOV/REL FEDERAL WEALTH PLURISM...GOV/COMP 20 LANDRAT. PAGE 126 F2478
LOC/G COLONIAL MGT TOP/EX

B50
LINCOLN G.,ECONOMICS OF NATIONAL SECURITY. USA+45 ELITES COM/IND DIST/IND INDUS NAT/G VOL/ASSN DELIB/GP EX/STRUC FOR/AID EDU/PROP COERCE NUC/PWR WAR ATTIT KNOWL ORD/FREE PWR TOT/POP VAL/FREE 20. PAGE 80 F1565
FORCES ECO/TAC AFR

B50
US DEPARTMENT OF STATE,POINT FOUR: COOPERATIVE PROGRAM FOR AID IN THE DEVELOPMENT OF ECONOMICALLY UNDERDEVELOPED AREAS. WOR+45 AGRI INDUS INT/ORG PLAN TEC/DEV DIPLOM EDU/PROP ADMIN PEACE PRODUC WEALTH 20 CONGRESS UN. PAGE 135 F2671
ECO/UNDEV FOR/AID FINAN INT/TRADE

S50
EBY K.,"RESEARCH IN LABOR UNIONS." EDU/PROP INGP/REL PWR...METH/CNCPT OBS. PAGE 36 F0693
RECORD QU LABOR PARTIC

B51
HARDMAN J.B.,THE HOUSE OF LABOR. LAW R+D NEIGH EDU/PROP LEAD ROUTINE REPRESENT GP/REL...POLICY STAT. PAGE 55 F1080
LABOR LOBBY ADMIN PRESS

B52
ANDREWS F.E.,CORPORATION GIVING. LAW TAX EDU/PROP ADMIN...POLICY STAT CHARTS. PAGE 5 F0101
LG/CO GIVE SML/CO FINAN

B52
EGLE W.P.,ECONOMIC STABILIZATION. USA+45 SOCIETY FINAN MARKET PLAN ECO/TAC DOMIN EDU/PROP LEGIT EXEC WEALTH...CONCPT METH/CNCPT TREND HYPO/EXP GEN/METH TOT/POP VAL/FREE 20. PAGE 36 F0708
NAT/G ECO/DEV CAP/ISM

L52
HUTH A.G.,"COMMUNICATION AND ECONOMIC DEVELOPMENT." FUT WOR+45 CULTURE SOCIETY INT/ORG PLAN TEC/DEV EDU/PROP DRIVE KNOWL WEALTH...POLICY CONCPT RECORD STERTYP GEN/LAWS COMMUN TOT/POP UNESCO 20 UN CMN/WLTH. PAGE 64 F1250
ECO/UNDEV

B53
DAHL R.A.,POLITICS, ECONOMICS AND WELFARE: PLANNING AND POLITICOECONOMIC SYSTEMS RESOLVED INTO BASIC SOCIAL PROCESSES. WOR+45 WOR-45 ECO/DEV ECO/UNDEV R+D CREATE PLAN TEC/DEV EDU/PROP HEALTH WEALTH ...SOC SELF/OBS TREND CHARTS GEN/METH 20. PAGE 29 F0571
ECO/TAC PHIL/SCI

B53
MENDE T.,WORLD POWER IN THE BALANCE. FUT USA+45 USSR WOR-45 ECO/DEV ECO/TAC INT/TRADE EDU/PROP UTOPIA ATTIT...HUM CONCPT TREND TOT/POP 20. PAGE 90 F1756
WOR+45 PWR BAL/PWR AFR

B53
ROBINSON E.A.G.,THE STRUCTURE OF COMPETITIVE INDUSTRY. UK ECO/DEV DIST/IND MARKET TEC/DEV DIPLOM EDU/PROP ADMIN EFFICIENCY WEALTH...MGT 19/20. PAGE 113 F2217
INDUS PRODUC WORKER OPTIMAL

B53
WOYTINSKY W.S.,WORLD POPULATION AND PRODUCTION: TRENDS AND OUTLOOK. FUT WOR+45 WOR-45 CULTURE SOCIETY ECO/DEV AGRI INDUS TEC/DEV EDU/PROP SKILL WEALTH...SOC TREND. PAGE 149 F2928
ECO/UNDEV METH/CNCPT GEOG PERSON

S53
GABLE R.W.,"NAM: INFLUENTIAL LOBBY OR KISS OF DEATH?" (BMR)" USA+45 LAW INSPECT EDU/PROP ADMIN CONTROL INGP/REL EFFICIENCY PWR 20 CONGRESS NAM TAFT/HART. PAGE 45 F0880
LOBBY LEGIS INDUS LG/CO

S53
LINCOLN G.,"FACTORS DETERMINING ARMS AID." COM FUT USA+45 USSR WOR+45 ECO/DEV NAT/G CONSULT PLAN TEC/DEV DIPLOM DOMIN EDU/PROP PERCEPT PWR ...DECISION CONCPT TREND MARX/KARL 20. PAGE 80 F1566
FORCES POLICY BAL/PWR FOR/AID

B54
KARTUN D.,AFRICA, AFRICA: A CONTINENT RISES TO ITS FEET. AFR SOUTH/AFR UK ELITES AGRI LABOR LOC/G POL/PAR EDU/PROP CONTROL COERCE DISCRIM AGE/Y NEGRO THIRD/WRLD GOLD/COAST. PAGE 69 F1358
COLONIAL ORD/FREE PROFIT EXTR/IND

B54
STALEY E.,THE FUTURE OF UNDERDEVELOPED COUNTRIES: POLITICAL IMPLICATIONS OF ECONOMIC DEVELOPMENT. AFR COM FUT USA+45 SOCIETY ECO/UNDEV CREATE PLAN CAP/ISM ATTIT DRIVE MARXISM SOCISM...POLICY CONCPT CHARTS 20. PAGE 125 F2466
EDU/PROP ECO/TAC FOR/AID

B54
WASHBURNE N.F.,INTERPRETING SOCIAL CHANGE IN AMERICA. USA+45 STRATA FAM NAT/G SECT OP/RES ECO/TAC EDU/PROP HABITAT...SOC TIME/SEQ TREND 20 BUREAUCRCY. PAGE 143 F2826
CULTURE STRUCT CREATE TEC/DEV

L54
OPLER M.E.,"SOCIAL ASPECTS OF TECHNICAL ASSISTANCE IN OPERATION." WOR+45 VOL/ASSN CREATE PLAN TEC/DEV EDU/PROP ALL/VALS...METH/CNCPT OBS RECORD TREND UN 20. PAGE 101 F1993
INT/ORG CONSULT FOR/AID

B55
COLE G.D.H.,STUDIES IN CLASS STRUCTURE. UK NAT/G WORKER TEC/DEV EDU/PROP...CLASSIF CHARTS 20. PAGE 26 F0501
STRUCT STRATA ELITES CONCPT

B55
US ADVISORY COMN INTERGOV REL,THE COMMISSION ON INTERGOVERNMENTAL RELATIONS; A REPORT TO THE PRESIDENT FOR TRANSMITTAL TO THE CONGRESS. USA+45 ECO/DEV AGRI COM/IND FINAN FORCES PLAN EDU/PROP HEALTH WEALTH...STAT MUNICH 20 CIV/DEFENS. PAGE 133 F2630
GOV/REL NAT/G LOC/G PROVS

B55
WRONG D.H.,AMERICAN AND CANADIAN VIEWPOINTS. CANADA USA+45 CONSTN STRATA FAM SECT WORKER ECO/TAC EDU/PROP ADJUD MARRIAGE...IDEA/COMP 20. PAGE 149 F2936
DIPLOM ATTIT NAT/COMP CULTURE

L55
KISER M.,"ORGANIZATION OF AMERICAN STATES." L/A+17C USA+45 ECO/UNDEV INT/ORG NAT/G PLAN TEC/DEV DIPLOM ECO/TAC INT/TRADE EDU/PROP ADMIN ALL/VALS...POLICY MGT RECORD ORG/CHARTS OAS COMMUN 20. PAGE 71 F1401
VOL/ASSN ECO/DEV REGION

B56
ATOMIC INDUSTRIAL FORUM,PUBLIC RELATIONS FOR THE ATOMIC INDUSTRY. WOR+45 PLAN PROB/SOLV EDU/PROP PRESS CONFER...AUD/VIS ANTHOL 20. PAGE 7 F0135
NUC/PWR INDUS GP/REL ATTIT

B56
GARDNER R.N.,STERLING-DOLLAR DIPLOMACY. EUR+WWI USA+45 INT/ORG NAT/G PLAN INT/TRADE EDU/PROP ADMIN KNOWL PWR WEALTH...POLICY SOC METH/CNCPT STAT CHARTS SIMUL GEN/LAWS 20. PAGE 46 F0902
ECO/DEV DIPLOM

B56
KNORR K.E.,RUBLE DIPLOMACY: CHALLENGE TO AMERICAN FOREIGN AID(PAMPHLET). AFR CHINA/COM USA+45 USSR PLAN TEC/DEV CAP/ISM INT/TRADE DOMIN EDU/PROP CONTROL LEAD 20. PAGE 72 F1413
ECO/UNDEV COM DIPLOM FOR/AID

B56
WHYTE W.H. JR.,THE ORGANIZATION MAN. CULTURE FINAN VOL/ASSN DOMIN EDU/PROP EXEC DISPL HABITAT ROLE ...PERS/TEST STERTYP. PAGE 146 F2875
ADMIN LG/CO PERSON CONSEN

B56
WOLFF R.L.,THE BALKANS IN OUR TIME. ALBANIA FUT MOD/EUR USSR YUGOSLAVIA CULTURE INT/ORG SECT DIPLOM EDU/PROP COERCE WAR ORD/FREE...CHARTS 4/20 BALKANS COMINFORM. PAGE 148 F2919
GEOG COM

B56
YABUKI K.,JAPAN BIBLIOGRAPHIC ANNUAL, 1956: THE LATEST LIST OF OLD AND NEW BOOKS ON JAPAN IN ENGLISH. EDU/PROP...LING 20 CHINJAP. PAGE 149 F2945
BIBLIOG SOC

S56
BONILLA F.,"WHEN IS PETITION 'PRESSURE?'" (BMR)" USA+45 ELITES INDUS LABOR CHIEF EDU/PROP LEGIT ATTIT...INT CHARTS 20 CONGRESS PRESIDENT EISNHWR/DD. PAGE 16 F0312
LEGIS EX/STRUC INT/TRADE TARIFFS

S56
GORDON L.,"THE ORGANIZATION FOR EUROPEAN ECONOMIC COOPERATION." EUR+WWI INDUS INT/ORG NAT/G CONSULT
VOL/ASSN ECO/DEV

DELIB/GP ACT/RES CREATE PLAN TEC/DEV EDU/PROP LEGIT WEALTH OEEC 20. PAGE 49 F0956

B57
DOWNS A.,AN ECONOMIC THEORY OF DEMOCRACY. NAT/G EDU/PROP RISK CHOOSE PERS/REL EQUILIB...SOC METH/CNCPT LOG STYLE. PAGE 34 F0659
DECISION RATIONAL

B57
LAVES W.H.C.,UNESCO. FUT WOR+45 NAT/G CONSULT DELIB/GP TEC/DEV ECO/TAC EDU/PROP PEACE ORD/FREE ...CONCPT TIME/SEQ TREND UNESCO VAL/FREE 20. PAGE 76 F1491
INT/ORG KNOWL

B57
NAUMANN R.,THEORIE UND PRAXIS DES NEOLIBERALISMUS; DAS MAERCHEN VON DER FREIEN ODER SOZIALEN MARKTWIRTSCHAFT. GERMANY/W FORCES PLAN EDU/PROP SOCISM...POLICY MARXIST IDEA/COMP BIBLIOG 18/20 ADENAUER/K. PAGE 97 F1903
MARXISM NEW/LIB ECO/TAC CAP/ISM

B57
WATSON G.,THE UNSERVILE STATE: ESSAYS IN LIBERTY AND WELFARE. UK LEGIS RECEIVE EDU/PROP COLONIAL ...WELF/ST 20 LIB/PARTY. PAGE 144 F2833
POL/PAR ORD/FREE CONTROL NEW/LIB

B58
MASON J.B.,THAILAND BIBLIOGRAPHY. S/ASIA THAILAND CULTURE EDU/PROP ADMIN...GEOG SOC LING 20. PAGE 87 F1701
BIBLIOG/A ECO/UNDEV DIPLOM NAT/G

B58
RUBIN B.,PUBLIC RELATIONS AND THE STATE, A CASE STUDY OF NEW YORK STATE ADMINISTRATION, 1943-54. USA+45 USA-45 COM/IND EDU/PROP GOV/REL...CHARTS 20 NEW/YORK DEWEY/THOM. PAGE 114 F2255
INGP/REL PRESS PROVS GP/REL

B58
SCOTT D.J.R.,RUSSIAN POLITICAL INSTITUTIONS. RUSSIA USSR CONSTN AGRI DELIB/GP PLAN EDU/PROP CONTROL CHOOSE EFFICIENCY ATTIT MARXISM...BIBLIOG/A IND 13/20. PAGE 118 F2332
NAT/G POL/PAR ADMIN DECISION

B58
US OPERATIONS MISSION TO VIET,BUILDING ECONOMIC STRENGTH (PAMPHLET). USA+45 VIETNAM/S INDUS TEC/DEV BUDGET ADMIN EATING HEALTH...STAT 20. PAGE 138 F2725
FOR/AID ECO/UNDEV AGRI EDU/PROP

L58
MASON E.S.,"ECONOMIC PLANNING IN UNDERDEVELOPED AREAS." FUT WOR+45 PLAN TEC/DEV EDU/PROP ATTIT RIGID/FLEX KNOWL...SOC CONCPT GEN/LAWS TOT/POP 20. PAGE 87 F1697
NAT/G ECO/UNDEV

B59
ALLEN R.L.,SOVIET INFLUENCE IN LATIN AMERICA. ECO/UNDEV FINAN PROC/MFG NAT/G TEC/DEV EDU/PROP EXEC ROUTINE ATTIT DRIVE PERSON ALL/VALS PWR...STAT CHARTS WORK FOR/TRADE 20. PAGE 4 F0071
L/A+17C ECO/TAC INT/TRADE USSR

B59
BONNETT C.E.,LABOR-MANAGEMENT RELATIONS. USA+45 OP/RES PROB/SOLV EDU/PROP...AUD/VIS CHARTS 20. PAGE 16 F0317
MGT LABOR INDUS GP/REL

B59
CHECCHI V.,HONDURAS: A PROBLEM IN ECONOMIC DEVELOPMENT. HONDURAS AGRI FINAN INDUS LABOR WORKER INT/TRADE EDU/PROP PRICE HEALTH...GEOG CHARTS BIBLIOG 20. PAGE 24 F0458
ECO/UNDEV ECO/TAC PROB/SOLV PLAN

B59
HOOVER C.B.,THE ECONOMY, LIBERTY AND THE STATE. COM EUR+WWI USA+45 USA-45 USSR CAP/ISM EDU/PROP COERCE TOTALISM ORD/FREE...POLICY OBS INT TREND NAZI 20. PAGE 61 F1206
ECO/DEV ECO/TAC

B59
KRIPALANI J.B.,CLASS STRUGGLE. INDIA WOR+45 ECO/UNDEV LABOR CAP/ISM EDU/PROP INGP/REL ...SOCIALIST IDEA/COMP 17/20. PAGE 73 F1440
MARXISM STRATA COERCE ECO/TAC

B59
PANIKKAR K.M.,THE AFRO-ASIAN STATES AND THEIR PROBLEMS. COM CULTURE KIN POL/PAR SECT DIPLOM EDU/PROP COLONIAL SOVEREIGN...TECHNIC GOV/COMP 20. PAGE 103 F2025
AFR S/ASIA ECO/UNDEV

B59
SERAPHIM H.J.,PROBLEME DER WILLENSBILDUNG UND DER WIRTSCHAFTSPOLITISCHEN FUEHRUNG. WOR+45 MARKET ACT/RES OP/RES PLAN EDU/PROP INGP/REL HABITAT PLURISM...MGT PERS/COMP METH 20. PAGE 119 F2357
POLICY DECISION PSY

B59
VINCENT W.S.,ROLES OF THE CITIZENS: PRINCIPLES AND PRACTICES. LOC/G POL/PAR VOL/ASSN CHOOSE ROLE ORD/FREE PWR...POLICY 20. PAGE 141 F2785
INGP/REL EDU/PROP CREATE LOBBY

B59
WORTHY J.C.,BIG BUSINESS AND FREE MEN. LG/CO EX/STRUC EDU/PROP LEAD CHOOSE GP/REL ATTIT DRIVE ROLE ORD/FREE...MAJORIT 20. PAGE 149 F2927
ELITES LOC/G TOP/EX PARTIC

S59
HOFFMAN P.,"OPERATION BREAKTHROUGH." AFR S/ASIA STRUCT INDUS CONSULT TEC/DEV ATTIT RIGID/FLEX SKILL WEALTH...TECHNIC CONCPT STYLE RECORD CHARTS ORG/CHARTS GEN/METH VAL/FREE 20. PAGE 61 F1190
ECO/UNDEV EDU/PROP FOR/AID

B60
BILLERBECK K.,SOVIET BLOC FOREIGN AID TO UNDERDEVELOPED COUNTRIES. COM FUT USSR FINAN FORCES TEC/DEV DIPLOM INT/TRADE EDU/PROP NUC/PWR...TREND 20. PAGE 15 F0285
FOR/AID ECO/UNDEV ECO/TAC MARXISM

B60
CAMPBELL R.W.,SOVIET ECONOMIC POWER. COM USA+45 DIST/IND MARKET TOP/EX ACT/RES CAP/ISM ECO/TAC DOMIN EDU/PROP ADMIN ROUTINE DRIVE...MATH TIME/SEQ CHARTS WORK 20. PAGE 21 F0409
ECO/DEV PLAN SOCISM USSR

B60
COPLAND D.,THE ADVENTURE OF GROWTH: ESSAYS ON THE AUSTRALIAN ECONOMY AND ITS INTERNATIONAL SETTING. WOR+45 DIST/IND ACADEM EDU/PROP ADMIN INCOME 20 AUSTRAL. PAGE 27 F0534
ECO/DEV ECO/UNDEV ECO/TAC INT/TRADE

B60
FORM W.H.,INDUSTRY, LABOR, AND COMMUNITY. STRUCT NEIGH SECT BAL/PWR EDU/PROP PARTIC ATTIT ROLE PWR WEALTH...METH/CNCPT CHARTS. PAGE 42 F0828
LABOR MGT GP/REL CONTROL

B60
GRANICK D.,THE RED EXECUTIVE. COM USA+45 SOCIETY ECO/DEV INDUS NAT/G POL/PAR EX/STRUC PLAN ECO/TAC EDU/PROP ADMIN EXEC ATTIT DRIVE...GP/COMP 20. PAGE 50 F0976
PWR STRATA USSR ELITES

B60
LISTER L.,EUROPE'S COAL AND STEEL COMMUNITY. FRANCE GERMANY STRUCT ECO/DEV EXTR/IND INDUS MARKET NAT/G DELIB/GP ECO/TAC INT/TRADE EDU/PROP ATTIT RIGID/FLEX ORD/FREE PWR WEALTH...CONCPT STAT TIME/SEQ CHARTS ECSC TERR/GP 20. PAGE 81 F1582
EUR+WWI INT/ORG REGION

B60
ROEPKE W.,A HUMANE ECONOMY: THE SOCIAL FRAMEWORK OF THE FREE MARKET. FUT USSR WOR+45 CULTURE SOCIETY ECO/DEV PLAN ECO/TAC ADMIN ATTIT PERSON RIGID/FLEX SUPEGO MORAL WEALTH SOCISM...POLICY OLD/LIB CONCPT TREND GEN/LAWS 20. PAGE 113 F2232
DRIVE EDU/PROP CAP/ISM

B60
SHONFIELD A.,THE ATTACK ON WORLD POVERTY. WOR+45 ECO/DEV ECO/UNDEV FINAN VOL/ASSN PLAN EDU/PROP DRIVE KNOWL WEALTH...CONT/OBS STAND/INT ORG/CHARTS TOT/POP UNESCO 20. PAGE 121 F2383
INT/ORG ECO/TAC FOR/AID INT/TRADE

B60
STEVENSON A.E.,PUTTING FIRST THINGS FIRST. USA+45 INT/ORG NEIGH FOR/AID DISCRIM...ANTHOL 20. PAGE 126 F2483
DIPLOM ECO/UNDEV ORD/FREE EDU/PROP

L60
SPENGLER J.J.,"ECONOMIC DEVELOPMENT: POLITICAL PRECONDITIONS AND POLITICAL CONSEQUENCE." WOR+45 STRUCT ECO/UNDEV NAT/G PLAN ECO/TAC EDU/PROP ATTIT ORD/FREE WEALTH SOCISM...SOC CONCPT TREND SIMUL GEN/METH WORK 20. PAGE 124 F2452
TEC/DEV METH/CNCPT CAP/ISM

S60
BAUM M.,"THE CASE FOR BUSINESS CIVILIZATION." R+D CAP/ISM GIVE EDU/PROP HAPPINESS...SOC TREND. PAGE 12 F0218
MGT CULTURE WEALTH

S60
GROSSMAN G.,"SOVIET GROWTH: ROUTINE, INERTIA, AND PRESSURE." COM STRATA NAT/G DELIB/GP PLAN TEC/DEV ECO/TAC EDU/PROP ADMIN ROUTINE DRIVE WEALTH 20. PAGE 52 F1007
POL/PAR ECO/DEV AFR USSR

S60
JAFFEE A.J.,"POPULATION TRENDS AND CONTROLS IN UNDERDEVELOPED COUNTRIES." AFR FUT ISLAM L/A+17C S/ASIA CULTURE R+D FAM ACT/RES PLAN EDU/PROP BIO/SOC RIGID/FLEX HEALTH...SOC STAT OBS CHARTS 20. PAGE 66 F1303
ECO/UNDEV GEOG

S60
MIKESELL R.F.,"AMERICA'S ECONOMIC RESPONSIBILITY AS A GREAT POWER." COM FUT USA+45 USSR WOR+45 INT/ORG PLAN ECO/TAC FOR/AID EDU/PROP CHOOSE WEALTH ...POLICY 20. PAGE 91 F1781
ECO/UNDEV BAL/PWR CAP/ISM

S60
POLLARD J.A.,"EMERGING PATTERNS OF CORPORATE GIVING." FINAN DELIB/GP PLAN EDU/PROP CENTRAL TREND. PAGE 107 F2098
GIVE LG/CO ADMIN MGT

B61
BENOIT E.,EUROPE AT SIXES AND SEVENS: THE COMMON MARKET, THE FREE TRADE ASSOCIATION AND THE UNITED STATES. EUR+WWI FUT USA+45 INDUS CONSULT DELIB/GP EX/STRUC TOP/EX ACT/RES ECO/TAC EDU/PROP ROUTINE CHOOSE PERCEPT WEALTH...MGT TREND EEC FOR/TRADE TOT/POP 20 EFTA. PAGE 13 F0249
FINAN ECO/DEV VOL/ASSN

B61
CAMPAIGNE J.G.,CHECK-OFF: LABOR BOSSES AND WORKING MEN. LEGIS WORKER EDU/PROP DEBATE COERCE REPRESENT GP/REL ORD/FREE CONSERVE. PAGE 21 F0404
LABOR ELITES PWR CONTROL

B61
DE GRAZIA A.,AMERICAN WELFARE. CLIENT FINAN LABOR LOC/G NAT/G NEIGH EDU/PROP GP/REL...CLASSIF CON/ANAL CHARTS BIBLIOG. PAGE 31 F0598
GIVE WEALTH SECT VOL/ASSN

B61
DEWITT N.,EDUCATION AND PROFESSIONAL EMPLOYMENT IN THE USSR. USSR PROF/ORG WORKER PLAN ADMIN UTIL AGE/C AGE/Y MARXISM...STAT CHARTS 20. PAGE 32 F0629 EDU/PROP ACADEM SCHOOL INTELL

B61
ENGLER R.,THE POLITICS OF OIL. USA+45 CLIENT ELITES DOMIN EDU/PROP EXEC PWR 20. PAGE 38 F0734 LOBBY REPRESENT POLICY

B61
INDUSTRIAL COUN SOC-ECO STU,THE SWEDISH ECONOMY AND THE UNDERDEVELOPED COUNTRIES. SWEDEN INDUS DELIB/GP TEC/DEV INT/TRADE EDU/PROP COLONIAL DRIVE...CHARTS 20. PAGE 64 F1264 FOR/AID ECO/UNDEV PLAN FINAN

B61
INTL UNION LOCAL AUTHORITIES,METROPOLIS. WOR+45 DIST/IND FINAN GIVE EDU/PROP CRIME COST HEALTH WEALTH MUNICH 20. PAGE 65 F1286 GOV/COMP LOC/G BIBLIOG

B61
KOVNER M.,THE CHALLENGE OF COEXISTENCE: A STUDY OF SOVIET ECONOMIC DIPLOMACY. COM FUT ECO/DEV ECO/UNDEV PLAN EDU/PROP DETER SKILL...OBS VAL/FREE 20. PAGE 73 F1430 PWR DIPLOM USSR AFR

B61
LENIN V.I.,WHAT IS TO BE DONE? (1902). RUSSIA LABOR NAT/G POL/PAR WORKER CAP/ISM ECO/TAC ADMIN PARTIC ...MARXIST IDEA/COMP GEN/LAWS 19/20. PAGE 78 F1522 EDU/PROP PRESS MARXISM METH/COMP

B61
LENSKI G.,THE RELIGIOUS FACTOR: A SOCIOLOGICAL STUDY OF RELIGION'S IMPACT ON POLITICS, ECONOMICS, AND FAMILY LIFE. FAM PROF/ORG EDU/PROP ROLE CATHISM ...INT SAMP MUNICH. PAGE 78 F1524 SECT GP/REL

B61
LETHBRIDGE H.J.,CHINA'S URBAN COMMUNES. CHINA/COM FUT ECO/UNDEV DIPLOM EDU/PROP DEMAND INCOME MARXISM ...POLICY MUNICH 20. PAGE 78 F1534 CONTROL ECO/TAC NAT/G

B61
LHOSTE-LACHAUME P.,OU GIT LE DESACCORD ENTRE LIBERAUX ET SOCIALISTES. EUR+WWI USA+45 USA-45 USSR CAP/ISM EDU/PROP MARXISM...MAJORIT IDEA/COMP 20 KEYNES/JM NEW/DEAL DEPRESSION. PAGE 79 F1555 LAISSEZ SOCISM FINAN

B61
SHARP W.R.,FIELD ADMINISTRATION IN THE UNITED NATION SYSTEM: THE CONDUCT OF INTERNATIONAL ECONOMIC AND SOCIAL PROGRAMS. FUT WOR+45 CONSTN SOCIETY ECO/UNDEV R+D DELIB/GP ACT/RES PLAN TEC/DEV EDU/PROP EXEC ROUTINE HEALTH WEALTH...HUM CONCPT CHARTS METH ILO UNESCO GP VAL/FREE UN 20. PAGE 120 F2369 INT/ORG CONSULT

S61
DEUTSCH K.W.,"NATIONAL INDUSTRIALIZATION AND THE DECLINING SHARE OF THE INTERNATIONAL ECONOMIC SECTOR." EUR+WWI FUT WOR+45 WOR-45 MARKET PLAN EDU/PROP WEALTH...WELF/ST OBS TESTS 20. PAGE 32 F0624 DIST/IND ECO/DEV INT/TRADE

S61
GALBRAITH J.K.,"A POSITIVE APPROACH TO ECONOMIC AID." FUT USA+45 INTELL NAT/G CONSULT ACT/RES DIPLOM ECO/TAC EDU/PROP ATTIT KNOWL PWR WEALTH ...SOC STERTYP MID/EX METH/GP 20. PAGE 45 F0883 ECO/UNDEV ROUTINE FOR/AID

S61
NOVE A.,"THE SOVIET MODEL AND UNDERDEVELOPED COUNTRIES." COM FUT USSR WOR+45 CULTURE ECO/DEV POL/PAR FOR/AID EDU/PROP ADMIN MORAL WEALTH ...POLICY RECORD HIST/WRIT 20. PAGE 99 F1942 ECO/UNDEV PLAN

N61
VINER J.,THE INTELLECTUAL HISTORY OF LAISSEZ FAIRE (PAMPHLET). WOR+45 WOR-45 LAW INTELL...POLICY LING LOG 19/20. PAGE 141 F2787 ATTIT EDU/PROP LAISSEZ ECO/TAC

B62
ARNOLD H.J.P.,AID FOR DEVELOPING COUNTRIES. COM EUR+WWI USA+45 USSR WOR+45 EDU/PROP ATTIT DRIVE PWR WEALTH...TREND CHARTS STERTYP NAT/ 20. PAGE 6 F0115 ECO/UNDEV ECO/TAC FOR/AID

B62
ARNOLD T.W.,THE FOLKLORE OF CAPITALISM. USA+45 USA-45 SOCIETY LG/CO SML/CO EX/STRUC ECO/TAC EDU/PROP ADJUST INCOME...MYTH CHARTS 20. PAGE 6 F0116 CAP/ISM ATTIT STERTYP ECO/DEV

B62
BARTELS R.,THE DEVELOPMENT OF MARKETING THOUGHT. USA+45 USA-45 FINAN ECO/TAC...CONCPT TREND. PAGE 11 F0199 ECO/DEV MARKET MGT EDU/PROP

B62
BRANCH M.C.,THE CORPORATE PLANNING PROCESS. FINAN EX/STRUC EDU/PROP CONTROL LEAD GP/REL PERS/REL RATIONAL PERCEPT...MGT MATH PROBABIL STAT GAME. PAGE 18 F0338 PROF/ORG PLAN DECISION PERSON

B62
BROOKINGS INSTITUTION,DEVELOPMENT OF THE EMERGING COUNTRIES; AN AGENDA FOR RESEARCH. WOR+45 AGRI TEC/DEV FOR/AID EDU/PROP ADJUST HABITAT KNOWL...PSY SOC ANTHOL 20 THIRD/WRLD. PAGE 19 F0362 ECO/UNDEV R+D SOCIETY PROB/SOLV

B62
DEBUYST F.,LAS CLASES SOCIALES EN AMERICA LATINA. L/A+17C SOCIETY STRUCT WORKER EDU/PROP RACE/REL ATTIT HABITAT ROLE...GEOG SOC NAT/COMP SOC/INTEG 20. PAGE 32 F0612 STRATA GP/REL WEALTH

B62
ELLIOTT J.R.,THE APPEAL OF COMMUNISM IN THE UNDERDEVELOPED NATIONS. AFR USSR WOR+45 INT/ORG NAT/G DIPLOM DOMIN EDU/PROP ROUTINE ATTIT RIGID/FLEX ORD/FREE PWR WEALTH MARXISM...POLICY SOC METH/CNCPT MYTH TOT/POP METH/GP 20. PAGE 37 F0722 COM ECO/UNDEV

B62
FRIEDMAN M.,CAPITALISM AND FREEDOM. USA+45 FINAN LG/CO WORKER INT/TRADE RECEIVE EDU/PROP CONTROL DISCRIM INCOME WEALTH POLICY. PAGE 44 F0859 CAP/ISM ORD/FREE NAT/G ECO/DEV

B62
HUMPHREY D.D.,THE UNITED STATES AND THE COMMON MARKET. USA+45 INDUS MARKET INT/ORG PLAN EDU/PROP BAL/PAY DRIVE PWR WEALTH...TREND STERTYP FOR/TRADE EEC 20. PAGE 63 F1241 ATTIT ECO/TAC

B62
INTERNAT CONGRESS OF JURISTS,EXECUTIVE ACTION AND THE RULE OF RULE: REPORTION PROCEEDINGS OF INT'T CONGRESS OF JURISTS,-RIO DE JANEIRO, BRAZIL. WOR+45 ACADEM CONSULT JUDGE EDU/PROP ADJUD CT/SYS INGP/REL PERSON DEPT/DEFEN. PAGE 64 F1269 JURID EXEC ORD/FREE CONTROL

B62
KAUTSKY J.H.,POLITICAL CHANGE IN UNDERDEVELOPED COUNTRIES: NATIONALISM AND COMMUNISM. WOR+45 AGRI TEC/DEV EDU/PROP ATTIT...POLICY METH/CNCPT STYLE INT QU CENSUS TREND SOC/EXP GEN/LAWS 20. PAGE 69 F1365 ECO/UNDEV SOCIETY CAP/ISM REV

B62
LEVENSTEIN A.,WHY PEOPLE WORK; CHANGING INCENTIVES IN A TROUBLED WORLD. USA+45 SOCIETY PROB/SOLV TEC/DEV EDU/PROP ADJUST...CENSUS BIBLIOG 20. PAGE 79 F1538 DRIVE WORKER ECO/DEV ANOMIE

B62
RIMALOV V.V.,ECONOMIC COOPERATION BETWEEN USSR AND UNDERDEVELOPED COUNTRIES. USSR FINAN TEC/DEV INT/TRADE DOMIN EDU/PROP COLONIAL NAT/LISM DRIVE SOVEREIGN...AUD/VIS 20. PAGE 111 F2194 FOR/AID PLAN ECO/UNDEV DIPLOM

B62
ROBINSON A.D.,DUTCH ORGANIZED AGRICULTURE IN INTERNATIONAL POLITICS, 1945-1960. EUR+WWI NETHERLAND STRUCT ECO/DEV NAT/G VOL/ASSN CONSULT DELIB/GP PLAN TEC/DEV INT/TRADE EDU/PROP ATTIT RIGID/FLEX ALL/VALS...NEW/IDEA TREND EEC COMMUN 20. PAGE 112 F2215 AGRI INT/ORG

B62
SELOSOEMARDJAN O.,SOCIAL CHANGES IN JOGJAKARTA. INDONESIA NETHERLAND ELITES STRATA STRUCT FAM POL/PAR CREATE DIPLOM INT/TRADE EDU/PROP ADMIN GOV/REL...SOC 20 JAVA CHINJAP. PAGE 119 F2352 ECO/UNDEV CULTURE REV COLONIAL

B62
US LIBRARY OF CONGRESS,A LIST OF AMERICAN DOCTORAL DISSERTATIONS ON AFRICA. SOCIETY SECT DIPLOM EDU/PROP ADMIN...GEOG 19/20. PAGE 138 F2717 BIBLIOG AFR ACADEM CULTURE

B62
WARD B.,THE RICH NATIONS AND THE POOR NATIONS. FUT WOR+45 CULTURE ECO/DEV ECO/UNDEV PLAN CAP/ISM EDU/PROP REV NAT/LISM ATTIT DRIVE SOCISM...POLICY CONCPT TIME/SEQ 20. PAGE 143 F2816 ECO/TAC GEN/LAWS

L62
"BIBLIOGRAPHY ON EDUCATION AND ECONOMIC AND SOCIAL DEVELOPMENT (AMERICAN SOURCES)" L/A+17C ECO/UNDEV PROB/SOLV...SOC 20. PAGE 1 F0015 BIBLIOG/A ACADEM EDU/PROP INTELL

L62
"HIGHER EDUCATION AND ECONOMIC AND SOCIAL DEVELOPMENT IN LATIN AMERICA: A BIBLIOGRAPHY." L/A+17C SOCIETY ECO/UNDEV PROF/ORG DIPLOM CONFER ...SOC 20. PAGE 1 F0016 BIBLIOG/A ACADEM INTELL EDU/PROP

L62
SCHULTZ T.W.,"INVESTMENT IN HUMAN BEINGS." ECO/DEV ECO/TAC CONFER COST INCOME PRODUC HEALTH...GEOG ANTHOL. PAGE 117 F2315 FINAN WORKER EDU/PROP SKILL

S62
ADISESHIAN M.,"EDUCATION AND DEVELOPMENT." FUT WOR+45 SOCIETY ACT/RES INT/TRADE EDU/PROP KNOWL SKILL WEALTH...POLICY CONCPT CONT/OBS CENSUS CHARTS TOT/POP VAL/FREE APPLIC FAO FOR/TRADE 20. PAGE 2 F0041 SCHOOL ECO/UNDEV

S62
BOKOR-SZEGO H.,"LA CONVENTION DE BELGRADE ET LE REGIME DU DANUBE." COM EUR+WWI WOR+45 STRUCT POL/PAR VOL/ASSN PLAN EDU/PROP WEALTH...TIME/SEQ METH/GP COMMUN 20. PAGE 16 F0308 INT/ORG TOTALISM YUGOSLAVIA

S62
IOVTCHOUK M.T.,"ON SOME THEORETICAL PRINCIPLES AND METHODS OF SOCIOLOGICAL INVESTIGATIONS (IN RUSSIAN)." FUT USA+45 STRATA R+D NAT/G POL/PAR TOP/EX ACT/RES PLAN ECO/TAC EDU/PROP ROUTINE ATTIT COM ECO/DEV CAP/ISM USSR

RIGID/FLEX MARXISM SOCISM...MARXIST METH/CNCPT OBS TREND NAT/COMP GEN/LAWS 20. PAGE 65 F1288

S62
MORGENTHAU H.J.,"A POLITICAL THEORY OF FOREIGN AID." ECO/UNDEV NAT/G DELIB/GP PLAN ECO/TAC EDU/PROP EXEC ORD/FREE RESPECT WEALTH...METH/CNCPT TREND 20. PAGE 93 F1833 — USA+45 PHIL/SCI FOR/AID

S62
ZAUBERMAN A.,"SOVIET AND CHINESE STRATEGY FOR ECONOMIC GROWTH." ASIA CHINA/COM COM USSR STRATA VOL/ASSN PLAN ATTIT PWR...METH/CNCPT GEN/LAWS WORK TERR/GP 20. PAGE 150 F2959 — ECO/DEV EDU/PROP

B63
BAUER R.A.,AMERICAN BUSINESS AND PUBLIC POLICY: THE POLITICS OF FOREIGN TRADE. USA+45 COM/IND LG/CO NAT/G PROF/ORG SML/CO VOL/ASSN LEGIS TOP/EX ECO/TAC EDU/PROP CHOOSE HEALTH PWR WEALTH...CONCPT METH/CNCPT OBS INT QU SAMP FOR/TRADE TRUE/GP VAL/FREE HI. PAGE 11 F0217 — ECO/DEV ATTIT

B63
BONINI C.P.,SIMULATION OF INFORMATION AND DECISION SYSTEMS IN THE FIRM. MARKET BUDGET DOMIN EDU/PROP ADMIN COST ATTIT HABITAT PERCEPT PWR...CONCPT PROBABIL QUANT PREDICT HYPO/EXP BIBLIOG. PAGE 16 F0313 — INDUS SIMUL DECISION MGT

B63
CHOJNACKI S.,REGISTER ON CURRENT RESEARCH ON ETHIOPIA AND THE HORN OF AFRICA. ETHIOPIA LAW CULTURE AGRI SECT EDU/PROP ADMIN...GEOG HEAL LING 20. PAGE 24 F0470 — BIBLIOG ACT/RES INTELL ACADEM

B63
CONF ON FUTURE OF COMMONWEALTH,THE FUTURE OF THE COMMONWEALTH. AFR UK ECO/UNDEV AGRI EDU/PROP ADMIN SOC/INTEG 20. PAGE 27 F0522 — DIPLOM RACE/REL ORD/FREE TEC/DEV

B63
DE VRIES E.,SOCIAL ASPECTS OF ECONOMIC DEVELOPMENT IN LATIN AMERICA. CULTURE SOCIETY STRATA FINAN INDUS INT/ORG DELIB/GP ACT/RES ECO/TAC EDU/PROP ADMIN ATTIT SUPEGO HEALTH KNOWL ORD/FREE...SOC STAT TREND ANTHOL TOT/POP VAL/FREE. PAGE 31 F0608 — L/A+17C ECO/UNDEV

B63
DEUTSCH K.W.,THE POLITICAL ROLE OF LABOR IN DEVELOPING COUNTRIES. AFR ASIA S/ASIA USA+45 WOR+45 ECO/UNDEV POL/PAR ECO/TAC EDU/PROP LEGIT COERCE ORD/FREE PWR WEALTH...OBS INT TREND VAL/FREE 20. PAGE 32 F0625 — LABOR NAT/LISM

B63
FREITAG R.S.,AGRICULTURAL DEVELOPMENT SCHEMES IN SUB-SAHARAN AFRICA. AFR EDU/PROP 20. PAGE 44 F0852 — BIBLIOG/A AGRI TEC/DEV KNOWL

B63
GAMBLE S.D.,NORTH CHINA VILLAGES: SOCIAL, POLITICAL, AND ECONOMIC ACTIVITIES BEFORE 1933. ASIA CULTURE STRUCT FAM DOMIN EDU/PROP MUNICH WORSHIP 20. PAGE 46 F0891 — AGRI LEAD FINAN

B63
HOOPES R.,THE STEEL CRISIS. USA+45 INDUS ECO/TAC EDU/PROP PRICE CONTROL ATTIT...POLICY 20 KENNEDY/JF. PAGE 61 F1205 — PROC/MFG NAT/G RATION CHIEF

B63
IANNI O.,INDUSTRIALIZACAO E DESENVOLVIMENTO SOCIAL NO BRASIL. BRAZIL L/A+17C STRATA STRUCT ECO/UNDEV EDU/PROP LEAD LOBBY NAT/LISM 20. PAGE 64 F1257 — WORKER GP/REL INDUS PARTIC

B63
KAPP W.K.,HINDU CULTURE: ECONOMIC DEVELOPMENT AND ECONOMIC PLANNING IN INDIA. INDIA S/ASIA CULTURE ECO/TAC EDU/PROP ADMIN ALL/VALS...POLICY MGT TIME/SEQ TRUE/GP VAL/FREE 20. PAGE 69 F1353 — SECT ECO/UNDEV

B63
KATZ S.M.,A SELECTED LIST OF US READINGS ON DEVELOPMENT. AGRI COM/IND DIST/IND INDUS LABOR PLAN FOR/AID EDU/PROP HEALTH...POLICY SOC/WK 20. PAGE 69 F1361 — BIBLIOG/A ECO/UNDEV TEC/DEV ACT/RES

B63
LAIRD R.D.,SOVIET AGRICULTURAL AND PEASANT AFFAIRS. FUT STRATA LOC/G DELIB/GP ACT/RES TEC/DEV ECO/TAC EDU/PROP ATTIT RIGID/FLEX ORD/FREE SKILL WEALTH ...STAT CON/ANAL ANTHOL MUNICH WORK VAL/FREE 20. PAGE 74 F1461 — COM AGRI POLICY

B63
LEWIS G.K.,PUERTO RICO: FREEDOM AND POWER IN THE CARIBBEAN. PUERT/RICO USA+45 CULTURE STRUCT INDUS POL/PAR WORKER EDU/PROP CATHISM 20. PAGE 79 F1548 — ECO/UNDEV COLONIAL NAT/LISM GEOG

B63
MINER J.,SOCIAL AND ECONOMIC FACTORS IN SPENDING FOR PUBLIC EDUCATION. USA+45 FINAN SCHOOL OPTIMAL ...POLICY DECISION REGRESS PREDICT CHARTS SIMUL 20. PAGE 92 F1801 — EDU/PROP NAT/G COST ACT/RES

B63
PERLO V.,MILITARISM AND INDUSTRY. USA+45 INT/TRADE EDU/PROP DETER KNOWL...CHARTS MAPS 20. PAGE 105 F2064 — CIVMIL/REL INDUS LOBBY ARMS/CONT

B63
US ECON SURVEY TEAM INDONESIA,INDONESIA - PERSPECTIVE AND PROPOSALS FOR UNITED STATES ECONOMIC AID. INDONESIA AGRI MARKET TEC/DEV DIPLOM INT/TRADE EDU/PROP 20. PAGE 136 F2678 — FOR/AID ECO/UNDEV PLAN INDUS

B63
WIGHTMAN D.,TOWARD ECONOMIC CO-OPERATION IN ASIA. ASIA S/ASIA VOL/ASSN ACT/RES PLAN TEC/DEV ECO/TAC EDU/PROP RIGID/FLEX SKILL...POLICY METH/CNCPT OBS INT GEN/LAWS UN 20 ECAFE. PAGE 146 F2877 — ECO/UNDEV CREATE

L63
ADERBIGDE A.,"SYMPOSIUM ON WEST AFRICA INTEGRATION." AFR EUR+WWI FUT CULTURE SOCIETY STRATA DIST/IND INDUS MARKET SERV/IND DELIB/GP PLAN TEC/DEV DOMIN EDU/PROP LEGIT COERCE ATTIT ALL/VALS ...POLICY STAT TREND CHARTS VAL/FREE. PAGE 2 F0040 — FINAN ECO/TAC REGION

L63
NASH M.,"PSYCHO-CULTURAL FACTORS IN ASIAN ECONOMIC GROWTH." ASIA ISLAM S/ASIA CULTURE ECO/UNDEV DELIB/GP EDU/PROP COERCE ATTIT PERSON HEALTH KNOWL ORD/FREE...PSY SOC STAT TREND ANTHOL VAL/FREE 20. PAGE 96 F1893 — SOCIETY ECO/TAC

L63
RIDAH A.,"LE NEO-DESTOUR DEPUIS L'INDEPENDANCE." FUT ISLAM WOR+45 ECO/UNDEV INT/ORG SCHOOL DELIB/GP TOP/EX ACT/RES EDU/PROP LEGIT ATTIT ALL/VALS 20 TUNIS. PAGE 111 F2189 — NAT/G CONSTN

S63
DIEBOLD W. JR.,"THE NEW SITUATION OF INTERNATIONAL TRADE POLICY." EUR+WWI FRANCE FUT UK USA+45 WOR+45 DIST/IND PLAN INT/TRADE EDU/PROP PWR WEALTH ...RECORD TREND GEN/LAWS EEC TRUE/GP VAL/FREE APPLIC 20. PAGE 33 F0636 — MARKET ECO/TAC

S63
EMERSON R.,"THE ATLANTIC COMMUNITY AND THE EMERGING COUNTRIES." FUT WOR+45 ECO/DEV ECO/UNDEV R+D NAT/G DELIB/GP BAL/PWR ECO/TAC EDU/PROP ROUTINE ORD/FREE PWR WEALTH...POLICY CONCPT TREND GEN/METH EEC 20 NATO. PAGE 37 F0729 — ATTIT INT/TRADE

S63
FLOREA I.,"CU PRIVIRE LA OBIECTUL MATERIALISMULUI ISTORIC SI AL COMUNISMULUI STIINTIFIC SI LA RAPORTUL DINTRE ELE." EUR+WWI WOR+45 WOR-45 INTELL NAT/G POL/PAR WORKER EDU/PROP PERCEPT MARXISM ...MARXIST PHIL/SCI CONCPT TOT/POP 20. PAGE 42 F0812 — COM ATTIT TOTALISM

S63
GRUSHIN B.A.,"PROBLEMS OF THE MOVEMENT OF COMMUNIST LABOR IN THE USSR." COM SOCIETY LABOR ECO/TAC EDU/PROP COERCE RIGID/FLEX ORD/FREE...POLICY MARXIST STAT QU WORK 20. PAGE 52 F1011 — ATTIT USSR

S63
NADLER E.B.,"SOME ECONOMIC DISADVANTAGES OF THE ARMS RACE." AFR USA+45 INDUS R+D FORCES PLAN TEC/DEV ECO/TAC FOR/AID EDU/PROP PWR WEALTH...TREND FOR/TRADE 20. PAGE 96 F1886 — ECO/DEV MGT BAL/PAY

S63
PINCUS J.,"THE COST OF FOREIGN AID." WOR+45 ECO/DEV FINAN NAT/G VOL/ASSN CREATE ECO/TAC EDU/PROP WEALTH ...METH/CNCPT STAT CHARTS HYPO/EXP TOT/POP VAL/FREE 20. PAGE 106 F2087 — USA+45 ECO/UNDEV FOR/AID

S63
POLYANOV N.,"THE DOLLAR'S VENTURES IN EUROPE." EUR+WWI FRANCE USA+45 ECO/DEV MARKET POL/PAR TEC/DEV ECO/TAC EDU/PROP DRIVE PWR WEALTH...MARXIST MYTH STAT TREND EEC 20. PAGE 107 F2100 — FINAN PLAN BAL/PAY CAP/ISM

S63
RAMERIE L.,"TENSION AU SEIN DU COMECON: LE CAS ROUMAIN." COM EUR+WWI USSR WOR+45 ECO/DEV DIST/IND NAT/G POL/PAR VOL/ASSN EDU/PROP TOTALISM ATTIT WEALTH...TIME/SEQ 20 COMECON. PAGE 109 F2142 — INT/ORG ECO/TAC INT/TRADE ROMANIA

B64
BASTIAT F.,ECONOMIC SOPHISMS (1845). FINAN MARKET INT/TRADE TAX EDU/PROP LAISSEZ. PAGE 11 F0207 — TARIFFS INDUS ECO/TAC CAP/ISM

B64
BLACKSTOCK P.W.,THE STRATEGY OF SUBVERSION. USA+45 FORCES EDU/PROP ADMIN COERCE GOV/REL...DECISION MGT 20 DEPT/DEFEN CIA DEPT/STATE. PAGE 15 F0292 — ORD/FREE DIPLOM CONTROL

B64
BOWEN W.G.,ECONOMIC ASPECTS OF EDUCATION (NO. 104). EUR+WWI UK USA+45 PROF/ORG PLAN TEC/DEV PAY ...POLICY STAT 20. PAGE 17 F0329 — EDU/PROP ACADEM FINAN METH/COMP

B64
DE BARY W.T.,APPROACHES TO ASIAN CIVILIZATIONS. INDIA ISLAM USA+45 CULTURE ACADEM...SOC ANTHOL 20 CHINJAP ARABS. PAGE 31 F0595 — ASIA EDU/PROP SOCIETY

B64
GARDNER L.C.,ECONOMIC ASPECTS OF NEW DEAL DIPLOMACY. USA-45 WOR-45 LAW ECO/DEV INT/ORG NAT/G VOL/ASSN LEGIS TOP/EX EDU/PROP ORD/FREE PWR WEALTH ...POLICY TIME/SEQ VAL/FREE 20 ROOSEVLT/F. PAGE 46 — ECO/TAC DIPLOM

F0901

B64
HAMBRIDGE G.,DYNAMICS OF DEVELOPMENT. AGRI FINAN INDUS LABOR INT/TRADE EDU/PROP ADMIN LEAD OWN HEALTH...ANTHOL BIBLIOG 20. PAGE 54 F1054
ECO/UNDEV ECO/TAC OP/RES ACT/RES

B64
HARBISON F.H.,EDUCATION, MANPOWER, AND ECONOMIC GROWTH. WOR+45 ECO/DEV ECO/UNDEV ACADEM LABOR SCHOOL WORKER UTIL...IDEA/COMP NAT/COMP. PAGE 55 F1075
PLAN TEC/DEV EDU/PROP SKILL

B64
LAFONT P.B.,BIBLIOGRAPHIE DU LAOS. LAOS S/ASIA EDU/PROP...GEOG 20. PAGE 74 F1458
BIBLIOG LAW SOC

B64
MELADY T.,FACES OF AFRICA. AFR FUT ISLAM NAT/G POL/PAR SCHOOL DELIB/GP PLAN ECO/TAC EDU/PROP ATTIT ALL/VALS...CHARTS TOT/POP TERR/GP VAL/FREE 20. PAGE 89 F1752
ECO/UNDEV TREND NAT/LISM

B64
MEZERIK A.G.,TRADE, AID AND ECONOMIC DEVELOPMENT. WOR+45 FINAN INDUS MARKET PLAN BAL/PWR BARGAIN FOR/AID TARIFFS EDU/PROP WEALTH...GP/COMP 20 UN GATT IMF IBRD. PAGE 91 F1777
ECO/TAC ECO/DEV INT/ORG INT/TRADE

B64
NAGEL P.C.,ONE NATION INDIVISIBLE: THE UNION IN AMERICAN THOUGHT 1776-1861. USA-45 INDUS TEC/DEV EDU/PROP DREAM...IDEA/COMP 18/19. PAGE 96 F1887
FEDERAL NAT/G ATTIT INGP/REL

B64
NATIONAL COUN APPLIED ECO RES,A STRATEGY FOR THE FOURTH PLAN. INDIA DIST/IND EXTR/IND SERV/IND ECO/TAC RATION EDU/PROP EATING HEALTH...CHARTS 20. PAGE 97 F1900
ECO/UNDEV PLAN AGRI WORKER

B64
RAISON T.,WHY CONSERVATIVE? UK FORCES DIPLOM ECO/TAC GIVE EDU/PROP ORD/FREE WEALTH LAISSEZ ...GOV/COMP 20 TORY/PARTY CONSRV/PAR. PAGE 109 F2137
PLURISM CONSERVE POL/PAR NAT/G

B64
SANDEE J.,EUROPE'S FUTURE CONSUMPTION. EUR+WWI FUT EDU/PROP...IDEA/COMP NAT/COMP ANTHOL 20 EUROPE. PAGE 115 F2277
MARKET ECO/DEV PREDICT PRICE

B64
SEERS D.,CUBA: THE ECONOMIC AND SOCIAL REVOLUTION. L/A+17C USSR YUGOSLAVIA STRATA AGRI INDUS SCHOOL DELIB/GP PLAN ECO/TAC DOMIN EDU/PROP ATTIT RIGID/FLEX ALL/VALS...STAT OBS TIME/SEQ WORK VAL/FREE 20. PAGE 119 F2341
ACT/RES COERCE CUBA REV

B64
SINGER H.W.,INTERNATIONAL DEVELOPMENT: GROWTH AND CHANGE. AFR BRAZIL L/A+17C WOR+45 CULTURE AGRI INDUS NAT/G ACT/RES ECO/TAC EDU/PROP WEALTH...GEOG CONCPT METH/CNCPT STAT HYPO/EXP WORK TOT/POP 20. PAGE 122 F2412
FINAN ECO/UNDEV FOR/AID INT/TRADE

B64
STRONG A.L.,THE RISE OF THE CHINESE PEOPLE'S COMMUNES - AND SIX YEARS AFTER (2ND ED.). CHINA/COM AGRI INDUS FORCES WORKER PROB/SOLV EDU/PROP EFFICIENCY ISOLAT 20. PAGE 127 F2503
NEIGH ECO/TAC MARXISM METH/COMP

B64
SULLIVAN G.,THE STORY OF THE PEACE CORPS. USA+45 WOR+45 INTELL FACE/GP NAT/G SCHOOL VOL/ASSN CONSULT EX/STRUC PLAN EDU/PROP ADMIN ATTIT DRIVE ALL/VALS ...POLICY HEAL SOC CONCPT INT QU BIOG TREND SOC/EXP WORK. PAGE 127 F2511
INT/ORG ECO/UNDEV FOR/AID PEACE

B64
TAWNEY R.H.,EQUALITY. UK CULTURE STRATA ECO/TAC EDU/PROP REPRESENT OWN NEW/LIB...MAJORIT WELF/ST SOC 20. PAGE 129 F2538
WEALTH STRUCT ELITES POPULISM

B64
US AGENCY INTERNATIONAL DEV,A.I.D. PROJECTS IN FISCAL YEAR 1963: BY COUNTRY AND FIELD OF ACTIVITY. USA+45 ECO/UNDEV ECO/TAC EDU/PROP GOV/REL...CHARTS 20 AID. PAGE 134 F2639
FINAN FOR/AID COST STAT

B64
WRIGHT G.,RURAL REVOLUTION IN FRANCE: THE PEASANTRY IN THE TWENTIETH CENTURY. EUR+WWI MOD/EUR LAW CULTURE AGRI POL/PAR DELIB/GP LEGIS ECO/TAC EDU/PROP COERCE CHOOSE ATTIT RIGID/FLEX HEALTH ...STAT CENSUS CHARTS VAL/FREE 20. PAGE 149 F2932
PWR STRATA FRANCE REV

B64
ZOBER M.,MARKETING MANAGEMENT. FINAN BUDGET EDU/PROP PRICE PRODUC ATTIT...POLICY TREND CHARTS METH/COMP EQULIB 20. PAGE 150 F2966
ECO/DEV MGT CONTROL MARKET

S64
FYFE J.,"LIST OF CURRENT ACQUISITIONS OF PERIODICALS AND NEWSPAPERS DEALING WITH THE SOVIET UNION AND EAST EUROPEAN COUNTRIES." USSR WRITING GP/REL INGP/REL MARXISM 20. PAGE 45 F0879
BIBLIOG COM EDU/PROP PRESS

S64
GARDNER R.N.,"GATT AND THE UNITED NATIONS CONFERENCE ON TRADE AND DEVELOPMENT." USA+45 WOR+45 SOCIETY ECO/UNDEV MARKET NAT/G DELIB/GP ACT/RES PLAN ECO/TAC TARIFFS EDU/PROP ROUTINE DRIVE RIGID/FLEX WEALTH...DECISION MGT TREND UN TOT/POP 20 GATT. PAGE 46 F0905
INT/ORG INT/TRADE

S64
GERBET P.,"LA MISE EN OEUVRE DU MARCHE COMMUN AGRICOLE." ECO/DEV MARKET INT/ORG NAT/G PLAN EDU/PROP NAT/LISM WEALTH...OBS EEC VAL/FREE 20. PAGE 47 F0917
EUR+WWI AGRI REGION

S64
NASH M.,"SOCIAL PREREQUISITES TO ECONOMIC GROWTH IN LATIN AMERICA AND SOUTHEAST ASIA." L/A+17C S/ASIA CULTURE SOCIETY ECO/UNDEV AGRI INDUS NAT/G PLAN TEC/DEV EDU/PROP ROUTINE ALL/VALS...POLICY RELATIV SOC NAT/COMP WORK TOT/POP 20. PAGE 96 F1894
ECO/DEV PERCEPT

S64
PESELT B.M.,"COMMUNIST ECONOMIC OFFENSIVE." WOR+45 SOCIETY INT/ORG PLAN ECO/TAC DOMIN EDU/PROP ATTIT PERSON PWR WEALTH...TREND CHARTS METH/GP 20. PAGE 105 F2067
COM ECO/UNDEV FOR/AID USSR

B65
ACHTERBERG E.,BERLINER HOCHFINANZ - KAISER, FURSTEN, MILLIONARE UM 1900. GERMANY NAT/G EDU/PROP PERSON...MGT MUNICH 19/20. PAGE 2 F0033
FINAN BIOG ECO/TAC

B65
ALDERSON W.,DYNAMIC MARKETING BEHAVIOR. USA+45 FINAN CREATE TEC/DEV EDU/PROP PRICE COST 20. PAGE 3 F0057
MGT MARKET ATTIT CAP/ISM

B65
ANDERSON C.A.,EDUCATION AND ECONOMIC DEVELOPMENT. INDUS R+D SCHOOL TEC/DEV ECO/TAC EDU/PROP AGE HEREDITY PERCEPT SKILL 20. PAGE 5 F0092
ANTHOL ECO/DEV ECO/UNDEV WORKER

B65
BOWEN W.G.,UNEMPLOYMENT IN A PROSPEROUS ECONOMY. USA+45 ECO/DEV NAT/G ACT/RES PLAN PAY EDU/PROP DEMAND...POLICY IDEA/COMP ANTHOL 20. PAGE 17 F0330
WORKER ECO/TAC WEALTH PROB/SOLV

B65
BROOKINGS INSTITUTION,BROOKINGS PAPERS ON PUBLIC POLICY. USA+45 ECO/UNDEV LEGIS CAP/ISM ECO/TAC TAX EDU/PROP CONTROL APPORT 20. PAGE 19 F0363
DIPLOM FOR/AID POLICY FINAN

B65
CHANDRASEKHAR S.,AMERICAN AID AND INDIA'S ECONOMIC DEVELOPMENT. AFR CHINA/COM INDIA USA+45 GIVE EDU/PROP EATING HEALTH ORD/FREE 20 AID. PAGE 23 F0449
FOR/AID PEACE DIPLOM ECO/UNDEV

B65
CLARK T.D.,THREE PATHS TO THE MODERN SOUTH: EDUCATION, AGRICULTURE, AND CONSERVATION. FUT USA-45 ECO/DEV ECO/TAC PEACE WEALTH...POLICY 20 SOUTH/US. PAGE 25 F0485
AGRI EDU/PROP GOV/REL REGION

B65
CONLEY R.W.,THE ECONOMICS OF VOCATIONAL REHABILITATION. USA+45 VOL/ASSN CREATE EDU/PROP COST EFFICIENCY SOC/INTEG 20. PAGE 27 F0527
PUB/INST HEALTH GIVE GP/REL

B65
COOMBS P.H.,EDUCATION AND FOREIGN AID. AFR USA+45 DIPLOM EFFICIENCY KNOWL ORD/FREE...ANTHOL 20 AID. PAGE 27 F0532
EDU/PROP FOR/AID SCHOOL ECO/UNDEV

B65
CRANE E.,MARKETING COMMUNICATION: A BEHAVIORAL APPROACH TO MEN, MESSAGES, AND MEDIA. STRATA R+D VOL/ASSN CROWD DRIVE PERSON SKILL WEALTH. PAGE 28 F0551
EDU/PROP MARKET PERCEPT ATTIT

B65
HARBISON F.,MANPOWER AND EDUCATION. AFR CHINA/COM IRAN L/A+17C S/ASIA TEC/DEV ADJUST OPTIMAL SKILL ...ANTHOL 20. PAGE 55 F1073
ECO/UNDEV EDU/PROP WORKER NAT/COMP

B65
LAZARUS S.,RESOLVING BUSINESS DISPUTES: THE POTENTIAL OF COMMERCIAL ARBITRATION. USA+45 INDUS LG/CO ACT/RES PROB/SOLV EDU/PROP CONSEN UTIL ...TREND 20. PAGE 76 F1496
FINAN DELIB/GP CONSULT ADJUD

B65
MELMANS S.,OUR DEPLETED SOCIETY. AFR SPACE USA+45 ECO/DEV FORCES BUDGET ECO/TAC ADMIN WEAPON EFFICIENCY 20. PAGE 89 F1753
CIVMIL/REL INDUS EDU/PROP CONTROL

B65
MONCRIEFF A.,SECOND THOUGHTS ON AID. WOR+45 ECO/UNDEV AGRI FINAN VOL/ASSN PLAN TEC/DEV GIVE EDU/PROP ROLE WEALTH 20. PAGE 93 F1816
FOR/AID ECO/TAC INT/ORG IDEA/COMP

B65
MORTON H.C.,BROOKINGS PAPERS ON PUBLIC POLICY. USA+45 WOR+45 INDUS ACADEM INT/ORG LOC/G PROVS EDU/PROP MUNICH. PAGE 94 F1840
FINAN ECO/DEV TOP/EX NAT/G

B65
NKRUMAH K.,NEO-COLONIALISM: THE LAST STAGE OF IMPERIALISM. AFR INT/ORG WORKER FOR/AID INT/TRADE EDU/PROP GOV/REL NAT/LISM SOVEREIGN POPULISM SOCISM ...SOCIALIST 20 THIRD/WRLD INTRVN/ECO. PAGE 98 F1929
COLONIAL DIPLOM ECO/UNDEV ECO/TAC

B65
OECD,MEDITERRANEAN REGIONAL PROJECT: TURKEY; EDUCATION AND DEVELOPMENT. FUT TURKEY SOCIETY STRATA FINAN NAT/G PROF/ORG PLAN PROB/SOLV ADMIN COST...STAT CHARTS 20 OECD. PAGE 100 F1969
EDU/PROP ACADEM SCHOOL ECO/UNDEV

B65
OECD,THE MEDITERRANEAN REGIONAL PROJECT: PORTUGAL; EDUCATION AND DEVELOPMENT. PORTUGAL SOCIETY STRATA FINAN PROF/ORG WORKER PLAN PROB/SOLV ADMIN...POLICY STAT CHARTS METH 20 OECD. PAGE 100 F1970
EDU/PROP SCHOOL ACADEM ECO/UNDEV

B65
OECD,THE MEDITERRANEAN REGIONAL PROJECT: ITALY; EDUCATION AND DEVELOPMENT. ITALY SOCIETY STRATA FINAN NAT/G PROF/ORG WORKER PLAN PROB/SOLV ADMIN ...STAT CHARTS METH 20 OECD. PAGE 100 F1971
SCHOOL EDU/PROP ECO/UNDEV ACADEM

B65
OECD,THE MEDITERRANEAN REGIONAL PROJECT: GREECE; EDUCATION AND DEVELOPMENT. FUT GREECE SOCIETY AGRI FINAN NAT/G PROF/ORG WORKER PLAN PROB/SOLV ADMIN DEMAND ATTIT 20 OECD. PAGE 100 F1972
EDU/PROP SCHOOL ACADEM ECO/UNDEV

B65
OECD,THE MEDITERRANEAN REGIONAL PROJECT: SPAIN; EDUCATION AND DEVELOPMENT. FUT SPAIN STRATA FINAN NAT/G WORKER PLAN PROB/SOLV ADMIN COST...POLICY STAT CHARTS 20 OECD. PAGE 100 F1973
ECO/UNDEV EDU/PROP ACADEM SCHOOL

B65
ORG FOR ECO COOP AND DEVEL,THE MEDITERRANEAN REGIONAL PROJECT: AN EXPERIMENT IN PLANNING BY SIX COUNTRIES. FUT GREECE SPAIN TURKEY YUGOSLAVIA SOCIETY FINAN NAT/G PROF/ORG EDU/PROP ADMIN REGION COST...POLICY STAT CHARTS 20 OECD. PAGE 102 F1995
PLAN ECO/UNDEV ACADEM SCHOOL

B65
ORG FOR ECO COOP AND DEVEL,THE MEDITERRANEAN REGIONAL PROJECT: YUGOSLAVIA; EDUCATION AND DEVELOPMENT. YUGOSLAVIA SOCIETY FINAN PROF/ORG PLAN ADMIN COST DEMAND MARXISM...STAT TREND CHARTS METH 20 OECD. PAGE 102 F1996
EDU/PROP ACADEM SCHOOL ECO/UNDEV

B65
PEARL A.,NEW CAREERS FOR THE POOR: THE NON-PROFESSIONAL IN HUMAN SERVICE. USA+45 SERV/IND NAT/G NEIGH WORKER EDU/PROP AUTOMAT SKILL...WELF/ST NEW/IDEA BIBLIOG SOC/INTEG 20. PAGE 104 F2044
SOC/WK WEALTH STRATA POLICY

B65
RANSOM H.H.,AN AMERICAN FOREIGN POLICY READER. USA+45 FORCES EDU/PROP COERCE NUC/PWR WAR PEACE ...DECISION 20. PAGE 109 F2146
NAT/G DIPLOM POLICY

B65
ROSS A.M.,EMPLOYMENT POLICY AND THE LABOR MARKET. USA+45 MARKET LABOR NAT/G PROB/SOLV PAY EDU/PROP PARTIC UTIL...POLICY 20. PAGE 114 F2242
ECO/DEV WORKER WEALTH DEMAND

B65
SCHULER E.A.,THE PAKISTAN ACADEMIES FOR RURAL DEVELOPMENT COMILLA AND PESHAWAR 1959-1964. PAKISTAN S/ASIA SOCIETY STRUCT AGRI NAT/G TEC/DEV EDU/PROP 20. PAGE 117 F2314
BIBLIOG PLAN ECO/TAC ECO/UNDEV

B65
SCOTT A.M.,THE REVOLUTION IN STATECRAFT: INFORMAL PENETRATION. WOR+45 WOR-45 CULTURE INT/ORG FORCES ECO/TAC ROUTINE...BIBLIOG 20. PAGE 118 F2331
DIPLOM EDU/PROP FOR/AID

B65
SHAFFER H.G.,THE SOVIET SYSTEM IN THEORY AND PRACTICE: SELECTED WESTERN AND SOVIET VIEWS. USSR LAW SOCIETY CREATE FOR/AID EDU/PROP PRESS CHOOSE PEACE ORD/FREE...ANTHOL 20 STALIN/J. PAGE 120 F2362
MARXISM SOCISM IDEA/COMP

B65
SIMON B.,EDUCATION AND THE LABOR MOVEMENT, 1870-1920. UK SOCIETY STRATA LABOR POL/PAR SCHOOL CONTROL PARTIC SOCISM...BIBLIOG 19/20. PAGE 122 F2406
EDU/PROP WORKER ADJUST LAW

B65
US BUREAU EDUC CULTURAL AFF,RESOURCES SURVEY FOR LATIN AMERICAN COUNTRIES. L/A+17C USA+45 CULTURE INDUS INT/ORG SECT PLAN EDU/PROP POLICY. PAGE 134 F2643
NAT/G ECO/UNDEV FOR/AID DIPLOM

S65
GOLDMAN M.I.,"A BALANCE SHEET OF SOVIET FOREIGN AID." USA+45 ECO/UNDEV BAL/PWR ECO/TAC RENT GIVE EDU/PROP CONTROL COST PROFIT GEN/METH. PAGE 48 F0939
USSR FOR/AID NAT/COMP EFFICIENCY

S65
JOHNSON H.G.,"A THEORETICAL MODEL OF ECONOMIC NATIONALISM IN NEW AND DEVELOPING STATES." ELITES INDUS INT/TRADE EDU/PROP COST OPTIMAL RATIONAL PWR WEALTH SOCISM STERTYP. PAGE 67 F1325
NAT/LISM ECO/UNDEV GEN/LAWS

S65
KORBONSKI A.,"USA POLICY IN EAST EUROPE." COM EUR+WWI GERMANY USA+45 CULTURE ECO/UNDEV EDU/PROP RIGID/FLEX WEALTH FOR/TRADE 20. PAGE 73 F1426
ACT/RES ECO/TAC FOR/AID

S65
MALHERBE E.G.,"MANPOWER TRAINING: EDUCATIONAL REQUIREMENTS FOR ECONOMIC EXPANSION." SOUTH/AFR ECO/DEV INDUS EDU/PROP...MGT STAT CHARTS 20. PAGE 84 F1646
LABOR SKILL SCHOOL ACADEM

S65
SPAAK P.H.,"THE SEARCH FOR CONSENSUS: A NEW EFFORT TO BUILD EUROPE." FRANCE GERMANY ECO/DEV NAT/G CONSULT FORCES PLAN EDU/PROP REGION CONSEN ATTIT ...SOC METH/CNCPT OBS TREND EEC NATO WORK TERR/GP METH/GP 20. PAGE 124 F2447
EUR+WWI INT/ORG

B66
ALEXANDER Y.,INTERNATIONAL TECHNICAL ASSISTANCE EXPERTS: A CASE STUDY OF THE U.N. EXPERIENCE. USA+45 WOR+45 WORKER CREATE PLAN PROB/SOLV ECO/TAC FOR/AID GIVE EDU/PROP...CHARTS BIBLIOG 20 UN. PAGE 3 F0062
SKILL INT/ORG TEC/DEV CONSULT

B66
BROEKMEIJER M.W.J.,FICTION AND TRUTH ABOUT THE "DECADE OF DEVELOPMENT" WOR+45 AGRI FINAN INDUS NAT/G TEC/DEV DIPLOM EDU/PROP LEAD SKILL 20 THIRD/WRLD. PAGE 19 F0358
FOR/AID POLICY ECO/UNDEV PLAN

B66
EBONY,THE NEGRO HANDBOOK. ACADEM LABOR LOC/G SECT FORCES WORKER CT/SYS CRIME DISCRIM ORD/FREE...BIOG SOC/INTEG 19/20 NEGRO CIV/RIGHTS. PAGE 36 F0692
RACE/REL EDU/PROP LAW STAT

B66
ECONOMIC RESEARCH SERVICE,RESEARCH DATA ON MINORITY GROUPS: AN ANNOTATED BIBLIOGRAPHY OF ECONOMIC RESEARCH SERVICE REPORTS: 1955-1965 (PAMPHLET). USA+45 STRATA ECO/DEV AGRI SCHOOL WORKER EDU/PROP HEALTH NEW/LIB SOC. PAGE 36 F0697
BIBLIOG/A DISCRIM WEALTH RACE/REL

B66
HO YHI-MIN,AGRICULTURAL DEVELOPMENT OF TAIWAN: 1903-1960. FINAN WORKER EDU/PROP...STAT CHARTS BIBLIOG 20. PAGE 60 F1181
ECO/UNDEV AGRI PRODUC PLAN

B66
HOWE R.W.,BLACK AFRICA: FROM PRE-HISTORY TO THE EVE OF THE COLONIAL ERA. ECO/UNDEV KIN PROVS SECT INT/TRADE EDU/PROP COLONIAL...BIBLIOG WORSHIP. PAGE 62 F1226
AFR CULTURE SOC

B66
HUNT C.L.,SOCIAL ASPECTS OF ECONOMIC DEVELOPMENT. S/ASIA AGRI FAM TEC/DEV RECEIVE EDU/PROP OWN...GEOG MUNICH 20. PAGE 63 F1243
SOC STRATA ATTIT ECO/UNDEV

B66
KAREFA-SMART J.,AFRICA: PROGRESS THROUGH COOPERATION. AFR FINAN TEC/DEV DIPLOM FOR/AID EDU/PROP CONFER REGION GP/REL WEALTH...HEAL SOC/INTEG 20. PAGE 69 F1356
ORD/FREE ECO/UNDEV VOL/ASSN PLAN

B66
MACFARQUHAR R.,CHINA UNDER MAO: POLITICS TAKES COMMAND. CHINA/COM COM AGRI INDUS CHIEF FORCES DIPLOM INT/TRADE EDU/PROP TASK REV ADJUST...ANTHOL 20 MAO. PAGE 83 F1628
ECO/UNDEV TEC/DEV ECO/TAC ADMIN

B66
MOSKOW M.H.,TEACHERS AND UNIONS. SCHOOL WORKER ADJUD LOBBY ATTIT ORD/FREE 20. PAGE 94 F1844
EDU/PROP PROF/ORG LABOR BARGAIN

B66
NICOSIA F.N.,CONSUMER DECISION PROCESSES* MARKETING AND ADVERTISING IMPLICATIONS. DIST/IND INDUS CONSULT EDU/PROP ATTIT. PAGE 98 F1925
MARKET PROB/SOLV SERV/IND

B66
OECD DEVELOPMENT CENTRE,CATALOGUE OF SOCIAL AND ECONOMIC DEVELOPMENT INSTITUTES AND PROGRAMMES* RESEARCH. ACT/RES PLAN TEC/DEV EDU/PROP...SOC GP/COMP NAT/COMP. PAGE 101 F1976
ECO/UNDEV ECO/DEV R+D ACADEM

B66
RAO Y.V.L.,COMMUNICATION AND DEVELOPMENT. INDIA S/ASIA SOCIETY ACT/RES EDU/PROP PARTIC ATTIT...SOC GP/COMP BIBLIOG MUNICH MUNICH 20. PAGE 109 F2149
COM/IND ECO/UNDEV OBS

B66
ROBINSON E.A.,THE ECONOMICS OF EDUCATION. WOR+45 CULTURE ECO/UNDEV FINAN SCHOOL DIPLOM PRICE COST DEMAND...CHARTS METH/COMP 20. PAGE 112 F2216
EDU/PROP ADJUST CONFER

B66
SHULTZ G.P.,STRATEGIES FOR THE DISPLACED WORKER. USA+45 COMPUTER TEC/DEV BARGAIN RECEIVE EDU/PROP CONFER GP/REL...MGT METH/COMP 20. PAGE 121 F2391
ECO/DEV WORKER PLAN AUTOMAT

B66
US DEPARTMENT OF STATE,RESEARCH ON THE USSR AND EASTERN EUROPE (EXTERNAL RESEARCH LIST NO 1-25). USSR LAW CULTURE SOCIETY NAT/G TEC/DEV DIPLOM EDU/PROP REGION...GEOG LING. PAGE 136 F2675
BIBLIOG/A EUR+WWI COM MARXISM

B66
US DEPARTMENT OF STATE,RESEARCH ON WESTERN EUROPE, GREAT BRITAIN, AND CANADA (EXTERNAL RESEARCH LIST NO 3-25). CANADA GERMANY/W UK LAW CULTURE NAT/G POL/PAR FORCES EDU/PROP REGION MARXISM...GEOG SOC WORSHIP 20 CMN/WLTH. PAGE 136 F2676
BIBLIOG/A EUR+WWI DIPLOM

B66
US SENATE COMM GOVT OPERATIONS,HEARINGS BEFORE SUBCOMMITTEE ON FOREIGN AID EXPENDITURES: POPULATION CRISIS VOLUMES 1-5 JUNE-SEPT 1965. STRATA ECO/UNDEV PLAN TEC/DEV EDU/PROP ATTIT HEALTH ...GEOG CHARTS 20 CONGRESS BIRTH/CON CASEBOOK. PAGE 138 F2729
ECO/DEV CENSUS FAM CONTROL

B66
US SENATE COMM GOVT OPERATIONS,INTERGOVERNMENTAL PERSONNEL ACT OF 1966. USA+45 NAT/G CONSULT DELIB/GP WORKER TEC/DEV PAY AUTOMAT UTIL 20 CONGRESS. PAGE 139 F2730
ADMIN LEGIS EFFICIENCY EDU/PROP

S66
KLEIN S.,"A SURVEY OF SINO-JAPANESE TRADE, 1950-1966" TAIWAN EDU/PROP 20 CHINJAP. PAGE 72 F1409
INT/TRADE DIPLOM MARXISM

S66
VERSLUYS J.D.N.,"SOME NOTES ON THE SOCIAL AND ECONOMIC EFFECTS OF RURAL ELECTRIFICATION IN BURMA" BURMA EDU/PROP PRODUC ORD/FREE...SOC QU MUNICH TIME 20. PAGE 141 F2782
TEC/DEV SOCIETY CREATE

B67
ALEXANDER G.J.,HONESTY AND COMPETITION: FALSE-ADVERTISING LAW AND POLICY UNDER FTC ADMINISTRATION. USA+45 INDUS NAT/G PRICE GP/REL 20 FTC. PAGE 3 F0058
EDU/PROP SERV/IND CONTROL DELIB/GP

B67
BALDWIN G.B.,PLANNING AND DEVELOPMENT IN IRAN. IRAN AGRI INDUS CONSULT WORKER EDU/PROP BAL/PAY...CHARTS 20. PAGE 9 F0164
PLAN ECO/UNDEV ADMIN PROB/SOLV

B67
BARANSON J.,TECHNOLOGY FOR UNDERDEVELOPED AREAS: AN ANNOTATED BIBLIOGRAPHY. FUT WOR+45 CULTURE INDUS INT/ORG CREATE PROB/SOLV INT/TRADE EDU/PROP AUTOMAT ...CONCPT METH. PAGE 10 F0181
BIBLIOG/A ECO/UNDEV TEC/DEV R+D

B67
BIRMINGHAM W.,A STUDY OF CONTEMPORARY GHANA VOL. I: SOME ASPECTS OF SOCIAL STRUCTURE. AFR GHANA AGRI FAM SECT PLAN EDU/PROP MARRIAGE OWN...POLICY STAT CHARTS MUNICH 20. PAGE 15 F0287
SOCIETY STRUCT CENSUS ECO/UNDEV

B67
BLAUG M.,ECONOMICS OF EDUCATION: A SELECTED ANNOTATED BIBLIOGRAPHY. EUR+WWI INTELL ECO/DEV ECO/UNDEV ACADEM INT/ORG NAT/G CREATE ADMIN EFFICIENCY ROLE PREDICT. PAGE 16 F0298
BIBLIOG/A EDU/PROP FINAN PLAN

B67
BURDEN H.T.,THE NUREMBERG PARTY RALLIES 1923-39. GERMANY POL/PAR SECT CREATE DOMIN WAR ATTIT ...AUD/VIS FILM 20. PAGE 20 F0384
EDU/PROP CONTROL CROWD TOTALISM

B67
DIEGUES M.,SOCIAL SCIENCE IN LATIN AMERICA. L/A+17C ...JURID SOC ANTHOL 20. PAGE 33 F0637
METH ACADEM EDU/PROP ACT/RES

B67
DIXON W.,SOCIETY, SCHOOLS AND PROGRESS IN SCANDINAVIA. DENMARK NORWAY SWEDEN 20. PAGE 33 F0644
EDU/PROP SOCIETY ADJUST PLAN

B67
FILENE P.G.,AMERICANS AND THE SOVIET EXPERIMENT, 1917-1933. USA-45 USSR INTELL NAT/G CAP/ISM DIPLOM EDU/PROP PRESS REV SOCISM...PSY 20. PAGE 41 F0793
ATTIT RIGID/FLEX MARXISM SOCIETY

B67
FONER P.S.,THE BOLSHEVIK REVOLUTION. USA-45 POL/PAR WORKER DIPLOM EDU/PROP MARXISM...STERTYP 20. PAGE 42 F0821
LABOR INTELL REV PRESS

B67
GOODMAN J.S.,THE DEMOCRATS AND LABOR IN RHODE ISLAND 9152-1962; CHANGES IN THE OLD ALLIANCE. USA+45 EDU/PROP LEAD GP/REL ROLE RHODE/ISL DEMOCRAT. PAGE 49 F0948
LABOR LOBBY POL/PAR LEGIS

B67
GOODMAN P.,LIKE A CONQUERED PROVINCE: THE MORAL AMBIGUITY OF AMERICA. AFR USA+45 NAT/G PROB/SOLV EDU/PROP ADJUST EFFICIENCY 20. PAGE 49 F0950
SOCIETY TEC/DEV WAR MORAL

B67
HANNAH H.W.,THE LEGAL BASE FOR UNIVERSITIES IN DEVELOPING COUNTRIES. AFR ASIA L/A+17C S/ASIA USA+45 FINAN CREATE EDU/PROP TASK EFFICIENCY ...JURID METH/COMP 20. PAGE 54 F1060
ADMIN LAW ACADEM LEGIS

B67
LEWIS L.J.,SOCIETY, SCHOOLS AND PROGRESS IN NIGERIA. NIGERIA WORKER ECO/TAC ADJUST 20. PAGE 79 F1550
EDU/PROP ECO/UNDEV SKILL SOCIETY

B67
MURTY B.S.,PROPAGANDA AND WORLD PUBLIC ORDER. FUT WOR+45 COM/IND INT/ORG PROB/SOLV ATTIT KNOWL ORD/FREE...POLICY UN. PAGE 95 F1868
EDU/PROP DIPLOM CONTROL JURID

B67
O'LEARY M.K.,THE POLITICS OF AMERICAN FOREIGN AID. USA+45 POL/PAR CHIEF BUDGET EDU/PROP LOBBY CONGRESS. PAGE 100 F1958
FOR/AID DIPLOM PARL/PROC ATTIT

B67
PEDLEY F.H.,EDUCATION AND SOCIAL WORK. USA+45 INTELL TEC/DEV. PAGE 104 F2047
GP/REL EDU/PROP SOC/WK EFFICIENCY

B67
PELTASON J.W.,FUNCTIONS AND POLICIES OF AMERICAN GOVERNMENT (3RD ED.). USA+45 FINAN INDUS EDU/PROP CIVMIL/REL RACE/REL ORD/FREE...ANTHOL T 20 JOHNSON/LB. PAGE 104 F2052
NAT/G GOV/REL POLICY PLAN

B67
PIKE F.B.,FREEDOM AND REFORM IN LATIN AMERICA. BRAZIL URUGUAY CONSTN CULTURE SECT DIPLOM EDU/PROP PARTIC DRIVE ALL/VALS CATHISM...GEOG ANTHOL BIBLIOG REFORMERS BOLIV. PAGE 106 F2086
L/A+17C ORD/FREE ECO/UNDEV REV

B67
PRINCE C.E.,NEW JERSEY'S JEFFERSONIAN REPUBLICANS; THE GENESIS OF AN EARLY PARTY MACHINE (1789-1817). USA-45 LOC/G EDU/PROP PRESS CONTROL CHOOSE...CHARTS 18/19 NEW/JERSEY REPUBLICAN. PAGE 108 F2117
POL/PAR CONSTN ADMIN PROVS

B67
REHMUS C.M.,LABOR AND AMERICAN POLITICS. POL/PAR WORKER EDU/PROP PARTIC ATTIT PWR. PAGE 110 F2175
LABOR ROLE LOBBY

B67
ROSS A.M.,EMPLOYMENT, RACE, AND POVERTY. USA+45 LAW STRATA MARKET LABOR EDU/PROP ISOLAT SKILL...MGT ANTHOL 20 NEGRO. PAGE 114 F2244
RACE/REL WORKER WEALTH DISCRIM

B67
SAPARINA Y.,CYBERNETICS WITHIN US. WOR+45 EDU/PROP FEEDBACK PERCEPT HEALTH...DECISION METH/CNCPT NEW/IDEA 20. PAGE 116 F2281
COMPUTER METH/COMP CONTROL SIMUL

B67
SPECTOR S.D.,CHECKLIST OF ITEMS IN THE NDEA INSTITUTE LIBRARY (PAMPHLET). USA+45 NAT/G SECT EDU/PROP ATTIT ALL/IDEOS...SOC BIOG. PAGE 124 F2448
BIBLIOG/A COM MARXISM

B67
THOMAS M.J.,PRESIDENTIAL STATEMENTS ON EDUCATION: EXCERPTS FROM INAUGURAL AND STATE OF THE UNION MESSAGES 1789-1967. USA+45 USA-45 NAT/G BUDGET ...IDEA/COMP 18/20 PRESIDENT. PAGE 130 F2562
EDU/PROP TOP/EX LEGIS SCHOOL

L67
BARRON J.A.,"ACCESS TO THE PRESS." USA+45 TEC/DEV PRESS TV ADJUD AUD/VIS. PAGE 10 F0196
ORD/FREE COM/IND EDU/PROP LAW

L67
COSTANZA J.F.,"WHOLESOME NEUTRALITY: LAW AND EDUCATION." USA+45 GIVE EDU/PROP ADJUD CONTROL GP/REL...DECISION JURID. PAGE 28 F0540
SECT PROVS ACADEM

S67
ALPANDER G.G.,"ENTREPRENEURS AND PRIVATE ENTERPRISE IN TURKEY." TURKEY INDUS PROC/MFG EDU/PROP ATTIT DRIVE WEALTH...GEOG MGT SOC STAT TREND CHARTS 20. PAGE 4 F0077
ECO/UNDEV LG/CO NAT/G POLICY

S67
BAGDKIAN B.H.,"NEWS AS A BYPRODUCT: WHAT HAPPENS WHEN JOURNALISM IS HITCHED TO GREAT, DIVERSIFIED CORPORATIONS?" USA+45 INDUS EDU/PROP PARTIC PROFIT ATTIT. PAGE 8 F0152
COM/IND PRESS CONTROL LG/CO

S67
BASOV V.,"THE DEVELOPMENT OF PUBLIC EDUCATION AND THE BUDGET." USSR NAT/G CONTROL REV COST AGE...STAT 20. PAGE 11 F0204
BUDGET GIVE EDU/PROP SCHOOL

S67
BENN W.,"TECHNOLOGY HAS AN INEXORABLE EFFECT." FUT UK ECO/DEV INT/ORG CONSULT PLAN EDU/PROP ADMIN LEAD GP/REL PRODUC...INT 20 EEC. PAGE 13 F0246
R+D LG/CO TEC/DEV INDUS

S67
DEMUTH J.,"GE: PROFILE OF A CORPORATION." USA+45 USA-45 LABOR ACT/RES RATION EDU/PROP ADJUD CT/SYS FASCISM 20. PAGE 32 F0619
LG/CO CONSERVE PRICE

S67
EDWARDS N.,"EDUCATION IN THE FEDERAL-STATE STRUCTURE OF GOVERNMENT." USA+45 SECT CONTROL GOV/REL RACE/REL DISCRIM FEDERAL ROLE PWR SOVEREIGN. PAGE 36 F0705
EDU/PROP NAT/G PROVS POLICY

S67
HILL L.W.,"FINANCING URBAN RENEWAL PROGRAMS." USA+45 ECO/DEV LOC/G EDU/PROP MUNICH 20. PAGE 60 F1171
FINAN NAT/G WEALTH

S67
JANSSEN P.,"NEA: THE RELUCTANT DRAGON." NAT/G EXEC LOBBY PARTIC SANCTION RACE/REL ROLE TREND. PAGE 66 F1305
EDU/PROP PROF/ORG MGT POLICY

S67
JEDLICKI W.,"THE FREE SPEECH MOVEMENT IN WARSAW." POLAND FORCES EDU/PROP LEAD ATTIT MARXISM ...IDEA/COMP 20. PAGE 67 F1310
COERCE CROWD ORD/FREE ACADEM

S67
KINGSLEY R.E.,"THE US BUSINESS IMAGE IN LATIN AMERICA." L/A+17C USA+45 NAT/G TEC/DEV CAP/ISM FOR/AID DOMIN EDU/PROP...CONCPT LING IDEA/COMP 20. PAGE 71 F1396
ATTIT LOVE DIPLOM ECO/UNDEV

S67
LANGLEY L.D.,"THE DEMOCRATIC TRADITION AND MILITARY REFORM, 1878-1885." USA-45 SECT EDU/PROP CROWD EFFICIENCY NAT/LISM 19 INDIAN/AM. PAGE 75 F1480
ATTIT FORCES POPULISM

S67
NUSENBAUM A.A.,"ON THE QUESTION OF TENDENCIES IN AMERICAN EDUCATION." USA+45 USSR SOCIETY SCHOOL RATIONAL 20. PAGE 99 F1946
MARXIST IDEA/COMP GEN/LAWS EDU/PROP

S67
PEMBERTON J., JR.,"CONSTITUTIONAL PROBLEMS IN RESTRAINT ON THE MEDIA." CONSTN PROB/SOLV EDU/PROP CONFER CONTROL JURID. PAGE 104 F2054
LAW PRESS ORD/FREE

S67
PETRAS J.,"MINERS AND AGRARIAN RADICALISM." CHILE AGRI EXTR/IND WORKER CHOOSE ATTIT SOCISM MUNICH 20. PAGE 105 F2073
PARTIC EDU/PROP LABOR

S67
POWELL D.,"THE EFFECTIVENESS OF SOVIET ANTI-RELIGIOUS PROPAGANDA." USSR NAT/G DOMIN LEGIT NAT/LISM 20. PAGE 107 F2109
EDU/PROP ATTIT SECT CONTROL

S67
RAGAN S.,"THE ABA RECOMMENDATIONS: A NEWSPAPERMAN'S CRITIQUE." EDU/PROP CONTROL GP/REL...JURID ABA. PAGE 109 F2136
LAW PRESS ADJUD ORD/FREE

S67
SCRIPP J.,"CONTROLLING PREJUDICIAL PUBLICITY BY THE CONTEMPT POWER: THE BRITISH PRACTICE AND ITS PROSPECT IN AMERICAN LAW." UK USA+45 EDU/PROP CONTROL GP/REL ORD/FREE JURID. PAGE 119 F2338
METH/COMP LAW PRESS ADJUD

S67
SMITH W.H.T.,"THE IMPLICATIONS OF THE AMERICAN BAR ASSOCIATION ADVISORY COMMITTEE RECOMMENDATIONS FOR POLICE ADMINISTRATION." AFR ADMIN...JURID 20. PAGE 123 F2435
EDU/PROP CONTROL GP/REL ORD/FREE

S67
WASSERMAN M.,"BEYOND TOKENISM: REVERSE INTEGRATION IN ALBANY, GEORGIA." USA+45 PLAN BUDGET EDU/PROP LEAD AGE/C AGE/Y GEORGIA NEGRO. PAGE 144 F2827
REGION RACE/REL DISCRIM SCHOOL

S67
WOLFSON M.,"GOVERNMENT'S ROLE IN TOURISM DEVELOPMENT." WOR+45 ECO/DEV ECO/UNDEV FINAN BUDGET DIPLOM EDU/PROP. PAGE 148 F2920
SERV/IND NAT/G CONTROL PLAN

N67
US HOUSE COMM FOREIGN AFFAIRS,COMMUNIST ACTIVITIES IN LATIN AMERICA 1967 (PAMPHLET). CUBA USA+45 DIPLOM INT/TRADE EDU/PROP COERCE GUERRILLA HOUSE/REP OAS. PAGE 137 F2696
L/A+17C MARXISM ORD/FREE ECO/TAC

B92
COULANGES F D.E.,THE ORIGIN OF PROPERTY IN LAND. LAW STRATA AGRI ACADEM EDU/PROP ORD/FREE 19. PAGE 28 F0543
OWN HIST/WRIT IDEA/COMP SOCISM

EDUCATION....SEE EDU/PROP

EDUCATIONAL INSTITUTIONS....SEE ACADEM, SCHOOL

EDWARDS C.D. F0703

EDWARDS E.O. F0704

EDWARDS N. F0705

EEC....EUROPEAN ECONOMIC COMMUNITY; SEE ALSO VOL/ASSN, INT/ORG

N
PEN I.,PRIMER ON INTERNATIONAL TRADE. WOR+45 WOR-45 ECO/DEV DIPLOM EFFICIENCY 16/20 EEC. PAGE 104 F2055
INT/TRADE BAL/PAY ECO/TAC EQUILIB

NCO
CARRINGTON C.E.,THE COMMONWEALTH IN AFRICA (PAMPHLET). UK STRUCT NAT/G COLONIAL REPRESENT GOV/REL RACE/REL NAT/LISM...MAJORIT 20 EEC NEGRO. PAGE 22 F0421
ECO/UNDEV AFR DIPLOM PLAN

N19
CASSELL F.,INTERNATIONAL MONETARY PROBLEMS (PAMPHLET). AFR BAL/PWR CONTROL EFFICIENCY WEALTH 20 EEC. PAGE 22 F0427
INT/TRADE FINAN DIPLOM TREND

B52
ALEXANDROWICZ C.H.,INTERNATIONAL ECONOMIC ORGANIZATION. WOR+45 ECO/DEV ECO/UNDEV DIST/IND FINAN MARKET PLAN ECO/TAC LEGIT DRIVE WEALTH ...POLICY CONCPT QUANT OBS TIME/SEQ GEN/LAWS WORK METH/GP EEC ILO OEEC UNESCO 20. PAGE 4 F0063
INT/ORG INT/TRADE

B55
FLORINSKY M.T.,INTEGRATED EUROPE. EUR+WWI FRANCE ITALY NETHERLAND UK ECO/DEV INT/ORG FORCES LEGIT FEDERAL ATTIT PWR WEALTH...POLICY GEOG CONCPT GEN/LAWS TOT/POP EEC OEEC 20. PAGE 42 F0816
FUT ECO/TAC REGION

B57
ARON R.,L'UNIFICATION ECONOMIQUE DE L'EUROPE. EUR+WWI SWITZERLND UK INT/ORG NAT/G REGION NAT/LISM ORD/FREE PWR...CONCPT METH/CNCPT OBS TREND STERTYP GEN/LAWS EEC FOR/TRADE 20. PAGE 6 F0118
VOL/ASSN ECO/TAC

B57
TRIFFIN R.,EUROPE AND THE MONEY MUDDLE. USA+45 INT/ORG NAT/G CONSULT PLAN ECO/TAC EXEC ROUTINE BAL/PAY WEALTH...METH/CNCPT OBS TREND CHARTS STERTYP GEN/METH EEC TERR/GP VAL/FREE ECSC. PAGE 131 F2587
EUR+WWI ECO/DEV REGION

B58
KINDLEBERGER C.P.,INTERNATIONAL ECONOMICS. WOR+45 WOR-45 ECO/DEV ECO/UNDEV FINAN VOL/ASSN ACT/RES DIPLOM ECO/TAC LEGIT REGION ATTIT DRIVE ORD/FREE WEALTH...POLICY STAT TREND GEN/LAWS EEC ECSC OEEC 20. PAGE 71 F1391
INT/ORG BAL/PWR TARIFFS

B58
MIKESELL R.F.,FINANCING FREE WORLD TRADE WITH THE SINO-SOVIET BLOC. CHINA/COM COM USSR WOR+45 ECO/DEV AGRI DIST/IND EXTR/IND FINAN INDUS MARKET PROC/MFG NAT/G PLAN TEC/DEV ECO/TAC...CHARTS METH/GP EEC FOR/TRADE 20. PAGE 91 F1780
STAT BAL/PAY

B58
SCITOUSKY T.,ECONOMIC THEORY AND WESTERN EUROPEAN INTEGRATION. EUR+WWI INT/ORG ACT/RES INT/TRADE REGION BAL/PAY WEALTH...METH/CNCPT STAT CHARTS GEN/METH ECSC TOT/POP EEC OEEC 20. PAGE 118 F2328
ECO/TAC

B59
ROBERTSON A.H.,EUROPEAN INSTITUTIONS: COOPERATION, INTEGRATION, UNIFICATION. EUR+WWI FINAN INT/ORG FORCES INT/TRADE TARIFFS 20 EEC EURATOM ECSC NATO TREATY. PAGE 112 F2208
ECO/DEV DIPLOM INDUS ECO/TAC

B59
ROPKE W.,INTERNATIONAL ORDER AND ECONOMIC INTEGRATION. ECO/DEV ECO/UNDEV AGRI FINAN INDUS INT/ORG WAR PEACE ORD/FREE...SOC METH/COMP 20 EEC. PAGE 114 F2238
INT/TRADE DIPLOM BAL/PAY ALL/IDEOS

B59
SANNWALD R.E.,ECONOMIC INTEGRATION: THEORETICAL ASSUMPTIONS AND CONSEQUENCES OF EUROPEAN UNIFICATION. EUR+WWI FUT FINAN INDUS VOL/ASSN ACT/RES ECO/TAC...PLURIST EEC FOR/TRADE OEEC 20. PAGE 116 F2279
INT/ORG ECO/DEV INT/TRADE

B59
WENTHOLT W.,SOME COMMENTS ON THE LIQUIDATION OF THE EUROPEAN PAYMENT UNION AND RELATED PROBLEMS (PAMPHLET). AFR WOR+45 PLAN BUDGET PRICE CONTROL 20 EEC. PAGE 145 F2857
FINAN ECO/DEV INT/ORG ECO/TAC

L59
MURPHY J.C.,"SOME IMPLICATIONS OF EUROPE'S COMMON MARKET. IN (COOK P, ECONOMIC DEVELOPMENT AND INTERNATIONAL TRADE.," EUR+WWI ECO/DEV DIST/IND INDUS NAT/G PLAN ECO/TAC INT/TRADE WEALTH...STAT TREND OEEC TOT/POP 20 EEC. PAGE 95 F1866
MARKET INT/ORG REGION

S59
SOLDATI A.,"EOCNOMIC DISINTEGRATION IN EUROPE." EUR+WWI FUT WOR+45 INDUS INT/ORG NAT/G CAP/ISM WEALTH...NEW/IDEA OBS TREND CHARTS EEC 20. PAGE 124 F2438
FINAN ECO/TAC

B60
ROPKE W.,A HUMANE ECONOMY. CULTURE ECO/DEV FINAN INDUS GP/REL CENTRAL WEALTH...GEOG SOC IDEA/COMP 20 EEC. PAGE 114 F2239
ECO/TAC INT/ORG DIPLOM ORD/FREE

B60
STEIN E.,AMERICAN ENTERPRISE IN THE EUROPEAN COMMON MARKET: A LEGAL PROFILE. EUR+WWI FUT USA+45 SOCIETY STRUCT ECO/DEV NAT/G VOL/ASSN CONSULT PLAN TEC/DEV ECO/TAC INT/TRADE ADMIN ATTIT RIGID/FLEX PWR...MGT NEW/IDEA STAT TREND COMPUT/IR SIMUL EEC 20. PAGE 125 F2475
MARKET ADJUD INT/LAW

B60
THE ECONOMIST (LONDON),THE COMMONWEALTH AND EUROPE. EUR+WWI WOR+45 AGRI FINAN INCOME...STAT CENSUS CHARTS CMN/WLTH EEC. PAGE 129 F2550
INT/TRADE INDUS INT/ORG NAT/COMP

B60
WENTHOLT W.,INFLATION OR SECURITY? EUR+WWI USA+45 INDUS CONSULT TEC/DEV CAP/ISM DIPLOM FOR/AID INT/TRADE MARXISM 20 EEC. PAGE 145 F2858
ECO/DEV ECO/TAC FINAN ORD/FREE

S60
KREININ M.E.,"THE 'OUTER-SEVEN' AND EUROPEAN INTEGRATION." EUR+WWI FRANCE GERMANY ITALY UK
ECO/TAC GEN/LAWS

ECO/DEV DIST/IND INT/TRADE DRIVE WEALTH...MYTH CHARTS EEC OEEC 20. PAGE 73 F1436

S60
NANES A.,"THE EUROPEAN COMMUNITY AND THE UNITED STATES: EVOLVING RELATIONS." EUR+WWI USA+45 WOR+45 ECO/UNDEV MARKET NAT/G DELIB/GP PLAN LEGIT ATTIT PWR WEALTH...CONCPT STAT TIME/SEQ CON/ANAL EEC METH/GP OEEC 20 EURATOM. PAGE 96 F1889 — INT/ORG REGION

N60
ERDMAN P.E.,COMMON MARKETS AND FREE TRADE AREAS (PAMPHLET). USA+45 MARKET INT/ORG TEC/DEV DIPLOM UTIL...CON/ANAL CHARTS BIBLIOG 20 EEC OEEC. PAGE 38 F0743 — TREND PROB/SOLV INT/TRADE ECO/DEV

B61
BENOIT E.,EUROPE AT SIXES AND SEVENS: THE COMMON MARKET, THE FREE TRADE ASSOCIATION AND THE UNITED STATES. EUR+WWI FUT USA+45 INDUS CONSULT DELIB/GP EX/STRUC TOP/EX ACT/RES ECO/TAC EDU/PROP ROUTINE CHOOSE PERCEPT WEALTH...MGT TREND EEC FOR/TRADE TOT/POP 20 EFTA. PAGE 13 F0249 — FINAN ECO/DEV VOL/ASSN

B61
FEARN H.,AN AFRICAN ECONOMY. AFR EUR+WWI PLAN COLONIAL WEALTH...CONT/OBS TREND EEC VAL/FREE 20. PAGE 39 F0770 — ECO/UNDEV

B61
FELLNER W.,THE PROBLEM OF RISING PRICES. AGRI INDUS WORKER BUDGET CAP/ISM ECO/TAC INT/TRADE PAY DEMAND ...POLICY 20 EEC. PAGE 40 F0780 — PRICE MARKET ECO/DEV COST

B61
INTL BANKING SUMMER SCHOOL,TRENDS IN BANK CREDIT AND FINANCE. EUR+WWI NETHERLAND ECO/DEV PROF/ORG PLAN BUDGET 20 EEC. PAGE 65 F1283 — FINAN ECO/TAC NAT/G LG/CO

B61
KITZINGER V.W.,THE CHALLENGE OF THE COMMON MARKET. EUR+WWI ECO/DEV DIST/IND PLAN ECO/TAC INT/TRADE LEGIT ATTIT PWR WEALTH...TIME/SEQ TREND CHARTS EEC 20. PAGE 71 F1403 — MARKET INT/ORG UK

S61
LANFALUSSY A.,"EUROPE'S PROGRESS: DUE TO COMMON MARKET." EUR+WWI ECO/DEV DELIB/GP PLAN ECO/TAC ROUTINE WEALTH...GEOG TREND EEC TERR/GP 20. PAGE 75 F1473 — INT/ORG MARKET

S61
OCHENG D.,"ECONOMIC FORCES AND UGANDA'S FOREIGN POLICY." AFR UGANDA INT/TRADE TARIFFS INCOME SOVEREIGN WEALTH 20 EACM EEC TANGANYIKA. PAGE 100 F1961 — ECO/TAC DIPLOM ECO/UNDEV INT/ORG

S61
RAY J.,"THE EUROPEAN FREE-TRADE ASSOCIATION AND ITS IMPACT ON INDIA'S TRADE." EUR+WWI FRANCE GERMANY INDIA S/ASIA UK NAT/G VOL/ASSN PLAN INT/TRADE ROUTINE WEALTH...STAT CHARTS TERR/GP CMN/WLTH EEC FOR/TRADE OEEC 20 EFTA. PAGE 109 F2155 — ECO/DEV ECO/TAC

B62
ALEXANDROWICZ C.H.,WORLD ECONOMIC AGENCIES: LAW AND PRACTICE. WOR+45 DIST/IND FINAN LABOR CONSULT INT/TRADE TARIFFS REPRESENT HEALTH...JURID 20 UN GATT EEC OAS ECSC. PAGE 4 F0064 — INT/LAW INT/ORG DIPLOM ADJUD

B62
FRIEDMANN W.,METHODS AND POLICIES OF PRINCIPAL DONOR COUNTRIES IN PUBLIC INTERNATIONAL DEVELOPMENT FINANCING: PRELIMINARY APPRAISAL. FRANCE GERMANY/W UK USA+45 USSR WOR+45 FINAN TEC/DEV CAP/ISM DIPLOM ECO/TAC ATTIT 20 EEC. PAGE 44 F0864 — INT/ORG FOR/AID NAT/COMP ADMIN

B62
HENDERSON W.O.,THE GENESIS OF THE COMMON MARKET. EUR+WWI FRANCE MOD/EUR UK SEA COM/IND EXTR/IND COLONIAL DISCRIM...TIME/SEQ CHARTS BIBLIOG 18/20 EEC TREATY. PAGE 58 F1149 — ECO/DEV INT/TRADE DIPLOM

B62
HUMPHREY D.D.,THE UNITED STATES AND THE COMMON MARKET. USA+45 INDUS MARKET INT/ORG PLAN EDU/PROP BAL/PAY DRIVE PWR WEALTH...TREND STERTYP FOR/TRADE EEC 20. PAGE 63 F1241 — ATTIT ECO/TAC

B62
LIPPMANN W.,WESTERN UNITY AND THE COMMON MARKET. EUR+WWI FRANCE GERMANY/W UK USA+45 ECO/DEV AGRI FINAN MARKET INT/ORG NAT/G FOR/AID AGREE WEALTH 20 EEC. PAGE 80 F1575 — DIPLOM INT/TRADE VOL/ASSN

B62
MCCRONE G.,THE ECONOMICS OF SUBSIDING AGRICULTURE. UK ECO/DEV MARKET PLAN TARIFFS PROFIT 20 EEC. PAGE 88 F1725 — AGRI BAL/PAY INT/TRADE LABOR

B62
MEADE J.E.,CASE STUDIES IN EUROPEAN ECONOMIC UNION. BELGIUM EUR+WWI LUXEMBOURG NAT/G INT/TRADE REGION ROUTINE WEALTH...METH/CNCPT STAT CHARTS ECSC TOT/POP OEEC EEC FOR/TRADE 20. PAGE 89 F1738 — INT/ORG ECO/TAC

B62
ROBERTSON B.C.,REGIONAL DEVELOPMENT IN THE EUROPEAN ECONOMIC COMMUNITY. EUR+WWI FRANCE FUT ITALY UK ECO/UNDEV WORKER ACT/RES PROB/SOLV TEC/DEV ECO/TAC INT/TRADE EEC. PAGE 112 F2209 — PLAN ECO/DEV INT/ORG REGION

B62
ROBINSON A.D.,DUTCH ORGANIZED AGRICULTURE IN INTERNATIONAL POLITICS, 1945-1960. EUR+WWI NETHERLAND STRUCT ECO/DEV NAT/G VOL/ASSN CONSULT DELIB/GP PLAN TEC/DEV INT/TRADE EDU/PROP ATTIT RIGID/FLEX ALL/VALS...NEW/IDEA TREND EEC COMMUN 20. PAGE 112 F2215 — AGRI INT/ORG

B62
SCHMITT H.A.,THE PATH TO EUROPEAN UNITY. EUR+WWI USA+45 PLAN TEC/DEV DIPLOM FOR/AID CONFER...INT/LAW 20 EEC EURCOALSTL MARSHL/PLN UNIFICA. PAGE 117 F2300 — INT/ORG INT/TRADE REGION ECO/DEV

B63
BELOFF M.,THE UNITED STATES AND THE UNITY OF EUROPE. EUR+WWI UK USA+45 WOR+45 VOL/ASSN DIPLOM REGION ATTIT PWR...CONCPT EEC OEEC 20 NATO. PAGE 13 F0239 — ECO/DEV INT/ORG

B63
CERAMI C.A.,ALLIANCE BORN OF DANGER. EUR+WWI USA+45 USSR ECO/DEV INDUS VOL/ASSN ECO/TAC REGION ATTIT MARXISM ATLAN/ALL 20 NATO EEC. PAGE 22 F0437 — DIPLOM INT/ORG NAT/G POLICY

B63
FATEMI N.S.,THE DOLLAR CRISIS. USA+45 INDUS NAT/G LEGIS BUDGET TAX COST...CHARTS METH/COMP 20 EEC. PAGE 39 F0766 — PROB/SOLV BAL/PAY FOR/AID PLAN

B63
KRAVIS I.B.,DOMESTIC INTERESTS AND INTERNATIONAL OBLIGATIONS: SAFEGUARDS IN INTERNATIONAL TRADE ORGANIZATIONS. EUR+WWI USA+45 WOR+45 FINAN DELIB/GP ATTIT RIGID/FLEX HEALTH...STAT EEC VAL/FREE OEEC ECSC 20. PAGE 73 F1435 — INT/ORG ECO/TAC INT/TRADE

B63
LICHTHEIM G.,THE NEW EUROPE: TODAY AND TOMORROW. EUR+WWI FINAN 20 EEC EUROPE/W. PAGE 80 F1560 — DIPLOM ECO/DEV INT/ORG INT/TRADE

B63
LINDBERG L.,POLITICAL DYNAMICS OF EUROPEAN ECONOMIC INTEGRATION. EUR+WWI ECO/DEV INT/ORG VOL/ASSN DELIB/GP ADMIN WEALTH...DECISION EEC TERR/GP 20. PAGE 80 F1567 — MARKET ECO/TAC

B63
PAN AMERICAN UNION,THE EFFECTS OF THE EUROPEAN ECONOMIC COMMUNITY ON THE LATIN AMERICAN ECONOMIES (BMR). EUR+WWI L/A+17C ECO/UNDEV AGRI INDUS MARKET REGION 20 EEC TREATY. PAGE 103 F2024 — INT/TRADE INT/ORG AGREE POLICY

B63
SALENT W.S.,THE UNITED STATES BALANCE OF PAYMENTS IN 1968. EUR+WWI UK USA+45 AGRI R+D LABOR FORCES PRODUC...GEOG CONCPT CHARTS 20 CHINJAP EEC. PAGE 115 F2274 — BAL/PAY DEMAND FINAN INT/TRADE

B63
US CONGRESS JOINT ECO COMM,OUTLOOK FOR UNITED STATES BALANCE OF PAYMENTS. AFR USA+45 ECO/DEV NAT/G FORCES DIPLOM FOR/AID COST EFFICIENCY ...POLICY CONGRESS EEC. PAGE 135 F2657 — BAL/PAY FINAN INT/TRADE PROB/SOLV

L63
MOUSKHELY M.,"LE BLOC COMMUNISTE ET LA COMMUNAUTE ECONOMIQUE EUROPEENNE." AFR COM EUR+WWI FUT USSR WOR+45 INTELL ECO/UNDEV LABOR POL/PAR NUC/PWR RIGID/FLEX...TIME/SEQ ORG/CHARTS EEC TOT/POP 20. PAGE 94 F1849 — INT/ORG ECO/DEV

S63
ADAMS F.G.,"ECONOMIC CONSIDERATIONS OF AN ATLANTIC ENERGY POLICY." EUR+WWI FUT USA+45 DIST/IND EXTR/IND MARKET CONSULT LEGIS ECO/TAC WEALTH ...POLICY EEC FOR/TRADE OEEC 20. PAGE 2 F0037 — ECO/DEV TEC/DEV NUC/PWR

S63
APPERT K.,"BERECHTIGE VORBEHALTE DER SCHWEIZERISCHEN ZUR INTEGRATION." EUR+WWI UK MARKET SERV/IND NAT/G PLAN RIGID/FLEX OEEC 20 EEC. PAGE 6 F0108 — FINAN ATTIT SWITZERLND

S63
BALOGH T.,"L'INFLUENCE DES INSTITUTIONS MONETAIRES ET COMMERCIALES SUR LA STRUCTURE ECONOMIQUE AFRICAIN." AFR EUR+WWI FUT USA+45 USA-45 WOR+45 SERV/IND INT/ORG NAT/G TOP/EX ROUTINE...INDEX EEC METH/GP 20. PAGE 9 F0168 — FINAN

S63
BARZANSKI S.,"REGIONAL UNDERDEVELOPMENT IN THE EUROPEAN ECONOMIC COMMUNITY." EUR+WWI ELITES DIST/IND MARKET VOL/ASSN CONSULT EX/STRUC ECO/TAC RIGID/FLEX WEALTH EEC OEEC 20. PAGE 11 F0202 — ECO/UNDEV PLAN

S63
BELOFF M.,"BRITAIN, EUROPE AND THE ATLANTIC COMMUNITY." EUR+WWI ELITES NAT/G VOL/ASSN TOP/EX ATTIT ORD/FREE PWR SOVEREIGN WEALTH EEC TOT/POP VAL/FREE CMN/WLTH 20. PAGE 13 F0240 — INT/ORG ECO/DEV UK

S63
DIEBOLD W. JR.,"THE NEW SITUATION OF INTERNATIONAL TRADE POLICY." EUR+WWI FRANCE FUT UK USA+45 WOR+45 DIST/IND PLAN INT/TRADE EDU/PROP PWR WEALTH ...RECORD TREND GEN/LAWS EEC TRUE/GP VAL/FREE APPLIC 20. PAGE 33 F0636 — MARKET ECO/TAC

S63
EMERSON R.,"THE ATLANTIC COMMUNITY AND THE EMERGING COUNTRIES." FUT WOR+45 ECO/DEV ECO/UNDEV R+D NAT/G DELIB/GP BAL/PWR ECO/TAC EDU/PROP ROUTINE ORD/FREE PWR WEALTH...POLICY CONCPT TREND GEN/METH EEC 20 NATO. PAGE 37 F0729
ATTIT INT/TRADE

S63
HALLSTEIN W.,"THE EUROPEAN COMMUNITY AND ATLANTIC PARTNERSHIP." EUR+WWI USA+45 MARKET NAT/G VOL/ASSN DELIB/GP ARMS/CONT NUC/PWR ATTIT PWR...CONCPT STAT TIME/SEQ TREND OEEC 20 EEC. PAGE 54 F1053
INT/ORG ECO/TAC UK

S63
MONROE A.D.,"BRITAIN AND THE EUROPEAN COMMUNITY." EUR+WWI FRANCE NAT/G DELIB/GP TOP/EX ECO/TAC DOMIN PWR...POLICY RECORD GEN/LAWS EEC EFTA 20 EFTA CMN/WLTH. PAGE 93 F1817
VOL/ASSN ATTIT UK

S63
POLYANOV N.,"THE DOLLAR'S VENTURES IN EUROPE." EUR+WWI FRANCE USA+45 ECO/DEV MARKET POL/PAR TEC/DEV ECO/TAC EDU/PROP DRIVE PWR WEALTH...MARXIST MYTH STAT TREND EEC 20. PAGE 107 F2100
FINAN PLAN BAL/PAY CAP/ISM

S63
SCHOFLING J.A.,"EFTA: THE OTHER EUROPE." ECO/DEV MARKET CONSULT ECO/TAC WEALTH...TIME/SEQ EEC OEEC 20 EFTA. PAGE 117 F2310
EUR+WWI INT/ORG REGION

S63
SHONFIELD A.,"AFTER BRUSSELS." EUR+WWI FRANCE GERMANY UK ECO/DEV DIST/IND MARKET VOL/ASSN DELIB/GP CREATE INT/TRADE ATTIT RIGID/FLEX...RECORD TREND GEN/LAWS EEC COMMUN CMN/WLTH 20. PAGE 121 F2385
PLAN ECO/TAC

S63
SHWADRAN B.,"MIDDLE EAST OIL, 1962." ISLAM USSR ECO/DEV DIST/IND INDUS PLAN BAL/PWR DISPL DRIVE ...POLICY STAT TREND GEN/LAWS TERR/GP METH/GP EEC OEEC 20 OIL. PAGE 121 F2394
MARKET ECO/TAC INT/TRADE

S63
TENNYSON L.B.,"THE USA IN ATLANTIC COMMUNITY." EUR+WWI FRANCE UK USA+45 ECO/UNDEV VOL/ASSN DELIB/GP TOP/EX DIPLOM DOMIN PWR...POLICY CONCPT TREND GEN/LAWS EEC 20. PAGE 129 F2545
ATTIT ECO/TAC BAL/PWR

S63
WOLFERS A.,"INTEGRATION IN THE WEST: THE CONFLICT OF PERSPECTIVES." AFR EUR+WWI USA+45 ECO/DEV INT/ORG DELIB/GP CREATE TEC/DEV DIPLOM ATTIT PWR ...CONCPT HIST/WRIT TREND GEN/LAWS EEC 20. PAGE 148 F2918
RIGID/FLEX ECO/TAC

B64
CASEY R.G.,THE FUTURE OF THE COMMONWEALTH. INDIA PAKISTAN UK ECO/UNDEV INT/ORG TEC/DEV COLONIAL SUPEGO 20 EEC AUSTRAL. PAGE 22 F0425
DIPLOM SOVEREIGN NAT/LISM FOR/AID

B64
ECONOMIDES C.P.,LE POUVOIR DE DECISION DES ORGANISATIONS INTERNATIONALES EUROPEENNES. DIPLOM DOMIN INGP/REL EFFICIENCY...INT/LAW JURID 20 NATO OEEC EEC COUNCL/EUR EURATOM. PAGE 36 F0698
INT/ORG PWR DECISION GP/COMP

B64
FREYMOND J.,WESTERN EUROPE SINCE THE WAR. COM EUR+WWI USA+45 DIPLOM...BIBLIOG 20 NATO UN EEC. PAGE 44 F0854
INT/ORG POLICY ECO/DEV ECO/TAC

B64
HINSHAW R.,THE EUROPEAN COMMUNITY AND AMERICAN TRADE: A STUDY IN ATLANTIC ECONOMICS AND POLICY. EUR+WWI UK USA+45 ECO/DEV ECO/UNDEV AGRI INDUS INT/ORG NAT/G ECO/TAC TARIFFS REGION...STAT CHARTS EEC 20. PAGE 60 F1174
MARKET TREND INT/TRADE

B64
KRAUSE L.B.,THE COMMON MARKET: PROGRESS AND CONTROVERSY. EUR+WWI UK ECO/DEV REGION...ANTHOL NATO EEC. PAGE 73 F1433
DIPLOM MARKET INT/TRADE INT/ORG

B64
LISKA G.,EUROPE ASCENDANT. EUR+WWI ECO/DEV FORCES INT/TRADE MARXISM 20 EEC. PAGE 81 F1579
DIPLOM BAL/PWR TARIFFS CENTRAL

B64
MARKHAM J.W.,THE COMMON MARKET: FRIEND OR COMPETITOR. AFR EUR+WWI FUT USA+45 INT/ORG LG/CO NAT/G VOL/ASSN DELIB/GP EX/STRUC PLAN TARIFFS ORD/FREE PWR WEALTH...POLICY STAT TREND EEC VAL/FREE 20. PAGE 85 F1671
ECO/DEV ECO/TAC

B64
RAMAZANI R.K.,THE MIDDLE EAST AND THE EUROPEAN COMMON MARKET. EUR+WWI ISLAM ECO/DEV EXTR/IND MARKET PROC/MFG INT/ORG NAT/G TEC/DEV ECO/TAC REGION DRIVE WEALTH...STAT CHARTS EEC TOT/POP 20. PAGE 109 F2141
ECO/UNDEV ATTIT INT/TRADE

B64
RIVKIN A.,AFRICA AND THE EUROPEAN COMMON MARKET (PAMPHLET). AFR MOD/EUR WOR+45 TEC/DEV FOR/AID TARIFFS BAL/PAY...POLICY 20 EEC. PAGE 111 F2196
INT/ORG INT/TRADE ECO/TAC ECO/UNDEV

B64
STEWART C.F.,A BIBLIOGRAPHY OF INTERNATIONAL BUSINESS. WOR+45 FINAN LG/CO NAT/G PLAN ECO/TAC TARIFFS...DECISION MGT GP/COMP NAT/COMP 20 EEC. PAGE 126 F2484
BIBLIOG INT/ORG OP/RES INT/TRADE

S64
GALBRAITH V.,"JAPAN'S POSITION IN WORLD TRADE." ASIA AGRI INDUS CREATE ECO/TAC LEGIT DRIVE WEALTH ...TREND EEC GATT FOR/TRADE 20 CHINJAP. PAGE 45 F0885
ECO/DEV DELIB/GP

S64
GERBET P.,"LA MISE EN OEUVRE DU MARCHE COMMUN AGRICOLE." ECO/DEV MARKET INT/ORG NAT/G PLAN EDU/PROP NAT/LISM WEALTH...OBS EEC VAL/FREE 20. PAGE 47 F0917
EUR+WWI AGRI REGION

S64
KOJIMA K.,"THE PATTERN OF INTERNATIONAL TRADE AMONG ADVANCED COUNTRIES." EUR+WWI UK USA+45 WOR+45 MARKET NAT/G ECO/TAC WEALTH...MATH STAT CON/ANAL CHARTS METH/GP EEC CHINJAP 20 CHINJAP. PAGE 72 F1419
ECO/DEV TREND INT/TRADE

S64
SALVADORI M.,"EL CAPITALISMO EN LA EUROPA DE LA POSGUERRA." AFR INT/ORG NAT/G POL/PAR PLAN ECO/TAC ATTIT ORD/FREE WEALTH...HIST/WRIT EEC 20. PAGE 115 F2275
EUR+WWI ECO/DEV CAP/ISM

S64
SCHMITT H.D.,"POLITICAL CONDITIONS FOR INTERNATIONAL CURRENCY REFORM." WOR+45 SOCIETY ECO/DEV PLAN ECO/TAC BAL/PAY ATTIT ORD/FREE WEALTH ...SOC CONCPT OBS TREND EEC VAL/FREE ECSC 20. PAGE 117 F2301
FINAN VOL/ASSN REGION

B65
LYONS G.M.,AMERICA: PURPOSE AND POWER. UK USA+45 FINAN INDUS MARKET WORKER TEC/DEV DIPLOM AUTOMAT NUC/PWR WAR RACE/REL ORD/FREE 20 EEC CONGRESS SUPREME/CT CIV/RIGHTS. PAGE 82 F1617
PWR PROB/SOLV ECO/DEV TASK

B65
PROCHNOW H.V.,WORLD ECONOMIC PROBLEMS AND POLICIES. INDIA ISRAEL WOR+45 AGRI LABOR PROB/SOLV FOR/AID TARIFFS CONTROL BAL/PAY NAT/LISM WEALTH...TREND CHARTS 20 CHINJAP EEC. PAGE 108 F2124
MARKET ECO/TAC PRODUC IDEA/COMP

B65
WEIL G.L.,A HANDBOOK ON THE EUROPEAN ECONOMIC COMMUNITY. BELGIUM EUR+WWI FRANCE GERMANY/W ITALY CONSTN ECO/DEV CREATE PARTIC GP/REL...DECISION MGT CHARTS 20 EEC. PAGE 144 F2846
INT/TRADE INT/ORG TEC/DEV INT/LAW

L65
LETICHE J.M.,"EUROPEAN INTEGRATION: AN AMERICAN VIEW." EUR+WWI FRANCE WOR+45 ECO/DEV DIST/IND EXTR/IND NAT/G DELIB/GP TOP/EX PLAN ECO/TAC ATTIT ...STAT CON/ANAL CHARTS EEC 20. PAGE 78 F1537
INDUS AGRI

S65
CAMPOLONGO A.,"EUROPEAN INVESTMENT BANK* ACTIVITY AND PROSPECTS." FUT ECO/UNDEV FINAN PLAN DIPLOM ...STAT EEC LOAN EIB. PAGE 21 F0410
ECO/TAC PREDICT

S65
HAYTER T.,"FRENCH AID TO AFRICA* ITS SCOPE AND ACHIEVEMENTS." CULTURE ECO/TAC INT/TRADE ADMIN REGION CENTRAL FEDERAL LOVE PWR SOVEREIGN EEC. PAGE 57 F1127
AFR FRANCE FOR/AID COLONIAL

S65
KINDLEBERGER C.P.,"MASS MIGRATION, THEN AND NOW." LAW ECO/DEV ECO/UNDEV INDUS LABOR INT/TRADE FEEDBACK REGION RIGID/FLEX...SOC NAT/COMP EEC. PAGE 71 F1394
EUR+WWI USA-45 WORKER IDEA/COMP

S65
MUNZI U.,"THE EUROPEAN SOCIAL FUND IN THE DEVELOPMENT OF THE MEDITERRANEAN REGIONS OF THE EEC." FUT GREECE ITALY PORTUGAL SPAIN TURKEY WORKER TEC/DEV ECO/TAC REGION...STAT EEC. PAGE 95 F1862
ECO/UNDEV PREDICT RECORD

S65
RUSINOW D.I.,"YUGOSLAV DEVELOPMENT BETWEEN EAST AND WEST." AGRI VOL/ASSN PLAN CAP/ISM ECO/TAC FOR/AID INT/TRADE BAL/PAY...MARXIST EEC COMECON. PAGE 115 F2262
YUGOSLAVIA ECO/UNDEV STAT

S65
SOPER T.,"THE EEC AND AID TO AFRICA." FRANCE UK ECO/UNDEV INT/TRADE TARIFFS REGION ROUTINE CENTRAL DISCRIM...DECISION RECORD EEC. PAGE 124 F2443
AFR FOR/AID COLONIAL

S65
SPAAK P.H.,"THE SEARCH FOR CONSENSUS: A NEW EFFORT TO BUILD EUROPE." FRANCE GERMANY ECO/DEV NAT/G CONSULT FORCES PLAN EDU/PROP REGION CONSEN ATTIT ...SOC METH/CNCPT OBS TREND EEC NATO WORK TERR/GP METH/GP 20. PAGE 124 F2447
EUR+WWI INT/ORG

B66
BEUGEL E.V.D.,FROM MARSHALL AID TO ATLANTIC PARTNERSHIP* EUROPEAN INTEGRATION AS A CONCERN OF AMERICAN FOREIGN POLICY. USA+45 INT/ORG FORCES PERSON EEC NATO. PAGE 14 F0272
REGION DIPLOM EUR+WWI VOL/ASSN

B66
EDWARDS C.D.,TRADE REGULATIONS OVERSEAS. IRELAND NEW/ZEALND SOUTH/AFR NAT/G CAP/ISM TARIFFS CONTROL ...POLICY JURID 20 EEC CHINJAP. PAGE 36 F0703
INT/TRADE DIPLOM INT/LAW ECO/TAC

B66
FRIEDMANN W.G.,INTERNATIONAL FINANCIAL AID. USA+45 ECO/DEV ECO/UNDEV NAT/G VOL/ASSN EX/STRUC PLAN RENT GIVE BAL/PAY PWR...GEOG INT/LAW STAT TREND UN EEC COMECON. PAGE 44 F0866
INT/ORG FOR/AID TEC/DEV ECO/TAC

B66
INGRAM J.C.,INTERNATIONAL ECONOMIC PROBLEMS. ECO/DEV ECO/UNDEV INDUS MARKET TEC/DEV TARIFFS BAL/PAY CENTRAL...POLICY 20 EEC. PAGE 64 F1265
INT/TRADE INT/ORG FINAN

B66
MEERHAEGHE M.,INTERNATIONAL ECONOMIC INSTITUTIONS. EUR+WWI FINAN INDUS MARKET PLAN TARIFFS BAL/PAY EQUILIB...POLICY BIBLIOG/A 20 GATT OEEC EEC IBRD EURCOALSTL. PAGE 89 F1745
ECO/TAC ECO/DEV INT/TRADE INT/ORG

B66
TRIFFIN R.,THE WORLD MONEY MAZE. AFR INT/ORG ECO/TAC PRICE OPTIMAL WEALTH...METH/COMP 20 EEC OEEC SILVER. PAGE 131 F2589
BAL/PAY FINAN INT/TRADE DIPLOM

S66
FELD W.,"EXTERNAL RELATIONS OF THE COMMON MARKET AND GROUP LEADERSHIP ATTITUDES IN THE MEMBER STATES." COM USA+45 ELITES AGRI NAT/G ATTIT...OBS EEC GATT. PAGE 40 F0776
DIPLOM CENTRAL TARIFFS INT/TRADE

S66
FELD W.,"NATIONAL ECONOMIC INTEREST GROUPS AND POLICY FORMATION IN THE EEC." NAT/G POL/PAR REGION CENTRAL SOVEREIGN...INT NET/THEORY EEC. PAGE 40 F0777
LOBBY ELITES DECISION

B67
GORZ A.,STRATEGY FOR LABOR: A RADICAL PROPOSAL (TRANS. BY MARTIN NICOLAUS AND VICTORIA ORTIZ). EUR+WWI FRANCE ITALY ECO/DEV POL/PAR OP/RES PLAN GP/REL ALL/IDEOS...SOC 20 EEC. PAGE 49 F0965
LABOR PWR STRUCT ECO/TAC

B67
HOGAN J.,THE US BALANCE OF PAYMENTS AND CAPITAL FLOWS. MARKET INT/ORG ECO/TAC PRICE CONTROL WEALTH ...METH/COMP 20 EEC. PAGE 61 F1192
BAL/PAY FINAN DIPLOM INT/TRADE

B67
KREININ M.E.,ALTERNATIVE COMMERCIAL POLICIES - THEIR EFFECT ON THE AMERICAN ECONOMY. USA+45 LAW ECO/DEV MARKET INT/ORG DIPLOM ECO/TAC TARIFFS PRICE DEMAND WEALTH...QUANT EEC AFTA. PAGE 73 F1437
INT/TRADE BAL/PAY NAT/G POLICY

B67
ROACH J.R.,THE UNITED STATES AND THE ATLANTIC COMMUNITY; ISSUES AND PROSPECTS. AFR WOR+45 TEC/DEV ECO/TAC COLONIAL REGION PEACE ROLE...ANTHOL NATO EEC. PAGE 112 F2199
INT/ORG POLICY ADJUST DIPLOM

L67
DROBNIG U.,"CONFLICT OF LAWS AND THE EUROPEAN ECONOMIC COMMUNITY." EUR+WWI PROB/SOLV DIPLOM ...JURID EEC. PAGE 34 F0663
INT/LAW ADJUD INT/ORG MARKET

L67
MESTMACKER E.J.,"STATE TRADING MONOPOLIES IN THE EUROPEAN ECONOMIC COMMUNITY. DIPLOM ECO/TAC ADJUD CONTROL DISCRIM 20 EEC. PAGE 90 F1764
INT/TRADE INT/ORG LAW TARIFFS

S67
APEL H.,"LES NOUVEAUX ASPECTS DE LA POLITIQUE ETRANGERE ALLEMANDE." AFR EUR+WWI GERMANY POL/PAR BAL/PWR ECO/TAC INT/TRADE NUC/PWR NAT/LISM PEACE ...POLICY 20 EEC. PAGE 6 F0107
DIPLOM INT/ORG FEDERAL

S67
AUBERT DE LA RUE P.,"PERSPECTIVES ECONOMIQUES ENTRE LES ETATS-UNIS ET L'EUROPE." FUT INDUS R+D INT/ORG ACT/RES ECO/TAC AGREE BAL/PAY PRODUC...CHARTS 20 EEC GATT WORLD/BANK. PAGE 7 F0138
INT/TRADE ECO/DEV FINAN TARIFFS

S67
BARTLETT J.L.,"AMERICAN BOND ISSUES IN THE EUROPEAN ECONOMIC COMMUNITY." EUR+WWI LUXEMBOURG USA+45 DIPLOM CONTROL BAL/PAY EEC. PAGE 11 F0201
LAW ECO/TAC FINAN TAX

S67
BENN W.,"TECHNOLOGY HAS AN INEXORABLE EFFECT." FUT UK ECO/DEV INT/ORG CONSULT PLAN EDU/PROP ADMIN LEAD GP/REL PRODUC...INT 20 EEC. PAGE 13 F0246
R+D LG/CO TEC/DEV INDUS

S67
BUTT R.,"THE COMMON MARKET AND CONSERVATIVE POLITICS, 1961-2." UK CHIEF DIPLOM ECO/TAC INT/TRADE CONFER DEBATE REGION ATTIT...POLICY 20 EEC. PAGE 21 F0398
EUR+WWI INT/ORG POL/PAR

S67
COSGROVE C.A.,"AGRICULTURE, FINANCE AND POLITICS IN THE EUROPEAN COMMUNITY." EUR+WWI DIST/IND MARKET INT/ORG VOL/ASSN DELIB/GP TEC/DEV BAL/PWR BARGAIN ECO/TAC RATION CONFER 20 EEC. PAGE 28 F0538
ECO/DEV DIPLOM AGRI INT/TRADE

S67
CROMER EARL OF,"STERLING AND THE COMMON MARKET." UK ECO/DEV INT/ORG 20 EEC. PAGE 29 F0554
ECO/TAC FINAN CHARTS INT/TRADE

S67
SMALL A.H.,"THE EFFECT OF TARIFF REDUCTIONS ON US IMPORT VOLUME." USA+45 INT/ORG NAT/G DIPLOM CONFER DEMAND...POLICY INT/LAW STAT CHARTS GATT EEC. PAGE 123 F2424
TARIFFS INT/TRADE PRICE ECO/TAC

S67
WARNER G.,"FRANCE, BRITAIN AND THE EEC." FRANCE UK INT/ORG DELIB/GP ECO/TAC CONTROL 20 EEC. PAGE 143 F2822
INT/TRADE BAL/PWR DIPLOM

S67
WEIL G.L.,"THE MERGER OF THE INSTITUTIONS OF THE EUROPEAN COMMUNITIES" EUR+WWI ECO/DEV INT/TRADE CONSEN PLURISM...DECISION MGT 20 EEC EURATOM ECSC TREATY. PAGE 145 F2847
ECO/TAC INT/ORG CENTRAL INT/LAW

S67
WILLMANN J.,"LA COMMUNAUTE EUROPEENNE ET LA GRANDE-BRETAGNE." UK PROB/SOLV TEC/DEV CAP/ISM DIPLOM CONFER FEDERAL...POLICY 20 EEC. PAGE 147 F2898
INT/ORG DRIVE NAT/LISM INT/TRADE

N67
US HOUSE COMM FOREIGN AFFAIRS,THE FOREIGN POLICY ASPECTS OF THE KENNEDY ROUND (PAMPHLET). USA+45 INDUS KENNEDY/JF CONGRESS HOUSE/REP EEC. PAGE 137 F2693
POLICY INT/TRADE FOR/AID ECO/DEV

EELLS R.S.F. F0706

EFFECTIVENESS....SEE EFFICIENCY, PRODUC

EFFICIENCY....EFFECTIVENESS

N
PEN I.,PRIMER ON INTERNATIONAL TRADE. WOR+45 WOR-45 ECO/DEV DIPLOM EFFICIENCY 16/20 EEC. PAGE 104 F2055
INT/TRADE BAL/PAY ECO/TAC EQUILIB

LCA
GODFREY E.M.,"THE ECONOMICS OF AN AFRICAN UNIVERSITY." AFR SCHOOL PRICE EFFICIENCY INCOME WEALTH...ECOMETRIC CHARTS 20. PAGE 48 F0930
ACADEM ECO/TAC COST EDU/PROP

N19
ARNDT H.W.,AUSTRALIAN FOREIGN AID POLICY (PAMPHLET). ECO/UNDEV DIPLOM GIVE GOV/REL COST UTIL PWR...CHARTS 20 AUSTRAL PAPUA NEW/GUINEA. PAGE 6 F0114
FOR/AID POLICY ECO/TAC EFFICIENCY

N19
ARNOW K.,SELF-INSURANCE IN THE TREASURY (PAMPHLET). USA+45 LAW RIGID/FLEX...POLICY METH/COMP 20 DEPT/TREAS. PAGE 6 F0117
ADMIN PLAN EFFICIENCY NAT/G

N19
BLOOMFIELD A.,MONETARY POLICY UNDER THE INTERNATIONAL GOLD STANDARD: 18801914 (PAMPHLET). AFR USA-45 DIPLOM CONTROL...POLICY 19. PAGE 16 F0300
FINAN ROLE EFFICIENCY

N19
BROWN W.M.,THE DESIGN AND PERFORMANCE OF "OPTIMUM" BLAST SHELTER PROGRAMS (PAMPHLET). USA+45 ACT/RES PLAN DEATH COST EFFICIENCY OPTIMAL...POLICY CHARTS 20. PAGE 19 F0375
HABITAT NUC/PWR WAR HEALTH

N19
CASSELL F.,INTERNATIONAL MONETARY PROBLEMS (PAMPHLET). AFR BAL/PWR CONTROL EFFICIENCY WEALTH 20 EEC. PAGE 22 F0427
INT/TRADE FINAN DIPLOM TREND

N19
DOTSON A.,PRODUCTION PLANNING IN THE PATENT OFFICE (PAMPHLET). USA+45 DIST/IND PROB/SOLV PRODUC...MGT PHIL/SCI 20 BUR/BUDGET PATENT/OFF. PAGE 34 F0655
EFFICIENCY PLAN NAT/G ADMIN

N19
DWYER J.W.,YARDSTICKS FOR PERFORMANCE (PAMPHLET). USA+45 FINAN CONTROL...CONCPT METH/COMP MUNICH. PAGE 35 F0688
BUDGET LOC/G EFFICIENCY

N19
HATANAKA M.,A SPECTRAL ANALYSIS OF BUSINESS CYCLE INDICATORS: LEAD-LAG IN TERMS OF ALL TIME POINTS (PAMPHLET). UNIV WORKER EFFICIENCY...REGRESS STAT CHARTS TIME 20. PAGE 56 F1110
ECOMETRIC ADJUST PRODUC CON/ANAL

N19
JACKSON R.G.A.,THE CASE FOR AN INTERNATIONAL DEVELOPMENT AUTHORITY (PAMPHLET). WOR+45 ECO/DEV DIPLOM GIVE CONTROL GP/REL EFFICIENCY NAT/LISM SOVEREIGN 20. PAGE 66 F1295
FOR/AID INT/ORG ECO/UNDEV ADMIN

N19
MORGENSTERN O.,A NEW LOOK AT ECONOMIC TIMES SERIES ANALYSIS (PAMPHLET). WEALTH...BIBLIOG 20 NSF NAVAL/RES. PAGE 93 F1831
TREND IDEA/COMP EFFICIENCY

N19
WILSON T.,FINANCIAL ASSISTANCE WITH REGIONAL DEVELOPMENT (PAMPHLET). CANADA INDUS NAT/G PLAN TAX CONTROL COST EFFICIENCY...POLICY CHARTS 20. PAGE 147 F2902
FINAN ECO/TAC REGION GOV/REL

B23
HOBSON J.A.,INCENTIVES IN THE NEW INDUSTRIAL ORDER. USA-45 NAT/G PAY COST EFFICIENCY PRODUC WEALTH ...MAJORIT PSY SOC/WK 20. PAGE 60 F1186
INDUS LABOR INCOME

OPTIMAL

B35
HICKS J.R.,THE THEORY OF WAGES. INDUS NAT/G PAY PRICE CONTROL COST EFFICIENCY WEALTH 19/20 MARSHALL/A CLARK/JB. PAGE 59 F1164 — INCOME WORKER LABOR PRODUC

B41
MACMAHON A.W.,THE ADMINISTRATION OF FEDERAL WORK RELIEF. USA-45 EX/STRUC WORKER BUDGET EFFICIENCY ...CONT/OBS CHARTS 20 WPA. PAGE 84 F1636 — ADMIN NAT/G MGT GIVE

B41
SLICHTER S.H.,UNION POLICIES AND INDUSTRIAL MANAGEMENT. USA-45 INDUS TEC/DEV PAY GP/REL INGP/REL COST EFFICIENCY PRODUC...POLICY 20. PAGE 123 F2420 — BARGAIN LABOR MGT WORKER

B42
US LIBRARY OF CONGRESS,THE WAR PRODUCTION PROGRAM: SELECTED DOCUMENTATION ON THE ECONOMICS OF WAR (PAMPHLET). USA-45 ECO/DEV AGRI FINAN NAT/G ECO/TAC RATION PRICE EFFICIENCY 20. PAGE 138 F2713 — BIBLIOG/A WAR PRODUC INDUS

B44
MERRIAM C.E.,PUBLIC AND PRIVATE GOVERNMENT. VOL/ASSN EDU/PROP ADMIN REPRESENT EFFICIENCY PWR PLURISM...MAJORIT CONCPT. PAGE 90 F1762 — NAT/G NEIGH MGT POLICY

B47
LEVER E.A.,ADVERTISING AND ECONOMIC THEORY. FINAN ECO/TAC DEMAND EFFICIENCY ATTIT...MGT PSY SAMP/SIZ CHARTS 20. PAGE 79 F1539 — EDU/PROP MARKET COM/IND ECO/DEV

B48
NOYES C.R.,ECONOMIC MAN IN RELATION TO HIS NATURAL ENVIRONMENT (2 VOLS.). UNIV COST DEMAND EFFICIENCY HAPPINESS INCOME PRODUC PROFIT HEREDITY...CHARTS BIBLIOG. PAGE 99 F1944 — HABITAT METH/CNCPT GEN/METH

B49
MACGREGOR D.H.,ECONOMIC THOUGHT AND POLICY. WOR-45 WORKER WAR DEMAND EFFICIENCY WEALTH LAISSEZ SOCISM ...MAJORIT BIBLIOG 19/20. PAGE 83 F1629 — CONCPT POLICY ECO/TAC

S49
HART C.W.M.,"INDUSTRIAL RELATIONS RESEARCH AND SOCIAL THEORY." CANADA VOL/ASSN WORKER LEAD EFFICIENCY...MGT SOC METH/CNCPT METH/COMP MUNICH 20. PAGE 56 F1099 — GEN/LAWS LABOR GP/REL

B50
CHAMBERLIN E.,THE THEORY OF MONOPOLISTIC COMPETITION (1933). INDUS PAY GP/REL COST DEMAND EFFICIENCY OPTIMAL PRODUC WEALTH...GEN/LAWS 20. PAGE 23 F0443 — MARKET PRICE ECO/TAC EQUILIB

S50
DALTON M.,"CONFLICTS BETWEEN STAFF AND LINE MANAGERIAL OFFICERS" (BMR). USA+45 USA-45 ELITES LG/CO WORKER PROB/SOLV ADMIN EXEC EFFICIENCY PRODUC ...GP/COMP 20. PAGE 30 F0576 — MGT ATTIT GP/REL INDUS

S50
DREYFUS S.,"THE INDUSTRIAL DESIGNER AND THE BUSINESSMAN." SERV/IND PROB/SOLV ECO/TAC COST EFFICIENCY PROFIT RATIONAL...DECISION MGT. PAGE 34 F0662 — CONSULT INDUS PRODUC UTIL

B51
DIMOCK M.E.,FREE ENTERPRISE AND THE ADMINISTRATIVE STATE. FINAN LG/CO BARGAIN BUDGET DOMIN CONTROL INGP/REL EFFICIENCY 20. PAGE 33 F0640 — CAP/ISM ADMIN MGT MARKET

B51
ROEPKE W.,THE PROBLEM OF ECONOMIC ORDER. WOR+45 SOCIETY PROB/SOLV CONTROL EFFICIENCY...CON/ANAL IDEA/COMP GEN/METH 20. PAGE 113 F2231 — ECO/TAC ORD/FREE MARKET PROC/MFG

C51
HOMANS G.C.,"THE WESTERN ELECTRIC RESEARCHES" IN S. HOSLETT, ED., HUMAN FACTORS IN MANAGEMENT (BMR)" ACT/RES GP/REL HAPPINESS PRODUC DRIVE...MGT OBS 20. PAGE 61 F1202 — OP/RES EFFICIENCY SOC/EXP WORKER

B52
WU Y.,ECONOMIC WARFARE. MARKET PLAN PROB/SOLV FOR/AID CONTROL EFFICIENCY WEALTH...METH/COMP 20. PAGE 149 F2937 — ECO/TAC WAR INT/TRADE DIPLOM

S52
PHILLIPS C.,"THE HIGH COST OF OUR LOW-PAID CONGRESS" (NYT MAG. 2/24/52)" USA+45 FINAN WRITING TASK TIME CONGRESS. PAGE 106 F2082 — LEGIS INCOME COST EFFICIENCY

B53
FLORENCE P.S.,THE LOGIC OF BRITISH AND AMERICAN INDUSTRY; A REALISTIC ANALYSIS OF ECONOMIC STRUCTURE AND GOVERNMENT. UK USA+45 USA-45 FINAN LABOR CAP/ISM INGP/REL EFFICIENCY...MGT CONCPT STAT CHARTS METH 20. PAGE 42 F0813 — INDUS ECO/DEV NAT/G NAT/COMP

B53
MILLIKAN M.F.,INCOME STABILIZATION FOR A DEVELOPING DEMOCRACY. USA+45 ECO/DEV LABOR BUDGET ECO/TAC TAX ADMIN ADJUST PRODUC WEALTH...POLICY TREND 20. PAGE 91 F1794 — ANTHOL MARKET EQUILIB EFFICIENCY

B53
ROBINSON E.A.G.,THE STRUCTURE OF COMPETITIVE INDUSTRY. UK ECO/DEV DIST/IND MARKET TEC/DEV DIPLOM EDU/PROP ADMIN EFFICIENCY WEALTH...MGT 19/20. PAGE 113 F2217 — INDUS PRODUC WORKER OPTIMAL

B53
WILLIAMS J.H.,ECONOMIC STABILITY IN A CHANGING WORLD. FRANCE USA+45 USSR AGRI WORKER BUDGET INT/TRADE TAX WAR BAL/PAY COST EFFICIENCY ALL/IDEOS EQULIB 20 KEYNES/JM. PAGE 147 F2892 — POLICY FINAN ECO/TAC WEALTH

S53
GABLE R.W.,"NAM: INFLUENTIAL LOBBY OR KISS OF DEATH?" (BMR)" USA+45 LAW INSPECT EDU/PROP ADMIN CONTROL INGP/REL EFFICIENCY PWR 20 CONGRESS NAM TAFT/HART. PAGE 45 F0880 — LOBBY LEGIS INDUS LG/CO

S53
LAWTON F.J.,"LEGISLATIVE-EXECUTIVE RELATIONS IN BUDGETING AS VIEWED BY THE EXECUTIVE." NAT/G LEGIS ADMIN REPRESENT EFFICIENCY 20. PAGE 76 F1495 — BUDGET EX/STRUC EXEC CONTROL

S53
SIMON H.A.,"BIRTH OF AN ORGANIZATION: THE ECONOMIC COOPERATION ADMINISTRATION." USA+45 PROB/SOLV INGP/REL EFFICIENCY 20. PAGE 122 F2408 — ADMIN EX/STRUC EXEC MGT

B55
BLOOM G.F.,ECONOMICS OF LABOR RELATIONS. USA+45 LAW CONSULT WORKER CAP/ISM PAY ADJUD CONTROL EFFICIENCY ORD/FREE...CHARTS 19/20 AFL/CIO NLRB DEPT/LABOR. PAGE 16 F0299 — ECO/DEV ECO/TAC LABOR GOV/REL

B55
PEDLER F.J.,ECONOMIC GEOGRAPHY OF WEST AFRICA. GAMBIA NIGER SIER/LEONE STRATA EXTR/IND MARKET LABOR INT/TRADE DEMAND HABITAT WEALTH...CHARTS 20. PAGE 104 F2046 — ECO/UNDEV GEOG PRODUC EFFICIENCY

B55
SMITHIES A.,THE BUDGETARY PROCESS IN THE UNITED STATES. AFR ECO/DEV AGRI EX/STRUC FORCES LEGIS PROB/SOLV TAX ROUTINE EFFICIENCY...MGT CONGRESS PRESIDENT. PAGE 124 F2436 — NAT/G ADMIN BUDGET GOV/REL

S55
DIESING P.,"NONECONOMIC DECISION-MAKING" (BMR)" PROB/SOLV GP/REL ORD/FREE...STAT METH/COMP SIMUL 20. PAGE 33 F0638 — DECISION METH EFFICIENCY SOC

S55
KELLY W.E.,"HOW SALES EXECUTIVES USE FACTORING TO BOOST SALES AND PROFITS TODAY." FINAN LG/CO BUDGET EFFICIENCY PROFIT...MGT PRODUCT. PAGE 70 F1372 — INDUS ECO/DEV CONSULT MARKET

B56
BURKHEAD J.,GOVERNMENT BUDGETING. ECO/DEV PROB/SOLV ECO/TAC ADMIN ROUTINE GOV/REL EFFICIENCY...DECISION MGT. PAGE 20 F0388 — BUDGET NAT/G PROVS EX/STRUC

S56
BROWN J.S.,"UNION SIZE AS A FUNCTION OF INTRA-UNION CONFLICT." CLIENT CONTROL CHOOSE EFFICIENCY ATTIT TREND. PAGE 19 F0370 — LABOR INGP/REL CONSEN DRIVE

S56
LANDAUER J.D.,"PROFESSIONAL CONSULTANTS: A NEW FACTOR IN REAL ESTATE." USA+45 PROB/SOLV ECO/TAC PERS/REL DEMAND EFFICIENCY DECISION. PAGE 75 F1467 — CONSULT CONSTRUC CLIENT

S56
MARGOLIS J.,"ON MUNICIPAL LAND POLICY FOR FISCAL GAINS." USA+45 PLAN TAX COST EFFICIENCY HABITAT KNOWL...MGT MUNICH 20. PAGE 85 F1667 — BUDGET POLICY GEOG LOC/G

B57
GOLD N.L.,REGIONAL ECONOMIC DEVELOPMENT AND NUCLEAR POWER IN INDIA. FUT INDIA FINAN FOR/AID INT/TRADE BAL/PAY EFFICIENCY OPTIMAL PRODUC WEALTH...PREDICT 20. PAGE 48 F0934 — ECO/UNDEV TEC/DEV NUC/PWR INDUS

S57
ANSHEN M.,"BUSINESS, LAWYERS, AND ECONOMISTS." PROB/SOLV ECO/TAC CONFER PROFIT RIGID/FLEX OBJECTIVE...MGT GP/COMP. PAGE 6 F0106 — INDUS CONSULT ROUTINE EFFICIENCY

S57
DETAMBEL M.H.,"PROBABILITY AND WORK AS DETERMINERS OF MULTICHOICE BEHAVIOR." PLAN TASK EFFICIENCY ...DECISION GAME. PAGE 32 F0622 — HYPO/EXP PROB/SOLV GEN/LAWS PROBABIL

S57
ROURKE F.E.,"THE POLITICS OF ADMINISTRATIVE ORGANIZATION: A CASE HISTORY." USA+45 LABOR WORKER PLAN ADMIN TASK EFFICIENCY 20 DEPT/LABOR CONGRESS. PAGE 114 F2251 — POLICY ATTIT MGT GP/COMP

B58
CHEEK G.,ECONOMIC AND SOCIAL IMPLICATIONS OF AUTOMATION: A BIBLIOGRAPHIC REVIEW (PAMPHLET). USA+45 LG/CO WORKER CREATE PLAN CONTROL ROUTINE PERS/REL EFFICIENCY PRODUC...METH/COMP 20. PAGE 24 F0459 — BIBLIOG/A SOCIETY INDUS AUTOMAT

B58
COOK P.L.,EFFECTS OF MERGERS: SIX STUDIES. USA+45 ECO/DEV LABOR LG/CO SML/CO VOL/ASSN ADMIN EFFICIENCY 20 CASEBOOK. PAGE 27 F0529
INDUS FINAN EX/STRUC GP/REL

B58
DOWNIE J.,THE COMPETITIVE PROCESS. ECO/TAC PRICE EFFICIENCY OPTIMAL PRODUC WEALTH...IDEA/COMP METH/COMP 20 MONOPOLY. PAGE 34 F0658
EQUILIB MARKET INDUS ECO/DEV

B58
SCOTT D.J.R.,RUSSIAN POLITICAL INSTITUTIONS. RUSSIA USSR CONSTN AGRI DELIB/GP PLAN EDU/PROP CONTROL CHOOSE EFFICIENCY ATTIT MARXISM...BIBLIOG/A IND 13/20. PAGE 118 F2332
NAT/G POL/PAR ADMIN DECISION

B58
SILOW R.A.,THE POTENTIAL CONTRIBUTION OF ATOMIC ENERGY TO DEVELOPMENT IN AGRICULTURE AND RELATED INDUSTRIES (PAMPHLET). WOR+45 R+D TEC/DEV EFFICIENCY 20 UN. PAGE 122 F2403
NUC/PWR ECO/UNDEV AGRI

B58
THEIL H.,ECONOMIC FORECASTS AND POLICY. UNIV CAP/ISM PRICE EFFICIENCY...DECISION CONCPT STAT 20. PAGE 129 F2551
SIMUL MATH ECOMETRIC PREDICT

B58
US HOUSE COMM POST OFFICE,MANPOWER UTILIZATION IN THE FEDERAL GOVERNMENT. USA+45 DIST/IND EX/STRUC LEGIS CONFER EFFICIENCY 20 CONGRESS CIVIL/SERV. PAGE 137 F2702
ADMIN WORKER DELIB/GP NAT/G

B58
US HOUSE COMM POST OFFICE,MANPOWER UTILIZATION IN THE FEDERAL GOVERNMENT. USA+45 DIST/IND EX/STRUC LEGIS CONFER EFFICIENCY 20 CONGRESS CIVIL/SERV. PAGE 137 F2703
ADMIN WORKER DELIB/GP NAT/G

S58
MANSFIELD E.,"A STUDY OF DECISION-MAKING WITHIN THE FIRM." LG/CO WORKER INGP/REL COST EFFICIENCY PRODUC ...CHARTS 20. PAGE 85 F1658
OP/RES PROB/SOLV AUTOMAT ROUTINE

B59
BAUER P.T.,UNITED STATES AID AND INDIAN ECONOMIC DEVELOPMENT. INDIA STRATA FINAN PLAN BUDGET DIPLOM INGP/REL EFFICIENCY SOCISM 20 AID. PAGE 11 F0215
FOR/AID ECO/UNDEV ECO/TAC POLICY

B59
NOVE A.,COMMUNIST ECONOMIC STRATEGY: SOVIET GROWTH AND CAPABILITIES. USSR AGRI LABOR PLAN TEC/DEV CAP/ISM INT/TRADE EFFICIENCY MARXISM 20 THIRD/WRLD. PAGE 99 F1941
FOR/AID ECO/TAC DIPLOM INDUS

B59
SELIGSOHN I.J.,"USING COMPUTER SERVICES IN SMALL BUSINESS" MANAGEMENT AIDS FOR SMALL MANUFACTURERS 109 (PAMPHLET). DIST/IND MARKET PROC/MFG COST EFFICIENCY PRODUC...DECISION IDEA/COMP. PAGE 119 F2350
SML/CO COMPUTER MGT PROB/SOLV

B59
SHUBIK M.,STRATEGY AND MARKET STRUCTURE: COMPETITION, OLIGOPOLY, AND THE THEORY OF GAMES. ELITES STRUCT MARKET OP/RES EXEC EFFICIENCY INCOME ...MGT MATH STAT CHARTS 20. PAGE 121 F2389
ECO/DEV ECO/TAC DECISION GAME

B59
US GENERAL ACCOUNTING OFFICE,EXAM OF ECONOMIC AND TECHNICAL ASSISTANCE PROGRAM FOR INDIA INT'NAT'L COOP ADMIN REPORT TO CONGRESS 1955-1958. INDIA USA+45 ECO/UNDEV FINAN PLAN DIPLOM COST UTIL WEALTH ...CHARTS 20 CONGRESS AID. PAGE 136 F2679
FOR/AID EFFICIENCY ECO/TAC TEC/DEV

S59
BENDIX R.,"INDUSTRIALIZATION, IDEOLOGIES, AND SOCIAL STRUCTURE" (BMR)" UK USA-45 USSR STRUCT WORKER GP/REL EFFICIENCY...IDEA/COMP 20. PAGE 13 F0243
INDUS ATTIT MGT ADMIN

S59
SHEENAN D.,"PUBLIC CORPORATIONS AND PUBLIC ACTION." UK ADMIN CONTROL REPRESENT SOCISM 20. PAGE 120 F2372
ECO/DEV EFFICIENCY EX/STRUC EXEC

B60
BHAMBHRI C.P.,PARLIAMENTARY CONTROL OVER STATE ENTERPRISE IN INDIA. INDIA DELIB/GP ADMIN CONTROL INGP/REL EFFICIENCY 20 PARLIAMENT. PAGE 14 F0277
NAT/G OWN INDUS PARL/PROC

B60
BRYCE M.D.,INDUSTRIAL DEVELOPMENT: A GUIDE FOR ACCELERATING ECONOMIC GROWTH. WOR+45 FINAN MARKET COST EFFICIENCY PRODUC. PAGE 20 F0378
INDUS PLAN ECO/UNDEV TEC/DEV

B60
FRYE R.J.,GOVERNMENT AND LABOR: THE ALABAMA PROGRAM. USA+45 INDUS R+D LABOR WORKER BUDGET EFFICIENCY AGE/Y HEALTH...CHARTS 20 ALABAMA. PAGE 45 F0870
ADMIN LEGIS LOC/G PROVS

B60
HUGHES R.,THE CHINESE COMMUNES; A BACKGROUND BOOK. CHINA/COM SOCIETY CONTROL ROUTINE ADJUST EFFICIENCY PRODUC 20. PAGE 63 F1234
AGRI INDUS STRUCT

MARXISM

B60
NEALE A.D.,THE FLOW OF RESOURCES FROM RICH TO POOR. WOR+45 ECO/DEV ECO/UNDEV FINAN INDUS NAT/G PLAN EFFICIENCY WEALTH...POLICY NAT/COMP 20 RESOURCE/N. PAGE 97 F1905
FOR/AID DIPLOM METH/CNCPT

B60
PENNSYLVANIA ECONOMY LEAGUE,URBAN RENEWAL IMPACT STUDY: ADMINISTRATIVE-LEGAL-FISCAL. USA+45 FINAN LOC/G NEIGH ADMIN EFFICIENCY...CENSUS CHARTS MUNICH 20 PENNSYLVAN. PAGE 105 F2059
PLAN BUDGET ADJUD

B60
RAO V.K.R.,INTERNATIONAL AID FOR ECONOMIC DEVELOPMENT - POSSIBILITIES AND LIMITATIONS. FINAN PLAN TEC/DEV ADMIN TASK EFFICIENCY...POLICY SOC METH/CNCPT CHARTS 20 UN. PAGE 109 F2147
FOR/AID DIPLOM INT/ORG ECO/UNDEV

B60
ROBINSON E.A.G.,ECONOMIC CONSEQUENCES OF THE SIZE OF NATIONS. AGRI INDUS DELIB/GP FOR/AID ADMIN EFFICIENCY...METH/COMP 20. PAGE 113 F2218
CONCPT INT/ORG NAT/COMP

B60
SIEGEL S.,BARGAINING AND GROUP DECISION-MAKING: EXPERIMENTS IN BILATERAL MONOPOLY. EFFICIENCY...PSY CHARTS. PAGE 122 F2397
DECISION PERS/REL PROB/SOLV BARGAIN

B60
US HOUSE COMM GOVT OPERATIONS,OPERATIONS OF THE DEVELOPMENT LOAN FUND: HEARINGS (COMMITTEE ON GOVERNMENT OPERATIONS). USA+45 PLAN BUDGET DIPLOM GOV/REL COST...CHARTS 20 CONGRESS DEPT/STATE AID. PAGE 137 F2698
FINAN FOR/AID ECO/TAC EFFICIENCY

L60
FUCHS R.F.,"FAIRNESS AND EFFECTIVENESS IN ADMINISTRATIVE AGENCY ORGANIZATION AND PROCEDURES." USA+45 ADJUD ADMIN REPRESENT. PAGE 45 F0872
EFFICIENCY EX/STRUC EXEC POLICY

S60
FRENCH J.R.P. JR.,"AN EXPERIMENT ON PARTICIPATION IN A NORWEGIAN FACTORY:INTERPERSONAL DIMENSIONS OF DECISION-MAKING." LABOR LEAD PERS/REL EFFICIENCY PRODUC...DECISION SOC CHARTS SOC/EXP. PAGE 44 F0853
INDUS PLAN RIGID/FLEX GP/REL

B61
ALFRED H.,PUBLIC OWNERSHIP IN THE USA: GOALS AND PRIORITIES. LAW INDUS INT/TRADE ADJUD GOV/REL EFFICIENCY PEACE SOCISM...POLICY ANTHOL 20 TVA. PAGE 4 F0065
CONTROL OWN ECO/DEV ECO/TAC

B61
BAUER P.T.,INDIAN ECONOMIC POLICY AND DEVELOPMENT. INDIA STRATA AGRI FINAN POL/PAR BUDGET FOR/AID GOV/REL EFFICIENCY...CENSUS 20. PAGE 11 F0216
ECO/UNDEV ECO/TAC POLICY PLAN

B61
DOIG J.W.,THE POLITICS OF METROPOLITAN TRANSPORTATION. DELIB/GP WORKER DIPLOM TASK EFFICIENCY UTIL...CHARTS BIBLIOG MUNICH 20 NEW/YORK NEW/JERSEY PUB/TRANS RAILROAD. PAGE 34 F0652
PROB/SOLV STRATA DIST/IND

B61
FILLOL T.R.,SOCIAL FACTORS IN ECONOMIC DEVELOPMENT: THE ARGENTINE CASE. STRUCT INDUS LABOR CREATE TEC/DEV EFFICIENCY PRODUC DRIVE...METH/CNCPT METH/COMP BIBLIOG/A 20 ARGEN. PAGE 41 F0795
ECO/UNDEV MGT PERS/REL TREND

B61
GOODWIN C.D.W.,CANADIAN ECONOMIC THOUGHT. CANADA STRATA TEC/DEV CAP/ISM TARIFFS TAX COST EFFICIENCY WEALTH...METH/CNCPT TREND 20 MARITIME ONTARIO. PAGE 49 F0952
INT/TRADE ECO/DEV FINAN DEMAND

B61
MACMAHON A.W.,DELEGATION AND AUTONOMY. INDIA STRUCT LEGIS BARGAIN BUDGET ECO/TAC LEGIT EXEC REPRESENT GOV/REL CENTRAL DEMAND EFFICIENCY PRODUC. PAGE 84 F1637
ADMIN PLAN FEDERAL

B61
MCCRACKEN H.L.,KEYNESIAN ECONOMICS IN THE STREAM OF ECONOMIC THOUGHT. FINAN MARKET BARGAIN EFFICIENCY OPTIMAL...PHIL/SCI CONCPT IDEA/COMP BIBLIOG 18/20 KEYNES/JM. PAGE 88 F1724
ECO/TAC DEMAND ECOMETRIC

B61
NOVE A.,THE SOVIET ECONOMY. USSR ECO/DEV FINAN NAT/G ECO/TAC PRICE ADMIN EFFICIENCY MARXISM ...TREND BIBLIOG 20. PAGE 99 F1943
PLAN PRODUC POLICY

B61
PETCH G.A.,ECONOMIC DEVELOPMENT AND MODERN WEST AFRICA. AFR CONGO/BRAZ GHANA NIGER SIER/LEONE AGRI MARKET LABOR FOR/AID TAX COST EFFICIENCY EQUILIB PRODUC...GEOG TREND 20. PAGE 105 F2068
ECO/UNDEV TEC/DEV EXTR/IND ECO/TAC

L61
CHENERY H.B.,"COMPARATIVE ADVANTAGE AND DEVELOPMENT POLICY." FINAN INT/TRADE RATION OPTIMAL...CHARTS METH/COMP GEN/LAWS BIBLIOG 20 RESOURCE/N. PAGE 24 F0463
ECO/UNDEV ECO/TAC PLAN EFFICIENCY

S61
CYERT R.M.,"TWO EXPERIMENTS ON BIAS AND CONFLICT IN ORGANIZATIONAL ESTIMATION." WORKER PROB/SOLV EFFICIENCY...MGT PSY STAT CHARTS. PAGE 29 F0568
LAB/EXP ROUTINE ADMIN DECISION

C61
FILLOL T.R.,"SOCIAL FACTORS IN ECONOMIC DEVELOPMENT: THE ARGENTINE CASE" INDUS LABOR CREATE TEC/DEV PERS/REL EFFICIENCY PRODUC DRIVE ...METH/CNCPT METH/COMP 20 ARGEN. PAGE 41 F0794
BIBLIOG ECO/UNDEV MGT TREND

B62
BRIEFS H.W.,PRICING POWER AND "ADMINISTRATIVE" INFLATION (PAMPHLET). AFR USA+45 PROC/MFG CONTROL EFFICIENCY MONEY. PAGE 18 F0349
ECO/DEV PRICE POLICY EXEC

B62
COPPOCK J.D.,INTERNATIONAL ECONOMIC INSTABILITY: THE EXPERIENCE AFTER WORLD WAR II. WOR+45 FINAN CAP/ISM CONTROL EFFICIENCY...CHARTS 20. PAGE 28 F0536
ECO/TAC ECOMETRIC INT/TRADE STAT

B62
DUPRE J.S.,SCIENCE AND THE NATION: POLICY AND POLITICS. USA+45 LAW ACADEM FORCES ADMIN CIVMIL/REL GOV/REL EFFICIENCY PEACE...TREND 20 SCI/ADVSRY. PAGE 35 F0682
R+D INDUS TEC/DEV NUC/PWR

B62
FAO,FOOD AND AGRICULTURE ORGANIZATION AFRICAN SURVEY. AFR CONGO/BRAZ GHANA STRATA AGRI INT/ORG TEC/DEV FOR/AID INT/TRADE RACE/REL DEMAND EFFICIENCY PRODUC...GEOG 20 UN CONGO/LEOP. PAGE 39 F0763
ECO/TAC WEALTH EXTR/IND ECO/UNDEV

B62
FORD A.G.,THE GOLD STANDARD 1880-1914: BRITAIN AND ARGENTINA. AFR UK ECO/UNDEV INT/TRADE ADMIN GOV/REL DEMAND EFFICIENCY...STAT CHARTS 19/20 ARGEN. PAGE 42 F0823
FINAN ECO/TAC BUDGET BAL/PAY

B62
HATTERY L.H.,INFORMATION RETRIEVAL MANAGEMENT. CLIENT INDUS TOP/EX COMPUTER OP/RES TEC/DEV ROUTINE COST EFFICIENCY RIGID/FLEX...METH/COMP ANTHOL 20. PAGE 57 F1113
R+D COMPUT/IR MGT CREATE

B62
KUHN T.E.,PUBLIC ENTERPRISES, PROJECT PLANNING AND ECONOMIC DEVELOPMENT (PAMPHLET). ECO/UNDEV FINAN PLAN ADMIN EFFICIENCY OWN...MGT STAT CHARTS ANTHOL 20. PAGE 74 F1447
ECO/DEV ECO/TAC LG/CO NAT/G

B62
MARTINS A.F.,REVOLUCAO BRANCA NO CAMPO. L/A+17C SERV/IND DEMAND EFFICIENCY PRODUC...POLICY METH/COMP. PAGE 86 F1685
AGRI ECO/UNDEV TEC/DEV NAT/COMP

B62
MEANS G.C.,PRICING POWER AND THE PUBLIC INTEREST. PLAN PROB/SOLV COST EFFICIENCY PROFIT RIGID/FLEX WEALTH. PAGE 89 F1741
LG/CO EX/STRUC PRICE ECO/TAC

B62
NATIONAL BUREAU ECONOMIC RES,THE RATE AND DIRECTION OF INVENTIVE ACTIVITY: ECONOMIC AND SOCIAL FACTORS. STRUCT INDUS MARKET R+D CREATE OP/RES TEC/DEV EFFICIENCY PRODUC RATIONAL UTIL...WELF/ST PHIL/SCI METH/CNCPT TIME. PAGE 97 F1895
DECISION PROB/SOLV MGT

B62
PONCET J.,LA COLONISATION ET L'AGRICULTURE EUROPEENNES EN TUNISIE DEPUIS 1881. FRANCE WORKER TEC/DEV ECO/TAC CONTROL EFFICIENCY ROLE WEALTH 19/20 TUNIS. PAGE 107 F2101
ECO/UNDEV AGRI COLONIAL FINAN

B62
PRAKASH O.M.,THE THEORY AND WORKING OF STATE CORPORATIONS: WITH SPECIAL REFERENCE TO INDIA. INDIA UK USA+45 TOP/EX PRICE ADMIN EFFICIENCY...MGT METH/COMP 20 TVA. PAGE 107 F2112
LG/CO ECO/UNDEV GOV/REL SOCISM

B62
SHINOHARA M.,GROWTH AND CYCLES IN THE JAPANESE ECONOMY. INDUS LABOR TEC/DEV CAP/ISM INT/TRADE PAY COST EFFICIENCY INCOME WEALTH...METH/COMP 20 CHINJAP. PAGE 121 F2380
PRODUC ECO/DEV EQUILIB ECOMETRIC

B62
SIEVERS A.M.,REVOLUTION, EVOLUTION AND THE ECONOMIC ORDER. INDUS LABOR TAX CONTROL REV WAR DEMAND PRODUC WEALTH...IDEA/COMP 19/20 KEYNES/JM. PAGE 122 F2399
EFFICIENCY ALL/IDEOS ECO/DEV WELF/ST

B62
SMITH G.A. JR.,POLICY FORMULATION AND ADMINISTRATION: A CASEBOOK OF TOPMANAGEMENT PROBLEMS IN BUSINESS. EX/STRUC PLAN PROB/SOLV ADMIN CONTROL EXEC LEAD ROUTINE EFFICIENCY ATTIT MGT. PAGE 123 F2430
INDUS SOC/EXP TOP/EX DECISION

B62
SRIVASTAVA G.L.,COLLECTIVE BARGAINING AND LABOR-MANAGEMENT RELATIONS IN INDIA. INDIA UK USA+45 INDUS LEGIS WORKER ADJUD EFFICIENCY PRODUC ...METH/COMP 20. PAGE 125 F2462
LABOR MGT BARGAIN GP/REL

B62
US CONGRESS JOINT ECO COMM,ECONOMIC DEVELOPMENTS IN SOUTH AMERICA. USA+45 SOCIETY FINAN NAT/G PROB/SOLV TEC/DEV INT/TRADE TAX EFFICIENCY PRODUC ATTIT ...POLICY 20 ALL/PROG CONGRESS SOUTH/AMER. PAGE 135 F2654
L/A+17C ECO/UNDEV FOR/AID DIPLOM

B62
WRIGHT D.M.,THE KEYNESIAN SYSTEM. WOR+45 WOR-45 LABOR NAT/G CONTROL COST DEMAND EFFICIENCY...POLICY CONCPT CHARTS SIMUL 20 KEYNES/JM. PAGE 149 F2931
INCOME ECO/DEV FINAN ECO/TAC

S62
BIERMAN H.,"PROBABILITY, STATISTICAL DECISION THEORY, AND ACCOUNTING." ACADEM TASK EFFICIENCY ...METH/CNCPT GEN/METH 20. PAGE 15 F0283
FINAN QUANT DECISION STAT

S62
GILL P.J.,"FUTURE TAXATION POLICY IN AN INDEPENDENT EAST AFRICA" UGANDA LOC/G ECO/TAC ADMIN EFFICIENCY INCOME PRODUC...CHARTS 20. PAGE 47 F0923
ECO/UNDEV TAX AFR COLONIAL

N62
BANK INTERNATIONAL SETTLEMENTS,AUSTRIA: MONETARY AND ECONOMIC SITUATION 1952-61 (PAMPHLET). AUSTRIA WORKER BUDGET INT/TRADE PRICE BAL/PAY DEMAND EFFICIENCY INCOME PRODUC...STAT 20 SILVER. PAGE 9 F0174
FINAN ECO/DEV CHARTS WEALTH

B63
CALKINS R.D.,ECONOMICS AS AN AID TO POLICY (PAMPHLET). USA+45 NAT/G LEAD 20. PAGE 21 F0401
CONSULT DECISION EFFICIENCY

B63
COLUMBIA U SCHOOL OF LAW,PUBLIC INTERNATIONAL DEVELOPMENT FINANCING IN SENEGAL. SENEGAL FINAN DELIB/GP GIVE EFFICIENCY...CHARTS GOV/COMP ANTHOL 20. PAGE 26 F0511
FOR/AID PLAN RECEIVE ECO/UNDEV

B63
DUE J.F.,STATE SALES TAX ADMINISTRATION. OP/RES BUDGET PAY ADMIN EXEC ROUTINE COST EFFICIENCY PROFIT...CHARTS METH/COMP 20. PAGE 34 F0671
PROVS TAX STAT GOV/COMP

B63
GANGULY D.S.,PUBLIC CORPORATIONS IN A NATIONAL ECONOMY. INDIA WOR+45 FINAN INDUS TOP/EX PRICE EFFICIENCY...MGT STAT CHARTS BIBLIOG 20. PAGE 46 F0897
ECO/UNDEV LG/CO SOCISM GOV/REL

B63
LETHBRIDGE H.J.,THE PEASANT AND THE COMMUNES. CHINA/COM COM USSR NEIGH PROB/SOLV ADJUST EFFICIENCY...POLICY METH/COMP NAT/COMP 20. PAGE 78 F1535
MARXISM ECO/TAC AGRI WORKER

B63
MCDONOUGH A.M.,INFORMATION ECONOMICS AND MANAGEMENT SYSTEMS. ECO/DEV OP/RES AUTOMAT EFFICIENCY 20. PAGE 88 F1726
COMPUT/IR MGT CONCPT COMPUTER

B63
MEYNAUD J.,PLANIFICATION ET POLITIQUE. FRANCE ITALY FINAN LABOR DELIB/GP LEGIS ADMIN EFFICIENCY ...MAJORIT DECISION 20. PAGE 90 F1773
PLAN ECO/TAC PROB/SOLV

B63
ROPKE W.,ECONOMICS OF THE FREE SOCIETY. FINAN INT/TRADE BAL/PAY COST DEMAND EFFICIENCY ORD/FREE WEALTH...CON/ANAL METH/COMP T 20 KEYNES/JM. PAGE 114 F2240
SOCIETY BUDGET ECO/DEV ECO/TAC

B63
STIFEL L.D.,THE TEXTILE INDUSTRY - A CASE STUDY OF INDUSTRIAL DEVELOPMENT IN THE PHILIPPINES (PAPER). PHILIPPINE WORKER CAP/ISM INT/TRADE TARIFFS RECEIVE PRICE ADMIN COST EFFICIENCY WEALTH...BIBLIOG 20. PAGE 126 F2486
S/ASIA ECO/UNDEV PROC/MFG NAT/G

B63
US CONGRESS JOINT ECO COMM,OUTLOOK FOR UNITED STATES BALANCE OF PAYMENTS. AFR USA+45 ECO/DEV NAT/G FORCES DIPLOM FOR/AID COST EFFICIENCY ...POLICY CONGRESS EEC. PAGE 135 F2657
BAL/PAY FINAN INT/TRADE PROB/SOLV

B63
US GOVERNMENT,REPORT TO INTER-AMERICAN ECONOMIC AND SOCIAL COUNCIL AT SECOND ANNUAL MEETING. L/A+17C USA+45 VOL/ASSN TEC/DEV DIPLOM TAX EATING EFFICIENCY HEALTH...STAT CHARTS 20 AID. PAGE 136 F2682
ECO/TAC FOR/AID FINAN PLAN

B63
US SENATE COMM GOVT OPERATIONS,REPORT OF A STUDY OF US FOREIGN AID IN TEN MIDDLE EASTERN AND AFRICAN COUNTRIES. AFR ISLAM USA+45 FORCES PLAN BUDGET DIPLOM TAX DETER WEALTH...STAT CHARTS 20 CONGRESS AID MID/EAST. PAGE 138 F2728
FOR/AID EFFICIENCY ECO/TAC FINAN

B63
VON BECKERATH E.,PROBLEME DER NORMATIVEN OKONOMIK UND DER WIRTSCHAFTSPOLITISCHEN BERATUNG. GERMANY UK ELITES CAP/ISM EFFICIENCY...CONCPT GOV/COMP IDEA/COMP 20. PAGE 142 F2789
ECO/TAC DELIB/GP ECO/DEV CONSULT

B63
WALKER F.V.,GROWTH, EMPLOYMENT, AND THE PRICE LEVEL. USA+45 NAT/G PLAN ECO/TAC DEMAND EFFICIENCY CHARTS. PAGE 142 F2803
ECO/DEV FINAN PRICE WORKER

S63
CLARK P.G.,"TOWARDS MORE COMPREHENSIVE PLANNING IN EAST AFRICA" AFR OP/RES ECO/TAC RATION TAX EFFICIENCY INCOME...MATH TREND CHARTS 20 AFRICA/E. PAGE 25 F0484
ECO/UNDEV PLAN STAT METH/COMP

S63
NYE J.,"TANGANYIKA'S SELF-HELP." TANZANIA NAT/G GIVE COST EFFICIENCY NAT/LISM 20. PAGE 99 F1948
ECO/TAC POL/PAR ECO/UNDEV WORKER

N63
US AGENCY INTERNATIONAL DEV,PRINCIPLES OF FOREIGN ECONOMIC ASSISTANCE (PAMPHLET). USA+45 FINAN GP/REL BAL/PAY EFFICIENCY 20 AID. PAGE 134 F2638
FOR/AID PLAN ECO/UNDEV ATTIT

B64
CENTRO ESTUDIOS MONETARIOS LAT,PROBLEMAS DE PAGOS EN AMERICA LATINA. L/A+17C MARKET BUDGET ECO/TAC EFFICIENCY WEALTH 20 CENTRAL/AM. PAGE 22 F0434
FINAN INT/TRADE BAL/PAY ECO/UNDEV

B64
COMMISSION ON MONEY AND CREDIT,INFLATION, GROWTH, AND EMPLOYMENT. AFR USA+45 PLAN PROB/SOLV PAY PRICE EFFICIENCY PRODUC WEALTH 20. PAGE 26 F0514
WORKER ECO/TAC OPTIMAL

B64
ECONOMIDES C.P.,LE POUVOIR DE DECISION DES ORGANISATIONS INTERNATIONALES EUROPEENNES. DIPLOM DOMIN INGP/REL EFFICIENCY...INT/LAW JURID 20 NATO OEEC EEC COUNCL/EUR EURATOM. PAGE 36 F0698
INT/ORG PWR DECISION GP/COMP

B64
FITCH L.C.,URBAN TRANSPORTATION AND PUBLIC POLICY. FINAN NAT/G LEGIS PROB/SOLV TEC/DEV PRICE COST EFFICIENCY...DECISION STAT CHARTS METH/COMP MUNICH 20 NEWYORK/C PHILADELPH LOS/ANG CHICAGO WASHING/DC. PAGE 41 F0806
DIST/IND PLAN LOC/G

B64
HAAR C.M.,LAW AND LAND: ANGLO-AMERICAN PLANNING PRACTICE. UK USA+45 NAT/G TEC/DEV BUDGET CT/SYS INGP/REL EFFICIENCY OWN...JURID MUNICH 20. PAGE 52 F1019
LAW PLAN NAT/COMP

B64
HATHAWAY D.E.,PROBLEMS OF PROGRESS IN THE AGRICULTURAL ECONOMY. USA+45 USA-45 ECO/DEV NAT/G INT/TRADE PRICE DEMAND EFFICIENCY OPTIMAL 20. PAGE 57 F1112
AGRI ECO/TAC MARKET PLAN

B64
LETICHE J.M.,A HISTORY OF RUSSIAN ECONOMIC THOUGHT: NINTH THROUGH EIGHTEENTH CENTURIES. RUSSIA FINAN SECT CAP/ISM DOMIN DEMAND EFFICIENCY OWN MARXISM ...TECHNIC ANTHOL BIBLIOG 9/18. PAGE 78 F1536
ECO/TAC TIME/SEQ IDEA/COMP ECO/UNDEV

B64
LITVAK I.A.,MARKETING: CANADA. CANADA STRATA PROC/MFG LEGIS TEC/DEV DIPLOM INT/TRADE PRICE AUTOMAT ATTIT WEALTH...ANTHOL 20. PAGE 81 F1587
ECO/TAC MARKET ECO/DEV EFFICIENCY

B64
MANSFIELD E.,MONOPOLY POWER AND ECONOMIC PERFORMANCE: AN INTRODUCTION TO A CURRENT ISSUE OF PUBLIC POLICY. ECO/DEV INDUS NAT/G PLAN CAP/ISM PRICE CONTROL LOBBY EFFICIENCY PRODUC...POLICY 20 CONGRESS KENNEDY/JF MONOPOLY. PAGE 85 F1659
LG/CO PWR ECO/TAC MARKET

B64
MEISEL J.,PAPERS ON THE 1962 ELECTION. CANADA PROVS SECT GP/REL CONSEN EFFICIENCY...MAJORIT 20. PAGE 89 F1751
POL/PAR RECORD CHOOSE STRATA

B64
STRONG A.L.,THE RISE OF THE CHINESE PEOPLE'S COMMUNES - AND SIX YEARS AFTER (2ND ED.). CHINA/COM AGRI INDUS FORCES WORKER PROB/SOLV EDU/PROP EFFICIENCY ISOLAT 20. PAGE 127 F2503
NEIGH ECO/TAC MARXISM METH/COMP

B64
THAILAND NATIONAL ECO DEV,THE NATIONAL ECONOMIC DEVELOPMENT PLAN: 1961-66: SECOND PHASE 1964-66. THAILAND AGRI FINAN BUDGET EFFICIENCY INCOME...STAT CHARTS 20. PAGE 129 F2547
ECO/UNDEV ECO/TAC PLAN NAT/G

B64
US HOUSE COMM BANKING-CURR,INTERNATIONAL DEVELOPMENT ASSOCIATION ACT AMENDMENT. CHINA/COM USA+45 USSR FINAN FORCES LEGIS DIPLOM CONFER EFFICIENCY...CHARTS GOV/COMP 20 PRESIDENT CONGRESS INTL/DEV. PAGE 136 F2689
BAL/PAY FOR/AID RECORD ECO/TAC

B64
US HOUSE COMM GOVT OPERATIONS,US OWNED FOREIGN CURRENCIES: HEARINGS (COMMITTEE ON GOVERNMENT OPERATIONS). INDIA ECO/DEV PLAN BUDGET TAX DEMAND EFFICIENCY 20 AID CONGRESS. PAGE 137 F2699
FINAN ECO/TAC FOR/AID OWN

B64
US SENATE COMM ON JUDICIARY,HEARINGS BEFORE SUBCOMMITTEE ON ANTITRUST AND MONOPOLY: ECONOMIC CONCENTRATION VOLUMES 1-5 JULY 1964-SEPT 1966. USA+45 LAW FINAN ECO/TAC ADJUD COST EFFICIENCY PRODUC...STAT CHARTS 20 CONGRESS MONOPOLY. PAGE 140 F2749
ECO/DEV CONTROL MARKET LG/CO

B64
WELLISZ S.,THE ECONOMICS OF THE SOVIET BLOC. COM USSR INDUS WORKER PLAN BUDGET INT/TRADE TAX PRICE PRODUC WEALTH MARXISM...METH/COMP 20. PAGE 145 F2854
EFFICIENCY ADMIN MARKET

B64
WILLIAMSON O.E.,THE ECONOMICS OF DISCRETIONARY BEHAVIOR: MANAGERIAL OBJECTIVES IN A THEORY OF THE FIRM. MARKET BUDGET CAP/ISM PRODUC DRIVE PERSON ...STAT CHARTS BIBLIOG METH 20. PAGE 147 F2897
EFFICIENCY MGT ECO/TAC CHOOSE

B65
ANALYSIS AND ASSESSMENT OF THE ECONOMIC EFFECTS: PUBLIC LAW 480 TITLE I PROGRAM TURKEY. INDIA TURKEY USA+45 AGRI NAT/G PLAN BUDGET DIPLOM COST EFFICIENCY...CHARTS 20. PAGE 1 F0021
ECO/TAC FOR/AID FINAN ECO/UNDEV

B65
COLLOQUE SUR LA PLANIFICATION,LA PLANIFICATION COMME PROCESSUS DE DECISION. FRANCE SOCIETY MARKET LABOR LEGIS GP/REL EFFICIENCY INCOME ATTIT TECHRACY ...MYTH IDEA/COMP 20. PAGE 26 F0508
PLAN ECO/TAC PROB/SOLV

B65
CONLEY R.W.,THE ECONOMICS OF VOCATIONAL REHABILITATION. USA+45 VOL/ASSN CREATE EDU/PROP COST EFFICIENCY SOC/INTEG 20. PAGE 27 F0527
PUB/INST HEALTH GIVE GP/REL

B65
COOMBS P.H.,EDUCATION AND FOREIGN AID. AFR USA+45 DIPLOM EFFICIENCY KNOWL ORD/FREE...ANTHOL 20 AID. PAGE 27 F0532
EDU/PROP FOR/AID SCHOOL ECO/UNDEV

B65
DELHI INSTITUTE OF ECO GROWTH,A STUDY IN THE WORKING OF THE INTENSIVE AREA SCHEME OF THE KHADI AND VILLAGE INDUSTRIES COMMISSION. INDIA AGRI FINAN DELIB/GP ECO/TAC EFFICIENCY...QU CHARTS MUNICH 20. PAGE 32 F0614
PLAN INDUS ECO/UNDEV

B65
DEMAS W.G.,THE ECONOMICS OF DEVELOPMENT IN SMALL COUNTRIES WITH SPECIAL REFERENCE TO THE CARIBBEAN. WOR+45 BAL/PAY DEMAND EFFICIENCY PRODUC...GEOG CARIBBEAN. PAGE 32 F0618
ECO/UNDEV PLAN WEALTH INT/TRADE

B65
HAEFELE E.T.,GOVERNMENT CONTROLS ON TRANSPORT. AFR RHODESIA TANZANIA DIPLOM ECO/TAC TARIFFS PRICE ADJUD CONTROL REGION EFFICIENCY...POLICY 20 CONGO. PAGE 53 F1031
ECO/UNDEV DIST/IND FINAN NAT/G

B65
KANTOROVICH L.V.,THE BEST USE OF ECONOMIC RESOURCES. USSR SOCIETY FINAN ACT/RES TEC/DEV ECO/TAC PRICE CONTROL COST DEMAND EFFICIENCY OPTIMAL...MGT STAT. PAGE 69 F1350
PLAN MATH DECISION

B65
MARCUS E.,INTERNATIONAL TRADE AND FINANCE. EFFICIENCY EQUILIB...CHARTS METH/COMP BIBLIOG METH T 20. PAGE 85 F1664
INT/TRADE FINAN MARKET WEALTH

B65
MARK S.M.,ECONOMICS IN ACTION (3RD ED.). USA+45 ECO/UNDEV AGRI INDUS FOR/AID INT/TRADE BAL/PAY COST ORD/FREE...ANTHOL 20 RESOURCE/N. PAGE 85 F1670
POLICY ECO/TAC EFFICIENCY PRICE

B65
MELMANS S.,OUR DEPLETED SOCIETY. AFR SPACE USA+45 ECO/DEV FORCES BUDGET ECO/TAC ADMIN WEAPON EFFICIENCY 20. PAGE 89 F1753
CIVMIL/REL INDUS EDU/PROP CONTROL

B65
MURUMBI J.,PROBLEMS OF ECONOMIC DEVELOPMENT IN EAST AFRICA. FINAN INDUS WORKER TEC/DEV INT/TRADE TAX DEMAND EFFICIENCY PRODUC SOCISM...TREND CHARTS 20 AFRICA/E. PAGE 95 F1869
AGRI ECO/TAC ECO/UNDEV PROC/MFG

B65
O'BRIEN F.,CRISIS IN WORLD COMMUNISM* MARXISM IN SEARCH OF EFFICIENCY. AFR COM ECO/DEV PLAN INT/TRADE WAR ADJUST PEACE...STAT TIME/SEQ GOV/COMP NAT/COMP. PAGE 99 F1951
MARXISM USSR DRIVE EFFICIENCY

B65
THAYER F.C. JR.,AIR TRANSPORT POLICY AND NATIONAL SECURITY: A POLITICAL, ECONOMIC, AND MILITARY ANALYSIS. DIST/IND OP/RES PLAN TEC/DEV DIPLOM DETER WAR COST EFFICIENCY...POLICY BIBLIOG 20 DEPT/DEFEN FAA CAB. PAGE 129 F2548
AIR FORCES CIVMIL/REL ORD/FREE

B65
WARD R.,BACKGROUND MATERIAL ON ECONOMIC IMPACT OF FEDERAL PROCUREMENT - 1965: FOR JOINT ECONOMIC COMMITTEE US CONGRESS. FINAN ROUTINE WEAPON CIVMIL/REL EFFICIENCY...STAT CHARTS 20 CONGRESS. PAGE 143 F2818
ECO/DEV NAT/G OWN GOV/REL

B65
WASSERMAN M.J.,THE BALANCE OF PAYMENTS: HISTORY, METHODOLOGY, THEORY. UK USA+45 USA-45 CAP/ISM DIPLOM EFFICIENCY...DECISION METH/CNCPT BIBLIOG 18/20 LEAGUE/NAT. PAGE 144 F2828
BAL/PAY ECO/TAC GEN/LAWS EQUILIB

B65
WU YUAN-LI,THE ECONOMY OF COMMUNIST CHINA. CHINA/COM USSR AGRI FINAN INDUS POL/PAR WORKER PROB/SOLV INT/TRADE PRICE EATING INCOME OWN WEALTH 20. PAGE 149 F2939
ECO/TAC MARXISM PLAN EFFICIENCY

L65
HAGE J.,"AN AXIOMATIC THEORY OF ORGANIZATIONS" USA+45 STRUCT LABOR PRODUC DRIVE PERSON RIGID/FLEX 20 WEBER/MAX. PAGE 53 F1032
GP/REL EFFICIENCY PROF/ORG ATTIT

S65
GOLDMAN M.I.,"A BALANCE SHEET OF SOVIET FOREIGN AID." USA+45 ECO/UNDEV BAL/PWR ECO/TAC RENT GIVE EDU/PROP CONTROL COST PROFIT GEN/METH. PAGE 48 F0939
USSR FOR/AID NAT/COMP EFFICIENCY

S65
GRENIEWSKI H.,"INTENTION AND PERFORMANCE: A PRIMER OF CYBERNETICS OF PLANNING." EFFICIENCY OPTIMAL KNOWL SKILL...DECISION MGT EQULIB. PAGE 51 F0995
SIMUL GAME GEN/METH PLAN

B66
ALEXANDER Y.,INTERNATIONAL TECHNICAL ASSISTANCE EXPERTS* A CASE STUDY OF THE U.N. EXPERIENCE. ECO/UNDEV CONSULT EX/STRUC CREATE PLAN DIPLOM FOR/AID TASK EFFICIENCY...ORG/CHARTS UN. PAGE 3 F0061
ECO/TAC INT/ORG ADMIN MGT

B66
CURRIE L.,ACCELERATING DEVELOPMENT: THE NECESSITY AND MEANS. COLOMBIA USA+45 INDUS DIPLOM EFFICIENCY WEALTH...METH/CNCPT NEW/IDEA 20. PAGE 29 F0564
PLAN ECO/UNDEV FOR/AID TEC/DEV

B66
GOODMAN L.H.,ECONOMIC PROGRESS AND SOCIAL WELFARE. USA+45 STRATA STRUCT ECO/TAC EFFICIENCY...MGT 20. PAGE 49 F0949
SOC/WK RECEIVE GP/COMP POLICY

B66
INARRITU A.L.,EL PATRON CAMBIO-ORO Y SUS REFORMAS. AFR L/A+17C WOR+45 PLAN PROB/SOLV BUDGET ECO/TAC INT/TRADE EFFICIENCY ORD/FREE 20 MEXIC/AMER. PAGE 64 F1262
ECO/UNDEV FINAN DIPLOM POLICY

B66
KUZNETS S.,MODERN ECONOMIC GROWTH. WOR+45 WOR-45 ECO/DEV ECO/UNDEV AGRI FINAN INDUS TEC/DEV EFFICIENCY INCOME...NAT/COMP 19/20. PAGE 74 F1456
TIME/SEQ WEALTH PRODUC

B66
LICHTMAN R.,TOWARD COMMUNITY (PAPER). PLAN PROB/SOLV WEALTH MARXISM...HEAL CONCPT 20. PAGE 80 F1561
NEW/LIB EFFICIENCY CAP/ISM ADJUST

B66
MANSFIELD E.,MANAGERIAL ECONOMICS AND OPERATIONS RESEARCH; A NONMATHEMATICAL INTRODUCTION. USA+45 ELITES ECO/DEV CONSULT EX/STRUC PROB/SOLV ROUTINE EFFICIENCY OPTIMAL...GAME T 20. PAGE 85 F1660
ECO/TAC OP/RES MGT COMPUTER

B66
NATIONAL COUN APPLIED ECO RES,DEVELOPMENT WITHOUT AID. INDIA FINAN TEC/DEV EFFICIENCY...ANTHOL 20. PAGE 97 F1901
FOR/AID PLAN SOVEREIGN ECO/UNDEV

B66
RAPHAEL J.S.,GOVERNMENTAL REGULATION OF BUSINESS. USA+45 LAW CONSTN TAX ADJUD ADMIN EFFICIENCY PWR 20. PAGE 109 F2150
LG/CO GOV/REL CONTROL ECO/DEV

B66
US SENATE COMM GOVT OPERATIONS,INTERGOVERNMENTAL PERSONNEL ACT OF 1966. USA+45 NAT/G CONSULT DELIB/GP WORKER TEC/DEV PAY AUTOMAT UTIL 20 CONGRESS. PAGE 139 F2730
ADMIN LEGIS EFFICIENCY EDU/PROP

B66
WESTON J.F.,THE SCOPE AND METHODOLOGY OF FINANCE. PLAN TEC/DEV CONTROL EFFICIENCY INCOME UTIL...MGT CONCPT MATH STAT TREND METH 20. PAGE 145 F2863
FINAN ECO/DEV POLICY PRICE

B66
WETTER G.A.,SOVIET IDEOLOGY TODAY. USSR ECO/UNDEV SECT WORKER CAP/ISM CONTROL TASK EFFICIENCY TOTALISM DRIVE WEALTH...TREND 18/20. PAGE 145 F2864
ALL/IDEOS MARXISM REV

B66
WOODMAN H.D.,SLAVERY AND THE SOUTHERN ECONOMY: SOURCES AND READINGS. USA-45 CULTURE STRUCT AGRI ECO/TAC LEAD RACE/REL DISCRIM EFFICIENCY...CHARTS ANTHOL MUNICH 18/19 NEGRO SOUTH/US. PAGE 148 F2922
ECO/DEV STRATA WORKER UTIL

B66
YOUNG S.,MANAGEMENT: A SYSTEMS ANALYSIS. DELIB/GP EX/STRUC ECO/TAC CONTROL EFFICIENCY...NET/THEORY 20. PAGE 150 F2952
PROB/SOLV MGT DECISION SIMUL

L66
AFRICAN BIBLIOGRAPHIC CENTER,"AFRICAN ECONOMIC AFFAIRS: A SELECT BIBLIOGRAPHICAL SURVEY, 1965-1966." AFR FINAN INDUS INT/ORG LABOR PLAN BUDGET DIPLOM INT/TRADE ADMIN EFFICIENCY WEALTH 20. PAGE 3 F0046
BIBLIOG ECO/UNDEV TEC/DEV FOR/AID

L66
CHENERY H.B.,"FOREIGN ASSISTANCE AND ECONOMIC DEVELOPMENT" FUT WOR+45 NAT/G DIPLOM GIVE PRODUC ...METH/CNCPT CHARTS 20. PAGE 24 F0464
FOR/AID EFFICIENCY ECO/UNDEV TEC/DEV

S66
DAVIS O.A.,"A THEORY OF THE BUDGETARY PROCESS." ECO/DEV FINAN LEGIS PROB/SOLV GOV/REL...ECOMETRIC METH/CNCPT STAT CONT/OBS TREND METH/COMP SIMUL 20 CONGRESS. PAGE 30 F0592
DECISION NAT/G BUDGET EFFICIENCY

S66
FLEMING W.G.,"AUTHORITY, EFFICIENCY, AND ROLE STRESS: PROBLEMS IN THE DEVELOPMENT OF EAST AFRICAN BUREAUCRACIES." AFR UGANDA STRUCT PROB/SOLV ROUTINE INGP/REL ROLE...MGT SOC GP/COMP GOV/COMP 20 TANGANYIKA AFRICA/E. PAGE 41 F0810
DOMIN EFFICIENCY COLONIAL ADMIN

S66
JAVITS J.K.,"POLITICAL ACTION VITAL FOR LATIN AMERICAN INTEGRATION." ECO/UNDEV INT/ORG POL/PAR VOL/ASSN PLAN PROB/SOLV INT/TRADE EFFICIENCY 20 OAS LAFTA ALL/PROG. PAGE 66 F1308
L/A+17C ECO/TAC REGION

B67
AARON H.J.,FINANCING URBAN DEVELOPMENT IN MEXICO CITY: A CASE STUDY OF PROPERTY TAX, LAND USE, HOUSING, AND URBAN PLANNING. LOC/G CREATE EFFICIENCY WEALTH...CHARTS MUNICH 20 MEXIC/AMER. PAGE 2 F0030
PLAN TAX PROB/SOLV

B67
BARNETT A.D.,CHINA AFTER MAO. ASIA CHINA/COM CULTURE ECO/UNDEV ECO/TAC CONTROL EFFICIENCY NAT/LISM MARXISM 20. PAGE 10 F0189
POL/PAR NAT/G TEC/DEV GP/REL

B67
BLAUG M.,ECONOMICS OF EDUCATION: A SELECTED ANNOTATED BIBLIOGRAPHY. EUR+WWI INTELL ECO/DEV ECO/UNDEV ACADEM INT/ORG NAT/G CREATE ADMIN EFFICIENCY ROLE PREDICT. PAGE 16 F0298
BIBLIOG/A EDU/PROP FINAN PLAN

B67
COTTAM R.W.,COMPETITIVE INTERFERENCE AND TWENTIETH CENTURY DIPLOMACY. IRAN ACT/RES CREATE PLAN ECO/TAC EFFICIENCY ATTIT...DECISION NEW/IDEA TREND 20 CIA. PAGE 28 F0541
DIPLOM DOMIN GAME

B67
DE JOUVENAL B.,THE ART OF CONJECTURE. WOR+45 EFFICIENCY PERCEPT KNOWL...DECISION PHIL/SCI CONCPT METH/COMP BIBLIOG 20. PAGE 31 F0600
FUT PREDICT SIMUL METH

B67
ELDREDGE H.W.,TAMING MEGALOPOLIS; HOW TO MANAGE AN URBANIZED WORLD. WOR+45 SOCIETY ECO/DEV ECO/UNDEV NAT/G COMPUTER CREATE PARTIC EFFICIENCY WEALTH ...MGT ANTHOL MUNICH. PAGE 37 F0716
TEC/DEV PLAN PROB/SOLV

B67
ENKE S.,DEFENSE MANAGEMENT. USA+45 R+D FORCES WORKER PLAN ECO/TAC ADMIN NUC/PWR BAL/PAY UTIL WEALTH...MGT DEPT/DEFEN. PAGE 38 F0738
DECISION DELIB/GP EFFICIENCY BUDGET

B67
GOODMAN P.,LIKE A CONQUERED PROVINCE: THE MORAL AMBIGUITY OF AMERICA. AFR USA+45 NAT/G PROB/SOLV EDU/PROP ADJUST EFFICIENCY 20. PAGE 49 F0950
SOCIETY TEC/DEV WAR MORAL

B67
GREEN C.,NEGATIVE TAXES AND THE POVERTY PROBLEM. COST EFFICIENCY INCOME NEW/LIB...METH/CNCPT CHARTS METH/COMP BIBLIOG 20. PAGE 50 F0983
TAX RECEIVE WEALTH PLAN

B67
HANNAH H.W.,THE LEGAL BASE FOR UNIVERSITIES IN DEVELOPING COUNTRIES. AFR ASIA L/A+17C S/ASIA USA+45 FINAN CREATE EDU/PROP TASK EFFICIENCY ...JURID METH/COMP 20. PAGE 54 F1060
ADMIN LAW ACADEM LEGIS

B67
HODGKINSON R.G.,THE ORIGINS OF THE NATIONAL HEALTH SERVICE: THE MEDICAL SERVICES OF THE NEW POOR LAW, 1834-1871. UK INDUS WORKER PROB/SOLV EFFICIENCY ATTIT HEALTH WEALTH SOCISM...JURID SOC/WK MUNICH 19/20. PAGE 60 F1189
HEAL NAT/G POLICY LAW

B67
MARRIS P.,DILEMMAS OF SOCIAL REFORM: POVERTY AND COMMUNITY ACTION IN THE UNITED STATES. USA+45 NAT/G OP/RES ADMIN PARTIC EFFICIENCY WEALTH...SOC METH/COMP T MUNICH 20 REFORMERS. PAGE 85 F1674
STRUCT PROB/SOLV COST

B67
MONTGOMERY J.D.,FOREIGN AID IN INTERNATIONAL POLITICS. USA+45 USA-45 WOR+45 ECO/TAC EFFICIENCY ...SOC TREND CHARTS BIBLIOG/A 20 AID. PAGE 93 F1818
DIPLOM FOR/AID

B67
PEDLEY F.H.,EDUCATION AND SOCIAL WORK. USA+45 INTELL TEC/DEV. PAGE 104 F2047
GP/REL EDU/PROP SOC/WK EFFICIENCY

B67
SCHON D.A.,TECHNOLOGY AND CHANGE* THE NEW HERACLITUS. TEC/DEV CONTROL COST DEMAND EFFICIENCY RIGID/FLEX...MYTH 20. PAGE 117 F2311
INDUS PROB/SOLV R+D CREATE

B67
US SENATE COMM ON FOREIGN REL,HARRISON E. SALISBURY'S TRIP TO NORTH VIETNAM. CHINA/COM USA+45 VIETNAM/N PRESS TASK GUERRILLA CONSEN EFFICIENCY PEACE DRIVE...OBS SENATE. PAGE 139 F2743
DIPLOM WAR FORCES ATTIT

B67
VENKATESWARAN R.J.,CABINET GOVERNMENT IN INDIA. INDIA UK SOCIETY OP/RES COLONIAL LEAD EFFICIENCY ORD/FREE 20. PAGE 141 F2776
DELIB/GP ADMIN CONSTN

NAT/G

B67
ZALESKI E.,PLANNING REFORMS IN THE SOVIET UNION 1962-1966. COM USSR NAT/G CONFER CONTROL EFFICIENCY MARXISM...POLICY DECISION 20. PAGE 150 F2957
ECO/DEV PLAN ADMIN CENTRAL

L67
BONFIELD A.E.,"THE SUBSTANCE OF AMERICAN FAIR EMPLOYMENT PRACTICES LEGISLA TION II - EMPLOYMENT AGENCIES, LABOR ORGANIZATIONS, ETC." ACT/RES DISCRIM EFFICIENCY. PAGE 16 F0311
LAW WORKER LABOR SERV/IND

L67
MACDONALD R.M.,"COLLECTIVE BARGAINING IN THE POSTWAR PERIOD." WORKER PROB/SOLV ECO/TAC PARTIC RISK CENTRAL EFFICIENCY DRIVE WEALTH...TREND 20. PAGE 83 F1624
LABOR INDUS BARGAIN CAP/ISM

L67
MACHLUP F.,"THEORIES OF THE FIRM* MARGINALIST, BEHAVIORALIST, MANAGERIAL." ADMIN EXEC EFFICIENCY PROFIT METH/CNCPT. PAGE 83 F1633
METH/COMP GEN/LAWS INDUS

S67
ALBAUM G.,"INFORMATION FLOW AND DECENTRALIZED DECISION MAKING IN MARKETING." EX/STRUC COMPUTER OP/RES PROB/SOLV EFFICIENCY OPTIMAL...METH/COMP ORG/CHARTS 20. PAGE 3 F0056
LG/CO ROUTINE KNOWL MARKET

S67
BRANCO R.,"LAND REFORM* THE ANSWER TO LATIN AMERICA'S AGRICULTURAL DEVELOPMENT?" L/A+17C NAT/G PLAN TEC/DEV BUDGET RENT EFFICIENCY 20. PAGE 18 F0339
ECO/UNDEV AGRI TAX OWN

S67
CHAMBERLAIN N.W.,"STRIKES IN CONTEMPORARY CONTEXT." LAW INDUS NAT/G CHIEF CONFER COST ATTIT ORD/FREE ...POLICY MGT 20. PAGE 23 F0442
LABOR BARGAIN EFFICIENCY PROB/SOLV

S67
DURIEZ P.,"THE IMPACT OF EX PARTE 230 (PIGGYBACKING) ON RAIL-MOTOR COMPETITION." USA+45 USA-45 LG/CO COST EFFICIENCY...CHARTS 20. PAGE 35 F0685
DIST/IND LAW CONTROL AGREE

S67
EDGEWORTH A.B. JR.,"CIVIL RIGHTS PLUS THREE YEARS: BANKS AND THE ANTI-DISCRIMINATION LAW" USA+45 SOCIETY DELIB/GP RACE/REL EFFICIENCY 20 NEGRO CIV/RIGHTS. PAGE 36 F0701
WORKER DISCRIM FINAN LAW

S67
FRANKEL T.,"ECONOMIC REFORM* A TENTATIVE APPRAISAL." COM USSR OP/RES BUDGET CONFER EFFICIENCY PRODUC MARXISM SOCISM...MGT 20. PAGE 43 F0847
ECO/DEV INDUS PLAN WEALTH

S67
GAUSSENS J.,"THE APPLICATIONS OF NUCLEAR ENERGY - TECHNICAL, ECONOMIC AND SOCIAL ASPECTS." WOR+45 INDUS R+D ACT/RES EFFICIENCY PRODUC SKILL PREDICT. PAGE 47 F0911
NUC/PWR TEC/DEV ECO/DEV ADJUST

S67
GOSALVEZ R.B.,"PERFIL DEL GENERAL VINCENTE ROJO." SPAIN DIPLOM CIVMIL/REL EFFICIENCY PERSON SKILL 20 BOLIV. PAGE 49 F0966
WAR FORCES ELITES BIOG

S67
HILDEBRAND G.H.,"SECOND THOUGHTS ON THE NEGATIVE INCOME TAX." PLAN BUDGET ECO/TAC GIVE RECEIVE DEBATE EFFICIENCY INCOME...METH/COMP COSTS. PAGE 59 F1169
TAX WEALTH SOC/WK ACT/RES

S67
KOTLER P.,"OPERATIONS RESEARCH IN MARKETING." USA+45 DIST/IND INDUS LG/CO CONSULT BUDGET TASK DEMAND EFFICIENCY PROFIT WEALTH DECISION. PAGE 73 F1429
ECOMETRIC OP/RES MARKET PLAN

S67
LANGLEY L.D.,"THE DEMOCRATIC TRADITION AND MILITARY REFORM, 1878-1885." USA-45 SECT EDU/PROP CROWD EFFICIENCY NAT/LISM 19 INDIAN/AM. PAGE 75 F1480
ATTIT FORCES POPULISM

S67
LEONTYEV L.,"THE LENINIST PRINCIPLES OF SOCIALIST ECONOMIC MANAGEMENT." USA+45 USSR POL/PAR WORKER PLAN ECO/TAC EFFICIENCY PRODUC MARXISM...POLICY SOCIALIST MGT TREND 20 LENIN/VI MARX/KARL. PAGE 78 F1529
SOCISM CAP/ISM IDEA/COMP ECO/DEV

S67
MAJSTRENKO I.W.,"PROBLEMS CONFRONTING SOVIET AGRICULTURE." COM USSR ECO/DEV ECO/TAC EFFICIENCY OPTIMAL WEALTH MARXISM 20. PAGE 84 F1643
AGRI PROB/SOLV CENTRAL TEC/DEV

S67
MERON T.,"THE UN'S 'COMMON SYSTEM' OF SALARY, ALLOWANCE, AND BENEFITS: CRITICAL APPR'SAL OF COORD IN PERSONNEL MATTERS." VOL/ASSN PAY EFFICIENCY ...CHARTS 20 UN. PAGE 90 F1761
ADMIN EX/STRUC INT/ORG BUDGET

S67
PAULY M.V.,"MIXED PUBLIC AND PRIVATE FINANCING OF EDUCATION." STRATA PAY RECEIVE COST INCOME OPTIMAL METH/COMP. PAGE 104 F2039
SCHOOL PLAN TAX EFFICIENCY

S67
PECCEI A.,"DEVELOPED-UNDERDEVELOPED AND EAST-WEST RELATIONS." ECO/UNDEV TEC/DEV DIPLOM LEAD EFFICIENCY GEOG. PAGE 104 F2045
FOR/AID TREND REGION ECO/DEV

S67
PENNEY N.,"BANK STATEMENTS, CANCELLED CHECKS, AND ARTICLE FOUR IN THE ELECTRONIC AGE." USA+45 TEC/DEV COST EFFICIENCY WEALTH. PAGE 104 F2056
CREATE LAW ADJUD FINAN

S67
PRATT R.C.,"THE ADMINISTRATION OF ECONOMIC PLANNING IN A NEWLY INDEPEND ENT STATE* THE TANZANIAN EXPERIENCE 1963-1966." AFR TANZANIA ECO/UNDEV PLAN CONTROL ROUTINE TASK EFFICIENCY 20. PAGE 107 F2114
NAT/G DELIB/GP ADMIN TEC/DEV

S67
PROBERT J.R.,"STREAMLINING THE FOREIGN POLICY MACHINE." USA+45 EFFICIENCY DEPT/STATE. PAGE 108 F2123
DIPLOM ADMIN EXEC GOV/REL

S67
RICHMAN B.M.,"CAPITALISTS & MANAGERS IN COMMUNIST CHINA." ASIA CHINA/COM ECO/UNDEV NAT/G CONSULT EX/STRUC PLAN EFFICIENCY PRODUC WEALTH MARXISM ...MGT CHARTS 20. PAGE 111 F2185
CAP/ISM INDUS

S67
RICHMAN B.M.,"SOVIET MANAGEMENT IN TRANSITION." USSR FINAN MARKET EX/STRUC PLAN PROB/SOLV TEC/DEV CONTROL LEAD CENTRAL EFFICIENCY...METH/COMP 20 REFORMERS. PAGE 111 F2186
MGT MARXISM POLICY AUTHORIT

S67
SEIDLER G.L.,"MARXIST LEGAL THOUGHT IN POLAND." POLAND SOCIETY R+D LOC/G NAT/G ACT/RES ADJUD CT/SYS SUPEGO PWR...SOC TREND 20 MARX/KARL. PAGE 119 F2343
MARXISM LAW CONCPT EFFICIENCY

S67
SHISTER J.,"THE DIRECTION OF UNIONISM 1947-1967: THRUST OF DRIFT?" INDUS CENTRAL EFFICIENCY INCOME ATTIT SOCISM...POLICY TREND 20 AFL/CIO. PAGE 121 F2382
LABOR PROF/ORG LEAD LAW

S67
SIMONE A.J.,"SCIENTIFIC PUBLIC POLICY, MARKET PERFORMANCE, AND SIZE OF FIRM." GP/REL COST EFFICIENCY OPTIMAL PRODUC PWR. PAGE 122 F2410
LAW INDUS NAT/G PROB/SOLV

S67
SPITTMANN I.,"EAST GERMANY: THE SWINGING PENDULUM." COM GERMANY/E NAT/G EFFICIENCY MARXISM 20. PAGE 125 F2458
PRODUC POL/PAR WEALTH ATTIT

S67
TELLER A.,"AIR-POLLUTION ABATEMENT: ECONOMIC RATIONALITY AND REALITY." NAT/G DELIB/GP ECO/TAC GOV/REL CENTRAL EFFICIENCY HEALTH...CHARTS METH MUNICH. PAGE 129 F2543
PROB/SOLV CONTROL COST AIR

S67
WALLACE H.M.,"AVAILABILITY AND USEFULNESS OF SELECTED HEALTH AND SOCIOECONOMIC DATA FOR COMMUNITY PLANNING." NEIGH EFFICIENCY...CORREL STAT CENSUS CHARTS. PAGE 142 F2806
HEALTH PLAN SOC/WK HEAL

S67
WILES P.J.,"THE POLITICAL AND SOCIAL PREREQUISITES FOR A SOVIET-TYPE ECONOMY." COM USSR LAW CULTURE CREATE ADMIN FEEDBACK ROUTINE COST OPTIMAL TOTALISM MARXISM 20. PAGE 146 F2883
ECO/DEV PLAN EX/STRUC EFFICIENCY

S67
ZOETEWEIJ B.,"INCOME POLICIES ABROAD: AN INTERIM REPORT." NAT/G PROB/SOLV BARGAIN BUDGET PRICE RISK CENTRAL EFFICIENCY EQUILIB...MGT NAT/COMP 20. PAGE 150 F2967
METH/COMP INCOME POLICY LABOR

N67
US CONGRESS JOINT ECO COMM,ECONOMY IN GOVERNMENT (PAMPHLET). USA+45 ECO/DEV FINAN NAT/G PLAN BUDGET SENATE. PAGE 135 F2662
ECO/TAC COST EFFICIENCY MGT

N67
US HOUSE COMM ON COMMERCE,PARTNERSHIP FOR HEALTH AMENDMENTS FOR 1967 (PAMPHLET). PUB/INST DELIB/GP PROB/SOLV BUDGET EFFICIENCY 20 CONGRESS. PAGE 137 F2701
HEAL PLAN NAT/G JURID

EFRON R. F1889

EFTA....EUROPEAN FREE TRADE ASSOCIATION

B61
BENOIT E.,EUROPE AT SIXES AND SEVENS: THE COMMON MARKET, THE FREE TRADE ASSOCIATION AND THE UNITED STATES. EUR+WWI FUT USA+45 INDUS CONSULT DELIB/GP EX/STRUC TOP/EX ACT/RES ECO/TAC EDU/PROP ROUTINE CHOOSE PERCEPT WEALTH...MGT TREND EEC FOR/TRADE TOT/POP 20 EFTA. PAGE 13 F0249
FINAN ECO/DEV VOL/ASSN

S61
RAY J.,"THE EUROPEAN FREE-TRADE ASSOCIATION AND ITS IMPACT ON INDIA'S TRADE." EUR+WWI FRANCE GERMANY INDIA S/ASIA UK NAT/G VOL/ASSN PLAN INT/TRADE
ECO/DEV ECO/TAC

ROUTINE WEALTH...STAT CHARTS TERR/GP CMN/WLTH EEC FOR/TRADE OEEC 20 EFTA. PAGE 109 F2155

S63

MONROE A.D.,"BRITAIN AND THE EUROPEAN COMMUNITY." EUR+WWI FRANCE NAT/G DELIB/GP TOP/EX ECO/TAC DOMIN PWR...POLICY RECORD GEN/LAWS EEC EFTA 20 EFTA CMN/WLTH. PAGE 93 F1817 — VOL/ASSN ATTIT UK

S63

MONROE A.D.,"BRITAIN AND THE EUROPEAN COMMUNITY." EUR+WWI FRANCE NAT/G DELIB/GP TOP/EX ECO/TAC DOMIN PWR...POLICY RECORD GEN/LAWS EEC EFTA 20 EFTA CMN/WLTH. PAGE 93 F1817 — VOL/ASSN ATTIT UK

S63

SCHOFLING J.A.,"EFTA: THE OTHER EUROPE." ECO/DEV MARKET CONSULT ECO/TAC WEALTH...TIME/SEQ EEC OEEC 20 EFTA. PAGE 117 F2310 — EUR+WWI INT/ORG REGION

B65

EUROPEAN FREE TRADE ASSN,REGIONAL DEVELOPMENT POLICIES IN EFTA. ECO/UNDEV INT/ORG PLAN REGION ...POLICY GEOG EFTA. PAGE 39 F0755 — EUR+WWI ECO/DEV NAT/COMP INT/TRADE

EGGERT G.G. F0707

EGLE W.P. F0708,F0709

EGYPT....SEE ALSO ISLAM, UAR, EGYPT/ANC

EGYPT/ANC....ANCIENT EGYPT

EHRHARD J. F0710

EHRLICH S. F0711

EHRMANN H.W. F0712

EIB....EUROPEAN INVESTMENT BANK

S65

CAMPOLONGO A.,"EUROPEAN INVESTMENT BANK* ACTIVITY AND PROSPECTS." FUT ECO/UNDEV FINAN PLAN DIPLOM ...STAT EEC LOAN EIB. PAGE 21 F0410 — ECO/TAC PREDICT

EICHMANN/A....ADOLF EICHMANN

EICHNER A.S. F2821

EINSTEIN/A....ALBERT EINSTEIN

EINZIG P. F0713,F0714,F0715

EISNER V. F2806

EISNHWR/DD....PRESIDENT DWIGHT DAVID EISENHOWER

N19

CARPER E.T.,LOBBYING AND THE NATURAL GAS BILL (PAMPHLET). USA+45 SERV/IND BARGAIN PAY DRIVE ROLE WEALTH 20 CONGRESS SENATE EISNHWR/DD. PAGE 22 F0418 — LOBBY ADJUD TRIBUTE NAT/G

N19

SILVERMAN C.,THE PRESIDENT'S ECONOMIC ADVISERS (PAMPHLET). USA+45 LAW ELITES ECO/DEV EX/STRUC ADMIN LEAD GOV/REL PERS/REL ROLE...POLICY DECISION 20 PRESIDENT CONGRESS EISNHWR/DD. PAGE 122 F2404 — CONSULT PROB/SOLV NAT/G PLAN

B56

US OFFICE OF THE PRESIDENT,REPORT TO CONGRESS ON THE MUTUAL SECURITY PROGRAM FOR THE SIX MONTHS ENDED DECEMBER 31, 1955. ASIA USSR ECO/DEV ECO/UNDEV INT/ORG CREATE TEC/DEV BAL/PWR ECO/TAC AGREE DETER COST ORD/FREE 20 DEPT/STATE DEPT/DEFEN EISNHWR/DD. PAGE 138 F2723 — DIPLOM FORCES PLAN FOR/AID

S56

BONILLA F.,"WHEN IS PETITION 'PRESSURE?'" (BMR)" USA+45 ELITES INDUS LABOR CHIEF EDU/PROP LEGIT ATTIT...INT CHARTS 20 CONGRESS PRESIDENT EISNHWR/DD. PAGE 16 F0312 — LEGIS EX/STRUC INT/TRADE TARIFFS

S59

GILPATRICK T.V.,"PRICE SUPPORT POLICY AND THE MIDWEST FARM VOTE" (BMR)" NAT/G PRICE CONTROL REGION...POLICY CHARTS 440 20 MIDWEST/US CONGRESS REPUBLICAN EISNHWR/DD 20. PAGE 47 F0925 — POL/PAR AGRI ATTIT CHOOSE

B60

CARPER E.T.,THE DEFENSE APPROPRIATIONS RIDER (PAMPHLET). USA+45 CONSTN CHIEF DELIB/GP LEGIS BUDGET LOBBY CIVMIL/REL...POLICY 20 CONGRESS EISNHWR/DD DEPT/DEFEN PRESIDENT BOSTON. PAGE 22 F0419 — GOV/REL ADJUD LAW CONTROL

B61

CANTERBERY E.R.,THE PRESIDENT'S COUNCIL OF ECONOMIC ADVISERS. AFR USA+45 FINAN LABOR NAT/G PLAN ADMIN OPTIMAL WEALTH 20 EISNHWR/DD PRESIDENT TRUMAN/HS KEYNES/JM. PAGE 21 F0413 — ECO/TAC OP/RES EXEC CHIEF

B62

HARRIS S.E.,THE ECONOMICS OF THE POLITICAL PARTIES. USA+45 FINAN CHIEF ACT/RES PLAN BUDGET GP/REL INGP/REL NEW/LIB...IDEA/COMP PERS/COMP 20 EISNHWR/DD KENNEDY/JF. PAGE 56 F1090 — POLICY ECO/DEV NAT/G POL/PAR

B62

SCHILLING W.R.,STRATEGY, POLITICS, AND DEFENSE BUDGETS. AFR USA+45 CHIEF LEGIS PLAN TEC/DEV BAL/PWR BUDGET NUC/PWR WAR CIVMIL/REL GOV/REL PWR 20 EISNHWR/DD. PAGE 117 F2297 — NAT/G POLICY FORCES DETER

B64

HARRIS S.E.,ECONOMICS OF THE KENNEDY YEARS AND A LOOK AHEAD. USA+45 PLAN BUDGET NEW/LIB...STAT RECORD IDEA/COMP PERS/COMP INDEX 20 KENNEDY/JF EISNHWR/DD JOHNSON/LB. PAGE 56 F1091 — ECO/TAC CHIEF POLICY NAT/G

EL/SALVADR....EL SALVADOR; SEE ALSO L/A+17C

ELDREDGE H.W. F0716,F0717

ELECT/COLL....ELECTORAL COLLEGE

ELECTIONS....SEE CHOOSE

ELIA O.H. F0748

ELITES....POWER-DOMINANT GROUPINGS OF A SOCIETY

N19

ADMINISTRATIVE STAFF COLLEGE,THE ACCOUNTABILITY OF GOVERNMENT DEPARTMENTS (PAMPHLET) (REV. ED.). UK CONSTN FINAN NAT/G CONSULT ADMIN INGP/REL CONSEN PRIVIL 20 PARLIAMENT. PAGE 2 F0043 — PARL/PROC ELITES SANCTION PROB/SOLV

N19

HOGARTY R.A.,NEW JERSEY FARMERS AND MIGRANT HOUSING RULES (PAMPHLET). USA+45 LAW ELITES FACE/GP LABOR PROF/ORG LOBBY PERS/REL RIGID/FLEX ROLE 20 NEW/JERSEY. PAGE 61 F1193 — AGRI PROVS WORKER HEALTH

N19

SENGHOR L.S.,AFRICAN SOCIALISM (PAMPHLET). AFR FRANCE MALI USSR ELITES ECO/UNDEV NAT/G DIPLOM DOMIN EDU/PROP ATTIT 20 NEGRO. PAGE 119 F2355 — SOCISM MARXISM ORD/FREE NAT/LISM

N19

SILVERMAN C.,THE PRESIDENT'S ECONOMIC ADVISERS (PAMPHLET). USA+45 LAW ELITES ECO/DEV EX/STRUC ADMIN LEAD GOV/REL PERS/REL ROLE...POLICY DECISION 20 PRESIDENT CONGRESS EISNHWR/DD. PAGE 122 F2404 — CONSULT PROB/SOLV NAT/G PLAN

B30

GREEN F.M.,CONSTITUTIONAL DEVELOPMENT IN THE SOUTH ATLANTIC STATES, 1776-1860; A STUDY IN THE EVOLUTION OF DEMOCRACY. USA-45 ELITES SOCIETY STRATA ECO/DEV AGRI POL/PAR EX/STRUC LEGIS CT/SYS REGION...BIBLIOG 18/19 MARYLAND VIRGINIA GEORGIA NORTH/CAR SOUTH/CAR. PAGE 50 F0984 — CONSTN PROVS PLURISM REPRESENT

B35

LASKI H.J.,THE STATE IN THEORY AND PRACTICE. ELITES ECO/TAC REPRESENT ORD/FREE PWR WEALTH POPULISM ...GOV/COMP GEN/LAWS 19/20. PAGE 76 F1483 — CAP/ISM COERCE NAT/G FASCISM

B38

DAVIES E.,"NATIONAL" CAPITALISM: THE GOVERNMENT'S RECORD AS PROTECTOR OF PRIVATE MONOPOLY. UK ELITES SOCIETY STRATA POL/PAR WORKER PROB/SOLV CONTROL SOCISM 20 MONOPOLY LABOR/PAR CHAMBRLN/N. PAGE 30 F0583 — CAP/ISM NAT/G INDUS POLICY

S41

LASSWELL H.D.,"THE GARRISON STATE" (BMR)" FUT WOR+45 ELITES INTELL FORCES ECO/TAC DOMIN EDU/PROP COERCE INGP/REL 20. PAGE 76 F1485 — NAT/G DIPLOM PWR CIVMIL/REL

B42

VEBLEN T.B.,THE THEORY OF THE LEISURE CLASS. USA-45 SOCIETY STRATA STRUCT NAT/G SECT WORKER CREATE EDU/PROP ATTIT...SOC GEN/LAWS 19. PAGE 141 F2772 — WEALTH ELITES LEISURE PRODUC

B48

MILLS C.W.,THE NEW MEN OF POWER. ELITES INTELL STRUCT WORKER ANOMIE ATTIT PWR POLICY. PAGE 92 F1799 — LABOR LEAD PLAN

B50

HUTCHISON K.,THE DECLINE AND FALL OF BRITISH CAPITALISM. UK ELITES STRATA ECO/DEV LABOR WORKER CONTROL WAR PWR...BIBLIOG/A 19/20. PAGE 63 F1249 — CAP/ISM SOCISM LAISSEZ DOMIN

B50

LINCOLN G.,ECONOMICS OF NATIONAL SECURITY. USA+45 ELITES COM/IND DIST/IND INDUS NAT/G VOL/ASSN DELIB/GP EX/STRUC FOR/AID EDU/PROP COERCE NUC/PWR WAR ATTIT KNOWL ORD/FREE PWR TOT/POP VAL/FREE 20. PAGE 80 F1565 — FORCES ECO/TAC AFR

S50

DALTON M.,"CONFLICTS BETWEEN STAFF AND LINE MANAGERIAL OFFICERS" (BMR). USA+45 USA-45 ELITES LG/CO WORKER PROB/SOLV ADMIN EXEC EFFICIENCY PRODUC ...GP/COMP 20. PAGE 30 F0576 — MGT ATTIT GP/REL INDUS

B52
DE JOUVENEL B.,THE ETHICS OF REDISTRIBUTION. UK ELITES MARKET WORKER GIVE PAY INCOME PERSON ...POLICY PSY GEN/LAWS 20. PAGE 31 F0602
WEALTH TAX SOCISM TRADIT

S53
BLOUGH R.,"THE ROLE OF THE ECONOMIST IN FEDERAL POLICY MAKING." USA+45 ELITES INTELL ECO/DEV NAT/G CONSULT EX/STRUC ACT/RES PLAN INT/TRADE BAL/PAY WEALTH...POLICY METH/GP CONGRESS 20. PAGE 16 F0301
DELIB/GP ECO/TAC

B54
KARTUN D.,AFRICA, AFRICA: A CONTINENT RISES TO ITS FEET. AFR SOUTH/AFR UK ELITES AGRI LABOR LOC/G POL/PAR EDU/PROP CONTROL COERCE DISCRIM AGE/Y NEGRO THIRD/WRLD GOLD/COAST. PAGE 69 F1358
COLONIAL ORD/FREE PROFIT EXTR/IND

B55
COLE G.D.H.,STUDIES IN CLASS STRUCTURE. UK NAT/G WORKER TEC/DEV EDU/PROP...CLASSIF CHARTS 20. PAGE 26 F0501
STRUCT STRATA ELITES CONCPT

B56
BROWN R.E.,CHARLES BEARD AND THE CONSTITUTION. USA-45 NAT/G ORD/FREE WEALTH...HUM TIME/SEQ METH/COMP 20 BEARD/CA. PAGE 19 F0372
CONSTN ELITES HIST/WRIT

S56
BONILLA F.,"WHEN IS PETITION 'PRESSURE?'" (BMR)" USA+45 ELITES INDUS LABOR CHIEF EDU/PROP LEGIT ATTIT...INT CHARTS 20 CONGRESS PRESIDENT EISNHWR/DD. PAGE 16 F0312
LEGIS EX/STRUC INT/TRADE TARIFFS

C56
MCKEE J.B.,"THE POWER TO DECIDE" IN M. WEINBERG AND O. SHABET, SOCIETY AND MAN." ELITES STRATA REPRESENT GP/REL ATTIT PWR MUNICH BUSINESS. PAGE 88 F1731
LABOR DECISION LEAD

B57
MASON E.S.,ECONOMIC CONCENTRATION AND THE MONOPOLY PROBLEM. USA+45 USA-45 LAW ELITES ECO/DEV LABOR RATION PRICE PWR WEALTH...CHARTS 20 MONOPOLY. PAGE 87 F1696
GP/REL LG/CO CONTROL MARKET

B58
PAYNO M.,LA REFORMA SOCIAL EN ESPANA Y MEXICO. SPAIN ECO/TAC TAX LOBBY COERCE REV OWN CATHISM 19/20 MEXIC/AMER. PAGE 104 F2043
SECT NAT/G LAW ELITES

B59
SHUBIK M.,STRATEGY AND MARKET STRUCTURE: COMPETITION, OLIGOPOLY, AND THE THEORY OF GAMES. ELITES STRUCT MARKET OP/RES EXEC EFFICIENCY INCOME ...MGT MATH STAT CHARTS 20. PAGE 121 F2389
ECO/DEV ECO/TAC DECISION GAME

B59
THE BROOKINGS INSTITUTION,ECONOMICS AND THE POLICY MAKER. USA+45 CREATE...ANTHOL 20. PAGE 129 F2549
ELITES ECO/TAC PROB/SOLV ECO/DEV

B59
WAHLKE J.C.,LEGISLATIVE BEHAVIOR: A READER IN THEORY AND RESEARCH. USA+45 CONSTN ELITES POL/PAR LOBBY REPRESENT PERS/REL PERSON ROLE...IDEA/COMP METH/COMP SIMUL. PAGE 142 F2800
LEGIS CHOOSE INGP/REL ATTIT

B59
WORTHY J.C.,BIG BUSINESS AND FREE MEN. LG/CO EX/STRUC EDU/PROP LEAD CHOOSE GP/REL ATTIT DRIVE ROLE ORD/FREE...MAJORIT 20. PAGE 149 F2927
ELITES LOC/G TOP/EX PARTIC

B60
FORBUSH D.R.,PROBLEMS OF CORPORATE POWER. CLIENT LAW ELITES ADJUD...DECISION MGT. PAGE 42 F0822
LG/CO PWR CONTROL GP/REL

B60
GRANICK D.,THE RED EXECUTIVE. COM USA+45 SOCIETY ECO/DEV INDUS NAT/G POL/PAR EX/STRUC PLAN ECO/TAC EDU/PROP ADMIN EXEC ATTIT DRIVE...GP/COMP 20. PAGE 50 F0976
PWR STRATA USSR ELITES

B60
HARBRECHT P.P.,TOWARD THE PARAPROPRIETAL SOCIETY. REPRESENT INCOME OWN PROFIT AGE/O. PAGE 55 F1076
PWR ADMIN ELITES CONTROL

B60
MC CLELLAN G.S.,INDIA. AFR CHINA/COM INDIA CONSTN ELITES STRATA AGRI POL/PAR FOR/AID ARMS/CONT REV MARXISM...CENSUS BIBLIOG 20 GANDHI/M NEHRU/J. PAGE 87 F1712
DIPLOM NAT/G SOCIETY ECO/UNDEV

B60
RAMA C.M.,LAS CLASES SOCIALES EN EL URUGUAY. L/A+17C URUGUAY ELITES SOCIETY STRATA INDUS ATTIT HABITAT PWR...GEOG SOC/INTEG MUNICH 20. PAGE 109 F2138
ECO/UNDEV STRUCT PARTIC

B61
CAMPAIGNE J.G.,CHECK-OFF: LABOR BOSSES AND WORKING MEN. LEGIS WORKER EDU/PROP DEBATE COERCE REPRESENT GP/REL ORD/FREE CONSERVE. PAGE 21 F0404
LABOR ELITES PWR CONTROL

B61
DELEFORTRIE-SOU N.,LES DIRIGEANTS DE L'INDUSTRIE FRANCAISE. FRANCE CULTURE ELITES PROB/SOLV ...DECISION STAT CHARTS 20. PAGE 32 F0613
INDUS STRATA TOP/EX LEAD

B61
ENGLER R.,THE POLITICS OF OIL. USA+45 CLIENT ELITES DOMIN EDU/PROP EXEC PWR 20. PAGE 38 F0734
LOBBY REPRESENT POLICY

B61
SCHWARTZ H.,THE RED PHOENIX: RUSSIA SINCE WORLD WAR II. USA+45 WOR+45 ELITES POL/PAR TEC/DEV ECO/TAC MARXISM. PAGE 118 F2325
DIPLOM NAT/G ECO/DEV

S61
VALLET R.,"IRAN: KEY TO THE MIDDLE EAST." COM IRAQ ISLAM KUWAIT LEBANON SAUDI/ARAB TURKEY ELITES SOCIETY INDUS PROC/MFG POL/PAR TOP/EX PLAN BAL/PWR DIPLOM ECO/TAC ALL/VALS...TREND FOR/TRADE CENTO 20. PAGE 140 F2760
NAT/G ECO/UNDEV IRAN

B62
SELOSOEMARDJAN O.,SOCIAL CHANGES IN JOGJAKARTA. INDONESIA NETHERLAND ELITES STRATA STRUCT FAM POL/PAR CREATE DIPLOM INT/TRADE EDU/PROP ADMIN GOV/REL...SOC 20 JAVA CHINJAP. PAGE 119 F2352
ECO/UNDEV CULTURE REV COLONIAL

B63
BRAYBROOKE D.,A STRATEGY OF DECISION: POLICY EVALUATION AS A SOCIAL PROCESS. UNIV ELITES OP/RES DOMIN CONFER FEEDBACK CONSEN PLURISM...CONCPT CENSUS. PAGE 18 F0343
DECISION POLICY CONTROL

B63
COPPOCK J.,NORTH ATLANTIC POLICY - THE AGRICULTURAL GAP. EUR+WWI ELITES ECO/DEV DIST/IND MARKET PLAN WEALTH...STAT TREND GEN/LAWS OEEC TOT/POP VAL/FREE FAO 20. PAGE 27 F0535
AGRI TEC/DEV INT/TRADE

B63
GEERTZ C.,PEDDLERS AND PRINCES: SOCIAL DEVELOPMENT AND ECONOMIC CHANGE IN TWO INDONESIAN TOWNS. S/ASIA CULTURE SOCIETY STRATA FACE/GP CREATE TEC/DEV ECO/TAC ORD/FREE WEALTH...OBS INT CENSUS CHARTS WORK TOT/POP METH/GP TERR/GP VAL/FREE 20 MUNICH. PAGE 47 F0913
ECO/UNDEV SOC ELITES INDONESIA

B63
MINGAY G.E.,ENGLISH LANDED SOCIETY IN THE EIGHTEENTH CENTURY. UK ELITES STRUCT AGRI INDUS CONTROL WEALTH 18. PAGE 92 F1802
OWN STRATA PWR

B63
PELLING H.M.,A HISTORY OF BRITISH TRADE UNIONISM. UK ELITES ECO/DEV POL/PAR GP/REL PWR NEW/LIB 19/20. PAGE 104 F2051
LABOR VOL/ASSN NAT/G

B63
SMITH R.A.,CORPORATIONS IN CRISIS. USA+45 LG/CO EX/STRUC ECO/TAC CONTROL LEAD PERS/REL...MGT 20. PAGE 123 F2432
ELITES INDUS PROB/SOLV METH/COMP

B63
VON BECKERATH E.,PROBLEME DER NORMATIVEN OKONOMIK UND DER WIRTSCHAFTSPOLITISCHEN BERATUNG. GERMANY UK ELITES CAP/ISM EFFICIENCY...CONCPT GOV/COMP IDEA/COMP 20. PAGE 142 F2789
ECO/TAC DELIB/GP ECO/DEV CONSULT

B63
WAGLEY C.,INTRODUCTION TO BRAZIL. BRAZIL L/A+17C FAM KIN SCHOOL SECT ATTIT WEALTH...GEOG SOC. PAGE 142 F2799
ECO/UNDEV ELITES HABITAT STRATA

B63
WILTZ J.E.,IN SEARCH OF PEACE: THE SENATE MUNITIONS INQUIRY, 1934-36. EUR+WWI USA-45 ELITES INDUS LG/CO LEGIS INT/TRADE LOBBY NEUTRAL ARMS/CONT...POLICY CONGRESS 20 LEAGUE/NAT PRESIDENT SENATE CONSCRIPTN. PAGE 147 F2905
DELIB/GP PROFIT WAR WEAPON

S63
BARZANSKI S.,"REGIONAL UNDERDEVELOPMENT IN THE EUROPEAN ECONOMIC COMMUNITY." EUR+WWI ELITES DIST/IND MARKET VOL/ASSN CONSULT EX/STRUC ECO/TAC RIGID/FLEX WEALTH EEC OEEC 20. PAGE 11 F0202
ECO/UNDEV PLAN

S63
BELOFF M.,"BRITAIN, EUROPE AND THE ATLANTIC COMMUNITY." EUR+WWI ELITES NAT/G VOL/ASSN TOP/EX ATTIT ORD/FREE PWR SOVEREIGN WEALTH EEC TOT/POP VAL/FREE CMN/WLTH 20. PAGE 13 F0240
INT/ORG ECO/DEV UK

S63
HOOVER C.B.,"ECONOMIC REFORM VERSUS ECONOMIC GROWTH IN UNDERDEVELOPED COUNTRIES." FUT WOR+45 ELITES STRATA ECO/UNDEV DIST/IND INDUS TEC/DEV CAP/ISM FOR/AID INT/TRADE ATTIT WEALTH...MYTH TREND STERTYP GEN/LAWS WORK 20. PAGE 61 F1209
ECO/DEV ECO/TAC

S63
SHWADRAN B.,"MIDDLE EAST OIL, 1962." ISLAM DIST/IND INDUS PLAN ATTIT DRIVE WEALTH...POLICY STAT CONT/OBS TREND CHARTS GEN/LAWS TERR/GP METH/GP 20 OIL. PAGE 121 F2393
PROC/MFG ECO/TAC ELITES REGION

B64
IMAZ J.L.,LOS QUE MANDAN. INDUS LABOR NAT/G POL/PAR PROVS SECT CHIEF TOP/EX CONTROL 20 ARGEN. PAGE 64 F1261
LEAD FORCES ELITES ATTIT

B64
REDLICH F.,THE GERMAN MILITARY ENTERPRISER AND HIS
EX/STRUC

WORK FORCE. CHRIST-17C GERMANY ELITES SOCIETY FINAN ECO/TAC CIVMIL/REL GP/REL INGP/REL...HIST/WRIT METH/COMP 14/17. PAGE 110 F2170 — FORCES PROFIT WORKER

B64
ROBINSON R.D.,INTERNATIONAL BUSINESS POLICY. AFR INDIA L/A+17C USA+45 ELITES AGRI FOR/AID COERCE BAL/PAY...DECISION INT/LAW MGT 20. PAGE 113 F2224 — ECO/TAC DIST/IND COLONIAL FINAN

B64
TAWNEY R.H.,EQUALITY. UK CULTURE STRATA ECO/TAC EDU/PROP REPRESENT OWN NEW/LIB...MAJORIT WELF/ST SOC 20. PAGE 129 F2538 — WEALTH STRUCT ELITES POPULISM

S64
CLELLAND D.A.,"ECONOMIC DOMINANTS AND COMMUNITY POWER: A COMPARATIVE ANALYSIS." ELITES ADJUST ATTIT WEALTH...DECISION MUNICH. PAGE 25 F0488 — LEAD MGT PWR

S64
LEFF N.H.,"ECONOMIC DEVELOPMENT THROUGH BUREAUCRATIC CORRUPTION." ELITES NAT/G ROUTINE REPRESENT GP/REL PERS/REL. PAGE 77 F1511 — ECO/UNDEV CLIENT EX/STRUC

B65
HAPGOOD D.,AFRICA: FROM INDEPENDENCE TO TOMARROW. AFR GUINEA SENEGAL CULTURE ELITES ECO/UNDEV AGRI SCHOOL FOR/AID COLONIAL MARXISM...TREND 20. PAGE 55 F1070 — ECO/TAC SOCIETY NAT/G

B65
STEINER G.A.,THE CREATIVE ORGANIZATION. ELITES LG/CO PLAN PROB/SOLV TEC/DEV INSPECT CAP/ISM CONTROL EXEC PERSON...METH/COMP HYPO/EXP 20. PAGE 126 F2476 — CREATE MGT ADMIN SOC

S65
JOHNSON H.G.,"A THEORETICAL MODEL OF ECONOMIC NATIONALISM IN NEW AND DEVELOPING STATES." ELITES INDUS INT/TRADE EDU/PROP COST OPTIMAL RATIONAL PWR WEALTH SOCISM STERTYP. PAGE 67 F1325 — NAT/LISM ECO/UNDEV GEN/LAWS

B66
BAKKE E.W.,MUTUAL SURVIVAL; THE GOAL OF UNION AND MANAGEMENT (2ND ED.). USA+45 ELITES ECO/DEV ECO/TAC CONFER ADMIN REPRESENT GP/REL INGP/REL ATTIT ...GP/COMP 20. PAGE 8 F0155 — MGT LABOR BARGAIN INDUS

B66
GOULD J.M.,THE TECHNICAL ELITE. INDUS LABOR TECHRACY...POLICY DECISION STAT CHARTS 20. PAGE 49 F0967 — ECO/DEV TEC/DEV ELITES TECHNIC

B66
KOMIYA R.,POSTWAR ECONOMIC GROWTH IN JAPAN. ELITES NAT/G EX/STRUC TEC/DEV BUDGET DIPLOM CONTROL BAL/PAY PRODUC...BIBLIOG 20 CHINJAP. PAGE 73 F1424 — ECO/DEV POLICY PLAN ADJUST

B66
MANSFIELD E.,MANAGERIAL ECONOMICS AND OPERATIONS RESEARCH; A NONMATHEMATICAL INTRODUCTION. USA+45 ELITES ECO/DEV CONSULT EX/STRUC PROB/SOLV ROUTINE EFFICIENCY OPTIMAL...GAME T 20. PAGE 85 F1660 — ECO/TAC OP/RES MGT COMPUTER

B66
THEIL H.,APPLIED ECONOMIC FORECASTING. UNIV USA+45 ELITES INTELL CONSULT PRODUC...DECISION MGT PREDICT CHARTS METH/COMP SIMUL 20. PAGE 129 F2552 — FUT OP/RES PLAN

S66
COHEN A.,"THE TECHNOLOGY/ELITE APPROACH TO THE DEVELOPMENTAL PROCESS* PERUVIAN CASE STUDY." L/A+17C STRUCT CREATE ECO/TAC FOR/AID CIVMIL/REL MARXISM TECHRACY HYPO/EXP. PAGE 26 F0496 — ECO/UNDEV ELITES PERU

S66
FELD W.,"EXTERNAL RELATIONS OF THE COMMON MARKET AND GROUP LEADERSHIP ATTITUDES IN THE MEMBER STATES." COM USA+45 ELITES AGRI NAT/G ATTIT...OBS EEC GATT. PAGE 40 F0776 — DIPLOM CENTRAL TARIFFS INT/TRADE

S66
FELD W.,"NATIONAL ECONOMIC INTEREST GROUPS AND POLICY FORMATION IN THE EEC." NAT/G POL/PAR REGION CENTRAL SOVEREIGN...INT NET/THEORY EEC. PAGE 40 F0777 — LOBBY ELITES DECISION

S66
LANGLEY D.,"POSTSCRIPT ON THE COLONIZATION OF THE INTERNATIONAL TRADE UNION MOVEMENT" USA+45 ELITES FINAN DOMIN LEGIT ADMIN PWR...SOCIALIST 20 AFL/CIO CIA LOVESTN/J. PAGE 75 F1479 — INT/TRADE LABOR NAT/G CONTROL

S66
MALENBAUM W.,"GOVERNMENT, ENTREPRENEURSHIP, AND ECONOMIC GROWTH IN POOR LANDS." ELITES ECO/UNDEV INDUS CREATE DRIVE. PAGE 84 F1645 — ECO/TAC PLAN CONSERVE NAT/G

S66
ROTHCHILD D.,"THE LIMITS OF FEDERALISM: AN EXAMINATION OF POLITICAL INSTITUTIONAL TRANSFER IN AFRICA." AFR CONSTN CULTURE ELITES ECO/UNDEV KIN PROB/SOLV ADMIN ORD/FREE PWR...POLICY 20. PAGE 114 F2250 — FEDERAL NAT/G NAT/LISM COLONIAL

B67
EGGERT G.G.,RAILROAD LABOR DISPUTES. USA+45 USA-45 ELITES DIST/IND DELIB/GP FORCES JUDGE WORKER PROB/SOLV DOMIN PWR...POLICY 20. PAGE 36 F0707 — GP/REL NAT/G LABOR BARGAIN

B67
FALL B.B.,HO CHI MINH ON REVOLUTION: SELECTED WRITINGS, 1920-66. COM VIETNAM ELITES NAT/G COERCE GUERRILLA RACE/REL MARXISM...MARXIST ANTHOL 20. PAGE 39 F0761 — REV COLONIAL ECO/UNDEV S/ASIA

B67
FANON F.,TOWARD THE AFRICAN REVOLUTION. AFR FRANCE CULTURE ELITES LEAD REV GP/REL ORD/FREE SOVEREIGN 20. PAGE 39 F0762 — COLONIAL DOMIN ECO/UNDEV RACE/REL

B67
GRIPP R.C.,PATTERNS OF SOVIET POLITICS (REV. ED.). USSR LAW ELITES LOC/G PLAN CONTROL CT/SYS CHOOSE ...POLICY BIBLIOG/A DICTIONARY 9/20. PAGE 51 F1003 — COM ADJUD POL/PAR

B67
HEILBRONER R.L.,THE LIMITS OF AMERICAN CAPITALISM. FUT ECO/DEV INDUS LG/CO EX/STRUC LEAD PWR TECHRACY 20. PAGE 58 F1137 — ELITES CREATE TEC/DEV CAP/ISM

L67
MANNE H.G.,"OUR TWO CORPORATION SYSTEMS* LAW AND ECONOMICS." LAW CONTROL SANCTION GP/REL...JURID 20. PAGE 85 F1657 — INDUS ELITES CAP/ISM ADMIN

S67
"THE SIERRA CLUB, POLITICAL ACTIVITY, AND TAX EXEMPT CHARITABLE STATUS." USA+45 LAW VOL/ASSN TAX PAY ADJUD LOBBY INGP/REL HABITAT 20. PAGE 2 F0027 — ELITES GOV/REL FACE/GP ORD/FREE

S67
CRAIG A.,"ARGENTINA: THE LATEST REVOLUTION." ELITES NAT/G CHIEF FORCES ECO/TAC CIVMIL/REL GOV/REL EQUILIB PRIVIL 20 ARGEN. PAGE 28 F0550 — ECO/UNDEV FINAN ATTIT REV

S67
DRAPER A.P.,"UNIONS AND THE WAR IN VIETNAM." USA+45 CONFER ADMIN LEAD WAR ORD/FREE PACIFIST 20. PAGE 34 F0660 — LABOR PACIFISM ATTIT ELITES

S67
FINER S.E.,"THE ONE-PARTY REGIMES IN AFRICA: RECONSIDERATIONS." AFR DOMIN CONSEN ORD/FREE 20. PAGE 41 F0798 — ELITES POL/PAR CONSTN ECO/UNDEV

S67
GORMAN W.,"ELLUL - A PROPHETIC VOICE." WOR+45 ELITES SOCIETY ACT/RES PLAN BAL/PWR DOMIN CONTROL PARTIC TOTALISM PWR 20. PAGE 49 F0963 — CREATE ORD/FREE EX/STRUC UTOPIA

S67
GOSALVEZ R.B.,"PERFIL DEL GENERAL VINCENTE ROJO." SPAIN DIPLOM CIVMIL/REL EFFICIENCY PERSON SKILL 20 BOLIV. PAGE 49 F0966 — WAR FORCES ELITES BIOG

S67
KRAUS J.,"A MARXIST IN GHANA." GHANA ELITES CHIEF PROB/SOLV TEC/DEV DIPLOM ECO/TAC COLONIAL PARTIC PWR 20 NKRUMAH/K. PAGE 73 F1432 — MARXISM PLAN ATTIT CREATE

S67
PAI G.A.,"TAXATION AND PLANNING IN INDIA: A BIRDS-EYE VIEW." INDIA ELITES NAT/G LEGIS BUDGET CONTROL LOBBY INCOME...STAT CHARTS 20. PAGE 102 F2015 — TAX PLAN WEALTH STRATA

S67
RAMA C.M.,"PASADO Y PRESENTE DE LA RELIGION EN AMERICA LATINA." L/A+17C ELITES SOCIETY STRATA MARXISM...STAT WORSHIP PROTESTANT. PAGE 109 F2139 — SECT CATHISM STRUCT NAT/COMP

B84
MILL J.,ELEMENTS OF POLITICAL ECONOMY. UK LAW ELITES FINAN WORKER ECO/TAC RENT OWN WEALTH ...POLICY GEN/LAWS 19. PAGE 91 F1785 — TAX TARIFFS NAT/G INCOME

B96
MARX K.,REVOLUTION AND COUNTER-REVOLUTION. GERMANY CONSTN ELITES INDUS NAT/G DIPLOM ECO/TAC WEALTH. PAGE 86 F1693 — MARXIST REV PWR STRATA

ELIZABTH/I....ELIZABETH I OF ENGLAND

EL-NAGGAR S. F0718

ELKIN A.B. F0719

ELKIN/AP....A.P. ELKIN

ELKOURI E.A. F0720

ELKOURI F. F0720

ELLENDER A.J. F0721

ELLIOTT J.E. F0996

ELLIOTT J.R. F0722

ELLIS H.S. F0380,F0723

ELLSWORTH P.T. F0724,F0725

ELSNER H. F0726

EMBREE A.T. F0595

EMERGENCY....SEE DECISION

EMERSON F.D. F0727,F0728

EMERSON R. F0729

EMPLOYMENT....SEE WORKER

ENG/CIV/WR....ENGLISH CIVIL WAR

ENGELS F. F0730,F0731,F0732,F0733,F1691

ENGELS/F....FRIEDRICH ENGELS

ENGLAND....SEE UK, ALSO APPROPRIATE TIME/SPACE/CULTURE INDEX

ENGLER R. F0734

ENGLISH H.E. F0348

ENGLSH/LAW....ENGLISH LAW

B24
HOLDSWORTH W.S.,A HISTORY OF ENGLISH LAW; THE COMMON LAW AND ITS RIVALS (VOL. VI). AFR UK STRATA EX/STRUC ADJUD ADMIN CONTROL CT/SYS...JURID CONCPT GEN/LAWS 17 PARLIAMENT ENGLSH/LAW COMMON/LAW. PAGE 61 F1194 — LAW CONSTN LEGIS CHIEF

B24
HOLDSWORTH W.S.,A HISTORY OF ENGLISH LAW; THE COMMON LAW AND ITS RIVALS (VOL. IV). UK SEA AGRI CHIEF ADJUD CONTROL CRIME GOV/REL...INT/LAW JURID NAT/COMP 16/17 PARLIAMENT COMMON/LAW CANON/LAW ENGLSH/LAW. PAGE 61 F1195 — LAW LEGIS CT/SYS CONSTN

B52
JENNINGS W.I.,CONSTITUTIONAL LAWS OF THE COMMONWEALTH. AFR UK LAW CHIEF LEGIS TAX CT/SYS PARL/PROC GOV/REL...INT/LAW 18/20 ENGLSH/LAW COMMON/LAW. PAGE 67 F1316 — CONSTN JURID ADJUD COLONIAL

ENKE S. F0735,F0736,F0737,F0738

ENLIGHTNMT....THE ENLIGHTENMENT

ENTHOVEN A.C. F0739

ENTREPRENEURSHIP....SEE OWN, INDUS, CAP/ISM

ENVY....SEE WEALTH, LOVE, AND VALUES INDEX

EPIST....EPISTEMOLOGY, SOCIOLOGY OF KNOWLEDGE

B66
BEQIRAJ M.,PEASANTRY IN REVOLUTION. STRATA ECO/UNDEV AGRI ROUTINE REV HABITAT RIGID/FLEX ...EPIST GEOG NEW/IDEA TREND MUNICH 20. PAGE 13 F0256 — WORKER KNOWL NAT/LISM SOC

B66
FUSFELD D.R.,THE AGE OF THE ECONOMIST. ECO/TAC WEALTH LAISSEZ MARXISM...EPIST 18/20 KEYNES/JM. PAGE 45 F0878 — PHIL/SCI CAP/ISM POLICY

EPISTEMOLOGY....SEE EPIST

EPTA....EXPANDED PROGRAM OF TECHNICAL ASSISTANCE

EQUILIB....EQUILIBRIUM; SEE ALSO BAL/PWR

N
PEN I.,PRIMER ON INTERNATIONAL TRADE. WOR+45 WOR-45 ECO/DEV DIPLOM EFFICIENCY 16/20 EEC. PAGE 104 F2055 — INT/TRADE BAL/PAY ECO/TAC EQUILIB

N19
BOS H.C.,A DISCUSSION ON METHODS OF MONETARY ANALYSIS AND NORMS FOR MONETARY POLICY (PAMPHLET). BAL/PAY COST INCOME...METH/COMP 20. PAGE 17 F0319 — FINAN POLICY EQUILIB SIMUL

N19
GROSECLOSE E.,THE DECAY OF MONEY; A SURVEY OF WESTERN CURRENCIES 1912-1962 (PAMPHLET). AFR FRANCE GERMANY UK LAW INT/TRADE BAL/PAY COST EQUILIB ...POLICY 20 DEPRESSION. PAGE 51 F1004 — FINAN NAT/G ECO/DEV ECO/TAC

N19
MIYASAWA K.,AN ECONOMIC SURVIVAL GAME (PAMPHLET). COST DEMAND EQUILIB INCOME PROFIT 20. PAGE 92 F1811 — ECOMETRIC GAME ECO/TAC DECISION

B27
BELLOC H.,THE SERVILE STATE (1912) (3RD ED.). PRUSSIA UK CULTURE STRATA INDUS NAT/G ECO/TAC CONTROL LEAD SUFF DISCRIM EQUILIB ORD/FREE WEALTH 20. PAGE 12 F0237 — WORKER CAP/ISM DOMIN CATH

B30
KEYNES J.M.,A TREATISE ON MONEY (2 VOLS.). UK USA-45 INDUS MARKET WORKER PRICE CONTROL COST OPTIMAL PROFIT WEALTH...POLICY 19/20 KEYNES/JM. PAGE 70 F1385 — EQUILIB ECO/TAC FINAN GEN/LAWS

B32
ROBBINS L.,AN ESSAY ON THE NATURE AND SIGNIFICANCE OF ECONOMIC SCIENCE. DEMAND EQUILIB PRODUC UTIL ...ECOMETRIC 20. PAGE 112 F2201 — GEN/LAWS METH/COMP ECO/DEV

B34
ROBINSON J.,THE ECONOMICS OF IMPERFECT COMPETITION. FINAN ECO/TAC PRICE COST DEMAND EQUILIB OPTIMAL WEALTH...METH MONOPOLY. PAGE 113 F2221 — MARKET WORKER INDUS

B35
KEYNES J.M.,THE GENERAL THEORY OF EMPLOYMENT, INTEREST, AND MONEY. AGRI INDUS WORKER ECO/TAC DEMAND EQUILIB INCOME PRODUC PROFIT ATTIT WEALTH 20. PAGE 71 F1386 — FINAN GEN/LAWS MARKET PRICE

B38
LAWLEY F.E.,THE GROWTH OF COLLECTIVE ECONOMY VOL. 2: INTERNATIONAL. WOR-45 AGRI INDUS EQUILIB OPTIMAL OWN WEALTH...NAT/COMP 19/20 NAZI NEW/DEAL MONOPOLY. PAGE 76 F1493 — ECO/TAC SOCISM NAT/LISM CONTROL

B40
TRIFFIN R.,MONOPOLISTIC COMPETITION AND GENERAL EQUILIBRIUM THEORY. DIST/IND PLAN TASK EQUILIB OPTIMAL...IDEA/COMP 20 MONOPOLY. PAGE 131 F2586 — INT/TRADE INDUS COST

B41
HAYEK F.A.,THE PURE THEORY OF CAPITAL. UNIV ECO/DEV ECO/TAC COST EQUILIB PROFIT WEALTH...SIMUL GEN/LAWS BIBLIOG INDEX TIME 20. PAGE 57 F1120 — CAP/ISM METH/CNCPT PRODUC FINAN

B48
HICKS J.R.,VALUE AND CAPITAL. FINAN PRICE EQUILIB INCOME PRODUC WEALTH...TIME/SEQ 20 MARSHALL/A PARETO/V SAMUELSN/P. PAGE 59 F1165 — ECOMETRIC MATH DEMAND PROB/SOLV

B48
SAMUELSON P.A.,FOUNDATIONS OF ECONOMIC ANALYSIS. MARKET RATION DEMAND UTIL...MATH METH T 20. PAGE 115 F2276 — EQUILIB GEN/LAWS ECO/DEV

B50
CHAMBERLIN E.,THE THEORY OF MONOPOLISTIC COMPETITION (1933). INDUS PAY GP/REL COST DEMAND EFFICIENCY OPTIMAL PRODUC WEALTH...GEN/LAWS 20. PAGE 23 F0443 — MARKET PRICE ECO/TAC EQUILIB

C50
ELLSWORTH P.T.,"INTERNATIONAL ECONOMY." ECO/DEV ECO/UNDEV FINAN LABOR DIPLOM FOR/AID TARIFFS BAL/PAY EQUILIB NAT/LISM OPTIMAL...INT/LAW 20 ILO GATT. PAGE 37 F0724 — BIBLIOG INT/TRADE ECO/TAC INT/ORG

C50
ROUSSEAU J.J.,"A DISCOURSE ON POLITICAL ECONOMY" (1755) IN THE SOCIAL CONTRACT AND DISCOURSES." UNIV SOCIETY STRATA STRUCT CONSEN EQUILIB HAPPINESS UTOPIA HEALTH WEALTH...POLICY WELF/ST. PAGE 114 F2252 — NAT/G ECO/TAC TAX GEN/LAWS

B51
HANSEN B.,A STUDY IN THE THEORY OF INFLATION. WOR-45 FINAN WAR DEMAND...CHARTS 20. PAGE 54 F1067 — PRICE ECO/TAC EQUILIB PRODUC

B52
EGLE W.P.,ECONOMIC STABILIZATION: OBJECTIVES, RULES, AND MECHANISMS. UNIV FINAN PROB/SOLV CAP/ISM ECO/TAC CONTROL...IDEA/COMP 20. PAGE 36 F0709 — EQUILIB PLAN NAT/G ECO/DEV

B52
REDFORD E.S.,ADMINISTRATION OF NATIONAL ECONOMIC CONTROL. ECO/DEV DELIB/GP ADJUD CONTROL EQUILIB 20. PAGE 110 F2166 — ADMIN ROUTINE GOV/REL LOBBY

B53
MILLIKAN M.F.,INCOME STABILIZATION FOR A DEVELOPING DEMOCRACY. USA+45 ECO/DEV LABOR BUDGET ECO/TAC TAX ADMIN ADJUST PRODUC WEALTH...POLICY TREND 20. PAGE 91 F1794 — ANTHOL MARKET EQUILIB EFFICIENCY

B53
NEISSER H.,NATIONAL INCOMES AND INTERNATIONAL TRADE. FRANCE GERMANY SWEDEN UK USA-45 EXTR/IND FINAN INDUS TEC/DEV PRICE BAL/PAY EQUILIB INCOME — INT/TRADE PRODUC MARKET

WEALTH...CHARTS METH 19 CHINJAP. PAGE 97 F1908 CON/ANAL

B54
MITCHELL W.G.,BUSINESS CYCLES. FINAN MARKET PRICE COST EQUILIB OPTIMAL PRODUC PROFIT...IDEA/COMP GEN/LAWS 19/20. PAGE 92 F1809
INDUS TIME/SEQ METH/COMP STAT

S54
SCITOVSKY T.,"TWO CONCEPTS OF EXTERNAL ECONOMIES." ECO/DEV IDEA/COMP. PAGE 118 F2329
SERV/IND GEN/LAWS INDUS EQUILIB

B55
GEORGE H.,PROGRESS AND POVERTY (1880). STRATA STRUCT INDUS TEC/DEV CAP/ISM EQUILIB INCOME OWN UTOPIA...WELF/ST CONCPT NEW/IDEA 19. PAGE 47 F0915
ECO/DEV ECO/TAC TAX WEALTH

B55
PALAMOUNTAIN JC J.R.,THE POLITICS OF DISTRIBUTION. USA+45 LG/CO SML/CO BAL/PWR CONTROL EQUILIB 20. PAGE 103 F2019
DIST/IND ECO/TAC CAP/ISM GP/REL

B56
FELLNER W.,TRENDS AND CYCLES IN ECONOMIC ACTIVITY: AN INTRODUCTION TO PROBLEMS OF ECONOMIC GROWTH. USA+45 INDUS ACT/RES CAP/ISM EQUILIB...MODAL METH/COMP BIBLIOG 20. PAGE 40 F0779
ECO/TAC TREND FINAN ECO/DEV

B56
ISARD W.,LOCATION AND SPACE-ECONOMY: GENERAL THEORY RELATING TO INDUSTRIAL LOCATION, MARKET AREAS, LAND USE, TRADE... UNIV DIST/IND MARKET LG/CO SML/CO TEC/DEV GP/REL EQUILIB HABITAT...NEW/IDEA MATH CHARTS 20. PAGE 66 F1290
GEN/LAWS GEOG INDUS REGION

B56
POOLE K.E.,PUBLIC FINANCE AND ECONOMIC WELFARE. STRUCT ECO/DEV LOC/G NAT/G BUDGET PAY ROUTINE COST EQUILIB WEALTH...SOC/WK METH/COMP 20. PAGE 107 F2103
FINAN TAX ORD/FREE

B57
DAY A.C.L.,OUTLINE OF MONETARY ECONOMICS. AFR WOR-45 INT/ORG WORKER DIPLOM BAL/PAY COST INCOME WEALTH...TIME/SEQ SIMUL 20. PAGE 31 F0594
FINAN NAT/G EQUILIB PRICE

B57
DOWNS A.,AN ECONOMIC THEORY OF DEMOCRACY. NAT/G EDU/PROP RISK CHOOSE PERS/REL EQUILIB...SOC METH/CNCPT LOG STYLE. PAGE 34 F0659
DECISION RATIONAL

B57
HARRIS S.E.,INTERNATIONAL AND INTERREGIONAL ECONOMICS. AFR WOR+45 WOR-45 NAT/G TARIFFS BAL/PAY EQUILIB...POLICY CONCPT STAT CHARTS IDEA/COMP 19/20. PAGE 55 F1088
INT/TRADE ECO/DEV MARKET FINAN

B57
HUTTON D.G.,INFLATION AND SOCIETY. AFR FINAN PLAN COST DEMAND EQUILIB...CONCPT 20. PAGE 64 F1254
ECO/DEV POLICY NAT/G ECO/TAC

B57
NANIWADA H.,STAAT UND WIRTSCHAFT; GRUNDLEGUNG DER NATIONALOEKONOMIE ALS DER LOGIK DER BURGERLICHEN GESELLSCHAFT. WOR+45 WOR-45 STRATA MARKET WORKER INGP/REL DEMAND EQUILIB WEALTH...POLICY IDEA/COMP GEN/LAWS 17/20 MARX/KARL KEYNES/JM LENIN/VI. PAGE 96 F1890
ALL/IDEOS ECO/TAC SOCIETY NAT/G

B58
DEFENSE AGAINST INFLATION. USA+45 LEGIS WORKER TAX PRICE DEMAND INCOME PRODUC...POLICY TREND METH/COMP 20 GOLD/STAND. PAGE 1 F0012
ECO/TAC EQUILIB WEALTH PROB/SOLV

B58
DOWNIE J.,THE COMPETITIVE PROCESS. ECO/TAC PRICE EFFICIENCY OPTIMAL PRODUC WEALTH...IDEA/COMP METH/COMP 20 MONOPOLY. PAGE 34 F0658
EQUILIB MARKET INDUS ECO/DEV

B58
US CONGRESS JOINT ECO COMM,THE RELATIONSHIP OF PRICES TO ECONOMIC STABILITY AND GROWTH. USA+45 MARKET TAX ADJUST COST DEMAND INCOME PRODUC ...POLICY TREND CHARTS ANTHOL 20 CONGRESS. PAGE 134 F2650
ECO/DEV PLAN EQUILIB PRICE

B58
WARNER A.W.,CONCEPTS AND CASES IN ECONOMIC ANALYSIS. PROB/SOLV BARGAIN CONTROL INCOME PRODUC ...ECOMETRIC MGT CONCPT CLASSIF CHARTS 20 KEYNES/JM. PAGE 143 F2820
ECO/TAC DEMAND EQUILIB COST

B59
ALLEN W.R.,FOREIGN TRADE AND FINANCE. ECO/DEV DIPLOM BAL/PAY...POLICY CONCPT ANTHOL 20. PAGE 4 F0073
INT/TRADE EQUILIB FINAN

B59
HARTOG F.,EUROPEAN TRADE CYCLE POLICY. WORKER TAX PRICE WAR CENTRAL DEMAND...TREND CHARTS 20 UN. PAGE 56 F1103
EQUILIB EUR+WWI INT/TRADE

B59
KOREAN MINISTRY RECONSTRUCTION,KOREAN ECONOMY AND ITS REQUIREMENTS. KOREA USA+45 ECO/TAC EQUILIB INCOME WEALTH...CHARTS 20. PAGE 73 F1427
FOR/AID WAR FINAN DIPLOM

B59
LINK R.G.,ENGLISH THEORIES OF ECONOMIC FLUCTUATIONS: 1815-1848. FRANCE UK AGRI WORKER DIPLOM PRICE TASK WAR DEMAND PRODUC...POLICY BIBLIOG 18 MALTHUS MILL/JS WILSON/J. PAGE 80 F1574
IDEA/COMP ECO/DEV WEALTH EQUILIB

S59
STREETEN P.,"UNBALANCED GROWTH" UK ECO/DEV AGRI MARKET TEC/DEV CAP/ISM ECO/TAC FOR/AID INT/TRADE DEMAND ORD/FREE...CONCPT 20. PAGE 127 F2502
IDEA/COMP FINAN PRODUC EQUILIB

B60
BAERWALD F.,ECONOMIC SYSTEM ANALYSIS: CONCEPTS AND PERSPECTIVES. USA+45 ECO/DEV NAT/G COMPUTER EQUILIB INCOME ATTIT...DECISION CONCPT IDEA/COMP. PAGE 8 F0151
ACT/RES ECO/TAC ROUTINE FINAN

B60
BELLAN R.C.,PRINCIPLES OF ECONOMICS AND THE CANADIAN ECONOMY (2ND ED.). CANADA UK USA+45 LABOR WORKER CAP/ISM INT/TRADE RISK BAL/PAY EQUILIB ALL/IDEOS 20. PAGE 12 F0236
ECO/DEV PRODUC WEALTH FINAN

B60
HARBERGER A.C.,THE DEMAND FOR DURABLE GOODS. AGRI FINAN COST EQUILIB...MATH STAT TIME/SEQ TREND CON/ANAL CHARTS SIMUL ANTHOL 20. PAGE 55 F1072
ECOMETRIC DEMAND PRICE

B60
RICHARDSON G.B.,INFORMATION AND INVESTMENT. PLAN PROB/SOLV CAP/ISM ECO/TAC KNOWL...CONCPT 20 MONEY. PAGE 111 F2184
ECO/DEV EQUILIB FINAN PHIL/SCI

B60
SIEGEL B.N.,AGGREGATE ECONOMICS AND PUBLIC POLICY. ECO/DEV TEC/DEV ECO/TAC TASK DEMAND EQUILIB INCOME ...CHARTS 20. PAGE 121 F2396
ECOMETRIC WEALTH PRODUC MARKET

B60
SILK L.S.,THE RESEARCH REVOLUTION. USA+45 FINAN CAP/ISM ECO/TAC PRICE EQUILIB PRODUC...STAT TREND CHARTS. PAGE 122 F2402
ECO/DEV R+D TEC/DEV PROB/SOLV

B61
BUSSCHAU W.J.,GOLD AND INTERNATIONAL LIQUIDITY. AFR WOR+45 PRICE EQUILIB WEALTH...CHARTS 20. PAGE 20 F0396
FINAN DIPLOM PROB/SOLV

B61
CLARK J.M.,COMPETITION AS A DYNAMIC PROCESS. ECO/DEV EXTR/IND INDUS LG/CO TEC/DEV ECO/TAC PRICE EQUILIB PRODUC...NEW/IDEA CAP 20. PAGE 25 F0483
WEALTH GP/REL FINAN PROFIT

B61
GANGULI B.N.,ECONOMIC INTEGRATION. FINAN LABOR CAP/ISM DIPLOM WEALTH...NAT/COMP 20. PAGE 46 F0895
ECO/TAC METH/CNCPT EQUILIB ECO/UNDEV

B61
MORRIS B.R.,PROBLEMS OF AMERICAN ECONOMIC GROWTH. USA+45 LABOR WORKER BUDGET ECO/TAC INT/TRADE EQUILIB 20. PAGE 94 F1836
ECO/DEV POLICY TEC/DEV DEMAND

B61
PETCH G.A.,ECONOMIC DEVELOPMENT AND MODERN WEST AFRICA. AFR CONGO/BRAZ GHANA NIGER SIER/LEONE AGRI MARKET LABOR FOR/AID TAX COST EFFICIENCY EQUILIB PRODUC...GEOG TREND 20. PAGE 105 F2068
ECO/UNDEV TEC/DEV EXTR/IND ECO/TAC

B61
PROUDHON P.J.,LA GUERRE ET LA PAIX (2 VOLS.). UNIV STRATA PROB/SOLV EQUILIB INCOME ATTIT...CONCPT 19. PAGE 108 F2125
WAR PEACE WEALTH

B62
HIRSCHFIELD R.S.,THE CONSTITUTION AND THE COURT. AFR SCHOOL WAR RACE/REL EQUILIB ORD/FREE...POLICY MAJORIT DECISION JURID 18/20 PRESIDENT CIVIL/LIB SUPREME/CT CONGRESS. PAGE 60 F1175
ADJUD PWR CONSTN LAW

B62
LUTZ F.A.,THE PROBLEM OF INTERNATIONAL ECONOMIC EQUILIBRIUM. FINAN PRODUC WEALTH 20 MONEY. PAGE 82 F1611
DIPLOM EQUILIB BAL/PAY PROB/SOLV

B62
MEYER F.V.,THE TERMS OF TRADE. WOR+45 AGRI MARKET PROC/MFG DIPLOM PRICE DEMAND PRODUC 20. PAGE 90 F1769
INT/TRADE BAL/PAY SIMUL EQUILIB

B62
SHINOHARA M.,GROWTH AND CYCLES IN THE JAPANESE ECONOMY. INDUS LABOR TEC/DEV CAP/ISM INT/TRADE PAY COST EFFICIENCY INCOME WEALTH...METH/COMP 20 CHINJAP. PAGE 121 F2380
PRODUC ECO/DEV EQUILIB ECOMETRIC

B63
CLARK J.J.,BUSINESS FLUCTUATIONS, GROWTH, AND ECONOMIC STABILIZATION. USA+45 FINAN INT/TRADE OPTIMAL...METH/CNCPT ANTHOL BIBLIOG 20. PAGE 25 F0479
CAP/ISM ECO/TAC EQUILIB POLICY

B63
FRIEDMAN M.,INFLATION: CAUSES AND CURES. AFR INDIA ECO/DEV ECO/TAC INT/TRADE RATION PRICE DEMAND
ECO/UNDEV PLAN

...POLICY 20. PAGE 44 F0860 FINAN EQUILIB B63

LEE M.W.,MACROECONOMICS: FLUCTUATIONS, GROWTH AND STABILITY (3RD ED.). MARKET LABOR TEC/DEV INT/TRADE TAX PRICE WAR PRODUC...POLICY ECOMETRIC CHARTS 19/20. PAGE 77 F1505 EQUILIB TREND WEALTH B63

MEEK R.L.,THE ECONOMICS OF PHYSIOCRACY. FRANCE UK AGRI FINAN WORKER CAP/ISM TAX DEMAND EQUILIB INCOME HABITAT...CHARTS ANTHOL 17. PAGE 89 F1744 PRODUC WEALTH MARKET B63

MEIER G.,INTERNATIONAL TRADE AND DEVELOPMENT. FINAN BAL/PAY COST DEMAND DISCRIM EQUILIB WEALTH...POLICY ECOMETRIC MATH STAT BIBLIOG/A 20. PAGE 89 F1747 ECO/UNDEV ECO/TAC INT/TRADE IDEA/COMP B63

RANGEL I.,A INFLACAO BRASILEIRA (2ND ED.). AFR BRAZIL AGRI INDUS MARKET INT/TRADE DEMAND EQUILIB ATTIT 20. PAGE 109 F2144 ECO/UNDEV FINAN PRICE TAX B63

VON MISES L.,HUMAN ACTION: A TREATISE ON ECONOMICS (2ND ED.). SOCIETY MARKET TAX PAY PRICE DEMAND EQUILIB RATIONAL...PSY 20. PAGE 142 F2794 PLAN DRIVE ATTIT S63

ANDREWS R.B.,"ECONOMIC PLANNING FOR SMALL AREAS: THE PLANNING PROCESS." INDUS PROC/MFG PROVS PROB/SOLV TAX EQUILIB...METH/COMP HYPO/EXP METH MUNICH 20. PAGE 5 F0103 ECO/TAC PLAN LOC/G N63

COMM ON FEDERAL TAX POLICY,FINANCING AMERICA'S FUTURE: TAXES, ECONOMIC STABILITY AND GROWTH (PAMPHLET). USA+45 LG/CO SML/CO DELIB/GP INCOME ...CHARTS 20. PAGE 26 F0513 TAX NAT/G EQUILIB PLAN B64

INTERNATIONAL MONETARY ARRANGEMENTS: THE PROBLEM OF CHOICE. PLAN PROB/SOLV INT/TRADE ADJUST COST EQUILIB 20. PAGE 1 F0020 POLICY DIPLOM FINAN ECO/DEV B64

BALL R.J.,INFLATION AND THE THEORY OF MONEY. MARKET TAX PAY PRICE TASK ADJUST BAL/PAY COST INCOME PRODUC WEALTH...METH/COMP 20 KEYNES/JM MONEY. PAGE 9 F0167 EQUILIB DEMAND POLICY B64

GEORGIADIS H.G.,BALANCE OF PAYMENTS EQUILIBRIUM. COST DEMAND...CONCPT MATH GEN/LAWS 20 KEYNES/JM. PAGE 47 F0916 BAL/PAY EQUILIB SIMUL INT/TRADE B64

HERSKOVITS M.J.,ECONOMIC TRANSITION IN AFRICA. FUT INT/ORG NAT/G WORKER PROB/SOLV TEC/DEV INT/TRADE EQUILIB INCOME...ANTHOL 20. PAGE 59 F1157 AFR ECO/UNDEV PLAN ADMIN B64

JACOBY N.H.,UNITED STATES MONETARY POLICY. UK USA+45 LAW NAT/G TEC/DEV TAX EQUILIB INCOME ...METH/COMP 20 FED/RESERV. PAGE 66 F1300 ECO/DEV POLICY ECO/TAC FINAN B64

STONIER A.W.,EXERCISES IN ECONOMICS. FINAN INDUS TEC/DEV RENT PAY EQUILIB PRODUC PROFIT...METH/COMP T. PAGE 127 F2498 PRICE MARKET WORKER B64

ZEBOT C.A.,THE ECONOMICS OF COMPETITIVE COEXISTENCE. CHINA/COM USSR WOR+45 FINAN MARKET FOR/AID PRICE DEMAND EQUILIB WEALTH ALL/IDEOS 20. PAGE 150 F2961 TEC/DEV DIPLOM METH/COMP B65

BAUMOL W.J.,ECONOMIC THEORY AND OPERATIONS ANALYSIS (2ND ED.). MARKET LG/CO BUDGET PRICE COST EQUILIB PRODUC...DECISION MATH CHARTS GAME 20. PAGE 12 F0219 OP/RES ECO/DEV METH/COMP STAT B65

BREAK G.F.,FEDERAL LENDING AND ECONOMIC STABILITY. USA+45 ECO/DEV LG/CO SML/CO EQUILIB...CHARTS 20. PAGE 18 F0344 BUDGET FINAN NAT/G ECO/TAC B65

MARCUS E.,INTERNATIONAL TRADE AND FINANCE. EFFICIENCY EQUILIB...CHARTS METH/COMP BIBLIOG METH T 20. PAGE 85 F1664 INT/TRADE FINAN MARKET WEALTH B65

MCCOLL G.D.,THE AUSTRALIAN BALANCE OF PAYMENTS. UK USA+45 AGRI WORKER DIPLOM EQUILIB PRODUC...STAT TREND CHARTS BIBLIOG/A 20 AUSTRAL. PAGE 88 F1719 ECO/DEV BAL/PAY INT/TRADE COST B65

ROLFE S.E.,GOLD AND WORLD POWER. AFR UK USA+45 WOR-45 INDUS WORKER INT/TRADE DEMAND...MGT CHARTS 20. PAGE 113 F2234 BAL/PAY EQUILIB ECO/TAC DIPLOM B65

ROOSA R.V.,MONETARY REFORM FOR THE WORLD ECONOMY. AFR EUR+WWI USA+45 WOR+45 CREATE BUDGET DIPLOM FOR/AID EQUILIB WEALTH IMF. PAGE 114 F2237 FINAN INT/ORG INT/TRADE BAL/PAY B65

SCITOVSKY T.,REQUIREMENTS OF AN INTERNATIONAL RESERVE SYSTEM. AFR ECO/TAC...PREDICT 20 SILVER MONEY. PAGE 118 F2330 BAL/PAY FINAN EQUILIB INT/TRADE B65

VANEK J.,GENERAL EQUILIBRIUM OF INTERNATIONAL DISCRIMINATION; THE CASE OF CUSTOMS UNIONS. LABOR PROB/SOLV ECO/TAC DISCRIM INCOME...MATH CHARTS METH 20. PAGE 140 F2767 INT/TRADE TARIFFS INT/ORG EQUILIB B65

WASSERMAN M.J.,THE BALANCE OF PAYMENTS: HISTORY, METHODOLOGY, THEORY. UK USA+45 USA-45 CAP/ISM DIPLOM EFFICIENCY...DECISION METH/CNCPT BIBLIOG 18/20 LEAGUE/NAT. PAGE 144 F2828 BAL/PAY ECO/TAC GEN/LAWS EQUILIB B65

ZAWADZKI K.K.F.,THE ECONOMICS OF INFLATIONARY PROCESSES. FINAN INT/TRADE PRICE CONTROL DEMAND EQUILIB PROFIT 20. PAGE 150 F2960 ECO/DEV COST ECO/TAC CAP/ISM S65

HUTT W.H.,"KEYNESIAN REVISIONS" SOUTH/AFR ECO/DEV FINAN NAT/G WORKER BUDGET TAX PRICE EQUILIB WEALTH 20 KEYNES/JM. PAGE 64 F1252 ECO/TAC GEN/LAWS LOG B66

FOX K.A.,THE THEORY OF QUANTITATIVE ECONOMIC POLICY WITH APPLICATIONS TO ECONOMIC GROWTH AND STABILIZATION. ECO/DEV AGRI NAT/G PLAN ADMIN RISK ...DECISION IDEA/COMP SIMUL T. PAGE 43 F0837 ECO/TAC ECOMETRIC EQUILIB GEN/LAWS B66

LEE M.W.,TOWARD ECONOMIC STABILITY. USA+45 BUDGET TAX PRICE EQUILIB INCOME. PAGE 77 F1506 ECO/TAC CONTROL POLICY NAT/G B66

MEERHAEGHE M.,INTERNATIONAL ECONOMIC INSTITUTIONS. EUR+WWI FINAN INDUS MARKET PLAN TARIFFS BAL/PAY EQUILIB...POLICY BIBLIOG/A 20 GATT OEEC EEC IBRD EURCOALSTL. PAGE 89 F1745 ECO/TAC ECO/DEV INT/TRADE INT/ORG B66

PIQUET H.S.,THE US BALANCE OF PAYMENTS AND INTERNATIONAL MONETARY RESERVES. AFR USA+45 PROB/SOLV INT/TRADE GOV/REL EQUILIB...POLICY STAT CHARTS 20. PAGE 106 F2090 BAL/PAY DIPLOM FINAN ECO/TAC N66

OECD,THE BALANCE OF PAYMENTS ADJUSTMENT PROCESS (PAMPHLET). EUR+WWI ECO/DEV FINAN CONSULT PLAN PROB/SOLV BUDGET CAP/ISM INT/TRADE PRICE CONTROL EQUILIB 20. PAGE 101 F1975 BAL/PAY ECO/TAC DIPLOM INT/ORG B67

ALLEN R.G.,MACRO-ECONOMIC THEORY: A MATHEMATICAL TREATMENT. UNIV...SIMUL T. PAGE 4 F0070 ECOMETRIC MATH EQUILIB GAME B67

BERGMANN D KAUN B.,STRUCTURAL UNEMPLOYMENT IN THE UNITED STATES. USA+45 ECO/DEV PRICE ADMIN INGP/REL DEMAND EQUILIB WEALTH...MATH REGRESS STAT 20 NEGRO. PAGE 13 F0258 ECOMETRIC METH WORKER ECO/TAC B67

KEWEN P.B.,INTERNATIONAL ECONOMICS (2ND ED.). USA+45 WOR+45 MARKET TARIFFS...BIBLIOG T 20. PAGE 70 F1384 INT/TRADE BAL/PAY FINAN EQUILIB B67

SPURRIER R.B.,THE OVERPOPULATED SOCIETY. WORKER EATING PERS/REL DEMAND EQUILIB ILLEGIT INCOME HABITAT 20. PAGE 125 F2461 BIO/SOC FOR/AID DRIVE RECEIVE B67

ULMAN L.,CHALLENGES TO COLLECTIVE BARGAINING. ECO/TAC DISCRIM EQUILIB ATTIT...JURID SOC/WK. PAGE 132 F2599 LABOR BARGAIN ADJUD POLICY S67

CRAIG A.,"ARGENTINA: THE LATEST REVOLUTION." ELITES NAT/G CHIEF FORCES ECO/TAC CIVMIL/REL GOV/REL EQUILIB PRIVIL 20 ARGEN. PAGE 28 F0550 ECO/UNDEV FINAN ATTIT REV S67

PLOTT C.R.,"A NOTION OF EQUILIBRIUM AND ITS POSSIBILITY UNDER MAJORITY RULE." CREATE...DECISION STAT CHARTS 20. PAGE 106 F2094 SIMUL EQUILIB CHOOSE MAJORITY S67

ZOETEWEIJ B.,"INCOME POLICIES ABROAD: AN INTERIM REPORT." NAT/G PROB/SOLV BARGAIN BUDGET PRICE RISK CENTRAL EFFICIENCY EQUILIB...MGT NAT/COMP 20. PAGE 150 F2967 METH/COMP INCOME POLICY LABOR B75

JEVONS W.S.,MONEY AND THE MECHANISM OF EXCHANGE. INDUS MARKET DIPLOM COST EQUILIB WEALTH LAISSEZ ...GEN/LAWS 19 MONEY. PAGE 67 F1319 PRICE FINAN ECO/TAC

POLICY

B76
TAINE H.A.,THE ANCIENT REGIME. FRANCE STRATA FORCES PARTIC EQUILIB WEALTH CONSERVE POPULISM...GOV/COMP SOC/INTEG 18/19. PAGE 128 F2527 — NAT/G GOV/REL TAX REV

B98
MARSHALL A.,PRINCIPLES OF ECONOMICS. INDUS WORKER PRICE COST EQUILIB INCOME OPTIMAL PRODUC...TIME/SEQ METH RICARDO/D. PAGE 86 F1678 — WEALTH GEN/LAWS MARKET

N19
PATRICK H.T.,CYCLICAL INSTABILITY AND FISCAL-MONETARY POLICY IN POST-WAR JAPAN (PAMPHLET). INDUS MARKET DIPLOM TAX PRICE BAL/PAY...TREND CHARTS EQULIB 20 CHINJAP. PAGE 104 F2036 — ECO/DEV PRODUC STAT

B53
WILLIAMS J.H.,ECONOMIC STABILITY IN A CHANGING WORLD. FRANCE USA+45 USSR AGRI WORKER BUDGET INT/TRADE TAX WAR BAL/PAY COST EFFICIENCY ALL/IDEOS EQULIB 20 KEYNES/JM. PAGE 147 F2892 — POLICY FINAN ECO/TAC WEALTH

B64
ZOBER M.,MARKETING MANAGEMENT. FINAN BUDGET EDU/PROP PRICE PRODUC ATTIT...POLICY TREND CHARTS METH/COMP EQULIB 20. PAGE 150 F2966 — ECO/DEV MGT CONTROL MARKET

S65
GRENIEWSKI H.,"INTENTION AND PERFORMANCE: A PRIMER OF CYBERNETICS OF PLANNING." EFFICIENCY OPTIMAL KNOWL SKILL...DECISION MGT EQULIB. PAGE 51 F0995 — SIMUL GAME GEN/METH PLAN

ERASMUS C.J. F0741

ERB GF F0742

ERDEMLI....ERDEMLI, TURKEY

ERDMAN P.E. F0743

ERDMANN H.H. F0744

ERHARD L. F0745

ERNST M.L. F0746

ESPIONAGE....ESPIONAGE

ESTEBAN J.C. F0747

ESTEVEZ A. F0748

ESTEY J.A. F0749

ESTEY M. F0750

ESTHUS R.A. F0751

ESTIMATION....SEE COST

ESTONIA....SEE ALSO USSR

ESTRANGEMENT....SEE STRANGE

ET A.L. F1381,F1765,F2274,F2962

ETHERINGTON D.M. F0752

ETHIC....PERSONAL ETHICS

ETHIOPIA....SEE ALSO AFR

B60
SIMOONS F.J.,NORTHWEST ETHIOPIA; PEOPLES AND ECONOMY. ETHIOPIA MARKET CREATE 20. PAGE 122 F2411 — SOCIETY STRUCT AGRI INDUS

B63
CHOJNACKI S.,REGISTER ON CURRENT RESEARCH ON ETHIOPIA AND THE HORN OF AFRICA. ETHIOPIA LAW CULTURE AGRI SECT EDU/PROP ADMIN...GEOG HEAL LING 20. PAGE 24 F0470 — BIBLIOG ACT/RES INTELL ACADEM

L67
MACDONALD R.S.J.,"THE RESORT TO ECONOMIC COERCION BY INTERNATIONAL POLITICAL ORGANIZATIONS." CUBA ETHIOPIA RHODESIA SOUTH/AFR NAT/G FOR/AID INT/TRADE DOMIN CONTROL SANCTION...DECISION LEAGUE/NAT UN OAS 20. PAGE 83 F1625 — INT/ORG COERCE ECO/TAC DIPLOM

ETHNICITY....SEE RACE/REL, CULTURE

ETHNOGRAPHY....SEE CULTURE

ETIQUET....ETIQUETTE, STYLING, FASHION, MANNERS

NCO
STOLPER W.,"SOCIAL FACTORS IN ECONOMIC PLANNING, WITH SPECIAL REFERENCE TO NIGERIA" AFR NIGER CULTURE FAM SECT RECEIVE ETIQUET ADMIN DEMAND 20. PAGE 126 F2494 — ECO/UNDEV PLAN ADJUST RISK

ETSCHMANN R. F0753

EUGENICS....SEE BIO/SOC+GEOG

EUGENIE....EMPRESS EUGENIE (FRANCE)

EULAU H. F2800

EUR+WWI....EUROPE SINCE WORLD WAR I

EURATOM....EUROPEAN ATOMIC ENERGY COMMUNITY

B59
ROBERTSON A.H.,EUROPEAN INSTITUTIONS: COOPERATION, INTEGRATION, UNIFICATION. EUR+WWI FINAN INT/ORG FORCES INT/TRADE TARIFFS 20 EEC EURATOM ECSC NATO TREATY. PAGE 112 F2208 — ECO/DEV DIPLOM INDUS ECO/TAC

S60
NANES A.,"THE EUROPEAN COMMUNITY AND THE UNITED STATES: EVOLVING RELATIONS." EUR+WWI USA+45 WOR+45 ECO/UNDEV MARKET NAT/G DELIB/GP PLAN LEGIT ATTIT PWR WEALTH...CONCPT STAT TIME/SEQ CON/ANAL EEC METH/GP OEEC 20 EURATOM. PAGE 96 F1889 — INT/ORG REGION

B64
ECONOMIDES C.P.,LE POUVOIR DE DECISION DES ORGANISATIONS INTERNATIONALES EUROPEENNES. DIPLOM DOMIN INGP/REL EFFICIENCY...INT/LAW JURID 20 NATO OEEC EEC COUNCL/EUR EURATOM. PAGE 36 F0698 — INT/ORG PWR DECISION GP/COMP

B65
HASSON J.A.,THE ECONOMICS OF NUCLEAR POWER. INDIA UK USA+45 WOR+45 INT/ORG TEC/DEV COST...SOC STAT CHARTS 20 EURATOM. PAGE 56 F1108 — NUC/PWR INDUS ECO/DEV METH

S67
WEIL G.L.,"THE MERGER OF THE INSTITUTIONS OF THE EUROPEAN COMMUNITIES" EUR+WWI ECO/DEV INT/TRADE CONSEN PLURISM...DECISION MGT 20 EEC EURATOM ECSC TREATY. PAGE 145 F2847 — ECO/TAC INT/ORG CENTRAL INT/LAW

EURCOALSTL....EUROPEAN COAL AND STEEL COMMUNITY; SEE ALSO VOL/ASSN, INT/ORG

B62
SCHMITT H.A.,THE PATH TO EUROPEAN UNITY. EUR+WWI USA+45 PLAN TEC/DEV DIPLOM FOR/AID CONFER...INT/LAW 20 EEC EURCOALSTL MARSHL/PLN UNIFICA. PAGE 117 F2300 — INT/ORG INT/TRADE REGION ECO/DEV

B66
MEERHAEGHE M.,INTERNATIONAL ECONOMIC INSTITUTIONS. EUR+WWI FINAN INDUS MARKET PLAN TARIFFS BAL/PAY EQUILIB...POLICY BIBLIOG/A 20 GATT OEEC EEC IBRD EURCOALSTL. PAGE 89 F1745 — ECO/TAC ECO/DEV INT/TRADE INT/ORG

EURCT/JUST....EUROPEAN COURT OF JUSTICE

EUROPE....SEE EUR+WWI, MOD/EUR

B39
MARQUAND H.A.,ORGANIZED LABOUR IN FOUR CONTINENTS. EUR+WWI USA-45 INDUS NAT/G PAY GP/REL TOTALISM ATTIT WEALTH ALL/IDEOS...TREND NAT/COMP 20 ILO AFL/CIO EUROPE CHINJAP MEXIC/AMER. PAGE 85 F1673 — LABOR WORKER CONCPT ANTHOL

B50
HUNT R.N.,THE THEORY AND PRACTICE OF COMMUNISM. STRUCT WORKER NAT/LISM TOTALISM...CONCPT TREND 19/20 STALIN/J EUROPE. PAGE 63 F1244 — MARXISM SOCISM REV STRATA

B52
MACARTHUR D.,REVITALIZING A NATION. ASIA COM FUT KOREA WOR+45 NAT/G FOR/AID TAX GIVE WAR ATTIT SOCISM 20 CHINJAP EUROPE. PAGE 83 F1619 — LEAD FORCES TOP/EX POLICY

B54
FRIEDMAN W.,THE PUBLIC CORPORATION: A COMPARATIVE SYMPOSIUM (UNIVERSITY OF TORONTO SCHOOL OF LAW COMPARATIVE LAW SERIES, VOL. I). AFR SWEDEN USA+45 INDUS INT/ORG NAT/G REGION CENTRAL FEDERAL...POLICY JURID IDEA/COMP NAT/COMP ANTHOL 20 MONOPOLY EUROPE. PAGE 44 F0861 — LAW SOCISM LG/CO OWN

B58
PALYI M.,MANAGED MONEY AT THE CROSSROADS: THE EUROPEAN EXPERIENCE. AFR WOR+45 WOR-45 TEC/DEV DIPLOM INT/TRADE DEMAND WEALTH...CHARTS BIBLIOG 19/20 EUROPE SILVER. PAGE 103 F2022 — FINAN ECO/TAC ECO/DEV PRODUC

N58
EUROPEAN COMM ECO-SOC PROG,EUROPEAN BUSINESS CYCLE POLICY (PAMPHLET). AFR EUR+WWI MARKET WORKER DIPLOM PRICE BAL/PAY 20 EUROPE. PAGE 39 F0754 — ECO/DEV FINAN ECO/TAC PROB/SOLV

B61
STARNER F.L.,GENERAL OBLIGATION BOND FINANCING BY LOCAL GOVERNMENTS: A SURVEY OF STATE CONTROLS. CANADA UK USA+45 CONSTN PROVS...POLICY JURID METH/COMP 20 EUROPE CALIFORNIA. PAGE 125 F2471 FINAN LOC/G GOV/REL ADJUD

B62
GEARY R.C.,EUROPE'S FUTURE IN FIGURES. FUT GOV/REL DEMAND PRODUC...STAT CHARTS METH/COMP ANTHOL METH 20 EUROPE. PAGE 47 F0912 FINAN ECO/DEV PREDICT WEALTH

B62
LUTZ F.A.,GELD UND WAHRUNG. AFR MARKET LABOR BUDGET 20 EUROPE. PAGE 82 F1610 ECO/TAC FINAN DIPLOM POLICY

B64
SANDEE J.,EUROPE'S FUTURE CONSUMPTION. EUR+WWI FUT EDU/PROP...IDEA/COMP NAT/COMP ANTHOL 20 EUROPE. PAGE 115 F2277 MARKET ECO/DEV PREDICT PRICE

B66
HARLOW J.S.,FRENCH ECONOMIC PLANNING: A CHALLENGE TO REASON. EUR+WWI FRANCE PROB/SOLV 20 EUROPE. PAGE 55 F1084 ECO/TAC PLAN STRUCT

N66
EOMMITTEE ECONOMIC DEVELOPMENT,THE DOLLAR AND THE WORLD MONETARY SYSTEM: A STATEMENT ON NATIONAL POLICY (PAMPHLET). AFR USA+45 NAT/G PLAN PROB/SOLV BUDGET ECO/TAC FOR/AID INCOME...POLICY 20 EUROPE. PAGE 38 F0740 FINAN BAL/PAY DIPLOM ECO/DEV

EUROPE/E....EASTERN EUROPE (ALL EUROPEAN COMMUNIST NATIONS)

B64
GRIFFITH W.E.,COMMUNISM IN EUROPE (2 VOLS.). CZECHOSLVK USSR WOR+45 WOR-45 YUGOSLAVIA INGP/REL MARXISM SOCISM...ANTHOL 20 EUROPE/E. PAGE 51 F1000 COM POL/PAR DIPLOM GOV/COMP

EUROPE/W....WESTERN EUROPE (NON-COMMUNIST EUROPE, EXCLUDING GREECE, TURKEY, SCANDINAVIA, AND THE BRITISH ISLES)

N19
HACKETT J.,ECONOMIC PLANNING IN FRANCE; ITS RELATION TO THE POLICIES OF THE DEVELOPED COUNTRIES OF WESTERN EUROPE (PAMPHLET). EUR+WWI FRANCE ECO/DEV PROB/SOLV CONTROL...POLICY 20 EUROPE/W. PAGE 52 F1026 ECO/TAC NAT/G PLAN INSPECT

B47
ISAAC J.,ECONOMICS OF MIGRATION. MOD/EUR CULTURE STRATA STRUCT NAT/G COLONIAL WEALTH...OLD/LIB TREND TIME 19/20 EUROPE/W MIGRATION. PAGE 65 F1289 HABITAT SOC GEOG

B63
LICHTHEIM G.,THE NEW EUROPE: TODAY AND TOMORROW. EUR+WWI FINAN 20 EEC EUROPE/W. PAGE 80 F1560 DIPLOM ECO/DEV INT/ORG INT/TRADE

B63
MYRDAL G.,CHALLENGE TO AFFLUENCE. USA+45 WOR+45 FINAN INT/ORG NAT/G PLAN ECO/TAC INT/TRADE BAL/PAY ORD/FREE 20 EUROPE/W. PAGE 96 F1882 ECO/DEV WEALTH DIPLOM PRODUC

B66
MUNBY D.,ECONOMIC GROWTH IN WORLD PERSPECTIVE. AFR WOR+45 SOCIETY INDUS PLAN TEC/DEV ECO/TAC FOR/AID INT/TRADE COST CATHISM...ANTHOL 20 EUROPE/W CHURCH/STA. PAGE 95 F1859 SECT ECO/UNDEV ECO/DEV

EUROPEAN ATOMIC ENERGY COMMUNITY....SEE EURATOM

EUROPEAN COAL AND STEEL COMMUNITY....SEE EURCOALSTL

EUROPEAN COURT OF JUSTICE....SEE EURCT/JUST

EUROPEAN ECONOMIC COMMUNITY....SEE EEC

EUROPEAN FREE TRADE ASSOCIATION....SEE EFTA

EUROPEAN INVESTMENT BANK....SEE EIB

EUROPEAN COMM ECO-SOC PROG F0754

EUROPEAN FREE TRADE ASSN F0755

EVANS R.H. F0756

EVERS/MED....MEDGAR EVERS

EX POST FACTO LAWS....SEE EXPOSTFACT

EX/IM/BANK....EXPORT-IMPORT BANK

EX/STRUC....EXECUTIVE ESTABLISHMENTS

N19
FIKS M.,PUBLIC ADMINISTRATION IN ISRAEL (PAMPHLET). ISRAEL SCHOOL EX/STRUC BUDGET PAY INGP/REL ...DECISION 20 CIVIL/SERV. PAGE 41 F0792 EDU/PROP NAT/G ADMIN WORKER

N19
MARSH J.F. JR.,THE FBI RETIREMENT BILL (PAMPHLET). USA+45 EX/STRUC WORKER PLAN PROB/SOLV BUDGET LEAD LOBBY PARL/PROC PERS/REL RIGID/FLEX...POLICY 20 FBI PRESIDENT BUR/BUDGET. PAGE 86 F1677 ADMIN NAT/G SENIOR GOV/REL

N19
MCCONNELL G.,THE STEEL SEIZURE OF 1952 (PAMPHLET). USA+45 FINAN INDUS PROC/MFG LG/CO EX/STRUC ADJUD CONTROL GP/REL ORD/FREE PWR 20 TRUMAN/HS PRESIDENT CONGRESS. PAGE 88 F1721 DELIB/GP LABOR PROB/SOLV NAT/G

N19
SILVERMAN C.,THE PRESIDENT'S ECONOMIC ADVISERS (PAMPHLET). USA+45 LAW ELITES ECO/DEV EX/STRUC ADMIN LEAD GOV/REL PERS/REL ROLE...POLICY DECISION 20 PRESIDENT CONGRESS EISNHWR/DD. PAGE 122 F2404 CONSULT PROB/SOLV NAT/G PLAN

B24
HOLDSWORTH W.S.,A HISTORY OF ENGLISH LAW; THE COMMON LAW AND ITS RIVALS (VOL. VI). AFR UK STRATA EX/STRUC ADJUD ADMIN CONTROL CT/SYS...JURID CONCPT GEN/LAWS 17 PARLIAMENT ENGLSH/LAW COMMON/LAW. PAGE 61 F1194 LAW CONSTN LEGIS CHIEF

B25
MATHEWS J.M.,AMERICAN STATE GOVERNMENT. USA-45 LOC/G CHIEF EX/STRUC LEGIS ADJUD CONTROL CT/SYS ROUTINE GOV/REL PWR 20 GOVERNOR. PAGE 87 F1703 PROVS ADMIN FEDERAL CONSTN

B28
FRANKFURTER F.,THE BUSINESS OF THE SUPREME COURT; A STUDY IN THE FEDERAL JUDICIAL SYSTEM. USA-45 CONSTN EX/STRUC PROB/SOLV GP/REL ATTIT PWR...POLICY JURID 18/20 SUPREME/CT CONGRESS. PAGE 43 F0848 CT/SYS ADJUD LAW FEDERAL

B30
GREEN F.M.,CONSTITUTIONAL DEVELOPMENT IN THE SOUTH ATLANTIC STATES, 1776-1860; A STUDY IN THE EVOLUTION OF DEMOCRACY. USA-45 ELITES SOCIETY STRATA ECO/DEV AGRI POL/PAR EX/STRUC LEGIS CT/SYS REGION...BIBLIOG 18/19 MARYLAND VIRGINIA GEORGIA NORTH/CAR SOUTH/CAR. PAGE 50 F0984 CONSTN PROVS PLURISM REPRESENT

B40
CAMPBELL P.,CONSUMER REPRESENTATION IN THE NEW DEAL. AGRI INDUS MARKET EX/STRUC PLAN CAP/ISM CONTROL GP/REL DEMAND POLICY. PAGE 21 F0408 CLIENT REPRESENT NAT/G

B40
GAUS J.M.,PUBLIC ADMINISTRATION AND THE UNITED STATES DEPARTMENT OF AGRICULTURE. USA-45 STRUCT DIST/IND FINAN MARKET EX/STRUC PROB/SOLV GIVE PRODUC...POLICY GEOG CHARTS 20 DEPT/AGRI. PAGE 47 F0909 ADMIN AGRI DELIB/GP OP/RES

B40
HELLMAN F.S.,THE NEW DEAL: SELECTED LIST OF REFERENCES. USA-45 FINAN LABOR EX/STRUC CREATE INT/TRADE ADMIN CT/SYS 20 SUPREME/CT. PAGE 58 F1145 BIBLIOG/A ECO/TAC PLAN POLICY

B41
MACMAHON A.W.,THE ADMINISTRATION OF FEDERAL WORK RELIEF. USA-45 EX/STRUC WORKER BUDGET EFFICIENCY ...CONT/OBS CHARTS 20 WPA. PAGE 84 F1636 ADMIN NAT/G MGT GIVE

B43
BRADY R.A.,BUSINESS AS A SYSTEM OF POWER. EX/STRUC PLAN ECO/TAC CONTROL GP/REL PWR...TREND GP/COMP. PAGE 17 F0334 VOL/ASSN LOBBY POLICY

B43
WILMERDING L. JR.,THE SPENDING POWER: A HISTORY OF THE EFFORTS OF CONGRESS TO CONTROL EXPENDITURES. USA-45 POL/PAR DELIB/GP EX/STRUC TOP/EX TARIFFS ADMIN GOV/REL...TIME/SEQ SENATE HOUSE/REP. PAGE 147 F2900 LEGIS BUDGET CONTROL

S45
MILLS C.W.,"THE TRADE UNION LEADER: A COLLECTIVE PORTRAIT." EX/STRUC TOP/EX INGP/REL...QU CON/ANAL CHARTS. PAGE 92 F1798 LABOR LEAD STAT STRATA

B46
DAVIES E.,NATIONAL ENTERPRISE: THE DEVELOPMENT OF THE PUBLIC CORPORATION. UK LG/CO EX/STRUC WORKER PROB/SOLV COST ATTIT SOCISM 20. PAGE 30 F0584 ADMIN NAT/G CONTROL INDUS

B48
SPERO S.D.,GOVERNMENT AS EMPLOYER. USA+45 NAT/G EX/STRUC ADMIN CONTROL EXEC 20. PAGE 124 F2453 SOVEREIGN INGP/REL REPRESENT CONFER

S48
NOURSE E.G.,"THE ROLE OF THE COUNCIL OF ECONOMIC ADVISERS." USA+45 DELIB/GP...DECISION PRESIDENT. PAGE 99 F1938 EX/STRUC CHIEF PROB/SOLV

B49
SELZNICK P.,TVA AND THE GRASS ROOTS: A STUDY IN THE SOCIOLOGY OF FORMAL ORGANIZATION. USA-45 EX/STRUC PROB/SOLV CONFER PARTIC ROUTINE PWR 20 TVA. REPRESENT LOBBY CONSULT

PAGE 119 F2353

B50
LINCOLN G.,ECONOMICS OF NATIONAL SECURITY. USA+45 ELITES COM/IND DIST/IND INDUS NAT/G VOL/ASSN DELIB/GP EX/STRUC FOR/AID EDU/PROP COERCE NUC/PWR WAR ATTIT KNOWL ORD/FREE PWR TOT/POP VAL/FREE 20. PAGE 80 F1565
FORCES ECO/TAC AFR

B51
LEONARD L.L.,INTERNATIONAL ORGANIZATION. WOR+45 WOR-45 EX/STRUC FORCES LEGIS ECO/TAC INT/TRADE COLONIAL ARMS/CONT...SOC/WK GOV/COMP BIBLIOG. PAGE 78 F1527
NAT/G DIPLOM INT/ORG DELIB/GP

B52
GOLDSTEIN J.,THE GOVERNMENT OF BRITISH TRADE UNIONS. UK ECO/DEV EX/STRUC INGP/REL...BIBLIOG 20. PAGE 48 F0940
LABOR PARTIC

S52
KLUMB S.,"EMPLOYEE DETERMINATION OF MANAGERIAL FUNCTIONS AND CHARACTERISTICS." DELIB/GP WORKER PARTIC ROUTINE INGP/REL...CLASSIF OBS QU. PAGE 72 F1410
MGT INDUS EX/STRUC CHOOSE

S53
BLOUGH R.,"THE ROLE OF THE ECONOMIST IN FEDERAL POLICY MAKING." USA+45 ELITES INTELL ECO/DEV NAT/G CONSULT EX/STRUC ACT/RES PLAN INT/TRADE BAL/PAY WEALTH...POLICY METH/GP CONGRESS 20. PAGE 16 F0301
DELIB/GP ECO/TAC

S53
LAWTON F.J.,"LEGISLATIVE-EXECUTIVE RELATIONS IN BUDGETING AS VIEWED BY THE EXECUTIVE." NAT/G LEGIS ADMIN REPRESENT EFFICIENCY 20. PAGE 76 F1495
BUDGET EX/STRUC EXEC CONTROL

S53
SIMON H.A.,"BIRTH OF AN ORGANIZATION: THE ECONOMIC COOPERATION ADMINISTRATION." USA+45 PROB/SOLV INGP/REL EFFICIENCY 20. PAGE 122 F2408
ADMIN EX/STRUC EXEC MGT

B54
EMERSON F.D.,SHAREHOLDER DEMOCRACY: A BROADER OUTLOOK FOR CORPORATIONS. DELIB/GP EX/STRUC LEGIS ADJUD CONTROL REPRESENT INGP/REL OWN PWR...POLICY STAT RECORD. PAGE 37 F0727
LG/CO PARTIC MAJORIT TREND

B54
HOBBS E.H.,BEHIND THE PRESIDENT - A STUDY OF EXECUTIVE OFFICE AGENCIES. USA+45 NAT/G PLAN BUDGET ECO/TAC EXEC ORD/FREE 20 BUR/BUDGET. PAGE 60 F1183
EX/STRUC DELIB/GP CONFER CONSULT

B54
LOCKLIN D.P.,ECONOMICS OF TRANSPORTATION (4TH ED.). USA+45 USA-45 SEA AIR LAW FINAN LG/CO EX/STRUC ADMIN CONTROL...STAT CHARTS 19/20 RAILROAD PUB/TRANS. PAGE 81 F1592
ECO/DEV DIST/IND ECO/TAC TEC/DEV

S54
EDELMAN M.J.,"LABOR'S INFLUENCE IN FOREIGN POLICY." NAT/G EXEC PWR 20. PAGE 36 F0700
LOBBY REPRESENT EX/STRUC LABOR

B55
RUSTOW D.A.,THE POLITICS OF COMPROMISE. SWEDEN LABOR EX/STRUC LEGIS PLAN REPRESENT SOCISM...SOC 19/20. PAGE 115 F2265
POL/PAR NAT/G POLICY ECO/TAC

B55
SMITHIES A.,THE BUDGETARY PROCESS IN THE UNITED STATES. AFR ECO/DEV AGRI EX/STRUC FORCES LEGIS PROB/SOLV TAX ROUTINE EFFICIENCY...MGT CONGRESS PRESIDENT. PAGE 124 F2436
NAT/G ADMIN BUDGET GOV/REL

B56
BURKHEAD J.,GOVERNMENT BUDGETING. ECO/DEV PROB/SOLV ECO/TAC ADMIN ROUTINE GOV/REL EFFICIENCY...DECISION MGT. PAGE 20 F0388
BUDGET NAT/G PROVS EX/STRUC

B56
REDFORD E.S.,PUBLIC ADMINISTRATION AND POLICY FORMATION: STUDIES IN OIL, GAS, BANKING, RIVER DEVELOPMENT AND CORPORATE INVESTIGATIONS. USA+45 CLIENT NAT/G ADMIN LOBBY REPRESENT GOV/REL INGP/REL 20. PAGE 110 F2167
EX/STRUC PROB/SOLV CONTROL EXEC

S56
BONILLA F.,"WHEN IS PETITION 'PRESSURE?'" (BMR)" USA+45 ELITES INDUS LABOR CHIEF EDU/PROP LEGIT ATTIT...INT CHARTS 20 CONGRESS PRESIDENT EISNHWR/DD. PAGE 16 F0312
LEGIS EX/STRUC INT/TRADE TARIFFS

S56
MILNE R.S.,"CONTROL OF GOVERNMENT CORPORATIONS IN THE UNITED STATES." USA+45 NAT/G CHIEF LEGIS BUDGET 20 GENACCOUNT. PAGE 92 F1800
CONTROL EX/STRUC GOV/REL PWR

B57
BERLE A.A. JR.,ECONOMIC POWER AND FREE SOCIETY (PAMPHLET). CLIENT CONSTN EX/STRUC ECO/TAC CONTROL PARTIC PWR WEALTH MAJORIT. PAGE 14 F0261
LG/CO CAP/ISM INGP/REL LEGIT

L57
SURREY S.S.,"THE CONGRESS AND THE TAX LOBBYIST - HOW SPECIAL TAX PROVISIONS GET ENACTED." LOBBY REPRESENT PRIVIL CONGRESS. PAGE 128 F2518
LEGIS TAX EX/STRUC

ROLE

B58
COOK P.L.,EFFECTS OF MERGERS: SIX STUDIES. USA+45 ECO/DEV LABOR LG/CO SML/CO VOL/ASSN ADMIN EFFICIENCY 20 CASEBOOK. PAGE 27 F0529
INDUS FINAN EX/STRUC GP/REL

B58
FINER S.E.,PRIVATE INDUSTRY AND POLITICAL POWER (PAMPHLET). UK INDUS CONTROL LOBBY PWR. PAGE 41 F0797
PLURISM REPRESENT EX/STRUC

B58
HENNING C.N.,INTERNATIONAL FINANCING. WOR+45 ECO/DEV INT/ORG EX/STRUC INSPECT CAP/ISM BAL/PAY COST PROFIT...MGT CHARTS T 20. PAGE 58 F1150
FINAN DIPLOM INT/TRADE

B58
US HOUSE COMM POST OFFICE,MANPOWER UTILIZATION IN THE FEDERAL GOVERNMENT. USA+45 DIST/IND EX/STRUC LEGIS CONFER EFFICIENCY 20 CONGRESS CIVIL/SERV. PAGE 137 F2702
ADMIN WORKER DELIB/GP NAT/G

B58
US HOUSE COMM POST OFFICE,MANPOWER UTILIZATION IN THE FEDERAL GOVERNMENT. USA+45 DIST/IND EX/STRUC LEGIS CONFER EFFICIENCY 20 CONGRESS CIVIL/SERV. PAGE 137 F2703
ADMIN WORKER DELIB/GP NAT/G

S58
ELKIN A.B.,"OEEC-ITS STRUCTURE AND POWERS." EUR+WWI CONSTN INDUS INT/ORG NAT/G VOL/ASSN DELIB/GP ACT/RES PLAN ORD/FREE WEALTH...CHARTS ORG/CHARTS OEEC 20. PAGE 37 F0719
ECO/DEV EX/STRUC

S58
LANE F.C.,"ECONOMIC CONSEQUENCES OF ORGANIZED VIOLENCE." FUT WOR+45 WOR-45 ECO/DEV DIST/IND SERV/IND NAT/G PROVS EX/STRUC CHOOSE ORD/FREE PWR ...TIME/SEQ GEN/LAWS MUNICH 20. PAGE 75 F1472
WEALTH COERCE

S58
O'NEAL F.H.,"RECENT LEGISLATION AFFECTING CLOSE CORPORATIONS." LAW EX/STRUC ECO/TAC ROUTINE CHOOSE RIGID/FLEX...MAJORIT MGT TREND. PAGE 100 F1959
LG/CO LEGIS REPRESENT PARTIC

B59
BROMWICH L.,UNION CONSTITUTIONS. CONSTN EX/STRUC PRESS ADJUD CONTROL CHOOSE REPRESENT PWR SAMP. PAGE 19 F0361
LABOR ROUTINE INGP/REL RACE/REL

B59
WORTHY J.C.,BIG BUSINESS AND FREE MEN. LG/CO EX/STRUC EDU/PROP LEAD CHOOSE GP/REL ATTIT DRIVE ROLE ORD/FREE...MAJORIT 20. PAGE 149 F2927
ELITES LOC/G TOP/EX PARTIC

S59
SEIDMAN H.,"THE GOVERNMENT CORPORATION IN THE UNITED STATES." USA+45 LEGIS ADMIN PLURISM 20. PAGE 119 F2344
CONTROL GOV/REL EX/STRUC EXEC

S59
SHEENAN D.,"PUBLIC CORPORATIONS AND PUBLIC ACTION." UK ADMIN CONTROL REPRESENT SOCISM 20. PAGE 120 F2372
ECO/DEV EFFICIENCY EX/STRUC EXEC

S59
STINCHCOMBE A.L.,"BUREAUCRATIC AND CRAFT ADMINISTRATION OF PRODUCTION: A COMPARATIVE STUDY" (BMR)" USA+45 STRUCT EX/STRUC ECO/TAC GP/REL ...CLASSIF GP/COMP IDEA/COMP GEN/LAWS 20 WEBER/MAX. PAGE 126 F2490
CONSTRUC PROC/MFG ADMIN PLAN

S59
STREAT R.,"GOVERNMENT CONSULTATION WITH INDUSTRY." UK 20. PAGE 127 F2501
REPRESENT ADMIN EX/STRUC INDUS

S59
WALLACE R.A.,"CONGRESSIONAL CONTROL OF THE BUDGET." USA+45 NAT/G CHIEF GP/REL FEDERAL OBJECTIVE...MGT CONGRESS. PAGE 143 F2807
LEGIS EX/STRUC BUDGET CONSTN

B60
EELLS R.S.F.,THE MEANING OF MODERN BUSINESS. LOC/G NAT/G NEIGH EX/STRUC PARTIC GP/REL INGP/REL DECISION. PAGE 36 F0706
LG/CO REPRESENT POLICY PLAN

B60
GRANICK D.,THE RED EXECUTIVE. COM USA+45 SOCIETY ECO/DEV INDUS NAT/G POL/PAR EX/STRUC PLAN ECO/TAC EDU/PROP ADMIN EXEC ATTIT DRIVE...GP/COMP 20. PAGE 50 F0976
PWR STRATA USSR ELITES

B60
THOMPSON V.A.,THE REGULATORY PROCESS IN OPA RATIONING. USA-45 CLIENT PROB/SOLV ADMIN LOBBY REPRESENT 20. PAGE 130 F2566
EX/STRUC GOV/REL INGP/REL

B60
WHEARE K.C.,THE CONSTITUTIONAL STRUCTURE OF THE COMMONWEALTH. UK EX/STRUC DIPLOM DOMIN ADMIN COLONIAL CONTROL LEAD INGP/REL SUPEGO 20 CMN/WLTH. PAGE 145 F2865
CONSTN INT/ORG VOL/ASSN SOVEREIGN

L60
FUCHS R.F.,"FAIRNESS AND EFFECTIVENESS IN
EFFICIENCY

ADMINISTRATIVE AGENCY ORGANIZATION AND PROCEDURES." USA+45 ADJUD ADMIN REPRESENT. PAGE 45 F0872
EX/STRUC EXEC POLICY

S60
MAIR L.P.,"SOCIAL CHANGE IN SOUTH AFRICA." MOD/EUR SOUTH/AFR WOR+45 ECO/UNDEV EX/STRUC TEC/DEV ATTIT DRIVE PERCEPT ORD/FREE...MGT CONCPT TIME/SEQ IND 20. PAGE 84 F1641
AFR NAT/G REV SOVEREIGN

S60
MANN S.Z.,"POLICY FORMULATION IN THE EXECUTIVE BRANCH: THE TAFT-HARTLEY EXPERIENCE." USA+45 LABOR CHIEF INGP/REL 20 NLRB. PAGE 85 F1656
EXEC GOV/REL EX/STRUC PROB/SOLV

B61
BARBASH J.,LABOR'S GRASS ROOTS. CONSTN NAT/G EX/STRUC LEGIS WORKER LEAD...MAJORIT BIBLIOG. PAGE 10 F0184
LABOR INGP/REL GP/REL LAW

B61
BENOIT E.,EUROPE AT SIXES AND SEVENS: THE COMMON MARKET, THE FREE TRADE ASSOCIATION AND THE UNITED STATES. EUR+WWI FUT USA+45 INDUS CONSULT DELIB/GP EX/STRUC TOP/EX ACT/RES ECO/TAC EDU/PROP ROUTINE CHOOSE PERCEPT WEALTH...MGT TREND EEC FOR/TRADE TOT/POP 20 EFTA. PAGE 13 F0249
FINAN ECO/DEV VOL/ASSN

B61
FRIEDMANN W.G.,JOINT INTERNATIONAL BUSINESS VENTURES. ASIA ISLAM L/A+17C ECO/DEV DIST/IND FINAN PROC/MFG FACE/GP LG/CO NAT/G VOL/ASSN CONSULT EX/STRUC PLAN ADMIN ROUTINE WEALTH...OLD/LIB FOR/TRADE WORK 20. PAGE 44 F0865
ECO/UNDEV INT/TRADE

B61
GARDNER R.N.,LEGAL-ECONOMIC PROBLEMS OF INTERNATIONAL TRADE. FUT WOR+45 INTELL ECO/DEV EX/STRUC INT/TRADE ROUTINE ATTIT WEALTH...GEN/LAWS ANTHOL FOR/TRADE 20. PAGE 46 F0904
FINAN ACT/RES

B61
GORDON R.A.,BUSINESS LEADERSHIP IN THE LARGE CORPORATION. USA+45 SOCIETY EX/STRUC ADMIN CONTROL ROUTINE GP/REL PWR...MGT 20. PAGE 49 F0960
LG/CO LEAD DECISION LOBBY

B61
HART W.R.,COLLECTIVE BARGAINING IN THE FEDERAL CIVIL SERVICE. NAT/G EX/STRUC ADMIN EXEC 20. PAGE 56 F1101
INGP/REL MGT REPRESENT LABOR

B61
QURESHI S.,INCENTIVES IN AMERICAN EMPLOYMENT (THESIS, UNIVERSITY OF PENNSYLVANIA). DELIB/GP TOP/EX BUDGET ROUTINE SANCTION COST TECHRACY MGT. PAGE 108 F2134
SERV/IND ADMIN PAY EX/STRUC

B61
ZEIGLER H.,THE POLITICS OF SMALL BUSINESS. USA+45 EX/STRUC ADMIN 20. PAGE 150 F2963
LOBBY REPRESENT EXEC VOL/ASSN

S61
BENNION E.G.,"ECONOMETRICS FOR MANAGEMENT." USA+45 INDUS EX/STRUC ACT/RES COMPUTER UTIL...MATH STAT PREDICT METH/COMP HYPO/EXP. PAGE 13 F0248
ECOMETRIC MGT SIMUL DECISION

S61
BRAFF A.J.,"WAGE-PRICE POLICIES UNDER PUBLIC PRESSURE." USA+45 EX/STRUC LOBBY REPRESENT PWR 20. PAGE 17 F0335
ATTIT PARTIC PROB/SOLV

S61
REAGAN M.D.,"THE POLITICAL STRUCTURE OF THE FEDERAL RESERVE SYSTEM." USA+45 FINAN NAT/G ADMIN 20. PAGE 110 F2163
PWR EX/STRUC EXEC LEAD

S61
SCHER S.,"REGULATORY AGENCY CONTROL THROUGH APPOINTMENT: THE CASE OF THE EISENHOWER ADMINISTRATION AND THE NLRB." USA+45 EX/STRUC GOV/REL 20 NLRB. PAGE 116 F2296
CHIEF LOBBY CONTROL TOP/EX

S61
WILDAVSKY A.,"POLITICAL IMPLICATIONS OF BUDGETARY REFORM." AFR NAT/G POL/PAR DELIB/GP EX/STRUC ATTIT PWR CONGRESS. PAGE 146 F2881
BUDGET PLAN LEGIS

B62
ARNOLD T.W.,THE FOLKLORE OF CAPITALISM. USA+45 USA-45 SOCIETY LG/CO SML/CO EX/STRUC ECO/TAC EDU/PROP ADJUST INCOME...MYTH CHARTS 20. PAGE 6 F0116
CAP/ISM ATTIT STERTYP ECO/DEV

B62
BRANCH M.C.,THE CORPORATE PLANNING PROCESS. FINAN EX/STRUC EDU/PROP CONTROL LEAD GP/REL PERS/REL RATIONAL PERCEPT...MGT MATH PROBABIL STAT GAME. PAGE 18 F0338
PROF/ORG PLAN DECISION PERSON

B62
CAIRNCROSS A.K.,FACTORS IN ECONOMIC DEVELOPMENT. WOR+45 ECO/UNDEV INDUS R+D LG/CO NAT/G EX/STRUC PLAN TEC/DEV ECO/TAC ATTIT HEALTH KNOWL PWR WEALTH ...TIME/SEQ GEN/LAWS TOT/POP TRUE/GP VAL/FREE 20. PAGE 21 F0399
MARKET ECO/DEV

B62
CHANDLER A.D.,STRATEGY AND STRUCTURE: CHAPTERS IN THE HISTORY OF THE INDUSTRIAL ENTERPRISE. USA+45 USA-45 ECO/DEV EX/STRUC ECO/TAC EXEC...DECISION 20. PAGE 23 F0446
LG/CO PLAN ADMIN FINAN

B62
COLLIER A.T.,MANAGEMENT, MEN, AND VALUES. INDUS FACE/GP EX/STRUC PLAN PROB/SOLV DEBATE SENIOR ADMIN PROFIT PERSON...PSY SOC 20. PAGE 26 F0505
MGT ATTIT PERS/REL DECISION

B62
GRANICK D.,THE EUROPEAN EXECUTIVE. BELGIUM FRANCE GERMANY/W UK INDUS LABOR LG/CO SML/CO EX/STRUC PLAN TEC/DEV CAP/ISM COST DEMAND...POLICY CHARTS 20. PAGE 50 F0977
MGT ECO/DEV ECO/TAC EXEC

B62
MEANS G.C.,PRICING POWER AND THE PUBLIC INTEREST. PLAN PROB/SOLV COST EFFICIENCY PROFIT RIGID/FLEX WEALTH. PAGE 89 F1741
LG/CO EX/STRUC PRICE ECO/TAC

B62
SMITH G.A. JR.,POLICY FORMULATION AND ADMINISTRATION: A CASEBOOK OF TOPMANAGEMENT PROBLEMS IN BUSINESS. EX/STRUC PLAN PROB/SOLV ADMIN CONTROL EXEC LEAD ROUTINE EFFICIENCY ATTIT MGT. PAGE 123 F2430
INDUS SOC/EXP TOP/EX DECISION

L62
WATERSTON A.,"PLANNING IN MOROCCO, ORGANIZATION AND IMPLEMENTATION. BALTIMORE: HOPKINS ECON. DEVELOP. INT. BANK FOR." ISLAM ECO/DEV AGRI DIST/IND INDUS PROC/MFG SERV/IND LOC/G EX/STRUC ECO/TAC PWR WEALTH TOT/POP TRUE/GP METH/GP TERR/GP VAL/FREE 20. PAGE 144 F2829
NAT/G PLAN MOROCCO

B63
BURRUS B.R.,ADMINSTRATIVE LAW AND LOCAL GOVERNMENT. USA+45 PROVS LEGIS LICENSE ADJUD ORD/FREE 20. PAGE 20 F0392
EX/STRUC LOC/G JURID CONSTN

B63
CHAMPION J.M.,CRITICAL INCIDENTS IN MANAGEMENT. MARKET LG/CO SML/CO OP/RES ADMIN CONTROL LEAD GP/REL PERS/REL COST ATTIT SUPEGO ALL/VALS...PSY PERS/TEST BIBLIOG. PAGE 23 F0445
MGT DECISION EX/STRUC INDUS

B63
HARVEY O.L.,THE ANVIL AND THE PLOW: A HISTORY OF THE UNITED STATES DEPARTMENT OF LABOR: 1913-1963. USA+45 USA-45 NAT/G CONFER NEW/LIB 20 DEPT/LABOR. PAGE 56 F1106
EX/STRUC REPRESENT GP/REL LABOR

B63
HATHAWAY D.A.,GOVERNMENT AND AGRICULTURE: PUBLIC POLICY IN A DEMOCRATIC SOCIETY. USA+45 LEGIS ADMIN EXEC LOBBY REPRESENT PWR 20. PAGE 57 F1111
AGRI GOV/REL PROB/SOLV EX/STRUC

B63
SMITH R.A.,CORPORATIONS IN CRISIS. USA+45 LG/CO EX/STRUC ECO/TAC CONTROL LEAD PERS/REL...MGT 20. PAGE 123 F2432
ELITES INDUS PROB/SOLV METH/COMP

S63
BARZANSKI S.,"REGIONAL UNDERDEVELOPMENT IN THE EUROPEAN ECONOMIC COMMUNITY." EUR+WWI ELITES DIST/IND MARKET VOL/ASSN CONSULT EX/STRUC ECO/TAC RIGID/FLEX WEALTH EEC OEEC 20. PAGE 11 F0202
ECO/UNDEV PLAN

B64
BLAKE R.R.,MANAGING INTERGROUP CONFLICT IN INDUSTRY. INDUS DELIB/GP EX/STRUC GP/REL PERS/REL GAME. PAGE 16 F0297
CREATE PROB/SOLV OP/RES ADJUD

B64
CHEIT E.F.,THE BUSINESS ESTABLISHMENT. FRANCE WOR+45 PROF/ORG TOP/EX PROB/SOLV CAP/ISM ADMIN SUPEGO MORAL PWR...METH/CNCPT MYTH NEW/IDEA 20. PAGE 24 F0460
PERSON EX/STRUC MGT INDUS

B64
JUCKER-FLEETWOOD E.,MONEY AND FINANCE IN AFRICA. ISLAM ECO/UNDEV SERV/IND NAT/G EX/STRUC PLAN ECO/TAC ROUTINE WEALTH...MGT TOT/POP 20. PAGE 68 F1344
AFR FINAN

B64
MARKHAM J.W.,THE COMMON MARKET: FRIEND OR COMPETITOR. AFR EUR+WWI FUT USA+45 INT/ORG LG/CO NAT/G VOL/ASSN DELIB/GP EX/STRUC PLAN TARIFFS ORD/FREE PWR WEALTH...POLICY STAT TREND EEC VAL/FREE 20. PAGE 85 F1671
ECO/DEV ECO/TAC

B64
MASON E.S.,FOREIGN AID AND FOREIGN POLICY. USA+45 AGRI INDUS NAT/G EX/STRUC ACT/RES RIGID/FLEX ALL/VALS...POLICY GEN/LAWS MARSHL/PLN ALL/PROG CONGRESS 20. PAGE 87 F1699
ECO/UNDEV ECO/TAC FOR/AID DIPLOM

B64
PAARLBERG D.,AMERICAN FARM POLICY: A CASE STUDY IN CENTRALIZED DECISION-MAKING. USA+45 NAT/G LEGIS LOBBY REPRESENT GOV/REL PWR LAISSEZ 20. PAGE 102 F2009
PROB/SOLV EX/STRUC AGRI

B64
REDLICH F.,THE GERMAN MILITARY ENTERPRISER AND HIS
EX/STRUC

WORK FORCE. CHRIST-17C GERMANY ELITES SOCIETY FINAN ECO/TAC CIVMIL/REL GP/REL INGP/REL...HIST/WRIT METH/COMP 14/17. PAGE 110 F2170
FORCES PROFIT WORKER

B64
STOESSINGER J.G.,FINANCING THE UNITED NATIONS SYSTEM. FUT WOR+45 CONSTN NAT/G VOL/ASSN DELIB/GP EX/STRUC ECO/TAC LEGIT CT/SYS PWR WEALTH...STAT TIME/SEQ TREND CHARTS TRUE/GP METH/GP TERR/GP VAL/FREE. PAGE 126 F2493
FINAN INT/ORG

B64
SULLIVAN G.,THE STORY OF THE PEACE CORPS. USA+45 WOR+45 INTELL FACE/GP NAT/G SCHOOL VOL/ASSN CONSULT EX/STRUC PLAN EDU/PROP ADMIN ATTIT DRIVE ALL/VALS ...POLICY HEAL SOC CONCPT INT QU BIOG TREND SOC/EXP WORK. PAGE 127 F2511
INT/ORG ECO/UNDEV FOR/AID PEACE

B64
WEIDENBAUM M.L.,CONGRESS AND THE FEDERAL BUDGET: FEDERAL BUDGETING AND THE RESPONSIBLE USE OF POWER. LOC/G PLAN TAX CONGRESS. PAGE 144 F2843
LEGIS EX/STRUC BUDGET ADMIN

B64
WHEARE K.C.,FEDERAL GOVERNMENT (4TH ED.). WOR+45 WOR-45 POL/PAR LEGIS BAL/PWR CT/SYS...POLICY JURID CONCPT GOV/COMP 17/20. PAGE 145 F2866
FEDERAL CONSTN EX/STRUC NAT/COMP

B64
ZOLLSCHAN G.K.,EXPLORATIONS IN SOCIAL CHANGE. SOCIETY STRATA STRUCT ECO/UNDEV EX/STRUC...PSY ANTHOL 20. PAGE 151 F2968
ORD/FREE SIMUL CONCPT CULTURE

S64
HUELIN D.,"ECONOMIC INTEGRATION IN LATIN AMERICAN: PROGRESS AND PROBLEMS." L/A+17C ECO/DEV AGRI DIST/IND FINAN INDUS NAT/G VOL/ASSN CONSULT DELIB/GP EX/STRUC ACT/RES PLAN TEC/DEV ECO/TAC ROUTINE BAL/PAY WEALTH FOR/TRADE WORK TERR/GP 20. PAGE 63 F1232
MARKET ECO/UNDEV INT/TRADE

S64
LEFF N.H.,"ECONOMIC DEVELOPMENT THROUGH BUREAUCRATIC CORRUPTION." ELITES NAT/G ROUTINE REPRESENT GP/REL PERS/REL. PAGE 77 F1511
ECO/UNDEV CLIENT EX/STRUC

B65
BOCK E.,GOVERNMENT REGULATION OF BUSINESS. USA+45 LAW EX/STRUC LEGIS EXEC ORD/FREE PWR...ANTHOL CONGRESS. PAGE 16 F0303
MGT ADMIN NAT/G CONTROL

B65
FLASH E.S. JR.,ECONOMIC ADVICE AND PRESIDENTIAL LEADERSHIP: THE COUNCIL OF ECONOMIC ADVISORS. USA+45 NAT/G EX/STRUC LEGIS TOP/EX ACT/RES ADMIN PRESIDENT CONGRESS. PAGE 41 F0808
PLAN CONSULT CHIEF

B65
INT. BANK RECONSTR. DEVELOP.,ECONOMIC DEVELOPMENT OF KUWAIT. ISLAM KUWAIT AGRI FINAN MARKET EX/STRUC TEC/DEV ECO/TAC ADMIN WEALTH...OBS CON/ANAL CHARTS 20. PAGE 64 F1266
INDUS NAT/G

B65
MUSOLF L.D.,PROMOTING THE GENERAL WELFARE: GOVERNMENT AND THE ECONOMY. USA+45 ECO/DEV CAP/ISM DEMAND OPTIMAL 20. PAGE 95 F1874
ECO/TAC NAT/G EX/STRUC NEW/LIB

B65
ONUOHA B.,THE ELEMENTS OF AFRICAN SOCIALISM. AFR FINAN SECT TEC/DEV FOR/AID GP/REL OWN LAISSEZ MARXISM...CONCPT BIBLIOG 20. PAGE 101 F1992
SOCISM ECO/UNDEV NAT/G EX/STRUC

B65
PAYNE J.L.,LABOR AND POLITICS IN PERU; THE SYSTEM OF POLITICAL BARGAINING. PERU CONSTN VOL/ASSN EX/STRUC LEAD PWR...CHARTS 20. PAGE 104 F2042
LABOR POL/PAR BARGAIN GP/REL

B65
SCHECHTER A.,THE BUSINESSMAN IN GOVERNMENT (THESIS, COLUMBIA UNIVERSITY). USA+45 CONFER GP/REL PERSON ...QU 20 PRESIDENT TRUMAN/HS CABINET. PAGE 116 F2291
INDUS NAT/G EX/STRUC DELIB/GP

L65
HAMMOND A.,"COMPREHENSIVE VERSUS INCREMENTAL BUDGETING IN THE DEPARTMENT OF AGRICULTURE" USA+45 GP/REL ATTIT...PSY INT 20 DEPT/AGRI. PAGE 54 F1057
TOP/EX EX/STRUC AGRI BUDGET

S65
LONG T.G.,"THE ADMINISTRATIVE PROCESS: AGONIZING REAPPRAISAL IN THE FTC." NAT/G REPRESENT 20 FTC. PAGE 82 F1598
ADJUD LOBBY ADMIN EX/STRUC

S65
WILDAVSKY A.,"TVA AND POWER POLITICS." USA+45 CLIENT PROB/SOLV EXEC GOV/REL 20. PAGE 146 F2882
PWR EX/STRUC LOBBY

B66
ALEXANDER Y.,INTERNATIONAL TECHNICAL ASSISTANCE EXPERTS* A CASE STUDY OF THE U.N. EXPERIENCE. ECO/UNDEV CONSULT EX/STRUC CREATE PLAN DIPLOM FOR/AID TASK EFFICIENCY...ORG/CHARTS UN. PAGE 3 F0061
ECO/TAC INT/ORG ADMIN MGT

B66
ANDERSON J.E.,POLITICS AND THE ECONOMY. NAT/G LOBBY PWR 20. PAGE 5 F0096
REPRESENT EX/STRUC CONTROL

B66
DAVIS K.,BUSINESS AND ITS ENVIRONMENT. LAW ECO/DEV INDUS OP/RES ADMIN CONTROL ROUTINE GP/REL PROFIT POLICY. PAGE 30 F0591
EX/STRUC PROB/SOLV CAP/ISM EXEC

B66
FRIEDMANN W.G.,INTERNATIONAL FINANCIAL AID. USA+45 ECO/DEV ECO/UNDEV NAT/G VOL/ASSN EX/STRUC PLAN RENT GIVE BAL/PAY PWR...GEOG INT/LAW STAT TREND UN EEC COMECON. PAGE 44 F0866
INT/ORG FOR/AID TEC/DEV ECO/TAC

B66
GREENE L.E.,GOVERNMENT IN TENNESSEE (2ND ED.). USA+45 DIST/IND INDUS POL/PAR EX/STRUC LEGIS PLAN BUDGET GIVE CT/SYS...MGT T 20 TENNESSEE. PAGE 51 F0989
PROVS LOC/G CONSTN ADMIN

B66
HACKETT J.,L'ECONOMIE BRITANNIQUE: PROBLEMES ET PERSPECTIVES. FRANCE UK LABOR NAT/G EX/STRUC PROB/SOLV BAL/PAY INCOME RIGID/FLEX...MGT PHIL/SCI CHARTS MUNICH 20. PAGE 53 F1027
ECO/DEV FINAN ECO/TAC PLAN

B66
HOLT R.T.,THE POLITICAL BASIS OF ECONOMIC DEVELOPMENT. STRATA STRUCT NAT/G DIPLOM ADMIN...SOC NAT/COMP BIBLIOG 20. PAGE 61 F1201
ECO/TAC GOV/COMP CONSTN EX/STRUC

B66
KIRDAR U.,THE STRUCTURE OF UNITED NATIONS ECONOMIC AID TO UNDERDEVELOPED COUNTRIES. AGRI FINAN INDUS NAT/G EX/STRUC PLAN GIVE TASK...POLICY 20 UN. PAGE 71 F1397
INT/ORG FOR/AID ECO/UNDEV ADMIN

B66
KOMIYA R.,POSTWAR ECONOMIC GROWTH IN JAPAN. ELITES NAT/G EX/STRUC TEC/DEV BUDGET DIPLOM CONTROL BAL/PAY PRODUC...BIBLIOG 20 CHINJAP. PAGE 73 F1424
ECO/DEV POLICY PLAN ADJUST

B66
MANSFIELD E.,MANAGERIAL ECONOMICS AND OPERATIONS RESEARCH; A NONMATHEMATICAL INTRODUCTION. USA+45 ELITES ECO/DEV CONSULT EX/STRUC PROB/SOLV ROUTINE EFFICIENCY OPTIMAL...GAME T 20. PAGE 85 F1660
ECO/TAC OP/RES MGT COMPUTER

B66
WALTON S.D.,AMERICAN BUSINESS AND ITS ENVIRONMENT. USA+45 LAW CONSTN FINAN MARKET LOC/G EX/STRUC CT/SYS COST PRODUC...STAT 20. PAGE 143 F2813
PRICE PROFIT

B66
YOUNG S.,MANAGEMENT: A SYSTEMS ANALYSIS. DELIB/GP EX/STRUC ECO/TAC CONTROL EFFICIENCY...NET/THEORY 20. PAGE 150 F2952
PROB/SOLV MGT DECISION SIMUL

S66
MARKSHAK J.,"ECONOMIC PLANNING AND THE COST OF THINKING." COM MARKET EX/STRUC...DECISION GEN/LAWS. PAGE 85 F1672
ECO/UNDEV ECO/TAC PLAN ECO/DEV

B67
BARROW T.C.,TRADE AND EMPIRE: THE BRITISH CUSTOMS SERVICE IN COLONIAL AMERICA, 1660-1775. UK USA-45 ECO/UNDEV NAT/G ECO/TAC DOMIN REV 17/18. PAGE 10 F0197
COLONIAL TARIFFS ADMIN EX/STRUC

B67
ESTEY M.,THE UNIONS: STRUCTURE, DEVELOPMENT, AND MANAGEMENT. FUT USA+45 ADJUD CONTROL INGP/REL DRIVE ...DECISION T 20 AFL/CIO. PAGE 38 F0750
LABOR EX/STRUC ADMIN GOV/REL

B67
GITTELL M.,PARTICIPANTS AND PARTICIPATION: A STUDY OF SCHOOL POLICY IN NEW YORK. USA+45 EX/STRUC BUDGET PAY ATTIT...POLICY MUNICH 20 NEWYORK/C. PAGE 47 F0926
SCHOOL DECISION PARTIC ADMIN

B67
GOLEMBIEWSKI R.T.,ORGANIZING MEN AND POWER: PATTERNS OF BEHAVIOR AND LINESTAFF MODELS. WOR+45 EX/STRUC ACT/RES DOMIN PERS/REL...NEW/IDEA 20. PAGE 48 F0943
ADMIN CONTROL SIMUL MGT

B67
HEILBRONER R.L.,THE LIMITS OF AMERICAN CAPITALISM. FUT ECO/DEV INDUS LG/CO EX/STRUC LEAD PWR TECHRACY 20. PAGE 58 F1137
ELITES CREATE TEC/DEV CAP/ISM

B67
LEIBY J.,CHARITY AND CORRECTION IN JERSEY; A HISTORY OF STATE WELFARE INSTITUTIONS. DELIB/GP EX/STRUC PROB/SOLV INSPECT LEAD ADJUST HEALTH ...POLICY PSY NEW/JERSEY. PAGE 77 F1514
PROVS PUB/INST ADMIN

L67
VIA J.W. JR.,"ANTITRUST AND THE AMENDED BANK MERGER AND HOLDING COMPANY ACTS: THE SEARCH FOR STANDARDS." USA+45 CONTROL GP/REL WEALTH SUPREME/CT. PAGE 141 F2783
FINAN CT/SYS LAW EX/STRUC

S67
ALBAUM G.,"INFORMATION FLOW AND DECENTRALIZED DECISION MAKING IN MARKETING." EX/STRUC COMPUTER
LG/CO ROUTINE

OP/RES PROB/SOLV EFFICIENCY OPTIMAL...METH/COMP ORG/CHARTS 20. PAGE 3 F0056 — KNOWL MARKET

S67
GORMAN W.,"ELLUL - A PROPHETIC VOICE." WOR+45 ELITES SOCIETY ACT/RES PLAN BAL/PWR DOMIN CONTROL PARTIC TOTALISM PWR 20. PAGE 49 F0963 — CREATE ORD/FREE EX/STRUC UTOPIA

S67
HALE G.E.,"EXPANDING ENTERPRISE: GEOGRAPHICAL CURBS ON MERGERS." USA+45 MARKET LG/CO ADJUD CONTROL GP/REL 20. PAGE 53 F1041 — LAW HABITAT INDUS EX/STRUC

S67
LINEBERRY R.L.,"REFORMISM AND PUBLIC POLICIES IN AMERICAN CITIES." USA+45 POL/PAR EX/STRUC LEGIS BUDGET TAX GP/REL...STAT CHARTS MUNICH. PAGE 80 F1573 — DECISION POLICY LOC/G

S67
MERON T.,"THE UN'S 'COMMON SYSTEM' OF SALARY, ALLOWANCE, AND BENEFITS: CRITICAL APPR'SAL OF COORD IN PERSONNEL MATTERS." VOL/ASSN PAY EFFICIENCY ...CHARTS 20 UN. PAGE 90 F1761 — ADMIN EX/STRUC INT/ORG BUDGET

S67
MITCHELL J.D.B.,"THE CONSTITUTIONAL IMPLICATIONS OF JUDICIAL CONTROL OF THE ADMINISTRATION IN THE UNITED KINGDOM." UK LAW ADJUD ADMIN GOV/REL ROLE ...GP/COMP 20. PAGE 92 F1808 — CONSTN CT/SYS CONTROL EX/STRUC

S67
RICHMAN B.M.,"CAPITALISTS & MANAGERS IN COMMUNIST CHINA." ASIA CHINA/COM ECO/UNDEV NAT/G CONSULT EX/STRUC PLAN EFFICIENCY PRODUC WEALTH MARXISM ...MGT CHARTS 20. PAGE 111 F2185 — CAP/ISM INDUS

S67
RICHMAN B.M.,"SOVIET MANAGEMENT IN TRANSITION." USSR FINAN MARKET EX/STRUC PLAN PROB/SOLV TEC/DEV CONTROL LEAD CENTRAL EFFICIENCY...METH/COMP 20 REFORMERS. PAGE 111 F2186 — MGT MARXISM POLICY AUTHORIT

S67
WILES P.J.,"THE POLITICAL AND SOCIAL PREREQUISITES FOR A SOVIET-TYPE ECONOMY." COM USSR LAW CULTURE CREATE ADMIN FEEDBACK ROUTINE COST OPTIMAL TOTALISM MARXISM 20. PAGE 146 F2883 — ECO/DEV PLAN EX/STRUC EFFICIENCY

S67
WILLIAMS C.,"REGIONAL MANAGEMENT OVERSEAS." USA+45 WOR+45 DIST/IND LG/CO EX/STRUC INT/TRADE TARIFFS ADMIN TASK CENTRAL. PAGE 147 F2889 — MGT EUR+WWI ECO/DEV PLAN

EXEC....EXECUTIVE PROCESS

B25
EDGEWORTH F.Y.,PAPERS RELATING TO POLITICAL ECONOMY. MOD/EUR SOCIETY STRATA DIST/IND INDUS MARKET NAT/G ACT/RES ECO/TAC EXEC WEALTH ...METH/CNCPT MATH TREND HYPO/EXP SIMUL GEN/METH FOR/TRADE VAL/FREE LOG/LING. PAGE 36 F0702 — ECO/DEV CAP/ISM

B30
FEIS H.,EUROPE, THE WORLD'S BANKER, 1871-1914. FRANCE GERMANY MOD/EUR UK WOR-45 NAT/G PLAN ECO/TAC EXEC ATTIT PWR WEALTH...CONCPT HIST/WRIT GEN/LAWS VAL/FREE 19/20. PAGE 40 F0773 — FINAN DIPLOM INT/TRADE

S30
CRAWFORD F.G.,"THE EXECUTIVE BUDGET DECISION IN NEW YORK." LEGIS EXEC PWR NEW/YORK. PAGE 28 F0552 — LEAD BUDGET PROVS PROB/SOLV

B41
YOUNG G.,FEDERALISM AND FREEDOM. EUR+WWI MOD/EUR RUSSIA USA-45 WOR-45 SOCIETY STRUCT ECO/DEV INT/ORG EXEC FEDERAL ATTIT PERSON ALL/VALS...OLD/LIB CONCPT OBS TREND LEAGUE/NAT TOT/POP. PAGE 150 F2950 — NAT/G WAR

S43
GOLDEN C.S.,"NEW PATTERNS OF DEMOCRACY." NEIGH DELIB/GP EDU/PROP EXEC PARTIC...MGT METH/CNCPT OBS TREND. PAGE 48 F0935 — LABOR REPRESENT LG/CO GP/REL

B46
CLOUGH S.B.,ECONOMIC HISTORY OF EUROPE. CHRIST-17C EUR+WWI MOD/EUR WOR-45 SOCIETY EXEC ATTIT WEALTH ...CONCPT GEN/LAWS WORK TOT/POP VAL/FREE 7/20. PAGE 25 F0493 — ECO/TAC CAP/ISM

B48
SPERO S.D.,GOVERNMENT AS EMPLOYER. USA+45 NAT/G EX/STRUC ADMIN CONTROL EXEC 20. PAGE 124 F2453 — SOVEREIGN INGP/REL REPRESENT CONFER

B49
SHISTER J.,ECONOMICS OF THE LABOR MARKET. LOC/G NAT/G WORKER TEC/DEV BARGAIN PAY PRICE EXEC GP/REL INCOME...MGT T 20. PAGE 121 F2381 — MARKET LABOR INDUS

S49
BANFIELD E.C.,"CONGRESS AND THE BUDGET: A PLANNER'S CRITICISM" USA+45 NAT/G PLAN LOBBY. PAGE 9 F0172 — LEGIS BUDGET EXEC POLICY

S50
DALTON M.,"CONFLICTS BETWEEN STAFF AND LINE MANAGERIAL OFFICERS" (BMR). USA+45 USA-45 ELITES LG/CO WORKER PROB/SOLV ADMIN EXEC EFFICIENCY PRODUC ...GP/COMP 20. PAGE 30 F0576 — MGT ATTIT GP/REL INDUS

B51
PETERSON F.,SURVEY OF LABOR ECONOMICS (REV. ED.). STRATA ECO/DEV LABOR INSPECT BARGAIN PAY PRICE EXEC ROUTINE GP/REL ALL/VALS ORD/FREE 20 AFL/CIO DEPT/LABOR. PAGE 105 F2069 — WORKER DEMAND IDEA/COMP T

B52
EGLE W.P.,ECONOMIC STABILIZATION. USA+45 SOCIETY FINAN MARKET PLAN ECO/TAC DOMIN EDU/PROP LEGIT EXEC WEALTH...CONCPT METH/CNCPT TREND HYPO/EXP GEN/METH TOT/POP VAL/FREE 20. PAGE 36 F0708 — NAT/G ECO/DEV CAP/ISM

S53
LAWTON F.J.,"LEGISLATIVE-EXECUTIVE RELATIONS IN BUDGETING AS VIEWED BY THE EXECUTIVE." NAT/G LEGIS ADMIN REPRESENT EFFICIENCY 20. PAGE 76 F1495 — BUDGET EX/STRUC EXEC CONTROL

S53
SIMON H.A.,"BIRTH OF AN ORGANIZATION: THE ECONOMIC COOPERATION ADMINISTRATION." USA+45 PROB/SOLV INGP/REL EFFICIENCY 20. PAGE 122 F2408 — ADMIN EX/STRUC EXEC MGT

B54
HOBBS E.H.,BEHIND THE PRESIDENT - A STUDY OF EXECUTIVE OFFICE AGENCIES. USA+45 NAT/G PLAN BUDGET ECO/TAC EXEC ORD/FREE 20 BUR/BUDGET. PAGE 60 F1183 — EX/STRUC DELIB/GP CONFER CONSULT

S54
EDELMAN M.J.,"LABOR'S INFLUENCE IN FOREIGN POLICY." NAT/G EXEC PWR 20. PAGE 36 F0700 — LOBBY REPRESENT EX/STRUC LABOR

B56
HICKMAN C.A.,INDIVIDUALS, GROUPS, AND ECONOMIC BEHAVIOR. WORKER PAY CONTROL EXEC GP/REL INGP/REL PERSON ROLE...PSY SOC PERS/COMP METH 20. PAGE 59 F1163 — MGT ADMIN ECO/TAC PLAN

B56
REDFORD E.S.,PUBLIC ADMINISTRATION AND POLICY FORMATION: STUDIES IN OIL, GAS, BANKING, RIVER DEVELOPMENT AND CORPORATE INVESTIGATIONS. USA+45 CLIENT NAT/G ADMIN LOBBY REPRESENT GOV/REL INGP/REL 20. PAGE 110 F2167 — EX/STRUC PROB/SOLV CONTROL EXEC

B56
WHYTE W.H. JR.,THE ORGANIZATION MAN. CULTURE FINAN VOL/ASSN DOMIN EDU/PROP EXEC DISPL HABITAT ROLE ...PERS/TEST STERTYP. PAGE 146 F2875 — ADMIN LG/CO PERSON CONSEN

B56
WILCOX W.W.,SOCIAL RESPONSIBILITY IN FARM LEADERSHIP. CLIENT LEGIS EXEC LOBBY GP/REL ATTIT WEALTH. PAGE 146 F2880 — AGRI LEAD VOL/ASSN WORKER

S56
MERRIAM R.E.,"THE BUREAU OF THE BUDGET AS PART OF THE PRESIDENT'S STAFF." 20 BUR/BUDGET 20 BOB. PAGE 90 F1763 — CHIEF CONTROL LEAD EXEC

B57
TRIFFIN R.,EUROPE AND THE MONEY MUDDLE. USA+45 INT/ORG NAT/G CONSULT PLAN ECO/TAC EXEC ROUTINE BAL/PAY WEALTH...METH/CNCPT OBS TREND CHARTS STERTYP GEN/METH EEC TERR/GP VAL/FREE ECSC. PAGE 131 F2587 — EUR+WWI ECO/DEV REGION

L58
CYERT R.M.,"THE ROLE OF EXPECTATIONS IN BUSINESS DECISION-MAKING." PROB/SOLV PRICE RIGID/FLEX. PAGE 29 F0566 — LG/CO DECISION ROUTINE EXEC

S58
EMERSON F.D.,"THE ROLES OF MANAGEMENT AND SHAREHOLDERS IN CORPORATE GOVERNMENT." CLIENT DELIB/GP CREATE ADMIN EXEC PARTIC PERS/REL PWR. PAGE 37 F0728 — LG/CO LAW INGP/REL REPRESENT

B59
ALLEN R.L.,SOVIET INFLUENCE IN LATIN AMERICA. ECO/UNDEV FINAN PROC/MFG NAT/G TEC/DEV EDU/PROP EXEC ROUTINE ATTIT DRIVE PERSON ALL/VALS PWR...STAT CHARTS WORK FOR/TRADE 20. PAGE 4 F0071 — L/A+17C ECO/TAC INT/TRADE USSR

B59
LEISERSON W.,AMERICAN TRADE UNION DEMOCRACY. CONSTN STRUCT ADJUD EXEC REPRESENT GP/REL INGP/REL MAJORITY ATTIT PWR. PAGE 77 F1516 — LABOR LEAD PARTIC DELIB/GP

B59
SHUBIK M.,STRATEGY AND MARKET STRUCTURE: COMPETITION, OLIGOPOLY, AND THE THEORY OF GAMES. ELITES STRUCT MARKET OP/RES EXEC EFFICIENCY INCOME ...MGT MATH STAT CHARTS 20. PAGE 121 F2389 — ECO/DEV ECO/TAC DECISION GAME

S59
SEIDMAN H.,"THE GOVERNMENT CORPORATION IN THE UNITED STATES." USA+45 LEGIS ADMIN PLURISM 20. PAGE 119 F2344 — CONTROL GOV/REL EX/STRUC

EXEC

S59
SHEENAN D.,"PUBLIC CORPORATIONS AND PUBLIC ACTION." UK ADMIN CONTROL REPRESENT SOCISM 20. PAGE 120 F2372 — ECO/DEV EFFICIENCY EX/STRUC EXEC

B60
GRANICK D.,THE RED EXECUTIVE. COM USA+45 SOCIETY ECO/DEV INDUS NAT/G POL/PAR EX/STRUC PLAN ECO/TAC EDU/PROP ADMIN EXEC ATTIT DRIVE...GP/COMP 20. PAGE 50 F0976 — PWR STRATA USSR ELITES

L60
FUCHS R.F.,"FAIRNESS AND EFFECTIVENESS IN ADMINISTRATIVE AGENCY ORGANIZATION AND PROCEDURES." USA+45 ADJUD ADMIN REPRESENT. PAGE 45 F0872 — EFFICIENCY EX/STRUC EXEC POLICY

S60
MANN S.Z.,"POLICY FORMULATION IN THE EXECUTIVE BRANCH: THE TAFT-HARTLEY EXPERIENCE." USA+45 LABOR CHIEF INGP/REL 20 NLRB. PAGE 85 F1656 — EXEC GOV/REL EX/STRUC PROB/SOLV

B61
AMERICAN MANAGEMENT ASSN,SUPERIOR-SUBORDINATE COMMUNICATION IN MANAGEMENT. STRATA FINAN INDUS SML/CO WORKER CONTROL EXEC ATTIT 20. PAGE 5 F0090 — MGT ACT/RES PERS/REL LG/CO

B61
BARRASH J.,LABOR'S GRASS ROOTS; A STUDY OF THE LOCAL UNION. STRATA BARGAIN LEAD REPRESENT DEMAND ATTIT PWR. PAGE 10 F0192 — LABOR USA+45 INGP/REL EXEC

B61
CANTERBERY E.R.,THE PRESIDENT'S COUNCIL OF ECONOMIC ADVISERS. AFR USA+45 FINAN LABOR NAT/G PLAN ADMIN OPTIMAL WEALTH 20 EISNHWR/DD PRESIDENT TRUMAN/HS KEYNES/JM. PAGE 21 F0413 — ECO/TAC OP/RES EXEC CHIEF

B61
ENGLER R.,THE POLITICS OF OIL. USA+45 CLIENT ELITES DOMIN EDU/PROP EXEC PWR 20. PAGE 38 F0734 — LOBBY REPRESENT POLICY

B61
HART W.R.,COLLECTIVE BARGAINING IN THE FEDERAL CIVIL SERVICE. NAT/G EX/STRUC ADMIN EXEC 20. PAGE 56 F1101 — INGP/REL MGT REPRESENT LABOR

B61
MACMAHON A.W.,DELEGATION AND AUTONOMY. INDIA STRUCT LEGIS BARGAIN BUDGET ECO/TAC LEGIT EXEC REPRESENT GOV/REL CENTRAL DEMAND EFFICIENCY PRODUC. PAGE 84 F1637 — ADMIN PLAN FEDERAL

B61
SHARP W.R.,FIELD ADMINISTRATION IN THE UNITED NATION SYSTEM: THE CONDUCT OF INTERNATIONAL ECONOMIC AND SOCIAL PROGRAMS. FUT WOR+45 CONSTN SOCIETY ECO/UNDEV R+D DELIB/GP ACT/RES PLAN TEC/DEV EDU/PROP EXEC ROUTINE HEALTH WEALTH...HUM CONCPT CHARTS METH ILO UNESCO GP VAL/FREE UN 20. PAGE 120 F2369 — INT/ORG CONSULT

B61
ZEIGLER H.,THE POLITICS OF SMALL BUSINESS. USA+45 EX/STRUC ADMIN 20. PAGE 150 F2963 — LOBBY REPRESENT EXEC VOL/ASSN

S61
REAGAN M.O.,"THE POLITICAL STRUCTURE OF THE FEDERAL RESERVE SYSTEM." USA+45 FINAN NAT/G ADMIN 20. PAGE 110 F2163 — PWR EX/STRUC EXEC LEAD

B62
BRIEFS H.W.,PRICING POWER AND "ADMINISTRATIVE" INFLATION (PAMPHLET). AFR USA+45 PROC/MFG CONTROL EFFICIENCY MONEY. PAGE 18 F0349 — ECO/DEV PRICE POLICY EXEC

B62
CHANDLER A.D.,STRATEGY AND STRUCTURE: CHAPTERS IN THE HISTORY OF THE INDUSTRIAL ENTERPRISE. USA+45 USA-45 ECO/DEV EX/STRUC ECO/TAC EXEC...DECISION 20. PAGE 23 F0446 — LG/CO PLAN ADMIN FINAN

B62
COX O.C.,CAPITALISM AND AMERICAN LEADERSHIP. WOR+45 WOR-45 STRATA INDUS SECT INT/TRADE EXEC INGP/REL RACE/REL RATIONAL PWR WEALTH. PAGE 28 F0548 — CAP/ISM LEAD ECO/DEV SOCIETY

B62
GRANICK D.,THE EUROPEAN EXECUTIVE. BELGIUM FRANCE GERMANY/W UK INDUS LABOR LG/CO SML/CO EX/STRUC PLAN TEC/DEV CAP/ISM COST DEMAND...POLICY CHARTS 20. PAGE 50 F0977 — MGT ECO/DEV ECO/TAC EXEC

B62
INTERNAT CONGRESS OF JURISTS,EXECUTIVE ACTION AND THE RULE OF RULE: REPORTION PROCEEDINGS OF INT'T CONGRESS OF JURISTS,-RIO DE JANEIRO, BRAZIL. WOR+45 ACADEM CONSULT JUDGE EDU/PROP ADJUD CT/SYS INGP/REL PERSON DEPT/DEFEN. PAGE 64 F1269 — JURID EXEC ORD/FREE CONTROL

B62
SMITH G.A. JR.,POLICY FORMULATION AND ADMINISTRATION: A CASEBOOK OF TOPMANAGEMENT PROBLEMS IN BUSINESS. EX/STRUC PLAN PROB/SOLV ADMIN CONTROL EXEC LEAD ROUTINE EFFICIENCY ATTIT MGT. PAGE 123 F2430 — INDUS SOC/EXP TOP/EX DECISION

S62
MORGENTHAU H.J.,"A POLITICAL THEORY OF FOREIGN AID." ECO/UNDEV NAT/G DELIB/GP PLAN ECO/TAC EDU/PROP EXEC ORD/FREE RESPECT WEALTH...METH/CNCPT TREND 20. PAGE 93 F1833 — USA+45 PHIL/SCI FOR/AID

S62
READ W.H.,"UPWARD COMMUNICATION IN INDUSTRIAL HIERARCHIES." LG/CO TOP/EX PROB/SOLV DOMIN EXEC PERS/REL ATTIT DRIVE PERCEPT...CORREL STAT CHARTS 20. PAGE 110 F2159 — ADMIN INGP/REL PSY MGT

B63
DUE J.F.,STATE SALES TAX ADMINISTRATION. OP/RES BUDGET PAY ADMIN EXEC ROUTINE COST EFFICIENCY PROFIT...CHARTS METH/COMP 20. PAGE 34 F0671 — PROVS TAX STAT GOV/COMP

B63
HATHAWAY D.A.,GOVERNMENT AND AGRICULTURE: PUBLIC POLICY IN A DEMOCRATIC SOCIETY. USA+45 LEGIS ADMIN EXEC LOBBY REPRESENT PWR 20. PAGE 57 F1111 — AGRI GOV/REL PROB/SOLV EX/STRUC

B63
ISSAWI C.,EGYPT IN REVOLUTION: AN ECONOMIC ANALYSIS. ISLAM STRUCT ECO/UNDEV AGRI FINAN INDUS PLAN EXEC REV NAT/LISM ATTIT RIGID/FLEX WEALTH SOCISM...STAT FOR/TRADE WORK 20. PAGE 66 F1292 — NAT/G UAR

S63
MASON E.S.,"INTERESTS, IDEOLOGIES AND THE PROBLEM OF STABILITY AND GROWTH." EUR+WWI USA+45 DELIB/GP CREATE PLAN EXEC ROUTINE BAL/PAY ATTIT PWR...MGT CONCPT OEEC 20. PAGE 87 F1698 — NAT/G ECO/DEV

B64
HACKER A.,THE CORPORATION TAKE-OVER. CONSTN LABOR PLAN BAL/PWR CONTROL EXEC LOBBY REPRESENT GP/REL ROLE ORD/FREE POLICY. PAGE 52 F1025 — LG/CO STRUCT PWR

B64
LI C.M.,INDUSTRIAL DEVELOPMENT IN COMMUNIST CHINA. CHINA/COM ECO/DEV ECO/UNDEV AGRI FINAN INDUS MARKET LABOR NAT/G ECO/TAC INT/TRADE EXEC ALL/VALS ...POLICY RELATIV TREND WORK TOT/POP VAL/FREE 20. PAGE 79 F1556 — ASIA TEC/DEV

B64
TINBERGEN J.,CENTRAL PLANNING. COM INTELL ECO/DEV ECO/UNDEV FINAN INT/ORG PROB/SOLV ECO/TAC CONTROL EXEC ROUTINE DECISION. PAGE 130 F2576 — PLAN INDUS MGT CENTRAL

L64
ARMENGALD A.,"ECONOMIE ET COEXISTENCE." COM EUR+WWI FUT USA+45 WOR+45 ECO/DEV ECO/UNDEV FINAN INT/ORG NAT/G EXEC CHOOSE ATTIT ALL/VALS...POLICY RELATIV DECISION TREND SOC/EXP WORK 20. PAGE 6 F0113 — MARKET ECO/TAC AFR CAP/ISM

S64
HOWE M.,"THE TRANSPORT ACT, 1962, AND THE CONSUMERS' CONSULTATIVE COMMITTEES." UK CONFER EXEC PWR 20. PAGE 62 F1225 — PARTIC REPRESENT DELIB/GP DIST/IND

B65
BOCK E.,GOVERNMENT REGULATION OF BUSINESS. USA+45 LAW EX/STRUC LEGIS EXEC ORD/FREE PWR...ANTHOL CONGRESS. PAGE 16 F0303 — MGT ADMIN NAT/G CONTROL

B65
DANIELSON M.N.,FEDERAL-METROPOLITAN POLITICS AND THE COMMUTER CRISIS. PROVS LEGIS EXEC LEAD PWR ...DECISION MUNICH. PAGE 30 F0580 — FEDERAL GOV/REL DIST/IND

B65
GOODSELL C.T.,ADMINISTRATION OF A REVOLUTION. PUERT/RICO ECO/UNDEV FINAN POL/PAR PROVS LEGIS PLAN BUDGET RECEIVE ADMIN COLONIAL LEAD MUNICH 20 ROOSEVLT/F. PAGE 49 F0951 — EXEC SOC

B65
STEINER G.A.,THE CREATIVE ORGANIZATION. ELITES LG/CO PLAN PROB/SOLV TEC/DEV INSPECT CAP/ISM CONTROL EXEC PERSON...METH/COMP HYPO/EXP 20. PAGE 126 F2476 — CREATE MGT ADMIN SOC

B65
WEIDENBAUM M.L.,CONGRESS AND THE FEDERAL BUDGET. FINAN ACT/RES DOMIN CONFER EXEC UTIL PWR NEW/LIB ...CHARTS CONGRESS. PAGE 144 F2844 — BUDGET LEGIS PLAN DECISION

S65
WILDAVSKY A.,"TVA AND POWER POLITICS." USA+45 CLIENT PROB/SOLV EXEC GOV/REL 20. PAGE 146 F2882 — PWR EX/STRUC LOBBY

C65
MANSFIELD H.C.,"THE CONGRESS AND ECONOMIC POLICY" IN C. TRUMAN ED., THE CONGRESS AND AMERICA'S FUTURE." USA+45 USA-45 CONSTN NAT/G BUDGET ADMIN CONTROL EXEC LOBBY. PAGE 85 F1661 — POLICY ECO/TAC PWR LEGIS

B66
DAVIS K.,BUSINESS AND ITS ENVIRONMENT. LAW ECO/DEV INDUS OP/RES ADMIN CONTROL ROUTINE GP/REL PROFIT POLICY. PAGE 30 F0591 — EX/STRUC PROB/SOLV CAP/ISM

EXEC

B66
ROSS A.M.,INDUSTRIAL RELATIONS AND ECONOMIC DEVELOPMENT. POL/PAR LEGIS WORKER BARGAIN PRICE EXEC LOBBY INCOME PWR...DECISION ANTHOL BIBLIOG 20. PAGE 114 F2243
ECO/UNDEV LABOR NAT/G GP/REL

B67
TOMA P.A.,THE POLITICS OF FOOD FOR PEACE; EXECUTIVE-LEGISLATIVE INTERACTION. USA+45 ECO/UNDEV POL/PAR DEBATE EXEC LOBBY CHOOSE PEACE...DECISION CHARTS. PAGE 131 F2580
FOR/AID POLICY LEGIS AGRI

L67
MACHLUP F.,"THEORIES OF THE FIRM* MARGINALIST, BEHAVIORALIST, MANAGERIAL." ADMIN EXEC EFFICIENCY PROFIT METH/CNCPT. PAGE 83 F1633
METH/COMP GEN/LAWS INDUS

S67
JANSSEN P.,"NEA: THE RELUCTANT DRAGON." NAT/G EXEC LOBBY PARTIC SANCTION RACE/REL ROLE TREND. PAGE 66 F1305
EDU/PROP PROF/ORG MGT POLICY

S67
JOHNSON L.B.,"BULLETS DO NOT DISCRIMINATE-LANDLORDS DO." PROB/SOLV EXEC LOBBY DEMAND...REALPOL SOC 20. PAGE 68 F1329
NAT/G DISCRIM POLICY

S67
PROBERT J.R.,"STREAMLINING THE FOREIGN POLICY MACHINE." USA+45 EFFICIENCY DEPT/STATE. PAGE 108 F2123
DIPLOM ADMIN EXEC GOV/REL

EXECUTIVE....SEE TOP/EX

EXECUTIVE ESTABLISHMENTS....SEE EX/STRUC

EXECUTIVE PROCESS....SEE EXEC

EXHIBIT....DISPLAY

EXPECTATIONS....SEE PROBABIL, SUPEGO, PREDICT

EXPERIMENTATION....SEE EXPERIMENTATION INDEX, P. XIV

EXPOSTFACT....EX POST FACTO LAWS

EXPROPRIAT....EXPROPRIATION

EXTR/IND....EXTRACTIVE INDUSTRY (FISHING, LUMBERING, ETC.)

N
US LIBRARY OF CONGRESS,SELECTED AND ANNOTATED BIBLIOGRAPHY ON AGRICULTURAL PROBLEMS AND POLICIES IN A WARTIME ECONOMY (PAMPHLET). R+D WORKER PRODUC 20. PAGE 137 F2706
BIBLIOG/A WAR AGRI EXTR/IND

N
US LIBRARY OF CONGRESS,SELECTED AND ANNOTATED BIBLIOGRAPHY ON RAW MATERIALS IN A WARTIME ECONOMY (PAMPHLET). WOR-45 NAT/G DEMAND PRODUC 20. PAGE 137 F2709
BIBLIOG/A ECO/DEV EXTR/IND WAR

B00
LIST F.,NATIONAL SYSTEM OF POLITICAL ECONOMY. ECO/DEV AGRI EXTR/IND FINAN INDUS TEC/DEV ECO/TAC ATTIT WEALTH...TREND GEN/LAWS FOR/TRADE 19. PAGE 81 F1581
MOD/EUR MARKET

B00
MILL J.S.,PRINCIPLES OF POLITICAL ECONOMY. WOR-45 CULTURE SOCIETY STRATA ECO/DEV AGRI EXTR/IND FINAN INDUS DELIB/GP ECO/TAC WEALTH...CONCPT MATH TREND 20. PAGE 91 F1786
MARKET INT/ORG INT/TRADE

N19
US BUREAU OF THE CENSUS,THE PROPORTION OF THE SHIPMENTS (OR EMPLOYEES) OF EACH INDUSTRY... (PAMPHLET). USA+45 ECO/DEV EXTR/IND INDUS CONTROL PROFIT...STAT 20 CONGRESS MONOPOLY. PAGE 134 F2645
PROC/MFG PRODUC MARKET CHARTS

B20
MOREL E.D.,THE BLACK MAN'S BURDEN. AFR MOD/EUR AGRI EXTR/IND PROB/SOLV INT/TRADE ADMIN CONTROL COERCE DISCRIM...POLICY 19/20 NEGRO LEAGUE/NAT. PAGE 93 F1828
ORD/FREE CAP/ISM RACE/REL DOMIN

B27
WEBER M.,GENERAL ECONOMIC HISTORY. CHRIST-17C MOD/EUR STRUCT AGRI EXTR/IND FINAN INDUS MARKET FAM NAT/G PROF/ORG SECT ECO/TAC MUNICH 8/20. PAGE 144 F2839
ECO/DEV CAP/ISM

B40
MEEK C.K.,EUROPE AND WEST AFRICA. AFR EUR+WWI EXTR/IND DIPLOM INT/TRADE EDU/PROP GP/REL...SOC 20. PAGE 89 F1743
CULTURE TEC/DEV ECO/UNDEV COLONIAL

B48
WHITE C.L.,HUMAN GEOGRAPHY: AN ECOLOGICAL STUDY OF GEOGRAPHY. UNIV SEA CULTURE AGRI EXTR/IND RACE/REL PRODUC...CHARTS HYPO/EXP SIMUL GEN/LAWS T. PAGE 146 F2868
SOC HABITAT GEOG SOCIETY

S49
ECKLER A.R.,"IMMIGRATION AND THE LABOR FORCE." USA+45 USA-45 EXTR/IND FINAN PROC/MFG AGE/Y SKILL ...CHARTS 19/20 MIGRATION. PAGE 36 F0694
WORKER STRANGE INDUS ECO/TAC

B52
SACHS E.S.,THE CHOICE BEFORE SOUTH AFRICA. SOUTH/AFR AGRI EXTR/IND PROC/MFG PROB/SOLV ORD/FREE SOVEREIGN 20 NEGRO. PAGE 115 F2267
NAT/LISM DISCRIM RACE/REL LABOR

B53
NEISSER H.,NATIONAL INCOMES AND INTERNATIONAL TRADE. FRANCE GERMANY SWEDEN UK USA-45 EXTR/IND FINAN INDUS TEC/DEV PRICE BAL/PAY EQUILIB INCOME WEALTH...CHARTS METH 19 CHINJAP. PAGE 97 F1908
INT/TRADE PRODUC MARKET CON/ANAL

B54
KARTUN D.,AFRICA, AFRICA: A CONTINENT RISES TO ITS FEET. AFR SOUTH/AFR UK ELITES AGRI LABOR LOC/G POL/PAR EDU/PROP CONTROL COERCE DISCRIM AGE/Y NEGRO THIRD/WRLD GOLD/COAST. PAGE 69 F1358
COLONIAL ORD/FREE PROFIT EXTR/IND

B55
JONES T.B.,A BIBLIOGRAPHY ON SOUTH AMERICAN ECONOMIC AFFAIRS: ARTICLES IN NINETEENTH CENTURY PERIODICALS (PAMPHLET). AGRI COM/IND DIST/IND EXTR/IND FINAN INDUS LABOR NAT/G 19. PAGE 68 F1340
BIBLIOG ECO/UNDEV L/A+17C TEC/DEV

B55
O'CONNOR H.,THE EMPIRE OF OIL. USA+45 DIST/IND FINAN MARKET CAP/ISM TAX CONTROL...POLICY MARXIST BIBLIOG/A 20. PAGE 100 F1955
EXTR/IND INT/TRADE CENTRAL NAT/G

B55
PEDLER F.J.,ECONOMIC GEOGRAPHY OF WEST AFRICA. GAMBIA NIGER SIER/LEONE STRATA EXTR/IND MARKET LABOR INT/TRADE DEMAND HABITAT WEALTH...CHARTS 20. PAGE 104 F2046
ECO/UNDEV GEOG PRODUC EFFICIENCY

B57
PALACIOS A.L.,PETROLEO, MONOPOLIOS, Y LATIFUNDIOS. L/A+17C EXTR/IND NAT/G TEC/DEV ECO/TAC CONTROL PRODUC 20 ARGEN MONOPOLY RESOURCE/N. PAGE 103 F2017
ECO/UNDEV NAT/LISM INDUS AGRI

B58
BIDWELL P.W.,RAW MATERIALS: A STUDY OF AMERICAN POLICY. USA+45 USA-45 ECO/UNDEV AGRI INDUS KIN CREATE PLAN ECO/TAC WAR PEACE ATTIT DRIVE WEALTH ...STAT CHARTS CONGRESS FOR/TRADE VAL/FREE. PAGE 15 F0279
EXTR/IND ECO/DEV

B58
MIKESELL R.F.,FINANCING FREE WORLD TRADE WITH THE SINO-SOVIET BLOC. CHINA/COM COM USSR WOR+45 ECO/DEV AGRI DIST/IND EXTR/IND FINAN INDUS MARKET PROC/MFG NAT/G PLAN TEC/DEV ECO/TAC...CHARTS METH/GP EEC FOR/TRADE 20. PAGE 91 F1780
STAT BAL/PAY

B59
BLACK J.D.,ECONOMICS FOR AGRICULTURE. USA+45 EXTR/IND FAM WORKER ACT/RES PLAN PRICE EATING INCOME...CENSUS BIBLIOG 20. PAGE 15 F0291
AGRI ECO/TAC MARKET POLICY

B59
DIEBOLD W. JR.,THE SCHUMAN PLAN: A STUDY IN ECONOMIC COOPERATION, 1950-1959. EUR+WWI FRANCE GERMANY USA+45 EXTR/IND CONSULT DELIB/GP PLAN DIPLOM ECO/TAC INT/TRADE ROUTINE ORD/FREE WEALTH ...METH/CNCPT STAT CONT/OBS INT TIME/SEQ ECSC 20. PAGE 33 F0635
INT/ORG REGION

B59
HAZLEWOOD A.,THE ECONOMICS OF "UNDER-DEVELOPED" AREAS. WOR+45 DIST/IND EXTR/IND FINAN INDUS MARKET PLAN FOR/AID...GEOG 20. PAGE 57 F1129
BIBLIOG/A ECO/UNDEV AGRI INT/TRADE

B59
LOPEZ VILLAMIL H.,A STATEMENT OF THE LAWS OF THE HONDURAS IN MATTERS AFFECTING BUSINESS (2ND ED.). HONDURAS DIST/IND EXTR/IND FINAN WORKER TAX DEATH MARRIAGE OWN MARITIME 20 MIGRATION. PAGE 82 F1600
CONSTN INDUS LEGIS NAT/G

B60
LENCZOWSKI G.,OIL AND STATE IN THE MIDDLE EAST. FUT IRAN LAW ECO/UNDEV EXTR/IND NAT/G TOP/EX PLAN TEC/DEV ECO/TAC LEGIT ADMIN COERCE ATTIT ALL/VALS PWR...CHARTS 20. PAGE 78 F1519
ISLAM INDUS NAT/LISM

B60
LISTER L.,EUROPE'S COAL AND STEEL COMMUNITY. FRANCE GERMANY STRUCT ECO/DEV EXTR/IND INDUS MARKET NAT/G DELIB/GP ECO/TAC INT/TRADE EDU/PROP ATTIT RIGID/FLEX ORD/FREE PWR WEALTH...CONCPT STAT TIME/SEQ CHARTS ECSC TERR/GP 20. PAGE 81 F1582
EUR+WWI INT/ORG REGION

B60
SMET G.,BIBLIOGRAPHIE DE LA CONTRIBUTION A L'ETUDE DE LA PROGRESSION ECONOMIQUE DE L'AFRIQUE. AFR DIST/IND EXTR/IND TEC/DEV 20. PAGE 123 F2427
BIBLIOG ECO/UNDEV INDUS AGRI

S60
NICHOLS J.P.,"HAZARDS OF AMERICAN PRIVATE INVESTMENT IN UNDERDEVELOPED COUNTRIES." FUT L/A+17C USA+45 USA-45 EXTR/IND CONSULT BAL/PWR ECO/TAC DOMIN ADJUD ATTIT SOVEREIGN WEALTH ...HIST/WRIT TIME/SEQ TREND TERR/GP VAL/FREE 20. PAGE 98 F1924
FINAN ECO/UNDEV CAP/ISM NAT/LISM

S60
OWEN C.F.,"US AND SOVIET RELATIONS WITH
ECO/UNDEV

UNDERDEVELOPED COUNTRIES: LATIN AMERICA-A CASE STUDY." AFR COM L/A+17C USA+45 USSR EXTR/IND MARKET TEC/DEV DIPLOM ECO/TAC NAT/LISM ORD/FREE PWR ...TREND WORK 20. PAGE 102 F2005
DRIVE INT/TRADE

S60
RIVKIN A.,"AFRICAN ECONOMIC DEVELOPMENT: ADVANCED TECHNOLOGY AND THE STAGES OF GROWTH." CULTURE ECO/UNDEV AGRI COM/IND EXTR/IND PLAN ECO/TAC ATTIT DRIVE RIGID/FLEX SKILL WEALTH...MGT SOC GEN/LAWS FOR/TRADE WORK TOT/POP 20. PAGE 111 F2195
AFR TEC/DEV FOR/AID

B61
CLARK J.M.,COMPETITION AS A DYNAMIC PROCESS. ECO/DEV EXTR/IND INDUS LG/CO TEC/DEV ECO/TAC PRICE EQUILIB PRODUC...NEW/IDEA CAP 20. PAGE 25 F0483
WEALTH GP/REL FINAN PROFIT

B61
HODGKINS J.A.,SOVIET POWER: ENERGY RESOURCES, PRODUCTION AND POTENTIALS. USSR ECO/DEV INDUS MARKET...POLICY STAT CHARTS 20 RESOURCE/N. PAGE 60 F1188
GEOG EXTR/IND TEC/DEV

B61
INTERNATIONAL BANK RECONST DEV,THE WORLD BANK IN AFRICA: SUMMARY OF ACTIVITIES. AGRI COM/IND DIST/IND EXTR/IND INDUS TAX COST...CHARTS 20. PAGE 65 F1271
FINAN ECO/UNDEV INT/ORG AFR

B61
LAHAYE R.,LES ENTREPRISES PUBLIQUES AU MAROC. FRANCE MOROCCO LAW DIST/IND EXTR/IND FINAN CONSULT PLAN TEC/DEV ADMIN AGREE CONTROL OWN...POLICY 20. PAGE 74 F1460
NAT/G INDUS ECO/UNDEV ECO/TAC

B61
LONGRIGG S.H.,OIL IN THE MIDDLE EAST: ITS DISCOVERY AND DEVELOPMENT. ECO/UNDEV LG/CO LOC/G TEC/DEV WEALTH...STAT TIME/SEQ 20 OIL. PAGE 82 F1599
ISLAM EXTR/IND

B61
PETCH G.A.,ECONOMIC DEVELOPMENT AND MODERN WEST AFRICA. AFR CONGO/BRAZ GHANA NIGER SIER/LEONE AGRI MARKET LABOR FOR/AID TAX COST EFFICIENCY EQUILIB PRODUC...GEOG TREND 20. PAGE 105 F2068
ECO/UNDEV TEC/DEV EXTR/IND ECO/TAC

B61
SCHNAPPER B.,LA POLITIQUE ET LE COMMERCE FRANCAIS DANS LE GOLFE DE GUINEE DE 1838 A 1871. FRANCE GUINEA UK SEA EXTR/IND NAT/G DELIB/GP LEGIS ADMIN ORD/FREE...POLICY GEOG CENSUS CHARTS BIBLIOG 19. PAGE 117 F2303
COLONIAL INT/TRADE DOMIN AFR

B61
SEPULVEDA C.,A STATEMENT OF THE LAWS OF MEXICO IN MATTERS AFFECTING BUSINESS (3RD ED.). AGRI DIST/IND EXTR/IND FINAN INDUS WORKER TAX MARRIAGE OWN ORD/FREE...BIBLIOG 20 MEXIC/AMER TREATY MIGRATION MONOPOLY. PAGE 119 F2356
CONSTN NAT/G JURID LEGIS

B62
CARPER E.T.,ILLINOIS GOES TO CONGRESS FOR ARMY LAND. USA+45 LAW EXTR/IND PROVS REGION CIVMIL/REL GOV/REL FEDERAL ATTIT 20 ILLINOIS SENATE CONGRESS DIRKSEN/E DOUGLAS/P. PAGE 22 F0420
ADMIN LOBBY GEOG LEGIS

B62
CHRISTENSON C.L.,ECONOMIC REDEVELOPMENT IN BITUMINOUS COAL: THE SPECIAL CASE OF TECHNOLOGICAL ADVANCE IN US COAL MINES 1930-1960. USA+45 USA-45 ECO/TAC AUTOMAT INCOME PRODUC...CHARTS 20. PAGE 24 F0471
EXTR/IND LABOR TEC/DEV ECO/DEV

B62
FAO,FOOD AND AGRICULTURE ORGANIZATION AFRICAN SURVEY. AFR CONGO/BRAZ GHANA STRATA AGRI INT/ORG TEC/DEV FOR/AID INT/TRADE RACE/REL DEMAND EFFICIENCY PRODUC...GEOG 20 UN CONGO/LEOP. PAGE 39 F0763
ECO/TAC WEALTH EXTR/IND ECO/UNDEV

B62
HENDERSON W.O.,THE GENESIS OF THE COMMON MARKET. EUR+WWI FRANCE MOD/EUR UK SEA COM/IND EXTR/IND COLONIAL DISCRIM...TIME/SEQ CHARTS BIBLIOG 18/20 EEC TREATY. PAGE 58 F1149
ECO/DEV INT/TRADE DIPLOM

B62
O'CONNOR H.,WORLD CRISES IN OIL (BMR). ISLAM L/A+17C INDUS LG/CO INT/TRADE 20. PAGE 100 F1956
EXTR/IND DIPLOM ECO/UNDEV SOCISM

B63
BATES J.L.,THE ORIGINS OF TEAPOT DOME: PROGRESSIVES, PARTIES, AND PETROLEUM, 1909-1921. USA-45 INDUS LG/CO POL/PAR DELIB/GP CONTROL GOV/REL CONSERVE...BIBLIOG 20 NAVY. PAGE 11 F0209
EXTR/IND CRIME NAT/G

B63
ELLENDER A.J.,A REPORT ON UNITED STATES FOREIGN OPERATIONS IN AFRICA. SOUTH/AFR USA+45 STRATA EXTR/IND FORCES RACE/REL ISOLAT SOVEREIGN...CHARTS 20 NEGRO. PAGE 37 F0721
FOR/AID DIPLOM WEALTH ECO/UNDEV

B63
FURTADO C.,THE ECONOMIC GROWTH OF BRAZIL: A SURVEY FROM COLONIAL TO MODERN TIMES. L/A+17C AGRI DIST/IND EXTR/IND INDUS WORKER COLONIAL RACE/REL OWN GOV/COMP. PAGE 45 F0877
ECO/UNDEV TEC/DEV LABOR DOMIN

B63
HUNTER A.,THE ECONOMICS OF AUSTRALIAN INDUSTRY. DIST/IND EXTR/IND FINAN PROC/MFG SERV/IND ACT/RES PLAN TARIFFS GP/REL INGP/REL 20 AUSTRAL. PAGE 63 F1245
INDUS ECO/DEV HABITAT GP/COMP

B63
MANN D.E.,THE POLITICS OF WATER IN ARIZONA. AGRI EXTR/IND PROVS ACT/RES CREATE PLAN GOV/REL COST HABITAT...MGT CHARTS 20 ARIZONA WATER. PAGE 84 F1655
POLICY ECO/TAC TEC/DEV

B63
NEUMARK S.D.,FOREIGN TRADE AND ECONOMIC DEVELOPMENT IN AFRICA: A HISTORICAL PERSPECTIVE. EUR+WWI MOD/EUR ECO/UNDEV AGRI COM/IND EXTR/IND PROC/MFG SKILL WEALTH...CONCPT TIME/SEQ TREND SIMUL FOR/TRADE WORK TOT/POP TERR/GP VAL/FREE 19/20. PAGE 98 F1916
AFR

S63
ADAMS F.G.,"ECONOMIC CONSIDERATIONS OF AN ATLANTIC ENERGY POLICY." EUR+WWI FUT USA+45 DIST/IND EXTR/IND MARKET CONSULT LEGIS ECO/TAC WEALTH ...POLICY EEC FOR/TRADE OEEC 20. PAGE 2 F0037
ECO/DEV TEC/DEV NUC/PWR

S63
DUCROS B.,"MOBILISATION DES RESSOURCES PRODUCTIVES ET DEVELOPPEMENT." FUT INTELL SOCIETY COM/IND DIST/IND EXTR/IND FINAN INDUS ROUTINE WEALTH ...METH/CNCPT OBS 20. PAGE 34 F0670
ECO/UNDEV TEC/DEV

B64
BALASSA B.,TRADE PROSPECTS FOR DEVELOPING COUNTRIES. WOR+45 ECO/DEV AGRI EXTR/IND INDUS CREATE PLAN PRICE...ECOMETRIC CLASSIF TIME/SEQ GEN/METH. PAGE 8 F0158
INT/TRADE ECO/UNDEV TREND STAT

B64
HUTT W.H.,THE ECONOMICS OF THE COLOUR BAR. SOUTH/AFR EXTR/IND LABOR ADJUD NEGRO. PAGE 64 F1251
INDUS DISCRIM RACE/REL ECO/UNDEV

B64
MYINT H.,THE ECONOMICS OF THE DEVELOPING COUNTRIES. WOR+45 AGRI PLAN COST...POLICY GEOG 20 MONEY. PAGE 96 F1878
ECO/UNDEV INT/TRADE EXTR/IND FINAN

B64
NATIONAL COUN APPLIED ECO RES,A STRATEGY FOR THE FOURTH PLAN. INDIA DIST/IND EXTR/IND SERV/IND ECO/TAC RATION EDU/PROP EATING HEALTH...CHARTS 20. PAGE 97 F1900
ECO/UNDEV PLAN AGRI WORKER

B64
RAMAZANI R.K.,THE MIDDLE EAST AND THE EUROPEAN COMMON MARKET. EUR+WWI ISLAM ECO/DEV EXTR/IND MARKET PROC/MFG INT/ORG NAT/G TEC/DEV ECO/TAC REGION DRIVE WEALTH...STAT CHARTS EEC TOT/POP 20. PAGE 109 F2141
ECO/UNDEV ATTIT INT/TRADE

B64
RENO P.,THE ORDEAL OF BRITISH GUIANA. L/A+17C USA+45 STRUCT AGRI EXTR/IND INDUS NAT/G FOR/AID ORD/FREE...GEOG 20 GUIANA/BR INTRVN/ECO. PAGE 111 F2178
COLONIAL ECO/UNDEV SOCISM PWR

B64
TELLADO A.,A STATEMENT OF THE LAWS OF THE DOMINICAN REPUBLIC IN MATTERS AFFECTING BUSINESS (3RD ED.). DOMIN/REP AGRI DIST/IND EXTR/IND FINAN FAM WORKER ECO/TAC TAX CT/SYS MARRIAGE OWN...BIBLIOG 20 MIGRATION. PAGE 129 F2542
CONSTN LEGIS NAT/G INDUS

B64
WITHERELL J.W.,OFFICIAL PUBLICATIONS OF FRENCH EQUATORIAL AFRICA, FRENCH CAMEROONS, AND TOGO, 1946-1958 (PAMPHLET). CAMEROON CHAD FRANCE GABON TOGO LAW ECO/UNDEV EXTR/IND INT/TRADE...GEOG HEAL 20. PAGE 148 F2913
BIBLIOG/A AFR NAT/G ADMIN

S64
HOOVER C.B.,"THE ROLE OF THE NATURAL AND DEVELOPED RESOURCES OF THE NATION STATES." FUT WOR+45 ECO/DEV ECO/UNDEV NAT/G PWR RESPECT SKILL WEALTH...POLICY GEOG TIME/SEQ TREND RESOURCE/N VAL/FREE 20. PAGE 62 F1210
EXTR/IND DOMIN

S64
KLEIN H.,"AMERICAN OIL COMPANIES IN LATIN AMERICA: THE BOLIVIAN EXPERIENCE." L/A+17C USA+45 USA-45 EXTR/IND LG/CO NAT/G ECO/TAC WEALTH...POLICY GEN/LAWS BOLIV TOT/POP 20 OIL. PAGE 72 F1405
MARKET ECO/UNDEV NAT/LISM

B65
BARRY E.E.,NATIONALISATION IN BRITISH POLITICS: THE HISTORICAL BACKGROUND. UK AGRI DIST/IND EXTR/IND LABOR LG/CO ATTIT CONSERVE SOCISM 19/20 LABOR/PAR. PAGE 10 F0198
NAT/G OWN INDUS POL/PAR

B65
LUGO-MARENCO J.J.,A STATEMENT OF THE LAWS OF NICARAGUA IN MATTERS AFFECTING BUSINESS. NICARAGUA AGRI DIST/IND EXTR/IND FINAN INDUS FAM WORKER INT/TRADE TAX MARRIAGE OWN BIO/SOC 20 TREATY RESOURCE/N MIGRATION. PAGE 82 F1606
CONSTN NAT/G LEGIS JURID

B65
WRIGHT L.B.,THE DREAM OF PROSPERITY IN COLONIAL AMERICA. USA-45 ECO/UNDEV AGRI EXTR/IND PARLIAMENT 17/18. PAGE 149 F2934
PROVS WEALTH MOD/EUR

L65
LETICHE J.M.,"EUROPEAN INTEGRATION: AN AMERICAN VIEW." EUR+WWI FRANCE WOR+45 ECO/DEV DIST/IND
INDUS AGRI

EXTR/IND NAT/G DELIB/GP TOP/EX PLAN ECO/TAC ATTIT ...STAT CON/ANAL CHARTS EEC 20. PAGE 78 F1537

S65
BERREBY J.J.,"IMPERATIFS STRATEGIQUES DU PETROLE." ECO/UNDEV VOL/ASSN ECO/TAC COLONIAL NUC/PWR WAR. PAGE 14 F0270 ISLAM EXTR/IND STAT OBS

S65
CECIL C.O.,"THE DETERMINANTS OF LIBYAN FOREIGN POLICY." AFR INTELL ECO/UNDEV EXTR/IND POL/PAR CREATE REGION SOVEREIGN CONSERVE MAGHREB NASSER/G. PAGE 22 F0431 LIBYA DIPLOM WEALTH ISLAM

B66
BALDWIN R.E.,ECONOMIC DEVELOPMENT AND EXPORT GROWTH: A STUDY OF NORTHERN RHODESIA, 1920-1960. AFR RHODESIA AGRI EXTR/IND FINAN MARKET LABOR WORKER ECO/TAC...CONCPT NEW/IDEA MUNICH 20. PAGE 9 F0166 ECO/UNDEV TEC/DEV INT/TRADE CAP/ISM

B66
FRANKEL P.H.,MATTEI; OIL AND POWER POLITICS. ITALY EXTR/IND MARKET GP/REL NAT/LISM SOCISM...POLICY MGT BIOG 20 MATTEI/E. PAGE 43 F0844 LEAD NAT/G CONTROL LG/CO

B66
KEENLEYSIDE H.L.,INTERNATIONAL AID: A SUMMARY. AFR INDIA S/ASIA UK STRATA EXTR/IND TEC/DEV ADMIN RACE/REL DEMAND NAT/LISM WEALTH...TREND CHINJAP. PAGE 70 F1367 ECO/UNDEV FOR/AID DIPLOM TASK

B66
O'CONNER A.M.,AN ECONOMIC GEOGRAPHY OF EAST AFRICA. AFR TANZANIA UGANDA AGRI WORKER INT/TRADE COLONIAL GOV/REL...CHARTS METH/COMP 20 AFRICA/E. PAGE 99 F1953 ECO/UNDEV EXTR/IND GEOG HABITAT

B67
ALNASRAWI A.,FINANCING ECONOMIC DEVELOPMENT IN IRAQ. IRAQ INDUS CAP/ISM COST PRODUC...STAT CHARTS BIBLIOG 20. PAGE 4 F0076 ECO/UNDEV EXTR/IND TEC/DEV INT/TRADE

B67
LANDEN R.G.,OMAN SINCE 1856: DISRUPTIVE MODERNIZATION IN A TRADITIONAL ARAB SOCIETY. UK DIST/IND EXTR/IND SECT DIPLOM INT/TRADE...SOC LING CHARTS BIBLIOG 19/20. PAGE 75 F1468 ISLAM CULTURE ECO/UNDEV NAT/G

S67
JENCKS C.E.,"COAL MINERS IN BRITAIN SINCE NATIONALIZATION." UK LABOR GP/REL ADJUST SOCISM ...INT 20. PAGE 67 F1311 EXTR/IND WORKER STRATA ATTIT

S67
JENCKS C.E.,"SOCIAL STATUS OF COAL MINERS IN BRITAIN SINCE NATIONALIZATION." UK STRATA STRUCT LABOR RECEIVE GP/REL INCOME OWN ATTIT HABITAT...MGT T 20. PAGE 67 F1312 EXTR/IND WORKER CONTROL NAT/G

S67
MILLER C.H.,"B. TRAVEN Y EL 'PROBLEMA PETROLERO'." USA-45 ECO/UNDEV INDUS TEC/DEV INT/TRADE ATTIT ORD/FREE SOVEREIGN 20 MEXIC/AMER. PAGE 91 F1791 EXTR/IND DIPLOM ECO/TAC DOMIN

S67
OLIVIER G.,"ASPECTS JURIDIQUES DE L'ADOPTION DU TRAITE CECA A LA CRISE CHARBONNIERE (SUITE ET FIN)" LAW DIST/IND PLAN DIPLOM RATION PRICE ADMIN COST DEMAND...POLICY CON/ANAL ECSC TREATY. PAGE 101 F1988 INT/TRADE INT/ORG EXTR/IND CONSTN

S67
PETRAS J.,"MINERS AND AGRARIAN RADICALISM." CHILE AGRI EXTR/IND WORKER CHOOSE ATTIT SOCISM MUNICH 20. PAGE 105 F2073 PARTIC EDU/PROP LABOR

EXTRACTIVE INDUSTRY....SEE EXTR/IND

F

FAA....U.S. FEDERAL AVIATION AGENCY

B65
THAYER F.C. JR.,AIR TRANSPORT POLICY AND NATIONAL SECURITY: A POLITICAL, ECONOMIC, AND MILITARY ANALYSIS. DIST/IND OP/RES PLAN TEC/DEV DIPLOM DETER WAR COST EFFICIENCY...POLICY BIBLIOG 20 DEPT/DEFEN FAA CAB. PAGE 129 F2548 AIR FORCES CIVMIL/REL ORD/FREE

FABIAN....FABIANS: MEMBERS AND/OR SUPPORTERS OF FABIAN SOCIETY

S47
DAHL R.A.,"WORKERS' CONTROL OF INDUSTRY AND THE BRITISH LABOUR PARTY." UK STRATA STRUCT DELIB/GP BARGAIN CAP/ISM DEBATE CONTROL CHOOSE GP/REL ATTIT ROLE PWR 19/20 PARLIAMENT LABOR/PAR FABIAN. PAGE 29 F0570 INDUS LABOR WORKER SOCISM

FABIAN SOCIETY F0757

FACE/GP....ACQUAINTANCE GROUP

N19
HOGARTY R.A.,NEW JERSEY FARMERS AND MIGRANT HOUSING RULES (PAMPHLET). USA+45 LAW ELITES FACE/GP LABOR PROF/ORG LOBBY PERS/REL RIGID/FLEX ROLE 20 NEW/JERSEY. PAGE 61 F1193 AGRI PROVS WORKER HEALTH

B56
LIPSET S.M.,UNION DEMOCRACY. STRUCT INDUS FACE/GP WORKER CONTROL LEAD PARTIC GP/REL ATTIT LAISSEZ ...INT QU CHARTS. PAGE 80 F1577 LABOR INGP/REL MAJORIT

B61
FRIEDMANN W.G.,JOINT INTERNATIONAL BUSINESS VENTURES. ASIA ISLAM L/A+17C ECO/DEV DIST/IND FINAN PROC/MFG FACE/GP LG/CO NAT/G VOL/ASSN CONSULT EX/STRUC PLAN ADMIN ROUTINE WEALTH...OLD/LIB FOR/TRADE WORK 20. PAGE 44 F0865 ECO/UNDEV INT/TRADE

B62
COLLIER A.T.,MANAGEMENT, MEN, AND VALUES. INDUS FACE/GP EX/STRUC PLAN PROB/SOLV DEBATE SENIOR ADMIN PROFIT PERSON...PSY SOC 20. PAGE 26 F0505 MGT ATTIT PERS/REL DECISION

B63
GEERTZ C.,PEDDLERS AND PRINCES: SOCIAL DEVELOPMENT AND ECONOMIC CHANGE IN TWO INDONESIAN TOWNS. S/ASIA CULTURE SOCIETY STRATA FACE/GP CREATE TEC/DEV ECO/TAC ORD/FREE WEALTH...OBS INT CENSUS CHARTS WORK TOT/POP METH/GP TERR/GP VAL/FREE 20 MUNICH. PAGE 47 F0913 ECO/UNDEV SOC ELITES INDONESIA

B64
SULLIVAN G.,THE STORY OF THE PEACE CORPS. USA+45 WOR+45 INTELL FACE/GP NAT/G SCHOOL VOL/ASSN CONSULT EX/STRUC PLAN EDU/PROP ADMIN ATTIT DRIVE ALL/VALS ...POLICY HEAL SOC CONCPT INT QU BIOG TREND SOC/EXP WORK. PAGE 127 F2511 INT/ORG ECO/UNDEV FOR/AID PEACE

S64
FINLEY D.D.,"A POLITICAL PERSPECTIVE OF ECONOMIC RELATIONS IN THE COMMUNIST CAMP." COM USSR FACE/GP NAT/G ACT/RES PLAN DOMIN COERCE ATTIT ORD/FREE WEALTH...TIME/SEQ 20. PAGE 41 F0800 VOL/ASSN ECO/TAC DIPLOM REGION

S67
"THE SIERRA CLUB, POLITICAL ACTIVITY, AND TAX EXEMPT CHARITABLE STATUS." USA+45 LAW VOL/ASSN TAX PAY ADJUD LOBBY INGP/REL HABITAT 20. PAGE 2 F0027 ELITES GOV/REL FACE/GP ORD/FREE

S67
FOX R.G.,"FAMILY, CASTE, AND COMMERCE IN A NORTH INDIAN MARKET TOWN." INDIA STRATA AGRI FACE/GP FAM NEIGH OP/RES BARGAIN ADMIN ROUTINE WEALTH...SOC CHARTS 20. PAGE 43 F0838 CULTURE GP/REL ECO/UNDEV DIST/IND

S67
ROY E.V.,"AN INTERPRETATION OF NORTHERN THAI PEASANT ECONOMY." THAILAND CLIENT CULTURE AGRI PROC/MFG FACE/GP DEMAND INCOME 20. PAGE 114 F2254 STRUCT STRATA ECO/UNDEV INGP/REL

FACTION....FACTION

FACTOR ANALYSIS....SEE CON/ANAL

FADDEYEV N. F0758

FAHRNKOPF N. F0759

FAINSOD M. F0760

FAIR T.J.D. F0987

FAIR EMPLOYMENT PRACTICES COMMISSION....SEE FEPC

FAIR/LABOR....FAIR LABOR STANDARD ACT

B63
BOWIE R.R.,GOVERNMENT REGULATION OF BUSINESS: CASES FROM THE NATIONAL REPORTER SYSTEM. USA+45 USA-45 NAT/G ECO/TAC ADJUD...ANTHOL 19/20 SUPREME/CT FTC FAIR/LABOR MONOPOLY. PAGE 17 F0331 LAW CONTROL INDUS CT/SYS

FAIRNESS, JUSTICE....SEE VALUES INDEX

FALANGE....FALANGE PARTY (SPAIN)

FALKLAND/I....FALKLAND ISLANDS

FALL B.B. F0761

FAM....FAMILY

NCO
STOLPER W.,"SOCIAL FACTORS IN ECONOMIC PLANNING, WITH SPECIAL REFERENCE TO NIGERIA" AFR NIGER CULTURE FAM SECT RECEIVE ETIQUET ADMIN DEMAND 20. PAGE 126 F2494 ECO/UNDEV PLAN ADJUST RISK

B02
MOREL E.D.,AFFAIRS OF WEST AFRICA. UK FINAN INDUS FAM KIN SECT CHIEF WORKER DIPLOM RACE/REL LITERACY HEALTH...CHARTS 18/20 AFRICA/W NEGRO. PAGE 93 F1826 COLONIAL ADMIN AFR

B27
WEBER M.,GENERAL ECONOMIC HISTORY. CHRIST-17C MOD/EUR STRUCT AGRI EXTR/IND FINAN INDUS MARKET FAM ECO/DEV CAP/ISM

NAT/G PROF/ORG SECT ECO/TAC MUNICH 8/20. PAGE 144
F2839

B39
ENGELS F.,HERRN EUGEN DUHRING'S REVOLUTION IN SCIENCE (1878). CULTURE STRATA STRUCT FAM SECT ECO/TAC REV WAR SOCISM...MARXIST 19. PAGE 37 F0731
PWR SOCIETY WEALTH GEN/LAWS

B51
HARROD R.F.,THE LIFE OF JOHN MAYNARD KEYNES. UK INTELL FAM CAP/ISM DIPLOM ECO/TAC WAR ATTIT PERSON ROLE 20 KEYNES/JM WWI. PAGE 56 F1094
BIOG FINAN GEN/LAWS

B54
WASHBURNE N.F.,INTERPRETING SOCIAL CHANGE IN AMERICA. USA+45 STRATA FAM NAT/G SECT OP/RES ECO/TAC EDU/PROP HABITAT...SOC TIME/SEQ TREND 20 BUREAUCRCY. PAGE 143 F2826
CULTURE STRUCT CREATE TEC/DEV

B55
WRONG D.H.,AMERICAN AND CANADIAN VIEWPOINTS. CANADA USA+45 CONSTN STRATA FAM SECT WORKER ECO/TAC EDU/PROP ADJUD MARRIAGE...IDEA/COMP 20. PAGE 149 F2936
DIPLOM ATTIT NAT/COMP CULTURE

B56
YUAN TUNG-LI,ECONOMIC AND SOCIAL DEVELOPMENT OF MODERN CHINA: A BIBLIOGRAPHIC GUIDE. COM/IND FINAN FAM LABOR SECT CRIME INCOME...STAT SAMP CON/ANAL. PAGE 150 F2954
BIBLIOG ASIA ECO/UNDEV SOC

B58
BUGEDA LANZAS J.,A STATEMENT OF THE LAWS OF CUBA IN MATTERS AFFECTING BUSINESS (2ND ED. REV., ENLARGED). CUBA L/A+17C LAW FINAN FAM LEGIS ACT/RES ADMIN GP/REL...BIBLIOG 20 OAS. PAGE 20 F0382
JURID NAT/G INDUS WORKER

B59
BLACK J.D.,ECONOMICS FOR AGRICULTURE. USA+45 EXTR/IND FAM WORKER ACT/RES PLAN PRICE EATING INCOME...CENSUS BIBLIOG 20. PAGE 15 F0291
AGRI ECO/TAC MARKET POLICY

B59
GOMEZ ROBLES J.,A STATEMENT OF THE LAWS OF GUATEMALA IN MATTERS AFFECTING BUSINESS (2ND ED. REV., ENLARGED). GUATEMALA L/A+17C LAW FINAN FAM WORKER ACT/RES DIPLOM ADJUD ADMIN GP/REL 20 OAS. PAGE 48 F0945
JURID NAT/G INDUS LEGIT

S60
ENKE S.,"THE ECONOMIES OF GOVERNMENT PAYMENTS TO LIMIT POPULATION." FUT INDIA WOR+45 CULTURE FINAN NAT/G CONSULT PLAN LEGIT CONTROL COST ATTIT RIGID/FLEX HEALTH WEALTH...STAT OBS CHARTS TOT/POP VAL/FREE 20. PAGE 38 F0736
FAM ACT/RES

S60
JAFFEE A.J.,"POPULATION TRENDS AND CONTROLS IN UNDERDEVELOPED COUNTRIES." AFR FUT ISLAM L/A+17C S/ASIA CULTURE R+D FAM ACT/RES PLAN EDU/PROP BIO/SOC RIGID/FLEX HEALTH...SOC STAT OBS CHARTS 20. PAGE 66 F1303
ECO/UNDEV GEOG

S60
STOCKWELL E.G.,"THE MEASUREMENT OF ECONOMIC DEVELOPMENT." WOR+45 SOCIETY ECO/DEV ECO/UNDEV INDUS ECO/TAC HEALTH WEALTH...WELF/ST GEOG METH/CNCPT CHARTS METH METH/GP 20. PAGE 126 F2492
FAM STAT

B61
DE VRIES E.,MAN IN RAPID SOCIAL CHANGE. WOR+45 SOCIETY ECO/DEV ECO/UNDEV AGRI INDUS FAM SECT TEC/DEV ATTIT...RECORD 20 CHRISTIAN. PAGE 31 F0607
CULTURE ALL/VALS SOC TASK

B61
LENSKI G.,THE RELIGIOUS FACTOR: A SOCIOLOGICAL STUDY OF RELIGION'S IMPACT ON POLITICS, ECONOMICS, AND FAMILY LIFE. FAM PROF/ORG EDU/PROP ROLE CATHISM ...INT SAMP MUNICH. PAGE 78 F1524
SECT GP/REL

B61
RUEDA B.,A STATEMENT OF THE LAWS OF COLOMBIA IN MATTERS AFFECTING BUSINESS (3RD ED.). INDUS FAM LABOR LG/CO NAT/G LEGIS TAX CONTROL MARRIAGE 20 COLOMB. PAGE 115 F2257
FINAN ECO/UNDEV LAW CONSTN

B62
PASTOR R.S.,A STATEMENT OF THE LAWS OF PARAGUAY IN MATTERS AFFECTING BUSINESS (2ND ED.). PARAGUAY INDUS FAM LABOR LG/CO NAT/G LEGIS TAX CONTROL MARRIAGE 20. PAGE 103 F2033
FINAN ECO/UNDEV LAW CONSTN

B62
SELOSOEMARDJAN O.,SOCIAL CHANGES IN JOGJAKARTA. INDONESIA NETHERLAND ELITES STRATA STRUCT FAM POL/PAR CREATE DIPLOM INT/TRADE EDU/PROP ADMIN GOV/REL...SOC 20 JAVA CHINJAP. PAGE 119 F2352
ECO/UNDEV CULTURE REV COLONIAL

B62
URQUIDI C.W.,A STATEMENT OF THE LAWS OF BOLIVIA IN MATTERS AFFECTING BUSINESS (3RD ED. REV., ENLARGED). L/A+17C LAW FINAN FAM WORKER ACT/RES DIPLOM ADJUD ADMIN GP/REL 20 BOLIV OAS. PAGE 133 F2626
JURID INDUS NAT/G LEGIT

B62
VACCARO J.R.,A STATEMENT OF THE LAWS OF CHILE IN MATTERS AFFECTING BUSINESS (3RD ED.). CHILE AGRI FINAN FAM LABOR ECO/TAC FOR/AID TAX ADJUD CONTROL MARRIAGE STRANGE...BIBLIOG 20. PAGE 140 F2756
CONSTN LAW INDUS MGT

B63
GAMBLE S.D.,NORTH CHINA VILLAGES: SOCIAL, POLITICAL, AND ECONOMIC ACTIVITIES BEFORE 1933. ASIA CULTURE STRUCT FAM DOMIN EDU/PROP MUNICH WORSHIP 20. PAGE 46 F0891
AGRI LEAD FINAN

B63
GRIGSBY W.G.,HOUSING MARKETS AND PUBLIC POLICY. USA+45 FAM NEIGH PRICE DEMAND WEALTH...POLICY CHARTS BIBLIOG METH MUNICH 20. PAGE 51 F1002
MARKET RENT HABITAT PLAN

B63
WAGLEY C.,INTRODUCTION TO BRAZIL. BRAZIL L/A+17C FAM KIN SCHOOL SECT ATTIT WEALTH...GEOG SOC. PAGE 142 F2799
ECO/UNDEV ELITES HABITAT STRATA

L63
OLSON M. JR.,"RAPID ECONOMIC GROWTH AS A DESTABILIZING FORCE." WOR+45 WOR-45 STRATA ECO/UNDEV FAM KIN CREATE TEC/DEV DIPLOM PEACE ATTIT PERSON RIGID/FLEX PWR RESPECT WEALTH...SOC 20. PAGE 101 F1989
SOCIETY FOR/AID

B64
BEARDSLEY R.K.,STUDIES ON ECONOMIC LIFE IN JAPAN (OCCASIONAL PAPERS NO. 8). INDUS FAM HABITAT...GEOG GOV/COMP 20 CHINJAP. PAGE 12 F0223
WEALTH PRESS PRODUC INCOME

B64
CEPEDE M.,POPULATION AND FOOD. USA+45 STRUCT ECO/UNDEV FAM PLAN TEC/DEV FOR/AID CONTROL...CATH SOC TREND 19/20. PAGE 22 F0436
FUT GEOG AGRI CENSUS

B64
COLSTON RESEARCH SOCIETY,ECONOMETRIC ANALYSIS FOR NATIONAL ECONOMIC PLANNING (PROCEEDINGS OF SIXTEENTH SYMPOSIUM OF COLSTON RESEARCH SOCIETY). UK USA+45 FINAN FAM LABOR NAT/G PLAN PRICE ...METH/CNCPT TREND CHARTS TIME 20. PAGE 26 F0510
ECOMETRIC DELIB/GP ECO/TAC PROB/SOLV

B64
FIRTH R.,CAPITAL, SAVING AND CREDIT IN PEASANT SOCIETIES. WOR+45 WOR-45 FAM ACT/RES ECO/TAC HEALTH ...SOC CONCPT STAT CHARTS ANTHOL CARIBBEAN VAL/FREE 20. PAGE 41 F0803
AGRI FINAN

B64
SAKAI R.K.,STUDIES ON ASIA, 1964. ASIA CHINA/COM ISRAEL MALAYSIA S/ASIA USA+45 USSR ECO/UNDEV FAM POL/PAR SECT CONSULT NAT/LISM...POLICY SOC 20 CHINJAP. PAGE 115 F2272
PWR DIPLOM

B64
TELLADO A.,A STATEMENT OF THE LAWS OF THE DOMINICAN REPUBLIC IN MATTERS AFFECTING BUSINESS (3RD ED.). DOMIN/REP AGRI DIST/IND EXTR/IND FINAN FAM WORKER ECO/TAC TAX CT/SYS MARRIAGE OWN...BIBLIOG 20 MIGRATION. PAGE 129 F2542
CONSTN LEGIS NAT/G INDUS

S64
WOOD N.,"THE FAMILY FIRM - BASE OF JAPAN'S GROWING ECONOMY." ECO/DEV ECO/UNDEV ECO/TAC WEALTH...POLICY TRADIT BIOG TREND 20 CHINJAP. PAGE 148 F2921
ASIA SML/CO FAM

B65
BEYER G.H.,HOUSING AND SOCIETY. USA+45 ECO/DEV FAM NAT/G PLAN RENT...CHARTS BIBLIOG MUNICH 20. PAGE 14 F0275
HABITAT AGE/O CONSTRUC

B65
LUGO-MARENCO J.J.,A STATEMENT OF THE LAWS OF NICARAGUA IN MATTERS AFFECTING BUSINESS. NICARAGUA AGRI DIST/IND EXTR/IND FINAN INDUS FAM WORKER INT/TRADE TAX MARRIAGE OWN BIO/SOC 20 TREATY RESOURCE/N MIGRATION. PAGE 82 F1606
CONSTN NAT/G LEGIS JURID

B66
HUNT C.L.,SOCIAL ASPECTS OF ECONOMIC DEVELOPMENT. S/ASIA AGRI FAM TEC/DEV RECEIVE EDU/PROP OWN...GEOG MUNICH 20. PAGE 63 F1243
SOC STRATA ATTIT ECO/UNDEV

B66
US SENATE COMM GOVT OPERATIONS,HEARINGS BEFORE SUBCOMMITTEE ON FOREIGN AID EXPENDITURES: POPULATION CRISIS VOLUMES 1-5 JUNE-SEPT 1965. STRATA ECO/UNDEV PLAN TEC/DEV EDU/PROP ATTIT HEALTH ...GEOG CHARTS 20 CONGRESS BIRTH/CON CASEBOOK. PAGE 138 F2729
ECO/DEV CENSUS FAM CONTROL

B66
WECHSBERG J.,THE MERCHANT BANKERS. EUR+WWI MOD/EUR CONTROL...BIOG GP/COMP PERS/COMP 16/20. PAGE 144 F2842
FINAN PWR WEALTH FAM

B67
BIRMINGHAM W.,A STUDY OF CONTEMPORARY GHANA VOL. I: SOME ASPECTS OF SOCIAL STRUCTURE. AFR GHANA AGRI FAM SECT PLAN EDU/PROP MARRIAGE OWN...POLICY STAT CHARTS MUNICH 20. PAGE 15 F0287
SOCIETY STRUCT CENSUS ECO/UNDEV

B67
DUN J.L.,THE ESSENCE OF CHINESE CIVILIZATION. ASIA FAM NAT/G TEC/DEV ADMIN SANCTION WAR HABITAT ...ANTHOL WORSHIP. PAGE 35 F0676
CULTURE SOCIETY

B67
WILLIAMS E.J.,LATIN AMERICAN CHRISTIAN DEMOCRATIC PARTIES. L/A+17C FAM LABOR FORCES...CATH TREND
POL/PAR GP/COMP

BIBLIOG 20. PAGE 147 F2890 CATHISM ALL/VALS

S67
FOX R.G.,"FAMILY, CASTE, AND COMMERCE IN A NORTH INDIAN MARKET TOWN." INDIA STRATA AGRI FACE/GP FAM NEIGH OP/RES BARGAIN ADMIN ROUTINE WEALTH...SOC CHARTS 20. PAGE 43 F0838 CULTURE GP/REL ECO/UNDEV DIST/IND

S67
MOONEY J.D.,"URBAN POVERTY AND LABOR FORCE PARTICIPATION." FAM DISCRIM...SOC/WK STAT CHARTS MUNICH. PAGE 93 F1820 INCOME WORKER WEALTH

S67
SCHWARZWELLER H.K.,"SOCIAL CLASS ORIGINS, RURAL-URBAN MIGRATION, AND ECONOMIC LIFE CHANGES." USA+45 SOCIETY STRUCT FAM NEIGH INCOME...SOC RECORD CHARTS MUNICH. PAGE 118 F2326 CLASSIF WEALTH AGRI

S67
STYCOS J.M.,"POLITICS AND POPULATION CONTROL IN LATIN AMERICA." USA+45 FAM NAT/G GP/REL AGE/C ATTIT CATHISM MARXISM...POLICY UN WHO. PAGE 127 F2509 PLAN CENSUS CONTROL L/A+17C

B96
SMITH A.,LECTURES ON JUSTICE, POLICE, REVENUE AND ARMS (1763). UK LAW FAM FORCES TARIFFS AGREE COERCE INCOME OWN WEALTH LAISSEZ...GEN/LAWS 17/18. PAGE 123 F2429 DIPLOM JURID OLD/LIB TAX

FAMILY....SEE FAM

FAMINE....SEE AGRI, HEALTH

FANON F. F0762

FAO F0763

FAO....FOOD AND AGRICULTURE ORGANIZATION; SEE ALSO UN, INT/ORG

S48
HARDIN L.M.,"REFLECTIONS ON AGRICULTURAL POLICY FORMATION IN THE UNITED STATES." LEGIS PLAN BUDGET ECO/TAC LEAD CENTRAL...MGT SOC NEW/IDEA STAT FAO. PAGE 55 F1078 AGRI POLICY ADMIN NEW/LIB

B57
WARRINER D.,LAND REFORM AND DEVELOPMENT IN THE MIDDLE EAST: A STUDY OF EGYPT, SYRIA AND IRAQ. IRAQ ISLAM SYRIA UAR AGRI DIST/IND PLAN TEC/DEV DOMIN REV ATTIT WEALTH...SOC METH/CNCPT STAT OBS RECORD HIST/WRIT TREND GEN/LAWS FAO 20. PAGE 143 F2825 ECO/UNDEV CONCPT

S62
ADISESHIAN M.,"EDUCATION AND DEVELOPMENT." FUT WOR+45 SOCIETY ACT/RES INT/TRADE EDU/PROP KNOWL SKILL WEALTH...POLICY CONCPT CONT/OBS CENSUS CHARTS TOT/POP VAL/FREE APPLIC FAO FOR/TRADE 20. PAGE 2 F0041 SCHOOL ECO/UNDEV

B63
COPPOCK J.,NORTH ATLANTIC POLICY - THE AGRICULTURAL GAP. EUR+WWI ELITES ECO/DEV DIST/IND MARKET PLAN WEALTH...STAT TREND GEN/LAWS OEEC TOT/POP VAL/FREE FAO 20. PAGE 27 F0535 AGRI TEC/DEV INT/TRADE

B67
JOHNSON D.G.,THE STRUGGLE AGAINST WORLD HUNGER (HEADLINE SERIES, NO. 184) (PAMPHLET). PLAN TEC/DEV FOR/AID...CHARTS 20 FAO MEXIC/AMER. PAGE 67 F1322 AGRI PROB/SOLV ECO/UNDEV HEALTH

FARER T.J. F0764

FARM/BUR....FARM BUREAU

FARMING....SEE AGRI

FARRIS M.T. F0765

FASCISM....FASCISM; SEE ALSO TOTALISM, FASCIST

N19
HAYEK FA V.O.N.,FREEDOM AND THE ECONOMIC SYSTEM. GERMANY USSR PLAN REPRESENT TOTALISM FASCISM POPULISM...MAJORIT METH/COMP GEN/LAWS 20. PAGE 57 F1123 ORD/FREE ECO/TAC CAP/ISM SOCISM

B35
LASKI H.J.,THE STATE IN THEORY AND PRACTICE. ELITES ECO/TAC REPRESENT ORD/FREE PWR WEALTH POPULISM ...GOV/COMP GEN/LAWS 19/20. PAGE 76 F1483 CAP/ISM COERCE NAT/G FASCISM

B38
HEIMANN E.,COMMUNISM, FASCISM, OR DEMOCRACY? WOR-45 CONSTN SOCIETY STRATA AGRI CAP/ISM MORAL ORD/FREE ...MAJORIT METH/COMP NAT/COMP 19/20. PAGE 58 F1141 SOCISM MARXISM FASCISM PLURISM

B38
REICH N.,LABOR RELATIONS IN REPUBLICAN GERMANY. GERMANY CONSTN ECO/DEV INDUS NAT/G ADMIN CONTROL GP/REL FASCISM POPULISM 20 WEIMAR/REP. PAGE 110 F2176 WORKER MGT LABOR BARGAIN

S39
COLE G.D.H.,"NAZI ECONOMICS: HOW DO THEY MANAGE IT?" GERMANY FORCES WORKER BUDGET INT/TRADE ROUTINE COERCE WAR 20 HITLER/A NAZI. PAGE 26 F0500 FASCISM ECO/TAC ATTIT PLAN

B40
HUNTER R.,REVOLUTION: WHY, HOW, WHEN? NAT/G ECO/TAC EDU/PROP COERCE ORD/FREE FASCISM POPULISM SOCISM 18/20 HITLER/A LENIN/VI. PAGE 63 F1246 REV METH/COMP LEAD CONSTN

B40
SIKES E.R.,CONTEMPORARY ECONOMIC SYSTEMS: THEIR ANALYSIS AND SOCIAL BACKGROUND. GERMANY ITALY USSR AGRI INDUS PLAN CAP/ISM ROUTINE TOTALISM FASCISM ...POLICY CON/ANAL BIBLIOG 20. PAGE 122 F2400 COM SOCISM CONCPT

B40
SPENCER H.,THE MAN VS. THE STATE (1892). UK POL/PAR LEGIS TARIFFS COERCE CRIME REPRESENT PWR SOCISM ...POLICY GEN/LAWS 19/20. PAGE 124 F2450 FASCISM POPULISM LAISSEZ ORD/FREE

B42
SWEEZY P.M.,THE THEORY OF CAPITALIST DEVELOPMENT. FUT NAT/G COST FASCISM BIBLIOG. PAGE 128 F2519 ECO/DEV CAP/ISM MARXISM COLONIAL

B60
BOHM F.,REDEN UND SCHRIFTEN UBER DIE ORDNUNG EINER FREIEN GESELLSCHAFT, EINER FREIEN WIRTSCHAFT, UND UBER DIE WIEDERGUTMACH. DIPLOM CRIME ORD/FREE RESPECT FASCISM 20 NAZI. PAGE 16 F0307 ECO/TAC NEW/LIB SUPEGO REPAR

B67
EBENSTEIN W.,TODAY'S ISMS: COMMUNISM, FASCISM, CAPITALISM, SOCIALISM (5TH ED.). COM WOR+45 PERCEPT PWR...SOC TREND IDEA/COMP NAT/COMP 20. PAGE 35 F0691 FASCISM MARXISM SOCISM CAP/ISM

B67
NYOMARKAY J.,CHARISMA AND FACTIONALISM IN THE NAZI PARTY. GERMANY POL/PAR LEGIT LEAD MARXISM ...NEW/IDEA METH/COMP GEN/LAWS BIBLIOG 20 HITLER/A. PAGE 99 F1949 FASCISM INGP/REL CHIEF PWR

L67
GREGORY A.J.,"AFRICAN SOCIALISM, SOCIALISM AND FASCISM: AN APPRAISAL." FUT LEAD REV GP/REL RACE/REL NAT/LISM ATTIT...IDEA/COMP STERTYP 20. PAGE 51 F0993 FASCISM MARXISM SOCISM AFR

S67
CAMMETT J.M.,"COMMUNIST THEORIES OF FASCISM, 1920-35." ITALY POL/PAR PROF/ORG VOL/ASSN WORKER COLONIAL TOTALISM...SOCIALIST 20. PAGE 21 F0403 MARXISM FASCISM ATTIT

S67
DEMUTH J.,"GE: PROFILE OF A CORPORATION." USA+45 USA-45 LABOR ACT/RES RATION EDU/PROP ADJUD CT/SYS FASCISM 20. PAGE 32 F0619 LG/CO CONSERVE PRICE

S67
MOLTMANN G.,"ZUR FORMULIERUNG DER AMERIKANISCHEN BESATZUNGSPOLITIK IN DEUTSCHLAND AM ENDE DES ZWEITEN WELTKRIEGES" GERMANY ECO/TAC ADMIN WAR CIVMIL/REL ORD/FREE FASCISM 20. PAGE 92 F1815 FORCES CONTROL POLICY INDUS

FASCIST....FASCIST

FASHION....SEE ETIQUET, MODAL

FATEMI N.S. F0766

FATHER/DIV....FATHER DIVINE AND HIS FOLLOWERS

FATOUROS A.A. F0767,F0768

FAULKNER H.U. F0769

FBI....U.S. FEDERAL BUREAU OF INVESTIGATION

N19
MARSH J.F. JR.,THE FBI RETIREMENT BILL (PAMPHLET). USA+45 EX/STRUC WORKER PLAN PROB/SOLV BUDGET LEAD LOBBY PARL/PROC PERS/REL RIGID/FLEX...POLICY 20 FBI PRESIDENT BUR/BUDGET. PAGE 86 F1677 ADMIN NAT/G SENIOR GOV/REL

FCC....U.S. FEDERAL COMMUNICATIONS COMMISSION

FDA....U.S. FOOD AND DRUG ADMINISTRATION

FDR....FRANKLIN D. ROOSEVELT

FEARN H. F0770

FEARS....SEE ANOMIE

FECHNER/GT....GUSTAV THEODOR FECHNER

FED/OPNMKT....FEDERAL OPEN MARKET COMMITTEE

FED/RESERV....U.S. FEDERAL RESERVE SYSTEM (INCLUDES FEDERAL

RESERVE BANK)

B48
HART A.G.,MONEY, DEBT, AND ECONOMIC ACTIVITY. AFR FINAN
WORKER DIPLOM PRICE CONTROL BAL/PAY COST OWN PRODUC WEALTH
...METH/COMP 20 FED/RESERV. PAGE 56 F1097 ECO/TAC
NAT/G

B50
HARTLAND P.C.,BALANCE OF INTERREGIONAL PAYMENTS OF ECO/DEV
NEW ENGLAND. USA+45 TEC/DEV ECO/TAC LEGIT ROUTINE FINAN
BAL/PAY PROFIT 20 NEW/ENGLND FED/RESERV. PAGE 56 REGION
F1102 PLAN

B50
SHAW E.S.,MONEY, INCOME, AND MONETARY POLICY. AFR FINAN
USA-45 NAT/G DIPLOM PAY CONTROL COST INCOME PRODUC ECO/TAC
WEALTH...T 20 FED/RESERV DEPT/TREAS. PAGE 120 F2370 ECO/DEV
PRICE

B53
HARROD R.,THE DOLLAR. AFR USA+45 USA-45 ECO/DEV FINAN
OPTIMAL WEALTH 18/20 FED/RESERV. PAGE 56 F1093 DIPLOM
BAL/PAY

N59
CHAMBER OF COMMERCE OF USA,ECONOMIC LESSONS OF ECO/DEV
POSTWAR RECESSIONS (PAMPHLET). AFR USA+45 LAW LEGIS PROB/SOLV
WORKER TAX...CHARTS 20 CONGRESS FED/RESERV. PAGE 23 FINAN
F0440 ECO/TAC

B63
US BD GOVERNORS FEDL RESRV,THE FEDERAL RESERVE AND FINAN
THE TREASURY. USA+45 WORKER PROB/SOLV PRICE COST GOV/REL
DEMAND WEALTH...STAT INT CHARTS 20 FED/RESERV CONTROL
DEPT/TREAS. PAGE 134 F2641 BUDGET

B64
JACOBY N.H.,UNITED STATES MONETARY POLICY. UK ECO/DEV
USA+45 LAW NAT/G TEC/DEV TAX EQUILIB INCOME POLICY
...METH/COMP 20 FED/RESERV. PAGE 66 F1300 ECO/TAC
FINAN

B65
KLEIN J.J.,MONEY AND THE ECONOMY. USA+45 NAT/G FINAN
DIPLOM CONTROL...POLICY T 20 FED/RESERV. PAGE 72 PLAN
F1406 WEALTH
BAL/PAY

B65
MACESICH G.,COMMERCIAL BANKING AND REGIONAL FINAN
DEVELOPMENT IN THE US, 1950-1960. USA+45 NAT/G PLAN ECO/DEV
ECO/TAC DEMAND...MGT 20 FED/RESERV SOUTH/US. INCOME
PAGE 83 F1627 COST

S66
FROMM G.,"RECENT MONETARY POLICY: AN ECONOMETRIC ECOMETRIC
VIEW" USA+45 ECO/DEV INDUS PAY PRICE PRODUC FINAN
ORD/FREE WEALTH...STAT 20 FED/RESERV. PAGE 45 F0869 POLICY
SIMUL

FEDERAL AVIATION AGENCY....SEE FAA

FEDERAL BUREAU OF INVESTIGATION....SEE FBI

FEDERAL COUNCIL FOR SCIENCE + TECHNOLOGY....SEE FEDSCI/TEC

FEDERAL HOUSING ADMINISTRATION...SEE FHA

FEDERAL RESERVE SYSTEM....SEE FED/RESERV

FEDERAL TRADE COMMISSION....SEE FTC

FEDERAL....FEDERALISM

N19
FREEMAN H.A.,COERCION OF STATES IN FEDERAL UNIONS FEDERAL
(PAMPHLET). WOR-45 DIPLOM CONTROL COERCE PEACE WAR
ORD/FREE...GOV/COMP METH/COMP NAT/COMP PACIFIST 20. INT/ORG
PAGE 43 F0850 PACIFISM

B25
MATHEWS J.M.,AMERICAN STATE GOVERNMENT. USA-45 PROVS
LOC/G CHIEF EX/STRUC LEGIS ADJUD CONTROL CT/SYS ADMIN
ROUTINE GOV/REL PWR 20 GOVERNOR. PAGE 87 F1703 FEDERAL
CONSTN

B28
FRANKFURTER F.,THE BUSINESS OF THE SUPREME COURT; A CT/SYS
STUDY IN THE FEDERAL JUDICIAL SYSTEM. USA-45 CONSTN ADJUD
EX/STRUC PROB/SOLV GP/REL ATTIT PWR...POLICY JURID LAW
18/20 SUPREME/CT CONGRESS. PAGE 43 F0848 FEDERAL

B41
YOUNG G.,FEDERALISM AND FREEDOM. EUR+WWI MOD/EUR NAT/G
RUSSIA USA-45 WOR-45 SOCIETY STRUCT ECO/DEV INT/ORG WAR
EXEC FEDERAL ATTIT PERSON ALL/VALS...OLD/LIB CONCPT
OBS TREND LEAGUE/NAT TOT/POP. PAGE 150 F2950

B48
VON HAYEK F.A.,INDIVIDUALISM AND ECONOMIC ORDER. SOCISM
GERMANY USA-45 USSR FINAN MARKET INT/ORG ECO/TAC CAP/ISM
INT/TRADE PRICE REPRESENT ORD/FREE...PLURIST POPULISM
GEN/LAWS 20. PAGE 142 F2793 FEDERAL

S49
STEINMETZ H.,"THE PROBLEMS OF THE LANDRAT: A STUDY LOC/G
OF COUNTY GOVERNMENT IN THE US ZONE OF GERMANY." COLONIAL
GERMANY/W USA+45 INDUS PLAN DIPLOM EDU/PROP CONTROL MGT
WAR GOV/REL FEDERAL WEALTH PLURISM...GOV/COMP 20 TOP/EX
LANDRAT. PAGE 126 F2478

B54
FRIEDMAN W.,THE PUBLIC CORPORATION: A COMPARATIVE LAW
SYMPOSIUM (UNIVERSITY OF TORONTO SCHOOL OF LAW SOCISM
COMPARATIVE LAW SERIES, VOL. I). AFR SWEDEN USA+45 LG/CO
INDUS INT/ORG NAT/G REGION CENTRAL FEDERAL...POLICY OWN
JURID IDEA/COMP NAT/COMP ANTHOL 20 MONOPOLY EUROPE.
PAGE 44 F0861

B55
FLORINSKY M.T.,INTEGRATED EUROPE. EUR+WWI FRANCE FUT
ITALY NETHERLAND UK ECO/DEV INT/ORG FORCES LEGIT ECO/TAC
FEDERAL ATTIT PWR WEALTH...POLICY GEOG CONCPT REGION
GEN/LAWS TOT/POP EEC OEEC 20. PAGE 42 F0816

B55
GOMES F.A.,OPERACAO MUNICIPIO. BRAZIL L/A+17C ECO/UNDEV
SERV/IND LOC/G BUDGET ECO/TAC COST DEMAND...POLICY FEDERAL
MUNICH 20. PAGE 48 F0944 GOV/REL

S59
WALLACE R.A.,"CONGRESSIONAL CONTROL OF THE BUDGET." LEGIS
USA+45 NAT/G CHIEF GP/REL FEDERAL OBJECTIVE...MGT EX/STRUC
CONGRESS. PAGE 143 F2807 BUDGET
CONSTN

B60
SANTHANAM K.,UNION-STATE RELATIONS IN INDIA. INDIA FEDERAL
FINAN PROVS PLAN ECO/TAC...LING 20. PAGE 116 F2280 GOV/REL
CONSTN
POLICY

B61
BREWIS T.N.,CANADIAN ECONOMIC POLICY. AFR CANADA ECO/DEV
BUDGET CAP/ISM INT/TRADE RATION TARIFFS TAX PRICE ECO/TAC
CONTROL ROUTINE FEDERAL INCOME PRODUC 20. PAGE 18 NAT/G
F0348 PLAN

B61
HICKS U.K.,FEDERALISM AND ECONOMIC GROWTH IN ECO/UNDEV
UNDERDEVELOPED COUNTRIES. WOR+45 WOR-45 FINAN NAT/G ECO/TAC
PLAN BUDGET DIPLOM INT/TRADE DEMAND WEALTH...ANTHOL FEDERAL
20. PAGE 59 F1167 CONSTN

B61
MACMAHON A.W.,DELEGATION AND AUTONOMY. INDIA STRUCT ADMIN
LEGIS BARGAIN BUDGET ECO/TAC LEGIT EXEC REPRESENT PLAN
GOV/REL CENTRAL DEMAND EFFICIENCY PRODUC. PAGE 84 FEDERAL
F1637

B61
UNIVS-NATL BUR COMM ECO RES,PUBLIC FINANCES: NEEDS, NAT/G
SOURCES, AND UTILIZATION. USA+45 FORCES PLAN TAX FINAN
CONFER PRICE FEDERAL UTIL...ANTHOL MUNICH 20. DECISION
PAGE 133 F2623 BUDGET

L61
GERWIG R.,"PUBLIC AUTHORITIES IN THE UNITED LOC/G
STATES." LAW CONSTN PROVS TAX ADMIN FEDERAL MUNICH. GOV/REL
PAGE 47 F0920 PWR

B62
CARPER E.T.,ILLINOIS GOES TO CONGRESS FOR ARMY ADMIN
LAND. USA+45 LAW EXTR/IND PROVS REGION CIVMIL/REL LOBBY
GOV/REL FEDERAL ATTIT 20 ILLINOIS SENATE CONGRESS GEOG
DIRKSEN/E DOUGLAS/P. PAGE 22 F0420 LEGIS

B62
DIMOCK M.E.,THE NEW AMERICAN POLITICAL ECONOMY: A FEDERAL
SYNTHESIS OF POLITICS AND ECONOMICS. USA+45 FINAN ECO/TAC
LG/CO PLAN ADMIN REGION GP/REL CENTRAL MORAL 20. NAT/G
PAGE 33 F0642 PARTIC

B62
URQUIDI V.L.,FREE TRADE AND ECONOMIC INTEGRATION IN INT/TRADE
LATIN AMERICA: THE EVOLUTION OF A COMMON MARKET REGION
POLICY. ECO/UNDEV MARKET DIPLOM BAL/PAY FEDERAL INT/ORG
...POLICY CHARTS 20 LAFTA. PAGE 133 F2627 L/A+17C

B63
DELL S.,TRADE BLOCS AND COMMON MARKETS. COM WOR+45 DIPLOM
ECO/DEV ECO/UNDEV GP/COMP. PAGE 32 F0615 ECO/TAC
INT/TRADE
FEDERAL

B64
NAGEL P.C.,ONE NATION INDIVISIBLE: THE UNION IN FEDERAL
AMERICAN THOUGHT 1776-1861. USA-45 INDUS TEC/DEV NAT/G
EDU/PROP DREAM...IDEA/COMP 18/19. PAGE 96 F1887 ATTIT
INGP/REL

B64
WHEARE K.C.,FEDERAL GOVERNMENT (4TH ED.). WOR+45 FEDERAL
WOR-45 POL/PAR LEGIS BAL/PWR CT/SYS...POLICY JURID CONSTN
CONCPT GOV/COMP 17/20. PAGE 145 F2866 EX/STRUC
NAT/COMP

S64
NEWLYN W.T.,"MONETARY SYSTEMS AND INTEGRATION" AFR ECO/UNDEV
BUDGET ADMIN FEDERAL PRODUC PROFIT UTIL...CHARTS 20 REGION
AFRICA/E. PAGE 98 F1922 METH/COMP
FINAN

B65
DANIELSON M.N.,FEDERAL-METROPOLITAN POLITICS AND FEDERAL
THE COMMUTER CRISIS. PROVS LEGIS EXEC LEAD PWR GOV/REL
...DECISION MUNICH. PAGE 30 F0580 DIST/IND

B65
GRIFFIN C.E.,THE FREE SOCIETY. CONSTN SOCIETY CONCPT
MARKET FEDERAL RATIONAL WEALTH...MAJORIT 20 ORD/FREE
CIVIL/LIB. PAGE 51 F0999 CAP/ISM

POPULISM
B65
LEYS C.T.,FEDERATION IN EAST AFRICA. LAW AGRI DIST/IND FINAN INT/ORG LABOR INT/TRADE CONFER ADMIN CONTROL GP/REL...ANTHOL 20 AFRICA/E. PAGE 79 F1554 FEDERAL REGION ECO/UNDEV PLAN
S65
HAYTER T.,"FRENCH AID TO AFRICA* ITS SCOPE AND ACHIEVEMENTS." CULTURE ECO/TAC INT/TRADE ADMIN REGION CENTRAL FEDERAL LOVE PWR SOVEREIGN EEC. PAGE 57 F1127 AFR FRANCE FOR/AID COLONIAL
B66
SASTRI K.V.S.,FEDERAL-STATE FISCAL RELATIONS IN INDIA: A STUDY OF THE FINANCE COMMISSION AND TECHNIQUES OF FINANCIAL ADJUSTMENT. INDIA PROVS DELIB/GP GOV/REL FEDERAL...MATH CHARTS 20. PAGE 116 F2283 TAX BUDGET FINAN NAT/G
S66
ROTHCHILD D.,"THE LIMITS OF FEDERALISM: AN EXAMINATION OF POLITICAL INSTITUTIONAL TRANSFER IN AFRICA." AFR CONSTN CULTURE ELITES ECO/UNDEV KIN PROB/SOLV ADMIN ORD/FREE PWR...POLICY 20. PAGE 114 F2250 FEDERAL NAT/G NAT/LISM COLONIAL
S67
APEL H.,"LES NOUVEAUX ASPECTS DE LA POLITIQUE ETRANGERE ALLEMANDE." AFR EUR+WWI GERMANY POL/PAR BAL/PWR ECO/TAC INT/TRADE NUC/PWR NAT/LISM PEACE ...POLICY 20 EEC. PAGE 6 F0107 DIPLOM INT/ORG FEDERAL
S67
EDWARDS N.,"EDUCATION IN THE FEDERAL-STATE STRUCTURE OF GOVERNMENT." USA+45 SECT CONTROL GOV/REL RACE/REL DISCRIM FEDERAL ROLE PWR SOVEREIGN. PAGE 36 F0705 EDU/PROP NAT/G PROVS POLICY
S67
WILLMANN J.,"LA COMMUNAUTE EUROPEENNE ET LA GRANDE-BRETAGNE." UK PROB/SOLV TEC/DEV CAP/ISM DIPLOM CONFER FEDERAL...POLICY 20 EEC. PAGE 147 F2898 INT/ORG DRIVE NAT/LISM INT/TRADE

FEDERALIST....FEDERALIST PARTY (ALL NATIONS)

B65
GRAMPP W.D.,ECONOMIC LIBERALISM; THE BEGINNINGS (VOL. I). USA-45 WOR-45 MARKET LABOR ATTIT WEALTH ...POLICY CONCPT BIBLIOG GREECE/ANC MERCANTLST REPUBLICAN FEDERALIST. PAGE 50 F0974 ECO/DEV CAP/ISM IDEA/COMP ECO/TAC

FEDSCI/TEC....FEDERAL COUNCIL FOR SCIENCE AND TECHNOLOGY

FEDYSHYN O.S. F0771

FEEDBACK....FEEDBACK PHENOMENA

B60
RAY D.D.,ACCOUNTING AND BUSINESS FLUCTUATIONS. LG/CO SML/CO FEEDBACK DEMAND...CHARTS IDEA/COMP BIBLIOG 20. PAGE 109 F2154 FINAN AFR CONTROL
B63
BRAYBROOKE D.,A STRATEGY OF DECISION: POLICY EVALUATION AS A SOCIAL PROCESS. UNIV ELITES OP/RES DOMIN CONFER FEEDBACK CONSEN PLURISM...CONCPT CENSUS. PAGE 18 F0343 DECISION POLICY CONTROL
S65
KINDLEBERGER C.P.,"MASS MIGRATION, THEN AND NOW." LAW ECO/DEV ECO/UNDEV INDUS LABOR INT/TRADE FEEDBACK REGION RIGID/FLEX...SOC NAT/COMP EEC. PAGE 71 F1394 EUR+WWI USA-45 WORKER IDEA/COMP
B66
SEWELL J.P.,FUNCTIONALISM AND WORLD POLITICS* A STUDY BASED ON UNITED NATIONS PROGRAMS FINANCING ECONOMICAL DEVELOPMENT. ECO/UNDEV FINAN PROB/SOLV DIPLOM ECO/TAC FEEDBACK REGION ADJUST ATTIT UN IBRD INTL/FINAN INTL/DEV UNSF. PAGE 120 F2360 TASK INT/ORG IDEA/COMP GEN/LAWS
B67
DONALD A.G.,MANAGEMENT, INFORMATION, AND SYSTEMS. WOR+45 LG/CO PROB/SOLV CONTROL FEEDBACK KNOWL MGT. PAGE 34 F0653 ROUTINE TEC/DEV CONCPT ADMIN
B67
JACOBY N.H.,US AID TO TAIWAN. CAP/ISM DIPLOM FEEDBACK COST PRODUC...OBS INT CHARTS 20. PAGE 66 F1301 FOR/AID OP/RES ECO/TAC ECO/UNDEV
B67
SAPARINA Y.,CYBERNETICS WITHIN US. WOR+45 EDU/PROP FEEDBACK PERCEPT HEALTH...DECISION METH/CNCPT NEW/IDEA 20. PAGE 116 F2281 COMPUTER METH/COMP CONTROL SIMUL
S67
WILES P.J.,"THE POLITICAL AND SOCIAL PREREQUISITES FOR A SOVIET-TYPE ECONOMY." COM USSR LAW CULTURE CREATE ADMIN FEEDBACK ROUTINE COST OPTIMAL TOTALISM MARXISM 20. PAGE 146 F2883 ECO/DEV PLAN EX/STRUC EFFICIENCY

FEI J.C.H. F0772

FEIGENBAUM E.A. F0567

FEIS H. F0773,F0774,F0775

FELD W. F0776,F0777

FELDMAN A.S. F1823

FELKER J.L. F0778

FELLNER W. F0779,F0780,F0781

FELS R. F0782

FEMALE/SEX....FEMALE SEX

S67
NEALE R.S.,"WORKING CLASS WOMEN AND WOMEN'S SUFFRAGE." UK LAW CONSTN LABOR NAT/G DELIB/GP LEGIS WORKER PAY PARTIC CHOOSE 19 FEMALE/SEX. PAGE 97 F1906 STRATA SEX SUFF DISCRIM

FEPC....FAIR EMPLOYMENT PRACTICES COMMISSION

B48
KESSELMAN L.C.,THE SOCIAL POLITICS OF THE FEPC. INDUS WORKER EDU/PROP GP/REL RACE/REL 20 NEGRO JEWS FEPC. PAGE 70 F1382 POLICY NAT/G ADMIN DISCRIM

FERBER R. F0783

FERGUSON D.E. F0784

FERMAN L.A. F0785

FERNANDES F. F0786

FERRY W.H. F0787

FERTIG L. F0788

FEUDALISM....FEUDALISM

FHA....U.S. FEDERAL HOUSING ADMINISTRATION

FICHTE/JG....JOHANN GOTTLIEB FICHTE

FICTIONS....SEE MYTH

FIELD G.C. F0789

FIELD G.L. F0790

FIELD/SJ....STEPHEN J. FIELD

B60
MENDELSON W.,CAPITALISM, DEMOCRACY, AND THE SUPREME COURT. USA+45 USA-45 CONSTN DIPLOM GOV/REL ATTIT ORD/FREE LAISSEZ...POLICY CHARTS PERS/COMP 18/20 SUPREME/CT MARSHALL/J HOLMES/OW TANEY/RB FIELD/JJ. PAGE 90 F1758 JUDGE CT/SYS JURID NAT/G

FIESER M.E. F0791

FIKS M. F0792

FILENE P.G. F0793

FILLMORE/M....PRESIDENT MILLARD FILLMORE

FILLOL T.R. F0794,F0795

FILM....FILM AND CINEMA

B67
BURDEN H.T.,THE NUREMBERG PARTY RALLIES 1923-39. GERMANY POL/PAR SECT CREATE DOMIN WAR ATTIT ...AUD/VIS FILM 20. PAGE 20 F0384 EDU/PROP CONTROL CROWD TOTALISM

FINAN....FINANCIAL SERVICE, BANKS, INSURANCE SYSTEMS, SECURITIES, EXCHANGES

N
JOHNSON R.B.,FINANCING A SUBURBAN CITY. USA+45 TAX COST...SAMP/SIZ MUNICH 20 COL. PAGE 68 F1331 FINAN PAY PROB/SOLV
N
NEW JERSEY STATE OF,SECOND REPORT TO GOVERNOR, SENATE, ASSEMBLY BY UNIFORM COMMERCIAL CODE STUDY COMMISSION. USA+45 INDUS LOC/G NAT/G PROF/ORG CONSULT ACT/RES LEGIT CT/SYS ATTIT NEW/JERSEY. PAGE 98 F1920 LAW FINAN CENTRAL PROVS

N
AMERICAN ECONOMIC REVIEW. FINAN INDUS LABOR OP/RES CAP/ISM INT/TRADE TAX WEALTH...CON/ANAL CHARTS 20. PAGE 1 F0001
BIBLIOG/A USA+45 ECO/DEV NAT/G

N
INTERNATIONAL BIBLIOGRAPHY OF ECONOMICS. WOR+45 FINAN MARKET ADMIN DEMAND INCOME PRODUC...POLICY IDEA/COMP METH. PAGE 1 F0002
BIBLIOG ECO/DEV ECO/UNDEV INT/TRADE

N
DOCUMENTATION ECONOMIQUE: REVUE BIBLIOGRAPHIQUE DE SYNTHESE. WOR+45 COM/IND FINAN BUDGET DIPLOM...GEOG 20. PAGE 1 F0004
BIBLIOG/A SOC

N
ECONOMIC ABSTRACTS. WOR+45 FINAN INDUS MARKET LABOR ACT/RES INT/TRADE WRITING GP/REL...MGT 20. PAGE 1 F0005
BIBLIOG/A EDU/PROP

N
ECONOMIC LIBRARY SELECTIONS. AGRI INDUS MARKET ADMIN...STAT NAT/COMP 20. PAGE 1 F0007
BIBLIOG/A WRITING FINAN

N
THE MIDDLE EAST AND NORTH AFRICA. AFR ISLAM CULTURE ECO/UNDEV AGRI NAT/G TEC/DEV FOR/AID INT/TRADE EDU/PROP...CHARTS 20. PAGE 1 F0008
INDEX INDUS FINAN STAT

N
SOUTH AFRICAN JOURNAL OF ECONOMICS. SOUTH/AFR FINAN MARKET ACT/RES OP/RES...PHIL/SCI STAT CON/ANAL METH/COMP BIBLIOG/A 20. PAGE 1 F0009
ECO/UNDEV ACADEM INTELL R+D

N
THE MIDDLE EAST. CULTURE...BIOG BIBLIOG. PAGE 1 F0010
ISLAM INDUS FINAN

N
AMERICAN ECONOMIC ASSOCIATION,THE JOURNAL OF ECONOMIC ABSTRACTS. ECO/UNDEV MARKET LABOR DIPLOM ...MGT CONCPT METH 20. PAGE 5 F0086
BIBLIOG/A R+D FINAN

N
US SUPERINTENDENT OF DOCUMENTS,CENSUS PUBLICATIONS (PRICE LIST 70). AGRI CONSTRUC DIST/IND FINAN LOC/G NAT/G PROVS INT/TRADE APPORT INCOME. PAGE 140 F2751
BIBLIOG/A CENSUS STAT USA+45

B00
LIST F.,NATIONAL SYSTEM OF POLITICAL ECONOMY. ECO/DEV AGRI EXTR/IND FINAN INDUS TEC/DEV ECO/TAC ATTIT WEALTH...TREND GEN/LAWS FOR/TRADE 19. PAGE 81 F1581
MOD/EUR MARKET

B00
MILL J.S.,PRINCIPLES OF POLITICAL ECONOMY. WOR-45 CULTURE SOCIETY STRATA ECO/DEV AGRI EXTR/IND FINAN INDUS DELIB/GP ECO/TAC WEALTH...CONCPT MATH TREND 20. PAGE 91 F1786
MARKET INT/ORG INT/TRADE

B02
MOREL E.D.,AFFAIRS OF WEST AFRICA. UK FINAN INDUS FAM KIN SECT CHIEF WORKER DIPLOM RACE/REL LITERACY HEALTH...CHARTS 18/20 AFRICA/W NEGRO. PAGE 93 F1826
COLONIAL ADMIN AFR

B04
MARX K.,A CONTRIBUTION TO THE CRITIQUE OF POLITICAL ECONOMY (TRANS. FROM 2ND ED. BY N.I. STONE). UK STRATA ECO/DEV FINAN MARKET PLAN BARGAIN CAP/ISM ECO/TAC ATTIT WEALTH...METH/CNCPT BIOG 19. PAGE 86 F1687
MARXIST NEW/IDEA MARXISM

B04
VEBLEN T.B.,THE THEORY OF BUSINESS ENTERPRISE. USA-45 FINAN WORKER ECO/TAC PRICE GP/REL COST ...POLICY 19/20. PAGE 141 F2770
TEC/DEV GEN/LAWS SOCIETY WEALTH

B13
DAVENPORT H.J.,THE ECONOMICS OF ENTERPRISE. UNIV FINAN SML/CO RENT COST WEALTH GEN/LAWS. PAGE 30 F0582
CAP/ISM PRICE ECO/TAC LG/CO

B14
HOBSON J.A.,WORK AND WEALTH. CULTURE FINAN INDUS WORKER TEC/DEV ECO/TAC GIVE PAY PRICE COST PRODUC UTIL. PAGE 60 F1185
WEALTH INCOME GEN/LAWS

B19
VEBLEN T.B.,THE VESTED INTERESTS AND THE STATE OF THE INDUSTRIAL ARTS. USA-45 LAW FINAN WORKER PAY DOMIN PRICE COST SOCISM...MARXIST 19/20. PAGE 141 F2771
INDUS CAP/ISM METH/COMP WEALTH

N19
ADMINISTRATIVE STAFF COLLEGE,THE ACCOUNTABILITY OF GOVERNMENT DEPARTMENTS (PAMPHLET) (REV. ED.). UK CONSTN FINAN NAT/G CONSULT ADMIN INGP/REL CONSEN PRIVIL 20 PARLIAMENT. PAGE 2 F0043
PARL/PROC ELITES SANCTION PROB/SOLV

N19
ANDERSON J.,THE ORGANIZATION OF ECONOMIC STUDIES IN RELATION TO THE PROBLEMS OF GOVERNMENT (PAMPHLET). UK FINAN INDUS DELIB/GP PLAN PROB/SOLV ADMIN 20. PAGE 5 F0095
ECO/TAC ACT/RES NAT/G CENTRAL

N19
BASCH A.,THE FUTURE OF FOREIGN LENDING FOR DEVELOPMENT (PAMPHLET). WOR+45 ECO/UNDEV FINAN INT/ORG ECO/TAC ATTIT...PREDICT 20. PAGE 11 F0203
FOR/AID ECO/DEV DIPLOM GIVE

N19
BASSIE V.L.,UNCERTAINTY IN FORECASTING AND POLICY FORMATION (PAMPHLET). UNIV MARKET ECO/TAC PRODUC ...POLICY DECISION MGT MATH CHARTS 20. PAGE 11 F0205
ECO/DEV FINAN PREDICT PROB/SOLV

N19
BLOOMFIELD A.,MONETARY POLICY UNDER THE INTERNATIONAL GOLD STANDARD: 18801914 (PAMPHLET). AFR USA-45 DIPLOM CONTROL...POLICY 19. PAGE 16 F0300
FINAN ROLE EFFICIENCY

N19
BOS H.C.,A DISCUSSION ON METHODS OF MONETARY ANALYSIS AND NORMS FOR MONETARY POLICY (PAMPHLET). BAL/PAY COST INCOME...METH/COMP 20. PAGE 17 F0319
FINAN POLICY EQUILIB SIMUL

N19
CASSELL F.,INTERNATIONAL MONETARY PROBLEMS (PAMPHLET). AFR BAL/PWR CONTROL EFFICIENCY WEALTH 20 EEC. PAGE 22 F0427
INT/TRADE FINAN DIPLOM TREND

N19
CONGRESSIONAL QUARTERLY SERV,FEDERAL ECONOMIC POLICY 1945-1965 (PAMPHLET). USA+45 FINAN OP/RES BAL/PWR ECO/TAC TAX BAL/PAY CENTRAL COST WEALTH ...CHARTS 20. PAGE 27 F0525
NAT/G ECO/DEV BUDGET POLICY

N19
DWYER J.W.,YARDSTICKS FOR PERFORMANCE (PAMPHLET). USA+45 FINAN CONTROL...CONCPT METH/COMP MUNICH. PAGE 35 F0688
BUDGET LOC/G EFFICIENCY

N19
GROSECLOSE E.,THE DECAY OF MONEY; A SURVEY OF WESTERN CURRENCIES 1912-1962 (PAMPHLET). AFR FRANCE GERMANY UK LAW INT/TRADE BAL/PAY COST EQUILIB ...POLICY 20 DEPRESSION. PAGE 51 F1004
FINAN NAT/G ECO/DEV ECO/TAC

N19
HABERLER G.,INFLATION; ITS CAUSES AND CURES (PAMPHLET). AFR USA+45 FINAN BUDGET PAY PRICE COST DEMAND 20. PAGE 52 F1021
ECO/DEV BAL/PAY POLICY NAT/G

N19
HABERLER G.,A SURVEY OF INTERNATIONAL TRADE THEORY (PAMPHLET). FINAN NAT/G COST INCOME 18/20 MONEY HUME/D MARSHALL/A. PAGE 52 F1022
INT/TRADE BAL/PAY GEN/LAWS POLICY

N19
HAGEN E.E.,AN ANALYTICAL MODEL OF THE TRANSITION TO ECONOMIC GROWTH (PAMPHLET). WOR+45 WOR-45 SOCIETY STRATA FINAN NAT/G CONTROL PARTIC PRODUC...PHIL/SCI BIBLIOG 17/20. PAGE 53 F1033
SIMUL ECO/DEV METH TEC/DEV

N19
HANSEN B.,INFLATION PROBLEMS IN SMALL COUNTRIES (PAMPHLET). AFR UNIV FOR/AID CONTROL BAL/PAY DEMAND PRODUC 20. PAGE 54 F1066
PRICE FINAN ECO/UNDEV ECO/TAC

N19
KINDLEBERGER C.P.,BALANCE-OF-PAYMENTS DEFICITS AND THE INTERNATIONAL MARKET FOR LIQUIDITY (PAMPHLET). ECO/DEV NAT/G PLAN DIPLOM ECO/TAC PRODUC...POLICY STAT CHARTS. PAGE 71 F1389
BAL/PAY INT/TRADE MARKET FINAN

N19
KRESSBACH T.W.,HE MICHIGAN CITY MANAGER IN BUDGETARY PROCEEDINGS (PAMPHLET). USA+45 PROVS DELIB/GP GP/REL SUPEGO...POLICY MUNICH. PAGE 73 F1438
LOC/G BUDGET FINAN

N19
KUWAIT ARABIA,KUWAIT FUND FOR ARAB ECONOMIC DEVELOPMENT (PAMPHLET). ISLAM KUWAIT UAR ECO/UNDEV LEGIS ECO/TAC WEALTH 20. PAGE 74 F1452
FOR/AID DIPLOM FINAN ADMIN

N19
KUWAIT FUND ARAB ECO DEVELOPMT,ANNUAL REPORTS 1962-65 (PAMPHLET). KUWAIT ECO/UNDEV DIPLOM ...POLICY 20 ARABS. PAGE 74 F1453
FOR/AID DELIB/GP FINAN ISLAM

N19
LUTZ F.A.,THE PROBLEM OF INTERNATIONAL LIQUIDITY AND THE MULTIPLECURRENCY STANDARD (PAMPHLET). WOR+45 MARKET INT/ORG PRICE BAL/PAY...NEW/IDEA METH/COMP BIBLIOG 20 IMF. PAGE 82 F1609
PROB/SOLV FINAN DIPLOM ECO/TAC

N19
MARCUS W.,US PRIVATE INVESTMENT AND ECONOMIC AID IN UNDERDEVELOPED COUNTRIES (PAMPHLET). USA+45 LG/CO NAT/G CAP/ISM EDU/PROP 20. PAGE 85 F1666
FOR/AID ECO/UNDEV FINAN PLAN

N19
MASON E.S.,THE DIPLOMACY OF ECONOMIC ASSISTANCE (PAMPHLET). INDIA PAKISTAN USA+45 ECO/UNDEV NAT/G BUDGET ATTIT...POLICY 20. PAGE 87 F1695
FOR/AID DIPLOM FINAN

N19
MCCONNELL G.,THE STEEL SEIZURE OF 1952 (PAMPHLET). USA+45 FINAN INDUS PROC/MFG LG/CO EX/STRUC ADJUD CONTROL GP/REL ORD/FREE PWR 20 TRUMAN/HS PRESIDENT CONGRESS. PAGE 88 F1721
DELIB/GP LABOR PROB/SOLV NAT/G

N19
MEZERIK A.G.,ECONOMIC AID FOR UNDERDEVELOPED COUNTRIES (PAMPHLET). AFR USSR WOR+45 FINAN LG/CO DELIB/GP NUC/PWR...GEOG CENSUS CHARTS 20 UN THIRD/WRLD. PAGE 90 F1775
FOR/AID ECO/UNDEV DIPLOM POLICY

N19
MUSHKIN S.J.,LOCAL SCHOOL EXPENDITURES: 1970 PROJECTIONS (PAMPHLET). FUT USA+45 CONSTRUC FINAN PROVS EDU/PROP COST...GEOG CENSUS PREDICT CHARTS SIMUL 20. PAGE 95 F1871
LOC/G SCHOOL BUDGET

N19
RIDLEY C.E.,MEASURING MUNICIPAL ACTIVITIES (PAMPHLET). FINAN SERV/IND FORCES RECEIVE INGP/REL HABITAT...POLICY SOC/WK 20. PAGE 111 F2191
MGT HEALTH WEALTH LOC/G

N19
ROBERTSON D.,GROWTH, WAGES, MONEY (PAMPHLET). UNIV WORKER BUDGET PRICE DEMAND PRODUC WEALTH...CONCPT MATH MONEY. PAGE 112 F2210
FINAN ECO/DEV ECO/TAC PAY

N19
STEUBER F.A.,THE CONTRIBUTION OF SWITZERLAND TO THE ECONOMIC AND SOCIAL DEVELOPMENT OF LOW-INCOME COUNTRIES (PAMPHLET). SWITZERLND FINAN NAT/G VOL/ASSN INT/TRADE DRIVE...CHARTS 20. PAGE 126 F2482
FOR/AID ECO/UNDEV PLAN DIPLOM

N19
US CHAMBER OF COMMERCE,THE SIGNIFICANCE OF CONCENTRATION RATIOS (PAMPHLET). USA+45 FINAN INDUS ADMIN...METH/CNCPT SAMP CHARTS 20. PAGE 134 F2647
MARKET PREDICT LG/CO CONTROL

N19
US MARITIME ADMINISTRATION,CONTRIBUTION OF FEDERAL AID PROGRAMS TO THE OCEANBORNE FOREIGN TRADE OF THE UNITED STATES: 1959-62 (PAMPHLET). USA+45 SEA FINAN NAT/G BUDGET...POLICY 20. PAGE 138 F2719
INT/TRADE ECO/TAC DIST/IND GIVE

N19
WILSON T.,FINANCIAL ASSISTANCE WITH REGIONAL DEVELOPMENT (PAMPHLET). CANADA INDUS NAT/G PLAN TAX CONTROL COST EFFICIENCY...POLICY CHARTS 20. PAGE 147 F2902
FINAN ECO/TAC REGION GOV/REL

B20
PIGOU A.C.,THE ECONOMICS OF WELFARE. UNIV INDUS WORKER ACT/RES RECEIVE INCOME NEW/LIB...MAJORIT SOC/WK. PAGE 106 F2085
ECO/TAC WEALTH FINAN CONTROL

B21
CLAPHAN J.H.,THE ECONOMIC DEVELOPMENT OF FRANCE AND GERMANY 1815-1914. FRANCE GERMANY MOD/EUR COM/IND DIST/IND FINAN INT/TRADE EDU/PROP 19/20. PAGE 24 F0476
ECO/UNDEV ECO/DEV AGRI INDUS

B26
MCPHEE A.,THE ECONOMIC REVOLUTION IN BRITISH WEST AFRICA. AFR UK CULTURE DIST/IND FINAN INDUS PLAN GP/REL RACE/REL 20 AFRICA/W. PAGE 88 F1735
ECO/UNDEV INT/TRADE COLONIAL GEOG

B27
WEBER M.,GENERAL ECONOMIC HISTORY. CHRIST-17C MOD/EUR STRUCT AGRI EXTR/IND FINAN INDUS MARKET FAM NAT/G PROF/ORG SECT ECO/TAC MUNICH 8/20. PAGE 144 F2839
ECO/DEV CAP/ISM

B28
CASSEL G.,FOREIGN INVESTMENTS. GERMANY UK USA-45 WOR-45 ECO/DEV NAT/G VOL/ASSN CAP/ISM REPAR ATTIT WEALTH...METH/CNCPT STAT SIMUL STERTYP ANTHOL FOR/TRADE TOT/POP VAL/FREE 20. PAGE 22 F0426
FINAN ECO/TAC BAL/PAY

B30
BIEL G.,TREATISE ON THE POWER AND UTILITY OF MONEY (1484). INDUS MARKET LOC/G NAT/G SECT ECO/TAC PRODUC WEALTH 15. PAGE 15 F0280
FINAN COST PRICE GEN/LAWS

B30
FEIS H.,EUROPE, THE WORLD'S BANKER, 1871-1914. FRANCE GERMANY MOD/EUR UK WOR-45 NAT/G PLAN ECO/TAC EXEC ATTIT PWR WEALTH...CONCPT HIST/WRIT GEN/LAWS VAL/FREE 19/20. PAGE 40 F0773
FINAN DIPLOM INT/TRADE

B30
KEYNES J.M.,A TREATISE ON MONEY (2 VOLS.). UK USA-45 INDUS MARKET WORKER PRICE CONTROL COST OPTIMAL PROFIT WEALTH...POLICY 19/20 KEYNES/JM. PAGE 70 F1385
EQUILIB ECO/TAC FINAN GEN/LAWS

B31
JEVONS W.S.,THE THEORY OF POLITICAL ECONOMY (4TH ED.; 1ST ED. 1871). WOR-45 FINAN MARKET RENT WEALTH ...LOG MATH QUANT CON/ANAL IDEA/COMP BIBLIOG METH 17/19. PAGE 67 F1318
GEN/LAWS UTIL LABOR

B32
DICKINSON H.D.,INSTITUTIONAL REVENUE: A STUDY OF THE INFLUENCE OF SOCIAL INSTITUTIONS ON THE DISTRIBUTION OF WEALTH. SOCIETY STRATA FINAN ...NEW/IDEA IDEA/COMP 20. PAGE 33 F0632
WEALTH CONCPT METH/CNCPT MARKET

B32
THOMPSON C.D.,CONFESSIONS OF THE POWER TRUST. MARKET ACT/RES EDU/PROP CONTROL GOV/REL INCOME OWN ...MGT 20 FTC MONOPOLY. PAGE 130 F2564
LG/CO SERV/IND PWR FINAN

B32
WRIGHT Q.,GOLD AND MONETARY STABILIZATION. FUT USA-45 WOR-45 INTELL ECO/DEV INT/ORG NAT/G CONSULT PLAN ECO/TAC ADMIN ATTIT WEALTH...CONCPT TREND 20. PAGE 149 F2935
FINAN POLICY

B34
ROBINSON J.,THE ECONOMICS OF IMPERFECT COMPETITION. FINAN ECO/TAC PRICE COST DEMAND EQUILIB OPTIMAL WEALTH...METH MONOPOLY. PAGE 113 F2221
MARKET WORKER INDUS

B35
KEYNES J.M.,THE GENERAL THEORY OF EMPLOYMENT, INTEREST, AND MONEY. AGRI INDUS WORKER ECO/TAC DEMAND EQUILIB INCOME PRODUC PROFIT ATTIT WEALTH 20. PAGE 71 F1386
FINAN GEN/LAWS MARKET PRICE

B35
STALEY E.,WAR AND THE PRIVATE INVESTOR. UNIV WOR-45 INTELL SOCIETY INT/ORG NAT/G TOP/EX CAP/ISM ECO/TAC WAR ATTIT ALL/VALS...INT TIME/SEQ TREND CON/ANAL WORK TOT/POP 20. PAGE 125 F2464
FINAN INT/TRADE DIPLOM

B35
WADE J.,HISTORY OF THE MIDDLE AND WORKING CLASSES; WITH A POPULAR EXPOSITION OF THE ECONOMICAL AND POLITICAL PRINCIPLES.... FRANCE UK CONSTN FINAN INDUS LABOR INCOME PROFIT KNOWL MORAL ORD/FREE WEALTH...CHARTS 14/19. PAGE 142 F2797
WORKER STRATA CONCPT

B37
BRESCIANI-TURRONI C,THE ECONOMICS OF INFLATION: A STUDY OF CURRENCY DEPRECIATION IN POST-WAR GERMANY. AFR GERMANY FINAN INT/TRADE PRICE TOTALISM...POLICY TIME/SEQ CHARTS GEN/LAWS 20 HITLER/A. PAGE 18 F0347
ECO/TAC WEALTH SOCIETY

B37
BROOKS R.R.,WHEN LABOR ORGANIZES. FINAN EDU/PROP ADMIN LOBBY PARTIC REPRESENT WEALTH TREND. PAGE 19 F0364
LABOR GP/REL POLICY

B37
HAMILTON W.H.,THE POWER TO GOVERN. ECO/DEV FINAN INDUS ECO/TAC INT/TRADE TARIFFS TAX CONTROL CT/SYS WAR COST PWR 18/20 SUPREME/CT. PAGE 54 F1056
LING CONSTN NAT/G POLICY

B37
MACKENZIE F.,PLANNED SOCIETY: YESTERDAY, TODAY, AND TOMORROW. ECO/DEV ECO/UNDEV AGRI FINAN INDUS PLAN INSPECT CONTROL ALL/IDEOS...TREND METH/COMP BIBLIOG 20 RESOURCE/N. PAGE 83 F1635
SOC CONCPT ANTHOL

B37
ROBBINS L.,ECONOMIC PLANNING AND INTERNATIONAL ORDER. WOR-45 SOCIETY FINAN INDUS NAT/G ECO/TAC ROUTINE WEALTH...SOC TIME/SEQ GEN/METH WORK 20 KEYNES/JM. PAGE 112 F2202
INT/ORG PLAN INT/TRADE

B37
VON HAYEK F.A.,MONETARY NATIONALISM AND INTERNATIONAL STABILITY. WOR-45 ECO/DEV NAT/G PROB/SOLV INT/TRADE...POLICY CONCPT METH/COMP NAT/COMP 20. PAGE 142 F2792
ECO/TAC FINAN DIPLOM NAT/LISM

B38
LANGE O.,ON THE ECONOMIC THEORY OF SOCIALISM. UNIV ECO/DEV FINAN INDUS INT/ORG PUB/INST ROUTINE ATTIT ALL/VALS...SOC CONCPT STAT TREND 20. PAGE 75 F1475
MARKET ECO/TAC INT/TRADE SOCISM

B38
MEADE J.E.,AN INTRODUCTION TO ECONOMIC ANALYSIS AND POLICY (AMERICAN EDITION EDITED BY C.J. HITCH). FINAN INDUS MARKET LABOR INT/TRADE CONTROL COST DEMAND INCOME...CLASSIF CHARTS T 20 KEYNES/JM MONOPOLY. PAGE 89 F1737
CONCPT PROFIT PRODUC

B39
CLARK J.M.,SOCIAL CONTROL OF BUSINESS (2ND ED.). ECO/DEV FINAN LG/CO PLAN ECO/TAC PRICE SUPEGO...T 20. PAGE 25 F0480
CAP/ISM CONTROL LAISSEZ METH/COMP

B39
THOMAS J.A.,THE HOUSE OF COMMONS, 1832-1901; A STUDY OF ITS ECONOMIC AND FUNCTIONAL CHARACTER. UK LAW STRATA FINAN DIPLOM CONTROL LEAD LOBBY REPRESENT WEALTH...POLICY STAT BIBLIOG 19/20 PARLIAMENT. PAGE 130 F2561
PARL/PROC LEGIS POL/PAR ECO/DEV

B40
GAUS J.M.,PUBLIC ADMINISTRATION AND THE UNITED STATES DEPARTMENT OF AGRICULTURE. USA-45 STRUCT DIST/IND FINAN MARKET EX/STRUC PROB/SOLV GIVE PRODUC...POLICY GEOG CHARTS 20 DEPT/AGRI. PAGE 47 F0909
ADMIN AGRI DELIB/GP OP/RES

B40
HELLMAN F.S.,THE NEW DEAL: SELECTED LIST OF REFERENCES. USA-45 FINAN LABOR EX/STRUC CREATE INT/TRADE ADMIN CT/SYS 20 SUPREME/CT. PAGE 58 F1145
BIBLIOG/A ECO/TAC PLAN POLICY

B41
ESTEY J.A.,BUSINESS CYCLES; THEIR NATURE, CAUSE, AND CONTROL. NAT/G BUDGET CAP/ISM TAX PRICE CONTROL INCOME...MODAL TIME/SEQ GEN/METH T 18/20 KEYNES/JM MONEY. PAGE 38 F0749
INDUS FINAN ECO/TAC POLICY

B41
HANSEN A.H.,FISCAL POLICY AND BUSINESS CYCLES. UK INDUS PROB/SOLV DIPLOM INT/TRADE OPTIMAL...POLICY TIME/SEQ CHARTS 19/20. PAGE 54 F1062
FINAN PLAN ECO/TAC

GOV/REL

B41
HAYEK F.A.,THE PURE THEORY OF CAPITAL. UNIV ECO/DEV ECO/TAC COST EQUILIB PROFIT WEALTH...SIMUL GEN/LAWS BIBLIOG INDEX TIME 20. PAGE 57 F1120
CAP/ISM METH/CNCPT PRODUC FINAN

B42
US LIBRARY OF CONGRESS,ECONOMICS OF WAR (APRIL 1941-MARCH 1942). WOR-45 FINAN INDUS LOC/G NAT/G PLAN BUDGET RATION COST DEMAND...POLICY 20. PAGE 138 F2712
BIBLIOG/A INT/TRADE ECO/TAC WAR

B42
US LIBRARY OF CONGRESS,THE WAR PRODUCTION PROGRAM: SELECTED DOCUMENTATION ON THE ECONOMICS OF WAR (PAMPHLET). USA-45 ECO/DEV AGRI FINAN NAT/G ECO/TAC RATION PRICE EFFICIENCY 20. PAGE 138 F2713
BIBLIOG/A WAR PRODUC INDUS

B42
WRIGHT D.M.,THE CREATION OF PURCHASING POWER. USA-45 NAT/G PRICE ADMIN WAR INCOME PRODUC...POLICY CONCPT IDEA/COMP BIBLIOG 20 MONEY. PAGE 149 F2930
FINAN ECO/TAC ECO/DEV CREATE

B44
LOCKE J.,FURTHER CONSIDERATIONS CONCERNING RAISING THE VALUE OF MONEY. AFR UK NAT/G ECO/TAC INCOME WEALTH...METH/COMP GEN/LAWS 17 SILVER. PAGE 81 F1591
COST FINAN PRICE CONTROL

B46
HARRISON S.M.,AMERICAN FOUNDATIONS FOR SOCIAL WELFARE. OP/RES CONTROL...POLICY MGT METH/CNCPT STAT TREND BIBLIOG. PAGE 56 F1092
GIVE FINAN CLASSIF ADMIN

B47
ENKE S.,INTERNATIONAL ECONOMICS. UK USA+45 USSR INT/ORG BAL/PWR BARGAIN CAP/ISM BAL/PAY...NAT/COMP 20 TREATY. PAGE 38 F0735
INT/TRADE FINAN TARIFFS ECO/TAC

B47
GORDON D.L.,THE HIDDEN WEAPON: THE STORY OF ECONOMIC WARFARE. EUR+WWI USA-45 LAW FINAN INDUS NAT/G CONSULT FORCES PLAN DOMIN PWR WEALTH ...INT/LAW CONCPT OBS TOT/POP NAZI 20. PAGE 49 F0955
INT/ORG ECO/TAC INT/TRADE WAR

B47
LEVER E.A.,ADVERTISING AND ECONOMIC THEORY. FINAN ECO/TAC DEMAND EFFICIENCY ATTIT...MGT PSY SAMP/SIZ CHARTS 20. PAGE 79 F1539
EDU/PROP MARKET COM/IND ECO/DEV

B47
TOWLE L.W.,INTERNATIONAL TRADE AND COMMERCIAL POLICY. WOR+45 LAW ECO/DEV FINAN INDUS NAT/G ECO/TAC WEALTH...TIME/SEQ ILO 20. PAGE 131 F2582
MARKET INT/ORG INT/TRADE

B48
GRAHAM F.D.,THE THEORY OF INTERNATIONAL VALUES. FUT WOR+45 WOR-45 ECO/DEV FINAN INT/ORG PLAN TEC/DEV CAP/ISM DIPLOM ECO/TAC TARIFFS ROUTINE BAL/PAY DRIVE PWR WEALTH SOCISM...POLICY STAT HYPO/EXP GEN/LAWS 20. PAGE 50 F0971
NEW/IDEA INT/TRADE

B48
HART A.G.,MONEY, DEBT, AND ECONOMIC ACTIVITY. AFR WORKER DIPLOM PRICE CONTROL BAL/PAY COST OWN PRODUC ...METH/COMP 20 FED/RESERV. PAGE 56 F1097
FINAN WEALTH ECO/TAC NAT/G

B48
HAYEK F.A.,INDIVIDUALISM AND ECONOMIC ORDER. FINAN PLAN MORAL LAISSEZ SOCISM...POLICY DECISION PHIL/SCI HIST/WRIT. PAGE 57 F1122
RATIONAL KNOWL PERSON

B48
HICKS J.R.,VALUE AND CAPITAL. FINAN PRICE EQUILIB INCOME PRODUC WEALTH...TIME/SEQ 20 MARSHALL/A PARETO/V SAMUELSN/P. PAGE 59 F1165
ECOMETRIC MATH DEMAND PROB/SOLV

B48
METZLER L.A.,INCOME, EMPLOYMENT, AND PUBLIC POLICY. FINAN INDUS LOC/G NAT/G TAX GIVE PAY COST PRODUC ...MGT TIME/SEQ 20. PAGE 90 F1765
INCOME WEALTH POLICY ECO/TAC

B48
ROBERTSON D.H.,MONEY. AFR ECO/DEV NAT/G DIPLOM INT/TRADE BAL/PAY INCOME WEALTH...TIME/SEQ 20 DEPRESSION. PAGE 112 F2212
FINAN MARKET COST PRICE

B48
TAYLOR P.E.,THE ECONOMICS OF PUBLIC FINANCE. USA+45 USA-45 ECO/DEV WORKER PLAN BUDGET WAR INCOME WEALTH ...CONCPT STAT BIBLIOG 20. PAGE 129 F2540
FINAN POLICY NAT/G TAX

B48
VON HAYEK F.A.,INDIVIDUALISM AND ECONOMIC ORDER. GERMANY USA-45 USSR FINAN MARKET INT/ORG ECO/TAC INT/TRADE PRICE REPRESENT ORD/FREE...PLURIST GEN/LAWS 20. PAGE 142 F2793
SOCISM CAP/ISM POPULISM FEDERAL

B49
HANSEN A.H.,MONETARY THEORY AND FISCAL POLICY. CONSULT PLAN INT/TRADE BAL/PAY OPTIMAL...TREND CHARTS METH/COMP BIBLIOG T 19/20 MONEY. PAGE 54 F1063
FINAN GEN/LAWS POLICY ECO/TAC

B49
SCHULTZ W.J.,AMERICAN PUBLIC FINANCE. USA+45 ECO/TAC TAX ADMIN GOV/REL GP/REL INCOME 20. PAGE 117 F2318
FINAN POLICY ECO/DEV NAT/G

S49
ECKLER A.R.,"IMMIGRATION AND THE LABOR FORCE." USA+45 USA-45 EXTR/IND FINAN PROC/MFG AGE/Y SKILL ...CHARTS 19/20 MIGRATION. PAGE 36 F0694
WORKER STRANGE INDUS ECO/TAC

B50
FEIS H.,THE DIPLOMACY OF THE DOLLAR: FIRST ERA 1919-32. EUR+WWI USA-45 FOR/AID REPAR ATTIT ...POLICY 20. PAGE 40 F0774
FINAN NAT/G DIPLOM ECO/TAC

B50
HARTLAND P.C.,BALANCE OF INTERREGIONAL PAYMENTS OF NEW ENGLAND. USA+45 TEC/DEV ECO/TAC LEGIT ROUTINE BAL/PAY PROFIT 20 NEW/ENGLND FED/RESERV. PAGE 56 F1102
ECO/DEV FINAN REGION PLAN

B50
HOOVER G.,TWENTIETH CENTURY ECONOMIC THOUGHT. USA+45 ECO/DEV AGRI FINAN INDUS MARKET SERV/IND LABOR NAT/G...STAT 20. PAGE 62 F1213
ECO/TAC CAP/ISM INT/TRADE

B50
SHAW E.S.,MONEY, INCOME, AND MONETARY POLICY. AFR USA-45 NAT/G DIPLOM PAY CONTROL COST INCOME PRODUC WEALTH...T 20 FED/RESERV DEPT/TREAS. PAGE 120 F2370
FINAN ECO/TAC ECO/DEV PRICE

B50
SURANYI-UNGER T.,PRIVATE ENTERPRISE AND GOVERNMENTAL PLANNING. STRUCT FINAN BAL/PWR HAPPINESS DRIVE NEW/LIB PLURISM...MATH QUANT STAT TREND BIBLIOG. PAGE 127 F2516
PLAN NAT/G LAISSEZ POLICY

B50
US DEPARTMENT OF STATE,POINT FOUR: COOPERATIVE PROGRAM FOR AID IN THE DEVELOPMENT OF ECONOMICALLY UNDERDEVELOPED AREAS. WOR+45 AGRI INDUS INT/ORG PLAN TEC/DEV DIPLOM EDU/PROP ADMIN PEACE PRODUC WEALTH 20 CONGRESS UN. PAGE 135 F2671
ECO/UNDEV FOR/AID FINAN INT/TRADE

C50
ELLSWORTH P.T.,"INTERNATIONAL ECONOMY." ECO/DEV ECO/UNDEV FINAN LABOR DIPLOM FOR/AID TARIFFS BAL/PAY EQUILIB NAT/LISM OPTIMAL...INT/LAW 20 ILO GATT. PAGE 37 F0724
BIBLIOG INT/TRADE ECO/TAC INT/ORG

B51
CHANDLER L.V.,INFLATION IN THE UNITED STATES 1940-1948. AFR NAT/G BUDGET PAY PRICE CONTROL WAR INCOME PRODUC...POLICY BIBLIOG 20. PAGE 23 F0448
ECO/TAC FINAN PROB/SOLV WEALTH

B51
COOKE C.A.,CORPORATION TRUST AND COMPANY: AN ESSAY IN LEGAL HISTORY. UK STRUCT LEGIS CAP/ISM GP/REL PROFIT 13/20 COMPNY/ACT. PAGE 27 F0531
LG/CO FINAN ECO/TAC JURID

B51
DIMOCK M.E.,FREE ENTERPRISE AND THE ADMINISTRATIVE STATE. FINAN LG/CO BARGAIN BUDGET DOMIN CONTROL INGP/REL EFFICIENCY 20. PAGE 33 F0640
CAP/ISM ADMIN MGT MARKET

B51
HANSEN B.,A STUDY IN THE THEORY OF INFLATION. WOR-45 FINAN WAR DEMAND...CHARTS 20. PAGE 54 F1067
PRICE ECO/TAC EQUILIB PRODUC

B51
HARROD R.F.,THE LIFE OF JOHN MAYNARD KEYNES. UK INTELL FAM CAP/ISM DIPLOM ECO/TAC WAR ATTIT PERSON ROLE 20 KEYNES/JM WWI. PAGE 56 F1094
BIOG FINAN GEN/LAWS

B51
HART A.G.,DEFENSE WITHOUT INFLATION. AFR KOREA FINAN INDUS NAT/G WORKER DIPLOM RATION TAX PRICE COST OPTIMAL 20 RESOURCE/N. PAGE 56 F1098
ECO/TAC CONTROL WAR PLAN

B51
LUXEMBORG R.,THE ACCUMULATION OF CAPITAL (TRANS. BY AGNES SCHWARZSCHILD). ECO/TAC DOMIN COLONIAL ATTIT LAISSEZ 19 MONEY. PAGE 82 F1614
MARXIST INT/TRADE CAP/ISM FINAN

B51
POOLE K.,FISCAL POLICIES AND THE AMERICAN ECONOMY. AFR ECO/DEV FINAN INDUS WORKER OP/RES INT/TRADE TAX COST INCOME PROFIT WEALTH...GP/COMP 20. PAGE 107 F2102
NAT/G POLICY ANTHOL

B51
US DEPARTMENT OF STATE,POINT FOUR, NEAR EAST AND AFRICA, A SELECTED BIBLIOGRAPHY OF STUDIES ON ECONOMICALLY UNDERDEVELOPED COUNTRIES. AGRI COM/IND FINAN INDUS PLAN INT/TRADE...SOC TREND 20. PAGE 135 F2672
BIBLIOG/A AFR S/ASIA ISLAM

S51
HAWLEY A.H.,"METROPOLITAN POPULATION AND MUNICIPAL GOVERNMENT EXPENDITURES IN CENTRAL CITIES" (BMR)" USA+45 FINAN TAX...STAT CON/ANAL CHARTS MUNICH 20. PAGE 57 F1117
GEOG LOC/G COST BUDGET

B52
ALEXANDROWICZ C.H.,INTERNATIONAL ECONOMIC ORGANIZATION. WOR+45 ECO/DEV ECO/UNDEV DIST/IND FINAN MARKET PLAN ECO/TAC LEGIT DRIVE WEALTH ...POLICY CONCPT QUANT OBS TIME/SEQ GEN/LAWS WORK METH/GP EEC ILO OEEC UNESCO 20. PAGE 4 F0063
INT/ORG INT/TRADE

B52
ANDREWS F.E.,CORPORATION GIVING. LAW TAX EDU/PROP ADMIN...POLICY STAT CHARTS. PAGE 5 F0101
LG/CO GIVE SML/CO FINAN

B52
ASHWORTH W.,A SHORT HISTORY OF THE INTERNATIONAL ECONOMY 1850-1950. WOR+45 WOR-45 AGRI FINAN INDUS MARKET LABOR ECO/TAC...CONCPT STAT HIST/WRIT FOR/TRADE ILO 19/20. PAGE 7 F0131
ECO/DEV TEC/DEV INT/TRADE

B52
AYRES C.E.,THE INDUSTRIAL ECONOMY. USA+45 FINAN MARKET NAT/G PUB/INST PLAN ECO/TAC TAX DEMAND INCOME...BIBLIOG/A 20. PAGE 8 F0146
ECO/DEV INDUS FUT PROB/SOLV

B52
EGLE W.P.,ECONOMIC STABILIZATION. USA+45 SOCIETY FINAN MARKET PLAN ECO/TAC DOMIN EDU/PROP LEGIT EXEC WEALTH...CONCPT METH/CNCPT TREND HYPO/EXP GEN/METH TOT/POP VAL/FREE 20. PAGE 36 F0708
NAT/G ECO/DEV CAP/ISM

B52
EGLE W.P.,ECONOMIC STABILIZATION: OBJECTIVES, RULES, AND MECHANISMS. UNIV FINAN PROB/SOLV CAP/ISM ECO/TAC CONTROL...IDEA/COMP 20. PAGE 36 F0709
EQUILIB PLAN NAT/G ECO/DEV

B52
GALBRAITH J.K.,AMERICAN CAPITALISM: THE CONCEPT OF COUNTERVAILING POWER. AFR FUT USA+45 FINAN PRICE CENTRAL INCOME PEACE WEALTH...POLICY DECISION 20. PAGE 45 F0881
ECO/TAC CAP/ISM TREND NAT/G

B52
SURANYI-UNGER T.,COMPARATIVE ECONOMIC SYSTEMS. FINAN MARKET DIPLOM PRICE WEALTH...GEOG SOC BIBLIOG METH T 20. PAGE 128 F2517
LAISSEZ PLAN ECO/DEV IDEA/COMP

S52
PHILLIPS C.,"THE HIGH COST OF OUR LOW-PAID CONGRESS" (NYT MAG. 2/24/52)" USA+45 FINAN WRITING TASK TIME CONGRESS. PAGE 106 F2082
LEGIS INCOME COST EFFICIENCY

C52
HUME D.,"OF TAXES" IN D. HUME, POLITICAL DISCOURSES (1752)" UK NAT/G COST INCOME LAISSEZ...GEN/LAWS 18. PAGE 63 F1236
TAX FINAN WEALTH POLICY

C52
HUME D.,"OF THE BALANCE OF TRADE" IN D. HUME, POLITICAL DISCOURSES (1752)" UK FINAN NAT/G TARIFFS PRICE PWR LAISSEZ...POLICY GEN/LAWS 18. PAGE 63 F1237
BAL/PAY INT/TRADE DIPLOM WEALTH

C52
HUME D.,"OF COMMERCE" IN D. HUME, POLITICAL DISCOURSES (1752)" UK FINAN DIPLOM WEALTH ...GEN/LAWS 18 MONEY. PAGE 63 F1238
INDUS INT/TRADE PWR AGRI

C52
HUME D.,"OF INTEREST" IN D. HUME, POLITICAL DISCOURSES (1752)" UK INDUS WORKER DIPLOM PAY DEMAND INCOME WEALTH...GEN/LAWS 18 MONEY. PAGE 63 F1239
PRICE COST FINAN INT/TRADE

C52
HUME D.,"OF MONEY" IN D. HUME, POLITICAL DISCOURSES (1752)" UK INDUS DIPLOM INT/TRADE...GEN/LAWS 18 MONEY. PAGE 63 F1240
FINAN COST PRICE WEALTH

B53
BOWEN H.R.,SOCIAL RESPONSIBILITIES OF THE BUSINESSMAN (FIRST EDITION). LAW FINAN ACT/RES CAP/ISM ROUTINE DRIVE PWR LAISSEZ...DECISION BIBLIOG. PAGE 17 F0326
MGT PERSON SUPEGO MORAL

B53
BURNS A.E.,MODERN ECONOMICS. UNIV ECO/DEV INT/TRADE PRICE INCOME WEALTH...POLICY CHARTS T 20 KEYNES/JM. PAGE 20 F0389
NAT/G ECO/TAC FINAN

B53
FLORENCE P.S.,THE LOGIC OF BRITISH AND AMERICAN INDUSTRY; A REALISTIC ANALYSIS OF ECONOMIC STRUCTURE AND GOVERNMENT. UK USA+45 USA-45 FINAN LABOR CAP/ISM INGP/REL EFFICIENCY...MGT CONCPT STAT CHARTS METH 20. PAGE 42 F0813
INDUS ECO/DEV NAT/G NAT/COMP

B53
FRANKEL S.H.,THE ECONOMIC IMPACT ON UNDERDEVELOPED SOCIETIES: ESSAYS ON INTERNATIONAL INVESTMENT AND SOCIAL CHANGE. AFR WOR+45 ECO/DEV FINAN INDUS NAT/G ACT/RES TEC/DEV COLONIAL ATTIT...CONCPT OBS TREND 20. PAGE 43 F0845
ECO/UNDEV FOR/AID INT/TRADE

B53
HARROD R.,THE DOLLAR. AFR USA+45 USA-45 ECO/DEV OPTIMAL WEALTH 18/20 FED/RESERV. PAGE 56 F1093
FINAN DIPLOM BAL/PAY

B53
NEISSER H.,NATIONAL INCOMES AND INTERNATIONAL TRADE. FRANCE GERMANY SWEDEN UK USA-45 EXTR/IND FINAN INDUS TEC/DEV PRICE BAL/PAY EQUILIB INCOME WEALTH...CHARTS METH 19 CHINJAP. PAGE 97 F1908
INT/TRADE PRODUC MARKET CON/ANAL

B53
WILLIAMS J.H.,ECONOMIC STABILITY IN A CHANGING WORLD. FRANCE USA+45 USSR AGRI WORKER BUDGET INT/TRADE TAX WAR BAL/PAY COST EFFICIENCY ALL/IDEOS EQULIB 20 KEYNES/JM. PAGE 147 F2892
POLICY FINAN ECO/TAC WEALTH

L53
NELSON J.R.,"UNITED STATES FOREIGN ECONOMIC POLICY AND THE STERLING AREA." USA-45 WOR+45 WOR-45 NAT/G ECO/TAC WEALTH...STAT TIME/SEQ TREND CHARTS METH/GP TERR/GP CMN/WLTH 20. PAGE 97 F1911
FINAN DIPLOM UK

B54
LOCKLIN D.P.,ECONOMICS OF TRANSPORTATION (4TH ED.). USA+45 USA-45 SEA AIR LAW FINAN LG/CO EX/STRUC ADMIN CONTROL...STAT CHARTS 19/20 RAILROAD PUB/TRANS. PAGE 81 F1592
ECO/DEV DIST/IND ECO/TAC TEC/DEV

B54
MEYER F.V.,INFLATION AND CAPITAL. AFR UK WOR+45 BUDGET GOV/REL INCOME PRODUC PROFIT WEALTH...CONCPT CHARTS 20. PAGE 90 F1768
ECO/DEV FINAN ECO/TAC DEMAND

B54
MITCHELL W.G.,BUSINESS CYCLES. FINAN MARKET PRICE COST EQUILIB OPTIMAL PRODUC PROFIT...IDEA/COMP GEN/LAWS 19/20. PAGE 92 F1809
INDUS TIME/SEQ METH/COMP STAT

B54
O.E.E.C.,PRIVATE UNITED STATES INVESTMENT IN EUROPE AND THE OVERSEAS TERRITORIES. EUR+WWI WOR+45 ECO/DEV ECO/UNDEV INT/ORG NAT/G VOL/ASSN ECO/TAC ATTIT WEALTH...GEOG STAT SYS/QU CHARTS VAL/FREE 20. PAGE 99 F1950
USA+45 FINAN BAL/PAY FOR/AID

B54
RECK D.,GOVERNMENT PURCHASING AND COMPETITION. USA+45 LEGIS CAP/ISM ECO/TAC GOV/REL CENTRAL ...POLICY 20 CONGRESS. PAGE 110 F2164
NAT/G FINAN MGT COST

B54
TAFT P.,THE STRUCTURE AND GOVERNMENT OF LABOR UNIONS. SANCTION INGP/REL ORD/FREE PWR MARXISM ...MAJORIT STAT TREND. PAGE 128 F2524
LABOR ADJUD WORKER FINAN

B55
FOGARTY M.P.,ECONOMIC CONTROL. FUT UK ECO/DEV FINAN CONSULT INT/TRADE...CHARTS BIBLIOG/A 20. PAGE 42 F0819
ECO/TAC NAT/G CONTROL PROB/SOLV

B55
JONES T.B.,A BIBLIOGRAPHY ON SOUTH AMERICAN ECONOMIC AFFAIRS: ARTICLES IN NINETEENTH CENTURY PERIODICALS (PAMPHLET). AGRI COM/IND DIST/IND EXTR/IND FINAN INDUS LABOR NAT/G 19. PAGE 68 F1340
BIBLIOG ECO/UNDEV L/A+17C TEC/DEV

B55
O'CONNOR H.,THE EMPIRE OF OIL. USA+45 DIST/IND FINAN MARKET CAP/ISM TAX CONTROL...POLICY MARXIST BIBLIOG/A 20. PAGE 100 F1955
EXTR/IND INT/TRADE CENTRAL NAT/G

B55
SERRANO MOSCOSO E.,A STATEMENT OF THE LAWS OF ECUADOR IN MATTERS AFFECTING BUSINESS (2ND ED.). ECUADOR INDUS LABOR LG/CO NAT/G LEGIS TAX CONTROL MARRIAGE 20. PAGE 120 F2359
FINAN ECO/UNDEV LAW CONSTN

B55
UN ECONOMIC COMN ASIA & FAR E,ECONOMIC SURVEY OF ASIA AND THE FAR EAST, 1954. AFGHANISTN CEYLON INDIA PHILIPPINE S/ASIA ECO/DEV FINAN INDUS INT/TRADE PRODUC WEALTH...STAT CHARTS 20 CHINJAP. PAGE 132 F2600
ECO/UNDEV PRICE NAT/COMP ASIA

B55
US ADVISORY COMN INTERGOV REL,THE COMMISSION ON INTERGOVERNMENTAL RELATIONS; A REPORT TO THE PRESIDENT FOR TRANSMITTAL TO THE CONGRESS. USA+45 ECO/DEV AGRI COM/IND FINAN FORCES PLAN EDU/PROP HEALTH WEALTH...STAT MUNICH 20 CIV/DEFENS. PAGE 133 F2630
GOV/REL NAT/G LOC/G PROVS

B55
WOYTINSKY W.S.,WORLD COMMERCE AND GOVERNMENTS: TRENDS AND OUTLOOK. WOR+45 FINAN POL/PAR DIPLOM ECO/TAC FOR/AID DOMIN WAR CHOOSE...CHARTS BIBLIOG 20 LEAGUE/NAT UN ILO. PAGE 149 F2929
INT/TRADE DIST/IND NAT/COMP NAT/G

S55
KELLY W.E.,"HOW SALES EXECUTIVES USE FACTORING TO BOOST SALES AND PROFITS TODAY." FINAN LG/CO BUDGET EFFICIENCY PROFIT...MGT PRODUCT. PAGE 70 F1372
INDUS ECO/DEV CONSULT MARKET

B56
BELL P.W.,THE STERLING AREA IN THE POSTWAR WORLD. EUR+WWI FUT S/ASIA UK ECO/DEV PLAN DIPLOM WEALTH ...STAT RECORD CHARTS GEN/LAWS FOR/TRADE TOT/POP 20. PAGE 12 F0235
FINAN ECO/TAC

B56
FELLNER W.,TRENDS AND CYCLES IN ECONOMIC ACTIVITY:
ECO/TAC

AN INTRODUCTION TO PROBLEMS OF ECONOMIC GROWTH. USA+45 INDUS ACT/RES CAP/ISM EQUILIB...MODAL METH/COMP BIBLIOG 20. PAGE 40 F0779 — TREND FINAN ECO/DEV

B56
JUAN T.L.,ECONOMIC AND SOCIAL DEVELOPMENT OF MODERN CHINA: A BIBLIOGRAPHICAL GUIDE. ASIA AGRI COM/IND DIST/IND FINAN INDUS DIPLOM...STAT 20. PAGE 68 F1342 — BIBLIOG SOC

B56
KOHLER E.L.,ACCOUNTING IN THE FEDERAL GOVERNMENT. USA+45 LOC/G PLAN TAX CONTROL COST 20. PAGE 72 F1416 — BUDGET AFR NAT/G FINAN

B56
POOLE K.E.,PUBLIC FINANCE AND ECONOMIC WELFARE. STRUCT ECO/DEV LOC/G NAT/G BUDGET PAY ROUTINE COST EQUILIB WEALTH...SOC/WK METH/COMP 20. PAGE 107 F2103 — FINAN TAX ORD/FREE

B56
US DEPARTMENT OF STATE,ECONOMIC PROBLEMS OF UNDERDEVELOPED AREAS (PAMPHLET). AFR ASIA ISLAM L/A+17C AGRI FINAN INDUS INT/ORG LABOR INT/TRADE ...PSY SOC 20. PAGE 136 F2673 — BIBLIOG ECO/UNDEV TEC/DEV R+D

B56
WHYTE W.H. JR.,THE ORGANIZATION MAN. CULTURE FINAN VOL/ASSN DOMIN EDU/PROP EXEC DISPL HABITAT ROLE ...PERS/TEST STERTYP. PAGE 146 F2875 — ADMIN LG/CO PERSON CONSEN

B56
YUAN TUNG-LI,ECONOMIC AND SOCIAL DEVELOPMENT OF MODERN CHINA: A BIBLIOGRAPHIC GUIDE. COM/IND FINAN FAM LABOR SECT CRIME INCOME...STAT SAMP CON/ANAL. PAGE 150 F2954 — BIBLIOG ASIA ECO/UNDEV SOC

S56
SPENGLER J.J.,"POPULATION THREATENS PROSPERITY" (BMR)" WOR+45 SOCIETY FINAN RATION COST INCOME ...SOC CHARTS 20 RESOURCE/N. PAGE 124 F2451 — CENSUS GEOG WEALTH TREND

B57
ASHER R.E.,THE UNITED NATIONS AND ECONOMIC AND SOCIAL COOPERATION. ECO/UNDEV COM/IND DIST/IND FINAN PLAN PROB/SOLV INT/TRADE TASK WEALTH...SOC 20 UN. PAGE 7 F0129 — INT/ORG DIPLOM FOR/AID

B57
ASSN U BUREAUS BUS-ECO RES,INDEX OF PUBLICATIONS OF BUREAUS OF BUSINESS AND ECONOMIC RESEARCH 1950-56 AND YEARLY SUPPLEMENTS THROUGH 1967. FINAN OP/RES PLAN GOV/REL INCOME AGE...POLICY 20. PAGE 7 F0133 — BIBLIOG ECO/DEV ECO/TAC LG/CO

B57
BARAN P.A.,THE POLITICAL ECONOMY OF GROWTH. MOD/EUR USA+45 USA-45 TEC/DEV TAX SOCISM...MGT CONCPT GOV/COMP. PAGE 9 F0178 — CAP/ISM CONTROL ECO/UNDEV FINAN

B57
BAUER P.T.,THE ECONOMICS OF UNDERDEVELOPED COUNTRIES. WOR+45 AGRI FINAN INDUS PROC/MFG WORKER CAP/ISM PAY PRICE INCOME MARXISM...METH/COMP 20 RESOURCE/N. PAGE 11 F0213 — ECO/UNDEV ECO/TAC PROB/SOLV NAT/G

B57
BEHRMAN J.N.,INTERNATIONAL ECONOMICS: THEORY, PRACTICE, POLICY. AGRI INDUS NAT/G TARIFFS CONTROL BAL/PAY...POLICY METH/CNCPT T 19/20. PAGE 12 F0230 — INT/TRADE FINAN DIPLOM FOR/AID

B57
COMMITTEE ECONOMIC DEVELOPMENT,ECONOMIC DEVELOPMENT ASSISTANCE. USA+45 WOR+45 AGRI CONFER ORD/FREE ...MGT CHARTS 20. PAGE 27 F0515 — FOR/AID ECO/UNDEV FINAN PLAN

B57
DAY A.C.L.,OUTLINE OF MONETARY ECONOMICS. AFR WOR-45 INT/ORG WORKER DIPLOM BAL/PAY COST INCOME WEALTH...TIME/SEQ SIMUL 20. PAGE 31 F0594 — FINAN NAT/G EQUILIB PRICE

B57
FOUSEK P.G.,FOREIGN CENTRAL BANKING: THE INSTRUMENTS OF MONETARY POLICY. WOR+45 CONTROL ...TREND CHARTS 20 MONEY. PAGE 43 F0836 — FINAN ECO/TAC ECO/DEV MARKET

B57
GOLD N.L.,REGIONAL ECONOMIC DEVELOPMENT AND NUCLEAR POWER IN INDIA. FUT INDIA FINAN FOR/AID INT/TRADE BAL/PAY EFFICIENCY OPTIMAL PRODUC WEALTH...PREDICT 20. PAGE 48 F0934 — ECO/UNDEV TEC/DEV NUC/PWR INDUS

B57
HARRIS S.E.,INTERNATIONAL AND INTERREGIONAL ECONOMICS. AFR WOR+45 WOR-45 NAT/G TARIFFS BAL/PAY EQUILIB...POLICY CONCPT STAT CHARTS IDEA/COMP 19/20. PAGE 55 F1088 — INT/TRADE ECO/DEV MARKET FINAN

B57
HARWOOD E.C.,CAUSE AND CONTROL OF THE BUSINESS CYCLE (5TH ED.). AFR USA-45 PRICE CONTROL WAR DEMAND INCOME WEALTH...TREND CHARTS 19. PAGE 56 F1107 — PRODUC MARKET FINAN

B57
HUTTON D.G.,INFLATION AND SOCIETY. AFR FINAN PLAN COST DEMAND EQUILIB...CONCPT 20. PAGE 64 F1254 — ECO/DEV POLICY NAT/G ECO/TAC

B57
INTL BANKING SUMMER SCHOOL,RELATIONS BETWEEN THE CENTRAL BANKS AND COMMERCIAL BANKS. EUR+WWI FRANCE GERMANY/W ITALY UK USA+45 USSR INDUS INT/ORG CAP/ISM CONTROL MONEY. PAGE 65 F1282 — FINAN NAT/G GP/REL LG/CO

B57
LUNDBERG E.,BUSINESS CYCLES AND ECONOMIC POLICY (TRANS. BY J. POTTER). SWEDEN ECO/DEV FINAN DELIB/GP PLAN PRICE CONTROL BAL/PAY 20 INTRVN/ECO. PAGE 82 F1607 — ECO/TAC INDUS INT/TRADE BUDGET

B57
MILLIKAN M.F.,A PROPOSAL: KEY TO AN EFFECTIVE FOREIGN POLICY. USA+45 AGRI FINAN DELIB/GP DIPLOM REPRESENT MAJORITY...NEW/IDEA CHARTS. PAGE 91 F1795 — FOR/AID GIVE ECO/UNDEV PLAN

B57
OLIVECRONA K.,THE PROBLEM OF THE MONETARY UNIT. AFR UNIV PAY PRICE UTIL...MATH 20 MONEY SILVER. PAGE 101 F1986 — FINAN ECO/TAC ECO/DEV CONCPT

B57
OLIVER H.M. JR.,ECONOMIC OPINION AND POLICY IN CEYLON. CEYLON FINAN POL/PAR WORKER INT/TRADE INCOME WEALTH...GEOG UNPLAN/INT BIBLIOG 20 CMN/WLTH. PAGE 101 F1987 — ECO/UNDEV NAT/LISM POLICY COLONIAL

B57
SINGH D.B.,INFLATIONARY PRICE TRENDS IN INDIA SINCE 1939. AFR INDIA ECO/TAC RATION CONTROL WAR GOV/REL BAL/PAY DEMAND INCOME PEACE PRODUC...POLICY CHARTS 20. PAGE 122 F2413 — BUDGET ECO/UNDEV PRICE FINAN

B57
THOMAS R.G.,OUR MODERN BANKING AND MONETARY SYSTEM (3RD ED.). AFR USA+45 USA-45 ACT/RES PLAN PROB/SOLV INT/TRADE PRICE WAR BAL/PAY INCOME...POLICY METH/CNCPT 20 DEPRESSION. PAGE 130 F2563 — FINAN SERV/IND ECO/TAC

B58
AVRAMOVIC D.,POSTWAR GROWTH IN INTERNATIONAL INDEBTEDNESS. AFR WOR+45 AGRI INDUS CAP/ISM PRICE INCOME...NAT/COMP 20 SILVER. PAGE 8 F0143 — INT/TRADE FINAN COST BAL/PAY

B58
BARRERE A.,POLITIQUE FINANCIERE. FRANCE BUDGET ECO/TAC TAX BAL/PAY INCOME PRODUC...MGT BIBLIOG T 20. PAGE 10 F0193 — FINAN NAT/G PLAN

B58
BERLINER J.S.,SOVIET ECONOMIC AID: THE AID AND TRADE POLICY IN UNDERDEVELOPED COUNTRIES. AFR COM ISLAM L/A+17C S/ASIA USSR ECO/DEV DIST/IND FINAN MARKET INT/ORG ACT/RES PLAN BAL/PWR WEAPON PWR WEALTH...CHARTS FOR/TRADE 20. PAGE 14 F0263 — ECO/UNDEV ECO/TAC FOR/AID

B58
BUGEDA LANZAS J.,A STATEMENT OF THE LAWS OF CUBA IN MATTERS AFFECTING BUSINESS (2ND ED. REV., ENLARGED). CUBA L/A+17C LAW FINAN FAM LEGIS ACT/RES ADMIN GP/REL...BIBLIOG 20 OAS. PAGE 20 F0382 — JURID NAT/G INDUS WORKER

B58
CHANG C.,THE INFLATIONARY SPIRAL: THE EXPERIENCE IN CHINA 1939-50. CHINA/COM BUDGET INT/TRADE PRICE ADMIN CONTROL WAR DEMAND...POLICY CHARTS 20. PAGE 23 F0451 — FINAN ECO/TAC BAL/PAY GOV/REL

B58
CLAIRMONTE F.,LE LIBERALISME ECONOMIQUE ET LES PAYS SOUS-DEVELOPPES: ETUDES SUR L'EVOLUTION D'UNE IDEE. ASIA INDIA UK FINAN INDUS PLAN CAP/ISM ECO/TAC COLONIAL NEW/LIB...BIBLIOG 20 THIRD/WRLD. PAGE 24 F0475 — LAISSEZ ECO/UNDEV

B58
COOK P.L.,EFFECTS OF MERGERS: SIX STUDIES. USA+45 ECO/DEV LABOR LG/CO SML/CO VOL/ASSN ADMIN EFFICIENCY 20 CASEBOOK. PAGE 27 F0529 — INDUS FINAN EX/STRUC GP/REL

B58
DAVIS E.H.,OF THE PEOPLE, BY THE PEOPLE, FOR THE PEOPLE. INCOME WEALTH...METH/COMP MUNICH 20. PAGE 30 F0587 — FINAN LOC/G TAX

B58
DUESENBERRY J.S.,BUSINESS CYCLES AND ECONOMIC GROWTH. USA+45 PROB/SOLV PAY PRICE...CONCPT MATH CHARTS IDEA/COMP 20 DEPRESSION KEYNES/JM. PAGE 34 F0672 — FINAN ECO/DEV ECO/TAC INCOME

B58
EHRHARD J.,LE DESTIN DU COLONIALISME. AFR FRANCE ECO/UNDEV AGRI FINAN MARKET CREATE PLAN TEC/DEV BUDGET DIPLOM PRICE 20. PAGE 36 F0710 — COLONIAL FOR/AID INT/TRADE INDUS

B58
HENNING C.N.,INTERNATIONAL FINANCING. WOR+45 ECO/DEV INT/ORG EX/STRUC INSPECT CAP/ISM BAL/PAY COST PROFIT...MGT CHARTS T 20. PAGE 58 F1150 — FINAN DIPLOM INT/TRADE

B58
HOOD W.C.,FINANCING OF ECONOMIC ACTIVITY IN CANADA. CANADA FUT VOL/ASSN WORKER ECO/TAC ADJUD ADMIN ...CHARTS 20. PAGE 61 F1204 — BUDGET FINAN GP/REL ECO/DEV

B58
INTERNATIONAL ECONOMIC ASSN,ECONOMICS OF INTERNATIONAL MIGRATION. WOR+45 WOR-45 ECO/UNDEV FINAN NAT/G REGION...NAT/COMP METH 20. PAGE 65 F1275
CENSUS GEOG DIPLOM ECO/TAC

B58
JACOBSSON P.,SOME MONETARY PROBLEMS, INTERNATIONAL AND NATIONAL. WOR+45 WOR-45 ECO/DEV FORCES WORKER PROB/SOLV DIPLOM INT/TRADE...ANTHOL 20. PAGE 66 F1299
FINAN PLAN ECO/TAC NAT/COMP

B58
JUCKER-FLEETWOOD E.,ECONOMIC THEORY AND POLICY IN FINLAND 1914-1925. FINLAND INT/TRADE PRICE COST 20 MONEY. PAGE 68 F1343
FINAN GEN/LAWS ECO/TAC PLAN

B58
KINDLEBERGER C.P.,INTERNATIONAL ECONOMICS. WOR+45 WOR-45 ECO/DEV ECO/UNDEV FINAN VOL/ASSN ACT/RES DIPLOM ECO/TAC LEGIT REGION ATTIT DRIVE ORD/FREE WEALTH...POLICY STAT TREND GEN/LAWS EEC ECSC OEEC 20. PAGE 71 F1391
INT/ORG BAL/PWR TARIFFS

B58
MCIVOR R.C.,CANADIAN MONETARY, BANKING, AND FISCAL DEVELOPMENT. CANADA INDUS LG/CO NAT/G SML/CO CONTROL WAR...GEN/LAWS BIBLIOG 17/20. PAGE 88 F1729
ECO/TAC FINAN ECO/DEV WEALTH

B58
MIKESELL R.F.,FINANCING FREE WORLD TRADE WITH THE SINO-SOVIET BLOC. CHINA/COM COM USSR WOR+45 ECO/DEV AGRI DIST/IND EXTR/IND FINAN INDUS MARKET PROC/MFG NAT/G PLAN TEC/DEV ECO/TAC...CHARTS METH/GP EEC FOR/TRADE 20. PAGE 91 F1780
STAT BAL/PAY

B58
MOULTON H.G.,CAN INFLATION BE CONTROLLED? ECO/DEV INDUS CAP/ISM RATION GOV/REL COST INCOME PEACE WEALTH...CHARTS TIME 20 KEYNES/JM MONEY. PAGE 94 F1847
ECO/TAC CONTROL DEMAND FINAN

B58
MUSGRAVE R.A.,CLASSICS IN THE THEORY OF PUBLIC FINANCE. UNIV MARKET LG/CO NAT/G CAP/ISM PRICE OPTIMAL...IDEA/COMP ANTHOL 19/20 SAY/EMIL EDGEWORTH LINDAHL/E RITSCHL/H. PAGE 95 F1870
TAX FINAN ECO/TAC GP/REL

B58
PALYI M.,MANAGED MONEY AT THE CROSSROADS: THE EUROPEAN EXPERIENCE. AFR WOR+45 WOR-45 TEC/DEV DIPLOM INT/TRADE DEMAND WEALTH...CHARTS BIBLIOG 19/20 EUROPE SILVER. PAGE 103 F2022
FINAN ECO/TAC ECO/DEV PRODUC

B58
SHAW S.J.,THE FINANCIAL AND ADMINISTRATIVE ORGANIZATION AND DEVELOPMENT OF OTTOMAN EGYPT 1517-1798. UAR LOC/G FORCES BUDGET INT/TRADE TAX EATING INCOME WEALTH...CHARTS BIBLIOG 16/18 OTTOMAN NAPOLEON/B. PAGE 120 F2371
FINAN ADMIN GOV/REL CULTURE

B58
TANNENBAUM A.S.,PARTICIPATION IN UNION LOCALS. SOCIETY FINAN CONTROL LEAD GP/REL...BIBLIOG 20. PAGE 128 F2531
LABOR MGT PARTIC INGP/REL

L58
TRAGER F.N.,"A SELECTED AND ANNOTATED BIBLIOGRAPHY ON ECONOMIC DEVELOPMENT, 1953-1957." WOR+45 AGRI FINAN INDUS MARKET LABOR WORKER PLAN INT/TRADE PRODUC...CENSUS MUNICH. PAGE 131 F2583
BIBLIOG/A ECO/UNDEV ECO/DEV

S58
LATTIN N.D.,"MINORITY AND DISSENTING SHAREHOLDERS' RIGHTS IN FUNDAMENTAL CHANGES." FINAN LEGIS ADJUD PARTIC ROUTINE CHOOSE REPRESENT INGP/REL TREND. PAGE 76 F1487
MAJORIT LG/CO LAW CREATE

S58
LOCKWOOD W.W.,"THE SOCIALISTIC SOCIETY: INDIA AND JAPAN." INDIA ECO/DEV ECO/UNDEV INDUS NAT/G CONTROL LEAD PRODUC WEALTH 20 CHINJAP. PAGE 81 F1593
ECO/TAC NAT/COMP FINAN SOCISM

N58
EUROPEAN COMM ECO-SOC PROG,EUROPEAN BUSINESS CYCLE POLICY (PAMPHLET). AFR EUR+WWI MARKET WORKER DIPLOM PRICE BAL/PAY 20 EUROPE. PAGE 39 F0754
ECO/DEV FINAN ECO/TAC PROB/SOLV

B59
AITKEN H.,THE STATE AND ECONOMIC GROWTH. COM EUR+WWI MOD/EUR S/ASIA USA+45 FINAN NAT/G DELIB/GP PLAN PWR WEALTH 20. PAGE 3 F0054
DIST/IND ECO/DEV

B59
AITKEN H.G.,THE AMERICAN ECONOMIC IMPACT ON CANADA. CANADA USA+45 AGRI FINAN INDUS LABOR INT/TRADE BAL/PAY...INT/LAW TREND 20. PAGE 3 F0055
DIPLOM ECO/TAC POLICY NAT/G

B59
ALLEN R.L.,SOVIET INFLUENCE IN LATIN AMERICA. ECO/UNDEV FINAN PROC/MFG NAT/G TEC/DEV EDU/PROP EXEC ROUTINE ATTIT DRIVE PERSON ALL/VALS PWR...STAT CHARTS WORK FOR/TRADE 20. PAGE 4 F0071
L/A+17C ECO/TAC INT/TRADE USSR

B59
ALLEN W.R.,FOREIGN TRADE AND FINANCE. ECO/DEV DIPLOM BAL/PAY...POLICY CONCPT ANTHOL 20. PAGE 4 F0073
INT/TRADE EQUILIB FINAN

B59
BAUER P.T.,UNITED STATES AID AND INDIAN ECONOMIC DEVELOPMENT. INDIA STRATA FINAN PLAN BUDGET DIPLOM INGP/REL EFFICIENCY SOCISM 20 AID. PAGE 11 F0215
FOR/AID ECO/UNDEV ECO/TAC POLICY

B59
CHECCHI V.,HONDURAS: A PROBLEM IN ECONOMIC DEVELOPMENT. HONDURAS AGRI FINAN INDUS LABOR WORKER INT/TRADE EDU/PROP PRICE HEALTH...GEOG CHARTS BIBLIOG 20. PAGE 24 F0458
ECO/UNDEV ECO/TAC PROB/SOLV PLAN

B59
CUCCORESE H.J.,HISTORIA DE LA CONVERSION DEL PAPEL MONEDA EN BUENOS AIRES, 1861-1867. AFR LAW LOC/G NAT/G ATTIT...POLICY BIBLIOG 19 ARGEN BUENOS/AIR. PAGE 29 F0560
FINAN PLAN LEGIS

B59
ETSCHMANN R.,DIE WAHRUNGS- UND DEVISENPOLITIK DES OSTBLOCKS UND IHRE AUSWIRKUNGEN AUF DIE WIRTSCHAFTSBEZIEHUNGEN ZWISCHEN OST U WEST. BULGARIA CZECHOSLVK HUNGARY POLAND USSR MARKET NAT/G PLAN DIPLOM...NAT/COMP 20. PAGE 39 F0753
ECO/TAC FINAN POLICY INT/TRADE

B59
FELS R.,AMERICAN BUSINESS CYCLES 1865-1897. USA+45 ECO/DEV LG/CO SML/CO PROB/SOLV TEC/DEV CAP/ISM INT/TRADE DEMAND...POLICY CHARTS METH 19 DEPRESSION. PAGE 40 F0782
FINAN INDUS TREND ECO/TAC

B59
GOMEZ ROBLES J.,A STATEMENT OF THE LAWS OF GUATEMALA IN MATTERS AFFECTING BUSINESS (2ND ED. REV., ENLARGED). GUATEMALA L/A+17C LAW FINAN FAM WORKER ACT/RES DIPLOM ADJUD ADMIN GP/REL 20 OAS. PAGE 48 F0945
JURID NAT/G INDUS LEGIT

B59
GUDIN E.,INFLACAO (2ND ED.). INDUS NAT/G PLAN ECO/TAC CONTROL COST 20. PAGE 52 F1012
ECO/UNDEV INT/TRADE BAL/PAY FINAN

B59
HARVARD UNIVERSITY LAW SCHOOL,INTERNATIONAL PROBLEMS OF FINANCIAL PROTECTION AGAINST NUCLEAR RISK. WOR+45 NAT/G DELIB/GP PROB/SOLV DIPLOM CONTROL ATTIT...POLICY INT/LAW MATH 20. PAGE 56 F1105
NUC/PWR ADJUD INDUS FINAN

B59
HAX K.,DIE HOCHSCHULLEHRER DER WIRTSCHAFTSWISSENSCHAFTEN IN DER BUNDESREPUBLIK DEUTSCHLAND EINSCHL. WESTBERLIN, OSTERREICH. AUSTRIA GERMANY/W SWITZERLND FINAN MARKET PROF/ORG BUDGET ECO/TAC INT/TRADE PRICE COST 20. PAGE 57 F1119
BIBLIOG ACADEM INTELL

B59
HAZLEWOOD A.,THE ECONOMICS OF "UNDER-DEVELOPED" AREAS. WOR+45 DIST/IND EXTR/IND FINAN INDUS MARKET PLAN FOR/AID...GEOG 20. PAGE 57 F1129
BIBLIOG/A ECO/UNDEV AGRI INT/TRADE

B59
KOREAN MINISTRY RECONSTRUCTION,KOREAN ECONOMY AND ITS REQUIREMENTS. KOREA USA+45 ECO/TAC EQUILIB INCOME WEALTH...CHARTS 20. PAGE 73 F1427
FOR/AID WAR FINAN DIPLOM

B59
LEWIS J.P.,BUSINESS CONDITIONS ANALYSIS. USA+45 MARKET LABOR BUDGET TAX AUTOMAT WAR DEMAND PRODUC ...ECOMETRIC CHARTS BIBLIOG 19/20. PAGE 79 F1549
FINAN PRICE TREND

B59
LI CHOH-MING,ECONOMIC DEVELOPMENT OF COMMUNIST CHINA. ASIA CHINA/COM AGRI FINAN TAX INCOME MARXISM ...MGT 20. PAGE 80 F1557
ECO/UNDEV INDUS ORD/FREE TEC/DEV

B59
LOPEZ VILLAMIL H.,A STATEMENT OF THE LAWS OF THE HONDURAS IN MATTERS AFFECTING BUSINESS (2ND ED.). HONDURAS DIST/IND EXTR/IND FINAN WORKER TAX DEATH MARRIAGE OWN MARITIME 20 MIGRATION. PAGE 82 F1600
CONSTN INDUS LEGIS NAT/G

B59
MARTIN D.D.,MERGERS AND THE CLAYTON ACT. FINAN LEGIS GP/REL...DECISION METH/COMP BIBLIOG 20. PAGE 86 F1681
OWN ECO/TAC LG/CO POLICY

B59
MATTHEWS R.C.O.,THE BUSINESS CYCLE. AFR LABOR INT/TRADE TAX PRICE RISK ADJUST WEALTH...POLICY ECOMETRIC CHARTS SIMUL TIME 20. PAGE 87 F1705
FINAN DEMAND TASK

B59
MEZERK A.G.,FINANCIAL ASSISTANCE FOR ECONOMIC DEVELOPMENT. WOR+45 INDUS DIPLOM INT/TRADE...CHARTS GOV/COMP UN. PAGE 91 F1778
FOR/AID FINAN ECO/TAC ECO/UNDEV

B59
MORGENSTERN O.,INTERNATIONAL FINANCIAL TRANSACTIONS AND BUSINESS CYCLES. FRANCE GERMANY UK USA+45 USA-45 WOR+45 WOR-45 ECO/DEV ECO/TAC WEALTH ...CONCPT STAT CON/ANAL CHARTS 19/20. PAGE 93 F1832
FINAN TIME/SEQ INT/TRADE

B59
OGBURN C.,ECONOMIC PLAN AND ACTION. USA+45 FINAN LABOR DIPLOM ECO/TAC FOR/AID 20. PAGE 101 F1981
ECO/DEV INT/TRADE

PLAN
BAL/PAY

B59
RAMANADHAM V.V.,PROBLEMS OF PUBLIC ENTERPRISE: THOUGHTS ON BRITISH EXPERIENCE. UK FINAN INDUS PLAN PRICE CENTRAL...POLICY 20. PAGE 109 F2140 — SOCISM LG/CO ECO/DEV GOV/REL

B59
ROBERTSON A.H.,EUROPEAN INSTITUTIONS: COOPERATION, INTEGRATION, UNIFICATION. EUR+WWI FINAN INT/ORG FORCES INT/TRADE TARIFFS 20 EEC EURATOM ECSC NATO TREATY. PAGE 112 F2208 — ECO/DEV DIPLOM INDUS ECO/TAC

B59
ROPKE W.,INTERNATIONAL ORDER AND ECONOMIC INTEGRATION. ECO/DEV ECO/UNDEV AGRI FINAN INDUS INT/ORG WAR PEACE ORD/FREE...SOC METH/COMP 20 EEC. PAGE 114 F2238 — INT/TRADE DIPLOM BAL/PAY ALL/IDEOS

B59
SANNWALD R.E.,ECONOMIC INTEGRATION: THEORETICAL ASSUMPTIONS AND CONSEQUENCES OF EUROPEAN UNIFICATION. EUR+WWI FUT FINAN INDUS VOL/ASSN ACT/RES ECO/TAC...PLURIST EEC FOR/TRADE OEEC 20. PAGE 116 F2279 — INT/ORG ECO/DEV INT/TRADE

B59
SHACKLE G.L.S.,ECONOMICS FOR PLEASURE. FINAN MARKET NAT/G WORKER PLAN INT/TRADE TARIFFS PAY BAL/PAY COST PRODUC 20. PAGE 120 F2361 — METH/CNCPT WEALTH INCOME

B59
STANFORD U, BOARD OF TRUSTEES,THE ALLOCATION OF ECONOMIC RESOURCES. WORKER PLAN BUDGET ECO/TAC TAX RECEIVE COST PRODUC...POLICY IDEA/COMP SIMUL ANTHOL 20. PAGE 125 F2468 — INCOME PRICE FINAN

B59
STOVEL J.A.,CANADA IN THE WORLD ECONOMY. CANADA PRICE DEMAND...STAT CHARTS BIBLIOG 20 VINER/J. PAGE 127 F2499 — INT/TRADE BAL/PAY FINAN ECO/TAC

B59
US DEPARTMENT OF STATE,THE UNITED STATES ECONOMY AND THE MUTUAL SECURITY PROGRAM. USA+45 ECO/UNDEV FINAN INDUS DIPLOM INT/TRADE DETER 20. PAGE 136 F2674 — ECO/DEV FORCES BUDGET FOR/AID

B59
US GENERAL ACCOUNTING OFFICE,EXAM OF ECONOMIC AND TECHNICAL ASSISTANCE PROGRAM FOR INDIA INT'NAT'L COOP ADMIN REPORT TO CONGRESS 1955-1958. INDIA USA+45 ECO/UNDEV FINAN PLAN DIPLOM COST UTIL WEALTH ...CHARTS 20 CONGRESS AID. PAGE 136 F2679 — FOR/AID EFFICIENCY ECO/TAC TEC/DEV

B59
WENTHOLT W.,SOME COMMENTS ON THE LIQUIDATION OF THE EUROPEAN PAYMENT UNION AND RELATED PROBLEMS (PAMPHLET). AFR WOR+45 PLAN BUDGET PRICE CONTROL 20 EEC. PAGE 145 F2857 — FINAN ECO/DEV INT/ORG ECO/TAC

B59
WIBBERLEY G.P.,AGRICULTURE AND URBAN GROWTH. UK USA+45 ECO/DEV FINAN PROB/SOLV INT/TRADE COST ...GEOG STAT CHARTS METH/COMP HYPO/EXP METH MUNICH 20. PAGE 146 F2876 — AGRI PLAN

S59
ALKHIMOV V.S.,"SOVIET FOREIGN TRADE CHANNELS." COM FUT USA+45 USSR ECO/DEV MARKET CONSULT PLAN WEALTH ...MARXIST OBS CON/ANAL FOR/TRADE 20. PAGE 4 F0068 — FINAN ECO/TAC DIPLOM

S59
KINDLEBERGER C.P.,"UNITED STATES ECONOMIC FOREIGN POLICY: RESEARCH REQUIREMENTS FOR 1965." FUT USA+45 WOR+45 DIST/IND MARKET INT/ORG ECO/TAC INT/TRADE WEALTH...OBS TREND CON/ANAL GEN/LAWS FOR/TRADE VAL/FREE 20. PAGE 71 F1392 — FINAN ECO/DEV FOR/AID

S59
SOLDATI A.,"EOCNOMIC DISINTEGRATION IN EUROPE." EUR+WWI FUT WOR+45 INDUS INT/ORG NAT/G CAP/ISM WEALTH...NEW/IDEA OBS TREND CHARTS EEC 20. PAGE 124 F2438 — FINAN ECO/TAC

S59
STREETEN P.,"UNBALANCED GROWTH" UK ECO/DEV AGRI MARKET TEC/DEV CAP/ISM ECO/TAC FOR/AID INT/TRADE DEMAND ORD/FREE...CONCPT 20. PAGE 127 F2502 — IDEA/COMP FINAN PRODUC EQUILIB

N59
CHAMBER OF COMMERCE OF USA,ECONOMIC LESSONS OF POSTWAR RECESSIONS (PAMPHLET). AFR USA+45 LAW LEGIS WORKER TAX...CHARTS 20 CONGRESS FED/RESERV. PAGE 23 F0440 — ECO/DEV PROB/SOLV FINAN ECO/TAC

B60
ALLEN R.L.,SOVIET ECONOMIC WARFARE. USSR FINAN INDUS NAT/G PLAN TEC/DEV FOR/AID DETER WEALTH ...TREND GEN/LAWS FOR/TRADE 20. PAGE 4 F0072 — COM ECO/TAC

B60
AMERICAN U BEIRUT ECO RES INST,A SELECTED AND ANNOTATED BIBLIOGRAPHY OF ECONOMIC LITERATURE ON THE ARABIC SPEAKING COUNTRIES OF THE MIDDLE EAST. ISLAM AGRI COM/IND DIST/IND FINAN INDUS LABOR ...GEOG 20. PAGE 5 F0091 — BIBLIOG/A ECO/UNDEV STAT

B60
APTHEKER H.,DISARMAMENT AND THE AMERICAN ECONOMY: A SYMPOSIUM. FUT USA+45 ECO/DEV DIST/IND FINAN INDUS PROC/MFG LABOR NAT/G POL/PAR CONSULT PLAN CAP/ISM INT/TRADE PEACE ATTIT MORAL WEALTH...TREND GEN/LAWS TOT/POP 20. PAGE 6 F0110 — MARXIST ARMS/CONT

B60
ATOMIC INDUSTRIAL FORUM,ATOMS FOR INDUSTRY: WORLD FORUM. WOR+45 FINAN COST UTIL...JURID ANTHOL 20. PAGE 7 F0137 — NUC/PWR INDUS PLAN PROB/SOLV

B60
BAERWALD F.,ECONOMIC SYSTEM ANALYSIS: CONCEPTS AND PERSPECTIVES. USA+45 ECO/DEV NAT/G COMPUTER EQUILIB INCOME ATTIT...DECISION CONCPT IDEA/COMP. PAGE 8 F0151 — ACT/RES ECO/TAC ROUTINE FINAN

B60
BATOR F.M.,QUESTION OF GOVERNMENT SPENDING. USA+45 DIST/IND FINAN BAL/PAY...STAT CENSUS CHARTS CONGRESS 20. PAGE 11 F0210 — ECO/DEV

B60
BAYER H.,WIRTSCHAFTSPROGNOSE UND WIRTSCHAFTSGESTALTUNG. GERMANY NETHERLAND MARKET PLAN CAP/ISM DEBATE...NAT/COMP 20. PAGE 12 F0220 — ECO/DEV ECO/UNDEV FINAN POLICY

B60
BELLAN R.C.,PRINCIPLES OF ECONOMICS AND THE CANADIAN ECONOMY (2ND ED.). CANADA UK USA+45 LABOR WORKER CAP/ISM INT/TRADE RISK BAL/PAY EQUILIB ALL/IDEOS 20. PAGE 12 F0236 — ECO/DEV PRODUC WEALTH FINAN

B60
BIERMAN H.,THE CAPITAL BUDGETING DECISION. AFR ECO/DEV MARKET TAX PRICE RISK COST INCOME TIME 20. PAGE 15 F0282 — FINAN OPTIMAL BUDGET PROFIT

B60
BILLERBECK K.,SOVIET BLOC FOREIGN AID TO UNDERDEVELOPED COUNTRIES. COM FUT USSR FINAN FORCES TEC/DEV DIPLOM INT/TRADE EDU/PROP NUC/PWR...TREND 20. PAGE 15 F0285 — FOR/AID ECO/UNDEV ECO/TAC MARXISM

B60
BISSON A.,INSTITUTIONS FINANCIERES ET ECONOMIQUES EN FRANCE. FRANCE INDUS OP/RES TAX COST PRODUC ...CHARTS 20. PAGE 15 F0289 — FINAN BUDGET PLAN

B60
BRYCE M.D.,INDUSTRIAL DEVELOPMENT: A GUIDE FOR ACCELERATING ECONOMIC GROWTH. WOR+45 FINAN MARKET COST EFFICIENCY PRODUC. PAGE 20 F0378 — INDUS PLAN ECO/UNDEV TEC/DEV

B60
COMMITTEE ECONOMIC DEVELOPMENT,NATIONAL OBJECTIVES AND THE BALANCE OF PAYMENTS PROBLEM: A STATEMENT ON NATIONAL POLICY. USA+45 WOR+45 DIST/IND FINAN INDUS LABOR NAT/G DELIB/GP ACT/RES FOR/AID INT/TRADE ...STAT CHARTS FOR/TRADE 20. PAGE 27 F0516 — ECO/DEV ECO/TAC BAL/PAY

B60
CROSSER P.K.,STATE CAPITALISM IN THE ECONOMY OF THE UNITED STATES. USA+45 USA-45 AGRI FINAN INDUS LABOR WORKER RATION CONTROL GOV/REL DEMAND...NEW/IDEA 20. PAGE 29 F0557 — CAP/ISM ECO/DEV ECO/TAC NAT/G

B60
DALE W.B.,THE FOREIGN DEFICIT OF THE UNITED STATES. ECO/TAC TARIFFS PAY PRICE CONTROL COST WEALTH POLICY. PAGE 30 F0573 — BAL/PAY DIPLOM FINAN INT/TRADE

B60
FIRESTONE J.M.,FEDERAL RECEIPTS AND EXPENDITURES DURING BUSINESS CYCLES, 1879-1958. USA+45 USA-45 INDUS PLAN ECO/TAC TAX WAR COST...CHARTS 19/20. PAGE 41 F0801 — FINAN INCOME BUDGET NAT/G

B60
GARBARINO J.W.,HEALTH PLANS AND COLLECTIVE BARGAINING. USA+45 LABOR BARGAIN GP/REL WEALTH ...WELF/ST CHARTS 20 DEPT/HEW SAN/FRAN. PAGE 46 F0900 — HEAL PLAN FINAN SERV/IND

B60
GILMORE D.R.,DEVELOPING THE "LITTLE" ECONOMIES. USA+45 FINAN LG/CO PROF/ORG VOL/ASSN CREATE ADMIN. PAGE 47 F0924 — ECO/TAC LOC/G PROVS PLAN

B60
GRIER E.,PRIVATELY DEVELOPED INTERRACIAL HOUSING: AN ANALYSIS OF EXPERIENCE. FINAN MARKET COST DISCRIM PROFIT SOC/INTEG 20. PAGE 51 F0997 — RACE/REL CONSTRUC HABITAT

B60
HALL C.A. JR.,FISCAL POLICY FOR STABLE GROWTH. USA+45 FINAN TEC/DEV TAX COST DEMAND INCOME ...BIBLIOG 20. PAGE 53 F1045 — ECO/TAC BUDGET NAT/G POLICY

B60
HARBERGER A.C.,THE DEMAND FOR DURABLE GOODS. AGRI FINAN COST EQUILIB...MATH STAT TIME/SEQ TREND CON/ANAL CHARTS SIMUL ANTHOL 20. PAGE 55 F1072 — ECOMETRIC DEMAND PRICE

B60
HUGHES J.,NATIONALISED INDUSTRIES IN THE MIXED ECONOMY (PAMPHLET). FINAN PROB/SOLV CAP/ISM OWN ...SOCIALIST STAT METH/COMP 20. PAGE 63 F1233 — SOCISM LG/CO GOV/REL ECO/DEV

B60
ILLINOIS U BUR COMMUNITY PLAN,PROCEEDINGS OF ILLINOIS STATEWIDE PLANNING CONFERENCE 1960. USA+45 FINAN LOC/G ACT/RES LEAD GOV/REL GP/REL WEALTH MUNICH 20 ILLINOIS. PAGE 64 F1260
PLAN DELIB/GP VOL/ASSN

B60
KENEN P.B.,GIANT AMONG NATIONS: PROBLEMS IN UNITED STATES FOREIGN ECONOMIC POLICY. AFR USA+45 FINAN DIPLOM TARIFFS BAL/PAY WEALTH 20. PAGE 70 F1376
FOR/AID ECO/UNDEV INT/TRADE PLAN

B60
KENEN P.B.,BRITISH MONETARY POLICY AND THE BALANCE OF PAYMENTS 1951-57. UK PLAN BUDGET ECO/TAC INT/TRADE PAY PRICE COST ATTIT 20. PAGE 70 F1377
BAL/PAY PROB/SOLV FINAN NAT/G

B60
LATIFI D.,INDIA AND UNITED STATES AID. ASIA INDIA UK USA+45 AGRI FINAN INDUS COLONIAL ORD/FREE SOVEREIGN WEALTH...METH/COMP 20. PAGE 76 F1486
FOR/AID DIPLOM ECO/UNDEV

B60
MARSHALL A.H.,FINANCIAL ADMINISTRATION IN LOCAL GOVERNMENT. UK DELIB/GP CONFER COST INCOME PERSON ...JURID 20. PAGE 86 F1679
FINAN LOC/G BUDGET ADMIN

B60
NEALE A.D.,THE FLOW OF RESOURCES FROM RICH TO POOR. WOR+45 ECO/DEV ECO/UNDEV FINAN INDUS NAT/G PLAN EFFICIENCY WEALTH...POLICY NAT/COMP 20 RESOURCE/N. PAGE 97 F1905
FOR/AID DIPLOM METH/CNCPT

B60
OEEC,STATISTICS OF SOURCES AND USES OF FINANCE. NAT/G CAP/ISM TAX PRICE COST 20 OEEC. PAGE 101 F1978
FINAN PRODUC INCOME NAT/COMP

B60
PENNSYLVANIA ECONOMY LEAGUE,URBAN RENEWAL IMPACT STUDY: ADMINISTRATIVE-LEGAL-FISCAL. USA+45 FINAN LOC/G NEIGH ADMIN EFFICIENCY...CENSUS CHARTS MUNICH 20 PENNSYLVAN. PAGE 105 F2059
PLAN BUDGET ADJUD

B60
RAO V.K.R.,INTERNATIONAL AID FOR ECONOMIC DEVELOPMENT - POSSIBILITIES AND LIMITATIONS. FINAN PLAN TEC/DEV ADMIN TASK EFFICIENCY...POLICY SOC METH/CNCPT CHARTS 20 UN. PAGE 109 F2147
FOR/AID DIPLOM INT/ORG ECO/UNDEV

B60
RAPKIN C.,THE DEMAND FOR HOUSING IN RACIALLY MIXED AREAS: A STUDY OF THE NATURE OF NEIGHBORHOOD CHANGE. USA+45 FINAN PRICE COST DRIVE...GEOG 20. PAGE 109 F2151
RACE/REL NEIGH DISCRIM MARKET

B60
RAY D.D.,ACCOUNTING AND BUSINESS FLUCTUATIONS. LG/CO SML/CO FEEDBACK DEMAND...CHARTS IDEA/COMP BIBLIOG 20. PAGE 109 F2154
FINAN AFR CONTROL

B60
RICHARDSON G.B.,INFORMATION AND INVESTMENT. PLAN PROB/SOLV CAP/ISM ECO/TAC KNOWL...CONCPT 20 MONEY. PAGE 111 F2184
ECO/DEV EQUILIB FINAN PHIL/SCI

B60
ROBERTSON D.,THE CONTROL OF INDUSTRY. UK MARKET LABOR WORKER PRICE CONTROL GP/REL COST DEMAND ORD/FREE WEALTH NEW/LIB SOCISM 20. PAGE 112 F2211
INDUS FINAN NAT/G ECO/DEV

B60
ROBINSON R.I.,FINANCIAL INSTITUTIONS. USA+45 PRICE GOV/REL DEMAND WEALTH...CHARTS T 20 MONEY. PAGE 113 F2226
FINAN ECO/TAC ECO/DEV BUDGET

B60
ROBSON W.A.,NATIONALIZED INDUSTRY AND PUBLIC OWNERSHIP. UK ECO/DEV FINAN LABOR LG/CO POL/PAR LEGIS ACT/RES GP/REL...TREND IDEA/COMP 20. PAGE 113 F2227
NAT/G OWN INDUS ATTIT

B60
ROPKE W.,A HUMANE ECONOMY. CULTURE ECO/DEV FINAN INDUS GP/REL CENTRAL WEALTH...GEOG SOC IDEA/COMP 20 EEC. PAGE 114 F2239
ECO/TAC INT/ORG DIPLOM ORD/FREE

B60
SANTHANAM K.,UNION-STATE RELATIONS IN INDIA. INDIA FINAN PROVS PLAN ECO/TAC...LING 20. PAGE 116 F2280
FEDERAL GOV/REL CONSTN POLICY

B60
SHANNON D.A.,THE GREAT DEPRESSION. USA-45 FINAN LG/CO SCHOOL SML/CO DELIB/GP RECEIVE REV EATING INCOME...ANTHOL MUNICH 20 ROOSEVLT/F CONGRESS. PAGE 120 F2365
WEALTH NAT/G AGRI INDUS

B60
SHONFIELD A.,THE ATTACK ON WORLD POVERTY. WOR+45 ECO/DEV ECO/UNDEV FINAN VOL/ASSN PLAN EDU/PROP DRIVE KNOWL WEALTH...CONT/OBS STAND/INT ORG/CHARTS TOT/POP UNESCO 20. PAGE 121 F2383
INT/ORG ECO/TAC FOR/AID INT/TRADE

B60
SILK L.S.,THE RESEARCH REVOLUTION. USA+45 FINAN CAP/ISM ECO/TAC PRICE EQUILIB PRODUC...STAT TREND CHARTS. PAGE 122 F2402
ECO/DEV R+D TEC/DEV PROB/SOLV

B60
STANFORD RESEARCH INSTITUTE,AFRICAN DEVELOPMENT: A TEST FOR INTERNATIONAL COOPERATION. AFR USA+45 WOR+45 FINAN INT/ORG PLAN PROB/SOLV ECO/TAC INT/TRADE ADMIN...CHARTS 20. PAGE 125 F2467
FOR/AID ECO/UNDEV ATTIT DIPLOM

B60
STOLPER W.F.,GERMANY BETWEEN EAST AND WEST: THE ECONOMICS OF COMPETITIVE COEXISTENCE. AFR FUT GERMANY/E GERMANY/W WOR+45 FINAN POL/PAR BUDGET ECO/TAC FOR/AID INT/TRADE...STAT CHARTS METH/COMP 20. PAGE 126 F2495
ECO/DEV DIPLOM GOV/COMP BAL/PWR

B60
THE ECONOMIST (LONDON),THE COMMONWEALTH AND EUROPE. EUR+WWI WOR+45 AGRI FINAN INCOME...STAT CENSUS CHARTS CMN/WLTH EEC. PAGE 129 F2550
INT/TRADE INDUS INT/ORG NAT/COMP

B60
THORBECKE E.,THE TENDENCY TOWARDS REGIONALIZATION IN INTERNATIONAL TRADE, 1928-1956. WOR+45 WOR-45 ECO/DEV FINAN ECO/TAC WEALTH...GEOG CHARTS TOT/POP FOR/TRADE 20. PAGE 130 F2569
STAT BAL/PAY REGION

B60
US GENERAL ACCOUNTING OFFICE,EXAMINATION OF ECONOMIC AND TECHNICAL ASSISTANCE PROGRAM FOR GUATEMALA. GUATEMALA L/A+17C USA+45 FINAN INDUS PLAN...POLICY STAT CHARTS 20 DEPT/STATE. PAGE 136 F2680
FOR/AID ECO/UNDEV TEC/DEV NAT/G

B60
US HOUSE COMM GOVT OPERATIONS,OPERATIONS OF THE DEVELOPMENT LOAN FUND: HEARINGS (COMMITTEE ON GOVERNMENT OPERATIONS). USA+45 PLAN BUDGET DIPLOM GOV/REL COST...CHARTS 20 CONGRESS DEPT/STATE AID. PAGE 137 F2698
FINAN FOR/AID ECO/TAC EFFICIENCY

B60
US OPERATIONS MISSION - TURKEY,SOME POSSIBILITIES FOR ACCELERATING TURKEY'S ECONOMIC GROWTH. TURKEY USA+45 AGRI FINAN INDUS NAT/G ACT/RES BUDGET COST ...CHARTS 20. PAGE 138 F2724
ECO/UNDEV ECO/TAC FOR/AID PRODUC

B60
US SENATE COMM ON COMMERCE,URBAN MASS TRANSPORTATION. FUT USA+45 AIR ECO/DEV FINAN LOC/G LEGIS CREATE PROB/SOLV TEC/DEV MUNICH 20 PUB/TRANS. PAGE 139 F2732
DIST/IND PLAN NAT/G LAW

B60
WATSON D.S.,ECONOMIC POLICY: BUSINESS AND GOVERNMENT. USA+45 FINAN LABOR PLAN BUDGET INT/TRADE GP/REL WEALTH LAISSEZ...CHARTS T. PAGE 144 F2832
ECO/TAC NAT/G POLICY ECO/DEV

B60
WENTHOLT W.,INFLATION OR SECURITY? EUR+WWI USA+45 INDUS CONSULT TEC/DEV CAP/ISM DIPLOM FOR/AID INT/TRADE MARXISM 20 EEC. PAGE 145 F2858
ECO/DEV ECO/TAC FINAN ORD/FREE

S60
"THE EMERGING COMMON MARKETS IN LATIN AMERICA." FUT L/A+17C STRATA DIST/IND INDUS LABOR NAT/G LEGIS ECO/TAC ADMIN RIGID/FLEX HEALTH...NEW/IDEA TIME/SEQ OAS 20. PAGE 1 F0013
FINAN ECO/UNDEV INT/TRADE

S60
BUTLER W.F.,"ECONOMIC PROGRESS IN LATIN AMERICA." L/A+17C USA+45 ECO/UNDEV AGRI FINAN NAT/G PLAN ECO/TAC FOR/AID ADMIN WEALTH...OLD/LIB TOT/POP 20. PAGE 21 F0397
INDUS ACT/RES

S60
ENKE S.,"THE ECONOMIES OF GOVERNMENT PAYMENTS TO LIMIT POPULATION." FUT INDIA WOR+45 CULTURE FINAN NAT/G CONSULT PLAN LEGIT CONTROL COST ATTIT RIGID/FLEX HEALTH WEALTH...STAT OBS CHARTS TOT/POP VAL/FREE 20. PAGE 38 F0736
FAM ACT/RES

S60
FRANKEL S.H.,"ECONOMIC ASPECTS OF POLITICAL INDEPENDENCE IN AFRICA." AFR FUT SOCIETY ECO/UNDEV COM/IND FINAN LEGIS PLAN TEC/DEV CAP/ISM ECO/TAC INT/TRADE ADMIN ATTIT DRIVE RIGID/FLEX PWR WEALTH ...MGT NEW/IDEA MATH TIME/SEQ VAL/FREE 20. PAGE 43 F0846
NAT/G FOR/AID

S60
HERRERA F.,"THE INTER-AMERICAN DEVELOPMENT BANK." USA+45 ECO/UNDEV INT/ORG CONSULT DELIB/GP PLAN ECO/TAC INT/TRADE ROUTINE WEALTH...STAT TERR/GP 20. PAGE 59 F1153
L/A+17C FINAN FOR/AID REGION

S60
HERZ J.H.,"EAST GERMANY: PROGRESS AND PROSPECTS." COM AGRI FINAN INDUS LOC/G NAT/G FORCES PLAN TEC/DEV DOMIN ADMIN COERCE DRIVE PERCEPT RIGID/FLEX MORAL ORD/FREE PWR...MARXIST PSY SOC RECORD STERTYP WORK. PAGE 59 F1158
POL/PAR STRUCT GERMANY

S60
LINDHOLM R.W.,"ACCELERATED DEVELOPMENT WITH A MINIMUM OF FOREIGN AID AND ECONOMIC CONTROLS." SOCIETY INDUS ECO/TAC WEALTH...CONCPT 20. PAGE 80 F1570
ECO/DEV FINAN FOR/AID

S60
MORALES C.J.,"TRADE AND ECONOMIC INTEGRATION IN
FINAN

LATIN AMERICA." FUT L/A+17C LAW STRATA ECO/UNDEV DIST/IND INDUS LABOR NAT/G LEGIS ECO/TAC ADMIN RIGID/FLEX WEALTH...CONCPT NEW/IDEA CONT/OBS TIME/SEQ WORK 20. PAGE 93 F1825 — INT/TRADE REGION

S60
MURPHY J.C.,"INTERNATIONAL INVESTMENT AND THE NATIONAL INTEREST." AFR WOR+45 WOR-45 ECO/DEV ECO/UNDEV NAT/G ACT/RES...CHARTS TOT/POP FOR/TRADE 20. PAGE 95 F1867 — FINAN WEALTH FOR/AID

S60
NICHOLS J.P.,"HAZARDS OF AMERICAN PRIVATE INVESTMENT IN UNDERDEVELOPED COUNTRIES." FUT L/A+17C USA+45 USA-45 EXTR/IND CONSULT BAL/PWR ECO/TAC DOMIN ADJUD ATTIT SOVEREIGN WEALTH ...HIST/WRIT TIME/SEQ TREND TERR/GP VAL/FREE 20. PAGE 98 F1924 — FINAN ECO/UNDEV CAP/ISM NAT/LISM

S60
POLLARD J.A.,"EMERGING PATTERNS OF CORPORATE GIVING." FINAN DELIB/GP PLAN EDU/PROP CENTRAL TREND. PAGE 107 F2098 — GIVE LG/CO ADMIN MGT

C60
FAULKNER H.U.,"AMERICAN ECONOMIC HISTORY (8TH ED.)" USA+45 USA-45 FINAN...CHARTS BIBLIOG/A T 17/20. PAGE 39 F0769 — AGRI INDUS ECO/DEV CAP/ISM

B61
ACKLEY G.,MACROECONOMIC THEORY. AFR FINAN WORKER ECO/TAC PRICE COST INCOME PRODUC...MATH TREND CHARTS IDEA/COMP T KEYNES/JM. PAGE 2 F0034 — SIMUL ECOMETRIC WEALTH

B61
AGARWAL R.C.,STATE ENTERPRISE IN INDIA. FUT INDIA UK FINAN INDUS ADMIN CONTROL OWN...POLICY CHARTS BIBLIOG 20 RAILROAD. PAGE 3 F0048 — ECO/UNDEV SOCISM GOV/REL LG/CO

B61
AMERICAN MANAGEMENT ASSN,SUPERIOR-SUBORDINATE COMMUNICATION IN MANAGEMENT. STRATA FINAN INDUS SML/CO WORKER CONTROL EXEC ATTIT 20. PAGE 5 F0090 — MGT ACT/RES PERS/REL LG/CO

B61
ASCHHEIM J.,TECHNIQUES OF MONETARY CONTROL. UK USA+45 CONTROL WAR DEMAND INCOME WEALTH...TREND CHARTS 20 MONEY. PAGE 7 F0127 — FINAN MARKET BUDGET CENTRAL

B61
ASHER R.E.,GRANTS, LOANS, AND LOCAL CURRENCIES; THEIR ROLE IN FOREIGN AID. AFR USA+45 ECO/UNDEV INT/ORG ACT/RES PLAN ECO/TAC GIVE CONTROL WEALTH 20. PAGE 7 F0130 — FOR/AID FINAN NAT/G BUDGET

B61
BAUER P.T.,INDIAN ECONOMIC POLICY AND DEVELOPMENT. INDIA STRATA AGRI FINAN POL/PAR BUDGET FOR/AID GOV/REL EFFICIENCY...CENSUS 20. PAGE 11 F0216 — ECO/UNDEV ECO/TAC POLICY PLAN

B61
BEASLEY K.E.,STATE SUPERVISION OF MUNICIPAL DEBT IN KANSAS - A CASE STUDY. USA+45 USA-45 FINAN PROVS BUDGET TAX ADJUD ADMIN CONTROL SUPEGO MUNICH. PAGE 12 F0224 — LOC/G LEGIS JURID

B61
BENHAM F.,ECONOMIC AID TO UNDERDEVELOPED COUNTRIES. WOR+45 INDUS BAL/PAY ALL/VALS 20. PAGE 13 F0244 — ECO/UNDEV FOR/AID INT/TRADE FINAN

B61
BENOIT E.,EUROPE AT SIXES AND SEVENS: THE COMMON MARKET, THE FREE TRADE ASSOCIATION AND THE UNITED STATES. EUR+WWI FUT USA+45 INDUS CONSULT DELIB/GP EX/STRUC TOP/EX ACT/RES ECO/TAC EDU/PROP ROUTINE CHOOSE PERCEPT WEALTH...MGT TREND EEC FOR/TRADE TOT/POP 20 EFTA. PAGE 13 F0249 — FINAN ECO/DEV VOL/ASSN

B61
BUSSCHAU W.J.,GOLD AND INTERNATIONAL LIQUIDITY. AFR WOR+45 PRICE EQUILIB WEALTH...CHARTS 20. PAGE 20 F0396 — FINAN DIPLOM PROB/SOLV

B61
CANTERBERY E.R.,THE PRESIDENT'S COUNCIL OF ECONOMIC ADVISERS. AFR USA+45 FINAN LABOR NAT/G PLAN ADMIN OPTIMAL WEALTH 20 EISNHWR/DD PRESIDENT TRUMAN/HS KEYNES/JM. PAGE 21 F0413 — ECO/TAC OP/RES EXEC CHIEF

B61
CLARK J.M.,COMPETITION AS A DYNAMIC PROCESS. ECO/DEV EXTR/IND INDUS LG/CO TEC/DEV ECO/TAC PRICE EQUILIB PRODUC...NEW/IDEA CAP 20. PAGE 25 F0483 — WEALTH GP/REL FINAN PROFIT

B61
DE GRAZIA A.,AMERICAN WELFARE. CLIENT FINAN LABOR LOC/G NAT/G NEIGH EDU/PROP GP/REL...CLASSIF CON/ANAL CHARTS BIBLIOG. PAGE 31 F0598 — GIVE WEALTH SECT VOL/ASSN

B61
DETHINE P.,BIBLIOGRAPHIE DES ASPECTS ECONOMIQUES ET SOCIAUX DE L'INDUSTRIALISATION EN AFRIQUE. AFR FINAN LABOR FOR/AID...SOC 20. PAGE 32 F0623 — BIBLIOG/A ECO/UNDEV INDUS TEC/DEV

B61
DIMOCK M.E.,BUSINESS AND GOVERNMENT (4TH ED.). AGRI FINAN OP/RES PLAN BUDGET DIPLOM LOBBY NUC/PWR NEW/LIB SOCISM...POLICY BIBLIOG 20. PAGE 33 F0641 — NAT/G INDUS LABOR ECO/TAC

B61
EINZIG P.,A DYNAMIC THEORY OF FORWARD EXCHANGE. FUT WOR+45 WOR-45 INT/TRADE BAL/PAY WEALTH...OLD/LIB NEW/IDEA OBS TREND FOR/TRADE 20. PAGE 37 F0713 — FINAN ECO/TAC

B61
ELLIS H.S.,ECONOMIC DEVELOPMENT FOR LATIN AMERICA. L/A+17C AGRI FINAN INDUS FOR/AID GP/REL BAL/PAY DEMAND...ANTHOL 20 INTL/ECON. PAGE 37 F0723 — ECO/UNDEV ECO/TAC PLAN INT/TRADE

B61
ESTEBAN J.C.,IMPERIALISMO Y DESARROLLO ECONOMICO. L/A+17C FINAN INDUS NAT/G ECO/TAC CONTROL ROLE. PAGE 38 F0747 — ECO/UNDEV NAT/LISM DIPLOM BAL/PAY

B61
ESTEVEZ A.,ASPECTOS ECONOMICO-FINANCIEROS DE LA CAMPANA SANMARITANA. L/A+17C SPAIN FINAN COLONIAL LEAD ROLE ORD/FREE WEALTH 19 SOUTH/AMER SAN/MARTIN. PAGE 38 F0748 — ECO/UNDEV REV BUDGET NAT/G

B61
FRIEDMANN W.G.,JOINT INTERNATIONAL BUSINESS VENTURES. ASIA ISLAM L/A+17C ECO/DEV DIST/IND FINAN PROC/MFG FACE/GP LG/CO NAT/G VOL/ASSN CONSULT EX/STRUC PLAN ADMIN ROUTINE WEALTH...OLD/LIB FOR/TRADE WORK 20. PAGE 44 F0865 — ECO/UNDEV INT/TRADE

B61
GANGULI B.N.,ECONOMIC INTEGRATION. FINAN LABOR CAP/ISM DIPLOM WEALTH...NAT/COMP 20. PAGE 46 F0895 — ECO/TAC METH/CNCPT EQUILIB ECO/UNDEV

B61
GARDNER R.N.,LEGAL-ECONOMIC PROBLEMS OF INTERNATIONAL TRADE. FUT WOR+45 INTELL ECO/DEV EX/STRUC INT/TRADE ROUTINE ATTIT WEALTH...GEN/LAWS ANTHOL FOR/TRADE 20. PAGE 46 F0904 — FINAN ACT/RES

B61
GOODWIN C.D.W.,CANADIAN ECONOMIC THOUGHT. CANADA STRATA TEC/DEV CAP/ISM TARIFFS TAX COST EFFICIENCY WEALTH...METH/CNCPT TREND 20 MARITIME ONTARIO. PAGE 49 F0952 — INT/TRADE ECO/DEV FINAN DEMAND

B61
GREY A.L.,ECONOMIC ISSUES AND POLICIES; READINGS IN INTRODUCTORY ECONOMICS (2ND ED.). WOR+45 ECO/UNDEV FINAN MARKET LABOR LG/CO INT/TRADE BAL/PAY WEALTH ...ANTHOL T. PAGE 51 F0996 — ECO/TAC PROB/SOLV METH/COMP

B61
GURTOO D.H.N.,INDIA'S BALANCE OF PAYMENTS (1920-1960). INDIA FINAN DIPLOM FOR/AID INT/TRADE PRICE COLONIAL...CHARTS BIBLIOG 20. PAGE 52 F1014 — BAL/PAY STAT ECO/TAC ECO/UNDEV

B61
HARRIS S.E.,THE DOLLAR IN CRISIS. AFR USA+45 MARKET INT/ORG ECO/TAC PRICE CONTROL WEALTH...METH/COMP ANTHOL 20. PAGE 55 F1089 — BAL/PAY DIPLOM FINAN INT/TRADE

B61
HAUSER M.,DIE URSACHEN DER FRANZOSISCHEN INFLATION IN DEN JAHREN 1946-1952. AFR FRANCE INDUS NAT/G BUDGET DIPLOM ECO/TAC FOR/AID COST MONEY 20. PAGE 57 F1114 — ECO/DEV FINAN PRICE

B61
HICKS U.K.,FEDERALISM AND ECONOMIC GROWTH IN UNDERDEVELOPED COUNTRIES. WOR+45 WOR-45 FINAN NAT/G PLAN BUDGET DIPLOM INT/TRADE DEMAND WEALTH...ANTHOL 20. PAGE 59 F1167 — ECO/UNDEV ECO/TAC FEDERAL CONSTN

B61
INDUSTRIAL COUN SOC-ECO STU,THE SWEDISH ECONOMY AND THE UNDERDEVELOPED COUNTRIES. SWEDEN INDUS DELIB/GP TEC/DEV INT/TRADE EDU/PROP COLONIAL DRIVE...CHARTS 20. PAGE 64 F1264 — FOR/AID ECO/UNDEV PLAN FINAN

B61
INTERNATIONAL BANK RECONST DEV,THE WORLD BANK IN AFRICA: SUMMARY OF ACTIVITIES. AGRI COM/IND DIST/IND EXTR/IND INDUS TAX COST...CHARTS 20. PAGE 65 F1271 — FINAN ECO/UNDEV INT/ORG AFR

B61
INTL BANKING SUMMER SCHOOL,TRENDS IN BANK CREDIT AND FINANCE. EUR+WWI NETHERLAND ECO/DEV PROF/ORG PLAN BUDGET 20 EEC. PAGE 65 F1283 — FINAN ECO/TAC NAT/G LG/CO

B61
INTL UNION LOCAL AUTHORITIES,METROPOLIS. WOR+45 DIST/IND FINAN GIVE EDU/PROP CRIME COST HEALTH WEALTH MUNICH 20. PAGE 65 F1286 — GOV/COMP LOC/G BIBLIOG

B61
KELSO L.O.,THE NEW CAPITALISTS: A PROPOSAL TO FREE ECONOMIC GROWTH FROM THE SLAVERY OF SAVINGS. UNIV USA+45 ECO/DEV CAP/ISM PRODUC WEALTH SOCISM ...NEW/IDEA 20. PAGE 70 F1373 — ECO/TAC WORKER FINAN GEN/LAWS

B61
LAHAYE R.,LES ENTREPRISES PUBLIQUES AU MAROC. — NAT/G

FRANCE MOROCCO LAW DIST/IND EXTR/IND FINAN CONSULT PLAN TEC/DEV ADMIN AGREE CONTROL OWN...POLICY 20. PAGE 74 F1460
INDUS ECO/UNDEV ECO/TAC

B61
LAMFALUSSY A.,INVESTMENT AND GROWTH IN MATURE ECONOMIES. BELGIUM EUR+WWI LABOR PRICE PRODUC PROFIT...STAT CONT/OBS CHARTS 20. PAGE 75 F1464
FINAN INDUS ECO/DEV CAP/ISM

B61
LEE R.R.,ENGINEERING-ECONOMIC PLANNING MISCELLANEOUS SUBJECTS: A SELECTED BIBLIOGRAPHY (MIMEOGRAPHED). FINAN LOC/G NEIGH ADMIN CONTROL INGP/REL HABITAT...GEOG MGT SOC/WK MUNICH 20 RESOURCE/N. PAGE 77 F1509
BIBLIOG/A PLAN REGION

B61
LHOSTE-LACHAUME P.,OU GIT LE DESACCORD ENTRE LIBERAUX ET SOCIALISTES. EUR+WWI USA+45 USA-45 USSR CAP/ISM EDU/PROP MARXISM...MAJORIT IDEA/COMP 20 KEYNES/JM NEW/DEAL DEPRESSION. PAGE 79 F1555
LAISSEZ SOCISM FINAN

B61
MARX K.,THE COMMUNIST MANIFESTO. IN (MENDEL A. ESSENTIAL WORKS OF MARXISM, NEW YORK: BANTAM. FUT MOD/EUR CULTURE ECO/DEV ECO/UNDEV AGRI FINAN INDUS MARKET PROC/MFG LABOR POL/PAR CONSULT FORCES CREATE PLAN ADMIN ATTIT DRIVE RIGID/FLEX ORD/FREE PWR RESPECT MARX/KARL MUNICH WORK. PAGE 86 F1691
COM NEW/IDEA CAP/ISM REV

B61
MCCRACKEN H.L.,KEYNESIAN ECONOMICS IN THE STREAM OF ECONOMIC THOUGHT. FINAN MARKET BARGAIN EFFICIENCY OPTIMAL...PHIL/SCI CONCPT IDEA/COMP BIBLIOG 18/20 KEYNES/JM. PAGE 88 F1724
ECO/TAC DEMAND ECOMETRIC

B61
MEZERIK A.G.,ECONOMIC DEVELOPMENT AIDS FOR UNDERDEVELOPED COUNTRIES. WOR+45 FINAN LEGIS PROB/SOLV TEC/DEV DIPLOM FOR/AID GIVE TASK WAR 20 UN. PAGE 91 F1776
ECO/UNDEV INT/ORG WEALTH PLAN

B61
MIT CENTER INTERNATIONAL STU,OFFICIAL SERIAL PUBLICATIONS RELATING TO ECONOMIC DEVELOPMENT IN AFRICA SOUTH OF THE SAHARA. AFR SOCIETY AGRI FINAN INDUS LG/CO ADMIN 20. PAGE 92 F1806
BIBLIOG ECO/UNDEV ECO/TAC NAT/G

B61
MOORE G.H.,BUSINESS CYCLE INDICATORS (TWO VOLS.). LABOR DIPLOM PRICE RISK TASK WAR PRODUC...CHARTS BIBLIOG 20. PAGE 93 F1822
MARKET FINAN WEALTH

B61
MORLEY L.,THE PATCHWORK HISTORY OF FOREIGN AID. AFR KOREA/S USA+45 USSR LAW FINAN INT/ORG TEC/DEV BAL/PWR GIVE 20 NATO. PAGE 93 F1834
FOR/AID ECO/UNDEV FORCES DIPLOM

B61
MYRDAL G.,THE POLITICAL ELEMENT IN THE DEVELOPMENT OF ECONOMIC THEORY. FINAN LOBBY ATTIT...WELF/ST CONCPT IDEA/COMP GEN/LAWS 20. PAGE 95 F1875
ECO/DEV ECO/TAC SOCIETY

B61
NEW JERSEY LEGISLATURE-SENATE,PUBLIC HEARINGS BEFORE COMMITTEE ON REVISION AND AMENDMENT OF LAWS ON SENATE BILL NO. 8. USA+45 FINAN PROVS WORKER ACT/RES PLAN BUDGET TAX CRIME...IDEA/COMP MUNICH 20 NEW/JERSEY URBAN/RNWL. PAGE 98 F1919
LEGIS INDUS PROB/SOLV

B61
NOVE A.,THE SOVIET ECONOMY. USSR ECO/DEV FINAN NAT/G ECO/TAC PRICE ADMIN EFFICIENCY MARXISM ...TREND BIBLIOG 20. PAGE 99 F1943
PLAN PRODUC POLICY

B61
OECD,STATISTICS OF BALANCE OF PAYMENTS 1950-61. WOR+45 FINAN ECO/TAC INT/TRADE DEMAND WEALTH...STAT NAT/COMP 20 OEEC OECD. PAGE 100 F1965
BAL/PAY ECO/DEV INT/ORG CHARTS

B61
PAUNIO J.J.,A STUDY IN THE THEORY OF OPEN INFLATION. AFR FINAN CAP/ISM PRICE DEMAND INCOME ...CHARTS BIBLIOG 20. PAGE 104 F2040
ACT/RES ECO/DEV ECO/TAC COST

B61
PERLO V.,EL IMPERIALISMO NORTHEAMERICANO. USA+45 USA-45 FINAN CAP/ISM DIPLOM DOMIN CONTROL DISCRIM 19/20. PAGE 105 F2063
SOCIALIST ECO/DEV INT/TRADE ECO/TAC

B61
RUEDA B.,A STATEMENT OF THE LAWS OF COLOMBIA IN MATTERS AFFECTING BUSINESS (3RD ED.). INDUS FAM LABOR LG/CO NAT/G LEGIS TAX CONTROL MARRIAGE 20 COLOMB. PAGE 115 F2257
FINAN ECO/UNDEV LAW CONSTN

B61
SACKS S.,FINANCING GOVERNMENT IN A METROPOLITAN GOVERNMENT. USA+45 ECO/DEV R+D LOC/G GOV/REL ...BIBLIOG MUNICH 20 CLEVELAND. PAGE 115 F2269
FINAN PLAN BUDGET

B61
SAKAI R.K.,STUDIES ON ASIA, 1961. ASIA BURMA INDIA S/ASIA FINAN ECO/TAC NAT/LISM SOCISM...POLICY ANTHOL 19/20 CHINJAP. PAGE 115 F2271
ECO/UNDEV SECT

B61
SCAMMEL W.M.,INTERNATIONAL MONETARY POLICY. WOR+45 WOR-45 ACT/RES ECO/TAC LEGIT WEALTH...GEN/METH UN 20. PAGE 116 F2286
INT/ORG FINAN BAL/PAY

B61
SEPULVEDA C.,A STATEMENT OF THE LAWS OF MEXICO IN MATTERS AFFECTING BUSINESS (3RD ED.). AGRI DIST/IND EXTR/IND FINAN INDUS WORKER TAX MARRIAGE OWN ORD/FREE...BIBLIOG 20 MEXIC/AMER TREATY MIGRATION MONOPOLY. PAGE 119 F2356
CONSTN NAT/G JURID LEGIS

B61
STANLEY C.J.,LATE CH'ING FINANCE: HU KUANG-YUNG AS AN INNOVATOR. ASIA NAT/G FORCES BUDGET TAX WAR GOV/REL COST...POLICY BIOG CHARTS BIBLIOG 19. PAGE 125 F2469
FINAN ECO/TAC CIVMIL/REL ADMIN

B61
STARNER F.L.,GENERAL OBLIGATION BOND FINANCING BY LOCAL GOVERNMENTS: A SURVEY OF STATE CONTROLS. CANADA UK USA+45 CONSTN PROVS...POLICY JURID METH/COMP 20 EUROPE CALIFORNIA. PAGE 125 F2471
FINAN LOC/G GOV/REL ADJUD

B61
TRIFFIN R.,GOLD AND THE DOLLAR CRISIS: THE FUTURE OF CONVERTIBILITY. AFR USA+45 USA-45 INT/ORG PROB/SOLV BUDGET INT/TRADE PRICE...STAT CHARTS 19/20. PAGE 131 F2588
FINAN ECO/DEV ECO/TAC BAL/PAY

B61
UNIVS-NATL BUR COMM ECO RES,PUBLIC FINANCES: NEEDS, SOURCES, AND UTILIZATION. USA+45 FORCES PLAN TAX CONFER PRICE FEDERAL UTIL...ANTHOL MUNICH 20. PAGE 133 F2623
NAT/G FINAN DECISION BUDGET

B61
US CONGRESS JOINT ECO COMM,INTERNATIONAL PAYMENTS IMBALANCES AND NEED FOR STRENGTHENING INTERNATIONAL FINANCIAL ARRANGEMENTS. USA+45 WOR+45 DELIB/GP DIPLOM INT/TRADE...CHARTS 20 CONGRESS OEEC. PAGE 134 F2651
BAL/PAY INT/ORG FINAN PROB/SOLV

B61
US SENATE COMM ON FOREIGN RELS,INTERNATIONAL DEVELOPMENT AND SECURITY: HEARINGS ON BILL (2 VOLS.). ECO/UNDEV FINAN FORCES REV COST WEALTH ...CHARTS 20 AID PRESIDENT. PAGE 139 F2747
FOR/AID CIVMIL/REL ORD/FREE ECO/TAC

B61
VEIT O.,GRUNDRISS DER WAHRUNGSPOLITIK. AFR FRANCE GERMANY USSR DIPLOM INT/TRADE...NAT/COMP 19/20 SILVER. PAGE 141 F2773
FINAN POLICY ECO/TAC CAP/ISM

B61
WESTON J.F.,THE ROLE OF MERGERS IN THE GROWTH OF LARGE FIRMS. USA+45 USA-45 LEGIS CONTROL...CONCPT STAT CHARTS 19/20. PAGE 145 F2862
LG/CO CENTRAL INDUS FINAN

B61
WILSON T.,INFLATION. FINAN PLAN CAP/ISM PRICE CONTROL...CHARTS 20. PAGE 147 F2903
ECO/DEV ECO/TAC POLICY COST

B61
WRIGHT H.M.,THE "NEW IMPERIALISM": ANALYSIS OF LATE NINETEENTH-CENTURY EXPANSION. MOD/EUR WOR-45 SOCIETY FINAN ECO/TAC INT/TRADE NAT/LISM...ANTHOL BIBLIOG/A 19. PAGE 149 F2933
HIST/WRIT IDEA/COMP COLONIAL DOMIN

L61
CHENERY H.B.,"COMPARATIVE ADVANTAGE AND DEVELOPMENT POLICY." FINAN INT/TRADE RATION OPTIMAL...CHARTS METH/COMP GEN/LAWS BIBLIOG 20 RESOURCE/N. PAGE 24 F0463
ECO/UNDEV ECO/TAC PLAN EFFICIENCY

L61
JOHNSTON B.F.,"THE ROLE OF AGRICULTURE IN ECONOMIC DEVELOPMENT." FINAN PRODUC ROLE BIBLIOG. PAGE 68 F1332
AGRI ECO/UNDEV PLAN INDUS

S61
REAGAN M.O.,"THE POLITICAL STRUCTURE OF THE FEDERAL RESERVE SYSTEM." USA+45 FINAN NAT/G ADMIN 20. PAGE 110 F2163
PWR EX/STRUC EXEC LEAD

S61
VERNON R.,"A TRADE POLICY FOR THE 1960'S." COM FUT USA+45 WOR+45 ECO/DEV ECO/UNDEV FINAN TOP/EX ACT/RES...WELF/ST METH/CNCPT CONT/OBS TOT/POP 20. PAGE 141 F2781
PLAN INT/TRADE

S61
VINER J.,"ECONOMIC FOREIGN POLICY ON THE NEW FRONTIER." USA+45 ECO/UNDEV AGRI FINAN INDUS MARKET INT/ORG NAT/G FOR/AID INT/TRADE ADMIN ATTIT PWR 20 KENNEDY/JF. PAGE 141 F2786
TOP/EX ECO/TAC BAL/PAY TARIFFS

B62
ROUND TABLE ON EUROPE'S ROLE IN LATIN AMERICAN DEVELOPMENT. EUR+WWI L/A+17C PLAN BAL/PAY UTIL ROLE WEALTH...CHARTS ANTHOL 20 UN INT/AM/DEV. PAGE 1 F0017
ECO/UNDEV FINAN TEC/DEV FOR/AID

B62
ALEXANDROWICZ C.H.,WORLD ECONOMIC AGENCIES: LAW AND PRACTICE. WOR+45 DIST/IND FINAN LABOR CONSULT INT/TRADE TARIFFS REPRESENT HEALTH...JURID 20 UN GATT EEC OAS ECSC. PAGE 4 F0064
INT/LAW INT/ORG DIPLOM ADJUD

B62
ALTMAN G.T.,INVISIBLE BARRIER: THE OPTIMUM GROWTH CURVE. USA+45 USA-45 ECO/DEV PLAN PAY CONTROL DEMAND OPTIMAL PRODUC WEALTH...STAT CHARTS 20.
INDUS FINAN ECO/TAC

PAGE 4 F0080
TAX

B62
BARTELS R.,THE DEVELOPMENT OF MARKETING THOUGHT. USA+45 USA-45 FINAN ECO/TAC...CONCPT TREND. PAGE 11 F0199
ECO/DEV MARKET MGT EDU/PROP

B62
BOGARDUS J.,OUTLINE FOR THE COURSE IN BUSINESS AND ECONOMICS LITERATURE (REV. ED; PAMPHLET). USA+45 FINAN INDUS NAT/G VOL/ASSN PRESS WRITING INDEX. PAGE 16 F0305
BIBLIOG/A STAT

B62
BRANCH M.C.,THE CORPORATE PLANNING PROCESS. FINAN EX/STRUC EDU/PROP CONTROL LEAD GP/REL PERS/REL RATIONAL PERCEPT...MGT MATH PROBABIL STAT GAME. PAGE 18 F0338
PROF/ORG PLAN DECISION PERSON

B62
CHANDLER A.D.,STRATEGY AND STRUCTURE: CHAPTERS IN THE HISTORY OF THE INDUSTRIAL ENTERPRISE. USA+45 USA-45 ECO/DEV EX/STRUC ECO/TAC EXEC...DECISION 20. PAGE 23 F0446
LG/CO PLAN ADMIN FINAN

B62
CONGRES ECONOMISTES LANG FRAN,MONNAIE ET EXPANSION. AFR FRANCE PROB/SOLV BUDGET CENTRAL COST OPTIMAL PRODUC WEALTH 20. PAGE 27 F0524
FINAN PLAN EUR+WWI

B62
COPPOCK J.D.,INTERNATIONAL ECONOMIC INSTABILITY: THE EXPERIENCE AFTER WORLD WAR II. WOR+45 FINAN CAP/ISM CONTROL EFFICIENCY...CHARTS 20. PAGE 28 F0536
ECO/TAC ECOMETRIC INT/TRADE STAT

B62
DE LAVALLE H.,A STATEMENT OF THE LAWS OF PERU IN MATTERS AFFECTING BUSINESS (3RD ED.). PERU WORKER INT/TRADE INCOME ORD/FREE...INT/LAW 20. PAGE 31 F0603
CONSTN JURID FINAN TAX

B62
DIMOCK M.E.,THE NEW AMERICAN POLITICAL ECONOMY: A SYNTHESIS OF POLITICS AND ECONOMICS. USA+45 FINAN LG/CO PLAN ADMIN REGION GP/REL CENTRAL MORAL 20. PAGE 33 F0642
FEDERAL ECO/TAC NAT/G PARTIC

B62
EINZIG P.,THE HISTORY OF FOREIGN EXCHANGE. CHRIST-17C ISLAM MEDIT-7 PRE/AMER WOR+45 ECO/DEV FINAN PLAN ECO/TAC ATTIT KNOWL WEALTH...SIMUL GEN/LAWS. PAGE 37 F0714
MARKET TIME/SEQ INT/TRADE

B62
FATOUROS A.A.,GOVERNMENT GUARANTEES TO FOREIGN INVESTORS. WOR+45 ECO/UNDEV INDUS WORKER ADJUD ...NAT/COMP BIBLIOG TREATY. PAGE 39 F0767
NAT/G FINAN INT/TRADE ECO/DEV

B62
FERBER R.,RESEARCH METHODS IN ECONOMICS AND BUSINESS. AFR ECO/DEV FINAN MARKET LG/CO SML/CO CONSULT CONTROL COST...STAT METH/COMP 20. PAGE 40 F0783
ACT/RES PROB/SOLV ECO/TAC MGT

B62
FORD A.G.,THE GOLD STANDARD 1880-1914: BRITAIN AND ARGENTINA. AFR UK ECO/UNDEV INT/TRADE ADMIN GOV/REL DEMAND EFFICIENCY...STAT CHARTS 19/20 ARGEN. PAGE 42 F0823
FINAN ECO/TAC BUDGET BAL/PAY

B62
FRIEDMAN M.,CAPITALISM AND FREEDOM. USA+45 FINAN LG/CO WORKER INT/TRADE RECEIVE EDU/PROP CONTROL DISCRIM INCOME WEALTH POLICY. PAGE 44 F0859
CAP/ISM ORD/FREE NAT/G ECO/DEV

B62
FRIEDMANN W.,METHODS AND POLICIES OF PRINCIPAL DONOR COUNTRIES IN PUBLIC INTERNATIONAL DEVELOPMENT FINANCING: PRELIMINARY APPRAISAL. FRANCE GERMANY/W UK USA+45 USSR WOR+45 FINAN TEC/DEV CAP/ISM DIPLOM ECO/TAC ATTIT 20 EEC. PAGE 44 F0864
INT/ORG FOR/AID NAT/COMP ADMIN

B62
GEARY R.C.,EUROPE'S FUTURE IN FIGURES. FUT GOV/REL DEMAND PRODUC...STAT CHARTS METH/COMP ANTHOL METH 20 EUROPE. PAGE 47 F0912
FINAN ECO/DEV PREDICT WEALTH

B62
GROVE J.W.,GOVERNMENT AND INDUSTRY IN BRITAIN. UK FINAN LOC/G CONSULT DELIB/GP INT/TRADE ADMIN CONTROL...BIBLIOG 20. PAGE 52 F1008
ECO/TAC INDUS NAT/G GP/REL

B62
HAGUE D.C.,INFLATION. AFR ECO/DEV ECO/UNDEV LABOR BUDGET CAP/ISM INT/TRADE TARIFFS SOCISM 20. PAGE 53 F1036
FINAN NAT/COMP BARGAIN ECO/TAC

B62
HARRIS S.E.,THE ECONOMICS OF THE POLITICAL PARTIES. USA+45 FINAN CHIEF ACT/RES PLAN BUDGET GP/REL INGP/REL NEW/LIB...IDEA/COMP PERS/COMP 20 EISNHWR/DD KENNEDY/JF. PAGE 56 F1090
POLICY ECO/DEV NAT/G POL/PAR

B62
HOLMAN A.G.,SOME MEASURES AND INTERPRETATIONS OF EFFECTS OF US FOREIGN ENTERPRISES ON US BALANCE OF PAYMENTS. USA+45 COST INCOME WEALTH...MATH CHARTS 20. PAGE 61 F1199
BAL/PAY INT/TRADE FINAN ECO/TAC

B62
HUHNE L.H.,FINANCING ECONOMIC DEVELOPMENT THROUGH NATIONAL AND INTERNATIONAL ORGANIZATIONS (THESIS; U OF WIS.). USA+45 INT/ORG PLAN GIVE GOV/REL WEALTH 20. PAGE 63 F1235
RATION FINAN FOR/AID ECO/UNDEV

B62
INTERNATIONAL BANK RECONST DEV,THE WORLD BANK AND IDA IN ASIA. ASIA S/ASIA COM/IND DIST/IND...CHARTS 20. PAGE 65 F1272
FINAN ECO/UNDEV AGRI INDUS

B62
JOHNSON H.G.,MONEY, TRADE AND ECONOMIC GROWTH. ECO/DEV ECO/UNDEV FINAN COST WEALTH...POLICY SOC IDEA/COMP 20 KEYNES/JM MONEY. PAGE 67 F1324
PLAN BAL/PAY INT/TRADE ECO/TAC

B62
JORDAN A.A. JR.,FOREIGN AID AND THE DEFENSE OF SOUTHEAST ASIA. PAKISTAN VIETNAM/S FINAN PLAN BUDGET ECO/TAC DETER WAR ORD/FREE...POLICY DECISION CENSUS CHARTS BIBLIOG 20. PAGE 68 F1341
FOR/AID S/ASIA FORCES ECO/UNDEV

B62
KUHN T.E.,PUBLIC ENTERPRISES, PROJECT PLANNING AND ECONOMIC DEVELOPMENT (PAMPHLET). ECO/UNDEV FINAN PLAN ADMIN EFFICIENCY OWN...MGT STAT CHARTS ANTHOL 20. PAGE 74 F1447
ECO/DEV ECO/TAC LG/CO NAT/G

B62
LIPPMANN W.,WESTERN UNITY AND THE COMMON MARKET. EUR+WWI FRANCE GERMANY/W UK USA+45 ECO/DEV AGRI FINAN MARKET INT/ORG NAT/G FOR/AID AGREE WEALTH 20 EEC. PAGE 80 F1575
DIPLOM INT/TRADE VOL/ASSN

B62
LUTZ F.A.,GELD UND WAHRUNG. AFR MARKET LABOR BUDGET 20 EUROPE. PAGE 82 F1610
ECO/TAC FINAN DIPLOM POLICY

B62
LUTZ F.A.,THE PROBLEM OF INTERNATIONAL ECONOMIC EQUILIBRIUM. FINAN PRODUC WEALTH 20 MONEY. PAGE 82 F1611
DIPLOM EQUILIB BAL/PAY PROB/SOLV

B62
MICHAELY M.,CONCENTRATION IN INTERNATIONAL TRADE. ECO/DEV ECO/UNDEV PRICE INCOME...CHARTS NAT/COMP 20. PAGE 91 F1779
INT/TRADE MARKET FINAN GEOG

B62
MOUSSA P.,THE UNDERPRIVILEGED NATIONS. FINAN INT/ORG PLAN PROB/SOLV CAP/ISM GIVE TASK WEALTH ...POLICY SOC IND 20. PAGE 94 F1850
ECO/UNDEV NAT/G DIPLOM FOR/AID

B62
PAKISTAN MINISTRY OF FINANCE,FOREIGN ECONOMIC AID: A REVIEW OF FOREIGN ECONOMIC AID TO PAKISTAN. EUR+WWI PAKISTAN UK USA+45 USSR ECO/UNDEV INT/ORG DELIB/GP DIPLOM ECO/TAC...CHARTS CMN/WLTH CHINJAP. PAGE 103 F2016
FOR/AID RECEIVE WEALTH FINAN

B62
PASTOR R.S.,A STATEMENT OF THE LAWS OF PARAGUAY IN MATTERS AFFECTING BUSINESS (2ND ED.). PARAGUAY INDUS FAM LABOR LG/CO NAT/G LEGIS TAX CONTROL MARRIAGE 20. PAGE 103 F2033
FINAN ECO/UNDEV LAW CONSTN

B62
PERROUX F.,L'ECONOMIE DES JEUNES NATIONS. EUR+WWI SOUTH/AFR FINAN MARKET TEC/DEV CAP/ISM FOR/AID INT/TRADE 20. PAGE 105 F2065
INDUS ECO/UNDEV ECO/TAC DIPLOM

B62
PHELPS E.S.,THE GOAL OF ECONOMIC GROWTH: SOURCES, COSTS, BENEFITS. USA+45 USSR FINAN TAX CONTROL DEMAND WEALTH...POLICY NAT/COMP ANTHOL BIBLIOG 20. PAGE 106 F2079
ECO/TAC ECO/DEV NAT/G FUT

B62
PONCET J.,LA COLONISATION ET L'AGRICULTURE EUROPEENNES EN TUNISIE DEPUIS 1881. FRANCE WORKER TEC/DEV ECO/TAC CONTROL EFFICIENCY ROLE WEALTH 19/20 TUNIS. PAGE 107 F2101
ECO/UNDEV AGRI COLONIAL FINAN

B62
RIMALOV V.V.,ECONOMIC COOPERATION BETWEEN USSR AND UNDERDEVELOPED COUNTRIES. USSR FINAN TEC/DEV INT/TRADE DOMIN EDU/PROP COLONIAL NAT/LISM DRIVE SOVEREIGN...AUD/VIS 20. PAGE 111 F2194
FOR/AID PLAN ECO/UNDEV DIPLOM

B62
ROBINSON M.A.,AN INTRODUCTION TO ECONOMIC REASONING. FINAN MARKET LABOR DIPLOM INT/TRADE BAL/PAY INCOME PRODUC WEALTH...POLICY MGT 20. PAGE 113 F2223
ECO/TAC METH/CNCPT NAT/G

B62
ROTHBARD M.N.,THE PANIC OF 1819; REACTIONS AND POLICIES. AFR USA-45 LAW FINAN BUDGET TARIFFS DEMAND 19 DEPRESSION. PAGE 114 F2247
ECO/UNDEV POLICY ATTIT ECO/TAC

B62
SCHALLER H.G.,PUBLIC EXPENDITURE DECISIONS IN THE URBAN COMMUNITY: PREPARED FOR RESOURCES FOR THE FUTURE, INC. INDUS SERV/IND LOC/G PUB/INST PLAN PROB/SOLV BUDGET DEMAND PRODUC...CHARTS MUNICH.
FINAN DECISION

PAGE 116 F2289

B62
SCHNEIDER E.,MONEY, INCOME AND EMPLOYMENT. TAX PAY DEMAND...CHARTS BIBLIOG 20. PAGE 117 F2305
ECO/DEV FINAN INCOME

B62
SEN S.R.,THE STRATEGY FOR AGRICULTURAL DEVELOPMENT AND OTHER ESSAYS ON ECONOMIC POLICY AND PLANNING. INDIA FINAN ACT/RES TEC/DEV CAP/ISM PRICE...STAT 20. PAGE 119 F2354
ECO/UNDEV PLAN AGRI POLICY

B62
SHANNON I.,THE ECONOMIC FUNCTIONS OF GOLD. AFR FUT WOR+45 WOR-45 INT/ORG BUDGET INT/TRADE BAL/PAY DEMAND PEACE 20 MONEY. PAGE 120 F2366
FINAN PRICE ECO/DEV ECO/TAC

B62
URQUIDI C.W.,A STATEMENT OF THE LAWS OF BOLIVIA IN MATTERS AFFECTING BUSINESS (3RD ED. REV., ENLARGED). L/A+17C LAW FINAN FAM WORKER ACT/RES DIPLOM ADJUD ADMIN GP/REL 20 BOLIV OAS. PAGE 133 F2626
JURID INDUS NAT/G LEGIT

B62
US AGENCY INTERNATIONAL DEV,OPERATIONS REPORT - 1962 (PAMPHLET). AFR ASIA L/A+17C USA+45 ECO/UNDEV FINAN INT/ORG NAT/G 20 MICHIGAN. PAGE 134 F2636
FOR/AID CHARTS STAT BUDGET

B62
US CONGRESS JOINT ECO COMM,INVENTORY FLUCTUATIONS AND ECONOMIC STABILIZATION. USA+45 LG/CO...MATH CHARTS CONGRESS. PAGE 134 F2652
ECO/TAC FINAN INDUS PROB/SOLV

B62
US CONGRESS JOINT ECO COMM,FACTORS AFFECTING THE UNITED STATES BALANCE OF PAYMENTS. USA+45 DELIB/GP PLAN DIPLOM FOR/AID PRODUC WEALTH...CHARTS 20 CONGRESS OEEC. PAGE 134 F2653
BAL/PAY INT/TRADE ECO/TAC FINAN

B62
US CONGRESS JOINT ECO COMM,ECONOMIC DEVELOPMENTS IN SOUTH AMERICA. USA+45 SOCIETY FINAN NAT/G PROB/SOLV TEC/DEV INT/TRADE TAX EFFICIENCY PRODUC ATTIT ...POLICY 20 ALL/PROG CONGRESS SOUTH/AMER. PAGE 135 F2654
L/A+17C ECO/UNDEV FOR/AID DIPLOM

B62
VACCARO J.R.,A STATEMENT OF THE LAWS OF CHILE IN MATTERS AFFECTING BUSINESS (3RD ED.). CHILE AGRI FINAN FAM LABOR ECO/TAC FOR/AID TAX ADJUD CONTROL MARRIAGE STRANGE...BIBLIOG 20. PAGE 140 F2756
CONSTN LAW INDUS MGT

B62
VANEK J.,THE BALANCE OF PAYMENTS, LEVEL OF ECONOMIC ACTIVITY AND THE VALUE OF CURRENCY: THEORY AND SOME RECENT EXPERIENCES. UNIV PRICE INCOME...MATH 20 KEYNES/JM. PAGE 140 F2766
BAL/PAY ECO/TAC FINAN GEN/LAWS

B62
WRIGHT D.M.,THE KEYNESIAN SYSTEM. WOR+45 WOR-45 LABOR NAT/G CONTROL COST DEMAND EFFICIENCY...POLICY CONCPT CHARTS SIMUL 20 KEYNES/JM. PAGE 149 F2931
INCOME ECO/DEV FINAN ECO/TAC

B62
ZOOK P.D.,FOREIGN TRADE AND HUMAN CAPITAL. L/A+17C USA+45 FINAN DIPLOM ECO/TAC PRODUC...POLICY 20. PAGE 151 F2970
INT/TRADE ECO/UNDEV FOR/AID BAL/PAY

L62
DURAND-REVILLE L.,"LE REGIME DES INVESTISSEMENTS DANS LES ETATS AFRICAINS D'EXPRESSION FRANCAISE ET A MADAGASCAR." MADAGASCAR ECO/UNDEV CAP/ISM ECO/TAC WEALTH...SOC TREND CHARTS 20. PAGE 35 F0683
AFR FINAN

L62
N,"UNION INVESTMENT IN BUSINESS: A SOURCE OF UNION CONFLICT OF INTEREST." LAW NAT/G LEGIS CONTROL GP/REL INGP/REL DECISION. PAGE 96 F1884
LABOR POLICY FINAN LG/CO

L62
SCHULTZ T.W.,"INVESTMENT IN HUMAN BEINGS." ECO/DEV ECO/TAC CONFER COST INCOME PRODUC HEALTH...GEOG ANTHOL. PAGE 117 F2315
FINAN WORKER EDU/PROP SKILL

S62
BIERMAN H.,"PROBABILITY, STATISTICAL DECISION THEORY, AND ACCOUNTING." ACADEM TASK EFFICIENCY ...METH/CNCPT GEN/METH 20. PAGE 15 F0283
FINAN QUANT DECISION STAT

S62
PIQUEMAL M.,"LA COOPERATION FINANCIERE ENTRE LA FRANCE ET LES ETATS AFRICAINS ET MALGACHE." ISLAM INT/ORG TOP/EX ECO/TAC...JURID CHARTS 20. PAGE 106 F2089
AFR FINAN FRANCE MADAGASCAR

N62
BANK INTERNATIONAL SETTLEMENTS,AUSTRIA: MONETARY AND ECONOMIC SITUATION 1952-61 (PAMPHLET). AUSTRIA WORKER BUDGET INT/TRADE PRICE BAL/PAY DEMAND EFFICIENCY INCOME PRODUC...STAT 20 SILVER. PAGE 9 F0174
FINAN ECO/DEV CHARTS WEALTH

B63
BRITISH AID. UK AGRI DIST/IND INDUS SCHOOL TEC/DEV INT/TRADE COLONIAL DEMAND...TREND CHARTS 20. PAGE 1 F0018
FOR/AID ECO/UNDEV NAT/G FINAN

B63
AHN L.A.,FUNFZIG JAHRE ZWISCHEN INFLATION UND DEFLATION. AFR GERMANY DIPLOM PRICE...CONCPT 20. PAGE 3 F0053
FINAN CAP/ISM NAT/COMP ECO/TAC

B63
ALPERT P.,ECONOMIC DEVELOPMENT. WOR+45 FINAN TEC/DEV ECO/TAC PRICE GOV/REL HABITAT...GEOG BIBLIOG T 20 THIRD/WRLD. PAGE 4 F0079
ECO/DEV ECO/UNDEV INT/TRADE FOR/AID

B63
BANERJI A.K.,INDIA'S BALANCE OF PAYMENTS. INDIA NAT/G PRICE BAL/PAY COST INCOME 20. PAGE 9 F0171
INT/TRADE DIPLOM FINAN BUDGET

B63
BARBOUR V.,CAPITALISM IN AMSTERDAM IN THE 17TH CENTURY. NETHERLAND FINAN ECO/TAC...METH/COMP BIBLIOG MUNICH 16. PAGE 10 F0185
CAP/ISM INT/TRADE MARKET WEALTH

B63
BERLE A.A. JR.,THE AMERICAN ECONOMIC REPUBLIC. STRUCT FINAN MARKET LABOR NAT/G PLAN...POLICY WELF/ST DECISION. PAGE 14 F0262
CAP/ISM ECO/TAC TREND CONCPT

B63
BURNS T.G.,DEVELOPMENT BANKING BIBLIOGRAPHY (PAPER). WOR+45 SML/CO VOL/ASSN PLAN BUDGET. PAGE 20 F0391
BIBLIOG/A ECO/DEV FINAN ECO/UNDEV

B63
CENTRO ESTUDIOS MONETARIOS LAT,COOPERACION FINANCIERA EN AMERICA LATINA. L/A+17C PLAN PROB/SOLV CONTROL REGION DEMAND...POLICY ANTHOL 20. PAGE 22 F0433
ECO/UNDEV INT/TRADE MARKET FINAN

B63
CHATTERJEE I.K.,ECONOMIC DEVELOPMENT PAYMENTS DEFICIT AND PAYMENT RESTRICTION. INDIA WOR+45 FINAN INT/TRADE CONTROL BAL/PAY WEALTH...POLICY CONCPT STAT CHARTS IDEA/COMP BIBLIOG 20. PAGE 23 F0456
ECO/DEV ECO/TAC PAY GOV/REL

B63
CLARK J.J.,BUSINESS FLUCTUATIONS, GROWTH, AND ECONOMIC STABILIZATION. USA+45 FINAN INT/TRADE OPTIMAL...METH/CNCPT ANTHOL BIBLIOG 20. PAGE 25 F0479
CAP/ISM ECO/TAC EQUILIB POLICY

B63
COLUMBIA U SCHOOL OF LAW,PUBLIC INTERNATIONAL DEVELOPMENT FINANCING IN SENEGAL. SENEGAL FINAN DELIB/GP GIVE EFFICIENCY...CHARTS GOV/COMP ANTHOL 20. PAGE 26 F0511
FOR/AID PLAN RECEIVE ECO/UNDEV

B63
COSSA L.,SAGGI BIBLIOGRAFICI DI ECONOMIA POLITICA. MOD/EUR LABOR PRICE COST INCOME 18/19. PAGE 28 F0539
BIBLIOG FINAN WEALTH

B63
DE VRIES E.,SOCIAL ASPECTS OF ECONOMIC DEVELOPMENT IN LATIN AMERICA. CULTURE SOCIETY STRATA FINAN INDUS INT/ORG DELIB/GP ACT/RES ECO/TAC EDU/PROP ADMIN ATTIT SUPEGO HEALTH KNOWL ORD/FREE...SOC STAT TREND ANTHOL TOT/POP VAL/FREE. PAGE 31 F0608
L/A+17C ECO/UNDEV

B63
EL-NAGGAR S.,FOREIGN AID TO UNITED ARAB REPUBLIC. UAR USA+45 USSR AGRI FINAN INDUS FORCES EATING DEMAND...CHARTS METH/COMP 20 RESOURCE/N AID. PAGE 37 F0718
FOR/AID ECO/UNDEV RECEIVE PLAN

B63
FOX S.,ECONOMIC CONTROL AND FREE ENTERPRISE. PLAN BUDGET INT/TRADE TAX...TREND 20. PAGE 43 F0839
CONTROL FINAN ECO/TAC

B63
FRIEDMAN M.,INFLATION: CAUSES AND CURES. AFR INDIA ECO/DEV ECO/TAC INT/TRADE RATION PRICE DEMAND ...POLICY 20. PAGE 44 F0860
ECO/UNDEV PLAN FINAN EQUILIB

B63
GAMBLE S.D.,NORTH CHINA VILLAGES: SOCIAL, POLITICAL, AND ECONOMIC ACTIVITIES BEFORE 1933. ASIA CULTURE STRUCT FAM DOMIN EDU/PROP MUNICH WORSHIP 20. PAGE 46 F0891
AGRI LEAD FINAN

B63
GANGULY D.S.,PUBLIC CORPORATIONS IN A NATIONAL ECONOMY. INDIA WOR+45 FINAN INDUS TOP/EX PRICE EFFICIENCY...MGT STAT CHARTS BIBLIOG 20. PAGE 46 F0897
ECO/UNDEV LG/CO SOCISM GOV/REL

B63
GLADE W.P. JR.,THE POLITICAL ECONOMY OF MEXICO. FUT L/A+17C CULTURE SOCIETY AGRI INDUS DELIB/GP ACT/RES ECO/TAC ATTIT HEALTH ORD/FREE...STAT TIME/SEQ TREND MEXIC/AMER TOT/POP VAL/FREE 20. PAGE 48 F0928
FINAN ECO/UNDEV

B63
GOLDMAN M.I.,SOVIET MARKETING. USSR DIST/IND FINAN RATION OWN WEALTH...SOC BIBLIOG 20. PAGE 48 F0937
MARKET ECO/TAC CONTROL MARXISM

B63
GRUBEL H.G.,WORLD MONETARY REFORM: PLANS AND ISSUES. FUT WOR+45 ECO/DEV ECO/UNDEV R+D DELIB/GP CREATE ECO/TAC ATTIT RIGID/FLEX WEALTH...STAT ANTHOL VAL/FREE 20. PAGE 52 F1009 FINAN INT/ORG BAL/PAY INT/TRADE

B63
HAHN L.A.,DIE AMERIKANISCHE KONJUNKTURPOLITIK DER DOLLAR UND DIE DMARK. GERMANY/W USA+45 DIPLOM PRICE BAL/PAY COST...POLICY MONEY. PAGE 53 F1038 FINAN BUDGET ECO/TAC LABOR

B63
HAQ M.,THE STRATEGY OF ECONOMIC PLANNING. PAKISTAN AGRI FINAN INDUS NAT/G FOR/AID TAX CONTROL REGION PRODUC...POLICY CHARTS 20. PAGE 55 F1071 ECO/TAC ECO/UNDEV PLAN PROB/SOLV

B63
HAUSMAN W.H.,MANAGING ECONOMIC DEVELOPMENT IN AFRICA. AFR USA+45 LAW FINAN WORKER TEC/DEV WEALTH ...ANTHOL 20. PAGE 57 F1116 ECO/UNDEV PLAN FOR/AID MGT

B63
HIRSCHMAN A.O.,JOURNEYS TOWARD PROGRESS: STUDIES OF ECONOMIC POLICYMAKING IN LATIN AMERICA. CHILE FUT ECO/UNDEV AGRI FINAN INDUS CONSULT DELIB/GP PLAN ATTIT HEALTH ORD/FREE WEALTH...POLICY STAT VAL/FREE COLOMB 20. PAGE 60 F1177 L/A+17C ECO/TAC BRAZIL

B63
HOLLAND E.P.,EXPERIMENTS ON A SIMULATED UNDERDEVELOPED ECONOMY: DEVELOPMENT PLANS AND BALANCE-OF-PAYMENTS POLICIES. WOR+45 ECO/UNDEV FINAN PLAN ECO/TAC...MATH STAT CHARTS SIMUL VAL/FREE. PAGE 61 F1196 AFR BAL/PAY

B63
HUNTER A.,THE ECONOMICS OF AUSTRALIAN INDUSTRY. DIST/IND EXTR/IND FINAN PROC/MFG SERV/IND ACT/RES PLAN TARIFFS GP/REL INGP/REL 20 AUSTRAL. PAGE 63 F1245 INDUS ECO/DEV HABITAT GP/COMP

B63
INTERNATIONAL BANK RECONST DEV,THE WORLD BANK GROUP IN ASIA. ASIA S/ASIA INDUS TEC/DEV ECO/TAC...RECORD 20 IBRD WORLD/BANK. PAGE 65 F1273 INT/ORG DIPLOM ECO/UNDEV FINAN

B63
INTERNATIONAL MONETARY FUND,COMPENSATORY FINANCING OF EXPORT FLUCTUATIONS (PAMPHLET). WOR+45 ECO/DEV ECO/UNDEV INT/ORG WEALTH...TREND 20 IMF MONEY. PAGE 65 F1281 BAL/PAY FINAN BUDGET INT/TRADE

B63
ISSAWI C.,EGYPT IN REVOLUTION: AN ECONOMIC ANALYSIS. ISLAM STRUCT ECO/UNDEV AGRI FINAN INDUS PLAN EXEC REV NAT/LISM ATTIT RIGID/FLEX WEALTH SOCISM...STAT FOR/TRADE WORK 20. PAGE 66 F1292 NAT/G UAR

B63
KOLKO G.,THE TRIUMPH OF CONSERVATISM. USA-45 INDUS LG/CO NAT/G PWR 20 PRESIDENT CONGRESS MONOPOLY PROGRSV/M. PAGE 72 F1421 CONSERVE CAP/ISM FINAN MARKET

B63
KRAVIS I.B.,DOMESTIC INTERESTS AND INTERNATIONAL OBLIGATIONS: SAFEGUARDS IN INTERNATIONAL TRADE ORGANIZATIONS. EUR+WWI USA+45 WOR+45 FINAN DELIB/GP ATTIT RIGID/FLEX HEALTH...STAT EEC VAL/FREE OEEC ECSC 20. PAGE 73 F1435 INT/ORG ECO/TAC INT/TRADE

B63
LANGE O.,ECONOMIC DEVELOPMENT, PLANNING, AND INTERNATIONAL COOPERATION. UAR WOR+45 FINAN CAP/ISM PERS/REL 20. PAGE 75 F1476 ECO/UNDEV DIPLOM INT/TRADE PLAN

B63
LARY M.B.,PROBLEMS OF THE UNITED STATES AS WORLD TRADER AND BANKER. USA+45 NAT/G PLAN DIPLOM FOR/AID ...TREND CHARTS. PAGE 76 F1482 ECO/DEV FINAN BAL/PAY INT/TRADE

B63
LICHTHEIM G.,THE NEW EUROPE: TODAY AND TOMORROW. EUR+WWI FINAN 20 EEC EUROPE/W. PAGE 80 F1560 DIPLOM ECO/DEV INT/ORG INT/TRADE

B63
LUTZ F.A.,DAS PROBLEM DES INTERNATIONALEN WIRTSCHAFTLICHEN GLEICHGEWICHTS. DIPLOM INT/TRADE COST INCOME 20. PAGE 82 F1612 FINAN CAP/ISM ECO/TAC PRODUC

B63
MACHLUP F.,ESSAYS ON ECONOMIC SEMANTICS. UNIV ECO/DEV FINAN COST DEMAND PRODUC...POLICY STAT CHARTS BIBLIOG. PAGE 83 F1632 LING CONCPT METH

B63
MAIZELS A.,INDUSTRIAL GROWTH AND WORLD TRADE. FUT WOR+45 ECO/DEV FINAN INT/ORG PLAN TEC/DEV ECO/TAC WEALTH...MATH STAT CHARTS VAL/FREE 19/20. PAGE 84 F1642 INDUS ECO/UNDEV INT/TRADE

B63
MARCHAL J.,EXPANSION ET RECESSION. FRANCE OP/RES PROB/SOLV ROLE ORD/FREE...TREND SIMUL 20 DEPRESSION. PAGE 85 F1663 FINAN PLAN ECO/DEV

B63
MEEK R.L.,THE ECONOMICS OF PHYSIOCRACY. FRANCE UK AGRI FINAN WORKER CAP/ISM TAX DEMAND EQUILIB INCOME HABITAT...CHARTS ANTHOL 17. PAGE 89 F1744 PRODUC WEALTH MARKET

B63
MEIER G.,INTERNATIONAL TRADE AND DEVELOPMENT. FINAN BAL/PAY COST DEMAND DISCRIM EQUILIB WEALTH...POLICY ECOMETRIC MATH STAT BIBLIOG/A 20. PAGE 89 F1747 ECO/UNDEV ECO/TAC INT/TRADE IDEA/COMP

B63
MEYNAUD J.,PLANIFICATION ET POLITIQUE. FRANCE ITALY FINAN LABOR DELIB/GP LEGIS ADMIN EFFICIENCY ...MAJORIT DECISION 20. PAGE 90 F1773 PLAN ECO/TAC PROB/SOLV

B63
MINER J.,SOCIAL AND ECONOMIC FACTORS IN SPENDING FOR PUBLIC EDUCATION. USA+45 FINAN SCHOOL OPTIMAL ...POLICY DECISION REGRESS PREDICT CHARTS SIMUL 20. PAGE 92 F1801 EDU/PROP NAT/G COST ACT/RES

B63
MULLENBACH P.,CIVILIAN NUCLEAR POWER: ECONOMIC ISSUES AND POLICY FORMATION. AFR FINAN INT/ORG DELIB/GP ACT/RES ECO/TAC ATTIT SUPEGO HEALTH ORD/FREE PWR...POLICY CONCPT MATH STAT CHARTS VAL/FREE 20. PAGE 94 F1855 USA+45 ECO/DEV NUC/PWR

B63
MYRDAL G.,CHALLENGE TO AFFLUENCE. USA+45 WOR+45 FINAN INT/ORG NAT/G PLAN ECO/TAC INT/TRADE BAL/PAY ORD/FREE 20 EUROPE/W. PAGE 96 F1882 ECO/DEV WEALTH DIPLOM PRODUC

B63
OECD,FOOD AID: ITS ROLE IN ECONOMIC DEVELOPMENT. FINAN NAT/G PLAN DIPLOM GIVE TASK WEALTH ...METH/COMP METH 20. PAGE 100 F1966 ECO/UNDEV FOR/AID INT/ORG POLICY

B63
PAENSON I.,SYSTEMATIC GLOSSARY ENGLISH, FRENCH, SPANISH, RUSSIAN OF SELECTED ECONOMIC AND SOCIAL TERMS. WOR+45 FINAN LABOR INT/TRADE DEMAND PRODUC 20. PAGE 102 F2014 DICTIONARY SOC LING

B63
PREST A.R.,PUBLIC FINANCE IN UNDERDEVELOPED COUNTRIES. UK WOR+45 WOR-45 SOCIETY INT/ORG NAT/G LEGIS ACT/RES PLAN ECO/TAC ADMIN ROUTINE...CHARTS 20. PAGE 108 F2115 FINAN ECO/UNDEV NIGERIA

B63
RANGEL I.,A INFLACAO BRASILEIRA (2ND ED.). AFR BRAZIL AGRI INDUS MARKET INT/TRADE DEMAND EQUILIB ATTIT 20. PAGE 109 F2144 ECO/UNDEV FINAN PRICE TAX

B63
ROBBINS L.,POLITICS AND ECONOMICS. ECO/DEV FINAN BUDGET DIPLOM BAL/PAY ORD/FREE 20. PAGE 112 F2204 NAT/G ATTIT

B63
ROPKE W.,ECONOMICS OF THE FREE SOCIETY. FINAN INT/TRADE BAL/PAY COST DEMAND EFFICIENCY ORD/FREE WEALTH...CON/ANAL METH/COMP T 20 KEYNES/JM. PAGE 114 F2240 SOCIETY BUDGET ECO/DEV ECO/TAC

B63
ROTHBARD M.N.,AMERICA'S GREAT DEPRESSION. USA-45 NAT/G ECO/TAC LAISSEZ...POLICY IDEA/COMP 20. PAGE 114 F2248 FINAN CAP/ISM MARKET GEN/LAWS

B63
SALANT W.S.,THE UNITED STATES BALANCE OF PAYMENTS IN 1968. USA+45 ECO/DEV ECO/UNDEV INT/ORG DELIB/GP ECO/TAC...POLICY STAT SIMUL 20. PAGE 115 F2273 FUT FINAN BAL/PAY

B63
SALENT W.S.,THE UNITED STATES BALANCE OF PAYMENTS IN 1968. EUR+WWI UK USA+45 AGRI R+D LABOR FORCES PRODUC...GEOG CONCPT CHARTS 20 CHINJAP EEC. PAGE 115 F2274 BAL/PAY DEMAND FINAN INT/TRADE

B63
UN SECRETARY GENERAL,PLANNING FOR ECONOMIC DEVELOPMENT. ECO/UNDEV FINAN BUDGET INT/TRADE TARIFFS TAX ADMIN 20 UN. PAGE 132 F2603 PLAN ECO/TAC MGT NAT/COMP

B63
US AGENCY INTERNATIONAL DEV,OPERATIONS REPORT - 1963. AFR ASIA L/A+17C USA+45 ECO/UNDEV FINAN INT/ORG NAT/G. PAGE 134 F2637 FOR/AID CHARTS STAT BUDGET

B63
US BD GOVERNORS FEDL RESRV,THE FEDERAL RESERVE AND THE TREASURY. USA+45 WORKER PROB/SOLV PRICE COST DEMAND WEALTH...STAT INT CHARTS 20 FED/RESERV DEPT/TREAS. PAGE 134 F2641 FINAN GOV/REL CONTROL BUDGET

B63
US CONGRESS JOINT ECO COMM,THE UNITED STATES BALANCE OF PAYMENTS. AFR USA+45 DELIB/GP BUDGET PRICE PRODUC 20 CONGRESS MONEY. PAGE 135 F2655 BAL/PAY INT/TRADE FINAN ECO/TAC

B63
US CONGRESS JOINT ECO COMM,OUTLOOK FOR UNITED STATES BALANCE OF PAYMENTS. AFR USA+45 ECO/DEV NAT/G FORCES DIPLOM FOR/AID COST EFFICIENCY ...POLICY CONGRESS EEC. PAGE 135 F2657 BAL/PAY FINAN INT/TRADE PROB/SOLV

B63
US GOVERNMENT,REPORT TO INTER-AMERICAN ECONOMIC AND SOCIAL COUNCIL AT SECOND ANNUAL MEETING. L/A+17C USA+45 VOL/ASSN TEC/DEV DIPLOM TAX EATING EFFICIENCY HEALTH...STAT CHARTS 20 AID. PAGE 136 F2682
ECO/TAC FOR/AID FINAN PLAN

B63
US HOUSE,URBAN RENEWAL: HOUSE COMMITTEE ON BANKING AND CURRENCY. USA+45 FINAN LOC/G NAT/G NEIGH DELIB/GP TEC/DEV BUDGET GOV/REL COST...CHARTS MUNICH 20 CONGRESS URBAN/RNWL. PAGE 136 F2684
PLAN PROB/SOLV LEGIS

B63
US HOUSE COMM BANKING-CURR,RECENT CHANGES IN MONETARY POLICY AND BALANCE OF PAYMENTS PROBLEMS. USA+45 DELIB/GP PLAN DIPLOM...CHARTS 20 CONGRESS. PAGE 136 F2688
BAL/PAY FINAN ECO/TAC POLICY

B63
US SENATE COMM GOVT OPERATIONS,REPORT OF A STUDY OF US FOREIGN AID IN TEN MIDDLE EASTERN AND AFRICAN COUNTRIES. AFR ISLAM USA+45 FORCES PLAN BUDGET DIPLOM TAX DETER WEALTH...STAT CHARTS 20 CONGRESS AID MID/EAST. PAGE 138 F2728
FOR/AID EFFICIENCY ECO/TAC FINAN

B63
VELEZ GARCIA J.,DEVALUACION 1962; HISTORIA DOCUMENTAL DE UN PROCESO ECONOMICO. AFR L/A+17C USA+45 FINAN FOR/AID PRODUC WEALTH...POLICY STAT CHARTS ANTHOL 20 COLOMB. PAGE 141 F2774
ECO/UNDEV ECO/TAC PLAN NAT/G

B63
WALKER F.V.,GROWTH, EMPLOYMENT, AND THE PRICE LEVEL. USA+45 NAT/G PLAN ECO/TAC DEMAND EFFICIENCY CHARTS. PAGE 142 F2803
ECO/DEV FINAN PRICE WORKER

L63
ADERBIGDE A.,"SYMPOSIUM ON WEST AFRICA INTEGRATION." AFR EUR+WWI FUT CULTURE SOCIETY STRATA DIST/IND INDUS MARKET SERV/IND DELIB/GP PLAN TEC/DEV DOMIN EDU/PROP LEGIT COERCE ATTIT ALL/VALS ...POLICY STAT TREND CHARTS VAL/FREE. PAGE 2 F0040
FINAN ECO/TAC REGION

L63
KUZNETS S.,"QUANTITATIVE ASPECTS OF THE ECONOMIC GROWTH OF NATIONS: DISTRIBUTION OF INCOME BY SIZE." WOR+45 FINAN ACT/RES HEALTH...MATH STAT VAL/FREE 20. PAGE 74 F1454
WEALTH ECO/TAC

L63
PADELFORD N.J.,"FINANCIAL CRISIS AND THE UNITED NATIONS." FUT USSR WOR+45 LAW CONSTN FINAN INT/ORG DELIB/GP FORCES PLAN BUDGET DIPLOM COST WEALTH ...STAT CHARTS UN CONGO 20. PAGE 102 F2012
CREATE ECO/TAC

S63
APPERT K.,"BERECHTIGE VORBEHALTE DER SCHWEIZERISCHEN ZUR INTEGRATION." EUR+WWI UK MARKET SERV/IND NAT/G PLAN RIGID/FLEX OEEC 20 EEC. PAGE 6 F0108
FINAN ATTIT SWITZERLND

S63
BALOGH T.,"L'INFLUENCE DES INSTITUTIONS MONETAIRES ET COMMERCIALES SUR LA STRUCTURE ECONOMIQUE AFRICAIN." AFR EUR+WWI FUT USA+45 USA-45 WOR+45 SERV/IND INT/ORG NAT/G TOP/EX ROUTINE...INDEX EEC METH/GP 20. PAGE 9 F0168
FINAN

S63
BARTHELEMY G.,"LE NOUVEAU FRANC (CFA) ET LA BANQUE CENTRALE DES ETATS DE L'AFRIQUE DE L'OUEST." FUT STRUCT INT/ORG PLAN ATTIT ALL/VALS FOR/TRADE 20. PAGE 11 F0200
AFR FINAN

S63
BEGUIN H.,"ASPECTS STRUCTURELS DU COMMERCE EXTERIEUR DES PAYS SOUS-DEVELOPPES." FUT WOR+45 STRUCT FINAN SERV/IND POL/PAR TEC/DEV PERCEPT WEALTH FOR/TRADE 20. PAGE 12 F0229
MARKET ECO/UNDEV FOR/AID

S63
DELWERT J.,"L'ECONOMIE CAMBODGIENNE ET SON EVOLUTION ACTUELLE." FUT S/ASIA ECO/UNDEV ACT/RES PLAN WEALTH...CONCPT OBS TIME/SEQ TREND 20. PAGE 32 F0617
FINAN ATTIT CAMBODIA

S63
DOSSER D.,"TOWARD A THEORY OF INTERNATIONAL PUBLIC FINANCE." WOR+45 ECO/DEV PLAN ECO/TAC WEALTH ...WELF/ST TREND GEN/LAWS TRUE/GP METH/GP 20. PAGE 34 F0654
FINAN INT/ORG FOR/AID

S63
DUCROS B.,"MOBILISATION DES RESSOURCES PRODUCTIVES ET DEVELOPPEMENT." FUT INTELL SOCIETY COM/IND DIST/IND EXTR/IND FINAN INDUS ROUTINE WEALTH ...METH/CNCPT OBS 20. PAGE 34 F0670
ECO/UNDEV TEC/DEV

S63
LEDUC G.,"L'AIDE INTERNATIONALE AU DEVELOPPEMENT." FUT WOR+45 ECO/DEV ECO/UNDEV R+D PROF/ORG TEC/DEV ECO/TAC ROUTINE ATTIT ALL/VALS...MGT TIME/SEQ FOR/TRADE TOT/POP 20. PAGE 77 F1503
FINAN PLAN FOR/AID

S63
MATHUR P.N.,"GAINS IN ECONOMIC GROWTH FROM INTERNATIONAL TRADE." USA-45 ECO/DEV FINAN INDUS ATTIT WEALTH...MATH QUANT STAT BIOG TREND GEN/LAWS WORK 20. PAGE 87 F1704
MARKET ECO/TAC CAP/ISM INT/TRADE

S63
MIKESELL R.F.,"COMMODITY AGREEMENTS AND AID TO DEVELOPING COUNTRIES." WOR+45 WOR-45 INT/ORG ECO/TAC ATTIT WEALTH WORK FOR/TRADE 20. PAGE 91 F1782
FINAN ECO/UNDEV BAL/PAY FOR/AID

S63
PINCUS J.,"THE COST OF FOREIGN AID." WOR+45 ECO/DEV FINAN NAT/G VOL/ASSN CREATE ECO/TAC EDU/PROP WEALTH ...METH/CNCPT STAT CHARTS HYPO/EXP TOT/POP VAL/FREE 20. PAGE 106 F2087
USA+45 ECO/UNDEV FOR/AID

S63
POLYANOV N.,"THE DOLLAR'S VENTURES IN EUROPE." EUR+WWI FRANCE USA+45 ECO/DEV MARKET POL/PAR TEC/DEV ECO/TAC EDU/PROP DRIVE PWR WEALTH...MARXIST MYTH STAT TREND EEC 20. PAGE 107 F2100
FINAN PLAN BAL/PAY CAP/ISM

S63
WALKER H.,"THE INTERNATIONAL LAW OF COMMODITY AGREEMENTS." FUT WOR+45 ECO/DEV ECO/UNDEV FINAN INT/ORG NAT/G CONSULT CREATE PLAN ECO/TAC ATTIT PERCEPT...CONCPT GEN/LAWS TOT/POP GATT 20. PAGE 142 F2804
MARKET VOL/ASSN INT/LAW INT/TRADE

N63
COMMITTEE ECONOMIC DEVELOPMENT,TAXES AND TRADE: 20 YEARS OF CED POLICY (PAMPHLET). USA+45 ECO/DEV PLAN BUDGET LEAD...POLICY KENNEDY/JF PRESIDENT. PAGE 27 F0518
FINAN ECO/TAC NAT/G DELIB/GP

N63
LEDERER W.,THE BALANCE ON FOREIGN TRANSACTIONS: PROBLEMS OF DEFINITION AND MEASUREMENT (PAMPHLET). USA+45 BUDGET DIPLOM ECO/TAC PRICE GOV/REL...POLICY STAT NAT/COMP METH 20. PAGE 77 F1502
FINAN BAL/PAY INT/TRADE ECO/DEV

N63
NORTH CAROLINA U INST GOVT,COSTING URBAN DEVELOPMENT AND REDEVELOPMENT (PAMPHLET). USA+45 USA-45 NEIGH PLAN TEC/DEV TAX OWN...GEOG MUNICH 20. PAGE 98 F1934
BIBLIOG COST FINAN

N63
US AGENCY INTERNATIONAL DEV,PRINCIPLES OF FOREIGN ECONOMIC ASSISTANCE (PAMPHLET). USA+45 FINAN GP/REL BAL/PAY EFFICIENCY 20 AID. PAGE 134 F2638
FOR/AID PLAN ECO/UNDEV ATTIT

B64
THE SPECIAL COMMONWEALTH AFRICAN ASSISTANCE PLAN. AFR CANADA INDIA NIGERIA UK FINAN SCHOOL...CHARTS 20 COMMONWLTH. PAGE 1 F0019
ECO/UNDEV TREND FOR/AID ADMIN

B64
INTERNATIONAL MONETARY ARRANGEMENTS: THE PROBLEM OF CHOICE. PLAN PROB/SOLV INT/TRADE ADJUST COST EQUILIB 20. PAGE 1 F0020
POLICY DIPLOM FINAN ECO/DEV

B64
AUBREY H.G.,THE DOLLAR IN WORLD AFFAIRS. FUT USA+45 WOR+45 ECO/DEV CAP/ISM INT/TRADE BAL/PAY...CHARTS 20. PAGE 7 F0140
FINAN ECO/TAC DIPLOM POLICY

B64
BALOGH T.,THE ECONOMIC IMPACT OF MONETARY AND COMMERCIAL INSTITUTIONS OF A EUROPEAN ORIGIN IN AFRICA. AFR UAR INDUS FOR/AID COLONIAL CONTROL ...NAT/COMP 20. PAGE 9 F0169
TEC/DEV FINAN ECO/UNDEV ECO/TAC

B64
BARKSDALE H.C.,MARKETING: CHANGE AND EXCHANGE. USA+45 FINAN ACADEM TEC/DEV PRICE AUTOMAT WEALTH ...CHARTS 20. PAGE 10 F0187
MARKET ECO/DEV DEMAND TREND

B64
BASTIAT F.,ECONOMIC SOPHISMS (1845). FINAN MARKET INT/TRADE TAX EDU/PROP LAISSEZ. PAGE 11 F0207
TARIFFS INDUS ECO/TAC CAP/ISM

B64
BERRILL K.,ECONOMIC DEVELOPMENT WITH SPECIAL REFERENCE TO EAST ASIA. ASIA INDIA S/ASIA AGRI INDUS LABOR DELIB/GP PLAN INT/TRADE COST PRODUC 20 CHINJAP. PAGE 14 F0271
FINAN ECO/UNDEV INT/ORG CAP/ISM

B64
BOARMAN P.M.,GERMANY'S ECONOMIC DILEMMA - INFLATION AND THE BALANCE OF PAYMENTS. AFR GERMANY/W LABOR CAP/ISM PRICE BAL/PAY COST INCOME 20. PAGE 16 F0302
ECO/DEV FINAN INT/TRADE BUDGET

B64
BOGEN J.I.,FINANCIAL HANDBOOK (4TH ED.). UNIV LAW PLAN TAX RISK 20. PAGE 16 F0306
FINAN DICTIONARY

B64
BOWEN W.G.,ECONOMIC ASPECTS OF EDUCATION (NO. 104). EUR+WWI UK USA+45 PROF/ORG PLAN TEC/DEV PAY ...POLICY STAT 20. PAGE 17 F0329
EDU/PROP ACADEM FINAN METH/COMP

B64
BROWN C.V.,GOVERNMENT AND BANKING IN WESTERN NIGERIA. AFR NIGERIA GOV/REL GP/REL...POLICY 20. PAGE 19 F0367
ADMIN ECO/UNDEV FINAN NAT/G

B64
BROWN E.H.P.,A COURSE IN APPLIED ECONOMICS (2ND ED.). ECO/DEV FINAN MARKET WORKER INT/TRADE RATION RENT PAY PRICE BAL/PAY...DECISION T RESOURCE/N.
POLICY ECO/TAC PROB/SOLV

PAGE 19 F0368

B64
BROWN W.M.,THE EXTERNAL LIQUIDITY OF AN ADVANCED COUNTRY. CANADA FRANCE GERMANY/W SWEDEN UK USA+45 ECO/DEV DIPLOM PRICE...CONCPT STAT NAT/COMP 20. PAGE 20 F0376
FINAN INT/TRADE COST INCOME

B64
CENTRO ESTUDIOS MONETARIOS LAT,PROBLEMAS DE PAGOS EN AMERICA LATINA. L/A+17C MARKET BUDGET ECO/TAC EFFICIENCY WEALTH 20 CENTRAL/AM. PAGE 22 F0434
FINAN INT/TRADE BAL/PAY ECO/UNDEV

B64
CHANDLER A.D. JR.,GIANT ENTERPRISE: FORD, GENERAL MOTORS, AND THE AUTOMOBILE INDUSTRY; SOURCES AND READINGS. USA+45 USA-45 FINAN MARKET CREATE ADMIN ...TIME/SEQ ANTHOL 20 AUTOMOBILE. PAGE 23 F0447
LG/CO DIST/IND LABOR MGT

B64
CLAIRBORN E.L.,FORECASTING THE BALANCE OF PAYMENTS: AN EVALUATION. AFR FUT UK USA+45 WOR+45 FINAN PLAN BUDGET PAY CONTROL...STAT CHARTS BIBLIOG 20. PAGE 24 F0474
PREDICT BAL/PAY ECO/DEV ECO/TAC

B64
COLSTON RESEARCH SOCIETY,ECONOMETRIC ANALYSIS FOR NATIONAL ECONOMIC PLANNING (PROCEEDINGS OF SIXTEENTH SYMPOSIUM OF COLSTON RESEARCH SOCIETY). UK USA+45 FINAN FAM LABOR NAT/G PLAN PRICE ...METH/CNCPT TREND CHARTS TIME 20. PAGE 26 F0510
ECOMETRIC DELIB/GP ECO/TAC PROB/SOLV

B64
COLUMBIA U SCHOOL OF LAW,PUBLIC INTERNATIONAL DEVELOPMENT FINANCING IN INDIA. GERMANY/W INDIA UK USA+45 INDUS PLAN TEC/DEV DIPLOM ECO/TAC GIVE ADMIN UTIL ATTIT 20. PAGE 26 F0512
ECO/UNDEV FINAN FOR/AID INT/ORG

B64
COMMITTEE ECONOMIC DEVELOPMENT,COMMUNITY ECONOMIC DEVELOPMENT PROGRAMS. USA+45 FINAN INDUS LG/CO PROF/ORG CREATE GP/REL MUNICH NEW/YORK VERMONT PENNSYLVAN IN ARKANSAS. PAGE 27 F0519
LOC/G LABOR PLAN

B64
COMPOS R.O.,A MOEDA, O GOVERNO E O TEMPO. AFR BRAZIL WOR+45 FINAN TEC/DEV FOR/AID REGION DEMAND ...ANTHOL 20. PAGE 27 F0520
ECO/UNDEV PLAN DIPLOM INT/TRADE

B64
EINZIG P.,MONETARY POLICY: ENDS AND MEANS. AFR UK INDUS WORKER PLAN DIPLOM PRICE BAL/PAY COST WEALTH ...DECISION TIME/SEQ 20. PAGE 37 F0715
FINAN POLICY ECO/TAC BUDGET

B64
FATOUROS A.A.,CANADA'S OVERSEAS AID. CANADA WOR+45 ECO/DEV FINAN NAT/G BUDGET ECO/TAC CONFER ADMIN 20. PAGE 39 F0768
FOR/AID DIPLOM ECO/UNDEV POLICY

B64
FIRTH R.,CAPITAL, SAVING AND CREDIT IN PEASANT SOCIETIES. WOR+45 WOR-45 FAM ACT/RES ECO/TAC HEALTH ...SOC CONCPT STAT CHARTS ANTHOL CARIBBEAN VAL/FREE 20. PAGE 41 F0803
AGRI FINAN

B64
FITCH L.C.,URBAN TRANSPORTATION AND PUBLIC POLICY. FINAN NAT/G LEGIS PROB/SOLV TEC/DEV PRICE COST EFFICIENCY...DECISION STAT CHARTS METH/COMP MUNICH 20 NEWYORK/C PHILADELPH LOS/ANG CHICAGO WASHING/DC. PAGE 41 F0806
DIST/IND PLAN LOC/G

B64
GARFIELD PJ LOVEJOY WF,PUBLIC UTILITY ECONOMICS. DIST/IND FINAN MARKET ADMIN COST DEMAND ...TECHNIC JURID MUNICH 20 MONOPOLY. PAGE 46 F0906
T ECO/TAC OWN SERV/IND

B64
GOWDA K.V.,INTERNATIONAL CURRENCY PLANS AND EXPANSION OF WORLD TRADE. INT/ORG CREATE BUDGET CONTROL BAL/PAY WEALTH 20 KEYNES/JM. PAGE 50 F0969
INT/TRADE FINAN METH/COMP

B64
GUTMANN P.M.,ECONOMIC GROWTH: AN AMERICAN PROBLEM. USA+45 FINAN R+D...POLICY NAT/COMP ANTHOL BIBLIOG 20. PAGE 52 F1016
WEALTH ECO/DEV CAP/ISM ORD/FREE

B64
HAGGER A.J.,THE THEORY OF INFLATION. AFR PLAN PROB/SOLV PAY COST INCOME 20. PAGE 53 F1035
DEMAND TEC/DEV FINAN

B64
HAMBRIDGE G.,DYNAMICS OF DEVELOPMENT. AGRI FINAN INDUS LABOR INT/TRADE EDU/PROP ADMIN LEAD OWN HEALTH...ANTHOL BIBLIOG 20. PAGE 54 F1054
ECO/UNDEV ECO/TAC OP/RES ACT/RES

B64
HANSEN A.H.,BUSINESS CYCLES AND NATIONAL INCOME. USA+45 FINAN ECO/TAC COST OPTIMAL...POLICY METH 20 KEYNES/JM. PAGE 54 F1065
INCOME WEALTH PRODUC INDUS

B64
HANSEN B.,INTERNATIONAL LIQUIDITY. USA+45 INT/ORG ECO/TAC PRICE CONTROL WEALTH...POLICY 20. PAGE 54 F1068
BAL/PAY INT/TRADE DIPLOM FINAN

B64
HAZLEWOOD A.,THE ECONOMICS OF DEVELOPMENT: AN ANNOTATED LIST OF BOOKS AND ARTICLES PUBLISHED 1958-1962. AGRI FINAN INDUS LABOR NAT/G DIPLOM INT/TRADE INCOME...MGT 20. PAGE 58 F1130
BIBLIOG/A ECO/UNDEV TEC/DEV

B64
INTL INF CTR LOCAL CREDIT,GOVERNMENT MEASURES FOR THE PROMOTION OF REGIONAL ECONOMIC DEVELOPMENT. WOR+45 ECO/UNDEV FINAN INT/ORG DIPLOM ORD/FREE ...POLICY GEOG 20. PAGE 65 F1285
FOR/AID PLAN ECO/TAC REGION

B64
JACOBY N.H.,UNITED STATES MONETARY POLICY. UK USA+45 LAW NAT/G TEC/DEV TAX EQUILIB INCOME ...METH/COMP 20 FED/RESERV. PAGE 66 F1300
ECO/DEV POLICY ECO/TAC FINAN

B64
JUCKER-FLEETWOOD E.,MONEY AND FINANCE IN AFRICA. ISLAM ECO/UNDEV SERV/IND NAT/G EX/STRUC PLAN ECO/TAC ROUTINE WEALTH...MGT TOT/POP 20. PAGE 68 F1344
AFR FINAN

B64
KALDOR N.,ESSAYS ON ECONOMIC POLICY (VOL. II). CHILE GERMANY INDIA FINAN...GOV/COMP METH/COMP 20 KEYNES/JM. PAGE 69 F1348
BAL/PAY INT/TRADE METH/CNCPT ECO/UNDEV

B64
KAPLAN A.D.H.,BIG ENTERPRISE IN A COMPETITIVE SYSTEM (REV. ED.). USA+45 INDUS MARKET WORKER TEC/DEV ECO/TAC PRICE ADJUD ADMIN CONTROL...MGT CHARTS 20 MONOPOLY. PAGE 69 F1351
FINAN GP/REL NAT/G LG/CO

B64
KEMP M.C.,THE PURE THEORY OF INTERNATIONAL TRADE. WOR+45 WOR-45 ECO/DEV ECO/UNDEV DIST/IND ECO/TAC ...MATH CON/ANAL CHARTS VAL/FREE. PAGE 70 F1374
FINAN CREATE INT/TRADE

B64
KNIGHT R.,BIBLIOGRAPHY ON INCOME AND WEALTH, 1957-1960 (VOL VIII). WOR+45 ECO/DEV FINAN INT/TRADE...GOV/COMP METH/COMP. PAGE 72 F1412
BIBLIOG/A ECO/UNDEV WEALTH INCOME

B64
KUZNETS S.,POSTWAR ECONOMIC GROWTH: FOUR LECTURES. WOR+45 INDUS NAT/G WORKER TEC/DEV ECO/TAC RATION TARIFFS PRICE BAL/PAY COST DEMAND 20. PAGE 74 F1455
ECO/DEV ECO/UNDEV TREND FINAN

B64
LAURSEN K.,THE GERMAN INFLATION, 1918-23. EUR+WWI GERMANY/E GERMANY/W WOR-45 BUDGET TAX GOV/REL BAL/PAY DEMAND PEACE...POLICY CHARTS 20 WEIMAR/REP. PAGE 76 F1489
ECO/DEV FINAN REPAR ECO/TAC

B64
LEKACHMAN R.,KEYNES' GENERAL THEORY: REPORTS OF THREE DECADES. FINAN ATTIT...POLICY 20 KEYNES/JM. PAGE 77 F1517
PHIL/SCI GEN/METH IDEA/COMP

B64
LETICHE J.M.,A HISTORY OF RUSSIAN ECONOMIC THOUGHT: NINTH THROUGH EIGHTEENTH CENTURIES. RUSSIA FINAN SECT CAP/ISM DOMIN DEMAND EFFICIENCY OWN MARXISM ...TECHNIC ANTHOL BIBLIOG 9/18. PAGE 78 F1536
ECO/TAC TIME/SEQ IDEA/COMP ECO/UNDEV

B64
LI C.M.,INDUSTRIAL DEVELOPMENT IN COMMUNIST CHINA. CHINA/COM ECO/DEV ECO/UNDEV AGRI FINAN INDUS MARKET LABOR NAT/G ECO/TAC INT/TRADE EXEC ALL/VALS ...POLICY RELATIV TREND WORK TOT/POP VAL/FREE 20. PAGE 79 F1556
ASIA TEC/DEV

B64
LINDHOLM R.W.,ECONOMIC DEVELOPMENT POLICY WITH EMPHASIS ON VIET-NAM. KOREA/S PAKISTAN VIETNAM/S AGRI INDUS CONSULT DELIB/GP FOR/AID...METH 20. PAGE 80 F1571
ECO/UNDEV TAX FINAN ECO/TAC

B64
MANN B.,STATE CONSTITUTIONAL RESTRICTIONS ON LOCAL BORROWING AND PROPERTY TAXING POWERS. USA+45 CONSTN PROVS CT/SYS GOV/REL PWR...DECISION JURID CHARTS 20. PAGE 84 F1654
LOC/G TAX FINAN LAW

B64
MAZA ZAVALA D.F.,VENEZUELA; UNA ECONOMIA DEPENDIENTE. L/A+17C VENEZUELA FINAN INDUS ...ECOMETRIC STAT TREND 20. PAGE 87 F1710
ECO/UNDEV BAL/PAY INT/TRADE PRICE

B64
MEYER J.R.,INVESTMENT DECISIONS, ECONOMIC FORECASTING, AND PUBLIC POLICY. ECO/DEV ECO/TAC ...DECISION REGRESS TIME/SEQ CHARTS GP/COMP SIMUL 20. PAGE 90 F1771
FINAN PROB/SOLV PREDICT LG/CO

B64
MEZERIK A.G.,TRADE, AID AND ECONOMIC DEVELOPMENT. WOR+45 FINAN INDUS MARKET PLAN BAL/PWR BARGAIN FOR/AID TARIFFS EDU/PROP WEALTH...GP/COMP 20 UN GATT IMF IBRD. PAGE 91 F1777
ECO/TAC ECO/DEV INT/ORG INT/TRADE

B64
MITAU G.T.,INSOLUBLE PROBLEMS: CASE PROBLEMS ON THE FUNCTIONS OF STATE AND LOCAL GOVERNMENT. USA+45 AIR FINAN LABOR POL/PAR PROB/SOLV TAX RECEIVE CONTROL GP/REL 20 CASEBOOK ZONING. PAGE 92 F1807
ADJUD LOC/G PROVS

B64
MYINT H.,THE ECONOMICS OF THE DEVELOPING COUNTRIES.
ECO/UNDEV

WOR+45 AGRI PLAN COST...POLICY GEOG 20 MONEY. PAGE 96 F1878 — INT/TRADE EXTR/IND FINAN

B64
NEWCOMER H.A.,INTERNATIONAL AIDS TO OVERSEAS INVESTMENTS AND TRADE. ECO/UNDEV TARIFFS PROFIT ...BIBLIOG 20 GATT UN. PAGE 98 F1921 — INT/TRADE FINAN DIPLOM FOR/AID

B64
NOSSITER B.D.,THE MYTHMAKERS: AN ESSAY ON POWER AND WEALTH. USA+45 LG/CO NAT/G TOP/EX PROB/SOLV ADMIN GP/REL ORD/FREE 20. PAGE 99 F1937 — ECO/TAC WEALTH FINAN PLAN

B64
ODEH H.S.,THE IMPACT OF INFLATION ON THE LEVEL OF ECONOMIC ACTIVITY. AFR BRAZIL CHILE BUDGET GOV/REL COST DEMAND INCOME WEALTH...STAT METH 20 MONEY. PAGE 100 F1963 — ECOMETRIC ECO/TAC ECO/UNDEV FINAN

B64
OECD,THE FLOW OF FINANCIAL RESOURCES TO LESS DEVELOPED COUNTRIES 1956-1963. WOR+45 FINAN CAP/ISM ...POLICY STAT 20. PAGE 100 F1968 — FOR/AID BUDGET INT/ORG ECO/UNDEV

B64
RANIS G.,THE UNITED STATES AND THE DEVELOPING ECONOMIES. COM USA+45 AGRI FINAN TEC/DEV CAP/ISM ECO/TAC INT/TRADE...POLICY METH/COMP ANTHOL 20 AID. PAGE 109 F2145 — ECO/UNDEV DIPLOM FOR/AID

B64
REDLICH F.,THE GERMAN MILITARY ENTERPRISER AND HIS WORK FORCE. CHRIST-17C GERMANY ELITES SOCIETY FINAN ECO/TAC CIVMIL/REL GP/REL INGP/REL...HIST/WRIT METH/COMP 14/17. PAGE 110 F2170 — EX/STRUC FORCES PROFIT WORKER

B64
REUSS H.S.,THE CRITICAL DECADE - AN ECONOMIC POLICY FOR AMERICA AND THE FREE WORLD. AFR USA+45 FINAN POL/PAR WORKER PLAN DIPLOM ECO/TAC TARIFFS BAL/PAY ...POLICY 20 CONGRESS. PAGE 111 F2181 — FOR/AID INT/TRADE LABOR LEGIS

B64
ROBINSON R.D.,INTERNATIONAL BUSINESS POLICY. AFR INDIA L/A+17C USA+45 ELITES AGRI FOR/AID COERCE BAL/PAY...DECISION INT/LAW MGT 20. PAGE 113 F2224 — ECO/TAC DIST/IND COLONIAL FINAN

B64
SCHULTZ T.W.,TRANSFORMING TRADITIONAL AGRICULTURE. WOR+45 WOR-45 CULTURE STRATA FINAN ACT/RES ECO/TAC ATTIT KNOWL SKILL...MATH STAT TIME/SEQ GEN/LAWS VAL/FREE. PAGE 117 F2316 — AGRI ECO/UNDEV

B64
SHANNON I.,INTERNATIONAL LIQUIDITY. AFR FUT USA+45 WOR+45 ECO/TAC PRICE DEMAND WEALTH...CONCPT 20. PAGE 120 F2367 — FINAN DIPLOM BAL/PAY ECO/DEV

B64
SINGER H.W.,INTERNATIONAL DEVELOPMENT: GROWTH AND CHANGE. AFR BRAZIL L/A+17C WOR+45 CULTURE AGRI INDUS NAT/G ACT/RES ECO/TAC EDU/PROP WEALTH...GEOG CONCPT METH/CNCPT STAT HYPO/EXP WORK TOT/POP 20. PAGE 122 F2412 — FINAN ECO/UNDEV FOR/AID INT/TRADE

B64
STEWART C.F.,A BIBLIOGRAPHY OF INTERNATIONAL BUSINESS. WOR+45 FINAN LG/CO NAT/G PLAN ECO/TAC TARIFFS...DECISION MGT GP/COMP NAT/COMP 20 EEC. PAGE 126 F2484 — BIBLIOG INT/ORG OP/RES INT/TRADE

B64
STOESSINGER J.G.,FINANCING THE UNITED NATIONS SYSTEM. FUT WOR+45 CONSTN NAT/G VOL/ASSN DELIB/GP EX/STRUC ECO/TAC LEGIT CT/SYS PWR WEALTH...STAT TIME/SEQ TREND CHARTS TRUE/GP METH/GP TERR/GP VAL/FREE. PAGE 126 F2493 — FINAN INT/ORG

B64
STONIER A.W.,EXERCISES IN ECONOMICS. FINAN INDUS TEC/DEV RENT PAY EQUILIB PRODUC PROFIT...METH/COMP T. PAGE 127 F2498 — PRICE MARKET WORKER

B64
TELLADO A.,A STATEMENT OF THE LAWS OF THE DOMINICAN REPUBLIC IN MATTERS AFFECTING BUSINESS (3RD ED.). DOMIN/REP AGRI DIST/IND EXTR/IND FINAN FAM WORKER ECO/TAC TAX CT/SYS MARRIAGE OWN...BIBLIOG 20 MIGRATION. PAGE 129 F2542 — CONSTN LEGIS NAT/G INDUS

B64
THAILAND NATIONAL ECO DEV,THE NATIONAL ECONOMIC DEVELOPMENT PLAN: 1961-66: SECOND PHASE 1964-66. THAILAND AGRI FINAN BUDGET EFFICIENCY INCOME...STAT CHARTS 20. PAGE 129 F2547 — ECO/UNDEV ECO/TAC PLAN NAT/G

B64
TINBERGEN J.,CENTRAL PLANNING. COM INTELL ECO/DEV ECO/UNDEV FINAN INT/ORG PROB/SOLV ECO/TAC CONTROL EXEC ROUTINE DECISION. PAGE 130 F2576 — PLAN INDUS MGT CENTRAL

B64
URQUIDI V.L.,THE CHALLENGE OF DEVELOPMENT IN LATIN AMERICA. L/A+17C FINAN INT/ORG TEC/DEV DIPLOM INT/TRADE PRICE REGION PRODUC...CHARTS 20 ALL/PROG. PAGE 133 F2628 — ECO/UNDEV ECO/TAC NAT/G TREND

B64
US AGENCY INTERNATIONAL DEV,A.I.D. PROJECTS IN FISCAL YEAR 1963: BY COUNTRY AND FIELD OF ACTIVITY. USA+45 ECO/UNDEV ECO/TAC EDU/PROP GOV/REL...CHARTS 20 AID. PAGE 134 F2639 — FINAN FOR/AID COST STAT

B64
US CONGRESS JOINT ECO COMM,PRIVATE INVESTMENT IN LATIN AMERICA. L/A+17C USA+45 INT/ORG PROB/SOLV ECO/TAC ATTIT...INT 20 CONGRESS. PAGE 135 F2658 — FINAN ECO/UNDEV PARL/PROC LEGIS

B64
US HOUSE COMM BANKING-CURR,INTERNATIONAL DEVELOPMENT ASSOCIATION ACT AMENDMENT. CHINA/COM USA+45 USSR FINAN FORCES LEGIS DIPLOM CONFER EFFICIENCY...CHARTS GOV/COMP 20 PRESIDENT CONGRESS INTL/DEV. PAGE 136 F2689 — BAL/PAY FOR/AID RECORD ECO/TAC

B64
US HOUSE COMM GOVT OPERATIONS,US OWNED FOREIGN CURRENCIES: HEARINGS (COMMITTEE ON GOVERNMENT OPERATIONS). INDIA ECO/DEV PLAN BUDGET TAX DEMAND EFFICIENCY 20 AID CONGRESS. PAGE 137 F2699 — FINAN ECO/TAC FOR/AID OWN

B64
US SENATE COMM ON FOREIGN REL,HEARING ON BILLS RELATING TO FOREIGN ASSISTANCE. USA+45 WOR+45 ECO/UNDEV FINAN INDUS 20 UN CONGRESS. PAGE 139 F2733 — FOR/AID DIPLOM TEC/DEV INT/ORG

B64
US SENATE COMM ON JUDICIARY,HEARINGS BEFORE SUBCOMMITTEE ON ANTITRUST AND MONOPOLY: ECONOMIC CONCENTRATION VOLUMES 1-5 JULY 1964-SEPT 1966. USA+45 LAW FINAN ECO/TAC ADJUD COST EFFICIENCY PRODUC...STAT CHARTS 20 CONGRESS MONOPOLY. PAGE 140 F2749 — ECO/DEV CONTROL MARKET LG/CO

B64
WERNETTE J.P.,GOVERNMENT AND BUSINESS. LABOR CAP/ISM ECO/TAC INT/TRADE TAX ADMIN AUTOMAT NUC/PWR CIVMIL/REL DEMAND...MGT 20 MONOPOLY. PAGE 145 F2859 — NAT/G FINAN ECO/DEV CONTROL

B64
WILLIAMSON J.G.,AMERICAN GROWTH AND THE BALANCE OF PAYMENTS, 1820-1913: A STUDY OF THE LONG SWING. EUR+WWI MOD/EUR USA+45 USA-45 ECO/DEV NAT/G ECO/TAC ROUTINE ORD/FREE WEALTH...MATH STAT TIME/SEQ CHARTS SIMUL GEN/LAWS TRUE/GP METH/GP VAL/FREE 19/20. PAGE 147 F2896 — FINAN BAL/PAY

B64
WILSON T.,POLICIES FOR REGIONAL DEVELOPMENT. CANADA UK FINAN INDUS NAT/G BUDGET TAX GIVE COST ...NAT/COMP 20. PAGE 147 F2904 — REGION PLAN ECO/DEV ECO/TAC

B64
ZEBOT C.A.,THE ECONOMICS OF COMPETITIVE COEXISTENCE. CHINA/COM USSR WOR+45 FINAN MARKET FOR/AID PRICE DEMAND EQUILIB WEALTH ALL/IDEOS 20. PAGE 150 F2961 — TEC/DEV DIPLOM METH/COMP

B64
ZOBER M.,MARKETING MANAGEMENT. FINAN BUDGET EDU/PROP PRICE PRODUC ATTIT...POLICY TREND CHARTS METH/COMP EQULIB 20. PAGE 150 F2966 — ECO/DEV MGT CONTROL MARKET

L64
ARMENGALD A.,"ECONOMIE ET COEXISTENCE." COM EUR+WWI FUT USA+45 WOR+45 ECO/DEV ECO/UNDEV FINAN INT/ORG NAT/G EXEC CHOOSE ATTIT ALL/VALS...POLICY RELATIV DECISION TREND SOC/EXP WORK 20. PAGE 6 F0113 — MARKET ECO/TAC AFR CAP/ISM

L64
BHAGWATI J.,"THE PURE THEORY OF INTERNATIONAL TRADE: A SURVEY." WOR+45 ECO/DEV ECO/UNDEV FINAN MARKET PROC/MFG INT/ORG LABOR LG/CO NAT/G TEC/DEV ECO/TAC SKILL WEALTH...POLICY RELATIV MGT CONCPT NEW/IDEA MATH QUANT GEN/LAWS FOR/TRADE 20. PAGE 14 F0276 — INDUS HYPO/EXP

L64
STERN R.M.,"POLICIES FOR TRADE AND DEVELOPMENT." AFR FUT WOR+45 DIST/IND FINAN NAT/G DELIB/GP PLAN ECO/TAC ORD/FREE WEALTH...POLICY STAT TIME/SEQ CHARTS METH/GP 20. PAGE 126 F2480 — MARKET ECO/UNDEV INT/TRADE

S64
CARNEGIE ENDOWMENT INT. PEACE,"ADMINISTRATION AND BUDGET (ISSUES BEFORE THE NINETEENTH GENERAL ASSEMBLY)." WOR+45 FINAN BUDGET ECO/TAC ROUTINE COST...STAT RECORD UN. PAGE 21 F0415 — INT/ORG ADMIN

S64
DOE J.F.,"TROPICAL AFRICAN CONTRIBUTIONS TO FEDERAL FINANCE." AFR NAT/G PROVS CENTRAL RIGID/FLEX PWR WEALTH...STAT VAL/FREE 20 CMN/WLTH. PAGE 33 F0650 — FINAN ECO/TAC

S64
HUELIN D.,"ECONOMIC INTEGRATION IN LATIN AMERICAN: PROGRESS AND PROBLEMS." L/A+17C ECO/DEV AGRI DIST/IND FINAN INDUS NAT/G VOL/ASSN CONSULT DELIB/GP EX/STRUC ACT/RES PLAN TEC/DEV ECO/TAC ROUTINE BAL/PAY WEALTH FOR/TRADE WORK TERR/GP 20. PAGE 63 F1232 — MARKET ECO/UNDEV INT/TRADE

S64
NEISSER H.,"THE EXTERNAL EQUILIBRIUM OF THE UNITED STATES ECONOMY." FUT USA+45 NAT/G ACT/RES PLAN — FINAN ECO/DEV

ECO/TAC ATTIT WEALTH...METH/CNCPT GEN/METH VAL/FREE FOR/TRADE 20. PAGE 97 F1910
BAL/PAY INT/TRADE

S64
NEWLYN W.T.,"MONETARY SYSTEMS AND INTEGRATION" AFR BUDGET ADMIN FEDERAL PRODUC PROFIT UTIL...CHARTS 20 AFRICA/E. PAGE 98 F1922
ECO/UNDEV REGION METH/COMP FINAN

S64
PATEL S.J.,"THE ECONOMIC DISTANCE BETWEEN NATIONS: ITS ORIGIN, MEASUREMENT AND OUTLOOK." WOR+45 ECO/DEV AGRI FINAN INDUS MARKET LABOR NAT/G CONSULT TEC/DEV ECO/TAC WEALTH...POLICY RELATIV MGT TREND WORK 20. PAGE 103 F2035
ECO/UNDEV PLAN

S64
SCHMITT H.D.,"POLITICAL CONDITIONS FOR INTERNATIONAL CURRENCY REFORM." WOR+45 SOCIETY ECO/DEV PLAN ECO/TAC BAL/PAY ATTIT ORD/FREE WEALTH ...SOC CONCPT OBS TREND EEC VAL/FREE ECSC 20. PAGE 117 F2301
FINAN VOL/ASSN REGION

S64
TOBIN J.,"ECONOMIC GROWTH AS AN OBJECTIVE OF GOVERNMENT POLICY." FUT WOR+45 FINAN WORKER BUDGET INCOME...SOC 20. PAGE 131 F2579
ECO/DEV POLICY ECO/TAC IDEA/COMP

C64
LOUFTY A.,"LA PLANIFICATION DE L'ECONOMIE." FRANCE USSR FINAN INDUS BUDGET INCOME PRODUC...BIBLIOG 20. PAGE 82 F1604
PLAN ECO/UNDEV ECO/DEV

N64
US BOARD GOVERNORS FEDL RESRV,SELECTED BIBLIOGRAPHY ON MONETARY POLICY AND MANAGEMENT OF THE PUBLIC DEBT 1947-1960 AND 1961-1963 SUPPLEMENT (PAMPH.). USA+45 PLAN...POLICY MGT OWE 20. PAGE 134 F2642
BIBLIOG FINAN NAT/G

B65
ANALYSIS AND ASSESSMENT OF THE ECONOMIC EFFECTS: PUBLIC LAW 480 TITLE I PROGRAM TURKEY. INDIA TURKEY USA+45 AGRI NAT/G PLAN BUDGET DIPLOM COST EFFICIENCY...CHARTS 20. PAGE 1 F0021
ECO/TAC FOR/AID FINAN ECO/UNDEV

B65
ACHTERBERG E.,BERLINER HOCHFINANZ - KAISER, FURSTEN, MILLIONARE UM 1900. GERMANY NAT/G EDU/PROP PERSON...MGT MUNICH 19/20. PAGE 2 F0033
FINAN BIOG ECO/TAC

B65
ALDERSON W.,DYNAMIC MARKETING BEHAVIOR. USA+45 FINAN CREATE TEC/DEV EDU/PROP PRICE COST 20. PAGE 3 F0057
MGT MARKET ATTIT CAP/ISM

B65
ALLEN W.R.,INTERNATIONAL TRADE THEORY: HUME TO OHLIN. FINAN LABOR TARIFFS TAX PRICE DEMAND PRODUC PROFIT...ANTHOL 18/20. PAGE 4 F0074
INT/TRADE WEALTH METH/CNCPT

B65
AMERICAN ECONOMIC ASSOCIATION,INDEX OF ECONOMIC JOURNALS 1886-1965 (7 VOLS.). UK USA+45 USA-45 AGRI FINAN PLAN ECO/TAC INT/TRADE ADMIN...STAT CENSUS 19/20. PAGE 5 F0087
BIBLIOG WRITING INDUS

B65
BALDWIN D.A.,SOFT LOANS AND AMERICAN FOREIGN POLICY: 1943-1962 (THESIS). USA+45 WOR+45 FINAN NAT/G FOR/AID BAL/PAY ATTIT...POLICY METH/COMP 20 UN CONGRESS. PAGE 9 F0161
DIPLOM ECO/TAC ECO/UNDEV

B65
BARRERE A.,ECONOMIE ET INSTITUTIONS FINANCIERES (VOL. I). AFR FRANCE PLAN...BIBLIOG T 20. PAGE 10 F0194
ECO/DEV BUDGET NAT/G FINAN

B65
BLAIR T.L.V.,AFRICA: A MARKET PROFILE. AFR COM/IND DIST/IND FINAN UTIL...DECISION CHARTS BIBLIOG 20. PAGE 15 F0295
MARKET OP/RES ECO/UNDEV INDUS

B65
BREAK G.F.,FEDERAL LENDING AND ECONOMIC STABILITY. USA+45 ECO/DEV LG/CO SML/CO EQUILIB...CHARTS 20. PAGE 18 F0344
BUDGET FINAN NAT/G ECO/TAC

B65
BRENNAN M.J.,PATTERNS OF MARKET BEHAVIOR. AFR USA+45 OP/RES CAP/ISM ECO/TAC INT/TRADE...CHARTS METH/COMP ANTHOL TIME 20. PAGE 18 F0346
MARKET LABOR FINAN ECOMETRIC

B65
BROOKINGS INSTITUTION,BROOKINGS PAPERS ON PUBLIC POLICY. USA+45 ECO/UNDEV LEGIS CAP/ISM ECO/TAC TAX EDU/PROP CONTROL APPORT 20. PAGE 19 F0363
DIPLOM FOR/AID POLICY FINAN

B65
BRYCE M.D.,POLICIES AND METHODS FOR INDUSTRIAL DEVELOPMENT. WOR+45 FINAN MARKET CONSULT TARIFFS TAX COST. PAGE 20 F0379
INDUS PLAN ECO/DEV TEC/DEV

B65
CASSELL F.,GOLD OR CREDIT? THE ECONOMICS AND POLITICS OF INTERNATIONAL MONEY. AFR WOR+45 PLAN PROB/SOLV BAL/PAY SOVEREIGN WEALTH 20 OEEC. PAGE 22 F0428
FINAN INT/ORG DIPLOM ECO/TAC

B65
COPELAND M.A.,OUR FREE ENTERPRISE ECONOMY. USA+45 INDUS LABOR ADMIN CONTROL GP/REL MGT. PAGE 27 F0533
CAP/ISM PLAN FINAN ECO/DEV

B65
DELHI INSTITUTE OF ECO GROWTH,A STUDY IN THE WORKING OF THE INTENSIVE AREA SCHEME OF THE KHADI AND VILLAGE INDUSTRIES COMMISSION. INDIA AGRI FINAN DELIB/GP ECO/TAC EFFICIENCY...QU CHARTS MUNICH 20. PAGE 32 F0614
PLAN INDUS ECO/UNDEV

B65
DODDY F.S.,INTRODUCTION TO THE USE OF ECONOMIC INDICATORS. FINAN LABOR PLAN COST...ECOMETRIC INDICATOR MATH PREDICT CHARTS METH 20. PAGE 33 F0649
TEC/DEV STAT PRODUC PRICE

B65
DOWD L.P.,PRINCIPLES OF WORLD BUSINESS. SERV/IND NAT/G DIPLOM ECO/TAC TARIFFS...INT/LAW JURID 20. PAGE 34 F0657
INT/TRADE MGT FINAN MARKET

B65
FARER T.J.,FINANCING AFRICAN DEVELOPMENT. AFR ECO/TAC FOR/AID SOCISM 20. PAGE 39 F0764
ECO/UNDEV FINAN CAP/ISM PLAN

B65
GOETZ-GIREY R.,LE MOUVEMENT DES GREVES EN FRANCE. FRANCE FINAN OP/RES PROB/SOLV ECO/TAC INCOME HABITAT...STAT CHARTS 19/20. PAGE 48 F0932
LABOR WORKER GP/REL INDUS

B65
GOODSELL C.T.,ADMINISTRATION OF A REVOLUTION. PUERT/RICO ECO/UNDEV FINAN POL/PAR PROVS LEGIS PLAN BUDGET RECEIVE ADMIN COLONIAL LEAD MUNICH 20 ROOSEVLT/F. PAGE 49 F0951
EXEC SOC

B65
GORDON W.,THE POLITICAL ECONOMY OF LATIN AMERICA. L/A+17C FINAN MARKET PROB/SOLV TEC/DEV RECEIVE ADMIN WEALTH 20. PAGE 49 F0962
ECO/UNDEV INT/TRADE REGION POLICY

B65
GREENFIELD K.R.,ECONOMICS AND LIBERALISM IN THE RISORGIMENTO (REV. ED.). ITALY AGRI FINAN PROC/MFG PLAN INT/TRADE CONTROL PWR 19. PAGE 51 F0990
NAT/LISM PRESS POLICY

B65
HAEFELE E.T.,GOVERNMENT CONTROLS ON TRANSPORT. AFR RHODESIA TANZANIA DIPLOM ECO/TAC TARIFFS PRICE ADJUD CONTROL REGION EFFICIENCY...POLICY 20 CONGO. PAGE 53 F1031
ECO/UNDEV DIST/IND FINAN NAT/G

B65
HLA MYINT U.,THE ECONOMICS OF THE DEVELOPING COUNTRIES. USA+45 WOR+45 AGRI FINAN NAT/G INT/TRADE ...CLASSIF CENSUS TREND NAT/COMP SIMUL GEN/LAWS. PAGE 60 F1180
ECO/UNDEV FOR/AID GEOG

B65
IANNI O.,ESTADO E CAPITALISMO. L/A+17C FINAN TEC/DEV ECO/TAC ORD/FREE WEALTH POLICY. PAGE 64 F1258
ECO/UNDEV STRUCT INDUS NAT/G

B65
INT. BANK RECONSTR. DEVELOP.,ECONOMIC DEVELOPMENT OF KUWAIT. ISLAM KUWAIT AGRI FINAN MARKET EX/STRUC TEC/DEV ECO/TAC ADMIN WEALTH...OBS CON/ANAL CHARTS 20. PAGE 64 F1266
INDUS NAT/G

B65
INTERAMERICAN ECO AND SOC COUN,THE ALLIANCE FOR PROGRESS: ITS THIRD YEAR 1963-1964. FUT L/A+17C WOR+45 ECO/DEV INT/ORG PLAN CONTROL ADJUST...STAT ANTHOL SOC/INTEG 20 ALL/PROG. PAGE 64 F1268
ECO/UNDEV ECO/TAC FINAN FOR/AID

B65
JOHNSON H.G.,THE WORLD ECONOMY AT THE CROSSROADS. COM WOR-45 ECO/DEV AGRI INDUS INT/TRADE REGION NAT/LISM 20. PAGE 67 F1326
FINAN DIPLOM INT/ORG ECO/UNDEV

B65
JOHNSTONE A.,UNITED STATES DIRECT INVESTMENT IN FRANCE: AN INVESTIGATION OF THE FRENCH CHARGES. FRANCE USA+45 ECO/DEV INDUS LG/CO NAT/G ECO/TAC CONTROL WEALTH...BIBLIOG 20 INTERVENT. PAGE 68 F1335
FINAN DIPLOM POLICY SOVEREIGN

B65
KANTOROVICH L.V.,THE BEST USE OF ECONOMIC RESOURCES. USSR SOCIETY FINAN ACT/RES TEC/DEV ECO/TAC PRICE CONTROL COST DEMAND EFFICIENCY OPTIMAL...MGT STAT. PAGE 69 F1350
PLAN MATH DECISION

B65
KLEIN J.J.,MONEY AND THE ECONOMY. USA+45 NAT/G DIPLOM CONTROL...POLICY T 20 FED/RESERV. PAGE 72 F1406
FINAN PLAN WEALTH BAL/PAY

B65
KRAUSE W.,ECONOMIC DEVELOPMENT: THE UNDERDEVELOPED WORLD AND THE AMERICAN INTEREST. USA+45 AGRI PLAN MARXISM...CHARTS 20. PAGE 73 F1434
FOR/AID ECO/UNDEV FINAN PROB/SOLV

B65
LAZARUS S.,RESOLVING BUSINESS DISPUTES: THE POTENTIAL OF COMMERCIAL ARBITRATION. USA+45 INDUS LG/CO ACT/RES PROB/SOLV EDU/PROP CONSEN UTIL ...TREND 20. PAGE 76 F1496
FINAN DELIB/GP CONSULT ADJUD

B65
LEYS C.T.,FEDERATION IN EAST AFRICA. LAW AGRI DIST/IND FINAN INT/ORG LABOR INT/TRADE CONFER ADMIN CONTROL GP/REL...ANTHOL 20 AFRICA/E. PAGE 79 F1554
FEDERAL REGION ECO/UNDEV PLAN

B65
LUGO-MARENCO J.J.,A STATEMENT OF THE LAWS OF NICARAGUA IN MATTERS AFFECTING BUSINESS. NICARAGUA AGRI DIST/IND EXTR/IND FINAN INDUS FAM WORKER INT/TRADE TAX MARRIAGE OWN BIO/SOC 20 TREATY RESOURCE/N MIGRATION. PAGE 82 F1606
CONSTN NAT/G LEGIS JURID

B65
LYONS G.M.,AMERICA: PURPOSE AND POWER. UK USA+45 FINAN INDUS MARKET WORKER TEC/DEV DIPLOM AUTOMAT NUC/PWR WAR RACE/REL ORD/FREE 20 EEC CONGRESS SUPREME/CT CIV/RIGHTS. PAGE 82 F1617
PWR PROB/SOLV ECO/DEV TASK

B65
MACDONALD R.W.,THE LEAGUE OF ARAB STATES: A STUDY IN THE DYNAMICS OF REGIONAL ORGANIZATION. ISRAEL UAR USSR FINAN INT/ORG DELIB/GP ECO/TAC AGREE NEUTRAL ORD/FREE PWR...DECISION BIBLIOG 20 TREATY UN. PAGE 83 F1626
ISLAM REGION DIPLOM ADMIN

B65
MACESICH G.,COMMERCIAL BANKING AND REGIONAL DEVELOPMENT IN THE US, 1950-1960. USA+45 NAT/G PLAN ECO/TAC DEMAND...MGT 20 FED/RESERV SOUTH/US. PAGE 83 F1627
FINAN ECO/DEV INCOME COST

B65
MAO J.C.T.,EFFICIENCY IN PUBLIC URBAN RENEWAL EXPENDITURES THROUGH CAPITAL BUDGETING. USA+45 FINAN LOC/G NAT/G NEIGH REGION UTIL...GEOG METH/CNCPT STAT SIMUL GEN/LAWS MUNICH 20 URBAN/RNWL. PAGE 85 F1662
TEC/DEV BUDGET PROB/SOLV

B65
MARCUS E.,INTERNATIONAL TRADE AND FINANCE. EFFICIENCY EQUILIB...CHARTS METH/COMP BIBLIOG METH T 20. PAGE 85 F1664
INT/TRADE FINAN MARKET WEALTH

B65
MARGOLIS J.,THE PUBLIC ECONOMY OF URBAN COMMUNITIES. USA+45 LEGIS PROB/SOLV TAX LOBBY CHOOSE ATTIT MUNICH. PAGE 85 F1668
LOC/G DECISION FINAN

B65
MEAGHER R.F.,PUBLIC INTERNATIONAL DEVELOPMENT FINANCING IN SUDAN. SUDAN FINAN DELIB/GP GIVE ...CHARTS GOV/COMP 20. PAGE 89 F1740
FOR/AID PLAN RECEIVE ECO/UNDEV

B65
MONCRIEFF A.,SECOND THOUGHTS ON AID. WOR+45 ECO/UNDEV AGRI FINAN VOL/ASSN PLAN TEC/DEV GIVE EDU/PROP ROLE WEALTH 20. PAGE 93 F1816
FOR/AID ECO/TAC INT/ORG IDEA/COMP

B65
MORTON H.C.,BROOKINGS PAPERS ON PUBLIC POLICY. USA+45 WOR+45 INDUS ACADEM INT/ORG LOC/G PROVS EDU/PROP MUNICH. PAGE 94 F1840
FINAN ECO/DEV TOP/EX NAT/G

B65
MURUMBI J.,PROBLEMS OF ECONOMIC DEVELOPMENT IN EAST AFRICA. FINAN INDUS WORKER TEC/DEV INT/TRADE TAX DEMAND EFFICIENCY PRODUC SOCISM...TREND CHARTS 20 AFRICA/E. PAGE 95 F1869
AGRI ECO/TAC ECO/UNDEV PROC/MFG

B65
MUSHKIN S.J.,PROPERTY TAXES: THE 1970 OUTLOOK (PAMPHLET). FUT USA+45 ECO/DEV MARKET PROVS PLAN ...PROBABIL STAT CENSUS PREDICT CHARTS METH 20. PAGE 95 F1872
TAX OWN FINAN LOC/G

B65
OECD,MEDITERRANEAN REGIONAL PROJECT: TURKEY; EDUCATION AND DEVELOPMENT. FUT TURKEY SOCIETY STRATA FINAN NAT/G PROF/ORG PLAN PROB/SOLV ADMIN COST...STAT CHARTS 20 OECD. PAGE 100 F1969
EDU/PROP ACADEM SCHOOL ECO/UNDEV

B65
OECD,THE MEDITERRANEAN REGIONAL PROJECT: PORTUGAL; EDUCATION AND DEVELOPMENT. PORTUGAL SOCIETY STRATA FINAN PROF/ORG WORKER PLAN PROB/SOLV ADMIN...POLICY STAT CHARTS METH 20 OECD. PAGE 100 F1970
EDU/PROP SCHOOL ACADEM ECO/UNDEV

B65
OECD,THE MEDITERRANEAN REGIONAL PROJECT: ITALY; EDUCATION AND DEVELOPMENT. ITALY SOCIETY STRATA FINAN NAT/G PROF/ORG WORKER PLAN PROB/SOLV ADMIN ...STAT CHARTS METH 20 OECD. PAGE 100 F1971
SCHOOL EDU/PROP ECO/UNDEV ACADEM

B65
OECD,THE MEDITERRANEAN REGIONAL PROJECT: GREECE; EDUCATION AND DEVELOPMENT. FUT GREECE SOCIETY AGRI FINAN NAT/G PROF/ORG WORKER PLAN PROB/SOLV ADMIN DEMAND ATTIT 20 OECD. PAGE 100 F1972
EDU/PROP SCHOOL ACADEM ECO/UNDEV

B65
OECD,THE MEDITERRANEAN REGIONAL PROJECT: SPAIN; EDUCATION AND DEVELOPMENT. FUT SPAIN STRATA FINAN NAT/G WORKER PLAN PROB/SOLV ADMIN COST...POLICY STAT CHARTS 20 OECD. PAGE 100 F1973
ECO/UNDEV EDU/PROP ACADEM SCHOOL

B65
ONUOHA B.,THE ELEMENTS OF AFRICAN SOCIALISM. AFR FINAN SECT TEC/DEV FOR/AID GP/REL OWN LAISSEZ MARXISM...CONCPT BIBLIOG 20. PAGE 101 F1992
SOCISM ECO/UNDEV NAT/G EX/STRUC

B65
ORG FOR ECO COOP AND DEVEL,THE MEDITERRANEAN REGIONAL PROJECT: AN EXPERIMENT IN PLANNING BY SIX COUNTRIES. FUT GREECE SPAIN TURKEY YUGOSLAVIA SOCIETY FINAN NAT/G PROF/ORG EDU/PROP ADMIN REGION COST...POLICY STAT CHARTS 20 OECD. PAGE 102 F1995
PLAN ECO/UNDEV ACADEM SCHOOL

B65
ORG FOR ECO COOP AND DEVEL,THE MEDITERRANEAN REGIONAL PROJECT: YUGOSLAVIA; EDUCATION AND DEVELOPMENT. YUGOSLAVIA SOCIETY FINAN PROF/ORG PLAN ADMIN COST DEMAND MARXISM...STAT TREND CHARTS METH 20 OECD. PAGE 102 F1996
EDU/PROP ACADEM SCHOOL ECO/UNDEV

B65
PHELPS E.S.,FISCAL NEUTRALITY TOWARD ECONOMIC GROWTH. FINAN NAT/G BUDGET CAP/ISM CONTROL INCOME 20. PAGE 106 F2080
ECO/DEV POLICY ECO/TAC TAX

B65
ROOSA R.V.,MONETARY REFORM FOR THE WORLD ECONOMY. AFR EUR+WWI USA+45 WOR+45 CREATE BUDGET DIPLOM FOR/AID EQUILIB WEALTH IMF. PAGE 114 F2237
FINAN INT/ORG INT/TRADE BAL/PAY

B65
RUEFF J.,THE ROLE AND THE RULE OF GOLD: AN ARGUMENT (PAMPHLET). AFR FRANCE USA+45 WOR+45 MARKET NAT/G PLAN DIPLOM ATTIT...POLICY INT 20 DEGAULLE/C. PAGE 115 F2258
FINAN ECO/DEV INT/TRADE BAL/PAY

B65
SCITOVSKY T.,REQUIREMENTS OF AN INTERNATIONAL RESERVE SYSTEM. AFR ECO/TAC...PREDICT 20 SILVER MONEY. PAGE 118 F2330
BAL/PAY FINAN EQUILIB INT/TRADE

B65
SHARIF A.,THE BALANCE OF PAYMENTS OF PAKISTAN, 1948-1958 (THESIS, UNIVERSITY OF TORONTO). PAKISTAN FINAN INDUS FOR/AID PRICE WEALTH...TREND CHARTS 20. PAGE 120 F2368
BAL/PAY BUDGET INT/TRADE ECO/UNDEV

B65
SHEPHERD W.G.,ECONOMIC PERFORMANCE UNDER PUBLIC OWNERSHIP: BRITISH FUEL AND POWER. UK BUDGET GP/REL ...METH/CNCPT CHARTS BIBLIOG 20. PAGE 120 F2375
PROC/MFG NAT/G OWN FINAN

B65
SMERK G.M.,URBAN TRANSPORTATION; THE FEDERAL ROLE. FUT USA+45 FINAN PROB/SOLV TEC/DEV AUTOMAT GOV/REL COST...STAT BIBLIOG MUNICH 20 PUB/TRANS. PAGE 123 F2426
PLAN DIST/IND NAT/G

B65
STEWART I.G.,AFRICAN PRIMARY PRODUCTS AND INTERNATIONAL TRADE. ECO/UNDEV AGRI FINAN DIPLOM CONTROL 20. PAGE 126 F2485
AFR INT/TRADE INT/ORG

B65
TEW B.,WEALTH AND INCOME. UK BUDGET INT/TRADE PRICE BAL/PAY DEMAND...CHARTS GOV/COMP 20 AUSTRAL. PAGE 129 F2546
FINAN ECO/DEV WEALTH INCOME

B65
US BUREAU OF THE BUDGET,THE BALANCE OF PAYMENTS STATISTICS OF THE UNITED STATES: A REVIEW AND APPRAISAL. USA+45 FINAN NAT/G PROB/SOLV DIPLOM. PAGE 134 F2644
BAL/PAY STAT METH/COMP BUDGET

B65
US CONGRESS JOINT ECO COMM,GUIDELINES FOR INTERNATIONAL MONETARY REFORM. USA+45 WOR+45 DELIB/GP BAL/PAY 20 CONGRESS IMF MONEY. PAGE 135 F2659
DIPLOM FINAN PLAN INT/ORG

B65
US SENATE COMM ON JUDICIARY,ANTITRUST EXEMPTIONS FOR AGREEMENTS RELATING TO BALANCE OF PAYMENTS. FINAN ECO/TAC CONTROL WEALTH...POLICY 20 CONGRESS. PAGE 140 F2750
BAL/PAY ADJUD MARKET INT/TRADE

B65
WALTON R.E.,A BEHAVIORAL THEORY OF LABOR NEGOTIATIONS: AN ANALYSIS OF A SOCIAL INTERACTION SYSTEM. USA+45 FINAN PROB/SOLV ECO/TAC GP/REL INGP/REL...DECISION BIBLIOG. PAGE 143 F2812
SOC LABOR BARGAIN ADMIN

B65
WARD R.,BACKGROUND MATERIAL ON ECONOMIC IMPACT OF FEDERAL PROCUREMENT - 1965: FOR JOINT ECONOMIC COMMITTEE US CONGRESS. FINAN ROUTINE WEAPON CIVMIL/REL EFFICIENCY...STAT CHARTS 20 CONGRESS. PAGE 143 F2818
ECO/DEV NAT/G OWN GOV/REL

B65
WARD R.J.,INTERNATIONAL FINANCE. INT/ORG DIPLOM DEMAND INCOME...POLICY METH/COMP 20. PAGE 143 F2819
INT/TRADE ECO/TAC FINAN BAL/PAY

B65
WEAVER J.N.,THE INTERNATIONAL DEVELOPMENT ASSOCIATION: A NEW APPROACH TO FOREIGN AID. USA+45
FOR/AID INT/ORG

NAT/G OP/RES PLAN PROB/SOLV WEALTH...CHARTS BIBLIOG 20 UN. PAGE 144 F2836
ECO/UNDEV FINAN

B65
WEIDENBAUM M.L.,CONGRESS AND THE FEDERAL BUDGET. FINAN ACT/RES DOMIN CONFER EXEC UTIL PWR NEW/LIB ...CHARTS CONGRESS. PAGE 144 F2844
BUDGET LEGIS PLAN DECISION

B65
WEILER J.,L'ECONOMIE INTERNATIONALE DEPUIS 1950. WOR+45 DIPLOM TARIFFS CONFER...POLICY TREATY. PAGE 145 F2848
FINAN INT/TRADE REGION FOR/AID

B65
WHITE J.,GERMAN AID. GERMANY/W FINAN PLAN TEC/DEV INT/TRADE ADMIN ATTIT...POLICY 20. PAGE 146 F2870
FOR/AID ECO/UNDEV DIPLOM ECO/TAC

B65
WU YUAN-LI,THE ECONOMY OF COMMUNIST CHINA. CHINA/COM USSR AGRI FINAN INDUS POL/PAR WORKER PROB/SOLV INT/TRADE PRICE EATING INCOME OWN WEALTH 20. PAGE 149 F2939
ECO/TAC MARXISM PLAN EFFICIENCY

B65
WURFEL S.W.,FOREIGN ENTERPRISE IN COLOMBIA. FINAN LABOR NAT/G ECO/TAC TAX REGION 20 COLOMB. PAGE 149 F2944
ECO/UNDEV INT/TRADE JURID CAP/ISM

B65
YOUNG A.N.,CHINA'S WARTIME FINANCE AND INFLATION. ASIA AGRI INDUS NAT/G ECO/TAC CONFER PRICE WAR COST 20. PAGE 150 F2949
FINAN FOR/AID TAX BUDGET

B65
ZAWADZKI K.K.F.,THE ECONOMICS OF INFLATIONARY PROCESSES. FINAN INT/TRADE PRICE CONTROL DEMAND EQUILIB PROFIT 20. PAGE 150 F2960
ECO/DEV COST ECO/TAC CAP/ISM

L65
LOFTUS M.L.,"INTERNATIONAL MONETARY FUND, 1962-1965: A SELECTED BIBLIOGRAPHY." WOR+45 PLAN BUDGET INCOME PROFIT WEALTH. PAGE 81 F1596
BIBLIOG FINAN INT/TRADE INT/ORG

L65
WILLIAMS S.,"NEGOTIATING INVESTMENT IN EMERGING COUNTRIES." USA+45 WOR+45 INDUS MARKET NAT/G TOP/EX TEC/DEV CAP/ISM ECO/TAC ADMIN SKILL WEALTH...POLICY RELATIV MGT WORK 20. PAGE 147 F2894
FINAN ECO/UNDEV

L65
WIONCZEK M.,"LATIN AMERICA FREE TRADE ASSOCIATION." AGRI DIST/IND FINAN INDUS INT/ORG LABOR NAT/G TEC/DEV ECO/TAC HEALTH SKILL WEALTH...POLICY RELATIV MGT LAFTA 20. PAGE 148 F2909
L/A+17C MARKET REGION

S65
BALDWIN D.A.,"THE INTERNATIONAL BANK IN POLITICAL PERSPECTIVE" USA+45 TEC/DEV FOR/AID RENT GIVE COST ...IDEA/COMP GAME IBRD. PAGE 9 F0160
FINAN INT/ORG

S65
CAMPOLONGO A.,"EUROPEAN INVESTMENT BANK* ACTIVITY AND PROSPECTS." FUT ECO/UNDEV FINAN PLAN DIPLOM ...STAT EEC LOAN EIB. PAGE 21 F0410
ECO/TAC PREDICT

S65
DICKMAN A.B.,"SOUTH AFRICAN MONEY MARKET - PROGRESS AND PROBLEMS SINCE 1960." SOUTH/AFR PROB/SOLV ROLE ...PREDICT CHARTS 20. PAGE 33 F0633
FINAN PLAN MARKET

S65
HUTT W.H.,"KEYNESIAN REVISIONS" SOUTH/AFR ECO/DEV FINAN NAT/G WORKER BUDGET TAX PRICE EQUILIB WEALTH 20 KEYNES/JM. PAGE 64 F1252
ECO/TAC GEN/LAWS LOG

S65
KAUFMAN R.H.,"THE ASIAN GOLD TRADE." ASIA LAOS THAILAND UK CHARTS. PAGE 69 F1362
S/ASIA FINAN STAT INT/TRADE

N65
STUDY GP CREATE RESERVE ASSETS,REPORT TO DEPUTIES (PAMPHLET). AFR FUT PLAN CONTROL DEMAND WEALTH ...ANTHOL METH 20. PAGE 127 F2507
INT/ORG INT/TRADE FINAN BUDGET

B66
AGGARWALA R.N.,FINANCIAL COMMITTEES OF THE INDIAN PARLIAMENT: A STUDY IN PARLIAMENTARY CONTROL OVER PUBLIC EXPENDITURE. INDIA FINAN NAT/G ROLE...CHARTS METH/COMP METH 20 PARLIAMENT. PAGE 3 F0049
PARL/PROC BUDGET CONTROL DELIB/GP

B66
ALIBER R.Z.,THE FUTURE OF THE DOLLAR AS AN INTERNATIONAL CURRENCY. AFR USA+45 USA-45 ECO/DEV PRICE COST INCOME...POLICY 20. PAGE 4 F0067
FINAN DIPLOM INT/ORG INT/TRADE

B66
AMER ENTERPRISE INST FOR PUBL,INTERNATIONAL PAYMENTS PROBLEM. MARKET DIPLOM DEBATE PRICE COST INCOME 20. PAGE 4 F0082
FINAN INT/TRADE POLICY

B66
AMER ENTERPRISE INST PUB POL,SIGNIFICANT ISSUES IN ECONOMIC AID TO DEVELOPING COUNTRIES. FINAN INT/ORG NAT/G PLAN PROB/SOLV GIVE TASK WEALTH...DECISION 20. PAGE 4 F0083
ECO/UNDEV FOR/AID DIPLOM POLICY

B66
BALDWIN D.A.,ECONOMIC DEVELOPMENT AND AMERICAN FOREIGN POLICY. USA+45 FINAN LG/CO LEGIS DIPLOM GIVE 20. PAGE 9 F0163
ECO/TAC FOR/AID ECO/UNDEV POLICY

B66
BALDWIN R.E.,ECONOMIC DEVELOPMENT AND EXPORT GROWTH: A STUDY OF NORTHERN RHODESIA, 1920-1960. AFR RHODESIA AGRI EXTR/IND FINAN MARKET LABOR WORKER ECO/TAC...CONCPT NEW/IDEA MUNICH 20. PAGE 9 F0166
ECO/UNDEV TEC/DEV INT/TRADE CAP/ISM

B66
BARAN P.A.,MONOPOLY CAPITAL; AN ESSAY ON THE AMERICAN ECONOMIC AND SOCIAL ORDER. USA+45 USA-45 ECO/UNDEV FINAN MARKET PLAN DIPLOM COLONIAL RACE/REL DEMAND MARXISM...CHARTS 20. PAGE 9 F0179
LG/CO CAP/ISM PRICE CONTROL

B66
BROEKMEIJER M.W.J.,FICTION AND TRUTH ABOUT THE "DECADE OF DEVELOPMENT" WOR+45 AGRI FINAN INDUS NAT/G TEC/DEV DIPLOM EDU/PROP LEAD SKILL 20 THIRD/WRLD. PAGE 19 F0358
FOR/AID POLICY ECO/UNDEV PLAN

B66
CANNON M.,THE LAND BOOMERS....BIBLIOG/A 19 AUSTRAL. PAGE 21 F0412
FINAN HABITAT LAISSEZ ECO/UNDEV

B66
CHASE S.B. JR.,PROBLEMS IN PUBLIC EXPENDITURE ANALYSIS. DIST/IND INDUS OP/RES PLAN BUDGET RECEIVE PRICE RISK COST INCOME...CHARTS ANTHOL 20. PAGE 23 F0455
ECO/DEV FINAN NAT/G INSPECT

B66
CONAN A.R.,THE PROBLEM OF STERLING. UK WOR+45 BUDGET ECO/TAC...POLICY STAT CHARTS 20 SILVER. PAGE 27 F0521
FINAN ECO/DEV BAL/PAY DIPLOM

B66
CONGRESSIONAL QUARTERLY SERV,FEDERAL ECONOMIC POLICY 1945-1965. USA+45 FINAN NAT/G CHIEF CONSULT TAX...CHARTS 20 PRESIDENT DEBT. PAGE 27 F0526
ECO/TAC BUDGET LEGIS

B66
COOK P.W. JR.,PROBLEMS OF CORPORATE POWER. WOR+45 FINAN INDUS BARGAIN GP/REL...MGT ANTHOL. PAGE 27 F0530
ADMIN LG/CO PWR ECO/TAC

B66
DUNCAN O.,METROPOLIS AND REGION (PREPARED FOR RESOURCES FOR THE FUTURE INC., WASHINGTON, D.C.). FINAN INDUS ECO/TAC TAX...CHARTS GOV/COMP MUNICH. PAGE 35 F0677
REGION GEOG

B66
DUNCOMBE H.S.,COUNTY GOVERNMENT IN AMERICA. USA+45 FINAN ADMIN ROUTINE GOV/REL...GOV/COMP MUNICH 20. PAGE 35 F0678
LOC/G PROVS CT/SYS TOP/EX

B66
FELLNER W.,MAINTAINING AND RESTORING BALANCE IN INTERNATIONAL PAYMENTS. ECO/UNDEV MARKET ECO/TAC PRICE INCOME WEALTH...POLICY METH/COMP 20 MONEY. PAGE 40 F0781
BAL/PAY DIPLOM FINAN INT/TRADE

B66
FRANCK L.R.,LA POLITIQUE ECONOMIQUE DES ETATS-UNIS. USA+45 USA-45 FINAN INDUS CONTROL CROWD GOV/REL GP/REL...POLICY SOC CHARTS 18/20. PAGE 43 F0841
NAT/G INT/TRADE GEOG

B66
FREIDEL F.,AMERICAN ISSUES IN THE TWENTIETH CENTURY. SOCIETY FINAN ECO/TAC FOR/AID CONTROL NUC/PWR WAR RACE/REL PEACE ATTIT...ANTHOL T 20 WILSON/W ROOSEVLT/F KENNEDY/JF TRUMAN/HS. PAGE 44 F0851
DIPLOM POLICY NAT/G ORD/FREE

B66
GROSS H.,MAKE OR BUY. AFR USA+45 FINAN INDUS CREATE PRICE PRODUC 20. PAGE 51 F1006
ECO/TAC PLAN MGT COST

B66
HACKETT J.,L'ECONOMIE BRITANNIQUE: PROBLEMES ET PERSPECTIVES. FRANCE UK LABOR NAT/G EX/STRUC PROB/SOLV BAL/PAY INCOME RIGID/FLEX...MGT PHIL/SCI CHARTS MUNICH 20. PAGE 53 F1027
ECO/DEV FINAN ECO/TAC PLAN

B66
HAINES W.W.,MONEY PRICES AND POLICY. WOR+45 ECO/DEV BUDGET CONTROL INCOME...POLICY STAT CHARTS BIBLIOG T 20. PAGE 53 F1039
PRICE FINAN ECO/TAC GOV/REL

B66
HALLER H.,DAS PROBLEM DER GELDWERTSTABILITAT. MARKET LABOR INCOME PRODUC...POLICY 20. PAGE 54 F1049
PRICE COST FINAN ECO/TAC

B66
HASTINGS P.G.,THE MANAGEMENT OF BUSINESS FINANCE. ECO/DEV PLAN BUDGET CONTROL COST...DECISION CHARTS BIBLIOG T 20. PAGE 56 F1109
FINAN MGT INDUS ECO/TAC

B66
HAYER T.,FRENCH AID. AFR FRANCE AGRI FINAN BUDGET ADMIN WAR PRODUC...CHARTS 18/20 THIRD/WRLD OVRSEA/DEV. PAGE 57 F1125
TEC/DEV COLONIAL FOR/AID ECO/UNDEV

B66
HEVESY P.D.,THE UNIFICATION OF THE WORLD. FUT USA+45 WOR+45 ECO/DEV ECO/UNDEV LEGIS PROB/SOLV BAL/PWR ECO/TAC INT/TRADE PEACE. PAGE 59 F1160
DIPLOM FINAN INT/ORG

B66
HO YHI-MIN,AGRICULTURAL DEVELOPMENT OF TAIWAN: 1903-1960. FINAN WORKER EDU/PROP...STAT CHARTS BIBLIOG 20. PAGE 60 F1181
ECO/UNDEV AGRI PRODUC PLAN

B66
INARRITU A.L.,EL PATRON CAMBIO-ORO Y SUS REFORMAS. AFR L/A+17C WOR+45 PLAN PROB/SOLV BUDGET ECO/TAC INT/TRADE EFFICIENCY ORD/FREE 20 MEXIC/AMER. PAGE 64 F1262
ECO/UNDEV FINAN DIPLOM POLICY

B66
INGRAM J.C.,INTERNATIONAL ECONOMIC PROBLEMS. ECO/DEV ECO/UNDEV INDUS MARKET TEC/DEV TARIFFS BAL/PAY CENTRAL...POLICY 20 EEC. PAGE 64 F1265
INT/TRADE INT/ORG FINAN

B66
INTERNATIONAL ECO POLICY ASSN,THE UNITED STATES BALANCE OF PAYMENTS. INT/ORG NAT/G PROB/SOLV BUDGET DIPLOM INT/TRADE WEALTH 20. PAGE 65 F1274
BAL/PAY ECO/TAC POLICY FINAN

B66
JENSEN F.B.,READINGS IN INTERNATIONAL ECONOMIC RELATIONS. COM ECO/UNDEV MARKET NAT/G FOR/AID ...ANTHOL 20. PAGE 67 F1317
BAL/PAY INT/TRADE FINAN

B66
KAREFA-SMART J.,AFRICA: PROGRESS THROUGH COOPERATION. AFR FINAN TEC/DEV DIPLOM FOR/AID EDU/PROP CONFER REGION GP/REL WEALTH...HEAL SOC/INTEG 20. PAGE 69 F1356
ORD/FREE ECO/UNDEV VOL/ASSN PLAN

B66
KINDLEBERGER C.P.,EUROPE AND THE DOLLAR. AFR EUR+WWI FRANCE GERMANY/W USA+45 CONSTN INT/ORG DIPLOM INT/TRADE...ANTHOL 20. PAGE 71 F1395
BAL/PAY BUDGET FINAN ECO/DEV

B66
KIRDAR U.,THE STRUCTURE OF UNITED NATIONS ECONOMIC AID TO UNDERDEVELOPED COUNTRIES. AGRI FINAN INDUS NAT/G EX/STRUC PLAN GIVE TASK...POLICY 20 UN. PAGE 71 F1397
INT/ORG FOR/AID ECO/UNDEV ADMIN

B66
KUZNETS S.,MODERN ECONOMIC GROWTH. WOR+45 WOR-45 ECO/DEV ECO/UNDEV AGRI FINAN INDUS TEC/DEV EFFICIENCY INCOME...NAT/COMP 19/20. PAGE 74 F1456
TIME/SEQ WEALTH PRODUC

B66
LERNER E.M.,A THEORY OF FINANCIAL ANALYSIS. UNIV LG/CO COST DEMAND INCOME PROFIT...MATH STAT CHARTS SIMUL T 20. PAGE 78 F1531
CONCPT FINAN ECO/DEV OPTIMAL

B66
LEWIS W.A.,DEVELOPMENT PLANNING; THE ESSENTIALS OF ECONOMIC POLICY. USA+45 FINAN INDUS NAT/G WORKER FOR/AID INT/TRADE ADMIN ROUTINE WEALTH...CONCPT STAT. PAGE 79 F1552
PLAN ECO/DEV POLICY CREATE

B66
MADAN G.R.,ECONOMIC THINKING IN INDIA. INDIA ECO/UNDEV AGRI FINAN INDUS LABOR PLAN CAP/ISM INT/TRADE MARXISM SOCISM...POLICY 1/20. PAGE 84 F1638
ECO/TAC PHIL/SCI NAT/G POL/PAR

B66
MASON E.S.,ECONOMIC DEVELOPMENT IN INDIA AND PAKISTAN. INDIA PAKISTAN AGRI FINAN PLAN BUDGET INT/TRADE WEALTH...POLICY STAT TREND CHARTS 20. PAGE 87 F1700
NAT/COMP ECO/UNDEV ECO/TAC FOR/AID

B66
MEERHAEGHE M.,INTERNATIONAL ECONOMIC INSTITUTIONS. EUR+WWI FINAN INDUS MARKET PLAN TARIFFS BAL/PAY EQUILIB...POLICY BIBLIOG/A 20 GATT OEEC EEC IBRD EURCOALSTL. PAGE 89 F1745
ECO/TAC ECO/DEV INT/TRADE INT/ORG

B66
MIKESELL R.F.,PUBLIC INTERNATIONAL LENDING FOR DEVELOPMENT. WOR+45 WOR-45 DELIB/GP...TIME/SEQ CHARTS BIBLIOG 20. PAGE 91 F1783
INT/ORG FOR/AID ECO/UNDEV FINAN

B66
NATIONAL COUN APPLIED ECO RES,DEVELOPMENT WITHOUT AID. INDIA FINAN TEC/DEV EFFICIENCY...ANTHOL 20. PAGE 97 F1901
FOR/AID PLAN SOVEREIGN ECO/UNDEV

B66
NATIONAL INDUSTRIAL CONF BOARD,GOLD AND WORLD MONETARY PROBLEMS. AFR FUT WOR+45 PROB/SOLV BUDGET INT/TRADE PAY GOV/REL...POLICY ANTHOL 20. PAGE 97 F1902
FINAN ECO/TAC PRICE BAL/PAY

B66
NEVITT A.A.,HOUSING, TAXATION AND SUBSIDIES; A STUDY OF HOUSING IN THE UNITED KINGDOM. UK FINAN GIVE CONTROL COST INCOME...CHARTS 20. PAGE 98 F1918
PLAN TAX HABITAT RENT

B66
OHLIN G.,AID AND INDEBTEDNESS. AUSTRIA FINAN INT/ORG PLAN DIPLOM GIVE...POLICY MATH CHARTS 20. PAGE 101 F1984
FOR/AID ECO/UNDEV ADMIN WEALTH

B66
ORG FOR ECO COOP AND DEVEL,GEOGRAPHICAL DISTRIBUTION OF FINANCIAL FLOWS TO LESS DEVELOPED COUNTRIES. WOR+45 DIPLOM INT/TRADE GIVE RECEIVE REPAR REGION WEALTH...GEOG STAT CHARTS 20 OECD. PAGE 102 F1997
FINAN ECO/UNDEV INT/ORG FOR/AID

B66
PERSALL E.S.,AN ECONOMETRIC STUDY OF FINANCIAL MARKETS. COMPUTER PROB/SOLV TEC/DEV...MATH STAT CHARTS METH/COMP BIBLIOG 20. PAGE 105 F2066
ECOMETRIC FINAN MARKET METH

B66
PIQUET H.S.,THE US BALANCE OF PAYMENTS AND INTERNATIONAL MONETARY RESERVES. AFR USA+45 PROB/SOLV INT/TRADE GOV/REL EQUILIB...POLICY STAT CHARTS 20. PAGE 106 F2090
BAL/PAY DIPLOM FINAN ECO/TAC

B66
POLK J.,U S PRODUCTION ABROAD AND THE BALANCE OF PAYMENTS* A SURVEY OF CORPORATE INVESTMENT EXPERIENCE. USA+45 SERV/IND NAT/G OP/RES COST PROFIT ATTIT...ECOMETRIC STAT INT QU GEN/METH. PAGE 107 F2096
BAL/PAY FINAN INT/TRADE INDUS

B66
REDFORD E.S.,THE ROLE OF GOVERNMENT IN THE AMERICAN ECONOMY. USA+45 USA-45 FINAN INDUS LG/CO PROB/SOLV ADMIN INGP/REL INCOME PRODUC 18/20. PAGE 110 F2169
NAT/G ECO/DEV CAP/ISM ECO/TAC

B66
ROBERTSON D.J.,THE BRITISH BALANCE OF PAYMENTS. UK WOR+45 INDUS BUDGET TAX ADJUST...CHARTS ANTHOL 20. PAGE 112 F2213
FINAN BAL/PAY ECO/DEV INT/TRADE

B66
ROBINSON E.A.,THE ECONOMICS OF EDUCATION. WOR+45 CULTURE ECO/UNDEV FINAN SCHOOL DIPLOM PRICE COST DEMAND...CHARTS METH/COMP 20. PAGE 112 F2216
EDU/PROP ADJUST CONFER

B66
SASTRI K.V.S.,FEDERAL-STATE FISCAL RELATIONS IN INDIA: A STUDY OF THE FINANCE COMMISSION AND TECHNIQUES OF FINANCIAL ADJUSTMENT. INDIA PROVS DELIB/GP GOV/REL FEDERAL...MATH CHARTS 20. PAGE 116 F2283
TAX BUDGET FINAN NAT/G

B66
SCHNEIDER E.,WIRTSCHAFTSKREISLAUF UND WIRTSCHAFTSWACHSTUM. ECO/DEV MARKET...CONCPT 20 MONEY. PAGE 117 F2306
ECO/TAC FINAN INCOME COST

B66
SEWELL J.P.,FUNCTIONALISM AND WORLD POLITICS* A STUDY BASED ON UNITED NATIONS PROGRAMS FINANCING ECONOMICAL DEVELOPMENT. ECO/UNDEV FINAN PROB/SOLV DIPLOM ECO/TAC FEEDBACK REGION ADJUST ATTIT UN IBRD INTL/FINAN INTL/DEV UNSF. PAGE 120 F2360
TASK INT/ORG IDEA/COMP GEN/LAWS

B66
SHULTZ G.P.,GUIDELINES, INFORMAL CONTROLS, AND THE MARKET PLACE: POLICY CHOICES IN A FULL EMPLOYMENT ECONOMY. UK ECO/DEV LABOR INT/TRADE CONFER GOV/REL BAL/PAY DEMAND INCOME...POLICY ANTHOL 20 PRESIDENT. PAGE 121 F2392
ECO/TAC CONTROL FINAN RATION

B66
SMITH H.E.,READINGS IN ECONOMIC DEVELOPMENT AND ADMINISTRATION IN TANZANIA. TANZANIA FINAN INDUS LABOR NAT/G PLAN PROB/SOLV INT/TRADE COLONIAL REGION...ANTHOL BIBLIOG 20 AFRICA/E. PAGE 123 F2431
TEC/DEV ADMIN GOV/REL

B66
SOMMERFELD R.M.,TAX REFORM AND THE ALLIANCE FOR PROGRESS. USA+45 ECO/DEV ECO/UNDEV FINAN NAT/G INCOME ORD/FREE WEALTH...STAT CHARTS 20 ALL/PROG. PAGE 124 F2442
TAX INT/ORG L/A+17C FOR/AID

B66
SPICER K.,A SAMARITAN STATE? AFR CANADA INDIA PAKISTAN UK USA+45 FINAN INDUS PRODUC...CHARTS 20 NATO. PAGE 124 F2455
DIPLOM FOR/AID ECO/DEV ADMIN

B66
TRIFFIN R.,THE WORLD MONEY MAZE. AFR INT/ORG ECO/TAC PRICE OPTIMAL WEALTH...METH/COMP 20 EEC OEEC SILVER. PAGE 131 F2589
BAL/PAY FINAN INT/TRADE DIPLOM

B66
TRIFFIN R.,THE BALANCE OF PAYMENTS AND THE FOREIGN INVESTMENT POSITION OF THE UNITED STATES. AFR USA+45 INT/ORG INT/TRADE PRICE CONTROL...POLICY 20. PAGE 131 F2590
BAL/PAY DIPLOM FINAN ECO/TAC

B66
US CONGRESS JOINT ECO COMM,NEW APPROACH TO UNITED STATES INTERNATIONAL ECONOMIC POLICY. USA+45 WOR+45 CHIEF DELIB/GP CONFER...CHARTS 20 CONGRESS MONEY. PAGE 135 F2660
DIPLOM ECO/TAC BAL/PAY FINAN

B66
US HOUSE COMM BANKING CURRENCY,HEARINGS BEFORE
FINAN

HOUSE COMMITTEE ON BANKING AND CURRENCY: SALE OF SBA LOAN POOL PARTICIPATIONS. USA+45 LAW LEGIS ECO/TAC RATION 20 CONGRESS. PAGE 136 F2687
SML/CO ADJUD GOV/REL

B66
US SENATE COMM ON FOREIGN REL,ASIAN DEVELOPMENT BANK ACT. USA+45 LAW DIPLOM...CHARTS 20 BLACK/EUG S/EASTASIA. PAGE 139 F2736
FOR/AID FINAN ECO/UNDEV S/ASIA

B66
WALTON S.D.,AMERICAN BUSINESS AND ITS ENVIRONMENT. USA+45 LAW CONSTN FINAN MARKET LOC/G EX/STRUC CT/SYS COST PRODUC...STAT 20. PAGE 143 F2813
PRICE PROFIT

B66
WECHSBERG J.,THE MERCHANT BANKERS. EUR+WWI MOD/EUR CONTROL...BIOG GP/COMP PERS/COMP 16/20. PAGE 144 F2842
FINAN PWR WEALTH FAM

B66
WESTON J.F.,THE SCOPE AND METHODOLOGY OF FINANCE. PLAN TEC/DEV CONTROL EFFICIENCY INCOME UTIL...MGT CONCPT MATH STAT TREND METH 20. PAGE 145 F2863
FINAN ECO/DEV POLICY PRICE

B66
YEAGER L.B.,INTERNATIONAL MONETARY RELATIONS: THEORY, HISTORY, AND POLICY. WOR+45 WOR-45 INT/TRADE BAL/PAY...NAT/COMP 18/20 MONEY. PAGE 150 F2947
FINAN DIPLOM ECO/TAC IDEA/COMP

B66
ZINKIN T.,CHALLENGES IN INDIA. INDIA PAKISTAN LAW AGRI FINAN INDUS TOP/EX TEC/DEV CONTROL ROUTINE ORD/FREE PWR 20 NEHRU/J SHASTRI/LB CIVIL/SERV. PAGE 150 F2964
NAT/G ECO/TAC POLICY ADMIN

B66
ZISCHKA A.,WAR ES EIN WUNDER? GERMANY/W ECO/DEV FINAN LG/CO BARGAIN CAP/ISM FOR/AID RATION 20 MARSHL/PLN. PAGE 150 F2965
ECO/TAC INT/TRADE INDUS WAR

L66
AFRICAN BIBLIOGRAPHIC CENTER,"AFRICAN ECONOMIC AFFAIRS: A SELECT BIBLIOGRAPHICAL SURVEY, 1965-1966." AFR FINAN INDUS INT/ORG LABOR PLAN BUDGET DIPLOM INT/TRADE ADMIN EFFICIENCY WEALTH 20. PAGE 3 F0046
BIBLIOG ECO/UNDEV TEC/DEV FOR/AID

L66
AFRICAN BIBLIOGRAPHIC CENTER,"AFRICAN ECONOMIC AFFAIRS: A SELECT BIBLIOGRAPHICAL SURVEY, 1965-1966; SUPPLEMENTS NUMBERS 1-3." AFR FINAN INDUS LABOR PLAN BUDGET CAP/ISM DIPLOM INT/TRADE ADMIN...GEOG 20. PAGE 3 F0047
BIBLIOG/A ECO/UNDEV FOR/AID TEC/DEV

L66
AMERICAN ECONOMIC REVIEW,"SIXTY-THIRD LIST OF DOCTORAL DISSERTATIONS IN POLITICAL ECONOMY IN AMERICAN UNIVERSITIES AND COLLEGES." ECO/DEV AGRI FINAN LABOR WORKER PLAN BUDGET INT/TRADE ADMIN DEMAND...MGT STAT 20. PAGE 5 F0088
BIBLIOG/A CONCPT ACADEM

S66
ANGELL J.W.,"THE LONGER RUN PROSPECTS FOR THE US BALANCE OF PAYMENTS." USA+45 DIPLOM FOR/AID RATION ORD/FREE WEALTH...IDEA/COMP GATT. PAGE 6 F0104
BAL/PAY ECO/TAC INT/TRADE FINAN

S66
DAVIS O.A.,"A THEORY OF THE BUDGETARY PROCESS." ECO/DEV FINAN LEGIS PROB/SOLV GOV/REL...ECOMETRIC METH/CNCPT STAT CONT/OBS TREND METH/COMP SIMUL 20 CONGRESS. PAGE 30 F0592
DECISION NAT/G BUDGET EFFICIENCY

S66
ERB GF,"THE UNITED NATIONS CONFERENCE ON TRADE AND DEVELOPMENT (UNCTAD): A SELECTED CURRENT READING LIST." FINAN FOR/AID CONFER 20 UN. PAGE 38 F0742
BIBLIOG/A INT/TRADE ECO/UNDEV INT/ORG

S66
FROMM G.,"RECENT MONETARY POLICY: AN ECONOMETRIC VIEW" USA+45 ECO/DEV INDUS PAY PRICE PRODUC ORD/FREE WEALTH...STAT 20 FED/RESERV. PAGE 45 F0869
ECOMETRIC FINAN POLICY SIMUL

S66
JACOBS P.,"RE-RADICALIZING THE DE-RADICALIZED." USA+45 SOCIETY STRUCT FINAN PLAN PROB/SOLV CAP/ISM WEALTH CONSERVE NEW/LIB 20. PAGE 66 F1297
NAT/G POLICY MARXIST ADMIN

S66
LANGLEY D.,"POSTSCRIPT ON THE COLONIZATION OF THE INTERNATIONAL TRADE UNION MOVEMENT" USA+45 ELITES FINAN DOMIN LEGIT ADMIN PWR...SOCIALIST 20 AFL/CIO CIA LOVESTN/J. PAGE 75 F1479
INT/TRADE LABOR NAT/G CONTROL

S66
NEWLYN W.T.,"MONEY MARKETS IN EAST AFRICA." AFR TANZANIA UGANDA UK DIPLOM CENTRAL 20. PAGE 98 F1923
FINAN WEALTH BAL/PAY ECO/UNDEV

S66
VENTRE F.T.,"LOCAL INITIATIVES IN URBAN INDUSTRIAL DEVELOPMENT." FINAN SERV/IND TOP/EX PLAN BUDGET RENT TAX...GP/COMP MUNICH 20. PAGE 141 F2777
ECO/TAC LOC/G INDUS

N66
EOMMITTEE ECONOMIC DEVELOPMENT,THE DOLLAR AND THE WORLD MONETARY SYSTEM: A STATEMENT ON NATIONAL POLICY (PAMPHLET). AFR USA+45 NAT/G PLAN PROB/SOLV BUDGET ECO/TAC FOR/AID INCOME...POLICY 20 EUROPE. PAGE 38 F0740
FINAN BAL/PAY DIPLOM ECO/DEV

N66
OECD,THE BALANCE OF PAYMENTS ADJUSTMENT PROCESS (PAMPHLET). EUR+WWI ECO/DEV FINAN CONSULT PLAN PROB/SOLV BUDGET CAP/ISM INT/TRADE PRICE CONTROL EQUILIB 20. PAGE 101 F1975
BAL/PAY ECO/TAC DIPLOM INT/ORG

N66
US ADVISORY COMN INTERGOV REL,CATALOGS AND OTHER INFORMATION SOURCES ON FEDERAL AND STATE AID PROGRAMS: A SECTED BIBLIOGRAPHY (PAPER). USA+45 LAW LOC/G NAT/G PROVS VOL/ASSN TEC/DEV ADMIN HEALTH ...WELF/ST SOC/WK MUNICH. PAGE 134 F2635
BIBLIOG/A GOV/REL FINAN ECO/DEV

B67
ADLER J.H.,CAPITAL MOVEMENTS AND ECONOMIC DEVELOPMENT. WOR+45 FINAN NAT/G BARGAIN ECO/TAC FOR/AID INT/TRADE ANTHOL. PAGE 2 F0042
DIPLOM ECO/DEV ECO/UNDEV

B67
BLAUG M.,ECONOMICS OF EDUCATION: A SELECTED ANNOTATED BIBLIOGRAPHY. EUR+WWI INTELL ECO/DEV ECO/UNDEV ACADEM INT/ORG NAT/G CREATE ADMIN EFFICIENCY ROLE PREDICT. PAGE 16 F0298
BIBLIOG/A EDU/PROP FINAN PLAN

B67
BREAK G.F.,INTERGOVERNMENTAL FISCAL RELATIONS IN THE UNITED STATES. USA+45 USA-45 DELIB/GP PLAN BUDGET TAX GOV/REL CENTRAL...TREND CHARTS MUNICH. PAGE 18 F0345
LOC/G NAT/G PROVS FINAN

B67
BRIEFS H.W.,REGAINING BALANCE IN A HIGH EMPLOYMENT ECONOMY: UNRESOLVED ISSUES FOR 1967 AND BEYOND. USA+45 NAT/G PLAN PROB/SOLV FOR/AID...CHARTS 20. PAGE 18 F0350
ECO/DEV FINAN BAL/PAY BUDGET

B67
CARNEY D.,PATTERNS AND MECHANICS OF ECONOMIC GROWTH: A GENERAL THEORETICAL APPROACH. WOR+45 OP/RES INCOME...MATH TREND CHARTS 20. PAGE 21 F0416
PLAN ECO/DEV FINAN

B67
CLEGERN W.M.,BRITISH HONDURAS: COLONIAL DEAD END, 1859-1900. HONDURAS AGRI FINAN PROB/SOLV INT/TRADE PWR WEALTH...BIBLIOG/A 19. PAGE 25 F0487
COLONIAL POLICY ECO/UNDEV DOMIN

B67
CLEMENT M.O.,THEORETICAL ISSUES IN INTERNATIONAL ECONOMICS. WOR+45 PLAN PROB/SOLV TEC/DEV ...ECOMETRIC METH/CNCPT MATH BIBLIOG T MONEY. PAGE 25 F0489
INT/TRADE FINAN CREATE BAL/PAY

B67
GOLDMAN M.,CONTROLLING POLLUTION: THE ECONOMICS OF A CLEANER AMERICA. USA+45 SOCIETY PROB/SOLV CONTROL COST ANTHOL. PAGE 48 F0936
HEALTH ECO/DEV NAT/G FINAN

B67
HAGUE D.C.,PRICE FORMATION IN VARIOUS ECONOMIES; PROCEEDINGS OF A CONFERENCE HELD BY THE INTERNATIONAL ECONOMIC ASSOCIATION. WOR+45 FINAN MARKET PLAN CONFER COST...DECISION MATH PREDICT CHARTS SIMUL 20 INTL/ECON. PAGE 53 F1037
PRICE CAP/ISM SOCISM METH/COMP

B67
HANNAH H.W.,THE LEGAL BASE FOR UNIVERSITIES IN DEVELOPING COUNTRIES. AFR ASIA L/A+17C S/ASIA USA+45 FINAN CREATE EDU/PROP TASK EFFICIENCY ...JURID METH/COMP 20. PAGE 54 F1060
ADMIN LAW ACADEM LEGIS

B67
HOGAN J.,THE US BALANCE OF PAYMENTS AND CAPITAL FLOWS. MARKET INT/ORG ECO/TAC PRICE CONTROL WEALTH ...METH/COMP 20 EEC. PAGE 61 F1192
BAL/PAY FINAN DIPLOM INT/TRADE

B67
KANNER L.,THE NEW YORK TIMES WORLD ECONOMIC REVIEW AND FORECAST: 1967. WOR+45 ECO/DEV ECO/UNDEV TEC/DEV...STAT PREDICT CHARTS 20. PAGE 69 F1349
INDUS FINAN TREND ECO/TAC

B67
KARDOUCHE G.K.,THE UAR IN DEVELOPMENT. UAR ECO/TAC INT/TRADE BAL/PAY...STAT CHARTS BIBLIOG 20. PAGE 69 F1355
FINAN MGT CAP/ISM ECO/UNDEV

B67
KEWEN P.B.,INTERNATIONAL ECONOMICS (2ND ED.). USA+45 WOR+45 MARKET TARIFFS...BIBLIOG T 20. PAGE 70 F1384
INT/TRADE BAL/PAY FINAN EQUILIB

B67
MARCUS S.,COMPETITION AND THE LAW. USA+45 INDUS LG/CO NAT/G CONSERVE LAISSEZ...BIBLIOG 20 FTC SUPREME/CT. PAGE 85 F1665
LAW ECO/DEV FINAN JURID

B67
MAZOUR A.G.,SOVIET ECONOMIC DEVELOPMENT: OPERATION OUTSTRIP: 1921-1965. USSR ECO/UNDEV FINAN CHIEF WORKER PROB/SOLV CONTROL PRODUC MARXISM...CHARTS ORG/CHARTS 20 STALIN/J. PAGE 87 F1711
ECO/TAC AGRI INDUS PLAN

B67
PELTASON J.W.,FUNCTIONS AND POLICIES OF AMERICAN
NAT/G

GOVERNMENT (3RD ED.). USA+45 FINAN INDUS EDU/PROP CIVMIL/REL RACE/REL ORD/FREE...ANTHOL T 20 JOHNSON/LB. PAGE 104 F2052
GOV/REL POLICY PLAN

B67
RUEFF J.,BALANCE OF PAYMENTS: PROPOSALS FOR RESOLVING THE CRITICAL WORLD ECONOMIC PROBLEM OF OUR TIME. USA+45 INDUS FOR/AID REPAR DEMAND OPTIMAL ...ECOMETRIC CHARTS METH/COMP 20. PAGE 115 F2259
BAL/PAY INT/TRADE FINAN NEW/IDEA

B67
TANSKY L.,US AND USSR AID TO DEVELOPING COUNTRIES. INDIA TURKEY UAR USA+45 USSR FINAN PLAN TEC/DEV ADMIN WEALTH...TREND METH/COMP 20. PAGE 128 F2535
FOR/AID ECO/UNDEV MARXISM CAP/ISM

B67
UNIVERSAL REFERENCE SYSTEM,ECONOMIC REGULATION, BUSINESS, AND GOVERNMENT (VOLUME VIII). WOR+45 WOR-45 ECO/DEV ECO/UNDEV FINAN LABOR TEC/DEV ECO/TAC INT/TRADE GOV/REL...POLICY COMPUT/IR. PAGE 133 F2617
BIBLIOG/A CONTROL NAT/G

B67
US CONGRESS JOINT ECO COMM,REPORT ON JANUARY 1967 ECONOMIC REPORT OF THE PRESIDENT. FINAN LABOR NAT/G LEGIS BUDGET INT/TRADE COST DEMAND INCOME PRODUC ...POLICY IDEA/COMP 20 CONGRESS. PAGE 135 F2663
CHIEF ECO/TAC PLAN DELIB/GP

B67
US CONGRESS JOINT ECO COMM,AN ECONOMIC PROFILE OF MAINLAND CHINA, VOLUMES I AND II. CHINA/COM AGRI DIST/IND FINAN INDUS LABOR FORCES ACT/RES PLAN INT/TRADE INGP/REL BAL/PAY 20 CONGRESS. PAGE 135 F2664
ECO/UNDEV WEALTH ECO/TAC DELIB/GP

B67
US CONGRESS SENATE,SURVEY OF THE ALLIANCE FOR PROGRESS; INFLATION IN LATIN AMERICA (PAMPHLET). USA+45 MARKET INT/ORG DIPLOM INT/TRADE BAL/PAY SENATE ALL/PROG. PAGE 135 F2666
L/A+17C FINAN POLICY FOR/AID

B67
US SENATE COMM ON FOREIGN REL,LATIN AMERICAN SUMMIT CONFERENCE. L/A+17C USA+45 FINAN PLAN SENATE ALL/PROG. PAGE 139 F2740
FOR/AID BUDGET DIPLOM INT/ORG

B67
US SENATE COMM ON FOREIGN REL,INTER-AMERICAN DEVELOPMENT BANK ACT AMENDMENT. L/A+17C USA+45 DELIB/GP DIPLOM FOR/AID BAL/PAY...CHARTS SENATE. PAGE 139 F2741
LAW FINAN INT/ORG ECO/UNDEV

B67
YAMAMURA K.,ECONOMIC POLICY IN POSTWAR JAPAN. ASIA FINAN POL/PAR DIPLOM LEAD NAT/LISM ATTIT NEW/LIB POPULISM 20 CHINJAP. PAGE 149 F2946
ECO/DEV POLICY NAT/G TEC/DEV

B67
ZUPNICK E.,UNDERSTANDING THE INTERNATIONAL MONEY SYSTEM (HEADLINE SERIES, NO. 182) (PAMPHLET). ECO/DEV NAT/G DIPLOM INT/TRADE...METH/COMP 20 IMF. PAGE 151 F2971
FINAN PLAN INT/ORG PROB/SOLV

L67
DEALEY S.,"MONETARY RECOVERY UNDER FEDERAL TRANSPORTATION STATUTES." USA+45 SEA WORKER TAX PAY ADJUD DEATH GOV/REL OWN HEALTH ORD/FREE 20. PAGE 31 F0609
DIST/IND LAW CONTROL FINAN

L67
HUBBARD P.H.,"MONETARY RECOVERY UNDER THE COPYRIGHT, PATENT, AND TRADEMARK ACTS." PROC/MFG TAX PAY LEGIT ADJUD GOV/REL OWN ORD/FREE 20. PAGE 62 F1228
CREATE LAW CONTROL FINAN

L67
LAMBERT J.D.,"CORPORATE POLITICAL SPENDING AND CAMPAIGN FINANCE." LAW CONSTN FINAN LABOR LG/CO LOC/G NAT/G VOL/ASSN TEC/DEV ADJUD ADMIN PARTIC. PAGE 75 F1463
USA+45 POL/PAR CHOOSE COST

L67
LENT G.E.,"TAX INCENTIVES FOR INVESTMENT IN DEVELOPING COUNTRIES" WOR+45 LAW INDUS PLAN BUDGET TARIFFS ADMIN...METH/COMP 20. PAGE 78 F1526
ECO/UNDEV TAX FINAN ECO/TAC

L67
MEIER G.M.,"UNCTAD PROPOSALS FOR INTERNATIONAL ECONOMIC REFORM." WOR+45 MARKET INT/ORG TARIFFS CONFER UN GATT IMF. PAGE 89 F1749
INT/TRADE FINAN INT/LAW ECO/UNDEV

L67
PARKER G.P. JR.,"MONETARY RECOVERY UNDER THE FEDERAL LABOR STATUTES." USA+45 USA-45 INDUS ADJUD CT/SYS GOV/REL HEALTH ORD/FREE 20 DEPT/LABOR NLRB. PAGE 103 F2027
LABOR CONTROL LAW FINAN

L67
SCHNEIDER C.W.,"REFORM OF THE FEDERAL SECURITIES LAWS." FUT USA+45 LAW FINAN INDUS DELIB/GP ACT/RES PROB/SOLV GP/REL. PAGE 117 F2304
NAT/G LG/CO ADMIN CONTROL

L67
STILL C.H.,"MONETARY RECOVERY UNDER THE FAIR LABOR STANDARDS ACT." USA+45 USA-45 WORKER PAY ADJUD GOV/REL HEALTH ORD/FREE...MATH 20 NLRB. PAGE 126 F2487
LABOR CONTROL LAW FINAN

L67
TANDON Y.,"CONSENSUS AND AUTHORITY BEHIND UNITED NATIONS PEACEKEEPING OPERATIONS." FINAN VOL/ASSN BUDGET DIPLOM PAY DOMIN...CHARTS 20 UN. PAGE 128 F2528
CONSEN INT/ORG PWR PEACE

L67
VIA J.W. JR.,"ANTITRUST AND THE AMENDED BANK MERGER AND HOLDING COMPANY ACTS: THE SEARCH FOR STANDARDS." USA+45 CONTROL GP/REL WEALTH SUPREME/CT. PAGE 141 F2783
FINAN CT/SYS LAW EX/STRUC

L67
WATKINS J.B.,"MONETARY RECOVERY UNDER FEDERAL ANTITRUST STATUTES." USA+45 PROB/SOLV ADJUD CT/SYS GOV/REL ORD/FREE 20. PAGE 144 F2831
LG/CO CONTROL LAW FINAN

L67
WILKINSON J.H. JR.,"THE NET OPERATING LOSS DEDUCTION AND RELATED INCOME TAX DEVICES." PROB/SOLV BUDGET PAY GOV/REL ORD/FREE...MATH CHARTS METH 20. PAGE 146 F2886
TAX FINAN LAW ADJUD

S67
ADAMS E.S.,"THE EXPANDING ROLE OF BANKS IN PUBLIC AFFAIRS." USA+45 GIVE LEAD ROLE...QU 20. PAGE 2 F0036
PARTIC FINAN LOC/G ATTIT

S67
ALVES V.,"FOREIGN CAPITAL IN BRAZIL." BRAZIL USA+45 CAP/ISM DIPLOM ECO/TAC INT/TRADE CONTROL PWR ...POLICY 20. PAGE 4 F0081
ECO/UNDEV FINAN SOCIALIST SOCISM

S67
AUBERT DE LA RUE P.,"PERSPECTIVES ECONOMIQUES ENTRE LES ETATS-UNIS ET L'EUROPE." FUT INDUS R+D INT/ORG ACT/RES ECO/TAC AGREE BAL/PAY PRODUC...CHARTS 20 EEC GATT WORLD/BANK. PAGE 7 F0138
INT/TRADE ECO/DEV FINAN TARIFFS

S67
BARRO S.,"ECONOMIC IMPACT OF SPACE EXPENDITURES: SOME BROAD ISSUES DEALING WITH COSTS AND BENEFITS." USA+45 PROC/MFG R+D LG/CO CONSULT COST PRODUC 20. PAGE 10 F0195
SPACE FINAN ECO/TAC NAT/G

S67
BARTLETT J.L.,"AMERICAN BOND ISSUES IN THE EUROPEAN ECONOMIC COMMUNITY." EUR+WWI LUXEMBOURG USA+45 DIPLOM CONTROL BAL/PAY EEC. PAGE 11 F0201
LAW ECO/TAC FINAN TAX

S67
BELISLE J.,"FOREIGN RESTRAINTS ON US BANKS ABROAD" WOR+45 LAW. PAGE 12 F0233
DIPLOM FINAN CONTROL LICENSE

S67
BOSHER J.F.,"GOVERNMENT AND PRIVATE INTERESTS IN NEW FRANCE." CANADA FRANCE INDUS LG/CO SML/CO CAP/ISM INT/TRADE COLONIAL GP/REL...HIST/WRIT 17/18. PAGE 17 F0320
NAT/G FINAN ADMIN CONTROL

S67
BRAUCHER R.,"RECLAMATION OF GOODS FROM A FRAUDULENT BUYER." USA+45 CLIENT FINAN CT/SYS PERS/REL COST WEALTH. PAGE 18 F0341
LAW ADJUD GOV/REL INT/TRADE

S67
CRAIG A.,"ARGENTINA: THE LATEST REVOLUTION." ELITES NAT/G CHIEF FORCES ECO/TAC CIVMIL/REL GOV/REL EQUILIB PRIVIL 20 ARGEN. PAGE 28 F0550
ECO/UNDEV FINAN ATTIT REV

S67
CROMER EARL OF,"STERLING AND THE COMMON MARKET." UK ECO/DEV INT/ORG 20 EEC. PAGE 29 F0554
ECO/TAC FINAN CHARTS INT/TRADE

S67
EDGEWORTH A.B. JR.,"CIVIL RIGHTS PLUS THREE YEARS: BANKS AND THE ANTI-DISCRIMINATION LAW" USA+45 SOCIETY DELIB/GP RACE/REL EFFICIENCY 20 NEGRO CIV/RIGHTS. PAGE 36 F0701
WORKER DISCRIM FINAN LAW

S67
FERGUSON D.E.,"DETERMINING CAPACITY FOR CAPITAL EXPENDITURES." USA+45 LOC/G BUDGET TAX ADMIN CONTROL...TREND MUNICH 20. PAGE 40 F0784
FINAN PAY COST

S67
GAUSE M.E.,"ELEMENTS OF FINANCE DEPARTMENT ORGANIZATION FOR SMALL GOVERNMENTAL UNITS." USA+45 PROB/SOLV CONTROL CENTRAL...METH MUNICH. PAGE 47 F0910
ADMIN LOC/G FINAN

S67
HERRERA F.,"EUROPEAN PARTICIPATION IN THE LATIN AMERICAN REGIONAL INTEGRATION" EUR+WWI L/A+17C GP/REL INGP/REL 20. PAGE 59 F1154
DIPLOM REGION INT/ORG FINAN

S67
HILL L.W.,"FINANCING URBAN RENEWAL PROGRAMS." USA+45 ECO/DEV LOC/G EDU/PROP MUNICH 20. PAGE 60 F1171
FINAN NAT/G WEALTH

S67
HILTON G.W.,"FEDERAL PARTICIPATION IN THE SUPERSONIC TRANSPORT PROGRAM." USA+45 LEGIS
DIST/IND TEC/DEV

PROB/SOLV BUDGET ATTIT 20. PAGE 60 F1172 — FINAN NAT/G

S67
LEVI M.,"LES RELATIONS ECONOMIQUES ENTRE L'EST ET L'OUEST EN EUROPE" INDUS...STAT CHARTS 20 OECD COMECON. PAGE 79 F1540 — INT/TRADE INT/ORG FINAN PRODUC

S67
LIFLAND W.T.,"BANKING PRACTICE AND THE ANTITRUST LAWS." NAT/G GP/REL...CONCPT IDEA/COMP 20. PAGE 80 F1563 — FINAN CAP/ISM JURID

S67
MALKIN A.,"BUSINESS BOOKS OF 1966." INDUS LABOR OP/RES TEC/DEV CAP/ISM ECO/TAC INCOME WEALTH 20. PAGE 84 F1649 — BIBLIOG/A FINAN MARKET

S67
MODESITT L.E.,"THE MUTUAL FUND - A CORPORATE ANOMALY." USA+45 CONTROL...MGT 20. PAGE 92 F1813 — SERV/IND FINAN ADMIN LAW

S67
MUNDHEIM R.H.,"SOME THOUGHTS ON THE DUTIES AND RESPONSIBILITIES OF UNAFFILIATED DIRECTORS OF MUTUAL FUNDS." USA+45 LG/CO SML/CO CONSULT LEAD PARTIC. PAGE 95 F1861 — FINAN WEALTH ECO/TAC ADMIN

S67
MYERS S.,"TECHNOLOGY AND URBAN TRANSIT: THE ENORMOUS POTENTIAL OF BUS AND RAIL SYSTEMS." USA+45 FINAN LOC/G WORKER PLAN PROB/SOLV PRICE AUTOMAT MUNICH 20. PAGE 96 F1877 — R+D TEC/DEV DIST/IND ACT/RES

S67
NILES J.G.,"CIVIL ACTIONS FOR DAMAGES UNDER THE FEDERAL CIVIL RIGHTS STATUTES." CONSTN FINAN ADJUD CT/SYS GOV/REL RACE/REL 20. PAGE 98 F1928 — DISCRIM LAW CONTROL ORD/FREE

S67
PENNEY N.,"BANK STATEMENTS, CANCELLED CHECKS, AND ARTICLE FOUR IN THE ELECTRONIC AGE." USA+45 TEC/DEV COST EFFICIENCY WEALTH. PAGE 104 F2056 — CREATE LAW ADJUD FINAN

S67
RICHMAN B.M.,"SOVIET MANAGEMENT IN TRANSITION." USSR FINAN MARKET EX/STRUC PLAN PROB/SOLV TEC/DEV CONTROL LEAD CENTRAL EFFICIENCY...METH/COMP 20 REFORMERS. PAGE 111 F2186 — MGT MARXISM POLICY AUTHORIT

S67
SCOVILLE W.J.,"GOVERNMENT REGULATION AND GROWTH IN THE FRENCH PAPER INDUSTRY DURING THE EIGHTEENTH CENTURY." FRANCE MOD/EUR FINAN CAP/ISM TAX ADMIN CONTROL PRIVIL LAISSEZ...POLICY 18. PAGE 118 F2337 — NAT/G PROC/MFG ECO/DEV INGP/REL

S67
SHEFFTZ M.C.,"THE TRADE DISPUTES AND TRADE UNIONS ACT OF 1927: THE AFTERMATH OF THE GENERAL STRIKE." UK FINAN WORKER ADJUD LEAD PARL/PROC 20. PAGE 120 F2373 — LEGIS ATTIT LABOR GP/REL

S67
SKILTON R.M.,"PROTECTION OF THE INSTALLMENT BUYER OF GOODS UNDER THE UNIFORM COMMERCIAL CODE." USA+45 NAT/G COST. PAGE 123 F2418 — LAW ADJUD LEGIT FINAN

S67
STEINHEIMER R.L. JR.,"THE UNIFORM COMMERCIAL CODE COMES OF AGE." USA+45 FINAN ACADEM JUDGE. PAGE 126 F2477 — ADJUD LEGIS INT/TRADE GOV/REL

S67
STILL J.F.,"THE FUTURE OF METROPOLITAN GOVERNMENT ORGANIZATION." USA+45 LOC/G BUDGET COST ATTIT MUNICH 20. PAGE 126 F2488 — ADMIN FINAN CONTROL

S67
STRANGE S.,"DEBTS, DEFAULTERS AND DEVELOPMENT." WOR+45 PROB/SOLV FOR/AID INT/TRADE. PAGE 127 F2500 — NAT/G FINAN ECO/UNDEV

S67
WARNER K.O.,"FINANCIAL IMPLICATION OF EMPLOYEE BARGAINING IN THE PUBLIC SERVICE." CANADA USA+45 FINAN ADMIN...MGT 20. PAGE 143 F2823 — BARGAIN LABOR COST LOC/G

S67
WHITE W.L.,"THE TREASURY BOARD AND PARLIAMENT." CANADA CONSTN CONSULT LEGIS LEAD PARL/PROC GP/REL ...DECISION 20. PAGE 146 F2871 — FINAN DELIB/GP NAT/G ADMIN

S67
WOLFSON M.,"GOVERNMENT'S ROLE IN TOURISM DEVELOPMENT." WOR+45 ECO/DEV ECO/UNDEV FINAN BUDGET DIPLOM EDU/PROP. PAGE 148 F2920 — SERV/IND NAT/G CONTROL PLAN

N67
US CONGRESS JOINT ECO COMM,ECONOMY IN GOVERNMENT (PAMPHLET). USA+45 ECO/DEV FINAN NAT/G PLAN BUDGET SENATE. PAGE 135 F2662 — ECO/TAC COST EFFICIENCY MGT

N67
US HOUSE COMM FOREIGN AFFAIRS,FOREIGN ASSISTANCE ACT OF 1967 (PAMPHLET). USA+45 WOR+45 FINAN CONGRESS HOUSE/REP UN. PAGE 137 F2695 — FOR/AID POLICY INT/ORG ECO/UNDEV

N67
US SENATE COMM ON FOREIGN REL,ARMS SALES AND FOREIGN POLICY (PAMPHLET). FINAN FOR/AID CONTROL 20. PAGE 139 F2737 — ARMS/CONT ADMIN OP/RES DIPLOM

B75
JEVONS W.S.,MONEY AND THE MECHANISM OF EXCHANGE. INDUS MARKET DIPLOM COST EQUILIB WEALTH LAISSEZ ...GEN/LAWS 19 MONEY. PAGE 67 F1319 — PRICE FINAN ECO/TAC POLICY

B82
CUNNINGHAM W.,THE GROWTH OF ENGLISH INDUSTRY AND COMMERCE. FUT UK FINAN NAT/G CAP/ISM...POLICY 20 MERCANTLST CHRISTIAN POPE. PAGE 29 F0562 — INDUS INT/TRADE SML/CO CONSERVE

B84
MILL J.,ELEMENTS OF POLITICAL ECONOMY. UK LAW ELITES FINAN WORKER ECO/TAC RENT OWN WEALTH ...POLICY GEN/LAWS 19. PAGE 91 F1785 — TAX TARIFFS NAT/G INCOME

S86
SMITH R.M.,"THE NATIONAL BUREAU OF LABOR AND INDUSTRIAL DEPRESSIONS" USA-45 DELIB/GP BARGAIN CONTROL COST INCOME WEALTH...STAT 19 DEPRESSION. PAGE 123 F2433 — LABOR INDUS FINAN GOV/REL

B88
BENTHAM J.,DEFENCE OF USURY (1787). UK LAW NAT/G TEC/DEV ECO/TAC CONTROL ATTIT...CONCPT IDEA/COMP 18 SMITH/ADAM. PAGE 13 F0255 — TAX FINAN ECO/DEV POLICY

FINANCE....SEE FINAN

FINCH/D....DANIEL FINCH

FINCH/ER....E.R. FINCH

FINE ARTS....SEE ART/METH

FINER H. F0796

FINER S.E. F0797,F0798

FINKLE J.L. F0799

FINLAND....SEE ALSO APPROPRIATE TIME/SPACE/CULTURE INDEX

B58
JUCKER-FLEETWOOD E.,ECONOMIC THEORY AND POLICY IN FINLAND 1914-1925. FINLAND INT/TRADE PRICE COST 20 MONEY. PAGE 68 F1343 — FINAN GEN/LAWS ECO/TAC PLAN

C65
WUORINEN J.H.,"SCANDINAVIA." DENMARK FINLAND ICELAND NORWAY SWEDEN SOCIETY AGRI POL/PAR DELIB/GP DIPLOM INT/TRADE NEUTRAL WAR...CHARTS IND TREATY 20. PAGE 149 F2942 — BIBLIOG NAT/G POLICY

B67
ANDERSON S.V.,THE NORDIC COUNCIL: A STUDY OF SCANDINAVIAN REGIONALISM. DENMARK FINLAND ICELAND NORWAY SWEDEN MARKET NAT/G VOL/ASSN CONSULT PARL/PROC ATTIT...TIME/SEQ BIBLIOG 20. PAGE 5 F0098 — INT/ORG REGION DIPLOM LEGIS

FINLEY D.D. F0800

FIRESTONE J.M. F0801

FIRM....SEE INDUS

FIRTH R. F0802,F0803

FISCAL POLICY....SEE ECO, NAT/G, BUDGET

FISHING INDUSTRY....SEE EXTR/IND

FISK E.K. F0804

FISK W.M. F0805

FITCH L.C. F0806

FLACKS R. F0807

FLANDERS....FLANDERS

FLASH E.S. F0808

FLEISCHER G.A. F1509

FLEMING R.W. F0699,F0809

FLEMING W.G. F0810

FLINN M.W. F0811

FLOREA I. F0812

FLORENCE P.S. F0813,F0814

FLORENCE....MEDIEVAL AND RENAISSANCE

FLORES E. F0815

FLORIDA....FLORIDA

FLORINSKY M.T. F0816,F0817

FLOURNOY H.I. F0293

FLOYD D. F0818

FLYNN/BOSS....BOSS FLYNN

FNMA....FEDERAL NATIONAL MORTGAGE ASSOCIATION

FOCH/F....FERDINAND FOCH

FOGARTY M.P. F0819

FOLDES L. F0820

FOLKLORE....SEE MYTH

FONER P.S. F0821

FONTANE/T....THEODORE FONTANE

FOOD....SEE AGRI, ALSO EATING

FOOD AND AGRICULTURAL ORGANIZATION....SEE FAO

FOOD/PEACE....OFFICE OF FOOD FOR PEACE

B64
MC GOVERN G.S.,WAR AGAINST WANT. USA+45 AGRI DIPLOM INT/TRADE GIVE RECEIVE DEMAND HEALTH 20 KENNEDY/JF FOOD/PEACE. PAGE 87 F1714
FOR/AID ECO/DEV POLICY EATING

FOR/AID....FOREIGN AID

N
THE MIDDLE EAST AND NORTH AFRICA. AFR ISLAM CULTURE ECO/UNDEV AGRI NAT/G TEC/DEV FOR/AID INT/TRADE EDU/PROP...CHARTS 20. PAGE 1 F0008
INDEX INDUS FINAN STAT

N
MINISTRY OF OVERSEAS DEVELOPME,TECHNICAL CO-OPERATION -- A BIBLIOGRAPHY. UK LAW SOCIETY DIPLOM ECO/TAC FOR/AID...STAT 20 CMN/WLTH. PAGE 92 F1803
BIBLIOG TEC/DEV ECO/DEV NAT/G

N19
ARNDT H.W.,AUSTRALIAN FOREIGN AID POLICY (PAMPHLET). ECO/UNDEV DIPLOM GIVE GOV/REL COST UTIL PWR...CHARTS 20 AUSTRAL PAPUA NEW/GUINEA. PAGE 6 F0114
FOR/AID POLICY ECO/TAC EFFICIENCY

N19
BASCH A.,THE FUTURE OF FOREIGN LENDING FOR DEVELOPMENT (PAMPHLET). WOR+45 ECO/UNDEV FINAN INT/ORG ECO/TAC ATTIT...PREDICT 20. PAGE 11 F0203
FOR/AID ECO/DEV DIPLOM GIVE

N19
FRANCK P.G.,AFGHANISTAN BETWEEN EAST AND WEST: THE ECONOMICS OF COMPETITIVE COEXISTENCE (PAMPHLET). AFGHANISTN USA+45 USA-45 USSR INDUS ECO/TAC INT/TRADE CONTROL NEUTRAL ORD/FREE MARXISM...GEOG 20 UN. PAGE 43 F0842
FOR/AID PLAN DIPLOM ECO/UNDEV

N19
HANSEN B.,INFLATION PROBLEMS IN SMALL COUNTRIES (PAMPHLET). AFR UNIV FOR/AID CONTROL BAL/PAY DEMAND PRODUC 20. PAGE 54 F1066
PRICE FINAN ECO/UNDEV ECO/TAC

N19
JACKSON R.G.A.,THE CASE FOR AN INTERNATIONAL DEVELOPMENT AUTHORITY (PAMPHLET). WOR+45 ECO/DEV DIPLOM GIVE CONTROL GP/REL EFFICIENCY NAT/LISM SOVEREIGN 20. PAGE 66 F1295
FOR/AID INT/ORG ECO/UNDEV ADMIN

N19
KUWAIT ARABIA,KUWAIT FUND FOR ARAB ECONOMIC DEVELOPMENT (PAMPHLET). ISLAM KUWAIT UAR ECO/UNDEV LEGIS ECO/TAC WEALTH 20. PAGE 74 F1452
FOR/AID DIPLOM FINAN ADMIN

N19
KUWAIT FUND ARAB ECO DEVELOPMT,ANNUAL REPORTS 1962-65 (PAMPHLET). KUWAIT ECO/UNDEV DIPLOM ...POLICY 20 ARABS. PAGE 74 F1453
FOR/AID DELIB/GP FINAN ISLAM

N19
MARCUS W.,US PRIVATE INVESTMENT AND ECONOMIC AID IN UNDERDEVELOPED COUNTRIES (PAMPHLET). USA+45 LG/CO NAT/G CAP/ISM EDU/PROP 20. PAGE 85 F1666
FOR/AID ECO/UNDEV FINAN PLAN

N19
MASON E.S.,THE DIPLOMACY OF ECONOMIC ASSISTANCE (PAMPHLET). INDIA PAKISTAN USA+45 ECO/UNDEV NAT/G BUDGET ATTIT...POLICY 20. PAGE 87 F1695
FOR/AID DIPLOM FINAN

N19
MEZERIK A.G.,ECONOMIC AID FOR UNDERDEVELOPED COUNTRIES (PAMPHLET). AFR USSR WOR+45 FINAN LG/CO DELIB/GP NUC/PWR...GEOG CENSUS CHARTS 20 UN THIRD/WRLD. PAGE 90 F1775
FOR/AID ECO/UNDEV DIPLOM POLICY

N19
STALEY E.,SCIENTIFIC RESEARCH AND PROGRESS IN NEWLY DEVELOPING COUNTRIES (PAMPHLET). AFR ASIA L/A+17C CONSULT DIPLOM...METH/COMP 20. PAGE 125 F2463
ECO/UNDEV ACT/RES FOR/AID TEC/DEV

N19
STEUBER F.A.,THE CONTRIBUTION OF SWITZERLAND TO THE ECONOMIC AND SOCIAL DEVELOPMENT OF LOW-INCOME COUNTRIES (PAMPHLET). SWITZERLND FINAN NAT/G VOL/ASSN INT/TRADE DRIVE...CHARTS 20. PAGE 126 F2482
FOR/AID ECO/UNDEV PLAN DIPLOM

B50
FEIS H.,THE DIPLOMACY OF THE DOLLAR: FIRST ERA 1919-32. EUR+WWI USA-45 FOR/AID REPAR ATTIT ...POLICY 20. PAGE 40 F0774
FINAN NAT/G DIPLOM ECO/TAC

B50
LINCOLN G.,ECONOMICS OF NATIONAL SECURITY. USA+45 ELITES COM/IND DIST/IND INDUS NAT/G VOL/ASSN DELIB/GP EX/STRUC FOR/AID EDU/PROP COERCE NUC/PWR WAR ATTIT KNOWL ORD/FREE PWR TOT/POP VAL/FREE 20. PAGE 80 F1565
FORCES ECO/TAC AFR

B50
US DEPARTMENT OF STATE,POINT FOUR: COOPERATIVE PROGRAM FOR AID IN THE DEVELOPMENT OF ECONOMICALLY UNDERDEVELOPED AREAS. WOR+45 AGRI INDUS INT/ORG PLAN TEC/DEV DIPLOM EDU/PROP ADMIN PEACE PRODUC WEALTH 20 CONGRESS UN. PAGE 135 F2671
ECO/UNDEV FOR/AID FINAN INT/TRADE

C50
ELLSWORTH P.T.,"INTERNATIONAL ECONOMY." ECO/DEV ECO/UNDEV FINAN LABOR DIPLOM FOR/AID TARIFFS BAL/PAY EQUILIB NAT/LISM OPTIMAL...INT/LAW 20 ILO GATT. PAGE 37 F0724
BIBLIOG INT/TRADE ECO/TAC INT/ORG

B51
US HOUSE COMM APPROPRIATIONS,MUTUAL SECURITY PROGRAM APPROPRIATIONS FOR 1952: HEARINGS BEFORE A SUBCOMMITTEE OF THE COMMITTEE ON APPROPRIATIONS. AFR KOREA L/A+17C ECO/DEV ECO/UNDEV INT/ORG INSPECT BAL/PWR DIPLOM DEBATE WAR...POLICY STAT ASIA/S 20 CONGRESS NATO MID/EAST. PAGE 136 F2686
LEGIS FORCES BUDGET FOR/AID

B52
HOSELITZ B.F.,THE PROGRESS OF UNDERDEVELOPED AREAS. AFR FUT WOR+45 WOR-45 ECO/DEV ECO/TAC INT/TRADE WEALTH...SOC TREND GEN/LAWS TOT/POP VAL/FREE FOR/TRADE 20. PAGE 62 F1219
ECO/UNDEV PLAN FOR/AID

B52
MACARTHUR D.,REVITALIZING A NATION. ASIA COM FUT KOREA WOR+45 NAT/G FOR/AID TAX GIVE WAR ATTIT SOCISM 20 CHINJAP EUROPE. PAGE 83 F1619
LEAD FORCES TOP/EX POLICY

B52
WU Y.,ECONOMIC WARFARE. MARKET PLAN PROB/SOLV FOR/AID CONTROL EFFICIENCY WEALTH...METH/COMP 20. PAGE 149 F2937
ECO/TAC WAR INT/TRADE DIPLOM

B53
FRANKEL S.H.,THE ECONOMIC IMPACT ON UNDERDEVELOPED SOCIETIES: ESSAYS ON INTERNATIONAL INVESTMENT AND SOCIAL CHANGE. AFR WOR+45 ECO/DEV FINAN INDUS NAT/G ACT/RES TEC/DEV COLONIAL ATTIT...CONCPT OBS TREND 20. PAGE 43 F0845
ECO/UNDEV FOR/AID INT/TRADE

S53
LINCOLN G.,"FACTORS DETERMINING ARMS AID." COM FUT USA+45 USSR WOR+45 ECO/DEV NAT/G CONSULT PLAN TEC/DEV DIPLOM DOMIN EDU/PROP PERCEPT PWR ...DECISION CONCPT TREND MARX/KARL 20. PAGE 80 F1566
FORCES POLICY BAL/PWR FOR/AID

B54
O.E.E.C.,PRIVATE UNITED STATES INVESTMENT IN EUROPE AND THE OVERSEAS TERRITORIES. EUR+WWI WOR+45 ECO/DEV ECO/UNDEV INT/ORG NAT/G VOL/ASSN ECO/TAC ATTIT WEALTH...GEOG STAT SYS/QU CHARTS VAL/FREE 20. PAGE 99 F1950
USA+45 FINAN BAL/PAY FOR/AID

B54
STALEY E.,THE FUTURE OF UNDERDEVELOPED COUNTRIES: POLITICAL IMPLICATIONS OF ECONOMIC DEVELOPMENT. AFR COM FUT USA+45 SOCIETY ECO/UNDEV CREATE PLAN CAP/ISM ATTIT DRIVE MARXISM SOCISM...POLICY CONCPT CHARTS 20. PAGE 125 F2466
EDU/PROP ECO/TAC FOR/AID

L54
OPLER M.E.,"SOCIAL ASPECTS OF TECHNICAL ASSISTANCE IN OPERATION." WOR+45 VOL/ASSN CREATE PLAN TEC/DEV EDU/PROP ALL/VALS...METH/CNCPT OBS RECORD TREND UN 20. PAGE 101 F1993
INT/ORG CONSULT FOR/AID

B55
BUCHANAN N.S.,APPROACHES TO ECONOMIC DEVELOPMENT. FUT USA+45 WOR+45 STRATA ECO/DEV INT/ORG NAT/G TEC/DEV DIPLOM FOR/AID ATTIT KNOWL PWR WEALTH ...RELATIV METH/CNCPT SELF/OBS TREND CON/ANAL STERTYP GEN/LAWS FOR/TRADE COMMUN 20. PAGE 20 F0380
ECO/UNDEV ECO/TAC INT/TRADE

B55
OECD,MARSHALL PLAN IN TURKEY. TURKEY USA+45 COM/IND CONSTRUC SERV/IND FORCES BUDGET...STAT 20 MARSHL/PLN. PAGE 100 F1964
FOR/AID ECO/UNDEV AGRI INDUS

B55
US OFFICE OF THE PRESIDENT,REPORT TO CONGRESS ON THE MUTUAL SECURITY PROGRAM FOR THE SIX MONTHS ENDED JUNE 30, 1955. ECO/DEV INT/ORG NAT/G CREATE TEC/DEV BAL/PWR ECO/TAC AGREE DETER COST ORD/FREE 20 DEPT/STATE DEPT/DEFEN. PAGE 138 F2722
DIPLOM FORCES PLAN FOR/AID

B55
WOYTINSKY W.S.,WORLD COMMERCE AND GOVERNMENTS: TRENDS AND OUTLOOK. WOR+45 FINAN POL/PAR DIPLOM ECO/TAC FOR/AID DOMIN WAR CHOOSE...CHARTS BIBLIOG 20 LEAGUE/NAT UN ILO. PAGE 149 F2929
INT/TRADE DIST/IND NAT/COMP NAT/G

B56
KNORR K.E.,RUBLE DIPLOMACY: CHALLENGE TO AMERICAN FOREIGN AID(PAMPHLET). AFR CHINA/COM USA+45 USSR PLAN TEC/DEV CAP/ISM INT/TRADE DOMIN EDU/PROP CONTROL LEAD 20. PAGE 72 F1413
ECO/UNDEV COM DIPLOM FOR/AID

B56
UNITED NATIONS,BIBLIOGRAPHY ON INDUSTRIALIZATION IN UNDER-DEVELOPED COUNTRIES. WOR+45 R+D INT/ORG NAT/G FOR/AID ADMIN LEAD 20 UN. PAGE 132 F2612
BIBLIOG ECO/UNDEV INDUS TEC/DEV

B56
US LIBRARY OF CONGRESS,UNITED STATES DIRECT ECONOMIC AID TO FOREIGN COUNTRIES: A COLLECTION OF EXCERPTS AND A BIBLIOGRAPHY (PAMPHLET). USA+45 PRESS DEBATE...ANTHOL BIBLIOG/A CONGRESS. PAGE 138 F2716
FOR/AID POLICY DIPLOM ECO/UNDEV

B56
US OFFICE OF THE PRESIDENT,REPORT TO CONGRESS ON THE MUTUAL SECURITY PROGRAM FOR THE SIX MONTHS ENDED DECEMBER 31, 1955. ASIA USSR ECO/DEV ECO/UNDEV INT/ORG CREATE TEC/DEV BAL/PWR ECO/TAC AGREE DETER COST ORD/FREE 20 DEPT/STATE DEPT/DEFEN EISNHWR/DD. PAGE 138 F2723
DIPLOM FORCES PLAN FOR/AID

N56
US HOUSE COMM FOREIGN AFFAIRS,REPORT OF THE SPECIAL STUDY MISSION TO AFRICA, SOUTH AND EAST OF THE SAHARA (PAMPHLET). AFR SOUTH/AFR USA+45 STRUCT INT/TRADE PARL/PROC NAT/LISM ATTIT ALL/VALS HEALTH ...POLICY 20 CONGRESS. PAGE 136 F2691
FOR/AID COLONIAL ECO/UNDEV DIPLOM

B57
ASHER R.E.,THE UNITED NATIONS AND ECONOMIC AND SOCIAL COOPERATION. ECO/UNDEV COM/IND DIST/IND FINAN PLAN PROB/SOLV INT/TRADE TASK WEALTH...SOC 20 UN. PAGE 7 F0129
INT/ORG DIPLOM FOR/AID

B57
BEHRMAN J.N.,INTERNATIONAL ECONOMICS: THEORY, PRACTICE, POLICY. AGRI INDUS NAT/G TARIFFS CONTROL BAL/PAY...POLICY METH/CNCPT T 19/20. PAGE 12 F0230
INT/TRADE FINAN DIPLOM FOR/AID

B57
COMMITTEE ECONOMIC DEVELOPMENT,ECONOMIC DEVELOPMENT ASSISTANCE. USA+45 WOR+45 AGRI CONFER ORD/FREE ...MGT CHARTS 20. PAGE 27 F0515
FOR/AID ECO/UNDEV FINAN PLAN

B57
DRUCKER P.F.,AMERICA'S NEXT TWENTY YEARS. USA+45 DIST/IND ACADEM SCHOOL DIPLOM ECO/TAC AUTOMAT HABITAT HEALTH...SOC/WK TREND MUNICH 20 URBAN/RNWL PUB/TRANS. PAGE 34 F0667
WORKER FOR/AID CENSUS GEOG

B57
GOLD N.L.,REGIONAL ECONOMIC DEVELOPMENT AND NUCLEAR POWER IN INDIA. FUT INDIA FINAN FOR/AID INT/TRADE BAL/PAY EFFICIENCY OPTIMAL PRODUC WEALTH...PREDICT 20. PAGE 48 F0934
ECO/UNDEV TEC/DEV NUC/PWR INDUS

B57
HALD M.,A SELECTED BIBLIOGRAPHY ON ECONOMIC DEVELOPMENT AND FOREIGN AID. INT/ORG PROB/SOLV ...SOC 20. PAGE 53 F1040
BIBLIOG ECO/UNDEV TEC/DEV FOR/AID

B57
LEIBENSTEIN H.,ECONOMIC BACKWARDNESS AND ECONOMIC GROWTH. WOR+45 SOCIETY AGRI INDUS TEC/DEV CAP/ISM FOR/AID COST DEMAND WEALTH...CHARTS IDEA/COMP 20. PAGE 77 F1513
ECO/UNDEV ECO/TAC PRODUC POLICY

B57
MILLIKAN M.F.,A PROPOSAL: KEY TO AN EFFECTIVE FOREIGN POLICY. USA+45 AGRI FINAN DELIB/GP DIPLOM REPRESENT MAJORITY...NEW/IDEA CHARTS. PAGE 91 F1795
FOR/AID GIVE ECO/UNDEV PLAN

B58
BERLINER J.S.,SOVIET ECONOMIC AID: THE AID AND TRADE POLICY IN UNDERDEVELOPED COUNTRIES. AFR COM ISLAM L/A+17C S/ASIA USSR ECO/DEV DIST/IND FINAN MARKET INT/ORG ACT/RES PLAN BAL/PWR WEAPON PWR WEALTH...CHARTS FOR/TRADE 20. PAGE 14 F0263
ECO/UNDEV ECO/TAC FOR/AID

B58
EHRHARD J.,LE DESTIN DU COLONIALISME. AFR FRANCE ECO/UNDEV AGRI FINAN MARKET CREATE PLAN TEC/DEV BUDGET DIPLOM PRICE 20. PAGE 36 F0710
COLONIAL FOR/AID INT/TRADE INDUS

B58
ELLSWORTH P.T.,THE INTERNATIONAL ECONOMY. EUR+WWI MOD/EUR INT/ORG CAP/ISM FOR/AID BAL/PAY LAISSEZ 16/20. PAGE 37 F0725
INT/TRADE TARIFFS ECO/DEV

B58
HANCE W.A.,AFRICAN ECONOMIC DEVELOPMENT. AGRI DIST/IND INDUS R+D ACT/RES PLAN CAP/ISM FOR/AID ...GOV/COMP BIBLIOG 20. PAGE 54 F1058
AFR ECO/UNDEV PROB/SOLV TEC/DEV

B58
JENNINGS I.,PROBLEMS OF THE NEW COMMONWEALTH. AFR CEYLON INDIA PAKISTAN S/ASIA ECO/UNDEV INT/ORG LOC/G DIPLOM ECO/TAC INT/TRADE COLONIAL RACE/REL DISCRIM 20 PARLIAMENT. PAGE 67 F1314
NAT/LISM NEUTRAL FOR/AID POL/PAR

B58
MYRDAL G.,RICH LANDS AND POOR: THE ROAD TO WORLD PROSPERITY. FUT WOR+45 WOR-45 ECO/DEV ECO/UNDEV INT/ORG PLAN ECO/TAC REGION...GEOG TIME/SEQ GEN/LAWS TOT/POP 20. PAGE 96 F1880
WEALTH TREND FOR/AID INT/TRADE

B58
US OPERATIONS MISSION TO VIET,BUILDING ECONOMIC STRENGTH (PAMPHLET). USA+45 VIETNAM/S INDUS TEC/DEV BUDGET ADMIN EATING HEALTH...STAT 20. PAGE 138 F2725
FOR/AID ECO/UNDEV AGRI EDU/PROP

B59
BARNETT A.D.,COMMUNIST ECONOMIC STRATEGY: THE RISE OF MAINLAND CHINA. CHINA/COM USSR WOR+45 AGRI INDUS FOR/AID INGP/REL ATTIT. PAGE 10 F0188
ECO/UNDEV INT/TRADE TOTALISM BAL/PWR

B59
BAUER P.T.,UNITED STATES AID AND INDIAN ECONOMIC DEVELOPMENT. INDIA STRATA FINAN PLAN BUDGET DIPLOM INGP/REL EFFICIENCY SOCISM 20 AID. PAGE 11 F0215
FOR/AID ECO/UNDEV ECO/TAC POLICY

B59
HAZLEWOOD A.,THE ECONOMICS OF "UNDER-DEVELOPED" AREAS. WOR+45 DIST/IND EXTR/IND FINAN INDUS MARKET PLAN FOR/AID...GEOG 20. PAGE 57 F1129
BIBLIOG/A ECO/UNDEV AGRI INT/TRADE

B59
KOREAN MINISTRY RECONSTRUCTION,KOREAN ECONOMY AND ITS REQUIREMENTS. KOREA USA+45 ECO/TAC EQUILIB INCOME WEALTH...CHARTS 20. PAGE 73 F1427
FOR/AID WAR FINAN DIPLOM

B59
MEZERK A.G.,FINANCIAL ASSISTANCE FOR ECONOMIC DEVELOPMENT. WOR+45 INDUS DIPLOM INT/TRADE...CHARTS GOV/COMP UN. PAGE 91 F1778
FOR/AID FINAN ECO/TAC ECO/UNDEV

B59
NOVE A.,COMMUNIST ECONOMIC STRATEGY: SOVIET GROWTH AND CAPABILITIES. USSR AGRI LABOR PLAN TEC/DEV CAP/ISM INT/TRADE EFFICIENCY MARXISM 20 THIRD/WRLD. PAGE 99 F1941
FOR/AID ECO/TAC DIPLOM INDUS

B59
NUNEZ JIMENEZ A.,LA LIBERACION DE LAS ISLAS. CUBA L/A+17C USA+45 LAW CHIEF PLAN DIPLOM FOR/AID OWN WEALTH 20 CASTRO/F. PAGE 99 F1945
AGRI REV ECO/UNDEV NAT/G

B59
OGBURN C.,ECONOMIC PLAN AND ACTION. USA+45 FINAN LABOR DIPLOM ECO/TAC FOR/AID 20. PAGE 101 F1981
ECO/DEV INT/TRADE PLAN BAL/PAY

B59
US DEPARTMENT OF STATE,THE UNITED STATES ECONOMY AND THE MUTUAL SECURITY PROGRAM. USA+45 ECO/UNDEV FINAN INDUS DIPLOM INT/TRADE DETER 20. PAGE 136 F2674
ECO/DEV FORCES BUDGET FOR/AID

B59
US GENERAL ACCOUNTING OFFICE,EXAM OF ECONOMIC AND TECHNICAL ASSISTANCE PROGRAM FOR INDIA INT'NAT'L COOP ADMIN REPORT TO CONGRESS 1955-1958. INDIA USA+45 ECO/UNDEV FINAN PLAN DIPLOM COST UTIL WEALTH ...CHARTS 20 CONGRESS AID. PAGE 136 F2679
FOR/AID EFFICIENCY ECO/TAC TEC/DEV

B59
US HOUSE COMM GOVT OPERATIONS,UNITED STATES AID OPERATIONS IN LAOS. LAOS USA+45 PLAN INSPECT HOUSE/REP. PAGE 137 F2697
FOR/AID ADMIN FORCES ECO/UNDEV

L59
GARDNER R.N.,"NEW DIRECTIONS IN UNITED STATES FOREIGN ECONOMIC POLICY." AFR USA+45 CONSULT ...GEN/LAWS GEN/METH FOR/TRADE 20. PAGE 46 F0903
ECO/UNDEV ECO/TAC FOR/AID DIPLOM

L59
WURFEL D.,"FOREIGN AID AND SOCIAL REFORM IN POLITICAL DEVELOPMENT" (BMR)" PHILIPPINE USA+45 WOR+45 SOCIETY POL/PAR ACT/RES TEC/DEV DIPLOM 20. PAGE 149 F2943
FOR/AID PROB/SOLV ECO/TAC ECO/UNDEV

S59
HOFFMAN P.,"OPERATION BREAKTHROUGH." AFR S/ASIA STRUCT INDUS CONSULT TEC/DEV ATTIT RIGID/FLEX SKILL WEALTH...TECHNIC CONCPT STYLE RECORD CHARTS ORG/CHARTS GEN/METH VAL/FREE 20. PAGE 61 F1190
ECO/UNDEV EDU/PROP FOR/AID

S59
KINDLEBERGER C.P.,"UNITED STATES ECONOMIC FOREIGN POLICY: RESEARCH REQUIREMENTS FOR 1965." FUT USA+45 WOR+45 DIST/IND MARKET INT/ORG ECO/TAC INT/TRADE WEALTH...OBS TREND CON/ANAL GEN/LAWS FOR/TRADE VAL/FREE 20. PAGE 71 F1392
FINAN ECO/DEV FOR/AID

S59
REUBENS E.D.,"THE BASIS FOR REORIENATION OF AMERICAN FOREIGN AID POLICY." USA+45 USSR STRUCT INT/ORG CONSULT ECO/TAC ADMIN DRIVE MORAL ORD/FREE PWR WEALTH...RELATIV MATH STAT TREND GEN/LAWS VAL/FREE 20. PAGE 111 F2180
ECO/UNDEV PLAN FOR/AID DIPLOM

S59
STREETEN P.,"UNBALANCED GROWTH" UK ECO/DEV AGRI MARKET TEC/DEV CAP/ISM ECO/TAC FOR/AID INT/TRADE DEMAND ORD/FREE...CONCPT 20. PAGE 127 F2502
IDEA/COMP FINAN PRODUC EQUILIB

B60
ALLEN R.L.,SOVIET ECONOMIC WARFARE. USSR FINAN INDUS NAT/G PLAN TEC/DEV FOR/AID DETER WEALTH ...TREND GEN/LAWS FOR/TRADE 20. PAGE 4 F0072
COM ECO/TAC

B60
BILLERBECK K.,SOVIET BLOC FOREIGN AID TO UNDERDEVELOPED COUNTRIES. COM FUT USSR FINAN FORCES TEC/DEV DIPLOM INT/TRADE EDU/PROP NUC/PWR...TREND 20. PAGE 15 F0285
FOR/AID ECO/UNDEV ECO/TAC MARXISM

B60
BLACK E.R.,THE DIPLOMACY OF ECONOMIC DEVELOPMENT. WOR+45 CONSULT PLAN TEC/DEV DIPLOM ECO/TAC FOR/AID ...CONCPT TREND 20. PAGE 15 F0290
ECO/UNDEV ACT/RES

B60
COMMITTEE ECONOMIC DEVELOPMENT,NATIONAL OBJECTIVES AND THE BALANCE OF PAYMENTS PROBLEM: A STATEMENT ON NATIONAL POLICY. USA+45 WOR+45 DIST/IND FINAN INDUS LABOR NAT/G DELIB/GP ACT/RES FOR/AID INT/TRADE ...STAT CHARTS FOR/TRADE 20. PAGE 27 F0516
ECO/DEV ECO/TAC BAL/PAY

B60
FRANCK P.G.,AFGHANISTAN: BETWEEN EAST AND WEST. AFGHANISTN AFR USA+45 USSR ECO/UNDEV PLAN ADMIN ROUTINE ATTIT PWR...STAT OBS CHARTS TOT/POP FOR/TRADE 20. PAGE 43 F0843
ECO/TAC TREND FOR/AID

B60
HOFFMANN P.G.,ONE HUNDRED COUNTRIES, ONE AND ONE QUARTER BILLION PEOPLE. MARKET INT/ORG TEC/DEV CAP/ISM...GEOG CHARTS METH/COMP 20 UN. PAGE 61 F1191
FOR/AID ECO/TAC ECO/UNDEV INT/TRADE

B60
KENEN P.B.,GIANT AMONG NATIONS: PROBLEMS IN UNITED STATES FOREIGN ECONOMIC POLICY. AFR USA+45 FINAN DIPLOM TARIFFS BAL/PAY WEALTH 20. PAGE 70 F1376
FOR/AID ECO/UNDEV INT/TRADE PLAN

B60
KILLOUGH H.B.,INTERNATIONAL ECONOMICS. PLAN PROB/SOLV FOR/AID TARIFFS CONTROL BAL/PAY...POLICY CHARTS T 20. PAGE 71 F1388
CONCPT ECO/UNDEV INT/ORG INT/TRADE

B60
KRISTENSEN T.,THE ECONOMIC WORLD BALANCE. FUT WOR+45 CULTURE ECO/DEV BAL/PWR INT/TRADE REGION PWR WEALTH...STAT TREND CHARTS 20. PAGE 73 F1442
ECO/UNDEV ECO/TAC FOR/AID

B60
LATIFI D.,INDIA AND UNITED STATES AID. ASIA INDIA UK USA+45 AGRI FINAN INDUS COLONIAL ORD/FREE SOVEREIGN WEALTH...METH/COMP 20. PAGE 76 F1486
FOR/AID DIPLOM ECO/UNDEV

B60
MC CLELLAN G.S.,INDIA. AFR CHINA/COM INDIA CONSTN ELITES STRATA AGRI POL/PAR FOR/AID ARMS/CONT REV MARXISM...CENSUS BIBLIOG 20 GANDHI/M NEHRU/J. PAGE 87 F1712
DIPLOM NAT/G SOCIETY ECO/UNDEV

B60
NEALE A.D.,THE FLOW OF RESOURCES FROM RICH TO POOR. WOR+45 ECO/DEV ECO/UNDEV FINAN INDUS NAT/G PLAN EFFICIENCY WEALTH...POLICY NAT/COMP 20 RESOURCE/N. PAGE 97 F1905
FOR/AID DIPLOM METH/CNCPT

B60
PENTONY D.E.,UNITED STATES FOREIGN AID. INDIA LAOS USA+45 ECO/UNDEV INT/TRADE ADMIN PEACE ATTIT ...POLICY METH/COMP ANTHOL 20. PAGE 105 F2060
FOR/AID DIPLOM ECO/TAC

B60
RAO V.K.R.,INTERNATIONAL AID FOR ECONOMIC DEVELOPMENT - POSSIBILITIES AND LIMITATIONS. FINAN PLAN TEC/DEV ADMIN TASK EFFICIENCY...POLICY SOC METH/CNCPT CHARTS 20 UN. PAGE 109 F2147
FOR/AID DIPLOM INT/ORG ECO/UNDEV

B60
ROBINSON E.A.G.,ECONOMIC CONSEQUENCES OF THE SIZE OF NATIONS. AGRI INDUS DELIB/GP FOR/AID ADMIN EFFICIENCY...METH/COMP 20. PAGE 113 F2218
CONCPT INT/ORG NAT/COMP

B60
SHONFIELD A.,THE ATTACK ON WORLD POVERTY. WOR+45 ECO/DEV ECO/UNDEV FINAN VOL/ASSN PLAN EDU/PROP DRIVE KNOWL WEALTH...CONT/OBS STAND/INT ORG/CHARTS TOT/POP UNESCO 20. PAGE 121 F2383
INT/ORG ECO/TAC FOR/AID INT/TRADE

B60
STANFORD RESEARCH INSTITUTE,AFRICAN DEVELOPMENT: A TEST FOR INTERNATIONAL COOPERATION. AFR USA+45 WOR+45 FINAN INT/ORG PLAN PROB/SOLV ECO/TAC INT/TRADE ADMIN...CHARTS 20. PAGE 125 F2467
FOR/AID ECO/UNDEV ATTIT DIPLOM

B60
STEVENSON A.E.,PUTTING FIRST THINGS FIRST. USA+45 INT/ORG NEIGH FOR/AID DISCRIM...ANTHOL 20. PAGE 126 F2483
DIPLOM ECO/UNDEV ORD/FREE EDU/PROP

B60
STOLPER W.F.,GERMANY BETWEEN EAST AND WEST: THE ECONOMICS OF COMPETITIVE COEXISTENCE. AFR FUT GERMANY/E GERMANY/W WOR+45 FINAN POL/PAR BUDGET ECO/TAC FOR/AID INT/TRADE...STAT CHARTS METH/COMP 20. PAGE 126 F2495
ECO/DEV DIPLOM GOV/COMP BAL/PWR

B60
THEOBALD R.,THE RICH AND THE POOR: A STUDY OF THE ECONOMICS OF RISING EXPECTATIONS. WOR+45 CONSTN ECO/DEV ECO/UNDEV INT/ORG NAT/G PLAN FOR/AID ROUTINE BAL/PAY ORD/FREE PWR WEALTH...GEOG TREND WORK FOR/TRADE 20. PAGE 129 F2553
ECO/TAC INT/TRADE

B60
US GENERAL ACCOUNTING OFFICE,EXAMINATION OF ECONOMIC AND TECHNICAL ASSISTANCE PROGRAM FOR GUATEMALA. GUATEMALA L/A+17C USA+45 FINAN INDUS PLAN...POLICY STAT CHARTS 20 DEPT/STATE. PAGE 136 F2680
FOR/AID ECO/UNDEV TEC/DEV NAT/G

B60
US HOUSE COMM GOVT OPERATIONS,OPERATIONS OF THE DEVELOPMENT LOAN FUND: HEARINGS (COMMITTEE ON GOVERNMENT OPERATIONS). USA+45 PLAN BUDGET DIPLOM GOV/REL COST...CHARTS 20 CONGRESS DEPT/STATE AID. PAGE 137 F2698
FINAN FOR/AID ECO/TAC EFFICIENCY

B60
US OPERATIONS MISSION - TURKEY,SOME POSSIBILITIES FOR ACCELERATING TURKEY'S ECONOMIC GROWTH. TURKEY USA+45 AGRI FINAN INDUS NAT/G ACT/RES BUDGET COST ...CHARTS 20. PAGE 138 F2724
ECO/UNDEV ECO/TAC FOR/AID PRODUC

B60
WENTHOLT W.,INFLATION OR SECURITY? EUR+WWI USA+45 INDUS CONSULT TEC/DEV CAP/ISM DIPLOM FOR/AID INT/TRADE MARXISM 20 EEC. PAGE 145 F2858
ECO/DEV ECO/TAC FINAN ORD/FREE

S60
BUTLER W.F.,"ECONOMIC PROGRESS IN LATIN AMERICA." L/A+17C USA+45 ECO/UNDEV AGRI FINAN NAT/G PLAN ECO/TAC FOR/AID ADMIN WEALTH...OLD/LIB TOT/POP 20. PAGE 21 F0397
INDUS ACT/RES

S60
FRANKEL S.H.,"ECONOMIC ASPECTS OF POLITICAL INDEPENDENCE IN AFRICA." AFR FUT SOCIETY ECO/UNDEV COM/IND FINAN LEGIS PLAN TEC/DEV CAP/ISM ECO/TAC INT/TRADE ADMIN ATTIT DRIVE RIGID/FLEX PWR WEALTH ...MGT NEW/IDEA MATH TIME/SEQ VAL/FREE 20. PAGE 43 F0846
NAT/G FOR/AID

S60
HERRERA F.,"THE INTER-AMERICAN DEVELOPMENT BANK." USA+45 ECO/UNDEV INT/ORG CONSULT DELIB/GP PLAN ECO/TAC INT/TRADE ROUTINE WEALTH...STAT TERR/GP 20. PAGE 59 F1153
L/A+17C FINAN FOR/AID REGION

S60
LINDHOLM R.W.,"ACCELERATED DEVELOPMENT WITH A MINIMUM OF FOREIGN AID AND ECONOMIC CONTROLS." SOCIETY INDUS ECO/TAC WEALTH...CONCPT 20. PAGE 80 F1570
ECO/DEV FINAN FOR/AID

S60
MARTIN E.M.,"NEW TRENDS IN UNITED STATES ECONOMIC FOREIGN POLICY." USA+45 INTELL DELIB/GP FOR/AID INT/TRADE ROUTINE BAL/PAY...RELATIV TRUE/GP 20. PAGE 86 F1682
NAT/G PLAN DIPLOM

S60
MIKESELL R.F.,"AMERICA'S ECONOMIC RESPONSIBILITY AS A GREAT POWER." COM FUT USA+45 USSR WOR+45 INT/ORG PLAN ECO/TAC FOR/AID EDU/PROP CHOOSE WEALTH ...POLICY 20. PAGE 91 F1781
ECO/UNDEV BAL/PWR CAP/ISM

S60
MURPHY J.C.,"INTERNATIONAL INVESTMENT AND THE NATIONAL INTEREST." AFR WOR+45 WOR-45 ECO/DEV ECO/UNDEV NAT/G ACT/RES...CHARTS TOT/POP FOR/TRADE 20. PAGE 95 F1867
FINAN WEALTH FOR/AID

S60
PYE L.W.,"SOVIET AND AMERICAN STYLES IN FOREIGN AID." COM USA+45 USSR WOR+45 NAT/G PLAN ECO/TAC ROUTINE RIGID/FLEX...POLICY CONCPT TREND GEN/LAWS TOT/POP 20. PAGE 108 F2132
ECO/UNDEV ATTIT FOR/AID

S60
RIVKIN A.,"AFRICAN ECONOMIC DEVELOPMENT: ADVANCED TECHNOLOGY AND THE STAGES OF GROWTH." CULTURE ECO/UNDEV AGRI COM/IND EXTR/IND PLAN ECO/TAC ATTIT DRIVE RIGID/FLEX SKILL WEALTH...MGT SOC GEN/LAWS FOR/TRADE WORK TOT/POP 20. PAGE 111 F2195
AFR TEC/DEV FOR/AID

B61
ASHER R.E.,GRANTS, LOANS, AND LOCAL CURRENCIES; THEIR ROLE IN FOREIGN AID. AFR USA+45 ECO/UNDEV
FOR/AID FINAN

INT/ORG ACT/RES PLAN ECO/TAC GIVE CONTROL WEALTH 20. PAGE 7 F0130
NAT/G BUDGET

B61
AUBREY H.G.,COEXISTENCE: ECONOMIC CHALLENGE AND RESPONSE. AFR USSR WOR+45 ACT/RES BAL/PWR CAP/ISM DIPLOM ECO/TAC FOR/AID INT/TRADE PEACE SOCISM ...METH/COMP NAT/COMP. PAGE 7 F0139
POLICY ECO/UNDEV PLAN COM

B61
BAUER P.T.,INDIAN ECONOMIC POLICY AND DEVELOPMENT. INDIA STRATA AGRI FINAN POL/PAR BUDGET FOR/AID GOV/REL EFFICIENCY...CENSUS 20. PAGE 11 F0216
ECO/UNDEV ECO/TAC POLICY PLAN

B61
BENHAM F.,ECONOMIC AID TO UNDERDEVELOPED COUNTRIES. WOR+45 INDUS BAL/PAY ALL/VALS 20. PAGE 13 F0244
ECO/UNDEV FOR/AID INT/TRADE FINAN

B61
BONNEFOUS M.,EUROPE ET TIERS MONDE. EUR+WWI SOCIETY INT/ORG NAT/G VOL/ASSN ACT/RES TEC/DEV CAP/ISM ECO/TAC ATTIT ORD/FREE SOVEREIGN...POLICY CONCPT TREND TERR/GP COMMUN 20. PAGE 16 F0314
AFR ECO/UNDEV FOR/AID INT/TRADE

B61
DETHINE P.,BIBLIOGRAPHIE DES ASPECTS ECONOMIQUES ET SOCIAUX DE L'INDUSTRIALISATION EN AFRIQUE. AFR FINAN LABOR FOR/AID...SOC 20. PAGE 32 F0623
BIBLIOG/A ECO/UNDEV INDUS TEC/DEV

B61
ELLIS H.S.,ECONOMIC DEVELOPMENT FOR LATIN AMERICA. L/A+17C AGRI FINAN INDUS FOR/AID GP/REL BAL/PAY DEMAND...ANTHOL 20 INTL/ECON. PAGE 37 F0723
ECO/UNDEV ECO/TAC PLAN INT/TRADE

B61
GURTOO D.H.N.,INDIA'S BALANCE OF PAYMENTS (1920-1960). INDIA FINAN DIPLOM FOR/AID INT/TRADE PRICE COLONIAL...CHARTS BIBLIOG 20. PAGE 52 F1014
BAL/PAY STAT ECO/TAC ECO/UNDEV

B61
HAUSER M.,DIE URSACHEN DER FRANZOSISCHEN INFLATION IN DEN JAHREN 1946-1952. AFR FRANCE INDUS NAT/G BUDGET DIPLOM ECO/TAC FOR/AID COST MONEY 20. PAGE 57 F1114
ECO/DEV FINAN PRICE

B61
INDUSTRIAL COUN SOC-ECO STU,THE SWEDISH ECONOMY AND THE UNDERDEVELOPED COUNTRIES. SWEDEN INDUS DELIB/GP TEC/DEV INT/TRADE EDU/PROP COLONIAL DRIVE...CHARTS 20. PAGE 64 F1264
FOR/AID ECO/UNDEV PLAN FINAN

B61
JAVITS B.A.,THE PEACE BY INVESTMENT CORPORATION. WOR+45 NAT/G LEGIS PROB/SOLV PERS/REL WEALTH ...POLICY 20. PAGE 66 F1307
ECO/UNDEV DIPLOM FOR/AID PEACE

B61
MEZERIK A.G.,ECONOMIC DEVELOPMENT AIDS FOR UNDERDEVELOPED COUNTRIES. WOR+45 FINAN LEGIS PROB/SOLV TEC/DEV DIPLOM FOR/AID GIVE TASK WAR 20 UN. PAGE 91 F1776
ECO/UNDEV INT/ORG WEALTH PLAN

B61
MORLEY L.,THE PATCHWORK HISTORY OF FOREIGN AID. AFR KOREA/S USA+45 USSR LAW FINAN INT/ORG TEC/DEV BAL/PWR GIVE 20 NATO. PAGE 93 F1834
FOR/AID ECO/UNDEV FORCES DIPLOM

B61
PETCH G.A.,ECONOMIC DEVELOPMENT AND MODERN WEST AFRICA. AFR CONGO/BRAZ GHANA NIGER SIER/LEONE AGRI MARKET LABOR FOR/AID TAX COST EFFICIENCY EQUILIB PRODUC...GEOG TREND 20. PAGE 105 F2068
ECO/UNDEV TEC/DEV EXTR/IND ECO/TAC

B61
THEOBALD R.,THE CHALLENGE OF ABUNDANCE. USA+45 WOR+45 MARKET DIPLOM FOR/AID REV PRODUC UTOPIA SUPEGO...POLICY TREND BIBLIOG/A 20. PAGE 129 F2554
WELF/ST ECO/UNDEV PROB/SOLV ECO/TAC

B61
US GENERAL ACCOUNTING OFFICE,EXAMINATION OF ECONOMIC AND TECHNICAL ASSISTANCE PROGRAM FOR IRAN. IRAN USA+45 AGRI INDUS DIPLOM CONTROL COST 20. PAGE 136 F2681
FOR/AID ADMIN TEC/DEV ECO/UNDEV

B61
US SENATE COMM ON FOREIGN RELS,INTERNATIONAL DEVELOPMENT AND SECURITY: HEARINGS ON BILL (2 VOLS.). ECO/UNDEV FINAN FORCES REV COST WEALTH ...CHARTS 20 AID PRESIDENT. PAGE 139 F2747
FOR/AID CIVMIL/REL ORD/FREE ECO/TAC

B61
WARD B.J.,INDIA AND THE WEST. INDIA UK USA+45 INT/TRADE GIVE COLONIAL ATTIT MARXISM 19/20. PAGE 143 F2817
PLAN ECO/UNDEV ECO/TAC FOR/AID

S61
BARALL M.,"THE UNITED STATES GOVERNMENT RESPONDS." L/A+17C USA+45 SOCIETY NAT/G CREATE PLAN DIPLOM ECO/TAC ATTIT DRIVE RIGID/FLEX KNOWL SKILL WEALTH ...METH/CNCPT TIME/SEQ GEN/METH 20. PAGE 9 F0176
ECO/UNDEV ACT/RES FOR/AID

S61
DELLA PORT G.,"PROBLEMI E PROSPETTIVE DI COESISTENZA FRA ORIENTE ED OCCIDENTE, (PART 3)." COM FUT WOR+45 NAT/G BAL/PWR FOR/AID BAL/PAY PWR WEALTH...SOC CONCPT GEN/LAWS 20. PAGE 32 F0616
AFR INT/TRADE

S61
GALBRAITH J.K.,"A POSITIVE APPROACH TO ECONOMIC AID." FUT USA+45 INTELL NAT/G CONSULT ACT/RES DIPLOM ECO/TAC EDU/PROP ATTIT KNOWL PWR WEALTH ...SOC STERTYP MID/EX METH/GP 20. PAGE 45 F0883
ECO/UNDEV ROUTINE FOR/AID

S61
HEILBRONER R.L.,"DYNAMICS OF FOREIGN AID: PROBLEMS OF UNDERDEVELOPED NATIONS PLAGUE ASSISTANCE PROGRAM." FUT USA+45 WOR+45 STRATA NAT/G PLAN TEC/DEV ATTIT DRIVE WEALTH WORK 20. PAGE 58 F1135
ECO/UNDEV ECO/TAC FOR/AID

S61
NOVE A.,"THE SOVIET MODEL AND UNDERDEVELOPED COUNTRIES." COM FUT USSR WOR+45 CULTURE ECO/DEV POL/PAR FOR/AID EDU/PROP ADMIN MORAL WEALTH ...POLICY RECORD HIST/WRIT 20. PAGE 99 F1942
ECO/UNDEV PLAN

S61
VINER J.,"ECONOMIC FOREIGN POLICY ON THE NEW FRONTIER." USA+45 ECO/UNDEV AGRI FINAN INDUS MARKET INT/ORG NAT/G FOR/AID INT/TRADE ADMIN ATTIT PWR 20 KENNEDY/JF. PAGE 141 F2786
TOP/EX ECO/TAC BAL/PAY TARIFFS

B62
ROUND TABLE ON EUROPE'S ROLE IN LATIN AMERICAN DEVELOPMENT. EUR+WWI L/A+17C PLAN BAL/PAY UTIL ROLE WEALTH...CHARTS ANTHOL 20 UN INT/AM/DEV. PAGE 1 F0017
ECO/UNDEV FINAN TEC/DEV FOR/AID

B62
ARNOLD H.J.P.,AID FOR DEVELOPING COUNTRIES. COM EUR+WWI USA+45 USSR WOR+45 EDU/PROP ATTIT DRIVE PWR WEALTH...TREND CHARTS STERTYP NAT/ 20. PAGE 6 F0115
ECO/UNDEV ECO/TAC FOR/AID

B62
BROOKINGS INSTITUTION,DEVELOPMENT OF THE EMERGING COUNTRIES; AN AGENDA FOR RESEARCH. WOR+45 AGRI TEC/DEV FOR/AID EDU/PROP ADJUST HABITAT KNOWL...PSY SOC ANTHOL 20 THIRD/WRLD. PAGE 19 F0362
ECO/UNDEV R+D SOCIETY PROB/SOLV

B62
DREIER J.C.,THE ALLIANCE FOR PROGRESS. L/A+17C USA+45 CULTURE ECO/DEV ECO/UNDEV NAT/G PLAN DIPLOM PWR 20 OAS ALL/PROG. PAGE 34 F0661
FOR/AID INT/ORG ECO/TAC POLICY

B62
FAO,FOOD AND AGRICULTURE ORGANIZATION AFRICAN SURVEY. AFR CONGO/BRAZ GHANA STRATA AGRI INT/ORG TEC/DEV FOR/AID INT/TRADE RACE/REL DEMAND EFFICIENCY PRODUC...GEOG 20 UN CONGO/LEOP. PAGE 39 F0763
ECO/TAC WEALTH EXTR/IND ECO/UNDEV

B62
FRIEDMANN W.,METHODS AND POLICIES OF PRINCIPAL DONOR COUNTRIES IN PUBLIC INTERNATIONAL DEVELOPMENT FINANCING: PRELIMINARY APPRAISAL. FRANCE GERMANY/W UK USA+45 USSR WOR+45 FINAN TEC/DEV CAP/ISM DIPLOM ECO/TAC ATTIT 20 EEC. PAGE 44 F0864
INT/ORG FOR/AID NAT/COMP ADMIN

B62
FRIEDRICH-EBERT-STIFTUNG,THE SOVIET BLOC AND DEVELOPING COUNTRIES. CHINA/COM COM GERMANY/E USSR WOR+45 ECO/UNDEV INT/ORG NAT/G TEC/DEV NEUTRAL PWR ...POLICY 20. PAGE 44 F0868
MARXISM DIPLOM ECO/TAC FOR/AID

B62
GOLDWIN R.A.,WHY FOREIGN AID? - TWO MESSAGES BY PRESIDENT KENNEDY AND ESSAYS. S/ASIA USA+45 ECO/UNDEV 20 KENNEDY/JF THIRD/WRLD. PAGE 48 F0942
DIPLOM FOR/AID POLICY

B62
HIGGANS B.,UNITED NATIONS AND U.S. FOREIGN ECONOMIC POLICY. FUT USA+45 WOR+45 ECO/DEV ECO/UNDEV NAT/G ECO/TAC WEALTH...TIME/SEQ TOT/POP UN 20. PAGE 59 F1168
INT/ORG ACT/RES FOR/AID DIPLOM

B62
HUHNE L.H.,FINANCING ECONOMIC DEVELOPMENT THROUGH NATIONAL AND INTERNATIONAL ORGANIZATIONS (THESIS; U OF WIS.). USA+45 INT/ORG PLAN GIVE GOV/REL WEALTH 20. PAGE 63 F1235
RATION FINAN FOR/AID ECO/UNDEV

B62
JORDAN A.A. JR.,FOREIGN AID AND THE DEFENSE OF SOUTHEAST ASIA. PAKISTAN VIETNAM/S FINAN PLAN BUDGET ECO/TAC DETER WAR ORD/FREE...POLICY DECISION CENSUS CHARTS BIBLIOG 20. PAGE 68 F1341
FOR/AID S/ASIA FORCES ECO/UNDEV

B62
LIPPMANN W.,WESTERN UNITY AND THE COMMON MARKET. EUR+WWI FRANCE GERMANY/W UK USA+45 ECO/DEV AGRI FINAN MARKET INT/ORG NAT/G FOR/AID AGREE WEALTH 20 EEC. PAGE 80 F1575
DIPLOM INT/TRADE VOL/ASSN

B62
MOUSSA P.,THE UNDERPRIVILEGED NATIONS. FINAN INT/ORG PLAN PROB/SOLV CAP/ISM GIVE TASK WEALTH ...POLICY SOC IND 20. PAGE 94 F1850
ECO/UNDEV NAT/G DIPLOM FOR/AID

B62
PAKISTAN MINISTRY OF FINANCE,FOREIGN ECONOMIC AID: A REVIEW OF FOREIGN ECONOMIC AID TO PAKISTAN. EUR+WWI PAKISTAN UK USA+45 USSR ECO/UNDEV INT/ORG DELIB/GP DIPLOM ECO/TAC...CHARTS CMN/WLTH CHINJAP. PAGE 103 F2016
FOR/AID RECEIVE WEALTH FINAN

B62
PERROUX F.,L'ECONOMIE DES JEUNES NATIONS. EUR+WWI SOUTH/AFR FINAN MARKET TEC/DEV CAP/ISM FOR/AID INT/TRADE 20. PAGE 105 F2065
INDUS ECO/UNDEV ECO/TAC

DIPLOM

B62
RIMALOV V.V.,ECONOMIC COOPERATION BETWEEN USSR AND UNDERDEVELOPED COUNTRIES. USSR FINAN TEC/DEV INT/TRADE DOMIN EDU/PROP COLONIAL NAT/LISM DRIVE SOVEREIGN...AUD/VIS 20. PAGE 111 F2194 FOR/AID PLAN ECO/UNDEV DIPLOM

B62
SCHMITT H.A.,THE PATH TO EUROPEAN UNITY. EUR+WWI USA+45 PLAN TEC/DEV DIPLOM FOR/AID CONFER...INT/LAW 20 EEC EURCOALSTL MARSHL/PLN UNIFICA. PAGE 117 F2300 INT/ORG INT/TRADE REGION ECO/DEV

B62
THEOBALD R.,NATIONAL DEVELOPMENT EFFORTS (PAMPHLET). WOR+45 AGRI BUDGET FOR/AID INT/TRADE TAX 20. PAGE 129 F2555 ECO/UNDEV PLAN BAL/PAY WEALTH

B62
UNIVERSITY OF TENNESSEE,GOVERNMENT AND WORLD CRISIS. USA+45 FOR/AID ORD/FREE...ANTHOL 20 UN ALL/PROG. PAGE 133 F2622 ECO/DEV DIPLOM NAT/G INT/ORG

B62
US AGENCY INTERNATIONAL DEV,OPERATIONS REPORT - 1962 (PAMPHLET). AFR ASIA L/A+17C USA+45 ECO/UNDEV FINAN INT/ORG NAT/G 20 MICHIGAN. PAGE 134 F2636 FOR/AID CHARTS STAT BUDGET

B62
US CONGRESS JOINT ECO COMM,FACTORS AFFECTING THE UNITED STATES BALANCE OF PAYMENTS. USA+45 DELIB/GP PLAN DIPLOM FOR/AID PRODUC WEALTH...CHARTS 20 CONGRESS OEEC. PAGE 134 F2653 BAL/PAY INT/TRADE ECO/TAC FINAN

B62
US CONGRESS JOINT ECO COMM,ECONOMIC DEVELOPMENTS IN SOUTH AMERICA. USA+45 SOCIETY FINAN NAT/G PROB/SOLV TEC/DEV INT/TRADE TAX EFFICIENCY PRODUC ATTIT ...POLICY 20 ALL/PROG CONGRESS SOUTH/AMER. PAGE 135 F2654 L/A+17C ECO/UNDEV FOR/AID DIPLOM

B62
VACCARO J.R.,A STATEMENT OF THE LAWS OF CHILE IN MATTERS AFFECTING BUSINESS (3RD ED.). CHILE AGRI FINAN FAM LABOR ECO/TAC FOR/AID TAX ADJUD CONTROL MARRIAGE STRANGE...BIBLIOG 20. PAGE 140 F2756 CONSTN LAW INDUS MGT

B62
VIET J.,INTERNATIONAL COOPERATION AND PROGRAMMES OF ECONOMIC AND SOCIAL DEVELOPMENT. TEC/DEV FOR/AID DOMIN COLONIAL PEACE WEALTH 20 UNESCO. PAGE 141 F2784 BIBLIOG/A INT/ORG DIPLOM ECO/UNDEV

B62
ZOOK P.D.,FOREIGN TRADE AND HUMAN CAPITAL. L/A+17C USA+45 FINAN DIPLOM ECO/TAC PRODUC...POLICY 20. PAGE 151 F2970 INT/TRADE ECO/UNDEV FOR/AID BAL/PAY

S62
MILLIKEN M.,"NEW AND OLD CRITERIA FOR AID." WOR+45 ECO/DEV ECO/UNDEV ACT/RES PLAN ATTIT KNOWL...TREND CON/ANAL SIMUL GEN/METH TERR/GP 20. PAGE 92 F1796 USA+45 ECO/TAC FOR/AID

S62
MORGENTHAU H.J.,"A POLITICAL THEORY OF FOREIGN AID." ECO/UNDEV NAT/G DELIB/GP PLAN ECO/TAC EDU/PROP EXEC ORD/FREE RESPECT WEALTH...METH/CNCPT TREND 20. PAGE 93 F1833 USA+45 PHIL/SCI FOR/AID

S62
PYE L.W.,"THE POLITICAL IMPULSES AND FANTASIES BEHIND FOREIGN AID." FUT USA+45 ECO/UNDEV DIPLOM ECO/TAC ROUTINE DRIVE KNOWL...SOC METH/CNCPT NEW/IDEA TREND HYPO/EXP STERTYP GEN/METH 20. PAGE 108 F2133 ACT/RES ATTIT FOR/AID

B63
BRITISH AID. UK AGRI DIST/IND INDUS SCHOOL TEC/DEV INT/TRADE COLONIAL DEMAND...TREND CHARTS 20. PAGE 1 F0018 FOR/AID ECO/UNDEV NAT/G FINAN

B63
ALPERT P.,ECONOMIC DEVELOPMENT. WOR+45 FINAN TEC/DEV ECO/TAC PRICE GOV/REL HABITAT...GEOG BIBLIOG T 20 THIRD/WRLD. PAGE 4 F0079 ECO/DEV ECO/UNDEV INT/TRADE FOR/AID

B63
CENTRO PARA EL DESARROLLO,LA ALIANZA PARA EL PROGRESO Y EL DESARROLLO SOCIAL DE AMERICA LATINA. L/A+17C INT/ORG DIPLOM ECO/TAC INT/TRADE ATTIT 20 ALL/PROG. PAGE 22 F0435 ECO/UNDEV FOR/AID PLAN REGION

B63
COLUMBIA U SCHOOL OF LAW,PUBLIC INTERNATIONAL DEVELOPMENT FINANCING IN SENEGAL. SENEGAL FINAN DELIB/GP GIVE EFFICIENCY...CHARTS GOV/COMP ANTHOL 20. PAGE 26 F0511 FOR/AID PLAN RECEIVE ECO/UNDEV

B63
EL-NAGGAR S.,FOREIGN AID TO UNITED ARAB REPUBLIC. UAR USA+45 USSR AGRI FINAN INDUS FORCES EATING DEMAND...CHARTS METH/COMP 20 RESOURCE/N AID. PAGE 37 F0718 FOR/AID ECO/UNDEV RECEIVE PLAN

B63
ELLENDER A.J.,A REPORT ON UNITED STATES FOREIGN OPERATIONS IN AFRICA. SOUTH/AFR USA+45 STRATA EXTR/IND FORCES RACE/REL ISOLAT SOVEREIGN...CHARTS 20 NEGRO. PAGE 37 F0721 FOR/AID DIPLOM WEALTH ECO/UNDEV

B63
FATEMI N.S.,THE DOLLAR CRISIS. USA+45 INDUS NAT/G LEGIS BUDGET TAX COST...CHARTS METH/COMP 20 EEC. PAGE 39 F0766 PROB/SOLV BAL/PAY FOR/AID PLAN

B63
GORDON L.,A NEW DEAL FOR LATIN AMERICA. L/A+17C USA+45 CULTURE NAT/G TEC/DEV DIPLOM FOR/AID REGION TASK...POLICY 20 ALL/PROG DEPT/STATE. PAGE 49 F0958 ECO/UNDEV ECO/TAC INT/ORG PLAN

B63
HAQ M.,THE STRATEGY OF ECONOMIC PLANNING. PAKISTAN AGRI FINAN INDUS NAT/G FOR/AID TAX CONTROL REGION PRODUC...POLICY CHARTS 20. PAGE 55 F1071 ECO/TAC ECO/UNDEV PLAN PROB/SOLV

B63
HARROD R.F.,INTERNATIONAL TRADE THEORY IN A DEVELOPING WORLD. COM WOR+45 FOR/AID REGION COST DEMAND WEALTH...POLICY 20 INTL/ECON. PAGE 56 F1095 INT/TRADE BAL/PAY ECO/UNDEV METH/COMP

B63
HAUSMAN W.H.,MANAGING ECONOMIC DEVELOPMENT IN AFRICA. AFR USA+45 LAW FINAN WORKER TEC/DEV WEALTH ...ANTHOL 20. PAGE 57 F1116 ECO/UNDEV PLAN FOR/AID MGT

B63
KATZ S.M.,A SELECTED LIST OF US READINGS ON DEVELOPMENT. AGRI COM/IND DIST/IND INDUS LABOR PLAN FOR/AID EDU/PROP HEALTH...POLICY SOC/WK 20. PAGE 69 F1361 BIBLIOG/A ECO/UNDEV TEC/DEV ACT/RES

B63
LARY M.B.,PROBLEMS OF THE UNITED STATES AS WORLD TRADER AND BANKER. USA+45 NAT/G PLAN DIPLOM FOR/AID ...TREND CHARTS. PAGE 76 F1482 ECO/DEV FINAN BAL/PAY INT/TRADE

B63
MANGER W.,THE ALLIANCE FOR PROGRESS: A CRITICAL APPRAISAL. FUT L/A+17C USA+45 CULTURE ECO/UNDEV ACADEM NAT/G SCHOOL PLAN FOR/AID...POLICY OAS ALL/PROG. PAGE 84 F1651 DIPLOM INT/ORG ECO/TAC REGION

B63
MARITANO N.,AN ALLIANCE FOR PROGRESS. FUT L/A+17C USA+45 CULTURE ECO/UNDEV NAT/G PLAN CONTROL ...POLICY ALL/PROG. PAGE 85 F1669 DIPLOM INT/ORG ECO/TAC FOR/AID

B63
OECD,FOOD AID: ITS ROLE IN ECONOMIC DEVELOPMENT. FINAN NAT/G PLAN DIPLOM GIVE TASK WEALTH ...METH/COMP METH 20. PAGE 100 F1966 ECO/UNDEV FOR/AID INT/ORG POLICY

B63
RAO V.K.R.,FOREIGN AID AND INDIA'S ECONOMIC DEVELOPMENT. INDIA INT/ORG PROB/SOLV TEC/DEV ECO/TAC CONTROL WEALTH...TREND 20. PAGE 109 F2148 FOR/AID ECO/UNDEV RECEIVE DIPLOM

B63
SCHOECK H.,THE NEW ARGUMENT IN ECONOMICS. UK USA+45 INDUS MARKET LABOR NAT/G ECO/TAC ADMIN ROUTINE BAL/PAY PWR...POLICY BOLIV. PAGE 117 F2309 WELF/ST FOR/AID ECO/DEV ALL/IDEOS

B63
US AGENCY INTERNATIONAL DEV,OPERATIONS REPORT - 1963. AFR ASIA L/A+17C USA+45 ECO/UNDEV FINAN INT/ORG NAT/G. PAGE 134 F2637 FOR/AID CHARTS STAT BUDGET

B63
US CONGRESS JOINT ECO COMM,OUTLOOK FOR UNITED STATES BALANCE OF PAYMENTS. AFR USA+45 ECO/DEV NAT/G FORCES DIPLOM FOR/AID COST EFFICIENCY ...POLICY CONGRESS EEC. PAGE 135 F2657 BAL/PAY FINAN INT/TRADE PROB/SOLV

B63
US ECON SURVEY TEAM INDONESIA,INDONESIA - PERSPECTIVE AND PROPOSALS FOR UNITED STATES ECONOMIC AID. INDONESIA AGRI MARKET TEC/DEV DIPLOM INT/TRADE EDU/PROP 20. PAGE 136 F2678 FOR/AID ECO/UNDEV PLAN INDUS

B63
US GOVERNMENT,REPORT TO INTER-AMERICAN ECONOMIC AND SOCIAL COUNCIL AT SECOND ANNUAL MEETING. L/A+17C USA+45 VOL/ASSN TEC/DEV DIPLOM TAX EATING EFFICIENCY HEALTH...STAT CHARTS 20 AID. PAGE 136 F2682 ECO/TAC FOR/AID FINAN PLAN

B63
US SENATE COMM GOVT OPERATIONS,REPORT OF A STUDY OF US FOREIGN AID IN TEN MIDDLE EASTERN AND AFRICAN COUNTRIES. AFR ISLAM USA+45 FORCES PLAN BUDGET DIPLOM TAX DETER WEALTH...STAT CHARTS 20 CONGRESS AID MID/EAST. PAGE 138 F2728 FOR/AID EFFICIENCY ECO/TAC FINAN

B63
VELEZ GARCIA J.,DEVALUACION 1962; HISTORIA DOCUMENTAL DE UN PROCESO ECONOMICO. AFR L/A+17C USA+45 FINAN FOR/AID PRODUC WEALTH...POLICY STAT CHARTS ANTHOL 20 COLOMB. PAGE 141 F2774 ECO/UNDEV ECO/TAC PLAN NAT/G

L63
OLSON M. JR.,"RAPID ECONOMIC GROWTH AS A DESTABILIZING FORCE." WOR+45 WOR-45 STRATA SOCIETY FOR/AID

ECO/UNDEV FAM KIN CREATE TEC/DEV DIPLOM PEACE ATTIT PERSON RIGID/FLEX PWR RESPECT WEALTH...SOC 20. PAGE 101 F1989

S63
BEGUIN H.,"ASPECTS STRUCTURELS DU COMMERCE EXTERIEUR DES PAYS SOUS-DEVELOPPES." FUT WOR+45 STRUCT FINAN SERV/IND POL/PAR TEC/DEV PERCEPT WEALTH FOR/TRADE 20. PAGE 12 F0229
MARKET ECO/UNDEV FOR/AID

S63
CARTER A.G.T.,"THE BALANCE OF PAYMENTS OF EAST AFRICA" AFR ECO/TAC FOR/AID RATION TARIFFS TAX ADMIN...STAT 20 AFRICA/E. PAGE 22 F0423
BUDGET ECO/UNDEV BAL/PAY INT/TRADE

S63
DOSSER D.,"TOWARD A THEORY OF INTERNATIONAL PUBLIC FINANCE." WOR+45 ECO/DEV PLAN ECO/TAC WEALTH ...WELF/ST TREND GEN/LAWS TRUE/GP METH/GP 20. PAGE 34 F0654
FINAN INT/ORG FOR/AID

S63
ETHERINGTON D.M.,"LAND RESETTLEMENT IN KENYA; POLICY AND PRACTICE" AFR TEC/DEV ECO/TAC FOR/AID TAX PRODUC...CHARTS 20. PAGE 39 F0752
ECO/UNDEV AGRI WORKER PLAN

S63
GANDILHON J.,"LA SCIENCE ET LA TECHNIQUE A L'AIDE DES REGIONS PEU DEVELOPPEES." FRANCE FUT WOR+45 ECO/DEV R+D PROF/ORG ACT/RES PLAN...MGT TOT/POP VAL/FREE 20 UN. PAGE 46 F0893
ECO/UNDEV TEC/DEV FOR/AID

S63
HINDLEY D.,"FOREIGN AID TO INDONESIA AND ITS POLITICAL IMPLICATIONS." INDONESIA POL/PAR ATTIT SOVEREIGN...CHARTS 20. PAGE 60 F1173
FOR/AID NAT/G WEALTH ECO/TAC

S63
HOOVER C.B.,"ECONOMIC REFORM VERSUS ECONOMIC GROWTH IN UNDERDEVELOPED COUNTRIES." FUT WOR+45 ELITES STRATA ECO/UNDEV DIST/IND INDUS TEC/DEV CAP/ISM FOR/AID INT/TRADE ATTIT WEALTH...MYTH TREND STERTYP GEN/LAWS WORK 20. PAGE 61 F1209
ECO/DEV ECO/TAC

S63
LEDUC G.,"L'AIDE INTERNATIONALE AU DEVELOPPEMENT." FUT WOR+45 ECO/DEV ECO/UNDEV R+D PROF/ORG TEC/DEV ECO/TAC ROUTINE ATTIT ALL/VALS...MGT TIME/SEQ FOR/TRADE TOT/POP 20. PAGE 77 F1503
FINAN PLAN FOR/AID

S63
MARTHELOT P.,"PROGRES DE LA REFORME AGRAIRE." INTELL ECO/DEV R+D FOR/AID ADMIN KNOWL...OBS VAL/FREE UN 20. PAGE 86 F1680
AGRI INT/ORG

S63
MIKESELL R.F.,"COMMODITY AGREEMENTS AND AID TO DEVELOPING COUNTRIES." WOR+45 WOR-45 INT/ORG ECO/TAC ATTIT WEALTH WORK FOR/TRADE 20. PAGE 91 F1782
FINAN ECO/UNDEV BAL/PAY FOR/AID

S63
NADLER E.B.,"SOME ECONOMIC DISADVANTAGES OF THE ARMS RACE." AFR USA+45 INDUS R+D FORCES PLAN TEC/DEV ECO/TAC FOR/AID EDU/PROP PWR WEALTH...TREND FOR/TRADE 20. PAGE 96 F1886
ECO/DEV MGT BAL/PAY

S63
PINCUS J.,"THE COST OF FOREIGN AID." WOR+45 ECO/DEV FINAN NAT/G VOL/ASSN CREATE ECO/TAC EDU/PROP WEALTH ...METH/CNCPT STAT CHARTS HYPO/EXP TOT/POP VAL/FREE 20. PAGE 106 F2087
USA+45 ECO/UNDEV FOR/AID

S63
REDDAWAY W.B.,"THE ECONOMICS OF UNDERDEVELOPED COUNTRIES." S/ASIA WOR+45 WOR-45 STRATA AGRI COM/IND DIST/IND MARKET PROC/MFG PLAN TEC/DEV FOR/AID BAL/PAY ATTIT DRIVE SKILL WORK FOR/TRADE 20. PAGE 110 F2165
ECO/TAC ECO/UNDEV INDIA

S63
VINER J.,"REPORT OF THE CLAY COMMITTEE ON FOREIGN AID: A SYMPOSIUM." USA+45 WOR+45 NAT/G CONSULT PLAN BAL/PWR ATTIT WEALTH...MGT CONCPT TOT/POP 20. PAGE 142 F2788
ACT/RES ECO/TAC FOR/AID

N63
US AGENCY INTERNATIONAL DEV,PRINCIPLES OF FOREIGN ECONOMIC ASSISTANCE (PAMPHLET). USA+45 FINAN GP/REL BAL/PAY EFFICIENCY 20 AID. PAGE 134 F2638
FOR/AID PLAN ECO/UNDEV ATTIT

N63
US COMM STRENG SEC FREE WORLD,THE SCOPE AND DISTRIBUTION OF UNITED STATES MILITARY AND ECONOMIC ASSISTANCE PROGRAMS (PAMPHLET). USA+45 PLAN BAL/PWR BUDGET DIPLOM CONTROL CIVMIL/REL ATTIT. PAGE 134 F2648
DELIB/GP POLICY FOR/AID ORD/FREE

B64
THE SPECIAL COMMONWEALTH AFRICAN ASSISTANCE PLAN. AFR CANADA INDIA NIGERIA UK FINAN SCHOOL...CHARTS 20 COMMONWLTH. PAGE 1 F0019
ECO/UNDEV TREND FOR/AID ADMIN

B64
BALOGH T.,THE ECONOMIC IMPACT OF MONETARY AND COMMERCIAL INSTITUTIONS OF A EUROPEAN ORIGIN IN AFRICA. AFR UAR INDUS FOR/AID COLONIAL CONTROL ...NAT/COMP 20. PAGE 9 F0169
TEC/DEV FINAN ECO/UNDEV ECO/TAC

B64
CALDER R.,TWO-WAY PASSAGE. INT/ORG TEC/DEV WAR PERSON ORD/FREE 20. PAGE 21 F0400
FOR/AID ECO/UNDEV ECO/TAC DIPLOM

B64
CASEY R.G.,THE FUTURE OF THE COMMONWEALTH. INDIA PAKISTAN UK ECO/UNDEV INT/ORG TEC/DEV COLONIAL SUPEGO 20 EEC AUSTRAL. PAGE 22 F0425
DIPLOM SOVEREIGN NAT/LISM FOR/AID

B64
CEPEDE M.,POPULATION AND FOOD. USA+45 STRUCT ECO/UNDEV FAM PLAN TEC/DEV FOR/AID CONTROL...CATH SOC TREND 19/20. PAGE 22 F0436
FUT GEOG AGRI CENSUS

B64
COLUMBIA U SCHOOL OF LAW,PUBLIC INTERNATIONAL DEVELOPMENT FINANCING IN INDIA. GERMANY/W INDIA UK USA+45 INDUS PLAN TEC/DEV DIPLOM ECO/TAC GIVE ADMIN UTIL ATTIT 20. PAGE 26 F0512
ECO/UNDEV FINAN FOR/AID INT/ORG

B64
COMPOS R.O.,A MOEDA, O GOVERNO E O TEMPO. AFR BRAZIL WOR+45 FINAN TEC/DEV FOR/AID REGION DEMAND ...ANTHOL 20. PAGE 27 F0520
ECO/UNDEV PLAN DIPLOM INT/TRADE

B64
ESTHUS R.A.,FROM ENMITY TO ALLIANCE: US AUSTRALIAN RELATIONS. S/ASIA DIST/IND VOL/ASSN FORCES ATTIT 20 AUSTRAL TREATY CMN/WLTH. PAGE 39 F0751
DIPLOM WAR INT/TRADE FOR/AID

B64
FATOUROS A.A.,CANADA'S OVERSEAS AID. CANADA WOR+45 ECO/DEV FINAN NAT/G BUDGET ECO/TAC CONFER ADMIN 20. PAGE 39 F0768
FOR/AID DIPLOM ECO/UNDEV POLICY

B64
FEIS H.,FOREIGN AID AND FOREIGN POLICY. USA+45 WOR+45 NAT/G VOL/ASSN ACT/RES TEC/DEV ATTIT HEALTH WEALTH...SOC GEN/LAWS 20. PAGE 40 F0775
ECO/UNDEV ECO/TAC FOR/AID DIPLOM

B64
HALLOWELL J.H.,DEVELOPMENT: FOR WHAT. WOR+45 POL/PAR SECT FOR/AID INT/TRADE CT/SYS PARTIC PRODUC PLURISM. PAGE 54 F1052
ECO/UNDEV CONSTN NAT/LISM ECO/TAC

B64
INTL INF CTR LOCAL CREDIT,GOVERNMENT MEASURES FOR THE PROMOTION OF REGIONAL ECONOMIC DEVELOPMENT. WOR+45 ECO/UNDEV FINAN INT/ORG DIPLOM ORD/FREE ...POLICY GEOG 20. PAGE 65 F1285
FOR/AID PLAN ECO/TAC REGION

B64
LEWIN P.,THE FOREIGN TRADE OF COMMUNIST CHINA* ITS IMPACT ON THE FREE WORLD. AFR EUR+WWI L/A+17C S/ASIA ECO/UNDEV CREATE FOR/AID...STAT NET/THEORY TREND CHARTS. PAGE 79 F1546
ASIA INT/TRADE NAT/COMP USSR

B64
LINDHOLM R.W.,ECONOMIC DEVELOPMENT POLICY WITH EMPHASIS ON VIET-NAM. KOREA/S PAKISTAN VIETNAM/S AGRI INDUS CONSULT DELIB/GP FOR/AID...METH 20. PAGE 80 F1571
ECO/UNDEV TAX FINAN ECO/TAC

B64
LITTLE I.M.D.,AID TO AFRICA. AFR UK TEC/DEV DIPLOM ECO/TAC INCOME WEALTH 20. PAGE 81 F1583
FOR/AID ECO/UNDEV ADMIN POLICY

B64
MASON E.S.,FOREIGN AID AND FOREIGN POLICY. USA+45 AGRI INDUS NAT/G EX/STRUC ACT/RES RIGID/FLEX ALL/VALS...POLICY GEN/LAWS MARSHL/PLN ALL/PROG CONGRESS 20. PAGE 87 F1699
ECO/UNDEV ECO/TAC FOR/AID DIPLOM

B64
MC GOVERN G.S.,WAR AGAINST WANT. USA+45 AGRI DIPLOM INT/TRADE GIVE RECEIVE DEMAND HEALTH 20 KENNEDY/JF FOOD/PEACE. PAGE 87 F1714
FOR/AID ECO/DEV POLICY EATING

B64
MEZERIK A.G.,TRADE, AID AND ECONOMIC DEVELOPMENT. WOR+45 FINAN INDUS MARKET PLAN BAL/PWR BARGAIN FOR/AID TARIFFS EDU/PROP WEALTH...GP/COMP 20 UN GATT IMF IBRD. PAGE 91 F1777
ECO/TAC ECO/DEV INT/ORG INT/TRADE

B64
MILIBAND R.,THE SOCIALIST REGISTER: 1964. GERMANY/W ITALY UK LABOR POL/PAR ECO/TAC FOR/AID NUC/PWR ...POLICY SOCIALIST IDEA/COMP 20 MAO NASSER/G. PAGE 91 F1784
MARXISM SOCISM CAP/ISM PROB/SOLV

B64
NEWCOMER H.A.,INTERNATIONAL AIDS TO OVERSEAS INVESTMENTS AND TRADE. ECO/UNDEV TARIFFS PROFIT ...BIBLIOG 20 GATT UN. PAGE 98 F1921
INT/TRADE FINAN DIPLOM FOR/AID

B64
OECD,DEVELOPMENT ASSISTANCE EFFORTS - POLICIES OF THE MEMBERS. AGRI INDUS BUDGET...GEOG NAT/COMP 20 OECD. PAGE 100 F1967
INT/ORG FOR/AID ECO/UNDEV TEC/DEV

B64
OECD,THE FLOW OF FINANCIAL RESOURCES TO LESS DEVELOPED COUNTRIES 1956-1963. WOR+45 FINAN CAP/ISM ...POLICY STAT 20. PAGE 100 F1968
FOR/AID BUDGET INT/ORG ECO/UNDEV

B64
RANIS G.,THE UNITED STATES AND THE DEVELOPING ECONOMIES. COM USA+45 AGRI FINAN TEC/DEV CAP/ISM ECO/TAC INT/TRADE...POLICY METH/COMP ANTHOL 20 AID. PAGE 109 F2145
ECO/UNDEV DIPLOM FOR/AID

B64
RENO P.,THE ORDEAL OF BRITISH GUIANA. L/A+17C USA+45 STRUCT AGRI EXTR/IND INDUS NAT/G FOR/AID ORD/FREE...GEOG 20 GUIANA/BR INTRVN/ECO. PAGE 111 F2178
COLONIAL ECO/UNDEV SOCISM PWR

B64
REUSS H.S.,THE CRITICAL DECADE - AN ECONOMIC POLICY FOR AMERICA AND THE FREE WORLD. AFR USA+45 FINAN POL/PAR WORKER PLAN DIPLOM ECO/TAC TARIFFS BAL/PAY ...POLICY 20 CONGRESS. PAGE 111 F2181
FOR/AID INT/TRADE LABOR LEGIS

B64
RIVKIN A.,AFRICA AND THE EUROPEAN COMMON MARKET (PAMPHLET). AFR MOD/EUR WOR+45 TEC/DEV FOR/AID TARIFFS BAL/PAY...POLICY 20 EEC. PAGE 111 F2196
INT/ORG INT/TRADE ECO/TAC ECO/UNDEV

B64
ROBINSON R.D.,INTERNATIONAL BUSINESS POLICY. AFR INDIA L/A+17C USA+45 ELITES AGRI FOR/AID COERCE BAL/PAY...DECISION INT/LAW MGT 20. PAGE 113 F2224
ECO/TAC DIST/IND COLONIAL FINAN

B64
SINGER H.W.,INTERNATIONAL DEVELOPMENT: GROWTH AND CHANGE. AFR BRAZIL L/A+17C WOR+45 CULTURE AGRI INDUS NAT/G ACT/RES ECO/TAC EDU/PROP WEALTH...GEOG CONCPT METH/CNCPT STAT HYPO/EXP WORK TOT/POP 20. PAGE 122 F2412
FINAN ECO/UNDEV FOR/AID INT/TRADE

B64
SULLIVAN G.,THE STORY OF THE PEACE CORPS. USA+45 WOR+45 INTELL FACE/GP NAT/G SCHOOL VOL/ASSN CONSULT EX/STRUC PLAN EDU/PROP ADMIN ATTIT DRIVE ALL/VALS ...POLICY HEAL SOC CONCPT INT QU BIOG TREND SOC/EXP WORK. PAGE 127 F2511
INT/ORG ECO/UNDEV FOR/AID PEACE

B64
US AGENCY INTERNATIONAL DEV,A.I.D. PROJECTS IN FISCAL YEAR 1963: BY COUNTRY AND FIELD OF ACTIVITY. USA+45 ECO/UNDEV ECO/TAC EDU/PROP GOV/REL...CHARTS 20 AID. PAGE 134 F2639
FINAN FOR/AID COST STAT

B64
US HOUSE COMM BANKING-CURR,INTERNATIONAL DEVELOPMENT ASSOCIATION ACT AMENDMENT. CHINA/COM USA+45 USSR FINAN FORCES LEGIS DIPLOM CONFER EFFICIENCY...CHARTS GOV/COMP 20 PRESIDENT CONGRESS INTL/DEV. PAGE 136 F2689
BAL/PAY FOR/AID RECORD ECO/TAC

B64
US HOUSE COMM GOVT OPERATIONS,US OWNED FOREIGN CURRENCIES: HEARINGS (COMMITTEE ON GOVERNMENT OPERATIONS). INDIA ECO/DEV PLAN BUDGET TAX DEMAND EFFICIENCY 20 AID CONGRESS. PAGE 137 F2699
FINAN ECO/TAC FOR/AID OWN

B64
US SENATE COMM ON FOREIGN REL,HEARING ON BILLS RELATING TO FOREIGN ASSISTANCE. USA+45 WOR+45 ECO/UNDEV FINAN INDUS 20 UN CONGRESS. PAGE 139 F2733
FOR/AID DIPLOM TEC/DEV INT/ORG

B64
WITHERS W.,THE ECONOMIC CRISIS IN LATIN AMERICA. BRAZIL CHILE STRATA AGRI DIPLOM FOR/AID PWR SOCISM ...POLICY 20 MEXIC/AMER ARGEN ALL/PROG. PAGE 148 F2914
L/A+17C ECO/UNDEV CAP/ISM ALL/IDEOS

B64
ZEBOT C.A.,THE ECONOMICS OF COMPETITIVE COEXISTENCE. CHINA/COM USSR WOR+45 FINAN MARKET FOR/AID PRICE DEMAND EQUILIB WEALTH ALL/IDEOS 20. PAGE 150 F2961
TEC/DEV DIPLOM METH/COMP

L64
CARNEGIE ENDOWMENT INT. PEACE,"ECONOMIC AND SOCIAL QUESTION (ISSUES BEFORE THE NINETEENTH GENERAL ASSEMBLY)." WOR+45 ECO/DEV ECO/UNDEV INDUS R+D DELIB/GP CREATE PLAN TEC/DEV ECO/TAC FOR/AID BAL/PAY...RECORD UN 20. PAGE 21 F0414
INT/ORG INT/TRADE

S64
BEIM D.,"THE COMMUNIST BLOC AND THE FOREIGN-AID GAME." AFR WOR+45 NAT/G PLAN ROUTINE ATTIT KNOWL ORD/FREE...DECISION QUANT CONT/OBS TIME/SEQ CHARTS GAME SIMUL LOG/LING 20. PAGE 12 F0231
COM ECO/UNDEV ECO/TAC FOR/AID

S64
HUTCHINSON E.C.,"AMERICAN AID TO AFRICA." FUT USA+45 MARKET INT/ORG LOC/G NAT/G PUB/INST PLAN ECO/TAC ATTIT RIGID/FLEX...POLICY CONCPT TREND TERR/GP 20. PAGE 63 F1248
AFR ECO/UNDEV FOR/AID

S64
PESELT B.M.,"COMMUNIST ECONOMIC OFFENSIVE." WOR+45 SOCIETY INT/ORG PLAN ECO/TAC DOMIN EDU/PROP ATTIT PERSON PWR WEALTH...TREND CHARTS METH/GP 20. PAGE 105 F2067
COM ECO/UNDEV FOR/AID USSR

N64
GREAT BRITAIN CENTRAL OFF INF,THE COLOMBO PLAN (PAMPHLET). AFR ASIA S/ASIA USA+45 VOL/ASSN ...CHARTS 20 RESOURCE/N. PAGE 50 F0980
FOR/AID PLAN INT/ORG ECO/UNDEV

B65
ANALYSIS AND ASSESSMENT OF THE ECONOMIC EFFECTS: PUBLIC LAW 480 TITLE I PROGRAM TURKEY. INDIA TURKEY USA+45 AGRI NAT/G PLAN BUDGET DIPLOM COST EFFICIENCY...CHARTS 20. PAGE 1 F0021
ECO/TAC FOR/AID FINAN ECO/UNDEV

B65
PEACE RESEARCH ABSTRACTS. FUT WOR+45 R+D INT/ORG NAT/G PLAN TEC/DEV BAL/PWR DIPLOM FOR/AID NUC/PWR HEALTH. PAGE 1 F0022
BIBLIOG/A PEACE ARMS/CONT WAR

B65
BALDWIN D.A.,SOFT LOANS AND AMERICAN FOREIGN POLICY: 1943-1962 (THESIS). USA+45 WOR+45 FINAN NAT/G FOR/AID BAL/PAY ATTIT...POLICY METH/COMP 20 UN CONGRESS. PAGE 9 F0161
DIPLOM ECO/TAC ECO/UNDEV

B65
BROOKINGS INSTITUTION,BROOKINGS PAPERS ON PUBLIC POLICY. USA+45 ECO/UNDEV LEGIS CAP/ISM ECO/TAC TAX EDU/PROP CONTROL APPORT 20. PAGE 19 F0363
DIPLOM FOR/AID POLICY FINAN

B65
CHANDRASEKHAR S.,AMERICAN AID AND INDIA'S ECONOMIC DEVELOPMENT. AFR CHINA/COM INDIA USA+45 GIVE EDU/PROP EATING HEALTH ORD/FREE 20 AID. PAGE 23 F0449
FOR/AID PEACE DIPLOM ECO/UNDEV

B65
COOMBS P.H.,EDUCATION AND FOREIGN AID. AFR USA+45 DIPLOM EFFICIENCY KNOWL ORD/FREE...ANTHOL 20 AID. PAGE 27 F0532
EDU/PROP FOR/AID SCHOOL ECO/UNDEV

B65
FARER T.J.,FINANCING AFRICAN DEVELOPMENT. AFR ECO/TAC FOR/AID SOCISM 20. PAGE 39 F0764
ECO/UNDEV FINAN CAP/ISM PLAN

B65
HAPGOOD D.,AFRICA: FROM INDEPENDENCE TO TOMARROW. AFR GUINEA SENEGAL CULTURE ELITES ECO/UNDEV AGRI SCHOOL FOR/AID COLONIAL MARXISM...TREND 20. PAGE 55 F1070
ECO/TAC SOCIETY NAT/G

B65
HLA MYINT U.,THE ECONOMICS OF THE DEVELOPING COUNTRIES. USA+45 WOR+45 AGRI FINAN NAT/G INT/TRADE ...CLASSIF CENSUS TREND NAT/COMP SIMUL GEN/LAWS. PAGE 60 F1180
ECO/UNDEV FOR/AID GEOG

B65
INTERAMERICAN ECO AND SOC COUN,THE ALLIANCE FOR PROGRESS: ITS THIRD YEAR 1963-1964. FUT L/A+17C WOR+45 ECO/DEV INT/ORG PLAN CONTROL ADJUST...STAT ANTHOL SOC/INTEG 20 ALL/PROG. PAGE 64 F1268
ECO/UNDEV ECO/TAC FINAN FOR/AID

B65
KRAUSE W.,ECONOMIC DEVELOPMENT: THE UNDERDEVELOPED WORLD AND THE AMERICAN INTEREST. USA+45 AGRI PLAN MARXISM...CHARTS 20. PAGE 73 F1434
FOR/AID ECO/UNDEV FINAN PROB/SOLV

B65
LITTLE I.M.D.,INTERNATIONAL AID. UK WOR+45 AGRI INDUS GIVE RECEIVE COLONIAL BAL/PAY WEALTH...POLICY GOV/COMP METH/COMP 20. PAGE 81 F1584
FOR/AID DIPLOM ECO/UNDEV NAT/G

B65
MARK S.M.,ECONOMICS IN ACTION (3RD ED.). USA+45 ECO/UNDEV AGRI INDUS FOR/AID INT/TRADE BAL/PAY COST ORD/FREE...ANTHOL 20 RESOURCE/N. PAGE 85 F1670
POLICY ECO/TAC EFFICIENCY PRICE

B65
MEAGHER R.F.,PUBLIC INTERNATIONAL DEVELOPMENT FINANCING IN SUDAN. SUDAN FINAN DELIB/GP GIVE ...CHARTS GOV/COMP 20. PAGE 89 F1740
FOR/AID PLAN RECEIVE ECO/UNDEV

B65
MONCRIEFF A.,SECOND THOUGHTS ON AID. WOR+45 ECO/UNDEV AGRI FINAN VOL/ASSN PLAN TEC/DEV GIVE EDU/PROP ROLE WEALTH 20. PAGE 93 F1816
FOR/AID ECO/TAC INT/ORG IDEA/COMP

B65
NKRUMAH K.,NEO-COLONIALISM: THE LAST STAGE OF IMPERIALISM. AFR INT/ORG WORKER FOR/AID INT/TRADE EDU/PROP GOV/REL NAT/LISM SOVEREIGN POPULISM SOCISM ...SOCIALIST 20 THIRD/WRLD INTRVN/ECO. PAGE 98 F1929
COLONIAL DIPLOM ECO/UNDEV ECO/TAC

B65
ONSLOW C.,ASIAN ECONOMIC DEVELOPMENT. BURMA CEYLON INDIA MALAYSIA PAKISTAN S/ASIA AGRI INDUS MARKET PROB/SOLV CAP/ISM FOR/AID INT/TRADE DEMAND WEALTH ...POLICY ANTHOL 20. PAGE 101 F1991
ECO/UNDEV ECO/TAC PLAN NAT/G

B65
ONUOHA B.,THE ELEMENTS OF AFRICAN SOCIALISM. AFR FINAN SECT TEC/DEV FOR/AID GP/REL OWN LAISSEZ MARXISM...CONCPT BIBLIOG 20. PAGE 101 F1992
SOCISM ECO/UNDEV NAT/G EX/STRUC

B65
PINCUS J.A.,ECONOMIC AID AND INTERNATIONAL COST
ECO/UNDEV

SHARING* A RAND CORPORATION RESEARCH STUDY. INT/ORG BUDGET CENTRAL...ECOMETRIC MATH QUANT STAT SIMUL. PAGE 106 F2088
COST FOR/AID INT/TRADE

B65

PROCHNOW H.V.,WORLD ECONOMIC PROBLEMS AND POLICIES. INDIA ISRAEL WOR+45 AGRI LABOR PROB/SOLV FOR/AID TARIFFS CONTROL BAL/PAY NAT/LISM WEALTH...TREND CHARTS 20 CHINJAP EEC. PAGE 108 F2124
MARKET ECO/TAC PRODUC IDEA/COMP

B65

ROOSA R.V.,MONETARY REFORM FOR THE WORLD ECONOMY. AFR EUR+WWI USA+45 WOR+45 CREATE BUDGET DIPLOM FOR/AID EQUILIB WEALTH IMF. PAGE 114 F2237
FINAN INT/ORG INT/TRADE BAL/PAY

B65

SCOTT A.M.,THE REVOLUTION IN STATECRAFT: INFORMAL PENETRATION. WOR+45 WOR-45 CULTURE INT/ORG FORCES ECO/TAC ROUTINE...BIBLIOG 20. PAGE 118 F2331
DIPLOM EDU/PROP FOR/AID

B65

SHAFFER H.G.,THE SOVIET SYSTEM IN THEORY AND PRACTICE: SELECTED WESTERN AND SOVIET VIEWS. USSR LAW SOCIETY CREATE FOR/AID EDU/PROP PRESS CHOOSE PEACE ORD/FREE...ANTHOL 20 STALIN/J. PAGE 120 F2362
MARXISM SOCISM IDEA/COMP

B65

SHARIF A.,THE BALANCE OF PAYMENTS OF PAKISTAN, 1948-1958 (THESIS, UNIVERSITY OF TORONTO). PAKISTAN FINAN INDUS FOR/AID PRICE WEALTH...TREND CHARTS 20. PAGE 120 F2368
BAL/PAY BUDGET INT/TRADE ECO/UNDEV

B65

US BUREAU EDUC CULTURAL AFF,RESOURCES SURVEY FOR LATIN AMERICAN COUNTRIES. L/A+17C USA+45 CULTURE INDUS INT/ORG SECT PLAN EDU/PROP POLICY. PAGE 134 F2643
NAT/G ECO/UNDEV FOR/AID DIPLOM

B65

US SENATE COMM ON FOREIGN REL,HEARINGS ON THE FOREIGN ASSISTANCE PROGRAM. AFR ASIA L/A+17C USA+45 WOR+45 FORCES TEC/DEV BUDGET CONTROL WEAPON ORD/FREE 20 UN CONGRESS SEC/STATE. PAGE 139 F2734
FOR/AID DIPLOM INT/ORG ECO/UNDEV

B65

WEAVER J.N.,THE INTERNATIONAL DEVELOPMENT ASSOCIATION: A NEW APPROACH TO FOREIGN AID. USA+45 NAT/G OP/RES PLAN PROB/SOLV WEALTH...CHARTS BIBLIOG 20 UN. PAGE 144 F2836
FOR/AID INT/ORG ECO/UNDEV FINAN

B65

WEILER J.,L'ECONOMIE INTERNATIONALE DEPUIS 1950. WOR+45 DIPLOM TARIFFS CONFER...POLICY TREATY. PAGE 145 F2848
FINAN INT/TRADE REGION FOR/AID

B65

WHITE J.,GERMAN AID. GERMANY/W FINAN PLAN TEC/DEV INT/TRADE ADMIN ATTIT...POLICY 20. PAGE 146 F2870
FOR/AID ECO/UNDEV DIPLOM ECO/TAC

B65

YOUNG A.N.,CHINA'S WARTIME FINANCE AND INFLATION. ASIA AGRI INDUS NAT/G ECO/TAC CONFER PRICE WAR COST 20. PAGE 150 F2949
FINAN FOR/AID TAX BUDGET

L65

DAANE J.D.,"THE EVOLVING INTERNATIONAL MONETARY MECHANISM." VOL/ASSN CREATE PLAN FOR/AID INT/TRADE CONFER BAL/PAY...RECORD PREDICT IMF. PAGE 29 F0569
INT/ORG ECO/TAC TREND GP/COMP

S65

BALDWIN D.A.,"THE INTERNATIONAL BANK IN POLITICAL PERSPECTIVE" USA+45 TEC/DEV FOR/AID RENT GIVE COST ...IDEA/COMP GAME IBRD. PAGE 9 F0160
FINAN INT/ORG

S65

DUMONT R.,"SURPEUPLEMENT CHINOIS ET SES CONSEQUENCES." AFR ECO/UNDEV AGRI PLAN PROB/SOLV ECO/TAC FOR/AID NUC/PWR...OBS INT PREDICT. PAGE 35 F0675
GEOG ASIA STAT

S65

GOLDMAN M.I.,"A BALANCE SHEET OF SOVIET FOREIGN AID." USA+45 ECO/UNDEV BAL/PWR ECO/TAC RENT GIVE EDU/PROP CONTROL COST PROFIT GEN/METH. PAGE 48 F0939
USSR FOR/AID NAT/COMP EFFICIENCY

S65

HAYTER T.,"FRENCH AID TO AFRICA* ITS SCOPE AND ACHIEVEMENTS." CULTURE ECO/TAC INT/TRADE ADMIN REGION CENTRAL FEDERAL LOVE PWR SOVEREIGN EEC. PAGE 57 F1127
AFR FRANCE FOR/AID COLONIAL

S65

KORBONSKI A.,"USA POLICY IN EAST EUROPE." COM EUR+WWI GERMANY USA+45 CULTURE ECO/UNDEV EDU/PROP RIGID/FLEX WEALTH FOR/TRADE 20. PAGE 73 F1426
ACT/RES ECO/TAC FOR/AID

S65

RUSINOW D.I.,"YUGOSLAV DEVELOPMENT BETWEEN EAST AND WEST." AGRI VOL/ASSN PLAN CAP/ISM ECO/TAC FOR/AID INT/TRADE BAL/PAY...MARXIST EEC COMECON. PAGE 115 F2262
YUGOSLAVIA ECO/UNDEV STAT

S65

SOPER T.,"THE EEC AND AID TO AFRICA." FRANCE UK ECO/UNDEV INT/TRADE TARIFFS REGION ROUTINE CENTRAL DISCRIM...DECISION RECORD EEC. PAGE 124 F2443
AFR FOR/AID COLONIAL

S65

WHITE J.,"WEST GERMAN AID TO DEVELOPING COUNTRIES."
GERMANY

AFR INT/ORG OP/RES GIVE CENTRAL ATTIT DRIVE...STAT NAT/COMP. PAGE 146 F2869
FOR/AID ECO/UNDEV CAP/ISM

B66

ALEXANDER Y.,INTERNATIONAL TECHNICAL ASSISTANCE EXPERTS* A CASE STUDY OF THE U.N. EXPERIENCE. ECO/UNDEV CONSULT EX/STRUC CREATE PLAN DIPLOM FOR/AID TASK EFFICIENCY...ORG/CHARTS UN. PAGE 3 F0061
ECO/TAC INT/ORG ADMIN MGT

B66

ALEXANDER Y.,INTERNATIONAL TECHNICAL ASSISTANCE EXPERTS: A CASE STUDY OF THE U.N. EXPERIENCE. USA+45 WOR+45 WORKER CREATE PLAN PROB/SOLV ECO/TAC FOR/AID GIVE EDU/PROP...CHARTS BIBLIOG 20 UN. PAGE 3 F0062
SKILL INT/ORG TEC/DEV CONSULT

B66

AMER ENTERPRISE INST PUB POL,SIGNIFICANT ISSUES IN ECONOMIC AID TO DEVELOPING COUNTRIES. FINAN INT/ORG NAT/G PLAN PROB/SOLV GIVE TASK WEALTH...DECISION 20. PAGE 4 F0083
ECO/UNDEV FOR/AID DIPLOM POLICY

B66

BALDWIN D.A.,FOREIGN AID AND AMERICAN FOREIGN POLICY; A DOCUMENTARY ANALYSIS. USA+45 ECO/UNDEV ADMIN...ECOMETRIC STAT STYLE CHARTS PROG/TEAC GEN/LAWS ANTHOL. PAGE 9 F0162
FOR/AID DIPLOM IDEA/COMP

B66

BALDWIN D.A.,ECONOMIC DEVELOPMENT AND AMERICAN FOREIGN POLICY. USA+45 FINAN LG/CO LEGIS DIPLOM GIVE 20. PAGE 9 F0163
ECO/TAC FOR/AID ECO/UNDEV POLICY

B66

BROEKMEIJER M.W.J.,FICTION AND TRUTH ABOUT THE "DECADE OF DEVELOPMENT" WOR+45 AGRI FINAN INDUS NAT/G TEC/DEV DIPLOM EDU/PROP LEAD SKILL 20 THIRD/WRLD. PAGE 19 F0358
FOR/AID POLICY ECO/UNDEV PLAN

B66

CURRIE L.,ACCELERATING DEVELOPMENT: THE NECESSITY AND MEANS. COLOMBIA USA+45 INDUS DIPLOM EFFICIENCY WEALTH...METH/CNCPT NEW/IDEA 20. PAGE 29 F0564
PLAN ECO/UNDEV FOR/AID TEC/DEV

B66

ECKSTEIN A.,COMMUNIST CHINA'S ECONOMIC GROWTH AND FOREIGN TRADE* IMPLICATIONS FOR US POLICY. COM USA+45 USSR STRUCT INDUS MARKET DIPLOM ECO/TAC FOR/AID INT/TRADE...STAT CHARTS. PAGE 36 F0696
ASIA ECO/UNDEV CREATE PWR

B66

FREIDEL F.,AMERICAN ISSUES IN THE TWENTIETH CENTURY. SOCIETY FINAN ECO/TAC FOR/AID CONTROL NUC/PWR WAR RACE/REL PEACE ATTIT...ANTHOL T 20 WILSON/W ROOSEVLT/F KENNEDY/JF TRUMAN/HS. PAGE 44 F0851
DIPLOM POLICY NAT/G ORD/FREE

B66

FRIEDMANN W.G.,INTERNATIONAL FINANCIAL AID. USA+45 ECO/DEV ECO/UNDEV NAT/G VOL/ASSN EX/STRUC PLAN RENT GIVE BAL/PAY PWR...GEOG INT/LAW STAT TREND UN EEC COMECON. PAGE 44 F0866
INT/ORG FOR/AID TEC/DEV ECO/TAC

B66

HALLET R.,PEOPLE AND PROGRESS IN WEST AFRICA: AN INTRODUCTION TO THE PROBLEMS OF DEVELOPMENT. COM/IND INDUS KIN DIPLOM FOR/AID INT/TRADE HEALTH ...GEOG TREND CHARTS BIBLIOG/A 20 AFRICA/W. PAGE 54 F1050
AFR SOCIETY ECO/UNDEV ECO/TAC

B66

HAYER T.,FRENCH AID. AFR FRANCE AGRI FINAN BUDGET ADMIN WAR PRODUC...CHARTS 18/20 THIRD/WRLD OVRSEA/DEV. PAGE 57 F1125
TEC/DEV COLONIAL FOR/AID ECO/UNDEV

B66

HOROWITZ D.,HEMISPHERES NORTH AND SOUTH: ECONOMIC DISPARITY AMONG NATIONS. WOR+45 ECO/DEV ECO/UNDEV INT/ORG PLAN DIPLOM INT/TRADE GIVE PARTIC GP/REL ...WELF/ST 20. PAGE 62 F1215
ECO/TAC FOR/AID STRATA WEALTH

B66

INTERNATIONAL ECONOMIC ASSN,STABILITY AND PROGRESS IN THE WORLD ECONOMY: THE FIRST CONGRESS OF THE INTERNATIONAL ECONOMIC ASSOCIATION. WOR+45 ECO/DEV ECO/UNDEV DELIB/GP FOR/AID BAL/PAY...TREND CMN/WLTH 20. PAGE 65 F1276
INT/TRADE

B66

JENSEN F.B.,READINGS IN INTERNATIONAL ECONOMIC RELATIONS. COM ECO/UNDEV MARKET NAT/G FOR/AID ...ANTHOL 20. PAGE 67 F1317
BAL/PAY INT/TRADE FINAN

B66

KAREFA-SMART J.,AFRICA: PROGRESS THROUGH COOPERATION. AFR FINAN TEC/DEV DIPLOM FOR/AID EDU/PROP CONFER REGION GP/REL WEALTH...HEAL SOC/INTEG 20. PAGE 69 F1356
ORD/FREE ECO/UNDEV VOL/ASSN PLAN

B66

KEENLEYSIDE H.L.,INTERNATIONAL AID: A SUMMARY. AFR INDIA S/ASIA UK STRATA EXTR/IND TEC/DEV ADMIN RACE/REL DEMAND NAT/LISM WEALTH...TREND CHINJAP. PAGE 70 F1367
ECO/UNDEV FOR/AID DIPLOM TASK

B66

KIRDAR U.,THE STRUCTURE OF UNITED NATIONS ECONOMIC AID TO UNDERDEVELOPED COUNTRIES. AGRI FINAN INDUS NAT/G EX/STRUC PLAN GIVE TASK...POLICY 20 UN.
INT/ORG FOR/AID ECO/UNDEV

PAGE 71 F1397
ADMIN

B66
LAMBERG R.F.,PRAG UND DIE DRITTE WELT. AFR ASIA CZECHOSLVK L/A+17C MARKET TEC/DEV ECO/TAC REV ATTIT 20 TREATY. PAGE 75 F1462
DIPLOM ECO/UNDEV INT/TRADE FOR/AID

B66
LEAGUE OF WOMEN VOTERS OF US,FOREIGN AID AT THE CROSSROADS. USA+45 WOR+45 DELIB/GP PROB/SOLV DIPLOM INT/TRADE RECEIVE BAL/PAY...CHARTS 20 UN ALL/PROG. PAGE 76 F1498
FOR/AID GIVE ECO/UNDEV PLAN

B66
LECHT L.,GOAL, PRIORITIES, AND DOLLARS: THE NEXT DECADE. SPACE USA+45 SOCIETY AGRI BUDGET FOR/AID ...HEAL SOC/WK STAT CHARTS 20 URBAN/RNWL PUB/TRANS. PAGE 76 F1499
IDEA/COMP POLICY CONSEN PLAN

B66
LEONTIEF W.,ESSAYS IN ECONOMICS. ECO/UNDEV INDUS NAT/G CAP/ISM FOR/AID AUTOMAT MARXISM...ECOMETRIC CHARTS ANTHOL METH 20 KEYNES/JM. PAGE 78 F1528
CONCPT METH/CNCPT METH/COMP

B66
LEWIS W.A.,DEVELOPMENT PLANNING; THE ESSENTIALS OF ECONOMIC POLICY. USA+45 FINAN INDUS NAT/G WORKER FOR/AID INT/TRADE ADMIN ROUTINE WEALTH...CONCPT STAT. PAGE 79 F1552
PLAN ECO/DEV POLICY CREATE

B66
MASON E.S.,ECONOMIC DEVELOPMENT IN INDIA AND PAKISTAN. INDIA PAKISTAN AGRI FINAN PLAN BUDGET INT/TRADE WEALTH...POLICY STAT TREND CHARTS 20. PAGE 87 F1700
NAT/COMP ECO/UNDEV ECO/TAC FOR/AID

B66
MIKESELL R.F.,PUBLIC INTERNATIONAL LENDING FOR DEVELOPMENT. WOR+45 WOR-45 DELIB/GP...TIME/SEQ CHARTS BIBLIOG 20. PAGE 91 F1783
INT/ORG FOR/AID ECO/UNDEV FINAN

B66
MUNBY D.,ECONOMIC GROWTH IN WORLD PERSPECTIVE. AFR WOR+45 SOCIETY INDUS PLAN TEC/DEV ECO/TAC FOR/AID INT/TRADE COST CATHISM...ANTHOL 20 EUROPE/W CHURCH/STA. PAGE 95 F1859
SECT ECO/UNDEV ECO/DEV

B66
NATIONAL COUN APPLIED ECO RES,DEVELOPMENT WITHOUT AID. INDIA FINAN TEC/DEV EFFICIENCY...ANTHOL 20. PAGE 97 F1901
FOR/AID PLAN SOVEREIGN ECO/UNDEV

B66
OHLIN G.,AID AND INDEBTEDNESS. AUSTRIA FINAN INT/ORG PLAN DIPLOM GIVE...POLICY MATH CHARTS 20. PAGE 101 F1984
FOR/AID ECO/UNDEV ADMIN WEALTH

B66
OHLIN G.,FOREIGN AID POLICIES RECONSIDERED. ECO/DEV ECO/UNDEV VOL/ASSN CONSULT PLAN CONTROL ATTIT ...CONCPT CHARTS BIBLIOG 20. PAGE 101 F1985
FOR/AID DIPLOM GIVE

B66
ORG FOR ECO COOP AND DEVEL,GEOGRAPHICAL DISTRIBUTION OF FINANCIAL FLOWS TO LESS DEVELOPED COUNTRIES. WOR+45 DIPLOM INT/TRADE GIVE RECEIVE REPAR REGION WEALTH...GEOG STAT CHARTS 20 OECD. PAGE 102 F1997
FINAN ECO/UNDEV INT/ORG FOR/AID

B66
RUBIN S.J.,THE CONSCIENCE OF THE RICH NATIONS: THE DEVELOPMENT ASSISTANCE COMMITTEE AND THE COMMON AID EFFORT. EUR+WWI USA+45 ECO/UNDEV INT/ORG NAT/G VOL/ASSN ECO/TAC INT/TRADE...OBS UN AID DEV/ASSIST IBRD OECD. PAGE 114 F2256
FOR/AID ECO/DEV CONFER CENTRAL

B66
SOMMERFELD R.M.,TAX REFORM AND THE ALLIANCE FOR PROGRESS. USA+45 ECO/DEV ECO/UNDEV FINAN NAT/G INCOME ORD/FREE WEALTH...STAT CHARTS 20 ALL/PROG. PAGE 124 F2442
TAX INT/ORG L/A+17C FOR/AID

B66
SPICER K.,A SAMARITAN STATE? AFR CANADA INDIA PAKISTAN UK USA+45 FINAN INDUS PRODUC...CHARTS 20 NATO. PAGE 124 F2455
DIPLOM FOR/AID ECO/DEV ADMIN

B66
US HOUSE COMM FOREIGN AFFAIRS,HEARINGS ON HR 12449 A BILL TO AMEND FURTHER THE FOREIGN ASSISTANCE ACT OF 1961. AFR ASIA L/A+17C USA+45 VIETNAM INT/ORG TEC/DEV INT/TRADE ATTIT ORD/FREE 20 UN NATO CONGRESS AID. PAGE 137 F2692
FOR/AID ECO/TAC ECO/UNDEV DIPLOM

B66
US SENATE COMM APPROPRIATIONS,FOREIGN ASSISTANCE AND RELATED AGENCIES APPROPRIATIONS FOR FISCAL YEAR 1967: HEARINGS... ON H. R. 17788. ECO/UNDEV INT/ORG FORCES INSPECT ECO/TAC GIVE DEBATE WEAPON CIVMIL/REL WEALTH...INT 20 CONGRESS DEPT/DEFEN DEPT/STATE DEPT/HEW AID. PAGE 138 F2727
BUDGET FOR/AID DIPLOM COST

B66
US SENATE COMM ON FOREIGN REL,HEARINGS ON S 2859 AND S 2861. USA+45 WOR+45 FORCES BUDGET CAP/ISM ADMIN DETER WEAPON TOTALISM...NAT/COMP 20 UN CONGRESS. PAGE 139 F2735
FOR/AID DIPLOM ORD/FREE ECO/UNDEV

B66
US SENATE COMM ON FOREIGN REL,ASIAN DEVELOPMENT BANK ACT. USA+45 LAW DIPLOM...CHARTS 20 BLACK/EUG S/EASTASIA. PAGE 139 F2736
FOR/AID FINAN ECO/UNDEV S/ASIA

B66
ZISCHKA A.,WAR ES EIN WUNDER? GERMANY/W ECO/DEV FINAN LG/CO BARGAIN CAP/ISM FOR/AID RATION 20 MARSHL/PLN. PAGE 150 F2965
ECO/TAC INT/TRADE INDUS WAR

L66
AFRICAN BIBLIOGRAPHIC CENTER,"AFRICAN ECONOMIC AFFAIRS: A SELECT BIBLIOGRAPHICAL SURVEY, 1965-1966." AFR FINAN INDUS INT/ORG LABOR PLAN BUDGET DIPLOM INT/TRADE ADMIN EFFICIENCY WEALTH 20. PAGE 3 F0046
BIBLIOG ECO/UNDEV TEC/DEV FOR/AID

L66
AFRICAN BIBLIOGRAPHIC CENTER,"AFRICAN ECONOMIC AFFAIRS: A SELECT BIBLIOGRAPHICAL SURVEY, 1965-1966; SUPPLEMENTS NUMBERS 1-3." AFR FINAN INDUS LABOR PLAN BUDGET CAP/ISM DIPLOM INT/TRADE ADMIN...GEOG 20. PAGE 3 F0047
BIBLIOG/A ECO/UNDEV FOR/AID TEC/DEV

L66
CHENERY H.B.,"FOREIGN ASSISTANCE AND ECONOMIC DEVELOPMENT" FUT WOR+45 NAT/G DIPLOM GIVE PRODUC ...METH/CNCPT CHARTS 20. PAGE 24 F0464
FOR/AID EFFICIENCY ECO/UNDEV TEC/DEV

L66
PACKENHAM R.A.,"POLITICAL-DEVELOPMENT DOCTRINES IN THE AMERICAN FOREIGN AID PROGRAM." STRUCT R+D CREATE DIPLOM AID. PAGE 102 F2011
FOR/AID ECO/UNDEV GEN/LAWS

S66
ANGELL J.W.,"THE LONGER RUN PROSPECTS FOR THE US BALANCE OF PAYMENTS." USA+45 DIPLOM FOR/AID RATION ORD/FREE WEALTH...IDEA/COMP GATT. PAGE 6 F0104
BAL/PAY ECO/TAC INT/TRADE FINAN

S66
COHEN A.,"THE TECHNOLOGY/ELITE APPROACH TO THE DEVELOPMENTAL PROCESS* PERUVIAN CASE STUDY." L/A+17C STRUCT CREATE ECO/TAC FOR/AID CIVMIL/REL MARXISM TECHRACY HYPO/EXP. PAGE 26 F0496
ECO/UNDEV ELITES PERU

S66
ERB GF,"THE UNITED NATIONS CONFERENCE ON TRADE AND DEVELOPMENT (UNCTAD): A SELECTED CURRENT READING LIST." FINAN FOR/AID CONFER 20 UN. PAGE 38 F0742
BIBLIOG/A INT/TRADE ECO/UNDEV INT/ORG

N66
BRITISH DEVELOPMENT POLICIES: 1966 (PAMPHLET). UK AGRI TARIFFS BAL/PAY...TREND CHARTS 20 OVRSEA/DEV. PAGE 1 F0023
WEALTH DIPLOM INT/TRADE FOR/AID

N66
EOMMITTEE ECONOMIC DEVELOPMENT,THE DOLLAR AND THE WORLD MONETARY SYSTEM: A STATEMENT ON NATIONAL POLICY (PAMPHLET). AFR USA+45 NAT/G PLAN PROB/SOLV BUDGET ECO/TAC FOR/AID INCOME...POLICY 20 EUROPE. PAGE 38 F0740
FINAN BAL/PAY DIPLOM ECO/DEV

B67
ADLER J.H.,CAPITAL MOVEMENTS AND ECONOMIC DEVELOPMENT. WOR+45 FINAN NAT/G BARGAIN ECO/TAC FOR/AID INT/TRADE ANTHOL. PAGE 2 F0042
DIPLOM ECO/DEV ECO/UNDEV

B67
BRIEFS H.W.,REGAINING BALANCE IN A HIGH EMPLOYMENT ECONOMY: UNRESOLVED ISSUES FOR 1967 AND BEYOND. USA+45 NAT/G PLAN PROB/SOLV FOR/AID...CHARTS 20. PAGE 18 F0350
ECO/DEV FINAN BAL/PAY BUDGET

B67
CHO S.S.,KOREA IN WORLD POLITICS 1940-1950; AN EVALUATION OF AMERICAN RESPONSIBILITY. KOREA USA+45 USSR CONSTN INT/ORG NAT/G FORCES FOR/AID ANOMIE SUPEGO MARXISM...DECISION BIBLIOG 20. PAGE 24 F0469
POLICY DIPLOM PROB/SOLV WAR

B67
DAVIS F.M.,COME AS A CONQUEROR: THE UNITED STATES ARMY'S OCCUPATION OF GERMANY: 1945-1949. EUR+WWI GERMANY USA+45 SOCIETY PLAN BAL/PWR DIPLOM FOR/AID PERS/REL DEMAND PEACE ORD/FREE 20. PAGE 30 F0588
FORCES CIVMIL/REL ECO/TAC CONTROL

B67
HALLE L.J.,THE COLD WAR AS HISTORY. AFR USSR WOR+45 ECO/TAC FOR/AID NUC/PWR WAR PEACE ORD/FREE ...MAJORIT TREND 20 KENNEDY/JF KHRUSH/N BERLIN/BLO. PAGE 54 F1048
DIPLOM BAL/PWR

B67
HUMPHREY R.A.,UNIVERSITIES...AND DEVELOPMENT ASSISTANCE ABROAD. USA+45 OP/RES ECO/TAC FOR/AID ...ANTHOL 20. PAGE 63 F1242
ACADEM DIPLOM KNOWL ECO/UNDEV

B67
JACOBY N.H.,US AID TO TAIWAN. CAP/ISM DIPLOM FEEDBACK COST PRODUC...OBS INT CHARTS 20. PAGE 66 F1301
FOR/AID OP/RES ECO/TAC ECO/UNDEV

B67
JOHNSON D.G.,THE STRUGGLE AGAINST WORLD HUNGER (HEADLINE SERIES, NO. 184) (PAMPHLET). PLAN TEC/DEV FOR/AID...CHARTS 20 FAO MEXIC/AMER. PAGE 67 F1322
AGRI PROB/SOLV ECO/UNDEV HEALTH

B67
JOHNSON H.G.,ECONOMIC POLICY TOWARD LESS DEVELOPED
ECO/UNDEV

COUNTRIES. USA+45 ECO/DEV INT/ORG PLAN CAP/ISM FOR/AID TARIFFS GIVE WEALTH...NEW/IDEA CHARTS 20 UN GATT. PAGE 67 F1327
ECO/TAC METH/COMP

B67
KAPLAN J.J.,CHALLENGE OF FOREIGN AID. USA+45 CONTROL BAL/PAY COST ATTIT ALL/VALS...METH/COMP 20. PAGE 69 F1352
FOR/AID PLAN GIVE POLICY

B67
MARTIN P.,CANADA AND THE QUEST FOR PEACE. CANADA VIETNAM ECO/UNDEV PLAN FOR/AID WAR 20 UN. PAGE 86 F1684
DIPLOM PEACE INT/ORG POLICY

B67
MONTGOMERY J.D.,FOREIGN AID IN INTERNATIONAL POLITICS. USA+45 USA-45 WOR+45 ECO/TAC EFFICIENCY ...SOC TREND CHARTS BIBLIOG/A 20 AID. PAGE 93 F1818
DIPLOM FOR/AID

B67
NKRUMAH K.,CHALLENGE OF THE CONGO. FORCES ECO/TAC FOR/AID REGION MURDER REPRESENT 20 CONGO/LEOP UN. PAGE 98 F1930
REV ECO/UNDEV ORD/FREE DIPLOM

B67
O'LEARY M.K.,THE POLITICS OF AMERICAN FOREIGN AID. USA+45 POL/PAR CHIEF BUDGET EDU/PROP LOBBY CONGRESS. PAGE 100 F1958
FOR/AID DIPLOM PARL/PROC ATTIT

B67
OGLESBY C.,CONTAINMENT AND CHANGE. AFR COM USA+45 ECO/UNDEV TEC/DEV ECO/TAC FOR/AID INT/TRADE DOMIN GUERRILLA REV PEACE 20 STALIN/J. PAGE 101 F1983
DIPLOM BAL/PWR MARXISM CULTURE

B67
OVERSEAS DEVELOPMENT INSTIT,EFFECTIVE AID. WOR+45 INT/ORG TEC/DEV DIPLOM INT/TRADE ADMIN. PAGE 102 F2004
FOR/AID ECO/UNDEV ECO/TAC NAT/COMP

B67
RUEFF J.,BALANCE OF PAYMENTS: PROPOSALS FOR RESOLVING THE CRITICAL WORLD ECONOMIC PROBLEM OF OUR TIME. USA+45 INDUS FOR/AID REPAR DEMAND OPTIMAL ...ECOMETRIC CHARTS METH/COMP 20. PAGE 115 F2259
BAL/PAY INT/TRADE FINAN NEW/IDEA

B67
SPURRIER R.B.,THE OVERPOPULATED SOCIETY. WORKER EATING PERS/REL DEMAND EQUILIB ILLEGIT INCOME HABITAT 20. PAGE 125 F2461
BIO/SOC FOR/AID DRIVE RECEIVE

B67
TANSKY L.,US AND USSR AID TO DEVELOPING COUNTRIES. INDIA TURKEY USA+45 USSR INDUS PLAN CAP/ISM WAR PWR WEALTH MARXISM...CHARTS NAT/COMP BIBLIOG 20. PAGE 128 F2534
ECO/UNDEV FOR/AID DIPLOM ECO/TAC

B67
TANSKY L.,US AND USSR AID TO DEVELOPING COUNTRIES. INDIA TURKEY UAR USA+45 USSR FINAN PLAN TEC/DEV ADMIN WEALTH...TREND METH/COMP 20. PAGE 128 F2535
FOR/AID ECO/UNDEV MARXISM CAP/ISM

B67
TOMA P.A.,THE POLITICS OF FOOD FOR PEACE; EXECUTIVE-LEGISLATIVE INTERACTION. USA+45 ECO/UNDEV POL/PAR DEBATE EXEC LOBBY CHOOSE PEACE...DECISION CHARTS. PAGE 131 F2580
FOR/AID POLICY LEGIS AGRI

B67
US AGENCY INTERNATIONAL DEV,PROPOSED FOREIGN AID PROGRAM FOR 1968: SUMMARY PRESENTATION TO THE CONGRESS. AFR S/ASIA USA+45 AGRI TEC/DEV DIPLOM ECO/TAC BAL/PAY COST HEALTH KNOWL SKILL 20 AID CONGRESS ALL/PROG. PAGE 134 F2640
ECO/UNDEV BUDGET FOR/AID STAT

B67
US CONGRESS SENATE,SURVEY OF THE ALLIANCE FOR PROGRESS; INFLATION IN LATIN AMERICA (PAMPHLET). USA+45 MARKET INT/ORG DIPLOM INT/TRADE BAL/PAY SENATE ALL/PROG. PAGE 135 F2666
L/A+17C FINAN POLICY FOR/AID

B67
US GOVERNMENT,SECTION-BY-SECTION ANALYSIS OF THE PROPOSED FOREIGN ASSISTANCE ACT OF 1967 (PAMPHLET). USA+45 ECO/UNDEV NAT/G CONGRESS. PAGE 136 F2683
FOR/AID POLICY FORCES INT/TRADE

B67
US SENATE COMM ON FOREIGN REL,LATIN AMERICAN SUMMIT CONFERENCE. L/A+17C USA+45 FINAN PLAN SENATE ALL/PROG. PAGE 139 F2740
FOR/AID BUDGET DIPLOM INT/ORG

B67
US SENATE COMM ON FOREIGN REL,INTER-AMERICAN DEVELOPMENT BANK ACT AMENDMENT. L/A+17C USA+45 DELIB/GP DIPLOM FOR/AID BAL/PAY...CHARTS SENATE. PAGE 139 F2741
LAW FINAN INT/ORG ECO/UNDEV

B67
US SENATE COMM ON FOREIGN REL,ARMS SALES TO NEAR EAST AND SOUTH ASIAN COUNTRIES. INDIA IRAN PAKISTAN WOR+45 PROC/MFG BAL/PWR DIPLOM...DECISION SENATE. PAGE 139 F2742
WEAPON FOR/AID FORCES POLICY

B67
US SENATE COMM ON FOREIGN REL,FOREIGN ASSISTANCE ACT OF 1967. VIETNAM WOR+45 DELIB/GP CONFER CONTROL WAR WEAPON BAL/PAY...CENSUS CHARTS SENATE. PAGE 139 F2744
FOR/AID LAW DIPLOM POLICY

B67
WATT A.,THE EVOLUTION OF AUSTRALIAN FOREIGN POLICY 1938-65. ASIA S/ASIA USA+45 USA-45 INT/ORG NAT/G FORCES FOR/AID TREATY 20 AUSTRAL. PAGE 144 F2834
DIPLOM WAR

B67
WOLF C. JR.,UNITED STATES POLICY AND THE THIRD WORLD. USA+45 WOR+45 FORCES ACT/RES BAL/PWR ECO/TAC FOR/AID DETER GUERRILLA NUC/PWR REV...CHARTS 20. PAGE 148 F2916
DIPLOM ECO/UNDEV POLICY NAT/G

B67
ZONDAG C.H.,THE BOLIVIAN ECONOMY 1952-65. L/A+17C TEC/DEV FOR/AID ADMIN...OBS TREND CHARTS BIBLIOG 20 BOLIV. PAGE 151 F2969
ECO/UNDEV INDUS PRODUC

L67
MACDONALD R.S.J.,"THE RESORT TO ECONOMIC COERCION BY INTERNATIONAL POLITICAL ORGANIZATIONS." CUBA ETHIOPIA RHODESIA SOUTH/AFR NAT/G FOR/AID INT/TRADE DOMIN CONTROL SANCTION...DECISION LEAGUE/NAT UN OAS 20. PAGE 83 F1625
INT/ORG COERCE ECO/TAC DIPLOM

S67
BELL D.E.,"THE QUALITY OF AID." USA+45 R+D DIPLOM GP/REL. PAGE 12 F0234
POLICY FOR/AID PROB/SOLV INSPECT

S67
FADDEYEV N.,"CMEA CO-OPERATION OF EQUAL NATIONS." COM R+D PLAN CAP/ISM DIPLOM FOR/AID WEALTH...POLICY MARXIST. PAGE 39 F0758
MARXISM ECO/TAC INT/ORG ECO/UNDEV

S67
FRIEDENBERG D.M.,"THE US IN LATIN AMERICA; A RECKONING OF SHAME." L/A+17C USA+45 USA-45 INT/ORG CAP/ISM FOR/AID 17/20 OAS. PAGE 44 F0857
DIPLOM POLICY DOMIN COLONIAL

S67
GUPTA S.,"FOREIGN POLICY IN THE 1967 MANIFESTOS." ASIA COM INDIA USA+45 FORCES FOR/AID TAX ATTIT ...DECISION 20. PAGE 52 F1013
IDEA/COMP POL/PAR POLICY DIPLOM

S67
ISELIN J.J.,"THE TRUMAN DOCTRINE: ITS PASSAGE THROUGH CONGRESS AND THE AFTERMATH." USA+45 ECO/UNDEV R+D INT/ORG DELIB/GP BAL/PWR REV PEACE ...POLICY UN. PAGE 66 F1291
DIPLOM COM FOR/AID AFR

S67
KINGSLEY R.E.,"THE US BUSINESS IMAGE IN LATIN AMERICA." L/A+17C USA+45 NAT/G TEC/DEV CAP/ISM FOR/AID DOMIN EDU/PROP...CONCPT LING IDEA/COMP 20. PAGE 71 F1396
ATTIT LOVE DIPLOM ECO/UNDEV

S67
LOSMAN D.L.,"FOREIGN AID, SOCIALISM AND THE EMERGING COUNTRIES" WOR+45 ADMIN CONTROL PWR 20. PAGE 82 F1602
ECO/UNDEV FOR/AID SOC

S67
MCCORD W.,"ARMIES AND POLITICS; A PROBLEM IN THE THIRD WORLD." AFR ISLAM USA+45 ECO/UNDEV TOTALISM 20. PAGE 88 F1723
FOR/AID POLICY NAT/G FORCES

S67
MEADE J.E.,"POPULATION EXPLOSION, THE STANDARD OF LIVING AND SOCIAL CONFLICT." DIPLOM FOR/AID OWN ...PREDICT TREND 20. PAGE 89 F1739
GEOG WEALTH PRODUC INCOME

S67
MEHTA A.,"INDIA* POVERTY AND CHANGE." STRATA INDUS CREATE ECO/TAC FOR/AID NEUTRAL GP/REL ADJUST INCOME ...NEW/IDEA 20. PAGE 89 F1746
INDIA SOCIETY ECO/UNDEV TEC/DEV

S67
PECCEI A.,"DEVELOPED-UNDERDEVELOPED AND EAST-WEST RELATIONS." ECO/UNDEV TEC/DEV DIPLOM LEAD EFFICIENCY GEOG. PAGE 104 F2045
FOR/AID TREND REGION ECO/DEV

S67
PETRAS J.,"U.S. HEGEMONY AND LATIN AMERICAN RULING CLASSES." L/A+17C USA+45 ECO/UNDEV FOR/AID REV SOC. PAGE 105 F2071
NAT/G ATTIT DIPLOM POLICY

S67
STRANGE S.,"DEBTS, DEFAULTERS AND DEVELOPMENT." WOR+45 PROB/SOLV FOR/AID INT/TRADE. PAGE 127 F2500
NAT/G FINAN ECO/UNDEV

S67
TABORSKY E.,"THE CLASS STRUGGLE, THE PROLETARIAT, AND THE DEVELOPING NATIONS." USSR LABOR POL/PAR FOR/AID COLONIAL GP/REL 20. PAGE 128 F2521
DIPLOM MARXISM ECO/UNDEV WORKER

S67
WALZER M.,"THE CONDITION OF GREECE; TWENTY YEARS AFTER THE TRUMAN DOCTRINE." AFR GREECE FORCES CAP/ISM 20 TRUMAN/HS. PAGE 143 F2814
DIPLOM POLICY FOR/AID TOTALISM

N67
US HOUSE COMM FOREIGN AFFAIRS,THE FOREIGN POLICY
POLICY

ASPECTS OF THE KENNEDY ROUND (PAMPHLET). USA+45 INDUS KENNEDY/JF CONGRESS HOUSE/REP EEC. PAGE 137 F2693 — INT/TRADE FOR/AID ECO/DEV — N67

US HOUSE COMM FOREIGN AFFAIRS,REPORT OF SPECIAL STUDY MISSION TO THE NEAR EAST (PAMPHLET). ISRAEL USA+45 YEMEN ECO/UNDEV INT/ORG FOR/AID ARMS/CONT WAR WEAPON NAT/LISM PEACE...GEOG 20 UN HOUSE/REP. PAGE 137 F2694 — ISLAM DIPLOM FORCES — N67

US HOUSE COMM FOREIGN AFFAIRS,FOREIGN ASSISTANCE ACT OF 1967 (PAMPHLET). USA+45 WOR+45 FINAN CONGRESS HOUSE/REP UN. PAGE 137 F2695 — FOR/AID POLICY INT/ORG ECO/UNDEV — N67

US HOUSE COMM SCI ASTRONAUT,GOVERNMENT, SCIENCE, AND INTERNATIONAL POLICY (PAMPHLET). INDIA NETHERLAND ECO/DEV ECO/UNDEV R+D ACADEM PLAN DIPLOM FOR/AID CONFER...PREDICT 20 CHINJAP. PAGE 137 F2705 — NAT/G POLICY CREATE TEC/DEV — N67

US SENATE COMM ON FOREIGN REL,ARMS SALES AND FOREIGN POLICY (PAMPHLET). FINAN FOR/AID CONTROL 20. PAGE 139 F2737 — ARMS/CONT ADMIN OP/RES DIPLOM — N67

US SENATE COMM ON FOREIGN REL,WAR OR PEACE IN THE MIDDLE EAST (PAMPHLET). GREECE ISLAM ISRAEL JORDAN UAR CHIEF PROB/SOLV FOR/AID WAR PWR 20 SENATE. PAGE 139 F2739 — DIPLOM FORCES PLAN

FOR/TRADE....FOREIGN TRADE; SEE ALSO INT/TRADE

B00

LIST F.,NATIONAL SYSTEM OF POLITICAL ECONOMY. ECO/DEV AGRI EXTR/IND FINAN INDUS TEC/DEV ECO/TAC ATTIT WEALTH...TREND GEN/LAWS FOR/TRADE 19. PAGE 81 F1581 — MOD/EUR MARKET — B25

EDGEWORTH F.Y.,PAPERS RELATING TO POLITICAL ECONOMY. MOD/EUR SOCIETY STRATA DIST/IND INDUS MARKET NAT/G ACT/RES ECO/TAC EXEC WEALTH ...METH/CNCPT MATH TREND HYPO/EXP SIMUL GEN/METH FOR/TRADE VAL/FREE LOG/LING. PAGE 36 F0702 — ECO/DEV CAP/ISM — B28

CASSEL G.,FOREIGN INVESTMENTS. GERMANY UK USA-45 WOR-45 ECO/DEV NAT/G VOL/ASSN CAP/ISM REPAR ATTIT WEALTH...METH/CNCPT STAT SIMUL STERTYP ANTHOL FOR/TRADE TOT/POP VAL/FREE 20. PAGE 22 F0426 — FINAN ECO/TAC BAL/PAY — B34

GRAHAM F.D.,PROTECTIVE TARIFFS. FUT USA+45 WOR-45 INDUS MARKET VOL/ASSN PLAN CAP/ISM ECO/TAC PEACE ATTIT DRIVE HEALTH ORD/FREE...OBS TREND GEN/LAWS FOR/TRADE 20. PAGE 50 F0970 — INT/ORG TARIFFS — B52

ASHWORTH W.,A SHORT HISTORY OF THE INTERNATIONAL ECONOMY 1850-1950. WOR+45 WOR-45 AGRI FINAN INDUS MARKET LABOR ECO/TAC...CONCPT STAT HIST/WRIT FOR/TRADE ILO 19/20. PAGE 7 F0131 — ECO/DEV TEC/DEV INT/TRADE — B52

HOSELITZ B.F.,THE PROGRESS OF UNDERDEVELOPED AREAS. AFR FUT WOR+45 WOR-45 ECO/DEV ECO/TAC INT/TRADE WEALTH...SOC TREND GEN/LAWS TOT/POP VAL/FREE FOR/TRADE 20. PAGE 62 F1219 — ECO/UNDEV PLAN FOR/AID — B54

WILLIAMSON H.F.,ECONOMIC DEVELOPMENT - PRINCIPLES AND PATTERNS. INDIA KOREA CULTURE ECO/DEV ECO/UNDEV TEC/DEV...CENSUS NAT/COMP FOR/TRADE 20 CHINJAP MEXIC/AMER RESOURCE/N. PAGE 147 F2895 — ECO/TAC GEOG LABOR — B55

BUCHANAN N.S.,APPROACHES TO ECONOMIC DEVELOPMENT. FUT USA+45 WOR+45 STRATA ECO/DEV INT/ORG NAT/G TEC/DEV DIPLOM FOR/AID ATTIT KNOWL PWR WEALTH ...RELATIV METH/CNCPT SELF/OBS TREND CON/ANAL STERTYP GEN/LAWS FOR/TRADE COMMUN 20. PAGE 20 F0380 — ECO/UNDEV ECO/TAC INT/TRADE — B55

HELANDER S.,DAS AUTARKIEPROBLEM IN DER WELTWIRTSCHAFT. PROB/SOLV BAL/PWR BARGAIN CAP/ISM ECO/TAC SOVEREIGN FOR/TRADE 20. PAGE 58 F1144 — NAT/COMP COLONIAL DIPLOM — B56

BELL P.W.,THE STERLING AREA IN THE POSTWAR WORLD. EUR+WWI FUT S/ASIA UK ECO/DEV PLAN DIPLOM WEALTH ...STAT RECORD CHARTS GEN/LAWS FOR/TRADE TOT/POP 20. PAGE 12 F0235 — FINAN ECO/TAC — B56

KINDLEBERGER C.P.,THE TERMS OF TRADE: A EUROPEAN CASE-STUDY. EUR+WWI MOD/EUR ECO/DEV ECO/UNDEV AGRI INDUS BAL/PAY...METH/CNCPT STAT CONT/OBS CON/ANAL SOC/EXP SIMUL FOR/TRADE 20. PAGE 71 F1390 — PLAN ECO/TAC — B57

ARON R.,L'UNIFICATION ECONOMIQUE DE L'EUROPE. EUR+WWI SWITZERLND UK INT/ORG NAT/G REGION NAT/LISM ORD/FREE PWR...CONCPT METH/CNCPT OBS TREND STERTYP GEN/LAWS EEC FOR/TRADE 20. PAGE 6 F0118 — VOL/ASSN ECO/TAC — B57

MEIER G.M.,ECONOMIC DEVELOPMENT: THEORY, HISTORY, AND POLICY. WOR+45 WOR-45 ECO/DEV ECO/UNDEV PLAN CAP/ISM BAL/PAY ATTIT PWR WEALTH SOCISM...CHARTS TOT/POP FOR/TRADE 20. PAGE 89 F1748 — ECO/TAC GEN/LAWS — L57

MASS. INST. TECH.,"THE CENTER FOR INTERNATIONAL STUDIES." AFR ASIA COM EUR+WWI ISLAM L/A+17C S/ASIA USA+45 USA-45 DIST/IND CONSULT FORCES ACT/RES TEC/DEV DIPLOM REV ATTIT WEALTH...CONCPT FOR/TRADE 20. PAGE 87 F1702 — R+D ECO/UNDEV — B58

BERLINER J.S.,SOVIET ECONOMIC AID: THE AID AND TRADE POLICY IN UNDERDEVELOPED COUNTRIES. AFR COM ISLAM L/A+17C S/ASIA USSR ECO/DEV DIST/IND FINAN MARKET INT/ORG ACT/RES PLAN BAL/PWR WEAPON PWR WEALTH...CHARTS FOR/TRADE 20. PAGE 14 F0263 — ECO/UNDEV ECO/TAC FOR/AID — B58

BIDWELL P.W.,RAW MATERIALS: A STUDY OF AMERICAN POLICY. USA+45 USA-45 ECO/UNDEV AGRI INDUS KIN CREATE PLAN ECO/TAC WAR PEACE ATTIT DRIVE WEALTH ...STAT CHARTS CONGRESS FOR/TRADE VAL/FREE. PAGE 15 F0279 — EXTR/IND ECO/DEV — B58

MIKESELL R.F.,FINANCING FREE WORLD TRADE WITH THE SINO-SOVIET BLOC. CHINA/COM COM USSR WOR+45 ECO/DEV AGRI DIST/IND EXTR/IND FINAN INDUS MARKET PROC/MFG NAT/G PLAN TEC/DEV ECO/TAC...CHARTS METH/GP EEC FOR/TRADE 20. PAGE 91 F1780 — STAT BAL/PAY — B59

ALLEN R.L.,SOVIET INFLUENCE IN LATIN AMERICA. ECO/UNDEV FINAN PROC/MFG NAT/G TEC/DEV EDU/PROP EXEC ROUTINE ATTIT DRIVE PERSON ALL/VALS PWR...STAT CHARTS WORK FOR/TRADE 20. PAGE 4 F0071 — L/A+17C ECO/TAC INT/TRADE USSR — B59

SANNWALD R.E.,ECONOMIC INTEGRATION: THEORETICAL ASSUMPTIONS AND CONSEQUENCES OF EUROPEAN UNIFICATION. EUR+WWI FUT FINAN INDUS VOL/ASSN ACT/RES ECO/TAC...PLURIST EEC FOR/TRADE OEEC 20. PAGE 116 F2279 — INT/ORG ECO/DEV INT/TRADE — L59

GARDNER R.N.,"NEW DIRECTIONS IN UNITED STATES FOREIGN ECONOMIC POLICY." AFR USA+45 CONSULT ...GEN/LAWS GEN/METH FOR/TRADE 20. PAGE 46 F0903 — ECO/UNDEV ECO/TAC FOR/AID DIPLOM — S59

ALKHIMOV V.S.,"SOVIET FOREIGN TRADE CHANNELS." COM FUT USA+45 USSR ECO/DEV MARKET CONSULT PLAN WEALTH ...MARXIST OBS CON/ANAL FOR/TRADE 20. PAGE 4 F0068 — FINAN ECO/TAC DIPLOM — S59

KINDLEBERGER C.P.,"UNITED STATES ECONOMIC FOREIGN POLICY: RESEARCH REQUIREMENTS FOR 1965." FUT USA+45 WOR+45 DIST/IND MARKET INT/ORG ECO/TAC INT/TRADE WEALTH...OBS TREND CON/ANAL GEN/LAWS FOR/TRADE VAL/FREE 20. PAGE 71 F1392 — FINAN ECO/DEV FOR/AID — B60

ALLEN R.L.,SOVIET ECONOMIC WARFARE. USSR FINAN INDUS NAT/G PLAN TEC/DEV FOR/AID DETER WEALTH ...TREND GEN/LAWS FOR/TRADE 20. PAGE 4 F0072 — COM ECO/TAC — B60

COMMITTEE ECONOMIC DEVELOPMENT,NATIONAL OBJECTIVES AND THE BALANCE OF PAYMENTS PROBLEM: A STATEMENT ON NATIONAL POLICY. USA+45 WOR+45 DIST/IND FINAN INDUS LABOR NAT/G DELIB/GP ACT/RES FOR/AID INT/TRADE ...STAT CHARTS FOR/TRADE 20. PAGE 27 F0516 — ECO/DEV ECO/TAC BAL/PAY — B60

FRANCK P.G.,AFGHANISTAN: BETWEEN EAST AND WEST. AFGHANISTN AFR USA+45 USSR ECO/UNDEV PLAN ADMIN ROUTINE ATTIT PWR...STAT OBS CHARTS TOT/POP FOR/TRADE 20. PAGE 43 F0843 — ECO/TAC TREND FOR/AID — B60

MYRDAL G.,BEYOND THE WELFARE STATE: ECONOMIC PLANNING AND ITS IMPLICATIONS. EUR+WWI FUT USA+45 USSR ECO/DEV ECO/UNDEV TEC/DEV SKILL WEALTH...PSY TREND FOR/TRADE 20. PAGE 96 F1881 — PLAN ECO/TAC CAP/ISM — B60

THEOBALD R.,THE RICH AND THE POOR: A STUDY OF THE ECONOMICS OF RISING EXPECTATIONS. WOR+45 CONSTN ECO/DEV ECO/UNDEV INT/ORG NAT/G PLAN FOR/AID ROUTINE BAL/PAY ORD/FREE PWR WEALTH...GEOG TREND WORK FOR/TRADE 20. PAGE 129 F2553 — ECO/TAC INT/TRADE — B60

THORBECKE E.,THE TENDENCY TOWARDS REGIONALIZATION IN INTERNATIONAL TRADE, 1928-1956. WOR+45 WOR-45 ECO/DEV FINAN ECO/TAC WEALTH...GEOG CHARTS TOT/POP FOR/TRADE 20. PAGE 130 F2569 — STAT BAL/PAY REGION — S60

BERG E.J.,"ECONOMIC BASIS OF POLITICAL CHOICE IN FRENCH WEST AFRICA." FRANCE ECO/UNDEV AGRI INDUS NAT/G PLAN LEGIT COLONIAL REGION ATTIT PWR WEALTH ...CONCPT FOR/TRADE 20. PAGE 13 F0257 — AFR ECO/TAC — S60

DUNN J.M.,"AMERICAN DEPENDENCE ON MATERIALS IMPORTS: THE WORLD-WIDE RESOURCE BASE." USA+45 WOR+45 NAT/G ATTIT WEALTH...RECORD TIME/SEQ CHARTS FOR/TRADE 20. PAGE 35 F0680 — ACT/RES ECO/TAC — S60

MURPHY J.C.,"INTERNATIONAL INVESTMENT AND THE NATIONAL INTEREST." AFR WOR+45 WOR-45 ECO/DEV — FINAN WEALTH

ECO/UNDEV NAT/G ACT/RES...CHARTS TOT/POP FOR/TRADE FOR/AID
20. PAGE 95 F1867

S60
RIVKIN A.,"AFRICAN ECONOMIC DEVELOPMENT: ADVANCED TECHNOLOGY AND THE STAGES OF GROWTH." CULTURE ECO/UNDEV AGRI COM/IND EXTR/IND PLAN ECO/TAC ATTIT DRIVE RIGID/FLEX SKILL WEALTH...MGT SOC GEN/LAWS FOR/TRADE WORK TOT/POP 20. PAGE 111 F2195
AFR
TEC/DEV
FOR/AID

B61
BALASSA B.,THE THEORY OF ECONOMIC INTEGRATION. EUR+WWI L/A+17C MOD/EUR WOR+45 ECO/UNDEV MARKET INT/ORG NAT/G VOL/ASSN DELIB/GP PLAN CAP/ISM ECO/TAC...MAJORIT FOR/TRADE OEEC 20. PAGE 8 F0157
ECO/DEV
ACT/RES
INT/TRADE

B61
BENOIT E.,EUROPE AT SIXES AND SEVENS: THE COMMON MARKET, THE FREE TRADE ASSOCIATION AND THE UNITED STATES. EUR+WWI FUT USA+45 INDUS CONSULT DELIB/GP EX/STRUC TOP/EX ACT/RES ECO/TAC EDU/PROP ROUTINE CHOOSE PERCEPT WEALTH...MGT TREND EEC FOR/TRADE TOT/POP 20 EFTA. PAGE 13 F0249
FINAN
ECO/DEV
VOL/ASSN

B61
EINZIG P.,A DYNAMIC THEORY OF FORWARD EXCHANGE. FUT WOR+45 WOR-45 INT/TRADE BAL/PAY WEALTH...OLD/LIB NEW/IDEA OBS TREND FOR/TRADE 20. PAGE 37 F0713
FINAN
ECO/TAC

B61
FRIEDMANN W.G.,JOINT INTERNATIONAL BUSINESS VENTURES. ASIA ISLAM L/A+17C ECO/DEV DIST/IND FINAN PROC/MFG FACE/GP LG/CO NAT/G VOL/ASSN CONSULT EX/STRUC PLAN ADMIN ROUTINE WEALTH...OLD/LIB FOR/TRADE WORK 20. PAGE 44 F0865
ECO/UNDEV
INT/TRADE

B61
GARDNER R.N.,LEGAL-ECONOMIC PROBLEMS OF INTERNATIONAL TRADE. FUT WOR+45 INTELL ECO/DEV EX/STRUC INT/TRADE ROUTINE ATTIT WEALTH...GEN/LAWS ANTHOL FOR/TRADE 20. PAGE 46 F0904
FINAN
ACT/RES

S61
HAYTES W.,"THREE VIEWS ON THE SOVIET ECONOMIC THREAT." AFR COM USA+45 USA-45 USSR WOR+45 WOR-45 INDUS TEC/DEV ECO/TAC DOMIN ATTIT PERCEPT PWR FOR/TRADE 20. PAGE 57 F1128
ECO/DEV
PLAN
TOTALISM

S61
RAY J.,"THE EUROPEAN FREE-TRADE ASSOCIATION AND ITS IMPACT ON INDIA'S TRADE." EUR+WWI FRANCE GERMANY INDIA S/ASIA UK NAT/G VOL/ASSN PLAN INT/TRADE ROUTINE WEALTH...STAT CHARTS TERR/GP CMN/WLTH EEC FOR/TRADE OEEC 20 EFTA. PAGE 109 F2155
ECO/DEV
ECO/TAC

S61
VALLET R.,"IRAN: KEY TO THE MIDDLE EAST." COM IRAQ ISLAM KUWAIT LEBANON SAUDI/ARAB TURKEY ELITES SOCIETY INDUS PROC/MFG POL/PAR TOP/EX PLAN BAL/PWR DIPLOM ECO/TAC ALL/VALS...TREND FOR/TRADE CENTO 20. PAGE 140 F2760
NAT/G
ECO/UNDEV
IRAN

B62
HUMPHREY D.D.,THE UNITED STATES AND THE COMMON MARKET. USA+45 INDUS MARKET INT/ORG PLAN EDU/PROP BAL/PAY DRIVE PWR WEALTH...TREND STERTYP FOR/TRADE EEC 20. PAGE 63 F1241
ATTIT
ECO/TAC

B62
MEADE J.E.,CASE STUDIES IN EUROPEAN ECONOMIC UNION. BELGIUM EUR+WWI LUXEMBOURG NAT/G INT/TRADE REGION ROUTINE WEALTH...METH/CNCPT STAT CHARTS ECSC TOT/POP OEEC EEC FOR/TRADE 20. PAGE 89 F1738
INT/ORG
ECO/TAC

L62
PRYOR F.L.,"FOREIGN TRADE IN THE COMMUNIST BLOC." COM ECO/DEV VOL/ASSN...METH/CNCPT GEN/LAWS FOR/TRADE TERR/GP 20. PAGE 108 F2129
ECO/TAC
STERTYP
USSR

S62
ADISESHIAN M.,"EDUCATION AND DEVELOPMENT." FUT WOR+45 SOCIETY ACT/RES INT/TRADE EDU/PROP KNOWL SKILL WEALTH...POLICY CONCPT CONT/OBS CENSUS CHARTS TOT/POP VAL/FREE APPLIC FAO FOR/TRADE 20. PAGE 2 F0041
SCHOOL
ECO/UNDEV

S62
BOONE A.,"THE FOREIGN TRADE OF CHINA." AFR ECO/DEV ECO/UNDEV INDUS MARKET NAT/G TEC/DEV WEALTH ...POLICY STAT TREND CHARTS FOR/TRADE. PAGE 17 F0318
ASIA
ECO/TAC

S62
SCOTT J.B.,"ANGLO-SOVIET TRADE AND ITS EFFECTS ON THE COMMONWEALTH." COM FUT UK USSR WOR+45 ECO/DEV MARKET INT/ORG CONSULT WEALTH...POLICY TREND CMN/WLTH FOR/TRADE 20. PAGE 118 F2333
NAT/G
ECO/TAC

B63
BAUER R.A.,AMERICAN BUSINESS AND PUBLIC POLICY: THE POLITICS OF FOREIGN TRADE. USA+45 COM/IND LG/CO NAT/G PROF/ORG SML/CO VOL/ASSN LEGIS TOP/EX ECO/TAC EDU/PROP CHOOSE HEALTH PWR WEALTH...CONCPT METH/CNCPT OBS INT QU SAMP FOR/TRADE TRUE/GP VAL/FREE HI. PAGE 11 F0217
ECO/DEV
ATTIT

B63
ISSAWI C.,EGYPT IN REVOLUTION: AN ECONOMIC ANALYSIS. ISLAM STRUCT ECO/UNDEV AGRI FINAN INDUS PLAN EXEC REV NAT/LISM ATTIT RIGID/FLEX WEALTH SOCISM...STAT FOR/TRADE WORK 20. PAGE 66 F1292
NAT/G
UAR

B63
NEUMARK S.D.,FOREIGN TRADE AND ECONOMIC DEVELOPMENT IN AFRICA: A HISTORICAL PERSPECTIVE. EUR+WWI MOD/EUR ECO/UNDEV AGRI COM/IND EXTR/IND PROC/MFG SKILL WEALTH...CONCPT TIME/SEQ TREND SIMUL FOR/TRADE WORK TOT/POP TERR/GP VAL/FREE 19/20. PAGE 98 F1916
AFR

B63
OLSON M. JR.,THE ECONOMICS OF WARTIME SHORTAGE. FRANCE GERMANY MOD/EUR UK AGRI PROB/SOLV ADMIN DEMAND WEALTH...POLICY OLD/LIB FOR/TRADE 17/20. PAGE 101 F1990
WAR
ADJUST
ECO/TAC
NAT/COMP

B63
PRYOR F.L.,THE COMMUNIST FOREIGN TRADE SYSTEM. COM CZECHOSLVK GERMANY YUGOSLAVIA LAW ECO/DEV DIST/IND POL/PAR PLAN DOMIN TOTALISM DRIVE RIGID/FLEX WEALTH ...STAT STAND/INT CHARTS FOR/TRADE 20. PAGE 108 F2130
ATTIT
ECO/TAC

S63
ADAMS F.G.,"ECONOMIC CONSIDERATIONS OF AN ATLANTIC ENERGY POLICY." EUR+WWI FUT USA+45 DIST/IND EXTR/IND MARKET CONSULT LEGIS ECO/TAC WEALTH ...POLICY EEC FOR/TRADE OEEC 20. PAGE 2 F0037
ECO/DEV
TEC/DEV
NUC/PWR

S63
BARTHELEMY G.,"LE NOUVEAU FRANC (CFA) ET LA BANQUE CENTRALE DES ETATS DE L'AFRIQUE DE L'OUEST." FUT STRUCT INT/ORG PLAN ATTIT ALL/VALS FOR/TRADE 20. PAGE 11 F0200
AFR
FINAN

S63
BEGUIN H.,"ASPECTS STRUCTURELS DU COMMERCE EXTERIEUR DES PAYS SOUS-DEVELOPPES." FUT WOR+45 STRUCT FINAN SERV/IND POL/PAR TEC/DEV PERCEPT WEALTH FOR/TRADE 20. PAGE 12 F0229
MARKET
ECO/UNDEV
FOR/AID

S63
CLEMHOUT S.,"PRODUCTION FUNCTION ANALYSIS APPLIED TO THE LEONTIEF SCARCE-FACTOR PARADOX OF INTERNATIONAL TRADE." EUR+WWI USA+45 DIST/IND NAT/G PLAN TEC/DEV DIPLOM PWR WEALTH...MGT METH/CNCPT CONT/OBS CON/ANAL CHARTS SIMUL GEN/LAWS FOR/TRADE 20. PAGE 25 F0490
ECO/DEV
ECO/TAC

S63
LEDUC G.,"L'AIDE INTERNATIONALE AU DEVELOPPEMENT." FUT WOR+45 ECO/DEV ECO/UNDEV R+D PROF/ORG TEC/DEV ECO/TAC ROUTINE ATTIT ALL/VALS...MGT TIME/SEQ FOR/TRADE TOT/POP 20. PAGE 77 F1503
FINAN
PLAN
FOR/AID

S63
MIKESELL R.F.,"COMMODITY AGREEMENTS AND AID TO DEVELOPING COUNTRIES." WOR+45 WOR-45 INT/ORG ECO/TAC ATTIT WEALTH WORK FOR/TRADE 20. PAGE 91 F1782
FINAN
ECO/UNDEV
BAL/PAY
FOR/AID

S63
MILLEN B.H.,"INTERNATIONAL TRADE AND POLITICAL INDEPENDENCE." WOR+45 ECO/DEV WEALTH...STAT CHARTS FOR/TRADE METH/GP TERR/GP VAL/FREE 20. PAGE 91 F1788
ECO/UNDEV
ECO/TAC
INT/TRADE

S63
NADLER E.B.,"SOME ECONOMIC DISADVANTAGES OF THE ARMS RACE." AFR USA+45 INDUS R+D FORCES PLAN TEC/DEV ECO/TAC FOR/AID EDU/PROP PWR WEALTH...TREND FOR/TRADE 20. PAGE 96 F1886
ECO/DEV
MGT
BAL/PAY

S63
POPPINO R.E.,"IMBALANCE IN BRAZIL." L/A+17C NAT/G TOP/EX PLAN DIPLOM LEGIT DRIVE WEALTH...CON/ANAL FOR/TRADE LAFTA 20. PAGE 107 F2105
POL/PAR
ECO/TAC
BRAZIL

S63
REDDAWAY W.B.,"THE ECONOMICS OF UNDERDEVELOPED COUNTRIES." S/ASIA WOR+45 WOR-45 STRATA AGRI COM/IND DIST/IND MARKET PROC/MFG PLAN TEC/DEV FOR/AID BAL/PAY ATTIT DRIVE SKILL WORK FOR/TRADE 20. PAGE 110 F2165
ECO/TAC
ECO/UNDEV
INDIA

L64
BHAGWATI J.,"THE PURE THEORY OF INTERNATIONAL TRADE: A SURVEY." WOR+45 ECO/DEV ECO/UNDEV FINAN MARKET PROC/MFG INT/ORG LABOR LG/CO NAT/G TEC/DEV ECO/TAC SKILL WEALTH...POLICY RELATIV MGT CONCPT NEW/IDEA MATH QUANT GEN/LAWS FOR/TRADE 20. PAGE 14 F0276
INDUS
HYPO/EXP

L64
KORBONSKI A.,"COMECON." ASIA ECO/DEV ECO/UNDEV ECO/TAC BAL/PAY NAT/LISM FOR/TRADE 20 COMECON. PAGE 73 F1425
COM
INT/ORG
INT/TRADE

S64
GALBRAITH V.,"JAPAN'S POSITION IN WORLD TRADE." ASIA AGRI INDUS CREATE ECO/TAC LEGIT DRIVE WEALTH ...TREND EEC GATT FOR/TRADE 20 CHINJAP. PAGE 45 F0885
ECO/DEV
DELIB/GP

S64
HUELIN D.,"ECONOMIC INTEGRATION IN LATIN AMERICAN: PROGRESS AND PROBLEMS." L/A+17C ECO/DEV AGRI DIST/IND FINAN INDUS NAT/G VOL/ASSN CONSULT DELIB/GP EX/STRUC ACT/RES PLAN TEC/DEV ECO/TAC ROUTINE BAL/PAY WEALTH FOR/TRADE WORK TERR/GP 20. PAGE 63 F1232
MARKET
ECO/UNDEV
INT/TRADE

S64
NEISSER H.,"THE EXTERNAL EQUILIBRIUM OF THE UNITED STATES ECONOMY." FUT USA+45 NAT/G ACT/RES PLAN ECO/TAC ATTIT WEALTH...METH/CNCPT GEN/METH VAL/FREE FOR/TRADE 20. PAGE 97 F1910
FINAN
ECO/DEV
BAL/PAY
INT/TRADE

S64
POLARIS J.,"THE SINO-SOVIET DISPUTE: ITS ECONOMIC IMPACT ON CHINA." ASIA CHINA/COM COM WOR+45 NAT/G ATTIT PWR WEALTH...STAT TREND FOR/TRADE 20. PAGE 107 F2095 ECO/UNDEV ECO/TAC

S64
WU Y.,"CHINA'S ECONOMY AND ITS PROSPECTS." ASIA CHINA/COM FUT USSR AGRI INDUS PLAN ECO/TAC LEGIT WEALTH...STAT CON/ANAL CHARTS GEN/LAWS FOR/TRADE 20. PAGE 149 F2938 ECO/DEV

S65
KORBONSKI A.,"USA POLICY IN EAST EUROPE." COM EUR+WWI GERMANY USA+45 CULTURE ECO/UNDEV EDU/PROP RIGID/FLEX WEALTH FOR/TRADE 20. PAGE 73 F1426 ACT/RES ECO/TAC FOR/AID

S65
WHITAKER A.P.,"ARGENTINA: STRUGGLE FOR RECOVERY." L/A+17C USA+45 NAT/G TOP/EX PLAN LEGIT COERCE REV RIGID/FLEX PWR WEALTH...RECORD ALL/PROG ARGEN FOR/TRADE 20. PAGE 146 F2867 POL/PAR ECO/TAC NAT/LISM

FORBUSH D.R. F0822

FORCE AND VIOLENCE....SEE COERCE

FORCES....ARMED FORCES AND POLICE

B14
DE BLOCH J.,THE FUTURE OF WAR IN ITS TECHNICAL, ECONOMIC, AND POLITICAL RELATIONS (1899). MOD/EUR TEC/DEV BUDGET INT/TRADE DETER GUERRILLA WEAPON COST PEACE 20. PAGE 31 F0596 WAR BAL/PWR PREDICT FORCES

N19
RIDLEY C.E.,MEASURING MUNICIPAL ACTIVITIES (PAMPHLET). FINAN SERV/IND FORCES RECEIVE INGP/REL HABITAT...POLICY SOC/WK 20. PAGE 111 F2191 MGT HEALTH WEALTH LOC/G

B30
HAWTREY R.G.,ECONOMIC ASPECTS OF SOVEREIGNTY. UNIV WOR+45 WOR-45 ECO/DEV ECO/UNDEV AGRI COM/IND INDUS MARKET NAT/G TEC/DEV ECO/TAC EDU/PROP COERCE ATTIT KNOWL WEALTH...CONCPT CON/ANAL GEN/LAWS 20. PAGE 57 F1118 FORCES PWR SOVEREIGN WAR

B37
UNION OF SOUTH AFRICA,REPORT CONCERNING ADMINISTRATION OF SOUTH WEST AFRICA (6 VOLS.). SOUTH/AFR INDUS PUB/INST FORCES LEGIS BUDGET DIPLOM EDU/PROP ADJUD CT/SYS...GEOG CHARTS 20 AFRICA/SW LEAGUE/NAT. PAGE 132 F2610 NAT/G ADMIN COLONIAL CONSTN

S39
COLE G.D.H.,"NAZI ECONOMICS: HOW DO THEY MANAGE IT?" GERMANY FORCES WORKER BUDGET INT/TRADE ROUTINE COERCE WAR 20 HITLER/A NAZI. PAGE 26 F0500 FASCISM ECO/TAC ATTIT PLAN

S41
LASSWELL H.D.,"THE GARRISON STATE" (BMR)" FUT WOR+45 ELITES INTELL FORCES ECO/TAC DOMIN EDU/PROP COERCE INGP/REL 20. PAGE 76 F1485 NAT/G DIPLOM PWR CIVMIL/REL

B42
JACKSON M.V.,EUROPEAN POWERS AND SOUTH-EAST AFRICA: A STUDY OF INTERNATIONAL RELATIONS ON SOUTH-EAST COAST OF AFRICA, 1796-1856. AFR FRANCE PORTUGAL SOUTH/AFR UK USA-45 FORCES INT/TRADE PWR...CHARTS BIBLIOG 18/19 TREATY. PAGE 66 F1294 DOMIN POLICY ORD/FREE DIPLOM

S43
HUZAR E.,"CONGRESS AND THE ARMY: APPROPRIATIONS." USA-45 CONFER CONTROL ATTIT SUPEGO SKILL CONGRESS. PAGE 64 F1255 LEGIS FORCES BUDGET DELIB/GP

B47
BALDWIN H.W.,THE PRICE OF POWER. USA+45 FORCES PLAN NUC/PWR ADJUST COST ORD/FREE...POLICY PSY BIBLIOG 20. PAGE 9 F0165 PROB/SOLV PWR POPULISM PRICE

B47
GORDON D.L.,THE HIDDEN WEAPON: THE STORY OF ECONOMIC WARFARE. EUR+WWI USA-45 LAW FINAN INDUS NAT/G CONSULT FORCES PLAN DOMIN PWR WEALTH ...INT/LAW CONCPT OBS TOT/POP NAZI 20. PAGE 49 F0955 INT/ORG ECO/TAC INT/TRADE WAR

B50
LINCOLN G.,ECONOMICS OF NATIONAL SECURITY. USA+45 ELITES COM/IND DIST/IND INDUS NAT/G VOL/ASSN DELIB/GP EX/STRUC FOR/AID EDU/PROP COERCE NUC/PWR WAR ATTIT KNOWL ORD/FREE PWR TOT/POP VAL/FREE 20. PAGE 80 F1565 FORCES ECO/TAC AFR

B51
LEONARD L.L.,INTERNATIONAL ORGANIZATION. WOR+45 WOR-45 EX/STRUC FORCES LEGIS ECO/TAC INT/TRADE COLONIAL ARMS/CONT...SOC/WK GOV/COMP BIBLIOG. PAGE 78 F1527 NAT/G DIPLOM INT/ORG DELIB/GP

B51
US HOUSE COMM APPROPRIATIONS,MUTUAL SECURITY PROGRAM APPROPRIATIONS FOR 1952: HEARINGS BEFORE A SUBCOMMITTEE OF THE COMMITTEE ON APPROPRIATIONS. AFR KOREA L/A+17C ECO/DEV ECO/UNDEV INT/ORG INSPECT BAL/PWR DIPLOM DEBATE WAR...POLICY STAT ASIA/S 20 CONGRESS NATO MID/EAST. PAGE 136 F2686 LEGIS FORCES BUDGET FOR/AID

B52
MACARTHUR D.,REVITALIZING A NATION. ASIA COM FUT KOREA WOR+45 NAT/G FOR/AID TAX GIVE WAR ATTIT SOCISM 20 CHINJAP EUROPE. PAGE 83 F1619 LEAD FORCES TOP/EX POLICY

S53
LINCOLN G.,"FACTORS DETERMINING ARMS AID." COM FUT USA+45 USSR WOR+45 ECO/DEV NAT/G CONSULT PLAN TEC/DEV DIPLOM DOMIN EDU/PROP PERCEPT PWR ...DECISION CONCPT TREND MARX/KARL 20. PAGE 80 F1566 FORCES POLICY BAL/PWR FOR/AID

B54
REYNOLDS P.A.,BRITISH FOREIGN POLICY IN THE INTER-WAR YEARS. CZECHOSLVK GERMANY POLAND UK USA-45 POL/PAR FORCES ECO/TAC ARMS/CONT WAR ATTIT 20. PAGE 111 F2182 DIPLOM POLICY NAT/G

B55
FLORINSKY M.T.,INTEGRATED EUROPE. EUR+WWI FRANCE ITALY NETHERLAND UK ECO/DEV INT/ORG FORCES LEGIT FEDERAL ATTIT PWR WEALTH...POLICY GEOG CONCPT GEN/LAWS TOT/POP EEC OEEC 20. PAGE 42 F0816 FUT ECO/TAC REGION

B55
OECD,MARSHALL PLAN IN TURKEY. TURKEY USA+45 COM/IND CONSTRUC SERV/IND FORCES BUDGET...STAT 20 MARSHL/PLN. PAGE 100 F1964 FOR/AID ECO/UNDEV AGRI INDUS

B55
SMITHIES A.,THE BUDGETARY PROCESS IN THE UNITED STATES. AFR ECO/DEV AGRI EX/STRUC FORCES LEGIS PROB/SOLV TAX ROUTINE EFFICIENCY...MGT CONGRESS PRESIDENT. PAGE 124 F2436 NAT/G ADMIN BUDGET GOV/REL

B55
US ADVISORY COMN INTERGOV REL,THE COMMISSION ON INTERGOVERNMENTAL RELATIONS; A REPORT TO THE PRESIDENT FOR TRANSMITTAL TO THE CONGRESS. USA+45 ECO/DEV AGRI COM/IND FINAN FORCES PLAN EDU/PROP HEALTH WEALTH...STAT MUNICH 20 CIV/DEFENS. PAGE 133 F2630 GOV/REL NAT/G LOC/G PROVS

B55
US OFFICE OF THE PRESIDENT,REPORT TO CONGRESS ON THE MUTUAL SECURITY PROGRAM FOR THE SIX MONTHS ENDED JUNE 30, 1955. ECO/DEV INT/ORG NAT/G CREATE TEC/DEV BAL/PWR ECO/TAC AGREE DETER COST ORD/FREE 20 DEPT/STATE DEPT/DEFEN. PAGE 138 F2722 DIPLOM FORCES PLAN FOR/AID

B56
US OFFICE OF THE PRESIDENT,REPORT TO CONGRESS ON THE MUTUAL SECURITY PROGRAM FOR THE SIX MONTHS ENDED DECEMBER 31, 1955. ASIA USSR ECO/DEV ECO/UNDEV INT/ORG CREATE TEC/DEV BAL/PWR ECO/TAC AGREE DETER COST ORD/FREE 20 DEPT/STATE DEPT/DEFEN EISNHWR/DD. PAGE 138 F2723 DIPLOM FORCES PLAN FOR/AID

B57
NAUMANN R.,THEORIE UND PRAXIS DES NEOLIBERALISMUS; DAS MAERCHEN VON DER FREIEN ODER SOZIALEN MARKTWIRTSCHAFT. GERMANY/W FORCES PLAN EDU/PROP SOCISM...POLICY MARXIST IDEA/COMP BIBLIOG 18/20 ADENAUER/K. PAGE 97 F1903 MARXISM NEW/LIB ECO/TAC CAP/ISM

B57
NEUMARK S.D.,ECONOMIC INFLUENCES ON THE SOUTH AFRICAN FRONTIER, 1652-1836. SOUTH/AFR SEA AGRI NAT/G FORCES WORKER DIPLOM INT/TRADE PRICE DEMAND PRODUC...STAT CHARTS 17/19 FRONTIER. PAGE 97 F1915 COLONIAL ECO/UNDEV ECO/TAC MARKET

L57
MASS. INST. TECH.,"THE CENTER FOR INTERNATIONAL STUDIES." AFR ASIA COM EUR+WWI ISLAM L/A+17C S/ASIA USA+45 USA-45 DIST/IND CONSULT FORCES ACT/RES TEC/DEV DIPLOM REV ATTIT WEALTH...CONCPT FOR/TRADE 20. PAGE 87 F1702 R+D ECO/UNDEV

S57
HOAG M.W.,"ECONOMIC PROBLEMS OF ALLIANCE." AFR COM EUR+WWI WOR+45 ECO/DEV ECO/UNDEV NAT/G VOL/ASSN FORCES PLAN TEC/DEV DIPLOM COERCE ORD/FREE PWR WEALTH...DECISION GEN/LAWS NATO TERR/GP. PAGE 60 F1182 INT/ORG ECO/TAC

B58
JACOBSSON P.,SOME MONETARY PROBLEMS, INTERNATIONAL AND NATIONAL. WOR+45 WOR-45 ECO/DEV FORCES WORKER PROB/SOLV DIPLOM INT/TRADE...ANTHOL 20. PAGE 66 F1299 FINAN PLAN ECO/TAC NAT/COMP

B58
SHAW S.J.,THE FINANCIAL AND ADMINISTRATIVE ORGANIZATION AND DEVELOPMENT OF OTTOMAN EGYPT 1517-1798. UAR LOC/G FORCES BUDGET INT/TRADE TAX EATING INCOME WEALTH...CHARTS BIBLIOG 16/18 OTTOMAN NAPOLEON/B. PAGE 120 F2371 FINAN ADMIN GOV/REL CULTURE

B59
ROBERTSON A.H.,EUROPEAN INSTITUTIONS: COOPERATION, INTEGRATION, UNIFICATION. EUR+WWI FINAN INT/ORG FORCES INT/TRADE TARIFFS 20 EEC EURATOM ECSC NATO TREATY. PAGE 112 F2208 ECO/DEV DIPLOM INDUS ECO/TAC

B59
STERNBERG F.,THE MILITARY AND INDUSTRIAL REVOLUTION OF OUR TIME. USA+45 USSR WOR+45 WORKER COMPUTER PLAN TEC/DEV NUC/PWR GP/REL...POLICY NAT/COMP 20. DIPLOM FORCES INDUS

PAGE 126 F2481 — CIVMIL/REL

B59
US DEPARTMENT OF STATE,THE UNITED STATES ECONOMY AND THE MUTUAL SECURITY PROGRAM. USA+45 ECO/UNDEV FINAN INDUS DIPLOM INT/TRADE DETER 20. PAGE 136 F2674 — ECO/DEV FORCES BUDGET FOR/AID

B59
US HOUSE COMM GOVT OPERATIONS,UNITED STATES AID OPERATIONS IN LAOS. LAOS USA+45 PLAN INSPECT HOUSE/REP. PAGE 137 F2697 — FOR/AID ADMIN FORCES ECO/UNDEV

B59
WARD B.,5 IDEAS THAT CHANGE THE WORLD. WOR+45 WOR-45 SOCIETY STRUCT AGRI INDUS INT/ORG NAT/G FORCES ACT/RES ARMS/CONT TOTALISM ATTIT DRIVE GEN/LAWS. PAGE 143 F2815 — ECO/UNDEV ALL/VALS NAT/LISM COLONIAL

B60
BILLERBECK K.,SOVIET BLOC FOREIGN AID TO UNDERDEVELOPED COUNTRIES. COM FUT USSR FINAN FORCES TEC/DEV DIPLOM INT/TRADE EDU/PROP NUC/PWR...TREND 20. PAGE 15 F0285 — FOR/AID ECO/UNDEV ECO/TAC MARXISM

B60
HITCH C.J.,THE ECONOMICS OF DEFENSE IN THE NUCLEAR AGE. USA+45 WOR+45 CREATE PLAN NUC/PWR ATTIT ...CON/ANAL CHARTS HYPO/EXP NATO 20. PAGE 60 F1179 — R+D FORCES

S60
HERZ J.H.,"EAST GERMANY: PROGRESS AND PROSPECTS." COM AGRI FINAN INDUS LOC/G NAT/G FORCES PLAN TEC/DEV DOMIN ADMIN COERCE DRIVE PERCEPT RIGID/FLEX MORAL ORD/FREE PWR...MARXIST PSY SOC RECORD STERTYP WORK. PAGE 59 F1158 — POL/PAR STRUCT GERMANY

B61
HARDT J.P.,THE COLD WAR ECONOMIC GAP. AFR USA+45 USSR ECO/DEV FORCES INT/TRADE NUC/PWR PWR 20. PAGE 55 F1081 — DIPLOM ECO/TAC NAT/COMP POLICY

B61
MARX K.,THE COMMUNIST MANIFESTO. IN (MENDEL A. ESSENTIAL WORKS OF MARXISM, NEW YORK: BANTAM. FUT MOD/EUR CULTURE ECO/DEV ECO/UNDEV AGRI FINAN INDUS MARKET PROC/MFG LABOR POL/PAR CONSULT FORCES CREATE PLAN ADMIN ATTIT DRIVE RIGID/FLEX ORD/FREE PWR RESPECT MARX/KARL MUNICH WORK. PAGE 86 F1691 — COM NEW/IDEA CAP/ISM REV

B61
MORLEY L.,THE PATCHWORK HISTORY OF FOREIGN AID. AFR KOREA/S USA+45 USSR LAW FINAN INT/ORG TEC/DEV BAL/PWR GIVE 20 NATO. PAGE 93 F1834 — FOR/AID ECO/UNDEV FORCES DIPLOM

B61
STANLEY C.J.,LATE CH'ING FINANCE: HU KUANG-YUNG AS AN INNOVATOR. ASIA NAT/G FORCES BUDGET TAX WAR GOV/REL COST...POLICY BIOG CHARTS BIBLIOG 19. PAGE 125 F2469 — FINAN ECO/TAC CIVMIL/REL ADMIN

B61
UNIVS-NATL BUR COMM ECO RES,PUBLIC FINANCES: NEEDS, SOURCES, AND UTILIZATION. USA+45 FORCES PLAN TAX CONFER PRICE FEDERAL UTIL...ANTHOL MUNICH 20. PAGE 133 F2623 — NAT/G FINAN DECISION BUDGET

B61
US SENATE COMM ON FOREIGN RELS,INTERNATIONAL DEVELOPMENT AND SECURITY: HEARINGS ON BILL (2 VOLS.). ECO/UNDEV FINAN FORCES REV COST WEALTH ...CHARTS 20 AID PRESIDENT. PAGE 139 F2747 — FOR/AID CIVMIL/REL ORD/FREE ECO/TAC

B62
DUPRE J.S.,SCIENCE AND THE NATION: POLICY AND POLITICS. USA+45 LAW ACADEM FORCES ADMIN CIVMIL/REL GOV/REL EFFICIENCY PEACE...TREND 20 SCI/ADVSRY. PAGE 35 F0682 — R+D INDUS TEC/DEV NUC/PWR

B62
JORDAN A.A. JR.,FOREIGN AID AND THE DEFENSE OF SOUTHEAST ASIA. PAKISTAN VIETNAM/S FINAN PLAN BUDGET ECO/TAC DETER WAR ORD/FREE...POLICY DECISION CENSUS CHARTS BIBLIOG 20. PAGE 68 F1341 — FOR/AID S/ASIA FORCES ECO/UNDEV

B62
SCHILLING W.R.,STRATEGY, POLITICS, AND DEFENSE BUDGETS. AFR USA+45 CHIEF LEGIS PLAN TEC/DEV BAL/PWR BUDGET NUC/PWR WAR CIVMIL/REL GOV/REL PWR 20 EISNHWR/DD. PAGE 117 F2297 — NAT/G POLICY FORCES DETER

C62
JOINT ECONOMIC COMMITTEE,"DIMENSIONS OF SOVIET ECONOMIC POWER." USSR R+D FORCES ACT/RES OP/RES TEC/DEV...GEOG STAT BIBLIOG 20. PAGE 68 F1337 — ECO/DEV PLAN PRODUC LABOR

B63
ABSHIRE D.M.,NATIONAL SECURITY: POLITICAL, MILITARY, AND ECONOMIC STRATEGIES IN THE DECADE AHEAD. ASIA COM USA+45 WOR+45 ECO/DEV ECO/UNDEV INT/ORG DELIB/GP FORCES ECO/TAC COERCE ATTIT RIGID/FLEX HEALTH ORD/FREE PWR WEALTH...POLICY STAT CHARTS ANTHOL COLD/WAR VAL/FREE APP/SCI. PAGE 2 F0032 — FUT ACT/RES BAL/PWR

B63
BERGSON A.,ECONOMIC TRENDS IN THE SOVIET UNION. USSR ECO/UNDEV AGRI NAT/G FORCES PLAN TEC/DEV INT/TRADE BAL/PAY...POLICY ANTHOL 20. PAGE 14 F0259 — ECO/DEV NAT/COMP INDUS LABOR

B63
EL-NAGGAR S.,FOREIGN AID TO UNITED ARAB REPUBLIC. UAR USA+45 USSR AGRI FINAN INDUS FORCES EATING DEMAND...CHARTS METH/COMP 20 RESOURCE/N AID. PAGE 37 F0718 — FOR/AID ECO/UNDEV RECEIVE PLAN

B63
ELLENDER A.J.,A REPORT ON UNITED STATES FOREIGN OPERATIONS IN AFRICA. SOUTH/AFR USA+45 STRATA EXTR/IND FORCES RACE/REL ISOLAT SOVEREIGN...CHARTS 20 NEGRO. PAGE 37 F0721 — FOR/AID DIPLOM WEALTH ECO/UNDEV

B63
GANGULI B.N.,ECONOMIC CONSEQUENCES OF DISARMAMENT. EUR+WWI ECO/DEV ECO/UNDEV FORCES ACT/RES BUDGET DIPLOM INT/TRADE...STAT CHARTS NAT/COMP. PAGE 46 F0896 — ECOMETRIC ARMS/CONT COST HYPO/EXP

B63
SALENT W.S.,THE UNITED STATES BALANCE OF PAYMENTS IN 1968. EUR+WWI UK USA+45 AGRI R+D LABOR FORCES PRODUC...GEOG CONCPT CHARTS 20 CHINJAP EEC. PAGE 115 F2274 — BAL/PAY DEMAND FINAN INT/TRADE

B63
US CONGRESS JOINT ECO COMM,OUTLOOK FOR UNITED STATES BALANCE OF PAYMENTS. AFR USA+45 ECO/DEV NAT/G FORCES DIPLOM FOR/AID COST EFFICIENCY ...POLICY CONGRESS EEC. PAGE 135 F2657 — BAL/PAY FINAN INT/TRADE PROB/SOLV

B63
US SENATE COMM GOVT OPERATIONS,REPORT OF A STUDY OF US FOREIGN AID IN TEN MIDDLE EASTERN AND AFRICAN COUNTRIES. AFR ISLAM USA+45 FORCES PLAN BUDGET DIPLOM TAX DETER WEALTH...STAT CHARTS 20 CONGRESS AID MID/EAST. PAGE 138 F2728 — FOR/AID EFFICIENCY ECO/TAC FINAN

L63
PADELFORD N.J.,"FINANCIAL CRISIS AND THE UNITED NATIONS." FUT USSR WOR+45 LAW CONSTN FINAN INT/ORG DELIB/GP FORCES PLAN BUDGET DIPLOM COST WEALTH ...STAT CHARTS UN CONGO 20. PAGE 102 F2012 — CREATE ECO/TAC

S63
ENTHOVEN A.C.,"ECONOMIC ANALYSIS IN THE DEPARTMENT OF DEFENSE." USA+45 NAT/G DELIB/GP PROB/SOLV RATION NUC/PWR WEAPON COST...DECISION 20 DEPT/DEFEN RESOURCE/N. PAGE 38 F0739 — PLAN BUDGET ECO/TAC FORCES

S63
NADLER E.B.,"SOME ECONOMIC DISADVANTAGES OF THE ARMS RACE." AFR USA+45 INDUS R+D FORCES PLAN TEC/DEV ECO/TAC FOR/AID EDU/PROP PWR WEALTH...TREND FOR/TRADE 20. PAGE 96 F1886 — ECO/DEV MGT BAL/PAY

B64
BLACKSTOCK P.W.,THE STRATEGY OF SUBVERSION. USA+45 FORCES EDU/PROP ADMIN COERCE GOV/REL...DECISION MGT 20 DEPT/DEFEN CIA DEPT/STATE. PAGE 15 F0292 — ORD/FREE DIPLOM CONTROL

B64
DUSCHA J.,ARMS, MONEY, AND POLITICS. USA+45 INDUS POL/PAR ECO/TAC TAX DETER NUC/PWR WAR WEAPON GOV/REL ATTIT...BIBLIOG/A 20 CONGRESS MONEY DEPT/DEFEN. PAGE 35 F0687 — NAT/G FORCES POLICY BUDGET

B64
ESTHUS R.A.,FROM ENMITY TO ALLIANCE: US AUSTRALIAN RELATIONS. S/ASIA DIST/IND VOL/ASSN FORCES ATTIT 20 AUSTRAL TREATY CMN/WLTH. PAGE 39 F0751 — DIPLOM WAR INT/TRADE FOR/AID

B64
FIESER M.E.,ECONOMIC POLICY AND WAR POTENTIAL. AFR WOR+45 ECO/DEV INDUS NAT/G FORCES TEC/DEV NUC/PWR CIVMIL/REL ORD/FREE 20. PAGE 40 F0791 — INT/TRADE POLICY ECO/TAC DETER

B64
HEKHUIS D.J.,INTERNATIONAL STABILITY: MILITARY, ECONOMIC AND POLITICAL DIMENSIONS. FUT WOR+45 LAW ECO/UNDEV INT/ORG NAT/G VOL/ASSN FORCES ACT/RES BAL/PWR PWR WEALTH...STAT UN 20. PAGE 58 F1143 — TEC/DEV DETER REGION

B64
HOLLEY I.B. JR.,US ARMY IN WORLD WAR II: SPECIAL STUDIES: BUYING AIRCRAFT: MATERIEL PROCUREMENT FOR THE ARMY AIR FORCES. USA+45 USA-45 BUDGET WEAPON GOV/REL PRODUC 20. PAGE 61 F1198 — FORCES COST DIST/IND CIVMIL/REL

B64
IMAZ J.L.,LOS QUE MANDAN. INDUS LABOR NAT/G POL/PAR PROVS SECT CHIEF TOP/EX CONTROL 20 ARGEN. PAGE 64 F1261 — LEAD FORCES ELITES ATTIT

B64
LISKA G.,EUROPE ASCENDANT. EUR+WWI ECO/DEV FORCES INT/TRADE MARXISM 20 EEC. PAGE 81 F1579 — DIPLOM BAL/PWR TARIFFS CENTRAL

B64
RAISON T.,WHY CONSERVATIVE? UK FORCES DIPLOM ECO/TAC GIVE EDU/PROP ORD/FREE WEALTH LAISSEZ ...GOV/COMP 20 TORY/PARTY CONSRV/PAR. PAGE 109 F2137 — PLURISM CONSERVE POL/PAR NAT/G

B64
REDLICH F.,THE GERMAN MILITARY ENTERPRISER AND HIS WORK FORCE. CHRIST-17C GERMANY ELITES SOCIETY FINAN ECO/TAC CIVMIL/REL GP/REL INGP/REL...HIST/WRIT METH/COMP 14/17. PAGE 110 F2170 — EX/STRUC FORCES PROFIT WORKER

B64
STRONG A.L.,THE RISE OF THE CHINESE PEOPLE'S COMMUNES - AND SIX YEARS AFTER (2ND ED.). CHINA/COM AGRI INDUS FORCES WORKER PROB/SOLV EDU/PROP EFFICIENCY ISOLAT 20. PAGE 127 F2503
NEIGH ECO/TAC MARXISM METH/COMP

B64
US HOUSE COMM BANKING-CURR,INTERNATIONAL DEVELOPMENT ASSOCIATION ACT AMENDMENT. CHINA/COM USA+45 USSR FINAN FORCES LEGIS DIPLOM CONFER EFFICIENCY...CHARTS GOV/COMP 20 PRESIDENT CONGRESS INTL/DEV. PAGE 136 F2689
BAL/PAY FOR/AID RECORD ECO/TAC

C64
NORGREN P.H.,"TOWARD FAIR EMPLOYMENT." USA+45 LAW STRATA LABOR NAT/G FORCES ACT/RES ADMIN ATTIT ...POLICY BIBLIOG 20 NEGRO. PAGE 98 F1932
RACE/REL DISCRIM WORKER MGT

B65
BEAUFRE A.,AN INTRODUCTION TO STRATEGY, WITH PARTICULAR REFERENCE TO PROBLEMS OF DEFENSE, POLITICS, ECONOMICS IN THE NUCLEAR AGE. WOR+45 FORCES DIPLOM DETER CIVMIL/REL GP/REL...NEW/IDEA IDEA/COMP 20. PAGE 12 F0226
PLAN NUC/PWR WEAPON DECISION

B65
CERNY K.H.,NATO IN QUEST OF COHESION* A CONFRONTATION OF VIEWPOINTS. COM EUR+WWI USA+45 FORCES LEAD REGION DETER...ANTHOL NATO. PAGE 22 F0438
CENTRAL NUC/PWR VOL/ASSN

B65
COX D.W.,THE PERILS OF PEACE* CONVERSION TO WHAT? FUT USA+45 ECO/DEV NAT/G ACT/RES CREATE PLAN NUC/PWR WAR DEMAND MGT. PAGE 28 F0546
PEACE WORKER FORCES MARKET

B65
MELMANS S.,OUR DEPLETED SOCIETY. AFR SPACE USA+45 ECO/DEV FORCES BUDGET ECO/TAC ADMIN WEAPON EFFICIENCY 20. PAGE 89 F1753
CIVMIL/REL INDUS EDU/PROP CONTROL

B65
RANSOM H.H.,AN AMERICAN FOREIGN POLICY READER. USA+45 FORCES EDU/PROP COERCE NUC/PWR WAR PEACE ...DECISION 20. PAGE 109 F2146
NAT/G DIPLOM POLICY

B65
SCOTT A.M.,THE REVOLUTION IN STATECRAFT: INFORMAL PENETRATION. WOR+45 WOR-45 CULTURE INT/ORG FORCES ECO/TAC ROUTINE...BIBLIOG 20. PAGE 118 F2331
DIPLOM EDU/PROP FOR/AID

B65
THAYER F.C. JR.,AIR TRANSPORT POLICY AND NATIONAL SECURITY: A POLITICAL, ECONOMIC, AND MILITARY ANALYSIS. DIST/IND OP/RES PLAN TEC/DEV DIPLOM DETER WAR COST EFFICIENCY...POLICY BIBLIOG 20 DEPT/DEFEN FAA CAB. PAGE 129 F2548
AIR FORCES CIVMIL/REL ORD/FREE

B65
TYBOUT R.A.,ECONOMICS OF RESEARCH AND DEVELOPMENT. ECO/DEV ECO/UNDEV INDUS PROFIT DECISION. PAGE 131 F2594
R+D FORCES ADMIN DIPLOM

B65
US SENATE COMM ON FOREIGN REL,HEARINGS ON THE FOREIGN ASSISTANCE PROGRAM. AFR ASIA L/A+17C USA+45 WOR+45 FORCES TEC/DEV BUDGET CONTROL WEAPON ORD/FREE 20 UN CONGRESS SEC/STATE. PAGE 139 F2734
FOR/AID DIPLOM INT/ORG ECO/UNDEV

S65
SPAAK P.H.,"THE SEARCH FOR CONSENSUS: A NEW EFFORT TO BUILD EUROPE." FRANCE GERMANY ECO/DEV NAT/G CONSULT FORCES PLAN EDU/PROP REGION CONSEN ATTIT ...SOC METH/CNCPT OBS TREND EEC NATO WORK TERR/GP METH/GP 20. PAGE 124 F2447
EUR+WWI INT/ORG

B66
AMERICAN ASSEMBLY COLUMBIA U,THE UNITED STATES AND THE PHILIPPINES. PHILIPPINE S/ASIA USA+45 USA-45 SOCIETY FORCES INT/TRADE...POLICY 20. PAGE 5 F0085
COLONIAL DIPLOM NAT/LISM

B66
BEUGEL E.V.D.,FROM MARSHALL AID TO ATLANTIC PARTNERSHIP* EUROPEAN INTEGRATION AS A CONCERN OF AMERICAN FOREIGN POLICY. USA+45 INT/ORG FORCES PERSON EEC NATO. PAGE 14 F0272
REGION DIPLOM EUR+WWI VOL/ASSN

B66
BOLTON R.E.,DEFENSE AND DISARMAMENT: THE ECONOMICS OF TRANSITION. USA+45 R+D FORCES PLAN LOBBY DETER WAR COST PEACE...ANTHOL BIBLIOG 20. PAGE 16 F0310
ARMS/CONT POLICY INDUS

B66
EBONY,THE NEGRO HANDBOOK. ACADEM LABOR LOC/G SECT FORCES WORKER CT/SYS CRIME DISCRIM ORD/FREE...BIOG SOC/INTEG 19/20 NEGRO CIV/RIGHTS. PAGE 36 F0692
RACE/REL EDU/PROP LAW STAT

B66
GYORGY A.,ISSUES OF WORLD COMMUNISM. ALBANIA CHINA/COM COM USSR YUGOSLAVIA STRATA AGRI INT/ORG CHIEF FORCES WORKER WAR ALL/IDEOS...GEOG 20 MAO. PAGE 52 F1018
ECO/UNDEV REV MARXISM CON/ANAL

B66
KUENNE R.E.,THE POLARIS MISSILE STRIKE* A GENERAL ECONOMIC SYSTEMS ANALYSIS. USA+45 USSR NAT/G BAL/PWR ARMS/CONT WAR...MATH PROBABIL COMPUT/IR CHARTS HYPO/EXP SIMUL. PAGE 74 F1446
NUC/PWR FORCES DETER DIPLOM

B66
MACFARQUHAR R.,CHINA UNDER MAO: POLITICS TAKES COMMAND. CHINA/COM COM AGRI INDUS CHIEF FORCES DIPLOM INT/TRADE EDU/PROP TASK REV ADJUST...ANTHOL 20 MAO. PAGE 83 F1628
ECO/UNDEV TEC/DEV ECO/TAC ADMIN

B66
RUPPENTHAL K.M.,TRANSPORTATION AND TOMORROW. FUT SPACE USA+45 SEA AIR FORCES TEC/DEV INT/TRADE ...ANTHOL 20 RAILROAD. PAGE 115 F2261
DIST/IND PLAN CIVMIL/REL PREDICT

B66
US DEPARTMENT OF STATE,RESEARCH ON WESTERN EUROPE, GREAT BRITAIN, AND CANADA (EXTERNAL RESEARCH LIST NO 3-25). CANADA GERMANY/W UK LAW CULTURE NAT/G POL/PAR FORCES EDU/PROP REGION MARXISM...GEOG SOC WORSHIP 20 CMN/WLTH. PAGE 136 F2676
BIBLIOG/A EUR+WWI DIPLOM

B66
US PRES COMM ECO IMPACT DEFENS,REPORT* JULY 1965. USA+45 ECO/DEV INDUS DELIB/GP FORCES OP/RES ARMS/CONT NUC/PWR WEAPON BAL/PAY...PREDICT SIMUL. PAGE 138 F2726
ACT/RES STAT WAR BUDGET

B66
US SENATE COMM APPROPRIATIONS,FOREIGN ASSISTANCE AND RELATED AGENCIES APPROPRIATIONS FOR FISCAL YEAR 1967: HEARINGS... ON H. R. 17788. ECO/UNDEV INT/ORG FORCES INSPECT ECO/TAC GIVE DEBATE WEAPON CIVMIL/REL WEALTH...INT 20 CONGRESS DEPT/DEFEN DEPT/STATE DEPT/HEW AID. PAGE 138 F2727
BUDGET FOR/AID DIPLOM COST

B66
US SENATE COMM ON FOREIGN REL,HEARINGS ON S 2859 AND S 2861. USA+45 WOR+45 FORCES BUDGET CAP/ISM ADMIN DETER WEAPON TOTALISM...NAT/COMP 20 UN CONGRESS. PAGE 139 F2735
FOR/AID DIPLOM ORD/FREE ECO/UNDEV

S66
BENOIT J.,"WORLD DEFENSE EXPENDITURES." WOR+45 WEAPON COST PRODUC. PAGE 13 F0253
FORCES STAT NAT/COMP BUDGET

B67
BEATON L.,THE STRUGGLE FOR PEACE. INT/ORG FORCES NUC/PWR COST PWR...POLICY TREND 20. PAGE 12 F0225
PEACE BAL/PWR DIPLOM WAR

B67
CHO S.S.,KOREA IN WORLD POLITICS 1940-1950; AN EVALUATION OF AMERICAN RESPONSIBILITY. KOREA USA+45 USSR CONSTN INT/ORG NAT/G FORCES FOR/AID ANOMIE SUPEGO MARXISM...DECISION BIBLIOG 20. PAGE 24 F0469
POLICY DIPLOM PROB/SOLV WAR

B67
DAVIS F.M.,COME AS A CONQUEROR: THE UNITED STATES ARMY'S OCCUPATION OF GERMANY: 1945-1949. EUR+WWI GERMANY USA+45 SOCIETY PLAN BAL/PWR DIPLOM FOR/AID PERS/REL DEMAND PEACE ORD/FREE 20. PAGE 30 F0588
FORCES CIVMIL/REL ECO/TAC CONTROL

B67
EGGERT G.G.,RAILROAD LABOR DISPUTES. USA+45 USA-45 ELITES DIST/IND DELIB/GP FORCES JUDGE WORKER PROB/SOLV DOMIN PWR...POLICY 20. PAGE 36 F0707
GP/REL NAT/G LABOR BARGAIN

B67
ENKE S.,DEFENSE MANAGEMENT. USA+45 R+D FORCES WORKER PLAN ECO/TAC ADMIN NUC/PWR BAL/PAY UTIL WEALTH...MGT DEPT/DEFEN. PAGE 38 F0738
DECISION DELIB/GP EFFICIENCY BUDGET

B67
GIAP V.N.,BIG VICTORY, GREAT TASK. VIETNAM WOR+45 FORCES PLAN DOMIN LEGIT RISK PEACE 20. PAGE 47 F0921
WAR LEAD ATTIT INSPECT

B67
LYTLE C.M.,THE WARREN COURT AND ITS CRITICS. USA+45 NAT/G PROVS FORCES LOBBY RACE/REL DISCRIM SOVEREIGN 20 SUPREME/CT WARRN/EARL. PAGE 83 F1618
CT/SYS ADJUD PROB/SOLV ATTIT

B67
MACCLOSKEY M.,PACTS FOR PEACE: UN, NATO, SEATO, CENTO, OAS. WOR+45 PLAN DIPLOM CONTROL PEACE ORD/FREE...ORG/CHARTS UN NATO SEATO OAS CENTO. PAGE 83 F1623
FORCES INT/ORG LEAD POLICY

B67
NKRUMAH K.,CHALLENGE OF THE CONGO. FORCES ECO/TAC FOR/AID REGION MURDER REPRESENT 20 CONGO/LEOP UN. PAGE 98 F1930
REV ECO/UNDEV ORD/FREE DIPLOM

B67
SCHAEFER W.V.,THE SUSPECT AND SOCIETY: CRIMINAL PROCEDURE AND CONVERGING CONSTITUTIONAL DOCTRINES. USA+45 TEC/DEV LOBBY ROUTINE SANCTION...INT 20. PAGE 116 F2288
CRIME FORCES CONSTN JURID

B67
US CONGRESS JOINT ECO COMM,AN ECONOMIC PROFILE OF MAINLAND CHINA, VOLUMES I AND II. CHINA/COM AGRI DIST/IND FINAN INDUS LABOR FORCES ACT/RES PLAN INT/TRADE INGP/REL BAL/PAY 20 CONGRESS. PAGE 135 F2664
ECO/UNDEV WEALTH ECO/TAC DELIB/GP

B67
US GOVERNMENT,SECTION-BY-SECTION ANALYSIS OF THE
FOR/AID

PROPOSED FOREIGN ASSISTANCE ACT OF 1967 (PAMPHLET). USA+45 ECO/UNDEV NAT/G CONGRESS. PAGE 136 F2683
POLICY FORCES INT/TRADE

B67
US SENATE COMM ON FOREIGN REL,ARMS SALES TO NEAR EAST AND SOUTH ASIAN COUNTRIES. INDIA IRAN PAKISTAN WOR+45 PROC/MFG BAL/PWR DIPLOM...DECISION SENATE. PAGE 139 F2742
WEAPON FOR/AID FORCES POLICY

B67
US SENATE COMM ON FOREIGN REL,HARRISON E. SALISBURY'S TRIP TO NORTH VIETNAM. CHINA/COM USA+45 VIETNAM/N PRESS TASK GUERRILLA CONSEN EFFICIENCY PEACE DRIVE...OBS SENATE. PAGE 139 F2743
DIPLOM WAR FORCES ATTIT

B67
VAN SLYKE L.P.,ENEMIES AND FRIENDS; THE UNITED FRONT IN CHINESE COMMUNIST HISTORY. CHINA/COM SOCIETY FORCES PLAN ADJUST 20 MAO. PAGE 140 F2764
INGP/REL MARXISM ATTIT GP/REL

B67
WATT A.,THE EVOLUTION OF AUSTRALIAN FOREIGN POLICY 1938-65. ASIA S/ASIA USA+45 USA-45 INT/ORG NAT/G FORCES FOR/AID TREATY 20 AUSTRAL. PAGE 144 F2834
DIPLOM WAR

B67
WILLIAMS E.J.,LATIN AMERICAN CHRISTIAN DEMOCRATIC PARTIES. L/A+17C FAM LABOR FORCES...CATH TREND BIBLIOG 20. PAGE 147 F2890
POL/PAR GP/COMP CATHISM ALL/VALS

B67
WOLF C. JR.,UNITED STATES POLICY AND THE THIRD WORLD. USA+45 WOR+45 FORCES ACT/RES BAL/PWR ECO/TAC FOR/AID DETER GUERRILLA NUC/PWR REV...CHARTS 20. PAGE 148 F2916
DIPLOM ECO/UNDEV POLICY NAT/G

B67
YOUNG J.M.,THE BRAZILIAN REVOLUTION OF 1930 AND THE AFTERMATH. BRAZIL COLONIAL PWR...BIBLIOG/A 16/20. PAGE 150 F2951
PLAN CHIEF FORCES REV

L67
JOHNSTON J.D. JR.,"CONSTITUTION OF SUBDIVISION CONTROL EXACTIONS: THE QUEST FOR A RATIONALE." USA+45 PROVS PUB/INST ADJUD CT/SYS GP/REL MUNICH. PAGE 68 F1334
PLAN CONTROL LOC/G FORCES

S67
AGUILAR M.A.,"?UNA OEA MAS FUERTE O UNA AMERICA LATINA MAS DEBIL?" L/A+17C USA+45 USA-45 ECO/UNDEV INDUS CHIEF DELIB/GP FORCES CONTROL PWR 20 OAS KENNEDY/JF JOHNSON/LB. PAGE 3 F0050
INT/ORG DIPLOM POLICY COLONIAL

S67
CRAIG A.,"ARGENTINA: THE LATEST REVOLUTION." ELITES NAT/G CHIEF FORCES ECO/TAC CIVMIL/REL GOV/REL EQUILIB PRIVIL 20 ARGEN. PAGE 28 F0550
ECO/UNDEV FINAN ATTIT REV

S67
CROKER F.P.U.,"ECONOMIC PEACEKEEPING." UK PLAN PROB/SOLV TEC/DEV BAL/PWR DIPLOM COERCE PEACE ...POLICY DECISION 20. PAGE 28 F0553
FORCES WEAPON COST WAR

S67
FLACKS R.,"CONSCRIPTION IN A DEMOCRATIC SOCIETY." USA+45 WORKER CONTROL SUFF SUPEGO. PAGE 41 F0807
POLICY FORCES ORD/FREE CIVMIL/REL

S67
GONZALEZ M.P.,"CUBA, UNA REVOLUCION EN MARCHA." CUBA L/A+17C USA+45 VIETNAM ECO/UNDEV FORCES DIPLOM DOMIN...POLICY MARXIST NAT/COMP CASTRO/F. PAGE 48 F0946
REV NAT/G COLONIAL SOVEREIGN

S67
GOSALVEZ R.B.,"PERFIL DEL GENERAL VINCENTE ROJO." SPAIN DIPLOM CIVMIL/REL EFFICIENCY PERSON SKILL 20 BOLIV. PAGE 49 F0966
WAR FORCES ELITES BIOG

S67
GUPTA S.,"FOREIGN POLICY IN THE 1967 MANIFESTOS." ASIA COM INDIA USA+45 FORCES FOR/AID TAX ATTIT ...DECISION 20. PAGE 52 F1013
IDEA/COMP POL/PAR POLICY DIPLOM

S67
JEDLICKI W.,"THE FREE SPEECH MOVEMENT IN WARSAW." POLAND FORCES EDU/PROP LEAD ATTIT MARXISM ...IDEA/COMP 20. PAGE 67 F1310
COERCE CROWD ORD/FREE ACADEM

S67
KENNY L.M.,"THE AFTERMATH OF DEFEAT IN EGYPT." ISLAM ISRAEL UAR UK USA+45 USSR INDUS FORCES ECO/TAC PRICE COERCE WEAPON COST ATTIT. PAGE 70 F1378
WAR ECO/UNDEV DIPLOM POLICY

S67
LANGLEY L.D.,"THE DEMOCRATIC TRADITION AND MILITARY REFORM, 1878-1885." USA-45 SECT EDU/PROP CROWD EFFICIENCY NAT/LISM 19 INDIAN/AM. PAGE 75 F1480
ATTIT FORCES POPULISM

S67
LEIFER M.,"ASTRIDE THE STRAITS OF JAHORE: THE BRITISH PRESENCE AND COMMONWEALTH RIVALRY IN SOUTHEAST ASIA." MALAYSIA UK FORCES PLAN ECO/TAC ...DECISION 20 CMN/WLTH. PAGE 77 F1515
DIPLOM NAT/LISM COLONIAL

S67
MCCOLL R.W.,"A POLITICAL GEOGRAPHY OF REVOLUTION: CHINA, VIETNAM, AND THAILAND." ASIA THAILAND VIETNAM FORCES CONTROL 20. PAGE 88 F1720
REV GEOG PLAN DECISION

S67
MCCORD W.,"ARMIES AND POLITICS; A PROBLEM IN THE THIRD WORLD." AFR ISLAM USA+45 ECO/UNDEV TOTALISM 20. PAGE 88 F1723
FOR/AID POLICY NAT/G FORCES

S67
MOLTMANN G.,"ZUR FORMULIERUNG DER AMERIKANISCHEN BESATZUNGSPOLITIK IN DEUTSCHLAND AM ENDE DES ZWEITEN WELTKRIEGES" GERMANY ECO/TAC ADMIN WAR CIVMIL/REL ORD/FREE FASCISM 20. PAGE 92 F1815
FORCES CONTROL POLICY INDUS

S67
SCHELLING T.C.,"ECONOMICS AND CRIMINAL ENTERPRISE." LAW FORCES BARGAIN ECO/TAC CONTROL GAMBLE ROUTINE ADJUST DEMAND INCOME PROFIT CRIMLGY. PAGE 116 F2295
CRIME PROB/SOLV CONCPT

S67
STOLTE S.C.,"THREE PROBLEMS FACING THE SOVIET BLOC." ASIA COM USA+45 USSR FORCES MARXISM ...IDEA/COMP METH/COMP 20 NATO WARSAW/P. PAGE 127 F2496
ECO/TAC DIPLOM INT/ORG POLICY

S67
WALZER M.,"THE CONDITION OF GREECE; TWENTY YEARS AFTER THE TRUMAN DOCTRINE." AFR GREECE FORCES CAP/ISM 20 TRUMAN/HS. PAGE 143 F2814
DIPLOM POLICY FOR/AID TOTALISM

S67
WOLFE T.W.,"SOVIET MILITARY POLICY AT THE FIFTY YEAR MARK." USSR VIETNAM WOR+45 RATION AGREE WAR WEAPON CIVMIL/REL TREATY. PAGE 148 F2917
FORCES POLICY TIME/SEQ PLAN

N67
US HOUSE COMM FOREIGN AFFAIRS,REPORT OF SPECIAL STUDY MISSION TO THE NEAR EAST (PAMPHLET). ISRAEL USA+45 YEMEN ECO/UNDEV INT/ORG FOR/AID ARMS/CONT WAR WEAPON NAT/LISM PEACE...GEOG 20 UN HOUSE/REP. PAGE 137 F2694
ISLAM DIPLOM FORCES

N67
US SENATE COMM ON FOREIGN REL,WAR OR PEACE IN THE MIDDLE EAST (PAMPHLET). GREECE ISLAM ISRAEL JORDAN UAR CHIEF PROB/SOLV FOR/AID WAR PWR 20 SENATE. PAGE 139 F2739
DIPLOM FORCES PLAN

N67
US SENATE COMM ON FOREIGN REL,SURVEY OF THE ALLIANCE FOR PROGRESS: THE LATIN AMERICAN MILITARY (PAMPHLET). USA+45 INT/ORG POL/PAR DIPLOM AGREE GP/REL ROLE ORD/FREE 20. PAGE 139 F2746
L/A+17C FORCES CIVMIL/REL POLICY

B76
TAINE H.A.,THE ANCIENT REGIME. FRANCE STRATA FORCES PARTIC EQUILIB WEALTH CONSERVE POPULISM...GOV/COMP SOC/INTEG 18/19. PAGE 128 F2527
NAT/G GOV/REL TAX REV

C83
BURKE E.,"RESOLUTIONS FOR CONCILIATION WITH AMERICA" (1775), IN E. BURKE, COLLECTED WORKS, VOL. 2." UK USA-45 FORCES INT/TRADE TARIFFS TAX SANCTION PEACE...POLICY 18 PRE/US/AM. PAGE 20 F0387
COLONIAL WAR SOVEREIGN ECO/TAC

B96
SMITH A.,LECTURES ON JUSTICE, POLICE, REVENUE AND ARMS (1763). UK LAW FAM FORCES TARIFFS AGREE COERCE INCOME OWN WEALTH LAISSEZ...GEN/LAWS 17/18. PAGE 123 F2429
DIPLOM JURID OLD/LIB TAX

FORD A.G. F0823

FORD J.L. F0824

FORD P. F0825

FORD/FOUND....FORD FOUNDATION

FORDE D. F0826

FOREIGN AID....SEE FOR/AID

FOREIGN TRADE....SEE INT/TRADE

FOREIGNREL....UNITED STATES SENATE COMMITTEE ON FOREIGN RELATIONS

FORGN/SERV....FOREIGN SERVICE

FORM W.H. F0488,F0827,F0828,F0829

FORMOSA....FORMOSA, PRE-1949; FOR POST-1949, SEE TAIWAN; SEE ALSO ASIA.

FORRESTER J.W. F0830

FORTE W.E. F0831

FORTRAN....FORTRAN - COMPUTER LANGUAGE

FOSTER/G....G. FOSTER

FOUAD M. F0832

FOURAKER L.E. F2397

FOURASTIE J. F0833

FOURIER C. F0834,F0835

FOURIER/FM....FRANCOIS MARIE CHARLES FOURIER

FOUSEK P.G. F0836

FOWLER E.P. F1573

FOX K.A. F0837

FOX R.G. F0838

FOX S. F0839

FOX/CJ....CHARLES J. FOX

FOX/INDIAN....FOX INDIANS

FPC....U.S. FEDERAL POWER COMMISSION

FRANCE....SEE ALSO APPROPRIATE TIME/SPACE/CULTURE INDEX

B03
MOREL E.D.,THE BRITISH CASE IN FRENCH CONGO. DIPLOM
CONGO/BRAZ FRANCE UK COERCE MORAL WEALTH...POLICY INT/TRADE
INT/LAW 20 CONGO/LEOP. PAGE 93 F1827 COLONIAL
AFR

B14
LEVINE L.,SYNDICALISM IN FRANCE (2ND ED.). FRANCE LABOR
LAW SOCIETY ECO/DEV NAT/G ECO/TAC LEAD ATTIT INDUS
...POLICY CONCPT STAT BIBLIOG 18/20 REFORMERS. SOCISM
PAGE 79 F1542 REV

N19
ENGELS F.,THE BRITISH LABOUR MOVEMENT (PAMPHLET). ECO/TAC
FRANCE GERMANY MOD/EUR UK USA-45 POL/PAR WORKER PAY MARXISM
EDU/PROP PRICE REPRESENT GP/REL 19. PAGE 37 F0730 LABOR
STRATA

N19
GROSECLOSE E.,THE DECAY OF MONEY; A SURVEY OF FINAN
WESTERN CURRENCIES 1912-1962 (PAMPHLET). AFR FRANCE NAT/G
GERMANY UK LAW INT/TRADE BAL/PAY COST EQUILIB ECO/DEV
...POLICY 20 DEPRESSION. PAGE 51 F1004 ECO/TAC

N19
HACKETT J.,ECONOMIC PLANNING IN FRANCE; ITS ECO/TAC
RELATION TO THE POLICIES OF THE DEVELOPED COUNTRIES NAT/G
OF WESTERN EUROPE (PAMPHLET). EUR+WWI FRANCE PLAN
ECO/DEV PROB/SOLV CONTROL...POLICY 20 EUROPE/W. INSPECT
PAGE 52 F1026

N19
SENGHOR L.S.,AFRICAN SOCIALISM (PAMPHLET). AFR SOCISM
FRANCE MALI USSR ELITES ECO/UNDEV NAT/G DIPLOM MARXISM
DOMIN EDU/PROP ATTIT 20 NEGRO. PAGE 119 F2355 ORD/FREE
NAT/LISM

B21
CLAPHAN J.H.,THE ECONOMIC DEVELOPMENT OF FRANCE AND ECO/UNDEV
GERMANY 1815-1914. FRANCE GERMANY MOD/EUR COM/IND ECO/DEV
DIST/IND FINAN INT/TRADE EDU/PROP 19/20. PAGE 24 AGRI
F0476 INDUS

B27
SIEGFRIED A.,AMERICA COMES OF AGE: A FRENCH USA-45
ANALYSIS (TRANS. BY H.H. HEMMING AND DORIS CULTURE
HEMMING). FRANCE UK POL/PAR WORKER TEC/DEV DIPLOM ECO/DEV
REGION RACE/REL ADJUST PRODUC HEREDITY...TIME/SEQ SOC
GP/COMP SOC/INTEG 20 DEMOCRAT REPUBLICAN KKK.
PAGE 122 F2398

B28
CROS L.,AFRIQUE FRANCAISE POUR TOUS. EUR+WWI FRANCE COLONIAL
PLAN TEC/DEV ATTIT 20. PAGE 29 F0556 DOMIN
ECO/TAC
AFR

B30
FEIS H.,EUROPE, THE WORLD'S BANKER, 1871-1914. FINAN
FRANCE GERMANY MOD/EUR UK WOR-45 NAT/G PLAN ECO/TAC DIPLOM
EXEC ATTIT PWR WEALTH...CONCPT HIST/WRIT GEN/LAWS INT/TRADE
VAL/FREE 19/20. PAGE 40 F0773

B31
CROOK W.H.,THE GENERAL STRIKE: A STUDY OF LABOR'S LABOR
TRAGIC WEAPON IN THEORY AND PRACTICE. BELGIUM WORKER
FRANCE SWEDEN UK WOR-45 PROB/SOLV ECO/TAC DOMIN PWR LG/CO
...POLICY TIME/SEQ NAT/COMP GEN/LAWS 19/20 STRIKE. BARGAIN
PAGE 29 F0555

B31
LORWIN L.L.,ADVISORY ECONOMIC COUNCILS. EUR+WWI CONSULT
FRANCE GERMANY PROB/SOLV INGP/REL...CLASSIF DELIB/GP
GP/COMP. PAGE 82 F1601 ECO/TAC
NAT/G

B34
MARX K.,THE CLASS STRUGGLES IN FRANCE. FRANCE INDUS MARXIST
WORKER CONSERVE...TREND GEN/LAWS 19. PAGE 86 F1689 STRATA
REV
INT/TRADE

B35
WADE J.,HISTORY OF THE MIDDLE AND WORKING CLASSES; WORKER
WITH A POPULAR EXPOSITION OF THE ECONOMICAL AND STRATA
POLITICAL PRINCIPLES.... FRANCE UK CONSTN FINAN CONCPT
INDUS LABOR INCOME PROFIT KNOWL MORAL ORD/FREE
WEALTH...CHARTS 14/19. PAGE 142 F2797

B42
JACKSON M.V.,EUROPEAN POWERS AND SOUTH-EAST AFRICA: DOMIN
A STUDY OF INTERNATIONAL RELATIONS ON SOUTH-EAST POLICY
COAST OF AFRICA, 1796-1856. AFR FRANCE PORTUGAL ORD/FREE
SOUTH/AFR UK USA-45 FORCES INT/TRADE PWR...CHARTS DIPLOM
BIBLIOG 18/19 TREATY. PAGE 66 F1294

B51
BROGAN D.W.,THE PRICE OF REVOLUTION. FRANCE USA+45 REV
USA-45 USSR CONSTN NAT/G DIPLOM COLONIAL NAT/LISM METH/COMP
ORD/FREE POPULISM...CONCPT 18/20 PRE/US/AM. PAGE 19 COST
F0359 MARXISM

B53
NEISSER H.,NATIONAL INCOMES AND INTERNATIONAL INT/TRADE
TRADE. FRANCE GERMANY SWEDEN UK USA-45 EXTR/IND PRODUC
FINAN INDUS TEC/DEV PRICE BAL/PAY EQUILIB INCOME MARKET
WEALTH...CHARTS METH 19 CHINJAP. PAGE 97 F1908 CON/ANAL

B53
WILLIAMS J.H.,ECONOMIC STABILITY IN A CHANGING POLICY
WORLD. FRANCE USA+45 USSR AGRI WORKER BUDGET FINAN
INT/TRADE TAX WAR BAL/PAY COST EFFICIENCY ALL/IDEOS ECO/TAC
EQULIB 20 KEYNES/JM. PAGE 147 F2892 WEALTH

B55
FLORINSKY M.T.,INTEGRATED EUROPE. EUR+WWI FRANCE FUT
ITALY NETHERLAND UK ECO/DEV INT/ORG FORCES LEGIT ECO/TAC
FEDERAL ATTIT PWR WEALTH...POLICY GEOG CONCPT REGION
GEN/LAWS TOT/POP EEC OEEC 20. PAGE 42 F0816

B57
EHRMANN H.W.,ORGANIZED BUSINESS IN FRANCE. EUR+WWI PROF/ORG
MOD/EUR ECO/DEV VOL/ASSN LEGIT ATTIT PERCEPT PWR ECO/TAC
RESPECT...PLURIST SOC INT TOT/POP 20. PAGE 36 F0712 FRANCE

B57
INTL BANKING SUMMER SCHOOL,RELATIONS BETWEEN THE FINAN
CENTRAL BANKS AND COMMERCIAL BANKS. EUR+WWI FRANCE NAT/G
GERMANY/W ITALY UK USA+45 USSR INDUS INT/ORG GP/REL
CAP/ISM CONTROL MONEY. PAGE 65 F1282 LG/CO

B57
MURDESHWAR A.K.,ADMINISTRATIVE PROBLEMS RELATING TO NAT/G
NATIONALISATION: WITH SPECIAL REFERENCE TO INDIAN OWN
STATE ENTERPRISES. CZECHOSLVK FRANCE INDIA UK INDUS
USA+45 LEGIS WORKER PROB/SOLV BUDGET PRICE CONTROL ADMIN
...MGT GEN/LAWS 20 PARLIAMENT. PAGE 95 F1863

S57
LEWIS E.G.,"PARLIAMENTARY CONTROL OF NATIONALIZED PWR
INDUSTRY IN FRANCE." FRANCE NAT/G DELIB/GP ACT/RES LEGIS
PLAN PROB/SOLV ECO/TAC DOMIN CENTRAL. PAGE 79 F1547 INDUS
CONTROL

B58
BARRERE A.,POLITIQUE FINANCIERE. FRANCE BUDGET FINAN
ECO/TAC TAX BAL/PAY INCOME PRODUC...MGT BIBLIOG T NAT/G
20. PAGE 10 F0193 PLAN

B58
EHRHARD J.,LE DESTIN DU COLONIALISME. AFR FRANCE COLONIAL
ECO/UNDEV AGRI FINAN MARKET CREATE PLAN TEC/DEV FOR/AID
BUDGET DIPLOM PRICE 20. PAGE 36 F0710 INT/TRADE
INDUS

B58
TILLION G.,ALGERIA: THE REALITIES. ALGERIA FRANCE ECO/UNDEV
ISLAM CULTURE STRATA PROB/SOLV DOMIN REV NAT/LISM SOC
WEALTH MARXISM...GEOG 20. PAGE 130 F2573 COLONIAL
DIPLOM

S58
SCHUMM S.,"INTEREST REPRESENTATION IN FRANCE AND LOBBY
GERMANY." EUR+WWI FRANCE GERMANY INSPECT PARL/PROC DELIB/GP
REPRESENT 20 WEIMAR/REP. PAGE 118 F2320 NAT/G

B59
DIEBOLD W. JR.,THE SCHUMAN PLAN: A STUDY IN INT/ORG
ECONOMIC COOPERATION, 1950-1959. EUR+WWI FRANCE REGION
GERMANY USA+45 EXTR/IND CONSULT DELIB/GP PLAN
DIPLOM ECO/TAC INT/TRADE ROUTINE ORD/FREE WEALTH
...METH/CNCPT STAT CONT/OBS INT TIME/SEQ ECSC 20.
PAGE 33 F0635

B59
LINK R.G.,ENGLISH THEORIES OF ECONOMIC IDEA/COMP
FLUCTUATIONS: 1815-1848. FRANCE UK AGRI WORKER ECO/DEV
DIPLOM PRICE TASK WAR DEMAND PRODUC...POLICY WEALTH
BIBLIOG 18 MALTHUS MILL/JS WILSON/J. PAGE 80 F1574 EQUILIB

B59
MARTIN K.,WAR, HISTORY, AND HUMAN NATURE. FRANCE PERSON
GERMANY INDIA UK UNIV POL/PAR COLONIAL DETER REV WAR
MARXISM PACIFISM...PSY CONCPT PREDICT LENIN/VI ATTIT
GANDHI/M. PAGE 86 F1683 IDEA/COMP

B59
MORGENSTERN O.,INTERNATIONAL FINANCIAL TRANSACTIONS FINAN
AND BUSINESS CYCLES. FRANCE GERMANY UK USA+45 TIME/SEQ
USA-45 WOR+45 WOR-45 ECO/DEV ECO/TAC WEALTH INT/TRADE

...CONCPT STAT CON/ANAL CHARTS 19/20. PAGE 93 F1832

B60
BISSON A.,INSTITUTIONS FINANCIERES ET ECONOMIQUES EN FRANCE. FRANCE INDUS OP/RES TAX COST PRODUC ...CHARTS 20. PAGE 15 F0289
FINAN BUDGET PLAN

B60
LISTER L.,EUROPE'S COAL AND STEEL COMMUNITY. FRANCE GERMANY STRUCT ECO/DEV EXTR/IND INDUS MARKET NAT/G DELIB/GP ECO/TAC INT/TRADE EDU/PROP ATTIT RIGID/FLEX ORD/FREE PWR WEALTH...CONCPT STAT TIME/SEQ CHARTS ECSC TERR/GP 20. PAGE 81 F1582
EUR+WWI INT/ORG REGION

B60
PETERSON W.C.,THE WELFARE STATE IN FRANCE. EUR+WWI FRANCE FUT STRATA PROB/SOLV TAX GIVE RECEIVE INCOME ORD/FREE PWR...CHARTS 20. PAGE 105 F2070
NEW/LIB ECO/TAC WEALTH NAT/G

S60
BERG E.J.,"ECONOMIC BASIS OF POLITICAL CHOICE IN FRENCH WEST AFRICA." FRANCE ECO/UNDEV AGRI INDUS NAT/G PLAN LEGIT COLONIAL REGION ATTIT PWR WEALTH ...CONCPT FOR/TRADE 20. PAGE 13 F0257
AFR ECO/TAC

S60
KREININ M.E.,"THE 'OUTER-SEVEN' AND EUROPEAN INTEGRATION." EUR+WWI FRANCE GERMANY ITALY UK ECO/DEV DIST/IND INT/TRADE DRIVE WEALTH...MYTH CHARTS EEC OEEC 20. PAGE 73 F1436
ECO/TAC GEN/LAWS

B61
DELEFORTRIE-SOU N.,LES DIRIGEANTS DE L'INDUSTRIE FRANCAISE. FRANCE CULTURE ELITES PROB/SOLV ...DECISION STAT CHARTS 20. PAGE 32 F0613
INDUS STRATA TOP/EX LEAD

B61
HAUSER M.,DIE URSACHEN DER FRANZOSISCHEN INFLATION IN DEN JAHREN 1946-1952. AFR FRANCE INDUS NAT/G BUDGET DIPLOM ECO/TAC FOR/AID COST MONEY 20. PAGE 57 F1114
ECO/DEV FINAN PRICE

B61
HENDERSON W.O.,THE INDUSTRIAL REVOLUTION IN EUROPE. FRANCE GERMANY MOD/EUR RUSSIA WORKER PROFIT PWR MARXISM SOCISM...SOC HIST/WRIT 19 INDUS/REV. PAGE 58 F1148
INDUS REV CAP/ISM TEC/DEV

B61
LAHAYE R.,LES ENTREPRISES PUBLIQUES AU MAROC. FRANCE MOROCCO LAW DIST/IND EXTR/IND FINAN CONSULT PLAN TEC/DEV ADMIN AGREE CONTROL OWN...POLICY 20. PAGE 74 F1460
NAT/G INDUS ECO/UNDEV ECO/TAC

B61
SCHNAPPER B.,LA POLITIQUE ET LE COMMERCE FRANCAIS DANS LE GOLFE DE GUINEE DE 1838 A 1871. FRANCE GUINEA UK SEA EXTR/IND NAT/G DELIB/GP LEGIS ADMIN ORD/FREE...POLICY GEOG CENSUS CHARTS BIBLIOG 19. PAGE 117 F2303
COLONIAL INT/TRADE DOMIN AFR

B61
VEIT O.,GRUNDRISS DER WAHRUNGSPOLITIK. AFR FRANCE GERMANY USSR DIPLOM INT/TRADE...NAT/COMP 19/20 SILVER. PAGE 141 F2773
FINAN POLICY ECO/TAC CAP/ISM

S61
RAY J.,"THE EUROPEAN FREE-TRADE ASSOCIATION AND ITS IMPACT ON INDIA'S TRADE." EUR+WWI FRANCE GERMANY INDIA S/ASIA UK NAT/G VOL/ASSN PLAN INT/TRADE ROUTINE WEALTH...STAT CHARTS TERR/GP CMN/WLTH EEC FOR/TRADE OEEC 20 EFTA. PAGE 109 F2155
ECO/DEV ECO/TAC

B62
CONGRES ECONOMISTES LANG FRAN,MONNAIE ET EXPANSION. AFR FRANCE PROB/SOLV BUDGET CENTRAL COST OPTIMAL PRODUC WEALTH 20. PAGE 27 F0524
FINAN PLAN EUR+WWI

B62
FRIEDMANN W.,METHODS AND POLICIES OF PRINCIPAL DONOR COUNTRIES IN PUBLIC INTERNATIONAL DEVELOPMENT FINANCING: PRELIMINARY APPRAISAL. FRANCE GERMANY/W UK USA+45 USSR WOR+45 FINAN TEC/DEV CAP/ISM DIPLOM ECO/TAC ATTIT 20 EEC. PAGE 44 F0864
INT/ORG FOR/AID NAT/COMP ADMIN

B62
GRANICK D.,THE EUROPEAN EXECUTIVE. BELGIUM FRANCE GERMANY/W UK INDUS LABOR LG/CO SML/CO EX/STRUC PLAN TEC/DEV CAP/ISM COST DEMAND...POLICY CHARTS 20. PAGE 50 F0977
MGT ECO/DEV ECO/TAC EXEC

B62
HENDERSON W.O.,THE GENESIS OF THE COMMON MARKET. EUR+WWI FRANCE MOD/EUR UK SEA COM/IND EXTR/IND COLONIAL DISCRIM...TIME/SEQ CHARTS BIBLIOG 18/20 EEC TREATY. PAGE 58 F1149
ECO/DEV INT/TRADE DIPLOM

B62
KENT R.K.,FROM MADAGASCAR TO THE MALAGASY REPUBLIC. FRANCE MADAGASCAR DIPLOM NAT/LISM ORD/FREE...MGT 18/20. PAGE 70 F1379
COLONIAL SOVEREIGN REV POL/PAR

B62
LIPPMANN W.,WESTERN UNITY AND THE COMMON MARKET. EUR+WWI FRANCE GERMANY/W UK USA+45 ECO/DEV AGRI FINAN MARKET INT/ORG NAT/G FOR/AID AGREE WEALTH 20 EEC. PAGE 80 F1575
DIPLOM INT/TRADE VOL/ASSN

B62
PONCET J.,LA COLONISATION ET L'AGRICULTURE EUROPEENNES EN TUNISIE DEPUIS 1881. FRANCE WORKER TEC/DEV ECO/TAC CONTROL EFFICIENCY ROLE WEALTH 19/20 TUNIS. PAGE 107 F2101
ECO/UNDEV AGRI COLONIAL FINAN

B62
ROBERTSON B.C.,REGIONAL DEVELOPMENT IN THE EUROPEAN ECONOMIC COMMUNITY. EUR+WWI FRANCE FUT ITALY UK ECO/UNDEV WORKER ACT/RES PROB/SOLV TEC/DEV ECO/TAC INT/TRADE EEC. PAGE 112 F2209
PLAN ECO/DEV INT/ORG REGION

S62
PIQUEMAL M.,"LA COOPERATION FINANCIERE ENTRE LA FRANCE ET LES ETATS AFRICAINS ET MALGACHE." ISLAM INT/ORG TOP/EX ECO/TAC...JURID CHARTS 20. PAGE 106 F2089
AFR FINAN FRANCE MADAGASCAR

B63
MARCHAL J.,EXPANSION ET RECESSION. FRANCE OP/RES PROB/SOLV ROLE ORD/FREE...TREND SIMUL 20 DEPRESSION. PAGE 85 F1663
FINAN PLAN ECO/DEV

B63
MEEK R.L.,THE ECONOMICS OF PHYSIOCRACY. FRANCE UK AGRI FINAN WORKER CAP/ISM TAX DEMAND EQUILIB INCOME HABITAT...CHARTS ANTHOL 17. PAGE 89 F1744
PRODUC WEALTH MARKET

B63
MEYNAUD J.,PLANIFICATION ET POLITIQUE. FRANCE ITALY FINAN LABOR DELIB/GP LEGIS ADMIN EFFICIENCY ...MAJORIT DECISION 20. PAGE 90 F1773
PLAN ECO/TAC PROB/SOLV

B63
OLSON M. JR.,THE ECONOMICS OF WARTIME SHORTAGE. FRANCE GERMANY MOD/EUR UK AGRI PROB/SOLV ADMIN DEMAND WEALTH...POLICY OLD/LIB FOR/TRADE 17/20. PAGE 101 F1990
WAR ADJUST ECO/TAC NAT/COMP

S63
DIEBOLD W. JR.,"THE NEW SITUATION OF INTERNATIONAL TRADE POLICY." EUR+WWI FRANCE FUT UK USA+45 WOR+45 DIST/IND PLAN INT/TRADE EDU/PROP PWR WEALTH ...RECORD TREND GEN/LAWS EEC TRUE/GP VAL/FREE APPLIC 20. PAGE 33 F0636
MARKET ECO/TAC

S63
GANDILHON J.,"LA SCIENCE ET LA TECHNIQUE A L'AIDE DES REGIONS PEU DEVELOPPEES." FRANCE FUT WOR+45 ECO/DEV R+D PROF/ORG ACT/RES PLAN...MGT TOT/POP VAL/FREE 20 UN. PAGE 46 F0893
ECO/UNDEV TEC/DEV FOR/AID

S63
GANDOLFI A.,"LES ACCORDS DE COOPERATION EN MATIERE DE POLITIQUE ETRANGERE ENTRE LA FRANCE ET LES NOUVEAUX ETATS AFRICAINS ET." AFR ISLAM MADAGASCAR WOR+45 ECO/DEV INT/ORG NAT/G DELIB/GP ECO/TAC ALL/VALS...CON/ANAL 20. PAGE 46 F0894
VOL/ASSN ECO/UNDEV DIPLOM FRANCE

S63
MONROE A.D.,"BRITAIN AND THE EUROPEAN COMMUNITY." EUR+WWI FRANCE NAT/G DELIB/GP TOP/EX ECO/TAC DOMIN PWR...POLICY RECORD GEN/LAWS EEC EFTA 20 EFTA CMN/WLTH. PAGE 93 F1817
VOL/ASSN ATTIT UK

S63
POLYANOV N.,"THE DOLLAR'S VENTURES IN EUROPE." EUR+WWI FRANCE USA+45 ECO/DEV MARKET POL/PAR TEC/DEV ECO/TAC EDU/PROP DRIVE PWR WEALTH...MARXIST MYTH STAT TREND EEC 20. PAGE 107 F2100
FINAN PLAN BAL/PAY CAP/ISM

S63
SHONFIELD A.,"AFTER BRUSSELS." EUR+WWI FRANCE GERMANY UK ECO/DEV DIST/IND MARKET VOL/ASSN DELIB/GP CREATE INT/TRADE ATTIT RIGID/FLEX...RECORD TREND GEN/LAWS EEC COMMUN CMN/WLTH 20. PAGE 121 F2385
PLAN ECO/TAC

S63
TENNYSON L.B.,"THE USA IN ATLANTIC COMMUNITY." EUR+WWI FRANCE UK USA+45 ECO/UNDEV VOL/ASSN DELIB/GP TOP/EX DIPLOM DOMIN PWR...POLICY CONCPT TREND GEN/LAWS EEC 20. PAGE 129 F2545
ATTIT ECO/TAC BAL/PWR

B64
BAUCHET P.,ECONOMIC PLANNING. FRANCE STRATA LG/CO CAP/ISM ADMIN PARL/PROC DEMAND OPTIMAL ATTIT PWR SOCISM...POLICY CHARTS 20. PAGE 11 F0212
ECO/DEV NAT/G PLAN ECO/TAC

B64
BROWN W.M.,THE EXTERNAL LIQUIDITY OF AN ADVANCED COUNTRY. CANADA FRANCE GERMANY/W SWEDEN UK USA+45 ECO/DEV DIPLOM PRICE...CONCPT STAT NAT/COMP 20. PAGE 20 F0376
FINAN INT/TRADE COST INCOME

B64
CHEIT E.F.,THE BUSINESS ESTABLISHMENT. FRANCE WOR+45 PROF/ORG TOP/EX PROB/SOLV CAP/ISM ADMIN SUPEGO MORAL PWR...METH/CNCPT MYTH NEW/IDEA 20. PAGE 24 F0460
PERSON EX/STRUC MGT INDUS

B64
MORRISSENS L.,ECONOMIC POLICY IN OUR TIME: COUNTRY STUDIES. BELGIUM EUR+WWI FRANCE GERMANY/W ITALY NETHERLAND INDUS BARGAIN BUDGET GOV/REL BAL/PAY PRODUC...CON/ANAL CHARTS COSTS 20. PAGE 94 F1839
ECO/DEV ECO/TAC METH/COMP PLAN

B64
WITHERELL J.W.,OFFICIAL PUBLICATIONS OF FRENCH EQUATORIAL AFRICA, FRENCH CAMEROONS, AND TOGO, 1946-1958 (PAMPHLET). CAMEROON CHAD FRANCE GABON TOGO LAW ECO/UNDEV EXTR/IND INT/TRADE...GEOG HEAL 20. PAGE 148 F2913
BIBLIOG/A AFR NAT/G ADMIN

B64
WRIGHT G.,RURAL REVOLUTION IN FRANCE: THE PEASANTRY IN THE TWENTIETH CENTURY. EUR+WWI MOD/EUR LAW
PWR STRATA

CULTURE AGRI POL/PAR DELIB/GP LEGIS ECO/TAC EDU/PROP COERCE CHOOSE ATTIT RIGID/FLEX HEALTH ...STAT CENSUS CHARTS VAL/FREE 20. PAGE 149 F2932 — FRANCE REV

C64
LOUFTY A.,"LA PLANIFICATION DE L'ECONOMIE." FRANCE USSR FINAN INDUS BUDGET INCOME PRODUC...BIBLIOG 20. PAGE 82 F1604 — PLAN ECO/UNDEV ECO/DEV

B65
BARRERE A.,ECONOMIE ET INSTITUTIONS FINANCIERES (VOL. I). AFR FRANCE PLAN...BIBLIOG T 20. PAGE 10 F0194 — ECO/DEV BUDGET NAT/G FINAN

B65
COLLINS H.,KARL MARX AND THE BRITISH LABOUR MOVEMENT; YEARS OF THE FIRST INTERNATIONAL. FRANCE SWITZERLND UK CAP/ISM WAR...MARXIST IDEA/COMP BIBLIOG 19. PAGE 26 F0506 — MARXISM LABOR INT/ORG REV

B65
COLLOQUE SUR LA PLANIFICATION,LA PLANIFICATION COMME PROCESSUS DE DECISION. FRANCE SOCIETY MARKET LABOR LEGIS GP/REL EFFICIENCY INCOME ATTIT TECHRACY ...MYTH IDEA/COMP 20. PAGE 26 F0508 — PLAN ECO/TAC PROB/SOLV

B65
GOETZ-GIREY R.,LE MOUVEMENT DES GREVES EN FRANCE. FRANCE FINAN OP/RES PROB/SOLV ECO/TAC INCOME HABITAT...STAT CHARTS 19/20. PAGE 48 F0932 — LABOR WORKER GP/REL INDUS

B65
HABERLER G.,A SURVEY OF INTERNATIONAL TRADE THEORY. CANADA FRANCE GERMANY ECO/TAC TARIFFS AGREE COST DEMAND WEALTH...ECOMETRIC 19/20 MONOPOLY TREATY. PAGE 52 F1024 — INT/TRADE BAL/PAY DIPLOM POLICY

B65
HICKMAN B.G.,QUANTITATIVE PLANNING OF ECONOMIC POLICY. FRANCE NETHERLAND OP/RES PRICE ROUTINE UTIL ...POLICY DECISION ECOMETRIC METH/CNCPT STAT STYLE CHINJAP. PAGE 59 F1162 — PROB/SOLV PLAN QUANT

B65
JOHNSTONE A.,UNITED STATES DIRECT INVESTMENT IN FRANCE: AN INVESTIGATION OF THE FRENCH CHARGES. FRANCE USA+45 ECO/DEV INDUS LG/CO NAT/G ECO/TAC CONTROL WEALTH...BIBLIOG 20 INTERVENT. PAGE 68 F1335 — FINAN DIPLOM POLICY SOVEREIGN

B65
KISSINGER H.A.,THE TROUBLED PARTNERSHIP* RE-APPRAISAL OF THE WESTERN ALLIANCE. EUR+WWI USA+45 INT/ORG NAT/G VOL/ASSN TOP/EX DIPLOM ORD/FREE PWR NATO. PAGE 71 F1402 — FRANCE NUC/PWR ECO/DEV

B65
LUTZ V.,FRENCH PLANNING. FRANCE TEC/DEV RIGID/FLEX ORD/FREE 20. PAGE 82 F1613 — PLAN ADMIN FUT

B65
OECD,TECHNIQUES OF ECONOMIC FORECASTING. CANADA FRANCE NETHERLAND SWEDEN UK USA+45 PROB/SOLV ROUTINE...CONCPT MATH CHARTS BIBLIOG METH 20. PAGE 100 F1974 — PREDICT METH/COMP PLAN

B65
OXENFELDT A.R.,ECONOMIC SYSTEMS IN ACTION. FRANCE USA+45 USSR CULTURE PLAN PROB/SOLV TEC/DEV INCOME PRODUC WEALTH...METH/COMP 20. PAGE 102 F2007 — ECO/DEV CAP/ISM MARXISM ECO/TAC

B65
RUEFF J.,THE ROLE AND THE RULE OF GOLD: AN ARGUMENT (PAMPHLET). AFR FRANCE USA+45 WOR+45 MARKET NAT/G PLAN DIPLOM ATTIT...POLICY INT 20 DEGAULLE/C. PAGE 115 F2258 — FINAN ECO/DEV INT/TRADE BAL/PAY

B65
SHONFIELD A.,MODERN CAPITALISM: THE CHANGING BALANCE OF PUBLIC AND PRIVATE POWER. FRANCE GERMANY/W UK USA+45 WOR+45 ECO/DEV INT/ORG NAT/G CONSULT INT/TRADE PRODUC...POLICY CONCPT METH/COMP 20. PAGE 121 F2386 — CAP/ISM CONTROL BAL/PWR CREATE

B65
WEIL G.L.,A HANDBOOK ON THE EUROPEAN ECONOMIC COMMUNITY. BELGIUM EUR+WWI FRANCE GERMANY/W ITALY CONSTN ECO/DEV CREATE PARTIC GP/REL...DECISION MGT CHARTS 20 EEC. PAGE 144 F2846 — INT/TRADE INT/ORG TEC/DEV INT/LAW

L65
LETICHE J.M.,"EUROPEAN INTEGRATION: AN AMERICAN VIEW." EUR+WWI FRANCE WOR+45 ECO/DEV DIST/IND EXTR/IND NAT/G DELIB/GP TOP/EX PLAN ECO/TAC ATTIT ...STAT CON/ANAL CHARTS EEC 20. PAGE 78 F1537 — INDUS AGRI

S65
HAYTER T.,"FRENCH AID TO AFRICA* ITS SCOPE AND ACHIEVEMENTS." CULTURE ECO/TAC INT/TRADE ADMIN REGION CENTRAL FEDERAL LOVE PWR SOVEREIGN EEC. PAGE 57 F1127 — AFR FRANCE FOR/AID COLONIAL

S65
SOPER T.,"THE EEC AND AID TO AFRICA." FRANCE UK ECO/UNDEV INT/TRADE TARIFFS REGION ROUTINE CENTRAL DISCRIM...DECISION RECORD EEC. PAGE 124 F2443 — AFR FOR/AID COLONIAL

S65
SPAAK P.H.,"THE SEARCH FOR CONSENSUS: A NEW EFFORT TO BUILD EUROPE." FRANCE GERMANY ECO/DEV NAT/G CONSULT FORCES PLAN EDU/PROP REGION CONSEN ATTIT ...SOC METH/CNCPT OBS TREND EEC NATO WORK TERR/GP METH/GP 20. PAGE 124 F2447 — EUR+WWI INT/ORG

B66
HACKETT J.,L'ECONOMIE BRITANNIQUE: PROBLEMES ET PERSPECTIVES. FRANCE UK LABOR NAT/G EX/STRUC PROB/SOLV BAL/PAY INCOME RIGID/FLEX...MGT PHIL/SCI CHARTS MUNICH 20. PAGE 53 F1027 — ECO/DEV FINAN ECO/TAC PLAN

B66
HARLOW J.S.,FRENCH ECONOMIC PLANNING: A CHALLENGE TO REASON. EUR+WWI FRANCE PROB/SOLV 20 EUROPE. PAGE 55 F1084 — ECO/TAC PLAN STRUCT

B66
HAYER T.,FRENCH AID. AFR FRANCE AGRI FINAN BUDGET ADMIN WAR PRODUC...CHARTS 18/20 THIRD/WRLD OVRSEA/DEV. PAGE 57 F1125 — TEC/DEV COLONIAL FOR/AID ECO/UNDEV

B66
KINDLEBERGER C.P.,EUROPE AND THE DOLLAR. AFR EUR+WWI FRANCE GERMANY/W USA+45 CONSTN INT/ORG DIPLOM INT/TRADE...ANTHOL 20. PAGE 71 F1395 — BAL/PAY BUDGET FINAN ECO/DEV

B67
FANON F.,TOWARD THE AFRICAN REVOLUTION. AFR FRANCE CULTURE ELITES LEAD REV GP/REL ORD/FREE SOVEREIGN 20. PAGE 39 F0762 — COLONIAL DOMIN ECO/UNDEV RACE/REL

B67
FIELD G.L.,COMPARATIVE POLITICAL DEVELOPMENT: THE PRECEDENT OF THE WEST. FRANCE GERMANY SWEDEN UK USSR STRATA STRUCT POL/PAR...METH 20. PAGE 40 F0790 — NAT/COMP CONCPT ECO/DEV SOCIETY

B67
GORZ A.,STRATEGY FOR LABOR: A RADICAL PROPOSAL (TRANS. BY MARTIN NICOLAUS AND VICTORIA ORTIZ). EUR+WWI FRANCE ITALY ECO/DEV POL/PAR OP/RES PLAN GP/REL ALL/IDEOS...SOC 20 EEC. PAGE 49 F0965 — LABOR PWR STRUCT ECO/TAC

S67
BOSHER J.F.,"GOVERNMENT AND PRIVATE INTERESTS IN NEW FRANCE." CANADA FRANCE INDUS LG/CO SML/CO CAP/ISM INT/TRADE COLONIAL GP/REL...HIST/WRIT 17/18. PAGE 17 F0320 — NAT/G FINAN ADMIN CONTROL

S67
GRUN C.,"DEUX ETUDES ALLEMANDES SUR LES PREJUGES NATIONAUX ET LES MOYENS DE LES COMBATTRE." FRANCE GERMANY DIST/IND PROB/SOLV GP/REL AGE/Y RIGID/FLEX ...PSY STAT INT SAMP. PAGE 52 F1010 — ATTIT REGION DISCRIM STERTYP

S67
SCOVILLE W.J.,"GOVERNMENT REGULATION AND GROWTH IN THE FRENCH PAPER INDUSTRY DURING THE EIGHTEENTH CENTURY." FRANCE MOD/EUR FINAN CAP/ISM TAX ADMIN CONTROL PRIVIL LAISSEZ...POLICY 18. PAGE 118 F2337 — NAT/G PROC/MFG ECO/DEV INGP/REL

S67
WARNER G.,"FRANCE, BRITAIN AND THE EEC." FRANCE UK INT/ORG DELIB/GP ECO/TAC CONTROL 20 EEC. PAGE 143 F2822 — INT/TRADE BAL/PWR DIPLOM

B76
TAINE H.A.,THE ANCIENT REGIME. FRANCE STRATA FORCES PARTIC EQUILIB WEALTH CONSERVE POPULISM...GOV/COMP SOC/INTEG 18/19. PAGE 128 F2527 — NAT/G GOV/REL TAX REV

FRANCHISE....FRANCHISE

FRANCIS R.G. F0840

FRANCK L.R. F0841

FRANCK P.G. F0842,F0843

FRANCO/F....FRANCISCO FRANCO

FRANK/PARL....FRANKFURT PARLIAMENT

B58
HAMEROW T.S.,RESTORATION, REVOLUTION, REACTION: ECONOMICS AND POLITICS IN GERMANY, 1815-1871. CAP/ISM ADJUST ATTIT PWR...BIBLIOG/A 19 GER/CONFED FRANK/PARL. PAGE 54 F1055 — REV ORD/FREE ECO/DEV

FRANKEL P.H. F0844

FRANKEL S.H. F0845,F0846

FRANKEL T. F0847

FRANKFUR/F....FELIX FRANKFURTER

FRANKFURT PARLIAMENT....SEE FRANK/PARL

FRANKFURTER F. F0848

FRANKLIN N.N. F0849

FRANKLIN/B....BENJAMIN FRANKLIN

FREDERICK....FREDERICK THE GREAT

FREDRKSBRG....FREDERICKSBURG, VIRGINIA

FREE/SOIL....FREE-SOIL DEBATE (U.S.)

FREE/SPEE....FREE SPEECH MOVEMENT; SEE ALSO AMEND/I

FREEDOM....SEE ORD/FREE

FREEDOM/HS....FREEDOM HOUSE

FREEMAN H.A. F0850

FREIDEL F. F0851

FREITAG R.S. F0852

FRELIMO....MOZAMBIQUE LIBERATION FRONT

FRENCH J.R.P. F0853

FRENCH CIVIL CODE....SEE CIVIL/CODE

FRENCH/CAN....FRENCH CANADA

FREUD/S....SIGMUND FREUD

FREYMOND J. F0854

FRIEDEN B.J. F0855,F0856

FRIEDENBERG D.M. F0857

FRIEDLANDER S.L. F0858

FRIEDMAN M. F0859,F0860

FRIEDMANN G. F0862

FRIEDMANN J. F0863

FRIEDMANN W. F0861,F0864

FRIEDMANN W.G. F0865,F0866

FRIEDRICH C.J. F0867

FRIEDRICH-EBERT-STIFTUNG F0868

FRIENDSHIP....SEE LOVE

FRNCO/PRUS....FRANCO-PRUSSIAN WAR

FROMM G. F0869

FROMM/E....ERICH FROMM

FRONTIER....FRONTIER

B57
NEUMARK S.D.,ECONOMIC INFLUENCES ON THE SOUTH AFRICAN FRONTIER, 1652-1836. SOUTH/AFR SEA AGRI NAT/G FORCES WORKER DIPLOM INT/TRADE PRICE DEMAND PRODUC...STAT CHARTS 17/19 FRONTIER. PAGE 97 F1915 — COLONIAL ECO/UNDEV ECO/TAC MARKET

FRUSTRATION....SEE BIO/SOC, ANOMIE, DRIVE

FRYE R.J. F0870,F0871

FTC....FEDERAL TRADE COMMISSION

N19
LAWRENCE S.A.,THE BATTERY ADDITIVE CONTROVERSY (PAMPHLET). USA+45 LAW MARKET PROC/MFG R+D CAP/ISM CT/SYS GOV/REL OWN FTC CONGRESS BUR/STNDRD RITCHIE/JM. PAGE 76 F1494 — PHIL/SCI LOBBY INSPECT

N19
PALAMOUNTAIN JC J.R.,THE DOLCIN CASE AND THE FEDERAL TRADE COMMISSION (PAMPHLET). USA+45 LAW MARKET SERV/IND LG/CO NAT/G BIO/SOC 20 FTC. PAGE 103 F2018 — ADJUD PROB/SOLV EDU/PROP HEALTH

B32
THOMPSON C.D.,CONFESSIONS OF THE POWER TRUST. MARKET ACT/RES EDU/PROP CONTROL GOV/REL INCOME OWN ...MGT 20 FTC MONOPOLY. PAGE 130 F2564 — LG/CO SERV/IND PWR FINAN

B63
BOWIE R.R.,GOVERNMENT REGULATION OF BUSINESS: CASES FROM THE NATIONAL REPORTER SYSTEM. USA+45 USA-45 NAT/G ECO/TAC ADJUD...ANTHOL 19/20 SUPREME/CT FTC FAIR/LABOR MONOPOLY. PAGE 17 F0331 — LAW CONTROL INDUS CT/SYS

L65
FORTE W.E.,"THE FOOD AND DRUG ADMINISTRATION, THE FEDERAL TRADE COMMISSION AND THE DECEPTIVE PACKAGING." ROUTINE...JURID 20 FTC. PAGE 43 F0831 — CONTROL HEALTH ADJUD INDUS

S65
LONG T.G.,"THE ADMINISTRATIVE PROCESS: AGONIZING REAPPRAISAL IN THE FTC." NAT/G REPRESENT 20 FTC. PAGE 82 F1598 — ADJUD LOBBY ADMIN EX/STRUC

B67
ALEXANDER G.J.,HONESTY AND COMPETITION: FALSE-ADVERTISING LAW AND POLICY UNDER FTC ADMINISTRATION. USA+45 INDUS NAT/G PRICE GP/REL 20 FTC. PAGE 3 F0058 — EDU/PROP SERV/IND CONTROL DELIB/GP

B67
MARCUS S.,COMPETITION AND THE LAW. USA+45 INDUS LG/CO NAT/G CONSERVE LAISSEZ...BIBLIOG 20 FTC SUPREME/CT. PAGE 85 F1665 — LAW ECO/DEV FINAN JURID

FUCHS R.F. F0872

FUCHS V.R. F0873,F2820

FULBRGHT/J....J. WILLIAM FULBRIGHT

FULLER G.H. F0874

FULLER/MW....MELVILLE WESTON FULLER

FULTON D.C. F2463

FUNCTIONAL ANALYSIS....SEE OP/RES

FURASH E.A. F0875

FURNIVAL/J....J.S. FURNIVALL

FURNIVALL J.S. F0876

FURTADO C. F0877

FUSFELD D.R. F0878

FUT....FUTURE (PAST AND PRESENT ATTEMPTS TO DEPICT IT)

B18
MARX K.,CAPITAL. FUT MOD/EUR STRATA DIST/IND PROC/MFG TEC/DEV WEALTH...MARXIST WORK 19. PAGE 86 F1688 — ECO/DEV CAP/ISM SOCISM

N19
MUSHKIN S.J.,LOCAL SCHOOL EXPENDITURES: 1970 PROJECTIONS (PAMPHLET). FUT USA+45 CONSTRUC FINAN PROVS EDU/PROP COST...GEOG CENSUS PREDICT CHARTS SIMUL 20. PAGE 95 F1871 — LOC/G SCHOOL BUDGET

B25
WILLIAMS B.,THE SELBORNE MEMORANDUM. AFR FUT SOUTH/AFR UK NAT/G BUDGET DIPLOM REGION GOV/REL SOVEREIGN...POLICY CHARTS 20 UNIFICA SELBORNE/W. PAGE 147 F2888 — COLONIAL PROVS

B30
THOMPSON W.R.,POPULATION PROBLEMS. FUT UNIV WOR-45 STRUCT DIST/IND ACT/RES ECO/TAC BIO/SOC...CONCPT OBS TIME/SEQ TOT/POP 20. PAGE 130 F2567 — ECO/UNDEV GEOG

B32
WRIGHT Q.,GOLD AND MONETARY STABILIZATION. FUT USA-45 WOR-45 INTELL ECO/DEV INT/ORG NAT/G CONSULT PLAN ECO/TAC ADMIN ATTIT WEALTH...CONCPT TREND 20. PAGE 149 F2935 — FINAN POLICY

B34
GRAHAM F.D.,PROTECTIVE TARIFFS. FUT USA+45 WOR-45 INDUS MARKET VOL/ASSN PLAN CAP/ISM ECO/TAC PEACE ATTIT DRIVE HEALTH ORD/FREE...OBS TREND GEN/LAWS FOR/TRADE 20. PAGE 50 F0970 — INT/ORG TARIFFS

S41
LASSWELL H.D.,"THE GARRISON STATE" (BMR)" FUT WOR+45 ELITES INTELL FORCES ECO/TAC DOMIN EDU/PROP COERCE INGP/REL 20. PAGE 76 F1485 — NAT/G DIPLOM PWR CIVMIL/REL

B42
SWEEZY P.M.,THE THEORY OF CAPITALIST DEVELOPMENT. FUT NAT/G COST FASCISM BIBLIOG. PAGE 128 F2519 — ECO/DEV CAP/ISM MARXISM COLONIAL

B44
HAYEK F.A.,THE ROAD TO SERFDOM. NAT/G POL/PAR CREATE EDU/PROP ATTIT WEALTH LAISSEZ...OLD/LIB CONCPT TREND 20. PAGE 57 F1121 — FUT PLAN ECO/TAC SOCISM

B48
GRAHAM F.D.,THE THEORY OF INTERNATIONAL VALUES. FUT WOR+45 WOR-45 ECO/DEV FINAN INT/ORG PLAN TEC/DEV CAP/ISM DIPLOM ECO/TAC TARIFFS ROUTINE BAL/PAY — NEW/IDEA INT/TRADE

DRIVE PWR WEALTH SOCISM...POLICY STAT HYPO/EXP GEN/LAWS 20. PAGE 50 F0971

B49
PARMELEE M.,GEO-ECONOMIC REGIONAL AND WORLD FEDERATION. FUT WOR+45 WOR-45 SOCIETY VOL/ASSN PLAN ...METH/CNCPT SIMUL GEN/METH TERR/GP TOT/POP 20. PAGE 103 F2028 — INT/ORG GEOG REGION

S49
SHEPHARD H.A.,"DEMOCRATIC CONTROL IN A LABOR UNION." FUT CONSTN STRUCT TEC/DEV LEAD PARTIC RACE/REL CENTRAL DRIVE HABITAT RECORD. PAGE 120 F2374 — LABOR MAJORIT CONTROL PWR

B52
AYRES C.E.,THE INDUSTRIAL ECONOMY. USA+45 FINAN MARKET NAT/G PUB/INST PLAN ECO/TAC TAX DEMAND INCOME...BIBLIOG/A 20. PAGE 8 F0146 — ECO/DEV INDUS FUT PROB/SOLV

B52
GALBRAITH J.K.,AMERICAN CAPITALISM: THE CONCEPT OF COUNTERVAILING POWER. AFR FUT USA+45 FINAN PRICE CENTRAL INCOME PEACE WEALTH...POLICY DECISION 20. PAGE 45 F0881 — ECO/TAC CAP/ISM TREND NAT/G

B52
HOSELITZ B.F.,THE PROGRESS OF UNDERDEVELOPED AREAS. AFR FUT WOR+45 WOR-45 ECO/DEV ECO/TAC INT/TRADE WEALTH...SOC TREND GEN/LAWS TOT/POP VAL/FREE FOR/TRADE 20. PAGE 62 F1219 — ECO/UNDEV PLAN FOR/AID

B52
MACARTHUR D.,REVITALIZING A NATION. ASIA COM FUT KOREA WOR+45 NAT/G FOR/AID TAX GIVE WAR ATTIT SOCISM 20 CHINJAP EUROPE. PAGE 83 F1619 — LEAD FORCES TOP/EX POLICY

L52
HUTH A.G.,"COMMUNICATION AND ECONOMIC DEVELOPMENT." FUT WOR+45 CULTURE SOCIETY INT/ORG PLAN TEC/DEV EDU/PROP DRIVE KNOWL WEALTH...POLICY CONCPT RECORD STERTYP GEN/LAWS COMMUN TOT/POP UNESCO 20 UN CMN/WLTH. PAGE 64 F1250 — ECO/UNDEV

B53
BOULDING K.E.,THE ORGANIZATIONAL REVOLUTION. FUT CULTURE ECO/DEV LABOR PROF/ORG ECO/TAC MORAL...SOC CONCPT RECORD INT SOC/EXP 20. PAGE 17 F0321 — SOCIETY TREND

B53
MENDE T.,WORLD POWER IN THE BALANCE. FUT USA+45 USSR WOR-45 ECO/DEV ECO/TAC INT/TRADE EDU/PROP UTOPIA ATTIT...HUM CONCPT TREND TOT/POP 20. PAGE 90 F1756 — WOR+45 PWR BAL/PWR AFR

B53
WOYTINSKY W.S.,WORLD POPULATION AND PRODUCTION: TRENDS AND OUTLOOK. FUT WOR+45 WOR-45 CULTURE SOCIETY ECO/DEV AGRI INDUS TEC/DEV EDU/PROP SKILL WEALTH...SOC TREND. PAGE 149 F2928 — ECO/UNDEV METH/CNCPT GEOG PERSON

S53
LINCOLN G.,"FACTORS DETERMINING ARMS AID." COM FUT USA+45 USSR WOR+45 ECO/DEV NAT/G CONSULT PLAN TEC/DEV DIPLOM DOMIN EDU/PROP PERCEPT PWR ...DECISION CONCPT TREND MARX/KARL 20. PAGE 80 F1566 — FORCES POLICY BAL/PWR FOR/AID

B54
STALEY E.,THE FUTURE OF UNDERDEVELOPED COUNTRIES: POLITICAL IMPLICATIONS OF ECONOMIC DEVELOPMENT. AFR COM FUT USA+45 SOCIETY ECO/UNDEV CREATE PLAN CAP/ISM ATTIT DRIVE MARXISM SOCISM...POLICY CONCPT CHARTS 20. PAGE 125 F2466 — EDU/PROP ECO/TAC FOR/AID

B55
BUCHANAN N.S.,APPROACHES TO ECONOMIC DEVELOPMENT. FUT USA+45 WOR+45 STRATA ECO/DEV INT/ORG NAT/G TEC/DEV DIPLOM FOR/AID ATTIT KNOWL PWR WEALTH ...RELATIV METH/CNCPT SELF/OBS TREND CON/ANAL STERTYP GEN/LAWS FOR/TRADE COMMUN 20. PAGE 20 F0380 — ECO/UNDEV ECO/TAC INT/TRADE

B55
FLORINSKY M.T.,INTEGRATED EUROPE. EUR+WWI FRANCE ITALY NETHERLAND UK ECO/DEV INT/ORG FORCES LEGIT FEDERAL ATTIT PWR WEALTH...POLICY GEOG CONCPT GEN/LAWS TOT/POP EEC OEEC 20. PAGE 42 F0816 — FUT ECO/TAC REGION

B55
FOGARTY M.P.,ECONOMIC CONTROL. FUT UK ECO/DEV FINAN CONSULT INT/TRADE...CHARTS BIBLIOG/A 20. PAGE 42 F0819 — ECO/TAC NAT/G CONTROL PROB/SOLV

B56
BELL P.W.,THE STERLING AREA IN THE POSTWAR WORLD. EUR+WWI FUT S/ASIA UK ECO/DEV PLAN DIPLOM WEALTH ...STAT RECORD CHARTS GEN/LAWS FOR/TRADE TOT/POP 20. PAGE 12 F0235 — FINAN ECO/TAC

B56
WOLFF R.L.,THE BALKANS IN OUR TIME. ALBANIA FUT MOD/EUR USSR YUGOSLAVIA CULTURE INT/ORG SECT DIPLOM EDU/PROP COERCE WAR ORD/FREE...CHARTS 4/20 BALKANS COMINFORM. PAGE 148 F2919 — GEOG COM

B57
GOLD N.L.,REGIONAL ECONOMIC DEVELOPMENT AND NUCLEAR POWER IN INDIA. FUT INDIA FINAN FOR/AID INT/TRADE BAL/PAY EFFICIENCY OPTIMAL PRODUC WEALTH...PREDICT 20. PAGE 48 F0934 — ECO/UNDEV TEC/DEV NUC/PWR INDUS

B57
LAVES W.H.C.,UNESCO. FUT WOR+45 NAT/G CONSULT DELIB/GP TEC/DEV ECO/TAC EDU/PROP PEACE ORD/FREE ...CONCPT TIME/SEQ TREND UNESCO VAL/FREE 20. PAGE 76 F1491 — INT/ORG KNOWL

B58
BANCROFT G.,THE AMERICAN LABOR FORCE: ITS GROWTH AND CHANGING COMPOSITION. FUT USA+45 USA-45 ECO/DEV INDUS WORKER...GEOG CHARTS 19/20. PAGE 9 F0170 — LABOR STAT TREND CENSUS

B58
GALBRAITH J.K.,THE AFFLUENT SOCIETY. EUR+WWI FUT USA+45 USSR CULTURE SERV/IND PEACE WEALTH SOCISM ...NEW/IDEA TREND VAL/FREE 20. PAGE 45 F0882 — ATTIT ECO/TAC CAP/ISM

B58
HOOD W.C.,FINANCING OF ECONOMIC ACTIVITY IN CANADA. CANADA FUT VOL/ASSN WORKER ECO/TAC ADJUD ADMIN ...CHARTS 20. PAGE 61 F1204 — BUDGET FINAN GP/REL ECO/DEV

B58
MYRDAL G.,RICH LANDS AND POOR: THE ROAD TO WORLD PROSPERITY. FUT WOR+45 WOR-45 ECO/DEV ECO/UNDEV INT/ORG PLAN ECO/TAC REGION...GEOG TIME/SEQ GEN/LAWS TOT/POP 20. PAGE 96 F1880 — WEALTH TREND FOR/AID INT/TRADE

B58
POLLOCK F.,AUTOMATION: A STUDY OF ITS ECONOMIC AND SOCIAL CONSEQUENCES. FUT USA+45 USA-45 SOCIETY ECO/DEV LABOR ACT/RES PLAN ECO/TAC AUTOMAT ROUTINE ALL/VALS...STAT TREND COMPUT/IR CHARTS SOC/EXP WORK 20. PAGE 107 F2099 — TEC/DEV SOC CAP/ISM

L58
MASON E.S.,"ECONOMIC PLANNING IN UNDERDEVELOPED AREAS." FUT WOR+45 PLAN TEC/DEV EDU/PROP ATTIT RIGID/FLEX KNOWL...SOC CONCPT GEN/LAWS TOT/POP 20. PAGE 87 F1697 — NAT/G ECO/UNDEV

S58
LANE F.C.,"ECONOMIC CONSEQUENCES OF ORGANIZED VIOLENCE." FUT WOR+45 WOR-45 ECO/DEV DIST/IND SERV/IND NAT/G PROVS EX/STRUC CHOOSE ORD/FREE PWR ...TIME/SEQ GEN/LAWS MUNICH 20. PAGE 75 F1472 — WEALTH COERCE

B59
SANNWALD R.E.,ECONOMIC INTEGRATION: THEORETICAL ASSUMPTIONS AND CONSEQUENCES OF EUROPEAN UNIFICATION. EUR+WWI FUT FINAN INDUS VOL/ASSN ACT/RES ECO/TAC...PLURIST EEC FOR/TRADE OEEC 20. PAGE 116 F2279 — INT/ORG ECO/DEV INT/TRADE

B59
VERNEY D.V.,PUBLIC ENTERPRISE IN SWEDEN. FUT SWEDEN UK INDUS POL/PAR LEGIS PROB/SOLV CAP/ISM INT/TRADE CONTROL SOCISM...MGT CONCPT NAT/COMP 20 SOCDEM/PAR CIVIL/SERV. PAGE 141 F2778 — ECO/DEV POLICY LG/CO NAT/G

S59
ALKHIMOV V.S.,"SOVIET FOREIGN TRADE CHANNELS." COM FUT USA+45 USSR ECO/DEV MARKET CONSULT PLAN WEALTH ...MARXIST OBS CON/ANAL FOR/TRADE 20. PAGE 4 F0068 — FINAN ECO/TAC DIPLOM

S59
KINDLEBERGER C.P.,"UNITED STATES ECONOMIC FOREIGN POLICY: RESEARCH REQUIREMENTS FOR 1965." FUT USA+45 WOR+45 DIST/IND MARKET INT/ORG ECO/TAC INT/TRADE WEALTH...OBS TREND CON/ANAL GEN/LAWS FOR/TRADE VAL/FREE 20. PAGE 71 F1392 — FINAN ECO/DEV FOR/AID

S59
PLAZA G.,"FOR A REGIONAL MARKET IN LATIN AMERICA." FUT L/A+17C CULTURE INDUS NAT/G ECO/TAC INT/TRADE ATTIT WEALTH...NEW/IDEA TREND OAS 20. PAGE 106 F2092 — MARKET INT/ORG REGION

S59
SOLDATI A.,"EOCNOMIC DISINTEGRATION IN EUROPE." EUR+WWI FUT WOR+45 INDUS INT/ORG NAT/G CAP/ISM WEALTH...NEW/IDEA OBS TREND CHARTS EEC 20. PAGE 124 F2438 — FINAN ECO/TAC

B60
APTHEKER H.,DISARMAMENT AND THE AMERICAN ECONOMY: A SYMPOSIUM. FUT USA+45 ECO/DEV DIST/IND FINAN INDUS PROC/MFG LABOR NAT/G POL/PAR CONSULT PLAN CAP/ISM INT/TRADE PEACE ATTIT MORAL WEALTH...TREND GEN/LAWS TOT/POP 20. PAGE 6 F0110 — MARXIST ARMS/CONT

B60
BILLERBECK K.,SOVIET BLOC FOREIGN AID TO UNDERDEVELOPED COUNTRIES. COM FUT USSR FINAN FORCES TEC/DEV DIPLOM INT/TRADE EDU/PROP NUC/PWR...TREND 20. PAGE 15 F0285 — FOR/AID ECO/UNDEV ECO/TAC MARXISM

B60
KRISTENSEN T.,THE ECONOMIC WORLD BALANCE. FUT WOR+45 CULTURE ECO/DEV BAL/PWR INT/TRADE REGION PWR WEALTH...STAT TREND CHARTS 20. PAGE 73 F1442 — ECO/UNDEV ECO/TAC FOR/AID

B60
LENCZOWSKI G.,OIL AND STATE IN THE MIDDLE EAST. FUT IRAN LAW ECO/UNDEV EXTR/IND NAT/G TOP/EX PLAN TEC/DEV ECO/TAC LEGIT ADMIN COERCE ATTIT ALL/VALS PWR...CHARTS 20. PAGE 78 F1519 — ISLAM INDUS NAT/LISM

B60
MYRDAL G.,BEYOND THE WELFARE STATE: ECONOMIC PLANNING AND ITS IMPLICATIONS. EUR+WWI FUT USA+45 USSR ECO/DEV ECO/UNDEV TEC/DEV SKILL WEALTH...PSY TREND FOR/TRADE 20. PAGE 96 F1881 — PLAN ECO/TAC CAP/ISM

B60
PETERSON W.C.,THE WELFARE STATE IN FRANCE. EUR+WWI FRANCE FUT STRATA PROB/SOLV TAX GIVE RECEIVE INCOME ORD/FREE PWR...CHARTS 20. PAGE 105 F2070 NEW/LIB ECO/TAC WEALTH NAT/G

B60
ROEPKE W.,A HUMANE ECONOMY: THE SOCIAL FRAMEWORK OF THE FREE MARKET. FUT USSR WOR+45 CULTURE SOCIETY ECO/DEV PLAN ECO/TAC ADMIN ATTIT PERSON RIGID/FLEX SUPEGO MORAL WEALTH SOCISM...POLICY OLD/LIB CONCPT TREND GEN/LAWS 20. PAGE 113 F2232 DRIVE EDU/PROP CAP/ISM

B60
STEIN E.,AMERICAN ENTERPRISE IN THE EUROPEAN COMMON MARKET: A LEGAL PROFILE. EUR+WWI FUT USA+45 SOCIETY STRUCT ECO/DEV NAT/G VOL/ASSN CONSULT PLAN TEC/DEV ECO/TAC INT/TRADE ADMIN ATTIT RIGID/FLEX PWR...MGT NEW/IDEA STAT TREND COMPUT/IR SIMUL EEC 20. PAGE 125 F2475 MARKET ADJUD INT/LAW

B60
STOLPER W.F.,GERMANY BETWEEN EAST AND WEST: THE ECONOMICS OF COMPETITIVE COEXISTENCE. AFR FUT GERMANY/E GERMANY/W WOR+45 FINAN POL/PAR BUDGET ECO/TAC FOR/AID INT/TRADE...STAT CHARTS METH/COMP 20. PAGE 126 F2495 ECO/DEV DIPLOM GOV/COMP BAL/PWR

B60
US SENATE COMM ON COMMERCE,URBAN MASS TRANSPORTATION. FUT USA+45 AIR ECO/DEV FINAN LOC/G LEGIS CREATE PROB/SOLV TEC/DEV MUNICH 20 PUB/TRANS. PAGE 139 F2732 DIST/IND PLAN NAT/G LAW

S60
"THE EMERGING COMMON MARKETS IN LATIN AMERICA." FUT L/A+17C STRATA DIST/IND INDUS LABOR NAT/G LEGIS ECO/TAC ADMIN RIGID/FLEX HEALTH...NEW/IDEA TIME/SEQ OAS 20. PAGE 1 F0013 FINAN ECO/UNDEV INT/TRADE

S60
ENKE S.,"THE ECONOMIES OF GOVERNMENT PAYMENTS TO LIMIT POPULATION." FUT INDIA WOR+45 CULTURE FINAN NAT/G CONSULT PLAN LEGIT CONTROL COST ATTIT RIGID/FLEX HEALTH WEALTH...STAT OBS CHARTS TOT/POP VAL/FREE 20. PAGE 38 F0736 FAM ACT/RES

S60
FRANKEL S.H.,"ECONOMIC ASPECTS OF POLITICAL INDEPENDENCE IN AFRICA." AFR FUT SOCIETY ECO/UNDEV COM/IND FINAN LEGIS PLAN TEC/DEV CAP/ISM ECO/TAC INT/TRADE ADMIN ATTIT DRIVE RIGID/FLEX PWR WEALTH ...MGT NEW/IDEA MATH TIME/SEQ VAL/FREE 20. PAGE 43 F0846 NAT/G FOR/AID

S60
JAFFEE A.J.,"POPULATION TRENDS AND CONTROLS IN UNDERDEVELOPED COUNTRIES." AFR FUT ISLAM L/A+17C S/ASIA CULTURE R+D FAM ACT/RES PLAN EDU/PROP BIO/SOC RIGID/FLEX HEALTH...SOC STAT OBS CHARTS 20. PAGE 66 F1303 ECO/UNDEV GEOG

S60
KELLOGG C.E.,"TRANSFER OF BASIC SKILLS OF FOOD PRODUCTION." AFR FUT S/ASIA STRATA ECO/UNDEV LABOR VOL/ASSN RIGID/FLEX...OLD/LIB SOCIALIST NEW/IDEA STAT PROJ/TEST GEN/LAWS 20. PAGE 70 F1370 AGRI PLAN

S60
MIKESELL R.F.,"AMERICA'S ECONOMIC RESPONSIBILITY AS A GREAT POWER." COM FUT USA+45 USSR WOR+45 INT/ORG PLAN ECO/TAC FOR/AID EDU/PROP CHOOSE WEALTH ...POLICY 20. PAGE 91 F1781 ECO/UNDEV BAL/PWR CAP/ISM

S60
MILLER A.S.,"SOME OBSERVATIONS ON THE POLITICAL ECONOMY OF POPULATION GROWTH." FUT USA+45 ECO/DEV R+D CONSULT PLAN TEC/DEV ECO/TAC ROUTINE BIO/SOC WEALTH...POLICY OBS. PAGE 91 F1790 SOCIETY GEOG

S60
MORALES C.J.,"TRADE AND ECONOMIC INTEGRATION IN LATIN AMERICA." FUT L/A+17C LAW STRATA ECO/UNDEV DIST/IND INDUS LABOR NAT/G LEGIS ECO/TAC ADMIN RIGID/FLEX WEALTH...CONCPT NEW/IDEA CONT/OBS TIME/SEQ WORK 20. PAGE 93 F1825 FINAN INT/TRADE REGION

S60
NICHOLS J.P.,"HAZARDS OF AMERICAN PRIVATE INVESTMENT IN UNDERDEVELOPED COUNTRIES." FUT L/A+17C USA+45 USA-45 EXTR/IND CONSULT BAL/PWR ECO/TAC DOMIN ADJUD ATTIT SOVEREIGN WEALTH ...HIST/WRIT TIME/SEQ TREND TERR/GP VAL/FREE 20. PAGE 98 F1924 FINAN ECO/UNDEV CAP/ISM NAT/LISM

B61
AGARWAL R.C.,STATE ENTERPRISE IN INDIA. FUT INDIA UK FINAN INDUS ADMIN CONTROL OWN...POLICY CHARTS BIBLIOG 20 RAILROAD. PAGE 3 F0048 ECO/UNDEV SOCISM GOV/REL LG/CO

B61
BENOIT E.,EUROPE AT SIXES AND SEVENS: THE COMMON MARKET, THE FREE TRADE ASSOCIATION AND THE UNITED STATES. EUR+WWI FUT USA+45 INDUS CONSULT DELIB/GP EX/STRUC TOP/EX ACT/RES ECO/TAC EDU/PROP ROUTINE CHOOSE PERCEPT WEALTH...MGT TREND EEC FOR/TRADE TOT/POP 20 EFTA. PAGE 13 F0249 FINAN ECO/DEV VOL/ASSN

B61
EINZIG P.,A DYNAMIC THEORY OF FORWARD EXCHANGE. FUT WOR+45 WOR-45 INT/TRADE BAL/PAY WEALTH...OLD/LIB NEW/IDEA OBS TREND FOR/TRADE 20. PAGE 37 F0713 FINAN ECO/TAC

B61
GARDNER R.N.,LEGAL-ECONOMIC PROBLEMS OF INTERNATIONAL TRADE. FUT WOR+45 INTELL ECO/DEV EX/STRUC INT/TRADE ROUTINE ATTIT WEALTH...GEN/LAWS ANTHOL FOR/TRADE 20. PAGE 46 F0904 FINAN ACT/RES

B61
KOVNER M.,THE CHALLENGE OF COEXISTENCE: A STUDY OF SOVIET ECONOMIC DIPLOMACY. COM FUT ECO/DEV ECO/UNDEV PLAN EDU/PROP DETER SKILL...OBS VAL/FREE 20. PAGE 73 F1430 PWR DIPLOM USSR AFR

B61
LETHBRIDGE H.J.,CHINA'S URBAN COMMUNES. CHINA/COM FUT ECO/UNDEV DIPLOM EDU/PROP DEMAND INCOME MARXISM ...POLICY MUNICH 20. PAGE 78 F1534 CONTROL ECO/TAC NAT/G

B61
MARX K.,THE COMMUNIST MANIFESTO. IN (MENDEL A. ESSENTIAL WORKS OF MARXISM, NEW YORK: BANTAM. FUT MOD/EUR CULTURE ECO/DEV ECO/UNDEV AGRI FINAN INDUS MARKET PROC/MFG LABOR POL/PAR CONSULT FORCES CREATE PLAN ADMIN ATTIT DRIVE RIGID/FLEX ORD/FREE PWR RESPECT MARX/KARL MUNICH WORK. PAGE 86 F1691 COM NEW/IDEA CAP/ISM REV

B61
SHARP W.R.,FIELD ADMINISTRATION IN THE UNITED NATION SYSTEM: THE CONDUCT OF INTERNATIONAL ECONOMIC AND SOCIAL PROGRAMS. FUT WOR+45 CONSTN SOCIETY ECO/UNDEV R+D DELIB/GP ACT/RES PLAN TEC/DEV EDU/PROP EXEC ROUTINE HEALTH WEALTH...HUM CONCPT CHARTS METH ILO UNESCO GP VAL/FREE UN 20. PAGE 120 F2369 INT/ORG CONSULT

B61
SLICHTER S.H.,ECONOMIC GROWTH IN THE UNITED STATES. FUT USA+45 USA-45 LABOR PAY INCOME PRODUC...MGT 19/20. PAGE 123 F2422 ECO/DEV TEC/DEV CAP/ISM DEMAND

B61
SPOONER F.P.,SOUTH AFRICAN PREDICAMENT. FUT SOUTH/AFR INDUS POL/PAR RACE/REL INCOME...CHARTS 20 NEGRO. PAGE 125 F2459 ECO/DEV DISCRIM ECO/TAC POLICY

B61
STARK H.,SOCIAL AND ECONOMIC FRONTIERS IN LATIN AMERICA (2ND ED.). CUBA FUT CULTURE AGRI INDUS ECO/TAC PRODUC ATTIT MARXISM...NAT/COMP BIBLIOG T 20. PAGE 125 F2470 L/A+17C SOCIETY DIPLOM ECO/UNDEV

S61
BENOIT E.,"THE PROPENSITY TO REDUCE THE NATIONAL DEBT OUT OF DEFENSE SAVINGS." FUT USA+45 SOCIETY R+D PLAN...WELF/ST SOC REC/INT STERTYP TOT/POP 20. PAGE 13 F0250 WEALTH ECO/TAC

S61
DELLA PORT G.,"PROBLEMI E PROSPETTIVE DI COESISTENZA FRA ORIENTE ED OCCIDENTE, (PART 3)." COM FUT WOR+45 NAT/G BAL/PWR FOR/AID BAL/PAY PWR WEALTH...SOC CONCPT GEN/LAWS 20. PAGE 32 F0616 AFR INT/TRADE

S61
DEUTSCH K.W.,"NATIONAL INDUSTRIALIZATION AND THE DECLINING SHARE OF THE INTERNATIONAL ECONOMIC SECTOR." EUR+WWI FUT WOR+45 WOR-45 MARKET PLAN EDU/PROP WEALTH...WELF/ST OBS TESTS 20. PAGE 32 F0624 DIST/IND ECO/DEV INT/TRADE

S61
GALBRAITH J.K.,"A POSITIVE APPROACH TO ECONOMIC AID." FUT USA+45 INTELL NAT/G CONSULT ACT/RES DIPLOM ECO/TAC EDU/PROP ATTIT KNOWL PWR WEALTH ...SOC STERTYP MID/EX METH/GP 20. PAGE 45 F0883 ECO/UNDEV ROUTINE FOR/AID

S61
GORDON L.,"ECONOMIC REGIONALISM RECONSIDERED." FUT USA+45 WOR+45 INDUS NAT/G TEC/DEV DIPLOM ROUTINE PERCEPT WEALTH...WELF/ST METH/CNCPT WORK 20. PAGE 49 F0957 ECO/DEV ATTIT CAP/ISM REGION

S61
HEILBRONER R.L.,"DYNAMICS OF FOREIGN AID: PROBLEMS OF UNDERDEVELOPED NATIONS PLAGUE ASSISTANCE PROGRAM." FUT USA+45 STRATA NAT/G PLAN TEC/DEV ATTIT DRIVE WEALTH WORK 20. PAGE 58 F1135 ECO/UNDEV ECO/TAC FOR/AID

S61
LINDSAY F.A.,"PLANNING IN FOREIGN AFFAIRS: THE MISSING ELEMENT." FUT USA+45 ROUTINE SKILL...MGT TOT/POP 20. PAGE 80 F1572 ECO/DEV PLAN DIPLOM

S61
NEAL A.C.,"NEW ECONOMIC POLICIES FOR THE WEST." COM EUR+WWI FUT USA+45 WOR+45 ECO/DEV ECO/UNDEV INDUS MARKET ROUTINE HEALTH ORD/FREE PWR...OLD/LIB METH/CNCPT 20. PAGE 97 F1904 PLAN ECO/TAC

S61
NOVE A.,"THE SOVIET MODEL AND UNDERDEVELOPED COUNTRIES." COM FUT USSR WOR+45 CULTURE ECO/DEV POL/PAR FOR/AID EDU/PROP ADMIN MORAL WEALTH ...POLICY RECORD HIST/WRIT 20. PAGE 99 F1942 ECO/UNDEV PLAN

S61
VERNON R.,"A TRADE POLICY FOR THE 1960'S." COM FUT USA+45 WOR+45 ECO/DEV ECO/UNDEV FINAN TOP/EX ACT/RES...WELF/ST METH/CNCPT CONT/OBS TOT/POP 20. PAGE 141 F2781 PLAN INT/TRADE

B62
BRUMBERG A.,RUSSIA UNDER KHRUSHCHEV. FUT USSR SOCIETY ECO/DEV AGRI PERF/ART WORKER PWR...SOC ANTHOL 20 KHRUSH/N. PAGE 20 F0377
COM MARXISM NAT/G CHIEF

B62
GEARY R.C.,EUROPE'S FUTURE IN FIGURES. FUT GOV/REL DEMAND PRODUC...STAT CHARTS METH/COMP ANTHOL METH 20 EUROPE. PAGE 47 F0912
FINAN ECO/DEV PREDICT WEALTH

B62
HEILBRONER R.L.,THE MAKING OF ECONOMIC SOCIETY. FUT WOR-45 SOCIETY STRATA ECO/DEV ECO/UNDEV ECO/TAC LEGIT ROUTINE...SOC RECORD REC/INT KNO/TEST CENSUS STERTYP GEN/LAWS. PAGE 58 F1136
CAP/ISM SOCISM

B62
HIGGANS B.,UNITED NATIONS AND U.S. FOREIGN ECONOMIC POLICY. FUT USA+45 WOR+45 ECO/DEV ECO/UNDEV NAT/G ECO/TAC WEALTH...TIME/SEQ TOT/POP UN 20. PAGE 59 F1168
INT/ORG ACT/RES FOR/AID DIPLOM

B62
HOOVER E.M.,ANATOMY OF A METROPOLIS. FUT USA+45 SOCIETY ECO/DEV DIST/IND INDUS WORKER ECO/TAC TAX GP/REL COST WEALTH MUNICH 20 NEWYORK/C. PAGE 62 F1212
ROUTINE TREND INCOME

B62
PHELPS E.S.,THE GOAL OF ECONOMIC GROWTH: SOURCES, COSTS, BENEFITS. USA+45 USSR FINAN TAX CONTROL DEMAND WEALTH...POLICY NAT/COMP ANTHOL BIBLIOG 20. PAGE 106 F2079
ECO/TAC ECO/DEV NAT/G FUT

B62
REES A.,THE ECONOMICS OF TRADE UNIONS. FUT ECO/DEV INDUS BARGAIN CAP/ISM PRICE SENIOR CONTROL GP/REL COST...TREND 20 AFL/CIO. PAGE 110 F2172
LABOR WORKER ECO/TAC

B62
ROBERTSON B.C.,REGIONAL DEVELOPMENT IN THE EUROPEAN ECONOMIC COMMUNITY. EUR+WWI FRANCE FUT ITALY UK ECO/UNDEV WORKER ACT/RES PROB/SOLV TEC/DEV ECO/TAC INT/TRADE EEC. PAGE 112 F2209
PLAN ECO/DEV INT/ORG REGION

B62
SHANNON I.,THE ECONOMIC FUNCTIONS OF GOLD. AFR FUT WOR+45 WOR-45 INT/ORG BUDGET INT/TRADE BAL/PAY DEMAND PEACE 20 MONEY. PAGE 120 F2366
FINAN PRICE ECO/DEV ECO/TAC

B62
WARD B.,THE RICH NATIONS AND THE POOR NATIONS. FUT WOR+45 CULTURE ECO/DEV ECO/UNDEV PLAN CAP/ISM EDU/PROP REV NAT/LISM ATTIT DRIVE SOCISM...POLICY CONCPT TIME/SEQ 20. PAGE 143 F2816
ECO/TAC GEN/LAWS

B62
WOODS H.D.,LABOUR POLICY AND LABOUR ECONOMICS IN CANADA. CANADA FUT NAT/G VOL/ASSN WORKER BARGAIN ECO/TAC PAY CONFER GP/REL 20. PAGE 148 F2924
LABOR POLICY INDUS ECO/DEV

S62
ADISESHIAN M.,"EDUCATION AND DEVELOPMENT." FUT WOR+45 SOCIETY ACT/RES INT/TRADE EDU/PROP KNOWL SKILL WEALTH...POLICY CONCPT CONT/OBS CENSUS CHARTS TOT/POP VAL/FREE APPLIC FAO FOR/TRADE 20. PAGE 2 F0041
SCHOOL ECO/UNDEV

S62
IOVTCHOUK M.T.,"ON SOME THEORETICAL PRINCIPLES AND METHODS OF SOCIOLOGICAL INVESTIGATIONS (IN RUSSIAN)." FUT USA+45 STRATA R+D NAT/G POL/PAR TOP/EX ACT/RES PLAN ECO/TAC EDU/PROP ROUTINE ATTIT RIGID/FLEX MARXISM SOCISM...MARXIST METH/CNCPT OBS TREND NAT/COMP GEN/LAWS 20. PAGE 65 F1288
COM ECO/DEV CAP/ISM USSR

S62
PYE L.W.,"THE POLITICAL IMPULSES AND FANTASIES BEHIND FOREIGN AID." FUT USA+45 ECO/UNDEV DIPLOM ECO/TAC ROUTINE DRIVE KNOWL...SOC METH/CNCPT NEW/IDEA TREND HYPO/EXP STERTYP GEN/METH 20. PAGE 108 F2133
ACT/RES ATTIT FOR/AID

S62
SCOTT J.B.,"ANGLO-SOVIET TRADE AND ITS EFFECTS ON THE COMMONWEALTH." COM FUT UK USSR WOR+45 ECO/DEV MARKET INT/ORG CONSULT WEALTH...POLICY TREND CMN/WLTH FOR/TRADE 20. PAGE 118 F2333
NAT/G ECO/TAC

B63
ABSHIRE D.M.,NATIONAL SECURITY: POLITICAL, MILITARY, AND ECONOMIC STRATEGIES IN THE DECADE AHEAD. ASIA COM USA+45 WOR+45 ECO/DEV ECO/UNDEV INT/ORG DELIB/GP FORCES ECO/TAC COERCE ATTIT RIGID/FLEX HEALTH ORD/FREE PWR WEALTH...POLICY STAT CHARTS ANTHOL COLD/WAR VAL/FREE APP/SCI. PAGE 2 F0032
FUT ACT/RES BAL/PWR

B63
BARNETT H.J.,SCARCITY AND GROWTH: THE ECONOMICS OF NATURAL RESOURCE AVAILABILITY. FUT WOR+45 AGRI INDUS PROB/SOLV TEC/DEV CONTROL PRODUC...SOC/WK IDEA/COMP METH/COMP SIMUL 20 RESOURCE/N MALTHUS RICARDO/D MILL/JS DARWIN/C. PAGE 10 F0191
DEMAND HABITAT CENSUS GEOG

B63
GLADE W.P. JR.,THE POLITICAL ECONOMY OF MEXICO. FUT L/A+17C CULTURE SOCIETY AGRI INDUS DELIB/GP ACT/RES ECO/TAC ATTIT HEALTH ORD/FREE...STAT TIME/SEQ TREND MEXIC/AMER TOT/POP VAL/FREE 20. PAGE 48 F0928
FINAN ECO/UNDEV

B63
GRUBEL H.G.,WORLD MONETARY REFORM: PLANS AND ISSUES. FUT WOR+45 ECO/DEV ECO/UNDEV R+D DELIB/GP CREATE ECO/TAC ATTIT RIGID/FLEX WEALTH...STAT ANTHOL VAL/FREE 20. PAGE 52 F1009
FINAN INT/ORG BAL/PAY INT/TRADE

B63
HIRSCHMAN A.O.,JOURNEYS TOWARD PROGRESS: STUDIES OF ECONOMIC POLICYMAKING IN LATIN AMERICA. CHILE FUT ECO/UNDEV AGRI FINAN INDUS CONSULT DELIB/GP PLAN ATTIT HEALTH ORD/FREE WEALTH...POLICY STAT VAL/FREE COLOMB 20. PAGE 60 F1177
L/A+17C ECO/TAC BRAZIL

B63
LAIRD R.D.,SOVIET AGRICULTURAL AND PEASANT AFFAIRS. FUT STRATA LOC/G DELIB/GP ACT/RES TEC/DEV ECO/TAC EDU/PROP ATTIT RIGID/FLEX ORD/FREE SKILL WEALTH ...STAT CON/ANAL ANTHOL MUNICH WORK VAL/FREE 20. PAGE 74 F1461
COM AGRI POLICY

B63
MAIZELS A.,INDUSTRIAL GROWTH AND WORLD TRADE. FUT WOR+45 ECO/DEV FINAN INT/ORG PLAN TEC/DEV ECO/TAC WEALTH...MATH STAT CHARTS VAL/FREE 19/20. PAGE 84 F1642
INDUS ECO/UNDEV INT/TRADE

B63
MANGER W.,THE ALLIANCE FOR PROGRESS: A CRITICAL APPRAISAL. FUT L/A+17C USA+45 CULTURE ECO/UNDEV ACADEM NAT/G SCHOOL PLAN FOR/AID...POLICY OAS ALL/PROG. PAGE 84 F1651
DIPLOM INT/ORG ECO/TAC REGION

B63
MARITANO N.,AN ALLIANCE FOR PROGRESS. FUT L/A+17C USA+45 CULTURE ECO/UNDEV NAT/G PLAN CONTROL ...POLICY ALL/PROG. PAGE 85 F1669
DIPLOM INT/ORG ECO/TAC FOR/AID

B63
SALANT W.S.,THE UNITED STATES BALANCE OF PAYMENTS IN 1968. USA+45 ECO/DEV ECO/UNDEV INT/ORG DELIB/GP ECO/TAC...POLICY STAT SIMUL 20. PAGE 115 F2273
FUT FINAN BAL/PAY

L63
ADERBIGDE A.,"SYMPOSIUM ON WEST AFRICA INTEGRATION." AFR EUR+WWI FUT CULTURE SOCIETY STRATA DIST/IND INDUS MARKET SERV/IND DELIB/GP PLAN TEC/DEV DOMIN EDU/PROP LEGIT COERCE ATTIT ALL/VALS ...POLICY STAT TREND CHARTS VAL/FREE. PAGE 2 F0040
FINAN ECO/TAC REGION

L63
MOUSKHELY M.,"LE BLOC COMMUNISTE ET LA COMMUNAUTE ECONOMIQUE EUROPEENNE." AFR COM EUR+WWI FUT USSR WOR+45 INTELL ECO/UNDEV LABOR POL/PAR NUC/PWR RIGID/FLEX...TIME/SEQ ORG/CHARTS EEC TOT/POP 20. PAGE 94 F1849
INT/ORG ECO/DEV

L63
PADELFORD N.J.,"FINANCIAL CRISIS AND THE UNITED NATIONS." FUT USSR WOR+45 LAW CONSTN FINAN INT/ORG DELIB/GP FORCES PLAN BUDGET DIPLOM COST WEALTH ...STAT CHARTS UN CONGO 20. PAGE 102 F2012
CREATE ECO/TAC

L63
RIDAH A.,"LE NEO-DESTOUR DEPUIS L'INDEPENDANCE." FUT ISLAM WOR+45 ECO/UNDEV INT/ORG SCHOOL DELIB/GP TOP/EX ACT/RES EDU/PROP LEGIT ATTIT ALL/VALS 20 TUNIS. PAGE 111 F2189
NAT/G CONSTN

S63
ADAMS F.G.,"ECONOMIC CONSIDERATIONS OF AN ATLANTIC ENERGY POLICY." EUR+WWI FUT USA+45 DIST/IND EXTR/IND MARKET CONSULT LEGIS ECO/TAC WEALTH ...POLICY EEC FOR/TRADE OEEC 20. PAGE 2 F0037
ECO/DEV TEC/DEV NUC/PWR

S63
ARDANT G.,"A PLAN FOR FULL EMPLOYMENT IN THE DEVELOPING COUNTRIES." AFR FUT WOR+45 DELIB/GP ACT/RES PLAN ECO/TAC ATTIT ALL/VALS...POLICY STAT CHARTS TUNIS VAL/FREE 20. PAGE 6 F0112
ECO/UNDEV SOCIETY MOROCCO

S63
BALOGH T.,"L'INFLUENCE DES INSTITUTIONS MONETAIRES ET COMMERCIALES SUR LA STRUCTURE ECONOMIQUE AFRICAIN." AFR EUR+WWI FUT USA+45 USA-45 WOR+45 SERV/IND INT/ORG NAT/G TOP/EX ROUTINE...INDEX EEC METH/GP 20. PAGE 9 F0168
FINAN

S63
BARTHELEMY G.,"LE NOUVEAU FRANC (CFA) ET LA BANQUE CENTRALE DES ETATS DE L'AFRIQUE DE L'OUEST." FUT STRUCT INT/ORG PLAN ATTIT ALL/VALS FOR/TRADE 20. PAGE 11 F0200
AFR FINAN

S63
BEGUIN H.,"ASPECTS STRUCTURELS DU COMMERCE EXTERIEUR DES PAYS SOUS-DEVELOPPES." FUT WOR+45 STRUCT FINAN SERV/IND POL/PAR TEC/DEV PERCEPT WEALTH FOR/TRADE 20. PAGE 12 F0229
MARKET ECO/UNDEV FOR/AID

S63
BENOIT E.,"ECONOMIC ADJUSTMENTS TO ARMS CONTROL." FUT USA+45 NAT/G NUC/PWR WAR WEAPON 20. PAGE 13 F0251
ECO/DEV PWR ARMS/CONT

S63
DELWERT J.,"L'ECONOMIE CAMBODGIENNE ET SON EVOLUTION ACTUELLE." FUT S/ASIA ECO/UNDEV ACT/RES PLAN WEALTH...CONCPT OBS TIME/SEQ TREND 20. PAGE 32 F0617
FINAN ATTIT CAMBODIA

S63
DIEBOLD W. JR.,"THE NEW SITUATION OF INTERNATIONAL
MARKET

TRADE POLICY." EUR+WWI FRANCE FUT UK USA+45 WOR+45 DIST/IND PLAN INT/TRADE EDU/PROP PWR WEALTH ...RECORD TREND GEN/LAWS EEC TRUE/GP VAL/FREE APPLIC 20. PAGE 33 F0636
ECO/TAC

S63
DUCROS B.,"MOBILISATION DES RESSOURCES PRODUCTIVES ET DEVELOPPEMENT." FUT INTELL SOCIETY COM/IND DIST/IND EXTR/IND FINAN INDUS ROUTINE WEALTH ...METH/CNCPT OBS 20. PAGE 34 F0670
ECO/UNDEV TEC/DEV

S63
EMERSON R.,"THE ATLANTIC COMMUNITY AND THE EMERGING COUNTRIES." FUT WOR+45 ECO/DEV ECO/UNDEV R+D NAT/G DELIB/GP BAL/PWR ECO/TAC EDU/PROP ROUTINE ORD/FREE PWR WEALTH...POLICY CONCPT TREND GEN/METH EEC 20 NATO. PAGE 37 F0729
ATTIT INT/TRADE

S63
FOURASTIE J.,"LES SCIENCES ECONOMIQUES ET SOCIALES EN EUROPE." EUR+WWI FUT MOD/EUR WOR+45 WOR-45 INTELL SOCIETY R+D PLAN ROUTINE ATTIT RIGID/FLEX KNOWL...OBS TREND. PAGE 43 F0833
ACT/RES CULTURE

S63
GALENSON W.,"ECONOMIC DEVELOPMENT AND THE SECTORAL EXPANSION OF EMPLOYMENT, INT." FUT WOR+45 ECO/UNDEV DIST/IND PROC/MFG SERV/IND ACT/RES HEALTH SKILL WEALTH...STAT TIME/SEQ VAL/FREE 20. PAGE 46 F0889
INDUS ECO/TAC

S63
GANDILHON J.,"LA SCIENCE ET LA TECHNIQUE A L'AIDE DES REGIONS PEU DEVELOPPEES." FRANCE FUT WOR+45 ECO/DEV R+D PROF/ORG ACT/RES PLAN...MGT TOT/POP VAL/FREE 20 UN. PAGE 46 F0893
ECO/UNDEV TEC/DEV FOR/AID

S63
GORDON B.,"ECONOMIC IMPEDIMENTS TO REGIONALISM IN SOUTH EAST ASIA." BURMA FUT S/ASIA THAILAND USA+45 AGRI INDUS R+D NAT/G PLAN ECO/TAC WEALTH...STAT CONT/OBS 20. PAGE 49 F0954
VOL/ASSN ECO/UNDEV INT/TRADE REGION

S63
HOOVER C.B.,"ECONOMIC REFORM VERSUS ECONOMIC GROWTH IN UNDERDEVELOPED COUNTRIES." FUT WOR+45 ELITES STRATA ECO/UNDEV DIST/IND INDUS TEC/DEV CAP/ISM FOR/AID INT/TRADE ATTIT WEALTH...MYTH TREND STERTYP GEN/LAWS WORK 20. PAGE 61 F1209
ECO/DEV ECO/TAC

S63
LEDUC G.,"L'AIDE INTERNATIONALE AU DEVELOPPEMENT." FUT WOR+45 ECO/DEV ECO/UNDEV R+D PROF/ORG TEC/DEV ECO/TAC ROUTINE ATTIT ALL/VALS...MGT TIME/SEQ FOR/TRADE TOT/POP 20. PAGE 77 F1503
FINAN PLAN FOR/AID

S63
PRYBYLA J.,"THE QUEST FOR ECONOMIC RATIONALITY IN THE SOVIET BLOC." COM FUT WOR+45 WOR-45 DIST/IND MARKET PLAN ECO/TAC ATTIT...METH/CNCPT TOT/POP 20. PAGE 108 F2128
ECO/DEV TREND USSR

S63
WALKER H.,"THE INTERNATIONAL LAW OF COMMODITY AGREEMENTS." FUT WOR+45 ECO/DEV ECO/UNDEV FINAN INT/ORG NAT/G CONSULT CREATE PLAN ECO/TAC ATTIT PERCEPT...CONCPT GEN/LAWS TOT/POP GATT 20. PAGE 142 F2804
MARKET VOL/ASSN INT/LAW INT/TRADE

S63
WILES P.J.D.,"WILL CAPITALISM AND COMMUNISM SPONTANEOUSLY CONVERGE." COM FUT USA+45 ECO/DEV DIST/IND MARKET CAP/ISM ECO/TAC RIGID/FLEX WEALTH MARXISM SOCISM...MATH STAT TREND COMPUT/IR 20. PAGE 146 F2885
PLAN TEC/DEV USSR

B64
AUBREY H.G.,THE DOLLAR IN WORLD AFFAIRS. FUT USA+45 WOR+45 ECO/DEV CAP/ISM INT/TRADE BAL/PAY...CHARTS 20. PAGE 7 F0140
FINAN ECO/TAC DIPLOM POLICY

B64
CEPEDE M.,POPULATION AND FOOD. USA+45 STRUCT ECO/UNDEV FAM PLAN TEC/DEV FOR/AID CONTROL...CATH SOC TREND 19/20. PAGE 22 F0436
FUT GEOG AGRI CENSUS

B64
CLAIRBORN E.L.,FORECASTING THE BALANCE OF PAYMENTS: AN EVALUATION. AFR FUT UK USA+45 WOR+45 FINAN PLAN BUDGET PAY CONTROL...STAT CHARTS BIBLIOG 20. PAGE 24 F0474
PREDICT BAL/PAY ECO/DEV ECO/TAC

B64
HEKHUIS D.J.,INTERNATIONAL STABILITY: MILITARY, ECONOMIC AND POLITICAL DIMENSIONS. FUT WOR+45 LAW ECO/UNDEV INT/ORG NAT/G VOL/ASSN FORCES ACT/RES BAL/PWR PWR WEALTH...STAT UN 20. PAGE 58 F1143
TEC/DEV DETER REGION

B64
HERSKOVITS M.J.,ECONOMIC TRANSITION IN AFRICA. FUT INT/ORG NAT/G WORKER PROB/SOLV TEC/DEV INT/TRADE EQUILIB INCOME...ANTHOL 20. PAGE 59 F1157
AFR ECO/UNDEV PLAN ADMIN

B64
KOHNSTAMM M.,THE EUROPEAN COMMUNITY AND ITS ROLE IN THE WORLD. FUT MOD/EUR UK USA+45 ECO/DEV 20. PAGE 72 F1418
INT/ORG NAT/G REGION DIPLOM

B64
MARKHAM J.W.,THE COMMON MARKET: FRIEND OR COMPETITOR. AFR EUR+WWI FUT USA+45 INT/ORG LG/CO NAT/G VOL/ASSN DELIB/GP EX/STRUC PLAN TARIFFS ORD/FREE PWR WEALTH...POLICY STAT TREND EEC VAL/FREE 20. PAGE 85 F1671
ECO/DEV ECO/TAC

B64
MELADY T.,FACES OF AFRICA. AFR FUT ISLAM NAT/G POL/PAR SCHOOL DELIB/GP PLAN ECO/TAC EDU/PROP ATTIT ALL/VALS...CHARTS TOT/POP TERR/GP VAL/FREE 20. PAGE 89 F1752
ECO/UNDEV TREND NAT/LISM

B64
SANDEE J.,EUROPE'S FUTURE CONSUMPTION. EUR+WWI FUT EDU/PROP...IDEA/COMP NAT/COMP ANTHOL 20 EUROPE. PAGE 115 F2277
MARKET ECO/DEV PREDICT PRICE

B64
SHANNON I.,INTERNATIONAL LIQUIDITY. AFR FUT USA+45 WOR+45 ECO/TAC PRICE DEMAND WEALTH...CONCPT 20. PAGE 120 F2367
FINAN DIPLOM BAL/PAY ECO/DEV

B64
STOESSINGER J.G.,FINANCING THE UNITED NATIONS SYSTEM. FUT WOR+45 CONSTN NAT/G VOL/ASSN DELIB/GP EX/STRUC ECO/TAC LEGIT CT/SYS PWR WEALTH...STAT TIME/SEQ TREND CHARTS TRUE/GP METH/GP TERR/GP VAL/FREE. PAGE 126 F2493
FINAN INT/ORG

L64
ARMENGALD A.,"ECONOMIE ET COEXISTENCE." COM EUR+WWI FUT USA+45 WOR+45 ECO/DEV ECO/UNDEV FINAN INT/ORG NAT/G EXEC CHOOSE ATTIT ALL/VALS...POLICY RELATIV DECISION TREND SOC/EXP WORK 20. PAGE 6 F0113
MARKET ECO/TAC AFR CAP/ISM

L64
STERN R.M.,"POLICIES FOR TRADE AND DEVELOPMENT." AFR FUT WOR+45 DIST/IND FINAN NAT/G DELIB/GP PLAN ECO/TAC ORD/FREE WEALTH...POLICY STAT TIME/SEQ CHARTS METH/GP 20. PAGE 126 F2480
MARKET ECO/UNDEV INT/TRADE

S64
HABERLER G.,"INTEGRATION AND GROWTH OF THE WORLD ECONOMY IN HISTORICAL PERSPECTIVE." FUT WOR+45 WOR-45 ECO/DEV ECO/UNDEV...TIME/SEQ TREND VAL/FREE 20. PAGE 52 F1023
WEALTH INT/TRADE

S64
HOOVER C.B.,"THE ROLE OF THE NATURAL AND DEVELOPED RESOURCES OF THE NATION STATES." FUT WOR+45 ECO/DEV ECO/UNDEV NAT/G PWR RESPECT SKILL WEALTH...POLICY GEOG TIME/SEQ TREND RESOURCE/N VAL/FREE 20. PAGE 62 F1210
EXTR/IND DOMIN

S64
HUTCHINSON E.C.,"AMERICAN AID TO AFRICA." FUT USA+45 MARKET INT/ORG LOC/G NAT/G PUB/INST PLAN ECO/TAC ATTIT RIGID/FLEX...POLICY CONCPT TREND TERR/GP 20. PAGE 63 F1248
AFR ECO/UNDEV FOR/AID

S64
NEISSER H.,"THE EXTERNAL EQUILIBRIUM OF THE UNITED STATES ECONOMY." FUT USA+45 NAT/G ACT/RES PLAN ECO/TAC ATTIT WEALTH...METH/CNCPT GEN/METH VAL/FREE FOR/TRADE 20. PAGE 97 F1910
FINAN ECO/DEV BAL/PAY INT/TRADE

S64
TOBIN J.,"ECONOMIC GROWTH AS AN OBJECTIVE OF GOVERNMENT POLICY." FUT WOR+45 FINAN WORKER BUDGET INCOME...SOC 20. PAGE 131 F2579
ECO/DEV POLICY ECO/TAC IDEA/COMP

S64
WU Y.,"CHINA'S ECONOMY AND ITS PROSPECTS." ASIA CHINA/COM FUT USSR AGRI INDUS PLAN ECO/TAC LEGIT WEALTH...STAT CON/ANAL CHARTS GEN/LAWS FOR/TRADE 20. PAGE 149 F2938
ECO/DEV

B65
PEACE RESEARCH ABSTRACTS. FUT WOR+45 R+D INT/ORG NAT/G PLAN TEC/DEV BAL/PWR DIPLOM FOR/AID NUC/PWR HEALTH. PAGE 1 F0022
BIBLIOG/A PEACE ARMS/CONT WAR

B65
CLARK T.D.,THREE PATHS TO THE MODERN SOUTH: EDUCATION, AGRICULTURE, AND CONSERVATION. FUT USA-45 ECO/DEV ECO/TAC PEACE WEALTH...POLICY 20 SOUTH/US. PAGE 25 F0485
AGRI EDU/PROP GOV/REL REGION

B65
COX D.W.,THE PERILS OF PEACE* CONVERSION TO WHAT? FUT USA+45 ECO/DEV NAT/G ACT/RES CREATE PLAN NUC/PWR WAR DEMAND MGT. PAGE 28 F0546
PEACE WORKER FORCES MARKET

B65
INTERAMERICAN ECO AND SOC COUN,THE ALLIANCE FOR PROGRESS: ITS THIRD YEAR 1963-1964. FUT L/A+17C WOR+45 ECO/DEV INT/ORG PLAN CONTROL ADJUST...STAT ANTHOL SOC/INTEG 20 ALL/PROG. PAGE 64 F1268
ECO/UNDEV ECO/TAC FINAN FOR/AID

B65
LUTZ V.,FRENCH PLANNING. FRANCE TEC/DEV RIGID/FLEX ORD/FREE 20. PAGE 82 F1613
PLAN ADMIN FUT

B65
MUSHKIN S.J.,PROPERTY TAXES: THE 1970 OUTLOOK (PAMPHLET). FUT USA+45 ECO/DEV MARKET PROVS PLAN ...PROBABIL STAT CENSUS PREDICT CHARTS METH 20. PAGE 95 F1872
TAX OWN FINAN LOC/G

B65
OECD,MEDITERRANEAN REGIONAL PROJECT: TURKEY;
EDU/PROP

EDUCATION AND DEVELOPMENT. FUT TURKEY SOCIETY STRATA FINAN NAT/G PROF/ORG PLAN PROB/SOLV ADMIN COST...STAT CHARTS 20 OECD. PAGE 100 F1969
ACADEM SCHOOL ECO/UNDEV

B65
OECD,THE MEDITERRANEAN REGIONAL PROJECT: GREECE; EDUCATION AND DEVELOPMENT. FUT GREECE SOCIETY AGRI FINAN NAT/G PROF/ORG WORKER PLAN PROB/SOLV ADMIN DEMAND ATTIT 20 OECD. PAGE 100 F1972
EDU/PROP SCHOOL ACADEM ECO/UNDEV

B65
OECD,THE MEDITERRANEAN REGIONAL PROJECT: SPAIN; EDUCATION AND DEVELOPMENT. FUT SPAIN STRATA FINAN NAT/G WORKER PLAN PROB/SOLV ADMIN COST...POLICY STAT CHARTS 20 OECD. PAGE 100 F1973
ECO/UNDEV EDU/PROP ACADEM SCHOOL

B65
ORG FOR ECO COOP AND DEVEL,THE MEDITERRANEAN REGIONAL PROJECT: AN EXPERIMENT IN PLANNING BY SIX COUNTRIES. FUT GREECE SPAIN TURKEY YUGOSLAVIA SOCIETY FINAN NAT/G PROF/ORG EDU/PROP ADMIN REGION COST...POLICY STAT CHARTS 20 OECD. PAGE 102 F1995
PLAN ECO/UNDEV ACADEM SCHOOL

B65
REDFORD E.S.,AMERICAN GOVERNMENT AND THE ECONOMY. FUT USA+45 USA-45 INDUS PROB/SOLV GOV/REL...POLICY DECISION METH/COMP BIBLIOG T 18/20. PAGE 110 F2168
CONSTN NAT/G

B65
SINHA M.R.,THE ECONOMICS OF MANPOWER PLANNING. FUT HUNGARY NAT/G CONTROL...POLICY GEOG ANTHOL 20 CHINJAP. PAGE 122 F2415
ECO/UNDEV PLAN WORKER ECO/TAC

B65
SMERK G.M.,URBAN TRANSPORTATION: THE FEDERAL ROLE. FUT USA+45 FINAN PROB/SOLV TEC/DEV AUTOMAT GOV/REL COST...STAT BIBLIOG MUNICH 20 PUB/TRANS. PAGE 123 F2426
PLAN DIST/IND NAT/G

S65
CAMPOLONGO A.,"EUROPEAN INVESTMENT BANK* ACTIVITY AND PROSPECTS." FUT ECO/UNDEV FINAN PLAN DIPLOM ...STAT EEC LOAN EIB. PAGE 21 F0410
ECO/TAC PREDICT

S65
MUNZI U.,"THE EUROPEAN SOCIAL FUND IN THE DEVELOPMENT OF THE MEDITERRANEAN REGIONS OF THE EEC." FUT GREECE ITALY PORTUGAL SPAIN TURKEY WORKER TEC/DEV ECO/TAC REGION...STAT EEC. PAGE 95 F1862
ECO/UNDEV PREDICT RECORD

N65
STUDY GP CREATE RESERVE ASSETS,REPORT TO DEPUTIES (PAMPHLET). AFR FUT PLAN CONTROL DEMAND WEALTH ...ANTHOL METH 20. PAGE 127 F2507
INT/ORG INT/TRADE FINAN BUDGET

B66
HEVESY P.D.,THE UNIFICATION OF THE WORLD. FUT USA+45 WOR+45 ECO/DEV ECO/UNDEV LEGIS PROB/SOLV BAL/PWR ECO/TAC INT/TRADE PEACE. PAGE 59 F1160
DIPLOM FINAN INT/ORG

B66
NATIONAL INDUSTRIAL CONF BOARD,GOLD AND WORLD MONETARY PROBLEMS. AFR FUT WOR+45 PROB/SOLV BUDGET INT/TRADE PAY GOV/REL...POLICY ANTHOL 20. PAGE 97 F1902
FINAN ECO/TAC PRICE BAL/PAY

B66
RUPPENTHAL K.M.,TRANSPORTATION AND TOMORROW. FUT SPACE USA+45 SEA AIR FORCES TEC/DEV INT/TRADE ...ANTHOL 20 RAILROAD. PAGE 115 F2261
DIST/IND PLAN CIVMIL/REL PREDICT

B66
THEIL H.,APPLIED ECONOMIC FORECASTING. UNIV USA+45 ELITES INTELL CONSULT PRODUC...DECISION MGT PREDICT CHARTS METH/COMP SIMUL 20. PAGE 129 F2552
FUT OP/RES PLAN

B66
THOMPSON J.H.,MODERNIZATION OF THE ARAB WORLD. FUT ISRAEL STRUCT ECO/UNDEV DIPLOM INGP/REL ATTIT ...CENSUS ANTHOL 20 ARABS. PAGE 130 F2565
ADJUST ISLAM PROB/SOLV NAT/COMP

L66
CHENERY H.B.,"FOREIGN ASSISTANCE AND ECONOMIC DEVELOPMENT" FUT WOR+45 NAT/G DIPLOM GIVE PRODUC ...METH/CNCPT CHARTS 20. PAGE 24 F0464
FOR/AID EFFICIENCY ECO/UNDEV TEC/DEV

S66
DUROSELLE J.B.,"THE FUTURE OF THE ATLANTIC COMMUNITY." EUR+WWI USA+45 USSR NAT/G CAP/ISM REGION DETER NUC/PWR ATTIT MARXISM...INT/LAW 20 NATO. PAGE 35 F0686
FUT DIPLOM MYTH POLICY

S66
LAURENS H.,"LES PAYS OCCIDENTAUX ET LE MARCHE CHINOIS." EUR+WWI FUT S/ASIA AGRI INDUS VOL/ASSN ECO/TAC BAL/PAY...RECORD PREDICT TREATY. PAGE 76 F1488
ASIA INT/TRADE TREND STAT

S66
LINDBLOOM C.E.,"HAS INDIA AN ECONOMIC FUTURE?" FUT INDIA NAT/G PROB/SOLV...POLICY 20. PAGE 80 F1568
AGRI PRODUC PLAN ECO/UNDEV

B67
BARANSON J.,TECHNOLOGY FOR UNDERDEVELOPED AREAS: AN ANNOTATED BIBLIOGRAPHY. FUT WOR+45 CULTURE INDUS INT/ORG CREATE PROB/SOLV INT/TRADE EDU/PROP AUTOMAT ...CONCPT METH. PAGE 10 F0181
BIBLIOG/A ECO/UNDEV TEC/DEV R+D

B67
DE JOUVENAL B.,THE ART OF CONJECTURE. WOR+45 EFFICIENCY PERCEPT KNOWL...DECISION PHIL/SCI CONCPT METH/COMP BIBLIOG 20. PAGE 31 F0600
FUT PREDICT SIMUL METH

B67
ELDREDGE H.W.,TAMING MEGALOPOLIS; WHAT IT IS AND WHAT COULD BE (VOL. I). FUT USA+45 WOR+45 SOCIETY STRUCT ECO/DEV INDUS LEISURE WEALTH...ANTHOL MUNICH. PAGE 37 F0717
PROB/SOLV PLAN TEC/DEV

B67
ESTEY M.,THE UNIONS: STRUCTURE, DEVELOPMENT, AND MANAGEMENT. FUT USA+45 ADJUD CONTROL INGP/REL DRIVE ...DECISION T 20 AFL/CIO. PAGE 38 F0750
LABOR EX/STRUC ADMIN GOV/REL

B67
HEILBRONER R.L.,THE LIMITS OF AMERICAN CAPITALISM. FUT ECO/DEV INDUS LG/CO EX/STRUC LEAD PWR TECHRACY 20. PAGE 58 F1137
ELITES CREATE TEC/DEV CAP/ISM

B67
LISS S.B.,THE CANAL, ASPECTS OF UNITED STATES-PANAMANIAN RELATIONS. AFR FUT PANAMA DOMIN COERCE ATTIT SOVEREIGN MARXISM 20 JOHNSON/LB KENNEDY/JF. PAGE 81 F1580
DIPLOM POLICY

B67
MURTY B.S.,PROPAGANDA AND WORLD PUBLIC ORDER. FUT WOR+45 COM/IND INT/ORG PROB/SOLV ATTIT KNOWL ORD/FREE...POLICY UN. PAGE 95 F1868
EDU/PROP DIPLOM CONTROL JURID

B67
UNIVERSAL REFERENCE SYSTEM,PUBLIC POLICY AND THE MANAGEMENT OF SCIENCE (VOLUME IX). FUT SPACE WOR+45 LAW NAT/G TEC/DEV CONTROL NUC/PWR GOV/REL ...COMPUT/IR GEN/METH. PAGE 133 F2618
BIBLIOG/A POLICY MGT PHIL/SCI

B67
WALLBANK T.W.,CIVILIZATION PAST AND PRESENT (3RD ED.). FUT WOR+45 WOR-45 SOCIETY...SOC CONCPT TIME/SEQ CHARTS BIBLIOG T. PAGE 143 F2809
CULTURE STRUCT TREND

B67
WISEMAN H.V.,BRITAIN AND THE COMMONWEALTH. EUR+WWI FUT UK ECO/DEV POL/PAR TEC/DEV INT/TRADE LEAD ROLE SOVEREIGN...SOC TREND 20 CMN/WLTH. PAGE 148 F2911
INT/ORG DIPLOM NAT/G NAT/COMP

L67
GREGORY A.J.,"AFRICAN SOCIALISM, SOCIALISM AND FASCISM: AN APPRAISAL." FUT LEAD REV GP/REL RACE/REL NAT/LISM ATTIT...IDEA/COMP STERTYP 20. PAGE 51 F0993
FASCISM MARXISM SOCISM AFR

L67
MIXON J.,"JANE JACOBS AND THE LAW - ZONING FOR DIVERSITY EXAMINED." FUT USA+45 CONSTN NEIGH PROB/SOLV CONTROL CT/SYS PARTIC ATTIT...POLICY CENSUS METH/COMP MUNICH. PAGE 92 F1810
IDEA/COMP PLAN LAW

L67
SCHNEIDER C.W.,"REFORM OF THE FEDERAL SECURITIES LAWS." FUT USA+45 LAW FINAN INDUS DELIB/GP ACT/RES PROB/SOLV GP/REL. PAGE 117 F2304
NAT/G LG/CO ADMIN CONTROL

S67
AUBERT DE LA RUE P.,"PERSPECTIVES ECONOMIQUES ENTRE LES ETATS-UNIS ET L'EUROPE." FUT INDUS R+D INT/ORG ACT/RES ECO/TAC AGREE BAL/PAY PRODUC...CHARTS 20 EEC GATT WORLD/BANK. PAGE 7 F0138
INT/TRADE ECO/DEV FINAN TARIFFS

S67
BARAN P.,"THE FUTURE COMPUTER UTILITY." USA+45 NAT/G PLAN CONTROL COST...POLICY 20. PAGE 9 F0177
COMPUTER UTIL FUT TEC/DEV

S67
BENN W.,"TECHNOLOGY HAS AN INEXORABLE EFFECT." FUT UK ECO/DEV INT/ORG CONSULT PLAN EDU/PROP ADMIN LEAD GP/REL PRODUC...INT 20 EEC. PAGE 13 F0246
R+D LG/CO TEC/DEV INDUS

S67
GRAHAM R.,"BRAZIL'S DILEMMA." BRAZIL FUT L/A+17C NAT/G CHIEF PROB/SOLV ECO/TAC PWR 20. PAGE 50 F0972
ECO/UNDEV CONSTN POL/PAR POLICY

S67
KELLY F.K.,"A PROPOSAL FOR AN ANNUAL REPORT ON THE STATE OF MANKIND." FUT INTELL COM/IND INT/ORG CREATE PROB/SOLV PERS/REL...CONCPT 20 UN. PAGE 70 F1371
SOCIETY UNIV ATTIT NEW/IDEA

S67
PERKINS D.H.,"ECONOMIC GROWTH IN CHINA AND THE CULTURAL REVOLUTION(1960APRIL 1967)" CHINA/COM FUT AGRI INDUS PLAN LEAD MARXISM...CHARTS 20 MAO. PAGE 105 F2062
ECO/TAC CULTURE REV ECO/UNDEV

S67
SHERWOOD W.B.,"THE RISE OF THE JUSTICE PARTY IN TURKEY." FUT TURKEY LEAD ATTIT 20. PAGE 121 F2378
POL/PAR ECO/UNDEV STRUCT SOCIETY

B82
CUNNINGHAM W.,THE GROWTH OF ENGLISH INDUSTRY AND
INDUS

COMMERCE. FUT UK FINAN NAT/G CAP/ISM...POLICY 20 MERCANTLST CHRISTIAN POPE. PAGE 29 F0562 — INT/TRADE SML/CO CONSERVE

FUTURE....SEE FUT

FYFE J. F0879

G

GABLE R.W. F0492,F0880

GABON....SEE ALSO AFR

B64
WITHERELL J.W.,OFFICIAL PUBLICATIONS OF FRENCH EQUATORIAL AFRICA, FRENCH CAMEROONS, AND TOGO, 1946-1958 (PAMPHLET). CAMEROON CHAD FRANCE GABON TOGO LAW ECO/UNDEV EXTR/IND INT/TRADE...GEOG HEAL 20. PAGE 148 F2913 — BIBLIOG/A AFR NAT/G ADMIN

GALBRAITH J.K. F0881,F0882,F0883,F0884

GALBRAITH V. F0885

GALBRTH/JK....JOHN KENNETH GALBRAITH

GALENSON W. F0886,F0887,F0888,F0889

GAMARNIKOW M. F0890

GAMBIA....SEE ALSO AFR

B55
PEDLER F.J.,ECONOMIC GEOGRAPHY OF WEST AFRICA. GAMBIA NIGER SIER/LEONE STRATA EXTR/IND MARKET LABOR INT/TRADE DEMAND HABITAT WEALTH...CHARTS 20. PAGE 104 F2046 — ECO/UNDEV GEOG PRODUC EFFICIENCY

B61
CARNEY D.E.,GOVERNMENT AND ECONOMY IN BRITISH WEST AFRICA. GAMBIA GHANA NIGERIA SIER/LEONE DOMIN ADMIN GOV/REL SOVEREIGN WEALTH LAISSEZ...BIBLIOG 20 CMN/WLTH. PAGE 21 F0417 — METH/COMP COLONIAL ECO/TAC ECO/UNDEV

GAMBLE S.D. F0891

GAMBLE....SPECULATION ON AN UNCERTAIN EVENT

S59
HARING J.E.,"UTILITY THEORY, DECISION THEORY, AND PROFIT MAXIMIZATION." PROB/SOLV GAMBLE UTIL ...DECISION CHARTS IDEA/COMP HYPO/EXP SIMUL GEN/METH. PAGE 55 F1083 — PROBABIL RISK GAME

S67
SCHELLING T.C.,"ECONOMICS AND CRIMINAL ENTERPRISE." LAW FORCES BARGAIN ECO/TAC CONTROL GAMBLE ROUTINE ADJUST DEMAND INCOME PROFIT CRIMLGY. PAGE 116 F2295 — CRIME PROB/SOLV CONCPT

GAMBLING....SEE RISK, GAMBLE

GAME....GAME THEORY AND DECISION THEORY IN MODELS

N19
MASCHLER M.,STABLE PAYOFF CONFIGURATIONS FOR QUOTA GAMES (PAMPHLET). PLAN PERS/REL 20. PAGE 87 F1694 — ECOMETRIC GAME COMPUTER DECISION

N19
MIYASAWA K.,AN ECONOMIC SURVIVAL GAME (PAMPHLET). COST DEMAND EQUILIB INCOME PROFIT 20. PAGE 92 F1811 — ECOMETRIC GAME ECO/TAC DECISION

B54
RICHTER R.,DAS KONKURRENZ PROBLEM IM OLIGOPOL. LG/CO BARGAIN PRICE COST...CONCPT 20 MONOPOLY. PAGE 111 F2188 — CONTROL GAME ECO/TAC GP/REL

L56
SCHELLING T.C.,"AN ESSAY ON BARGAINING" (BMR)" OP/RES PROB/SOLV PRICE CHOOSE PWR...DECISION MODELS 20. PAGE 116 F2294 — BARGAIN MARKET ECO/TAC GAME

S56
HARSANYI J.C.,"APPROACHES TO THE BARGAINING PROBLEM BEFORE AND AFTER THE THEORY OF GAMES."...DECISION CON/ANAL SIMUL GEN/LAWS. PAGE 56 F1096 — NEW/IDEA GAME IDEA/COMP

S57
DETAMBEL M.H.,"PROBABILITY AND WORK AS DETERMINERS OF MULTICHOICE BEHAVIOR." PLAN TASK EFFICIENCY ...DECISION GAME. PAGE 32 F0622 — HYPO/EXP PROB/SOLV GEN/LAWS PROBABIL

S58
FOLDES L.,"UNCERTAINTY, PROBABILITY AND POTENTIAL SURPRISE." MARKET PROB/SOLV RISK PERSON...DECISION MGT HYPO/EXP GAME. PAGE 42 F0820 — PROBABIL ADMIN ROUTINE

B59
CONTY J.M.,PSYCHOLOGIE DE LA DECISION....PSY GAME 20. PAGE 27 F0528 — DECISION PROB/SOLV OP/RES METH/COMP

B59
KARLIN S.,MATHEMATICAL METHODS AND THEORY IN GAMES, PROGRAMMING, AND ECONOMICS. COMPUTER PLAN CONTROL TASK...MATH 20. PAGE 69 F1357 — GAME METH/COMP ACT/RES DECISION

B59
SHUBIK M.,STRATEGY AND MARKET STRUCTURE: COMPETITION, OLIGOPOLY, AND THE THEORY OF GAMES. ELITES STRUCT MARKET OP/RES EXEC EFFICIENCY INCOME ...MGT MATH STAT CHARTS 20. PAGE 121 F2389 — ECO/DEV ECO/TAC DECISION GAME

S59
CYERT R.M.,"MODELS IN A BEHAVIORAL THEORY OF THE FIRM." ROUTINE...DECISION MGT METH/CNCPT MATH. PAGE 29 F0567 — SIMUL GAME PREDICT INDUS

S59
HARING J.E.,"UTILITY THEORY, DECISION THEORY, AND PROFIT MAXIMIZATION." PROB/SOLV GAMBLE UTIL ...DECISION CHARTS IDEA/COMP HYPO/EXP SIMUL GEN/METH. PAGE 55 F1083 — PROBABIL RISK GAME

B60
MORRIS W.T.,ENGINEERING ECONOMY. AUTOMAT RISK RATIONAL...PROBABIL STAT CHARTS GAME SIMUL BIBLIOG T 20. PAGE 94 F1838 — OP/RES DECISION MGT PROB/SOLV

S61
HIRSHLEIFER J.,"THE BAYESIAN APPROACH TO STATISTICAL DECISION: AN EXPOSITION." OP/RES PROB/SOLV UTIL...PROBABIL CHARTS IDEA/COMP HYPO/EXP 20. PAGE 60 F1178 — DECISION GAME SIMUL STAT

S61
SHUBIK M.,"APPROACHES TO THE STUDY OF DECISION-MAKING RELEVANT TO THE FIRM." INDUS COMPUTER OP/RES ...PROBABIL STAT 20. PAGE 121 F2390 — GAME DECISION MGT SIMUL

B62
BRANCH M.C.,THE CORPORATE PLANNING PROCESS. FINAN EX/STRUC EDU/PROP CONTROL LEAD GP/REL PERS/REL RATIONAL PERCEPT...MGT MATH PROBABIL STAT GAME. PAGE 18 F0338 — PROF/ORG PLAN DECISION PERSON

S62
LIPSON H.A.,"FORMAL REASONING AND MARKETING STRATEGY." ECO/DEV PROB/SOLV PRICE ALL/VALS CONT/OBS. PAGE 81 F1578 — MARKET DECISION GAME ECO/TAC

B64
BLAKE R.R.,MANAGING INTERGROUP CONFLICT IN INDUSTRY. INDUS DELIB/GP EX/STRUC GP/REL PERS/REL GAME. PAGE 16 F0297 — CREATE PROB/SOLV OP/RES ADJUD

B64
JUSTER F.T.,ANTICIPATIONS AND PURCHASES; AN ANALYSIS OF CONSUMER BEHAVIOR. PROB/SOLV RISK COST PRODUC DRIVE...STAT STYLE SAMP CON/ANAL CHARTS HYPO/EXP GAME SIMUL. PAGE 68 F1345 — PROBABIL DECISION PREDICT DEMAND

S64
BEIM D.,"THE COMMUNIST BLOC AND THE FOREIGN-AID GAME." AFR WOR+45 NAT/G PLAN ROUTINE ATTIT KNOWL ORD/FREE...DECISION QUANT CONT/OBS TIME/SEQ CHARTS GAME SIMUL LOG/LING 20. PAGE 12 F0231 — COM ECO/UNDEV ECO/TAC FOR/AID

B65
BAUMOL W.J.,ECONOMIC THEORY AND OPERATIONS ANALYSIS (2ND ED.). MARKET LG/CO BUDGET PRICE COST EQUILIB PRODUC...DECISION MATH CHARTS GAME 20. PAGE 12 F0219 — OP/RES ECO/DEV METH/COMP STAT

B65
OZGA S.A.,EXPECTATIONS IN ECONOMIC THEORY. MORAL ...ECOMETRIC MATH STAT IDEA/COMP 20. PAGE 102 F2008 — RISK GAME CONCPT PREDICT

S65
BALDWIN D.A.,"THE INTERNATIONAL BANK IN POLITICAL PERSPECTIVE" USA+45 TEC/DEV FOR/AID RENT GIVE COST ...IDEA/COMP GAME IBRD. PAGE 9 F0160 — FINAN INT/ORG

S65
CHU K.,"A DYNAMIC MODEL OF THE FIRM." OP/RES PROB/SOLV...DECISION ECOMETRIC NEW/IDEA STAT GAME ORG/CHARTS SIMUL. PAGE 24 F0472 — INDUS COMPUTER TEC/DEV

S65
GRENIEWSKI H.,"INTENTION AND PERFORMANCE: A PRIMER OF CYBERNETICS OF PLANNING." EFFICIENCY OPTIMAL KNOWL SKILL...DECISION MGT EQULIB. PAGE 51 F0995 — SIMUL GAME GEN/METH PLAN

B66
HEISS K.P.,GAME THEORY AND HUMAN CONFLICTS (RESEARCH MEMORANDUM). UNIV ACT/RES...DECISION SOC MATH PROBABIL SIMUL 20 DEFINETT/B. PAGE 58 F1142 — GAME ECOMETRIC PLAN PROB/SOLV

B66
MANSFIELD E.,MANAGERIAL ECONOMICS AND OPERATIONS RESEARCH; A NONMATHEMATICAL INTRODUCTION. USA+45 — ECO/TAC OP/RES

ELITES ECO/DEV CONSULT EX/STRUC PROB/SOLV ROUTINE EFFICIENCY OPTIMAL...GAME T 20. PAGE 85 F1660 MGT COMPUTER

B67
ALLEN R.G.,MACRO-ECONOMIC THEORY: A MATHEMATICAL TREATMENT. UNIV...SIMUL T. PAGE 4 F0070 ECOMETRIC MATH EQUILIB GAME

B67
COTTAM R.W.,COMPETITIVE INTERFERENCE AND TWENTIETH CENTURY DIPLOMACY. IRAN ACT/RES CREATE PLAN ECO/TAC EFFICIENCY ATTIT...DECISION NEW/IDEA TREND 20 CIA. PAGE 28 F0541 DIPLOM DOMIN GAME

B67
MALINVAUD E.,ACTIVITY ANALYSIS IN THE THEORY OF GROWTH AND PLANNING. UNIV AGRI COMPUTER OP/RES REGION...CHARTS ANTHOL METH. PAGE 84 F1648 MATH GAME SIMUL

S67
LEMIEUX V.,"LA DIMENSION POLITIQUE DE L'ACTION RATIONNELLE." CONTROL GP/REL PERS/REL...DECISION NEW/IDEA GAME 20. PAGE 77 F1518 GEN/LAWS RATIONAL PWR

GANDHI M.K. F0892

GANDHI/I....MME. INDIRA GANDHI

GANDHI/M....MAHATMA GANDHI

B59
MADHOK B.,POLITICAL TRENDS IN INDIA. INDIA PAKISTAN UK STRATA ECO/UNDEV POL/PAR LEGIS CAP/ISM DIPLOM COLONIAL CHOOSE MARXISM...SOC TREND 20 GANDHI/M NEHRU/J. PAGE 84 F1639 GEOG NAT/G

B59
MARTIN K.,WAR, HISTORY, AND HUMAN NATURE. FRANCE GERMANY INDIA UK UNIV POL/PAR COLONIAL DETER REV MARXISM PACIFISM...PSY CONCPT PREDICT LENIN/VI GANDHI/M. PAGE 86 F1683 PERSON WAR ATTIT IDEA/COMP

B60
MC CLELLAN G.S.,INDIA. AFR CHINA/COM INDIA CONSTN ELITES STRATA AGRI POL/PAR FOR/AID ARMS/CONT REV MARXISM...CENSUS BIBLIOG 20 GANDHI/M NEHRU/J. PAGE 87 F1712 DIPLOM NAT/G SOCIETY ECO/UNDEV

B63
GANDHI M.K.,THE WAY TO COMMUNAL HARMONY. INDIA MAJORITY RIGID/FLEX ROLE RESPECT 20 GANDHI/M. PAGE 46 F0892 RACE/REL DISCRIM ATTIT ADJUST

GANDILHON J. F0893

GANDOLFI A. F0894

GANGULI B.N. F0895,F0896

GANGULY D.S. F0897

GANZ G. F0898

GAO....THE EMPIRE OF GAO

GARAUDY R. F0899

GARBARINO J.W. F0900

GARDNER L.C. F0901

GARDNER R.N. F0902,F0903,F0904,F0905

GARFIELD P.J. F0906

GARFIELD/J....PRESIDENT JAMES A. GARFIELD

GARIBALD/G....GUISEPPE GARIBALDI

GARNICK D.H. F0907

GARY....GARY, INDIANA

GAS/NATURL....GAS, NATURAL

GATELL F.O. F0908

GATT....GENERAL AGREEMENT ON TARIFFS AND TRADE; SEE ALSO VOL/ASSN, INT/ORG

N
US SUPERINTENDENT OF DOCUMENTS,TARIFF AND TAXATION (PRICE LIST 37). USA+45 LAW INT/TRADE ADJUD ADMIN CT/SYS INCOME OWN...DECISION GATT. PAGE 140 F2754 BIBLIOG/A TAX TARIFFS NAT/G

C50
ELLSWORTH P.T.,"INTERNATIONAL ECONOMY." ECO/DEV ECO/UNDEV FINAN LABOR DIPLOM FOR/AID TARIFFS BAL/PAY EQUILIB NAT/LISM OPTIMAL...INT/LAW 20 ILO GATT. PAGE 37 F0724 BIBLIOG INT/TRADE ECO/TAC INT/ORG

B59
SILCOCK T.H.,THE COMMONWEALTH ECONOMY IN SOUTHEAST ASIA. AFR INDIA MALAYSIA S/ASIA ECO/DEV AGRI LOC/G PLAN TARIFFS COLONIAL BAL/PAY DEMAND...BIBLIOG/A 20 GATT. PAGE 122 F2401 ECO/TAC INT/TRADE RACE/REL DIPLOM

B62
ALEXANDROWICZ C.H.,WORLD ECONOMIC AGENCIES: LAW AND PRACTICE. WOR+45 DIST/IND FINAN LABOR CONSULT INT/TRADE TARIFFS REPRESENT HEALTH...JURID 20 UN GATT EEC OAS ECSC. PAGE 4 F0064 INT/LAW INT/ORG DIPLOM ADJUD

S63
WALKER H.,"THE INTERNATIONAL LAW OF COMMODITY AGREEMENTS." FUT WOR+45 ECO/DEV ECO/UNDEV FINAN INT/ORG NAT/G CONSULT CREATE PLAN ECO/TAC ATTIT PERCEPT...CONCPT GEN/LAWS TOT/POP GATT 20. PAGE 142 F2804 MARKET VOL/ASSN INT/LAW INT/TRADE

B64
MEZERIK A.G.,TRADE, AID AND ECONOMIC DEVELOPMENT. WOR+45 FINAN INDUS MARKET PLAN BAL/PWR BARGAIN FOR/AID TARIFFS EDU/PROP WEALTH...GP/COMP 20 UN GATT IMF IBRD. PAGE 91 F1777 ECO/TAC ECO/DEV INT/ORG INT/TRADE

B64
NEWCOMER H.A.,INTERNATIONAL AIDS TO OVERSEAS INVESTMENTS AND TRADE. ECO/UNDEV TARIFFS PROFIT ...BIBLIOG 20 GATT UN. PAGE 98 F1921 INT/TRADE FINAN DIPLOM FOR/AID

S64
GALBRAITH V.,"JAPAN'S POSITION IN WORLD TRADE." ASIA AGRI INDUS CREATE ECO/TAC LEGIT DRIVE WEALTH ...TREND EEC GATT FOR/TRADE 20 CHINJAP. PAGE 45 F0885 ECO/DEV DELIB/GP

S64
GARDNER R.N.,"GATT AND THE UNITED NATIONS CONFERENCE ON TRADE AND DEVELOPMENT." USA+45 WOR+45 SOCIETY ECO/UNDEV MARKET NAT/G DELIB/GP ACT/RES PLAN ECO/TAC TARIFFS EDU/PROP ROUTINE DRIVE RIGID/FLEX WEALTH...DECISION MGT TREND UN TOT/POP 20 GATT. PAGE 46 F0905 INT/ORG INT/TRADE

B66
MEERHAEGHE M.,INTERNATIONAL ECONOMIC INSTITUTIONS. EUR+WWI FINAN INDUS MARKET PLAN TARIFFS BAL/PAY EQUILIB...POLICY BIBLIOG/A 20 GATT OEEC EEC IBRD EURCOALSTL. PAGE 89 F1745 ECO/TAC ECO/DEV INT/TRADE INT/ORG

S66
ANGELL J.W.,"THE LONGER RUN PROSPECTS FOR THE US BALANCE OF PAYMENTS." USA+45 DIPLOM FOR/AID RATION ORD/FREE WEALTH...IDEA/COMP GATT. PAGE 6 F0104 BAL/PAY ECO/TAC INT/TRADE FINAN

S66
FELD W.,"EXTERNAL RELATIONS OF THE COMMON MARKET AND GROUP LEADERSHIP ATTITUDES IN THE MEMBER STATES." COM USA+45 ELITES AGRI NAT/G ATTIT...OBS EEC GATT. PAGE 40 F0776 DIPLOM CENTRAL TARIFFS INT/TRADE

B67
JOHNSON H.G.,ECONOMIC POLICY TOWARD LESS DEVELOPED COUNTRIES. USA+45 ECO/DEV INT/ORG PLAN CAP/ISM FOR/AID TARIFFS GIVE WEALTH...NEW/IDEA CHARTS 20 UN GATT. PAGE 67 F1327 ECO/UNDEV ECO/TAC METH/COMP

L67
MEIER G.M.,"UNCTAD PROPOSALS FOR INTERNATIONAL ECONOMIC REFORM." WOR+45 MARKET INT/ORG TARIFFS CONFER UN GATT IMF. PAGE 89 F1749 INT/TRADE FINAN INT/LAW ECO/UNDEV

S67
AUBERT DE LA RUE P.,"PERSPECTIVES ECONOMIQUES ENTRE LES ETATS-UNIS ET L'EUROPE." FUT INDUS R+D INT/ORG ACT/RES ECO/TAC AGREE BAL/PAY PRODUC...CHARTS 20 EEC GATT WORLD/BANK. PAGE 7 F0138 INT/TRADE ECO/DEV FINAN TARIFFS

S67
SMALL A.H.,"THE EFFECT OF TARIFF REDUCTIONS ON US IMPORT VOLUME." USA+45 INT/ORG NAT/G DIPLOM CONFER DEMAND...POLICY INT/LAW STAT CHARTS GATT EEC. PAGE 123 F2424 TARIFFS INT/TRADE PRICE ECO/TAC

GAUS J.M. F0909

GAUSE M.E. F0910

GAUSSENS J. F0911

GEARY R.C. F0912

GEARY....GEARY ACT

GEERTZ C. F0913

GEIGER T. F0509

GEISS I. F0914

GEN/DYNMCS....GENERAL DYNAMICS CORPORATION

GEN/ELCTRC....GENERAL ELECTRIC CO.

GEN/LAWS....SYSTEMS AND APPROACHES BASED ON SUBSTANTIVE RELATIONS

GEN/METH....SYSTEMS BASED ON METHODOLGY

GEN/MOTORS....GENERAL MOTORS CORPORATION

GENACCOUNT....GENERAL ACCOUNTING OFFICE

S56
MILNE R.S.,"CONTROL OF GOVERNMENT CORPORATIONS IN THE UNITED STATES." USA+45 NAT/G CHIEF LEGIS BUDGET 20 GENACCOUNT. PAGE 92 F1800 — CONTROL EX/STRUC GOV/REL PWR

GENERAL AGREEMENT ON TARIFFS AND TRADE....SEE GATT

GENERAL AND COMPLETE DISARMAMENT....SEE ARMS/CONT

GENERAL DYNAMICS CORPORATION....SEE GEN/DYNMCS

GENERAL ELECTRIC COMPANY....SEE GEN/ELCTRC

GENERAL MOTORS CORPORATION....SEE GEN/MOTORS

GENEVA/CON....GENEVA CONFERENCES (ANY OR ALL)

GEOG....DEMOGRAPHY AND GEOGRAPHY

B
BRITISH COMMONWEALTH BUR AGRI,WORLD AGRICULTURAL ECONOMICS AND RURAL SOCIOLOGY ABSTRACTS. NAT/G OP/RES PLAN TEC/DEV LEAD PRODUC...GEOG MGT NAT/COMP 20. PAGE 18 F0354 — BIBLIOG/A AGRI SOC WORKER

N
DOCUMENTATION ECONOMIQUE: REVUE BIBLIOGRAPHIQUE DE SYNTHESE. WOR+45 COM/IND FINAN BUDGET DIPLOM...GEOG 20. PAGE 1 F0004 — BIBLIOG/A SOC

N
SCIENTIFIC COUNCIL FOR AFRICA,INVENTORY OF ECONOMIC STUDIES CONCERNING AFRICA SOUTH OF THE SAHARA. AFR ...PHIL/SCI 20. PAGE 118 F2327 — BIBLIOG/A GEOG ECO/UNDEV

N
UNIVERSITY OF FLORIDA,CARIBBEAN ACQUISITIONS: MATERIALS ACQUIRED BY THE UNIVERSITY OF FLORIDA 1957-1960. L/A+17C...ART/METH GEOG MGT 20. PAGE 133 F2620 — BIBLIOG ECO/UNDEV EDU/PROP JURID

N
US LIBRARY OF CONGRESS,SOUTHERN ASIA ACCESSIONS LIST. BURMA CEYLON INDIA NEPAL PAKISTAN S/ASIA THAILAND AGRI INDUS SCHOOL WORKER...ART/METH GEOG HEAL PHIL/SCI LING 20. PAGE 137 F2710 — BIBLIOG/A SOCIETY CULTURE ECO/UNDEV

N19
FRANCK P.G.,AFGHANISTAN BETWEEN EAST AND WEST: THE ECONOMICS OF COMPETITIVE COEXISTENCE (PAMPHLET). AFGHANISTN USA+45 USA-45 USSR INDUS ECO/TAC INT/TRADE CONTROL NEUTRAL ORD/FREE MARXISM...GEOG 20 UN. PAGE 43 F0842 — FOR/AID PLAN DIPLOM ECO/UNDEV

N19
MEZERIK A.G.,ECONOMIC AID FOR UNDERDEVELOPED COUNTRIES (PAMPHLET). AFR USSR WOR+45 FINAN LG/CO DELIB/GP NUC/PWR...GEOG CENSUS CHARTS 20 UN THIRD/WRLD. PAGE 90 F1775 — FOR/AID ECO/UNDEV DIPLOM POLICY

N19
MUSHKIN S.J.,LOCAL SCHOOL EXPENDITURES: 1970 PROJECTIONS (PAMPHLET). FUT USA+45 CONSTRUC FINAN PROVS EDU/PROP COST...GEOG CENSUS PREDICT CHARTS SIMUL 20. PAGE 95 F1871 — LOC/G SCHOOL BUDGET

N19
PEGRUM D.F.,URBAN TRANSPORT AND THE LOCATION OF INDUSTRY IN METROPOLITAN LOS ANGELES (PAMPHLET). USA+45 WORKER...GEOG CHARTS MUNICH. PAGE 104 F2049 — DIST/IND REGION INDUS

B20
BUCK S.J.,THE AGRARIAN CRUSADE: A CHRONICLE OF THE FARMER IN POLITICS. USA-45 INDUS PROB/SOLV PWR WEALTH...GEOG CENSUS 19/20 GREENBACK GRANGE SILVER. PAGE 20 F0381 — AGRI POPULISM VOL/ASSN POL/PAR

B22
VON ENGELIN O.D.,INHERITING THE EARTH, THE GEOGRAPHICAL FACTOR IN NATIONAL DEVELOPMENT. WOR-45 CULTURE DIPLOM BIO/SOC HABITAT PERSON...PSY SOC CONCPT IDEA/COMP. PAGE 142 F2791 — INGP/REL GEOG SOCIETY ROLE

B26
MCPHEE A.,THE ECONOMIC REVOLUTION IN BRITISH WEST AFRICA. AFR UK CULTURE DIST/IND FINAN INDUS PLAN GP/REL RACE/REL 20 AFRICA/W. PAGE 88 F1735 — ECO/UNDEV INT/TRADE COLONIAL GEOG

B30
THOMPSON W.R.,POPULATION PROBLEMS. FUT UNIV WOR-45 STRUCT DIST/IND ACT/RES ECO/TAC BIO/SOC...CONCPT OBS TIME/SEQ TOT/POP 20. PAGE 130 F2567 — ECO/UNDEV GEOG

B37
UNION OF SOUTH AFRICA,REPORT CONCERNING ADMINISTRATION OF SOUTH WEST AFRICA (6 VOLS.). SOUTH/AFR INDUS PUB/INST FORCES LEGIS BUDGET DIPLOM EDU/PROP ADJUD CT/SYS...GEOG CHARTS 20 AFRICA/SW LEAGUE/NAT. PAGE 132 F2610 — NAT/G ADMIN COLONIAL CONSTN

B38
CARVALHO C.M.,GEOGRAPHIA HUMANA; POLITICA E ECONOMICA (3RD ED.). BRAZIL CULTURE AGRI INDUS DIPLOM COLONIAL GP/REL RACE/REL...LING 20 RESOURCE/N. PAGE 22 F0424 — GEOG HABITAT

B40
GAUS J.M.,PUBLIC ADMINISTRATION AND THE UNITED STATES DEPARTMENT OF AGRICULTURE. USA-45 STRUCT DIST/IND FINAN MARKET EX/STRUC PROB/SOLV GIVE PRODUC...POLICY GEOG CHARTS 20 DEPT/AGRI. PAGE 47 F0909 — ADMIN AGRI DELIB/GP OP/RES

S41
MUKERJEE R.,"POPULATION THEORY AND POLITICS (BMR)" WOR-45 NAT/G PLAN PROB/SOLV ECO/TAC INT/TRADE CONTROL WAR PEACE...CENSUS 20 BIRTH/CON RESOURCE/N. PAGE 94 F1854 — GEOG OPTIMAL CONCPT

B47
ISAAC J.,ECONOMICS OF MIGRATION. MOD/EUR CULTURE STRATA STRUCT NAT/G COLONIAL WEALTH...OLD/LIB TREND TIME 19/20 EUROPE/W MIGRATION. PAGE 65 F1289 — HABITAT SOC GEOG

B47
MILLETT J.D.,THE PROCESS AND ORGANIZATION OF GOVERNMENT PLANNING. USA+45 DELIB/GP ACT/RES LEAD LOBBY TASK...POLICY GEOG TIME 20 RESOURCE/N. PAGE 91 F1793 — ADMIN NAT/G PLAN CONSULT

B48
HOOVER E.M.,THE LOCATION OF ECONOMIC ACTIVITY. WOR+45 MARKET WORKER PROB/SOLV INT/TRADE ADMIN COST ...POLICY CHARTS T MUNICH 20. PAGE 62 F1211 — HABITAT INDUS ECO/TAC GEOG

B48
OSBORN F.,OUR PLUNDERED PLANET. UNIV DEATH WAR ...BIBLIOG RESOURCE/N. PAGE 102 F2001 — HABITAT GEOG ADJUST AGRI

B48
WHITE C.L.,HUMAN GEOGRAPHY: AN ECOLOGICAL STUDY OF GEOGRAPHY. UNIV SEA CULTURE AGRI EXTR/IND RACE/REL PRODUC...CHARTS HYPO/EXP SIMUL GEN/LAWS T. PAGE 146 F2868 — SOC HABITAT GEOG SOCIETY

B49
PARMELEE M.,GEO-ECONOMIC REGIONAL AND WORLD FEDERATION. FUT WOR+45 WOR-45 SOCIETY VOL/ASSN PLAN ...METH/CNCPT SIMUL GEN/METH TERR/GP TOT/POP 20. PAGE 103 F2028 — INT/ORG GEOG REGION

B49
PELZER K.J.,SELECTED BIBLIOGRAPHY ON THE GEOGRAPHY OF SOUTHEAST ASIA (3 VOLS., 1949-1956). PHILIPPINE CULTURE...SOC 20 MALAYA. PAGE 104 F2053 — BIBLIOG S/ASIA GEOG

B49
US DEPARTMENT OF STATE,SOVIET BIBLIOGRAPHY (PAMPHLET). CHINA/COM COM USSR LAW AGRI INT/ORG ECO/TAC EDU/PROP...POLICY GEOG IND 20. PAGE 135 F2670 — BIBLIOG/A MARXISM CULTURE DIPLOM

S51
HAWLEY A.H.,"METROPOLITAN POPULATION AND MUNICIPAL GOVERNMENT EXPENDITURES IN CENTRAL CITIES" (BMR)" USA+45 FINAN TAX...STAT CON/ANAL CHARTS MUNICH 20. PAGE 57 F1117 — GEOG LOC/G COST BUDGET

B52
SURANYI-UNGER T.,COMPARATIVE ECONOMIC SYSTEMS. FINAN MARKET DIPLOM PRICE WEALTH...GEOG SOC BIBLIOG METH T 20. PAGE 128 F2517 — LAISSEZ PLAN ECO/DEV IDEA/COMP

S52
HEBERLE R.,"ON POLITICAL ECOLOGY" (BMR)" INCOME ATTIT WEALTH...GEOG METH SOC/INTEG 20. PAGE 58 F1133 — HABITAT STRATA CHOOSE

B53
WOYTINSKY W.S.,WORLD POPULATION AND PRODUCTION: TRENDS AND OUTLOOK. FUT WOR+45 WOR-45 CULTURE SOCIETY ECO/DEV AGRI INDUS TEC/DEV EDU/PROP SKILL WEALTH...SOC TREND. PAGE 149 F2928 — ECO/UNDEV METH/CNCPT GEOG PERSON

S53
HANSER P.M.,"EXPLODING POPULATIONS: INTERNATIONAL AND REGIONAL ASPECTS." AFR S/ASIA ECO/TAC WEAPON BIO/SOC LOVE ORD/FREE...NEW/IDEA CENSUS TOT/POP 20. PAGE 55 F1069 — ECO/UNDEV GEOG

B54
BATTEN T.R.,PROBLEMS OF AFRICAN DEVELOPMENT (2ND ED.). AFR LAW SOCIETY SCHOOL ECO/TAC TAX...GEOG HEAL SOC 20. PAGE 11 F0211 — ECO/UNDEV AGRI LOC/G PROB/SOLV

B54
O.E.E.C.,PRIVATE UNITED STATES INVESTMENT IN EUROPE AND THE OVERSEAS TERRITORIES. EUR+WWI WOR+45 ECO/DEV ECO/UNDEV INT/ORG NAT/G VOL/ASSN ECO/TAC ATTIT WEALTH...GEOG STAT SYS/QU CHARTS VAL/FREE 20. PAGE 99 F1950 — USA+45 FINAN BAL/PAY FOR/AID

B54
WILLIAMSON H.F.,ECONOMIC DEVELOPMENT - PRINCIPLES AND PATTERNS. INDIA KOREA CULTURE ECO/DEV ECO/UNDEV TEC/DEV...CENSUS NAT/COMP FOR/TRADE 20 CHINJAP MEXIC/AMER RESOURCE/N. PAGE 147 F2895 — ECO/TAC GEOG LABOR

S54
FORM W.H.,"THE PLACE OF SOCIAL STRUCTURE IN THE DETERMINATION OF LAND USE: SOME IMPLICATIONS FOR A THEORY OF URBAN ECOLOGY" (BMR)" STRUCT...GEOG PHIL/SCI SOC MUNICH 20. PAGE 42 F0827
HABITAT MARKET ORD/FREE

B55
FLORINSKY M.T.,INTEGRATED EUROPE. EUR+WWI FRANCE ITALY NETHERLAND UK ECO/DEV INT/ORG FORCES LEGIT FEDERAL ATTIT PWR WEALTH...POLICY GEOG CONCPT GEN/LAWS TOT/POP EEC OEEC 20. PAGE 42 F0816
FUT ECO/TAC REGION

B55
PEDLER F.J.,ECONOMIC GEOGRAPHY OF WEST AFRICA. GAMBIA NIGER SIER/LEONE STRATA EXTR/IND MARKET LABOR INT/TRADE DEMAND HABITAT WEALTH...CHARTS 20. PAGE 104 F2046
ECO/UNDEV GEOG PRODUC EFFICIENCY

B56
ISARD W.,LOCATION AND SPACE-ECONOMY: GENERAL THEORY RELATING TO INDUSTRIAL LOCATION, MARKET AREAS, LAND USE, TRADE... UNIV DIST/IND MARKET LG/CO SML/CO TEC/DEV GP/REL EQUILIB HABITAT...NEW/IDEA MATH CHARTS 20. PAGE 66 F1290
GEN/LAWS GEOG INDUS REGION

B56
WOLFF R.L.,THE BALKANS IN OUR TIME. ALBANIA FUT MOD/EUR USSR YUGOSLAVIA CULTURE INT/ORG SECT DIPLOM EDU/PROP COERCE WAR ORD/FREE...CHARTS 4/20 BALKANS COMINFORM. PAGE 148 F2919
GEOG COM

S56
MARGOLIS J.,"ON MUNICIPAL LAND POLICY FOR FISCAL GAINS." USA+45 PLAN TAX COST EFFICIENCY HABITAT KNOWL...MGT MUNICH 20. PAGE 85 F1667
BUDGET POLICY GEOG LOC/G

S56
SPENGLER J.J.,"POPULATION THREATENS PROSPERITY" (BMR) WOR+45 SOCIETY FINAN RATION COST INCOME ...SOC CHARTS 20 RESOURCE/N. PAGE 124 F2451
CENSUS GEOG WEALTH TREND

B57
BOUSTEDT O.,REGIONALE STRUKTUR- UND WIRTSCHAFTSFORSCHUNG. WOR+45 WOR-45 PROVS...STAT MUNICH. PAGE 17 F0325
GEOG CONCPT NAT/COMP

B57
DRUCKER P.F.,AMERICA'S NEXT TWENTY YEARS. USA+45 DIST/IND ACADEM SCHOOL DIPLOM ECO/TAC AUTOMAT HABITAT HEALTH...SOC/WK TREND MUNICH 20 URBAN/RNWL PUB/TRANS. PAGE 34 F0667
WORKER FOR/AID CENSUS GEOG

B57
OLIVER H.M. JR.,ECONOMIC OPINION AND POLICY IN CEYLON. CEYLON FINAN POL/PAR WORKER INT/TRADE INCOME WEALTH...GEOG UNPLAN/INT BIBLIOG 20 CMN/WLTH. PAGE 101 F1987
ECO/UNDEV NAT/LISM POLICY COLONIAL

B57
PATAI R.,JORDAN, LEBANON AND SYRIA: AN ANNOTATED BIBLIOGRAPHY. ISLAM JORDAN LEBANON SYRIA...GEOG 20. PAGE 103 F2034
BIBLIOG/A SOC

B57
WEIGERT H.W.,PRINCIPLES OF POLITICAL GEOGRAPHY. WOR+45 ECO/DEV ECO/UNDEV SECT ECO/TAC COLONIAL HABITAT...CHARTS T 20. PAGE 144 F2845
GEOG CULTURE

B58
BANCROFT G.,THE AMERICAN LABOR FORCE: ITS GROWTH AND CHANGING COMPOSITION. FUT USA+45 USA-45 ECO/DEV INDUS WORKER...GEOG CHARTS 19/20. PAGE 9 F0170
LABOR STAT TREND CENSUS

B58
BROWN B.,INCOME TRENDS IN THE UNITED STATES THROUGH 1975. USA+45 NAT/G WEALTH...GEOG CENSUS PREDICT CHARTS METH 20. PAGE 19 F0366
STAT INCOME TREND TAX

B58
COALE A.J.,POPULATION GROWTH AND ECONOMIC DEVELOPMENT IN LOW-INCOME COUNTRIES: A CASE STUDY OF INDIA'S PROSPECTS. INDIA AGRI WORKER INCOME AGE WEALTH...CHARTS 20 MEXIC/AMER. PAGE 25 F0495
ECO/UNDEV GEOG CENSUS SEX

B58
INTERNATIONAL ECONOMIC ASSN,ECONOMICS OF INTERNATIONAL MIGRATION. WOR+45 WOR-45 ECO/UNDEV FINAN NAT/G REGION...NAT/COMP METH 20. PAGE 65 F1275
CENSUS GEOG DIPLOM ECO/TAC

B58
MASON J.B.,THAILAND BIBLIOGRAPHY. S/ASIA THAILAND CULTURE EDU/PROP ADMIN...GEOG SOC LING 20. PAGE 87 F1701
BIBLIOG/A ECO/UNDEV DIPLOM NAT/G

B58
MYRDAL G.,RICH LANDS AND POOR: THE ROAD TO WORLD PROSPERITY. FUT WOR+45 WOR-45 ECO/DEV ECO/UNDEV INT/ORG PLAN ECO/TAC REGION...GEOG TIME/SEQ GEN/LAWS TOT/POP 20. PAGE 96 F1880
WEALTH TREND FOR/AID INT/TRADE

B58
TILLION G.,ALGERIA: THE REALITIES. ALGERIA FRANCE ISLAM CULTURE STRATA PROB/SOLV DOMIN REV NAT/LISM WEALTH MARXISM...GEOG 20. PAGE 130 F2573
ECO/UNDEV SOC COLONIAL DIPLOM

S58
THOMAS D.S.,"AGE AND ECONOMIC DIFFERENTIALS IN INTERSTATE MIGRATION." SEX...GEOG SAMP/SIZ TREND CON/ANAL CHARTS BIBLIOG. PAGE 130 F2560
AGE WEALTH HABITAT CENSUS

B59
CHECCHI V.,HONDURAS: A PROBLEM IN ECONOMIC DEVELOPMENT. HONDURAS AGRI FINAN INDUS LABOR WORKER INT/TRADE EDU/PROP PRICE HEALTH...GEOG CHARTS BIBLIOG 20. PAGE 24 F0458
ECO/UNDEV ECO/TAC PROB/SOLV PLAN

B59
HAZLEWOOD A.,THE ECONOMICS OF "UNDER-DEVELOPED" AREAS. WOR+45 DIST/IND EXTR/IND FINAN INDUS MARKET PLAN FOR/AID...GEOG 20. PAGE 57 F1129
BIBLIOG/A ECO/UNDEV AGRI INT/TRADE

B59
MADHOK B.,POLITICAL TRENDS IN INDIA. INDIA PAKISTAN UK STRATA ECO/UNDEV POL/PAR LEGIS CAP/ISM DIPLOM COLONIAL CHOOSE MARXISM...SOC TREND 20 GANDHI/M NEHRU/J. PAGE 84 F1639
GEOG NAT/G

B59
MAYER H.M.,READINGS IN URBAN GEOGRAPHY. WOR+45 SOCIETY DIST/IND INDUS MARKET HABITAT...CLASSIF CENSUS CHARTS ANTHOL MUNICH 20 WATER. PAGE 87 F1706
GEOG STRUCT

B59
ROCHE J.,LA COLONISATION ALLEMANDE ET LE RIO GRANDE DO SUL. BRAZIL L/A+17C NAT/G PROVS INGP/REL RACE/REL DISCRIM HABITAT...GEOG SOC/INTEG 19/20 MIGRATION. PAGE 113 F2228
ECO/UNDEV GP/REL ATTIT

B59
WIBBERLEY G.P.,AGRICULTURE AND URBAN GROWTH. UK USA+45 ECO/DEV FINAN PROB/SOLV INT/TRADE COST ...GEOG STAT CHARTS METH/COMP HYPO/EXP METH MUNICH 20. PAGE 146 F2876
AGRI PLAN

S59
THOMPSON W.S.,"POPULATION AND PROGRESS IN THE FAR EAST." ASIA S/ASIA DIST/IND CREATE ECO/TAC WAR LOVE SKILL WEALTH...CONT/OBS TOT/POP 20. PAGE 130 F2568
ECO/UNDEV BIO/SOC GEOG

C59
MINTZ S.W.,"INTERNAL MARKET SYS AS MECHANISMS OF SOCIAL ARTIC," IN V.F. RAY, INTERMED SOCIETIES, SOCIAL MOBILITY, AND COMMUNIC (BMR). UNIV STRATA GP/REL INGP/REL...GEOG SOC BIBLIOG. PAGE 92 F1804
MARKET SOCIETY ECO/UNDEV STRUCT

B60
AMERICAN U BEIRUT ECO RES INST,A SELECTED AND ANNOTATED BIBLIOGRAPHY OF ECONOMIC LITERATURE ON THE ARABIC SPEAKING COUNTRIES OF THE MIDDLE EAST. ISLAM AGRI COM/IND DIST/IND FINAN INDUS LABOR ...GEOG 20. PAGE 5 F0091
BIBLIOG/A ECO/UNDEV STAT

B60
ASPREMONT-LYNDEN H.,RAPPORT SUR L'ADMINISTRATION BELGE DU RUANDA-URUNDI PENDANT L'ANNEE 1959. BELGIUM RWANDA AGRI INDUS DIPLOM ECO/TAC INT/TRADE DOMIN ADMIN RACE/REL...GEOG CENSUS 20 UN. PAGE 7 F0132
AFR COLONIAL ECO/UNDEV INT/ORG

B60
GONZALEZ NAVARRO M.,LA COLONIZACION EN MEXICO, 1877-1910. AGRI NAT/G PLAN PROB/SOLV INCOME ...POLICY JURID CENSUS 19/20 MEXIC/AMER MIGRATION. PAGE 48 F0947
ECO/UNDEV GEOG HABITAT COLONIAL

B60
HEYSE T.,PROBLEMS FONCIERS ET REGIME DES TERRES (ASPECTS ECONOMIQUES, JURIDIQUES ET SOCIAUX). AFR CONGO/BRAZ INT/ORG DIPLOM SOVEREIGN...GEOG TREATY 20. PAGE 59 F1161
BIBLIOG AGRI ECO/UNDEV LEGIS

B60
HOFFMANN P.G.,ONE HUNDRED COUNTRIES, ONE AND ONE QUARTER BILLION PEOPLE. MARKET INT/ORG TEC/DEV CAP/ISM...GEOG CHARTS METH/COMP 20 UN. PAGE 61 F1191
FOR/AID ECO/TAC ECO/UNDEV INT/TRADE

B60
RAMA C.M.,LAS CLASES SOCIALES EN EL URUGUAY. L/A+17C URUGUAY ELITES SOCIETY STRATA INDUS ATTIT HABITAT PWR...GEOG SOC/INTEG MUNICH 20. PAGE 109 F2138
ECO/UNDEV STRUCT PARTIC

B60
RAPKIN C.,THE DEMAND FOR HOUSING IN RACIALLY MIXED AREAS: A STUDY OF THE NATURE OF NEIGHBORHOOD CHANGE. USA+45 FINAN PRICE COST DRIVE...GEOG 20. PAGE 109 F2151
RACE/REL NEIGH DISCRIM MARKET

B60
ROPKE W.,A HUMANE ECONOMY. CULTURE ECO/DEV FINAN INDUS GP/REL CENTRAL WEALTH...GEOG SOC IDEA/COMP 20 EEC. PAGE 114 F2239
ECO/TAC INT/ORG DIPLOM ORD/FREE

B60
THEOBALD R.,THE RICH AND THE POOR: A STUDY OF THE ECONOMICS OF RISING EXPECTATIONS. WOR+45 CONSTN ECO/DEV ECO/UNDEV INT/ORG NAT/G PLAN FOR/AID ROUTINE BAL/PAY ORD/FREE PWR WEALTH...GEOG TREND WORK FOR/TRADE 20. PAGE 129 F2553
ECO/TAC INT/TRADE

B60
THORBECKE E.,THE TENDENCY TOWARDS REGIONALIZATION IN INTERNATIONAL TRADE, 1928-1956. WOR+45 WOR-45 ECO/DEV FINAN ECO/TAC WEALTH...GEOG CHARTS TOT/POP FOR/TRADE 20. PAGE 130 F2569
STAT BAL/PAY REGION

S60
JAFFEE A.J.,"POPULATION TRENDS AND CONTROLS IN UNDERDEVELOPED COUNTRIES." AFR FUT ISLAM L/A+17C
ECO/UNDEV GEOG

S/ASIA CULTURE R+D FAM ACT/RES PLAN EDU/PROP BIO/SOC RIGID/FLEX HEALTH...SOC STAT OBS CHARTS 20. PAGE 66 F1303

S60
MILLER A.S.,"SOME OBSERVATIONS ON THE POLITICAL ECONOMY OF POPULATION GROWTH." FUT USA+45 ECO/DEV R+D CONSULT PLAN TEC/DEV ECO/TAC ROUTINE BIO/SOC WEALTH...POLICY OBS. PAGE 91 F1790
SOCIETY GEOG

S60
STOCKWELL E.G.,"THE MEASUREMENT OF ECONOMIC DEVELOPMENT." WOR+45 SOCIETY ECO/DEV ECO/UNDEV INDUS ECO/TAC HEALTH WEALTH...WELF/ST GEOG METH/CNCPT CHARTS METH METH/GP 20. PAGE 126 F2492
FAM STAT

N60
COMMITTEE ECONOMIC DEVELOPMENT,GUIDING METROPOLITAN GROWTH (PAMPHLET). USA+45 LOC/G NAT/G PROF/ORG ACT/RES PLAN...SOC/WK MUNICH. PAGE 27 F0517
GEOG INDUS HEALTH

B61
HODGKINS J.A.,SOVIET POWER: ENERGY RESOURCES, PRODUCTION AND POTENTIALS. USSR ECO/DEV INDUS MARKET...POLICY STAT CHARTS 20 RESOURCE/N. PAGE 60 F1188
GEOG EXTR/IND TEC/DEV

B61
LEE R.R.,ENGINEERING-ECONOMIC PLANNING MISCELLANEOUS SUBJECTS: A SELECTED BIBLIOGRAPHY (MIMEOGRAPHED). FINAN LOC/G NEIGH ADMIN CONTROL INGP/REL HABITAT...GEOG MGT SOC/WK MUNICH 20 RESOURCE/N. PAGE 77 F1509
BIBLIOG/A PLAN REGION

B61
PETCH G.A.,ECONOMIC DEVELOPMENT AND MODERN WEST AFRICA. AFR CONGO/BRAZ GHANA NIGER SIER/LEONE AGRI MARKET LABOR FOR/AID TAX COST EFFICIENCY EQUILIB PRODUC...GEOG TREND 20. PAGE 105 F2068
ECO/UNDEV TEC/DEV EXTR/IND ECO/TAC

B61
SCHNAPPER B.,LA POLITIQUE ET LE COMMERCE FRANCAIS DANS LE GOLFE DE GUINEE DE 1838 A 1871. FRANCE GUINEA UK SEA EXTR/IND NAT/G DELIB/GP LEGIS ADMIN ORD/FREE...POLICY GEOG CENSUS CHARTS BIBLIOG 19. PAGE 117 F2303
COLONIAL INT/TRADE DOMIN AFR

S61
LANFALUSSY A.,"EUROPE'S PROGRESS: DUE TO COMMON MARKET." EUR+WWI ECO/DEV DELIB/GP PLAN ECO/TAC ROUTINE WEALTH...GEOG TREND EEC TERR/GP 20. PAGE 75 F1473
INT/ORG MARKET

B62
CARPER E.T.,ILLINOIS GOES TO CONGRESS FOR ARMY LAND. USA+45 LAW EXTR/IND PROVS REGION CIVMIL/REL GOV/REL FEDERAL ATTIT 20 ILLINOIS SENATE CONGRESS DIRKSEN/E DOUGLAS/P. PAGE 22 F0420
ADMIN LOBBY GEOG LEGIS

B62
CHAPIN F.S.,URBAN GROWTH DYNAMICS IN A REGIONAL CLUSTER OF CITIES. TEC/DEV ECO/TAC HABITAT...GEOG SOC MUNICH. PAGE 23 F0453
REGION PLAN

B62
DEBUYST F.,LAS CLASES SOCIALES EN AMERICA LATINA. L/A+17C SOCIETY STRUCT WORKER EDU/PROP RACE/REL ATTIT HABITAT ROLE...GEOG SOC NAT/COMP SOC/INTEG 20. PAGE 32 F0612
STRATA GP/REL WEALTH

B62
FAO,FOOD AND AGRICULTURE ORGANIZATION AFRICAN SURVEY. AFR CONGO/BRAZ GHANA STRATA AGRI INT/ORG TEC/DEV FOR/AID INT/TRADE RACE/REL DEMAND EFFICIENCY PRODUC...GEOG 20 UN CONGO/LEOP. PAGE 39 F0763
ECO/TAC WEALTH EXTR/IND ECO/UNDEV

B62
GREEN L.P.,DEVELOPMENT IN AFRICA. AFR CENTRL/AFR GHANA RHODESIA SOUTH/AFR AGRI PROC/MFG INT/TRADE DEMAND NAT/LISM PRODUC WEALTH...GEOG METH/CNCPT CHARTS BIBLIOG 20. PAGE 50 F0987
CULTURE ECO/UNDEV GOV/REL TREND

B62
MICHAELY M.,CONCENTRATION IN INTERNATIONAL TRADE. ECO/DEV ECO/UNDEV PRICE INCOME...CHARTS NAT/COMP 20. PAGE 91 F1779
INT/TRADE MARKET FINAN GEOG

B62
UNECA LIBRARY,NEW ACQUISITIONS IN THE UNECA LIBRARY. LAW NAT/G PLAN PROB/SOLV TEC/DEV ADMIN REGION...GEOG SOC 20 UN. PAGE 132 F2606
BIBLIOG AFR ECO/UNDEV INT/ORG

B62
US LIBRARY OF CONGRESS,A LIST OF AMERICAN DOCTORAL DISSERTATIONS ON AFRICA. SOCIETY SECT DIPLOM EDU/PROP ADMIN...GEOG 19/20. PAGE 138 F2717
BIBLIOG AFR ACADEM CULTURE

L62
SCHULTZ T.W.,"INVESTMENT IN HUMAN BEINGS." ECO/DEV ECO/TAC CONFER COST INCOME PRODUC HEALTH...GEOG ANTHOL. PAGE 117 F2315
FINAN WORKER EDU/PROP SKILL

S62
MUELLER E.,"LOCATION DECISIONS OF MANUFACTURERS." USA+45 MARKET ATTIT...POLICY STAT INT CHARTS 20. PAGE 94 F1852
DECISION PROC/MFG GEOG TOP/EX

C62
GREEN L.P.,"DEVELOPMENT IN AFRICA." RHODESIA SOUTH/AFR UGANDA MARKET PROC/MFG PRODUC WEALTH ...GEOG 20. PAGE 50 F0986
BIBLIOG ECO/UNDEV AFR AGRI

C62
JOINT ECONOMIC COMMITTEE,"DIMENSIONS OF SOVIET ECONOMIC POWER." USSR R+D FORCES ACT/RES OP/RES TEC/DEV...GEOG STAT BIBLIOG 20. PAGE 68 F1337
ECO/DEV PLAN PRODUC LABOR

B63
ALPERT P.,ECONOMIC DEVELOPMENT. WOR+45 FINAN TEC/DEV ECO/TAC PRICE GOV/REL HABITAT...GEOG BIBLIOG T 20 THIRD/WRLD. PAGE 4 F0079
ECO/DEV ECO/UNDEV INT/TRADE FOR/AID

B63
BARNETT H.J.,SCARCITY AND GROWTH: THE ECONOMICS OF NATURAL RESOURCE AVAILABILITY. FUT WOR+45 AGRI INDUS PROB/SOLV TEC/DEV CONTROL PRODUC...SOC/WK IDEA/COMP METH/COMP SIMUL 20 RESOURCE/N MALTHUS RICARDO/D MILL/JS DARWIN/C. PAGE 10 F0191
DEMAND HABITAT CENSUS GEOG

B63
CHOJNACKI S.,REGISTER ON CURRENT RESEARCH ON ETHIOPIA AND THE HORN OF AFRICA. ETHIOPIA LAW CULTURE AGRI SECT EDU/PROP ADMIN...GEOG HEAL LING 20. PAGE 24 F0470
BIBLIOG ACT/RES INTELL ACADEM

B63
LEWIS G.K.,PUERTO RICO: FREEDOM AND POWER IN THE CARIBBEAN. PUERT/RICO USA+45 CULTURE STRUCT INDUS POL/PAR WORKER EDU/PROP CATHISM 20. PAGE 79 F1548
ECO/UNDEV COLONIAL NAT/LISM GEOG

B63
OTERO L.M.,HONDURAS. HONDURAS SPAIN STRUCT SECT COLONIAL REV WAR ATTIT PWR...GEOG WORSHIP 16/20. PAGE 102 F2003
NAT/G SOCIETY NAT/LISM ECO/UNDEV

B63
SALENT W.S.,THE UNITED STATES BALANCE OF PAYMENTS IN 1968. EUR+WWI UK USA+45 AGRI R+D LABOR FORCES PRODUC...GEOG CONCPT CHARTS 20 CHINJAP EEC. PAGE 115 F2274
BAL/PAY DEMAND FINAN INT/TRADE

B63
STUCKI C.W.,AMERICAN DOCTORAL DISSERTATIONS ON ASIA 1933-62 (A PAPER). PREHIST INDUS NAT/G GOV/REL ALL/IDEOS...ART/METH GEOG SOC LING 20. PAGE 127 F2506
BIBLIOG ASIA SOCIETY S/ASIA

B63
WAGLEY C.,INTRODUCTION TO BRAZIL. BRAZIL L/A+17C FAM KIN SCHOOL SECT ATTIT WEALTH...GEOG SOC. PAGE 142 F2799
ECO/UNDEV ELITES HABITAT STRATA

S63
LOEWENSTEIN L.K.,"THE LOCATION OF URBAN LAND USES." USA+45 LOC/G HABITAT...STAT CHARTS MUNICH 20. PAGE 81 F1595
GEOG PLAN INDUS

S63
STEFANIAK N.J.,"A REFINEMENT OF HAIG'S THEORY." USA+45 INDUS PROB/SOLV TEC/DEV...CONCPT CHARTS MUNICH 20 HAIG. PAGE 125 F2474
GEOG GEN/LAWS PLAN

N63
NORTH CAROLINA U INST GOVT,COSTING URBAN DEVELOPMENT AND REDEVELOPMENT (PAMPHLET). USA+45 USA-45 NEIGH PLAN TEC/DEV TAX OWN...GEOG MUNICH 20. PAGE 98 F1934
BIBLIOG COST FINAN

B64
BEARDSLEY R.K.,STUDIES ON ECONOMIC LIFE IN JAPAN (OCCASIONAL PAPERS NO. 8). INDUS FAM HABITAT...GEOG GOV/COMP 20 CHINJAP. PAGE 12 F0223
WEALTH PRESS PRODUC INCOME

B64
CEPEDE M.,POPULATION AND FOOD. USA+45 STRUCT ECO/UNDEV FAM PLAN TEC/DEV FOR/AID CONTROL...CATH SOC TREND 19/20. PAGE 22 F0436
FUT GEOG AGRI CENSUS

B64
FLORENCE P.S.,ECONOMICS AND SOCIOLOGY OF INDUSTRY; A REALISTIC ANALYSIS OF DEVELOPMENT. ECO/UNDEV LG/CO NAT/G PLAN...GEOG MGT BIBLIOG 20. PAGE 42 F0814
INDUS SOC ADMIN

B64
FRIEDMANN J.,REGIONAL DEVELOPMENT AND PLANNING: A READER. AGRI MARKET NAT/G ECO/TAC INCOME...GEOG STAT CENSUS CHARTS ANTHOL BIBLIOG MUNICH 20 OPEN/SPACE. PAGE 44 F0863
PLAN REGION INDUS ECO/DEV

B64
INTL INF CTR LOCAL CREDIT,GOVERNMENT MEASURES FOR THE PROMOTION OF REGIONAL ECONOMIC DEVELOPMENT. WOR+45 ECO/UNDEV FINAN INT/ORG DIPLOM ORD/FREE ...POLICY GEOG 20. PAGE 65 F1285
FOR/AID PLAN ECO/TAC REGION

B64
LAFONT P.B.,BIBLIOGRAPHIE DU LAOS. LAOS S/ASIA EDU/PROP...GEOG 20. PAGE 74 F1458
BIBLIOG LAW SOC

B64
MYINT H.,THE ECONOMICS OF THE DEVELOPING COUNTRIES. WOR+45 AGRI PLAN COST...POLICY GEOG 20 MONEY. PAGE 96 F1878
ECO/UNDEV INT/TRADE EXTR/IND FINAN

B64
OECD,DEVELOPMENT ASSISTANCE EFFORTS - POLICIES OF THE MEMBERS. AGRI INDUS BUDGET...GEOG NAT/COMP 20 OECD. PAGE 100 F1967
INT/ORG FOR/AID ECO/UNDEV TEC/DEV

B64
RENO P.,THE ORDEAL OF BRITISH GUIANA. L/A+17C USA+45 STRUCT AGRI EXTR/IND INDUS NAT/G FOR/AID ORD/FREE...GEOG 20 GUIANA/BR INTRVN/ECO. PAGE 111 F2178
COLONIAL ECO/UNDEV SOCISM PWR

B64
ROBINSON E.A.G.,ECONOMIC DEVELOPMENT FOR AFRICA SOUTH OF THE SAHARA. AFR AGRI INDUS LABOR BUDGET INT/TRADE PRICE...POLICY GEOG ANTHOL 20. PAGE 113 F2219
ECO/UNDEV ECO/TAC ACT/RES PLAN

B64
SINGER H.W.,INTERNATIONAL DEVELOPMENT: GROWTH AND CHANGE. AFR BRAZIL L/A+17C WOR+45 CULTURE AGRI INDUS NAT/G ACT/RES ECO/TAC EDU/PROP WEALTH...GEOG CONCPT METH/CNCPT STAT HYPO/EXP WORK TOT/POP 20. PAGE 122 F2412
FINAN ECO/UNDEV FOR/AID INT/TRADE

B64
TAEUBER I.B.,POPULATION TRENDS IN THE UNITED STATES: 1900 TO 1960. USA+45 USA-45 PROVS INCOME AGE...SOC TIME/SEQ TREND CHARTS MUNICH TIME 20 NEGRO. PAGE 128 F2522
CENSUS GEOG STRATA STRUCT

B64
WITHERELL J.W.,OFFICIAL PUBLICATIONS OF FRENCH EQUATORIAL AFRICA, FRENCH CAMEROONS, AND TOGO, 1946-1958 (PAMPHLET). CAMEROON CHAD FRANCE GABON TOGO LAW ECO/UNDEV EXTR/IND INT/TRADE...GEOG HEAL 20. PAGE 148 F2913
BIBLIOG/A AFR NAT/G ADMIN

S64
HOOVER C.B.,"THE ROLE OF THE NATURAL AND DEVELOPED RESOURCES OF THE NATION STATES." FUT WOR+45 ECO/DEV ECO/UNDEV NAT/G PWR RESPECT SKILL WEALTH...POLICY GEOG TIME/SEQ TREND RESOURCE/N VAL/FREE 20. PAGE 62 F1210
EXTR/IND DOMIN

S64
READER D.H.,"A SURVEY OF CATEGORIES OF ECONOMIC ACTIVITIES AMONG THE PEOPLES OF AFRICA." AGRI INDUS MARKET KIN HEALTH SKILL WEALTH...GEOG METH/CNCPT CHARTS TERR/GP WORK TOT/POP VAL/FREE 20. PAGE 110 F2160
TEC/DEV ECO/UNDEV AFR

S64
RUSSETT B.M.,"INEQUALITY AND INSTABILITY: THE RELATION OF LAND TENURE TO POLITICS." WOR+45 ECO/DEV ECO/UNDEV AGRI NAT/G COERCE PWR...MATH STAT CHARTS GEN/LAWS TERR/GP TRUE/GP METH/GP VAL/FREE 20. PAGE 115 F2263
WEALTH GEOG ECO/TAC ORD/FREE

B65
AMERICAN FOREST PRODUCTS INDUS,GOVERNMENT LAND ACQUISITION: A SUMMARY OF LAND ACQUISITION BY FEDERAL, STATE, AND LOCAL GOVERNMENTS UP TO 1964. USA+45 USA-45 TAX...POLICY GEOG CHARTS 20. PAGE 5 F0089
NAT/G OWN ECO/TAC GOV/REL

B65
BOLLENS J.C.,THE METROPOLIS: ITS PEOPLE, POLITICS, AND ECONOMIC LIFE. USA+45 PLAN PROB/SOLV PERS/REL PWR...DECISION GEOG CENSUS TREND CON/ANAL MUNICH 20 NEWYORK/C LOS/ANG SAN/FRAN CHICAGO PHILADELPH. PAGE 16 F0309
HABITAT SOC LOC/G

B65
CAMERON W.J.,NEW ZEALAND. NEW/ZEALND S/ASIA DIPLOM INT/TRADE WRITING COLONIAL PARL/PROC...GEOG CMN/WLTH. PAGE 21 F0402
SOCIETY GP/REL STRUCT

B65
DEMAS W.G.,THE ECONOMICS OF DEVELOPMENT IN SMALL COUNTRIES WITH SPECIAL REFERENCE TO THE CARIBBEAN. WOR+45 BAL/PAY DEMAND EFFICIENCY PRODUC...GEOG CARIBBEAN. PAGE 32 F0618
ECO/UNDEV PLAN WEALTH INT/TRADE

B65
EUROPEAN FREE TRADE ASSN,REGIONAL DEVELOPMENT POLICIES IN EFTA. ECO/UNDEV INT/ORG PLAN REGION ...POLICY GEOG EFTA. PAGE 39 F0755
EUR+WWI ECO/DEV NAT/COMP INT/TRADE

B65
FRIEDLANDER S.L.,LABOR MIGRATION AND ECONOMIC GROWTH: A CASE STUDY OF PUERTO RICO. PUERT/RICO AGRI WORKER PLAN PROB/SOLV...ECOMETRIC STAT PREDICT CHARTS HYPO/EXP SIMUL 20. PAGE 44 F0858
CENSUS GEOG ECO/UNDEV WEALTH

B65
GREEN J.L.,METROPOLITAN ECONOMIC REPUBLICS. USA+45 ECO/TAC INCOME...GEOG SOC CONCPT SIMUL MUNICH 20 ATLANTA. PAGE 50 F0985
SOC/WK PLAN LABOR

B65
HAUSER P.M.,THE STUDY OF URBANIZATION. S/ASIA ECO/DEV ECO/UNDEV NEIGH ACT/RES...GEOG MUNICH. PAGE 57 F1115
CULTURE SOC

B65
HERRICK B.H.,URBAN MIGRATION AND ECONOMIC DEVELOPMENT IN CHILE. CHILE AGRI INDUS LABOR NAT/G CENTRAL PRODUC...STAT SAMP CHARTS BIBLIOG/A MUNICH 20 MIGRATION. PAGE 59 F1156
HABITAT GEOG ECO/UNDEV

B65
HLA MYINT U.,THE ECONOMICS OF THE DEVELOPING COUNTRIES. USA+45 WOR+45 AGRI FINAN NAT/G INT/TRADE ...CLASSIF CENSUS TREND NAT/COMP SIMUL GEN/LAWS. PAGE 60 F1180
ECO/UNDEV FOR/AID GEOG

B65
MAO J.C.T.,EFFICIENCY IN PUBLIC URBAN RENEWAL EXPENDITURES THROUGH CAPITAL BUDGETING. USA+45 FINAN LOC/G NAT/G NEIGH REGION UTIL...GEOG METH/CNCPT STAT SIMUL GEN/LAWS MUNICH 20 URBAN/RNWL. PAGE 85 F1662
TEC/DEV BUDGET PROB/SOLV

B65
SINHA M.R.,THE ECONOMICS OF MANPOWER PLANNING. FUT HUNGARY NAT/G CONTROL...POLICY GEOG ANTHOL 20 CHINJAP. PAGE 122 F2415
ECO/UNDEV PLAN WORKER ECO/TAC

B65
US ADVISORY COMN INTERGOV REL,METROPOLITAN SOCIAL AND ECONOMIC DISPARITIES: IMPLICATIONS FOR INTERGOVERNMENTAL RELATIONS IN CENT'L CITIES AND SUBURBS. CULTURE STRATA DIST/IND LOC/G PLAN GP/REL DISCRIM HABITAT MUNICH. PAGE 134 F2634
GOV/REL GEOG

B65
WILKINSON T.O.,THE URBANIZATION OF JAPANESE LABOR, 1868-1955. AGRI PROC/MFG CAP/ISM PRODUC PROFIT ...SOC CLASSIF CENSUS CHARTS MUNICH 19/20 CHINJAP. PAGE 146 F2887
LABOR INDUS GEOG

B65
WINT G.,ASIA: A HANDBOOK. ASIA COM INDIA USSR CULTURE INTELL NAT/G...GEOG STAT CENSUS NAT/COMP WORSHIP 20 TREATY CHINJAP. PAGE 148 F2907
DIPLOM SOC

S65
DUMONT R.,"SURPEUPLEMENT CHINOIS ET SES CONSEQUENCES." AFR ECO/UNDEV AGRI PLAN PROB/SOLV ECO/TAC FOR/AID NUC/PWR...OBS INT PREDICT. PAGE 35 F0675
GEOG ASIA STAT

B66
BAKLANOFF E.N.,NEW PERSPECTIVES ON BRAZIL. BRAZIL SOCIETY INDUS DOMIN LEAD REV CIVMIL/REL...GEOG PSY LING ANTHOL 20. PAGE 8 F0156
ECO/UNDEV TEC/DEV DIPLOM ORD/FREE

B66
BEN-PORATH Y.,THE ARAB LABOR FORCE IN ISRAEL. ISLAM ISRAEL AGRI INDUS SCHOOL CAP/ISM PAY DEMAND...GEOG REGRESS STAT CHARTS 20 ARABS. PAGE 13 F0245
WORKER CENSUS GP/REL STRUCT

B66
BEQIRAJ M.,PEASANTRY IN REVOLUTION. STRATA ECO/UNDEV AGRI ROUTINE REV HABITAT RIGID/FLEX ...EPIST GEOG NEW/IDEA TREND MUNICH 20. PAGE 13 F0256
WORKER KNOWL NAT/LISM SOC

B66
BROWN R.T.,TRANSPORT AND THE ECONOMIC INTEGRATION OF SOUTH AMERICA. L/A+17C ECO/UNDEV NAT/G OP/RES DIPLOM INT/TRADE REGION WEALTH...ECOMETRIC GEOG STAT LAFTA TIME. PAGE 19 F0373
MARKET DIST/IND SIMUL

B66
CROWDER M.,A SHORT HISTORY OF NIGERIA. AFR NIGERIA UK ECO/UNDEV CHIEF INT/TRADE RACE/REL NAT/LISM ORD/FREE...GEOG SOC CHARTS BIBLIOG 14/20. PAGE 29 F0558
COLONIAL NAT/G CULTURE

B66
DUNCAN O.,METROPOLIS AND REGION (PREPARED FOR RESOURCES FOR THE FUTURE INC., WASHINGTON, D.C.). FINAN INDUS ECO/TAC TAX...CHARTS GOV/COMP MUNICH. PAGE 35 F0677
REGION GEOG

B66
FRANCK L.R.,LA POLITIQUE ECONOMIQUE DES ETATS-UNIS. USA+45 USA-45 FINAN INDUS CONTROL CROWD GOV/REL GP/REL...POLICY SOC CHARTS 18/20. PAGE 43 F0841
NAT/G INT/TRADE GEOG

B66
FRIEDMANN W.G.,INTERNATIONAL FINANCIAL AID. USA+45 ECO/DEV ECO/UNDEV NAT/G VOL/ASSN EX/STRUC PLAN RENT GIVE BAL/PAY PWR...GEOG INT/LAW STAT TREND UN EEC COMECON. PAGE 44 F0866
INT/ORG FOR/AID TEC/DEV ECO/TAC

B66
GYORGY A.,ISSUES OF WORLD COMMUNISM. ALBANIA CHINA/COM COM USSR YUGOSLAVIA STRATA AGRI INT/ORG CHIEF FORCES WORKER WAR ALL/IDEOS...GEOG 20 MAO. PAGE 52 F1018
ECO/UNDEV REV MARXISM CON/ANAL

B66
HALLET R.,PEOPLE AND PROGRESS IN WEST AFRICA: AN INTRODUCTION TO THE PROBLEMS OF DEVELOPMENT. COM/IND INDUS KIN DIPLOM FOR/AID INT/TRADE HEALTH ...GEOG TREND CHARTS BIBLIOG/A 20 AFRICA/W. PAGE 54 F1050
AFR SOCIETY ECO/UNDEV ECO/TAC

B66
HUNT C.L.,SOCIAL ASPECTS OF ECONOMIC DEVELOPMENT. S/ASIA AGRI FAM TEC/DEV RECEIVE EDU/PROP OWN...GEOG MUNICH 20. PAGE 63 F1243
SOC STRATA ATTIT ECO/UNDEV

B66
MOUNTJOY A.B.,INDUSTRIALIZATION AND UNDER-DEVELOPED COUNTRIES (2ND REV. ED.). CHILE GHANA INDIA NIGERIA WOR+45 SOCIETY PROB/SOLV ECO/TAC...SOC CHARTS 20 INDUS/REV. PAGE 94 F1848
ECO/UNDEV INDUS GEOG HABITAT

B66
O'CONNER A.M.,AN ECONOMIC GEOGRAPHY OF EAST AFRICA.
ECO/UNDEV

AFR TANZANIA UGANDA AGRI WORKER INT/TRADE COLONIAL GOV/REL...CHARTS METH/COMP 20 AFRICA/E. PAGE 99 F1953
EXTR/IND GEOG HABITAT

B66
ODEGARD P.H.,POLITICAL POWER AND SOCIAL CHANGE. UNIV NAT/G CREATE ALL/IDEOS...POLICY GEOG SOC CENSUS TREND. PAGE 100 F1962
PWR TEC/DEV IDEA/COMP

B66
ORG FOR ECO COOP AND DEVEL,GEOGRAPHICAL DISTRIBUTION OF FINANCIAL FLOWS TO LESS DEVELOPED COUNTRIES. WOR+45 DIPLOM INT/TRADE GIVE RECEIVE REPAR REGION WEALTH...GEOG STAT CHARTS 20 OECD. PAGE 102 F1997
FINAN ECO/UNDEV INT/ORG FOR/AID

B66
UN STATISTICAL OFFICE,STATISTICAL YEARBOOK (17TH ED.). WOR+45 AGRI...GEOG CHARTS 20. PAGE 132 F2604
STAT INDEX SOCIETY INDUS

B66
UREN P.E.,EAST - WEST TRADE* A SYMPOSIUM. COM AGRI INT/ORG PRICE HABITAT RIGID/FLEX...GEOG INT/LAW ANTHOL NATO. PAGE 133 F2625
INT/TRADE BAL/PWR AFR CANADA

B66
US DEPARTMENT OF STATE,RESEARCH ON THE USSR AND EASTERN EUROPE (EXTERNAL RESEARCH LIST NO 1-25). USSR LAW CULTURE SOCIETY NAT/G TEC/DEV DIPLOM EDU/PROP REGION...GEOG LING. PAGE 136 F2675
BIBLIOG/A EUR+WWI COM MARXISM

B66
US DEPARTMENT OF STATE,RESEARCH ON WESTERN EUROPE, GREAT BRITAIN, AND CANADA (EXTERNAL RESEARCH LIST NO 3-25). CANADA GERMANY/W UK LAW CULTURE NAT/G POL/PAR FORCES EDU/PROP REGION MARXISM...GEOG SOC WORSHIP 20 CMN/WLTH. PAGE 136 F2676
BIBLIOG/A EUR+WWI DIPLOM

B66
US SENATE COMM GOVT OPERATIONS,HEARINGS BEFORE SUBCOMMITTEE ON FOREIGN AID EXPENDITURES: POPULATION CRISIS VOLUMES 1-5 JUNE-SEPT 1965. STRATA ECO/UNDEV PLAN TEC/DEV EDU/PROP ATTIT HEALTH ...GEOG CHARTS 20 CONGRESS BIRTH/CON CASEBOOK. PAGE 138 F2729
ECO/DEV CENSUS FAM CONTROL

L66
AFRICAN BIBLIOGRAPHIC CENTER,"AFRICAN ECONOMIC AFFAIRS: A SELECT BIBLIOGRAPHICAL SURVEY, 1965-1966; SUPPLEMENTS NUMBERS 1-3." AFR FINAN INDUS LABOR PLAN BUDGET CAP/ISM DIPLOM INT/TRADE ADMIN...GEOG 20. PAGE 3 F0047
BIBLIOG/A ECO/UNDEV FOR/AID TEC/DEV

S66
SHORTE F.C.,"THE APPLICATION OF DEVELOPMENT HYPOTHESES IN MIDDLE EASTERN STUDIES." STRUCT AGRI CREATE DEMAND...GEOG STAT CON/ANAL CHARTS. PAGE 121 F2387
ECO/UNDEV ISLAM SOC HYPO/EXP

B67
BLAIR P.W.,THE MINISTATE DILEMMA. WOR+45 AGREE COLONIAL ORD/FREE...GEOG CHARTS MUNICH LEAGUE/NAT UN. PAGE 15 F0294
INT/ORG NAT/G CENSUS

B67
CHANDRASEKHAR S.,PROBLEMS OF ECONOMIC DEVELOPMENT. AFR INDIA PHILIPPINE UAR WOR+45 INDUS...GEOG SOC ANTHOL BIBLIOG 20 CHINJAP. PAGE 23 F0450
ECO/UNDEV PLAN AGRI PROB/SOLV

B67
MOSS F.M.,THE WATER CRISIS. PROB/SOLV CONTROL ...POLICY NEW/IDEA. PAGE 94 F1846
GEOG ACT/RES PRODUC WEALTH

B67
PIKE F.B.,FREEDOM AND REFORM IN LATIN AMERICA. BRAZIL URUGUAY CONSTN CULTURE SECT DIPLOM EDU/PROP PARTIC DRIVE ALL/VALS CATHISM...GEOG ANTHOL BIBLIOG REFORMERS BOLIV. PAGE 106 F2086
L/A+17C ORD/FREE ECO/UNDEV REV

B67
SYMONS L.,AGRICULTURAL GEOGRAPHY. OP/RES SKILL ...CONCPT CHARTS BIBLIOG T 20. PAGE 128 F2520
AGRI GEOG METH/COMP OBS

B67
THOMAN R.S.,GEOGRAPHY OF INTERNATIONAL TRADE. WOR+45 ECO/DEV ECO/UNDEV INT/ORG LG/CO PLAN BAL/PAY ...STAT CHARTS NAT/COMP 20. PAGE 130 F2559
INT/TRADE GEOG ECO/TAC DIPLOM

L67
HOSHII I.,"JAPAN'S STAKE IN ASIA." ASIA S/ASIA CAP/ISM ECO/TAC ROLE...GEOG 20 CHINJAP. PAGE 62 F1224
DIPLOM REGION NAT/G INT/ORG

L67
ZEIDBERG L.D.,"THE NASHVILLE AIR POLLUTION STUDY" (PARTS V-VII)" USA+45 PLAN AGE HEALTH...GEOG STAT CENSUS SAMP/SIZ CHARTS BIBLIOG MUNICH. PAGE 150 F2962
DEATH HABITAT AIR BIO/SOC

S67
"PROTEST AGAINST SOVIET INDUSTRIALIZATION ILLS IN LITHUANIA* A MEMORANDUM." USSR LITHUANIA NAT/G PROVS COST GEOG. PAGE 1 F0024
INDUS COLONIAL NAT/LISM PLAN

S67
ALPANDER G.G.,"ENTREPRENEURS AND PRIVATE ENTERPRISE IN TURKEY." TURKEY INDUS PROC/MFG EDU/PROP ATTIT DRIVE WEALTH...GEOG MGT SOC STAT TREND CHARTS 20. PAGE 4 F0077
ECO/UNDEV LG/CO NAT/G POLICY

S67
BAILEY S.L.,"THE ITALIANS AND ORGANIZED LABOR IN THE UNITED STATES AND ARGENTINA: 1880-1910." ITALY USA-45 PARTIC HABITAT PWR...GEOG GP/COMP 19/20 ARGEN. PAGE 8 F0153
LABOR LEAD WEALTH GP/REL

S67
GREGORY R.,"THE MINISTER'S LINE: OR, THE M4 COMES TO BERKSHIRE. PART I." UK CONSTN DIST/IND LEGIS TOP/EX PLAN ADJUD...GEOG 20. PAGE 51 F0994
DECISION CONSTRUC NAT/G DELIB/GP

S67
HUTCHINGS R.,"THE ENDING OF UNEMPLOYMENT IN THE USSR" USSR PLAN ECO/TAC PRICE INGP/REL...GEOG STAT CHARTS 20 MIGRATION. PAGE 63 F1247
WORKER AGRI INDUS MARXISM

S67
MCCOLL R.W.,"A POLITICAL GEOGRAPHY OF REVOLUTION: CHINA, VIETNAM, AND THAILAND." ASIA THAILAND VIETNAM FORCES CONTROL 20. PAGE 88 F1720
REV GEOG PLAN DECISION

S67
MEADE J.E.,"POPULATION EXPLOSION, THE STANDARD OF LIVING AND SOCIAL CONFLICT." DIPLOM FOR/AID OWN ...PREDICT TREND 20. PAGE 89 F1739
GEOG WEALTH PRODUC INCOME

S67
PECCEI A.,"DEVELOPED-UNDERDEVELOPED AND EAST-WEST RELATIONS." ECO/UNDEV TEC/DEV DIPLOM LEAD EFFICIENCY GEOG. PAGE 104 F2045
FOR/AID TREND REGION ECO/DEV

S67
THEROUX P.,"HATING THE ASIANS." TANZANIA UGANDA CONSTN INDUS NAT/G POL/PAR WORKER ECO/TAC HABITAT LOVE...POLICY GEOG 20 MIGRATION. PAGE 130 F2557
AFR RACE/REL SOVEREIGN ATTIT

S67
VAN KLAVEREN J.,"DIE WIRTSCHAFTLICHEN AUSWIRKUNGEN DES SCHWARZEN TODES" GERMANY PRICE DEMAND PRODUC MUNICH 14/15 DEPRESSION. PAGE 140 F2762
HEALTH AGRI GEOG

N67
US HOUSE COMM FOREIGN AFFAIRS,REPORT OF SPECIAL STUDY MISSION TO THE NEAR EAST (PAMPHLET). ISRAEL USA+45 YEMEN ECO/UNDEV INT/ORG FOR/AID ARMS/CONT WAR WEAPON NAT/LISM PEACE...GEOG 20 UN HOUSE/REP. PAGE 137 F2694
ISLAM DIPLOM FORCES

N67
US HOUSE COMM GOVT OPERATIONS,FEDERALLY FINANCED SOCIAL RESEARCH, EXPENDITURES, STATUS, AND OBJECTIVES (PAMPHLET). WOR+45 CREATE LEAD GP/REL ATTIT...GEOG PSY SOC. PAGE 137 F2700
ACT/RES NAT/G GIVE BUDGET

GEOGRAPHY....SEE GEOG

GEOPOLITIC....GEOPOLITICS

GEOPOLITICS....SEE GEOG

GEORGE H. F0915

GEORGE/DL....DAVID LLOYD GEORGE

GEORGE/III....GEORGE THE THIRD OF ENGLAND

GEORGIA....GEORGIA

B30
GREEN F.M.,CONSTITUTIONAL DEVELOPMENT IN THE SOUTH ATLANTIC STATES, 1776-1860; A STUDY IN THE EVOLUTION OF DEMOCRACY. USA-45 ELITES SOCIETY STRATA ECO/DEV AGRI POL/PAR EX/STRUC LEGIS CT/SYS REGION...BIBLIOG 18/19 MARYLAND VIRGINIA GEORGIA NORTH/CAR SOUTH/CAR. PAGE 50 F0984
CONSTN PROVS PLURISM REPRESENT

S67
WASSERMAN M.,"BEYOND TOKENISM: REVERSE INTEGRATION IN ALBANY, GEORGIA." USA+45 PLAN BUDGET EDU/PROP LEAD AGE/C AGE/Y GEORGIA NEGRO. PAGE 144 F2827
REGION RACE/REL DISCRIM SCHOOL

GEORGIADIS H.G. F0916

GER/CONFED....GERMAN CONFEDERATION

B58
HAMEROW T.S.,RESTORATION, REVOLUTION, REACTION: ECONOMICS AND POLITICS IN GERMANY, 1815-1871. CAP/ISM ADJUST ATTIT PWR...BIBLIOG/A 19 GER/CONFED FRANK/PARL. PAGE 54 F1055
REV ORD/FREE ECO/DEV

GERBET P. F0917

GERHARD H. F0918

GERMAN CONFEDERATION....SEE GER/CONFED

GERMAN/AM....GERMAN-AMERICANS

GERMANS/PA....GERMANS IN PENNSYLVANIA

GERMANY....GERMANY IN GENERAL; SEE ALSO APPROPRIATE TIME/SPACE/CULTURE INDEX

N
DEUTSCHE BUCHEREI,DEUTSCHES BUCHERVERZEICHNIS. GERMANY LAW CULTURE POL/PAR ADMIN LEAD ATTIT PERSON ...SOC 20. PAGE 32 F0626 — BIBLIOG NAT/G DIPLOM ECO/DEV

B15
VEBLEN T.,IMPERIAL GERMANY AND THE INDUSTRIAL REVOLUTION. GERMANY MOD/EUR UK USA-45 NAT/G TEC/DEV CAP/ISM...MAJORIT NAT/COMP 19/20 CHINJAP. PAGE 141 F2769 — ECO/DEV INDUS TECHNIC BAL/PWR

N19
ENGELS F.,THE BRITISH LABOUR MOVEMENT (PAMPHLET). FRANCE GERMANY MOD/EUR UK USA-45 POL/PAR WORKER PAY EDU/PROP PRICE REPRESENT GP/REL 19. PAGE 37 F0730 — ECO/TAC MARXISM LABOR STRATA

N19
GROSECLOSE E.,THE DECAY OF MONEY; A SURVEY OF WESTERN CURRENCIES 1912-1962 (PAMPHLET). AFR FRANCE GERMANY UK LAW INT/TRADE BAL/PAY COST EQUILIB ...POLICY 20 DEPRESSION. PAGE 51 F1004 — FINAN NAT/G ECO/DEV ECO/TAC

N19
HAYEK FA V.O.N.,FREEDOM AND THE ECONOMIC SYSTEM. GERMANY USSR PLAN REPRESENT TOTALISM FASCISM POPULISM...MAJORIT METH/COMP GEN/LAWS 20. PAGE 57 F1123 — ORD/FREE ECO/TAC CAP/ISM SOCISM

B21
CLAPHAN J.H.,THE ECONOMIC DEVELOPMENT OF FRANCE AND GERMANY 1815-1914. FRANCE GERMANY MOD/EUR COM/IND DIST/IND FINAN INT/TRADE EDU/PROP 19/20. PAGE 24 F0476 — ECO/UNDEV ECO/DEV AGRI INDUS

B23
FINER H.,REPRESENTATIVE GOVERNMENT AND A PARLIAMENT OF INDUSTRY. A STUDY OF THE GERMAN FEDERAL ECONOMIC COUNCIL. GERMANY UK CONSTN INDUS PARL/PROC ...NAT/COMP 20. PAGE 41 F0796 — DELIB/GP ECO/TAC WAR REV

B28
CASSEL G.,FOREIGN INVESTMENTS. GERMANY UK USA-45 WOR-45 ECO/DEV NAT/G VOL/ASSN CAP/ISM REPAR ATTIT WEALTH...METH/CNCPT STAT SIMUL STERTYP ANTHOL FOR/TRADE TOT/POP VAL/FREE 20. PAGE 22 F0426 — FINAN ECO/TAC BAL/PAY

B30
FEIS H.,EUROPE, THE WORLD'S BANKER, 1871-1914. FRANCE GERMANY MOD/EUR UK WOR-45 NAT/G PLAN ECO/TAC EXEC ATTIT PWR WEALTH...CONCPT HIST/WRIT GEN/LAWS VAL/FREE 19/20. PAGE 40 F0773 — FINAN DIPLOM INT/TRADE

B31
LORWIN L.L.,ADVISORY ECONOMIC COUNCILS. EUR+WWI FRANCE GERMANY PROB/SOLV INGP/REL...CLASSIF GP/COMP. PAGE 82 F1601 — CONSULT DELIB/GP ECO/TAC NAT/G

B37
BRESCIANI-TURRONI C,THE ECONOMICS OF INFLATION: A STUDY OF CURRENCY DEPRECIATION IN POST-WAR GERMANY. AFR GERMANY FINAN INT/TRADE PRICE TOTALISM...POLICY TIME/SEQ CHARTS GEN/LAWS 20 HITLER/A. PAGE 18 F0347 — ECO/TAC WEALTH SOCIETY

B38
REICH N.,LABOR RELATIONS IN REPUBLICAN GERMANY. GERMANY CONSTN ECO/DEV INDUS NAT/G ADMIN CONTROL GP/REL FASCISM POPULISM 20 WEIMAR/REP. PAGE 110 F2176 — WORKER MGT LABOR BARGAIN

S39
COLE G.D.H.,"NAZI ECONOMICS: HOW DO THEY MANAGE IT?" GERMANY FORCES WORKER BUDGET INT/TRADE ROUTINE COERCE WAR 20 HITLER/A NAZI. PAGE 26 F0500 — FASCISM ECO/TAC ATTIT PLAN

B40
SIKES E.R.,CONTEMPORARY ECONOMIC SYSTEMS: THEIR ANALYSIS AND SOCIAL BACKGROUND. GERMANY ITALY USSR AGRI INDUS PLAN CAP/ISM ROUTINE TOTALISM FASCISM ...POLICY CON/ANAL BIBLIOG 20. PAGE 122 F2400 — COM SOCISM CONCPT

B40
WUNDERLICH F.,LABOR UNDER GERMAN DEMOCRACY, ARBITRATION 1918-1933. GERMANY NAT/G PAY REPAR ADJUD CT/SYS GP/REL...MAJORIT 20. PAGE 149 F2941 — LABOR WORKER INDUS BARGAIN

B47
BOWEN R.H.,GERMAN THEORIES OF THE CORPORATIVE STATE, WITH SPECIAL REFERENCES TO THE PERIOD 1870-1919. GERMANY INDUS LG/CO CATHISM SOCISM...SOC 18/20. PAGE 17 F0328 — IDEA/COMP CENTRAL NAT/G POLICY

B48
VON HAYEK F.A.,INDIVIDUALISM AND ECONOMIC ORDER. GERMANY USA-45 USSR FINAN MARKET INT/ORG ECO/TAC INT/TRADE PRICE REPRESENT ORD/FREE...PLURIST GEN/LAWS 20. PAGE 142 F2793 — SOCISM CAP/ISM POPULISM FEDERAL

B53
NEISSER H.,NATIONAL INCOMES AND INTERNATIONAL TRADE. FRANCE GERMANY SWEDEN UK USA-45 EXTR/IND FINAN INDUS TEC/DEV PRICE BAL/PAY EQUILIB INCOME WEALTH...CHARTS METH 19 CHINJAP. PAGE 97 F1908 — INT/TRADE PRODUC MARKET CON/ANAL

B54
REYNOLDS P.A.,BRITISH FOREIGN POLICY IN THE INTER-WAR YEARS. CZECHOSLVK GERMANY POLAND UK USA-45 POL/PAR FORCES ECO/TAC ARMS/CONT WAR ATTIT 20. PAGE 111 F2182 — DIPLOM POLICY NAT/G

B58
COLE G.D.H.,COMMUNISM AND SOCIAL DEMOCRACY (VOL. IV OF "HISTORY OF SOCIAL THOUGHT"). COM GERMANY ITALY UK AGRI INT/ORG WORKER DIPLOM COLONIAL NAT/LISM ALL/IDEOS...BIBLIOG 20 LEAGUE/NAT AUST/HUNG. PAGE 26 F0502 — MARXISM REV POL/PAR SOCISM

B58
ROBERTS B.C.,NATIONAL WAGES POLICY IN WAR AND PEACE. EUR+WWI GERMANY S/ASIA SWEDEN UK USA+45 USA-45 STRATA ECO/DEV LABOR NAT/G DELIB/GP PLAN INT/TRADE WEALTH...STAT TREND CHARTS 20. PAGE 112 F2205 — CREATE ECO/TAC

S58
SCHUMM S.,"INTEREST REPRESENTATION IN FRANCE AND GERMANY." EUR+WWI FRANCE GERMANY INSPECT PARL/PROC REPRESENT 20 WEIMAR/REP. PAGE 118 F2320 — LOBBY DELIB/GP NAT/G

B59
DIEBOLD W. JR.,THE SCHUMAN PLAN: A STUDY IN ECONOMIC COOPERATION, 1950-1959. EUR+WWI FRANCE GERMANY USA+45 EXTR/IND CONSULT DELIB/GP PLAN DIPLOM ECO/TAC INT/TRADE ROUTINE ORD/FREE WEALTH ...METH/CNCPT STAT CONT/OBS INT TIME/SEQ ECSC 20. PAGE 33 F0635 — INT/ORG REGION

B59
MARTIN K.,WAR, HISTORY, AND HUMAN NATURE. FRANCE GERMANY INDIA UK UNIV POL/PAR COLONIAL DETER REV MARXISM PACIFISM...PSY CONCPT PREDICT LENIN/VI GANDHI/M. PAGE 86 F1683 — PERSON WAR ATTIT IDEA/COMP

B59
MORGENSTERN O.,INTERNATIONAL FINANCIAL TRANSACTIONS AND BUSINESS CYCLES. FRANCE GERMANY UK USA+45 USA-45 WOR+45 WOR-45 ECO/DEV ECO/TAC WEALTH ...CONCPT STAT CON/ANAL CHARTS 19/20. PAGE 93 F1832 — FINAN TIME/SEQ INT/TRADE

B60
BAYER H.,WIRTSCHAFTSPROGNOSE UND WIRTSCHAFTSGESTALTUNG. GERMANY NETHERLAND MARKET PLAN CAP/ISM DEBATE...NAT/COMP 20. PAGE 12 F0220 — ECO/DEV ECO/UNDEV FINAN POLICY

B60
LISTER L.,EUROPE'S COAL AND STEEL COMMUNITY. FRANCE GERMANY STRUCT ECO/DEV EXTR/IND INDUS MARKET NAT/G DELIB/GP ECO/TAC INT/TRADE EDU/PROP ATTIT RIGID/FLEX ORD/FREE PWR WEALTH...CONCPT STAT TIME/SEQ CHARTS ECSC TERR/GP 20. PAGE 81 F1582 — EUR+WWI INT/ORG REGION

S60
HERZ J.H.,"EAST GERMANY: PROGRESS AND PROSPECTS." COM AGRI FINAN INDUS LOC/G NAT/G FORCES PLAN TEC/DEV DOMIN ADMIN COERCE DRIVE PERCEPT RIGID/FLEX MORAL ORD/FREE PWR...MARXIST PSY SOC RECORD STERTYP WORK. PAGE 59 F1158 — POL/PAR STRUCT GERMANY

S60
KREININ M.E.,"THE 'OUTER-SEVEN' AND EUROPEAN INTEGRATION." EUR+WWI FRANCE GERMANY ITALY UK ECO/DEV DIST/IND INT/TRADE DRIVE WEALTH...MYTH CHARTS EEC OEEC 20. PAGE 73 F1436 — ECO/TAC GEN/LAWS

B61
HENDERSON W.O.,THE INDUSTRIAL REVOLUTION IN EUROPE. FRANCE GERMANY MOD/EUR RUSSIA WORKER PROFIT PWR MARXISM SOCISM...SOC HIST/WRIT 19 INDUS/REV. PAGE 58 F1148 — INDUS REV CAP/ISM TEC/DEV

B61
LICHTHEIM G.,MARXISM. GERMANY SOCIETY WORKER CAP/ISM ECO/TAC NAT/LISM POPULISM...TIME/SEQ GOV/COMP NAT/COMP 18/20 COM/PARTY. PAGE 80 F1559 — MARXISM SOCISM IDEA/COMP CULTURE

B61
VEIT O.,GRUNDRISS DER WAHRUNGSPOLITIK. AFR FRANCE GERMANY USSR DIPLOM INT/TRADE...NAT/COMP 19/20 SILVER. PAGE 141 F2773 — FINAN POLICY ECO/TAC CAP/ISM

S61
RAY J.,"THE EUROPEAN FREE-TRADE ASSOCIATION AND ITS IMPACT ON INDIA'S TRADE." EUR+WWI FRANCE GERMANY INDIA S/ASIA UK NAT/G VOL/ASSN PLAN INT/TRADE ROUTINE WEALTH...STAT CHARTS TERR/GP CMN/WLTH EEC FOR/TRADE OEEC 20 EFTA. PAGE 109 F2155 — ECO/DEV ECO/TAC

B63
AHN L.A.,FUNFZIG JAHRE ZWISCHEN INFLATION UND DEFLATION. AFR GERMANY DIPLOM PRICE...CONCPT 20. PAGE 3 F0053 — FINAN CAP/ISM NAT/COMP ECO/TAC

B63
OLSON M. JR.,THE ECONOMICS OF WARTIME SHORTAGE. FRANCE GERMANY MOD/EUR UK AGRI PROB/SOLV ADMIN DEMAND WEALTH...POLICY OLD/LIB FOR/TRADE 17/20. PAGE 101 F1990 — WAR ADJUST ECO/TAC NAT/COMP

B63
PRYOR F.L.,THE COMMUNIST FOREIGN TRADE SYSTEM. COM — ATTIT

CZECHOSLVK GERMANY YUGOSLAVIA LAW ECO/DEV DIST/IND POL/PAR PLAN DOMIN TOTALISM DRIVE RIGID/FLEX WEALTH ...STAT STAND/INT CHARTS FOR/TRADE 20. PAGE 108 F2130 — ECO/TAC

B63
VON BECKERATH E.,PROBLEME DER NORMATIVEN OKONOMIK UND DER WIRTSCHAFTSPOLITISCHEN BERATUNG. GERMANY UK ELITES CAP/ISM EFFICIENCY...CONCPT GOV/COMP IDEA/COMP 20. PAGE 142 F2789 — ECO/TAC DELIB/GP ECO/DEV CONSULT

S63
SHONFIELD A.,"AFTER BRUSSELS." EUR+WWI FRANCE GERMANY UK ECO/DEV DIST/IND MARKET VOL/ASSN DELIB/GP CREATE INT/TRADE ATTIT RIGID/FLEX...RECORD TREND GEN/LAWS EEC COMMUN CMN/WLTH 20. PAGE 121 F2385 — PLAN ECO/TAC

B64
KALDOR N.,ESSAYS ON ECONOMIC POLICY (VOL. II). CHILE GERMANY INDIA FINAN...GOV/COMP METH/COMP 20 KEYNES/JM. PAGE 69 F1348 — BAL/PAY INT/TRADE METH/CNCPT ECO/UNDEV

B64
REDLICH F.,THE GERMAN MILITARY ENTERPRISER AND HIS WORK FORCE. CHRIST-17C GERMANY ELITES SOCIETY FINAN ECO/TAC CIVMIL/REL GP/REL INGP/REL...HIST/WRIT METH/COMP 14/17. PAGE 110 F2170 — EX/STRUC FORCES PROFIT WORKER

B65
ACHTERBERG E.,BERLINER HOCHFINANZ - KAISER, FURSTEN, MILLIONARE UM 1900. GERMANY NAT/G EDU/PROP PERSON...MGT MUNICH 19/20. PAGE 2 F0033 — FINAN BIOG ECO/TAC

B65
EDELMAN M.,THE POLITICS OF WAGE-PRICE DECISIONS. GERMANY ITALY NETHERLAND UK INDUS LABOR POL/PAR PROB/SOLV BARGAIN PRICE ROUTINE BAL/PAY COST DEMAND 20. PAGE 36 F0699 — GOV/COMP CONTROL ECO/TAC PLAN

B65
HABERLER G.,A SURVEY OF INTERNATIONAL TRADE THEORY. CANADA FRANCE GERMANY ECO/TAC TARIFFS AGREE COST DEMAND WEALTH...ECOMETRIC 19/20 MONOPOLY TREATY. PAGE 52 F1024 — INT/TRADE BAL/PAY DIPLOM POLICY

S65
KORBONSKI A.,"USA POLICY IN EAST EUROPE." COM EUR+WWI GERMANY USA+45 CULTURE ECO/UNDEV EDU/PROP RIGID/FLEX WEALTH FOR/TRADE 20. PAGE 73 F1426 — ACT/RES ECO/TAC FOR/AID

S65
SPAAK P.H.,"THE SEARCH FOR CONSENSUS: A NEW EFFORT TO BUILD EUROPE." FRANCE GERMANY ECO/DEV NAT/G CONSULT FORCES PLAN EDU/PROP REGION CONSEN ATTIT ...SOC METH/CNCPT OBS TREND EEC NATO WORK TERR/GP METH/GP 20. PAGE 124 F2447 — EUR+WWI INT/ORG

S65
WHITE J.,"WEST GERMAN AID TO DEVELOPING COUNTRIES." AFR INT/ORG OP/RES GIVE CENTRAL ATTIT DRIVE...STAT NAT/COMP. PAGE 146 F2869 — GERMANY FOR/AID ECO/UNDEV CAP/ISM

B67
BROMKE A.,POLAND'S POLITICS: IDEALISM VS. REALISM. COM GERMANY POLAND RUSSIA USSR POL/PAR CATHISM ...BIBLIOG 19/20. PAGE 19 F0360 — NAT/G DIPLOM MARXISM

B67
BURDEN H.T.,THE NUREMBERG PARTY RALLIES 1923-39. GERMANY POL/PAR SECT CREATE DOMIN WAR ATTIT ...AUD/VIS FILM 20. PAGE 20 F0384 — EDU/PROP CONTROL CROWD TOTALISM

B67
DAVIS F.M.,COME AS A CONQUEROR: THE UNITED STATES ARMY'S OCCUPATION OF GERMANY: 1945-1949. EUR+WWI GERMANY USA+45 SOCIETY PLAN BAL/PWR DIPLOM FOR/AID PERS/REL DEMAND PEACE ORD/FREE 20. PAGE 30 F0588 — FORCES CIVMIL/REL ECO/TAC CONTROL

B67
FIELD G.L.,COMPARATIVE POLITICAL DEVELOPMENT: THE PRECEDENT OF THE WEST. FRANCE GERMANY SWEDEN UK USSR STRATA STRUCT POL/PAR...METH 20. PAGE 40 F0790 — NAT/COMP CONCPT ECO/DEV SOCIETY

B67
NYOMARKAY J.,CHARISMA AND FACTIONALISM IN THE NAZI PARTY. GERMANY POL/PAR LEGIT LEAD MARXISM ...NEW/IDEA METH/COMP GEN/LAWS BIBLIOG 20 HITLER/A. PAGE 99 F1949 — FASCISM INGP/REL CHIEF PWR

S67
APEL H.,"LES NOUVEAUX ASPECTS DE LA POLITIQUE ETRANGERE ALLEMANDE." AFR EUR+WWI GERMANY POL/PAR BAL/PWR ECO/TAC INT/TRADE NUC/PWR NAT/LISM PEACE ...POLICY 20 EEC. PAGE 6 F0107 — DIPLOM INT/ORG FEDERAL

S67
GRUN C.,"DEUX ETUDES ALLEMANDES SUR LES PREJUGES NATIONAUX ET LES MOYENS DE LES COMBATTRE." FRANCE GERMANY DIST/IND PROB/SOLV GP/REL AGE/Y RIGID/FLEX ...PSY STAT INT SAMP. PAGE 52 F1010 — ATTIT REGION DISCRIM STERTYP

S67
MOLTMANN G.,"ZUR FORMULIERUNG DER AMERIKANISCHEN BESATZUNGSPOLITIK IN DEUTSCHLAND AM ENDE DES ZWEITEN WELTKRIEGES" GERMANY ECO/TAC ADMIN WAR CIVMIL/REL ORD/FREE FASCISM 20. PAGE 92 F1815 — FORCES CONTROL POLICY INDUS

S67
VAN KLAVEREN J.,"DIE WIRTSCHAFTLICHEN AUSWIRKUNGEN DES SCHWARZEN TODES" GERMANY PRICE DEMAND PRODUC MUNICH 14/15 DEPRESSION. PAGE 140 F2762 — HEALTH AGRI GEOG

L86
OSGOOD H.L.,"SCIENTIFIC SOCIALISM: RODBERTUS" GERMANY CAP/ISM COST WEALTH...MAJORIT BIOG IDEA/COMP 19 RODBRTUS/C. PAGE 102 F2002 — SOCISM MARXISM ECO/DEV ECO/TAC

B96
MARX K.,REVOLUTION AND COUNTER-REVOLUTION. GERMANY CONSTN ELITES INDUS NAT/G DIPLOM ECO/TAC WEALTH. PAGE 86 F1693 — MARXIST REV PWR STRATA

GERMANY/E....EAST GERMANY; SEE ALSO COM

B60
STOLPER W.F.,GERMANY BETWEEN EAST AND WEST: THE ECONOMICS OF COMPETITIVE COEXISTENCE. AFR FUT GERMANY/E GERMANY/W WOR+45 FINAN POL/PAR BUDGET ECO/TAC FOR/AID INT/TRADE...STAT CHARTS METH/COMP 20. PAGE 126 F2495 — ECO/DEV DIPLOM GOV/COMP BAL/PWR

B62
FRIEDRICH-EBERT-STIFTUNG,THE SOVIET BLOC AND DEVELOPING COUNTRIES. CHINA/COM COM GERMANY/E USSR WOR+45 ECO/UNDEV INT/ORG NAT/G TEC/DEV NEUTRAL PWR ...POLICY 20. PAGE 44 F0868 — MARXISM DIPLOM ECO/TAC FOR/AID

B64
LAURSEN K.,THE GERMAN INFLATION, 1918-23. EUR+WWI GERMANY/E GERMANY/W WOR-45 BUDGET TAX GOV/REL BAL/PAY DEMAND PEACE...POLICY CHARTS 20 WEIMAR/REP. PAGE 76 F1489 — ECO/DEV FINAN REPAR ECO/TAC

S67
SPITTMANN I.,"EAST GERMANY: THE SWINGING PENDULUM." COM GERMANY/E NAT/G EFFICIENCY MARXISM 20. PAGE 125 F2458 — PRODUC POL/PAR WEALTH ATTIT

GERMANY/W....WEST GERMANY

S49
STEINMETZ H.,"THE PROBLEMS OF THE LANDRAT: A STUDY OF COUNTY GOVERNMENT IN THE US ZONE OF GERMANY." GERMANY/W USA+45 INDUS PLAN DIPLOM EDU/PROP CONTROL WAR GOV/REL FEDERAL WEALTH PLURISM...GOV/COMP 20 LANDRAT. PAGE 126 F2478 — LOC/G COLONIAL MGT TOP/EX

B57
INTL BANKING SUMMER SCHOOL,RELATIONS BETWEEN THE CENTRAL BANKS AND COMMERCIAL BANKS. EUR+WWI FRANCE GERMANY/W ITALY UK USA+45 USSR INDUS INT/ORG CAP/ISM CONTROL MONEY. PAGE 65 F1282 — FINAN NAT/G GP/REL LG/CO

B57
NAUMANN R.,THEORIE UND PRAXIS DES NEOLIBERALISMUS; DAS MAERCHEN VON DER FREIEN ODER SOZIALEN MARKTWIRTSCHAFT. GERMANY/W FORCES PLAN EDU/PROP SOCISM...POLICY MARXIST IDEA/COMP BIBLIOG 18/20 ADENAUER/K. PAGE 97 F1903 — MARXISM NEW/LIB ECO/TAC CAP/ISM

B59
HAX K.,DIE HOCHSCHULLEHRER DER WIRTSCHAFTSWISSENSCHAFTEN IN DER BUNDESREPUBLIK DEUTSCHLAND EINSCHL. WESTBERLIN, OSTERREICH. AUSTRIA GERMANY/W SWITZERLND FINAN MARKET PROF/ORG BUDGET ECO/TAC INT/TRADE PRICE COST 20. PAGE 57 F1119 — BIBLIOG ACADEM INTELL

B59
KOLLAI H.R.,DIE EINGLIEDERUNG DER VERTRIEBENEN UND ZUWANDERER IN NIEDERSACHSEN. GERMANY/W SOCIETY STRATA STRUCT LABOR SOC/INTEG 20. PAGE 72 F1422 — GP/REL INGP/REL

B60
SERAPHIM H.J.,ZUR GRUNDLEGUNG WIRTSCHAFTSPOLITISCHER KONZEPTIONEN (SCHRIFTEN DES VEREINS FUR SOZIALPOLITIK, N.F. BAND 18). GERMANY/W WOR+45 ECO/DEV DELIB/GP ACT/RES ECO/TAC INGP/REL ORD/FREE...CONCPT IDEA/COMP GEN/LAWS 20. PAGE 120 F2358 — POLICY PHIL/SCI PLAN

B60
STOLPER W.F.,GERMANY BETWEEN EAST AND WEST: THE ECONOMICS OF COMPETITIVE COEXISTENCE. AFR FUT GERMANY/E GERMANY/W WOR+45 FINAN POL/PAR BUDGET ECO/TAC FOR/AID INT/TRADE...STAT CHARTS METH/COMP 20. PAGE 126 F2495 — ECO/DEV DIPLOM GOV/COMP BAL/PWR

B62
FRIEDMANN W.,METHODS AND POLICIES OF PRINCIPAL DONOR COUNTRIES IN PUBLIC INTERNATIONAL DEVELOPMENT FINANCING: PRELIMINARY APPRAISAL. FRANCE GERMANY/W UK USA+45 USSR WOR+45 FINAN TEC/DEV CAP/ISM DIPLOM ECO/TAC ATTIT 20 EEC. PAGE 44 F0864 — INT/ORG FOR/AID NAT/COMP ADMIN

B62
GRANICK D.,THE EUROPEAN EXECUTIVE. BELGIUM FRANCE GERMANY/W UK INDUS LABOR LG/CO SML/CO EX/STRUC PLAN TEC/DEV CAP/ISM COST DEMAND...POLICY CHARTS 20. PAGE 50 F0977 — MGT ECO/DEV ECO/TAC EXEC

B62
LIPPMANN W.,WESTERN UNITY AND THE COMMON MARKET. EUR+WWI FRANCE GERMANY/W UK USA+45 ECO/DEV AGRI FINAN MARKET INT/ORG NAT/G FOR/AID AGREE WEALTH 20 EEC. PAGE 80 F1575 — DIPLOM INT/TRADE VOL/ASSN

B62
MULLER E.,DIE HEIMATVERTRIEBENEN IN BADEN-WURTTEMBERG. GERMANY/W AGRI INDUS LABOR PROVS SOC/INTEG 20 MIGRATION. PAGE 95 F1858
GP/REL INGP/REL

B62
WENDT P.F.,HOUSING POLICY - THE SEARCH FOR SOLUTIONS. GERMANY/W SWEDEN UK USA+45 OP/RES HABITAT WEALTH...SOC/WK CHARTS 20. PAGE 145 F2856
PLAN ADMIN METH/COMP NAT/G

B63
ERHARD L.,THE ECONOMICS OF SUCCESS. GERMANY/W WOR+45 LABOR CHIEF TAX REGION COST DEMAND ANTHOL. PAGE 38 F0745
ECO/DEV INT/TRADE PLAN DIPLOM

B63
HAHN L.A.,DIE AMERIKANISCHE KONJUNKTURPOLITIK DER DOLLAR UND DIE DMARK. GERMANY/W USA+45 DIPLOM PRICE BAL/PAY COST...POLICY MONEY. PAGE 53 F1038
FINAN BUDGET ECO/TAC LABOR

B64
BOARMAN P.M.,GERMANY'S ECONOMIC DILEMMA - INFLATION AND THE BALANCE OF PAYMENTS. AFR GERMANY/W LABOR CAP/ISM PRICE BAL/PAY COST INCOME 20. PAGE 16 F0302
ECO/DEV FINAN INT/TRADE BUDGET

B64
BROWN W.M.,THE EXTERNAL LIQUIDITY OF AN ADVANCED COUNTRY. CANADA FRANCE GERMANY/W SWEDEN UK USA+45 ECO/DEV DIPLOM PRICE...CONCPT STAT NAT/COMP 20. PAGE 20 F0376
FINAN INT/TRADE COST INCOME

B64
COLUMBIA U SCHOOL OF LAW,PUBLIC INTERNATIONAL DEVELOPMENT FINANCING IN INDIA. GERMANY/W INDIA UK USA+45 INDUS PLAN TEC/DEV DIPLOM ECO/TAC GIVE ADMIN UTIL ATTIT 20. PAGE 26 F0512
ECO/UNDEV FINAN FOR/AID INT/ORG

B64
LAURSEN K.,THE GERMAN INFLATION, 1918-23. EUR+WWI GERMANY/E GERMANY/W WOR-45 BUDGET TAX GOV/REL BAL/PAY DEMAND PEACE...POLICY CHARTS 20 WEIMAR/REP. PAGE 76 F1489
ECO/DEV FINAN REPAR ECO/TAC

B64
MILIBAND R.,THE SOCIALIST REGISTER: 1964. GERMANY/W ITALY UK LABOR POL/PAR ECO/TAC FOR/AID NUC/PWR ...POLICY SOCIALIST IDEA/COMP 20 MAO NASSER/G. PAGE 91 F1784
MARXISM SOCISM CAP/ISM PROB/SOLV

B64
MORRISSENS L.,ECONOMIC POLICY IN OUR TIME: COUNTRY STUDIES. BELGIUM EUR+WWI FRANCE GERMANY/W ITALY NETHERLAND INDUS BARGAIN BUDGET GOV/REL BAL/PAY PRODUC...CON/ANAL CHARTS COSTS 20. PAGE 94 F1839
ECO/DEV ECO/TAC METH/COMP PLAN

B65
SHONFIELD A.,MODERN CAPITALISM: THE CHANGING BALANCE OF PUBLIC AND PRIVATE POWER. FRANCE GERMANY/W UK USA+45 WOR+45 ECO/DEV INT/ORG NAT/G CONSULT INT/TRADE PRODUC...POLICY CONCPT METH/COMP 20. PAGE 121 F2386
CAP/ISM CONTROL BAL/PWR CREATE

B65
WEIL G.L.,A HANDBOOK ON THE EUROPEAN ECONOMIC COMMUNITY. BELGIUM EUR+WWI FRANCE GERMANY/W ITALY CONSTN ECO/DEV CREATE PARTIC GP/REL...DECISION MGT CHARTS 20 EEC. PAGE 144 F2846
INT/TRADE INT/ORG TEC/DEV INT/LAW

B65
WHITE J.,GERMAN AID. GERMANY/W FINAN PLAN TEC/DEV INT/TRADE ADMIN ATTIT...POLICY 20. PAGE 146 F2870
FOR/AID ECO/UNDEV DIPLOM ECO/TAC

B66
KAESTNER K.,GESAMTWIRTSCHAFTLICHE PLANUNG IN EINER GEMISCHTEN WIRTSCHAFTSORDNUNG (WIRTSCHAFTSPOLITISCHE STUDIEN 5). GERMANY/W WOR+45 WOR-45 INDUS MARKET NAT/G ACT/RES GP/REL INGP/REL PRODUC...ECOMETRIC MGT BIBLIOG 20. PAGE 68 F1346
ECO/TAC PLAN POLICY PREDICT

B66
KINDLEBERGER C.P.,EUROPE AND THE DOLLAR. AFR EUR+WWI FRANCE GERMANY/W USA+45 CONSTN INT/ORG DIPLOM INT/TRADE...ANTHOL 20. PAGE 71 F1395
BAL/PAY BUDGET FINAN ECO/DEV

B66
US DEPARTMENT OF STATE,RESEARCH ON WESTERN EUROPE, GREAT BRITAIN, AND CANADA (EXTERNAL RESEARCH LIST NO 3-25). CANADA GERMANY/W UK LAW CULTURE NAT/G POL/PAR FORCES EDU/PROP REGION MARXISM...GEOG SOC WORSHIP 20 CMN/WLTH. PAGE 136 F2676
BIBLIOG/A EUR+WWI DIPLOM

B66
ZISCHKA A.,WAR ES EIN WUNDER? GERMANY/W ECO/DEV FINAN LG/CO BARGAIN CAP/ISM FOR/AID RATION 20 MARSHL/PLN. PAGE 150 F2965
ECO/TAC INT/TRADE INDUS WAR

B67
HANRIEDER W.F.,WEST GERMAN FOREIGN POLICY 1949-1963: INTERNATIONAL PRESSURE AND DOMESTIC RESPONSE. EUR+WWI GERMANY/W POL/PAR LOBBY CONSEN 20. PAGE 54 F1061
DIPLOM POLICY NAT/G ATTIT

S67
GEISS I.,"THE GERMANS AND THE MIDDLE EAST CRISIS." GERMANY/W ISLAM ISRAEL USSR POL/PAR RACE/REL MARXISM...GP/COMP 20 JEWS. PAGE 47 F0914
ATTIT DIPLOM WAR

POLICY

GERSCHENKRON A. F0919

GERWIG R. F0920

GETTYSBURG....BATTLE OF GETTYSBURG

GHANA....SEE ALSO AFR

N
BROCKWAY A.F.,AFRICAN SOCIALISM. EUR+WWI GHANA ISLAM UAR ECO/UNDEV CAP/ISM INT/TRADE COLONIAL COERCE GOV/REL DISCRIM 20 NEGRO NKRUMAH/K NASSER/G. PAGE 19 F0356
AFR SOCISM MARXISM

B60
PITCHER G.M.,BIBLIOGRAPHY OF GHANA. AFR GHANA NAT/G 20. PAGE 106 F2091
BIBLIOG/A SOC

B61
CARNEY D.E.,GOVERNMENT AND ECONOMY IN BRITISH WEST AFRICA. GAMBIA GHANA NIGERIA SIER/LEONE DOMIN ADMIN GOV/REL SOVEREIGN WEALTH LAISSEZ...BIBLIOG 20 CMN/WLTH. PAGE 21 F0417
METH/COMP COLONIAL ECO/TAC ECO/UNDEV

B61
PETCH G.A.,ECONOMIC DEVELOPMENT AND MODERN WEST AFRICA. AFR CONGO/BRAZ GHANA NIGER SIER/LEONE AGRI MARKET LABOR FOR/AID TAX COST EFFICIENCY EQUILIB PRODUC...GEOG TREND 20. PAGE 105 F2068
ECO/UNDEV TEC/DEV EXTR/IND ECO/TAC

B62
FAO,FOOD AND AGRICULTURE ORGANIZATION AFRICAN SURVEY. AFR CONGO/BRAZ GHANA STRATA AGRI INT/ORG TEC/DEV FOR/AID INT/TRADE RACE/REL DEMAND EFFICIENCY PRODUC...GEOG 20 UN CONGO/LEOP. PAGE 39 F0763
ECO/TAC WEALTH EXTR/IND ECO/UNDEV

B62
GREEN L.P.,DEVELOPMENT IN AFRICA. AFR CENTRL/AFR GHANA RHODESIA SOUTH/AFR AGRI PROC/MFG INT/TRADE DEMAND NAT/LISM PRODUC WEALTH...GEOG METH/CNCPT CHARTS BIBLIOG 20. PAGE 50 F0987
CULTURE ECO/UNDEV GOV/REL TREND

B66
BIRMINGHAM W.,A STUDY OF CONTEMPORARY GHANA VOL I: THE ECONOMY OF GHANA. AFR GHANA PLAN...POLICY STAT CHARTS ANTHOL BIBLIOG 20. PAGE 15 F0286
ECO/UNDEV ECO/TAC NAT/G PRODUC

B66
BOYD H.W.,MARKETING MANAGEMENT: CASES FROM EMERGING COUNTRIES. BRAZIL GHANA ISRAEL WOR+45 ADMIN PERS/REL ATTIT HABITAT WEALTH...ANTHOL 20 ARGEN CASEBOOK. PAGE 17 F0332
MGT ECO/UNDEV PROB/SOLV MARKET

B66
MOUNTJOY A.B.,INDUSTRIALIZATION AND UNDER-DEVELOPED COUNTRIES (2ND REV. ED.). CHILE GHANA INDIA NIGERIA WOR+45 SOCIETY PROB/SOLV ECO/TAC...SOC CHARTS 20 INDUS/REV. PAGE 94 F1848
ECO/UNDEV INDUS GEOG HABITAT

B67
BIRMINGHAM W.,A STUDY OF CONTEMPORARY GHANA VOL. I: SOME ASPECTS OF SOCIAL STRUCTURE. AFR GHANA AGRI FAM SECT PLAN EDU/PROP MARRIAGE OWN...POLICY STAT CHARTS MUNICH 20. PAGE 15 F0287
SOCIETY STRUCT CENSUS ECO/UNDEV

S67
KRAUS J.,"A MARXIST IN GHANA." GHANA ELITES CHIEF PROB/SOLV TEC/DEV DIPLOM ECO/TAC COLONIAL PARTIC PWR 20 NKRUMAH/K. PAGE 73 F1432
MARXISM PLAN ATTIT CREATE

GIAP V.N. F0921

GIBBON/EDW....EDWARD GIBBON

GIBRALTAR....SEE UK

GIBSON D.M.T. F0332

GIERSCH H. F2789

GILBERT L.D. F0922

GILBERT M. F0780

GILL P.J. F0923

GILLESPIE R.W. F1196

GILMORE D.R. F0924

GILPATRICK T.V. F0925

GITTELL M. F0926

GITTINGER J.P. F0927

GIVE....GIVING, PHILANTHROPY

B14
HOBSON J.A.,WORK AND WEALTH. CULTURE FINAN INDUS WORKER TEC/DEV ECO/TAC GIVE PAY PRICE COST PRODUC
WEALTH INCOME

UTIL. PAGE 60 F1185 GEN/LAWS

N19
ARNDT H.W.,AUSTRALIAN FOREIGN AID POLICY (PAMPHLET). ECO/UNDEV DIPLOM GIVE GOV/REL COST UTIL PWR...CHARTS 20 AUSTRAL PAPUA NEW/GUINEA. PAGE 6 F0114
FOR/AID POLICY ECO/TAC EFFICIENCY

N19
BASCH A.,THE FUTURE OF FOREIGN LENDING FOR DEVELOPMENT (PAMPHLET). WOR+45 ECO/UNDEV FINAN INT/ORG ECO/TAC ATTIT...PREDICT 20. PAGE 11 F0203
FOR/AID ECO/DEV DIPLOM GIVE

N19
JACKSON R.G.A.,THE CASE FOR AN INTERNATIONAL DEVELOPMENT AUTHORITY (PAMPHLET). WOR+45 ECO/DEV DIPLOM GIVE CONTROL GP/REL EFFICIENCY NAT/LISM SOVEREIGN 20. PAGE 66 F1295
FOR/AID INT/ORG ECO/UNDEV ADMIN

N19
LANGE O.R.,"DISARMAMENT ECONOMIC GROWTH AND INTERNATIONAL CO-OPERATION" (PAMPHLET). WOR+45 DIST/IND PLAN INT/TRADE GIVE TASK DETER WEALTH SOCISM 18/19 BOLIVAR/S. PAGE 75 F1477
ARMS/CONT DIPLOM ECO/DEV ECO/UNDEV

N19
US MARITIME ADMINISTRATION,CONTRIBUTION OF FEDERAL AID PROGRAMS TO THE OCEANBORNE FOREIGN TRADE OF THE UNITED STATES: 1959-62 (PAMPHLET). USA+45 SEA FINAN NAT/G BUDGET...POLICY 20. PAGE 138 F2719
INT/TRADE ECO/TAC DIST/IND GIVE

B29
JONES M.M.,CORPORATION CONTRIBUTIONS TO COMMUNITY WELFARE AGENCIES (PAMPHLET). DELIB/GP TAX CONTROL PARTIC RATIONAL POLICY. PAGE 68 F1339
LG/CO GIVE NEIGH SOC/WK

S32
DODD E.M. JR.,"FOR WHOM ARE CORPORATE MANAGERS TRUSTEES'." SERV/IND CAP/ISM GIVE LEAD REPRESENT ORD/FREE WEALTH. PAGE 33 F0648
LG/CO ROLE NAT/G PLAN

B40
BLAISDELL D.C.,GOVERNMENT AND AGRICULTURE; THE GROWTH OF FEDERAL FARM AID. USA-45 MARKET PLAN PROB/SOLV TEC/DEV ECO/TAC GOV/REL ADJUST ATTIT ...CHARTS 20 DEPT/AGRI. PAGE 15 F0296
NAT/G GIVE AGRI DELIB/GP

B40
GAUS J.M.,PUBLIC ADMINISTRATION AND THE UNITED STATES DEPARTMENT OF AGRICULTURE. USA-45 STRUCT DIST/IND FINAN MARKET EX/STRUC PROB/SOLV GIVE PRODUC...POLICY GEOG CHARTS 20 DEPT/AGRI. PAGE 47 F0909
ADMIN AGRI DELIB/GP OP/RES

B41
MACMAHON A.W.,THE ADMINISTRATION OF FEDERAL WORK RELIEF. USA-45 EX/STRUC WORKER BUDGET EFFICIENCY ...CONT/OBS CHARTS 20 WPA. PAGE 84 F1636
ADMIN NAT/G MGT GIVE

B45
DAVIS J.,AFRICA ADVANCING. AFR CONGO/BRAZ LIBERIA NIGER INT/ORG SCHOOL DIPLOM GIVE KNOWL SKILL 20. PAGE 30 F0590
SECT COLONIAL AGRI ECO/UNDEV

B46
HARRISON S.M.,AMERICAN FOUNDATIONS FOR SOCIAL WELFARE. OP/RES CONTROL...POLICY MGT METH/CNCPT STAT TREND BIBLIOG. PAGE 56 F1092
GIVE FINAN CLASSIF ADMIN

B48
METZLER L.A.,INCOME, EMPLOYMENT, AND PUBLIC POLICY. FINAN INDUS LOC/G NAT/G TAX GIVE PAY COST PRODUC ...MGT TIME/SEQ 20. PAGE 90 F1765
INCOME WEALTH POLICY ECO/TAC

B52
ANDREWS F.E.,CORPORATION GIVING. LAW TAX EDU/PROP ADMIN...POLICY STAT CHARTS. PAGE 5 F0101
LG/CO GIVE SML/CO FINAN

B52
DE JOUVENEL B.,THE ETHICS OF REDISTRIBUTION. UK ELITES MARKET WORKER GIVE PAY INCOME PERSON ...POLICY PSY GEN/LAWS 20. PAGE 31 F0602
WEALTH TAX SOCISM TRADIT

B52
MACARTHUR D.,REVITALIZING A NATION. ASIA COM FUT KOREA WOR+45 NAT/G FOR/AID TAX GIVE WAR ATTIT SOCISM 20 CHINJAP EUROPE. PAGE 83 F1619
LEAD FORCES TOP/EX POLICY

B53
BOEKE J.H.,ECONOMICS AND ECONOMIC POLICY OF DUAL SOCIETIES AS EXEMPLIFIED BY INDONESIA. INDIA INDONESIA SOCIETY CAP/ISM INT/TRADE GIVE PRICE GP/REL WEALTH SOCISM...POLICY NAT/COMP GEN/LAWS 20. PAGE 16 F0304
ECO/TAC ECO/UNDEV NAT/G CONTROL

B53
DAHL R.A.,POLITICS, ECONOMICS, AND WELFARE. TEC/DEV BARGAIN ECO/TAC RECEIVE PRICE CONTROL LEAD INGP/REL ...POLICY GEN/LAWS. PAGE 29 F0572
SOCIETY GIVE

B57
MILLIKAN M.F.,A PROPOSAL: KEY TO AN EFFECTIVE FOREIGN POLICY. USA+45 AGRI FINAN DELIB/GP DIPLOM REPRESENT MAJORITY...NEW/IDEA CHARTS. PAGE 91 F1795
FOR/AID GIVE ECO/UNDEV

PLAN

B60
PETERSON W.C.,THE WELFARE STATE IN FRANCE. EUR+WWI FRANCE FUT STRATA PROB/SOLV TAX GIVE RECEIVE INCOME ORD/FREE PWR...CHARTS 20. PAGE 105 F2070
NEW/LIB ECO/TAC WEALTH NAT/G

S60
BAUM M.,"THE CASE FOR BUSINESS CIVILIZATION." R+D CAP/ISM GIVE EDU/PROP HAPPINESS...SOC TREND. PAGE 12 F0218
MGT CULTURE WEALTH

S60
POLLARD J.A.,"EMERGING PATTERNS OF CORPORATE GIVING." FINAN DELIB/GP PLAN EDU/PROP CENTRAL TREND. PAGE 107 F2098
GIVE LG/CO ADMIN MGT

B61
ASHER R.E.,GRANTS, LOANS, AND LOCAL CURRENCIES; THEIR ROLE IN FOREIGN AID. AFR USA+45 ECO/UNDEV INT/ORG ACT/RES PLAN ECO/TAC GIVE CONTROL WEALTH 20. PAGE 7 F0130
FOR/AID FINAN NAT/G BUDGET

B61
DE GRAZIA A.,AMERICAN WELFARE. CLIENT FINAN LABOR LOC/G NAT/G NEIGH EDU/PROP GP/REL...CLASSIF CON/ANAL CHARTS BIBLIOG. PAGE 31 F0598
GIVE WEALTH SECT VOL/ASSN

B61
INTL UNION LOCAL AUTHORITIES,METROPOLIS. WOR+45 DIST/IND FINAN GIVE EDU/PROP CRIME COST HEALTH WEALTH MUNICH 20. PAGE 65 F1286
GOV/COMP LOC/G BIBLIOG

B61
MEZERIK A.G.,ECONOMIC DEVELOPMENT AIDS FOR UNDERDEVELOPED COUNTRIES. WOR+45 FINAN LEGIS PROB/SOLV TEC/DEV DIPLOM FOR/AID GIVE TASK WAR 20 UN. PAGE 91 F1776
ECO/UNDEV INT/ORG WEALTH PLAN

B61
MORLEY L.,THE PATCHWORK HISTORY OF FOREIGN AID. AFR KOREA/S USA+45 USSR LAW FINAN INT/ORG TEC/DEV BAL/PWR GIVE 20 NATO. PAGE 93 F1834
FOR/AID ECO/UNDEV FORCES DIPLOM

B61
WARD B.J.,INDIA AND THE WEST. INDIA UK USA+45 INT/TRADE GIVE COLONIAL ATTIT MARXISM 19/20. PAGE 143 F2817
PLAN ECO/UNDEV ECO/TAC FOR/AID

B62
HUHNE L.H.,FINANCING ECONOMIC DEVELOPMENT THROUGH NATIONAL AND INTERNATIONAL ORGANIZATIONS (THESIS; U OF WIS.). USA+45 INT/ORG PLAN GIVE GOV/REL WEALTH 20. PAGE 63 F1235
RATION FINAN FOR/AID ECO/UNDEV

B62
MOUSSA P.,THE UNDERPRIVILEGED NATIONS. FINAN INT/ORG PLAN PROB/SOLV CAP/ISM GIVE TASK WEALTH ...POLICY SOC IND 20. PAGE 94 F1850
ECO/UNDEV NAT/G DIPLOM FOR/AID

B63
COLUMBIA U SCHOOL OF LAW,PUBLIC INTERNATIONAL DEVELOPMENT FINANCING IN SENEGAL. SENEGAL FINAN DELIB/GP GIVE EFFICIENCY...CHARTS GOV/COMP ANTHOL 20. PAGE 26 F0511
FOR/AID PLAN RECEIVE ECO/UNDEV

B63
INTERAMERICAN ECO AND SOC COUN,THE ALLIANCE FOR PROGRESS: ITS FIRST YEAR: 1961-1962. AGRI SCHOOL PLAN TEC/DEV INT/TRADE TAX GIVE ADMIN WEALTH...SOC 20 ALL/PROG SOUTH/AMER. PAGE 64 F1267
INT/ORG PROB/SOLV ECO/TAC L/A+17C

B63
OECD,FOOD AID: ITS ROLE IN ECONOMIC DEVELOPMENT. FINAN NAT/G PLAN DIPLOM GIVE TASK WEALTH ...METH/COMP METH 20. PAGE 100 F1966
ECO/UNDEV FOR/AID INT/ORG POLICY

S63
NYE J.,"TANGANYIKA'S SELF-HELP." TANZANIA NAT/G GIVE COST EFFICIENCY NAT/LISM 20. PAGE 99 F1948
ECO/TAC POL/PAR ECO/UNDEV WORKER

B64
COLUMBIA U SCHOOL OF LAW,PUBLIC INTERNATIONAL DEVELOPMENT FINANCING IN INDIA. GERMANY/W INDIA UK USA+45 INDUS PLAN TEC/DEV DIPLOM ECO/TAC GIVE ADMIN UTIL ATTIT 20. PAGE 26 F0512
ECO/UNDEV FINAN FOR/AID INT/ORG

B64
MC GOVERN G.S.,WAR AGAINST WANT. USA+45 AGRI DIPLOM INT/TRADE GIVE RECEIVE DEMAND HEALTH 20 KENNEDY/JF FOOD/PEACE. PAGE 87 F1714
FOR/AID ECO/DEV POLICY EATING

B64
RAISON T.,WHY CONSERVATIVE? UK FORCES DIPLOM ECO/TAC GIVE EDU/PROP ORD/FREE WEALTH LAISSEZ ...GOV/COMP 20 TORY/PARTY CONSRV/PAR. PAGE 109 F2137
PLURISM CONSERVE POL/PAR NAT/G

B64
WILSON T.,POLICIES FOR REGIONAL DEVELOPMENT. CANADA UK FINAN INDUS NAT/G BUDGET TAX GIVE COST ...NAT/COMP 20. PAGE 147 F2904
REGION PLAN ECO/DEV ECO/TAC

B65
CHANDRASEKHAR S.,AMERICAN AID AND INDIA'S ECONOMIC
FOR/AID

DEVELOPMENT. AFR CHINA/COM INDIA USA+45 GIVE EDU/PROP EATING HEALTH ORD/FREE 20 AID. PAGE 23 F0449
PEACE DIPLOM ECO/UNDEV
B65

CONLEY R.W.,THE ECONOMICS OF VOCATIONAL REHABILITATION. USA+45 VOL/ASSN CREATE EDU/PROP COST EFFICIENCY SOC/INTEG 20. PAGE 27 F0527
PUB/INST HEALTH GIVE GP/REL
B65

COUGHLIN B.J.,CHURCH AND STATE IN SOCIAL WELFARE. USA+45 RECEIVE GP/REL ORD/FREE WEALTH NEW/LIB. PAGE 28 F0542
CULTURE SECT VOL/ASSN GIVE
B65

LITTLE I.M.D.,INTERNATIONAL AID. UK WOR+45 AGRI INDUS GIVE RECEIVE COLONIAL BAL/PAY WEALTH...POLICY GOV/COMP METH/COMP 20. PAGE 81 F1584
FOR/AID DIPLOM ECO/UNDEV NAT/G
B65

MEAGHER R.F.,PUBLIC INTERNATIONAL DEVELOPMENT FINANCING IN SUDAN. SUDAN FINAN DELIB/GP GIVE ...CHARTS GOV/COMP 20. PAGE 89 F1740
FOR/AID PLAN RECEIVE ECO/UNDEV
B65

MONCRIEFF A.,SECOND THOUGHTS ON AID. WOR+45 ECO/UNDEV AGRI FINAN VOL/ASSN PLAN TEC/DEV GIVE EDU/PROP ROLE WEALTH 20. PAGE 93 F1816
FOR/AID ECO/TAC INT/ORG IDEA/COMP
B65

US OFFICE ECONOMIC OPPORTUNITY,CATALOG OF FEDERAL PROGRAMS FOR INDIVIDUAL AND COMMUNITY IMPROVEMENT. USA+45 GIVE RECEIVE ADMIN HEALTH KNOWL SKILL WEALTH ...CHARTS MUNICH. PAGE 138 F2721
BIBLIOG CLIENT ECO/TAC
S65

BALDWIN D.A.,"THE INTERNATIONAL BANK IN POLITICAL PERSPECTIVE" USA+45 TEC/DEV FOR/AID RENT GIVE COST ...IDEA/COMP GAME IBRD. PAGE 9 F0160
FINAN INT/ORG
S65

GOLDMAN M.I.,"A BALANCE SHEET OF SOVIET FOREIGN AID." USA+45 ECO/UNDEV BAL/PWR ECO/TAC RENT GIVE EDU/PROP CONTROL COST PROFIT GEN/METH. PAGE 48 F0939
USSR FOR/AID NAT/COMP EFFICIENCY
S65

HADDAD W.F.,"MR. SHRIVER AND THE SAVAGE POLITICS OF POVERTY" USA+45 LAW NAT/G DELIB/GP LEGIS GIVE LEAD CENTRAL PWR...SOC/WK CHARTS 20 CONGRESS POVRTY/WAR SHRIVER/S OEO. PAGE 53 F1028
WEALTH GOV/REL CONTROL TOP/EX
S65

WHITE J.,"WEST GERMAN AID TO DEVELOPING COUNTRIES." AFR INT/ORG OP/RES GIVE CENTRAL ATTIT DRIVE...STAT NAT/COMP. PAGE 146 F2869
GERMANY FOR/AID ECO/UNDEV CAP/ISM
B66

ALEXANDER Y.,INTERNATIONAL TECHNICAL ASSISTANCE EXPERTS: A CASE STUDY OF THE U.N. EXPERIENCE. USA+45 WOR+45 WORKER CREATE PLAN PROB/SOLV ECO/TAC FOR/AID GIVE EDU/PROP...CHARTS BIBLIOG 20 UN. PAGE 3 F0062
SKILL INT/ORG TEC/DEV CONSULT
B66

AMER ENTERPRISE INST PUB POL,SIGNIFICANT ISSUES IN ECONOMIC AID TO DEVELOPING COUNTRIES. FINAN INT/ORG NAT/G PLAN PROB/SOLV GIVE TASK WEALTH...DECISION 20. PAGE 4 F0083
ECO/UNDEV FOR/AID DIPLOM POLICY
B66

BALDWIN D.A.,ECONOMIC DEVELOPMENT AND AMERICAN FOREIGN POLICY. USA+45 FINAN LG/CO LEGIS DIPLOM GIVE 20. PAGE 9 F0163
ECO/TAC FOR/AID ECO/UNDEV POLICY
B66

FRIEDMANN W.G.,INTERNATIONAL FINANCIAL AID. USA+45 ECO/DEV ECO/UNDEV NAT/G VOL/ASSN EX/STRUC PLAN RENT GIVE BAL/PAY PWR...GEOG INT/LAW STAT TREND UN EEC COMECON. PAGE 44 F0866
INT/ORG FOR/AID TEC/DEV ECO/TAC
B66

GREENE L.E.,GOVERNMENT IN TENNESSEE (2ND ED.). USA+45 DIST/IND INDUS POL/PAR EX/STRUC LEGIS PLAN BUDGET GIVE CT/SYS...MGT T 20 TENNESSEE. PAGE 51 F0989
PROVS LOC/G CONSTN ADMIN
B66

HOROWITZ D.,HEMISPHERES NORTH AND SOUTH: ECONOMIC DISPARITY AMONG NATIONS. WOR+45 ECO/DEV ECO/UNDEV INT/ORG PLAN DIPLOM INT/TRADE GIVE PARTIC GP/REL ...WELF/ST 20. PAGE 62 F1215
ECO/TAC FOR/AID STRATA WEALTH
B66

KIRDAR U.,THE STRUCTURE OF UNITED NATIONS ECONOMIC AID TO UNDERDEVELOPED COUNTRIES. AGRI FINAN INDUS NAT/G EX/STRUC PLAN GIVE TASK...POLICY 20 UN. PAGE 71 F1397
INT/ORG FOR/AID ECO/UNDEV ADMIN
B66

KIRKENDALL R.S.,SOCIAL SCIENTISTS AND FARM POLITICS IN THE AGE OF ROOSEVELT. ACADEM PLAN ECO/TAC GIVE ADMIN CONTROL PRODUC...SOC 20 NEW/DEAL ROOSEVLT/F BURAGR/ECO. PAGE 71 F1399
AGRI INTELL POLICY NAT/G
B66

LEAGUE OF WOMEN VOTERS OF US,FOREIGN AID AT THE CROSSROADS. USA+45 WOR+45 DELIB/GP PROB/SOLV DIPLOM INT/TRADE RECEIVE BAL/PAY...CHARTS 20 UN ALL/PROG. PAGE 76 F1498
FOR/AID GIVE ECO/UNDEV PLAN
B66

NEVITT A.A.,HOUSING, TAXATION AND SUBSIDIES; A STUDY OF HOUSING IN THE UNITED KINGDOM. UK FINAN GIVE CONTROL COST INCOME...CHARTS 20. PAGE 98 F1918
PLAN TAX HABITAT RENT
B66

OHLIN G.,AID AND INDEBTEDNESS. AUSTRIA FINAN INT/ORG PLAN DIPLOM GIVE...POLICY MATH CHARTS 20. PAGE 101 F1984
FOR/AID ECO/UNDEV ADMIN WEALTH
B66

OHLIN G.,FOREIGN AID POLICIES RECONSIDERED. ECO/DEV ECO/UNDEV VOL/ASSN CONSULT PLAN CONTROL ATTIT ...CONCPT CHARTS BIBLIOG 20. PAGE 101 F1985
FOR/AID DIPLOM GIVE
B66

ORG FOR ECO COOP AND DEVEL,GEOGRAPHICAL DISTRIBUTION OF FINANCIAL FLOWS TO LESS DEVELOPED COUNTRIES. WOR+45 DIPLOM INT/TRADE GIVE RECEIVE REPAR REGION WEALTH...GEOG STAT CHARTS 20 OECD. PAGE 102 F1997
FINAN ECO/UNDEV INT/ORG FOR/AID
B66

US SENATE COMM APPROPRIATIONS,FOREIGN ASSISTANCE AND RELATED AGENCIES APPROPRIATIONS FOR FISCAL YEAR 1967: HEARINGS... ON H. R. 17788. ECO/UNDEV INT/ORG FORCES INSPECT ECO/TAC GIVE DEBATE WEAPON CIVMIL/REL WEALTH...INT 20 CONGRESS DEPT/DEFEN DEPT/STATE DEPT/HEW AID. PAGE 138 F2727
BUDGET FOR/AID DIPLOM COST
L66

CHENERY H.B.,"FOREIGN ASSISTANCE AND ECONOMIC DEVELOPMENT" FUT WOR+45 NAT/G DIPLOM GIVE PRODUC ...METH/CNCPT CHARTS 20. PAGE 24 F0464
FOR/AID EFFICIENCY ECO/UNDEV TEC/DEV
B67

DE TORRES J.,FINANCING LOCAL GOVERNMENT. USA+45 USA-45 NAT/G PROVS GIVE ADJUST PWR...TIME/SEQ CHARTS MUNICH 20. PAGE 31 F0606
LOC/G BUDGET TAX TREND
B67

JOHNSON H.G.,ECONOMIC POLICY TOWARD LESS DEVELOPED COUNTRIES. USA+45 ECO/DEV INT/ORG PLAN CAP/ISM FOR/AID TARIFFS GIVE WEALTH...NEW/IDEA CHARTS 20 UN GATT. PAGE 67 F1327
ECO/UNDEV ECO/TAC METH/COMP
B67

KAPLAN J.J.,CHALLENGE OF FOREIGN AID. USA+45 CONTROL BAL/PAY COST ATTIT ALL/VALS...METH/COMP 20. PAGE 69 F1352
FOR/AID PLAN GIVE POLICY
L67

COSTANZA J.F.,"WHOLESOME NEUTRALITY: LAW AND EDUCATION." USA+45 GIVE EDU/PROP ADJUD CONTROL GP/REL...DECISION JURID. PAGE 28 F0540
SECT PROVS ACADEM
S67

ADAMS E.S.,"THE EXPANDING ROLE OF BANKS IN PUBLIC AFFAIRS." USA+45 GIVE LEAD ROLE...QU 20. PAGE 2 F0036
PARTIC FINAN LOC/G ATTIT
S67

BASOV V.,"THE DEVELOPMENT OF PUBLIC EDUCATION AND THE BUDGET." USSR NAT/G CONTROL REV COST AGE...STAT 20. PAGE 11 F0204
BUDGET GIVE EDU/PROP SCHOOL
S67

FUCHS V.R.,"REDEFINING POVERTY AND REDISTRIBUTING INCOME." USA+45 NAT/G ECO/TAC GIVE COST...NEW/IDEA CHARTS. PAGE 45 F0873
WEALTH INCOME STRATA PROB/SOLV
S67

GREEN C.,"SCHEMES FOR TRANSFERRING INCOME TO THE POOR." BUDGET GIVE RECEIVE DEBATE COST INCOME ...SOC/WK METH/COMP. PAGE 50 F0982
TAX WEALTH PLAN ACT/RES
S67

HILDEBRAND G.H.,"SECOND THOUGHTS ON THE NEGATIVE INCOME TAX." PLAN BUDGET ECO/TAC GIVE RECEIVE DEBATE EFFICIENCY INCOME...METH/COMP COSTS. PAGE 59 F1169
TAX WEALTH SOC/WK ACT/RES
N67

US HOUSE COMM GOVT OPERATIONS,FEDERALLY FINANCED SOCIAL RESEARCH, EXPENDITURES, STATUS, AND OBJECTIVES (PAMPHLET). WOR+45 CREATE LEAD GP/REL ATTIT...GEOG PSY SOC. PAGE 137 F2700
ACT/RES NAT/G GIVE BUDGET

GLADE W.P. F0928

GLADSTON/W....WILLIAM GLADSTONE

GLAUBER R.R. F1771

GLAZER N. F0929

GMP/REG....GOOD MANUFACTURING PRACTICE REGULATIONS

GODFREY E.M. F0930

GODWIN F.W. F0931

GOEBBELS/J....JOSEPH GOEBBELS

GOETHE/J....JOHANN WOLFGANG VON GOETHE

GOETZ-GIREY R. F0932

GOLD J. F0933

GOLD N.L. F0934

GOLD....GOLD

GOLD/COAST....GOLD COAST (PRE-GHANA)

B54
KARTUN D.,AFRICA, AFRICA: A CONTINENT RISES TO ITS FEET. AFR SOUTH/AFR UK ELITES AGRI LABOR LOC/G POL/PAR EDU/PROP CONTROL COERCE DISCRIM AGE/Y NEGRO THIRD/WRLD GOLD/COAST. PAGE 69 F1358
COLONIAL ORD/FREE PROFIT EXTR/IND

GOLD/STAND....GOLD STANDARD

B58
DEFENSE AGAINST INFLATION. USA+45 LEGIS WORKER TAX PRICE DEMAND INCOME PRODUC...POLICY TREND METH/COMP 20 GOLD/STAND. PAGE 1 F0012
ECO/TAC EQUILIB WEALTH PROB/SOLV

GOLDEN C.S. F0935

GOLDMAN M. F0936

GOLDMAN M.I. F0937,F0938,F0939

GOLDMAN/E....ERIC GOLDMAN

GOLDSTEIN J. F0940

GOLDSTEIN W. F0941

GOLDWATR/B....BARRY GOLDWATER

GOLDWIN R.A. F0942

GOLEMBIEWSKI R.T. F0943

GOMBERG W. F2388

GOMES F.A. F0944

GOMEZ ROBLES J. F0945

GOMILLN/CG....C.G. GOMILLION

GONZALEZ M.P. F0946

GONZALEZ NAVARRO M. F0947

GOODMAN J.S. F0948

GOODMAN L.H. F0949

GOODMAN P. F0950

GOODSELL C.T. F0951

GOODWIN C.D.W. F0952,F0953

GOODWIN R.N. F0931

GORDON B. F0954

GORDON D.L. F0955

GORDON L. F0760,F0956,F0957,F0958

GORDON M.S. F0959,F0961

GORDON R.A. F0960,F0961

GORDON W. F0962

GORDON/K....K. GORDON

GORDON/W....WILLIAM GORDON

GORMAN W. F0963

GORT M. F0964

GORZ A. F0965

GOSALVEZ R.B. F0966

GOULD J.M. F0967

GOULD W.B. F0968

GOV/COMP....COMPARISON OF GOVERNMENTS

B08
LLOYD H.D.,THE SWISS DEMOCRACY. SWITZERLND INDUS NAT/G WORKER CHOOSE OWN ORD/FREE SOCISM...PLURIST 19/20 MONOPOLY. PAGE 81 F1590
NAT/COMP GOV/COMP REPRESENT POPULISM

N19
BUSINESS ECONOMISTS' GROUP,INCOME POLICIES (PAMPHLET). UK INDUS LABOR TOP/EX PAY COST PRODUC ...ECOMETRIC GOV/COMP SIMUL ANTHOL 20. PAGE 20 F0395
INCOME WORKER WEALTH POLICY

N19
FREEMAN H.A.,COERCION OF STATES IN FEDERAL UNIONS (PAMPHLET). WOR-45 DIPLOM CONTROL COERCE PEACE ORD/FREE...GOV/COMP METH/COMP NAT/COMP PACIFIST 20. PAGE 43 F0850
FEDERAL WAR INT/ORG PACIFISM

B35
LASKI H.J.,THE STATE IN THEORY AND PRACTICE. ELITES ECO/TAC REPRESENT ORD/FREE PWR WEALTH POPULISM ...GOV/COMP GEN/LAWS 19/20. PAGE 76 F1483
CAP/ISM COERCE NAT/G FASCISM

B38
LAWLEY F.E.,THE GROWTH OF COLLECTIVE ECONOMY VOL. 1: NATIONAL. EUR+WWI AGRI INDUS NAT/G BARGAIN CAP/ISM ECO/TAC WAR OPTIMAL WEALTH...GOV/COMP METH/COMP 19/20 MONOPOLY. PAGE 76 F1492
SOCISM PRICE CONTROL OWN

B48
LAUTERBACH A.,ECONOMIC SECURITY AND INDIVIDUAL FREEDOM: CAN WE HAVE BOTH? COM EUR+WWI MOD/EUR UNIV WOR+45 CAP/ISM TOTALISM ALL/VALS...GOV/COMP BIBLIOG 20. PAGE 76 F1490
ORD/FREE ECO/DEV DECISION INGP/REL

S49
STEINMETZ H.,"THE PROBLEMS OF THE LANDRAT: A STUDY OF COUNTY GOVERNMENT IN THE US ZONE OF GERMANY." GERMANY/W USA+45 INDUS PLAN DIPLOM EDU/PROP CONTROL WAR GOV/REL FEDERAL WEALTH PLURISM...GOV/COMP 20 LANDRAT. PAGE 126 F2478
LOC/G COLONIAL MGT TOP/EX

B51
LEONARD L.L.,INTERNATIONAL ORGANIZATION. WOR+45 WOR-45 EX/STRUC FORCES LEGIS ECO/TAC INT/TRADE COLONIAL ARMS/CONT...SOC/WK GOV/COMP BIBLIOG. PAGE 78 F1527
NAT/G DIPLOM INT/ORG DELIB/GP

B57
BARAN P.A.,THE POLITICAL ECONOMY OF GROWTH. MOD/EUR USA+45 USA-45 TEC/DEV TAX SOCISM...MGT CONCPT GOV/COMP. PAGE 9 F0178
CAP/ISM CONTROL ECO/UNDEV FINAN

N57
U WISCONSIN BUREAU OF GOVT,SERVICE SALES OF THE CITY OF MADISON TO METROPOLITAN COMMUNITIES AND NONRESIDENTS (PAMPHLET). DIST/IND LOC/G ADMIN ...DECISION GOV/COMP MUNICH. PAGE 132 F2597
REGION ECO/TAC PLAN

B58
HANCE W.A.,AFRICAN ECONOMIC DEVELOPMENT. AGRI DIST/IND INDUS R+D ACT/RES PLAN CAP/ISM FOR/AID ...GOV/COMP BIBLIOG 20. PAGE 54 F1058
AFR ECO/UNDEV PROB/SOLV TEC/DEV

B58
OGDEN F.D.,THE POLL TAX IN THE SOUTH. USA+45 USA-45 CONSTN ADJUD ADMIN PARTIC CRIME...TIME/SEQ GOV/COMP METH/COMP 18/20 SOUTH/US. PAGE 101 F1982
TAX CHOOSE RACE/REL DISCRIM

B58
WOODS H.D.,PATTERNS OF INDUSTRIAL DISPUTE SETTLEMENT IN FIVE CANADIAN INDUSTRIES. CANADA USA+45 CONSULT ADJUD GP/REL...JURID GOV/COMP METH/COMP ANTHOL 20. PAGE 148 F2923
BARGAIN INDUS LABOR NAT/G

B59
KELF-COHEN R.,NATIONALISATION IN BRITAIN: THE END OF DOGMA. EUR+WWI UK NAT/G POL/PAR WORKER ECO/TAC PARL/PROC WEALTH SOCISM...GOV/COMP 20. PAGE 70 F1369
NEW/LIB ECO/DEV INDUS OWN

B59
MEZERK A.G.,FINANCIAL ASSISTANCE FOR ECONOMIC DEVELOPMENT. WOR+45 INDUS DIPLOM INT/TRADE...CHARTS GOV/COMP UN. PAGE 91 F1778
FOR/AID FINAN ECO/TAC ECO/UNDEV

B59
PANIKKAR K.M.,THE AFRO-ASIAN STATES AND THEIR PROBLEMS. COM CULTURE KIN POL/PAR SECT DIPLOM EDU/PROP COLONIAL SOVEREIGN...TECHNIC GOV/COMP 20. PAGE 103 F2025
AFR S/ASIA ECO/UNDEV

B60
STOLPER W.F.,GERMANY BETWEEN EAST AND WEST: THE ECONOMICS OF COMPETITIVE COEXISTENCE. AFR FUT GERMANY/E GERMANY/W WOR+45 FINAN POL/PAR BUDGET ECO/TAC FOR/AID INT/TRADE...STAT CHARTS METH/COMP
ECO/DEV DIPLOM GOV/COMP BAL/PWR

20. PAGE 126 F2495

B61
INTL UNION LOCAL AUTHORITIES,METROPOLIS. WOR+45 GOV/COMP
DIST/IND FINAN GIVE EDU/PROP CRIME COST HEALTH LOC/G
WEALTH MUNICH 20. PAGE 65 F1286 BIBLIOG

B61
LICHTHEIM G.,MARXISM. GERMANY SOCIETY WORKER MARXISM
CAP/ISM ECO/TAC NAT/LISM POPULISM...TIME/SEQ SOCISM
GOV/COMP NAT/COMP 18/20 COM/PARTY. PAGE 80 F1559 IDEA/COMP
CULTURE

B62
KINDLEBERGER C.P.,FOREIGN TRADE AND THE NATIONAL INT/TRADE
ECONOMY. WOR+45 ECO/DEV ECO/UNDEV ECO/TAC COST GOV/COMP
DEMAND 20. PAGE 71 F1393 BAL/PAY
POLICY

B63
COLUMBIA U SCHOOL OF LAW,PUBLIC INTERNATIONAL FOR/AID
DEVELOPMENT FINANCING IN SENEGAL. SENEGAL FINAN PLAN
DELIB/GP GIVE EFFICIENCY...CHARTS GOV/COMP ANTHOL RECEIVE
20. PAGE 26 F0511 ECO/UNDEV

B63
DUE J.F.,STATE SALES TAX ADMINISTRATION. OP/RES PROVS
BUDGET PAY ADMIN EXEC ROUTINE COST EFFICIENCY TAX
PROFIT...CHARTS METH/COMP 20. PAGE 34 F0671 STAT
GOV/COMP

B63
ENKE S.,ECONOMICS FOR DEVELOPMENT. AGRI TEC/DEV ECO/UNDEV
CAP/ISM DIPLOM ECO/TAC TAX ATTIT DRIVE HABITAT PHIL/SCI
WEALTH...GOV/COMP BIBLIOG 20. PAGE 38 F0737 CON/ANAL

B63
FURTADO C.,THE ECONOMIC GROWTH OF BRAZIL: A SURVEY ECO/UNDEV
FROM COLONIAL TO MODERN TIMES. L/A+17C AGRI TEC/DEV
DIST/IND EXTR/IND INDUS WORKER COLONIAL RACE/REL LABOR
OWN GOV/COMP. PAGE 45 F0877 DOMIN

B63
US ADVISORY COMN INTERGOV REL,PERFORMANCE OF URBAN REGION
FUNCTIONS: LOCAL AND AREAWIDE. TEC/DEV PARTIC LOC/G
REPRESENT PWR...DECISION GOV/COMP MUNICH. PAGE 133 ECO/TAC
F2633

B63
VON BECKERATH E.,PROBLEME DER NORMATIVEN OKONOMIK ECO/TAC
UND DER WIRTSCHAFTSPOLITISCHEN BERATUNG. GERMANY UK DELIB/GP
ELITES CAP/ISM EFFICIENCY...CONCPT GOV/COMP ECO/DEV
IDEA/COMP 20. PAGE 142 F2789 CONSULT

B64
BEARDSLEY R.K.,STUDIES ON ECONOMIC LIFE IN JAPAN WEALTH
(OCCASIONAL PAPERS NO. 8). INDUS FAM HABITAT...GEOG PRESS
GOV/COMP 20 CHINJAP. PAGE 12 F0223 PRODUC
INCOME

B64
GRIFFITH W.E.,COMMUNISM IN EUROPE (2 VOLS.). COM
CZECHOSLVK USSR WOR+45 WOR-45 YUGOSLAVIA INGP/REL POL/PAR
MARXISM SOCISM...ANTHOL 20 EUROPE/E. PAGE 51 F1000 DIPLOM
GOV/COMP

B64
KALDOR N.,ESSAYS ON ECONOMIC POLICY (VOL. II). BAL/PAY
CHILE GERMANY INDIA FINAN...GOV/COMP METH/COMP 20 INT/TRADE
KEYNES/JM. PAGE 69 F1348 METH/CNCPT
ECO/UNDEV

B64
KNIGHT R.,BIBLIOGRAPHY ON INCOME AND WEALTH, BIBLIOG/A
1957-1960 (VOL VIII). WOR+45 ECO/DEV FINAN ECO/UNDEV
INT/TRADE...GOV/COMP METH/COMP. PAGE 72 F1412 WEALTH
INCOME

B64
RAISON T.,WHY CONSERVATIVE? UK FORCES DIPLOM PLURISM
ECO/TAC GIVE EDU/PROP ORD/FREE WEALTH LAISSEZ CONSERVE
...GOV/COMP 20 TORY/PARTY CONSRV/PAR. PAGE 109 POL/PAR
F2137 NAT/G

B64
US HOUSE COMM BANKING-CURR,INTERNATIONAL BAL/PAY
DEVELOPMENT ASSOCIATION ACT AMENDMENT. CHINA/COM FOR/AID
USA+45 USSR FINAN FORCES LEGIS DIPLOM CONFER RECORD
EFFICIENCY...CHARTS GOV/COMP 20 PRESIDENT CONGRESS ECO/TAC
INTL/DEV. PAGE 136 F2689

B64
WHEARE K.C.,FEDERAL GOVERNMENT (4TH ED.). WOR+45 FEDERAL
WOR-45 POL/PAR LEGIS BAL/PWR CT/SYS...POLICY JURID CONSTN
CONCPT GOV/COMP 17/20. PAGE 145 F2866 EX/STRUC
NAT/COMP

B65
EDELMAN M.,THE POLITICS OF WAGE-PRICE DECISIONS. GOV/COMP
GERMANY ITALY NETHERLAND UK INDUS LABOR POL/PAR CONTROL
PROB/SOLV BARGAIN PRICE ROUTINE BAL/PAY COST DEMAND ECO/TAC
20. PAGE 36 F0699 PLAN

B65
LITTLE I.M.D.,INTERNATIONAL AID. UK WOR+45 AGRI FOR/AID
INDUS GIVE RECEIVE COLONIAL BAL/PAY WEALTH...POLICY DIPLOM
GOV/COMP METH/COMP 20. PAGE 81 F1584 ECO/UNDEV
NAT/G

B65
MEAGHER R.F.,PUBLIC INTERNATIONAL DEVELOPMENT FOR/AID
FINANCING IN SUDAN. SUDAN FINAN DELIB/GP GIVE PLAN
...CHARTS GOV/COMP 20. PAGE 89 F1740 RECEIVE
ECO/UNDEV

B65
O'BRIEN F.,CRISIS IN WORLD COMMUNISM* MARXISM IN MARXISM
SEARCH OF EFFICIENCY. AFR COM ECO/DEV PLAN USSR
INT/TRADE WAR ADJUST PEACE...STAT TIME/SEQ GOV/COMP DRIVE
NAT/COMP. PAGE 99 F1951 EFFICIENCY

B65
TEW B.,WEALTH AND INCOME. UK BUDGET INT/TRADE PRICE FINAN
BAL/PAY DEMAND...CHARTS GOV/COMP 20 AUSTRAL. ECO/DEV
PAGE 129 F2546 WEALTH
INCOME

S65
BRANDENBURG F.,"THE RELEVANCE OF MEXICAN EXPERIENCE L/A+17C
TO LATIN AMERICAN DEVELOPMENT." BRAZIL CHILE GOV/COMP
VENEZUELA STRUCT ECO/UNDEV AGRI CREATE ECO/TAC
...STAT RECORD MEXIC/AMER ARGEN COLOMB. PAGE 18
F0340

S65
KEE W.S.,"CENTRAL CITY EXPENDITURES AND LOC/G
METROPOLITAN AREAS." PLAN BUDGET ECO/TAC TAX GP/REL GOV/COMP
WEALTH...CHARTS MUNICH 20. PAGE 70 F1366 NEIGH

B66
ANDRESKI S.,PARASITISM AND SUBVERSION* THE CASE OF L/A+17C
LATIN AMERICA. CULTURE ECO/UNDEV LABOR NAT/G SECT GOV/COMP
PROB/SOLV RACE/REL TOTALISM ATTIT WEALTH ALL/IDEOS. STRATA
PAGE 5 F0100 REV

B66
DUNCAN O.,METROPOLIS AND REGION (PREPARED FOR REGION
RESOURCES FOR THE FUTURE INC., WASHINGTON, D.C.). GEOG
FINAN INDUS ECO/TAC TAX...CHARTS GOV/COMP MUNICH.
PAGE 35 F0677

B66
DUNCOMBE H.S.,COUNTY GOVERNMENT IN AMERICA. USA+45 LOC/G
FINAN ADMIN ROUTINE GOV/REL...GOV/COMP MUNICH 20. PROVS
PAGE 35 F0678 CT/SYS
TOP/EX

B66
HOLT R.T.,THE POLITICAL BASIS OF ECONOMIC ECO/TAC
DEVELOPMENT. STRATA STRUCT NAT/G DIPLOM ADMIN...SOC GOV/COMP
NAT/COMP BIBLIOG 20. PAGE 61 F1201 CONSTN
EX/STRUC

S66
FLEMING W.G.,"AUTHORITY, EFFICIENCY, AND ROLE DOMIN
STRESS: PROBLEMS IN THE DEVELOPMENT OF EAST AFRICAN EFFICIENCY
BUREAUCRACIES." AFR UGANDA STRUCT PROB/SOLV ROUTINE COLONIAL
INGP/REL ROLE...MGT SOC GP/COMP GOV/COMP 20 ADMIN
TANGANYIKA AFRICA/E. PAGE 41 F0810

B67
CAMPBELL A.K.,METROPOLITAN AMERICA* FISCAL PATTERNS USA+45
AND GOVERNMENTAL SYSTEMS. PROVS PLAN COST...POLICY NAT/G
DECISION GOV/COMP METH/COMP BIBLIOG. PAGE 21 F0405 LOC/G
BUDGET

B76
TAINE H.A.,THE ANCIENT REGIME. FRANCE STRATA FORCES NAT/G
PARTIC EQUILIB WEALTH CONSERVE POPULISM...GOV/COMP GOV/REL
SOC/INTEG 18/19. PAGE 128 F2527 TAX
REV

B91
MILL J.S.,SOCIALISM (1859). MOD/EUR AGRI INDUS WEALTH
NAT/G REV INCOME PRODUC ORD/FREE POPULISM SOCISM SOCIALIST
...GOV/COMP METH/COMP 19. PAGE 91 F1787 ECO/TAC
OWN

B95
SELIGMAN E.R.A.,ESSAYS IN TAXATION. NEW/ZEALND TAX
PRUSSIA UK USA-45 MARKET LOC/G CREATE PRICE CONTROL TARIFFS
INCOME OWN WEALTH...GOV/COMP METH/COMP 19. PAGE 119 INDUS
F2349 NAT/G

GOV/REL....RELATIONS BETWEEN GOVERNMENTS

N
BROCKWAY A.F.,AFRICAN SOCIALISM. EUR+WWI GHANA AFR
ISLAM UAR ECO/UNDEV CAP/ISM INT/TRADE COLONIAL SOCISM
COERCE GOV/REL DISCRIM 20 NEGRO NKRUMAH/K NASSER/G. MARXISM
PAGE 19 F0356

N
US SUPERINTENDENT OF DOCUMENTS,INTERSTATE COMMERCE BIBLIOG/A
(PRICE LIST 59). USA+45 LAW LOC/G NAT/G LEGIS DIST/IND
TARIFFS TAX ADMIN CONTROL HEALTH DECISION. PAGE 140 GOV/REL
F2752 PROVS

NCO
CARRINGTON C.E.,THE COMMONWEALTH IN AFRICA ECO/UNDEV
(PAMPHLET). UK STRUCT NAT/G COLONIAL REPRESENT AFR
GOV/REL RACE/REL NAT/LISM...MAJORIT 20 EEC NEGRO. DIPLOM
PAGE 22 F0421 PLAN

B03
GRIFFIN A.P.C.,LISTS PUBLISHED 1902-03: GOVERNMENT BIBLIOG
OWNERSHIP OF RAILROADS (PAMPHLET). USA-45 LAW NAT/G DIST/IND
RATION GOV/REL CENTRAL SOCISM...POLICY 19/20. CONTROL
PAGE 51 F0998 ADJUD

N19
ARNDT H.W.,AUSTRALIAN FOREIGN AID POLICY FOR/AID
(PAMPHLET). ECO/UNDEV DIPLOM GIVE GOV/REL COST UTIL POLICY
PWR...CHARTS 20 AUSTRAL PAPUA NEW/GUINEA. PAGE 6 ECO/TAC
F0114 EFFICIENCY

N19
EAST KENTUCKY REGIONAL PLAN,PROGRAM 60: A DECADE OF REGION

ACTION FOR PROGRESS IN EASTERN KENTUCKY (PAMPHLET). ADMIN
USA+45 AGRI CONSTRUC INDUS CONSULT ACT/RES PLAN
PROB/SOLV EDU/PROP GOV/REL HEALTH KENTUCKY. PAGE 35 ECO/UNDEV
F0689

N19
EAST KENTUCKY REGIONAL PLAN,PROGRAM 60 REPORT: REGION
ACTION FOR PORGRESS IN EASTERN KENTUCKY (PAMPHLET). PLAN
USA+45 CONSTRUC INDUS ACT/RES PROB/SOLV EDU/PROP ECO/UNDEV
ADMIN GOV/REL KENTUCKY. PAGE 35 F0690 CONSULT

N19
FAHRNKOPF N.,STATE AND LOCAL GOVERNMENT IN ILLINOIS BIBLIOG
(PAMPHLET). CONSTN ADMIN PARTIC CHOOSE REPRESENT LOC/G
GOV/REL...JURID MGT 20 ILLINOIS. PAGE 39 F0759 LEGIS
CT/SYS

N19
HERZBERG D.G.,A BUDGET FOR NEW YORK STATE, POL/PAR
1956-1957 (PAMPHLET). USA+45 ADMIN GOV/REL 20 PROVS
NEW/YORK HARRIMAN/A. PAGE 59 F1159 BUDGET
LEGIS

N19
KRIESBERG M.,CANCELLATION OF THE RATION STAMPS RATION
(PAMPHLET). USA+45 USA-45 MARKET PROB/SOLV PRICE DECISION
GOV/REL RIGID/FLEX 20 OPA. PAGE 73 F1439 ADMIN
NAT/G

N19
LAWRENCE S.A.,THE BATTERY ADDITIVE CONTROVERSY PHIL/SCI
(PAMPHLET). USA+45 LAW MARKET PROC/MFG R+D CAP/ISM LOBBY
CT/SYS GOV/REL OWN FTC CONGRESS BUR/STNDRD INSPECT
RITCHIE/JM. PAGE 76 F1494

N19
MARSH J.F. JR.,THE FBI RETIREMENT BILL (PAMPHLET). ADMIN
USA+45 EX/STRUC WORKER PLAN PROB/SOLV BUDGET LEAD NAT/G
LOBBY PARL/PROC PERS/REL RIGID/FLEX...POLICY 20 FBI SENIOR
PRESIDENT BUR/BUDGET. PAGE 86 F1677 GOV/REL

N19
SAPIR H.M.,JAPAN, CHINA, AND THE WEST (PAMPHLET). ECO/UNDEV
AFR ASIA CHINA/COM PROB/SOLV GOV/REL 20 CHINJAP. INT/TRADE
PAGE 116 F2282 DECISION
PLAN

N19
SILVERMAN C.,THE PRESIDENT'S ECONOMIC ADVISERS CONSULT
(PAMPHLET). USA+45 LAW ELITES ECO/DEV EX/STRUC PROB/SOLV
ADMIN LEAD GOV/REL PERS/REL ROLE...POLICY DECISION NAT/G
20 PRESIDENT CONGRESS EISNHWR/DD. PAGE 122 F2404 PLAN

N19
WILSON T.,FINANCIAL ASSISTANCE WITH REGIONAL FINAN
DEVELOPMENT (PAMPHLET). CANADA INDUS NAT/G PLAN TAX ECO/TAC
CONTROL COST EFFICIENCY...POLICY CHARTS 20. REGION
PAGE 147 F2902 GOV/REL

N19
YLVISAKER P.N.,THE NATURAL CEMENT ISSUE (PAMPHLET). POLICY
USA+45 USA-45 CONSTRUC PROVS CAP/ISM ADMIN LOBBY NAT/G
PERS/REL OWN RIGID/FLEX ROLE 20 MINNESOTA. PAGE 150 PLAN
F2948 GOV/REL

B24
HOLDSWORTH W.S.,A HISTORY OF ENGLISH LAW; THE LAW
COMMON LAW AND ITS RIVALS (VOL. IV). UK SEA AGRI LEGIS
CHIEF ADJUD CONTROL CRIME GOV/REL...INT/LAW JURID CT/SYS
NAT/COMP 16/17 PARLIAMENT COMMON/LAW CANON/LAW CONSTN
ENGLSH/LAW. PAGE 61 F1195

B25
MATHEWS J.M.,AMERICAN STATE GOVERNMENT. USA-45 PROVS
LOC/G CHIEF EX/STRUC LEGIS ADJUD CONTROL CT/SYS ADMIN
ROUTINE GOV/REL PWR 20 GOVERNOR. PAGE 87 F1703 FEDERAL
CONSTN

B25
WILLIAMS B.,THE SELBORNE MEMORANDUM. AFR FUT COLONIAL
SOUTH/AFR UK NAT/G BUDGET DIPLOM REGION GOV/REL PROVS
SOVEREIGN...POLICY CHARTS 20 UNIFICA SELBORNE/W.
PAGE 147 F2888

B32
THOMPSON C.D.,CONFESSIONS OF THE POWER TRUST. LG/CO
MARKET ACT/RES EDU/PROP CONTROL GOV/REL INCOME OWN SERV/IND
...MGT 20 FTC MONOPOLY. PAGE 130 F2564 PWR
FINAN

B35
SCHATTSCHNEIDER E.E.,POLITICS, PRESSURES AND THE LOBBY
TARIFF: A STUDY OF FREE PRIVATE ENTERPRISE IN LEGIS
PRESSURE POLITICS IN TARIFF REVISION 1929-1930. TARIFFS
NAT/G BARGAIN ECO/TAC ROUTINE REPRESENT GOV/REL
GP/REL PWR POLICY. PAGE 116 F2290

B40
BLAISDELL D.C.,GOVERNMENT AND AGRICULTURE; THE NAT/G
GROWTH OF FEDERAL FARM AID. USA-45 MARKET PLAN GIVE
PROB/SOLV TEC/DEV ECO/TAC GOV/REL ADJUST ATTIT AGRI
...CHARTS 20 DEPT/AGRI. PAGE 15 F0296 DELIB/GP

B41
HANSEN A.H.,FISCAL POLICY AND BUSINESS CYCLES. UK FINAN
INDUS PROB/SOLV DIPLOM INT/TRADE OPTIMAL...POLICY PLAN
TIME/SEQ CHARTS 19/20. PAGE 54 F1062 ECO/TAC
GOV/REL

B43
WILMERDING L. JR.,THE SPENDING POWER: A HISTORY OF LEGIS
THE EFFORTS OF CONGRESS TO CONTROL EXPENDITURES. BUDGET
USA-45 POL/PAR DELIB/GP EX/STRUC TOP/EX TARIFFS CONTROL
ADMIN GOV/REL...TIME/SEQ SENATE HOUSE/REP. PAGE 147
F2900

B48
KEIR D.L.,CASES IN CONSTITUTIONAL LAW. UK CHIEF CONSTN
LEGIS DIPLOM TAX PARL/PROC CRIME GOV/REL...INT/LAW LAW
JURID 17/20. PAGE 70 F1368 ADJUD
CT/SYS

B49
SCHULTZ W.J.,AMERICAN PUBLIC FINANCE. USA+45 FINAN
ECO/TAC TAX ADMIN GOV/REL GP/REL INCOME 20. POLICY
PAGE 117 F2318 ECO/DEV
NAT/G

S49
STEINMETZ H.,"THE PROBLEMS OF THE LANDRAT: A STUDY LOC/G
OF COUNTY GOVERNMENT IN THE US ZONE OF GERMANY." COLONIAL
GERMANY/W USA+45 INDUS PLAN DIPLOM EDU/PROP CONTROL MGT
WAR GOV/REL FEDERAL WEALTH PLURISM...GOV/COMP 20 TOP/EX
LANDRAT. PAGE 126 F2478

B50
KOENIG L.W.,THE SALE OF THE TANKERS. USA+45 SEA NAT/G
DIST/IND POL/PAR DIPLOM ADMIN CIVMIL/REL ATTIT POLICY
...DECISION 20 PRESIDENT DEPT/STATE. PAGE 72 F1414 PLAN
GOV/REL

B52
HARDIN C.M.,THE POLITICS OF AGRICULTURE. USA+45 AGRI
NAT/G PROF/ORG LEGIS LOBBY 20 DEPT/AGRI. PAGE 55 POLICY
F1077 ECO/TAC
GOV/REL

B52
JENNINGS W.I.,CONSTITUTIONAL LAWS OF THE CONSTN
COMMONWEALTH. AFR UK LAW CHIEF LEGIS TAX CT/SYS JURID
PARL/PROC GOV/REL...INT/LAW 18/20 ENGLSH/LAW ADJUD
COMMON/LAW. PAGE 67 F1316 COLONIAL

B52
REDFORD E.S.,ADMINISTRATION OF NATIONAL ECONOMIC ADMIN
CONTROL. ECO/DEV DELIB/GP ADJUD CONTROL EQUILIB 20. ROUTINE
PAGE 110 F2166 GOV/REL
LOBBY

B54
MEYER F.V.,INFLATION AND CAPITAL. AFR UK WOR+45 ECO/DEV
BUDGET GOV/REL INCOME PRODUC PROFIT WEALTH...CONCPT FINAN
CHARTS 20. PAGE 90 F1768 ECO/TAC
DEMAND

B54
RECK D.,GOVERNMENT PURCHASING AND COMPETITION. NAT/G
USA+45 LEGIS CAP/ISM ECO/TAC GOV/REL CENTRAL FINAN
...POLICY 20 CONGRESS. PAGE 110 F2164 MGT
COST

B55
BLOOM G.F.,ECONOMICS OF LABOR RELATIONS. USA+45 LAW ECO/DEV
CONSULT WORKER CAP/ISM PAY ADJUD CONTROL EFFICIENCY ECO/TAC
ORD/FREE...CHARTS 19/20 AFL/CIO NLRB DEPT/LABOR. LABOR
PAGE 16 F0299 GOV/REL

B55
GOMES F.A.,OPERACAO MUNICIPIO. BRAZIL L/A+17C ECO/UNDEV
SERV/IND LOC/G BUDGET ECO/TAC COST DEMAND...POLICY FEDERAL
MUNICH 20. PAGE 48 F0944 GOV/REL

B55
SMITHIES A.,THE BUDGETARY PROCESS IN THE UNITED NAT/G
STATES. AFR ECO/DEV AGRI EX/STRUC FORCES LEGIS ADMIN
PROB/SOLV TAX ROUTINE EFFICIENCY...MGT CONGRESS BUDGET
PRESIDENT. PAGE 124 F2436 GOV/REL

B55
STILLMAN C.W.,AFRICA IN THE MODERN WORLD. AFR ECO/UNDEV
USA+45 WOR+45 INT/TRADE COLONIAL PARTIC REGION DIPLOM
GOV/REL RACE/REL 20. PAGE 126 F2489 POLICY
STRUCT

B55
US ADVISORY COMN INTERGOV REL,THE COMMISSION ON GOV/REL
INTERGOVERNMENTAL RELATIONS; A REPORT TO THE NAT/G
PRESIDENT FOR TRANSMITTAL TO THE CONGRESS. USA+45 LOC/G
ECO/DEV AGRI COM/IND FINAN FORCES PLAN EDU/PROP PROVS
HEALTH WEALTH...STAT MUNICH 20 CIV/DEFENS. PAGE 133
F2630

B56
BURKHEAD J.,GOVERNMENT BUDGETING. ECO/DEV PROB/SOLV BUDGET
ECO/TAC ADMIN ROUTINE GOV/REL EFFICIENCY...DECISION NAT/G
MGT. PAGE 20 F0388 PROVS
EX/STRUC

B56
REDFORD E.S.,PUBLIC ADMINISTRATION AND POLICY EX/STRUC
FORMATION: STUDIES IN OIL, GAS, BANKING, RIVER PROB/SOLV
DEVELOPMENT AND CORPORATE INVESTIGATIONS. USA+45 CONTROL
CLIENT NAT/G ADMIN LOBBY REPRESENT GOV/REL INGP/REL EXEC
20. PAGE 110 F2167

S56
MILNE R.S.,"CONTROL OF GOVERNMENT CORPORATIONS IN CONTROL
THE UNITED STATES." USA+45 NAT/G CHIEF LEGIS BUDGET EX/STRUC
20 GENACCOUNT. PAGE 92 F1800 GOV/REL
PWR

S56
TYLER G.,"THE PRESIDENCY AND LABOR." USA+45 USA-45 LABOR
NAT/G LOBBY GOV/REL PWR 20 PRESIDENT. PAGE 131 REPRESENT
F2595 CHIEF

B57
ASSN U BUREAUS BUS-ECO RES,INDEX OF PUBLICATIONS OF BIBLIOG
BUREAUS OF BUSINESS AND ECONOMIC RESEARCH 1950-56 ECO/DEV

AND YEARLY SUPPLEMENTS THROUGH 1967. FINAN OP/RES PLAN GOV/REL INCOME AGE...POLICY 20. PAGE 7 F0133
ECO/TAC LG/CO

B57
SINGH D.B.,INFLATIONARY PRICE TRENDS IN INDIA SINCE 1939. AFR INDIA ECO/TAC RATION CONTROL WAR GOV/REL BAL/PAY DEMAND INCOME PEACE PRODUC...POLICY CHARTS 20. PAGE 122 F2413
BUDGET ECO/UNDEV PRICE FINAN

B58
CHANG C.,THE INFLATIONARY SPIRAL: THE EXPERIENCE IN CHINA 1939-50. CHINA/COM BUDGET INT/TRADE PRICE ADMIN CONTROL WAR DEMAND...POLICY CHARTS 20. PAGE 23 F0451
FINAN ECO/TAC BAL/PAY GOV/REL

B58
MOULTON H.G.,CAN INFLATION BE CONTROLLED? ECO/DEV INDUS CAP/ISM RATION GOV/REL COST INCOME PEACE WEALTH...CHARTS TIME 20 KEYNES/JM MONEY. PAGE 94 F1847
ECO/TAC CONTROL DEMAND FINAN

B58
PAN AMERICAN UNION,REPERTORIO DE PUBLICACIONES PERIODICAS ACTUALES LATINO-AMERICANAS. CULTURE ECO/UNDEV ADMIN LEAD GOV/REL 20 OAS. PAGE 103 F2023
BIBLIOG L/A+17C NAT/G DIPLOM

B58
RUBIN B.,PUBLIC RELATIONS AND THE STATE, A CASE STUDY OF NEW YORK STATE ADMINISTRATION, 1943-54. USA+45 USA-45 COM/IND EDU/PROP GOV/REL...CHARTS 20 NEW/YORK DEWEY/THOM. PAGE 114 F2255
INGP/REL PRESS PROVS GP/REL

B58
SHAW S.J.,THE FINANCIAL AND ADMINISTRATIVE ORGANIZATION AND DEVELOPMENT OF OTTOMAN EGYPT 1517-1798. UAR LOC/G FORCES BUDGET INT/TRADE TAX EATING INCOME WEALTH...CHARTS BIBLIOG 16/18 OTTOMAN NAPOLEON/B. PAGE 120 F2371
FINAN ADMIN GOV/REL CULTURE

B59
RAMANADHAM V.V.,PROBLEMS OF PUBLIC ENTERPRISE: THOUGHTS ON BRITISH EXPERIENCE. UK FINAN INDUS PLAN PRICE CENTRAL...POLICY 20. PAGE 109 F2140
SOCISM LG/CO ECO/DEV GOV/REL

B59
U OF MICHIGAN LAW SCHOOL,ATOMS AND THE LAW. USA+45 PROVS WORKER PROB/SOLV DIPLOM ADMIN GOV/REL ANTHOL. PAGE 132 F2596
NUC/PWR NAT/G CONTROL LAW

S59
SCHEEHAN D.,"PUBLIC AND PRIVATE GROUPS AS IDENTIFIED IN THE FIELD OF TRADE REGULATIONS." USA+45 ADMIN REPRESENT GOV/REL. PAGE 116 F2293
LAW CONTROL ADJUD LOBBY

S59
SEIDMAN H.,"THE GOVERNMENT CORPORATION IN THE UNITED STATES." USA+45 LEGIS ADMIN PLURISM 20. PAGE 119 F2344
CONTROL GOV/REL EX/STRUC EXEC

B60
CARPER E.T.,THE DEFENSE APPROPRIATIONS RIDER (PAMPHLET). USA+45 CONSTN CHIEF DELIB/GP LEGIS BUDGET LOBBY CIVMIL/REL...POLICY 20 CONGRESS EISNHWR/DD DEPT/DEFEN PRESIDENT BOSTON. PAGE 22 F0419
GOV/REL ADJUD LAW CONTROL

B60
CROSSER P.K.,STATE CAPITALISM IN THE ECONOMY OF THE UNITED STATES. USA+45 USA-45 AGRI FINAN INDUS LABOR WORKER RATION CONTROL GOV/REL DEMAND...NEW/IDEA 20. PAGE 29 F0557
CAP/ISM ECO/DEV ECO/TAC NAT/G

B60
FINKLE J.L.,THE PRESIDENT MAKES A DECISION: A STUDY OF DIXON-YATES. OP/RES PROB/SOLV BUDGET ADMIN GOV/REL...POLICY BIBLIOG/A 20 PRESIDENT. PAGE 41 F0799
DECISION CHIEF PWR POL/PAR

B60
HUGHES J.,NATIONALISED INDUSTRIES IN THE MIXED ECONOMY (PAMPHLET). FINAN PROB/SOLV CAP/ISM OWN ...SOCIALIST STAT METH/COMP 20. PAGE 63 F1233
SOCISM LG/CO GOV/REL ECO/DEV

B60
ILLINOIS U BUR COMMUNITY PLAN,PROCEEDINGS OF ILLINOIS STATEWIDE PLANNING CONFERENCE 1960. USA+45 FINAN LOC/G ACT/RES LEAD GOV/REL GP/REL WEALTH MUNICH 20 ILLINOIS. PAGE 64 F1260
PLAN DELIB/GP VOL/ASSN

B60
MENDELSON W.,CAPITALISM, DEMOCRACY, AND THE SUPREME COURT. USA+45 USA-45 CONSTN DIPLOM GOV/REL ATTIT ORD/FREE LAISSEZ...POLICY CHARTS PERS/COMP 18/20 SUPREME/CT MARSHALL/J HOLMES/OW TANEY/RB FIELD/JJ. PAGE 90 F1758
JUDGE CT/SYS JURID NAT/G

B60
ROBINSON R.I.,FINANCIAL INSTITUTIONS. USA+45 PRICE GOV/REL DEMAND WEALTH...CHARTS T 20 MONEY. PAGE 113 F2226
FINAN ECO/TAC ECO/DEV BUDGET

B60
SANTHANAM K.,UNION-STATE RELATIONS IN INDIA. INDIA FINAN PROVS PLAN ECO/TAC...LING 20. PAGE 116 F2280
FEDERAL GOV/REL CONSTN POLICY

B60
THOMPSON V.A.,THE REGULATORY PROCESS IN OPA RATIONING. USA-45 CLIENT PROB/SOLV ADMIN LOBBY REPRESENT 20. PAGE 130 F2566
EX/STRUC GOV/REL INGP/REL

B60
US HOUSE COMM GOVT OPERATIONS,OPERATIONS OF THE DEVELOPMENT LOAN FUND: HEARINGS (COMMITTEE ON GOVERNMENT OPERATIONS). USA+45 PLAN BUDGET DIPLOM GOV/REL COST...CHARTS 20 CONGRESS DEPT/STATE AID. PAGE 137 F2698
FINAN FOR/AID ECO/TAC EFFICIENCY

S60
MANN S.Z.,"POLICY FORMULATION IN THE EXECUTIVE BRANCH: THE TAFT-HARTLEY EXPERIENCE." USA+45 LABOR CHIEF INGP/REL 20 NLRB. PAGE 85 F1656
EXEC GOV/REL EX/STRUC PROB/SOLV

B61
AGARWAL R.C.,STATE ENTERPRISE IN INDIA. FUT INDIA UK FINAN INDUS ADMIN CONTROL OWN...POLICY CHARTS BIBLIOG 20 RAILROAD. PAGE 3 F0048
ECO/UNDEV SOCISM GOV/REL LG/CO

B61
ALFRED H.,PUBLIC OWNERSHIP IN THE USA: GOALS AND PRIORITIES. LAW INDUS INT/TRADE ADJUD GOV/REL EFFICIENCY PEACE SOCISM...POLICY ANTHOL 20 TVA. PAGE 4 F0065
CONTROL OWN ECO/DEV ECO/TAC

B61
BAUER P.T.,INDIAN ECONOMIC POLICY AND DEVELOPMENT. INDIA STRATA AGRI FINAN POL/PAR BUDGET FOR/AID GOV/REL EFFICIENCY...CENSUS 20. PAGE 11 F0216
ECO/UNDEV ECO/TAC POLICY PLAN

B61
CARNEY D.E.,GOVERNMENT AND ECONOMY IN BRITISH WEST AFRICA. GAMBIA GHANA NIGERIA SIER/LEONE DOMIN ADMIN GOV/REL SOVEREIGN WEALTH LAISSEZ...BIBLIOG 20 CMN/WLTH. PAGE 21 F0417
METH/COMP COLONIAL ECO/TAC ECO/UNDEV

B61
HUBBARD P.J.,ORIGINS OF THE TVA: THE MUSCLE SHOALS CONTROVERSY, 1920-1932. USA-45 DELIB/GP LEGIS LEAD LOBBY GOV/REL GP/REL INGP/REL OWN PERSON...BIBLIOG 20 TVA CONGRESS WATER. PAGE 62 F1229
SEA CONTROL NAT/G INDUS

B61
MACMAHON A.W.,DELEGATION AND AUTONOMY. INDIA STRUCT LEGIS BARGAIN BUDGET ECO/TAC LEGIT EXEC REPRESENT GOV/REL CENTRAL DEMAND EFFICIENCY PRODUC. PAGE 84 F1637
ADMIN PLAN FEDERAL

B61
SACKS S.,FINANCING GOVERNMENT IN A METROPOLITAN GOVERNMENT. USA+45 ECO/DEV R+D LOC/G GOV/REL ...BIBLIOG MUNICH 20 CLEVELAND. PAGE 115 F2269
FINAN PLAN BUDGET

B61
STANLEY C.J.,LATE CH'ING FINANCE: HU KUANG-YUNG AS AN INNOVATOR. ASIA NAT/G FORCES BUDGET TAX WAR GOV/REL COST...POLICY BIOG CHARTS BIBLIOG 19. PAGE 125 F2469
FINAN ECO/TAC CIVMIL/REL ADMIN

B61
STARNER F.L.,GENERAL OBLIGATION BOND FINANCING BY LOCAL GOVERNMENTS: A SURVEY OF STATE CONTROLS. CANADA UK USA+45 CONSTN PROVS...POLICY JURID METH/COMP 20 EUROPE CALIFORNIA. PAGE 125 F2471
FINAN LOC/G GOV/REL ADJUD

B61
STOCKING G.W.,WORKABLE COMPETITION AND ANTITRUST POLICY. USA+45 NAT/G CONSULT PLAN PRICE GOV/REL COST DEMAND PROFIT...POLICY 20. PAGE 126 F2491
LG/CO INDUS ECO/TAC CONTROL

L61
GERWIG R.,"PUBLIC AUTHORITIES IN THE UNITED STATES." LAW CONSTN PROVS TAX ADMIN FEDERAL MUNICH. PAGE 47 F0920
LOC/G GOV/REL PWR

S61
SCHER S.,"REGULATORY AGENCY CONTROL THROUGH APPOINTMENT: THE CASE OF THE EISENHOWER ADMINISTRATION AND THE NLRB." USA+45 EX/STRUC GOV/REL 20 NLRB. PAGE 116 F2296
CHIEF LOBBY CONTROL TOP/EX

N61
US ADVISORY COMM INTERGOV REL,STATE AND LOCAL TAXATION ON PRIVATELY OWNED PROPERTY LOCATED ON FEDERAL AREAS: PROPOSED AMENDMENT OF BUCK ACT (PAMPHLET). USA+45 ACT/RES PLAN CONTROL GOV/REL INGP/REL OWN...POLICY JURID CHARTS GP/COMP 20. PAGE 133 F2629
PROVS LOC/G NAT/G TAX

N61
US ADVISORY COMN INTERGOV REL,STATE CONSTITUTIONAL AND STATUTORY RESTRICTIONS ON LOCAL GOVERNMENT DEBT (PAMPHLET). LAW CONSTN CHOOSE PWR...DECISION MUNICH. PAGE 133 F2631
TAX PROVS GOV/REL

B62
CARPER E.T.,ILLINOIS GOES TO CONGRESS FOR ARMY LAND. USA+45 LAW EXTR/IND PROVS REGION CIVMIL/REL GOV/REL FEDERAL ATTIT 20 ILLINOIS SENATE CONGRESS DIRKSEN/E DOUGLAS/P. PAGE 22 F0420
ADMIN LOBBY GEOG LEGIS

B62
DUPRE J.S.,SCIENCE AND THE NATION: POLICY AND POLITICS. USA+45 LAW ACADEM FORCES ADMIN CIVMIL/REL GOV/REL EFFICIENCY PEACE...TREND 20 SCI/ADVSRY. PAGE 35 F0682
R+D INDUS TEC/DEV NUC/PWR

B62
FORD A.G.,THE GOLD STANDARD 1880-1914: BRITAIN AND ARGENTINA. AFR UK ECO/UNDEV INT/TRADE ADMIN GOV/REL DEMAND EFFICIENCY...STAT CHARTS 19/20 ARGEN. PAGE 42 F0823 — FINAN ECO/TAC BUDGET BAL/PAY

B62
GEARY R.C.,EUROPE'S FUTURE IN FIGURES. FUT GOV/REL DEMAND PRODUC...STAT CHARTS METH/COMP ANTHOL METH 20 EUROPE. PAGE 47 F0912 — FINAN ECO/DEV PREDICT WEALTH

B62
GREEN L.P.,DEVELOPMENT IN AFRICA. AFR CENTRL/AFR GHANA RHODESIA SOUTH/AFR AGRI PROC/MFG INT/TRADE DEMAND NAT/LISM PRODUC WEALTH...GEOG METH/CNCPT CHARTS BIBLIOG 20. PAGE 50 F0987 — CULTURE ECO/UNDEV GOV/REL TREND

B62
HUHNE L.H.,FINANCING ECONOMIC DEVELOPMENT THROUGH NATIONAL AND INTERNATIONAL ORGANIZATIONS (THESIS; U OF WIS.). USA+45 INT/ORG PLAN GIVE GOV/REL WEALTH 20. PAGE 63 F1235 — RATION FINAN FOR/AID ECO/UNDEV

B62
LICHFIELD N.,COST-BENEFIT ANALYSIS IN URBAN REDEVELOPMENT. CONSTRUC LOC/G NEIGH ACT/RES PROB/SOLV TEC/DEV BUDGET TAX...DECISION STAT CHARTS SOC/EXP MUNICH 20. PAGE 80 F1558 — PLAN COST GOV/REL

B62
MORGAN C.A.,LABOR ECONOMICS. LAW INDUS MARKET WORKER PLAN PROB/SOLV GOV/REL INCOME ROLE...T 20 DEPT/LABOR NLRB. PAGE 93 F1829 — LABOR ECO/TAC ECO/DEV CAP/ISM

B62
PRAKASH O.M.,THE THEORY AND WORKING OF STATE CORPORATIONS: WITH SPECIAL REFERENCE TO INDIA. INDIA UK USA+45 TOP/EX PRICE ADMIN EFFICIENCY...MGT METH/COMP 20 TVA. PAGE 107 F2112 — LG/CO ECO/UNDEV GOV/REL SOCISM

B62
SCHILLING W.R.,STRATEGY, POLITICS, AND DEFENSE BUDGETS. AFR USA+45 CHIEF LEGIS PLAN TEC/DEV BAL/PWR BUDGET NUC/PWR WAR CIVMIL/REL GOV/REL PWR 20 EISNHWR/DD. PAGE 117 F2297 — NAT/G POLICY FORCES DETER

B62
SELOSOEMARDJAN O.,SOCIAL CHANGES IN JOGJAKARTA. INDONESIA NETHERLAND ELITES STRATA STRUCT FAM POL/PAR CREATE DIPLOM INT/TRADE EDU/PROP ADMIN GOV/REL...SOC 20 JAVA CHINJAP. PAGE 119 F2352 — ECO/UNDEV CULTURE REV COLONIAL

B62
US ADVISORY COMN INTERGOV REL,STATE CONSTITUTIONAL AND STATUTORY RESTRICTIONS ON LOCAL TAXING POWERS. USA+45 USA-45 LAW CONSTN ACT/RES CONTROL WEALTH ...JURID CHARTS 20. PAGE 133 F2632 — LOC/G PROVS GOV/REL TAX

B62
US BUREAU OF THE CENSUS,REPORT FOR SUBCOMMITTEE ON ANTITRUST AND MONOPOLY: CONCENTRATION RATIOS IN MANUFACTURING INDUSTRY 1958. USA+45 ECO/DEV CONTROL GOV/REL OWN PRODUC PROFIT...STAT 20 CONGRESS MONOPOLY. PAGE 134 F2646 — CHARTS PROC/MFG MARKET LG/CO

B63
ALPERT P.,ECONOMIC DEVELOPMENT. WOR+45 FINAN TEC/DEV ECO/TAC PRICE GOV/REL HABITAT...GEOG BIBLIOG T 20 THIRD/WRLD. PAGE 4 F0079 — ECO/DEV ECO/UNDEV INT/TRADE FOR/AID

B63
BATES J.L.,THE ORIGINS OF TEAPOT DOME: PROGRESSIVES, PARTIES, AND PETROLEUM, 1909-1921. USA-45 INDUS LG/CO POL/PAR DELIB/GP CONTROL GOV/REL CONSERVE...BIBLIOG 20 NAVY. PAGE 11 F0209 — EXTR/IND CRIME NAT/G

B63
CHATTERJEE I.K.,ECONOMIC DEVELOPMENT PAYMENTS DEFICIT AND PAYMENT RESTRICTION. INDIA WOR+45 FINAN INT/TRADE CONTROL BAL/PAY WEALTH...POLICY CONCPT STAT CHARTS IDEA/COMP BIBLIOG 20. PAGE 23 F0456 — ECO/DEV ECO/TAC PAY GOV/REL

B63
GANGULY D.S.,PUBLIC CORPORATIONS IN A NATIONAL ECONOMY. INDIA WOR+45 FINAN INDUS TOP/EX PRICE EFFICIENCY...MGT STAT CHARTS BIBLIOG 20. PAGE 46 F0897 — ECO/UNDEV LG/CO SOCISM GOV/REL

B63
HATHAWAY D.A.,GOVERNMENT AND AGRICULTURE: PUBLIC POLICY IN A DEMOCRATIC SOCIETY. USA+45 LEGIS ADMIN EXEC LOBBY REPRESENT PWR 20. PAGE 57 F1111 — AGRI GOV/REL PROB/SOLV EX/STRUC

B63
MANN D.E.,THE POLITICS OF WATER IN ARIZONA. AGRI EXTR/IND PROVS ACT/RES CREATE PLAN GOV/REL COST HABITAT...MGT CHARTS 20 ARIZONA WATER. PAGE 84 F1655 — POLICY ECO/TAC TEC/DEV

B63
PRITCHETT C.H.,THE THIRD BRANCH OF GOVERNMENT. USA+45 USA-45 CONSTN SOCIETY INDUS SECT LEGIS JUDGE PROB/SOLV GOV/REL 20 SUPREME/CT CHURCH/STA. PAGE 108 F2122 — JURID NAT/G ADJUD CT/SYS

B63
SHANKS M.,THE LESSONS OF PUBLIC ENTERPRISE. UK LEGIS WORKER ECO/TAC ADMIN PARL/PROC GOV/REL ATTIT ...POLICY MGT METH/COMP NAT/COMP ANTHOL 20 PARLIAMENT. PAGE 120 F2364 — SOCISM OWN NAT/G INDUS

B63
STUCKI C.W.,AMERICAN DOCTORAL DISSERTATIONS ON ASIA 1933-62 (A PAPER). PREHIST INDUS NAT/G GOV/REL ALL/IDEOS...ART/METH GEOG SOC LING 20. PAGE 127 F2506 — BIBLIOG ASIA SOCIETY S/ASIA

B63
TREVES G.,GOVERNMENT ORGANIZATION FOR ECONOMIC DEVELOPMENT (PAMPHLET). WOR+45 LAW BUDGET ECO/TAC GOV/REL...DECISION 20. PAGE 131 F2585 — ECO/DEV ECO/UNDEV PLAN POLICY

B63
US BD GOVERNORS FEDL RESRV,THE FEDERAL RESERVE AND THE TREASURY. USA+45 WORKER PROB/SOLV PRICE COST DEMAND WEALTH...STAT INT CHARTS 20 FED/RESERV DEPT/TREAS. PAGE 134 F2641 — FINAN GOV/REL CONTROL BUDGET

B63
US HOUSE,URBAN RENEWAL: HOUSE COMMITTEE ON BANKING AND CURRENCY. USA+45 FINAN LOC/G NAT/G NEIGH DELIB/GP TEC/DEV BUDGET GOV/REL COST...CHARTS MUNICH 20 CONGRESS URBAN/RNWL. PAGE 136 F2684 — PLAN PROB/SOLV LEGIS

N63
LEDERER W.,THE BALANCE ON FOREIGN TRANSACTIONS: PROBLEMS OF DEFINITION AND MEASUREMENT (PAMPHLET). USA+45 BUDGET DIPLOM ECO/TAC PRICE GOV/REL...POLICY STAT NAT/COMP METH 20. PAGE 77 F1502 — FINAN BAL/PAY INT/TRADE ECO/DEV

B64
BLACKSTOCK P.W.,THE STRATEGY OF SUBVERSION. USA+45 FORCES EDU/PROP ADMIN COERCE GOV/REL...DECISION MGT 20 DEPT/DEFEN CIA DEPT/STATE. PAGE 15 F0292 — ORD/FREE DIPLOM CONTROL

B64
BROWN C.V.,GOVERNMENT AND BANKING IN WESTERN NIGERIA. AFR NIGERIA GOV/REL GP/REL...POLICY 20. PAGE 19 F0367 — ADMIN ECO/UNDEV FINAN NAT/G

B64
CHINITZ B.,CITY AND SUBURB: THE ECONOMICS OF METROPOLITAN GROWTH. DIST/IND BUDGET GOV/REL DEMAND ATTIT HABITAT MUNICH PHILADELPH. PAGE 24 F0467 — TEC/DEV PLAN

B64
DUSCHA J.,ARMS, MONEY, AND POLITICS. USA+45 INDUS POL/PAR ECO/TAC TAX DETER NUC/PWR WAR WEAPON GOV/REL ATTIT...BIBLIOG/A 20 CONGRESS MONEY DEPT/DEFEN. PAGE 35 F0687 — NAT/G FORCES POLICY BUDGET

B64
HOLLEY I.B. JR.,US ARMY IN WORLD WAR II: SPECIAL STUDIES: BUYING AIRCRAFT: MATERIEL PROCUREMENT FOR THE ARMY AIR FORCES. USA+45 USA-45 BUDGET WEAPON GOV/REL PRODUC 20. PAGE 61 F1198 — FORCES COST DIST/IND CIVMIL/REL

B64
LAURSEN K.,THE GERMAN INFLATION, 1918-23. EUR+WWI GERMANY/E GERMANY/W WOR-45 BUDGET TAX GOV/REL BAL/PAY DEMAND PEACE...POLICY CHARTS 20 WEIMAR/REP. PAGE 76 F1489 — ECO/DEV FINAN REPAR ECO/TAC

B64
MANN B.,STATE CONSTITUTIONAL RESTRICTIONS ON LOCAL BORROWING AND PROPERTY TAXING POWERS. USA+45 CONSTN PROVS CT/SYS GOV/REL PWR...DECISION JURID CHARTS 20. PAGE 84 F1654 — LOC/G TAX FINAN LAW

B64
MORRISSENS L.,ECONOMIC POLICY IN OUR TIME: COUNTRY STUDIES. BELGIUM EUR+WWI FRANCE GERMANY/W ITALY NETHERLAND INDUS BARGAIN BUDGET GOV/REL BAL/PAY PRODUC...CON/ANAL CHARTS COSTS 20. PAGE 94 F1839 — ECO/DEV ECO/TAC METH/COMP PLAN

B64
ODEH H.S.,THE IMPACT OF INFLATION ON THE LEVEL OF ECONOMIC ACTIVITY. AFR BRAZIL CHILE BUDGET GOV/REL COST DEMAND INCOME WEALTH...STAT METH 20 MONEY. PAGE 100 F1963 — ECOMETRIC ECO/TAC ECO/UNDEV FINAN

B64
PAARLBERG D.,AMERICAN FARM POLICY: A CASE STUDY IN CENTRALIZED DECISION-MAKING. USA+45 NAT/G LEGIS LOBBY REPRESENT GOV/REL PWR LAISSEZ 20. PAGE 102 F2009 — PROB/SOLV EX/STRUC AGRI

B64
US AGENCY INTERNATIONAL DEV,A.I.D. PROJECTS IN FISCAL YEAR 1963: BY COUNTRY AND FIELD OF ACTIVITY. USA+45 ECO/UNDEV ECO/TAC EDU/PROP GOV/REL...CHARTS 20 AID. PAGE 134 F2639 — FINAN FOR/AID COST STAT

B64
US DEPT LABOR OFF SOLICITOR,LEGISLATIVE HISTORY OF THE LABOR-MANAGEMENT AND DISCLOSURE ACT OF 1959. DELIB/GP WORKER ADMIN LOBBY PARL/PROC SANCTION CHOOSE GOV/REL 20 CONGRESS PRESIDENT. PAGE 136 F2677 — LABOR LEGIS DEBATE POLICY

S64
HORECKY P.L.,"LIBRARY OF CONGRESS PUBLICATIONS IN AID OF USSR AND EAST EUROPEAN RESEARCH." BULGARIA CZECHOSLVK POLAND USSR YUGOSLAVIA NAT/G POL/PAR DIPLOM ADMIN GOV/REL...CLASSIF 20. PAGE 62 F1214 — BIBLIOG/A COM MARXISM

B65
AMERICAN FOREST PRODUCTS INDUS,GOVERNMENT LAND ACQUISITION: A SUMMARY OF LAND ACQUISITION BY FEDERAL, STATE, AND LOCAL GOVERNMENTS UP TO 1964. USA+45 USA-45 TAX...POLICY GEOG CHARTS 20. PAGE 5 F0089 — NAT/G OWN ECO/TAC GOV/REL

B65
CLARK T.D.,THREE PATHS TO THE MODERN SOUTH: EDUCATION, AGRICULTURE, AND CONSERVATION. FUT USA-45 ECO/DEV ECO/TAC PEACE WEALTH...POLICY 20 SOUTH/US. PAGE 25 F0485
AGRI EDU/PROP GOV/REL REGION

B65
DANIELSON M.N.,FEDERAL-METROPOLITAN POLITICS AND THE COMMUTER CRISIS. PROVS LEGIS EXEC LEAD PWR ...DECISION MUNICH. PAGE 30 F0580
FEDERAL GOV/REL DIST/IND

B65
DUGGAR G.S.,RENEWAL OF TOWN AND VILLAGE I: A WORLD-WIDE SURVEY OF LOCAL GOVERNMENT EXPERIENCE. WOR+45 CONSTRUC INDUS CREATE BUDGET REGION GOV/REL...QU NAT/COMP MUNICH 20 URBAN/RNWL. PAGE 35 F0673
NEIGH PLAN ADMIN

B65
FRYE R.J.,HOUSING AND URBAN RENEWAL IN ALABAMA. USA+45 NEIGH LEGIS BUDGET ADJUD ADMIN PARTIC...MGT MUNICH 20 ALABAMA URBAN/RNWL. PAGE 45 F0871
PROB/SOLV PLAN GOV/REL

B65
GREER S.,URBAN RENEWAL AND AMERICAN CITIES: THE DILEMMA OF DEMOCRATIC INTERVENTION. USA+45 R+D LOC/G VOL/ASSN ACT/RES BUDGET ADMIN GOV/REL...SOC INT SAMP MUNICH 20 BOSTON CHICAGO LOS/ANG MIAMI URBAN/RNWL. PAGE 51 F0992
PROB/SOLV PLAN NAT/G

B65
NKRUMAH K.,NEO-COLONIALISM: THE LAST STAGE OF IMPERIALISM. AFR INT/ORG WORKER FOR/AID INT/TRADE EDU/PROP GOV/REL NAT/LISM SOVEREIGN POPULISM SOCISM ...SOCIALIST 20 THIRD/WRLD INTRVN/ECO. PAGE 98 F1929
COLONIAL DIPLOM ECO/UNDEV ECO/TAC

B65
RATNAM K.J.,COMMUNALISM AND THE POLITICAL PROCESS IN MALAYA. MALAYSIA WOR+45 ECO/UNDEV PARTIC CHOOSE REPRESENT GP/REL CENTRAL ATTIT...CHARTS WORSHIP 20. PAGE 109 F2152
CONSTN GOV/REL REGION

B65
REDFORD E.S.,AMERICAN GOVERNMENT AND THE ECONOMY. FUT USA+45 USA-45 INDUS PROB/SOLV GOV/REL...POLICY DECISION METH/COMP BIBLIOG T 18/20. PAGE 110 F2168
CONSTN NAT/G

B65
SMERK G.M.,URBAN TRANSPORTATION; THE FEDERAL ROLE. FUT USA+45 FINAN PROB/SOLV TEC/DEV AUTOMAT GOV/REL COST...STAT BIBLIOG MUNICH 20 PUB/TRANS. PAGE 123 F2426
PLAN DIST/IND NAT/G

B65
SPENCE J.E.,REPUBLIC UNDER PRESSURE: A STUDY OF SOUTH AFRICAN FOREIGN POLICY. SOUTH/AFR ADMIN COLONIAL GOV/REL RACE/REL DISCRIM NAT/LISM ATTIT ROLE...TREND 20 NEGRO. PAGE 124 F2449
DIPLOM POLICY AFR

B65
US ADVISORY COMN INTERGOV REL,METROPOLITAN SOCIAL AND ECONOMIC DISPARITIES: IMPLICATIONS FOR INTERGOVERNMENTAL RELATIONS IN CENT'L CITIES AND SUBURBS. CULTURE STRATA DIST/IND LOC/G PLAN GP/REL DISCRIM HABITAT MUNICH. PAGE 134 F2634
GOV/REL GEOG

B65
WARD R.,BACKGROUND MATERIAL ON ECONOMIC IMPACT OF FEDERAL PROCUREMENT - 1965: FOR JOINT ECONOMIC COMMITTEE US CONGRESS. FINAN ROUTINE WEAPON CIVMIL/REL EFFICIENCY...STAT CHARTS 20 CONGRESS. PAGE 143 F2818
ECO/DEV NAT/G OWN GOV/REL

S65
BANOVETZ J.M.,"METROPOLITAN SUBSIDIES: AN APPRAISAL." LEAD GP/REL DISCRIM MUNICH. PAGE 9 F0175
REGION TAX GOV/REL

S65
HADDAD W.F.,"MR. SHRIVER AND THE SAVAGE POLITICS OF POVERTY" USA+45 LAW NAT/G DELIB/GP LEGIS GIVE LEAD CENTRAL PWR...SOC/WK CHARTS 20 CONGRESS POVRTY/WAR SHRIVER/S OEO. PAGE 53 F1028
WEALTH GOV/REL CONTROL TOP/EX

S65
WILDAVSKY A.,"TVA AND POWER POLITICS." USA+45 CLIENT PROB/SOLV EXEC GOV/REL 20. PAGE 146 F2882
PWR EX/STRUC LOBBY

B66
CONFERENCE REGIONAL ACCOUNTS,REGIONAL ACCOUNTS FOR POLICY DECISIONS. PROB/SOLV CONTROL RATIONAL KNOWL ORD/FREE...POLICY DECISION MATH STAT ANTHOL 20. PAGE 27 F0523
GOV/REL REGION PLAN ECO/TAC

B66
DUNCOMBE H.S.,COUNTY GOVERNMENT IN AMERICA. USA+45 FINAN ADMIN ROUTINE GOV/REL...GOV/COMP MUNICH 20. PAGE 35 F0678
LOC/G PROVS CT/SYS TOP/EX

B66
FRANCK L.R.,LA POLITIQUE ECONOMIQUE DES ETATS-UNIS. USA+45 USA-45 FINAN INDUS CONTROL CROWD GOV/REL GP/REL...POLICY SOC CHARTS 18/20. PAGE 43 F0841
NAT/G INT/TRADE GEOG

B66
GOODWIN C.D.W.,ECONOMIC INQUIRY IN AUSTRALIA. ECO/DEV ECO/UNDEV ACADEM INT/TRADE RENT TARIFFS TAX PRESS GOV/REL SOCISM 18/20 AUSTRAL. PAGE 49 F0953
ECO/TAC IDEA/COMP BUDGET COLONIAL

B66
HAINES W.W.,MONEY PRICES AND POLICY. WOR+45 ECO/DEV BUDGET CONTROL INCOME...POLICY STAT CHARTS BIBLIOG T 20. PAGE 53 F1039
PRICE FINAN ECO/TAC GOV/REL

B66
LEE R.A.,TRUMAN AND TAFT-HARTLEY: A QUESTION OF MANDATE. USA+45 LAW CONSTN LG/CO CONTROL LOBBY GOV/REL PEACE NEW/LIB 20 TRUMAN/HS CONGRESS. PAGE 77 F1507
LEGIS TOP/EX ADJUD LABOR

B66
NATIONAL INDUSTRIAL CONF BOARD,GOLD AND WORLD MONETARY PROBLEMS. AFR FUT WOR+45 PROB/SOLV BUDGET INT/TRADE PAY GOV/REL...POLICY ANTHOL 20. PAGE 97 F1902
FINAN ECO/TAC PRICE BAL/PAY

B66
O'CONNER A.M.,AN ECONOMIC GEOGRAPHY OF EAST AFRICA. AFR TANZANIA UGANDA AGRI WORKER INT/TRADE COLONIAL GOV/REL...CHARTS METH/COMP 20 AFRICA/E. PAGE 99 F1953
ECO/UNDEV EXTR/IND GEOG HABITAT

B66
PIQUET H.S.,THE US BALANCE OF PAYMENTS AND INTERNATIONAL MONETARY RESERVES. AFR USA+45 PROB/SOLV INT/TRADE GOV/REL EQUILIB...POLICY STAT CHARTS 20. PAGE 106 F2090
BAL/PAY DIPLOM FINAN ECO/TAC

B66
RAPHAEL J.S.,GOVERNMENTAL REGULATION OF BUSINESS. USA+45 LAW CONSTN TAX ADJUD ADMIN EFFICIENCY PWR 20. PAGE 109 F2150
LG/CO GOV/REL CONTROL ECO/DEV

B66
SASTRI K.V.S.,FEDERAL-STATE FISCAL RELATIONS IN INDIA: A STUDY OF THE FINANCE COMMISSION AND TECHNIQUES OF FINANCIAL ADJUSTMENT. INDIA PROVS DELIB/GP GOV/REL FEDERAL...MATH CHARTS 20. PAGE 116 F2283
TAX BUDGET FINAN NAT/G

B66
SHULTZ G.P.,GUIDELINES, INFORMAL CONTROLS, AND THE MARKET PLACE: POLICY CHOICES IN A FULL EMPLOYMENT ECONOMY. UK ECO/DEV LABOR INT/TRADE CONFER GOV/REL BAL/PAY DEMAND INCOME...POLICY ANTHOL 20 PRESIDENT. PAGE 121 F2392
ECO/TAC CONTROL FINAN RATION

B66
SMITH H.E.,READINGS IN ECONOMIC DEVELOPMENT AND ADMINISTRATION IN TANZANIA. TANZANIA FINAN INDUS LABOR NAT/G PLAN PROB/SOLV INT/TRADE COLONIAL REGION...ANTHOL BIBLIOG 20 AFRICA/E. PAGE 123 F2431
TEC/DEV ADMIN GOV/REL

B66
THIESENHUSEN W.C.,CHILE'S EXPERIMENTS IN AGRARIAN REFORM. CHILE STRUCT NAT/G ACT/RES ECO/TAC GOV/REL COST SOCISM...TREND CHARTS SOC/EXP 20. PAGE 130 F2558
AGRI ECO/UNDEV SOC TEC/DEV

B66
US HOUSE COMM BANKING CURRENCY,HEARINGS BEFORE HOUSE COMMITTEE ON BANKING AND CURRENCY: SALE OF SBA LOAN POOL PARTICIPATIONS. USA+45 LAW LEGIS ECO/TAC RATION 20 CONGRESS. PAGE 136 F2687
FINAN SML/CO ADJUD GOV/REL

S66
DAVIS O.A.,"A THEORY OF THE BUDGETARY PROCESS." ECO/DEV FINAN LEGIS PROB/SOLV GOV/REL...ECOMETRIC METH/CNCPT STAT CONT/OBS TREND METH/COMP SIMUL 20 CONGRESS. PAGE 30 F0592
DECISION NAT/G BUDGET EFFICIENCY

N66
PRINCETON U INDUSTRIAL REL SEC,RECENT MATERIAL ON COLLECTIVE BARGAINING IN GOVERNMENT (PAMPHLET NO. 130). USA+45 ECO/DEV LABOR WORKER ECO/TAC GOV/REL ...MGT 20. PAGE 108 F2120
BIBLIOG/A BARGAIN NAT/G GP/REL

N66
PRINCETON U INDUSTRIAL REL SEC,THE ROLE OF THE PUBLIC EMPLOYMENT SERVICE (PAMPHLET NO. 129). USA+45 ECO/DEV PLAN ECO/TAC GOV/REL 20. PAGE 108 F2121
BIBLIOG/A NAT/G POLICY LABOR

N66
US ADVISORY COMN INTERGOV REL,CATALOGS AND OTHER INFORMATION SOURCES ON FEDERAL AND STATE AID PROGRAMS: A SECTED BIBLIOGRAPHY (PAPER). USA+45 LAW LOC/G NAT/G PROVS VOL/ASSN TEC/DEV ADMIN HEALTH ...WELF/ST SOC/WK MUNICH. PAGE 134 F2635
BIBLIOG/A GOV/REL FINAN ECO/DEV

B67
BARDENS D.,CHURCHILL IN PARLIAMENT. UK DIPLOM ADJUD CONTROL AUTHORIT PERSON ORD/FREE 20 CHURCHLL/W PARLIAMENT. PAGE 10 F0186
TOP/EX LEGIS GOV/REL

B67
BIBBY J.,ON CAPITOL HILL. POL/PAR LOBBY PARL/PROC GOV/REL PERS/REL...JURID PHIL/SCI OBS INT BIBLIOG 20 CONGRESS PRESIDENT. PAGE 15 F0278
CONFER LEGIS CREATE LEAD

B67
BREAK G.F.,INTERGOVERNMENTAL FISCAL RELATIONS IN THE UNITED STATES. USA+45 USA-45 DELIB/GP PLAN BUDGET TAX GOV/REL CENTRAL...TREND CHARTS MUNICH. PAGE 18 F0345
LOC/G NAT/G PROVS FINAN

B67
ESTEY M.,THE UNIONS: STRUCTURE, DEVELOPMENT, AND MANAGEMENT. FUT USA+45 ADJUD CONTROL INGP/REL DRIVE ...DECISION T 20 AFL/CIO. PAGE 38 F0750
LABOR EX/STRUC ADMIN GOV/REL

B67
HEADLEY J.C.,PESTICIDE PROBLEM: AN ECONOMIC
HABITAT

APPROACH TO PUBLIC POLICY. AGRI TEC/DEV GOV/REL COST ATTIT CHARTS. PAGE 58 F1131 — POLICY BIO/SOC CONTROL

B67
PELTASON J.W.,FUNCTIONS AND POLICIES OF AMERICAN GOVERNMENT (3RD ED.). USA+45 FINAN INDUS EDU/PROP CIVMIL/REL RACE/REL ORD/FREE...ANTHOL T 20 JOHNSON/LB. PAGE 104 F2052 — NAT/G GOV/REL POLICY PLAN

B67
UNIVERSAL REFERENCE SYSTEM,ADMINISTRATIVE MANAGEMENT: PUBLIC AND PRIVATE BUREAUCRACY (VOLUME IV). WOR+45 WOR-45 ECO/DEV LG/CO LOC/G PUB/INST VOL/ASSN GOV/REL...COMPUT/IR GEN/METH. PAGE 133 F2616 — BIBLIOG/A MGT ADMIN NAT/G

B67
UNIVERSAL REFERENCE SYSTEM,ECONOMIC REGULATION, BUSINESS, AND GOVERNMENT (VOLUME VIII). WOR+45 WOR-45 ECO/DEV ECO/UNDEV FINAN LABOR TEC/DEV ECO/TAC INT/TRADE GOV/REL...POLICY COMPUT/IR. PAGE 133 F2617 — BIBLIOG/A CONTROL NAT/G

B67
UNIVERSAL REFERENCE SYSTEM,PUBLIC POLICY AND THE MANAGEMENT OF SCIENCE (VOLUME IX). FUT SPACE WOR+45 LAW NAT/G TEC/DEV CONTROL NUC/PWR GOV/REL ...COMPUT/IR GEN/METH. PAGE 133 F2618 — BIBLIOG/A POLICY MGT PHIL/SCI

L67
DEALEY S.,"MONETARY RECOVERY UNDER FEDERAL TRANSPORTATION STATUTES." USA+45 SEA WORKER TAX PAY ADJUD DEATH GOV/REL OWN HEALTH ORD/FREE 20. PAGE 31 F0609 — DIST/IND LAW CONTROL FINAN

L67
DOERFER G.L.,"THE LIMITS ON TRADE SECRET LAW IMPOSED BY FEDERAL PATENT & ANTITRUST SUPREMACY." USA+45 LAW R+D CAP/ISM LICENSE CONTROL SANCTION ORD/FREE. PAGE 33 F0651 — JURID GOV/REL POLICY LEGIT

L67
HUBBARD P.H.,"MONETARY RECOVERY UNDER THE COPYRIGHT, PATENT, AND TRADEMARK ACTS." PROC/MFG TAX PAY LEGIT ADJUD GOV/REL OWN ORD/FREE 20. PAGE 62 F1228 — CREATE LAW CONTROL FINAN

L67
PARKER G.P. JR.,"MONETARY RECOVERY UNDER THE FEDERAL LABOR STATUTES." USA+45 USA-45 INDUS ADJUD CT/SYS GOV/REL HEALTH ORD/FREE 20 DEPT/LABOR NLRB. PAGE 103 F2027 — LABOR CONTROL LAW FINAN

L67
STILL C.H.,"MONETARY RECOVERY UNDER THE FAIR LABOR STANDARDS ACT." USA+45 USA-45 WORKER PAY ADJUD GOV/REL HEALTH ORD/FREE...MATH 20 NLRB. PAGE 126 F2487 — LABOR CONTROL LAW FINAN

L67
WATKINS J.B.,"MONETARY RECOVERY UNDER FEDERAL ANTITRUST STATUTES." USA+45 PROB/SOLV ADJUD CT/SYS GOV/REL ORD/FREE 20. PAGE 144 F2831 — LG/CO CONTROL LAW FINAN

L67
WILKINSON J.H. JR.,"THE NET OPERATING LOSS DEDUCTION AND RELATED INCOME TAX DEVICES." PROB/SOLV BUDGET PAY GOV/REL ORD/FREE...MATH CHARTS METH 20. PAGE 146 F2886 — TAX FINAN LAW ADJUD

S67
"THE SIERRA CLUB, POLITICAL ACTIVITY, AND TAX EXEMPT CHARITABLE STATUS." USA+45 LAW VOL/ASSN TAX PAY ADJUD LOBBY INGP/REL HABITAT 20. PAGE 2 F0027 — ELITES GOV/REL FACE/GP ORD/FREE

S67
BRAUCHER R.,"RECLAMATION OF GOODS FROM A FRAUDULENT BUYER." USA+45 CLIENT FINAN CT/SYS PERS/REL COST WEALTH. PAGE 18 F0341 — LAW ADJUD GOV/REL INT/TRADE

S67
CRAIG A.,"ARGENTINA: THE LATEST REVOLUTION." ELITES NAT/G CHIEF FORCES ECO/TAC CIVMIL/REL GOV/REL EQUILIB PRIVIL 20 ARGEN. PAGE 28 F0550 — ECO/UNDEV FINAN ATTIT REV

S67
EDWARDS N.,"EDUCATION IN THE FEDERAL-STATE STRUCTURE OF GOVERNMENT." USA+45 SECT CONTROL GOV/REL RACE/REL DISCRIM FEDERAL ROLE PWR SOVEREIGN. PAGE 36 F0705 — EDU/PROP NAT/G PROVS POLICY

S67
MITCHELL J.D.B.,"THE CONSTITUTIONAL IMPLICATIONS OF JUDICIAL CONTROL OF THE ADMINISTRATION IN THE UNITED KINGDOM." UK LAW ADJUD ADMIN GOV/REL ROLE ...GP/COMP 20. PAGE 92 F1808 — CONSTN CT/SYS CONTROL EX/STRUC

S67
NILES J.G.,"CIVIL ACTIONS FOR DAMAGES UNDER THE FEDERAL CIVIL RIGHTS STATUTES." CONSTN FINAN ADJUD CT/SYS GOV/REL RACE/REL 20. PAGE 98 F1928 — DISCRIM LAW CONTROL ORD/FREE

S67
NOURSE E.G.,"EARLY FLOWERING OF THE EMPLOYMENT ACT" USA+45 LABOR CONSULT DELIB/GP LEGIS BUDGET GOV/REL PRODUC WEALTH 20 INTRVN/ECO. PAGE 99 F1939 — NAT/G WORKER ECO/TAC CONTROL

S67
PROBERT J.R.,"STREAMLINING THE FOREIGN POLICY MACHINE." USA+45 EFFICIENCY DEPT/STATE. PAGE 108 F2123 — DIPLOM ADMIN EXEC GOV/REL

S67
SIDDIQ M.M.,"LOCAL GOVERNMENT IN PAKISTAN." PAKISTAN PROB/SOLV TAX COLONIAL GOV/REL MUNICH 20. PAGE 121 F2395 — ADMIN LOC/G DELIB/GP BUDGET

S67
STEINHEIMER R.L. JR.,"THE UNIFORM COMMERCIAL CODE COMES OF AGE." USA+45 FINAN ACADEM JUDGE. PAGE 126 F2477 — ADJUD LEGIS INT/TRADE GOV/REL

S67
TELLER A.,"AIR-POLLUTION ABATEMENT: ECONOMIC RATIONALITY AND REALITY." NAT/G DELIB/GP ECO/TAC GOV/REL CENTRAL EFFICIENCY HEALTH...CHARTS METH MUNICH. PAGE 129 F2543 — PROB/SOLV CONTROL COST AIR

B76
TAINE H.A.,THE ANCIENT REGIME. FRANCE STRATA FORCES PARTIC EQUILIB WEALTH CONSERVE POPULISM...GOV/COMP SOC/INTEG 18/19. PAGE 128 F2527 — NAT/G GOV/REL TAX REV

S86
SMITH R.M.,"THE NATIONAL BUREAU OF LABOR AND INDUSTRIAL DEPRESSIONS" USA-45 DELIB/GP BARGAIN CONTROL COST INCOME WEALTH...STAT 19 DEPRESSION. PAGE 123 F2433 — LABOR INDUS FINAN GOV/REL

GOVERNMENT....SEE NAT/G, LOC/G

GOVERNOR....GOVERNOR; SEE ALSO PROVS, CHIEF, LEAD

B25
MATHEWS J.M.,AMERICAN STATE GOVERNMENT. USA-45 LOC/G CHIEF EX/STRUC LEGIS ADJUD CONTROL CT/SYS ROUTINE GOV/REL PWR 20 GOVERNOR. PAGE 87 F1703 — PROVS ADMIN FEDERAL CONSTN

GOWDA K.V. F0969

GP/ADMIN....ADMINISTRATIVE GROUP; SEE ALSO ADMIN

B61
SHARP W.R.,FIELD ADMINISTRATION IN THE UNITED NATION SYSTEM: THE CONDUCT OF INTERNATIONAL ECONOMIC AND SOCIAL PROGRAMS. FUT WOR+45 CONSTN SOCIETY ECO/UNDEV R+D DELIB/GP ACT/RES PLAN TEC/DEV EDU/PROP EXEC ROUTINE HEALTH WEALTH...HUM CONCPT CHARTS METH ILO UNESCO GP VAL/FREE UN 20. PAGE 120 F2369 — INT/ORG CONSULT

GP/COMP....COMPARISON OF GROUPS

B27
SIEGFRIED A.,AMERICA COMES OF AGE: A FRENCH ANALYSIS (TRANS. BY H.H. HEMMING AND DORIS HEMMING). FRANCE UK POL/PAR WORKER TEC/DEV DIPLOM REGION RACE/REL ADJUST PRODUC HEREDITY...TIME/SEQ GP/COMP SOC/INTEG 20 DEMOCRAT REPUBLICAN KKK. PAGE 122 F2398 — USA-45 CULTURE ECO/DEV SOC

B31
LORWIN L.L.,ADVISORY ECONOMIC COUNCILS. EUR+WWI FRANCE GERMANY PROB/SOLV INGP/REL...CLASSIF GP/COMP. PAGE 82 F1601 — CONSULT DELIB/GP ECO/TAC NAT/G

B43
BRADY R.A.,BUSINESS AS A SYSTEM OF POWER. EX/STRUC PLAN ECO/TAC CONTROL GP/REL PWR...TREND GP/COMP. PAGE 17 F0334 — VOL/ASSN LOBBY POLICY

S50
DALTON M.,"CONFLICTS BETWEEN STAFF AND LINE MANAGERIAL OFFICERS" (BMR). USA+45 USA-45 ELITES LG/CO WORKER PROB/SOLV ADMIN EXEC EFFICIENCY PRODUC ...GP/COMP 20. PAGE 30 F0576 — MGT ATTIT GP/REL INDUS

B51
OWENS R.N.,BUSINESS, ORGANIZATION, AND COMBINATION. USA+45 USA-45 LAW NAT/G LEGIS ECO/TAC CONTROL INGP/REL...JURID GP/COMP 20 NEW/DEAL. PAGE 102 F2006 — SML/CO LG/CO STRUCT GP/REL

B51
POOLE K.,FISCAL POLICIES AND THE AMERICAN ECONOMY. AFR ECO/DEV FINAN INDUS WORKER OP/RES INT/TRADE TAX COST INCOME PROFIT WEALTH...GP/COMP 20. PAGE 107 F2102 — NAT/G POLICY ANTHOL

S57
ANSHEN M.,"BUSINESS, LAWYERS, AND ECONOMISTS." PROB/SOLV ECO/TAC CONFER PROFIT RIGID/FLEX OBJECTIVE...MGT GP/COMP. PAGE 6 F0106 — INDUS CONSULT ROUTINE EFFICIENCY

S57
ROURKE F.E.,"THE POLITICS OF ADMINISTRATIVE ORGANIZATION: A CASE HISTORY." USA+45 LABOR WORKER PLAN ADMIN TASK EFFICIENCY 20 DEPT/LABOR CONGRESS. — POLICY ATTIT MGT

PAGE 114 F2251 — GP/COMP

L59
FURASH E.A.,"PROBLEMS IN REVIEW: INDUSTRIAL ESPIONAGE." WORKER ECO/TAC PERS/REL OPTIMAL AGE ATTIT KNOWL...MGT DEEP/INT DEEP/QU GP/COMP IDEA/COMP. PAGE 45 F0875
INDUS TOP/EX MAJORITY

S59
STINCHCOMBE A.L.,"BUREAUCRATIC AND CRAFT ADMINISTRATION OF PRODUCTION: A COMPARATIVE STUDY" (BMR)" USA+45 STRUCT EX/STRUC ECO/TAC GP/REL ...CLASSIF GP/COMP IDEA/COMP GEN/LAWS 20 WEBER/MAX. PAGE 126 F2490
CONSTRUC PROC/MFG ADMIN PLAN

B60
GRANICK D.,THE RED EXECUTIVE. COM USA+45 SOCIETY ECO/DEV INDUS NAT/G POL/PAR EX/STRUC PLAN ECO/TAC EDU/PROP ADMIN EXEC ATTIT DRIVE...GP/COMP 20. PAGE 50 F0976
PWR STRATA USSR ELITES

L60
CHENERY H.B.,"PATTERNS OF INDUSTRIAL GROWTH." INT/TRADE DEMAND PRODUC...MATH REGRESS CHARTS SIMUL METH 20. PAGE 24 F0462
ECO/TAC ECO/DEV GP/COMP CON/ANAL

N61
US ADVISORY COMM INTERGOV REL,STATE AND LOCAL TAXATION ON PRIVATELY OWNED PROPERTY LOCATED ON FEDERAL AREAS: PROPOSED AMENDMENT OF BUCK ACT (PAMPHLET). USA+45 ACT/RES PLAN CONTROL GOV/REL INGP/REL OWN...POLICY JURID CHARTS GP/COMP 20. PAGE 133 F2629
PROVS LOC/G NAT/G TAX

B62
GORT M.,DIVERSIFICATION AND INTEGRATION IN AMERICAN INDUSTRY. CLIENT DIST/IND PROC/MFG SERV/IND LG/CO CONTROL DEMAND PWR...METH/CNCPT STAT TREND CON/ANAL GP/COMP. PAGE 49 F0964
CONCPT GP/REL CLASSIF

B63
DELL S.,TRADE BLOCS AND COMMON MARKETS. COM WOR+45 ECO/DEV ECO/UNDEV GP/COMP. PAGE 32 F0615
DIPLOM ECO/TAC INT/TRADE FEDERAL

B63
HUNTER A.,THE ECONOMICS OF AUSTRALIAN INDUSTRY. DIST/IND EXTR/IND FINAN PROC/MFG SERV/IND ACT/RES PLAN TARIFFS GP/REL INGP/REL 20 AUSTRAL. PAGE 63 F1245
INDUS ECO/DEV HABITAT GP/COMP

B63
MILLER W.,REVENUE-COST RATIOS OF RURAL TOWNSHIPS WITH CHANGING LAND USES. USA+45 INDUS SERV/IND PROVS GP/REL HABITAT...CHARTS GP/COMP MUNICH 20 NEW/JERSEY. PAGE 91 F1792
TAX COST AGRI

L63
LIVERNASH E.R.,"THE RELATION OF POWER TO THE STRUCTURE AND PROCESS OF COLLECTIVE BARGAINING." ADJUD ORD/FREE...POLICY MGT CLASSIF GP/COMP. PAGE 81 F1589
LABOR GP/REL PWR ECO/TAC

L63
MCKERSIE R.B.,"NONPROFESSIONAL HOSPITAL WORKERS AND A UNION ORGANIZING DRIVE." PLAN GP/REL RACE/REL ATTIT DRIVE...CORREL STAT INT GP/COMP. PAGE 88 F1732
VOL/ASSN HEALTH INGP/REL LABOR

B64
ECONOMIDES C.P.,LE POUVOIR DE DECISION DES ORGANISATIONS INTERNATIONALES EUROPEENNES. DIPLOM DOMIN INGP/REL EFFICIENCY...INT/LAW JURID 20 NATO OEEC EEC COUNCL/EUR EURATOM. PAGE 36 F0698
INT/ORG PWR DECISION GP/COMP

B64
MEYER J.R.,INVESTMENT DECISIONS, ECONOMIC FORECASTING, AND PUBLIC POLICY. ECO/DEV ECO/TAC ...DECISION REGRESS TIME/SEQ CHARTS GP/COMP SIMUL 20. PAGE 90 F1771
FINAN PROB/SOLV PREDICT LG/CO

B64
MEZERIK A.G.,TRADE, AID AND ECONOMIC DEVELOPMENT. WOR+45 FINAN INDUS MARKET PLAN BAL/PWR BARGAIN FOR/AID TARIFFS EDU/PROP WEALTH...GP/COMP 20 UN GATT IMF IBRD. PAGE 91 F1777
ECO/TAC ECO/DEV INT/ORG INT/TRADE

B64
STEWART C.F.,A BIBLIOGRAPHY OF INTERNATIONAL BUSINESS. WOR+45 FINAN LG/CO NAT/G PLAN ECO/TAC TARIFFS...DECISION MGT GP/COMP NAT/COMP 20 EEC. PAGE 126 F2484
BIBLIOG INT/ORG OP/RES INT/TRADE

B65
RIVKIN M.D.,AREA DEVELOPMENT FOR NATIONAL GROWTH; THE TURKISH PRECEDENT. ISLAM TURKEY ACT/RES INGP/REL...POLICY CHARTS GP/COMP MUNICH 20 ATATURK/MK INONU/I. PAGE 112 F2197
ECO/UNDEV REGION ECO/TAC PLAN

L65
DAANE J.D.,"THE EVOLVING INTERNATIONAL MONETARY MECHANISM." VOL/ASSN CREATE PLAN FOR/AID INT/TRADE CONFER BAL/PAY...RECORD PREDICT IMF. PAGE 29 F0569
INT/ORG ECO/TAC TREND GP/COMP

B66
BAKKE E.W.,MUTUAL SURVIVAL; THE GOAL OF UNION AND MANAGEMENT (2ND ED.). USA+45 ELITES ECO/DEV ECO/TAC CONFER ADMIN REPRESENT GP/REL INGP/REL ATTIT ...GP/COMP 20. PAGE 8 F0155
MGT LABOR BARGAIN INDUS

B66
GOODMAN L.H.,ECONOMIC PROGRESS AND SOCIAL WELFARE. USA+45 STRATA STRUCT ECO/TAC EFFICIENCY...MGT 20. PAGE 49 F0949
SOC/WK RECEIVE GP/COMP POLICY

B66
OECD DEVELOPMENT CENTRE,CATALOGUE OF SOCIAL AND ECONOMIC DEVELOPMENT INSTITUTES AND PROGRAMMES* RESEARCH. ACT/RES PLAN TEC/DEV EDU/PROP...SOC GP/COMP NAT/COMP. PAGE 101 F1976
ECO/UNDEV ECO/DEV R+D ACADEM

B66
RAO Y.V.L.,COMMUNICATION AND DEVELOPMENT. INDIA S/ASIA SOCIETY ACT/RES EDU/PROP PARTIC ATTIT...SOC GP/COMP BIBLIOG MUNICH MUNICH 20. PAGE 109 F2149
COM/IND ECO/UNDEV OBS

B66
SINGH L.P.,THE POLITICS OF ECONOMIC COOPERATION IN ASIA; A STUDY OF ASIAN INTERNATIONAL ORGANIZATIONS. ASIA INT/ORG ACT/RES PLAN GP/REL...POLICY GP/COMP BIBLIOG 20 UN SEATO. PAGE 122 F2414
ECO/UNDEV ECO/TAC REGION DIPLOM

B66
WECHSBERG J.,THE MERCHANT BANKERS. EUR+WWI MOD/EUR CONTROL...BIOG GP/COMP PERS/COMP 16/20. PAGE 144 F2842
FINAN PWR WEALTH FAM

S66
FLEMING W.G.,"AUTHORITY, EFFICIENCY, AND ROLE STRESS: PROBLEMS IN THE DEVELOPMENT OF EAST AFRICAN BUREAUCRACIES." AFR UGANDA STRUCT PROB/SOLV ROUTINE INGP/REL ROLE...MGT SOC GP/COMP GOV/COMP 20 TANGANYIKA AFRICA/E. PAGE 41 F0810
DOMIN EFFICIENCY COLONIAL ADMIN

S66
VENTRE F.T.,"LOCAL INITIATIVES IN URBAN INDUSTRIAL DEVELOPMENT." FINAN SERV/IND TOP/EX PLAN BUDGET RENT TAX...GP/COMP MUNICH 20. PAGE 141 F2777
ECO/TAC LOC/G INDUS

B67
WILLIAMS E.J.,LATIN AMERICAN CHRISTIAN DEMOCRATIC PARTIES. L/A+17C FAM LABOR FORCES...CATH TREND BIBLIOG 20. PAGE 147 F2890
POL/PAR GP/COMP CATHISM ALL/VALS

S67
BAILEY S.L.,"THE ITALIANS AND ORGANIZED LABOR IN THE UNITED STATES AND ARGENTINA: 1880-1910." ITALY USA-45 PARTIC HABITAT PWR...GEOG GP/COMP 19/20 ARGEN. PAGE 8 F0153
LABOR LEAD WEALTH GP/REL

S67
GEISS I.,"THE GERMANS AND THE MIDDLE EAST CRISIS." GERMANY/W ISLAM ISRAEL USSR POL/PAR RACE/REL MARXISM...GP/COMP 20 JEWS. PAGE 47 F0914
ATTIT DIPLOM WAR POLICY

S67
LASLETT J.H.M.,"SOCIALISM AND THE AMERICAN LABOR MOVEMENT* SOME NEW REFLECTIONS." USA-45 VOL/ASSN LOBBY PARTIC CENTRAL ALL/VALS SOCISM...GP/COMP 20. PAGE 76 F1484
LABOR ROUTINE ATTIT GP/REL

S67
MITCHELL J.D.B.,"THE CONSTITUTIONAL IMPLICATIONS OF JUDICIAL CONTROL OF THE ADMINISTRATION IN THE UNITED KINGDOM." UK LAW ADJUD ADMIN GOV/REL ROLE ...GP/COMP 20. PAGE 92 F1808
CONSTN CT/SYS CONTROL EX/STRUC

S67
MULLER A.L.,"ECONOMIC GROWTH AND MINORITIES." USA+45 SKILL...SOC GP/COMP NEGRO. PAGE 95 F1857
INCOME WORKER ECO/DEV RACE/REL

S67
SCOTT R.,"TRADE UNIONS IN AFRICA." AFR UGANDA USA-45 ECO/UNDEV INDUS INT/ORG POL/PAR ECO/TAC WEALTH...GP/COMP 20 NKRUMAH/K. PAGE 118 F2335
LABOR WORKER NAT/G

GP/REL....RELATIONS AMONG GROUPS

N
ECONOMIC ABSTRACTS. WOR+45 FINAN INDUS MARKET LABOR ACT/RES INT/TRADE WRITING GP/REL...MGT 20. PAGE 1 F0005
BIBLIOG/A EDU/PROP

N
RAND SCHOOL OF SOCIAL SCIENCE,INDEX TO LABOR ARTICLES. ECO/DEV INT/ORG LEGIS DIPLOM GP/REL ...NAT/COMP 20. PAGE 109 F2143
BIBLIOG LABOR MGT ADJUD

N
US LIBRARY OF CONGRESS,SELECTED AND ANNOTATED BIBLIOGRAPHY ON LABOR PROBLEMS AND POLICIES IN A WARTIME ECONOMY (PAMPHLET). USA-45 INDUS LEGIS GP/REL DISCRIM PRODUC...SOC 20. PAGE 137 F2708
BIBLIOG/A WAR LABOR WORKER

B02
SELIGMAN E.R.,THE ECONOMIC INTERPRETATION OF HISTORY. ECO/TAC MARXISM SOCISM...PHIL/SCI METH/CNCPT 18/20. PAGE 119 F2348
IDEA/COMP HIST/WRIT GP/REL

B02
WEBB S.,THE HISTORY OF TRADE UNIONISM. UK PARTIC ...OBS CHARTS BIBLIOG/A 15/19 CASEBOOK. PAGE 144 F2837
LABOR VOL/ASSN GP/REL

B04
VEBLEN T.B.,THE THEORY OF BUSINESS ENTERPRISE. USA-45 FINAN WORKER ECO/TAC PRICE GP/REL COST ...POLICY 19/20. PAGE 141 F2770
TEC/DEV GEN/LAWS SOCIETY WEALTH

B11
SOREL G.,LES ILLUSIONS DU PROGRES (1906). UNIV SOCIETY STRATA INDUS GP/REL OWN PRODUC SOCISM 17/20. PAGE 124 F2444
WORKER POPULISM ECO/DEV ATTIT

N19
ENGELS F.,THE BRITISH LABOUR MOVEMENT (PAMPHLET). FRANCE GERMANY MOD/EUR UK USA-45 POL/PAR WORKER PAY EDU/PROP PRICE REPRESENT GP/REL 19. PAGE 37 F0730
ECO/TAC MARXISM LABOR STRATA

N19
JACKSON R.G.A.,THE CASE FOR AN INTERNATIONAL DEVELOPMENT AUTHORITY (PAMPHLET). WOR+45 ECO/DEV DIPLOM GIVE CONTROL GP/REL EFFICIENCY NAT/LISM SOVEREIGN 20. PAGE 66 F1295
FOR/AID INT/ORG ECO/UNDEV ADMIN

N19
KRESSBACH T.W.,HE MICHIGAN CITY MANAGER IN BUDGETARY PROCEEDINGS (PAMPHLET). USA+45 PROVS DELIB/GP GP/REL SUPEGO...POLICY MUNICH. PAGE 73 F1438
LOC/G BUDGET FINAN

N19
MCCONNELL G.,THE STEEL SEIZURE OF 1952 (PAMPHLET). USA+45 FINAN INDUS PROC/MFG LG/CO EX/STRUC ADJUD CONTROL GP/REL ORD/FREE PWR 20 TRUMAN/HS PRESIDENT CONGRESS. PAGE 88 F1721
DELIB/GP LABOR PROB/SOLV NAT/G

B20
TAWNEY R.H.,THE ACQUISITIVE SOCIETY. STRATA WORKER PROB/SOLV CAP/ISM ECO/TAC CONTROL GP/REL OWN PRIVIL ATTIT ORD/FREE WEALTH 20. PAGE 128 F2536
INDUS SOCIETY PRODUC MORAL

B20
WEBB S.,INDUSTRIAL DEMOCRACY. UK PARTIC GP/REL ...SOC OBS RECORD CHARTS 18/20. PAGE 144 F2838
LABOR NAT/G VOL/ASSN MAJORIT

B26
MCPHEE A.,THE ECONOMIC REVOLUTION IN BRITISH WEST AFRICA. AFR UK CULTURE DIST/IND FINAN INDUS PLAN GP/REL RACE/REL 20 AFRICA/W. PAGE 88 F1735
ECO/UNDEV INT/TRADE COLONIAL GEOG

B26
SUFRIN S.C.,A BRIEF ANNOTATED BIBLIOGRAPHY ON LABOR IN EMERGING SOCIETIES. WOR+45 CULTURE SOCIETY INDUS EDU/PROP GP/REL INGP/REL. PAGE 127 F2510
BIBLIOG/A LABOR ECO/UNDEV WORKER

B28
FRANKFURTER F.,THE BUSINESS OF THE SUPREME COURT; A STUDY IN THE FEDERAL JUDICIAL SYSTEM. USA-45 CONSTN EX/STRUC PROB/SOLV GP/REL ATTIT PWR...POLICY JURID 18/20 SUPREME/CT CONGRESS. PAGE 43 F0848
CT/SYS ADJUD LAW FEDERAL

B28
HARDMAN J.B.,AMERICAN LABOR DYNAMICS. WORKER ECO/TAC DOMIN ADJUD LEAD LOBBY PWR...POLICY MGT. PAGE 55 F1079
LABOR INGP/REL ATTIT GP/REL

B35
O'CONNOR H.,REVOLUTION IN SEATTLE. USA-45 STRATA WORKER GP/REL ATTIT SOCISM...OBS BIBLIOG/A 20 SEATTLE STRIKE COM/PARTY. PAGE 99 F1954
REV EDU/PROP LABOR MARXISM

B35
SCHATTSCHNEIDER E.E.,POLITICS, PRESSURES AND THE TARIFF: A STUDY OF FREE PRIVATE ENTERPRISE IN PRESSURE POLITICS IN TARIFF REVISION 1929-1930. NAT/G BARGAIN ECO/TAC ROUTINE REPRESENT GOV/REL GP/REL PWR POLICY. PAGE 116 F2290
LOBBY LEGIS TARIFFS

S35
BONNETT C.E.,"THE EVOLUTION OF BUSINESS GROUPINGS." ECO/TAC EDU/PROP PRICE LOBBY ORD/FREE. PAGE 16 F0315
VOL/ASSN GP/REL PROB/SOLV

B36
BURNS A.R.,THE DECLINE OF COMPETITION. LAW LG/CO NAT/G SML/CO LEGIS PRICE AGREE CONTROL GP/REL INCOME PRODUC...POLICY 19/20 NRA. PAGE 20 F0390
MARKET GEN/LAWS INDUS

B37
BROOKS R.R.,WHEN LABOR ORGANIZES. FINAN EDU/PROP ADMIN LOBBY PARTIC REPRESENT WEALTH TREND. PAGE 19 F0364
LABOR GP/REL POLICY

B37
DALTON J.E.,SUGAR: A CASE STUDY OF GOVERNMENT CONTROL. USA-45 AGRI PROC/MFG LG/CO LEGIS PROB/SOLV ECO/TAC GP/REL...CHARTS 19/20. PAGE 30 F0575
CONTROL NAT/G INDUS POLICY

B38
CARVALHO C.M.,GEOGRAPHIA HUMANA; POLITICA E ECONOMICA (3RD ED.). BRAZIL CULTURE AGRI INDUS DIPLOM COLONIAL GP/REL RACE/REL...LING 20 RESOURCE/N. PAGE 22 F0424
GEOG HABITAT

B38
REICH N.,LABOR RELATIONS IN REPUBLICAN GERMANY. GERMANY CONSTN ECO/DEV INDUS NAT/G ADMIN CONTROL GP/REL FASCISM POPULISM 20 WEIMAR/REP. PAGE 110 F2176
WORKER MGT LABOR BARGAIN

B39
JENNINGS W.I.,PARLIAMENT. UK POL/PAR OP/RES BUDGET LEAD CHOOSE GP/REL...MGT 20 PARLIAMENT HOUSE/LORD HOUSE/CMNS. PAGE 67 F1315
PARL/PROC LEGIS CONSTN NAT/G

B39
MARQUAND H.A.,ORGANIZED LABOUR IN FOUR CONTINENTS. EUR+WWI USA-45 INDUS NAT/G PAY GP/REL TOTALISM ATTIT WEALTH ALL/IDEOS...TREND NAT/COMP 20 ILO AFL/CIO EUROPE CHINJAP MEXIC/AMER. PAGE 85 F1673
LABOR WORKER CONCPT ANTHOL

B40
BATCHELOR B.,THE NEW OUTLOOK IN BUSINESS. LAW WORKER TAX LEAD ORD/FREE...POLICY TREND. PAGE 11 F0208
LG/CO GP/REL CAP/ISM LABOR

B40
CAMPBELL P.,CONSUMER REPRESENTATION IN THE NEW DEAL. AGRI INDUS MARKET EX/STRUC PLAN CAP/ISM CONTROL GP/REL DEMAND POLICY. PAGE 21 F0408
CLIENT REPRESENT NAT/G

B40
MEEK C.K.,EUROPE AND WEST AFRICA. AFR EUR+WWI EXTR/IND DIPLOM INT/TRADE EDU/PROP GP/REL...SOC 20. PAGE 89 F1743
CULTURE TEC/DEV ECO/UNDEV COLONIAL

B40
WUNDERLICH F.,LABOR UNDER GERMAN DEMOCRACY, ARBITRATION 1918-1933. GERMANY NAT/G PAY REPAR ADJUD CT/SYS GP/REL...MAJORIT 20. PAGE 149 F2941
LABOR WORKER INDUS BARGAIN

B41
DAUGHERTY C.R.,LABOR PROBLEMS IN AMERICAN INDUSTRY (5TH ED.). USA-45 SOCIETY OP/RES ECO/TAC...MGT PSY T 20. PAGE 30 F0581
LABOR INDUS GP/REL PROB/SOLV

B41
SLICHTER S.H.,UNION POLICIES AND INDUSTRIAL MANAGEMENT. USA-45 INDUS TEC/DEV PAY GP/REL INGP/REL COST EFFICIENCY PRODUC...POLICY 20. PAGE 123 F2420
BARGAIN LABOR MGT WORKER

S41
BRITT S.H.,"CONFORMITY OF LABOR NEWSPAPERS WITH RESPECT TO THE AFL-CIO CONFLICT." BAL/PWR CONSEN ATTIT. PAGE 18 F0355
LABOR PRESS DOMIN GP/REL

B42
ROBBINS J.J.,THE GOVERNMENT OF LABOR RELATIONS IN SWEDEN. SWEDEN LAW CONSTN ADJUD CT/SYS GP/REL ...JURID 20. PAGE 112 F2200
NAT/G BARGAIN LABOR INDUS

L42
GRANT J.A.C.,"THE GUILD RETURNS TO AMERICA." CHRIST-17C USA-45 LEGIS LICENSE ADJUD CONTROL GP/REL. PAGE 50 F0978
PROF/ORG JURID LABOR PWR

B43
BRADY R.A.,BUSINESS AS A SYSTEM OF POWER. EX/STRUC PLAN ECO/TAC CONTROL GP/REL PWR...TREND GP/COMP. PAGE 17 F0334
VOL/ASSN LOBBY POLICY

S43
GOLDEN C.S.,"NEW PATTERNS OF DEMOCRACY." NEIGH DELIB/GP EDU/PROP EXEC PARTIC...MGT METH/CNCPT OBS TREND. PAGE 48 F0935
LABOR REPRESENT LG/CO GP/REL

B45
MILLIS H.A.,ORGANIZED LABOR (FIRST ED.). LAW STRUCT DELIB/GP WORKER ECO/TAC ADJUD CONTROL REPRESENT INGP/REL INCOME MGT. PAGE 92 F1797
LABOR POLICY ROUTINE GP/REL

B46
DRUCKER P.F.,CONCEPT OF CORPORATION. LAW LABOR WORKER PRICE CONTROL LEAD GP/REL POLICY. PAGE 34 F0665
LG/CO CENTRAL INGP/REL

B47
BAERWALD F.,FUNDAMENTALS OF LABOR ECONOMICS. LAW INDUS LABOR LG/CO CONTROL GP/REL INCOME TOTALISM ...MGT CHARTS GEN/LAWS BIBLIOG 20. PAGE 8 F0150
ECO/DEV WORKER MARKET

B47
SLICHTER S.H.,THE CHALLENGE OF INDUSTRIAL RELATIONS: TRADE UNIONS, MANAGEMENT AND THE PUBLIC INTEREST. PLAN ECO/TAC ADJUD CONTROL LEAD SANCTION GP/REL INGP/REL INCOME. PAGE 123 F2421
LABOR MGT CLIENT POLICY

B47
WARNER W.L.,THE SOCIAL SYSTEM OF THE MODERN FACTORY; THE STRIKE: AN ANALYSIS. USA-45 STRATA WORKER ECO/TAC GP/REL INGP/REL...MGT SOC CHARTS 20 YANKEE/C. PAGE 143 F2824
ROLE STRUCT LABOR PROC/MFG

S47
DAHL R.A.,"WORKERS' CONTROL OF INDUSTRY AND THE BRITISH LABOUR PARTY." UK STRATA STRUCT DELIB/GP BARGAIN CAP/ISM DEBATE CONTROL CHOOSE GP/REL ATTIT ROLE PWR 19/20 PARLIAMENT LABOR/PAR FABIAN. PAGE 29 F0570
INDUS LABOR WORKER SOCISM

B48
KESSELMAN L.C.,THE SOCIAL POLITICS OF THE FEPC. INDUS WORKER EDU/PROP GP/REL RACE/REL 20 NEGRO JEWS FEPC. PAGE 70 F1382
POLICY NAT/G ADMIN DISCRIM

B48
KILE O.M.,THE FARM BUREAU MOVEMENT: THE FARM BUREAU
AGRI

THROUGH THREE DECADES. NAT/G LEGIS LEAD LOBBY GP/REL INCOME POLICY. PAGE 71 F1387 STRUCT VOL/ASSN DOMIN

B48
WHYTE W.F.,HUMAN RELATIONS IN THE RESTAURANT INDUSTRY (1ST ED). CLIENT WORKER WAR ATTIT...MGT OBS INT. PAGE 146 F2874 INGP/REL GP/REL SERV/IND LABOR

B49
SCHULTZ W.J.,AMERICAN PUBLIC FINANCE. USA+45 ECO/TAC TAX ADMIN GOV/REL GP/REL INCOME 20. PAGE 117 F2318 FINAN POLICY ECO/DEV NAT/G

B49
SHISTER J.,ECONOMICS OF THE LABOR MARKET. LOC/G NAT/G WORKER TEC/DEV BARGAIN PAY PRICE EXEC GP/REL INCOME...MGT T 20. PAGE 121 F2381 MARKET LABOR INDUS

S49
HART C.W.M.,"INDUSTRIAL RELATIONS RESEARCH AND SOCIAL THEORY." CANADA VOL/ASSN WORKER LEAD EFFICIENCY...MGT SOC METH/CNCPT METH/COMP MUNICH 20. PAGE 56 F1099 GEN/LAWS LABOR GP/REL

B50
CHAMBERLIN E.,THE THEORY OF MONOPOLISTIC COMPETITION (1933). INDUS PAY GP/REL COST DEMAND EFFICIENCY OPTIMAL PRODUC WEALTH...GEN/LAWS 20. PAGE 23 F0443 MARKET PRICE ECO/TAC EQUILIB

B50
CLARK J.M.,ALTERNATIVE TO SERFDOM. SOCIETY STRATA INDUS MARKET WORKER PRICE GP/REL PROFIT BIO/SOC PWR WEALTH...GEN/LAWS 20 KEYNES/JM. PAGE 25 F0481 ORD/FREE POPULISM ECO/TAC REPRESENT

S50
DALTON M.,"CONFLICTS BETWEEN STAFF AND LINE MANAGERIAL OFFICERS" (BMR). USA+45 USA-45 ELITES LG/CO WORKER PROB/SOLV ADMIN EXEC EFFICIENCY PRODUC ...GP/COMP 20. PAGE 30 F0576 MGT ATTIT GP/REL INDUS

B51
COOKE C.A.,CORPORATION TRUST AND COMPANY: AN ESSAY IN LEGAL HISTORY. UK STRUCT LEGIS CAP/ISM GP/REL PROFIT 13/20 COMPNY/ACT. PAGE 27 F0531 LG/CO FINAN ECO/TAC JURID

B51
HARBISON F.H.,GOALS AND STRATEGY IN COLLECTIVE BARGAINING. WORKER BAL/PWR PARTIC DRIVE...POLICY MGT. PAGE 55 F1074 LABOR BARGAIN GP/REL ADMIN

B51
HARDMAN J.B.,THE HOUSE OF LABOR. LAW R+D NEIGH EDU/PROP LEAD ROUTINE REPRESENT GP/REL...POLICY STAT. PAGE 55 F1080 LABOR LOBBY ADMIN PRESS

B51
OWENS R.N.,BUSINESS, ORGANIZATION, AND COMBINATION. USA+45 USA-45 LAW NAT/G LEGIS ECO/TAC CONTROL INGP/REL...JURID GP/COMP 20 NEW/DEAL. PAGE 102 F2006 SML/CO LG/CO STRUCT GP/REL

B51
PETERSON F.,SURVEY OF LABOR ECONOMICS (REV. ED.). STRATA ECO/DEV LABOR INSPECT BARGAIN PAY PRICE EXEC ROUTINE GP/REL ALL/VALS ORD/FREE 20 AFL/CIO DEPT/LABOR. PAGE 105 F2069 WORKER DEMAND IDEA/COMP T

C51
HOMANS G.C.,"THE WESTERN ELECTRIC RESEARCHES" IN S. HOSLETT, ED., HUMAN FACTORS IN MANAGEMENT (BMR)" ACT/RES GP/REL HAPPINESS PRODUC DRIVE...MGT OBS 20. PAGE 61 F1202 OP/RES EFFICIENCY SOC/EXP WORKER

B52
ROSE A.M.,UNION SOLIDARITY: THE INTERNAL COHESION OF A LABOR UNION. SECT GP/REL RACE/REL ATTIT ROLE HEALTH WEALTH...INT QU. PAGE 114 F2241 LABOR INGP/REL PARTIC SUPEGO

B53
BOEKE J.H.,ECONOMICS AND ECONOMIC POLICY OF DUAL SOCIETIES AS EXEMPLIFIED BY INDONESIA. INDIA INDONESIA SOCIETY CAP/ISM INT/TRADE GIVE PRICE GP/REL WEALTH SOCISM...POLICY NAT/COMP GEN/LAWS 20. PAGE 16 F0304 ECO/TAC ECO/UNDEV NAT/G CONTROL

B53
SAYLES L.R.,THE LOCAL UNION. CONSTN CULTURE DELIB/GP PARTIC CHOOSE GP/REL INGP/REL ATTIT ROLE ...MAJORIT DECISION MGT. PAGE 116 F2284 LABOR LEAD ADJUD ROUTINE

S53
BERNSTEIN M.H.,"POLITICAL IDEAS OF SELECTED AMERICAN BUSINESS JOURNALS (BMR)" USA+45 GP/REL ATTIT RIGID/FLEX ROLE ORD/FREE POLICY. PAGE 14 F0267 IDEA/COMP NAT/G LEAD

S53
MCKEE J.B.,"STATUS AND POWER IN THE INDUSTRIAL COMMUNITY; A COMMENT ON DRUCKER'S THESIS." LABOR LEGIT LEAD GP/REL PWR...MGT CONCPT. PAGE 88 F1730 SOC STRATA NEIGH PARTIC

B54
CHILDS M.W.,ETHICS IN A BUSINESS SOCIETY. PROF/ORG LEAD WAR GP/REL ATTIT DRIVE PERSON KNOWL MORAL PWR ...WELF/ST BIBLIOG. PAGE 24 F0466 MGT SOCIETY

B54
HAYEK FA V.O.N.,CAPITALISM AND THE HISTORIANS. MOD/EUR TEC/DEV GP/REL WEALTH...HIST/WRIT ANTHOL 19. PAGE 57 F1124 CAP/ISM LABOR STRATA ECO/TAC

B54
RICHTER R.,DAS KONKURRENZ PROBLEM IM OLIGOPOL. LG/CO BARGAIN PRICE COST...CONCPT 20 MONOPOLY. PAGE 111 F2188 CONTROL GAME ECO/TAC GP/REL

S54
MACK R.W.,"ECOLOGICAL PATTERNS IN AN INDUSTRIAL SHOP" (BMR)" USA+45 CULTURE SOCIETY STRATA STRUCT LABOR NEIGH GP/REL ADJUST HABITAT...SOC SOC/INTEG 20. PAGE 83 F1634 INDUS DISCRIM WORKER

B55
BERNAYS E.L.,THE ENGINEERING OF CONSENT. VOL/ASSN OP/RES ROUTINE INGP/REL ATTIT RESPECT...POLICY METH/CNCPT METH/COMP 20. PAGE 14 F0264 GP/REL PLAN ACT/RES ADJUST

B55
BERNSTEIN M.H.,REGULATING BUSINESS BY INDEPENDENT COMMISSION. USA+45 USA-45 LG/CO CHIEF LEGIS PROB/SOLV ADJUD SANCTION GP/REL ATTIT...TIME/SEQ 19/20 MONOPOLY PRESIDENT CONGRESS. PAGE 14 F0268 DELIB/GP CONTROL CONSULT

B55
BRAUN K.,LABOR DISPUTES AND THEIR SETTLEMENT. ECO/TAC ROUTINE TASK GP/REL...DECISION GEN/LAWS. PAGE 18 F0342 INDUS LABOR BARGAIN ADJUD

B55
JOHR W.A.,THE ROLE OF THE ECONOMIST AS OFFICIAL ADVISER. WOR+45 INTELL ECO/DEV NAT/G PLAN GP/REL ROLE...DECISION PREDICT IDEA/COMP. PAGE 68 F1336 CONSULT ECO/TAC POLICY INGP/REL

B55
PALAMOUNTAIN JC J.R.,THE POLITICS OF DISTRIBUTION. USA+45 LG/CO SML/CO BAL/PWR CONTROL EQUILIB 20. PAGE 103 F2019 DIST/IND ECO/TAC CAP/ISM GP/REL

S55
BUNZEL J.H.,"THE GENERAL IDEOLOGY OF AMERICAN SMALL BUSINESS"(BMR)" USA+45 USA-45 AGRI GP/REL INGP/REL PERSON...MGT IDEA/COMP 18/20. PAGE 20 F0383 ALL/IDEOS ATTIT SML/CO INDUS

S55
DIESING P.,"NONECONOMIC DECISION-MAKING" (BMR)" PROB/SOLV GP/REL ORD/FREE...STAT METH/COMP SIMUL 20. PAGE 33 F0638 DECISION METH EFFICIENCY SOC

B56
ATOMIC INDUSTRIAL FORUM,PUBLIC RELATIONS FOR THE ATOMIC INDUSTRY. WOR+45 PLAN PROB/SOLV EDU/PROP PRESS CONFER...AUD/VIS ANTHOL 20. PAGE 7 F0135 NUC/PWR INDUS GP/REL ATTIT

B56
BARBASH J.,THE PRACTICE OF UNIONISM. ECO/TAC LEAD LOBBY GP/REL INGP/REL DRIVE MARXISM BIBLIOG. PAGE 10 F0182 LABOR REPRESENT CONTROL ADMIN

B56
BONNETT C.E.,HISTORY OF EMPLOYERS' ASSOCIATIONS IN THE UNITED STATES (1ST ED.). MARKET DETER GP/REL ADJUST. PAGE 16 F0316 LABOR VOL/ASSN LG/CO

B56
HICKMAN C.A.,INDIVIDUALS, GROUPS, AND ECONOMIC BEHAVIOR. WORKER PAY CONTROL EXEC GP/REL INGP/REL PERSON ROLE...PSY SOC PERS/COMP METH 20. PAGE 59 F1163 MGT ADMIN ECO/TAC PLAN

B56
ISARD W.,LOCATION AND SPACE-ECONOMY: GENERAL THEORY RELATING TO INDUSTRIAL LOCATION, MARKET AREAS, LAND USE, TRADE... UNIV DIST/IND MARKET LG/CO SML/CO TEC/DEV GP/REL EQUILIB HABITAT...NEW/IDEA MATH CHARTS 20. PAGE 66 F1290 GEN/LAWS GEOG INDUS REGION

B56
LIPSET S.M.,UNION DEMOCRACY. STRUCT INDUS FACE/GP WORKER CONTROL LEAD PARTIC GP/REL ATTIT LAISSEZ ...INT QU CHARTS. PAGE 80 F1577 LABOR INGP/REL MAJORIT

B56
WILCOX W.W.,SOCIAL RESPONSIBILITY IN FARM LEADERSHIP. CLIENT LEGIS EXEC LOBBY GP/REL ATTIT WEALTH. PAGE 146 F2880 AGRI LEAD VOL/ASSN WORKER

L56
TAGLIACOZZO D.L.,"TRADE-UNION GOVERNMENT, ITS NATURE AND ITS PROBLEMS: A BIBLIOGRAPHICAL REVIEW, 1945-1955." STRUCT LEAD PARTIC CHOOSE ATTIT ...MAJORIT METH/CNCPT BIBLIOG. PAGE 128 F2526 CLASSIF LABOR INGP/REL GP/REL

S56
MYERS C.A.,"LINE AND STAFF IN INDUSTRIAL RELATIONS." INDUS LABOR GP/REL PWR...MGT INT. PAGE 96 F1876 ROLE PROB/SOLV ADMIN CONSULT

S56
TANNENBAUM A.S.,"CONTROL OF STRUCTURE AND UNION FUNCTIONS." PARTIC GP/REL INGP/REL CONSEN ATTIT PWR ...QU SAMP. PAGE 128 F2529
LABOR STRUCT CONTROL LEAD

C56
MCKEE J.B.,"THE POWER TO DECIDE" IN M. WEINBERG AND O. SHABET, SOCIETY AND MAN." ELITES STRATA REPRESENT GP/REL ATTIT PWR MUNICH BUSINESS. PAGE 88 F1731
LABOR DECISION LEAD

B57
INTL BANKING SUMMER SCHOOL,RELATIONS BETWEEN THE CENTRAL BANKS AND COMMERCIAL BANKS. EUR+WWI FRANCE GERMANY/W ITALY UK USA+45 USSR INDUS INT/ORG CAP/ISM CONTROL MONEY. PAGE 65 F1282
FINAN NAT/G GP/REL LG/CO

B57
MASON E.S.,ECONOMIC CONCENTRATION AND THE MONOPOLY PROBLEM. USA+45 USA-45 LAW ELITES ECO/DEV LABOR RATION PRICE PWR WEALTH...CHARTS 20 MONOPOLY. PAGE 87 F1696
GP/REL LG/CO CONTROL MARKET

B57
SCHNEIDER E.V.,INDUSTRIAL SOCIOLOGY: THE SOCIAL RELATIONS OF INDUSTRY AND COMMUNITY. STRATA INDUS NAT/G NEIGH CREATE ADMIN PARTIC GP/REL RACE/REL ROLE PWR...POLICY BIBLIOG. PAGE 117 F2308
LABOR MGT INGP/REL STRUCT

S57
DUBIN R.,"POWER AND UNION-MANAGEMENT RELATIONS." PROB/SOLV ADJUD ROUTINE ATTIT ORD/FREE...MGT STERTYP. PAGE 34 F0668
PWR LABOR BARGAIN GP/REL

B58
BUGEDA LANZAS J.,A STATEMENT OF THE LAWS OF CUBA IN MATTERS AFFECTING BUSINESS (2ND ED. REV., ENLARGED). CUBA L/A+17C LAW FINAN FAM LEGIS ACT/RES ADMIN GP/REL...BIBLIOG 20 OAS. PAGE 20 F0382
JURID NAT/G INDUS WORKER

B58
CLAUNCH J.M.,THE PROBLEM OF GOVERNMENT IN METROPOLITAN AREAS. CULTURE INDUS POL/PAR PLAN REGION GP/REL...CENSUS ANTHOL MUNICH 20. PAGE 25 F0486
PROB/SOLV SOC

B58
COOK P.L.,EFFECTS OF MERGERS: SIX STUDIES. USA+45 ECO/DEV LABOR LG/CO SML/CO VOL/ASSN ADMIN EFFICIENCY 20 CASEBOOK. PAGE 27 F0529
INDUS FINAN EX/STRUC GP/REL

B58
CUNNINGHAM W.B.,COMPULSORY CONCILIATION AND COLLECTIVE BARGAINING. CANADA NAT/G LEGIS ADJUD CT/SYS GP/REL...MGT 20 NEW/BRUNS STRIKE CASEBOOK. PAGE 29 F0563
POLICY BARGAIN LABOR INDUS

B58
DUBIN R.,WORKING UNION-MANAGEMENT RELATIONS. LAW PLAN ECO/TAC CHOOSE REPRESENT INGP/REL PWR...POLICY SOC BIBLIOG. PAGE 34 F0669
LABOR MGT AUTHORIT GP/REL

B58
HOOD W.C.,FINANCING OF ECONOMIC ACTIVITY IN CANADA. CANADA FUT VOL/ASSN WORKER ECO/TAC ADJUD ADMIN ...CHARTS 20. PAGE 61 F1204
BUDGET FINAN GP/REL ECO/DEV

B58
INDIAN INST OF PUBLIC ADMIN,IMPROVING CITY GOVERNMENT. INDIA ECO/UNDEV PLAN BUDGET PARTIC GP/REL MUNICH 20. PAGE 64 F1263
LOC/G PROB/SOLV ADMIN

B58
LESTER R.A.,AS UNIONS MATURE. POL/PAR BARGAIN LEAD PARTIC GP/REL CENTRAL...MAJORIT TIME/SEQ METH/COMP. PAGE 78 F1533
LABOR INDUS POLICY MGT

B58
MOSKOWITZ M.,HUMAN RIGHTS AND WORLD ORDER. INT/ORG PLAN GP/REL NAT/LISM SOVEREIGN...CONCPT 20 UN TREATY CIV/RIGHTS. PAGE 94 F1845
DIPLOM INT/LAW ORD/FREE

B58
MUSGRAVE R.A.,CLASSICS IN THE THEORY OF PUBLIC FINANCE. UNIV MARKET LG/CO NAT/G CAP/ISM PRICE OPTIMAL...IDEA/COMP ANTHOL 19/20 SAY/EMIL EDGEWORTH LINDAHL/E RITSCHL/H. PAGE 95 F1870
TAX FINAN ECO/TAC GP/REL

B58
RUBIN B.,PUBLIC RELATIONS AND THE STATE, A CASE STUDY OF NEW YORK STATE ADMINISTRATION, 1943-54. USA+45 USA-45 COM/IND EDU/PROP GOV/REL...CHARTS 20 NEW/YORK DEWEY/THOM. PAGE 114 F2255
INGP/REL PRESS PROVS GP/REL

B58
TAFT P.,CORRUPTION AND RACKETEERING IN THE LABOR MOVEMENT (PAMPHLET). ADMIN SANCTION CENTRAL ROLE WEALTH...POLICY CLASSIF. PAGE 128 F2525
LABOR INGP/REL GP/REL CRIME

B58
TANNENBAUM A.S.,PARTICIPATION IN UNION LOCALS. SOCIETY FINAN CONTROL LEAD GP/REL...BIBLIOG 20. PAGE 128 F2531
LABOR MGT PARTIC INGP/REL

B58
WOODS H.D.,PATTERNS OF INDUSTRIAL DISPUTE SETTLEMENT IN FIVE CANADIAN INDUSTRIES. CANADA USA+45 CONSULT ADJUD GP/REL...JURID GOV/COMP METH/COMP ANTHOL 20. PAGE 148 F2923
BARGAIN INDUS LABOR NAT/G

S58
JOHNSON D.G.,"GOVERNMENT AND AGRICULTURE: IS AGRICULTURE A SPECIAL CASE?" PLAN ECO/TAC LOBBY WEALTH POLICY. PAGE 67 F1321
INDUS GP/REL INCOME NAT/G

B59
BARBASH J.,UNIONS AND UNION LEADERSHIP. NAT/G WORKER TEC/DEV ECO/TAC PARTIC GP/REL RACE/REL ORD/FREE CLASSIF. PAGE 10 F0183
LABOR VOL/ASSN CAP/ISM LEAD

B59
BONNETT C.E.,LABOR-MANAGEMENT RELATIONS. USA+45 OP/RES PROB/SOLV EDU/PROP...AUD/VIS CHARTS 20. PAGE 16 F0317
MGT LABOR INDUS GP/REL

B59
GOMEZ ROBLES J.,A STATEMENT OF THE LAWS OF GUATEMALA IN MATTERS AFFECTING BUSINESS (2ND ED. REV., ENLARGED). GUATEMALA L/A+17C LAW FINAN FAM WORKER ACT/RES DIPLOM ADJUD ADMIN GP/REL 20 OAS. PAGE 48 F0945
JURID NAT/G INDUS LEGIT

B59
KOLLAI H.R.,DIE EINGLIEDERUNG DER VERTRIEBENEN UND ZUWANDERER IN NIEDERSACHSEN. GERMANY/W SOCIETY STRATA STRUCT LABOR SOC/INTEG 20. PAGE 72 F1422
GP/REL INGP/REL

B59
LEISERSON W.,AMERICAN TRADE UNION DEMOCRACY. CONSTN STRUCT ADJUD EXEC REPRESENT GP/REL INGP/REL MAJORITY ATTIT PWR. PAGE 77 F1516
LABOR LEAD PARTIC DELIB/GP

B59
MARTIN D.D.,MERGERS AND THE CLAYTON ACT. FINAN LEGIS GP/REL...DECISION METH/COMP BIBLIOG 20. PAGE 86 F1681
OWN ECO/TAC LG/CO POLICY

B59
ROCHE J.,LA COLONISATION ALLEMANDE ET LE RIO GRANDE DO SUL. BRAZIL L/A+17C NAT/G PROVS INGP/REL RACE/REL DISCRIM HABITAT...GEOG SOC/INTEG 19/20 MIGRATION. PAGE 113 F2228
ECO/UNDEV GP/REL ATTIT

B59
STERNBERG F.,THE MILITARY AND INDUSTRIAL REVOLUTION OF OUR TIME. USA+45 USSR WOR+45 WORKER COMPUTER PLAN TEC/DEV NUC/PWR GP/REL...POLICY NAT/COMP 20. PAGE 126 F2481
DIPLOM FORCES INDUS CIVMIL/REL

B59
US NATIONAL LABOR RELATIONS BD,LEGISLATIVE HISTORY OF THE LABOR-MANAGEMENT REPORTING AND DISCLOSURE ACT OF 1959 (2 VOLS.). USA+45 LEGIS...MGT CHARTS. PAGE 138 F2720
LAW LABOR GP/REL

B59
WORTHY J.C.,BIG BUSINESS AND FREE MEN. LG/CO EX/STRUC EDU/PROP LEAD CHOOSE GP/REL ATTIT DRIVE ROLE ORD/FREE...MAJORIT 20. PAGE 149 F2927
ELITES LOC/G TOP/EX PARTIC

S59
BENDIX R.,"INDUSTRIALIZATION, IDEOLOGIES, AND SOCIAL STRUCTURE" (BMR)" UK USA-45 USSR STRUCT WORKER GP/REL EFFICIENCY...IDEA/COMP 20. PAGE 13 F0243
INDUS ATTIT MGT ADMIN

S59
STINCHCOMBE A.L.,"BUREAUCRATIC AND CRAFT ADMINISTRATION OF PRODUCTION: A COMPARATIVE STUDY" (BMR)" USA+45 STRUCT EX/STRUC ECO/TAC GP/REL ...CLASSIF GP/COMP IDEA/COMP GEN/LAWS 20 WEBER/MAX. PAGE 126 F2490
CONSTRUC PROC/MFG ADMIN PLAN

S59
WALLACE R.A.,"CONGRESSIONAL CONTROL OF THE BUDGET." USA+45 NAT/G CHIEF GP/REL FEDERAL OBJECTIVE...MGT CONGRESS. PAGE 143 F2807
LEGIS EX/STRUC BUDGET CONSTN

C59
MINTZ S.W.,"INTERNAL MARKET SYS AS MECHANISMS OF SOCIAL ARTIC," IN V.F. RAY, INTERMED SOCIETIES, SOCIAL MOBILITY, AND COMMUNIC (BMR). UNIV STRATA GP/REL INGP/REL...GEOG SOC BIBLIOG. PAGE 92 F1804
MARKET SOCIETY ECO/UNDEV STRUCT

B60
EELLS R.S.F.,THE MEANING OF MODERN BUSINESS. LOC/G NAT/G NEIGH EX/STRUC PARTIC GP/REL INGP/REL DECISION. PAGE 36 F0706
LG/CO REPRESENT POLICY PLAN

B60
ELKOURI F.,HOW ARBITRATION WORKS (REV. ED.). LAW INDUS BARGAIN 20. PAGE 37 F0720
MGT LABOR ADJUD GP/REL

B60
FERNANDES F.,MUDANCAS SOCIAIS NO BRASIL. BRAZIL L/A+17C SOCIETY AGRI PROVS LEAD GP/REL RACE/REL ORD/FREE...SOC SOC/INTEG 20 SAO/PAULO. PAGE 40 F0786
ECO/UNDEV STRATA INDUS

B60
FORBUSH D.R.,PROBLEMS OF CORPORATE POWER. CLIENT LAW ELITES ADJUD...DECISION MGT. PAGE 42 F0822
LG/CO PWR

CONTROL
GP/REL

B60
FORM W.H.,INDUSTRY, LABOR, AND COMMUNITY. STRUCT NEIGH SECT BAL/PWR EDU/PROP PARTIC ATTIT ROLE PWR WEALTH...METH/CNCPT CHARTS. PAGE 42 F0828
LABOR MGT GP/REL CONTROL

B60
GARBARINO J.W.,HEALTH PLANS AND COLLECTIVE BARGAINING. USA+45 LABOR BARGAIN GP/REL WEALTH ...WELF/ST CHARTS 20 DEPT/HEW SAN/FRAN. PAGE 46 F0900
HEAL PLAN FINAN SERV/IND

B60
ILLINOIS U BUR COMMUNITY PLAN,PROCEEDINGS OF ILLINOIS STATEWIDE PLANNING CONFERENCE 1960. USA+45 FINAN LOC/G ACT/RES LEAD GOV/REL GP/REL WEALTH MUNICH 20 ILLINOIS. PAGE 64 F1260
PLAN DELIB/GP VOL/ASSN

B60
ROBERTSON D.,THE CONTROL OF INDUSTRY. UK MARKET LABOR WORKER PRICE CONTROL GP/REL COST DEMAND ORD/FREE WEALTH NEW/LIB SOCISM 20. PAGE 112 F2211
INDUS FINAN NAT/G ECO/DEV

B60
ROBSON W.A.,NATIONALIZED INDUSTRY AND PUBLIC OWNERSHIP. UK ECO/DEV FINAN LABOR LG/CO POL/PAR LEGIS ACT/RES GP/REL...TREND IDEA/COMP 20. PAGE 113 F2227
NAT/G OWN INDUS ATTIT

B60
ROPKE W.,A HUMANE ECONOMY. CULTURE ECO/DEV FINAN INDUS GP/REL CENTRAL WEALTH...GEOG SOC IDEA/COMP 20 EEC. PAGE 114 F2239
ECO/TAC INT/ORG DIPLOM ORD/FREE

B60
WATSON D.S.,ECONOMIC POLICY: BUSINESS AND GOVERNMENT. USA+45 FINAN LABOR PLAN BUDGET INT/TRADE GP/REL WEALTH LAISSEZ...CHARTS T. PAGE 144 F2832
ECO/TAC NAT/G POLICY ECO/DEV

S60
FORM W.H.,"ORGANIZED LABOR'S IMAGE OF COMMUNITY POWER STRUCTURE." LABOR LG/CO CONTROL LEAD REPRESENT...DECISION METH/CNCPT INT QU SAMP. PAGE 42 F0829
NEIGH PARTIC PWR GP/REL

S60
FRENCH J.R.P. JR.,"AN EXPERIMENT ON PARTICIPATION IN A NORWEGIAN FACTORY:INTERPERSONAL DIMENSIONS OF DECISION-MAKING." LABOR LEAD PERS/REL EFFICIENCY PRODUC...DECISION SOC CHARTS SOC/EXP. PAGE 44 F0853
INDUS PLAN RIGID/FLEX GP/REL

B61
MEXICO: CINCUENTA ANOS DE REVOLUCION VOL. II. L/A+17C SOCIETY LABOR RECEIVE GP/REL AGE/Y HEALTH ...SOC/WK ANTHOL MUNICH 20 MEXIC/AMER. PAGE 1 F0014
ECO/UNDEV STRUCT INDUS POL/PAR

B61
BARBASH J.,LABOR'S GRASS ROOTS. CONSTN NAT/G EX/STRUC LEGIS WORKER LEAD...MAJORIT BIBLIOG. PAGE 10 F0184
LABOR INGP/REL GP/REL LAW

B61
CAMPAIGNE J.G.,CHECK-OFF: LABOR BOSSES AND WORKING MEN. LEGIS WORKER EDU/PROP DEBATE COERCE REPRESENT GP/REL ORD/FREE CONSERVE. PAGE 21 F0404
LABOR ELITES PWR CONTROL

B61
CARROTHERS A.W.R.,LABOR ARBITRATION IN CANADA. CANADA LAW NAT/G CONSULT LEGIS WORKER ADJUD ADMIN CT/SYS 20. PAGE 22 F0422
LABOR MGT GP/REL BARGAIN

B61
CLARK J.M.,COMPETITION AS A DYNAMIC PROCESS. ECO/DEV EXTR/IND INDUS LG/CO TEC/DEV ECO/TAC PRICE EQUILIB PRODUC...NEW/IDEA CAP 20. PAGE 25 F0483
WEALTH GP/REL FINAN PROFIT

B61
DE GRAZIA A.,AMERICAN WELFARE. CLIENT FINAN LABOR LOC/G NAT/G NEIGH EDU/PROP GP/REL...CLASSIF CON/ANAL CHARTS BIBLIOG. PAGE 31 F0598
GIVE WEALTH SECT VOL/ASSN

B61
ELLIS H.S.,ECONOMIC DEVELOPMENT FOR LATIN AMERICA. L/A+17C AGRI FINAN INDUS FOR/AID GP/REL BAL/PAY DEMAND...ANTHOL 20 INTL/ECON. PAGE 37 F0723
ECO/UNDEV ECO/TAC PLAN INT/TRADE

B61
GALENSON W.,TRADE UNION DEMOCRACY IN WESTERN EUROPE. ECO/DEV INDUS PROF/ORG WORKER INCOME ...METH/COMP 20. PAGE 45 F0886
LABOR GP/REL ECO/TAC EUR+WWI

B61
GORDON R.A.,BUSINESS LEADERSHIP IN THE LARGE CORPORATION. USA+45 SOCIETY EX/STRUC ADMIN CONTROL ROUTINE GP/REL PWR...MGT 20. PAGE 49 F0960
LG/CO LEAD DECISION LOBBY

B61
HUBBARD P.J.,ORIGINS OF THE TVA: THE MUSCLE SHOALS CONTROVERSY, 1920-1932. USA-45 DELIB/GP LEGIS LEAD LOBBY GOV/REL GP/REL INGP/REL OWN PERSON...BIBLIOG 20 TVA CONGRESS WATER. PAGE 62 F1229
SEA CONTROL NAT/G INDUS

B61
LENSKI G.,THE RELIGIOUS FACTOR: A SOCIOLOGICAL STUDY OF RELIGION'S IMPACT ON POLITICS, ECONOMICS, AND FAMILY LIFE. FAM PROF/ORG EDU/PROP ROLE CATHISM ...INT SAMP MUNICH. PAGE 78 F1524
SECT GP/REL

B61
ROEPKE W.,JENSEITS VON ANGEBOT UND NACHFRAGE (DRITTE VERAENDERTE AUFLAGE). WOR+45 MARKET TEC/DEV ECO/TAC GP/REL INGP/REL NEW/LIB...POLICY SOC IDEA/COMP PERS/COMP 20. PAGE 113 F2233
SOCIETY STRANGE ECO/DEV STRUCT

B61
STROUD G.S.,LABOR HISTORY IN THE UNITED STATES: A GENERAL BIBLIOGRAPHY. USA+45 USA-45 STRATA VOL/ASSN AUTOMAT GP/REL INGP/REL ATTIT HEALTH 18/20. PAGE 127 F2504
BIBLIOG WORKER LABOR

S61
HOSELITZ B.F.,"ECONOMIC DEVELOPMENT AND POLITICAL STABILITY IN INDIA" INDIA NAT/G GP/REL...POLICY 20. PAGE 62 F1222
ECO/UNDEV GEN/LAWS PROB/SOLV

B62
BRANCH M.C.,THE CORPORATE PLANNING PROCESS. FINAN EX/STRUC EDU/PROP CONTROL LEAD GP/REL PERS/REL RATIONAL PERCEPT...MGT MATH PROBABIL STAT GAME. PAGE 18 F0338
PROF/ORG PLAN DECISION PERSON

B62
DEBUYST F.,LAS CLASES SOCIALES EN AMERICA LATINA. L/A+17C SOCIETY STRUCT WORKER EDU/PROP RACE/REL ATTIT HABITAT ROLE...GEOG SOC NAT/COMP SOC/INTEG 20. PAGE 32 F0612
STRATA GP/REL WEALTH

B62
DIMOCK M.E.,THE NEW AMERICAN POLITICAL ECONOMY: A SYNTHESIS OF POLITICS AND ECONOMICS. USA+45 FINAN LG/CO PLAN ADMIN REGION GP/REL CENTRAL MORAL 20. PAGE 33 F0642
FEDERAL ECO/TAC NAT/G PARTIC

B62
DOUGLAS A.,INDUSTRIAL PEACEMAKING. CONSULT ACT/RES ...MGT PSY METH 20. PAGE 34 F0656
BARGAIN INDUS LABOR GP/REL

B62
GALENSON W.,LABOR IN DEVELOPING COUNTRIES. BRAZIL INDONESIA ISRAEL PAKISTAN TURKEY AGRI INDUS WORKER PAY PRICE GP/REL WEALTH...MGT CHARTS METH/COMP NAT/COMP 20. PAGE 45 F0888
LABOR ECO/UNDEV BARGAIN POL/PAR

B62
GORT M.,DIVERSIFICATION AND INTEGRATION IN AMERICAN INDUSTRY. CLIENT DIST/IND PROC/MFG SERV/IND LG/CO CONTROL DEMAND PWR...METH/CNCPT STAT TREND CON/ANAL GP/COMP. PAGE 49 F0964
CONCPT GP/REL CLASSIF

B62
GROVE J.W.,GOVERNMENT AND INDUSTRY IN BRITAIN. UK FINAN LOC/G CONSULT DELIB/GP INT/TRADE ADMIN CONTROL...BIBLIOG 20. PAGE 52 F1008
ECO/TAC INDUS NAT/G GP/REL

B62
HARRINGTON M.,THE RETAIL CLERKS. ECO/TAC LEAD PARTIC CHOOSE GP/REL INGP/REL CENTRAL POLICY. PAGE 55 F1087
LABOR SERV/IND STRUCT DELIB/GP

B62
HARRIS S.E.,THE ECONOMICS OF THE POLITICAL PARTIES. USA+45 FINAN CHIEF ACT/RES PLAN BUDGET GP/REL INGP/REL NEW/LIB...IDEA/COMP PERS/COMP 20 EISNHWR/DD KENNEDY/JF. PAGE 56 F1090
POLICY ECO/DEV NAT/G POL/PAR

B62
HOOVER E.M.,ANATOMY OF A METROPOLIS. FUT USA+45 SOCIETY ECO/DEV DIST/IND INDUS WORKER ECO/TAC TAX GP/REL COST WEALTH MUNICH 20 NEWYORK/C. PAGE 62 F1212
ROUTINE TREND INCOME

B62
LEVY H.V.,LIBERDADE E JUSTICA SOCIAL (2ND ED.). BRAZIL COM L/A+17C USSR INT/ORG PARTIC GP/REL WEALTH 20 UN COM/PARTY. PAGE 79 F1544
ORD/FREE MARXISM CAP/ISM LAW

B62
LITTLEFIELD N.,METROPOLITAN AREA PROBLEMS AND MUNICIPAL HOME RULE. USA+45 PROVS ADMIN CONTROL GP/REL PWR. PAGE 81 F1586
LOC/G SOVEREIGN JURID LEGIS

B62
LITWACK L.,THE AMERICAN LABOR MOVEMENT. USA-45 NAT/G CREATE TEC/DEV CAP/ISM ECO/TAC ADJUD AUTOMAT SKILL...TREND ANTHOL 19/20. PAGE 81 F1588
INDUS LABOR GP/REL METH/COMP

B62
MCCLELLAN J.L.,CRIME WITHOUT PUNISHMENT. USA+45 LAW SOCIETY DELIB/GP TRIBUTE CONTROL LOBBY COERCE GP/REL ANOMIE MORAL...CRIMLGY 20 CONGRESS HOFFA/J. PAGE 88 F1718
CRIME ACT/RES LABOR PWR

B62
MOWITZ R.J.,PROFILE OF A METROPOLIS: A CASE BOOK. COM/IND CONSTRUC INDUS PUB/INST PLAN TEC/DEV LEAD GP/REL...POLICY TECHNIC WELF/ST MUNICH. PAGE 94 F1851
DECISION ADMIN

B62
MULLER E.,DIE HEIMATVERTRIEBENEN IN BADEN-WURTTEMBERG. GERMANY/W AGRI INDUS LABOR PROVS SOC/INTEG 20 MIGRATION. PAGE 95 F1858
GP/REL INGP/REL

B62
REES A.,THE ECONOMICS OF TRADE UNIONS. FUT ECO/DEV INDUS BARGAIN CAP/ISM PRICE SENIOR CONTROL GP/REL COST...TREND 20 AFL/CIO. PAGE 110 F2172
LABOR WORKER ECO/TAC

B62
SHERIF M.,INTERGROUP RELATIONS AND LEADERSHIP: APPROACHES AND RESEARCH IN INDUSTRIAL, ETHNIC, CULTURAL AND POLITICAL AREAS. CULTURE R+D LABOR DIPLOM GP/REL RACE/REL PERCEPT...PSY CONCPT. PAGE 121 F2377
LEAD REPRESENT PWR INGP/REL

B62
SRIVASTAVA G.L.,COLLECTIVE BARGAINING AND LABOR-MANAGEMENT RELATIONS IN INDIA. INDIA UK USA+45 INDUS LEGIS WORKER ADJUD EFFICIENCY PRODUC ...METH/COMP 20. PAGE 125 F2462
LABOR MGT BARGAIN GP/REL

B62
URQUIDI C.W.,A STATEMENT OF THE LAWS OF BOLIVIA IN MATTERS AFFECTING BUSINESS (3RD ED. REV., ENLARGED). L/A+17C LAW FINAN FAM WORKER ACT/RES DIPLOM ADJUD ADMIN GP/REL 20 BOLIV OAS. PAGE 133 F2626
JURID INDUS NAT/G LEGIT

B62
WOODS H.D.,LABOUR POLICY AND LABOUR ECONOMICS IN CANADA. CANADA FUT NAT/G VOL/ASSN WORKER BARGAIN ECO/TAC PAY CONFER GP/REL 20. PAGE 148 F2924
LABOR POLICY INDUS ECO/DEV

L62
N,"UNION INVESTMENT IN BUSINESS: A SOURCE OF UNION CONFLICT OF INTEREST." LAW NAT/G LEGIS CONTROL GP/REL INGP/REL DECISION. PAGE 96 F1884
LABOR POLICY FINAN LG/CO

B63
BURTT E.J. JR.,LABOR MARKETS, UNIONS, AND GOVERNMENT POLICIES. USA+45 MARKET NAT/G DELIB/GP CREATE BARGAIN GP/REL ORD/FREE PWR...POLICY CHARTS 20 AFL/CIO. PAGE 20 F0393
LABOR ECO/DEV CONTROL WORKER

B63
CHAMBERLAIN E.H.,THE ECONOMIC ANALYSIS OF LABOR UNION POWER (PAMPHLET). WORKER ECO/TAC DOMIN COERCE GP/REL DRIVE WEALTH POLICY. PAGE 23 F0441
LABOR PWR CONTROL

B63
CHAMPION J.M.,CRITICAL INCIDENTS IN MANAGEMENT. MARKET LG/CO SML/CO OP/RES ADMIN CONTROL LEAD GP/REL PERS/REL COST ATTIT SUPEGO ALL/VALS...PSY PERS/TEST BIBLIOG. PAGE 23 F0445
MGT DECISION EX/STRUC INDUS

B63
HARVEY O.L.,THE ANVIL AND THE PLOW: A HISTORY OF THE UNITED STATES DEPARTMENT OF LABOR: 1913-1963. USA+45 USA-45 NAT/G CONFER NEW/LIB 20 DEPT/LABOR. PAGE 56 F1106
EX/STRUC REPRESENT GP/REL LABOR

B63
HUNTER A.,THE ECONOMICS OF AUSTRALIAN INDUSTRY. DIST/IND EXTR/IND FINAN PROC/MFG SERV/IND ACT/RES PLAN TARIFFS GP/REL INGP/REL 20 AUSTRAL. PAGE 63 F1245
INDUS ECO/DEV HABITAT GP/COMP

B63
IANNI O.,INDUSTRIALIZACAO E DESENVOLVIMENTO SOCIAL NO BRASIL. BRAZIL L/A+17C STRATA STRUCT ECO/UNDEV EDU/PROP LEAD LOBBY NAT/LISM 20. PAGE 64 F1257
WORKER GP/REL INDUS PARTIC

B63
JACOBS P.,STATE OF UNIONS. USA+45 STRATA TOP/EX GP/REL RACE/REL DEMAND DISCRIM ATTIT PWR 20 CONGRESS NEGRO HOFFA/J. PAGE 66 F1296
LABOR ECO/TAC BARGAIN DECISION

B63
LEWIN J.,POLITICS AND LAW IN SOUTH AFRICA. SOUTH/AFR UK POL/PAR BAL/PWR ECO/TAC COLONIAL CONTROL GP/REL DISCRIM PWR 20 NEGRO. PAGE 79 F1545
NAT/LISM POLICY LAW RACE/REL

B63
MILLER W.,REVENUE-COST RATIOS OF RURAL TOWNSHIPS WITH CHANGING LAND USES. USA+45 INDUS SERV/IND PROVS GP/REL HABITAT...CHARTS GP/COMP MUNICH 20 NEW/JERSEY. PAGE 91 F1792
TAX COST AGRI

B63
PELLING H.M.,A HISTORY OF BRITISH TRADE UNIONISM. UK ELITES ECO/DEV POL/PAR GP/REL PWR NEW/LIB 19/20. PAGE 104 F2051
LABOR VOL/ASSN NAT/G

B63
REAGAN M.D.,THE MANAGED ECONOMY. USA+45 INDUS LG/CO BUDGET GP/REL ORD/FREE PWR WEALTH 20. PAGE 110 F2161
PLAN ECO/DEV NAT/G ROLE

B63
RILEY J.W. JR.,THE CORPORATION AND ITS PUBLICS. ESSAYS ON THE CORPORATE IMAGE. CLIENT ISOLAT AGE ATTIT...POLICY SOC METH/CNCPT INT. PAGE 111 F2193
LG/CO CLASSIF GP/REL NEIGH

B63
SELF P.,THE STATE AND THE FARMER. UK ECO/DEV MARKET WORKER PRICE CONTROL GP/REL...WELF/ST 20 DEPT/AGRI.
AGRI NAT/G

PAGE 119 F2346
ADMIN VOL/ASSN

L63
LIVERNASH E.R.,"THE RELATION OF POWER TO THE STRUCTURE AND PROCESS OF COLLECTIVE BARGAINING." ADJUD ORD/FREE...POLICY MGT CLASSIF GP/COMP. PAGE 81 F1589
LABOR GP/REL PWR ECO/TAC

L63
MCKERSIE R.B.,"NONPROFESSIONAL HOSPITAL WORKERS AND A UNION ORGANIZING DRIVE." PLAN GP/REL RACE/REL ATTIT DRIVE...CORREL STAT INT GP/COMP. PAGE 88 F1732
VOL/ASSN HEALTH INGP/REL LABOR

S63
REES A.,"THE EFFECTS OF UNIONS ON RESOURCE ALLOCATION." USA+45 WORKER PRICE CONTROL GP/REL ...MGT METH/COMP 20. PAGE 110 F2173
LABOR BARGAIN RATION INCOME

N63
US AGENCY INTERNATIONAL DEV,PRINCIPLES OF FOREIGN ECONOMIC ASSISTANCE (PAMPHLET). USA+45 FINAN GP/REL BAL/PAY EFFICIENCY 20 AID. PAGE 134 F2638
FOR/AID PLAN ECO/UNDEV ATTIT

B64
ASH W.,MARXISM AND MORAL CONCEPTS. CAP/ISM GP/REL ORD/FREE...BIBLIOG 20. PAGE 7 F0128
MARXISM CONCPT MORAL SOCIETY

B64
BLAKE R.R.,MANAGING INTERGROUP CONFLICT IN INDUSTRY. INDUS DELIB/GP EX/STRUC GP/REL PERS/REL GAME. PAGE 16 F0297
CREATE PROB/SOLV OP/RES ADJUD

B64
BROWN C.V.,GOVERNMENT AND BANKING IN WESTERN NIGERIA. AFR NIGERIA GOV/REL GP/REL...POLICY 20. PAGE 19 F0367
ADMIN ECO/UNDEV FINAN NAT/G

B64
COMMITTEE ECONOMIC DEVELOPMENT,COMMUNITY ECONOMIC DEVELOPMENT PROGRAMS. USA+45 FINAN INDUS LG/CO PROF/ORG CREATE GP/REL MUNICH NEW/YORK VERMONT PENNSYLVAN IN ARKANSAS. PAGE 27 F0519
LOC/G LABOR PLAN

B64
FISK W.M.,ADMINISTRATIVE PROCEDURE IN A REGULATORY AGENCY: THE CAB AND THE NEW YORK-CHICAGO CASE (PAMPHLET). USA+45 DIST/IND ADMIN CONTROL LOBBY GP/REL ROLE ORD/FREE NEWYORK/C CHICAGO CAB. PAGE 41 F0805
SERV/IND ECO/DEV AIR JURID

B64
HACKER A.,THE CORPORATION TAKE-OVER. CONSTN LABOR PLAN BAL/PWR CONTROL EXEC LOBBY REPRESENT GP/REL ROLE ORD/FREE POLICY. PAGE 52 F1025
LG/CO STRUCT PWR

B64
KAPLAN A.D.H.,BIG ENTERPRISE IN A COMPETITIVE SYSTEM (REV. ED.). USA+45 INDUS MARKET WORKER TEC/DEV ECO/TAC PRICE ADJUD ADMIN CONTROL...MGT CHARTS 20 MONOPOLY. PAGE 69 F1351
FINAN GP/REL NAT/G LG/CO

B64
MEISEL J.,PAPERS ON THE 1962 ELECTION. CANADA PROVS SECT GP/REL CONSEN EFFICIENCY...MAJORIT 20. PAGE 89 F1751
POL/PAR RECORD CHOOSE STRATA

B64
MITAU G.T.,INSOLUBLE PROBLEMS: CASE PROBLEMS ON THE FUNCTIONS OF STATE AND LOCAL GOVERNMENT. USA+45 AIR FINAN LABOR POL/PAR PROB/SOLV TAX RECEIVE CONTROL GP/REL 20 CASEBOOK ZONING. PAGE 92 F1807
ADJUD LOC/G PROVS

B64
MOAK L.L.,A MANUAL OF SUGGESTED PRACTICE FOR THE PREPARATION AND ADOPTION OF CAPITAL PROGRAMS AND CAPITAL BUDGETS BY LOCAL GOVERN. USA+45 DELIB/GP PLAN TAX GP/REL COST DECISION. PAGE 92 F1812
LOC/G BUDGET LEGIS PROB/SOLV

B64
MORGAN H.W.,AMERICAN SOCIALISM 1900-1960. AFR USA+45 USA-45 INTELL AGRI LABOR WORKER BARGAIN ECO/TAC GP/REL RACE/REL 20 NEGRO MIGRATION. PAGE 93 F1830
SOCISM POL/PAR ECO/DEV STRATA

B64
NOSSITER B.D.,THE MYTHMAKERS: AN ESSAY ON POWER AND WEALTH. USA+45 LG/CO NAT/G TOP/EX PROB/SOLV ADMIN GP/REL ORD/FREE 20. PAGE 99 F1937
ECO/TAC WEALTH FINAN PLAN

B64
NOVACK D.E.,DEVELOPMENT AND SOCIETY; THE DYNAMICS OF ECONOMIC CHANGE. WOR+45 STRATA STRUCT ECO/TAC CONTROL CROWD REV GP/REL ADJUST PRODUC WEALTH PSY. PAGE 99 F1940
SOCIETY CULTURE SOC ECO/UNDEV

B64
REDLICH F.,THE GERMAN MILITARY ENTERPRISER AND HIS WORK FORCE. CHRIST-17C GERMANY ELITES SOCIETY FINAN ECO/TAC CIVMIL/REL GP/REL INGP/REL...HIST/WRIT METH/COMP 14/17. PAGE 110 F2170
EX/STRUC FORCES PROFIT WORKER

B64
RUSTAMJI R.F.,THE LAW OF INDUSTRIAL DISPUTES IN INDIA. INDIA LEGIS WORKER CONTROL GP/REL...JURID MGT TIME/SEQ 20. PAGE 115 F2264
INDUS ADJUD BARGAIN

LABOR

B64
TAX S.,EL CAPITALISMO DEL CENTAVO; UNA ECONOMIA INDIGENA DE GUATEMALA (2 VOLS.). GUATEMALA L/A+17C SOCIETY GP/REL DEMAND INCOME HABITAT...SOC MUNICH 20 INDIAN/AM. PAGE 129 F2539
ECO/UNDEV AGRI WEALTH COST

B64
TONG T.,UNITED STATES DIPLOMACY IN CHINA, 1844-1860. ASIA USA-45 ECO/UNDEV ECO/TAC COERCE GP/REL...INT/LAW 19 TREATY. PAGE 131 F2581
DIPLOM INT/TRADE COLONIAL

S64
FYFE J.,"LIST OF CURRENT ACQUISITIONS OF PERIODICALS AND NEWSPAPERS DEALING WITH THE SOVIET UNION AND EAST EUROPEAN COUNTRIES." USSR WRITING GP/REL INGP/REL MARXISM 20. PAGE 45 F0879
BIBLIOG COM EDU/PROP PRESS

S64
LEFF N.H.,"ECONOMIC DEVELOPMENT THROUGH BUREAUCRATIC CORRUPTION." ELITES NAT/G ROUTINE REPRESENT GP/REL PERS/REL. PAGE 77 F1511
ECO/UNDEV CLIENT EX/STRUC

S64
N,"QUASI-LEGISLATIVE ARBITRATION AGREEMENTS." LAW LG/CO ECO/TAC SANCTION ATTIT POLICY. PAGE 96 F1885
ADJUD ADJUST LABOR GP/REL

C64
LANDAUER C.,"CONTEMPORARY ECONOMIC SYSTEMS." COM WOR+45 ECO/UNDEV PLAN GP/REL...BIBLIOG 20. PAGE 75 F1466
CAP/ISM SOCISM MARXISM IDEA/COMP

B65
BEAUFRE A.,AN INTRODUCTION TO STRATEGY, WITH PARTICULAR REFERENCE TO PROBLEMS OF DEFENSE, POLITICS, ECONOMICS IN THE NUCLEAR AGE. WOR+45 FORCES DIPLOM DETER CIVMIL/REL GP/REL...NEW/IDEA IDEA/COMP 20. PAGE 12 F0226
PLAN NUC/PWR WEAPON DECISION

B65
BRADLEY J.F.,THE ROLE OF TRADE ASSOCIATIONS AND PROFESSIONAL BUSINESS SOCIETIES IN AMERICA. USA+45 USA-45 STRUCT CONSULT DELIB/GP CREATE LOBBY GP/REL 20. PAGE 17 F0333
ECO/DEV PROF/ORG VOL/ASSN SOCIETY

B65
CAMERON W.J.,NEW ZEALAND. NEW/ZEALND S/ASIA DIPLOM INT/TRADE WRITING COLONIAL PARL/PROC...GEOG CMN/WLTH. PAGE 21 F0402
SOCIETY GP/REL STRUCT

B65
COLBERG M.R.,HUMAN CAPITAL IN SOUTHERN DEVELOPMENT. USA+45 AGRI ACADEM LABOR SCHOOL WORKER CAP/ISM DISCRIM. PAGE 26 F0498
PROVS RACE/REL GP/REL

B65
COLLOQUE SUR LA PLANIFICATION,LA PLANIFICATION COMME PROCESSUS DE DECISION. FRANCE SOCIETY MARKET LABOR LEGIS GP/REL EFFICIENCY INCOME ATTIT TECHRACY ...MYTH IDEA/COMP 20. PAGE 26 F0508
PLAN ECO/TAC PROB/SOLV

B65
CONLEY R.W.,THE ECONOMICS OF VOCATIONAL REHABILITATION. USA+45 VOL/ASSN CREATE EDU/PROP COST EFFICIENCY SOC/INTEG 20. PAGE 27 F0527
PUB/INST HEALTH GIVE GP/REL

B65
COPELAND M.A.,OUR FREE ENTERPRISE ECONOMY. USA+45 INDUS LABOR ADMIN CONTROL GP/REL MGT. PAGE 27 F0533
CAP/ISM PLAN FINAN ECO/DEV

B65
COUGHLIN B.J.,CHURCH AND STATE IN SOCIAL WELFARE. USA+45 RECEIVE GP/REL ORD/FREE WEALTH NEW/LIB. PAGE 28 F0542
CULTURE SECT VOL/ASSN GIVE

B65
DERBER M.,PLANT UNION-MANAGEMENT RELATIONS: FROM PRACTICE TO THEORY. PROC/MFG NEIGH PROB/SOLV ORD/FREE...DECISION MGT OBS QU SAMP. PAGE 32 F0621
LG/CO LABOR GP/REL ATTIT

B65
FLEMING R.W.,THE LABOR ARBITRATION PROCESS. USA+45 LAW BARGAIN ADJUD ROUTINE SANCTION COST...PREDICT CHARTS TIME 20. PAGE 41 F0809
GP/REL LABOR CONSULT DELIB/GP

B65
GOETZ-GIREY R.,LE MOUVEMENT DES GREVES EN FRANCE. FRANCE FINAN OP/RES PROB/SOLV ECO/TAC INCOME HABITAT...STAT CHARTS 19/20. PAGE 48 F0932
LABOR WORKER GP/REL INDUS

B65
HADWIGER D.F.,PRESSURES AND PROTEST. NAT/G LEGIS PLAN LEAD PARTIC ROUTINE ATTIT POLICY. PAGE 53 F1030
AGRI GP/REL LOBBY CHOOSE

B65
LEYS C.T.,FEDERATION IN EAST AFRICA. LAW AGRI DIST/IND FINAN INT/ORG LABOR INT/TRADE CONFER ADMIN CONTROL GP/REL...ANTHOL 20 AFRICA/E. PAGE 79 F1554
FEDERAL REGION ECO/UNDEV PLAN

B65
ONUOHA B.,THE ELEMENTS OF AFRICAN SOCIALISM. AFR FINAN SECT TEC/DEV FOR/AID GP/REL OWN LAISSEZ MARXISM...CONCPT BIBLIOG 20. PAGE 101 F1992
SOCISM ECO/UNDEV NAT/G EX/STRUC

B65
PARRIS H.W.,GOVERNMENT AND THE RAILWAYS IN NINETEENTH-CENTURY BRITAIN. UK DELIB/GP CONTROL LEAD CENTRAL 19 RAILROAD. PAGE 103 F2029
DIST/IND NAT/G PLAN GP/REL

B65
PAYNE J.L.,LABOR AND POLITICS IN PERU; THE SYSTEM OF POLITICAL BARGAINING. PERU CONSTN VOL/ASSN EX/STRUC LEAD PWR...CHARTS 20. PAGE 104 F2042
LABOR POL/PAR BARGAIN GP/REL

B65
RATNAM K.J.,COMMUNALISM AND THE POLITICAL PROCESS IN MALAYA. MALAYSIA WOR+45 ECO/UNDEV PARTIC CHOOSE REPRESENT GP/REL CENTRAL ATTIT...CHARTS WORSHIP 20. PAGE 109 F2152
CONSTN GOV/REL REGION

B65
ROSS P.,THE GOVERNMENT AS A SOURCE OF UNION POWER. USA+45 LAW ECO/DEV PROB/SOLV ECO/TAC LEAD GP/REL ...MGT 20. PAGE 114 F2245
LABOR BARGAIN POLICY NAT/G

B65
SCHECHTER A.,THE BUSINESSMAN IN GOVERNMENT (THESIS, COLUMBIA UNIVERSITY). USA+45 CONFER GP/REL PERSON ...QU 20 PRESIDENT TRUMAN/HS CABINET. PAGE 116 F2291
INDUS NAT/G EX/STRUC DELIB/GP

B65
SHEPHERD W.G.,ECONOMIC PERFORMANCE UNDER PUBLIC OWNERSHIP: BRITISH FUEL AND POWER. UK BUDGET GP/REL ...METH/CNCPT CHARTS BIBLIOG 20. PAGE 120 F2375
PROC/MFG NAT/G OWN FINAN

B65
US ADVISORY COMN INTERGOV REL,METROPOLITAN SOCIAL AND ECONOMIC DISPARITIES: IMPLICATIONS FOR INTERGOVERNMENTAL RELATIONS IN CENT'L CITIES AND SUBURBS. CULTURE STRATA DIST/IND LOC/G PLAN GP/REL DISCRIM HABITAT MUNICH. PAGE 134 F2634
GOV/REL GEOG

B65
VAID K.N.,STATE AND LABOR IN INDIA. INDIA INDUS WORKER PAY PRICE ADJUD CONTROL PARL/PROC GP/REL ORD/FREE 20. PAGE 140 F2757
LAW LABOR MGT NEW/LIB

B65
WALTON R.E.,A BEHAVIORAL THEORY OF LABOR NEGOTIATIONS: AN ANALYSIS OF A SOCIAL INTERACTION SYSTEM. USA+45 FINAN PROB/SOLV ECO/TAC GP/REL INGP/REL...DECISION BIBLIOG. PAGE 143 F2812
SOC LABOR BARGAIN ADMIN

B65
WEIL G.L.,A HANDBOOK ON THE EUROPEAN ECONOMIC COMMUNITY. BELGIUM EUR+WWI FRANCE GERMANY/W ITALY CONSTN ECO/DEV CREATE PARTIC GP/REL...DECISION MGT CHARTS 20 EEC. PAGE 144 F2846
INT/TRADE INT/ORG TEC/DEV INT/LAW

L65
HAGE J.,"AN AXIOMATIC THEORY OF ORGANIZATIONS" USA+45 STRUCT LABOR PRODUC DRIVE PERSON RIGID/FLEX 20 WEBER/MAX. PAGE 53 F1032
GP/REL EFFICIENCY PROF/ORG ATTIT

L65
HAMMOND A.,"COMPREHENSIVE VERSUS INCREMENTAL BUDGETING IN THE DEPARTMENT OF AGRICULTURE" USA+45 GP/REL ATTIT...PSY INT 20 DEPT/AGRI. PAGE 54 F1057
TOP/EX EX/STRUC AGRI BUDGET

S65
BANOVETZ J.M.,"METROPOLITAN SUBSIDIES: AN APPRAISAL." LEAD GP/REL DISCRIM MUNICH. PAGE 9 F0175
REGION TAX GOV/REL

S65
KEE W.S.,"CENTRAL CITY EXPENDITURES AND METROPOLITAN AREAS." PLAN BUDGET ECO/TAC TAX GP/REL WEALTH...CHARTS MUNICH 20. PAGE 70 F1366
LOC/G GOV/COMP NEIGH

S65
MULLER A.L.,"THE ECONOMIC POSITION OF THE ASIANS IN AFRICA." AFR SOUTH/AFR ECO/UNDEV MARKET ECO/TAC GP/REL INCOME...CHARTS IND 20 MONOPOLY ASIANS. PAGE 95 F1856
WORKER RACE/REL CAP/ISM DISCRIM

S65
SELLERS C.,"THE EQUILIBRIUM CYCLE IN TWO-PARTY POLITICS." USA+45 USA-45 CULTURE R+D GP/REL MAJORITY DECISION. PAGE 119 F2351
CHOOSE TREND POL/PAR

B66
BAKKE E.W.,MUTUAL SURVIVAL; THE GOAL OF UNION AND MANAGEMENT (2ND ED.). USA+45 ELITES ECO/DEV ECO/TAC CONFER ADMIN REPRESENT GP/REL INGP/REL ATTIT ...GP/COMP 20. PAGE 8 F0155
MGT LABOR BARGAIN INDUS

B66
BEN-PORATH Y.,THE ARAB LABOR FORCE IN ISRAEL. ISLAM ISRAEL AGRI INDUS SCHOOL CAP/ISM PAY DEMAND...GEOG REGRESS STAT CHARTS 20 ARABS. PAGE 13 F0245
WORKER CENSUS GP/REL STRUCT

B66
COOK P.W. JR.,PROBLEMS OF CORPORATE POWER. WOR+45 FINAN INDUS BARGAIN GP/REL...MGT ANTHOL. PAGE 27 F0530
ADMIN LG/CO PWR ECO/TAC

B66
DAVIES I.,AFRICAN TRADE UNIONS. AFR ECO/UNDEV INT/ORG GP/REL ORD/FREE SOVEREIGN SOCISM 20. PAGE 30 F0585 LABOR COLONIAL PWR INDUS

B66
DAVIS K.,BUSINESS AND ITS ENVIRONMENT. LAW ECO/DEV INDUS OP/RES ADMIN CONTROL ROUTINE GP/REL PROFIT POLICY. PAGE 30 F0591 EX/STRUC PROB/SOLV CAP/ISM EXEC

B66
DILLEY M.R.,BRITISH POLICY IN KENYA COLONY (2ND ED.). AFR INDIA UK LABOR BUDGET TAX ADMIN PARL/PROC GP/REL...BIBLIOG 20 PARLIAMENT. PAGE 33 F0639 COLONIAL REPRESENT SOVEREIGN

B66
FELKER J.L.,SOVIET ECONOMIC CONTROVERSIES. USSR INDUS PLAN INT/TRADE GP/REL MARXISM SOCISM...POLICY 20. PAGE 40 F0778 ECO/DEV MARKET PROFIT PRICE

B66
FRANCK L.R.,LA POLITIQUE ECONOMIQUE DES ETATS-UNIS. USA+45 USA-45 FINAN INDUS CONTROL CROWD GOV/REL GP/REL...POLICY SOC CHARTS 18/20. PAGE 43 F0841 NAT/G INT/TRADE GEOG

B66
FRANKEL P.H.,MATTEI; OIL AND POWER POLITICS. ITALY EXTR/IND MARKET GP/REL NAT/LISM SOCISM...POLICY MGT BIOG 20 MATTEI/E. PAGE 43 F0844 LEAD NAT/G CONTROL LG/CO

B66
HAYS P.R.,LABOR ARBITRATION: A DISSENTING VIEW. USA+45 LAW DELIB/GP BARGAIN ADJUD...PREDICT 20. PAGE 57 F1126 GP/REL LABOR CONSULT CT/SYS

B66
HOROWITZ D.,HEMISPHERES NORTH AND SOUTH: ECONOMIC DISPARITY AMONG NATIONS. WOR+45 ECO/DEV ECO/UNDEV INT/ORG PLAN DIPLOM INT/TRADE GIVE PARTIC GP/REL ...WELF/ST 20. PAGE 62 F1215 ECO/TAC FOR/AID STRATA WEALTH

B66
KAESTNER K.,GESAMTWIRTSCHAFTLICHE PLANUNG IN EINER GEMISCHTEN WIRTSCHAFTSORDNUNG (WIRTSCHAFTSPOLITISCHE STUDIEN 5). GERMANY/W WOR+45 WOR-45 INDUS MARKET NAT/G ACT/RES GP/REL INGP/REL PRODUC...ECOMETRIC MGT BIBLIOG 20. PAGE 68 F1346 ECO/TAC PLAN POLICY PREDICT

B66
KAREFA-SMART J.,AFRICA: PROGRESS THROUGH COOPERATION. AFR FINAN TEC/DEV DIPLOM FOR/AID EDU/PROP CONFER REGION GP/REL WEALTH...HEAL SOC/INTEG 20. PAGE 69 F1356 ORD/FREE ECO/UNDEV VOL/ASSN PLAN

B66
LANDERS D.S.,RISE OF CAPITALISM. LABOR AUTOMAT GP/REL CENTRAL COST PROFIT...SOC CONCPT ANTHOL 19/20. PAGE 75 F1469 CAP/ISM INDUS AGRI

B66
MC CONNELL J.P.,LAW AND BUSINESS: PATTERNS AND ISSUES IN COMMERCIAL LAW. USA+45 USA-45 LOC/G WORKER LICENSE CRIME REPRESENT GP/REL 20. PAGE 87 F1713 ECO/DEV JURID ADJUD MGT

B66
RIZK C.,LE REGIME POLITIQUE LIBANAIS. ISLAM LEBANON STRUCT POL/PAR SECT LOBBY GP/REL 20 ARABS MUSLIM CHRISTIAN. PAGE 112 F2198 ECO/UNDEV NAT/G CULTURE

B66
ROSS A.M.,INDUSTRIAL RELATIONS AND ECONOMIC DEVELOPMENT. POL/PAR LEGIS WORKER BARGAIN PRICE EXEC LOBBY INCOME PWR...DECISION ANTHOL BIBLIOG 20. PAGE 114 F2243 ECO/UNDEV LABOR NAT/G GP/REL

B66
SHULTZ G.P.,STRATEGIES FOR THE DISPLACED WORKER. USA+45 COMPUTER TEC/DEV BARGAIN RECEIVE EDU/PROP CONFER GP/REL...MGT METH/COMP 20. PAGE 121 F2391 ECO/DEV WORKER PLAN AUTOMAT

B66
SINGH L.P.,THE POLITICS OF ECONOMIC COOPERATION IN ASIA; A STUDY OF ASIAN INTERNATIONAL ORGANIZATIONS. ASIA INT/ORG ACT/RES PLAN GP/REL...POLICY GP/COMP BIBLIOG 20 UN SEATO. PAGE 122 F2414 ECO/UNDEV ECO/TAC REGION DIPLOM

B66
TIVEY L.J.,NATIONALISATION IN BRITISH INDUSTRY. UK LEGIS PARL/PROC GP/REL OWN ATTIT SOCISM 20. PAGE 131 F2578 NAT/G INDUS CONTROL LG/CO

B66
US DEPARTMENT OF LABOR,TECHNOLOGICAL TRENDS IN MAJOR AMERICAN INDUSTRIES. USA+45 R+D LABOR GP/REL PRODUC...MGT BIBLIOG 20. PAGE 135 F2669 TEC/DEV INDUS TREND AUTOMAT

B66
US SENATE COMM LABOR-PUB WELF,AMEND THE RAILWAY LABOR ACT. USA+45 CONSTN CONSULT DELIB/GP ADJUD CONGRESS RAILROAD. PAGE 139 F2731 GP/REL LABOR DIST/IND LAW

N66
PRINCETON U INDUSTRIAL REL SEC,RECENT MATERIAL ON COLLECTIVE BARGAINING IN GOVERNMENT (PAMPHLET NO. 130). USA+45 ECO/DEV LABOR WORKER ECO/TAC GOV/REL ...MGT 20. PAGE 108 F2120 BIBLIOG/A BARGAIN NAT/G GP/REL

B67
ALEXANDER G.J.,HONESTY AND COMPETITION: FALSE-ADVERTISING LAW AND POLICY UNDER FTC ADMINISTRATION. USA+45 INDUS NAT/G PRICE GP/REL 20 FTC. PAGE 3 F0058 EDU/PROP SERV/IND CONTROL DELIB/GP

B67
BADGLEY R.F.,DOCTORS' STRIKE; MEDICAL CARE AND CONFLICT IN SASKATCHEWAN. CANADA NAT/G PROF/ORG GP/REL ADJUST ATTIT...HEAL SOC 20. PAGE 8 F0148 HEALTH PLAN LABOR BARGAIN

B67
BAILY S.L.,LABOR, NATIONALISM, AND POLITICS IN ARGENTINA. POL/PAR TOP/EX GP/REL...BIBLIOG/A 19/20 MIGRATION PERON/JUAN ARGEN. PAGE 8 F0154 LABOR NAT/LISM

B67
BARNETT A.D.,CHINA AFTER MAO. ASIA CHINA/COM CULTURE ECO/UNDEV ECO/TAC CONTROL EFFICIENCY NAT/LISM MARXISM 20. PAGE 10 F0189 POL/PAR NAT/G TEC/DEV GP/REL

B67
BEAL E.F.,THE PRACTICE OF COLLECTIVE BARGAINING (3RD ED.). USA+45 WOR+45 ECO/DEV INDUS LG/CO PROF/ORG WORKER ECO/TAC GP/REL WEALTH...JURID METH/CNCPT. PAGE 12 F0221 BARGAIN MGT LABOR ADJUD

B67
BLAIR G.S.,LEGISLATIVE BODIES IN CALIFORNIA. USA+45 LAW POL/PAR LOBBY APPORT CHOOSE REPRESENT GP/REL ...T CALIFORNIA. PAGE 15 F0293 LEGIS PROVS LOC/G ADJUD

B67
COWLING M.,1867 DISRAELI, GLADSTONE, AND REVOLUTION; THE PASSING OF THE SECOND REFORM BILL. UK LEGIS LEAD LOBBY GP/REL INGP/REL...DECISION BIBLIOG 19 REFORMERS. PAGE 28 F0545 PARL/PROC POL/PAR ATTIT LAW

B67
EGGERT G.G.,RAILROAD LABOR DISPUTES. USA+45 USA-45 ELITES DIST/IND DELIB/GP FORCES JUDGE WORKER PROB/SOLV DOMIN PWR...POLICY 20. PAGE 36 F0707 GP/REL NAT/G LABOR BARGAIN

B67
FANON F.,TOWARD THE AFRICAN REVOLUTION. AFR FRANCE CULTURE ELITES LEAD REV GP/REL ORD/FREE SOVEREIGN 20. PAGE 39 F0762 COLONIAL DOMIN ECO/UNDEV RACE/REL

B67
GOODMAN J.S.,THE DEMOCRATS AND LABOR IN RHODE ISLAND 9152-1962; CHANGES IN THE OLD ALLIANCE. USA+45 EDU/PROP LEAD GP/REL ROLE RHODE/ISL DEMOCRAT. PAGE 49 F0948 LABOR LOBBY POL/PAR LEGIS

B67
GORZ A.,STRATEGY FOR LABOR: A RADICAL PROPOSAL (TRANS. BY MARTIN NICOLAUS AND VICTORIA ORTIZ). EUR+WWI FRANCE ITALY ECO/DEV POL/PAR OP/RES PLAN GP/REL ALL/IDEOS...SOC 20 EEC. PAGE 49 F0965 LABOR PWR STRUCT ECO/TAC

B67
NELSON R.R.,TECHNOLOGY, ECONOMIC GROWTH, AND PUBLIC POLICY. USA+45 PLAN GP/REL UTIL KNOWL...POLICY PHIL/SCI CHARTS BIBLIOG 20. PAGE 97 F1912 R+D CONSULT CREATE ACT/RES

B67
PEDLEY F.H.,EDUCATION AND SOCIAL WORK. USA+45 INTELL TEC/DEV. PAGE 104 F2047 GP/REL EDU/PROP SOC/WK EFFICIENCY

B67
POWLEDGE F.,BLACK POWER WHITE RESISTANCE. USA+45 STRUCT PLAN GP/REL DISCRIM HABITAT ORD/FREE WEALTH ...METH/COMP SOC/INTEG NEGRO. PAGE 107 F2111 RACE/REL ATTIT PWR

B67
RIDKER R.G.,ECONOMIC COSTS OF AIR POLLUTION* STUDIES IN MEASUREMENT. R+D GP/REL KNOWL...OBS MUNICH 20. PAGE 111 F2190 OP/RES HABITAT PHIL/SCI

B67
ROBERTS B.C.,COLLECTIVE BARGAINING IN AFRICAN COUNTRIES. AFR LAW ECO/UNDEV BARGAIN GP/REL ...DECISION METH/COMP 20. PAGE 112 F2206 LABOR MGT PLAN ECO/TAC

B67
SMITH T.L.,THE PROCESS OF RURAL DEVELOPMENT IN LATIN AMERICA (A MONOGRAPH). L/A+17C STRATA INDUS PLAN GP/REL PERS/REL RIGID/FLEX WEALTH...OBS CHARTS ORG/CHARTS ANTHOL 20 COLOMB. PAGE 123 F2434 IDEA/COMP SOC AGRI ECO/UNDEV

B67
VAN SLYKE L.P.,ENEMIES AND FRIENDS; THE UNITED FRONT IN CHINESE COMMUNIST HISTORY. CHINA/COM SOCIETY FORCES PLAN ADJUST 20 MAO. PAGE 140 F2764 INGP/REL MARXISM ATTIT GP/REL

B67
WILLIAMS M.,THE EAST IS RED: THE VIEW INSIDE CHINA. CHINA/COM CONSTN COERCE AGE/Y ATTIT PERSON...OBS 20 MAO. PAGE 147 F2893 REV MARXIST GP/REL DIPLOM

B67
WOOTON G.,WORKERS, UNIONS, AND THE STATE. INDUS PROB/SOLV GP/REL DRIVE SUPEGO RESPECT...PSY SOC. PARTIC WORKER

PAGE 148 F2925
NAT/G LABOR

L67
AFFELDT R.J.,"THE INDEPENDENT LABOR UNION AND THE GOOD LIFE." USA+45 ADJUD CONTROL SANCTION GP/REL ORD/FREE JURID. PAGE 3 F0045
LABOR CT/SYS PWR SOVEREIGN

L67
COSTANZA J.F.,"WHOLESOME NEUTRALITY: LAW AND EDUCATION." USA+45 GIVE EDU/PROP ADJUD CONTROL GP/REL...DECISION JURID. PAGE 28 F0540
SECT PROVS ACADEM

L67
GOULD W.B.,"THE STATUS OF UNAUTHORIZED AND 'WILDCAT' STRIKES UNDER THE NATIONAL LABOR RELATIONS ACT." USA+45 ACT/RES BARGAIN ECO/TAC LEGIT ADJUD ADMIN GP/REL MGT. PAGE 50 F0968
ECO/DEV INDUS LABOR POLICY

L67
GREGORY A.J.,"AFRICAN SOCIALISM, SOCIALISM AND FASCISM: AN APPRAISAL." FUT LEAD REV GP/REL RACE/REL NAT/LISM ATTIT...IDEA/COMP STERTYP 20. PAGE 51 F0993
FASCISM MARXISM SOCISM AFR

L67
JOHNSTON J.D. JR.,"CONSTITUTION OF SUBDIVISION CONTROL EXACTIONS: THE QUEST FOR A RATIONALE." USA+45 PROVS PUB/INST ADJUD CT/SYS GP/REL MUNICH. PAGE 68 F1334
PLAN CONTROL LOC/G FORCES

L67
MANNE H.G.,"OUR TWO CORPORATION SYSTEMS* LAW AND ECONOMICS." LAW CONTROL SANCTION GP/REL...JURID 20. PAGE 85 F1657
INDUS ELITES CAP/ISM ADMIN

L67
SCHNEIDER C.W.,"REFORM OF THE FEDERAL SECURITIES LAWS." FUT USA+45 LAW FINAN INDUS DELIB/GP ACT/RES PROB/SOLV GP/REL. PAGE 117 F2304
NAT/G LG/CO ADMIN CONTROL

L67
VIA J.W. JR.,"ANTITRUST AND THE AMENDED BANK MERGER AND HOLDING COMPANY ACTS: THE SEARCH FOR STANDARDS." USA+45 CONTROL GP/REL WEALTH SUPREME/CT. PAGE 141 F2783
FINAN CT/SYS LAW EX/STRUC

L67
WHITNEY S.N.,"MERGERS, CONGLOMERATES, AND OLIGOPOLIES* A WIDENING OF ANTI TRUST TARGETS." LAW NAT/G TEC/DEV CAP/ISM GP/REL PWR...OLD/LIB 20. PAGE 146 F2873
ECO/TAC INDUS JURID

S67
AMERASINGHE C.F.,"SOME LEGAL PROBLEMS OF STATE TRADING IN SOUTHEAST ASIA." PROB/SOLV ADJUD CONTROL CT/SYS GP/REL 20. PAGE 5 F0084
INT/TRADE NAT/G INT/LAW PRIVIL

S67
BAILEY S.L.,"THE ITALIANS AND ORGANIZED LABOR IN THE UNITED STATES AND ARGENTINA: 1880-1910." ITALY USA-45 PARTIC HABITAT PWR...GEOG GP/COMP 19/20 ARGEN. PAGE 8 F0153
LABOR LEAD WEALTH GP/REL

S67
BELL D.E.,"THE QUALITY OF AID." USA+45 R+D DIPLOM GP/REL. PAGE 12 F0234
POLICY FOR/AID PROB/SOLV INSPECT

S67
BENN W.,"TECHNOLOGY HAS AN INEXORABLE EFFECT." FUT UK ECO/DEV INT/ORG CONSULT PLAN EDU/PROP ADMIN LEAD GP/REL PRODUC...INT 20 EEC. PAGE 13 F0246
R+D LG/CO TEC/DEV INDUS

S67
BOSHER J.F.,"GOVERNMENT AND PRIVATE INTERESTS IN NEW FRANCE." CANADA FRANCE INDUS LG/CO SML/CO CAP/ISM INT/TRADE COLONIAL GP/REL...HIST/WRIT 17/18. PAGE 17 F0320
NAT/G FINAN ADMIN CONTROL

S67
BROWN M.B.,"THE TRADE UNION QUESTION." UK INDUS OP/RES PRICE PROFIT 20. PAGE 19 F0371
WORKER LABOR GP/REL LAW

S67
EHRLICH S.,"INTERNATIONAL PRESSURE GROUPS: A CONTRIBUTION TO THE SOCIOLOGY OF INTERNATIONAL RELATIONS IN THE CAPITALIST WORLD." GP/REL...METH 20. PAGE 36 F0711
INT/ORG LOBBY DIPLOM DECISION

S67
FEDYSHYN O.S.,"KHRUSHCHEV'S 'LEAP FORWARD': NATIONAL ASSIMILATION IN THE USSR AFTER STALIN." USSR PLAN NAT/LISM PERSON...POLICY 20 KHRUSH/N STALIN/J. PAGE 39 F0771
GP/REL INGP/REL MARXISM METH

S67
FOX R.G.,"FAMILY, CASTE, AND COMMERCE IN A NORTH INDIAN MARKET TOWN." INDIA STRATA AGRI FACE/GP FAM NEIGH OP/RES BARGAIN ADMIN ROUTINE WEALTH...SOC CHARTS 20. PAGE 43 F0838
CULTURE GP/REL ECO/UNDEV DIST/IND

S67
GOLDSTEIN W.,"THE SCIENCE ESTABLISHMENT AND ITS POLITICAL CONTROL." WOR+45 SOCIETY GP/REL RATIONAL ORD/FREE. PAGE 48 F0941
CREATE ADJUST CONTROL

S67
GRUN C.,"DEUX ETUDES ALLEMANDES SUR LES PREJUGES NATIONAUX ET LES MOYENS DE LES COMBATTRE." FRANCE GERMANY DIST/IND PROB/SOLV GP/REL AGE/Y RIGID/FLEX ...PSY STAT INT SAMP. PAGE 52 F1010
ATTIT REGION DISCRIM STERTYP

S67
HALE G.E.,"EXPANDING ENTERPRISE: GEOGRAPHICAL CURBS ON MERGERS." USA+45 MARKET LG/CO ADJUD CONTROL GP/REL 20. PAGE 53 F1041
LAW HABITAT INDUS EX/STRUC

S67
HALL B.,"THE COALITION AGAINST DISHWASHERS." USA+45 POL/PAR PROB/SOLV BARGAIN LEAD CHOOSE REPRESENT GP/REL ORD/FREE PWR...POLICY 20. PAGE 53 F1044
LABOR ADMIN DOMIN WORKER

S67
HERRERA F.,"EUROPEAN PARTICIPATION IN THE LATIN AMERICAN REGIONAL INTEGRATION" EUR+WWI L/A+17C GP/REL INGP/REL 20. PAGE 59 F1154
DIPLOM REGION INT/ORG FINAN

S67
JENCKS C.E.,"COAL MINERS IN BRITAIN SINCE NATIONALIZATION." UK LABOR GP/REL ADJUST SOCISM ...INT 20. PAGE 67 F1311
EXTR/IND WORKER STRATA ATTIT

S67
JENCKS C.E.,"SOCIAL STATUS OF COAL MINERS IN BRITAIN SINCE NATIONALIZATION." UK STRATA STRUCT LABOR RECEIVE GP/REL INCOME OWN ATTIT HABITAT...MGT T 20. PAGE 67 F1312
EXTR/IND WORKER CONTROL NAT/G

S67
LANDES W.M.,"THE EFFECT OF STATE FAIR EMPLOYMENT LAWS ON THE ECONOMIC POSITION OF NONWHITES." USA+45 PROVS SECT LEGIS ADMIN GP/REL RACE/REL...JURID CONCPT CHARTS HYPO/EXP NEGRO. PAGE 75 F1470
DISCRIM LAW WORKER

S67
LASLETT J.H.M.,"SOCIALISM AND THE AMERICAN LABOR MOVEMENT* SOME NEW REFLECTIONS." USA-45 VOL/ASSN LOBBY PARTIC CENTRAL ALL/VALS SOCISM...GP/COMP 20. PAGE 76 F1484
LABOR ROUTINE ATTIT GP/REL

S67
LEMIEUX V.,"LA DIMENSION POLITIQUE DE L'ACTION RATIONNELLE." CONTROL GP/REL PERS/REL...DECISION NEW/IDEA GAME 20. PAGE 77 F1518
GEN/LAWS RATIONAL PWR

S67
LIFLAND W.T.,"BANKING PRACTICE AND THE ANTITRUST LAWS." NAT/G GP/REL...CONCPT IDEA/COMP 20. PAGE 80 F1563
FINAN CAP/ISM JURID

S67
LINEBERRY R.L.,"REFORMISM AND PUBLIC POLICIES IN AMERICAN CITIES." USA+45 POL/PAR EX/STRUC LEGIS BUDGET TAX GP/REL...STAT CHARTS MUNICH. PAGE 80 F1573
DECISION POLICY LOC/G

S67
MEHTA A.,"INDIA* POVERTY AND CHANGE." STRATA INDUS CREATE ECO/TAC FOR/AID NEUTRAL GP/REL ADJUST INCOME ...NEW/IDEA 20. PAGE 89 F1746
INDIA SOCIETY ECO/UNDEV TEC/DEV

S67
PRASOW P.,"THE DEVELOPMENT OF JUDICIAL ARBITRATION IN LABOR-MANAGEMENT DISPUTES." LAW INDUS WORKER GP/REL ROLE...HIST/WRIT 20. PAGE 107 F2113
LABOR BARGAIN ADJUD TREND

S67
RAGAN S.,"THE ABA RECOMMENDATIONS: A NEWSPAPERMAN'S CRITIQUE." EDU/PROP CONTROL GP/REL...JURID ABA. PAGE 109 F2136
LAW PRESS ADJUD ORD/FREE

S67
RAZA M.A.,"EMERGING TRENDS IN PUBLIC LABOR POLICIES AND UNION - GOVERN MENT RELATIONS IN ASIA AND AFRICA." LAW NAT/G POL/PAR COLONIAL COERCE GP/REL ATTIT 20. PAGE 110 F2157
LABOR CONTROL TREND

S67
ROCKE J.R.M.,"THE BRITISH EXPORT BATTLE FOR THE CARIBBEAN" GP/REL...POLICY 20 CMN/WLTH. PAGE 113 F2229
INT/TRADE DIPLOM MARKET ECO/TAC

S67
RONY V.,"HEARTBREAK IN TENNESSEE* POOR WHITES AND THE UNIONS." LAW STRUCT CAP/ISM ADJUD GP/REL. PAGE 113 F2236
LABOR LOC/G WORKER PWR

S67
SCRIPP J.,"CONTROLLING PREJUDICIAL PUBLICITY BY THE CONTEMPT POWER: THE BRITISH PRACTICE AND ITS PROSPECT IN AMERICAN LAW." UK USA+45 EDU/PROP CONTROL GP/REL ORD/FREE JURID. PAGE 119 F2338
METH/COMP LAW PRESS ADJUD

S67
SHEFFTZ M.C.,"THE TRADE DISPUTES AND TRADE UNIONS ACT OF 1927: THE AFTERMATH OF THE GENERAL STRIKE." UK FINAN WORKER ADJUD LEAD PARL/PROC 20. PAGE 120 F2373
LEGIS ATTIT LABOR GP/REL

S67
SIMONE A.J.,"SCIENTIFIC PUBLIC POLICY, MARKET PERFORMANCE, AND SIZE OF FIRM." GP/REL COST
LAW INDUS

EFFICIENCY OPTIMAL PRODUC PWR. PAGE 122 F2410 NAT/G PROB/SOLV

S67
SMITH W.H.T.,"THE IMPLICATIONS OF THE AMERICAN BAR ASSOCIATION ADVISORY COMMITTEE RECOMMENDATIONS FOR POLICE ADMINISTRATION." AFR ADMIN...JURID 20. PAGE 123 F2435 EDU/PROP CONTROL GP/REL ORD/FREE

S67
SOLT L.F.,"PURITANISM, CAPITALISM, DEMOCRACY, AND THE NEW SCIENCE." NAT/G GP/REL CONSERVE...IDEA/COMP GEN/LAWS. PAGE 124 F2440 SECT CAP/ISM RATIONAL POPULISM

S67
STEMPEL GH I.I.I.,"A NEW ANALYSIS OF MONOPOLY AND COMPETITION." USA+45 INDUS TV ATTIT MUNICH. PAGE 126 F2479 PRESS COM/IND GP/REL

S67
STYCOS J.M.,"POLITICS AND POPULATION CONTROL IN LATIN AMERICA." USA+45 FAM NAT/G GP/REL AGE/C ATTIT CATHISM MARXISM...POLICY UN WHO. PAGE 127 F2509 PLAN CENSUS CONTROL L/A+17C

S67
TABORSKY E.,"THE CLASS STRUGGLE, THE PROLETARIAT, AND THE DEVELOPING NATIONS." USSR LABOR POL/PAR FOR/AID COLONIAL GP/REL 20. PAGE 128 F2521 DIPLOM MARXISM ECO/UNDEV WORKER

S67
WAITS C.R.,"CRAFT GILDS AS AN INSTITUTIONAL BARRIER TO THE INDUSTRIAL REVOLUTION." CHRIST-17C MOD/EUR ECO/UNDEV CONTROL GP/REL ATTIT 16/19. PAGE 142 F2801 TEC/DEV INDUS REV PROF/ORG

S67
WHITE W.L.,"THE TREASURY BOARD AND PARLIAMENT." CANADA CONSTN CONSULT LEGIS LEAD PARL/PROC GP/REL ...DECISION 20. PAGE 146 F2871 FINAN DELIB/GP NAT/G ADMIN

S67
ZACK A.M.,"ARE STRIKES OF PUBLIC EMPLOYEES NECESSARY?" USA+45 DELIB/GP PROB/SOLV REPRESENT GP/REL MGT. PAGE 150 F2956 LABOR NAT/G WORKER BARGAIN

N67
NATIONAL COMN COMMUNITY HEALTH,ACTION - PLANNING FOR COMMUNITY HEALTH SERVICES (PAMPHLET). USA+45 PROF/ORG DELIB/GP BUDGET ROUTINE GP/REL ATTIT ...HEAL SOC SOC/WK CHARTS MUNICH TIME 20. PAGE 97 F1898 PLAN HEALTH ADJUST

N67
US HOUSE COMM GOVT OPERATIONS,FEDERALLY FINANCED SOCIAL RESEARCH, EXPENDITURES, STATUS, AND OBJECTIVES (PAMPHLET). WOR+45 CREATE LEAD GP/REL ATTIT...GEOG PSY SOC. PAGE 137 F2700 ACT/RES NAT/G GIVE BUDGET

N67
US SENATE COMM ON FOREIGN REL,SURVEY OF THE ALLIANCE FOR PROGRESS: THE LATIN AMERICAN MILITARY (PAMPHLET). USA+45 INT/ORG POL/PAR DIPLOM AGREE GP/REL ROLE ORD/FREE 20. PAGE 139 F2746 L/A+17C FORCES CIVMIL/REL POLICY

B68
PROUDHON P.J.,SYSTEME DES CONTRADICTIONS ECONOMIQUES, OU PHILOSOPHIE DA LA MISERE (2 VOLS.) (1846). SECT WORKER GP/REL ISOLAT PRODUC IDEA/COMP. PAGE 108 F2126 SOCIETY STRATA MORAL

B76
PROUDHON P.J.,WHAT IS PROPERTY? (TRANS. BY B.R. TUCKER). SOCIETY AGRI CAP/ISM CRIME GP/REL PERSON MORAL ORD/FREE WEALTH. PAGE 108 F2127 OWN WORKER PRODUC ANARCH

GRAFT....SEE TRIBUTE

GRAHAM F.D. F0970,F0971

GRAHAM R. F0972

GRAMPP W.D. F0973,F0974,F0975

GRAND/JURY....GRAND JURIES

GRANGE....GRANGE AND GRANGERS

B20
BUCK S.J.,THE AGRARIAN CRUSADE: A CHRONICLE OF THE FARMER IN POLITICS. USA-45 INDUS PROB/SOLV PWR WEALTH...GEOG CENSUS 19/20 GREENBACK GRANGE SILVER. PAGE 20 F0381 AGRI POPULISM VOL/ASSN POL/PAR

GRANICK D. F0976,F0977

GRANT J.A.C. F0978

GRANT/US....PRESIDENT ULYSSES S. GRANT

GRANTS....SEE GIVE+FOR/AID

GRAYSON D.K. F0979

GRAYSON L.E. F0037

GREAT BRITAIN....SEE UK

GREAT BRITAIN CENTRAL OFF INF F0980

GREAT/SOC....GREAT SOCIETY

GREBLER L. F0981

GRECO/ROMN....GRECO-ROMAN CIVILIZATION

B54
SCHUMPETER J.A.,HISTORY OF ECONOMIC ANALYSIS. WOR-45...PHIL/SCI METH/CNCPT STAT IDEA/COMP GRECO/ROMN. PAGE 118 F2322 KNOWL GEN/LAWS METH

GREECE....MODERN GREECE

B65
OECD,THE MEDITERRANEAN REGIONAL PROJECT: GREECE; EDUCATION AND DEVELOPMENT. FUT GREECE SOCIETY AGRI FINAN NAT/G PROF/ORG WORKER PLAN PROB/SOLV ADMIN DEMAND ATTIT 20 OECD. PAGE 100 F1972 EDU/PROP SCHOOL ACADEM ECO/UNDEV

B65
ORG FOR ECO COOP AND DEVEL,THE MEDITERRANEAN REGIONAL PROJECT: AN EXPERIMENT IN PLANNING BY SIX COUNTRIES. FUT GREECE SPAIN TURKEY YUGOSLAVIA SOCIETY FINAN NAT/G PROF/ORG EDU/PROP ADMIN REGION COST...POLICY STAT CHARTS 20 OECD. PAGE 102 F1995 PLAN ECO/UNDEV ACADEM SCHOOL

S65
MUNZI U.,"THE EUROPEAN SOCIAL FUND IN THE DEVELOPMENT OF THE MEDITERRANEAN REGIONS OF THE EEC." FUT GREECE ITALY PORTUGAL SPAIN TURKEY WORKER TEC/DEV ECO/TAC REGION...STAT EEC. PAGE 95 F1862 ECO/UNDEV PREDICT RECORD

B67
DINERSTEIN H.S.,INTERVENTION AGAINST COMMUNISM (STUDIES IN INTERNATIONAL AFFAIRS NO. 1). CUBA DOMIN/REP GREECE USA+45 USSR VIETNAM OP/RES COERCE WAR 20. PAGE 33 F0643 MARXISM DIPLOM NAT/LISM

S67
WALZER M.,"THE CONDITION OF GREECE; TWENTY YEARS AFTER THE TRUMAN DOCTRINE." AFR GREECE FORCES CAP/ISM 20 TRUMAN/HS. PAGE 143 F2814 DIPLOM POLICY FOR/AID TOTALISM

N67
US SENATE COMM ON FOREIGN REL,WAR OR PEACE IN THE MIDDLE EAST (PAMPHLET). GREECE ISLAM ISRAEL JORDAN UAR CHIEF PROB/SOLV FOR/AID WAR PWR 20 SENATE. PAGE 139 F2739 DIPLOM FORCES PLAN

GREECE/ANC....ANCIENT GREECE

B65
GRAMPP W.D.,ECONOMIC LIBERALISM; THE BEGINNINGS (VOL. I). USA-45 WOR-45 MARKET LABOR ATTIT WEALTH ...POLICY CONCPT BIBLIOG GREECE/ANC MERCANTLST REPUBLICAN FEDERALIST. PAGE 50 F0974 ECO/DEV CAP/ISM IDEA/COMP ECO/TAC

GREEN C. F0982,F0983

GREEN F.M. F0984

GREEN J.L. F0985

GREEN L.P. F0986,F0987

GREEN P.E. F0988

GREEN/TH....T.H. GREEN

GREENBACK....GREENBACK PARTY

B20
BUCK S.J.,THE AGRARIAN CRUSADE: A CHRONICLE OF THE FARMER IN POLITICS. USA-45 INDUS PROB/SOLV PWR WEALTH...GEOG CENSUS 19/20 GREENBACK GRANGE SILVER. PAGE 20 F0381 AGRI POPULISM VOL/ASSN POL/PAR

GREENE L.E. F0989

GREENFIELD K.R. F0990

GREENHUT M.L. F0991

GREENWICH....GREENWICH, ENGLAND

GREER S. F0992

GREGORY A.J. F0993

GREGORY R. F0994

GREGORY T.E. F0426

GRENADA....GRENADA (WEST INDIES)

GRENIEWSKI H. F0995

GRENVILLES....GRENVILLES - ENGLISH FAMILY; SEE ALSO UK

GRESHAM-YANG TREATY....SEE GRESHMYANG

GRESHM/LAW....GRESHAM'S LAW

GREY A.L. F0996

GRIER E. F0997

GRIER G. F0997

GRIFFIN A.P.C. F0998

GRIFFIN C.E. F0999

GRIFFITH W.E. F1000,F1001

GRIGSBY W.G. F1002,F2151

GRIPP R.C. F1003

GRNWCH/VIL....GREENWICH VILLAGE

GROND L. F0436

GROSECLOSE E. F1004

GROSS B.H. F1938

GROSS B.M. F1005,F1938

GROSS H. F1006

GROSS NATIONAL PRODUCT....WEALTH+ECO+PRODUC

GROSSMAN G. F1007

GROUP RELATIONS....SEE GP/REL

GROVE J.W. F1008

GROWTH....SEE CREATE+ECO/UNDEV

GRUBEL H.G. F1009

GRUN C. F1010

GRUNWALD J. F0149

GRUSHIN B.A. F1011
GT BRIT MIN OF OVERSEAS DEV F1803
GUAM....GUAM

GUATEMALA....SEE ALSO L/A+17C

B59
GOMEZ ROBLES J.,A STATEMENT OF THE LAWS OF GUATEMALA IN MATTERS AFFECTING BUSINESS (2ND ED. REV., ENLARGED). GUATEMALA L/A+17C LAW FINAN FAM WORKER ACT/RES DIPLOM ADJUD ADMIN GP/REL 20 OAS. PAGE 48 F0945 — JURID NAT/G INDUS LEGIT

B60
US GENERAL ACCOUNTING OFFICE,EXAMINATION OF ECONOMIC AND TECHNICAL ASSISTANCE PROGRAM FOR GUATEMALA. GUATEMALA L/A+17C USA+45 FINAN INDUS PLAN...POLICY STAT CHARTS 20 DEPT/STATE. PAGE 136 F2680 — FOR/AID ECO/UNDEV TEC/DEV NAT/G

B64
TAX S.,EL CAPITALISMO DEL CENTAVO; UNA ECONOMIA INDIGENA DE GUATEMALA (2 VOLS.). GUATEMALA L/A+17C SOCIETY GP/REL DEMAND INCOME HABITAT...SOC MUNICH 20 INDIAN/AM. PAGE 129 F2539 — ECO/UNDEV AGRI WEALTH COST

S67
PETRAS J.,"GUERRILLA MOVEMENTS IN LATIN AMERICA - I." GUATEMALA PERU VENEZUELA NAT/G COLONIAL LEAD ATTIT PWR...TIME/SEQ METH/COMP 20 COLOMB. PAGE 105 F2072 — GUERRILLA REV L/A+17C MARXISM

GUDIN E. F1012

GUEMES/M....MARTIN GUEMES

GUERRILLA....GUERRILLA WARFARE

B14
DE BLOCH J.,THE FUTURE OF WAR IN ITS TECHNICAL, ECONOMIC, AND POLITICAL RELATIONS (1899). MOD/EUR TEC/DEV BUDGET INT/TRADE DETER GUERRILLA WEAPON COST PEACE 20. PAGE 31 F0596 — WAR BAL/PWR PREDICT FORCES

B67
FALL B.B.,HO CHI MINH ON REVOLUTION: SELECTED WRITINGS, 1920-66. COM VIETNAM ELITES NAT/G COERCE GUERRILLA RACE/REL MARXISM...MARXIST ANTHOL 20. PAGE 39 F0761 — REV COLONIAL ECO/UNDEV S/ASIA

B67
OGLESBY C.,CONTAINMENT AND CHANGE. AFR COM USA+45 ECO/UNDEV TEC/DEV ECO/TAC FOR/AID INT/TRADE DOMIN GUERRILLA REV PEACE 20 STALIN/J. PAGE 101 F1983 — DIPLOM BAL/PWR MARXISM CULTURE

B67
US SENATE COMM ON FOREIGN REL,HARRISON E. SALISBURY'S TRIP TO NORTH VIETNAM. CHINA/COM USA+45 VIETNAM/N PRESS TASK GUERRILLA CONSEN EFFICIENCY PEACE DRIVE...OBS SENATE. PAGE 139 F2743 — DIPLOM WAR FORCES ATTIT

B67
WOLF C. JR.,UNITED STATES POLICY AND THE THIRD WORLD. USA+45 WOR+45 FORCES ACT/RES BAL/PWR ECO/TAC FOR/AID DETER GUERRILLA NUC/PWR REV...CHARTS 20. PAGE 148 F2916 — DIPLOM ECO/UNDEV POLICY NAT/G

S67
PETRAS J.,"GUERRILLA MOVEMENTS IN LATIN AMERICA - I." GUATEMALA PERU VENEZUELA NAT/G COLONIAL LEAD ATTIT PWR...TIME/SEQ METH/COMP 20 COLOMB. PAGE 105 F2072 — GUERRILLA REV L/A+17C MARXISM

N67
US HOUSE COMM FOREIGN AFFAIRS,COMMUNIST ACTIVITIES IN LATIN AMERICA 1967 (PAMPHLET). CUBA USA+45 DIPLOM INT/TRADE EDU/PROP COERCE GUERRILLA HOUSE/REP OAS. PAGE 137 F2696 — L/A+17C MARXISM ORD/FREE ECO/TAC

GUEVARA/E....ERNESTO GUEVARA

GUIANA/BR....BRITISH GUIANA;

B64
RENO P.,THE ORDEAL OF BRITISH GUIANA. L/A+17C USA+45 STRUCT AGRI EXTR/IND INDUS NAT/G FOR/AID ORD/FREE...GEOG 20 GUIANA/BR INTRVN/ECO. PAGE 111 F2178 — COLONIAL ECO/UNDEV SOCISM PWR

GUIANA/FR....FRENCH GUIANA

GUILDS....SEE PROF/ORG

GUINEA....SEE ALSO AFR

B61
SCHNAPPER B.,LA POLITIQUE ET LE COMMERCE FRANCAIS DANS LE GOLFE DE GUINEE DE 1838 A 1871. FRANCE GUINEA UK SEA EXTR/IND NAT/G DELIB/GP LEGIS ADMIN ORD/FREE...POLICY GEOG CENSUS CHARTS BIBLIOG 19. PAGE 117 F2303 — COLONIAL INT/TRADE DOMIN AFR

B65
HAPGOOD D.,AFRICA: FROM INDEPENDENCE TO TOMARROW. AFR GUINEA SENEGAL CULTURE ELITES ECO/UNDEV AGRI SCHOOL FOR/AID COLONIAL MARXISM...TREND 20. PAGE 55 F1070 — ECO/TAC SOCIETY NAT/G

GUJARAT....GUJARAT (STATE OF INDIA)

GUPTA S. F1013

GURR T. F0598

GURTOO D.H.N. F1014

GUTKIND E.A. F1015

GUTMANN P.M. F1016

GUTTMAN/L....LOUIS GUTTMAN (AND GUTTMAN SCALE)

GUYANA....GUYANA; SEE ALSO GUIANA/BR, L/A+17C

GWYN W.B. F1017

GYORGY A. F1018

H

HAAR C.M. F1019

HAAS E.B. F1020

HABER A. F0785

HABERLER G. F1021,F1022,F1023,F1024

HABITAT....ECOLOGY

N19
BROWN W.M.,THE DESIGN AND PERFORMANCE OF "OPTIMUM" — HABITAT

BLAST SHELTER PROGRAMS (PAMPHLET). USA+45 ACT/RES PLAN DEATH COST EFFICIENCY OPTIMAL...POLICY CHARTS 20. PAGE 19 F0375
NUC/PWR WAR HEALTH

N19
CHATTERS C.H.,NEW MUNICIPAL REVENUES FOR NEW MUNICIPAL EXPENDITURES (PAMPHLET). PLAN PRICE UTIL HABITAT...IDEA/COMP MUNICH 20. PAGE 23 F0457
LOC/G BUDGET TAX

N19
RIDLEY C.E.,MEASURING MUNICIPAL ACTIVITIES (PAMPHLET). FINAN SERV/IND FORCES RECEIVE INGP/REL HABITAT...POLICY SOC/WK 20. PAGE 111 F2191
MGT HEALTH WEALTH LOC/G

B22
VON ENGELIN O.D.,INHERITING THE EARTH, THE GEOGRAPHICAL FACTOR IN NATIONAL DEVELOPMENT. WOR-45 CULTURE DIPLOM BIO/SOC HABITAT PERSON...PSY SOC CONCPT IDEA/COMP. PAGE 142 F2791
INGP/REL GEOG SOCIETY ROLE

B37
COLE W.E.,RECENT TRENDS IN RURAL PLANNING. USA-45 LAW ECO/DEV LOC/G SECT EDU/PROP CRIME LEISURE AGE/Y HABITAT...SOC/WK MUNICH 20. PAGE 26 F0503
AGRI NEIGH PLAN ACT/RES

B38
CARVALHO C.M.,GEOGRAPHIA HUMANA; POLITICA E ECONOMICA (3RD ED.). BRAZIL CULTURE AGRI INDUS DIPLOM COLONIAL GP/REL RACE/REL...LING 20 RESOURCE/N. PAGE 22 F0424
GEOG HABITAT

B47
ISAAC J.,ECONOMICS OF MIGRATION. MOD/EUR CULTURE STRATA STRUCT NAT/G COLONIAL WEALTH...OLD/LIB TREND TIME 19/20 EUROPE/W MIGRATION. PAGE 65 F1289
HABITAT SOC GEOG

B48
HOOVER E.M.,THE LOCATION OF ECONOMIC ACTIVITY. WOR+45 MARKET WORKER PROB/SOLV INT/TRADE ADMIN COST ...POLICY CHARTS T MUNICH 20. PAGE 62 F1211
HABITAT INDUS ECO/TAC GEOG

B48
NOYES C.R.,ECONOMIC MAN IN RELATION TO HIS NATURAL ENVIRONMENT (2 VOLS.). UNIV COST DEMAND EFFICIENCY HAPPINESS INCOME PRODUC PROFIT HEREDITY...CHARTS BIBLIOG. PAGE 99 F1944
HABITAT METH/CNCPT GEN/METH

B48
OSBORN F.,OUR PLUNDERED PLANET. UNIV DEATH WAR ...BIBLIOG RESOURCE/N. PAGE 102 F2001
HABITAT GEOG ADJUST AGRI

B48
WHITE C.L.,HUMAN GEOGRAPHY: AN ECOLOGICAL STUDY OF GEOGRAPHY. UNIV SEA CULTURE AGRI EXTR/IND RACE/REL PRODUC...CHARTS HYPO/EXP SIMUL GEN/LAWS T. PAGE 146 F2868
SOC HABITAT GEOG SOCIETY

S49
SHEPHARD H.A.,"DEMOCRATIC CONTROL IN A LABOR UNION." FUT CONSTN STRUCT TEC/DEV LEAD PARTIC RACE/REL CENTRAL DRIVE HABITAT RECORD. PAGE 120 F2374
LABOR MAJORIT CONTROL PWR

S52
HEBERLE R.,"ON POLITICAL ECOLOGY" (BMR)" INCOME ATTIT WEALTH...GEOG METH SOC/INTEG 20. PAGE 58 F1133
HABITAT STRATA CHOOSE

B54
WASHBURNE N.F.,INTERPRETING SOCIAL CHANGE IN AMERICA. USA+45 STRATA FAM NAT/G SECT OP/RES ECO/TAC EDU/PROP HABITAT...SOC TIME/SEQ TREND 20 BUREAUCRCY. PAGE 143 F2826
CULTURE STRUCT CREATE TEC/DEV

S54
FORM W.H.,"THE PLACE OF SOCIAL STRUCTURE IN THE DETERMINATION OF LAND USE: SOME IMPLICATIONS FOR A THEORY OF URBAN ECOLOGY" (BMR)" STRUCT...GEOG PHIL/SCI SOC MUNICH 20. PAGE 42 F0827
HABITAT MARKET ORD/FREE

S54
MACK R.W.,"ECOLOGICAL PATTERNS IN AN INDUSTRIAL SHOP" (BMR)" USA+45 CULTURE SOCIETY STRATA STRUCT LABOR NEIGH GP/REL ADJUST HABITAT...SOC SOC/INTEG 20. PAGE 83 F1634
INDUS DISCRIM WORKER

B55
PEDLER F.J.,ECONOMIC GEOGRAPHY OF WEST AFRICA. GAMBIA NIGER SIER/LEONE STRATA EXTR/IND MARKET LABOR INT/TRADE DEMAND HABITAT WEALTH...CHARTS 20. PAGE 104 F2046
ECO/UNDEV GEOG PRODUC EFFICIENCY

B56
ISARD W.,LOCATION AND SPACE-ECONOMY: GENERAL THEORY RELATING TO INDUSTRIAL LOCATION, MARKET AREAS, LAND USE, TRADE... UNIV DIST/IND MARKET LG/CO SML/CO TEC/DEV GP/REL EQUILIB HABITAT...NEW/IDEA MATH CHARTS 20. PAGE 66 F1290
GEN/LAWS GEOG INDUS REGION

B56
WHYTE W.H. JR.,THE ORGANIZATION MAN. CULTURE FINAN VOL/ASSN DOMIN EDU/PROP EXEC DISPL HABITAT ROLE ...PERS/TEST STERTYP. PAGE 146 F2875
ADMIN LG/CO PERSON CONSEN

S56
MARGOLIS J.,"ON MUNICIPAL LAND POLICY FOR FISCAL GAINS." USA+45 PLAN TAX COST EFFICIENCY HABITAT KNOWL...MGT MUNICH 20. PAGE 85 F1667
BUDGET POLICY GEOG LOC/G

B57
DRUCKER P.F.,AMERICA'S NEXT TWENTY YEARS. USA+45 DIST/IND ACADEM SCHOOL DIPLOM ECO/TAC AUTOMAT HABITAT HEALTH...SOC/WK TREND MUNICH 20 URBAN/RNWL PUB/TRANS. PAGE 34 F0667
WORKER FOR/AID CENSUS GEOG

B57
WEIGERT H.W.,PRINCIPLES OF POLITICAL GEOGRAPHY. WOR+45 ECO/DEV ECO/UNDEV SECT ECO/TAC COLONIAL HABITAT...CHARTS T 20. PAGE 144 F2845
GEOG CULTURE

S57
VERNON R.,"PRODUCTION AND DISTRIBUTION IN THE LARGE METROPOLIS" (BMR)" USA+45 PROC/MFG ECO/TAC HABITAT ...CENSUS TREND MUNICH 20. PAGE 141 F2779
PRODUC DIST/IND PROB/SOLV

B58
CROWE S.,THE LANDSCAPE OF POWER. UK CULTURE SERV/IND NAT/G CONSULT PARTIC NUC/PWR LEISURE...SOC EXHIBIT 20. PAGE 29 F0559
HABITAT TEC/DEV PLAN CONTROL

S58
THOMAS D.S.,"AGE AND ECONOMIC DIFFERENTIALS IN INTERSTATE MIGRATION." SEX...GEOG SAMP/SIZ TREND CON/ANAL CHARTS BIBLIOG. PAGE 130 F2560
AGE WEALTH HABITAT CENSUS

B59
MAYER H.M.,READINGS IN URBAN GEOGRAPHY. WOR+45 SOCIETY DIST/IND INDUS MARKET HABITAT...CLASSIF CENSUS CHARTS ANTHOL MUNICH 20 WATER. PAGE 87 F1706
GEOG STRUCT

B59
NORTON P.L.,URBAN PROBLEMS AND TECHNIQUES. AIR AGRI INDUS MARKET TEC/DEV BUDGET LEISURE ALL/VALS ...ANTHOL MUNICH 20 URBAN/RNWL. PAGE 99 F1936
PLAN LOC/G HABITAT

B59
ROCHE J.,LA COLONISATION ALLEMANDE ET LE RIO GRANDE DO SUL. BRAZIL L/A+17C NAT/G PROVS INGP/REL RACE/REL DISCRIM HABITAT...GEOG SOC/INTEG 19/20 MIGRATION. PAGE 113 F2228
ECO/UNDEV GP/REL ATTIT

B59
SERAPHIM H.J.,PROBLEME DER WILLENSBILDUNG UND DER WIRTSCHAFTSPOLITISCHEN FUEHRUNG. WOR+45 MARKET ACT/RES OP/RES PLAN EDU/PROP INGP/REL HABITAT PLURISM...MGT PERS/COMP METH 20. PAGE 119 F2357
POLICY DECISION PSY

B60
GONZALEZ NAVARRO M.,LA COLONIZACION EN MEXICO, 1877-1910. AGRI NAT/G PLAN PROB/SOLV INCOME ...POLICY JURID CENSUS 19/20 MEXIC/AMER MIGRATION. PAGE 48 F0947
ECO/UNDEV GEOG HABITAT COLONIAL

B60
GRIER E.,PRIVATELY DEVELOPED INTERRACIAL HOUSING: AN ANALYSIS OF EXPERIENCE. FINAN MARKET COST DISCRIM PROFIT SOC/INTEG 20. PAGE 51 F0997
RACE/REL CONSTRUC HABITAT

B60
RAMA C.M.,LAS CLASES SOCIALES EN EL URUGUAY. L/A+17C URUGUAY ELITES SOCIETY STRATA INDUS ATTIT HABITAT PWR...GEOG SOC/INTEG MUNICH 20. PAGE 109 F2138
ECO/UNDEV STRUCT PARTIC

B60
SLOTKIN J.S.,FROM FIELD TO FACTORY; NEW INDUSTRIAL EMPLOYEES. HABITAT...MGT NEW/IDEA NAT/COMP BIBLIOG SOC/INTEG 20. PAGE 123 F2423
INDUS LABOR CULTURE WORKER

S60
SPINRAD W.,"CORRELATES OF TRADE UNION PARTICIPATION: A SUMMARY OF LITERATURE." ACT/RES PERS/REL HAPPINESS HABITAT...BIBLIOG WORK. PAGE 125 F2456
LABOR PARTIC CORREL ROLE

B61
LEE R.R.,ENGINEERING-ECONOMIC PLANNING MISCELLANEOUS SUBJECTS: A SELECTED BIBLIOGRAPHY (MIMEOGRAPHED). FINAN LOC/G NEIGH ADMIN CONTROL INGP/REL HABITAT...GEOG MGT SOC/WK MUNICH 20 RESOURCE/N. PAGE 77 F1509
BIBLIOG/A PLAN REGION

B61
WEISBROD B.A.,ECONOMICS OF PUBLIC HEALTH. USA+45 INGP/REL HABITAT...POLICY STAT COSTS 20. PAGE 145 F2851
SOCIETY HEALTH NEW/IDEA ECO/DEV

S61
DALTON G.,"ECONOMIC THEORY AND PRIMITIVE SOCIETY" (BMR)" UNIV AGRI KIN TEC/DEV ECO/TAC REGION HABITAT SKILL...METH/COMP BIBLIOG. PAGE 30 F0574
ECO/UNDEV METH PHIL/SCI SOC

B62
BROOKINGS INSTITUTION,DEVELOPMENT OF THE EMERGING COUNTRIES; AN AGENDA FOR RESEARCH. WOR+45 AGRI TEC/DEV FOR/AID EDU/PROP ADJUST HABITAT KNOWL...PSY SOC ANTHOL 20 THIRD/WRLD. PAGE 19 F0362
ECO/UNDEV R+D SOCIETY PROB/SOLV

B62
CHAPIN F.S.,URBAN GROWTH DYNAMICS IN A REGIONAL CLUSTER OF CITIES. TEC/DEV ECO/TAC HABITAT...GEOG SOC MUNICH. PAGE 23 F0453
REGION PLAN

B62
DEBUYST F.,LAS CLASES SOCIALES EN AMERICA LATINA. L/A+17C SOCIETY STRUCT WORKER EDU/PROP RACE/REL ATTIT HABITAT ROLE...GEOG SOC NAT/COMP SOC/INTEG 20. PAGE 32 F0612
STRATA GP/REL WEALTH

B62
TIEBOUT C.M.,THE COMMUNITY ECONOMIC BASE STUDY (PAMPHLET). USA+45 ECO/TAC LEAD DEMAND HABITAT 20. PAGE 130 F2572
NEIGH INCOME ACT/RES

B62
WENDT P.F.,HOUSING POLICY - THE SEARCH FOR SOLUTIONS. GERMANY/W SWEDEN UK USA+45 OP/RES HABITAT WEALTH...SOC/WK CHARTS 20. PAGE 145 F2856
PLAN ADMIN METH/COMP NAT/G

B63
ALPERT P.,ECONOMIC DEVELOPMENT. WOR+45 FINAN TEC/DEV ECO/TAC PRICE GOV/REL HABITAT...GEOG BIBLIOG T 20 THIRD/WRLD. PAGE 4 F0079
ECO/DEV ECO/UNDEV INT/TRADE FOR/AID

B63
BARNETT H.J.,SCARCITY AND GROWTH: THE ECONOMICS OF NATURAL RESOURCE AVAILABILITY. FUT WOR+45 AGRI INDUS PROB/SOLV TEC/DEV CONTROL PRODUC...SOC/WK IDEA/COMP METH/COMP SIMUL 20 RESOURCE/N MALTHUS RICARDO/D MILL/JS DARWIN/C. PAGE 10 F0191
DEMAND HABITAT CENSUS GEOG

B63
BONINI C.P.,SIMULATION OF INFORMATION AND DECISION SYSTEMS IN THE FIRM. MARKET BUDGET DOMIN EDU/PROP ADMIN COST ATTIT HABITAT PERCEPT PWR...CONCPT PROBABIL QUANT PREDICT HYPO/EXP BIBLIOG. PAGE 16 F0313
INDUS SIMUL DECISION MGT

B63
ENKE S.,ECONOMICS FOR DEVELOPMENT. AGRI TEC/DEV CAP/ISM DIPLOM ECO/TAC TAX ATTIT DRIVE HABITAT WEALTH...GOV/COMP BIBLIOG 20. PAGE 38 F0737
ECO/UNDEV PHIL/SCI CON/ANAL

B63
GRIGSBY W.G.,HOUSING MARKETS AND PUBLIC POLICY. USA+45 FAM NEIGH PRICE DEMAND WEALTH...POLICY CHARTS BIBLIOG METH MUNICH 20. PAGE 51 F1002
MARKET RENT HABITAT PLAN

B63
HUNTER A.,THE ECONOMICS OF AUSTRALIAN INDUSTRY. DIST/IND EXTR/IND FINAN PROC/MFG SERV/IND ACT/RES PLAN TARIFFS GP/REL INGP/REL 20 AUSTRAL. PAGE 63 F1245
INDUS ECO/DEV HABITAT GP/COMP

B63
KAPP W.K.,SOCIAL COSTS OF BUSINESS ENTERPRISE. WOR+45 LABOR TEC/DEV CAP/ISM HABITAT...PHIL/SCI NEW/IDEA CON/ANAL 20. PAGE 69 F1354
COST SOCIETY INDUS RIGID/FLEX

B63
MANN D.E.,THE POLITICS OF WATER IN ARIZONA. AGRI EXTR/IND PROVS ACT/RES CREATE PLAN GOV/REL COST HABITAT...MGT CHARTS 20 ARIZONA WATER. PAGE 84 F1655
POLICY ECO/TAC TEC/DEV

B63
MEEK R.L.,THE ECONOMICS OF PHYSIOCRACY. FRANCE UK AGRI FINAN WORKER CAP/ISM TAX DEMAND EQUILIB INCOME HABITAT...CHARTS ANTHOL 17. PAGE 89 F1744
PRODUC WEALTH MARKET

B63
MILLER W.,REVENUE-COST RATIOS OF RURAL TOWNSHIPS WITH CHANGING LAND USES. USA+45 INDUS SERV/IND PROVS GP/REL HABITAT...CHARTS GP/COMP MUNICH 20 NEW/JERSEY. PAGE 91 F1792
TAX COST AGRI

B63
WAGLEY C.,INTRODUCTION TO BRAZIL. BRAZIL L/A+17C FAM KIN SCHOOL SECT ATTIT WEALTH...GEOG SOC. PAGE 142 F2799
ECO/UNDEV ELITES HABITAT STRATA

S63
LOEWENSTEIN L.K.,"THE LOCATION OF URBAN LAND USES." USA+45 LOC/G HABITAT...STAT CHARTS MUNICH 20. PAGE 81 F1595
GEOG PLAN INDUS

B64
BEARDSLEY R.K.,STUDIES ON ECONOMIC LIFE IN JAPAN (OCCASIONAL PAPERS NO. 8). INDUS FAM HABITAT...GEOG GOV/COMP 20 CHINJAP. PAGE 12 F0223
WEALTH PRESS PRODUC INCOME

B64
CHINITZ B.,CITY AND SUBURB: THE ECONOMICS OF METROPOLITAN GROWTH. DIST/IND BUDGET GOV/REL DEMAND ATTIT HABITAT MUNICH PHILADELPH. PAGE 24 F0467
TEC/DEV PLAN

B64
TAX S.,EL CAPITALISMO DEL CENTAVO; UNA ECONOMIA INDIGENA DE GUATEMALA (2 VOLS.). GUATEMALA L/A+17C SOCIETY GP/REL DEMAND INCOME HABITAT...SOC MUNICH 20 INDIAN/AM. PAGE 129 F2539
ECO/UNDEV AGRI WEALTH COST

B65
BEYER G.H.,HOUSING AND SOCIETY. USA+45 ECO/DEV FAM NAT/G PLAN RENT...CHARTS BIBLIOG MUNICH 20. PAGE 14 F0275
HABITAT AGE/O CONSTRUC

B65
BOLLENS J.C.,THE METROPOLIS: ITS PEOPLE, POLITICS, AND ECONOMIC LIFE. USA+45 PLAN PROB/SOLV PERS/REL PWR...DECISION GEOG CENSUS TREND CON/ANAL MUNICH 20 NEWYORK/C LOS/ANG SAN/FRAN CHICAGO PHILADELPH. PAGE 16 F0309
HABITAT SOC LOC/G

B65
GOETZ-GIREY R.,LE MOUVEMENT DES GREVES EN FRANCE. FRANCE FINAN OP/RES PROB/SOLV ECO/TAC INCOME HABITAT...STAT CHARTS 19/20. PAGE 48 F0932
LABOR WORKER GP/REL INDUS

B65
HERRICK B.H.,URBAN MIGRATION AND ECONOMIC DEVELOPMENT IN CHILE. CHILE AGRI INDUS LABOR NAT/G CENTRAL PRODUC...STAT SAMP CHARTS BIBLIOG/A MUNICH 20 MIGRATION. PAGE 59 F1156
HABITAT GEOG ECO/UNDEV

B65
US ADVISORY COMN INTERGOV REL,METROPOLITAN SOCIAL AND ECONOMIC DISPARITIES: IMPLICATIONS FOR INTERGOVERNMENTAL RELATIONS IN CENT'L CITIES AND SUBURBS. CULTURE STRATA DIST/IND LOC/G PLAN GP/REL DISCRIM HABITAT MUNICH. PAGE 134 F2634
GOV/REL GEOG

B66
BEQIRAJ M.,PEASANTRY IN REVOLUTION. STRATA ECO/UNDEV AGRI ROUTINE REV HABITAT RIGID/FLEX ...EPIST GEOG NEW/IDEA TREND MUNICH 20. PAGE 13 F0256
WORKER KNOWL NAT/LISM SOC

B66
BOYD H.W.,MARKETING MANAGEMENT: CASES FROM EMERGING COUNTRIES. BRAZIL GHANA ISRAEL WOR+45 ADMIN PERS/REL ATTIT HABITAT WEALTH...ANTHOL 20 ARGEN CASEBOOK. PAGE 17 F0332
MGT ECO/UNDEV PROB/SOLV MARKET

B66
CANNON M.,THE LAND BOOMERS....BIBLIOG/A 19 AUSTRAL. PAGE 21 F0412
FINAN HABITAT LAISSEZ ECO/UNDEV

B66
MOUNTJOY A.B.,INDUSTRIALIZATION AND UNDER-DEVELOPED COUNTRIES (2ND REV. ED.). CHILE GHANA INDIA NIGERIA WOR+45 SOCIETY PROB/SOLV ECO/TAC...SOC CHARTS 20 INDUS/REV. PAGE 94 F1848
ECO/UNDEV INDUS GEOG HABITAT

B66
NEVITT A.A.,THE ECONOMIC PROBLEMS OF HOUSING. WOR+45 ECO/DEV ECO/UNDEV ACT/RES PROB/SOLV ECO/TAC RENT...OBS CHARTS 20. PAGE 98 F1917
HABITAT PROC/MFG DELIB/GP NAT/COMP

B66
NEVITT A.A.,HOUSING, TAXATION AND SUBSIDIES; A STUDY OF HOUSING IN THE UNITED KINGDOM. UK FINAN GIVE CONTROL COST INCOME...CHARTS 20. PAGE 98 F1918
PLAN TAX HABITAT RENT

B66
O'CONNER A.M.,AN ECONOMIC GEOGRAPHY OF EAST AFRICA. AFR TANZANIA UGANDA AGRI WORKER INT/TRADE COLONIAL GOV/REL...CHARTS METH/COMP 20 AFRICA/E. PAGE 99 F1953
ECO/UNDEV EXTR/IND GEOG HABITAT

B66
UREN P.E.,EAST - WEST TRADE* A SYMPOSIUM. COM AGRI INT/ORG PRICE HABITAT RIGID/FLEX...GEOG INT/LAW ANTHOL NATO. PAGE 133 F2625
INT/TRADE BAL/PWR AFR CANADA

B67
DUN J.L.,THE ESSENCE OF CHINESE CIVILIZATION. ASIA FAM NAT/G TEC/DEV ADMIN SANCTION WAR HABITAT ...ANTHOL WORSHIP. PAGE 35 F0676
CULTURE SOCIETY

B67
GROSS B.M.,ACTION UNDER PLANNING: THE GUIDANCE OF ECONOMIC DEVELOPMENT. STRUCT R+D NAT/G ACT/RES HABITAT...DECISION 20. PAGE 51 F1005
ECO/UNDEV PLAN ADMIN MGT

B67
HEADLEY J.C.,PESTICIDE PROBLEM: AN ECONOMIC APPROACH TO PUBLIC POLICY. AGRI TEC/DEV GOV/REL COST ATTIT CHARTS. PAGE 58 F1131
HABITAT POLICY BIO/SOC CONTROL

B67
POWLEDGE F.,BLACK POWER WHITE RESISTANCE. USA+45 STRUCT PLAN GP/REL DISCRIM HABITAT ORD/FREE WEALTH ...METH/COMP SOC/INTEG NEGRO. PAGE 107 F2111
RACE/REL ATTIT PWR

B67
RIDKER R.G.,ECONOMIC COSTS OF AIR POLLUTION* STUDIES IN MEASUREMENT. R+D GP/REL KNOWL...OBS MUNICH 20. PAGE 111 F2190
OP/RES HABITAT PHIL/SCI

B67
SPURRIER R.B.,THE OVERPOPULATED SOCIETY. WORKER EATING PERS/REL DEMAND EQUILIB ILLEGIT INCOME HABITAT 20. PAGE 125 F2461
BIO/SOC FOR/AID DRIVE RECEIVE

L67
"GOVERNMENT CONTROL OF LAND: PROTECTING THE I-KNOW-IT-WHENI-SEE-IT INTEREST." USA+45 LAW CONSTN DELIB/GP CT/SYS HABITAT ILLINOIS. PAGE 2 F0026
PLAN LOC/G CONTROL ADJUD

L67
GLAZER N.,"HOUSING PROBLEMS AND HOUSING POLICIES." USA+45 PLAN RENT ADJUST CONSEN DEMAND DISCRIM AGE ATTIT HEALTH WEALTH MUNICH NEGRO. PAGE 48 F0929
POLICY CONSTRUC CREATE HABITAT

L67
ZEIDBERG L.D.,"THE NASHVILLE AIR POLLUTION STUDY" (PARTS V-VII)" USA+45 PLAN AGE HEALTH...GEOG STAT CENSUS SAMP/SIZ CHARTS BIBLIOG MUNICH. PAGE 150 F2962
DEATH HABITAT AIR BIO/SOC

S67
"THE SIERRA CLUB, POLITICAL ACTIVITY, AND TAX
ELITES

EXEMPT CHARITABLE STATUS." USA+45 LAW VOL/ASSN TAX PAY ADJUD LOBBY INGP/REL HABITAT 20. PAGE 2 F0027 — GOV/REL FACE/GP ORD/FREE

S67
BAILEY S.L.,"THE ITALIANS AND ORGANIZED LABOR IN THE UNITED STATES AND ARGENTINA: 1880-1910." ITALY USA-45 PARTIC HABITAT PWR...GEOG GP/COMP 19/20 ARGEN. PAGE 8 F0153 — LABOR LEAD WEALTH GP/REL

S67
HALE G.E.,"EXPANDING ENTERPRISE: GEOGRAPHICAL CURBS ON MERGERS." USA+45 MARKET LG/CO ADJUD CONTROL GP/REL 20. PAGE 53 F1041 — LAW HABITAT INDUS EX/STRUC

S67
JENCKS C.E.,"SOCIAL STATUS OF COAL MINERS IN BRITAIN SINCE NATIONALIZATION." UK STRATA STRUCT LABOR RECEIVE GP/REL INCOME OWN ATTIT HABITAT...MGT T 20. PAGE 67 F1312 — EXTR/IND WORKER CONTROL NAT/G

S67
ORAZEM F.,"THE NEW SOVIET PLAN FOR AGRICULTURE (1960-1970)" USSR WORKER CAP/ISM ECO/TAC PRICE OWN HABITAT MARXISM...CHARTS 20. PAGE 101 F1994 — AGRI PLAN COM ECO/DEV

S67
THEROUX P.,"HATING THE ASIANS." TANZANIA UGANDA CONSTN INDUS NAT/G POL/PAR WORKER ECO/TAC HABITAT LOVE...POLICY GEOG 20 MIGRATION. PAGE 130 F2557 — AFR RACE/REL SOVEREIGN ATTIT

HACKER A. F1025

HACKETT A.M. F1027

HACKETT J. F1026,F1027

HADDAD W.F. F0931,F1028

HADDOCK G.B. F1029

HADWIGER D.F. F1030

HAEFELE E.T. F1031

HAGE J. F1032

HAGEN E.E. F1033

HAGGER A.J. F1035

HAGUE D. F1095

HAGUE D.C. F1036,F1037,F2498

HAGUE/F....FRANK HAGUE

HAHN L.A. F1038

HAIG

S63
STEFANIAK N.J.,"A REFINEMENT OF HAIG'S THEORY." USA+45 INDUS PROB/SOLV TEC/DEV...CONCPT CHARTS MUNICH 20 HAIG. PAGE 125 F2474 — GEOG GEN/LAWS PLAN

HAINES W.W. F1039

HAITI....SEE ALSO L/A+17C

HAKLUYT/R....RICHARD HAKLUYT

HALD M. F1040

HALE G.E. F1041

HALE R.D. F1041

HALEVY E. F1042

HALL B. F1043,F1044

HALL C.A. F1045

HALL G. F1046

HALL R.C. F1047

HALLE L.J. F1048

HALLECK/C....CHARLES HALLECK

HALLER H. F1049

HALLET R. F1050

HALLETT D. F1051

HALLOWELL J.H. F1052

HALLSTEIN W. F1053

HAMBRIDGE G. F1054

HAMBURG....HAMBURG, GERMANY

HAMEROW T.S. F1055

HAMILTON W.H. F1056

HAMILTON/A....ALEXANDER HAMILTON

HAMMARSK/D....DAG HAMMARSKJOLD

HAMMOND A. F1057

HAMMOND P.Y. F2297

HANCE W.A. F1058

HANCOCK J.L. F1059

HANNA/MARK....MARK HANNA

HANNAH H.W. F1060

HANRIEDER W.F. F1061

HANSEN A.H. F1062,F1063,F1065

HANSEN B. F1066,F1067,F1068

HANSER P.M. F1069

HAPGOOD D. F1070

HAPPINESS.... HAPPINESS AS A CONDITION (UNHAPPINESS)

B13
KROPOTKIN P.,THE CONQUEST OF BREAD. SOCIETY STRATA AGRI INDUS WORKER REV HAPPINESS INCOME PRODUC HEALTH MORAL ORD/FREE. PAGE 74 F1444 — ANARCH SOCIALIST OWN AGREE

B29
DE MAN H.,JOY IN WORK. STRATA ECO/DEV ECO/TAC PRODUC ANOMIE ROLE SOCISM...IDEA/COMP 20. PAGE 31 F0605 — SOC WORKER HAPPINESS RESPECT

C43
BENTHAM J.,"THE RATIONALE OF REWARD" IN J. BOWRING, ED., THE WORKS OF JEREMY BENTHAM (VOL. 2)" LAW WORKER CREATE INSPECT PAY ROUTINE HAPPINESS PRODUC SUPEGO WEALTH METH/CNCPT. PAGE 13 F0254 — SANCTION ECO/TAC INCOME PWR

B48
NOYES C.R.,ECONOMIC MAN IN RELATION TO HIS NATURAL ENVIRONMENT (2 VOLS.). UNIV COST DEMAND EFFICIENCY HAPPINESS INCOME PRODUC PROFIT HEREDITY...CHARTS BIBLIOG. PAGE 99 F1944 — HABITAT METH/CNCPT GEN/METH

B50
SURANYI-UNGER T.,PRIVATE ENTERPRISE AND GOVERNMENTAL PLANNING. STRUCT FINAN BAL/PWR HAPPINESS DRIVE NEW/LIB PLURISM...MATH QUANT STAT TREND BIBLIOG. PAGE 127 F2516 — PLAN NAT/G LAISSEZ POLICY

C50
ROUSSEAU J.J.,"A DISCOURSE ON POLITICAL ECONOMY" (1755) IN THE SOCIAL CONTRACT AND DISCOURSES." UNIV SOCIETY STRATA STRUCT CONSEN EQUILIB HAPPINESS UTOPIA HEALTH WEALTH...POLICY WELF/ST. PAGE 114 F2252 — NAT/G ECO/TAC TAX GEN/LAWS

C51
HOMANS G.C.,"THE WESTERN ELECTRIC RESEARCHES" IN S. HOSLETT, ED., HUMAN FACTORS IN MANAGEMENT (BMR)" ACT/RES GP/REL HAPPINESS PRODUC DRIVE...MGT OBS 20. PAGE 61 F1202 — OP/RES EFFICIENCY SOC/EXP WORKER

B53
PURCELL T.V.,THE WORKER SPEAKS HIS MIND ON COMPANY AND UNION. WORKER ADJUD LEAD RACE/REL ATTIT DRIVE MARXISM...MGT CLASSIF STAT OBS INT SAMP BIBLIOG. PAGE 108 F2131 — LABOR PARTIC INGP/REL HAPPINESS

S60
BAUM M.,"THE CASE FOR BUSINESS CIVILIZATION." R+D CAP/ISM GIVE EDU/PROP HAPPINESS...SOC TREND. PAGE 12 F0218 — MGT CULTURE WEALTH

S60
SPINRAD W.,"CORRELATES OF TRADE UNION PARTICIPATION: A SUMMARY OF LITERATURE." ACT/RES PERS/REL HAPPINESS HABITAT...BIBLIOG WORK. PAGE 125 F2456 — LABOR PARTIC CORREL ROLE

B62
DE GRAZIA S.,OF TIME, WORK, AND LEISURE. USA+45 ECO/DEV WORKER HAPPINESS UTOPIA ALL/VALS...SOC NEW/IDEA TIME. PAGE 31 F0599 — CULTURE LEISURE CONCPT

COOPERATION. AFR FINAN TEC/DEV DIPLOM FOR/AID EDU/PROP CONFER REGION GP/REL WEALTH...HEAL SOC/INTEG 20. PAGE 69 F1356
ECO/UNDEV VOL/ASSN PLAN

B66
LECHT L.,GOAL, PRIORITIES, AND DOLLARS: THE NEXT DECADE. SPACE USA+45 SOCIETY AGRI BUDGET FOR/AID ...HEAL SOC/WK STAT CHARTS 20 URBAN/RNWL PUB/TRANS. PAGE 76 F1499
IDEA/COMP POLICY CONSEN PLAN

B66
LICHTMAN R.,TOWARD COMMUNITY (PAPER). PLAN PROB/SOLV WEALTH MARXISM...HEAL CONCPT 20. PAGE 80 F1561
NEW/LIB EFFICIENCY CAP/ISM ADJUST

B67
BADGLEY R.F.,DOCTORS' STRIKE; MEDICAL CARE AND CONFLICT IN SASKATCHEWAN. CANADA NAT/G PROF/ORG GP/REL ADJUST ATTIT...HEAL SOC 20. PAGE 8 F0148
HEALTH PLAN LABOR BARGAIN

B67
HODGKINSON R.G.,THE ORIGINS OF THE NATIONAL HEALTH SERVICE: THE MEDICAL SERVICES OF THE NEW POOR LAW, 1834-1871. UK INDUS WORKER PROB/SOLV EFFICIENCY ATTIT HEALTH WEALTH SOCISM...JURID SOC/WK MUNICH 19/20. PAGE 60 F1189
HEAL NAT/G POLICY LAW

S67
WALLACE H.M.,"AVAILABILITY AND USEFULNESS OF SELECTED HEALTH AND SOCIOECONOMIC DATA FOR COMMUNITY PLANNING." NEIGH EFFICIENCY...CORREL STAT CENSUS CHARTS. PAGE 142 F2806
HEALTH PLAN SOC/WK HEAL

N67
NATIONAL COMN COMMUNITY HEALTH,ACTION - PLANNING FOR COMMUNITY HEALTH SERVICES (PAMPHLET). USA+45 PROF/ORG DELIB/GP BUDGET ROUTINE GP/REL ATTIT ...HEAL SOC SOC/WK CHARTS MUNICH TIME 20. PAGE 97 F1898
PLAN HEALTH ADJUST

N67
US HOUSE COMM ON COMMERCE,PARTNERSHIP FOR HEALTH AMENDMENTS FOR 1967 (PAMPHLET). PUB/INST DELIB/GP PROB/SOLV BUDGET EFFICIENCY 20 CONGRESS. PAGE 137 F2701
HEAL PLAN NAT/G JURID

HEALEY/D....DOROTHY HEALEY

HEALTH....WELL-BEING, BODILY AND PSYCHIC INTEGRITY

N
US SUPERINTENDENT OF DOCUMENTS,INTERSTATE COMMERCE (PRICE LIST 59). USA+45 LAW LOC/G NAT/G LEGIS TARIFFS TAX ADMIN CONTROL HEALTH DECISION. PAGE 140 F2752
BIBLIOG/A DIST/IND GOV/REL PROVS

B02
MOREL E.D.,AFFAIRS OF WEST AFRICA. UK FINAN INDUS FAM KIN SECT CHIEF WORKER DIPLOM RACE/REL LITERACY HEALTH...CHARTS 18/20 AFRICA/W NEGRO. PAGE 93 F1826
COLONIAL ADMIN AFR

B13
KROPOTKIN P.,THE CONQUEST OF BREAD. SOCIETY STRATA AGRI INDUS WORKER REV HAPPINESS INCOME PRODUC HEALTH MORAL ORD/FREE. PAGE 74 F1444
ANARCH SOCIALIST OWN AGREE

N19
BROWN W.M.,THE DESIGN AND PERFORMANCE OF "OPTIMUM" BLAST SHELTER PROGRAMS (PAMPHLET). USA+45 ACT/RES PLAN DEATH COST EFFICIENCY OPTIMAL...POLICY CHARTS 20. PAGE 19 F0375
HABITAT NUC/PWR WAR HEALTH

N19
EAST KENTUCKY REGIONAL PLAN,PROGRAM 60: A DECADE OF ACTION FOR PROGRESS IN EASTERN KENTUCKY (PAMPHLET). USA+45 AGRI CONSTRUC INDUS CONSULT ACT/RES PROB/SOLV EDU/PROP GOV/REL HEALTH KENTUCKY. PAGE 35 F0689
REGION ADMIN PLAN ECO/UNDEV

N19
HOGARTY R.A.,NEW JERSEY FARMERS AND MIGRANT HOUSING RULES (PAMPHLET). USA+45 LAW ELITES FACE/GP LABOR PROF/ORG LOBBY PERS/REL RIGID/FLEX ROLE 20 NEW/JERSEY. PAGE 61 F1193
AGRI PROVS WORKER HEALTH

N19
PALAMOUNTAIN JC J.R.,THE DOLCIN CASE AND THE FEDERAL TRADE COMMISSION (PAMPHLET). USA+45 LAW MARKET SERV/IND LG/CO NAT/G BIO/SOC 20 FTC. PAGE 103 F2018
ADJUD PROB/SOLV EDU/PROP HEALTH

N19
RIDLEY C.E.,MEASURING MUNICIPAL ACTIVITIES (PAMPHLET). FINAN SERV/IND FORCES RECEIVE INGP/REL HABITAT...POLICY SOC/WK 20. PAGE 111 F2191
MGT HEALTH WEALTH LOC/G

B34
GRAHAM F.D.,PROTECTIVE TARIFFS. FUT USA+45 WOR-45 INDUS MARKET VOL/ASSN PLAN CAP/ISM ECO/TAC PEACE ATTIT DRIVE HEALTH ORD/FREE...OBS TREND GEN/LAWS FOR/TRADE 20. PAGE 50 F0970
INT/ORG TARIFFS

C50
ROUSSEAU J.J.,"A DISCOURSE ON POLITICAL ECONOMY" (1755) IN THE SOCIAL CONTRACT AND DISCOURSES." UNIV SOCIETY STRATA STRUCT CONSEN EQUILIB HAPPINESS UTOPIA HEALTH WEALTH...POLICY WELF/ST. PAGE 114 F2252
NAT/G ECO/TAC TAX GEN/LAWS

B52
ROSE A.M.,UNION SOLIDARITY: THE INTERNAL COHESION OF A LABOR UNION. SECT GP/REL RACE/REL ATTIT ROLE HEALTH WEALTH...INT QU. PAGE 114 F2241
LABOR INGP/REL PARTIC SUPEGO

B53
DAHL R.A.,POLITICS, ECONOMICS AND WELFARE: PLANNING AND POLITICOECONOMIC SYSTEMS RESOLVED INTO BASIC SOCIAL PROCESSES. WOR+45 WOR-45 ECO/DEV ECO/UNDEV R+D CREATE PLAN TEC/DEV EDU/PROP HEALTH WEALTH ...SOC SELF/OBS TREND CHARTS GEN/METH 20. PAGE 29 F0571
ECO/TAC PHIL/SCI

B55
US ADVISORY COMN INTERGOV REL,THE COMMISSION ON INTERGOVERNMENTAL RELATIONS; A REPORT TO THE PRESIDENT FOR TRANSMITTAL TO THE CONGRESS. USA+45 ECO/DEV AGRI COM/IND FINAN FORCES PLAN EDU/PROP HEALTH WEALTH...STAT MUNICH 20 CIV/DEFENS. PAGE 133 F2630
GOV/REL NAT/G LOC/G PROVS

N56
US HOUSE COMM FOREIGN AFFAIRS,REPORT OF THE SPECIAL STUDY MISSION TO AFRICA, SOUTH AND EAST OF THE SAHARA (PAMPHLET). AFR SOUTH/AFR USA+45 STRUCT INT/TRADE PARL/PROC NAT/LISM ATTIT ALL/VALS HEALTH ...POLICY 20 CONGRESS. PAGE 136 F2691
FOR/AID COLONIAL ECO/UNDEV DIPLOM

B57
DRUCKER P.F.,AMERICA'S NEXT TWENTY YEARS. USA+45 DIST/IND ACADEM SCHOOL DIPLOM ECO/TAC AUTOMAT HABITAT HEALTH...SOC/WK TREND MUNICH 20 URBAN/RNWL PUB/TRANS. PAGE 34 F0667
WORKER FOR/AID CENSUS GEOG

B58
ATOMIC INDUSTRIAL FORUM,MANAGEMENT AND ATOMIC ENERGY. WOR+45 SEA LAW MARKET NAT/G TEC/DEV INSPECT INT/TRADE CONFER PEACE HEALTH...ANTHOL 20. PAGE 7 F0136
NUC/PWR INDUS MGT ECO/TAC

B58
US OPERATIONS MISSION TO VIET,BUILDING ECONOMIC STRENGTH (PAMPHLET). USA+45 VIETNAM/S INDUS TEC/DEV BUDGET ADMIN EATING HEALTH...STAT 20. PAGE 138 F2725
FOR/AID ECO/UNDEV AGRI EDU/PROP

B59
CHECCHI V.,HONDURAS: A PROBLEM IN ECONOMIC DEVELOPMENT. HONDURAS AGRI FINAN INDUS LABOR WORKER INT/TRADE EDU/PROP PRICE HEALTH...GEOG CHARTS BIBLIOG 20. PAGE 24 F0458
ECO/UNDEV ECO/TAC PROB/SOLV PLAN

B60
FRYE R.J.,GOVERNMENT AND LABOR: THE ALABAMA PROGRAM. USA+45 INDUS R+D LABOR WORKER BUDGET EFFICIENCY AGE/Y HEALTH...CHARTS 20 ALABAMA. PAGE 45 F0870
ADMIN LEGIS LOC/G PROVS

S60
"THE EMERGING COMMON MARKETS IN LATIN AMERICA." FUT L/A+17C STRATA DIST/IND INDUS LABOR NAT/G LEGIS ECO/TAC ADMIN RIGID/FLEX HEALTH...NEW/IDEA TIME/SEQ OAS 20. PAGE 1 F0013
FINAN ECO/UNDEV INT/TRADE

S60
ENKE S.,"THE ECONOMIES OF GOVERNMENT PAYMENTS TO LIMIT POPULATION." FUT INDIA WOR+45 CULTURE FINAN NAT/G CONSULT PLAN LEGIT CONTROL COST ATTIT RIGID/FLEX HEALTH WEALTH...STAT OBS CHARTS TOT/POP VAL/FREE 20. PAGE 38 F0736
FAM ACT/RES

S60
JAFFEE A.J.,"POPULATION TRENDS AND CONTROLS IN UNDERDEVELOPED COUNTRIES." AFR FUT ISLAM L/A+17C S/ASIA CULTURE R+D FAM ACT/RES PLAN EDU/PROP BIO/SOC RIGID/FLEX HEALTH...SOC STAT OBS CHARTS 20. PAGE 66 F1303
ECO/UNDEV GEOG

S60
STOCKWELL E.G.,"THE MEASUREMENT OF ECONOMIC DEVELOPMENT." WOR+45 SOCIETY ECO/DEV ECO/UNDEV INDUS ECO/TAC HEALTH WEALTH...WELF/ST GEOG METH/CNCPT CHARTS METH METH/GP 20. PAGE 126 F2492
FAM STAT

N60
COMMITTEE ECONOMIC DEVELOPMENT,GUIDING METROPOLITAN GROWTH (PAMPHLET). USA+45 LOC/G NAT/G PROF/ORG ACT/RES PLAN...SOC/WK MUNICH. PAGE 27 F0517
GEOG INDUS HEALTH

B61
MEXICO: CINCUENTA ANOS DE REVOLUCION VOL. II. L/A+17C SOCIETY LABOR RECEIVE GP/REL AGE/Y HEALTH ...SOC/WK ANTHOL MUNICH 20 MEXIC/AMER. PAGE 1 F0014
ECO/UNDEV STRUCT INDUS POL/PAR

B61
INTL UNION LOCAL AUTHORITIES,METROPOLIS. WOR+45 DIST/IND FINAN GIVE EDU/PROP CRIME COST HEALTH WEALTH MUNICH 20. PAGE 65 F1286
GOV/COMP LOC/G BIBLIOG

B61
SHARP W.R.,FIELD ADMINISTRATION IN THE UNITED NATION SYSTEM: THE CONDUCT OF INTERNATIONAL ECONOMIC AND SOCIAL PROGRAMS. FUT WOR+45 CONSTN SOCIETY ECO/UNDEV R+D DELIB/GP ACT/RES PLAN TEC/DEV EDU/PROP EXEC ROUTINE HEALTH WEALTH...HUM CONCPT CHARTS METH ILO UNESCO GP VAL/FREE UN 20. PAGE 120 F2369
INT/ORG CONSULT

B61
STROUD G.S.,LABOR HISTORY IN THE UNITED STATES: A GENERAL BIBLIOGRAPHY. USA+45 USA-45 STRATA VOL/ASSN
BIBLIOG WORKER

AUTOMAT GP/REL INGP/REL ATTIT HEALTH 18/20. PAGE 127 F2504 — LABOR

B61
WEISBROD B.A.,ECONOMICS OF PUBLIC HEALTH. USA+45 INGP/REL HABITAT...POLICY STAT COSTS 20. PAGE 145 F2851 — SOCIETY HEALTH NEW/IDEA ECO/DEV

S61
NEAL A.C.,"NEW ECONOMIC POLICIES FOR THE WEST." COM EUR+WWI FUT USA+45 WOR+45 ECO/DEV ECO/UNDEV INDUS MARKET ROUTINE HEALTH ORD/FREE PWR...OLD/LIB METH/CNCPT 20. PAGE 97 F1904 — PLAN ECO/TAC

B62
ALEXANDROWICZ C.H.,WORLD ECONOMIC AGENCIES: LAW AND PRACTICE. WOR+45 DIST/IND FINAN LABOR CONSULT INT/TRADE TARIFFS REPRESENT HEALTH...JURID 20 UN GATT EEC OAS ECSC. PAGE 4 F0064 — INT/LAW INT/ORG DIPLOM ADJUD

B62
CAIRNCROSS A.K.,FACTORS IN ECONOMIC DEVELOPMENT. WOR+45 ECO/UNDEV INDUS R+D LG/CO NAT/G EX/STRUC PLAN TEC/DEV ECO/TAC ATTIT HEALTH KNOWL PWR WEALTH ...TIME/SEQ GEN/LAWS TOT/POP TRUE/GP VAL/FREE 20. PAGE 21 F0399 — MARKET ECO/DEV

L62
MACHLUP F.,"PLANS FOR REFORM OF THE INTERNATIONAL MONETARY SYSTEM. PRINCETON: U. PR., 1962, 70 PP., $0.25." WOR+45 INT/ORG ECO/TAC BAL/PAY HEALTH ORD/FREE WEALTH MID/EX TERR/GP VAL/FREE APPLIC 20. PAGE 83 F1631 — ECO/DEV STAT

L62
SCHULTZ T.W.,"INVESTMENT IN HUMAN BEINGS." ECO/DEV ECO/TAC CONFER COST INCOME PRODUC HEALTH...GEOG ANTHOL. PAGE 117 F2315 — FINAN WORKER EDU/PROP SKILL

B63
ABSHIRE D.M.,NATIONAL SECURITY: POLITICAL, MILITARY, AND ECONOMIC STRATEGIES IN THE DECADE AHEAD. ASIA COM USA+45 WOR+45 ECO/DEV ECO/UNDEV INT/ORG DELIB/GP FORCES ECO/TAC COERCE ATTIT RIGID/FLEX HEALTH ORD/FREE PWR WEALTH...POLICY STAT CHARTS ANTHOL COLD/WAR VAL/FREE APP/SCI. PAGE 2 F0032 — FUT ACT/RES BAL/PWR

B63
BAUER R.A.,AMERICAN BUSINESS AND PUBLIC POLICY: THE POLITICS OF FOREIGN TRADE. USA+45 COM/IND LG/CO NAT/G PROF/ORG SML/CO VOL/ASSN LEGIS TOP/EX ECO/TAC EDU/PROP CHOOSE HEALTH PWR WEALTH...CONCPT METH/CNCPT OBS INT QU SAMP FOR/TRADE TRUE/GP VAL/FREE HI. PAGE 11 F0217 — ECO/DEV ATTIT

B63
DE VRIES E.,SOCIAL ASPECTS OF ECONOMIC DEVELOPMENT IN LATIN AMERICA. CULTURE SOCIETY STRATA FINAN INDUS INT/ORG DELIB/GP ACT/RES ECO/TAC EDU/PROP ADMIN ATTIT SUPEGO HEALTH KNOWL ORD/FREE...SOC STAT TREND ANTHOL TOT/POP VAL/FREE. PAGE 31 F0608 — L/A+17C ECO/UNDEV

B63
GLADE W.P. JR.,THE POLITICAL ECONOMY OF MEXICO. FUT L/A+17C CULTURE SOCIETY AGRI INDUS DELIB/GP ACT/RES ECO/TAC ATTIT HEALTH ORD/FREE...STAT TIME/SEQ TREND MEXIC/AMER TOT/POP VAL/FREE 20. PAGE 48 F0928 — FINAN ECO/UNDEV

B63
HIRSCHMAN A.O.,JOURNEYS TOWARD PROGRESS: STUDIES OF ECONOMIC POLICYMAKING IN LATIN AMERICA. CHILE FUT ECO/UNDEV AGRI FINAN INDUS CONSULT DELIB/GP PLAN ATTIT HEALTH ORD/FREE WEALTH...POLICY STAT VAL/FREE COLOMB 20. PAGE 60 F1177 — L/A+17C ECO/TAC BRAZIL

B63
KATZ S.M.,A SELECTED LIST OF US READINGS ON DEVELOPMENT. AGRI COM/IND DIST/IND INDUS LABOR PLAN FOR/AID EDU/PROP HEALTH...POLICY SOC/WK 20. PAGE 69 F1361 — BIBLIOG/A ECO/UNDEV TEC/DEV ACT/RES

B63
KRAVIS I.B.,DOMESTIC INTERESTS AND INTERNATIONAL OBLIGATIONS: SAFEGUARDS IN INTERNATIONAL TRADE ORGANIZATIONS. EUR+WWI USA+45 WOR+45 FINAN DELIB/GP ATTIT RIGID/FLEX HEALTH...STAT EEC VAL/FREE OEEC ECSC 20. PAGE 73 F1435 — INT/ORG ECO/TAC INT/TRADE

B63
MULLENBACH P.,CIVILIAN NUCLEAR POWER: ECONOMIC ISSUES AND POLICY FORMATION. AFR FINAN INT/ORG DELIB/GP ACT/RES ECO/TAC ATTIT SUPEGO HEALTH ORD/FREE PWR...POLICY CONCPT MATH STAT CHARTS VAL/FREE 20. PAGE 94 F1855 — USA+45 ECO/DEV NUC/PWR

B63
US GOVERNMENT,REPORT TO INTER-AMERICAN ECONOMIC AND SOCIAL COUNCIL AT SECOND ANNUAL MEETING. L/A+17C USA+45 VOL/ASSN TEC/DEV DIPLOM TAX EATING EFFICIENCY HEALTH...STAT CHARTS 20 AID. PAGE 136 F2682 — ECO/TAC FOR/AID FINAN PLAN

L63
KUZNETS S.,"QUANTITATIVE ASPECTS OF THE ECONOMIC GROWTH OF NATIONS: DISTRIBUTION OF INCOME BY SIZE." WOR+45 FINAN ACT/RES HEALTH...MATH STAT VAL/FREE 20. PAGE 74 F1454 — WEALTH ECO/TAC

L63
MCKERSIE R.B.,"NONPROFESSIONAL HOSPITAL WORKERS AND A UNION ORGANIZING DRIVE." PLAN GP/REL RACE/REL ATTIT DRIVE...CORREL STAT INT GP/COMP. PAGE 88 F1732 — VOL/ASSN HEALTH INGP/REL LABOR

L63
NASH M.,"PSYCHO-CULTURAL FACTORS IN ASIAN ECONOMIC GROWTH." ASIA ISLAM S/ASIA CULTURE ECO/UNDEV DELIB/GP EDU/PROP COERCE ATTIT PERSON HEALTH KNOWL ORD/FREE...PSY SOC STAT TREND ANTHOL VAL/FREE 20. PAGE 96 F1893 — SOCIETY ECO/TAC

S63
GALENSON W.,"ECONOMIC DEVELOPMENT AND THE SECTORAL EXPANSION OF EMPLOYMENT, INT." FUT WOR+45 ECO/UNDEV DIST/IND PROC/MFG SERV/IND ACT/RES HEALTH SKILL WEALTH...STAT TIME/SEQ VAL/FREE 20. PAGE 46 F0889 — INDUS ECO/TAC

B64
FEIS H.,FOREIGN AID AND FOREIGN POLICY. USA+45 WOR+45 NAT/G VOL/ASSN ACT/RES TEC/DEV ATTIT HEALTH WEALTH...SOC GEN/LAWS 20. PAGE 40 F0775 — ECO/UNDEV ECO/TAC FOR/AID DIPLOM

B64
FIRTH R.,CAPITAL, SAVING AND CREDIT IN PEASANT SOCIETIES. WOR+45 WOR-45 FAM ACT/RES ECO/TAC HEALTH ...SOC CONCPT STAT CHARTS ANTHOL CARIBBEAN VAL/FREE 20. PAGE 41 F0803 — AGRI FINAN

B64
HAMBRIDGE G.,DYNAMICS OF DEVELOPMENT. AGRI FINAN INDUS LABOR INT/TRADE EDU/PROP ADMIN LEAD OWN HEALTH...ANTHOL BIBLIOG 20. PAGE 54 F1054 — ECO/UNDEV ECO/TAC OP/RES ACT/RES

B64
MC GOVERN G.S.,WAR AGAINST WANT. USA+45 AGRI DIPLOM INT/TRADE GIVE RECEIVE DEMAND HEALTH 20 KENNEDY/JF FOOD/PEACE. PAGE 87 F1714 — FOR/AID ECO/DEV POLICY EATING

B64
NATIONAL COUN APPLIED ECO RES,A STRATEGY FOR THE FOURTH PLAN. INDIA DIST/IND EXTR/IND SERV/IND ECO/TAC RATION EDU/PROP EATING HEALTH...CHARTS 20. PAGE 97 F1900 — ECO/UNDEV PLAN AGRI WORKER

B64
WRIGHT G.,RURAL REVOLUTION IN FRANCE: THE PEASANTRY IN THE TWENTIETH CENTURY. EUR+WWI MOD/EUR LAW CULTURE AGRI POL/PAR DELIB/GP LEGIS ECO/TAC EDU/PROP COERCE CHOOSE ATTIT RIGID/FLEX HEALTH ...STAT CENSUS CHARTS VAL/FREE 20. PAGE 149 F2932 — PWR STRATA FRANCE REV

S64
READER D.H.,"A SURVEY OF CATEGORIES OF ECONOMIC ACTIVITIES AMONG THE PEOPLES OF AFRICA." AGRI INDUS MARKET KIN HEALTH SKILL WEALTH...GEOG METH/CNCPT CHARTS TERR/GP WORK TOT/POP VAL/FREE 20. PAGE 110 F2160 — TEC/DEV ECO/UNDEV AFR

B65
PEACE RESEARCH ABSTRACTS. FUT WOR+45 R+D INT/ORG NAT/G PLAN TEC/DEV BAL/PWR DIPLOM FOR/AID NUC/PWR HEALTH. PAGE 1 F0022 — BIBLIOG/A PEACE ARMS/CONT WAR

B65
CHANDRASEKHAR S.,AMERICAN AID AND INDIA'S ECONOMIC DEVELOPMENT. AFR CHINA/COM INDIA USA+45 GIVE EDU/PROP EATING HEALTH ORD/FREE 20 AID. PAGE 23 F0449 — FOR/AID PEACE DIPLOM ECO/UNDEV

B65
CONLEY R.W.,THE ECONOMICS OF VOCATIONAL REHABILITATION. USA+45 VOL/ASSN CREATE EDU/PROP COST EFFICIENCY SOC/INTEG 20. PAGE 27 F0527 — PUB/INST HEALTH GIVE GP/REL

B65
SHOSTAK A.B.,NEW PERSPECTIVES ON POVERTY. USA+45 SCHOOL WORKER INGP/REL RACE/REL AGE/C AGE/Y ATTIT HEALTH...ANTHOL BIBLIOG 20 JOHNSON/LB POVRTY/WAR. PAGE 121 F2388 — WEALTH NAT/G RECEIVE INCOME

B65
US OFFICE ECONOMIC OPPORTUNITY,CATALOG OF FEDERAL PROGRAMS FOR INDIVIDUAL AND COMMUNITY IMPROVEMENT. USA+45 GIVE RECEIVE ADMIN HEALTH KNOWL SKILL WEALTH ...CHARTS MUNICH. PAGE 138 F2721 — BIBLIOG CLIENT ECO/TAC

L65
FORTE W.E.,"THE FOOD AND DRUG ADMINISTRATION, THE FEDERAL TRADE COMMISSION AND THE DECEPTIVE PACKAGING." ROUTINE...JURID 20 FTC. PAGE 43 F0831 — CONTROL HEALTH ADJUD INDUS

L65
WIONCZEK M.,"LATIN AMERICA FREE TRADE ASSOCIATION." AGRI DIST/IND FINAN INDUS INT/ORG LABOR NAT/G TEC/DEV ECO/TAC HEALTH SKILL WEALTH...POLICY RELATIV MGT LAFTA 20. PAGE 148 F2909 — L/A+17C MARKET REGION

B66
ECONOMIC RESEARCH SERVICE,RESEARCH DATA ON MINORITY GROUPS: AN ANNOTATED BIBLIOGRAPHY OF ECONOMIC RESEARCH SERVICE REPORTS: 1955-1965 (PAMPHLET). USA+45 STRATA ECO/DEV AGRI SCHOOL WORKER EDU/PROP HEALTH NEW/LIB SOC. PAGE 36 F0697 — BIBLIOG/A DISCRIM WEALTH RACE/REL

B66
HALLET R.,PEOPLE AND PROGRESS IN WEST AFRICA: AN INTRODUCTION TO THE PROBLEMS OF DEVELOPMENT. COM/IND INDUS KIN DIPLOM FOR/AID INT/TRADE HEALTH — AFR SOCIETY ECO/UNDEV

...GEOG TREND CHARTS BIBLIOG/A 20 AFRICA/W. PAGE 54 F1050 ECO/TAC

B66
US SENATE COMM GOVT OPERATIONS,HEARINGS BEFORE SUBCOMMITTEE ON FOREIGN AID EXPENDITURES: POPULATION CRISIS VOLUMES 1-5 JUNE-SEPT 1965. STRATA ECO/UNDEV PLAN TEC/DEV EDU/PROP ATTIT HEALTH ...GEOG CHARTS 20 CONGRESS BIRTH/CON CASEBOOK. PAGE 138 F2729 ECO/DEV CENSUS FAM CONTROL

N66
US ADVISORY COMN INTERGOV REL,CATALOGS AND OTHER INFORMATION SOURCES ON FEDERAL AND STATE AID PROGRAMS: A SECTED BIBLIOGRAPHY (PAPER). USA+45 LAW LOC/G NAT/G PROVS VOL/ASSN TEC/DEV ADMIN HEALTH ...WELF/ST SOC/WK MUNICH. PAGE 134 F2635 BIBLIOG/A GOV/REL FINAN ECO/DEV

B67
BADGLEY R.F.,DOCTORS' STRIKE; MEDICAL CARE AND CONFLICT IN SASKATCHEWAN. CANADA NAT/G PROF/ORG GP/REL ADJUST ATTIT...HEAL SOC 20. PAGE 8 F0148 HEALTH PLAN LABOR BARGAIN

B67
GOLDMAN M.,CONTROLLING POLLUTION: THE ECONOMICS OF A CLEANER AMERICA. USA+45 SOCIETY PROB/SOLV CONTROL COST ANTHOL. PAGE 48 F0936 HEALTH ECO/DEV NAT/G FINAN

B67
HODGKINSON R.G.,THE ORIGINS OF THE NATIONAL HEALTH SERVICE: THE MEDICAL SERVICES OF THE NEW POOR LAW, 1834-1871. UK INDUS WORKER PROB/SOLV EFFICIENCY ATTIT HEALTH WEALTH SOCISM...JURID SOC/WK MUNICH 19/20. PAGE 60 F1189 HEAL NAT/G POLICY LAW

B67
JOHNSON D.G.,THE STRUGGLE AGAINST WORLD HUNGER (HEADLINE SERIES, NO. 184) (PAMPHLET). PLAN TEC/DEV FOR/AID...CHARTS 20 FAO MEXIC/AMER. PAGE 67 F1322 AGRI PROB/SOLV ECO/UNDEV HEALTH

B67
LEIBY J.,CHARITY AND CORRECTION IN JERSEY; A HISTORY OF STATE WELFARE INSTITUTIONS. DELIB/GP EX/STRUC PROB/SOLV INSPECT LEAD ADJUST HEALTH ...POLICY PSY NEW/JERSEY. PAGE 77 F1514 PROVS PUB/INST ADMIN

B67
SAPARINA Y.,CYBERNETICS WITHIN US. WOR+45 EDU/PROP FEEDBACK PERCEPT HEALTH...DECISION METH/CNCPT NEW/IDEA 20. PAGE 116 F2281 COMPUTER METH/COMP CONTROL SIMUL

B67
US AGENCY INTERNATIONAL DEV,PROPOSED FOREIGN AID PROGRAM FOR 1968: SUMMARY PRESENTATION TO THE CONGRESS. AFR S/ASIA USA+45 AGRI TEC/DEV DIPLOM ECO/TAC BAL/PAY COST HEALTH KNOWL SKILL 20 AID CONGRESS ALL/PROG. PAGE 134 F2640 ECO/UNDEV BUDGET FOR/AID STAT

L67
DEALEY S.,"MONETARY RECOVERY UNDER FEDERAL TRANSPORTATION STATUTES." USA+45 SEA WORKER TAX PAY ADJUD DEATH GOV/REL OWN HEALTH ORD/FREE 20. PAGE 31 F0609 DIST/IND LAW CONTROL FINAN

L67
GLAZER N.,"HOUSING PROBLEMS AND HOUSING POLICIES." USA+45 PLAN RENT ADJUST CONSEN DEMAND DISCRIM AGE ATTIT HEALTH WEALTH MUNICH NEGRO. PAGE 48 F0929 POLICY CONSTRUC CREATE HABITAT

L67
PARKER G.P. JR.,"MONETARY RECOVERY UNDER THE FEDERAL LABOR STATUTES." USA+45 USA-45 INDUS ADJUD CT/SYS GOV/REL HEALTH ORD/FREE 20 DEPT/LABOR NLRB. PAGE 103 F2027 LABOR CONTROL LAW FINAN

L67
STILL C.H.,"MONETARY RECOVERY UNDER THE FAIR LABOR STANDARDS ACT." USA+45 USA-45 WORKER PAY ADJUD GOV/REL HEALTH ORD/FREE...MATH 20 NLRB. PAGE 126 F2487 LABOR CONTROL LAW FINAN

L67
ZEIDBERG L.D.,"THE NASHVILLE AIR POLLUTION STUDY" (PARTS V-VII)" USA+45 PLAN AGE HEALTH...GEOG STAT CENSUS SAMP/SIZ CHARTS BIBLIOG MUNICH. PAGE 150 F2962 DEATH HABITAT AIR BIO/SOC

S67
TELLER A.,"AIR-POLLUTION ABATEMENT: ECONOMIC RATIONALITY AND REALITY." NAT/G DELIB/GP ECO/TAC GOV/REL CENTRAL EFFICIENCY HEALTH...CHARTS METH MUNICH. PAGE 129 F2543 PROB/SOLV CONTROL COST AIR

S67
VAN KLAVEREN J.,"DIE WIRTSCHAFTLICHEN AUSWIRKUNGEN DES SCHWARZEN TODES" GERMANY PRICE DEMAND PRODUC MUNICH 14/15 DEPRESSION. PAGE 140 F2762 HEALTH AGRI GEOG

S67
WALLACE H.M.,"AVAILABILITY AND USEFULNESS OF SELECTED HEALTH AND SOCIOECONOMIC DATA FOR COMMUNITY PLANNING." NEIGH EFFICIENCY...CORREL STAT CENSUS CHARTS. PAGE 142 F2806 HEALTH PLAN SOC/WK HEAL

N67
NATIONAL COMN COMMUNITY HEALTH,ACTION - PLANNING FOR COMMUNITY HEALTH SERVICES (PAMPHLET). USA+45 PROF/ORG DELIB/GP BUDGET ROUTINE GP/REL ATTIT ...HEAL SOC SOC/WK CHARTS MUNICH TIME 20. PAGE 97 F1898 PLAN HEALTH ADJUST

B92
ENGELS F.,THE CONDITION OF THE WORKING-CLASS IN ENGLAND (1848). UK INDUS LABOR PRICE CONTROL COST INCOME HEALTH MARXISM MUNICH 19. PAGE 38 F0733 WORKER WEALTH MARXIST CAP/ISM

HEATH D.B. F1132

HEBERLE R. F1133

HEGEL/G....GEORG WILHELM FRIEDRICH HEGEL

HEILBRNR/R....ROBERT HEILBRONER

HEILBRONER R.L. F1135,F1136,F1137,F1138

HEILPERIN M.A. F1139,F1140

HEIMANN E. F1141

HEISS K.P. F1142

HEKHUIS D.J. F1143

HELANDER S. F1144

HELLMAN F.S. F0874,F1145

HELLMUTH W.F. F2269

HELSTAD O.L. F2418

HEMPSTONE S. F1146

HENDEL S. F1147

HENDERSON W.O. F1148,F1149

HENNING C.N. F1150

HERBERG W. F1151

HERDER/J....JOHANN GOTTFRIED VON HERDER

HEREDITY....GENETIC INFLUENCES ON PERSONALITY DEVELOPMENT AND SOCIAL GROWTH

B27
SIEGFRIED A.,AMERICA COMES OF AGE: A FRENCH ANALYSIS (TRANS. BY H.H. HEMMING AND DORIS HEMMING). FRANCE UK POL/PAR WORKER TEC/DEV DIPLOM REGION RACE/REL ADJUST PRODUC HEREDITY...TIME/SEQ GP/COMP SOC/INTEG 20 DEMOCRAT REPUBLICAN KKK. PAGE 122 F2398 USA-45 CULTURE ECO/DEV SOC

B48
NOYES C.R.,ECONOMIC MAN IN RELATION TO HIS NATURAL ENVIRONMENT (2 VOLS.). UNIV COST DEMAND EFFICIENCY HAPPINESS INCOME PRODUC PROFIT HEREDITY...CHARTS BIBLIOG. PAGE 99 F1944 HABITAT METH/CNCPT GEN/METH

B65
ANDERSON C.A.,EDUCATION AND ECONOMIC DEVELOPMENT. INDUS R+D SCHOOL TEC/DEV ECO/TAC EDU/PROP AGE HEREDITY PERCEPT SKILL 20. PAGE 5 F0092 ANTHOL ECO/DEV ECO/UNDEV WORKER

HERESY....HERESY

HERMAN L.M. F1152

HERRERA F. F1153,F1154

HERRESHOFF D. F1155

HERRICK B.H. F1156

HERSKOVITS M.J. F1157

HERZ J.H. F1158

HERZBERG D.G. F1159

HEVESY P.D. F1160

HEYSE T. F1161

HI

B63
BAUER R.A.,AMERICAN BUSINESS AND PUBLIC POLICY: THE POLITICS OF FOREIGN TRADE. USA+45 COM/IND LG/CO NAT/G PROF/ORG SML/CO VOL/ASSN LEGIS TOP/EX ECO/TAC EDU/PROP CHOOSE HEALTH PWR WEALTH...CONCPT METH/CNCPT OBS INT QU SAMP FOR/TRADE TRUE/GP VAL/FREE HI. PAGE 11 F0217 ECO/DEV ATTIT

HICKMAN B.G. F1162

HICKMAN C.A. F1163

HICKS J.R. F1164,F1165,F1166

HICKS U.K. F1167

HIESTAND/F....FRED J. HIESTAND

HIGGINS B. F1168

HIGGINS/G....GODFREY HIGGINS

HIGHWAY....HIGHWAY PLANNING AND DEVELOPMENT

HILDEBRAND G.H. F1169

HILDEBRAND J.R. F1170

HILL H. F2244

HILL L.W. F1171

HILL S.E. F1932

HILTON G.W. F1172

HINDLEY D. F1173

HINDU....HINDUISM AND HINDU PEOPLE

HINSHAW R. F1174

HIROSHIMA....SEE WAR, NUC/PWR, PLAN, PROB/SOLV, CONSULT

HIRSCH F. F2258

HIRSCH W. F2968

HIRSCHFIELD R.S. F1175

HIRSCHMAN A.O. F1176,F1177

HIRSHLEIFER J. F1178

HISS/ALGER....ALGER HISS

HIST....HISTORY, INCLUDING CURRENT EVENTS

HIST/WRIT....HISTORIOGRAPHY

B02
SELIGMAN E.R.,THE ECONOMIC INTERPRETATION OF HISTORY. ECO/TAC MARXISM SOCISM...PHIL/SCI METH/CNCPT 18/20. PAGE 119 F2348 — IDEA/COMP HIST/WRIT GP/REL

B13
BEARD C.A.,AN ECONOMIC INTERPRETATION OF THE CONSTITUTION OF THE UNITED STATES. USA-45 AGRI INT/TRADE SUFF OWN ATTIT...CONCPT MYTH BIOG HIST/WRIT 18. PAGE 12 F0222 — CONSTN ECO/TAC CHOOSE

B30
FEIS H.,EUROPE, THE WORLD'S BANKER, 1871-1914. FRANCE GERMANY MOD/EUR UK WOR-45 NAT/G PLAN ECO/TAC EXEC ATTIT PWR WEALTH...CONCPT HIST/WRIT GEN/LAWS VAL/FREE 19/20. PAGE 40 F0773 — FINAN DIPLOM INT/TRADE

B48
HAYEK F.A.,INDIVIDUALISM AND ECONOMIC ORDER. FINAN PLAN MORAL LAISSEZ SOCISM...POLICY DECISION PHIL/SCI HIST/WRIT. PAGE 57 F1122 — RATIONAL KNOWL PERSON

B52
ASHWORTH W.,A SHORT HISTORY OF THE INTERNATIONAL ECONOMY 1850-1950. WOR+45 WOR-45 AGRI FINAN INDUS MARKET LABOR ECO/TAC...CONCPT STAT HIST/WRIT FOR/TRADE ILO 19/20. PAGE 7 F0131 — ECO/DEV TEC/DEV INT/TRADE

B54
HAYEK FA V.O.N.,CAPITALISM AND THE HISTORIANS. MOD/EUR TEC/DEV GP/REL WEALTH...HIST/WRIT ANTHOL 19. PAGE 57 F1124 — CAP/ISM LABOR STRATA ECO/TAC

B55
MAYO H.B.,DEMOCRACY AND MARXISM. COM USSR STRATA NAT/G WORKER ECO/TAC REV MORAL...PHIL/SCI HIST/WRIT IDEA/COMP WORSHIP 20 MARX/KARL LENIN/VI STALIN/J TROTSKY/L. PAGE 87 F1708 — MARXISM CAP/ISM

B56
BROWN R.E.,CHARLES BEARD AND THE CONSTITUTION. USA-45 NAT/G ORD/FREE WEALTH...HUM TIME/SEQ METH/COMP 20 BEARD/CA. PAGE 19 F0372 — CONSTN ELITES HIST/WRIT

B57
WARRINER D.,LAND REFORM AND DEVELOPMENT IN THE MIDDLE EAST: A STUDY OF EGYPT, SYRIA AND IRAQ. IRAQ ISLAM SYRIA UAR AGRI DIST/IND PLAN TEC/DEV DOMIN REV ATTIT WEALTH...SOC METH/CNCPT STAT OBS RECORD HIST/WRIT TREND GEN/LAWS FAO 20. PAGE 143 F2825 — ECO/UNDEV CONCPT

S59
TIPTON J.B.,"PARTICIPATION OF THE UNITED STATES IN THE INTERNATIONAL LABOR ORGANIZATION." USA+45 LAW STRUCT ECO/DEV ECO/UNDEV INDUS TEC/DEV ECO/TAC ADMIN PERCEPT ORD/FREE SKILL...STAT HIST/WRIT GEN/METH ILO WORK 20. PAGE 131 F2577 — LABOR INT/ORG

S60
NICHOLS J.P.,"HAZARDS OF AMERICAN PRIVATE INVESTMENT IN UNDERDEVELOPED COUNTRIES." FUT L/A+17C USA+45 USA-45 EXTR/IND CONSULT BAL/PWR ECO/TAC DOMIN ADJUD ATTIT SOVEREIGN WEALTH ...HIST/WRIT TIME/SEQ TREND TERR/GP VAL/FREE 20. PAGE 98 F1924 — FINAN ECO/UNDEV CAP/ISM NAT/LISM

B61
HENDERSON W.O.,THE INDUSTRIAL REVOLUTION IN EUROPE. FRANCE GERMANY MOD/EUR RUSSIA WORKER PROFIT PWR MARXISM SOCISM...SOC HIST/WRIT 19 INDUS/REV. PAGE 58 F1148 — INDUS REV CAP/ISM TEC/DEV

B61
WRIGHT H.M.,THE "NEW IMPERIALISM": ANALYSIS OF LATE NINETEENTH-CENTURY EXPANSION. MOD/EUR WOR-45 SOCIETY FINAN ECO/TAC INT/TRADE NAT/LISM...ANTHOL BIBLIOG/A 19. PAGE 149 F2933 — HIST/WRIT IDEA/COMP COLONIAL DOMIN

S61
NOVE A.,"THE SOVIET MODEL AND UNDERDEVELOPED COUNTRIES." COM FUT USSR WOR+45 CULTURE ECO/DEV POL/PAR FOR/AID EDU/PROP ADMIN MORAL WEALTH ...POLICY RECORD HIST/WRIT 20. PAGE 99 F1942 — ECO/UNDEV PLAN

S63
SCHURMANN F.,"ECONOMIC POLICY AND POLITICAL POWER IN COMMUNIST CHINA." ASIA CHINA/COM USSR SOCIETY ECO/UNDEV AGRI INDUS CREATE ADMIN ROUTINE ATTIT DRIVE RIGID/FLEX PWR WEALTH...HIST/WRIT TREND CHARTS WORK 20. PAGE 118 F2323 — PLAN ECO/TAC

S63
WOLFERS A.,"INTEGRATION IN THE WEST: THE CONFLICT OF PERSPECTIVES." AFR EUR+WWI USA+45 ECO/DEV INT/ORG DELIB/GP CREATE TEC/DEV DIPLOM ATTIT PWR ...CONCPT HIST/WRIT TREND GEN/LAWS EEC 20. PAGE 148 F2918 — RIGID/FLEX ECO/TAC

B64
REDLICH F.,THE GERMAN MILITARY ENTERPRISER AND HIS WORK FORCE. CHRIST-17C GERMANY ELITES SOCIETY FINAN ECO/TAC CIVMIL/REL GP/REL INGP/REL...HIST/WRIT METH/COMP 14/17. PAGE 110 F2170 — EX/STRUC FORCES PROFIT WORKER

S64
SALVADORI M.,"EL CAPITALISMO EN LA EUROPA DE LA POSGUERRA." AFR INT/ORG NAT/G POL/PAR PLAN ECO/TAC ATTIT ORD/FREE WEALTH...HIST/WRIT EEC 20. PAGE 115 F2275 — EUR+WWI ECO/DEV CAP/ISM

B67
ELSNER H.,THE TECHNOCRATS, PROPHETS OF AUTOMATION. SOCIETY INDUS VOL/ASSN COST INCOME ATTIT 20. PAGE 37 F0726 — AUTOMAT TECHRACY PRODUC HIST/WRIT

B67
POLLACK N.,THE POPULIST MIND. USA-45 STRATA AGRI NAT/G POL/PAR LEGIS WORKER RACE/REL WEALTH...ANTHOL BIBLIOG 19 NEGRO. PAGE 107 F2097 — POPULISM HIST/WRIT ATTIT INGP/REL

S67
BOSHER J.F.,"GOVERNMENT AND PRIVATE INTERESTS IN NEW FRANCE." CANADA FRANCE INDUS LG/CO SML/CO CAP/ISM INT/TRADE COLONIAL GP/REL...HIST/WRIT 17/18. PAGE 17 F0320 — NAT/G FINAN ADMIN CONTROL

S67
PRASOW P.,"THE DEVELOPMENT OF JUDICIAL ARBITRATION IN LABOR-MANAGEMENT DISPUTES." LAW INDUS WORKER GP/REL ROLE...HIST/WRIT 20. PAGE 107 F2113 — LABOR BARGAIN ADJUD TREND

B92
COULANGES F D.E.,THE ORIGIN OF PROPERTY IN LAND. LAW STRATA AGRI ACADEM EDU/PROP ORD/FREE 19. PAGE 28 F0543 — OWN HIST/WRIT IDEA/COMP SOCISM

HITCH C.J. F1179

HITLER/A....ADOLF HITLER

B37
BRESCIANI-TURRONI C,THE ECONOMICS OF INFLATION: A STUDY OF CURRENCY DEPRECIATION IN POST-WAR GERMANY. AFR GERMANY FINAN INT/TRADE PRICE TOTALISM...POLICY TIME/SEQ CHARTS GEN/LAWS 20 HITLER/A. PAGE 18 F0347 — ECO/TAC WEALTH SOCIETY

S39
COLE G.D.H.,"NAZI ECONOMICS: HOW DO THEY MANAGE IT?" GERMANY FORCES WORKER BUDGET INT/TRADE ROUTINE COERCE WAR 20 HITLER/A NAZI. PAGE 26 F0500 — FASCISM ECO/TAC ATTIT PLAN

B40
HUNTER R.,REVOLUTION: WHY, HOW, WHEN? NAT/G ECO/TAC EDU/PROP COERCE ORD/FREE FASCISM POPULISM SOCISM 18/20 HITLER/A LENIN/VI. PAGE 63 F1246 — REV METH/COMP LEAD CONSTN

B42
DRUCKER P.F.,THE FUTURE OF INDUSTRIAL MAN; A CONSERVATIVE APPROACH. USA-45 LOC/G PLAN WAR CENTRAL RATIONAL TOTALISM ORD/FREE LAISSEZ ...PLURIST IDEA/COMP 19/20 HITLER/A. PAGE 34 F0664 — INDUS SOCIETY REGION PROB/SOLV

B67
NYOMARKAY J.,CHARISMA AND FACTIONALISM IN THE NAZI PARTY. GERMANY POL/PAR LEGIT LEAD MARXISM ...NEW/IDEA METH/COMP GEN/LAWS BIBLIOG 20 HITLER/A. PAGE 99 F1949 — FASCISM INGP/REL CHIEF PWR

HLA MYINT U. F1180

HO YHI-MIN F1181

HO/CHI/MIN....HO CHI MINH

HOAG M.W. F1182

HOBBES/T....THOMAS HOBBES

HOBBS E.H. F1183

HOBSON J.A. F1184,F1185,F1186,F1187

HODGKINS J.A. F1188

HODGKINSON R.G. F1189

HOFFA/J....JAMES HOFFA

B62
MCCLELLAN J.L.,CRIME WITHOUT PUNISHMENT. USA+45 LAW SOCIETY DELIB/GP TRIBUTE CONTROL LOBBY COERCE GP/REL ANOMIE MORAL...CRIMLGY 20 CONGRESS HOFFA/J. PAGE 88 F1718 — CRIME ACT/RES LABOR PWR

B63
JACOBS P.,STATE OF UNIONS. USA+45 STRATA TOP/EX GP/REL RACE/REL DEMAND DISCRIM ATTIT PWR 20 CONGRESS NEGRO HOFFA/J. PAGE 66 F1296 — LABOR ECO/TAC BARGAIN DECISION

HOFFENBERG M. F1082

HOFFMAN P. F1190

HOGAN J. F1192

HOGARTY R.A. F1193

HOLDSWORTH W.S. F1194,F1195

HOLIFLD/C....CHET HOLIFIELD

HOLLAND E.P. F1196

HOLLAND....SEE NETHERLAND

HOLLER J.E. F1197

HOLLEY I.B. F1198

HOLMANS A.E. F1200

HOLMES/OW....OLIVER WENDELL HOLMES

B60
MENDELSON W.,CAPITALISM, DEMOCRACY, AND THE SUPREME COURT. USA+45 USA-45 CONSTN DIPLOM GOV/REL ATTIT ORD/FREE LAISSEZ...POLICY CHARTS PERS/COMP 18/20 SUPREME/CT MARSHALL/J HOLMES/OW TANEY/RB FIELD/JJ. PAGE 90 F1758 — JUDGE CT/SYS JURID NAT/G

HOLMES/OWJ....OLIVER WENDELL HOLMES, JR.

HOLSTI/KJ....K.J. HOLSTI

HOLT R.T. F1201

HOLUMNYCHY V. F2007

HOMANS G.C. F1202

HOMEOSTASIS....SEE FEEDBACK

HOMER....HOMER

HOMEST/ACT....HOMESTEAD ACT OF 1862

HOMICIDE....SEE MURDER

HOMOSEXUAL....HOMOSEXUALITY; SEE ALSO BIO/SOC, CRIME, SEX

HOMOSEXUALITY....SEE BIO/SOC, SEX, CRIME,

HONDURAS....SEE ALSO L/A+17C

B59
CHECCHI V.,HONDURAS: A PROBLEM IN ECONOMIC DEVELOPMENT. HONDURAS AGRI FINAN INDUS LABOR WORKER INT/TRADE EDU/PROP PRICE HEALTH...GEOG CHARTS BIBLIOG 20. PAGE 24 F0458 — ECO/UNDEV ECO/TAC PROB/SOLV PLAN

B59
LOPEZ VILLAMIL H.,A STATEMENT OF THE LAWS OF THE HONDURAS IN MATTERS AFFECTING BUSINESS (2ND ED.). HONDURAS DIST/IND EXTR/IND FINAN WORKER TAX DEATH MARRIAGE OWN MARITIME 20 MIGRATION. PAGE 82 F1600 — CONSTN INDUS LEGIS NAT/G

B63
OTERO L.M.,HONDURAS. HONDURAS SPAIN STRUCT SECT COLONIAL REV WAR ATTIT PWR...GEOG WORSHIP 16/20. PAGE 102 F2003 — NAT/G SOCIETY NAT/LISM ECO/UNDEV

B65
HONDURAS CONSEJO NAC DE ECO,PLAN NACIONAL DE DESARROLLO ECONOMICO Y SOCIAL DE HONDURAS 1965-69. HONDURAS AGRI INDUS BAL/PAY INCOME 20. PAGE 61 F1203 — ECO/UNDEV NAT/G PLAN POLICY

B67
CLEGERN W.M.,BRITISH HONDURAS: COLONIAL DEAD END, 1859-1900. HONDURAS AGRI FINAN PROB/SOLV INT/TRADE PWR WEALTH...BIBLIOG/A 19. PAGE 25 F0487 — COLONIAL POLICY ECO/UNDEV DOMIN

HONDURAS CONSEJO NAC DE ECO F1203

HONG/KONG....HONG KONG

B65
HOLLER J.E.,POPULATION TRENDS AND ECONOMIC DEVELOPMENT IN THE FAR EAST (PAMPHLET). KOREA S/ASIA AGRI INDUS DELIB/GP PROB/SOLV RATIONAL ...POLICY CHARTS BIBLIOG 20 OUTER/MONG CHINJAP HONG/KONG. PAGE 61 F1197 — CENSUS TREND ECO/UNDEV ASIA

HOOD W.C. F1204

HOOPES R. F1205

HOOVER C.B. F1206,F1207,F1208,F1209,F1210

HOOVER E.M. F0495,F1211,F1212

HOOVER G. F1213

HOOVER/H....HERBERT HOOVER

HOPI....HOPI INDIANS

HOPKINS/H....HARRY HOPKINS

HORECKY P.L. F1214

HOROWITZ D. F1215

HOROWITZ I.L. F1216

HOSELITZ B.F. F1218,F1219,F1220,F1221,F1222.F1223

HOSHII I. F1224

HOSPITALS....SEE PUB/INST

HOUSE OF REPRESENTATIVES....SEE HOUSE/REP

HOUSE RULES COMMITTEE....SEE HOUSE/REP

HOUSE/CMNS....HOUSE OF COMMONS (ALL NATIONS)

S38
HALL R.C.,"REPRESENTATION OF BIG BUSINESS IN THE HOUSE OF COMMONS." UK ECO/DEV INDUS PROF/ORG LEGIS CAP/ISM ECO/TAC LAISSEZ...POLICY OLD/LIB PLURIST MGT 20 HOUSE/CMNS. PAGE 53 F1047 — LOBBY NAT/G

B39
JENNINGS W.I.,PARLIAMENT. UK POL/PAR OP/RES BUDGET LEAD CHOOSE GP/REL...MGT 20 PARLIAMENT HOUSE/LORD HOUSE/CMNS. PAGE 67 F1315 — PARL/PROC LEGIS CONSTN NAT/G

HOUSE/LORD....HOUSE OF LORDS (ALL NATIONS)

B39
JENNINGS W.I.,PARLIAMENT. UK POL/PAR OP/RES BUDGET LEAD CHOOSE GP/REL...MGT 20 PARLIAMENT HOUSE/LORD HOUSE/CMNS. PAGE 67 F1315 — PARL/PROC LEGIS CONSTN NAT/G

HOUSE/REP....HOUSE OF REPRESENTATIVES (ALL NATIONS) SEE ALSO CONGRESS, LEGIS

B43
WILMERDING L. JR.,THE SPENDING POWER: A HISTORY OF THE EFFORTS OF CONGRESS TO CONTROL EXPENDITURES. USA-45 POL/PAR DELIB/GP EX/STRUC TOP/EX TARIFFS ADMIN GOV/REL...TIME/SEQ SENATE HOUSE/REP. PAGE 147 F2900 — LEGIS BUDGET CONTROL

B59
US HOUSE COMM GOVT OPERATIONS,UNITED STATES AID OPERATIONS IN LAOS. LAOS USA+45 PLAN INSPECT HOUSE/REP. PAGE 137 F2697 — FOR/AID ADMIN FORCES ECO/UNDEV

N67
US HOUSE COMM FOREIGN AFFAIRS,THE FOREIGN POLICY ASPECTS OF THE KENNEDY ROUND (PAMPHLET). USA+45 INDUS KENNEDY/JF CONGRESS HOUSE/REP EEC. PAGE 137 F2693 — POLICY INT/TRADE FOR/AID ECO/DEV

N67
US HOUSE COMM FOREIGN AFFAIRS,REPORT OF SPECIAL STUDY MISSION TO THE NEAR EAST (PAMPHLET). ISRAEL USA+45 YEMEN ECO/UNDEV INT/ORG FOR/AID ARMS/CONT WAR WEAPON NAT/LISM PEACE...GEOG 20 UN HOUSE/REP. PAGE 137 F2694 — ISLAM DIPLOM FORCES

N67
US HOUSE COMM FOREIGN AFFAIRS,FOREIGN ASSISTANCE ACT OF 1967 (PAMPHLET). USA+45 WOR+45 FINAN CONGRESS HOUSE/REP UN. PAGE 137 F2695 — FOR/AID POLICY INT/ORG ECO/UNDEV

N67
US HOUSE COMM FOREIGN AFFAIRS,COMMUNIST ACTIVITIES IN LATIN AMERICA 1967 (PAMPHLET). CUBA USA+45 DIPLOM INT/TRADE EDU/PROP COERCE GUERRILLA HOUSE/REP OAS. PAGE 137 F2696 — L/A+17C MARXISM ORD/FREE ECO/TAC

N67
US HOUSE COMM SCI ASTRONAUT,AUTHORIZING APPROPRIATIONS TO THE NATIONAL AERONAUTICS AND SPACE ADMINISTRATION (PAMPHLET). USA+45 NAT/G OP/RES TEC/DEV BUDGET NASA HOUSE/REP. PAGE 137 F2704 — SPACE R+D PHIL/SCI NUC/PWR

HOUSTON....HOUSTON, TEXAS

HOUTART F. F0436

HOWE M. F1225

HOWE R.W. F1226

HS/SCIASTR....HOUSE COMMITTEE ON SCIENCE AND ASTRONAUTICS

HU/FENG....HU FENG

HUAC....HOUSE UNAMERICAN ACTIVITIES COMMITTEE

HUBBARD P.H. F1228

HUBBARD P.J. F1229

HUBERMAN L. F1230,F1231

HUELIN D. F1232

HUGHES J. F1233

HUGHES R. F1234

HUHNE L.H. F1235

HUKS....HUKS (PHILIPPINES)

HULTMAN C.W. F0450

HUM....METHODS OF HUMANITIES, LITERARY ANALYSIS

B14
VEBLEN T.,THE INSTINCT OF WORKMANSHIP. UNIV SOCIETY ECO/DEV ECO/UNDEV CREATE TEC/DEV ECO/TAC EDU/PROP ROUTINE PERSON...HUM CONCPT TIME/SEQ GEN/LAWS. PAGE 140 F2768 — DRIVE SKILL

B53
MENDE T.,WORLD POWER IN THE BALANCE. FUT USA+45 USSR WOR-45 ECO/DEV ECO/TAC INT/TRADE EDU/PROP UTOPIA ATTIT...HUM CONCPT TREND TOT/POP 20. PAGE 90 F1756 — WOR+45 PWR BAL/PWR AFR

B56
BROWN R.E.,CHARLES BEARD AND THE CONSTITUTION. USA-45 NAT/G ORD/FREE WEALTH...HUM TIME/SEQ METH/COMP 20 BEARD/CA. PAGE 19 F0372 — CONSTN ELITES HIST/WRIT

B61
SHARP W.R.,FIELD ADMINISTRATION IN THE UNITED NATION SYSTEM: THE CONDUCT OF INTERNATIONAL ECONOMIC AND SOCIAL PROGRAMS. FUT WOR+45 CONSTN SOCIETY ECO/UNDEV R+D DELIB/GP ACT/RES PLAN TEC/DEV EDU/PROP EXEC ROUTINE HEALTH WEALTH...HUM CONCPT CHARTS METH ILO UNESCO GP VAL/FREE UN 20. PAGE 120 F2369 — INT/ORG CONSULT

HUM/RIGHTS....HUMAN RIGHTS, DECLARATIONS OF HUMAN RIGHTS, AND HUMAN RIGHTS COMMISSIONS (OFFICIAL ORGANIZATIONS)

HUMAN NATURE....SEE PERSON

HUMAN RELATIONS....SEE RELATIONS INDEX

HUMAN RIGHTS, DECLARATIONS OF HUMAN RIGHTS, AND HUMAN RIGHTS COMMISSIONS (OFFICIAL ORGANIZATIONS)....SEE HUM/RIGHTS

HUMANISM....HUMANISM AND HUMANISTS

HUMANITIES....SEE HUM

HUME D. F1236,F1237,F1238,F1239,F1240

HUME/D....DAVID HUME

N19
HABERLER G.,A SURVEY OF INTERNATIONAL TRADE THEORY (PAMPHLET). FINAN NAT/G COST INCOME 18/20 MONEY HUME/D MARSHALL/A. PAGE 52 F1022 — INT/TRADE BAL/PAY GEN/LAWS POLICY

B65
GRAMPP W.D.,ECONOMIC LIBERALISM; THE CLASSICAL VIEW (VOL. II). MOD/EUR SOCIETY MARKET INT/TRADE NAT/LISM WEALTH LAISSEZ...POLICY PSY CONCPT BIBLIOG 19 SMITH/ADAM HUME/D MILL/JS. PAGE 50 F0975 — ECO/DEV CAP/ISM IDEA/COMP ECO/TAC

HUMPHREY D.D. F1241

HUMPHREY R.A. F1242

HUMPHREY/H....HUBERT HORATIO HUMPHREY

HUNGARY....SEE ALSO COM

B59
ETSCHMANN R.,DIE WAHRUNGS- UND DEVISENPOLITIK DES OSTBLOCKS UND IHRE AUSWIRKUNGEN AUF DIE WIRTSCHAFTSBEZIEHUNGEN ZWISCHEN OST U WEST. BULGARIA CZECHOSLVK HUNGARY POLAND USSR MARKET NAT/G PLAN DIPLOM...NAT/COMP 20. PAGE 39 F0753 — ECO/TAC FINAN POLICY INT/TRADE

B65
SINHA M.R.,THE ECONOMICS OF MANPOWER PLANNING. FUT HUNGARY NAT/G CONTROL...POLICY GEOG ANTHOL 20 CHINJAP. PAGE 122 F2415 — ECO/UNDEV PLAN WORKER ECO/TAC

B66
BROWN J.F.,THE NEW EASTERN EUROPE. ALBANIA BULGARIA HUNGARY POLAND ROMANIA CULTURE AGRI POL/PAR WAR NAT/LISM MARXISM...CHARTS BIBLIOG 20. PAGE 19 F0369 — DIPLOM COM NAT/G ECO/UNDEV

B66
SPULBER N.,THE STATE AND ECONOMIC DEVELOPMENT IN EASTERN EUROPE. BULGARIA COM CZECHOSLVK HUNGARY POLAND YUGOSLAVIA CULTURE PLAN CAP/ISM INT/TRADE CONTROL...POLICY CHARTS METH/COMP BIBLIOG/A 19/20. PAGE 125 F2460 — ECO/DEV ECO/UNDEV NAT/G TOTALISM

HUNT C.L. F1243

HUNT R.N. F1244

HUNTER A. F1245

HUNTER R. F1246

HUNTNGTN/S....SAMUEL P. HUNTINGTON

HUNTON/P....PHILIP HUNTON

HURLEY/PJ....PATRICK J. HURLEY

HURWICZ L. F0122,F0124

HUSSEIN....KING HUSSEIN I, KING OF JORDAN

HUSSEY E.R. F1743

HUTCHINGS R. F1247

HUTCHINS/R....ROBERT HUTCHINS

HUTCHINSON E.C. F1248

HUTCHISON K. F1249

HUTH A.G. F1250

HUTT W.H. F1251,F1252

HUTTENBACH R.A. F1253

HUTTON D.G. F1254

HUZAR E. F1255

HYDE D. F1256

HYPO/EXP....INTELLECTUAL CONSTRUCTS

B25
EDGEWORTH F.Y.,PAPERS RELATING TO POLITICAL ECONOMY. MOD/EUR SOCIETY STRATA DIST/IND INDUS MARKET NAT/G ACT/RES ECO/TAC EXEC WEALTH ...METH/CNCPT MATH TREND HYPO/EXP SIMUL GEN/METH FOR/TRADE VAL/FREE LOG/LING. PAGE 36 F0702
ECO/DEV CAP/ISM

B48
GRAHAM F.D.,THE THEORY OF INTERNATIONAL VALUES. FUT WOR+45 WOR-45 ECO/DEV FINAN INT/ORG PLAN TEC/DEV CAP/ISM DIPLOM ECO/TAC TARIFFS ROUTINE BAL/PAY DRIVE PWR WEALTH SOCISM...POLICY STAT HYPO/EXP GEN/LAWS 20. PAGE 50 F0971
NEW/IDEA INT/TRADE

B48
WHITE C.L.,HUMAN GEOGRAPHY: AN ECOLOGICAL STUDY OF GEOGRAPHY. UNIV SEA CULTURE AGRI EXTR/IND RACE/REL PRODUC...CHARTS HYPO/EXP SIMUL GEN/LAWS T. PAGE 146 F2868
SOC HABITAT GEOG SOCIETY

B52
EGLE W.P.,ECONOMIC STABILIZATION. USA+45 SOCIETY FINAN MARKET PLAN ECO/TAC DOMIN EDU/PROP LEGIT EXEC WEALTH...CONCPT METH/CNCPT TREND HYPO/EXP GEN/METH TOT/POP VAL/FREE 20. PAGE 36 F0708
NAT/G ECO/DEV CAP/ISM

B56
GREENHUT M.L.,PLANT LOCATION IN THEORY AND PRACTICE; THE ECONOMICS OF SPACE. WOR+45 WOR-45 MARKET WORKER COST DEMAND...CONCPT STAT CHARTS HYPO/EXP BIBLIOG 19/20. PAGE 51 F0991
SML/CO ECO/DEV CAP/ISM IDEA/COMP

S57
DETAMBEL M.H.,"PROBABILITY AND WORK AS DETERMINERS OF MULTICHOICE BEHAVIOR." PLAN TASK EFFICIENCY ...DECISION GAME. PAGE 32 F0622
HYPO/EXP PROB/SOLV GEN/LAWS PROBABIL

S58
ARROW K.J.,"UTILITIES, ATTITUDES, CHOICES: A REVIEW NOTE." USA+45 PLAN...METH/CNCPT MATH STAT CHARTS HYPO/EXP. PAGE 6 F0121
DECISION DIST/IND MARKET CREATE

S58
ARROW K.J.,"A NOTE ON EXPECTATIONS AND STABILITY." WOR+45...METH/CNCPT MATH STAT CHARTS HYPO/EXP. PAGE 7 F0123
DECISION MARKET ECO/DEV ECO/TAC

S58
FOLDES L.,"UNCERTAINTY, PROBABILITY AND POTENTIAL SURPRISE." MARKET PROB/SOLV RISK PERSON...DECISION MGT HYPO/EXP GAME. PAGE 42 F0820
PROBABIL ADMIN ROUTINE

B59
WIBBERLEY G.P.,AGRICULTURE AND URBAN GROWTH. UK USA+45 ECO/DEV FINAN PROB/SOLV INT/TRADE COST ...GEOG STAT CHARTS METH/COMP HYPO/EXP METH MUNICH 20. PAGE 146 F2876
AGRI PLAN

L59
ARROW K.J.,"ON THE STABILITY OF THE COMPETITIVE EQUILIBRIUM: II." WOR+45...METH/CNCPT MATH STAT CHARTS HYPO/EXP. PAGE 7 F0124
DECISION MARKET ECO/DEV ECO/TAC

L59
SIMON H.A.,"THEORIES OF DECISION-MAKING IN ECONOMICS AND BEHAVIORAL SCIENCE" (BMR)" MARKET BARGAIN UTIL DRIVE...DECISION MGT PROBABIL HYPO/EXP SIMUL 20 BEHAVIORSM. PAGE 122 F2409
PSY GEN/LAWS PROB/SOLV

S59
HARING J.E.,"UTILITY THEORY, DECISION THEORY, AND PROFIT MAXIMIZATION." PROB/SOLV GAMBLE UTIL ...DECISION CHARTS IDEA/COMP HYPO/EXP SIMUL GEN/METH. PAGE 55 F1083
PROBABIL RISK GAME

B60
HITCH C.J.,THE ECONOMICS OF DEFENSE IN THE NUCLEAR AGE. USA+45 WOR+45 CREATE PLAN NUC/PWR ATTIT ...CON/ANAL CHARTS HYPO/EXP NATO 20. PAGE 60 F1179
R+D FORCES

S61
ANDREWS R.B.,"URBAN ECONOMICS: AN APPRAISAL OF PROGRESS." LOC/G PROB/SOLV TEC/DEV...CONCPT OBS/ENVIR METH/COMP HYPO/EXP SOC/EXP SIMUL GEN/METH METH MUNICH 20. PAGE 5 F0102
PHIL/SCI ECOMETRIC

S61
BENNION E.G.,"ECONOMETRICS FOR MANAGEMENT." USA+45 INDUS EX/STRUC ACT/RES COMPUTER UTIL...MATH STAT PREDICT METH/COMP HYPO/EXP. PAGE 13 F0248
ECOMETRIC MGT SIMUL DECISION

S61
HIRSHLEIFER J.,"THE BAYESIAN APPROACH TO STATISTICAL DECISION: AN EXPOSITION." OP/RES PROB/SOLV UTIL...PROBABIL CHARTS IDEA/COMP HYPO/EXP 20. PAGE 60 F1178
DECISION GAME SIMUL STAT

S62
PYE L.W.,"THE POLITICAL IMPULSES AND FANTASIES BEHIND FOREIGN AID." FUT USA+45 ECO/UNDEV DIPLOM ECO/TAC ROUTINE DRIVE KNOWL...SOC METH/CNCPT NEW/IDEA TREND HYPO/EXP STERTYP GEN/METH 20. PAGE 108 F2133
ACT/RES ATTIT FOR/AID

B63
BONINI C.P.,SIMULATION OF INFORMATION AND DECISION SYSTEMS IN THE FIRM. MARKET BUDGET DOMIN EDU/PROP ADMIN COST ATTIT HABITAT PERCEPT PWR...CONCPT PROBABIL QUANT PREDICT HYPO/EXP BIBLIOG. PAGE 16 F0313
INDUS SIMUL DECISION MGT

B63
GANGULI B.N.,ECONOMIC CONSEQUENCES OF DISARMAMENT. EUR+WWI ECO/DEV ECO/UNDEV FORCES ACT/RES BUDGET DIPLOM INT/TRADE...STAT CHARTS NAT/COMP. PAGE 46 F0896
ECOMETRIC ARMS/CONT COST HYPO/EXP

S63
ANDREWS R.B.,"ECONOMIC PLANNING FOR SMALL AREAS: THE PLANNING PROCESS." INDUS PROC/MFG PROVS PROB/SOLV TAX EQUILIB...METH/COMP HYPO/EXP METH MUNICH 20. PAGE 5 F0103
ECO/TAC PLAN LOC/G

S63
PINCUS J.,"THE COST OF FOREIGN AID." WOR+45 ECO/DEV FINAN NAT/G VOL/ASSN CREATE ECO/TAC EDU/PROP WEALTH ...METH/CNCPT STAT CHARTS HYPO/EXP TOT/POP VAL/FREE 20. PAGE 106 F2087
USA+45 ECO/UNDEV FOR/AID

B64
JUSTER F.T.,ANTICIPATIONS AND PURCHASES; AN ANALYSIS OF CONSUMER BEHAVIOR. PROB/SOLV RISK COST PRODUC DRIVE...STAT STYLE SAMP CON/ANAL CHARTS HYPO/EXP GAME SIMUL. PAGE 68 F1345
PROBABIL DECISION PREDICT DEMAND

B64
SINGER H.W.,INTERNATIONAL DEVELOPMENT: GROWTH AND CHANGE. AFR BRAZIL L/A+17C WOR+45 CULTURE AGRI INDUS NAT/G ACT/RES ECO/TAC EDU/PROP WEALTH...GEOG CONCPT METH/CNCPT STAT HYPO/EXP WORK TOT/POP 20. PAGE 122 F2412
FINAN ECO/UNDEV FOR/AID INT/TRADE

L64
BHAGWATI J.,"THE PURE THEORY OF INTERNATIONAL TRADE: A SURVEY." WOR+45 ECO/DEV ECO/UNDEV FINAN MARKET PROC/MFG INT/ORG LABOR LG/CO NAT/G TEC/DEV ECO/TAC SKILL WEALTH...POLICY RELATIV MGT CONCPT NEW/IDEA MATH QUANT GEN/LAWS FOR/TRADE 20. PAGE 14 F0276
INDUS HYPO/EXP

B65
FRIEDLANDER S.L.,LABOR MIGRATION AND ECONOMIC GROWTH: A CASE STUDY OF PUERTO RICO. PUERT/RICO AGRI WORKER PLAN PROB/SOLV...ECOMETRIC STAT PREDICT CHARTS HYPO/EXP SIMUL 20. PAGE 44 F0858
CENSUS GEOG ECO/UNDEV WEALTH

B65
STEINER G.A.,THE CREATIVE ORGANIZATION. ELITES LG/CO PLAN PROB/SOLV TEC/DEV INSPECT CAP/ISM CONTROL EXEC PERSON...METH/COMP HYPO/EXP 20. PAGE 126 F2476
CREATE MGT ADMIN SOC

S65
KUNKEL J.H.,"VALUES AND BEHAVIOR IN ECONOMIC DEVELOPMENT." INDIA PERU CULTURE STRUCT CREATE PERS/REL ATTIT PERSON...CHARTS HYPO/EXP ARGEN. PAGE 74 F1449
SIMUL ECO/UNDEV PSY STERTYP

B66
KUENNE R.E.,THE POLARIS MISSILE STRIKE* A GENERAL ECONOMIC SYSTEMS ANALYSIS. USA+45 USSR NAT/G BAL/PWR ARMS/CONT WAR...MATH PROBABIL COMPUT/IR CHARTS HYPO/EXP SIMUL. PAGE 74 F1446
NUC/PWR FORCES DETER DIPLOM

B66
LENSKI G.E.,POWER AND PRIVILEGE: A THEORY OF SOCIAL STRATIFICATION. SWEDEN UK UNIV USSR CULTURE ECO/UNDEV PRIVIL PWR...PHIL/SCI CONCPT CHARTS IDEA/COMP HYPO/EXP METH MARX/KARL. PAGE 78 F1525
SOC STRATA STRUCT SOCIETY

S66
COHEN A.,"THE TECHNOLOGY/ELITE APPROACH TO THE DEVELOPMENTAL PROCESS* PERUVIAN CASE STUDY." L/A+17C STRUCT CREATE ECO/TAC FOR/AID CIVMIL/REL MARXISM TECHRACY HYPO/EXP. PAGE 26 F0496
ECO/UNDEV ELITES PERU

S66
SHORTE F.C.,"THE APPLICATION OF DEVELOPMENT HYPOTHESES IN MIDDLE EASTERN STUDIES." STRUCT AGRI CREATE DEMAND...GEOG STAT CON/ANAL CHARTS. PAGE 121 F2387
ECO/UNDEV ISLAM SOC HYPO/EXP

B67
BANFIELD E.C.,THE MORAL BASIS OF A BACKWARD SOCIETY. EUR+WWI ITALY STRATA NEIGH PARTIC INGP/REL ...SOC QU PREDICT TREND HYPO/EXP MUNICH 20. PAGE 9 F0173
MORAL WEALTH ATTIT

S67
GATELL F.O.,"MONEY AND PARTY IN JACKSONIAN AMERICA* A QUANTITATIVE LOOK AT NEW YORK CITY'S MEN OF QUALITY." USA-45 STRATA SECT SUFF CONSEN MAJORITY ATTIT...CHARTS HYPO/EXP 19. PAGE 46 F0908 — WEALTH POL/PAR PERSON IDEA/COMP

S67
LANDES W.M.,"THE EFFECT OF STATE FAIR EMPLOYMENT LAWS ON THE ECONOMIC POSITION OF NONWHITES." USA+45 PROVS SECT LEGIS ADMIN GP/REL RACE/REL...JURID CONCPT CHARTS HYPO/EXP NEGRO. PAGE 75 F1470 — DISCRIM LAW WORKER

HYPOTHETICAL EXPERIMENTS....SEE HYPO/EXP

IADB....INTER-ASIAN DEVELOPMENT BANK

IAEA....INTERNATIONAL ATOMIC ENERGY AGENCY

IANNI O. F1257,F1258

IBARRA J. F1259

IBO....IBO TRIBE

IBRD....INTERNATIONAL BANK FOR RECONSTRUCTION AND DEVELOPMENT

B63
INTERNATIONAL BANK RECONST DEV,THE WORLD BANK GROUP IN ASIA. ASIA S/ASIA INDUS TEC/DEV ECO/TAC...RECORD 20 IBRD WORLD/BANK. PAGE 65 F1273 — INT/ORG DIPLOM ECO/UNDEV FINAN

B64
MEZERIK A.G.,TRADE, AID AND ECONOMIC DEVELOPMENT. WOR+45 FINAN INDUS MARKET PLAN BAL/PWR BARGAIN FOR/AID TARIFFS EDU/PROP WEALTH...GP/COMP 20 UN GATT IMF IBRD. PAGE 91 F1777 — ECO/TAC ECO/DEV INT/ORG INT/TRADE

S65
BALDWIN D.A.,"THE INTERNATIONAL BANK IN POLITICAL PERSPECTIVE" USA+45 TEC/DEV FOR/AID RENT GIVE COST ...IDEA/COMP GAME IBRD. PAGE 9 F0160 — FINAN INT/ORG

B66
MEERHAEGHE M.,INTERNATIONAL ECONOMIC INSTITUTIONS. EUR+WWI FINAN INDUS MARKET PLAN TARIFFS BAL/PAY EQUILIB...POLICY BIBLIOG/A 20 GATT OEEC EEC IBRD EURCOALSTL. PAGE 89 F1745 — ECO/TAC ECO/DEV INT/TRADE INT/ORG

B66
RUBIN S.J.,THE CONSCIENCE OF THE RICH NATIONS: THE DEVELOPMENT ASSISTANCE COMMITTEE AND THE COMMON AID EFFORT. EUR+WWI USA+45 ECO/UNDEV INT/ORG NAT/G VOL/ASSN ECO/TAC INT/TRADE...OBS UN AID DEV/ASSIST IBRD OECD. PAGE 114 F2256 — FOR/AID ECO/DEV CONFER CENTRAL

B66
SEWELL J.P.,FUNCTIONALISM AND WORLD POLITICS* A STUDY BASED ON UNITED NATIONS PROGRAMS FINANCING ECONOMICAL DEVELOPMENT. ECO/UNDEV FINAN PROB/SOLV DIPLOM ECO/TAC FEEDBACK REGION ADJUST ATTIT UN IBRD INTL/FINAN INTL/DEV UNSF. PAGE 120 F2360 — TASK INT/ORG IDEA/COMP GEN/LAWS

ICA....INTERNATIONAL COOPERATION ADMINISTRATION

ICC....U.S. INTERSTATE COMMERCE COMMISSION

ICELAND....ICELAND

C65
WUORINEN J.H.,"SCANDINAVIA." DENMARK FINLAND ICELAND NORWAY SWEDEN SOCIETY AGRI POL/PAR DELIB/GP DIPLOM INT/TRADE NEUTRAL WAR...CHARTS IND TREATY 20. PAGE 149 F2942 — BIBLIOG NAT/G POLICY

B67
ANDERSON S.V.,THE NORDIC COUNCIL: A STUDY OF SCANDINAVIAN REGIONALISM. DENMARK FINLAND ICELAND NORWAY SWEDEN MARKET NAT/G VOL/ASSN CONSULT PARL/PROC ATTIT...TIME/SEQ BIBLIOG 20. PAGE 5 F0098 — INT/ORG REGION DIPLOM LEGIS

ICJ....INTERNATIONAL COURT OF JUSTICE;

ICSU....INTERNATIONAL COUNCIL OF SCIENTIFIC UNIONS

IDA....INTERNATIONAL DEVELOPMENT ASSOCIATION

IDAHO....IDAHO

IDEA/COMP....COMPARISON OF IDEAS

N
INTERNATIONAL BIBLIOGRAPHY OF ECONOMICS. WOR+45 FINAN MARKET ADMIN DEMAND INCOME PRODUC...POLICY IDEA/COMP METH. PAGE 1 F0002 — BIBLIOG ECO/DEV ECO/UNDEV INT/TRADE

B02
SELIGMAN E.R.,THE ECONOMIC INTERPRETATION OF HISTORY. ECO/TAC MARXISM SOCISM...PHIL/SCI METH/CNCPT 18/20. PAGE 119 F2348 — IDEA/COMP HIST/WRIT GP/REL

N19
CHATTERS C.H.,NEW MUNICIPAL REVENUES FOR NEW MUNICIPAL EXPENDITURES (PAMPHLET). PLAN PRICE UTIL HABITAT...IDEA/COMP MUNICH 20. PAGE 23 F0457 — LOC/G BUDGET TAX

N19
MORGENSTERN O.,A NEW LOOK AT ECONOMIC TIMES SERIES ANALYSIS (PAMPHLET). WEALTH...BIBLIOG 20 NSF NAVAL/RES. PAGE 93 F1831 — TREND IDEA/COMP EFFICIENCY

B22
VON ENGELIN O.D.,INHERITING THE EARTH, THE GEOGRAPHICAL FACTOR IN NATIONAL DEVELOPMENT. WOR-45 CULTURE DIPLOM BIO/SOC HABITAT PERSON...PSY SOC CONCPT IDEA/COMP. PAGE 142 F2791 — INGP/REL GEOG SOCIETY ROLE

B24
CLARK J.B.,THE DISTRIBUTION OF WEALTH (1899). WORKER OWN PRODUC PROFIT WEALTH LAISSEZ...IDEA/COMP GEN/LAWS. PAGE 25 F0478 — ECO/TAC INDUS LABOR INCOME

B29
DE MAN H.,JOY IN WORK. STRATA ECO/DEV ECO/TAC PRODUC ANOMIE ROLE SOCISM...IDEA/COMP 20. PAGE 31 F0605 — SOC WORKER HAPPINESS RESPECT

B31
JEVONS W.S.,THE THEORY OF POLITICAL ECONOMY (4TH ED.; 1ST ED. 1871). WOR-45 FINAN MARKET RENT WEALTH ...LOG MATH QUANT CON/ANAL IDEA/COMP BIBLIOG METH 17/19. PAGE 67 F1318 — GEN/LAWS UTIL LABOR

B32
DICKINSON H.D.,INSTITUTIONAL REVENUE: A STUDY OF THE INFLUENCE OF SOCIAL INSTITUTIONS ON THE DISTRIBUTION OF WEALTH. SOCIETY STRATA FINAN ...NEW/IDEA IDEA/COMP 20. PAGE 33 F0632 — WEALTH CONCPT METH/CNCPT MARKET

B40
TRIFFIN R.,MONOPOLISTIC COMPETITION AND GENERAL EQUILIBRIUM THEORY. DIST/IND PLAN TASK EQUILIB OPTIMAL...IDEA/COMP 20 MONOPOLY. PAGE 131 F2586 — INT/TRADE INDUS COST

B42
DRUCKER P.F.,THE FUTURE OF INDUSTRIAL MAN; A CONSERVATIVE APPROACH. USA-45 LOC/G PLAN WAR CENTRAL RATIONAL TOTALISM ORD/FREE LAISSEZ ...PLURIST IDEA/COMP 19/20 HITLER/A. PAGE 34 F0664 — INDUS SOCIETY REGION PROB/SOLV

B42
WRIGHT D.M.,THE CREATION OF PURCHASING POWER. USA-45 NAT/G PRICE ADMIN WAR INCOME PRODUC...POLICY CONCPT IDEA/COMP BIBLIOG 20 MONEY. PAGE 149 F2930 — FINAN ECO/TAC ECO/DEV CREATE

B46
ERNST M.L.,THE FIRST FREEDOM. USA-45 CONSTN PRESS PRIVIL...CHARTS IDEA/COMP BIBLIOG 20 AMEND/I. PAGE 38 F0746 — EDU/PROP COM/IND ORD/FREE CONTROL

B47
BOWEN R.H.,GERMAN THEORIES OF THE CORPORATIVE STATE, WITH SPECIAL REFERENCES TO THE PERIOD 1870-1919. GERMANY INDUS LG/CO CATHISM SOCISM...SOC 18/20. PAGE 17 F0328 — IDEA/COMP CENTRAL NAT/G POLICY

B48
WINSLOW E.M.,THE PATTERN OF IMPERIALISM; A STUDY IN THE THEORIES OF POWER. DOMIN WAR PWR MARXISM ...IDEA/COMP METH/COMP BIBLIOG 20. PAGE 147 F2906 — SOCISM CAP/ISM COLONIAL ECO/TAC

B50
SCHUMPETER J.A.,CAPITALISM, SOCIALISM, AND DEMOCRACY (3RD ED.). USA-45 USSR WOR+45 WOR-45 INTELL ECO/DEV ECO/UNDEV ECO/TAC WAR PRODUC ORD/FREE...MGT SOC 20 MARX/KARL. PAGE 118 F2321 — SOCIALIST CAP/ISM MARXISM IDEA/COMP

B51
PETERSON F.,SURVEY OF LABOR ECONOMICS (REV. ED.). STRATA ECO/DEV LABOR INSPECT BARGAIN PAY PRICE EXEC ROUTINE GP/REL ALL/VALS ORD/FREE 20 AFL/CIO DEPT/LABOR. PAGE 105 F2069 — WORKER DEMAND IDEA/COMP T

B51
ROEPKE W.,THE PROBLEM OF ECONOMIC ORDER. WOR+45 SOCIETY PROB/SOLV CONTROL EFFICIENCY...CON/ANAL IDEA/COMP GEN/METH 20. PAGE 113 F2231 — ECO/TAC ORD/FREE MARKET PROC/MFG

B52
EGLE W.P.,ECONOMIC STABILIZATION: OBJECTIVES, RULES, AND MECHANISMS. UNIV FINAN PROB/SOLV CAP/ISM ECO/TAC CONTROL...IDEA/COMP 20. PAGE 36 F0709 — EQUILIB PLAN NAT/G ECO/DEV

B52
SURANYI-UNGER T.,COMPARATIVE ECONOMIC SYSTEMS. FINAN MARKET DIPLOM PRICE WEALTH...GEOG SOC BIBLIOG METH T 20. PAGE 128 F2517 — LAISSEZ PLAN ECO/DEV IDEA/COMP

S52
LEWIS V.B.,"TOWARD A THEORY OF BUDGETING" (BMR)" USA+45 NAT/G PLAN PROB/SOLV...IDEA/COMP METH 20 SUPREME/CT. PAGE 79 F1551 — BUDGET CONCPT CREATE

B53
SCHLEIFFER H.,INDEX TO ECONOMIC HISTORY ESSAYS IN FESTSCHRIFTEN (PAMPHLET). WOR+45 WOR-45...CONCPT IDEA/COMP ANTHOL. PAGE 117 F2299 — BIBLIOG NAT/G

S53
BERNSTEIN M.H.,"POLITICAL IDEAS OF SELECTED AMERICAN BUSINESS JOURNALS (BMR)" USA+45 GP/REL ATTIT RIGID/FLEX ROLE ORD/FREE POLICY. PAGE 14 F0267
IDEA/COMP NAT/G LEAD

S53
BIRNBAUM N.,"CONFLICTING INTERPRETATIONS OF THE RISE OF CAPITALISM: MARX AND WEBER" (BMR)" WOR-45 INTELL SOCIETY STRUCT INDUS WORKER...PHIL/SCI SOC PERS/COMP 19/20 MARX/KARL WEBER/MAX. PAGE 15 F0288
CAP/ISM IDEA/COMP ECO/DEV MARXISM

B54
FRIEDMAN W.,THE PUBLIC CORPORATION: A COMPARATIVE SYMPOSIUM (UNIVERSITY OF TORONTO SCHOOL OF LAW COMPARATIVE LAW SERIES, VOL. I). AFR SWEDEN USA+45 INDUS INT/ORG NAT/G REGION CENTRAL FEDERAL...POLICY JURID IDEA/COMP NAT/COMP ANTHOL 20 MONOPOLY EUROPE. PAGE 44 F0861
LAW SOCISM LG/CO OWN

B54
MITCHELL W.G.,BUSINESS CYCLES. FINAN MARKET PRICE COST EQUILIB OPTIMAL PRODUC PROFIT...IDEA/COMP GEN/LAWS 19/20. PAGE 92 F1809
INDUS TIME/SEQ METH/COMP STAT

B54
SCHUMPETER J.A.,HISTORY OF ECONOMIC ANALYSIS. WOR-45...PHIL/SCI METH/CNCPT STAT IDEA/COMP GRECO/ROMN. PAGE 118 F2322
KNOWL GEN/LAWS METH

S54
SCITOVSKY T.,"TWO CONCEPTS OF EXTERNAL ECONOMIES." ECO/DEV IDEA/COMP. PAGE 118 F2329
SERV/IND GEN/LAWS INDUS EQUILIB

B55
JOHR W.A.,THE ROLE OF THE ECONOMIST AS OFFICIAL ADVISER. WOR+45 INTELL ECO/DEV NAT/G PLAN GP/REL ROLE...DECISION PREDICT IDEA/COMP. PAGE 68 F1336
CONSULT ECO/TAC POLICY INGP/REL

B55
MAYO H.B.,DEMOCRACY AND MARXISM. COM USSR STRATA NAT/G WORKER ECO/TAC REV MORAL...PHIL/SCI HIST/WRIT IDEA/COMP WORSHIP 20 MARX/KARL LENIN/VI STALIN/J TROTSKY/L. PAGE 87 F1708
MARXISM CAP/ISM

B55
UYEHARA C.H.,COMPARATIVE PLATFORMS OF JAPAN'S MAJOR PARTIES... USA+45 AGRI LEGIS WORKER CAP/ISM ORD/FREE MARXISM SOCISM...IDEA/COMP 20 CHINJAP. PAGE 140 F2755
POLICY POL/PAR DIPLOM NAT/G

B55
WRONG D.H.,AMERICAN AND CANADIAN VIEWPOINTS. CANADA USA+45 CONSTN STRATA FAM SECT WORKER ECO/TAC EDU/PROP ADJUD MARRIAGE...IDEA/COMP 20. PAGE 149 F2936
DIPLOM ATTIT NAT/COMP CULTURE

S55
BUNZEL J.H.,"THE GENERAL IDEOLOGY OF AMERICAN SMALL BUSINESS"(BMR)" USA+45 USA-45 AGRI GP/REL INGP/REL PERSON...MGT IDEA/COMP 18/20. PAGE 20 F0383
ALL/IDEOS ATTIT SML/CO INDUS

B56
FIELD G.C.,POLITICAL THEORY. POL/PAR REPRESENT MORAL SOVEREIGN...JURID IDEA/COMP. PAGE 40 F0789
CONCPT NAT/G ORD/FREE DIPLOM

B56
GREENHUT M.L.,PLANT LOCATION IN THEORY AND PRACTICE; THE ECONOMICS OF SPACE. WOR+45 WOR-45 MARKET WORKER COST DEMAND...CONCPT STAT CHARTS HYPO/EXP BIBLIOG 19/20. PAGE 51 F0991
SML/CO ECO/DEV CAP/ISM IDEA/COMP

B56
PARSONS T.,ECONOMY AND SOCIETY: A STUDY IN THE INTEGRATION OF ECONOMIC AND SOCIAL THEORY. UNIV ACT/RES...SOC CHARTS IDEA/COMP BIBLIOG/A. PAGE 103 F2031
STRUCT METH/CNCPT UTIL PHIL/SCI

B56
WEBER M.,WIRTSCHAFT UND GESELLSCHAFT (2ND VOL.). STRUCT NAT/G POL/PAR LEAD PWR OBJECTIVE IDEA/COMP. PAGE 144 F2841
LEGIT JURID SOC

S56
HARSANYI J.C.,"APPROACHES TO THE BARGAINING PROBLEM BEFORE AND AFTER THE THEORY OF GAMES."...DECISION CON/ANAL SIMUL GEN/LAWS. PAGE 56 F1096
NEW/IDEA GAME IDEA/COMP

B57
HARRIS S.E.,INTERNATIONAL AND INTERREGIONAL ECONOMICS. AFR WOR+45 WOR-45 NAT/G TARIFFS BAL/PAY EQUILIB...POLICY CONCPT STAT CHARTS IDEA/COMP 19/20. PAGE 55 F1088
INT/TRADE ECO/DEV MARKET FINAN

B57
LEIBENSTEIN H.,ECONOMIC BACKWARDNESS AND ECONOMIC GROWTH. WOR+45 SOCIETY AGRI INDUS TEC/DEV CAP/ISM FOR/AID COST DEMAND WEALTH...CHARTS IDEA/COMP 20. PAGE 77 F1513
ECO/UNDEV ECO/TAC PRODUC POLICY

B57
LOUCKS W.N.,COMPARATIVE ECONOMIC SYSTEMS (5TH ED.). COM UK USSR INDUS POL/PAR PLAN CAP/ISM TOTALISM MARXISM...PHIL/SCI BIBLIOG 19/20. PAGE 82 F1603
NAT/COMP IDEA/COMP SOCISM

B57
NANIWADA H.,STAAT UND WIRTSCHAFT; GRUNDLEGUNG DER NATIONALOEKONOMIE ALS DER LOGIK DER BURGERLICHEN GESELLSCHAFT. WOR+45 WOR-45 STRATA MARKET WORKER INGP/REL DEMAND EQUILIB WEALTH...POLICY IDEA/COMP GEN/LAWS 17/20 MARX/KARL KEYNES/JM LENIN/VI. PAGE 96 F1890
ALL/IDEOS ECO/TAC SOCIETY NAT/G

B57
NAUMANN R.,THEORIE UND PRAXIS DES NEOLIBERALISMUS; DAS MAERCHEN VON DER FREIEN ODER SOZIALEN MARKTWIRTSCHAFT. GERMANY/W FORCES PLAN EDU/PROP SOCISM...POLICY MARXIST IDEA/COMP BIBLIOG 18/20 ADENAUER/K. PAGE 97 F1903
MARXISM NEW/LIB ECO/TAC CAP/ISM

B58
DOWNIE J.,THE COMPETITIVE PROCESS. ECO/TAC PRICE EFFICIENCY OPTIMAL PRODUC WEALTH...IDEA/COMP METH/COMP 20 MONOPOLY. PAGE 34 F0658
EQUILIB MARKET INDUS ECO/DEV

B58
DUESENBERRY J.S.,BUSINESS CYCLES AND ECONOMIC GROWTH. USA+45 PROB/SOLV PAY PRICE...CONCPT MATH CHARTS IDEA/COMP 20 DEPRESSION KEYNES/JM. PAGE 34 F0672
FINAN ECO/DEV ECO/TAC INCOME

B58
MOONEY R.E.,INFLATION AND RECESSION? AFR USA+45 LABOR LG/CO PRESS LEAD...IDEA/COMP ANTHOL 20. PAGE 93 F1821
PRICE ECO/TAC NAT/G PRODUC

B58
MUSGRAVE R.A.,CLASSICS IN THE THEORY OF PUBLIC FINANCE. UNIV MARKET LG/CO NAT/G CAP/ISM PRICE OPTIMAL...IDEA/COMP ANTHOL 19/20 SAY/EMIL EDGEWORTH LINDAHL/E RITSCHL/H. PAGE 95 F1870
TAX FINAN ECO/TAC GP/REL

B59
ENGELS F.,SOCIALISM: UTOPIAN AND SCIENTIFIC (2ND ED.). SOCISM...CONCPT CON/ANAL GEN/LAWS 19 DUHRING/E. PAGE 38 F0732
MARXISM PHIL/SCI UTOPIA IDEA/COMP

B59
KRIPALANI J.B.,CLASS STRUGGLE. INDIA WOR+45 ECO/UNDEV LABOR CAP/ISM EDU/PROP INGP/REL ...SOCIALIST IDEA/COMP 17/20. PAGE 73 F1440
MARXISM STRATA COERCE ECO/TAC

B59
LINK R.G.,ENGLISH THEORIES OF ECONOMIC FLUCTUATIONS: 1815-1848. FRANCE UK AGRI WORKER DIPLOM PRICE TASK WAR DEMAND PRODUC...POLICY BIBLIOG 18 MALTHUS MILL/JS WILSON/J. PAGE 80 F1574
IDEA/COMP ECO/DEV WEALTH EQUILIB

B59
MARTIN K.,WAR, HISTORY, AND HUMAN NATURE. FRANCE GERMANY INDIA UK UNIV POL/PAR COLONIAL DETER REV MARXISM PACIFISM...PSY CONCPT PREDICT LENIN/VI GANDHI/M. PAGE 86 F1683
PERSON WAR ATTIT IDEA/COMP

B59
SELIGSOHN I.J.,"USING COMPUTER SERVICES IN SMALL BUSINESS" MANAGEMENT AIDS FOR SMALL MANUFACTURERS 109 (PAMPHLET). DIST/IND MARKET PROC/MFG COST EFFICIENCY PRODUC...DECISION IDEA/COMP. PAGE 119 F2350
SML/CO COMPUTER MGT PROB/SOLV

B59
STANFORD U, BOARD OF TRUSTEES,THE ALLOCATION OF ECONOMIC RESOURCES. WORKER PLAN BUDGET ECO/TAC TAX RECEIVE COST PRODUC...POLICY IDEA/COMP SIMUL ANTHOL 20. PAGE 125 F2468
INCOME PRICE FINAN

B59
WAHLKE J.C.,LEGISLATIVE BEHAVIOR: A READER IN THEORY AND RESEARCH. USA+45 CONSTN ELITES POL/PAR LOBBY REPRESENT PERS/REL PERSON ROLE...IDEA/COMP METH/COMP SIMUL. PAGE 142 F2800
LEGIS CHOOSE INGP/REL ATTIT

B59
WELTON H.,THE THIRD WORLD WAR; TRADE AND INDUSTRY, THE NEW BATTLEGROUND. AFR WOR+45 ECO/DEV INDUS MARKET TASK...MGT IDEA/COMP. PAGE 145 F2855
INT/TRADE PLAN DIPLOM

L59
FURASH E.A.,"PROBLEMS IN REVIEW: INDUSTRIAL ESPIONAGE." WORKER ECO/TAC PERS/REL OPTIMAL AGE ATTIT KNOWL...MGT DEEP/INT DEEP/QU GP/COMP IDEA/COMP. PAGE 45 F0875
INDUS TOP/EX MAJORITY

S59
BENDIX R.,"INDUSTRIALIZATION, IDEOLOGIES, AND SOCIAL STRUCTURE" (BMR)" UK USA-45 USSR STRUCT WORKER GP/REL EFFICIENCY...IDEA/COMP 20. PAGE 13 F0243
INDUS ATTIT MGT ADMIN

S59
HARING J.E.,"UTILITY THEORY, DECISION THEORY, AND PROFIT MAXIMIZATION." PROB/SOLV GAMBLE UTIL ...DECISION CHARTS IDEA/COMP HYPO/EXP SIMUL GEN/METH. PAGE 55 F1083
PROBABIL RISK GAME

S59
STINCHCOMBE A.L.,"BUREAUCRATIC AND CRAFT ADMINISTRATION OF PRODUCTION: A COMPARATIVE STUDY" (BMR)" USA+45 STRUCT EX/STRUC ECO/TAC GP/REL ...CLASSIF GP/COMP IDEA/COMP GEN/LAWS 20 WEBER/MAX. PAGE 126 F2490
CONSTRUC PROC/MFG ADMIN PLAN

S59
STREETEN P.,"UNBALANCED GROWTH" UK ECO/DEV AGRI MARKET TEC/DEV CAP/ISM ECO/TAC FOR/AID INT/TRADE DEMAND ORD/FREE...CONCPT 20. PAGE 127 F2502
IDEA/COMP FINAN PRODUC EQUILIB

B60
ANGERS F.A.,ESSAI SUR LA CENTRALISATION: ANALYSE DES PRINCIPES ET PERSPECTIVES CANADIENNES. CANADA ECO/TAC CONTROL...SOC IDEA/COMP BIBLIOG 20. PAGE 6 F0105
CENTRAL ADMIN

B60
BAERWALD F.,ECONOMIC SYSTEM ANALYSIS: CONCEPTS AND PERSPECTIVES. USA+45 ECO/DEV NAT/G COMPUTER EQUILIB INCOME ATTIT...DECISION CONCPT IDEA/COMP. PAGE 8 F0151
ACT/RES ECO/TAC ROUTINE FINAN

B60
GRAMPP W.D.,THE MANCHESTER SCHOOL OF ECONOMICS. UK LAW ECO/DEV COERCE ATTIT ORD/FREE LAISSEZ ...PHIL/SCI IDEA/COMP 19/20 MANCHESTER CORN/LAWS. PAGE 50 F0973
ECO/TAC VOL/ASSN LOBBY NAT/G

B60
MAYO H.B.,INTRODUCTION TO MARXIST THEORY. SECT WORKER POPULISM SOCISM 19/20. PAGE 87 F1709
MARXISM STRATA IDEA/COMP PHIL/SCI

B60
PFOUTS R.W.,THE TECHNIQUES OF URBAN ECONOMIC ANALYSIS. USA+45...ECOMETRIC CONCPT CHARTS IDEA/COMP ANTHOL MUNICH 20. PAGE 106 F2078
METH ECO/DEV METH/COMP

B60
RAY D.D.,ACCOUNTING AND BUSINESS FLUCTUATIONS. LG/CO SML/CO FEEDBACK DEMAND...CHARTS IDEA/COMP BIBLIOG 20. PAGE 109 F2154
FINAN AFR CONTROL

B60
ROBINSON J.,AN ESSAY ON MARXIAN ECONOMICS. USA+45 STRATA INDUS MARKET CAP/ISM...METH/COMP 19/20 MARX/KARL. PAGE 113 F2222
IDEA/COMP MARXISM ACADEM

B60
ROBSON W.A.,NATIONALIZED INDUSTRY AND PUBLIC OWNERSHIP. UK ECO/DEV FINAN LABOR LG/CO POL/PAR LEGIS ACT/RES GP/REL...TREND IDEA/COMP 20. PAGE 113 F2227
NAT/G OWN INDUS ATTIT

B60
ROPKE W.,A HUMANE ECONOMY. CULTURE ECO/DEV FINAN INDUS GP/REL CENTRAL WEALTH...GEOG SOC IDEA/COMP 20 EEC. PAGE 114 F2239
ECO/TAC INT/ORG DIPLOM ORD/FREE

B60
SERAPHIM H.J.,ZUR GRUNDLEGUNG WIRTSCHAFTSPOLITISCHER KONZEPTIONEN (SCHRIFTEN DES VEREINS FUR SOZIALPOLITIK, N.F. BAND 18). GERMANY/W WOR+45 ECO/DEV DELIB/GP ACT/RES ECO/TAC INGP/REL ORD/FREE...CONCPT IDEA/COMP GEN/LAWS 20. PAGE 120 F2358
POLICY PHIL/SCI PLAN

B60
WALLICH H.C.,THE COST OF FREEDOM: A NEW LOOK AT CAPITALISM. USA+45 SOCIETY ECO/DEV INGP/REL CONSEN LAISSEZ SOCISM...OLD/LIB IDEA/COMP. PAGE 143 F2810
CAP/ISM ORD/FREE POLICY ECO/TAC

C60
HOSELITZ B.,"THE ROLE OF CITIES IN THE ECONOMIC GROWTH OF UNDERDEVELOPED COUNTRIES" IN "SOCIOLOGICAL ASPECTS OF ECONOMIC GROWTH"(BMR). CULTURE LOC/G ACT/RES...SOC IDEA/COMP METH/COMP METH MUNICH IND 14/20 REDFIELD/R. PAGE 62 F1218
METH/CNCPT TEC/DEV ECO/UNDEV

B61
ACKLEY G.,MACROECONOMIC THEORY. AFR FINAN WORKER ECO/TAC PRICE COST INCOME PRODUC...MATH TREND CHARTS IDEA/COMP T KEYNES/JM. PAGE 2 F0034
SIMUL ECOMETRIC WEALTH

B61
LENIN V.I.,WHAT IS TO BE DONE? (1902). RUSSIA LABOR NAT/G POL/PAR WORKER CAP/ISM ECO/TAC ADMIN PARTIC ...MARXIST IDEA/COMP GEN/LAWS 19/20. PAGE 78 F1522
EDU/PROP PRESS MARXISM METH/COMP

B61
LHOSTE-LACHAUME P.,OU GIT LE DESACCORD ENTRE LIBERAUX ET SOCIALISTES. EUR+WWI USA+45 USA-45 USSR CAP/ISM EDU/PROP MARXISM...MAJORIT IDEA/COMP 20 KEYNES/JM NEW/DEAL DEPRESSION. PAGE 79 F1555
LAISSEZ SOCISM FINAN

B61
LICHTHEIM G.,MARXISM. GERMANY SOCIETY WORKER CAP/ISM ECO/TAC NAT/LISM POPULISM...TIME/SEQ GOV/COMP NAT/COMP 18/20 COM/PARTY. PAGE 80 F1559
MARXISM SOCISM IDEA/COMP CULTURE

B61
MCCRACKEN H.L.,KEYNESIAN ECONOMICS IN THE STREAM OF ECONOMIC THOUGHT. FINAN MARKET BARGAIN EFFICIENCY OPTIMAL...PHIL/SCI CONCPT IDEA/COMP BIBLIOG 18/20 KEYNES/JM. PAGE 88 F1724
ECO/TAC DEMAND ECOMETRIC

B61
MYBDAL G.,THE POLITICAL ELEMENT IN THE DEVELOPMENT OF ECONOMIC THEORY. FINAN LOBBY ATTIT...WELF/ST CONCPT IDEA/COMP GEN/LAWS 20. PAGE 95 F1875
ECO/DEV ECO/TAC SOCIETY

B61
NEW JERSEY LEGISLATURE-SENATE,PUBLIC HEARINGS BEFORE COMMITTEE ON REVISION AND AMENDMENT OF LAWS ON SENATE BILL NO. 8. USA+45 FINAN PROVS WORKER ACT/RES PLAN BUDGET TAX CRIME...IDEA/COMP MUNICH 20 NEW/JERSEY URBAN/RNWL. PAGE 98 F1919
LEGIS INDUS PROB/SOLV

B61
ROEPKE W.,JENSEITS VON ANGEBOT UND NACHFRAGE (DRITTE VERAENDERTE AUFLAGE). WOR+45 MARKET TEC/DEV ECO/TAC GP/REL INGP/REL NEW/LIB...POLICY SOC IDEA/COMP PERS/COMP 20. PAGE 113 F2233
SOCIETY STRANGE ECO/DEV STRUCT

B61
WRIGHT H.M.,THE "NEW IMPERIALISM": ANALYSIS OF LATE NINETEENTH-CENTURY EXPANSION. MOD/EUR WOR-45 SOCIETY FINAN ECO/TAC INT/TRADE NAT/LISM...ANTHOL BIBLIOG/A 19. PAGE 149 F2933
HIST/WRIT IDEA/COMP COLONIAL DOMIN

S61
HIRSHLEIFER J.,"THE BAYESIAN APPROACH TO STATISTICAL DECISION: AN EXPOSITION." OP/RES PROB/SOLV UTIL...PROBABIL CHARTS IDEA/COMP HYPO/EXP 20. PAGE 60 F1178
DECISION GAME SIMUL STAT

B62
HARRIS S.E.,THE ECONOMICS OF THE POLITICAL PARTIES. USA+45 FINAN CHIEF ACT/RES PLAN BUDGET GP/REL INGP/REL NEW/LIB...IDEA/COMP PERS/COMP 20 EISNHWR/DD KENNEDY/JF. PAGE 56 F1090
POLICY ECO/DEV NAT/G POL/PAR

B62
JOHNSON H.G.,MONEY, TRADE AND ECONOMIC GROWTH. ECO/DEV ECO/UNDEV FINAN COST WEALTH...POLICY SOC IDEA/COMP 20 KEYNES/JM MONEY. PAGE 67 F1324
PLAN BAL/PAY INT/TRADE ECO/TAC

B62
MEANS G.C.,THE CORPORATE REVOLUTION IN AMERICA: ECONOMIC REALITY VS. ECONOMIC THEORY. USA+45 USA-45 INDUS WORKER PLAN CAP/ISM ADMIN...IDEA/COMP 20. PAGE 89 F1742
LG/CO MARKET CONTROL PRICE

B62
SIEVERS A.M.,REVOLUTION, EVOLUTION AND THE ECONOMIC ORDER. INDUS LABOR TAX CONTROL REV WAR DEMAND PRODUC WEALTH...IDEA/COMP 19/20 KEYNES/JM. PAGE 122 F2399
EFFICIENCY ALL/IDEOS ECO/DEV WELF/ST

B63
BARNETT H.J.,SCARCITY AND GROWTH: THE ECONOMICS OF NATURAL RESOURCE AVAILABILITY. FUT WOR+45 AGRI INDUS PROB/SOLV TEC/DEV CONTROL PRODUC...SOC/WK IDEA/COMP METH/COMP SIMUL 20 RESOURCE/N MALTHUS RICARDO/D MILL/JS DARWIN/C. PAGE 10 F0191
DEMAND HABITAT CENSUS GEOG

B63
CHATTERJEE I.K.,ECONOMIC DEVELOPMENT PAYMENTS DEFICIT AND PAYMENT RESTRICTION. INDIA WOR+45 FINAN INT/TRADE CONTROL BAL/PAY WEALTH...POLICY CONCPT STAT CHARTS IDEA/COMP BIBLIOG 20. PAGE 23 F0456
ECO/DEV ECO/TAC PAY GOV/REL

B63
MEIER G.,INTERNATIONAL TRADE AND DEVELOPMENT. FINAN BAL/PAY COST DEMAND DISCRIM EQUILIB WEALTH...POLICY ECOMETRIC MATH STAT BIBLIOG/A 20. PAGE 89 F1747
ECO/UNDEV ECO/TAC INT/TRADE IDEA/COMP

B63
NOMAD M.,POLITICAL HERETICS: FROM PLATO TO MAO TSE-TUNG. UNIV INGP/REL...SOC IDEA/COMP. PAGE 98 F1931
SOCIETY UTOPIA ALL/IDEOS CONCPT

B63
ROTHBARD M.N.,AMERICA'S GREAT DEPRESSION. USA-45 NAT/G ECO/TAC LAISSEZ...POLICY IDEA/COMP 20. PAGE 114 F2248
FINAN CAP/ISM MARKET GEN/LAWS

B63
SMELSER N.J.,THE SOCIOLOGY OF ECONOMIC LIFE. UNIV CULTURE PERCEPT...PSY T 18/20. PAGE 123 F2425
SOC METH/COMP IDEA/COMP

B63
VON BECKERATH E.,PROBLEME DER NORMATIVEN OKONOMIK UND DER WIRTSCHAFTSPOLITISCHEN BERATUNG. GERMANY UK ELITES CAP/ISM EFFICIENCY...CONCPT GOV/COMP IDEA/COMP 20. PAGE 142 F2789
ECO/TAC DELIB/GP ECO/DEV CONSULT

L63
MEYER J.R.,"REGIONAL ECONOMICS: A SURVEY." INTELL ACADEM CREATE...IDEA/COMP BIBLIOG. PAGE 90 F1770
REGION ECO/TAC GEN/LAWS PROB/SOLV

B64
HARBISON F.H.,EDUCATION, MANPOWER, AND ECONOMIC GROWTH. WOR+45 ECO/DEV ECO/UNDEV ACADEM LABOR SCHOOL WORKER UTIL...IDEA/COMP NAT/COMP. PAGE 55 F1075
PLAN TEC/DEV EDU/PROP SKILL

B64
HARRIS S.E.,ECONOMICS OF THE KENNEDY YEARS AND A LOOK AHEAD. USA+45 PLAN BUDGET NEW/LIB...STAT RECORD IDEA/COMP PERS/COMP INDEX 20 KENNEDY/JF EISNHWR/DD JOHNSON/LB. PAGE 56 F1091
ECO/TAC CHIEF POLICY NAT/G

B64
LEKACHMAN R.,KEYNES' GENERAL THEORY: REPORTS OF THREE DECADES. FINAN ATTIT...POLICY 20 KEYNES/JM. PAGE 77 F1517
PHIL/SCI GEN/METH IDEA/COMP

B64
LETICHE J.M.,A HISTORY OF RUSSIAN ECONOMIC THOUGHT: NINTH THROUGH EIGHTEENTH CENTURIES. RUSSIA FINAN SECT CAP/ISM DOMIN DEMAND EFFICIENCY OWN MARXISM ...TECHNIC ANTHOL BIBLIOG 9/18. PAGE 78 F1536
ECO/TAC TIME/SEQ IDEA/COMP ECO/UNDEV

B64
MILIBAND R.,THE SOCIALIST REGISTER: 1964. GERMANY/W ITALY UK LABOR POL/PAR ECO/TAC FOR/AID NUC/PWR ...POLICY SOCIALIST IDEA/COMP 20 MAO NASSER/G.
MARXISM SOCISM CAP/ISM

PAGE 91 F1784 PROB/SOLV

B64
NAGEL P.C.,ONE NATION INDIVISIBLE: THE UNION IN AMERICAN THOUGHT 1776-1861. USA-45 INDUS TEC/DEV EDU/PROP DREAM...IDEA/COMP 18/19. PAGE 96 F1887
FEDERAL NAT/G ATTIT INGP/REL

B64
RESOURCES FOR THE FUTURE,URBAN AND REGIONAL STUDIES AT US UNIVERSITIES; A REPORT BASED ON A 1963 SURVEY OF URBAN AND REGIONAL RESEARCH. USA+45 SOCIETY CONSTRUC DIST/IND ACADEM NAT/G ACT/RES ECO/TAC ...CENSUS IDEA/COMP MUNICH. PAGE 111 F2179
BIBLIOG/A REGION PLAN

B64
SANDEE J.,EUROPE'S FUTURE CONSUMPTION. EUR+WWI FUT EDU/PROP...IDEA/COMP NAT/COMP ANTHOL 20 EUROPE. PAGE 115 F2277
MARKET ECO/DEV PREDICT PRICE

S64
TOBIN J.,"ECONOMIC GROWTH AS AN OBJECTIVE OF GOVERNMENT POLICY." FUT WOR+45 FINAN WORKER BUDGET INCOME...SOC 20. PAGE 131 F2579
ECO/DEV POLICY ECO/TAC IDEA/COMP

C64
GOLDMAN M.I.,"COMPARATIVE ECONOMIC SYSTEMS: A READER." COM ECO/UNDEV NAT/G BUDGET CAP/ISM ADMIN TOTALISM MARXISM SOCISM...MGT ANTHOL BIBLIOG 19/20. PAGE 48 F0938
NAT/COMP CONTROL IDEA/COMP

C64
LANDAUER C.,"CONTEMPORARY ECONOMIC SYSTEMS." COM WOR+45 ECO/UNDEV PLAN GP/REL...BIBLIOG 20. PAGE 75 F1466
CAP/ISM SOCISM MARXISM IDEA/COMP

B65
BEAUFRE A.,AN INTRODUCTION TO STRATEGY, WITH PARTICULAR REFERENCE TO PROBLEMS OF DEFENSE, POLITICS, ECONOMICS IN THE NUCLEAR AGE. WOR+45 FORCES DIPLOM DETER CIVMIL/REL GP/REL...NEW/IDEA IDEA/COMP 20. PAGE 12 F0226
PLAN NUC/PWR WEAPON DECISION

B65
BOWEN W.G.,UNEMPLOYMENT IN A PROSPEROUS ECONOMY. USA+45 ECO/DEV NAT/G ACT/RES PLAN PAY EDU/PROP DEMAND...POLICY IDEA/COMP ANTHOL 20. PAGE 17 F0330
WORKER ECO/TAC WEALTH PROB/SOLV

B65
COLLINS H.,KARL MARX AND THE BRITISH LABOUR MOVEMENT; YEARS OF THE FIRST INTERNATIONAL. FRANCE SWITZERLND UK CAP/ISM WAR...MARXIST IDEA/COMP BIBLIOG 19. PAGE 26 F0506
MARXISM LABOR INT/ORG REV

B65
COLLOQUE SUR LA PLANIFICATION,LA PLANIFICATION COMME PROCESSUS DE DECISION. FRANCE SOCIETY MARKET LABOR LEGIS GP/REL EFFICIENCY INCOME ATTIT TECHRACY ...MYTH IDEA/COMP 20. PAGE 26 F0508
PLAN ECO/TAC PROB/SOLV

B65
GRAMPP W.D.,ECONOMIC LIBERALISM; THE BEGINNINGS (VOL. I). USA-45 WOR-45 MARKET LABOR ATTIT WEALTH ...POLICY CONCPT BIBLIOG GREECE/ANC MERCANTLST REPUBLICAN FEDERALIST. PAGE 50 F0974
ECO/DEV CAP/ISM IDEA/COMP ECO/TAC

B65
GRAMPP W.D.,ECONOMIC LIBERALISM; THE CLASSICAL VIEW (VOL. II). MOD/EUR SOCIETY MARKET INT/TRADE NAT/LISM WEALTH LAISSEZ...POLICY PSY CONCPT BIBLIOG 19 SMITH/ADAM HUME/D MILL/JS. PAGE 50 F0975
ECO/DEV CAP/ISM IDEA/COMP ECO/TAC

B65
MONCRIEFF A.,SECOND THOUGHTS ON AID. WOR+45 ECO/UNDEV AGRI FINAN VOL/ASSN PLAN TEC/DEV GIVE EDU/PROP ROLE WEALTH 20. PAGE 93 F1816
FOR/AID ECO/TAC INT/ORG IDEA/COMP

B65
NARASIMHAN V.K.,DEMOCRACY AND MIXED ECONOMY. INDIA CONTROL...CENSUS IDEA/COMP 20. PAGE 96 F1891
CAP/ISM MARXISM ORD/FREE NEW/LIB

B65
OZGA S.A.,EXPECTATIONS IN ECONOMIC THEORY. MORAL ...ECOMETRIC MATH STAT IDEA/COMP 20. PAGE 102 F2008
RISK GAME CONCPT PREDICT

B65
PROCHNOW H.V.,WORLD ECONOMIC PROBLEMS AND POLICIES. INDIA ISRAEL WOR+45 AGRI LABOR PROB/SOLV FOR/AID TARIFFS CONTROL BAL/PAY NAT/LISM WEALTH...TREND CHARTS 20 CHINJAP EEC. PAGE 108 F2124
MARKET ECO/TAC PRODUC IDEA/COMP

B65
REAGAN M.D.,POLITICS, ECONOMICS, AND THE GENERAL WELFARE. USA+45 INDUS ECO/TAC TAX WEALTH...POLICY IDEA/COMP ANTHOL 20. PAGE 110 F2162
NAT/G ECO/DEV R+D ACADEM

B65
SHAFFER H.G.,THE SOVIET SYSTEM IN THEORY AND PRACTICE: SELECTED WESTERN AND SOVIET VIEWS. USSR LAW SOCIETY CREATE FOR/AID EDU/PROP PRESS CHOOSE PEACE ORD/FREE...ANTHOL 20 STALIN/J. PAGE 120 F2362
MARXISM SOCISM IDEA/COMP

B65
THORNTON A.P.,DOCTRINES OF IMPERIALISM. WOR+45 WOR-45 DOMIN NAT/LISM PROFIT ATTIT PERSON PWR
IDEA/COMP COLONIAL

RESPECT SOVEREIGN...CONCPT STERTYP. PAGE 130 F2571 DRIVE

S65
BALDWIN D.A.,"THE INTERNATIONAL BANK IN POLITICAL PERSPECTIVE" USA+45 TEC/DEV FOR/AID RENT GIVE COST ...IDEA/COMP GAME IBRD. PAGE 9 F0160
FINAN INT/ORG

S65
KINDLEBERGER C.P.,"MASS MIGRATION, THEN AND NOW." LAW ECO/DEV ECO/UNDEV INDUS LABOR INT/TRADE FEEDBACK REGION RIGID/FLEX...SOC NAT/COMP EEC. PAGE 71 F1394
EUR+WWI USA-45 WORKER IDEA/COMP

B66
BALDWIN D.A.,FOREIGN AID AND AMERICAN FOREIGN POLICY; A DOCUMENTARY ANALYSIS. USA+45 ECO/UNDEV ADMIN...ECOMETRIC STAT STYLE CHARTS PROG/TEAC GEN/LAWS ANTHOL. PAGE 9 F0162
FOR/AID DIPLOM IDEA/COMP

B66
FOX K.A.,THE THEORY OF QUANTITATIVE ECONOMIC POLICY WITH APPLICATIONS TO ECONOMIC GROWTH AND STABILIZATION. ECO/DEV AGRI NAT/G PLAN ADMIN RISK ...DECISION IDEA/COMP SIMUL T. PAGE 43 F0837
ECO/TAC ECOMETRIC EQUILIB GEN/LAWS

B66
GOODWIN C.D.W.,ECONOMIC INQUIRY IN AUSTRALIA. ECO/DEV ECO/UNDEV ACADEM INT/TRADE RENT TARIFFS TAX PRESS GOV/REL SOCISM 18/20 AUSTRAL. PAGE 49 F0953
ECO/TAC IDEA/COMP BUDGET COLONIAL

B66
HOROWITZ I.L.,THREE WORLDS OF DEVELOPMENT. COM USA+45 STRUCT ECO/DEV PLAN PROB/SOLV TEC/DEV CIVMIL/REL...PHIL/SCI IDEA/COMP 20. PAGE 62 F1216
ECO/UNDEV BAL/PWR POL/PAR REV

B66
LANSING J.B.,TRANSPORTATION AND ECONOMIC POLICY. USA+45 COST DEMAND...ECOMETRIC TREND CHARTS IDEA/COMP T 20. PAGE 76 F1481
DIST/IND OP/RES ECO/DEV UTIL

B66
LECHT L.,GOAL, PRIORITIES, AND DOLLARS: THE NEXT DECADE. SPACE USA+45 SOCIETY AGRI BUDGET FOR/AID ...HEAL SOC/WK STAT CHARTS 20 URBAN/RNWL PUB/TRANS. PAGE 76 F1499
IDEA/COMP POLICY CONSEN PLAN

B66
LENSKI G.E.,POWER AND PRIVILEGE: A THEORY OF SOCIAL STRATIFICATION. SWEDEN UK UNIV USSR CULTURE ECO/UNDEV PRIVIL PWR...PHIL/SCI CONCPT CHARTS IDEA/COMP HYPO/EXP METH MARX/KARL. PAGE 78 F1525
SOC STRATA STRUCT SOCIETY

B66
ODEGARD P.H.,POLITICAL POWER AND SOCIAL CHANGE. UNIV NAT/G CREATE ALL/IDEOS...POLICY GEOG SOC CENSUS TREND. PAGE 100 F1962
PWR TEC/DEV IDEA/COMP

B66
SEWELL J.P.,FUNCTIONALISM AND WORLD POLITICS* A STUDY BASED ON UNITED NATIONS PROGRAMS FINANCING ECONOMICAL DEVELOPMENT. ECO/UNDEV FINAN PROB/SOLV DIPLOM ECO/TAC FEEDBACK REGION ADJUST ATTIT UN IBRD INTL/FINAN INTL/DEV UNSF. PAGE 120 F2360
TASK INT/ORG IDEA/COMP GEN/LAWS

B66
YEAGER L.B.,INTERNATIONAL MONETARY RELATIONS: THEORY, HISTORY, AND POLICY. WOR+45 WOR-45 INT/TRADE BAL/PAY...NAT/COMP 18/20 MONEY. PAGE 150 F2947
FINAN DIPLOM ECO/TAC IDEA/COMP

S66
ANGELL J.W.,"THE LONGER RUN PROSPECTS FOR THE US BALANCE OF PAYMENTS." USA+45 DIPLOM FOR/AID RATION ORD/FREE WEALTH...IDEA/COMP GATT. PAGE 6 F0104
BAL/PAY ECO/TAC INT/TRADE FINAN

B67
CHILCOTE R.H.,PORTUGUESE AFRICA. PORTUGAL CULTURE SOCIETY ECO/UNDEV DOMIN NAT/LISM...TREND IDEA/COMP NAT/COMP BIBLIOG 15/20. PAGE 24 F0465
AFR COLONIAL ORD/FREE PROB/SOLV

B67
COHEN M.R.,LAW AND THE SOCIAL ORDER: ESSAYS IN LEGAL PHILOSOPHY. USA-45 CONSULT WORKER ECO/TAC ATTIT WEALTH...POLICY WELF/ST SOC 20 NEW/DEAL DEPRESSION. PAGE 26 F0497
JURID LABOR IDEA/COMP

B67
DAVIS H.B.,NATIONALISM AND SOCIALISM: MARXIST AND LABOR THEORIES OF NATIONALISM TO 1917. WOR-45 PROB/SOLV SOVEREIGN...CONCPT IDEA/COMP 19/20. PAGE 30 F0589
MARXISM ATTIT NAT/LISM SOCISM

B67
EBENSTEIN W.,TODAY'S ISMS: COMMUNISM, FASCISM, CAPITALISM, SOCIALISM (5TH ED.). COM WOR+45 PERCEPT PWR...SOC TREND IDEA/COMP NAT/COMP 20. PAGE 35 F0691
FASCISM MARXISM SOCISM CAP/ISM

B67
LYND S.,RECONSTRUCTION. USA-45 PROB/SOLV RACE/REL ...IDEA/COMP ANTHOL 19. PAGE 82 F1616
SUFF ECO/TAC ADJUST

B67
SHAFFER H.G.,THE COMMUNIST WORLD: MARXIST AND NON-MARXIST VIEWS. WOR+45 SOCIETY DIPLOM ECO/TAC CONTROL SOCISM...MARXIST ANTHOL BIBLIOG/A 20. PAGE 120 F2363
MARXISM NAT/COMP IDEA/COMP COM

B67
SMITH T.L.,THE PROCESS OF RURAL DEVELOPMENT IN
IDEA/COMP

LATIN AMERICA (A MONOGRAPH). L/A+17C STRATA INDUS PLAN GP/REL PERS/REL RIGID/FLEX WEALTH...OBS CHARTS ORG/CHARTS ANTHOL 20 COLOMB. PAGE 123 F2434 — SOC AGRI ECO/UNDEV

B67
THOMAS M.J.,PRESIDENTIAL STATEMENTS ON EDUCATION: EXCERPTS FROM INAUGURAL AND STATE OF THE UNION MESSAGES 1789-1967. USA+45 USA-45 NAT/G BUDGET ...IDEA/COMP 18/20 PRESIDENT. PAGE 130 F2562 — EDU/PROP TOP/EX LEGIS SCHOOL

B67
US CONGRESS JOINT ECO COMM,REPORT ON JANUARY 1967 ECONOMIC REPORT OF THE PRESIDENT. FINAN LABOR NAT/G LEGIS BUDGET INT/TRADE COST DEMAND INCOME PRODUC ...POLICY IDEA/COMP 20 CONGRESS. PAGE 135 F2663 — CHIEF ECO/TAC PLAN DELIB/GP

L67
BERNHARD R.C.,"COMPETITION IN LAW AND ECONOMICS." LAW PLAN PRICE CONTROL PRODUC PROFIT...METH/CNCPT IDEA/COMP GEN/LAWS 20. PAGE 14 F0265 — MARKET POLICY NAT/G CT/SYS

L67
GREGORY A.J.,"AFRICAN SOCIALISM, SOCIALISM AND FASCISM: AN APPRAISAL." FUT LEAD REV GP/REL RACE/REL NAT/LISM ATTIT...IDEA/COMP STERTYP 20. PAGE 51 F0993 — FASCISM MARXISM SOCISM AFR

L67
MIXON J.,"JANE JACOBS AND THE LAW - ZONING FOR DIVERSITY EXAMINED." FUT USA+45 CONSTN NEIGH PROB/SOLV CONTROL CT/SYS PARTIC ATTIT...POLICY CENSUS METH/COMP MUNICH. PAGE 92 F1810 — IDEA/COMP PLAN LAW

S67
DAVIS O.A.,"ON THE DISTINCTION BETWEEN PUBLIC AND PRIVATE GOODS." USA+45 COM/IND LG/CO NAT/G TV DEBATE PRICE ADMIN ROLE...MATH IDEA/COMP. PAGE 31 F0593 — MARKET OWN CONCPT

S67
GAMARNIKOW M.,"THE NEW ROLE OF PRIVATE ENTERPRISE." ECO/DEV INDUS NAT/G SML/CO CREATE PROB/SOLV MARXISM ...POLICY TREND IDEA/COMP 20. PAGE 46 F0890 — ECO/TAC ATTIT CAP/ISM COM

S67
GATELL F.O.,"MONEY AND PARTY IN JACKSONIAN AMERICA* A QUANTITATIVE LOOK AT NEW YORK CITY'S MEN OF QUALITY." USA-45 STRATA SECT SUFF CONSEN MAJORITY ATTIT...CHARTS HYPO/EXP 19. PAGE 46 F0908 — WEALTH POL/PAR PERSON IDEA/COMP

S67
GUPTA S.,"FOREIGN POLICY IN THE 1967 MANIFESTOS." ASIA COM INDIA USA+45 FORCES FOR/AID TAX ATTIT ...DECISION 20. PAGE 52 F1013 — IDEA/COMP POL/PAR POLICY DIPLOM

S67
JEDLICKI W.,"THE FREE SPEECH MOVEMENT IN WARSAW." POLAND FORCES EDU/PROP LEAD ATTIT MARXISM ...IDEA/COMP 20. PAGE 67 F1310 — COERCE CROWD ORD/FREE ACADEM

S67
KINGSLEY R.E.,"THE US BUSINESS IMAGE IN LATIN AMERICA." L/A+17C USA+45 NAT/G TEC/DEV CAP/ISM FOR/AID DOMIN EDU/PROP...CONCPT LING IDEA/COMP 20. PAGE 71 F1396 — ATTIT LOVE DIPLOM ECO/UNDEV

S67
LEE R.L.,"THE PARADOX OF EQUALITY: A THREAT TO INDIVIDUAL AND SYSTEM FUNCTIONING." CHINA/COM ECO/UNDEV WORKER...SIMUL GEN/LAWS 20. PAGE 77 F1508 — SOCIETY STRATA MARXISM IDEA/COMP

S67
LEONTYEV L.,"THE LENINIST PRINCIPLES OF SOCIALIST ECONOMIC MANAGEMENT." USA+45 USSR POL/PAR WORKER PLAN ECO/TAC EFFICIENCY PRODUC MARXISM...POLICY SOCIALIST MGT TREND 20 LENIN/VI MARX/KARL. PAGE 78 F1529 — SOCISM CAP/ISM IDEA/COMP ECO/DEV

S67
LIFLAND W.T.,"BANKING PRACTICE AND THE ANTITRUST LAWS." NAT/G GP/REL...CONCPT IDEA/COMP 20. PAGE 80 F1563 — FINAN CAP/ISM JURID

S67
NUSENBAUM A.A.,"ON THE QUESTION OF TENDENCIES IN AMERICAN EDUCATION." USA+45 USSR SOCIETY SCHOOL RATIONAL 20. PAGE 99 F1946 — MARXIST IDEA/COMP GEN/LAWS EDU/PROP

S67
PETROVICH M.B.,"UNITED STATES POLICY IN EAST EUROPE." ECO/DEV ECO/TAC IDEA/COMP. PAGE 105 F2075 — COM INT/TRADE USA+45 DIPLOM

S67
SOLT L.F.,"PURITANISM, CAPITALISM, DEMOCRACY, AND THE NEW SCIENCE." NAT/G GP/REL CONSERVE...IDEA/COMP GEN/LAWS. PAGE 124 F2440 — SECT CAP/ISM RATIONAL POPULISM

S67
STOLTE S.C.,"THREE PROBLEMS FACING THE SOVIET BLOC." ASIA COM USA+45 USSR FORCES MARXISM ...IDEA/COMP METH/COMP 20 NATO WARSAW/P. PAGE 127 F2496 — ECO/TAC DIPLOM INT/ORG POLICY

S67
WEISSKOPF W.A.,"THE DIALECTICS OF ABUNDANCE." UNIV CAP/ISM ATTIT MARXISM...CONCPT 20. PAGE 145 F2853 — INDUS SOCIETY IDEA/COMP ALL/VALS

S67
WILSON C.E.,"AMERICAN INVESTMENT IN PORTUGUESE AFRICA: A PROBLEM OF "DEMOCRATIC" COLONIALISM." AFR ECO/UNDEV DIPLOM MORAL...IDEA/COMP 20 ANGOLA MOZAMBIQUE. PAGE 147 F2901 — COLONIAL DOMIN ORD/FREE POLICY

B68
PROUDHON P.J.,SYSTEME DES CONTRADICTIONS ECONOMIQUES, OU PHILOSOPHIE DA LA MISERE (2 VOLS.) (1846). SECT WORKER GP/REL ISOLAT PRODUC IDEA/COMP. PAGE 108 F2126 — SOCIETY STRATA MORAL

L86
OSGOOD H.L.,"SCIENTIFIC SOCIALISM: RODBERTUS" GERMANY CAP/ISM COST WEALTH...MAJORIT BIOG IDEA/COMP 19 RODBRTUS/C. PAGE 102 F2002 — SOCISM MARXISM ECO/DEV ECO/TAC

B88
BENTHAM J.,DEFENCE OF USURY (1787). UK LAW NAT/G TEC/DEV ECO/TAC CONTROL ATTIT...CONCPT IDEA/COMP 18 SMITH/ADAM. PAGE 13 F0255 — TAX FINAN ECO/DEV POLICY

B92
COULANGES F D.E.,THE ORIGIN OF PROPERTY IN LAND. LAW STRATA AGRI ACADEM EDU/PROP ORD/FREE 19. PAGE 28 F0543 — OWN HIST/WRIT IDEA/COMP SOCISM

IDEOLOGY....SEE ATTIT, STERTYP, ALSO IDEOLOGICAL TOPIC INDEX, P. XIII

IFC....INTERNATIONAL FINANCE CORPORATION

IFFLAND C.P. F0332

IGNORANCE....SEE KNOWL

IGY....INTERNATIONAL GEOPHYSICAL YEAR

ILLEGIT....BASTARDY

B67
SPURRIER R.B.,THE OVERPOPULATED SOCIETY. WORKER EATING PERS/REL DEMAND EQUILIB ILLEGIT INCOME HABITAT 20. PAGE 125 F2461 — BIO/SOC FOR/AID DRIVE RECEIVE

ILLEGITIMACY....SEE ILLEGIT

ILLINOIS....ILLINOIS

N19
FAHRNKOPF N.,STATE AND LOCAL GOVERNMENT IN ILLINOIS (PAMPHLET). CONSTN ADMIN PARTIC CHOOSE REPRESENT GOV/REL...JURID MGT 20 ILLINOIS. PAGE 39 F0759 — BIBLIOG LOC/G LEGIS CT/SYS

B60
ILLINOIS U BUR COMMUNITY PLAN,PROCEEDINGS OF ILLINOIS STATEWIDE PLANNING CONFERENCE 1960. USA+45 FINAN LOC/G ACT/RES LEAD GOV/REL GP/REL WEALTH MUNICH 20 ILLINOIS. PAGE 64 F1260 — PLAN DELIB/GP VOL/ASSN

B62
CARPER E.T.,ILLINOIS GOES TO CONGRESS FOR ARMY LAND. USA+45 LAW EXTR/IND PROVS REGION CIVMIL/REL GOV/REL FEDERAL ATTIT 20 ILLINOIS SENATE CONGRESS DIRKSEN/E DOUGLAS/P. PAGE 22 F0420 — ADMIN LOBBY GEOG LEGIS

L67
"GOVERNMENT CONTROL OF LAND: PROTECTING THE I-KNOW-IT-WHENI-SEE-IT INTEREST." USA+45 LAW CONSTN DELIB/GP CT/SYS HABITAT ILLINOIS. PAGE 2 F0026 — PLAN LOC/G CONTROL ADJUD

ILLINOIS U BUR COMMUNITY PLAN F1260

ILO....INTERNATIONAL LABOR ORGANIZATION; SEE ALSO INT/ORG

N19
INTERNATIONAL LABOUR OFFICE,EMPLOYMENT, UNEMPLOYMENT AND LABOUR FORCE STATISTICS (PAMPHLET). EUR+WWI STRATA AGRI INDUS NAT/G PROB/SOLV PAY AGE SEX...SAMP NAT/COMP METH 20 ILO. PAGE 65 F1278 — WORKER LABOR STAT ECO/DEV

B39
MARQUAND H.A.,ORGANIZED LABOUR IN FOUR CONTINENTS. EUR+WWI USA-45 INDUS NAT/G PAY GP/REL TOTALISM ATTIT WEALTH ALL/IDEOS...TREND NAT/COMP 20 ILO AFL/CIO EUROPE CHINJAP MEXIC/AMER. PAGE 85 F1673 — LABOR WORKER CONCPT ANTHOL

B47
TOWLE L.W.,INTERNATIONAL TRADE AND COMMERCIAL POLICY. WOR+45 LAW ECO/DEV FINAN INDUS NAT/G ECO/TAC WEALTH...TIME/SEQ ILO 20. PAGE 131 F2582 — MARKET INT/ORG INT/TRADE

C50
ELLSWORTH P.T.,"INTERNATIONAL ECONOMY." ECO/DEV ECO/UNDEV FINAN LABOR DIPLOM FOR/AID TARIFFS BAL/PAY EQUILIB NAT/LISM OPTIMAL...INT/LAW 20 ILO GATT. PAGE 37 F0724 — BIBLIOG INT/TRADE ECO/TAC INT/ORG

B52
ALEXANDROWICZ C.H.,INTERNATIONAL ECONOMIC ORGANIZATION. WOR+45 ECO/DEV ECO/UNDEV DIST/IND FINAN MARKET PLAN ECO/TAC LEGIT DRIVE WEALTH ...POLICY CONCPT QUANT OBS TIME/SEQ GEN/LAWS WORK METH/GP EEC ILO OEEC UNESCO 20. PAGE 4 F0063
INT/ORG INT/TRADE

B52
ASHWORTH W.,A SHORT HISTORY OF THE INTERNATIONAL ECONOMY 1850-1950. WOR+45 WOR-45 AGRI FINAN INDUS MARKET LABOR ECO/TAC...CONCPT STAT HIST/WRIT FOR/TRADE ILO 19/20. PAGE 7 F0131
ECO/DEV TEC/DEV INT/TRADE

B55
WOYTINSKY W.S.,WORLD COMMERCE AND GOVERNMENTS: TRENDS AND OUTLOOK. WOR+45 FINAN POL/PAR DIPLOM ECO/TAC FOR/AID DOMIN WAR CHOOSE...CHARTS BIBLIOG 20 LEAGUE/NAT UN ILO. PAGE 149 F2929
INT/TRADE DIST/IND NAT/COMP NAT/G

L59
BEGUIN B.,"ILO AND THE TRIPARTITE SYSTEM." EUR+WWI WOR+45 WOR-45 CONSTN ECO/DEV ECO/UNDEV INDUS INT/ORG NAT/G VOL/ASSN DELIB/GP PLAN TEC/DEV LEGIT ORD/FREE WEALTH...CONCPT TIME/SEQ WORK ILO 20. PAGE 12 F0228
LABOR

S59
TIPTON J.B.,"PARTICIPATION OF THE UNITED STATES IN THE INTERNATIONAL LABOR ORGANIZATION." USA+45 LAW STRUCT ECO/DEV ECO/UNDEV INDUS TEC/DEV ECO/TAC ADMIN PERCEPT ORD/FREE SKILL...STAT HIST/WRIT GEN/METH ILO WORK 20. PAGE 131 F2577
LABOR INT/ORG

S60
JACOBSON H.K.,"THE USSR AND ILO." AFR COM STRUCT ECO/DEV ECO/UNDEV CONSULT DELIB/GP ECO/TAC ILO WORK 20. PAGE 66 F1298
INT/ORG LABOR USSR

B61
SHARP W.R.,FIELD ADMINISTRATION IN THE UNITED NATION SYSTEM: THE CONDUCT OF INTERNATIONAL ECONOMIC AND SOCIAL PROGRAMS. FUT WOR+45 CONSTN SOCIETY ECO/UNDEV R+D DELIB/GP ACT/RES PLAN TEC/DEV EDU/PROP EXEC ROUTINE HEALTH WEALTH...HUM CONCPT CHARTS METH ILO UNESCO GP VAL/FREE UN 20. PAGE 120 F2369
INT/ORG CONSULT

B64
INTERNATIONAL LABOUR OFFICE,EMPLOYMENT AND ECONOMIC GROWTH. ECO/DEV ECO/UNDEV NAT/G PLAN DIPLOM INT/TRADE CONTROL INCOME PRODUC WEALTH...STAT NAT/COMP 20 ILO. PAGE 65 F1279
WORKER METH/COMP ECO/TAC OPTIMAL

B67
MEYNAUD J.,TRADE UNIONISM IN AFRICA; A STUDY OF ITS GROWTH AND ORIENTATION (TRANS. BY ANGELA BRENCH). INT/ORG PROB/SOLV COLONIAL PWR...TIME/SEQ TREND ILO. PAGE 90 F1774
LABOR AFR NAT/LISM ORD/FREE

IMAZ J.L. F1261

IMF....INTERNATIONAL MONETARY FUND

N19
LUTZ F.A.,THE PROBLEM OF INTERNATIONAL LIQUIDITY AND THE MULTIPLECURRENCY STANDARD (PAMPHLET). WOR+45 MARKET INT/ORG PRICE BAL/PAY...NEW/IDEA METH/COMP BIBLIOG 20 IMF. PAGE 82 F1609
PROB/SOLV FINAN DIPLOM ECO/TAC

B63
INTERNATIONAL MONETARY FUND,COMPENSATORY FINANCING OF EXPORT FLUCTUATIONS (PAMPHLET). WOR+45 ECO/DEV ECO/UNDEV INT/ORG WEALTH...TREND 20 IMF MONEY. PAGE 65 F1281
BAL/PAY FINAN BUDGET INT/TRADE

B64
MEZERIK A.G.,TRADE, AID AND ECONOMIC DEVELOPMENT. WOR+45 FINAN INDUS MARKET PLAN BAL/PWR BARGAIN FOR/AID TARIFFS EDU/PROP WEALTH...GP/COMP 20 UN GATT IMF IBRD. PAGE 91 F1777
ECO/TAC ECO/DEV INT/ORG INT/TRADE

B65
ROOSA R.V.,MONETARY REFORM FOR THE WORLD ECONOMY. AFR EUR+WWI USA+45 WOR+45 CREATE BUDGET DIPLOM FOR/AID EQUILIB WEALTH IMF. PAGE 114 F2237
FINAN INT/ORG INT/TRADE BAL/PAY

B65
US CONGRESS JOINT ECO COMM,GUIDELINES FOR INTERNATIONAL MONETARY REFORM. USA+45 WOR+45 DELIB/GP BAL/PAY 20 CONGRESS IMF MONEY. PAGE 135 F2659
DIPLOM FINAN PLAN INT/ORG

L65
DAANE J.D.,"THE EVOLVING INTERNATIONAL MONETARY MECHANISM." VOL/ASSN CREATE PLAN FOR/AID INT/TRADE CONFER BAL/PAY...RECORD PREDICT IMF. PAGE 29 F0569
INT/ORG ECO/TAC TREND GP/COMP

B67
ZUPNICK E.,UNDERSTANDING THE INTERNATIONAL MONEY SYSTEM (HEADLINE SERIES, NO. 182) (PAMPHLET). ECO/DEV NAT/G DIPLOM INT/TRADE...METH/COMP 20 IMF. PAGE 151 F2971
FINAN PLAN INT/ORG PROB/SOLV

L67
MEIER G.M.,"UNCTAD PROPOSALS FOR INTERNATIONAL ECONOMIC REFORM." WOR+45 MARKET INT/ORG TARIFFS CONFER UN GATT IMF. PAGE 89 F1749
INT/TRADE FINAN INT/LAW ECO/UNDEV

IMITATION....SEE NEW/IDEA, CONSEN, CREATE

IMMUNITY....SEE PRIVIL

IMPERIALISM....SEE COLONIAL, SOVEREIGN, DOMIN

IMPERSONALITY....SEE STRANGE

IMPROMPTU INTERVIEW....SEE UNPLAN/INT

IN....INDIANA

B64
COMMITTEE ECONOMIC DEVELOPMENT,COMMUNITY ECONOMIC DEVELOPMENT PROGRAMS. USA+45 FINAN INDUS LG/CO PROF/ORG CREATE GP/REL MUNIC NEW/YORK VERMONT PENNSYLVAN IN ARKANSAS. PAGE 27 F0519
LOC/G LABOR PLAN

INARRITU A.L. F1262

INAUGURATE....INAUGURATIONS AND CORONATIONS

INCOME....SEE ALSO FINAN, WEALTH

N
INTERNATIONAL BIBLIOGRAPHY OF ECONOMICS. WOR+45 FINAN MARKET ADMIN DEMAND INCOME PRODUC...POLICY IDEA/COMP METH. PAGE 1 F0002
BIBLIOG ECO/DEV ECO/UNDEV INT/TRADE

N
US SUPERINTENDENT OF DOCUMENTS,CENSUS PUBLICATIONS (PRICE LIST 70). AGRI CONSTRUC DIST/IND FINAN LOC/G NAT/G PROVS INT/TRADE APPORT INCOME. PAGE 140 F2751
BIBLIOG/A CENSUS STAT USA+45

N
US SUPERINTENDENT OF DOCUMENTS,TARIFF AND TAXATION (PRICE LIST 37). USA+45 LAW INT/TRADE ADJUD ADMIN CT/SYS INCOME OWN...DECISION GATT. PAGE 140 F2754
BIBLIOG/A TAX TARIFFS NAT/G

LCA
GODFREY E.M.,"THE ECONOMICS OF AN AFRICAN UNIVERSITY." AFR SCHOOL PRICE EFFICIENCY INCOME WEALTH...ECOMETRIC CHARTS 20. PAGE 48 F0930
ACADEM ECO/TAC COST EDU/PROP

B12
HOBSON J.A.,THE EVOLUTION OF MODERN CAPITALISM. MOD/EUR UK STRATA ECO/DEV INDUS INCOME UTIL WEALTH ...SOC GEN/LAWS 7/20. PAGE 60 F1184
CAP/ISM WORKER TEC/DEV TIME/SEQ

B13
KROPOTKIN P.,THE CONQUEST OF BREAD. SOCIETY STRATA AGRI INDUS WORKER REV HAPPINESS INCOME PRODUC HEALTH MORAL ORD/FREE. PAGE 74 F1444
ANARCH SOCIALIST OWN AGREE

B14
HOBSON J.A.,WORK AND WEALTH. CULTURE FINAN INDUS WORKER TEC/DEV ECO/TAC GIVE PAY PRICE COST PRODUC UTIL. PAGE 60 F1185
WEALTH INCOME GEN/LAWS

N19
BOS H.C.,A DISCUSSION ON METHODS OF MONETARY ANALYSIS AND NORMS FOR MONETARY POLICY (PAMPHLET). BAL/PAY COST INCOME...METH/COMP 20. PAGE 17 F0319
FINAN POLICY EQUILIB SIMUL

N19
BUSINESS ECONOMISTS' GROUP,INCOME POLICIES (PAMPHLET). UK INDUS LABOR TOP/EX PAY COST PRODUC ...ECOMETRIC GOV/COMP SIMUL ANTHOL 20. PAGE 20 F0395
INCOME WORKER WEALTH POLICY

N19
HABERLER G.,A SURVEY OF INTERNATIONAL TRADE THEORY (PAMPHLET). FINAN NAT/G COST INCOME 18/20 MONEY HUME/D MARSHALL/A. PAGE 52 F1022
INT/TRADE BAL/PAY GEN/LAWS POLICY

N19
HALL G.,MAIN STREET TO WALL STREET: END THE COLD WAR (PAMPHLET). AFR USA+45 LAW STRUCT POL/PAR WORKER INT/TRADE DOMIN INCOME...POLICY 20 COM/PARTY. PAGE 53 F1046
MARXIST CAP/ISM DIPLOM NAT/G

N19
MIYASAWA K.,AN ECONOMIC SURVIVAL GAME (PAMPHLET). COST DEMAND EQUILIB INCOME PROFIT 20. PAGE 92 F1811
ECOMETRIC GAME ECO/TAC DECISION

B20
PIGOU A.C.,THE ECONOMICS OF WELFARE. UNIV INDUS WORKER ACT/RES RECEIVE INCOME NEW/LIB...MAJORIT SOC/WK. PAGE 106 F2085
ECO/TAC WEALTH FINAN CONTROL

B23
HOBSON J.A.,INCENTIVES IN THE NEW INDUSTRIAL ORDER. USA-45 NAT/G PAY COST EFFICIENCY PRODUC WEALTH ...MAJORIT PSY SOC/WK 20. PAGE 60 F1186
INDUS LABOR INCOME OPTIMAL

B24
CLARK J.B.,THE DISTRIBUTION OF WEALTH (1899). WORKER OWN PRODUC PROFIT WEALTH LAISSEZ...IDEA/COMP
ECO/TAC INDUS

GEN/LAWS. PAGE 25 F0478 LABOR INCOME

B30
BEVERIDGE W.H.,UNEMPLOYMENT: A PROBLEM OF INDUSTRY (1909-1930). USA-45 LAW ECO/DEV MARKET DELIB/GP WAR DEMAND INCOME...POLICY STAT CHARTS 20. PAGE 14 F0274 WORKER ECO/TAC GEN/LAWS

B32
THOMPSON C.D.,CONFESSIONS OF THE POWER TRUST. MARKET ACT/RES EDU/PROP CONTROL GOV/REL INCOME OWN ...MGT 20 FTC MONOPOLY. PAGE 130 F2564 LG/CO SERV/IND PWR FINAN

B35
HICKS J.R.,THE THEORY OF WAGES. INDUS NAT/G PAY PRICE CONTROL COST EFFICIENCY WEALTH 19/20 MARSHALL/A CLARK/JB. PAGE 59 F1164 INCOME WORKER LABOR PRODUC

B35
KEYNES J.M.,THE GENERAL THEORY OF EMPLOYMENT, INTEREST, AND MONEY. AGRI INDUS WORKER ECO/TAC DEMAND EQUILIB INCOME PRODUC PROFIT ATTIT WEALTH 20. PAGE 71 F1386 FINAN GEN/LAWS MARKET PRICE

B35
MARX K.,WAGE-LABOR AND CAPITAL -- VALUE, PRICE AND PROFIT. LABOR PAY PRICE COST INCOME OWN PROFIT WEALTH 19. PAGE 86 F1690 STRATA WORKER MARXIST MARXISM

B35
WADE J.,HISTORY OF THE MIDDLE AND WORKING CLASSES; WITH A POPULAR EXPOSITION OF THE ECONOMICAL AND POLITICAL PRINCIPLES.... FRANCE UK CONSTN FINAN INDUS LABOR INCOME PROFIT KNOWL MORAL ORD/FREE WEALTH...CHARTS 14/19. PAGE 142 F2797 WORKER STRATA CONCPT

B36
BURNS A.R.,THE DECLINE OF COMPETITION. LAW LG/CO NAT/G SML/CO LEGIS PRICE AGREE CONTROL GP/REL INCOME PRODUC...POLICY 19/20 NRA. PAGE 20 F0390 MARKET GEN/LAWS INDUS

B38
LEVINSON E.,LABOR ON THE MARCH. WORKER CREATE ECO/TAC ADJUD LEAD PARL/PROC PARTIC INGP/REL SKILL POLICY. PAGE 79 F1543 LABOR INCOME NAT/G PLAN

B38
MEADE J.E.,AN INTRODUCTION TO ECONOMIC ANALYSIS AND POLICY (AMERICAN EDITION EDITED BY C.J. HITCH). FINAN INDUS MARKET LABOR INT/TRADE CONTROL COST DEMAND INCOME...CLASSIF CHARTS T 20 KEYNES/JM MONOPOLY. PAGE 89 F1737 CONCPT PROFIT PRODUC

B41
ESTEY J.A.,BUSINESS CYCLES; THEIR NATURE, CAUSE, AND CONTROL. NAT/G BUDGET CAP/ISM TAX PRICE CONTROL INCOME...MODAL TIME/SEQ GEN/METH T 18/20 KEYNES/JM MONEY. PAGE 38 F0749 INDUS FINAN ECO/TAC POLICY

B41
LESTER R.A.,ECONOMICS OF LABOR. UK USA-45 TEC/DEV BARGAIN PAY INGP/REL INCOME...MGT 19/20. PAGE 78 F1532 LABOR ECO/DEV INDUS WORKER

B42
WRIGHT D.M.,THE CREATION OF PURCHASING POWER. USA-45 NAT/G PRICE ADMIN WAR INCOME PRODUC...POLICY CONCPT IDEA/COMP BIBLIOG 20 MONEY. PAGE 149 F2930 FINAN ECO/TAC ECO/DEV CREATE

C43
BENTHAM J.,"THE RATIONALE OF REWARD" IN J. BOWRING, ED., THE WORKS OF JEREMY BENTHAM (VOL. 2)" LAW WORKER CREATE INSPECT PAY ROUTINE HAPPINESS PRODUC SUPEGO WEALTH METH/CNCPT. PAGE 13 F0254 SANCTION ECO/TAC INCOME PWR

B44
LOCKE J.,FURTHER CONSIDERATIONS CONCERNING RAISING THE VALUE OF MONEY. AFR UK NAT/G ECO/TAC INCOME WEALTH...METH/COMP GEN/LAWS 17 SILVER. PAGE 81 F1591 COST FINAN PRICE CONTROL

B45
MILLIS H.A.,ORGANIZED LABOR (FIRST ED.). LAW STRUCT DELIB/GP WORKER ECO/TAC ADJUD CONTROL REPRESENT INGP/REL INCOME MGT. PAGE 92 F1797 LABOR POLICY ROUTINE GP/REL

B47
BAERWALD F.,FUNDAMENTALS OF LABOR ECONOMICS. LAW INDUS LABOR LG/CO CONTROL GP/REL INCOME TOTALISM ...MGT CHARTS GEN/LAWS BIBLIOG 20. PAGE 8 F0150 ECO/DEV WORKER MARKET

B47
SLICHTER S.H.,THE CHALLENGE OF INDUSTRIAL RELATIONS: TRADE UNIONS, MANAGEMENT AND THE PUBLIC INTEREST. PLAN ECO/TAC ADJUD CONTROL LEAD SANCTION GP/REL INGP/REL INCOME. PAGE 123 F2421 LABOR MGT CLIENT POLICY

B48
HICKS J.R.,VALUE AND CAPITAL. FINAN PRICE EQUILIB INCOME PRODUC WEALTH...TIME/SEQ 20 MARSHALL/A PARETO/V SAMUELSN/P. PAGE 59 F1165 ECOMETRIC MATH DEMAND PROB/SOLV

B48
KILE O.M.,THE FARM BUREAU MOVEMENT: THE FARM BUREAU THROUGH THREE DECADES. NAT/G LEGIS LEAD LOBBY GP/REL INCOME POLICY. PAGE 71 F1387 AGRI STRUCT VOL/ASSN DOMIN

B48
METZLER L.A.,INCOME, EMPLOYMENT, AND PUBLIC POLICY. FINAN INDUS LOC/G NAT/G TAX GIVE PAY COST PRODUC ...MGT TIME/SEQ 20. PAGE 90 F1765 INCOME WEALTH POLICY ECO/TAC

B48
NOYES C.R.,ECONOMIC MAN IN RELATION TO HIS NATURAL ENVIRONMENT (2 VOLS.). UNIV COST DEMAND EFFICIENCY HAPPINESS INCOME PRODUC PROFIT HEREDITY...CHARTS BIBLIOG. PAGE 99 F1944 HABITAT METH/CNCPT GEN/METH

B48
ROBERTSON D.H.,MONEY. AFR ECO/DEV NAT/G DIPLOM INT/TRADE BAL/PAY INCOME WEALTH...TIME/SEQ 20 DEPRESSION. PAGE 112 F2212 FINAN MARKET COST PRICE

B48
TAYLOR P.E.,THE ECONOMICS OF PUBLIC FINANCE. USA+45 USA-45 ECO/DEV WORKER PLAN BUDGET WAR INCOME WEALTH ...CONCPT STAT BIBLIOG 20. PAGE 129 F2540 FINAN POLICY NAT/G TAX

S48
CLEVELAND A.S.,"NAM: SPOKESMAN FOR INDUSTRY?" LEGIS PLAN LEAD LOBBY PARTIC CONSEN INCOME ATTIT ROLE ORD/FREE POLICY. PAGE 25 F0491 VOL/ASSN CLIENT REPRESENT INDUS

B49
SCHULTZ W.J.,AMERICAN PUBLIC FINANCE. USA+45 ECO/TAC TAX ADMIN GOV/REL GP/REL INCOME 20. PAGE 117 F2318 FINAN POLICY ECO/DEV NAT/G

B49
SHISTER J.,ECONOMICS OF THE LABOR MARKET. LOC/G NAT/G WORKER TEC/DEV BARGAIN PAY PRICE EXEC GP/REL INCOME...MGT T 20. PAGE 121 F2381 MARKET LABOR INDUS

B50
SHAW E.S.,MONEY, INCOME, AND MONETARY POLICY. AFR USA-45 NAT/G DIPLOM PAY CONTROL COST INCOME PRODUC WEALTH...T 20 FED/RESERV DEPT/TREAS. PAGE 120 F2370 FINAN ECO/TAC ECO/DEV PRICE

B51
CHANDLER L.V.,INFLATION IN THE UNITED STATES 1940-1948. AFR NAT/G BUDGET PAY PRICE CONTROL WAR INCOME PRODUC...POLICY BIBLIOG 20. PAGE 23 F0448 ECO/TAC FINAN PROB/SOLV WEALTH

B51
POOLE K.,FISCAL POLICIES AND THE AMERICAN ECONOMY. AFR ECO/DEV FINAN INDUS WORKER OP/RES INT/TRADE TAX COST INCOME PROFIT WEALTH...GP/COMP 20. PAGE 107 F2102 NAT/G POLICY ANTHOL

B52
AYRES C.E.,THE INDUSTRIAL ECONOMY. USA+45 FINAN MARKET NAT/G PUB/INST PLAN ECO/TAC TAX DEMAND INCOME...BIBLIOG/A 20. PAGE 8 F0146 ECO/DEV INDUS FUT PROB/SOLV

B52
DE JOUVENEL B.,THE ETHICS OF REDISTRIBUTION. UK ELITES MARKET WORKER GIVE PAY INCOME PERSON ...POLICY PSY GEN/LAWS 20. PAGE 31 F0602 WEALTH TAX SOCISM TRADIT

B52
GALBRAITH J.K.,AMERICAN CAPITALISM: THE CONCEPT OF COUNTERVAILING POWER. AFR FUT USA+45 FINAN PRICE CENTRAL INCOME PEACE WEALTH...POLICY DECISION 20. PAGE 45 F0881 ECO/TAC CAP/ISM TREND NAT/G

S52
HEBERLE R.,"ON POLITICAL ECOLOGY" (BMR)" INCOME ATTIT WEALTH...GEOG METH SOC/INTEG 20. PAGE 58 F1133 HABITAT STRATA CHOOSE

S52
PHILLIPS C.,"THE HIGH COST OF OUR LOW-PAID CONGRESS" (NYT MAG. 2/24/52)" USA+45 FINAN WRITING TASK TIME CONGRESS. PAGE 106 F2082 LEGIS INCOME COST EFFICIENCY

C52
HUME D.,"OF TAXES" IN D. HUME, POLITICAL DISCOURSES (1752)" UK NAT/G COST INCOME LAISSEZ...GEN/LAWS 18. PAGE 63 F1236 TAX FINAN WEALTH POLICY

C52
HUME D.,"OF INTEREST" IN D. HUME, POLITICAL DISCOURSES (1752)" UK INDUS WORKER DIPLOM PAY DEMAND INCOME WEALTH...GEN/LAWS 18 MONEY. PAGE 63 F1239 PRICE COST FINAN INT/TRADE

B53
BURNS A.E.,MODERN ECONOMICS. UNIV ECO/DEV INT/TRADE PRICE INCOME WEALTH...POLICY CHARTS T 20 KEYNES/JM. PAGE 20 F0389 NAT/G ECO/TAC FINAN

B53
NEISSER H.,NATIONAL INCOMES AND INTERNATIONAL TRADE. FRANCE GERMANY SWEDEN UK USA-45 EXTR/IND FINAN INDUS TEC/DEV PRICE BAL/PAY EQUILIB INCOME WEALTH...CHARTS METH 19 CHINJAP. PAGE 97 F1908 INT/TRADE PRODUC MARKET CON/ANAL

B54
MEYER F.V.,INFLATION AND CAPITAL. AFR UK WOR+45 BUDGET GOV/REL INCOME PRODUC PROFIT WEALTH...CONCPT ECO/DEV FINAN

CHARTS 20. PAGE 90 F1768 ECO/TAC
DEMAND

B55
BOULDING K.E.,ECONOMIC ANALYSIS (3RD ED.). USA+45 PHIL/SCI
PLAN ECO/TAC COST DEMAND INCOME...POLICY STAT ECO/DEV
CHARTS SIMUL T. PAGE 17 F0322 CAP/ISM

B55
GEORGE H.,PROGRESS AND POVERTY (1880). STRATA ECO/DEV
STRUCT INDUS TEC/DEV CAP/ISM EQUILIB INCOME OWN ECO/TAC
UTOPIA...WELF/ST CONCPT NEW/IDEA 19. PAGE 47 F0915 TAX
WEALTH

B56
YUAN TUNG-LI,ECONOMIC AND SOCIAL DEVELOPMENT OF BIBLIOG
MODERN CHINA: A BIBLIOGRAPHIC GUIDE. COM/IND FINAN ASIA
FAM LABOR SECT CRIME INCOME...STAT SAMP CON/ANAL. ECO/UNDEV
PAGE 150 F2954 SOC

S56
SPENGLER J.J.,"POPULATION THREATENS PROSPERITY" CENSUS
(BMR)" WOR+45 SOCIETY FINAN RATION COST INCOME GEOG
...SOC CHARTS 20 RESOURCE/N. PAGE 124 F2451 WEALTH
TREND

B57
ASSN U BUREAUS BUS-ECO RES,INDEX OF PUBLICATIONS OF BIBLIOG
BUREAUS OF BUSINESS AND ECONOMIC RESEARCH 1950-56 ECO/DEV
AND YEARLY SUPPLEMENTS THROUGH 1967. FINAN OP/RES ECO/TAC
PLAN GOV/REL INCOME AGE...POLICY 20. PAGE 7 F0133 LG/CO

B57
BAUER P.T.,THE ECONOMICS OF UNDERDEVELOPED ECO/UNDEV
COUNTRIES. WOR+45 AGRI FINAN INDUS PROC/MFG WORKER ECO/TAC
CAP/ISM PAY PRICE INCOME MARXISM...METH/COMP 20 PROB/SOLV
RESOURCE/N. PAGE 11 F0213 NAT/G

B57
DAY A.C.L.,OUTLINE OF MONETARY ECONOMICS. AFR FINAN
WOR-45 INT/ORG WORKER DIPLOM BAL/PAY COST INCOME NAT/G
WEALTH...TIME/SEQ SIMUL 20. PAGE 31 F0594 EQUILIB
PRICE

B57
DUNLOP J.T.,THE THEORY OF WAGE DETERMINATION; PRICE
PROCEEDINGS OF CONFERENCE HELD BY INTERNATIONAL WORKER
ECONOMIC ASSOCIATION. AFR ECO/DEV LABOR BARGAIN PAY GEN/LAWS
CONFER...CHARTS ANTHOL 20. PAGE 35 F0679 INCOME

B57
HARWOOD E.C.,CAUSE AND CONTROL OF THE BUSINESS PRODUC
CYCLE (5TH ED.). AFR USA-45 PRICE CONTROL WAR MARKET
DEMAND INCOME WEALTH...TREND CHARTS 19. PAGE 56 FINAN
F1107

B57
OLIVER H.M. JR.,ECONOMIC OPINION AND POLICY IN ECO/UNDEV
CEYLON. CEYLON FINAN POL/PAR WORKER INT/TRADE NAT/LISM
INCOME WEALTH...GEOG UNPLAN/INT BIBLIOG 20 POLICY
CMN/WLTH. PAGE 101 F1987 COLONIAL

B57
SINGH D.B.,INFLATIONARY PRICE TRENDS IN INDIA SINCE BUDGET
1939. AFR INDIA ECO/TAC RATION CONTROL WAR GOV/REL ECO/UNDEV
BAL/PAY DEMAND INCOME PEACE PRODUC...POLICY CHARTS PRICE
20. PAGE 122 F2413 FINAN

B57
THOMAS R.G.,OUR MODERN BANKING AND MONETARY SYSTEM FINAN
(3RD ED.). AFR USA+45 USA-45 ACT/RES PLAN PROB/SOLV SERV/IND
INT/TRADE PRICE WAR BAL/PAY INCOME...POLICY ECO/TAC
METH/CNCPT 20 DEPRESSION. PAGE 130 F2563

B58
DEFENSE AGAINST INFLATION. USA+45 LEGIS WORKER TAX ECO/TAC
PRICE DEMAND INCOME PRODUC...POLICY TREND METH/COMP EQUILIB
20 GOLD/STAND. PAGE 1 F0012 WEALTH
PROB/SOLV

B58
AVRAMOVIC D.,POSTWAR GROWTH IN INTERNATIONAL INT/TRADE
INDEBTEDNESS. AFR WOR+45 AGRI INDUS CAP/ISM PRICE FINAN
INCOME...NAT/COMP 20 SILVER. PAGE 8 F0143 COST
BAL/PAY

B58
BARRERE A.,POLITIQUE FINANCIERE. FRANCE BUDGET FINAN
ECO/TAC TAX BAL/PAY INCOME PRODUC...MGT BIBLIOG T NAT/G
20. PAGE 10 F0193 PLAN

B58
BROWN B.,INCOME TRENDS IN THE UNITED STATES THROUGH STAT
1975. USA+45 NAT/G WEALTH...GEOG CENSUS PREDICT INCOME
CHARTS METH 20. PAGE 19 F0366 TREND
TAX

B58
COALE A.J.,POPULATION GROWTH AND ECONOMIC ECO/UNDEV
DEVELOPMENT IN LOW-INCOME COUNTRIES: A CASE STUDY GEOG
OF INDIA'S PROSPECTS. INDIA AGRI WORKER INCOME AGE CENSUS
WEALTH...CHARTS 20 MEXIC/AMER. PAGE 25 F0495 SEX

B58
COLM G.,THE ECONOMY OF THE AMERICAN PEOPLE: WEALTH
PROGRESS, PROBLEMS, PROSPECTS. USA+45 INDUS MARKET PRODUC
LABOR TEC/DEV INCOME 20. PAGE 26 F0509 CAP/ISM
MGT

B58
DAVIS E.H.,OF THE PEOPLE, BY THE PEOPLE, FOR THE FINAN
PEOPLE. INCOME WEALTH...METH/COMP MUNICH 20. LOC/G
PAGE 30 F0587 TAX

B58
DUESENBERRY J.S.,BUSINESS CYCLES AND ECONOMIC FINAN
GROWTH. USA+45 PROB/SOLV PAY PRICE...CONCPT MATH ECO/DEV
CHARTS IDEA/COMP 20 DEPRESSION KEYNES/JM. PAGE 34 ECO/TAC
F0672 INCOME

B58
MOULTON H.G.,CAN INFLATION BE CONTROLLED? ECO/DEV ECO/TAC
INDUS CAP/ISM RATION GOV/REL COST INCOME PEACE CONTROL
WEALTH...CHARTS TIME 20 KEYNES/JM MONEY. PAGE 94 DEMAND
F1847 FINAN

B58
SHAW S.J.,THE FINANCIAL AND ADMINISTRATIVE FINAN
ORGANIZATION AND DEVELOPMENT OF OTTOMAN EGYPT ADMIN
1517-1798. UAR LOC/G FORCES BUDGET INT/TRADE TAX GOV/REL
EATING INCOME WEALTH...CHARTS BIBLIOG 16/18 OTTOMAN CULTURE
NAPOLEON/B. PAGE 120 F2371

B58
US CONGRESS JOINT ECO COMM,THE RELATIONSHIP OF ECO/DEV
PRICES TO ECONOMIC STABILITY AND GROWTH. USA+45 PLAN
MARKET TAX ADJUST COST DEMAND INCOME PRODUC EQUILIB
...POLICY TREND CHARTS ANTHOL 20 CONGRESS. PAGE 134 PRICE
F2650

B58
WARNER A.W.,CONCEPTS AND CASES IN ECONOMIC ECO/TAC
ANALYSIS. PROB/SOLV BARGAIN CONTROL INCOME PRODUC DEMAND
...ECOMETRIC MGT CONCPT CLASSIF CHARTS 20 EQUILIB
KEYNES/JM. PAGE 143 F2820 COST

S58
JOHNSON D.G.,"GOVERNMENT AND AGRICULTURE: IS INDUS
AGRICULTURE A SPECIAL CASE?" PLAN ECO/TAC LOBBY GP/REL
WEALTH POLICY. PAGE 67 F1321 INCOME
NAT/G

B59
BLACK J.D.,ECONOMICS FOR AGRICULTURE. USA+45 AGRI
EXTR/IND FAM WORKER ACT/RES PLAN PRICE EATING ECO/TAC
INCOME...CENSUS BIBLIOG 20. PAGE 15 F0291 MARKET
POLICY

B59
KOREAN MINISTRY RECONSTRUCTION,KOREAN ECONOMY AND FOR/AID
ITS REQUIREMENTS. KOREA USA+45 ECO/TAC EQUILIB WAR
INCOME WEALTH...CHARTS 20. PAGE 73 F1427 FINAN
DIPLOM

B59
LI CHOH-MING,ECONOMIC DEVELOPMENT OF COMMUNIST ECO/UNDEV
CHINA. ASIA CHINA/COM AGRI FINAN TAX INCOME MARXISM INDUS
...MGT 20. PAGE 80 F1557 ORD/FREE
TEC/DEV

B59
SHACKLE G.L.S.,ECONOMICS FOR PLEASURE. FINAN MARKET METH/CNCPT
NAT/G WORKER PLAN INT/TRADE TARIFFS PAY BAL/PAY WEALTH
COST PRODUC 20. PAGE 120 F2361 INCOME

B59
SHUBIK M.,STRATEGY AND MARKET STRUCTURE: ECO/DEV
COMPETITION, OLIGOPOLY, AND THE THEORY OF GAMES. ECO/TAC
ELITES STRUCT MARKET OP/RES EXEC EFFICIENCY INCOME DECISION
...MGT MATH STAT CHARTS 20. PAGE 121 F2389 GAME

B59
STANFORD U, BOARD OF TRUSTEES,THE ALLOCATION OF INCOME
ECONOMIC RESOURCES. WORKER PLAN BUDGET ECO/TAC TAX PRICE
RECEIVE COST PRODUC...POLICY IDEA/COMP SIMUL ANTHOL FINAN
20. PAGE 125 F2468

S59
ALLEN G.,"NATIONAL FARMERS UNION AS A PRESSURE DIST/IND
GROUP: II." UK ECO/DEV MARKET POL/PAR DELIB/GP AGRI
PROB/SOLV ECO/TAC LOBBY INCOME...POLICY METH/COMP PROF/ORG
19/20 NAT/FARMER. PAGE 4 F0069 TREND

S59
CLONER A.,"THE CALIFORNIA LEGISLATOR AND THE INCOME
PROBLEM OF COMPENSATION." USA+45 WORKER REPRESENT. PROVS
PAGE 25 F0492 LEGIS
SUPEGO

B60
BAERWALD F.,ECONOMIC SYSTEM ANALYSIS: CONCEPTS AND ACT/RES
PERSPECTIVES. USA+45 ECO/DEV NAT/G COMPUTER EQUILIB ECO/TAC
INCOME ATTIT...DECISION CONCPT IDEA/COMP. PAGE 8 ROUTINE
F0151 FINAN

B60
BIERMAN H.,THE CAPITAL BUDGETING DECISION. AFR FINAN
ECO/DEV MARKET TAX PRICE RISK COST INCOME TIME 20. OPTIMAL
PAGE 15 F0282 BUDGET
PROFIT

B60
COPLAND D.,THE ADVENTURE OF GROWTH: ESSAYS ON THE ECO/DEV
AUSTRALIAN ECONOMY AND ITS INTERNATIONAL SETTING. ECO/UNDEV
WOR+45 DIST/IND ACADEM EDU/PROP ADMIN INCOME 20 ECO/TAC
AUSTRAL. PAGE 27 F0534 INT/TRADE

B60
FIRESTONE J.M.,FEDERAL RECEIPTS AND EXPENDITURES FINAN
DURING BUSINESS CYCLES, 1879-1958. USA+45 USA-45 INCOME
INDUS PLAN ECO/TAC TAX WAR COST...CHARTS 19/20. BUDGET
PAGE 41 F0801 NAT/G

B60
GONZALEZ NAVARRO M.,LA COLONIZACION EN MEXICO, ECO/UNDEV
1877-1910. AGRI NAT/G PLAN PROB/SOLV INCOME GEOG
...POLICY JURID CENSUS 19/20 MEXIC/AMER MIGRATION. HABITAT
PAGE 48 F0947 COLONIAL

B60
HALL C.A. JR.,FISCAL POLICY FOR STABLE GROWTH. ECO/TAC

USA+45 FINAN TEC/DEV TAX COST DEMAND INCOME ...BIBLIOG 20. PAGE 53 F1045
BUDGET NAT/G POLICY

B60
HARBRECHT P.P.,TOWARD THE PARAPROPRIETAL SOCIETY. REPRESENT INCOME OWN PROFIT AGE/O. PAGE 55 F1076
PWR ADMIN ELITES CONTROL

B60
MARSHALL A.H.,FINANCIAL ADMINISTRATION IN LOCAL GOVERNMENT. UK DELIB/GP CONFER COST INCOME PERSON ...JURID 20. PAGE 86 F1679
FINAN LOC/G BUDGET ADMIN

B60
OEEC,STATISTICS OF SOURCES AND USES OF FINANCE. NAT/G CAP/ISM TAX PRICE COST 20 OEEC. PAGE 101 F1978
FINAN PRODUC INCOME NAT/COMP

B60
PETERSON W.C.,THE WELFARE STATE IN FRANCE. EUR+WWI FRANCE FUT STRATA PROB/SOLV TAX GIVE RECEIVE INCOME ORD/FREE PWR...CHARTS 20. PAGE 105 F2070
NEW/LIB ECO/TAC WEALTH NAT/G

B60
SHANNON D.A.,THE GREAT DEPRESSION. USA-45 FINAN LG/CO SCHOOL SML/CO DELIB/GP RECEIVE REV EATING INCOME...ANTHOL MUNICH 20 ROOSEVLT/F CONGRESS. PAGE 120 F2365
WEALTH NAT/G AGRI INDUS

B60
SIEGEL B.N.,AGGREGATE ECONOMICS AND PUBLIC POLICY. ECO/DEV TEC/DEV ECO/TAC TASK DEMAND EQUILIB INCOME ...CHARTS 20. PAGE 121 F2396
ECOMETRIC WEALTH PRODUC MARKET

B60
THE ECONOMIST (LONDON),THE COMMONWEALTH AND EUROPE. EUR+WWI WOR+45 AGRI FINAN INCOME...STAT CENSUS CHARTS CMN/WLTH EEC. PAGE 129 F2550
INT/TRADE INDUS INT/ORG NAT/COMP

B61
ACKLEY G.,MACROECONOMIC THEORY. AFR FINAN WORKER ECO/TAC PRICE COST INCOME PRODUC...MATH TREND CHARTS IDEA/COMP T KEYNES/JM. PAGE 2 F0034
SIMUL ECOMETRIC WEALTH

B61
ASCHHEIM J.,TECHNIQUES OF MONETARY CONTROL. UK USA+45 CONTROL WAR DEMAND INCOME WEALTH...TREND CHARTS 20 MONEY. PAGE 7 F0127
FINAN MARKET BUDGET CENTRAL

B61
BREWIS T.N.,CANADIAN ECONOMIC POLICY. AFR CANADA BUDGET CAP/ISM INT/TRADE RATION TARIFFS TAX PRICE CONTROL ROUTINE FEDERAL INCOME PRODUC 20. PAGE 18 F0348
ECO/DEV ECO/TAC NAT/G PLAN

B61
GALENSON W.,TRADE UNION DEMOCRACY IN WESTERN EUROPE. ECO/DEV INDUS PROF/ORG WORKER INCOME ...METH/COMP 20. PAGE 45 F0886
LABOR GP/REL ECO/TAC EUR+WWI

B61
LETHBRIDGE H.J.,CHINA'S URBAN COMMUNES. CHINA/COM FUT ECO/UNDEV DIPLOM EDU/PROP DEMAND INCOME MARXISM ...POLICY MUNICH 20. PAGE 78 F1534
CONTROL ECO/TAC NAT/G

B61
LIEFMANN-KEIL E.,OKONOMISCHE THEORIE DER SOZIALPOLITIK. INT/ORG LABOR WORKER COST INCOME NEW/LIB...CONCPT SOC/INTEG 20. PAGE 80 F1562
ECO/DEV INDUS NAT/G SOC/WK

B61
PAUNIO J.J.,A STUDY IN THE THEORY OF OPEN INFLATION. AFR FINAN CAP/ISM PRICE DEMAND INCOME ...CHARTS BIBLIOG 20. PAGE 104 F2040
ACT/RES ECO/DEV ECO/TAC COST

B61
PROUDHON P.J.,LA GUERRE ET LA PAIX (2 VOLS.). UNIV STRATA PROB/SOLV EQUILIB INCOME ATTIT...CONCPT 19. PAGE 108 F2125
WAR PEACE WEALTH

B61
SLICHTER S.H.,ECONOMIC GROWTH IN THE UNITED STATES. FUT USA+45 USA-45 LABOR PAY INCOME PRODUC...MGT 19/20. PAGE 123 F2422
ECO/DEV TEC/DEV CAP/ISM DEMAND

B61
SPOONER F.P.,SOUTH AFRICAN PREDICAMENT. FUT SOUTH/AFR INDUS POL/PAR RACE/REL INCOME...CHARTS 20 NEGRO. PAGE 125 F2459
ECO/DEV DISCRIM ECO/TAC POLICY

B61
WAGLE S.S.,TECHNIQUE OF PLANNING FOR ACCELERATED ECONOMIC GROWTH OF UNDERDEVELOPED COUNTRIES. WOR+45 ACT/RES PROB/SOLV RATION BAL/PAY DEMAND INCOME 20. PAGE 142 F2798
ECO/UNDEV PLAN INDUS ECO/TAC

S61
OCHENG D.,"ECONOMIC FORCES AND UGANDA'S FOREIGN POLICY." AFR UGANDA INT/TRADE TARIFFS INCOME SOVEREIGN WEALTH 20 EACM EEC TANGANYIKA. PAGE 100 F1961
ECO/TAC DIPLOM ECO/UNDEV INT/ORG

B62
ARNOLD T.W.,THE FOLKLORE OF CAPITALISM. USA+45 USA-45 SOCIETY LG/CO SML/CO EX/STRUC ECO/TAC EDU/PROP ADJUST INCOME...MYTH CHARTS 20. PAGE 6 F0116
CAP/ISM ATTIT STERTYP ECO/DEV

B62
CHRISTENSON C.L.,ECONOMIC REDEVELOPMENT IN BITUMINOUS COAL: THE SPECIAL CASE OF TECHNOLOGICAL ADVANCE IN US COAL MINES 1930-1960. USA+45 USA-45 ECO/TAC AUTOMAT INCOME PRODUC...CHARTS 20. PAGE 24 F0471
EXTR/IND LABOR TEC/DEV ECO/DEV

B62
DE LAVALLE H.,A STATEMENT OF THE LAWS OF PERU IN MATTERS AFFECTING BUSINESS (3RD ED.). PERU WORKER INT/TRADE INCOME ORD/FREE...INT/LAW 20. PAGE 31 F0603
CONSTN JURID FINAN TAX

B62
FRIEDMAN M.,CAPITALISM AND FREEDOM. USA+45 FINAN LG/CO WORKER INT/TRADE RECEIVE EDU/PROP CONTROL DISCRIM INCOME WEALTH POLICY. PAGE 44 F0859
CAP/ISM ORD/FREE NAT/G ECO/DEV

B62
HARRINGTON M.,THE OTHER AMERICA: POVERTY IN THE UNITED STATES. WORKER CREATE REPRESENT RACE/REL AGE/O DRIVE POLICY. PAGE 55 F1086
WEALTH WELF/ST INCOME CULTURE

B62
HOLMAN A.G.,SOME MEASURES AND INTERPRETATIONS OF EFFECTS OF US FOREIGN ENTERPRISES ON US BALANCE OF PAYMENTS. USA+45 COST INCOME WEALTH...MATH CHARTS 20. PAGE 61 F1199
BAL/PAY INT/TRADE FINAN ECO/TAC

B62
HOOVER E.M.,ANATOMY OF A METROPOLIS. FUT USA+45 SOCIETY ECO/DEV DIST/IND INDUS WORKER ECO/TAC TAX GP/REL COST WEALTH MUNICH 20 NEWYORK/C. PAGE 62 F1212
ROUTINE TREND INCOME

B62
KOLKO G.,WEALTH AND POWER IN AMERICA. USA+45 SOCIETY STRATA LG/CO ECO/TAC TAX PWR...SOC BIBLIOG 20 DEPRESSION. PAGE 72 F1420
STRUCT INCOME ECO/DEV WEALTH

B62
MICHAELY M.,CONCENTRATION IN INTERNATIONAL TRADE. ECO/DEV ECO/UNDEV PRICE INCOME...CHARTS NAT/COMP 20. PAGE 91 F1779
INT/TRADE MARKET FINAN GEOG

B62
MORGAN C.A.,LABOR ECONOMICS. LAW INDUS MARKET WORKER PLAN PROB/SOLV GOV/REL INCOME ROLE...T 20 DEPT/LABOR NLRB. PAGE 93 F1829
LABOR ECO/TAC ECO/DEV CAP/ISM

B62
ROBINSON M.A.,AN INTRODUCTION TO ECONOMIC REASONING. FINAN MARKET LABOR DIPLOM INT/TRADE BAL/PAY INCOME PRODUC WEALTH...POLICY MGT 20. PAGE 113 F2223
ECO/TAC METH/CNCPT NAT/G

B62
SCHNEIDER E.,MONEY, INCOME AND EMPLOYMENT. TAX PAY DEMAND...CHARTS BIBLIOG 20. PAGE 117 F2305
ECO/DEV FINAN INCOME

B62
SHINOHARA M.,GROWTH AND CYCLES IN THE JAPANESE ECONOMY. INDUS LABOR TEC/DEV CAP/ISM INT/TRADE PAY COST EFFICIENCY INCOME WEALTH...METH/COMP 20 CHINJAP. PAGE 121 F2380
PRODUC ECO/DEV EQUILIB ECOMETRIC

B62
TIEBOUT C.M.,THE COMMUNITY ECONOMIC BASE STUDY (PAMPHLET). USA+45 ECO/TAC LEAD DEMAND HABITAT 20. PAGE 130 F2572
NEIGH INCOME ACT/RES

B62
VANEK J.,THE BALANCE OF PAYMENTS, LEVEL OF ECONOMIC ACTIVITY AND THE VALUE OF CURRENCY: THEORY AND SOME RECENT EXPERIENCES. UNIV PRICE INCOME...MATH 20 KEYNES/JM. PAGE 140 F2766
BAL/PAY ECO/TAC FINAN GEN/LAWS

B62
WRIGHT D.M.,THE KEYNESIAN SYSTEM. WOR+45 WOR-45 LABOR NAT/G CONTROL COST DEMAND EFFICIENCY...POLICY CONCPT CHARTS SIMUL 20 KEYNES/JM. PAGE 149 F2931
INCOME ECO/DEV FINAN ECO/TAC

L62
SCHULTZ T.W.,"INVESTMENT IN HUMAN BEINGS." ECO/DEV ECO/TAC CONFER COST INCOME PRODUC HEALTH...GEOG ANTHOL. PAGE 117 F2315
FINAN WORKER EDU/PROP SKILL

S62
GILL P.J.,"FUTURE TAXATION POLICY IN AN INDEPENDENT EAST AFRICA" UGANDA LOC/G ECO/TAC ADMIN EFFICIENCY INCOME PRODUC...CHARTS 20. PAGE 47 F0923
ECO/UNDEV TAX AFR COLONIAL

N62
BANK INTERNATIONAL SETTLEMENTS,AUSTRIA: MONETARY AND ECONOMIC SITUATION 1952-61 (PAMPHLET). AUSTRIA WORKER BUDGET INT/TRADE PRICE BAL/PAY DEMAND EFFICIENCY INCOME PRODUC...STAT 20 SILVER. PAGE 9 F0174
FINAN ECO/DEV CHARTS WEALTH

B63
BANERJI A.K.,INDIA'S BALANCE OF PAYMENTS. INDIA NAT/G PRICE BAL/PAY COST INCOME 20. PAGE 9 F0171 — INT/TRADE DIPLOM FINAN BUDGET

B63
COSSA L.,SAGGI BIBLIOGRAFICI DI ECONOMIA POLITICA. MOD/EUR LABOR PRICE COST INCOME 18/19. PAGE 28 F0539 — BIBLIOG FINAN WEALTH

B63
COURNOT A.A.,RESEARCHES INTO THE MATHEMATICAL PRINCIPLES OF THE THEORY OF WEALTH (1838). UNIV ECO/DEV ECO/UNDEV AGRI INDUS MARKET PAY CONTROL COST INCOME 19. PAGE 28 F0544 — ECOMETRIC GEN/LAWS WEALTH

B63
GORDON M.S.,THE ECONOMICS OF WELFARE POLICIES. INDUS LOC/G NAT/G LEGIS WORKER INCOME AGE/O SKILL WEALTH...METH/COMP NAT/COMP 20. PAGE 49 F0959 — METH/CNCPT ECO/TAC POLICY

B63
INTERNATIONAL ASSOCIATION RES,AFRICAN STUDIES IN INCOME AND WEALTH. AFR NAT/G PROB/SOLV DEMAND INCOME...ECOMETRIC METH/COMP 20. PAGE 64 F1270 — WEALTH PLAN ECO/UNDEV BUDGET

B63
LUTZ F.A.,DAS PROBLEM DES INTERNATIONALEN WIRTSCHAFTLICHEN GLEICHGEWICHTS. DIPLOM INT/TRADE COST INCOME 20. PAGE 82 F1612 — FINAN CAP/ISM ECO/TAC PRODUC

B63
MEEK R.L.,THE ECONOMICS OF PHYSIOCRACY. FRANCE UK AGRI FINAN WORKER CAP/ISM TAX DEMAND EQUILIB INCOME HABITAT...CHARTS ANTHOL 17. PAGE 89 F1744 — PRODUC WEALTH MARKET

B63
THEOBALD R.,FREE MEN AND FREE MARKETS. USA+45 USA-45 ECO/DEV NAT/G TEC/DEV DIPLOM INT/TRADE INCOME ORD/FREE WEALTH...TREND 19/20 KEYNES/JM. PAGE 130 F2556 — CONCPT ECO/TAC CAP/ISM MARKET

S63
CLARK P.G.,"TOWARDS MORE COMPREHENSIVE PLANNING IN EAST AFRICA" AFR OP/RES ECO/TAC RATION TAX EFFICIENCY INCOME...MATH TREND CHARTS 20 AFRICA/E. PAGE 25 F0484 — ECO/UNDEV PLAN STAT METH/COMP

S63
REES A.,"THE EFFECTS OF UNIONS ON RESOURCE ALLOCATION." USA+45 WORKER PRICE CONTROL GP/REL ...MGT METH/COMP 20. PAGE 110 F2173 — LABOR BARGAIN RATION INCOME

N63
COMM ON FEDERAL TAX POLICY,FINANCING AMERICA'S FUTURE: TAXES, ECONOMIC STABILITY AND GROWTH (PAMPHLET). USA+45 LG/CO SML/CO DELIB/GP INCOME ...CHARTS 20. PAGE 26 F0513 — TAX NAT/G EQUILIB PLAN

B64
BALL R.J.,INFLATION AND THE THEORY OF MONEY. MARKET TAX PAY PRICE TASK ADJUST BAL/PAY COST INCOME PRODUC WEALTH...METH/COMP 20 KEYNES/JM MONEY. PAGE 9 F0167 — EQUILIB DEMAND POLICY

B64
BEARDSLEY R.K.,STUDIES ON ECONOMIC LIFE IN JAPAN (OCCASIONAL PAPERS NO. 8). INDUS FAM HABITAT...GEOG GOV/COMP 20 CHINJAP. PAGE 12 F0223 — WEALTH PRESS PRODUC INCOME

B64
BOARMAN P.M.,GERMANY'S ECONOMIC DILEMMA - INFLATION AND THE BALANCE OF PAYMENTS. AFR GERMANY/W LABOR CAP/ISM PRICE BAL/PAY COST INCOME 20. PAGE 16 F0302 — ECO/DEV FINAN INT/TRADE BUDGET

B64
BROWN W.M.,THE EXTERNAL LIQUIDITY OF AN ADVANCED COUNTRY. CANADA FRANCE GERMANY/W SWEDEN UK USA+45 ECO/DEV DIPLOM PRICE...CONCPT STAT NAT/COMP 20. PAGE 20 F0376 — FINAN INT/TRADE COST INCOME

B64
FRIEDMANN J.,REGIONAL DEVELOPMENT AND PLANNING: A READER. AGRI MARKET NAT/G ECO/TAC INCOME...GEOG STAT CENSUS CHARTS ANTHOL BIBLIOG MUNICH 20 OPEN/SPACE. PAGE 44 F0863 — PLAN REGION INDUS ECO/DEV

B64
HAGGER A.J.,THE THEORY OF INFLATION. AFR PLAN PROB/SOLV PAY COST INCOME 20. PAGE 53 F1035 — DEMAND TEC/DEV FINAN

B64
HANSEN A.H.,BUSINESS CYCLES AND NATIONAL INCOME. USA+45 FINAN ECO/TAC COST OPTIMAL...POLICY METH 20 KEYNES/JM. PAGE 54 F1065 — INCOME WEALTH PRODUC INDUS

B64
HAZLEWOOD A.,THE ECONOMICS OF DEVELOPMENT: AN ANNOTATED LIST OF BOOKS AND ARTICLES PUBLISHED 1958-1962. AGRI FINAN INDUS LABOR NAT/G DIPLOM INT/TRADE INCOME...MGT 20. PAGE 58 F1130 — BIBLIOG/A ECO/UNDEV TEC/DEV

B64
HERSKOVITS M.J.,ECONOMIC TRANSITION IN AFRICA. FUT INT/ORG NAT/G WORKER PROB/SOLV TEC/DEV INT/TRADE EQUILIB INCOME...ANTHOL 20. PAGE 59 F1157 — AFR ECO/UNDEV PLAN ADMIN

B64
INTERNATIONAL LABOUR OFFICE,EMPLOYMENT AND ECONOMIC GROWTH. ECO/DEV ECO/UNDEV NAT/G PLAN DIPLOM INT/TRADE CONTROL INCOME PRODUC WEALTH...STAT NAT/COMP 20 ILO. PAGE 65 F1279 — WORKER METH/COMP ECO/TAC OPTIMAL

B64
JACOBY N.H.,UNITED STATES MONETARY POLICY. UK USA+45 LAW NAT/G TEC/DEV TAX EQUILIB INCOME ...METH/COMP 20 FED/RESERV. PAGE 66 F1300 — ECO/DEV POLICY ECO/TAC FINAN

B64
KNIGHT R.,BIBLIOGRAPHY ON INCOME AND WEALTH, 1957-1960 (VOL VIII). WOR+45 ECO/DEV FINAN INT/TRADE...GOV/COMP METH/COMP. PAGE 72 F1412 — BIBLIOG/A ECO/UNDEV WEALTH INCOME

B64
LITTLE I.M.D.,AID TO AFRICA. AFR UK TEC/DEV DIPLOM ECO/TAC INCOME WEALTH 20. PAGE 81 F1583 — FOR/AID ECO/UNDEV ADMIN POLICY

B64
ODEH H.S.,THE IMPACT OF INFLATION ON THE LEVEL OF ECONOMIC ACTIVITY. AFR BRAZIL CHILE BUDGET GOV/REL COST DEMAND INCOME WEALTH...STAT METH 20 MONEY. PAGE 100 F1963 — ECOMETRIC ECO/TAC ECO/UNDEV FINAN

B64
TAEUBER I.B.,POPULATION TRENDS IN THE UNITED STATES: 1900 TO 1960. USA+45 USA-45 PROVS INCOME AGE...SOC TIME/SEQ TREND CHARTS MUNICH TIME 20 NEGRO. PAGE 128 F2522 — CENSUS GEOG STRATA STRUCT

B64
TAX S.,EL CAPITALISMO DEL CENTAVO; UNA ECONOMIA INDIGENA DE GUATEMALA (2 VOLS.). GUATEMALA L/A+17C SOCIETY GP/REL DEMAND INCOME HABITAT...SOC MUNICH 20 INDIAN/AM. PAGE 129 F2539 — ECO/UNDEV AGRI WEALTH COST

B64
THAILAND NATIONAL ECO DEV,THE NATIONAL ECONOMIC DEVELOPMENT PLAN: 1961-66: SECOND PHASE 1964-66. THAILAND AGRI FINAN BUDGET EFFICIENCY INCOME...STAT CHARTS 20. PAGE 129 F2547 — ECO/UNDEV ECO/TAC PLAN NAT/G

S64
TOBIN J.,"ECONOMIC GROWTH AS AN OBJECTIVE OF GOVERNMENT POLICY." FUT WOR+45 FINAN WORKER BUDGET INCOME...SOC 20. PAGE 131 F2579 — ECO/DEV POLICY ECO/TAC IDEA/COMP

C64
LOUFTY A.,"LA PLANIFICATION DE L'ECONOMIE." FRANCE USSR FINAN INDUS BUDGET INCOME PRODUC...BIBLIOG 20. PAGE 82 F1604 — PLAN ECO/UNDEV ECO/DEV

B65
COLLOQUE SUR LA PLANIFICATION,LA PLANIFICATION COMME PROCESSUS DE DECISION. FRANCE SOCIETY MARKET LABOR LEGIS GP/REL EFFICIENCY INCOME ATTIT TECHRACY ...MYTH IDEA/COMP 20. PAGE 26 F0508 — PLAN ECO/TAC PROB/SOLV

B65
FORD J.L.,THE OHLIN-HECKSCHER THEORY OF THE BASIS AND EFFECTS OF COMMODITY TRADE. WOR+45 ECO/TAC DEMAND INCOME...CONCPT GEN/METH 20 OHLIN/HECK. PAGE 42 F0824 — ECOMETRIC INT/TRADE NEW/IDEA SIMUL

B65
GOETZ-GIREY R.,LE MOUVEMENT DES GREVES EN FRANCE. FRANCE FINAN OP/RES PROB/SOLV ECO/TAC INCOME HABITAT...STAT CHARTS 19/20. PAGE 48 F0932 — LABOR WORKER GP/REL INDUS

B65
GREEN J.L.,METROPOLITAN ECONOMIC REPUBLICS. USA+45 ECO/TAC INCOME...GEOG SOC CONCPT SIMUL MUNICH 20 ATLANTA. PAGE 50 F0985 — SOC/WK PLAN LABOR

B65
HONDURAS CONSEJO NAC DE ECO,PLAN NACIONAL DE DESARROLLO ECONOMICO Y SOCIAL DE HONDURAS 1965-69. HONDURAS AGRI INDUS BAL/PAY INCOME 20. PAGE 61 F1203 — ECO/UNDEV NAT/G PLAN POLICY

B65
MACESICH G.,COMMERCIAL BANKING AND REGIONAL DEVELOPMENT IN THE US, 1950-1960. USA+45 NAT/G PLAN ECO/TAC DEMAND...MGT 20 FED/RESERV SOUTH/US. PAGE 83 F1627 — FINAN ECO/DEV INCOME COST

B65
OXENFELDT A.R.,ECONOMIC SYSTEMS IN ACTION. FRANCE USA+45 USSR CULTURE PLAN PROB/SOLV TEC/DEV INCOME PRODUC WEALTH...METH/COMP 20. PAGE 102 F2007 — ECO/DEV CAP/ISM MARXISM ECO/TAC

B65
PHELPS E.S.,FISCAL NEUTRALITY TOWARD ECONOMIC GROWTH. FINAN NAT/G BUDGET CAP/ISM CONTROL INCOME 20. PAGE 106 F2080 — ECO/DEV POLICY ECO/TAC TAX

B65
SCHULTZ T.W.,ECONOMIC CRISES IN WORLD AGRICULTURE. ASIA INDIA USSR ECO/DEV ECO/UNDEV INDUS VOL/ASSN CAP/ISM RATION COLONIAL 20. PAGE 117 F2317 — AGRI ECO/TAC INCOME WORKER

B65
SELIGMAN B.B.,POVERTY AS A PUBLIC ISSUE. USA+45 ECO/DEV NAT/G PAY RECEIVE PERS/REL INCOME NEW/LIB — LEGIS ECO/TAC

20. PAGE 119 F2347 STRATA DISCRIM

B65
SHOSTAK A.B.,NEW PERSPECTIVES ON POVERTY. USA+45 SCHOOL WORKER INGP/REL RACE/REL AGE/C AGE/Y ATTIT HEALTH...ANTHOL BIBLIOG 20 JOHNSON/LB POVRTY/WAR. PAGE 121 F2388 WEALTH NAT/G RECEIVE INCOME

B65
TEW B.,WEALTH AND INCOME. UK BUDGET INT/TRADE PRICE BAL/PAY DEMAND...CHARTS GOV/COMP 20 AUSTRAL. PAGE 129 F2546 FINAN ECO/DEV WEALTH INCOME

B65
VANEK J.,GENERAL EQUILIBRIUM OF INTERNATIONAL DISCRIMINATION; THE CASE OF CUSTOMS UNIONS. LABOR PROB/SOLV ECO/TAC DISCRIM INCOME...MATH CHARTS METH 20. PAGE 140 F2767 INT/TRADE TARIFFS INT/ORG EQUILIB

B65
WARD R.J.,INTERNATIONAL FINANCE. INT/ORG DIPLOM DEMAND INCOME...POLICY METH/COMP 20. PAGE 143 F2819 INT/TRADE ECO/TAC FINAN BAL/PAY

B65
WU YUAN-LI,THE ECONOMY OF COMMUNIST CHINA. CHINA/COM USSR AGRI FINAN INDUS POL/PAR WORKER PROB/SOLV INT/TRADE PRICE EATING INCOME OWN WEALTH 20. PAGE 149 F2939 ECO/TAC MARXISM PLAN EFFICIENCY

L65
LOFTUS M.L.,"INTERNATIONAL MONETARY FUND, 1962-1965: A SELECTED BIBLIOGRAPHY." WOR+45 PLAN BUDGET INCOME PROFIT WEALTH. PAGE 81 F1596 BIBLIOG FINAN INT/TRADE INT/ORG

S65
MULLER A.L.,"THE ECONOMIC POSITION OF THE ASIANS IN AFRICA." AFR SOUTH/AFR ECO/UNDEV MARKET ECO/TAC GP/REL INCOME...CHARTS IND 20 MONOPOLY ASIANS. PAGE 95 F1856 WORKER RACE/REL CAP/ISM DISCRIM

B66
ALIBER R.Z.,THE FUTURE OF THE DOLLAR AS AN INTERNATIONAL CURRENCY. AFR USA+45 USA-45 ECO/DEV PRICE COST INCOME...POLICY 20. PAGE 4 F0067 FINAN DIPLOM INT/ORG INT/TRADE

B66
AMER ENTERPRISE INST FOR PUBL,INTERNATIONAL PAYMENTS PROBLEM. MARKET DIPLOM DEBATE PRICE COST INCOME 20. PAGE 4 F0082 FINAN INT/TRADE POLICY

B66
BOWEN H.R.,AUTOMATION AND ECONOMIC PROGRESS. EUR+WWI USA+45 ECO/DEV INCOME ORD/FREE WEALTH ...POLICY ANTHOL 20. PAGE 17 F0327 AUTOMAT TEC/DEV WORKER LEISURE

B66
CHASE S.B. JR.,PROBLEMS IN PUBLIC EXPENDITURE ANALYSIS. DIST/IND INDUS OP/RES PLAN BUDGET RECEIVE PRICE RISK COST INCOME...CHARTS ANTHOL 20. PAGE 23 F0455 ECO/DEV FINAN NAT/G INSPECT

B66
FELLNER W.,MAINTAINING AND RESTORING BALANCE IN INTERNATIONAL PAYMENTS. ECO/UNDEV MARKET ECO/TAC PRICE INCOME WEALTH...POLICY METH/COMP 20 MONEY. PAGE 40 F0781 BAL/PAY DIPLOM FINAN INT/TRADE

B66
HACKETT J.,L'ECONOMIE BRITANNIQUE: PROBLEMES ET PERSPECTIVES. FRANCE UK LABOR NAT/G EX/STRUC PROB/SOLV BAL/PAY INCOME RIGID/FLEX...MGT PHIL/SCI CHARTS MUNICH 20. PAGE 53 F1027 ECO/DEV FINAN ECO/TAC PLAN

B66
HAINES W.W.,MONEY PRICES AND POLICY. WOR+45 ECO/DEV BUDGET CONTROL INCOME...POLICY STAT CHARTS BIBLIOG T 20. PAGE 53 F1039 PRICE FINAN ECO/TAC GOV/REL

B66
HALLER H.,DAS PROBLEM DER GELDWERTSTABILITAT. MARKET LABOR INCOME PRODUC...POLICY 20. PAGE 54 F1049 PRICE COST FINAN ECO/TAC

B66
KUZNETS S.,MODERN ECONOMIC GROWTH. WOR+45 WOR-45 ECO/DEV ECO/UNDEV AGRI FINAN INDUS TEC/DEV EFFICIENCY INCOME...NAT/COMP 19/20. PAGE 74 F1456 TIME/SEQ WEALTH PRODUC

B66
LEE M.W.,TOWARD ECONOMIC STABILITY. USA+45 BUDGET TAX PRICE EQUILIB INCOME. PAGE 77 F1506 ECO/TAC CONTROL POLICY NAT/G

B66
LERNER E.M.,A THEORY OF FINANCIAL ANALYSIS. UNIV LG/CO COST DEMAND INCOME PROFIT...MATH STAT CHARTS SIMUL T 20. PAGE 78 F1531 CONCPT FINAN ECO/DEV OPTIMAL

B66
MURPHY G.G.,SOVIET MONGOLIA: A STUDY OF THE OLDEST POLITICAL SATELLITE. USSR STRATA STRUCT COST INCOME ATTIT SOCISM 20. PAGE 95 F1865 DIPLOM ECO/TAC PLAN DOMIN

B66
NEVITT A.A.,HOUSING, TAXATION AND SUBSIDIES; A STUDY OF HOUSING IN THE UNITED KINGDOM. UK FINAN GIVE CONTROL COST INCOME...CHARTS 20. PAGE 98 F1918 PLAN TAX HABITAT RENT

B66
REDFORD E.S.,THE ROLE OF GOVERNMENT IN THE AMERICAN ECONOMY. USA+45 USA-45 FINAN INDUS LG/CO PROB/SOLV ADMIN INGP/REL INCOME PRODUC 18/20. PAGE 110 F2169 NAT/G ECO/DEV CAP/ISM ECO/TAC

B66
ROSS A.M.,INDUSTRIAL RELATIONS AND ECONOMIC DEVELOPMENT. POL/PAR LEGIS WORKER BARGAIN PRICE EXEC LOBBY INCOME PWR...DECISION ANTHOL BIBLIOG 20. PAGE 114 F2243 ECO/UNDEV LABOR NAT/G GP/REL

B66
SCHNEIDER E.,WIRTSCHAFTSKREISLAUF UND WIRTSCHAFTSWACHSTUM. ECO/DEV MARKET...CONCPT 20 MONEY. PAGE 117 F2306 ECO/TAC FINAN INCOME COST

B66
SHULTZ G.P.,GUIDELINES, INFORMAL CONTROLS, AND THE MARKET PLACE: POLICY CHOICES IN A FULL EMPLOYMENT ECONOMY. UK ECO/DEV LABOR INT/TRADE CONFER GOV/REL BAL/PAY DEMAND INCOME...POLICY ANTHOL 20 PRESIDENT. PAGE 121 F2392 ECO/TAC CONTROL FINAN RATION

B66
SOMMERFELD R.M.,TAX REFORM AND THE ALLIANCE FOR PROGRESS. USA+45 ECO/DEV ECO/UNDEV FINAN NAT/G INCOME ORD/FREE WEALTH...STAT CHARTS 20 ALL/PROG. PAGE 124 F2442 TAX INT/ORG L/A+17C FOR/AID

B66
TURNER H.A.,PRICES, WAGES, AND INCOME POLICIES IN INDUSTRIALIZED MARKET ECONOMIES. AFR WOR+45 ECO/DEV INDUS PROB/SOLV ECO/TAC CONTROL WEALTH...CHARTS 20 INTRVN/ECO. PAGE 131 F2593 PRICE PAY MARKET INCOME

B66
WESTON J.F.,THE SCOPE AND METHODOLOGY OF FINANCE. PLAN TEC/DEV CONTROL EFFICIENCY INCOME UTIL...MGT CONCPT MATH STAT TREND METH 20. PAGE 145 F2863 FINAN ECO/DEV POLICY PRICE

N66
EOMMITTEE ECONOMIC DEVELOPMENT,THE DOLLAR AND THE WORLD MONETARY SYSTEM: A STATEMENT ON NATIONAL POLICY (PAMPHLET). AFR USA+45 NAT/G PLAN PROB/SOLV BUDGET ECO/TAC FOR/AID INCOME...POLICY 20 EUROPE. PAGE 38 F0740 FINAN BAL/PAY DIPLOM ECO/DEV

B67
CARNEY D.,PATTERNS AND MECHANICS OF ECONOMIC GROWTH: A GENERAL THEORETICAL APPROACH. WOR+45 OP/RES INCOME...MATH TREND CHARTS 20. PAGE 21 F0416 PLAN ECO/DEV FINAN

B67
ELSNER H.,THE TECHNOCRATS, PROPHETS OF AUTOMATION. SOCIETY INDUS VOL/ASSN COST INCOME ATTIT 20. PAGE 37 F0726 AUTOMAT TECHRACY PRODUC HIST/WRIT

B67
GREEN C.,NEGATIVE TAXES AND THE POVERTY PROBLEM. COST EFFICIENCY INCOME NEW/LIB...METH/CNCPT CHARTS METH/COMP BIBLIOG 20. PAGE 50 F0983 TAX RECEIVE WEALTH PLAN

B67
SPURRIER R.B.,THE OVERPOPULATED SOCIETY. WORKER EATING PERS/REL DEMAND EQUILIB ILLEGIT INCOME HABITAT 20. PAGE 125 F2461 BIO/SOC FOR/AID DRIVE RECEIVE

B67
US CONGRESS JOINT ECO COMM,REPORT ON JANUARY 1967 ECONOMIC REPORT OF THE PRESIDENT. FINAN LABOR NAT/G LEGIS BUDGET INT/TRADE COST DEMAND INCOME PRODUC ...POLICY IDEA/COMP 20 CONGRESS. PAGE 135 F2663 CHIEF ECO/TAC PLAN DELIB/GP

S67
"IMPORT-EXPORT CLAUSE: A BLANKET PROHIBITION MISAPPLIED." USA+45 INT/TRADE ADJUD INCOME PWR 20. PAGE 2 F0029 CONSTN TAX PROVS LAW

S67
BENNETT J.T.,"POLITICAL IMPLICATIONS OF ECONOMIC CHANGE: SOUTH VIETNAM." VIETNAM/S INGP/REL INCOME ATTIT 20 AID. PAGE 13 F0247 ECO/UNDEV INDUS AGRI PRODUC

S67
DANIEL C.,"FREEDOM, EQUITY, AND THE WAR ON POVERTY." USA+45 WORKER ECO/TAC JURID. PAGE 30 F0578 WEALTH INCOME SOCIETY ORD/FREE

S67
FRANKLIN N.N.,"THE CONCEPT AND MEASUREMENT OF 'MINIMUM LIVING STANDARDS'." UNIV OP/RES PAY INGP/REL DEMAND INCOME DRIVE WEALTH...SOC CHARTS METH/COMP. PAGE 43 F0849 CONCPT PHIL/SCI ALL/VALS HAPPINESS

S67
FUCHS V.R.,"REDEFINING POVERTY AND REDISTRIBUTING INCOME." USA+45 NAT/G ECO/TAC GIVE COST...NEW/IDEA CHARTS. PAGE 45 F0873 WEALTH INCOME STRATA PROB/SOLV

S67
GREEN C.,"SCHEMES FOR TRANSFERRING INCOME TO THE POOR." BUDGET GIVE RECEIVE DEBATE COST INCOME ...SOC/WK METH/COMP. PAGE 50 F0982
TAX WEALTH PLAN ACT/RES

S67
HILDEBRAND G.H.,"SECOND THOUGHTS ON THE NEGATIVE INCOME TAX." PLAN BUDGET ECO/TAC GIVE RECEIVE DEBATE EFFICIENCY INCOME...METH/COMP COSTS. PAGE 59 F1169
TAX WEALTH SOC/WK ACT/RES

S67
JENCKS C.E.,"SOCIAL STATUS OF COAL MINERS IN BRITAIN SINCE NATIONALIZATION." UK STRATA STRUCT LABOR RECEIVE GP/REL INCOME OWN ATTIT HABITAT...MGT T 20. PAGE 67 F1312
EXTR/IND WORKER CONTROL NAT/G

S67
LEDEBUR L.C.,"THE PROBLEM OF SOCIAL COST." STRUCT PROB/SOLV...CHARTS GEN/LAWS. PAGE 77 F1501
COST INCOME SOCIETY ECO/TAC

S67
MALKIN A.,"BUSINESS BOOKS OF 1966." INDUS LABOR OP/RES TEC/DEV CAP/ISM ECO/TAC INCOME WEALTH 20. PAGE 84 F1649
BIBLIOG/A FINAN MARKET

S67
MEADE J.E.,"POPULATION EXPLOSION, THE STANDARD OF LIVING AND SOCIAL CONFLICT." DIPLOM FOR/AID OWN ...PREDICT TREND 20. PAGE 89 F1739
GEOG WEALTH PRODUC INCOME

S67
MEHTA A.,"INDIA* POVERTY AND CHANGE." STRATA INDUS CREATE ECO/TAC FOR/AID NEUTRAL GP/REL ADJUST INCOME ...NEW/IDEA 20. PAGE 89 F1746
INDIA SOCIETY ECO/UNDEV TEC/DEV

S67
MOONEY J.D.,"URBAN POVERTY AND LABOR FORCE PARTICIPATION." FAM DISCRIM...SOC/WK STAT CHARTS MUNICH. PAGE 93 F1820
INCOME WORKER WEALTH

S67
MULLER A.L.,"ECONOMIC GROWTH AND MINORITIES." USA+45 SKILL...SOC GP/COMP NEGRO. PAGE 95 F1857
INCOME WORKER ECO/DEV RACE/REL

S67
PAI G.A.,"TAXATION AND PLANNING IN INDIA: A BIRDS-EYE VIEW." INDIA ELITES NAT/G LEGIS BUDGET CONTROL LOBBY INCOME...STAT CHARTS 20. PAGE 102 F2015
TAX PLAN WEALTH STRATA

S67
PAULY M.V.,"MIXED PUBLIC AND PRIVATE FINANCING OF EDUCATION." STRATA PAY RECEIVE COST INCOME OPTIMAL METH/COMP. PAGE 104 F2039
SCHOOL PLAN TAX EFFICIENCY

S67
ROY E.V.,"AN INTERPRETATION OF NORTHERN THAI PEASANT ECONOMY." THAILAND CLIENT CULTURE AGRI PROC/MFG FACE/GP DEMAND INCOME 20. PAGE 114 F2254
STRUCT STRATA ECO/UNDEV INGP/REL

S67
SCHACHTER G.,"REGIONAL DEVELOPMENT IN THE ITALIAN DUAL ECONOMY" ITALY AGRI INDUS MARKET WORKER ECO/TAC CONTROL INCOME PRODUC 20. PAGE 116 F2287
REGION ECO/UNDEV NAT/G PROB/SOLV

S67
SCHELLING T.C.,"ECONOMICS AND CRIMINAL ENTERPRISE." LAW FORCES BARGAIN ECO/TAC CONTROL GAMBLE ROUTINE ADJUST DEMAND INCOME PROFIT CRIMLGY. PAGE 116 F2295
CRIME PROB/SOLV CONCPT

S67
SCHWARZWELLER H.K.,"SOCIAL CLASS ORIGINS, RURAL-URBAN MIGRATION, AND ECONOMIC LIFE CHANGES." USA+45 SOCIETY STRUCT FAM NEIGH INCOME...SOC RECORD CHARTS MUNICH. PAGE 118 F2326
CLASSIF WEALTH AGRI

S67
SHISTER J.,"THE DIRECTION OF UNIONISM 1947-1967: THRUST OF DRIFT?" INDUS CENTRAL EFFICIENCY INCOME ATTIT SOCISM...POLICY TREND 20 AFL/CIO. PAGE 121 F2382
LABOR PROF/ORG LEAD LAW

S67
ZOETEWEIJ B.,"INCOME POLICIES ABROAD: AN INTERIM REPORT." NAT/G PROB/SOLV BARGAIN BUDGET PRICE RISK CENTRAL EFFICIENCY EQUILIB...MGT NAT/COMP 20. PAGE 150 F2967
METH/COMP INCOME POLICY LABOR

B84
MILL J.,ELEMENTS OF POLITICAL ECONOMY. UK LAW ELITES FINAN WORKER ECO/TAC RENT OWN WEALTH ...POLICY GEN/LAWS 19. PAGE 91 F1785
TAX TARIFFS NAT/G INCOME

S86
SMITH R.M.,"THE NATIONAL BUREAU OF LABOR AND INDUSTRIAL DEPRESSIONS" USA-45 DELIB/GP BARGAIN CONTROL COST INCOME WEALTH...STAT 19 DEPRESSION. PAGE 123 F2433
LABOR INDUS FINAN GOV/REL

B91
MILL J.S.,SOCIALISM (1859). MOD/EUR AGRI INDUS NAT/G REV INCOME PRODUC ORD/FREE POPULISM SOCISM ...GOV/COMP METH/COMP 19. PAGE 91 F1787
WEALTH SOCIALIST ECO/TAC OWN

B92
ENGELS F.,THE CONDITION OF THE WORKING-CLASS IN ENGLAND (1848). UK INDUS LABOR PRICE CONTROL COST INCOME HEALTH MARXISM MUNICH 19. PAGE 38 F0733
WORKER WEALTH MARXIST CAP/ISM

B95
SELIGMAN E.R.A.,ESSAYS IN TAXATION. NEW/ZEALND PRUSSIA UK USA-45 MARKET LOC/G CREATE PRICE CONTROL INCOME OWN WEALTH...GOV/COMP METH/COMP 19. PAGE 119 F2349
TAX TARIFFS INDUS NAT/G

B96
SMITH A.,LECTURES ON JUSTICE, POLICE, REVENUE AND ARMS (1763). UK LAW FAM FORCES TARIFFS AGREE COERCE INCOME OWN WEALTH LAISSEZ...GEN/LAWS 17/18. PAGE 123 F2429
DIPLOM JURID OLD/LIB TAX

B98
MARSHALL A.,PRINCIPLES OF ECONOMICS. INDUS WORKER PRICE COST EQUILIB INCOME OPTIMAL PRODUC...TIME/SEQ METH RICARDO/D. PAGE 86 F1678
WEALTH GEN/LAWS MARKET

INCOMPETENCE....SEE SKILL

IND....INDUSTRY; SEE ALSO INDUS

B49
US DEPARTMENT OF STATE,SOVIET BIBLIOGRAPHY (PAMPHLET). CHINA/COM COM USSR LAW AGRI INT/ORG ECO/TAC EDU/PROP...POLICY GEOG IND 20. PAGE 135 F2670
BIBLIOG/A MARXISM CULTURE DIPLOM

B58
SCOTT D.J.R.,RUSSIAN POLITICAL INSTITUTIONS. RUSSIA USSR CONSTN AGRI DELIB/GP PLAN EDU/PROP CONTROL CHOOSE EFFICIENCY ATTIT MARXISM...BIBLIOG/A IND 13/20. PAGE 118 F2332
NAT/G POL/PAR ADMIN DECISION

S60
MAIR L.P.,"SOCIAL CHANGE IN SOUTH AFRICA." MOD/EUR SOUTH/AFR WOR+45 ECO/UNDEV EX/STRUC TEC/DEV ATTIT DRIVE PERCEPT ORD/FREE...MGT CONCPT TIME/SEQ IND 20. PAGE 84 F1641
AFR NAT/G REV SOVEREIGN

C60
HOSELITZ B.,"THE ROLE OF CITIES IN THE ECONOMIC GROWTH OF UNDERDEVELOPED COUNTRIES" IN "SOCIOLOGICAL ASPECTS OF ECONOMIC GROWTH"(BMR). CULTURE LOC/G ACT/RES...SOC IDEA/COMP METH/COMP METH MUNICH IND 14/20 REDFIELD/R. PAGE 62 F1218
METH/CNCPT TEC/DEV ECO/UNDEV

B62
MOUSSA P.,THE UNDERPRIVILEGED NATIONS. FINAN INT/ORG PLAN PROB/SOLV CAP/ISM GIVE TASK WEALTH ...POLICY SOC IND 20. PAGE 94 F1850
ECO/UNDEV NAT/G DIPLOM FOR/AID

S65
MULLER A.L.,"THE ECONOMIC POSITION OF THE ASIANS IN AFRICA." AFR SOUTH/AFR ECO/UNDEV MARKET ECO/TAC GP/REL INCOME...CHARTS IND 20 MONOPOLY ASIANS. PAGE 95 F1856
WORKER RACE/REL CAP/ISM DISCRIM

C65
WUORINEN J.H.,"SCANDINAVIA." DENMARK FINLAND ICELAND NORWAY SWEDEN SOCIETY AGRI POL/PAR DELIB/GP DIPLOM INT/TRADE NEUTRAL WAR...CHARTS IND TREATY 20. PAGE 149 F2942
BIBLIOG NAT/G POLICY

IND/WRK/AF....INDUSTRIAL AND WORKERS' COMMERCIAL UNION OF AFRICA

INDEX....INDEX SYSTEM

N
LONDON TIMES OFFICIAL INDEX. UK LAW ECO/DEV NAT/G DIPLOM LEAD ATTIT 20. PAGE 1 F0006
BIBLIOG INDEX PRESS WRITING

N
THE MIDDLE EAST AND NORTH AFRICA. AFR ISLAM CULTURE ECO/UNDEV AGRI NAT/G TEC/DEV FOR/AID INT/TRADE EDU/PROP...CHARTS 20. PAGE 1 F0008
INDEX INDUS FINAN STAT

B41
HAYEK F.A.,THE PURE THEORY OF CAPITAL. UNIV ECO/DEV ECO/TAC COST EQUILIB PROFIT WEALTH...SIMUL GEN/LAWS BIBLIOG INDEX TIME 20. PAGE 57 F1120
CAP/ISM METH/CNCPT PRODUC FINAN

B56
HISTORICAL ABSTRACTS. NAT/G CREATE DIPLOM ATTIT ...SOC DICTIONARY INDEX 18/20. PAGE 1 F0011
WOR-45 COMPUT/IR BIBLIOG/A

B60
LERNER A.P.,THE ECONOMICS OF CONTROL. USA+45 ECO/UNDEV INT/ORG ACT/RES PLAN CAP/ISM INT/TRADE ATTIT WEALTH...SOC MATH STAT GEN/LAWS INDEX 20. PAGE 78 F1530
ECO/DEV ROUTINE ECO/TAC SOCISM

B62
BOGARDUS J.,OUTLINE FOR THE COURSE IN BUSINESS AND ECONOMICS LITERATURE (REV. ED; PAMPHLET). USA+45 FINAN INDUS NAT/G VOL/ASSN PRESS WRITING INDEX. PAGE 16 F0305
BIBLIOG/A STAT

S63
BALOGH T.,"L'INFLUENCE DES INSTITUTIONS MONETAIRES ET COMMERCIALES SUR LA STRUCTURE ECONOMIQUE AFRICAIN." AFR EUR+WWI FUT USA+45 USA-45 WOR+45 SERV/IND INT/ORG NAT/G TOP/EX ROUTINE...INDEX EEC METH/GP 20. PAGE 9 F0168
FINAN

B64
HARRIS S.E.,ECONOMICS OF THE KENNEDY YEARS AND A LOOK AHEAD. USA+45 PLAN BUDGET NEW/LIB...STAT RECORD IDEA/COMP PERS/COMP INDEX 20 KENNEDY/JF EISNHWR/DD JOHNSON/LB. PAGE 56 F1091
ECO/TAC CHIEF POLICY NAT/G

B65
CHAO K.,THE RATE AND PATTERN OF INDUSTRIAL GROWTH IN COMMUNIST CHINA. CHINA/COM ECO/UNDEV TEC/DEV PRICE...NAT/COMP BIBLIOG 20. PAGE 23 F0452
INDUS INDEX STAT PRODUC

B65
OFFICE OF ECONOMIC OPPORTUNITY,CATALOG OF FEDERAL PROGRAMS FOR INDIVIDUAL AND COMMUNITY IMPROVEMENT. USA+45 WEALTH NEW/LIB 20. PAGE 101 F1980
INDEX ECO/UNDEV RECEIVE NAT/G

B66
UN STATISTICAL OFFICE,STATISTICAL YEARBOOK (17TH ED.). WOR+45 AGRI...GEOG CHARTS 20. PAGE 132 F2604
STAT INDEX SOCIETY INDUS

INDIA....SEE ALSO S/ASIA

N
UNESCO,SOUTH ASIA SOCIAL SCIENCES ABSTRACTS. BURMA CEYLON INDIA S/ASIA PRESS...PSY 20. PAGE 132 F2608
BIBLIOG/A SOC

N
US LIBRARY OF CONGRESS,SOUTHERN ASIA ACCESSIONS LIST. BURMA CEYLON INDIA NEPAL PAKISTAN S/ASIA THAILAND AGRI INDUS SCHOOL WORKER...ART/METH GEOG HEAL PHIL/SCI LING 20. PAGE 137 F2710
BIBLIOG/A SOCIETY CULTURE ECO/UNDEV

N19
MASON E.S.,THE DIPLOMACY OF ECONOMIC ASSISTANCE (PAMPHLET). INDIA PAKISTAN USA+45 ECO/UNDEV NAT/G BUDGET ATTIT...POLICY 20. PAGE 87 F1695
FOR/AID DIPLOM FINAN

B39
FURNIVALL J.S.,NETHERLANDS INDIA. INDIA NETHERLAND CULTURE INDUS NAT/G DIPLOM ADMIN WEALTH...POLICY CHARTS 17/20. PAGE 45 F0876
COLONIAL ECO/UNDEV SOVEREIGN PLURISM

B53
BOEKE J.H.,ECONOMICS AND ECONOMIC POLICY OF DUAL SOCIETIES AS EXEMPLIFIED BY INDONESIA. INDIA INDONESIA SOCIETY CAP/ISM INT/TRADE GIVE PRICE GP/REL WEALTH SOCISM...POLICY NAT/COMP GEN/LAWS 20. PAGE 16 F0304
ECO/TAC ECO/UNDEV NAT/G CONTROL

B54
WILLIAMSON H.F.,ECONOMIC DEVELOPMENT - PRINCIPLES AND PATTERNS. INDIA KOREA CULTURE ECO/DEV ECO/UNDEV TEC/DEV...CENSUS NAT/COMP FOR/TRADE 20 CHINJAP MEXIC/AMER RESOURCE/N. PAGE 147 F2895
ECO/TAC GEOG LABOR

B55
PANT Y.P.,PLANNING IN UNDERDEVELOPED ECONOMIES. INDIA NEPAL INT/TRADE COLONIAL SOVEREIGN ALL/IDEOS ...TIME/SEQ METH/COMP 20. PAGE 103 F2026
ECO/UNDEV PLAN ECO/TAC DIPLOM

B55
UN ECONOMIC COMN ASIA & FAR E,ECONOMIC SURVEY OF ASIA AND THE FAR EAST, 1954. AFGHANISTN CEYLON INDIA PHILIPPINE S/ASIA ECO/DEV FINAN INDUS INT/TRADE PRODUC WEALTH...STAT CHARTS 20 CHINJAP. PAGE 132 F2600
ECO/UNDEV PRICE NAT/COMP ASIA

B56
VAKIL C.N.,PLANNING FOR AN EXPANDING ECONOMY. INDIA TAX COST 20. PAGE 140 F2759
TEC/DEV LABOR BUDGET CAP/ISM

B57
GOLD N.L.,REGIONAL ECONOMIC DEVELOPMENT AND NUCLEAR POWER IN INDIA. FUT INDIA FINAN FOR/AID INT/TRADE BAL/PAY EFFICIENCY OPTIMAL PRODUC WEALTH...PREDICT 20. PAGE 48 F0934
ECO/UNDEV TEC/DEV NUC/PWR INDUS

B57
MURDESHWAR A.K.,ADMINISTRATIVE PROBLEMS RELATING TO NATIONALISATION: WITH SPECIAL REFERENCE TO INDIAN STATE ENTERPRISES. CZECHOSLVK FRANCE INDIA UK USA+45 LEGIS WORKER PROB/SOLV BUDGET PRICE CONTROL ...MGT GEN/LAWS 20 PARLIAMENT. PAGE 95 F1863
NAT/G OWN INDUS ADMIN

B57
SINGH D.B.,INFLATIONARY PRICE TRENDS IN INDIA SINCE 1939. AFR INDIA ECO/TAC RATION CONTROL WAR GOV/REL BAL/PAY DEMAND INCOME PEACE PRODUC...POLICY CHARTS 20. PAGE 122 F2413
BUDGET ECO/UNDEV PRICE FINAN

B58
CLAIRMONTE F.,LE LIBERALISME ECONOMIQUE ET LES PAYS SOUS-DEVELOPPES: ETUDES SUR L'EVOLUTION D'UNE IDEE. ASIA INDIA UK FINAN INDUS PLAN CAP/ISM ECO/TAC COLONIAL NEW/LIB...BIBLIOG 20 THIRD/WRLD. PAGE 24 F0475
LAISSEZ ECO/UNDEV

B58
COALE A.J.,POPULATION GROWTH AND ECONOMIC DEVELOPMENT IN LOW-INCOME COUNTRIES: A CASE STUDY OF INDIA'S PROSPECTS. INDIA AGRI WORKER INCOME AGE WEALTH...CHARTS 20 MEXIC/AMER. PAGE 25 F0495
ECO/UNDEV GEOG CENSUS SEX

B58
INDIAN INST OF PUBLIC ADMIN,IMPROVING CITY GOVERNMENT. INDIA ECO/UNDEV PLAN BUDGET PARTIC GP/REL MUNICH 20. PAGE 64 F1263
LOC/G PROB/SOLV ADMIN

B58
JENNINGS I.,PROBLEMS OF THE NEW COMMONWEALTH. AFR CEYLON INDIA PAKISTAN S/ASIA ECO/UNDEV INT/ORG LOC/G DIPLOM ECO/TAC INT/TRADE COLONIAL RACE/REL DISCRIM 20 PARLIAMENT. PAGE 67 F1314
NAT/LISM NEUTRAL FOR/AID POL/PAR

S58
LOCKWOOD W.W.,"THE SOCIALISTIC SOCIETY: INDIA AND JAPAN." INDIA ECO/DEV ECO/UNDEV INDUS NAT/G CONTROL LEAD PRODUC WEALTH 20 CHINJAP. PAGE 81 F1593
ECO/TAC NAT/COMP FINAN SOCISM

B59
BAUER P.T.,UNITED STATES AID AND INDIAN ECONOMIC DEVELOPMENT. INDIA STRATA FINAN PLAN BUDGET DIPLOM INGP/REL EFFICIENCY SOCISM 20 AID. PAGE 11 F0215
FOR/AID ECO/UNDEV ECO/TAC POLICY

B59
KRIPALANI J.B.,CLASS STRUGGLE. INDIA WOR+45 ECO/UNDEV LABOR CAP/ISM EDU/PROP INGP/REL ...SOCIALIST IDEA/COMP 17/20. PAGE 73 F1440
MARXISM STRATA COERCE ECO/TAC

B59
MADHOK B.,POLITICAL TRENDS IN INDIA. INDIA PAKISTAN UK STRATA ECO/UNDEV POL/PAR LEGIS CAP/ISM DIPLOM COLONIAL CHOOSE MARXISM...SOC TREND 20 GANDHI/M NEHRU/J. PAGE 84 F1639
GEOG NAT/G

B59
MARTIN K.,WAR, HISTORY, AND HUMAN NATURE. FRANCE GERMANY INDIA UK UNIV POL/PAR COLONIAL DETER REV MARXISM PACIFISM...PSY CONCPT PREDICT LENIN/VI GANDHI/M. PAGE 86 F1683
PERSON WAR ATTIT IDEA/COMP

B59
SILCOCK T.H.,THE COMMONWEALTH ECONOMY IN SOUTHEAST ASIA. AFR INDIA MALAYSIA S/ASIA ECO/DEV AGRI LOC/G PLAN TARIFFS COLONIAL BAL/PAY DEMAND...BIBLIOG/A 20 GATT. PAGE 122 F2401
ECO/TAC INT/TRADE RACE/REL DIPLOM

B59
US GENERAL ACCOUNTING OFFICE,EXAM OF ECONOMIC AND TECHNICAL ASSISTANCE PROGRAM FOR INDIA INT'NAT'L COOP ADMIN REPORT TO CONGRESS 1955-1958. INDIA USA+45 ECO/UNDEV FINAN PLAN DIPLOM COST UTIL WEALTH ...CHARTS 20 CONGRESS AID. PAGE 136 F2679
FOR/AID EFFICIENCY ECO/TAC TEC/DEV

B60
BHAMBHRI C.P.,PARLIAMENTARY CONTROL OVER STATE ENTERPRISE IN INDIA. INDIA DELIB/GP ADMIN CONTROL INGP/REL EFFICIENCY 20 PARLIAMENT. PAGE 14 F0277
NAT/G OWN INDUS PARL/PROC

B60
LATIFI D.,INDIA AND UNITED STATES AID. ASIA INDIA UK USA+45 AGRI FINAN INDUS COLONIAL ORD/FREE SOVEREIGN WEALTH...METH/COMP 20. PAGE 76 F1486
FOR/AID DIPLOM ECO/UNDEV

B60
MC CLELLAN G.S.,INDIA. AFR CHINA/COM INDIA CONSTN ELITES STRATA AGRI POL/PAR FOR/AID ARMS/CONT REV MARXISM...CENSUS BIBLIOG 20 GANDHI/M NEHRU/J. PAGE 87 F1712
DIPLOM NAT/G SOCIETY ECO/UNDEV

B60
PENTONY D.E.,UNITED STATES FOREIGN AID. INDIA LAOS USA+45 ECO/UNDEV INT/TRADE ADMIN PEACE ATTIT ...POLICY METH/COMP ANTHOL 20. PAGE 105 F2060
FOR/AID DIPLOM ECO/TAC

B60
SANTHANAM K.,UNION-STATE RELATIONS IN INDIA. INDIA FINAN PROVS PLAN ECO/TAC...LING 20. PAGE 116 F2280
FEDERAL GOV/REL CONSTN POLICY

S60
ENKE S.,"THE ECONOMIES OF GOVERNMENT PAYMENTS TO LIMIT POPULATION." FUT INDIA WOR+45 CULTURE FINAN NAT/G CONSULT PLAN LEGIT CONTROL COST ATTIT RIGID/FLEX HEALTH WEALTH...STAT OBS CHARTS TOT/POP VAL/FREE 20. PAGE 38 F0736
FAM ACT/RES

B61
AGARWAL R.C.,STATE ENTERPRISE IN INDIA. FUT INDIA UK FINAN INDUS ADMIN CONTROL OWN...POLICY CHARTS BIBLIOG 20 RAILROAD. PAGE 3 F0048
ECO/UNDEV SOCISM GOV/REL LG/CO

B61
BAUER P.T.,INDIAN ECONOMIC POLICY AND DEVELOPMENT. INDIA STRATA AGRI FINAN POL/PAR BUDGET FOR/AID GOV/REL EFFICIENCY...CENSUS 20. PAGE 11 F0216
ECO/UNDEV ECO/TAC POLICY PLAN

B61
GURTOO D.H.N.,INDIA'S BALANCE OF PAYMENTS (1920-1960). INDIA FINAN DIPLOM FOR/AID INT/TRADE PRICE COLONIAL...CHARTS BIBLIOG 20. PAGE 52 F1014
BAL/PAY STAT ECO/TAC ECO/UNDEV

B61
MACMAHON A.W.,DELEGATION AND AUTONOMY. INDIA STRUCT
ADMIN

LEGIS BARGAIN BUDGET ECO/TAC LEGIT EXEC REPRESENT GOV/REL CENTRAL DEMAND EFFICIENCY PRODUC. PAGE 84 F1637 PLAN FEDERAL

B61
SAKAI R.K.,STUDIES ON ASIA, 1961. ASIA BURMA INDIA S/ASIA FINAN ECO/TAC NAT/LISM SOCISM...POLICY ANTHOL 19/20 CHINJAP. PAGE 115 F2271 ECO/UNDEV SECT

B61
SHONFIELD A.,ECONOMIC GROWTH AND INFLATION: A STUDY OF INDIAN PLANNING. AFR INDIA AGRI INDUS TEC/DEV CONTROL DEMAND UTIL 20. PAGE 121 F2384 ECO/UNDEV PRICE PLAN BUDGET

B61
WARD B.J.,INDIA AND THE WEST. INDIA UK USA+45 INT/TRADE GIVE COLONIAL ATTIT MARXISM 19/20. PAGE 143 F2817 PLAN ECO/UNDEV ECO/TAC FOR/AID

S61
HOSELITZ B.F.,"ECONOMIC DEVELOPMENT AND POLITICAL STABILITY IN INDIA" INDIA NAT/G GP/REL...POLICY 20. PAGE 62 F1222 ECO/UNDEV GEN/LAWS PROB/SOLV

S61
RAY J.,"THE EUROPEAN FREE-TRADE ASSOCIATION AND ITS IMPACT ON INDIA'S TRADE." EUR+WWI FRANCE GERMANY INDIA S/ASIA UK NAT/G VOL/ASSN PLAN INT/TRADE ROUTINE WEALTH...STAT CHARTS TERR/GP CMN/WLTH EEC FOR/TRADE OEEC 20 EFTA. PAGE 109 F2155 ECO/DEV ECO/TAC

B62
BROWN S.D.,STUDIES ON ASIA, 1962. ASIA BURMA INDIA ISLAM ISRAEL S/ASIA ECO/UNDEV POL/PAR SECT ECO/TAC ...ANTHOL 20 CHINJAP. PAGE 19 F0374 PWR PARL/PROC

B62
HOOVER C.B.,ECONOMIC SYSTEMS OF THE COMMONWEALTH. AFR CANADA INDIA UK ECO/DEV ECO/UNDEV AGRI INDUS TEC/DEV TARIFFS PRICE BAL/PAY DEMAND...SIMUL 20 AUSTRAL. PAGE 61 F1208 CAP/ISM SOCISM ECO/TAC PLAN

B62
PRAKASH O.M.,THE THEORY AND WORKING OF STATE CORPORATIONS: WITH SPECIAL REFERENCE TO INDIA. INDIA UK USA+45 TOP/EX PRICE ADMIN EFFICIENCY...MGT METH/COMP 20 TVA. PAGE 107 F2112 LG/CO ECO/UNDEV GOV/REL SOCISM

B62
SEN S.R.,THE STRATEGY FOR AGRICULTURAL DEVELOPMENT AND OTHER ESSAYS ON ECONOMIC POLICY AND PLANNING. INDIA FINAN ACT/RES TEC/DEV CAP/ISM PRICE...STAT 20. PAGE 119 F2354 ECO/UNDEV PLAN AGRI POLICY

B62
SRIVASTAVA G.L.,COLLECTIVE BARGAINING AND LABOR-MANAGEMENT RELATIONS IN INDIA. INDIA UK USA+45 INDUS LEGIS WORKER ADJUD EFFICIENCY PRODUC ...METH/COMP 20. PAGE 125 F2462 LABOR MGT BARGAIN GP/REL

B63
BANERJI A.K.,INDIA'S BALANCE OF PAYMENTS. INDIA NAT/G PRICE BAL/PAY COST INCOME 20. PAGE 9 F0171 INT/TRADE DIPLOM FINAN BUDGET

B63
BRAIBANTI R.J.D.,ADMINISTRATION AND ECONOMIC DEVELOPMENT IN INDIA. INDIA S/ASIA SOCIETY STRATA ECO/TAC PERSON WEALTH...MGT GEN/LAWS TOT/POP VAL/FREE 20. PAGE 18 F0337 ECO/UNDEV ADMIN

B63
CHATTERJEE I.K.,ECONOMIC DEVELOPMENT PAYMENTS DEFICIT AND PAYMENT RESTRICTION. INDIA WOR+45 FINAN INT/TRADE CONTROL BAL/PAY WEALTH...POLICY CONCPT STAT CHARTS IDEA/COMP BIBLIOG 20. PAGE 23 F0456 ECO/DEV ECO/TAC PAY GOV/REL

B63
FRIEDMAN M.,INFLATION: CAUSES AND CURES. AFR INDIA ECO/DEV ECO/TAC INT/TRADE RATION PRICE DEMAND ...POLICY 20. PAGE 44 F0860 ECO/UNDEV PLAN FINAN EQUILIB

B63
GANDHI M.K.,THE WAY TO COMMUNAL HARMONY. INDIA MAJORITY RIGID/FLEX ROLE RESPECT 20 GANDHI/M. PAGE 46 F0892 RACE/REL DISCRIM ATTIT ADJUST

B63
GANGULY D.S.,PUBLIC CORPORATIONS IN A NATIONAL ECONOMY. INDIA WOR+45 FINAN INDUS TOP/EX PRICE EFFICIENCY...MGT STAT CHARTS BIBLIOG 20. PAGE 46 F0897 ECO/UNDEV LG/CO SOCISM GOV/REL

B63
KAPP W.K.,HINDU CULTURE: ECONOMIC DEVELOPMENT AND ECONOMIC PLANNING IN INDIA. INDIA S/ASIA CULTURE ECO/TAC EDU/PROP ADMIN ALL/VALS...POLICY MGT TIME/SEQ TRUE/GP VAL/FREE 20. PAGE 69 F1353 SECT ECO/UNDEV

B63
RAO V.K.R.,FOREIGN AID AND INDIA'S ECONOMIC DEVELOPMENT. INDIA INT/ORG PROB/SOLV TEC/DEV ECO/TAC CONTROL WEALTH...TREND 20. PAGE 109 F2148 FOR/AID ECO/UNDEV RECEIVE DIPLOM

S63
REDDAWAY W.B.,"THE ECONOMICS OF UNDERDEVELOPED COUNTRIES." S/ASIA WOR+45 WOR-45 STRATA AGRI COM/IND DIST/IND MARKET PROC/MFG PLAN TEC/DEV FOR/AID BAL/PAY ATTIT DRIVE SKILL WORK FOR/TRADE 20. PAGE 110 F2165 ECO/TAC ECO/UNDEV INDIA

B64
THE SPECIAL COMMONWEALTH AFRICAN ASSISTANCE PLAN. AFR CANADA INDIA NIGERIA UK FINAN SCHOOL...CHARTS 20 COMMONWLTH. PAGE 1 F0019 ECO/UNDEV TREND FOR/AID ADMIN

B64
BERRILL K.,ECONOMIC DEVELOPMENT WITH SPECIAL REFERENCE TO EAST ASIA. ASIA INDIA S/ASIA AGRI INDUS LABOR DELIB/GP PLAN INT/TRADE COST PRODUC 20 CHINJAP. PAGE 14 F0271 FINAN ECO/UNDEV INT/ORG CAP/ISM

B64
CASEY R.G.,THE FUTURE OF THE COMMONWEALTH. INDIA PAKISTAN UK ECO/UNDEV INT/ORG TEC/DEV COLONIAL SUPEGO 20 EEC AUSTRAL. PAGE 22 F0425 DIPLOM SOVEREIGN NAT/LISM FOR/AID

B64
COLUMBIA U SCHOOL OF LAW,PUBLIC INTERNATIONAL DEVELOPMENT FINANCING IN INDIA. GERMANY/W INDIA UK USA+45 INDUS PLAN TEC/DEV DIPLOM ECO/TAC GIVE ADMIN UTIL ATTIT 20. PAGE 26 F0512 ECO/UNDEV FINAN FOR/AID INT/ORG

B64
DE BARY W.T.,APPROACHES TO ASIAN CIVILIZATIONS. INDIA ISLAM USA+45 CULTURE ACADEM...SOC ANTHOL 20 CHINJAP ARABS. PAGE 31 F0595 ASIA EDU/PROP SOCIETY

B64
KALDOR N.,ESSAYS ON ECONOMIC POLICY (VOL. II). CHILE GERMANY INDIA FINAN...GOV/COMP METH/COMP 20 KEYNES/JM. PAGE 69 F1348 BAL/PAY INT/TRADE METH/CNCPT ECO/UNDEV

B64
NATIONAL COUN APPLIED ECO RES,A STRATEGY FOR THE FOURTH PLAN. INDIA DIST/IND EXTR/IND SERV/IND ECO/TAC RATION EDU/PROP EATING HEALTH...CHARTS 20. PAGE 97 F1900 ECO/UNDEV PLAN AGRI WORKER

B64
ROBINSON R.D.,INTERNATIONAL BUSINESS POLICY. AFR INDIA L/A+17C USA+45 ELITES AGRI FOR/AID COERCE BAL/PAY...DECISION INT/LAW MGT 20. PAGE 113 F2224 ECO/TAC DIST/IND COLONIAL FINAN

B64
RUSTAMJI R.F.,THE LAW OF INDUSTRIAL DISPUTES IN INDIA. INDIA LEGIS WORKER CONTROL GP/REL...JURID MGT TIME/SEQ 20. PAGE 115 F2264 INDUS ADJUD BARGAIN LABOR

B64
US HOUSE COMM GOVT OPERATIONS,US OWNED FOREIGN CURRENCIES: HEARINGS (COMMITTEE ON GOVERNMENT OPERATIONS). INDIA ECO/DEV PLAN BUDGET TAX DEMAND EFFICIENCY 20 AID CONGRESS. PAGE 137 F2699 FINAN ECO/TAC FOR/AID OWN

B65
ANALYSIS AND ASSESSMENT OF THE ECONOMIC EFFECTS: PUBLIC LAW 480 TITLE I PROGRAM TURKEY. INDIA TURKEY USA+45 AGRI NAT/G PLAN BUDGET DIPLOM COST EFFICIENCY...CHARTS 20. PAGE 1 F0021 ECO/TAC FOR/AID FINAN ECO/UNDEV

B65
CHANDRASEKHAR S.,AMERICAN AID AND INDIA'S ECONOMIC DEVELOPMENT. AFR CHINA/COM INDIA USA+45 GIVE EDU/PROP EATING HEALTH ORD/FREE 20 AID. PAGE 23 F0449 FOR/AID PEACE DIPLOM ECO/UNDEV

B65
CRABB C.V. JR.,THE ELEPHANTS AND THE GRASS* A STUDY OF NONALIGNMENT. ASIA INDIA S/ASIA USA+45 USSR BAL/PWR NEUTRAL ATTIT...TREND NAT/COMP. PAGE 28 F0549 ECO/UNDEV AFR DIPLOM CONCPT

B65
DELHI INSTITUTE OF ECO GROWTH,A STUDY IN THE WORKING OF THE INTENSIVE AREA SCHEME OF THE KHADI AND VILLAGE INDUSTRIES COMMISSION. INDIA AGRI FINAN DELIB/GP ECO/TAC EFFICIENCY...QU CHARTS MUNICH 20. PAGE 32 F0614 PLAN INDUS ECO/UNDEV

B65
HASSON J.A.,THE ECONOMICS OF NUCLEAR POWER. INDIA UK USA+45 WOR+45 INT/ORG TEC/DEV COST...SOC STAT CHARTS 20 EURATOM. PAGE 56 F1108 NUC/PWR INDUS ECO/DEV METH

B65
JAIN S.C.,THE STATE AND AGRICULTURE. INDIA S/ASIA ECO/UNDEV PROB/SOLV CAP/ISM MARXISM SOCISM 20. PAGE 66 F1304 NAT/G POLICY AGRI ECO/TAC

B65
MORRIS M.D.,THE EMERGENCE OF AN INDUSTRIAL LABOR FORCE IN INDIA: A STUDY OF THE BOMBAY COTTON MILLS, 1854-1947. INDIA WORKER OP/RES ADMIN 19/20. PAGE 94 F1837 INDUS LABOR ECO/UNDEV CAP/ISM

B65
NARASIMHAN V.K.,DEMOCRACY AND MIXED ECONOMY. INDIA CONTROL...CENSUS IDEA/COMP 20. PAGE 96 F1891 CAP/ISM MARXISM ORD/FREE NEW/LIB

B65
ONSLOW C.,ASIAN ECONOMIC DEVELOPMENT. BURMA CEYLON INDIA MALAYSIA PAKISTAN S/ASIA AGRI INDUS MARKET PROB/SOLV CAP/ISM FOR/AID INT/TRADE DEMAND WEALTH ...POLICY ANTHOL 20. PAGE 101 F1991 ECO/UNDEV ECO/TAC PLAN NAT/G

B65
PROCHNOW H.V.,WORLD ECONOMIC PROBLEMS AND POLICIES. MARKET
INDIA ISRAEL WOR+45 AGRI LABOR PROB/SOLV FOR/AID ECO/TAC
TARIFFS CONTROL BAL/PAY NAT/LISM WEALTH...TREND PRODUC
CHARTS 20 CHINJAP EEC. PAGE 108 F2124 IDEA/COMP

B65
SCHULTZ T.W.,ECONOMIC CRISES IN WORLD AGRICULTURE. AGRI
ASIA INDIA USSR ECO/DEV ECO/UNDEV INDUS VOL/ASSN ECO/TAC
CAP/ISM RATION COLONIAL 20. PAGE 117 F2317 INCOME
WORKER

B65
VAID K.N.,STATE AND LABOR IN INDIA. INDIA INDUS LAW
WORKER PAY PRICE ADJUD CONTROL PARL/PROC GP/REL LABOR
ORD/FREE 20. PAGE 140 F2757 MGT
NEW/LIB

B65
WINT G.,ASIA: A HANDBOOK. ASIA COM INDIA USSR DIPLOM
CULTURE INTELL NAT/G...GEOG STAT CENSUS NAT/COMP SOC
WORSHIP 20 TREATY CHINJAP. PAGE 148 F2907

S65
KUNKEL J.H.,"VALUES AND BEHAVIOR IN ECONOMIC SIMUL
DEVELOPMENT." INDIA PERU CULTURE STRUCT CREATE ECO/UNDEV
PERS/REL ATTIT PERSON...CHARTS HYPO/EXP ARGEN. PSY
PAGE 74 F1449 STERTYP

B66
AGGARWALA R.N.,FINANCIAL COMMITTEES OF THE INDIAN PARL/PROC
PARLIAMENT: A STUDY IN PARLIAMENTARY CONTROL OVER BUDGET
PUBLIC EXPENDITURE. INDIA FINAN NAT/G ROLE...CHARTS CONTROL
METH/COMP METH 20 PARLIAMENT. PAGE 3 F0049 DELIB/GP

B66
DEBENKO E.,RESEARCH SOURCES FOR SOUTH ASIAN STUDIES BIBLIOG
IN ECONOMIC DEVELOPMENT: A SELECT BIBLIOGRAPHY OF ECO/UNDEV
SERIAL PUBLICATIONS. CEYLON INDIA NEPAL PAKISTAN S/ASIA
PROB/SOLV ADMIN...POLICY 20. PAGE 32 F0611 PLAN

B66
DILLEY M.R.,BRITISH POLICY IN KENYA COLONY (2ND COLONIAL
ED.). AFR INDIA UK LABOR BUDGET TAX ADMIN PARL/PROC REPRESENT
GP/REL...BIBLIOG 20 PARLIAMENT. PAGE 33 F0639 SOVEREIGN

B66
KEENLEYSIDE H.L.,INTERNATIONAL AID: A SUMMARY. AFR ECO/UNDEV
INDIA S/ASIA UK STRATA EXTR/IND TEC/DEV ADMIN FOR/AID
RACE/REL DEMAND NAT/LISM WEALTH...TREND CHINJAP. DIPLOM
PAGE 70 F1367 TASK

B66
KOH S.J.,STAGES OF INDUSTRIAL DEVELOPMENT IN ASIA. INDUS
ASIA INDIA KOREA STRATA STRUCT NAT/G INT/TRADE ECO/UNDEV
...CHARTS 19/20 CHINJAP. PAGE 72 F1415 ECO/DEV
LABOR

B66
MADAN G.R.,ECONOMIC THINKING IN INDIA. INDIA ECO/TAC
ECO/UNDEV AGRI FINAN INDUS LABOR PLAN CAP/ISM PHIL/SCI
INT/TRADE MARXISM SOCISM...POLICY 1/20. PAGE 84 NAT/G
F1638 POL/PAR

B66
MASON E.S.,ECONOMIC DEVELOPMENT IN INDIA AND NAT/COMP
PAKISTAN. INDIA PAKISTAN AGRI FINAN PLAN BUDGET ECO/UNDEV
INT/TRADE WEALTH...POLICY STAT TREND CHARTS 20. ECO/TAC
PAGE 87 F1700 FOR/AID

B66
MOUNTJOY A.B.,INDUSTRIALIZATION AND UNDER-DEVELOPED ECO/UNDEV
COUNTRIES (2ND REV. ED.). CHILE GHANA INDIA NIGERIA INDUS
WOR+45 SOCIETY PROB/SOLV ECO/TAC...SOC CHARTS 20 GEOG
INDUS/REV. PAGE 94 F1848 HABITAT

B66
NAMBOODIRIPAD E.M.,ECONOMICS AND POLITICS OF ECO/UNDEV
INDIA'S SOCIALIST PATTERN. INDIA STRATA AGRI INDUS PLAN
NAT/G PRICE ORD/FREE SOVEREIGN 20. PAGE 96 F1888 SOCISM
CAP/ISM

B66
NATIONAL COUN APPLIED ECO RES,DEVELOPMENT WITHOUT FOR/AID
AID. INDIA FINAN TEC/DEV EFFICIENCY...ANTHOL 20. PLAN
PAGE 97 F1901 SOVEREIGN
ECO/UNDEV

B66
RAO Y.V.L.,COMMUNICATION AND DEVELOPMENT. INDIA COM/IND
S/ASIA SOCIETY ACT/RES EDU/PROP PARTIC ATTIT...SOC ECO/UNDEV
GP/COMP BIBLIOG MUNICH MUNICH 20. PAGE 109 F2149 OBS

B66
SASTRI K.V.S.,FEDERAL-STATE FISCAL RELATIONS IN TAX
INDIA: A STUDY OF THE FINANCE COMMISSION AND BUDGET
TECHNIQUES OF FINANCIAL ADJUSTMENT. INDIA PROVS FINAN
DELIB/GP GOV/REL FEDERAL...MATH CHARTS 20. PAGE 116 NAT/G
F2283

B66
SPICER K.,A SAMARITAN STATE? AFR CANADA INDIA DIPLOM
PAKISTAN UK USA+45 FINAN INDUS PRODUC...CHARTS 20 FOR/AID
NATO. PAGE 124 F2455 ECO/DEV
ADMIN

B66
WILCOX C.,ECONOMIES OF THE WORLD TODAY: THEIR ECO/DEV
ORGANIZATION, DEVELOPMENT, AND PERFORMANCE (2ND ECO/UNDEV
ED.). CHINA/COM COM INDIA NIGERIA UK WOR+45 WOR-45 MARXISM
INDUS MARKET PLAN ECO/TAC SOCISM...CHARTS METH/COMP CAP/ISM
20. PAGE 146 F2878

B66
ZINKIN T.,CHALLENGES IN INDIA. INDIA PAKISTAN LAW NAT/G
AGRI FINAN INDUS TOP/EX TEC/DEV CONTROL ROUTINE ECO/TAC
ORD/FREE PWR 20 NEHRU/J SHASTRI/LB CIVIL/SERV. POLICY
PAGE 150 F2964 ADMIN

S66
LINDBLOOM C.E.,"HAS INDIA AN ECONOMIC FUTURE?" FUT AGRI
INDIA NAT/G PROB/SOLV...POLICY 20. PAGE 80 F1568 PRODUC
PLAN
ECO/UNDEV

B67
CHANDRASEKHAR S.,PROBLEMS OF ECONOMIC DEVELOPMENT. ECO/UNDEV
AFR INDIA PHILIPPINE UAR WOR+45 INDUS...GEOG SOC PLAN
ANTHOL BIBLIOG 20 CHINJAP. PAGE 23 F0450 AGRI
PROB/SOLV

B67
JHANGIANI M.A.,JANA SANGH AND SWATANTRA: A PROFILE POL/PAR
OF THE RIGHTIST PARTIES IN INDIA. INDIA ADMIN LAISSEZ
CHOOSE MARXISM SOCISM...INT CHARTS BIBLIOG 20. NAT/LISM
PAGE 67 F1320 ATTIT

B67
TANSKY L.,US AND USSR AID TO DEVELOPING COUNTRIES. ECO/UNDEV
INDIA TURKEY USA+45 USSR INDUS PLAN CAP/ISM WAR PWR FOR/AID
WEALTH MARXISM...CHARTS NAT/COMP BIBLIOG 20. DIPLOM
PAGE 128 F2534 ECO/TAC

B67
TANSKY L.,US AND USSR AID TO DEVELOPING COUNTRIES. FOR/AID
INDIA TURKEY UAR USA+45 USSR FINAN PLAN TEC/DEV ECO/UNDEV
ADMIN WEALTH...TREND METH/COMP 20. PAGE 128 F2535 MARXISM
CAP/ISM

B67
US SENATE COMM ON FOREIGN REL,ARMS SALES TO NEAR WEAPON
EAST AND SOUTH ASIAN COUNTRIES. INDIA IRAN PAKISTAN FOR/AID
WOR+45 PROC/MFG BAL/PWR DIPLOM...DECISION SENATE. FORCES
PAGE 139 F2742 POLICY

B67
VENKATESWARAN R.J.,CABINET GOVERNMENT IN INDIA. DELIB/GP
INDIA UK SOCIETY OP/RES COLONIAL LEAD EFFICIENCY ADMIN
ORD/FREE 20. PAGE 141 F2776 CONSTN
NAT/G

S67
FOX R.G.,"FAMILY, CASTE, AND COMMERCE IN A NORTH CULTURE
INDIAN MARKET TOWN." INDIA STRATA AGRI FACE/GP FAM GP/REL
NEIGH OP/RES BARGAIN ADMIN ROUTINE WEALTH...SOC ECO/UNDEV
CHARTS 20. PAGE 43 F0838 DIST/IND

S67
GUPTA S.,"FOREIGN POLICY IN THE 1967 MANIFESTOS." IDEA/COMP
ASIA COM INDIA USA+45 FORCES FOR/AID TAX ATTIT POL/PAR
...DECISION 20. PAGE 52 F1013 POLICY
DIPLOM

S67
MEHTA A.,"INDIA* POVERTY AND CHANGE." STRATA INDUS INDIA
CREATE ECO/TAC FOR/AID NEUTRAL GP/REL ADJUST INCOME SOCIETY
...NEW/IDEA 20. PAGE 89 F1746 ECO/UNDEV
TEC/DEV

S67
PAI G.A.,"TAXATION AND PLANNING IN INDIA: A BIRDS- TAX
EYE VIEW." INDIA ELITES NAT/G LEGIS BUDGET CONTROL PLAN
LOBBY INCOME...STAT CHARTS 20. PAGE 102 F2015 WEALTH
STRATA

S67
SIPPEL D.,"INDIENS UNSICHERE ZUKUNFT." INDIA SOCIETY
CULTURE ACADEM POL/PAR LEGIS COLONIAL CHOOSE STRUCT
SOVEREIGN...JURID 20. PAGE 122 F2416 ECO/UNDEV
NAT/G

N67
US HOUSE COMM SCI ASTRONAUT,GOVERNMENT, SCIENCE, NAT/G
AND INTERNATIONAL POLICY (PAMPHLET). INDIA POLICY
NETHERLAND ECO/DEV ECO/UNDEV R+D ACADEM PLAN DIPLOM CREATE
FOR/AID CONFER...PREDICT 20 CHINJAP. PAGE 137 F2705 TEC/DEV

INDIAN INST OF PUBLIC ADMIN F1263

INDIAN/AM....AMERICAN INDIANS

B33
TANNENBAUM F.,PEACE BY REVOLUTION. ECO/UNDEV AGRI CULTURE
SECT WORKER DIPLOM EDU/PROP DISCRIM OWN WEALTH COLONIAL
POPULISM 17/20 MEXIC/AMER INDIAN/AM. PAGE 128 F2532 RACE/REL
REV

B64
TAX S.,EL CAPITALISMO DEL CENTAVO; UNA ECONOMIA ECO/UNDEV
INDIGENA DE GUATEMALA (2 VOLS.). GUATEMALA L/A+17C AGRI
SOCIETY GP/REL DEMAND INCOME HABITAT...SOC MUNICH WEALTH
20 INDIAN/AM. PAGE 129 F2539 COST

B67
WEINBERG M.,SCHOOL INTEGRATION: A COMPREHENSIVE BIBLIOG
CLASSIFIED BIBLIOGRAPHY OF 3,100 REFERENCES. USA+45 SCHOOL
LAW NAT/G NEIGH SECT PLAN ROUTINE AGE/C WEALTH DISCRIM
SOC/INTEG INDIAN/AM. PAGE 145 F2849 RACE/REL

S67
LANGLEY L.D.,"THE DEMOCRATIC TRADITION AND MILITARY ATTIT
REFORM, 1878-1885." USA-45 SECT EDU/PROP CROWD FORCES
EFFICIENCY NAT/LISM 19 INDIAN/AM. PAGE 75 F1480 POPULISM

INDIANA....INDIANA

INDICATOR....NUMERICAL INDICES AND INDICATORS

B65
DODDY F.S.,INTRODUCTION TO THE USE OF ECONOMIC INDICATORS. FINAN LABOR PLAN COST...ECOMETRIC INDICATOR MATH PREDICT CHARTS METH 20. PAGE 33 F0649
TEC/DEV STAT PRODUC PRICE

S65
BRIGHAM E.F.,"THE DETERMINANTS OF RESIDENTIAL LAND VALUES." USA+45 ECO/DEV PROB/SOLV RENT PRICE ...REGRESS STAT CHARTS GEN/METH MUNICH 20 LOS/ANG. PAGE 18 F0351
COST INDICATOR SIMUL ECOMETRIC

INDIVIDUAL....SEE PERSON

INDOCTRINATION....SEE EDU/PROP

INDONESIA....SEE ALSO S/ASIA

B53
BOEKE J.H.,ECONOMICS AND ECONOMIC POLICY OF DUAL SOCIETIES AS EXEMPLIFIED BY INDONESIA. INDIA INDONESIA SOCIETY CAP/ISM INT/TRADE GIVE PRICE GP/REL WEALTH SOCISM...POLICY NAT/COMP GEN/LAWS 20. PAGE 16 F0304
ECO/TAC ECO/UNDEV NAT/G CONTROL

B53
MIT CENTER INTERNATIONAL STU,BIBLIOGRAPHY OF THE ECONOMIC AND POLITICAL DEVELOPMENT OF INDONESIA. INDONESIA STRUCT NAT/G COLONIAL LEAD...STAT 20. PAGE 92 F1805
BIBLIOG ECO/UNDEV TEC/DEV S/ASIA

B62
GALENSON W.,LABOR IN DEVELOPING COUNTRIES. BRAZIL INDONESIA ISRAEL PAKISTAN TURKEY AGRI INDUS WORKER PAY PRICE GP/REL WEALTH...MGT CHARTS METH/COMP NAT/COMP 20. PAGE 45 F0888
LABOR ECO/UNDEV BARGAIN POL/PAR

B62
SELOSOEMARDJAN O.,SOCIAL CHANGES IN JOGJAKARTA. INDONESIA NETHERLAND ELITES STRATA STRUCT FAM POL/PAR CREATE DIPLOM INT/TRADE EDU/PROP ADMIN GOV/REL...SOC 20 JAVA CHINJAP. PAGE 119 F2352
ECO/UNDEV CULTURE REV COLONIAL

B63
GEERTZ C.,PEDDLERS AND PRINCES: SOCIAL DEVELOPMENT AND ECONOMIC CHANGE IN TWO INDONESIAN TOWNS. S/ASIA CULTURE SOCIETY STRATA FACE/GP CREATE TEC/DEV ECO/TAC ORD/FREE WEALTH...OBS INT CENSUS CHARTS WORK TOT/POP METH/GP TERR/GP VAL/FREE 20 MUNICH. PAGE 47 F0913
ECO/UNDEV SOC ELITES INDONESIA

B63
US ECON SURVEY TEAM INDONESIA,INDONESIA - PERSPECTIVE AND PROPOSALS FOR UNITED STATES ECONOMIC AID. INDONESIA AGRI MARKET TEC/DEV DIPLOM INT/TRADE EDU/PROP 20. PAGE 136 F2678
FOR/AID ECO/UNDEV PLAN INDUS

S63
HINDLEY D.,"FOREIGN AID TO INDONESIA AND ITS POLITICAL IMPLICATIONS." INDONESIA POL/PAR ATTIT SOVEREIGN...CHARTS 20. PAGE 60 F1173
FOR/AID NAT/G WEALTH ECO/TAC

B64
WERTHEIM W.F.,EAST-WEST PARALLELS. INDONESIA S/ASIA NAT/G SECT...TIME/SEQ METH REFORMERS S/EASTASIA. PAGE 145 F2860
SOC ECO/UNDEV CULTURE NAT/LISM

INDUS....ALL OR MOST INDUSTRY; SEE ALSO SPECIFIC INDUSTRIES, INSTITUTIONAL INDEX, PART C, P. XII; SEE ALSO IND

N
NEW JERSEY STATE OF,SECOND REPORT TO GOVERNOR, SENATE, ASSEMBLY BY UNIFORM COMMERCIAL CODE STUDY COMMISSION. USA+45 INDUS LOC/G NAT/G PROF/ORG CONSULT ACT/RES LEGIT CT/SYS ATTIT NEW/JERSEY. PAGE 98 F1920
LAW FINAN CENTRAL PROVS

N
AMERICAN ECONOMIC REVIEW. FINAN INDUS LABOR OP/RES CAP/ISM INT/TRADE TAX WEALTH...CON/ANAL CHARTS 20. PAGE 1 F0001
BIBLIOG/A USA+45 ECO/DEV NAT/G

N
ECONOMIC ABSTRACTS. WOR+45 FINAN INDUS MARKET LABOR ACT/RES INT/TRADE WRITING GP/REL...MGT 20. PAGE 1 F0005
BIBLIOG/A EDU/PROP

N
ECONOMIC LIBRARY SELECTIONS. AGRI INDUS MARKET ADMIN...STAT NAT/COMP 20. PAGE 1 F0007
BIBLIOG/A WRITING FINAN

N
THE MIDDLE EAST AND NORTH AFRICA. AFR ISLAM CULTURE ECO/UNDEV AGRI NAT/G TEC/DEV FOR/AID INT/TRADE EDU/PROP...CHARTS 20. PAGE 1 F0008
INDEX INDUS FINAN STAT

N
THE MIDDLE EAST. CULTURE...BIOG BIBLIOG. PAGE 1 F0010
ISLAM INDUS FINAN

N
UNESCO,INTERNATIONAL BIBLIOGRAPHY OF ECONOMICS (VOLUMES 1-8). WOR+45 AGRI INDUS LABOR PLAN TEC/DEV 20. PAGE 132 F2607
BIBLIOG ECO/DEV ECO/UNDEV

N
US LIBRARY OF CONGRESS,SELECTED AND ANNOTATED BIBLIOGRAPHY ON INDUSTRIAL PROBLEMS AND POLICIES IN WARTIME (PAMPHLET). WOR-45 CONSTRUC NAT/G PROB/SOLV COST DEMAND PRODUC 20. PAGE 137 F2707
BIBLIOG/A ECO/DEV INDUS WAR

N
US LIBRARY OF CONGRESS,SELECTED AND ANNOTATED BIBLIOGRAPHY ON LABOR PROBLEMS AND POLICIES IN A WARTIME ECONOMY (PAMPHLET). USA-45 INDUS LEGIS GP/REL DISCRIM PRODUC...SOC 20. PAGE 137 F2708
BIBLIOG/A WAR LABOR WORKER

N
US LIBRARY OF CONGRESS,SOUTHERN ASIA ACCESSIONS LIST. BURMA CEYLON INDIA NEPAL PAKISTAN S/ASIA THAILAND AGRI INDUS SCHOOL WORKER...ART/METH GEOG HEAL PHIL/SCI LING 20. PAGE 137 F2710
BIBLIOG/A SOCIETY CULTURE ECO/UNDEV

N
US SUPERINTENDENT OF DOCUMENTS,LABOR (PRICE LIST 33). USA+45 LAW AGRI CONSTRUC INDUS NAT/G BARGAIN PRICE ADMIN AUTOMAT PRODUC MGT. PAGE 140 F2753
BIBLIOG/A WORKER LABOR LEGIS

B00
LIST F.,NATIONAL SYSTEM OF POLITICAL ECONOMY. ECO/DEV AGRI EXTR/IND FINAN INDUS TEC/DEV ECO/TAC ATTIT WEALTH...TREND GEN/LAWS FOR/TRADE 19. PAGE 81 F1581
MOD/EUR MARKET

B00
MILL J.S.,PRINCIPLES OF POLITICAL ECONOMY. WOR-45 CULTURE SOCIETY STRATA ECO/DEV AGRI EXTR/IND FINAN INDUS DELIB/GP ECO/TAC WEALTH...CONCPT MATH TREND 20. PAGE 91 F1786
MARKET INT/ORG INT/TRADE

B02
MOREL E.D.,AFFAIRS OF WEST AFRICA. UK FINAN INDUS FAM KIN SECT CHIEF WORKER DIPLOM RACE/REL LITERACY HEALTH...CHARTS 18/20 AFRICA/W NEGRO. PAGE 93 F1826
COLONIAL ADMIN AFR

B08
LLOYD H.D.,THE SWISS DEMOCRACY. SWITZERLND INDUS NAT/G WORKER CHOOSE OWN ORD/FREE SOCISM...PLURIST 19/20 MONOPOLY. PAGE 81 F1590
NAT/COMP GOV/COMP REPRESENT POPULISM

B11
SOREL G.,LES ILLUSIONS DU PROGRES (1906). UNIV SOCIETY STRATA INDUS GP/REL OWN PRODUC SOCISM 17/20. PAGE 124 F2444
WORKER POPULISM ECO/DEV ATTIT

B12
HOBSON J.A.,THE EVOLUTION OF MODERN CAPITALISM. MOD/EUR UK STRATA ECO/DEV INDUS INCOME UTIL WEALTH ...SOC GEN/LAWS 7/20. PAGE 60 F1184
CAP/ISM WORKER TEC/DEV TIME/SEQ

B13
KROPOTKIN P.,THE CONQUEST OF BREAD. SOCIETY STRATA AGRI INDUS WORKER REV HAPPINESS INCOME PRODUC HEALTH MORAL ORD/FREE. PAGE 74 F1444
ANARCH SOCIALIST OWN AGREE

B14
HOBSON J.A.,WORK AND WEALTH. CULTURE FINAN INDUS WORKER TEC/DEV ECO/TAC GIVE PAY PRICE COST PRODUC UTIL. PAGE 60 F1185
WEALTH INCOME GEN/LAWS

B14
LEVINE L.,SYNDICALISM IN FRANCE (2ND ED.). FRANCE LAW SOCIETY ECO/DEV NAT/G ECO/TAC LEAD ATTIT ...POLICY CONCPT STAT BIBLIOG 18/20 REFORMERS. PAGE 79 F1542
LABOR INDUS SOCISM REV

B15
VEBLEN T.,IMPERIAL GERMANY AND THE INDUSTRIAL REVOLUTION. GERMANY MOD/EUR UK USA-45 NAT/G TEC/DEV CAP/ISM...MAJORIT NAT/COMP 19/20 CHINJAP. PAGE 141 F2769
ECO/DEV INDUS TECHNIC BAL/PWR

B19
VEBLEN T.B.,THE VESTED INTERESTS AND THE STATE OF THE INDUSTRIAL ARTS. USA-45 LAW FINAN WORKER PAY DOMIN PRICE COST SOCISM...MARXIST 19/20. PAGE 141 F2771
INDUS CAP/ISM METH/COMP WEALTH

N19
ANDERSON J.,THE ORGANIZATION OF ECONOMIC STUDIES IN RELATION TO THE PROBLEMS OF GOVERNMENT (PAMPHLET). UK FINAN INDUS DELIB/GP PLAN PROB/SOLV ADMIN 20. PAGE 5 F0095
ECO/TAC ACT/RES NAT/G CENTRAL

N19
ATOMIC INDUSTRIAL FORUM,COMMENTARY ON LEGISLATION TO PERMIT PRIVATE OWNERSHIP OF SPECIAL NUCLEAR MATERIAL (PAMPHLET). USA+45 DELIB/GP LEGIS PLAN OWN ...POLICY 20 AEC CONGRESS. PAGE 7 F0134
NUC/PWR MARKET INDUS LAW

N19
BUSINESS ECONOMISTS' GROUP,INCOME POLICIES (PAMPHLET). UK INDUS LABOR TOP/EX PAY COST PRODUC ...ECOMETRIC GOV/COMP SIMUL ANTHOL 20. PAGE 20 F0395
INCOME WORKER WEALTH POLICY

N19
EAST KENTUCKY REGIONAL PLAN,PROGRAM 60: A DECADE OF ACTION FOR PROGRESS IN EASTERN KENTUCKY (PAMPHLET). USA+45 AGRI CONSTRUC INDUS CONSULT ACT/RES PROB/SOLV EDU/PROP GOV/REL HEALTH KENTUCKY. PAGE 35 F0689
REGION ADMIN PLAN ECO/UNDEV

N19
EAST KENTUCKY REGIONAL PLAN,PROGRAM 60 REPORT:
REGION

ACTION FOR PORGRESS IN EASTERN KENTUCKY (PAMPHLET). USA+45 CONSTRUC INDUS ACT/RES PROB/SOLV EDU/PROP ADMIN GOV/REL KENTUCKY. PAGE 35 F0690 PLAN ECO/UNDEV CONSULT N19

FRANCK P.G.,AFGHANISTAN BETWEEN EAST AND WEST: THE ECONOMICS OF COMPETITIVE COEXISTENCE (PAMPHLET). AFGHANISTN USA+45 USA-45 USSR INDUS ECO/TAC INT/TRADE CONTROL NEUTRAL ORD/FREE MARXISM...GEOG 20 UN. PAGE 43 F0842 FOR/AID PLAN DIPLOM ECO/UNDEV N19

INTERNATIONAL LABOUR OFFICE,EMPLOYMENT, UNEMPLOYMENT AND LABOUR FORCE STATISTICS (PAMPHLET). EUR+WWI STRATA AGRI INDUS NAT/G PROB/SOLV PAY AGE SEX...SAMP NAT/COMP METH 20 ILO. PAGE 65 F1278 WORKER LABOR STAT ECO/DEV N19

MCCONNELL G.,THE STEEL SEIZURE OF 1952 (PAMPHLET). USA+45 FINAN INDUS PROC/MFG LG/CO EX/STRUC ADJUD CONTROL GP/REL ORD/FREE PWR 20 TRUMAN/HS PRESIDENT CONGRESS. PAGE 88 F1721 DELIB/GP LABOR PROB/SOLV NAT/G N19

PATRICK H.T.,CYCLICAL INSTABILITY AND FISCAL-MONETARY POLICY IN POST-WAR JAPAN (PAMPHLET). INDUS MARKET DIPLOM TAX PRICE BAL/PAY...TREND CHARTS EQULIB 20 CHINJAP. PAGE 104 F2036 ECO/DEV PRODUC STAT N19

PEGRUM D.F.,URBAN TRANSPORT AND THE LOCATION OF INDUSTRY IN METROPOLITAN LOS ANGELES (PAMPHLET). USA+45 WORKER...GEOG CHARTS MUNICH. PAGE 104 F2049 DIST/IND REGION INDUS N19

US BUREAU OF THE CENSUS,THE PROPORTION OF THE SHIPMENTS (OR EMPLOYEES) OF EACH INDUSTRY... (PAMPHLET). USA+45 ECO/DEV EXTR/IND INDUS CONTROL PROFIT...STAT 20 CONGRESS MONOPOLY. PAGE 134 F2645 PROC/MFG PRODUC MARKET CHARTS N19

US CHAMBER OF COMMERCE,THE SIGNIFICANCE OF CONCENTRATION RATIOS (PAMPHLET). USA+45 FINAN INDUS ADMIN...METH/CNCPT SAMP CHARTS 20. PAGE 134 F2647 MARKET PREDICT LG/CO CONTROL N19

WILSON T.,FINANCIAL ASSISTANCE WITH REGIONAL DEVELOPMENT (PAMPHLET). CANADA INDUS NAT/G PLAN TAX CONTROL COST EFFICIENCY...POLICY CHARTS 20. PAGE 147 F2902 FINAN ECO/TAC REGION GOV/REL B20

BUCK S.J.,THE AGRARIAN CRUSADE: A CHRONICLE OF THE FARMER IN POLITICS. USA-45 INDUS PROB/SOLV PWR WEALTH...GEOG CENSUS 19/20 GREENBACK GRANGE SILVER. PAGE 20 F0381 AGRI POPULISM VOL/ASSN POL/PAR B20

MALTHUS T.R.,PRINCIPLES OF POLITICAL ECONOMY. UK AGRI INDUS MARKET NAT/G DIPLOM PRICE CONTROL BAL/PAY COST OWN PWR LAISSEZ 18/19. PAGE 84 F1650 GEN/LAWS DEMAND WEALTH B20

PIGOU A.C.,THE ECONOMICS OF WELFARE. UNIV INDUS WORKER ACT/RES RECEIVE INCOME NEW/LIB...MAJORIT SOC/WK. PAGE 106 F2085 ECO/TAC WEALTH FINAN CONTROL B20

TAWNEY R.H.,THE ACQUISITIVE SOCIETY. STRATA WORKER PROB/SOLV CAP/ISM ECO/TAC CONTROL GP/REL OWN PRIVIL ATTIT ORD/FREE WEALTH 20. PAGE 128 F2536 INDUS SOCIETY PRODUC MORAL B21

CLAPHAN J.H.,THE ECONOMIC DEVELOPMENT OF FRANCE AND GERMANY 1815-1914. FRANCE GERMANY MOD/EUR COM/IND DIST/IND FINAN INT/TRADE EDU/PROP 19/20. PAGE 24 F0476 ECO/UNDEV ECO/DEV AGRI INDUS B22

FOURIER C.,TRAITE DE L'ASSOCIATION DOMESTIQUE-AGRICOLE (2 VOLS.). UNIV SOCIETY INDUS ECO/TAC PERSON MORAL ANARCH. PAGE 43 F0834 VOL/ASSN AGRI UTOPIA CONCPT B23

FINER H.,REPRESENTATIVE GOVERNMENT AND A PARLIAMENT OF INDUSTRY. A STUDY OF THE GERMAN FEDERAL ECONOMIC COUNCIL. GERMANY UK CONSTN INDUS PARL/PROC ...NAT/COMP 20. PAGE 41 F0796 DELIB/GP ECO/TAC WAR REV B23

HOBSON J.A.,INCENTIVES IN THE NEW INDUSTRIAL ORDER. USA-45 NAT/G PAY COST EFFICIENCY PRODUC WEALTH ...MAJORIT PSY SOC/WK 20. PAGE 60 F1186 INDUS LABOR INCOME OPTIMAL B24

CLARK J.B.,THE DISTRIBUTION OF WEALTH (1899). WORKER OWN PRODUC PROFIT WEALTH LAISSEZ...IDEA/COMP GEN/LAWS. PAGE 25 F0478 ECO/TAC INDUS LABOR INCOME B25

EDGEWORTH F.Y.,PAPERS RELATING TO POLITICAL ECONOMY. MOD/EUR SOCIETY STRATA DIST/IND INDUS MARKET NAT/G ACT/RES ECO/TAC EXEC WEALTH ...METH/CNCPT MATH TREND HYPO/EXP SIMUL GEN/METH FOR/TRADE VAL/FREE LOG/LING. PAGE 36 F0702 ECO/DEV CAP/ISM B26

MCPHEE A.,THE ECONOMIC REVOLUTION IN BRITISH WEST AFRICA. AFR UK CULTURE DIST/IND FINAN INDUS PLAN GP/REL RACE/REL 20 AFRICA/W. PAGE 88 F1735 ECO/UNDEV INT/TRADE COLONIAL GEOG B26

SUFRIN S.C.,A BRIEF ANNOTATED BIBLIOGRAPHY ON LABOR IN EMERGING SOCIETIES. WOR+45 CULTURE SOCIETY INDUS EDU/PROP GP/REL INGP/REL. PAGE 127 F2510 BIBLIOG/A LABOR ECO/UNDEV WORKER B26

TAWNEY R.H.,RELIGION AND THE RISE OF CAPITALISM. UK CULTURE NAT/G TEC/DEV OWN LAISSEZ...POLICY SOC TIME/SEQ 16/19. PAGE 129 F2537 SECT WEALTH INDUS CAP/ISM B27

BELLOC H.,THE SERVILE STATE (1912) (3RD ED.). PRUSSIA UK CULTURE STRATA INDUS NAT/G ECO/TAC CONTROL LEAD SUFF DISCRIM EQUILIB ORD/FREE WEALTH 20. PAGE 12 F0237 WORKER CAP/ISM DOMIN CATH B27

WEBER M.,GENERAL ECONOMIC HISTORY. CHRIST-17C MOD/EUR STRUCT AGRI EXTR/IND FINAN INDUS MARKET FAM NAT/G PROF/ORG SECT ECO/TAC MUNICH 8/20. PAGE 144 F2839 ECO/DEV CAP/ISM B30

BIEL G.,TREATISE ON THE POWER AND UTILITY OF MONEY (1484). INDUS MARKET LOC/G NAT/G SECT ECO/TAC PRODUC WEALTH 15. PAGE 15 F0280 FINAN COST PRICE GEN/LAWS B30

HAWTREY R.G.,ECONOMIC ASPECTS OF SOVEREIGNTY. UNIV WOR+45 WOR-45 ECO/DEV ECO/UNDEV AGRI COM/IND INDUS MARKET NAT/G TEC/DEV ECO/TAC EDU/PROP COERCE ATTIT KNOWL WEALTH...CONCPT CON/ANAL GEN/LAWS 20. PAGE 57 F1118 FORCES PWR SOVEREIGN WAR B30

KEYNES J.M.,A TREATISE ON MONEY (2 VOLS.). UK USA-45 INDUS MARKET WORKER PRICE CONTROL COST OPTIMAL PROFIT WEALTH...POLICY 19/20 KEYNES/JM. PAGE 70 F1385 EQUILIB ECO/TAC FINAN GEN/LAWS B34

GRAHAM F.D.,PROTECTIVE TARIFFS. FUT USA+45 WOR-45 INDUS MARKET VOL/ASSN PLAN CAP/ISM ECO/TAC PEACE ATTIT DRIVE HEALTH ORD/FREE...OBS TREND GEN/LAWS FOR/TRADE 20. PAGE 50 F0970 INT/ORG TARIFFS B34

MARX K.,THE CLASS STRUGGLES IN FRANCE. FRANCE INDUS WORKER CONSERVE...TREND GEN/LAWS 19. PAGE 86 F1689 MARXIST STRATA REV INT/TRADE B34

ROBINSON J.,THE ECONOMICS OF IMPERFECT COMPETITION. FINAN ECO/TAC PRICE COST DEMAND EQUILIB OPTIMAL WEALTH...METH MONOPOLY. PAGE 113 F2221 MARKET WORKER INDUS B35

HICKS J.R.,THE THEORY OF WAGES. INDUS NAT/G PAY PRICE CONTROL COST EFFICIENCY WEALTH 19/20 MARSHALL/A CLARK/JB. PAGE 59 F1164 INCOME WORKER LABOR PRODUC B35

KEYNES J.M.,THE GENERAL THEORY OF EMPLOYMENT, INTEREST, AND MONEY. AGRI INDUS WORKER ECO/TAC DEMAND EQUILIB INCOME PRODUC PROFIT ATTIT WEALTH 20. PAGE 71 F1386 FINAN GEN/LAWS MARKET PRICE B35

WADE J.,HISTORY OF THE MIDDLE AND WORKING CLASSES; WITH A POPULAR EXPOSITION OF THE ECONOMICAL AND POLITICAL PRINCIPLES.... FRANCE UK CONSTN FINAN INDUS LABOR INCOME PROFIT KNOWL MORAL ORD/FREE WEALTH...CHARTS 14/19. PAGE 142 F2797 WORKER STRATA CONCPT B36

BURNS A.R.,THE DECLINE OF COMPETITION. LAW LG/CO NAT/G SML/CO LEGIS PRICE AGREE CONTROL GP/REL INCOME PRODUC...POLICY 19/20 NRA. PAGE 20 F0390 MARKET GEN/LAWS INDUS B37

DALTON J.E.,SUGAR: A CASE STUDY OF GOVERNMENT CONTROL. USA-45 AGRI PROC/MFG LG/CO LEGIS PROB/SOLV ECO/TAC GP/REL...CHARTS 19/20. PAGE 30 F0575 CONTROL NAT/G INDUS POLICY B37

HAMILTON W.H.,THE POWER TO GOVERN. ECO/DEV FINAN INDUS ECO/TAC INT/TRADE TARIFFS TAX CONTROL CT/SYS WAR COST PWR 18/20 SUPREME/CT. PAGE 54 F1056 LING CONSTN NAT/G POLICY B37

MACKENZIE F.,PLANNED SOCIETY: YESTERDAY, TODAY, AND TOMORROW. ECO/DEV ECO/UNDEV AGRI FINAN INDUS PLAN INSPECT CONTROL ALL/IDEOS...TREND METH/COMP BIBLIOG 20 RESOURCE/N. PAGE 83 F1635 SOC CONCPT ANTHOL B37

ROBBINS L.,ECONOMIC PLANNING AND INTERNATIONAL ORDER. WOR-45 SOCIETY FINAN INDUS NAT/G ECO/TAC ROUTINE WEALTH...SOC TIME/SEQ GEN/METH WORK 20 KEYNES/JM. PAGE 112 F2202 INT/ORG PLAN INT/TRADE B37

UNION OF SOUTH AFRICA,REPORT CONCERNING ADMINISTRATION OF SOUTH WEST AFRICA (6 VOLS.). NAT/G ADMIN

SOUTH/AFR INDUS PUB/INST FORCES LEGIS BUDGET DIPLOM EDU/PROP ADJUD CT/SYS...GEOG CHARTS 20 AFRICA/SW LEAGUE/NAT. PAGE 132 F2610
COLONIAL CONSTN

B38
CARVALHO C.M.,GEOGRAPHIA HUMANA; POLITICA E ECONOMICA (3RD ED.). BRAZIL CULTURE AGRI INDUS DIPLOM COLONIAL GP/REL RACE/REL...LING 20 RESOURCE/N. PAGE 22 F0424
GEOG HABITAT

B38
DAVIES E.,"NATIONAL" CAPITALISM: THE GOVERNMENT'S RECORD AS PROTECTOR OF PRIVATE MONOPOLY. UK ELITES SOCIETY STRATA POL/PAR WORKER PROB/SOLV CONTROL SOCISM 20 MONOPOLY LABOR/PAR CHAMBRLN/N. PAGE 30 F0583
CAP/ISM NAT/G INDUS POLICY

B38
LANGE O.,ON THE ECONOMIC THEORY OF SOCIALISM. UNIV ECO/DEV FINAN INDUS INT/ORG PUB/INST ROUTINE ATTIT ALL/VALS...SOC CONCPT STAT TREND 20. PAGE 75 F1475
MARKET ECO/TAC INT/TRADE SOCISM

B38
LAWLEY F.E.,THE GROWTH OF COLLECTIVE ECONOMY VOL. 1: NATIONAL. EUR+WWI AGRI INDUS NAT/G BARGAIN CAP/ISM ECO/TAC WAR OPTIMAL WEALTH...GOV/COMP METH/COMP 19/20 MONOPOLY. PAGE 76 F1492
SOCISM PRICE CONTROL OWN

B38
LAWLEY F.E.,THE GROWTH OF COLLECTIVE ECONOMY VOL. 2: INTERNATIONAL. WOR-45 AGRI INDUS EQUILIB OPTIMAL OWN WEALTH...NAT/COMP 19/20 NAZI NEW/DEAL MONOPOLY. PAGE 76 F1493
ECO/TAC SOCISM NAT/LISM CONTROL

B38
MEADE J.E.,AN INTRODUCTION TO ECONOMIC ANALYSIS AND POLICY (AMERICAN EDITION EDITED BY C.J. HITCH). FINAN INDUS MARKET LABOR INT/TRADE CONTROL COST DEMAND INCOME...CLASSIF CHARTS T 20 KEYNES/JM MONOPOLY. PAGE 89 F1737
CONCPT PROFIT PRODUC

B38
REICH N.,LABOR RELATIONS IN REPUBLICAN GERMANY. GERMANY CONSTN ECO/DEV INDUS NAT/G ADMIN CONTROL GP/REL FASCISM POPULISM 20 WEIMAR/REP. PAGE 110 F2176
WORKER MGT LABOR BARGAIN

S38
HALL R.C.,"REPRESENTATION OF BIG BUSINESS IN THE HOUSE OF COMMONS." UK ECO/DEV INDUS PROF/ORG LEGIS CAP/ISM ECO/TAC LAISSEZ...POLICY OLD/LIB PLURIST MGT 20 HOUSE/CMNS. PAGE 53 F1047
LOBBY NAT/G

B39
FURNIVALL J.S.,NETHERLANDS INDIA. INDIA NETHERLAND CULTURE INDUS NAT/G DIPLOM ADMIN WEALTH...POLICY CHARTS 17/20. PAGE 45 F0876
COLONIAL ECO/UNDEV SOVEREIGN PLURISM

B39
MARQUAND H.A.,ORGANIZED LABOUR IN FOUR CONTINENTS. EUR+WWI USA-45 INDUS NAT/G PAY GP/REL TOTALISM ATTIT WEALTH ALL/IDEOS...TREND NAT/COMP 20 ILO AFL/CIO EUROPE CHINJAP MEXIC/AMER. PAGE 85 F1673
LABOR WORKER CONCPT ANTHOL

B40
CAMPBELL P.,CONSUMER REPRESENTATION IN THE NEW DEAL. AGRI INDUS MARKET EX/STRUC PLAN CAP/ISM CONTROL GP/REL DEMAND POLICY. PAGE 21 F0408
CLIENT REPRESENT NAT/G

B40
SIKES E.R.,CONTEMPORARY ECONOMIC SYSTEMS: THEIR ANALYSIS AND SOCIAL BACKGROUND. GERMANY ITALY USSR AGRI INDUS PLAN CAP/ISM ROUTINE TOTALISM FASCISM ...POLICY CON/ANAL BIBLIOG 20. PAGE 122 F2400
COM SOCISM CONCPT

B40
TRIFFIN R.,MONOPOLISTIC COMPETITION AND GENERAL EQUILIBRIUM THEORY. DIST/IND PLAN TASK EQUILIB OPTIMAL...IDEA/COMP 20 MONOPOLY. PAGE 131 F2586
INT/TRADE INDUS COST

B40
WUNDERLICH F.,LABOR UNDER GERMAN DEMOCRACY, ARBITRATION 1918-1933. GERMANY NAT/G PAY REPAR ADJUD CT/SYS GP/REL...MAJORIT 20. PAGE 149 F2941
LABOR WORKER INDUS BARGAIN

B41
DAUGHERTY C.R.,LABOR PROBLEMS IN AMERICAN INDUSTRY (5TH ED.). USA-45 SOCIETY OP/RES ECO/TAC...MGT PSY T 20. PAGE 30 F0581
LABOR INDUS GP/REL PROB/SOLV

B41
ESTEY J.A.,BUSINESS CYCLES; THEIR NATURE, CAUSE, AND CONTROL. NAT/G BUDGET CAP/ISM TAX PRICE CONTROL INCOME...MODAL TIME/SEQ GEN/METH T 18/20 KEYNES/JM MONEY. PAGE 38 F0749
INDUS FINAN ECO/TAC POLICY

B41
HANSEN A.H.,FISCAL POLICY AND BUSINESS CYCLES. UK INDUS PROB/SOLV DIPLOM INT/TRADE OPTIMAL...POLICY TIME/SEQ CHARTS 19/20. PAGE 54 F1062
FINAN PLAN ECO/TAC GOV/REL

B41
LESTER R.A.,ECONOMICS OF LABOR. UK USA-45 TEC/DEV BARGAIN PAY INGP/REL INCOME...MGT 19/20. PAGE 78 F1532
LABOR ECO/DEV INDUS WORKER

B41
SLICHTER S.H.,UNION POLICIES AND INDUSTRIAL MANAGEMENT. USA-45 INDUS TEC/DEV PAY GP/REL INGP/REL COST EFFICIENCY PRODUC...POLICY 20. PAGE 123 F2420
BARGAIN LABOR MGT WORKER

B42
DRUCKER P.F.,THE FUTURE OF INDUSTRIAL MAN; A CONSERVATIVE APPROACH. USA-45 LOC/G PLAN WAR CENTRAL RATIONAL TOTALISM ORD/FREE LAISSEZ ...PLURIST IDEA/COMP 19/20 HITLER/A. PAGE 34 F0664
INDUS SOCIETY REGION PROB/SOLV

B42
ROBBINS J.J.,THE GOVERNMENT OF LABOR RELATIONS IN SWEDEN. SWEDEN LAW CONSTN ADJUD CT/SYS GP/REL ...JURID 20. PAGE 112 F2200
NAT/G BARGAIN LABOR INDUS

B42
US LIBRARY OF CONGRESS,ECONOMICS OF WAR (APRIL 1941-MARCH 1942). WOR-45 FINAN INDUS LOC/G NAT/G PLAN BUDGET RATION COST DEMAND...POLICY 20. PAGE 138 F2712
BIBLIOG/A INT/TRADE ECO/TAC WAR

B42
US LIBRARY OF CONGRESS,THE WAR PRODUCTION PROGRAM: SELECTED DOCUMENTATION ON THE ECONOMICS OF WAR (PAMPHLET). USA-45 ECO/DEV AGRI FINAN NAT/G ECO/TAC RATION PRICE EFFICIENCY 20. PAGE 138 F2713
BIBLIOG/A WAR PRODUC INDUS

B44
FABIAN SOCIETY,CAN PLANNING BE DEMOCRATIC? UK CULTURE INDUS NAT/G BUDGET ORD/FREE...GEN/LAWS ANTHOL 20. PAGE 39 F0757
PLAN MAJORIT SOCIALIST ECO/DEV

B44
LANDAUER C.,THEORY OF NATIONAL ECONOMIC PLANNING. USA-45 INDUS MARKET WORKER PROB/SOLV DIPLOM RATION PRICE CONTROL WAR COST 20. PAGE 75 F1465
ECO/TAC PLAN NAT/G ECO/DEV

B44
MCFADYEAN A.,GOVERNMENT AND INDUSTRY (PAMPHLET). UK INDUS CONTROL REPRESENT 20. PAGE 88 F1728
POL/PAR SOCISM

B46
DAVIES E.,NATIONAL ENTERPRISE: THE DEVELOPMENT OF THE PUBLIC CORPORATION. UK LG/CO EX/STRUC WORKER PROB/SOLV COST ATTIT SOCISM 20. PAGE 30 F0584
ADMIN NAT/G CONTROL INDUS

B47
BAERWALD F.,FUNDAMENTALS OF LABOR ECONOMICS. LAW INDUS LABOR LG/CO CONTROL GP/REL INCOME TOTALISM ...MGT CHARTS GEN/LAWS BIBLIOG 20. PAGE 8 F0150
ECO/DEV WORKER MARKET

B47
BOWEN R.H.,GERMAN THEORIES OF THE CORPORATIVE STATE, WITH SPECIAL REFERENCES TO THE PERIOD 1870-1919. GERMANY INDUS LG/CO CATHISM SOCISM...SOC 18/20. PAGE 17 F0328
IDEA/COMP CENTRAL NAT/G POLICY

B47
GORDON D.L.,THE HIDDEN WEAPON: THE STORY OF ECONOMIC WARFARE. EUR+WWI USA-45 LAW FINAN INDUS NAT/G CONSULT FORCES PLAN DOMIN PWR WEALTH ...INT/LAW CONCPT OBS TOT/POP NAZI 20. PAGE 49 F0955
INT/ORG ECO/TAC INT/TRADE WAR

B47
TOWLE L.W.,INTERNATIONAL TRADE AND COMMERCIAL POLICY. WOR+45 LAW ECO/DEV FINAN INDUS NAT/G ECO/TAC WEALTH...TIME/SEQ ILO 20. PAGE 131 F2582
MARKET INT/ORG INT/TRADE

B47
WHITEHEAD T.N.,LEADERSHIP IN A FREE SOCIETY; A STUDY IN HUMAN RELATIONS BASED ON AN ANALYSIS OF PRESENT-DAY INDUSTRIAL CIVILIZATION. WOR-45 STRUCT R+D LABOR LG/CO SML/CO WORKER PLAN PROB/SOLV TEC/DEV DRIVE...MGT 20. PAGE 146 F2872
INDUS LEAD ORD/FREE SOCIETY

S47
DAHL R.A.,"WORKERS' CONTROL OF INDUSTRY AND THE BRITISH LABOUR PARTY." UK STRATA STRUCT DELIB/GP BARGAIN CAP/ISM DEBATE CONTROL CHOOSE GP/REL ATTIT ROLE PWR 19/20 PARLIAMENT LABOR/PAR FABIAN. PAGE 29 F0570
INDUS LABOR WORKER SOCISM

B48
HOOVER E.M.,THE LOCATION OF ECONOMIC ACTIVITY. WOR+45 MARKET WORKER PROB/SOLV INT/TRADE ADMIN COST ...POLICY CHARTS T MUNICH 20. PAGE 62 F1211
HABITAT INDUS ECO/TAC GEOG

B48
KESSELMAN L.C.,THE SOCIAL POLITICS OF THE FEPC. INDUS WORKER EDU/PROP GP/REL RACE/REL 20 NEGRO JEWS FEPC. PAGE 70 F1382
POLICY NAT/G ADMIN DISCRIM

B48
METZLER L.A.,INCOME, EMPLOYMENT, AND PUBLIC POLICY. FINAN INDUS LOC/G NAT/G TAX GIVE PAY COST PRODUC ...MGT TIME/SEQ 20. PAGE 90 F1765
INCOME WEALTH POLICY ECO/TAC

S48
CLEVELAND A.S.,"NAM: SPOKESMAN FOR INDUSTRY?" LEGIS PLAN LEAD LOBBY PARTIC CONSEN INCOME ATTIT ROLE ORD/FREE POLICY. PAGE 25 F0491
VOL/ASSN CLIENT REPRESENT INDUS

B49
SHISTER J.,ECONOMICS OF THE LABOR MARKET. LOC/G NAT/G WORKER TEC/DEV BARGAIN PAY PRICE EXEC GP/REL INCOME...MGT T 20. PAGE 121 F2381
MARKET LABOR INDUS

S49
ECKLER A.R.,"IMMIGRATION AND THE LABOR FORCE." USA+45 USA-45 EXTR/IND FINAN PROC/MFG AGE/Y SKILL ...CHARTS 19/20 MIGRATION. PAGE 36 F0694
WORKER STRANGE INDUS ECO/TAC

S49
STEINMETZ H.,"THE PROBLEMS OF THE LANDRAT: A STUDY OF COUNTY GOVERNMENT IN THE US ZONE OF GERMANY." GERMANY/W USA+45 INDUS PLAN DIPLOM EDU/PROP CONTROL WAR GOV/REL FEDERAL WEALTH PLURISM...GOV/COMP 20 LANDRAT. PAGE 126 F2478
LOC/G COLONIAL MGT TOP/EX

B50
CHAMBERLIN E.,THE THEORY OF MONOPOLISTIC COMPETITION (1933). INDUS PAY GP/REL COST DEMAND EFFICIENCY OPTIMAL PRODUC WEALTH...GEN/LAWS 20. PAGE 23 F0443
MARKET PRICE ECO/TAC EQUILIB

B50
CLARK J.M.,ALTERNATIVE TO SERFDOM. SOCIETY STRATA INDUS MARKET WORKER PRICE GP/REL PROFIT BIO/SOC PWR WEALTH...GEN/LAWS 20 KEYNES/JM. PAGE 25 F0481
ORD/FREE POPULISM ECO/TAC REPRESENT

B50
HOOVER G.,TWENTIETH CENTURY ECONOMIC THOUGHT. USA+45 ECO/DEV AGRI FINAN INDUS MARKET SERV/IND LABOR NAT/G...STAT 20. PAGE 62 F1213
ECO/TAC CAP/ISM INT/TRADE

B50
LINCOLN G.,ECONOMICS OF NATIONAL SECURITY. USA+45 ELITES COM/IND DIST/IND INDUS NAT/G VOL/ASSN DELIB/GP EX/STRUC FOR/AID EDU/PROP COERCE NUC/PWR WAR ATTIT KNOWL ORD/FREE PWR TOT/POP VAL/FREE 20. PAGE 80 F1565
FORCES ECO/TAC AFR

B50
MARX H.L.,THE WELFARE STATE. USA+45 USA-45 CHIEF CAP/ISM CENTRAL ORD/FREE LAISSEZ...SOC ANTHOL 20. PAGE 86 F1686
ECO/DEV INDUS WEALTH WELF/ST

B50
US DEPARTMENT OF STATE,POINT FOUR: COOPERATIVE PROGRAM FOR AID IN THE DEVELOPMENT OF ECONOMICALLY UNDERDEVELOPED AREAS. WOR+45 AGRI INDUS INT/ORG PLAN TEC/DEV DIPLOM EDU/PROP ADMIN PEACE PRODUC WEALTH 20 CONGRESS UN. PAGE 135 F2671
ECO/UNDEV FOR/AID FINAN INT/TRADE

S50
DALTON M.,"CONFLICTS BETWEEN STAFF AND LINE MANAGERIAL OFFICERS" (BMR). USA+45 USA-45 ELITES LG/CO WORKER PROB/SOLV ADMIN EXEC EFFICIENCY PRODUC ...GP/COMP 20. PAGE 30 F0576
MGT ATTIT GP/REL INDUS

S50
DREYFUS S.,"THE INDUSTRIAL DESIGNER AND THE BUSINESSMAN." SERV/IND PROB/SOLV ECO/TAC COST EFFICIENCY PROFIT RATIONAL...DECISION MGT. PAGE 34 F0662
CONSULT INDUS PRODUC UTIL

B51
CLARK C.,THE CONDITIONS OF ECONOMIC PROGRESS. EUR+WWI WOR+45 WOR-45 ECO/DEV INDUS CAP/ISM MORAL ...WELF/ST METH/CNCPT STAT TOT/POP VAL/FREE 20. PAGE 25 F0477
MARKET WEALTH

B51
HART A.G.,DEFENSE WITHOUT INFLATION. AFR KOREA FINAN INDUS NAT/G WORKER DIPLOM RATION TAX PRICE COST OPTIMAL 20 RESOURCE/N. PAGE 56 F1098
ECO/TAC CONTROL WAR PLAN

B51
POOLE K.,FISCAL POLICIES AND THE AMERICAN ECONOMY. AFR ECO/DEV FINAN INDUS WORKER OP/RES INT/TRADE TAX COST INCOME PROFIT WEALTH...GP/COMP 20. PAGE 107 F2102
NAT/G POLICY ANTHOL

B51
PRINCETON U INDUSTRIAL REL SEC,COMPULSORY ARBITRATION OF UTILITY DISPUTES IN NEW JERSEY AND PENNSYLVANIA. USA+45 LEGIS WORKER ADJUD ORD/FREE ...POLICY MGT METH/COMP 20 NEW/JERSEY PENNSYLVAN. PAGE 108 F2118
BARGAIN PROVS INDUS LABOR

B51
US DEPARTMENT OF STATE,POINT FOUR, NEAR EAST AND AFRICA, A SELECTED BIBLIOGRAPHY OF STUDIES ON ECONOMICALLY UNDERDEVELOPED COUNTRIES. AGRI COM/IND FINAN INDUS PLAN INT/TRADE...SOC TREND 20. PAGE 135 F2672
BIBLIOG/A AFR S/ASIA ISLAM

B52
ASHWORTH W.,A SHORT HISTORY OF THE INTERNATIONAL ECONOMY 1850-1950. WOR+45 WOR-45 AGRI FINAN INDUS MARKET LABOR ECO/TAC...CONCPT STAT HIST/WRIT FOR/TRADE ILO 19/20. PAGE 7 F0131
ECO/DEV TEC/DEV INT/TRADE

B52
AYRES C.E.,THE INDUSTRIAL ECONOMY. USA+45 FINAN MARKET NAT/G PUB/INST PLAN ECO/TAC TAX DEMAND INCOME...BIBLIOG/A 20. PAGE 8 F0146
ECO/DEV INDUS FUT PROB/SOLV

B52
TANNENBAUM F.,A PHILOSOPHY OF LABOR. SOCIETY STRATA INDUS LG/CO AGREE ADJUST OWN ORD/FREE PWR...CONCPT 20. PAGE 128 F2533
LABOR PHIL/SCI WORKER CREATE

S52
CHINOY E.,"THE TRADITION OF OPPORTUNITY AND THE ASPIRATIONS OF AUTOMOBILE WORKERS" (BMR)" STRATA ACT/RES ALL/VALS SKILL...INT 20. PAGE 24 F0468
WORKER ECO/DEV DRIVE INDUS

S52
KLUMB S.,"EMPLOYEE DETERMINATION OF MANAGERIAL FUNCTIONS AND CHARACTERISTICS." DELIB/GP WORKER PARTIC ROUTINE INGP/REL...CLASSIF OBS QU. PAGE 72 F1410
MGT INDUS EX/STRUC CHOOSE

C52
HUME D.,"OF COMMERCE" IN D. HUME, POLITICAL DISCOURSES (1752)" UK FINAN DIPLOM WEALTH ...GEN/LAWS 18 MONEY. PAGE 63 F1238
INDUS INT/TRADE PWR AGRI

C52
HUME D.,"OF INTEREST" IN D. HUME, POLITICAL DISCOURSES (1752)" UK INDUS WORKER DIPLOM PAY DEMAND INCOME WEALTH...GEN/LAWS 18 MONEY. PAGE 63 F1239
PRICE COST FINAN INT/TRADE

C52
HUME D.,"OF MONEY" IN D. HUME, POLITICAL DISCOURSES (1752)" UK INDUS DIPLOM INT/TRADE...GEN/LAWS 18 MONEY. PAGE 63 F1240
FINAN COST PRICE WEALTH

B53
FLORENCE P.S.,THE LOGIC OF BRITISH AND AMERICAN INDUSTRY; A REALISTIC ANALYSIS OF ECONOMIC STRUCTURE AND GOVERNMENT. UK USA+45 USA-45 FINAN LABOR CAP/ISM INGP/REL EFFICIENCY...MGT CONCPT STAT CHARTS METH 20. PAGE 42 F0813
INDUS ECO/DEV NAT/G NAT/COMP

B53
FRANKEL S.H.,THE ECONOMIC IMPACT ON UNDERDEVELOPED SOCIETIES: ESSAYS ON INTERNATIONAL INVESTMENT AND SOCIAL CHANGE. AFR WOR+45 ECO/DEV FINAN INDUS NAT/G ACT/RES TEC/DEV COLONIAL ATTIT...CONCPT OBS TREND 20. PAGE 43 F0845
ECO/UNDEV FOR/AID INT/TRADE

B53
NEISSER H.,NATIONAL INCOMES AND INTERNATIONAL TRADE. FRANCE GERMANY SWEDEN UK USA-45 EXTR/IND FINAN INDUS TEC/DEV PRICE BAL/PAY EQUILIB INCOME WEALTH...CHARTS METH 19 CHINJAP. PAGE 97 F1908
INT/TRADE PRODUC MARKET CON/ANAL

B53
ROBINSON E.A.G.,THE STRUCTURE OF COMPETITIVE INDUSTRY. UK ECO/DEV DIST/IND MARKET TEC/DEV DIPLOM EDU/PROP ADMIN EFFICIENCY WEALTH...MGT 19/20. PAGE 113 F2217
INDUS PRODUC WORKER OPTIMAL

B53
WOYTINSKY W.S.,WORLD POPULATION AND PRODUCTION: TRENDS AND OUTLOOK. FUT WOR+45 WOR-45 CULTURE SOCIETY ECO/DEV AGRI INDUS TEC/DEV EDU/PROP SKILL WEALTH...SOC TREND. PAGE 149 F2928
ECO/UNDEV METH/CNCPT GEOG PERSON

S53
BIRNBAUM N.,"CONFLICTING INTERPRETATIONS OF THE RISE OF CAPITALISM: MARX AND WEBER" (BMR)" WOR-45 INTELL SOCIETY STRUCT INDUS WORKER...PHIL/SCI SOC PERS/COMP 19/20 MARX/KARL WEBER/MAX. PAGE 15 F0288
CAP/ISM IDEA/COMP ECO/DEV MARXISM

S53
GABLE R.W.,"NAM: INFLUENTIAL LOBBY OR KISS OF DEATH?" (BMR)" USA+45 LAW INSPECT EDU/PROP ADMIN CONTROL INGP/REL EFFICIENCY PWR 20 CONGRESS NAM TAFT/HART. PAGE 45 F0880
LOBBY LEGIS INDUS LG/CO

B54
FRIEDMAN W.,THE PUBLIC CORPORATION: A COMPARATIVE SYMPOSIUM (UNIVERSITY OF TORONTO SCHOOL OF LAW COMPARATIVE LAW SERIES, VOL. I). AFR SWEDEN USA+45 INDUS INT/ORG NAT/G REGION CENTRAL FEDERAL...POLICY JURID IDEA/COMP NAT/COMP ANTHOL 20 MONOPOLY EUROPE. PAGE 44 F0861
LAW SOCISM LG/CO OWN

B54
MITCHELL W.G.,BUSINESS CYCLES. FINAN MARKET PRICE COST EQUILIB OPTIMAL PRODUC PROFIT...IDEA/COMP GEN/LAWS 19/20. PAGE 92 F1809
INDUS TIME/SEQ METH/COMP STAT

B54
MOSK S.A.,INDUSTRIAL REVOLUTION IN MEXICO. MARKET LABOR CREATE CAP/ISM ADMIN ATTIT SOCISM...POLICY 20 MEXIC/AMER. PAGE 94 F1843
INDUS TEC/DEV ECO/UNDEV NAT/G

S54
MACK R.W.,"ECOLOGICAL PATTERNS IN AN INDUSTRIAL SHOP" (BMR)" USA+45 CULTURE SOCIETY STRATA STRUCT LABOR NEIGH GP/REL ADJUST HABITAT...SOC SOC/INTEG 20. PAGE 83 F1634
INDUS DISCRIM WORKER

S54
SCITOVSKY T.,"TWO CONCEPTS OF EXTERNAL ECONOMIES." ECO/DEV IDEA/COMP. PAGE 118 F2329
SERV/IND GEN/LAWS INDUS EQUILIB

B55
BRAUN K.,LABOR DISPUTES AND THEIR SETTLEMENT. ECO/TAC ROUTINE TASK GP/REL...DECISION GEN/LAWS. PAGE 18 F0342
INDUS LABOR BARGAIN ADJUD

B55
GEORGE H.,PROGRESS AND POVERTY (1880). STRATA STRUCT INDUS TEC/DEV CAP/ISM EQUILIB INCOME OWN UTOPIA...WELF/ST CONCPT NEW/IDEA 19. PAGE 47 F0915
ECO/DEV ECO/TAC TAX

WEALTH

B55
JONES T.B.,A BIBLIOGRAPHY ON SOUTH AMERICAN ECONOMIC AFFAIRS: ARTICLES IN NINETEENTH CENTURY PERIODICALS (PAMPHLET). AGRI COM/IND DIST/IND EXTR/IND FINAN INDUS LABOR NAT/G 19. PAGE 68 F1340
BIBLIOG ECO/UNDEV L/A+17C TEC/DEV

B55
OECD,MARSHALL PLAN IN TURKEY. TURKEY USA+45 COM/IND CONSTRUC SERV/IND FORCES BUDGET...STAT 20 MARSHL/PLN. PAGE 100 F1964
FOR/AID ECO/UNDEV AGRI INDUS

B55
SERRANO MOSCOSO E.,A STATEMENT OF THE LAWS OF ECUADOR IN MATTERS AFFECTING BUSINESS (2ND ED.). ECUADOR INDUS LABOR LG/CO NAT/G LEGIS TAX CONTROL MARRIAGE 20. PAGE 120 F2359
FINAN ECO/UNDEV LAW CONSTN

B55
UN ECONOMIC COMN ASIA & FAR E,ECONOMIC SURVEY OF ASIA AND THE FAR EAST, 1954. AFGHANISTN CEYLON INDIA PHILIPPINE S/ASIA ECO/DEV FINAN INDUS INT/TRADE PRODUC WEALTH...STAT CHARTS 20 CHINJAP. PAGE 132 F2600
ECO/UNDEV PRICE NAT/COMP ASIA

S55
BUNZEL J.H.,"THE GENERAL IDEOLOGY OF AMERICAN SMALL BUSINESS"(BMR)" USA+45 USA-45 AGRI GP/REL INGP/REL PERSON...MGT IDEA/COMP 18/20. PAGE 20 F0383
ALL/IDEOS ATTIT SML/CO INDUS

S55
HALLETT D.,"THE HISTORY AND STRUCTURE OF OEEC." EUR+WWI USA+45 CONSTN INDUS INT/ORG NAT/G DELIB/GP ACT/RES PLAN ORD/FREE WEALTH...CONCPT OEEC 20 CMN/WLTH. PAGE 54 F1051
VOL/ASSN ECO/DEV

S55
KELLY W.E.,"HOW SALES EXECUTIVES USE FACTORING TO BOOST SALES AND PROFITS TODAY." FINAN LG/CO BUDGET EFFICIENCY PROFIT...MGT PRODUCT. PAGE 70 F1372
INDUS ECO/DEV CONSULT MARKET

B56
ATOMIC INDUSTRIAL FORUM,PUBLIC RELATIONS FOR THE ATOMIC INDUSTRY. WOR+45 PLAN PROB/SOLV EDU/PROP PRESS CONFER...AUD/VIS ANTHOL 20. PAGE 7 F0135
NUC/PWR INDUS GP/REL ATTIT

B56
FELLNER W.,TRENDS AND CYCLES IN ECONOMIC ACTIVITY: AN INTRODUCTION TO PROBLEMS OF ECONOMIC GROWTH. USA+45 INDUS ACT/RES CAP/ISM EQUILIB...MODAL METH/COMP BIBLIOG 20. PAGE 40 F0779
ECO/TAC TREND FINAN ECO/DEV

B56
ISARD W.,LOCATION AND SPACE-ECONOMY: GENERAL THEORY RELATING TO INDUSTRIAL LOCATION, MARKET AREAS, LAND USE, TRADE... UNIV DIST/IND MARKET LG/CO SML/CO TEC/DEV GP/REL EQUILIB HABITAT...NEW/IDEA MATH CHARTS 20. PAGE 66 F1290
GEN/LAWS GEOG INDUS REGION

B56
JUAN T.L.,ECONOMIC AND SOCIAL DEVELOPMENT OF MODERN CHINA: A BIBLIOGRAPHICAL GUIDE. ASIA AGRI COM/IND DIST/IND FINAN INDUS DIPLOM...STAT 20. PAGE 68 F1342
BIBLIOG SOC

B56
KINDLEBERGER C.P.,THE TERMS OF TRADE: A EUROPEAN CASE-STUDY. EUR+WWI MOD/EUR ECO/DEV ECO/UNDEV AGRI INDUS BAL/PAY...METH/CNCPT STAT CONT/OBS CON/ANAL SOC/EXP SIMUL FOR/TRADE 20. PAGE 71 F1390
PLAN ECO/TAC

B56
LIPSET S.M.,UNION DEMOCRACY. STRUCT INDUS FACE/GP WORKER CONTROL LEAD PARTIC GP/REL ATTIT LAISSEZ ...INT QU CHARTS. PAGE 80 F1577
LABOR INGP/REL MAJORIT

B56
UNITED NATIONS,BIBLIOGRAPHY ON INDUSTRIALIZATION IN UNDER-DEVELOPED COUNTRIES. WOR+45 R+D INT/ORG NAT/G FOR/AID ADMIN LEAD 20 UN. PAGE 132 F2612
BIBLIOG ECO/UNDEV INDUS TEC/DEV

B56
US DEPARTMENT OF STATE,ECONOMIC PROBLEMS OF UNDERDEVELOPED AREAS (PAMPHLET). AFR ASIA ISLAM L/A+17C AGRI FINAN INDUS INT/ORG LABOR INT/TRADE ...PSY SOC 20. PAGE 136 F2673
BIBLIOG ECO/UNDEV TEC/DEV R+D

S56
BONILLA F.,"WHEN IS PETITION 'PRESSURE?'" (BMR)" USA+45 ELITES INDUS LABOR CHIEF EDU/PROP LEGIT ATTIT...INT CHARTS 20 CONGRESS PRESIDENT EISNHWR/DD. PAGE 16 F0312
LEGIS EX/STRUC INT/TRADE TARIFFS

S56
GORDON L.,"THE ORGANIZATION FOR EUROPEAN ECONOMIC COOPERATION." EUR+WWI INDUS INT/ORG NAT/G CONSULT DELIB/GP ACT/RES CREATE PLAN TEC/DEV EDU/PROP LEGIT WEALTH OEEC 20. PAGE 49 F0956
VOL/ASSN ECO/DEV

S56
MYERS C.A.,"LINE AND STAFF IN INDUSTRIAL RELATIONS." INDUS LABOR GP/REL PWR...MGT INT. PAGE 96 F1876
ROLE PROB/SOLV ADMIN CONSULT

B57
BAUER P.T.,THE ECONOMICS OF UNDERDEVELOPED COUNTRIES. WOR+45 AGRI FINAN INDUS PROC/MFG WORKER CAP/ISM PAY PRICE INCOME MARXISM...METH/COMP 20 RESOURCE/N. PAGE 11 F0213
ECO/UNDEV ECO/TAC PROB/SOLV NAT/G

B57
BEHRMAN J.N.,INTERNATIONAL ECONOMICS: THEORY, PRACTICE, POLICY. AGRI INDUS NAT/G TARIFFS CONTROL BAL/PAY...POLICY METH/CNCPT T 19/20. PAGE 12 F0230
INT/TRADE FINAN DIPLOM FOR/AID

B57
GOLD N.L.,REGIONAL ECONOMIC DEVELOPMENT AND NUCLEAR POWER IN INDIA. FUT INDIA FINAN FOR/AID INT/TRADE BAL/PAY EFFICIENCY OPTIMAL PRODUC WEALTH...PREDICT 20. PAGE 48 F0934
ECO/UNDEV TEC/DEV NUC/PWR INDUS

B57
INTL BANKING SUMMER SCHOOL,RELATIONS BETWEEN THE CENTRAL BANKS AND COMMERCIAL BANKS. EUR+WWI FRANCE GERMANY/W ITALY UK USA+45 USSR INDUS INT/ORG CAP/ISM CONTROL MONEY. PAGE 65 F1282
FINAN NAT/G GP/REL LG/CO

B57
LEIBENSTEIN H.,ECONOMIC BACKWARDNESS AND ECONOMIC GROWTH. WOR+45 SOCIETY AGRI INDUS TEC/DEV CAP/ISM FOR/AID COST DEMAND WEALTH...CHARTS IDEA/COMP 20. PAGE 77 F1513
ECO/UNDEV ECO/TAC PRODUC POLICY

B57
LENIN V.I.,THE DEVELOPMENT OF CAPITALISM IN RUSSIA. MOD/EUR USSR AGRI MARKET POL/PAR TEC/DEV...CONCPT 19/20. PAGE 78 F1521
COM INDUS CAP/ISM

B57
LOUCKS W.N.,COMPARATIVE ECONOMIC SYSTEMS (5TH ED.). COM UK USSR INDUS POL/PAR PLAN CAP/ISM TOTALISM MARXISM...PHIL/SCI BIBLIOG 19/20. PAGE 82 F1603
NAT/COMP IDEA/COMP SOCISM

B57
LUNDBERG E.,BUSINESS CYCLES AND ECONOMIC POLICY (TRANS. BY J. POTTER). SWEDEN ECO/DEV FINAN DELIB/GP PLAN PRICE CONTROL BAL/PAY 20 INTRVN/ECO. PAGE 82 F1607
ECO/TAC INDUS INT/TRADE BUDGET

B57
MURDESHWAR A.K.,ADMINISTRATIVE PROBLEMS RELATING TO NATIONALISATION: WITH SPECIAL REFERENCE TO INDIAN STATE ENTERPRISES. CZECHOSLVK FRANCE INDIA UK USA+45 LEGIS WORKER PROB/SOLV BUDGET PRICE CONTROL ...MGT GEN/LAWS 20 PARLIAMENT. PAGE 95 F1863
NAT/G OWN INDUS ADMIN

B57
PALACIOS A.L.,PETROLEO, MONOPOLIOS, Y LATIFUNDIOS. L/A+17C EXTR/IND NAT/G TEC/DEV ECO/TAC CONTROL PRODUC 20 ARGEN MONOPOLY RESOURCE/N. PAGE 103 F2017
ECO/UNDEV NAT/LISM INDUS AGRI

B57
SCHNEIDER E.V.,INDUSTRIAL SOCIOLOGY: THE SOCIAL RELATIONS OF INDUSTRY AND COMMUNITY. STRATA INDUS NAT/G NEIGH CREATE ADMIN PARTIC GP/REL RACE/REL ROLE PWR...POLICY BIBLIOG. PAGE 117 F2308
LABOR MGT INGP/REL STRUCT

S57
ANSHEN M.,"BUSINESS, LAWYERS, AND ECONOMISTS." PROB/SOLV ECO/TAC CONFER PROFIT RIGID/FLEX OBJECTIVE...MGT GP/COMP. PAGE 6 F0106
INDUS CONSULT ROUTINE EFFICIENCY

S57
LEWIS E.G.,"PARLIAMENTARY CONTROL OF NATIONALIZED INDUSTRY IN FRANCE." FRANCE NAT/G DELIB/GP ACT/RES PLAN PROB/SOLV ECO/TAC DOMIN CENTRAL. PAGE 79 F1547
PWR LEGIS INDUS CONTROL

B58
ATOMIC INDUSTRIAL FORUM,MANAGEMENT AND ATOMIC ENERGY. WOR+45 SEA LAW MARKET NAT/G TEC/DEV INSPECT INT/TRADE CONFER PEACE HEALTH...ANTHOL 20. PAGE 7 F0136
NUC/PWR INDUS MGT ECO/TAC

B58
AVRAMOVIC D.,POSTWAR GROWTH IN INTERNATIONAL INDEBTEDNESS. AFR WOR+45 AGRI INDUS CAP/ISM PRICE INCOME...NAT/COMP 20 SILVER. PAGE 8 F0143
INT/TRADE FINAN COST BAL/PAY

B58
BANCROFT G.,THE AMERICAN LABOR FORCE: ITS GROWTH AND CHANGING COMPOSITION. FUT USA+45 USA-45 ECO/DEV INDUS WORKER...GEOG CHARTS 19/20. PAGE 9 F0170
LABOR STAT TREND CENSUS

B58
BIDWELL P.W.,RAW MATERIALS: A STUDY OF AMERICAN POLICY. USA+45 USA-45 ECO/UNDEV AGRI INDUS KIN CREATE PLAN ECO/TAC WAR PEACE ATTIT DRIVE WEALTH ...STAT CHARTS CONGRESS FOR/TRADE VAL/FREE. PAGE 15 F0279
EXTR/IND ECO/DEV

B58
BUGEDA LANZAS J.,A STATEMENT OF THE LAWS OF CUBA IN MATTERS AFFECTING BUSINESS (2ND ED. REV., ENLARGED). CUBA L/A+17C LAW FINAN FAM LEGIS ACT/RES ADMIN GP/REL...BIBLIOG 20 OAS. PAGE 20 F0382
JURID NAT/G INDUS WORKER

B58
CHEEK G.,ECONOMIC AND SOCIAL IMPLICATIONS OF AUTOMATION: A BIBLIOGRAPHIC REVIEW (PAMPHLET). USA+45 LG/CO WORKER CREATE PLAN CONTROL ROUTINE PERS/REL EFFICIENCY PRODUC...METH/COMP 20. PAGE 24 F0459
BIBLIOG/A SOCIETY INDUS AUTOMAT

B58
CLAIRMONTE F.,LE LIBERALISME ECONOMIQUE ET LES PAYS SOUS-DEVELOPPES: ETUDES SUR L'EVOLUTION D'UNE IDEE. ASIA INDIA UK FINAN INDUS PLAN CAP/ISM ECO/TAC
LAISSEZ ECO/UNDEV

COLONIAL NEW/LIB...BIBLIOG 20 THIRD/WRLD. PAGE 24 F0475

B58
CLAUNCH J.M.,THE PROBLEM OF GOVERNMENT IN METROPOLITAN AREAS. CULTURE INDUS POL/PAR PLAN REGION GP/REL...CENSUS ANTHOL MUNICH 20. PAGE 25 F0486 PROB/SOLV SOC

B58
COLM G.,THE ECONOMY OF THE AMERICAN PEOPLE: PROGRESS, PROBLEMS, PROSPECTS. USA+45 INDUS MARKET LABOR TEC/DEV INCOME 20. PAGE 26 F0509 WEALTH PRODUC CAP/ISM MGT

B58
COOK P.L.,EFFECTS OF MERGERS: SIX STUDIES. USA+45 ECO/DEV LABOR LG/CO SML/CO VOL/ASSN ADMIN EFFICIENCY 20 CASEBOOK. PAGE 27 F0529 INDUS FINAN EX/STRUC GP/REL

B58
CUNNINGHAM W.B.,COMPULSORY CONCILIATION AND COLLECTIVE BARGAINING. CANADA NAT/G LEGIS ADJUD CT/SYS GP/REL...MGT 20 NEW/BRUNS STRIKE CASEBOOK. PAGE 29 F0563 POLICY BARGAIN LABOR INDUS

B58
DOWNIE J.,THE COMPETITIVE PROCESS. ECO/TAC PRICE EFFICIENCY OPTIMAL PRODUC WEALTH...IDEA/COMP METH/COMP 20 MONOPOLY. PAGE 34 F0658 EQUILIB MARKET INDUS ECO/DEV

B58
EHRHARD J.,LE DESTIN DU COLONIALISME. AFR FRANCE ECO/UNDEV AGRI FINAN MARKET CREATE PLAN TEC/DEV BUDGET DIPLOM PRICE 20. PAGE 36 F0710 COLONIAL FOR/AID INT/TRADE INDUS

B58
FINER S.E.,PRIVATE INDUSTRY AND POLITICAL POWER (PAMPHLET). UK INDUS CONTROL LOBBY PWR. PAGE 41 F0797 PLURISM REPRESENT EX/STRUC

B58
HANCE W.A.,AFRICAN ECONOMIC DEVELOPMENT. AGRI DIST/IND INDUS R+D ACT/RES PLAN CAP/ISM FOR/AID ...GOV/COMP BIBLIOG 20. PAGE 54 F1058 AFR ECO/UNDEV PROB/SOLV TEC/DEV

B58
LESTER R.A.,AS UNIONS MATURE. POL/PAR BARGAIN LEAD PARTIC GP/REL CENTRAL...MAJORIT TIME/SEQ METH/COMP. PAGE 78 F1533 LABOR INDUS POLICY MGT

B58
MCIVOR R.C.,CANADIAN MONETARY, BANKING, AND FISCAL DEVELOPMENT. CANADA INDUS LG/CO NAT/G SML/CO CONTROL WAR...GEN/LAWS BIBLIOG 17/20. PAGE 88 F1729 ECO/TAC FINAN ECO/DEV WEALTH

B58
MIKESELL R.F.,FINANCING FREE WORLD TRADE WITH THE SINO-SOVIET BLOC. CHINA/COM COM USSR WOR+45 ECO/DEV AGRI DIST/IND EXTR/IND FINAN INDUS MARKET PROC/MFG NAT/G PLAN TEC/DEV ECO/TAC...CHARTS METH/GP EEC FOR/TRADE 20. PAGE 91 F1780 STAT BAL/PAY

B58
MOULTON H.G.,CAN INFLATION BE CONTROLLED? ECO/DEV INDUS CAP/ISM RATION GOV/REL COST INCOME PEACE WEALTH...CHARTS TIME 20 KEYNES/JM MONEY. PAGE 94 F1847 ECO/TAC CONTROL DEMAND FINAN

B58
OEEC,THE INDUSTRIAL CHALLENGE OF NUCLEAR ENERGY. EUR+WWI ECO/DEV INDUS OP/RES CONFER RISK PWR ...AUD/VIS CHARTS ANTHOL 20 OEEC. PAGE 101 F1977 NUC/PWR ACT/RES ECO/TAC INT/ORG

B58
PALMER E.E.,INDUSTRIAL MAN. USA+45 PERSON ORD/FREE POPULISM...PREDICT TREND ANTHOL 20. PAGE 103 F2020 INDUS ECO/UNDEV CULTURE WEALTH

B58
US OPERATIONS MISSION TO VIET,BUILDING ECONOMIC STRENGTH (PAMPHLET). USA+45 VIETNAM/S INDUS TEC/DEV BUDGET ADMIN EATING HEALTH...STAT 20. PAGE 138 F2725 FOR/AID ECO/UNDEV AGRI EDU/PROP

B58
WOODS H.D.,PATTERNS OF INDUSTRIAL DISPUTE SETTLEMENT IN FIVE CANADIAN INDUSTRIES. CANADA USA+45 CONSULT ADJUD GP/REL...JURID GOV/COMP METH/COMP ANTHOL 20. PAGE 148 F2923 BARGAIN INDUS LABOR NAT/G

L58
FORRESTER J.W.,"INDUSTRIAL DYNAMICS* A MAJOR BREAKTHROUGH FOR DECISION MAKERS." COMPUTER OP/RES ...DECISION CONCPT NEW/IDEA. PAGE 42 F0830 INDUS ACT/RES MGT PROB/SOLV

L58
TRAGER F.N.,"A SELECTED AND ANNOTATED BIBLIOGRAPHY ON ECONOMIC DEVELOPMENT, 1953-1957." WOR+45 AGRI FINAN INDUS MARKET LABOR WORKER PLAN INT/TRADE PRODUC...CENSUS MUNICH. PAGE 131 F2583 BIBLIOG/A ECO/UNDEV ECO/DEV

S58
ELKIN A.B.,"OEEC-ITS STRUCTURE AND POWERS." EUR+WWI CONSTN INDUS INT/ORG NAT/G VOL/ASSN DELIB/GP ACT/RES PLAN ORD/FREE WEALTH...CHARTS ORG/CHARTS OEEC 20. PAGE 37 F0719 ECO/DEV EX/STRUC

S58
JOHNSON D.G.,"GOVERNMENT AND AGRICULTURE: IS AGRICULTURE A SPECIAL CASE?" PLAN ECO/TAC LOBBY WEALTH POLICY. PAGE 67 F1321 INDUS GP/REL INCOME NAT/G

S58
LOCKWOOD W.W.,"THE SOCIALISTIC SOCIETY: INDIA AND JAPAN." INDIA ECO/DEV ECO/UNDEV INDUS NAT/G CONTROL LEAD PRODUC WEALTH 20 CHINJAP. PAGE 81 F1593 ECO/TAC NAT/COMP FINAN SOCISM

B59
AITKEN H.G.,THE AMERICAN ECONOMIC IMPACT ON CANADA. CANADA USA+45 AGRI FINAN INDUS LABOR INT/TRADE BAL/PAY...INT/LAW TREND 20. PAGE 3 F0055 DIPLOM ECO/TAC POLICY NAT/G

B59
BARNETT A.D.,COMMUNIST ECONOMIC STRATEGY: THE RISE OF MAINLAND CHINA. CHINA/COM USSR WOR+45 AGRI INDUS FOR/AID INGP/REL ATTIT. PAGE 10 F0188 ECO/UNDEV INT/TRADE TOTALISM BAL/PWR

B59
BONNETT C.E.,LABOR-MANAGEMENT RELATIONS. USA+45 OP/RES PROB/SOLV EDU/PROP...AUD/VIS CHARTS 20. PAGE 16 F0317 MGT LABOR INDUS GP/REL

B59
CHECCHI V.,HONDURAS: A PROBLEM IN ECONOMIC DEVELOPMENT. HONDURAS AGRI FINAN INDUS LABOR WORKER INT/TRADE EDU/PROP PRICE HEALTH...GEOG CHARTS BIBLIOG 20. PAGE 24 F0458 ECO/UNDEV ECO/TAC PROB/SOLV PLAN

B59
FELS R.,AMERICAN BUSINESS CYCLES 1865-1897. USA+45 ECO/DEV LG/CO SML/CO PROB/SOLV TEC/DEV CAP/ISM INT/TRADE DEMAND...POLICY CHARTS METH 19 DEPRESSION. PAGE 40 F0782 FINAN INDUS TREND ECO/TAC

B59
GOMEZ ROBLES J.,A STATEMENT OF THE LAWS OF GUATEMALA IN MATTERS AFFECTING BUSINESS (2ND ED. REV., ENLARGED). GUATEMALA L/A+17C LAW FINAN FAM WORKER ACT/RES DIPLOM ADJUD ADMIN GP/REL 20 OAS. PAGE 48 F0945 JURID NAT/G INDUS LEGIT

B59
GUDIN E.,INFLACAO (2ND ED.). INDUS NAT/G PLAN ECO/TAC CONTROL COST 20. PAGE 52 F1012 ECO/UNDEV INT/TRADE BAL/PAY FINAN

B59
HARVARD UNIVERSITY LAW SCHOOL,INTERNATIONAL PROBLEMS OF FINANCIAL PROTECTION AGAINST NUCLEAR RISK. WOR+45 NAT/G DELIB/GP PROB/SOLV DIPLOM CONTROL ATTIT...POLICY INT/LAW MATH 20. PAGE 56 F1105 NUC/PWR ADJUD INDUS FINAN

B59
HAZLEWOOD A.,THE ECONOMICS OF "UNDER-DEVELOPED" AREAS. WOR+45 DIST/IND EXTR/IND FINAN INDUS MARKET PLAN FOR/AID...GEOG 20. PAGE 57 F1129 BIBLIOG/A ECO/UNDEV AGRI INT/TRADE

B59
JENKINS C.,POWER AT THE TOP: A CRITICAL SURVEY OF THE NATIONALIZED INDUSTRIES. UK POL/PAR CONTROL ...WELF/ST CHARTS 20 LABOR/PAR. PAGE 67 F1313 NAT/G OWN INDUS NEW/LIB

B59
KELF-COHEN R.,NATIONALISATION IN BRITAIN: THE END OF DOGMA. EUR+WWI UK NAT/G POL/PAR WORKER ECO/TAC PARL/PROC WEALTH SOCISM...GOV/COMP 20. PAGE 70 F1369 NEW/LIB ECO/DEV INDUS OWN

B59
LI CHOH-MING,ECONOMIC DEVELOPMENT OF COMMUNIST CHINA. ASIA CHINA/COM AGRI FINAN TAX INCOME MARXISM ...MGT 20. PAGE 80 F1557 ECO/UNDEV INDUS ORD/FREE TEC/DEV

B59
LOPEZ VILLAMIL H.,A STATEMENT OF THE LAWS OF THE HONDURAS IN MATTERS AFFECTING BUSINESS (2ND ED.). HONDURAS DIST/IND EXTR/IND FINAN WORKER TAX DEATH MARRIAGE OWN MARITIME 20 MIGRATION. PAGE 82 F1600 CONSTN INDUS LEGIS NAT/G

B59
MAYER H.M.,READINGS IN URBAN GEOGRAPHY. WOR+45 SOCIETY DIST/IND INDUS MARKET HABITAT...CLASSIF CENSUS CHARTS ANTHOL MUNICH 20 WATER. PAGE 87 F1706 GEOG STRUCT

B59
MEYER A.J.,MIDDLE EASTERN CAPITALISM: NINE ESSAYS. ISLAM CULTURE ECO/UNDEV INDUS MARKET NAT/G PLAN ATTIT RIGID/FLEX...STAT OBS TREND GEN/LAWS. PAGE 90 F1767 TEC/DEV ECO/TAC ANTHOL

B59
MEZERK A.G.,FINANCIAL ASSISTANCE FOR ECONOMIC DEVELOPMENT. WOR+45 INDUS DIPLOM INT/TRADE...CHARTS GOV/COMP UN. PAGE 91 F1778 FOR/AID FINAN ECO/TAC ECO/UNDEV

B59
MUSOLF L.D.,PUBLIC OWNERSHIP AND ACCOUNTABILITY: THE CANADIAN EXPERIENCE. CANADA REPRESENT PWR 20. PAGE 95 F1873 MGT CONTROL INDUS

B59
NORTON P.L.,URBAN PROBLEMS AND TECHNIQUES. AIR AGRI INDUS MARKET TEC/DEV BUDGET LEISURE ALL/VALS ...ANTHOL MUNICH 20 URBAN/RNWL. PAGE 99 F1936
PLAN LOC/G HABITAT

B59
NOVE A.,COMMUNIST ECONOMIC STRATEGY: SOVIET GROWTH AND CAPABILITIES. USSR AGRI LABOR PLAN TEC/DEV CAP/ISM INT/TRADE EFFICIENCY MARXISM 20 THIRD/WRLD. PAGE 99 F1941
FOR/AID ECO/TAC DIPLOM INDUS

B59
RAMANADHAM V.V.,PROBLEMS OF PUBLIC ENTERPRISE: THOUGHTS ON BRITISH EXPERIENCE. UK FINAN INDUS PLAN PRICE CENTRAL...POLICY 20. PAGE 109 F2140
SOCISM LG/CO ECO/DEV GOV/REL

B59
ROBERTSON A.H.,EUROPEAN INSTITUTIONS: COOPERATION, INTEGRATION, UNIFICATION. EUR+WWI FINAN INT/ORG FORCES INT/TRADE TARIFFS 20 EEC EURATOM ECSC NATO TREATY. PAGE 112 F2208
ECO/DEV DIPLOM INDUS ECO/TAC

B59
ROPKE W.,INTERNATIONAL ORDER AND ECONOMIC INTEGRATION. ECO/DEV ECO/UNDEV AGRI FINAN INDUS INT/ORG WAR PEACE ORD/FREE...SOC METH/COMP 20 EEC. PAGE 114 F2238
INT/TRADE DIPLOM BAL/PAY ALL/IDEOS

B59
SANNWALD R.E.,ECONOMIC INTEGRATION: THEORETICAL ASSUMPTIONS AND CONSEQUENCES OF EUROPEAN UNIFICATION. EUR+WWI FUT FINAN INDUS VOL/ASSN ACT/RES ECO/TAC...PLURIST EEC FOR/TRADE OEEC 20. PAGE 116 F2279
INT/ORG ECO/DEV INT/TRADE

B59
STERNBERG F.,THE MILITARY AND INDUSTRIAL REVOLUTION OF OUR TIME. USA+45 USSR WOR+45 WORKER COMPUTER PLAN TEC/DEV NUC/PWR GP/REL...POLICY NAT/COMP 20. PAGE 126 F2481
DIPLOM FORCES INDUS CIVMIL/REL

B59
US DEPARTMENT OF STATE,THE UNITED STATES ECONOMY AND THE MUTUAL SECURITY PROGRAM. USA+45 ECO/UNDEV FINAN INDUS DIPLOM INT/TRADE DETER 20. PAGE 136 F2674
ECO/DEV FORCES BUDGET FOR/AID

B59
VERNEY D.V.,PUBLIC ENTERPRISE IN SWEDEN. FUT SWEDEN UK INDUS POL/PAR LEGIS PROB/SOLV CAP/ISM INT/TRADE CONTROL SOCISM...MGT CONCPT NAT/COMP 20 SOCDEM/PAR CIVIL/SERV. PAGE 141 F2778
ECO/DEV POLICY LG/CO NAT/G

B59
WARD B.,5 IDEAS THAT CHANGE THE WORLD. WOR+45 WOR-45 SOCIETY STRUCT AGRI INDUS INT/ORG NAT/G FORCES ACT/RES ARMS/CONT TOTALISM ATTIT DRIVE GEN/LAWS. PAGE 143 F2815
ECO/UNDEV ALL/VALS NAT/LISM COLONIAL

B59
WELTON H.,THE THIRD WORLD WAR; TRADE AND INDUSTRY, THE NEW BATTLEGROUND. AFR WOR+45 ECO/DEV INDUS MARKET TASK...MGT IDEA/COMP. PAGE 145 F2855
INT/TRADE PLAN DIPLOM

B59
YRARRAZAVAL E.,AMERICA LATINE EN LA GUERRA FRIA. AFR EUR+WWI L/A+17C USA+45 USSR WOR+45 INDUS INT/ORG NAT/LISM POLICY. PAGE 150 F2953
REGION DIPLOM ECO/UNDEV INT/TRADE

L59
BEGUIN B.,"ILO AND THE TRIPARTITE SYSTEM." EUR+WWI WOR+45 WOR-45 CONSTN ECO/DEV ECO/UNDEV INDUS INT/ORG NAT/G VOL/ASSN DELIB/GP PLAN TEC/DEV LEGIT ORD/FREE WEALTH...CONCPT TIME/SEQ WORK ILO 20. PAGE 12 F0228
LABOR

L59
FURASH E.A.,"PROBLEMS IN REVIEW: INDUSTRIAL ESPIONAGE." WORKER ECO/TAC PERS/REL OPTIMAL AGE ATTIT KNOWL...MGT DEEP/INT DEEP/QU GP/COMP IDEA/COMP. PAGE 45 F0875
INDUS TOP/EX MAJORITY

L59
MURPHY J.C.,"SOME IMPLICATIONS OF EUROPE'S COMMON MARKET. IN (COOK P, ECONOMIC DEVELOPMENT AND INTERNATIONAL TRADE.." EUR+WWI ECO/DEV DIST/IND INDUS NAT/G PLAN ECO/TAC INT/TRADE WEALTH...STAT TREND OEEC TOT/POP 20 EEC. PAGE 95 F1866
MARKET INT/ORG REGION

S59
BENDIX R.,"INDUSTRIALIZATION, IDEOLOGIES, AND SOCIAL STRUCTURE" (BMR)" UK USA-45 USSR STRUCT WORKER GP/REL EFFICIENCY...IDEA/COMP 20. PAGE 13 F0243
INDUS ATTIT MGT ADMIN

S59
CYERT R.M.,"MODELS IN A BEHAVIORAL THEORY OF THE FIRM." ROUTINE...DECISION MGT METH/CNCPT MATH. PAGE 29 F0567
SIMUL GAME PREDICT INDUS

S59
HOFFMAN P.,"OPERATION BREAKTHROUGH." AFR S/ASIA STRUCT INDUS CONSULT TEC/DEV ATTIT RIGID/FLEX SKILL WEALTH...TECHNIC CONCPT STYLE RECORD CHARTS ORG/CHARTS GEN/METH VAL/FREE 20. PAGE 61 F1190
ECO/UNDEV EDU/PROP FOR/AID

S59
PLAZA G.,"FOR A REGIONAL MARKET IN LATIN AMERICA." FUT L/A+17C CULTURE INDUS NAT/G ECO/TAC INT/TRADE ATTIT WEALTH...NEW/IDEA TREND OAS 20. PAGE 106 F2092
MARKET INT/ORG REGION

S59
SOLDATI A.,"EOCNOMIC DISINTEGRATION IN EUROPE." EUR+WWI FUT WOR+45 INDUS INT/ORG NAT/G CAP/ISM WEALTH...NEW/IDEA OBS TREND CHARTS EEC 20. PAGE 124 F2438
FINAN ECO/TAC

S59
STREAT R.,"GOVERNMENT CONSULTATION WITH INDUSTRY." UK 20. PAGE 127 F2501
REPRESENT ADMIN EX/STRUC INDUS

S59
TEITSWORTH C.S.,"GROWING ROLE OF THE COMPANY ECONOMIST." USA+45 PLAN PROB/SOLV CAP/ISM ECO/TAC ADMIN ATTIT MGT. PAGE 129 F2541
INDUS CONSULT UTIL DECISION

S59
TIPTON J.B.,"PARTICIPATION OF THE UNITED STATES IN THE INTERNATIONAL LABOR ORGANIZATION." USA+45 LAW STRUCT ECO/DEV ECO/UNDEV INDUS TEC/DEV ECO/TAC ADMIN PERCEPT ORD/FREE SKILL...STAT HIST/WRIT GEN/METH ILO WORK 20. PAGE 131 F2577
LABOR INT/ORG

S59
ZAUBERMAN A.,"SOVIET BLOC ECONOMIC INTEGRATION." COM CULTURE INTELL ECO/DEV INDUS TOP/EX ACT/RES PLAN ECO/TAC INT/TRADE ROUTINE CHOOSE ATTIT ...TIME/SEQ 20. PAGE 150 F2958
MARKET INT/ORG USSR TOTALISM

C59
FAINSOD M.,"GOVERNMENT AND THE AMERICAN ECONOMY." USA+45 USA-45 INDUS LABOR OP/RES PROB/SOLV ECO/TAC CONTROL...CHARTS BIBLIOG T 20. PAGE 39 F0760
CONSTN ECO/DEV CAP/ISM NAT/G

B60
AHMED J.,NATURAL RESOURCES IN LOW INCOME COUNTRIES: AN ANALYTICAL SURVEY OF SOCIO-ECONOMIC RESEARCH (PAMPHLET). WOR+45 20. PAGE 3 F0052
BIBLIOG/A ECO/UNDEV INDUS AGRI

B60
ALLEN R.L.,SOVIET ECONOMIC WARFARE. USSR FINAN INDUS NAT/G PLAN TEC/DEV FOR/AID DETER WEALTH ...TREND GEN/LAWS FOR/TRADE 20. PAGE 4 F0072
COM ECO/TAC

B60
AMERICAN U BEIRUT ECO RES INST,A SELECTED AND ANNOTATED BIBLIOGRAPHY OF ECONOMIC LITERATURE ON THE ARABIC SPEAKING COUNTRIES OF THE MIDDLE EAST. ISLAM AGRI COM/IND DIST/IND FINAN INDUS LABOR ...GEOG 20. PAGE 5 F0091
BIBLIOG/A ECO/UNDEV STAT

B60
APTHEKER H.,DISARMAMENT AND THE AMERICAN ECONOMY: A SYMPOSIUM. FUT USA+45 ECO/DEV DIST/IND FINAN INDUS PROC/MFG LABOR NAT/G POL/PAR CONSULT PLAN CAP/ISM INT/TRADE PEACE ATTIT MORAL WEALTH...TREND GEN/LAWS TOT/POP 20. PAGE 6 F0110
MARXIST ARMS/CONT

B60
ASPREMONT-LYNDEN H.,RAPPORT SUR L'ADMINISTRATION BELGE DU RUANDA-URUNDI PENDANT L'ANNEE 1959. BELGIUM RWANDA AGRI INDUS DIPLOM ECO/TAC INT/TRADE DOMIN ADMIN RACE/REL...GEOG CENSUS 20 UN. PAGE 7 F0132
AFR COLONIAL ECO/UNDEV INT/ORG

B60
ATOMIC INDUSTRIAL FORUM,ATOMS FOR INDUSTRY: WORLD FORUM. WOR+45 FINAN COST UTIL...JURID ANTHOL 20. PAGE 7 F0137
NUC/PWR INDUS PLAN PROB/SOLV

B60
BHAMBHRI C.P.,PARLIAMENTARY CONTROL OVER STATE ENTERPRISE IN INDIA. INDIA DELIB/GP ADMIN CONTROL INGP/REL EFFICIENCY 20 PARLIAMENT. PAGE 14 F0277
NAT/G OWN INDUS PARL/PROC

B60
BISSON A.,INSTITUTIONS FINANCIERES ET ECONOMIQUES EN FRANCE. FRANCE INDUS OP/RES TAX COST PRODUC ...CHARTS 20. PAGE 15 F0289
FINAN BUDGET PLAN

B60
BRYCE M.D.,INDUSTRIAL DEVELOPMENT: A GUIDE FOR ACCELERATING ECONOMIC GROWTH. WOR+45 FINAN MARKET COST EFFICIENCY PRODUC. PAGE 20 F0378
INDUS PLAN ECO/UNDEV TEC/DEV

B60
COMMITTEE ECONOMIC DEVELOPMENT,NATIONAL OBJECTIVES AND THE BALANCE OF PAYMENTS PROBLEM: A STATEMENT ON NATIONAL POLICY. USA+45 WOR+45 DIST/IND FINAN INDUS LABOR NAT/G DELIB/GP ACT/RES FOR/AID INT/TRADE ...STAT CHARTS FOR/TRADE 20. PAGE 27 F0516
ECO/DEV ECO/TAC BAL/PAY

B60
CROSSER P.K.,STATE CAPITALISM IN THE ECONOMY OF THE UNITED STATES. USA+45 USA-45 AGRI FINAN INDUS LABOR WORKER RATION CONTROL GOV/REL DEMAND...NEW/IDEA 20. PAGE 29 F0557
CAP/ISM ECO/DEV ECO/TAC NAT/G

B60
ELKOURI F.,HOW ARBITRATION WORKS (REV. ED.). LAW INDUS BARGAIN 20. PAGE 37 F0720
MGT LABOR ADJUD GP/REL

B60
FERNANDES F.,MUDANCAS SOCIAIS NO BRASIL. BRAZIL L/A+17C SOCIETY AGRI PROVS LEAD GP/REL RACE/REL
ECO/UNDEV STRATA

ORD/FREE...SOC SOC/INTEG 20 SAO/PAULO. PAGE 40 F0786 INDUS

B60
FIRESTONE J.M.,FEDERAL RECEIPTS AND EXPENDITURES DURING BUSINESS CYCLES, 1879-1958. USA+45 USA-45 INDUS PLAN ECO/TAC TAX WAR COST...CHARTS 19/20. PAGE 41 F0801
FINAN INCOME BUDGET NAT/G

B60
FRYE R.J.,GOVERNMENT AND LABOR: THE ALABAMA PROGRAM. USA+45 INDUS R+D LABOR WORKER BUDGET EFFICIENCY AGE/Y HEALTH...CHARTS 20 ALABAMA. PAGE 45 F0870
ADMIN LEGIS LOC/G PROVS

B60
GRANICK D.,THE RED EXECUTIVE. COM USA+45 SOCIETY ECO/DEV INDUS NAT/G POL/PAR EX/STRUC PLAN ECO/TAC EDU/PROP ADMIN EXEC ATTIT DRIVE...GP/COMP 20. PAGE 50 F0976
PWR STRATA USSR ELITES

B60
HUGHES R.,THE CHINESE COMMUNES; A BACKGROUND BOOK. CHINA/COM SOCIETY CONTROL ROUTINE ADJUST EFFICIENCY PRODUC 20. PAGE 63 F1234
AGRI INDUS STRUCT MARXISM

B60
KERR C.,INDUSTRIALISM AND INDUSTRIAL MAN. CULTURE SOCIETY ECO/UNDEV NAT/G ADMIN PRODUC WEALTH ...PREDICT TREND NAT/COMP 19/20. PAGE 70 F1381
WORKER MGT ECO/DEV INDUS

B60
LATIFI D.,INDIA AND UNITED STATES AID. ASIA INDIA UK USA+45 AGRI FINAN INDUS COLONIAL ORD/FREE SOVEREIGN WEALTH...METH/COMP 20. PAGE 76 F1486
FOR/AID DIPLOM ECO/UNDEV

B60
LENCZOWSKI G.,OIL AND STATE IN THE MIDDLE EAST. FUT IRAN LAW ECO/UNDEV EXTR/IND NAT/G TOP/EX PLAN TEC/DEV ECO/TAC LEGIT ADMIN COERCE ATTIT ALL/VALS PWR...CHARTS 20. PAGE 78 F1519
ISLAM INDUS NAT/LISM

B60
LISTER L.,EUROPE'S COAL AND STEEL COMMUNITY. FRANCE GERMANY STRUCT ECO/DEV EXTR/IND INDUS MARKET NAT/G DELIB/GP ECO/TAC INT/TRADE EDU/PROP ATTIT RIGID/FLEX ORD/FREE PWR WEALTH...CONCPT STAT TIME/SEQ CHARTS ECSC TERR/GP 20. PAGE 81 F1582
EUR+WWI INT/ORG REGION

B60
MOORE W.E.,LABOR COMMITMENT AND SOCIAL CHANGE IN DEVELOPING AREAS. SOCIETY STRATA ECO/UNDEV MARKET VOL/ASSN WORKER AUTHORIT SKILL...MGT NAT/COMP SOC/INTEG 20. PAGE 93 F1823
LABOR ORD/FREE ATTIT INDUS

B60
NEALE A.D.,THE FLOW OF RESOURCES FROM RICH TO POOR. WOR+45 ECO/DEV ECO/UNDEV FINAN INDUS NAT/G PLAN EFFICIENCY WEALTH...POLICY NAT/COMP 20 RESOURCE/N. PAGE 97 F1905
FOR/AID DIPLOM METH/CNCPT

B60
RAMA C.M.,LAS CLASES SOCIALES EN EL URUGUAY. L/A+17C URUGUAY ELITES SOCIETY STRATA INDUS ATTIT HABITAT PWR...GEOG SOC/INTEG MUNICH 20. PAGE 109 F2138
ECO/UNDEV STRUCT PARTIC

B60
ROBERTSON D.,THE CONTROL OF INDUSTRY. UK MARKET LABOR WORKER PRICE CONTROL GP/REL COST DEMAND ORD/FREE WEALTH NEW/LIB SOCISM 20. PAGE 112 F2211
INDUS FINAN NAT/G ECO/DEV

B60
ROBINSON E.A.G.,ECONOMIC CONSEQUENCES OF THE SIZE OF NATIONS. AGRI INDUS DELIB/GP FOR/AID ADMIN EFFICIENCY...METH/COMP 20. PAGE 113 F2218
CONCPT INT/ORG NAT/COMP

B60
ROBINSON J.,AN ESSAY ON MARXIAN ECONOMICS. USA+45 STRATA INDUS MARKET CAP/ISM...METH/COMP 19/20 MARX/KARL. PAGE 113 F2222
IDEA/COMP MARXISM ACADEM

B60
ROBSON W.A.,NATIONALIZED INDUSTRY AND PUBLIC OWNERSHIP. UK ECO/DEV FINAN LABOR LG/CO POL/PAR LEGIS ACT/RES GP/REL...TREND IDEA/COMP 20. PAGE 113 F2227
NAT/G OWN INDUS ATTIT

B60
ROPKE W.,A HUMANE ECONOMY. CULTURE ECO/DEV FINAN INDUS GP/REL CENTRAL WEALTH...GEOG SOC IDEA/COMP 20 EEC. PAGE 114 F2239
ECO/TAC INT/ORG DIPLOM ORD/FREE

B60
SHANNON D.A.,THE GREAT DEPRESSION. USA-45 FINAN LG/CO SCHOOL SML/CO DELIB/GP RECEIVE REV EATING INCOME...ANTHOL MUNICH 20 ROOSEVLT/F CONGRESS. PAGE 120 F2365
WEALTH NAT/G AGRI INDUS

B60
SIMOONS F.J.,NORTHWEST ETHIOPIA; PEOPLES AND ECONOMY. ETHIOPIA MARKET CREATE 20. PAGE 122 F2411
SOCIETY STRUCT AGRI INDUS

B60
SLOTKIN J.S.,FROM FIELD TO FACTORY; NEW INDUSTRIAL EMPLOYEES. HABITAT...MGT NEW/IDEA NAT/COMP BIBLIOG SOC/INTEG 20. PAGE 123 F2423
INDUS LABOR CULTURE WORKER

B60
SMET G.,BIBLIOGRAPHIE DE LA CONTRIBUTION A L'ETUDE DE LA PROGRESSION ECONOMIQUE DE L'AFRIQUE. AFR DIST/IND EXTR/IND TEC/DEV 20. PAGE 123 F2427
BIBLIOG ECO/UNDEV INDUS AGRI

B60
THE ECONOMIST (LONDON),THE COMMONWEALTH AND EUROPE. EUR+WWI WOR+45 AGRI FINAN INCOME...STAT CENSUS CHARTS CMN/WLTH EEC. PAGE 129 F2550
INT/TRADE INDUS INT/ORG NAT/COMP

B60
UNESCO,SOUTHERN ASIA SOCIAL SCIENCE BIBLIOGRAPHY (WITH ANNOTATIONS AND ABSTRACTS), 1959 (PAMPHLET). S/ASIA...SOC 20. PAGE 132 F2609
BIBLIOG/A ECO/UNDEV TEC/DEV INDUS

B60
US GENERAL ACCOUNTING OFFICE,EXAMINATION OF ECONOMIC AND TECHNICAL ASSISTANCE PROGRAM FOR GUATEMALA. GUATEMALA L/A+17C USA+45 FINAN INDUS PLAN...POLICY STAT CHARTS 20 DEPT/STATE. PAGE 136 F2680
FOR/AID ECO/UNDEV TEC/DEV NAT/G

B60
US OPERATIONS MISSION - TURKEY,SOME POSSIBILITIES FOR ACCELERATING TURKEY'S ECONOMIC GROWTH. TURKEY USA+45 AGRI FINAN INDUS NAT/G ACT/RES BUDGET COST ...CHARTS 20. PAGE 138 F2724
ECO/UNDEV ECO/TAC FOR/AID PRODUC

B60
WEINER H.E.,BRITISH LABOR AND PUBLIC OWNERSHIP. UK SERV/IND LG/CO WORKER CONTROL OWN 20. PAGE 145 F2850
LABOR NAT/G INDUS ATTIT

B60
WENTHOLT W.,INFLATION OR SECURITY? EUR+WWI USA+45 INDUS CONSULT TEC/DEV CAP/ISM DIPLOM FOR/AID INT/TRADE MARXISM 20 EEC. PAGE 145 F2858
ECO/DEV ECO/TAC FINAN ORD/FREE

S60
"THE EMERGING COMMON MARKETS IN LATIN AMERICA." FUT L/A+17C STRATA DIST/IND INDUS LABOR NAT/G LEGIS ECO/TAC ADMIN RIGID/FLEX HEALTH...NEW/IDEA TIME/SEQ OAS 20. PAGE 1 F0013
FINAN ECO/UNDEV INT/TRADE

S60
BECKER A.S.,"COMPARISIONS OF UNITED STATES AND USSR NATIONAL OUTPUT: SOME RULES OF THE GAME." COM USA+45 ECO/DEV AGRI DIST/IND INDUS R+D CONSULT PLAN ECO/TAC RIGID/FLEX KNOWL...METH/CNCPT CHARTS 20. PAGE 12 F0227
STAT USSR

S60
BERG E.J.,"ECONOMIC BASIS OF POLITICAL CHOICE IN FRENCH WEST AFRICA." FRANCE ECO/UNDEV AGRI INDUS NAT/G PLAN LEGIT COLONIAL REGION ATTIT PWR WEALTH ...CONCPT FOR/TRADE 20. PAGE 13 F0257
AFR ECO/TAC

S60
BUTLER W.F.,"ECONOMIC PROGRESS IN LATIN AMERICA." L/A+17C USA+45 ECO/UNDEV AGRI FINAN NAT/G PLAN ECO/TAC FOR/AID ADMIN WEALTH...OLD/LIB TOT/POP 20. PAGE 21 F0397
INDUS ACT/RES

S60
FRENCH J.R.P. JR.,"AN EXPERIMENT ON PARTICIPATION IN A NORWEGIAN FACTORY:INTERPERSONAL DIMENSIONS OF DECISION-MAKING." LABOR LEAD PERS/REL EFFICIENCY PRODUC...DECISION SOC CHARTS SOC/EXP. PAGE 44 F0853
INDUS PLAN RIGID/FLEX GP/REL

S60
GARNICK D.H.,"ON THE ECONOMIC FEASIBILITY OF A MIDDLE EASTERN COMMON MARKET." AFR ISLAM CULTURE INDUS NAT/G PLAN TEC/DEV ECO/TAC ADMIN ATTIT DRIVE RIGID/FLEX...PLURIST STAT TREND GEN/LAWS 20. PAGE 46 F0907
MARKET INT/TRADE

S60
HERZ J.H.,"EAST GERMANY: PROGRESS AND PROSPECTS." COM AGRI FINAN INDUS LOC/G NAT/G FORCES PLAN TEC/DEV DOMIN ADMIN COERCE DRIVE PERCEPT RIGID/FLEX MORAL ORD/FREE PWR...MARXIST PSY SOC RECORD STERTYP WORK. PAGE 59 F1158
POL/PAR STRUCT GERMANY

S60
LINDHOLM R.W.,"ACCELERATED DEVELOPMENT WITH A MINIMUM OF FOREIGN AID AND ECONOMIC CONTROLS." SOCIETY INDUS ECO/TAC WEALTH...CONCPT 20. PAGE 80 F1570
ECO/DEV FINAN FOR/AID

S60
MORALES C.J.,"TRADE AND ECONOMIC INTEGRATION IN LATIN AMERICA." FUT L/A+17C LAW STRATA ECO/UNDEV DIST/IND INDUS LABOR NAT/G LEGIS ECO/TAC ADMIN RIGID/FLEX WEALTH...CONCPT NEW/IDEA CONT/OBS TIME/SEQ WORK 20. PAGE 93 F1825
FINAN INT/TRADE REGION

S60
STOCKWELL E.G.,"THE MEASUREMENT OF ECONOMIC DEVELOPMENT." WOR+45 SOCIETY ECO/DEV ECO/UNDEV INDUS ECO/TAC HEALTH WEALTH...WELF/ST GEOG METH/CNCPT CHARTS METH METH/GP 20. PAGE 126 F2492
FAM STAT

C60
FAULKNER H.U.,"AMERICAN ECONOMIC HISTORY (8TH ED.)" USA+45 USA-45 FINAN...CHARTS BIBLIOG/A T 17/20. PAGE 39 F0769
AGRI INDUS ECO/DEV CAP/ISM

N60
COMMITTEE ECONOMIC DEVELOPMENT,GUIDING METROPOLITAN GROWTH (PAMPHLET). USA+45 LOC/G NAT/G PROF/ORG ACT/RES PLAN...SOC/WK MUNICH. PAGE 27 F0517
GEOG INDUS HEALTH

B61
MEXICO; CINCUENTA ANOS DE REVOLUCION VOL. II. L/A+17C SOCIETY LABOR RECEIVE GP/REL AGE/Y HEALTH ...SOC/WK ANTHOL MUNICH 20 MEXIC/AMER. PAGE 1 F0014
ECO/UNDEV STRUCT INDUS POL/PAR

B61
AGARWAL R.C.,STATE ENTERPRISE IN INDIA. FUT INDIA UK FINAN INDUS ADMIN CONTROL OWN...POLICY CHARTS BIBLIOG 20 RAILROAD. PAGE 3 F0048
ECO/UNDEV SOCISM GOV/REL LG/CO

B61
ALFRED H.,PUBLIC OWNERSHIP IN THE USA: GOALS AND PRIORITIES. LAW INDUS INT/TRADE ADJUD GOV/REL EFFICIENCY PEACE SOCISM...POLICY ANTHOL 20 TVA. PAGE 4 F0065
CONTROL OWN ECO/DEV ECO/TAC

B61
AMERICAN MANAGEMENT ASSN,SUPERIOR-SUBORDINATE COMMUNICATION IN MANAGEMENT. STRATA FINAN INDUS SML/CO WORKER CONTROL EXEC ATTIT 20. PAGE 5 F0090
MGT ACT/RES PERS/REL LG/CO

B61
BENHAM F.,ECONOMIC AID TO UNDERDEVELOPED COUNTRIES. WOR+45 INDUS BAL/PAY ALL/VALS 20. PAGE 13 F0244
ECO/UNDEV FOR/AID INT/TRADE FINAN

B61
BENOIT E.,EUROPE AT SIXES AND SEVENS: THE COMMON MARKET, THE FREE TRADE ASSOCIATION AND THE UNITED STATES. EUR+WWI FUT USA+45 INDUS CONSULT DELIB/GP EX/STRUC TOP/EX ACT/RES ECO/TAC EDU/PROP ROUTINE CHOOSE PERCEPT WEALTH...MGT TREND EEC FOR/TRADE TOT/POP 20 EFTA. PAGE 13 F0249
FINAN ECO/DEV VOL/ASSN

B61
CLARK J.M.,COMPETITION AS A DYNAMIC PROCESS. ECO/DEV EXTR/IND INDUS LG/CO TEC/DEV ECO/TAC PRICE EQUILIB PRODUC...NEW/IDEA CAP 20. PAGE 25 F0483
WEALTH GP/REL FINAN PROFIT

B61
DE VRIES E.,MAN IN RAPID SOCIAL CHANGE. WOR+45 SOCIETY ECO/DEV ECO/UNDEV AGRI INDUS FAM SECT TEC/DEV ATTIT...RECORD 20 CHRISTIAN. PAGE 31 F0607
CULTURE ALL/VALS SOC TASK

B61
DELEFORTRIE-SOU N.,LES DIRIGEANTS DE L'INDUSTRIE FRANCAISE. FRANCE CULTURE ELITES PROB/SOLV ...DECISION STAT CHARTS 20. PAGE 32 F0613
INDUS STRATA TOP/EX LEAD

B61
DETHINE P.,BIBLIOGRAPHIE DES ASPECTS ECONOMIQUES ET SOCIAUX DE L'INDUSTRIALISATION EN AFRIQUE. AFR FINAN LABOR FOR/AID...SOC 20. PAGE 32 F0623
BIBLIOG/A ECO/UNDEV INDUS TEC/DEV

B61
DIMOCK M.E.,BUSINESS AND GOVERNMENT (4TH ED.). AGRI FINAN OP/RES PLAN BUDGET DIPLOM LOBBY NUC/PWR NEW/LIB SOCISM...POLICY BIBLIOG 20. PAGE 33 F0641
NAT/G INDUS LABOR ECO/TAC

B61
ELLIS H.S.,ECONOMIC DEVELOPMENT FOR LATIN AMERICA. L/A+17C AGRI FINAN INDUS FOR/AID GP/REL BAL/PAY DEMAND...ANTHOL 20 INTL/ECON. PAGE 37 F0723
ECO/UNDEV ECO/TAC PLAN INT/TRADE

B61
ESTEBAN J.C.,IMPERIALISMO Y DESARROLLO ECONOMICO. L/A+17C FINAN INDUS NAT/G ECO/TAC CONTROL ROLE. PAGE 38 F0747
ECO/UNDEV NAT/LISM DIPLOM BAL/PAY

B61
FELLNER W.,THE PROBLEM OF RISING PRICES. AGRI INDUS WORKER BUDGET CAP/ISM ECO/TAC INT/TRADE PAY DEMAND ...POLICY 20 EEC. PAGE 40 F0780
PRICE MARKET ECO/DEV COST

B61
FERTIG L.,PROSPERITY THROUGH FREEDOM. COM INDUS LABOR CAP/ISM ECO/TAC PRODUC PROFIT ORD/FREE WEALTH SOCISM...METH/CNCPT 20. PAGE 40 F0788
NAT/G CONTROL POLICY

B61
FILLOL T.R.,SOCIAL FACTORS IN ECONOMIC DEVELOPMENT: THE ARGENTINE CASE. STRUCT INDUS LABOR CREATE TEC/DEV EFFICIENCY PRODUC DRIVE...METH/CNCPT METH/COMP BIBLIOG/A 20 ARGEN. PAGE 41 F0795
ECO/UNDEV MGT PERS/REL TREND

B61
FLINN M.W.,AN ECONOMIC AND SOCIAL HISTORY OF BRITAIN, 1066-1939. UK LAW STRATA STRUCT AGRI DIST/IND INDUS WORKER INT/TRADE WAR...CENSUS 11/20. PAGE 42 F0811
SOCIETY SOC

B61
FRIEDMANN G.,THE ANATOMY OF WORK. USA+45 SOCIETY CONTROL ROUTINE DRIVE SKILL...PSY SOC STAT OBS METH/COMP PERS/COMP 20. PAGE 44 F0862
AUTOMAT WORKER INDUS PERSON

B61
GALENSON W.,TRADE UNION DEMOCRACY IN WESTERN EUROPE. ECO/DEV INDUS PROF/ORG WORKER INCOME ...METH/COMP 20. PAGE 45 F0886
LABOR GP/REL ECO/TAC EUR+WWI

B61
HAUSER M.,DIE URSACHEN DER FRANZOSISCHEN INFLATION IN DEN JAHREN 1946-1952. AFR FRANCE INDUS NAT/G BUDGET DIPLOM ECO/TAC FOR/AID COST MONEY 20. PAGE 57 F1114
ECO/DEV FINAN PRICE

B61
HEMPSTONE S.,THE NEW AFRICA. AGRI INDUS KIN NAT/G COLONIAL MARXISM...SOC INT TREND NAT/COMP BIBLIOG/A 20. PAGE 58 F1146
AFR ORD/FREE PERSON CULTURE

B61
HENDERSON W.O.,THE INDUSTRIAL REVOLUTION IN EUROPE. FRANCE GERMANY MOD/EUR RUSSIA WORKER PROFIT PWR MARXISM SOCISM...SOC HIST/WRIT 19 INDUS/REV. PAGE 58 F1148
INDUS REV CAP/ISM TEC/DEV

B61
HODGKINS J.A.,SOVIET POWER: ENERGY RESOURCES, PRODUCTION AND POTENTIALS. USSR ECO/DEV INDUS MARKET...POLICY STAT CHARTS 20 RESOURCE/N. PAGE 60 F1188
GEOG EXTR/IND TEC/DEV

B61
HORVATH B.,THE CHARACTERISTICS OF YUGOSLAV ECONOMIC DEVELOPMENT. COM ECO/UNDEV AGRI INDUS PLAN CAP/ISM ECO/TAC ROUTINE WEALTH...SOCIALIST STAT CHARTS STERTYP WORK 20. PAGE 62 F1217
ACT/RES YUGOSLAVIA

B61
HUBBARD P.J.,ORIGINS OF THE TVA: THE MUSCLE SHOALS CONTROVERSY, 1920-1932. USA-45 DELIB/GP LEGIS LEAD LOBBY GOV/REL GP/REL INGP/REL OWN PERSON...BIBLIOG 20 TVA CONGRESS WATER. PAGE 62 F1229
SEA CONTROL NAT/G INDUS

B61
INDUSTRIAL COUN SOC-ECO STU,THE SWEDISH ECONOMY AND THE UNDERDEVELOPED COUNTRIES. SWEDEN INDUS DELIB/GP TEC/DEV INT/TRADE EDU/PROP COLONIAL DRIVE...CHARTS 20. PAGE 64 F1264
FOR/AID ECO/UNDEV PLAN FINAN

B61
INTERNATIONAL BANK RECONST DEV,THE WORLD BANK IN AFRICA: SUMMARY OF ACTIVITIES. AGRI COM/IND DIST/IND EXTR/IND INDUS TAX COST...CHARTS 20. PAGE 65 F1271
FINAN ECO/UNDEV INT/ORG AFR

B61
LAHAYE R.,LES ENTREPRISES PUBLIQUES AU MAROC. FRANCE MOROCCO LAW DIST/IND EXTR/IND FINAN CONSULT PLAN TEC/DEV ADMIN AGREE CONTROL OWN...POLICY 20. PAGE 74 F1460
NAT/G INDUS ECO/UNDEV ECO/TAC

B61
LAMFALUSSY A.,INVESTMENT AND GROWTH IN MATURE ECONOMIES. BELGIUM EUR+WWI LABOR PRICE PRODUC PROFIT...STAT CONT/OBS CHARTS 20. PAGE 75 F1464
FINAN INDUS ECO/DEV CAP/ISM

B61
LIEFMANN-KEIL E.,OKONOMISCHE THEORIE DER SOZIALPOLITIK. INT/ORG LABOR WORKER COST INCOME NEW/LIB...CONCPT SOC/INTEG 20. PAGE 80 F1562
ECO/DEV INDUS NAT/G SOC/WK

B61
LUZ N.V.,A LUTA PELA INDUSTRIALIZACAO DO BRAZIL. BRAZIL L/A+17C AGRI NAT/G TEC/DEV COLONIAL 19/20. PAGE 82 F1615
ECO/UNDEV INDUS NAT/LISM POLICY

B61
MARX K.,THE COMMUNIST MANIFESTO. IN (MENDEL A. ESSENTIAL WORKS OF MARXISM, NEW YORK: BANTAM. FUT MOD/EUR CULTURE ECO/DEV ECO/UNDEV AGRI FINAN INDUS MARKET PROC/MFG LABOR POL/PAR CONSULT FORCES CREATE PLAN ADMIN ATTIT DRIVE RIGID/FLEX ORD/FREE PWR RESPECT MARX/KARL MUNICH WORK. PAGE 86 F1691
COM NEW/IDEA CAP/ISM REV

B61
MIT CENTER INTERNATIONAL STU,OFFICIAL SERIAL PUBLICATIONS RELATING TO ECONOMIC DEVELOPMENT IN AFRICA SOUTH OF THE SAHARA. AFR SOCIETY AGRI FINAN INDUS LG/CO ADMIN 20. PAGE 92 F1806
BIBLIOG ECO/UNDEV ECO/TAC NAT/G

B61
NEW JERSEY LEGISLATURE-SENATE,PUBLIC HEARINGS BEFORE COMMITTEE ON REVISION AND AMENDMENT OF LAWS ON SENATE BILL NO. 8. USA+45 FINAN PROVS WORKER ACT/RES PLAN BUDGET TAX CRIME...IDEA/COMP MUNICH 20 NEW/JERSEY URBAN/RNWL. PAGE 98 F1919
LEGIS INDUS PROB/SOLV

B61
NORTH D.C.,THE ECONOMIC GROWTH OF THE UNITED STATES 1790-1860. USA-45 INDUS TEC/DEV CAP/ISM ECO/TAC PRICE COST DEMAND LAISSEZ...ECOMETRIC STAT TREND 19. PAGE 98 F1933
AGRI ECO/UNDEV

B61
RUEDA B.,A STATEMENT OF THE LAWS OF COLOMBIA IN MATTERS AFFECTING BUSINESS (3RD ED.). INDUS FAM LABOR LG/CO NAT/G LEGIS TAX CONTROL MARRIAGE 20 COLOMB. PAGE 115 F2257
FINAN ECO/UNDEV LAW CONSTN

B61
SEPULVEDA C.,A STATEMENT OF THE LAWS OF MEXICO IN MATTERS AFFECTING BUSINESS (3RD ED.). AGRI DIST/IND
CONSTN NAT/G

EXTR/IND FINAN INDUS WORKER TAX MARRIAGE OWN ORD/FREE...BIBLIOG 20 MEXIC/AMER TREATY MIGRATION MONOPOLY. PAGE 119 F2356 — JURID LEGIS

B61
SHONFIELD A.,ECONOMIC GROWTH AND INFLATION; A STUDY OF INDIAN PLANNING. AFR INDIA AGRI INDUS TEC/DEV CONTROL DEMAND UTIL 20. PAGE 121 F2384 — ECO/UNDEV PRICE PLAN BUDGET

B61
SPOONER F.P.,SOUTH AFRICAN PREDICAMENT. FUT SOUTH/AFR INDUS POL/PAR RACE/REL INCOME...CHARTS 20 NEGRO. PAGE 125 F2459 — ECO/DEV DISCRIM ECO/TAC POLICY

B61
STARK H.,SOCIAL AND ECONOMIC FRONTIERS IN LATIN AMERICA (2ND ED.). CUBA FUT CULTURE AGRI INDUS ECO/TAC PRODUC ATTIT MARXISM...NAT/COMP BIBLIOG T 20. PAGE 125 F2470 — L/A+17C SOCIETY DIPLOM ECO/UNDEV

B61
STOCKING G.W.,WORKABLE COMPETITION AND ANTITRUST POLICY. USA+45 NAT/G CONSULT PLAN PRICE GOV/REL COST DEMAND PROFIT...POLICY 20. PAGE 126 F2491 — LG/CO INDUS ECO/TAC CONTROL

B61
US GENERAL ACCOUNTING OFFICE,EXAMINATION OF ECONOMIC AND TECHNICAL ASSISTANCE PROGRAM FOR IRAN. IRAN USA+45 AGRI INDUS DIPLOM CONTROL COST 20. PAGE 136 F2681 — FOR/AID ADMIN TEC/DEV ECO/UNDEV

B61
WAGLE S.S.,TECHNIQUE OF PLANNING FOR ACCELERATED ECONOMIC GROWTH OF UNDERDEVELOPED COUNTRIES. WOR+45 ACT/RES PROB/SOLV RATION BAL/PAY DEMAND INCOME 20. PAGE 142 F2798 — ECO/UNDEV PLAN INDUS ECO/TAC

B61
WESTON J.F.,THE ROLE OF MERGERS IN THE GROWTH OF LARGE FIRMS. USA+45 USA-45 LEGIS CONTROL...CONCPT STAT CHARTS 19/20. PAGE 145 F2862 — LG/CO CENTRAL INDUS FINAN

L61
JOHNSTON B.F.,"THE ROLE OF AGRICULTURE IN ECONOMIC DEVELOPMENT." FINAN PRODUC ROLE BIBLIOG. PAGE 68 F1332 — AGRI ECO/UNDEV PLAN INDUS

S61
BENNION E.G.,"ECONOMETRICS FOR MANAGEMENT." USA+45 INDUS EX/STRUC ACT/RES COMPUTER UTIL...MATH STAT PREDICT METH/COMP HYPO/EXP. PAGE 13 F0248 — ECOMETRIC MGT SIMUL DECISION

S61
DICKS-MIREAUX L.A.,"THE INTERRELATIONSHIP BETWEEN COST AND PRICE CHANGES 19461959: A STUDY OF INFLATION IN POST-WAR BRITAIN" AFR UK ECO/DEV INDUS WORKER ECO/TAC ORD/FREE WEALTH...ECOMETRIC REGRESS STAT TREND CHARTS 20. PAGE 33 F0634 — PRICE PAY DEMAND

S61
GORDON L.,"ECONOMIC REGIONALISM RECONSIDERED." FUT USA+45 WOR+45 INDUS NAT/G TEC/DEV DIPLOM ROUTINE PERCEPT WEALTH...WELF/ST METH/CNCPT WORK 20. PAGE 49 F0957 — ECO/DEV ATTIT CAP/ISM REGION

S61
HAYTES W.,"THREE VIEWS ON THE SOVIET ECONOMIC THREAT." AFR COM USA+45 USA-45 USSR WOR+45 WOR-45 INDUS TEC/DEV ECO/TAC DOMIN ATTIT PERCEPT PWR FOR/TRADE 20. PAGE 57 F1128 — ECO/DEV PLAN TOTALISM

S61
NEAL A.C.,"NEW ECONOMIC POLICIES FOR THE WEST." COM EUR+WWI FUT USA+45 WOR+45 ECO/DEV ECO/UNDEV INDUS MARKET ROUTINE HEALTH ORD/FREE PWR...OLD/LIB METH/CNCPT 20. PAGE 97 F1904 — PLAN ECO/TAC

S61
SHUBIK M.,"APPROACHES TO THE STUDY OF DECISION-MAKING RELEVANT TO THE FIRM." INDUS COMPUTER OP/RES ...PROBABIL STAT 20. PAGE 121 F2390 — GAME DECISION MGT SIMUL

S61
VALLET R.,"IRAN: KEY TO THE MIDDLE EAST." COM IRAQ ISLAM KUWAIT LEBANON SAUDI/ARAB TURKEY ELITES SOCIETY INDUS PROC/MFG POL/PAR TOP/EX PLAN BAL/PWR DIPLOM ECO/TAC ALL/VALS...TREND FOR/TRADE CENTO 20. PAGE 140 F2760 — NAT/G ECO/UNDEV IRAN

S61
VINER J.,"ECONOMIC FOREIGN POLICY ON THE NEW FRONTIER." USA+45 ECO/UNDEV AGRI FINAN INDUS MARKET INT/ORG NAT/G FOR/AID INT/TRADE ADMIN ATTIT PWR 20 KENNEDY/JF. PAGE 141 F2786 — TOP/EX ECO/TAC BAL/PAY TARIFFS

C61
FILLOL T.R.,"SOCIAL FACTORS IN ECONOMIC DEVELOPMENT: THE ARGENTINE CASE" INDUS LABOR CREATE TEC/DEV PERS/REL EFFICIENCY PRODUC DRIVE ...METH/CNCPT METH/COMP 20 ARGEN. PAGE 41 F0794 — BIBLIOG ECO/UNDEV MGT TREND

B62
ALTMAN G.T.,INVISIBLE BARRIER: THE OPTIMUM GROWTH CURVE. USA+45 USA-45 ECO/DEV PLAN PAY CONTROL DEMAND OPTIMAL PRODUC WEALTH...STAT CHARTS 20. PAGE 4 F0080 — INDUS FINAN ECO/TAC TAX

B62
BOGARDUS J.,OUTLINE FOR THE COURSE IN BUSINESS AND ECONOMICS LITERATURE (REV. ED; PAMPHLET). USA+45 FINAN INDUS NAT/G VOL/ASSN PRESS WRITING INDEX. PAGE 16 F0305 — BIBLIOG/A STAT

B62
CAIRNCROSS A.K.,FACTORS IN ECONOMIC DEVELOPMENT. WOR+45 ECO/UNDEV INDUS R+D LG/CO NAT/G EX/STRUC PLAN TEC/DEV ECO/TAC ATTIT HEALTH KNOWL PWR WEALTH ...TIME/SEQ GEN/LAWS TOT/POP TRUE/GP VAL/FREE 20. PAGE 21 F0399 — MARKET ECO/DEV

B62
COLLIER A.T.,MANAGEMENT, MEN, AND VALUES. INDUS FACE/GP EX/STRUC PLAN PROB/SOLV DEBATE SENIOR ADMIN PROFIT PERSON...PSY SOC 20. PAGE 26 F0505 — MGT ATTIT PERS/REL DECISION

B62
COX O.C.,CAPITALISM AND AMERICAN LEADERSHIP. WOR+45 WOR-45 STRATA INDUS SECT INT/TRADE EXEC INGP/REL RACE/REL RATIONAL PWR WEALTH. PAGE 28 F0548 — CAP/ISM LEAD ECO/DEV SOCIETY

B62
DENISON E.F.,THE SOURCES OF ECONOMIC GROWTH IN THE UNITED STATES AND THE ALTERNATIVES BEFORE US. AGRI INDUS SCHOOL TEC/DEV CAP/ISM ECO/TAC PRICE COST WEALTH...STAT TREND CHARTS 20. PAGE 32 F0620 — ECO/DEV WORKER PRODUC

B62
DOUGLAS A.,INDUSTRIAL PEACEMAKING. CONSULT ACT/RES ...MGT PSY METH 20. PAGE 34 F0656 — BARGAIN INDUS LABOR GP/REL

B62
DUPRE J.S.,SCIENCE AND THE NATION: POLICY AND POLITICS. USA+45 LAW ACADEM FORCES ADMIN CIVMIL/REL GOV/REL EFFICIENCY PEACE...TREND 20 SCI/ADVSRY. PAGE 35 F0682 — R+D INDUS TEC/DEV NUC/PWR

B62
FATOUROS A.A.,GOVERNMENT GUARANTEES TO FOREIGN INVESTORS. WOR+45 ECO/UNDEV INDUS WORKER ADJUD ...NAT/COMP BIBLIOG TREATY. PAGE 39 F0767 — NAT/G FINAN INT/TRADE ECO/DEV

B62
GALENSON W.,LABOR IN DEVELOPING COUNTRIES. BRAZIL INDONESIA ISRAEL PAKISTAN TURKEY AGRI INDUS WORKER PAY PRICE GP/REL WEALTH...MGT CHARTS METH/COMP NAT/COMP 20. PAGE 45 F0888 — LABOR ECO/UNDEV BARGAIN POL/PAR

B62
GERSCHENKRON A.,ECONOMIC BACKWARDNESS IN HISTORICAL PERSPECTIVE. WOR+45 WOR-45 ECO/DEV ECO/UNDEV INDUS NAT/G LEGIT DRIVE...WELF/ST DECISION QUANT TREND CHARTS 20. PAGE 47 F0919 — TEC/DEV USSR

B62
GRANICK D.,THE EUROPEAN EXECUTIVE. BELGIUM FRANCE GERMANY/W UK INDUS LABOR LG/CO SML/CO EX/STRUC PLAN TEC/DEV CAP/ISM COST DEMAND...POLICY CHARTS 20. PAGE 50 F0977 — MGT ECO/DEV ECO/TAC EXEC

B62
GROVE J.W.,GOVERNMENT AND INDUSTRY IN BRITAIN. UK FINAN LOC/G CONSULT DELIB/GP INT/TRADE ADMIN CONTROL...BIBLIOG 20. PAGE 52 F1008 — ECO/TAC INDUS NAT/G GP/REL

B62
HATTERY L.H.,INFORMATION RETRIEVAL MANAGEMENT. CLIENT INDUS TOP/EX COMPUTER OP/RES TEC/DEV ROUTINE COST EFFICIENCY RIGID/FLEX...METH/COMP ANTHOL 20. PAGE 57 F1113 — R+D COMPUT/IR MGT CREATE

B62
HOOVER C.B.,ECONOMIC SYSTEMS OF THE COMMONWEALTH. AFR CANADA INDIA UK ECO/DEV ECO/UNDEV AGRI INDUS TEC/DEV TARIFFS PRICE BAL/PAY DEMAND...SIMUL 20 AUSTRAL. PAGE 61 F1208 — CAP/ISM SOCISM ECO/TAC PLAN

B62
HOOVER E.M.,ANATOMY OF A METROPOLIS. FUT USA+45 SOCIETY ECO/DEV DIST/IND INDUS WORKER ECO/TAC TAX GP/REL COST WEALTH MUNICH 20 NEWYORK/C. PAGE 62 F1212 — ROUTINE TREND INCOME

B62
HUMPHREY D.D.,THE UNITED STATES AND THE COMMON MARKET. USA+45 INDUS MARKET INT/ORG PLAN EDU/PROP BAL/PAY DRIVE PWR WEALTH...TREND STERTYP FOR/TRADE EEC 20. PAGE 63 F1241 — ATTIT ECO/TAC

B62
INTERNATIONAL BANK RECONST DEV,THE WORLD BANK AND IDA IN ASIA. ASIA S/ASIA COM/IND DIST/IND...CHARTS 20. PAGE 65 F1272 — FINAN ECO/UNDEV AGRI INDUS

B62
LITWACK L.,THE AMERICAN LABOR MOVEMENT. USA-45 NAT/G CREATE TEC/DEV CAP/ISM ECO/TAC ADJUD AUTOMAT SKILL...TREND ANTHOL 19/20. PAGE 81 F1588 — INDUS LABOR GP/REL METH/COMP

B62
MEANS G.C.,THE CORPORATE REVOLUTION IN AMERICA: ECONOMIC REALITY VS. ECONOMIC THEORY. USA+45 USA-45 INDUS WORKER PLAN CAP/ISM ADMIN...IDEA/COMP 20. PAGE 89 F1742 — LG/CO MARKET CONTROL PRICE

B62
MORGAN C.A.,LABOR ECONOMICS. LAW INDUS MARKET WORKER PLAN PROB/SOLV GOV/REL INCOME ROLE...T 20 DEPT/LABOR NLRB. PAGE 93 F1829
LABOR
ECO/TAC
ECO/DEV
CAP/ISM

B62
MOWITZ R.J.,PROFILE OF A METROPOLIS: A CASE BOOK. COM/IND CONSTRUC INDUS PUB/INST PLAN TEC/DEV LEAD GP/REL...POLICY TECHNIC WELF/ST MUNICH. PAGE 94 F1851
DECISION
ADMIN

B62
MULLER E.,DIE HEIMATVERTRIEBENEN IN BADEN-WURTTEMBERG. GERMANY/W AGRI INDUS LABOR PROVS SOC/INTEG 20 MIGRATION. PAGE 95 F1858
GP/REL
INGP/REL

B62
NATIONAL BUREAU ECONOMIC RES,THE RATE AND DIRECTION OF INVENTIVE ACTIVITY: ECONOMIC AND SOCIAL FACTORS. STRUCT INDUS MARKET R+D CREATE OP/RES TEC/DEV EFFICIENCY PRODUC RATIONAL UTIL...WELF/ST PHIL/SCI METH/CNCPT TIME. PAGE 97 F1895
DECISION
PROB/SOLV
MGT

B62
O'CONNOR H.,WORLD CRISES IN OIL (BMR). ISLAM L/A+17C INDUS LG/CO INT/TRADE 20. PAGE 100 F1956
EXTR/IND
DIPLOM
ECO/UNDEV
SOCISM

B62
PASTOR R.S.,A STATEMENT OF THE LAWS OF PARAGUAY IN MATTERS AFFECTING BUSINESS (2ND ED.). PARAGUAY INDUS FAM LABOR LG/CO NAT/G LEGIS TAX CONTROL MARRIAGE 20. PAGE 103 F2033
FINAN
ECO/UNDEV
LAW
CONSTN

B62
PERROUX F.,L'ECONOMIE DES JEUNES NATIONS. EUR+WWI SOUTH/AFR FINAN MARKET TEC/DEV CAP/ISM FOR/AID INT/TRADE 20. PAGE 105 F2065
INDUS
ECO/UNDEV
ECO/TAC
DIPLOM

B62
REES A.,THE ECONOMICS OF TRADE UNIONS. FUT ECO/DEV INDUS BARGAIN CAP/ISM PRICE SENIOR CONTROL GP/REL COST...TREND 20 AFL/CIO. PAGE 110 F2172
LABOR
WORKER
ECO/TAC

B62
SCHALLER H.G.,PUBLIC EXPENDITURE DECISIONS IN THE URBAN COMMUNITY: PREPARED FOR RESOURCES FOR THE FUTURE, INC. INDUS SERV/IND LOC/G PUB/INST PLAN PROB/SOLV BUDGET DEMAND PRODUC...CHARTS MUNICH. PAGE 116 F2289
FINAN
DECISION

B62
SHINOHARA M.,GROWTH AND CYCLES IN THE JAPANESE ECONOMY. INDUS LABOR TEC/DEV CAP/ISM INT/TRADE PAY COST EFFICIENCY INCOME WEALTH...METH/COMP 20 CHINJAP. PAGE 121 F2380
PRODUC
ECO/DEV
EQUILIB
ECOMETRIC

B62
SIEVERS A.M.,REVOLUTION, EVOLUTION AND THE ECONOMIC ORDER. INDUS LABOR TAX CONTROL REV WAR DEMAND PRODUC WEALTH...IDEA/COMP 19/20 KEYNES/JM. PAGE 122 F2399
EFFICIENCY
ALL/IDEOS
ECO/DEV
WELF/ST

B62
SMITH G.A. JR.,POLICY FORMULATION AND ADMINISTRATION: A CASEBOOK OF TOPMANAGEMENT PROBLEMS IN BUSINESS. EX/STRUC PLAN PROB/SOLV ADMIN CONTROL EXEC LEAD ROUTINE EFFICIENCY ATTIT MGT. PAGE 123 F2430
INDUS
SOC/EXP
TOP/EX
DECISION

B62
SRIVASTAVA G.L.,COLLECTIVE BARGAINING AND LABOR-MANAGEMENT RELATIONS IN INDIA. INDIA UK USA+45 INDUS LEGIS WORKER ADJUD EFFICIENCY PRODUC ...METH/COMP 20. PAGE 125 F2462
LABOR
MGT
BARGAIN
GP/REL

B62
URQUIDI C.W.,A STATEMENT OF THE LAWS OF BOLIVIA IN MATTERS AFFECTING BUSINESS (3RD ED. REV., ENLARGED). L/A+17C LAW FINAN FAM WORKER ACT/RES DIPLOM ADJUD ADMIN GP/REL 20 BOLIV OAS. PAGE 133 F2626
JURID
INDUS
NAT/G
LEGIT

B62
US CONGRESS JOINT ECO COMM,INVENTORY FLUCTUATIONS AND ECONOMIC STABILIZATION. USA+45 LG/CO...MATH CHARTS CONGRESS. PAGE 134 F2652
ECO/TAC
FINAN
INDUS
PROB/SOLV

B62
VACCARO J.R.,A STATEMENT OF THE LAWS OF CHILE IN MATTERS AFFECTING BUSINESS (3RD ED.). CHILE AGRI FINAN FAM LABOR ECO/TAC FOR/AID TAX ADJUD CONTROL MARRIAGE STRANGE...BIBLIOG 20. PAGE 140 F2756
CONSTN
LAW
INDUS
MGT

B62
WOODS H.D.,LABOUR POLICY AND LABOUR ECONOMICS IN CANADA. CANADA FUT NAT/G VOL/ASSN WORKER BARGAIN ECO/TAC PAY CONFER GP/REL 20. PAGE 148 F2924
LABOR
POLICY
INDUS
ECO/DEV

L62
BELSHAW D.G.R.,"PUBLIC INVESTMENT IN AGRICULTURE AND ECONOMIC DEVELOPMENT OF UGANDA" UGANDA AGRI INDUS R+D ECO/TAC RATION TAX PAY COLONIAL 20 WORLD/BANK. PAGE 13 F0242
ECO/UNDEV
PLAN
ADMIN
CENTRAL

L62
WATERSTON A.,"PLANNING IN MOROCCO, ORGANIZATION AND IMPLEMENTATION. BALTIMORE: HOPKINS ECON. DEVELOP. INT. BANK FOR." ISLAM ECO/DEV AGRI DIST/IND INDUS PROC/MFG SERV/IND LOC/G EX/STRUC ECO/TAC PWR WEALTH TOT/POP TRUE/GP METH/GP TERR/GP VAL/FREE 20. PAGE 144 F2829
NAT/G
PLAN
MOROCCO

S62
BOONE A.,"THE FOREIGN TRADE OF CHINA." AFR ECO/DEV ECO/UNDEV INDUS MARKET NAT/G TEC/DEV WEALTH ...POLICY STAT TREND CHARTS FOR/TRADE. PAGE 17 F0318
ASIA
ECO/TAC

S62
KRISHNA K.G.V.,"PLANNING AND ECONOMIC DEVELOPMENT" AFR UGANDA AGRI INDUS R+D BUDGET RATION TAX COLONIAL 20. PAGE 73 F1441
ECO/UNDEV
ECO/TAC
NAT/LISM
PLAN

N62
US SENATE COMM ON JUDICIARY,LEGISLATION TO STRENGTHEN PENALTIES UNDER THE ANTITRUST LAWS (PAMPHLET). USA+45 LG/CO CONFER CONTROL SANCTION ORD/FREE 20 SENATE MONOPOLY. PAGE 139 F2748
LEAD
ADJUD
INDUS
ECO/TAC

B63
BRITISH AID. UK AGRI DIST/IND INDUS SCHOOL TEC/DEV INT/TRADE COLONIAL DEMAND...TREND CHARTS 20. PAGE 1 F0018
FOR/AID
ECO/UNDEV
NAT/G
FINAN

B63
BARNETT H.J.,SCARCITY AND GROWTH: THE ECONOMICS OF NATURAL RESOURCE AVAILABILITY. FUT WOR+45 AGRI INDUS PROB/SOLV TEC/DEV CONTROL PRODUC...SOC/WK IDEA/COMP METH/COMP SIMUL 20 RESOURCE/N MALTHUS RICARDO/D MILL/JS DARWIN/C. PAGE 10 F0191
DEMAND
HABITAT
CENSUS
GEOG

B63
BATES J.L.,THE ORIGINS OF TEAPOT DOME: PROGRESSIVES, PARTIES, AND PETROLEUM, 1909-1921. USA-45 INDUS LG/CO POL/PAR DELIB/GP CONTROL GOV/REL CONSERVE...BIBLIOG 20 NAVY. PAGE 11 F0209
EXTR/IND
CRIME
NAT/G

B63
BERGSON A.,ECONOMIC TRENDS IN THE SOVIET UNION. USSR ECO/UNDEV AGRI NAT/G FORCES PLAN TEC/DEV INT/TRADE BAL/PAY...POLICY ANTHOL 20. PAGE 14 F0259
ECO/DEV
NAT/COMP
INDUS
LABOR

B63
BONINI C.P.,SIMULATION OF INFORMATION AND DECISION SYSTEMS IN THE FIRM. MARKET BUDGET DOMIN EDU/PROP ADMIN COST ATTIT HABITAT PERCEPT PWR...CONCPT PROBABIL QUANT PREDICT HYPO/EXP BIBLIOG. PAGE 16 F0313
INDUS
SIMUL
DECISION
MGT

B63
BOWIE R.R.,GOVERNMENT REGULATION OF BUSINESS: CASES FROM THE NATIONAL REPORTER SYSTEM. USA+45 USA-45 NAT/G ECO/TAC ADJUD...ANTHOL 19/20 SUPREME/CT FTC FAIR/LABOR MONOPOLY. PAGE 17 F0331
LAW
CONTROL
INDUS
CT/SYS

B63
CERAMI C.A.,ALLIANCE BORN OF DANGER. EUR+WWI USA+45 USSR ECO/DEV INDUS VOL/ASSN ECO/TAC REGION ATTIT MARXISM ATLAN/ALL 20 NATO EEC. PAGE 22 F0437
DIPLOM
INT/ORG
NAT/G
POLICY

B63
CHAMPION J.M.,CRITICAL INCIDENTS IN MANAGEMENT. MARKET LG/CO SML/CO OP/RES ADMIN CONTROL LEAD GP/REL PERS/REL COST ATTIT SUPEGO ALL/VALS...PSY PERS/TEST BIBLIOG. PAGE 23 F0445
MGT
DECISION
EX/STRUC
INDUS

B63
CORLEY R.N.,THE LEGAL ENVIRONMENT OF BUSINESS. CONSTN LEGIS TAX ADMIN CT/SYS DISCRIM ATTIT PWR ...TREND 18/20. PAGE 28 F0537
NAT/G
INDUS
JURID
DECISION

B63
COURNOT A.A.,RESEARCHES INTO THE MATHEMATICAL PRINCIPLES OF THE THEORY OF WEALTH (1838). UNIV ECO/DEV ECO/UNDEV AGRI INDUS MARKET PAY CONTROL COST INCOME 19. PAGE 28 F0544
ECOMETRIC
GEN/LAWS
WEALTH

B63
DE VRIES E.,SOCIAL ASPECTS OF ECONOMIC DEVELOPMENT IN LATIN AMERICA. CULTURE SOCIETY STRATA FINAN INDUS INT/ORG DELIB/GP ACT/RES ECO/TAC EDU/PROP ADMIN ATTIT SUPEGO HEALTH KNOWL ORD/FREE...SOC STAT TREND ANTHOL TOT/POP VAL/FREE. PAGE 31 F0608
L/A+17C
ECO/UNDEV

B63
EL-NAGGAR S.,FOREIGN AID TO UNITED ARAB REPUBLIC. UAR USA+45 USSR AGRI FINAN INDUS FORCES EATING DEMAND...CHARTS METH/COMP 20 RESOURCE/N AID. PAGE 37 F0718
FOR/AID
ECO/UNDEV
RECEIVE
PLAN

B63
FATEMI N.S.,THE DOLLAR CRISIS. USA+45 INDUS NAT/G LEGIS BUDGET TAX COST...CHARTS METH/COMP 20 EEC. PAGE 39 F0766
PROB/SOLV
BAL/PAY
FOR/AID
PLAN

B63
FURTADO C.,THE ECONOMIC GROWTH OF BRAZIL: A SURVEY FROM COLONIAL TO MODERN TIMES. L/A+17C AGRI DIST/IND EXTR/IND INDUS WORKER COLONIAL RACE/REL OWN GOV/COMP. PAGE 45 F0877
ECO/UNDEV
TEC/DEV
LABOR
DOMIN

B63
GANGULY D.S.,PUBLIC CORPORATIONS IN A NATIONAL ECONOMY. INDIA WOR+45 FINAN INDUS TOP/EX PRICE EFFICIENCY...MGT STAT CHARTS BIBLIOG 20. PAGE 46 F0897
ECO/UNDEV
LG/CO
SOCISM
GOV/REL

B63
GLADE W.P. JR.,THE POLITICAL ECONOMY OF MEXICO. FUT L/A+17C CULTURE SOCIETY AGRI INDUS DELIB/GP ACT/RES ECO/TAC ATTIT HEALTH ORD/FREE...STAT TIME/SEQ TREND MEXIC/AMER TOT/POP VAL/FREE 20. PAGE 48 F0928 FINAN ECO/UNDEV

B63
GORDON M.S.,THE ECONOMICS OF WELFARE POLICIES. INDUS LOC/G NAT/G LEGIS WORKER INCOME AGE/O SKILL WEALTH...METH/COMP NAT/COMP 20. PAGE 49 F0959 METH/CNCPT ECO/TAC POLICY

B63
HAQ M.,THE STRATEGY OF ECONOMIC PLANNING. PAKISTAN AGRI FINAN INDUS NAT/G FOR/AID TAX CONTROL REGION PRODUC...POLICY CHARTS 20. PAGE 55 F1071 ECO/TAC ECO/UNDEV PLAN PROB/SOLV

B63
HIRSCHMAN A.O.,JOURNEYS TOWARD PROGRESS: STUDIES OF ECONOMIC POLICYMAKING IN LATIN AMERICA. CHILE FUT ECO/UNDEV AGRI FINAN INDUS CONSULT DELIB/GP PLAN ATTIT HEALTH ORD/FREE WEALTH...POLICY STAT VAL/FREE COLOMB 20. PAGE 60 F1177 L/A+17C ECO/TAC BRAZIL

B63
HOOPES R.,THE STEEL CRISIS. USA+45 INDUS ECO/TAC EDU/PROP PRICE CONTROL ATTIT...POLICY 20 KENNEDY/JF. PAGE 61 F1205 PROC/MFG NAT/G RATION CHIEF

B63
HUNTER A.,THE ECONOMICS OF AUSTRALIAN INDUSTRY. DIST/IND EXTR/IND FINAN PROC/MFG SERV/IND ACT/RES PLAN TARIFFS GP/REL INGP/REL 20 AUSTRAL. PAGE 63 F1245 INDUS ECO/DEV HABITAT GP/COMP

B63
IANNI O.,INDUSTRIALIZACAO E DESENVOLVIMENTO SOCIAL NO BRASIL. BRAZIL L/A+17C STRATA STRUCT ECO/UNDEV EDU/PROP LEAD LOBBY NAT/LISM 20. PAGE 64 F1257 WORKER GP/REL INDUS PARTIC

B63
INTERNATIONAL BANK RECONST DEV,THE WORLD BANK GROUP IN ASIA. ASIA S/ASIA INDUS TEC/DEV ECO/TAC...RECORD 20 IBRD WORLD/BANK. PAGE 65 F1273 INT/ORG DIPLOM ECO/UNDEV FINAN

B63
ISSAWI C.,EGYPT IN REVOLUTION: AN ECONOMIC ANALYSIS. ISLAM STRUCT ECO/UNDEV AGRI FINAN INDUS PLAN EXEC REV NAT/LISM ATTIT RIGID/FLEX WEALTH SOCISM...STAT FOR/TRADE WORK 20. PAGE 66 F1292 NAT/G UAR

B63
KAPP W.K.,SOCIAL COSTS OF BUSINESS ENTERPRISE. WOR+45 LABOR TEC/DEV CAP/ISM HABITAT...PHIL/SCI NEW/IDEA CON/ANAL 20. PAGE 69 F1354 COST SOCIETY INDUS RIGID/FLEX

B63
KATZ S.M.,A SELECTED LIST OF US READINGS ON DEVELOPMENT. AGRI COM/IND DIST/IND INDUS LABOR PLAN FOR/AID EDU/PROP HEALTH...POLICY SOC/WK 20. PAGE 69 F1361 BIBLIOG/A ECO/UNDEV TEC/DEV ACT/RES

B63
KOLKO G.,THE TRIUMPH OF CONSERVATISM. USA-45 INDUS LG/CO NAT/G PWR 20 PRESIDENT CONGRESS MONOPOLY PROGRSV/M. PAGE 72 F1421 CONSERVE CAP/ISM FINAN MARKET

B63
LAFEBER W.,THE NEW EMPIRE: AN INTERPRETATION OF AMERICAN EXPANSION, 1860-1898. USA-45 CONSTN NAT/LISM SOVEREIGN...TREND BIBLIOG 19/20. PAGE 74 F1457 INDUS NAT/G DIPLOM CAP/ISM

B63
LEWIS G.K.,PUERTO RICO: FREEDOM AND POWER IN THE CARIBBEAN. PUERT/RICO USA+45 CULTURE STRUCT INDUS POL/PAR WORKER EDU/PROP CATHISM 20. PAGE 79 F1548 ECO/UNDEV COLONIAL NAT/LISM GEOG

B63
MAIZELS A.,INDUSTRIAL GROWTH AND WORLD TRADE. FUT WOR+45 ECO/DEV FINAN INT/ORG PLAN TEC/DEV ECO/TAC WEALTH...MATH STAT CHARTS VAL/FREE 19/20. PAGE 84 F1642 INDUS ECO/UNDEV INT/TRADE

B63
MARX K.,THE POVERTY OF PHILOSOPHY (1847). SOCIETY STRATA INDUS WORKER OWN UTOPIA SOCISM...GEN/LAWS MARX/KARL. PAGE 86 F1692 MARXIST PRODUC

B63
MCCONNELL G.,STEEL AND THE PRESIDENCY, 1962. USA+45 INDUS PROB/SOLV CONFER ROLE...POLICY 20 PRESIDENT. PAGE 88 F1722 PWR CHIEF REPRESENT DOMIN

B63
MILLER W.,REVENUE-COST RATIOS OF RURAL TOWNSHIPS WITH CHANGING LAND USES. USA+45 INDUS SERV/IND PROVS GP/REL HABITAT...CHARTS GP/COMP MUNICH 20 NEW/JERSEY. PAGE 91 F1792 TAX COST AGRI

B63
MINGAY G.E.,ENGLISH LANDED SOCIETY IN THE EIGHTEENTH CENTURY. UK ELITES STRUCT AGRI INDUS CONTROL WEALTH 18. PAGE 92 F1802 OWN STRATA PWR

B63
PAN AMERICAN UNION,THE EFFECTS OF THE EUROPEAN ECONOMIC COMMUNITY ON THE LATIN AMERICAN ECONOMIES (BMR). EUR+WWI L/A+17C ECO/UNDEV AGRI INDUS MARKET REGION 20 EEC TREATY. PAGE 103 F2024 INT/TRADE INT/ORG AGREE POLICY

B63
PATTON R.,THE DEVELOPMENT OF THE AMERICAN ECONOMY: REVISED. USA+45 USA-45 INDUS LABOR NAT/G CAP/ISM DIPLOM INT/TRADE WAR WEALTH 16/20. PAGE 104 F2038 ECO/TAC ECO/DEV DEMAND

B63
PERLO V.,MILITARISM AND INDUSTRY. USA+45 INT/TRADE EDU/PROP DETER KNOWL...CHARTS MAPS 20. PAGE 105 F2064 CIVMIL/REL INDUS LOBBY ARMS/CONT

B63
PRITCHETT C.H.,THE THIRD BRANCH OF GOVERNMENT. USA+45 USA-45 CONSTN SOCIETY INDUS SECT LEGIS JUDGE PROB/SOLV GOV/REL 20 SUPREME/CT CHURCH/STA. PAGE 108 F2122 JURID NAT/G ADJUD CT/SYS

B63
RANGEL I.,A INFLACAO BRASILEIRA (2ND ED.). AFR BRAZIL AGRI INDUS MARKET INT/TRADE DEMAND EQUILIB ATTIT 20. PAGE 109 F2144 ECO/UNDEV FINAN PRICE TAX

B63
REAGAN M.D.,THE MANAGED ECONOMY. USA+45 INDUS LG/CO BUDGET GP/REL ORD/FREE PWR WEALTH 20. PAGE 110 F2161 PLAN ECO/DEV NAT/G ROLE

B63
RICARDO D.,THE PRINCIPLES OF POLITICAL ECONOMY AND TAXATION (1817). UK INDUS MARKET ECO/TAC INT/TRADE TARIFFS PRICE COST DEMAND OPTIMAL WEALTH...CONCPT 19 INTRVN/ECO. PAGE 111 F2183 GEN/LAWS TAX LAISSEZ

B63
SCHOECK H.,THE NEW ARGUMENT IN ECONOMICS. UK USA+45 INDUS MARKET LABOR NAT/G ECO/TAC ADMIN ROUTINE BAL/PAY PWR...POLICY BOLIV. PAGE 117 F2309 WELF/ST FOR/AID ECO/DEV ALL/IDEOS

B63
SHANKS M.,THE LESSONS OF PUBLIC ENTERPRISE. UK LEGIS WORKER ECO/TAC ADMIN PARL/PROC GOV/REL ATTIT ...POLICY MGT METH/COMP NAT/COMP ANTHOL 20 PARLIAMENT. PAGE 120 F2364 SOCISM OWN NAT/G INDUS

B63
SMITH R.A.,CORPORATIONS IN CRISIS. USA+45 LG/CO EX/STRUC ECO/TAC CONTROL LEAD PERS/REL...MGT 20. PAGE 123 F2432 ELITES INDUS PROB/SOLV METH/COMP

B63
STUCKI C.W.,AMERICAN DOCTORAL DISSERTATIONS ON ASIA 1933-62 (A PAPER). PREHIST INDUS NAT/G GOV/REL ALL/IDEOS...ART/METH GEOG SOC LING 20. PAGE 127 F2506 BIBLIOG ASIA SOCIETY S/ASIA

B63
UN FAO,BIBLIOGRAPHY ON THE ANALYSIS AND PROJECTION OF DEMAND AND PRODUCTION, 1963. WOR+45 ECO/DEV ECO/UNDEV...PREDICT TREND 20. PAGE 132 F2601 BIBLIOG/A AGRI INDUS

B63
UNITED NATIONS,THE GROWTH OF WORLD INDUSTRY, 1938-1961: NATIONAL TABLES. WOR+45 STRUCT ECO/DEV ECO/UNDEV NAT/G COST...CHARTS UN. PAGE 132 F2613 STAT INDUS PRODUC ORD/FREE

B63
US DEPARTMENT OF LABOR,THE ANVIL AND THE PLOW. KOREA USA+45 USA-45 INDUS WORKER BUDGET WAR ...POLICY AUD/VIS CHARTS 20 DEPT/LABOR. PAGE 135 F2667 ECO/DEV LABOR ECO/TAC NAT/G

B63
US ECON SURVEY TEAM INDONESIA,INDONESIA - PERSPECTIVE AND PROPOSALS FOR UNITED STATES ECONOMIC AID. INDONESIA AGRI MARKET TEC/DEV DIPLOM INT/TRADE EDU/PROP 20. PAGE 136 F2678 FOR/AID ECO/UNDEV PLAN INDUS

B63
WILTZ J.E.,IN SEARCH OF PEACE: THE SENATE MUNITIONS INQUIRY, 1934-36. EUR+WWI USA-45 ELITES INDUS LG/CO LEGIS INT/TRADE LOBBY NEUTRAL ARMS/CONT...POLICY CONGRESS 20 LEAGUE/NAT PRESIDENT SENATE CONSCRIPTN. PAGE 147 F2905 DELIB/GP PROFIT WAR WEAPON

L63
ADERBIGDE A.,"SYMPOSIUM ON WEST AFRICA INTEGRATION." AFR EUR+WWI FUT CULTURE SOCIETY STRATA DIST/IND INDUS MARKET SERV/IND DELIB/GP PLAN TEC/DEV DOMIN EDU/PROP LEGIT COERCE ATTIT ALL/VALS ...POLICY STAT TREND CHARTS VAL/FREE. PAGE 2 F0040 FINAN ECO/TAC REGION

S63
ANDREWS R.B.,"ECONOMIC PLANNING FOR SMALL AREAS: THE PLANNING PROCESS." INDUS PROC/MFG PROVS PROB/SOLV TAX EQUILIB...METH/COMP HYPO/EXP METH MUNICH 20. PAGE 5 F0103 ECO/TAC PLAN LOC/G

S63
DUCROS B.,"MOBILISATION DES RESSOURCES PRODUCTIVES ET DEVELOPPEMENT." FUT INTELL SOCIETY COM/IND DIST/IND EXTR/IND FINAN INDUS ROUTINE WEALTH ...METH/CNCPT OBS 20. PAGE 34 F0670 ECO/UNDEV TEC/DEV

S63
GALENSON W.,"ECONOMIC DEVELOPMENT AND THE SECTORAL EXPANSION OF EMPLOYMENT, INT." FUT WOR+45 ECO/UNDEV DIST/IND PROC/MFG SERV/IND ACT/RES HEALTH SKILL INDUS ECO/TAC

WEALTH...STAT TIME/SEQ VAL/FREE 20. PAGE 46 F0889

S63
GORDON B.,"ECONOMIC IMPEDIMENTS TO REGIONALISM IN SOUTH EAST ASIA." BURMA FUT S/ASIA THAILAND USA+45 AGRI INDUS R+D NAT/G PLAN ECO/TAC WEALTH...STAT CONT/OBS 20. PAGE 49 F0954
VOL/ASSN ECO/UNDEV INT/TRADE REGION

S63
HOOVER C.B.,"ECONOMIC REFORM VERSUS ECONOMIC GROWTH IN UNDERDEVELOPED COUNTRIES." FUT WOR+45 ELITES STRATA ECO/UNDEV DIST/IND INDUS TEC/DEV CAP/ISM FOR/AID INT/TRADE ATTIT WEALTH...MYTH TREND STERTYP GEN/LAWS WORK 20. PAGE 61 F1209
ECO/DEV ECO/TAC

S63
LOEWENSTEIN L.K.,"THE LOCATION OF URBAN LAND USES." USA+45 LOC/G HABITAT...STAT CHARTS MUNICH 20. PAGE 81 F1595
GEOG PLAN INDUS

S63
MATHUR P.N.,"GAINS IN ECONOMIC GROWTH FROM INTERNATIONAL TRADE." USA-45 ECO/DEV FINAN INDUS ATTIT WEALTH...MATH QUANT STAT BIOG TREND GEN/LAWS WORK 20. PAGE 87 F1704
MARKET ECO/TAC CAP/ISM INT/TRADE

S63
NADLER E.B.,"SOME ECONOMIC DISADVANTAGES OF THE ARMS RACE." AFR USA+45 INDUS R+D FORCES PLAN TEC/DEV ECO/TAC FOR/AID EDU/PROP PWR WEALTH...TREND FOR/TRADE 20. PAGE 96 F1886
ECO/DEV MGT BAL/PAY

S63
PAAUW D.S.,"ECONOMIC PROGRESS IN SOUTHEAST ASIA." S/ASIA AGRI INDUS PROC/MFG ACT/RES ECO/TAC...CHARTS VAL/FREE 20. PAGE 102 F2010
ECO/UNDEV STAT

S63
SCHURMANN F.,"ECONOMIC POLICY AND POLITICAL POWER IN COMMUNIST CHINA." ASIA CHINA/COM USSR SOCIETY ECO/UNDEV AGRI INDUS CREATE ADMIN ROUTINE ATTIT DRIVE RIGID/FLEX PWR WEALTH...HIST/WRIT TREND CHARTS WORK 20. PAGE 118 F2323
PLAN ECO/TAC

S63
SHWADRAN B.,"MIDDLE EAST OIL, 1962." ISLAM DIST/IND INDUS PLAN ATTIT DRIVE WEALTH...POLICY STAT CONT/OBS TREND CHARTS GEN/LAWS TERR/GP METH/GP 20 OIL. PAGE 121 F2393
PROC/MFG ECO/TAC ELITES REGION

S63
SHWADRAN B.,"MIDDLE EAST OIL, 1962." ISLAM USSR ECO/DEV DIST/IND INDUS PLAN BAL/PWR DISPL DRIVE ...POLICY STAT TREND GEN/LAWS TERR/GP METH/GP EEC OEEC 20 OIL. PAGE 121 F2394
MARKET ECO/TAC INT/TRADE

S63
STEFANIAK N.J.,"A REFINEMENT OF HAIG'S THEORY." USA+45 INDUS PROB/SOLV TEC/DEV...CONCPT CHARTS MUNICH 20 HAIG. PAGE 125 F2474
GEOG GEN/LAWS PLAN

B64
BALASSA B.,TRADE PROSPECTS FOR DEVELOPING COUNTRIES. WOR+45 ECO/DEV AGRI EXTR/IND INDUS CREATE PLAN PRICE...ECOMETRIC CLASSIF TIME/SEQ GEN/METH. PAGE 8 F0158
INT/TRADE ECO/UNDEV TREND STAT

B64
BALOGH T.,THE ECONOMIC IMPACT OF MONETARY AND COMMERCIAL INSTITUTIONS OF A EUROPEAN ORIGIN IN AFRICA. AFR UAR INDUS FOR/AID COLONIAL CONTROL ...NAT/COMP 20. PAGE 9 F0169
TEC/DEV FINAN ECO/UNDEV ECO/TAC

B64
BASTIAT F.,ECONOMIC SOPHISMS (1845). FINAN MARKET INT/TRADE TAX EDU/PROP LAISSEZ. PAGE 11 F0207
TARIFFS INDUS ECO/TAC CAP/ISM

B64
BEARDSLEY R.K.,STUDIES ON ECONOMIC LIFE IN JAPAN (OCCASIONAL PAPERS NO. 8). INDUS FAM HABITAT...GEOG GOV/COMP 20 CHINJAP. PAGE 12 F0223
WEALTH PRESS PRODUC INCOME

B64
BERRILL K.,ECONOMIC DEVELOPMENT WITH SPECIAL REFERENCE TO EAST ASIA. ASIA INDIA S/ASIA AGRI INDUS LABOR DELIB/GP PLAN INT/TRADE COST PRODUC 20 CHINJAP. PAGE 14 F0271
FINAN ECO/UNDEV INT/ORG CAP/ISM

B64
BLAKE R.R.,MANAGING INTERGROUP CONFLICT IN INDUSTRY. INDUS DELIB/GP EX/STRUC GP/REL PERS/REL GAME. PAGE 16 F0297
CREATE PROB/SOLV OP/RES ADJUD

B64
BRIGHT J.R.,RESEARCH, DEVELOPMENT AND TECHNOLOGICAL INNOVATION. CULTURE R+D CREATE PLAN PROB/SOLV AUTOMAT RISK PERSON...DECISION CONCPT PREDICT BIBLIOG. PAGE 18 F0352
TEC/DEV NEW/IDEA INDUS MGT

B64
CHEIT E.F.,THE BUSINESS ESTABLISHMENT. FRANCE WOR+45 PROF/ORG TOP/EX PROB/SOLV CAP/ISM ADMIN SUPEGO MORAL PWR...METH/CNCPT MYTH NEW/IDEA 20. PAGE 24 F0460
PERSON EX/STRUC MGT INDUS

B64
COLUMBIA U SCHOOL OF LAW,PUBLIC INTERNATIONAL DEVELOPMENT FINANCING IN INDIA. GERMANY/W INDIA UK USA+45 INDUS PLAN TEC/DEV DIPLOM ECO/TAC GIVE ADMIN UTIL ATTIT 20. PAGE 26 F0512
ECO/UNDEV FINAN FOR/AID INT/ORG

B64
COMMITTEE ECONOMIC DEVELOPMENT,COMMUNITY ECONOMIC DEVELOPMENT PROGRAMS. USA+45 FINAN INDUS LG/CO PROF/ORG CREATE GP/REL MUNICH NEW/YORK VERMONT PENNSYLVAN IN ARKANSAS. PAGE 27 F0519
LOC/G LABOR PLAN

B64
DUSCHA J.,ARMS, MONEY, AND POLITICS. USA+45 INDUS POL/PAR ECO/TAC TAX DETER NUC/PWR WAR WEAPON GOV/REL ATTIT...BIBLIOG/A 20 CONGRESS MONEY DEPT/DEFEN. PAGE 35 F0687
NAT/G FORCES POLICY BUDGET

B64
EDWARDS E.O.,THE NATION'S ECONOMIC OBJECTIVES. INDUS WORKER BUDGET DIPLOM CONTROL ORD/FREE ...POLICY SOC METH/CNCPT ANTHOL 20. PAGE 36 F0704
NAT/G ECO/TAC

B64
EINZIG P.,MONETARY POLICY: ENDS AND MEANS. AFR UK INDUS WORKER PLAN DIPLOM PRICE BAL/PAY COST WEALTH ...DECISION TIME/SEQ 20. PAGE 37 F0715
FINAN POLICY ECO/TAC BUDGET

B64
FEI J.C.H.,DEVELOPMENT OF THE LABOR SURPLUS ECONOMY: THEORY AND POLICY. WOR+45 AGRI INDUS MARKET PROB/SOLV TEC/DEV...STAT CHARTS GEN/LAWS METH 20 THIRD/WRLD. PAGE 40 F0772
ECO/TAC POLICY WORKER ECO/UNDEV

B64
FIESER M.E.,ECONOMIC POLICY AND WAR POTENTIAL. AFR WOR+45 ECO/DEV INDUS NAT/G FORCES TEC/DEV NUC/PWR CIVMIL/REL ORD/FREE 20. PAGE 40 F0791
INT/TRADE POLICY ECO/TAC DETER

B64
FLORENCE P.S.,ECONOMICS AND SOCIOLOGY OF INDUSTRY; A REALISTIC ANALYSIS OF DEVELOPMENT. ECO/UNDEV LG/CO NAT/G PLAN...GEOG MGT BIBLIOG 20. PAGE 42 F0814
INDUS SOC ADMIN

B64
FRIEDMANN J.,REGIONAL DEVELOPMENT AND PLANNING: A READER. AGRI MARKET NAT/G ECO/TAC INCOME...GEOG STAT CENSUS CHARTS ANTHOL BIBLIOG MUNICH 20 OPEN/SPACE. PAGE 44 F0863
PLAN REGION INDUS ECO/DEV

B64
HAMBRIDGE G.,DYNAMICS OF DEVELOPMENT. AGRI FINAN INDUS LABOR INT/TRADE EDU/PROP ADMIN LEAD OWN HEALTH...ANTHOL BIBLIOG 20. PAGE 54 F1054
ECO/UNDEV ECO/TAC OP/RES ACT/RES

B64
HANSEN A.H.,BUSINESS CYCLES AND NATIONAL INCOME. USA+45 FINAN ECO/TAC COST OPTIMAL...POLICY METH 20 KEYNES/JM. PAGE 54 F1065
INCOME WEALTH PRODUC INDUS

B64
HART P.E.,ECONOMETRIC ANALYSIS FOR NATIONAL ECONOMIC PLANNING. INDUS OP/RES PRICE PRODUC ...SIMUL ANTHOL MODELS 20. PAGE 56 F1100
PLAN ECOMETRIC STAT

B64
HAZLEWOOD A.,THE ECONOMICS OF DEVELOPMENT: AN ANNOTATED LIST OF BOOKS AND ARTICLES PUBLISHED 1958-1962. AGRI FINAN INDUS LABOR NAT/G DIPLOM INT/TRADE INCOME...MGT 20. PAGE 58 F1130
BIBLIOG/A ECO/UNDEV TEC/DEV

B64
HINSHAW R.,THE EUROPEAN COMMUNITY AND AMERICAN TRADE: A STUDY IN ATLANTIC ECONOMICS AND POLICY. EUR+WWI UK USA+45 ECO/DEV ECO/UNDEV AGRI INDUS INT/ORG NAT/G ECO/TAC TARIFFS REGION...STAT CHARTS EEC 20. PAGE 60 F1174
MARKET TREND INT/TRADE

B64
HUTT W.H.,THE ECONOMICS OF THE COLOUR BAR. SOUTH/AFR EXTR/IND LABOR ADJUD NEGRO. PAGE 64 F1251
INDUS DISCRIM RACE/REL ECO/UNDEV

B64
IMAZ J.L.,LOS QUE MANDAN. INDUS LABOR NAT/G POL/PAR PROVS SECT CHIEF TOP/EX CONTROL 20 ARGEN. PAGE 64 F1261
LEAD FORCES ELITES ATTIT

B64
KAPLAN A.D.H.,BIG ENTERPRISE IN A COMPETITIVE SYSTEM (REV. ED.). USA+45 INDUS MARKET WORKER TEC/DEV ECO/TAC PRICE ADJUD ADMIN CONTROL...MGT CHARTS 20 MONOPOLY. PAGE 69 F1351
FINAN GP/REL NAT/G LG/CO

B64
KUZNETS S.,POSTWAR ECONOMIC GROWTH: FOUR LECTURES. WOR+45 INDUS NAT/G WORKER TEC/DEV ECO/TAC RATION TARIFFS PRICE BAL/PAY COST DEMAND 20. PAGE 74 F1455
ECO/DEV ECO/UNDEV TREND FINAN

B64
LI C.M.,INDUSTRIAL DEVELOPMENT IN COMMUNIST CHINA. CHINA/COM ECO/DEV ECO/UNDEV AGRI FINAN INDUS MARKET LABOR NAT/G ECO/TAC INT/TRADE EXEC ALL/VALS ...POLICY RELATIV TREND WORK TOT/POP VAL/FREE 20. PAGE 79 F1556
ASIA TEC/DEV

B64
LINDHOLM R.W.,ECONOMIC DEVELOPMENT POLICY WITH EMPHASIS ON VIET-NAM. KOREA/S PAKISTAN VIETNAM/S AGRI INDUS CONSULT DELIB/GP FOR/AID...METH 20. PAGE 80 F1571
ECO/UNDEV TAX FINAN ECO/TAC

B64
MAGALHAES S.,PRATICA DA EMANCIPACAO NACIONAL. L/A+17C INDUS PLAN ECO/TAC CONTROL NAT/LISM ORD/FREE. PAGE 84 F1640
BAL/PAY ECO/UNDEV DIPLOM WEALTH

B64
MANSFIELD E.,MONOPOLY POWER AND ECONOMIC PERFORMANCE: AN INTRODUCTION TO A CURRENT ISSUE OF PUBLIC POLICY. ECO/DEV INDUS NAT/G PLAN CAP/ISM PRICE CONTROL LOBBY EFFICIENCY PRODUC...POLICY 20 CONGRESS KENNEDY/JF MONOPOLY. PAGE 85 F1659
LG/CO PWR ECO/TAC MARKET

B64
MASON E.S.,FOREIGN AID AND FOREIGN POLICY. USA+45 AGRI INDUS NAT/G EX/STRUC ACT/RES RIGID/FLEX ALL/VALS...POLICY GEN/LAWS MARSHL/PLN ALL/PROG CONGRESS 20. PAGE 87 F1699
ECO/UNDEV ECO/TAC FOR/AID DIPLOM

B64
MAZA ZAVALA D.F.,VENEZUELA; UNA ECONOMIA DEPENDIENTE. L/A+17C VENEZUELA FINAN INDUS ...ECOMETRIC STAT TREND 20. PAGE 87 F1710
ECO/UNDEV BAL/PAY INT/TRADE PRICE

B64
MEZERIK A.G.,TRADE, AID AND ECONOMIC DEVELOPMENT. WOR+45 FINAN INDUS MARKET PLAN BAL/PWR BARGAIN FOR/AID TARIFFS EDU/PROP WEALTH...GP/COMP 20 UN GATT IMF IBRD. PAGE 91 F1777
ECO/TAC ECO/DEV INT/ORG INT/TRADE

B64
MORRISSENS L.,ECONOMIC POLICY IN OUR TIME: COUNTRY STUDIES. BELGIUM EUR+WWI FRANCE GERMANY/W ITALY NETHERLAND INDUS BARGAIN BUDGET GOV/REL BAL/PAY PRODUC...CON/ANAL CHARTS COSTS 20. PAGE 94 F1839
ECO/DEV ECO/TAC METH/COMP PLAN

B64
NAGEL P.C.,ONE NATION INDIVISIBLE: THE UNION IN AMERICAN THOUGHT 1776-1861. USA-45 INDUS TEC/DEV EDU/PROP DREAM...IDEA/COMP 18/19. PAGE 96 F1887
FEDERAL NAT/G ATTIT INGP/REL

B64
NEHEMKIS P.,LATIN AMERICA: MYTH AND REALITY. INDUS INT/ORG PROB/SOLV CAP/ISM DIPLOM REV...SOC MUNICH 20. PAGE 97 F1907
REGION MYTH L/A+17C ECO/UNDEV

B64
NEUFIELD M.F.,A REPRESENTATIVE BIBLIOGRAPHY OF AMERICAN LABOR HISTORY. USA+45 USA-45 20. PAGE 97 F1914
BIBLIOG LABOR WORKER INDUS

B64
OECD,DEVELOPMENT ASSISTANCE EFFORTS - POLICIES OF THE MEMBERS. AGRI INDUS BUDGET...GEOG NAT/COMP 20 OECD. PAGE 100 F1967
INT/ORG FOR/AID ECO/UNDEV TEC/DEV

B64
ORGANIZATION AMERICAN STATES,ECONOMIC SURVEY OF LATIN AMERICA, 1962. L/A+17C AGRI DIST/IND INDUS MARKET PROC/MFG R+D PLAN TEC/DEV ECO/TAC REGION BAL/PAY ALL/VALS...CON/ANAL ORG/CHARTS GEN/METH OAS ALL/PROG 20 ALL/PROG. PAGE 102 F1998
ECO/UNDEV CHARTS

B64
PAWERA J.C.,ALGERIA'S INFRASTRUCTURE. ALGERIA PLAN WEALTH...METH/CNCPT 20. PAGE 104 F2041
ECO/UNDEV INDUS TEC/DEV COM/IND

B64
POWELSON J.P.,LATIN AMERICA: TODAY'S ECONOMIC AND SOCIAL REVOLUTION. L/A+17C INTELL SOCIETY STRUCT AGRI INDUS NAT/G DIPLOM ECO/TAC REV...POLICY 20. PAGE 107 F2110
ECO/UNDEV WEALTH ADJUST PLAN

B64
RENO P.,THE ORDEAL OF BRITISH GUIANA. L/A+17C USA+45 STRUCT AGRI EXTR/IND INDUS NAT/G FOR/AID ORD/FREE...GEOG 20 GUIANA/BR INTRVN/ECO. PAGE 111 F2178
COLONIAL ECO/UNDEV SOCISM PWR

B64
ROBINSON E.A.G.,ECONOMIC DEVELOPMENT FOR AFRICA SOUTH OF THE SAHARA. AFR AGRI INDUS LABOR BUDGET INT/TRADE PRICE...POLICY GEOG ANTHOL 20. PAGE 113 F2219
ECO/UNDEV ECO/TAC ACT/RES PLAN

B64
RUSTAMJI R.F.,THE LAW OF INDUSTRIAL DISPUTES IN INDIA. INDIA LEGIS WORKER CONTROL GP/REL...JURID MGT TIME/SEQ 20. PAGE 115 F2264
INDUS ADJUD BARGAIN LABOR

B64
SEERS D.,CUBA: THE ECONOMIC AND SOCIAL REVOLUTION. L/A+17C USSR YUGOSLAVIA STRATA AGRI INDUS SCHOOL DELIB/GP PLAN ECO/TAC DOMIN EDU/PROP ATTIT RIGID/FLEX ALL/VALS...STAT OBS TIME/SEQ WORK VAL/FREE 20. PAGE 119 F2341
ACT/RES COERCE CUBA REV

B64
SINGER H.W.,INTERNATIONAL DEVELOPMENT: GROWTH AND CHANGE. AFR BRAZIL L/A+17C WOR+45 CULTURE AGRI INDUS NAT/G ACT/RES ECO/TAC EDU/PROP WEALTH...GEOG CONCPT METH/CNCPT STAT HYPO/EXP WORK TOT/POP 20. PAGE 122 F2412
FINAN ECO/UNDEV FOR/AID INT/TRADE

B64
SOLOW R.M.,THE NATURE AND SOURCES OF UNEMPLOYMENT IN THE UNITED STATES (PAMPHLET). USA+45 INDUS LABOR TEC/DEV ECO/TAC SKILL WEALTH...TREND NAT/COMP 20. PAGE 124 F2439
ECO/DEV WORKER STAT PRODUC

B64
STONIER A.W.,EXERCISES IN ECONOMICS. FINAN INDUS TEC/DEV RENT PAY EQUILIB PRODUC PROFIT...METH/COMP T. PAGE 127 F2498
PRICE MARKET WORKER

B64
STRONG A.L.,THE RISE OF THE CHINESE PEOPLE'S COMMUNES - AND SIX YEARS AFTER (2ND ED.). CHINA/COM AGRI INDUS FORCES WORKER PROB/SOLV EDU/PROP EFFICIENCY ISOLAT 20. PAGE 127 F2503
NEIGH ECO/TAC MARXISM METH/COMP

B64
TELLADO A.,A STATEMENT OF THE LAWS OF THE DOMINICAN REPUBLIC IN MATTERS AFFECTING BUSINESS (3RD ED.). DOMIN/REP AGRI DIST/IND EXTR/IND FINAN FAM WORKER ECO/TAC TAX CT/SYS MARRIAGE OWN...BIBLIOG 20 MIGRATION. PAGE 129 F2542
CONSTN LEGIS NAT/G INDUS

B64
TINBERGEN J.,CENTRAL PLANNING. COM INTELL ECO/DEV ECO/UNDEV FINAN INT/ORG PROB/SOLV ECO/TAC CONTROL EXEC ROUTINE DECISION. PAGE 130 F2576
PLAN INDUS MGT CENTRAL

B64
US SENATE COMM ON FOREIGN REL,HEARING ON BILLS RELATING TO FOREIGN ASSISTANCE. USA+45 WOR+45 ECO/UNDEV FINAN INDUS 20 UN CONGRESS. PAGE 139 F2733
FOR/AID DIPLOM TEC/DEV INT/ORG

B64
WELLISZ S.,THE ECONOMICS OF THE SOVIET BLOC. COM USSR INDUS WORKER PLAN BUDGET INT/TRADE TAX PRICE PRODUC WEALTH MARXISM...METH/COMP 20. PAGE 145 F2854
EFFICIENCY ADMIN MARKET

B64
WILSON T.,POLICIES FOR REGIONAL DEVELOPMENT. CANADA UK FINAN INDUS NAT/G BUDGET TAX GIVE COST ...NAT/COMP 20. PAGE 147 F2904
REGION PLAN ECO/DEV ECO/TAC

L64
BHAGWATI J.,"THE PURE THEORY OF INTERNATIONAL TRADE: A SURVEY." WOR+45 ECO/DEV ECO/UNDEV FINAN MARKET PROC/MFG INT/ORG LABOR LG/CO NAT/G TEC/DEV ECO/TAC SKILL WEALTH...POLICY RELATIV MGT CONCPT NEW/IDEA MATH QUANT GEN/LAWS FOR/TRADE 20. PAGE 14 F0276
INDUS HYPO/EXP

L64
CARNEGIE ENDOWMENT INT. PEACE,"ECONOMIC AND SOCIAL QUESTION (ISSUES BEFORE THE NINETEENTH GENERAL ASSEMBLY)." WOR+45 ECO/DEV ECO/UNDEV INDUS R+D DELIB/GP CREATE PLAN TEC/DEV ECO/TAC FOR/AID BAL/PAY...RECORD UN 20. PAGE 21 F0414
INT/ORG INT/TRADE

S64
FLORINSKY M.T.,"TRENDS IN THE SOVIET ECONOMY." COM USA+45 USSR INDUS LABOR NAT/G PLAN TEC/DEV ECO/TAC ALL/VALS SOCISM...MGT METH/CNCPT STYLE CON/ANAL GEN/METH WORK 20. PAGE 42 F0817
ECO/DEV AGRI

S64
GALBRAITH V.,"JAPAN'S POSITION IN WORLD TRADE." ASIA AGRI INDUS CREATE ECO/TAC LEGIT DRIVE WEALTH ...TREND EEC GATT FOR/TRADE 20 CHINJAP. PAGE 45 F0885
ECO/DEV DELIB/GP

S64
HERMAN L.M.,"THE ECONOMIC CONTENT OF SOVIET TRADE WITH THE WEST." WOR+45 ECO/DEV ECO/UNDEV AGRI COM/IND INDUS CAP/ISM ECO/TAC ATTIT RIGID/FLEX WEALTH...OBS TREND VAL/FREE MARX/KARL 20. PAGE 59 F1152
COM MARKET INT/TRADE USSR

S64
HUELIN D.,"ECONOMIC INTEGRATION IN LATIN AMERICAN: PROGRESS AND PROBLEMS." L/A+17C ECO/DEV AGRI DIST/IND FINAN INDUS NAT/G VOL/ASSN CONSULT DELIB/GP EX/STRUC ACT/RES PLAN TEC/DEV ECO/TAC ROUTINE BAL/PAY WEALTH FOR/TRADE WORK TERR/GP 20. PAGE 63 F1232
MARKET ECO/UNDEV INT/TRADE

S64
NASH M.,"SOCIAL PREREQUISITES TO ECONOMIC GROWTH IN LATIN AMERICA AND SOUTHEAST ASIA." L/A+17C S/ASIA CULTURE SOCIETY ECO/UNDEV AGRI INDUS NAT/G PLAN TEC/DEV EDU/PROP ROUTINE ALL/VALS...POLICY RELATIV SOC NAT/COMP WORK TOT/POP 20. PAGE 96 F1894
ECO/DEV PERCEPT

S64
PATEL S.J.,"THE ECONOMIC DISTANCE BETWEEN NATIONS: ITS ORIGIN, MEASUREMENT AND OUTLOOK." WOR+45 ECO/DEV AGRI FINAN INDUS MARKET LABOR NAT/G CONSULT TEC/DEV ECO/TAC WEALTH...POLICY RELATIV MGT TREND WORK 20. PAGE 103 F2035
ECO/UNDEV PLAN

S64
READER D.H.,"A SURVEY OF CATEGORIES OF ECONOMIC ACTIVITIES AMONG THE PEOPLES OF AFRICA." AGRI INDUS MARKET KIN HEALTH SKILL WEALTH...GEOG METH/CNCPT CHARTS TERR/GP WORK TOT/POP VAL/FREE 20. PAGE 110 F2160
TEC/DEV ECO/UNDEV AFR

S64
ROTHCHILD D.,"EAST AFRICAN FEDERATION." AFR TANZANIA UGANDA INDUS REGION 20. PAGE 114 F2249
INT/ORG DIPLOM ECO/UNDEV

ECO/TAC

S64
WU Y.,"CHINA'S ECONOMY AND ITS PROSPECTS." ASIA CHINA/COM FUT USSR AGRI INDUS PLAN ECO/TAC LEGIT WEALTH...STAT CON/ANAL CHARTS GEN/LAWS FOR/TRADE 20. PAGE 149 F2938 ECO/DEV

C64
LOUFTY A.,"LA PLANIFICATION DE L'ECONOMIE." FRANCE USSR FINAN INDUS BUDGET INCOME PRODUC...BIBLIOG 20. PAGE 82 F1604 PLAN ECO/UNDEV ECO/DEV

N64
KENYA MINISTRY ECO PLAN DEV,AFRICAN SOCIALISM AND ITS APPLICATION TO PLANNING IN KENYA (PAMPHLET). AFR AGRI INDUS WORKER TAX COLONIAL WEALTH 20. PAGE 70 F1380 NAT/G SOCISM PLAN ECO/UNDEV

B65
AMERICAN ECONOMIC ASSOCIATION,INDEX OF ECONOMIC JOURNALS 1886-1965 (7 VOLS.). UK USA+45 USA-45 AGRI FINAN PLAN ECO/TAC INT/TRADE ADMIN...STAT CENSUS 19/20. PAGE 5 F0087 BIBLIOG WRITING INDUS

B65
ANDERSON C.A.,EDUCATION AND ECONOMIC DEVELOPMENT. INDUS R+D SCHOOL TEC/DEV ECO/TAC EDU/PROP AGE HEREDITY PERCEPT SKILL 20. PAGE 5 F0092 ANTHOL ECO/DEV ECO/UNDEV WORKER

B65
BAERRESEN D.W.,LATIN AMERICAN TRADE PATTERNS. L/A+17C ECO/UNDEV AGRI INDUS MARKET CREATE ...NET/THEORY CHARTS LAFTA. PAGE 8 F0149 INT/TRADE STAT REGION

B65
BARRY E.E.,NATIONALISATION IN BRITISH POLITICS: THE HISTORICAL BACKGROUND. UK AGRI DIST/IND EXTR/IND LABOR LG/CO ATTIT CONSERVE SOCISM 19/20 LABOR/PAR. PAGE 10 F0198 NAT/G OWN INDUS POL/PAR

B65
BELASSA B.,ECONOMIC DEVELOPMENT AND INTEGRATION. LG/CO PROB/SOLV TEC/DEV INT/TRADE TARIFFS COST WEALTH...POLICY METH/COMP 20. PAGE 12 F0232 ECO/UNDEV ECO/TAC INT/ORG INDUS

B65
BLAIR T.L.V.,AFRICA: A MARKET PROFILE. AFR COM/IND DIST/IND FINAN UTIL...DECISION CHARTS BIBLIOG 20. PAGE 15 F0295 MARKET OP/RES ECO/UNDEV INDUS

B65
BRYCE M.D.,POLICIES AND METHODS FOR INDUSTRIAL DEVELOPMENT. WOR+45 FINAN MARKET CONSULT TARIFFS TAX COST. PAGE 20 F0379 INDUS PLAN ECO/DEV TEC/DEV

B65
CHAO K.,THE RATE AND PATTERN OF INDUSTRIAL GROWTH IN COMMUNIST CHINA. CHINA/COM ECO/UNDEV TEC/DEV PRICE...NAT/COMP BIBLIOG 20. PAGE 23 F0452 INDUS INDEX STAT PRODUC

B65
COLLINS H.,KARL MARX AND THE BRITISH LABOR MOVEMENT, YEARS OF THE FIRST INTERNATIONAL. EUR+WWI MOD/EUR UK STRATA INDUS NAT/G POL/PAR SOCISM ...CONCPT 19/20 MARX/KARL. PAGE 26 F0507 MARXISM LABOR INT/ORG WORKER

B65
COPELAND M.A.,OUR FREE ENTERPRISE ECONOMY. USA+45 INDUS LABOR ADMIN CONTROL GP/REL MGT. PAGE 27 F0533 CAP/ISM PLAN FINAN ECO/DEV

B65
DELHI INSTITUTE OF ECO GROWTH,A STUDY IN THE WORKING OF THE INTENSIVE AREA SCHEME OF THE KHADI AND VILLAGE INDUSTRIES COMMISSION. INDIA AGRI FINAN DELIB/GP ECO/TAC EFFICIENCY...QU CHARTS MUNICH 20. PAGE 32 F0614 PLAN INDUS ECO/UNDEV

B65
DUGGAR G.S.,RENEWAL OF TOWN AND VILLAGE I: A WORLD-WIDE SURVEY OF LOCAL GOVERNMENT EXPERIENCE. WOR+45 CONSTRUC INDUS CREATE BUDGET REGION GOV/REL...QU NAT/COMP MUNICH 20 URBAN/RNWL. PAGE 35 F0673 NEIGH PLAN ADMIN

B65
EDELMAN M.,THE POLITICS OF WAGE-PRICE DECISIONS. GERMANY ITALY NETHERLAND UK INDUS LABOR POL/PAR PROB/SOLV BARGAIN PRICE ROUTINE BAL/PAY COST DEMAND 20. PAGE 36 F0699 GOV/COMP CONTROL ECO/TAC PLAN

B65
GOETZ-GIREY R.,LE MOUVEMENT DES GREVES EN FRANCE. FRANCE FINAN OP/RES PROB/SOLV ECO/TAC INCOME HABITAT...STAT CHARTS 19/20. PAGE 48 F0932 LABOR WORKER GP/REL INDUS

B65
HASSON J.A.,THE ECONOMICS OF NUCLEAR POWER. INDIA UK USA+45 WOR+45 INT/ORG TEC/DEV COST...SOC STAT CHARTS 20 EURATOM. PAGE 56 F1108 NUC/PWR INDUS ECO/DEV METH

B65
HERRICK B.H.,URBAN MIGRATION AND ECONOMIC DEVELOPMENT IN CHILE. CHILE AGRI INDUS LABOR NAT/G CENTRAL PRODUC...STAT SAMP CHARTS BIBLIOG/A MUNICH 20 MIGRATION. PAGE 59 F1156 HABITAT GEOG ECO/UNDEV

B65
HOLLER J.E.,POPULATION TRENDS AND ECONOMIC DEVELOPMENT IN THE FAR EAST (PAMPHLET). KOREA S/ASIA AGRI INDUS DELIB/GP PROB/SOLV RATIONAL ...POLICY CHARTS BIBLIOG 20 OUTER/MONG CHINJAP HONG/KONG. PAGE 61 F1197 CENSUS TREND ECO/UNDEV ASIA

B65
HONDURAS CONSEJO NAC DE ECO,PLAN NACIONAL DE DESARROLLO ECONOMICO Y SOCIAL DE HONDURAS 1965-69. HONDURAS AGRI INDUS BAL/PAY INCOME 20. PAGE 61 F1203 ECO/UNDEV NAT/G PLAN POLICY

B65
HOSELITZ B.F.,ECONOMICS AND THE IDEA OF MANKIND. UNIV ECO/DEV ECO/UNDEV DIST/IND INDUS INT/ORG NAT/G ACT/RES ECO/TAC WEALTH...CONCPT STAT. PAGE 62 F1223 CREATE INT/TRADE

B65
IANNI O.,ESTADO E CAPITALISMO. L/A+17C FINAN TEC/DEV ECO/TAC ORD/FREE WEALTH POLICY. PAGE 64 F1258 ECO/UNDEV STRUCT INDUS NAT/G

B65
INT. BANK RECONSTR. DEVELOP.,ECONOMIC DEVELOPMENT OF KUWAIT. ISLAM KUWAIT AGRI FINAN MARKET EX/STRUC TEC/DEV ECO/TAC ADMIN WEALTH...OBS CON/ANAL CHARTS 20. PAGE 64 F1266 INDUS NAT/G

B65
JOHNSON H.G.,THE WORLD ECONOMY AT THE CROSSROADS. COM WOR-45 ECO/DEV AGRI INDUS INT/TRADE REGION NAT/LISM 20. PAGE 67 F1326 FINAN DIPLOM INT/ORG ECO/UNDEV

B65
JOHNSTONE A.,UNITED STATES DIRECT INVESTMENT IN FRANCE: AN INVESTIGATION OF THE FRENCH CHARGES. FRANCE USA+45 ECO/DEV INDUS LG/CO NAT/G ECO/TAC CONTROL WEALTH...BIBLIOG 20 INTERVENT. PAGE 68 F1335 FINAN DIPLOM POLICY SOVEREIGN

B65
KLASSEN L.H.,AREA ECONOMIC AND SOCIAL REDEVELOPMENT. ECO/UNDEV INDUS NAT/G PLAN CAP/ISM TAX...ECOMETRIC SIMUL 20. PAGE 72 F1404 OPTIMAL WORKER METH ECO/TAC

B65
LAZARUS S.,RESOLVING BUSINESS DISPUTES: THE POTENTIAL OF COMMERCIAL ARBITRATION. USA+45 INDUS LG/CO ACT/RES PROB/SOLV EDU/PROP CONSEN UTIL ...TREND 20. PAGE 76 F1496 FINAN DELIB/GP CONSULT ADJUD

B65
LITTLE I.M.D.,INTERNATIONAL AID. UK WOR+45 AGRI INDUS GIVE RECEIVE COLONIAL BAL/PAY WEALTH...POLICY GOV/COMP METH/COMP 20. PAGE 81 F1584 FOR/AID DIPLOM ECO/UNDEV NAT/G

B65
THE STATE AND ECONOMIC ENTERPRISE IN JAPAN; ESSAYS IN THE POLITICAL ECONOMY OF GROWTH. AGRI INDUS DRIVE POPULISM...CHARTS NAT/COMP ANTHOL 19/20 CHINJAP. PAGE 81 F1594 ECO/UNDEV ECO/DEV CAP/ISM ECO/TAC

B65
LUGO-MARENCO J.J.,A STATEMENT OF THE LAWS OF NICARAGUA IN MATTERS AFFECTING BUSINESS. NICARAGUA AGRI DIST/IND EXTR/IND FINAN INDUS FAM WORKER INT/TRADE TAX MARRIAGE OWN BIO/SOC 20 TREATY RESOURCE/N MIGRATION. PAGE 82 F1606 CONSTN NAT/G LEGIS JURID

B65
LYONS G.M.,AMERICA: PURPOSE AND POWER. UK USA+45 FINAN INDUS MARKET WORKER TEC/DEV DIPLOM AUTOMAT NUC/PWR WAR RACE/REL ORD/FREE 20 EEC CONGRESS SUPREME/CT CIV/RIGHTS. PAGE 82 F1617 PWR PROB/SOLV ECO/DEV TASK

B65
MARK S.M.,ECONOMICS IN ACTION (3RD ED.). USA+45 ECO/UNDEV AGRI INDUS FOR/AID INT/TRADE BAL/PAY COST ORD/FREE...ANTHOL 20 RESOURCE/N. PAGE 85 F1670 POLICY ECO/TAC EFFICIENCY PRICE

B65
MELMANS S.,OUR DEPLETED SOCIETY. AFR SPACE USA+45 ECO/DEV FORCES BUDGET ECO/TAC ADMIN WEAPON EFFICIENCY 20. PAGE 89 F1753 CIVMIL/REL INDUS EDU/PROP CONTROL

B65
MOORE W.E.,THE IMPACT OF INDUSTRY. CULTURE STRUCT ORD/FREE...TREND 20. PAGE 93 F1824 INDUS MGT TEC/DEV ECO/UNDEV

B65
MORRIS M.D.,THE EMERGENCE OF AN INDUSTRIAL LABOR FORCE IN INDIA: A STUDY OF THE BOMBAY COTTON MILLS, 1854-1947. INDIA WORKER OP/RES ADMIN 19/20. PAGE 94 F1837 INDUS LABOR ECO/UNDEV CAP/ISM

B65
MORTON H.C.,BROOKINGS PAPERS ON PUBLIC POLICY. USA+45 WOR+45 INDUS ACADEM INT/ORG LOC/G PROVS EDU/PROP MUNICH. PAGE 94 F1840 FINAN ECO/DEV TOP/EX NAT/G

B65
MUND V.A.,GOVERNMENT AND BUSINESS (4TH ED.). USA+45 INDUS LG/CO SML/CO LEGIS INT/TRADE LICENSE PRICE ADJUD. PAGE 95 F1860 NAT/G ECO/TAC BUDGET

CONTROL

B65
MURUMBI J.,PROBLEMS OF ECONOMIC DEVELOPMENT IN EAST AFRICA. FINAN INDUS WORKER TEC/DEV INT/TRADE TAX DEMAND EFFICIENCY PRODUC SOCISM...TREND CHARTS 20 AFRICA/E. PAGE 95 F1869
AGRI ECO/TAC ECO/UNDEV PROC/MFG

B65
ONSLOW C.,ASIAN ECONOMIC DEVELOPMENT. BURMA CEYLON INDIA MALAYSIA PAKISTAN S/ASIA AGRI INDUS MARKET PROB/SOLV CAP/ISM FOR/AID INT/TRADE DEMAND WEALTH ...POLICY ANTHOL 20. PAGE 101 F1991
ECO/UNDEV ECO/TAC PLAN NAT/G

B65
REAGAN M.D.,POLITICS, ECONOMICS, AND THE GENERAL WELFARE. USA+45 INDUS ECO/TAC TAX WEALTH...POLICY IDEA/COMP ANTHOL 20. PAGE 110 F2162
NAT/G ECO/DEV R+D ACADEM

B65
REDFORD E.S.,AMERICAN GOVERNMENT AND THE ECONOMY. FUT USA+45 USA-45 INDUS PROB/SOLV GOV/REL...POLICY DECISION METH/COMP BIBLIOG T 18/20. PAGE 110 F2168
CONSTN NAT/G

B65
RIGBY P.H.,CONCEPTUAL FOUNDATIONS OF BUSINESS RESEARCH. COMPUTER PROB/SOLV OPTIMAL...MGT CONCPT MATH STAT TESTS SIMUL GEN/METH. PAGE 111 F2192
PROFIT R+D INDUS DECISION

B65
ROLFE S.E.,GOLD AND WORLD POWER. AFR UK USA+45 WOR-45 INDUS WORKER INT/TRADE DEMAND...MGT CHARTS 20. PAGE 113 F2234
BAL/PAY EQUILIB ECO/TAC DIPLOM

B65
SCHECHTER A.,THE BUSINESSMAN IN GOVERNMENT (THESIS, COLUMBIA UNIVERSITY). USA+45 CONFER GP/REL PERSON ...QU 20 PRESIDENT TRUMAN/HS CABINET. PAGE 116 F2291
INDUS NAT/G EX/STRUC DELIB/GP

B65
SCHULTZ T.W.,ECONOMIC CRISES IN WORLD AGRICULTURE. ASIA INDIA USSR ECO/DEV ECO/UNDEV INDUS VOL/ASSN CAP/ISM RATION COLONIAL 20. PAGE 117 F2317
AGRI ECO/TAC INCOME WORKER

B65
SHARIF A.,THE BALANCE OF PAYMENTS OF PAKISTAN, 1948-1958 (THESIS, UNIVERSITY OF TORONTO). PAKISTAN FINAN INDUS FOR/AID PRICE WEALTH...TREND CHARTS 20. PAGE 120 F2368
BAL/PAY BUDGET INT/TRADE ECO/UNDEV

B65
TYBOUT R.A.,ECONOMICS OF RESEARCH AND DEVELOPMENT. ECO/DEV ECO/UNDEV INDUS PROFIT DECISION. PAGE 131 F2594
R+D FORCES ADMIN DIPLOM

B65
US BUREAU EDUC CULTURAL AFF,RESOURCES SURVEY FOR LATIN AMERICAN COUNTRIES. L/A+17C USA+45 CULTURE INDUS INT/ORG SECT PLAN EDU/PROP POLICY. PAGE 134 F2643
NAT/G ECO/UNDEV FOR/AID DIPLOM

B65
VAID K.N.,STATE AND LABOR IN INDIA. INDIA INDUS WORKER PAY PRICE ADJUD CONTROL PARL/PROC GP/REL ORD/FREE 20. PAGE 140 F2757
LAW LABOR MGT NEW/LIB

B65
WILKINSON T.O.,THE URBANIZATION OF JAPANESE LABOR, 1868-1955. AGRI PROC/MFG CAP/ISM PRODUC PROFIT ...SOC CLASSIF CENSUS CHARTS MUNICH 19/20 CHINJAP. PAGE 146 F2887
LABOR INDUS GEOG

B65
WU YUAN-LI,THE ECONOMY OF COMMUNIST CHINA. CHINA/COM USSR AGRI FINAN INDUS POL/PAR WORKER PROB/SOLV INT/TRADE PRICE EATING INCOME OWN WEALTH 20. PAGE 149 F2939
ECO/TAC MARXISM PLAN EFFICIENCY

B65
YOUNG A.N.,CHINA'S WARTIME FINANCE AND INFLATION. ASIA AGRI INDUS NAT/G ECO/TAC CONFER PRICE WAR COST 20. PAGE 150 F2949
FINAN FOR/AID TAX BUDGET

L65
FORTE W.E.,"THE FOOD AND DRUG ADMINISTRATION, THE FEDERAL TRADE COMMISSION AND THE DECEPTIVE PACKAGING." ROUTINE...JURID 20 FTC. PAGE 43 F0831
CONTROL HEALTH ADJUD INDUS

L65
LETICHE J.M.,"EUROPEAN INTEGRATION: AN AMERICAN VIEW." EUR+WWI FRANCE WOR+45 ECO/DEV DIST/IND EXTR/IND NAT/G DELIB/GP TOP/EX PLAN ECO/TAC ATTIT ...STAT CON/ANAL CHARTS EEC 20. PAGE 78 F1537
INDUS AGRI

L65
WILLIAMS S.,"NEGOTIATING INVESTMENT IN EMERGING COUNTRIES." USA+45 WOR+45 INDUS MARKET NAT/G TOP/EX TEC/DEV CAP/ISM ECO/TAC ADMIN SKILL WEALTH...POLICY RELATIV MGT WORK 20. PAGE 147 F2894
FINAN ECO/UNDEV

L65
WIONCZEK M.,"LATIN AMERICA FREE TRADE ASSOCIATION." AGRI DIST/IND FINAN INDUS INT/ORG LABOR NAT/G TEC/DEV ECO/TAC HEALTH SKILL WEALTH...POLICY RELATIV MGT LAFTA 20. PAGE 148 F2909
L/A+17C MARKET REGION

S65
CHU K.,"A DYNAMIC MODEL OF THE FIRM." OP/RES PROB/SOLV...DECISION ECOMETRIC NEW/IDEA STAT GAME ORG/CHARTS SIMUL. PAGE 24 F0472
INDUS COMPUTER TEC/DEV

S65
JOHNSON H.G.,"A THEORETICAL MODEL OF ECONOMIC NATIONALISM IN NEW AND DEVELOPING STATES." ELITES INDUS INT/TRADE EDU/PROP COST OPTIMAL RATIONAL PWR WEALTH SOCISM STERTYP. PAGE 67 F1325
NAT/LISM ECO/UNDEV GEN/LAWS

S65
JOHNSON L.L.,"US BUSINESS INTERESTS IN CUBA AND THE RISE OF CASTRO." L/A+17C USA+45 ECO/UNDEV INDUS NAT/G VOL/ASSN ATTIT ORD/FREE PWR WEALTH ALL/PROG. PAGE 68 F1330
DIPLOM CUBA ECO/TAC INT/TRADE

S65
KINDLEBERGER C.P.,"MASS MIGRATION, THEN AND NOW." LAW ECO/DEV ECO/UNDEV INDUS LABOR INT/TRADE FEEDBACK REGION RIGID/FLEX...SOC NAT/COMP EEC. PAGE 71 F1394
EUR+WWI USA-45 WORKER IDEA/COMP

S65
MALHERBE E.G.,"MANPOWER TRAINING: EDUCATIONAL REQUIREMENTS FOR ECONOMIC EXPANSION." SOUTH/AFR ECO/DEV INDUS EDU/PROP...MGT STAT CHARTS 20. PAGE 84 F1646
LABOR SKILL SCHOOL ACADEM

S65
SCHROEDER G.,"LABOR PLANNING IN THE USSR." COM USSR ECO/DEV INDUS SCHOOL PRODUC WEALTH...PREDICT TIME/SEQ TREND TIME 20. PAGE 117 F2313
WORKER PLAN CENSUS

S65
TENDLER J.D.,"TECHNOLOGY AND ECONOMIC DEVELOPMENT* THE CASE OF HYDRO VS THERMAL POWER." CONSTRUC DIST/IND CREATE TEC/DEV INT/TRADE CENTRAL PWR SKILL WEALTH...MGT NAT/COMP ARGEN. PAGE 129 F2544
BRAZIL INDUS ECO/UNDEV

S65
VAN DER HORST S.T.,"THE ECONOMICS OF DECENTRALISATION OF INDUSTRY." SOUTH/AFR ECO/DEV LG/CO AUTOMAT DISCRIM...POLICY MUNICH 20. PAGE 140 F2761
PLAN INDUS CENTRAL TEC/DEV

C65
PEGRUM D.E.,"PUBLIC REGULATION OF BUSINESS (REV ED)" LAW CONSTN DIST/IND SERV/IND LG/CO LEGIS OWN LAISSEZ SOCISM...POLICY DECISION BIBLIOG 20. PAGE 104 F2048
INDUS PLAN NEW/LIB PRICE

B66
BAKKE E.W.,MUTUAL SURVIVAL; THE GOAL OF UNION AND MANAGEMENT (2ND ED.). USA+45 ELITES ECO/DEV ECO/TAC CONFER ADMIN REPRESENT GP/REL INGP/REL ATTIT ...GP/COMP 20. PAGE 8 F0155
MGT LABOR BARGAIN INDUS

B66
BAKLANOFF E.N.,NEW PERSPECTIVES ON BRAZIL. BRAZIL SOCIETY INDUS DOMIN LEAD REV CIVMIL/REL...GEOG PSY LING ANTHOL 20. PAGE 8 F0156
ECO/UNDEV TEC/DEV DIPLOM ORD/FREE

B66
BEN-PORATH Y.,THE ARAB LABOR FORCE IN ISRAEL. ISLAM ISRAEL AGRI INDUS SCHOOL CAP/ISM PAY DEMAND...GEOG REGRESS STAT CHARTS 20 ARABS. PAGE 13 F0245
WORKER CENSUS GP/REL STRUCT

B66
BOLTON R.E.,DEFENSE AND DISARMAMENT: THE ECONOMICS OF TRANSITION. USA+45 R+D FORCES PLAN LOBBY DETER WAR COST PEACE...ANTHOL BIBLIOG 20. PAGE 16 F0310
ARMS/CONT POLICY INDUS

B66
BRODERSEN A.,THE SOVIET WORKER: LABOR AND GOVERNMENT IN SOVIET SOCIETY. USSR STRUCT INDUS LABOR PLAN PAY INGP/REL PRODUC...POLICY GEN/LAWS BIBLIOG 20 STALIN/J LENIN/VI BOLSHEVISM KHRUSH/N. PAGE 19 F0357
WORKER ROLE NAT/G MARXISM

B66
BROEKMEIJER M.W.J.,FICTION AND TRUTH ABOUT THE "DECADE OF DEVELOPMENT" WOR+45 AGRI FINAN INDUS NAT/G TEC/DEV DIPLOM EDU/PROP LEAD SKILL 20 THIRD/WRLD. PAGE 19 F0358
FOR/AID POLICY ECO/UNDEV PLAN

B66
CHASE S.B. JR.,PROBLEMS IN PUBLIC EXPENDITURE ANALYSIS. DIST/IND INDUS OP/RES PLAN BUDGET RECEIVE PRICE RISK COST INCOME...CHARTS ANTHOL 20. PAGE 23 F0455
ECO/DEV FINAN NAT/G INSPECT

B66
COOK P.W. JR.,PROBLEMS OF CORPORATE POWER. WOR+45 FINAN INDUS BARGAIN GP/REL...MGT ANTHOL. PAGE 27 F0530
ADMIN LG/CO PWR ECO/TAC

B66
CURRIE L.,ACCELERATING DEVELOPMENT: THE NECESSITY AND MEANS. COLOMBIA USA+45 INDUS DIPLOM EFFICIENCY WEALTH...METH/CNCPT NEW/IDEA 20. PAGE 29 F0564
PLAN ECO/UNDEV FOR/AID TEC/DEV

B66
DAVIES I.,AFRICAN TRADE UNIONS. AFR ECO/UNDEV INT/ORG GP/REL ORD/FREE SOVEREIGN SOCISM 20. PAGE 30 F0585
LABOR COLONIAL PWR INDUS

B66
DAVIS K.,BUSINESS AND ITS ENVIRONMENT. LAW ECO/DEV INDUS OP/RES ADMIN CONTROL ROUTINE GP/REL PROFIT
EX/STRUC PROB/SOLV

POLICY. PAGE 30 F0591
CAP/ISM EXEC

B66
DOBB M.,SOVIET ECONOMIC DEVELOPMENT SINCE 1917. USSR ECO/DEV ECO/UNDEV LABOR NAT/G TEC/DEV ECO/TAC ROUTINE PRODUC MARXISM 20. PAGE 33 F0647
PLAN INDUS WORKER

B66
DUNCAN O.,METROPOLIS AND REGION (PREPARED FOR RESOURCES FOR THE FUTURE INC., WASHINGTON, D.C.). FINAN INDUS ECO/TAC TAX...CHARTS GOV/COMP MUNICH. PAGE 35 F0677
REGION GEOG

B66
ECKSTEIN A.,COMMUNIST CHINA'S ECONOMIC GROWTH AND FOREIGN TRADE* IMPLICATIONS FOR US POLICY. COM USA+45 USSR STRUCT INDUS MARKET DIPLOM ECO/TAC FOR/AID INT/TRADE...STAT CHARTS. PAGE 36 F0696
ASIA ECO/UNDEV CREATE PWR

B66
FELKER J.L.,SOVIET ECONOMIC CONTROVERSIES. USSR INDUS PLAN INT/TRADE GP/REL MARXISM SOCISM...POLICY 20. PAGE 40 F0778
ECO/DEV MARKET PROFIT PRICE

B66
FRANCK L.R.,LA POLITIQUE ECONOMIQUE DES ETATS-UNIS. USA+45 USA-45 FINAN INDUS CONTROL CROWD GOV/REL GP/REL...POLICY SOC CHARTS 18/20. PAGE 43 F0841
NAT/G INT/TRADE GEOG

B66
GORDON R.A.,PROSPERITY AND UNEMPLOYMENT. USA+45 PLAN ECO/TAC ADJUST DEMAND ALL/VALS...POLICY DECISION TREND CHARTS ANTHOL 20. PAGE 49 F0961
WORKER INDUS ECO/DEV WEALTH

B66
GOULD J.M.,THE TECHNICAL ELITE. INDUS LABOR TECHRACY...POLICY DECISION STAT CHARTS 20. PAGE 49 F0967
ECO/DEV TEC/DEV ELITES TECHNIC

B66
GREENE L.E.,GOVERNMENT IN TENNESSEE (2ND ED.). USA+45 DIST/IND INDUS POL/PAR EX/STRUC LEGIS PLAN BUDGET GIVE CT/SYS...MGT T 20 TENNESSEE. PAGE 51 F0989
PROVS LOC/G CONSTN ADMIN

B66
GROSS H.,MAKE OR BUY. AFR USA+45 FINAN INDUS CREATE PRICE PRODUC 20. PAGE 51 F1006
ECO/TAC PLAN MGT COST

B66
HALLET R.,PEOPLE AND PROGRESS IN WEST AFRICA: AN INTRODUCTION TO THE PROBLEMS OF DEVELOPMENT. COM/IND INDUS KIN DIPLOM FOR/AID INT/TRADE HEALTH ...GEOG TREND CHARTS BIBLIOG/A 20 AFRICA/W. PAGE 54 F1050
AFR SOCIETY ECO/UNDEV ECO/TAC

B66
HASTINGS P.G.,THE MANAGEMENT OF BUSINESS FINANCE. ECO/DEV PLAN BUDGET CONTROL COST...DECISION CHARTS BIBLIOG T 20. PAGE 56 F1109
FINAN MGT INDUS ECO/TAC

B66
INGRAM J.C.,INTERNATIONAL ECONOMIC PROBLEMS. ECO/DEV ECO/UNDEV INDUS MARKET TEC/DEV TARIFFS BAL/PAY CENTRAL...POLICY 20 EEC. PAGE 64 F1265
INT/TRADE INT/ORG FINAN

B66
KAESTNER K.,GESAMTWIRTSCHAFTLICHE PLANUNG IN EINER GEMISCHTEN WIRTSCHAFTSORDNUNG (WIRTSCHAFTSPOLITISCHE STUDIEN 5). GERMANY/W WOR+45 WOR-45 INDUS MARKET NAT/G ACT/RES GP/REL INGP/REL PRODUC...ECOMETRIC MGT BIBLIOG 20. PAGE 68 F1346
ECO/TAC PLAN POLICY PREDICT

B66
KIRDAR U.,THE STRUCTURE OF UNITED NATIONS ECONOMIC AID TO UNDERDEVELOPED COUNTRIES. AGRI FINAN INDUS NAT/G EX/STRUC PLAN GIVE TASK...POLICY 20 UN. PAGE 71 F1397
INT/ORG FOR/AID ECO/UNDEV ADMIN

B66
KOH S.J.,STAGES OF INDUSTRIAL DEVELOPMENT IN ASIA. ASIA INDIA KOREA STRATA STRUCT NAT/G INT/TRADE ...CHARTS 19/20 CHINJAP. PAGE 72 F1415
INDUS ECO/UNDEV ECO/DEV LABOR

B66
KROOSS H.E.,AMERICAN ECONOMIC DEVELOPMENT (2ND ED.). USA+45 USA-45 AGRI INDUS LABOR WORKER INT/TRADE TAX WAR...CHARTS 18/20. PAGE 73 F1443
ECO/TAC NAT/G CAP/ISM ECO/DEV

B66
KURAKOV I.G.,SCIENCE, TECHNOLOGY AND COMMUNISM; SOME QUESTIONS OF DEVELOPMENT (TRANS. BY CARIN DEDIJER). USSR INDUS PLAN PROB/SOLV COST PRODUC ...MGT MATH CHARTS METH 20. PAGE 74 F1450
CREATE TEC/DEV MARXISM ECO/TAC

B66
KUZNETS S.,MODERN ECONOMIC GROWTH. WOR+45 WOR-45 ECO/DEV ECO/UNDEV AGRI FINAN INDUS TEC/DEV EFFICIENCY INCOME...NAT/COMP 19/20. PAGE 74 F1456
TIME/SEQ WEALTH PRODUC

B66
LANDERS D.S.,RISE OF CAPITALISM. LABOR AUTOMAT GP/REL CENTRAL COST PROFIT...SOC CONCPT ANTHOL 19/20. PAGE 75 F1469
CAP/ISM INDUS AGRI

B66
LEONTIEF W.,ESSAYS IN ECONOMICS. ECO/UNDEV INDUS NAT/G CAP/ISM FOR/AID AUTOMAT MARXISM...ECOMETRIC CHARTS ANTHOL METH 20 KEYNES/JM. PAGE 78 F1528
CONCPT METH/CNCPT METH/COMP

B66
LEWIS W.A.,DEVELOPMENT PLANNING; THE ESSENTIALS OF ECONOMIC POLICY. USA+45 FINAN INDUS NAT/G WORKER FOR/AID INT/TRADE ADMIN ROUTINE WEALTH...CONCPT STAT. PAGE 79 F1552
PLAN ECO/DEV POLICY CREATE

B66
MACFARQUHAR R.,CHINA UNDER MAO: POLITICS TAKES COMMAND. CHINA/COM COM AGRI INDUS CHIEF FORCES DIPLOM INT/TRADE EDU/PROP TASK REV ADJUST...ANTHOL 20 MAO. PAGE 83 F1628
ECO/UNDEV TEC/DEV ECO/TAC ADMIN

B66
MADAN G.R.,ECONOMIC THINKING IN INDIA. INDIA ECO/UNDEV AGRI FINAN INDUS LABOR PLAN CAP/ISM INT/TRADE MARXISM SOCISM...POLICY 1/20. PAGE 84 F1638
ECO/TAC PHIL/SCI NAT/G POL/PAR

B66
MEERHAEGHE M.,INTERNATIONAL ECONOMIC INSTITUTIONS. EUR+WWI FINAN INDUS MARKET PLAN TARIFFS BAL/PAY EQUILIB...POLICY BIBLIOG/A 20 GATT OEEC EEC IBRD EURCOALSTL. PAGE 89 F1745
ECO/TAC ECO/DEV INT/TRADE INT/ORG

B66
MOUNTJOY A.B.,INDUSTRIALIZATION AND UNDER-DEVELOPED COUNTRIES (2ND REV. ED.). CHILE GHANA INDIA NIGERIA WOR+45 SOCIETY PROB/SOLV ECO/TAC...SOC CHARTS 20 INDUS/REV. PAGE 94 F1848
ECO/UNDEV INDUS GEOG HABITAT

B66
MUNBY D.,ECONOMIC GROWTH IN WORLD PERSPECTIVE. AFR WOR+45 SOCIETY INDUS PLAN TEC/DEV ECO/TAC FOR/AID INT/TRADE COST CATHISM...ANTHOL 20 EUROPE/W CHURCH/STA. PAGE 95 F1859
SECT ECO/UNDEV ECO/DEV

B66
NAMBOODIRIPAD E.M.,ECONOMICS AND POLITICS OF INDIA'S SOCIALIST PATTERN. INDIA STRATA AGRI INDUS NAT/G PRICE ORD/FREE SOVEREIGN 20. PAGE 96 F1888
ECO/UNDEV PLAN SOCISM CAP/ISM

B66
NICOSIA F.N.,CONSUMER DECISION PROCESSES* MARKETING AND ADVERTISING IMPLICATIONS. DIST/IND INDUS CONSULT EDU/PROP ATTIT. PAGE 98 F1925
MARKET PROB/SOLV SERV/IND

B66
PASSIN H.,THE UNITED STATES AND JAPAN. USA+45 INDUS CAP/ISM...TREND 20 CHINJAP TREATY. PAGE 103 F2032
DIPLOM INT/TRADE ECO/DEV ECO/TAC

B66
PFEFFER K.H.,WELT IM UMBRUCH. SOCIETY STRUCT INDUS PROF/ORG SECT TEC/DEV PARTIC SUPEGO WORSHIP 20 CHRISTIAN. PAGE 106 F2076
ORD/FREE STRATA CREATE

B66
POLK J.,U S PRODUCTION ABROAD AND THE BALANCE OF PAYMENTS* A SURVEY OF CORPORATE INVESTMENT EXPERIENCE. USA+45 SERV/IND NAT/G OP/RES COST PROFIT ATTIT...ECOMETRIC STAT INT QU GEN/METH. PAGE 107 F2096
BAL/PAY FINAN INT/TRADE INDUS

B66
REDFORD E.S.,THE ROLE OF GOVERNMENT IN THE AMERICAN ECONOMY. USA+45 USA-45 FINAN INDUS LG/CO PROB/SOLV ADMIN INGP/REL INCOME PRODUC 18/20. PAGE 110 F2169
NAT/G ECO/DEV CAP/ISM ECO/TAC

B66
ROBERTSON D.J.,THE BRITISH BALANCE OF PAYMENTS. UK WOR+45 INDUS BUDGET TAX ADJUST...CHARTS ANTHOL 20. PAGE 112 F2213
FINAN BAL/PAY ECO/DEV INT/TRADE

B66
SMITH H.E.,READINGS IN ECONOMIC DEVELOPMENT AND ADMINISTRATION IN TANZANIA. TANZANIA FINAN INDUS LABOR NAT/G PLAN PROB/SOLV INT/TRADE COLONIAL REGION...ANTHOL BIBLIOG 20 AFRICA/E. PAGE 123 F2431
TEC/DEV ADMIN GOV/REL

B66
SOVERN M.I.,LEGAL RESTRAINTS ON RACIAL DISCRIMINATION IN EMPLOYMENT. USA+45 LAW INDUS LG/CO SML/CO DELIB/GP LEGIS SANCTION 20 NLRB PRESIDENT NEGRO CIV/RIGHTS RAILROAD. PAGE 124 F2446
DISCRIM RACE/REL WORKER JURID

B66
SPICER K.,A SAMARITAN STATE? AFR CANADA INDIA PAKISTAN UK USA+45 FINAN INDUS PRODUC...CHARTS 20 NATO. PAGE 124 F2455
DIPLOM FOR/AID ECO/DEV ADMIN

B66
TIVEY L.J.,NATIONALISATION IN BRITISH INDUSTRY. UK LEGIS PARL/PROC GP/REL OWN ATTIT SOCISM 20. PAGE 131 F2578
NAT/G INDUS CONTROL LG/CO

B66
TURNER H.A.,PRICES, WAGES, AND INCOME POLICIES IN INDUSTRIALIZED MARKET ECONOMIES. AFR WOR+45 ECO/DEV INDUS PROB/SOLV ECO/TAC CONTROL WEALTH...CHARTS 20 INTRVN/ECO. PAGE 131 F2593
PRICE PAY MARKET INCOME

B66
UN STATISTICAL OFFICE,STATISTICAL YEARBOOK (17TH ED.). WOR+45 AGRI...GEOG CHARTS 20. PAGE 132 F2604
STAT INDEX SOCIETY INDUS

B66
US DEPARTMENT OF LABOR,PRODUCTIVITY: A BIBLIOGRAPHY. ECO/DEV INDUS MARKET OP/RES AUTOMAT COST...STAT 20. PAGE 135 F2668
BIBLIOG/A PRODUC LABOR PLAN

B66
US DEPARTMENT OF LABOR,TECHNOLOGICAL TRENDS IN MAJOR AMERICAN INDUSTRIES. USA+45 R+D LABOR GP/REL PRODUC...MGT BIBLIOG 20. PAGE 135 F2669
TEC/DEV INDUS TREND AUTOMAT

B66
US PRES COMM ECO IMPACT DEFENS,REPORT* JULY 1965. USA+45 ECO/DEV INDUS DELIB/GP FORCES OP/RES ARMS/CONT NUC/PWR WEAPON BAL/PAY...PREDICT SIMUL. PAGE 138 F2726
ACT/RES STAT WAR BUDGET

B66
WILCOX C.,ECONOMIES OF THE WORLD TODAY: THEIR ORGANIZATION, DEVELOPMENT, AND PERFORMANCE (2ND ED.). CHINA/COM COM INDIA NIGERIA UK WOR+45 WOR-45 INDUS MARKET PLAN ECO/TAC SOCISM...CHARTS METH/COMP 20. PAGE 146 F2878
ECO/DEV ECO/UNDEV MARXISM CAP/ISM

B66
WILLIAMS G.,MERTHYR POLITICS: THE MAKING OF A WORKING-CLASS TRADITION. UK CHIEF WORKER LEAD SOCISM...ANTHOL MUNICH 19/20 MERTHYR RICHARD/H. PAGE 147 F2891
LOC/G POL/PAR INDUS

B66
ZINKIN T.,CHALLENGES IN INDIA. INDIA PAKISTAN LAW AGRI FINAN INDUS TOP/EX TEC/DEV CONTROL ROUTINE ORD/FREE PWR 20 NEHRU/J SHASTRI/LB CIVIL/SERV. PAGE 150 F2964
NAT/G ECO/TAC POLICY ADMIN

B66
ZISCHKA A.,WAR ES EIN WUNDER? GERMANY/W ECO/DEV FINAN LG/CO BARGAIN CAP/ISM FOR/AID RATION 20 MARSHL/PLN. PAGE 150 F2965
ECO/TAC INT/TRADE INDUS WAR

L66
AFRICAN BIBLIOGRAPHIC CENTER,"AFRICAN ECONOMIC AFFAIRS: A SELECT BIBLIOGRAPHICAL SURVEY, 1965-1966." AFR FINAN INDUS INT/ORG LABOR PLAN BUDGET DIPLOM INT/TRADE ADMIN EFFICIENCY WEALTH 20. PAGE 3 F0046
BIBLIOG ECO/UNDEV TEC/DEV FOR/AID

L66
AFRICAN BIBLIOGRAPHIC CENTER,"AFRICAN ECONOMIC AFFAIRS: A SELECT BIBLIOGRAPHICAL SURVEY, 1965-1966; SUPPLEMENTS NUMBERS 1-3." AFR FINAN INDUS LABOR PLAN BUDGET CAP/ISM DIPLOM INT/TRADE ADMIN...GEOG 20. PAGE 3 F0047
BIBLIOG/A ECO/UNDEV FOR/AID TEC/DEV

S66
FROMM G.,"RECENT MONETARY POLICY: AN ECONOMETRIC VIEW" USA+45 ECO/DEV INDUS PAY PRICE PRODUC ORD/FREE WEALTH...STAT 20 FED/RESERV. PAGE 45 F0869
ECOMETRIC FINAN POLICY SIMUL

S66
LAURENS H.,"LES PAYS OCCIDENTAUX ET LE MARCHE CHINOIS." EUR+WWI FUT S/ASIA AGRI INDUS VOL/ASSN ECO/TAC BAL/PAY...RECORD PREDICT TREATY. PAGE 76 F1488
ASIA INT/TRADE TREND STAT

S66
MALENBAUM W.,"GOVERNMENT, ENTREPRENEURSHIP, AND ECONOMIC GROWTH IN POOR LANDS." ELITES ECO/UNDEV INDUS CREATE DRIVE. PAGE 84 F1645
ECO/TAC PLAN CONSERVE NAT/G

S66
POSEN G.S.,"RECENT TRENDS IN SOVIET ECONOMIC THOUGHT." USSR ECO/DEV PLAN CONTROL CENTRAL 20. PAGE 107 F2107
ECO/TAC MARXISM INDUS PROFIT

S66
VENTRE F.T.,"LOCAL INITIATIVES IN URBAN INDUSTRIAL DEVELOPMENT." FINAN SERV/IND TOP/EX PLAN BUDGET RENT TAX...GP/COMP MUNICH 20. PAGE 141 F2777
ECO/TAC LOC/G INDUS

C66
WINT G.,"ASIA: A HANDBOOK." ASIA S/ASIA INDUS LABOR SECT PRESS RACE/REL MARXISM...STAT CHARTS BIBLIOG 20. PAGE 148 F2908
ECO/UNDEV DIPLOM NAT/G SOCIETY

N66
PRINCETON U INDUSTRIAL REL SEC,PUBLIC PROGRAMS TO CREATE JOBS (PAMPHLET NO. 125). USA+45 ECO/DEV INDUS PLAN ECO/TAC AGE/Y 20. PAGE 108 F2119
BIBLIOG/A NAT/G POLICY WORKER

B67
ALEXANDER G.J.,HONESTY AND COMPETITION: FALSE-ADVERTISING LAW AND POLICY UNDER FTC ADMINISTRATION. USA+45 INDUS NAT/G PRICE GP/REL 20 FTC. PAGE 3 F0058
EDU/PROP SERV/IND CONTROL DELIB/GP

B67
ALNASRAWI A.,FINANCING ECONOMIC DEVELOPMENT IN IRAQ. IRAQ INDUS CAP/ISM COST PRODUC...STAT CHARTS BIBLIOG 20. PAGE 4 F0076
ECO/UNDEV EXTR/IND TEC/DEV INT/TRADE

B67
ANDERSON C.W.,POLITICS AND ECONOMIC CHANGE IN LATIN AMERICA. L/A+17C INDUS NAT/G OP/RES ADMIN DEMAND ...POLICY STAT CHARTS NAT/COMP 20. PAGE 5 F0093
ECO/UNDEV PROB/SOLV PLAN
ECO/TAC

B67
BALDWIN G.B.,PLANNING AND DEVELOPMENT IN IRAN. IRAN AGRI INDUS CONSULT WORKER EDU/PROP BAL/PAY...CHARTS 20. PAGE 9 F0164
PLAN ECO/UNDEV ADMIN PROB/SOLV

B67
BARANSON J.,TECHNOLOGY FOR UNDERDEVELOPED AREAS: AN ANNOTATED BIBLIOGRAPHY. FUT WOR+45 CULTURE INDUS INT/ORG CREATE PROB/SOLV INT/TRADE EDU/PROP AUTOMAT ...CONCPT METH. PAGE 10 F0181
BIBLIOG/A ECO/UNDEV TEC/DEV R+D

B67
BEAL E.F.,THE PRACTICE OF COLLECTIVE BARGAINING (3RD ED.). USA+45 WOR+45 ECO/DEV INDUS LG/CO PROF/ORG WORKER ECO/TAC GP/REL WEALTH...JURID METH/CNCPT. PAGE 12 F0221
BARGAIN MGT LABOR ADJUD

B67
CHANDRASEKHAR S.,PROBLEMS OF ECONOMIC DEVELOPMENT. AFR INDIA PHILIPPINE UAR WOR+45 INDUS...GEOG SOC ANTHOL BIBLIOG 20 CHINJAP. PAGE 23 F0450
ECO/UNDEV PLAN AGRI PROB/SOLV

B67
ELDREDGE H.W.,TAMING MEGALOPOLIS; WHAT IT IS AND WHAT COULD BE (VOL. I). FUT USA+45 WOR+45 SOCIETY STRUCT ECO/DEV INDUS LEISURE WEALTH...ANTHOL MUNICH. PAGE 37 F0717
PROB/SOLV PLAN TEC/DEV

B67
ELSNER H.,THE TECHNOCRATS, PROPHETS OF AUTOMATION. SOCIETY INDUS VOL/ASSN COST INCOME ATTIT 20. PAGE 37 F0726
AUTOMAT TECHRACY PRODUC HIST/WRIT

B67
HEILBRONER R.L.,THE LIMITS OF AMERICAN CAPITALISM. FUT ECO/DEV INDUS LG/CO EX/STRUC LEAD PWR TECHRACY 20. PAGE 58 F1137
ELITES CREATE TEC/DEV CAP/ISM

B67
HODGKINSON R.G.,THE ORIGINS OF THE NATIONAL HEALTH SERVICE: THE MEDICAL SERVICES OF THE NEW POOR LAW, 1834-1871. UK INDUS WORKER PROB/SOLV EFFICIENCY ATTIT HEALTH WEALTH SOCISM...JURID SOC/WK MUNICH 19/20. PAGE 60 F1189
HEAL NAT/G POLICY LAW

B67
KANNER L.,THE NEW YORK TIMES WORLD ECONOMIC REVIEW AND FORECAST: 1967. WOR+45 ECO/DEV ECO/UNDEV TEC/DEV...STAT PREDICT CHARTS 20. PAGE 69 F1349
INDUS FINAN TREND ECO/TAC

B67
KRANZBERG M.,TECHNOLOGY IN WESTERN CIVILIZATION VOLUME ONE. UNIV INDUS SKILL. PAGE 73 F1431
TEC/DEV ACT/RES AUTOMAT POLICY

B67
MARCUS S.,COMPETITION AND THE LAW. USA+45 INDUS LG/CO NAT/G CONSERVE LAISSEZ...BIBLIOG 20 FTC SUPREME/CT. PAGE 85 F1665
LAW ECO/DEV FINAN JURID

B67
MAZOUR A.G.,SOVIET ECONOMIC DEVELOPMENT: OPERATION OUTSTRIP: 1921-1965. USSR ECO/UNDEV FINAN CHIEF WORKER PROB/SOLV CONTROL PRODUC MARXISM...CHARTS ORG/CHARTS 20 STALIN/J. PAGE 87 F1711
ECO/TAC AGRI INDUS PLAN

B67
MORRIS A.J.A.,PARLIAMENTARY DEMOCRACY IN THE NINETEENTH CENTURY. UK INDUS LOC/G NAT/G POL/PAR CONSULT LEGIS INT/TRADE ADMIN CHOOSE SUFF SOVEREIGN 19 PARLIAMENT. PAGE 93 F1835
TIME/SEQ CONSTN PARL/PROC POPULISM

B67
PELTASON J.W.,FUNCTIONS AND POLICIES OF AMERICAN GOVERNMENT (3RD ED.). USA+45 FINAN INDUS EDU/PROP CIVMIL/REL RACE/REL ORD/FREE...ANTHOL T 20 JOHNSON/LB. PAGE 104 F2052
NAT/G GOV/REL POLICY PLAN

B67
RAVKIN A.,THE NEW STATES OF AFRICA (HEADLINE SERIES, NO. 183((PAMPHLET). CULTURE STRUCT INDUS COLONIAL NAT/LISM...SOC 20. PAGE 109 F2153
AFR ECO/UNDEV SOCIETY ADMIN

B67
ROBINSON E.A.G.,ECONOMIC PLANNING IN THE UNITED KINGDOM. UK WORKER PLAN PROB/SOLV BAL/PAY 20. PAGE 113 F2220
ECO/DEV INDUS PRODUC BUDGET

B67
RUEFF J.,BALANCE OF PAYMENTS: PROPOSALS FOR RESOLVING THE CRITICAL WORLD ECONOMIC PROBLEM OF OUR TIME. USA+45 INDUS FOR/AID REPAR DEMAND OPTIMAL ...ECOMETRIC CHARTS METH/COMP 20. PAGE 115 F2259
BAL/PAY INT/TRADE FINAN NEW/IDEA

B67
SCHON D.A.,TECHNOLOGY AND CHANGE* THE NEW HERACLITUS. TEC/DEV CONTROL COST DEMAND EFFICIENCY RIGID/FLEX...MYTH 20. PAGE 117 F2311
INDUS PROB/SOLV R+D CREATE

B67
SCOTT J.C.,ANTITRUST AND TRADE REGULATION TODAY: 1967. USA+45 MARKET LG/CO DELIB/GP LEGIS CAP/ISM INT/TRADE TAX PRICE INGP/REL WEALTH 20 SUPREME/CT.
NAT/G INDUS CONTROL

PAGE 118 F2334 JURID
B67

SMITH T.L.,THE PROCESS OF RURAL DEVELOPMENT IN IDEA/COMP
LATIN AMERICA (A MONOGRAPH). L/A+17C STRATA INDUS SOC
PLAN GP/REL PERS/REL RIGID/FLEX WEALTH...OBS CHARTS AGRI
ORG/CHARTS ANTHOL 20 COLOMB. PAGE 123 F2434 ECO/UNDEV
B67

STEARNS P.N.,EUROPEAN SOCIETY IN UPHEAVAL* SOCIAL REGION
HISTORY SINCE 1800. EUR+WWI MOD/EUR STRATA SECT ECO/DEV
WORKER TEC/DEV WAR...WELF/ST SOC TREND BIBLIOG SOCIETY
19/20. PAGE 125 F2472 INDUS
B67

TANSKY L.,US AND USSR AID TO DEVELOPING COUNTRIES. ECO/UNDEV
INDIA TURKEY USA+45 USSR INDUS PLAN CAP/ISM WAR PWR FOR/AID
WEALTH MARXISM...CHARTS NAT/COMP BIBLIOG 20. DIPLOM
PAGE 128 F2534 ECO/TAC
B67

US CONGRESS JOINT ECO COMM,AN ECONOMIC PROFILE OF ECO/UNDEV
MAINLAND CHINA, VOLUMES I AND II. CHINA/COM AGRI WEALTH
DIST/IND FINAN INDUS LABOR FORCES ACT/RES PLAN ECO/TAC
INT/TRADE INGP/REL BAL/PAY 20 CONGRESS. PAGE 135 DELIB/GP
F2664
B67

WOOTON G.,WORKERS, UNIONS, AND THE STATE. INDUS PARTIC
PROB/SOLV GP/REL DRIVE SUPEGO RESPECT...PSY SOC. WORKER
PAGE 148 F2925 NAT/G
LABOR
B67

ZONDAG C.H.,THE BOLIVIAN ECONOMY 1952-65. L/A+17C ECO/UNDEV
TEC/DEV FOR/AID ADMIN...OBS TREND CHARTS BIBLIOG 20 INDUS
BOLIV. PAGE 151 F2969 PRODUC
L67

GOULD W.B.,"THE STATUS OF UNAUTHORIZED AND ECO/DEV
'WILDCAT' STRIKES UNDER THE NATIONAL LABOR INDUS
RELATIONS ACT." USA+45 ACT/RES BARGAIN ECO/TAC LABOR
LEGIT ADJUD ADMIN GP/REL MGT. PAGE 50 F0968 POLICY
L67

LENT G.E.,"TAX INCENTIVES FOR INVESTMENT IN ECO/UNDEV
DEVELOPING COUNTRIES" WOR+45 LAW INDUS PLAN BUDGET TAX
TARIFFS ADMIN...METH/COMP 20. PAGE 78 F1526 FINAN
ECO/TAC
L67

MACDONALD R.M.,"COLLECTIVE BARGAINING IN THE LABOR
POSTWAR PERIOD." WORKER PROB/SOLV ECO/TAC PARTIC INDUS
RISK CENTRAL EFFICIENCY DRIVE WEALTH...TREND 20. BARGAIN
PAGE 83 F1624 CAP/ISM
L67

MACHLUP F.,"THEORIES OF THE FIRM* MARGINALIST, METH/COMP
BEHAVIORALIST, MANAGERIAL." ADMIN EXEC EFFICIENCY GEN/LAWS
PROFIT METH/CNCPT. PAGE 83 F1633 INDUS
L67

MANNE H.G.,"OUR TWO CORPORATION SYSTEMS* LAW AND INDUS
ECONOMICS." LAW CONTROL SANCTION GP/REL...JURID 20. ELITES
PAGE 85 F1657 CAP/ISM
ADMIN
L67

PARKER G.P. JR.,"MONETARY RECOVERY UNDER THE LABOR
FEDERAL LABOR STATUTES." USA+45 USA-45 INDUS ADJUD CONTROL
CT/SYS GOV/REL HEALTH ORD/FREE 20 DEPT/LABOR NLRB. LAW
PAGE 103 F2027 FINAN
L67

SCHNEIDER C.W.,"REFORM OF THE FEDERAL SECURITIES NAT/G
LAWS." FUT USA+45 LAW FINAN INDUS DELIB/GP ACT/RES LG/CO
PROB/SOLV GP/REL. PAGE 117 F2304 ADMIN
CONTROL
L67

WHITNEY S.N.,"MERGERS, CONGLOMERATES, AND ECO/TAC
OLIGOPOLIES* A WIDENING OF ANTI TRUST TARGETS." LAW INDUS
NAT/G TEC/DEV CAP/ISM GP/REL PWR...OLD/LIB 20. JURID
PAGE 146 F2873
S67

"PROTEST AGAINST SOVIET INDUSTRIALIZATION ILLS IN INDUS
LITHUANIA* A MEMORANDUM." USSR LITHUANIA NAT/G COLONIAL
PROVS COST GEOG. PAGE 1 F0024 NAT/LISM
PLAN
S67

AGUILAR M.A.,"?UNA OEA MAS FUERTE O UNA AMERICA INT/ORG
LATINA MAS DEBIL?" L/A+17C USA+45 USA-45 ECO/UNDEV DIPLOM
INDUS CHIEF DELIB/GP FORCES CONTROL PWR 20 OAS POLICY
KENNEDY/JF JOHNSON/LB. PAGE 3 F0050 COLONIAL
S67

ALLISON D.,"THE GROWTH OF IDEAS." USA+45 LG/CO R+D
ADMIN. PAGE 4 F0075 OP/RES
INDUS
TEC/DEV
S67

ALPANDER G.G.,"ENTREPRENEURS AND PRIVATE ENTERPRISE ECO/UNDEV
IN TURKEY." TURKEY INDUS PROC/MFG EDU/PROP ATTIT LG/CO
DRIVE WEALTH...GEOG MGT SOC STAT TREND CHARTS 20. NAT/G
PAGE 4 F0077 POLICY
S67

ASCH P.,"CONGLOMERATE MERGERS AND PUBLIC POLICY." INDUS
USA+45 ECO/DEV LG/CO NAT/G ECO/TAC ADJUD CENTRAL CAP/ISM
20. PAGE 7 F0126 BARGAIN
S67

AUBERT DE LA RUE P.,"PERSPECTIVES ECONOMIQUES ENTRE INT/TRADE
LES ETATS-UNIS ET L'EUROPE." FUT INDUS R+D INT/ORG ECO/DEV
ACT/RES ECO/TAC AGREE BAL/PAY PRODUC...CHARTS 20 FINAN
EEC GATT WORLD/BANK. PAGE 7 F0138 TARIFFS
S67

BAGDKIAN B.H.,"NEWS AS A BYPRODUCT: WHAT HAPPENS COM/IND
WHEN JOURNALISM IS HITCHED TO GREAT, DIVERSIFIED PRESS
CORPORATIONS?" USA+45 INDUS EDU/PROP PARTIC PROFIT CONTROL
ATTIT. PAGE 8 F0152 LG/CO
S67

BENN W.,"TECHNOLOGY HAS AN INEXORABLE EFFECT." FUT R+D
UK ECO/DEV INT/ORG CONSULT PLAN EDU/PROP ADMIN LEAD LG/CO
GP/REL PRODUC...INT 20 EEC. PAGE 13 F0246 TEC/DEV
INDUS
S67

BENNETT J.T.,"POLITICAL IMPLICATIONS OF ECONOMIC ECO/UNDEV
CHANGE: SOUTH VIETNAM." VIETNAM/S INGP/REL INCOME INDUS
ATTIT 20 AID. PAGE 13 F0247 AGRI
PRODUC
S67

BOSHER J.F.,"GOVERNMENT AND PRIVATE INTERESTS IN NAT/G
NEW FRANCE." CANADA FRANCE INDUS LG/CO SML/CO FINAN
CAP/ISM INT/TRADE COLONIAL GP/REL...HIST/WRIT ADMIN
17/18. PAGE 17 F0320 CONTROL
S67

BROWN M.B.,"THE TRADE UNION QUESTION." UK INDUS WORKER
OP/RES PRICE PROFIT 20. PAGE 19 F0371 LABOR
GP/REL
LAW
S67

CHADWELL J.T.,"ANTITRUST ASPECTS OF DEALER LAW
LICENSING AND FRANCHISING." ACT/RES LICENSE ADJUD PRIVIL
CONTROL OWN. PAGE 23 F0439 INDUS
S67

CHAMBERLAIN N.W.,"STRIKES IN CONTEMPORARY CONTEXT." LABOR
LAW INDUS NAT/G CHIEF CONFER COST ATTIT ORD/FREE BARGAIN
...POLICY MGT 20. PAGE 23 F0442 EFFICIENCY
PROB/SOLV
S67

CLABAULT J.M.,"PRACTICALITIES IN COMPETITOR INDUS
EXCHANGING PRICE INFORMATION." ECO/DEV PLAN LAW
...CONCPT 20. PAGE 24 F0473 METH/COMP
S67

CURTIN W.J.,"NATIONAL EMERGENCY DISPUTES JURID
LEGISLATION* ITS NEED AND ITS PROSPECTS IN THE LABOR
TRANSPORTATION INDUSTRIES." USA+45 ECO/DEV INDUS ADJUD
NAT/G LEGIS ACT/RES BARGAIN POLICY. PAGE 29 F0565 DIST/IND
S67

DEWHURST A.,"THE WAGE MOVEMENT IN CANADA." CANADA WORKER
AGRI NAT/G PARTIC COST PRODUC PROFIT 20. PAGE 32 MARXIST
F0627 INDUS
LABOR
S67

DEYRUP F.J.,"SOCIAL MOBILITY AS A MAJOR FACTOR IN STRATA
ECONOMIC DEVELOPMENT." CHRIST-17C EUR+WWI MOD/EUR ECO/DEV
ECO/UNDEV DEMAND 20. PAGE 32 F0630 INDUS
WORKER
S67

FRANKEL T.,"ECONOMIC REFORM* A TENTATIVE ECO/DEV
APPRAISAL." COM USSR OP/RES BUDGET CONFER INDUS
EFFICIENCY PRODUC MARXISM SOCISM...MGT 20. PAGE 43 PLAN
F0847 WEALTH
S67

GAMARNIKOW M.,"THE NEW ROLE OF PRIVATE ENTERPRISE." ECO/TAC
ECO/DEV INDUS NAT/G SML/CO CREATE PROB/SOLV MARXISM ATTIT
...POLICY TREND IDEA/COMP 20. PAGE 46 F0890 CAP/ISM
COM
S67

GANZ G.,"THE CONTROL OF INDUSTRY BY ADMINISTRATIVE INDUS
PROCESS." UK DELIB/GP WORKER 20. PAGE 46 F0898 LAW
ADMIN
CONTROL
S67

GAUSSENS J.,"THE APPLICATIONS OF NUCLEAR ENERGY - NUC/PWR
TECHNICAL, ECONOMIC AND SOCIAL ASPECTS." WOR+45 TEC/DEV
INDUS R+D ACT/RES EFFICIENCY PRODUC SKILL PREDICT. ECO/DEV
PAGE 47 F0911 ADJUST
S67

HADDOCK G.B.,"CORPORATE GROWTH AS AFFECTED BY THE INDUS
FEDERAL ANTITRUST LAWS" ECO/DEV NAT/G PLAN TEC/DEV JURID
CAP/ISM ECO/TAC 20. PAGE 53 F1029 ADJUD
S67

HALE G.E.,"EXPANDING ENTERPRISE: GEOGRAPHICAL CURBS LAW
ON MERGERS." USA+45 MARKET LG/CO ADJUD CONTROL HABITAT
GP/REL 20. PAGE 53 F1041 INDUS
EX/STRUC
S67

HUTCHINGS R.,"THE ENDING OF UNEMPLOYMENT IN THE WORKER
USSR" USSR PLAN ECO/TAC PRICE INGP/REL...GEOG STAT AGRI
CHARTS 20 MIGRATION. PAGE 63 F1247 INDUS
MARXISM
S67

KENNY L.M.,"THE AFTERMATH OF DEFEAT IN EGYPT." WAR
ISLAM ISRAEL UAR UK USA+45 USSR INDUS FORCES ECO/UNDEV
ECO/TAC PRICE COERCE WEAPON COST ATTIT. PAGE 70 DIPLOM
F1378 POLICY

S67
KESTENBAUM L.,"PRIMARY JURISDICTION TO DECIDE ANTITRUST JURISDICTION* A PRACTICAL APPROACH TO THE ALLOCATION OF FUNCTIONS." USA+45 ECO/DEV INDUS VOL/ASSN ECO/TAC. PAGE 70 F1383
JURID CT/SYS LABOR ADJUD

S67
KOTLER P.,"OPERATIONS RESEARCH IN MARKETING." USA+45 DIST/IND INDUS LG/CO CONSULT BUDGET TASK DEMAND EFFICIENCY PROFIT WEALTH DECISION. PAGE 73 F1429
ECOMETRIC OP/RES MARKET PLAN

S67
LEVI M.,"LES RELATIONS ECONOMIQUES ENTRE L'EST ET L'OUEST EN EUROPE" INDUS...STAT CHARTS 20 OECD COMECON. PAGE 79 F1540
INT/TRADE INT/ORG FINAN PRODUC

S67
MALKIN A.,"BUSINESS BOOKS OF 1966." INDUS LABOR OP/RES TEC/DEV CAP/ISM ECO/TAC INCOME WEALTH 20. PAGE 84 F1649
BIBLIOG/A FINAN MARKET

S67
MEHTA A.,"INDIA* POVERTY AND CHANGE." STRATA INDUS CREATE ECO/TAC FOR/AID NEUTRAL GP/REL ADJUST INCOME ...NEW/IDEA 20. PAGE 89 F1746
INDIA SOCIETY ECO/UNDEV TEC/DEV

S67
MILLER C.H.,"B. TRAVEN Y EL 'PROBLEMA PETROLERO'." USA-45 ECO/UNDEV INDUS TEC/DEV INT/TRADE ATTIT ORD/FREE SOVEREIGN 20 MEXIC/AMER. PAGE 91 F1791
EXTR/IND DIPLOM ECO/TAC DOMIN

S67
MOLTMANN G.,"ZUR FORMULIERUNG DER AMERIKANISCHEN BESATZUNGSPOLITIK IN DEUTSCHLAND AM ENDE DES ZWEITEN WELTKRIEGES" GERMANY ECO/TAC ADMIN WAR CIVMIL/REL ORD/FREE FASCISM 20. PAGE 92 F1815
FORCES CONTROL POLICY INDUS

S67
MORTON J.A.,"A SYSTEMS APPROACH TO THE INNOVATION PROCESS: ITS USE IN THE BELL SYSTEM." USA+45 INTELL INDUS LG/CO CONSULT WORKER COMPUTER AUTOMAT DEMAND ...MGT CHARTS 20. PAGE 94 F1841
TEC/DEV GEN/METH R+D COM/IND

S67
MYRDAL G.,"ECONOMIC DEVELOPMENT IN THE BACKWARD COUNTRIES." INT/ORG TEC/DEV CAP/ISM DIPLOM INT/TRADE PRODUC WEALTH 20. PAGE 96 F1883
ECO/UNDEV INDUS NAT/G ECO/TAC

S67
PERKINS D.H.,"ECONOMIC GROWTH IN CHINA AND THE CULTURAL REVOLUTION(1960APRIL 1967)" CHINA/COM FUT AGRI INDUS PLAN LEAD MARXISM...CHARTS 20 MAO. PAGE 105 F2062
ECO/TAC CULTURE REV ECO/UNDEV

S67
PFEFFERMANN G.,"TRADE UNIONS AND POLITICS IN FRENCH WEST AFRICA DURING THE FOURTH REPUBLIC." AFR INDUS POL/PAR COLONIAL ATTIT PWR 20. PAGE 106 F2077
PARTIC DRIVE INT/TRADE LABOR

S67
PRASOW P.,"THE DEVELOPMENT OF JUDICIAL ARBITRATION IN LABOR-MANAGEMENT DISPUTES." LAW INDUS WORKER GP/REL ROLE...HIST/WRIT 20. PAGE 107 F2113
LABOR BARGAIN ADJUD TREND

S67
RICHMAN B.M.,"CAPITALISTS & MANAGERS IN COMMUNIST CHINA." ASIA CHINA/COM ECO/UNDEV NAT/G CONSULT EX/STRUC PLAN EFFICIENCY PRODUC WEALTH MARXISM ...MGT CHARTS 20. PAGE 111 F2185
CAP/ISM INDUS

S67
SCHACHTER G.,"REGIONAL DEVELOPMENT IN THE ITALIAN DUAL ECONOMY" ITALY AGRI INDUS MARKET WORKER ECO/TAC CONTROL INCOME PRODUC 20. PAGE 116 F2287
REGION ECO/UNDEV NAT/G PROB/SOLV

S67
SCOTT R.,"TRADE UNIONS IN AFRICA." AFR UGANDA USA-45 ECO/UNDEV INDUS INT/ORG POL/PAR ECO/TAC WEALTH...GP/COMP 20 NKRUMAH/K. PAGE 118 F2335
LABOR WORKER NAT/G

S67
SHISTER J.,"THE DIRECTION OF UNIONISM 1947-1967: THRUST OF DRIFT?" INDUS CENTRAL EFFICIENCY INCOME ATTIT SOCISM...POLICY TREND 20 AFL/CIO. PAGE 121 F2382
LABOR PROF/ORG LEAD LAW

S67
SIMONE A.J.,"SCIENTIFIC PUBLIC POLICY, MARKET PERFORMANCE, AND SIZE OF FIRM." GP/REL COST EFFICIENCY OPTIMAL PRODUC PWR. PAGE 122 F2410
LAW INDUS NAT/G PROB/SOLV

S67
STEMPEL GH I.I.I.,"A NEW ANALYSIS OF MONOPOLY AND COMPETITION." USA+45 INDUS TV ATTIT MUNICH. PAGE 126 F2479
PRESS COM/IND GP/REL

S67
THEROUX P.,"HATING THE ASIANS." TANZANIA UGANDA CONSTN INDUS NAT/G POL/PAR WORKER ECO/TAC HABITAT LOVE...POLICY GEOG 20 MIGRATION. PAGE 130 F2557
AFR RACE/REL SOVEREIGN ATTIT

S67
WAITS C.R.,"CRAFT GILDS AS AN INSTITUTIONAL BARRIER TO THE INDUSTRIAL REVOLUTION." CHRIST-17C MOD/EUR ECO/UNDEV CONTROL GP/REL ATTIT 16/19. PAGE 142 F2801
TEC/DEV INDUS REV PROF/ORG

S67
WEISSKOPF W.A.,"THE DIALECTICS OF ABUNDANCE." UNIV CAP/ISM ATTIT MARXISM...CONCPT 20. PAGE 145 F2853
INDUS SOCIETY IDEA/COMP ALL/VALS

N67
US HOUSE COMM FOREIGN AFFAIRS,THE FOREIGN POLICY ASPECTS OF THE KENNEDY ROUND (PAMPHLET). USA+45 INDUS KENNEDY/JF CONGRESS HOUSE/REP EEC. PAGE 137 F2693
POLICY INT/TRADE FOR/AID ECO/DEV

B75
JEVONS W.S.,MONEY AND THE MECHANISM OF EXCHANGE. INDUS MARKET DIPLOM COST EQUILIB WEALTH LAISSEZ ...GEN/LAWS 19 MONEY. PAGE 67 F1319
PRICE FINAN ECO/TAC POLICY

B76
FOURIER C.,SOCIAL DESTINIES, IN A. BRISBANE, GENERAL INTRODUCTION TO SOCIAL SCIENCE. UNIV AGRI INDUS SECT PRODUC...PHIL/SCI CONCPT. PAGE 43 F0835
UTOPIA SOCIETY PERSON VOL/ASSN

B76
SMITH A.,THE WEALTH OF NATIONS. UK STRUCT WORKER DIPLOM ECO/TAC OPTIMAL DRIVE PERSON ORD/FREE ...OLD/LIB GEN/LAWS 17/18. PAGE 123 F2428
WEALTH PRODUC INDUS LAISSEZ

B82
CUNNINGHAM W.,THE GROWTH OF ENGLISH INDUSTRY AND COMMERCE. FUT UK FINAN NAT/G CAP/ISM...POLICY 20 MERCANTLST CHRISTIAN POPE. PAGE 29 F0562
INDUS INT/TRADE SML/CO CONSERVE

S86
SMITH R.M.,"THE NATIONAL BUREAU OF LABOR AND INDUSTRIAL DEPRESSIONS" USA-45 DELIB/GP BARGAIN CONTROL COST INCOME WEALTH...STAT 19 DEPRESSION. PAGE 123 F2433
LABOR INDUS FINAN GOV/REL

B91
MILL J.S.,SOCIALISM (1859). MOD/EUR AGRI INDUS NAT/G REV INCOME PRODUC ORD/FREE POPULISM SOCISM ...GOV/COMP METH/COMP 19. PAGE 91 F1787
WEALTH SOCIALIST ECO/TAC OWN

B92
ENGELS F.,THE CONDITION OF THE WORKING-CLASS IN ENGLAND (1848). UK INDUS LABOR PRICE CONTROL COST INCOME HEALTH MARXISM MUNICH 19. PAGE 38 F0733
WORKER WEALTH MARXIST CAP/ISM

B95
SELIGMAN E.R.A.,ESSAYS IN TAXATION. NEW/ZEALND PRUSSIA UK USA-45 MARKET LOC/G CREATE PRICE CONTROL INCOME OWN WEALTH...GOV/COMP METH/COMP 19. PAGE 119 F2349
TAX TARIFFS INDUS NAT/G

B96
MARX K.,REVOLUTION AND COUNTER-REVOLUTION. GERMANY CONSTN ELITES INDUS NAT/G DIPLOM ECO/TAC WEALTH. PAGE 86 F1693
MARXIST REV PWR STRATA

B96
SCHMOLLER G.,THE MERCANTILE SYSTEM AND ITS HISTORICAL SIGNIFICANCE: ILLUSTRATED CHIEFLY FROM PRUSSIAN HISTORY (TRANS.). PRUSSIA CULTURE INDUS KIN NAT/G PROVS OP/RES ECO/TAC INT/TRADE SUPEGO PWR WEALTH MUNICH 19 MERCANTLST. PAGE 117 F2302
GEN/METH INGP/REL CONCPT

B98
MARSHALL A.,PRINCIPLES OF ECONOMICS. INDUS WORKER PRICE COST EQUILIB INCOME OPTIMAL PRODUC...TIME/SEQ METH RICARDO/D. PAGE 86 F1678
WEALTH GEN/LAWS MARKET

B99
KROPOTKIN P.,FIELDS, FACTORIES, AND WORKSHOPS. UNIV INTELL ECO/DEV LG/CO SCHOOL SML/CO ECO/TAC PRODUC UTOPIA...NEW/IDEA MUNICH. PAGE 74 F1445
SOCIETY WORKER AGRI INDUS

INDUS/REV....INDUSTRIAL REVOLUTION

B61
HENDERSON W.O.,THE INDUSTRIAL REVOLUTION IN EUROPE. FRANCE GERMANY MOD/EUR RUSSIA WORKER PROFIT PWR MARXISM SOCISM...SOC HIST/WRIT 19 INDUS/REV. PAGE 58 F1148
INDUS REV CAP/ISM TEC/DEV

B66
MOUNTJOY A.B.,INDUSTRIALIZATION AND UNDER-DEVELOPED COUNTRIES (2ND REV. ED.). CHILE GHANA INDIA NIGERIA WOR+45 SOCIETY PROB/SOLV ECO/TAC...SOC CHARTS 20 INDUS/REV. PAGE 94 F1848
ECO/UNDEV INDUS GEOG HABITAT

INDUSTRIAL COUN SOC-ECO STU F1264

INDUSTRIAL RELATIONS....SEE LABOR, MGT, INDUS

INDUSTRIALIZATION....SEE ECO/DEV, ECO/UNDEV

INDUSTRY....SEE INDUS

INDUSTRY, COMMUNICATION....SEE COM/IND

INDUSTRY, CONSTRUCTION....SEE CONSTRUC

INDUSTRY, EXTRACTIVE....SEE EXTR/IND

INDUSTRY, MANUFACTURING....SEE PROC/MFG

INDUSTRY, PROCESSING....SEE PROC/MFG

INDUSTRY, SERVICE....SEE SERV/IND

INDUSTRY, TRANSPORTATION....SEE DIST/IND

INDUSTRY, WAREHOUSING....SEE DIST/IND

INFLATION....INFLATION

INFLUENCING....SEE MORE SPECIFIC FORMS, E.G., DOMIN, PWR, WEALTH, EDU/PROP, SKILL, CHANGE, LOBBY

INGP/REL....INTRAGROUP RELATIONS

N19
ADMINISTRATIVE STAFF COLLEGE,THE ACCOUNTABILITY OF GOVERNMENT DEPARTMENTS (PAMPHLET) (REV. ED.). UK CONSTN FINAN NAT/G CONSULT ADMIN INGP/REL CONSEN PRIVIL 20 PARLIAMENT. PAGE 2 F0043
PARL/PROC ELITES SANCTION PROB/SOLV

N19
FIKS M.,PUBLIC ADMINISTRATION IN ISRAEL (PAMPHLET). ISRAEL SCHOOL EX/STRUC BUDGET PAY INGP/REL ...DECISION 20 CIVIL/SERV. PAGE 41 F0792
EDU/PROP NAT/G ADMIN WORKER

N19
RIDLEY C.E.,MEASURING MUNICIPAL ACTIVITIES (PAMPHLET). FINAN SERV/IND FORCES RECEIVE INGP/REL HABITAT...POLICY SOC/WK 20. PAGE 111 F2191
MGT HEALTH WEALTH LOC/G

B22
VON ENGELIN O.D.,INHERITING THE EARTH, THE GEOGRAPHICAL FACTOR IN NATIONAL DEVELOPMENT. WOR-45 CULTURE DIPLOM BIO/SOC HABITAT PERSON...PSY SOC CONCPT IDEA/COMP. PAGE 142 F2791
INGP/REL GEOG SOCIETY ROLE

B26
SUFRIN S.C.,A BRIEF ANNOTATED BIBLIOGRAPHY ON LABOR IN EMERGING SOCIETIES. WOR+45 CULTURE SOCIETY INDUS EDU/PROP GP/REL INGP/REL. PAGE 127 F2510
BIBLIOG/A LABOR ECO/UNDEV WORKER

B28
HARDMAN J.B.,AMERICAN LABOR DYNAMICS. WORKER ECO/TAC DOMIN ADJUD LEAD LOBBY PWR...POLICY MGT. PAGE 55 F1079
LABOR INGP/REL ATTIT GP/REL

B31
LORWIN L.L.,ADVISORY ECONOMIC COUNCILS. EUR+WWI FRANCE GERMANY PROB/SOLV INGP/REL...CLASSIF GP/COMP. PAGE 82 F1601
CONSULT DELIB/GP ECO/TAC NAT/G

B38
LEVINSON E.,LABOR ON THE MARCH. WORKER CREATE ECO/TAC ADJUD LEAD PARL/PROC PARTIC INGP/REL SKILL POLICY. PAGE 79 F1543
LABOR INCOME NAT/G PLAN

B41
LESTER R.A.,ECONOMICS OF LABOR. UK USA-45 TEC/DEV BARGAIN PAY INGP/REL INCOME...MGT 19/20. PAGE 78 F1532
LABOR ECO/DEV INDUS WORKER

B41
SLICHTER S.H.,UNION POLICIES AND INDUSTRIAL MANAGEMENT. USA-45 INDUS TEC/DEV PAY GP/REL INGP/REL COST EFFICIENCY PRODUC...POLICY 20. PAGE 123 F2420
BARGAIN LABOR MGT WORKER

S41
LASSWELL H.D.,"THE GARRISON STATE" (BMR)" FUT WOR+45 ELITES INTELL FORCES ECO/TAC DOMIN EDU/PROP COERCE INGP/REL 20. PAGE 76 F1485
NAT/G DIPLOM PWR CIVMIL/REL

S43
HERBERG W.,"BUREAUCRACY AND DEMOCRACY IN LABOR UNIONS." LAW CONSTN STRUCT WORKER ADMIN CONTROL PARTIC RIGID/FLEX PWR TREND. PAGE 59 F1151
LABOR REPRESENT ROUTINE INGP/REL

B45
MILLIS H.A.,ORGANIZED LABOR (FIRST ED.). LAW STRUCT DELIB/GP WORKER ECO/TAC ADJUD CONTROL REPRESENT INGP/REL INCOME MGT. PAGE 92 F1797
LABOR POLICY ROUTINE GP/REL

S45
MILLS C.W.,"THE TRADE UNION LEADER: A COLLECTIVE PORTRAIT." EX/STRUC TOP/EX INGP/REL...QU CON/ANAL CHARTS. PAGE 92 F1798
LABOR LEAD STAT STRATA

B46
DRUCKER P.F.,CONCEPT OF CORPORATION. LAW LABOR WORKER PRICE CONTROL LEAD GP/REL POLICY. PAGE 34 F0665
LG/CO CENTRAL INGP/REL

B47
SLICHTER S.H.,THE CHALLENGE OF INDUSTRIAL RELATIONS: TRADE UNIONS, MANAGEMENT AND THE PUBLIC INTEREST. PLAN ECO/TAC ADJUD CONTROL LEAD SANCTION GP/REL INGP/REL INCOME. PAGE 123 F2421
LABOR MGT CLIENT POLICY

B47
WARNER W.L.,THE SOCIAL SYSTEM OF THE MODERN FACTORY; THE STRIKE: AN ANALYSIS. USA-45 STRATA WORKER ECO/TAC GP/REL INGP/REL...MGT SOC CHARTS 20 YANKEE/C. PAGE 143 F2824
ROLE STRUCT LABOR PROC/MFG

B48
LAUTERBACH A.,ECONOMIC SECURITY AND INDIVIDUAL FREEDOM: CAN WE HAVE BOTH? COM EUR+WWI MOD/EUR UNIV WOR+45 CAP/ISM TOTALISM ALL/VALS...GOV/COMP BIBLIOG 20. PAGE 76 F1490
ORD/FREE ECO/DEV DECISION INGP/REL

B48
SPERO S.D.,GOVERNMENT AS EMPLOYER. USA+45 NAT/G EX/STRUC ADMIN CONTROL EXEC 20. PAGE 124 F2453
SOVEREIGN INGP/REL REPRESENT CONFER

B48
WHYTE W.F.,HUMAN RELATIONS IN THE RESTAURANT INDUSTRY (1ST ED). CLIENT WORKER WAR ATTIT...MGT OBS INT. PAGE 146 F2874
INGP/REL GP/REL SERV/IND LABOR

S50
EBY K.,"RESEARCH IN LABOR UNIONS." EDU/PROP INGP/REL PWR...METH/CNCPT OBS. PAGE 36 F0693
RECORD QU LABOR PARTIC

B51
DIMOCK M.E.,FREE ENTERPRISE AND THE ADMINISTRATIVE STATE. FINAN LG/CO BARGAIN BUDGET DOMIN CONTROL INGP/REL EFFICIENCY 20. PAGE 33 F0640
CAP/ISM ADMIN MGT MARKET

B51
OWENS R.N.,BUSINESS, ORGANIZATION, AND COMBINATION. USA+45 USA-45 LAW NAT/G LEGIS ECO/TAC CONTROL INGP/REL...JURID GP/COMP 20 NEW/DEAL. PAGE 102 F2006
SML/CO LG/CO STRUCT GP/REL

L51
SUMMERS C.W.,"UNION POWERS AND WORKERS RIGHTS." WORKER PROB/SOLV ECO/TAC PARTIC INGP/REL PWR. PAGE 127 F2513
LABOR CONSTN LAW REPRESENT

B52
GOLDSTEIN J.,THE GOVERNMENT OF BRITISH TRADE UNIONS. UK ECO/DEV EX/STRUC INGP/REL...BIBLIOG 20. PAGE 48 F0940
LABOR PARTIC

B52
ROSE A.M.,UNION SOLIDARITY: THE INTERNAL COHESION OF A LABOR UNION. SECT GP/REL RACE/REL ATTIT ROLE HEALTH WEALTH...INT QU. PAGE 114 F2241
LABOR INGP/REL PARTIC SUPEGO

S52
KLUMB S.,"EMPLOYEE DETERMINATION OF MANAGERIAL FUNCTIONS AND CHARACTERISTICS." DELIB/GP WORKER PARTIC ROUTINE INGP/REL...CLASSIF OBS QU. PAGE 72 F1410
MGT INDUS EX/STRUC CHOOSE

B53
DAHL R.A.,POLITICS, ECONOMICS, AND WELFARE. TEC/DEV BARGAIN ECO/TAC RECEIVE PRICE CONTROL LEAD INGP/REL ...POLICY GEN/LAWS. PAGE 29 F0572
SOCIETY GIVE

B53
FLORENCE P.S.,THE LOGIC OF BRITISH AND AMERICAN INDUSTRY; A REALISTIC ANALYSIS OF ECONOMIC STRUCTURE AND GOVERNMENT. UK USA+45 USA-45 FINAN LABOR CAP/ISM INGP/REL EFFICIENCY...MGT CONCPT STAT CHARTS METH 20. PAGE 42 F0813
INDUS ECO/DEV NAT/G NAT/COMP

B53
PURCELL T.V.,THE WORKER SPEAKS HIS MIND ON COMPANY AND UNION. WORKER ADJUD LEAD RACE/REL ATTIT DRIVE MARXISM...MGT CLASSIF STAT OBS INT SAMP BIBLIOG. PAGE 108 F2131
LABOR PARTIC INGP/REL HAPPINESS

B53
SAYLES L.R.,THE LOCAL UNION. CONSTN CULTURE DELIB/GP PARTIC CHOOSE GP/REL INGP/REL ATTIT ROLE ...MAJORIT DECISION MGT. PAGE 116 F2284
LABOR LEAD ADJUD ROUTINE

S53
GABLE R.W.,"NAM: INFLUENTIAL LOBBY OR KISS OF DEATH?" (BMR)" USA+45 LAW INSPECT EDU/PROP ADMIN CONTROL INGP/REL EFFICIENCY PWR 20 CONGRESS NAM TAFT/HART. PAGE 45 F0880
LOBBY LEGIS INDUS LG/CO

S53
SIMON H.A.,"BIRTH OF AN ORGANIZATION: THE ECONOMIC COOPERATION ADMINISTRATION." USA+45 PROB/SOLV INGP/REL EFFICIENCY 20. PAGE 122 F2408
ADMIN EX/STRUC EXEC MGT

B54
EMERSON F.D.,SHAREHOLDER DEMOCRACY: A BROADER OUTLOOK FOR CORPORATIONS. DELIB/GP EX/STRUC LEGIS ADJUD CONTROL REPRESENT INGP/REL OWN PWR...POLICY STAT RECORD. PAGE 37 F0727
LG/CO PARTIC MAJORIT TREND

B54
TAFT P.,THE STRUCTURE AND GOVERNMENT OF LABOR UNIONS. SANCTION INGP/REL ORD/FREE PWR MARXISM ...MAJORIT STAT TREND. PAGE 128 F2524
LABOR ADJUD WORKER FINAN

B55
BERNAYS E.L.,THE ENGINEERING OF CONSENT. VOL/ASSN OP/RES ROUTINE INGP/REL ATTIT RESPECT...POLICY METH/CNCPT METH/COMP 20. PAGE 14 F0264
GP/REL PLAN ACT/RES ADJUST

B55
JOHR W.A.,THE ROLE OF THE ECONOMIST AS OFFICIAL ADVISER. WOR+45 INTELL ECO/DEV NAT/G PLAN GP/REL ROLE...DECISION PREDICT IDEA/COMP. PAGE 68 F1336
CONSULT ECO/TAC POLICY INGP/REL

S55
BUNZEL J.H.,"THE GENERAL IDEOLOGY OF AMERICAN SMALL BUSINESS"(BMR)" USA+45 USA-45 AGRI GP/REL INGP/REL PERSON...MGT IDEA/COMP 18/20. PAGE 20 F0383
ALL/IDEOS ATTIT SML/CO INDUS

B56
BARBASH J.,THE PRACTICE OF UNIONISM. ECO/TAC LEAD LOBBY GP/REL INGP/REL DRIVE MARXISM BIBLIOG. PAGE 10 F0182
LABOR REPRESENT CONTROL ADMIN

B56
GILBERT L.D.,DIVIDENDS AND DEMOCRACY. DELIB/GP LEGIS CAP/ISM ADJUD LOBBY OWN PWR LAISSEZ MAJORIT. PAGE 47 F0922
LG/CO INGP/REL CONTROL PARTIC

B56
HICKMAN C.A.,INDIVIDUALS, GROUPS, AND ECONOMIC BEHAVIOR. WORKER PAY CONTROL EXEC GP/REL INGP/REL PERSON ROLE...PSY SOC PERS/COMP METH 20. PAGE 59 F1163
MGT ADMIN ECO/TAC PLAN

B56
LIPSET S.M.,UNION DEMOCRACY. STRUCT INDUS FACE/GP WORKER CONTROL LEAD PARTIC GP/REL ATTIT LAISSEZ ...INT QU CHARTS. PAGE 80 F1577
LABOR INGP/REL MAJORIT

B56
REDFORD E.S.,PUBLIC ADMINISTRATION AND POLICY FORMATION: STUDIES IN OIL, GAS, BANKING, RIVER DEVELOPMENT AND CORPORATE INVESTIGATIONS. USA+45 CLIENT NAT/G ADMIN LOBBY REPRESENT GOV/REL INGP/REL 20. PAGE 110 F2167
EX/STRUC PROB/SOLV CONTROL EXEC

L56
TAGLIACOZZO D.L.,"TRADE-UNION GOVERNMENT, ITS NATURE AND ITS PROBLEMS: A BIBLIOGRAPHICAL REVIEW, 1945-1955." STRUCT LEAD PARTIC CHOOSE ATTIT ...MAJORIT METH/CNCPT BIBLIOG. PAGE 128 F2526
CLASSIF LABOR INGP/REL GP/REL

S56
BROWN J.S.,"UNION SIZE AS A FUNCTION OF INTRA-UNION CONFLICT." CLIENT CONTROL CHOOSE EFFICIENCY ATTIT TREND. PAGE 19 F0370
LABOR INGP/REL CONSEN DRIVE

S56
TANNENBAUM A.S.,"CONTROL OF STRUCTURE AND UNION FUNCTIONS." PARTIC GP/REL INGP/REL CONSEN ATTIT PWR ...QU SAMP. PAGE 128 F2529
LABOR STRUCT CONTROL LEAD

B57
BERLE A.A. JR.,ECONOMIC POWER AND FREE SOCIETY (PAMPHLET). CLIENT CONSTN EX/STRUC ECO/TAC CONTROL PARTIC PWR WEALTH MAJORIT. PAGE 14 F0261
LG/CO CAP/ISM INGP/REL LEGIT

B57
NANIWADA H.,STAAT UND WIRTSCHAFT; GRUNDLEGUNG DER NATIONALOEKONOMIE ALS DER LOGIK DER BURGERLICHEN GESELLSCHAFT. WOR+45 WOR-45 STRATA MARKET WORKER INGP/REL DEMAND EQUILIB WEALTH...POLICY IDEA/COMP GEN/LAWS 17/20 MARX/KARL KEYNES/JM LENIN/VI. PAGE 96 F1890
ALL/IDEOS ECO/TAC SOCIETY NAT/G

B57
SCHNEIDER E.V.,INDUSTRIAL SOCIOLOGY: THE SOCIAL RELATIONS OF INDUSTRY AND COMMUNITY. STRATA INDUS NAT/G NEIGH CREATE ADMIN PARTIC GP/REL RACE/REL ROLE PWR...POLICY BIBLIOG. PAGE 117 F2308
LABOR MGT INGP/REL STRUCT

S57
KAHN R.L.,"UNION PRACTICES AND MEMBER PARTICIPATION." PARTIC CHOOSE REPRESENT PERS/REL PERSON SKILL...DECISION METH/CNCPT QU. PAGE 69 F1347
INGP/REL LABOR ATTIT LEAD

B58
CHAMBERLIN E.H.,LABOR UNIONS AND PUBLIC POLICY. PLAN BARGAIN SANCTION INGP/REL JURID. PAGE 23 F0444
LABOR WEALTH PWR NAT/G

B58
DUBIN R.,WORKING UNION-MANAGEMENT RELATIONS. LAW PLAN ECO/TAC CHOOSE REPRESENT INGP/REL PWR...POLICY SOC BIBLIOG. PAGE 34 F0669
LABOR MGT AUTHORIT GP/REL

B58
RUBIN B.,PUBLIC RELATIONS AND THE STATE, A CASE STUDY OF NEW YORK STATE ADMINISTRATION, 1943-54. USA+45 USA-45 COM/IND EDU/PROP GOV/REL...CHARTS 20 NEW/YORK DEWEY/THOM. PAGE 114 F2255
INGP/REL PRESS PROVS GP/REL

B58
SEIDMAN J.I.,DEMOCRACY IN THE LABOR MOVEMENT (PAMPHLET). LAW CONSTN STRUCT DELIB/GP WORKER ADJUD PARTIC SANCTION POLICY. PAGE 119 F2345
LABOR INGP/REL PWR MAJORIT

B58
TAFT P.,CORRUPTION AND RACKETEERING IN THE LABOR MOVEMENT (PAMPHLET). ADMIN SANCTION CENTRAL ROLE WEALTH...POLICY CLASSIF. PAGE 128 F2525
LABOR INGP/REL GP/REL CRIME

B58
TANNENBAUM A.S.,PARTICIPATION IN UNION LOCALS. SOCIETY FINAN CONTROL LEAD GP/REL...BIBLIOG 20. PAGE 128 F2531
LABOR MGT PARTIC INGP/REL

S58
EMERSON F.D.,"THE ROLES OF MANAGEMENT AND SHAREHOLDERS IN CORPORATE GOVERNMENT." CLIENT DELIB/GP CREATE ADMIN EXEC PARTIC PERS/REL PWR. PAGE 37 F0728
LG/CO LAW INGP/REL REPRESENT

S58
LATTIN N.D.,"MINORITY AND DISSENTING SHAREHOLDERS' RIGHTS IN FUNDAMENTAL CHANGES." FINAN LEGIS ADJUD PARTIC ROUTINE CHOOSE REPRESENT INGP/REL TREND. PAGE 76 F1487
MAJORIT LG/CO LAW CREATE

S58
MANSFIELD E.,"A STUDY OF DECISION-MAKING WITHIN THE FIRM." LG/CO WORKER INGP/REL COST EFFICIENCY PRODUC ...CHARTS 20. PAGE 85 F1658
OP/RES PROB/SOLV AUTOMAT ROUTINE

B59
BARNETT A.D.,COMMUNIST ECONOMIC STRATEGY: THE RISE OF MAINLAND CHINA. CHINA/COM USSR WOR+45 AGRI INDUS FOR/AID INGP/REL ATTIT. PAGE 10 F0188
ECO/UNDEV INT/TRADE TOTALISM BAL/PWR

B59
BAUER P.T.,UNITED STATES AID AND INDIAN ECONOMIC DEVELOPMENT. INDIA STRATA FINAN PLAN BUDGET DIPLOM INGP/REL EFFICIENCY SOCISM 20 AID. PAGE 11 F0215
FOR/AID ECO/UNDEV ECO/TAC POLICY

B59
BROMWICH L.,UNION CONSTITUTIONS. CONSTN EX/STRUC PRESS ADJUD CONTROL CHOOSE REPRESENT PWR SAMP. PAGE 19 F0361
LABOR ROUTINE INGP/REL RACE/REL

B59
KOLLAI H.R.,DIE EINGLIEDERUNG DER VERTRIEBENEN UND ZUWANDERER IN NIEDERSACHSEN. GERMANY/W SOCIETY STRATA STRUCT LABOR SOC/INTEG 20. PAGE 72 F1422
GP/REL INGP/REL

B59
KRIPALANI J.B.,CLASS STRUGGLE. INDIA WOR+45 ECO/UNDEV LABOR CAP/ISM EDU/PROP INGP/REL ...SOCIALIST IDEA/COMP 17/20. PAGE 73 F1440
MARXISM STRATA COERCE ECO/TAC

B59
LEISERSON W.,AMERICAN TRADE UNION DEMOCRACY. CONSTN STRUCT ADJUD EXEC REPRESENT GP/REL INGP/REL MAJORITY ATTIT PWR. PAGE 77 F1516
LABOR LEAD PARTIC DELIB/GP

B59
ROCHE J.,LA COLONISATION ALLEMANDE ET LE RIO GRANDE DO SUL. BRAZIL L/A+17C NAT/G PROVS INGP/REL RACE/REL DISCRIM HABITAT...GEOG SOC/INTEG 19/20 MIGRATION. PAGE 113 F2228
ECO/UNDEV GP/REL ATTIT

B59
SERAPHIM H.J.,PROBLEME DER WILLENSBILDUNG UND DER WIRTSCHAFTSPOLITISCHEN FUEHRUNG. WOR+45 MARKET ACT/RES OP/RES PLAN EDU/PROP INGP/REL HABITAT PLURISM...MGT PERS/COMP METH 20. PAGE 119 F2357
POLICY DECISION PSY

B59
VINCENT W.S.,ROLES OF THE CITIZENS: PRINCIPLES AND PRACTICES. LOC/G POL/PAR VOL/ASSN CHOOSE ROLE ORD/FREE PWR...POLICY 20. PAGE 141 F2785
INGP/REL EDU/PROP CREATE LOBBY

B59
WAHLKE J.C.,LEGISLATIVE BEHAVIOR: A READER IN THEORY AND RESEARCH. USA+45 CONSTN ELITES POL/PAR LOBBY REPRESENT PERS/REL PERSON ROLE...IDEA/COMP METH/COMP SIMUL. PAGE 142 F2800
LEGIS CHOOSE INGP/REL ATTIT

L59
OBERER W.E.,"VOLUNTARY IMPARTIAL REVIEW OF LABOR: SOME REFLECTIONS." DELIB/GP LEGIS PROB/SOLV ADJUD CONTROL COERCE PWR PLURISM POLICY. PAGE 100 F1960
LABOR LAW PARTIC INGP/REL

S59
MILLER A.S.,"CONSTITUTIONALIZING THE CORPORATION." LABOR NAT/G WORKER PWR...POLICY MGT. PAGE 91 F1789
CONSTN INGP/REL LG/CO CONTROL

C59
MINTZ S.W.,"INTERNAL MARKET SYS AS MECHANISMS OF SOCIAL ARTIC," IN V.F. RAY, INTERMED SOCIETIES, SOCIAL MOBILITY, AND COMMUNIC (BMR). UNIV STRATA GP/REL INGP/REL...GEOG SOC BIBLIOG. PAGE 92 F1804
MARKET SOCIETY ECO/UNDEV STRUCT

B60
BHAMBHRI C.P.,PARLIAMENTARY CONTROL OVER STATE ENTERPRISE IN INDIA. INDIA DELIB/GP ADMIN CONTROL INGP/REL EFFICIENCY 20 PARLIAMENT. PAGE 14 F0277
NAT/G OWN INDUS PARL/PROC

B60
EELLS R.S.F.,THE MEANING OF MODERN BUSINESS. LOC/G NAT/G NEIGH EX/STRUC PARTIC GP/REL INGP/REL DECISION. PAGE 36 F0706
LG/CO REPRESENT POLICY PLAN

B60
SERAPHIM H.J.,ZUR GRUNDLEGUNG WIRTSCHAFTSPOLITISCHER KONZEPTIONEN (SCHRIFTEN DES VEREINS FUR SOZIALPOLITIK, N.F. BAND 18). GERMANY/W WOR+45 ECO/DEV DELIB/GP ACT/RES ECO/TAC INGP/REL ORD/FREE...CONCPT IDEA/COMP GEN/LAWS 20. PAGE 120 F2358
POLICY PHIL/SCI PLAN

B60
THOMPSON V.A.,THE REGULATORY PROCESS IN OPA RATIONING. USA-45 CLIENT PROB/SOLV ADMIN LOBBY REPRESENT 20. PAGE 130 F2566
EX/STRUC GOV/REL INGP/REL

B60
WALLICH H.C.,THE COST OF FREEDOM: A NEW LOOK AT CAPITALISM. USA+45 SOCIETY ECO/DEV INGP/REL CONSEN LAISSEZ SOCISM...OLD/LIB IDEA/COMP. PAGE 143 F2810
CAP/ISM ORD/FREE POLICY ECO/TAC

B60
WHEARE K.C.,THE CONSTITUTIONAL STRUCTURE OF THE COMMONWEALTH. UK EX/STRUC DIPLOM DOMIN ADMIN COLONIAL CONTROL LEAD INGP/REL SUPEGO 20 CMN/WLTH. PAGE 145 F2865
CONSTN INT/ORG VOL/ASSN SOVEREIGN

S60
MANN S.Z.,"POLICY FORMULATION IN THE EXECUTIVE BRANCH: THE TAFT-HARTLEY EXPERIENCE." USA+45 LABOR CHIEF INGP/REL 20 NLRB. PAGE 85 F1656
EXEC GOV/REL EX/STRUC PROB/SOLV

B61
BARBASH J.,LABOR'S GRASS ROOTS. CONSTN NAT/G EX/STRUC LEGIS WORKER LEAD...MAJORIT BIBLIOG. PAGE 10 F0184
LABOR INGP/REL GP/REL LAW

B61
BARRASH J.,LABOR'S GRASS ROOTS; A STUDY OF THE LOCAL UNION. STRATA BARGAIN LEAD REPRESENT DEMAND ATTIT PWR. PAGE 10 F0192
LABOR USA+45 INGP/REL EXEC

B61
DUKE UNIVERSITY,EXPULSION OR OPPRESSION OF BUSINESS ASSOCIATES: "SQUEEZE-OUTS" IN SMALL ENTERPRISES. LAW CONTROL PARTIC COERCE INGP/REL...POLICY RECORD INT. PAGE 35 F0674
PWR MGT SML/CO ECO/TAC

B61
HART W.R.,COLLECTIVE BARGAINING IN THE FEDERAL CIVIL SERVICE. NAT/G EX/STRUC ADMIN EXEC 20. PAGE 56 F1101
INGP/REL MGT REPRESENT LABOR

B61
HUBBARD P.J.,ORIGINS OF THE TVA: THE MUSCLE SHOALS CONTROVERSY, 1920-1932. USA-45 DELIB/GP LEGIS LEAD LOBBY GOV/REL GP/REL INGP/REL OWN PERSON...BIBLIOG 20 TVA CONGRESS WATER. PAGE 62 F1229
SEA CONTROL NAT/G INDUS

B61
LEE R.R.,ENGINEERING-ECONOMIC PLANNING MISCELLANEOUS SUBJECTS: A SELECTED BIBLIOGRAPHY (MIMEOGRAPHED). FINAN LOC/G NEIGH ADMIN CONTROL INGP/REL HABITAT...GEOG MGT SOC/WK MUNICH 20 RESOURCE/N. PAGE 77 F1509
BIBLIOG/A PLAN REGION

B61
ROEPKE W.,JENSEITS VON ANGEBOT UND NACHFRAGE (DRITTE VERAENDERTE AUFLAGE). WOR+45 MARKET TEC/DEV ECO/TAC GP/REL INGP/REL NEW/LIB...POLICY SOC IDEA/COMP PERS/COMP 20. PAGE 113 F2233
SOCIETY STRANGE ECO/DEV STRUCT

B61
STROUD G.S.,LABOR HISTORY IN THE UNITED STATES: A GENERAL BIBLIOGRAPHY. USA+45 USA-45 STRATA VOL/ASSN AUTOMAT GP/REL INGP/REL ATTIT HEALTH 18/20. PAGE 127 F2504
BIBLIOG WORKER LABOR

B61
WEISBROD B.A.,ECONOMICS OF PUBLIC HEALTH. USA+45 INGP/REL HABITAT...POLICY STAT COSTS 20. PAGE 145 F2851
SOCIETY HEALTH NEW/IDEA ECO/DEV

N61
US ADVISORY COMM INTERGOV REL,STATE AND LOCAL TAXATION ON PRIVATELY OWNED PROPERTY LOCATED ON FEDERAL AREAS: PROPOSED AMENDMENT OF BUCK ACT (PAMPHLET). USA+45 ACT/RES PLAN CONTROL GOV/REL INGP/REL OWN...POLICY JURID CHARTS GP/COMP 20. PAGE 133 F2629
PROVS LOC/G NAT/G TAX

B62
COX O.C.,CAPITALISM AND AMERICAN LEADERSHIP. WOR+45 WOR-45 STRATA INDUS SECT INT/TRADE EXEC INGP/REL RACE/REL RATIONAL PWR WEALTH. PAGE 28 F0548
CAP/ISM LEAD ECO/DEV SOCIETY

B62
GALENSON W.,TRADE UNIONS MONOGRAPH SERIES (A SERIES OF NINE TEXTS). DELIB/GP LEAD PARTIC...DECISION ORG/CHARTS. PAGE 45 F0887
LABOR INGP/REL CONSTN REPRESENT

B62
HARRINGTON M.,THE RETAIL CLERKS. ECO/TAC LEAD PARTIC CHOOSE GP/REL INGP/REL CENTRAL POLICY. PAGE 55 F1087
LABOR SERV/IND STRUCT DELIB/GP

B62
HARRIS S.E.,THE ECONOMICS OF THE POLITICAL PARTIES. USA+45 FINAN CHIEF ACT/RES PLAN BUDGET GP/REL INGP/REL NEW/LIB...IDEA/COMP PERS/COMP 20 EISNHWR/DD KENNEDY/JF. PAGE 56 F1090
POLICY ECO/DEV NAT/G POL/PAR

B62
INTERNAT CONGRESS OF JURISTS,EXECUTIVE ACTION AND THE RULE OF RULE: REPORTION PROCEEDINGS OF INT'T CONGRESS OF JURISTS,-RIO DE JANEIRO, BRAZIL. WOR+45 ACADEM CONSULT JUDGE EDU/PROP ADJUD CT/SYS INGP/REL PERSON DEPT/DEFEN. PAGE 64 F1269
JURID EXEC ORD/FREE CONTROL

B62
MULLER E.,DIE HEIMATVERTRIEBENEN IN BADEN-WURTTEMBERG. GERMANY/W AGRI INDUS LABOR PROVS SOC/INTEG 20 MIGRATION. PAGE 95 F1858
GP/REL INGP/REL

B62
SHERIF M.,INTERGROUP RELATIONS AND LEADERSHIP: APPROACHES AND RESEARCH IN INDUSTRIAL, ETHNIC, CULTURAL AND POLITICAL AREAS. CULTURE R+D LABOR DIPLOM GP/REL RACE/REL PERCEPT...PSY CONCPT. PAGE 121 F2377
LEAD REPRESENT PWR INGP/REL

L62
N,"UNION INVESTMENT IN BUSINESS: A SOURCE OF UNION CONFLICT OF INTEREST." LAW NAT/G LEGIS CONTROL GP/REL INGP/REL DECISION. PAGE 96 F1884
LABOR POLICY FINAN LG/CO

S62
READ W.H.,"UPWARD COMMUNICATION IN INDUSTRIAL HIERARCHIES." LG/CO TOP/EX PROB/SOLV DOMIN EXEC PERS/REL ATTIT DRIVE PERCEPT...CORREL STAT CHARTS 20. PAGE 110 F2159
ADMIN INGP/REL PSY MGT

B63
FRIEDRICH C.J.,MAN AND HIS GOVERNMENT: AN EMPIRICAL THEORY OF POLITICS. UNIV LOC/G NAT/G ADJUD REV INGP/REL DISCRIM PWR BIBLIOG. PAGE 44 F0867
PERSON ORD/FREE PARTIC CONTROL

B63
HUNTER A.,THE ECONOMICS OF AUSTRALIAN INDUSTRY. DIST/IND EXTR/IND FINAN PROC/MFG SERV/IND ACT/RES PLAN TARIFFS GP/REL INGP/REL 20 AUSTRAL. PAGE 63 F1245
INDUS ECO/DEV HABITAT GP/COMP

B63
NOMAD M.,POLITICAL HERETICS: FROM PLATO TO MAO TSE-TUNG. UNIV INGP/REL...SOC IDEA/COMP. PAGE 98 F1931
SOCIETY UTOPIA ALL/IDEOS CONCPT

L63
MCKERSIE R.B.,"NONPROFESSIONAL HOSPITAL WORKERS AND A UNION ORGANIZING DRIVE." PLAN GP/REL RACE/REL ATTIT DRIVE...CORREL STAT INT GP/COMP. PAGE 88 F1732
VOL/ASSN HEALTH INGP/REL LABOR

B64
AHMAD M.,THE CIVIL SERVANT IN PAKISTAN. PAKISTAN ECO/UNDEV COLONIAL INGP/REL...SOC CHARTS BIBLIOG 20 CIVIL/SERV. PAGE 3 F0051
WELF/ST ADMIN ATTIT STRATA

B64
ECONOMIDES C.P.,LE POUVOIR DE DECISION DES ORGANISATIONS INTERNATIONALES EUROPEENNES. DIPLOM DOMIN INGP/REL EFFICIENCY...INT/LAW JURID 20 NATO OEEC EEC COUNCL/EUR EURATOM. PAGE 36 F0698
INT/ORG PWR DECISION GP/COMP

B64
GRIFFITH W.E.,COMMUNISM IN EUROPE (2 VOLS.). CZECHOSLVK USSR WOR+45 WOR-45 YUGOSLAVIA INGP/REL MARXISM SOCISM...ANTHOL 20 EUROPE/E. PAGE 51 F1000
COM POL/PAR DIPLOM GOV/COMP

B64
HAAR C.M.,LAW AND LAND: ANGLO-AMERICAN PLANNING PRACTICE. UK USA+45 NAT/G TEC/DEV BUDGET CT/SYS INGP/REL EFFICIENCY OWN...JURID MUNICH 20. PAGE 52 F1019
LAW PLAN NAT/COMP

B64
NAGEL P.C.,ONE NATION INDIVISIBLE: THE UNION IN AMERICAN THOUGHT 1776-1861. USA-45 INDUS TEC/DEV EDU/PROP DREAM...IDEA/COMP 18/19. PAGE 96 F1887
FEDERAL NAT/G ATTIT INGP/REL

B64
REDLICH F.,THE GERMAN MILITARY ENTERPRISER AND HIS WORK FORCE. CHRIST-17C GERMANY ELITES SOCIETY FINAN ECO/TAC CIVMIL/REL GP/REL INGP/REL...HIST/WRIT METH/COMP 14/17. PAGE 110 F2170
EX/STRUC FORCES PROFIT WORKER

B64
SULTAN P.E.,THE DISENCHANTED UNIONIST. NAT/G ADJUD CONTROL SANCTION RACE/REL ANOMIE ATTIT ROLE ...METH/CNCPT INT. PAGE 127 F2512
LABOR INGP/REL CHARTS MAJORIT

S64
FYFE J.,"LIST OF CURRENT ACQUISITIONS OF
BIBLIOG

PERIODICALS AND NEWSPAPERS DEALING WITH THE SOVIET UNION AND EAST EUROPEAN COUNTRIES." USSR WRITING GP/REL INGP/REL MARXISM 20. PAGE 45 F0879 — COM EDU/PROP PRESS

B65
PHELPS E.S.,PRIVATE WANTS AND PUBLIC NEEDS - AN INTRODUCTION TO A CURRENT ISSUE OF PUBLIC POLICY (REV. ED.). USA+45 PLAN CAP/ISM INGP/REL ROLE ...DECISION TIME/SEQ 20. PAGE 106 F2081 — NAT/G POLICY DEMAND

B65
PLOSS S.I.,CONFLICT AND DECISION-MAKING IN SOVIET RUSSIA - A CASE STUDY OF AGRICULTURAL POLICY - 1953-1963. USSR DELIB/GP INGP/REL PWR MARXISM. PAGE 106 F2093 — AGRI DECISION ATTIT

B65
RIVKIN M.D.,AREA DEVELOPMENT FOR NATIONAL GROWTH; THE TURKISH PRECEDENT. ISLAM TURKEY ACT/RES INGP/REL...POLICY CHARTS GP/COMP MUNICH 20 ATATURK/MK INONU/I. PAGE 112 F2197 — ECO/UNDEV REGION ECO/TAC PLAN

B65
SHOSTAK A.B.,NEW PERSPECTIVES ON POVERTY. USA+45 SCHOOL WORKER INGP/REL RACE/REL AGE/C AGE/Y ATTIT HEALTH...ANTHOL BIBLIOG 20 JOHNSON/LB POVRTY/WAR. PAGE 121 F2388 — WEALTH NAT/G RECEIVE INCOME

B65
WALTON R.E.,A BEHAVIORAL THEORY OF LABOR NEGOTIATIONS: AN ANALYSIS OF A SOCIAL INTERACTION SYSTEM. USA+45 FINAN PROB/SOLV ECO/TAC GP/REL INGP/REL...DECISION BIBLIOG. PAGE 143 F2812 — SOC LABOR BARGAIN ADMIN

B65
WEISBROD B.A.,THE ECONOMICS OF POVERTY: AN AMERICAN PARADOX. USA+45 NAT/G WORKER TASK INGP/REL DISCRIM POLICY. PAGE 145 F2852 — ECO/DEV WEALTH RECEIVE STRATA

S65
KAUN D.E.,"THE FAIR LABOUR STANDARDS ACT: AN EVALUATION IN TERMS OF ITS STATED GOALS." SOUTH/AFR LAW LABOR BARGAIN PAY INGP/REL WEALTH 20. PAGE 69 F1364 — ECO/TAC PRICE WORKER LEGIS

S65
STEENKAMP W.F.J.,"THE PROBLEM OF WAGE REGULATION." SOUTH/AFR LAW ECO/DEV ECO/UNDEV LABOR NAT/G BARGAIN PAY INGP/REL DISCRIM WEALTH...METH/COMP 20. PAGE 125 F2473 — ECO/TAC PRICE WORKER RATION

B66
BAKKE E.W.,MUTUAL SURVIVAL; THE GOAL OF UNION AND MANAGEMENT (2ND ED.). USA+45 ELITES ECO/DEV ECO/TAC CONFER ADMIN REPRESENT GP/REL INGP/REL ATTIT ...GP/COMP 20. PAGE 8 F0155 — MGT LABOR BARGAIN INDUS

B66
BRODERSEN A.,THE SOVIET WORKER: LABOR AND GOVERNMENT IN SOVIET SOCIETY. USSR STRUCT INDUS LABOR PLAN PAY INGP/REL PRODUC...POLICY GEN/LAWS BIBLIOG 20 STALIN/J LENIN/VI BOLSHEVISM KHRUSH/N. PAGE 19 F0357 — WORKER ROLE NAT/G MARXISM

B66
KAESTNER K.,GESAMTWIRTSCHAFTLICHE PLANUNG IN EINER GEMISCHTEN WIRTSCHAFTSORDNUNG (WIRTSCHAFTSPOLITISCHE STUDIEN 5). GERMANY/W WOR+45 WOR-45 INDUS MARKET NAT/G ACT/RES GP/REL INGP/REL PRODUC...ECOMETRIC MGT BIBLIOG 20. PAGE 68 F1346 — ECO/TAC PLAN POLICY PREDICT

B66
RAYBACK J.G.,A HISTORY OF AMERICAN LABOR. USA+45 USA-45 ECO/DEV LEGIS COLONIAL WAR INGP/REL PWR WEALTH 17/20. PAGE 110 F2156 — LABOR LOBBY ECO/UNDEV NAT/G

B66
REDFORD E.S.,THE ROLE OF GOVERNMENT IN THE AMERICAN ECONOMY. USA+45 USA-45 FINAN INDUS LG/CO PROB/SOLV ADMIN INGP/REL INCOME PRODUC 18/20. PAGE 110 F2169 — NAT/G ECO/DEV CAP/ISM ECO/TAC

B66
THOMPSON J.H.,MODERNIZATION OF THE ARAB WORLD. FUT ISRAEL STRUCT ECO/UNDEV DIPLOM INGP/REL ATTIT ...CENSUS ANTHOL 20 ARABS. PAGE 130 F2565 — ADJUST ISLAM PROB/SOLV NAT/COMP

S66
FLEMING W.G.,"AUTHORITY, EFFICIENCY, AND ROLE STRESS: PROBLEMS IN THE DEVELOPMENT OF EAST AFRICAN BUREAUCRACIES." AFR UGANDA STRUCT PROB/SOLV ROUTINE INGP/REL ROLE...MGT SOC GP/COMP GOV/COMP 20 TANGANYIKA AFRICA/E. PAGE 41 F0810 — DOMIN EFFICIENCY COLONIAL ADMIN

B67
BANFIELD E.C.,THE MORAL BASIS OF A BACKWARD SOCIETY. EUR+WWI ITALY STRATA NEIGH PARTIC INGP/REL ...SOC QU PREDICT TREND HYPO/EXP MUNICH 20. PAGE 9 F0173 — MORAL WEALTH ATTIT

B67
BERGMANN D KAUN B.,STRUCTURAL UNEMPLOYMENT IN THE UNITED STATES. USA+45 ECO/DEV PRICE ADMIN INGP/REL DEMAND EQUILIB WEALTH...MATH REGRESS STAT 20 NEGRO. PAGE 13 F0258 — ECOMETRIC METH WORKER ECO/TAC

B67
BUREAU NATIONAL AFFAIRS,LABOR RELATIONS REFERENCE MANUAL VOL. 63. USA+45 CONSTN ECO/DEV PROVS WORKER DEBATE INGP/REL...DECISION 20. PAGE 20 F0385 — LABOR ADJUD CT/SYS NAT/G

B67
COWLING M.,1867 DISRAELI, GLADSTONE, AND REVOLUTION; THE PASSING OF THE SECOND REFORM BILL. UK LEGIS LEAD LOBBY GP/REL INGP/REL...DECISION BIBLIOG 19 REFORMERS. PAGE 28 F0545 — PARL/PROC POL/PAR ATTIT LAW

B67
ESTEY M.,THE UNIONS: STRUCTURE, DEVELOPMENT, AND MANAGEMENT. FUT USA+45 ADJUD CONTROL INGP/REL DRIVE ...DECISION T 20 AFL/CIO. PAGE 38 F0750 — LABOR EX/STRUC ADMIN GOV/REL

B67
NYOMARKAY J.,CHARISMA AND FACTIONALISM IN THE NAZI PARTY. GERMANY POL/PAR LEGIT LEAD MARXISM ...NEW/IDEA METH/COMP GEN/LAWS BIBLIOG 20 HITLER/A. PAGE 99 F1949 — FASCISM INGP/REL CHIEF PWR

B67
POLLACK N.,THE POPULIST MIND. USA-45 STRATA AGRI NAT/G POL/PAR LEGIS WORKER RACE/REL WEALTH...ANTHOL BIBLIOG 19 NEGRO. PAGE 107 F2097 — POPULISM HIST/WRIT ATTIT INGP/REL

B67
SCOTT J.C.,ANTITRUST AND TRADE REGULATION TODAY: 1967. USA+45 MARKET LG/CO DELIB/GP LEGIS CAP/ISM INT/TRADE TAX PRICE INGP/REL WEALTH 20 SUPREME/CT. PAGE 118 F2334 — NAT/G INDUS CONTROL JURID

B67
US CONGRESS JOINT ECO COMM,AN ECONOMIC PROFILE OF MAINLAND CHINA, VOLUMES I AND II. CHINA/COM AGRI DIST/IND FINAN INDUS LABOR FORCES ACT/RES PLAN INT/TRADE INGP/REL BAL/PAY 20 CONGRESS. PAGE 135 F2664 — ECO/UNDEV WEALTH ECO/TAC DELIB/GP

B67
VAN SLYKE L.P.,ENEMIES AND FRIENDS; THE UNITED FRONT IN CHINESE COMMUNIST HISTORY. CHINA/COM SOCIETY FORCES PLAN ADJUST 20 MAO. PAGE 140 F2764 — INGP/REL MARXISM ATTIT GP/REL

S67
"THE SIERRA CLUB, POLITICAL ACTIVITY, AND TAX EXEMPT CHARITABLE STATUS." USA+45 LAW VOL/ASSN TAX PAY ADJUD LOBBY INGP/REL HABITAT 20. PAGE 2 F0027 — ELITES GOV/REL FACE/GP ORD/FREE

S67
ALEXANDER R.J.,"'THIRD FORCE' IN WORLD COMMUNISM?" CHINA/COM CUBA USSR INT/ORG DIPLOM TASK INGP/REL ATTIT PWR 20 CASTRO/F. PAGE 3 F0060 — CHIEF MARXISM LEAD REV

S67
BENNETT J.T.,"POLITICAL IMPLICATIONS OF ECONOMIC CHANGE: SOUTH VIETNAM." VIETNAM/S INGP/REL INCOME ATTIT 20 AID. PAGE 13 F0247 — ECO/UNDEV INDUS AGRI PRODUC

S67
FEDYSHYN O.S.,"KHRUSHCHEV'S 'LEAP FORWARD': NATIONAL ASSIMILATION IN THE USSR AFTER STALIN." USSR PLAN NAT/LISM PERSON...POLICY 20 KHRUSH/N STALIN/J. PAGE 39 F0771 — GP/REL INGP/REL MARXISM METH

S67
FLOYD D.,"FIFTH AMENDMENT RIGHT TO COUNSEL IN FEDERAL INCOME TAX INVESTIGATIONS." USA+45 LAW OP/RES INGP/REL. PAGE 42 F0818 — JURID CT/SYS TAX CONSULT

S67
FRANKLIN N.N.,"THE CONCEPT AND MEASUREMENT OF 'MINIMUM LIVING STANDARDS'." UNIV OP/RES PAY INGP/REL DEMAND INCOME DRIVE WEALTH...SOC CHARTS METH/COMP. PAGE 43 F0849 — CONCPT PHIL/SCI ALL/VALS HAPPINESS

S67
HERRERA F.,"EUROPEAN PARTICIPATION IN THE LATIN AMERICAN REGIONAL INTEGRATION" EUR+WWI L/A+17C GP/REL INGP/REL 20. PAGE 59 F1154 — DIPLOM REGION INT/ORG FINAN

S67
HUTCHINGS R.,"THE ENDING OF UNEMPLOYMENT IN THE USSR" USSR PLAN ECO/TAC PRICE INGP/REL...GEOG STAT CHARTS 20 MIGRATION. PAGE 63 F1247 — WORKER AGRI INDUS MARXISM

S67
ROY E.V.,"AN INTERPRETATION OF NORTHERN THAI PEASANT ECONOMY." THAILAND CLIENT CULTURE AGRI PROC/MFG FACE/GP DEMAND INCOME 20. PAGE 114 F2254 — STRUCT STRATA ECO/UNDEV INGP/REL

S67
SCOVILLE W.J.,"GOVERNMENT REGULATION AND GROWTH IN THE FRENCH PAPER INDUSTRY DURING THE EIGHTEENTH CENTURY." FRANCE MOD/EUR FINAN CAP/ISM TAX ADMIN CONTROL PRIVIL LAISSEZ...POLICY 18. PAGE 118 F2337 — NAT/G PROC/MFG ECO/DEV INGP/REL

B96
SCHMOLLER G.,THE MERCANTILE SYSTEM AND ITS HISTORICAL SIGNIFICANCE: ILLUSTRATED CHIEFLY FROM PRUSSIAN HISTORY (TRANS.). PRUSSIA CULTURE INDUS KIN NAT/G PROVS OP/RES ECO/TAC INT/TRADE SUPEGO PWR WEALTH MUNICH 19 MERCANTLST. PAGE 117 F2302 — GEN/METH INGP/REL CONCPT

INGRAM J.C. F1265

INNIS/H....HAROLD ADAMS INNIS

INNOVATION....SEE CREATE

INONU/I....ISMET INONU

B65
RIVKIN M.D.,AREA DEVELOPMENT FOR NATIONAL GROWTH; THE TURKISH PRECEDENT. ISLAM TURKEY ACT/RES INGP/REL...POLICY CHARTS GP/COMP MUNICH 20 ATATURK/MK INONU/I. PAGE 112 F2197
ECO/UNDEV REGION ECO/TAC PLAN

INSPECT....EXAMINING FOR QUALITY, OUTPUT, LEGALITY

N19
HACKETT J.,ECONOMIC PLANNING IN FRANCE; ITS RELATION TO THE POLICIES OF THE DEVELOPED COUNTRIES OF WESTERN EUROPE (PAMPHLET). EUR+WWI FRANCE ECO/DEV PROB/SOLV CONTROL...POLICY 20 EUROPE/W. PAGE 52 F1026
ECO/TAC NAT/G PLAN INSPECT

N19
LAWRENCE S.A.,THE BATTERY ADDITIVE CONTROVERSY (PAMPHLET). USA+45 LAW MARKET PROC/MFG R+D CAP/ISM CT/SYS GOV/REL OWN FTC CONGRESS BUR/STNDRD RITCHIE/JM. PAGE 76 F1494
PHIL/SCI LOBBY INSPECT

B37
MACKENZIE F.,PLANNED SOCIETY: YESTERDAY, TODAY, AND TOMORROW. ECO/DEV ECO/UNDEV AGRI FINAN INDUS PLAN INSPECT CONTROL ALL/IDEOS...TREND METH/COMP BIBLIOG 20 RESOURCE/N. PAGE 83 F1635
SOC CONCPT ANTHOL

C43
BENTHAM J.,"THE RATIONALE OF REWARD" IN J. BOWRING, ED., THE WORKS OF JEREMY BENTHAM (VOL. 2)" LAW WORKER CREATE INSPECT PAY ROUTINE HAPPINESS PRODUC SUPEGO WEALTH METH/CNCPT. PAGE 13 F0254
SANCTION ECO/TAC INCOME PWR

B51
PETERSON F.,SURVEY OF LABOR ECONOMICS (REV. ED.). STRATA ECO/DEV LABOR INSPECT BARGAIN PAY PRICE EXEC ROUTINE GP/REL ALL/VALS ORD/FREE 20 AFL/CIO DEPT/LABOR. PAGE 105 F2069
WORKER DEMAND IDEA/COMP T

B51
US HOUSE COMM APPROPRIATIONS,MUTUAL SECURITY PROGRAM APPROPRIATIONS FOR 1952: HEARINGS BEFORE A SUBCOMMITTEE OF THE COMMITTEE ON APPROPRIATIONS. AFR KOREA L/A+17C ECO/DEV ECO/UNDEV INT/ORG INSPECT BAL/PWR DIPLOM DEBATE WAR...POLICY STAT ASIA/S 20 CONGRESS NATO MID/EAST. PAGE 136 F2686
LEGIS FORCES BUDGET FOR/AID

S53
GABLE R.W.,"NAM: INFLUENTIAL LOBBY OR KISS OF DEATH?" (BMR)" USA+45 LAW INSPECT EDU/PROP ADMIN CONTROL INGP/REL EFFICIENCY PWR 20 CONGRESS NAM TAFT/HART. PAGE 45 F0880
LOBBY LEGIS INDUS LG/CO

B58
ATOMIC INDUSTRIAL FORUM,MANAGEMENT AND ATOMIC ENERGY. WOR+45 SEA LAW MARKET NAT/G TEC/DEV INSPECT INT/TRADE CONFER PEACE HEALTH...ANTHOL 20. PAGE 7 F0136
NUC/PWR INDUS MGT ECO/TAC

B58
HENNING C.N.,INTERNATIONAL FINANCING. WOR+45 ECO/DEV INT/ORG EX/STRUC INSPECT CAP/ISM BAL/PAY COST PROFIT...MGT CHARTS T 20. PAGE 58 F1150
FINAN DIPLOM INT/TRADE

S58
SCHUMM S.,"INTEREST REPRESENTATION IN FRANCE AND GERMANY." EUR+WWI FRANCE GERMANY INSPECT PARL/PROC REPRESENT 20 WEIMAR/REP. PAGE 118 F2320
LOBBY DELIB/GP NAT/G

B59
US HOUSE COMM GOVT OPERATIONS,UNITED STATES AID OPERATIONS IN LAOS. LAOS USA+45 PLAN INSPECT HOUSE/REP. PAGE 137 F2697
FOR/AID ADMIN FORCES ECO/UNDEV

B64
MARSH D.C.,THE FUTURE OF THE WELFARE STATE. UK CONSTN NAT/G POL/PAR...POLICY WELF/ST 20. PAGE 86 F1676
NEW/LIB ADMIN CONCPT INSPECT

B65
STEINER G.A.,THE CREATIVE ORGANIZATION. ELITES LG/CO PLAN PROB/SOLV TEC/DEV INSPECT CAP/ISM CONTROL EXEC PERSON...METH/COMP HYPO/EXP 20. PAGE 126 F2476
CREATE MGT ADMIN SOC

B66
CHASE S.B. JR.,PROBLEMS IN PUBLIC EXPENDITURE ANALYSIS. DIST/IND INDUS OP/RES PLAN BUDGET RECEIVE PRICE RISK COST INCOME...CHARTS ANTHOL 20. PAGE 23 F0455
ECO/DEV FINAN NAT/G INSPECT

B66
MACBEAN A.I.,EXPORT INSTABILITY AND ECONOMIC DEVELOPMENT. CHILE PAKISTAN PUERT/RICO TANZANIA UGANDA WOR+45 MARKET ECO/TAC...POLICY REGRESS CHARTS BIBLIOG TIME 20. PAGE 83 F1622
INT/TRADE ECO/UNDEV ECOMETRIC INSPECT

B66
US SENATE COMM APPROPRIATIONS,FOREIGN ASSISTANCE AND RELATED AGENCIES APPROPRIATIONS FOR FISCAL YEAR 1967: HEARINGS... ON H. R. 17788. ECO/UNDEV INT/ORG FORCES INSPECT ECO/TAC GIVE DEBATE WEAPON CIVMIL/REL WEALTH...INT 20 CONGRESS DEPT/DEFEN DEPT/STATE DEPT/HEW AID. PAGE 138 F2727
BUDGET FOR/AID DIPLOM COST

B67
GIAP V.N.,BIG VICTORY, GREAT TASK. VIETNAM WOR+45 FORCES PLAN DOMIN LEGIT RISK PEACE 20. PAGE 47 F0921
WAR LEAD ATTIT INSPECT

B67
LEIBY J.,CHARITY AND CORRECTION IN JERSEY; A HISTORY OF STATE WELFARE INSTITUTIONS. DELIB/GP EX/STRUC PROB/SOLV INSPECT LEAD ADJUST HEALTH ...POLICY PSY NEW/JERSEY. PAGE 77 F1514
PROVS PUB/INST ADMIN

S67
BELL D.E.,"THE QUALITY OF AID." USA+45 R+D DIPLOM GP/REL. PAGE 12 F0234
POLICY FOR/AID PROB/SOLV INSPECT

INSTITUTION, EDUCATIONAL....SEE SCHOOL, ACADEM

INSTITUTION, MENTAL....SEE PUB/INST

INSTITUTION, RELIGIOUS....SEE SECT

INSTITUTIONS....SEE DESCRIPTORS IN INSTITUTIONAL INDEX (TOPICAL INDEX, NO. 2)

INSURANCE....SEE FINAN, SERV/IND

INSURRECTION....SEE REV

INT....INTERVIEW; SEE ALSO INTERVIEWS INDEX, P. XIV

B35
STALEY E.,WAR AND THE PRIVATE INVESTOR. UNIV WOR-45 INTELL SOCIETY INT/ORG NAT/G TOP/EX CAP/ISM ECO/TAC WAR ATTIT ALL/VALS...INT TIME/SEQ TREND CON/ANAL WORK TOT/POP 20. PAGE 125 F2464
FINAN INT/TRADE DIPLOM

B48
WHYTE W.F.,HUMAN RELATIONS IN THE RESTAURANT INDUSTRY (1ST ED). CLIENT WORKER WAR ATTIT...MGT OBS INT. PAGE 146 F2874
INGP/REL GP/REL SERV/IND LABOR

B50
ADORNO T.W.,THE AUTHORITARIAN PERSONALITY. STRATA SECT PROB/SOLV ECO/TAC DISCRIM ATTIT SEX...SOC INT CHARTS METH 20. PAGE 3 F0044
AUTHORIT PERSON ALL/IDEOS SOCIETY

B52
ROSE A.M.,UNION SOLIDARITY: THE INTERNAL COHESION OF A LABOR UNION. SECT GP/REL RACE/REL ATTIT ROLE HEALTH WEALTH...INT QU. PAGE 114 F2241
LABOR INGP/REL PARTIC SUPEGO

S52
CHINOY E.,"THE TRADITION OF OPPORTUNITY AND THE ASPIRATIONS OF AUTOMOBILE WORKERS" (BMR)" STRATA ACT/RES ALL/VALS SKILL...INT 20. PAGE 24 F0468
WORKER ECO/DEV DRIVE INDUS

B53
BOULDING K.E.,THE ORGANIZATIONAL REVOLUTION. FUT CULTURE ECO/DEV LABOR PROF/ORG ECO/TAC MORAL...SOC CONCPT RECORD INT SOC/EXP 20. PAGE 17 F0321
SOCIETY TREND

B53
PURCELL T.V.,THE WORKER SPEAKS HIS MIND ON COMPANY AND UNION. WORKER ADJUD LEAD RACE/REL ATTIT DRIVE MARXISM...MGT CLASSIF STAT OBS INT SAMP BIBLIOG. PAGE 108 F2131
LABOR PARTIC INGP/REL HAPPINESS

B56
LIPSET S.M.,UNION DEMOCRACY. STRUCT INDUS FACE/GP WORKER CONTROL LEAD PARTIC GP/REL ATTIT LAISSEZ ...INT QU CHARTS. PAGE 80 F1577
LABOR INGP/REL MAJORIT

S56
BONILLA F.,"WHEN IS PETITION 'PRESSURE?'" (BMR)" USA+45 ELITES INDUS LABOR CHIEF EDU/PROP LEGIT ATTIT...INT CHARTS 20 CONGRESS PRESIDENT EISNHWR/DD. PAGE 16 F0312
LEGIS EX/STRUC INT/TRADE TARIFFS

S56
KNAPP D.C.,"CONGRESSIONAL CONTROL OF AGRICULTURAL CONSERVATION POLICY: A CASE STUDY OF THE APPROPRIATIONS PROCESS." DELIB/GP PLAN PROB/SOLV CONFER PARL/PROC...POLICY INT CONGRESS. PAGE 72 F1411
LEGIS AGRI BUDGET CONTROL

S56
MYERS C.A.,"LINE AND STAFF IN INDUSTRIAL RELATIONS." INDUS LABOR GP/REL PWR...MGT INT. PAGE 96 F1876
ROLE PROB/SOLV ADMIN CONSULT

B57
EHRMANN H.W.,ORGANIZED BUSINESS IN FRANCE. EUR+WWI MOD/EUR ECO/DEV VOL/ASSN LEGIT ATTIT PERCEPT PWR RESPECT...PLURIST SOC INT TOT/POP 20. PAGE 36 F0712
PROF/ORG ECO/TAC FRANCE

B59
DIEBOLD W. JR.,THE SCHUMAN PLAN: A STUDY IN ECONOMIC COOPERATION, 1950-1959. EUR+WWI FRANCE GERMANY USA+45 EXTR/IND CONSULT DELIB/GP PLAN DIPLOM ECO/TAC INT/TRADE ROUTINE ORD/FREE WEALTH ...METH/CNCPT STAT CONT/OBS INT TIME/SEQ ECSC 20. PAGE 33 F0635
INT/ORG REGION

B59

HOOVER C.B.,THE ECONOMY, LIBERTY AND THE STATE. COM EUR+WWI USA+45 USA-45 USSR CAP/ISM EDU/PROP COERCE TOTALISM ORD/FREE...POLICY OBS INT TREND NAZI 20. PAGE 61 F1206 ECO/DEV ECO/TAC

S60

FORM W.H.,"ORGANIZED LABOR'S IMAGE OF COMMUNITY POWER STRUCTURE." LABOR LG/CO CONTROL LEAD REPRESENT...DECISION METH/CNCPT INT QU SAMP. PAGE 42 F0829 NEIGH PARTIC PWR GP/REL

B61

DUKE UNIVERSITY,EXPULSION OR OPPRESSION OF BUSINESS ASSOCIATES: "SQUEEZE-OUTS" IN SMALL ENTERPRISES. LAW CONTROL PARTIC COERCE INGP/REL...POLICY RECORD INT. PAGE 35 F0674 PWR MGT SML/CO ECO/TAC

B61

HEMPSTONE S.,THE NEW AFRICA. AGRI INDUS KIN NAT/G COLONIAL MARXISM...SOC INT TREND NAT/COMP BIBLIOG/A 20. PAGE 58 F1146 AFR ORD/FREE PERSON CULTURE

B61

LENSKI G.,THE RELIGIOUS FACTOR: A SOCIOLOGICAL STUDY OF RELIGION'S IMPACT ON POLITICS, ECONOMICS, AND FAMILY LIFE. FAM PROF/ORG EDU/PROP ROLE CATHISM ...INT SAMP MUNICH. PAGE 78 F1524 SECT GP/REL

B62

KAUTSKY J.H.,POLITICAL CHANGE IN UNDERDEVELOPED COUNTRIES: NATIONALISM AND COMMUNISM. WOR+45 AGRI TEC/DEV EDU/PROP ATTIT...POLICY METH/CNCPT STYLE INT QU CENSUS TREND SOC/EXP GEN/LAWS 20. PAGE 69 F1365 ECO/UNDEV SOCIETY CAP/ISM REV

S62

MUELLER E.,"LOCATION DECISIONS OF MANUFACTURERS." USA+45 MARKET ATTIT...POLICY STAT INT CHARTS 20. PAGE 94 F1852 DECISION PROC/MFG GEOG TOP/EX

B63

BAUER R.A.,AMERICAN BUSINESS AND PUBLIC POLICY: THE POLITICS OF FOREIGN TRADE. USA+45 COM/IND LG/CO NAT/G PROF/ORG SML/CO VOL/ASSN LEGIS TOP/EX ECO/TAC EDU/PROP CHOOSE HEALTH PWR WEALTH...CONCPT METH/CNCPT OBS INT QU SAMP FOR/TRADE TRUE/GP VAL/FREE HI. PAGE 11 F0217 ECO/DEV ATTIT

B63

DEUTSCH K.W.,THE POLITICAL ROLE OF LABOR IN DEVELOPING COUNTRIES. AFR ASIA S/ASIA USA+45 WOR+45 ECO/UNDEV POL/PAR ECO/TAC EDU/PROP LEGIT COERCE ORD/FREE PWR WEALTH...OBS INT TREND VAL/FREE 20. PAGE 32 F0625 LABOR NAT/LISM

B63

GEERTZ C.,PEDDLERS AND PRINCES: SOCIAL DEVELOPMENT AND ECONOMIC CHANGE IN TWO INDONESIAN TOWNS. S/ASIA CULTURE SOCIETY STRATA FACE/GP CREATE TEC/DEV ECO/TAC ORD/FREE WEALTH...OBS INT CENSUS CHARTS WORK TOT/POP METH/GP TERR/GP VAL/FREE 20 MUNICH. PAGE 47 F0913 ECO/UNDEV SOC ELITES INDONESIA

B63

RILEY J.W. JR.,THE CORPORATION AND ITS PUBLICS. ESSAYS ON THE CORPORATE IMAGE. CLIENT ISOLAT AGE ATTIT...POLICY SOC METH/CNCPT INT. PAGE 111 F2193 LG/CO CLASSIF GP/REL NEIGH

B63

US BD GOVERNORS FEDL RESRV,THE FEDERAL RESERVE AND THE TREASURY. USA+45 WORKER PROB/SOLV PRICE COST DEMAND WEALTH...STAT INT CHARTS 20 FED/RESERV DEPT/TREAS. PAGE 134 F2641 FINAN GOV/REL CONTROL BUDGET

B63

WIGHTMAN D.,TOWARD ECONOMIC CO-OPERATION IN ASIA. ASIA S/ASIA VOL/ASSN ACT/RES PLAN TEC/DEV ECO/TAC EDU/PROP RIGID/FLEX SKILL...POLICY METH/CNCPT OBS INT GEN/LAWS UN 20 ECAFE. PAGE 146 F2877 ECO/UNDEV CREATE

L63

MCKERSIE R.B.,"NONPROFESSIONAL HOSPITAL WORKERS AND A UNION ORGANIZING DRIVE." PLAN GP/REL RACE/REL ATTIT DRIVE...CORREL STAT INT GP/COMP. PAGE 88 F1732 VOL/ASSN HEALTH INGP/REL LABOR

B64

FRIEDEN B.J.,THE FUTURE OF OLD NEIGHBORHOODS: REBUILDING FOR A CHANGING POPULATION. CONSTRUC LOC/G NAT/G ACT/RES ECO/TAC REGION ATTIT...INT SAMP MUNICH 20 NEWYORK/C LOS/ANG HARTFORD URBAN/RNWL. PAGE 44 F0855 NEIGH PROB/SOLV PLAN BUDGET

B64

SULLIVAN G.,THE STORY OF THE PEACE CORPS. USA+45 WOR+45 INTELL FACE/GP NAT/G SCHOOL VOL/ASSN CONSULT EX/STRUC PLAN EDU/PROP ADMIN ATTIT DRIVE ALL/VALS ...POLICY HEAL SOC CONCPT INT QU BIOG TREND SOC/EXP WORK. PAGE 127 F2511 INT/ORG ECO/UNDEV FOR/AID PEACE

B64

SULTAN P.E.,THE DISENCHANTED UNIONIST. NAT/G ADJUD CONTROL SANCTION RACE/REL ANOMIE ATTIT ROLE ...METH/CNCPT INT. PAGE 127 F2512 LABOR INGP/REL CHARTS MAJORIT

B64

US CONGRESS JOINT ECO COMM,PRIVATE INVESTMENT IN LATIN AMERICA. L/A+17C USA+45 INT/ORG PROB/SOLV ECO/TAC ATTIT...INT 20 CONGRESS. PAGE 135 F2658 FINAN ECO/UNDEV PARL/PROC LEGIS

B65

GREER S.,URBAN RENEWAL AND AMERICAN CITIES: THE DILEMMA OF DEMOCRATIC INTERVENTION. USA+45 R+D LOC/G VOL/ASSN ACT/RES BUDGET ADMIN GOV/REL...SOC INT SAMP MUNICH 20 BOSTON CHICAGO LOS/ANG MIAMI URBAN/RNWL. PAGE 51 F0992 PROB/SOLV PLAN NAT/G

B65

RUEFF J.,THE ROLE AND THE RULE OF GOLD: AN ARGUMENT (PAMPHLET). AFR FRANCE USA+45 WOR+45 MARKET NAT/G PLAN DIPLOM ATTIT...POLICY INT 20 DEGAULLE/C. PAGE 115 F2258 FINAN ECO/DEV INT/TRADE BAL/PAY

L65

HAMMOND A.,"COMPREHENSIVE VERSUS INCREMENTAL BUDGETING IN THE DEPARTMENT OF AGRICULTURE" USA+45 GP/REL ATTIT...PSY INT 20 DEPT/AGRI. PAGE 54 F1057 TOP/EX EX/STRUC AGRI BUDGET

S65

DUMONT R.,"SURPEUPLEMENT CHINOIS ET SES CONSEQUENCES." AFR ECO/UNDEV AGRI PLAN PROB/SOLV ECO/TAC FOR/AID NUC/PWR...OBS INT PREDICT. PAGE 35 F0675 GEOG ASIA STAT

B66

DAVIES JC I.I.I.,NEIGHBORHOOD GROUPS AND URBAN RENEWAL. USA+45 PLAN LOBBY PARTIC CHOOSE RACE/REL ...POLICY DECISION SOC INT MUNICH SOC/INTEG 20 NEWYORK/C. PAGE 30 F0586 NEIGH CREATE PROB/SOLV

B66

POLK J.,U S PRODUCTION ABROAD AND THE BALANCE OF PAYMENTS* A SURVEY OF CORPORATE INVESTMENT EXPERIENCE. USA+45 SERV/IND NAT/G OP/RES COST PROFIT ATTIT...ECOMETRIC STAT INT QU GEN/METH. PAGE 107 F2096 BAL/PAY FINAN INT/TRADE INDUS

B66

US SENATE COMM APPROPRIATIONS,FOREIGN ASSISTANCE AND RELATED AGENCIES APPROPRIATIONS FOR FISCAL YEAR 1967: HEARINGS... ON H. R. 17788. ECO/UNDEV INT/ORG FORCES INSPECT ECO/TAC GIVE DEBATE WEAPON CIVMIL/REL WEALTH...INT 20 CONGRESS DEPT/DEFEN DEPT/STATE DEPT/HEW AID. PAGE 138 F2727 BUDGET FOR/AID DIPLOM COST

S66

FELD W.,"NATIONAL ECONOMIC INTEREST GROUPS AND POLICY FORMATION IN THE EEC." NAT/G POL/PAR REGION CENTRAL SOVEREIGN...INT NET/THEORY EEC. PAGE 40 F0777 LOBBY ELITES DECISION

B67

BIBBY J.,ON CAPITOL HILL. POL/PAR LOBBY PARL/PROC GOV/REL PERS/REL...JURID PHIL/SCI OBS INT BIBLIOG 20 CONGRESS PRESIDENT. PAGE 15 F0278 CONFER LEGIS CREATE LEAD

B67

JACOBY N.H.,US AID TO TAIWAN. CAP/ISM DIPLOM FEEDBACK COST PRODUC...OBS INT CHARTS 20. PAGE 66 F1301 FOR/AID OP/RES ECO/TAC ECO/UNDEV

B67

JHANGIANI M.A.,JANA SANGH AND SWATANTRA: A PROFILE OF THE RIGHTIST PARTIES IN INDIA. INDIA ADMIN CHOOSE MARXISM SOCISM...INT CHARTS BIBLIOG 20. PAGE 67 F1320 POL/PAR LAISSEZ NAT/LISM ATTIT

B67

PETRO S.,THE KINGSPORT STRIKE. USA+45 PROC/MFG NAT/G JUDGE PRESS PARTIC PERS/REL...OLD/LIB OBS INT 20 NLRB. PAGE 105 F2074 LABOR COERCE SANCTION ALL/VALS

B67

SCHAEFER W.V.,THE SUSPECT AND SOCIETY: CRIMINAL PROCEDURE AND CONVERGING CONSTITUTIONAL DOCTRINES. USA+45 TEC/DEV LOBBY ROUTINE SANCTION...INT 20. PAGE 116 F2288 CRIME FORCES CONSTN JURID

S67

BENN W.,"TECHNOLOGY HAS AN INEXORABLE EFFECT." FUT UK ECO/DEV INT/ORG CONSULT PLAN EDU/PROP ADMIN LEAD GP/REL PRODUC...INT 20 EEC. PAGE 13 F0246 R+D LG/CO TEC/DEV INDUS

S67

GRUN C.,"DEUX ETUDES ALLEMANDES SUR LES PREJUGES NATIONAUX ET LES MOYENS DE LES COMBATTRE." FRANCE GERMANY DIST/IND PROB/SOLV GP/REL AGE/Y RIGID/FLEX ...PSY STAT INT SAMP. PAGE 52 F1010 ATTIT REGION DISCRIM STERTYP

S67

JENCKS C.E.,"COAL MINERS IN BRITAIN SINCE NATIONALIZATION." UK LABOR GP/REL ADJUST SOCISM ...INT 20. PAGE 67 F1311 EXTR/IND WORKER STRATA ATTIT

INT. BANK RECONSTR. DEVELOP. F1266

INT/AM/DEV....INTER-AMERICAN DEVELOPMENT BANK

B62

ROUND TABLE ON EUROPE'S ROLE IN LATIN AMERICAN DEVELOPMENT. EUR+WWI L/A+17C PLAN BAL/PAY UTIL ROLE WEALTH...CHARTS ANTHOL 20 UN INT/AM/DEV. PAGE 1 F0017 ECO/UNDEV FINAN TEC/DEV FOR/AID

INT/AVIATN....INTERNATIONAL CIVIL AVIATION ORGANIZATION

INT/LAW....INTERNATIONAL LAW

B03
MOREL E.D.,THE BRITISH CASE IN FRENCH CONGO. CONGO/BRAZ FRANCE UK COERCE MORAL WEALTH...POLICY INT/LAW 20 CONGO/LEOP. PAGE 93 F1827
DIPLOM INT/TRADE COLONIAL AFR

B24
HOLDSWORTH W.S.,A HISTORY OF ENGLISH LAW; THE COMMON LAW AND ITS RIVALS (VOL. IV). UK SEA AGRI CHIEF ADJUD CONTROL CRIME GOV/REL...INT/LAW JURID NAT/COMP 16/17 PARLIAMENT COMMON/LAW CANON/LAW ENGLSH/LAW. PAGE 61 F1195
LAW LEGIS CT/SYS CONSTN

B47
GORDON D.L.,THE HIDDEN WEAPON: THE STORY OF ECONOMIC WARFARE. EUR+WWI USA-45 LAW FINAN INDUS NAT/G CONSULT FORCES PLAN DOMIN PWR WEALTH ...INT/LAW CONCPT OBS TOT/POP NAZI 20. PAGE 49 F0955
INT/ORG ECO/TAC INT/TRADE WAR

B48
KEIR D.L.,CASES IN CONSTITUTIONAL LAW. UK CHIEF LEGIS DIPLOM TAX PARL/PROC CRIME GOV/REL...INT/LAW JURID 17/20. PAGE 70 F1368
CONSTN LAW ADJUD CT/SYS

C50
ELLSWORTH P.T.,"INTERNATIONAL ECONOMY." ECO/DEV ECO/UNDEV FINAN LABOR DIPLOM FOR/AID TARIFFS BAL/PAY EQUILIB NAT/LISM OPTIMAL...INT/LAW 20 ILO GATT. PAGE 37 F0724
BIBLIOG INT/TRADE ECO/TAC INT/ORG

B52
JENNINGS W.I.,CONSTITUTIONAL LAWS OF THE COMMONWEALTH. AFR UK LAW CHIEF LEGIS TAX CT/SYS PARL/PROC GOV/REL...INT/LAW 18/20 ENGLSH/LAW COMMON/LAW. PAGE 67 F1316
CONSTN JURID ADJUD COLONIAL

B56
WATT D.C.,BRITAIN AND THE SUEZ CANAL. COM UAR UK ...INT/LAW 20 SUEZ TREATY. PAGE 144 F2835
DIPLOM INT/TRADE DIST/IND NAT/G

B58
MOSKOWITZ M.,HUMAN RIGHTS AND WORLD ORDER. INT/ORG PLAN GP/REL NAT/LISM SOVEREIGN...CONCPT 20 UN TREATY CIV/RIGHTS. PAGE 94 F1845
DIPLOM INT/LAW ORD/FREE

B59
AITKEN H.G.,THE AMERICAN ECONOMIC IMPACT ON CANADA. CANADA USA+45 AGRI FINAN INDUS LABOR INT/TRADE BAL/PAY...INT/LAW TREND 20. PAGE 3 F0055
DIPLOM ECO/TAC POLICY NAT/G

B59
HARVARD UNIVERSITY LAW SCHOOL,INTERNATIONAL PROBLEMS OF FINANCIAL PROTECTION AGAINST NUCLEAR RISK. WOR+45 NAT/G DELIB/GP PROB/SOLV DIPLOM CONTROL ATTIT...POLICY INT/LAW MATH 20. PAGE 56 F1105
NUC/PWR ADJUD INDUS FINAN

B60
STEIN E.,AMERICAN ENTERPRISE IN THE EUROPEAN COMMON MARKET: A LEGAL PROFILE. EUR+WWI FUT USA+45 SOCIETY STRUCT ECO/DEV NAT/G VOL/ASSN CONSULT PLAN TEC/DEV ECO/TAC INT/TRADE ADMIN ATTIT RIGID/FLEX PWR...MGT NEW/IDEA STAT TREND COMPUT/IR SIMUL EEC 20. PAGE 125 F2475
MARKET ADJUD INT/LAW

B62
ALEXANDROWICZ C.H.,WORLD ECONOMIC AGENCIES: LAW AND PRACTICE. WOR+45 DIST/IND FINAN LABOR CONSULT INT/TRADE TARIFFS REPRESENT HEALTH...JURID 20 UN GATT EEC OAS ECSC. PAGE 4 F0064
INT/LAW INT/ORG DIPLOM ADJUD

B62
DE LAVALLE H.,A STATEMENT OF THE LAWS OF PERU IN MATTERS AFFECTING BUSINESS (3RD ED.). PERU WORKER INT/TRADE INCOME ORD/FREE...INT/LAW 20. PAGE 31 F0603
CONSTN JURID FINAN TAX

B62
SCHMITT H.A.,THE PATH TO EUROPEAN UNITY. EUR+WWI USA+45 PLAN TEC/DEV DIPLOM FOR/AID CONFER...INT/LAW 20 EEC EURCOALSTL MARSHL/PLN UNIFICA. PAGE 117 F2300
INT/ORG INT/TRADE REGION ECO/DEV

S63
GERHARD H.,"COMMODITY TRADE STABILIZATION THROUGH INTERNATIONAL AGREEMENTS." WOR+45 ECO/DEV ECO/UNDEV NAT/G ROUTINE ORD/FREE...INT/LAW OBS TREND GEN/METH TOT/POP 20. PAGE 47 F0918
PLAN ECO/TAC INT/TRADE

S63
WALKER H.,"THE INTERNATIONAL LAW OF COMMODITY AGREEMENTS." FUT WOR+45 ECO/DEV ECO/UNDEV FINAN INT/ORG NAT/G CONSULT CREATE PLAN ECO/TAC ATTIT PERCEPT...CONCPT GEN/LAWS TOT/POP GATT 20. PAGE 142 F2804
MARKET VOL/ASSN INT/LAW INT/TRADE

B64
ECONOMIDES C.P.,LE POUVOIR DE DECISION DES ORGANISATIONS INTERNATIONALES EUROPEENNES. DIPLOM DOMIN INGP/REL EFFICIENCY...INT/LAW JURID 20 NATO OEEC EEC COUNCL/EUR EURATOM. PAGE 36 F0698
INT/ORG PWR DECISION GP/COMP

B64
ROBINSON R.D.,INTERNATIONAL BUSINESS POLICY. AFR INDIA L/A+17C USA+45 ELITES AGRI FOR/AID COERCE BAL/PAY...DECISION INT/LAW MGT 20. PAGE 113 F2224
ECO/TAC DIST/IND COLONIAL FINAN

B64
SEGAL R.,SANCTIONS AGAINST SOUTH AFRICA. AFR SOUTH/AFR NAT/G INT/TRADE RACE/REL PEACE PWR ...INT/LAW ANTHOL 20 UN. PAGE 119 F2342
SANCTION DISCRIM ECO/TAC POLICY

B64
TONG T.,UNITED STATES DIPLOMACY IN CHINA, 1844-1860. ASIA USA-45 ECO/UNDEV ECO/TAC COERCE GP/REL...INT/LAW 19 TREATY. PAGE 131 F2581
DIPLOM INT/TRADE COLONIAL

B65
DOWD L.P.,PRINCIPLES OF WORLD BUSINESS. SERV/IND NAT/G DIPLOM ECO/TAC TARIFFS...INT/LAW JURID 20. PAGE 34 F0657
INT/TRADE MGT FINAN MARKET

B65
O'CONNELL D.P.,INTERNATIONAL LAW (2 VOLS.). WOR+45 WOR-45 ECO/DEV ECO/UNDEV INT/ORG NAT/G AGREE ...POLICY JURID CONCPT NAT/COMP 20 TREATY. PAGE 99 F1952
INT/LAW DIPLOM CT/SYS

B65
WEIL G.L.,A HANDBOOK ON THE EUROPEAN ECONOMIC COMMUNITY. BELGIUM EUR+WWI FRANCE GERMANY/W ITALY CONSTN ECO/DEV CREATE PARTIC GP/REL...DECISION MGT CHARTS 20 EEC. PAGE 144 F2846
INT/TRADE INT/ORG TEC/DEV INT/LAW

B66
EDWARDS C.D.,TRADE REGULATIONS OVERSEAS. IRELAND NEW/ZEALND SOUTH/AFR NAT/G CAP/ISM TARIFFS CONTROL ...POLICY JURID 20 EEC CHINJAP. PAGE 36 F0703
INT/TRADE DIPLOM INT/LAW ECO/TAC

B66
FRIEDMANN W.G.,INTERNATIONAL FINANCIAL AID. USA+45 ECO/DEV ECO/UNDEV NAT/G VOL/ASSN EX/STRUC PLAN RENT GIVE BAL/PAY PWR...GEOG INT/LAW STAT TREND UN EEC COMECON. PAGE 44 F0866
INT/ORG FOR/AID TEC/DEV ECO/TAC

B66
UREN P.E.,EAST - WEST TRADE* A SYMPOSIUM. COM AGRI INT/ORG PRICE HABITAT RIGID/FLEX...GEOG INT/LAW ANTHOL NATO. PAGE 133 F2625
INT/TRADE BAL/PWR AFR CANADA

S66
DUROSELLE J.B.,"THE FUTURE OF THE ATLANTIC COMMUNITY." EUR+WWI USA+45 USSR NAT/G CAP/ISM REGION DETER NUC/PWR ATTIT MARXISM...INT/LAW 20 NATO. PAGE 35 F0686
FUT DIPLOM MYTH POLICY

B67
MCDOUGAL M.S.,THE INTERPRETATION OF AGREEMENTS AND WORLD PUBLIC ORDER: PRINCIPLES OF CONTENT AND PROCEDURE. WOR+45 CONSTN PROB/SOLV TEC/DEV ...CON/ANAL TREATY. PAGE 88 F1727
INT/LAW STRUCT ECO/UNDEV DIPLOM

L67
DROBNIG U.,"CONFLICT OF LAWS AND THE EUROPEAN ECONOMIC COMMUNITY." EUR+WWI PROB/SOLV DIPLOM ...JURID EEC. PAGE 34 F0663
INT/LAW ADJUD INT/ORG MARKET

L67
MEIER G.M.,"UNCTAD PROPOSALS FOR INTERNATIONAL ECONOMIC REFORM." WOR+45 MARKET INT/ORG TARIFFS CONFER UN GATT IMF. PAGE 89 F1749
INT/TRADE FINAN INT/LAW ECO/UNDEV

S67
AMERASINGHE C.F.,"SOME LEGAL PROBLEMS OF STATE TRADING IN SOUTHEAST ASIA." PROB/SOLV ADJUD CONTROL CT/SYS GP/REL 20. PAGE 5 F0084
INT/TRADE NAT/G INT/LAW PRIVIL

S67
SMALL A.H.,"THE EFFECT OF TARIFF REDUCTIONS ON US IMPORT VOLUME." USA+45 INT/ORG NAT/G DIPLOM CONFER DEMAND...POLICY INT/LAW STAT CHARTS GATT EEC. PAGE 123 F2424
TARIFFS INT/TRADE PRICE ECO/TAC

S67
WEIL G.L.,"THE MERGER OF THE INSTITUTIONS OF THE EUROPEAN COMMUNITIES" EUR+WWI ECO/DEV INT/TRADE CONSEN PLURISM...DECISION MGT 20 EEC EURATOM ECSC TREATY. PAGE 145 F2847
ECO/TAC INT/ORG CENTRAL INT/LAW

INT/ORG....INTERNATIONAL ORGANIZATIONS; SEE ALSO VOL/ASSN AND APPROPRIATE ORGANIZATION

N
RAND SCHOOL OF SOCIAL SCIENCE,INDEX TO LABOR ARTICLES. ECO/DEV INT/ORG LEGIS DIPLOM GP/REL ...NAT/COMP 20. PAGE 109 F2143
BIBLIOG LABOR MGT ADJUD

N
UNITED NATIONS,OFFICIAL RECORDS OF THE ECONOMIC AND SOCIAL COUNCIL OF THE UNITED NATIONS. WOR+45 DIPLOM INT/TRADE CONFER...SOC SOC/WK 20 UN UNESCO. PAGE 132 F2611
INT/ORG DELIB/GP WRITING

B00
MILL J.S.,PRINCIPLES OF POLITICAL ECONOMY. WOR-45 CULTURE SOCIETY STRATA ECO/DEV AGRI EXTR/IND FINAN INDUS DELIB/GP ECO/TAC WEALTH...CONCPT MATH TREND 20. PAGE 91 F1786
MARKET INT/ORG INT/TRADE

N19
BASCH A.,THE FUTURE OF FOREIGN LENDING FOR DEVELOPMENT (PAMPHLET). WOR+45 ECO/UNDEV FINAN INT/ORG ECO/TAC ATTIT...PREDICT 20. PAGE 11 F0203
FOR/AID ECO/DEV DIPLOM GIVE

N19
FREEMAN H.A.,COERCION OF STATES IN FEDERAL UNIONS (PAMPHLET). WOR-45 DIPLOM CONTROL COERCE PEACE ORD/FREE...GOV/COMP METH/COMP NAT/COMP PACIFIST 20. PAGE 43 F0850
FEDERAL WAR INT/ORG PACIFISM

N19
JACKSON R.G.A.,THE CASE FOR AN INTERNATIONAL DEVELOPMENT AUTHORITY (PAMPHLET). WOR+45 ECO/DEV DIPLOM GIVE CONTROL GP/REL EFFICIENCY NAT/LISM SOVEREIGN 20. PAGE 66 F1295
FOR/AID INT/ORG ECO/UNDEV ADMIN

N19
LUTZ F.A.,THE PROBLEM OF INTERNATIONAL LIQUIDITY AND THE MULTIPLECURRENCY STANDARD (PAMPHLET). WOR+45 MARKET INT/ORG PRICE BAL/PAY...NEW/IDEA METH/COMP BIBLIOG 20 IMF. PAGE 82 F1609
PROB/SOLV FINAN DIPLOM ECO/TAC

N19
VELYAMINOV G.,AFRICA AND THE COMMON MARKET (PAMPHLET). AFR MARKET VOL/ASSN ECO/TAC COLONIAL ORD/FREE...SOCIALIST 20 THIRD/WRLD. PAGE 141 F2775
INT/ORG INT/TRADE SOVEREIGN ECO/UNDEV

B32
WRIGHT Q.,GOLD AND MONETARY STABILIZATION. FUT USA-45 WOR-45 INTELL ECO/DEV INT/ORG NAT/G CONSULT PLAN ECO/TAC ADMIN ATTIT WEALTH...CONCPT TREND 20. PAGE 149 F2935
FINAN POLICY

B34
GRAHAM F.D.,PROTECTIVE TARIFFS. FUT USA+45 WOR-45 INDUS MARKET VOL/ASSN PLAN CAP/ISM ECO/TAC PEACE ATTIT DRIVE HEALTH ORD/FREE...OBS TREND GEN/LAWS FOR/TRADE 20. PAGE 50 F0970
INT/ORG TARIFFS

B35
STALEY E.,WAR AND THE PRIVATE INVESTOR. UNIV WOR-45 INTELL SOCIETY INT/ORG NAT/G TOP/EX CAP/ISM ECO/TAC WAR ATTIT ALL/VALS...INT TIME/SEQ TREND CON/ANAL WORK TOT/POP 20. PAGE 125 F2464
FINAN INT/TRADE DIPLOM

B37
ROBBINS L.,ECONOMIC PLANNING AND INTERNATIONAL ORDER. WOR-45 SOCIETY FINAN INDUS NAT/G ECO/TAC ROUTINE WEALTH...SOC TIME/SEQ GEN/METH WORK 20 KEYNES/JM. PAGE 112 F2202
INT/ORG PLAN INT/TRADE

B38
LANGE O.,ON THE ECONOMIC THEORY OF SOCIALISM. UNIV ECO/DEV FINAN INDUS INT/ORG PUB/INST ROUTINE ATTIT ALL/VALS...SOC CONCPT STAT TREND 20. PAGE 75 F1475
MARKET ECO/TAC INT/TRADE SOCISM

B39
ROBBINS L.,ECONOMIC CAUSES OF WAR. WOR-45 ECO/DEV ECO/UNDEV INT/ORG NAT/G TEC/DEV DIPLOM DOMIN COLONIAL ATTIT DRIVE PWR WEALTH...POLICY CONCPT OBS SAMP TREND CON/ANAL GEN/LAWS MARX/KARL 20. PAGE 112 F2203
COERCE ECO/TAC WAR

B39
STALEY E.,WORLD ECONOMY IN TRANSITION. WOR-45 SOCIETY INT/ORG PROF/ORG ECO/TAC ATTIT WEALTH ...METH/CNCPT TREND GEN/LAWS 20. PAGE 125 F2465
TEC/DEV INT/TRADE

B41
YOUNG G.,FEDERALISM AND FREEDOM. EUR+WWI MOD/EUR RUSSIA USA-45 WOR-45 SOCIETY STRUCT ECO/DEV INT/ORG EXEC FEDERAL ATTIT PERSON ALL/VALS...OLD/LIB CONCPT OBS TREND LEAGUE/NAT TOT/POP. PAGE 150 F2950
NAT/G WAR

B45
DAVIS J.,AFRICA ADVANCING. AFR CONGO/BRAZ LIBERIA NIGER INT/ORG SCHOOL DIPLOM GIVE KNOWL SKILL 20. PAGE 30 F0590
SECT COLONIAL AGRI ECO/UNDEV

B47
ENKE S.,INTERNATIONAL ECONOMICS. UK USA+45 USSR INT/ORG BAL/PWR BARGAIN CAP/ISM BAL/PAY...NAT/COMP 20 TREATY. PAGE 38 F0735
INT/TRADE FINAN TARIFFS ECO/TAC

B47
GORDON D.L.,THE HIDDEN WEAPON: THE STORY OF ECONOMIC WARFARE. EUR+WWI USA-45 LAW FINAN INDUS NAT/G CONSULT FORCES PLAN DOMIN PWR WEALTH ...INT/LAW CONCPT OBS TOT/POP NAZI 20. PAGE 49 F0955
INT/ORG ECO/TAC INT/TRADE WAR

B47
HEILPERIN M.A.,THE TRADE OF NATIONS. USA+45 USA-45 WOR+45 WOR-45 CULTURE ECO/DEV NAT/G DELIB/GP EDU/PROP ATTIT DISPL ORD/FREE PWR WEALTH TOT/POP 20. PAGE 58 F1139
MARKET INT/ORG INT/TRADE PEACE

B47
TOWLE L.W.,INTERNATIONAL TRADE AND COMMERCIAL POLICY. WOR+45 LAW ECO/DEV FINAN INDUS NAT/G ECO/TAC WEALTH...TIME/SEQ ILO 20. PAGE 131 F2582
MARKET INT/ORG INT/TRADE

B47
US LIBRARY OF CONGRESS,POSTWAR PLANNING AND RECONSTRUCTION: JANUARY-MARCH 1943. WOR+45 SOCIETY INT/ORG DIPLOM...SOC PREDICT 20. PAGE 138 F2714
BIBLIOG/A WAR PEACE PLAN

B48
GRAHAM F.D.,THE THEORY OF INTERNATIONAL VALUES. FUT WOR+45 WOR-45 ECO/DEV FINAN INT/ORG PLAN TEC/DEV CAP/ISM DIPLOM ECO/TAC TARIFFS ROUTINE BAL/PAY DRIVE PWR WEALTH SOCISM...POLICY STAT HYPO/EXP GEN/LAWS 20. PAGE 50 F0971
NEW/IDEA INT/TRADE

B48
VON HAYEK F.A.,INDIVIDUALISM AND ECONOMIC ORDER. GERMANY USA-45 USSR FINAN MARKET INT/ORG ECO/TAC INT/TRADE PRICE REPRESENT ORD/FREE...PLURIST GEN/LAWS 20. PAGE 142 F2793
SOCISM CAP/ISM POPULISM FEDERAL

B49
PARMELEE M.,GEO-ECONOMIC REGIONAL AND WORLD FEDERATION. FUT WOR+45 WOR-45 SOCIETY VOL/ASSN PLAN ...METH/CNCPT SIMUL GEN/METH TERR/GP TOT/POP 20. PAGE 103 F2028
INT/ORG GEOG REGION

B49
US DEPARTMENT OF STATE,SOVIET BIBLIOGRAPHY (PAMPHLET). CHINA/COM COM USSR LAW AGRI INT/ORG ECO/TAC EDU/PROP...POLICY GEOG IND 20. PAGE 135 F2670
BIBLIOG/A MARXISM CULTURE DIPLOM

B50
US DEPARTMENT OF STATE,POINT FOUR: COOPERATIVE PROGRAM FOR AID IN THE DEVELOPMENT OF ECONOMICALLY UNDERDEVELOPED AREAS. WOR+45 AGRI INDUS INT/ORG PLAN TEC/DEV DIPLOM EDU/PROP ADMIN PEACE PRODUC WEALTH 20 CONGRESS UN. PAGE 135 F2671
ECO/UNDEV FOR/AID FINAN INT/TRADE

C50
ELLSWORTH P.T.,"INTERNATIONAL ECONOMY." ECO/DEV ECO/UNDEV FINAN LABOR DIPLOM FOR/AID TARIFFS BAL/PAY EQUILIB NAT/LISM OPTIMAL...INT/LAW 20 ILO GATT. PAGE 37 F0724
BIBLIOG INT/TRADE ECO/TAC INT/ORG

B51
LEONARD L.L.,INTERNATIONAL ORGANIZATION. WOR+45 WOR-45 EX/STRUC FORCES LEGIS ECO/TAC INT/TRADE COLONIAL ARMS/CONT...SOC/WK GOV/COMP BIBLIOG. PAGE 78 F1527
NAT/G DIPLOM INT/ORG DELIB/GP

B51
US HOUSE COMM APPROPRIATIONS,MUTUAL SECURITY PROGRAM APPROPRIATIONS FOR 1952: HEARINGS BEFORE A SUBCOMMITTEE OF THE COMMITTEE ON APPROPRIATIONS. AFR KOREA L/A+17C ECO/DEV ECO/UNDEV INT/ORG INSPECT BAL/PWR DIPLOM DEBATE WAR...POLICY STAT ASIA/S 20 CONGRESS NATO MID/EAST. PAGE 136 F2686
LEGIS FORCES BUDGET FOR/AID

B52
ALEXANDROWICZ C.H.,INTERNATIONAL ECONOMIC ORGANIZATION. WOR+45 ECO/DEV ECO/UNDEV DIST/IND FINAN MARKET PLAN ECO/TAC LEGIT DRIVE WEALTH ...POLICY CONCPT QUANT OBS TIME/SEQ GEN/LAWS WORK METH/GP EEC ILO OEEC UNESCO 20. PAGE 4 F0063
INT/ORG INT/TRADE

B52
SECRETARIAT COUNCIL OF EUROPE,THE STRASBOURG PLAN. EUR+WWI CONSULT PLAN ECO/TAC TARIFFS DEBATE REGION 20 COUNCL/EUR STRASBOURG. PAGE 119 F2340
INT/ORG ECO/DEV INT/TRADE DIPLOM

L52
HUTH A.G.,"COMMUNICATION AND ECONOMIC DEVELOPMENT." FUT WOR+45 CULTURE SOCIETY INT/ORG PLAN TEC/DEV EDU/PROP DRIVE KNOWL WEALTH...POLICY CONCPT RECORD STERTYP GEN/LAWS COMMUN TOT/POP UNESCO 20 UN CMN/WLTH. PAGE 64 F1250
ECO/UNDEV

B54
FRIEDMAN W.,THE PUBLIC CORPORATION: A COMPARATIVE SYMPOSIUM (UNIVERSITY OF TORONTO SCHOOL OF LAW COMPARATIVE LAW SERIES, VOL. I). AFR SWEDEN USA+45 INDUS INT/ORG NAT/G REGION CENTRAL FEDERAL...POLICY JURID IDEA/COMP NAT/COMP ANTHOL 20 MONOPOLY EUROPE. PAGE 44 F0861
LAW SOCISM LG/CO OWN

B54
INTERNATIONAL LABOUR OFF LIB,BIBLIOGRAPHY ON THE INTERNATIONAL LABOUR ORGANISATION. WORKER 20. PAGE 65 F1277
BIBLIOG LABOR INT/ORG CONFER

B54
O.E.E.C.,PRIVATE UNITED STATES INVESTMENT IN EUROPE AND THE OVERSEAS TERRITORIES. EUR+WWI WOR+45 ECO/DEV ECO/UNDEV INT/ORG NAT/G VOL/ASSN ECO/TAC ATTIT WEALTH...GEOG STAT SYS/QU CHARTS VAL/FREE 20. PAGE 99 F1950
USA+45 FINAN BAL/PAY FOR/AID

B54
TINBERGEN J.,INTERNATIONAL ECONOMIC INTEGRATION. WOR+45 WOR-45 ECO/UNDEV NAT/G ECO/TAC BAL/PAY ...METH/CNCPT STAT TIME/SEQ GEN/METH OEEC 20. PAGE 130 F2574
INT/ORG ECO/DEV INT/TRADE

L54
OPLER M.E.,"SOCIAL ASPECTS OF TECHNICAL ASSISTANCE IN OPERATION." WOR+45 VOL/ASSN CREATE PLAN TEC/DEV EDU/PROP ALL/VALS...METH/CNCPT OBS RECORD TREND UN 20. PAGE 101 F1993
INT/ORG CONSULT FOR/AID

B55
BUCHANAN N.S.,APPROACHES TO ECONOMIC DEVELOPMENT. FUT USA+45 WOR+45 STRATA ECO/DEV INT/ORG NAT/G TEC/DEV DIPLOM FOR/AID ATTIT KNOWL PWR WEALTH ...RELATIV METH/CNCPT SELF/OBS TREND CON/ANAL STERTYP GEN/LAWS FOR/TRADE COMMUN 20. PAGE 20 F0380
ECO/UNDEV ECO/TAC INT/TRADE

B55
FLORINSKY M.T.,INTEGRATED EUROPE. EUR+WWI FRANCE ITALY NETHERLAND UK ECO/DEV INT/ORG FORCES LEGIT FEDERAL ATTIT PWR WEALTH...POLICY GEOG CONCPT GEN/LAWS TOT/POP EEC OEEC 20. PAGE 42 F0816
FUT
ECO/TAC
REGION

B55
US OFFICE OF THE PRESIDENT,REPORT TO CONGRESS ON THE MUTUAL SECURITY PROGRAM FOR THE SIX MONTHS ENDED JUNE 30, 1955. ECO/DEV INT/ORG NAT/G CREATE TEC/DEV BAL/PWR ECO/TAC AGREE DETER COST ORD/FREE 20 DEPT/STATE DEPT/DEFEN. PAGE 138 F2722
DIPLOM
FORCES
PLAN
FOR/AID

L55
KISER M.,"ORGANIZATION OF AMERICAN STATES." L/A+17C USA+45 ECO/UNDEV INT/ORG NAT/G PLAN TEC/DEV DIPLOM ECO/TAC INT/TRADE EDU/PROP ADMIN ALL/VALS...POLICY MGT RECORD ORG/CHARTS OAS COMMUN 20. PAGE 71 F1401
VOL/ASSN
ECO/DEV
REGION

S55
HALLETT D.,"THE HISTORY AND STRUCTURE OF OEEC." EUR+WWI USA+45 CONSTN INDUS INT/ORG NAT/G DELIB/GP ACT/RES PLAN ORD/FREE WEALTH...CONCPT OEEC 20 CMN/WLTH. PAGE 54 F1051
VOL/ASSN
ECO/DEV

B56
GARDNER R.N.,STERLING-DOLLAR DIPLOMACY. EUR+WWI USA+45 INT/ORG NAT/G PLAN INT/TRADE EDU/PROP ADMIN KNOWL PWR WEALTH...POLICY SOC METH/CNCPT STAT CHARTS SIMUL GEN/LAWS 20. PAGE 46 F0902
ECO/DEV
DIPLOM

B56
UN HEADQUARTERS LIBRARY,BIBLIOGRAPHY OF INDUSTRIALIZATION IN UNDERDEVELOPED COUNTRIES (BIBLIOGRAPHICAL SERIES NO. 6). WOR+45 R+D ACADEM INT/ORG NAT/G. PAGE 132 F2602
BIBLIOG
ECO/UNDEV
TEC/DEV

B56
UNITED NATIONS,BIBLIOGRAPHY ON INDUSTRIALIZATION IN UNDER-DEVELOPED COUNTRIES. WOR+45 R+D INT/ORG NAT/G FOR/AID ADMIN LEAD 20 UN. PAGE 132 F2612
BIBLIOG
ECO/UNDEV
INDUS
TEC/DEV

B56
US DEPARTMENT OF STATE,ECONOMIC PROBLEMS OF UNDERDEVELOPED AREAS (PAMPHLET). AFR ASIA ISLAM L/A+17C AGRI FINAN INDUS INT/ORG LABOR INT/TRADE ...PSY SOC 20. PAGE 136 F2673
BIBLIOG
ECO/UNDEV
TEC/DEV
R+D

B56
US OFFICE OF THE PRESIDENT,REPORT TO CONGRESS ON THE MUTUAL SECURITY PROGRAM FOR THE SIX MONTHS ENDED DECEMBER 31, 1955. ASIA USSR ECO/DEV ECO/UNDEV INT/ORG CREATE TEC/DEV BAL/PWR ECO/TAC AGREE DETER COST ORD/FREE 20 DEPT/STATE DEPT/DEFEN EISNHWR/DD. PAGE 138 F2723
DIPLOM
FORCES
PLAN
FOR/AID

B56
WOLFF R.L.,THE BALKANS IN OUR TIME. ALBANIA FUT MOD/EUR USSR YUGOSLAVIA CULTURE INT/ORG SECT DIPLOM EDU/PROP COERCE WAR ORD/FREE...CHARTS 4/20 BALKANS COMINFORM. PAGE 148 F2919
GEOG
COM

S56
GORDON L.,"THE ORGANIZATION FOR EUROPEAN ECONOMIC COOPERATION." EUR+WWI INDUS INT/ORG NAT/G CONSULT DELIB/GP ACT/RES CREATE PLAN TEC/DEV EDU/PROP LEGIT WEALTH OEEC 20. PAGE 49 F0956
VOL/ASSN
ECO/DEV

B57
ARON R.,L'UNIFICATION ECONOMIQUE DE L'EUROPE. EUR+WWI SWITZERLND UK INT/ORG NAT/G REGION NAT/LISM ORD/FREE PWR...CONCPT METH/CNCPT OBS TREND STERTYP GEN/LAWS EEC FOR/TRADE 20. PAGE 6 F0118
VOL/ASSN
ECO/TAC

B57
ASHER R.E.,THE UNITED NATIONS AND ECONOMIC AND SOCIAL COOPERATION. ECO/UNDEV COM/IND DIST/IND FINAN PLAN PROB/SOLV INT/TRADE TASK WEALTH...SOC 20 UN. PAGE 7 F0129
INT/ORG
DIPLOM
FOR/AID

B57
DAY A.C.L.,OUTLINE OF MONETARY ECONOMICS. AFR WOR-45 INT/ORG WORKER DIPLOM BAL/PAY COST INCOME WEALTH...TIME/SEQ SIMUL 20. PAGE 31 F0594
FINAN
NAT/G
EQUILIB
PRICE

B57
HALD M.,A SELECTED BIBLIOGRAPHY ON ECONOMIC DEVELOPMENT AND FOREIGN AID. INT/ORG PROB/SOLV ...SOC 20. PAGE 53 F1040
BIBLIOG
ECO/UNDEV
TEC/DEV
FOR/AID

B57
INTL BANKING SUMMER SCHOOL,RELATIONS BETWEEN THE CENTRAL BANKS AND COMMERCIAL BANKS. EUR+WWI FRANCE GERMANY/W ITALY UK USA+45 USSR INDUS INT/ORG CAP/ISM CONTROL MONEY. PAGE 65 F1282
FINAN
NAT/G
GP/REL
LG/CO

B57
LAVES W.H.C.,UNESCO. FUT WOR+45 NAT/G CONSULT DELIB/GP TEC/DEV ECO/TAC EDU/PROP PEACE ORD/FREE ...CONCPT TIME/SEQ TREND UNESCO VAL/FREE 20. PAGE 76 F1491
INT/ORG
KNOWL

B57
TRIFFIN R.,EUROPE AND THE MONEY MUDDLE. USA+45 INT/ORG NAT/G CONSULT PLAN ECO/TAC EXEC ROUTINE BAL/PAY WEALTH...METH/CNCPT OBS TREND CHARTS STERTYP GEN/METH EEC TERR/GP VAL/FREE ECSC. PAGE 131 F2587
EUR+WWI
ECO/DEV
REGION

S57
HOAG M.W.,"ECONOMIC PROBLEMS OF ALLIANCE." AFR COM EUR+WWI WOR+45 ECO/DEV ECO/UNDEV NAT/G VOL/ASSN FORCES PLAN TEC/DEV DIPLOM COERCE ORD/FREE PWR WEALTH...DECISION GEN/LAWS NATO TERR/GP. PAGE 60 F1182
INT/ORG
ECO/TAC

B58
BERLINER J.S.,SOVIET ECONOMIC AID: THE AID AND TRADE POLICY IN UNDERDEVELOPED COUNTRIES. AFR COM ISLAM L/A+17C S/ASIA USSR ECO/DEV DIST/IND FINAN MARKET INT/ORG ACT/RES PLAN BAL/PWR WEAPON PWR WEALTH...CHARTS FOR/TRADE 20. PAGE 14 F0263
ECO/UNDEV
ECO/TAC
FOR/AID

B58
COLE G.D.H.,COMMUNISM AND SOCIAL DEMOCRACY (VOL. IV OF "HISTORY OF SOCIAL THOUGHT"). COM GERMANY ITALY UK AGRI INT/ORG WORKER DIPLOM COLONIAL NAT/LISM ALL/IDEOS...BIBLIOG 20 LEAGUE/NAT AUST/HUNG. PAGE 26 F0502
MARXISM
REV
POL/PAR
SOCISM

B58
ELLSWORTH P.T.,THE INTERNATIONAL ECONOMY. EUR+WWI MOD/EUR INT/ORG CAP/ISM FOR/AID BAL/PAY LAISSEZ 16/20. PAGE 37 F0725
INT/TRADE
TARIFFS
ECO/DEV

B58
HENNING C.N.,INTERNATIONAL FINANCING. WOR+45 ECO/DEV INT/ORG EX/STRUC INSPECT CAP/ISM BAL/PAY COST PROFIT...MGT CHARTS T 20. PAGE 58 F1150
FINAN
DIPLOM
INT/TRADE

B58
JENNINGS I.,PROBLEMS OF THE NEW COMMONWEALTH. AFR CEYLON INDIA PAKISTAN S/ASIA ECO/UNDEV INT/ORG LOC/G DIPLOM ECO/TAC INT/TRADE COLONIAL RACE/REL DISCRIM 20 PARLIAMENT. PAGE 67 F1314
NAT/LISM
NEUTRAL
FOR/AID
POL/PAR

B58
KINDLEBERGER C.P.,INTERNATIONAL ECONOMICS. WOR+45 WOR-45 ECO/DEV ECO/UNDEV FINAN VOL/ASSN ACT/RES DIPLOM ECO/TAC LEGIT REGION ATTIT DRIVE ORD/FREE WEALTH...POLICY STAT TREND GEN/LAWS EEC ECSC OEEC 20. PAGE 71 F1391
INT/ORG
BAL/PWR
TARIFFS

B58
MOSKOWITZ M.,HUMAN RIGHTS AND WORLD ORDER. INT/ORG PLAN GP/REL NAT/LISM SOVEREIGN...CONCPT 20 UN TREATY CIV/RIGHTS. PAGE 94 F1845
DIPLOM
INT/LAW
ORD/FREE

B58
MYRDAL G.,RICH LANDS AND POOR: THE ROAD TO WORLD PROSPERITY. FUT WOR+45 WOR-45 ECO/DEV ECO/UNDEV INT/ORG PLAN ECO/TAC REGION...GEOG TIME/SEQ GEN/LAWS TOT/POP 20. PAGE 96 F1880
WEALTH
TREND
FOR/AID
INT/TRADE

B58
OEEC,THE INDUSTRIAL CHALLENGE OF NUCLEAR ENERGY. EUR+WWI ECO/DEV INDUS OP/RES CONFER RISK PWR ...AUD/VIS CHARTS ANTHOL 20 OEEC. PAGE 101 F1977
NUC/PWR
ACT/RES
ECO/TAC
INT/ORG

B58
SCITOUSKY T.,ECONOMIC THEORY AND WESTERN EUROPEAN INTEGRATION. EUR+WWI INT/ORG ACT/RES INT/TRADE REGION BAL/PAY WEALTH...METH/CNCPT STAT CHARTS GEN/METH ECSC TOT/POP EEC OEEC 20. PAGE 118 F2328
ECO/TAC

S58
ELKIN A.B.,"OEEC-ITS STRUCTURE AND POWERS." EUR+WWI CONSTN INDUS INT/ORG NAT/G VOL/ASSN DELIB/GP ACT/RES PLAN ORD/FREE WEALTH...CHARTS ORG/CHARTS OEEC 20. PAGE 37 F0719
ECO/DEV
EX/STRUC

B59
DIEBOLD W. JR.,THE SCHUMAN PLAN: A STUDY IN ECONOMIC COOPERATION, 1950-1959. EUR+WWI FRANCE GERMANY USA+45 EXTR/IND CONSULT DELIB/GP PLAN DIPLOM ECO/TAC INT/TRADE ROUTINE ORD/FREE WEALTH ...METH/CNCPT STAT CONT/OBS INT TIME/SEQ ECSC 20. PAGE 33 F0635
INT/ORG
REGION

B59
ROBERTSON A.H.,EUROPEAN INSTITUTIONS: COOPERATION, INTEGRATION, UNIFICATION. EUR+WWI FINAN INT/ORG FORCES INT/TRADE TARIFFS 20 EEC EURATOM ECSC NATO TREATY. PAGE 112 F2208
ECO/DEV
DIPLOM
INDUS
ECO/TAC

B59
ROPKE W.,INTERNATIONAL ORDER AND ECONOMIC INTEGRATION. ECO/DEV ECO/UNDEV AGRI FINAN INDUS INT/ORG WAR PEACE ORD/FREE...SOC METH/COMP 20 EEC. PAGE 114 F2238
INT/TRADE
DIPLOM
BAL/PAY
ALL/IDEOS

B59
SANNWALD R.E.,ECONOMIC INTEGRATION: THEORETICAL ASSUMPTIONS AND CONSEQUENCES OF EUROPEAN UNIFICATION. EUR+WWI FUT FINAN INDUS VOL/ASSN ACT/RES ECO/TAC...PLURIST EEC FOR/TRADE OEEC 20. PAGE 116 F2279
INT/ORG
ECO/DEV
INT/TRADE

B59
WARD B.,5 IDEAS THAT CHANGE THE WORLD. WOR+45 WOR-45 SOCIETY STRUCT AGRI INDUS INT/ORG NAT/G FORCES ACT/RES ARMS/CONT TOTALISM ATTIT DRIVE GEN/LAWS. PAGE 143 F2815
ECO/UNDEV
ALL/VALS
NAT/LISM
COLONIAL

B59
WENTHOLT W.,SOME COMMENTS ON THE LIQUIDATION OF THE EUROPEAN PAYMENT UNION AND RELATED PROBLEMS (PAMPHLET). AFR WOR+45 PLAN BUDGET PRICE CONTROL 20 EEC. PAGE 145 F2857
FINAN
ECO/DEV
INT/ORG
ECO/TAC

B59
YRARRAZAVAL E.,AMERICA LATINE EN LA GUERRA FRIA. AFR EUR+WWI L/A+17C USA+45 USSR WOR+45 INDUS INT/ORG NAT/LISM POLICY. PAGE 150 F2953
REGION
DIPLOM
ECO/UNDEV

INT/TRADE

L59

BEGUIN B.,"ILO AND THE TRIPARTITE SYSTEM." EUR+WWI WOR+45 WOR-45 CONSTN ECO/DEV ECO/UNDEV INDUS INT/ORG NAT/G VOL/ASSN DELIB/GP PLAN TEC/DEV LEGIT ORD/FREE WEALTH...CONCPT TIME/SEQ WORK ILO 20. PAGE 12 F0228
LABOR

L59

MURPHY J.C.,"SOME IMPLICATIONS OF EUROPE'S COMMON MARKET. IN (COOK P. ECONOMIC DEVELOPMENT AND INTERNATIONAL TRADE,." EUR+WWI ECO/DEV DIST/IND INDUS NAT/G PLAN ECO/TAC INT/TRADE WEALTH...STAT TREND OEEC TOT/POP 20 EEC. PAGE 95 F1866
MARKET
INT/ORG
REGION

S59

KINDLEBERGER C.P.,"UNITED STATES ECONOMIC FOREIGN POLICY: RESEARCH REQUIREMENTS FOR 1965." FUT USA+45 WOR+45 DIST/IND MARKET INT/ORG ECO/TAC INT/TRADE WEALTH...OBS TREND CON/ANAL GEN/LAWS FOR/TRADE VAL/FREE 20. PAGE 71 F1392
FINAN
ECO/DEV
FOR/AID

S59

PLAZA G.,"FOR A REGIONAL MARKET IN LATIN AMERICA." FUT L/A+17C CULTURE INDUS NAT/G ECO/TAC INT/TRADE ATTIT WEALTH...NEW/IDEA TREND OAS 20. PAGE 106 F2092
MARKET
INT/ORG
REGION

S59

REUBENS E.D.,"THE BASIS FOR REORIENATION OF AMERICAN FOREIGN AID POLICY." USA+45 USSR STRUCT INT/ORG CONSULT ECO/TAC ADMIN DRIVE MORAL ORD/FREE PWR WEALTH...RELATIV MATH STAT TREND GEN/LAWS VAL/FREE 20. PAGE 111 F2180
ECO/UNDEV
PLAN
FOR/AID
DIPLOM

S59

SOLDATI A.,"EOCNOMIC DISINTEGRATION IN EUROPE." EUR+WWI FUT WOR+45 INDUS INT/ORG NAT/G CAP/ISM WEALTH...NEW/IDEA OBS TREND CHARTS EEC 20. PAGE 124 F2438
FINAN
ECO/TAC

S59

TIPTON J.B.,"PARTICIPATION OF THE UNITED STATES IN THE INTERNATIONAL LABOR ORGANIZATION." USA+45 LAW STRUCT ECO/DEV ECO/UNDEV INDUS TEC/DEV ECO/TAC ADMIN PERCEPT ORD/FREE SKILL...STAT HIST/WRIT GEN/METH ILO WORK 20. PAGE 131 F2577
LABOR
INT/ORG

S59

ZAUBERMAN A.,"SOVIET BLOC ECONOMIC INTEGRATION." COM CULTURE INTELL ECO/DEV INDUS TOP/EX ACT/RES PLAN ECO/TAC INT/TRADE ROUTINE CHOOSE ATTIT ...TIME/SEQ 20. PAGE 150 F2958
MARKET
INT/ORG
USSR
TOTALISM

B60

ASPREMONT-LYNDEN H.,RAPPORT SUR L'ADMINISTRATION BELGE DU RUANDA-URUNDI PENDANT L'ANNEE 1959. BELGIUM RWANDA AGRI INDUS DIPLOM ECO/TAC INT/TRADE DOMIN ADMIN RACE/REL...GEOG CENSUS 20 UN. PAGE 7 F0132
AFR
COLONIAL
ECO/UNDEV
INT/ORG

B60

HEYSE T.,PROBLEMS FONCIERS ET REGIME DES TERRES (ASPECTS ECONOMIQUES, JURIDIQUES ET SOCIAUX). AFR CONGO/BRAZ INT/ORG DIPLOM SOVEREIGN...GEOG TREATY 20. PAGE 59 F1161
BIBLIOG
AGRI
ECO/UNDEV
LEGIS

B60

HOFFMANN P.G.,ONE HUNDRED COUNTRIES, ONE AND ONE QUARTER BILLION PEOPLE. MARKET INT/ORG TEC/DEV CAP/ISM...GEOG CHARTS METH/COMP 20 UN. PAGE 61 F1191
FOR/AID
ECO/TAC
ECO/UNDEV
INT/TRADE

B60

KILLOUGH H.B.,INTERNATIONAL ECONOMICS. PLAN PROB/SOLV FOR/AID TARIFFS CONTROL BAL/PAY...POLICY CHARTS T 20. PAGE 71 F1388
CONCPT
ECO/UNDEV
INT/ORG
INT/TRADE

B60

LERNER A.P.,THE ECONOMICS OF CONTROL. USA+45 ECO/UNDEV INT/ORG ACT/RES PLAN CAP/ISM INT/TRADE ATTIT WEALTH...SOC MATH STAT GEN/LAWS INDEX 20. PAGE 78 F1530
ECO/DEV
ROUTINE
ECO/TAC
SOCISM

B60

LISTER L.,EUROPE'S COAL AND STEEL COMMUNITY. FRANCE GERMANY STRUCT ECO/DEV EXTR/IND INDUS MARKET NAT/G DELIB/GP ECO/TAC INT/TRADE EDU/PROP ATTIT RIGID/FLEX ORD/FREE PWR WEALTH...CONCPT STAT TIME/SEQ CHARTS ECSC TERR/GP 20. PAGE 81 F1582
EUR+WWI
INT/ORG
REGION

B60

RAO V.K.R.,INTERNATIONAL AID FOR ECONOMIC DEVELOPMENT - POSSIBILITIES AND LIMITATIONS. FINAN PLAN TEC/DEV ADMIN TASK EFFICIENCY...POLICY SOC METH/CNCPT CHARTS 20 UN. PAGE 109 F2147
FOR/AID
DIPLOM
INT/ORG
ECO/UNDEV

B60

ROBINSON E.A.G.,ECONOMIC CONSEQUENCES OF THE SIZE OF NATIONS. AGRI INDUS DELIB/GP FOR/AID ADMIN EFFICIENCY...METH/COMP 20. PAGE 113 F2218
CONCPT
INT/ORG
NAT/COMP

B60

ROPKE W.,A HUMANE ECONOMY. CULTURE ECO/DEV FINAN INDUS GP/REL CENTRAL WEALTH...GEOG SOC IDEA/COMP 20 EEC. PAGE 114 F2239
ECO/TAC
INT/ORG
DIPLOM
ORD/FREE

B60

SHONFIELD A.,THE ATTACK ON WORLD POVERTY. WOR+45 ECO/DEV ECO/UNDEV FINAN VOL/ASSN PLAN EDU/PROP DRIVE KNOWL WEALTH...CONT/OBS STAND/INT ORG/CHARTS TOT/POP UNESCO 20. PAGE 121 F2383
INT/ORG
ECO/TAC
FOR/AID
INT/TRADE

B60

STANFORD RESEARCH INSTITUTE,AFRICAN DEVELOPMENT: A TEST FOR INTERNATIONAL COOPERATION. AFR USA+45 WOR+45 FINAN INT/ORG PLAN PROB/SOLV ECO/TAC INT/TRADE ADMIN...CHARTS 20. PAGE 125 F2467
FOR/AID
ECO/UNDEV
ATTIT
DIPLOM

B60

STEVENSON A.E.,PUTTING FIRST THINGS FIRST. USA+45 INT/ORG NEIGH FOR/AID DISCRIM...ANTHOL 20. PAGE 126 F2483
DIPLOM
ECO/UNDEV
ORD/FREE
EDU/PROP

B60

THE ECONOMIST (LONDON),THE COMMONWEALTH AND EUROPE. EUR+WWI WOR+45 AGRI FINAN INCOME...STAT CENSUS CHARTS CMN/WLTH EEC. PAGE 129 F2550
INT/TRADE
INDUS
INT/ORG
NAT/COMP

B60

THEOBALD R.,THE RICH AND THE POOR: A STUDY OF THE ECONOMICS OF RISING EXPECTATIONS. WOR+45 CONSTN ECO/DEV ECO/UNDEV INT/ORG NAT/G PLAN FOR/AID ROUTINE BAL/PAY ORD/FREE PWR WEALTH...GEOG TREND WORK FOR/TRADE 20. PAGE 129 F2553
ECO/TAC
INT/TRADE

B60

WHEARE K.C.,THE CONSTITUTIONAL STRUCTURE OF THE COMMONWEALTH. UK EX/STRUC DIPLOM DOMIN ADMIN COLONIAL CONTROL LEAD INGP/REL SUPEGO 20 CMN/WLTH. PAGE 145 F2865
CONSTN
INT/ORG
VOL/ASSN
SOVEREIGN

S60

HERRERA F.,"THE INTER-AMERICAN DEVELOPMENT BANK." USA+45 ECO/UNDEV INT/ORG CONSULT DELIB/GP PLAN ECO/TAC INT/TRADE ROUTINE WEALTH...STAT TERR/GP 20. PAGE 59 F1153
L/A+17C
FINAN
FOR/AID
REGION

S60

JACOBSON H.K.,"THE USSR AND ILO." AFR COM STRUCT ECO/DEV ECO/UNDEV CONSULT DELIB/GP ECO/TAC ILO WORK 20. PAGE 66 F1298
INT/ORG
LABOR
USSR

S60

MIKESELL R.F.,"AMERICA'S ECONOMIC RESPONSIBILITY AS A GREAT POWER." COM FUT USA+45 USSR WOR+45 INT/ORG PLAN ECO/TAC FOR/AID EDU/PROP CHOOSE WEALTH ...POLICY 20. PAGE 91 F1781
ECO/UNDEV
BAL/PWR
CAP/ISM

S60

NANES A.,"THE EUROPEAN COMMUNITY AND THE UNITED STATES: EVOLVING RELATIONS." EUR+WWI USA+45 WOR+45 ECO/UNDEV MARKET NAT/G DELIB/GP PLAN LEGIT ATTIT PWR WEALTH...CONCPT STAT TIME/SEQ CON/ANAL EEC METH/GP OEEC 20 EURATOM. PAGE 96 F1889
INT/ORG
REGION

S60

RICHTER J.H.,"TOWARDS AN INTERNATIONAL POLICY ON AGRICULTURAL TRADE." EUR+WWI USA+45 ECO/DEV NAT/G PLAN ECO/TAC ATTIT PWR WEALTH...CONCPT GEN/LAWS 20. PAGE 111 F2187
AGRI
INT/ORG

N60

ERDMAN P.E.,COMMON MARKETS AND FREE TRADE AREAS (PAMPHLET). USA+45 MARKET INT/ORG TEC/DEV DIPLOM UTIL...CON/ANAL CHARTS BIBLIOG 20 EEC OEEC. PAGE 38 F0743
TREND
PROB/SOLV
INT/TRADE
ECO/DEV

B61

ASHER R.E.,GRANTS, LOANS, AND LOCAL CURRENCIES; THEIR ROLE IN FOREIGN AID. AFR USA+45 ECO/UNDEV INT/ORG ACT/RES PLAN ECO/TAC GIVE CONTROL WEALTH 20. PAGE 7 F0130
FOR/AID
FINAN
NAT/G
BUDGET

B61

BALASSA B.,THE THEORY OF ECONOMIC INTEGRATION. EUR+WWI L/A+17C MOD/EUR WOR+45 ECO/UNDEV MARKET INT/ORG NAT/G VOL/ASSN DELIB/GP PLAN CAP/ISM ECO/TAC...MAJORIT FOR/TRADE OEEC 20. PAGE 8 F0157
ECO/DEV
ACT/RES
INT/TRADE

B61

BONNEFOUS M.,EUROPE ET TIERS MONDE. EUR+WWI SOCIETY INT/ORG NAT/G VOL/ASSN ACT/RES TEC/DEV CAP/ISM ECO/TAC ATTIT ORD/FREE SOVEREIGN...POLICY CONCPT TREND TERR/GP COMMUN 20. PAGE 16 F0314
AFR
ECO/UNDEV
FOR/AID
INT/TRADE

B61

HARRIS S.E.,THE DOLLAR IN CRISIS. AFR USA+45 MARKET INT/ORG ECO/TAC PRICE CONTROL WEALTH...METH/COMP ANTHOL 20. PAGE 55 F1089
BAL/PAY
DIPLOM
FINAN
INT/TRADE

B61

INTERNATIONAL BANK RECONST DEV,THE WORLD BANK IN AFRICA: SUMMARY OF ACTIVITIES. AGRI COM/IND DIST/IND EXTR/IND INDUS TAX COST...CHARTS 20. PAGE 65 F1271
FINAN
ECO/UNDEV
INT/ORG
AFR

B61

KITZINGER V.W.,THE CHALLENGE OF THE COMMON MARKET. EUR+WWI ECO/DEV DIST/IND PLAN ECO/TAC INT/TRADE LEGIT ATTIT PWR WEALTH...TIME/SEQ TREND CHARTS EEC 20. PAGE 71 F1403
MARKET
INT/ORG
UK

B61

LANDSKROY W.A.,OFFICIAL SERIAL PUBLICATIONS RELATING TO ECONOMIC DEVELOPMENT IN AFRICA SOUTH OF THE SAHARA (PAMPHLET). AFR UK R+D ACT/RES 20 UN. PAGE 75 F1471
BIBLIOG
ECO/UNDEV
COLONIAL
INT/ORG

B61

LIEFMANN-KEIL E.,OKONOMISCHE THEORIE DER SOZIALPOLITIK. INT/ORG LABOR WORKER COST INCOME NEW/LIB...CONCPT SOC/INTEG 20. PAGE 80 F1562
ECO/DEV
INDUS
NAT/G

SOC/WK

B61
MEZERIK A.G.,ECONOMIC DEVELOPMENT AIDS FOR UNDERDEVELOPED COUNTRIES. WOR+45 FINAN LEGIS PROB/SOLV TEC/DEV DIPLOM FOR/AID GIVE TASK WAR 20 UN. PAGE 91 F1776
ECO/UNDEV INT/ORG WEALTH PLAN

B61
MORLEY L.,THE PATCHWORK HISTORY OF FOREIGN AID. AFR KOREA/S USA+45 USSR LAW FINAN INT/ORG TEC/DEV BAL/PWR GIVE 20 NATO. PAGE 93 F1834
FOR/AID ECO/UNDEV FORCES DIPLOM

B61
OECD,STATISTICS OF BALANCE OF PAYMENTS 1950-61. WOR+45 FINAN ECO/TAC INT/TRADE DEMAND WEALTH...STAT NAT/COMP 20 OEEC OECD. PAGE 100 F1965
BAL/PAY ECO/DEV INT/ORG CHARTS

B61
SCAMMEL W.M.,INTERNATIONAL MONETARY POLICY. WOR+45 WOR-45 ACT/RES ECO/TAC LEGIT WEALTH...GEN/METH UN 20. PAGE 116 F2286
INT/ORG FINAN BAL/PAY

B61
SHARP W.R.,FIELD ADMINISTRATION IN THE UNITED NATION SYSTEM: THE CONDUCT OF INTERNATIONAL ECONOMIC AND SOCIAL PROGRAMS. FUT WOR+45 CONSTN SOCIETY ECO/UNDEV R+D DELIB/GP ACT/RES PLAN TEC/DEV EDU/PROP EXEC ROUTINE HEALTH WEALTH...HUM CONCPT CHARTS METH ILO UNESCO GP VAL/FREE UN 20. PAGE 120 F2369
INT/ORG CONSULT

B61
TRIFFIN R.,GOLD AND THE DOLLAR CRISIS: THE FUTURE OF CONVERTIBILITY. AFR USA+45 USA-45 INT/ORG PROB/SOLV BUDGET INT/TRADE PRICE...STAT CHARTS 19/20. PAGE 131 F2588
FINAN ECO/DEV ECO/TAC BAL/PAY

B61
US CONGRESS JOINT ECO COMM,INTERNATIONAL PAYMENTS IMBALANCES AND NEED FOR STRENGTHENING INTERNATIONAL FINANCIAL ARRANGEMENTS. USA+45 WOR+45 DELIB/GP DIPLOM INT/TRADE...CHARTS 20 CONGRESS OEEC. PAGE 134 F2651
BAL/PAY INT/ORG FINAN PROB/SOLV

S61
LANFALUSSY A.,"EUROPE'S PROGRESS: DUE TO COMMON MARKET." EUR+WWI ECO/DEV DELIB/GP PLAN ECO/TAC ROUTINE WEALTH...GEOG TREND EEC TERR/GP 20. PAGE 75 F1473
INT/ORG MARKET

S61
NYANZI S.,"THE EAST AFRICAN MARKET: FOR BETTER OF FOR WORSE." AFR TANZANIA UGANDA PROB/SOLV TARIFFS TAX BAL/PAY. PAGE 99 F1947
ECO/TAC ECO/UNDEV INT/ORG INT/TRADE

S61
OCHENG D.,"ECONOMIC FORCES AND UGANDA'S FOREIGN POLICY." AFR UGANDA INT/TRADE TARIFFS INCOME SOVEREIGN WEALTH 20 EACM EEC TANGANYIKA. PAGE 100 F1961
ECO/TAC DIPLOM ECO/UNDEV INT/ORG

S61
VINER J.,"ECONOMIC FOREIGN POLICY ON THE NEW FRONTIER." USA+45 ECO/UNDEV AGRI FINAN INDUS MARKET INT/ORG NAT/G FOR/AID INT/TRADE ADMIN ATTIT PWR 20 KENNEDY/JF. PAGE 141 F2786
TOP/EX ECO/TAC BAL/PAY TARIFFS

B62
ALEXANDROWICZ C.H.,WORLD ECONOMIC AGENCIES: LAW AND PRACTICE. WOR+45 DIST/IND FINAN LABOR CONSULT INT/TRADE TARIFFS REPRESENT HEALTH...JURID 20 UN GATT EEC OAS ECSC. PAGE 4 F0064
INT/LAW INT/ORG DIPLOM ADJUD

B62
DREIER J.C.,THE ALLIANCE FOR PROGRESS. L/A+17C USA+45 CULTURE ECO/DEV ECO/UNDEV NAT/G PLAN DIPLOM PWR 20 OAS ALL/PROG. PAGE 34 F0661
FOR/AID INT/ORG ECO/TAC POLICY

B62
ELLIOTT J.R.,THE APPEAL OF COMMUNISM IN THE UNDERDEVELOPED NATIONS. AFR USSR WOR+45 INT/ORG NAT/G DIPLOM DOMIN EDU/PROP ROUTINE ATTIT RIGID/FLEX ORD/FREE PWR WEALTH MARXISM...POLICY SOC METH/CNCPT MYTH TOT/POP METH/GP 20. PAGE 37 F0722
COM ECO/UNDEV

B62
FAO,FOOD AND AGRICULTURE ORGANIZATION AFRICAN SURVEY. AFR CONGO/BRAZ GHANA STRATA AGRI INT/ORG TEC/DEV FOR/AID INT/TRADE RACE/REL DEMAND EFFICIENCY PRODUC...GEOG 20 UN CONGO/LEOP. PAGE 39 F0763
ECO/TAC WEALTH EXTR/IND ECO/UNDEV

B62
FRIEDMANN W.,METHODS AND POLICIES OF PRINCIPAL DONOR COUNTRIES IN PUBLIC INTERNATIONAL DEVELOPMENT FINANCING: PRELIMINARY APPRAISAL. FRANCE GERMANY/W UK USA+45 USSR WOR+45 FINAN TEC/DEV CAP/ISM DIPLOM ECO/TAC ATTIT 20 EEC. PAGE 44 F0864
INT/ORG FOR/AID NAT/COMP ADMIN

B62
FRIEDRICH-EBERT-STIFTUNG,THE SOVIET BLOC AND DEVELOPING COUNTRIES. CHINA/COM COM GERMANY/E USSR WOR+45 ECO/UNDEV INT/ORG NAT/G TEC/DEV NEUTRAL PWR ...POLICY 20. PAGE 44 F0868
MARXISM DIPLOM ECO/TAC FOR/AID

B62
HIGGANS B.,UNITED NATIONS AND U.S. FOREIGN ECONOMIC POLICY. FUT USA+45 WOR+45 ECO/DEV ECO/UNDEV NAT/G ECO/TAC WEALTH...TIME/SEQ TOT/POP UN 20. PAGE 59 F1168
INT/ORG ACT/RES FOR/AID DIPLOM

B62
HUHNE L.H.,FINANCING ECONOMIC DEVELOPMENT THROUGH NATIONAL AND INTERNATIONAL ORGANIZATIONS (THESIS; U OF WIS.). USA+45 INT/ORG PLAN GIVE GOV/REL WEALTH 20. PAGE 63 F1235
RATION FINAN FOR/AID ECO/UNDEV

B62
HUMPHREY D.D.,THE UNITED STATES AND THE COMMON MARKET. USA+45 INDUS MARKET INT/ORG PLAN EDU/PROP BAL/PAY DRIVE PWR WEALTH...TREND STERTYP FOR/TRADE EEC 20. PAGE 63 F1241
ATTIT ECO/TAC

B62
LEVY H.V.,LIBERDADE E JUSTICA SOCIAL (2ND ED.). BRAZIL COM L/A+17C USSR INT/ORG PARTIC GP/REL WEALTH 20 UN COM/PARTY. PAGE 79 F1544
ORD/FREE MARXISM CAP/ISM LAW

B62
LIPPMANN W.,WESTERN UNITY AND THE COMMON MARKET. EUR+WWI FRANCE GERMANY/W UK USA+45 ECO/DEV AGRI FINAN MARKET INT/ORG NAT/G FOR/AID AGREE WEALTH 20 EEC. PAGE 80 F1575
DIPLOM INT/TRADE VOL/ASSN

B62
MEADE J.E.,CASE STUDIES IN EUROPEAN ECONOMIC UNION. BELGIUM EUR+WWI LUXEMBOURG NAT/G INT/TRADE REGION ROUTINE WEALTH...METH/CNCPT STAT CHARTS ECSC TOT/POP OEEC EEC FOR/TRADE 20. PAGE 89 F1738
INT/ORG ECO/TAC

B62
MOUSSA P.,THE UNDERPRIVILEGED NATIONS. FINAN INT/ORG PLAN PROB/SOLV CAP/ISM GIVE TASK WEALTH ...POLICY SOC IND 20. PAGE 94 F1850
ECO/UNDEV NAT/G DIPLOM FOR/AID

B62
PAKISTAN MINISTRY OF FINANCE,FOREIGN ECONOMIC AID: A REVIEW OF FOREIGN ECONOMIC AID TO PAKISTAN. EUR+WWI PAKISTAN UK USA+45 USSR ECO/UNDEV INT/ORG DELIB/GP DIPLOM ECO/TAC...CHARTS CMN/WLTH CHINJAP. PAGE 103 F2016
FOR/AID RECEIVE WEALTH FINAN

B62
ROBERTSON B.C.,REGIONAL DEVELOPMENT IN THE EUROPEAN ECONOMIC COMMUNITY. EUR+WWI FRANCE FUT ITALY UK ECO/UNDEV WORKER ACT/RES PROB/SOLV TEC/DEV ECO/TAC INT/TRADE EEC. PAGE 112 F2209
PLAN ECO/DEV INT/ORG REGION

B62
ROBINSON A.D.,DUTCH ORGANIZED AGRICULTURE IN INTERNATIONAL POLITICS, 1945-1960. EUR+WWI NETHERLAND STRUCT ECO/DEV NAT/G VOL/ASSN CONSULT DELIB/GP PLAN TEC/DEV INT/TRADE EDU/PROP ATTIT RIGID/FLEX ALL/VALS...NEW/IDEA TREND EEC COMMUN 20. PAGE 112 F2215
AGRI INT/ORG

B62
SCHMITT H.A.,THE PATH TO EUROPEAN UNITY. EUR+WWI USA+45 PLAN TEC/DEV DIPLOM FOR/AID CONFER...INT/LAW 20 EEC EURCOALSTL MARSHL/PLN UNIFICA. PAGE 117 F2300
INT/ORG INT/TRADE REGION ECO/DEV

B62
SHANNON I.,THE ECONOMIC FUNCTIONS OF GOLD. AFR FUT WOR+45 WOR-45 INT/ORG BUDGET INT/TRADE BAL/PAY DEMAND PEACE 20 MONEY. PAGE 120 F2366
FINAN PRICE ECO/DEV ECO/TAC

B62
UNECA LIBRARY,BOOKS ON AFRICA IN THE UNECA LIBRARY. WOR+45 AGRI INT/ORG NAT/G PLAN WRITING REGION...SOC STAT UN. PAGE 132 F2605
BIBLIOG AFR ECO/UNDEV TEC/DEV

B62
UNECA LIBRARY,NEW ACQUISITIONS IN THE UNECA LIBRARY. LAW NAT/G PLAN PROB/SOLV TEC/DEV ADMIN REGION...GEOG SOC 20 UN. PAGE 132 F2606
BIBLIOG AFR ECO/UNDEV INT/ORG

B62
UNIVERSITY OF TENNESSEE,GOVERNMENT AND WORLD CRISIS. USA+45 FOR/AID ORD/FREE...ANTHOL 20 UN ALL/PROG. PAGE 133 F2622
ECO/DEV DIPLOM NAT/G INT/ORG

B62
URQUIDI V.L.,FREE TRADE AND ECONOMIC INTEGRATION IN LATIN AMERICA: THE EVOLUTION OF A COMMON MARKET POLICY. ECO/UNDEV MARKET DIPLOM BAL/PAY FEDERAL ...POLICY CHARTS 20 LAFTA. PAGE 133 F2627
INT/TRADE REGION INT/ORG L/A+17C

B62
US AGENCY INTERNATIONAL DEV,OPERATIONS REPORT - 1962 (PAMPHLET). AFR ASIA L/A+17C USA+45 ECO/UNDEV FINAN INT/ORG NAT/G 20 MICHIGAN. PAGE 134 F2636
FOR/AID CHARTS STAT BUDGET

B62
VIET J.,INTERNATIONAL COOPERATION AND PROGRAMMES OF ECONOMIC AND SOCIAL DEVELOPMENT. TEC/DEV FOR/AID DOMIN COLONIAL PEACE WEALTH 20 UNESCO. PAGE 141 F2784
BIBLIOG/A INT/ORG DIPLOM ECO/UNDEV

L62
MACHLUP F.,"PLANS FOR REFORM OF THE INTERNATIONAL MONETARY SYSTEM. PRINCETON: U. PR., 1962, 70 PP., $0.25." WOR+45 INT/ORG ECO/TAC BAL/PAY HEALTH ORD/FREE WEALTH MID/EX TERR/GP VAL/FREE APPLIC 20. PAGE 83 F1631
ECO/DEV STAT

S62
BOKOR-SZEGO H.,"LA CONVENTION DE BELGRADE ET LE REGIME DU DANUBE." COM EUR+WWI WOR+45 STRUCT POL/PAR VOL/ASSN PLAN EDU/PROP WEALTH...TIME/SEQ METH/GP COMMUN 20. PAGE 16 F0308
INT/ORG TOTALISM YUGOSLAVIA

S62
PIQUEMAL M.,"LA COOPERATION FINANCIERE ENTRE LA FRANCE ET LES ETATS AFRICAINS ET MALGACHE." ISLAM INT/ORG TOP/EX ECO/TAC...JURID CHARTS 20. PAGE 106 F2089
AFR FINAN FRANCE MADAGASCAR

S62
RAZAFIMBAHINY J.,"L'ORGANISATION AFRICAINE ET MALGACHE DE COOPERATION ECONOMIQUE." AFR ISLAM MADAGASCAR NAT/G ACT/RES ECO/TAC ALL/VALS ...TIME/SEQ 20. PAGE 110 F2158
INT/ORG ECO/UNDEV

S62
SCOTT J.B.,"ANGLO-SOVIET TRADE AND ITS EFFECTS ON THE COMMONWEALTH." COM FUT UK USSR WOR+45 ECO/DEV MARKET INT/ORG CONSULT WEALTH...POLICY TREND CMN/WLTH FOR/TRADE 20. PAGE 118 F2333
NAT/G ECO/TAC

B63
ABSHIRE D.M.,NATIONAL SECURITY: POLITICAL, MILITARY, AND ECONOMIC STRATEGIES IN THE DECADE AHEAD. ASIA COM USA+45 WOR+45 ECO/DEV ECO/UNDEV INT/ORG DELIB/GP FORCES ECO/TAC COERCE ATTIT RIGID/FLEX HEALTH ORD/FREE PWR WEALTH...POLICY STAT CHARTS ANTHOL COLD/WAR VAL/FREE APP/SCI. PAGE 2 F0032
FUT ACT/RES BAL/PWR

B63
BELOFF M.,THE UNITED STATES AND THE UNITY OF EUROPE. EUR+WWI UK USA+45 WOR+45 VOL/ASSN DIPLOM REGION ATTIT PWR...CONCPT EEC OEEC 20 NATO. PAGE 13 F0239
ECO/DEV INT/ORG

B63
CENTRO PARA EL DESARROLLO,LA ALIANZA PARA EL PROGRESO Y EL DESARROLLO SOCIAL DE AMERICA LATINA. L/A+17C INT/ORG DIPLOM ECO/TAC INT/TRADE ATTIT 20 ALL/PROG. PAGE 22 F0435
ECO/UNDEV FOR/AID PLAN REGION

B63
CERAMI C.A.,ALLIANCE BORN OF DANGER. EUR+WWI USA+45 USSR ECO/DEV INDUS VOL/ASSN ECO/TAC REGION ATTIT MARXISM ATLAN/ALL 20 NATO EEC. PAGE 22 F0437
DIPLOM INT/ORG NAT/G POLICY

B63
DE VRIES E.,SOCIAL ASPECTS OF ECONOMIC DEVELOPMENT IN LATIN AMERICA. CULTURE SOCIETY STRATA FINAN INDUS INT/ORG DELIB/GP ACT/RES ECO/TAC EDU/PROP ADMIN ATTIT SUPEGO HEALTH KNOWL ORD/FREE...SOC STAT TREND ANTHOL TOT/POP VAL/FREE. PAGE 31 F0608
L/A+17C ECO/UNDEV

B63
FLORES E.,LAND REFORM AND THE ALLIANCE FOR PROGRESS (PAMPHLET). L/A+17C USA+45 STRUCT ECO/UNDEV NAT/G WORKER CREATE PLAN ECO/TAC COERCE REV 20 ALL/PROG. PAGE 42 F0815
AGRI INT/ORG DIPLOM POLICY

B63
GORDON L.,A NEW DEAL FOR LATIN AMERICA. L/A+17C USA+45 CULTURE NAT/G TEC/DEV DIPLOM FOR/AID REGION TASK...POLICY 20 ALL/PROG DEPT/STATE. PAGE 49 F0958
ECO/UNDEV ECO/TAC INT/ORG PLAN

B63
GRUBEL H.G.,WORLD MONETARY REFORM: PLANS AND ISSUES. FUT WOR+45 ECO/DEV ECO/UNDEV R+D DELIB/GP CREATE ECO/TAC ATTIT RIGID/FLEX WEALTH...STAT ANTHOL VAL/FREE 20. PAGE 52 F1009
FINAN INT/ORG BAL/PAY INT/TRADE

B63
INTERAMERICAN ECO AND SOC COUN,THE ALLIANCE FOR PROGRESS: ITS FIRST YEAR: 1961-1962. AGRI SCHOOL PLAN TEC/DEV INT/TRADE TAX GIVE ADMIN WEALTH...SOC 20 ALL/PROG SOUTH/AMER. PAGE 64 F1267
INT/ORG PROB/SOLV ECO/TAC L/A+17C

B63
INTERNATIONAL BANK RECONST DEV,THE WORLD BANK GROUP IN ASIA. ASIA S/ASIA INDUS TEC/DEV ECO/TAC...RECORD 20 IBRD WORLD/BANK. PAGE 65 F1273
INT/ORG DIPLOM ECO/UNDEV FINAN

B63
INTERNATIONAL MONETARY FUND,COMPENSATORY FINANCING OF EXPORT FLUCTUATIONS (PAMPHLET). WOR+45 ECO/DEV ECO/UNDEV INT/ORG WEALTH...TREND 20 IMF MONEY. PAGE 65 F1281
BAL/PAY FINAN BUDGET INT/TRADE

B63
KRAVIS I.B.,DOMESTIC INTERESTS AND INTERNATIONAL OBLIGATIONS: SAFEGUARDS IN INTERNATIONAL TRADE ORGANIZATIONS. EUR+WWI USA+45 WOR+45 FINAN DELIB/GP ATTIT RIGID/FLEX HEALTH...STAT EEC VAL/FREE OEEC ECSC 20. PAGE 73 F1435
INT/ORG ECO/TAC INT/TRADE

B63
LICHTHEIM G.,THE NEW EUROPE: TODAY AND TOMORROW. EUR+WWI FINAN 20 EEC EUROPE/W. PAGE 80 F1560
DIPLOM ECO/DEV INT/ORG INT/TRADE

B63
LINDBERG L.,POLITICAL DYNAMICS OF EUROPEAN ECONOMIC INTEGRATION. EUR+WWI ECO/DEV INT/ORG VOL/ASSN DELIB/GP ADMIN WEALTH...DECISION EEC TERR/GP 20. PAGE 80 F1567
MARKET ECO/TAC

B63
MAIZELS A.,INDUSTRIAL GROWTH AND WORLD TRADE. FUT WOR+45 ECO/DEV FINAN INT/ORG PLAN TEC/DEV ECO/TAC WEALTH...MATH STAT CHARTS VAL/FREE 19/20. PAGE 84 F1642
INDUS ECO/UNDEV INT/TRADE

B63
MANGER W.,THE ALLIANCE FOR PROGRESS: A CRITICAL APPRAISAL. FUT L/A+17C USA+45 CULTURE ECO/UNDEV ACADEM NAT/G SCHOOL PLAN FOR/AID...POLICY OAS ALL/PROG. PAGE 84 F1651
DIPLOM INT/ORG ECO/TAC REGION

B63
MARITANO N.,AN ALLIANCE FOR PROGRESS. FUT L/A+17C USA+45 CULTURE ECO/UNDEV NAT/G PLAN CONTROL ...POLICY ALL/PROG. PAGE 85 F1669
DIPLOM INT/ORG ECO/TAC FOR/AID

B63
MULLENBACH P.,CIVILIAN NUCLEAR POWER: ECONOMIC ISSUES AND POLICY FORMATION. AFR FINAN INT/ORG DELIB/GP ACT/RES ECO/TAC ATTIT SUPEGO HEALTH ORD/FREE PWR...POLICY CONCPT MATH STAT CHARTS VAL/FREE 20. PAGE 94 F1855
USA+45 ECO/DEV NUC/PWR

B63
MYRDAL G.,CHALLENGE TO AFFLUENCE. USA+45 WOR+45 FINAN INT/ORG NAT/G PLAN ECO/TAC INT/TRADE BAL/PAY ORD/FREE 20 EUROPE/W. PAGE 96 F1882
ECO/DEV WEALTH DIPLOM PRODUC

B63
OECD,FOOD AID: ITS ROLE IN ECONOMIC DEVELOPMENT. FINAN NAT/G PLAN DIPLOM GIVE TASK WEALTH ...METH/COMP METH 20. PAGE 100 F1966
ECO/UNDEV FOR/AID INT/ORG POLICY

B63
PAN AMERICAN UNION,THE EFFECTS OF THE EUROPEAN ECONOMIC COMMUNITY ON THE LATIN AMERICAN ECONOMIES (BMR). EUR+WWI L/A+17C ECO/UNDEV AGRI INDUS MARKET REGION 20 EEC TREATY. PAGE 103 F2024
INT/TRADE INT/ORG AGREE POLICY

B63
PREST A.R.,PUBLIC FINANCE IN UNDERDEVELOPED COUNTRIES. UK WOR+45 WOR-45 SOCIETY INT/ORG NAT/G LEGIS ACT/RES PLAN ECO/TAC ADMIN ROUTINE...CHARTS 20. PAGE 108 F2115
FINAN ECO/UNDEV NIGERIA

B63
RAO V.K.R.,FOREIGN AID AND INDIA'S ECONOMIC DEVELOPMENT. INDIA INT/ORG PROB/SOLV TEC/DEV ECO/TAC CONTROL WEALTH...TREND 20. PAGE 109 F2148
FOR/AID ECO/UNDEV RECEIVE DIPLOM

B63
SALANT W.S.,THE UNITED STATES BALANCE OF PAYMENTS IN 1968. USA+45 ECO/DEV ECO/UNDEV INT/ORG DELIB/GP ECO/TAC...POLICY STAT SIMUL 20. PAGE 115 F2273
FUT FINAN BAL/PAY

B63
US AGENCY INTERNATIONAL DEV,OPERATIONS REPORT - 1963. AFR ASIA L/A+17C USA+45 ECO/UNDEV FINAN INT/ORG NAT/G. PAGE 134 F2637
FOR/AID CHARTS STAT BUDGET

L63
MOUSKHELY M.,"LE BLOC COMMUNISTE ET LA COMMUNAUTE ECONOMIQUE EUROPEENNE." AFR COM EUR+WWI FUT USSR WOR+45 INTELL ECO/UNDEV LABOR POL/PAR NUC/PWR RIGID/FLEX...TIME/SEQ ORG/CHARTS EEC TOT/POP 20. PAGE 94 F1849
INT/ORG ECO/DEV

L63
PADELFORD N.J.,"FINANCIAL CRISIS AND THE UNITED NATIONS." FUT USSR WOR+45 LAW CONSTN FINAN INT/ORG DELIB/GP FORCES PLAN BUDGET DIPLOM COST WEALTH ...STAT CHARTS UN CONGO 20. PAGE 102 F2012
CREATE ECO/TAC

L63
RIDAH A.,"LE NEO-DESTOUR DEPUIS L'INDEPENDANCE." FUT ISLAM WOR+45 ECO/UNDEV INT/ORG SCHOOL DELIB/GP TOP/EX ACT/RES EDU/PROP LEGIT ATTIT ALL/VALS 20 TUNIS. PAGE 111 F2189
NAT/G CONSTN

S63
BALOGH T.,"L'INFLUENCE DES INSTITUTIONS MONETAIRES ET COMMERCIALES SUR LA STRUCTURE ECONOMIQUE AFRICAIN." AFR EUR+WWI FUT USA+45 USA-45 WOR+45 SERV/IND INT/ORG NAT/G TOP/EX ROUTINE...INDEX EEC METH/GP 20. PAGE 9 F0168
FINAN

S63
BARTHELEMY G.,"LE NOUVEAU FRANC (CFA) ET LA BANQUE CENTRALE DES ETATS DE L'AFRIQUE DE L'OUEST." FUT STRUCT INT/ORG PLAN ATTIT ALL/VALS FOR/TRADE 20. PAGE 11 F0200
AFR FINAN

S63
BELOFF M.,"BRITAIN, EUROPE AND THE ATLANTIC COMMUNITY." EUR+WWI ELITES NAT/G VOL/ASSN TOP/EX ATTIT ORD/FREE PWR SOVEREIGN WEALTH EEC TOT/POP VAL/FREE CMN/WLTH 20. PAGE 13 F0240
INT/ORG ECO/DEV UK

S63
DOSSER D.,"TOWARD A THEORY OF INTERNATIONAL PUBLIC FINANCE." WOR+45 ECO/DEV PLAN ECO/TAC WEALTH ...WELF/ST TREND GEN/LAWS TRUE/GP METH/GP 20. PAGE 34 F0654
FINAN INT/ORG FOR/AID

S63
GANDOLFI A.,"LES ACCORDS DE COOPERATION EN MATIERE DE POLITIQUE ETRANGERE ENTRE LA FRANCE ET LES NOUVEAUX ETATS AFRICAINS ET." AFR ISLAM MADAGASCAR
VOL/ASSN ECO/UNDEV DIPLOM

WOR+45 ECO/DEV INT/ORG NAT/G DELIB/GP ECO/TAC ALL/VALS...CON/ANAL 20. PAGE 46 F0894
FRANCE

S63
HALLSTEIN W.,"THE EUROPEAN COMMUNITY AND ATLANTIC PARTNERSHIP." EUR+WWI USA+45 MARKET NAT/G VOL/ASSN DELIB/GP ARMS/CONT NUC/PWR ATTIT PWR...CONCPT STAT TIME/SEQ TREND OEEC 20 EEC. PAGE 54 F1053
INT/ORG
ECO/TAC
UK

S63
MARTHELOT P.,"PROGRES DE LA REFORME AGRAIRE." INTELL ECO/DEV R+D FOR/AID ADMIN KNOWL...OBS VAL/FREE UN 20. PAGE 86 F1680
AGRI
INT/ORG

S63
MIKESELL R.F.,"COMMODITY AGREEMENTS AND AID TO DEVELOPING COUNTRIES." WOR+45 WOR-45 INT/ORG ECO/TAC ATTIT WEALTH WORK FOR/TRADE 20. PAGE 91 F1782
FINAN
ECO/UNDEV
BAL/PAY
FOR/AID

S63
RAMERIE L.,"TENSION AU SEIN DU COMECON: LE CAS ROUMAIN." COM EUR+WWI USSR WOR+45 ECO/DEV DIST/IND NAT/G POL/PAR VOL/ASSN EDU/PROP TOTALISM ATTIT WEALTH...TIME/SEQ 20 COMECON. PAGE 109 F2142
INT/ORG
ECO/TAC
INT/TRADE
ROMANIA

S63
SCHOFLING J.A.,"EFTA: THE OTHER EUROPE." ECO/DEV MARKET CONSULT ECO/TAC WEALTH...TIME/SEQ EEC OEEC 20 EFTA. PAGE 117 F2310
EUR+WWI
INT/ORG
REGION

S63
WALKER H.,"THE INTERNATIONAL LAW OF COMMODITY AGREEMENTS." FUT WOR+45 ECO/DEV ECO/UNDEV FINAN INT/ORG NAT/G CONSULT CREATE PLAN ECO/TAC ATTIT PERCEPT...CONCPT GEN/LAWS TOT/POP GATT 20. PAGE 142 F2804
MARKET
VOL/ASSN
INT/LAW
INT/TRADE

S63
WOLFERS A.,"INTEGRATION IN THE WEST: THE CONFLICT OF PERSPECTIVES." AFR EUR+WWI USA+45 ECO/DEV INT/ORG DELIB/GP CREATE TEC/DEV DIPLOM ATTIT PWR ...CONCPT HIST/WRIT TREND GEN/LAWS EEC 20. PAGE 148 F2918
RIGID/FLEX
ECO/TAC

B64
BERRILL K.,ECONOMIC DEVELOPMENT WITH SPECIAL REFERENCE TO EAST ASIA. ASIA INDIA S/ASIA AGRI INDUS LABOR DELIB/GP PLAN INT/TRADE COST PRODUC 20 CHINJAP. PAGE 14 F0271
FINAN
ECO/UNDEV
INT/ORG
CAP/ISM

B64
BOURGOIGNIE G.E.,JEUNE AFRIQUE MOBILISABLE; LES PROBLEMES DE LA JEUNESSE DESOEUVREE EN AFRIQUE NOIRE. INT/ORG VOL/ASSN ECO/TAC ROUTINE UTIL ATTIT 20. PAGE 17 F0324
AGE/Y
AFR
CREATE
ECO/UNDEV

B64
CALDER R.,TWO-WAY PASSAGE. INT/ORG TEC/DEV WAR PERSON ORD/FREE 20. PAGE 21 F0400
FOR/AID
ECO/UNDEV
ECO/TAC
DIPLOM

B64
CASEY R.G.,THE FUTURE OF THE COMMONWEALTH. INDIA PAKISTAN UK ECO/UNDEV INT/ORG TEC/DEV COLONIAL SUPEGO 20 EEC AUSTRAL. PAGE 22 F0425
DIPLOM
SOVEREIGN
NAT/LISM
FOR/AID

B64
COLUMBIA U SCHOOL OF LAW,PUBLIC INTERNATIONAL DEVELOPMENT FINANCING IN INDIA. GERMANY/W INDIA UK USA+45 INDUS PLAN TEC/DEV DIPLOM ECO/TAC GIVE ADMIN UTIL ATTIT 20. PAGE 26 F0512
ECO/UNDEV
FINAN
FOR/AID
INT/ORG

B64
ECONOMIDES C.P.,LE POUVOIR DE DECISION DES ORGANISATIONS INTERNATIONALES EUROPEENNES. DIPLOM DOMIN INGP/REL EFFICIENCY...INT/LAW JURID 20 NATO OEEC EEC COUNCL/EUR EURATOM. PAGE 36 F0698
INT/ORG
PWR
DECISION
GP/COMP

B64
FREYMOND J.,WESTERN EUROPE SINCE THE WAR. COM EUR+WWI USA+45 DIPLOM...BIBLIOG 20 NATO UN EEC. PAGE 44 F0854
INT/ORG
POLICY
ECO/DEV
ECO/TAC

B64
GARDNER L.C.,ECONOMIC ASPECTS OF NEW DEAL DIPLOMACY. USA-45 WOR-45 LAW ECO/DEV INT/ORG NAT/G VOL/ASSN LEGIS TOP/EX EDU/PROP ORD/FREE PWR WEALTH ...POLICY TIME/SEQ VAL/FREE 20 ROOSEVLT/F. PAGE 46 F0901
ECO/TAC
DIPLOM

B64
GOWDA K.V.,INTERNATIONAL CURRENCY PLANS AND EXPANSION OF WORLD TRADE. INT/ORG CREATE BUDGET CONTROL BAL/PAY WEALTH 20 KEYNES/JM. PAGE 50 F0969
INT/TRADE
FINAN
METH/COMP

B64
HANSEN B.,INTERNATIONAL LIQUIDITY. USA+45 INT/ORG ECO/TAC PRICE CONTROL WEALTH...POLICY 20. PAGE 54 F1068
BAL/PAY
INT/TRADE
DIPLOM
FINAN

B64
HEKHUIS D.J.,INTERNATIONAL STABILITY: MILITARY, ECONOMIC AND POLITICAL DIMENSIONS. FUT WOR+45 LAW ECO/UNDEV INT/ORG NAT/G VOL/ASSN FORCES ACT/RES BAL/PWR PWR WEALTH...STAT UN 20. PAGE 58 F1143
TEC/DEV
DETER
REGION

B64
HERSKOVITS M.J.,ECONOMIC TRANSITION IN AFRICA. FUT INT/ORG NAT/G WORKER PROB/SOLV TEC/DEV INT/TRADE EQUILIB INCOME...ANTHOL 20. PAGE 59 F1157
AFR
ECO/UNDEV
PLAN

ADMIN

B64
HINSHAW R.,THE EUROPEAN COMMUNITY AND AMERICAN TRADE: A STUDY IN ATLANTIC ECONOMICS AND POLICY. EUR+WWI UK USA+45 ECO/DEV ECO/UNDEV AGRI INDUS INT/ORG NAT/G ECO/TAC TARIFFS REGION...STAT CHARTS EEC 20. PAGE 60 F1174
MARKET
TREND
INT/TRADE

B64
INTL INF CTR LOCAL CREDIT,GOVERNMENT MEASURES FOR THE PROMOTION OF REGIONAL ECONOMIC DEVELOPMENT. WOR+45 ECO/UNDEV FINAN INT/ORG DIPLOM ORD/FREE ...POLICY GEOG 20. PAGE 65 F1285
FOR/AID
PLAN
ECO/TAC
REGION

B64
KOHNSTAMM M.,THE EUROPEAN COMMUNITY AND ITS ROLE IN THE WORLD. FUT MOD/EUR UK USA+45 ECO/DEV 20. PAGE 72 F1418
INT/ORG
NAT/G
REGION
DIPLOM

B64
KRAUSE L.B.,THE COMMON MARKET: PROGRESS AND CONTROVERSY. EUR+WWI UK ECO/DEV REGION...ANTHOL NATO EEC. PAGE 73 F1433
DIPLOM
MARKET
INT/TRADE
INT/ORG

B64
MARKHAM J.W.,THE COMMON MARKET: FRIEND OR COMPETITOR. AFR EUR+WWI FUT USA+45 INT/ORG LG/CO NAT/G VOL/ASSN DELIB/GP EX/STRUC PLAN TARIFFS ORD/FREE PWR WEALTH...POLICY STAT TREND EEC VAL/FREE 20. PAGE 85 F1671
ECO/DEV
ECO/TAC

B64
MEZERIK A.G.,TRADE, AID AND ECONOMIC DEVELOPMENT. WOR+45 FINAN INDUS MARKET PLAN BAL/PWR BARGAIN FOR/AID TARIFFS EDU/PROP WEALTH...GP/COMP 20 UN GATT IMF IBRD. PAGE 91 F1777
ECO/TAC
ECO/DEV
INT/ORG
INT/TRADE

B64
NEHEMKIS P.,LATIN AMERICA: MYTH AND REALITY. INDUS INT/ORG PROB/SOLV CAP/ISM DIPLOM REV...SOC MUNICH 20. PAGE 97 F1907
REGION
MYTH
L/A+17C
ECO/UNDEV

B64
OECD,DEVELOPMENT ASSISTANCE EFFORTS - POLICIES OF THE MEMBERS. AGRI INDUS BUDGET...GEOG NAT/COMP 20 OECD. PAGE 100 F1967
INT/ORG
FOR/AID
ECO/UNDEV
TEC/DEV

B64
OECD,THE FLOW OF FINANCIAL RESOURCES TO LESS DEVELOPED COUNTRIES 1956-1963. WOR+45 FINAN CAP/ISM ...POLICY STAT 20. PAGE 100 F1968
FOR/AID
BUDGET
INT/ORG
ECO/UNDEV

B64
RAMAZANI R.K.,THE MIDDLE EAST AND THE EUROPEAN COMMON MARKET. EUR+WWI ISLAM ECO/DEV EXTR/IND MARKET PROC/MFG INT/ORG NAT/G TEC/DEV ECO/TAC REGION DRIVE WEALTH...STAT CHARTS EEC TOT/POP 20. PAGE 109 F2141
ECO/UNDEV
ATTIT
INT/TRADE

B64
RIVKIN A.,AFRICA AND THE EUROPEAN COMMON MARKET (PAMPHLET). AFR MOD/EUR WOR+45 TEC/DEV FOR/AID TARIFFS BAL/PAY...POLICY 20 EEC. PAGE 111 F2196
INT/ORG
INT/TRADE
ECO/TAC
ECO/UNDEV

B64
STEWART C.F.,A BIBLIOGRAPHY OF INTERNATIONAL BUSINESS. WOR+45 FINAN LG/CO NAT/G PLAN ECO/TAC TARIFFS...DECISION MGT GP/COMP NAT/COMP 20 EEC. PAGE 126 F2484
BIBLIOG
INT/ORG
OP/RES
INT/TRADE

B64
STOESSINGER J.G.,FINANCING THE UNITED NATIONS SYSTEM. FUT WOR+45 CONSTN NAT/G VOL/ASSN DELIB/GP EX/STRUC ECO/TAC LEGIT CT/SYS PWR WEALTH...STAT TIME/SEQ TREND CHARTS TRUE/GP METH/GP TERR/GP VAL/FREE. PAGE 126 F2493
FINAN
INT/ORG

B64
SULLIVAN G.,THE STORY OF THE PEACE CORPS. USA+45 WOR+45 INTELL FACE/GP NAT/G SCHOOL VOL/ASSN CONSULT EX/STRUC PLAN EDU/PROP ADMIN ATTIT DRIVE ALL/VALS ...POLICY HEAL SOC CONCPT INT QU BIOG TREND SOC/EXP WORK. PAGE 127 F2511
INT/ORG
ECO/UNDEV
FOR/AID
PEACE

B64
TINBERGEN J.,CENTRAL PLANNING. COM INTELL ECO/DEV ECO/UNDEV FINAN INT/ORG PROB/SOLV ECO/TAC CONTROL EXEC ROUTINE DECISION. PAGE 130 F2576
PLAN
INDUS
MGT
CENTRAL

B64
URQUIDI V.L.,THE CHALLENGE OF DEVELOPMENT IN LATIN AMERICA. L/A+17C FINAN INT/ORG TEC/DEV DIPLOM INT/TRADE PRICE REGION PRODUC...CHARTS 20 ALL/PROG. PAGE 133 F2628
ECO/UNDEV
ECO/TAC
NAT/G
TREND

B64
US CONGRESS JOINT ECO COMM,PRIVATE INVESTMENT IN LATIN AMERICA. L/A+17C USA+45 INT/ORG PROB/SOLV ECO/TAC ATTIT...INT 20 CONGRESS. PAGE 135 F2658
FINAN
ECO/UNDEV
PARL/PROC
LEGIS

B64
US SENATE COMM ON FOREIGN REL,HEARING ON BILLS RELATING TO FOREIGN ASSISTANCE. USA+45 WOR+45 ECO/UNDEV FINAN INDUS 20 UN CONGRESS. PAGE 139 F2733
FOR/AID
DIPLOM
TEC/DEV
INT/ORG

L64
ARMENGALD A.,"ECONOMIE ET COEXISTENCE." COM EUR+WWI FUT USA+45 WOR+45 ECO/DEV ECO/UNDEV FINAN INT/ORG NAT/G EXEC CHOOSE ATTIT ALL/VALS...POLICY RELATIV DECISION TREND SOC/EXP WORK 20. PAGE 6 F0113
MARKET ECO/TAC AFR CAP/ISM

L64
BHAGWATI J.,"THE PURE THEORY OF INTERNATIONAL TRADE: A SURVEY." WOR+45 ECO/DEV ECO/UNDEV FINAN MARKET PROC/MFG INT/ORG LABOR LG/CO NAT/G TEC/DEV ECO/TAC SKILL WEALTH...POLICY RELATIV MGT CONCPT NEW/IDEA MATH QUANT GEN/LAWS FOR/TRADE 20. PAGE 14 F0276
INDUS HYPO/EXP

L64
CARNEGIE ENDOWMENT INT. PEACE,"ECONOMIC AND SOCIAL QUESTION (ISSUES BEFORE THE NINETEENTH GENERAL ASSEMBLY)." WOR+45 ECO/DEV ECO/UNDEV INDUS R+D DELIB/GP CREATE PLAN TEC/DEV ECO/TAC FOR/AID BAL/PAY...RECORD UN 20. PAGE 21 F0414
INT/ORG INT/TRADE

L64
HAAS E.B.,"ECONOMICS AND DIFFERENTIAL PATTERNS OF POLITICAL INTEGRATION: PROJECTIONS ABOUT UNITY IN LATIN AMERICA." SOCIETY NAT/G DELIB/GP ACT/RES CREATE PLAN ECO/TAC REGION ROUTINE ATTIT DRIVE PWR WEALTH...CONCPT TREND CHARTS LAFTA TERR/GP 20. PAGE 52 F1020
L/A+17C INT/ORG MARKET

L64
KORBONSKI A.,"COMECON." ASIA ECO/DEV ECO/UNDEV ECO/TAC BAL/PAY NAT/LISM FOR/TRADE 20 COMECON. PAGE 73 F1425
COM INT/ORG INT/TRADE

S64
CARNEGIE ENDOWMENT INT. PEACE,"ADMINISTRATION AND BUDGET (ISSUES BEFORE THE NINETEENTH GENERAL ASSEMBLY)." WOR+45 FINAN BUDGET ECO/TAC ROUTINE COST...STAT RECORD UN. PAGE 21 F0415
INT/ORG ADMIN

S64
GARDNER R.N.,"GATT AND THE UNITED NATIONS CONFERENCE ON TRADE AND DEVELOPMENT." USA+45 WOR+45 SOCIETY ECO/UNDEV MARKET NAT/G DELIB/GP ACT/RES PLAN ECO/TAC TARIFFS EDU/PROP ROUTINE DRIVE RIGID/FLEX WEALTH...DECISION MGT TREND UN TOT/POP 20 GATT. PAGE 46 F0905
INT/ORG INT/TRADE

S64
GERBET P.,"LA MISE EN OEUVRE DU MARCHE COMMUN AGRICOLE." ECO/DEV MARKET INT/ORG NAT/G PLAN EDU/PROP NAT/LISM WEALTH...OBS EEC VAL/FREE 20. PAGE 47 F0917
EUR+WWI AGRI REGION

S64
HUTCHINSON E.C.,"AMERICAN AID TO AFRICA." FUT USA+45 MARKET INT/ORG LOC/G NAT/G PUB/INST PLAN ECO/TAC ATTIT RIGID/FLEX...POLICY CONCPT TREND TERR/GP 20. PAGE 63 F1248
AFR ECO/UNDEV FOR/AID

S64
PADELFORD N.J.,"THE ORGANIZATION OF AFRICAN UNITY." ECO/UNDEV INT/ORG PLAN BAL/PWR DIPLOM ECO/TAC NAT/LISM ORD/FREE PWR WEALTH...CONCPT TREND STERTYP TERR/GP VAL/FREE 20. PAGE 102 F2013
AFR VOL/ASSN REGION

S64
PESELT B.M.,"COMMUNIST ECONOMIC OFFENSIVE." WOR+45 SOCIETY INT/ORG PLAN ECO/TAC DOMIN EDU/PROP ATTIT PERSON PWR WEALTH...TREND CHARTS METH/GP 20. PAGE 105 F2067
COM ECO/UNDEV FOR/AID USSR

S64
ROTHCHILD D.,"EAST AFRICAN FEDERATION." AFR TANZANIA UGANDA INDUS REGION 20. PAGE 114 F2249
INT/ORG DIPLOM ECO/UNDEV ECO/TAC

S64
SALVADORI M.,"EL CAPITALISMO EN LA EUROPA DE LA POSGUERRA." AFR INT/ORG NAT/G POL/PAR PLAN ECO/TAC ATTIT ORD/FREE WEALTH...HIST/WRIT EEC 20. PAGE 115 F2275
EUR+WWI ECO/DEV CAP/ISM

N64
GREAT BRITAIN CENTRAL OFF INF,THE COLOMBO PLAN (PAMPHLET). AFR ASIA S/ASIA USA+45 VOL/ASSN ...CHARTS 20 RESOURCE/N. PAGE 50 F0980
FOR/AID PLAN INT/ORG ECO/UNDEV

B65
PEACE RESEARCH ABSTRACTS. FUT WOR+45 R+D INT/ORG NAT/G PLAN TEC/DEV BAL/PWR DIPLOM FOR/AID NUC/PWR HEALTH. PAGE 1 F0022
BIBLIOG/A PEACE ARMS/CONT WAR

B65
ALEXANDER R.J.,ORGANIZED LABOR IN LATIN AMERICA. L/A+17C INT/ORG LEGIS WORKER TEC/DEV BARGAIN INT/TRADE REV...NAT/COMP BIBLIOG 20. PAGE 3 F0059
LABOR POL/PAR ECO/UNDEV POLICY

B65
BELASSA B.,ECONOMIC DEVELOPMENT AND INTEGRATION. LG/CO PROB/SOLV TEC/DEV INT/TRADE TARIFFS COST WEALTH...POLICY METH/COMP 20. PAGE 12 F0232
ECO/UNDEV ECO/TAC INT/ORG INDUS

B65
CASSELL F.,GOLD OR CREDIT? THE ECONOMICS AND POLITICS OF INTERNATIONAL MONEY. AFR WOR+45 PLAN PROB/SOLV BAL/PAY SOVEREIGN WEALTH 20 OEEC. PAGE 22 F0428
FINAN INT/ORG DIPLOM ECO/TAC

B65
COLLINS H.,KARL MARX AND THE BRITISH LABOUR MOVEMENT; YEARS OF THE FIRST INTERNATIONAL. FRANCE SWITZERLND UK CAP/ISM WAR...MARXIST IDEA/COMP BIBLIOG 19. PAGE 26 F0506
MARXISM LABOR INT/ORG REV

B65
COLLINS H.,KARL MARX AND THE BRITISH LABOR MOVEMENT, YEARS OF THE FIRST INTERNATIONAL. EUR+WWI MOD/EUR UK STRATA INDUS NAT/G POL/PAR SOCISM ...CONCPT 19/20 MARX/KARL. PAGE 26 F0507
MARXISM LABOR INT/ORG WORKER

B65
EUROPEAN FREE TRADE ASSN,REGIONAL DEVELOPMENT POLICIES IN EFTA. ECO/UNDEV INT/ORG PLAN REGION ...POLICY GEOG EFTA. PAGE 39 F0755
EUR+WWI ECO/DEV NAT/COMP INT/TRADE

B65
HASSON J.A.,THE ECONOMICS OF NUCLEAR POWER. INDIA UK USA+45 WOR+45 INT/ORG TEC/DEV COST...SOC STAT CHARTS 20 EURATOM. PAGE 56 F1108
NUC/PWR INDUS ECO/DEV METH

B65
HOSELITZ B.F.,ECONOMICS AND THE IDEA OF MANKIND. UNIV ECO/DEV ECO/UNDEV DIST/IND INDUS INT/ORG NAT/G ACT/RES ECO/TAC WEALTH...CONCPT STAT. PAGE 62 F1223
CREATE INT/TRADE

B65
INTERAMERICAN ECO AND SOC COUN,THE ALLIANCE FOR PROGRESS: ITS THIRD YEAR 1963-1964. FUT L/A+17C WOR+45 ECO/DEV INT/ORG PLAN CONTROL ADJUST...STAT ANTHOL SOC/INTEG 20 ALL/PROG. PAGE 64 F1268
ECO/UNDEV ECO/TAC FINAN FOR/AID

B65
JOHNSON H.G.,THE WORLD ECONOMY AT THE CROSSROADS. COM WOR-45 ECO/DEV AGRI INDUS INT/TRADE REGION NAT/LISM 20. PAGE 67 F1326
FINAN DIPLOM INT/ORG ECO/UNDEV

B65
KASER M.,COMECON* INTEGRATION PROBLEMS OF THE PLANNED ECONOMIES. INT/ORG TEC/DEV INT/TRADE PRICE ADMIN ADJUST CENTRAL...STAT TIME/SEQ ORG/CHARTS COMECON. PAGE 69 F1359
PLAN ECO/DEV COM REGION

B65
KISSINGER H.A.,THE TROUBLED PARTNERSHIP* RE-APPRAISAL OF THE WESTERN ALLIANCE. EUR+WWI USA+45 INT/ORG NAT/G VOL/ASSN TOP/EX DIPLOM ORD/FREE PWR NATO. PAGE 71 F1402
FRANCE NUC/PWR ECO/DEV

B65
LEYS C.T.,FEDERATION IN EAST AFRICA. LAW AGRI DIST/IND FINAN INT/ORG LABOR INT/TRADE CONFER ADMIN CONTROL GP/REL...ANTHOL 20 AFRICA/E. PAGE 79 F1554
FEDERAL REGION ECO/UNDEV PLAN

B65
MACDONALD R.W.,THE LEAGUE OF ARAB STATES: A STUDY IN THE DYNAMICS OF REGIONAL ORGANIZATION. ISRAEL UAR USSR FINAN INT/ORG DELIB/GP ECO/TAC AGREE NEUTRAL ORD/FREE PWR...DECISION BIBLIOG 20 TREATY UN. PAGE 83 F1626
ISLAM REGION DIPLOM ADMIN

B65
MONCRIEFF A.,SECOND THOUGHTS ON AID. WOR+45 ECO/UNDEV AGRI FINAN VOL/ASSN PLAN TEC/DEV GIVE EDU/PROP ROLE WEALTH 20. PAGE 93 F1816
FOR/AID ECO/TAC INT/ORG IDEA/COMP

B65
MORTON H.C.,BROOKINGS PAPERS ON PUBLIC POLICY. USA+45 WOR+45 INDUS ACADEM INT/ORG LOC/G PROVS EDU/PROP MUNICH. PAGE 94 F1840
FINAN ECO/DEV TOP/EX NAT/G

B65
NKRUMAH K.,NEO-COLONIALISM: THE LAST STAGE OF IMPERIALISM. AFR INT/ORG WORKER FOR/AID INT/TRADE EDU/PROP GOV/REL NAT/LISM SOVEREIGN POPULISM SOCISM ...SOCIALIST 20 THIRD/WRLD INTRVN/ECO. PAGE 98 F1929
COLONIAL DIPLOM ECO/UNDEV ECO/TAC

B65
O'CONNELL D.P.,INTERNATIONAL LAW (2 VOLS.). WOR+45 WOR-45 ECO/DEV ECO/UNDEV INT/ORG NAT/G AGREE ...POLICY JURID CONCPT NAT/COMP 20 TREATY. PAGE 99 F1952
INT/LAW DIPLOM CT/SYS

B65
PINCUS J.A.,ECONOMIC AID AND INTERNATIONAL COST SHARING* A RAND CORPORATION RESEARCH STUDY. INT/ORG BUDGET CENTRAL...ECOMETRIC MATH QUANT STAT SIMUL. PAGE 106 F2088
ECO/UNDEV COST FOR/AID INT/TRADE

B65
ROOSA R.V.,MONETARY REFORM FOR THE WORLD ECONOMY. AFR EUR+WWI USA+45 WOR+45 CREATE BUDGET DIPLOM FOR/AID EQUILIB WEALTH IMF. PAGE 114 F2237
FINAN INT/ORG INT/TRADE BAL/PAY

B65
SCOTT A.M.,THE REVOLUTION IN STATECRAFT: INFORMAL PENETRATION. WOR+45 WOR-45 CULTURE INT/ORG FORCES ECO/TAC ROUTINE...BIBLIOG 20. PAGE 118 F2331
DIPLOM EDU/PROP FOR/AID

B65
SHONFIELD A.,MODERN CAPITALISM: THE CHANGING BALANCE OF PUBLIC AND PRIVATE POWER. FRANCE GERMANY/W UK USA+45 WOR+45 ECO/DEV INT/ORG NAT/G CONSULT INT/TRADE PRODUC...POLICY CONCPT METH/COMP 20. PAGE 121 F2386
CAP/ISM CONTROL BAL/PWR CREATE

B65
STEWART I.G.,AFRICAN PRIMARY PRODUCTS AND INTERNATIONAL TRADE. ECO/UNDEV AGRI FINAN DIPLOM CONTROL 20. PAGE 126 F2485
AFR INT/TRADE INT/ORG

B65
US BUREAU EDUC CULTURAL AFF,RESOURCES SURVEY FOR LATIN AMERICAN COUNTRIES. L/A+17C USA+45 CULTURE INDUS INT/ORG SECT PLAN EDU/PROP POLICY. PAGE 134 F2643
NAT/G ECO/UNDEV FOR/AID DIPLOM

B65
US CONGRESS JOINT ECO COMM,GUIDELINES FOR INTERNATIONAL MONETARY REFORM. USA+45 WOR+45 DELIB/GP BAL/PAY 20 CONGRESS IMF MONEY. PAGE 135 F2659
DIPLOM FINAN PLAN INT/ORG

B65
US SENATE COMM ON FOREIGN REL,HEARINGS ON THE FOREIGN ASSISTANCE PROGRAM. AFR ASIA L/A+17C USA+45 WOR+45 FORCES TEC/DEV BUDGET CONTROL WEAPON ORD/FREE 20 UN CONGRESS SEC/STATE. PAGE 139 F2734
FOR/AID DIPLOM INT/ORG ECO/UNDEV

B65
VANEK J.,GENERAL EQUILIBRIUM OF INTERNATIONAL DISCRIMINATION; THE CASE OF CUSTOMS UNIONS. LABOR PROB/SOLV ECO/TAC DISCRIM INCOME...MATH CHARTS METH 20. PAGE 140 F2767
INT/TRADE TARIFFS INT/ORG EQUILIB

B65
WARD R.J.,INTERNATIONAL FINANCE. INT/ORG DIPLOM DEMAND INCOME...POLICY METH/COMP 20. PAGE 143 F2819
INT/TRADE ECO/TAC FINAN BAL/PAY

B65
WEAVER J.N.,THE INTERNATIONAL DEVELOPMENT ASSOCIATION: A NEW APPROACH TO FOREIGN AID. USA+45 NAT/G OP/RES PLAN PROB/SOLV WEALTH...CHARTS BIBLIOG 20 UN. PAGE 144 F2836
FOR/AID INT/ORG ECO/UNDEV FINAN

B65
WEIL G.L.,A HANDBOOK ON THE EUROPEAN ECONOMIC COMMUNITY. BELGIUM EUR+WWI FRANCE GERMANY/W ITALY CONSTN ECO/DEV CREATE PARTIC GP/REL...DECISION MGT CHARTS 20 EEC. PAGE 144 F2846
INT/TRADE INT/ORG TEC/DEV INT/LAW

L65
DAANE J.D.,"THE EVOLVING INTERNATIONAL MONETARY MECHANISM." VOL/ASSN CREATE PLAN FOR/AID INT/TRADE CONFER BAL/PAY...RECORD PREDICT IMF. PAGE 29 F0569
INT/ORG ECO/TAC TREND GP/COMP

L65
LOFTUS M.L.,"INTERNATIONAL MONETARY FUND, 1962-1965: A SELECTED BIBLIOGRAPHY." WOR+45 PLAN BUDGET INCOME PROFIT WEALTH. PAGE 81 F1596
BIBLIOG FINAN INT/TRADE INT/ORG

L65
WIONCZEK M.,"LATIN AMERICA FREE TRADE ASSOCIATION." AGRI DIST/IND FINAN INDUS INT/ORG LABOR NAT/G TEC/DEV ECO/TAC HEALTH SKILL WEALTH...POLICY RELATIV MGT LAFTA 20. PAGE 148 F2909
L/A+17C MARKET REGION

S65
BALDWIN D.A.,"THE INTERNATIONAL BANK IN POLITICAL PERSPECTIVE" USA+45 TEC/DEV FOR/AID RENT GIVE COST ...IDEA/COMP GAME IBRD. PAGE 9 F0160
FINAN INT/ORG

S65
LECLERCQ H.,"ECONOMIC RESEARCH AND DEVELOPMENT IN TROPICAL AFRICA." ECO/UNDEV INT/ORG CREATE PLAN UN. PAGE 77 F1500
AFR R+D ACADEM ECO/TAC

S65
SPAAK P.H.,"THE SEARCH FOR CONSENSUS: A NEW EFFORT TO BUILD EUROPE." FRANCE GERMANY ECO/DEV NAT/G CONSULT FORCES PLAN EDU/PROP REGION CONSEN ATTIT ...SOC METH/CNCPT OBS TREND EEC NATO WORK TERR/GP METH/GP 20. PAGE 124 F2447
EUR+WWI INT/ORG

S65
WHITE J.,"WEST GERMAN AID TO DEVELOPING COUNTRIES." AFR INT/ORG OP/RES GIVE CENTRAL ATTIT DRIVE...STAT NAT/COMP. PAGE 146 F2869
GERMANY FOR/AID ECO/UNDEV CAP/ISM

N65
STUDY GP CREATE RESERVE ASSETS,REPORT TO DEPUTIES (PAMPHLET). AFR FUT PLAN CONTROL DEMAND WEALTH ...ANTHOL METH 20. PAGE 127 F2507
INT/ORG INT/TRADE FINAN BUDGET

B66
ALEXANDER Y.,INTERNATIONAL TECHNICAL ASSISTANCE EXPERTS* A CASE STUDY OF THE U.N. EXPERIENCE. ECO/UNDEV CONSULT EX/STRUC CREATE PLAN DIPLOM FOR/AID TASK EFFICIENCY...ORG/CHARTS UN. PAGE 3 F0061
ECO/TAC INT/ORG ADMIN MGT

B66
ALEXANDER Y.,INTERNATIONAL TECHNICAL ASSISTANCE EXPERTS: A CASE STUDY OF THE U.N. EXPERIENCE. USA+45 WOR+45 WORKER CREATE PLAN PROB/SOLV ECO/TAC FOR/AID GIVE EDU/PROP...CHARTS BIBLIOG 20 UN. PAGE 3 F0062
SKILL INT/ORG TEC/DEV CONSULT

B66
ALIBER R.Z.,THE FUTURE OF THE DOLLAR AS AN INTERNATIONAL CURRENCY. AFR USA+45 USA-45 ECO/DEV PRICE COST INCOME...POLICY 20. PAGE 4 F0067
FINAN DIPLOM INT/ORG INT/TRADE

B66
AMER ENTERPRISE INST PUB POL,SIGNIFICANT ISSUES IN ECONOMIC AID TO DEVELOPING COUNTRIES. FINAN INT/ORG NAT/G PLAN PROB/SOLV GIVE TASK WEALTH...DECISION 20. PAGE 4 F0083
ECO/UNDEV FOR/AID DIPLOM POLICY

B66
BEUGEL E.V.D.,FROM MARSHALL AID TO ATLANTIC PARTNERSHIP* EUROPEAN INTEGRATION AS A CONCERN OF AMERICAN FOREIGN POLICY. USA+45 INT/ORG FORCES PERSON EEC NATO. PAGE 14 F0272
REGION DIPLOM EUR+WWI VOL/ASSN

B66
DAVIES I.,AFRICAN TRADE UNIONS. AFR ECO/UNDEV INT/ORG GP/REL ORD/FREE SOVEREIGN SOCISM 20. PAGE 30 F0585
LABOR COLONIAL PWR INDUS

B66
FRIEDMANN W.G.,INTERNATIONAL FINANCIAL AID. USA+45 ECO/DEV ECO/UNDEV NAT/G VOL/ASSN EX/STRUC PLAN RENT GIVE BAL/PAY PWR...GEOG INT/LAW STAT TREND UN EEC COMECON. PAGE 44 F0866
INT/ORG FOR/AID TEC/DEV ECO/TAC

B66
GITTINGER J.P.,THE LITERATURE OF AGRICULTURAL PLANNING. UNIV INT/ORG CONSULT WORKER TEC/DEV ECO/TAC OPTIMAL...POLICY METH/COMP BIBLIOG/A 20. PAGE 47 F0927
ECO/UNDEV AGRI PLAN WRITING

B66
GYORGY A.,ISSUES OF WORLD COMMUNISM. ALBANIA CHINA/COM COM USSR YUGOSLAVIA STRATA AGRI INT/ORG CHIEF FORCES WORKER WAR ALL/IDEOS...GEOG 20 MAO. PAGE 52 F1018
ECO/UNDEV REV MARXISM CON/ANAL

B66
HEVESY P.D.,THE UNIFICATION OF THE WORLD. FUT USA+45 WOR+45 ECO/DEV ECO/UNDEV LEGIS PROB/SOLV BAL/PWR ECO/TAC INT/TRADE PEACE. PAGE 59 F1160
DIPLOM FINAN INT/ORG

B66
HOROWITZ D.,HEMISPHERES NORTH AND SOUTH: ECONOMIC DISPARITY AMONG NATIONS. WOR+45 ECO/DEV ECO/UNDEV INT/ORG PLAN DIPLOM INT/TRADE GIVE PARTIC GP/REL ...WELF/ST 20. PAGE 62 F1215
ECO/TAC FOR/AID STRATA WEALTH

B66
HUTTENBACH R.A.,BRITISH IMPERIAL EXPERIENCE. AFR S/ASIA UK WOR-45 INT/ORG TEC/DEV...CHARTS 16/20 MERCANTLST. PAGE 64 F1253
COLONIAL TIME/SEQ INT/TRADE

B66
INGRAM J.C.,INTERNATIONAL ECONOMIC PROBLEMS. ECO/DEV ECO/UNDEV INDUS MARKET TEC/DEV TARIFFS BAL/PAY CENTRAL...POLICY 20 EEC. PAGE 64 F1265
INT/TRADE INT/ORG FINAN

B66
INTERNATIONAL ECO POLICY ASSN,THE UNITED STATES BALANCE OF PAYMENTS. INT/ORG NAT/G PROB/SOLV BUDGET DIPLOM INT/TRADE WEALTH 20. PAGE 65 F1274
BAL/PAY ECO/TAC POLICY FINAN

B66
JACKSON G.D.,COMINTERN AND PEASANT IN EAST EUROPE 1919-1930. BULGARIA COM CZECHOSLVK EUR+WWI POLAND ROMANIA YUGOSLAVIA STRATA AGRI VOL/ASSN DIPLOM CONTROL CROWD WEALTH...POLICY NAT/COMP 20. PAGE 66 F1293
MARXISM ECO/UNDEV WORKER INT/ORG

B66
KINDLEBERGER C.P.,EUROPE AND THE DOLLAR. AFR EUR+WWI FRANCE GERMANY/W USA+45 CONSTN INT/ORG DIPLOM INT/TRADE...ANTHOL 20. PAGE 71 F1395
BAL/PAY BUDGET FINAN ECO/DEV

B66
KIRDAR U.,THE STRUCTURE OF UNITED NATIONS ECONOMIC AID TO UNDERDEVELOPED COUNTRIES. AGRI FINAN INDUS NAT/G EX/STRUC PLAN GIVE TASK...POLICY 20 UN. PAGE 71 F1397
INT/ORG FOR/AID ECO/UNDEV ADMIN

B66
MEERHAEGHE M.,INTERNATIONAL ECONOMIC INSTITUTIONS. EUR+WWI FINAN INDUS MARKET PLAN TARIFFS BAL/PAY EQUILIB...POLICY BIBLIOG/A 20 GATT OEEC EEC IBRD EURCOALSTL. PAGE 89 F1745
ECO/TAC ECO/DEV INT/TRADE INT/ORG

B66
MIKESELL R.F.,PUBLIC INTERNATIONAL LENDING FOR DEVELOPMENT. WOR+45 WOR-45 DELIB/GP...TIME/SEQ CHARTS BIBLIOG 20. PAGE 91 F1783
INT/ORG FOR/AID ECO/UNDEV FINAN

B66
OHLIN G.,AID AND INDEBTEDNESS. AUSTRIA FINAN INT/ORG PLAN DIPLOM GIVE...POLICY MATH CHARTS 20. PAGE 101 F1984
FOR/AID ECO/UNDEV ADMIN WEALTH

B66
ORG FOR ECO COOP AND DEVEL,GEOGRAPHICAL DISTRIBUTION OF FINANCIAL FLOWS TO LESS DEVELOPED COUNTRIES. WOR+45 DIPLOM INT/TRADE GIVE RECEIVE REPAR REGION WEALTH...GEOG STAT CHARTS 20 OECD. PAGE 102 F1997
FINAN ECO/UNDEV INT/ORG FOR/AID

B66
RUBIN S.J.,THE CONSCIENCE OF THE RICH NATIONS: THE DEVELOPMENT ASSISTANCE COMMITTEE AND THE COMMON AID EFFORT. EUR+WWI USA+45 ECO/UNDEV INT/ORG NAT/G VOL/ASSN ECO/TAC INT/TRADE...OBS UN AID DEV/ASSIST IBRD OECD. PAGE 114 F2256
FOR/AID ECO/DEV CONFER CENTRAL

B66
SEWELL J.P.,FUNCTIONALISM AND WORLD POLITICS* A STUDY BASED ON UNITED NATIONS PROGRAMS FINANCING ECONOMICAL DEVELOPMENT. ECO/UNDEV FINAN PROB/SOLV DIPLOM ECO/TAC FEEDBACK REGION ADJUST ATTIT UN IBRD INTL/FINAN INTL/DEV UNSF. PAGE 120 F2360
TASK INT/ORG IDEA/COMP GEN/LAWS

B66
SINGH L.P.,THE POLITICS OF ECONOMIC COOPERATION IN ASIA; A STUDY OF ASIAN INTERNATIONAL ORGANIZATIONS. ASIA INT/ORG ACT/RES PLAN GP/REL...POLICY GP/COMP BIBLIOG 20 UN SEATO. PAGE 122 F2414
ECO/UNDEV ECO/TAC REGION DIPLOM

B66
SOMMERFELD R.M.,TAX REFORM AND THE ALLIANCE FOR PROGRESS. USA+45 ECO/DEV ECO/UNDEV FINAN NAT/G INCOME ORD/FREE WEALTH...STAT CHARTS 20 ALL/PROG. PAGE 124 F2442
TAX INT/ORG L/A+17C FOR/AID

B66
TRIFFIN R.,THE WORLD MONEY MAZE. AFR INT/ORG ECO/TAC PRICE OPTIMAL WEALTH...METH/COMP 20 EEC OEEC SILVER. PAGE 131 F2589
BAL/PAY FINAN INT/TRADE DIPLOM

B66
TRIFFIN R.,THE BALANCE OF PAYMENTS AND THE FOREIGN INVESTMENT POSITION OF THE UNITED STATES. AFR USA+45 INT/ORG INT/TRADE PRICE CONTROL...POLICY 20. PAGE 131 F2590
BAL/PAY DIPLOM FINAN ECO/TAC

B66
UREN P.E.,EAST - WEST TRADE* A SYMPOSIUM. COM AGRI INT/ORG PRICE HABITAT RIGID/FLEX...GEOG INT/LAW ANTHOL NATO. PAGE 133 F2625
INT/TRADE BAL/PWR AFR CANADA

B66
US HOUSE COMM FOREIGN AFFAIRS,HEARINGS ON HR 12449 A BILL TO AMEND FURTHER THE FOREIGN ASSISTANCE ACT OF 1961. AFR ASIA L/A+17C USA+45 VIETNAM INT/ORG TEC/DEV INT/TRADE ATTIT ORD/FREE 20 UN NATO CONGRESS AID. PAGE 137 F2692
FOR/AID ECO/TAC ECO/UNDEV DIPLOM

B66
US SENATE COMM APPROPRIATIONS,FOREIGN ASSISTANCE AND RELATED AGENCIES APPROPRIATIONS FOR FISCAL YEAR 1967: HEARINGS... ON H. R. 17788. ECO/UNDEV INT/ORG FORCES INSPECT ECO/TAC GIVE DEBATE WEAPON CIVMIL/REL WEALTH...INT 20 CONGRESS DEPT/DEFEN DEPT/STATE DEPT/HEW AID. PAGE 138 F2727
BUDGET FOR/AID DIPLOM COST

L66
AFRICAN BIBLIOGRAPHIC CENTER,"AFRICAN ECONOMIC AFFAIRS: A SELECT BIBLIOGRAPHICAL SURVEY, 1965-1966." AFR FINAN INDUS INT/ORG LABOR PLAN BUDGET DIPLOM INT/TRADE ADMIN EFFICIENCY WEALTH 20. PAGE 3 F0046
BIBLIOG ECO/UNDEV TEC/DEV FOR/AID

S66
ERB GF,"THE UNITED NATIONS CONFERENCE ON TRADE AND DEVELOPMENT (UNCTAD): A SELECTED CURRENT READING LIST." FINAN FOR/AID CONFER 20 UN. PAGE 38 F0742
BIBLIOG/A INT/TRADE ECO/UNDEV INT/ORG

S66
JAVITS J.K.,"POLITICAL ACTION VITAL FOR LATIN AMERICAN INTEGRATION." ECO/UNDEV INT/ORG POL/PAR VOL/ASSN PLAN PROB/SOLV INT/TRADE EFFICIENCY 20 OAS LAFTA ALL/PROG. PAGE 66 F1308
L/A+17C ECO/TAC REGION

N66
OECD,THE BALANCE OF PAYMENTS ADJUSTMENT PROCESS (PAMPHLET). EUR+WWI ECO/DEV FINAN CONSULT PLAN PROB/SOLV BUDGET CAP/ISM INT/TRADE PRICE CONTROL EQUILIB 20. PAGE 101 F1975
BAL/PAY ECO/TAC DIPLOM INT/ORG

B67
ANDERSON S.V.,THE NORDIC COUNCIL: A STUDY OF SCANDINAVIAN REGIONALISM. DENMARK FINLAND ICELAND NORWAY SWEDEN MARKET NAT/G VOL/ASSN CONSULT PARL/PROC ATTIT...TIME/SEQ BIBLIOG 20. PAGE 5 F0098
INT/ORG REGION DIPLOM LEGIS

B67
BARANSON J.,TECHNOLOGY FOR UNDERDEVELOPED AREAS: AN ANNOTATED BIBLIOGRAPHY. FUT WOR+45 CULTURE INDUS INT/ORG CREATE PROB/SOLV INT/TRADE EDU/PROP AUTOMAT ...CONCPT METH. PAGE 10 F0181
BIBLIOG/A ECO/UNDEV TEC/DEV R+D

B67
BEATON L.,THE STRUGGLE FOR PEACE. INT/ORG FORCES NUC/PWR COST PWR...POLICY TREND 20. PAGE 12 F0225
PEACE BAL/PWR DIPLOM WAR

B67
BLAIR P.W.,THE MINISTATE DILEMMA. WOR+45 AGREE COLONIAL ORD/FREE...GEOG CHARTS MUNICH LEAGUE/NAT UN. PAGE 15 F0294
INT/ORG NAT/G CENSUS

B67
BLAUG M.,ECONOMICS OF EDUCATION: A SELECTED ANNOTATED BIBLIOGRAPHY. EUR+WWI INTELL ECO/DEV ECO/UNDEV ACADEM INT/ORG NAT/G CREATE ADMIN EFFICIENCY ROLE PREDICT. PAGE 16 F0298
BIBLIOG/A EDU/PROP FINAN PLAN

B67
CHO S.S.,KOREA IN WORLD POLITICS 1940-1950; AN EVALUATION OF AMERICAN RESPONSIBILITY. KOREA USA+45 USSR CONSTN INT/ORG NAT/G FORCES FOR/AID ANOMIE SUPEGO MARXISM...DECISION BIBLIOG 20. PAGE 24 F0469
POLICY DIPLOM PROB/SOLV WAR

B67
HOGAN J.,THE US BALANCE OF PAYMENTS AND CAPITAL FLOWS. MARKET INT/ORG ECO/TAC PRICE CONTROL WEALTH ...METH/COMP 20 EEC. PAGE 61 F1192
BAL/PAY FINAN DIPLOM INT/TRADE

B67
INTERNATIONAL LABOUR OFFICE,SUBJECT GUIDE TO PUBLICATIONS OF THE INTERNATIONAL LABOUR OFFICE, 1919-1964. DIPLOM 20. PAGE 65 F1280
BIBLIOG LABOR INT/ORG WORKER

B67
JOHNSON H.G.,ECONOMIC POLICY TOWARD LESS DEVELOPED COUNTRIES. USA+45 ECO/DEV INT/ORG PLAN CAP/ISM FOR/AID TARIFFS GIVE WEALTH...NEW/IDEA CHARTS 20 UN GATT. PAGE 67 F1327
ECO/UNDEV ECO/TAC METH/COMP

B67
KREININ M.E.,ALTERNATIVE COMMERCIAL POLICIES - THEIR EFFECT ON THE AMERICAN ECONOMY. USA+45 LAW ECO/DEV MARKET INT/ORG DIPLOM ECO/TAC TARIFFS PRICE DEMAND WEALTH...QUANT EEC AFTA. PAGE 73 F1437
INT/TRADE BAL/PAY NAT/G POLICY

B67
MACCLOSKEY M.,PACTS FOR PEACE: UN, NATO, SEATO, CENTO, OAS. WOR+45 PLAN DIPLOM CONTROL PEACE ORD/FREE...ORG/CHARTS UN NATO SEATO OAS CENTO. PAGE 83 F1623
FORCES INT/ORG LEAD POLICY

B67
MARTIN P.,CANADA AND THE QUEST FOR PEACE. CANADA VIETNAM ECO/UNDEV PLAN FOR/AID WAR 20 UN. PAGE 86 F1684
DIPLOM PEACE INT/ORG POLICY

B67
MEYNAUD J.,TRADE UNIONISM IN AFRICA; A STUDY OF ITS GROWTH AND ORIENTATION (TRANS. BY ANGELA BRENCH). INT/ORG PROB/SOLV COLONIAL PWR...TIME/SEQ TREND ILO. PAGE 90 F1774
LABOR AFR NAT/LISM ORD/FREE

B67
MURTY B.S.,PROPAGANDA AND WORLD PUBLIC ORDER. FUT WOR+45 COM/IND INT/ORG PROB/SOLV ATTIT KNOWL ORD/FREE...POLICY UN. PAGE 95 F1868
EDU/PROP DIPLOM CONTROL JURID

B67
OVERSEAS DEVELOPMENT INSTIT,EFFECTIVE AID. WOR+45 INT/ORG TEC/DEV DIPLOM INT/TRADE ADMIN. PAGE 102 F2004
FOR/AID ECO/UNDEV ECO/TAC NAT/COMP

B67
ROACH J.R.,THE UNITED STATES AND THE ATLANTIC COMMUNITY; ISSUES AND PROSPECTS. AFR WOR+45 TEC/DEV ECO/TAC COLONIAL REGION PEACE ROLE...ANTHOL NATO EEC. PAGE 112 F2199
INT/ORG POLICY ADJUST DIPLOM

B67
THOMAN R.S.,GEOGRAPHY OF INTERNATIONAL TRADE. WOR+45 ECO/DEV ECO/UNDEV INT/ORG LG/CO PLAN BAL/PAY ...STAT CHARTS NAT/COMP 20. PAGE 130 F2559
INT/TRADE GEOG ECO/TAC DIPLOM

B67
US CONGRESS SENATE,SURVEY OF THE ALLIANCE FOR PROGRESS; INFLATION IN LATIN AMERICA (PAMPHLET). USA+45 MARKET INT/ORG DIPLOM INT/TRADE BAL/PAY SENATE ALL/PROG. PAGE 135 F2666
L/A+17C FINAN POLICY FOR/AID

B67
US SENATE COMM ON FOREIGN REL,LATIN AMERICAN SUMMIT CONFERENCE. L/A+17C USA+45 FINAN PLAN SENATE ALL/PROG. PAGE 139 F2740
FOR/AID BUDGET DIPLOM INT/ORG

B67
US SENATE COMM ON FOREIGN REL,INTER-AMERICAN DEVELOPMENT BANK ACT AMENDMENT. L/A+17C USA+45 DELIB/GP DIPLOM FOR/AID BAL/PAY...CHARTS SENATE. PAGE 139 F2741
LAW FINAN INT/ORG ECO/UNDEV

B67
WATT A.,THE EVOLUTION OF AUSTRALIAN FOREIGN POLICY 1938-65. ASIA S/ASIA USA+45 USA-45 INT/ORG NAT/G FORCES FOR/AID TREATY 20 AUSTRAL. PAGE 144 F2834
DIPLOM WAR

B67
WISEMAN H.V.,BRITAIN AND THE COMMONWEALTH. EUR+WWI FUT UK ECO/DEV POL/PAR TEC/DEV INT/TRADE LEAD ROLE SOVEREIGN...SOC TREND 20 CMN/WLTH. PAGE 148 F2911
INT/ORG DIPLOM NAT/G NAT/COMP

B67
ZUPNICK E.,UNDERSTANDING THE INTERNATIONAL MONEY SYSTEM (HEADLINE SERIES, NO. 182) (PAMPHLET). ECO/DEV NAT/G DIPLOM INT/TRADE...METH/COMP 20 IMF. PAGE 151 F2971
FINAN PLAN INT/ORG PROB/SOLV

L67
DROBNIG U.,"CONFLICT OF LAWS AND THE EUROPEAN ECONOMIC COMMUNITY." EUR+WWI PROB/SOLV DIPLOM ...JURID EEC. PAGE 34 F0663
INT/LAW ADJUD INT/ORG MARKET

L67
GOLD J.,"INTERPRETATION BY THE INTERNATIONAL MONETARY FUND OF ITS ARTICLES OF AGREEMENT." INT/TRADE ADJUD ATTIT...POLICY JURID. PAGE 48 F0933
CONSTN INT/ORG LAW DIPLOM

L67
HOSHII I.,"JAPAN'S STAKE IN ASIA." ASIA S/ASIA CAP/ISM ECO/TAC ROLE...GEOG 20 CHINJAP. PAGE 62 F1224
DIPLOM REGION NAT/G

INT/ORG

L67
MACDONALD R.S.J.,"THE RESORT TO ECONOMIC COERCION BY INTERNATIONAL POLITICAL ORGANIZATIONS." CUBA ETHIOPIA RHODESIA SOUTH/AFR NAT/G FOR/AID INT/TRADE DOMIN CONTROL SANCTION...DECISION LEAGUE/NAT UN OAS 20. PAGE 83 F1625
INT/ORG COERCE ECO/TAC DIPLOM

L67
MCALLISTER J.T. JR.,"THE POSSIBILITIES FOR DIPLOMACY IN SOUTHEAST ASIA." LAOS VIETNAM INT/ORG NAT/G PROVS BAL/PWR DOMIN AGREE COLONIAL WAR PWR 17/20 TREATY. PAGE 88 F1716
DIPLOM S/ASIA

L67
MEIER G.M.,"UNCTAD PROPOSALS FOR INTERNATIONAL ECONOMIC REFORM." WOR+45 MARKET INT/ORG TARIFFS CONFER UN GATT IMF. PAGE 89 F1749
INT/TRADE FINAN INT/LAW ECO/UNDEV

L67
MESTMACKER E.J.,"STATE TRADING MONOPOLIES IN THE EUROPEAN ECONOMIC COMMUNITY. DIPLOM ECO/TAC ADJUD CONTROL DISCRIM 20 EEC. PAGE 90 F1764
INT/TRADE INT/ORG LAW TARIFFS

L67
TANDON Y.,"CONSENSUS AND AUTHORITY BEHIND UNITED NATIONS PEACEKEEPING OPERATIONS." FINAN VOL/ASSN BUDGET DIPLOM PAY DOMIN...CHARTS 20 UN. PAGE 128 F2528
CONSEN INT/ORG PWR PEACE

S67
AGUILAR M.A.,"?UNA OEA MAS FUERTE O UNA AMERICA LATINA MAS DEBIL?" L/A+17C USA+45 USA-45 ECO/UNDEV INDUS CHIEF DELIB/GP FORCES CONTROL PWR 20 OAS KENNEDY/JF JOHNSON/LB. PAGE 3 F0050
INT/ORG DIPLOM POLICY COLONIAL

S67
ALEXANDER R.J.,"'THIRD FORCE' IN WORLD COMMUNISM?" CHINA/COM CUBA USSR INT/ORG DIPLOM TASK INGP/REL ATTIT PWR 20 CASTRO/F. PAGE 3 F0060
CHIEF MARXISM LEAD REV

S67
APEL H.,"LES NOUVEAUX ASPECTS DE LA POLITIQUE ETRANGERE ALLEMANDE." AFR EUR+WWI GERMANY POL/PAR BAL/PWR ECO/TAC INT/TRADE NUC/PWR NAT/LISM PEACE ...POLICY 20 EEC. PAGE 6 F0107
DIPLOM INT/ORG FEDERAL

S67
AUBERT DE LA RUE P.,"PERSPECTIVES ECONOMIQUES ENTRE LES ETATS-UNIS ET L'EUROPE." FUT INDUS R+D INT/ORG ACT/RES ECO/TAC AGREE BAL/PAY PRODUC...CHARTS 20 EEC GATT WORLD/BANK. PAGE 7 F0138
INT/TRADE ECO/DEV FINAN TARIFFS

S67
BENN W.,"TECHNOLOGY HAS AN INEXORABLE EFFECT." FUT UK ECO/DEV INT/ORG CONSULT PLAN EDU/PROP ADMIN LEAD GP/REL PRODUC...INT 20 EEC. PAGE 13 F0246
R+D LG/CO TEC/DEV INDUS

S67
BUTT R.,"THE COMMON MARKET AND CONSERVATIVE POLITICS, 1961-2." UK CHIEF DIPLOM ECO/TAC INT/TRADE CONFER DEBATE REGION ATTIT...POLICY 20 EEC. PAGE 21 F0398
EUR+WWI INT/ORG POL/PAR

S67
COSGROVE C.A.,"AGRICULTURE, FINANCE AND POLITICS IN THE EUROPEAN COMMUNITY." EUR+WWI DIST/IND MARKET INT/ORG VOL/ASSN DELIB/GP TEC/DEV BAL/PWR BARGAIN ECO/TAC RATION CONFER 20 EEC. PAGE 28 F0538
ECO/DEV DIPLOM AGRI INT/TRADE

S67
CROMER EARL OF,"STERLING AND THE COMMON MARKET." UK ECO/DEV INT/ORG 20 EEC. PAGE 29 F0554
ECO/TAC FINAN CHARTS INT/TRADE

S67
EHRLICH S.,"INTERNATIONAL PRESSURE GROUPS: A CONTRIBUTION TO THE SOCIOLOGY OF INTERNATIONAL RELATIONS IN THE CAPITALIST WORLD." GP/REL...METH 20. PAGE 36 F0711
INT/ORG LOBBY DIPLOM DECISION

S67
FADDEYEV N.,"CMEA CO-OPERATION OF EQUAL NATIONS." COM R+D PLAN CAP/ISM DIPLOM FOR/AID WEALTH...POLICY MARXIST. PAGE 39 F0758
MARXISM ECO/TAC INT/ORG ECO/UNDEV

S67
FRIEDENBERG D.M.,"THE US IN LATIN AMERICA; A RECKONING OF SHAME." L/A+17C USA+45 USA-45 INT/ORG CAP/ISM FOR/AID 17/20 OAS. PAGE 44 F0857
DIPLOM POLICY DOMIN COLONIAL

S67
HERRERA F.,"EUROPEAN PARTICIPATION IN THE LATIN AMERICAN REGIONAL INTEGRATION" EUR+WWI L/A+17C GP/REL INGP/REL 20. PAGE 59 F1154
DIPLOM REGION INT/ORG FINAN

S67
HILDEBRAND J.R.,"THE CENTRAL AMERICAN COMMON MARKET: ECONOMIC AND POLITICAL INTEGRATION." L/A+17C USA+45 ECO/DEV ECO/UNDEV AGRI SOVEREIGN. PAGE 59 F1170
DIPLOM ECO/TAC INT/TRADE INT/ORG

S67
ISELIN J.J.,"THE TRUMAN DOCTRINE: ITS PASSAGE THROUGH CONGRESS AND THE AFTERMATH." USA+45 ECO/UNDEV R+D INT/ORG DELIB/GP BAL/PWR REV PEACE ...POLICY UN. PAGE 66 F1291
DIPLOM COM FOR/AID AFR

S67
KELLY F.K.,"A PROPOSAL FOR AN ANNUAL REPORT ON THE STATE OF MANKIND." FUT INTELL COM/IND INT/ORG CREATE PROB/SOLV PERS/REL...CONCPT 20 UN. PAGE 70 F1371
SOCIETY UNIV ATTIT NEW/IDEA

S67
LEVI M.,"LES RELATIONS ECONOMIQUES ENTRE L'EST ET L'OUEST EN EUROPE" INDUS...STAT CHARTS 20 OECD COMECON. PAGE 79 F1540
INT/TRADE INT/ORG FINAN PRODUC

S67
MERON T.,"THE UN'S 'COMMON SYSTEM' OF SALARY, ALLOWANCE, AND BENEFITS: CRITICAL APPR'SAL OF COORD IN PERSONNEL MATTERS." VOL/ASSN PAY EFFICIENCY ...CHARTS 20 UN. PAGE 90 F1761
ADMIN EX/STRUC INT/ORG BUDGET

S67
MYRDAL G.,"ECONOMIC DEVELOPMENT IN THE BACKWARD COUNTRIES." INT/ORG TEC/DEV CAP/ISM DIPLOM INT/TRADE PRODUC WEALTH 20. PAGE 96 F1883
ECO/UNDEV INDUS NAT/G ECO/TAC

S67
OLIVIER G.,"ASPECTS JURIDIQUES DE L'ADOPTION DU TRAITE CECA A LA CRISE CHARBONNIERE (SUITE ET FIN)" LAW DIST/IND PLAN DIPLOM RATION PRICE ADMIN COST DEMAND...POLICY CON/ANAL ECSC TREATY. PAGE 101 F1988
INT/TRADE INT/ORG EXTR/IND CONSTN

S67
SCOTT R.,"TRADE UNIONS IN AFRICA." AFR UGANDA USA-45 ECO/UNDEV INDUS INT/ORG POL/PAR ECO/TAC WEALTH...GP/COMP 20 NKRUMAH/K. PAGE 118 F2335
LABOR WORKER NAT/G

S67
SMALL A.H.,"THE EFFECT OF TARIFF REDUCTIONS ON US IMPORT VOLUME." USA+45 INT/ORG NAT/G DIPLOM CONFER DEMAND...POLICY INT/LAW STAT CHARTS GATT EEC. PAGE 123 F2424
TARIFFS INT/TRADE PRICE ECO/TAC

S67
STOLTE S.C.,"THREE PROBLEMS FACING THE SOVIET BLOC." ASIA COM USA+45 USSR FORCES MARXISM ...IDEA/COMP METH/COMP 20 NATO WARSAW/P. PAGE 127 F2496
ECO/TAC DIPLOM INT/ORG POLICY

S67
WARNER G.,"FRANCE, BRITAIN AND THE EEC." FRANCE UK INT/ORG DELIB/GP ECO/TAC CONTROL 20 EEC. PAGE 143 F2822
INT/TRADE BAL/PWR DIPLOM

S67
WEIL G.L.,"THE MERGER OF THE INSTITUTIONS OF THE EUROPEAN COMMUNITIES" EUR+WWI ECO/DEV INT/TRADE CONSEN PLURISM...DECISION MGT 20 EEC EURATOM ECSC TREATY. PAGE 145 F2847
ECO/TAC INT/ORG CENTRAL INT/LAW

S67
WILLMANN J.,"LA COMMUNAUTE EUROPEENNE ET LA GRANDE-BRETAGNE." UK PROB/SOLV TEC/DEV CAP/ISM DIPLOM CONFER FEDERAL...POLICY 20 EEC. PAGE 147 F2898
INT/ORG DRIVE NAT/LISM INT/TRADE

N67
US HOUSE COMM FOREIGN AFFAIRS,REPORT OF SPECIAL STUDY MISSION TO THE NEAR EAST (PAMPHLET). ISRAEL USA+45 YEMEN ECO/UNDEV INT/ORG FOR/AID ARMS/CONT WAR WEAPON NAT/LISM PEACE...GEOG 20 UN HOUSE/REP. PAGE 137 F2694
ISLAM DIPLOM FORCES

N67
US HOUSE COMM FOREIGN AFFAIRS,FOREIGN ASSISTANCE ACT OF 1967 (PAMPHLET). USA+45 WOR+45 FINAN CONGRESS HOUSE/REP UN. PAGE 137 F2695
FOR/AID POLICY INT/ORG ECO/UNDEV

N67
US SENATE COMM ON FOREIGN REL,THE UNITED NATIONS AT TWENTY-ONE (PAMPHLET). WOR+45 BUDGET ADMIN SENATE UN. PAGE 139 F2738
INT/ORG DIPLOM PEACE

N67
US SENATE COMM ON FOREIGN REL,SURVEY OF THE ALLIANCE FOR PROGRESS: THE LATIN AMERICAN MILITARY (PAMPHLET). USA+45 INT/ORG POL/PAR DIPLOM AGREE GP/REL ROLE ORD/FREE 20. PAGE 139 F2746
L/A+17C FORCES CIVMIL/REL POLICY

INT/REL....INTERNATIONAL RELATIONS

INT/TRADE....INTERNATIONAL TRADE; SEE ALSO FOR/TRADE

N
BROCKWAY A.F.,AFRICAN SOCIALISM. EUR+WWI GHANA ISLAM UAR ECO/UNDEV CAP/ISM INT/TRADE COLONIAL COERCE GOV/REL DISCRIM 20 NEGRO NKRUMAH/K NASSER/G. PAGE 19 F0356
AFR SOCISM MARXISM

N
PEN I.,PRIMER ON INTERNATIONAL TRADE. WOR+45 WOR-45 ECO/DEV DIPLOM EFFICIENCY 16/20 EEC. PAGE 104 F2055
INT/TRADE BAL/PAY ECO/TAC EQUILIB

N
AMERICAN ECONOMIC REVIEW. FINAN INDUS LABOR OP/RES CAP/ISM INT/TRADE TAX WEALTH...CON/ANAL CHARTS 20. PAGE 1 F0001
BIBLIOG/A USA+45 ECO/DEV NAT/G

N
INTERNATIONAL BIBLIOGRAPHY OF ECONOMICS. WOR+45 FINAN MARKET ADMIN DEMAND INCOME PRODUC...POLICY IDEA/COMP METH. PAGE 1 F0002
BIBLIOG | ECO/DEV | ECO/UNDEV | INT/TRADE

N
ECONOMIC ABSTRACTS. WOR+45 FINAN INDUS MARKET LABOR ACT/RES INT/TRADE WRITING GP/REL...MGT 20. PAGE 1 F0005
BIBLIOG/A | EDU/PROP

N
THE MIDDLE EAST AND NORTH AFRICA. AFR ISLAM CULTURE ECO/UNDEV AGRI NAT/G TEC/DEV FOR/AID INT/TRADE EDU/PROP...CHARTS 20. PAGE 1 F0008
INDEX | INDUS | FINAN | STAT

N
UNITED NATIONS,OFFICIAL RECORDS OF THE ECONOMIC AND SOCIAL COUNCIL OF THE UNITED NATIONS. WOR+45 DIPLOM INT/TRADE CONFER...SOC SOC/WK 20 UN UNESCO. PAGE 132 F2611
INT/ORG | DELIB/GP | WRITING

N
US SUPERINTENDENT OF DOCUMENTS,CENSUS PUBLICATIONS (PRICE LIST 70). AGRI CONSTRUC DIST/IND FINAN LOC/G NAT/G PROVS INT/TRADE APPORT INCOME. PAGE 140 F2751
BIBLIOG/A | CENSUS | STAT | USA+45

N
US SUPERINTENDENT OF DOCUMENTS,TARIFF AND TAXATION (PRICE LIST 37). USA+45 LAW INT/TRADE ADJUD ADMIN CT/SYS INCOME OWN...DECISION GATT. PAGE 140 F2754
BIBLIOG/A | TAX | TARIFFS | NAT/G

B00
MILL J.S.,PRINCIPLES OF POLITICAL ECONOMY. WOR-45 CULTURE SOCIETY STRATA ECO/DEV AGRI EXTR/IND FINAN INDUS DELIB/GP ECO/TAC WEALTH...CONCPT MATH TREND 20. PAGE 91 F1786
MARKET | INT/ORG | INT/TRADE

B03
MOREL E.D.,THE BRITISH CASE IN FRENCH CONGO. CONGO/BRAZ FRANCE UK COERCE MORAL WEALTH...POLICY INT/LAW 20 CONGO/LEOP. PAGE 93 F1827
DIPLOM | INT/TRADE | COLONIAL | AFR

B13
BEARD C.A.,AN ECONOMIC INTERPRETATION OF THE CONSTITUTION OF THE UNITED STATES. USA-45 AGRI INT/TRADE SUFF OWN ATTIT...CONCPT MYTH BIOG HIST/WRIT 18. PAGE 12 F0222
CONSTN | ECO/TAC | CHOOSE

B14
DE BLOCH J.,THE FUTURE OF WAR IN ITS TECHNICAL, ECONOMIC, AND POLITICAL RELATIONS (1899). MOD/EUR TEC/DEV BUDGET INT/TRADE DETER GUERRILLA WEAPON COST PEACE 20. PAGE 31 F0596
WAR | BAL/PWR | PREDICT | FORCES

B19
SUMNER W.G.,WAR AND OTHER ESSAYS. USA-45 DELIB/GP DIPLOM TARIFFS COLONIAL PEACE SOVEREIGN 20. PAGE 127 F2514
INT/TRADE | ORD/FREE | CAP/ISM | ECO/TAC

N19
CASSELL F.,INTERNATIONAL MONETARY PROBLEMS (PAMPHLET). AFR BAL/PWR CONTROL EFFICIENCY WEALTH 20 EEC. PAGE 22 F0427
INT/TRADE | FINAN | DIPLOM | TREND

N19
FRANCK P.G.,AFGHANISTAN BETWEEN EAST AND WEST: THE ECONOMICS OF COMPETITIVE COEXISTENCE (PAMPHLET). AFGHANISTN USA+45 USA-45 USSR INDUS ECO/TAC INT/TRADE CONTROL NEUTRAL ORD/FREE MARXISM...GEOG 20 UN. PAGE 43 F0842
FOR/AID | PLAN | DIPLOM | ECO/UNDEV

N19
GROSECLOSE E.,THE DECAY OF MONEY; A SURVEY OF WESTERN CURRENCIES 1912-1962 (PAMPHLET). AFR FRANCE GERMANY UK LAW INT/TRADE BAL/PAY COST EQUILIB ...POLICY 20 DEPRESSION. PAGE 51 F1004
FINAN | NAT/G | ECO/DEV | ECO/TAC

N19
HABERLER G.,A SURVEY OF INTERNATIONAL TRADE THEORY (PAMPHLET). FINAN NAT/G COST INCOME 18/20 MONEY HUME/D MARSHALL/A. PAGE 52 F1022
INT/TRADE | BAL/PAY | GEN/LAWS | POLICY

N19
HALL G.,MAIN STREET TO WALL STREET: END THE COLD WAR (PAMPHLET). AFR USA+45 LAW STRUCT POL/PAR WORKER INT/TRADE DOMIN INCOME...POLICY 20 COM/PARTY. PAGE 53 F1046
MARXIST | CAP/ISM | DIPLOM | NAT/G

N19
KINDLEBERGER C.P.,BALANCE-OF-PAYMENTS DEFICITS AND THE INTERNATIONAL MARKET FOR LIQUIDITY (PAMPHLET). ECO/DEV NAT/G PLAN DIPLOM ECO/TAC PRODUC...POLICY STAT CHARTS. PAGE 71 F1389
BAL/PAY | INT/TRADE | MARKET | FINAN

N19
LANGE O.R.,"DISARMAMENT ECONOMIC GROWTH AND INTERNATIONAL CO-OPERATION" (PAMPHLET). WOR+45 DIST/IND PLAN INT/TRADE GIVE TASK DETER WEALTH SOCISM 18/19 BOLIVAR/S. PAGE 75 F1477
ARMS/CONT | DIPLOM | ECO/DEV | ECO/UNDEV

N19
SAPIR H.M.,JAPAN, CHINA, AND THE WEST (PAMPHLET). AFR ASIA CHINA/COM PROB/SOLV GOV/REL 20 CHINJAP. PAGE 116 F2282
ECO/UNDEV | INT/TRADE | DECISION | PLAN

N19
STEUBER F.A.,THE CONTRIBUTION OF SWITZERLAND TO THE ECONOMIC AND SOCIAL DEVELOPMENT OF LOW-INCOME COUNTRIES (PAMPHLET). SWITZERLND FINAN NAT/G VOL/ASSN INT/TRADE DRIVE...CHARTS 20. PAGE 126 F2482
FOR/AID | ECO/UNDEV | PLAN | DIPLOM

N19
US MARITIME ADMINISTRATION,CONTRIBUTION OF FEDERAL AID PROGRAMS TO THE OCEANBORNE FOREIGN TRADE OF THE UNITED STATES: 1959-62 (PAMPHLET). USA+45 SEA FINAN NAT/G BUDGET...POLICY 20. PAGE 138 F2719
INT/TRADE | ECO/TAC | DIST/IND | GIVE

N19
VELYAMINOV G.,AFRICA AND THE COMMON MARKET (PAMPHLET). AFR MARKET VOL/ASSN ECO/TAC COLONIAL ORD/FREE...SOCIALIST 20 THIRD/WRLD. PAGE 141 F2775
INT/ORG | INT/TRADE | SOVEREIGN | ECO/UNDEV

B20
COX H.,ECONOMIC LIBERTY. UNIV LAW INT/TRADE RATION TARIFFS RACE/REL SOCISM POLICY. PAGE 28 F0547
NAT/G | ORD/FREE | ECO/TAC | PERSON

B20
MOREL E.D.,THE BLACK MAN'S BURDEN. AFR MOD/EUR AGRI EXTR/IND PROB/SOLV INT/TRADE ADMIN CONTROL COERCE DISCRIM...POLICY 19/20 NEGRO LEAGUE/NAT. PAGE 93 F1828
ORD/FREE | CAP/ISM | RACE/REL | DOMIN

B21
CLAPHAN J.H.,THE ECONOMIC DEVELOPMENT OF FRANCE AND GERMANY 1815-1914. FRANCE GERMANY MOD/EUR COM/IND DIST/IND FINAN INT/TRADE EDU/PROP 19/20. PAGE 24 F0476
ECO/UNDEV | ECO/DEV | AGRI | INDUS

B26
MCPHEE A.,THE ECONOMIC REVOLUTION IN BRITISH WEST AFRICA. AFR UK CULTURE DIST/IND FINAN INDUS PLAN GP/REL RACE/REL 20 AFRICA/W. PAGE 88 F1735
ECO/UNDEV | INT/TRADE | COLONIAL | GEOG

B30
FEIS H.,EUROPE, THE WORLD'S BANKER, 1871-1914. FRANCE GERMANY MOD/EUR UK WOR-45 NAT/G PLAN ECO/TAC EXEC ATTIT PWR WEALTH...CONCPT HIST/WRIT GEN/LAWS VAL/FREE 19/20. PAGE 40 F0773
FINAN | DIPLOM | INT/TRADE

B34
MARX K.,THE CLASS STRUGGLES IN FRANCE. FRANCE INDUS WORKER CONSERVE...TREND GEN/LAWS 19. PAGE 86 F1689
MARXIST | STRATA | REV | INT/TRADE

B35
STALEY E.,WAR AND THE PRIVATE INVESTOR. UNIV WOR-45 INTELL SOCIETY INT/ORG NAT/G TOP/EX CAP/ISM ECO/TAC WAR ATTIT ALL/VALS...INT TIME/SEQ TREND CON/ANAL WORK TOT/POP 20. PAGE 125 F2464
FINAN | INT/TRADE | DIPLOM

B37
BRESCIANI-TURRONI C,THE ECONOMICS OF INFLATION: A STUDY OF CURRENCY DEPRECIATION IN POST-WAR GERMANY. AFR GERMANY FINAN INT/TRADE PRICE TOTALISM...POLICY TIME/SEQ CHARTS GEN/LAWS 20 HITLER/A. PAGE 18 F0347
ECO/TAC | WEALTH | SOCIETY

B37
HAMILTON W.H.,THE POWER TO GOVERN. ECO/DEV FINAN INDUS ECO/TAC INT/TRADE TARIFFS TAX CONTROL CT/SYS WAR COST PWR 18/20 SUPREME/CT. PAGE 54 F1056
LING | CONSTN | NAT/G | POLICY

B37
ROBBINS L.,ECONOMIC PLANNING AND INTERNATIONAL ORDER. WOR-45 SOCIETY FINAN INDUS NAT/G ECO/TAC ROUTINE WEALTH...SOC TIME/SEQ GEN/METH WORK 20 KEYNES/JM. PAGE 112 F2202
INT/ORG | PLAN | INT/TRADE

B37
VON HAYEK F.A.,MONETARY NATIONALISM AND INTERNATIONAL STABILITY. WOR-45 ECO/DEV NAT/G PROB/SOLV INT/TRADE...POLICY CONCPT METH/COMP NAT/COMP 20. PAGE 142 F2792
ECO/TAC | FINAN | DIPLOM | NAT/LISM

B38
HARPER S.N.,THE GOVERNMENT OF THE SOVIET UNION. COM USSR LAW CONSTN ECO/DEV PLAN TEC/DEV DIPLOM INT/TRADE ADMIN REV NAT/LISM...POLICY 20. PAGE 55 F1085
MARXISM | NAT/G | LEAD | POL/PAR

B38
LANGE O.,ON THE ECONOMIC THEORY OF SOCIALISM. UNIV ECO/DEV FINAN INDUS INT/ORG PUB/INST ROUTINE ATTIT ALL/VALS...SOC CONCPT STAT TREND 20. PAGE 75 F1475
MARKET | ECO/TAC | INT/TRADE | SOCISM

B38
MEADE J.E.,AN INTRODUCTION TO ECONOMIC ANALYSIS AND POLICY (AMERICAN EDITION EDITED BY C.J. HITCH). FINAN INDUS MARKET LABOR INT/TRADE CONTROL COST DEMAND INCOME...CLASSIF CHARTS T 20 KEYNES/JM MONOPOLY. PAGE 89 F1737
CONCPT | PROFIT | PRODUC

B39
STALEY E.,WORLD ECONOMY IN TRANSITION. WOR-45 SOCIETY INT/ORG PROF/ORG ECO/TAC ATTIT WEALTH ...METH/CNCPT TREND GEN/LAWS 20. PAGE 125 F2465
TEC/DEV | INT/TRADE

S39
COLE G.D.H.,"NAZI ECONOMICS: HOW DO THEY MANAGE IT?" GERMANY FORCES WORKER BUDGET INT/TRADE ROUTINE COERCE WAR 20 HITLER/A NAZI. PAGE 26 F0500
FASCISM | ECO/TAC | ATTIT | PLAN

B40
HELLMAN F.S.,THE NEW DEAL: SELECTED LIST OF REFERENCES. USA-45 FINAN LABOR EX/STRUC CREATE INT/TRADE ADMIN CT/SYS 20 SUPREME/CT. PAGE 58 F1145
BIBLIOG/A ECO/TAC PLAN POLICY

B40
MEEK C.K.,EUROPE AND WEST AFRICA. AFR EUR+WWI EXTR/IND DIPLOM INT/TRADE EDU/PROP GP/REL...SOC 20. PAGE 89 F1743
CULTURE TEC/DEV ECO/UNDEV COLONIAL

B40
TRIFFIN R.,MONOPOLISTIC COMPETITION AND GENERAL EQUILIBRIUM THEORY. DIST/IND PLAN TASK EQUILIB OPTIMAL...IDEA/COMP 20 MONOPOLY. PAGE 131 F2586
INT/TRADE INDUS COST

B41
HANSEN A.H.,FISCAL POLICY AND BUSINESS CYCLES. UK INDUS PROB/SOLV DIPLOM INT/TRADE OPTIMAL...POLICY TIME/SEQ CHARTS 19/20. PAGE 54 F1062
FINAN PLAN ECO/TAC GOV/REL

S41
MUKERJEE R.,"POPULATION THEORY AND POLITICS (BMR)" WOR-45 NAT/G PLAN PROB/SOLV ECO/TAC INT/TRADE CONTROL WAR PEACE...CENSUS 20 BIRTH/CON RESOURCE/N. PAGE 94 F1854
GEOG OPTIMAL CONCPT

B42
JACKSON M.V.,EUROPEAN POWERS AND SOUTH-EAST AFRICA: A STUDY OF INTERNATIONAL RELATIONS ON SOUTH-EAST COAST OF AFRICA, 1796-1856. AFR FRANCE PORTUGAL SOUTH/AFR UK USA-45 FORCES INT/TRADE PWR...CHARTS BIBLIOG 18/19 TREATY. PAGE 66 F1294
DOMIN POLICY ORD/FREE DIPLOM

B42
US LIBRARY OF CONGRESS,ECONOMICS OF WAR (APRIL 1941-MARCH 1942). WOR-45 FINAN INDUS LOC/G NAT/G PLAN BUDGET RATION COST DEMAND...POLICY 20. PAGE 138 F2712
BIBLIOG/A INT/TRADE ECO/TAC WAR

B44
INTL CHAMBER OF COMMERCE,TERMS COMMONLY USED IN DISTRIBUTION AND ADVERTISING. PORTUGAL SPAIN UK WOR-45 SERV/IND 20. PAGE 65 F1284
DICTIONARY EDU/PROP DIST/IND INT/TRADE

B47
ENKE S.,INTERNATIONAL ECONOMICS. UK USA+45 USSR INT/ORG BAL/PWR BARGAIN CAP/ISM BAL/PAY...NAT/COMP 20 TREATY. PAGE 38 F0735
INT/TRADE FINAN TARIFFS ECO/TAC

B47
GORDON D.L.,THE HIDDEN WEAPON: THE STORY OF ECONOMIC WARFARE. EUR+WWI USA-45 LAW FINAN INDUS NAT/G CONSULT FORCES PLAN DOMIN PWR WEALTH ...INT/LAW CONCPT OBS TOT/POP NAZI 20. PAGE 49 F0955
INT/ORG ECO/TAC INT/TRADE WAR

B47
HEILPERIN M.A.,THE TRADE OF NATIONS. USA+45 USA-45 WOR+45 WOR-45 CULTURE ECO/DEV NAT/G DELIB/GP EDU/PROP ATTIT DISPL ORD/FREE PWR WEALTH TOT/POP 20. PAGE 58 F1139
MARKET INT/ORG INT/TRADE PEACE

B47
TOWLE L.W.,INTERNATIONAL TRADE AND COMMERCIAL POLICY. WOR+45 LAW ECO/DEV FINAN INDUS NAT/G ECO/TAC WEALTH...TIME/SEQ ILO 20. PAGE 131 F2582
MARKET INT/ORG INT/TRADE

B48
CLYDE P.H.,THE FAR EAST: A HISTORY OF THE IMPACT OF THE WEST ON EASTERN ASIA. CHINA/COM CULTURE INT/TRADE DOMIN COLONIAL WAR PWR...CHARTS BIBLIOG 19/20 CHINJAP. PAGE 25 F0494
DIPLOM ASIA

B48
GRAHAM F.D.,THE THEORY OF INTERNATIONAL VALUES. FUT WOR+45 WOR-45 ECO/DEV FINAN INT/ORG PLAN TEC/DEV CAP/ISM DIPLOM ECO/TAC TARIFFS ROUTINE BAL/PAY DRIVE PWR WEALTH SOCISM...POLICY STAT HYPO/EXP GEN/LAWS 20. PAGE 50 F0971
NEW/IDEA INT/TRADE

B48
HOOVER E.M.,THE LOCATION OF ECONOMIC ACTIVITY. WOR+45 MARKET WORKER PROB/SOLV INT/TRADE ADMIN COST ...POLICY CHARTS T MUNICH 20. PAGE 62 F1211
HABITAT INDUS ECO/TAC GEOG

B48
ROBERTSON D.H.,MONEY. AFR ECO/DEV NAT/G DIPLOM INT/TRADE BAL/PAY INCOME WEALTH...TIME/SEQ 20 DEPRESSION. PAGE 112 F2212
FINAN MARKET COST PRICE

B48
VON HAYEK F.A.,INDIVIDUALISM AND ECONOMIC ORDER. GERMANY USA-45 USSR FINAN MARKET INT/ORG ECO/TAC INT/TRADE PRICE REPRESENT ORD/FREE...PLURIST GEN/LAWS 20. PAGE 142 F2793
SOCISM CAP/ISM POPULISM FEDERAL

B49
DE JOUVENEL B.,PROBLEMS OF SOCIALIST ENGLAND. AFR UK USSR BAL/PWR ECO/TAC INT/TRADE PRICE WAR BAL/PAY PEACE 20. PAGE 31 F0601
SOCISM NEW/LIB PROB/SOLV PLAN

B49
HANSEN A.H.,MONETARY THEORY AND FISCAL POLICY. CONSULT PLAN INT/TRADE BAL/PAY OPTIMAL...TREND CHARTS METH/COMP BIBLIOG T 19/20 MONEY. PAGE 54 F1063
FINAN GEN/LAWS POLICY ECO/TAC

B50
HOOVER G.,TWENTIETH CENTURY ECONOMIC THOUGHT. USA+45 ECO/DEV AGRI FINAN INDUS MARKET SERV/IND LABOR NAT/G...STAT 20. PAGE 62 F1213
ECO/TAC CAP/ISM INT/TRADE

B50
US DEPARTMENT OF STATE,POINT FOUR: COOPERATIVE PROGRAM FOR AID IN THE DEVELOPMENT OF ECONOMICALLY UNDERDEVELOPED AREAS. WOR+45 AGRI INDUS INT/ORG PLAN TEC/DEV DIPLOM EDU/PROP ADMIN PEACE PRODUC WEALTH 20 CONGRESS UN. PAGE 135 F2671
ECO/UNDEV FOR/AID FINAN INT/TRADE

C50
ELLSWORTH P.T.,"INTERNATIONAL ECONOMY." ECO/DEV ECO/UNDEV FINAN LABOR DIPLOM FOR/AID TARIFFS BAL/PAY EQUILIB NAT/LISM OPTIMAL...INT/LAW 20 ILO GATT. PAGE 37 F0724
BIBLIOG INT/TRADE ECO/TAC INT/ORG

B51
LEONARD L.L.,INTERNATIONAL ORGANIZATION. WOR+45 WOR-45 EX/STRUC FORCES LEGIS ECO/TAC INT/TRADE COLONIAL ARMS/CONT...SOC/WK GOV/COMP BIBLIOG. PAGE 78 F1527
NAT/G DIPLOM INT/ORG DELIB/GP

B51
LUXEMBORG R.,THE ACCUMULATION OF CAPITAL (TRANS. BY AGNES SCHWARZSCHILD). ECO/TAC DOMIN COLONIAL ATTIT LAISSEZ 19 MONEY. PAGE 82 F1614
MARXIST INT/TRADE CAP/ISM FINAN

B51
POOLE K.,FISCAL POLICIES AND THE AMERICAN ECONOMY. AFR ECO/DEV FINAN INDUS WORKER OP/RES INT/TRADE TAX COST INCOME PROFIT WEALTH...GP/COMP 20. PAGE 107 F2102
NAT/G POLICY ANTHOL

B51
US DEPARTMENT OF STATE,POINT FOUR, NEAR EAST AND AFRICA, A SELECTED BIBLIOGRAPHY OF STUDIES ON ECONOMICALLY UNDERDEVELOPED COUNTRIES. AGRI COM/IND FINAN INDUS PLAN INT/TRADE...SOC TREND 20. PAGE 135 F2672
BIBLIOG/A AFR S/ASIA ISLAM

B52
ALEXANDROWICZ C.H.,INTERNATIONAL ECONOMIC ORGANIZATION. WOR+45 ECO/DEV ECO/UNDEV DIST/IND FINAN MARKET PLAN ECO/TAC LEGIT DRIVE WEALTH ...POLICY CONCPT QUANT OBS TIME/SEQ GEN/LAWS WORK METH/GP EEC ILO OEEC UNESCO 20. PAGE 4 F0063
INT/ORG INT/TRADE

B52
ASHWORTH W.,A SHORT HISTORY OF THE INTERNATIONAL ECONOMY 1850-1950. WOR+45 WOR-45 AGRI FINAN INDUS MARKET LABOR ECO/TAC...CONCPT STAT HIST/WRIT FOR/TRADE ILO 19/20. PAGE 7 F0131
ECO/DEV TEC/DEV INT/TRADE

B52
HOSELITZ B.F.,THE PROGRESS OF UNDERDEVELOPED AREAS. AFR FUT WOR+45 WOR-45 ECO/DEV ECO/TAC INT/TRADE WEALTH...SOC TREND GEN/LAWS TOT/POP VAL/FREE FOR/TRADE 20. PAGE 62 F1219
ECO/UNDEV PLAN FOR/AID

B52
SECRETARIAT COUNCIL OF EUROPE,THE STRASBOURG PLAN. EUR+WWI CONSULT PLAN ECO/TAC TARIFFS DEBATE REGION 20 COUNCL/EUR STRASBOURG. PAGE 119 F2340
INT/ORG ECO/DEV INT/TRADE DIPLOM

B52
WU Y.,ECONOMIC WARFARE. MARKET PLAN PROB/SOLV FOR/AID CONTROL EFFICIENCY WEALTH...METH/COMP 20. PAGE 149 F2937
ECO/TAC WAR INT/TRADE DIPLOM

C52
HUME D.,"OF THE BALANCE OF TRADE" IN D. HUME, POLITICAL DISCOURSES (1752)" UK FINAN NAT/G TARIFFS PRICE PWR LAISSEZ...POLICY GEN/LAWS 18. PAGE 63 F1237
BAL/PAY INT/TRADE DIPLOM WEALTH

C52
HUME D.,"OF COMMERCE" IN D. HUME, POLITICAL DISCOURSES (1752)" UK FINAN DIPLOM WEALTH ...GEN/LAWS 18 MONEY. PAGE 63 F1238
INDUS INT/TRADE PWR AGRI

C52
HUME D.,"OF INTEREST" IN D. HUME, POLITICAL DISCOURSES (1752)" UK INDUS WORKER DIPLOM PAY DEMAND INCOME WEALTH...GEN/LAWS 18 MONEY. PAGE 63 F1239
PRICE COST FINAN INT/TRADE

C52
HUME D.,"OF MONEY" IN D. HUME, POLITICAL DISCOURSES (1752)" UK INDUS DIPLOM INT/TRADE...GEN/LAWS 18 MONEY. PAGE 63 F1240
FINAN COST PRICE WEALTH

B53
BOEKE J.H.,ECONOMICS AND ECONOMIC POLICY OF DUAL SOCIETIES AS EXEMPLIFIED BY INDONESIA. INDIA INDONESIA SOCIETY CAP/ISM INT/TRADE GIVE PRICE GP/REL WEALTH SOCISM...POLICY NAT/COMP GEN/LAWS 20. PAGE 16 F0304
ECO/TAC ECO/UNDEV NAT/G CONTROL

B53
BURNS A.E.,MODERN ECONOMICS. UNIV ECO/DEV INT/TRADE PRICE INCOME WEALTH...POLICY CHARTS T 20 KEYNES/JM. PAGE 20 F0389
NAT/G ECO/TAC FINAN

B53
FRANKEL S.H.,THE ECONOMIC IMPACT ON UNDERDEVELOPED SOCIETIES: ESSAYS ON INTERNATIONAL INVESTMENT AND SOCIAL CHANGE. AFR WOR+45 ECO/DEV FINAN INDUS NAT/G
ECO/UNDEV FOR/AID INT/TRADE

ACT/RES TEC/DEV COLONIAL ATTIT...CONCPT OBS TREND
20. PAGE 43 F0845

B53
MENDE T.,WORLD POWER IN THE BALANCE. FUT USA+45 WOR+45
USSR WOR-45 ECO/DEV ECO/TAC INT/TRADE EDU/PROP PWR
UTOPIA ATTIT...HUM CONCPT TREND TOT/POP 20. PAGE 90 BAL/PWR
F1756 AFR

B53
NEISSER H.,NATIONAL INCOMES AND INTERNATIONAL INT/TRADE
TRADE. FRANCE GERMANY SWEDEN UK USA-45 EXTR/IND PRODUC
FINAN INDUS TEC/DEV PRICE BAL/PAY EQUILIB INCOME MARKET
WEALTH...CHARTS METH 19 CHINJAP. PAGE 97 F1908 CON/ANAL

B53
WILLIAMS J.H.,ECONOMIC STABILITY IN A CHANGING POLICY
WORLD. FRANCE USA+45 USSR AGRI WORKER BUDGET FINAN
INT/TRADE TAX WAR BAL/PAY COST EFFICIENCY ALL/IDEOS ECO/TAC
EQULIB 20 KEYNES/JM. PAGE 147 F2892 WEALTH

S53
BLOUGH R.,"THE ROLE OF THE ECONOMIST IN FEDERAL DELIB/GP
POLICY MAKING." USA+45 ELITES INTELL ECO/DEV NAT/G ECO/TAC
CONSULT EX/STRUC ACT/RES PLAN INT/TRADE BAL/PAY
WEALTH...POLICY METH/GP CONGRESS 20. PAGE 16 F0301

B54
TINBERGEN J.,INTERNATIONAL ECONOMIC INTEGRATION. INT/ORG
WOR+45 WOR-45 ECO/UNDEV NAT/G ECO/TAC BAL/PAY ECO/DEV
...METH/CNCPT STAT TIME/SEQ GEN/METH OEEC 20. INT/TRADE
PAGE 130 F2574

B55
BUCHANAN N.S.,APPROACHES TO ECONOMIC DEVELOPMENT. ECO/UNDEV
FUT USA+45 WOR+45 STRATA ECO/DEV INT/ORG NAT/G ECO/TAC
TEC/DEV DIPLOM FOR/AID ATTIT KNOWL PWR WEALTH INT/TRADE
...RELATIV METH/CNCPT SELF/OBS TREND CON/ANAL
STERTYP GEN/LAWS FOR/TRADE COMMUN 20. PAGE 20 F0380

B55
FOGARTY M.P.,ECONOMIC CONTROL. FUT UK ECO/DEV FINAN ECO/TAC
CONSULT INT/TRADE...CHARTS BIBLIOG/A 20. PAGE 42 NAT/G
F0819 CONTROL
PROB/SOLV

B55
O'CONNOR H.,THE EMPIRE OF OIL. USA+45 DIST/IND EXTR/IND
FINAN MARKET CAP/ISM TAX CONTROL...POLICY MARXIST INT/TRADE
BIBLIOG/A 20. PAGE 100 F1955 CENTRAL
NAT/G

B55
PANT Y.P.,PLANNING IN UNDERDEVELOPED ECONOMIES. ECO/UNDEV
INDIA NEPAL INT/TRADE COLONIAL SOVEREIGN ALL/IDEOS PLAN
...TIME/SEQ METH/COMP 20. PAGE 103 F2026 ECO/TAC
DIPLOM

B55
PEDLER F.J.,ECONOMIC GEOGRAPHY OF WEST AFRICA. ECO/UNDEV
GAMBIA NIGER SIER/LEONE STRATA EXTR/IND MARKET GEOG
LABOR INT/TRADE DEMAND HABITAT WEALTH...CHARTS 20. PRODUC
PAGE 104 F2046 EFFICIENCY

B55
STILLMAN C.W.,AFRICA IN THE MODERN WORLD. AFR ECO/UNDEV
USA+45 WOR+45 INT/TRADE COLONIAL PARTIC REGION DIPLOM
GOV/REL RACE/REL 20. PAGE 126 F2489 POLICY
STRUCT

B55
UN ECONOMIC COMN ASIA & FAR E,ECONOMIC SURVEY OF ECO/UNDEV
ASIA AND THE FAR EAST, 1954. AFGHANISTN CEYLON PRICE
INDIA PHILIPPINE S/ASIA ECO/DEV FINAN INDUS NAT/COMP
INT/TRADE PRODUC WEALTH...STAT CHARTS 20 CHINJAP. ASIA
PAGE 132 F2600

B55
WOYTINSKY W.S.,WORLD COMMERCE AND GOVERNMENTS: INT/TRADE
TRENDS AND OUTLOOK. WOR+45 FINAN POL/PAR DIPLOM DIST/IND
ECO/TAC FOR/AID DOMIN WAR CHOOSE...CHARTS BIBLIOG NAT/COMP
20 LEAGUE/NAT UN ILO. PAGE 149 F2929 NAT/G

L55
KISER M.,"ORGANIZATION OF AMERICAN STATES." L/A+17C VOL/ASSN
USA+45 ECO/UNDEV INT/ORG NAT/G PLAN TEC/DEV DIPLOM ECO/DEV
ECO/TAC INT/TRADE EDU/PROP ADMIN ALL/VALS...POLICY REGION
MGT RECORD ORG/CHARTS OAS COMMUN 20. PAGE 71 F1401

B56
GARDNER R.N.,STERLING-DOLLAR DIPLOMACY. EUR+WWI ECO/DEV
USA+45 INT/ORG NAT/G PLAN INT/TRADE EDU/PROP ADMIN DIPLOM
KNOWL PWR WEALTH...POLICY SOC METH/CNCPT STAT
CHARTS SIMUL GEN/LAWS 20. PAGE 46 F0902

B56
KNORR K.E.,RUBLE DIPLOMACY: CHALLENGE TO AMERICAN ECO/UNDEV
FOREIGN AID(PAMPHLET). AFR CHINA/COM USA+45 USSR COM
PLAN TEC/DEV CAP/ISM INT/TRADE DOMIN EDU/PROP DIPLOM
CONTROL LEAD 20. PAGE 72 F1413 FOR/AID

B56
US DEPARTMENT OF STATE,ECONOMIC PROBLEMS OF BIBLIOG
UNDERDEVELOPED AREAS (PAMPHLET). AFR ASIA ISLAM ECO/UNDEV
L/A+17C AGRI FINAN INDUS INT/ORG LABOR INT/TRADE TEC/DEV
...PSY SOC 20. PAGE 136 F2673 R+D

B56
WATT D.C.,BRITAIN AND THE SUEZ CANAL. COM UAR UK DIPLOM
...INT/LAW 20 SUEZ TREATY. PAGE 144 F2835 INT/TRADE
DIST/IND
NAT/G

S56
BONILLA F.,"WHEN IS PETITION 'PRESSURE?'" (BMR)" LEGIS
USA+45 ELITES INDUS LABOR CHIEF EDU/PROP LEGIT EX/STRUC
ATTIT...INT CHARTS 20 CONGRESS PRESIDENT INT/TRADE
EISNHWR/DD. PAGE 16 F0312 TARIFFS

N56
US HOUSE COMM FOREIGN AFFAIRS,REPORT OF THE SPECIAL FOR/AID
STUDY MISSION TO AFRICA, SOUTH AND EAST OF THE COLONIAL
SAHARA (PAMPHLET). AFR SOUTH/AFR USA+45 STRUCT ECO/UNDEV
INT/TRADE PARL/PROC NAT/LISM ATTIT ALL/VALS HEALTH DIPLOM
...POLICY 20 CONGRESS. PAGE 136 F2691

B57
ASHER R.E.,THE UNITED NATIONS AND ECONOMIC AND INT/ORG
SOCIAL COOPERATION. ECO/UNDEV COM/IND DIST/IND DIPLOM
FINAN PLAN PROB/SOLV INT/TRADE TASK WEALTH...SOC 20 FOR/AID
UN. PAGE 7 F0129

B57
BAUER P.T.,ECONOMIC ANALYSIS AND POLICY IN ECO/UNDEV
UNDERDEVELOPED COUNTRIES. AFR WOR+45 AGRI INT/TRADE METH/COMP
TAX PRICE...GEN/METH BIBLIOG/A 20. PAGE 11 F0214 POLICY

B57
BEHRMAN J.N.,INTERNATIONAL ECONOMICS: THEORY, INT/TRADE
PRACTICE, POLICY. AGRI INDUS NAT/G TARIFFS CONTROL FINAN
BAL/PAY...POLICY METH/CNCPT T 19/20. PAGE 12 F0230 DIPLOM
FOR/AID

B57
GOLD N.L.,REGIONAL ECONOMIC DEVELOPMENT AND NUCLEAR ECO/UNDEV
POWER IN INDIA. FUT INDIA FINAN FOR/AID INT/TRADE TEC/DEV
BAL/PAY EFFICIENCY OPTIMAL PRODUC WEALTH...PREDICT NUC/PWR
20. PAGE 48 F0934 INDUS

B57
HARRIS S.E.,INTERNATIONAL AND INTERREGIONAL INT/TRADE
ECONOMICS. AFR WOR+45 WOR-45 NAT/G TARIFFS BAL/PAY ECO/DEV
EQUILIB...POLICY CONCPT STAT CHARTS IDEA/COMP MARKET
19/20. PAGE 55 F1088 FINAN

B57
LUNDBERG E.,BUSINESS CYCLES AND ECONOMIC POLICY ECO/TAC
(TRANS. BY J. POTTER). SWEDEN ECO/DEV FINAN INDUS
DELIB/GP PLAN PRICE CONTROL BAL/PAY 20 INTRVN/ECO. INT/TRADE
PAGE 82 F1607 BUDGET

B57
NEUMARK S.D.,ECONOMIC INFLUENCES ON THE SOUTH COLONIAL
AFRICAN FRONTIER, 1652-1836. SOUTH/AFR SEA AGRI ECO/UNDEV
NAT/G FORCES WORKER DIPLOM INT/TRADE PRICE DEMAND ECO/TAC
PRODUC...STAT CHARTS 17/19 FRONTIER. PAGE 97 F1915 MARKET

B57
OLIVER H.M. JR.,ECONOMIC OPINION AND POLICY IN ECO/UNDEV
CEYLON. CEYLON FINAN POL/PAR WORKER INT/TRADE NAT/LISM
INCOME WEALTH...GEOG UNPLAN/INT BIBLIOG 20 POLICY
CMN/WLTH. PAGE 101 F1987 COLONIAL

B57
THOMAS R.G.,OUR MODERN BANKING AND MONETARY SYSTEM FINAN
(3RD ED.). AFR USA+45 USA-45 ACT/RES PLAN PROB/SOLV SERV/IND
INT/TRADE PRICE WAR BAL/PAY INCOME...POLICY ECO/TAC
METH/CNCPT 20 DEPRESSION. PAGE 130 F2563

B58
ATOMIC INDUSTRIAL FORUM,MANAGEMENT AND ATOMIC NUC/PWR
ENERGY. WOR+45 SEA LAW MARKET NAT/G TEC/DEV INSPECT INDUS
INT/TRADE CONFER PEACE HEALTH...ANTHOL 20. PAGE 7 MGT
F0136 ECO/TAC

B58
AVRAMOVIC D.,POSTWAR GROWTH IN INTERNATIONAL INT/TRADE
INDEBTEDNESS. AFR WOR+45 AGRI INDUS CAP/ISM PRICE FINAN
INCOME...NAT/COMP 20 SILVER. PAGE 8 F0143 COST
BAL/PAY

B58
CHANG C.,THE INFLATIONARY SPIRAL: THE EXPERIENCE IN FINAN
CHINA 1939-50. CHINA/COM BUDGET INT/TRADE PRICE ECO/TAC
ADMIN CONTROL WAR DEMAND...POLICY CHARTS 20. BAL/PAY
PAGE 23 F0451 GOV/REL

B58
EHRHARD J.,LE DESTIN DU COLONIALISME. AFR FRANCE COLONIAL
ECO/UNDEV AGRI FINAN MARKET CREATE PLAN TEC/DEV FOR/AID
BUDGET DIPLOM PRICE 20. PAGE 36 F0710 INT/TRADE
INDUS

B58
ELLSWORTH P.T.,THE INTERNATIONAL ECONOMY. EUR+WWI INT/TRADE
MOD/EUR INT/ORG CAP/ISM FOR/AID BAL/PAY LAISSEZ TARIFFS
16/20. PAGE 37 F0725 ECO/DEV

B58
HENNING C.N.,INTERNATIONAL FINANCING. WOR+45 FINAN
ECO/DEV INT/ORG EX/STRUC INSPECT CAP/ISM BAL/PAY DIPLOM
COST PROFIT...MGT CHARTS T 20. PAGE 58 F1150 INT/TRADE

B58
HIRSCHMAN A.O.,STRATEGY OF ECONOMIC DEVELOPMENT. ECO/UNDEV
WOR+45 WOR-45 CULTURE ECO/DEV NAT/G PLAN TEC/DEV ECO/TAC
INT/TRADE BAL/PAY ATTIT DRIVE RIGID/FLEX WEALTH CAP/ISM
...CONCPT METH/CNCPT OBS CHARTS SIMUL GEN/LAWS
TOT/POP VAL/FREE. PAGE 60 F1176

B58
JACOBSSON P.,SOME MONETARY PROBLEMS, INTERNATIONAL FINAN
AND NATIONAL. WOR+45 WOR-45 ECO/DEV FORCES WORKER PLAN
PROB/SOLV DIPLOM INT/TRADE...ANTHOL 20. PAGE 66 ECO/TAC
F1299 NAT/COMP

B58
JENNINGS I.,PROBLEMS OF THE NEW COMMONWEALTH. AFR NAT/LISM
CEYLON INDIA PAKISTAN S/ASIA ECO/UNDEV INT/ORG NEUTRAL
LOC/G DIPLOM ECO/TAC INT/TRADE COLONIAL RACE/REL FOR/AID

DISCRIM 20 PARLIAMENT. PAGE 67 F1314 POL/PAR
B58

JOHNSON H.G.,INTERNATIONAL TRADE AND ECONOMIC GROWTH. WOR+45 BUDGET CAP/ISM ECO/TAC TARIFFS BAL/PAY 20. PAGE 67 F1323 INT/TRADE BAL/PWR BARGAIN DIPLOM
B58

JUCKER-FLEETWOOD E.,ECONOMIC THEORY AND POLICY IN FINLAND 1914-1925. FINLAND INT/TRADE PRICE COST 20 MONEY. PAGE 68 F1343 FINAN GEN/LAWS ECO/TAC PLAN
B58

MYRDAL G.,RICH LANDS AND POOR: THE ROAD TO WORLD PROSPERITY. FUT WOR+45 WOR-45 ECO/DEV ECO/UNDEV INT/ORG PLAN ECO/TAC REGION...GEOG TIME/SEQ GEN/LAWS TOT/POP 20. PAGE 96 F1880 WEALTH TREND FOR/AID INT/TRADE
B58

PALYI M.,MANAGED MONEY AT THE CROSSROADS: THE EUROPEAN EXPERIENCE. AFR WOR+45 WOR-45 TEC/DEV DIPLOM INT/TRADE DEMAND WEALTH...CHARTS BIBLIOG 19/20 EUROPE SILVER. PAGE 103 F2022 FINAN ECO/TAC ECO/DEV PRODUC
B58

ROBERTS B.C.,NATIONAL WAGES POLICY IN WAR AND PEACE. EUR+WWI GERMANY S/ASIA SWEDEN UK USA+45 USA-45 STRATA ECO/DEV LABOR NAT/G DELIB/GP PLAN INT/TRADE WEALTH...STAT TREND CHARTS 20. PAGE 112 F2205 CREATE ECO/TAC
B58

SCITOUSKY T.,ECONOMIC THEORY AND WESTERN EUROPEAN INTEGRATION. EUR+WWI INT/ORG ACT/RES INT/TRADE REGION BAL/PAY WEALTH...METH/CNCPT STAT CHARTS GEN/METH ECSC TOT/POP EEC OEEC 20. PAGE 118 F2328 ECO/TAC
B58

SHAW S.J.,THE FINANCIAL AND ADMINISTRATIVE ORGANIZATION AND DEVELOPMENT OF OTTOMAN EGYPT 1517-1798. UAR LOC/G FORCES BUDGET INT/TRADE TAX EATING INCOME WEALTH...CHARTS BIBLIOG 16/18 OTTOMAN NAPOLEON/B. PAGE 120 F2371 FINAN ADMIN GOV/REL CULTURE
L58

TRAGER F.N.,"A SELECTED AND ANNOTATED BIBLIOGRAPHY ON ECONOMIC DEVELOPMENT, 1953-1957." WOR+45 AGRI FINAN INDUS MARKET LABOR WORKER PLAN INT/TRADE PRODUC...CENSUS MUNICH. PAGE 131 F2583 BIBLIOG/A ECO/UNDEV ECO/DEV
B59

AITKEN H.G.,THE AMERICAN ECONOMIC IMPACT ON CANADA. CANADA USA+45 AGRI FINAN INDUS LABOR INT/TRADE BAL/PAY...INT/LAW TREND 20. PAGE 3 F0055 DIPLOM ECO/TAC POLICY NAT/G
B59

ALLEN R.L.,SOVIET INFLUENCE IN LATIN AMERICA. ECO/UNDEV FINAN PROC/MFG NAT/G TEC/DEV EDU/PROP EXEC ROUTINE ATTIT DRIVE PERSON ALL/VALS PWR...STAT CHARTS WORK FOR/TRADE 20. PAGE 4 F0071 L/A+17C ECO/TAC INT/TRADE USSR
B59

ALLEN W.R.,FOREIGN TRADE AND FINANCE. ECO/DEV DIPLOM BAL/PAY...POLICY CONCPT ANTHOL 20. PAGE 4 F0073 INT/TRADE EQUILIB FINAN
B59

BARNETT A.D.,COMMUNIST ECONOMIC STRATEGY: THE RISE OF MAINLAND CHINA. CHINA/COM USSR WOR+45 AGRI INDUS FOR/AID INGP/REL ATTIT. PAGE 10 F0188 ECO/UNDEV INT/TRADE TOTALISM BAL/PWR
B59

CHECCHI V.,HONDURAS: A PROBLEM IN ECONOMIC DEVELOPMENT. HONDURAS AGRI FINAN INDUS LABOR WORKER INT/TRADE EDU/PROP PRICE HEALTH...GEOG CHARTS BIBLIOG 20. PAGE 24 F0458 ECO/UNDEV ECO/TAC PROB/SOLV PLAN
B59

DIEBOLD W. JR.,THE SCHUMAN PLAN: A STUDY IN ECONOMIC COOPERATION, 1950-1959. EUR+WWI FRANCE GERMANY USA+45 EXTR/IND CONSULT DELIB/GP PLAN DIPLOM ECO/TAC INT/TRADE ROUTINE ORD/FREE WEALTH ...METH/CNCPT STAT CONT/OBS INT TIME/SEQ ECSC 20. PAGE 33 F0635 INT/ORG REGION
B59

ETSCHMANN R.,DIE WAHRUNGS- UND DEVISENPOLITIK DES OSTBLOCKS UND IHRE AUSWIRKUNGEN AUF DIE WIRTSCHAFTSBEZIEHUNGEN ZWISCHEN OST U WEST. BULGARIA CZECHOSLVK HUNGARY POLAND USSR MARKET NAT/G PLAN DIPLOM...NAT/COMP 20. PAGE 39 F0753 ECO/TAC FINAN POLICY INT/TRADE
B59

FELS R.,AMERICAN BUSINESS CYCLES 1865-1897. USA+45 ECO/DEV LG/CO SML/CO PROB/SOLV TEC/DEV CAP/ISM INT/TRADE DEMAND...POLICY CHARTS METH 19 DEPRESSION. PAGE 40 F0782 FINAN INDUS TREND ECO/TAC
B59

FERRY W.H.,THE CORPORATION AND THE ECONOMY. CLIENT LAW CONSTN LABOR NAT/G PLAN INT/TRADE PARTIC CONSEN ORD/FREE PWR POLICY. PAGE 40 F0787 LG/CO CONTROL REPRESENT
B59

GUDIN E.,INFLACAO (2ND ED.). INDUS NAT/G PLAN ECO/TAC CONTROL COST 20. PAGE 52 F1012 ECO/UNDEV INT/TRADE BAL/PAY FINAN
B59

HARTOG F.,EUROPEAN TRADE CYCLE POLICY. WORKER TAX PRICE WAR CENTRAL DEMAND...TREND CHARTS 20 UN. PAGE 56 F1103 EQUILIB EUR+WWI INT/TRADE
B59

HAX K.,DIE HOCHSCHULLEHRER DER WIRTSCHAFTSWISSENSCHAFTEN IN DER BUNDESREPUBLIK DEUTSCHLAND EINSCHL. WESTBERLIN, OSTERREICH. AUSTRIA GERMANY/W SWITZERLND FINAN MARKET PROF/ORG BUDGET ECO/TAC INT/TRADE PRICE COST 20. PAGE 57 F1119 BIBLIOG ACADEM INTELL
B59

HAZLEWOOD A.,THE ECONOMICS OF "UNDER-DEVELOPED" AREAS. WOR+45 DIST/IND EXTR/IND FINAN INDUS MARKET PLAN FOR/AID...GEOG 20. PAGE 57 F1129 BIBLIOG/A ECO/UNDEV AGRI INT/TRADE
B59

MATTHEWS R.C.O.,THE BUSINESS CYCLE. AFR LABOR INT/TRADE TAX PRICE RISK ADJUST WEALTH...POLICY ECOMETRIC CHARTS SIMUL TIME 20. PAGE 87 F1705 FINAN DEMAND TASK
B59

MEZERK A.G.,FINANCIAL ASSISTANCE FOR ECONOMIC DEVELOPMENT. WOR+45 INDUS DIPLOM INT/TRADE...CHARTS GOV/COMP UN. PAGE 91 F1778 FOR/AID FINAN ECO/TAC ECO/UNDEV
B59

MORGENSTERN O.,INTERNATIONAL FINANCIAL TRANSACTIONS AND BUSINESS CYCLES. FRANCE GERMANY UK USA+45 USA-45 WOR+45 WOR-45 ECO/DEV ECO/TAC WEALTH ...CONCPT STAT CON/ANAL CHARTS 19/20. PAGE 93 F1832 FINAN TIME/SEQ INT/TRADE
B59

NOVE A.,COMMUNIST ECONOMIC STRATEGY: SOVIET GROWTH AND CAPABILITIES. USSR AGRI LABOR PLAN TEC/DEV CAP/ISM INT/TRADE EFFICIENCY MARXISM 20 THIRD/WRLD. PAGE 99 F1941 FOR/AID ECO/TAC DIPLOM INDUS
B59

OGBURN C.,ECONOMIC PLAN AND ACTION. USA+45 FINAN LABOR DIPLOM ECO/TAC FOR/AID 20. PAGE 101 F1981 ECO/DEV INT/TRADE PLAN BAL/PAY
B59

ROBERTSON A.H.,EUROPEAN INSTITUTIONS: COOPERATION, INTEGRATION, UNIFICATION. EUR+WWI FINAN INT/ORG FORCES INT/TRADE TARIFFS 20 EEC EURATOM ECSC NATO TREATY. PAGE 112 F2208 ECO/DEV DIPLOM INDUS ECO/TAC
B59

ROPKE W.,INTERNATIONAL ORDER AND ECONOMIC INTEGRATION. ECO/DEV ECO/UNDEV AGRI FINAN INDUS INT/ORG WAR PEACE ORD/FREE...SOC METH/COMP 20 EEC. PAGE 114 F2238 INT/TRADE DIPLOM BAL/PAY ALL/IDEOS
B59

SANNWALD R.E.,ECONOMIC INTEGRATION: THEORETICAL ASSUMPTIONS AND CONSEQUENCES OF EUROPEAN UNIFICATION. EUR+WWI FUT FINAN INDUS VOL/ASSN ACT/RES ECO/TAC...PLURIST EEC FOR/TRADE OEEC 20. PAGE 116 F2279 INT/ORG ECO/DEV INT/TRADE
B59

SHACKLE G.L.S.,ECONOMICS FOR PLEASURE. FINAN MARKET NAT/G WORKER PLAN INT/TRADE TARIFFS PAY BAL/PAY COST PRODUC 20. PAGE 120 F2361 METH/CNCPT WEALTH INCOME
B59

SILCOCK T.H.,THE COMMONWEALTH ECONOMY IN SOUTHEAST ASIA. AFR INDIA MALAYSIA S/ASIA ECO/DEV AGRI LOC/G PLAN TARIFFS COLONIAL BAL/PAY DEMAND...BIBLIOG/A 20 GATT. PAGE 122 F2401 ECO/TAC INT/TRADE RACE/REL DIPLOM
B59

STOVEL J.A.,CANADA IN THE WORLD ECONOMY. CANADA PRICE DEMAND...STAT CHARTS BIBLIOG 20 VINER/J. PAGE 127 F2499 INT/TRADE BAL/PAY FINAN ECO/TAC
B59

US DEPARTMENT OF STATE,THE UNITED STATES ECONOMY AND THE MUTUAL SECURITY PROGRAM. USA+45 ECO/UNDEV FINAN INDUS DIPLOM INT/TRADE DETER 20. PAGE 136 F2674 ECO/DEV FORCES BUDGET FOR/AID
B59

VERNEY D.V.,PUBLIC ENTERPRISE IN SWEDEN. FUT SWEDEN UK INDUS POL/PAR LEGIS PROB/SOLV CAP/ISM INT/TRADE CONTROL SOCISM...MGT CONCPT NAT/COMP 20 SOCDEM/PAR CIVIL/SERV. PAGE 141 F2778 ECO/DEV POLICY LG/CO NAT/G
B59

WELTON H.,THE THIRD WORLD WAR; TRADE AND INDUSTRY, THE NEW BATTLEGROUND. AFR WOR+45 ECO/DEV INDUS MARKET TASK...MGT IDEA/COMP. PAGE 145 F2855 INT/TRADE PLAN DIPLOM
B59

WIBBERLEY G.P.,AGRICULTURE AND URBAN GROWTH. UK USA+45 ECO/DEV FINAN PROB/SOLV INT/TRADE COST ...GEOG STAT CHARTS METH/COMP HYPO/EXP METH MUNICH 20. PAGE 146 F2876 AGRI PLAN
B59

YRARRAZAVAL E.,AMERICA LATINE EN LA GUERRA FRIA. AFR EUR+WWI L/A+17C USA+45 USSR WOR+45 INDUS INT/ORG NAT/LISM POLICY. PAGE 150 F2953 REGION DIPLOM ECO/UNDEV INT/TRADE
L59

MURPHY J.C.,"SOME IMPLICATIONS OF EUROPE'S COMMON MARKET. IN (COOK P, ECONOMIC DEVELOPMENT AND INTERNATIONAL TRADE,." EUR+WWI ECO/DEV DIST/IND MARKET INT/ORG REGION

INDUS NAT/G PLAN ECO/TAC INT/TRADE WEALTH...STAT TREND OEEC TOT/POP 20 EEC. PAGE 95 F1866

S59
KINDLEBERGER C.P.,"UNITED STATES ECONOMIC FOREIGN POLICY: RESEARCH REQUIREMENTS FOR 1965." FUT USA+45 WOR+45 DIST/IND MARKET INT/ORG ECO/TAC INT/TRADE WEALTH...OBS TREND CON/ANAL GEN/LAWS FOR/TRADE VAL/FREE 20. PAGE 71 F1392
FINAN ECO/DEV FOR/AID

S59
PLAZA G.,"FOR A REGIONAL MARKET IN LATIN AMERICA." FUT L/A+17C CULTURE INDUS NAT/G ECO/TAC INT/TRADE ATTIT WEALTH...NEW/IDEA TREND OAS 20. PAGE 106 F2092
MARKET INT/ORG REGION

S59
STREETEN P.,"UNBALANCED GROWTH" UK ECO/DEV AGRI MARKET TEC/DEV CAP/ISM ECO/TAC FOR/AID INT/TRADE DEMAND ORD/FREE...CONCPT 20. PAGE 127 F2502
IDEA/COMP FINAN PRODUC EQUILIB

S59
ZAUBERMAN A.,"SOVIET BLOC ECONOMIC INTEGRATION." COM CULTURE INTELL ECO/DEV INDUS TOP/EX ACT/RES PLAN ECO/TAC INT/TRADE ROUTINE CHOOSE ATTIT ...TIME/SEQ 20. PAGE 150 F2958
MARKET INT/ORG USSR TOTALISM

B60
APTHEKER H.,DISARMAMENT AND THE AMERICAN ECONOMY: A SYMPOSIUM. FUT USA+45 ECO/DEV DIST/IND FINAN INDUS PROC/MFG LABOR NAT/G POL/PAR CONSULT PLAN CAP/ISM INT/TRADE PEACE ATTIT MORAL WEALTH...TREND GEN/LAWS TOT/POP 20. PAGE 6 F0110
MARXIST ARMS/CONT

B60
ASPREMONT-LYNDEN H.,RAPPORT SUR L'ADMINISTRATION BELGE DU RUANDA-URUNDI PENDANT L'ANNEE 1959. BELGIUM RWANDA AGRI INDUS DIPLOM ECO/TAC INT/TRADE DOMIN ADMIN RACE/REL...GEOG CENSUS 20 UN. PAGE 7 F0132
AFR COLONIAL ECO/UNDEV INT/ORG

B60
BELLAN R.C.,PRINCIPLES OF ECONOMICS AND THE CANADIAN ECONOMY (2ND ED.). CANADA UK USA+45 LABOR WORKER CAP/ISM INT/TRADE RISK BAL/PAY EQUILIB ALL/IDEOS 20. PAGE 12 F0236
ECO/DEV PRODUC WEALTH FINAN

B60
BILLERBECK K.,SOVIET BLOC FOREIGN AID TO UNDERDEVELOPED COUNTRIES. COM FUT USSR FINAN FORCES TEC/DEV DIPLOM INT/TRADE EDU/PROP NUC/PWR...TREND 20. PAGE 15 F0285
FOR/AID ECO/UNDEV ECO/TAC MARXISM

B60
COMMITTEE ECONOMIC DEVELOPMENT,NATIONAL OBJECTIVES AND THE BALANCE OF PAYMENTS PROBLEM: A STATEMENT ON NATIONAL POLICY. USA+45 WOR+45 DIST/IND FINAN INDUS LABOR NAT/G DELIB/GP ACT/RES FOR/AID INT/TRADE ...STAT CHARTS FOR/TRADE 20. PAGE 27 F0516
ECO/DEV ECO/TAC BAL/PAY

B60
COPLAND D.,THE ADVENTURE OF GROWTH: ESSAYS ON THE AUSTRALIAN ECONOMY AND ITS INTERNATIONAL SETTING. WOR+45 DIST/IND ACADEM EDU/PROP ADMIN INCOME 20 AUSTRAL. PAGE 27 F0534
ECO/DEV ECO/UNDEV ECO/TAC INT/TRADE

B60
DALE W.B.,THE FOREIGN DEFICIT OF THE UNITED STATES. ECO/TAC TARIFFS PAY PRICE CONTROL COST WEALTH POLICY. PAGE 30 F0573
BAL/PAY DIPLOM FINAN INT/TRADE

B60
DIA M.,REFLEXIONS SUR L'ECONOMIE DE L'AFRIQUE NOIRE (REV. ED.). CULTURE ECO/UNDEV CREATE TEC/DEV DIPLOM INT/TRADE OPTIMAL ATTIT...POLICY 20. PAGE 32 F0631
AFR ECO/TAC SOCISM PLAN

B60
HEILPERIN M.A.,STUDIES IN ECONOMIC NATIONALISM. EUR+WWI MOD/EUR USA+45 ECO/DEV PLAN INT/TRADE TARIFFS WAR PRODUC PROFIT 18/20 KEYNES/JM. PAGE 58 F1140
ECO/TAC NAT/G NAT/LISM POLICY

B60
HOFFMANN P.G.,ONE HUNDRED COUNTRIES, ONE AND ONE QUARTER BILLION PEOPLE. MARKET INT/ORG TEC/DEV CAP/ISM...GEOG CHARTS METH/COMP 20 UN. PAGE 61 F1191
FOR/AID ECO/TAC ECO/UNDEV INT/TRADE

B60
HOSELITZ B.F.,THEORIES OF ECONOMIC GROWTH. UK WOR+45 WOR-45 ECO/UNDEV PLAN INT/TRADE KNOWL ...CONCPT METH/CNCPT TIME/SEQ GEN/LAWS TOT/POP. PAGE 62 F1220
ECO/DEV INTELL

B60
KENEN P.B.,GIANT AMONG NATIONS: PROBLEMS IN UNITED STATES FOREIGN ECONOMIC POLICY. AFR USA+45 FINAN DIPLOM TARIFFS BAL/PAY WEALTH 20. PAGE 70 F1376
FOR/AID ECO/UNDEV INT/TRADE PLAN

B60
KENEN P.B.,BRITISH MONETARY POLICY AND THE BALANCE OF PAYMENTS 1951-57. UK PLAN BUDGET ECO/TAC INT/TRADE PAY PRICE COST ATTIT 20. PAGE 70 F1377
BAL/PAY PROB/SOLV FINAN NAT/G

B60
KILLOUGH H.B.,INTERNATIONAL ECONOMICS. PLAN PROB/SOLV FOR/AID TARIFFS CONTROL BAL/PAY...POLICY CHARTS T 20. PAGE 71 F1388
CONCPT ECO/UNDEV INT/ORG INT/TRADE

B60
KRISTENSEN T.,THE ECONOMIC WORLD BALANCE. FUT WOR+45 CULTURE ECO/DEV BAL/PWR INT/TRADE REGION PWR WEALTH...STAT TREND CHARTS 20. PAGE 73 F1442
ECO/UNDEV ECO/TAC FOR/AID

B60
LERNER A.P.,THE ECONOMICS OF CONTROL. USA+45 ECO/UNDEV INT/ORG ACT/RES PLAN CAP/ISM INT/TRADE ATTIT WEALTH...SOC MATH STAT GEN/LAWS INDEX 20. PAGE 78 F1530
ECO/DEV ROUTINE ECO/TAC SOCISM

B60
LISTER L.,EUROPE'S COAL AND STEEL COMMUNITY. FRANCE GERMANY STRUCT ECO/DEV EXTR/IND INDUS MARKET NAT/G DELIB/GP ECO/TAC INT/TRADE EDU/PROP ATTIT RIGID/FLEX ORD/FREE PWR WEALTH...CONCPT STAT TIME/SEQ CHARTS ECSC TERR/GP 20. PAGE 81 F1582
EUR+WWI INT/ORG REGION

B60
PENTONY D.E.,UNITED STATES FOREIGN AID. INDIA LAOS USA+45 ECO/UNDEV INT/TRADE ADMIN PEACE ATTIT ...POLICY METH/COMP ANTHOL 20. PAGE 105 F2060
FOR/AID DIPLOM ECO/TAC

B60
SHONFIELD A.,THE ATTACK ON WORLD POVERTY. WOR+45 ECO/DEV ECO/UNDEV FINAN VOL/ASSN PLAN EDU/PROP DRIVE KNOWL WEALTH...CONT/OBS STAND/INT ORG/CHARTS TOT/POP UNESCO 20. PAGE 121 F2383
INT/ORG ECO/TAC FOR/AID INT/TRADE

B60
STANFORD RESEARCH INSTITUTE,AFRICAN DEVELOPMENT: A TEST FOR INTERNATIONAL COOPERATION. AFR USA+45 WOR+45 FINAN INT/ORG PLAN PROB/SOLV ECO/TAC INT/TRADE ADMIN...CHARTS 20. PAGE 125 F2467
FOR/AID ECO/UNDEV ATTIT DIPLOM

B60
STEIN E.,AMERICAN ENTERPRISE IN THE EUROPEAN COMMON MARKET: A LEGAL PROFILE. EUR+WWI FUT USA+45 SOCIETY STRUCT ECO/DEV NAT/G VOL/ASSN CONSULT PLAN TEC/DEV ECO/TAC INT/TRADE ADMIN ATTIT RIGID/FLEX PWR...MGT NEW/IDEA STAT TREND COMPUT/IR SIMUL EEC 20. PAGE 125 F2475
MARKET ADJUD INT/LAW

B60
STOLPER W.F.,GERMANY BETWEEN EAST AND WEST: THE ECONOMICS OF COMPETITIVE COEXISTENCE. AFR FUT GERMANY/E GERMANY/W WOR+45 FINAN POL/PAR BUDGET ECO/TAC FOR/AID INT/TRADE...STAT CHARTS METH/COMP 20. PAGE 126 F2495
ECO/DEV DIPLOM GOV/COMP BAL/PWR

B60
THE ECONOMIST (LONDON),THE COMMONWEALTH AND EUROPE. EUR+WWI WOR+45 AGRI FINAN INCOME...STAT CENSUS CHARTS CMN/WLTH EEC. PAGE 129 F2550
INT/TRADE INDUS INT/ORG NAT/COMP

B60
THEOBALD R.,THE RICH AND THE POOR: A STUDY OF THE ECONOMICS OF RISING EXPECTATIONS. WOR+45 CONSTN ECO/DEV ECO/UNDEV INT/ORG NAT/G PLAN FOR/AID ROUTINE BAL/PAY ORD/FREE PWR WEALTH...GEOG TREND WORK FOR/TRADE 20. PAGE 129 F2553
ECO/TAC INT/TRADE

B60
WATSON D.S.,ECONOMIC POLICY: BUSINESS AND GOVERNMENT. USA+45 FINAN LABOR PLAN BUDGET INT/TRADE GP/REL WEALTH LAISSEZ...CHARTS T. PAGE 144 F2832
ECO/TAC NAT/G POLICY ECO/DEV

B60
WENTHOLT W.,INFLATION OR SECURITY? EUR+WWI USA+45 INDUS CONSULT TEC/DEV CAP/ISM DIPLOM FOR/AID INT/TRADE MARXISM 20 EEC. PAGE 145 F2858
ECO/DEV ECO/TAC FINAN ORD/FREE

B60
WODDIS J.,AFRICA: THE ROOTS OF REVOLT. SOUTH/AFR WORKER INT/TRADE RACE/REL DISCRIM ORD/FREE 20. PAGE 148 F2915
COLONIAL SOVEREIGN WAR ECO/UNDEV

L60
CHENERY H.B.,"PATTERNS OF INDUSTRIAL GROWTH." INT/TRADE DEMAND PRODUC...MATH REGRESS CHARTS SIMUL METH 20. PAGE 24 F0462
ECO/TAC ECO/DEV GP/COMP CON/ANAL

S60
"THE EMERGING COMMON MARKETS IN LATIN AMERICA." FUT L/A+17C STRATA DIST/IND INDUS LABOR NAT/G LEGIS ECO/TAC ADMIN RIGID/FLEX HEALTH...NEW/IDEA TIME/SEQ OAS 20. PAGE 1 F0013
FINAN ECO/UNDEV INT/TRADE

S60
FRANKEL S.H.,"ECONOMIC ASPECTS OF POLITICAL INDEPENDENCE IN AFRICA." AFR FUT SOCIETY ECO/UNDEV COM/IND FINAN LEGIS PLAN TEC/DEV CAP/ISM ECO/TAC INT/TRADE ADMIN ATTIT DRIVE RIGID/FLEX PWR WEALTH ...MGT NEW/IDEA MATH TIME/SEQ VAL/FREE 20. PAGE 43 F0846
NAT/G FOR/AID

S60
GARNICK D.H.,"ON THE ECONOMIC FEASIBILITY OF A MIDDLE EASTERN COMMON MARKET." AFR ISLAM CULTURE INDUS NAT/G PLAN TEC/DEV ECO/TAC ADMIN ATTIT DRIVE RIGID/FLEX...PLURIST STAT TREND GEN/LAWS 20. PAGE 46 F0907
MARKET INT/TRADE

S60
HERRERA F.,"THE INTER-AMERICAN DEVELOPMENT BANK." USA+45 ECO/UNDEV INT/ORG CONSULT DELIB/GP PLAN ECO/TAC INT/TRADE ROUTINE WEALTH...STAT TERR/GP 20. PAGE 59 F1153
L/A+17C FINAN FOR/AID REGION

S60
KREININ M.E.,"THE 'OUTER-SEVEN' AND EUROPEAN INTEGRATION." EUR+WWI FRANCE GERMANY ITALY UK ECO/DEV DIST/IND INT/TRADE DRIVE WEALTH...MYTH CHARTS EEC OEEC 20. PAGE 73 F1436
ECO/TAC GEN/LAWS

S60
MARTIN E.M.,"NEW TRENDS IN UNITED STATES ECONOMIC FOREIGN POLICY." USA+45 INTELL DELIB/GP FOR/AID INT/TRADE ROUTINE BAL/PAY...RELATIV TRUE/GP 20. PAGE 86 F1682
NAT/G PLAN DIPLOM

S60
MORALES C.J.,"TRADE AND ECONOMIC INTEGRATION IN LATIN AMERICA." FUT L/A+17C LAW STRATA ECO/UNDEV DIST/IND INDUS LABOR NAT/G LEGIS ECO/TAC ADMIN RIGID/FLEX WEALTH...CONCPT NEW/IDEA CONT/OBS TIME/SEQ WORK 20. PAGE 93 F1825
FINAN INT/TRADE REGION

S60
NEISSER H.,"ECONOMIC IMPERALISM RECONSIDERED." WOR+45 WOR-45 ECO/DEV ECO/UNDEV DIST/IND LEGIT COLONIAL PWR WEALTH SOCISM...MYTH MATH TIME/SEQ 20. PAGE 97 F1909
ACT/RES ECO/TAC CAP/ISM INT/TRADE

S60
OWEN C.F.,"US AND SOVIET RELATIONS WITH UNDERDEVELOPED COUNTRIES: LATIN AMERICA-A CASE STUDY." AFR COM L/A+17C USA+45 USSR EXTR/IND MARKET TEC/DEV DIPLOM ECO/TAC NAT/LISM ORD/FREE PWR ...TREND WORK 20. PAGE 102 F2005
ECO/UNDEV DRIVE INT/TRADE

N60
ERDMAN P.E.,COMMON MARKETS AND FREE TRADE AREAS (PAMPHLET). USA+45 MARKET INT/ORG TEC/DEV DIPLOM UTIL...CON/ANAL CHARTS BIBLIOG 20 EEC OEEC. PAGE 38 F0743
TREND PROB/SOLV INT/TRADE ECO/DEV

B61
ALFRED H.,PUBLIC OWNERSHIP IN THE USA: GOALS AND PRIORITIES. LAW INDUS INT/TRADE ADJUD GOV/REL EFFICIENCY PEACE SOCISM...POLICY ANTHOL 20 TVA. PAGE 4 F0065
CONTROL OWN ECO/DEV ECO/TAC

B61
AUBREY H.G.,COEXISTENCE: ECONOMIC CHALLENGE AND RESPONSE. AFR USSR WOR+45 ACT/RES BAL/PWR CAP/ISM DIPLOM ECO/TAC FOR/AID INT/TRADE PEACE SOCISM ...METH/COMP NAT/COMP. PAGE 7 F0139
POLICY ECO/UNDEV PLAN COM

B61
BALASSA B.,THE THEORY OF ECONOMIC INTEGRATION. EUR+WWI L/A+17C MOD/EUR WOR+45 ECO/UNDEV MARKET INT/ORG NAT/G VOL/ASSN DELIB/GP PLAN CAP/ISM ECO/TAC...MAJORIT FOR/TRADE OEEC 20. PAGE 8 F0157
ECO/DEV ACT/RES INT/TRADE

B61
BENHAM F.,ECONOMIC AID TO UNDERDEVELOPED COUNTRIES. WOR+45 INDUS BAL/PAY ALL/VALS 20. PAGE 13 F0244
ECO/UNDEV FOR/AID INT/TRADE FINAN

B61
BONNEFOUS M.,EUROPE ET TIERS MONDE. EUR+WWI SOCIETY INT/ORG NAT/G VOL/ASSN ACT/RES TEC/DEV CAP/ISM ECO/TAC ATTIT ORD/FREE SOVEREIGN...POLICY CONCPT TREND TERR/GP COMMUN 20. PAGE 16 F0314
AFR ECO/UNDEV FOR/AID INT/TRADE

B61
BREWIS T.N.,CANADIAN ECONOMIC POLICY. AFR CANADA BUDGET CAP/ISM INT/TRADE RATION TARIFFS TAX PRICE CONTROL ROUTINE FEDERAL INCOME PRODUC 20. PAGE 18 F0348
ECO/DEV ECO/TAC NAT/G PLAN

B61
EINZIG P.,A DYNAMIC THEORY OF FORWARD EXCHANGE. FUT WOR+45 WOR-45 INT/TRADE BAL/PAY WEALTH...OLD/LIB NEW/IDEA OBS TREND FOR/TRADE 20. PAGE 37 F0713
FINAN ECO/TAC

B61
ELLIS H.S.,ECONOMIC DEVELOPMENT FOR LATIN AMERICA. L/A+17C AGRI FINAN INDUS FOR/AID GP/REL BAL/PAY DEMAND...ANTHOL 20 INTL/ECON. PAGE 37 F0723
ECO/UNDEV ECO/TAC PLAN INT/TRADE

B61
FELLNER W.,THE PROBLEM OF RISING PRICES. AGRI INDUS WORKER BUDGET CAP/ISM ECO/TAC INT/TRADE PAY DEMAND ...POLICY 20 EEC. PAGE 40 F0780
PRICE MARKET ECO/DEV COST

B61
FLINN M.W.,AN ECONOMIC AND SOCIAL HISTORY OF BRITAIN, 1066-1939. UK LAW STRATA STRUCT AGRI DIST/IND INDUS WORKER INT/TRADE WAR...CENSUS 11/20. PAGE 42 F0811
SOCIETY SOC

B61
FRIEDMANN W.G.,JOINT INTERNATIONAL BUSINESS VENTURES. ASIA ISLAM L/A+17C ECO/DEV DIST/IND FINAN PROC/MFG FACE/GP LG/CO NAT/G VOL/ASSN CONSULT EX/STRUC PLAN ADMIN ROUTINE WEALTH...OLD/LIB FOR/TRADE WORK 20. PAGE 44 F0865
ECO/UNDEV INT/TRADE

B61
GARDNER R.N.,LEGAL-ECONOMIC PROBLEMS OF INTERNATIONAL TRADE. FUT WOR+45 INTELL ECO/DEV EX/STRUC INT/TRADE ROUTINE ATTIT WEALTH...GEN/LAWS ANTHOL FOR/TRADE 20. PAGE 46 F0904
FINAN ACT/RES

B61
GOODWIN C.D.W.,CANADIAN ECONOMIC THOUGHT. CANADA STRATA TEC/DEV CAP/ISM TARIFFS TAX COST EFFICIENCY WEALTH...METH/CNCPT TREND 20 MARITIME ONTARIO. PAGE 49 F0952
INT/TRADE ECO/DEV FINAN DEMAND

B61
GREY A.L.,ECONOMIC ISSUES AND POLICIES; READINGS IN INTRODUCTORY ECONOMICS (2ND ED.). WOR+45 ECO/UNDEV FINAN MARKET LABOR LG/CO INT/TRADE BAL/PAY WEALTH ...ANTHOL T. PAGE 51 F0996
ECO/TAC PROB/SOLV METH/COMP

B61
GURTOO D.H.N.,INDIA'S BALANCE OF PAYMENTS (1920-1960). INDIA FINAN DIPLOM FOR/AID INT/TRADE PRICE COLONIAL...CHARTS BIBLIOG 20. PAGE 52 F1014
BAL/PAY STAT ECO/TAC ECO/UNDEV

B61
HARDT J.P.,THE COLD WAR ECONOMIC GAP. AFR USA+45 USSR ECO/DEV FORCES INT/TRADE NUC/PWR PWR 20. PAGE 55 F1081
DIPLOM ECO/TAC NAT/COMP POLICY

B61
HARRIS S.E.,THE DOLLAR IN CRISIS. AFR USA+45 MARKET INT/ORG ECO/TAC PRICE CONTROL WEALTH...METH/COMP ANTHOL 20. PAGE 55 F1089
BAL/PAY DIPLOM FINAN INT/TRADE

B61
HICKS U.K.,FEDERALISM AND ECONOMIC GROWTH IN UNDERDEVELOPED COUNTRIES. WOR+45 WOR-45 FINAN NAT/G PLAN BUDGET DIPLOM INT/TRADE DEMAND WEALTH...ANTHOL 20. PAGE 59 F1167
ECO/UNDEV ECO/TAC FEDERAL CONSTN

B61
INDUSTRIAL COUN SOC-ECO STU,THE SWEDISH ECONOMY AND THE UNDERDEVELOPED COUNTRIES. SWEDEN INDUS DELIB/GP TEC/DEV INT/TRADE EDU/PROP COLONIAL DRIVE...CHARTS 20. PAGE 64 F1264
FOR/AID ECO/UNDEV PLAN FINAN

B61
KITZINGER V.W.,THE CHALLENGE OF THE COMMON MARKET. EUR+WWI ECO/DEV DIST/IND PLAN ECO/TAC INT/TRADE LEGIT ATTIT PWR WEALTH...TIME/SEQ TREND CHARTS EEC 20. PAGE 71 F1403
MARKET INT/ORG UK

B61
MORRIS B.R.,PROBLEMS OF AMERICAN ECONOMIC GROWTH. USA+45 LABOR WORKER BUDGET ECO/TAC INT/TRADE EQUILIB 20. PAGE 94 F1836
ECO/DEV POLICY TEC/DEV DEMAND

B61
OECD,STATISTICS OF BALANCE OF PAYMENTS 1950-61. WOR+45 FINAN ECO/TAC INT/TRADE DEMAND WEALTH...STAT NAT/COMP 20 OEEC OECD. PAGE 100 F1965
BAL/PAY ECO/DEV INT/ORG CHARTS

B61
PERKINS D.,THE UNITED STATES AND LATIN AMERICAN. L/A+17C USA+45 USA-45 STRUCT COLONIAL REV ORD/FREE 19/20. PAGE 105 F2061
DIPLOM INT/TRADE NAT/G

B61
PERLO V.,EL IMPERIALISMO NORTHEAMERICANO. USA+45 USA-45 FINAN CAP/ISM DIPLOM DOMIN CONTROL DISCRIM 19/20. PAGE 105 F2063
SOCIALIST ECO/DEV INT/TRADE ECO/TAC

B61
SCHNAPPER B.,LA POLITIQUE ET LE COMMERCE FRANCAIS DANS LE GOLFE DE GUINEE DE 1838 A 1871. FRANCE GUINEA UK SEA EXTR/IND NAT/G DELIB/GP LEGIS ADMIN ORD/FREE...POLICY GEOG CENSUS CHARTS BIBLIOG 19. PAGE 117 F2303
COLONIAL INT/TRADE DOMIN AFR

B61
TRIFFIN R.,GOLD AND THE DOLLAR CRISIS: THE FUTURE OF CONVERTIBILITY. AFR USA+45 USA-45 INT/ORG PROB/SOLV BUDGET INT/TRADE PRICE...STAT CHARTS 19/20. PAGE 131 F2588
FINAN ECO/DEV ECO/TAC BAL/PAY

B61
US CONGRESS JOINT ECO COMM,INTERNATIONAL PAYMENTS IMBALANCES AND NEED FOR STRENGTHENING INTERNATIONAL FINANCIAL ARRANGEMENTS. USA+45 WOR+45 DELIB/GP DIPLOM INT/TRADE...CHARTS 20 CONGRESS OEEC. PAGE 134 F2651
BAL/PAY INT/ORG FINAN PROB/SOLV

B61
VEIT O.,GRUNDRISS DER WAHRUNGSPOLITIK. AFR FRANCE GERMANY USSR DIPLOM INT/TRADE...NAT/COMP 19/20 SILVER. PAGE 141 F2773
FINAN POLICY ECO/TAC CAP/ISM

B61
WARD B.J.,INDIA AND THE WEST. INDIA UK USA+45 INT/TRADE GIVE COLONIAL ATTIT MARXISM 19/20. PAGE 143 F2817
PLAN ECO/UNDEV ECO/TAC FOR/AID

B61
WRIGHT H.M.,THE "NEW IMPERIALISM": ANALYSIS OF LATE NINETEENTH-CENTURY EXPANSION. MOD/EUR WOR-45 SOCIETY FINAN ECO/TAC INT/TRADE NAT/LISM...ANTHOL BIBLIOG/A 19. PAGE 149 F2933
HIST/WRIT IDEA/COMP COLONIAL DOMIN

L61
CHENERY H.B.,"COMPARATIVE ADVANTAGE AND DEVELOPMENT POLICY." FINAN INT/TRADE RATION OPTIMAL...CHARTS METH/COMP GEN/LAWS BIBLIOG 20 RESOURCE/N. PAGE 24 F0463
ECO/UNDEV ECO/TAC PLAN EFFICIENCY

S61
DELLA PORT G.,"PROBLEMI E PROSPETTIVE DI COESISTENZA FRA ORIENTE ED OCCIDENTE, (PART 3)." COM FUT WOR+45 NAT/G BAL/PWR FOR/AID BAL/PAY PWR
AFR INT/TRADE

WEALTH...SOC CONCPT GEN/LAWS 20. PAGE 32 F0616

S61

DEUTSCH K.W.,"NATIONAL INDUSTRIALIZATION AND THE DECLINING SHARE OF THE INTERNATIONAL ECONOMIC SECTOR." EUR+WWI FUT WOR+45 WOR-45 MARKET PLAN EDU/PROP WEALTH...WELF/ST OBS TESTS 20. PAGE 32 F0624
DIST/IND ECO/DEV INT/TRADE

S61

NYANZI S.,"THE EAST AFRICAN MARKET: FOR BETTER OF FOR WORSE." AFR TANZANIA UGANDA PROB/SOLV TARIFFS TAX BAL/PAY. PAGE 99 F1947
ECO/TAC ECO/UNDEV INT/ORG INT/TRADE

S61

OCHENG D.,"ECONOMIC FORCES AND UGANDA'S FOREIGN POLICY." AFR UGANDA INT/TRADE TARIFFS INCOME SOVEREIGN WEALTH 20 EACM EEC TANGANYIKA. PAGE 100 F1961
ECO/TAC DIPLOM ECO/UNDEV INT/ORG

S61

RAY J.,"THE EUROPEAN FREE-TRADE ASSOCIATION AND ITS IMPACT ON INDIA'S TRADE." EUR+WWI FRANCE GERMANY INDIA S/ASIA UK NAT/G VOL/ASSN PLAN INT/TRADE ROUTINE WEALTH...STAT CHARTS TERR/GP CMN/WLTH EEC FOR/TRADE OEEC 20 EFTA. PAGE 109 F2155
ECO/DEV ECO/TAC

S61

VERNON R.,"A TRADE POLICY FOR THE 1960'S." COM FUT USA+45 WOR+45 ECO/DEV ECO/UNDEV FINAN TOP/EX ACT/RES...WELF/ST METH/CNCPT CONT/OBS TOT/POP 20. PAGE 141 F2781
PLAN INT/TRADE

S61

VINER J.,"ECONOMIC FOREIGN POLICY ON THE NEW FRONTIER." USA+45 ECO/UNDEV AGRI FINAN INDUS MARKET INT/ORG NAT/G FOR/AID INT/TRADE ADMIN ATTIT PWR 20 KENNEDY/JF. PAGE 141 F2786
TOP/EX ECO/TAC BAL/PAY TARIFFS

B62

ALEXANDROWICZ C.H.,WORLD ECONOMIC AGENCIES: LAW AND PRACTICE. WOR+45 DIST/IND FINAN LABOR CONSULT INT/TRADE TARIFFS REPRESENT HEALTH...JURID 20 UN GATT EEC OAS ECSC. PAGE 4 F0064
INT/LAW INT/ORG DIPLOM ADJUD

B62

BACKMAN J.,THE ECONOMICS OF THE ELECTRICAL MACHINERY INDUSTRY. USA+45 PROC/MFG LABOR WORKER INT/TRADE TV PRICE COST...CHARTS 19/20. PAGE 8 F0147
PRODUC TEC/DEV TREND

B62

COPPOCK J.D.,INTERNATIONAL ECONOMIC INSTABILITY: THE EXPERIENCE AFTER WORLD WAR II. WOR+45 FINAN CAP/ISM CONTROL EFFICIENCY...CHARTS 20. PAGE 28 F0536
ECO/TAC ECOMETRIC INT/TRADE STAT

B62

COX O.C.,CAPITALISM AND AMERICAN LEADERSHIP. WOR+45 WOR-45 STRATA INDUS SECT INT/TRADE EXEC INGP/REL RACE/REL RATIONAL PWR WEALTH. PAGE 28 F0548
CAP/ISM LEAD ECO/DEV SOCIETY

B62

DE LAVALLE H.,A STATEMENT OF THE LAWS OF PERU IN MATTERS AFFECTING BUSINESS (3RD ED.). PERU WORKER INT/TRADE INCOME ORD/FREE...INT/LAW 20. PAGE 31 F0603
CONSTN JURID FINAN TAX

B62

EINZIG P.,THE HISTORY OF FOREIGN EXCHANGE. CHRIST-17C ISLAM MEDIT-7 PRE/AMER WOR+45 ECO/DEV FINAN PLAN ECO/TAC ATTIT KNOWL WEALTH...SIMUL GEN/LAWS. PAGE 37 F0714
MARKET TIME/SEQ INT/TRADE

B62

FAO,FOOD AND AGRICULTURE ORGANIZATION AFRICAN SURVEY. AFR CONGO/BRAZ GHANA STRATA AGRI INT/ORG TEC/DEV FOR/AID INT/TRADE RACE/REL DEMAND EFFICIENCY PRODUC...GEOG 20 UN CONGO/LEOP. PAGE 39 F0763
ECO/TAC WEALTH EXTR/IND ECO/UNDEV

B62

FATOUROS A.A.,GOVERNMENT GUARANTEES TO FOREIGN INVESTORS. WOR+45 ECO/UNDEV INDUS WORKER ADJUD ...NAT/COMP BIBLIOG TREATY. PAGE 39 F0767
NAT/G FINAN INT/TRADE ECO/DEV

B62

FORD A.G.,THE GOLD STANDARD 1880-1914: BRITAIN AND ARGENTINA. AFR UK ECO/UNDEV INT/TRADE ADMIN GOV/REL DEMAND EFFICIENCY...STAT CHARTS 19/20 ARGEN. PAGE 42 F0823
FINAN ECO/TAC BUDGET BAL/PAY

B62

FRIEDMAN M.,CAPITALISM AND FREEDOM. USA+45 FINAN LG/CO WORKER INT/TRADE RECEIVE EDU/PROP CONTROL DISCRIM INCOME WEALTH POLICY. PAGE 44 F0859
CAP/ISM ORD/FREE NAT/G ECO/DEV

B62

GREEN L.P.,DEVELOPMENT IN AFRICA. AFR CENTRL/AFR GHANA RHODESIA SOUTH/AFR AGRI PROC/MFG INT/TRADE DEMAND NAT/LISM PRODUC WEALTH...GEOG METH/CNCPT CHARTS BIBLIOG 20. PAGE 50 F0987
CULTURE ECO/UNDEV GOV/REL TREND

B62

GROVE J.W.,GOVERNMENT AND INDUSTRY IN BRITAIN. UK FINAN LOC/G CONSULT DELIB/GP INT/TRADE ADMIN CONTROL...BIBLIOG 20. PAGE 52 F1008
ECO/TAC INDUS NAT/G GP/REL

B62

HAGUE D.C.,INFLATION. AFR ECO/DEV ECO/UNDEV LABOR BUDGET CAP/ISM INT/TRADE TARIFFS SOCISM 20. PAGE 53 F1036
FINAN NAT/COMP BARGAIN ECO/TAC

B62

HENDERSON W.O.,THE GENESIS OF THE COMMON MARKET. EUR+WWI FRANCE MOD/EUR UK SEA COM/IND EXTR/IND COLONIAL DISCRIM...TIME/SEQ CHARTS BIBLIOG 18/20 EEC TREATY. PAGE 58 F1149
ECO/DEV INT/TRADE DIPLOM

B62

HOLMAN A.G.,SOME MEASURES AND INTERPRETATIONS OF EFFECTS OF US FOREIGN ENTERPRISES ON US BALANCE OF PAYMENTS. USA+45 COST INCOME WEALTH...MATH CHARTS 20. PAGE 61 F1199
BAL/PAY INT/TRADE FINAN ECO/TAC

B62

JOHNSON H.G.,MONEY, TRADE AND ECONOMIC GROWTH. ECO/DEV ECO/UNDEV FINAN COST WEALTH...POLICY SOC IDEA/COMP 20 KEYNES/JM MONEY. PAGE 67 F1324
PLAN BAL/PAY INT/TRADE ECO/TAC

B62

KINDLEBERGER C.P.,FOREIGN TRADE AND THE NATIONAL ECONOMY. WOR+45 ECO/DEV ECO/UNDEV ECO/TAC COST DEMAND 20. PAGE 71 F1393
INT/TRADE GOV/COMP BAL/PAY POLICY

B62

LIPPMANN W.,WESTERN UNITY AND THE COMMON MARKET. EUR+WWI FRANCE GERMANY/W UK USA+45 ECO/DEV AGRI FINAN MARKET INT/ORG NAT/G FOR/AID AGREE WEALTH 20 EEC. PAGE 80 F1575
DIPLOM INT/TRADE VOL/ASSN

B62

MCCRONE G.,THE ECONOMICS OF SUBSIDING AGRICULTURE. UK ECO/DEV MARKET PLAN TARIFFS PROFIT 20 EEC. PAGE 88 F1725
AGRI BAL/PAY INT/TRADE LABOR

B62

MEADE J.E.,CASE STUDIES IN EUROPEAN ECONOMIC UNION. BELGIUM EUR+WWI LUXEMBOURG NAT/G INT/TRADE REGION ROUTINE WEALTH...METH/CNCPT STAT CHARTS ECSC TOT/POP OEEC EEC FOR/TRADE 20. PAGE 89 F1738
INT/ORG ECO/TAC

B62

MEYER F.V.,THE TERMS OF TRADE. WOR+45 AGRI MARKET PROC/MFG DIPLOM PRICE DEMAND PRODUC 20. PAGE 90 F1769
INT/TRADE BAL/PAY SIMUL EQUILIB

B62

MICHAELY M.,CONCENTRATION IN INTERNATIONAL TRADE. ECO/DEV ECO/UNDEV PRICE INCOME...CHARTS NAT/COMP 20. PAGE 91 F1779
INT/TRADE MARKET FINAN GEOG

B62

O'CONNOR H.,WORLD CRISES IN OIL (BMR). ISLAM L/A+17C INDUS LG/CO INT/TRADE 20. PAGE 100 F1956
EXTR/IND DIPLOM ECO/UNDEV SOCISM

B62

PERROUX F.,L'ECONOMIE DES JEUNES NATIONS. EUR+WWI SOUTH/AFR FINAN MARKET TEC/DEV CAP/ISM FOR/AID INT/TRADE 20. PAGE 105 F2065
INDUS ECO/UNDEV ECO/TAC DIPLOM

B62

RIMALOV V.V.,ECONOMIC COOPERATION BETWEEN USSR AND UNDERDEVELOPED COUNTRIES. USSR FINAN TEC/DEV INT/TRADE DOMIN EDU/PROP COLONIAL NAT/LISM DRIVE SOVEREIGN...AUD/VIS 20. PAGE 111 F2194
FOR/AID PLAN ECO/UNDEV DIPLOM

B62

ROBERTSON B.C.,REGIONAL DEVELOPMENT IN THE EUROPEAN ECONOMIC COMMUNITY. EUR+WWI FRANCE FUT ITALY UK ECO/UNDEV WORKER ACT/RES PROB/SOLV TEC/DEV ECO/TAC INT/TRADE EEC. PAGE 112 F2209
PLAN ECO/DEV INT/ORG REGION

B62

ROBINSON A.D.,DUTCH ORGANIZED AGRICULTURE IN INTERNATIONAL POLITICS, 1945-1960. EUR+WWI NETHERLAND STRUCT ECO/DEV NAT/G VOL/ASSN CONSULT DELIB/GP PLAN TEC/DEV INT/TRADE EDU/PROP ATTIT RIGID/FLEX ALL/VALS...NEW/IDEA TREND EEC COMMUN 20. PAGE 112 F2215
AGRI INT/ORG

B62

ROBINSON M.A.,AN INTRODUCTION TO ECONOMIC REASONING. FINAN MARKET LABOR DIPLOM INT/TRADE BAL/PAY INCOME PRODUC WEALTH...POLICY MGT 20. PAGE 113 F2223
ECO/TAC METH/CNCPT NAT/G

B62

SCHMITT H.A.,THE PATH TO EUROPEAN UNITY. EUR+WWI USA+45 PLAN TEC/DEV DIPLOM FOR/AID CONFER...INT/LAW 20 EEC EURCOALSTL MARSHL/PLN UNIFICA. PAGE 117 F2300
INT/ORG INT/TRADE REGION ECO/DEV

B62

SELOSOEMARDJAN O.,SOCIAL CHANGES IN JOGJAKARTA. INDONESIA NETHERLAND ELITES STRATA STRUCT FAM POL/PAR CREATE DIPLOM INT/TRADE EDU/PROP ADMIN GOV/REL...SOC 20 JAVA CHINJAP. PAGE 119 F2352
ECO/UNDEV CULTURE REV COLONIAL

B62

SHANNON I.,THE ECONOMIC FUNCTIONS OF GOLD. AFR FUT WOR+45 WOR-45 INT/ORG BUDGET INT/TRADE BAL/PAY DEMAND PEACE 20 MONEY. PAGE 120 F2366
FINAN PRICE ECO/DEV ECO/TAC

B62
SHINOHARA M.,GROWTH AND CYCLES IN THE JAPANESE ECONOMY. INDUS LABOR TEC/DEV CAP/ISM INT/TRADE PAY COST EFFICIENCY INCOME WEALTH...METH/COMP 20 CHINJAP. PAGE 121 F2380
PRODUC ECO/DEV EQUILIB ECOMETRIC

B62
THEOBALD R.,NATIONAL DEVELOPMENT EFFORTS (PAMPHLET). WOR+45 AGRI BUDGET FOR/AID INT/TRADE TAX 20. PAGE 129 F2555
ECO/UNDEV PLAN BAL/PAY WEALTH

B62
URQUIDI V.L.,FREE TRADE AND ECONOMIC INTEGRATION IN LATIN AMERICA: THE EVOLUTION OF A COMMON MARKET POLICY. ECO/UNDEV MARKET DIPLOM BAL/PAY FEDERAL ...POLICY CHARTS 20 LAFTA. PAGE 133 F2627
INT/TRADE REGION INT/ORG L/A+17C

B62
US CONGRESS JOINT ECO COMM,FACTORS AFFECTING THE UNITED STATES BALANCE OF PAYMENTS. USA+45 DELIB/GP PLAN DIPLOM FOR/AID PRODUC WEALTH...CHARTS 20 CONGRESS OEEC. PAGE 134 F2653
BAL/PAY INT/TRADE ECO/TAC FINAN

B62
US CONGRESS JOINT ECO COMM,ECONOMIC DEVELOPMENTS IN SOUTH AMERICA. USA+45 SOCIETY FINAN NAT/G PROB/SOLV TEC/DEV INT/TRADE TAX EFFICIENCY PRODUC ATTIT ...POLICY 20 ALL/PROG CONGRESS SOUTH/AMER. PAGE 135 F2654
L/A+17C ECO/UNDEV FOR/AID DIPLOM

B62
VANEK J.,INTERNATIONAL TRADE - THEORY AND ECONOMIC POLICY. LABOR BAL/PWR ECO/TAC TARIFFS PRICE BAL/PAY COST DEMAND 20. PAGE 140 F2765
INT/TRADE DIPLOM BARGAIN MARKET

B62
ZOOK P.D.,FOREIGN TRADE AND HUMAN CAPITAL. L/A+17C USA+45 FINAN DIPLOM ECO/TAC PRODUC...POLICY 20. PAGE 151 F2970
INT/TRADE ECO/UNDEV FOR/AID BAL/PAY

S62
ADISESHIAN M.,"EDUCATION AND DEVELOPMENT." FUT WOR+45 SOCIETY ACT/RES INT/TRADE EDU/PROP KNOWL SKILL WEALTH...POLICY CONCPT CONT/OBS CENSUS CHARTS TOT/POP VAL/FREE APPLIC FAO FOR/TRADE 20. PAGE 2 F0041
SCHOOL ECO/UNDEV

N62
BANK INTERNATIONAL SETTLEMENTS,AUSTRIA: MONETARY AND ECONOMIC SITUATION 1952-61 (PAMPHLET). AUSTRIA WORKER BUDGET INT/TRADE PRICE BAL/PAY DEMAND EFFICIENCY INCOME PRODUC...STAT 20 SILVER. PAGE 9 F0174
FINAN ECO/DEV CHARTS WEALTH

B63
BRITISH AID. UK AGRI DIST/IND INDUS SCHOOL TEC/DEV INT/TRADE COLONIAL DEMAND...TREND CHARTS 20. PAGE 1 F0018
FOR/AID ECO/UNDEV NAT/G FINAN

B63
ALPERT P.,ECONOMIC DEVELOPMENT. WOR+45 FINAN TEC/DEV ECO/TAC PRICE GOV/REL HABITAT...GEOG BIBLIOG T 20 THIRD/WRLD. PAGE 4 F0079
ECO/DEV ECO/UNDEV INT/TRADE FOR/AID

B63
BANERJI A.K.,INDIA'S BALANCE OF PAYMENTS. INDIA NAT/G PRICE BAL/PAY COST INCOME 20. PAGE 9 F0171
INT/TRADE DIPLOM FINAN BUDGET

B63
BARBOUR V.,CAPITALISM IN AMSTERDAM IN THE 17TH CENTURY. NETHERLAND FINAN ECO/TAC...METH/COMP BIBLIOG MUNICH 16. PAGE 10 F0185
CAP/ISM INT/TRADE MARKET WEALTH

B63
BERGSON A.,ECONOMIC TRENDS IN THE SOVIET UNION. USSR ECO/UNDEV AGRI NAT/G FORCES PLAN TEC/DEV INT/TRADE BAL/PAY...POLICY ANTHOL 20. PAGE 14 F0259
ECO/DEV NAT/COMP INDUS LABOR

B63
CENTRO ESTUDIOS MONETARIOS LAT,COOPERACION FINANCIERA EN AMERICA LATINA. L/A+17C PLAN PROB/SOLV CONTROL REGION DEMAND...POLICY ANTHOL 20. PAGE 22 F0433
ECO/UNDEV INT/TRADE MARKET FINAN

B63
CENTRO PARA EL DESARROLLO,LA ALIANZA PARA EL PROGRESO Y EL DESARROLLO SOCIAL DE AMERICA LATINA. L/A+17C INT/ORG DIPLOM ECO/TAC INT/TRADE ATTIT 20 ALL/PROG. PAGE 22 F0435
ECO/UNDEV FOR/AID PLAN REGION

B63
CHATTERJEE I.K.,ECONOMIC DEVELOPMENT PAYMENTS DEFICIT AND PAYMENT RESTRICTION. INDIA WOR+45 FINAN INT/TRADE CONTROL BAL/PAY WEALTH...POLICY CONCPT STAT CHARTS IDEA/COMP BIBLIOG 20. PAGE 23 F0456
ECO/DEV ECO/TAC PAY GOV/REL

B63
CLARK J.J.,BUSINESS FLUCTUATIONS, GROWTH, AND ECONOMIC STABILIZATION. USA+45 FINAN INT/TRADE OPTIMAL...METH/CNCPT ANTHOL BIBLIOG 20. PAGE 25 F0479
CAP/ISM ECO/TAC EQUILIB POLICY

B63
COPPOCK J.,NORTH ATLANTIC POLICY - THE AGRICULTURAL GAP. EUR+WWI ELITES ECO/DEV DIST/IND MARKET PLAN WEALTH...STAT TREND GEN/LAWS OEEC TOT/POP VAL/FREE FAO 20. PAGE 27 F0535
AGRI TEC/DEV INT/TRADE

B63
DELL S.,TRADE BLOCS AND COMMON MARKETS. COM WOR+45 ECO/DEV ECO/UNDEV GP/COMP. PAGE 32 F0615
DIPLOM ECO/TAC INT/TRADE FEDERAL

B63
ERHARD L.,THE ECONOMICS OF SUCCESS. GERMANY/W WOR+45 LABOR CHIEF TAX REGION COST DEMAND ANTHOL. PAGE 38 F0745
ECO/DEV INT/TRADE PLAN DIPLOM

B63
FOX S.,ECONOMIC CONTROL AND FREE ENTERPRISE. PLAN BUDGET INT/TRADE TAX...TREND 20. PAGE 43 F0839
CONTROL FINAN ECO/TAC

B63
FRIEDMAN M.,INFLATION: CAUSES AND CURES. AFR INDIA ECO/DEV ECO/TAC INT/TRADE RATION PRICE DEMAND ...POLICY 20. PAGE 44 F0860
ECO/UNDEV PLAN FINAN EQUILIB

B63
GANGULI B.N.,ECONOMIC CONSEQUENCES OF DISARMAMENT. EUR+WWI ECO/DEV ECO/UNDEV FORCES ACT/RES BUDGET DIPLOM INT/TRADE...STAT CHARTS NAT/COMP. PAGE 46 F0896
ECOMETRIC ARMS/CONT COST HYPO/EXP

B63
GRUBEL H.G.,WORLD MONETARY REFORM: PLANS AND ISSUES. FUT WOR+45 ECO/DEV ECO/UNDEV R+D DELIB/GP CREATE ECO/TAC ATTIT RIGID/FLEX WEALTH...STAT ANTHOL VAL/FREE 20. PAGE 52 F1009
FINAN INT/ORG BAL/PAY INT/TRADE

B63
HARROD R.F.,INTERNATIONAL TRADE THEORY IN A DEVELOPING WORLD. COM WOR+45 FOR/AID REGION COST DEMAND WEALTH...POLICY 20 INTL/ECON. PAGE 56 F1095
INT/TRADE BAL/PAY ECO/UNDEV METH/COMP

B63
INTERAMERICAN ECO AND SOC COUN,THE ALLIANCE FOR PROGRESS: ITS FIRST YEAR: 1961-1962. AGRI SCHOOL PLAN TEC/DEV INT/TRADE TAX GIVE ADMIN WEALTH...SOC 20 ALL/PROG SOUTH/AMER. PAGE 64 F1267
INT/ORG PROB/SOLV ECO/TAC L/A+17C

B63
INTERNATIONAL MONETARY FUND,COMPENSATORY FINANCING OF EXPORT FLUCTUATIONS (PAMPHLET). WOR+45 ECO/DEV ECO/UNDEV INT/ORG WEALTH...TREND 20 IMF MONEY. PAGE 65 F1281
BAL/PAY FINAN BUDGET INT/TRADE

B63
KRAVIS I.B.,DOMESTIC INTERESTS AND INTERNATIONAL OBLIGATIONS: SAFEGUARDS IN INTERNATIONAL TRADE ORGANIZATIONS. EUR+WWI USA+45 WOR+45 FINAN DELIB/GP ATTIT RIGID/FLEX HEALTH...STAT EEC VAL/FREE OEEC ECSC 20. PAGE 73 F1435
INT/ORG ECO/TAC INT/TRADE

B63
LANGE O.,ECONOMIC DEVELOPMENT, PLANNING, AND INTERNATIONAL COOPERATION. UAR WOR+45 FINAN CAP/ISM PERS/REL 20. PAGE 75 F1476
ECO/UNDEV DIPLOM INT/TRADE PLAN

B63
LARY M.B.,PROBLEMS OF THE UNITED STATES AS WORLD TRADER AND BANKER. USA+45 NAT/G PLAN DIPLOM FOR/AID ...TREND CHARTS. PAGE 76 F1482
ECO/DEV FINAN BAL/PAY INT/TRADE

B63
LEE M.W.,MACROECONOMICS: FLUCTUATIONS, GROWTH AND STABILITY (3RD ED.). MARKET LABOR TEC/DEV INT/TRADE TAX PRICE WAR PRODUC...POLICY ECOMETRIC CHARTS 19/20. PAGE 77 F1505
EQUILIB TREND WEALTH

B63
LICHTHEIM G.,THE NEW EUROPE: TODAY AND TOMORROW. EUR+WWI FINAN 20 EEC EUROPE/W. PAGE 80 F1560
DIPLOM ECO/DEV INT/ORG INT/TRADE

B63
LUTZ F.A.,DAS PROBLEM DES INTERNATIONALEN WIRTSCHAFTLICHEN GLEICHGEWICHTS. DIPLOM INT/TRADE COST INCOME 20. PAGE 82 F1612
FINAN CAP/ISM ECO/TAC PRODUC

B63
MAIZELS A.,INDUSTRIAL GROWTH AND WORLD TRADE. FUT WOR+45 ECO/DEV FINAN INT/ORG PLAN TEC/DEV ECO/TAC WEALTH...MATH STAT CHARTS VAL/FREE 19/20. PAGE 84 F1642
INDUS ECO/UNDEV INT/TRADE

B63
MEIER G.,INTERNATIONAL TRADE AND DEVELOPMENT. FINAN BAL/PAY COST DEMAND DISCRIM EQUILIB WEALTH...POLICY ECOMETRIC MATH STAT BIBLIOG/A 20. PAGE 89 F1747
ECO/UNDEV ECO/TAC INT/TRADE IDEA/COMP

B63
MYRDAL G.,CHALLENGE TO AFFLUENCE. USA+45 WOR+45 FINAN INT/ORG NAT/G PLAN ECO/TAC INT/TRADE BAL/PAY ORD/FREE 20 EUROPE/W. PAGE 96 F1882
ECO/DEV WEALTH DIPLOM PRODUC

B63
PAENSON I.,SYSTEMATIC GLOSSARY ENGLISH, FRENCH, SPANISH, RUSSIAN OF SELECTED ECONOMIC AND SOCIAL TERMS. WOR+45 FINAN LABOR INT/TRADE DEMAND PRODUC
DICTIONARY SOC LING

20. PAGE 102 F2014

B63
PAN AMERICAN UNION,THE EFFECTS OF THE EUROPEAN ECONOMIC COMMUNITY ON THE LATIN AMERICAN ECONOMIES (BMR). EUR+WWI L/A+17C ECO/UNDEV AGRI INDUS MARKET REGION 20 EEC TREATY. PAGE 103 F2024 INT/TRADE INT/ORG AGREE POLICY

B63
PATTON R.,THE DEVELOPMENT OF THE AMERICAN ECONOMY: REVISED. USA+45 USA-45 INDUS LABOR NAT/G CAP/ISM DIPLOM INT/TRADE WAR WEALTH 16/20. PAGE 104 F2038 ECO/TAC ECO/DEV DEMAND

B63
PERLO V.,MILITARISM AND INDUSTRY. USA+45 INT/TRADE EDU/PROP DETER KNOWL...CHARTS MAPS 20. PAGE 105 F2064 CIVMIL/REL INDUS LOBBY ARMS/CONT

B63
RANGEL I.,A INFLACAO BRASILEIRA (2ND ED.). AFR BRAZIL AGRI INDUS MARKET INT/TRADE DEMAND EQUILIB ATTIT 20. PAGE 109 F2144 ECO/UNDEV FINAN PRICE TAX

B63
RICARDO D.,THE PRINCIPLES OF POLITICAL ECONOMY AND TAXATION (1817). UK INDUS MARKET ECO/TAC INT/TRADE TARIFFS PRICE COST DEMAND OPTIMAL WEALTH...CONCPT 19 INTRVN/ECO. PAGE 111 F2183 GEN/LAWS TAX LAISSEZ

B63
ROPKE W.,ECONOMICS OF THE FREE SOCIETY. FINAN INT/TRADE BAL/PAY COST DEMAND EFFICIENCY ORD/FREE WEALTH...CON/ANAL METH/COMP T 20 KEYNES/JM. PAGE 114 F2240 SOCIETY BUDGET ECO/DEV ECO/TAC

B63
SALENT W.S.,THE UNITED STATES BALANCE OF PAYMENTS IN 1968. EUR+WWI UK USA+45 AGRI R+D LABOR FORCES PRODUC...GEOG CONCPT CHARTS 20 CHINJAP EEC. PAGE 115 F2274 BAL/PAY DEMAND FINAN INT/TRADE

B63
STIFEL L.D.,THE TEXTILE INDUSTRY - A CASE STUDY OF INDUSTRIAL DEVELOPMENT IN THE PHILIPPINES (PAPER). PHILIPPINE WORKER CAP/ISM INT/TRADE TARIFFS RECEIVE PRICE ADMIN COST EFFICIENCY WEALTH...BIBLIOG 20. PAGE 126 F2486 S/ASIA ECO/UNDEV PROC/MFG NAT/G

B63
THEOBALD R.,FREE MEN AND FREE MARKETS. USA+45 USA-45 ECO/DEV NAT/G TEC/DEV DIPLOM INT/TRADE INCOME ORD/FREE WEALTH...TREND 19/20 KEYNES/JM. PAGE 130 F2556 CONCPT ECO/TAC CAP/ISM MARKET

B63
UN SECRETARY GENERAL,PLANNING FOR ECONOMIC DEVELOPMENT. ECO/UNDEV FINAN BUDGET INT/TRADE TARIFFS TAX ADMIN 20 UN. PAGE 132 F2603 PLAN ECO/TAC MGT NAT/COMP

B63
US CONGRESS JOINT ECO COMM,THE UNITED STATES BALANCE OF PAYMENTS. AFR USA+45 DELIB/GP BUDGET PRICE PRODUC 20 CONGRESS MONEY. PAGE 135 F2655 BAL/PAY INT/TRADE FINAN ECO/TAC

B63
US CONGRESS JOINT ECO COMM,THE UNITED STATES BALANCE OF PAYMENTS. USA+45 DELIB/GP CONFER...MATH PREDICT CHARTS 20 CONGRESS. PAGE 135 F2656 BAL/PAY ECO/TAC INT/TRADE CONSULT

B63
US CONGRESS JOINT ECO COMM,OUTLOOK FOR UNITED STATES BALANCE OF PAYMENTS. AFR USA+45 ECO/DEV NAT/G FORCES DIPLOM FOR/AID COST EFFICIENCY ...POLICY CONGRESS EEC. PAGE 135 F2657 BAL/PAY FINAN INT/TRADE PROB/SOLV

B63
US ECON SURVEY TEAM INDONESIA,INDONESIA - PERSPECTIVE AND PROPOSALS FOR UNITED STATES ECONOMIC AID. INDONESIA AGRI MARKET TEC/DEV DIPLOM INT/TRADE EDU/PROP 20. PAGE 136 F2678 FOR/AID ECO/UNDEV PLAN INDUS

B63
WILTZ J.E.,IN SEARCH OF PEACE: THE SENATE MUNITIONS INQUIRY, 1934-36. EUR+WWI USA-45 ELITES INDUS LG/CO LEGIS INT/TRADE LOBBY NEUTRAL ARMS/CONT...POLICY CONGRESS 20 LEAGUE/NAT PRESIDENT SENATE CONSCRIPTN. PAGE 147 F2905 DELIB/GP PROFIT WAR WEAPON

S63
CARTER A.G.T.,"THE BALANCE OF PAYMENTS OF EAST AFRICA" AFR ECO/TAC FOR/AID RATION TARIFFS TAX ADMIN...STAT 20 AFRICA/E. PAGE 22 F0423 BUDGET ECO/UNDEV BAL/PAY INT/TRADE

S63
COLLERY A.,"A FULL EMPLOYMENT, KEYNESIAN THEORY OF INTERNATIONAL TRADE." WOR+45 ECO/DEV ACT/RES ECO/TAC ROUTINE ORD/FREE WEALTH...MATH CHARTS 20 KEYNES/JM. PAGE 26 F0504 SIMUL INT/TRADE

S63
DIEBOLD W. JR.,"THE NEW SITUATION OF INTERNATIONAL TRADE POLICY." EUR+WWI FRANCE FUT UK USA+45 WOR+45 DIST/IND PLAN INT/TRADE EDU/PROP PWR WEALTH ...RECORD TREND GEN/LAWS EEC TRUE/GP VAL/FREE APPLIC 20. PAGE 33 F0636 MARKET ECO/TAC

S63
EMERSON R.,"THE ATLANTIC COMMUNITY AND THE EMERGING COUNTRIES." FUT WOR+45 ECO/DEV ECO/UNDEV R+D NAT/G DELIB/GP BAL/PWR ECO/TAC EDU/PROP ROUTINE ORD/FREE PWR WEALTH...POLICY CONCPT TREND GEN/METH EEC 20 NATO. PAGE 37 F0729 ATTIT INT/TRADE

S63
GERHARD H.,"COMMODITY TRADE STABILIZATION THROUGH INTERNATIONAL AGREEMENTS." WOR+45 ECO/DEV ECO/UNDEV NAT/G ROUTINE ORD/FREE...INT/LAW OBS TREND GEN/METH TOT/POP 20. PAGE 47 F0918 PLAN ECO/TAC INT/TRADE

S63
GORDON B.,"ECONOMIC IMPEDIMENTS TO REGIONALISM IN SOUTH EAST ASIA." BURMA FUT S/ASIA THAILAND USA+45 AGRI INDUS R+D NAT/G PLAN ECO/TAC WEALTH...STAT CONT/OBS 20. PAGE 49 F0954 VOL/ASSN ECO/UNDEV INT/TRADE REGION

S63
HOOVER C.B.,"ECONOMIC REFORM VERSUS ECONOMIC GROWTH IN UNDERDEVELOPED COUNTRIES." FUT WOR+45 ELITES STRATA ECO/UNDEV DIST/IND INDUS TEC/DEV CAP/ISM FOR/AID INT/TRADE ATTIT WEALTH...MYTH TREND STERTYP GEN/LAWS WORK 20. PAGE 61 F1209 ECO/DEV ECO/TAC

S63
MATHUR P.N.,"GAINS IN ECONOMIC GROWTH FROM INTERNATIONAL TRADE." USA-45 ECO/DEV FINAN INDUS ATTIT WEALTH...MATH QUANT STAT BIOG TREND GEN/LAWS WORK 20. PAGE 87 F1704 MARKET ECO/TAC CAP/ISM INT/TRADE

S63
MILLEN B.H.,"INTERNATIONAL TRADE AND POLITICAL INDEPENDENCE." WOR+45 ECO/DEV WEALTH...STAT CHARTS FOR/TRADE METH/GP TERR/GP VAL/FREE 20. PAGE 91 F1788 ECO/UNDEV ECO/TAC INT/TRADE

S63
RAMERIE L.,"TENSION AU SEIN DU COMECON: LE CAS ROUMAIN." COM EUR+WWI USSR WOR+45 ECO/DEV DIST/IND NAT/G POL/PAR VOL/ASSN EDU/PROP TOTALISM ATTIT WEALTH...TIME/SEQ 20 COMECON. PAGE 109 F2142 INT/ORG ECO/TAC INT/TRADE ROMANIA

S63
SHONFIELD A.,"AFTER BRUSSELS." EUR+WWI FRANCE GERMANY UK ECO/DEV DIST/IND MARKET VOL/ASSN DELIB/GP CREATE INT/TRADE ATTIT RIGID/FLEX...RECORD TREND GEN/LAWS EEC COMMUN CMN/WLTH 20. PAGE 121 F2385 PLAN ECO/TAC

S63
SHWADRAN B.,"MIDDLE EAST OIL, 1962." ISLAM USSR ECO/DEV DIST/IND INDUS PLAN BAL/PWR DISPL DRIVE ...POLICY STAT TREND GEN/LAWS TERR/GP METH/GP EEC OEEC 20 OIL. PAGE 121 F2394 MARKET ECO/TAC INT/TRADE

S63
WALKER H.,"THE INTERNATIONAL LAW OF COMMODITY AGREEMENTS." FUT WOR+45 ECO/DEV ECO/UNDEV FINAN INT/ORG NAT/G CONSULT CREATE PLAN ECO/TAC ATTIT PERCEPT...CONCPT GEN/LAWS TOT/POP GATT 20. PAGE 142 F2804 MARKET VOL/ASSN INT/LAW INT/TRADE

N63
LEDERER W.,THE BALANCE ON FOREIGN TRANSACTIONS: PROBLEMS OF DEFINITION AND MEASUREMENT (PAMPHLET). USA+45 BUDGET DIPLOM ECO/TAC PRICE GOV/REL...POLICY STAT NAT/COMP METH 20. PAGE 77 F1502 FINAN BAL/PAY INT/TRADE ECO/DEV

B64
INTERNATIONAL MONETARY ARRANGEMENTS: THE PROBLEM OF CHOICE. PLAN PROB/SOLV INT/TRADE ADJUST COST EQUILIB 20. PAGE 1 F0020 POLICY DIPLOM FINAN ECO/DEV

B64
AUBREY H.G.,THE DOLLAR IN WORLD AFFAIRS. FUT USA+45 WOR+45 ECO/DEV CAP/ISM INT/TRADE BAL/PAY...CHARTS 20. PAGE 7 F0140 FINAN ECO/TAC DIPLOM POLICY

B64
BALASSA B.,TRADE PROSPECTS FOR DEVELOPING COUNTRIES. WOR+45 ECO/DEV AGRI EXTR/IND INDUS CREATE PLAN PRICE...ECOMETRIC CLASSIF TIME/SEQ GEN/METH. PAGE 8 F0158 INT/TRADE ECO/UNDEV TREND STAT

B64
BALASSA B.,CHANGING PATTERNS IN FOREIGN TRADE AND PAYMENTS. AFR USA+45 USA-45 ECO/DEV NAT/G PLAN BAL/PWR...POLICY ANTHOL BIBLIOG 20. PAGE 8 F0159 ECO/TAC INT/TRADE BAL/PAY WEALTH

B64
BASTIAT F.,ECONOMIC HARMONIES (1850). STRATA STRUCT ECO/DEV BUDGET TAX PRICE LOBBY COST. PAGE 11 F0206 ECO/TAC PLAN INT/TRADE LAISSEZ

B64
BASTIAT F.,ECONOMIC SOPHISMS (1845). FINAN MARKET INT/TRADE TAX EDU/PROP LAISSEZ. PAGE 11 F0207 TARIFFS INDUS ECO/TAC CAP/ISM

B64
BERRILL K.,ECONOMIC DEVELOPMENT WITH SPECIAL REFERENCE TO EAST ASIA. ASIA INDIA S/ASIA AGRI INDUS LABOR DELIB/GP PLAN INT/TRADE COST PRODUC 20 CHINJAP. PAGE 14 F0271 FINAN ECO/UNDEV INT/ORG CAP/ISM

B64
BOARMAN P.M.,GERMANY'S ECONOMIC DILEMMA - INFLATION AND THE BALANCE OF PAYMENTS. AFR GERMANY/W LABOR CAP/ISM PRICE BAL/PAY COST INCOME 20. PAGE 16 F0302 ECO/DEV FINAN INT/TRADE BUDGET

B64
BROWN E.H.P.,A COURSE IN APPLIED ECONOMICS (2ND ED.). ECO/DEV FINAN MARKET WORKER INT/TRADE RATION RENT PAY PRICE BAL/PAY...DECISION T RESOURCE/N. PAGE 19 F0368
POLICY ECO/TAC PROB/SOLV

B64
BROWN W.M.,THE EXTERNAL LIQUIDITY OF AN ADVANCED COUNTRY. CANADA FRANCE GERMANY/W SWEDEN UK USA+45 ECO/DEV DIPLOM PRICE...CONCPT STAT NAT/COMP 20. PAGE 20 F0376
FINAN INT/TRADE COST INCOME

B64
CENTRO ESTUDIOS MONETARIOS LAT,PROBLEMAS DE PAGOS EN AMERICA LATINA. L/A+17C MARKET BUDGET ECO/TAC EFFICIENCY WEALTH 20 CENTRAL/AM. PAGE 22 F0434
FINAN INT/TRADE BAL/PAY ECO/UNDEV

B64
COMPOS R.O.,A MOEDA, O GOVERNO E O TEMPO. AFR BRAZIL WOR+45 FINAN TEC/DEV FOR/AID REGION DEMAND ...ANTHOL 20. PAGE 27 F0520
ECO/UNDEV PLAN DIPLOM INT/TRADE

B64
ESTHUS R.A.,FROM ENMITY TO ALLIANCE: US AUSTRALIAN RELATIONS. S/ASIA DIST/IND VOL/ASSN FORCES ATTIT 20 AUSTRAL TREATY CMN/WLTH. PAGE 39 F0751
DIPLOM WAR INT/TRADE FOR/AID

B64
FIESER M.E.,ECONOMIC POLICY AND WAR POTENTIAL. AFR WOR+45 ECO/DEV INDUS NAT/G FORCES TEC/DEV NUC/PWR CIVMIL/REL ORD/FREE 20. PAGE 40 F0791
INT/TRADE POLICY ECO/TAC DETER

B64
GEORGIADIS H.G.,BALANCE OF PAYMENTS EQUILIBRIUM. COST DEMAND...CONCPT MATH GEN/LAWS 20 KEYNES/JM. PAGE 47 F0916
BAL/PAY EQUILIB SIMUL INT/TRADE

B64
GOWDA K.V.,INTERNATIONAL CURRENCY PLANS AND EXPANSION OF WORLD TRADE. INT/ORG CREATE BUDGET CONTROL BAL/PAY WEALTH 20 KEYNES/JM. PAGE 50 F0969
INT/TRADE FINAN METH/COMP

B64
HALLOWELL J.H.,DEVELOPMENT: FOR WHAT. WOR+45 POL/PAR SECT FOR/AID INT/TRADE CT/SYS PARTIC PRODUC PLURISM. PAGE 54 F1052
ECO/UNDEV CONSTN NAT/LISM ECO/TAC

B64
HAMBRIDGE G.,DYNAMICS OF DEVELOPMENT. AGRI FINAN INDUS LABOR INT/TRADE EDU/PROP ADMIN LEAD OWN HEALTH...ANTHOL BIBLIOG 20. PAGE 54 F1054
ECO/UNDEV ECO/TAC OP/RES ACT/RES

B64
HANSEN B.,INTERNATIONAL LIQUIDITY. USA+45 INT/ORG ECO/TAC PRICE CONTROL WEALTH...POLICY 20. PAGE 54 F1068
BAL/PAY INT/TRADE DIPLOM FINAN

B64
HATHAWAY D.E.,PROBLEMS OF PROGRESS IN THE AGRICULTURAL ECONOMY. USA+45 USA-45 ECO/DEV NAT/G INT/TRADE PRICE DEMAND EFFICIENCY OPTIMAL 20. PAGE 57 F1112
AGRI ECO/TAC MARKET PLAN

B64
HAZLEWOOD A.,THE ECONOMICS OF DEVELOPMENT: AN ANNOTATED LIST OF BOOKS AND ARTICLES PUBLISHED 1958-1962. AGRI FINAN INDUS LABOR NAT/G DIPLOM INT/TRADE INCOME...MGT 20. PAGE 58 F1130
BIBLIOG/A ECO/UNDEV TEC/DEV

B64
HERSKOVITS M.J.,ECONOMIC TRANSITION IN AFRICA. FUT INT/ORG NAT/G WORKER PROB/SOLV TEC/DEV INT/TRADE EQUILIB INCOME...ANTHOL 20. PAGE 59 F1157
AFR ECO/UNDEV PLAN ADMIN

B64
HINSHAW R.,THE EUROPEAN COMMUNITY AND AMERICAN TRADE: A STUDY IN ATLANTIC ECONOMICS AND POLICY. EUR+WWI UK USA+45 ECO/DEV ECO/UNDEV AGRI INDUS INT/ORG NAT/G ECO/TAC TARIFFS REGION...STAT CHARTS EEC 20. PAGE 60 F1174
MARKET TREND INT/TRADE

B64
INTERNATIONAL LABOUR OFFICE,EMPLOYMENT AND ECONOMIC GROWTH. ECO/DEV ECO/UNDEV NAT/G PLAN DIPLOM INT/TRADE CONTROL INCOME PRODUC WEALTH...STAT NAT/COMP 20 ILO. PAGE 65 F1279
WORKER METH/COMP ECO/TAC OPTIMAL

B64
KALDOR N.,ESSAYS ON ECONOMIC POLICY (VOL. II). CHILE GERMANY INDIA FINAN...GOV/COMP METH/COMP 20 KEYNES/JM. PAGE 69 F1348
BAL/PAY INT/TRADE METH/CNCPT ECO/UNDEV

B64
KEMP M.C.,THE PURE THEORY OF INTERNATIONAL TRADE. WOR+45 WOR-45 ECO/DEV ECO/UNDEV DIST/IND ECO/TAC ...MATH CON/ANAL CHARTS VAL/FREE. PAGE 70 F1374
FINAN CREATE INT/TRADE

B64
KNIGHT R.,BIBLIOGRAPHY ON INCOME AND WEALTH, 1957-1960 (VOL VIII). WOR+45 ECO/DEV FINAN INT/TRADE...GOV/COMP METH/COMP. PAGE 72 F1412
BIBLIOG/A ECO/UNDEV WEALTH INCOME

B64
KRAUSE L.B.,THE COMMON MARKET: PROGRESS AND CONTROVERSY. EUR+WWI UK ECO/DEV REGION...ANTHOL NATO EEC. PAGE 73 F1433
DIPLOM MARKET INT/TRADE INT/ORG

B64
LEWIN P.,THE FOREIGN TRADE OF COMMUNIST CHINA* ITS IMPACT ON THE FREE WORLD. AFR EUR+WWI L/A+17C S/ASIA ECO/UNDEV CREATE FOR/AID...STAT NET/THEORY TREND CHARTS. PAGE 79 F1546
ASIA INT/TRADE NAT/COMP USSR

B64
LI C.M.,INDUSTRIAL DEVELOPMENT IN COMMUNIST CHINA. CHINA/COM ECO/DEV ECO/UNDEV AGRI FINAN INDUS MARKET LABOR NAT/G ECO/TAC INT/TRADE EXEC ALL/VALS ...POLICY RELATIV TREND WORK TOT/POP VAL/FREE 20. PAGE 79 F1556
ASIA TEC/DEV

B64
LISKA G.,EUROPE ASCENDANT. EUR+WWI ECO/DEV FORCES INT/TRADE MARXISM 20 EEC. PAGE 81 F1579
DIPLOM BAL/PWR TARIFFS CENTRAL

B64
LITVAK I.A.,MARKETING: CANADA. CANADA STRATA PROC/MFG LEGIS TEC/DEV DIPLOM INT/TRADE PRICE AUTOMAT ATTIT WEALTH...ANTHOL 20. PAGE 81 F1587
ECO/TAC MARKET ECO/DEV EFFICIENCY

B64
MAZA ZAVALA D.F.,VENEZUELA; UNA ECONOMIA DEPENDIENTE. L/A+17C VENEZUELA FINAN INDUS ...ECOMETRIC STAT TREND 20. PAGE 87 F1710
ECO/UNDEV BAL/PAY INT/TRADE PRICE

B64
MC GOVERN G.S.,WAR AGAINST WANT. USA+45 AGRI DIPLOM INT/TRADE GIVE RECEIVE DEMAND HEALTH 20 KENNEDY/JF FOOD/PEACE. PAGE 87 F1714
FOR/AID ECO/DEV POLICY EATING

B64
MEZERIK A.G.,TRADE, AID AND ECONOMIC DEVELOPMENT. WOR+45 FINAN INDUS MARKET PLAN BAL/PWR BARGAIN FOR/AID TARIFFS EDU/PROP WEALTH...GP/COMP 20 UN GATT IMF IBRD. PAGE 91 F1777
ECO/TAC ECO/DEV INT/ORG INT/TRADE

B64
MYINT H.,THE ECONOMICS OF THE DEVELOPING COUNTRIES. WOR+45 AGRI PLAN COST...POLICY GEOG 20 MONEY. PAGE 96 F1878
ECO/UNDEV INT/TRADE EXTR/IND FINAN

B64
NEWCOMER H.A.,INTERNATIONAL AIDS TO OVERSEAS INVESTMENTS AND TRADE. ECO/UNDEV TARIFFS PROFIT ...BIBLIOG 20 GATT UN. PAGE 98 F1921
INT/TRADE FINAN DIPLOM FOR/AID

B64
PIERSON J.H.,INSURING FULL EMPLOYMENT. USA+45 LABOR DIPLOM ECO/TAC PAY BAL/PAY 20. PAGE 106 F2084
ECO/DEV INT/TRADE POLICY WORKER

B64
RAMAZANI R.K.,THE MIDDLE EAST AND THE EUROPEAN COMMON MARKET. EUR+WWI ISLAM ECO/DEV EXTR/IND MARKET PROC/MFG INT/ORG NAT/G TEC/DEV ECO/TAC REGION DRIVE WEALTH...STAT CHARTS EEC TOT/POP 20. PAGE 109 F2141
ECO/UNDEV ATTIT INT/TRADE

B64
RANIS G.,THE UNITED STATES AND THE DEVELOPING ECONOMIES. COM USA+45 AGRI FINAN TEC/DEV CAP/ISM ECO/TAC INT/TRADE...POLICY METH/COMP ANTHOL 20 AID. PAGE 109 F2145
ECO/UNDEV DIPLOM FOR/AID

B64
REUSS H.S.,THE CRITICAL DECADE - AN ECONOMIC POLICY FOR AMERICA AND THE FREE WORLD. AFR USA+45 FINAN POL/PAR WORKER PLAN DIPLOM ECO/TAC TARIFFS BAL/PAY ...POLICY 20 CONGRESS. PAGE 111 F2181
FOR/AID INT/TRADE LABOR LEGIS

B64
RIVKIN A.,AFRICA AND THE EUROPEAN COMMON MARKET (PAMPHLET). AFR MOD/EUR WOR+45 TEC/DEV FOR/AID TARIFFS BAL/PAY...POLICY 20 EEC. PAGE 111 F2196
INT/ORG INT/TRADE ECO/TAC ECO/UNDEV

B64
ROBINSON E.A.G.,ECONOMIC DEVELOPMENT FOR AFRICA SOUTH OF THE SAHARA. AFR AGRI INDUS LABOR BUDGET INT/TRADE PRICE...POLICY GEOG ANTHOL 20. PAGE 113 F2219
ECO/UNDEV ECO/TAC ACT/RES PLAN

B64
SEGAL R.,SANCTIONS AGAINST SOUTH AFRICA. AFR SOUTH/AFR NAT/G INT/TRADE RACE/REL PEACE PWR ...INT/LAW ANTHOL 20 UN. PAGE 119 F2342
SANCTION DISCRIM ECO/TAC POLICY

B64
SINGER H.W.,INTERNATIONAL DEVELOPMENT: GROWTH AND CHANGE. AFR BRAZIL L/A+17C WOR+45 CULTURE AGRI INDUS NAT/G ACT/RES ECO/TAC EDU/PROP WEALTH...GEOG CONCPT METH/CNCPT STAT HYPO/EXP WORK TOT/POP 20. PAGE 122 F2412
FINAN ECO/UNDEV FOR/AID INT/TRADE

B64
STEWART C.F.,A BIBLIOGRAPHY OF INTERNATIONAL BUSINESS. WOR+45 FINAN LG/CO NAT/G PLAN ECO/TAC TARIFFS...DECISION MGT GP/COMP NAT/COMP 20 EEC. PAGE 126 F2484
BIBLIOG INT/ORG OP/RES INT/TRADE

B64
TONG T.,UNITED STATES DIPLOMACY IN CHINA, 1844-1860. ASIA USA-45 ECO/UNDEV ECO/TAC COERCE GP/REL...INT/LAW 19 TREATY. PAGE 131 F2581
DIPLOM INT/TRADE COLONIAL

B64
URQUIDI V.L.,THE CHALLENGE OF DEVELOPMENT IN LATIN AMERICA. L/A+17C FINAN INT/ORG TEC/DEV DIPLOM INT/TRADE PRICE REGION PRODUC...CHARTS 20 ALL/PROG. PAGE 133 F2628
ECO/UNDEV ECO/TAC NAT/G TREND

B64
WELLISZ S.,THE ECONOMICS OF THE SOVIET BLOC. COM USSR INDUS WORKER PLAN BUDGET INT/TRADE TAX PRICE PRODUC WEALTH MARXISM...METH/COMP 20. PAGE 145 F2854
EFFICIENCY ADMIN MARKET

B64
WERNETTE J.P.,GOVERNMENT AND BUSINESS. LABOR CAP/ISM ECO/TAC INT/TRADE TAX ADMIN AUTOMAT NUC/PWR CIVMIL/REL DEMAND...MGT 20 MONOPOLY. PAGE 145 F2859
NAT/G FINAN ECO/DEV CONTROL

B64
WITHERELL J.W.,OFFICIAL PUBLICATIONS OF FRENCH EQUATORIAL AFRICA, FRENCH CAMEROONS, AND TOGO, 1946-1958 (PAMPHLET). CAMEROON CHAD FRANCE GABON TOGO LAW ECO/UNDEV EXTR/IND INT/TRADE...GEOG HEAL 20. PAGE 148 F2913
BIBLIOG/A AFR NAT/G ADMIN

L64
CARNEGIE ENDOWMENT INT. PEACE,"ECONOMIC AND SOCIAL QUESTION (ISSUES BEFORE THE NINETEENTH GENERAL ASSEMBLY)." WOR+45 ECO/DEV ECO/UNDEV INDUS R+D DELIB/GP CREATE PLAN TEC/DEV ECO/TAC FOR/AID BAL/PAY...RECORD UN 20. PAGE 21 F0414
INT/ORG INT/TRADE

L64
KORBONSKI A.,"COMECON." ASIA ECO/DEV ECO/UNDEV ECO/TAC BAL/PAY NAT/LISM FOR/TRADE 20 COMECON. PAGE 73 F1425
COM INT/ORG INT/TRADE

L64
STERN R.M.,"POLICIES FOR TRADE AND DEVELOPMENT." AFR FUT WOR+45 DIST/IND FINAN NAT/G DELIB/GP PLAN ECO/TAC ORD/FREE WEALTH...POLICY STAT TIME/SEQ CHARTS METH/GP 20. PAGE 126 F2480
MARKET ECO/UNDEV INT/TRADE

S64
GARDNER R.N.,"GATT AND THE UNITED NATIONS CONFERENCE ON TRADE AND DEVELOPMENT." USA+45 WOR+45 SOCIETY ECO/UNDEV MARKET NAT/G DELIB/GP ACT/RES PLAN ECO/TAC TARIFFS EDU/PROP ROUTINE DRIVE RIGID/FLEX WEALTH...DECISION MGT TREND UN TOT/POP 20 GATT. PAGE 46 F0905
INT/ORG INT/TRADE

S64
HABERLER G.,"INTEGRATION AND GROWTH OF THE WORLD ECONOMY IN HISTORICAL PERSPECTIVE." FUT WOR+45 WOR-45 ECO/DEV ECO/UNDEV...TIME/SEQ TREND VAL/FREE 20. PAGE 52 F1023
WEALTH INT/TRADE

S64
HERMAN L.M.,"THE ECONOMIC CONTENT OF SOVIET TRADE WITH THE WEST." WOR+45 ECO/DEV ECO/UNDEV AGRI COM/IND INDUS CAP/ISM ECO/TAC ATTIT RIGID/FLEX WEALTH...OBS TREND VAL/FREE MARX/KARL 20. PAGE 59 F1152
COM MARKET INT/TRADE USSR

S64
HUELIN D.,"ECONOMIC INTEGRATION IN LATIN AMERICAN: PROGRESS AND PROBLEMS." L/A+17C ECO/DEV AGRI DIST/IND FINAN INDUS NAT/G VOL/ASSN CONSULT DELIB/GP EX/STRUC ACT/RES PLAN TEC/DEV ECO/TAC ROUTINE BAL/PAY WEALTH FOR/TRADE WORK TERR/GP 20. PAGE 63 F1232
MARKET ECO/UNDEV INT/TRADE

S64
KOJIMA K.,"THE PATTERN OF INTERNATIONAL TRADE AMONG ADVANCED COUNTRIES." EUR+WWI UK USA+45 WOR+45 MARKET NAT/G ECO/TAC WEALTH...MATH STAT CON/ANAL CHARTS METH/GP EEC CHINJAP 20 CHINJAP. PAGE 72 F1419
ECO/DEV TREND INT/TRADE

S64
NEISSER H.,"THE EXTERNAL EQUILIBRIUM OF THE UNITED STATES ECONOMY." FUT USA+45 NAT/G ACT/RES PLAN ECO/TAC ATTIT WEALTH...METH/CNCPT GEN/METH VAL/FREE FOR/TRADE 20. PAGE 97 F1910
FINAN ECO/DEV BAL/PAY INT/TRADE

B65
ALEXANDER R.J.,ORGANIZED LABOR IN LATIN AMERICA. L/A+17C INT/ORG LEGIS WORKER TEC/DEV BARGAIN INT/TRADE REV...NAT/COMP BIBLIOG 20. PAGE 3 F0059
LABOR POL/PAR ECO/UNDEV POLICY

B65
ALLEN W.R.,INTERNATIONAL TRADE THEORY: HUME TO OHLIN. FINAN LABOR TARIFFS TAX PRICE DEMAND PRODUC PROFIT...ANTHOL 18/20. PAGE 4 F0074
INT/TRADE WEALTH METH/CNCPT

B65
AMERICAN ECONOMIC ASSOCIATION,INDEX OF ECONOMIC JOURNALS 1886-1965 (7 VOLS.). UK USA+45 USA-45 AGRI FINAN PLAN ECO/TAC INT/TRADE ADMIN...STAT CENSUS 19/20. PAGE 5 F0087
BIBLIOG WRITING INDUS

B65
BAERRESEN D.W.,LATIN AMERICAN TRADE PATTERNS. L/A+17C ECO/UNDEV AGRI INDUS MARKET CREATE ...NET/THEORY CHARTS LAFTA. PAGE 8 F0149
INT/TRADE STAT REGION

B65
BELASSA B.,ECONOMIC DEVELOPMENT AND INTEGRATION. LG/CO PROB/SOLV TEC/DEV INT/TRADE TARIFFS COST WEALTH...POLICY METH/COMP 20. PAGE 12 F0232
ECO/UNDEV ECO/TAC INT/ORG INDUS

B65
BRENNAN M.J.,PATTERNS OF MARKET BEHAVIOR. AFR USA+45 OP/RES CAP/ISM ECO/TAC INT/TRADE...CHARTS METH/COMP ANTHOL TIME 20. PAGE 18 F0346
MARKET LABOR FINAN ECOMETRIC

B65
CAMERON W.J.,NEW ZEALAND. NEW/ZEALND S/ASIA DIPLOM INT/TRADE WRITING COLONIAL PARL/PROC...GEOG CMN/WLTH. PAGE 21 F0402
SOCIETY GP/REL STRUCT

B65
DEMAS W.G.,THE ECONOMICS OF DEVELOPMENT IN SMALL COUNTRIES WITH SPECIAL REFERENCE TO THE CARIBBEAN. WOR+45 BAL/PAY DEMAND EFFICIENCY PRODUC...GEOG CARIBBEAN. PAGE 32 F0618
ECO/UNDEV PLAN WEALTH INT/TRADE

B65
DOWD L.P.,PRINCIPLES OF WORLD BUSINESS. SERV/IND NAT/G DIPLOM ECO/TAC TARIFFS...INT/LAW JURID 20. PAGE 34 F0657
INT/TRADE MGT FINAN MARKET

B65
EUROPEAN FREE TRADE ASSN,REGIONAL DEVELOPMENT POLICIES IN EFTA. ECO/UNDEV INT/ORG PLAN REGION ...POLICY GEOG EFTA. PAGE 39 F0755
EUR+WWI ECO/DEV NAT/COMP INT/TRADE

B65
FORD J.L.,THE OHLIN-HECKSCHER THEORY OF THE BASIS AND EFFECTS OF COMMODITY TRADE. WOR+45 ECO/TAC DEMAND INCOME...CONCPT GEN/METH 20 OHLIN/HECK. PAGE 42 F0824
ECOMETRIC INT/TRADE NEW/IDEA SIMUL

B65
GORDON W.,THE POLITICAL ECONOMY OF LATIN AMERICA. L/A+17C FINAN MARKET PROB/SOLV TEC/DEV RECEIVE ADMIN WEALTH 20. PAGE 49 F0962
ECO/UNDEV INT/TRADE REGION POLICY

B65
GRAMPP W.D.,ECONOMIC LIBERALISM; THE CLASSICAL VIEW (VOL. II). MOD/EUR SOCIETY MARKET INT/TRADE NAT/LISM WEALTH LAISSEZ...POLICY PSY CONCPT BIBLIOG 19 SMITH/ADAM HUME/D MILL/JS. PAGE 50 F0975
ECO/DEV CAP/ISM IDEA/COMP ECO/TAC

B65
GREENFIELD K.R.,ECONOMICS AND LIBERALISM IN THE RISORGIMENTO (REV. ED.). ITALY AGRI FINAN PROC/MFG PLAN INT/TRADE CONTROL PWR 19. PAGE 51 F0990
NAT/LISM PRESS POLICY

B65
HABERLER G.,A SURVEY OF INTERNATIONAL TRADE THEORY. CANADA FRANCE GERMANY ECO/TAC TARIFFS AGREE COST DEMAND WEALTH...ECOMETRIC 19/20 MONOPOLY TREATY. PAGE 52 F1024
INT/TRADE BAL/PAY DIPLOM POLICY

B65
HLA MYINT U.,THE ECONOMICS OF THE DEVELOPING COUNTRIES. USA+45 WOR+45 AGRI FINAN NAT/G INT/TRADE ...CLASSIF CENSUS TREND NAT/COMP SIMUL GEN/LAWS. PAGE 60 F1180
ECO/UNDEV FOR/AID GEOG

B65
HOSELITZ B.F.,ECONOMICS AND THE IDEA OF MANKIND. UNIV ECO/DEV ECO/UNDEV DIST/IND INDUS INT/ORG NAT/G ACT/RES ECO/TAC WEALTH...CONCPT STAT. PAGE 62 F1223
CREATE INT/TRADE

B65
JOHNSON H.G.,THE WORLD ECONOMY AT THE CROSSROADS. COM WOR-45 ECO/DEV AGRI INDUS INT/TRADE REGION NAT/LISM 20. PAGE 67 F1326
FINAN DIPLOM INT/ORG ECO/UNDEV

B65
KASER M.,COMECON* INTEGRATION PROBLEMS OF THE PLANNED ECONOMIES. INT/ORG TEC/DEV INT/TRADE PRICE ADMIN ADJUST CENTRAL...STAT TIME/SEQ ORG/CHARTS COMECON. PAGE 69 F1359
PLAN ECO/DEV COM REGION

B65
LEYS C.T.,FEDERATION IN EAST AFRICA. LAW AGRI DIST/IND FINAN INT/ORG LABOR INT/TRADE CONFER ADMIN CONTROL GP/REL...ANTHOL 20 AFRICA/E. PAGE 79 F1554
FEDERAL REGION ECO/UNDEV PLAN

B65
LUGO-MARENCO J.J.,A STATEMENT OF THE LAWS OF NICARAGUA IN MATTERS AFFECTING BUSINESS. NICARAGUA AGRI DIST/IND EXTR/IND FINAN INDUS FAM WORKER INT/TRADE TAX MARRIAGE OWN BIO/SOC 20 TREATY RESOURCE/N MIGRATION. PAGE 82 F1606
CONSTN NAT/G LEGIS JURID

B65
MARCUS E.,INTERNATIONAL TRADE AND FINANCE. EFFICIENCY EQUILIB...CHARTS METH/COMP BIBLIOG METH T 20. PAGE 85 F1664
INT/TRADE FINAN MARKET WEALTH

B65
MARK S.M.,ECONOMICS IN ACTION (3RD ED.). USA+45 ECO/UNDEV AGRI INDUS FOR/AID INT/TRADE BAL/PAY COST ORD/FREE...ANTHOL 20 RESOURCE/N. PAGE 85 F1670
POLICY ECO/TAC EFFICIENCY PRICE

B65
MCCOLL G.D.,THE AUSTRALIAN BALANCE OF PAYMENTS. UK USA+45 AGRI WORKER DIPLOM EQUILIB PRODUC...STAT TREND CHARTS BIBLIOG/A 20 AUSTRAL. PAGE 88 F1719
ECO/DEV BAL/PAY INT/TRADE COST

B65
MUND V.A.,GOVERNMENT AND BUSINESS (4TH ED.). USA+45 INDUS LG/CO SML/CO LEGIS INT/TRADE LICENSE PRICE ADJUD. PAGE 95 F1860 — NAT/G ECO/TAC BUDGET CONTROL

B65
MURUMBI J.,PROBLEMS OF ECONOMIC DEVELOPMENT IN EAST AFRICA. FINAN INDUS WORKER TEC/DEV INT/TRADE TAX DEMAND EFFICIENCY PRODUC SOCISM...TREND CHARTS 20 AFRICA/E. PAGE 95 F1869 — AGRI ECO/TAC ECO/UNDEV PROC/MFG

B65
NATIONAL CENTRAL LIBRARY,LATIN AMERICAN ECONOMIC AND SOCIAL SERIALS. UK SOCIETY NAT/G PLAN PROB/SOLV ...SOC 20. PAGE 97 F1897 — BIBLIOG INT/TRADE ECO/UNDEV L/A+17C

B65
NKRUMAH K.,NEO-COLONIALISM: THE LAST STAGE OF IMPERIALISM. AFR INT/ORG WORKER FOR/AID INT/TRADE EDU/PROP GOV/REL NAT/LISM SOVEREIGN POPULISM SOCISM ...SOCIALIST 20 THIRD/WRLD INTRVN/ECO. PAGE 98 F1929 — COLONIAL DIPLOM ECO/UNDEV ECO/TAC

B65
O'BRIEN F.,CRISIS IN WORLD COMMUNISM* MARXISM IN SEARCH OF EFFICIENCY. AFR COM ECO/DEV PLAN INT/TRADE WAR ADJUST PEACE...STAT TIME/SEQ GOV/COMP NAT/COMP. PAGE 99 F1951 — MARXISM USSR DRIVE EFFICIENCY

B65
ONSLOW C.,ASIAN ECONOMIC DEVELOPMENT. BURMA CEYLON INDIA MALAYSIA PAKISTAN S/ASIA AGRI INDUS MARKET PROB/SOLV CAP/ISM FOR/AID INT/TRADE DEMAND WEALTH ...POLICY ANTHOL 20. PAGE 101 F1991 — ECO/UNDEV ECO/TAC PLAN NAT/G

B65
PINCUS J.A.,ECONOMIC AID AND INTERNATIONAL COST SHARING* A RAND CORPORATION RESEARCH STUDY. INT/ORG BUDGET CENTRAL...ECOMETRIC MATH QUANT STAT SIMUL. PAGE 106 F2088 — ECO/UNDEV COST FOR/AID INT/TRADE

B65
ROLFE S.E.,GOLD AND WORLD POWER. AFR UK USA+45 WOR-45 INDUS WORKER INT/TRADE DEMAND...MGT CHARTS 20. PAGE 113 F2234 — BAL/PAY EQUILIB ECO/TAC DIPLOM

B65
ROOSA R.V.,MONETARY REFORM FOR THE WORLD ECONOMY. AFR EUR+WWI USA+45 WOR+45 CREATE BUDGET DIPLOM FOR/AID EQUILIB WEALTH IMF. PAGE 114 F2237 — FINAN INT/ORG INT/TRADE BAL/PAY

B65
ROWE J.W.,PRIMARY COMMODITIES IN INTERNATIONAL TRADE. MARKET CAP/ISM ECO/TAC DEMAND...NAT/COMP 20. PAGE 114 F2253 — INT/TRADE AGRI RATION PRICE

B65
RUEFF J.,THE ROLE AND THE RULE OF GOLD: AN ARGUMENT (PAMPHLET). AFR FRANCE USA+45 WOR+45 MARKET NAT/G PLAN DIPLOM ATTIT...POLICY INT 20 DEGAULLE/C. PAGE 115 F2258 — FINAN ECO/DEV INT/TRADE BAL/PAY

B65
SABLE M.H.,PERIODICALS FOR LATIN AMERICAN ECONOMIC DEVELOPMENT, TRADE, AND FINANCE: AN ANNOTATED BIBLIOGRAPHY (A PAMPHLET). ECO/TAC PRODUC PROFIT ...STAT NAT/COMP 20 OAS. PAGE 115 F2266 — BIBLIOG/A L/A+17C ECO/UNDEV INT/TRADE

B65
SCHWARTZ G.,SCIENCE IN MARKETING. OP/RES PROB/SOLV INT/TRADE PRICE CONTROL ADJUST PRODUC...CONCPT 20. PAGE 118 F2324 — PHIL/SCI TREND ECO/DEV MARKET

B65
SCITOVSKY T.,REQUIREMENTS OF AN INTERNATIONAL RESERVE SYSTEM. AFR ECO/TAC...PREDICT 20 SILVER MONEY. PAGE 118 F2330 — BAL/PAY FINAN EQUILIB INT/TRADE

B65
SHARIF A.,THE BALANCE OF PAYMENTS OF PAKISTAN, 1948-1958 (THESIS, UNIVERSITY OF TORONTO). PAKISTAN FINAN INDUS FOR/AID PRICE WEALTH...TREND CHARTS 20. PAGE 120 F2368 — BAL/PAY BUDGET INT/TRADE ECO/UNDEV

B65
SHONFIELD A.,MODERN CAPITALISM: THE CHANGING BALANCE OF PUBLIC AND PRIVATE POWER. FRANCE GERMANY/W UK USA+45 WOR+45 ECO/DEV INT/ORG NAT/G CONSULT INT/TRADE PRODUC...POLICY CONCPT METH/COMP 20. PAGE 121 F2386 — CAP/ISM CONTROL BAL/PWR CREATE

B65
STEWART I.G.,AFRICAN PRIMARY PRODUCTS AND INTERNATIONAL TRADE. ECO/UNDEV AGRI FINAN DIPLOM CONTROL 20. PAGE 126 F2485 — AFR INT/TRADE INT/ORG

B65
TEW B.,WEALTH AND INCOME. UK BUDGET INT/TRADE PRICE BAL/PAY DEMAND...CHARTS GOV/COMP 20 AUSTRAL. PAGE 129 F2546 — FINAN ECO/DEV WEALTH INCOME

B65
US SENATE COMM ON JUDICIARY,ANTITRUST EXEMPTIONS FOR AGREEMENTS RELATING TO BALANCE OF PAYMENTS. FINAN ECO/TAC CONTROL WEALTH...POLICY 20 CONGRESS. PAGE 140 F2750 — BAL/PAY ADJUD MARKET INT/TRADE

B65
VANEK J.,GENERAL EQUILIBRIUM OF INTERNATIONAL DISCRIMINATION; THE CASE OF CUSTOMS UNIONS. LABOR PROB/SOLV ECO/TAC DISCRIM INCOME...MATH CHARTS METH 20. PAGE 140 F2767 — INT/TRADE TARIFFS INT/ORG EQUILIB

B65
WARD R.J.,INTERNATIONAL FINANCE. INT/ORG DIPLOM DEMAND INCOME...POLICY METH/COMP 20. PAGE 143 F2819 — INT/TRADE ECO/TAC FINAN BAL/PAY

B65
WEIL G.L.,A HANDBOOK ON THE EUROPEAN ECONOMIC COMMUNITY. BELGIUM EUR+WWI FRANCE GERMANY/W ITALY CONSTN ECO/DEV CREATE PARTIC GP/REL...DECISION MGT CHARTS 20 EEC. PAGE 144 F2846 — INT/TRADE INT/ORG TEC/DEV INT/LAW

B65
WEILER J.,L'ECONOMIE INTERNATIONALE DEPUIS 1950. WOR+45 DIPLOM TARIFFS CONFER...POLICY TREATY. PAGE 145 F2848 — FINAN INT/TRADE REGION FOR/AID

B65
WHITE J.,GERMAN AID. GERMANY/W FINAN PLAN TEC/DEV INT/TRADE ADMIN ATTIT...POLICY 20. PAGE 146 F2870 — FOR/AID ECO/UNDEV DIPLOM ECO/TAC

B65
WU YUAN-LI,THE ECONOMY OF COMMUNIST CHINA. CHINA/COM USSR AGRI FINAN INDUS POL/PAR WORKER PROB/SOLV INT/TRADE PRICE EATING INCOME OWN WEALTH 20. PAGE 149 F2939 — ECO/TAC MARXISM PLAN EFFICIENCY

B65
WURFEL S.W.,FOREIGN ENTERPRISE IN COLOMBIA. FINAN LABOR NAT/G ECO/TAC TAX REGION 20 COLOMB. PAGE 149 F2944 — ECO/UNDEV INT/TRADE JURID CAP/ISM

B65
ZAWADZKI K.K.F.,THE ECONOMICS OF INFLATIONARY PROCESSES. FINAN INT/TRADE PRICE CONTROL DEMAND EQUILIB PROFIT 20. PAGE 150 F2960 — ECO/DEV COST ECO/TAC CAP/ISM

L65
DAANE J.D.,"THE EVOLVING INTERNATIONAL MONETARY MECHANISM." VOL/ASSN CREATE PLAN FOR/AID INT/TRADE CONFER BAL/PAY...RECORD PREDICT IMF. PAGE 29 F0569 — INT/ORG ECO/TAC TREND GP/COMP

L65
LOFTUS M.L.,"INTERNATIONAL MONETARY FUND, 1962-1965: A SELECTED BIBLIOGRAPHY." WOR+45 PLAN BUDGET INCOME PROFIT WEALTH. PAGE 81 F1596 — BIBLIOG FINAN INT/TRADE INT/ORG

S65
HAYTER T.,"FRENCH AID TO AFRICA* ITS SCOPE AND ACHIEVEMENTS." CULTURE ECO/TAC INT/TRADE ADMIN REGION CENTRAL FEDERAL LOVE PWR SOVEREIGN EEC. PAGE 57 F1127 — AFR FRANCE FOR/AID COLONIAL

S65
JOHNSON H.G.,"A THEORETICAL MODEL OF ECONOMIC NATIONALISM IN NEW AND DEVELOPING STATES." ELITES INDUS INT/TRADE EDU/PROP COST OPTIMAL RATIONAL PWR WEALTH SOCISM STERTYP. PAGE 67 F1325 — NAT/LISM ECO/UNDEV GEN/LAWS

S65
JOHNSON L.L.,"US BUSINESS INTERESTS IN CUBA AND THE RISE OF CASTRO." L/A+17C USA+45 ECO/UNDEV INDUS NAT/G VOL/ASSN ATTIT ORD/FREE PWR WEALTH ALL/PROG. PAGE 68 F1330 — DIPLOM CUBA ECO/TAC INT/TRADE

S65
KAUFMAN R.H.,"THE ASIAN GOLD TRADE." ASIA LAOS THAILAND UK CHARTS. PAGE 69 F1362 — S/ASIA FINAN STAT INT/TRADE

S65
KINDLEBERGER C.P.,"MASS MIGRATION, THEN AND NOW." LAW ECO/DEV ECO/UNDEV INDUS LABOR INT/TRADE FEEDBACK REGION RIGID/FLEX...SOC NAT/COMP EEC. PAGE 71 F1394 — EUR+WWI USA-45 WORKER IDEA/COMP

S65
RUSINOW D.I.,"YUGOSLAV DEVELOPMENT BETWEEN EAST AND WEST." AGRI VOL/ASSN PLAN CAP/ISM ECO/TAC FOR/AID INT/TRADE BAL/PAY...MARXIST EEC COMECON. PAGE 115 F2262 — YUGOSLAVIA ECO/UNDEV STAT

S65
SOPER T.,"THE EEC AND AID TO AFRICA." FRANCE UK ECO/UNDEV INT/TRADE TARIFFS REGION ROUTINE CENTRAL DISCRIM...DECISION RECORD EEC. PAGE 124 F2443 — AFR FOR/AID COLONIAL

S65
TENDLER J.D.,"TECHNOLOGY AND ECONOMIC DEVELOPMENT* THE CASE OF HYDRO VS THERMAL POWER." CONSTRUC DIST/IND CREATE TEC/DEV INT/TRADE CENTRAL PWR SKILL WEALTH...MGT NAT/COMP ARGEN. PAGE 129 F2544 — BRAZIL INDUS ECO/UNDEV

C65
WUORINEN J.H.,"SCANDINAVIA." DENMARK FINLAND ICELAND NORWAY SWEDEN SOCIETY AGRI POL/PAR DELIB/GP DIPLOM INT/TRADE NEUTRAL WAR...CHARTS IND TREATY 20. PAGE 149 F2942 — BIBLIOG NAT/G POLICY

N65
STUDY GP CREATE RESERVE ASSETS,REPORT TO DEPUTIES — INT/ORG

(PAMPHLET). AFR FUT PLAN CONTROL DEMAND WEALTH ...ANTHOL METH 20. PAGE 127 F2507 INT/TRADE FINAN BUDGET

B66
ALIBER R.Z.,THE FUTURE OF THE DOLLAR AS AN INTERNATIONAL CURRENCY. AFR USA+45 USA-45 ECO/DEV PRICE COST INCOME...POLICY 20. PAGE 4 F0067 FINAN DIPLOM INT/ORG INT/TRADE

B66
AMER ENTERPRISE INST FOR PUBL,INTERNATIONAL PAYMENTS PROBLEM. MARKET DIPLOM DEBATE PRICE COST INCOME 20. PAGE 4 F0082 FINAN INT/TRADE POLICY

B66
AMERICAN ASSEMBLY COLUMBIA U,THE UNITED STATES AND THE PHILIPPINES. PHILIPPINE S/ASIA USA+45 USA-45 SOCIETY FORCES INT/TRADE...POLICY 20. PAGE 5 F0085 COLONIAL DIPLOM NAT/LISM

B66
BALDWIN R.E.,ECONOMIC DEVELOPMENT AND EXPORT GROWTH: A STUDY OF NORTHERN RHODESIA, 1920-1960. AFR RHODESIA AGRI EXTR/IND FINAN MARKET LABOR WORKER ECO/TAC...CONCPT NEW/IDEA MUNICH 20. PAGE 9 F0166 ECO/UNDEV TEC/DEV INT/TRADE CAP/ISM

B66
BROWN R.T.,TRANSPORT AND THE ECONOMIC INTEGRATION OF SOUTH AMERICA. L/A+17C ECO/UNDEV NAT/G OP/RES DIPLOM INT/TRADE REGION WEALTH...ECOMETRIC GEOG STAT LAFTA TIME. PAGE 19 F0373 MARKET DIST/IND SIMUL

B66
CROWDER M.,A SHORT HISTORY OF NIGERIA. AFR NIGERIA UK ECO/UNDEV CHIEF INT/TRADE RACE/REL NAT/LISM ORD/FREE...GEOG SOC CHARTS BIBLIOG 14/20. PAGE 29 F0558 COLONIAL NAT/G CULTURE

B66
ECKSTEIN A.,COMMUNIST CHINA'S ECONOMIC GROWTH AND FOREIGN TRADE* IMPLICATIONS FOR US POLICY. COM USA+45 USSR STRUCT INDUS MARKET DIPLOM ECO/TAC FOR/AID INT/TRADE...STAT CHARTS. PAGE 36 F0696 ASIA ECO/UNDEV CREATE PWR

B66
EDWARDS C.D.,TRADE REGULATIONS OVERSEAS. IRELAND NEW/ZEALND SOUTH/AFR NAT/G CAP/ISM TARIFFS CONTROL ...POLICY JURID 20 EEC CHINJAP. PAGE 36 F0703 INT/TRADE DIPLOM INT/LAW ECO/TAC

B66
FELKER J.L.,SOVIET ECONOMIC CONTROVERSIES. USSR INDUS PLAN INT/TRADE GP/REL MARXISM SOCISM...POLICY 20. PAGE 40 F0778 ECO/DEV MARKET PROFIT PRICE

B66
FELLNER W.,MAINTAINING AND RESTORING BALANCE IN INTERNATIONAL PAYMENTS. ECO/UNDEV MARKET ECO/TAC PRICE INCOME WEALTH...POLICY METH/COMP 20 MONEY. PAGE 40 F0781 BAL/PAY DIPLOM FINAN INT/TRADE

B66
FISK E.K.,NEW GUINEA ON THE THRESHOLD; ASPECTS OF SOCIAL, POLITICAL, AND ECONOMIC DEVELOPMENT. AGRI NAT/G INT/TRADE ADMIN ADJUST LITERACY ROLE...CHARTS ANTHOL 20 NEW/GUINEA. PAGE 41 F0804 ECO/UNDEV SOCIETY

B66
FRANCK L.R.,LA POLITIQUE ECONOMIQUE DES ETATS-UNIS. USA+45 USA-45 FINAN INDUS CONTROL CROWD GOV/REL GP/REL...POLICY SOC CHARTS 18/20. PAGE 43 F0841 NAT/G INT/TRADE GEOG

B66
GOODWIN C.D.W.,ECONOMIC INQUIRY IN AUSTRALIA. ECO/DEV ECO/UNDEV ACADEM INT/TRADE RENT TARIFFS TAX PRESS GOV/REL SOCISM 18/20 AUSTRAL. PAGE 49 F0953 ECO/TAC IDEA/COMP BUDGET COLONIAL

B66
HALLET R.,PEOPLE AND PROGRESS IN WEST AFRICA: AN INTRODUCTION TO THE PROBLEMS OF DEVELOPMENT. COM/IND INDUS KIN DIPLOM FOR/AID INT/TRADE HEALTH ...GEOG TREND CHARTS BIBLIOG/A 20 AFRICA/W. PAGE 54 F1050 AFR SOCIETY ECO/UNDEV ECO/TAC

B66
HEVESY P.D.,THE UNIFICATION OF THE WORLD. FUT USA+45 WOR+45 ECO/DEV ECO/UNDEV LEGIS PROB/SOLV BAL/PWR ECO/TAC INT/TRADE PEACE. PAGE 59 F1160 DIPLOM FINAN INT/ORG

B66
HOROWITZ D.,HEMISPHERES NORTH AND SOUTH: ECONOMIC DISPARITY AMONG NATIONS. WOR+45 ECO/DEV ECO/UNDEV INT/ORG PLAN DIPLOM INT/TRADE GIVE PARTIC GP/REL ...WELF/ST 20. PAGE 62 F1215 ECO/TAC FOR/AID STRATA WEALTH

B66
HOWE R.W.,BLACK AFRICA: FROM PRE-HISTORY TO THE EVE OF THE COLONIAL ERA. ECO/UNDEV KIN PROVS SECT INT/TRADE EDU/PROP COLONIAL...BIBLIOG WORSHIP. PAGE 62 F1226 AFR CULTURE SOC

B66
HUTTENBACH R.A.,BRITISH IMPERIAL EXPERIENCE. AFR S/ASIA UK WOR-45 INT/ORG TEC/DEV...CHARTS 16/20 MERCANTLST. PAGE 64 F1253 COLONIAL TIME/SEQ INT/TRADE

B66
INARRITU A.L.,EL PATRON CAMBIO-ORO Y SUS REFORMAS. AFR L/A+17C WOR+45 PLAN PROB/SOLV BUDGET ECO/TAC INT/TRADE EFFICIENCY ORD/FREE 20 MEXIC/AMER. PAGE 64 F1262 ECO/UNDEV FINAN DIPLOM POLICY

B66
INGRAM J.C.,INTERNATIONAL ECONOMIC PROBLEMS. ECO/DEV ECO/UNDEV INDUS MARKET TEC/DEV TARIFFS BAL/PAY CENTRAL...POLICY 20 EEC. PAGE 64 F1265 INT/TRADE INT/ORG FINAN

B66
INTERNATIONAL ECO POLICY ASSN,THE UNITED STATES BALANCE OF PAYMENTS. INT/ORG NAT/G PROB/SOLV BUDGET DIPLOM INT/TRADE WEALTH 20. PAGE 65 F1274 BAL/PAY ECO/TAC POLICY FINAN

B66
INTERNATIONAL ECONOMIC ASSN,STABILITY AND PROGRESS IN THE WORLD ECONOMY: THE FIRST CONGRESS OF THE INTERNATIONAL ECONOMIC ASSOCIATION. WOR+45 ECO/DEV ECO/UNDEV DELIB/GP FOR/AID BAL/PAY...TREND CMN/WLTH 20. PAGE 65 F1276 INT/TRADE

B66
JENSEN F.B.,READINGS IN INTERNATIONAL ECONOMIC RELATIONS. COM ECO/UNDEV MARKET NAT/G FOR/AID ...ANTHOL 20. PAGE 67 F1317 BAL/PAY INT/TRADE FINAN

B66
KINDLEBERGER C.P.,EUROPE AND THE DOLLAR. AFR EUR+WWI FRANCE GERMANY/W USA+45 CONSTN INT/ORG DIPLOM INT/TRADE...ANTHOL 20. PAGE 71 F1395 BAL/PAY BUDGET FINAN ECO/DEV

B66
KOH S.J.,STAGES OF INDUSTRIAL DEVELOPMENT IN ASIA. ASIA INDIA KOREA STRATA STRUCT NAT/G INT/TRADE ...CHARTS 19/20 CHINJAP. PAGE 72 F1415 INDUS ECO/UNDEV ECO/DEV LABOR

B66
KROOSS H.E.,AMERICAN ECONOMIC DEVELOPMENT (2ND ED.). USA+45 USA-45 AGRI INDUS LABOR WORKER INT/TRADE TAX WAR...CHARTS 18/20. PAGE 73 F1443 ECO/TAC NAT/G CAP/ISM ECO/DEV

B66
LAMBERG R.F.,PRAG UND DIE DRITTE WELT. AFR ASIA CZECHOSLVK L/A+17C MARKET TEC/DEV ECO/TAC REV ATTIT 20 TREATY. PAGE 75 F1462 DIPLOM ECO/UNDEV INT/TRADE FOR/AID

B66
LEAGUE OF WOMEN VOTERS OF US,FOREIGN AID AT THE CROSSROADS. USA+45 WOR+45 DELIB/GP PROB/SOLV DIPLOM INT/TRADE RECEIVE BAL/PAY...CHARTS 20 UN ALL/PROG. PAGE 76 F1498 FOR/AID GIVE ECO/UNDEV PLAN

B66
LEWIS W.A.,DEVELOPMENT PLANNING; THE ESSENTIALS OF ECONOMIC POLICY. USA+45 FINAN INDUS NAT/G WORKER FOR/AID INT/TRADE ADMIN ROUTINE WEALTH...CONCPT STAT. PAGE 79 F1552 PLAN ECO/DEV POLICY CREATE

B66
MACBEAN A.I.,EXPORT INSTABILITY AND ECONOMIC DEVELOPMENT. CHILE PAKISTAN PUERT/RICO TANZANIA UGANDA WOR+45 MARKET ECO/TAC...POLICY REGRESS CHARTS BIBLIOG TIME 20. PAGE 83 F1622 INT/TRADE ECO/UNDEV ECOMETRIC INSPECT

B66
MACFARQUHAR R.,CHINA UNDER MAO: POLITICS TAKES COMMAND. CHINA/COM COM AGRI INDUS CHIEF FORCES DIPLOM INT/TRADE EDU/PROP TASK REV ADJUST...ANTHOL 20 MAO. PAGE 83 F1628 ECO/UNDEV TEC/DEV ECO/TAC ADMIN

B66
MADAN G.R.,ECONOMIC THINKING IN INDIA. INDIA ECO/UNDEV AGRI FINAN INDUS LABOR PLAN CAP/ISM INT/TRADE MARXISM SOCISM...POLICY 1/20. PAGE 84 F1638 ECO/TAC PHIL/SCI NAT/G POL/PAR

B66
MANGONE G.J.,UN ADMINISTRATION OF ECONOMIC AND AOCIAL PROGRAMS. CONSULT BUDGET INT/TRADE REGION 20 UN. PAGE 84 F1653 ADMIN MGT ECO/TAC DELIB/GP

B66
MASON E.S.,ECONOMIC DEVELOPMENT IN INDIA AND PAKISTAN. INDIA PAKISTAN AGRI FINAN PLAN BUDGET INT/TRADE WEALTH...POLICY STAT TREND CHARTS 20. PAGE 87 F1700 NAT/COMP ECO/UNDEV ECO/TAC FOR/AID

B66
MEERHAEGHE M.,INTERNATIONAL ECONOMIC INSTITUTIONS. EUR+WWI FINAN INDUS MARKET PLAN TARIFFS BAL/PAY EQUILIB...POLICY BIBLIOG/A 20 GATT OEEC EEC IBRD EURCOALSTL. PAGE 89 F1745 ECO/TAC ECO/DEV INT/TRADE INT/ORG

B66
MUNBY D.,ECONOMIC GROWTH IN WORLD PERSPECTIVE. AFR WOR+45 SOCIETY INDUS PLAN TEC/DEV ECO/TAC FOR/AID INT/TRADE COST CATHISM...ANTHOL 20 EUROPE/W CHURCH/STA. PAGE 95 F1859 SECT ECO/UNDEV ECO/DEV

B66
NATIONAL INDUSTRIAL CONF BOARD,GOLD AND WORLD MONETARY PROBLEMS. AFR FUT WOR+45 PROB/SOLV BUDGET INT/TRADE PAY GOV/REL...POLICY ANTHOL 20. PAGE 97 F1902 FINAN ECO/TAC PRICE BAL/PAY

B66
O'CONNER A.M.,AN ECONOMIC GEOGRAPHY OF EAST AFRICA. AFR TANZANIA UGANDA AGRI WORKER INT/TRADE COLONIAL GOV/REL...CHARTS METH/COMP 20 AFRICA/E. PAGE 99 F1953 ECO/UNDEV EXTR/IND GEOG HABITAT

B66
ORG FOR ECO COOP AND DEVEL,GEOGRAPHICAL FINAN

DISTRIBUTION OF FINANCIAL FLOWS TO LESS DEVELOPED COUNTRIES. WOR+45 DIPLOM INT/TRADE GIVE RECEIVE REPAR REGION WEALTH...GEOG STAT CHARTS 20 OECD. PAGE 102 F1997
ECO/UNDEV INT/ORG FOR/AID

B66
PASSIN H.,THE UNITED STATES AND JAPAN. USA+45 INDUS CAP/ISM...TREND 20 CHINJAP TREATY. PAGE 103 F2032
DIPLOM INT/TRADE ECO/DEV ECO/TAC

B66
PIQUET H.S.,THE US BALANCE OF PAYMENTS AND INTERNATIONAL MONETARY RESERVES. AFR USA+45 PROB/SOLV INT/TRADE GOV/REL EQUILIB...POLICY STAT CHARTS 20. PAGE 106 F2090
BAL/PAY DIPLOM FINAN ECO/TAC

B66
POLK J.,U S PRODUCTION ABROAD AND THE BALANCE OF PAYMENTS* A SURVEY OF CORPORATE INVESTMENT EXPERIENCE. USA+45 SERV/IND NAT/G OP/RES COST PROFIT ATTIT...ECOMETRIC STAT INT QU GEN/METH. PAGE 107 F2096
BAL/PAY FINAN INT/TRADE INDUS

B66
ROBERTSON D.J.,THE BRITISH BALANCE OF PAYMENTS. UK WOR+45 INDUS BUDGET TAX ADJUST...CHARTS ANTHOL 20. PAGE 112 F2213
FINAN BAL/PAY ECO/DEV INT/TRADE

B66
RUBIN S.J.,THE CONSCIENCE OF THE RICH NATIONS: THE DEVELOPMENT ASSISTANCE COMMITTEE AND THE COMMON AID EFFORT. EUR+WWI USA+45 ECO/UNDEV INT/ORG NAT/G VOL/ASSN ECO/TAC INT/TRADE...OBS UN AID DEV/ASSIST IBRD OECD. PAGE 114 F2256
FOR/AID ECO/DEV CONFER CENTRAL

B66
RUPPENTHAL K.M.,TRANSPORTATION AND TOMORROW. FUT SPACE USA+45 SEA AIR FORCES TEC/DEV INT/TRADE ...ANTHOL 20 RAILROAD. PAGE 115 F2261
DIST/IND PLAN CIVMIL/REL PREDICT

B66
SHULTZ G.P.,GUIDELINES, INFORMAL CONTROLS, AND THE MARKET PLACE: POLICY CHOICES IN A FULL EMPLOYMENT ECONOMY. UK ECO/DEV LABOR INT/TRADE CONFER GOV/REL BAL/PAY DEMAND INCOME...POLICY ANTHOL 20 PRESIDENT. PAGE 121 F2392
ECO/TAC CONTROL FINAN RATION

B66
SMITH H.E.,READINGS IN ECONOMIC DEVELOPMENT AND ADMINISTRATION IN TANZANIA. TANZANIA FINAN INDUS LABOR NAT/G PLAN PROB/SOLV INT/TRADE COLONIAL REGION...ANTHOL BIBLIOG 20 AFRICA/E. PAGE 123 F2431
TEC/DEV ADMIN GOV/REL

B66
SPULBER N.,THE STATE AND ECONOMIC DEVELOPMENT IN EASTERN EUROPE. BULGARIA COM CZECHOSLVK HUNGARY POLAND YUGOSLAVIA CULTURE PLAN CAP/ISM INT/TRADE CONTROL...POLICY CHARTS METH/COMP BIBLIOG/A 19/20. PAGE 125 F2460
ECO/DEV ECO/UNDEV NAT/G TOTALISM

B66
TRIFFIN R.,THE WORLD MONEY MAZE. AFR INT/ORG ECO/TAC PRICE OPTIMAL WEALTH...METH/COMP 20 EEC OEEC SILVER. PAGE 131 F2589
BAL/PAY FINAN INT/TRADE DIPLOM

B66
TRIFFIN R.,THE BALANCE OF PAYMENTS AND THE FOREIGN INVESTMENT POSITION OF THE UNITED STATES. AFR USA+45 INT/ORG INT/TRADE PRICE CONTROL...POLICY 20. PAGE 131 F2590
BAL/PAY DIPLOM FINAN ECO/TAC

B66
UNITED NATIONS,YEARBOOK OF INTERNATIONAL TRADE STATISTICS, 1964 (15TH ISSUE). WOR+45 ECO/DEV ECO/UNDEV UN. PAGE 132 F2614
STAT INT/TRADE DIPLOM CHARTS

B66
UREN P.E.,EAST - WEST TRADE* A SYMPOSIUM. COM AGRI INT/ORG PRICE HABITAT RIGID/FLEX...GEOG INT/LAW ANTHOL NATO. PAGE 133 F2625
INT/TRADE BAL/PWR AFR CANADA

B66
US HOUSE COMM FOREIGN AFFAIRS,HEARINGS ON HR 12449 A BILL TO AMEND FURTHER THE FOREIGN ASSISTANCE ACT OF 1961. AFR ASIA L/A+17C USA+45 VIETNAM INT/ORG TEC/DEV INT/TRADE ATTIT ORD/FREE 20 UN NATO CONGRESS AID. PAGE 137 F2692
FOR/AID ECO/TAC ECO/UNDEV DIPLOM

B66
YEAGER L.B.,INTERNATIONAL MONETARY RELATIONS: THEORY, HISTORY, AND POLICY. WOR+45 WOR-45 INT/TRADE BAL/PAY...NAT/COMP 18/20 MONEY. PAGE 150 F2947
FINAN DIPLOM ECO/TAC IDEA/COMP

B66
ZISCHKA A.,WAR ES EIN WUNDER? GERMANY/W ECO/DEV FINAN LG/CO BARGAIN CAP/ISM FOR/AID RATION 20 MARSHL/PLN. PAGE 150 F2965
ECO/TAC INT/TRADE INDUS WAR

L66
AFRICAN BIBLIOGRAPHIC CENTER,"AFRICAN ECONOMIC AFFAIRS: A SELECT BIBLIOGRAPHICAL SURVEY, 1965-1966." AFR FINAN INDUS INT/ORG LABOR PLAN BUDGET DIPLOM INT/TRADE ADMIN EFFICIENCY WEALTH 20. PAGE 3 F0046
BIBLIOG ECO/UNDEV TEC/DEV FOR/AID

L66
AFRICAN BIBLIOGRAPHIC CENTER,"AFRICAN ECONOMIC AFFAIRS: A SELECT BIBLIOGRAPHICAL SURVEY, 1965-1966; SUPPLEMENTS NUMBERS 1-3." AFR FINAN INDUS LABOR PLAN BUDGET CAP/ISM DIPLOM INT/TRADE ADMIN...GEOG 20. PAGE 3 F0047
BIBLIOG/A ECO/UNDEV FOR/AID TEC/DEV

L66
AMERICAN ECONOMIC REVIEW,"SIXTY-THIRD LIST OF DOCTORAL DISSERTATIONS IN POLITICAL ECONOMY IN AMERICAN UNIVERSITIES AND COLLEGES." ECO/DEV AGRI FINAN LABOR WORKER PLAN BUDGET INT/TRADE ADMIN DEMAND...MGT STAT 20. PAGE 5 F0088
BIBLIOG/A CONCPT ACADEM

S66
ANGELL J.W.,"THE LONGER RUN PROSPECTS FOR THE US BALANCE OF PAYMENTS." USA+45 DIPLOM FOR/AID RATION ORD/FREE WEALTH...IDEA/COMP GATT. PAGE 6 F0104
BAL/PAY ECO/TAC INT/TRADE FINAN

S66
ERB GF,"THE UNITED NATIONS CONFERENCE ON TRADE AND DEVELOPMENT (UNCTAD): A SELECTED CURRENT READING LIST." FINAN FOR/AID CONFER 20 UN. PAGE 38 F0742
BIBLIOG/A INT/TRADE ECO/UNDEV INT/ORG

S66
FELD W.,"EXTERNAL RELATIONS OF THE COMMON MARKET AND GROUP LEADERSHIP ATTITUDES IN THE MEMBER STATES." COM USA+45 ELITES AGRI NAT/G ATTIT...OBS EEC GATT. PAGE 40 F0776
DIPLOM CENTRAL TARIFFS INT/TRADE

S66
JAVITS J.K.,"POLITICAL ACTION VITAL FOR LATIN AMERICAN INTEGRATION." ECO/UNDEV INT/ORG POL/PAR VOL/ASSN PLAN PROB/SOLV INT/TRADE EFFICIENCY 20 OAS LAFTA ALL/PROG. PAGE 66 F1308
L/A+17C ECO/TAC REGION

S66
KLEIN S.,"A SURVEY OF SINO-JAPANESE TRADE, 1950-1966" TAIWAN EDU/PROP 20 CHINJAP. PAGE 72 F1409
INT/TRADE DIPLOM MARXISM

S66
LANGLEY D.,"POSTSCRIPT ON THE COLONIZATION OF THE INTERNATIONAL TRADE UNION MOVEMENT" USA+45 ELITES FINAN DOMIN LEGIT ADMIN PWR...SOCIALIST 20 AFL/CIO CIA LOVESTN/J. PAGE 75 F1479
INT/TRADE LABOR NAT/G CONTROL

S66
LAURENS H.,"LES PAYS OCCIDENTAUX ET LE MARCHE CHINOIS." EUR+WWI FUT S/ASIA AGRI INDUS VOL/ASSN ECO/TAC BAL/PAY...RECORD PREDICT TREATY. PAGE 76 F1488
ASIA INT/TRADE TREND STAT

N66
BRITISH DEVELOPMENT POLICIES: 1966 (PAMPHLET). UK AGRI TARIFFS BAL/PAY...TREND CHARTS 20 OVRSEA/DEV. PAGE 1 F0023
WEALTH DIPLOM INT/TRADE FOR/AID

N66
OECD,THE BALANCE OF PAYMENTS ADJUSTMENT PROCESS (PAMPHLET). EUR+WWI ECO/DEV FINAN CONSULT PLAN PROB/SOLV BUDGET CAP/ISM INT/TRADE PRICE CONTROL EQUILIB 20. PAGE 101 F1975
BAL/PAY ECO/TAC DIPLOM INT/ORG

B67
ADLER J.H.,CAPITAL MOVEMENTS AND ECONOMIC DEVELOPMENT. WOR+45 FINAN NAT/G BARGAIN ECO/TAC FOR/AID INT/TRADE ANTHOL. PAGE 2 F0042
DIPLOM ECO/DEV ECO/UNDEV

B67
ALNASRAWI A.,FINANCING ECONOMIC DEVELOPMENT IN IRAQ. IRAQ INDUS CAP/ISM COST PRODUC...STAT CHARTS BIBLIOG 20. PAGE 4 F0076
ECO/UNDEV EXTR/IND TEC/DEV INT/TRADE

B67
BARANSON J.,TECHNOLOGY FOR UNDERDEVELOPED AREAS: AN ANNOTATED BIBLIOGRAPHY. FUT WOR+45 CULTURE INDUS INT/ORG CREATE PROB/SOLV INT/TRADE EDU/PROP AUTOMAT ...CONCPT METH. PAGE 10 F0181
BIBLIOG/A ECO/UNDEV TEC/DEV R+D

B67
CASTILLO C.M.,GROWTH AND INTEGRATION IN CENTRAL AMERICA. L/A+17C CREATE PROB/SOLV ECO/TAC REGION PRODUC...OBS BIBLIOG 20. PAGE 22 F0429
ECO/UNDEV INT/TRADE NAT/COMP

B67
CLEGERN W.M.,BRITISH HONDURAS: COLONIAL DEAD END, 1859-1900. HONDURAS AGRI FINAN PROB/SOLV INT/TRADE PWR WEALTH...BIBLIOG/A 19. PAGE 25 F0487
COLONIAL POLICY ECO/UNDEV DOMIN

B67
CLEMENT M.O.,THEORETICAL ISSUES IN INTERNATIONAL ECONOMICS. WOR+45 PLAN PROB/SOLV TEC/DEV ...ECOMETRIC METH/CNCPT MATH BIBLIOG T MONEY. PAGE 25 F0489
INT/TRADE FINAN CREATE BAL/PAY

B67
HOGAN J.,THE US BALANCE OF PAYMENTS AND CAPITAL FLOWS. MARKET INT/ORG ECO/TAC PRICE CONTROL WEALTH ...METH/COMP 20 EEC. PAGE 61 F1192
BAL/PAY FINAN DIPLOM INT/TRADE

B67
KARDOUCHE G.K.,THE UAR IN DEVELOPMENT. UAR ECO/TAC INT/TRADE BAL/PAY...STAT CHARTS BIBLIOG 20. PAGE 69 F1355
FINAN MGT CAP/ISM ECO/UNDEV

B67
KEWEN P.B.,INTERNATIONAL ECONOMICS (2ND ED.).
INT/TRADE

USA+45 WOR+45 MARKET TARIFFS...BIBLIOG T 20. PAGE 70 F1384
BAL/PAY FINAN EQUILIB

B67
KREININ M.E.,ALTERNATIVE COMMERCIAL POLICIES - THEIR EFFECT ON THE AMERICAN ECONOMY. USA+45 LAW ECO/DEV MARKET INT/ORG DIPLOM ECO/TAC TARIFFS PRICE DEMAND WEALTH...QUANT EEC AFTA. PAGE 73 F1437
INT/TRADE BAL/PAY NAT/G POLICY

B67
LANDEN R.G.,OMAN SINCE 1856: DISRUPTIVE MODERNIZATION IN A TRADITIONAL ARAB SOCIETY. UK DIST/IND EXTR/IND SECT DIPLOM INT/TRADE...SOC LING CHARTS BIBLIOG 19/20. PAGE 75 F1468
ISLAM CULTURE ECO/UNDEV NAT/G

B67
LINDER S.B.,TRADE AND TRADE POLICY FOR DEVELOPMENT. OP/RES DIPLOM TARIFFS UTIL WEALTH...BIBLIOG 20. PAGE 80 F1569
ECO/UNDEV ECO/TAC TEC/DEV INT/TRADE

B67
MORRIS A.J.A.,PARLIAMENTARY DEMOCRACY IN THE NINETEENTH CENTURY. UK INDUS LOC/G NAT/G POL/PAR CONSULT LEGIS INT/TRADE ADMIN CHOOSE SUFF SOVEREIGN 19 PARLIAMENT. PAGE 93 F1835
TIME/SEQ CONSTN PARL/PROC POPULISM

B67
OFER G.,THE SERVICE INDUSTRIES IN A DEVELOPING ECONOMY: ISRAEL AS A CASE STUDY. ISRAEL ECO/TAC INT/TRADE PRODUC WEALTH SOCISM...TIME/SEQ TREND CHARTS 20. PAGE 101 F1979
DIPLOM ECO/DEV SERV/IND

B67
OGLESBY C.,CONTAINMENT AND CHANGE. AFR COM USA+45 ECO/UNDEV TEC/DEV ECO/TAC FOR/AID INT/TRADE DOMIN GUERRILLA REV PEACE 20 STALIN/J. PAGE 101 F1983
DIPLOM BAL/PWR MARXISM CULTURE

B67
OVERSEAS DEVELOPMENT INSTIT,EFFECTIVE AID. WOR+45 INT/ORG TEC/DEV DIPLOM INT/TRADE ADMIN. PAGE 102 F2004
FOR/AID ECO/UNDEV ECO/TAC NAT/COMP

B67
RUEFF J.,BALANCE OF PAYMENTS: PROPOSALS FOR RESOLVING THE CRITICAL WORLD ECONOMIC PROBLEM OF OUR TIME. USA+45 INDUS FOR/AID REPAR DEMAND OPTIMAL ...ECOMETRIC CHARTS METH/COMP 20. PAGE 115 F2259
BAL/PAY INT/TRADE FINAN NEW/IDEA

B67
SCOTT J.C.,ANTITRUST AND TRADE REGULATION TODAY: 1967. USA+45 MARKET LG/CO DELIB/GP LEGIS CAP/ISM INT/TRADE TAX PRICE INGP/REL WEALTH 20 SUPREME/CT. PAGE 118 F2334
NAT/G INDUS CONTROL JURID

B67
THOMAN R.S.,GEOGRAPHY OF INTERNATIONAL TRADE. WOR+45 ECO/DEV ECO/UNDEV INT/ORG LG/CO PLAN BAL/PAY ...STAT CHARTS NAT/COMP 20. PAGE 130 F2559
INT/TRADE GEOG ECO/TAC DIPLOM

B67
UNIVERSAL REFERENCE SYSTEM,ECONOMIC REGULATION, BUSINESS, AND GOVERNMENT (VOLUME VIII). WOR+45 WOR-45 ECO/DEV ECO/UNDEV FINAN LABOR TEC/DEV ECO/TAC INT/TRADE GOV/REL...POLICY COMPUT/IR. PAGE 133 F2617
BIBLIOG/A CONTROL NAT/G

B67
US CONGRESS JOINT ECO COMM,REPORT ON JANUARY 1967 ECONOMIC REPORT OF THE PRESIDENT. FINAN LABOR NAT/G LEGIS BUDGET INT/TRADE COST DEMAND INCOME PRODUC ...POLICY IDEA/COMP 20 CONGRESS. PAGE 135 F2663
CHIEF ECO/TAC PLAN DELIB/GP

B67
US CONGRESS JOINT ECO COMM,AN ECONOMIC PROFILE OF MAINLAND CHINA, VOLUMES I AND II. CHINA/COM AGRI DIST/IND FINAN INDUS LABOR FORCES ACT/RES PLAN INT/TRADE INGP/REL BAL/PAY 20 CONGRESS. PAGE 135 F2664
ECO/UNDEV WEALTH ECO/TAC DELIB/GP

B67
US CONGRESS SENATE,SURVEY OF THE ALLIANCE FOR PROGRESS: INFLATION IN LATIN AMERICA (PAMPHLET). USA+45 MARKET INT/ORG DIPLOM INT/TRADE BAL/PAY SENATE ALL/PROG. PAGE 135 F2666
L/A+17C FINAN POLICY FOR/AID

B67
US GOVERNMENT,SECTION-BY-SECTION ANALYSIS OF THE PROPOSED FOREIGN ASSISTANCE ACT OF 1967 (PAMPHLET). USA+45 ECO/UNDEV NAT/G CONGRESS. PAGE 136 F2683
FOR/AID POLICY FORCES INT/TRADE

B67
WISEMAN H.V.,BRITAIN AND THE COMMONWEALTH. EUR+WWI FUT UK ECO/DEV POL/PAR TEC/DEV INT/TRADE LEAD ROLE SOVEREIGN...SOC TREND 20 CMN/WLTH. PAGE 148 F2911
INT/ORG DIPLOM NAT/G NAT/COMP

B67
ZUPNICK E.,UNDERSTANDING THE INTERNATIONAL MONEY SYSTEM (HEADLINE SERIES, NO. 182) (PAMPHLET). ECO/DEV NAT/G DIPLOM INT/TRADE...METH/COMP 20 IMF. PAGE 151 F2971
FINAN PLAN INT/ORG PROB/SOLV

L67
GOLD J.,"INTERPRETATION BY THE INTERNATIONAL MONETARY FUND OF ITS ARTICLES OF AGREEMENT." INT/TRADE ADJUD ATTIT...POLICY JURID. PAGE 48 F0933
CONSTN INT/ORG LAW DIPLOM

L67
MACDONALD R.S.J.,"THE RESORT TO ECONOMIC COERCION BY INTERNATIONAL POLITICAL ORGANIZATIONS." CUBA ETHIOPIA RHODESIA SOUTH/AFR NAT/G FOR/AID INT/TRADE DOMIN CONTROL SANCTION...DECISION LEAGUE/NAT UN OAS 20. PAGE 83 F1625
INT/ORG COERCE ECO/TAC DIPLOM

L67
MEIER G.M.,"UNCTAD PROPOSALS FOR INTERNATIONAL ECONOMIC REFORM." WOR+45 MARKET INT/ORG TARIFFS CONFER UN GATT IMF. PAGE 89 F1749
INT/TRADE FINAN INT/LAW ECO/UNDEV

L67
MESTMACKER E.J.,"STATE TRADING MONOPOLIES IN THE EUROPEAN ECONOMIC COMMUNITY. DIPLOM ECO/TAC ADJUD CONTROL DISCRIM 20 EEC. PAGE 90 F1764
INT/TRADE INT/ORG LAW TARIFFS

S67
"IMPORT-EXPORT CLAUSE: A BLANKET PROHIBITION MISAPPLIED." USA+45 INT/TRADE ADJUD INCOME PWR 20. PAGE 2 F0029
CONSTN TAX PROVS LAW

S67
ALVES V.,"FOREIGN CAPITAL IN BRAZIL." BRAZIL USA+45 CAP/ISM DIPLOM ECO/TAC INT/TRADE CONTROL PWR ...POLICY 20. PAGE 4 F0081
ECO/UNDEV FINAN SOCIALIST SOCISM

S67
AMERASINGHE C.F.,"SOME LEGAL PROBLEMS OF STATE TRADING IN SOUTHEAST ASIA." PROB/SOLV ADJUD CONTROL CT/SYS GP/REL 20. PAGE 5 F0084
INT/TRADE NAT/G INT/LAW PRIVIL

S67
APEL H.,"LES NOUVEAUX ASPECTS DE LA POLITIQUE ETRANGERE ALLEMANDE." AFR EUR+WWI GERMANY POL/PAR BAL/PWR ECO/TAC INT/TRADE NUC/PWR NAT/LISM PEACE ...POLICY 20 EEC. PAGE 6 F0107
DIPLOM INT/ORG FEDERAL

S67
AUBERT DE LA RUE P.,"PERSPECTIVES ECONOMIQUES ENTRE LES ETATS-UNIS ET L'EUROPE." FUT INDUS R+D INT/ORG ACT/RES ECO/TAC AGREE BAL/PAY PRODUC...CHARTS 20 EEC GATT WORLD/BANK. PAGE 7 F0138
INT/TRADE ECO/DEV FINAN TARIFFS

S67
BOSHER J.F.,"GOVERNMENT AND PRIVATE INTERESTS IN NEW FRANCE." CANADA FRANCE INDUS LG/CO SML/CO CAP/ISM INT/TRADE COLONIAL GP/REL...HIST/WRIT 17/18. PAGE 17 F0320
NAT/G FINAN ADMIN CONTROL

S67
BRAUCHER R.,"RECLAMATION OF GOODS FROM A FRAUDULENT BUYER." USA+45 CLIENT FINAN CT/SYS PERS/REL COST WEALTH. PAGE 18 F0341
LAW ADJUD GOV/REL INT/TRADE

S67
BUTT R.,"THE COMMON MARKET AND CONSERVATIVE POLITICS, 1961-2." UK CHIEF DIPLOM ECO/TAC INT/TRADE CONFER DEBATE REGION ATTIT...POLICY 20 EEC. PAGE 21 F0398
EUR+WWI INT/ORG POL/PAR

S67
COSGROVE C.A.,"AGRICULTURE, FINANCE AND POLITICS IN THE EUROPEAN COMMUNITY." EUR+WWI DIST/IND MARKET INT/ORG VOL/ASSN DELIB/GP TEC/DEV BAL/PWR BARGAIN ECO/TAC RATION CONFER 20 EEC. PAGE 28 F0538
ECO/DEV DIPLOM AGRI INT/TRADE

S67
CROMER EARL OF,"STERLING AND THE COMMON MARKET." UK ECO/DEV INT/ORG 20 EEC. PAGE 29 F0554
ECO/TAC FINAN CHARTS INT/TRADE

S67
HILDEBRAND J.R.,"THE CENTRAL AMERICAN COMMON MARKET: ECONOMIC AND POLITICAL INTEGRATION." L/A+17C USA+45 ECO/DEV ECO/UNDEV AGRI SOVEREIGN. PAGE 59 F1170
DIPLOM ECO/TAC INT/TRADE INT/ORG

S67
IBARRA J.,"EL EXPERIMENTO CUBANO." COM CUBA L/A+17C USA+45 ECO/UNDEV LEGIS INT/TRADE CONTROL REV NAT/LISM PWR 19/20 TREATY. PAGE 64 F1259
COLONIAL DIPLOM NAT/G POLICY

S67
LEVI M.,"LES RELATIONS ECONOMIQUES ENTRE L'EST ET L'OUEST EN EUROPE" INDUS...STAT CHARTS 20 OECD COMECON. PAGE 79 F1540
INT/TRADE INT/ORG FINAN PRODUC

S67
MILLER C.H.,"B. TRAVEN Y EL 'PROBLEMA PETROLERO'." USA-45 ECO/UNDEV INDUS TEC/DEV INT/TRADE ATTIT ORD/FREE SOVEREIGN 20 MEXIC/AMER. PAGE 91 F1791
EXTR/IND DIPLOM ECO/TAC DOMIN

S67
MYRDAL G.,"ECONOMIC DEVELOPMENT IN THE BACKWARD COUNTRIES." INT/ORG TEC/DEV CAP/ISM DIPLOM INT/TRADE PRODUC WEALTH 20. PAGE 96 F1883
ECO/UNDEV INDUS NAT/G ECO/TAC

S67
OLIVIER G.,"ASPECTS JURIDIQUES DE L'ADOPTION DU TRAITE CECA A LA CRISE CHARBONNIERE (SUITE ET FIN)" LAW DIST/IND PLAN DIPLOM RATION PRICE ADMIN COST DEMAND...POLICY CON/ANAL ECSC TREATY. PAGE 101
INT/TRADE INT/ORG EXTR/IND CONSTN

F1988

S67
PETROVICH M.B.,"UNITED STATES POLICY IN EAST EUROPE." ECO/DEV ECO/TAC IDEA/COMP. PAGE 105 F2075 — COM INT/TRADE USA+45 DIPLOM

S67
PFEFFERMANN G.,"TRADE UNIONS AND POLITICS IN FRENCH WEST AFRICA DURING THE FOURTH REPUBLIC." AFR INDUS POL/PAR COLONIAL ATTIT PWR 20. PAGE 106 F2077 — PARTIC DRIVE INT/TRADE LABOR

S67
ROCKE J.R.M.,"THE BRITISH EXPORT BATTLE FOR THE CARIBBEAN" GP/REL...POLICY 20 CMN/WLTH. PAGE 113 F2229 — INT/TRADE DIPLOM MARKET ECO/TAC

S67
SCHNEIDER E.,"DIE ENTPOLITISIERUNG DES DEUTSCHEN OSTHANDELS." AFR MARKET TEC/DEV OBJECTIVE 20. PAGE 117 F2307 — ATTIT INT/TRADE ECO/TAC DIPLOM

S67
SMALL A.H.,"THE EFFECT OF TARIFF REDUCTIONS ON US IMPORT VOLUME." USA+45 INT/ORG NAT/G DIPLOM CONFER DEMAND...POLICY INT/LAW STAT CHARTS GATT EEC. PAGE 123 F2424 — TARIFFS INT/TRADE PRICE ECO/TAC

S67
STEINHEIMER R.L. JR.,"THE UNIFORM COMMERCIAL CODE COMES OF AGE." USA+45 FINAN ACADEM JUDGE. PAGE 126 F2477 — ADJUD LEGIS INT/TRADE GOV/REL

S67
STRANGE S.,"DEBTS, DEFAULTERS AND DEVELOPMENT." WOR+45 PROB/SOLV FOR/AID INT/TRADE. PAGE 127 F2500 — NAT/G FINAN ECO/UNDEV

S67
WALKER R.L.,"THE WEST AND THE 'NEW ASIA'." CHINA/COM ECO/UNDEV DIPLOM...PREDICT 20. PAGE 142 F2805 — ASIA INT/TRADE COLONIAL REGION

S67
WARNER G.,"FRANCE, BRITAIN AND THE EEC." FRANCE UK INT/ORG DELIB/GP ECO/TAC CONTROL 20 EEC. PAGE 143 F2822 — INT/TRADE BAL/PWR DIPLOM

S67
WEIL G.L.,"THE MERGER OF THE INSTITUTIONS OF THE EUROPEAN COMMUNITIES" EUR+WWI ECO/DEV INT/TRADE CONSEN PLURISM...DECISION MGT 20 EEC EURATOM ECSC TREATY. PAGE 145 F2847 — ECO/TAC INT/ORG CENTRAL INT/LAW

S67
WILLIAMS C.,"REGIONAL MANAGEMENT OVERSEAS." USA+45 WOR+45 DIST/IND LG/CO EX/STRUC INT/TRADE TARIFFS ADMIN TASK CENTRAL. PAGE 147 F2889 — MGT EUR+WWI ECO/DEV PLAN

S67
WILLMANN J.,"LA COMMUNAUTE EUROPEENNE ET LA GRANDE-BRETAGNE." UK PROB/SOLV TEC/DEV CAP/ISM DIPLOM CONFER FEDERAL...POLICY 20 EEC. PAGE 147 F2898 — INT/ORG DRIVE NAT/LISM INT/TRADE

N67
US CONGRESS JOINT ECO COMM,MAINLAND CHINA IN THE WORLD ECONOMY (PAMPHLET). CHINA/COM USA+45 AGRI CHIEF MARXISM CONGRESS. PAGE 135 F2661 — ECO/UNDEV POLICY ECO/TAC INT/TRADE

N67
US HOUSE COMM FOREIGN AFFAIRS,THE FOREIGN POLICY ASPECTS OF THE KENNEDY ROUND (PAMPHLET). USA+45 INDUS KENNEDY/JF CONGRESS HOUSE/REP EEC. PAGE 137 F2693 — POLICY INT/TRADE FOR/AID ECO/DEV

N67
US HOUSE COMM FOREIGN AFFAIRS,COMMUNIST ACTIVITIES IN LATIN AMERICA 1967 (PAMPHLET). CUBA USA+45 DIPLOM INT/TRADE EDU/PROP COERCE GUERRILLA HOUSE/REP OAS. PAGE 137 F2696 — L/A+17C MARXISM ORD/FREE ECO/TAC

B82
CUNNINGHAM W.,THE GROWTH OF ENGLISH INDUSTRY AND COMMERCE. FUT UK FINAN NAT/G CAP/ISM...POLICY 20 MERCANTLST CHRISTIAN POPE. PAGE 29 F0562 — INDUS INT/TRADE SML/CO CONSERVE

C83
BURKE E.,"RESOLUTIONS FOR CONCILIATION WITH AMERICA" (1775), IN E. BURKE, COLLECTED WORKS, VOL. 2." UK USA-45 FORCES INT/TRADE TARIFFS TAX SANCTION PEACE...POLICY 18 PRE/US/AM. PAGE 20 F0387 — COLONIAL WAR SOVEREIGN ECO/TAC

B96
SCHMOLLER G.,THE MERCANTILE SYSTEM AND ITS HISTORICAL SIGNIFICANCE: ILLUSTRATED CHIEFLY FROM PRUSSIAN HISTORY (TRANS.). PRUSSIA CULTURE INDUS KIN NAT/G PROVS OP/RES ECO/TAC INT/TRADE SUPEGO PWR WEALTH MUNICH 19 MERCANTLST. PAGE 117 F2302 — GEN/METH INGP/REL CONCPT

INTEGRATION....SEE NEGRO, SOUTH/US, RACE/REL, SOC/INTEG, CIV/RIGHTS, DISCRIM, ISOLAT, SCHOOL, STRANGE

INTEGRATION, POLITICAL+ECONOMIC....SEE REGION+INT/ORG+VOL/ASSN+CENTRAL

INTELL....INTELLIGENTSIA

N
SOUTH AFRICAN JOURNAL OF ECONOMICS. SOUTH/AFR FINAN MARKET ACT/RES OP/RES...PHIL/SCI STAT CON/ANAL METH/COMP BIBLIOG/A 20. PAGE 1 F0009 — ECO/UNDEV ACADEM INTELL R+D

B32
WRIGHT Q.,GOLD AND MONETARY STABILIZATION. FUT USA-45 WOR-45 INTELL ECO/DEV INT/ORG NAT/G CONSULT PLAN ECO/TAC ADMIN ATTIT WEALTH...CONCPT TREND 20. PAGE 149 F2935 — FINAN POLICY

B35
STALEY E.,WAR AND THE PRIVATE INVESTOR. UNIV WOR-45 INTELL SOCIETY INT/ORG NAT/G TOP/EX CAP/ISM ECO/TAC WAR ATTIT ALL/VALS...INT TIME/SEQ TREND CON/ANAL WORK TOT/POP 20. PAGE 125 F2464 — FINAN INT/TRADE DIPLOM

S41
LASSWELL H.D.,"THE GARRISON STATE" (BMR)" FUT WOR+45 ELITES INTELL FORCES ECO/TAC DOMIN EDU/PROP COERCE INGP/REL 20. PAGE 76 F1485 — NAT/G DIPLOM PWR CIVMIL/REL

B48
MILLS C.W.,THE NEW MEN OF POWER. ELITES INTELL STRUCT WORKER ANOMIE ATTIT PWR POLICY. PAGE 92 F1799 — LABOR LEAD PLAN

B50
ORTON W.A.,THE ECONOMIC ROLE OF THE STATE. INTELL ECO/UNDEV PLAN CONTROL PWR SOVEREIGN...POLICY 17/20. PAGE 102 F2000 — ECO/DEV NAT/G ECO/TAC ORD/FREE

B50
SCHUMPETER J.A.,CAPITALISM, SOCIALISM, AND DEMOCRACY (3RD ED.). USA-45 USSR WOR+45 WOR-45 INTELL ECO/DEV ECO/UNDEV ECO/TAC WAR PRODUC ORD/FREE...MGT SOC 20 MARX/KARL. PAGE 118 F2321 — SOCIALIST CAP/ISM MARXISM IDEA/COMP

B51
HARROD R.F.,THE LIFE OF JOHN MAYNARD KEYNES. UK INTELL FAM CAP/ISM DIPLOM ECO/TAC WAR ATTIT PERSON ROLE 20 KEYNES/JM WWI. PAGE 56 F1094 — BIOG FINAN GEN/LAWS

B51
PARSONS T.,THE SOCIAL SYSTEM. UNIV INTELL SOCIETY ECO/DEV SECT PLAN PERCEPT...CONCPT METH/CNCPT. PAGE 103 F2030 — DRIVE SOC

S53
BIRNBAUM N.,"CONFLICTING INTERPRETATIONS OF THE RISE OF CAPITALISM: MARX AND WEBER" (BMR)" WOR-45 INTELL SOCIETY STRUCT INDUS WORKER...PHIL/SCI SOC PERS/COMP 19/20 MARX/KARL WEBER/MAX. PAGE 15 F0288 — CAP/ISM IDEA/COMP ECO/DEV MARXISM

S53
BLOUGH R.,"THE ROLE OF THE ECONOMIST IN FEDERAL POLICY MAKING." USA+45 ELITES INTELL ECO/DEV NAT/G CONSULT EX/STRUC ACT/RES PLAN INT/TRADE BAL/PAY WEALTH...POLICY METH/GP CONGRESS 20. PAGE 16 F0301 — DELIB/GP ECO/TAC

B54
LENIN V.I.,SELECTED WORKS (12 VOLS.). USSR INTELL SOCIETY STRATA STRUCT NAT/G POL/PAR WORKER CAP/ISM REV WAR...MARXIST PHIL/SCI 20 MARX/KARL LENIN/VI. PAGE 78 F1520 — COM MARXISM

B54
MEYER A.G.,MARXISM. INTELL ECO/DEV WORKER CAP/ISM LEAD WAR ATTIT ALL/IDEOS...SOC 19/20 MARX/KARL. PAGE 90 F1766 — MARXISM CONCPT ECO/TAC STRUCT

B55
JOHR W.A.,THE ROLE OF THE ECONOMIST AS OFFICIAL ADVISER. WOR+45 INTELL ECO/DEV NAT/G PLAN GP/REL ROLE...DECISION PREDICT IDEA/COMP. PAGE 68 F1336 — CONSULT ECO/TAC POLICY INGP/REL

B59
HAX K.,DIE HOCHSCHULLEHRER DER WIRTSCHAFTSWISSENSCHAFTEN IN DER BUNDESREPUBLIK DEUTSCHLAND EINSCHL. WESTBERLIN, OSTERREICH. AUSTRIA GERMANY/W SWITZERLND FINAN MARKET PROF/ORG BUDGET ECO/TAC INT/TRADE PRICE COST 20. PAGE 57 F1119 — BIBLIOG ACADEM INTELL

S59
ZAUBERMAN A.,"SOVIET BLOC ECONOMIC INTEGRATION." COM CULTURE INTELL ECO/DEV INDUS TOP/EX ACT/RES PLAN ECO/TAC INT/TRADE ROUTINE CHOOSE ATTIT ...TIME/SEQ 20. PAGE 150 F2958 — MARKET INT/ORG USSR TOTALISM

B60
HOSELITZ B.F.,THEORIES OF ECONOMIC GROWTH. UK WOR+45 WOR-45 ECO/UNDEV PLAN INT/TRADE KNOWL ...CONCPT METH/CNCPT TIME/SEQ GEN/LAWS TOT/POP. PAGE 62 F1220 — ECO/DEV INTELL

S60
MARTIN E.M.,"NEW TRENDS IN UNITED STATES ECONOMIC FOREIGN POLICY." USA+45 INTELL DELIB/GP FOR/AID INT/TRADE ROUTINE BAL/PAY...RELATIV TRUE/GP 20. PAGE 86 F1682 — NAT/G PLAN DIPLOM

S60
MURPHEY R.,"ECONOMIC CONFLICTS IN SOUTH ASIA." ASIA CULTURE INTELL ECO/TAC REGION ATTIT DRIVE KNOWL ...METH/CNCPT TIME/SEQ STERTYP TOT/POP METH/GP VAL/FREE 20. PAGE 95 F1864 — S/ASIA ECO/UNDEV

B61
DEWITT N.,EDUCATION AND PROFESSIONAL EMPLOYMENT IN THE USSR. USSR PROF/ORG WORKER PLAN ADMIN UTIL AGE/C AGE/Y MARXISM...STAT CHARTS 20. PAGE 32 F0629 EDU/PROP ACADEM SCHOOL INTELL

B61
GARDNER R.N.,LEGAL-ECONOMIC PROBLEMS OF INTERNATIONAL TRADE. FUT WOR+45 INTELL ECO/DEV EX/STRUC INT/TRADE ROUTINE ATTIT WEALTH...GEN/LAWS ANTHOL FOR/TRADE 20. PAGE 46 F0904 FINAN ACT/RES

B61
KATKOFF U.,SOVIET ECONOMY 1940-1965. COM WOR+45 WOR-45 INTELL NAT/G POL/PAR TOP/EX ATTIT PWR ...POLICY TIME/SEQ VAL/FREE 20. PAGE 69 F1360 AGRI PERSON TOTALISM USSR

S61
GALBRAITH J.K.,"A POSITIVE APPROACH TO ECONOMIC AID." FUT USA+45 INTELL NAT/G CONSULT ACT/RES DIPLOM ECO/TAC EDU/PROP ATTIT KNOWL PWR WEALTH ...SOC STERTYP MID/EX METH/GP 20. PAGE 45 F0883 ECO/UNDEV ROUTINE FOR/AID

N61
VINER J.,THE INTELLECTUAL HISTORY OF LAISSEZ FAIRE (PAMPHLET). WOR+45 WOR-45 LAW INTELL...POLICY LING LOG 19/20. PAGE 141 F2787 ATTIT EDU/PROP LAISSEZ ECO/TAC

B62
VAIZEY J.,THE ECONOMICS OF EDUCATION. INTELL ECO/TAC PAY COST PRODUC 20. PAGE 140 F2758 ECO/DEV SCHOOL ACADEM PROFIT

L62
"BIBLIOGRAPHY ON EDUCATION AND ECONOMIC AND SOCIAL DEVELOPMENT (AMERICAN SOURCES)" L/A+17C ECO/UNDEV PROB/SOLV...SOC 20. PAGE 1 F0015 BIBLIOG/A ACADEM EDU/PROP INTELL

L62
"HIGHER EDUCATION AND ECONOMIC AND SOCIAL DEVELOPMENT IN LATIN AMERICA: A BIBLIOGRAPHY." L/A+17C SOCIETY ECO/UNDEV PROF/ORG DIPLOM CONFER ...SOC 20. PAGE 1 F0016 BIBLIOG/A ACADEM INTELL EDU/PROP

B63
CHOJNACKI S.,REGISTER ON CURRENT RESEARCH ON ETHIOPIA AND THE HORN OF AFRICA. ETHIOPIA LAW CULTURE AGRI SECT EDU/PROP ADMIN...GEOG HEAL LING 20. PAGE 24 F0470 BIBLIOG ACT/RES INTELL ACADEM

L63
MEYER J.R.,"REGIONAL ECONOMICS: A SURVEY." INTELL ACADEM CREATE...IDEA/COMP BIBLIOG. PAGE 90 F1770 REGION ECO/TAC GEN/LAWS PROB/SOLV

L63
MOUSKHELY M.,"LE BLOC COMMUNISTE ET LA COMMUNAUTE ECONOMIQUE EUROPEENNE." AFR COM EUR+WWI FUT USSR WOR+45 INTELL ECO/UNDEV LABOR POL/PAR NUC/PWR RIGID/FLEX...TIME/SEQ ORG/CHARTS EEC TOT/POP 20. PAGE 94 F1849 INT/ORG ECO/DEV

S63
DUCROS B.,"MOBILISATION DES RESSOURCES PRODUCTIVES ET DEVELOPPEMENT." FUT INTELL SOCIETY COM/IND DIST/IND EXTR/IND FINAN INDUS ROUTINE WEALTH ...METH/CNCPT OBS 20. PAGE 34 F0670 ECO/UNDEV TEC/DEV

S63
FLOREA I.,"CU PRIVIRE LA OBIECTUL MATERIALISMULUI ISTORIC SI AL COMUNISMULUI STIINTIFIC SI LA RAPORTUL DINTRE ELE." EUR+WWI WOR+45 WOR-45 INTELL NAT/G POL/PAR WORKER EDU/PROP PERCEPT MARXISM ...MARXIST PHIL/SCI CONCPT TOT/POP 20. PAGE 42 F0812 COM ATTIT TOTALISM

S63
FOURASTIE J.,"LES SCIENCES ECONOMIQUES ET SOCIALES EN EUROPE." EUR+WWI FUT MOD/EUR WOR+45 WOR-45 INTELL SOCIETY R+D PLAN ROUTINE ATTIT RIGID/FLEX KNOWL...OBS TREND. PAGE 43 F0833 ACT/RES CULTURE

S63
MARTHELOT P.,"PROGRES DE LA REFORME AGRAIRE." INTELL ECO/DEV R+D FOR/AID ADMIN KNOWL...OBS VAL/FREE UN 20. PAGE 86 F1680 AGRI INT/ORG

B64
MORGAN H.W.,AMERICAN SOCIALISM 1900-1960. AFR USA+45 USA-45 INTELL AGRI LABOR WORKER BARGAIN ECO/TAC GP/REL RACE/REL 20 NEGRO MIGRATION. PAGE 93 F1830 SOCISM POL/PAR ECO/DEV STRATA

B64
POWELSON J.P.,LATIN AMERICA: TODAY'S ECONOMIC AND SOCIAL REVOLUTION. L/A+17C INTELL SOCIETY STRUCT AGRI INDUS NAT/G DIPLOM ECO/TAC REV...POLICY 20. PAGE 107 F2110 ECO/UNDEV WEALTH ADJUST PLAN

B64
SULLIVAN G.,THE STORY OF THE PEACE CORPS. USA+45 WOR+45 INTELL FACE/GP NAT/G SCHOOL VOL/ASSN CONSULT EX/STRUC PLAN EDU/PROP ADMIN ATTIT DRIVE ALL/VALS ...POLICY HEAL SOC CONCPT INT QU BIOG TREND SOC/EXP WORK. PAGE 127 F2511 INT/ORG ECO/UNDEV FOR/AID PEACE

B64
TINBERGEN J.,CENTRAL PLANNING. COM INTELL ECO/DEV ECO/UNDEV FINAN INT/ORG PROB/SOLV ECO/TAC CONTROL EXEC ROUTINE DECISION. PAGE 130 F2576 PLAN INDUS MGT CENTRAL

B65
WARNER A.W.,THE IMPACT OF SCIENCE ON TECHNOLOGY. UNIV INTELL SOCIETY NAT/G ACT/RES PLAN PROB/SOLV BUDGET OPTIMAL GEN/METH. PAGE 143 F2821 DECISION TEC/DEV CREATE POLICY

B65
WINT G.,ASIA: A HANDBOOK. ASIA COM INDIA USSR CULTURE INTELL NAT/G...GEOG STAT CENSUS NAT/COMP WORSHIP 20 TREATY CHINJAP. PAGE 148 F2907 DIPLOM SOC

S65
CECIL C.O.,"THE DETERMINANTS OF LIBYAN FOREIGN POLICY." AFR INTELL ECO/UNDEV EXTR/IND POL/PAR CREATE REGION SOVEREIGN CONSERVE MAGHREB NASSER/G. PAGE 22 F0431 LIBYA DIPLOM WEALTH ISLAM

B66
KIRKENDALL R.S.,SOCIAL SCIENTISTS AND FARM POLITICS IN THE AGE OF ROOSEVELT. ACADEM PLAN ECO/TAC GIVE ADMIN CONTROL PRODUC...SOC 20 NEW/DEAL ROOSEVLT/F BURAGR/ECO. PAGE 71 F1399 AGRI INTELL POLICY NAT/G

B66
THEIL H.,APPLIED ECONOMIC FORECASTING. UNIV USA+45 ELITES INTELL CONSULT PRODUC...DECISION MGT PREDICT CHARTS METH/COMP SIMUL 20. PAGE 129 F2552 FUT OP/RES PLAN

B67
BLAUG M.,ECONOMICS OF EDUCATION: A SELECTED ANNOTATED BIBLIOGRAPHY. EUR+WWI INTELL ECO/DEV ECO/UNDEV ACADEM INT/ORG NAT/G CREATE ADMIN EFFICIENCY ROLE PREDICT. PAGE 16 F0298 BIBLIOG/A EDU/PROP FINAN PLAN

B67
FILENE P.G.,AMERICANS AND THE SOVIET EXPERIMENT, 1917-1933. USA-45 USSR INTELL NAT/G CAP/ISM DIPLOM EDU/PROP PRESS REV SOCISM...PSY 20. PAGE 41 F0793 ATTIT RIGID/FLEX MARXISM SOCIETY

B67
FONER P.S.,THE BOLSHEVIK REVOLUTION. USA-45 POL/PAR WORKER DIPLOM EDU/PROP MARXISM...STERTYP 20. PAGE 42 F0821 LABOR INTELL REV PRESS

B67
ORLANS H.,CONTRACTING FOR ATOMS. AFR USA+45 LAW INTELL ACADEM LG/CO NAT/G PLAN TEC/DEV CONTROL DETER...TREND 20. PAGE 102 F1999 NUC/PWR R+D PRODUC PEACE

B67
PEDLEY F.H.,EDUCATION AND SOCIAL WORK. USA+45 INTELL TEC/DEV. PAGE 104 F2047 GP/REL EDU/PROP SOC/WK EFFICIENCY

S67
ADAMS R.N.,"ETHICS AND THE SOCIAL ANTHROPOLOGIST IN LATIN AMERICA." USA+45 INTELL PROB/SOLV ECO/TAC LEAD...DECISION SOC NAT/COMP PERS/COMP. PAGE 2 F0039 L/A+17C POLICY ECO/UNDEV CONSULT

S67
KELLY F.K.,"A PROPOSAL FOR AN ANNUAL REPORT ON THE STATE OF MANKIND." FUT INTELL COM/IND INT/ORG CREATE PROB/SOLV PERS/REL...CONCPT 20 UN. PAGE 70 F1371 SOCIETY UNIV ATTIT NEW/IDEA

S67
MORTON J.A.,"A SYSTEMS APPROACH TO THE INNOVATION PROCESS: ITS USE IN THE BELL SYSTEM." USA+45 INTELL INDUS LG/CO CONSULT WORKER COMPUTER AUTOMAT DEMAND ...MGT CHARTS 20. PAGE 94 F1841 TEC/DEV GEN/METH R+D COM/IND

B99
KROPOTKIN P.,FIELDS, FACTORIES, AND WORKSHOPS. UNIV INTELL ECO/DEV LG/CO SCHOOL SML/CO ECO/TAC PRODUC UTOPIA...NEW/IDEA MUNICH. PAGE 74 F1445 SOCIETY WORKER AGRI INDUS

INTELLIGENCE, MILITARY....SEE ACT/RES+FORCES+KNOWL

INTELLIGENTSIA....SEE INTELL

INTERAMERICAN ECO AND SOC COUN F1267,F1268

INTEREST....INTEREST

INTER-AMERICAN DEVELOPMENT BANK....SEE INT/AM/DEV

INTER-ASIAN DEVELOPMENT BANK....SEE IADB

INTERNAL WARFARE....SEE REV

INTERNAT CONGRESS OF JURISTS F1269

INTERNATIONAL ASSOCIATION RES F1270

INTERNATIONAL BANK RECONST DEV F1271,F1272,F1273

INTERNATIONAL ECO POLICY ASSN F1274

INTERNATIONAL ECONOMIC ASSN F1275,F1276

B61
US GENERAL ACCOUNTING OFFICE,EXAMINATION OF ECONOMIC AND TECHNICAL ASSISTANCE PROGRAM FOR IRAN. IRAN USA+45 AGRI INDUS DIPLOM CONTROL COST 20. PAGE 136 F2681 FOR/AID ADMIN TEC/DEV ECO/UNDEV

S61
VALLET R.,"IRAN: KEY TO THE MIDDLE EAST." COM IRAQ ISLAM KUWAIT LEBANON SAUDI/ARAB TURKEY ELITES SOCIETY INDUS PROC/MFG POL/PAR TOP/EX PLAN BAL/PWR DIPLOM ECO/TAC ALL/VALS...TREND FOR/TRADE CENTO 20. PAGE 140 F2760 NAT/G ECO/UNDEV IRAN

S63
BILL J.A.,"THE SOCIAL AND ECONOMIC FOUNDATIONS OF POWER IN CONTEMPORARY IRAN." ISLAM CULTURE NAT/G ECO/TAC DOMIN COERCE ATTIT PWR WEALTH...TREND VAL/FREE 20. PAGE 15 F0284 SOCIETY STRATA IRAN

B65
HARBISON F.,MANPOWER AND EDUCATION. AFR CHINA/COM IRAN L/A+17C S/ASIA TEC/DEV ADJUST OPTIMAL SKILL ...ANTHOL 20. PAGE 55 F1073 ECO/UNDEV EDU/PROP WORKER NAT/COMP

B67
BALDWIN G.B.,PLANNING AND DEVELOPMENT IN IRAN. IRAN AGRI INDUS CONSULT WORKER EDU/PROP BAL/PAY...CHARTS 20. PAGE 9 F0164 PLAN ECO/UNDEV ADMIN PROB/SOLV

B67
COTTAM R.W.,COMPETITIVE INTERFERENCE AND TWENTIETH CENTURY DIPLOMACY. IRAN ACT/RES CREATE PLAN ECO/TAC EFFICIENCY ATTIT...DECISION NEW/IDEA TREND 20 CIA. PAGE 28 F0541 DIPLOM DOMIN GAME

B67
US SENATE COMM ON FOREIGN REL,ARMS SALES TO NEAR EAST AND SOUTH ASIAN COUNTRIES. INDIA IRAN PAKISTAN WOR+45 PROC/MFG BAL/PWR DIPLOM...DECISION SENATE. PAGE 139 F2742 WEAPON FOR/AID FORCES POLICY

IRAQ....SEE ALSO ISLAM

B57
WARRINER D.,LAND REFORM AND DEVELOPMENT IN THE MIDDLE EAST: A STUDY OF EGYPT, SYRIA AND IRAQ. IRAQ ISLAM SYRIA UAR AGRI DIST/IND PLAN TEC/DEV DOMIN REV ATTIT WEALTH...SOC METH/CNCPT STAT OBS RECORD HIST/WRIT TREND GEN/LAWS FAO 20. PAGE 143 F2825 ECO/UNDEV CONCPT

S61
VALLET R.,"IRAN: KEY TO THE MIDDLE EAST." COM IRAQ ISLAM KUWAIT LEBANON SAUDI/ARAB TURKEY ELITES SOCIETY INDUS PROC/MFG POL/PAR TOP/EX PLAN BAL/PWR DIPLOM ECO/TAC ALL/VALS...TREND FOR/TRADE CENTO 20. PAGE 140 F2760 NAT/G ECO/UNDEV IRAN

B67
ALNASRAWI A.,FINANCING ECONOMIC DEVELOPMENT IN IRAQ. IRAQ INDUS CAP/ISM COST PRODUC...STAT CHARTS BIBLIOG 20. PAGE 4 F0076 ECO/UNDEV EXTR/IND TEC/DEV INT/TRADE

IRELAND....SEE ALSO UK

B66
EDWARDS C.D.,TRADE REGULATIONS OVERSEAS. IRELAND NEW/ZEALND SOUTH/AFR NAT/G CAP/ISM TARIFFS CONTROL ...POLICY JURID 20 EEC CHINJAP. PAGE 36 F0703 INT/TRADE DIPLOM INT/LAW ECO/TAC

B86
O'CONNOR T.P.,THE PARNELL MOVEMENT: WITH A SKETCH OF IRISH PARTIES FROM 1843. IRELAND UK USA-45 LEGIS WORKER ECO/TAC COERCE CRIME REV CHOOSE ORD/FREE CATHISM LAISSEZ...SOC 19/20 PARLIAMENT PARNELL/CS LAND/LEAG. PAGE 100 F1957 LEAD DOMIN POL/PAR POLICY

IRGUN....IRGUN - PALESTINE REVOLUTIONARY ORGANIZATION

IRISH/AMER....IRISH AMERICANS

IRS....U.S. INTERNAL REVENUE SERVICE

ISAAC J. F1289

ISARD W. F1290

ISELIN J.J. F1291

ISLAM....ISLAMIC WORLD; SEE ALSO APPROPRIATE NATIONS

N
BROCKWAY A.F.,AFRICAN SOCIALISM. EUR+WWI GHANA ISLAM UAR ECO/UNDEV CAP/ISM INT/TRADE COLONIAL COERCE GOV/REL DISCRIM 20 NEGRO NKRUMAH/K NASSER/G. PAGE 19 F0356 AFR SOCISM MARXISM

N
THE MIDDLE EAST AND NORTH AFRICA. AFR ISLAM CULTURE ECO/UNDEV AGRI NAT/G TEC/DEV FOR/AID INT/TRADE EDU/PROP...CHARTS 20. PAGE 1 F0008 INDEX INDUS FINAN STAT

N
THE MIDDLE EAST. CULTURE...BIOG BIBLIOG. PAGE 1 F0010 ISLAM INDUS FINAN

N19
KUWAIT ARABIA,KUWAIT FUND FOR ARAB ECONOMIC DEVELOPMENT (PAMPHLET). ISLAM KUWAIT UAR ECO/UNDEV LEGIS ECO/TAC WEALTH 20. PAGE 74 F1452 FOR/AID DIPLOM FINAN ADMIN

N19
KUWAIT FUND ARAB ECO DEVELOPMT,ANNUAL REPORTS 1962-65 (PAMPHLET). KUWAIT ECO/UNDEV DIPLOM ...POLICY 20 ARABS. PAGE 74 F1453 FOR/AID DELIB/GP FINAN ISLAM

B51
US DEPARTMENT OF STATE,POINT FOUR, NEAR EAST AND AFRICA, A SELECTED BIBLIOGRAPHY OF STUDIES ON ECONOMICALLY UNDERDEVELOPED COUNTRIES. AGRI COM/IND FINAN INDUS PLAN INT/TRADE...SOC TREND 20. PAGE 135 F2672 BIBLIOG/A AFR S/ASIA ISLAM

B56
US DEPARTMENT OF STATE,ECONOMIC PROBLEMS OF UNDERDEVELOPED AREAS (PAMPHLET). AFR ASIA ISLAM L/A+17C AGRI FINAN INDUS INT/ORG LABOR INT/TRADE ...PSY SOC 20. PAGE 136 F2673 BIBLIOG ECO/UNDEV TEC/DEV R+D

B57
PATAI R.,JORDAN, LEBANON AND SYRIA: AN ANNOTATED BIBLIOGRAPHY. ISLAM JORDAN LEBANON SYRIA...GEOG 20. PAGE 103 F2034 BIBLIOG/A SOC

B57
WARRINER D.,LAND REFORM AND DEVELOPMENT IN THE MIDDLE EAST: A STUDY OF EGYPT, SYRIA AND IRAQ. IRAQ ISLAM SYRIA UAR AGRI DIST/IND PLAN TEC/DEV DOMIN REV ATTIT WEALTH...SOC METH/CNCPT STAT OBS RECORD HIST/WRIT TREND GEN/LAWS FAO 20. PAGE 143 F2825 ECO/UNDEV CONCPT

L57
MASS. INST. TECH.,"THE CENTER FOR INTERNATIONAL STUDIES." AFR ASIA COM EUR+WWI ISLAM L/A+17C S/ASIA USA+45 USA-45 DIST/IND CONSULT FORCES ACT/RES TEC/DEV DIPLOM REV ATTIT WEALTH...CONCPT FOR/TRADE 20. PAGE 87 F1702 R+D ECO/UNDEV

B58
BERLINER J.S.,SOVIET ECONOMIC AID: THE AID AND TRADE POLICY IN UNDERDEVELOPED COUNTRIES. AFR COM ISLAM L/A+17C S/ASIA USSR ECO/DEV DIST/IND FINAN MARKET INT/ORG ACT/RES PLAN BAL/PWR WEAPON PWR WEALTH...CHARTS FOR/TRADE 20. PAGE 14 F0263 ECO/UNDEV ECO/TAC FOR/AID

B58
TILLION G.,ALGERIA: THE REALITIES. ALGERIA FRANCE ISLAM CULTURE STRATA PROB/SOLV DOMIN REV NAT/LISM WEALTH MARXISM...GEOG 20. PAGE 130 F2573 ECO/UNDEV SOC COLONIAL DIPLOM

B59
MEYER A.J.,MIDDLE EASTERN CAPITALISM: NINE ESSAYS. ISLAM CULTURE ECO/UNDEV INDUS MARKET NAT/G PLAN ATTIT RIGID/FLEX...STAT OBS TREND GEN/LAWS. PAGE 90 F1767 TEC/DEV ECO/TAC ANTHOL

B60
AMERICAN U BEIRUT ECO RES INST,A SELECTED AND ANNOTATED BIBLIOGRAPHY OF ECONOMIC LITERATURE ON THE ARABIC SPEAKING COUNTRIES OF THE MIDDLE EAST. ISLAM AGRI COM/IND DIST/IND FINAN INDUS LABOR ...GEOG 20. PAGE 5 F0091 BIBLIOG/A ECO/UNDEV STAT

B60
AUSTRUY J.,STRUCTURE ECONOMIQUE ET CIVILISATION: L'EGYPTE ET LE DESTIN ECONOMIQUE DE L'ISLAM. ISLAM UAR CREATE OP/RES ECO/TAC...SOC BIBLIOG 20 MUSLIM. PAGE 8 F0142 ECO/UNDEV CULTURE STRUCT

B60
LENCZOWSKI G.,OIL AND STATE IN THE MIDDLE EAST. FUT IRAN LAW ECO/UNDEV EXTR/IND NAT/G TOP/EX PLAN TEC/DEV ECO/TAC LEGIT ADMIN COERCE ATTIT ALL/VALS PWR...CHARTS 20. PAGE 78 F1519 ISLAM INDUS NAT/LISM

S60
GARNICK D.H.,"ON THE ECONOMIC FEASIBILITY OF A MIDDLE EASTERN COMMON MARKET." AFR ISLAM CULTURE INDUS NAT/G PLAN TEC/DEV ECO/TAC ADMIN ATTIT DRIVE RIGID/FLEX...PLURIST STAT TREND GEN/LAWS 20. PAGE 46 F0907 MARKET INT/TRADE

S60
JAFFEE A.J.,"POPULATION TRENDS AND CONTROLS IN UNDERDEVELOPED COUNTRIES." AFR FUT ISLAM L/A+17C S/ASIA CULTURE R+D FAM ACT/RES PLAN EDU/PROP BIO/SOC RIGID/FLEX HEALTH...SOC STAT OBS CHARTS 20. PAGE 66 F1303 ECO/UNDEV GEOG

B61
FRIEDMANN W.G.,JOINT INTERNATIONAL BUSINESS VENTURES. ASIA ISLAM L/A+17C ECO/DEV DIST/IND FINAN PROC/MFG FACE/GP LG/CO NAT/G VOL/ASSN CONSULT EX/STRUC PLAN ADMIN ROUTINE WEALTH...OLD/LIB FOR/TRADE WORK 20. PAGE 44 F0865 ECO/UNDEV INT/TRADE

B61
LONGRIGG S.H.,OIL IN THE MIDDLE EAST: ITS DISCOVERY AND DEVELOPMENT. ECO/UNDEV LG/CO LOC/G TEC/DEV WEALTH...STAT TIME/SEQ 20 OIL. PAGE 82 F1599 ISLAM EXTR/IND

S61
VALLET R.,"IRAN: KEY TO THE MIDDLE EAST." COM IRAQ ISLAM KUWAIT LEBANON SAUDI/ARAB TURKEY ELITES SOCIETY INDUS PROC/MFG POL/PAR TOP/EX PLAN BAL/PWR DIPLOM ECO/TAC ALL/VALS...TREND FOR/TRADE CENTO 20. PAGE 140 F2760
NAT/G ECO/UNDEV IRAN

B62
BROWN S.D.,STUDIES ON ASIA, 1962. ASIA BURMA INDIA ISLAM ISRAEL S/ASIA ECO/UNDEV POL/PAR SECT ECO/TAC ...ANTHOL 20 CHINJAP. PAGE 19 F0374
PWR PARL/PROC

B62
EINZIG P.,THE HISTORY OF FOREIGN EXCHANGE. CHRIST-17C ISLAM MEDIT-7 PRE/AMER WOR+45 ECO/DEV FINAN PLAN ECO/TAC ATTIT KNOWL WEALTH...SIMUL GEN/LAWS. PAGE 37 F0714
MARKET TIME/SEQ INT/TRADE

B62
O'CONNOR H.,WORLD CRISES IN OIL (BMR). ISLAM L/A+17C INDUS LG/CO INT/TRADE 20. PAGE 100 F1956
EXTR/IND DIPLOM ECO/UNDEV SOCISM

L62
WATERSTON A.,"PLANNING IN MOROCCO, ORGANIZATION AND IMPLEMENTATION. BALTIMORE: HOPKINS ECON. DEVELOP. INT. BANK FOR." ISLAM ECO/DEV AGRI DIST/IND INDUS PROC/MFG SERV/IND LOC/G EX/STRUC ECO/TAC PWR WEALTH TOT/POP TRUE/GP METH/GP TERR/GP VAL/FREE 20. PAGE 144 F2829
NAT/G PLAN MOROCCO

S62
PIQUEMAL M.,"LA COOPERATION FINANCIERE ENTRE LA FRANCE ET LES ETATS AFRICAINS ET MALGACHE." ISLAM INT/ORG TOP/EX ECO/TAC...JURID CHARTS 20. PAGE 106 F2089
AFR FINAN FRANCE MADAGASCAR

S62
RAZAFIMBAHINY J.,"L'ORGANISATION AFRICAINE ET MALGACHE DE COOPERATION ECONOMIQUE." AFR ISLAM MADAGASCAR NAT/G ACT/RES ECO/TAC ALL/VALS ...TIME/SEQ 20. PAGE 110 F2158
INT/ORG ECO/UNDEV

B63
ISSAWI C.,EGYPT IN REVOLUTION: AN ECONOMIC ANALYSIS. ISLAM STRUCT ECO/UNDEV AGRI FINAN INDUS PLAN EXEC REV NAT/LISM ATTIT RIGID/FLEX WEALTH SOCISM...STAT FOR/TRADE WORK 20. PAGE 66 F1292
NAT/G UAR

B63
US SENATE COMM GOVT OPERATIONS,REPORT OF A STUDY OF US FOREIGN AID IN TEN MIDDLE EASTERN AND AFRICAN COUNTRIES. AFR ISLAM USA+45 FORCES PLAN BUDGET DIPLOM TAX DETER WEALTH...STAT CHARTS 20 CONGRESS AID MID/EAST. PAGE 138 F2728
FOR/AID EFFICIENCY ECO/TAC FINAN

L63
NASH M.,"PSYCHO-CULTURAL FACTORS IN ASIAN ECONOMIC GROWTH." ASIA ISLAM S/ASIA CULTURE ECO/UNDEV DELIB/GP EDU/PROP COERCE ATTIT PERSON HEALTH KNOWL ORD/FREE...PSY SOC STAT TREND ANTHOL VAL/FREE 20. PAGE 96 F1893
SOCIETY ECO/TAC

L63
RIDAH A.,"LE NEO-DESTOUR DEPUIS L'INDEPENDANCE." FUT ISLAM WOR+45 ECO/UNDEV INT/ORG SCHOOL DELIB/GP TOP/EX ACT/RES EDU/PROP LEGIT ATTIT ALL/VALS 20 TUNIS. PAGE 111 F2189
NAT/G CONSTN

S63
BILL J.A.,"THE SOCIAL AND ECONOMIC FOUNDATIONS OF POWER IN CONTEMPORARY IRAN." ISLAM CULTURE NAT/G ECO/TAC DOMIN COERCE ATTIT PWR WEALTH...TREND VAL/FREE 20. PAGE 15 F0284
SOCIETY STRATA IRAN

S63
GANDOLFI A.,"LES ACCORDS DE COOPERATION EN MATIERE DE POLITIQUE ETRANGERE ENTRE LA FRANCE ET LES NOUVEAUX ETATS AFRICAINS ET." AFR ISLAM MADAGASCAR WOR+45 ECO/DEV INT/ORG NAT/G DELIB/GP ECO/TAC ALL/VALS...CON/ANAL 20. PAGE 46 F0894
VOL/ASSN ECO/UNDEV DIPLOM FRANCE

S63
SHWADRAN B.,"MIDDLE EAST OIL, 1962." ISLAM DIST/IND INDUS PLAN ATTIT DRIVE WEALTH...POLICY STAT CONT/OBS TREND CHARTS GEN/LAWS TERR/GP METH/GP 20 OIL. PAGE 121 F2393
PROC/MFG ECO/TAC ELITES REGION

S63
SHWADRAN B.,"MIDDLE EAST OIL, 1962." ISLAM USSR ECO/DEV DIST/IND INDUS PLAN BAL/PWR DISPL DRIVE ...POLICY STAT TREND GEN/LAWS TERR/GP METH/GP EEC OEEC 20 OIL. PAGE 121 F2394
MARKET ECO/TAC INT/TRADE

B64
DE BARY W.T.,APPROACHES TO ASIAN CIVILIZATIONS. INDIA ISLAM USA+45 CULTURE ACADEM...SOC ANTHOL 20 CHINJAP ARABS. PAGE 31 F0595
ASIA EDU/PROP SOCIETY

B64
JUCKER-FLEETWOOD E.,MONEY AND FINANCE IN AFRICA. ISLAM ECO/UNDEV SERV/IND NAT/G EX/STRUC PLAN ECO/TAC ROUTINE WEALTH...MGT TOT/POP 20. PAGE 68 F1344
AFR FINAN

B64
MELADY T.,FACES OF AFRICA. AFR FUT ISLAM NAT/G POL/PAR SCHOOL DELIB/GP PLAN ECO/TAC EDU/PROP ATTIT ALL/VALS...CHARTS TOT/POP TERR/GP VAL/FREE 20. PAGE 89 F1752
ECO/UNDEV TREND NAT/LISM

B64
RAMAZANI R.K.,THE MIDDLE EAST AND THE EUROPEAN COMMON MARKET. EUR+WWI ISLAM ECO/DEV EXTR/IND MARKET PROC/MFG INT/ORG NAT/G TEC/DEV ECO/TAC REGION DRIVE WEALTH...STAT CHARTS EEC TOT/POP 20. PAGE 109 F2141
ECO/UNDEV ATTIT INT/TRADE

B65
INT. BANK RECONSTR. DEVELOP.,ECONOMIC DEVELOPMENT OF KUWAIT. ISLAM KUWAIT AGRI FINAN MARKET EX/STRUC TEC/DEV ECO/TAC ADMIN WEALTH...OBS CON/ANAL CHARTS 20. PAGE 64 F1266
INDUS NAT/G

B65
MACDONALD R.W.,THE LEAGUE OF ARAB STATES: A STUDY IN THE DYNAMICS OF REGIONAL ORGANIZATION. ISRAEL UAR USSR FINAN INT/ORG DELIB/GP ECO/TAC AGREE NEUTRAL ORD/FREE PWR...DECISION BIBLIOG 20 TREATY UN. PAGE 83 F1626
ISLAM REGION DIPLOM ADMIN

B65
RIVKIN M.D.,AREA DEVELOPMENT FOR NATIONAL GROWTH; THE TURKISH PRECEDENT. ISLAM TURKEY ACT/RES INGP/REL...POLICY CHARTS GP/COMP MUNICH 20 ATATURK/MK INONU/I. PAGE 112 F2197
ECO/UNDEV REGION ECO/TAC PLAN

B65
VON RENESSE E.A.,UNVOLLENDETE DEMOKRATIEN. AFR ISLAM S/ASIA SOCIETY ACT/RES COLONIAL...JURID CHARTS BIBLIOG METH 13/20. PAGE 142 F2795
ECO/UNDEV NAT/COMP SOVEREIGN

S65
BERREBY J.J.,"IMPERATIFS STRATEGIQUES DU PETROLE." ECO/UNDEV VOL/ASSN ECO/TAC COLONIAL NUC/PWR WAR. PAGE 14 F0270
ISLAM EXTR/IND STAT OBS

S65
CECIL C.O.,"THE DETERMINANTS OF LIBYAN FOREIGN POLICY." AFR INTELL ECO/UNDEV EXTR/IND POL/PAR CREATE REGION SOVEREIGN CONSERVE MAGHREB NASSER/G. PAGE 22 F0431
LIBYA DIPLOM WEALTH ISLAM

B66
BEN-PORATH Y.,THE ARAB LABOR FORCE IN ISRAEL. ISLAM ISRAEL AGRI INDUS SCHOOL CAP/ISM PAY DEMAND...GEOG REGRESS STAT CHARTS 20 ARABS. PAGE 13 F0245
WORKER CENSUS GP/REL STRUCT

B66
RIZK C.,LE REGIME POLITIQUE LIBANAIS. ISLAM LEBANON STRUCT POL/PAR SECT LOBBY GP/REL 20 ARABS MUSLIM CHRISTIAN. PAGE 112 F2198
ECO/UNDEV NAT/G CULTURE

B66
THOMPSON J.H.,MODERNIZATION OF THE ARAB WORLD. FUT ISRAEL STRUCT ECO/UNDEV DIPLOM INGP/REL ATTIT ...CENSUS ANTHOL 20 ARABS. PAGE 130 F2565
ADJUST ISLAM PROB/SOLV NAT/COMP

S66
SHORTE F.C.,"THE APPLICATION OF DEVELOPMENT HYPOTHESES IN MIDDLE EASTERN STUDIES." STRUCT AGRI CREATE DEMAND...GEOG STAT CON/ANAL CHARTS. PAGE 121 F2387
ECO/UNDEV ISLAM SOC HYPO/EXP

B67
LANDEN R.G.,OMAN SINCE 1856: DISRUPTIVE MODERNIZATION IN A TRADITIONAL ARAB SOCIETY. UK DIST/IND EXTR/IND SECT DIPLOM INT/TRADE...SOC LING CHARTS BIBLIOG 19/20. PAGE 75 F1468
ISLAM CULTURE ECO/UNDEV NAT/G

S67
GEISS I.,"THE GERMANS AND THE MIDDLE EAST CRISIS." GERMANY/W ISLAM ISRAEL USSR POL/PAR RACE/REL MARXISM...GP/COMP 20 JEWS. PAGE 47 F0914
ATTIT DIPLOM WAR POLICY

S67
KENNY L.M.,"THE AFTERMATH OF DEFEAT IN EGYPT." ISLAM ISRAEL UAR UK USA+45 USSR INDUS FORCES ECO/TAC PRICE COERCE WEAPON COST ATTIT. PAGE 70 F1378
WAR ECO/UNDEV DIPLOM POLICY

S67
MCCORD W.,"ARMIES AND POLITICS; A PROBLEM IN THE THIRD WORLD." AFR ISLAM USA+45 ECO/UNDEV TOTALISM 20. PAGE 88 F1723
FOR/AID POLICY NAT/G FORCES

N67
US HOUSE COMM FOREIGN AFFAIRS,REPORT OF SPECIAL STUDY MISSION TO THE NEAR EAST (PAMPHLET). ISRAEL USA+45 YEMEN ECO/UNDEV INT/ORG FOR/AID ARMS/CONT WAR WEAPON NAT/LISM PEACE...GEOG 20 UN HOUSE/REP. PAGE 137 F2694
ISLAM DIPLOM FORCES

N67
US SENATE COMM ON FOREIGN REL,WAR OR PEACE IN THE MIDDLE EAST (PAMPHLET). GREECE ISLAM ISRAEL JORDAN UAR CHIEF PROB/SOLV FOR/AID WAR PWR 20 SENATE. PAGE 139 F2739
DIPLOM FORCES PLAN

ISOLAT....ISOLATION AND COMMUNITY, CONDITIONS OF HIGH GROUP SEGREGATION

N
US LIBRARY OF CONGRESS,EAST EUROPEAN ACCESSIONS INDEX. NAT/G ISOLAT ATTIT KNOWL...POLICY 20. PAGE 138 F2711
BIBLIOG COM MARXIST DIPLOM

B63
ELLENDER A.J.,A REPORT ON UNITED STATES FOREIGN OPERATIONS IN AFRICA. SOUTH/AFR USA+45 STRATA
FOR/AID DIPLOM

EXTR/IND FORCES RACE/REL ISOLAT SOVEREIGN...CHARTS 20 NEGRO. PAGE 37 F0721 WEALTH ECO/UNDEV B63

RILEY J.W. JR.,THE CORPORATION AND ITS PUBLICS. ESSAYS ON THE CORPORATE IMAGE. CLIENT ISOLAT AGE ATTIT...POLICY SOC METH/CNCPT INT. PAGE 111 F2193 LG/CO CLASSIF GP/REL NEIGH B64

STRONG A.L.,THE RISE OF THE CHINESE PEOPLE'S COMMUNES - AND SIX YEARS AFTER (2ND ED.). CHINA/COM AGRI INDUS FORCES WORKER PROB/SOLV EDU/PROP EFFICIENCY ISOLAT 20. PAGE 127 F2503 NEIGH ECO/TAC MARXISM METH/COMP B67

ROSS A.M.,EMPLOYMENT, RACE, AND POVERTY. USA+45 LAW STRATA MARKET LABOR EDU/PROP ISOLAT SKILL...MGT ANTHOL 20 NEGRO. PAGE 114 F2244 RACE/REL WORKER WEALTH DISCRIM B67

SACKS B.,SOUTH AFRICA: AN IMPERIAL DILEMMA. SOUTH/AFR UK ECO/UNDEV KIN DOMIN DEBATE CONTROL REV DISCRIM ISOLAT...POLICY STAT BIBLIOG 20. PAGE 115 F2268 COLONIAL RACE/REL DIPLOM ORD/FREE B68

PROUDHON P.J.,SYSTEME DES CONTRADICTIONS ECONOMIQUES, OU PHILOSOPHIE DA LA MISERE (2 VOLS.) (1846). SECT WORKER GP/REL ISOLAT PRODUC IDEA/COMP. PAGE 108 F2126 SOCIETY STRATA MORAL

ISOLATION....SEE ISOLAT

ISRAEL J. F0853

ISRAEL....SEE ALSO JEWS, ISLAM

N19

FIKS M.,PUBLIC ADMINISTRATION IN ISRAEL (PAMPHLET). ISRAEL SCHOOL EX/STRUC BUDGET PAY INGP/REL ...DECISION 20 CIVIL/SERV. PAGE 41 F0792 EDU/PROP NAT/G ADMIN WORKER B62

BROWN S.D.,STUDIES ON ASIA, 1962. ASIA BURMA INDIA ISLAM ISRAEL S/ASIA ECO/UNDEV POL/PAR SECT ECO/TAC ...ANTHOL 20 CHINJAP. PAGE 19 F0374 PWR PARL/PROC B62

GALENSON W.,LABOR IN DEVELOPING COUNTRIES. BRAZIL INDONESIA ISRAEL PAKISTAN TURKEY AGRI INDUS WORKER PAY PRICE GP/REL WEALTH...MGT CHARTS METH/COMP NAT/COMP 20. PAGE 45 F0888 LABOR ECO/UNDEV BARGAIN POL/PAR B64

SAKAI R.K.,STUDIES ON ASIA, 1964. ASIA CHINA/COM ISRAEL MALAYSIA S/ASIA USA+45 USSR ECO/UNDEV FAM POL/PAR SECT CONSULT NAT/LISM...POLICY SOC 20 CHINJAP. PAGE 115 F2272 PWR DIPLOM B65

MACDONALD R.W.,THE LEAGUE OF ARAB STATES: A STUDY IN THE DYNAMICS OF REGIONAL ORGANIZATION. ISRAEL UAR USSR FINAN INT/ORG DELIB/GP ECO/TAC AGREE NEUTRAL ORD/FREE PWR...DECISION BIBLIOG 20 TREATY UN. PAGE 83 F1626 ISLAM REGION DIPLOM ADMIN B65

PROCHNOW H.V.,WORLD ECONOMIC PROBLEMS AND POLICIES. INDIA ISRAEL WOR+45 AGRI LABOR PROB/SOLV FOR/AID TARIFFS CONTROL BAL/PAY NAT/LISM WEALTH...TREND CHARTS 20 CHINJAP EEC. PAGE 108 F2124 MARKET ECO/TAC PRODUC IDEA/COMP B66

BEN-PORATH Y.,THE ARAB LABOR FORCE IN ISRAEL. ISLAM ISRAEL AGRI INDUS SCHOOL CAP/ISM PAY DEMAND...GEOG REGRESS STAT CHARTS 20 ARABS. PAGE 13 F0245 WORKER CENSUS GP/REL STRUCT B66

BOYD H.W.,MARKETING MANAGEMENT: CASES FROM EMERGING COUNTRIES. BRAZIL GHANA ISRAEL WOR+45 ADMIN PERS/REL ATTIT HABITAT WEALTH...ANTHOL 20 ARGEN CASEBOOK. PAGE 17 F0332 MGT ECO/UNDEV PROB/SOLV MARKET B66

THOMPSON J.H.,MODERNIZATION OF THE ARAB WORLD. FUT ISRAEL STRUCT ECO/UNDEV DIPLOM INGP/REL ATTIT ...CENSUS ANTHOL 20 ARABS. PAGE 130 F2565 ADJUST ISLAM PROB/SOLV NAT/COMP B67

OFER G.,THE SERVICE INDUSTRIES IN A DEVELOPING ECONOMY: ISRAEL AS A CASE STUDY. ISRAEL ECO/TAC INT/TRADE PRODUC WEALTH SOCISM...TIME/SEQ TREND CHARTS 20. PAGE 101 F1979 DIPLOM ECO/DEV SERV/IND S67

GEISS I.,"THE GERMANS AND THE MIDDLE EAST CRISIS." GERMANY/W ISLAM ISRAEL USSR POL/PAR RACE/REL MARXISM...GP/COMP 20 JEWS. PAGE 47 F0914 ATTIT DIPLOM WAR POLICY S67

KENNY L.M.,"THE AFTERMATH OF DEFEAT IN EGYPT." ISLAM ISRAEL UAR UK USA+45 USSR INDUS FORCES ECO/TAC PRICE COERCE WEAPON COST ATTIT. PAGE 70 F1378 WAR ECO/UNDEV DIPLOM POLICY N67

US HOUSE COMM FOREIGN AFFAIRS,REPORT OF SPECIAL STUDY MISSION TO THE NEAR EAST (PAMPHLET). ISRAEL USA+45 YEMEN ECO/UNDEV INT/ORG FOR/AID ARMS/CONT WAR WEAPON NAT/LISM PEACE...GEOG 20 UN HOUSE/REP. PAGE 137 F2694 ISLAM DIPLOM FORCES N67

US SENATE COMM ON FOREIGN REL,WAR OR PEACE IN THE MIDDLE EAST (PAMPHLET). GREECE ISLAM ISRAEL JORDAN UAR CHIEF PROB/SOLV FOR/AID WAR PWR 20 SENATE. PAGE 139 F2739 DIPLOM FORCES PLAN

ISSAWI C. F1292

ITAL/AMER....ITALIAN-AMERICANS

ITALY....SEE ALSO APPROPRIATE TIME/SPACE/CULTURE INDEX

B40

SIKES E.R.,CONTEMPORARY ECONOMIC SYSTEMS: THEIR ANALYSIS AND SOCIAL BACKGROUND. GERMANY ITALY USSR AGRI INDUS PLAN CAP/ISM ROUTINE TOTALISM FASCISM ...POLICY CON/ANAL BIBLIOG 20. PAGE 122 F2400 COM SOCISM CONCPT B55

FLORINSKY M.T.,INTEGRATED EUROPE. EUR+WWI FRANCE ITALY NETHERLAND UK ECO/DEV INT/ORG FORCES LEGIT FEDERAL ATTIT PWR WEALTH...POLICY GEOG CONCPT GEN/LAWS TOT/POP EEC OEEC 20. PAGE 42 F0816 FUT ECO/TAC REGION B57

INTL BANKING SUMMER SCHOOL,RELATIONS BETWEEN THE CENTRAL BANKS AND COMMERCIAL BANKS. EUR+WWI FRANCE GERMANY/W ITALY UK USA+45 USSR INDUS INT/ORG CAP/ISM CONTROL MONEY. PAGE 65 F1282 FINAN NAT/G GP/REL LG/CO B58

COLE G.D.H.,COMMUNISM AND SOCIAL DEMOCRACY (VOL. IV OF "HISTORY OF SOCIAL THOUGHT"). COM GERMANY ITALY UK AGRI INT/ORG WORKER DIPLOM COLONIAL NAT/LISM ALL/IDEOS...BIBLIOG 20 LEAGUE/NAT AUST/HUNG. PAGE 26 F0502 MARXISM REV POL/PAR SOCISM S60

KREININ M.E.,"THE 'OUTER-SEVEN' AND EUROPEAN INTEGRATION." EUR+WWI FRANCE GERMANY ITALY UK ECO/DEV DIST/IND INT/TRADE DRIVE WEALTH...MYTH CHARTS EEC OEEC 20. PAGE 73 F1436 ECO/TAC GEN/LAWS B62

ROBERTSON B.C.,REGIONAL DEVELOPMENT IN THE EUROPEAN ECONOMIC COMMUNITY. EUR+WWI FRANCE FUT ITALY UK ECO/UNDEV WORKER ACT/RES PROB/SOLV TEC/DEV ECO/TAC INT/TRADE EEC. PAGE 112 F2209 PLAN ECO/DEV INT/ORG REGION B62

SIRUGO F.,L'ECONOMIA DEGLI STAT' ITALIANI PRIMA DELL' UNIFICAZIONE (10 VOLS.). ITALY...TIME/SEQ 18/19. PAGE 122 F2417 BIBLIOG PROVS NAT/G B63

MEYNAUD J.,PLANIFICATION ET POLITIQUE. FRANCE ITALY FINAN LABOR DELIB/GP LEGIS ADMIN EFFICIENCY ...MAJORIT DECISION 20. PAGE 90 F1773 PLAN ECO/TAC PROB/SOLV B64

MILIBAND R.,THE SOCIALIST REGISTER: 1964. GERMANY/W ITALY UK LABOR POL/PAR ECO/TAC FOR/AID NUC/PWR ...POLICY SOCIALIST IDEA/COMP 20 MAO NASSER/G. PAGE 91 F1784 MARXISM SOCISM CAP/ISM PROB/SOLV B64

MORRISSENS L.,ECONOMIC POLICY IN OUR TIME: COUNTRY STUDIES. BELGIUM EUR+WWI FRANCE GERMANY/W ITALY NETHERLAND INDUS BARGAIN BUDGET GOV/REL BAL/PAY PRODUC...CON/ANAL CHARTS COSTS 20. PAGE 94 F1839 ECO/DEV ECO/TAC METH/COMP PLAN B65

EDELMAN M.,THE POLITICS OF WAGE-PRICE DECISIONS. GERMANY ITALY NETHERLAND UK INDUS LABOR POL/PAR PROB/SOLV BARGAIN PRICE ROUTINE BAL/PAY COST DEMAND 20. PAGE 36 F0699 GOV/COMP CONTROL ECO/TAC PLAN B65

GREENFIELD K.R.,ECONOMICS AND LIBERALISM IN THE RISORGIMENTO (REV. ED.). ITALY AGRI FINAN PROC/MFG PLAN INT/TRADE CONTROL PWR 19. PAGE 51 F0990 NAT/LISM PRESS POLICY B65

OECD,THE MEDITERRANEAN REGIONAL PROJECT: ITALY; EDUCATION AND DEVELOPMENT. ITALY SOCIETY STRATA FINAN NAT/G PROF/ORG WORKER PLAN PROB/SOLV ADMIN ...STAT CHARTS METH 20 OECD. PAGE 100 F1971 SCHOOL EDU/PROP ECO/UNDEV ACADEM B65

WEIL G.L.,A HANDBOOK ON THE EUROPEAN ECONOMIC COMMUNITY. BELGIUM EUR+WWI FRANCE GERMANY/W ITALY CONSTN ECO/DEV CREATE PARTIC GP/REL...DECISION MGT CHARTS 20 EEC. PAGE 144 F2846 INT/TRADE INT/ORG TEC/DEV INT/LAW S65

MUNZI U.,"THE EUROPEAN SOCIAL FUND IN THE DEVELOPMENT OF THE MEDITERRANEAN REGIONS OF THE EEC." FUT GREECE ITALY PORTUGAL SPAIN TURKEY WORKER TEC/DEV ECO/TAC REGION...STAT EEC. PAGE 95 F1862 ECO/UNDEV PREDICT RECORD B66

FRANKEL P.H.,MATTEI: OIL AND POWER POLITICS. ITALY EXTR/IND MARKET GP/REL NAT/LISM SOCISM...POLICY MGT BIOG 20 MATTEI/E. PAGE 43 F0844 LEAD NAT/G CONTROL LG/CO

B67
BANFIELD E.C.,THE MORAL BASIS OF A BACKWARD SOCIETY. EUR+WWI ITALY STRATA NEIGH PARTIC INGP/REL ...SOC QU PREDICT TREND HYPO/EXP MUNICH 20. PAGE 9 F0173 MORAL WEALTH ATTIT

B67
EVANS R.H.,COEXISTENCE: COMMUNISM AND ITS PRACTICE IN BOLOGNA, 1945-1965. ITALY CAP/ISM ADMIN CHOOSE PEACE ORD/FREE...SOC STAT DEEP/INT SAMP CHARTS BIBLIOG MUNICH 20. PAGE 39 F0756 MARXISM CULTURE POL/PAR

B67
GORZ A.,STRATEGY FOR LABOR: A RADICAL PROPOSAL (TRANS. BY MARTIN NICOLAUS AND VICTORIA ORTIZ). EUR+WWI FRANCE ITALY ECO/DEV POL/PAR OP/RES PLAN GP/REL ALL/IDEOS...SOC 20 EEC. PAGE 49 F0965 LABOR PWR STRUCT ECO/TAC

S67
BAILEY S.L.,"THE ITALIANS AND ORGANIZED LABOR IN THE UNITED STATES AND ARGENTINA: 1880-1910." ITALY USA-45 PARTIC HABITAT PWR...GEOG GP/COMP 19/20 ARGEN. PAGE 8 F0153 LABOR LEAD WEALTH GP/REL

S67
CAMMETT J.M.,"COMMUNIST THEORIES OF FASCISM, 1920-35." ITALY POL/PAR PROF/ORG VOL/ASSN WORKER COLONIAL TOTALISM...SOCIALIST 20. PAGE 21 F0403 MARXISM FASCISM ATTIT

S67
SCHACHTER G.,"REGIONAL DEVELOPMENT IN THE ITALIAN DUAL ECONOMY" ITALY AGRI INDUS MARKET WORKER ECO/TAC CONTROL INCOME PRODUC 20. PAGE 116 F2287 REGION ECO/UNDEV NAT/G PROB/SOLV

ITO....INTERNATIONAL TRADE ORGANIZATION

ITU....INTERNATIONAL TELECOMMUNICATIONS UNION

IVORY COAST....SEE IVORY/CST

IVORY/CST....IVORY COAST; SEE ALSO AFR

IWW....INTERNATIONAL WORKERS OF THE WORLD

J

JACKSON G.D. F1293

JACKSON M.V. F1294

JACKSON R.G.A. F1295

JACKSON/A....PRESIDENT ANDREW JACKSON

JACKSON/RH....R.H. JACKSON

JACOBINISM....JACOBINISM: FRENCH DEMOCRATIC REVOLUTIONARY DOCTRINE, 1789

JACOBS P. F1296,F1297

JACOBSON H.K. F1298

JACOBSSON P. F1299

JACOBY N.H. F1300,F1301

JACOBY S.B. F1302

JAFFA/HU....H.U. JAFFA

JAFFEE A.J. F1303

JAIN S.C. F1304

JAKARTA....JAKARTA, INDONESIA

JAMAICA....SEE ALSO L/A+17C

JANET/P....PIERRE JANET

JANSSEN P. F1305

JAPAN....SEE ALSO ASIA

JARMO....JARMO, A PRE- OR EARLY HISTORIC SOCIETY

JASNY H. F1306

JASPERS/K....KARL JASPERS

JAT....A POLITICAL SYSTEM OF INDIA

JAURES/JL....JEAN LEON JAURES (FRENCH SOCIALIST 1859-1914)

JAVA....JAVA, INDONESIA; SEE ALSO INDONESIA

B62
SELOSOEMARDJAN O.,SOCIAL CHANGES IN JOGJAKARTA. INDONESIA NETHERLAND ELITES STRATA STRUCT FAM POL/PAR CREATE DIPLOM INT/TRADE EDU/PROP ADMIN GOV/REL...SOC 20 JAVA CHINJAP. PAGE 119 F2352 ECO/UNDEV CULTURE REV COLONIAL

JAVITS B.A. F1307

JAVITS J.K. F1308,F1309

JEDLICKI W. F1310

JEFFERSN/T....PRESIDENT THOMAS JEFFERSON

JEHOVA/WIT....JEHOVAHOS WITNESSES

JENCKS C.E. F1311,F1312

JENCKS/C....C. JENCKS

JENKINS C. F1313

JENNINGS W.I. F1314,F1315,F1316

JENSEN F.B. F1317

JEVONS W.S. F1318,F1319

JEWS....JEWS, JUDAISM

B48
KESSELMAN L.C.,THE SOCIAL POLITICS OF THE FEPC. INDUS WORKER EDU/PROP GP/REL RACE/REL 20 NEGRO JEWS FEPC. PAGE 70 F1382 POLICY NAT/G ADMIN DISCRIM

S67
GEISS I.,"THE GERMANS AND THE MIDDLE EAST CRISIS." GERMANY/W ISLAM ISRAEL USSR POL/PAR RACE/REL MARXISM...GP/COMP 20 JEWS. PAGE 47 F0914 ATTIT DIPLOM WAR POLICY

JHANGIANI M.A. F1320

JOHN/XXII....POPE JOHN XXII

JOHN/XXIII....POPE JOHN XXIII

JOHNSN/ALB....ALBERT JOHNSON

JOHNSN/AND....PRESIDENT ANDREW JOHNSON

JOHNSN/LB....PRESIDENT LYNDON BAINES JOHNSON

JOHNSON D.G. F1321,F1322

JOHNSON H.G. F1323,F1324,F1325,F1326,F1327,F1328

JOHNSON L.B. F1329

JOHNSON L.L. F1330

JOHNSON R.B. F1331

JOHNSON/D....D. JOHNSON

JOHNSON/LB....PRESIDENT LYNDON BAINES JOHNSON

B64
HARRIS S.E.,ECONOMICS OF THE KENNEDY YEARS AND A LOOK AHEAD. USA+45 PLAN BUDGET NEW/LIB...STAT RECORD IDEA/COMP PERS/COMP INDEX 20 KENNEDY/JF EISNHWR/DD JOHNSON/LB. PAGE 56 F1091 ECO/TAC CHIEF POLICY NAT/G

B65
SHOSTAK A.B.,NEW PERSPECTIVES ON POVERTY. USA+45 SCHOOL WORKER INGP/REL RACE/REL AGE/C AGE/Y ATTIT HEALTH...ANTHOL BIBLIOG 20 JOHNSON/LB POVRTY/WAR. PAGE 121 F2388 WEALTH NAT/G RECEIVE INCOME

B67
LISS S.B.,THE CANAL, ASPECTS OF UNITED STATES-PANAMANIAN RELATIONS. AFR FUT PANAMA DOMIN COERCE ATTIT SOVEREIGN MARXISM 20 JOHNSON/LB KENNEDY/JF. PAGE 81 F1580 DIPLOM POLICY

B67
PELTASON J.W.,FUNCTIONS AND POLICIES OF AMERICAN GOVERNMENT (3RD ED.). USA+45 FINAN INDUS EDU/PROP CIVMIL/REL RACE/REL ORD/FREE...ANTHOL T 20 JOHNSON/LB. PAGE 104 F2052 NAT/G GOV/REL POLICY PLAN

S67
AGUILAR M.A.,"?UNA OEA MAS FUERTE O UNA AMERICA LATINA MAS DEBIL?" L/A+17C USA+45 USA-45 ECO/UNDEV INDUS CHIEF DELIB/GP FORCES CONTROL PWR 20 OAS KENNEDY/JF JOHNSON/LB. PAGE 3 F0050 INT/ORG DIPLOM POLICY COLONIAL

JOHNSTN/GD....GEORGE D. JOHNSTON

JOHNSTON B.F. F1332

JOHNSTON J. F1333

JOHNSTON J.D. F1334

JOHNSTONE A. F1335

JOHR W.A. F1336

JOINT ECONOMIC COMMITTEE F1337

JONES G.N. F0066

JONES J.H. F1338

JONES M.M. F1339

JONES T.B. F1340

JONESVILLE....JONESVILLE: LOCATION OF W.L. WARNEROS "DEMOCRACY IN JONESVILLE"

JORDAN A.A. F1341

JORDAN....SEE ALSO ISLAM

B57
PATAI R.,JORDAN, LEBANON AND SYRIA: AN ANNOTATED BIBLIOGRAPHY. ISLAM JORDAN LEBANON SYRIA...GEOG 20. PAGE 103 F2034
BIBLIOG/A SOC

N67
US SENATE COMM ON FOREIGN REL,WAR OR PEACE IN THE MIDDLE EAST (PAMPHLET). GREECE ISLAM ISRAEL JORDAN UAR CHIEF PROB/SOLV FOR/AID WAR PWR 20 SENATE. PAGE 139 F2739
DIPLOM FORCES PLAN

JOURNALISM....SEE PRESS

JUAN T.L. F1342

JUCKER-FLEETWOOD E. F1343,F1344

JUDGE....JUDGES; SEE ALSO ADJUD

B60
MENDELSON W.,CAPITALISM, DEMOCRACY, AND THE SUPREME COURT. USA+45 USA-45 CONSTN DIPLOM GOV/REL ATTIT ORD/FREE LAISSEZ...POLICY CHARTS PERS/COMP 18/20 SUPREME/CT MARSHALL/J HOLMES/OW TANEY/RB FIELD/JJ. PAGE 90 F1758
JUDGE CT/SYS JURID NAT/G

B62
INTERNAT CONGRESS OF JURISTS,EXECUTIVE ACTION AND THE RULE OF RULE: REPORTION PROCEEDINGS OF INT'T CONGRESS OF JURISTS,-RIO DE JANEIRO, BRAZIL. WOR+45 ACADEM CONSULT JUDGE EDU/PROP ADJUD CT/SYS INGP/REL PERSON DEPT/DEFEN. PAGE 64 F1269
JURID EXEC ORD/FREE CONTROL

B63
PRITCHETT C.H.,THE THIRD BRANCH OF GOVERNMENT. USA+45 USA-45 CONSTN SOCIETY INDUS SECT LEGIS JUDGE PROB/SOLV GOV/REL 20 SUPREME/CT CHURCH/STA. PAGE 108 F2122
JURID NAT/G ADJUD CT/SYS

B67
EGGERT G.G.,RAILROAD LABOR DISPUTES. USA+45 USA-45 ELITES DIST/IND DELIB/GP FORCES JUDGE WORKER PROB/SOLV DOMIN PWR...POLICY 20. PAGE 36 F0707
GP/REL NAT/G LABOR BARGAIN

B67
PETRO S.,THE KINGSPORT STRIKE. USA+45 PROC/MFG NAT/G JUDGE PRESS PARTIC PERS/REL...OLD/LIB OBS INT 20 NLRB. PAGE 105 F2074
LABOR COERCE SANCTION ALL/VALS

L67
STRUVE G.M.,"THE LESS-RESTRICTIVE-ALTERNATIVE PRINCIPLE AND ECONOMIC DUE PROCESS." USA+45 ECO/DEV LABOR NAT/G CONSULT DELIB/GP OP/RES PLAN WEALTH. PAGE 127 F2505
JURID JUDGE SANCTION CAP/ISM

S67
STEINHEIMER R.L. JR.,"THE UNIFORM COMMERCIAL CODE COMES OF AGE." USA+45 FINAN ACADEM JUDGE. PAGE 126 F2477
ADJUD LEGIS INT/TRADE GOV/REL

JUDICIAL PROCESS....SEE ADJUD

JUGOSLAVIA....SEE YUGOSLAVIA

JUNKER ....JUNKER: REACTIONARY PRUSSIAN ARISTOCRACY

JURID....LAW

N
UNIVERSITY OF FLORIDA,CARIBBEAN ACQUISITIONS: MATERIALS ACQUIRED BY THE UNIVERSITY OF FLORIDA 1957-1960. L/A+17C...ART/METH GEOG MGT 20. PAGE 133 F2620
BIBLIOG ECO/UNDEV EDU/PROP JURID

B12
FOUAD M.,LE REGIME DE LA PRESSE EN EGYPTE: THESE POUR LE DOCTORAT. UAR LICENSE EDU/PROP ADMIN SANCTION CRIME SUPEGO PWR...ART/METH JURID 19/20. PAGE 43 F0832
ORD/FREE LEGIS CONTROL PRESS

N19
FAHRNKOPF N.,STATE AND LOCAL GOVERNMENT IN ILLINOIS (PAMPHLET). CONSTN ADMIN PARTIC CHOOSE REPRESENT GOV/REL...JURID MGT 20 ILLINOIS. PAGE 39 F0759
BIBLIOG LOC/G LEGIS CT/SYS

B24
HOLDSWORTH W.S.,A HISTORY OF ENGLISH LAW; THE COMMON LAW AND ITS RIVALS (VOL. VI). AFR UK STRATA EX/STRUC ADJUD ADMIN CONTROL CT/SYS...JURID CONCPT GEN/LAWS 17 PARLIAMENT ENGLSH/LAW COMMON/LAW. PAGE 61 F1194
LAW CONSTN LEGIS CHIEF

B24
HOLDSWORTH W.S.,A HISTORY OF ENGLISH LAW; THE COMMON LAW AND ITS RIVALS (VOL. IV). UK SEA AGRI CHIEF ADJUD CONTROL CRIME GOV/REL...INT/LAW JURID NAT/COMP 16/17 PARLIAMENT COMMON/LAW CANON/LAW ENGLSH/LAW. PAGE 61 F1195
LAW LEGIS CT/SYS CONSTN

B28
FRANKFURTER F.,THE BUSINESS OF THE SUPREME COURT; A STUDY IN THE FEDERAL JUDICIAL SYSTEM. USA-45 CONSTN EX/STRUC PROB/SOLV GP/REL ATTIT PWR...POLICY JURID 18/20 SUPREME/CT CONGRESS. PAGE 43 F0848
CT/SYS ADJUD LAW FEDERAL

B42
ROBBINS J.J.,THE GOVERNMENT OF LABOR RELATIONS IN SWEDEN. SWEDEN LAW CONSTN ADJUD CT/SYS GP/REL ...JURID 20. PAGE 112 F2200
NAT/G BARGAIN LABOR INDUS

L42
GRANT J.A.C.,"THE GUILD RETURNS TO AMERICA." CHRIST-17C USA-45 LEGIS LICENSE ADJUD CONTROL GP/REL. PAGE 50 F0978
PROF/ORG JURID LABOR PWR

B48
KEIR D.L.,CASES IN CONSTITUTIONAL LAW. UK CHIEF LEGIS DIPLOM TAX PARL/PROC CRIME GOV/REL...INT/LAW JURID 17/20. PAGE 70 F1368
CONSTN LAW ADJUD CT/SYS

B51
COOKE C.A.,CORPORATION TRUST AND COMPANY: AN ESSAY IN LEGAL HISTORY. UK STRUCT LEGIS CAP/ISM GP/REL PROFIT 13/20 COMPNY/ACT. PAGE 27 F0531
LG/CO FINAN ECO/TAC JURID

B51
OWENS R.N.,BUSINESS, ORGANIZATION, AND COMBINATION. USA+45 USA-45 LAW NAT/G LEGIS ECO/TAC CONTROL INGP/REL...JURID GP/COMP 20 NEW/DEAL. PAGE 102 F2006
SML/CO LG/CO STRUCT GP/REL

B52
JENNINGS W.I.,CONSTITUTIONAL LAWS OF THE COMMONWEALTH. AFR UK LAW CHIEF LEGIS TAX CT/SYS PARL/PROC GOV/REL...INT/LAW 18/20 ENGLSH/LAW COMMON/LAW. PAGE 67 F1316
CONSTN JURID ADJUD COLONIAL

B54
FRIEDMAN W.,THE PUBLIC CORPORATION: A COMPARATIVE SYMPOSIUM (UNIVERSITY OF TORONTO SCHOOL OF LAW COMPARATIVE LAW SERIES, VOL. I). AFR SWEDEN USA+45 INDUS INT/ORG NAT/G REGION CENTRAL FEDERAL...POLICY JURID IDEA/COMP NAT/COMP ANTHOL 20 MONOPOLY EUROPE. PAGE 44 F0861
LAW SOCISM LG/CO OWN

B55
MOHL R.V.,DIE GESCHICHTE UND LITERATUR DER STAATSWISSENSCHAFTEN (3 VOLS.). LAW NAT/G...JURID METH/COMP METH. PAGE 92 F1814
PHIL/SCI MOD/EUR

B56
FIELD G.C.,POLITICAL THEORY. POL/PAR REPRESENT MORAL SOVEREIGN...JURID IDEA/COMP. PAGE 40 F0789
CONCPT NAT/G ORD/FREE DIPLOM

B56
WEBER M.,WIRTSCHAFT UND GESELLSCHAFT (2ND VOL.). STRUCT NAT/G POL/PAR LEAD PWR OBJECTIVE IDEA/COMP. PAGE 144 F2841
LEGIT JURID SOC

S57
CUNNINGHAM E.M.,"THE BUSINESS MAN AND HIS LAWYER." USA+45 LG/CO SML/CO TOP/EX CHOOSE SKILL...JURID MGT 20. PAGE 29 F0561
CONSULT LAW DECISION SERV/IND

B58
BUGEDA LANZAS J.,A STATEMENT OF THE LAWS OF CUBA IN MATTERS AFFECTING BUSINESS (2ND ED. REV., ENLARGED). CUBA L/A+17C LAW FINAN FAM LEGIS ACT/RES ADMIN GP/REL...BIBLIOG 20 OAS. PAGE 20 F0382
JURID NAT/G INDUS WORKER

B58
CHAMBERLIN E.H.,LABOR UNIONS AND PUBLIC POLICY. PLAN BARGAIN SANCTION INGP/REL JURID. PAGE 23 F0444
LABOR WEALTH PWR NAT/G

B58
WOODS H.D.,PATTERNS OF INDUSTRIAL DISPUTE SETTLEMENT IN FIVE CANADIAN INDUSTRIES. CANADA USA+45 CONSULT ADJUD GP/REL...JURID GOV/COMP
BARGAIN INDUS LABOR

METH/COMP ANTHOL 20. PAGE 148 F2923 NAT/G

B59
GOMEZ ROBLES J.,A STATEMENT OF THE LAWS OF JURID
GUATEMALA IN MATTERS AFFECTING BUSINESS (2ND ED. NAT/G
REV., ENLARGED). GUATEMALA L/A+17C LAW FINAN FAM INDUS
WORKER ACT/RES DIPLOM ADJUD ADMIN GP/REL 20 OAS. LEGIT
PAGE 48 F0945

B60
ATOMIC INDUSTRIAL FORUM,ATOMS FOR INDUSTRY: WORLD NUC/PWR
FORUM. WOR+45 FINAN COST UTIL...JURID ANTHOL 20. INDUS
PAGE 7 F0137 PLAN
PROB/SOLV

B60
GONZALEZ NAVARRO M.,LA COLONIZACION EN MEXICO, ECO/UNDEV
1877-1910. AGRI NAT/G PLAN PROB/SOLV INCOME GEOG
...POLICY JURID CENSUS 19/20 MEXIC/AMER MIGRATION. HABITAT
PAGE 48 F0947 COLONIAL

B60
MARSHALL A.H.,FINANCIAL ADMINISTRATION IN LOCAL FINAN
GOVERNMENT. UK DELIB/GP CONFER COST INCOME PERSON LOC/G
...JURID 20. PAGE 86 F1679 BUDGET
ADMIN

B60
MENDELSON W.,CAPITALISM, DEMOCRACY, AND THE SUPREME JUDGE
COURT. USA+45 USA-45 CONSTN DIPLOM GOV/REL ATTIT CT/SYS
ORD/FREE LAISSEZ...POLICY CHARTS PERS/COMP 18/20 JURID
SUPREME/CT MARSHALL/J HOLMES/OW TANEY/RB FIELD/JJ. NAT/G
PAGE 90 F1758

B61
BEASLEY K.E.,STATE SUPERVISION OF MUNICIPAL DEBT IN LOC/G
KANSAS - A CASE STUDY. USA+45 USA-45 FINAN PROVS LEGIS
BUDGET TAX ADJUD ADMIN CONTROL SUPEGO MUNICH. JURID
PAGE 12 F0224

B61
SEPULVEDA C.,A STATEMENT OF THE LAWS OF MEXICO IN CONSTN
MATTERS AFFECTING BUSINESS (3RD ED.). AGRI DIST/IND NAT/G
EXTR/IND FINAN INDUS WORKER TAX MARRIAGE OWN JURID
ORD/FREE...BIBLIOG 20 MEXIC/AMER TREATY MIGRATION LEGIS
MONOPOLY. PAGE 119 F2356

B61
STARNER F.L.,GENERAL OBLIGATION BOND FINANCING BY FINAN
LOCAL GOVERNMENTS: A SURVEY OF STATE CONTROLS. LOC/G
CANADA UK USA+45 CONSTN PROVS...POLICY JURID GOV/REL
METH/COMP 20 EUROPE CALIFORNIA. PAGE 125 F2471 ADJUD

N61
US ADVISORY COMM INTERGOV REL,STATE AND LOCAL PROVS
TAXATION ON PRIVATELY OWNED PROPERTY LOCATED ON LOC/G
FEDERAL AREAS: PROPOSED AMENDMENT OF BUCK ACT NAT/G
(PAMPHLET). USA+45 ACT/RES PLAN CONTROL GOV/REL TAX
INGP/REL OWN...POLICY JURID CHARTS GP/COMP 20.
PAGE 133 F2629

B62
ALEXANDROWICZ C.H.,WORLD ECONOMIC AGENCIES: LAW AND INT/LAW
PRACTICE. WOR+45 DIST/IND FINAN LABOR CONSULT INT/ORG
INT/TRADE TARIFFS REPRESENT HEALTH...JURID 20 UN DIPLOM
GATT EEC OAS ECSC. PAGE 4 F0064 ADJUD

B62
DE LAVALLE H.,A STATEMENT OF THE LAWS OF PERU IN CONSTN
MATTERS AFFECTING BUSINESS (3RD ED.). PERU WORKER JURID
INT/TRADE INCOME ORD/FREE...INT/LAW 20. PAGE 31 FINAN
F0603 TAX

B62
HIRSCHFIELD R.S.,THE CONSTITUTION AND THE COURT. ADJUD
AFR SCHOOL WAR RACE/REL EQUILIB ORD/FREE...POLICY PWR
MAJORIT DECISION JURID 18/20 PRESIDENT CIVIL/LIB CONSTN
SUPREME/CT CONGRESS. PAGE 60 F1175 LAW

B62
INTERNAT CONGRESS OF JURISTS,EXECUTIVE ACTION AND JURID
THE RULE OF RULE: REPORTION PROCEEDINGS OF INT'T EXEC
CONGRESS OF JURISTS,-RIO DE JANEIRO, BRAZIL. WOR+45 ORD/FREE
ACADEM CONSULT JUDGE EDU/PROP ADJUD CT/SYS INGP/REL CONTROL
PERSON DEPT/DEFEN. PAGE 64 F1269

B62
LITTLEFIELD N.,METROPOLITAN AREA PROBLEMS AND LOC/G
MUNICIPAL HOME RULE. USA+45 PROVS ADMIN CONTROL SOVEREIGN
GP/REL PWR. PAGE 81 F1586 JURID
LEGIS

B62
URQUIDI C.W.,A STATEMENT OF THE LAWS OF BOLIVIA IN JURID
MATTERS AFFECTING BUSINESS (3RD ED. REV., INDUS
ENLARGED). L/A+17C LAW FINAN FAM WORKER ACT/RES NAT/G
DIPLOM ADJUD ADMIN GP/REL 20 BOLIV OAS. PAGE 133 LEGIT
F2626

B62
US ADVISORY COMN INTERGOV REL,STATE CONSTITUTIONAL LOC/G
AND STATUTORY RESTRICTIONS ON LOCAL TAXING POWERS. PROVS
USA+45 USA-45 LAW CONSTN ACT/RES CONTROL WEALTH GOV/REL
...JURID CHARTS 20. PAGE 133 F2632 TAX

S62
PIQUEMAL M.,"LA COOPERATION FINANCIERE ENTRE LA AFR
FRANCE ET LES ETATS AFRICAINS ET MALGACHE." ISLAM FINAN
INT/ORG TOP/EX ECO/TAC...JURID CHARTS 20. PAGE 106 FRANCE
F2089 MADAGASCAR

B63
BURRUS B.R.,ADMINSTRATIVE LAW AND LOCAL GOVERNMENT. EX/STRUC
USA+45 PROVS LEGIS LICENSE ADJUD ORD/FREE 20. LOC/G
PAGE 20 F0392 JURID
CONSTN

B63
CORLEY R.N.,THE LEGAL ENVIRONMENT OF BUSINESS. NAT/G
CONSTN LEGIS TAX ADMIN CT/SYS DISCRIM ATTIT PWR INDUS
...TREND 18/20. PAGE 28 F0537 JURID
DECISION

B63
PRITCHETT C.H.,THE THIRD BRANCH OF GOVERNMENT. JURID
USA+45 USA-45 CONSTN SOCIETY INDUS SECT LEGIS JUDGE NAT/G
PROB/SOLV GOV/REL 20 SUPREME/CT CHURCH/STA. ADJUD
PAGE 108 F2122 CT/SYS

B64
ECONOMIDES C.P.,LE POUVOIR DE DECISION DES INT/ORG
ORGANISATIONS INTERNATIONALES EUROPEENNES. DIPLOM PWR
DOMIN INGP/REL EFFICIENCY...INT/LAW JURID 20 NATO DECISION
OEEC EEC COUNCL/EUR EURATOM. PAGE 36 F0698 GP/COMP

B64
FISK W.M.,ADMINISTRATIVE PROCEDURE IN A REGULATORY SERV/IND
AGENCY: THE CAB AND THE NEW YORK-CHICAGO CASE ECO/DEV
(PAMPHLET). USA+45 DIST/IND ADMIN CONTROL LOBBY AIR
GP/REL ROLE ORD/FREE NEWYORK/C CHICAGO CAB. PAGE 41 JURID
F0805

B64
GARFIELD PJ LOVEJOY WF,PUBLIC UTILITY T
ECONOMICS. DIST/IND FINAN MARKET ADMIN COST DEMAND ECO/TAC
...TECHNIC JURID MUNICH 20 MONOPOLY. PAGE 46 F0906 OWN
SERV/IND

B64
HAAR C.M.,LAW AND LAND: ANGLO-AMERICAN PLANNING LAW
PRACTICE. UK USA+45 NAT/G TEC/DEV BUDGET CT/SYS PLAN
INGP/REL EFFICIENCY OWN...JURID MUNICH 20. PAGE 52 NAT/COMP
F1019

B64
MANN B.,STATE CONSTITUTIONAL RESTRICTIONS ON LOCAL LOC/G
BORROWING AND PROPERTY TAXING POWERS. USA+45 CONSTN TAX
PROVS CT/SYS GOV/REL PWR...DECISION JURID CHARTS FINAN
20. PAGE 84 F1654 LAW

B64
RUSTAMJI R.F.,THE LAW OF INDUSTRIAL DISPUTES IN INDUS
INDIA. INDIA LEGIS WORKER CONTROL GP/REL...JURID ADJUD
MGT TIME/SEQ 20. PAGE 115 F2264 BARGAIN
LABOR

B64
WHEARE K.C.,FEDERAL GOVERNMENT (4TH ED.). WOR+45 FEDERAL
WOR-45 POL/PAR LEGIS BAL/PWR CT/SYS...POLICY JURID CONSTN
CONCPT GOV/COMP 17/20. PAGE 145 F2866 EX/STRUC
NAT/COMP

B65
DOWD L.P.,PRINCIPLES OF WORLD BUSINESS. SERV/IND INT/TRADE
NAT/G DIPLOM ECO/TAC TARIFFS...INT/LAW JURID 20. MGT
PAGE 34 F0657 FINAN
MARKET

B65
LUGO-MARENCO J.J.,A STATEMENT OF THE LAWS OF CONSTN
NICARAGUA IN MATTERS AFFECTING BUSINESS. NICARAGUA NAT/G
AGRI DIST/IND EXTR/IND FINAN INDUS FAM WORKER LEGIS
INT/TRADE TAX MARRIAGE OWN BIO/SOC 20 TREATY JURID
RESOURCE/N MIGRATION. PAGE 82 F1606

B65
O'CONNELL D.P.,INTERNATIONAL LAW (2 VOLS.). WOR+45 INT/LAW
WOR-45 ECO/DEV ECO/UNDEV INT/ORG NAT/G AGREE DIPLOM
...POLICY JURID CONCPT NAT/COMP 20 TREATY. PAGE 99 CT/SYS
F1952

B65
VON RENESSE E.A.,UNVOLLENDETE DEMOKRATIEN. AFR ECO/UNDEV
ISLAM S/ASIA SOCIETY ACT/RES COLONIAL...JURID NAT/COMP
CHARTS BIBLIOG METH 13/20. PAGE 142 F2795 SOVEREIGN

B65
WURFEL S.W.,FOREIGN ENTERPRISE IN COLOMBIA. FINAN ECO/UNDEV
LABOR NAT/G ECO/TAC TAX REGION 20 COLOMB. PAGE 149 INT/TRADE
F2944 JURID
CAP/ISM

L65
FORTE W.E.,"THE FOOD AND DRUG ADMINISTRATION, THE CONTROL
FEDERAL TRADE COMMISSION AND THE DECEPTIVE HEALTH
PACKAGING." ROUTINE...JURID 20 FTC. PAGE 43 F0831 ADJUD
INDUS

B66
EDWARDS C.D.,TRADE REGULATIONS OVERSEAS. IRELAND INT/TRADE
NEW/ZEALND SOUTH/AFR NAT/G CAP/ISM TARIFFS CONTROL DIPLOM
...POLICY JURID 20 EEC CHINJAP. PAGE 36 F0703 INT/LAW
ECO/TAC

B66
MC CONNELL J.P.,LAW AND BUSINESS: PATTERNS AND ECO/DEV
ISSUES IN COMMERCIAL LAW. USA+45 USA-45 LOC/G JURID
WORKER LICENSE CRIME REPRESENT GP/REL 20. PAGE 87 ADJUD
F1713 MGT

B66
SOVERN M.I.,LEGAL RESTRAINTS ON RACIAL DISCRIM
DISCRIMINATION IN EMPLOYMENT. USA+45 LAW INDUS RACE/REL
LG/CO SML/CO DELIB/GP LEGIS SANCTION 20 NLRB WORKER
PRESIDENT NEGRO CIV/RIGHTS RAILROAD. PAGE 124 F2446 JURID

B67
BEAL E.F.,THE PRACTICE OF COLLECTIVE BARGAINING BARGAIN
(3RD ED.). USA+45 WOR+45 ECO/DEV INDUS LG/CO MGT

PROF/ORG WORKER ECO/TAC GP/REL WEALTH...JURID METH/CNCPT. PAGE 12 F0221 LABOR ADJUD

B67

BIBBY J.,ON CAPITOL HILL. POL/PAR LOBBY PARL/PROC GOV/REL PERS/REL...JURID PHIL/SCI OBS INT BIBLIOG 20 CONGRESS PRESIDENT. PAGE 15 F0278 CONFER LEGIS CREATE LEAD

B67

COHEN M.R.,LAW AND THE SOCIAL ORDER: ESSAYS IN LEGAL PHILOSOPHY. USA-45 CONSULT WORKER ECO/TAC ATTIT WEALTH...POLICY WELF/ST SOC 20 NEW/DEAL DEPRESSION. PAGE 26 F0497 JURID LABOR IDEA/COMP

B67

DIEGUES M.,SOCIAL SCIENCE IN LATIN AMERICA. L/A+17C ...JURID SOC ANTHOL 20. PAGE 33 F0637 METH ACADEM EDU/PROP ACT/RES

B67

HANNAH H.W.,THE LEGAL BASE FOR UNIVERSITIES IN DEVELOPING COUNTRIES. AFR ASIA L/A+17C S/ASIA USA+45 FINAN CREATE EDU/PROP TASK EFFICIENCY ...JURID METH/COMP 20. PAGE 54 F1060 ADMIN LAW ACADEM LEGIS

B67

HODGKINSON R.G.,THE ORIGINS OF THE NATIONAL HEALTH SERVICE: THE MEDICAL SERVICES OF THE NEW POOR LAW, 1834-1871. UK INDUS WORKER PROB/SOLV EFFICIENCY ATTIT HEALTH WEALTH SOCISM...JURID SOC/WK MUNICH 19/20. PAGE 60 F1189 HEAL NAT/G POLICY LAW

B67

MARCUS S.,COMPETITION AND THE LAW. USA+45 INDUS LG/CO NAT/G CONSERVE LAISSEZ...BIBLIOG 20 FTC SUPREME/CT. PAGE 85 F1665 LAW ECO/DEV FINAN JURID

B67

MEYERS M.,SOURCES OF THE AMERICAN REPUBLIC; A DOCUMENTARY HISTORY OF POLITICS, SOCIETY, AND THOUGHT (VOL. I, REV. ED.). USA-45 CULTURE STRUCT NAT/G LEGIS LEAD ATTIT...JURID SOC ANTHOL 17/19 PRESIDENT. PAGE 90 F1772 COLONIAL REV WAR

B67

MURTY B.S.,PROPAGANDA AND WORLD PUBLIC ORDER. FUT WOR+45 COM/IND INT/ORG PROB/SOLV ATTIT KNOWL ORD/FREE...POLICY UN. PAGE 95 F1868 EDU/PROP DIPLOM CONTROL JURID

B67

ROELOFS H.M.,THE LANGUAGE OF MODERN POLITICS: AN INTRODUCTION TO THE STUDY OF GOVERNMENT. DIPLOM ADMIN MARXISM NEW/LIB...JURID CONCPT METH/COMP T 20. PAGE 113 F2230 LEAD NAT/COMP PERS/REL NAT/G

B67

SCHAEFER W.V.,THE SUSPECT AND SOCIETY: CRIMINAL PROCEDURE AND CONVERGING CONSTITUTIONAL DOCTRINES. USA+45 TEC/DEV LOBBY ROUTINE SANCTION...INT 20. PAGE 116 F2288 CRIME FORCES CONSTN JURID

B67

SCOTT J.C.,ANTITRUST AND TRADE REGULATION TODAY: 1967. USA+45 MARKET LG/CO DELIB/GP LEGIS CAP/ISM INT/TRADE TAX PRICE INGP/REL WEALTH 20 SUPREME/CT. PAGE 118 F2334 NAT/G INDUS CONTROL JURID

B67

SPICER G.W.,THE SUPREME COURT AND FUNDAMENTAL FREEDOMS (2ND ED.). USA+45 CONSTN SOCIETY ATTIT 20 SUPREME/CT. PAGE 124 F2454 CT/SYS JURID CONTROL ORD/FREE

B67

ULMAN L.,CHALLENGES TO COLLECTIVE BARGAINING. ECO/TAC DISCRIM EQUILIB ATTIT...JURID SOC/WK. PAGE 132 F2599 LABOR BARGAIN ADJUD POLICY

L67

AFFELDT R.J.,"THE INDEPENDENT LABOR UNION AND THE GOOD LIFE." USA+45 ADJUD CONTROL SANCTION GP/REL ORD/FREE JURID. PAGE 3 F0045 LABOR CT/SYS PWR SOVEREIGN

L67

COSTANZA J.F.,"WHOLESOME NEUTRALITY: LAW AND EDUCATION." USA+45 GIVE EDU/PROP ADJUD CONTROL GP/REL...DECISION JURID. PAGE 28 F0540 SECT PROVS ACADEM

L67

DOERFER G.L.,"THE LIMITS ON TRADE SECRET LAW IMPOSED BY FEDERAL PATENT & ANTITRUST SUPREMACY." USA+45 LAW R+D CAP/ISM LICENSE CONTROL SANCTION ORD/FREE. PAGE 33 F0651 JURID GOV/REL POLICY LEGIT

L67

DROBNIG U.,"CONFLICT OF LAWS AND THE EUROPEAN ECONOMIC COMMUNITY." EUR+WWI PROB/SOLV DIPLOM ...JURID EEC. PAGE 34 F0663 INT/LAW ADJUD INT/ORG MARKET

L67

GOLD J.,"INTERPRETATION BY THE INTERNATIONAL MONETARY FUND OF ITS ARTICLES OF AGREEMENT." INT/TRADE ADJUD ATTIT...POLICY JURID. PAGE 48 F0933 CONSTN INT/ORG LAW DIPLOM

L67

JACOBY S.B.,"THE 89TH CONGRESS AND GOVERNMENT LITIGATION." USA+45 ADMIN COST...JURID 20 CONGRESS. PAGE 66 F1302 LAW NAT/G ADJUD SANCTION

L67

MANNE H.G.,"OUR TWO CORPORATION SYSTEMS* LAW AND ECONOMICS." LAW CONTROL SANCTION GP/REL...JURID 20. PAGE 85 F1657 INDUS ELITES CAP/ISM ADMIN

L67

STRUVE G.M.,"THE LESS-RESTRICTIVE-ALTERNATIVE PRINCIPLE AND ECONOMIC DUE PROCESS." USA+45 ECO/DEV LABOR NAT/G CONSULT DELIB/GP OP/RES PLAN WEALTH. PAGE 127 F2505 JURID JUDGE SANCTION CAP/ISM

L67

WHITNEY S.N.,"MERGERS, CONGLOMERATES, AND OLIGOPOLIES* A WIDENING OF ANTI TRUST TARGETS." LAW NAT/G TEC/DEV CAP/ISM GP/REL PWR...OLD/LIB 20. PAGE 146 F2873 ECO/TAC INDUS JURID

S67

CURTIN W.J.,"NATIONAL EMERGENCY DISPUTES LEGISLATION* ITS NEED AND ITS PROSPECTS IN THE TRANSPORTATION INDUSTRIES." USA+45 ECO/DEV INDUS NAT/G LEGIS ACT/RES BARGAIN POLICY. PAGE 29 F0565 JURID LABOR ADJUD DIST/IND

S67

DANIEL C.,"FREEDOM, EQUITY, AND THE WAR ON POVERTY." USA+45 WORKER ECO/TAC JURID. PAGE 30 F0578 WEALTH INCOME SOCIETY ORD/FREE

S67

FLOYD D.,"FIFTH AMENDMENT RIGHT TO COUNSEL IN FEDERAL INCOME TAX INVESTIGATIONS." USA+45 LAW OP/RES INGP/REL. PAGE 42 F0818 JURID CT/SYS TAX CONSULT

S67

HADDOCK G.B.,"CORPORATE GROWTH AS AFFECTED BY THE FEDERAL ANTITRUST LAWS" ECO/DEV NAT/G PLAN TEC/DEV CAP/ISM ECO/TAC 20. PAGE 53 F1029 INDUS JURID ADJUD

S67

KESTENBAUM L.,"PRIMARY JURISDICTION TO DECIDE ANTITRUST JURISDICTION* A PRACTICAL APPROACH TO THE ALLOCATION OF FUNCTIONS." USA+45 ECO/DEV INDUS VOL/ASSN ECO/TAC. PAGE 70 F1383 JURID CT/SYS LABOR ADJUD

S67

LANDES W.M.,"THE EFFECT OF STATE FAIR EMPLOYMENT LAWS ON THE ECONOMIC POSITION OF NONWHITES." USA+45 PROVS SECT LEGIS ADMIN GP/REL RACE/REL...JURID CONCPT CHARTS HYPO/EXP NEGRO. PAGE 75 F1470 DISCRIM LAW WORKER

S67

LIFLAND W.T.,"BANKING PRACTICE AND THE ANTITRUST LAWS." NAT/G GP/REL...CONCPT IDEA/COMP 20. PAGE 80 F1563 FINAN CAP/ISM JURID

S67

MELTZER B.D.,"RUMINATIONS ABOUT IDEOLOGY, LAW, AND LABOR ARBITRATION." USA+45 ECO/DEV PROB/SOLV CONFER MGT. PAGE 89 F1754 JURID ADJUD LABOR CONSULT

S67

PEMBERTON J., JR.,"CONSTITUTIONAL PROBLEMS IN RESTRAINT ON THE MEDIA." CONSTN PROB/SOLV EDU/PROP CONFER CONTROL JURID. PAGE 104 F2054 LAW PRESS ORD/FREE

S67

PIERPONT J.R.,"NEW STAGE IN THE LONGSHORE STRUGGLE." USA+45 SENIOR ADJUD RACE/REL...JURID 20 NEGRO. PAGE 106 F2083 LABOR DISCRIM WORKER CT/SYS

S67

RAGAN S.,"THE ABA RECOMMENDATIONS: A NEWSPAPERMAN'S CRITIQUE." EDU/PROP CONTROL GP/REL...JURID ABA. PAGE 109 F2136 LAW PRESS ADJUD ORD/FREE

S67

SCRIPP J.,"CONTROLLING PREJUDICIAL PUBLICITY BY THE CONTEMPT POWER: THE BRITISH PRACTICE AND ITS PROSPECT IN AMERICAN LAW." UK USA+45 EDU/PROP CONTROL GP/REL ORD/FREE JURID. PAGE 119 F2338 METH/COMP LAW PRESS ADJUD

S67

SIPPEL D.,"INDIENS UNSICHERE ZUKUNFT." INDIA CULTURE ACADEM POL/PAR LEGIS COLONIAL CHOOSE SOVEREIGN...JURID 20. PAGE 122 F2416 SOCIETY STRUCT ECO/UNDEV NAT/G

S67

SMITH W.H.T.,"THE IMPLICATIONS OF THE AMERICAN BAR ASSOCIATION ADVISORY COMMITTEE RECOMMENDATIONS FOR POLICE ADMINISTRATION." AFR ADMIN...JURID 20. PAGE 123 F2435 EDU/PROP CONTROL GP/REL ORD/FREE

N67

US HOUSE COMM ON COMMERCE,PARTNERSHIP FOR HEALTH AMENDMENTS FOR 1967 (PAMPHLET). PUB/INST DELIB/GP PROB/SOLV BUDGET EFFICIENCY 20 CONGRESS. PAGE 137 F2701 HEAL PLAN NAT/G JURID

B96

SMITH A.,LECTURES ON JUSTICE, POLICE, REVENUE AND ARMS (1763). UK LAW FAM FORCES TARIFFS AGREE COERCE INCOME OWN WEALTH LAISSEZ...GEN/LAWS 17/18. PAGE 123 F2429 DIPLOM JURID OLD/LIB TAX

JURISPRUDENCE....SEE LAW

K

USA+45 AGRI CONSTRUC INDUS CONSULT ACT/RES PROB/SOLV EDU/PROP GOV/REL HEALTH KENTUCKY. PAGE 35 F0689 — PLAN ECO/UNDEV

N19
EAST KENTUCKY REGIONAL PLAN,PROGRAM 60 REPORT: ACTION FOR PORGRESS IN EASTERN KENTUCKY (PAMPHLET). USA+45 CONSTRUC INDUS ACT/RES PROB/SOLV EDU/PROP ADMIN GOV/REL KENTUCKY. PAGE 35 F0690 — REGION PLAN ECO/UNDEV CONSULT

KENYA....KENYA

KENYA MINISTRY ECO PLAN DEV F1380

KENYATTA....JOMO KENYATTA

KERN A. F1772

KERR C. F1381

KESSELMAN L.C. F1382

KESTENBAUM L. F1383

KEWEN P.B. F1384

KEYNES J.M. F1385,F1386

KEYNES/G....GEOFFREY KEYNES

KEYNES/JM....JOHN MAYNARD KEYNES

B30
KEYNES J.M.,A TREATISE ON MONEY (2 VOLS.). UK USA-45 INDUS MARKET WORKER PRICE CONTROL COST OPTIMAL PROFIT WEALTH...POLICY 19/20 KEYNES/JM. PAGE 70 F1385 — EQUILIB ECO/TAC FINAN GEN/LAWS

B37
ROBBINS L.,ECONOMIC PLANNING AND INTERNATIONAL ORDER. WOR-45 SOCIETY FINAN INDUS NAT/G ECO/TAC ROUTINE WEALTH...SOC TIME/SEQ GEN/METH WORK 20 KEYNES/JM. PAGE 112 F2202 — INT/ORG PLAN INT/TRADE

B38
MEADE J.E.,AN INTRODUCTION TO ECONOMIC ANALYSIS AND POLICY (AMERICAN EDITION EDITED BY C.J. HITCH). FINAN INDUS MARKET LABOR INT/TRADE CONTROL COST DEMAND INCOME...CLASSIF CHARTS T 20 KEYNES/JM MONOPOLY. PAGE 89 F1737 — CONCPT PROFIT PRODUC

B41
ESTEY J.A.,BUSINESS CYCLES; THEIR NATURE, CAUSE, AND CONTROL. NAT/G BUDGET CAP/ISM TAX PRICE CONTROL INCOME...MODAL TIME/SEQ GEN/METH T 18/20 KEYNES/JM MONEY. PAGE 38 F0749 — INDUS FINAN ECO/TAC POLICY

B50
CLARK J.M.,ALTERNATIVE TO SERFDOM. SOCIETY STRATA INDUS MARKET WORKER PRICE GP/REL PROFIT BIO/SOC PWR WEALTH...GEN/LAWS 20 KEYNES/JM. PAGE 25 F0481 — ORD/FREE POPULISM ECO/TAC REPRESENT

B51
HARROD R.F.,THE LIFE OF JOHN MAYNARD KEYNES. UK INTELL FAM CAP/ISM DIPLOM ECO/TAC WAR ATTIT PERSON ROLE 20 KEYNES/JM WWI. PAGE 56 F1094 — BIOG FINAN GEN/LAWS

B53
BURNS A.E.,MODERN ECONOMICS. UNIV ECO/DEV INT/TRADE PRICE INCOME WEALTH...POLICY CHARTS T 20 KEYNES/JM. PAGE 20 F0389 — NAT/G ECO/TAC FINAN

B53
WILLIAMS J.H.,ECONOMIC STABILITY IN A CHANGING WORLD. FRANCE USA+45 USSR AGRI WORKER BUDGET INT/TRADE TAX WAR BAL/PAY COST EFFICIENCY ALL/IDEOS EQULIB 20 KEYNES/JM. PAGE 147 F2892 — POLICY FINAN ECO/TAC WEALTH

B57
NANIWADA H.,STAAT UND WIRTSCHAFT; GRUNDLEGUNG DER NATIONALOEKONOMIE ALS DER LOGIK DER BURGERLICHEN GESELLSCHAFT. WOR+45 WOR-45 STRATA MARKET WORKER INGP/REL DEMAND EQUILIB WEALTH...POLICY IDEA/COMP GEN/LAWS 17/20 MARX/KARL KEYNES/JM LENIN/VI. PAGE 96 F1890 — ALL/IDEOS ECO/TAC , SOCIETY NAT/G

B58
DUESENBERRY J.S.,BUSINESS CYCLES AND ECONOMIC GROWTH. USA+45 PROB/SOLV PAY PRICE...CONCPT MATH CHARTS IDEA/COMP 20 DEPRESSION KEYNES/JM. PAGE 34 F0672 — FINAN ECO/DEV ECO/TAC INCOME

B58
MOULTON H.G.,CAN INFLATION BE CONTROLLED? ECO/DEV INDUS CAP/ISM RATION GOV/REL COST INCOME PEACE WEALTH...CHARTS TIME 20 KEYNES/JM MONEY. PAGE 94 F1847 — ECO/TAC CONTROL DEMAND FINAN

B58
WARNER A.W.,CONCEPTS AND CASES IN ECONOMIC ANALYSIS. PROB/SOLV BARGAIN CONTROL INCOME PRODUC ...ECOMETRIC MGT CONCPT CLASSIF CHARTS 20 KEYNES/JM. PAGE 143 F2820 — ECO/TAC DEMAND EQUILIB COST

B60
HEILPERIN M.A.,STUDIES IN ECONOMIC NATIONALISM. EUR+WWI MOD/EUR USA+45 ECO/DEV PLAN INT/TRADE TARIFFS WAR PRODUC PROFIT 18/20 KEYNES/JM. PAGE 58 F1140 — ECO/TAC NAT/G NAT/LISM POLICY

B61
ACKLEY G.,MACROECONOMIC THEORY. AFR FINAN WORKER ECO/TAC PRICE COST INCOME PRODUC...MATH TREND CHARTS IDEA/COMP T KEYNES/JM. PAGE 2 F0034 — SIMUL ECOMETRIC WEALTH

B61
CANTERBERY E.R.,THE PRESIDENT'S COUNCIL OF ECONOMIC ADVISERS. AFR USA+45 FINAN LABOR NAT/G PLAN ADMIN OPTIMAL WEALTH 20 EISNHWR/DD PRESIDENT TRUMAN/HS KEYNES/JM. PAGE 21 F0413 — ECO/TAC OP/RES EXEC CHIEF

B61
LHOSTE-LACHAUME P.,OU GIT LE DESACCORD ENTRE LIBERAUX ET SOCIALISTES. EUR+WWI USA+45 USA-45 USSR CAP/ISM EDU/PROP MARXISM...MAJORIT IDEA/COMP 20 KEYNES/JM NEW/DEAL DEPRESSION. PAGE 79 F1555 — LAISSEZ SOCISM FINAN

B61
MCCRACKEN H.L.,KEYNESIAN ECONOMICS IN THE STREAM OF ECONOMIC THOUGHT. FINAN MARKET BARGAIN EFFICIENCY OPTIMAL...PHIL/SCI CONCPT IDEA/COMP BIBLIOG 18/20 KEYNES/JM. PAGE 88 F1724 — ECO/TAC DEMAND ECOMETRIC

B62
JOHNSON H.G.,MONEY, TRADE AND ECONOMIC GROWTH. ECO/DEV ECO/UNDEV FINAN COST WEALTH...POLICY SOC IDEA/COMP 20 KEYNES/JM MONEY. PAGE 67 F1324 — PLAN BAL/PAY INT/TRADE ECO/TAC

B62
SIEVERS A.M.,REVOLUTION, EVOLUTION AND THE ECONOMIC ORDER. INDUS LABOR TAX CONTROL REV WAR DEMAND PRODUC WEALTH...IDEA/COMP 19/20 KEYNES/JM. PAGE 122 F2399 — EFFICIENCY ALL/IDEOS ECO/DEV WELF/ST

B62
VANEK J.,THE BALANCE OF PAYMENTS, LEVEL OF ECONOMIC ACTIVITY AND THE VALUE OF CURRENCY: THEORY AND SOME RECENT EXPERIENCES. UNIV PRICE INCOME...MATH 20 KEYNES/JM. PAGE 140 F2766 — BAL/PAY ECO/TAC FINAN GEN/LAWS

B62
WRIGHT D.M.,THE KEYNESIAN SYSTEM. WOR+45 WOR-45 LABOR NAT/G CONTROL COST DEMAND EFFICIENCY...POLICY CONCPT CHARTS SIMUL 20 KEYNES/JM. PAGE 149 F2931 — INCOME ECO/DEV FINAN ECO/TAC

B63
ROPKE W.,ECONOMICS OF THE FREE SOCIETY. FINAN INT/TRADE BAL/PAY COST DEMAND EFFICIENCY ORD/FREE WEALTH...CON/ANAL METH/COMP T 20 KEYNES/JM. PAGE 114 F2240 — SOCIETY BUDGET ECO/DEV ECO/TAC

B63
THEOBALD R.,FREE MEN AND FREE MARKETS. USA+45 USA-45 ECO/DEV NAT/G TEC/DEV DIPLOM INT/TRADE INCOME ORD/FREE WEALTH...TREND 19/20 KEYNES/JM. PAGE 130 F2556 — CONCPT ECO/TAC CAP/ISM MARKET

S63
COLLERY A.,"A FULL EMPLOYMENT, KEYNESIAN THEORY OF INTERNATIONAL TRADE." WOR+45 ECO/DEV ACT/RES ECO/TAC ROUTINE ORD/FREE WEALTH...MATH CHARTS 20 KEYNES/JM. PAGE 26 F0504 — SIMUL INT/TRADE

B64
BALL R.J.,INFLATION AND THE THEORY OF MONEY. MARKET TAX PAY PRICE TASK ADJUST BAL/PAY COST INCOME PRODUC WEALTH...METH/COMP 20 KEYNES/JM MONEY. PAGE 9 F0167 — EQUILIB DEMAND POLICY

B64
GEORGIADIS H.G.,BALANCE OF PAYMENTS EQUILIBRIUM. COST DEMAND...CONCPT MATH GEN/LAWS 20 KEYNES/JM. PAGE 47 F0916 — BAL/PAY EQUILIB SIMUL INT/TRADE

B64
GOWDA K.V.,INTERNATIONAL CURRENCY PLANS AND EXPANSION OF WORLD TRADE. INT/ORG CREATE BUDGET CONTROL BAL/PAY WEALTH 20 KEYNES/JM. PAGE 50 F0969 — INT/TRADE FINAN METH/COMP

B64
HANSEN A.H.,BUSINESS CYCLES AND NATIONAL INCOME. USA+45 FINAN ECO/TAC COST OPTIMAL...POLICY METH 20 KEYNES/JM. PAGE 54 F1065 — INCOME WEALTH PRODUC INDUS

B64
KALDOR N.,ESSAYS ON ECONOMIC POLICY (VOL. II). CHILE GERMANY INDIA FINAN...GOV/COMP METH/COMP 20 KEYNES/JM. PAGE 69 F1348 — BAL/PAY INT/TRADE METH/CNCPT ECO/UNDEV

B64
LEKACHMAN R.,KEYNES' GENERAL THEORY: REPORTS OF THREE DECADES. FINAN ATTIT...POLICY 20 KEYNES/JM. PAGE 77 F1517 — PHIL/SCI GEN/METH IDEA/COMP

S65
HUTT W.H.,"KEYNESIAN REVISIONS" SOUTH/AFR ECO/DEV FINAN NAT/G WORKER BUDGET TAX PRICE EQUILIB WEALTH 20 KEYNES/JM. PAGE 64 F1252 — ECO/TAC GEN/LAWS LOG

B66
FUSFELD D.R.,THE AGE OF THE ECONOMIST. ECO/TAC WEALTH LAISSEZ MARXISM...EPIST 18/20 KEYNES/JM. PAGE 45 F0878 — PHIL/SCI CAP/ISM POLICY

B66
LEONTIEF W.,ESSAYS IN ECONOMICS. ECO/UNDEV INDUS NAT/G CAP/ISM FOR/AID AUTOMAT MARXISM...ECOMETRIC CHARTS ANTHOL METH 20 KEYNES/JM. PAGE 78 F1528 — CONCPT METH/CNCPT METH/COMP

KEYSERLING L.H. F1307

KHASAS....KHASAS (ANCIENT COMMUNITY)

KHRUSH/N....NIKITA KHRUSHCHEV

B62
BRUMBERG A.,RUSSIA UNDER KHRUSHCHEV. FUT USSR SOCIETY ECO/DEV AGRI PERF/ART WORKER PWR...SOC ANTHOL 20 KHRUSH/N. PAGE 20 F0377 COM MARXISM NAT/G CHIEF

B65
JASNY H.,KHRUSHCHEV'S CROP POLICY. USSR ECO/DEV PLAN MARXISM...STAT 20 KHRUSH/N RESOURCE/N. PAGE 66 F1306 AGRI NAT/G POLICY ECO/TAC

B66
BRODERSEN A.,THE SOVIET WORKER: LABOR AND GOVERNMENT IN SOVIET SOCIETY. USSR STRUCT INDUS LABOR PLAN PAY INGP/REL PRODUC...POLICY GEN/LAWS BIBLIOG 20 STALIN/J LENIN/VI BOLSHEVISM KHRUSH/N. PAGE 19 F0357 WORKER ROLE NAT/G MARXISM

B67
HALLE L.J.,THE COLD WAR AS HISTORY. AFR USSR WOR+45 ECO/TAC FOR/AID NUC/PWR WAR PEACE ORD/FREE ...MAJORIT TREND 20 KENNEDY/JF KHRUSH/N BERLIN/BLO. PAGE 54 F1048 DIPLOM BAL/PWR

S67
AVTORKHANOV A.,"A NEW AGRARIAN REVOLUTION." COM USSR ECO/DEV PLAN TEC/DEV ADMIN CONTROL OPTIMAL WEALTH SOCISM 20 KHRUSH/N STALIN/J. PAGE 8 F0144 AGRI METH/COMP MARXISM OWN

S67
CAMPBELL J.C.,"SOVIET-AMERICAN RELATIONS: CONFLICT AND COOPERATION." AFR USA+45 USSR AGREE WAR PEACE 20 KHRUSH/N KENNEDY/JF. PAGE 21 F0407 DIPLOM POLICY

S67
CATTELL D.T.,"THE FIFTIETH ANNIVERSARY: A SOVIET WATERSHED?" USSR CONSTN ECO/DEV NAT/G LEAD TOTALISM 20 KHRUSH/N. PAGE 22 F0430 MARXISM CHIEF POLICY ADJUST

S67
FEDYSHYN O.S.,"KHRUSHCHEV'S 'LEAP FORWARD': NATIONAL ASSIMILATION IN THE USSR AFTER STALIN." USSR PLAN NAT/LISM PERSON...POLICY 20 KHRUSH/N STALIN/J. PAGE 39 F0771 GP/REL INGP/REL MARXISM METH

KIERKE/S....SOREN KIERKEGAARD

KILE O.M. F1387

KILLIAN K.W. F1812

KILLOUGH H.B. F1388

KILLOUGH L.W. F1388

KIM/IL-SON....KIM IL-SON

KIN....KINSHIP (EXCEPT NUCLEAR FAMILY)

B02
MOREL E.D.,AFFAIRS OF WEST AFRICA. UK FINAN INDUS FAM KIN SECT CHIEF WORKER DIPLOM RACE/REL LITERACY HEALTH...CHARTS 18/20 AFRICA/W NEGRO. PAGE 93 F1826 COLONIAL ADMIN AFR

B49
LEE A.M.,SOCIAL PROBLEMS IN AMERICA: A SOURCE BOOK. STRATA STRUCT KIN NEIGH VOL/ASSN ACT/RES LEAD CRIME AGE SEX 20. PAGE 77 F1504 SOC SOCIETY PERSON EDU/PROP

B58
BIDWELL P.W.,RAW MATERIALS: A STUDY OF AMERICAN POLICY. USA+45 USA-45 ECO/UNDEV AGRI INDUS KIN CREATE PLAN ECO/TAC WAR PEACE ATTIT DRIVE WEALTH ...STAT CHARTS CONGRESS FOR/TRADE VAL/FREE. PAGE 15 F0279 EXTR/IND ECO/DEV

B59
PANIKKAR K.M.,THE AFRO-ASIAN STATES AND THEIR PROBLEMS. COM CULTURE KIN POL/PAR SECT DIPLOM EDU/PROP COLONIAL SOVEREIGN...TECHNIC GOV/COMP 20. PAGE 103 F2025 AFR S/ASIA ECO/UNDEV

B61
HEMPSTONE S.,THE NEW AFRICA. AGRI INDUS KIN NAT/G COLONIAL MARXISM...SOC INT TREND NAT/COMP BIBLIOG/A 20. PAGE 58 F1146 AFR ORD/FREE PERSON CULTURE

S61
DALTON G.,"ECONOMIC THEORY AND PRIMITIVE SOCIETY" (BMR)" UNIV AGRI KIN TEC/DEV ECO/TAC REGION HABITAT SKILL...METH/COMP BIBLIOG. PAGE 30 F0574 ECO/UNDEV METH PHIL/SCI SOC

B63
WAGLEY C.,INTRODUCTION TO BRAZIL. BRAZIL L/A+17C FAM KIN SCHOOL SECT ATTIT WEALTH...GEOG SOC. PAGE 142 F2799 ECO/UNDEV ELITES HABITAT STRATA

L63
OLSON M. JR.,"RAPID ECONOMIC GROWTH AS A DESTABILIZING FORCE." WOR+45 WOR-45 STRATA ECO/UNDEV FAM KIN CREATE TEC/DEV DIPLOM PEACE ATTIT PERSON RIGID/FLEX PWR RESPECT WEALTH...SOC 20. PAGE 101 F1989 SOCIETY FOR/AID

B64
LUTHULI A.,AFRICA'S FREEDOM. KIN LABOR POL/PAR SCHOOL DIPLOM NEUTRAL REGION REV NAT/LISM PWR WEALTH SOCISM SOC/INTEG 20. PAGE 82 F1608 AFR ECO/UNDEV COLONIAL

S64
READER D.H.,"A SURVEY OF CATEGORIES OF ECONOMIC ACTIVITIES AMONG THE PEOPLES OF AFRICA." AGRI INDUS MARKET KIN HEALTH SKILL WEALTH...GEOG METH/CNCPT CHARTS TERR/GP WORK TOT/POP VAL/FREE 20. PAGE 110 F2160 TEC/DEV ECO/UNDEV AFR

B66
HALLET R.,PEOPLE AND PROGRESS IN WEST AFRICA: AN INTRODUCTION TO THE PROBLEMS OF DEVELOPMENT. COM/IND INDUS KIN DIPLOM FOR/AID INT/TRADE HEALTH ...GEOG TREND CHARTS BIBLIOG/A 20 AFRICA/W. PAGE 54 F1050 AFR SOCIETY ECO/UNDEV ECO/TAC

B66
HOWE R.W.,BLACK AFRICA: FROM PRE-HISTORY TO THE EVE OF THE COLONIAL ERA. ECO/UNDEV KIN PROVS SECT INT/TRADE EDU/PROP COLONIAL...BIBLIOG WORSHIP. PAGE 62 F1226 AFR CULTURE SOC

S66
ROTHCHILD D.,"THE LIMITS OF FEDERALISM: AN EXAMINATION OF POLITICAL INSTITUTIONAL TRANSFER IN AFRICA." AFR CONSTN CULTURE ELITES ECO/UNDEV KIN PROB/SOLV ADMIN ORD/FREE PWR...POLICY 20. PAGE 114 F2250 FEDERAL NAT/G NAT/LISM COLONIAL

B67
FORDE D.,WEST AFRICAN KINGDOMS IN THE NINETEENTH CENTURY. ECO/UNDEV AGRI KIN...SOC CHARTS NAT/COMP 19. PAGE 42 F0826 AFR REGION CULTURE

B67
SACKS B.,SOUTH AFRICA: AN IMPERIAL DILEMMA. SOUTH/AFR UK ECO/UNDEV KIN DOMIN DEBATE CONTROL REV DISCRIM ISOLAT...POLICY STAT BIBLIOG 20. PAGE 115 F2268 COLONIAL RACE/REL DIPLOM ORD/FREE

B96
SCHMOLLER G.,THE MERCANTILE SYSTEM AND ITS HISTORICAL SIGNIFICANCE: ILLUSTRATED CHIEFLY FROM PRUSSIAN HISTORY (TRANS.). PRUSSIA CULTURE INDUS KIN NAT/G PROVS OP/RES ECO/TAC INT/TRADE SUPEGO PWR WEALTH MUNICH 19 MERCANTLST. PAGE 117 F2302 GEN/METH INGP/REL CONCPT

KINDLEBERGER C.P. F1389,F1390,F1391,F1392,F1393,F1394,F1395

KING....KING AND KINGSHIP; SEE ALSO CHIEF, CONSERVE, TRADIT

KING/MAR/L....REVEREND MARTIN LUTHER KING

KINGSLEY R.E. F1396

KINSEY/A....ALFRED KINSEY

KIPLING/R....RUDYARD KIPLING

KIRDAR U. F1397

KIRK R. F1398

KIRK/GRAY....GRAYSON KIRK

KIRKENDALL R.S. F1399

KIRPICEVA I.K. F1400

KISER M. F1401

KISSINGER H.A. F1402

KITZINGER V.W. F1403

KKK....KU KLUX KLAN

B27
SIEGFRIED A.,AMERICA COMES OF AGE: A FRENCH ANALYSIS (TRANS. BY H.H. HEMMING AND DORIS HEMMING). FRANCE UK POL/PAR WORKER TEC/DEV DIPLOM REGION RACE/REL ADJUST PRODUC HEREDITY...TIME/SEQ GP/COMP SOC/INTEG 20 DEMOCRAT REPUBLICAN KKK. PAGE 122 F2398 USA-45 CULTURE ECO/DEV SOC

KLASSEN L.H. F1404

KLEIN H. F1405

KLEIN J.J. F1406

KLEIN L.R. F1407,F1408

KLEIN S. F1409

KLUCKHN/C....CLYDE KLUCKHOHN

KLUMB S. F1410

KNAPP D.C. F1411

KNIGHT R. F1412

KNO/TEST....TESTS FOR FACTUAL KNOWLEDGE

B62
HEILBRONER R.L.,THE MAKING OF ECONOMIC SOCIETY. FUT WOR-45 SOCIETY STRATA ECO/DEV ECO/UNDEV ECO/TAC LEGIT ROUTINE...SOC RECORD REC/INT KNO/TEST CENSUS STERTYP GEN/LAWS. PAGE 58 F1136 — CAP/ISM SOCISM

KNORR K.E. F1413

KNOWL....ENLIGHTENMENT, KNOWLEDGE

N
TEXTBOOKS IN PRINT. WOR+45 WOR-45 LAW DIPLOM ALL/VALS ALL/IDEOS...SOC T 19/20. PAGE 1 F0003 — BIBLIOG SCHOOL KNOWL

N
US LIBRARY OF CONGRESS,EAST EUROPEAN ACCESSIONS INDEX. NAT/G ISOLAT ATTIT KNOWL...POLICY 20. PAGE 138 F2711 — BIBLIOG COM MARXIST DIPLOM

B30
HAWTREY R.G.,ECONOMIC ASPECTS OF SOVEREIGNTY. UNIV WOR+45 WOR-45 ECO/DEV ECO/UNDEV AGRI COM/IND INDUS MARKET NAT/G TEC/DEV ECO/TAC EDU/PROP COERCE ATTIT KNOWL WEALTH...CONCPT CON/ANAL GEN/LAWS 20. PAGE 57 F1118 — FORCES PWR SOVEREIGN WAR

B35
WADE J.,HISTORY OF THE MIDDLE AND WORKING CLASSES; WITH A POPULAR EXPOSITION OF THE ECONOMICAL AND POLITICAL PRINCIPLES.... FRANCE UK CONSTN FINAN INDUS LABOR INCOME PROFIT KNOWL MORAL ORD/FREE WEALTH...CHARTS 14/19. PAGE 142 F2797 — WORKER STRATA CONCPT

B45
DAVIS J.,AFRICA ADVANCING. AFR CONGO/BRAZ LIBERIA NIGER INT/ORG SCHOOL DIPLOM GIVE KNOWL SKILL 20. PAGE 30 F0590 — SECT COLONIAL AGRI ECO/UNDEV

B48
HAYEK F.A.,INDIVIDUALISM AND ECONOMIC ORDER. FINAN PLAN MORAL LAISSEZ SOCISM...POLICY DECISION PHIL/SCI HIST/WRIT. PAGE 57 F1122 — RATIONAL KNOWL PERSON

B50
LINCOLN G.,ECONOMICS OF NATIONAL SECURITY. USA+45 ELITES COM/IND DIST/IND INDUS NAT/G VOL/ASSN DELIB/GP EX/STRUC FOR/AID EDU/PROP COERCE NUC/PWR WAR ATTIT KNOWL ORD/FREE PWR TOT/POP VAL/FREE 20. PAGE 80 F1565 — FORCES ECO/TAC AFR

L52
HUTH A.G.,"COMMUNICATION AND ECONOMIC DEVELOPMENT." FUT WOR+45 CULTURE SOCIETY INT/ORG PLAN TEC/DEV EDU/PROP DRIVE KNOWL WEALTH...POLICY CONCPT RECORD STERTYP GEN/LAWS COMMUN TOT/POP UNESCO 20 UN CMN/WLTH. PAGE 64 F1250 — ECO/UNDEV

B54
CHILDS M.W.,ETHICS IN A BUSINESS SOCIETY. PROF/ORG LEAD WAR GP/REL ATTIT DRIVE PERSON KNOWL MORAL PWR ...WELF/ST BIBLIOG. PAGE 24 F0466 — MGT SOCIETY

B54
SCHUMPETER J.A.,HISTORY OF ECONOMIC ANALYSIS. WOR-45...PHIL/SCI METH/CNCPT STAT IDEA/COMP GRECO/ROMN. PAGE 118 F2322 — KNOWL GEN/LAWS METH

B55
BUCHANAN N.S.,APPROACHES TO ECONOMIC DEVELOPMENT. FUT USA+45 WOR+45 STRATA ECO/DEV INT/ORG NAT/G TEC/DEV DIPLOM FOR/AID ATTIT KNOWL PWR WEALTH ...RELATIV METH/CNCPT SELF/OBS TREND CON/ANAL STERTYP GEN/LAWS FOR/TRADE COMMUN 20. PAGE 20 F0380 — ECO/UNDEV ECO/TAC INT/TRADE

B56
GARDNER R.N.,STERLING-DOLLAR DIPLOMACY. EUR+WWI USA+45 INT/ORG NAT/G PLAN INT/TRADE EDU/PROP ADMIN KNOWL PWR WEALTH...POLICY SOC METH/CNCPT STAT CHARTS SIMUL GEN/LAWS 20. PAGE 46 F0902 — ECO/DEV DIPLOM

S56
MARGOLIS J.,"ON MUNICIPAL LAND POLICY FOR FISCAL GAINS." USA+45 PLAN TAX COST EFFICIENCY HABITAT KNOWL...MGT MUNICH 20. PAGE 85 F1667 — BUDGET POLICY GEOG LOC/G

B57
LAVES W.H.C.,UNESCO. FUT WOR+45 NAT/G CONSULT DELIB/GP TEC/DEV ECO/TAC EDU/PROP PEACE ORD/FREE ...CONCPT TIME/SEQ TREND UNESCO VAL/FREE 20. PAGE 76 F1491 — INT/ORG KNOWL

L58
MASON E.S.,"ECONOMIC PLANNING IN UNDERDEVELOPED AREAS." FUT WOR+45 PLAN TEC/DEV EDU/PROP ATTIT RIGID/FLEX KNOWL...SOC CONCPT GEN/LAWS TOT/POP 20. PAGE 87 F1697 — NAT/G ECO/UNDEV

L59
FURASH E.A.,"PROBLEMS IN REVIEW: INDUSTRIAL ESPIONAGE." WORKER ECO/TAC PERS/REL OPTIMAL AGE ATTIT KNOWL...MGT DEEP/INT DEEP/QU GP/COMP IDEA/COMP. PAGE 45 F0875 — INDUS TOP/EX MAJORITY

B60
HOSELITZ B.F.,THEORIES OF ECONOMIC GROWTH. UK WOR+45 WOR-45 ECO/UNDEV PLAN INT/TRADE KNOWL ...CONCPT METH/CNCPT TIME/SEQ GEN/LAWS TOT/POP. PAGE 62 F1220 — ECO/DEV INTELL

B60
RICHARDSON G.B.,INFORMATION AND INVESTMENT. PLAN PROB/SOLV CAP/ISM ECO/TAC KNOWL...CONCPT 20 MONEY. PAGE 111 F2184 — ECO/DEV EQUILIB FINAN PHIL/SCI

B60
SHONFIELD A.,THE ATTACK ON WORLD POVERTY. WOR+45 ECO/DEV ECO/UNDEV FINAN VOL/ASSN PLAN EDU/PROP DRIVE KNOWL WEALTH...CONT/OBS STAND/INT ORG/CHARTS TOT/POP UNESCO 20. PAGE 121 F2383 — INT/ORG ECO/TAC FOR/AID INT/TRADE

S60
BECKER A.S.,"COMPARISIONS OF UNITED STATES AND USSR NATIONAL OUTPUT: SOME RULES OF THE GAME." COM USA+45 ECO/DEV AGRI DIST/IND INDUS R+D CONSULT PLAN ECO/TAC RIGID/FLEX KNOWL...METH/CNCPT CHARTS 20. PAGE 12 F0227 — STAT USSR

S60
MURPHEY R.,"ECONOMIC CONFLICTS IN SOUTH ASIA." ASIA CULTURE INTELL ECO/TAC REGION ATTIT DRIVE KNOWL ...METH/CNCPT TIME/SEQ STERTYP TOT/POP METH/GP VAL/FREE 20. PAGE 95 F1864 — S/ASIA ECO/UNDEV

S61
BARALL M.,"THE UNITED STATES GOVERNMENT RESPONDS." L/A+17C USA+45 SOCIETY NAT/G CREATE PLAN DIPLOM ECO/TAC ATTIT DRIVE RIGID/FLEX KNOWL SKILL WEALTH ...METH/CNCPT TIME/SEQ GEN/METH 20. PAGE 9 F0176 — ECO/UNDEV ACT/RES FOR/AID

S61
GALBRAITH J.K.,"A POSITIVE APPROACH TO ECONOMIC AID." FUT USA+45 INTELL NAT/G CONSULT ACT/RES DIPLOM ECO/TAC EDU/PROP ATTIT KNOWL PWR WEALTH ...SOC STERTYP MID/EX METH/GP 20. PAGE 45 F0883 — ECO/UNDEV ROUTINE FOR/AID

B62
BROOKINGS INSTITUTION,DEVELOPMENT OF THE EMERGING COUNTRIES; AN AGENDA FOR RESEARCH. WOR+45 AGRI TEC/DEV FOR/AID EDU/PROP ADJUST HABITAT KNOWL...PSY SOC ANTHOL 20 THIRD/WRLD. PAGE 19 F0362 — ECO/UNDEV R+D SOCIETY PROB/SOLV

B62
CAIRNCROSS A.K.,FACTORS IN ECONOMIC DEVELOPMENT. WOR+45 ECO/UNDEV INDUS R+D LG/CO NAT/G EX/STRUC PLAN TEC/DEV ECO/TAC ATTIT HEALTH KNOWL PWR WEALTH ...TIME/SEQ GEN/LAWS TOT/POP TRUE/GP VAL/FREE 20. PAGE 21 F0399 — MARKET ECO/DEV

B62
EINZIG P.,THE HISTORY OF FOREIGN EXCHANGE. CHRIST-17C ISLAM MEDIT-7 PRE/AMER WOR+45 ECO/DEV FINAN PLAN ECO/TAC ATTIT KNOWL WEALTH...SIMUL GEN/LAWS. PAGE 37 F0714 — MARKET TIME/SEQ INT/TRADE

S62
ADISESHIAN M.,"EDUCATION AND DEVELOPMENT." FUT WOR+45 SOCIETY ACT/RES INT/TRADE EDU/PROP KNOWL SKILL WEALTH...POLICY CONCPT CONT/OBS CENSUS CHARTS TOT/POP VAL/FREE APPLIC FAO FOR/TRADE 20. PAGE 2 F0041 — SCHOOL ECO/UNDEV

S62
MILLIKEN M.,"NEW AND OLD CRITERIA FOR AID." WOR+45 ECO/DEV ECO/UNDEV ACT/RES PLAN ATTIT KNOWL...TREND CON/ANAL SIMUL GEN/METH TERR/GP 20. PAGE 92 F1796 — USA+45 ECO/TAC FOR/AID

S62
PYE L.W.,"THE POLITICAL IMPULSES AND FANTASIES BEHIND FOREIGN AID." FUT USA+45 ECO/UNDEV DIPLOM ECO/TAC ROUTINE DRIVE KNOWL...SOC METH/CNCPT NEW/IDEA TREND HYPO/EXP STERTYP GEN/METH 20. PAGE 108 F2133 — ACT/RES ATTIT FOR/AID

B63
DE VRIES E.,SOCIAL ASPECTS OF ECONOMIC DEVELOPMENT IN LATIN AMERICA. CULTURE SOCIETY STRATA FINAN INDUS INT/ORG DELIB/GP ACT/RES ECO/TAC EDU/PROP ADMIN ATTIT SUPEGO HEALTH KNOWL ORD/FREE...SOC STAT TREND ANTHOL TOT/POP VAL/FREE. PAGE 31 F0608 — L/A+17C ECO/UNDEV

B63
FREITAG R.S.,AGRICULTURAL DEVELOPMENT SCHEMES IN SUB-SAHARAN AFRICA. AFR EDU/PROP 20. PAGE 44 F0852 — BIBLIOG/A AGRI TEC/DEV KNOWL

B63
PERLO V.,MILITARISM AND INDUSTRY. USA+45 INT/TRADE EDU/PROP DETER KNOWL...CHARTS MAPS 20. PAGE 105 F2064 — CIVMIL/REL INDUS LOBBY ARMS/CONT

L63
NASH M.,"PSYCHO-CULTURAL FACTORS IN ASIAN ECONOMIC GROWTH." ASIA ISLAM S/ASIA CULTURE ECO/UNDEV DELIB/GP EDU/PROP COERCE ATTIT PERSON HEALTH KNOWL ORD/FREE...PSY SOC STAT TREND ANTHOL VAL/FREE 20. PAGE 96 F1893 — SOCIETY ECO/TAC

S63
FOURASTIE J.,"LES SCIENCES ECONOMIQUES ET SOCIALES EN EUROPE." EUR+WWI FUT MOD/EUR WOR+45 WOR-45 INTELL SOCIETY R+D PLAN ROUTINE ATTIT RIGID/FLEX KNOWL...OBS TREND. PAGE 43 F0833 — ACT/RES CULTURE

S63
MARTHELOT P.,"PROGRES DE LA REFORME AGRAIRE." INTELL ECO/DEV R+D FOR/AID ADMIN KNOWL...OBS VAL/FREE UN 20. PAGE 86 F1680 — AGRI INT/ORG

B64
SCHULTZ T.W.,TRANSFORMING TRADITIONAL AGRICULTURE. WOR+45 WOR-45 CULTURE STRATA FINAN ACT/RES ECO/TAC ATTIT KNOWL SKILL...MATH STAT TIME/SEQ GEN/LAWS VAL/FREE. PAGE 117 F2316 — AGRI ECO/UNDEV

S64
BEIM D.,"THE COMMUNIST BLOC AND THE FOREIGN-AID GAME." AFR WOR+45 NAT/G PLAN ROUTINE ATTIT KNOWL ORD/FREE...DECISION QUANT CONT/OBS TIME/SEQ CHARTS GAME SIMUL LOG/LING 20. PAGE 12 F0231 — COM ECO/UNDEV ECO/TAC FOR/AID

B65
COOMBS P.H.,EDUCATION AND FOREIGN AID. AFR USA+45 DIPLOM EFFICIENCY KNOWL ORD/FREE...ANTHOL 20 AID. PAGE 27 F0532 — EDU/PROP FOR/AID SCHOOL ECO/UNDEV

B65
US OFFICE ECONOMIC OPPORTUNITY,CATALOG OF FEDERAL PROGRAMS FOR INDIVIDUAL AND COMMUNITY IMPROVEMENT. USA+45 GIVE RECEIVE ADMIN HEALTH KNOWL SKILL WEALTH ...CHARTS MUNICH. PAGE 138 F2721 — BIBLIOG CLIENT ECO/TAC

S65
GRENIEWSKI H.,"INTENTION AND PERFORMANCE: A PRIMER OF CYBERNETICS OF PLANNING." EFFICIENCY OPTIMAL KNOWL SKILL...DECISION MGT EQULIB. PAGE 51 F0995 — SIMUL GAME GEN/METH PLAN

B66
BEQIRAJ M.,PEASANTRY IN REVOLUTION. STRATA ECO/UNDEV AGRI ROUTINE REV HABITAT RIGID/FLEX ...EPIST GEOG NEW/IDEA TREND MUNICH 20. PAGE 13 F0256 — WORKER KNOWL NAT/LISM SOC

B66
CONFERENCE REGIONAL ACCOUNTS,REGIONAL ACCOUNTS FOR POLICY DECISIONS. PROB/SOLV CONTROL RATIONAL KNOWL ORD/FREE...POLICY DECISION MATH STAT ANTHOL 20. PAGE 27 F0523 — GOV/REL REGION PLAN ECO/TAC

B66
MALASSIS L.,ECONOMIC DEVELOPMENT AND THE PROGRAMMING OF RURAL EDUCATION. CONSULT PROB/SOLV LITERACY KNOWL...CHARTS GEN/METH 20. PAGE 84 F1644 — AGRI ECO/UNDEV SCHOOL PLAN

B67
DE JOUVENAL B.,THE ART OF CONJECTURE. WOR+45 EFFICIENCY PERCEPT KNOWL...DECISION PHIL/SCI CONCPT METH/COMP BIBLIOG 20. PAGE 31 F0600 — FUT PREDICT SIMUL METH

B67
DONALD A.G.,MANAGEMENT, INFORMATION, AND SYSTEMS. WOR+45 LG/CO PROB/SOLV CONTROL FEEDBACK KNOWL MGT. PAGE 34 F0653 — ROUTINE TEC/DEV CONCPT ADMIN

B67
HUMPHREY R.A.,UNIVERSITIES...AND DEVELOPMENT ASSISTANCE ABROAD. USA+45 OP/RES ECO/TAC FOR/AID ...ANTHOL 20. PAGE 63 F1242 — ACADEM DIPLOM KNOWL ECO/UNDEV

B67
MURTY B.S.,PROPAGANDA AND WORLD PUBLIC ORDER. FUT WOR+45 COM/IND INT/ORG PROB/SOLV ATTIT KNOWL ORD/FREE...POLICY UN. PAGE 95 F1868 — EDU/PROP DIPLOM CONTROL JURID

B67
NELSON R.R.,TECHNOLOGY, ECONOMIC GROWTH, AND PUBLIC POLICY. USA+45 PLAN GP/REL UTIL KNOWL...POLICY PHIL/SCI CHARTS BIBLIOG 20. PAGE 97 F1912 — R+D CONSULT CREATE ACT/RES

B67
RIDKER R.G.,ECONOMIC COSTS OF AIR POLLUTION* STUDIES IN MEASUREMENT. R+D GP/REL KNOWL...OBS MUNICH 20. PAGE 111 F2190 — OP/RES HABITAT PHIL/SCI

B67
US AGENCY INTERNATIONAL DEV,PROPOSED FOREIGN AID PROGRAM FOR 1968: SUMMARY PRESENTATION TO THE CONGRESS. AFR S/ASIA USA+45 AGRI TEC/DEV DIPLOM ECO/TAC BAL/PAY COST HEALTH KNOWL SKILL 20 AID CONGRESS ALL/PROG. PAGE 134 F2640 — ECO/UNDEV BUDGET FOR/AID STAT

S67
ALBAUM G.,"INFORMATION FLOW AND DECENTRALIZED DECISION MAKING IN MARKETING." EX/STRUC COMPUTER OP/RES PROB/SOLV EFFICIENCY OPTIMAL...METH/COMP ORG/CHARTS 20. PAGE 3 F0056 — LG/CO ROUTINE KNOWL MARKET

KNOWLEDGE TEST....SEE KNO/TEST

KNOX/HENRY....HENRY KNOX (SECRETARY OF WAR 1789)

KOENIG L.W. F1414

KOH S.J. F1415

KOHLER E.L. F1416

KOHLER/J....JOSEF KOHLER

KOHN C.F. F1706

KOHN W.S.G. F1417

KOHNSTAMM M. F1418

KOJIMA K. F1419

KOLKO G. F1420,F1421

KOLLAI H.R. F1422

KOLODZIEJ E.A. F1423

KOMIYA R. F1424

KORBONSKI A. F1425,F1426

KOREA....KOREA IN GENERAL; SEE ALSO ASIA

B51
HART A.G.,DEFENSE WITHOUT INFLATION. AFR KOREA FINAN INDUS NAT/G WORKER DIPLOM RATION TAX PRICE COST OPTIMAL 20 RESOURCE/N. PAGE 56 F1098 — ECO/TAC CONTROL WAR PLAN

B51
US HOUSE COMM APPROPRIATIONS,MUTUAL SECURITY PROGRAM APPROPRIATIONS FOR 1952: HEARINGS BEFORE A SUBCOMMITTEE OF THE COMMITTEE ON APPROPRIATIONS. AFR KOREA L/A+17C ECO/DEV ECO/UNDEV INT/ORG INSPECT BAL/PWR DIPLOM DEBATE WAR...POLICY STAT ASIA/S 20 CONGRESS NATO MID/EAST. PAGE 136 F2686 — LEGIS FORCES BUDGET FOR/AID

B52
MACARTHUR D.,REVITALIZING A NATION. ASIA COM FUT KOREA WOR+45 NAT/G FOR/AID TAX GIVE WAR ATTIT SOCISM 20 CHINJAP EUROPE. PAGE 83 F1619 — LEAD FORCES TOP/EX POLICY

B54
WILLIAMSON H.F.,ECONOMIC DEVELOPMENT - PRINCIPLES AND PATTERNS. INDIA KOREA CULTURE ECO/DEV ECO/UNDEV TEC/DEV...CENSUS NAT/COMP FOR/TRADE 20 CHINJAP MEXIC/AMER RESOURCE/N. PAGE 147 F2895 — ECO/TAC GEOG LABOR

B59
KOREAN MINISTRY RECONSTRUCTION,KOREAN ECONOMY AND ITS REQUIREMENTS. KOREA USA+45 ECO/TAC EQUILIB INCOME WEALTH...CHARTS 20. PAGE 73 F1427 — FOR/AID WAR FINAN DIPLOM

B63
US DEPARTMENT OF LABOR,THE ANVIL AND THE PLOW. KOREA USA+45 USA-45 INDUS WORKER BUDGET WAR ...POLICY AUD/VIS CHARTS 20 DEPT/LABOR. PAGE 135 F2667 — ECO/DEV LABOR ECO/TAC NAT/G

B65
HOLLER J.E.,POPULATION TRENDS AND ECONOMIC DEVELOPMENT IN THE FAR EAST (PAMPHLET). KOREA S/ASIA AGRI INDUS DELIB/GP PROB/SOLV RATIONAL ...POLICY CHARTS BIBLIOG 20 OUTER/MONG CHINJAP HONG/KONG. PAGE 61 F1197 — CENSUS TREND ECO/UNDEV ASIA

B66
KOH S.J.,STAGES OF INDUSTRIAL DEVELOPMENT IN ASIA. ASIA INDIA KOREA STRATA STRUCT NAT/G INT/TRADE ...CHARTS 19/20 CHINJAP. PAGE 72 F1415 — INDUS ECO/UNDEV ECO/DEV LABOR

B67
CHO S.S.,KOREA IN WORLD POLITICS 1940-1950; AN EVALUATION OF AMERICAN RESPONSIBILITY. KOREA USA+45 USSR CONSTN INT/ORG NAT/G FORCES FOR/AID ANOMIE SUPEGO MARXISM...DECISION BIBLIOG 20. PAGE 24 F0469 — POLICY DIPLOM PROB/SOLV WAR

B67
MCNELLY T.,SOURCES IN MODERN EAST ASIAN HISTORY AND POLITICS. KOREA VIETNAM CULTURE DIPLOM COLONIAL REV WAR PWR ALL/IDEOS MARXISM...ANTHOL 20 CHINJAP. PAGE 88 F1733 — NAT/COMP ASIA S/ASIA SOCIETY

KOREA/N....NORTH KOREA

KOREA/S....SOUTH KOREA

B61
MORLEY L.,THE PATCHWORK HISTORY OF FOREIGN AID. AFR KOREA/S USA+45 USSR LAW FINAN INT/ORG TEC/DEV BAL/PWR GIVE 20 NATO. PAGE 93 F1834 — FOR/AID ECO/UNDEV FORCES DIPLOM

B64
LINDHOLM R.W.,ECONOMIC DEVELOPMENT POLICY WITH EMPHASIS ON VIET-NAM. KOREA/S PAKISTAN VIETNAM/S AGRI INDUS CONSULT DELIB/GP FOR/AID...METH 20. PAGE 80 F1571 — ECO/UNDEV TAX FINAN ECO/TAC

KOREAN MINISTRY RECONSTRUCTION F1427

KORNBLUH J.L. F0785

KORNHAUSER W. F1428

KORNILOV/L....LAVR GEORGIEVICH KORNILOV

KOTLER P. F1429

KOTSCHING W.M. F0129

KOVNER M. F1430

KRANZBERG M. F1431

KRAUS J. F1432

KRAUSE L.B. F1433

KRAUSE W. F1434

KRAVIS I.B. F1435

KRAWIETZ W. F2795

KREININ M.E. F1436,F1437

KRESSBACH T.W. F1438

KRIESBERG M. F1439

KRIPALANI J.B. F1440

KRISHNA K.G.V. F1441

KRISHNAN V.N. F0611

KRISTENSEN T. F1442

KROOSS H.E. F1443

KROPOTKIN P. F1444,F1445

KU KLUX KLAN....SEE KKK

KUCZYNSKI R. F0426

KUENNE R.E. F1446

KUHN M.H. F1163

KUHN T.E. F1447

KULSKI J.E. F1448

KUNKEL J.H. F1449

KUOMINTANG....KUOMINTANG

KURAKOV I.G. F1450

KURIHARA K.L. F1451

KUWAIT....SEE ALSO ISLAM

N19
KUWAIT ARABIA,KUWAIT FUND FOR ARAB ECONOMIC DEVELOPMENT (PAMPHLET). ISLAM KUWAIT UAR ECO/UNDEV LEGIS ECO/TAC WEALTH 20. PAGE 74 F1452 — FOR/AID DIPLOM FINAN ADMIN

N19
KUWAIT FUND ARAB ECO DEVELOPMT,ANNUAL REPORTS 1962-65 (PAMPHLET). KUWAIT ECO/UNDEV DIPLOM ...POLICY 20 ARABS. PAGE 74 F1453 — FOR/AID DELIB/GP FINAN ISLAM

S61
VALLET R.,"IRAN: KEY TO THE MIDDLE EAST." COM IRAQ ISLAM KUWAIT LEBANON SAUDI/ARAB TURKEY ELITES SOCIETY INDUS PROC/MFG POL/PAR TOP/EX PLAN BAL/PWR DIPLOM ECO/TAC ALL/VALS...TREND FOR/TRADE CENTO 20. PAGE 140 F2760 — NAT/G ECO/UNDEV IRAN

B65
INT. BANK RECONSTR. DEVELOP.,ECONOMIC DEVELOPMENT OF KUWAIT. ISLAM KUWAIT AGRI FINAN MARKET EX/STRUC TEC/DEV ECO/TAC ADMIN WEALTH...OBS CON/ANAL CHARTS 20. PAGE 64 F1266 — INDUS NAT/G

KUWAIT ARABIA F1452

KUWAIT FUND ARAB ECO DEVELOPMT F1453

KUZNETS S. F1454,F1455,F1456

KUZNETS....KUZNETS SCALE

KY/NGUYEN....NGUYEN KY

L/A+17C....LATIN AMERICA SINCE 1700; SEE ALSO APPROPRIATE NATIONS

N
UNIVERSITY OF FLORIDA,CARIBBEAN ACQUISITIONS: MATERIALS ACQUIRED BY THE UNIVERSITY OF FLORIDA 1957-1960. L/A+17C...ART/METH GEOG MGT 20. PAGE 133 F2620 — BIBLIOG ECO/UNDEV EDU/PROP JURID

N19
STALEY E.,SCIENTIFIC RESEARCH AND PROGRESS IN NEWLY DEVELOPING COUNTRIES (PAMPHLET). AFR ASIA L/A+17C CONSULT DIPLOM...METH/COMP 20. PAGE 125 F2463 — ECO/UNDEV ACT/RES FOR/AID TEC/DEV

B51
US HOUSE COMM APPROPRIATIONS,MUTUAL SECURITY PROGRAM APPROPRIATIONS FOR 1952: HEARINGS BEFORE A SUBCOMMITTEE OF THE COMMITTEE ON APPROPRIATIONS. AFR KOREA L/A+17C ECO/DEV ECO/UNDEV INT/ORG INSPECT BAL/PWR DIPLOM DEBATE WAR...POLICY STAT ASIA/S 20 CONGRESS NATO MID/EAST. PAGE 136 F2686 — LEGIS FORCES BUDGET FOR/AID

B55
GOMES F.A.,OPERACAO MUNICIPIO. BRAZIL L/A+17C SERV/IND LOC/G BUDGET ECO/TAC COST DEMAND...POLICY MUNICH 20. PAGE 48 F0944 — ECO/UNDEV FEDERAL GOV/REL

B55
JONES T.B.,A BIBLIOGRAPHY ON SOUTH AMERICAN ECONOMIC AFFAIRS: ARTICLES IN NINETEENTH CENTURY PERIODICALS (PAMPHLET). AGRI COM/IND DIST/IND EXTR/IND FINAN INDUS LABOR NAT/G 19. PAGE 68 F1340 — BIBLIOG ECO/UNDEV L/A+17C TEC/DEV

L55
KISER M.,"ORGANIZATION OF AMERICAN STATES." L/A+17C USA+45 ECO/UNDEV INT/ORG NAT/G PLAN TEC/DEV DIPLOM ECO/TAC INT/TRADE EDU/PROP ADMIN ALL/VALS...POLICY MGT RECORD ORG/CHARTS OAS COMMUN 20. PAGE 71 F1401 — VOL/ASSN ECO/DEV REGION

B56
US DEPARTMENT OF STATE,ECONOMIC PROBLEMS OF UNDERDEVELOPED AREAS (PAMPHLET). AFR ASIA ISLAM L/A+17C AGRI FINAN INDUS INT/ORG LABOR INT/TRADE ...PSY SOC 20. PAGE 136 F2673 — BIBLIOG ECO/UNDEV TEC/DEV R+D

B57
PALACIOS A.L.,PETROLEO, MONOPOLIOS, Y LATIFUNDIOS. L/A+17C EXTR/IND NAT/G TEC/DEV ECO/TAC CONTROL PRODUC 20 ARGEN MONOPOLY RESOURCE/N. PAGE 103 F2017 — ECO/UNDEV NAT/LISM INDUS AGRI

L57
MASS. INST. TECH.,"THE CENTER FOR INTERNATIONAL STUDIES." AFR ASIA COM EUR+WWI ISLAM L/A+17C S/ASIA USA+45 USA-45 DIST/IND CONSULT FORCES ACT/RES TEC/DEV DIPLOM REV ATTIT WEALTH...CONCPT FOR/TRADE 20. PAGE 87 F1702 — R+D ECO/UNDEV

B58
BERLINER J.S.,SOVIET ECONOMIC AID: THE AID AND TRADE POLICY IN UNDERDEVELOPED COUNTRIES. AFR COM ISLAM L/A+17C S/ASIA USSR ECO/DEV DIST/IND FINAN MARKET INT/ORG ACT/RES PLAN BAL/PWR WEAPON PWR WEALTH...CHARTS FOR/TRADE 20. PAGE 14 F0263 — ECO/UNDEV ECO/TAC FOR/AID

B58
BUGEDA LANZAS J.,A STATEMENT OF THE LAWS OF CUBA IN MATTERS AFFECTING BUSINESS (2ND ED. REV., ENLARGED). CUBA L/A+17C LAW FINAN FAM LEGIS ACT/RES ADMIN GP/REL...BIBLIOG 20 OAS. PAGE 20 F0382 — JURID NAT/G INDUS WORKER

B58
PAN AMERICAN UNION,REPERTORIO DE PUBLICACIONES PERIODICAS ACTUALES LATINO-AMERICANAS. CULTURE ECO/UNDEV ADMIN LEAD GOV/REL 20 OAS. PAGE 103 F2023 — BIBLIOG L/A+17C NAT/G DIPLOM

B59
ALLEN R.L.,SOVIET INFLUENCE IN LATIN AMERICA. ECO/UNDEV FINAN PROC/MFG NAT/G TEC/DEV EDU/PROP EXEC ROUTINE ATTIT DRIVE PERSON ALL/VALS PWR...STAT CHARTS WORK FOR/TRADE 20. PAGE 4 F0071 — L/A+17C ECO/TAC INT/TRADE USSR

B59
GOMEZ ROBLES J.,A STATEMENT OF THE LAWS OF GUATEMALA IN MATTERS AFFECTING BUSINESS (2ND ED. REV., ENLARGED). GUATEMALA L/A+17C LAW FINAN FAM WORKER ACT/RES DIPLOM ADJUD ADMIN GP/REL 20 OAS. PAGE 48 F0945 — JURID NAT/G INDUS LEGIT

B59
NUNEZ JIMENEZ A.,LA LIBERACION DE LAS ISLAS. CUBA L/A+17C USA+45 LAW CHIEF PLAN DIPLOM FOR/AID OWN WEALTH 20 CASTRO/F. PAGE 99 F1945 — AGRI REV ECO/UNDEV NAT/G

B59
ROCHE J.,LA COLONISATION ALLEMANDE ET LE RIO GRANDE DO SUL. BRAZIL L/A+17C NAT/G PROVS INGP/REL RACE/REL DISCRIM HABITAT...GEOG SOC/INTEG 19/20 MIGRATION. PAGE 113 F2228 — ECO/UNDEV GP/REL ATTIT

B59
YRARRAZAVAL E.,AMERICA LATINE EN LA GUERRA FRIA. AFR EUR+WWI L/A+17C USA+45 USSR WOR+45 INDUS INT/ORG NAT/LISM POLICY. PAGE 150 F2953 — REGION DIPLOM ECO/UNDEV INT/TRADE

S59
PLAZA G.,"FOR A REGIONAL MARKET IN LATIN AMERICA." FUT L/A+17C CULTURE INDUS NAT/G ECO/TAC INT/TRADE ATTIT WEALTH...NEW/IDEA TREND OAS 20. PAGE 106 — MARKET INT/ORG REGION

F2092

B60
FERNANDES F.,MUDANCAS SOCIAIS NO BRASIL. BRAZIL L/A+17C SOCIETY AGRI PROVS LEAD GP/REL RACE/REL ORD/FREE...SOC SOC/INTEG 20 SAO/PAULO. PAGE 40 F0786
ECO/UNDEV STRATA INDUS

B60
RAMA C.M.,LAS CLASES SOCIALES EN EL URUGUAY. L/A+17C URUGUAY ELITES SOCIETY STRATA INDUS ATTIT HABITAT PWR...GEOG SOC/INTEG MUNICH 20. PAGE 109 F2138
ECO/UNDEV STRUCT PARTIC

B60
US GENERAL ACCOUNTING OFFICE,EXAMINATION OF ECONOMIC AND TECHNICAL ASSISTANCE PROGRAM FOR GUATEMALA. GUATEMALA L/A+17C USA+45 FINAN INDUS PLAN...POLICY STAT CHARTS 20 DEPT/STATE. PAGE 136 F2680
FOR/AID ECO/UNDEV TEC/DEV NAT/G

S60
"THE EMERGING COMMON MARKETS IN LATIN AMERICA." FUT L/A+17C STRATA DIST/IND INDUS LABOR NAT/G LEGIS ECO/TAC ADMIN RIGID/FLEX HEALTH...NEW/IDEA TIME/SEQ OAS 20. PAGE 1 F0013
FINAN ECO/UNDEV INT/TRADE

S60
BUTLER W.F.,"ECONOMIC PROGRESS IN LATIN AMERICA." L/A+17C USA+45 ECO/UNDEV AGRI FINAN NAT/G PLAN ECO/TAC FOR/AID ADMIN WEALTH...OLD/LIB TOT/POP 20. PAGE 21 F0397
INDUS ACT/RES

S60
HERRERA F.,"THE INTER-AMERICAN DEVELOPMENT BANK." USA+45 ECO/UNDEV INT/ORG CONSULT DELIB/GP PLAN ECO/TAC INT/TRADE ROUTINE WEALTH...STAT TERR/GP 20. PAGE 59 F1153
L/A+17C FINAN FOR/AID REGION

S60
JAFFEE A.J.,"POPULATION TRENDS AND CONTROLS IN UNDERDEVELOPED COUNTRIES." AFR FUT ISLAM L/A+17C S/ASIA CULTURE R+D FAM ACT/RES PLAN EDU/PROP BIO/SOC RIGID/FLEX HEALTH...SOC STAT OBS CHARTS 20. PAGE 66 F1303
ECO/UNDEV GEOG

S60
MORALES C.J.,"TRADE AND ECONOMIC INTEGRATION IN LATIN AMERICA." FUT L/A+17C LAW STRATA ECO/UNDEV DIST/IND INDUS LABOR NAT/G LEGIS ECO/TAC ADMIN RIGID/FLEX WEALTH...CONCPT NEW/IDEA CONT/OBS TIME/SEQ WORK 20. PAGE 93 F1825
FINAN INT/TRADE REGION

S60
NICHOLS J.P.,"HAZARDS OF AMERICAN PRIVATE INVESTMENT IN UNDERDEVELOPED COUNTRIES." FUT L/A+17C USA+45 USA-45 EXTR/IND CONSULT BAL/PWR ECO/TAC DOMIN ADJUD ATTIT SOVEREIGN WEALTH ...HIST/WRIT TIME/SEQ TREND TERR/GP VAL/FREE 20. PAGE 98 F1924
FINAN ECO/UNDEV CAP/ISM NAT/LISM

S60
OWEN C.F.,"US AND SOVIET RELATIONS WITH UNDERDEVELOPED COUNTRIES: LATIN AMERICA-A CASE STUDY." AFR COM L/A+17C USA+45 USSR EXTR/IND MARKET TEC/DEV DIPLOM ECO/TAC NAT/LISM ORD/FREE PWR ...TREND WORK 20. PAGE 102 F2005
ECO/UNDEV DRIVE INT/TRADE

B61
MEXICO; CINCUENTA ANOS DE REVOLUCION VOL. II. L/A+17C SOCIETY LABOR RECEIVE GP/REL AGE/Y HEALTH ...SOC/WK ANTHOL MUNICH 20 MEXIC/AMER. PAGE 1 F0014
ECO/UNDEV STRUCT INDUS POL/PAR

B61
BALASSA B.,THE THEORY OF ECONOMIC INTEGRATION. EUR+WWI L/A+17C MOD/EUR WOR+45 ECO/UNDEV MARKET INT/ORG NAT/G VOL/ASSN DELIB/GP PLAN CAP/ISM ECO/TAC...MAJORIT FOR/TRADE OEEC 20. PAGE 8 F0157
ECO/DEV ACT/RES INT/TRADE

B61
ELLIS H.S.,ECONOMIC DEVELOPMENT FOR LATIN AMERICA. L/A+17C AGRI FINAN INDUS FOR/AID GP/REL BAL/PAY DEMAND...ANTHOL 20 INTL/ECON. PAGE 37 F0723
ECO/UNDEV ECO/TAC PLAN INT/TRADE

B61
ESTEBAN J.C.,IMPERIALISMO Y DESARROLLO ECONOMICO. L/A+17C FINAN INDUS NAT/G ECO/TAC CONTROL ROLE. PAGE 38 F0747
ECO/UNDEV NAT/LISM DIPLOM BAL/PAY

B61
ESTEVEZ A.,ASPECTOS ECONOMICO-FINANCIEROS DE LA CAMPANA SANMARITANA. L/A+17C SPAIN FINAN COLONIAL LEAD ROLE ORD/FREE WEALTH 19 SOUTH/AMER SAN/MARTIN. PAGE 38 F0748
ECO/UNDEV REV BUDGET NAT/G

B61
FRIEDMANN W.G.,JOINT INTERNATIONAL BUSINESS VENTURES. ASIA ISLAM L/A+17C ECO/DEV DIST/IND FINAN PROC/MFG FACE/GP LG/CO NAT/G VOL/ASSN CONSULT EX/STRUC PLAN ADMIN ROUTINE WEALTH...OLD/LIB FOR/TRADE WORK 20. PAGE 44 F0865
ECO/UNDEV INT/TRADE

B61
LUZ N.V.,A LUTA PELA INDUSTRIALIZACAO DO BRAZIL. BRAZIL L/A+17C AGRI NAT/G TEC/DEV COLONIAL 19/20. PAGE 82 F1615
ECO/UNDEV INDUS NAT/LISM POLICY

B61
PERKINS D.,THE UNITED STATES AND LATIN AMERICAN. L/A+17C USA+45 USA-45 STRUCT COLONIAL REV ORD/FREE 19/20. PAGE 105 F2061
DIPLOM INT/TRADE NAT/G

B61
STARK H.,SOCIAL AND ECONOMIC FRONTIERS IN LATIN AMERICA (2ND ED.). CUBA FUT CULTURE AGRI INDUS ECO/TAC PRODUC ATTIT MARXISM...NAT/COMP BIBLIOG T 20. PAGE 125 F2470
L/A+17C SOCIETY DIPLOM ECO/UNDEV

S61
BARALL M.,"THE UNITED STATES GOVERNMENT RESPONDS." L/A+17C USA+45 SOCIETY NAT/G CREATE PLAN DIPLOM ECO/TAC ATTIT DRIVE RIGID/FLEX KNOWL SKILL WEALTH ...METH/CNCPT TIME/SEQ GEN/METH 20. PAGE 9 F0176
ECO/UNDEV ACT/RES FOR/AID

B62
ROUND TABLE ON EUROPE'S ROLE IN LATIN AMERICAN DEVELOPMENT. EUR+WWI L/A+17C PLAN BAL/PAY UTIL ROLE WEALTH...CHARTS ANTHOL 20 UN INT/AM/DEV. PAGE 1 F0017
ECO/UNDEV FINAN TEC/DEV FOR/AID

B62
DEBUYST F.,LAS CLASES SOCIALES EN AMERICA LATINA. L/A+17C SOCIETY STRUCT WORKER EDU/PROP RACE/REL ATTIT HABITAT ROLE...GEOG SOC NAT/COMP SOC/INTEG 20. PAGE 32 F0612
STRATA GP/REL WEALTH

B62
DREIER J.C.,THE ALLIANCE FOR PROGRESS. L/A+17C USA+45 CULTURE ECO/DEV ECO/UNDEV NAT/G PLAN DIPLOM PWR 20 OAS ALL/PROG. PAGE 34 F0661
FOR/AID INT/ORG ECO/TAC POLICY

B62
LEVY H.V.,LIBERDADE E JUSTICA SOCIAL (2ND ED.). BRAZIL COM L/A+17C USSR INT/ORG PARTIC GP/REL WEALTH 20 UN COM/PARTY. PAGE 79 F1544
ORD/FREE MARXISM CAP/ISM LAW

B62
MARTINS A.F.,REVOLUCAO BRANCA NO CAMPO. L/A+17C SERV/IND DEMAND EFFICIENCY PRODUC...POLICY METH/COMP. PAGE 86 F1685
AGRI ECO/UNDEV TEC/DEV NAT/COMP

B62
O'CONNOR H.,WORLD CRISES IN OIL (BMR). ISLAM L/A+17C INDUS LG/CO INT/TRADE 20. PAGE 100 F1956
EXTR/IND DIPLOM ECO/UNDEV SOCISM

B62
URQUIDI C.W.,A STATEMENT OF THE LAWS OF BOLIVIA IN MATTERS AFFECTING BUSINESS (3RD ED. REV., ENLARGED). L/A+17C LAW FINAN FAM WORKER ACT/RES DIPLOM ADJUD ADMIN GP/REL 20 BOLIV OAS. PAGE 133 F2626
JURID INDUS NAT/G LEGIT

B62
URQUIDI V.L.,FREE TRADE AND ECONOMIC INTEGRATION IN LATIN AMERICA: THE EVOLUTION OF A COMMON MARKET POLICY. ECO/UNDEV MARKET DIPLOM BAL/PAY FEDERAL ...POLICY CHARTS 20 LAFTA. PAGE 133 F2627
INT/TRADE REGION INT/ORG L/A+17C

B62
US AGENCY INTERNATIONAL DEV,OPERATIONS REPORT - 1962 (PAMPHLET). AFR ASIA L/A+17C USA+45 ECO/UNDEV FINAN INT/ORG NAT/G 20 MICHIGAN. PAGE 134 F2636
FOR/AID CHARTS STAT BUDGET

B62
US CONGRESS JOINT ECO COMM,ECONOMIC DEVELOPMENTS IN SOUTH AMERICA. USA+45 SOCIETY FINAN NAT/G PROB/SOLV TEC/DEV INT/TRADE TAX EFFICIENCY PRODUC ATTIT ...POLICY 20 ALL/PROG CONGRESS SOUTH/AMER. PAGE 135 F2654
L/A+17C ECO/UNDEV FOR/AID DIPLOM

B62
ZOOK P.D.,FOREIGN TRADE AND HUMAN CAPITAL. L/A+17C USA+45 FINAN DIPLOM ECO/TAC PRODUC...POLICY 20. PAGE 151 F2970
INT/TRADE ECO/UNDEV FOR/AID BAL/PAY

L62
"BIBLIOGRAPHY ON EDUCATION AND ECONOMIC AND SOCIAL DEVELOPMENT (AMERICAN SOURCES)" L/A+17C ECO/UNDEV PROB/SOLV...SOC 20. PAGE 1 F0015
BIBLIOG/A ACADEM EDU/PROP INTELL

L62
"HIGHER EDUCATION AND ECONOMIC AND SOCIAL DEVELOPMENT IN LATIN AMERICA: A BIBLIOGRAPHY." L/A+17C SOCIETY ECO/UNDEV PROF/ORG DIPLOM CONFER ...SOC 20. PAGE 1 F0016
BIBLIOG/A ACADEM INTELL EDU/PROP

B63
CENTRO ESTUDIOS MONETARIOS LAT,COOPERACION FINANCIERA EN AMERICA LATINA. L/A+17C PLAN PROB/SOLV CONTROL REGION DEMAND...POLICY ANTHOL 20. PAGE 22 F0433
ECO/UNDEV INT/TRADE MARKET FINAN

B63
CENTRO PARA EL DESARROLLO,LA ALIANZA PARA EL PROGRESO Y EL DESARROLLO SOCIAL DE AMERICA LATINA. L/A+17C INT/ORG DIPLOM ECO/TAC INT/TRADE ATTIT 20 ALL/PROG. PAGE 22 F0435
ECO/UNDEV FOR/AID PLAN REGION

B63
DE VRIES E.,SOCIAL ASPECTS OF ECONOMIC DEVELOPMENT IN LATIN AMERICA. CULTURE SOCIETY STRATA FINAN INDUS INT/ORG DELIB/GP ACT/RES ECO/TAC EDU/PROP ADMIN ATTIT SUPEGO HEALTH KNOWL ORD/FREE...SOC STAT TREND ANTHOL TOT/POP VAL/FREE. PAGE 31 F0608
L/A+17C ECO/UNDEV

B63
FLORES E.,LAND REFORM AND THE ALLIANCE FOR PROGRESS
AGRI

(PAMPHLET). L/A+17C USA+45 STRUCT ECO/UNDEV NAT/G WORKER CREATE PLAN ECO/TAC COERCE REV 20 ALL/PROG. PAGE 42 F0815
INT/ORG DIPLOM POLICY

B63
FURTADO C.,THE ECONOMIC GROWTH OF BRAZIL: A SURVEY FROM COLONIAL TO MODERN TIMES. L/A+17C AGRI DIST/IND EXTR/IND INDUS WORKER COLONIAL RACE/REL OWN GOV/COMP. PAGE 45 F0877
ECO/UNDEV TEC/DEV LABOR DOMIN

B63
GLADE W.P. JR.,THE POLITICAL ECONOMY OF MEXICO. FUT L/A+17C CULTURE SOCIETY AGRI INDUS DELIB/GP ACT/RES ECO/TAC ATTIT HEALTH ORD/FREE...STAT TIME/SEQ TREND MEXIC/AMER TOT/POP VAL/FREE 20. PAGE 48 F0928
FINAN ECO/UNDEV

B63
GORDON L.,A NEW DEAL FOR LATIN AMERICA. L/A+17C USA+45 CULTURE NAT/G TEC/DEV DIPLOM FOR/AID REGION TASK...POLICY 20 ALL/PROG DEPT/STATE. PAGE 49 F0958
ECO/UNDEV ECO/TAC INT/ORG PLAN

B63
HIRSCHMAN A.O.,JOURNEYS TOWARD PROGRESS: STUDIES OF ECONOMIC POLICYMAKING IN LATIN AMERICA. CHILE FUT ECO/UNDEV AGRI FINAN INDUS CONSULT DELIB/GP PLAN ATTIT HEALTH ORD/FREE WEALTH...POLICY STAT VAL/FREE COLOMB 20. PAGE 60 F1177
L/A+17C ECO/TAC BRAZIL

B63
IANNI O.,INDUSTRIALIZACAO E DESENVOLVIMENTO SOCIAL NO BRASIL. BRAZIL L/A+17C STRATA STRUCT ECO/UNDEV EDU/PROP LEAD LOBBY NAT/LISM 20. PAGE 64 F1257
WORKER GP/REL INDUS PARTIC

B63
INTERAMERICAN ECO AND SOC COUN,THE ALLIANCE FOR PROGRESS: ITS FIRST YEAR: 1961-1962. AGRI SCHOOL PLAN TEC/DEV INT/TRADE TAX GIVE ADMIN WEALTH...SOC 20 ALL/PROG SOUTH/AMER. PAGE 64 F1267
INT/ORG PROB/SOLV ECO/TAC L/A+17C

B63
LAGOS G.,INTERNATIONAL STRATIFICATION AND UNDERDEVELOPED COUNTRIES. L/A+17C WOR+45 PLAN ECO/TAC PWR RESPECT WEALTH...METH/CNCPT STAT CHARTS SIMUL GEN/LAWS TRUE/GP METH/GP VAL/FREE 20. PAGE 74 F1459
ECO/UNDEV STRATA

B63
MANGER W.,THE ALLIANCE FOR PROGRESS: A CRITICAL APPRAISAL. FUT L/A+17C USA+45 CULTURE ECO/UNDEV ACADEM NAT/G SCHOOL PLAN FOR/AID...POLICY OAS ALL/PROG. PAGE 84 F1651
DIPLOM INT/ORG ECO/TAC REGION

B63
MARITANO N.,AN ALLIANCE FOR PROGRESS. FUT L/A+17C USA+45 CULTURE ECO/UNDEV NAT/G PLAN CONTROL ...POLICY ALL/PROG. PAGE 85 F1669
DIPLOM INT/ORG ECO/TAC FOR/AID

B63
PAN AMERICAN UNION,THE EFFECTS OF THE EUROPEAN ECONOMIC COMMUNITY ON THE LATIN AMERICAN ECONOMIES (BMR). EUR+WWI L/A+17C ECO/UNDEV AGRI INDUS MARKET REGION 20 EEC TREATY. PAGE 103 F2024
INT/TRADE INT/ORG AGREE POLICY

B63
US AGENCY INTERNATIONAL DEV,OPERATIONS REPORT - 1963. AFR ASIA L/A+17C USA+45 ECO/UNDEV FINAN INT/ORG NAT/G. PAGE 134 F2637
FOR/AID CHARTS STAT BUDGET

B63
US GOVERNMENT,REPORT TO INTER-AMERICAN ECONOMIC AND SOCIAL COUNCIL AT SECOND ANNUAL MEETING. L/A+17C USA+45 VOL/ASSN TEC/DEV DIPLOM TAX EATING EFFICIENCY HEALTH...STAT CHARTS 20 AID. PAGE 136 F2682
ECO/TAC FOR/AID FINAN PLAN

B63
VELEZ GARCIA J.,DEVALUACION 1962; HISTORIA DOCUMENTAL DE UN PROCESO ECONOMICO. AFR L/A+17C USA+45 FINAN FOR/AID PRODUC WEALTH...POLICY STAT CHARTS ANTHOL 20 COLOMB. PAGE 141 F2774
ECO/UNDEV ECO/TAC PLAN NAT/G

B63
WAGLEY C.,INTRODUCTION TO BRAZIL. BRAZIL L/A+17C FAM KIN SCHOOL SECT ATTIT WEALTH...GEOG SOC. PAGE 142 F2799
ECO/UNDEV ELITES HABITAT STRATA

S63
POPPINO R.E.,"IMBALANCE IN BRAZIL." L/A+17C NAT/G TOP/EX PLAN DIPLOM LEGIT DRIVE WEALTH...CON/ANAL FOR/TRADE LAFTA 20. PAGE 107 F2105
POL/PAR ECO/TAC BRAZIL

B64
CENTRO ESTUDIOS MONETARIOS LAT,PROBLEMAS DE PAGOS EN AMERICA LATINA. L/A+17C MARKET BUDGET ECO/TAC EFFICIENCY WEALTH 20 CENTRAL/AM. PAGE 22 F0434
FINAN INT/TRADE BAL/PAY ECO/UNDEV

B64
LEWIN P.,THE FOREIGN TRADE OF COMMUNIST CHINA* ITS IMPACT ON THE FREE WORLD. AFR EUR+WWI L/A+17C S/ASIA ECO/UNDEV CREATE FOR/AID...STAT NET/THEORY TREND CHARTS. PAGE 79 F1546
ASIA INT/TRADE NAT/COMP USSR

B64
MAGALHAES S.,PRATICA DA EMANCIPACAO NACIONAL. L/A+17C INDUS PLAN ECO/TAC CONTROL NAT/LISM ORD/FREE. PAGE 84 F1640
BAL/PAY ECO/UNDEV DIPLOM WEALTH

B64
MAZA ZAVALA D.F.,VENEZUELA; UNA ECONOMIA DEPENDIENTE. L/A+17C VENEZUELA FINAN INDUS ...ECOMETRIC STAT TREND 20. PAGE 87 F1710
ECO/UNDEV BAL/PAY INT/TRADE PRICE

B64
NEHEMKIS P.,LATIN AMERICA: MYTH AND REALITY. INDUS INT/ORG PROB/SOLV CAP/ISM DIPLOM REV...SOC MUNICH 20. PAGE 97 F1907
REGION MYTH L/A+17C ECO/UNDEV

B64
ORGANIZATION AMERICAN STATES,ECONOMIC SURVEY OF LATIN AMERICA, 1962. L/A+17C AGRI DIST/IND INDUS MARKET PROC/MFG R+D PLAN TEC/DEV ECO/TAC REGION BAL/PAY ALL/VALS...CON/ANAL ORG/CHARTS GEN/METH OAS ALL/PROG 20 ALL/PROG. PAGE 102 F1998
ECO/UNDEV CHARTS

B64
POWELSON J.P.,LATIN AMERICA: TODAY'S ECONOMIC AND SOCIAL REVOLUTION. L/A+17C INTELL SOCIETY STRUCT AGRI INDUS NAT/G DIPLOM ECO/TAC REV...POLICY 20. PAGE 107 F2110
ECO/UNDEV WEALTH ADJUST PLAN

B64
RENO P.,THE ORDEAL OF BRITISH GUIANA. L/A+17C USA+45 STRUCT AGRI EXTR/IND INDUS NAT/G FOR/AID ORD/FREE...GEOG 20 GUIANA/BR INTRVN/ECO. PAGE 111 F2178
COLONIAL ECO/UNDEV SOCISM PWR

B64
ROBINSON R.D.,INTERNATIONAL BUSINESS POLICY. AFR INDIA L/A+17C USA+45 ELITES AGRI FOR/AID COERCE BAL/PAY...DECISION INT/LAW MGT 20. PAGE 113 F2224
ECO/TAC DIST/IND COLONIAL FINAN

B64
SEERS D.,CUBA: THE ECONOMIC AND SOCIAL REVOLUTION. L/A+17C USSR YUGOSLAVIA STRATA AGRI INDUS SCHOOL DELIB/GP PLAN ECO/TAC DOMIN EDU/PROP ATTIT RIGID/FLEX ALL/VALS...STAT OBS TIME/SEQ WORK VAL/FREE 20. PAGE 119 F2341
ACT/RES COERCE CUBA REV

B64
SINGER H.W.,INTERNATIONAL DEVELOPMENT: GROWTH AND CHANGE. AFR BRAZIL L/A+17C WOR+45 CULTURE AGRI INDUS NAT/G ACT/RES ECO/TAC EDU/PROP WEALTH...GEOG CONCPT METH/CNCPT STAT HYPO/EXP WORK TOT/POP 20. PAGE 122 F2412
FINAN ECO/UNDEV FOR/AID INT/TRADE

B64
TAX S.,EL CAPITALISMO DEL CENTAVO; UNA ECONOMIA INDIGENA DE GUATEMALA (2 VOLS.). GUATEMALA L/A+17C SOCIETY GP/REL DEMAND INCOME HABITAT...SOC MUNICH 20 INDIAN/AM. PAGE 129 F2539
ECO/UNDEV AGRI WEALTH COST

B64
URQUIDI V.L.,THE CHALLENGE OF DEVELOPMENT IN LATIN AMERICA. L/A+17C FINAN INT/ORG TEC/DEV DIPLOM INT/TRADE PRICE REGION PRODUC...CHARTS 20 ALL/PROG. PAGE 133 F2628
ECO/UNDEV ECO/TAC NAT/G TREND

B64
US CONGRESS JOINT ECO COMM,PRIVATE INVESTMENT IN LATIN AMERICA. L/A+17C USA+45 INT/ORG PROB/SOLV ECO/TAC ATTIT...INT 20 CONGRESS. PAGE 135 F2658
FINAN ECO/UNDEV PARL/PROC LEGIS

B64
WITHERS W.,THE ECONOMIC CRISIS IN LATIN AMERICA. BRAZIL CHILE STRATA AGRI DIPLOM FOR/AID PWR SOCISM ...POLICY 20 MEXIC/AMER ARGEN ALL/PROG. PAGE 148 F2914
L/A+17C ECO/UNDEV CAP/ISM ALL/IDEOS

L64
HAAS E.B.,"ECONOMICS AND DIFFERENTIAL PATTERNS OF POLITICAL INTEGRATION: PROJECTIONS ABOUT UNITY IN LATIN AMERICA." SOCIETY NAT/G DELIB/GP ACT/RES CREATE PLAN ECO/TAC REGION ROUTINE ATTIT DRIVE PWR WEALTH...CONCPT TREND CHARTS LAFTA TERR/GP 20. PAGE 52 F1020
L/A+17C INT/ORG MARKET

S64
HUELIN D.,"ECONOMIC INTEGRATION IN LATIN AMERICAN: PROGRESS AND PROBLEMS." L/A+17C ECO/DEV AGRI DIST/IND FINAN INDUS NAT/G VOL/ASSN CONSULT DELIB/GP EX/STRUC ACT/RES PLAN TEC/DEV ECO/TAC ROUTINE BAL/PAY WEALTH FOR/TRADE WORK TERR/GP 20. PAGE 63 F1232
MARKET ECO/UNDEV INT/TRADE

S64
KLEIN H.,"AMERICAN OIL COMPANIES IN LATIN AMERICA: THE BOLIVIAN EXPERIENCE." L/A+17C USA+45 USA-45 EXTR/IND LG/CO NAT/G ECO/TAC WEALTH...POLICY GEN/LAWS BOLIV TOT/POP 20 OIL. PAGE 72 F1405
MARKET ECO/UNDEV NAT/LISM

S64
NASH M.,"SOCIAL PREREQUISITES TO ECONOMIC GROWTH IN LATIN AMERICA AND SOUTHEAST ASIA." L/A+17C S/ASIA CULTURE SOCIETY ECO/UNDEV AGRI INDUS NAT/G PLAN TEC/DEV EDU/PROP ROUTINE ALL/VALS...POLICY RELATIV SOC NAT/COMP WORK TOT/POP 20. PAGE 96 F1894
ECO/DEV PERCEPT

B65
ALEXANDER R.J.,ORGANIZED LABOR IN LATIN AMERICA. L/A+17C INT/ORG LEGIS WORKER TEC/DEV BARGAIN INT/TRADE REV...NAT/COMP BIBLIOG 20. PAGE 3 F0059
LABOR POL/PAR ECO/UNDEV POLICY

B65
APTER D.E.,THE POLITICS OF MODERNIZATION. AFR L/A+17C CULTURE NAT/G POL/PAR ADMIN COLONIAL
ECO/UNDEV GEN/LAWS

NAT/LISM ATTIT RIGID/FLEX PWR...SOC CONCPT. PAGE 6 F0109
STRATA CREATE

B65
BAERRESEN D.W.,LATIN AMERICAN TRADE PATTERNS. L/A+17C ECO/UNDEV AGRI INDUS MARKET CREATE ...NET/THEORY CHARTS LAFTA. PAGE 8 F0149
INT/TRADE STAT REGION

B65
GORDON W.,THE POLITICAL ECONOMY OF LATIN AMERICA. L/A+17C FINAN MARKET PROB/SOLV TEC/DEV RECEIVE ADMIN WEALTH 20. PAGE 49 F0962
ECO/UNDEV INT/TRADE REGION POLICY

B65
HARBISON F.,MANPOWER AND EDUCATION. AFR CHINA/COM IRAN L/A+17C S/ASIA TEC/DEV ADJUST OPTIMAL SKILL ...ANTHOL 20. PAGE 55 F1073
ECO/UNDEV EDU/PROP WORKER NAT/COMP

B65
IANNI O.,ESTADO E CAPITALISMO. L/A+17C FINAN TEC/DEV ECO/TAC ORD/FREE WEALTH POLICY. PAGE 64 F1258
ECO/UNDEV STRUCT INDUS NAT/G

B65
INTERAMERICAN ECO AND SOC COUN,THE ALLIANCE FOR PROGRESS: ITS THIRD YEAR 1963-1964. FUT L/A+17C WOR+45 ECO/DEV INT/ORG PLAN CONTROL ADJUST...STAT ANTHOL SOC/INTEG 20 ALL/PROG. PAGE 64 F1268
ECO/UNDEV ECO/TAC FINAN FOR/AID

B65
NATIONAL CENTRAL LIBRARY,LATIN AMERICAN ECONOMIC AND SOCIAL SERIALS. UK SOCIETY NAT/G PLAN PROB/SOLV ...SOC 20. PAGE 97 F1897
BIBLIOG INT/TRADE ECO/UNDEV L/A+17C

B65
SABLE M.H.,PERIODICALS FOR LATIN AMERICAN ECONOMIC DEVELOPMENT, TRADE, AND FINANCE: AN ANNOTATED BIBLIOGRAPHY (A PAMPHLET). ECO/TAC PRODUC PROFIT ...STAT NAT/COMP 20 OAS. PAGE 115 F2266
BIBLIOG/A L/A+17C ECO/UNDEV INT/TRADE

B65
US BUREAU EDUC CULTURAL AFF,RESOURCES SURVEY FOR LATIN AMERICAN COUNTRIES. L/A+17C USA+45 CULTURE INDUS INT/ORG SECT PLAN EDU/PROP POLICY. PAGE 134 F2643
NAT/G ECO/UNDEV FOR/AID DIPLOM

B65
US SENATE COMM ON FOREIGN REL,HEARINGS ON THE FOREIGN ASSISTANCE PROGRAM. AFR ASIA L/A+17C USA+45 WOR+45 FORCES TEC/DEV BUDGET CONTROL WEAPON ORD/FREE 20 UN CONGRESS SEC/STATE. PAGE 139 F2734
FOR/AID DIPLOM INT/ORG ECO/UNDEV

B65
WISH J.R.,ECONOMIC DEVELOPMENT IN LATIN AMERICA: AN ANNOTATED BIBLIOGRAPHY. L/A+17C COM/IND MARKET R+D CREATE CAP/ISM ATTIT...STAT METH 20. PAGE 148 F2912
BIBLIOG/A ECO/UNDEV TEC/DEV AGRI

L65
WIONCZEK M.,"LATIN AMERICA FREE TRADE ASSOCIATION." AGRI DIST/IND FINAN INDUS INT/ORG LABOR NAT/G TEC/DEV ECO/TAC HEALTH SKILL WEALTH...POLICY RELATIV MGT LAFTA 20. PAGE 148 F2909
L/A+17C MARKET REGION

S65
BRANDENBURG F.,"THE RELEVANCE OF MEXICAN EXPERIENCE TO LATIN AMERICAN DEVELOPMENT." BRAZIL CHILE VENEZUELA STRUCT ECO/UNDEV AGRI CREATE ECO/TAC ...STAT RECORD MEXIC/AMER ARGEN COLOMB. PAGE 18 F0340
L/A+17C GOV/COMP

S65
JOHNSON L.L.,"US BUSINESS INTERESTS IN CUBA AND THE RISE OF CASTRO." L/A+17C USA+45 ECO/UNDEV INDUS NAT/G VOL/ASSN ATTIT ORD/FREE PWR WEALTH ALL/PROG. PAGE 68 F1330
DIPLOM CUBA ECO/TAC INT/TRADE

S65
WHITAKER A.P.,"ARGENTINA: STRUGGLE FOR RECOVERY." L/A+17C USA+45 NAT/G TOP/EX PLAN LEGIT COERCE REV RIGID/FLEX PWR WEALTH...RECORD ALL/PROG ARGEN FOR/TRADE 20. PAGE 146 F2867
POL/PAR ECO/TAC NAT/LISM

B66
ANDRESKI S.,PARASITISM AND SUBVERSION* THE CASE OF LATIN AMERICA. CULTURE ECO/UNDEV LABOR NAT/G SECT PROB/SOLV RACE/REL TOTALISM ATTIT WEALTH ALL/IDEOS. PAGE 5 F0100
L/A+17C GOV/COMP STRATA REV

B66
BROWN R.T.,TRANSPORT AND THE ECONOMIC INTEGRATION OF SOUTH AMERICA. L/A+17C ECO/UNDEV NAT/G OP/RES DIPLOM INT/TRADE REGION WEALTH...ECOMETRIC GEOG STAT LAFTA TIME. PAGE 19 F0373
MARKET DIST/IND SIMUL

B66
CANNING HOUSE LIBRARY,AUTHOR AND SUBJECT CATALOGUES OF THE CANNING HOUSE LIBRARY (5 VOLS.). UK CULTURE LEAD...SOC 19/20. PAGE 21 F0411
BIBLIOG L/A+17C NAT/G DIPLOM

B66
INARRITU A.L.,EL PATRON CAMBIO-ORO Y SUS REFORMAS. AFR L/A+17C WOR+45 PLAN PROB/SOLV BUDGET ECO/TAC INT/TRADE EFFICIENCY ORD/FREE 20 MEXIC/AMER. PAGE 64 F1262
ECO/UNDEV FINAN DIPLOM POLICY

B66
LAMBERG R.F.,PRAG UND DIE DRITTE WELT. AFR ASIA CZECHOSLVK L/A+17C MARKET TEC/DEV ECO/TAC REV ATTIT 20 TREATY. PAGE 75 F1462
DIPLOM ECO/UNDEV INT/TRADE FOR/AID

B66
SOMMERFELD R.M.,TAX REFORM AND THE ALLIANCE FOR PROGRESS. USA+45 ECO/DEV ECO/UNDEV FINAN NAT/G INCOME ORD/FREE WEALTH...STAT CHARTS 20 ALL/PROG. PAGE 124 F2442
TAX INT/ORG L/A+17C FOR/AID

B66
US HOUSE COMM FOREIGN AFFAIRS,HEARINGS ON HR 12449 A BILL TO AMEND FURTHER THE FOREIGN ASSISTANCE ACT OF 1961. AFR ASIA L/A+17C USA+45 VIETNAM INT/ORG TEC/DEV INT/TRADE ATTIT ORD/FREE 20 UN NATO CONGRESS AID. PAGE 137 F2692
FOR/AID ECO/TAC ECO/UNDEV DIPLOM

S66
COHEN A.,"THE TECHNOLOGY/ELITE APPROACH TO THE DEVELOPMENTAL PROCESS* PERUVIAN CASE STUDY." L/A+17C STRUCT CREATE ECO/TAC FOR/AID CIVMIL/REL MARXISM TECHRACY HYPO/EXP. PAGE 26 F0496
ECO/UNDEV ELITES PERU

S66
JAVITS J.K.,"POLITICAL ACTION VITAL FOR LATIN AMERICAN INTEGRATION." ECO/UNDEV INT/ORG POL/PAR VOL/ASSN PLAN PROB/SOLV INT/TRADE EFFICIENCY 20 OAS LAFTA ALL/PROG. PAGE 66 F1308
L/A+17C ECO/TAC REGION

B67
ANDERSON C.W.,POLITICS AND ECONOMIC CHANGE IN LATIN AMERICA. L/A+17C INDUS NAT/G OP/RES ADMIN DEMAND ...POLICY STAT CHARTS NAT/COMP 20. PAGE 5 F0093
ECO/UNDEV PROB/SOLV PLAN ECO/TAC

B67
BUSEY J.L.,NOTES ON COSTA RICAN DEMOCRACY. COSTA/RICA L/A+17C NAT/G POL/PAR LEGIS CHOOSE OWN ATTIT...BIBLIOG 20. PAGE 20 F0394
CONSTN MAJORIT SOCIETY ECO/UNDEV

B67
CASTILLO C.M.,GROWTH AND INTEGRATION IN CENTRAL AMERICA. L/A+17C CREATE PROB/SOLV ECO/TAC REGION PRODUC...OBS BIBLIOG 20. PAGE 22 F0429
ECO/UNDEV INT/TRADE NAT/COMP

B67
DIEGUES M.,SOCIAL SCIENCE IN LATIN AMERICA. L/A+17C ...JURID SOC ANTHOL 20. PAGE 33 F0637
METH ACADEM EDU/PROP ACT/RES

B67
HANNAH H.W.,THE LEGAL BASE FOR UNIVERSITIES IN DEVELOPING COUNTRIES. AFR ASIA L/A+17C S/ASIA USA+45 FINAN CREATE EDU/PROP TASK EFFICIENCY ...JURID METH/COMP 20. PAGE 54 F1060
ADMIN LAW ACADEM LEGIS

B67
PIKE F.B.,FREEDOM AND REFORM IN LATIN AMERICA. BRAZIL URUGUAY CONSTN CULTURE SECT DIPLOM EDU/PROP PARTIC DRIVE ALL/VALS CATHISM...GEOG ANTHOL BIBLIOG REFORMERS BOLIV. PAGE 106 F2086
L/A+17C ORD/FREE ECO/UNDEV REV

B67
SMITH T.L.,THE PROCESS OF RURAL DEVELOPMENT IN LATIN AMERICA (A MONOGRAPH). L/A+17C STRATA INDUS PLAN GP/REL PERS/REL RIGID/FLEX WEALTH...OBS CHARTS ORG/CHARTS ANTHOL 20 COLOMB. PAGE 123 F2434
IDEA/COMP SOC AGRI ECO/UNDEV

B67
US CONGRESS SENATE,SURVEY OF THE ALLIANCE FOR PROGRESS; INFLATION IN LATIN AMERICA (PAMPHLET). USA+45 MARKET INT/ORG DIPLOM INT/TRADE BAL/PAY SENATE ALL/PROG. PAGE 135 F2666
L/A+17C FINAN POLICY FOR/AID

B67
US SENATE COMM ON FOREIGN REL,LATIN AMERICAN SUMMIT CONFERENCE. L/A+17C USA+45 FINAN PLAN SENATE ALL/PROG. PAGE 139 F2740
FOR/AID BUDGET DIPLOM INT/ORG

B67
US SENATE COMM ON FOREIGN REL,INTER-AMERICAN DEVELOPMENT BANK ACT AMENDMENT. L/A+17C USA+45 DELIB/GP DIPLOM FOR/AID BAL/PAY...CHARTS SENATE. PAGE 139 F2741
LAW FINAN INT/ORG ECO/UNDEV

B67
WILLIAMS E.J.,LATIN AMERICAN CHRISTIAN DEMOCRATIC PARTIES. L/A+17C FAM LABOR FORCES...CATH TREND BIBLIOG 20. PAGE 147 F2890
POL/PAR GP/COMP CATHISM ALL/VALS

B67
ZONDAG C.H.,THE BOLIVIAN ECONOMY 1952-65. L/A+17C TEC/DEV FOR/AID ADMIN...OBS TREND CHARTS BIBLIOG 20 BOLIV. PAGE 151 F2969
ECO/UNDEV INDUS PRODUC

S67
ADAMS R.N.,"ETHICS AND THE SOCIAL ANTHROPOLOGIST IN LATIN AMERICA." USA+45 INTELL PROB/SOLV ECO/TAC LEAD...DECISION SOC NAT/COMP PERS/COMP. PAGE 2 F0039
L/A+17C POLICY ECO/UNDEV CONSULT

S67
AGUILAR M.A.,"?UNA OEA MAS FUERTE O UNA AMERICA LATINA MAS DEBIL?" L/A+17C USA+45 USA-45 ECO/UNDEV INDUS CHIEF DELIB/GP FORCES CONTROL PWR 20 OAS KENNEDY/JF JOHNSON/LB. PAGE 3 F0050
INT/ORG DIPLOM POLICY COLONIAL

S67
BRANCO R.,"LAND REFORM* THE ANSWER TO LATIN AMERICA'S AGRICULTURAL DEVELOPMENT?" L/A+17C NAT/G PLAN TEC/DEV BUDGET RENT EFFICIENCY 20. PAGE 18 F0339
ECO/UNDEV AGRI TAX OWN

S67
FRIEDENBERG D.M.,"THE US IN LATIN AMERICA; A RECKONING OF SHAME." L/A+17C USA+45 USA-45 INT/ORG CAP/ISM FOR/AID 17/20 OAS. PAGE 44 F0857 DIPLOM POLICY DOMIN COLONIAL

S67
GONZALEZ M.P.,"CUBA, UNA REVOLUCION EN MARCHA." CUBA L/A+17C USA+45 VIETNAM ECO/UNDEV FORCES DIPLOM DOMIN...POLICY MARXIST NAT/COMP CASTRO/F. PAGE 48 F0946 REV NAT/G COLONIAL SOVEREIGN

S67
GRAHAM R.,"BRAZIL'S DILEMMA." BRAZIL FUT L/A+17C NAT/G CHIEF PROB/SOLV ECO/TAC PWR 20. PAGE 50 F0972 ECO/UNDEV CONSTN POL/PAR POLICY

S67
HEATH D.B.,"BOLIVIA UNDER BARRIENTOS." L/A+17C NAT/G CHIEF DIPLOM ECO/TAC...POLICY 20 BOLIV. PAGE 58 F1132 ECO/UNDEV POL/PAR REV CONSTN

S67
HERRERA F.,"EUROPEAN PARTICIPATION IN THE LATIN AMERICAN REGIONAL INTEGRATION" EUR+WWI L/A+17C GP/REL INGP/REL 20. PAGE 59 F1154 DIPLOM REGION INT/ORG FINAN

S67
HILDEBRAND J.R.,"THE CENTRAL AMERICAN COMMON MARKET: ECONOMIC AND POLITICAL INTEGRATION." L/A+17C USA+45 ECO/DEV ECO/UNDEV AGRI SOVEREIGN. PAGE 59 F1170 DIPLOM ECO/TAC INT/TRADE INT/ORG

S67
IBARRA J.,"EL EXPERIMENTO CUBANO." COM CUBA L/A+17C USA+45 ECO/UNDEV LEGIS INT/TRADE CONTROL REV NAT/LISM PWR 19/20 TREATY. PAGE 64 F1259 COLONIAL DIPLOM NAT/G POLICY

S67
KINGSLEY R.E.,"THE US BUSINESS IMAGE IN LATIN AMERICA." L/A+17C USA+45 NAT/G TEC/DEV CAP/ISM FOR/AID DOMIN EDU/PROP...CONCPT LING IDEA/COMP 20. PAGE 71 F1396 ATTIT LOVE DIPLOM ECO/UNDEV

S67
PETRAS J.,"U.S. HEGEMONY AND LATIN AMERICAN RULING CLASSES." L/A+17C USA+45 ECO/UNDEV FOR/AID REV SOC. PAGE 105 F2071 NAT/G ATTIT DIPLOM POLICY

S67
PETRAS J.,"GUERRILLA MOVEMENTS IN LATIN AMERICA - I." GUATEMALA PERU VENEZUELA NAT/G COLONIAL LEAD ATTIT PWR...TIME/SEQ METH/COMP 20 COLOMB. PAGE 105 F2072 GUERRILLA REV L/A+17C MARXISM

S67
RAMA C.M.,"PASADO Y PRESENTE DE LA RELIGION EN AMERICA LATINA." L/A+17C ELITES SOCIETY STRATA MARXISM...STAT WORSHIP PROTESTANT. PAGE 109 F2139 SECT CATHISM STRUCT NAT/COMP

S67
STYCOS J.M.,"POLITICS AND POPULATION CONTROL IN LATIN AMERICA." USA+45 FAM NAT/G GP/REL AGE/C ATTIT CATHISM MARXISM...POLICY UN WHO. PAGE 127 F2509 PLAN CENSUS CONTROL L/A+17C

N67
US HOUSE COMM FOREIGN AFFAIRS,COMMUNIST ACTIVITIES IN LATIN AMERICA 1967 (PAMPHLET). CUBA USA+45 DIPLOM INT/TRADE EDU/PROP COERCE GUERRILLA HOUSE/REP OAS. PAGE 137 F2696 L/A+17C MARXISM ORD/FREE ECO/TAC

N67
US SENATE COMM ON FOREIGN REL,SURVEY OF THE ALLIANCE FOR PROGRESS: THE LATIN AMERICAN MILITARY (PAMPHLET). USA+45 INT/ORG POL/PAR DIPLOM AGREE GP/REL ROLE ORD/FREE 20. PAGE 139 F2746 L/A+17C FORCES CIVMIL/REL POLICY

LAB/EXP....LABORATORY EXPERIMENTS

S61
CYERT R.M.,"TWO EXPERIMENTS ON BIAS AND CONFLICT IN ORGANIZATIONAL ESTIMATION." WORKER PROB/SOLV EFFICIENCY...MGT PSY STAT CHARTS. PAGE 29 F0568 LAB/EXP ROUTINE ADMIN DECISION

LABOR FORCE....SEE WORKER

LABOR RELATIONS....SEE LABOR, ALSO RELATIONS INDEX

LABOR UNIONS....SEE LABOR

LABOR....LABOR UNIONS (BUT NOT GUILDS)

N
AMERICAN ECONOMIC REVIEW. FINAN INDUS LABOR OP/RES CAP/ISM INT/TRADE TAX WEALTH...CON/ANAL CHARTS 20. PAGE 1 F0001 BIBLIOG/A USA+45 ECO/DEV NAT/G

N
ECONOMIC ABSTRACTS. WOR+45 FINAN INDUS MARKET LABOR ACT/RES INT/TRADE WRITING GP/REL...MGT 20. PAGE 1 F0005 BIBLIOG/A EDU/PROP

N
AMERICAN ECONOMIC ASSOCIATION,THE JOURNAL OF ECONOMIC ABSTRACTS. ECO/UNDEV MARKET LABOR DIPLOM ...MGT CONCPT METH 20. PAGE 5 F0086 BIBLIOG/A R+D FINAN

N
RAND SCHOOL OF SOCIAL SCIENCE,INDEX TO LABOR ARTICLES. ECO/DEV INT/ORG LEGIS DIPLOM GP/REL ...NAT/COMP 20. PAGE 109 F2143 BIBLIOG LABOR MGT ADJUD

N
UNESCO,INTERNATIONAL BIBLIOGRAPHY OF ECONOMICS (VOLUMES 1-8). WOR+45 AGRI INDUS LABOR PLAN TEC/DEV 20. PAGE 132 F2607 BIBLIOG ECO/DEV ECO/UNDEV

N
US LIBRARY OF CONGRESS,SELECTED AND ANNOTATED BIBLIOGRAPHY ON LABOR PROBLEMS AND POLICIES IN A WARTIME ECONOMY (PAMPHLET). USA-45 INDUS LEGIS GP/REL DISCRIM PRODUC...SOC 20. PAGE 137 F2708 BIBLIOG/A WAR LABOR WORKER

N
US SUPERINTENDENT OF DOCUMENTS,LABOR (PRICE LIST 33). USA+45 LAW AGRI CONSTRUC INDUS NAT/G BARGAIN PRICE ADMIN AUTOMAT PRODUC MGT. PAGE 140 F2753 BIBLIOG/A WORKER LABOR LEGIS

B02
WEBB S.,THE HISTORY OF TRADE UNIONISM. UK PARTIC ...OBS CHARTS BIBLIOG/A 15/19 CASEBOOK. PAGE 144 F2837 LABOR VOL/ASSN GP/REL

B14
LEVINE L.,SYNDICALISM IN FRANCE (2ND ED.). FRANCE LAW SOCIETY ECO/DEV NAT/G ECO/TAC LEAD ATTIT ...POLICY CONCPT STAT BIBLIOG 18/20 REFORMERS. PAGE 79 F1542 LABOR INDUS SOCISM REV

N19
BUSINESS ECONOMISTS' GROUP,INCOME POLICIES (PAMPHLET). UK INDUS LABOR TOP/EX PAY COST PRODUC ...ECOMETRIC GOV/COMP SIMUL ANTHOL 20. PAGE 20 F0395 INCOME WORKER WEALTH POLICY

N19
ENGELS F.,THE BRITISH LABOUR MOVEMENT (PAMPHLET). FRANCE GERMANY MOD/EUR UK USA-45 POL/PAR WORKER PAY EDU/PROP PRICE REPRESENT GP/REL 19. PAGE 37 F0730 ECO/TAC MARXISM LABOR STRATA

N19
HOGARTY R.A.,NEW JERSEY FARMERS AND MIGRANT HOUSING RULES (PAMPHLET). USA+45 LAW ELITES FACE/GP LABOR PROF/ORG LOBBY PERS/REL RIGID/FLEX ROLE 20 NEW/JERSEY. PAGE 61 F1193 AGRI PROVS WORKER HEALTH

N19
INTERNATIONAL LABOUR OFFICE,EMPLOYMENT, UNEMPLOYMENT AND LABOUR FORCE STATISTICS (PAMPHLET). EUR+WWI STRATA AGRI INDUS NAT/G PROB/SOLV PAY AGE SEX...SAMP NAT/COMP METH 20 ILO. PAGE 65 F1278 WORKER LABOR STAT ECO/DEV

N19
MCCONNELL G.,THE STEEL SEIZURE OF 1952 (PAMPHLET). USA+45 FINAN INDUS PROC/MFG LG/CO EX/STRUC ADJUD CONTROL GP/REL ORD/FREE PWR 20 TRUMAN/HS PRESIDENT CONGRESS. PAGE 88 F1721 DELIB/GP LABOR PROB/SOLV NAT/G

N19
STUTZ R.L.,COLLECTIVE DEALING BY UNITS OF LOCAL GOVERNMENT IN CONNECTICUT (PAMPHLET). USA+45 LOC/G PROVS...STAT MUNICH 20 CONNECTICT. PAGE 127 F2508 VOL/ASSN LABOR WORKER

B20
WEBB S.,INDUSTRIAL DEMOCRACY. UK PARTIC GP/REL ...SOC OBS RECORD CHARTS 18/20. PAGE 144 F2838 LABOR NAT/G VOL/ASSN MAJORIT

B23
HOBSON J.A.,INCENTIVES IN THE NEW INDUSTRIAL ORDER. USA-45 NAT/G PAY COST EFFICIENCY PRODUC WEALTH ...MAJORIT PSY SOC/WK 20. PAGE 60 F1186 INDUS LABOR INCOME OPTIMAL

B24
CLARK J.B.,THE DISTRIBUTION OF WEALTH (1899). WORKER OWN PRODUC PROFIT WEALTH LAISSEZ...IDEA/COMP GEN/LAWS. PAGE 25 F0478 ECO/TAC INDUS LABOR INCOME

B26
SUFRIN S.C.,A BRIEF ANNOTATED BIBLIOGRAPHY ON LABOR IN EMERGING SOCIETIES. WOR+45 CULTURE SOCIETY INDUS EDU/PROP GP/REL INGP/REL. PAGE 127 F2510 BIBLIOG/A LABOR ECO/UNDEV WORKER

B28
DE MAN H.,THE PSYCHOLOGY OF SOCIALISM. EUR+WWI USSR LABOR NAT/LISM PERSON WEALTH MARXISM...METH/COMP 20. PAGE 31 F0604 WORKER ATTIT SOC SOCISM

B28
HARDMAN J.B.,AMERICAN LABOR DYNAMICS. WORKER ECO/TAC DOMIN ADJUD LEAD LOBBY PWR...POLICY MGT. PAGE 55 F1079 LABOR INGP/REL ATTIT GP/REL

B31
CROOK W.H.,THE GENERAL STRIKE: A STUDY OF LABOR'S TRAGIC WEAPON IN THEORY AND PRACTICE. BELGIUM FRANCE SWEDEN UK WOR-45 PROB/SOLV ECO/TAC DOMIN PWR LABOR WORKER LG/CO

...POLICY TIME/SEQ NAT/COMP GEN/LAWS 19/20 STRIKE. PAGE 29 F0555 — BARGAIN

B31
JEVONS W.S.,THE THEORY OF POLITICAL ECONOMY (4TH ED.; 1ST ED. 1871). WOR-45 FINAN MARKET RENT WEALTH ...LOG MATH QUANT CON/ANAL IDEA/COMP BIBLIOG METH 17/19. PAGE 67 F1318 — GEN/LAWS UTIL LABOR

B35
HICKS J.R.,THE THEORY OF WAGES. INDUS NAT/G PAY PRICE CONTROL COST EFFICIENCY WEALTH 19/20 MARSHALL/A CLARK/JB. PAGE 59 F1164 — INCOME WORKER LABOR PRODUC

B35
MARX K.,WAGE-LABOR AND CAPITAL -- VALUE, PRICE AND PROFIT. LABOR PAY PRICE COST INCOME OWN PROFIT WEALTH 19. PAGE 86 F1690 — STRATA WORKER MARXIST MARXISM

B35
O'CONNOR H.,REVOLUTION IN SEATTLE. USA-45 STRATA WORKER GP/REL ATTIT SOCISM...OBS BIBLIOG/A 20 SEATTLE STRIKE COM/PARTY. PAGE 99 F1954 — REV EDU/PROP LABOR MARXISM

B35
WADE J.,HISTORY OF THE MIDDLE AND WORKING CLASSES; WITH A POPULAR EXPOSITION OF THE ECONOMICAL AND POLITICAL PRINCIPLES.... FRANCE UK CONSTN FINAN INDUS LABOR INCOME PROFIT KNOWL MORAL ORD/FREE WEALTH...CHARTS 14/19. PAGE 142 F2797 — WORKER STRATA CONCPT

B37
BROOKS R.R.,WHEN LABOR ORGANIZES. FINAN EDU/PROP ADMIN LOBBY PARTIC REPRESENT WEALTH TREND. PAGE 19 F0364 — LABOR GP/REL POLICY

B38
LEVINSON E.,LABOR ON THE MARCH. WORKER CREATE ECO/TAC ADJUD LEAD PARL/PROC PARTIC INGP/REL SKILL POLICY. PAGE 79 F1543 — LABOR INCOME NAT/G PLAN

B38
MEADE J.E.,AN INTRODUCTION TO ECONOMIC ANALYSIS AND POLICY (AMERICAN EDITION EDITED BY C.J. HITCH). FINAN INDUS MARKET LABOR INT/TRADE CONTROL COST DEMAND INCOME...CLASSIF CHARTS T 20 KEYNES/JM MONOPOLY. PAGE 89 F1737 — CONCPT PROFIT PRODUC

B38
REICH N.,LABOR RELATIONS IN REPUBLICAN GERMANY. GERMANY CONSTN ECO/DEV INDUS NAT/G ADMIN CONTROL GP/REL FASCISM POPULISM 20 WEIMAR/REP. PAGE 110 F2176 — WORKER MGT LABOR BARGAIN

B39
MARQUAND H.A.,ORGANIZED LABOUR IN FOUR CONTINENTS. EUR+WWI USA-45 INDUS NAT/G PAY GP/REL TOTALISM ATTIT WEALTH ALL/IDEOS...TREND NAT/COMP 20 ILO AFL/CIO EUROPE CHINJAP MEXIC/AMER. PAGE 85 F1673 — LABOR WORKER CONCPT ANTHOL

B40
BATCHELOR B.,THE NEW OUTLOOK IN BUSINESS. LAW WORKER TAX LEAD ORD/FREE...POLICY TREND. PAGE 11 F0208 — LG/CO GP/REL CAP/ISM LABOR

B40
HELLMAN F.S.,THE NEW DEAL: SELECTED LIST OF REFERENCES. USA-45 FINAN LABOR EX/STRUC CREATE INT/TRADE ADMIN CT/SYS 20 SUPREME/CT. PAGE 58 F1145 — BIBLIOG/A ECO/TAC PLAN POLICY

B40
WUNDERLICH F.,LABOR UNDER GERMAN DEMOCRACY, ARBITRATION 1918-1933. GERMANY NAT/G PAY REPAR ADJUD CT/SYS GP/REL...MAJORIT 20. PAGE 149 F2941 — LABOR WORKER INDUS BARGAIN

B41
DAUGHERTY C.R.,LABOR PROBLEMS IN AMERICAN INDUSTRY (5TH ED.). USA-45 SOCIETY OP/RES ECO/TAC...MGT PSY T 20. PAGE 30 F0581 — LABOR INDUS GP/REL PROB/SOLV

B41
LESTER R.A.,ECONOMICS OF LABOR. UK USA-45 TEC/DEV BARGAIN PAY INGP/REL INCOME...MGT 19/20. PAGE 78 F1532 — LABOR ECO/DEV INDUS WORKER

B41
SLICHTER S.H.,UNION POLICIES AND INDUSTRIAL MANAGEMENT. USA-45 INDUS TEC/DEV PAY GP/REL INGP/REL COST EFFICIENCY PRODUC...POLICY 20. PAGE 123 F2420 — BARGAIN LABOR MGT WORKER

S41
BRITT S.H.,"CONFORMITY OF LABOR NEWSPAPERS WITH RESPECT TO THE AFL-CIO CONFLICT." BAL/PWR CONSEN ATTIT. PAGE 18 F0355 — LABOR PRESS DOMIN GP/REL

B42
ROBBINS J.J.,THE GOVERNMENT OF LABOR RELATIONS IN SWEDEN. SWEDEN LAW CONSTN ADJUD CT/SYS GP/REL ...JURID 20. PAGE 112 F2200 — NAT/G BARGAIN LABOR INDUS

L42
GRANT J.A.C.,"THE GUILD RETURNS TO AMERICA." CHRIST-17C USA-45 LEGIS LICENSE ADJUD CONTROL GP/REL. PAGE 50 F0978 — PROF/ORG JURID LABOR PWR

S43
GOLDEN C.S.,"NEW PATTERNS OF DEMOCRACY." NEIGH DELIB/GP EDU/PROP EXEC PARTIC...MGT METH/CNCPT OBS TREND. PAGE 48 F0935 — LABOR REPRESENT LG/CO GP/REL

S43
HERBERG W.,"BUREAUCRACY AND DEMOCRACY IN LABOR UNIONS." LAW CONSTN STRUCT WORKER ADMIN CONTROL PARTIC RIGID/FLEX PWR TREND. PAGE 59 F1151 — LABOR REPRESENT ROUTINE INGP/REL

B45
MILLIS H.A.,ORGANIZED LABOR (FIRST ED.). LAW STRUCT DELIB/GP WORKER ECO/TAC ADJUD CONTROL REPRESENT INGP/REL INCOME MGT. PAGE 92 F1797 — LABOR POLICY ROUTINE GP/REL

S45
MILLS C.W.,"THE TRADE UNION LEADER: A COLLECTIVE PORTRAIT." EX/STRUC TOP/EX INGP/REL...QU CON/ANAL CHARTS. PAGE 92 F1798 — LABOR LEAD STAT STRATA

B46
DRUCKER P.F.,CONCEPT OF CORPORATION. LAW LABOR WORKER PRICE CONTROL LEAD GP/REL POLICY. PAGE 34 F0665 — LG/CO CENTRAL INGP/REL

B47
BAERWALD F.,FUNDAMENTALS OF LABOR ECONOMICS. LAW INDUS LABOR LG/CO CONTROL GP/REL INCOME TOTALISM ...MGT CHARTS GEN/LAWS BIBLIOG 20. PAGE 8 F0150 — ECO/DEV WORKER MARKET

B47
SLICHTER S.H.,THE CHALLENGE OF INDUSTRIAL RELATIONS: TRADE UNIONS, MANAGEMENT AND THE PUBLIC INTEREST. PLAN ECO/TAC ADJUD CONTROL LEAD SANCTION GP/REL INGP/REL INCOME. PAGE 123 F2421 — LABOR MGT CLIENT POLICY

B47
WARNER W.L.,THE SOCIAL SYSTEM OF THE MODERN FACTORY; THE STRIKE: AN ANALYSIS. USA-45 STRATA WORKER ECO/TAC GP/REL INGP/REL...MGT SOC CHARTS 20 YANKEE/C. PAGE 143 F2824 — ROLE STRUCT LABOR PROC/MFG

B47
WEBER M.,THE THEORY OF SOCIAL AND ECONOMIC ORGANIZATION. STRUCT LABOR POL/PAR ECO/TAC LEGIT PRODUC BIOG. PAGE 144 F2840 — ECO/DEV SOC PHIL/SCI LEAD

B47
WHITEHEAD T.N.,LEADERSHIP IN A FREE SOCIETY; A STUDY IN HUMAN RELATIONS BASED ON AN ANALYSIS OF PRESENT-DAY INDUSTRIAL CIVILIZATION. WOR-45 STRUCT R+D LABOR LG/CO SML/CO WORKER PLAN PROB/SOLV TEC/DEV DRIVE...MGT 20. PAGE 146 F2872 — INDUS LEAD ORD/FREE SOCIETY

S47
DAHL R.A.,"WORKERS' CONTROL OF INDUSTRY AND THE BRITISH LABOUR PARTY." UK STRATA STRUCT DELIB/GP BARGAIN CAP/ISM DEBATE CONTROL CHOOSE GP/REL ATTIT ROLE PWR 19/20 PARLIAMENT LABOR/PAR FABIAN. PAGE 29 F0570 — INDUS LABOR WORKER SOCISM

B48
MCCABE D.A.,LABOR AND SOCIAL ORGANIZATION. LEGIS WORKER CAP/ISM ECO/TAC PAY MARXISM SOCISM SOC/INTEG 20 INTRVN/ECO. PAGE 88 F1717 — LABOR STRATA NEW/LIB

B48
MILLS C.W.,THE NEW MEN OF POWER. ELITES INTELL STRUCT WORKER ANOMIE ATTIT PWR POLICY. PAGE 92 F1799 — LABOR LEAD PLAN

B48
WHYTE W.F.,HUMAN RELATIONS IN THE RESTAURANT INDUSTRY (1ST ED). CLIENT WORKER WAR ATTIT...MGT OBS INT. PAGE 146 F2874 — INGP/REL GP/REL SERV/IND LABOR

B49
SHISTER J.,ECONOMICS OF THE LABOR MARKET. LOC/G NAT/G WORKER TEC/DEV BARGAIN PAY PRICE EXEC GP/REL INCOME...MGT T 20. PAGE 121 F2381 — MARKET LABOR INDUS

S49
HART C.W.M.,"INDUSTRIAL RELATIONS RESEARCH AND SOCIAL THEORY." CANADA VOL/ASSN WORKER LEAD EFFICIENCY...MGT SOC METH/CNCPT METH/COMP MUNICH 20. PAGE 56 F1099 — GEN/LAWS LABOR GP/REL

S49
SHEPHARD H.A.,"DEMOCRATIC CONTROL IN A LABOR UNION." FUT CONSTN STRUCT TEC/DEV LEAD PARTIC RACE/REL CENTRAL DRIVE HABITAT RECORD. PAGE 120 F2374 — LABOR MAJORIT CONTROL PWR

B50
HOOVER G.,TWENTIETH CENTURY ECONOMIC THOUGHT. USA+45 ECO/DEV AGRI FINAN INDUS MARKET SERV/IND LABOR NAT/G...STAT 20. PAGE 62 F1213 — ECO/TAC CAP/ISM INT/TRADE

B50
HUTCHISON K.,THE DECLINE AND FALL OF BRITISH CAPITALISM. UK ELITES STRATA ECO/DEV LABOR WORKER CONTROL WAR PWR...BIBLIOG/A 19/20. PAGE 63 F1249 — CAP/ISM SOCISM LAISSEZ DOMIN

B50
SOREL G.,REFLECTIONS ON VIOLENCE (1908) (TRANS. BY T.E. HULME AND J. ROTH). UNIV SOCIETY LABOR UTOPIA — COERCE REV

MORAL SOCISM...ANARCH SOCIALIST CONCPT 20. PAGE 124 F2445 WORKER MYTH

S50
EBY K.,"RESEARCH IN LABOR UNIONS." EDU/PROP INGP/REL PWR...METH/CNCPT OBS. PAGE 36 F0693 RECORD QU LABOR PARTIC

C50
ELLSWORTH P.T.,"INTERNATIONAL ECONOMY." ECO/DEV ECO/UNDEV FINAN LABOR DIPLOM FOR/AID TARIFFS BAL/PAY EQUILIB NAT/LISM OPTIMAL...INT/LAW 20 ILO GATT. PAGE 37 F0724 BIBLIOG INT/TRADE ECO/TAC INT/ORG

B51
HALEVY E.,IMPERIALISM AND THE RISE OF LABOR (2ND ED.). UK NAT/G POL/PAR TOP/EX ATTIT ORD/FREE PWR 19/20 PARLIAMENT LABOR/PAR. PAGE 53 F1042 COLONIAL LABOR POLICY WAR

B51
HARBISON F.H.,GOALS AND STRATEGY IN COLLECTIVE BARGAINING. WORKER BAL/PWR PARTIC DRIVE...POLICY MGT. PAGE 55 F1074 LABOR BARGAIN GP/REL ADMIN

B51
HARDMAN J.B.,THE HOUSE OF LABOR. LAW R+D NEIGH EDU/PROP LEAD ROUTINE REPRESENT GP/REL...POLICY STAT. PAGE 55 F1080 LABOR LOBBY ADMIN PRESS

B51
PETERSON F.,SURVEY OF LABOR ECONOMICS (REV. ED.). STRATA ECO/DEV LABOR INSPECT BARGAIN PAY PRICE EXEC ROUTINE GP/REL ALL/VALS ORD/FREE 20 AFL/CIO DEPT/LABOR. PAGE 105 F2069 WORKER DEMAND IDEA/COMP T

B51
PRINCETON U INDUSTRIAL REL SEC,COMPULSORY ARBITRATION OF UTILITY DISPUTES IN NEW JERSEY AND PENNSYLVANIA. USA+45 LEGIS WORKER ADJUD ORD/FREE ...POLICY MGT METH/COMP 20 NEW/JERSEY PENNSYLVAN. PAGE 108 F2118 BARGAIN PROVS INDUS LABOR

L51
SUMMERS C.W.,"UNION POWERS AND WORKERS RIGHTS." WORKER PROB/SOLV ECO/TAC PARTIC INGP/REL PWR. PAGE 127 F2513 LABOR CONSTN LAW REPRESENT

B52
ASHWORTH W.,A SHORT HISTORY OF THE INTERNATIONAL ECONOMY 1850-1950. WOR+45 WOR-45 AGRI FINAN INDUS MARKET LABOR ECO/TAC...CONCPT STAT HIST/WRIT FOR/TRADE ILO 19/20. PAGE 7 F0131 ECO/DEV TEC/DEV INT/TRADE

B52
GOLDSTEIN J.,THE GOVERNMENT OF BRITISH TRADE UNIONS. UK ECO/DEV EX/STRUC INGP/REL...BIBLIOG 20. PAGE 48 F0940 LABOR PARTIC

B52
MACHLUP F.,THE POLITICAL ECONOMY OF MONOPOLY: BUSINESS, LABOR AND GOVERNMENT POLICIES. USA+45 USA-45 ECO/DEV LABOR NAT/G CAP/ISM PWR...POLICY CHARTS T 20. PAGE 83 F1630 ECO/TAC DOMIN LG/CO CONTROL

B52
ROSE A.M.,UNION SOLIDARITY: THE INTERNAL COHESION OF A LABOR UNION. SECT GP/REL RACE/REL ATTIT ROLE HEALTH WEALTH...INT QU. PAGE 114 F2241 LABOR INGP/REL PARTIC SUPEGO

B52
SACHS E.S.,THE CHOICE BEFORE SOUTH AFRICA. SOUTH/AFR AGRI EXTR/IND PROC/MFG PROB/SOLV ORD/FREE SOVEREIGN 20 NEGRO. PAGE 115 F2267 NAT/LISM DISCRIM RACE/REL LABOR

B52
TANNENBAUM F.,A PHILOSOPHY OF LABOR. SOCIETY STRATA INDUS LG/CO AGREE ADJUST OWN ORD/FREE PWR...CONCPT 20. PAGE 128 F2533 LABOR PHIL/SCI WORKER CREATE

S52
KORNHAUSER W.,"THE NEGRO UNION OFFICIAL: A STUDY OF SPONSORSHIP AND CONTROL" (BMR)" USA+45 CONTROL DISCRIM ROLE SUPEGO...OBS 20 NEGRO. PAGE 73 F1428 LABOR LEAD RACE/REL CHOOSE

B53
BOULDING K.E.,THE ORGANIZATIONAL REVOLUTION. FUT CULTURE ECO/DEV LABOR PROF/ORG ECO/TAC MORAL...SOC CONCPT RECORD INT SOC/EXP 20. PAGE 17 F0321 SOCIETY TREND

B53
FLORENCE P.S.,THE LOGIC OF BRITISH AND AMERICAN INDUSTRY; A REALISTIC ANALYSIS OF ECONOMIC STRUCTURE AND GOVERNMENT. UK USA+45 USA-45 FINAN LABOR CAP/ISM INGP/REL EFFICIENCY...MGT CONCPT STAT CHARTS METH 20. PAGE 42 F0813 INDUS ECO/DEV NAT/G NAT/COMP

B53
MILLIKAN M.F.,INCOME STABILIZATION FOR A DEVELOPING DEMOCRACY. USA+45 ECO/DEV LABOR BUDGET ECO/TAC TAX ADMIN ADJUST PRODUC WEALTH...POLICY TREND 20. PAGE 91 F1794 ANTHOL MARKET EQUILIB EFFICIENCY

B53
PURCELL T.V.,THE WORKER SPEAKS HIS MIND ON COMPANY AND UNION. WORKER ADJUD LEAD RACE/REL ATTIT DRIVE MARXISM...MGT CLASSIF STAT OBS INT SAMP BIBLIOG. PAGE 108 F2131 LABOR PARTIC INGP/REL HAPPINESS

B53
SAYLES L.R.,THE LOCAL UNION. CONSTN CULTURE DELIB/GP PARTIC CHOOSE GP/REL INGP/REL ATTIT ROLE ...MAJORIT DECISION MGT. PAGE 116 F2284 LABOR LEAD ADJUD ROUTINE

S53
DRUCKER P.F.,"THE EMPLOYEE SOCIETY." STRUCT BAL/PWR PARTIC REPRESENT PWR...DECISION CONCPT. PAGE 34 F0666 LABOR MGT WORKER CULTURE

S53
MCKEE J.B.,"STATUS AND POWER IN THE INDUSTRIAL COMMUNITY; A COMMENT ON DRUCKER'S THESIS." LABOR LEGIT LEAD GP/REL PWR...MGT CONCPT. PAGE 88 F1730 SOC STRATA NEIGH PARTIC

B54
HAYEK FA V.O.N.,CAPITALISM AND THE HISTORIANS. MOD/EUR TEC/DEV GP/REL WEALTH...HIST/WRIT ANTHOL 19. PAGE 57 F1124 CAP/ISM LABOR STRATA ECO/TAC

B54
INTERNATIONAL LABOUR OFF LIB,BIBLIOGRAPHY ON THE INTERNATIONAL LABOUR ORGANISATION. WORKER 20. PAGE 65 F1277 BIBLIOG LABOR INT/ORG CONFER

B54
KARTUN D.,AFRICA, AFRICA: A CONTINENT RISES TO ITS FEET. AFR SOUTH/AFR UK ELITES AGRI LABOR LOC/G POL/PAR EDU/PROP CONTROL COERCE DISCRIM AGE/Y NEGRO THIRD/WRLD GOLD/COAST. PAGE 69 F1358 COLONIAL ORD/FREE PROFIT EXTR/IND

B54
MOSK S.A.,INDUSTRIAL REVOLUTION IN MEXICO. MARKET LABOR CREATE CAP/ISM ADMIN ATTIT SOCISM...POLICY 20 MEXIC/AMER. PAGE 94 F1843 INDUS TEC/DEV ECO/UNDEV NAT/G

B54
TAFT P.,THE STRUCTURE AND GOVERNMENT OF LABOR UNIONS. SANCTION INGP/REL ORD/FREE PWR MARXISM ...MAJORIT STAT TREND. PAGE 128 F2524 LABOR ADJUD WORKER FINAN

B54
WILLIAMSON H.F.,ECONOMIC DEVELOPMENT - PRINCIPLES AND PATTERNS. INDIA KOREA CULTURE ECO/DEV ECO/UNDEV TEC/DEV...CENSUS NAT/COMP FOR/TRADE 20 CHINJAP MEXIC/AMER RESOURCE/N. PAGE 147 F2895 ECO/TAC GEOG LABOR

S54
EDELMAN M.J.,"LABOR'S INFLUENCE IN FOREIGN POLICY." NAT/G EXEC PWR 20. PAGE 36 F0700 LOBBY REPRESENT EX/STRUC LABOR

S54
MACK R.W.,"ECOLOGICAL PATTERNS IN AN INDUSTRIAL SHOP" (BMR)" USA+45 CULTURE SOCIETY STRATA STRUCT LABOR NEIGH GP/REL ADJUST HABITAT...SOC SOC/INTEG 20. PAGE 83 F1634 INDUS DISCRIM WORKER

B55
BLOOM G.F.,ECONOMICS OF LABOR RELATIONS. USA+45 LAW CONSULT WORKER CAP/ISM PAY ADJUD CONTROL EFFICIENCY ORD/FREE...CHARTS 19/20 AFL/CIO NLRB DEPT/LABOR. PAGE 16 F0299 ECO/DEV ECO/TAC LABOR GOV/REL

B55
BRAUN K.,LABOR DISPUTES AND THEIR SETTLEMENT. ECO/TAC ROUTINE TASK GP/REL...DECISION GEN/LAWS. PAGE 18 F0342 INDUS LABOR BARGAIN ADJUD

B55
JONES T.B.,A BIBLIOGRAPHY ON SOUTH AMERICAN ECONOMIC AFFAIRS: ARTICLES IN NINETEENTH CENTURY PERIODICALS (PAMPHLET). AGRI COM/IND DIST/IND EXTR/IND FINAN INDUS LABOR NAT/G 19. PAGE 68 F1340 BIBLIOG ECO/UNDEV L/A+17C TEC/DEV

B55
PEDLER F.J.,ECONOMIC GEOGRAPHY OF WEST AFRICA. GAMBIA NIGER SIER/LEONE STRATA EXTR/IND MARKET LABOR INT/TRADE DEMAND HABITAT WEALTH...CHARTS 20. PAGE 104 F2046 ECO/UNDEV GEOG PRODUC EFFICIENCY

B55
RUSTOW D.A.,THE POLITICS OF COMPROMISE. SWEDEN LABOR EX/STRUC LEGIS PLAN REPRESENT SOCISM...SOC 19/20. PAGE 115 F2265 POL/PAR NAT/G POLICY ECO/TAC

B55
SERRANO MOSCOSO E.,A STATEMENT OF THE LAWS OF ECUADOR IN MATTERS AFFECTING BUSINESS (2ND ED.). ECUADOR INDUS LABOR LG/CO NAT/G LEGIS TAX CONTROL MARRIAGE 20. PAGE 120 F2359 FINAN ECO/UNDEV LAW CONSTN

B56
BARBASH J.,THE PRACTICE OF UNIONISM. ECO/TAC LEAD LOBBY GP/REL INGP/REL DRIVE MARXISM BIBLIOG. PAGE 10 F0182 LABOR REPRESENT CONTROL ADMIN

B56
BONNETT C.E.,HISTORY OF EMPLOYERS' ASSOCIATIONS IN THE UNITED STATES (1ST ED.). MARKET DETER GP/REL ADJUST. PAGE 16 F0316 LABOR VOL/ASSN LG/CO

B56
LIPSET S.M.,UNION DEMOCRACY. STRUCT INDUS FACE/GP WORKER CONTROL LEAD PARTIC GP/REL ATTIT LAISSEZ ...INT QU CHARTS. PAGE 80 F1577
LABOR INGP/REL MAJORIT

B56
UPHOFF W.H.,UNDERSTANDING THE UNION MEMBER (PAMPHLET). STRATA R+D LEAD PARTIC...METH/CNCPT STAT QU. PAGE 133 F2624
LABOR WORKER ATTIT DRIVE

B56
US DEPARTMENT OF STATE,ECONOMIC PROBLEMS OF UNDERDEVELOPED AREAS (PAMPHLET). AFR ASIA ISLAM L/A+17C AGRI FINAN INDUS INT/ORG LABOR INT/TRADE ...PSY SOC 20. PAGE 136 F2673
BIBLIOG ECO/UNDEV TEC/DEV R+D

B56
VAKIL C.N.,PLANNING FOR AN EXPANDING ECONOMY. INDIA TAX COST 20. PAGE 140 F2759
TEC/DEV LABOR BUDGET CAP/ISM

B56
YUAN TUNG-LI,ECONOMIC AND SOCIAL DEVELOPMENT OF MODERN CHINA: A BIBLIOGRAPHIC GUIDE. COM/IND FINAN FAM LABOR SECT CRIME INCOME...STAT SAMP CON/ANAL. PAGE 150 F2954
BIBLIOG ASIA ECO/UNDEV SOC

L56
TAGLIACOZZO D.L.,"TRADE-UNION GOVERNMENT, ITS NATURE AND ITS PROBLEMS: A BIBLIOGRAPHICAL REVIEW, 1945-1955." STRUCT LEAD PARTIC CHOOSE ATTIT ...MAJORIT METH/CNCPT BIBLIOG. PAGE 128 F2526
CLASSIF LABOR INGP/REL GP/REL

S56
BONILLA F.,"WHEN IS PETITION 'PRESSURE?'" (BMR)" USA+45 ELITES INDUS LABOR CHIEF EDU/PROP LEGIT ATTIT...INT CHARTS 20 CONGRESS PRESIDENT EISNHWR/DD. PAGE 16 F0312
LEGIS EX/STRUC INT/TRADE TARIFFS

S56
BROWN J.S.,"UNION SIZE AS A FUNCTION OF INTRA-UNION CONFLICT." CLIENT CONTROL CHOOSE EFFICIENCY ATTIT TREND. PAGE 19 F0370
LABOR INGP/REL CONSEN DRIVE

S56
MYERS C.A.,"LINE AND STAFF IN INDUSTRIAL RELATIONS." INDUS LABOR GP/REL PWR...MGT INT. PAGE 96 F1876
ROLE PROB/SOLV ADMIN CONSULT

S56
TANNENBAUM A.S.,"CONTROL OF STRUCTURE AND UNION FUNCTIONS." PARTIC GP/REL INGP/REL CONSEN ATTIT PWR ...QU SAMP. PAGE 128 F2529
LABOR STRUCT CONTROL LEAD

S56
TYLER G.,"THE PRESIDENCY AND LABOR." USA+45 USA-45 NAT/G LOBBY GOV/REL PWR 20 PRESIDENT. PAGE 131 F2595
LABOR REPRESENT CHIEF

C56
MCKEE J.B.,"THE POWER TO DECIDE" IN M. WEINBERG AND O. SHABET, SOCIETY AND MAN." ELITES STRATA REPRESENT GP/REL ATTIT PWR MUNICH BUSINESS. PAGE 88 F1731
LABOR DECISION LEAD

B57
DUNLOP J.T.,THE THEORY OF WAGE DETERMINATION; PROCEEDINGS OF CONFERENCE HELD BY INTERNATIONAL ECONOMIC ASSOCIATION. AFR ECO/DEV LABOR BARGAIN PAY CONFER...CHARTS ANTHOL 20. PAGE 35 F0679
PRICE WORKER GEN/LAWS INCOME

B57
MASON E.S.,ECONOMIC CONCENTRATION AND THE MONOPOLY PROBLEM. USA+45 USA-45 LAW ELITES ECO/DEV LABOR RATION PRICE PWR WEALTH...CHARTS 20 MONOPOLY. PAGE 87 F1696
GP/REL LG/CO CONTROL MARKET

B57
SCHNEIDER E.V.,INDUSTRIAL SOCIOLOGY: THE SOCIAL RELATIONS OF INDUSTRY AND COMMUNITY. STRATA INDUS NAT/G NEIGH CREATE ADMIN PARTIC GP/REL RACE/REL ROLE PWR...POLICY BIBLIOG. PAGE 117 F2308
LABOR MGT INGP/REL STRUCT

S57
DUBIN R.,"POWER AND UNION-MANAGEMENT RELATIONS." PROB/SOLV ADJUD ROUTINE ATTIT ORD/FREE...MGT STERTYP. PAGE 34 F0668
PWR LABOR BARGAIN GP/REL

S57
KAHN R.L.,"UNION PRACTICES AND MEMBER PARTICIPATION." PARTIC CHOOSE REPRESENT PERS/REL PERSON SKILL...DECISION METH/CNCPT QU. PAGE 69 F1347
INGP/REL LABOR ATTIT LEAD

S57
ROURKE F.E.,"THE POLITICS OF ADMINISTRATIVE ORGANIZATION: A CASE HISTORY." USA+45 LABOR WORKER PLAN ADMIN TASK EFFICIENCY 20 DEPT/LABOR CONGRESS. PAGE 114 F2251
POLICY ATTIT MGT GP/COMP

S57
TANNENBAUM A.S.,"ORGANIZATIONAL CONTROL STRUCTURE: A GENERAL DESCRIPTIVE TECHNIQUE AS APPLIED TO FOUR LOCAL UNIONS." LABOR PWR...METH/CNCPT CLASSIF QU CHARTS. PAGE 128 F2530
WORKER PARTIC STRUCT CONTROL

B58
BANCROFT G.,THE AMERICAN LABOR FORCE: ITS GROWTH AND CHANGING COMPOSITION. FUT USA+45 USA-45 ECO/DEV INDUS WORKER...GEOG CHARTS 19/20. PAGE 9 F0170
LABOR STAT TREND CENSUS

B58
CHAMBERLIN E.H.,LABOR UNIONS AND PUBLIC POLICY. PLAN BARGAIN SANCTION INGP/REL JURID. PAGE 23 F0444
LABOR WEALTH PWR NAT/G

B58
COLM G.,THE ECONOMY OF THE AMERICAN PEOPLE: PROGRESS, PROBLEMS, PROSPECTS. USA+45 INDUS MARKET LABOR TEC/DEV INCOME 20. PAGE 26 F0509
WEALTH PRODUC CAP/ISM MGT

B58
COOK P.L.,EFFECTS OF MERGERS: SIX STUDIES. USA+45 ECO/DEV LABOR LG/CO SML/CO VOL/ASSN ADMIN EFFICIENCY 20 CASEBOOK. PAGE 27 F0529
INDUS FINAN EX/STRUC GP/REL

B58
CUNNINGHAM W.B.,COMPULSORY CONCILIATION AND COLLECTIVE BARGAINING. CANADA NAT/G LEGIS ADJUD CT/SYS GP/REL...MGT 20 NEW/BRUNS STRIKE CASEBOOK. PAGE 29 F0563
POLICY BARGAIN LABOR INDUS

B58
DUBIN R.,WORKING UNION-MANAGEMENT RELATIONS. LAW PLAN ECO/TAC CHOOSE REPRESENT INGP/REL PWR...POLICY SOC BIBLIOG. PAGE 34 F0669
LABOR MGT AUTHORIT GP/REL

B58
LESTER R.A.,AS UNIONS MATURE. POL/PAR BARGAIN LEAD PARTIC GP/REL CENTRAL...MAJORIT TIME/SEQ METH/COMP. PAGE 78 F1533
LABOR INDUS POLICY MGT

B58
MOONEY R.E.,INFLATION AND RECESSION? AFR USA+45 LABOR LG/CO PRESS LEAD...IDEA/COMP ANTHOL 20. PAGE 93 F1821
PRICE ECO/TAC NAT/G PRODUC

B58
POLLOCK F.,AUTOMATION: A STUDY OF ITS ECONOMIC AND SOCIAL CONSEQUENCES. FUT USA+45 USA-45 SOCIETY ECO/DEV LABOR ACT/RES PLAN ECO/TAC AUTOMAT ROUTINE ALL/VALS...STAT TREND COMPUT/IR CHARTS SOC/EXP WORK 20. PAGE 107 F2099
TEC/DEV SOC CAP/ISM

B58
ROBERTS B.C.,NATIONAL WAGES POLICY IN WAR AND PEACE. EUR+WWI GERMANY S/ASIA SWEDEN UK USA+45 USA-45 STRATA ECO/DEV LABOR NAT/G DELIB/GP PLAN INT/TRADE WEALTH...STAT TREND CHARTS 20. PAGE 112 F2205
CREATE ECO/TAC

B58
SEIDMAN J.I.,DEMOCRACY IN THE LABOR MOVEMENT (PAMPHLET). LAW CONSTN STRUCT DELIB/GP WORKER ADJUD PARTIC SANCTION POLICY. PAGE 119 F2345
LABOR INGP/REL PWR MAJORIT

B58
TAFT P.,CORRUPTION AND RACKETEERING IN THE LABOR MOVEMENT (PAMPHLET). ADMIN SANCTION CENTRAL ROLE WEALTH...POLICY CLASSIF. PAGE 128 F2525
LABOR INGP/REL GP/REL CRIME

B58
TANNENBAUM A.S.,PARTICIPATION IN UNION LOCALS. SOCIETY FINAN CONTROL LEAD GP/REL...BIBLIOG 20. PAGE 128 F2531
LABOR MGT PARTIC INGP/REL

B58
WOODS H.D.,PATTERNS OF INDUSTRIAL DISPUTE SETTLEMENT IN FIVE CANADIAN INDUSTRIES. CANADA USA+45 CONSULT ADJUD GP/REL...JURID GOV/COMP METH/COMP ANTHOL 20. PAGE 148 F2923
BARGAIN INDUS LABOR NAT/G

L58
TRAGER F.N.,"A SELECTED AND ANNOTATED BIBLIOGRAPHY ON ECONOMIC DEVELOPMENT, 1953-1957." WOR+45 AGRI FINAN INDUS MARKET LABOR WORKER PLAN INT/TRADE PRODUC...CENSUS MUNICH. PAGE 131 F2583
BIBLIOG/A ECO/UNDEV ECO/DEV

B59
AITKEN H.G.,THE AMERICAN ECONOMIC IMPACT ON CANADA. CANADA USA+45 AGRI FINAN INDUS LABOR INT/TRADE BAL/PAY...INT/LAW TREND 20. PAGE 3 F0055
DIPLOM ECO/TAC POLICY NAT/G

B59
BARBASH J.,UNIONS AND UNION LEADERSHIP. NAT/G WORKER TEC/DEV ECO/TAC PARTIC GP/REL RACE/REL ORD/FREE CLASSIF. PAGE 10 F0183
LABOR VOL/ASSN CAP/ISM LEAD

B59
BONNETT C.E.,LABOR-MANAGEMENT RELATIONS. USA+45 OP/RES PROB/SOLV EDU/PROP...AUD/VIS CHARTS 20. PAGE 16 F0317
MGT LABOR INDUS GP/REL

B59
BROMWICH L.,UNION CONSTITUTIONS. CONSTN EX/STRUC PRESS ADJUD CONTROL CHOOSE REPRESENT PWR SAMP. PAGE 19 F0361
LABOR ROUTINE INGP/REL RACE/REL

B59
CHECCHI V.,HONDURAS: A PROBLEM IN ECONOMIC
ECO/UNDEV

DEVELOPMENT. HONDURAS AGRI FINAN INDUS LABOR WORKER INT/TRADE EDU/PROP PRICE HEALTH...GEOG CHARTS BIBLIOG 20. PAGE 24 F0458
ECO/TAC PROB/SOLV PLAN

B59
FERRY W.H.,THE CORPORATION AND THE ECONOMY. CLIENT LAW CONSTN LABOR NAT/G PLAN INT/TRADE PARTIC CONSEN ORD/FREE PWR POLICY. PAGE 40 F0787
LG/CO CONTROL REPRESENT

B59
KOLLAI H.R.,DIE EINGLIEDERUNG DER VERTRIEBENEN UND ZUWANDERER IN NIEDERSACHSEN. GERMANY/W SOCIETY STRATA STRUCT LABOR SOC/INTEG 20. PAGE 72 F1422
GP/REL INGP/REL

B59
KRIPALANI J.B.,CLASS STRUGGLE. INDIA WOR+45 ECO/UNDEV LABOR CAP/ISM EDU/PROP INGP/REL ...SOCIALIST IDEA/COMP 17/20. PAGE 73 F1440
MARXISM STRATA COERCE ECO/TAC

B59
LEISERSON W.,AMERICAN TRADE UNION DEMOCRACY. CONSTN STRUCT ADJUD EXEC REPRESENT GP/REL INGP/REL MAJORITY ATTIT PWR. PAGE 77 F1516
LABOR LEAD PARTIC DELIB/GP

B59
LEWIS J.P.,BUSINESS CONDITIONS ANALYSIS. USA+45 MARKET LABOR BUDGET TAX AUTOMAT WAR DEMAND PRODUC ...ECOMETRIC CHARTS BIBLIOG 19/20. PAGE 79 F1549
FINAN PRICE TREND

B59
MATTHEWS R.C.O.,THE BUSINESS CYCLE. AFR LABOR INT/TRADE TAX PRICE RISK ADJUST WEALTH...POLICY ECOMETRIC CHARTS SIMUL TIME 20. PAGE 87 F1705
FINAN DEMAND TASK

B59
NOVE A.,COMMUNIST ECONOMIC STRATEGY: SOVIET GROWTH AND CAPABILITIES. USSR AGRI LABOR PLAN TEC/DEV CAP/ISM INT/TRADE EFFICIENCY MARXISM 20 THIRD/WRLD. PAGE 99 F1941
FOR/AID ECO/TAC DIPLOM INDUS

B59
OGBURN C.,ECONOMIC PLAN AND ACTION. USA+45 FINAN LABOR DIPLOM ECO/TAC FOR/AID 20. PAGE 101 F1981
ECO/DEV INT/TRADE PLAN BAL/PAY

B59
US NATIONAL LABOR RELATIONS BD,LEGISLATIVE HISTORY OF THE LABOR-MANAGEMENT REPORTING AND DISCLOSURE ACT OF 1959 (2 VOLS.). USA+45 LEGIS...MGT CHARTS. PAGE 138 F2720
LAW LABOR GP/REL

L59
BEGUIN B.,"ILO AND THE TRIPARTITE SYSTEM." EUR+WWI WOR+45 WOR-45 CONSTN ECO/DEV ECO/UNDEV INDUS INT/ORG NAT/G VOL/ASSN DELIB/GP PLAN TEC/DEV LEGIT ORD/FREE WEALTH...CONCPT TIME/SEQ WORK ILO 20. PAGE 12 F0228
LABOR

L59
OBERER W.E.,"VOLUNTARY IMPARTIAL REVIEW OF LABOR: SOME REFLECTIONS." DELIB/GP LEGIS PROB/SOLV ADJUD CONTROL COERCE PWR PLURISM POLICY. PAGE 100 F1960
LABOR LAW PARTIC INGP/REL

S59
MILLER A.S.,"CONSTITUTIONALIZING THE CORPORATION." LABOR NAT/G WORKER PWR...POLICY MGT. PAGE 91 F1789
CONSTN INGP/REL LG/CO CONTROL

S59
REES A.,"DO UNIONS CAUSE INFLATION?" CONTROL 20. PAGE 110 F2171
LABOR ECO/TAC PRICE WORKER

S59
SHEPPARD H.L.,"THE POLITICAL ATTITUDES AND PREFERENCES OF UNION MEMBERS: THE CASE OF THE DETROIT AUTO WORKERS." LOBBY CHOOSE ROLE...CLASSIF QU SAMP TREND. PAGE 120 F2376
LABOR ATTIT WORKER

S59
TIPTON J.B.,"PARTICIPATION OF THE UNITED STATES IN THE INTERNATIONAL LABOR ORGANIZATION." USA+45 LAW STRUCT ECO/DEV ECO/UNDEV INDUS TEC/DEV ECO/TAC ADMIN PERCEPT ORD/FREE SKILL...STAT HIST/WRIT GEN/METH ILO WORK 20. PAGE 131 F2577
LABOR INT/ORG

C59
FAINSOD M.,"GOVERNMENT AND THE AMERICAN ECONOMY." USA+45 USA-45 INDUS LABOR OP/RES PROB/SOLV ECO/TAC CONTROL...CHARTS BIBLIOG T 20. PAGE 39 F0760
CONSTN ECO/DEV CAP/ISM NAT/G

B60
AMERICAN U BEIRUT ECO RES INST,A SELECTED AND ANNOTATED BIBLIOGRAPHY OF ECONOMIC LITERATURE ON THE ARABIC SPEAKING COUNTRIES OF THE MIDDLE EAST. ISLAM AGRI COM/IND DIST/IND FINAN INDUS LABOR ...GEOG 20. PAGE 5 F0091
BIBLIOG/A ECO/UNDEV STAT

B60
APTHEKER H.,DISARMAMENT AND THE AMERICAN ECONOMY: A SYMPOSIUM. FUT USA+45 ECO/DEV DIST/IND FINAN INDUS PROC/MFG LABOR NAT/G POL/PAR CONSULT PLAN CAP/ISM INT/TRADE PEACE ATTIT MORAL WEALTH...TREND GEN/LAWS TOT/POP 20. PAGE 6 F0110
MARXIST ARMS/CONT

B60
BELLAN R.C.,PRINCIPLES OF ECONOMICS AND THE CANADIAN ECONOMY (2ND ED.). CANADA UK USA+45 LABOR WORKER CAP/ISM INT/TRADE RISK BAL/PAY EQUILIB ALL/IDEOS 20. PAGE 12 F0236
ECO/DEV PRODUC WEALTH FINAN

B60
COMMITTEE ECONOMIC DEVELOPMENT,NATIONAL OBJECTIVES AND THE BALANCE OF PAYMENTS PROBLEM: A STATEMENT ON NATIONAL POLICY. USA+45 WOR+45 DIST/IND FINAN INDUS LABOR NAT/G DELIB/GP ACT/RES FOR/AID INT/TRADE ...STAT CHARTS FOR/TRADE 20. PAGE 27 F0516
ECO/DEV ECO/TAC BAL/PAY

B60
CROSSER P.K.,STATE CAPITALISM IN THE ECONOMY OF THE UNITED STATES. USA+45 USA-45 AGRI FINAN INDUS LABOR WORKER RATION CONTROL GOV/REL DEMAND...NEW/IDEA 20. PAGE 29 F0557
CAP/ISM ECO/DEV ECO/TAC NAT/G

B60
ELKOURI F.,HOW ARBITRATION WORKS (REV. ED.). LAW INDUS BARGAIN 20. PAGE 37 F0720
MGT LABOR ADJUD GP/REL

B60
FORM W.H.,INDUSTRY, LABOR, AND COMMUNITY. STRUCT NEIGH SECT BAL/PWR EDU/PROP PARTIC ATTIT ROLE PWR WEALTH...METH/CNCPT CHARTS. PAGE 42 F0828
LABOR MGT GP/REL CONTROL

B60
FRYE R.J.,GOVERNMENT AND LABOR: THE ALABAMA PROGRAM. USA+45 INDUS R+D LABOR WORKER BUDGET EFFICIENCY AGE/Y HEALTH...CHARTS 20 ALABAMA. PAGE 45 F0870
ADMIN LEGIS LOC/G PROVS

B60
GARBARINO J.W.,HEALTH PLANS AND COLLECTIVE BARGAINING. USA+45 LABOR BARGAIN GP/REL WEALTH ...WELF/ST CHARTS 20 DEPT/HEW SAN/FRAN. PAGE 46 F0900
HEAL PLAN FINAN SERV/IND

B60
MOORE W.E.,LABOR COMMITMENT AND SOCIAL CHANGE IN DEVELOPING AREAS. SOCIETY STRATA ECO/UNDEV MARKET VOL/ASSN WORKER AUTHORIT SKILL...MGT NAT/COMP SOC/INTEG 20. PAGE 93 F1823
LABOR ORD/FREE ATTIT INDUS

B60
ROBERTSON D.,THE CONTROL OF INDUSTRY. UK MARKET LABOR WORKER PRICE CONTROL GP/REL COST DEMAND ORD/FREE WEALTH NEW/LIB SOCISM 20. PAGE 112 F2211
INDUS FINAN NAT/G ECO/DEV

B60
ROBSON W.A.,NATIONALIZED INDUSTRY AND PUBLIC OWNERSHIP. UK ECO/DEV FINAN LABOR LG/CO POL/PAR LEGIS ACT/RES GP/REL...TREND IDEA/COMP 20. PAGE 113 F2227
NAT/G OWN INDUS ATTIT

B60
SLOTKIN J.S.,FROM FIELD TO FACTORY; NEW INDUSTRIAL EMPLOYEES. HABITAT...MGT NEW/IDEA NAT/COMP BIBLIOG SOC/INTEG 20. PAGE 123 F2423
INDUS LABOR CULTURE WORKER

B60
WATSON D.S.,ECONOMIC POLICY: BUSINESS AND GOVERNMENT. USA+45 FINAN LABOR PLAN BUDGET INT/TRADE GP/REL WEALTH LAISSEZ...CHARTS T. PAGE 144 F2832
ECO/TAC NAT/G POLICY ECO/DEV

B60
WEINER H.E.,BRITISH LABOR AND PUBLIC OWNERSHIP. UK SERV/IND LG/CO WORKER CONTROL OWN 20. PAGE 145 F2850
LABOR NAT/G INDUS ATTIT

S60
"THE EMERGING COMMON MARKETS IN LATIN AMERICA." FUT L/A+17C STRATA DIST/IND INDUS LABOR NAT/G LEGIS ECO/TAC ADMIN RIGID/FLEX HEALTH...NEW/IDEA TIME/SEQ OAS 20. PAGE 1 F0013
FINAN ECO/UNDEV INT/TRADE

S60
FORM W.H.,"ORGANIZED LABOR'S IMAGE OF COMMUNITY POWER STRUCTURE." LABOR LG/CO CONTROL LEAD REPRESENT...DECISION METH/CNCPT INT QU SAMP. PAGE 42 F0829
NEIGH PARTIC PWR GP/REL

S60
FRENCH J.R.P. JR.,"AN EXPERIMENT ON PARTICIPATION IN A NORWEGIAN FACTORY:INTERPERSONAL DIMENSIONS OF DECISION-MAKING." LABOR LEAD PERS/REL EFFICIENCY PRODUC...DECISION SOC CHARTS SOC/EXP. PAGE 44 F0853
INDUS PLAN RIGID/FLEX GP/REL

S60
JACOBSON H.K.,"THE USSR AND ILO." AFR COM STRUCT ECO/DEV ECO/UNDEV CONSULT DELIB/GP ECO/TAC ILO WORK 20. PAGE 66 F1298
INT/ORG LABOR USSR

S60
KELLOGG C.E.,"TRANSFER OF BASIC SKILLS OF FOOD PRODUCTION." AFR FUT S/ASIA STRATA ECO/UNDEV LABOR VOL/ASSN RIGID/FLEX...OLD/LIB SOCIALIST NEW/IDEA STAT PROJ/TEST GEN/LAWS 20. PAGE 70 F1370
AGRI PLAN

S60
MANN S.Z.,"POLICY FORMULATION IN THE EXECUTIVE BRANCH: THE TAFT-HARTLEY EXPERIENCE." USA+45 LABOR CHIEF INGP/REL 20 NLRB. PAGE 85 F1656
EXEC GOV/REL EX/STRUC PROB/SOLV

S60
MORALES C.J.,"TRADE AND ECONOMIC INTEGRATION IN LATIN AMERICA." FUT L/A+17C LAW STRATA ECO/UNDEV DIST/IND INDUS LABOR NAT/G LEGIS ECO/TAC ADMIN
FINAN INT/TRADE REGION

RIGID/FLEX WEALTH...CONCPT NEW/IDEA CONT/OBS TIME/SEQ WORK 20. PAGE 93 F1825

S60
SPINRAD W.,"CORRELATES OF TRADE UNION PARTICIPATION: A SUMMARY OF LITERATURE." ACT/RES PERS/REL HAPPINESS HABITAT...BIBLIOG WORK. PAGE 125 F2456
LABOR PARTIC CORREL ROLE

B61
MEXICO; CINCUENTA ANOS DE REVOLUCION VOL. II. L/A+17C SOCIETY LABOR RECEIVE GP/REL AGE/Y HEALTH ...SOC/WK ANTHOL MUNICH 20 MEXIC/AMER. PAGE 1 F0014
ECO/UNDEV STRUCT INDUS POL/PAR

B61
BARBASH J.,LABOR'S GRASS ROOTS. CONSTN NAT/G EX/STRUC LEGIS WORKER LEAD...MAJORIT BIBLIOG. PAGE 10 F0184
LABOR INGP/REL GP/REL LAW

B61
BARRASH J.,LABOR'S GRASS ROOTS; A STUDY OF THE LOCAL UNION. STRATA BARGAIN LEAD REPRESENT DEMAND ATTIT PWR. PAGE 10 F0192
LABOR USA+45 INGP/REL EXEC

B61
CAMPAIGNE J.G.,CHECK-OFF: LABOR BOSSES AND WORKING MEN. LEGIS WORKER EDU/PROP DEBATE COERCE REPRESENT GP/REL ORD/FREE CONSERVE. PAGE 21 F0404
LABOR ELITES PWR CONTROL

B61
CANTERBERY E.R.,THE PRESIDENT'S COUNCIL OF ECONOMIC ADVISERS. AFR USA+45 FINAN LABOR NAT/G PLAN ADMIN OPTIMAL WEALTH 20 EISNHWR/DD PRESIDENT TRUMAN/HS KEYNES/JM. PAGE 21 F0413
ECO/TAC OP/RES EXEC CHIEF

B61
CARROTHERS A.W.R.,LABOR ARBITRATION IN CANADA. CANADA LAW NAT/G CONSULT LEGIS WORKER ADJUD ADMIN CT/SYS 20. PAGE 22 F0422
LABOR MGT GP/REL BARGAIN

B61
DE GRAZIA A.,AMERICAN WELFARE. CLIENT FINAN LABOR LOC/G NAT/G NEIGH EDU/PROP GP/REL...CLASSIF CON/ANAL CHARTS BIBLIOG. PAGE 31 F0598
GIVE WEALTH SECT VOL/ASSN

B61
DETHINE P.,BIBLIOGRAPHIE DES ASPECTS ECONOMIQUES ET SOCIAUX DE L'INDUSTRIALISATION EN AFRIQUE. AFR FINAN LABOR FOR/AID...SOC 20. PAGE 32 F0623
BIBLIOG/A ECO/UNDEV INDUS TEC/DEV

B61
DIMOCK M.E.,BUSINESS AND GOVERNMENT (4TH ED.). AGRI FINAN OP/RES PLAN BUDGET DIPLOM LOBBY NUC/PWR NEW/LIB SOCISM...POLICY BIBLIOG 20. PAGE 33 F0641
NAT/G INDUS LABOR ECO/TAC

B61
FERTIG L.,PROSPERITY THROUGH FREEDOM. COM INDUS LABOR CAP/ISM ECO/TAC PRODUC PROFIT ORD/FREE WEALTH SOCISM...METH/CNCPT 20. PAGE 40 F0788
NAT/G CONTROL POLICY

B61
FILLOL T.R.,SOCIAL FACTORS IN ECONOMIC DEVELOPMENT: THE ARGENTINE CASE. STRUCT INDUS LABOR CREATE TEC/DEV EFFICIENCY PRODUC DRIVE...METH/CNCPT METH/COMP BIBLIOG/A 20 ARGEN. PAGE 41 F0795
ECO/UNDEV MGT PERS/REL TREND

B61
GALENSON W.,TRADE UNION DEMOCRACY IN WESTERN EUROPE. ECO/DEV INDUS PROF/ORG WORKER INCOME ...METH/COMP 20. PAGE 45 F0886
LABOR GP/REL ECO/TAC EUR+WWI

B61
GANGULI B.N.,ECONOMIC INTEGRATION. FINAN LABOR CAP/ISM DIPLOM WEALTH...NAT/COMP 20. PAGE 46 F0895
ECO/TAC METH/CNCPT EQUILIB ECO/UNDEV

B61
GREY A.L.,ECONOMIC ISSUES AND POLICIES; READINGS IN INTRODUCTORY ECONOMICS (2ND ED.). WOR+45 ECO/UNDEV FINAN MARKET LABOR LG/CO INT/TRADE BAL/PAY WEALTH ...ANTHOL T. PAGE 51 F0996
ECO/TAC PROB/SOLV METH/COMP

B61
HART W.R.,COLLECTIVE BARGAINING IN THE FEDERAL CIVIL SERVICE. NAT/G EX/STRUC ADMIN EXEC 20. PAGE 56 F1101
INGP/REL MGT REPRESENT LABOR

B61
LAMFALUSSY A.,INVESTMENT AND GROWTH IN MATURE ECONOMIES. BELGIUM EUR+WWI LABOR PRICE PRODUC PROFIT...STAT CONT/OBS CHARTS 20. PAGE 75 F1464
FINAN INDUS ECO/DEV CAP/ISM

B61
LENIN V.I.,WHAT IS TO BE DONE? (1902). RUSSIA LABOR NAT/G POL/PAR WORKER CAP/ISM ECO/TAC ADMIN PARTIC ...MARXIST IDEA/COMP GEN/LAWS 19/20. PAGE 78 F1522
EDU/PROP PRESS MARXISM METH/COMP

B61
LIEFMANN-KEIL E.,OKONOMISCHE THEORIE DER SOZIALPOLITIK. INT/ORG LABOR WORKER COST INCOME NEW/LIB...CONCPT SOC/INTEG 20. PAGE 80 F1562
ECO/DEV INDUS NAT/G SOC/WK

B61
MARX K.,THE COMMUNIST MANIFESTO. IN (MENDEL A. ESSENTIAL WORKS OF MARXISM, NEW YORK: BANTAM. FUT MOD/EUR CULTURE ECO/DEV ECO/UNDEV AGRI FINAN INDUS MARKET PROC/MFG LABOR POL/PAR CONSULT FORCES CREATE PLAN ADMIN ATTIT DRIVE RIGID/FLEX ORD/FREE PWR RESPECT MARX/KARL MUNICH WORK. PAGE 86 F1691
COM NEW/IDEA CAP/ISM REV

B61
MOORE G.H.,BUSINESS CYCLE INDICATORS (TWO VOLS.). LABOR DIPLOM PRICE RISK TASK WAR PRODUC...CHARTS BIBLIOG 20. PAGE 93 F1822
MARKET FINAN WEALTH

B61
MORRIS B.R.,PROBLEMS OF AMERICAN ECONOMIC GROWTH. USA+45 LABOR WORKER BUDGET ECO/TAC INT/TRADE EQUILIB 20. PAGE 94 F1836
ECO/DEV POLICY TEC/DEV DEMAND

B61
PETCH G.A.,ECONOMIC DEVELOPMENT AND MODERN WEST AFRICA. AFR CONGO/BRAZ GHANA NIGER SIER/LEONE AGRI MARKET LABOR FOR/AID TAX COST EFFICIENCY EQUILIB PRODUC...GEOG TREND 20. PAGE 105 F2068
ECO/UNDEV TEC/DEV EXTR/IND ECO/TAC

B61
RUEDA B.,A STATEMENT OF THE LAWS OF COLOMBIA IN MATTERS AFFECTING BUSINESS (3RD ED.). INDUS FAM LABOR LG/CO NAT/G LEGIS TAX CONTROL MARRIAGE 20 COLOMB. PAGE 115 F2257
FINAN ECO/UNDEV LAW CONSTN

B61
SLICHTER S.H.,ECONOMIC GROWTH IN THE UNITED STATES. FUT USA+45 USA-45 LABOR PAY INCOME PRODUC...MGT 19/20. PAGE 123 F2422
ECO/DEV TEC/DEV CAP/ISM DEMAND

B61
STROUD G.S.,LABOR HISTORY IN THE UNITED STATES: A GENERAL BIBLIOGRAPHY. USA+45 USA-45 STRATA VOL/ASSN AUTOMAT GP/REL INGP/REL ATTIT HEALTH 18/20. PAGE 127 F2504
BIBLIOG WORKER LABOR

C61
FILLOL T.R.,"SOCIAL FACTORS IN ECONOMIC DEVELOPMENT: THE ARGENTINE CASE" INDUS LABOR CREATE TEC/DEV PERS/REL EFFICIENCY PRODUC DRIVE ...METH/CNCPT METH/COMP 20 ARGEN. PAGE 41 F0794
BIBLIOG ECO/UNDEV MGT TREND

B62
ALEXANDROWICZ C.H.,WORLD ECONOMIC AGENCIES: LAW AND PRACTICE. WOR+45 DIST/IND FINAN LABOR CONSULT INT/TRADE TARIFFS REPRESENT HEALTH...JURID 20 UN GATT EEC OAS ECSC. PAGE 4 F0064
INT/LAW INT/ORG DIPLOM ADJUD

B62
BACKMAN J.,THE ECONOMICS OF THE ELECTRICAL MACHINERY INDUSTRY. USA+45 PROC/MFG LABOR WORKER INT/TRADE TV PRICE COST...CHARTS 19/20. PAGE 8 F0147
PRODUC TEC/DEV TREND

B62
CHRISTENSON C.L.,ECONOMIC REDEVELOPMENT IN BITUMINOUS COAL: THE SPECIAL CASE OF TECHNOLOGICAL ADVANCE IN US COAL MINES 1930-1960. USA+45 USA-45 ECO/TAC AUTOMAT INCOME PRODUC...CHARTS 20. PAGE 24 F0471
EXTR/IND LABOR TEC/DEV ECO/DEV

B62
DOUGLAS A.,INDUSTRIAL PEACEMAKING. CONSULT ACT/RES ...MGT PSY METH 20. PAGE 34 F0656
BARGAIN INDUS LABOR GP/REL

B62
GALENSON W.,TRADE UNIONS MONOGRAPH SERIES (A SERIES OF NINE TEXTS). DELIB/GP LEAD PARTIC...DECISION ORG/CHARTS. PAGE 45 F0887
LABOR INGP/REL CONSTN REPRESENT

B62
GALENSON W.,LABOR IN DEVELOPING COUNTRIES. BRAZIL INDONESIA ISRAEL PAKISTAN TURKEY AGRI INDUS WORKER PAY PRICE GP/REL WEALTH...MGT CHARTS METH/COMP NAT/COMP 20. PAGE 45 F0888
LABOR ECO/UNDEV BARGAIN POL/PAR

B62
GRANICK D.,THE EUROPEAN EXECUTIVE. BELGIUM FRANCE GERMANY/W UK INDUS LABOR LG/CO SML/CO EX/STRUC PLAN TEC/DEV CAP/ISM COST DEMAND...POLICY CHARTS 20. PAGE 50 F0977
MGT ECO/DEV ECO/TAC EXEC

B62
HAGUE D.C.,INFLATION. AFR ECO/DEV ECO/UNDEV LABOR BUDGET CAP/ISM INT/TRADE TARIFFS SOCISM 20. PAGE 53 F1036
FINAN NAT/COMP BARGAIN ECO/TAC

B62
HARRINGTON M.,THE RETAIL CLERKS. ECO/TAC LEAD PARTIC CHOOSE GP/REL INGP/REL CENTRAL POLICY. PAGE 55 F1087
LABOR SERV/IND STRUCT DELIB/GP

B62
LITWACK L.,THE AMERICAN LABOR MOVEMENT. USA-45 NAT/G CREATE TEC/DEV CAP/ISM ECO/TAC ADJUD AUTOMAT SKILL...TREND ANTHOL 19/20. PAGE 81 F1588
INDUS LABOR GP/REL METH/COMP

B62
LUTZ F.A.,GELD UND WAHRUNG. AFR MARKET LABOR BUDGET 20 EUROPE. PAGE 82 F1610
ECO/TAC FINAN DIPLOM

POLICY

B62
MCCLELLAN J.L.,CRIME WITHOUT PUNISHMENT. USA+45 LAW SOCIETY DELIB/GP TRIBUTE CONTROL LOBBY COERCE GP/REL ANOMIE MORAL...CRIMLGY 20 CONGRESS HOFFA/J. PAGE 88 F1718
CRIME ACT/RES LABOR PWR

B62
MCCRONE G.,THE ECONOMICS OF SUBSIDING AGRICULTURE. UK ECO/DEV MARKET PLAN TARIFFS PROFIT 20 EEC. PAGE 88 F1725
AGRI BAL/PAY INT/TRADE LABOR

B62
MORGAN C.A.,LABOR ECONOMICS. LAW INDUS MARKET WORKER PLAN PROB/SOLV GOV/REL INCOME ROLE...T 20 DEPT/LABOR NLRB. PAGE 93 F1829
LABOR ECO/TAC ECO/DEV CAP/ISM

B62
MULLER E.,DIE HEIMATVERTRIEBENEN IN BADEN-WURTTEMBERG. GERMANY/W AGRI INDUS LABOR PROVS SOC/INTEG 20 MIGRATION. PAGE 95 F1858
GP/REL INGP/REL

B62
PASTOR R.S.,A STATEMENT OF THE LAWS OF PARAGUAY IN MATTERS AFFECTING BUSINESS (2ND ED.). PARAGUAY INDUS FAM LABOR LG/CO NAT/G LEGIS TAX CONTROL MARRIAGE 20. PAGE 103 F2033
FINAN ECO/UNDEV LAW CONSTN

B62
REES A.,THE ECONOMICS OF TRADE UNIONS. FUT ECO/DEV INDUS BARGAIN CAP/ISM PRICE SENIOR CONTROL GP/REL COST...TREND 20 AFL/CIO. PAGE 110 F2172
LABOR WORKER ECO/TAC

B62
ROBINSON M.A.,AN INTRODUCTION TO ECONOMIC REASONING. FINAN MARKET LABOR DIPLOM INT/TRADE BAL/PAY INCOME PRODUC WEALTH...POLICY MGT 20. PAGE 113 F2223
ECO/TAC METH/CNCPT NAT/G

B62
SHERIF M.,INTERGROUP RELATIONS AND LEADERSHIP: APPROACHES AND RESEARCH IN INDUSTRIAL, ETHNIC, CULTURAL AND POLITICAL AREAS. CULTURE R+D LABOR DIPLOM GP/REL RACE/REL PERCEPT...PSY CONCPT. PAGE 121 F2377
LEAD REPRESENT PWR INGP/REL

B62
SHINOHARA M.,GROWTH AND CYCLES IN THE JAPANESE ECONOMY. INDUS LABOR TEC/DEV CAP/ISM INT/TRADE PAY COST EFFICIENCY INCOME WEALTH...METH/COMP 20 CHINJAP. PAGE 121 F2380
PRODUC ECO/DEV EQUILIB ECOMETRIC

B62
SIEVERS A.M.,REVOLUTION, EVOLUTION AND THE ECONOMIC ORDER. INDUS LABOR TAX CONTROL REV WAR DEMAND PRODUC WEALTH...IDEA/COMP 19/20 KEYNES/JM. PAGE 122 F2399
EFFICIENCY ALL/IDEOS ECO/DEV WELF/ST

B62
SRIVASTAVA G.L.,COLLECTIVE BARGAINING AND LABOR-MANAGEMENT RELATIONS IN INDIA. INDIA UK USA+45 INDUS LEGIS WORKER ADJUD EFFICIENCY PRODUC ...METH/COMP 20. PAGE 125 F2462
LABOR MGT BARGAIN GP/REL

B62
VACCARO J.R.,A STATEMENT OF THE LAWS OF CHILE IN MATTERS AFFECTING BUSINESS (3RD ED.). CHILE AGRI FINAN FAM LABOR ECO/TAC FOR/AID TAX ADJUD CONTROL MARRIAGE STRANGE...BIBLIOG 20. PAGE 140 F2756
CONSTN LAW INDUS MGT

B62
VANEK J.,INTERNATIONAL TRADE - THEORY AND ECONOMIC POLICY. LABOR BAL/PWR ECO/TAC TARIFFS PRICE BAL/PAY COST DEMAND 20. PAGE 140 F2765
INT/TRADE DIPLOM BARGAIN MARKET

B62
WOODS H.D.,LABOUR POLICY AND LABOUR ECONOMICS IN CANADA. CANADA FUT NAT/G VOL/ASSN WORKER BARGAIN ECO/TAC PAY CONFER GP/REL 20. PAGE 148 F2924
LABOR POLICY INDUS ECO/DEV

B62
WRIGHT D.M.,THE KEYNESIAN SYSTEM. WOR+45 WOR-45 LABOR NAT/G CONTROL COST DEMAND EFFICIENCY...POLICY CONCPT CHARTS SIMUL 20 KEYNES/JM. PAGE 149 F2931
INCOME ECO/DEV FINAN ECO/TAC

L62
N,"UNION INVESTMENT IN BUSINESS: A SOURCE OF UNION CONFLICT OF INTEREST." LAW NAT/G LEGIS CONTROL GP/REL INGP/REL DECISION. PAGE 96 F1884
LABOR POLICY FINAN LG/CO

C62
JOINT ECONOMIC COMMITTEE,"DIMENSIONS OF SOVIET ECONOMIC POWER." USSR R+D FORCES ACT/RES OP/RES TEC/DEV...GEOG STAT BIBLIOG 20. PAGE 68 F1337
ECO/DEV PLAN PRODUC LABOR

B63
BERGSON A.,ECONOMIC TRENDS IN THE SOVIET UNION. USSR ECO/UNDEV AGRI NAT/G FORCES PLAN TEC/DEV INT/TRADE BAL/PAY...POLICY ANTHOL 20. PAGE 14 F0259
ECO/DEV NAT/COMP INDUS LABOR

B63
BERLE A.A. JR.,THE AMERICAN ECONOMIC REPUBLIC. STRUCT FINAN MARKET LABOR NAT/G PLAN...POLICY WELF/ST DECISION. PAGE 14 F0262
CAP/ISM ECO/TAC TREND CONCPT

B63
BURTT E.J. JR.,LABOR MARKETS, UNIONS, AND GOVERNMENT POLICIES. USA+45 MARKET NAT/G DELIB/GP CREATE BARGAIN GP/REL ORD/FREE PWR...POLICY CHARTS 20 AFL/CIO. PAGE 20 F0393
LABOR ECO/DEV CONTROL WORKER

B63
CHAMBERLAIN E.H.,THE ECONOMIC ANALYSIS OF LABOR UNION POWER (PAMPHLET). WORKER ECO/TAC DOMIN COERCE GP/REL DRIVE WEALTH POLICY. PAGE 23 F0441
LABOR PWR CONTROL

B63
COSSA L.,SAGGI BIBLIOGRAFICI DI ECONOMIA POLITICA. MOD/EUR LABOR PRICE COST INCOME 18/19. PAGE 28 F0539
BIBLIOG FINAN WEALTH

B63
DEUTSCH K.W.,THE POLITICAL ROLE OF LABOR IN DEVELOPING COUNTRIES. AFR ASIA S/ASIA USA+45 WOR+45 ECO/UNDEV POL/PAR ECO/TAC EDU/PROP LEGIT COERCE ORD/FREE PWR WEALTH...OBS INT TREND VAL/FREE 20. PAGE 32 F0625
LABOR NAT/LISM

B63
ERHARD L.,THE ECONOMICS OF SUCCESS. GERMANY/W WOR+45 LABOR CHIEF TAX REGION COST DEMAND ANTHOL. PAGE 38 F0745
ECO/DEV INT/TRADE PLAN DIPLOM

B63
FURTADO C.,THE ECONOMIC GROWTH OF BRAZIL: A SURVEY FROM COLONIAL TO MODERN TIMES. L/A+17C AGRI DIST/IND EXTR/IND INDUS WORKER COLONIAL RACE/REL OWN GOV/COMP. PAGE 45 F0877
ECO/UNDEV TEC/DEV LABOR DOMIN

B63
HAHN L.A.,DIE AMERIKANISCHE KONJUNKTURPOLITIK DER DOLLAR UND DIE DMARK. GERMANY/W USA+45 DIPLOM PRICE BAL/PAY COST...POLICY MONEY. PAGE 53 F1038
FINAN BUDGET ECO/TAC LABOR

B63
HARVEY O.L.,THE ANVIL AND THE PLOW: A HISTORY OF THE UNITED STATES DEPARTMENT OF LABOR: 1913-1963. USA+45 USA-45 NAT/G CONFER NEW/LIB 20 DEPT/LABOR. PAGE 56 F1106
EX/STRUC REPRESENT GP/REL LABOR

B63
JACOBS P.,STATE OF UNIONS. USA+45 STRATA TOP/EX GP/REL RACE/REL DEMAND DISCRIM ATTIT PWR 20 CONGRESS NEGRO HOFFA/J. PAGE 66 F1296
LABOR ECO/TAC BARGAIN DECISION

B63
KAPP W.K.,SOCIAL COSTS OF BUSINESS ENTERPRISE. WOR+45 LABOR TEC/DEV CAP/ISM HABITAT...PHIL/SCI NEW/IDEA CON/ANAL 20. PAGE 69 F1354
COST SOCIETY INDUS RIGID/FLEX

B63
KATZ S.M.,A SELECTED LIST OF US READINGS ON DEVELOPMENT. AGRI COM/IND DIST/IND INDUS LABOR PLAN FOR/AID EDU/PROP HEALTH...POLICY SOC/WK 20. PAGE 69 F1361
BIBLIOG/A ECO/UNDEV TEC/DEV ACT/RES

B63
LEE M.W.,MACROECONOMICS: FLUCTUATIONS, GROWTH AND STABILITY (3RD ED.). MARKET LABOR TEC/DEV INT/TRADE TAX PRICE WAR PRODUC...POLICY ECOMETRIC CHARTS 19/20. PAGE 77 F1505
EQUILIB TREND WEALTH

B63
MEYNAUD J.,PLANIFICATION ET POLITIQUE. FRANCE ITALY FINAN LABOR DELIB/GP LEGIS ADMIN EFFICIENCY ...MAJORIT DECISION 20. PAGE 90 F1773
PLAN ECO/TAC PROB/SOLV

B63
PAENSON I.,SYSTEMATIC GLOSSARY ENGLISH, FRENCH, SPANISH, RUSSIAN OF SELECTED ECONOMIC AND SOCIAL TERMS. WOR+45 FINAN LABOR INT/TRADE DEMAND PRODUC 20. PAGE 102 F2014
DICTIONARY SOC LING

B63
PATTON R.,THE DEVELOPMENT OF THE AMERICAN ECONOMY: REVISED. USA+45 USA-45 INDUS LABOR NAT/G CAP/ISM DIPLOM INT/TRADE WAR WEALTH 16/20. PAGE 104 F2038
ECO/TAC ECO/DEV DEMAND

B63
PELLING H.M.,A HISTORY OF BRITISH TRADE UNIONISM. UK ELITES ECO/DEV POL/PAR GP/REL PWR NEW/LIB 19/20. PAGE 104 F2051
LABOR VOL/ASSN NAT/G

B63
SALENT W.S.,THE UNITED STATES BALANCE OF PAYMENTS IN 1968. EUR+WWI UK USA+45 AGRI R+D LABOR FORCES PRODUC...GEOG CONCPT CHARTS 20 CHINJAP EEC. PAGE 115 F2274
BAL/PAY DEMAND FINAN INT/TRADE

B63
SCHOECK H.,THE NEW ARGUMENT IN ECONOMICS. UK USA+45 INDUS MARKET LABOR NAT/G ECO/TAC ADMIN ROUTINE BAL/PAY PWR...POLICY BOLIV. PAGE 117 F2309
WELF/ST FOR/AID ECO/DEV ALL/IDEOS

B63
US DEPARTMENT OF LABOR,THE ANVIL AND THE PLOW. KOREA USA+45 USA-45 INDUS WORKER BUDGET WAR ...POLICY AUD/VIS CHARTS 20 DEPT/LABOR. PAGE 135 F2667
ECO/DEV LABOR ECO/TAC NAT/G

L63
LIVERNASH E.R.,"THE RELATION OF POWER TO THE STRUCTURE AND PROCESS OF COLLECTIVE BARGAINING." ADJUD ORD/FREE...POLICY MGT CLASSIF GP/COMP. PAGE 81 F1589
LABOR GP/REL PWR ECO/TAC

L63
MCKERSIE R.B.,"NONPROFESSIONAL HOSPITAL WORKERS AND A UNION ORGANIZING DRIVE." PLAN GP/REL RACE/REL ATTIT DRIVE...CORREL STAT INT GP/COMP. PAGE 88 F1732
VOL/ASSN HEALTH INGP/REL LABOR

L63
MOUSKHELY M.,"LE BLOC COMMUNISTE ET LA COMMUNAUTE ECONOMIQUE EUROPEENNE." AFR COM EUR+WWI FUT USSR WOR+45 INTELL ECO/UNDEV LABOR POL/PAR NUC/PWR RIGID/FLEX...TIME/SEQ ORG/CHARTS EEC TOT/POP 20. PAGE 94 F1849
INT/ORG ECO/DEV

S63
GRUSHIN B.A.,"PROBLEMS OF THE MOVEMENT OF COMMUNIST LABOR IN THE USSR." COM SOCIETY LABOR ECO/TAC EDU/PROP COERCE RIGID/FLEX ORD/FREE...POLICY MARXIST STAT QU WORK 20. PAGE 52 F1011
ATTIT USSR

S63
REES A.,"THE EFFECTS OF UNIONS ON RESOURCE ALLOCATION." USA+45 WORKER PRICE CONTROL GP/REL ...MGT METH/COMP 20. PAGE 110 F2173
LABOR BARGAIN RATION INCOME

B64
BERRILL K.,ECONOMIC DEVELOPMENT WITH SPECIAL REFERENCE TO EAST ASIA. ASIA INDIA S/ASIA AGRI INDUS LABOR DELIB/GP PLAN INT/TRADE COST PRODUC 20 CHINJAP. PAGE 14 F0271
FINAN ECO/UNDEV INT/ORG CAP/ISM

B64
BOARMAN P.M.,GERMANY'S ECONOMIC DILEMMA - INFLATION AND THE BALANCE OF PAYMENTS. AFR GERMANY/W LABOR CAP/ISM PRICE BAL/PAY COST INCOME 20. PAGE 16 F0302
ECO/DEV FINAN INT/TRADE BUDGET

B64
CHANDLER A.D. JR.,GIANT ENTERPRISE: FORD, GENERAL MOTORS, AND THE AUTOMOBILE INDUSTRY; SOURCES AND READINGS. USA+45 USA-45 FINAN MARKET CREATE ADMIN ...TIME/SEQ ANTHOL 20 AUTOMOBILE. PAGE 23 F0447
LG/CO DIST/IND LABOR MGT

B64
COLSTON RESEARCH SOCIETY,ECONOMETRIC ANALYSIS FOR NATIONAL ECONOMIC PLANNING (PROCEEDINGS OF SIXTEENTH SYMPOSIUM OF COLSTON RESEARCH SOCIETY). UK USA+45 FINAN FAM LABOR NAT/G PLAN PRICE ...METH/CNCPT TREND CHARTS TIME 20. PAGE 26 F0510
ECOMETRIC DELIB/GP ECO/TAC PROB/SOLV

B64
COMMITTEE ECONOMIC DEVELOPMENT,COMMUNITY ECONOMIC DEVELOPMENT PROGRAMS. USA+45 FINAN INDUS LG/CO PROF/ORG CREATE GP/REL MUNICH NEW/YORK VERMONT PENNSYLVAN IN ARKANSAS. PAGE 27 F0519
LOC/G LABOR PLAN

B64
HACKER A.,THE CORPORATION TAKE-OVER. CONSTN LABOR PLAN BAL/PWR CONTROL EXEC LOBBY REPRESENT GP/REL ROLE ORD/FREE POLICY. PAGE 52 F1025
LG/CO STRUCT PWR

B64
HAMBRIDGE G.,DYNAMICS OF DEVELOPMENT. AGRI FINAN INDUS LABOR INT/TRADE EDU/PROP ADMIN LEAD OWN HEALTH...ANTHOL BIBLIOG 20. PAGE 54 F1054
ECO/UNDEV ECO/TAC OP/RES ACT/RES

B64
HARBISON F.H.,EDUCATION, MANPOWER, AND ECONOMIC GROWTH. WOR+45 ECO/DEV ECO/UNDEV ACADEM LABOR SCHOOL WORKER UTIL...IDEA/COMP NAT/COMP. PAGE 55 F1075
PLAN TEC/DEV EDU/PROP SKILL

B64
HAZLEWOOD A.,THE ECONOMICS OF DEVELOPMENT: AN ANNOTATED LIST OF BOOKS AND ARTICLES PUBLISHED 1958-1962. AGRI FINAN INDUS LABOR NAT/G DIPLOM INT/TRADE INCOME...MGT 20. PAGE 58 F1130
BIBLIOG/A ECO/UNDEV TEC/DEV

B64
HUTT W.H.,THE ECONOMICS OF THE COLOUR BAR. SOUTH/AFR EXTR/IND LABOR ADJUD NEGRO. PAGE 64 F1251
INDUS DISCRIM RACE/REL ECO/UNDEV

B64
IMAZ J.L.,LOS QUE MANDAN. INDUS LABOR NAT/G POL/PAR PROVS SECT CHIEF TOP/EX CONTROL 20 ARGEN. PAGE 64 F1261
LEAD FORCES ELITES ATTIT

B64
LI C.M.,INDUSTRIAL DEVELOPMENT IN COMMUNIST CHINA. CHINA/COM ECO/DEV ECO/UNDEV AGRI FINAN INDUS MARKET LABOR NAT/G ECO/TAC INT/TRADE EXEC ALL/VALS ...POLICY RELATIV TREND WORK TOT/POP VAL/FREE 20. PAGE 79 F1556
ASIA TEC/DEV

B64
LUTHULI A.,AFRICA'S FREEDOM. KIN LABOR POL/PAR SCHOOL DIPLOM NEUTRAL REGION REV NAT/LISM PWR WEALTH SOCISM SOC/INTEG 20. PAGE 82 F1608
AFR ECO/UNDEV COLONIAL

B64
MILIBAND R.,THE SOCIALIST REGISTER: 1964. GERMANY/W ITALY UK LABOR POL/PAR ECO/TAC FOR/AID NUC/PWR ...POLICY SOCIALIST IDEA/COMP 20 MAO NASSER/G. PAGE 91 F1784
MARXISM SOCISM CAP/ISM PROB/SOLV

B64
MITAU G.T.,INSOLUBLE PROBLEMS: CASE PROBLEMS ON THE FUNCTIONS OF STATE AND LOCAL GOVERNMENT. USA+45 AIR FINAN LABOR POL/PAR PROB/SOLV TAX RECEIVE CONTROL GP/REL 20 CASEBOOK ZONING. PAGE 92 F1807
ADJUD LOC/G PROVS

B64
MORGAN H.W.,AMERICAN SOCIALISM 1900-1960. AFR USA+45 USA-45 INTELL AGRI LABOR WORKER BARGAIN ECO/TAC GP/REL RACE/REL 20 NEGRO MIGRATION. PAGE 93 F1830
SOCISM POL/PAR ECO/DEV STRATA

B64
NEUFIELD M.F.,A REPRESENTATIVE BIBLIOGRAPHY OF AMERICAN LABOR HISTORY. USA+45 USA-45 20. PAGE 97 F1914
BIBLIOG LABOR WORKER INDUS

B64
PIERSON J.H.,INSURING FULL EMPLOYMENT. USA+45 LABOR DIPLOM ECO/TAC PAY BAL/PAY 20. PAGE 106 F2084
ECO/DEV INT/TRADE POLICY WORKER

B64
REUSS H.S.,THE CRITICAL DECADE - AN ECONOMIC POLICY FOR AMERICA AND THE FREE WORLD. AFR USA+45 FINAN POL/PAR WORKER PLAN DIPLOM ECO/TAC TARIFFS BAL/PAY ...POLICY 20 CONGRESS. PAGE 111 F2181
FOR/AID INT/TRADE LABOR LEGIS

B64
ROBINSON E.A.G.,ECONOMIC DEVELOPMENT FOR AFRICA SOUTH OF THE SAHARA. AFR AGRI INDUS LABOR BUDGET INT/TRADE PRICE...POLICY GEOG ANTHOL 20. PAGE 113 F2219
ECO/UNDEV ECO/TAC ACT/RES PLAN

B64
RUSTAMJI R.F.,THE LAW OF INDUSTRIAL DISPUTES IN INDIA. INDIA LEGIS WORKER CONTROL GP/REL...JURID MGT TIME/SEQ 20. PAGE 115 F2264
INDUS ADJUD BARGAIN LABOR

B64
SOLOW R.M.,THE NATURE AND SOURCES OF UNEMPLOYMENT IN THE UNITED STATES (PAMPHLET). USA+45 INDUS LABOR TEC/DEV ECO/TAC SKILL WEALTH...TREND NAT/COMP 20. PAGE 124 F2439
ECO/DEV WORKER STAT PRODUC

B64
SULTAN P.E.,THE DISENCHANTED UNIONIST. NAT/G ADJUD CONTROL SANCTION RACE/REL ANOMIE ATTIT ROLE ...METH/CNCPT INT. PAGE 127 F2512
LABOR INGP/REL CHARTS MAJORIT

B64
US DEPT LABOR OFF SOLICITOR,LEGISLATIVE HISTORY OF THE LABOR-MANAGEMENT AND DISCLOSURE ACT OF 1959. DELIB/GP WORKER ADMIN LOBBY PARL/PROC SANCTION CHOOSE GOV/REL 20 CONGRESS PRESIDENT. PAGE 136 F2677
LABOR LEGIS DEBATE POLICY

B64
WERNETTE J.P.,GOVERNMENT AND BUSINESS. LABOR CAP/ISM ECO/TAC INT/TRADE TAX ADMIN AUTOMAT NUC/PWR CIVMIL/REL DEMAND...MGT 20 MONOPOLY. PAGE 145 F2859
NAT/G FINAN ECO/DEV CONTROL

B64
YUDELMAN M.,AFRICANS ON THE LAND. RHODESIA MARKET LABOR OWN...ECOMETRIC TREND 20. PAGE 150 F2955
ECO/DEV AFR AGRI ECO/TAC

L64
BHAGWATI J.,"THE PURE THEORY OF INTERNATIONAL TRADE: A SURVEY." WOR+45 ECO/DEV ECO/UNDEV FINAN MARKET PROC/MFG INT/ORG LABOR LG/CO NAT/G TEC/DEV ECO/TAC SKILL WEALTH...POLICY RELATIV MGT CONCPT NEW/IDEA MATH QUANT GEN/LAWS FOR/TRADE 20. PAGE 14 F0276
INDUS HYPO/EXP

S64
FLORINSKY M.T.,"TRENDS IN THE SOVIET ECONOMY." COM USA+45 USSR INDUS LABOR NAT/G PLAN TEC/DEV ECO/TAC ALL/VALS SOCISM...MGT METH/CNCPT STYLE CON/ANAL GEN/METH WORK 20. PAGE 42 F0817
ECO/DEV AGRI

S64
N,"QUASI-LEGISLATIVE ARBITRATION AGREEMENTS." LAW LG/CO ECO/TAC SANCTION ATTIT POLICY. PAGE 96 F1885
ADJUD ADJUST LABOR GP/REL

S64
PATEL S.J.,"THE ECONOMIC DISTANCE BETWEEN NATIONS: ITS ORIGIN, MEASUREMENT AND OUTLOOK." WOR+45 ECO/DEV AGRI FINAN INDUS MARKET LABOR NAT/G CONSULT TEC/DEV ECO/TAC WEALTH...POLICY RELATIV MGT TREND WORK 20. PAGE 103 F2035
ECO/UNDEV PLAN

C64
NORGREN P.H.,"TOWARD FAIR EMPLOYMENT." USA+45 LAW STRATA LABOR NAT/G FORCES ACT/RES ADMIN ATTIT ...POLICY BIBLIOG 20 NEGRO. PAGE 98 F1932
RACE/REL DISCRIM WORKER MGT

B65
ALEXANDER R.J.,ORGANIZED LABOR IN LATIN AMERICA. L/A+17C INT/ORG LEGIS WORKER TEC/DEV BARGAIN INT/TRADE REV...NAT/COMP BIBLIOG 20. PAGE 3 F0059
LABOR POL/PAR ECO/UNDEV POLICY

B65
ALLEN W.R.,INTERNATIONAL TRADE THEORY: HUME TO OHLIN. FINAN LABOR TARIFFS TAX PRICE DEMAND PRODUC PROFIT...ANTHOL 18/20. PAGE 4 F0074
INT/TRADE WEALTH METH/CNCPT

B65
ARTEL R.,THE STRUCTURE OF THE STOCKHOLM ECONOMY. SWEDEN DIST/IND LABOR LOC/G TEC/DEV DEMAND MUNICH
ECO/DEV METH/COMP

LOUISIANA 20. PAGE 7 F0125
BAL/PAY

B65

BARRY E.E.,NATIONALISATION IN BRITISH POLITICS: THE HISTORICAL BACKGROUND. UK AGRI DIST/IND EXTR/IND LABOR LG/CO ATTIT CONSERVE SOCISM 19/20 LABOR/PAR. PAGE 10 F0198
NAT/G OWN INDUS POL/PAR

B65

BRENNAN M.J.,PATTERNS OF MARKET BEHAVIOR. AFR USA+45 OP/RES CAP/ISM ECO/TAC INT/TRADE...CHARTS METH/COMP ANTHOL TIME 20. PAGE 18 F0346
MARKET LABOR FINAN ECOMETRIC

B65

COLBERG M.R.,HUMAN CAPITAL IN SOUTHERN DEVELOPMENT. USA+45 AGRI ACADEM LABOR SCHOOL WORKER CAP/ISM DISCRIM. PAGE 26 F0498
PROVS RACE/REL GP/REL

B65

COLLINS H.,KARL MARX AND THE BRITISH LABOUR MOVEMENT; YEARS OF THE FIRST INTERNATIONAL. FRANCE SWITZERLND UK CAP/ISM WAR...MARXIST IDEA/COMP BIBLIOG 19. PAGE 26 F0506
MARXISM LABOR INT/ORG REV

B65

COLLINS H.,KARL MARX AND THE BRITISH LABOR MOVEMENT, YEARS OF THE FIRST INTERNATIONAL. EUR+WWI MOD/EUR UK STRATA INDUS NAT/G POL/PAR SOCISM ...CONCPT 19/20 MARX/KARL. PAGE 26 F0507
MARXISM LABOR INT/ORG WORKER

B65

COLLOQUE SUR LA PLANIFICATION,LA PLANIFICATION COMME PROCESSUS DE DECISION. FRANCE SOCIETY MARKET LABOR LEGIS GP/REL EFFICIENCY INCOME ATTIT TECHRACY ...MYTH IDEA/COMP 20. PAGE 26 F0508
PLAN ECO/TAC PROB/SOLV

B65

COPELAND M.A.,OUR FREE ENTERPRISE ECONOMY. USA+45 INDUS LABOR ADMIN CONTROL GP/REL MGT. PAGE 27 F0533
CAP/ISM PLAN FINAN ECO/DEV

B65

DERBER M.,PLANT UNION-MANAGEMENT RELATIONS: FROM PRACTICE TO THEORY. PROC/MFG NEIGH PROB/SOLV ORD/FREE...DECISION MGT OBS QU SAMP. PAGE 32 F0621
LG/CO LABOR GP/REL ATTIT

B65

DODDY F.S.,INTRODUCTION TO THE USE OF ECONOMIC INDICATORS. FINAN LABOR PLAN COST...ECOMETRIC INDICATOR MATH PREDICT CHARTS METH 20. PAGE 33 F0649
TEC/DEV STAT PRODUC PRICE

B65

EDELMAN M.,THE POLITICS OF WAGE-PRICE DECISIONS. GERMANY ITALY NETHERLAND UK INDUS LABOR POL/PAR PROB/SOLV BARGAIN PRICE ROUTINE BAL/PAY COST DEMAND 20. PAGE 36 F0699
GOV/COMP CONTROL ECO/TAC PLAN

B65

FLEMING R.W.,THE LABOR ARBITRATION PROCESS. USA+45 LAW BARGAIN ADJUD ROUTINE SANCTION COST...PREDICT CHARTS TIME 20. PAGE 41 F0809
GP/REL LABOR CONSULT DELIB/GP

B65

GOETZ-GIREY R.,LE MOUVEMENT DES GREVES EN FRANCE. FRANCE FINAN OP/RES PROB/SOLV ECO/TAC INCOME HABITAT...STAT CHARTS 19/20. PAGE 48 F0932
LABOR WORKER GP/REL INDUS

B65

GRAMPP W.D.,ECONOMIC LIBERALISM; THE BEGINNINGS (VOL. I). USA-45 WOR-45 MARKET LABOR ATTIT WEALTH ...POLICY CONCPT BIBLIOG GREECE/ANC MERCANTLST REPUBLICAN FEDERALIST. PAGE 50 F0974
ECO/DEV CAP/ISM IDEA/COMP ECO/TAC

B65

GREEN J.L.,METROPOLITAN ECONOMIC REPUBLICS. USA+45 ECO/TAC INCOME...GEOG SOC CONCPT SIMUL MUNICH 20 ATLANTA. PAGE 50 F0985
SOC/WK PLAN LABOR

B65

HERRICK B.H.,URBAN MIGRATION AND ECONOMIC DEVELOPMENT IN CHILE. CHILE AGRI INDUS LABOR NAT/G CENTRAL PRODUC...STAT SAMP CHARTS BIBLIOG/A MUNICH 20 MIGRATION. PAGE 59 F1156
HABITAT GEOG ECO/UNDEV

B65

LEYS C.T.,FEDERATION IN EAST AFRICA. LAW AGRI DIST/IND FINAN INT/ORG LABOR INT/TRADE CONFER ADMIN CONTROL GP/REL...ANTHOL 20 AFRICA/E. PAGE 79 F1554
FEDERAL REGION ECO/UNDEV PLAN

B65

MORRIS M.D.,THE EMERGENCE OF AN INDUSTRIAL LABOR FORCE IN INDIA: A STUDY OF THE BOMBAY COTTON MILLS, 1854-1947. INDIA WORKER OP/RES ADMIN 19/20. PAGE 94 F1837
INDUS LABOR ECO/UNDEV CAP/ISM

B65

PAYNE J.L.,LABOR AND POLITICS IN PERU; THE SYSTEM OF POLITICAL BARGAINING. PERU CONSTN VOL/ASSN EX/STRUC LEAD PWR...CHARTS 20. PAGE 104 F2042
LABOR POL/PAR BARGAIN GP/REL

B65

PROCHNOW H.V.,WORLD ECONOMIC PROBLEMS AND POLICIES. INDIA ISRAEL WOR+45 AGRI LABOR PROB/SOLV FOR/AID TARIFFS CONTROL BAL/PAY NAT/LISM WEALTH...TREND CHARTS 20 CHINJAP EEC. PAGE 108 F2124
MARKET ECO/TAC PRODUC IDEA/COMP

B65

ROSS A.M.,EMPLOYMENT POLICY AND THE LABOR MARKET. USA+45 MARKET LABOR NAT/G PROB/SOLV PAY EDU/PROP PARTIC UTIL...POLICY 20. PAGE 114 F2242
ECO/DEV WORKER WEALTH DEMAND

B65

ROSS P.,THE GOVERNMENT AS A SOURCE OF UNION POWER. USA+45 LAW ECO/DEV PROB/SOLV ECO/TAC LEAD GP/REL ...MGT 20. PAGE 114 F2245
LABOR BARGAIN POLICY NAT/G

B65

SIMON B.,EDUCATION AND THE LABOR MOVEMENT, 1870-1920. UK SOCIETY STRATA LABOR POL/PAR SCHOOL CONTROL PARTIC SOCISM...BIBLIOG 19/20. PAGE 122 F2406
EDU/PROP WORKER ADJUST LAW

B65

VAID K.N.,STATE AND LABOR IN INDIA. INDIA INDUS WORKER PAY PRICE ADJUD CONTROL PARL/PROC GP/REL ORD/FREE 20. PAGE 140 F2757
LAW LABOR MGT NEW/LIB

B65

VANEK J.,GENERAL EQUILIBRIUM OF INTERNATIONAL DISCRIMINATION; THE CASE OF CUSTOMS UNIONS. LABOR PROB/SOLV ECO/TAC DISCRIM INCOME...MATH CHARTS METH 20. PAGE 140 F2767
INT/TRADE TARIFFS INT/ORG EQUILIB

B65

WALTON R.E.,A BEHAVIORAL THEORY OF LABOR NEGOTIATIONS: AN ANALYSIS OF A SOCIAL INTERACTION SYSTEM. USA+45 FINAN PROB/SOLV ECO/TAC GP/REL INGP/REL...DECISION BIBLIOG. PAGE 143 F2812
SOC LABOR BARGAIN ADMIN

B65

WILKINSON T.O.,THE URBANIZATION OF JAPANESE LABOR, 1868-1955. AGRI PROC/MFG CAP/ISM PRODUC PROFIT ...SOC CLASSIF CENSUS CHARTS MUNICH 19/20 CHINJAP. PAGE 146 F2887
LABOR INDUS GEOG

B65

WISCONSIN HISTORICAL SOCIETY,LABOR PAPERS ON MICROFILM: A COMBINED LIST. USA+45 USA-45 WORKER 20. PAGE 148 F2910
BIBLIOG LABOR PRESS

B65

WURFEL S.W.,FOREIGN ENTERPRISE IN COLOMBIA. FINAN LABOR NAT/G ECO/TAC TAX REGION 20 COLOMB. PAGE 149 F2944
ECO/UNDEV INT/TRADE JURID CAP/ISM

L65

HAGE J.,"AN AXIOMATIC THEORY OF ORGANIZATIONS" USA+45 STRUCT LABOR PRODUC DRIVE PERSON RIGID/FLEX 20 WEBER/MAX. PAGE 53 F1032
GP/REL EFFICIENCY PROF/ORG ATTIT

L65

WIONCZEK M.,"LATIN AMERICA FREE TRADE ASSOCIATION." AGRI DIST/IND FINAN INDUS INT/ORG LABOR NAT/G TEC/DEV ECO/TAC HEALTH SKILL WEALTH...POLICY RELATIV MGT LAFTA 20. PAGE 148 F2909
L/A+17C MARKET REGION

S65

KAUN D.E.,"THE FAIR LABOUR STANDARDS ACT: AN EVALUATION IN TERMS OF ITS STATED GOALS." SOUTH/AFR LAW LABOR BARGAIN PAY INGP/REL WEALTH 20. PAGE 69 F1364
ECO/TAC PRICE WORKER LEGIS

S65

KINDLEBERGER C.P.,"MASS MIGRATION, THEN AND NOW." LAW ECO/DEV ECO/UNDEV INDUS LABOR INT/TRADE FEEDBACK REGION RIGID/FLEX...SOC NAT/COMP EEC. PAGE 71 F1394
EUR+WWI USA-45 WORKER IDEA/COMP

S65

MALHERBE E.G.,"MANPOWER TRAINING: EDUCATIONAL REQUIREMENTS FOR ECONOMIC EXPANSION." SOUTH/AFR ECO/DEV INDUS EDU/PROP...MGT STAT CHARTS 20. PAGE 84 F1646
LABOR SKILL SCHOOL ACADEM

S65

STEENKAMP W.F.J.,"THE PROBLEM OF WAGE REGULATION." SOUTH/AFR LAW ECO/DEV ECO/UNDEV LABOR NAT/G BARGAIN PAY INGP/REL DISCRIM WEALTH...METH/COMP 20. PAGE 125 F2473
ECO/TAC PRICE WORKER RATION

B66

ANDRESKI S.,PARASITISM AND SUBVERSION* THE CASE OF LATIN AMERICA. CULTURE ECO/UNDEV LABOR NAT/G SECT PROB/SOLV RACE/REL TOTALISM ATTIT WEALTH ALL/IDEOS. PAGE 5 F0100
L/A+17C GOV/COMP STRATA REV

B66

BAKKE E.W.,MUTUAL SURVIVAL; THE GOAL OF UNION AND MANAGEMENT (2ND ED.). USA+45 ELITES ECO/DEV ECO/TAC CONFER ADMIN REPRESENT GP/REL INGP/REL ATTIT ...GP/COMP 20. PAGE 8 F0155
MGT LABOR BARGAIN INDUS

B66

BALDWIN R.E.,ECONOMIC DEVELOPMENT AND EXPORT GROWTH: A STUDY OF NORTHERN RHODESIA, 1920-1960. AFR RHODESIA AGRI EXTR/IND FINAN MARKET LABOR WORKER ECO/TAC...CONCPT NEW/IDEA MUNICH 20. PAGE 9 F0166
ECO/UNDEV TEC/DEV INT/TRADE CAP/ISM

B66

BRODERSEN A.,THE SOVIET WORKER: LABOR AND GOVERNMENT IN SOVIET SOCIETY. USSR STRUCT INDUS LABOR PLAN PAY INGP/REL PRODUC...POLICY GEN/LAWS BIBLIOG 20 STALIN/J LENIN/VI BOLSHEVISM KHRUSH/N. PAGE 19 F0357
WORKER ROLE NAT/G MARXISM

B66

COLE A.B.,SOCIALIST PARTIES IN POSTWAR JAPAN.
POL/PAR

STRATA AGRI LABOR PLAN DIPLOM ECO/TAC AGREE LEAD CHOOSE ATTIT...CHARTS 20 CHINJAP SOC/DEMPAR. PAGE 26 F0499
POLICY SOCISM NAT/G

B66
DAVIES I.,AFRICAN TRADE UNIONS. AFR ECO/UNDEV INT/ORG GP/REL ORD/FREE SOVEREIGN SOCISM 20. PAGE 30 F0585
LABOR COLONIAL PWR INDUS

B66
DILLEY M.R.,BRITISH POLICY IN KENYA COLONY (2ND ED.). AFR INDIA UK LABOR BUDGET TAX ADMIN PARL/PROC GP/REL...BIBLIOG 20 PARLIAMENT. PAGE 33 F0639
COLONIAL REPRESENT SOVEREIGN

B66
DOBB M.,SOVIET ECONOMIC DEVELOPMENT SINCE 1917. USSR ECO/DEV ECO/UNDEV LABOR NAT/G TEC/DEV ECO/TAC ROUTINE PRODUC MARXISM 20. PAGE 33 F0647
PLAN INDUS WORKER

B66
EBONY,THE NEGRO HANDBOOK. ACADEM LABOR LOC/G SECT FORCES WORKER CT/SYS CRIME DISCRIM ORD/FREE...BIOG SOC/INTEG 19/20 NEGRO CIV/RIGHTS. PAGE 36 F0692
RACE/REL EDU/PROP LAW STAT

B66
FORD P.,CARDINAL MORAN AND THE A. L. P. NAT/G POL/PAR SECT DELIB/GP LOBBY REV CHOOSE ORD/FREE MARXISM 19/20 AUSTRAL PROTESTANT LABOR/PAR. PAGE 42 F0825
CATHISM SOCISM LABOR SOCIETY

B66
GOULD J.M.,THE TECHNICAL ELITE. INDUS LABOR TECHRACY...POLICY DECISION STAT CHARTS 20. PAGE 49 F0967
ECO/DEV TEC/DEV ELITES TECHNIC

B66
HACKETT J.,L'ECONOMIE BRITANNIQUE: PROBLEMES ET PERSPECTIVES. FRANCE UK LABOR NAT/G EX/STRUC PROB/SOLV BAL/PAY INCOME RIGID/FLEX...MGT PHIL/SCI CHARTS MUNICH 20. PAGE 53 F1027
ECO/DEV FINAN ECO/TAC PLAN

B66
HALLER H.,DAS PROBLEM DER GELDWERTSTABILITAT. MARKET LABOR INCOME PRODUC...POLICY 20. PAGE 54 F1049
PRICE COST FINAN ECO/TAC

B66
HAYS P.R.,LABOR ARBITRATION: A DISSENTING VIEW. USA+45 LAW DELIB/GP BARGAIN ADJUD...PREDICT 20. PAGE 57 F1126
GP/REL LABOR CONSULT CT/SYS

B66
KOH S.J.,STAGES OF INDUSTRIAL DEVELOPMENT IN ASIA. ASIA INDIA KOREA STRATA STRUCT NAT/G INT/TRADE ...CHARTS 19/20 CHINJAP. PAGE 72 F1415
INDUS ECO/UNDEV ECO/DEV LABOR

B66
KROOSS H.E.,AMERICAN ECONOMIC DEVELOPMENT (2ND ED.). USA+45 USA-45 AGRI INDUS LABOR WORKER INT/TRADE TAX WAR...CHARTS 18/20. PAGE 73 F1443
ECO/TAC NAT/G CAP/ISM ECO/DEV

B66
LANDERS D.S.,RISE OF CAPITALISM. LABOR AUTOMAT GP/REL CENTRAL COST PROFIT...SOC CONCPT ANTHOL 19/20. PAGE 75 F1469
CAP/ISM INDUS AGRI

B66
LEE R.A.,TRUMAN AND TAFT-HARTLEY: A QUESTION OF MANDATE. USA+45 LAW CONSTN LG/CO CONTROL LOBBY GOV/REL PEACE NEW/LIB 20 TRUMAN/HS CONGRESS. PAGE 77 F1507
LEGIS TOP/EX ADJUD LABOR

B66
MADAN G.R.,ECONOMIC THINKING IN INDIA. INDIA ECO/UNDEV AGRI FINAN INDUS LABOR PLAN CAP/ISM INT/TRADE MARXISM SOCISM...POLICY 1/20. PAGE 84 F1638
ECO/TAC PHIL/SCI NAT/G POL/PAR

B66
MOSKOW M.H.,TEACHERS AND UNIONS. SCHOOL WORKER ADJUD LOBBY ATTIT ORD/FREE 20. PAGE 94 F1844
EDU/PROP PROF/ORG LABOR BARGAIN

B66
PEIRCE W.S.,SELECTIVE MANPOWER POLICIES AND THE TRADE-OFF BETWEEN RISING PRICES AND UNEMPLOYMENT (DISSERTATION). ECO/DEV WORKER ACT/RES...PHIL/SCI 20. PAGE 104 F2050
PRICE LABOR POLICY ECO/TAC

B66
RAYBACK J.G.,A HISTORY OF AMERICAN LABOR. USA+45 USA-45 ECO/DEV LEGIS COLONIAL WAR INGP/REL PWR WEALTH 17/20. PAGE 110 F2156
LABOR LOBBY ECO/UNDEV NAT/G

B66
ROSS A.M.,INDUSTRIAL RELATIONS AND ECONOMIC DEVELOPMENT. POL/PAR LEGIS WORKER BARGAIN PRICE EXEC LOBBY INCOME PWR...DECISION ANTHOL BIBLIOG 20. PAGE 114 F2243
ECO/UNDEV LABOR NAT/G GP/REL

B66
SHULTZ G.P.,GUIDELINES, INFORMAL CONTROLS, AND THE MARKET PLACE: POLICY CHOICES IN A FULL EMPLOYMENT ECONOMY. UK ECO/DEV LABOR INT/TRADE CONFER GOV/REL BAL/PAY DEMAND INCOME...POLICY ANTHOL 20 PRESIDENT. PAGE 121 F2392
ECO/TAC CONTROL FINAN RATION

B66
SMITH H.E.,READINGS IN ECONOMIC DEVELOPMENT AND ADMINISTRATION IN TANZANIA. TANZANIA FINAN INDUS LABOR NAT/G PLAN PROB/SOLV INT/TRADE COLONIAL REGION...ANTHOL BIBLIOG 20 AFRICA/E. PAGE 123 F2431
TEC/DEV ADMIN GOV/REL

B66
US DEPARTMENT OF LABOR,PRODUCTIVITY: A BIBLIOGRAPHY. ECO/DEV INDUS MARKET OP/RES AUTOMAT COST...STAT 20. PAGE 135 F2668
BIBLIOG/A PRODUC LABOR PLAN

B66
US DEPARTMENT OF LABOR,TECHNOLOGICAL TRENDS IN MAJOR AMERICAN INDUSTRIES. USA+45 R+D LABOR GP/REL PRODUC...MGT BIBLIOG 20. PAGE 135 F2669
TEC/DEV INDUS TREND AUTOMAT

B66
US SENATE COMM LABOR-PUB WELF,AMEND THE RAILWAY LABOR ACT. USA+45 CONSTN CONSULT DELIB/GP ADJUD CONGRESS RAILROAD. PAGE 139 F2731
GP/REL LABOR DIST/IND LAW

L66
AFRICAN BIBLIOGRAPHIC CENTER,"AFRICAN ECONOMIC AFFAIRS: A SELECT BIBLIOGRAPHICAL SURVEY, 1965-1966." AFR FINAN INDUS INT/ORG LABOR PLAN BUDGET DIPLOM INT/TRADE ADMIN EFFICIENCY WEALTH 20. PAGE 3 F0046
BIBLIOG ECO/UNDEV TEC/DEV FOR/AID

L66
AFRICAN BIBLIOGRAPHIC CENTER,"AFRICAN ECONOMIC AFFAIRS: A SELECT BIBLIOGRAPHICAL SURVEY, 1965-1966; SUPPLEMENTS NUMBERS 1-3." AFR FINAN INDUS LABOR PLAN BUDGET CAP/ISM DIPLOM INT/TRADE ADMIN...GEOG 20. PAGE 3 F0047
BIBLIOG/A ECO/UNDEV FOR/AID TEC/DEV

L66
AMERICAN ECONOMIC REVIEW,"SIXTY-THIRD LIST OF DOCTORAL DISSERTATIONS IN POLITICAL ECONOMY IN AMERICAN UNIVERSITIES AND COLLEGES." ECO/DEV AGRI FINAN LABOR WORKER PLAN BUDGET INT/TRADE ADMIN DEMAND...MGT STAT 20. PAGE 5 F0088
BIBLIOG/A CONCPT ACADEM

S66
LANGLEY D.,"POSTSCRIPT ON THE COLONIZATION OF THE INTERNATIONAL TRADE UNION MOVEMENT" USA+45 ELITES FINAN DOMIN LEGIT ADMIN PWR...SOCIALIST 20 AFL/CIO CIA LOVESTN/J. PAGE 75 F1479
INT/TRADE LABOR NAT/G CONTROL

C66
WINT G.,"ASIA: A HANDBOOK." ASIA S/ASIA INDUS LABOR SECT PRESS RACE/REL MARXISM...STAT CHARTS BIBLIOG 20. PAGE 148 F2908
ECO/UNDEV DIPLOM NAT/G SOCIETY

N66
PRINCETON U INDUSTRIAL REL SEC,RECENT MATERIAL ON COLLECTIVE BARGAINING IN GOVERNMENT (PAMPHLET NO. 130). USA+45 ECO/DEV LABOR WORKER ECO/TAC GOV/REL ...MGT 20. PAGE 108 F2120
BIBLIOG/A BARGAIN NAT/G GP/REL

N66
PRINCETON U INDUSTRIAL REL SEC,THE ROLE OF THE PUBLIC EMPLOYMENT SERVICE (PAMPHLET NO. 129). USA+45 ECO/DEV PLAN ECO/TAC GOV/REL 20. PAGE 108 F2121
BIBLIOG/A NAT/G POLICY LABOR

B67
BADGLEY R.F.,DOCTORS' STRIKE; MEDICAL CARE AND CONFLICT IN SASKATCHEWAN. CANADA NAT/G PROF/ORG GP/REL ADJUST ATTIT...HEAL SOC 20. PAGE 8 F0148
HEALTH PLAN LABOR BARGAIN

B67
BAILY S.L.,LABOR, NATIONALISM, AND POLITICS IN ARGENTINA. POL/PAR TOP/EX GP/REL...BIBLIOG/A 19/20 MIGRATION PERON/JUAN ARGEN. PAGE 8 F0154
LABOR NAT/LISM

B67
BEAL E.F.,THE PRACTICE OF COLLECTIVE BARGAINING (3RD ED.). USA+45 WOR+45 ECO/DEV INDUS LG/CO PROF/ORG WORKER ECO/TAC GP/REL WEALTH...JURID METH/CNCPT. PAGE 12 F0221
BARGAIN MGT LABOR ADJUD

B67
BUREAU NATIONAL AFFAIRS,LABOR RELATIONS REFERENCE MANUAL VOL. 63. USA+45 CONSTN ECO/DEV PROVS WORKER DEBATE INGP/REL...DECISION 20. PAGE 20 F0385
LABOR ADJUD CT/SYS NAT/G

B67
COHEN M.R.,LAW AND THE SOCIAL ORDER: ESSAYS IN LEGAL PHILOSOPHY. USA-45 CONSULT WORKER ECO/TAC ATTIT WEALTH...POLICY WELF/ST SOC 20 NEW/DEAL DEPRESSION. PAGE 26 F0497
JURID LABOR IDEA/COMP

B67
EGGERT G.G.,RAILROAD LABOR DISPUTES. USA+45 USA-45 ELITES DIST/IND DELIB/GP FORCES JUDGE WORKER PROB/SOLV DOMIN PWR...POLICY 20. PAGE 36 F0707
GP/REL NAT/G LABOR BARGAIN

B67
ESTEY M.,THE UNIONS: STRUCTURE, DEVELOPMENT, AND MANAGEMENT. FUT USA+45 ADJUD CONTROL INGP/REL DRIVE ...DECISION T 20 AFL/CIO. PAGE 38 F0750
LABOR EX/STRUC ADMIN GOV/REL

B67
FONER P.S.,THE BOLSHEVIK REVOLUTION. USA-45 POL/PAR WORKER DIPLOM EDU/PROP MARXISM...STERTYP 20. PAGE 42 F0821
LABOR INTELL REV

PRESS

B67

GOODMAN J.S.,THE DEMOCRATS AND LABOR IN RHODE ISLAND 9152-1962; CHANGES IN THE OLD ALLIANCE. USA+45 EDU/PROP LEAD GP/REL ROLE RHODE/ISL DEMOCRAT. PAGE 49 F0948 — LABOR LOBBY POL/PAR LEGIS

B67

GORZ A.,STRATEGY FOR LABOR: A RADICAL PROPOSAL (TRANS. BY MARTIN NICOLAUS AND VICTORIA ORTIZ). EUR+WWI FRANCE ITALY ECO/DEV POL/PAR OP/RES PLAN GP/REL ALL/IDEOS...SOC 20 EEC. PAGE 49 F0965 — LABOR PWR STRUCT ECO/TAC

B67

INTERNATIONAL LABOUR OFFICE,SUBJECT GUIDE TO PUBLICATIONS OF THE INTERNATIONAL LABOUR OFFICE, 1919-1964. DIPLOM 20. PAGE 65 F1280 — BIBLIOG LABOR INT/ORG WORKER

B67

KIRK R.,THE POLITICAL PRINCIPLES OF ROBERT A. TAFT. USA+45 LABOR DIPLOM ADJUD ADJUST ORD/FREE TAFT/RA. PAGE 71 F1398 — POL/PAR LEAD LEGIS ATTIT

B67

MEYNAUD J.,TRADE UNIONISM IN AFRICA; A STUDY OF ITS GROWTH AND ORIENTATION (TRANS. BY ANGELA BRENCH). INT/ORG PROB/SOLV COLONIAL PWR...TIME/SEQ TREND ILO. PAGE 90 F1774 — LABOR AFR NAT/LISM ORD/FREE

B67

PETRO S.,THE KINGSPORT STRIKE. USA+45 PROC/MFG NAT/G JUDGE PRESS PARTIC PERS/REL...OLD/LIB OBS INT 20 NLRB. PAGE 105 F2074 — LABOR COERCE SANCTION ALL/VALS

B67

REHMUS C.M.,LABOR AND AMERICAN POLITICS. POL/PAR WORKER EDU/PROP PARTIC ATTIT PWR. PAGE 110 F2175 — LABOR ROLE LOBBY

B67

ROBERTS B.C.,COLLECTIVE BARGAINING IN AFRICAN COUNTRIES. AFR LAW ECO/UNDEV BARGAIN GP/REL ...DECISION METH/COMP 20. PAGE 112 F2206 — LABOR MGT PLAN ECO/TAC

B67

ROBINSON R.D.,INTERNATIONAL MANAGEMENT. LAW MARKET LABOR PRICE CONTROL COST DEMAND OWN PRODUC WEALTH 20. PAGE 113 F2225 — T OP/RES MGT DIPLOM

B67

ROSS A.M.,EMPLOYMENT, RACE, AND POVERTY. USA+45 LAW STRATA MARKET LABOR EDU/PROP ISOLAT SKILL...MGT ANTHOL 20 NEGRO. PAGE 114 F2244 — RACE/REL WORKER WEALTH DISCRIM

B67

ULMAN L.,CHALLENGES TO COLLECTIVE BARGAINING. ECO/TAC DISCRIM EQUILIB ATTIT...JURID SOC/WK. PAGE 132 F2599 — LABOR BARGAIN ADJUD POLICY

B67

UNIVERSAL REFERENCE SYSTEM,ECONOMIC REGULATION, BUSINESS, AND GOVERNMENT (VOLUME VIII). WOR+45 WOR-45 ECO/DEV ECO/UNDEV FINAN LABOR TEC/DEV ECO/TAC INT/TRADE GOV/REL...POLICY COMPUT/IR. PAGE 133 F2617 — BIBLIOG/A CONTROL NAT/G

B67

US CONGRESS JOINT ECO COMM,REPORT ON JANUARY 1967 ECONOMIC REPORT OF THE PRESIDENT. FINAN LABOR NAT/G LEGIS BUDGET INT/TRADE COST DEMAND INCOME PRODUC ...POLICY IDEA/COMP 20 CONGRESS. PAGE 135 F2663 — CHIEF ECO/TAC PLAN DELIB/GP

B67

US CONGRESS JOINT ECO COMM,AN ECONOMIC PROFILE OF MAINLAND CHINA, VOLUMES I AND II. CHINA/COM AGRI DIST/IND FINAN INDUS LABOR FORCES ACT/RES PLAN INT/TRADE INGP/REL BAL/PAY 20 CONGRESS. PAGE 135 F2664 — ECO/UNDEV WEALTH ECO/TAC DELIB/GP

B67

WILLIAMS E.J.,LATIN AMERICAN CHRISTIAN DEMOCRATIC PARTIES. L/A+17C FAM LABOR FORCES...CATH TREND BIBLIOG 20. PAGE 147 F2890 — POL/PAR GP/COMP CATHISM ALL/VALS

B67

WOOTON G.,WORKERS, UNIONS, AND THE STATE. INDUS PROB/SOLV GP/REL DRIVE SUPEGO RESPECT...PSY SOC. PAGE 148 F2925 — PARTIC WORKER NAT/G LABOR

L67

AFFELDT R.J.,"THE INDEPENDENT LABOR UNION AND THE GOOD LIFE." USA+45 ADJUD CONTROL SANCTION GP/REL ORD/FREE JURID. PAGE 3 F0045 — LABOR CT/SYS PWR SOVEREIGN

L67

BONFIELD A.E.,"THE SUBSTANCE OF AMERICAN FAIR EMPLOYMENT PRACTICES LEGISLA TION II - EMPLOYMENT AGENCIES, LABOR ORGANIZATIONS, ETC." ACT/RES DISCRIM EFFICIENCY. PAGE 16 F0311 — LAW WORKER LABOR SERV/IND

L67

GOULD W.B.,"THE STATUS OF UNAUTHORIZED AND 'WILDCAT' STRIKES UNDER THE NATIONAL LABOR RELATIONS ACT." USA+45 ACT/RES BARGAIN ECO/TAC LEGIT ADJUD ADMIN GP/REL MGT. PAGE 50 F0968 — ECO/DEV INDUS LABOR POLICY

L67

LAMBERT J.D.,"CORPORATE POLITICAL SPENDING AND CAMPAIGN FINANCE." LAW CONSTN FINAN LABOR LG/CO LOC/G NAT/G VOL/ASSN TEC/DEV ADJUD ADMIN PARTIC. PAGE 75 F1463 — USA+45 POL/PAR CHOOSE COST

L67

MACDONALD R.M.,"COLLECTIVE BARGAINING IN THE POSTWAR PERIOD." WORKER PROB/SOLV ECO/TAC PARTIC RISK CENTRAL EFFICIENCY DRIVE WEALTH...TREND 20. PAGE 83 F1624 — LABOR INDUS BARGAIN CAP/ISM

L67

PARKER G.P. JR.,"MONETARY RECOVERY UNDER THE FEDERAL LABOR STATUTES." USA+45 USA-45 INDUS ADJUD CT/SYS GOV/REL HEALTH ORD/FREE 20 DEPT/LABOR NLRB. PAGE 103 F2027 — LABOR CONTROL LAW FINAN

L67

STILL C.H.,"MONETARY RECOVERY UNDER THE FAIR LABOR STANDARDS ACT." USA+45 USA-45 WORKER PAY ADJUD GOV/REL HEALTH ORD/FREE...MATH 20 NLRB. PAGE 126 F2487 — LABOR CONTROL LAW FINAN

L67

STRUVE G.M.,"THE LESS-RESTRICTIVE-ALTERNATIVE PRINCIPLE AND ECONOMIC DUE PROCESS." USA+45 ECO/DEV LABOR NAT/G CONSULT DELIB/GP OP/RES PLAN WEALTH. PAGE 127 F2505 — JURID JUDGE SANCTION CAP/ISM

S67

BAILEY S.L.,"THE ITALIANS AND ORGANIZED LABOR IN THE UNITED STATES AND ARGENTINA: 1880-1910." ITALY USA-45 PARTIC HABITAT PWR...GEOG GP/COMP 19/20 ARGEN. PAGE 8 F0153 — LABOR LEAD WEALTH GP/REL

S67

BROWN M.B.,"THE TRADE UNION QUESTION." UK INDUS OP/RES PRICE PROFIT 20. PAGE 19 F0371 — WORKER LABOR GP/REL LAW

S67

CHAMBERLAIN N.W.,"STRIKES IN CONTEMPORARY CONTEXT." LAW INDUS NAT/G CHIEF CONFER COST ATTIT ORD/FREE ...POLICY MGT 20. PAGE 23 F0442 — LABOR BARGAIN EFFICIENCY PROB/SOLV

S67

CURTIN W.J.,"NATIONAL EMERGENCY DISPUTES LEGISLATION* ITS NEED AND ITS PROSPECTS IN THE TRANSPORTATION INDUSTRIES." USA+45 ECO/DEV INDUS NAT/G LEGIS ACT/RES BARGAIN POLICY. PAGE 29 F0565 — JURID LABOR ADJUD DIST/IND

S67

DEMUTH J.,"GE: PROFILE OF A CORPORATION." USA+45 USA-45 LABOR ACT/RES RATION EDU/PROP ADJUD CT/SYS FASCISM 20. PAGE 32 F0619 — LG/CO CONSERVE PRICE

S67

DEWHURST A.,"THE WAGE MOVEMENT IN CANADA." CANADA AGRI NAT/G PARTIC COST PRODUC PROFIT 20. PAGE 32 F0627 — WORKER MARXIST INDUS LABOR

S67

DRAPER A.P.,"UNIONS AND THE WAR IN VIETNAM." USA+45 CONFER ADMIN LEAD WAR ORD/FREE PACIFIST 20. PAGE 34 F0660 — LABOR PACIFISM ATTIT ELITES

S67

HALL B.,"THE PAINTER'S UNION: A PARTIAL VICTORY." USA+45 PROB/SOLV LEGIT ADMIN REPRESENT 20. PAGE 53 F1043 — LABOR CHIEF CHOOSE CRIME

S67

HALL B.,"THE COALITION AGAINST DISHWASHERS." USA+45 POL/PAR PROB/SOLV BARGAIN LEAD CHOOSE REPRESENT GP/REL ORD/FREE PWR...POLICY 20. PAGE 53 F1044 — LABOR ADMIN DOMIN WORKER

S67

JENCKS C.E.,"COAL MINERS IN BRITAIN SINCE NATIONALIZATION." UK LABOR GP/REL ADJUST SOCISM ...INT 20. PAGE 67 F1311 — EXTR/IND WORKER STRATA ATTIT

S67

JENCKS C.E.,"SOCIAL STATUS OF COAL MINERS IN BRITAIN SINCE NATIONALIZATION." UK STRATA STRUCT LABOR RECEIVE GP/REL INCOME OWN ATTIT HABITAT...MGT T 20. PAGE 67 F1312 — EXTR/IND WORKER CONTROL NAT/G

S67

KESTENBAUM L.,"PRIMARY JURISDICTION TO DECIDE ANTITRUST JURISDICTION* A PRACTICAL APPROACH TO THE ALLOCATION OF FUNCTIONS." USA+45 ECO/DEV INDUS VOL/ASSN ECO/TAC. PAGE 70 F1383 — JURID CT/SYS LABOR ADJUD

S67

LASLETT J.H.M.,"SOCIALISM AND THE AMERICAN LABOR MOVEMENT* SOME NEW REFLECTIONS." USA-45 VOL/ASSN LOBBY PARTIC CENTRAL ALL/VALS SOCISM...GP/COMP 20. PAGE 76 F1484 — LABOR ROUTINE ATTIT GP/REL

S67

LENS S.,"WALTER REUTHER TRIES TO BUILD A FIRE." WORKER LEAD DISCRIM AGE ORD/FREE NEW/LIB SOC. PAGE 78 F1523 — LABOR PARTIC NEIGH PLAN

S67
LEWIS W.A.,"THE STATUTORY LANGUAGE OF LABOR DISQUALIFICATION IN STATE EMPLOYMENT SECURITY LAWS." LABOR WORKER WORK 20. PAGE 79 F1553
METH/COMP LEGIS SOC PROVS

S67
MALKIN A.,"BUSINESS BOOKS OF 1966." INDUS LABOR OP/RES TEC/DEV CAP/ISM ECO/TAC INCOME WEALTH 20. PAGE 84 F1649
BIBLIOG/A FINAN MARKET

S67
MELTZER B.D.,"RUMINATIONS ABOUT IDEOLOGY, LAW, AND LABOR ARBITRATION." USA+45 ECO/DEV PROB/SOLV CONFER MGT. PAGE 89 F1754
JURID ADJUD LABOR CONSULT

S67
NEALE R.S.,"WORKING CLASS WOMEN AND WOMEN'S SUFFRAGE." UK LAW CONSTN LABOR NAT/G DELIB/GP LEGIS WORKER PAY PARTIC CHOOSE 19 FEMALE/SEX. PAGE 97 F1906
STRATA SEX SUFF DISCRIM

S67
NOURSE E.G.,"EARLY FLOWERING OF THE EMPLOYMENT ACT" USA+45 LABOR CONSULT DELIB/GP LEGIS BUDGET GOV/REL PRODUC WEALTH 20 INTRVN/ECO. PAGE 99 F1939
NAT/G WORKER ECO/TAC CONTROL

S67
PETRAS J.,"MINERS AND AGRARIAN RADICALISM." CHILE AGRI EXTR/IND WORKER CHOOSE ATTIT SOCISM MUNICH 20. PAGE 105 F2073
PARTIC EDU/PROP LABOR

S67
PFEFFERMANN G.,"TRADE UNIONS AND POLITICS IN FRENCH WEST AFRICA DURING THE FOURTH REPUBLIC." AFR INDUS POL/PAR COLONIAL ATTIT PWR 20. PAGE 106 F2077
PARTIC DRIVE INT/TRADE LABOR

S67
PIERPONT J.R.,"NEW STAGE IN THE LONGSHORE STRUGGLE." USA+45 SENIOR ADJUD RACE/REL...JURID 20 NEGRO. PAGE 106 F2083
LABOR DISCRIM WORKER CT/SYS

S67
PRASOW P.,"THE DEVELOPMENT OF JUDICIAL ARBITRATION IN LABOR-MANAGEMENT DISPUTES." LAW INDUS WORKER GP/REL ROLE...HIST/WRIT 20. PAGE 107 F2113
LABOR BARGAIN ADJUD TREND

S67
RAZA M.A.,"EMERGING TRENDS IN PUBLIC LABOR POLICIES AND UNION - GOVERN MENT RELATIONS IN ASIA AND AFRICA." LAW NAT/G POL/PAR COLONIAL COERCE GP/REL ATTIT 20. PAGE 110 F2157
LABOR CONTROL TREND

S67
RONY V.,"HEARTBREAK IN TENNESSEE* POOR WHITES AND THE UNIONS." LAW STRUCT CAP/ISM ADJUD GP/REL. PAGE 113 F2236
LABOR LOC/G WORKER PWR

S67
SCOTT R.,"TRADE UNIONS IN AFRICA." AFR UGANDA USA-45 ECO/UNDEV INDUS INT/ORG POL/PAR ECO/TAC WEALTH...GP/COMP 20 NKRUMAH/K. PAGE 118 F2335
LABOR WORKER NAT/G

S67
SHEFFTZ M.C.,"THE TRADE DISPUTES AND TRADE UNIONS ACT OF 1927: THE AFTERMATH OF THE GENERAL STRIKE." UK FINAN WORKER ADJUD LEAD PARL/PROC 20. PAGE 120 F2373
LEGIS ATTIT LABOR GP/REL

S67
SHISTER J.,"THE DIRECTION OF UNIONISM 1947-1967: THRUST OF DRIFT?" INDUS CENTRAL EFFICIENCY INCOME ATTIT SOCISM...POLICY TREND 20 AFL/CIO. PAGE 121 F2382
LABOR PROF/ORG LEAD LAW

S67
TABORSKY E.,"THE CLASS STRUGGLE, THE PROLETARIAT, AND THE DEVELOPING NATIONS." USSR LABOR POL/PAR FOR/AID COLONIAL GP/REL 20. PAGE 128 F2521
DIPLOM MARXISM ECO/UNDEV WORKER

S67
WARNER K.O.,"FINANCIAL IMPLICATION OF EMPLOYEE BARGAINING IN THE PUBLIC SERVICE." CANADA USA+45 FINAN ADMIN...MGT 20. PAGE 143 F2823
BARGAIN LABOR COST LOC/G

S67
ZACK A.M.,"ARE STRIKES OF PUBLIC EMPLOYEES NECESSARY?" USA+45 DELIB/GP PROB/SOLV REPRESENT GP/REL MGT. PAGE 150 F2956
LABOR NAT/G WORKER BARGAIN

S67
ZOETEWEIJ B.,"INCOME POLICIES ABROAD: AN INTERIM REPORT." NAT/G PROB/SOLV BARGAIN BUDGET PRICE RISK CENTRAL EFFICIENCY EQUILIB...MGT NAT/COMP 20. PAGE 150 F2967
METH/COMP INCOME POLICY LABOR

S86
SMITH R.M.,"THE NATIONAL BUREAU OF LABOR AND INDUSTRIAL DEPRESSIONS" USA-45 DELIB/GP BARGAIN CONTROL COST INCOME WEALTH...STAT 19 DEPRESSION. PAGE 123 F2433
LABOR INDUS FINAN GOV/REL

B92
ENGELS F.,THE CONDITION OF THE WORKING-CLASS IN ENGLAND (1848). UK INDUS LABOR PRICE CONTROL COST INCOME HEALTH MARXISM MUNICH 19. PAGE 38 F0733
WORKER WEALTH MARXIST CAP/ISM

LABOR/PAR....LABOR PARTY (ALL NATIONS)

B38
DAVIES E.,"NATIONAL" CAPITALISM: THE GOVERNMENT'S RECORD AS PROTECTOR OF PRIVATE MONOPOLY. UK ELITES SOCIETY STRATA POL/PAR WORKER PROB/SOLV CONTROL SOCISM 20 MONOPOLY LABOR/PAR CHAMBRLN/N. PAGE 30 F0583
CAP/ISM NAT/G INDUS POLICY

S47
DAHL R.A.,"WORKERS' CONTROL OF INDUSTRY AND THE BRITISH LABOUR PARTY." UK STRATA STRUCT DELIB/GP BARGAIN CAP/ISM DEBATE CONTROL CHOOSE GP/REL ATTIT ROLE PWR 19/20 PARLIAMENT LABOR/PAR FABIAN. PAGE 29 F0570
INDUS LABOR WORKER SOCISM

B51
HALEVY E.,IMPERIALISM AND THE RISE OF LABOR (2ND ED.). UK NAT/G POL/PAR TOP/EX ATTIT ORD/FREE PWR 19/20 PARLIAMENT LABOR/PAR. PAGE 53 F1042
COLONIAL LABOR POLICY WAR

B59
JENKINS C.,POWER AT THE TOP: A CRITICAL SURVEY OF THE NATIONALIZED INDUSTRIES. UK POL/PAR CONTROL ...WELF/ST CHARTS 20 LABOR/PAR. PAGE 67 F1313
NAT/G OWN INDUS NEW/LIB

B65
BARRY E.E.,NATIONALISATION IN BRITISH POLITICS: THE HISTORICAL BACKGROUND. UK AGRI DIST/IND EXTR/IND LABOR LG/CO ATTIT CONSERVE SOCISM 19/20 LABOR/PAR. PAGE 10 F0198
NAT/G OWN INDUS POL/PAR

B66
FORD P.,CARDINAL MORAN AND THE A. L. P. NAT/G POL/PAR SECT DELIB/GP LOBBY REV CHOOSE ORD/FREE MARXISM 19/20 AUSTRAL PROTESTANT LABOR/PAR. PAGE 42 F0825
CATHISM SOCISM LABOR SOCIETY

LABORATORY EXPERIMENTS....SEE LAB/EXP

LAFEBER W. F1457

LAFONT P.B. F1458

LAFTA....LATIN AMERICAN FREE TRADE ASSOCIATION; SEE ALSO INT/ORG, VOL/ASSN, INT/TRADE

B62
URQUIDI V.L.,FREE TRADE AND ECONOMIC INTEGRATION IN LATIN AMERICA: THE EVOLUTION OF A COMMON MARKET POLICY. ECO/UNDEV MARKET DIPLOM BAL/PAY FEDERAL ...POLICY CHARTS 20 LAFTA. PAGE 133 F2627
INT/TRADE REGION INT/ORG L/A+17C

S63
POPPINO R.E.,"IMBALANCE IN BRAZIL." L/A+17C NAT/G TOP/EX PLAN DIPLOM LEGIT DRIVE WEALTH...CON/ANAL FOR/TRADE LAFTA 20. PAGE 107 F2105
POL/PAR ECO/TAC BRAZIL

L64
HAAS E.B.,"ECONOMICS AND DIFFERENTIAL PATTERNS OF POLITICAL INTEGRATION: PROJECTIONS ABOUT UNITY IN LATIN AMERICA." SOCIETY NAT/G DELIB/GP ACT/RES CREATE PLAN ECO/TAC REGION ROUTINE ATTIT DRIVE PWR WEALTH...CONCPT TREND CHARTS LAFTA TERR/GP 20. PAGE 52 F1020
L/A+17C INT/ORG MARKET

B65
BAERRESEN D.W.,LATIN AMERICAN TRADE PATTERNS. L/A+17C ECO/UNDEV AGRI INDUS MARKET CREATE ...NET/THEORY CHARTS LAFTA. PAGE 8 F0149
INT/TRADE STAT REGION

L65
WIONCZEK M.,"LATIN AMERICA FREE TRADE ASSOCIATION." AGRI DIST/IND FINAN INDUS INT/ORG LABOR NAT/G TEC/DEV ECO/TAC HEALTH SKILL WEALTH...POLICY RELATIV MGT LAFTA 20. PAGE 148 F2909
L/A+17C MARKET REGION

B66
BROWN R.T.,TRANSPORT AND THE ECONOMIC INTEGRATION OF SOUTH AMERICA. L/A+17C ECO/UNDEV NAT/G OP/RES DIPLOM INT/TRADE REGION WEALTH...ECOMETRIC GEOG STAT LAFTA TIME. PAGE 19 F0373
MARKET DIST/IND SIMUL

S66
JAVITS J.K.,"POLITICAL ACTION VITAL FOR LATIN AMERICAN INTEGRATION." ECO/UNDEV INT/ORG POL/PAR VOL/ASSN PLAN PROB/SOLV INT/TRADE EFFICIENCY 20 OAS LAFTA ALL/PROG. PAGE 66 F1308
L/A+17C ECO/TAC REGION

LAGOS G. F1459

LAGUARD/F....FIORELLO LAGUARDIA

LAHAYE R. F1460

LAIRD R.D. F1461

LAISSEZ....LAISSEZ-FAIRE-ISM; SEE ALSO OLD/LIB

B20
MALTHUS T.R.,PRINCIPLES OF POLITICAL ECONOMY. UK AGRI INDUS MARKET NAT/G DIPLOM PRICE CONTROL BAL/PAY COST OWN PWR LAISSEZ 18/19. PAGE 84 F1650
GEN/LAWS DEMAND WEALTH

B24
CLARK J.B.,THE DISTRIBUTION OF WEALTH (1899). WORKER OWN PRODUC PROFIT WEALTH LAISSEZ...IDEA/COMP GEN/LAWS. PAGE 25 F0478
ECO/TAC INDUS LABOR INCOME

B26
TAWNEY R.H.,RELIGION AND THE RISE OF CAPITALISM. UK CULTURE NAT/G TEC/DEV OWN LAISSEZ...POLICY SOC TIME/SEQ 16/19. PAGE 129 F2537
SECT WEALTH INDUS CAP/ISM

S38
HALL R.C.,"REPRESENTATION OF BIG BUSINESS IN THE HOUSE OF COMMONS." UK ECO/DEV INDUS PROF/ORG LEGIS CAP/ISM ECO/TAC LAISSEZ...POLICY OLD/LIB PLURIST MGT 20 HOUSE/CMNS. PAGE 53 F1047
LOBBY NAT/G

B39
CLARK J.M.,SOCIAL CONTROL OF BUSINESS (2ND ED.). ECO/DEV FINAN LG/CO PLAN ECO/TAC PRICE SUPEGO...T 20. PAGE 25 F0480
CAP/ISM CONTROL LAISSEZ METH/COMP

B40
SPENCER H.,THE MAN VS. THE STATE (1892). UK POL/PAR LEGIS TARIFFS COERCE CRIME REPRESENT PWR SOCISM ...POLICY GEN/LAWS 19/20. PAGE 124 F2450
FASCISM POPULISM LAISSEZ ORD/FREE

B42
DRUCKER P.F.,THE FUTURE OF INDUSTRIAL MAN; A CONSERVATIVE APPROACH. USA-45 LOC/G PLAN WAR CENTRAL RATIONAL TOTALISM ORD/FREE LAISSEZ ...PLURIST IDEA/COMP 19/20 HITLER/A. PAGE 34 F0664
INDUS SOCIETY REGION PROB/SOLV

B44
HAYEK F.A.,THE ROAD TO SERFDOM. NAT/G POL/PAR CREATE EDU/PROP ATTIT WEALTH LAISSEZ...OLD/LIB CONCPT TREND 20. PAGE 57 F1121
FUT PLAN ECO/TAC SOCISM

B48
HAYEK F.A.,INDIVIDUALISM AND ECONOMIC ORDER. FINAN PLAN MORAL LAISSEZ SOCISM...POLICY DECISION PHIL/SCI HIST/WRIT. PAGE 57 F1122
RATIONAL KNOWL PERSON

B49
MACGREGOR D.H.,ECONOMIC THOUGHT AND POLICY. WOR-45 WORKER WAR DEMAND EFFICIENCY WEALTH LAISSEZ SOCISM ...MAJORIT BIBLIOG 19/20. PAGE 83 F1629
CONCPT POLICY ECO/TAC

B50
HUTCHISON K.,THE DECLINE AND FALL OF BRITISH CAPITALISM. UK ELITES STRATA ECO/DEV LABOR WORKER CONTROL WAR PWR...BIBLIOG/A 19/20. PAGE 63 F1249
CAP/ISM SOCISM LAISSEZ DOMIN

B50
MARX H.L.,THE WELFARE STATE. USA+45 USA-45 CHIEF CAP/ISM CENTRAL ORD/FREE LAISSEZ...SOC ANTHOL 20. PAGE 86 F1686
ECO/DEV INDUS WEALTH WELF/ST

B50
SURANYI-UNGER T.,PRIVATE ENTERPRISE AND GOVERNMENTAL PLANNING. STRUCT FINAN BAL/PWR HAPPINESS DRIVE NEW/LIB PLURISM...MATH QUANT STAT TREND BIBLIOG. PAGE 127 F2516
PLAN NAT/G LAISSEZ POLICY

B51
LUXEMBORG R.,THE ACCUMULATION OF CAPITAL (TRANS. BY AGNES SCHWARZSCHILD). ECO/TAC DOMIN COLONIAL ATTIT LAISSEZ 19 MONEY. PAGE 82 F1614
MARXIST INT/TRADE CAP/ISM FINAN

B52
SURANYI-UNGER T.,COMPARATIVE ECONOMIC SYSTEMS. FINAN MARKET DIPLOM PRICE WEALTH...GEOG SOC BIBLIOG METH T 20. PAGE 128 F2517
LAISSEZ PLAN ECO/DEV IDEA/COMP

C52
HUME D.,"OF TAXES" IN D. HUME, POLITICAL DISCOURSES (1752)" UK NAT/G COST INCOME LAISSEZ...GEN/LAWS 18. PAGE 63 F1236
TAX FINAN WEALTH POLICY

C52
HUME D.,"OF THE BALANCE OF TRADE" IN D. HUME, POLITICAL DISCOURSES (1752)" UK FINAN NAT/G TARIFFS PRICE PWR LAISSEZ...POLICY GEN/LAWS 18. PAGE 63 F1237
BAL/PAY INT/TRADE DIPLOM WEALTH

B53
BOWEN H.R.,SOCIAL RESPONSIBILITIES OF THE BUSINESSMAN (FIRST EDITION). LAW FINAN ACT/RES CAP/ISM ROUTINE DRIVE PWR LAISSEZ...DECISION BIBLIOG. PAGE 17 F0326
MGT PERSON SUPEGO MORAL

B56
GILBERT L.D.,DIVIDENDS AND DEMOCRACY. DELIB/GP LEGIS CAP/ISM ADJUD LOBBY OWN PWR LAISSEZ MAJORIT. PAGE 47 F0922
LG/CO INGP/REL CONTROL PARTIC

B56
LIPSET S.M.,UNION DEMOCRACY. STRUCT INDUS FACE/GP WORKER CONTROL LEAD PARTIC GP/REL ATTIT LAISSEZ ...INT QU CHARTS. PAGE 80 F1577
LABOR INGP/REL MAJORIT

B58
CLAIRMONTE F.,LE LIBERALISME ECONOMIQUE ET LES PAYS SOUS-DEVELOPPES: ETUDES SUR L'EVOLUTION D'UNE IDEE. ASIA INDIA UK FINAN INDUS PLAN CAP/ISM ECO/TAC COLONIAL NEW/LIB...BIBLIOG 20 THIRD/WRLD. PAGE 24 F0475
LAISSEZ ECO/UNDEV

B58
ELLSWORTH P.T.,THE INTERNATIONAL ECONOMY. EUR+WWI MOD/EUR INT/ORG CAP/ISM FOR/AID BAL/PAY LAISSEZ 16/20. PAGE 37 F0725
INT/TRADE TARIFFS ECO/DEV

B60
GRAMPP W.D.,THE MANCHESTER SCHOOL OF ECONOMICS. UK LAW ECO/DEV COERCE ATTIT ORD/FREE LAISSEZ ...PHIL/SCI IDEA/COMP 19/20 MANCHESTER CORN/LAWS. PAGE 50 F0973
ECO/TAC VOL/ASSN LOBBY NAT/G

B60
MENDELSON W.,CAPITALISM, DEMOCRACY, AND THE SUPREME COURT. USA+45 USA-45 CONSTN DIPLOM GOV/REL ATTIT ORD/FREE LAISSEZ...POLICY CHARTS PERS/COMP 18/20 SUPREME/CT MARSHALL/J HOLMES/OW TANEY/RB FIELD/JJ. PAGE 90 F1758
JUDGE CT/SYS JURID NAT/G

B60
WALLICH H.C.,THE COST OF FREEDOM: A NEW LOOK AT CAPITALISM. USA+45 SOCIETY ECO/DEV INGP/REL CONSEN LAISSEZ SOCISM...OLD/LIB IDEA/COMP. PAGE 143 F2810
CAP/ISM ORD/FREE POLICY ECO/TAC

B60
WATSON D.S.,ECONOMIC POLICY: BUSINESS AND GOVERNMENT. USA+45 FINAN LABOR PLAN BUDGET INT/TRADE GP/REL WEALTH LAISSEZ...CHARTS T. PAGE 144 F2832
ECO/TAC NAT/G POLICY ECO/DEV

B61
CARNEY D.E.,GOVERNMENT AND ECONOMY IN BRITISH WEST AFRICA. GAMBIA GHANA NIGERIA SIER/LEONE DOMIN ADMIN GOV/REL SOVEREIGN WEALTH LAISSEZ...BIBLIOG 20 CMN/WLTH. PAGE 21 F0417
METH/COMP COLONIAL ECO/TAC ECO/UNDEV

B61
LHOSTE-LACHAUME P.,OU GIT LE DESACCORD ENTRE LIBERAUX ET SOCIALISTES. EUR+WWI USA+45 USA-45 USSR CAP/ISM EDU/PROP MARXISM...MAJORIT IDEA/COMP 20 KEYNES/JM NEW/DEAL DEPRESSION. PAGE 79 F1555
LAISSEZ SOCISM FINAN

B61
NORTH D.C.,THE ECONOMIC GROWTH OF THE UNITED STATES 1790-1860. USA-45 INDUS TEC/DEV CAP/ISM ECO/TAC PRICE COST DEMAND LAISSEZ...ECOMETRIC STAT TREND 19. PAGE 98 F1933
AGRI ECO/UNDEV

N61
VINER J.,THE INTELLECTUAL HISTORY OF LAISSEZ FAIRE (PAMPHLET). WOR+45 WOR-45 LAW INTELL...POLICY LING LOG 19/20. PAGE 141 F2787
ATTIT EDU/PROP LAISSEZ ECO/TAC

B63
RICARDO D.,THE PRINCIPLES OF POLITICAL ECONOMY AND TAXATION (1817). UK INDUS MARKET ECO/TAC INT/TRADE TARIFFS PRICE COST DEMAND OPTIMAL WEALTH...CONCPT 19 INTRVN/ECO. PAGE 111 F2183
GEN/LAWS TAX LAISSEZ

B63
ROTHBARD M.N.,AMERICA'S GREAT DEPRESSION. USA-45 NAT/G ECO/TAC LAISSEZ...POLICY IDEA/COMP 20. PAGE 114 F2248
FINAN CAP/ISM MARKET GEN/LAWS

B64
BASTIAT F.,ECONOMIC HARMONIES (1850). STRATA STRUCT ECO/DEV BUDGET TAX PRICE LOBBY COST. PAGE 11 F0206
ECO/TAC PLAN INT/TRADE LAISSEZ

B64
BASTIAT F.,ECONOMIC SOPHISMS (1845). FINAN MARKET INT/TRADE TAX EDU/PROP LAISSEZ. PAGE 11 F0207
TARIFFS INDUS ECO/TAC CAP/ISM

B64
PAARLBERG D.,AMERICAN FARM POLICY: A CASE STUDY IN CENTRALIZED DECISION-MAKING. USA+45 NAT/G LEGIS LOBBY REPRESENT GOV/REL PWR LAISSEZ 20. PAGE 102 F2009
PROB/SOLV EX/STRUC AGRI

B64
RAISON T.,WHY CONSERVATIVE? UK FORCES DIPLOM ECO/TAC GIVE EDU/PROP ORD/FREE WEALTH LAISSEZ ...GOV/COMP 20 TORY/PARTY CONSRV/PAR. PAGE 109 F2137
PLURISM CONSERVE POL/PAR NAT/G

B65
GRAMPP W.D.,ECONOMIC LIBERALISM; THE CLASSICAL VIEW (VOL. II). MOD/EUR SOCIETY MARKET INT/TRADE NAT/LISM WEALTH LAISSEZ...POLICY PSY CONCPT BIBLIOG 19 SMITH/ADAM HUME/D MILL/JS. PAGE 50 F0975
ECO/DEV CAP/ISM IDEA/COMP ECO/TAC

B65
ONUOHA B.,THE ELEMENTS OF AFRICAN SOCIALISM. AFR FINAN SECT TEC/DEV FOR/AID GP/REL OWN LAISSEZ MARXISM...CONCPT BIBLIOG 20. PAGE 101 F1992
SOCISM ECO/UNDEV NAT/G EX/STRUC

C65
PEGRUM D.E.,"PUBLIC REGULATION OF BUSINESS (REV ED)" LAW CONSTN DIST/IND SERV/IND LG/CO LEGIS OWN LAISSEZ SOCISM...POLICY DECISION BIBLIOG 20. PAGE 104 F2048
INDUS PLAN NEW/LIB PRICE

B66
CANNON M.,THE LAND BOOMERS....BIBLIOG/A 19 AUSTRAL. PAGE 21 F0412
FINAN HABITAT LAISSEZ

ECO/UNDEV

B66
FUSFELD D.R.,THE AGE OF THE ECONOMIST. ECO/TAC WEALTH LAISSEZ MARXISM...EPIST 18/20 KEYNES/JM. PAGE 45 F0878 — PHIL/SCI CAP/ISM POLICY

B67
JHANGIANI M.A.,JANA SANGH AND SWATANTRA: A PROFILE OF THE RIGHTIST PARTIES IN INDIA. INDIA ADMIN CHOOSE MARXISM SOCISM...INT CHARTS BIBLIOG 20. PAGE 67 F1320 — POL/PAR LAISSEZ NAT/LISM ATTIT

B67
MARCUS S.,COMPETITION AND THE LAW. USA+45 INDUS LG/CO NAT/G CONSERVE LAISSEZ...BIBLIOG 20 FTC SUPREME/CT. PAGE 85 F1665 — LAW ECO/DEV FINAN JURID

S67
SCOVILLE W.J.,"GOVERNMENT REGULATION AND GROWTH IN THE FRENCH PAPER INDUSTRY DURING THE EIGHTEENTH CENTURY." FRANCE MOD/EUR FINAN CAP/ISM TAX ADMIN CONTROL PRIVIL LAISSEZ...POLICY 18. PAGE 118 F2337 — NAT/G PROC/MFG ECO/DEV INGP/REL

B75
JEVONS W.S.,MONEY AND THE MECHANISM OF EXCHANGE. INDUS MARKET DIPLOM COST EQUILIB WEALTH LAISSEZ ...GEN/LAWS 19 MONEY. PAGE 67 F1319 — PRICE FINAN ECO/TAC POLICY

B76
SMITH A.,THE WEALTH OF NATIONS. UK STRUCT WORKER DIPLOM ECO/TAC OPTIMAL DRIVE PERSON ORD/FREE ...OLD/LIB GEN/LAWS 17/18. PAGE 123 F2428 — WEALTH PRODUC INDUS LAISSEZ

B86
O'CONNOR T.P.,THE PARNELL MOVEMENT: WITH A SKETCH OF IRISH PARTIES FROM 1843. IRELAND UK USA-45 LEGIS WORKER ECO/TAC COERCE CRIME REV CHOOSE ORD/FREE CATHISM LAISSEZ...SOC 19/20 PARLIAMENT PARNELL/CS LAND/LEAG. PAGE 100 F1957 — LEAD DOMIN POL/PAR POLICY

B96
SMITH A.,LECTURES ON JUSTICE, POLICE, REVENUE AND ARMS (1763). UK LAW FAM FORCES TARIFFS AGREE COERCE INCOME OWN WEALTH LAISSEZ...GEN/LAWS 17/18. PAGE 123 F2429 — DIPLOM JURID OLD/LIB TAX

LAKEWOOD....LAKEWOOD, CALIFORNIA

LAKOFF/SA....SANFORD A. LAKOFF

LAMBERG R.F. F1462

LAMBERT J.D. F1463

LAMFALUSSY A. F1464

LAMPMAN R.J. F0982

LAND REFORM....SEE AGRI + CREATE

LAND/LEAG....LAND LEAGUE (IRELAND)

B86
O'CONNOR T.P.,THE PARNELL MOVEMENT: WITH A SKETCH OF IRISH PARTIES FROM 1843. IRELAND UK USA-45 LEGIS WORKER ECO/TAC COERCE CRIME REV CHOOSE ORD/FREE CATHISM LAISSEZ...SOC 19/20 PARLIAMENT PARNELL/CS LAND/LEAG. PAGE 100 F1957 — LEAD DOMIN POL/PAR POLICY

LAND/VALUE....LAND VALUE TAX

LANDAUER C. F1465,F1466

LANDAUER J.D. F1467

LANDEN R.G. F1468

LANDERS D.S. F1469

LANDES W.M. F1470

LANDIS J.M. F0848

LANDRAT....COUNTY CHIEF EXECUTIVE (GERMANY)

S49
STEINMETZ H.,"THE PROBLEMS OF THE LANDRAT: A STUDY OF COUNTY GOVERNMENT IN THE US ZONE OF GERMANY." GERMANY/W USA+45 INDUS PLAN DIPLOM EDU/PROP CONTROL WAR GOV/REL FEDERAL WEALTH PLURISM...GOV/COMP 20 LANDRAT. PAGE 126 F2478 — LOC/G COLONIAL MGT TOP/EX

LANDRM/GRF....LANDRUM-GRIFFIN ACT

LANDRUM-GRIFFIN ACT....SEE LANDRM/GRF

LANDSKROY W.A. F1471

LANE F.C. F1472

LANFALUSSY A. F1473

LANG A.S. F1474

LANGE O. F1475,F1476

LANGE O.R. F1477

LANGHOFF P. F1478

LANGLEY D. F1479

LANGLEY L.D. F1480

LANGLEY....LANGLEY-PORTER NEUROPSYCHIATRIC INSTITUTE

LANGUAGE....SEE LING, ALSO LOGIC, MATHEMATICS, AND LANGUAGE INDEX, P. XIV

LANGUEDOC....LANGUEDOC, SOUTHERN FRANCE

LANSING J.B. F1481

LAO/TZU....LAO TZU

LAOS....SEE ALSO S/ASIA

B59
US HOUSE COMM GOVT OPERATIONS,UNITED STATES AID OPERATIONS IN LAOS. LAOS USA+45 PLAN INSPECT HOUSE/REP. PAGE 137 F2697 — FOR/AID ADMIN FORCES ECO/UNDEV

B60
PENTONY D.E.,UNITED STATES FOREIGN AID. INDIA LAOS USA+45 ECO/UNDEV INT/TRADE ADMIN PEACE ATTIT ...POLICY METH/COMP ANTHOL 20. PAGE 105 F2060 — FOR/AID DIPLOM ECO/TAC

B64
LAFONT P.B.,BIBLIOGRAPHIE DU LAOS. LAOS S/ASIA EDU/PROP...GEOG 20. PAGE 74 F1458 — BIBLIOG LAW SOC

S65
KAUFMAN R.H.,"THE ASIAN GOLD TRADE." ASIA LAOS THAILAND UK CHARTS. PAGE 69 F1362 — S/ASIA FINAN STAT INT/TRADE

L67
MCALLISTER J.T. JR.,"THE POSSIBILITIES FOR DIPLOMACY IN SOUTHEAST ASIA." LAOS VIETNAM INT/ORG NAT/G PROVS BAL/PWR DOMIN AGREE COLONIAL WAR PWR 17/20 TREATY. PAGE 88 F1716 — DIPLOM S/ASIA

LARCENY....LARCENY

LARTEH....LARTEH, GHANA

LARY M.B. F1482

LASKI H.J. F1483

LASKI/H....HAROLD LASKI

LASLETT J.H.M. F1484

LASSALLE/F....FERDINAND LASSALLE

LASSWELL H.D. F1485,F1727

LASSWELL/H....HAROLD D. LASSWELL

LATCHAM F.C. F0727

LATIFI D. F1486

LATIN AMERICA....SEE L/A+17C

LATIN AMERICAN FREE TRADE ASSOCIATION....SEE LAFTA

LATTIN N.D. F1487

LATVIA....SEE ALSO USSR

LAURENS H. F1488

LAURIER/W....SIR WILFRED LAURIER

LAURSEN K. F1489

LAUTERBACH A. F1490

LAVES W.H.C. F1491

LAW....LAW, ETHICAL DIRECTIVES IN A COMMUNITY; SEE ALSO JURID

N
NEW JERSEY STATE OF,SECOND REPORT TO GOVERNOR, — LAW

SENATE, ASSEMBLY BY UNIFORM COMMERCIAL CODE STUDY COMMISSION. USA+45 INDUS LOC/G NAT/G PROF/ORG CONSULT ACT/RES LEGIT CT/SYS ATTIT NEW/JERSEY. PAGE 98 F1920 FINAN CENTRAL PROVS

N

TEXTBOOKS IN PRINT. WOR+45 WOR-45 LAW DIPLOM ALL/VALS ALL/IDEOS...SOC T 19/20. PAGE 1 F0003 BIBLIOG SCHOOL KNOWL

N

LONDON TIMES OFFICIAL INDEX. UK LAW ECO/DEV NAT/G DIPLOM LEAD ATTIT 20. PAGE 1 F0006 BIBLIOG INDEX PRESS WRITING

N

DEUTSCHE BUCHEREI,DEUTSCHES BUCHERVERZEICHNIS. GERMANY LAW CULTURE POL/PAR ADMIN LEAD ATTIT PERSON ...SOC 20. PAGE 32 F0626 BIBLIOG NAT/G DIPLOM ECO/DEV

N

MINISTRY OF OVERSEAS DEVELOPME,TECHNICAL CO-OPERATION -- A BIBLIOGRAPHY. UK LAW SOCIETY DIPLOM ECO/TAC FOR/AID...STAT 20 CMN/WLTH. PAGE 92 F1803 BIBLIOG TEC/DEV ECO/DEV NAT/G

N

US SUPERINTENDENT OF DOCUMENTS,INTERSTATE COMMERCE (PRICE LIST 59). USA+45 LAW LOC/G NAT/G LEGIS TARIFFS TAX ADMIN CONTROL HEALTH DECISION. PAGE 140 F2752 BIBLIOG/A DIST/IND GOV/REL PROVS

N

US SUPERINTENDENT OF DOCUMENTS,LABOR (PRICE LIST 33). USA+45 LAW AGRI CONSTRUC INDUS NAT/G BARGAIN PRICE ADMIN AUTOMAT PRODUC MGT. PAGE 140 F2753 BIBLIOG/A WORKER LABOR LEGIS

N

US SUPERINTENDENT OF DOCUMENTS,TARIFF AND TAXATION (PRICE LIST 37). USA+45 LAW INT/TRADE ADJUD ADMIN CT/SYS INCOME OWN...DECISION GATT. PAGE 140 F2754 BIBLIOG/A TAX TARIFFS NAT/G

B03

GRIFFIN A.P.C.,LISTS PUBLISHED 1902-03: GOVERNMENT OWNERSHIP OF RAILROADS (PAMPHLET). USA-45 LAW NAT/G RATION GOV/REL CENTRAL SOCISM...POLICY 19/20. PAGE 51 F0998 BIBLIOG DIST/IND CONTROL ADJUD

B14

LEVINE L.,SYNDICALISM IN FRANCE (2ND ED.). FRANCE LAW SOCIETY ECO/DEV NAT/G ECO/TAC LEAD ATTIT ...POLICY CONCPT STAT BIBLIOG 18/20 REFORMERS. PAGE 79 F1542 LABOR INDUS SOCISM REV

B19

VEBLEN T.B.,THE VESTED INTERESTS AND THE STATE OF THE INDUSTRIAL ARTS. USA-45 LAW FINAN WORKER PAY DOMIN PRICE COST SOCISM...MARXIST 19/20. PAGE 141 F2771 INDUS CAP/ISM METH/COMP WEALTH

N19

ARNOW K.,SELF-INSURANCE IN THE TREASURY (PAMPHLET). USA+45 LAW RIGID/FLEX...POLICY METH/COMP 20 DEPT/TREAS. PAGE 6 F0117 ADMIN PLAN EFFICIENCY NAT/G

N19

ATOMIC INDUSTRIAL FORUM,COMMENTARY ON LEGISLATION TO PERMIT PRIVATE OWNERSHIP OF SPECIAL NUCLEAR MATERIAL (PAMPHLET). USA+45 DELIB/GP LEGIS PLAN OWN ...POLICY 20 AEC CONGRESS. PAGE 7 F0134 NUC/PWR MARKET INDUS LAW

N19

GROSECLOSE E.,THE DECAY OF MONEY; A SURVEY OF WESTERN CURRENCIES 1912-1962 (PAMPHLET). AFR FRANCE GERMANY UK LAW INT/TRADE BAL/PAY COST EQUILIB ...POLICY 20 DEPRESSION. PAGE 51 F1004 FINAN NAT/G ECO/DEV ECO/TAC

N19

HALL G.,MAIN STREET TO WALL STREET: END THE COLD WAR (PAMPHLET). AFR USA+45 LAW STRUCT POL/PAR WORKER INT/TRADE DOMIN INCOME...POLICY 20 COM/PARTY. PAGE 53 F1046 MARXIST CAP/ISM DIPLOM NAT/G

N19

HOGARTY R.A.,NEW JERSEY FARMERS AND MIGRANT HOUSING RULES (PAMPHLET). USA+45 LAW ELITES FACE/GP LABOR PROF/ORG LOBBY PERS/REL RIGID/FLEX ROLE 20 NEW/JERSEY. PAGE 61 F1193 AGRI PROVS WORKER HEALTH

N19

LAWRENCE S.A.,THE BATTERY ADDITIVE CONTROVERSY (PAMPHLET). USA+45 LAW MARKET PROC/MFG R+D CAP/ISM CT/SYS GOV/REL OWN FTC CONGRESS BUR/STNDRD RITCHIE/JM. PAGE 76 F1494 PHIL/SCI LOBBY INSPECT

N19

PALAMOUNTAIN JC J.R.,THE DOLCIN CASE AND THE FEDERAL TRADE COMMISSION (PAMPHLET). USA+45 LAW MARKET SERV/IND LG/CO NAT/G BIO/SOC 20 FTC. PAGE 103 F2018 ADJUD PROB/SOLV EDU/PROP HEALTH

N19

SILVERMAN C.,THE PRESIDENT'S ECONOMIC ADVISERS (PAMPHLET). USA+45 LAW ELITES ECO/DEV EX/STRUC ADMIN LEAD GOV/REL PERS/REL ROLE...POLICY DECISION 20 PRESIDENT CONGRESS EISNHWR/DD. PAGE 122 F2404 CONSULT PROB/SOLV NAT/G PLAN

B20

COX H.,ECONOMIC LIBERTY. UNIV LAW INT/TRADE RATION TARIFFS RACE/REL SOCISM POLICY. PAGE 28 F0547 NAT/G ORD/FREE ECO/TAC PERSON

B24

HOLDSWORTH W.S.,A HISTORY OF ENGLISH LAW; THE COMMON LAW AND ITS RIVALS (VOL. VI). AFR UK STRATA EX/STRUC ADJUD ADMIN CONTROL CT/SYS...JURID CONCPT GEN/LAWS 17 PARLIAMENT ENGLSH/LAW COMMON/LAW. PAGE 61 F1194 LAW CONSTN LEGIS CHIEF

B24

HOLDSWORTH W.S.,A HISTORY OF ENGLISH LAW; THE COMMON LAW AND ITS RIVALS (VOL. IV). UK SEA AGRI CHIEF ADJUD CONTROL CRIME GOV/REL...INT/LAW JURID NAT/COMP 16/17 PARLIAMENT COMMON/LAW CANON/LAW ENGLSH/LAW. PAGE 61 F1195 LAW LEGIS CT/SYS CONSTN

B28

FRANKFURTER F.,THE BUSINESS OF THE SUPREME COURT; A STUDY IN THE FEDERAL JUDICIAL SYSTEM. USA-45 CONSTN EX/STRUC PROB/SOLV GP/REL ATTIT PWR...POLICY JURID 18/20 SUPREME/CT CONGRESS. PAGE 43 F0848 CT/SYS ADJUD LAW FEDERAL

B28

TRUE A.C.,A HISTORY OF AGRICULTURAL EXTENSION WORK IN THE UNITED STATES, 1785-1923. USA-45 LAW SCHOOL WAR ADJUST...CHARTS BIBLIOG 18/20 SMITH/LEVR COUNTY/AGT. PAGE 131 F2591 EDU/PROP AGRI VOL/ASSN PLAN

B30

BEVERIDGE W.H.,UNEMPLOYMENT: A PROBLEM OF INDUSTRY (1909-1930). USA-45 LAW ECO/DEV MARKET DELIB/GP WAR DEMAND INCOME...POLICY STAT CHARTS 20. PAGE 14 F0274 WORKER ECO/TAC GEN/LAWS

B36

BURNS A.R.,THE DECLINE OF COMPETITION. LAW LG/CO NAT/G SML/CO LEGIS PRICE AGREE CONTROL GP/REL INCOME PRODUC...POLICY 19/20 NRA. PAGE 20 F0390 MARKET GEN/LAWS INDUS

B37

COLE W.E.,RECENT TRENDS IN RURAL PLANNING. USA-45 LAW ECO/DEV LOC/G SECT EDU/PROP CRIME LEISURE AGE/Y HABITAT...SOC/WK MUNICH 20. PAGE 26 F0503 AGRI NEIGH PLAN ACT/RES

B38

HARPER S.N.,THE GOVERNMENT OF THE SOVIET UNION. COM USSR LAW CONSTN ECO/DEV PLAN TEC/DEV DIPLOM INT/TRADE ADMIN REV NAT/LISM...POLICY 20. PAGE 55 F1085 MARXISM NAT/G LEAD POL/PAR

B39

THOMAS J.A.,THE HOUSE OF COMMONS, 1832-1901; A STUDY OF ITS ECONOMIC AND FUNCTIONAL CHARACTER. UK LAW STRATA FINAN DIPLOM CONTROL LEAD LOBBY REPRESENT WEALTH...POLICY STAT BIBLIOG 19/20 PARLIAMENT. PAGE 130 F2561 PARL/PROC LEGIS POL/PAR ECO/DEV

B40

BATCHELOR B.,THE NEW OUTLOOK IN BUSINESS. LAW WORKER TAX LEAD ORD/FREE...POLICY TREND. PAGE 11 F0208 LG/CO GP/REL CAP/ISM LABOR

B42

ROBBINS J.J.,THE GOVERNMENT OF LABOR RELATIONS IN SWEDEN. SWEDEN LAW CONSTN ADJUD CT/SYS GP/REL ...JURID 20. PAGE 112 F2200 NAT/G BARGAIN LABOR INDUS

S43

HERBERG W.,"BUREAUCRACY AND DEMOCRACY IN LABOR UNIONS." LAW CONSTN STRUCT WORKER ADMIN CONTROL PARTIC RIGID/FLEX PWR TREND. PAGE 59 F1151 LABOR REPRESENT ROUTINE INGP/REL

C43

BENTHAM J.,"THE RATIONALE OF REWARD" IN J. BOWRING, ED., THE WORKS OF JEREMY BENTHAM (VOL. 2)" LAW WORKER CREATE INSPECT PAY ROUTINE HAPPINESS PRODUC SUPEGO WEALTH METH/CNCPT. PAGE 13 F0254 SANCTION ECO/TAC INCOME PWR

B45

MILLIS H.A.,ORGANIZED LABOR (FIRST ED.). LAW STRUCT DELIB/GP WORKER ECO/TAC ADJUD CONTROL REPRESENT INGP/REL INCOME MGT. PAGE 92 F1797 LABOR POLICY ROUTINE GP/REL

B46

DRUCKER P.F.,CONCEPT OF CORPORATION. LAW LABOR WORKER PRICE CONTROL LEAD GP/REL POLICY. PAGE 34 F0665 LG/CO CENTRAL INGP/REL

B47

BAERWALD F.,FUNDAMENTALS OF LABOR ECONOMICS. LAW INDUS LABOR LG/CO CONTROL GP/REL INCOME TOTALISM ...MGT CHARTS GEN/LAWS BIBLIOG 20. PAGE 8 F0150 ECO/DEV WORKER MARKET

B47

GORDON D.L.,THE HIDDEN WEAPON: THE STORY OF ECONOMIC WARFARE. EUR+WWI USA-45 LAW FINAN INDUS NAT/G CONSULT FORCES PLAN DOMIN PWR WEALTH ...INT/LAW CONCPT OBS TOT/POP NAZI 20. PAGE 49 F0955 INT/ORG ECO/TAC INT/TRADE WAR

B47

TOWLE L.W.,INTERNATIONAL TRADE AND COMMERCIAL POLICY. WOR+45 LAW ECO/DEV FINAN INDUS NAT/G ECO/TAC WEALTH...TIME/SEQ ILO 20. PAGE 131 F2582 MARKET INT/ORG INT/TRADE

B48

KEIR D.L.,CASES IN CONSTITUTIONAL LAW. UK CHIEF LEGIS DIPLOM TAX PARL/PROC CRIME GOV/REL...INT/LAW JURID 17/20. PAGE 70 F1368 CONSTN LAW ADJUD

CT/SYS

B49
US DEPARTMENT OF STATE,SOVIET BIBLIOGRAPHY (PAMPHLET). CHINA/COM COM USSR LAW AGRI INT/ORG ECO/TAC EDU/PROP...POLICY GEOG IND 20. PAGE 135 F2670
BIBLIOG/A MARXISM CULTURE DIPLOM

B51
HARDMAN J.B.,THE HOUSE OF LABOR. LAW R+D NEIGH EDU/PROP LEAD ROUTINE REPRESENT GP/REL...POLICY STAT. PAGE 55 F1080
LABOR LOBBY ADMIN PRESS

B51
OWENS R.N.,BUSINESS, ORGANIZATION, AND COMBINATION. USA+45 USA-45 LAW NAT/G LEGIS ECO/TAC CONTROL INGP/REL...JURID GP/COMP 20 NEW/DEAL. PAGE 102 F2006
SML/CO LG/CO STRUCT GP/REL

L51
SUMMERS C.W.,"UNION POWERS AND WORKERS RIGHTS." WORKER PROB/SOLV ECO/TAC PARTIC INGP/REL PWR. PAGE 127 F2513
LABOR CONSTN LAW REPRESENT

B52
ANDREWS F.E.,CORPORATION GIVING. LAW TAX EDU/PROP ADMIN...POLICY STAT CHARTS. PAGE 5 F0101
LG/CO GIVE SML/CO FINAN

B52
JENNINGS W.I.,CONSTITUTIONAL LAWS OF THE COMMONWEALTH. AFR UK LAW CHIEF LEGIS TAX CT/SYS PARL/PROC GOV/REL...INT/LAW 18/20 ENGLSH/LAW COMMON/LAW. PAGE 67 F1316
CONSTN JURID ADJUD COLONIAL

B53
BOWEN H.R.,SOCIAL RESPONSIBILITIES OF THE BUSINESSMAN (FIRST EDITION). LAW FINAN ACT/RES CAP/ISM ROUTINE DRIVE PWR LAISSEZ...DECISION BIBLIOG. PAGE 17 F0326
MGT PERSON SUPEGO MORAL

S53
GABLE R.W.,"NAM: INFLUENTIAL LOBBY OR KISS OF DEATH?" (BMR)" USA+45 LAW INSPECT EDU/PROP ADMIN CONTROL INGP/REL EFFICIENCY PWR 20 CONGRESS NAM TAFT/HART. PAGE 45 F0880
LOBBY LEGIS INDUS LG/CO

B54
BATTEN T.R.,PROBLEMS OF AFRICAN DEVELOPMENT (2ND ED.). AFR LAW SOCIETY SCHOOL ECO/TAC TAX...GEOG HEAL SOC 20. PAGE 11 F0211
ECO/UNDEV AGRI LOC/G PROB/SOLV

B54
FRIEDMAN W.,THE PUBLIC CORPORATION: A COMPARATIVE SYMPOSIUM (UNIVERSITY OF TORONTO SCHOOL OF LAW COMPARATIVE LAW SERIES, VOL. I). AFR SWEDEN USA+45 INDUS INT/ORG NAT/G REGION CENTRAL FEDERAL...POLICY JURID IDEA/COMP NAT/COMP ANTHOL 20 MONOPOLY EUROPE. PAGE 44 F0861
LAW SOCISM LG/CO OWN

B54
LOCKLIN D.P.,ECONOMICS OF TRANSPORTATION (4TH ED.). USA+45 USA-45 SEA AIR LAW FINAN LG/CO EX/STRUC ADMIN CONTROL...STAT CHARTS 19/20 RAILROAD PUB/TRANS. PAGE 81 F1592
ECO/DEV DIST/IND ECO/TAC TEC/DEV

B55
BLOOM G.F.,ECONOMICS OF LABOR RELATIONS. USA+45 LAW CONSULT WORKER CAP/ISM PAY ADJUD CONTROL EFFICIENCY ORD/FREE...CHARTS 19/20 AFL/CIO NLRB DEPT/LABOR. PAGE 16 F0299
ECO/DEV ECO/TAC LABOR GOV/REL

B55
MOHL R.V.,DIE GESCHICHTE UND LITERATUR DER STAATSWISSENSCHAFTEN (3 VOLS.). LAW NAT/G...JURID METH/COMP METH. PAGE 92 F1814
PHIL/SCI MOD/EUR

B55
SERRANO MOSCOSO E.,A STATEMENT OF THE LAWS OF ECUADOR IN MATTERS AFFECTING BUSINESS (2ND ED.). ECUADOR INDUS LABOR LG/CO NAT/G LEGIS TAX CONTROL MARRIAGE 20. PAGE 120 F2359
FINAN ECO/UNDEV LAW CONSTN

B57
MASON E.S.,ECONOMIC CONCENTRATION AND THE MONOPOLY PROBLEM. USA+45 USA-45 LAW ELITES ECO/DEV LABOR RATION PRICE PWR WEALTH...CHARTS 20 MONOPOLY. PAGE 87 F1696
GP/REL LG/CO CONTROL MARKET

S57
CUNNINGHAM E.M.,"THE BUSINESS MAN AND HIS LAWYER." USA+45 LG/CO SML/CO TOP/EX CHOOSE SKILL...JURID MGT 20. PAGE 29 F0561
CONSULT LAW DECISION SERV/IND

B58
ATOMIC INDUSTRIAL FORUM,MANAGEMENT AND ATOMIC ENERGY. WOR+45 SEA LAW MARKET NAT/G TEC/DEV INSPECT INT/TRADE CONFER PEACE HEALTH...ANTHOL 20. PAGE 7 F0136
NUC/PWR INDUS MGT ECO/TAC

B58
BUGEDA LANZAS J.,A STATEMENT OF THE LAWS OF CUBA IN MATTERS AFFECTING BUSINESS (2ND ED. REV., ENLARGED). CUBA L/A+17C LAW FINAN FAM LEGIS ACT/RES ADMIN GP/REL...BIBLIOG 20 OAS. PAGE 20 F0382
JURID NAT/G INDUS WORKER

B58
DUBIN R.,WORKING UNION-MANAGEMENT RELATIONS. LAW PLAN ECO/TAC CHOOSE REPRESENT INGP/REL PWR...POLICY SOC BIBLIOG. PAGE 34 F0669
LABOR MGT AUTHORIT

GP/REL

B58
PAYNO M.,LA REFORMA SOCIAL EN ESPANA Y MEXICO. SPAIN ECO/TAC TAX LOBBY COERCE REV OWN CATHISM 19/20 MEXIC/AMER. PAGE 104 F2043
SECT NAT/G LAW ELITES

B58
SEIDMAN J.I.,DEMOCRACY IN THE LABOR MOVEMENT (PAMPHLET). LAW CONSTN STRUCT DELIB/GP WORKER ADJUD PARTIC SANCTION POLICY. PAGE 119 F2345
LABOR INGP/REL PWR MAJORIT

B58
UNIVERSITY OF LONDON,THE FAR EAST AND SOUTH-EAST ASIA: A CUMULATED LIST OF PERIODICAL ARTICLES, MAY 1956-APRIL 1957. ASIA S/ASIA LAW ADMIN...LING 20. PAGE 133 F2621
BIBLIOG SOC

S58
EMERSON F.D.,"THE ROLES OF MANAGEMENT AND SHAREHOLDERS IN CORPORATE GOVERNMENT." CLIENT DELIB/GP CREATE ADMIN EXEC PARTIC PERS/REL PWR. PAGE 37 F0728
LG/CO LAW INGP/REL REPRESENT

S58
LATTIN N.D.,"MINORITY AND DISSENTING SHAREHOLDERS' RIGHTS IN FUNDAMENTAL CHANGES." FINAN LEGIS ADJUD PARTIC ROUTINE CHOOSE REPRESENT INGP/REL TREND. PAGE 76 F1487
MAJORIT LG/CO LAW CREATE

S58
O'NEAL F.H.,"RECENT LEGISLATION AFFECTING CLOSE CORPORATIONS." LAW EX/STRUC ECO/TAC ROUTINE CHOOSE RIGID/FLEX...MAJORIT MGT TREND. PAGE 100 F1959
LG/CO LEGIS REPRESENT PARTIC

B59
CUCCORESE H.J.,HISTORIA DE LA CONVERSION DEL PAPEL MONEDA EN BUENOS AIRES, 1861-1867. AFR LAW LOC/G NAT/G ATTIT...POLICY BIBLIOG 19 ARGEN BUENOS/AIR. PAGE 29 F0560
FINAN PLAN LEGIS

B59
FERRY W.H.,THE CORPORATION AND THE ECONOMY. CLIENT LAW CONSTN LABOR NAT/G PLAN INT/TRADE PARTIC CONSEN ORD/FREE PWR POLICY. PAGE 40 F0787
LG/CO CONTROL REPRESENT

B59
GOMEZ ROBLES J.,A STATEMENT OF THE LAWS OF GUATEMALA IN MATTERS AFFECTING BUSINESS (2ND ED. REV., ENLARGED). GUATEMALA L/A+17C LAW FINAN FAM WORKER ACT/RES DIPLOM ADJUD ADMIN GP/REL 20 OAS. PAGE 48 F0945
JURID NAT/G INDUS LEGIT

B59
NUNEZ JIMENEZ A.,LA LIBERACION DE LAS ISLAS. CUBA L/A+17C USA+45 LAW CHIEF PLAN DIPLOM FOR/AID OWN WEALTH 20 CASTRO/F. PAGE 99 F1945
AGRI REV ECO/UNDEV NAT/G

B59
U OF MICHIGAN LAW SCHOOL,ATOMS AND THE LAW. USA+45 PROVS WORKER PROB/SOLV DIPLOM ADMIN GOV/REL ANTHOL. PAGE 132 F2596
NUC/PWR NAT/G CONTROL LAW

B59
US NATIONAL LABOR RELATIONS BD,LEGISLATIVE HISTORY OF THE LABOR-MANAGEMENT REPORTING AND DISCLOSURE ACT OF 1959 (2 VOLS.). USA+45 LEGIS...MGT CHARTS. PAGE 138 F2720
LAW LABOR GP/REL

B59
VOSE C.E.,CAUCASIANS ONLY: THE SUPREME COURT, THE NAACP, AND THE RESTRICTIVE COVENANT CASES. USA+45 LAW CONSTN LOBBY...SOC 20 NAACP SUPREME/CT NEGRO. PAGE 142 F2796
CT/SYS RACE/REL DISCRIM

L59
OBERER W.E.,"VOLUNTARY IMPARTIAL REVIEW OF LABOR: SOME REFLECTIONS." DELIB/GP LEGIS PROB/SOLV ADJUD CONTROL COERCE PWR PLURISM POLICY. PAGE 100 F1960
LABOR LAW PARTIC INGP/REL

S59
SCHEEHAN D.,"PUBLIC AND PRIVATE GROUPS AS IDENTIFIED IN THE FIELD OF TRADE REGULATIONS." USA+45 ADMIN REPRESENT GOV/REL. PAGE 116 F2293
LAW CONTROL ADJUD LOBBY

S59
TIPTON J.B.,"PARTICIPATION OF THE UNITED STATES IN THE INTERNATIONAL LABOR ORGANIZATION." USA+45 LAW STRUCT ECO/DEV ECO/UNDEV INDUS TEC/DEV ECO/TAC ADMIN PERCEPT ORD/FREE SKILL...STAT HIST/WRIT GEN/METH ILO WORK 20. PAGE 131 F2577
LABOR INT/ORG

N59
CHAMBER OF COMMERCE OF USA,ECONOMIC LESSONS OF POSTWAR RECESSIONS (PAMPHLET). AFR USA+45 LAW LEGIS WORKER TAX...CHARTS 20 CONGRESS FED/RESERV. PAGE 23 F0440
ECO/DEV PROB/SOLV FINAN ECO/TAC

B60
CARPER E.T.,THE DEFENSE APPROPRIATIONS RIDER (PAMPHLET). USA+45 CONSTN CHIEF DELIB/GP LEGIS BUDGET LOBBY CIVMIL/REL...POLICY 20 CONGRESS EISNHWR/DD DEPT/DEFEN PRESIDENT BOSTON. PAGE 22 F0419
GOV/REL ADJUD LAW CONTROL

B60
ELKOURI F.,HOW ARBITRATION WORKS (REV. ED.). LAW INDUS BARGAIN 20. PAGE 37 F0720
MGT LABOR

ADJUD GP/REL

B60
FORBUSH D.R.,PROBLEMS OF CORPORATE POWER. CLIENT LAW ELITES ADJUD...DECISION MGT. PAGE 42 F0822
LG/CO PWR CONTROL GP/REL

B60
GRAMPP W.D.,THE MANCHESTER SCHOOL OF ECONOMICS. UK LAW ECO/DEV COERCE ATTIT ORD/FREE LAISSEZ ...PHIL/SCI IDEA/COMP 19/20 MANCHESTER CORN/LAWS. PAGE 50 F0973
ECO/TAC VOL/ASSN LOBBY NAT/G

B60
LENCZOWSKI G.,OIL AND STATE IN THE MIDDLE EAST. FUT IRAN LAW ECO/UNDEV EXTR/IND NAT/G TOP/EX PLAN TEC/DEV ECO/TAC LEGIT ADMIN COERCE ATTIT ALL/VALS PWR...CHARTS 20. PAGE 78 F1519
ISLAM INDUS NAT/LISM

B60
US SENATE COMM ON COMMERCE,URBAN MASS TRANSPORTATION. FUT USA+45 AIR ECO/DEV FINAN LOC/G LEGIS CREATE PROB/SOLV TEC/DEV MUNICH 20 PUB/TRANS. PAGE 139 F2732
DIST/IND PLAN NAT/G LAW

S60
MORALES C.J.,"TRADE AND ECONOMIC INTEGRATION IN LATIN AMERICA." FUT L/A+17C LAW STRATA ECO/UNDEV DIST/IND INDUS LABOR NAT/G LEGIS ECO/TAC ADMIN RIGID/FLEX WEALTH...CONCPT NEW/IDEA CONT/OBS TIME/SEQ WORK 20. PAGE 93 F1825
FINAN INT/TRADE REGION

B61
ALFRED H.,PUBLIC OWNERSHIP IN THE USA: GOALS AND PRIORITIES. LAW INDUS INT/TRADE ADJUD GOV/REL EFFICIENCY PEACE SOCISM...POLICY ANTHOL 20 TVA. PAGE 4 F0065
CONTROL OWN ECO/DEV ECO/TAC

B61
BARBASH J.,LABOR'S GRASS ROOTS. CONSTN NAT/G EX/STRUC LEGIS WORKER LEAD...MAJORIT BIBLIOG. PAGE 10 F0184
LABOR INGP/REL GP/REL LAW

B61
CARROTHERS A.W.R.,LABOR ARBITRATION IN CANADA. CANADA LAW NAT/G CONSULT LEGIS WORKER ADJUD ADMIN CT/SYS 20. PAGE 22 F0422
LABOR MGT GP/REL BARGAIN

B61
DUKE UNIVERSITY,EXPULSION OR OPPRESSION OF BUSINESS ASSOCIATES: "SQUEEZE-OUTS" IN SMALL ENTERPRISES. LAW CONTROL PARTIC COERCE INGP/REL...POLICY RECORD INT. PAGE 35 F0674
PWR MGT SML/CO ECO/TAC

B61
FLINN M.W.,AN ECONOMIC AND SOCIAL HISTORY OF BRITAIN, 1066-1939. UK LAW STRATA STRUCT AGRI DIST/IND INDUS WORKER INT/TRADE WAR...CENSUS 11/20. PAGE 42 F0811
SOCIETY SOC

B61
LAHAYE R.,LES ENTREPRISES PUBLIQUES AU MAROC. FRANCE MOROCCO LAW DIST/IND EXTR/IND FINAN CONSULT PLAN TEC/DEV ADMIN AGREE CONTROL OWN...POLICY 20. PAGE 74 F1460
NAT/G INDUS ECO/UNDEV ECO/TAC

B61
MORLEY L.,THE PATCHWORK HISTORY OF FOREIGN AID. AFR KOREA/S USA+45 USSR LAW FINAN INT/ORG TEC/DEV BAL/PWR GIVE 20 NATO. PAGE 93 F1834
FOR/AID ECO/UNDEV FORCES DIPLOM

B61
RUEDA B.,A STATEMENT OF THE LAWS OF COLOMBIA IN MATTERS AFFECTING BUSINESS (3RD ED.). INDUS FAM LABOR LG/CO NAT/G LEGIS TAX CONTROL MARRIAGE 20 COLOMB. PAGE 115 F2257
FINAN ECO/UNDEV LAW CONSTN

L61
GERWIG R.,"PUBLIC AUTHORITIES IN THE UNITED STATES." LAW CONSTN PROVS TAX ADMIN FEDERAL MUNICH. PAGE 47 F0920
LOC/G GOV/REL PWR

N61
US ADVISORY COMN INTERGOV REL,STATE CONSTITUTIONAL AND STATUTORY RESTRICTIONS ON LOCAL GOVERNMENT DEBT (PAMPHLET). LAW CONSTN CHOOSE PWR...DECISION MUNICH. PAGE 133 F2631
TAX PROVS GOV/REL

N61
VINER J.,THE INTELLECTUAL HISTORY OF LAISSEZ FAIRE (PAMPHLET). WOR+45 WOR-45 LAW INTELL...POLICY LING LOG 19/20. PAGE 141 F2787
ATTIT EDU/PROP LAISSEZ ECO/TAC

B62
BUREAU OF NATIONAL AFFAIRS,FEDERAL-STATE REGULATION OF WELFARE FUNDS (REV. ED.). USA+45 LAW LEGIS DEBATE AGE/O 20 CONGRESS. PAGE 20 F0386
WELF/ST WEALTH PLAN SOC/WK

B62
CARPER E.T.,ILLINOIS GOES TO CONGRESS FOR ARMY LAND. USA+45 LAW EXTR/IND PROVS REGION CIVMIL/REL GOV/REL FEDERAL ATTIT 20 ILLINOIS SENATE CONGRESS DIRKSEN/E DOUGLAS/P. PAGE 22 F0420
ADMIN LOBBY GEOG LEGIS

B62
DUPRE J.S.,SCIENCE AND THE NATION: POLICY AND POLITICS. USA+45 LAW ACADEM FORCES ADMIN CIVMIL/REL GOV/REL EFFICIENCY PEACE...TREND 20 SCI/ADVSRY. PAGE 35 F0682
R+D INDUS TEC/DEV NUC/PWR

B62
HIRSCHFIELD R.S.,THE CONSTITUTION AND THE COURT. AFR SCHOOL WAR RACE/REL EQUILIB ORD/FREE...POLICY MAJORIT DECISION JURID 18/20 PRESIDENT CIVIL/LIB SUPREME/CT CONGRESS. PAGE 60 F1175
ADJUD PWR CONSTN LAW

B62
INTNTL COTTON ADVISORY COMMITT,GOVERNMENT REGULATIONS ON COTTON, 1962 (PAMPHLET). WOR+45 RATION PRODUC...CHARTS 20. PAGE 65 F1287
ECO/TAC LAW CONTROL AGRI

B62
LEVY H.V.,LIBERDADE E JUSTICA SOCIAL (2ND ED.). BRAZIL COM L/A+17C USSR INT/ORG PARTIC GP/REL WEALTH 20 UN COM/PARTY. PAGE 79 F1544
ORD/FREE MARXISM CAP/ISM LAW

B62
MCCLELLAN J.L.,CRIME WITHOUT PUNISHMENT. USA+45 LAW SOCIETY DELIB/GP TRIBUTE CONTROL LOBBY COERCE GP/REL ANOMIE MORAL...CRIMLGY 20 CONGRESS HOFFA/J. PAGE 88 F1718
CRIME ACT/RES LABOR PWR

B62
MORGAN C.A.,LABOR ECONOMICS. LAW INDUS MARKET WORKER PLAN PROB/SOLV GOV/REL INCOME ROLE...T 20 DEPT/LABOR NLRB. PAGE 93 F1829
LABOR ECO/TAC ECO/DEV CAP/ISM

B62
PASTOR R.S.,A STATEMENT OF THE LAWS OF PARAGUAY IN MATTERS AFFECTING BUSINESS (2ND ED.). PARAGUAY INDUS FAM LABOR LG/CO NAT/G LEGIS TAX CONTROL MARRIAGE 20. PAGE 103 F2033
FINAN ECO/UNDEV LAW CONSTN

B62
ROTHBARD M.N.,THE PANIC OF 1819; REACTIONS AND POLICIES. AFR USA-45 LAW FINAN BUDGET TARIFFS DEMAND 19 DEPRESSION. PAGE 114 F2247
ECO/UNDEV POLICY ATTIT ECO/TAC

B62
UNECA LIBRARY,NEW ACQUISITIONS IN THE UNECA LIBRARY. LAW NAT/G PLAN PROB/SOLV TEC/DEV ADMIN REGION...GEOG SOC 20 UN. PAGE 132 F2606
BIBLIOG AFR ECO/UNDEV INT/ORG

B62
URQUIDI C.W.,A STATEMENT OF THE LAWS OF BOLIVIA IN MATTERS AFFECTING BUSINESS (3RD ED. REV., ENLARGED). L/A+17C LAW FINAN FAM WORKER ACT/RES DIPLOM ADJUD ADMIN GP/REL 20 BOLIV OAS. PAGE 133 F2626
JURID INDUS NAT/G LEGIT

B62
US ADVISORY COMN INTERGOV REL,STATE CONSTITUTIONAL AND STATUTORY RESTRICTIONS ON LOCAL TAXING POWERS. USA+45 USA-45 LAW CONSTN ACT/RES CONTROL WEALTH ...JURID CHARTS 20. PAGE 133 F2632
LOC/G PROVS GOV/REL TAX

B62
US CONGRESS,LEGISLATIVE HISTORY OF UNITED STATES TAX CONVENTIONS(VOL. 1). USA+45 USA-45 DELIB/GP WEALTH...CHARTS 20 CONGRESS. PAGE 134 F2649
TAX LEGIS LAW DIPLOM

B62
VACCARO J.R.,A STATEMENT OF THE LAWS OF CHILE IN MATTERS AFFECTING BUSINESS (3RD ED.). CHILE AGRI FINAN FAM LABOR ECO/TAC FOR/AID TAX ADJUD CONTROL MARRIAGE STRANGE...BIBLIOG 20. PAGE 140 F2756
CONSTN LAW INDUS MGT

L62
N,"UNION INVESTMENT IN BUSINESS: A SOURCE OF UNION CONFLICT OF INTEREST." LAW NAT/G LEGIS CONTROL GP/REL INGP/REL DECISION. PAGE 96 F1884
LABOR POLICY FINAN LG/CO

B63
BOWIE R.R.,GOVERNMENT REGULATION OF BUSINESS: CASES FROM THE NATIONAL REPORTER SYSTEM. USA+45 USA-45 NAT/G ECO/TAC ADJUD...ANTHOL 19/20 SUPREME/CT FTC FAIR/LABOR MONOPOLY. PAGE 17 F0331
LAW CONTROL INDUS CT/SYS

B63
CHOJNACKI S.,REGISTER ON CURRENT RESEARCH ON ETHIOPIA AND THE HORN OF AFRICA. ETHIOPIA LAW CULTURE AGRI SECT EDU/PROP ADMIN...GEOG HEAL LING 20. PAGE 24 F0470
BIBLIOG ACT/RES INTELL ACADEM

B63
HAUSMAN W.H.,MANAGING ECONOMIC DEVELOPMENT IN AFRICA. AFR USA+45 LAW FINAN WORKER TEC/DEV WEALTH ...ANTHOL 20. PAGE 57 F1116
ECO/UNDEV PLAN FOR/AID MGT

B63
LEWIN J.,POLITICS AND LAW IN SOUTH AFRICA. SOUTH/AFR UK POL/PAR BAL/PWR ECO/TAC COLONIAL CONTROL GP/REL DISCRIM PWR 20 NEGRO. PAGE 79 F1545
NAT/LISM POLICY LAW RACE/REL

B63
PRYOR F.L.,THE COMMUNIST FOREIGN TRADE SYSTEM. COM CZECHOSLVK GERMANY YUGOSLAVIA LAW ECO/DEV DIST/IND POL/PAR PLAN DOMIN TOTALISM DRIVE RIGID/FLEX WEALTH ...STAT STAND/INT CHARTS FOR/TRADE 20. PAGE 108 F2130
ATTIT ECO/TAC

B63
TREVES G.,GOVERNMENT ORGANIZATION FOR ECONOMIC DEVELOPMENT (PAMPHLET). WOR+45 LAW BUDGET ECO/TAC
ECO/DEV ECO/UNDEV

GOV/REL...DECISION 20. PAGE 131 F2585 PLAN POLICY

L63
PADELFORD N.J.,"FINANCIAL CRISIS AND THE UNITED NATIONS." FUT USSR WOR+45 LAW CONSTN FINAN INT/ORG DELIB/GP FORCES PLAN BUDGET DIPLOM COST WEALTH ...STAT CHARTS UN CONGO 20. PAGE 102 F2012 CREATE ECO/TAC

B64
BOGEN J.I.,FINANCIAL HANDBOOK (4TH ED.). UNIV LAW PLAN TAX RISK 20. PAGE 16 F0306 FINAN DICTIONARY

B64
GARDNER L.C.,ECONOMIC ASPECTS OF NEW DEAL DIPLOMACY. USA-45 WOR-45 LAW ECO/DEV INT/ORG NAT/G VOL/ASSN LEGIS TOP/EX EDU/PROP ORD/FREE PWR WEALTH ...POLICY TIME/SEQ VAL/FREE 20 ROOSEVLT/F. PAGE 46 F0901 ECO/TAC DIPLOM

B64
HAAR C.M.,LAW AND LAND: ANGLO-AMERICAN PLANNING PRACTICE. UK USA+45 NAT/G TEC/DEV BUDGET CT/SYS INGP/REL EFFICIENCY OWN...JURID MUNICH 20. PAGE 52 F1019 LAW PLAN NAT/COMP

B64
HEKHUIS D.J.,INTERNATIONAL STABILITY: MILITARY, ECONOMIC AND POLITICAL DIMENSIONS. FUT WOR+45 LAW ECO/UNDEV INT/ORG NAT/G VOL/ASSN FORCES ACT/RES BAL/PWR PWR WEALTH...STAT UN 20. PAGE 58 F1143 TEC/DEV DETER REGION

B64
JACOBY N.H.,UNITED STATES MONETARY POLICY. UK USA+45 LAW NAT/G TEC/DEV TAX EQUILIB INCOME ...METH/COMP 20 FED/RESERV. PAGE 66 F1300 ECO/DEV POLICY ECO/TAC FINAN

B64
LAFONT P.B.,BIBLIOGRAPHIE DU LAOS. LAOS S/ASIA EDU/PROP...GEOG 20. PAGE 74 F1458 BIBLIOG LAW SOC

B64
MANN B.,STATE CONSTITUTIONAL RESTRICTIONS ON LOCAL BORROWING AND PROPERTY TAXING POWERS. USA+45 CONSTN PROVS CT/SYS GOV/REL PWR...DECISION JURID CHARTS 20. PAGE 84 F1654 LOC/G TAX FINAN LAW

B64
US SENATE COMM ON JUDICIARY,HEARINGS BEFORE SUBCOMMITTEE ON ANTITRUST AND MONOPOLY: ECONOMIC CONCENTRATION VOLUMES 1-5 JULY 1964-SEPT 1966. USA+45 LAW FINAN ECO/TAC ADJUD COST EFFICIENCY PRODUC...STAT CHARTS 20 CONGRESS MONOPOLY. PAGE 140 F2749 ECO/DEV CONTROL MARKET LG/CO

B64
WITHERELL J.W.,OFFICIAL PUBLICATIONS OF FRENCH EQUATORIAL AFRICA, FRENCH CAMEROONS, AND TOGO, 1946-1958 (PAMPHLET). CAMEROON CHAD FRANCE GABON TOGO LAW ECO/UNDEV EXTR/IND INT/TRADE...GEOG HEAL 20. PAGE 148 F2913 BIBLIOG/A AFR NAT/G ADMIN

B64
WRIGHT G.,RURAL REVOLUTION IN FRANCE: THE PEASANTRY IN THE TWENTIETH CENTURY. EUR+WWI MOD/EUR LAW CULTURE AGRI POL/PAR DELIB/GP LEGIS ECO/TAC EDU/PROP COERCE CHOOSE ATTIT RIGID/FLEX HEALTH ...STAT CENSUS CHARTS VAL/FREE 20. PAGE 149 F2932 PWR STRATA FRANCE REV

S64
N,"QUASI-LEGISLATIVE ARBITRATION AGREEMENTS." LAW LG/CO ECO/TAC SANCTION ATTIT POLICY. PAGE 96 F1885 ADJUD ADJUST LABOR GP/REL

C64
NORGREN P.H.,"TOWARD FAIR EMPLOYMENT." USA+45 LAW STRATA LABOR NAT/G FORCES ACT/RES ADMIN ATTIT ...POLICY BIBLIOG 20 NEGRO. PAGE 98 F1932 RACE/REL DISCRIM WORKER MGT

B65
BOCK E.,GOVERNMENT REGULATION OF BUSINESS. USA+45 LAW EX/STRUC LEGIS EXEC ORD/FREE PWR...ANTHOL CONGRESS. PAGE 16 F0303 MGT ADMIN NAT/G CONTROL

B65
FLEMING R.W.,THE LABOR ARBITRATION PROCESS. USA+45 LAW BARGAIN ADJUD ROUTINE SANCTION COST...PREDICT CHARTS TIME 20. PAGE 41 F0809 GP/REL LABOR CONSULT DELIB/GP

B65
LEYS C.T.,FEDERATION IN EAST AFRICA. LAW AGRI DIST/IND FINAN INT/ORG LABOR INT/TRADE CONFER ADMIN CONTROL GP/REL...ANTHOL 20 AFRICA/E. PAGE 79 F1554 FEDERAL REGION ECO/UNDEV PLAN

B65
NATIONAL CONF SOCIAL WELFARE,THE SOCIAL WELFARE FORUM, 1965. LAW CULTURE VOL/ASSN CONTROL PERS/REL ADJUST POLICY. PAGE 97 F1899 CONSTN WEALTH ORD/FREE NEIGH

B65
ROSS P.,THE GOVERNMENT AS A SOURCE OF UNION POWER. USA+45 LAW ECO/DEV PROB/SOLV ECO/TAC LEAD GP/REL ...MGT 20. PAGE 114 F2245 LABOR BARGAIN POLICY NAT/G

B65
SHAFFER H.G.,THE SOVIET SYSTEM IN THEORY AND PRACTICE: SELECTED WESTERN AND SOVIET VIEWS. USSR LAW SOCIETY CREATE FOR/AID EDU/PROP PRESS CHOOSE PEACE ORD/FREE...ANTHOL 20 STALIN/J. PAGE 120 F2362 MARXISM SOCISM IDEA/COMP

B65
SIMON B.,EDUCATION AND THE LABOR MOVEMENT, 1870-1920. UK SOCIETY STRATA LABOR POL/PAR SCHOOL CONTROL PARTIC SOCISM...BIBLIOG 19/20. PAGE 122 F2406 EDU/PROP WORKER ADJUST LAW

B65
VAID K.N.,STATE AND LABOR IN INDIA. INDIA INDUS WORKER PAY PRICE ADJUD CONTROL PARL/PROC GP/REL ORD/FREE 20. PAGE 140 F2757 LAW LABOR MGT NEW/LIB

S65
HADDAD W.F.,"MR. SHRIVER AND THE SAVAGE POLITICS OF POVERTY" USA+45 LAW NAT/G DELIB/GP LEGIS GIVE LEAD CENTRAL PWR...SOC/WK CHARTS 20 CONGRESS POVRTY/WAR SHRIVER/S OEO. PAGE 53 F1028 WEALTH GOV/REL CONTROL TOP/EX

S65
KAUN D.E.,"THE FAIR LABOUR STANDARDS ACT: AN EVALUATION IN TERMS OF ITS STATED GOALS." SOUTH/AFR LAW LABOR BARGAIN PAY INGP/REL WEALTH 20. PAGE 69 F1364 ECO/TAC PRICE WORKER LEGIS

S65
KINDLEBERGER C.P.,"MASS MIGRATION, THEN AND NOW." LAW ECO/DEV ECO/UNDEV INDUS LABOR INT/TRADE FEEDBACK REGION RIGID/FLEX...SOC NAT/COMP EEC. PAGE 71 F1394 EUR+WWI USA-45 WORKER IDEA/COMP

S65
STEENKAMP W.F.J.,"THE PROBLEM OF WAGE REGULATION." SOUTH/AFR LAW ECO/DEV ECO/UNDEV LABOR NAT/G BARGAIN PAY INGP/REL DISCRIM WEALTH...METH/COMP 20. PAGE 125 F2473 ECO/TAC PRICE WORKER RATION

C65
PEGRUM D.E.,"PUBLIC REGULATION OF BUSINESS (REV ED)" LAW CONSTN DIST/IND SERV/IND LG/CO LEGIS OWN LAISSEZ SOCISM...POLICY DECISION BIBLIOG 20. PAGE 104 F2048 INDUS PLAN NEW/LIB PRICE

B66
DAVIS K.,BUSINESS AND ITS ENVIRONMENT. LAW ECO/DEV INDUS OP/RES ADMIN CONTROL ROUTINE GP/REL PROFIT POLICY. PAGE 30 F0591 EX/STRUC PROB/SOLV CAP/ISM EXEC

B66
EBONY,THE NEGRO HANDBOOK. ACADEM LABOR LOC/G SECT FORCES WORKER CT/SYS CRIME DISCRIM ORD/FREE...BIOG SOC/INTEG 19/20 NEGRO CIV/RIGHTS. PAGE 36 F0692 RACE/REL EDU/PROP LAW STAT

B66
HAYS P.R.,LABOR ARBITRATION: A DISSENTING VIEW. USA+45 LAW DELIB/GP BARGAIN ADJUD...PREDICT 20. PAGE 57 F1126 GP/REL LABOR CONSULT CT/SYS

B66
LEE R.A.,TRUMAN AND TAFT-HARTLEY: A QUESTION OF MANDATE. USA+45 LAW CONSTN LG/CO CONTROL LOBBY GOV/REL PEACE NEW/LIB 20 TRUMAN/HS CONGRESS. PAGE 77 F1507 LEGIS TOP/EX ADJUD LABOR

B66
RAPHAEL J.S.,GOVERNMENTAL REGULATION OF BUSINESS. USA+45 LAW CONSTN TAX ADJUD ADMIN EFFICIENCY PWR 20. PAGE 109 F2150 LG/CO GOV/REL CONTROL ECO/DEV

B66
SOCIAL SCIENCE RESEARCH COUN,BIBLIOGRAPHY OF RESEARCH IN THE SOCIAL SCIENCES IN AUSTRALIA 1957-1960. LAW R+D DIPLOM 20 AUSTRAL. PAGE 124 F2437 BIBLIOG SOC PSY

B66
SOVERN M.I.,LEGAL RESTRAINTS ON RACIAL DISCRIMINATION IN EMPLOYMENT. USA+45 LAW INDUS LG/CO SML/CO DELIB/GP LEGIS SANCTION 20 NLRB PRESIDENT NEGRO CIV/RIGHTS RAILROAD. PAGE 124 F2446 DISCRIM RACE/REL WORKER JURID

B66
US DEPARTMENT OF STATE,RESEARCH ON THE USSR AND EASTERN EUROPE (EXTERNAL RESEARCH LIST NO 1-25). USSR LAW CULTURE SOCIETY NAT/G TEC/DEV DIPLOM EDU/PROP REGION...GEOG LING. PAGE 136 F2675 BIBLIOG/A EUR+WWI COM MARXISM

B66
US DEPARTMENT OF STATE,RESEARCH ON WESTERN EUROPE, GREAT BRITAIN, AND CANADA (EXTERNAL RESEARCH LIST NO 3-25). CANADA GERMANY/W UK LAW CULTURE NAT/G POL/PAR FORCES EDU/PROP REGION MARXISM...GEOG SOC WORSHIP 20 CMN/WLTH. PAGE 136 F2676 BIBLIOG/A EUR+WWI DIPLOM

B66
US HOUSE COMM BANKING CURRENCY,HEARINGS BEFORE HOUSE COMMITTEE ON BANKING AND CURRENCY: SALE OF SBA LOAN POOL PARTICIPATIONS. USA+45 LAW LEGIS ECO/TAC RATION 20 CONGRESS. PAGE 136 F2687 FINAN SML/CO ADJUD GOV/REL

B66
US SENATE COMM LABOR-PUB WELF,AMEND THE RAILWAY LABOR ACT. USA+45 CONSTN CONSULT DELIB/GP ADJUD CONGRESS RAILROAD. PAGE 139 F2731 GP/REL LABOR DIST/IND LAW

B66
US SENATE COMM ON FOREIGN REL,ASIAN DEVELOPMENT FOR/AID

BANK ACT. USA+45 LAW DIPLOM...CHARTS 20 BLACK/EUG S/EASTASIA. PAGE 139 F2736 FINAN ECO/UNDEV S/ASIA B66

WALTON S.D.,AMERICAN BUSINESS AND ITS ENVIRONMENT. USA+45 LAW CONSTN FINAN MARKET LOC/G EX/STRUC CT/SYS COST PRODUC...STAT 20. PAGE 143 F2813 PRICE PROFIT B66

ZINKIN T.,CHALLENGES IN INDIA. INDIA PAKISTAN LAW AGRI FINAN INDUS TOP/EX TEC/DEV CONTROL ROUTINE ORD/FREE PWR 20 NEHRU/J SHASTRI/LB CIVIL/SERV. PAGE 150 F2964 NAT/G ECO/TAC POLICY ADMIN N66

US ADVISORY COMN INTERGOV REL,CATALOGS AND OTHER INFORMATION SOURCES ON FEDERAL AND STATE AID PROGRAMS: A SECTED BIBLIOGRAPHY (PAPER). USA+45 LAW LOC/G NAT/G PROVS VOL/ASSN TEC/DEV ADMIN HEALTH ...WELF/ST SOC/WK MUNICH. PAGE 134 F2635 BIBLIOG/A GOV/REL FINAN ECO/DEV B67

BLAIR G.S.,LEGISLATIVE BODIES IN CALIFORNIA. USA+45 LAW POL/PAR LOBBY APPORT CHOOSE REPRESENT GP/REL ...T CALIFORNIA. PAGE 15 F0293 LEGIS PROVS LOC/G ADJUD B67

CHAPIN F.S. JR.,SELECTED REFERENCES ON URBAN PLANNING METHODS AND TECHNIQUES. USA+45 LAW ECO/DEV LOC/G NAT/G SCHOOL CONSULT CREATE PROB/SOLV TEC/DEV ...SOC/WK MUNICH. PAGE 23 F0454 BIBLIOG NEIGH PLAN B67

COWLING M.,1867 DISRAELI, GLADSTONE, AND REVOLUTION; THE PASSING OF THE SECOND REFORM BILL. UK LEGIS LEAD LOBBY GP/REL INGP/REL...DECISION BIBLIOG 19 REFORMERS. PAGE 28 F0545 PARL/PROC POL/PAR ATTIT LAW B67

GRIPP R.C.,PATTERNS OF SOVIET POLITICS (REV. ED.). USSR LAW ELITES LOC/G PLAN CONTROL CT/SYS CHOOSE ...POLICY BIBLIOG/A DICTIONARY 9/20. PAGE 51 F1003 COM ADJUD POL/PAR B67

HANNAH H.W.,THE LEGAL BASE FOR UNIVERSITIES IN DEVELOPING COUNTRIES. AFR ASIA L/A+17C S/ASIA USA+45 FINAN CREATE EDU/PROP TASK EFFICIENCY ...JURID METH/COMP 20. PAGE 54 F1060 ADMIN LAW ACADEM LEGIS B67

HODGKINSON R.G.,THE ORIGINS OF THE NATIONAL HEALTH SERVICE: THE MEDICAL SERVICES OF THE NEW POOR LAW, 1834-1871. UK INDUS WORKER PROB/SOLV EFFICIENCY ATTIT HEALTH WEALTH SOCISM...JURID SOC/WK MUNICH 19/20. PAGE 60 F1189 HEAL NAT/G POLICY LAW B67

KREININ M.E.,ALTERNATIVE COMMERCIAL POLICIES - THEIR EFFECT ON THE AMERICAN ECONOMY. USA+45 LAW ECO/DEV MARKET INT/ORG DIPLOM ECO/TAC TARIFFS PRICE DEMAND WEALTH...QUANT EEC AFTA. PAGE 73 F1437 INT/TRADE BAL/PAY NAT/G POLICY B67

MARCUS S.,COMPETITION AND THE LAW. USA+45 INDUS LG/CO NAT/G CONSERVE LAISSEZ...BIBLIOG 20 FTC SUPREME/CT. PAGE 85 F1665 LAW ECO/DEV FINAN JURID B67

NARVER J.C.,CONGLOMERATE MERGERS AND MARKET COMPETITION. USA+45 LAW STRUCT ADMIN LEAD RISK COST PROFIT WEALTH...POLICY CHARTS BIBLIOG. PAGE 96 F1892 DEMAND LG/CO MARKET MGT B67

ORLANS H.,CONTRACTING FOR ATOMS. AFR USA+45 LAW INTELL ACADEM LG/CO NAT/G PLAN TEC/DEV CONTROL DETER...TREND 20. PAGE 102 F1999 NUC/PWR R+D PRODUC PEACE B67

ROBERTS B.C.,COLLECTIVE BARGAINING IN AFRICAN COUNTRIES. AFR LAW ECO/UNDEV BARGAIN GP/REL ...DECISION METH/COMP 20. PAGE 112 F2206 LABOR MGT PLAN ECO/TAC B67

ROBINSON R.D.,INTERNATIONAL MANAGEMENT. LAW MARKET LABOR PRICE CONTROL COST DEMAND OWN PRODUC WEALTH 20. PAGE 113 F2225 T OP/RES MGT DIPLOM B67

ROSS A.M.,EMPLOYMENT, RACE, AND POVERTY. USA+45 LAW STRATA MARKET LABOR EDU/PROP ISOLAT SKILL...MGT ANTHOL 20 NEGRO. PAGE 114 F2244 RACE/REL WORKER WEALTH DISCRIM B67

UNIVERSAL REFERENCE SYSTEM,BIBLIOGRAPHY OF BIBLIOGRAPHIES IN POLITICAL SCIENCE, GOVERNMENT, AND PUBLIC POLICY (VOLUME III). WOR+45 WOR-45 LAW ADMIN...SOC CON/ANAL COMPUT/IR GEN/METH. PAGE 133 F2615 BIBLIOG/A NAT/G DIPLOM POLICY B67

UNIVERSAL REFERENCE SYSTEM,PUBLIC POLICY AND THE MANAGEMENT OF SCIENCE (VOLUME IX). FUT SPACE WOR+45 LAW NAT/G TEC/DEV CONTROL NUC/PWR GOV/REL ...COMPUT/IR GEN/METH. PAGE 133 F2618 BIBLIOG/A POLICY MGT PHIL/SCI B67

US SENATE COMM ON FOREIGN REL,INTER-AMERICAN DEVELOPMENT BANK ACT AMENDMENT. L/A+17C USA+45 DELIB/GP DIPLOM FOR/AID BAL/PAY...CHARTS SENATE. PAGE 139 F2741 LAW FINAN INT/ORG ECO/UNDEV B67

US SENATE COMM ON FOREIGN REL,FOREIGN ASSISTANCE ACT OF 1967. VIETNAM WOR+45 DELIB/GP CONFER CONTROL WAR WEAPON BAL/PAY...CENSUS CHARTS SENATE. PAGE 139 F2744 FOR/AID LAW DIPLOM POLICY B67

WEINBERG M.,SCHOOL INTEGRATION: A COMPREHENSIVE CLASSIFIED BIBLIOGRAPHY OF 3,100 REFERENCES. USA+45 LAW NAT/G NEIGH SECT PLAN ROUTINE AGE/C WEALTH SOC/INTEG INDIAN/AM. PAGE 145 F2849 BIBLIOG SCHOOL DISCRIM RACE/REL L67

"GOVERNMENT CONTROL OF LAND: PROTECTING THE I-KNOW-IT-WHENI-SEE-IT INTEREST." USA+45 LAW CONSTN DELIB/GP CT/SYS HABITAT ILLINOIS. PAGE 2 F0026 PLAN LOC/G CONTROL ADJUD L67

BARRON J.A.,"ACCESS TO THE PRESS." USA+45 TEC/DEV PRESS TV ADJUD AUD/VIS. PAGE 10 F0196 ORD/FREE COM/IND EDU/PROP LAW L67

BERNHARD R.C.,"COMPETITION IN LAW AND ECONOMICS." LAW PLAN PRICE CONTROL PRODUC PROFIT...METH/CNCPT IDEA/COMP GEN/LAWS 20. PAGE 14 F0265 MARKET POLICY NAT/G CT/SYS L67

BONFIELD A.E.,"THE SUBSTANCE OF AMERICAN FAIR EMPLOYMENT PRACTICES LEGISLA TION II - EMPLOYMENT AGENCIES, LABOR ORGANIZATIONS, ETC." ACT/RES DISCRIM EFFICIENCY. PAGE 16 F0311 LAW WORKER LABOR SERV/IND L67

DEALEY S.,"MONETARY RECOVERY UNDER FEDERAL TRANSPORTATION STATUTES." USA+45 SEA WORKER TAX PAY ADJUD DEATH GOV/REL OWN HEALTH ORD/FREE 20. PAGE 31 F0609 DIST/IND LAW CONTROL FINAN L67

DOERFER G.L.,"THE LIMITS ON TRADE SECRET LAW IMPOSED BY FEDERAL PATENT & ANTITRUST SUPREMACY." USA+45 LAW R+D CAP/ISM LICENSE CONTROL SANCTION ORD/FREE. PAGE 33 F0651 JURID GOV/REL POLICY LEGIT L67

GOLD J.,"INTERPRETATION BY THE INTERNATIONAL MONETARY FUND OF ITS ARTICLES OF AGREEMENT." INT/TRADE ADJUD ATTIT...POLICY JURID. PAGE 48 F0933 CONSTN INT/ORG LAW DIPLOM L67

HUBBARD P.H.,"MONETARY RECOVERY UNDER THE COPYRIGHT, PATENT, AND TRADEMARK ACTS." PROC/MFG TAX PAY LEGIT ADJUD GOV/REL OWN ORD/FREE 20. PAGE 62 F1228 CREATE LAW CONTROL FINAN L67

JACOBY S.B.,"THE 89TH CONGRESS AND GOVERNMENT LITIGATION." USA+45 ADMIN COST...JURID 20 CONGRESS. PAGE 66 F1302 LAW NAT/G ADJUD SANCTION L67

LAMBERT J.D.,"CORPORATE POLITICAL SPENDING AND CAMPAIGN FINANCE." LAW CONSTN FINAN LABOR LG/CO LOC/G NAT/G VOL/ASSN TEC/DEV ADJUD ADMIN PARTIC. PAGE 75 F1463 USA+45 POL/PAR CHOOSE COST L67

LENT G.E.,"TAX INCENTIVES FOR INVESTMENT IN DEVELOPING COUNTRIES" WOR+45 LAW INDUS PLAN BUDGET TARIFFS ADMIN...METH/COMP 20. PAGE 78 F1526 ECO/UNDEV TAX FINAN ECO/TAC L67

MANNE H.G.,"OUR TWO CORPORATION SYSTEMS* LAW AND ECONOMICS." LAW CONTROL SANCTION GP/REL...JURID 20. PAGE 85 F1657 INDUS ELITES CAP/ISM ADMIN L67

MESTMACKER E.J.,"STATE TRADING MONOPOLIES IN THE EUROPEAN ECONOMIC COMMUNITY. DIPLOM ECO/TAC ADJUD CONTROL DISCRIM 20 EEC. PAGE 90 F1764 INT/TRADE INT/ORG LAW TARIFFS L67

MIXON J.,"JANE JACOBS AND THE LAW - ZONING FOR DIVERSITY EXAMINED." FUT USA+45 CONSTN NEIGH PROB/SOLV CONTROL CT/SYS PARTIC ATTIT...POLICY CENSUS METH/COMP MUNICH. PAGE 92 F1810 IDEA/COMP PLAN LAW L67

PARKER G.P. JR.,"MONETARY RECOVERY UNDER THE FEDERAL LABOR STATUTES." USA+45 USA-45 INDUS ADJUD CT/SYS GOV/REL HEALTH ORD/FREE 20 DEPT/LABOR NLRB. PAGE 103 F2027 LABOR CONTROL LAW FINAN L67

ROBERTS E.F.,"THE CASE OF THE UNWARY HOME BUYER: THE HOUSING MERCHANT DID IT." USA+45 CLIENT DIST/IND MARKET LG/CO SML/CO PROB/SOLV LEGIT COST PROFIT. PAGE 112 F2207 ADJUD CONSTRUC OWN LAW L67

SCHNEIDER C.W.,"REFORM OF THE FEDERAL SECURITIES LAWS." FUT USA+45 LAW FINAN INDUS DELIB/GP ACT/RES NAT/G LG/CO

PROB/SOLV GP/REL. PAGE 117 F2304 — ADMIN CONTROL

L67
SEABERG G.P.,"THE DRUG ABUSE PROBLEMS AND SOME PROPOSALS." UK USA+45 MARKET SANCTION CRIME ...POLICY NEW/IDEA. PAGE 119 F2339
BIO/SOC LAW ADJUD PROB/SOLV

L67
STILL C.H.,"MONETARY RECOVERY UNDER THE FAIR LABOR STANDARDS ACT." USA+45 USA-45 WORKER PAY ADJUD GOV/REL HEALTH ORD/FREE...MATH 20 NLRB. PAGE 126 F2487
LABOR CONTROL LAW FINAN

L67
TRAVERS H. JR.,"AN EXAMINATION OF THE CAB'S MERGER POLICY." USA+45 USA-45 LAW NAT/G LEGIS PLAN ADMIN ...DECISION 20 CONGRESS. PAGE 131 F2584
ADJUD LG/CO POLICY DIST/IND

L67
VIA J.W. JR.,"ANTITRUST AND THE AMENDED BANK MERGER AND HOLDING COMPANY ACTS: THE SEARCH FOR STANDARDS." USA+45 CONTROL GP/REL WEALTH SUPREME/CT. PAGE 141 F2783
FINAN CT/SYS LAW EX/STRUC

L67
WATKINS J.B.,"MONETARY RECOVERY UNDER FEDERAL ANTITRUST STATUTES." USA+45 PROB/SOLV ADJUD CT/SYS GOV/REL ORD/FREE 20. PAGE 144 F2831
LG/CO CONTROL LAW FINAN

L67
WHITNEY S.N.,"MERGERS, CONGLOMERATES, AND OLIGOPOLIES* A WIDENING OF ANTI TRUST TARGETS." LAW NAT/G TEC/DEV CAP/ISM GP/REL PWR...OLD/LIB 20. PAGE 146 F2873
ECO/TAC INDUS JURID

L67
WILKINSON J.H. JR.,"THE NET OPERATING LOSS DEDUCTION AND RELATED INCOME TAX DEVICES." PROB/SOLV BUDGET PAY GOV/REL ORD/FREE...MATH CHARTS METH 20. PAGE 146 F2886
TAX FINAN LAW ADJUD

S67
"THE FEDERAL AGRICULTURAL STABILIZATION PROGRAM AND THE NEGRO." LAW CONSTN PLAN REPRESENT DISCRIM ORD/FREE 20 NEGRO CONGRESS. PAGE 2 F0025
AGRI CONTROL NAT/G RACE/REL

S67
"THE SIERRA CLUB, POLITICAL ACTIVITY, AND TAX EXEMPT CHARITABLE STATUS." USA+45 LAW VOL/ASSN TAX PAY ADJUD LOBBY INGP/REL HABITAT 20. PAGE 2 F0027
ELITES GOV/REL FACE/GP ORD/FREE

S67
"ANTITRUST VENUE: TRANSACTING BUSINESS UNDER THE CLAYTON ACT." USA+45 DIST/IND PROB/SOLV ECO/TAC ADJUD CT/SYS 20. PAGE 2 F0028
LAW LG/CO CONTROL NAT/G

S67
"IMPORT-EXPORT CLAUSE: A BLANKET PROHIBITION MISAPPLIED." USA+45 INT/TRADE ADJUD INCOME PWR 20. PAGE 2 F0029
CONSTN TAX PROVS LAW

S67
BARTLETT J.L.,"AMERICAN BOND ISSUES IN THE EUROPEAN ECONOMIC COMMUNITY." EUR+WWI LUXEMBOURG USA+45 DIPLOM CONTROL BAL/PAY EEC. PAGE 11 F0201
LAW ECO/TAC FINAN TAX

S67
BELISLE J.,"FOREIGN RESTRAINTS ON US BANKS ABROAD" WOR+45 LAW. PAGE 12 F0233
DIPLOM FINAN CONTROL LICENSE

S67
BRAUCHER R.,"RECLAMATION OF GOODS FROM A FRAUDULENT BUYER." USA+45 CLIENT FINAN CT/SYS PERS/REL COST WEALTH. PAGE 18 F0341
LAW ADJUD GOV/REL INT/TRADE

S67
BROWN M.B.,"THE TRADE UNION QUESTION." UK INDUS OP/RES PRICE PROFIT 20. PAGE 19 F0371
WORKER LABOR GP/REL LAW

S67
CHADWELL J.T.,"ANTITRUST ASPECTS OF DEALER LICENSING AND FRANCHISING." ACT/RES LICENSE ADJUD CONTROL OWN. PAGE 23 F0439
LAW PRIVIL INDUS

S67
CHAMBERLAIN N.W.,"STRIKES IN CONTEMPORARY CONTEXT." LAW INDUS NAT/G CHIEF CONFER COST ATTIT ORD/FREE ...POLICY MGT 20. PAGE 23 F0442
LABOR BARGAIN EFFICIENCY PROB/SOLV

S67
CLABAULT J.M.,"PRACTICALITIES IN COMPETITOR EXCHANGING PRICE INFORMATION." ECO/DEV PLAN ...CONCPT 20. PAGE 24 F0473
INDUS LAW METH/COMP

S67
DANIEL C.,"THE REGULATION OF PRIVATE ENTERPRISES AS PUBLIC UTILITIES." WOR+45 LAW LICENSE POLICY. PAGE 30 F0577
LOC/G NAT/G CONTROL SERV/IND

S67
DURIEZ P.,"THE IMPACT OF EX PARTE 230 (PIGGYBACKING) ON RAIL-MOTOR COMPETITION." USA+45 USA-45 LG/CO COST EFFICIENCY...CHARTS 20. PAGE 35 F0685
DIST/IND LAW CONTROL AGREE

S67
EDGEWORTH A.B. JR.,"CIVIL RIGHTS PLUS THREE YEARS: BANKS AND THE ANTI-DISCRIMINATION LAW" USA+45 SOCIETY DELIB/GP RACE/REL EFFICIENCY 20 NEGRO CIV/RIGHTS. PAGE 36 F0701
WORKER DISCRIM FINAN LAW

S67
FLOYD D.,"FIFTH AMENDMENT RIGHT TO COUNSEL IN FEDERAL INCOME TAX INVESTIGATIONS." USA+45 LAW OP/RES INGP/REL. PAGE 42 F0818
JURID CT/SYS TAX CONSULT

S67
GANZ G.,"THE CONTROL OF INDUSTRY BY ADMINISTRATIVE PROCESS." UK DELIB/GP WORKER 20. PAGE 46 F0898
INDUS LAW ADMIN CONTROL

S67
GRAYSON D.K.,"RISK ALLOCATIONS UNDER THE PERMITS AND RESPONSIBILITIES CLAUSE OF THE STANDARD GOVERNMENT CONSTRUCTION CONTRACT." USA+45 LAW WORKER. PAGE 50 F0979
CONSTRUC CONTROL RISK NAT/G

S67
HALE G.E.,"EXPANDING ENTERPRISE: GEOGRAPHICAL CURBS ON MERGERS." USA+45 MARKET LG/CO ADJUD CONTROL GP/REL 20. PAGE 53 F1041
LAW HABITAT INDUS EX/STRUC

S67
KENDALL R.J.,"CHANGED CONDITIONS AS MISREPRESENTATION IN GOVERNMENT CONSTRUCTION CONTRACTS." USA+45 BARGAIN ADJUD COST. PAGE 70 F1375
CONTROL CONSTRUC NAT/G LAW

S67
LANDES W.M.,"THE EFFECT OF STATE FAIR EMPLOYMENT LAWS ON THE ECONOMIC POSITION OF NONWHITES." USA+45 PROVS SECT LEGIS ADMIN GP/REL RACE/REL...JURID CONCPT CHARTS HYPO/EXP NEGRO. PAGE 75 F1470
DISCRIM LAW WORKER

S67
MITCHELL J.D.B.,"THE CONSTITUTIONAL IMPLICATIONS OF JUDICIAL CONTROL OF THE ADMINISTRATION IN THE UNITED KINGDOM." UK LAW ADJUD ADMIN GOV/REL ROLE ...GP/COMP 20. PAGE 92 F1808
CONSTN CT/SYS CONTROL EX/STRUC

S67
MODESITT L.E.,"THE MUTUAL FUND - A CORPORATE ANOMALY." USA+45 CONTROL...MGT 20. PAGE 92 F1813
SERV/IND FINAN ADMIN LAW

S67
NEALE R.S.,"WORKING CLASS WOMEN AND WOMEN'S SUFFRAGE." UK LAW CONSTN LABOR NAT/G DELIB/GP LEGIS WORKER PAY PARTIC CHOOSE 19 FEMALE/SEX. PAGE 97 F1906
STRATA SEX SUFF DISCRIM

S67
NILES J.G.,"CIVIL ACTIONS FOR DAMAGES UNDER THE FEDERAL CIVIL RIGHTS STATUTES." CONSTN FINAN ADJUD CT/SYS GOV/REL RACE/REL 20. PAGE 98 F1928
DISCRIM LAW CONTROL ORD/FREE

S67
OLIVIER G.,"ASPECTS JURIDIQUES DE L'ADOPTION DU TRAITE CECA A LA CRISE CHARBONNIERE (SUITE ET FIN)" LAW DIST/IND PLAN DIPLOM RATION PRICE ADMIN COST DEMAND...POLICY CON/ANAL ECSC TREATY. PAGE 101 F1988
INT/TRADE INT/ORG EXTR/IND CONSTN

S67
PEMBERTON J., JR.,"CONSTITUTIONAL PROBLEMS IN RESTRAINT ON THE MEDIA." CONSTN PROB/SOLV EDU/PROP CONFER CONTROL JURID. PAGE 104 F2054
LAW PRESS ORD/FREE

S67
PENNEY N.,"BANK STATEMENTS, CANCELLED CHECKS, AND ARTICLE FOUR IN THE ELECTRONIC AGE." USA+45 TEC/DEV COST EFFICIENCY WEALTH. PAGE 104 F2056
CREATE LAW ADJUD FINAN

S67
PRASOW P.,"THE DEVELOPMENT OF JUDICIAL ARBITRATION IN LABOR-MANAGEMENT DISPUTES." LAW INDUS WORKER GP/REL ROLE...HIST/WRIT 20. PAGE 107 F2113
LABOR BARGAIN ADJUD TREND

S67
RAGAN S.,"THE ABA RECOMMENDATIONS: A NEWSPAPERMAN'S CRITIQUE." EDU/PROP CONTROL GP/REL...JURID ABA. PAGE 109 F2136
LAW PRESS ADJUD ORD/FREE

S67
RAZA M.A.,"EMERGING TRENDS IN PUBLIC LABOR POLICIES AND UNION - GOVERN MENT RELATIONS IN ASIA AND AFRICA." LAW NAT/G POL/PAR COLONIAL COERCE GP/REL ATTIT 20. PAGE 110 F2157
LABOR CONTROL TREND

S67
REILLY T.J.,"FREEZING AND CONFISCATION OF CUBAN PROPERTY." CUBA USA+45 LAW DIPLOM LEGIT ADJUD CONTROL. PAGE 111 F2177
STRANGE OWN ECO/TAC

S67
RONY V.,"HEARTBREAK IN TENNESSEE* POOR WHITES AND
LABOR

THE UNIONS." LAW STRUCT CAP/ISM ADJUD GP/REL. PAGE 113 F2236 LOC/G WORKER PWR

S67
SCHELLING T.C.,"ECONOMICS AND CRIMINAL ENTERPRISE." LAW FORCES BARGAIN ECO/TAC CONTROL GAMBLE ROUTINE ADJUST DEMAND INCOME PROFIT CRIMLGY. PAGE 116 F2295 CRIME PROB/SOLV CONCPT

S67
SCRIPP J.,"CONTROLLING PREJUDICIAL PUBLICITY BY THE CONTEMPT POWER: THE BRITISH PRACTICE AND ITS PROSPECT IN AMERICAN LAW." UK USA+45 EDU/PROP CONTROL GP/REL ORD/FREE JURID. PAGE 119 F2338 METH/COMP LAW PRESS ADJUD

S67
SEIDLER G.L.,"MARXIST LEGAL THOUGHT IN POLAND." POLAND SOCIETY R+D LOC/G NAT/G ACT/RES ADJUD CT/SYS SUPEGO PWR...SOC TREND 20 MARX/KARL. PAGE 119 F2343 MARXISM LAW CONCPT EFFICIENCY

S67
SHISTER J.,"THE DIRECTION OF UNIONISM 1947-1967: THRUST OF DRIFT?" INDUS CENTRAL EFFICIENCY INCOME ATTIT SOCISM...POLICY TREND 20 AFL/CIO. PAGE 121 F2382 LABOR PROF/ORG LEAD LAW

S67
SIMONE A.J.,"SCIENTIFIC PUBLIC POLICY, MARKET PERFORMANCE, AND SIZE OF FIRM." GP/REL COST EFFICIENCY OPTIMAL PRODUC PWR. PAGE 122 F2410 LAW INDUS NAT/G PROB/SOLV

S67
SKILTON R.M.,"PROTECTION OF THE INSTALLMENT BUYER OF GOODS UNDER THE UNIFORM COMMERCIAL CODE." USA+45 NAT/G COST. PAGE 123 F2418 LAW ADJUD LEGIT FINAN

S67
THORKELSON H.,"FOOD STAMPS AND HUNGER IN AMERICA." USA+45 LAW DELIB/GP ADMIN COST DEMAND POLICY. PAGE 130 F2570 WEALTH RECEIVE EATING PLAN

S67
WILES P.J.,"THE POLITICAL AND SOCIAL PREREQUISITES FOR A SOVIET-TYPE ECONOMY." COM USSR LAW CULTURE CREATE ADMIN FEEDBACK ROUTINE COST OPTIMAL TOTALISM MARXISM 20. PAGE 146 F2883 ECO/DEV PLAN EX/STRUC EFFICIENCY

B84
MILL J.,ELEMENTS OF POLITICAL ECONOMY. UK LAW ELITES FINAN WORKER ECO/TAC RENT OWN WEALTH ...POLICY GEN/LAWS 19. PAGE 91 F1785 TAX TARIFFS NAT/G INCOME

B88
BENTHAM J.,DEFENCE OF USURY (1787). UK LAW NAT/G TEC/DEV ECO/TAC CONTROL ATTIT...CONCPT IDEA/COMP 18 SMITH/ADAM. PAGE 13 F0255 TAX FINAN ECO/DEV POLICY

B92
COULANGES F D.E.,THE ORIGIN OF PROPERTY IN LAND. LAW STRATA AGRI ACADEM EDU/PROP ORD/FREE 19. PAGE 28 F0543 OWN HIST/WRIT IDEA/COMP SOCISM

B96
SMITH A.,LECTURES ON JUSTICE, POLICE, REVENUE AND ARMS (1763). UK LAW FAM FORCES TARIFFS AGREE COERCE INCOME OWN WEALTH LAISSEZ...GEN/LAWS 17/18. PAGE 123 F2429 DIPLOM JURID OLD/LIB TAX

LAW/ETHIC....ETHICS OF LAW AND COURT PROCESSES

LAWLEY F.E. F1492,F1493

LAWRENC/TE....THOMAS EDWARD LAWRENCE

LAWRENCE S.A. F1494

LAWSON F.H. F1368

LAWTON F.J. F1495

LAZARUS S. F1496

LAZRSFLD/P....PAUL LAZARSFELD (AND LAZARSFELD SCALE)

LAZUTKIN Y. F1497

LEAD....LEADING, CONTRIBUTING MORE THAN AVERAGE

B
BRITISH COMMONWEALTH BUR AGRI,WORLD AGRICULTURAL ECONOMICS AND RURAL SOCIOLOGY ABSTRACTS. NAT/G OP/RES PLAN TEC/DEV LEAD PRODUC...GEOG MGT NAT/COMP 20. PAGE 18 F0354 BIBLIOG/A AGRI SOC WORKER

N
LONDON TIMES OFFICIAL INDEX. UK LAW ECO/DEV NAT/G DIPLOM LEAD ATTIT 20. PAGE 1 F0006 BIBLIOG INDEX PRESS WRITING

N
DEUTSCHE BUCHEREI,DEUTSCHES BUCHERVERZEICHNIS. GERMANY LAW CULTURE POL/PAR ADMIN LEAD ATTIT PERSON ...SOC 20. PAGE 32 F0626 BIBLIOG NAT/G DIPLOM ECO/DEV

B14
LEVINE L.,SYNDICALISM IN FRANCE (2ND ED.). FRANCE LAW SOCIETY ECO/DEV NAT/G ECO/TAC LEAD ATTIT ...POLICY CONCPT STAT BIBLIOG 18/20 REFORMERS. PAGE 79 F1542 LABOR INDUS SOCISM REV

N19
MARSH J.F. JR.,THE FBI RETIREMENT BILL (PAMPHLET). USA+45 EX/STRUC WORKER PLAN PROB/SOLV BUDGET LEAD LOBBY PARL/PROC PERS/REL RIGID/FLEX...POLICY 20 FBI PRESIDENT BUR/BUDGET. PAGE 86 F1677 ADMIN NAT/G SENIOR GOV/REL

N19
SILVERMAN C.,THE PRESIDENT'S ECONOMIC ADVISERS (PAMPHLET). USA+45 LAW ELITES ECO/DEV EX/STRUC ADMIN LEAD GOV/REL PERS/REL ROLE...POLICY DECISION 20 PRESIDENT CONGRESS EISNHWR/DD. PAGE 122 F2404 CONSULT PROB/SOLV NAT/G PLAN

S21
MALINOWSKI B.,"THE PRIMITIVE ECONOMICS OF THE TROBRIAND ISLANDERS" (BMR)" CULTURE SOCIETY NAT/G CHIEF LEAD OWN...SOC MYTH WORSHIP 20 NEW/GUINEA TROBRIAND RESOURCE/N. PAGE 84 F1647 ECO/UNDEV AGRI PRODUC STRUCT

B27
BELLOC H.,THE SERVILE STATE (1912) (3RD ED.). PRUSSIA UK CULTURE STRATA INDUS NAT/G ECO/TAC CONTROL LEAD SUFF DISCRIM EQUILIB ORD/FREE WEALTH 20. PAGE 12 F0237 WORKER CAP/ISM DOMIN CATH

B28
HARDMAN J.B.,AMERICAN LABOR DYNAMICS. WORKER ECO/TAC DOMIN ADJUD LEAD LOBBY PWR...POLICY MGT. PAGE 55 F1079 LABOR INGP/REL ATTIT GP/REL

S30
CRAWFORD F.G.,"THE EXECUTIVE BUDGET DECISION IN NEW YORK." LEGIS EXEC PWR NEW/YORK. PAGE 28 F0552 LEAD BUDGET PROVS PROB/SOLV

S32
DODD E.M. JR.,"FOR WHOM ARE CORPORATE MANAGERS TRUSTEES'." SERV/IND CAP/ISM GIVE LEAD REPRESENT ORD/FREE WEALTH. PAGE 33 F0648 LG/CO ROLE NAT/G PLAN

B38
HARPER S.N.,THE GOVERNMENT OF THE SOVIET UNION. COM USSR LAW CONSTN ECO/DEV PLAN TEC/DEV DIPLOM INT/TRADE ADMIN REV NAT/LISM...POLICY 20. PAGE 55 F1085 MARXISM NAT/G LEAD POL/PAR

B38
LEVINSON E.,LABOR ON THE MARCH. WORKER CREATE ECO/TAC ADJUD LEAD PARL/PROC PARTIC INGP/REL SKILL POLICY. PAGE 79 F1543 LABOR INCOME NAT/G PLAN

B39
JENNINGS W.I.,PARLIAMENT. UK POL/PAR OP/RES BUDGET LEAD CHOOSE GP/REL...MGT 20 PARLIAMENT HOUSE/LORD HOUSE/CMNS. PAGE 67 F1315 PARL/PROC LEGIS CONSTN NAT/G

B39
THOMAS J.A.,THE HOUSE OF COMMONS, 1832-1901; A STUDY OF ITS ECONOMIC AND FUNCTIONAL CHARACTER. UK LAW STRATA FINAN DIPLOM CONTROL LEAD LOBBY REPRESENT WEALTH...POLICY STAT BIBLIOG 19/20 PARLIAMENT. PAGE 130 F2561 PARL/PROC LEGIS POL/PAR ECO/DEV

B40
BATCHELOR B.,THE NEW OUTLOOK IN BUSINESS. LAW WORKER TAX LEAD ORD/FREE...POLICY TREND. PAGE 11 F0208 LG/CO GP/REL CAP/ISM LABOR

B40
HUNTER R.,REVOLUTION: WHY, HOW, WHEN? NAT/G ECO/TAC EDU/PROP COERCE ORD/FREE FASCISM POPULISM SOCISM 18/20 HITLER/A LENIN/VI. PAGE 63 F1246 REV METH/COMP LEAD CONSTN

B44
BIENSTOCK G.,MANAGEMENT IN RUSSIAN INDUSTRY AND AGRICULTURE. USSR CONSULT WORKER LEAD COST PROFIT ATTIT DRIVE PWR...MGT METH/COMP DICTIONARY ACCT 20. PAGE 15 F0281 ADMIN MARXISM SML/CO AGRI

S45
MILLS C.W.,"THE TRADE UNION LEADER: A COLLECTIVE PORTRAIT." EX/STRUC TOP/EX INGP/REL...QU CON/ANAL CHARTS. PAGE 92 F1798 LABOR LEAD STAT STRATA

B46
DRUCKER P.F.,CONCEPT OF CORPORATION. LAW LABOR WORKER PRICE CONTROL LEAD GP/REL POLICY. PAGE 34 F0665 LG/CO CENTRAL INGP/REL

B47
MILLETT J.D.,THE PROCESS AND ORGANIZATION OF GOVERNMENT PLANNING. USA+45 DELIB/GP ACT/RES LEAD LOBBY TASK...POLICY GEOG TIME 20 RESOURCE/N. PAGE 91 F1793 ADMIN NAT/G PLAN CONSULT

B47
SLICHTER S.H.,THE CHALLENGE OF INDUSTRIAL RELATIONS: TRADE UNIONS, MANAGEMENT AND THE PUBLIC INTEREST. PLAN ECO/TAC ADJUD CONTROL LEAD SANCTION LABOR MGT CLIENT

GP/REL INGP/REL INCOME. PAGE 123 F2421 — POLICY

B47 WEBER M.,THE THEORY OF SOCIAL AND ECONOMIC ORGANIZATION. STRUCT LABOR POL/PAR ECO/TAC LEGIT PRODUC BIOG. PAGE 144 F2840 — ECO/DEV SOC PHIL/SCI LEAD

B47 WHITEHEAD T.N.,LEADERSHIP IN A FREE SOCIETY; A STUDY IN HUMAN RELATIONS BASED ON AN ANALYSIS OF PRESENT-DAY INDUSTRIAL CIVILIZATION. WOR-45 STRUCT R+D LABOR LG/CO SML/CO WORKER PLAN PROB/SOLV TEC/DEV DRIVE...MGT 20. PAGE 146 F2872 — INDUS LEAD ORD/FREE SOCIETY

B48 KILE O.M.,THE FARM BUREAU MOVEMENT: THE FARM BUREAU THROUGH THREE DECADES. NAT/G LEGIS LEAD LOBBY GP/REL INCOME POLICY. PAGE 71 F1387 — AGRI STRUCT VOL/ASSN DOMIN

B48 MILLS C.W.,THE NEW MEN OF POWER. ELITES INTELL STRUCT WORKER ANOMIE ATTIT PWR POLICY. PAGE 92 F1799 — LABOR LEAD PLAN

S48 CLEVELAND A.S.,"NAM: SPOKESMAN FOR INDUSTRY?" LEGIS PLAN LEAD LOBBY PARTIC CONSEN INCOME ATTIT ROLE ORD/FREE POLICY. PAGE 25 F0491 — VOL/ASSN CLIENT REPRESENT INDUS

S48 HARDIN L.M.,"REFLECTIONS ON AGRICULTURAL POLICY FORMATION IN THE UNITED STATES." LEGIS PLAN BUDGET ECO/TAC LEAD CENTRAL...MGT SOC NEW/IDEA STAT FAO. PAGE 55 F1078 — AGRI POLICY ADMIN NEW/LIB

B49 LEE A.M.,SOCIAL PROBLEMS IN AMERICA: A SOURCE BOOK. STRATA STRUCT KIN NEIGH VOL/ASSN ACT/RES LEAD CRIME AGE SEX 20. PAGE 77 F1504 — SOC SOCIETY PERSON EDU/PROP

S49 HART C.W.M.,"INDUSTRIAL RELATIONS RESEARCH AND SOCIAL THEORY." CANADA VOL/ASSN WORKER LEAD EFFICIENCY...MGT SOC METH/CNCPT METH/COMP MUNICH 20. PAGE 56 F1099 — GEN/LAWS LABOR GP/REL

S49 SHEPHARD H.A.,"DEMOCRATIC CONTROL IN A LABOR UNION." FUT CONSTN STRUCT TEC/DEV LEAD PARTIC RACE/REL CENTRAL DRIVE HABITAT RECORD. PAGE 120 F2374 — LABOR MAJORIT CONTROL PWR

B51 HARDMAN J.B.,THE HOUSE OF LABOR. LAW R+D NEIGH EDU/PROP LEAD ROUTINE REPRESENT GP/REL...POLICY STAT. PAGE 55 F1080 — LABOR LOBBY ADMIN PRESS

B51 US LIBRARY OF CONGRESS,EAST EUROPEAN ACCESSIONS LIST (VOL. I). POL/PAR DIPLOM ADMIN LEAD 20. PAGE 138 F2715 — BIBLIOG/A COM SOCIETY NAT/G

B52 MACARTHUR D.,REVITALIZING A NATION. ASIA COM FUT KOREA WOR+45 NAT/G FOR/AID TAX GIVE WAR ATTIT SOCISM 20 CHINJAP EUROPE. PAGE 83 F1619 — LEAD FORCES TOP/EX POLICY

S52 KORNHAUSER W.,"THE NEGRO UNION OFFICIAL: A STUDY OF SPONSORSHIP AND CONTROL" (BMR)" USA+45 CONTROL DISCRIM ROLE SUPEGO...OBS 20 NEGRO. PAGE 73 F1428 — LABOR LEAD RACE/REL CHOOSE

B53 DAHL R.A.,POLITICS, ECONOMICS, AND WELFARE. TEC/DEV BARGAIN ECO/TAC RECEIVE PRICE CONTROL LEAD INGP/REL ...POLICY GEN/LAWS. PAGE 29 F0572 — SOCIETY GIVE

B53 MIT CENTER INTERNATIONAL STU,BIBLIOGRAPHY OF THE ECONOMIC AND POLITICAL DEVELOPMENT OF INDONESIA. INDONESIA STRUCT NAT/G COLONIAL LEAD...STAT 20. PAGE 92 F1805 — BIBLIOG ECO/UNDEV TEC/DEV S/ASIA

B53 PURCELL T.V.,THE WORKER SPEAKS HIS MIND ON COMPANY AND UNION. WORKER ADJUD LEAD RACE/REL ATTIT DRIVE MARXISM...MGT CLASSIF STAT OBS INT SAMP BIBLIOG. PAGE 108 F2131 — LABOR PARTIC INGP/REL HAPPINESS

B53 SAYLES L.R.,THE LOCAL UNION. CONSTN CULTURE DELIB/GP PARTIC CHOOSE GP/REL INGP/REL ATTIT ROLE ...MAJORIT DECISION MGT. PAGE 116 F2284 — LABOR LEAD ADJUD ROUTINE

S53 BERNSTEIN M.H.,"POLITICAL IDEAS OF SELECTED AMERICAN BUSINESS JOURNALS (BMR)" USA+45 GP/REL ATTIT RIGID/FLEX ROLE ORD/FREE POLICY. PAGE 14 F0267 — IDEA/COMP NAT/G LEAD

S53 MCKEE J.B.,"STATUS AND POWER IN THE INDUSTRIAL COMMUNITY; A COMMENT ON DRUCKER'S THESIS." LABOR LEGIT LEAD GP/REL PWR...MGT CONCPT. PAGE 88 F1730 — SOC STRATA NEIGH PARTIC

B54 CHILDS M.W.,ETHICS IN A BUSINESS SOCIETY. PROF/ORG LEAD WAR GP/REL ATTIT DRIVE PERSON KNOWL MORAL PWR ...WELF/ST BIBLIOG. PAGE 24 F0466 — MGT SOCIETY

B54 MEYER A.G.,MARXISM. INTELL ECO/DEV WORKER CAP/ISM LEAD WAR ATTIT ALL/IDEOS...SOC 19/20 MARX/KARL. PAGE 90 F1766 — MARXISM CONCPT ECO/TAC STRUCT

B56 BARBASH J.,THE PRACTICE OF UNIONISM. ECO/TAC LEAD LOBBY GP/REL INGP/REL DRIVE MARXISM BIBLIOG. PAGE 10 F0182 — LABOR REPRESENT CONTROL ADMIN

B56 KNORR K.E.,RUBLE DIPLOMACY: CHALLENGE TO AMERICAN FOREIGN AID(PAMPHLET). AFR CHINA/COM USA+45 USSR PLAN TEC/DEV CAP/ISM INT/TRADE DOMIN EDU/PROP CONTROL LEAD 20. PAGE 72 F1413 — ECO/UNDEV COM DIPLOM FOR/AID

B56 LIPSET S.M.,UNION DEMOCRACY. STRUCT INDUS FACE/GP WORKER CONTROL LEAD PARTIC GP/REL ATTIT LAISSEZ ...INT QU CHARTS. PAGE 80 F1577 — LABOR INGP/REL MAJORIT

B56 UNITED NATIONS,BIBLIOGRAPHY ON INDUSTRIALIZATION IN UNDER-DEVELOPED COUNTRIES. WOR+45 R+D INT/ORG NAT/G FOR/AID ADMIN LEAD 20 UN. PAGE 132 F2612 — BIBLIOG ECO/UNDEV INDUS TEC/DEV

B56 UPHOFF W.H.,UNDERSTANDING THE UNION MEMBER (PAMPHLET). STRATA R+D LEAD PARTIC...METH/CNCPT STAT QU. PAGE 133 F2624 — LABOR WORKER ATTIT DRIVE

B56 WEBER M.,WIRTSCHAFT UND GESELLSCHAFT (2ND VOL.). STRUCT NAT/G POL/PAR LEAD PWR OBJECTIVE IDEA/COMP. PAGE 144 F2841 — LEGIT JURID SOC

B56 WILCOX W.W.,SOCIAL RESPONSIBILITY IN FARM LEADERSHIP. CLIENT LEGIS EXEC LOBBY GP/REL ATTIT WEALTH. PAGE 146 F2880 — AGRI LEAD VOL/ASSN WORKER

L56 TAGLIACOZZO D.L.,"TRADE-UNION GOVERNMENT, ITS NATURE AND ITS PROBLEMS: A BIBLIOGRAPHICAL REVIEW, 1945-1955." STRUCT LEAD PARTIC CHOOSE ATTIT ...MAJORIT METH/CNCPT BIBLIOG. PAGE 128 F2526 — CLASSIF LABOR INGP/REL GP/REL

S56 MERRIAM R.E.,"THE BUREAU OF THE BUDGET AS PART OF THE PRESIDENT'S STAFF." 20 BUR/BUDGET 20 BOB. PAGE 90 F1763 — CHIEF CONTROL LEAD EXEC

S56 TANNENBAUM A.S.,"CONTROL OF STRUCTURE AND UNION FUNCTIONS." PARTIC GP/REL INGP/REL CONSEN ATTIT PWR ...QU SAMP. PAGE 128 F2529 — LABOR STRUCT CONTROL LEAD

C56 MCKEE J.B.,"THE POWER TO DECIDE" IN M. WEINBERG AND O. SHABET, SOCIETY AND MAN." ELITES STRATA REPRESENT GP/REL ATTIT PWR MUNICH BUSINESS. PAGE 88 F1731 — LABOR DECISION LEAD

S57 KAHN R.L.,"UNION PRACTICES AND MEMBER PARTICIPATION." PARTIC CHOOSE REPRESENT PERS/REL PERSON SKILL...DECISION METH/CNCPT QU. PAGE 69 F1347 — INGP/REL LABOR ATTIT LEAD

B58 LESTER R.A.,AS UNIONS MATURE. POL/PAR BARGAIN LEAD PARTIC GP/REL CENTRAL...MAJORIT TIME/SEQ METH/COMP. PAGE 78 F1533 — LABOR INDUS POLICY MGT

B58 MOONEY R.E.,INFLATION AND RECESSION? AFR USA+45 LABOR LG/CO PRESS LEAD...IDEA/COMP ANTHOL 20. PAGE 93 F1821 — PRICE ECO/TAC NAT/G PRODUC

B58 PAN AMERICAN UNION,REPERTORIO DE PUBLICACIONES PERIODICAS ACTUALES LATINO-AMERICANAS. CULTURE ECO/UNDEV ADMIN LEAD GOV/REL 20 OAS. PAGE 103 F2023 — BIBLIOG L/A+17C NAT/G DIPLOM

B58 TANNENBAUM A.S.,PARTICIPATION IN UNION LOCALS. SOCIETY FINAN CONTROL LEAD GP/REL...BIBLIOG 20. PAGE 128 F2531 — LABOR MGT PARTIC INGP/REL

S58 LOCKWOOD W.W.,"THE SOCIALISTIC SOCIETY: INDIA AND JAPAN." INDIA ECO/DEV ECO/UNDEV INDUS NAT/G CONTROL LEAD PRODUC WEALTH 20 CHINJAP. PAGE 81 F1593 — ECO/TAC NAT/COMP FINAN SOCISM

B59 BARBASH J.,UNIONS AND UNION LEADERSHIP. NAT/G WORKER TEC/DEV ECO/TAC PARTIC GP/REL RACE/REL ORD/FREE CLASSIF. PAGE 10 F0183 — LABOR VOL/ASSN CAP/ISM

LEAD

B59
HENDEL S.,THE SOVIET CRUCIBLE. USSR LEAD COERCE NAT/LISM UTOPIA PWR...POLICY CONCPT ANTHOL 20 STALIN/J LENIN/VI MARX/KARL BOLSHEVIK. PAGE 58 F1147
COM MARXISM REV TOTALISM

B59
LEISERSON W.,AMERICAN TRADE UNION DEMOCRACY. CONSTN STRUCT ADJUD EXEC REPRESENT GP/REL INGP/REL MAJORITY ATTIT PWR. PAGE 77 F1516
LABOR LEAD PARTIC DELIB/GP

B59
WORTHY J.C.,BIG BUSINESS AND FREE MEN. LG/CO EX/STRUC EDU/PROP LEAD CHOOSE GP/REL ATTIT DRIVE ROLE ORD/FREE...MAJORIT 20. PAGE 149 F2927
ELITES LOC/G TOP/EX PARTIC

B60
FERNANDES F.,MUDANCAS SOCIAIS NO BRASIL. BRAZIL L/A+17C SOCIETY AGRI PROVS LEAD GP/REL RACE/REL ORD/FREE...SOC SOC/INTEG 20 SAO/PAULO. PAGE 40 F0786
ECO/UNDEV STRATA INDUS

B60
ILLINOIS U BUR COMMUNITY PLAN,PROCEEDINGS OF ILLINOIS STATEWIDE PLANNING CONFERENCE 1960. USA+45 FINAN LOC/G ACT/RES LEAD GOV/REL GP/REL WEALTH MUNICH 20 ILLINOIS. PAGE 64 F1260
PLAN DELIB/GP VOL/ASSN

B60
VERNON R.,METROPOLIS 1985. LOC/G PLAN TAX LEAD PWR MUNICH. PAGE 141 F2780
REGION ECO/TAC DECISION

B60
WHEARE K.C.,THE CONSTITUTIONAL STRUCTURE OF THE COMMONWEALTH. UK EX/STRUC DIPLOM DOMIN ADMIN COLONIAL CONTROL LEAD INGP/REL SUPEGO 20 CMN/WLTH. PAGE 145 F2865
CONSTN INT/ORG VOL/ASSN SOVEREIGN

S60
FORM W.H.,"ORGANIZED LABOR'S IMAGE OF COMMUNITY POWER STRUCTURE." LABOR LG/CO CONTROL LEAD REPRESENT...DECISION METH/CNCPT INT QU SAMP. PAGE 42 F0829
NEIGH PARTIC PWR GP/REL

S60
FRENCH J.R.P. JR.,"AN EXPERIMENT ON PARTICIPATION IN A NORWEGIAN FACTORY:INTERPERSONAL DIMENSIONS OF DECISION-MAKING." LABOR LEAD PERS/REL EFFICIENCY PRODUC...DECISION SOC CHARTS SOC/EXP. PAGE 44 F0853
INDUS PLAN RIGID/FLEX GP/REL

B61
BARBASH J.,LABOR'S GRASS ROOTS. CONSTN NAT/G EX/STRUC LEGIS WORKER LEAD...MAJORIT BIBLIOG. PAGE 10 F0184
LABOR INGP/REL GP/REL LAW

B61
BARRASH J.,LABOR'S GRASS ROOTS; A STUDY OF THE LOCAL UNION. STRATA BARGAIN LEAD REPRESENT DEMAND ATTIT PWR. PAGE 10 F0192
LABOR USA+45 INGP/REL EXEC

B61
DELEFORTRIE-SOU N.,LES DIRIGEANTS DE L'INDUSTRIE FRANCAISE. FRANCE CULTURE ELITES PROB/SOLV ...DECISION STAT CHARTS 20. PAGE 32 F0613
INDUS STRATA TOP/EX LEAD

B61
ESTEVEZ A.,ASPECTOS ECONOMICO-FINANCIEROS DE LA CAMPANA SANMARITANA. L/A+17C SPAIN FINAN COLONIAL LEAD ROLE ORD/FREE WEALTH 19 SOUTH/AMER SAN/MARTIN. PAGE 38 F0748
ECO/UNDEV REV BUDGET NAT/G

B61
GORDON R.A.,BUSINESS LEADERSHIP IN THE LARGE CORPORATION. USA+45 SOCIETY EX/STRUC ADMIN CONTROL ROUTINE GP/REL PWR...MGT 20. PAGE 49 F0960
LG/CO LEAD DECISION LOBBY

B61
HUBBARD P.J.,ORIGINS OF THE TVA: THE MUSCLE SHOALS CONTROVERSY, 1920-1932. USA-45 DELIB/GP LEGIS LEAD LOBBY GOV/REL GP/REL INGP/REL OWN PERSON...BIBLIOG 20 TVA CONGRESS WATER. PAGE 62 F1229
SEA CONTROL NAT/G INDUS

S61
REAGAN M.O.,"THE POLITICAL STRUCTURE OF THE FEDERAL RESERVE SYSTEM." USA+45 FINAN NAT/G ADMIN 20. PAGE 110 F2163
PWR EX/STRUC EXEC LEAD

B62
BRANCH M.C.,THE CORPORATE PLANNING PROCESS. FINAN EX/STRUC EDU/PROP CONTROL LEAD GP/REL PERS/REL RATIONAL PERCEPT...MGT MATH PROBABIL STAT GAME. PAGE 18 F0338
PROF/ORG PLAN DECISION PERSON

B62
COX O.C.,CAPITALISM AND AMERICAN LEADERSHIP. WOR+45 WOR-45 STRATA INDUS SECT INT/TRADE EXEC INGP/REL RACE/REL RATIONAL PWR WEALTH. PAGE 28 F0548
CAP/ISM LEAD ECO/DEV SOCIETY

B62
GALENSON W.,TRADE UNIONS MONOGRAPH SERIES (A SERIES OF NINE TEXTS). DELIB/GP LEAD PARTIC...DECISION ORG/CHARTS. PAGE 45 F0887
LABOR INGP/REL CONSTN REPRESENT

B62
HARRINGTON M.,THE RETAIL CLERKS. ECO/TAC LEAD PARTIC CHOOSE GP/REL INGP/REL CENTRAL POLICY. PAGE 55 F1087
LABOR SERV/IND STRUCT DELIB/GP

B62
KIRPICEVA I.K.,HANDBUCH DER RUSSISCHEN UND SOWJETISCHEN BIBLIOGRAPHIEN (5 VOLS.). USSR STRUCT ECO/DEV DIPLOM LEAD ATTIT 18/20. PAGE 71 F1400
BIBLIOG/A NAT/G MARXISM COM

B62
MOWITZ R.J.,PROFILE OF A METROPOLIS: A CASE BOOK. COM/IND CONSTRUC INDUS PUB/INST PLAN TEC/DEV LEAD GP/REL...POLICY TECHNIC WELF/ST MUNICH. PAGE 94 F1851
DECISION ADMIN

B62
SHERIF M.,INTERGROUP RELATIONS AND LEADERSHIP: APPROACHES AND RESEARCH IN INDUSTRIAL, ETHNIC, CULTURAL AND POLITICAL AREAS. CULTURE R+D LABOR DIPLOM GP/REL RACE/REL PERCEPT...PSY CONCPT. PAGE 121 F2377
LEAD REPRESENT PWR INGP/REL

B62
SMITH G.A. JR.,POLICY FORMULATION AND ADMINISTRATION: A CASEBOOK OF TOPMANAGEMENT PROBLEMS IN BUSINESS. EX/STRUC PLAN PROB/SOLV ADMIN CONTROL EXEC LEAD ROUTINE EFFICIENCY ATTIT MGT. PAGE 123 F2430
INDUS SOC/EXP TOP/EX DECISION

B62
TIEBOUT C.M.,THE COMMUNITY ECONOMIC BASE STUDY (PAMPHLET). USA+45 ECO/TAC LEAD DEMAND HABITAT 20. PAGE 130 F2572
NEIGH INCOME ACT/RES

N62
US SENATE COMM ON JUDICIARY,LEGISLATION TO STRENGTHEN PENALTIES UNDER THE ANTITRUST LAWS (PAMPHLET). USA+45 LG/CO CONFER CONTROL SANCTION ORD/FREE 20 SENATE MONOPOLY. PAGE 139 F2748
LEAD ADJUD INDUS ECO/TAC

B63
CALKINS R.D.,ECONOMICS AS AN AID TO POLICY (PAMPHLET). USA+45 NAT/G LEAD 20. PAGE 21 F0401
CONSULT DECISION EFFICIENCY

B63
CHAMPION J.M.,CRITICAL INCIDENTS IN MANAGEMENT. MARKET LG/CO SML/CO OP/RES ADMIN CONTROL LEAD GP/REL PERS/REL COST ATTIT SUPEGO ALL/VALS...PSY PERS/TEST BIBLIOG. PAGE 23 F0445
MGT DECISION EX/STRUC INDUS

B63
GAMBLE S.D.,NORTH CHINA VILLAGES: SOCIAL, POLITICAL, AND ECONOMIC ACTIVITIES BEFORE 1933. ASIA CULTURE STRUCT FAM DOMIN EDU/PROP MUNICH WORSHIP 20. PAGE 46 F0891
AGRI LEAD FINAN

B63
IANNI O.,INDUSTRIALIZACAO E DESENVOLVIMENTO SOCIAL NO BRASIL. BRAZIL L/A+17C STRATA STRUCT ECO/UNDEV EDU/PROP LEAD LOBBY NAT/LISM 20. PAGE 64 F1257
WORKER GP/REL INDUS PARTIC

B63
MENEZES A.J.,SUBDESENVOLVIMENTO E POLITICA INTERNACIONAL. BRAZIL WOR+45 PLAN CONTROL LEAD NAT/LISM ORD/FREE 20 THIRD/WRLD. PAGE 90 F1759
ECO/UNDEV DIPLOM POLICY BAL/PWR

B63
SMITH R.A.,CORPORATIONS IN CRISIS. USA+45 LG/CO EX/STRUC ECO/TAC CONTROL LEAD PERS/REL...MGT 20. PAGE 123 F2432
ELITES INDUS PROB/SOLV METH/COMP

N63
COMMITTEE ECONOMIC DEVELOPMENT,TAXES AND TRADE: 20 YEARS OF CED POLICY (PAMPHLET). USA+45 ECO/DEV PLAN BUDGET LEAD...POLICY KENNEDY/JF PRESIDENT. PAGE 27 F0518
FINAN ECO/TAC NAT/G DELIB/GP

B64
HAMBRIDGE G.,DYNAMICS OF DEVELOPMENT. AGRI FINAN INDUS LABOR INT/TRADE EDU/PROP ADMIN LEAD OWN HEALTH...ANTHOL BIBLIOG 20. PAGE 54 F1054
ECO/UNDEV ECO/TAC OP/RES ACT/RES

B64
IMAZ J.L.,LOS QUE MANDAN. INDUS LABOR NAT/G POL/PAR PROVS SECT CHIEF TOP/EX CONTROL 20 ARGEN. PAGE 64 F1261
LEAD FORCES ELITES ATTIT

S64
CLELLAND D.A.,"ECONOMIC DOMINANTS AND COMMUNITY POWER: A COMPARATIVE ANALYSIS." ELITES ADJUST ATTIT WEALTH...DECISION MUNICH. PAGE 25 F0488
LEAD MGT PWR

B65
CERNY K.H.,NATO IN QUEST OF COHESION* A CONFRONTATION OF VIEWPOINTS. COM EUR+WWI USA+45 FORCES LEAD REGION DETER...ANTHOL NATO. PAGE 22 F0438
CENTRAL NUC/PWR VOL/ASSN

B65
DANIELSON M.N.,FEDERAL-METROPOLITAN POLITICS AND THE COMMUTER CRISIS. PROVS LEGIS EXEC LEAD PWR ...DECISION MUNICH. PAGE 30 F0580
FEDERAL GOV/REL DIST/IND

B65
GOODSELL C.T.,ADMINISTRATION OF A REVOLUTION. PUERT/RICO ECO/UNDEV FINAN POL/PAR PROVS LEGIS PLAN
EXEC SOC

BUDGET RECEIVE ADMIN COLONIAL LEAD MUNICH 20 ROOSEVLT/F. PAGE 49 F0951

B65
HADWIGER D.F.,PRESSURES AND PROTEST. NAT/G LEGIS PLAN LEAD PARTIC ROUTINE ATTIT POLICY. PAGE 53 F1030
AGRI GP/REL LOBBY CHOOSE

B65
PARRIS H.W.,GOVERNMENT AND THE RAILWAYS IN NINETEENTH-CENTURY BRITAIN. UK DELIB/GP CONTROL LEAD CENTRAL 19 RAILROAD. PAGE 103 F2029
DIST/IND NAT/G PLAN GP/REL

B65
PAYNE J.L.,LABOR AND POLITICS IN PERU; THE SYSTEM OF POLITICAL BARGAINING. PERU CONSTN VOL/ASSN EX/STRUC LEAD PWR...CHARTS 20. PAGE 104 F2042
LABOR POL/PAR BARGAIN GP/REL

B65
ROSS P.,THE GOVERNMENT AS A SOURCE OF UNION POWER. USA+45 LAW ECO/DEV PROB/SOLV ECO/TAC LEAD GP/REL ...MGT 20. PAGE 114 F2245
LABOR BARGAIN POLICY NAT/G

S65
BANOVETZ J.M.,"METROPOLITAN SUBSIDIES: AN APPRAISAL." LEAD GP/REL DISCRIM MUNICH. PAGE 9 F0175
REGION TAX GOV/REL

S65
HADDAD W.F.,"MR. SHRIVER AND THE SAVAGE POLITICS OF POVERTY" USA+45 LAW NAT/G DELIB/GP LEGIS GIVE LEAD CENTRAL PWR...SOC/WK CHARTS 20 CONGRESS POVRTY/WAR SHRIVER/S OEO. PAGE 53 F1028
WEALTH GOV/REL CONTROL TOP/EX

B66
BAKLANOFF E.N.,NEW PERSPECTIVES ON BRAZIL. BRAZIL SOCIETY INDUS DOMIN LEAD REV CIVMIL/REL...GEOG PSY LING ANTHOL 20. PAGE 8 F0156
ECO/UNDEV TEC/DEV DIPLOM ORD/FREE

B66
BROEKMEIJER M.W.J.,FICTION AND TRUTH ABOUT THE "DECADE OF DEVELOPMENT" WOR+45 AGRI FINAN INDUS NAT/G TEC/DEV DIPLOM EDU/PROP LEAD SKILL 20 THIRD/WRLD. PAGE 19 F0358
FOR/AID POLICY ECO/UNDEV PLAN

B66
CANNING HOUSE LIBRARY,AUTHOR AND SUBJECT CATALOGUES OF THE CANNING HOUSE LIBRARY (5 VOLS.). UK CULTURE LEAD...SOC 19/20. PAGE 21 F0411
BIBLIOG L/A+17C NAT/G DIPLOM

B66
COLE A.B.,SOCIALIST PARTIES IN POSTWAR JAPAN. STRATA AGRI LABOR PLAN DIPLOM ECO/TAC AGREE LEAD CHOOSE ATTIT...CHARTS 20 CHINJAP SOC/DEMPAR. PAGE 26 F0499
POL/PAR POLICY SOCISM NAT/G

B66
FRANKEL P.H.,MATTEI; OIL AND POWER POLITICS. ITALY EXTR/IND MARKET GP/REL NAT/LISM SOCISM...POLICY MGT BIOG 20 MATTEI/E. PAGE 43 F0844
LEAD NAT/G CONTROL LG/CO

B66
WILLIAMS G.,MERTHYR POLITICS: THE MAKING OF A WORKING-CLASS TRADITION. UK CHIEF WORKER LEAD SOCISM...ANTHOL MUNICH 19/20 MERTHYR RICHARD/H. PAGE 147 F2891
LOC/G POL/PAR INDUS

B66
WOODMAN H.D.,SLAVERY AND THE SOUTHERN ECONOMY: SOURCES AND READINGS. USA-45 CULTURE STRUCT AGRI ECO/TAC LEAD RACE/REL DISCRIM EFFICIENCY...CHARTS ANTHOL MUNICH 18/19 NEGRO SOUTH/US. PAGE 148 F2922
ECO/DEV STRATA WORKER UTIL

B67
BIBBY J.,ON CAPITOL HILL. POL/PAR LOBBY PARL/PROC GOV/REL PERS/REL...JURID PHIL/SCI OBS INT BIBLIOG 20 CONGRESS PRESIDENT. PAGE 15 F0278
CONFER LEGIS CREATE LEAD

B67
COWLING M.,1867 DISRAELI, GLADSTONE, AND REVOLUTION; THE PASSING OF THE SECOND REFORM BILL. UK LEGIS LEAD LOBBY GP/REL INGP/REL...DECISION BIBLIOG 19 REFORMERS. PAGE 28 F0545
PARL/PROC POL/PAR ATTIT LAW

B67
FANON F.,TOWARD THE AFRICAN REVOLUTION. AFR FRANCE CULTURE ELITES LEAD REV GP/REL ORD/FREE SOVEREIGN 20. PAGE 39 F0762
COLONIAL DOMIN ECO/UNDEV RACE/REL

B67
GIAP V.N.,BIG VICTORY, GREAT TASK. VIETNAM WOR+45 FORCES PLAN DOMIN LEGIT RISK PEACE 20. PAGE 47 F0921
WAR LEAD ATTIT INSPECT

B67
GOODMAN J.S.,THE DEMOCRATS AND LABOR IN RHODE ISLAND 9152-1962; CHANGES IN THE OLD ALLIANCE. USA+45 EDU/PROP LEAD GP/REL ROLE RHODE/ISL DEMOCRAT. PAGE 49 F0948
LABOR LOBBY POL/PAR LEGIS

B67
HEILBRONER R.L.,THE LIMITS OF AMERICAN CAPITALISM. FUT ECO/DEV INDUS LG/CO EX/STRUC LEAD PWR TECHRACY 20. PAGE 58 F1137
ELITES CREATE TEC/DEV CAP/ISM

B67
KIRK R.,THE POLITICAL PRINCIPLES OF ROBERT A. TAFT. USA+45 LABOR DIPLOM ADJUD ADJUST ORD/FREE TAFT/RA. PAGE 71 F1398
POL/PAR LEAD LEGIS ATTIT

B67
LEIBY J.,CHARITY AND CORRECTION IN JERSEY; A HISTORY OF STATE WELFARE INSTITUTIONS. DELIB/GP EX/STRUC PROB/SOLV INSPECT LEAD ADJUST HEALTH ...POLICY PSY NEW/JERSEY. PAGE 77 F1514
PROVS PUB/INST ADMIN

B67
MACCLOSKEY M.,PACTS FOR PEACE: UN, NATO, SEATO, CENTO, OAS. WOR+45 PLAN DIPLOM CONTROL PEACE ORD/FREE...ORG/CHARTS UN NATO SEATO OAS CENTO. PAGE 83 F1623
FORCES INT/ORG LEAD POLICY

B67
MENDEL A.P.,POLITICAL MEMOIRS 1905-1917 BY PAUL MILIUKOV (TRANS. BY CARL GOLDBERG). USSR AGRI DIPLOM ECO/TAC POPULISM...MAJORIT 20. PAGE 90 F1757
BIOG LEAD NAT/G CONSTN

B67
MEYERS M.,SOURCES OF THE AMERICAN REPUBLIC; A DOCUMENTARY HISTORY OF POLITICS, SOCIETY, AND THOUGHT (VOL. I, REV. ED.). USA-45 CULTURE STRUCT NAT/G LEGIS LEAD ATTIT...JURID SOC ANTHOL 17/19 PRESIDENT. PAGE 90 F1772
COLONIAL REV WAR

B67
NARVER J.C.,CONGLOMERATE MERGERS AND MARKET COMPETITION. USA+45 LAW STRUCT ADMIN LEAD RISK COST PROFIT WEALTH...POLICY CHARTS BIBLIOG. PAGE 96 F1892
DEMAND LG/CO MARKET MGT

B67
NORTON H.S.,NATIONAL TRANSPORTATION POLICY: FORMATION AND IMPLEMENTATION. USA+45 USA-45 DELIB/GP LEAD...DECISION TIME/SEQ 19/20 PRESIDENT CONGRESS. PAGE 98 F1935
POLICY DIST/IND NAT/G PROB/SOLV

B67
NYOMARKAY J.,CHARISMA AND FACTIONALISM IN THE NAZI PARTY. GERMANY POL/PAR LEGIT LEAD MARXISM ...NEW/IDEA METH/COMP GEN/LAWS BIBLIOG 20 HITLER/A. PAGE 99 F1949
FASCISM INGP/REL CHIEF PWR

B67
ROELOFS H.M.,THE LANGUAGE OF MODERN POLITICS: AN INTRODUCTION TO THE STUDY OF GOVERNMENT. DIPLOM ADMIN MARXISM NEW/LIB...JURID CONCPT METH/COMP T 20. PAGE 113 F2230
LEAD NAT/COMP PERS/REL NAT/G

B67
SCHECTER J.,THE NEW FACE OF BUDDHA: BUDDHISM AND POLITICAL POWER IN SOUTHEAST ASIA. S/ASIA NAT/G POL/PAR NAT/LISM ATTIT MARXISM...BIBLIOG 20. PAGE 116 F2292
SECT POLICY PWR LEAD

B67
VENKATESWARAN R.J.,CABINET GOVERNMENT IN INDIA. INDIA UK SOCIETY OP/RES COLONIAL LEAD EFFICIENCY ORD/FREE 20. PAGE 141 F2776
DELIB/GP ADMIN CONSTN NAT/G

B67
WESSON R.G.,THE IMPERIAL ORDER. WOR-45 STRUCT SECT DOMIN ADMIN COLONIAL LEAD CONSERVE...CONCPT BIBLIOG 20. PAGE 145 F2861
PWR CHIEF CONTROL SOCIETY

B67
WISEMAN H.V.,BRITAIN AND THE COMMONWEALTH. EUR+WWI FUT UK ECO/DEV POL/PAR TEC/DEV INT/TRADE LEAD ROLE SOVEREIGN...SOC TREND 20 CMN/WLTH. PAGE 140 F2911
INT/ORG DIPLOM NAT/G NAT/COMP

B67
YAMAMURA K.,ECONOMIC POLICY IN POSTWAR JAPAN. ASIA FINAN POL/PAR DIPLOM LEAD NAT/LISM ATTIT NEW/LIB POPULISM 20 CHINJAP. PAGE 149 F2946
ECO/DEV POLICY NAT/G TEC/DEV

L67
GREGORY A.J.,"AFRICAN SOCIALISM, SOCIALISM AND FASCISM: AN APPRAISAL." FUT LEAD REV GP/REL RACE/REL NAT/LISM ATTIT...IDEA/COMP STERTYP 20. PAGE 51 F0993
FASCISM MARXISM SOCISM AFR

S67
ADAMS E.S.,"THE EXPANDING ROLE OF BANKS IN PUBLIC AFFAIRS." USA+45 GIVE LEAD ROLE...QU 20. PAGE 2 F0036
PARTIC FINAN LOC/G ATTIT

S67
ADAMS R.N.,"ETHICS AND THE SOCIAL ANTHROPOLOGIST IN LATIN AMERICA." USA+45 INTELL PROB/SOLV ECO/TAC LEAD...DECISION SOC NAT/COMP PERS/COMP. PAGE 2 F0039
L/A+17C POLICY ECO/UNDEV CONSULT

S67
ALEXANDER R.J.,"'THIRD FORCE' IN WORLD COMMUNISM?" CHINA/COM CUBA USSR INT/ORG DIPLOM TASK INGP/REL ATTIT PWR 20 CASTRO/F. PAGE 3 F0060
CHIEF MARXISM LEAD REV

S67
BAILEY S.L.,"THE ITALIANS AND ORGANIZED LABOR IN THE UNITED STATES AND ARGENTINA: 1880-1910." ITALY USA-45 PARTIC HABITAT PWR...GEOG GP/COMP 19/20 ARGEN. PAGE 8 F0153
LABOR LEAD WEALTH GP/REL

S67
BENN W.,"TECHNOLOGY HAS AN INEXORABLE EFFECT." FUT UK ECO/DEV INT/ORG CONSULT PLAN EDU/PROP ADMIN LEAD GP/REL PRODUC...INT 20 EEC. PAGE 13 F0246 — R+D LG/CO TEC/DEV INDUS

S67
CATTELL D.T.,"THE FIFTIETH ANNIVERSARY: A SOVIET WATERSHED?" USSR CONSTN ECO/DEV NAT/G LEAD TOTALISM 20 KHRUSH/N. PAGE 22 F0430 — MARXISM CHIEF POLICY ADJUST

S67
DRAPER A.P.,"UNIONS AND THE WAR IN VIETNAM." USA+45 CONFER ADMIN LEAD WAR ORD/FREE PACIFIST 20. PAGE 34 F0660 — LABOR PACIFISM ATTIT ELITES

S67
HALL B.,"THE COALITION AGAINST DISHWASHERS." USA+45 POL/PAR PROB/SOLV BARGAIN LEAD CHOOSE REPRESENT GP/REL ORD/FREE PWR...POLICY 20. PAGE 53 F1044 — LABOR ADMIN DOMIN WORKER

S67
JEDLICKI W.,"THE FREE SPEECH MOVEMENT IN WARSAW." POLAND FORCES EDU/PROP LEAD ATTIT MARXISM ...IDEA/COMP 20. PAGE 67 F1310 — COERCE CROWD ORD/FREE ACADEM

S67
LENS S.,"WALTER REUTHER TRIES TO BUILD A FIRE." WORKER LEAD DISCRIM AGE ORD/FREE NEW/LIB SOC. PAGE 78 F1523 — LABOR PARTIC NEIGH PLAN

S67
MUNDHEIM R.H.,"SOME THOUGHTS ON THE DUTIES AND RESPONSIBILITIES OF UNAFFILIATED DIRECTORS OF MUTUAL FUNDS." USA+45 LG/CO SML/CO CONSULT LEAD PARTIC. PAGE 95 F1861 — FINAN WEALTH ECO/TAC ADMIN

S67
PECCEI A.,"DEVELOPED-UNDERDEVELOPED AND EAST-WEST RELATIONS." ECO/UNDEV TEC/DEV DIPLOM LEAD EFFICIENCY GEOG. PAGE 104 F2045 — FOR/AID TREND REGION ECO/DEV

S67
PERKINS D.H.,"ECONOMIC GROWTH IN CHINA AND THE CULTURAL REVOLUTION(1960APRIL 1967)" CHINA/COM FUT AGRI INDUS PLAN LEAD MARXISM...CHARTS 20 MAO. PAGE 105 F2062 — ECO/TAC CULTURE REV ECO/UNDEV

S67
PETRAS J.,"GUERRILLA MOVEMENTS IN LATIN AMERICA - I." GUATEMALA PERU VENEZUELA NAT/G COLONIAL LEAD ATTIT PWR...TIME/SEQ METH/COMP 20 COLOMB. PAGE 105 F2072 — GUERRILLA REV L/A+17C MARXISM

S67
RICHMAN B.M.,"SOVIET MANAGEMENT IN TRANSITION." USSR FINAN MARKET EX/STRUC PLAN PROB/SOLV TEC/DEV CONTROL LEAD CENTRAL EFFICIENCY...METH/COMP 20 REFORMERS. PAGE 111 F2186 — MGT MARXISM POLICY AUTHORIT

S67
SHEFFTZ M.C.,"THE TRADE DISPUTES AND TRADE UNIONS ACT OF 1927: THE AFTERMATH OF THE GENERAL STRIKE." UK FINAN WORKER ADJUD LEAD PARL/PROC 20. PAGE 120 F2373 — LEGIS ATTIT LABOR GP/REL

S67
SHERWOOD W.B.,"THE RISE OF THE JUSTICE PARTY IN TURKEY." FUT TURKEY LEAD ATTIT 20. PAGE 121 F2378 — POL/PAR ECO/UNDEV STRUCT SOCIETY

S67
SHISTER J.,"THE DIRECTION OF UNIONISM 1947-1967: THRUST OF DRIFT?" INDUS CENTRAL EFFICIENCY INCOME ATTIT SOCISM...POLICY TREND 20 AFL/CIO. PAGE 121 F2382 — LABOR PROF/ORG LEAD LAW

S67
WASSERMAN M.,"BEYOND TOKENISM: REVERSE INTEGRATION IN ALBANY, GEORGIA." USA+45 PLAN BUDGET EDU/PROP LEAD AGE/C AGE/Y GEORGIA NEGRO. PAGE 144 F2827 — REGION RACE/REL DISCRIM SCHOOL

S67
WHITE W.L.,"THE TREASURY BOARD AND PARLIAMENT." CANADA CONSTN CONSULT LEGIS LEAD PARL/PROC GP/REL ...DECISION 20. PAGE 146 F2871 — FINAN DELIB/GP NAT/G ADMIN

N67
US HOUSE COMM GOVT OPERATIONS,FEDERALLY FINANCED SOCIAL RESEARCH, EXPENDITURES, STATUS, AND OBJECTIVES (PAMPHLET). WOR+45 CREATE LEAD GP/REL ATTIT...GEOG PSY SOC. PAGE 137 F2700 — ACT/RES NAT/G GIVE BUDGET

B86
O'CONNOR T.P.,THE PARNELL MOVEMENT: WITH A SKETCH OF IRISH PARTIES FROM 1843. IRELAND UK USA-45 LEGIS WORKER ECO/TAC COERCE CRIME REV CHOOSE ORD/FREE CATHISM LAISSEZ...SOC 19/20 PARLIAMENT PARNELL/CS LAND/LEAG. PAGE 100 F1957 — LEAD DOMIN POL/PAR POLICY

LEADING....SEE LEAD

LEAGUE OF WOMEN VOTERS....SEE LEAGUE/WV

LEAGUE OF WOMEN VOTERS OF US F1498

LEAGUE/NAT....LEAGUE OF NATIONS; SEE ALSO INT/ORG

B20
MOREL E.D.,THE BLACK MAN'S BURDEN. AFR MOD/EUR AGRI EXTR/IND PROB/SOLV INT/TRADE ADMIN CONTROL COERCE DISCRIM...POLICY 19/20 NEGRO LEAGUE/NAT. PAGE 93 F1828 — ORD/FREE CAP/ISM RACE/REL DOMIN

B37
UNION OF SOUTH AFRICA,REPORT CONCERNING ADMINISTRATION OF SOUTH WEST AFRICA (6 VOLS.). SOUTH/AFR INDUS PUB/INST FORCES LEGIS BUDGET DIPLOM EDU/PROP ADJUD CT/SYS...GEOG CHARTS 20 AFRICA/SW LEAGUE/NAT. PAGE 132 F2610 — NAT/G ADMIN COLONIAL CONSTN

B41
YOUNG G.,FEDERALISM AND FREEDOM. EUR+WWI MOD/EUR RUSSIA USA-45 WOR-45 SOCIETY STRUCT ECO/DEV INT/ORG EXEC FEDERAL ATTIT PERSON ALL/VALS...OLD/LIB CONCPT OBS TREND LEAGUE/NAT TOT/POP. PAGE 150 F2950 — NAT/G WAR

B55
WOYTINSKY W.S.,WORLD COMMERCE AND GOVERNMENTS: TRENDS AND OUTLOOK. WOR+45 FINAN POL/PAR DIPLOM ECO/TAC FOR/AID DOMIN WAR CHOOSE...CHARTS BIBLIOG 20 LEAGUE/NAT UN ILO. PAGE 149 F2929 — INT/TRADE DIST/IND NAT/COMP NAT/G

B58
COLE G.D.H.,COMMUNISM AND SOCIAL DEMOCRACY (VOL. IV OF "HISTORY OF SOCIAL THOUGHT"). COM GERMANY ITALY UK AGRI INT/ORG WORKER DIPLOM COLONIAL NAT/LISM ALL/IDEOS...BIBLIOG 20 LEAGUE/NAT AUST/HUNG. PAGE 26 F0502 — MARXISM REV POL/PAR SOCISM

B63
WILTZ J.E.,IN SEARCH OF PEACE: THE SENATE MUNITIONS INQUIRY, 1934-36. EUR+WWI USA-45 ELITES INDUS LG/CO LEGIS INT/TRADE LOBBY NEUTRAL ARMS/CONT...POLICY CONGRESS 20 LEAGUE/NAT PRESIDENT SENATE CONSCRIPTN. PAGE 147 F2905 — DELIB/GP PROFIT WAR WEAPON

B65
WASSERMAN M.J.,THE BALANCE OF PAYMENTS: HISTORY, METHODOLOGY, THEORY. UK USA+45 USA-45 CAP/ISM DIPLOM EFFICIENCY...DECISION METH/CNCPT BIBLIOG 18/20 LEAGUE/NAT. PAGE 144 F2828 — BAL/PAY ECO/TAC GEN/LAWS EQUILIB

B67
BLAIR P.W.,THE MINISTATE DILEMMA. WOR+45 AGREE COLONIAL ORD/FREE...GEOG CHARTS MUNICH LEAGUE/NAT UN. PAGE 15 F0294 — INT/ORG NAT/G CENSUS

L67
MACDONALD R.S.J.,"THE RESORT TO ECONOMIC COERCION BY INTERNATIONAL POLITICAL ORGANIZATIONS." CUBA ETHIOPIA RHODESIA SOUTH/AFR NAT/G FOR/AID INT/TRADE DOMIN CONTROL SANCTION...DECISION LEAGUE/NAT UN OAS 20. PAGE 83 F1625 — INT/ORG COERCE ECO/TAC DIPLOM

LEAGUE/WV....LEAGUE OF WOMEN VOTERS

LEARNING....SEE PERCEPT

LEASE....SEE RENT

LEBANON....SEE ALSO ISLAM

B57
PATAI R.,JORDAN, LEBANON AND SYRIA: AN ANNOTATED BIBLIOGRAPHY. ISLAM JORDAN LEBANON SYRIA...GEOG 20. PAGE 103 F2034 — BIBLIOG/A SOC

S61
VALLET R.,"IRAN: KEY TO THE MIDDLE EAST." COM IRAQ ISLAM KUWAIT LEBANON SAUDI/ARAB TURKEY ELITES SOCIETY INDUS PROC/MFG POL/PAR TOP/EX PLAN BAL/PWR DIPLOM ECO/TAC ALL/VALS...TREND FOR/TRADE CENTO 20. PAGE 140 F2760 — NAT/G ECO/UNDEV IRAN

B66
RIZK C.,LE REGIME POLITIQUE LIBANAIS. ISLAM LEBANON STRUCT POL/PAR SECT LOBBY GP/REL 20 ARABS MUSLIM CHRISTIAN. PAGE 112 F2198 — ECO/UNDEV NAT/G CULTURE

LECHT L. F1499

LECLERCQ H. F1500

LEDEBUR L.C. F1501

LEDERER W. F1502

LEDUC G. F1503

LEDYARD/J....JOHN LEDYARD

LEE A.M. F1504

LEE E.B. F1504

LEE M.W. F1505,F1506

LEE R.A. F1507

LEE R.L. F1508

LEE R.R. F1509

LEE/IVY....IVY LEE

LEEVILLE....LEEVILLE, TEXAS

LEFCOE G. F1510

LEFF N.H. F1511

LEGAL SYSTEM....SEE LAW

LEGAL PERMIT....SEE LICENSE

LEGION OF DECENCY....SEE LEGION/DCY

LEGION/DCY....LEGION OF DECENCY

LEGIS....LEGISLATURES; SEE ALSO PARLIAMENT, CONGRESS

N
RAND SCHOOL OF SOCIAL SCIENCE,INDEX TO LABOR ARTICLES. ECO/DEV INT/ORG LEGIS DIPLOM GP/REL ...NAT/COMP 20. PAGE 109 F2143 — BIBLIOG LABOR MGT ADJUD

N
US LIBRARY OF CONGRESS,SELECTED AND ANNOTATED BIBLIOGRAPHY ON LABOR PROBLEMS AND POLICIES IN A WARTIME ECONOMY (PAMPHLET). USA-45 INDUS LEGIS GP/REL DISCRIM PRODUC...SOC 20. PAGE 137 F2708 — BIBLIOG/A WAR LABOR WORKER

N
US SUPERINTENDENT OF DOCUMENTS,INTERSTATE COMMERCE (PRICE LIST 59). USA+45 LAW LOC/G NAT/G LEGIS TARIFFS TAX ADMIN CONTROL HEALTH DECISION. PAGE 140 F2752 — BIBLIOG/A DIST/IND GOV/REL PROVS

N
US SUPERINTENDENT OF DOCUMENTS,LABOR (PRICE LIST 33). USA+45 LAW AGRI CONSTRUC INDUS NAT/G BARGAIN PRICE ADMIN AUTOMAT PRODUC MGT. PAGE 140 F2753 — BIBLIOG/A WORKER LABOR LEGIS

C01
LOWELL A.L.,"THE INFLUENCE OF PARTY UPON LEGISLATION IN ENGLAND AND AMERICA" IN ANNUAL REPORT OF AMER HISTORICAL ASSN." LEGIS CONTROL ...CON/ANAL CHARTS 19/20 CONGRESS PARLIAMENT. PAGE 82 F1605 — PARL/PROC POL/PAR DECISION OP/RES

B12
FOUAD M.,LE REGIME DE LA PRESSE EN EGYPTE: THESE POUR LE DOCTORAT. UAR LICENSE EDU/PROP ADMIN SANCTION CRIME SUPEGO PWR...ART/METH JURID 19/20. PAGE 43 F0832 — ORD/FREE LEGIS CONTROL PRESS

N19
ATOMIC INDUSTRIAL FORUM,COMMENTARY ON LEGISLATION TO PERMIT PRIVATE OWNERSHIP OF SPECIAL NUCLEAR MATERIAL (PAMPHLET). USA+45 DELIB/GP LEGIS PLAN OWN ...POLICY 20 AEC CONGRESS. PAGE 7 F0134 — NUC/PWR MARKET INDUS LAW

N19
FAHRNKOPF N.,STATE AND LOCAL GOVERNMENT IN ILLINOIS (PAMPHLET). CONSTN ADMIN PARTIC CHOOSE REPRESENT GOV/REL...JURID MGT 20 ILLINOIS. PAGE 39 F0759 — BIBLIOG LOC/G LEGIS CT/SYS

N19
HERZBERG D.G.,A BUDGET FOR NEW YORK STATE, 1956-1957 (PAMPHLET). USA+45 ADMIN GOV/REL 20 NEW/YORK HARRIMAN/A. PAGE 59 F1159 — POL/PAR PROVS BUDGET LEGIS

N19
KUWAIT ARABIA,KUWAIT FUND FOR ARAB ECONOMIC DEVELOPMENT (PAMPHLET). ISLAM KUWAIT UAR ECO/UNDEV LEGIS ECO/TAC WEALTH 20. PAGE 74 F1452 — FOR/AID DIPLOM FINAN ADMIN

B24
HOLDSWORTH W.S.,A HISTORY OF ENGLISH LAW; THE COMMON LAW AND ITS RIVALS (VOL. VI). AFR UK STRATA EX/STRUC ADJUD ADMIN CONTROL CT/SYS...JURID CONCPT GEN/LAWS 17 PARLIAMENT ENGLSH/LAW COMMON/LAW. PAGE 61 F1194 — LAW CONSTN LEGIS CHIEF

B24
HOLDSWORTH W.S.,A HISTORY OF ENGLISH LAW; THE COMMON LAW AND ITS RIVALS (VOL. IV). UK SEA AGRI CHIEF ADJUD CONTROL CRIME GOV/REL...INT/LAW JURID NAT/COMP 16/17 PARLIAMENT COMMON/LAW CANON/LAW ENGLSH/LAW. PAGE 61 F1195 — LAW LEGIS CT/SYS CONSTN

B25
MATHEWS J.M.,AMERICAN STATE GOVERNMENT. USA-45 LOC/G CHIEF EX/STRUC LEGIS ADJUD CONTROL CT/SYS ROUTINE GOV/REL PWR 20 GOVERNOR. PAGE 87 F1703 — PROVS ADMIN FEDERAL CONSTN

B30
GREEN F.M.,CONSTITUTIONAL DEVELOPMENT IN THE SOUTH ATLANTIC STATES, 1776-1860; A STUDY IN THE EVOLUTION OF DEMOCRACY. USA-45 ELITES SOCIETY STRATA ECO/DEV AGRI POL/PAR EX/STRUC LEGIS CT/SYS REGION...BIBLIOG 18/19 MARYLAND VIRGINIA GEORGIA NORTH/CAR SOUTH/CAR. PAGE 50 F0984 — CONSTN PROVS PLURISM REPRESENT

S30
CRAWFORD F.G.,"THE EXECUTIVE BUDGET DECISION IN NEW YORK." LEGIS EXEC PWR NEW/YORK. PAGE 28 F0552 — LEAD BUDGET PROVS PROB/SOLV

B35
SCHATTSCHNEIDER E.E.,POLITICS, PRESSURES AND THE TARIFF: A STUDY OF FREE PRIVATE ENTERPRISE IN PRESSURE POLITICS IN TARIFF REVISION 1929-1930. NAT/G BARGAIN ECO/TAC ROUTINE REPRESENT GOV/REL GP/REL PWR POLICY. PAGE 116 F2290 — LOBBY LEGIS TARIFFS

B36
BURNS A.R.,THE DECLINE OF COMPETITION. LAW LG/CO NAT/G SML/CO LEGIS PRICE AGREE CONTROL GP/REL INCOME PRODUC...POLICY 19/20 NRA. PAGE 20 F0390 — MARKET GEN/LAWS INDUS

B37
DALTON J.E.,SUGAR: A CASE STUDY OF GOVERNMENT CONTROL. USA-45 AGRI PROC/MFG LG/CO LEGIS PROB/SOLV ECO/TAC GP/REL...CHARTS 19/20. PAGE 30 F0575 — CONTROL NAT/G INDUS POLICY

B37
UNION OF SOUTH AFRICA,REPORT CONCERNING ADMINISTRATION OF SOUTH WEST AFRICA (6 VOLS.). SOUTH/AFR INDUS PUB/INST FORCES LEGIS BUDGET DIPLOM EDU/PROP ADJUD CT/SYS...GEOG CHARTS 20 AFRICA/SW LEAGUE/NAT. PAGE 132 F2610 — NAT/G ADMIN COLONIAL CONSTN

S38
HALL R.C.,"REPRESENTATION OF BIG BUSINESS IN THE HOUSE OF COMMONS." UK ECO/DEV INDUS PROF/ORG LEGIS CAP/ISM ECO/TAC LAISSEZ...POLICY OLD/LIB PLURIST MGT 20 HOUSE/CMNS. PAGE 53 F1047 — LOBBY NAT/G

B39
JENNINGS W.I.,PARLIAMENT. UK POL/PAR OP/RES BUDGET LEAD CHOOSE GP/REL...MGT 20 PARLIAMENT HOUSE/LORD HOUSE/CMNS. PAGE 67 F1315 — PARL/PROC LEGIS CONSTN NAT/G

B39
THOMAS J.A.,THE HOUSE OF COMMONS, 1832-1901; A STUDY OF ITS ECONOMIC AND FUNCTIONAL CHARACTER. UK LAW STRATA FINAN DIPLOM CONTROL LEAD LOBBY REPRESENT WEALTH...POLICY STAT BIBLIOG 19/20 PARLIAMENT. PAGE 130 F2561 — PARL/PROC LEGIS POL/PAR ECO/DEV

B40
SPENCER H.,THE MAN VS. THE STATE (1892). UK POL/PAR LEGIS TARIFFS COERCE CRIME REPRESENT PWR SOCISM ...POLICY GEN/LAWS 19/20. PAGE 124 F2450 — FASCISM POPULISM LAISSEZ ORD/FREE

L42
GRANT J.A.C.,"THE GUILD RETURNS TO AMERICA." CHRIST-17C USA-45 LEGIS LICENSE ADJUD CONTROL GP/REL. PAGE 50 F0978 — PROF/ORG JURID LABOR PWR

B43
WILMERDING L. JR.,THE SPENDING POWER: A HISTORY OF THE EFFORTS OF CONGRESS TO CONTROL EXPENDITURES. USA-45 POL/PAR DELIB/GP EX/STRUC TOP/EX TARIFFS ADMIN GOV/REL...TIME/SEQ SENATE HOUSE/REP. PAGE 147 F2900 — LEGIS BUDGET CONTROL

S43
HUZAR E.,"CONGRESS AND THE ARMY: APPROPRIATIONS." USA-45 CONFER CONTROL ATTIT SUPEGO SKILL CONGRESS. PAGE 64 F1255 — LEGIS FORCES BUDGET DELIB/GP

B48
KEIR D.L.,CASES IN CONSTITUTIONAL LAW. UK CHIEF LEGIS DIPLOM TAX PARL/PROC CRIME GOV/REL...INT/LAW JURID 17/20. PAGE 70 F1368 — CONSTN LAW ADJUD CT/SYS

B48
KILE O.M.,THE FARM BUREAU MOVEMENT: THE FARM BUREAU THROUGH THREE DECADES. NAT/G LEGIS LEAD LOBBY GP/REL INCOME POLICY. PAGE 71 F1387 — AGRI STRUCT VOL/ASSN DOMIN

B48
MCCABE D.A.,LABOR AND SOCIAL ORGANIZATION. LEGIS WORKER CAP/ISM ECO/TAC PAY MARXISM SOCISM SOC/INTEG 20 INTRVN/ECO. PAGE 88 F1717 — LABOR STRATA NEW/LIB

S48
CLEVELAND A.S.,"NAM: SPOKESMAN FOR INDUSTRY?" LEGIS PLAN LEAD LOBBY PARTIC CONSEN INCOME ATTIT ROLE ORD/FREE POLICY. PAGE 25 F0491 — VOL/ASSN CLIENT REPRESENT INDUS

S48
HARDIN L.M.,"REFLECTIONS ON AGRICULTURAL POLICY FORMATION IN THE UNITED STATES." LEGIS PLAN BUDGET ECO/TAC LEAD CENTRAL...MGT SOC NEW/IDEA STAT FAO. PAGE 55 F1078 — AGRI POLICY ADMIN NEW/LIB

S49
BANFIELD E.C.,"CONGRESS AND THE BUDGET: A PLANNER'S CRITICISM" USA+45 NAT/G PLAN LOBBY. PAGE 9 F0172 — LEGIS BUDGET EXEC POLICY

B51
COOKE C.A.,CORPORATION TRUST AND COMPANY: AN ESSAY IN LEGAL HISTORY. UK STRUCT LEGIS CAP/ISM GP/REL PROFIT 13/20 COMPNY/ACT. PAGE 27 F0531
LG/CO FINAN ECO/TAC JURID

B51
LEONARD L.L.,INTERNATIONAL ORGANIZATION. WOR+45 WOR-45 EX/STRUC FORCES LEGIS ECO/TAC INT/TRADE COLONIAL ARMS/CONT...SOC/WK GOV/COMP BIBLIOG. PAGE 78 F1527
NAT/G DIPLOM INT/ORG DELIB/GP

B51
OWENS R.N.,BUSINESS, ORGANIZATION, AND COMBINATION. USA+45 USA-45 LAW NAT/G LEGIS ECO/TAC CONTROL INGP/REL...JURID GP/COMP 20 NEW/DEAL. PAGE 102 F2006
SML/CO LG/CO STRUCT GP/REL

B51
PRINCETON U INDUSTRIAL REL SEC,COMPULSORY ARBITRATION OF UTILITY DISPUTES IN NEW JERSEY AND PENNSYLVANIA. USA+45 LEGIS WORKER ADJUD ORD/FREE ...POLICY MGT METH/COMP 20 NEW/JERSEY PENNSYLVAN. PAGE 108 F2118
BARGAIN PROVS INDUS LABOR

B51
US HOUSE COMM APPROPRIATIONS,MUTUAL SECURITY PROGRAM APPROPRIATIONS FOR 1952: HEARINGS BEFORE A SUBCOMMITTEE OF THE COMMITTEE ON APPROPRIATIONS. AFR KOREA L/A+17C ECO/DEV ECO/UNDEV INT/ORG INSPECT BAL/PWR DIPLOM DEBATE WAR...POLICY STAT ASIA/S 20 CONGRESS NATO MID/EAST. PAGE 136 F2686
LEGIS FORCES BUDGET FOR/AID

B52
BEVAN A.,IN PLACE OF FEAR. WOR+45 STRATA LEGIS REPRESENT OWN NEW/LIB POPULISM...CHARTS 20. PAGE 14 F0273
SOCISM SOCIALIST WEALTH MAJORIT

B52
HARDIN C.M.,THE POLITICS OF AGRICULTURE. USA+45 NAT/G PROF/ORG LEGIS LOBBY 20 DEPT/AGRI. PAGE 55 F1077
AGRI POLICY ECO/TAC GOV/REL

B52
JENNINGS W.I.,CONSTITUTIONAL LAWS OF THE COMMONWEALTH. AFR UK LAW CHIEF LEGIS TAX CT/SYS PARL/PROC GOV/REL...INT/LAW 18/20 ENGLSH/LAW COMMON/LAW. PAGE 67 F1316
CONSTN JURID ADJUD COLONIAL

S52
PHILLIPS C.,"THE HIGH COST OF OUR LOW-PAID CONGRESS" (NYT MAG. 2/24/52)" USA+45 FINAN WRITING TASK TIME CONGRESS. PAGE 106 F2082
LEGIS INCOME COST EFFICIENCY

S53
GABLE R.W.,"NAM: INFLUENTIAL LOBBY OR KISS OF DEATH?" (BMR)" USA+45 LAW INSPECT EDU/PROP ADMIN CONTROL INGP/REL EFFICIENCY PWR 20 CONGRESS NAM TAFT/HART. PAGE 45 F0880
LOBBY LEGIS INDUS LG/CO

S53
LAWTON F.J.,"LEGISLATIVE-EXECUTIVE RELATIONS IN BUDGETING AS VIEWED BY THE EXECUTIVE." NAT/G LEGIS ADMIN REPRESENT EFFICIENCY 20. PAGE 76 F1495
BUDGET EX/STRUC EXEC CONTROL

B54
EMERSON F.D.,SHAREHOLDER DEMOCRACY: A BROADER OUTLOOK FOR CORPORATIONS. DELIB/GP EX/STRUC LEGIS ADJUD CONTROL REPRESENT INGP/REL OWN PWR...POLICY STAT RECORD. PAGE 37 F0727
LG/CO PARTIC MAJORIT TREND

B54
RECK D.,GOVERNMENT PURCHASING AND COMPETITION. USA+45 LEGIS CAP/ISM ECO/TAC GOV/REL CENTRAL ...POLICY 20 CONGRESS. PAGE 110 F2164
NAT/G FINAN MGT COST

B55
BERNSTEIN M.H.,REGULATING BUSINESS BY INDEPENDENT COMMISSION. USA+45 USA-45 LG/CO CHIEF LEGIS PROB/SOLV ADJUD SANCTION GP/REL ATTIT...TIME/SEQ 19/20 MONOPOLY PRESIDENT CONGRESS. PAGE 14 F0268
DELIB/GP CONTROL CONSULT

B55
RUSTOW D.A.,THE POLITICS OF COMPROMISE. SWEDEN LABOR EX/STRUC LEGIS PLAN REPRESENT SOCISM...SOC 19/20. PAGE 115 F2265
POL/PAR NAT/G POLICY ECO/TAC

B55
SERRANO MOSCOSO E.,A STATEMENT OF THE LAWS OF ECUADOR IN MATTERS AFFECTING BUSINESS (2ND ED.). ECUADOR INDUS LABOR LG/CO NAT/G LEGIS TAX CONTROL MARRIAGE 20. PAGE 120 F2359
FINAN ECO/UNDEV LAW CONSTN

B55
SMITHIES A.,THE BUDGETARY PROCESS IN THE UNITED STATES. AFR ECO/DEV AGRI EX/STRUC FORCES LEGIS PROB/SOLV TAX ROUTINE EFFICIENCY...MGT CONGRESS PRESIDENT. PAGE 124 F2436
NAT/G ADMIN BUDGET GOV/REL

B55
UYEHARA C.H.,COMPARATIVE PLATFORMS OF JAPAN'S MAJOR PARTIES... USA+45 AGRI LEGIS WORKER CAP/ISM ORD/FREE MARXISM SOCISM...IDEA/COMP 20 CHINJAP. PAGE 140 F2755
POLICY POL/PAR DIPLOM NAT/G

B56
GILBERT L.D.,DIVIDENDS AND DEMOCRACY. DELIB/GP LEGIS CAP/ISM ADJUD LOBBY OWN PWR LAISSEZ MAJORIT. PAGE 47 F0922
LG/CO INGP/REL CONTROL PARTIC

B56
WILCOX W.W.,SOCIAL RESPONSIBILITY IN FARM LEADERSHIP. CLIENT LEGIS EXEC LOBBY GP/REL ATTIT WEALTH. PAGE 146 F2880
AGRI LEAD VOL/ASSN WORKER

L56
PENNOCK J.R.,"PARTY AND CONSTITUENCY IN POSTWAR AGRICULTURAL PRICE SUPPORT LEGISLATION." USA+45 LEGIS DEBATE LOBBY RIGID/FLEX. PAGE 105 F2057
POL/PAR REPRESENT AGRI CHOOSE

S56
BONILLA F.,"WHEN IS PETITION 'PRESSURE?'" (BMR)" USA+45 ELITES INDUS LABOR CHIEF EDU/PROP LEGIT ATTIT...INT CHARTS 20 CONGRESS PRESIDENT EISNHWR/DD. PAGE 16 F0312
LEGIS EX/STRUC INT/TRADE TARIFFS

S56
KNAPP D.C.,"CONGRESSIONAL CONTROL OF AGRICULTURAL CONSERVATION POLICY: A CASE STUDY OF THE APPROPRIATIONS PROCESS." DELIB/GP PLAN PROB/SOLV CONFER PARL/PROC...POLICY INT CONGRESS. PAGE 72 F1411
LEGIS AGRI BUDGET CONTROL

S56
MILNE R.S.,"CONTROL OF GOVERNMENT CORPORATIONS IN THE UNITED STATES." USA+45 NAT/G CHIEF LEGIS BUDGET 20 GENACCOUNT. PAGE 92 F1800
CONTROL EX/STRUC GOV/REL PWR

B57
MURDESHWAR A.K.,ADMINISTRATIVE PROBLEMS RELATING TO NATIONALISATION: WITH SPECIAL REFERENCE TO INDIAN STATE ENTERPRISES. CZECHOSLVK FRANCE INDIA UK USA+45 LEGIS WORKER PROB/SOLV BUDGET PRICE CONTROL ...MGT GEN/LAWS 20 PARLIAMENT. PAGE 95 F1863
NAT/G OWN INDUS ADMIN

B57
ROBERTSON H.M.,SOUTH AFRICA, ECONOMIC AND POLITICAL ASPECTS. SOUTH/AFR CONSTN CULTURE POL/PAR LEGIS DIPLOM DOMIN COLONIAL...SOC BIBLIOG 19/20. PAGE 112 F2214
RACE/REL ECO/UNDEV ECO/TAC DISCRIM

B57
WATSON G.,THE UNSERVILE STATE: ESSAYS IN LIBERTY AND WELFARE. UK LEGIS RECEIVE EDU/PROP COLONIAL ...WELF/ST 20 LIB/PARTY. PAGE 144 F2833
POL/PAR ORD/FREE CONTROL NEW/LIB

L57
SURREY S.S.,"THE CONGRESS AND THE TAX LOBBYIST - HOW SPECIAL TAX PROVISIONS GET ENACTED." LOBBY REPRESENT PRIVIL CONGRESS. PAGE 128 F2518
LEGIS TAX EX/STRUC ROLE

S57
LEWIS E.G.,"PARLIAMENTARY CONTROL OF NATIONALIZED INDUSTRY IN FRANCE." FRANCE NAT/G DELIB/GP ACT/RES PLAN PROB/SOLV ECO/TAC DOMIN CENTRAL. PAGE 79 F1547
PWR LEGIS INDUS CONTROL

B58
DEFENSE AGAINST INFLATION. USA+45 LEGIS WORKER TAX PRICE DEMAND INCOME PRODUC...POLICY TREND METH/COMP 20 GOLD/STAND. PAGE 1 F0012
ECO/TAC EQUILIB WEALTH PROB/SOLV

B58
BUGEDA LANZAS J.,A STATEMENT OF THE LAWS OF CUBA IN MATTERS AFFECTING BUSINESS (2ND ED. REV., ENLARGED). CUBA L/A+17C LAW FINAN FAM LEGIS ACT/RES ADMIN GP/REL...BIBLIOG 20 OAS. PAGE 20 F0382
JURID NAT/G INDUS WORKER

B58
CUNNINGHAM W.B.,COMPULSORY CONCILIATION AND COLLECTIVE BARGAINING. CANADA NAT/G LEGIS ADJUD CT/SYS GP/REL...MGT 20 NEW/BRUNS STRIKE CASEBOOK. PAGE 29 F0563
POLICY BARGAIN LABOR INDUS

B58
US HOUSE COMM POST OFFICE,MANPOWER UTILIZATION IN THE FEDERAL GOVERNMENT. USA+45 DIST/IND EX/STRUC LEGIS CONFER EFFICIENCY 20 CONGRESS CIVIL/SERV. PAGE 137 F2702
ADMIN WORKER DELIB/GP NAT/G

B58
US HOUSE COMM POST OFFICE,MANPOWER UTILIZATION IN THE FEDERAL GOVERNMENT. USA+45 DIST/IND EX/STRUC LEGIS CONFER EFFICIENCY 20 CONGRESS CIVIL/SERV. PAGE 137 F2703
ADMIN WORKER DELIB/GP NAT/G

S58
LATTIN N.D.,"MINORITY AND DISSENTING SHAREHOLDERS' RIGHTS IN FUNDAMENTAL CHANGES." FINAN LEGIS ADJUD PARTIC ROUTINE CHOOSE REPRESENT INGP/REL TREND. PAGE 76 F1487
MAJORIT LG/CO LAW CREATE

S58
O'NEAL F.H.,"RECENT LEGISLATION AFFECTING CLOSE CORPORATIONS." LAW EX/STRUC ECO/TAC ROUTINE CHOOSE RIGID/FLEX...MAJORIT MGT TREND. PAGE 100 F1959
LG/CO LEGIS REPRESENT PARTIC

B59
CUCCORESE H.J.,HISTORIA DE LA CONVERSION DEL PAPEL MONEDA EN BUENOS AIRES, 1861-1867. AFR LAW LOC/G NAT/G ATTIT...POLICY BIBLIOG 19 ARGEN BUENOS/AIR. PAGE 29 F0560
FINAN PLAN LEGIS

B59
LOPEZ VILLAMIL H.,A STATEMENT OF THE LAWS OF THE
CONSTN

HONDURAS IN MATTERS AFFECTING BUSINESS (2ND ED.). HONDURAS DIST/IND EXTR/IND FINAN WORKER TAX DEATH MARRIAGE OWN MARITIME 20 MIGRATION. PAGE 82 F1600 — INDUS LEGIS NAT/G

B59
MADHOK B.,POLITICAL TRENDS IN INDIA. INDIA PAKISTAN UK STRATA ECO/UNDEV POL/PAR LEGIS CAP/ISM DIPLOM COLONIAL CHOOSE MARXISM...SOC TREND 20 GANDHI/M NEHRU/J. PAGE 84 F1639 — GEOG NAT/G

B59
MARTIN D.D.,MERGERS AND THE CLAYTON ACT. FINAN LEGIS GP/REL...DECISION METH/COMP BIBLIOG 20. PAGE 86 F1681 — OWN ECO/TAC LG/CO POLICY

B59
US NATIONAL LABOR RELATIONS BD,LEGISLATIVE HISTORY OF THE LABOR-MANAGEMENT REPORTING AND DISCLOSURE ACT OF 1959 (2 VOLS.). USA+45 LEGIS...MGT CHARTS. PAGE 138 F2720 — LAW LABOR GP/REL

B59
VERNEY D.V.,PUBLIC ENTERPRISE IN SWEDEN. FUT SWEDEN UK INDUS POL/PAR LEGIS PROB/SOLV CAP/ISM INT/TRADE CONTROL SOCISM...MGT CONCPT NAT/COMP 20 SOCDEM/PAR CIVIL/SERV. PAGE 141 F2778 — ECO/DEV POLICY LG/CO NAT/G

B59
WAHLKE J.C.,LEGISLATIVE BEHAVIOR: A READER IN THEORY AND RESEARCH. USA+45 CONSTN ELITES POL/PAR LOBBY REPRESENT PERS/REL PERSON ROLE...IDEA/COMP METH/COMP SIMUL. PAGE 142 F2800 — LEGIS CHOOSE INGP/REL ATTIT

L59
OBERER W.E.,"VOLUNTARY IMPARTIAL REVIEW OF LABOR: SOME REFLECTIONS." DELIB/GP LEGIS PROB/SOLV ADJUD CONTROL COERCE PWR PLURISM POLICY. PAGE 100 F1960 — LABOR LAW PARTIC INGP/REL

S59
CLONER A.,"THE CALIFORNIA LEGISLATOR AND THE PROBLEM OF COMPENSATION." USA+45 WORKER REPRESENT. PAGE 25 F0492 — INCOME PROVS LEGIS SUPEGO

S59
SEIDMAN H.,"THE GOVERNMENT CORPORATION IN THE UNITED STATES." USA+45 LEGIS ADMIN PLURISM 20. PAGE 119 F2344 — CONTROL GOV/REL EX/STRUC EXEC

S59
WALLACE R.A.,"CONGRESSIONAL CONTROL OF THE BUDGET." USA+45 NAT/G CHIEF GP/REL FEDERAL OBJECTIVE...MGT CONGRESS. PAGE 143 F2807 — LEGIS EX/STRUC BUDGET CONSTN

N59
CHAMBER OF COMMERCE OF USA,ECONOMIC LESSONS OF POSTWAR RECESSIONS (PAMPHLET). AFR USA+45 LAW LEGIS WORKER TAX...CHARTS 20 CONGRESS FED/RESERV. PAGE 23 F0440 — ECO/DEV PROB/SOLV FINAN ECO/TAC

B60
CARPER E.T.,THE DEFENSE APPROPRIATIONS RIDER (PAMPHLET). USA+45 CONSTN CHIEF DELIB/GP LEGIS BUDGET LOBBY CIVMIL/REL...POLICY 20 CONGRESS EISNHWR/DD DEPT/DEFEN PRESIDENT BOSTON. PAGE 22 F0419 — GOV/REL ADJUD LAW CONTROL

B60
FRYE R.J.,GOVERNMENT AND LABOR: THE ALABAMA PROGRAM. USA+45 INDUS R+D LABOR WORKER BUDGET EFFICIENCY AGE/Y HEALTH...CHARTS 20 ALABAMA. PAGE 45 F0870 — ADMIN LEGIS LOC/G PROVS

B60
HEYSE T.,PROBLEMS FONCIERS ET REGIME DES TERRES (ASPECTS ECONOMIQUES, JURIDIQUES ET SOCIAUX). AFR CONGO/BRAZ INT/ORG DIPLOM SOVEREIGN...GEOG TREATY 20. PAGE 59 F1161 — BIBLIOG AGRI ECO/UNDEV LEGIS

B60
POOLEY B.J.,THE EVOLUTION OF BRITISH PLANNING LEGISLATION. UK ECO/DEV LOC/G CONSULT DELIB/GP ADMIN MUNICH 20 URBAN/RNWL. PAGE 107 F2104 — PLAN LEGIS PROB/SOLV

B60
ROBSON W.A.,NATIONALIZED INDUSTRY AND PUBLIC OWNERSHIP. UK ECO/DEV FINAN LABOR LG/CO POL/PAR LEGIS ACT/RES GP/REL...TREND IDEA/COMP 20. PAGE 113 F2227 — NAT/G OWN INDUS ATTIT

B60
US SENATE COMM ON COMMERCE,URBAN MASS TRANSPORTATION. FUT USA+45 AIR ECO/DEV FINAN LOC/G LEGIS CREATE PROB/SOLV TEC/DEV MUNICH 20 PUB/TRANS. PAGE 139 F2732 — DIST/IND PLAN NAT/G LAW

B60
WALLACE R.A.,CONGRESSIONAL CONTROL OF FEDERAL SPENDING. USA+45 CONSTN NAT/G OP/RES CONFER DEBATE PERS/REL UTIL RIGID/FLEX PWR OBJECTIVE...OBS CHARTS. PAGE 143 F2808 — LEGIS DELIB/GP BUDGET

S60
"THE EMERGING COMMON MARKETS IN LATIN AMERICA." FUT L/A+17C STRATA DIST/IND INDUS LABOR NAT/G LEGIS ECO/TAC ADMIN RIGID/FLEX HEALTH...NEW/IDEA TIME/SEQ OAS 20. PAGE 1 F0013 — FINAN ECO/UNDEV INT/TRADE

S60
FRANKEL S.H.,"ECONOMIC ASPECTS OF POLITICAL INDEPENDENCE IN AFRICA." AFR FUT SOCIETY ECO/UNDEV COM/IND FINAN LEGIS PLAN TEC/DEV CAP/ISM ECO/TAC INT/TRADE ADMIN ATTIT DRIVE RIGID/FLEX PWR WEALTH ...MGT NEW/IDEA MATH TIME/SEQ VAL/FREE 20. PAGE 43 F0846 — NAT/G FOR/AID

S60
MORALES C.J.,"TRADE AND ECONOMIC INTEGRATION IN LATIN AMERICA." FUT L/A+17C LAW STRATA ECO/UNDEV DIST/IND INDUS LABOR NAT/G LEGIS ECO/TAC ADMIN RIGID/FLEX WEALTH...CONCPT NEW/IDEA CONT/OBS TIME/SEQ WORK 20. PAGE 93 F1825 — FINAN INT/TRADE REGION

B61
BARBASH J.,LABOR'S GRASS ROOTS. CONSTN NAT/G EX/STRUC LEGIS WORKER LEAD...MAJORIT BIBLIOG. PAGE 10 F0184 — LABOR INGP/REL GP/REL LAW

B61
BEASLEY K.E.,STATE SUPERVISION OF MUNICIPAL DEBT IN KANSAS - A CASE STUDY. USA+45 USA-45 FINAN PROVS BUDGET TAX ADJUD ADMIN CONTROL SUPEGO MUNICH. PAGE 12 F0224 — LOC/G LEGIS JURID

B61
CAMPAIGNE J.G.,CHECK-OFF: LABOR BOSSES AND WORKING MEN. LEGIS WORKER EDU/PROP DEBATE COERCE REPRESENT GP/REL ORD/FREE CONSERVE. PAGE 21 F0404 — LABOR ELITES PWR CONTROL

B61
CARROTHERS A.W.R.,LABOR ARBITRATION IN CANADA. CANADA LAW NAT/G CONSULT LEGIS WORKER ADJUD ADMIN CT/SYS 20. PAGE 22 F0422 — LABOR MGT GP/REL BARGAIN

B61
HUBBARD P.J.,ORIGINS OF THE TVA: THE MUSCLE SHOALS CONTROVERSY, 1920-1932. USA-45 DELIB/GP LEGIS LEAD LOBBY GOV/REL GP/REL INGP/REL OWN PERSON...BIBLIOG 20 TVA CONGRESS WATER. PAGE 62 F1229 — SEA CONTROL NAT/G INDUS

B61
JAVITS B.A.,THE PEACE BY INVESTMENT CORPORATION. WOR+45 NAT/G LEGIS PROB/SOLV PERS/REL WEALTH ...POLICY 20. PAGE 66 F1307 — ECO/UNDEV DIPLOM FOR/AID PEACE

B61
MACMAHON A.W.,DELEGATION AND AUTONOMY. INDIA STRUCT LEGIS BARGAIN BUDGET ECO/TAC LEGIT EXEC REPRESENT GOV/REL CENTRAL DEMAND EFFICIENCY PRODUC. PAGE 84 F1637 — ADMIN PLAN FEDERAL

B61
MEZERIK A.G.,ECONOMIC DEVELOPMENT AIDS FOR UNDERDEVELOPED COUNTRIES. WOR+45 FINAN LEGIS PROB/SOLV TEC/DEV DIPLOM FOR/AID GIVE TASK WAR 20 UN. PAGE 91 F1776 — ECO/UNDEV INT/ORG WEALTH PLAN

B61
NEW JERSEY LEGISLATURE-SENATE,PUBLIC HEARINGS BEFORE COMMITTEE ON REVISION AND AMENDMENT OF LAWS ON SENATE BILL NO. 8. USA+45 FINAN PROVS WORKER ACT/RES PLAN BUDGET TAX CRIME...IDEA/COMP MUNICH 20 NEW/JERSEY URBAN/RNWL. PAGE 98 F1919 — LEGIS INDUS PROB/SOLV

B61
RUEDA B.,A STATEMENT OF THE LAWS OF COLOMBIA IN MATTERS AFFECTING BUSINESS (3RD ED.). INDUS FAM LABOR LG/CO NAT/G LEGIS TAX CONTROL MARRIAGE 20 COLOMB. PAGE 115 F2257 — FINAN ECO/UNDEV LAW CONSTN

B61
SCHNAPPER B.,LA POLITIQUE ET LE COMMERCE FRANCAIS DANS LE GOLFE DE GUINEE DE 1838 A 1871. FRANCE GUINEA UK SEA EXTR/IND NAT/G DELIB/GP LEGIS ADMIN ORD/FREE...POLICY GEOG CENSUS CHARTS BIBLIOG 19. PAGE 117 F2303 — COLONIAL INT/TRADE DOMIN AFR

B61
SEPULVEDA C.,A STATEMENT OF THE LAWS OF MEXICO IN MATTERS AFFECTING BUSINESS (3RD ED.). AGRI DIST/IND EXTR/IND FINAN INDUS WORKER TAX MARRIAGE OWN ORD/FREE...BIBLIOG 20 MEXIC/AMER TREATY MIGRATION MONOPOLY. PAGE 119 F2356 — CONSTN NAT/G JURID LEGIS

B61
WESTON J.F.,THE ROLE OF MERGERS IN THE GROWTH OF LARGE FIRMS. USA+45 USA-45 LEGIS CONTROL...CONCPT STAT CHARTS 19/20. PAGE 145 F2862 — LG/CO CENTRAL INDUS FINAN

S61
WILDAVSKY A.,"POLITICAL IMPLICATIONS OF BUDGETARY REFORM." AFR NAT/G POL/PAR DELIB/GP EX/STRUC ATTIT PWR CONGRESS. PAGE 146 F2881 — BUDGET PLAN LEGIS

B62
BUREAU OF NATIONAL AFFAIRS,FEDERAL-STATE REGULATION OF WELFARE FUNDS (REV. ED.). USA+45 LAW LEGIS DEBATE AGE/O 20 CONGRESS. PAGE 20 F0386 — WELF/ST WEALTH PLAN SOC/WK

B62
CARPER E.T.,ILLINOIS GOES TO CONGRESS FOR ARMY LAND. USA+45 LAW EXTR/IND PROVS REGION CIVMIL/REL GOV/REL FEDERAL ATTIT 20 ILLINOIS SENATE CONGRESS DIRKSEN/E DOUGLAS/P. PAGE 22 F0420 — ADMIN LOBBY GEOG LEGIS

B62
LITTLEFIELD N.,METROPOLITAN AREA PROBLEMS AND MUNICIPAL HOME RULE. USA+45 PROVS ADMIN CONTROL GP/REL PWR. PAGE 81 F1586 — LOC/G SOVEREIGN JURID

LEGIS

B62
PASTOR R.S.,A STATEMENT OF THE LAWS OF PARAGUAY IN MATTERS AFFECTING BUSINESS (2ND ED.). PARAGUAY INDUS FAM LABOR LG/CO NAT/G LEGIS TAX CONTROL MARRIAGE 20. PAGE 103 F2033 FINAN ECO/UNDEV LAW CONSTN

B62
SCHILLING W.R.,STRATEGY, POLITICS, AND DEFENSE BUDGETS. AFR USA+45 CHIEF LEGIS PLAN TEC/DEV BAL/PWR BUDGET NUC/PWR WAR CIVMIL/REL GOV/REL PWR 20 EISNHWR/DD. PAGE 117 F2297 NAT/G POLICY FORCES DETER

B62
SRIVASTAVA G.L.,COLLECTIVE BARGAINING AND LABOR-MANAGEMENT RELATIONS IN INDIA. INDIA UK USA+45 INDUS LEGIS WORKER ADJUD EFFICIENCY PRODUC ...METH/COMP 20. PAGE 125 F2462 LABOR MGT BARGAIN GP/REL

B62
US CONGRESS,LEGISLATIVE HISTORY OF UNITED STATES TAX CONVENTIONS(VOL. 1). USA+45 USA-45 DELIB/GP WEALTH...CHARTS 20 CONGRESS. PAGE 134 F2649 TAX LEGIS LAW DIPLOM

L62
N,"UNION INVESTMENT IN BUSINESS: A SOURCE OF UNION CONFLICT OF INTEREST." LAW NAT/G LEGIS CONTROL GP/REL INGP/REL DECISION. PAGE 96 F1884 LABOR POLICY FINAN LG/CO

B63
BAUER R.A.,AMERICAN BUSINESS AND PUBLIC POLICY: THE POLITICS OF FOREIGN TRADE. USA+45 COM/IND LG/CO NAT/G PROF/ORG SML/CO VOL/ASSN LEGIS TOP/EX ECO/TAC EDU/PROP CHOOSE HEALTH PWR WEALTH...CONCPT METH/CNCPT OBS INT QU SAMP FOR/TRADE TRUE/GP VAL/FREE HI. PAGE 11 F0217 ECO/DEV ATTIT

B63
BURRUS B.R.,ADMINSTRATIVE LAW AND LOCAL GOVERNMENT. USA+45 PROVS LEGIS LICENSE ADJUD ORD/FREE 20. PAGE 20 F0392 EX/STRUC LOC/G JURID CONSTN

B63
CORLEY R.N.,THE LEGAL ENVIRONMENT OF BUSINESS. CONSTN LEGIS TAX ADMIN CT/SYS DISCRIM ATTIT PWR ...TREND 18/20. PAGE 28 F0537 NAT/G INDUS JURID DECISION

B63
FATEMI N.S.,THE DOLLAR CRISIS. USA+45 INDUS NAT/G LEGIS BUDGET TAX COST...CHARTS METH/COMP 20 EEC. PAGE 39 F0766 PROB/SOLV BAL/PAY FOR/AID PLAN

B63
GORDON M.S.,THE ECONOMICS OF WELFARE POLICIES. INDUS LOC/G NAT/G LEGIS WORKER INCOME AGE/O SKILL WEALTH...METH/COMP NAT/COMP 20. PAGE 49 F0959 METH/CNCPT ECO/TAC POLICY

B63
HATHAWAY D.A.,GOVERNMENT AND AGRICULTURE: PUBLIC POLICY IN A DEMOCRATIC SOCIETY. USA+45 LEGIS ADMIN EXEC LOBBY REPRESENT PWR 20. PAGE 57 F1111 AGRI GOV/REL PROB/SOLV EX/STRUC

B63
MEYNAUD J.,PLANIFICATION ET POLITIQUE. FRANCE ITALY FINAN LABOR DELIB/GP LEGIS ADMIN EFFICIENCY ...MAJORIT DECISION 20. PAGE 90 F1773 PLAN ECO/TAC PROB/SOLV

B63
PREST A.R.,PUBLIC FINANCE IN UNDERDEVELOPED COUNTRIES. UK WOR+45 WOR-45 SOCIETY INT/ORG NAT/G LEGIS ACT/RES PLAN ECO/TAC ADMIN ROUTINE...CHARTS 20. PAGE 108 F2115 FINAN ECO/UNDEV NIGERIA

B63
PRITCHETT C.H.,THE THIRD BRANCH OF GOVERNMENT. USA+45 USA-45 CONSTN SOCIETY INDUS SECT LEGIS JUDGE PROB/SOLV GOV/REL 20 SUPREME/CT CHURCH/STA. PAGE 108 F2122 JURID NAT/G ADJUD CT/SYS

B63
SHANKS M.,THE LESSONS OF PUBLIC ENTERPRISE. UK LEGIS WORKER ECO/TAC ADMIN PARL/PROC GOV/REL ATTIT ...POLICY MGT METH/COMP NAT/COMP ANTHOL 20 PARLIAMENT. PAGE 120 F2364 SOCISM OWN NAT/G INDUS

B63
US HOUSE,URBAN RENEWAL: HOUSE COMMITTEE ON BANKING AND CURRENCY. USA+45 FINAN LOC/G NAT/G NEIGH DELIB/GP TEC/DEV BUDGET GOV/REL COST...CHARTS MUNICH 20 CONGRESS URBAN/RNWL. PAGE 136 F2684 PLAN PROB/SOLV LEGIS

B63
WILTZ J.E.,IN SEARCH OF PEACE: THE SENATE MUNITIONS INQUIRY, 1934-36. EUR+WWI USA-45 ELITES INDUS LG/CO LEGIS INT/TRADE LOBBY NEUTRAL ARMS/CONT...POLICY CONGRESS 20 LEAGUE/NAT PRESIDENT SENATE CONSCRIPTN. PAGE 147 F2905 DELIB/GP PROFIT WAR WEAPON

S63
ADAMS F.G.,"ECONOMIC CONSIDERATIONS OF AN ATLANTIC ENERGY POLICY." EUR+WWI FUT USA+45 DIST/IND EXTR/IND MARKET CONSULT LEGIS ECO/TAC WEALTH ...POLICY EEC FOR/TRADE OEEC 20. PAGE 2 F0037 ECO/DEV TEC/DEV NUC/PWR

B64
FITCH L.C.,URBAN TRANSPORTATION AND PUBLIC POLICY. FINAN NAT/G LEGIS PROB/SOLV TEC/DEV PRICE COST EFFICIENCY...DECISION STAT CHARTS METH/COMP MUNICH 20 NEWYORK/C PHILADELPH LOS/ANG CHICAGO WASHING/DC. PAGE 41 F0806 DIST/IND PLAN LOC/G

B64
GARDNER L.C.,ECONOMIC ASPECTS OF NEW DEAL DIPLOMACY. USA-45 WOR-45 LAW ECO/DEV INT/ORG NAT/G VOL/ASSN LEGIS TOP/EX EDU/PROP ORD/FREE PWR WEALTH ...POLICY TIME/SEQ VAL/FREE 20 ROOSEVLT/F. PAGE 46 F0901 ECO/TAC DIPLOM

B64
LITVAK I.A.,MARKETING: CANADA. CANADA STRATA PROC/MFG LEGIS TEC/DEV DIPLOM INT/TRADE PRICE AUTOMAT ATTIT WEALTH...ANTHOL 20. PAGE 81 F1587 ECO/TAC MARKET ECO/DEV EFFICIENCY

B64
MOAK L.L.,A MANUAL OF SUGGESTED PRACTICE FOR THE PREPARATION AND ADOPTION OF CAPITAL PROGRAMS AND CAPITAL BUDGETS BY LOCAL GOVERN. USA+45 DELIB/GP PLAN TAX GP/REL COST DECISION. PAGE 92 F1812 LOC/G BUDGET LEGIS PROB/SOLV

B64
PAARLBERG D.,AMERICAN FARM POLICY: A CASE STUDY IN CENTRALIZED DECISION-MAKING. USA+45 NAT/G LEGIS LOBBY REPRESENT GOV/REL PWR LAISSEZ 20. PAGE 102 F2009 PROB/SOLV EX/STRUC AGRI

B64
REUSS H.S.,THE CRITICAL DECADE - AN ECONOMIC POLICY FOR AMERICA AND THE FREE WORLD. AFR USA+45 FINAN POL/PAR WORKER PLAN DIPLOM ECO/TAC TARIFFS BAL/PAY ...POLICY 20 CONGRESS. PAGE 111 F2181 FOR/AID INT/TRADE LABOR LEGIS

B64
RUSTAMJI R.F.,THE LAW OF INDUSTRIAL DISPUTES IN INDIA. INDIA LEGIS WORKER CONTROL GP/REL...JURID MGT TIME/SEQ 20. PAGE 115 F2264 INDUS ADJUD BARGAIN LABOR

B64
TELLADO A.,A STATEMENT OF THE LAWS OF THE DOMINICAN REPUBLIC IN MATTERS AFFECTING BUSINESS (3RD ED.). DOMIN/REP AGRI DIST/IND EXTR/IND FINAN FAM WORKER ECO/TAC TAX CT/SYS MARRIAGE OWN...BIBLIOG 20 MIGRATION. PAGE 129 F2542 CONSTN LEGIS NAT/G INDUS

B64
US CONGRESS JOINT ECO COMM,PRIVATE INVESTMENT IN LATIN AMERICA. L/A+17C USA+45 INT/ORG PROB/SOLV ECO/TAC ATTIT...INT 20 CONGRESS. PAGE 135 F2658 FINAN ECO/UNDEV PARL/PROC LEGIS

B64
US DEPT LABOR OFF SOLICITOR,LEGISLATIVE HISTORY OF THE LABOR-MANAGEMENT AND DISCLOSURE ACT OF 1959. DELIB/GP WORKER ADMIN LOBBY PARL/PROC SANCTION CHOOSE GOV/REL 20 CONGRESS PRESIDENT. PAGE 136 F2677 LABOR LEGIS DEBATE POLICY

B64
US HOUSE COMM BANKING-CURR,INTERNATIONAL DEVELOPMENT ASSOCIATION ACT AMENDMENT. CHINA/COM USA+45 USSR FINAN FORCES LEGIS DIPLOM CONFER EFFICIENCY...CHARTS GOV/COMP 20 PRESIDENT CONGRESS INTL/DEV. PAGE 136 F2689 BAL/PAY FOR/AID RECORD ECO/TAC

B64
WEIDENBAUM M.L.,CONGRESS AND THE FEDERAL BUDGET: FEDERAL BUDGETING AND THE RESPONSIBLE USE OF POWER. LOC/G PLAN TAX CONGRESS. PAGE 144 F2843 LEGIS EX/STRUC BUDGET ADMIN

B64
WHEARE K.C.,FEDERAL GOVERNMENT (4TH ED.). WOR+45 WOR-45 POL/PAR LEGIS BAL/PWR CT/SYS...POLICY JURID CONCPT GOV/COMP 17/20. PAGE 145 F2866 FEDERAL CONSTN EX/STRUC NAT/COMP

B64
WRIGHT G.,RURAL REVOLUTION IN FRANCE: THE PEASANTRY IN THE TWENTIETH CENTURY. EUR+WWI MOD/EUR LAW CULTURE AGRI POL/PAR DELIB/GP LEGIS ECO/TAC EDU/PROP COERCE CHOOSE ATTIT RIGID/FLEX HEALTH ...STAT CENSUS CHARTS VAL/FREE 20. PAGE 149 F2932 PWR STRATA FRANCE REV

L64
KOLODZIEJ E.A.,"RATIONAL CONSENT AND DEFENSE BUDGETS: THE ROLE OF CONGRESS, 1945-1962." LEGIS DIPLOM CONTROL PARL/PROC 20 CONGRESS. PAGE 72 F1423 DECISION PLAN CIVMIL/REL BUDGET

B65
ALEXANDER R.J.,ORGANIZED LABOR IN LATIN AMERICA. L/A+17C INT/ORG LEGIS WORKER TEC/DEV BARGAIN INT/TRADE REV...NAT/COMP BIBLIOG 20. PAGE 3 F0059 LABOR POL/PAR ECO/UNDEV POLICY

B65
BOCK E.,GOVERNMENT REGULATION OF BUSINESS. USA+45 LAW EX/STRUC LEGIS EXEC ORD/FREE PWR...ANTHOL CONGRESS. PAGE 16 F0303 MGT ADMIN NAT/G CONTROL

B65
BROOKINGS INSTITUTION,BROOKINGS PAPERS ON PUBLIC POLICY. USA+45 ECO/UNDEV LEGIS CAP/ISM ECO/TAC TAX EDU/PROP CONTROL APPORT 20. PAGE 19 F0363 DIPLOM FOR/AID POLICY FINAN

B65
COLLOQUE SUR LA PLANIFICATION,LA PLANIFICATION COMME PROCESSUS DE DECISION. FRANCE SOCIETY MARKET LABOR LEGIS GP/REL EFFICIENCY INCOME ATTIT TECHRACY PLAN ECO/TAC PROB/SOLV

...MYTH IDEA/COMP 20. PAGE 26 F0508

B65
DANIELSON M.N.,FEDERAL-METROPOLITAN POLITICS AND THE COMMUTER CRISIS. PROVS LEGIS EXEC LEAD PWR ...DECISION MUNICH. PAGE 30 F0580
FEDERAL GOV/REL DIST/IND

B65
FLASH E.S. JR.,ECONOMIC ADVICE AND PRESIDENTIAL LEADERSHIP: THE COUNCIL OF ECONOMIC ADVISORS. USA+45 NAT/G EX/STRUC LEGIS TOP/EX ACT/RES ADMIN PRESIDENT CONGRESS. PAGE 41 F0808
PLAN CONSULT CHIEF

B65
FRYE R.J.,HOUSING AND URBAN RENEWAL IN ALABAMA. USA+45 NEIGH LEGIS BUDGET ADJUD ADMIN PARTIC...MGT MUNICH 20 ALABAMA URBAN/RNWL. PAGE 45 F0871
PROB/SOLV PLAN GOV/REL

B65
GOODSELL C.T.,ADMINISTRATION OF A REVOLUTION. PUERT/RICO ECO/UNDEV FINAN POL/PAR PROVS LEGIS PLAN BUDGET RECEIVE ADMIN COLONIAL LEAD MUNICH 20 ROOSEVLT/F. PAGE 49 F0951
EXEC SOC

B65
HADWIGER D.F.,PRESSURES AND PROTEST. NAT/G LEGIS PLAN LEAD PARTIC ROUTINE ATTIT POLICY. PAGE 53 F1030
AGRI GP/REL LOBBY CHOOSE

B65
LUGO-MARENCO J.J.,A STATEMENT OF THE LAWS OF NICARAGUA IN MATTERS AFFECTING BUSINESS. NICARAGUA AGRI DIST/IND EXTR/IND FINAN INDUS FAM WORKER INT/TRADE TAX MARRIAGE OWN BIO/SOC 20 TREATY RESOURCE/N MIGRATION. PAGE 82 F1606
CONSTN NAT/G LEGIS JURID

B65
MARGOLIS J.,THE PUBLIC ECONOMY OF URBAN COMMUNITIES. USA+45 LEGIS PROB/SOLV TAX LOBBY CHOOSE ATTIT MUNICH. PAGE 85 F1668
LOC/G DECISION FINAN

B65
MUND V.A.,GOVERNMENT AND BUSINESS (4TH ED.). USA+45 INDUS LG/CO SML/CO LEGIS INT/TRADE LICENSE PRICE ADJUD. PAGE 95 F1860
NAT/G ECO/TAC BUDGET CONTROL

B65
SELIGMAN B.B.,POVERTY AS A PUBLIC ISSUE. USA+45 ECO/DEV NAT/G PAY RECEIVE PERS/REL INCOME NEW/LIB 20. PAGE 119 F2347
LEGIS ECO/TAC STRATA DISCRIM

B65
WEIDENBAUM M.L.,CONGRESS AND THE FEDERAL BUDGET. FINAN ACT/RES DOMIN CONFER EXEC UTIL PWR NEW/LIB ...CHARTS CONGRESS. PAGE 144 F2844
BUDGET LEGIS PLAN DECISION

S65
HADDAD W.F.,"MR. SHRIVER AND THE SAVAGE POLITICS OF POVERTY" USA+45 LAW NAT/G DELIB/GP LEGIS GIVE LEAD CENTRAL PWR...SOC/WK CHARTS 20 CONGRESS POVRTY/WAR SHRIVER/S OEO. PAGE 53 F1028
WEALTH GOV/REL CONTROL TOP/EX

S65
KAUN D.E.,"THE FAIR LABOUR STANDARDS ACT: AN EVALUATION IN TERMS OF ITS STATED GOALS." SOUTH/AFR LAW LABOR BARGAIN PAY INGP/REL WEALTH 20. PAGE 69 F1364
ECO/TAC PRICE WORKER LEGIS

C65
MANSFIELD H.C.,"THE CONGRESS AND ECONOMIC POLICY" IN C. TRUMAN ED., THE CONGRESS AND AMERICA'S FUTURE." USA+45 USA-45 CONSTN NAT/G BUDGET ADMIN CONTROL EXEC LOBBY. PAGE 85 F1661
POLICY ECO/TAC PWR LEGIS

C65
PEGRUM D.E.,"PUBLIC REGULATION OF BUSINESS (REV ED)" LAW CONSTN DIST/IND SERV/IND LG/CO LEGIS OWN LAISSEZ SOCISM...POLICY DECISION BIBLIOG 20. PAGE 104 F2048
INDUS PLAN NEW/LIB PRICE

B66
BALDWIN D.A.,ECONOMIC DEVELOPMENT AND AMERICAN FOREIGN POLICY. USA+45 FINAN LG/CO LEGIS DIPLOM GIVE 20. PAGE 9 F0163
ECO/TAC FOR/AID ECO/UNDEV POLICY

B66
CONGRESSIONAL QUARTERLY SERV,FEDERAL ECONOMIC POLICY 1945-1965. USA+45 FINAN NAT/G CHIEF CONSULT TAX...CHARTS 20 PRESIDENT DEBT. PAGE 27 F0526
ECO/TAC BUDGET LEGIS

B66
GREENE L.E.,GOVERNMENT IN TENNESSEE (2ND ED.). USA+45 DIST/IND INDUS POL/PAR EX/STRUC LEGIS PLAN BUDGET GIVE CT/SYS...MGT T 20 TENNESSEE. PAGE 51 F0989
PROVS LOC/G CONSTN ADMIN

B66
HEVESY P.D.,THE UNIFICATION OF THE WORLD. FUT USA+45 WOR+45 ECO/DEV ECO/UNDEV LEGIS PROB/SOLV BAL/PWR ECO/TAC INT/TRADE PEACE. PAGE 59 F1160
DIPLOM FINAN INT/ORG

B66
LEE R.A.,TRUMAN AND TAFT-HARTLEY: A QUESTION OF MANDATE. USA+45 LAW CONSTN LG/CO CONTROL LOBBY GOV/REL PEACE NEW/LIB 20 TRUMAN/HS CONGRESS. PAGE 77 F1507
LEGIS TOP/EX ADJUD LABOR

B66
RAYBACK J.G.,A HISTORY OF AMERICAN LABOR. USA+45 USA-45 ECO/DEV LEGIS COLONIAL WAR INGP/REL PWR WEALTH 17/20. PAGE 110 F2156
LABOR LOBBY ECO/UNDEV

NAT/G

B66
ROSS A.M.,INDUSTRIAL RELATIONS AND ECONOMIC DEVELOPMENT. POL/PAR LEGIS WORKER BARGAIN PRICE EXEC LOBBY INCOME PWR...DECISION ANTHOL BIBLIOG 20. PAGE 114 F2243
ECO/UNDEV LABOR NAT/G GP/REL

B66
SOVERN M.I.,LEGAL RESTRAINTS ON RACIAL DISCRIMINATION IN EMPLOYMENT. USA+45 LAW INDUS LG/CO SML/CO DELIB/GP LEGIS SANCTION 20 NLRB PRESIDENT NEGRO CIV/RIGHTS RAILROAD. PAGE 124 F2446
DISCRIM RACE/REL WORKER JURID

B66
TIVEY L.J.,NATIONALISATION IN BRITISH INDUSTRY. UK LEGIS PARL/PROC GP/REL OWN ATTIT SOCISM 20. PAGE 131 F2578
NAT/G INDUS CONTROL LG/CO

B66
US HOUSE COMM BANKING CURRENCY,HEARINGS BEFORE HOUSE COMMITTEE ON BANKING AND CURRENCY: SALE OF SBA LOAN POOL PARTICIPATIONS. USA+45 LAW LEGIS ECO/TAC RATION 20 CONGRESS. PAGE 136 F2687
FINAN SML/CO ADJUD GOV/REL

B66
US SENATE COMM GOVT OPERATIONS,INTERGOVERNMENTAL PERSONNEL ACT OF 1966. USA+45 NAT/G CONSULT DELIB/GP WORKER TEC/DEV PAY AUTOMAT UTIL 20 CONGRESS. PAGE 139 F2730
ADMIN LEGIS EFFICIENCY EDU/PROP

S66
DAVIS O.A.,"A THEORY OF THE BUDGETARY PROCESS." ECO/DEV FINAN LEGIS PROB/SOLV GOV/REL...ECOMETRIC METH/CNCPT STAT CONT/OBS TREND METH/COMP SIMUL 20 CONGRESS. PAGE 30 F0592
DECISION NAT/G BUDGET EFFICIENCY

B67
ANDERSON S.V.,THE NORDIC COUNCIL: A STUDY OF SCANDINAVIAN REGIONALISM. DENMARK FINLAND ICELAND NORWAY SWEDEN MARKET NAT/G VOL/ASSN CONSULT PARL/PROC ATTIT...TIME/SEQ BIBLIOG 20. PAGE 5 F0098
INT/ORG REGION DIPLOM LEGIS

B67
BARDENS D.,CHURCHILL IN PARLIAMENT. UK DIPLOM ADJUD CONTROL AUTHORIT PERSON ORD/FREE 20 CHURCHLL/W PARLIAMENT. PAGE 10 F0186
TOP/EX LEGIS GOV/REL

B67
BIBBY J.,ON CAPITOL HILL. POL/PAR LOBBY PARL/PROC GOV/REL PERS/REL...JURID PHIL/SCI OBS INT BIBLIOG 20 CONGRESS PRESIDENT. PAGE 15 F0278
CONFER LEGIS CREATE LEAD

B67
BLAIR G.S.,LEGISLATIVE BODIES IN CALIFORNIA. USA+45 LAW POL/PAR LOBBY APPORT CHOOSE REPRESENT GP/REL ...T CALIFORNIA. PAGE 15 F0293
LEGIS PROVS LOC/G ADJUD

B67
BUSEY J.L.,NOTES ON COSTA RICAN DEMOCRACY. COSTA/RICA L/A+17C NAT/G POL/PAR LEGIS CHOOSE OWN ATTIT...BIBLIOG 20. PAGE 20 F0394
CONSTN MAJORIT SOCIETY ECO/UNDEV

B67
COWLING M.,1867 DISRAELI, GLADSTONE, AND REVOLUTION; THE PASSING OF THE SECOND REFORM BILL. UK LEGIS LEAD LOBBY GP/REL INGP/REL...DECISION BIBLIOG 19 REFORMERS. PAGE 28 F0545
PARL/PROC POL/PAR ATTIT LAW

B67
GOODMAN J.S.,THE DEMOCRATS AND LABOR IN RHODE ISLAND 9152-1962; CHANGES IN THE OLD ALLIANCE. USA+45 EDU/PROP LEAD GP/REL ROLE RHODE/ISL DEMOCRAT. PAGE 49 F0948
LABOR LOBBY POL/PAR LEGIS

B67
HANNAH H.W.,THE LEGAL BASE FOR UNIVERSITIES IN DEVELOPING COUNTRIES. AFR ASIA L/A+17C S/ASIA USA+45 FINAN CREATE EDU/PROP TASK EFFICIENCY ...JURID METH/COMP 20. PAGE 54 F1060
ADMIN LAW ACADEM LEGIS

B67
KIRK R.,THE POLITICAL PRINCIPLES OF ROBERT A. TAFT. USA+45 LABOR DIPLOM ADJUD ADJUST ORD/FREE TAFT/RA. PAGE 71 F1398
POL/PAR LEAD LEGIS ATTIT

B67
MEYERS M.,SOURCES OF THE AMERICAN REPUBLIC; A DOCUMENTARY HISTORY OF POLITICS, SOCIETY, AND THOUGHT (VOL. I, REV. ED.). USA-45 CULTURE STRUCT NAT/G LEGIS LEAD ATTIT...JURID SOC ANTHOL 17/19 PRESIDENT. PAGE 90 F1772
COLONIAL REV WAR

B67
MORRIS A.J.A.,PARLIAMENTARY DEMOCRACY IN THE NINETEENTH CENTURY. UK INDUS LOC/G NAT/G POL/PAR CONSULT LEGIS INT/TRADE ADMIN CHOOSE SUFF SOVEREIGN 19 PARLIAMENT. PAGE 93 F1835
TIME/SEQ CONSTN PARL/PROC POPULISM

B67
POLLACK N.,THE POPULIST MIND. USA-45 STRATA AGRI NAT/G POL/PAR LEGIS WORKER RACE/REL WEALTH...ANTHOL BIBLIOG 19 NEGRO. PAGE 107 F2097
POPULISM HIST/WRIT ATTIT INGP/REL

B67
SCOTT J.C.,ANTITRUST AND TRADE REGULATION TODAY: 1967. USA+45 MARKET LG/CO DELIB/GP LEGIS CAP/ISM INT/TRADE TAX PRICE INGP/REL WEALTH 20 SUPREME/CT. PAGE 118 F2334
NAT/G INDUS CONTROL JURID

B67
THOMAS M.J.,PRESIDENTIAL STATEMENTS ON EDUCATION: EXCERPTS FROM INAUGURAL AND STATE OF THE UNION MESSAGES 1789-1967. USA+45 USA-45 NAT/G BUDGET ...IDEA/COMP 18/20 PRESIDENT. PAGE 130 F2562 EDU/PROP TOP/EX LEGIS SCHOOL

B67
TOMA P.A.,THE POLITICS OF FOOD FOR PEACE; EXECUTIVE-LEGISLATIVE INTERACTION. USA+45 ECO/UNDEV POL/PAR DEBATE EXEC LOBBY CHOOSE PEACE...DECISION CHARTS. PAGE 131 F2580 FOR/AID POLICY LEGIS AGRI

B67
US CONGRESS JOINT ECO COMM,REPORT ON JANUARY 1967 ECONOMIC REPORT OF THE PRESIDENT. FINAN LABOR NAT/G LEGIS BUDGET INT/TRADE COST DEMAND INCOME PRODUC ...POLICY IDEA/COMP 20 CONGRESS. PAGE 135 F2663 CHIEF ECO/TAC PLAN DELIB/GP

L67
TRAVERS H. JR.,"AN EXAMINATION OF THE CAB'S MERGER POLICY." USA+45 USA-45 LAW NAT/G LEGIS PLAN ADMIN ...DECISION 20 CONGRESS. PAGE 131 F2584 ADJUD LG/CO POLICY DIST/IND

S67
CURTIN W.J.,"NATIONAL EMERGENCY DISPUTES LEGISLATION* ITS NEED AND ITS PROSPECTS IN THE TRANSPORTATION INDUSTRIES." USA+45 ECO/DEV INDUS NAT/G LEGIS ACT/RES BARGAIN POLICY. PAGE 29 F0565 JURID LABOR ADJUD DIST/IND

S67
GREGORY R.,"THE MINISTER'S LINE: OR, THE M4 COMES TO BERKSHIRE. PART I." UK CONSTN DIST/IND LEGIS TOP/EX PLAN ADJUD...GEOG 20. PAGE 51 F0994 DECISION CONSTRUC NAT/G DELIB/GP

S67
HILTON G.W.,"FEDERAL PARTICIPATION IN THE SUPERSONIC TRANSPORT PROGRAM." USA+45 LEGIS PROB/SOLV BUDGET ATTIT 20. PAGE 60 F1172 DIST/IND TEC/DEV FINAN NAT/G

S67
IBARRA J.,"EL EXPERIMENTO CUBANO." COM CUBA L/A+17C USA+45 ECO/UNDEV LEGIS INT/TRADE CONTROL REV NAT/LISM PWR 19/20 TREATY. PAGE 64 F1259 COLONIAL DIPLOM NAT/G POLICY

S67
LANDES W.M.,"THE EFFECT OF STATE FAIR EMPLOYMENT LAWS ON THE ECONOMIC POSITION OF NONWHITES." USA+45 PROVS SECT LEGIS ADMIN GP/REL RACE/REL...JURID CONCPT CHARTS HYPO/EXP NEGRO. PAGE 75 F1470 DISCRIM LAW WORKER

S67
LEWIS W.A.,"THE STATUTORY LANGUAGE OF LABOR DISQUALIFICATION IN STATE EMPLOYMENT SECURITY LAWS." LABOR WORKER WORK 20. PAGE 79 F1553 METH/COMP LEGIS SOC PROVS

S67
LINEBERRY R.L.,"REFORMISM AND PUBLIC POLICIES IN AMERICAN CITIES." USA+45 POL/PAR EX/STRUC LEGIS BUDGET TAX GP/REL...STAT CHARTS MUNICH. PAGE 80 F1573 DECISION POLICY LOC/G

S67
NEALE R.S.,"WORKING CLASS WOMEN AND WOMEN'S SUFFRAGE." UK LAW CONSTN LABOR NAT/G DELIB/GP LEGIS WORKER PAY PARTIC CHOOSE 19 FEMALE/SEX. PAGE 97 F1906 STRATA SEX SUFF DISCRIM

S67
NOURSE E.G.,"EARLY FLOWERING OF THE EMPLOYMENT ACT" USA+45 LABOR CONSULT DELIB/GP LEGIS BUDGET GOV/REL PRODUC WEALTH 20 INTRVN/ECO. PAGE 99 F1939 NAT/G WORKER ECO/TAC CONTROL

S67
PAI G.A.,"TAXATION AND PLANNING IN INDIA: A BIRDS-EYE VIEW." INDIA ELITES NAT/G LEGIS BUDGET CONTROL LOBBY INCOME...STAT CHARTS 20. PAGE 102 F2015 TAX PLAN WEALTH STRATA

S67
SHEFFTZ M.C.,"THE TRADE DISPUTES AND TRADE UNIONS ACT OF 1927: THE AFTERMATH OF THE GENERAL STRIKE." UK FINAN WORKER ADJUD LEAD PARL/PROC 20. PAGE 120 F2373 LEGIS ATTIT LABOR GP/REL

S67
SIPPEL D.,"INDIENS UNSICHERE ZUKUNFT." INDIA CULTURE ACADEM POL/PAR LEGIS COLONIAL CHOOSE SOVEREIGN...JURID 20. PAGE 122 F2416 SOCIETY STRUCT ECO/UNDEV NAT/G

S67
STEINHEIMER R.L. JR.,"THE UNIFORM COMMERCIAL CODE COMES OF AGE." USA+45 FINAN ACADEM JUDGE. PAGE 126 F2477 ADJUD LEGIS INT/TRADE GOV/REL

S67
WHITE W.L.,"THE TREASURY BOARD AND PARLIAMENT." CANADA CONSTN CONSULT LEGIS LEAD PARL/PROC GP/REL ...DECISION 20. PAGE 146 F2871 FINAN DELIB/GP NAT/G ADMIN

B86
O'CONNOR T.P.,THE PARNELL MOVEMENT: WITH A SKETCH OF IRISH PARTIES FROM 1843. IRELAND UK USA-45 LEGIS WORKER ECO/TAC COERCE CRIME REV CHOOSE ORD/FREE CATHISM LAISSEZ...SOC 19/20 PARLIAMENT PARNELL/CS LAND/LEAG. PAGE 100 F1957 LEAD DOMIN POL/PAR POLICY

LEGISLATION....SEE CONGRESS, LEGIS, SENATE, HOUSE/REP

LEGISLATIVE APPORTIONMENT....SEE APPORT

LEGISLATURES....SEE LEGIS

LEGIT....LEGITIMACY

N
NEW JERSEY STATE OF,SECOND REPORT TO GOVERNOR, SENATE, ASSEMBLY BY UNIFORM COMMERCIAL CODE STUDY COMMISSION. USA+45 INDUS LOC/G NAT/G PROF/ORG CONSULT ACT/RES LEGIT CT/SYS ATTIT NEW/JERSEY. PAGE 98 F1920 LAW FINAN CENTRAL PROVS

B38
HOBSON J.A.,IMPERIALISM. MOD/EUR UK WOR-45 CULTURE ECO/UNDEV NAT/G VOL/ASSN PLAN EDU/PROP LEGIT REGION COERCE ATTIT PWR...POLICY PLURIST TIME/SEQ GEN/LAWS TERR/GP 19/20. PAGE 60 F1187 DOMIN ECO/TAC BAL/PWR COLONIAL

B47
WEBER M.,THE THEORY OF SOCIAL AND ECONOMIC ORGANIZATION. STRUCT LABOR POL/PAR ECO/TAC LEGIT PRODUC BIOG. PAGE 144 F2840 ECO/DEV SOC PHIL/SCI LEAD

B50
HARTLAND P.C.,BALANCE OF INTERREGIONAL PAYMENTS OF NEW ENGLAND. USA+45 TEC/DEV ECO/TAC LEGIT ROUTINE BAL/PAY PROFIT 20 NEW/ENGLND FED/RESERV. PAGE 56 F1102 ECO/DEV FINAN REGION PLAN

B52
ALEXANDROWICZ C.H.,INTERNATIONAL ECONOMIC ORGANIZATION. WOR+45 ECO/DEV ECO/UNDEV DIST/IND FINAN MARKET PLAN ECO/TAC LEGIT DRIVE WEALTH ...POLICY CONCPT QUANT OBS TIME/SEQ GEN/LAWS WORK METH/GP EEC ILO OEEC UNESCO 20. PAGE 4 F0063 INT/ORG INT/TRADE

B52
EGLE W.P.,ECONOMIC STABILIZATION. USA+45 SOCIETY FINAN MARKET PLAN ECO/TAC DOMIN EDU/PROP LEGIT EXEC WEALTH...CONCPT METH/CNCPT TREND HYPO/EXP GEN/METH TOT/POP VAL/FREE 20. PAGE 36 F0708 NAT/G ECO/DEV CAP/ISM

S53
MCKEE J.B.,"STATUS AND POWER IN THE INDUSTRIAL COMMUNITY; A COMMENT ON DRUCKER'S THESIS." LABOR LEGIT LEAD GP/REL PWR...MGT CONCPT. PAGE 88 F1730 SOC STRATA NEIGH PARTIC

B55
FLORINSKY M.T.,INTEGRATED EUROPE. EUR+WWI FRANCE ITALY NETHERLAND UK ECO/DEV INT/ORG FORCES LEGIT FEDERAL ATTIT PWR WEALTH...POLICY GEOG CONCPT GEN/LAWS TOT/POP EEC OEEC 20. PAGE 42 F0816 FUT ECO/TAC REGION

B56
ABELS J.,THE TRUMAN SCANDALS. USA+45 USA-45 POL/PAR TAX LEGIT CT/SYS CHOOSE PRIVIL MORAL WEALTH 20 TRUMAN/HS PRESIDENT CONGRESS. PAGE 2 F0031 CRIME ADMIN CHIEF TRIBUTE

B56
WEBER M.,WIRTSCHAFT UND GESELLSCHAFT (2ND VOL.). STRUCT NAT/G POL/PAR LEAD PWR OBJECTIVE IDEA/COMP. PAGE 144 F2841 LEGIT JURID SOC

S56
BONILLA F.,"WHEN IS PETITION 'PRESSURE?'" (BMR)" USA+45 ELITES INDUS LABOR CHIEF EDU/PROP LEGIT ATTIT...INT CHARTS 20 CONGRESS PRESIDENT EISNHWR/DD. PAGE 16 F0312 LEGIS EX/STRUC INT/TRADE TARIFFS

S56
GORDON L.,"THE ORGANIZATION FOR EUROPEAN ECONOMIC COOPERATION." EUR+WWI INDUS INT/ORG NAT/G CONSULT DELIB/GP ACT/RES CREATE PLAN TEC/DEV EDU/PROP LEGIT WEALTH OEEC 20. PAGE 49 F0956 VOL/ASSN ECO/DEV

B57
BERLE A.A. JR.,ECONOMIC POWER AND FREE SOCIETY (PAMPHLET). CLIENT CONSTN EX/STRUC ECO/TAC CONTROL PARTIC PWR WEALTH MAJORIT. PAGE 14 F0261 LG/CO CAP/ISM INGP/REL LEGIT

B57
EHRMANN H.W.,ORGANIZED BUSINESS IN FRANCE. EUR+WWI MOD/EUR ECO/DEV VOL/ASSN LEGIT ATTIT PERCEPT PWR RESPECT...PLURIST SOC INT TOT/POP 20. PAGE 36 F0712 PROF/ORG ECO/TAC FRANCE

B58
KINDLEBERGER C.P.,INTERNATIONAL ECONOMICS. WOR+45 WOR-45 ECO/DEV ECO/UNDEV FINAN VOL/ASSN ACT/RES DIPLOM ECO/TAC LEGIT REGION ATTIT DRIVE ORD/FREE WEALTH...POLICY STAT TREND GEN/LAWS EEC ECSC OEEC 20. PAGE 71 F1391 INT/ORG BAL/PWR TARIFFS

B59
GOMEZ ROBLES J.,A STATEMENT OF THE LAWS OF GUATEMALA IN MATTERS AFFECTING BUSINESS (2ND ED. REV., ENLARGED). GUATEMALA L/A+17C LAW FINAN FAM WORKER ACT/RES DIPLOM ADJUD ADMIN GP/REL 20 OAS. PAGE 48 F0945 JURID NAT/G INDUS LEGIT

L59
BEGUIN B.,"ILO AND THE TRIPARTITE SYSTEM." EUR+WWI WOR+45 WOR-45 CONSTN ECO/DEV ECO/UNDEV INDUS INT/ORG NAT/G VOL/ASSN DELIB/GP PLAN TEC/DEV LEGIT ORD/FREE WEALTH...CONCPT TIME/SEQ WORK ILO 20. PAGE 12 F0228 LABOR

B60
LENCZOWSKI G.,OIL AND STATE IN THE MIDDLE EAST. FUT ISLAM
IRAN LAW ECO/UNDEV EXTR/IND NAT/G TOP/EX PLAN INDUS
TEC/DEV ECO/TAC LEGIT ADMIN COERCE ATTIT ALL/VALS NAT/LISM
PWR...CHARTS 20. PAGE 78 F1519

S60
BERG E.J.,"ECONOMIC BASIS OF POLITICAL CHOICE IN AFR
FRENCH WEST AFRICA." FRANCE ECO/UNDEV AGRI INDUS ECO/TAC
NAT/G PLAN LEGIT COLONIAL REGION ATTIT PWR WEALTH
...CONCPT FOR/TRADE 20. PAGE 13 F0257

S60
ENKE S.,"THE ECONOMIES OF GOVERNMENT PAYMENTS TO FAM
LIMIT POPULATION." FUT INDIA WOR+45 CULTURE FINAN ACT/RES
NAT/G CONSULT PLAN LEGIT CONTROL COST ATTIT
RIGID/FLEX HEALTH WEALTH...STAT OBS CHARTS TOT/POP
VAL/FREE 20. PAGE 38 F0736

S60
NANES A.,"THE EUROPEAN COMMUNITY AND THE UNITED INT/ORG
STATES: EVOLVING RELATIONS." EUR+WWI USA+45 WOR+45 REGION
ECO/UNDEV MARKET NAT/G DELIB/GP PLAN LEGIT ATTIT
PWR WEALTH...CONCPT STAT TIME/SEQ CON/ANAL EEC
METH/GP OEEC 20 EURATOM. PAGE 96 F1889

S60
NEISSER H.,"ECONOMIC IMPERALISM RECONSIDERED." ACT/RES
WOR+45 WOR-45 ECO/DEV ECO/UNDEV DIST/IND LEGIT ECO/TAC
COLONIAL PWR WEALTH SOCISM...MYTH MATH TIME/SEQ 20. CAP/ISM
PAGE 97 F1909 INT/TRADE

B61
KITZINGER V.W.,THE CHALLENGE OF THE COMMON MARKET. MARKET
EUR+WWI ECO/DEV DIST/IND PLAN ECO/TAC INT/TRADE INT/ORG
LEGIT ATTIT PWR WEALTH...TIME/SEQ TREND CHARTS EEC UK
20. PAGE 71 F1403

B61
MACMAHON A.W.,DELEGATION AND AUTONOMY. INDIA STRUCT ADMIN
LEGIS BARGAIN BUDGET ECO/TAC LEGIT EXEC REPRESENT PLAN
GOV/REL CENTRAL DEMAND EFFICIENCY PRODUC. PAGE 84 FEDERAL
F1637

B61
SCAMMEL W.M.,INTERNATIONAL MONETARY POLICY. WOR+45 INT/ORG
WOR-45 ACT/RES ECO/TAC LEGIT WEALTH...GEN/METH UN FINAN
20. PAGE 116 F2286 BAL/PAY

B62
GERSCHENKRON A.,ECONOMIC BACKWARDNESS IN HISTORICAL TEC/DEV
PERSPECTIVE. WOR+45 WOR-45 ECO/DEV ECO/UNDEV INDUS USSR
NAT/G LEGIT DRIVE...WELF/ST DECISION QUANT TREND
CHARTS 20. PAGE 47 F0919

B62
HEILBRONER R.L.,THE MAKING OF ECONOMIC SOCIETY. FUT CAP/ISM
WOR-45 SOCIETY STRATA ECO/DEV ECO/UNDEV ECO/TAC SOCISM
LEGIT ROUTINE...SOC RECORD REC/INT KNO/TEST CENSUS
STERTYP GEN/LAWS. PAGE 58 F1136

B62
URQUIDI C.W.,A STATEMENT OF THE LAWS OF BOLIVIA IN JURID
MATTERS AFFECTING BUSINESS (3RD ED. REV., INDUS
ENLARGED). L/A+17C LAW FINAN FAM WORKER ACT/RES NAT/G
DIPLOM ADJUD ADMIN GP/REL 20 BOLIV OAS. PAGE 133 LEGIT
F2626

B63
DEUTSCH K.W.,THE POLITICAL ROLE OF LABOR IN LABOR
DEVELOPING COUNTRIES. AFR ASIA S/ASIA USA+45 NAT/LISM
WOR+45 ECO/UNDEV POL/PAR ECO/TAC EDU/PROP LEGIT
COERCE ORD/FREE PWR WEALTH...OBS INT TREND VAL/FREE
20. PAGE 32 F0625

L63
ADERBIGDE A.,"SYMPOSIUM ON WEST AFRICA FINAN
INTEGRATION." AFR EUR+WWI FUT CULTURE SOCIETY ECO/TAC
STRATA DIST/IND INDUS MARKET SERV/IND DELIB/GP PLAN REGION
TEC/DEV DOMIN EDU/PROP LEGIT COERCE ATTIT ALL/VALS
...POLICY STAT TREND CHARTS VAL/FREE. PAGE 2 F0040

L63
RIDAH A.,"LE NEO-DESTOUR DEPUIS L'INDEPENDANCE." NAT/G
FUT ISLAM WOR+45 ECO/UNDEV INT/ORG SCHOOL DELIB/GP CONSTN
TOP/EX ACT/RES EDU/PROP LEGIT ATTIT ALL/VALS 20
TUNIS. PAGE 111 F2189

S63
POPPINO R.E.,"IMBALANCE IN BRAZIL." L/A+17C NAT/G POL/PAR
TOP/EX PLAN DIPLOM LEGIT DRIVE WEALTH...CON/ANAL ECO/TAC
FOR/TRADE LAFTA 20. PAGE 107 F2105 BRAZIL

B64
STOESSINGER J.G.,FINANCING THE UNITED NATIONS FINAN
SYSTEM. FUT WOR+45 CONSTN NAT/G VOL/ASSN DELIB/GP INT/ORG
EX/STRUC ECO/TAC LEGIT CT/SYS PWR WEALTH...STAT
TIME/SEQ TREND CHARTS TRUE/GP METH/GP TERR/GP
VAL/FREE. PAGE 126 F2493

S64
GALBRAITH V.,"JAPAN'S POSITION IN WORLD TRADE." ECO/DEV
ASIA AGRI INDUS CREATE ECO/TAC LEGIT DRIVE WEALTH DELIB/GP
...TREND EEC GATT FOR/TRADE 20 CHINJAP. PAGE 45
F0885

S64
WU Y.,"CHINA'S ECONOMY AND ITS PROSPECTS." ASIA ECO/DEV
CHINA/COM FUT USSR AGRI INDUS PLAN ECO/TAC LEGIT
WEALTH...STAT CON/ANAL CHARTS GEN/LAWS FOR/TRADE
20. PAGE 149 F2938

S65
WHITAKER A.P.,"ARGENTINA: STRUGGLE FOR RECOVERY." POL/PAR
L/A+17C USA+45 NAT/G TOP/EX PLAN LEGIT COERCE REV ECO/TAC
RIGID/FLEX PWR WEALTH...RECORD ALL/PROG ARGEN NAT/LISM
FOR/TRADE 20. PAGE 146 F2867

S66
LANGLEY D.,"POSTSCRIPT ON THE COLONIZATION OF THE INT/TRADE
INTERNATIONAL TRADE UNION MOVEMENT" USA+45 ELITES LABOR
FINAN DOMIN LEGIT ADMIN PWR...SOCIALIST 20 AFL/CIO NAT/G
CIA LOVESTN/J. PAGE 75 F1479 CONTROL

B67
GIAP V.N.,BIG VICTORY, GREAT TASK. VIETNAM WOR+45 WAR
FORCES PLAN DOMIN LEGIT RISK PEACE 20. PAGE 47 LEAD
F0921 ATTIT
INSPECT

B67
NYOMARKAY J.,CHARISMA AND FACTIONALISM IN THE NAZI FASCISM
PARTY. GERMANY POL/PAR LEGIT LEAD MARXISM INGP/REL
...NEW/IDEA METH/COMP GEN/LAWS BIBLIOG 20 HITLER/A. CHIEF
PAGE 99 F1949 PWR

L67
DOERFER G.L.,"THE LIMITS ON TRADE SECRET LAW JURID
IMPOSED BY FEDERAL PATENT & ANTITRUST SUPREMACY." GOV/REL
USA+45 LAW R+D CAP/ISM LICENSE CONTROL SANCTION POLICY
ORD/FREE. PAGE 33 F0651 LEGIT

L67
GOULD W.B.,"THE STATUS OF UNAUTHORIZED AND ECO/DEV
'WILDCAT' STRIKES UNDER THE NATIONAL LABOR INDUS
RELATIONS ACT." USA+45 ACT/RES BARGAIN ECO/TAC LABOR
LEGIT ADJUD ADMIN GP/REL MGT. PAGE 50 F0968 POLICY

L67
HUBBARD P.H.,"MONETARY RECOVERY UNDER THE CREATE
COPYRIGHT, PATENT, AND TRADEMARK ACTS." PROC/MFG LAW
TAX PAY LEGIT ADJUD GOV/REL OWN ORD/FREE 20. CONTROL
PAGE 62 F1228 FINAN

L67
ROBERTS E.F.,"THE CASE OF THE UNWARY HOME BUYER: ADJUD
THE HOUSING MERCHANT DID IT." USA+45 CLIENT CONSTRUC
DIST/IND MARKET LG/CO SML/CO PROB/SOLV LEGIT COST OWN
PROFIT. PAGE 112 F2207 LAW

S67
HALL B.,"THE PAINTER'S UNION: A PARTIAL VICTORY." LABOR
USA+45 PROB/SOLV LEGIT ADMIN REPRESENT 20. PAGE 53 CHIEF
F1043 CHOOSE
CRIME

S67
POWELL D.,"THE EFFECTIVENESS OF SOVIET ANTI- EDU/PROP
RELIGIOUS PROPAGANDA." USSR NAT/G DOMIN LEGIT ATTIT
NAT/LISM 20. PAGE 107 F2109 SECT
CONTROL

S67
REILLY T.J.,"FREEZING AND CONFISCATION OF CUBAN STRANGE
PROPERTY." CUBA USA+45 LAW DIPLOM LEGIT ADJUD OWN
CONTROL. PAGE 111 F2177 ECO/TAC

S67
SKILTON R.M.,"PROTECTION OF THE INSTALLMENT BUYER LAW
OF GOODS UNDER THE UNIFORM COMMERCIAL CODE." USA+45 ADJUD
NAT/G COST. PAGE 123 F2418 LEGIT
FINAN

LEHMAN R.L. F1512

LEIBENSTEIN H. F1513

LEIBNITZ/G....GOTTFRIED WILHELM VON LEIBNITZ

LEIBY J. F1514

LEIFER M. F1515

LEISERSON W. F1516

LEISURE....UNOBLIGATED TIME EXPENDITURES

B37
COLE W.E.,RECENT TRENDS IN RURAL PLANNING. USA-45 AGRI
LAW ECO/DEV LOC/G SECT EDU/PROP CRIME LEISURE AGE/Y NEIGH
HABITAT...SOC/WK MUNICH 20. PAGE 26 F0503 PLAN
ACT/RES

B42
VEBLEN T.B.,THE THEORY OF THE LEISURE CLASS. USA-45 WEALTH
SOCIETY STRATA STRUCT NAT/G SECT WORKER CREATE ELITES
EDU/PROP ATTIT...SOC GEN/LAWS 19. PAGE 141 F2772 LEISURE
PRODUC

B58
CROWE S.,THE LANDSCAPE OF POWER. UK CULTURE HABITAT
SERV/IND NAT/G CONSULT PARTIC NUC/PWR LEISURE...SOC TEC/DEV
EXHIBIT 20. PAGE 29 F0559 PLAN
CONTROL

B59
NORTON P.L.,URBAN PROBLEMS AND TECHNIQUES. AIR AGRI PLAN
INDUS MARKET TEC/DEV BUDGET LEISURE ALL/VALS LOC/G
...ANTHOL MUNICH 20 URBAN/RNWL. PAGE 99 F1936 HABITAT

B62
DE GRAZIA S.,OF TIME, WORK, AND LEISURE. USA+45 CULTURE
ECO/DEV WORKER HAPPINESS UTOPIA ALL/VALS...SOC LEISURE
NEW/IDEA TIME. PAGE 31 F0599 CONCPT

B66
BOWEN H.R.,AUTOMATION AND ECONOMIC PROGRESS. EUR+WWI USA+45 ECO/DEV INCOME ORD/FREE WEALTH ...POLICY ANTHOL 20. PAGE 17 F0327 AUTOMAT TEC/DEV WORKER LEISURE

B67
ELDREDGE H.W.,TAMING MEGALOPOLIS; WHAT IT IS AND WHAT COULD BE (VOL. I). FUT USA+45 WOR+45 SOCIETY STRUCT ECO/DEV INDUS LEISURE WEALTH...ANTHOL MUNICH. PAGE 37 F0717 PROB/SOLV PLAN TEC/DEV

S67
LAZUTKIN Y.,"SOCIALISM AND SPARE TIME." ECO/DEV WORKER CREATE TEC/DEV ROUTINE TIME. PAGE 76 F1497 LEISURE PRODUC SOCISM SOCIALIST

LEKACHMAN R. F1517,F1940

LEMIEUX V. F1518

LENCZOWSKI G. F1519

LEND/LEASE....LEND-LEASE PROGRAM(S)

LENIN V.I. F1520,F1521,F1522

LENIN/VI....VLADIMIR ILYICH LENIN

B40
HUNTER R.,REVOLUTION: WHY, HOW, WHEN? NAT/G ECO/TAC EDU/PROP COERCE ORD/FREE FASCISM POPULISM SOCISM 18/20 HITLER/A LENIN/VI. PAGE 63 F1246 REV METH/COMP LEAD CONSTN

B54
LENIN V.I.,SELECTED WORKS (12 VOLS.). USSR INTELL SOCIETY STRATA STRUCT NAT/G POL/PAR WORKER CAP/ISM REV WAR...MARXIST PHIL/SCI 20 MARX/KARL LENIN/VI. PAGE 78 F1520 COM MARXISM

B55
MAYO H.B.,DEMOCRACY AND MARXISM. COM USSR STRATA NAT/G WORKER ECO/TAC REV MORAL...PHIL/SCI HIST/WRIT IDEA/COMP WORSHIP 20 MARX/KARL LENIN/VI STALIN/J TROTSKY/L. PAGE 87 F1708 MARXISM CAP/ISM

B57
NANIWADA H.,STAAT UND WIRTSCHAFT; GRUNDLEGUNG DER NATIONALOEKONOMIE ALS DER LOGIK DER BURGERLICHEN GESELLSCHAFT. WOR+45 WOR-45 STRATA MARKET WORKER INGP/REL DEMAND EQUILIB WEALTH...POLICY IDEA/COMP GEN/LAWS 17/20 MARX/KARL KEYNES/JM LENIN/VI. PAGE 96 F1890 ALL/IDEOS ECO/TAC SOCIETY NAT/G

B59
HENDEL S.,THE SOVIET CRUCIBLE. USSR LEAD COERCE NAT/LISM UTOPIA PWR...POLICY CONCPT ANTHOL 20 STALIN/J LENIN/VI MARX/KARL BOLSHEVIK. PAGE 58 F1147 COM MARXISM REV TOTALISM

B59
MARTIN K.,WAR, HISTORY, AND HUMAN NATURE. FRANCE GERMANY INDIA UK UNIV POL/PAR COLONIAL DETER REV MARXISM PACIFISM...PSY CONCPT PREDICT LENIN/VI GANDHI/M. PAGE 86 F1683 PERSON WAR ATTIT IDEA/COMP

B66
BRODERSEN A.,THE SOVIET WORKER: LABOR AND GOVERNMENT IN SOVIET SOCIETY. USSR STRUCT INDUS LABOR PLAN PAY INGP/REL PRODUC...POLICY GEN/LAWS BIBLIOG 20 STALIN/J LENIN/VI BOLSHEVISM KHRUSH/N. PAGE 19 F0357 WORKER ROLE NAT/G MARXISM

S67
LEONTYEV L.,"THE LENINIST PRINCIPLES OF SOCIALIST ECONOMIC MANAGEMENT." USA+45 USSR POL/PAR WORKER PLAN ECO/TAC EFFICIENCY PRODUC MARXISM...POLICY SOCIALIST MGT TREND 20 LENIN/VI MARX/KARL. PAGE 78 F1529 SOCISM CAP/ISM IDEA/COMP ECO/DEV

LENS S. F1523

LENSKI G. F1524

LENSKI G.E. F1525

LENT G.E. F1526

LEONARD L.L. F1527

LEONTIEF W. F1528

LEONTYEV L. F1529

LERNER A.P. F1530

LERNER E.M. F1531

LESAGE/J....J. LESAGE

LESTER R.A. F1532,F1533,F1717

LETHBRIDGE H.J. F1534,F1535

LETICHE J.M. F1536,F1537

LEUTHOLD D.A. F2471

LEVELLERS....LEVELLERS PARTY

LEVENSTEIN A. F1538

LEVER E.A. F1539

LEVI M. F1540

LEVIN T. F1541

LEVINE L. F1542

LEVINSON E. F1543

LEVY H.V. F1544

LEVY M.F. F2193

LEWIN J. F1545

LEWIN P. F1546

LEWIS E.G. F1547

LEWIS G.K. F1548

LEWIS J.N. F1131

LEWIS J.P. F1549

LEWIS L.J. F1550

LEWIS V.B. F0909,F1551

LEWIS W.A. F1552,F1553

LEWIS/A....ARTHUR LEWIS

LEWIS/JL....JOHN L. LEWIS

LEYS C.T. F1554

LFNA....LEAGUE OF FREE NATIONS ASSOCIATION

LG/CO....LARGE COMPANY

B13
DAVENPORT H.J.,THE ECONOMICS OF ENTERPRISE. UNIV FINAN SML/CO RENT COST WEALTH GEN/LAWS. PAGE 30 F0582 CAP/ISM PRICE ECO/TAC LG/CO

N19
MARCUS W.,US PRIVATE INVESTMENT AND ECONOMIC AID IN UNDERDEVELOPED COUNTRIES (PAMPHLET). USA+45 LG/CO NAT/G CAP/ISM EDU/PROP 20. PAGE 85 F1666 FOR/AID ECO/UNDEV FINAN PLAN

N19
MCCONNELL G.,THE STEEL SEIZURE OF 1952 (PAMPHLET). USA+45 FINAN INDUS PROC/MFG LG/CO EX/STRUC ADJUD CONTROL GP/REL ORD/FREE PWR 20 TRUMAN/HS PRESIDENT CONGRESS. PAGE 88 F1721 DELIB/GP LABOR PROB/SOLV NAT/G

N19
MEZERIK A.G.,ECONOMIC AID FOR UNDERDEVELOPED COUNTRIES (PAMPHLET). AFR USSR WOR+45 FINAN LG/CO DELIB/GP NUC/PWR...GEOG CENSUS CHARTS 20 UN THIRD/WRLD. PAGE 90 F1775 FOR/AID ECO/UNDEV DIPLOM POLICY

N19
PALAMOUNTAIN JC J.R.,THE DOLCIN CASE AND THE FEDERAL TRADE COMMISSION (PAMPHLET). USA+45 LAW MARKET SERV/IND LG/CO NAT/G BIO/SOC 20 FTC. PAGE 103 F2018 ADJUD PROB/SOLV EDU/PROP HEALTH

N19
US CHAMBER OF COMMERCE,THE SIGNIFICANCE OF CONCENTRATION RATIOS (PAMPHLET). USA+45 FINAN INDUS ADMIN...METH/CNCPT SAMP CHARTS 20. PAGE 134 F2647 MARKET PREDICT LG/CO CONTROL

B29
JONES M.M.,CORPORATION CONTRIBUTIONS TO COMMUNITY WELFARE AGENCIES (PAMPHLET). DELIB/GP TAX CONTROL PARTIC RATIONAL POLICY. PAGE 68 F1339 LG/CO GIVE NEIGH SOC/WK

B31
CROOK W.H.,THE GENERAL STRIKE: A STUDY OF LABOR'S TRAGIC WEAPON IN THEORY AND PRACTICE. BELGIUM FRANCE SWEDEN UK WOR-45 PROB/SOLV ECO/TAC DOMIN PWR ...POLICY TIME/SEQ NAT/COMP GEN/LAWS 19/20 STRIKE. PAGE 29 F0555 LABOR WORKER LG/CO BARGAIN

B32
THOMPSON C.D.,CONFESSIONS OF THE POWER TRUST. MARKET ACT/RES EDU/PROP CONTROL GOV/REL INCOME OWN ...MGT 20 FTC MONOPOLY. PAGE 130 F2564 LG/CO SERV/IND PWR FINAN

S32
DODD E.M. JR.,"FOR WHOM ARE CORPORATE MANAGERS TRUSTEES'." SERV/IND CAP/ISM GIVE LEAD REPRESENT ORD/FREE WEALTH. PAGE 33 F0648
LG/CO ROLE NAT/G PLAN

B36
BURNS A.R.,THE DECLINE OF COMPETITION. LAW LG/CO NAT/G SML/CO LEGIS PRICE AGREE CONTROL GP/REL INCOME PRODUC...POLICY 19/20 NRA. PAGE 20 F0390
MARKET GEN/LAWS INDUS

B37
DALTON J.E.,SUGAR: A CASE STUDY OF GOVERNMENT CONTROL. USA-45 AGRI PROC/MFG LG/CO LEGIS PROB/SOLV ECO/TAC GP/REL...CHARTS 19/20. PAGE 30 F0575
CONTROL NAT/G INDUS POLICY

B39
CLARK J.M.,SOCIAL CONTROL OF BUSINESS (2ND ED.). ECO/DEV FINAN LG/CO PLAN ECO/TAC PRICE SUPEGO...T 20. PAGE 25 F0480
CAP/ISM CONTROL LAISSEZ METH/COMP

B40
BATCHELOR B.,THE NEW OUTLOOK IN BUSINESS. LAW WORKER TAX LEAD ORD/FREE...POLICY TREND. PAGE 11 F0208
LG/CO GP/REL CAP/ISM LABOR

S43
GOLDEN C.S.,"NEW PATTERNS OF DEMOCRACY." NEIGH DELIB/GP EDU/PROP EXEC PARTIC...MGT METH/CNCPT OBS TREND. PAGE 48 F0935
LABOR REPRESENT LG/CO GP/REL

B46
DAVIES E.,NATIONAL ENTERPRISE: THE DEVELOPMENT OF THE PUBLIC CORPORATION. UK LG/CO EX/STRUC WORKER PROB/SOLV COST ATTIT SOCISM 20. PAGE 30 F0584
ADMIN NAT/G CONTROL INDUS

B46
DRUCKER P.F.,CONCEPT OF CORPORATION. LAW LABOR WORKER PRICE CONTROL LEAD GP/REL POLICY. PAGE 34 F0665
LG/CO CENTRAL INGP/REL

B47
BAERWALD F.,FUNDAMENTALS OF LABOR ECONOMICS. LAW INDUS LABOR LG/CO CONTROL GP/REL INCOME TOTALISM ...MGT CHARTS GEN/LAWS BIBLIOG 20. PAGE 8 F0150
ECO/DEV WORKER MARKET

B47
BOWEN R.H.,GERMAN THEORIES OF THE CORPORATIVE STATE, WITH SPECIAL REFERENCES TO THE PERIOD 1870-1919. GERMANY INDUS LG/CO CATHISM SOCISM...SOC 18/20. PAGE 17 F0328
IDEA/COMP CENTRAL NAT/G POLICY

B47
WHITEHEAD T.N.,LEADERSHIP IN A FREE SOCIETY; A STUDY IN HUMAN RELATIONS BASED ON AN ANALYSIS OF PRESENT-DAY INDUSTRIAL CIVILIZATION. WOR-45 STRUCT R+D LABOR LG/CO SML/CO WORKER PLAN PROB/SOLV TEC/DEV DRIVE...MGT 20. PAGE 146 F2872
INDUS LEAD ORD/FREE SOCIETY

S50
DALTON M.,"CONFLICTS BETWEEN STAFF AND LINE MANAGERIAL OFFICERS" (BMR). USA+45 USA-45 ELITES LG/CO WORKER PROB/SOLV ADMIN EXEC EFFICIENCY PRODUC ...GP/COMP 20. PAGE 30 F0576
MGT ATTIT GP/REL INDUS

B51
COOKE C.A.,CORPORATION TRUST AND COMPANY: AN ESSAY IN LEGAL HISTORY. UK STRUCT LEGIS CAP/ISM GP/REL PROFIT 13/20 COMPNY/ACT. PAGE 27 F0531
LG/CO FINAN ECO/TAC JURID

B51
DIMOCK M.E.,FREE ENTERPRISE AND THE ADMINISTRATIVE STATE. FINAN LG/CO BARGAIN BUDGET DOMIN CONTROL INGP/REL EFFICIENCY 20. PAGE 33 F0640
CAP/ISM ADMIN MGT MARKET

B51
OWENS R.N.,BUSINESS, ORGANIZATION, AND COMBINATION. USA+45 USA-45 LAW NAT/G LEGIS ECO/TAC CONTROL INGP/REL...JURID GP/COMP 20 NEW/DEAL. PAGE 102 F2006
SML/CO LG/CO STRUCT GP/REL

B52
ANDREWS F.E.,CORPORATION GIVING. LAW TAX EDU/PROP ADMIN...POLICY STAT CHARTS. PAGE 5 F0101
LG/CO GIVE SML/CO FINAN

B52
MACHLUP F.,THE POLITICAL ECONOMY OF MONOPOLY: BUSINESS, LABOR AND GOVERNMENT POLICIES. USA+45 USA-45 ECO/DEV LABOR NAT/G CAP/ISM PWR...POLICY CHARTS T 20. PAGE 83 F1630
ECO/TAC DOMIN LG/CO CONTROL

B52
TANNENBAUM F.,A PHILOSOPHY OF LABOR. SOCIETY STRATA INDUS LG/CO AGREE ADJUST OWN ORD/FREE PWR...CONCPT 20. PAGE 128 F2533
LABOR PHIL/SCI WORKER CREATE

S53
GABLE R.W.,"NAM: INFLUENTIAL LOBBY OR KISS OF DEATH?" (BMR)" USA+45 LAW INSPECT EDU/PROP ADMIN CONTROL INGP/REL EFFICIENCY PWR 20 CONGRESS NAM TAFT/HART. PAGE 45 F0880
LOBBY LEGIS INDUS LG/CO

B54
EMERSON F.D.,SHAREHOLDER DEMOCRACY: A BROADER OUTLOOK FOR CORPORATIONS. DELIB/GP EX/STRUC LEGIS ADJUD CONTROL REPRESENT INGP/REL OWN PWR...POLICY STAT RECORD. PAGE 37 F0727
LG/CO PARTIC MAJORIT TREND

B54
FRIEDMAN W.,THE PUBLIC CORPORATION: A COMPARATIVE SYMPOSIUM (UNIVERSITY OF TORONTO SCHOOL OF LAW COMPARATIVE LAW SERIES, VOL. I). AFR SWEDEN USA+45 INDUS INT/ORG NAT/G REGION CENTRAL FEDERAL...POLICY JURID IDEA/COMP NAT/COMP ANTHOL 20 MONOPOLY EUROPE. PAGE 44 F0861
LAW SOCISM LG/CO OWN

B54
LOCKLIN D.P.,ECONOMICS OF TRANSPORTATION (4TH ED.). USA+45 USA-45 SEA AIR LAW FINAN LG/CO EX/STRUC ADMIN CONTROL...STAT CHARTS 19/20 RAILROAD PUB/TRANS. PAGE 81 F1592
ECO/DEV DIST/IND ECO/TAC TEC/DEV

B54
RICHTER R.,DAS KONKURRENZ PROBLEM IM OLIGOPOL. LG/CO BARGAIN PRICE COST...CONCPT 20 MONOPOLY. PAGE 111 F2188
CONTROL GAME ECO/TAC GP/REL

C54
BERLE A.A. JR.,"THE 20TH CENTURY CAPITALIST REVOLUTION." ECO/DEV NAT/G DIPLOM PRICE CONTROL ATTIT...BIBLIOG/A 20. PAGE 14 F0260
LG/CO CAP/ISM MGT PWR

B55
BERNSTEIN M.H.,REGULATING BUSINESS BY INDEPENDENT COMMISSION. USA+45 USA-45 LG/CO CHIEF LEGIS PROB/SOLV ADJUD SANCTION GP/REL ATTIT...TIME/SEQ 19/20 MONOPOLY PRESIDENT CONGRESS. PAGE 14 F0268
DELIB/GP CONTROL CONSULT

B55
PALAMOUNTAIN JC J.R.,THE POLITICS OF DISTRIBUTION. USA+45 LG/CO SML/CO BAL/PWR CONTROL EQUILIB 20. PAGE 103 F2019
DIST/IND ECO/TAC CAP/ISM GP/REL

B55
SERRANO MOSCOSO E.,A STATEMENT OF THE LAWS OF ECUADOR IN MATTERS AFFECTING BUSINESS (2ND ED.). ECUADOR INDUS LABOR LG/CO NAT/G LEGIS TAX CONTROL MARRIAGE 20. PAGE 120 F2359
FINAN ECO/UNDEV LAW CONSTN

S55
KELLY W.E.,"HOW SALES EXECUTIVES USE FACTORING TO BOOST SALES AND PROFITS TODAY." FINAN LG/CO BUDGET EFFICIENCY PROFIT...MGT PRODUCT. PAGE 70 F1372
INDUS ECO/DEV CONSULT MARKET

B56
BONNETT C.E.,HISTORY OF EMPLOYERS' ASSOCIATIONS IN THE UNITED STATES (1ST ED.). MARKET DETER GP/REL ADJUST. PAGE 16 F0316
LABOR VOL/ASSN LG/CO

B56
GILBERT L.D.,DIVIDENDS AND DEMOCRACY. DELIB/GP LEGIS CAP/ISM ADJUD LOBBY OWN PWR LAISSEZ MAJORIT. PAGE 47 F0922
LG/CO INGP/REL CONTROL PARTIC

B56
ISARD W.,LOCATION AND SPACE-ECONOMY: GENERAL THEORY RELATING TO INDUSTRIAL LOCATION, MARKET AREAS, LAND USE, TRADE... UNIV DIST/IND MARKET LG/CO SML/CO TEC/DEV GP/REL EQUILIB HABITAT...NEW/IDEA MATH CHARTS 20. PAGE 66 F1290
GEN/LAWS GEOG INDUS REGION

B56
WHYTE W.H. JR.,THE ORGANIZATION MAN. CULTURE FINAN VOL/ASSN DOMIN EDU/PROP EXEC DISPL HABITAT ROLE ...PERS/TEST STERTYP. PAGE 146 F2875
ADMIN LG/CO PERSON CONSEN

B57
ASSN U BUREAUS BUS-ECO RES,INDEX OF PUBLICATIONS OF BUREAUS OF BUSINESS AND ECONOMIC RESEARCH 1950-56 AND YEARLY SUPPLEMENTS THROUGH 1967. FINAN OP/RES PLAN GOV/REL INCOME AGE...POLICY 20. PAGE 7 F0133
BIBLIOG ECO/DEV ECO/TAC LG/CO

B57
BERLE A.A. JR.,ECONOMIC POWER AND FREE SOCIETY (PAMPHLET). CLIENT CONSTN EX/STRUC ECO/TAC CONTROL PARTIC PWR WEALTH MAJORIT. PAGE 14 F0261
LG/CO CAP/ISM INGP/REL LEGIT

B57
INTL BANKING SUMMER SCHOOL,RELATIONS BETWEEN THE CENTRAL BANKS AND COMMERCIAL BANKS. EUR+WWI FRANCE GERMANY/W ITALY UK USA+45 USSR INDUS INT/ORG CAP/ISM CONTROL MONEY. PAGE 65 F1282
FINAN NAT/G GP/REL LG/CO

B57
MASON E.S.,ECONOMIC CONCENTRATION AND THE MONOPOLY PROBLEM. USA+45 USA-45 LAW ELITES ECO/DEV LABOR RATION PRICE PWR WEALTH...CHARTS 20 MONOPOLY. PAGE 87 F1696
GP/REL LG/CO CONTROL MARKET

S57
CUNNINGHAM E.M.,"THE BUSINESS MAN AND HIS LAWYER." USA+45 LG/CO SML/CO TOP/EX CHOOSE SKILL...JURID MGT 20. PAGE 29 F0561
CONSULT LAW DECISION SERV/IND

B58
CHEEK G.,ECONOMIC AND SOCIAL IMPLICATIONS OF AUTOMATION: A BIBLIOGRAPHIC REVIEW (PAMPHLET). USA+45 LG/CO WORKER CREATE PLAN CONTROL ROUTINE PERS/REL EFFICIENCY PRODUC...METH/COMP 20. PAGE 24 F0459
BIBLIOG/A SOCIETY INDUS AUTOMAT

B58
COOK P.L.,EFFECTS OF MERGERS: SIX STUDIES. USA+45 ECO/DEV LABOR LG/CO SML/CO VOL/ASSN ADMIN EFFICIENCY 20 CASEBOOK. PAGE 27 F0529
INDUS FINAN EX/STRUC GP/REL

B58
MCIVOR R.C.,CANADIAN MONETARY, BANKING, AND FISCAL DEVELOPMENT. CANADA INDUS LG/CO NAT/G SML/CO CONTROL WAR...GEN/LAWS BIBLIOG 17/20. PAGE 88 F1729
ECO/TAC FINAN ECO/DEV WEALTH

B58
MOONEY R.E.,INFLATION AND RECESSION? AFR USA+45 LABOR LG/CO PRESS LEAD...IDEA/COMP ANTHOL 20. PAGE 93 F1821
PRICE ECO/TAC NAT/G PRODUC

B58
MUSGRAVE R.A.,CLASSICS IN THE THEORY OF PUBLIC FINANCE. UNIV MARKET LG/CO NAT/G CAP/ISM PRICE OPTIMAL...IDEA/COMP ANTHOL 19/20 SAY/EMIL EDGEWORTH LINDAHL/E RITSCHL/H. PAGE 95 F1870
TAX FINAN ECO/TAC GP/REL

L58
CYERT R.M.,"THE ROLE OF EXPECTATIONS IN BUSINESS DECISION-MAKING." PROB/SOLV PRICE RIGID/FLEX. PAGE 29 F0566
LG/CO DECISION ROUTINE EXEC

S58
EMERSON F.D.,"THE ROLES OF MANAGEMENT AND SHAREHOLDERS IN CORPORATE GOVERNMENT." CLIENT DELIB/GP CREATE ADMIN EXEC PARTIC PERS/REL PWR. PAGE 37 F0728
LG/CO LAW INGP/REL REPRESENT

S58
LATTIN N.D.,"MINORITY AND DISSENTING SHAREHOLDERS' RIGHTS IN FUNDAMENTAL CHANGES." FINAN LEGIS ADJUD PARTIC ROUTINE CHOOSE REPRESENT INGP/REL TREND. PAGE 76 F1487
MAJORIT LG/CO LAW CREATE

S58
MANSFIELD E.,"A STUDY OF DECISION-MAKING WITHIN THE FIRM." LG/CO WORKER INGP/REL COST EFFICIENCY PRODUC ...CHARTS 20. PAGE 85 F1658
OP/RES PROB/SOLV AUTOMAT ROUTINE

S58
O'NEAL F.H.,"RECENT LEGISLATION AFFECTING CLOSE CORPORATIONS." LAW EX/STRUC ECO/TAC ROUTINE CHOOSE RIGID/FLEX...MAJORIT MGT TREND. PAGE 100 F1959
LG/CO LEGIS REPRESENT PARTIC

B59
FELS R.,AMERICAN BUSINESS CYCLES 1865-1897. USA+45 ECO/DEV LG/CO SML/CO PROB/SOLV TEC/DEV CAP/ISM INT/TRADE DEMAND...POLICY CHARTS METH 19 DEPRESSION. PAGE 40 F0782
FINAN INDUS TREND ECO/TAC

B59
FERRY W.H.,THE CORPORATION AND THE ECONOMY. CLIENT LAW CONSTN LABOR NAT/G PLAN INT/TRADE PARTIC CONSEN ORD/FREE PWR POLICY. PAGE 40 F0787
LG/CO CONTROL REPRESENT

B59
MARTIN D.D.,MERGERS AND THE CLAYTON ACT. FINAN LEGIS GP/REL...DECISION METH/COMP BIBLIOG 20. PAGE 86 F1681
OWN ECO/TAC LG/CO POLICY

B59
RAMANADHAM V.V.,PROBLEMS OF PUBLIC ENTERPRISE: THOUGHTS ON BRITISH EXPERIENCE. UK FINAN INDUS PLAN PRICE CENTRAL...POLICY 20. PAGE 109 F2140
SOCISM LG/CO ECO/DEV GOV/REL

B59
VERNEY D.V.,PUBLIC ENTERPRISE IN SWEDEN. FUT SWEDEN UK INDUS POL/PAR LEGIS PROB/SOLV CAP/ISM INT/TRADE CONTROL SOCISM...MGT CONCPT NAT/COMP 20 SOCDEM/PAR CIVIL/SERV. PAGE 141 F2778
ECO/DEV POLICY LG/CO NAT/G

B59
WORTHY J.C.,BIG BUSINESS AND FREE MEN. LG/CO EX/STRUC EDU/PROP LEAD CHOOSE GP/REL ATTIT DRIVE ROLE ORD/FREE...MAJORIT 20. PAGE 149 F2927
ELITES LOC/G TOP/EX PARTIC

S59
MILLER A.S.,"CONSTITUTIONALIZING THE CORPORATION." LABOR NAT/G WORKER PWR...POLICY MGT. PAGE 91 F1789
CONSTN INGP/REL LG/CO CONTROL

B60
BOULDING K.E.,LINEAR PROGRAMMING AND THE THEORY OF THE FIRM. ACT/RES PLAN...MGT MATH. PAGE 17 F0323
LG/CO NEW/IDEA COMPUTER

B60
EELLS R.S.F.,THE MEANING OF MODERN BUSINESS. LOC/G NAT/G NEIGH EX/STRUC PARTIC GP/REL INGP/REL DECISION. PAGE 36 F0706
LG/CO REPRESENT POLICY PLAN

B60
FORBUSH D.R.,PROBLEMS OF CORPORATE POWER. CLIENT LAW ELITES ADJUD...DECISION MGT. PAGE 42 F0822
LG/CO PWR CONTROL GP/REL

B60
GILMORE D.R.,DEVELOPING THE "LITTLE" ECONOMIES. USA+45 FINAN LG/CO PROF/ORG VOL/ASSN CREATE ADMIN. PAGE 47 F0924
ECO/TAC LOC/G PROVS PLAN

B60
HUGHES J.,NATIONALISED INDUSTRIES IN THE MIXED ECONOMY (PAMPHLET). FINAN PROB/SOLV CAP/ISM OWN ...SOCIALIST STAT METH/COMP 20. PAGE 63 F1233
SOCISM LG/CO GOV/REL ECO/DEV

B60
RAY D.D.,ACCOUNTING AND BUSINESS FLUCTUATIONS. LG/CO SML/CO FEEDBACK DEMAND...CHARTS IDEA/COMP BIBLIOG 20. PAGE 109 F2154
FINAN AFR CONTROL

B60
ROBSON W.A.,NATIONALIZED INDUSTRY AND PUBLIC OWNERSHIP. UK ECO/DEV FINAN LABOR LG/CO POL/PAR LEGIS ACT/RES GP/REL...TREND IDEA/COMP 20. PAGE 113 F2227
NAT/G OWN INDUS ATTIT

B60
SHANNON D.A.,THE GREAT DEPRESSION. USA-45 FINAN LG/CO SCHOOL SML/CO DELIB/GP RECEIVE REV EATING INCOME...ANTHOL MUNICH 20 ROOSEVLT/F CONGRESS. PAGE 120 F2365
WEALTH NAT/G AGRI INDUS

B60
WEINER H.E.,BRITISH LABOR AND PUBLIC OWNERSHIP. UK SERV/IND LG/CO WORKER CONTROL OWN 20. PAGE 145 F2850
LABOR NAT/G INDUS ATTIT

S60
FORM W.H.,"ORGANIZED LABOR'S IMAGE OF COMMUNITY POWER STRUCTURE." LABOR LG/CO CONTROL LEAD REPRESENT...DECISION METH/CNCPT INT QU SAMP. PAGE 42 F0829
NEIGH PARTIC PWR GP/REL

S60
POLLARD J.A.,"EMERGING PATTERNS OF CORPORATE GIVING." FINAN DELIB/GP PLAN EDU/PROP CENTRAL TREND. PAGE 107 F2098
GIVE LG/CO ADMIN MGT

B61
AGARWAL R.C.,STATE ENTERPRISE IN INDIA. FUT INDIA UK FINAN INDUS ADMIN CONTROL OWN...POLICY CHARTS BIBLIOG 20 RAILROAD. PAGE 3 F0048
ECO/UNDEV SOCISM GOV/REL LG/CO

B61
AMERICAN MANAGEMENT ASSN,SUPERIOR-SUBORDINATE COMMUNICATION IN MANAGEMENT. STRATA FINAN INDUS SML/CO WORKER CONTROL EXEC ATTIT 20. PAGE 5 F0090
MGT ACT/RES PERS/REL LG/CO

B61
CLARK J.M.,COMPETITION AS A DYNAMIC PROCESS. ECO/DEV EXTR/IND INDUS LG/CO TEC/DEV ECO/TAC PRICE EQUILIB PRODUC...NEW/IDEA CAP 20. PAGE 25 F0483
WEALTH GP/REL FINAN PROFIT

B61
FRIEDMANN W.G.,JOINT INTERNATIONAL BUSINESS VENTURES. ASIA ISLAM L/A+17C ECO/DEV DIST/IND FINAN PROC/MFG FACE/GP LG/CO NAT/G VOL/ASSN CONSULT EX/STRUC PLAN ADMIN ROUTINE WEALTH...OLD/LIB FOR/TRADE WORK 20. PAGE 44 F0865
ECO/UNDEV INT/TRADE

B61
GORDON R.A.,BUSINESS LEADERSHIP IN THE LARGE CORPORATION. USA+45 SOCIETY EX/STRUC ADMIN CONTROL ROUTINE GP/REL PWR...MGT 20. PAGE 49 F0960
LG/CO LEAD DECISION LOBBY

B61
GREY A.L.,ECONOMIC ISSUES AND POLICIES; READINGS IN INTRODUCTORY ECONOMICS (2ND ED.). WOR+45 ECO/UNDEV FINAN MARKET LABOR LG/CO INT/TRADE BAL/PAY WEALTH ...ANTHOL T. PAGE 51 F0996
ECO/TAC PROB/SOLV METH/COMP

B61
INTL BANKING SUMMER SCHOOL,TRENDS IN BANK CREDIT AND FINANCE. EUR+WWI NETHERLAND ECO/DEV PROF/ORG PLAN BUDGET 20 EEC. PAGE 65 F1283
FINAN ECO/TAC NAT/G LG/CO

B61
LONGRIGG S.H.,OIL IN THE MIDDLE EAST: ITS DISCOVERY AND DEVELOPMENT. ECO/UNDEV LG/CO LOC/G TEC/DEV WEALTH...STAT TIME/SEQ 20 OIL. PAGE 82 F1599
ISLAM EXTR/IND

B61
MIT CENTER INTERNATIONAL STU,OFFICIAL SERIAL PUBLICATIONS RELATING TO ECONOMIC DEVELOPMENT IN AFRICA SOUTH OF THE SAHARA. AFR SOCIETY AGRI FINAN INDUS LG/CO ADMIN 20. PAGE 92 F1806
BIBLIOG ECO/UNDEV ECO/TAC NAT/G

B61
RUEDA B.,A STATEMENT OF THE LAWS OF COLOMBIA IN MATTERS AFFECTING BUSINESS (3RD ED.). INDUS FAM LABOR LG/CO NAT/G LEGIS TAX CONTROL MARRIAGE 20 COLOMB. PAGE 115 F2257
FINAN ECO/UNDEV LAW CONSTN

B61
STOCKING G.W.,WORKABLE COMPETITION AND ANTITRUST POLICY. USA+45 NAT/G CONSULT PLAN PRICE GOV/REL COST DEMAND PROFIT...POLICY 20. PAGE 126 F2491
LG/CO INDUS ECO/TAC CONTROL

B61
WESTON J.F.,THE ROLE OF MERGERS IN THE GROWTH OF LARGE FIRMS. USA+45 USA-45 LEGIS CONTROL...CONCPT STAT CHARTS 19/20. PAGE 145 F2862
LG/CO CENTRAL INDUS FINAN

B62
ARNOLD T.W.,THE FOLKLORE OF CAPITALISM. USA+45 USA-45 SOCIETY LG/CO SML/CO EX/STRUC ECO/TAC EDU/PROP ADJUST INCOME...MYTH CHARTS 20. PAGE 6 F0116
CAP/ISM ATTIT STERTYP ECO/DEV

B62
CAIRNCROSS A.K.,FACTORS IN ECONOMIC DEVELOPMENT. WOR+45 ECO/UNDEV INDUS R+D LG/CO NAT/G EX/STRUC PLAN TEC/DEV ECO/TAC ATTIT HEALTH KNOWL PWR WEALTH ...TIME/SEQ GEN/LAWS TOT/POP TRUE/GP VAL/FREE 20. PAGE 21 F0399
MARKET ECO/DEV

B62
CHANDLER A.D.,STRATEGY AND STRUCTURE: CHAPTERS IN THE HISTORY OF THE INDUSTRIAL ENTERPRISE. USA+45 USA-45 ECO/DEV EX/STRUC ECO/TAC EXEC...DECISION 20. PAGE 23 F0446
LG/CO PLAN ADMIN FINAN

B62
DIMOCK M.E.,THE NEW AMERICAN POLITICAL ECONOMY: A SYNTHESIS OF POLITICS AND ECONOMICS. USA+45 FINAN LG/CO PLAN ADMIN REGION GP/REL CENTRAL MORAL 20. PAGE 33 F0642
FEDERAL ECO/TAC NAT/G PARTIC

B62
FERBER R.,RESEARCH METHODS IN ECONOMICS AND BUSINESS. AFR ECO/DEV FINAN MARKET LG/CO SML/CO CONSULT CONTROL COST...STAT METH/COMP 20. PAGE 40 F0783
ACT/RES PROB/SOLV ECO/TAC MGT

B62
FRIEDMAN M.,CAPITALISM AND FREEDOM. USA+45 FINAN LG/CO WORKER INT/TRADE RECEIVE EDU/PROP CONTROL DISCRIM INCOME WEALTH POLICY. PAGE 44 F0859
CAP/ISM ORD/FREE NAT/G ECO/DEV

B62
GORT M.,DIVERSIFICATION AND INTEGRATION IN AMERICAN INDUSTRY. CLIENT DIST/IND PROC/MFG SERV/IND LG/CO CONTROL DEMAND PWR...METH/CNCPT STAT TREND CON/ANAL GP/COMP. PAGE 49 F0964
CONCPT GP/REL CLASSIF

B62
GRANICK D.,THE EUROPEAN EXECUTIVE. BELGIUM FRANCE GERMANY/W UK INDUS LABOR LG/CO SML/CO EX/STRUC PLAN TEC/DEV CAP/ISM COST DEMAND...POLICY CHARTS 20. PAGE 50 F0977
MGT ECO/DEV ECO/TAC EXEC

B62
KOLKO G.,WEALTH AND POWER IN AMERICA. USA+45 SOCIETY STRATA LG/CO ECO/TAC TAX PWR...SOC BIBLIOG 20 DEPRESSION. PAGE 72 F1420
STRUCT INCOME ECO/DEV WEALTH

B62
KUHN T.E.,PUBLIC ENTERPRISES, PROJECT PLANNING AND ECONOMIC DEVELOPMENT (PAMPHLET). ECO/UNDEV FINAN PLAN ADMIN EFFICIENCY OWN...MGT STAT CHARTS ANTHOL 20. PAGE 74 F1447
ECO/DEV ECO/TAC LG/CO NAT/G

B62
MEANS G.C.,PRICING POWER AND THE PUBLIC INTEREST. PLAN PROB/SOLV COST EFFICIENCY PROFIT RIGID/FLEX WEALTH. PAGE 89 F1741
LG/CO EX/STRUC PRICE ECO/TAC

B62
MEANS G.C.,THE CORPORATE REVOLUTION IN AMERICA: ECONOMIC REALITY VS. ECONOMIC THEORY. USA+45 USA-45 INDUS WORKER PLAN CAP/ISM ADMIN...IDEA/COMP 20. PAGE 89 F1742
LG/CO MARKET CONTROL PRICE

B62
O'CONNOR H.,WORLD CRISES IN OIL (BMR). ISLAM L/A+17C INDUS LG/CO INT/TRADE 20. PAGE 100 F1956
EXTR/IND DIPLOM ECO/UNDEV SOCISM

B62
PASTOR R.S.,A STATEMENT OF THE LAWS OF PARAGUAY IN MATTERS AFFECTING BUSINESS (2ND ED.). PARAGUAY INDUS FAM LABOR LG/CO NAT/G LEGIS TAX CONTROL MARRIAGE 20. PAGE 103 F2033
FINAN ECO/UNDEV LAW CONSTN

B62
PRAKASH O.M.,THE THEORY AND WORKING OF STATE CORPORATIONS: WITH SPECIAL REFERENCE TO INDIA. INDIA UK USA+45 TOP/EX PRICE ADMIN EFFICIENCY...MGT METH/COMP 20 TVA. PAGE 107 F2112
LG/CO ECO/UNDEV GOV/REL SOCISM

B62
US BUREAU OF THE CENSUS,REPORT FOR SUBCOMMITTEE ON ANTITRUST AND MONOPOLY: CONCENTRATION RATIOS IN MANUFACTURING INDUSTRY 1958. USA+45 ECO/DEV CONTROL GOV/REL OWN PRODUC PROFIT...STAT 20 CONGRESS MONOPOLY. PAGE 134 F2646
CHARTS PROC/MFG MARKET LG/CO

B62
US CONGRESS JOINT ECO COMM,INVENTORY FLUCTUATIONS AND ECONOMIC STABILIZATION. USA+45 LG/CO...MATH CHARTS CONGRESS. PAGE 134 F2652
ECO/TAC FINAN INDUS PROB/SOLV

L62
N,"UNION INVESTMENT IN BUSINESS: A SOURCE OF UNION CONFLICT OF INTEREST." LAW NAT/G LEGIS CONTROL GP/REL INGP/REL DECISION. PAGE 96 F1884
LABOR POLICY FINAN LG/CO

S62
READ W.H.,"UPWARD COMMUNICATION IN INDUSTRIAL HIERARCHIES." LG/CO TOP/EX PROB/SOLV DOMIN EXEC PERS/REL ATTIT DRIVE PERCEPT...CORREL STAT CHARTS 20. PAGE 110 F2159
ADMIN INGP/REL PSY MGT

N62
US SENATE COMM ON JUDICIARY,LEGISLATION TO STRENGTHEN PENALTIES UNDER THE ANTITRUST LAWS (PAMPHLET). USA+45 LG/CO CONFER CONTROL SANCTION ORD/FREE 20 SENATE MONOPOLY. PAGE 139 F2748
LEAD ADJUD INDUS ECO/TAC

B63
BATES J.L.,THE ORIGINS OF TEAPOT DOME: PROGRESSIVES, PARTIES, AND PETROLEUM, 1909-1921. USA-45 INDUS LG/CO POL/PAR DELIB/GP CONTROL GOV/REL CONSERVE...BIBLIOG 20 NAVY. PAGE 11 F0209
EXTR/IND CRIME NAT/G

B63
BAUER R.A.,AMERICAN BUSINESS AND PUBLIC POLICY: THE POLITICS OF FOREIGN TRADE. USA+45 COM/IND LG/CO NAT/G PROF/ORG SML/CO VOL/ASSN LEGIS TOP/EX ECO/TAC EDU/PROP CHOOSE HEALTH PWR WEALTH...CONCPT METH/CNCPT OBS INT QU SAMP FOR/TRADE TRUE/GP VAL/FREE HI. PAGE 11 F0217
ECO/DEV ATTIT

B63
BROUDE H.W.,STEEL DECISIONS AND THE NATIONAL ECONOMY. USA+45 LG/CO PLAN ADMIN COST DECISION. PAGE 19 F0365
PROC/MFG NAT/G CONTROL ECO/TAC

B63
CHAMPION J.M.,CRITICAL INCIDENTS IN MANAGEMENT. MARKET LG/CO SML/CO OP/RES ADMIN CONTROL LEAD GP/REL PERS/REL COST ATTIT SUPEGO ALL/VALS...PSY PERS/TEST BIBLIOG. PAGE 23 F0445
MGT DECISION EX/STRUC INDUS

B63
GANGULY D.S.,PUBLIC CORPORATIONS IN A NATIONAL ECONOMY. INDIA WOR+45 FINAN INDUS TOP/EX PRICE EFFICIENCY...MGT STAT CHARTS BIBLIOG 20. PAGE 46 F0897
ECO/UNDEV LG/CO SOCISM GOV/REL

B63
KOLKO G.,THE TRIUMPH OF CONSERVATISM. USA-45 INDUS LG/CO NAT/G PWR 20 PRESIDENT CONGRESS MONOPOLY PROGRSV/M. PAGE 72 F1421
CONSERVE CAP/ISM FINAN MARKET

B63
REAGAN M.D.,THE MANAGED ECONOMY. USA+45 INDUS LG/CO BUDGET GP/REL ORD/FREE PWR WEALTH 20. PAGE 110 F2161
PLAN ECO/DEV NAT/G ROLE

B63
RILEY J.W. JR.,THE CORPORATION AND ITS PUBLICS. ESSAYS ON THE CORPORATE IMAGE. CLIENT ISOLAT AGE ATTIT...POLICY SOC METH/CNCPT INT. PAGE 111 F2193
LG/CO CLASSIF GP/REL NEIGH

B63
SMITH R.A.,CORPORATIONS IN CRISIS. USA+45 LG/CO EX/STRUC ECO/TAC CONTROL LEAD PERS/REL...MGT 20. PAGE 123 F2432
ELITES INDUS PROB/SOLV METH/COMP

B63
WILTZ J.E.,IN SEARCH OF PEACE: THE SENATE MUNITIONS INQUIRY, 1934-36. EUR+WWI USA-45 ELITES INDUS LG/CO LEGIS INT/TRADE LOBBY NEUTRAL ARMS/CONT...POLICY CONGRESS 20 LEAGUE/NAT PRESIDENT SENATE CONSCRIPTN. PAGE 147 F2905
DELIB/GP PROFIT WAR WEAPON

N63
COMM ON FEDERAL TAX POLICY,FINANCING AMERICA'S FUTURE: TAXES, ECONOMIC STABILITY AND GROWTH (PAMPHLET). USA+45 LG/CO SML/CO DELIB/GP INCOME ...CHARTS 20. PAGE 26 F0513
TAX NAT/G EQUILIB PLAN

B64
BAUCHET P.,ECONOMIC PLANNING. FRANCE STRATA LG/CO CAP/ISM ADMIN PARL/PROC DEMAND OPTIMAL ATTIT PWR SOCISM...POLICY CHARTS 20. PAGE 11 F0212
ECO/DEV NAT/G PLAN ECO/TAC

B64
CHANDLER A.D. JR.,GIANT ENTERPRISE: FORD, GENERAL MOTORS, AND THE AUTOMOBILE INDUSTRY; SOURCES AND READINGS. USA+45 USA-45 FINAN MARKET CREATE ADMIN ...TIME/SEQ ANTHOL 20 AUTOMOBILE. PAGE 23 F0447
LG/CO DIST/IND LABOR MGT

B64
COMMITTEE ECONOMIC DEVELOPMENT,COMMUNITY ECONOMIC DEVELOPMENT PROGRAMS. USA+45 FINAN INDUS LG/CO PROF/ORG CREATE GP/REL MUNICH NEW/YORK VERMONT PENNSYLVAN IN ARKANSAS. PAGE 27 F0519
LOC/G LABOR PLAN

B64
FLORENCE P.S.,ECONOMICS AND SOCIOLOGY OF INDUSTRY; A REALISTIC ANALYSIS OF DEVELOPMENT. ECO/UNDEV LG/CO NAT/G PLAN...GEOG MGT BIBLIOG 20. PAGE 42 F0814
INDUS SOC ADMIN

B64
HACKER A.,THE CORPORATION TAKE-OVER. CONSTN LABOR PLAN BAL/PWR CONTROL EXEC LOBBY REPRESENT GP/REL ROLE ORD/FREE POLICY. PAGE 52 F1025
LG/CO STRUCT PWR

B64
KAPLAN A.D.H.,BIG ENTERPRISE IN A COMPETITIVE SYSTEM (REV. ED.). USA+45 INDUS MARKET WORKER TEC/DEV ECO/TAC PRICE ADJUD ADMIN CONTROL...MGT CHARTS 20 MONOPOLY. PAGE 69 F1351
FINAN GP/REL NAT/G LG/CO

B64
MANSFIELD E.,MONOPOLY POWER AND ECONOMIC PERFORMANCE: AN INTRODUCTION TO A CURRENT ISSUE OF
LG/CO PWR

PUBLIC POLICY. ECO/DEV INDUS NAT/G PLAN CAP/ISM PRICE CONTROL LOBBY EFFICIENCY PRODUC...POLICY 20 CONGRESS KENNEDY/JF MONOPOLY. PAGE 85 F1659 — ECO/TAC MARKET

B64
MARKHAM J.W.,THE COMMON MARKET: FRIEND OR COMPETITOR. AFR EUR+WWI FUT USA+45 INT/ORG LG/CO NAT/G VOL/ASSN DELIB/GP EX/STRUC PLAN TARIFFS ORD/FREE PWR WEALTH...POLICY STAT TREND EEC VAL/FREE 20. PAGE 85 F1671 — ECO/DEV ECO/TAC

B64
MARRIS R.,THE ECONOMIC THEORY OF "MANAGERIAL" CAPITALISM. USA+45 ECO/DEV LG/CO ECO/TAC DEMAND ...CHARTS BIBLIOG 20. PAGE 86 F1675 — CAP/ISM MGT CONTROL OP/RES

B64
MCNULTY J.E.,SOME ECONOMIC ASPECTS OF BUSINESS ORGANIZATION. ECO/DEV UTIL...MGT CHARTS BIBLIOG METH 20. PAGE 88 F1734 — ADMIN LG/CO GEN/LAWS

B64
MEYER J.R.,INVESTMENT DECISIONS, ECONOMIC FORECASTING, AND PUBLIC POLICY. ECO/DEV ECO/TAC ...DECISION REGRESS TIME/SEQ CHARTS GP/COMP SIMUL 20. PAGE 90 F1771 — FINAN PROB/SOLV PREDICT LG/CO

B64
NOSSITER B.D.,THE MYTHMAKERS: AN ESSAY ON POWER AND WEALTH. USA+45 LG/CO NAT/G TOP/EX PROB/SOLV ADMIN GP/REL ORD/FREE 20. PAGE 99 F1937 — ECO/TAC WEALTH FINAN PLAN

B64
PRESTHUS R.,MEN AT THE TOP; A STUDY IN COMMUNITY POWER. USA+45 STRUCT ACT/RES REPRESENT CONSEN ALL/VALS ORD/FREE...SAMP/SIZ 20. PAGE 108 F2116 — PLURISM LG/CO PWR ADMIN

B64
STEWART C.F.,A BIBLIOGRAPHY OF INTERNATIONAL BUSINESS. WOR+45 FINAN LG/CO NAT/G PLAN ECO/TAC TARIFFS...DECISION MGT GP/COMP NAT/COMP 20 EEC. PAGE 126 F2484 — BIBLIOG INT/ORG OP/RES INT/TRADE

B64
US SENATE COMM ON JUDICIARY,HEARINGS BEFORE SUBCOMMITTEE ON ANTITRUST AND MONOPOLY: ECONOMIC CONCENTRATION VOLUMES 1-5 JULY 1964-SEPT 1966. USA+45 LAW FINAN ECO/TAC ADJUD COST EFFICIENCY PRODUC...STAT CHARTS 20 CONGRESS MONOPOLY. PAGE 140 F2749 — ECO/DEV CONTROL MARKET LG/CO

L64
BHAGWATI J.,"THE PURE THEORY OF INTERNATIONAL TRADE: A SURVEY." WOR+45 ECO/DEV ECO/UNDEV FINAN MARKET PROC/MFG INT/ORG LABOR LG/CO NAT/G TEC/DEV ECO/TAC SKILL WEALTH...POLICY RELATIV MGT CONCPT NEW/IDEA MATH QUANT GEN/LAWS FOR/TRADE 20. PAGE 14 F0276 — INDUS HYPO/EXP

S64
KLEIN H.,"AMERICAN OIL COMPANIES IN LATIN AMERICA: THE BOLIVIAN EXPERIENCE." L/A+17C USA+45 USA-45 EXTR/IND LG/CO NAT/G ECO/TAC WEALTH...POLICY GEN/LAWS BOLIV TOT/POP 20 OIL. PAGE 72 F1405 — MARKET ECO/UNDEV NAT/LISM

S64
N,"QUASI-LEGISLATIVE ARBITRATION AGREEMENTS." LAW LG/CO ECO/TAC SANCTION ATTIT POLICY. PAGE 96 F1885 — ADJUD ADJUST LABOR GP/REL

B65
BARRY E.E.,NATIONALISATION IN BRITISH POLITICS: THE HISTORICAL BACKGROUND. UK AGRI DIST/IND EXTR/IND LABOR LG/CO ATTIT CONSERVE SOCISM 19/20 LABOR/PAR. PAGE 10 F0198 — NAT/G OWN INDUS POL/PAR

B65
BAUMOL W.J.,ECONOMIC THEORY AND OPERATIONS ANALYSIS (2ND ED.). MARKET LG/CO BUDGET PRICE COST EQUILIB PRODUC...DECISION MATH CHARTS GAME 20. PAGE 12 F0219 — OP/RES ECO/DEV METH/COMP STAT

B65
BELASSA B.,ECONOMIC DEVELOPMENT AND INTEGRATION. LG/CO PROB/SOLV TEC/DEV INT/TRADE TARIFFS COST WEALTH...POLICY METH/COMP 20. PAGE 12 F0232 — ECO/UNDEV ECO/TAC INT/ORG INDUS

B65
BREAK G.F.,FEDERAL LENDING AND ECONOMIC STABILITY. USA+45 ECO/DEV LG/CO SML/CO EQUILIB...CHARTS 20. PAGE 18 F0344 — BUDGET FINAN NAT/G ECO/TAC

B65
DERBER M.,PLANT UNION-MANAGEMENT RELATIONS: FROM PRACTICE TO THEORY. PROC/MFG NEIGH PROB/SOLV ORD/FREE...DECISION MGT OBS QU SAMP. PAGE 32 F0621 — LG/CO LABOR GP/REL ATTIT

B65
JOHNSTONE A.,UNITED STATES DIRECT INVESTMENT IN FRANCE: AN INVESTIGATION OF THE FRENCH CHARGES. FRANCE USA+45 ECO/DEV INDUS LG/CO NAT/G ECO/TAC CONTROL WEALTH...BIBLIOG 20 INTERVENT. PAGE 68 F1335 — FINAN DIPLOM POLICY SOVEREIGN

B65
LAZARUS S.,RESOLVING BUSINESS DISPUTES: THE POTENTIAL OF COMMERCIAL ARBITRATION. USA+45 INDUS LG/CO ACT/RES PROB/SOLV EDU/PROP CONSEN UTIL ...TREND 20. PAGE 76 F1496 — FINAN DELIB/GP CONSULT ADJUD

B65
MUND V.A.,GOVERNMENT AND BUSINESS (4TH ED.). USA+45 INDUS LG/CO SML/CO LEGIS INT/TRADE LICENSE PRICE ADJUD. PAGE 95 F1860 — NAT/G ECO/TAC BUDGET CONTROL

B65
STEINER G.A.,THE CREATIVE ORGANIZATION. ELITES LG/CO PLAN PROB/SOLV TEC/DEV INSPECT CAP/ISM CONTROL EXEC PERSON...METH/COMP HYPO/EXP 20. PAGE 126 F2476 — CREATE MGT ADMIN SOC

S65
VAN DER HORST S.T.,"THE ECONOMICS OF DECENTRALISATION OF INDUSTRY." SOUTH/AFR ECO/DEV LG/CO AUTOMAT DISCRIM...POLICY MUNICH 20. PAGE 140 F2761 — PLAN INDUS CENTRAL TEC/DEV

C65
PEGRUM D.E.,"PUBLIC REGULATION OF BUSINESS (REV ED)" LAW CONSTN DIST/IND SERV/IND LG/CO LEGIS OWN LAISSEZ SOCISM...POLICY DECISION BIBLIOG 20. PAGE 104 F2048 — INDUS PLAN NEW/LIB PRICE

B66
BALDWIN D.A.,ECONOMIC DEVELOPMENT AND AMERICAN FOREIGN POLICY. USA+45 FINAN LG/CO LEGIS DIPLOM GIVE 20. PAGE 9 F0163 — ECO/TAC FOR/AID ECO/UNDEV POLICY

B66
BARAN P.A.,MONOPOLY CAPITAL; AN ESSAY ON THE AMERICAN ECONOMIC AND SOCIAL ORDER. USA+45 USA-45 ECO/UNDEV FINAN MARKET PLAN DIPLOM COLONIAL RACE/REL DEMAND MARXISM...CHARTS 20. PAGE 9 F0179 — LG/CO CAP/ISM PRICE CONTROL

B66
COOK P.W. JR.,PROBLEMS OF CORPORATE POWER. WOR+45 FINAN INDUS BARGAIN GP/REL...MGT ANTHOL. PAGE 27 F0530 — ADMIN LG/CO PWR ECO/TAC

B66
FRANKEL P.H.,MATTEI; OIL AND POWER POLITICS. ITALY EXTR/IND MARKET GP/REL NAT/LISM SOCISM...POLICY MGT BIOG 20 MATTEI/E. PAGE 43 F0844 — LEAD NAT/G CONTROL LG/CO

B66
LEE R.A.,TRUMAN AND TAFT-HARTLEY: A QUESTION OF MANDATE. USA+45 LAW CONSTN LG/CO CONTROL LOBBY GOV/REL PEACE NEW/LIB 20 TRUMAN/HS CONGRESS. PAGE 77 F1507 — LEGIS TOP/EX ADJUD LABOR

B66
LERNER E.M.,A THEORY OF FINANCIAL ANALYSIS. UNIV LG/CO COST DEMAND INCOME PROFIT...MATH STAT CHARTS SIMUL T 20. PAGE 78 F1531 — CONCPT FINAN ECO/DEV OPTIMAL

B66
RAPHAEL J.S.,GOVERNMENTAL REGULATION OF BUSINESS. USA+45 LAW CONSTN TAX ADJUD ADMIN EFFICIENCY PWR 20. PAGE 109 F2150 — LG/CO GOV/REL CONTROL ECO/DEV

B66
REDFORD E.S.,THE ROLE OF GOVERNMENT IN THE AMERICAN ECONOMY. USA+45 USA-45 FINAN INDUS LG/CO PROB/SOLV ADMIN INGP/REL INCOME PRODUC 18/20. PAGE 110 F2169 — NAT/G ECO/DEV CAP/ISM ECO/TAC

B66
SOVERN M.I.,LEGAL RESTRAINTS ON RACIAL DISCRIMINATION IN EMPLOYMENT. USA+45 LAW INDUS LG/CO SML/CO DELIB/GP LEGIS SANCTION 20 NLRB PRESIDENT NEGRO CIV/RIGHTS RAILROAD. PAGE 124 F2446 — DISCRIM RACE/REL WORKER JURID

B66
TIVEY L.J.,NATIONALISATION IN BRITISH INDUSTRY. UK LEGIS PARL/PROC GP/REL OWN ATTIT SOCISM 20. PAGE 131 F2578 — NAT/G INDUS CONTROL LG/CO

B66
ZISCHKA A.,WAR ES EIN WUNDER? GERMANY/W ECO/DEV FINAN LG/CO BARGAIN CAP/ISM FOR/AID RATION 20 MARSHL/PLN. PAGE 150 F2965 — ECO/TAC INT/TRADE INDUS WAR

B67
BEAL E.F.,THE PRACTICE OF COLLECTIVE BARGAINING (3RD ED.). USA+45 WOR+45 ECO/DEV INDUS LG/CO PROF/ORG WORKER ECO/TAC GP/REL WEALTH...JURID METH/CNCPT. PAGE 12 F0221 — BARGAIN MGT LABOR ADJUD

B67
DONALD A.G.,MANAGEMENT, INFORMATION, AND SYSTEMS. WOR+45 LG/CO PROB/SOLV CONTROL FEEDBACK KNOWL MGT. PAGE 34 F0653 — ROUTINE TEC/DEV CONCPT ADMIN

B67
HEILBRONER R.L.,THE LIMITS OF AMERICAN CAPITALISM. FUT ECO/DEV INDUS LG/CO EX/STRUC LEAD PWR TECHRACY 20. PAGE 58 F1137 — ELITES CREATE TEC/DEV CAP/ISM

B67
MARCUS S.,COMPETITION AND THE LAW. USA+45 INDUS LG/CO NAT/G CONSERVE LAISSEZ...BIBLIOG 20 FTC SUPREME/CT. PAGE 85 F1665 — LAW ECO/DEV FINAN

JURID

B67
NARVER J.C.,CONGLOMERATE MERGERS AND MARKET COMPETITION. USA+45 LAW STRUCT ADMIN LEAD RISK COST PROFIT WEALTH...POLICY CHARTS BIBLIOG. PAGE 96 F1892
DEMAND LG/CO MARKET MGT

B67
ORLANS H.,CONTRACTING FOR ATOMS. AFR USA+45 LAW INTELL ACADEM LG/CO NAT/G PLAN TEC/DEV CONTROL DETER...TREND 20. PAGE 102 F1999
NUC/PWR R+D PRODUC PEACE

B67
SCOTT J.C.,ANTITRUST AND TRADE REGULATION TODAY: 1967. USA+45 MARKET LG/CO DELIB/GP LEGIS CAP/ISM INT/TRADE TAX PRICE INGP/REL WEALTH 20 SUPREME/CT. PAGE 118 F2334
NAT/G INDUS CONTROL JURID

B67
THOMAN R.S.,GEOGRAPHY OF INTERNATIONAL TRADE. WOR+45 ECO/DEV ECO/UNDEV INT/ORG LG/CO PLAN BAL/PAY ...STAT CHARTS NAT/COMP 20. PAGE 130 F2559
INT/TRADE GEOG ECO/TAC DIPLOM

B67
UNIVERSAL REFERENCE SYSTEM,ADMINISTRATIVE MANAGEMENT: PUBLIC AND PRIVATE BUREAUCRACY (VOLUME IV). WOR+45 WOR-45 ECO/DEV LG/CO LOC/G PUB/INST VOL/ASSN GOV/REL...COMPUT/IR GEN/METH. PAGE 133 F2616
BIBLIOG/A MGT ADMIN NAT/G

L67
LAMBERT J.D.,"CORPORATE POLITICAL SPENDING AND CAMPAIGN FINANCE." LAW CONSTN FINAN LABOR LG/CO LOC/G NAT/G VOL/ASSN TEC/DEV ADJUD ADMIN PARTIC. PAGE 75 F1463
USA+45 POL/PAR CHOOSE COST

L67
ROBERTS E.F.,"THE CASE OF THE UNWARY HOME BUYER: THE HOUSING MERCHANT DID IT." USA+45 CLIENT DIST/IND MARKET LG/CO SML/CO PROB/SOLV LEGIT COST PROFIT. PAGE 112 F2207
ADJUD CONSTRUC OWN LAW

L67
SCHNEIDER C.W.,"REFORM OF THE FEDERAL SECURITIES LAWS." FUT USA+45 LAW FINAN INDUS DELIB/GP ACT/RES PROB/SOLV GP/REL. PAGE 117 F2304
NAT/G LG/CO ADMIN CONTROL

L67
TRAVERS H. JR.,"AN EXAMINATION OF THE CAB'S MERGER POLICY." USA+45 USA-45 LAW NAT/G LEGIS PLAN ADMIN ...DECISION 20 CONGRESS. PAGE 131 F2584
ADJUD LG/CO POLICY DIST/IND

L67
WATKINS J.B.,"MONETARY RECOVERY UNDER FEDERAL ANTITRUST STATUTES." USA+45 PROB/SOLV ADJUD CT/SYS GOV/REL ORD/FREE 20. PAGE 144 F2831
LG/CO CONTROL LAW FINAN

S67
"ANTITRUST VENUE: TRANSACTING BUSINESS UNDER THE CLAYTON ACT." USA+45 DIST/IND PROB/SOLV ECO/TAC ADJUD CT/SYS 20. PAGE 2 F0028
LAW LG/CO CONTROL NAT/G

S67
ALBAUM G.,"INFORMATION FLOW AND DECENTRALIZED DECISION MAKING IN MARKETING." EX/STRUC COMPUTER OP/RES PROB/SOLV EFFICIENCY OPTIMAL...METH/COMP ORG/CHARTS 20. PAGE 3 F0056
LG/CO ROUTINE KNOWL MARKET

S67
ALLISON D.,"THE GROWTH OF IDEAS." USA+45 LG/CO ADMIN. PAGE 4 F0075
R+D OP/RES INDUS TEC/DEV

S67
ALPANDER G.G.,"ENTREPRENEURS AND PRIVATE ENTERPRISE IN TURKEY." TURKEY INDUS PROC/MFG EDU/PROP ATTIT DRIVE WEALTH...GEOG MGT SOC STAT TREND CHARTS 20. PAGE 4 F0077
ECO/UNDEV LG/CO NAT/G POLICY

S67
ASCH P.,"CONGLOMERATE MERGERS AND PUBLIC POLICY." USA+45 ECO/DEV LG/CO NAT/G ECO/TAC ADJUD CENTRAL 20. PAGE 7 F0126
INDUS CAP/ISM BARGAIN

S67
BAGDKIAN B.H.,"NEWS AS A BYPRODUCT: WHAT HAPPENS WHEN JOURNALISM IS HITCHED TO GREAT, DIVERSIFIED CORPORATIONS?" USA+45 INDUS EDU/PROP PARTIC PROFIT ATTIT. PAGE 8 F0152
COM/IND PRESS CONTROL LG/CO

S67
BARRO S.,"ECONOMIC IMPACT OF SPACE EXPENDITURES: SOME BROAD ISSUES DEALING WITH COSTS AND BENEFITS." USA+45 PROC/MFG R+D LG/CO CONSULT COST PRODUC 20. PAGE 10 F0195
SPACE FINAN ECO/TAC NAT/G

S67
BENN W.,"TECHNOLOGY HAS AN INEXORABLE EFFECT." FUT UK ECO/DEV INT/ORG CONSULT PLAN EDU/PROP ADMIN LEAD GP/REL PRODUC...INT 20 EEC. PAGE 13 F0246
R+D LG/CO TEC/DEV INDUS

S67
BOSHER J.F.,"GOVERNMENT AND PRIVATE INTERESTS IN NEW FRANCE." CANADA FRANCE INDUS LG/CO SML/CO CAP/ISM INT/TRADE COLONIAL GP/REL...HIST/WRIT 17/18. PAGE 17 F0320
NAT/G FINAN ADMIN CONTROL

S67
DAVIS O.A.,"ON THE DISTINCTION BETWEEN PUBLIC AND PRIVATE GOODS." USA+45 COM/IND LG/CO NAT/G TV DEBATE PRICE ADMIN ROLE...MATH IDEA/COMP. PAGE 31 F0593
MARKET OWN CONCPT

S67
DEMUTH J.,"GE: PROFILE OF A CORPORATION." USA+45 USA-45 LABOR ACT/RES RATION EDU/PROP ADJUD CT/SYS FASCISM 20. PAGE 32 F0619
LG/CO CONSERVE PRICE

S67
DURIEZ P.,"THE IMPACT OF EX PARTE 230 (PIGGYBACKING) ON RAIL-MOTOR COMPETITION." USA+45 USA-45 LG/CO COST EFFICIENCY...CHARTS 20. PAGE 35 F0685
DIST/IND LAW CONTROL AGREE

S67
HALE G.E.,"EXPANDING ENTERPRISE: GEOGRAPHICAL CURBS ON MERGERS." USA+45 MARKET LG/CO ADJUD CONTROL GP/REL 20. PAGE 53 F1041
LAW HABITAT INDUS EX/STRUC

S67
KOTLER P.,"OPERATIONS RESEARCH IN MARKETING." USA+45 DIST/IND INDUS LG/CO CONSULT BUDGET TASK DEMAND EFFICIENCY PROFIT WEALTH DECISION. PAGE 73 F1429
ECOMETRIC OP/RES MARKET PLAN

S67
MORTON J.A.,"A SYSTEMS APPROACH TO THE INNOVATION PROCESS: ITS USE IN THE BELL SYSTEM." USA+45 INTELL INDUS LG/CO CONSULT WORKER COMPUTER AUTOMAT DEMAND ...MGT CHARTS 20. PAGE 94 F1841
TEC/DEV GEN/METH R+D COM/IND

S67
MUNDHEIM R.H.,"SOME THOUGHTS ON THE DUTIES AND RESPONSIBILITIES OF UNAFFILIATED DIRECTORS OF MUTUAL FUNDS." USA+45 LG/CO SML/CO CONSULT LEAD PARTIC. PAGE 95 F1861
FINAN WEALTH ECO/TAC ADMIN

S67
WILLIAMS C.,"REGIONAL MANAGEMENT OVERSEAS." USA+45 WOR+45 DIST/IND LG/CO EX/STRUC INT/TRADE TARIFFS ADMIN TASK CENTRAL. PAGE 147 F2889
MGT EUR+WWI ECO/DEV PLAN

B99
KROPOTKIN P.,FIELDS, FACTORIES, AND WORKSHOPS. UNIV INTELL ECO/DEV LG/CO SCHOOL SML/CO ECO/TAC PRODUC UTOPIA...NEW/IDEA MUNICH. PAGE 74 F1445
SOCIETY WORKER AGRI INDUS

LHOSTE-LACHAUME P. F1555

LI CHOH-MING F1557, F1556

LIB/INTRNT....LIBERAL INTERNATIONAL

LIB/PARTY....LIBERAL PARTY (ALL NATIONS)

B57
WATSON G.,THE UNSERVILE STATE: ESSAYS IN LIBERTY AND WELFARE. UK LEGIS RECEIVE EDU/PROP COLONIAL ...WELF/ST 20 LIB/PARTY. PAGE 144 F2833
POL/PAR ORD/FREE CONTROL NEW/LIB

LIBERALISM....SEE NEW/LIB, WELF/ST, OLD/LIB, LAISSEZ

LIBERIA....SEE ALSO AFR

B45
DAVIS J.,AFRICA ADVANCING. AFR CONGO/BRAZ LIBERIA NIGER INT/ORG SCHOOL DIPLOM GIVE KNOWL SKILL 20. PAGE 30 F0590
SECT COLONIAL AGRI ECO/UNDEV

LIBERTY....SEE ORD/FREE

LIBYA....SEE ALSO ISLAM

S65
CECIL C.O.,"THE DETERMINANTS OF LIBYAN FOREIGN POLICY." AFR INTELL ECO/UNDEV EXTR/IND POL/PAR CREATE REGION SOVEREIGN CONSERVE MAGHREB NASSER/G. PAGE 22 F0431
LIBYA DIPLOM WEALTH ISLAM

LICENSE....LEGAL PERMIT

B12
FOUAD M.,LE REGIME DE LA PRESSE EN EGYPTE: THESE POUR LE DOCTORAT. UAR LICENSE EDU/PROP ADMIN SANCTION CRIME SUPEGO PWR...ART/METH JURID 19/20. PAGE 43 F0832
ORD/FREE LEGIS CONTROL PRESS

L42
GRANT J.A.C.,"THE GUILD RETURNS TO AMERICA." CHRIST-17C USA-45 LEGIS LICENSE ADJUD CONTROL GP/REL. PAGE 50 F0978
PROF/ORG JURID LABOR PWR

B63
BURRUS B.R.,ADMINSTRATIVE LAW AND LOCAL GOVERNMENT. USA+45 PROVS LEGIS LICENSE ADJUD ORD/FREE 20. PAGE 20 F0392
EX/STRUC LOC/G JURID CONSTN

B65
MUND V.A.,GOVERNMENT AND BUSINESS (4TH ED.). USA+45 INDUS LG/CO SML/CO LEGIS INT/TRADE LICENSE PRICE ADJUD. PAGE 95 F1860
NAT/G ECO/TAC BUDGET CONTROL

B66
MC CONNELL J.P.,LAW AND BUSINESS: PATTERNS AND ISSUES IN COMMERCIAL LAW. USA+45 USA-45 LOC/G WORKER LICENSE CRIME REPRESENT GP/REL 20. PAGE 87 F1713
ECO/DEV JURID ADJUD MGT

L67
DOERFER G.L.,"THE LIMITS ON TRADE SECRET LAW IMPOSED BY FEDERAL PATENT & ANTITRUST SUPREMACY." USA+45 LAW R+D CAP/ISM LICENSE CONTROL SANCTION ORD/FREE. PAGE 33 F0651
JURID GOV/REL POLICY LEGIT

S67
BELISLE J.,"FOREIGN RESTRAINTS ON US BANKS ABROAD" WOR+45 LAW. PAGE 12 F0233
DIPLOM FINAN CONTROL LICENSE

S67
CHADWELL J.T.,"ANTITRUST ASPECTS OF DEALER LICENSING AND FRANCHISING." ACT/RES LICENSE ADJUD CONTROL OWN. PAGE 23 F0439
LAW PRIVIL INDUS

S67
DANIEL C.,"THE REGULATION OF PRIVATE ENTERPRISES AS PUBLIC UTILITIES." WOR+45 LAW LICENSE POLICY. PAGE 30 F0577
LOC/G NAT/G CONTROL SERV/IND

S67
LEFCOE G.,"CONSTRUCTION LENDING AND THE EQUITABLE LIEN." LICENSE CT/SYS OWN...STAT 20. PAGE 77 F1510
CONSTRUC RENT ADJUD

LICHFIELD N. F1558

LICHTHEIM G. F1559,F1560

LICHTMAN R. F1561

LIECHTENST....LIECHTENSTEIN; SEE ALSO APPROPRIATE TIME/SPACE/CULTURE INDEX

S67
KOHN W.S.G.,"THE SOVEREIGNTY OF LIECHTENSTEIN." LIECHTENST SWITZERLND USSR CONSTN DEBATE WAR CONSERVE 18/20 UN. PAGE 72 F1417
SOVEREIGN NAT/G PWR DIPLOM

LIEFMANN-KEIL E. F1562

LIESNER H.H. F1738

LIFLAND W.T. F1563

LIGHTFT/PM....PHIL M. LIGHTFOOT

LIKERT/R....RENSIS LIKERT

LILLEY S. F1564

LIN/PIAO....LIN PIAO

LINCOLN G. F1565,F1566

LINCOLN/A....PRESIDENT ABRAHAM LINCOLN

LINDAHL/E....ERIK LINDAHL

B58
MUSGRAVE R.A.,CLASSICS IN THE THEORY OF PUBLIC FINANCE. UNIV MARKET LG/CO NAT/G CAP/ISM PRICE OPTIMAL...IDEA/COMP ANTHOL 19/20 SAY/EMIL EDGEWORTH LINDAHL/E RITSCHL/H. PAGE 95 F1870
TAX FINAN ECO/TAC GP/REL

LINDBERG L. F1567

LINDBLOM C.E. F0343,F0572

LINDBLOOM C.E. F1568

LINDER S.B. F1569

LINDHOLM R.W. F1570,F1571

LINDSAY F.A. F1572

LINEBERRY R.L. F1573

LING....LINGUISTICS, LANGUAGE

N
US LIBRARY OF CONGRESS,SOUTHERN ASIA ACCESSIONS LIST. BURMA CEYLON INDIA NEPAL PAKISTAN S/ASIA THAILAND AGRI INDUS SCHOOL WORKER...ART/METH GEOG HEAL PHIL/SCI LING 20. PAGE 137 F2710
BIBLIOG/A SOCIETY CULTURE ECO/UNDEV

B37
HAMILTON W.H.,THE POWER TO GOVERN. ECO/DEV FINAN INDUS ECO/TAC INT/TRADE TARIFFS TAX CONTROL CT/SYS WAR COST PWR 18/20 SUPREME/CT. PAGE 54 F1056
LING CONSTN NAT/G POLICY

B38
CARVALHO C.M.,GEOGRAPHIA HUMANA; POLITICA E ECONOMICA (3RD ED.). BRAZIL CULTURE AGRI INDUS DIPLOM COLONIAL GP/REL RACE/REL...LING 20 RESOURCE/N. PAGE 22 F0424
GEOG HABITAT

B44
KAUFMANN F.,METHODOLOGY OF THE SOCIAL SCIENCES. PERSON...RELATIV PSY CONCPT LING METH 20. PAGE 69 F1363
SOC PHIL/SCI GEN/LAWS METH/CNCPT

B56
YABUKI K.,JAPAN BIBLIOGRAPHIC ANNUAL, 1956: THE LATEST LIST OF OLD AND NEW BOOKS ON JAPAN IN ENGLISH. EDU/PROP...LING 20 CHINJAP. PAGE 149 F2945
BIBLIOG SOC

B58
MASON J.B.,THAILAND BIBLIOGRAPHY. S/ASIA THAILAND CULTURE EDU/PROP ADMIN...GEOG SOC LING 20. PAGE 87 F1701
BIBLIOG/A ECO/UNDEV DIPLOM NAT/G

B58
UNIVERSITY OF LONDON,THE FAR EAST AND SOUTH-EAST ASIA: A CUMULATED LIST OF PERIODICAL ARTICLES, MAY 1956-APRIL 1957. ASIA S/ASIA LAW ADMIN...LING 20. PAGE 133 F2621
BIBLIOG SOC

B60
SANTHANAM K.,UNION-STATE RELATIONS IN INDIA. INDIA FINAN PROVS PLAN ECO/TAC...LING 20. PAGE 116 F2280
FEDERAL GOV/REL CONSTN POLICY

N61
VINER J.,THE INTELLECTUAL HISTORY OF LAISSEZ FAIRE (PAMPHLET). WOR+45 WOR-45 LAW INTELL...POLICY LING LOG 19/20. PAGE 141 F2787
ATTIT EDU/PROP LAISSEZ ECO/TAC

B63
CHOJNACKI S.,REGISTER ON CURRENT RESEARCH ON ETHIOPIA AND THE HORN OF AFRICA. ETHIOPIA LAW CULTURE AGRI SECT EDU/PROP ADMIN...GEOG HEAL LING 20. PAGE 24 F0470
BIBLIOG ACT/RES INTELL ACADEM

B63
MACHLUP F.,ESSAYS ON ECONOMIC SEMANTICS. UNIV ECO/DEV FINAN COST DEMAND PRODUC...POLICY STAT CHARTS BIBLIOG. PAGE 83 F1632
LING CONCPT METH

B63
PAENSON I.,SYSTEMATIC GLOSSARY ENGLISH, FRENCH, SPANISH, RUSSIAN OF SELECTED ECONOMIC AND SOCIAL TERMS. WOR+45 FINAN LABOR INT/TRADE DEMAND PRODUC 20. PAGE 102 F2014
DICTIONARY SOC LING

B63
STUCKI C.W.,AMERICAN DOCTORAL DISSERTATIONS ON ASIA 1933-62 (A PAPER). PREHIST INDUS NAT/G GOV/REL ALL/IDEOS...ART/METH GEOG SOC LING 20. PAGE 127 F2506
BIBLIOG ASIA SOCIETY S/ASIA

B66
BAKLANOFF E.N.,NEW PERSPECTIVES ON BRAZIL. BRAZIL SOCIETY INDUS DOMIN LEAD REV CIVMIL/REL...GEOG PSY LING ANTHOL 20. PAGE 8 F0156
ECO/UNDEV TEC/DEV DIPLOM ORD/FREE

B66
US DEPARTMENT OF STATE,RESEARCH ON THE USSR AND EASTERN EUROPE (EXTERNAL RESEARCH LIST NO 1-25). USSR LAW CULTURE SOCIETY NAT/G TEC/DEV DIPLOM EDU/PROP REGION...GEOG LING. PAGE 136 F2675
BIBLIOG/A EUR+WWI COM MARXISM

B67
LANDEN R.G.,OMAN SINCE 1856: DISRUPTIVE MODERNIZATION IN A TRADITIONAL ARAB SOCIETY. UK DIST/IND EXTR/IND SECT DIPLOM INT/TRADE...SOC LING CHARTS BIBLIOG 19/20. PAGE 75 F1468
ISLAM CULTURE ECO/UNDEV NAT/G

S67
KINGSLEY R.E.,"THE US BUSINESS IMAGE IN LATIN AMERICA." L/A+17C USA+45 NAT/G TEC/DEV CAP/ISM FOR/AID DOMIN EDU/PROP...CONCPT LING IDEA/COMP 20. PAGE 71 F1396
ATTIT LOVE DIPLOM ECO/UNDEV

LINGUISTICS....SEE LING

LINK R.G. F1574

LINK/AS....ARTHUR S. LINK

LIPPMANN W. F1575

LIPPMANN/W....WALTER LIPPMANN

LIPSET S.M. F1576,F1577

LIPSON H.A. F1578

LISKA G. F1579

LISS S.B. F1580

LIST F. F1581

LISTER L. F1582

LITERACY....ABILITY TO READ AND WRITE

B02
MOREL E.D.,AFFAIRS OF WEST AFRICA. UK FINAN INDUS FAM KIN SECT CHIEF WORKER DIPLOM RACE/REL LITERACY HEALTH...CHARTS 18/20 AFRICA/W NEGRO. PAGE 93 F1826
COLONIAL ADMIN AFR

B66
FISK E.K.,NEW GUINEA ON THE THRESHOLD; ASPECTS OF SOCIAL, POLITICAL, AND ECONOMIC DEVELOPMENT. AGRI NAT/G INT/TRADE ADMIN ADJUST LITERACY ROLE...CHARTS ANTHOL 20 NEW/GUINEA. PAGE 41 F0804
ECO/UNDEV SOCIETY

B66
MALASSIS L.,ECONOMIC DEVELOPMENT AND THE PROGRAMMING OF RURAL EDUCATION. CONSULT PROB/SOLV LITERACY KNOWL...CHARTS GEN/METH 20. PAGE 84 F1644
AGRI ECO/UNDEV SCHOOL PLAN

LITERARY ANALYSIS....SEE HUM

LITHUANIA....SEE ALSO USSR

S67
"PROTEST AGAINST SOVIET INDUSTRIALIZATION ILLS IN LITHUANIA* A MEMORANDUM." USSR LITHUANIA NAT/G PROVS COST GEOG. PAGE 1 F0024
INDUS COLONIAL NAT/LISM PLAN

LITTLE I.M.D. F1583,F1584

LITTLE AD, INC. F1585

LITTLEFIELD N. F1586

LITVAK I.A. F1587

LITWACK L. F1588

LIU/SHAO....LIU SHAO-CHI

LIVERNASH E.R. F1589

LIVNGSTN/D....DAVID LIVINGSTON

LIVY....LIVY

LLOYD H.D. F1590

LLOYD/HD....HENRY D. LLOYD

LLOYD-GEO/D....DAVID LLOYD GEORGE

LOAN....LOANS; SEE ALSO RENT+GIVE+FOR/AID+FINAN

S65
CAMPOLONGO A.,"EUROPEAN INVESTMENT BANK* ACTIVITY AND PROSPECTS." FUT ECO/UNDEV FINAN PLAN DIPLOM ...STAT EEC LOAN EIB. PAGE 21 F0410
ECO/TAC PREDICT

LOBBY....PRESSURE GROUP

N19
CARPER E.T.,LOBBYING AND THE NATURAL GAS BILL (PAMPHLET). USA+45 SERV/IND BARGAIN PAY DRIVE ROLE WEALTH 20 CONGRESS SENATE EISNHWR/DD. PAGE 22 F0418
LOBBY ADJUD TRIBUTE NAT/G

N19
HOGARTY R.A.,NEW JERSEY FARMERS AND MIGRANT HOUSING RULES (PAMPHLET). USA+45 LAW ELITES FACE/GP LABOR PROF/ORG LOBBY PERS/REL RIGID/FLEX ROLE 20 NEW/JERSEY. PAGE 61 F1193
AGRI PROVS WORKER HEALTH

N19
LAWRENCE S.A.,THE BATTERY ADDITIVE CONTROVERSY (PAMPHLET). USA+45 LAW MARKET PROC/MFG R+D CAP/ISM CT/SYS GOV/REL OWN FTC CONGRESS BUR/STNDRD RITCHIE/JM. PAGE 76 F1494
PHIL/SCI LOBBY INSPECT

N19
MARSH J.F. JR.,THE FBI RETIREMENT BILL (PAMPHLET). USA+45 EX/STRUC WORKER PLAN PROB/SOLV BUDGET LEAD LOBBY PARL/PROC PERS/REL RIGID/FLEX...POLICY 20 FBI PRESIDENT BUR/BUDGET. PAGE 86 F1677
ADMIN NAT/G SENIOR GOV/REL

N19
YLVISAKER P.N.,THE NATURAL CEMENT ISSUE (PAMPHLET). USA+45 USA-45 CONSTRUC PROVS CAP/ISM ADMIN LOBBY PERS/REL OWN RIGID/FLEX ROLE 20 MINNESOTA. PAGE 150 F2948
POLICY NAT/G PLAN GOV/REL

B28
HARDMAN J.B.,AMERICAN LABOR DYNAMICS. WORKER ECO/TAC DOMIN ADJUD LEAD LOBBY PWR...POLICY MGT. PAGE 55 F1079
LABOR INGP/REL ATTIT GP/REL

B35
SCHATTSCHNEIDER E.E.,POLITICS, PRESSURES AND THE TARIFF: A STUDY OF FREE PRIVATE ENTERPRISE IN PRESSURE POLITICS IN TARIFF REVISION 1929-1930. NAT/G BARGAIN ECO/TAC ROUTINE REPRESENT GOV/REL GP/REL PWR POLICY. PAGE 116 F2290
LOBBY LEGIS TARIFFS

S35
BONNETT C.E.,"THE EVOLUTION OF BUSINESS GROUPINGS." ECO/TAC EDU/PROP PRICE LOBBY ORD/FREE. PAGE 16 F0315
VOL/ASSN GP/REL PROB/SOLV

B37
BROOKS R.R.,WHEN LABOR ORGANIZES. FINAN EDU/PROP ADMIN LOBBY PARTIC REPRESENT WEALTH TREND. PAGE 19 F0364
LABOR GP/REL POLICY

S38
HALL R.C.,"REPRESENTATION OF BIG BUSINESS IN THE HOUSE OF COMMONS." UK ECO/DEV INDUS PROF/ORG LEGIS CAP/ISM ECO/TAC LAISSEZ...POLICY OLD/LIB PLURIST MGT 20 HOUSE/CMNS. PAGE 53 F1047
LOBBY NAT/G

B39
THOMAS J.A.,THE HOUSE OF COMMONS, 1832-1901; A STUDY OF ITS ECONOMIC AND FUNCTIONAL CHARACTER. UK LAW STRATA FINAN DIPLOM CONTROL LEAD LOBBY REPRESENT WEALTH...POLICY STAT BIBLIOG 19/20 PARLIAMENT. PAGE 130 F2561
PARL/PROC LEGIS POL/PAR ECO/DEV

B43
BRADY R.A.,BUSINESS AS A SYSTEM OF POWER. EX/STRUC PLAN ECO/TAC CONTROL GP/REL PWR...TREND GP/COMP. PAGE 17 F0334
VOL/ASSN LOBBY POLICY

B47
MILLETT J.D.,THE PROCESS AND ORGANIZATION OF GOVERNMENT PLANNING. USA+45 DELIB/GP ACT/RES LEAD LOBBY TASK...POLICY GEOG TIME 20 RESOURCE/N. PAGE 91 F1793
ADMIN NAT/G PLAN CONSULT

B48
KILE O.M.,THE FARM BUREAU MOVEMENT: THE FARM BUREAU THROUGH THREE DECADES. NAT/G LEGIS LEAD LOBBY GP/REL INCOME POLICY. PAGE 71 F1387
AGRI STRUCT VOL/ASSN DOMIN

S48
CLEVELAND A.S.,"NAM: SPOKESMAN FOR INDUSTRY?" LEGIS PLAN LEAD LOBBY PARTIC CONSEN INCOME ATTIT ROLE ORD/FREE POLICY. PAGE 25 F0491
VOL/ASSN CLIENT REPRESENT INDUS

B49
SELZNICK P.,TVA AND THE GRASS ROOTS: A STUDY IN THE SOCIOLOGY OF FORMAL ORGANIZATION. USA-45 EX/STRUC PROB/SOLV CONFER PARTIC ROUTINE PWR 20 TVA. PAGE 119 F2353
REPRESENT LOBBY CONSULT

S49
BANFIELD E.C.,"CONGRESS AND THE BUDGET: A PLANNER'S CRITICISM" USA+45 NAT/G PLAN LOBBY. PAGE 9 F0172
LEGIS BUDGET EXEC POLICY

B51
HARDMAN J.B.,THE HOUSE OF LABOR. LAW R+D NEIGH EDU/PROP LEAD ROUTINE REPRESENT GP/REL...POLICY STAT. PAGE 55 F1080
LABOR LOBBY ADMIN PRESS

B52
HARDIN C.M.,THE POLITICS OF AGRICULTURE. USA+45 NAT/G PROF/ORG LEGIS LOBBY 20 DEPT/AGRI. PAGE 55 F1077
AGRI POLICY ECO/TAC GOV/REL

B52
REDFORD E.S.,ADMINISTRATION OF NATIONAL ECONOMIC CONTROL. ECO/DEV DELIB/GP ADJUD CONTROL EQUILIB 20. PAGE 110 F2166
ADMIN ROUTINE GOV/REL LOBBY

S53
GABLE R.W.,"NAM: INFLUENTIAL LOBBY OR KISS OF DEATH?" (BMR)" USA+45 LAW INSPECT EDU/PROP ADMIN CONTROL INGP/REL EFFICIENCY PWR 20 CONGRESS NAM TAFT/HART. PAGE 45 F0880
LOBBY LEGIS INDUS LG/CO

S54
EDELMAN M.J.,"LABOR'S INFLUENCE IN FOREIGN POLICY." NAT/G EXEC PWR 20. PAGE 36 F0700
LOBBY REPRESENT EX/STRUC LABOR

B56
BARBASH J.,THE PRACTICE OF UNIONISM. ECO/TAC LEAD LOBBY GP/REL INGP/REL DRIVE MARXISM BIBLIOG. PAGE 10 F0182
LABOR REPRESENT CONTROL ADMIN

B56
GILBERT L.D.,DIVIDENDS AND DEMOCRACY. DELIB/GP LEGIS CAP/ISM ADJUD LOBBY OWN PWR LAISSEZ MAJORIT. PAGE 47 F0922
LG/CO INGP/REL CONTROL PARTIC

B56
REDFORD E.S.,PUBLIC ADMINISTRATION AND POLICY FORMATION: STUDIES IN OIL, GAS, BANKING, RIVER DEVELOPMENT AND CORPORATE INVESTIGATIONS. USA+45 CLIENT NAT/G ADMIN LOBBY REPRESENT GOV/REL INGP/REL 20. PAGE 110 F2167 — EX/STRUC PROB/SOLV CONTROL EXEC

B56
WILCOX W.W.,SOCIAL RESPONSIBILITY IN FARM LEADERSHIP. CLIENT LEGIS EXEC LOBBY GP/REL ATTIT WEALTH. PAGE 146 F2880 — AGRI LEAD VOL/ASSN WORKER

L56
PENNOCK J.R.,"PARTY AND CONSTITUENCY IN POSTWAR AGRICULTURAL PRICE SUPPORT LEGISLATION." USA+45 LEGIS DEBATE LOBBY RIGID/FLEX. PAGE 105 F2057 — POL/PAR REPRESENT AGRI CHOOSE

S56
TYLER G.,"THE PRESIDENCY AND LABOR." USA+45 USA-45 NAT/G LOBBY GOV/REL PWR 20 PRESIDENT. PAGE 131 F2595 — LABOR REPRESENT CHIEF

L57
SURREY S.S.,"THE CONGRESS AND THE TAX LOBBYIST - HOW SPECIAL TAX PROVISIONS GET ENACTED." LOBBY REPRESENT PRIVIL CONGRESS. PAGE 128 F2518 — LEGIS TAX EX/STRUC ROLE

B58
FINER S.E.,PRIVATE INDUSTRY AND POLITICAL POWER (PAMPHLET). UK INDUS CONTROL LOBBY PWR. PAGE 41 F0797 — PLURISM REPRESENT EX/STRUC

B58
PAYNO M.,LA REFORMA SOCIAL EN ESPANA Y MEXICO. SPAIN ECO/TAC TAX LOBBY COERCE REV OWN CATHISM 19/20 MEXIC/AMER. PAGE 104 F2043 — SECT NAT/G LAW ELITES

S58
JOHNSON D.G.,"GOVERNMENT AND AGRICULTURE: IS AGRICULTURE A SPECIAL CASE?" PLAN ECO/TAC LOBBY WEALTH POLICY. PAGE 67 F1321 — INDUS GP/REL INCOME NAT/G

S58
SCHUMM S.,"INTEREST REPRESENTATION IN FRANCE AND GERMANY." EUR+WWI FRANCE GERMANY INSPECT PARL/PROC REPRESENT 20 WEIMAR/REP. PAGE 118 F2320 — LOBBY DELIB/GP NAT/G

B59
VINCENT W.S.,ROLES OF THE CITIZENS: PRINCIPLES AND PRACTICES. LOC/G POL/PAR VOL/ASSN CHOOSE ROLE ORD/FREE PWR...POLICY 20. PAGE 141 F2785 — INGP/REL EDU/PROP CREATE LOBBY

B59
VOSE C.E.,CAUCASIANS ONLY: THE SUPREME COURT, THE NAACP, AND THE RESTRICTIVE COVENANT CASES. USA+45 LAW CONSTN LOBBY...SOC 20 NAACP SUPREME/CT NEGRO. PAGE 142 F2796 — CT/SYS RACE/REL DISCRIM

B59
WAHLKE J.C.,LEGISLATIVE BEHAVIOR: A READER IN THEORY AND RESEARCH. USA+45 CONSTN ELITES POL/PAR LOBBY REPRESENT PERS/REL PERSON ROLE...IDEA/COMP METH/COMP SIMUL. PAGE 142 F2800 — LEGIS CHOOSE INGP/REL ATTIT

B59
WUERTHNER J.J.,THE BUSINESSMAN'S GUIDE TO PRACTICAL POLITICS. USA+45 PWR 20. PAGE 149 F2940 — LOBBY CHOOSE REPRESENT

S59
ALLEN G.,"NATIONAL FARMERS UNION AS A PRESSURE GROUP: II." UK ECO/DEV MARKET POL/PAR DELIB/GP PROB/SOLV ECO/TAC LOBBY INCOME...POLICY METH/COMP 19/20 NAT/FARMER. PAGE 4 F0069 — DIST/IND AGRI PROF/ORG TREND

S59
SCHEEHAN D.,"PUBLIC AND PRIVATE GROUPS AS IDENTIFIED IN THE FIELD OF TRADE REGULATIONS." USA+45 ADMIN REPRESENT GOV/REL. PAGE 116 F2293 — LAW CONTROL ADJUD LOBBY

S59
SHEPPARD H.L.,"THE POLITICAL ATTITUDES AND PREFERENCES OF UNION MEMBERS: THE CASE OF THE DETROIT AUTO WORKERS." LOBBY CHOOSE ROLE...CLASSIF QU SAMP TREND. PAGE 120 F2376 — LABOR ATTIT WORKER

B60
CARPER E.T.,THE DEFENSE APPROPRIATIONS RIDER (PAMPHLET). USA+45 CONSTN CHIEF DELIB/GP LEGIS BUDGET LOBBY CIVMIL/REL...POLICY 20 CONGRESS EISNHWR/DD DEPT/DEFEN PRESIDENT BOSTON. PAGE 22 F0419 — GOV/REL ADJUD LAW CONTROL

B60
GRAMPP W.D.,THE MANCHESTER SCHOOL OF ECONOMICS. UK LAW ECO/DEV COERCE ATTIT ORD/FREE LAISSEZ ...PHIL/SCI IDEA/COMP 19/20 MANCHESTER CORN/LAWS. PAGE 50 F0973 — ECO/TAC VOL/ASSN LOBBY NAT/G

B60
THOMPSON V.A.,THE REGULATORY PROCESS IN OPA RATIONING. USA-45 CLIENT PROB/SOLV ADMIN LOBBY REPRESENT 20. PAGE 130 F2566 — EX/STRUC GOV/REL INGP/REL

B61
DIMOCK M.E.,BUSINESS AND GOVERNMENT (4TH ED.). AGRI FINAN OP/RES PLAN BUDGET DIPLOM LOBBY NUC/PWR NEW/LIB SOCISM...POLICY BIBLIOG 20. PAGE 33 F0641 — NAT/G INDUS LABOR ECO/TAC

B61
ENGLER R.,THE POLITICS OF OIL. USA+45 CLIENT ELITES DOMIN EDU/PROP EXEC PWR 20. PAGE 38 F0734 — LOBBY REPRESENT POLICY

B61
GORDON R.A.,BUSINESS LEADERSHIP IN THE LARGE CORPORATION. USA+45 SOCIETY EX/STRUC ADMIN CONTROL ROUTINE GP/REL PWR...MGT 20. PAGE 49 F0960 — LG/CO LEAD DECISION LOBBY

B61
HUBBARD P.J.,ORIGINS OF THE TVA: THE MUSCLE SHOALS CONTROVERSY, 1920-1932. USA-45 DELIB/GP LEGIS LEAD LOBBY GOV/REL GP/REL INGP/REL OWN PERSON...BIBLIOG 20 TVA CONGRESS WATER. PAGE 62 F1229 — SEA CONTROL NAT/G INDUS

B61
MYRDAL G.,THE POLITICAL ELEMENT IN THE DEVELOPMENT OF ECONOMIC THEORY. FINAN LOBBY ATTIT...WELF/ST CONCPT IDEA/COMP GEN/LAWS 20. PAGE 95 F1875 — ECO/DEV ECO/TAC SOCIETY

B61
ZEIGLER H.,THE POLITICS OF SMALL BUSINESS. USA+45 EX/STRUC ADMIN 20. PAGE 150 F2963 — LOBBY REPRESENT EXEC VOL/ASSN

S61
BRAFF A.J.,"WAGE-PRICE POLICIES UNDER PUBLIC PRESSURE." USA+45 EX/STRUC LOBBY REPRESENT PWR 20. PAGE 17 F0335 — ATTIT PARTIC PROB/SOLV

S61
SCHER S.,"REGULATORY AGENCY CONTROL THROUGH APPOINTMENT: THE CASE OF THE EISENHOWER ADMINISTRATION AND THE NLRB." USA+45 EX/STRUC GOV/REL 20 NLRB. PAGE 116 F2296 — CHIEF LOBBY CONTROL TOP/EX

B62
CARPER E.T.,ILLINOIS GOES TO CONGRESS FOR ARMY LAND. USA+45 LAW EXTR/IND PROVS REGION CIVMIL/REL GOV/REL FEDERAL ATTIT 20 ILLINOIS SENATE CONGRESS DIRKSEN/E DOUGLAS/P. PAGE 22 F0420 — ADMIN LOBBY GEOG LEGIS

B62
MCCLELLAN J.L.,CRIME WITHOUT PUNISHMENT. USA+45 LAW SOCIETY DELIB/GP TRIBUTE CONTROL LOBBY COERCE GP/REL ANOMIE MORAL...CRIMLGY 20 CONGRESS HOFFA/J. PAGE 88 F1718 — CRIME ACT/RES LABOR PWR

L62
ERDMANN H.H.,"ADMINISTRATIVE LAW AND FARM ECONOMICS." USA+45 LOC/G NAT/G PLAN PROB/SOLV LOBBY ...DECISION ANTHOL 20. PAGE 38 F0744 — AGRI ADMIN ADJUD POLICY

B63
HATHAWAY D.A.,GOVERNMENT AND AGRICULTURE: PUBLIC POLICY IN A DEMOCRATIC SOCIETY. USA+45 LEGIS ADMIN EXEC LOBBY REPRESENT PWR 20. PAGE 57 F1111 — AGRI GOV/REL PROB/SOLV EX/STRUC

B63
IANNI O.,INDUSTRIALIZACAO E DESENVOLVIMENTO SOCIAL NO BRASIL. BRAZIL L/A+17C STRATA STRUCT ECO/UNDEV EDU/PROP LEAD LOBBY NAT/LISM 20. PAGE 64 F1257 — WORKER GP/REL INDUS PARTIC

B63
PERLO V.,MILITARISM AND INDUSTRY. USA+45 INT/TRADE EDU/PROP DETER KNOWL...CHARTS MAPS 20. PAGE 105 F2064 — CIVMIL/REL INDUS LOBBY ARMS/CONT

B63
WILTZ J.E.,IN SEARCH OF PEACE: THE SENATE MUNITIONS INQUIRY, 1934-36. EUR+WWI USA-45 ELITES INDUS LG/CO LEGIS INT/TRADE LOBBY NEUTRAL ARMS/CONT...POLICY CONGRESS 20 LEAGUE/NAT PRESIDENT SENATE CONSCRIPTN. PAGE 147 F2905 — DELIB/GP PROFIT WAR WEAPON

B64
BASTIAT F.,ECONOMIC HARMONIES (1850). STRATA STRUCT ECO/DEV BUDGET TAX PRICE LOBBY COST. PAGE 11 F0206 — ECO/TAC PLAN INT/TRADE LAISSEZ

B64
FISK W.M.,ADMINISTRATIVE PROCEDURE IN A REGULATORY AGENCY: THE CAB AND THE NEW YORK-CHICAGO CASE (PAMPHLET). USA+45 DIST/IND ADMIN CONTROL LOBBY GP/REL ROLE ORD/FREE NEWYORK/C CHICAGO CAB. PAGE 41 F0805 — SERV/IND ECO/DEV AIR JURID

B64
HACKER A.,THE CORPORATION TAKE-OVER. CONSTN LABOR PLAN BAL/PWR CONTROL EXEC LOBBY REPRESENT GP/REL ROLE ORD/FREE POLICY. PAGE 52 F1025 — LG/CO STRUCT PWR

B64
MANSFIELD E.,MONOPOLY POWER AND ECONOMIC PERFORMANCE: AN INTRODUCTION TO A CURRENT ISSUE OF PUBLIC POLICY. ECO/DEV INDUS NAT/G PLAN CAP/ISM PRICE CONTROL LOBBY EFFICIENCY PRODUC...POLICY 20 CONGRESS KENNEDY/JF MONOPOLY. PAGE 85 F1659 — LG/CO PWR ECO/TAC MARKET

B64
PAARLBERG D.,AMERICAN FARM POLICY: A CASE STUDY IN CENTRALIZED DECISION-MAKING. USA+45 NAT/G LEGIS LOBBY REPRESENT GOV/REL PWR LAISSEZ 20. PAGE 102 F2009 — PROB/SOLV EX/STRUC AGRI

B64
US DEPT LABOR OFF SOLICITOR,LEGISLATIVE HISTORY OF THE LABOR-MANAGEMENT AND DISCLOSURE ACT OF 1959. DELIB/GP WORKER ADMIN LOBBY PARL/PROC SANCTION CHOOSE GOV/REL 20 CONGRESS PRESIDENT. PAGE 136 F2677
LABOR LEGIS DEBATE POLICY

B65
BRADLEY J.F.,THE ROLE OF TRADE ASSOCIATIONS AND PROFESSIONAL BUSINESS SOCIETIES IN AMERICA. USA+45 USA-45 STRUCT CONSULT DELIB/GP CREATE LOBBY GP/REL 20. PAGE 17 F0333
ECO/DEV PROF/ORG VOL/ASSN SOCIETY

B65
HADWIGER D.F.,PRESSURES AND PROTEST. NAT/G LEGIS PLAN LEAD PARTIC ROUTINE ATTIT POLICY. PAGE 53 F1030
AGRI GP/REL LOBBY CHOOSE

B65
MARGOLIS J.,THE PUBLIC ECONOMY OF URBAN COMMUNITIES. USA+45 LEGIS PROB/SOLV TAX LOBBY CHOOSE ATTIT MUNICH. PAGE 85 F1668
LOC/G DECISION FINAN

S65
LONG T.G.,"THE ADMINISTRATIVE PROCESS: AGONIZING REAPPRAISAL IN THE FTC." NAT/G REPRESENT 20 FTC. PAGE 82 F1598
ADJUD LOBBY ADMIN EX/STRUC

S65
WILDAVSKY A.,"TVA AND POWER POLITICS." USA+45 CLIENT PROB/SOLV EXEC GOV/REL 20. PAGE 146 F2882
PWR EX/STRUC LOBBY

C65
MANSFIELD H.C.,"THE CONGRESS AND ECONOMIC POLICY" IN C. TRUMAN ED., THE CONGRESS AND AMERICA'S FUTURE." USA+45 USA-45 CONSTN NAT/G BUDGET ADMIN CONTROL EXEC LOBBY. PAGE 85 F1661
POLICY ECO/TAC PWR LEGIS

B66
ANDERSON J.E.,POLITICS AND THE ECONOMY. NAT/G LOBBY PWR 20. PAGE 5 F0096
REPRESENT EX/STRUC CONTROL

B66
BOLTON R.E.,DEFENSE AND DISARMAMENT: THE ECONOMICS OF TRANSITION. USA+45 R+D FORCES PLAN LOBBY DETER WAR COST PEACE...ANTHOL BIBLIOG 20. PAGE 16 F0310
ARMS/CONT POLICY INDUS

B66
DAVIES JC I.I.I.,NEIGHBORHOOD GROUPS AND URBAN RENEWAL. USA+45 PLAN LOBBY PARTIC CHOOSE RACE/REL ...POLICY DECISION SOC INT MUNICH SOC/INTEG 20 NEWYORK/C. PAGE 30 F0586
NEIGH CREATE PROB/SOLV

B66
FORD P.,CARDINAL MORAN AND THE A. L. P. NAT/G POL/PAR SECT DELIB/GP LOBBY REV CHOOSE ORD/FREE MARXISM 19/20 AUSTRAL PROTESTANT LABOR/PAR. PAGE 42 F0825
CATHISM SOCISM LABOR SOCIETY

B66
LEE R.A.,TRUMAN AND TAFT-HARTLEY: A QUESTION OF MANDATE. USA+45 LAW CONSTN LG/CO CONTROL LOBBY GOV/REL PEACE NEW/LIB 20 TRUMAN/HS CONGRESS. PAGE 77 F1507
LEGIS TOP/EX ADJUD LABOR

B66
MOSKOW M.H.,TEACHERS AND UNIONS. SCHOOL WORKER ADJUD LOBBY ATTIT ORD/FREE 20. PAGE 94 F1844
EDU/PROP PROF/ORG LABOR BARGAIN

B66
RAYBACK J.G.,A HISTORY OF AMERICAN LABOR. USA+45 USA-45 ECO/DEV LEGIS COLONIAL WAR INGP/REL PWR WEALTH 17/20. PAGE 110 F2156
LABOR LOBBY ECO/UNDEV NAT/G

B66
RIZK C.,LE REGIME POLITIQUE LIBANAIS. ISLAM LEBANON STRUCT POL/PAR SECT LOBBY GP/REL 20 ARABS MUSLIM CHRISTIAN. PAGE 112 F2198
ECO/UNDEV NAT/G CULTURE

B66
ROSS A.M.,INDUSTRIAL RELATIONS AND ECONOMIC DEVELOPMENT. POL/PAR LEGIS WORKER BARGAIN PRICE EXEC LOBBY INCOME PWR...DECISION ANTHOL BIBLIOG 20. PAGE 114 F2243
ECO/UNDEV LABOR NAT/G GP/REL

S66
FELD W.,"NATIONAL ECONOMIC INTEREST GROUPS AND POLICY FORMATION IN THE EEC." NAT/G POL/PAR REGION CENTRAL SOVEREIGN...INT NET/THEORY EEC. PAGE 40 F0777
LOBBY ELITES DECISION

B67
BIBBY J.,ON CAPITOL HILL. POL/PAR LOBBY PARL/PROC GOV/REL PERS/REL...JURID PHIL/SCI OBS INT BIBLIOG 20 CONGRESS PRESIDENT. PAGE 15 F0278
CONFER LEGIS CREATE LEAD

B67
BLAIR G.S.,LEGISLATIVE BODIES IN CALIFORNIA. USA+45 LAW POL/PAR LOBBY APPORT CHOOSE REPRESENT GP/REL ...T CALIFORNIA. PAGE 15 F0293
LEGIS PROVS LOC/G ADJUD

B67
COWLING M.,1867 DISRAELI, GLADSTONE, AND REVOLUTION; THE PASSING OF THE SECOND REFORM BILL. UK LEGIS LEAD LOBBY GP/REL INGP/REL...DECISION BIBLIOG 19 REFORMERS. PAGE 28 F0545
PARL/PROC POL/PAR ATTIT LAW

B67
GOODMAN J.S.,THE DEMOCRATS AND LABOR IN RHODE ISLAND 9152-1962; CHANGES IN THE OLD ALLIANCE. USA+45 EDU/PROP LEAD GP/REL ROLE RHODE/ISL DEMOCRAT. PAGE 49 F0948
LABOR LOBBY POL/PAR LEGIS

B67
HANRIEDER W.F.,WEST GERMAN FOREIGN POLICY 1949-1963: INTERNATIONAL PRESSURE AND DOMESTIC RESPONSE. EUR+WWI GERMANY/W POL/PAR LOBBY CONSEN 20. PAGE 54 F1061
DIPLOM POLICY NAT/G ATTIT

B67
LYTLE C.M.,THE WARREN COURT AND ITS CRITICS. USA+45 NAT/G PROVS FORCES LOBBY RACE/REL DISCRIM SOVEREIGN 20 SUPREME/CT WARRN/EARL. PAGE 83 F1618
CT/SYS ADJUD PROB/SOLV ATTIT

B67
O'LEARY M.K.,THE POLITICS OF AMERICAN FOREIGN AID. USA+45 POL/PAR CHIEF BUDGET EDU/PROP LOBBY CONGRESS. PAGE 100 F1958
FOR/AID DIPLOM PARL/PROC ATTIT

B67
REHMUS C.M.,LABOR AND AMERICAN POLITICS. POL/PAR WORKER EDU/PROP PARTIC ATTIT PWR. PAGE 110 F2175
LABOR ROLE LOBBY

B67
SCHAEFER W.V.,THE SUSPECT AND SOCIETY: CRIMINAL PROCEDURE AND CONVERGING CONSTITUTIONAL DOCTRINES. USA+45 TEC/DEV LOBBY ROUTINE SANCTION...INT 20. PAGE 116 F2288
CRIME FORCES CONSTN JURID

B67
TOMA P.A.,THE POLITICS OF FOOD FOR PEACE; EXECUTIVE-LEGISLATIVE INTERACTION. USA+45 ECO/UNDEV POL/PAR DEBATE EXEC LOBBY CHOOSE PEACE...DECISION CHARTS. PAGE 131 F2580
FOR/AID POLICY LEGIS AGRI

S67
"THE SIERRA CLUB, POLITICAL ACTIVITY, AND TAX EXEMPT CHARITABLE STATUS." USA+45 LAW VOL/ASSN TAX PAY ADJUD LOBBY INGP/REL HABITAT 20. PAGE 2 F0027
ELITES GOV/REL FACE/GP ORD/FREE

S67
EHRLICH S.,"INTERNATIONAL PRESSURE GROUPS: A CONTRIBUTION TO THE SOCIOLOGY OF INTERNATIONAL RELATIONS IN THE CAPITALIST WORLD." GP/REL...METH 20. PAGE 36 F0711
INT/ORG LOBBY DIPLOM DECISION

S67
JANSSEN P.,"NEA: THE RELUCTANT DRAGON." NAT/G EXEC LOBBY PARTIC SANCTION RACE/REL ROLE TREND. PAGE 66 F1305
EDU/PROP PROF/ORG MGT POLICY

S67
JOHNSON L.B.,"BULLETS DO NOT DISCRIMINATE-LANDLORDS DO." PROB/SOLV EXEC LOBBY DEMAND...REALPOL SOC 20. PAGE 68 F1329
NAT/G DISCRIM POLICY

S67
LASLETT J.H.M.,"SOCIALISM AND THE AMERICAN LABOR MOVEMENT* SOME NEW REFLECTIONS." USA-45 VOL/ASSN LOBBY PARTIC CENTRAL ALL/VALS SOCISM...GP/COMP 20. PAGE 76 F1484
LABOR ROUTINE ATTIT GP/REL

S67
PAI G.A.,"TAXATION AND PLANNING IN INDIA: A BIRDS-EYE VIEW." INDIA ELITES NAT/G LEGIS BUDGET CONTROL LOBBY INCOME...STAT CHARTS 20. PAGE 102 F2015
TAX PLAN WEALTH STRATA

LOBBYING....SEE LOBBY

LOC/G....LOCAL GOVERNMENT

N
NEW JERSEY STATE OF,SECOND REPORT TO GOVERNOR, SENATE, ASSEMBLY BY UNIFORM COMMERCIAL CODE STUDY COMMISSION. USA+45 INDUS LOC/G NAT/G PROF/ORG CONSULT ACT/RES LEGIT CT/SYS ATTIT NEW/JERSEY. PAGE 98 F1920
LAW FINAN CENTRAL PROVS

N
US SUPERINTENDENT OF DOCUMENTS,CENSUS PUBLICATIONS (PRICE LIST 70). AGRI CONSTRUC DIST/IND FINAN LOC/G NAT/G PROVS INT/TRADE APPORT INCOME. PAGE 140 F2751
BIBLIOG/A CENSUS STAT USA+45

N
US SUPERINTENDENT OF DOCUMENTS,INTERSTATE COMMERCE (PRICE LIST 59). USA+45 LAW LOC/G NAT/G LEGIS TARIFFS TAX ADMIN CONTROL HEALTH DECISION. PAGE 140 F2752
BIBLIOG/A DIST/IND GOV/REL PROVS

N19
CHATTERS C.H.,NEW MUNICIPAL REVENUES FOR NEW MUNICIPAL EXPENDITURES (PAMPHLET). PLAN PRICE UTIL HABITAT...IDEA/COMP MUNICH 20. PAGE 23 F0457
LOC/G BUDGET TAX

N19
DWYER J.W.,YARDSTICKS FOR PERFORMANCE (PAMPHLET). USA+45 FINAN CONTROL...CONCPT METH/COMP MUNICH. PAGE 35 F0688
BUDGET LOC/G EFFICIENCY

N19
FAHRNKOPF N.,STATE AND LOCAL GOVERNMENT IN ILLINOIS (PAMPHLET). CONSTN ADMIN PARTIC CHOOSE REPRESENT GOV/REL...JURID MGT 20 ILLINOIS. PAGE 39 F0759
BIBLIOG LOC/G LEGIS

CT/SYS

N19
KRESSBACH T.W.,HE MICHIGAN CITY MANAGER IN BUDGETARY PROCEEDINGS (PAMPHLET). USA+45 PROVS DELIB/GP GP/REL SUPEGO...POLICY MUNICH. PAGE 73 F1438
LOC/G BUDGET FINAN

N19
MUSHKIN S.J.,LOCAL SCHOOL EXPENDITURES: 1970 PROJECTIONS (PAMPHLET). FUT USA+45 CONSTRUC FINAN PROVS EDU/PROP COST...GEOG CENSUS PREDICT CHARTS SIMUL 20. PAGE 95 F1871
LOC/G SCHOOL BUDGET

N19
RIDLEY C.E.,MEASURING MUNICIPAL ACTIVITIES (PAMPHLET). FINAN SERV/IND FORCES RECEIVE INGP/REL HABITAT...POLICY SOC/WK 20. PAGE 111 F2191
MGT HEALTH WEALTH LOC/G

N19
STUTZ R.L.,COLLECTIVE DEALING BY UNITS OF LOCAL GOVERNMENT IN CONNECTICUT (PAMPHLET). USA+45 LOC/G PROVS...STAT MUNICH 20 CONNECTICT. PAGE 127 F2508
VOL/ASSN LABOR WORKER

B25
MATHEWS J.M.,AMERICAN STATE GOVERNMENT. USA-45 LOC/G CHIEF EX/STRUC LEGIS ADJUD CONTROL CT/SYS ROUTINE GOV/REL PWR 20 GOVERNOR. PAGE 87 F1703
PROVS ADMIN FEDERAL CONSTN

B30
BIEL G.,TREATISE ON THE POWER AND UTILITY OF MONEY (1484). INDUS MARKET LOC/G NAT/G SECT ECO/TAC PRODUC WEALTH 15. PAGE 15 F0280
FINAN COST PRICE GEN/LAWS

B37
COLE W.E.,RECENT TRENDS IN RURAL PLANNING. USA-45 LAW ECO/DEV LOC/G SECT EDU/PROP CRIME LEISURE AGE/Y HABITAT...SOC/WK MUNICH 20. PAGE 26 F0503
AGRI NEIGH PLAN ACT/RES

B42
DRUCKER P.F.,THE FUTURE OF INDUSTRIAL MAN; A CONSERVATIVE APPROACH. USA-45 LOC/G PLAN WAR CENTRAL RATIONAL TOTALISM ORD/FREE LAISSEZ ...PLURIST IDEA/COMP 19/20 HITLER/A. PAGE 34 F0664
INDUS SOCIETY REGION PROB/SOLV

B42
US LIBRARY OF CONGRESS,ECONOMICS OF WAR (APRIL 1941-MARCH 1942). WOR-45 FINAN INDUS LOC/G NAT/G PLAN BUDGET RATION COST DEMAND...POLICY 20. PAGE 138 F2712
BIBLIOG/A INT/TRADE ECO/TAC WAR

B48
METZLER L.A.,INCOME, EMPLOYMENT, AND PUBLIC POLICY. FINAN INDUS LOC/G NAT/G TAX GIVE PAY COST PRODUC ...MGT TIME/SEQ 20. PAGE 90 F1765
INCOME WEALTH POLICY ECO/TAC

B49
SHISTER J.,ECONOMICS OF THE LABOR MARKET. LOC/G NAT/G WORKER TEC/DEV BARGAIN PAY PRICE EXEC GP/REL INCOME...MGT T 20. PAGE 121 F2381
MARKET LABOR INDUS

S49
STEINMETZ H.,"THE PROBLEMS OF THE LANDRAT: A STUDY OF COUNTY GOVERNMENT IN THE US ZONE OF GERMANY." GERMANY/W USA+45 INDUS PLAN DIPLOM EDU/PROP CONTROL WAR GOV/REL FEDERAL WEALTH PLURISM...GOV/COMP 20 LANDRAT. PAGE 126 F2478
LOC/G COLONIAL MGT TOP/EX

S51
HAWLEY A.H.,"METROPOLITAN POPULATION AND MUNICIPAL GOVERNMENT EXPENDITURES IN CENTRAL CITIES" (BMR)" USA+45 FINAN TAX...STAT CON/ANAL CHARTS MUNICH 20. PAGE 57 F1117
GEOG LOC/G COST BUDGET

B54
BATTEN T.R.,PROBLEMS OF AFRICAN DEVELOPMENT (2ND ED.). AFR LAW SOCIETY SCHOOL ECO/TAC TAX...GEOG HEAL SOC 20. PAGE 11 F0211
ECO/UNDEV AGRI LOC/G PROB/SOLV

B54
KARTUN D.,AFRICA, AFRICA: A CONTINENT RISES TO ITS FEET. AFR SOUTH/AFR UK ELITES AGRI LABOR LOC/G POL/PAR EDU/PROP CONTROL COERCE DISCRIM AGE/Y NEGRO THIRD/WRLD GOLD/COAST. PAGE 69 F1358
COLONIAL ORD/FREE PROFIT EXTR/IND

B55
GOMES F.A.,OPERACAO MUNICIPIO. BRAZIL L/A+17C SERV/IND LOC/G BUDGET ECO/TAC COST DEMAND...POLICY MUNICH 20. PAGE 48 F0944
ECO/UNDEV FEDERAL GOV/REL

B55
US ADVISORY COMN INTERGOV REL,THE COMMISSION ON INTERGOVERNMENTAL RELATIONS; A REPORT TO THE PRESIDENT FOR TRANSMITTAL TO THE CONGRESS. USA+45 ECO/DEV AGRI COM/IND FINAN FORCES PLAN EDU/PROP HEALTH WEALTH...STAT MUNICH 20 CIV/DEFENS. PAGE 133 F2630
GOV/REL NAT/G LOC/G PROVS

B56
KOHLER E.L.,ACCOUNTING IN THE FEDERAL GOVERNMENT. USA+45 LOC/G PLAN TAX CONTROL COST 20. PAGE 72 F1416
BUDGET AFR NAT/G FINAN

B56
POOLE K.E.,PUBLIC FINANCE AND ECONOMIC WELFARE. STRUCT ECO/DEV LOC/G NAT/G BUDGET PAY ROUTINE COST EQUILIB WEALTH...SOC/WK METH/COMP 20. PAGE 107 F2103
FINAN TAX ORD/FREE

S56
MARGOLIS J.,"ON MUNICIPAL LAND POLICY FOR FISCAL GAINS." USA+45 PLAN TAX COST EFFICIENCY HABITAT KNOWL...MGT MUNICH 20. PAGE 85 F1667
BUDGET POLICY GEOG LOC/G

N57
U WISCONSIN BUREAU OF GOVT,SERVICE SALES OF THE CITY OF MADISON TO METROPOLITAN COMMUNITIES AND NONRESIDENTS (PAMPHLET). DIST/IND LOC/G ADMIN ...DECISION GOV/COMP MUNICH. PAGE 132 F2597
REGION ECO/TAC PLAN

B58
DAVIS E.H.,OF THE PEOPLE, BY THE PEOPLE, FOR THE PEOPLE. INCOME WEALTH...METH/COMP MUNICH 20. PAGE 30 F0587
FINAN LOC/G TAX

B58
INDIAN INST OF PUBLIC ADMIN,IMPROVING CITY GOVERNMENT. INDIA ECO/UNDEV PLAN BUDGET PARTIC GP/REL MUNICH 20. PAGE 64 F1263
LOC/G PROB/SOLV ADMIN

B58
JENNINGS I.,PROBLEMS OF THE NEW COMMONWEALTH. AFR CEYLON INDIA PAKISTAN S/ASIA ECO/UNDEV INT/ORG LOC/G DIPLOM ECO/TAC INT/TRADE COLONIAL RACE/REL DISCRIM 20 PARLIAMENT. PAGE 67 F1314
NAT/LISM NEUTRAL FOR/AID POL/PAR

B58
NICULESCU B.,COLONIAL PLANNING: A COMPARATIVE STUDY. AFR AGRI LOC/G NAT/G DELIB/GP COLONIAL MUNICH 20. PAGE 98 F1927
PLAN ECO/UNDEV TEC/DEV NAT/COMP

B58
SHAW S.J.,THE FINANCIAL AND ADMINISTRATIVE ORGANIZATION AND DEVELOPMENT OF OTTOMAN EGYPT 1517-1798. UAR LOC/G FORCES BUDGET INT/TRADE TAX EATING INCOME WEALTH...CHARTS BIBLIOG 16/18 OTTOMAN NAPOLEON/B. PAGE 120 F2371
FINAN ADMIN GOV/REL CULTURE

B59
CUCCORESE H.J.,HISTORIA DE LA CONVERSION DEL PAPEL MONEDA EN BUENOS AIRES, 1861-1867. AFR LAW LOC/G NAT/G ATTIT...POLICY BIBLIOG 19 ARGEN BUENOS/AIR. PAGE 29 F0560
FINAN PLAN LEGIS

B59
NORTON P.L.,URBAN PROBLEMS AND TECHNIQUES. AIR AGRI INDUS MARKET TEC/DEV BUDGET LEISURE ALL/VALS ...ANTHOL MUNICH 20 URBAN/RNWL. PAGE 99 F1936
PLAN LOC/G HABITAT

B59
SILCOCK T.H.,THE COMMONWEALTH ECONOMY IN SOUTHEAST ASIA. AFR INDIA MALAYSIA S/ASIA ECO/DEV AGRI LOC/G PLAN TARIFFS COLONIAL BAL/PAY DEMAND...BIBLIOG/A 20 GATT. PAGE 122 F2401
ECO/TAC INT/TRADE RACE/REL DIPLOM

B59
VINCENT W.S.,ROLES OF THE CITIZENS: PRINCIPLES AND PRACTICES. LOC/G POL/PAR VOL/ASSN CHOOSE ROLE ORD/FREE PWR...POLICY 20. PAGE 141 F2785
INGP/REL EDU/PROP CREATE LOBBY

B59
WORTHY J.C.,BIG BUSINESS AND FREE MEN. LG/CO EX/STRUC EDU/PROP LEAD CHOOSE GP/REL ATTIT DRIVE ROLE ORD/FREE...MAJORIT 20. PAGE 149 F2927
ELITES LOC/G TOP/EX PARTIC

B60
EELLS R.S.F.,THE MEANING OF MODERN BUSINESS. LOC/G NAT/G NEIGH EX/STRUC PARTIC GP/REL INGP/REL DECISION. PAGE 36 F0706
LG/CO REPRESENT POLICY PLAN

B60
FRYE R.J.,GOVERNMENT AND LABOR: THE ALABAMA PROGRAM. USA+45 INDUS R+D LABOR WORKER BUDGET EFFICIENCY AGE/Y HEALTH...CHARTS 20 ALABAMA. PAGE 45 F0870
ADMIN LEGIS LOC/G PROVS

B60
GILMORE D.R.,DEVELOPING THE "LITTLE" ECONOMIES. USA+45 FINAN LG/CO PROF/ORG VOL/ASSN CREATE ADMIN. PAGE 47 F0924
ECO/TAC LOC/G PROVS PLAN

B60
ILLINOIS U BUR COMMUNITY PLAN,PROCEEDINGS OF ILLINOIS STATEWIDE PLANNING CONFERENCE 1960. USA+45 FINAN LOC/G ACT/RES LEAD GOV/REL GP/REL WEALTH MUNICH 20 ILLINOIS. PAGE 64 F1260
PLAN DELIB/GP VOL/ASSN

B60
MARSHALL A.H.,FINANCIAL ADMINISTRATION IN LOCAL GOVERNMENT. UK DELIB/GP CONFER COST INCOME PERSON ...JURID 20. PAGE 86 F1679
FINAN LOC/G BUDGET ADMIN

B60
PENNSYLVANIA ECONOMY LEAGUE,URBAN RENEWAL IMPACT STUDY: ADMINISTRATIVE-LEGAL-FISCAL. USA+45 FINAN LOC/G NEIGH ADMIN EFFICIENCY...CENSUS CHARTS MUNICH 20 PENNSYLVAN. PAGE 105 F2059
PLAN BUDGET ADJUD

B60
POOLEY B.J.,THE EVOLUTION OF BRITISH PLANNING LEGISLATION. UK ECO/DEV LOC/G CONSULT DELIB/GP ADMIN MUNICH 20 URBAN/RNWL. PAGE 107 F2104
PLAN LEGIS PROB/SOLV

B60
US SENATE COMM ON COMMERCE,URBAN MASS TRANSPORTATION. FUT USA+45 AIR ECO/DEV FINAN LOC/G LEGIS CREATE PROB/SOLV TEC/DEV MUNICH 20 PUB/TRANS.
DIST/IND PLAN NAT/G

PAGE 139 F2732 LAW

B60
VERNON R.,METROPOLIS 1985. LOC/G PLAN TAX LEAD PWR MUNICH. PAGE 141 F2780
REGION ECO/TAC DECISION

S60
HERZ J.H.,"EAST GERMANY: PROGRESS AND PROSPECTS." COM AGRI FINAN INDUS LOC/G NAT/G FORCES PLAN TEC/DEV DOMIN ADMIN COERCE DRIVE PERCEPT RIGID/FLEX MORAL ORD/FREE PWR...MARXIST PSY SOC RECORD STERTYP WORK. PAGE 59 F1158
POL/PAR STRUCT GERMANY

C60
HOSELITZ B.,"THE ROLE OF CITIES IN THE ECONOMIC GROWTH OF UNDERDEVELOPED COUNTRIES" IN "SOCIOLOGICAL ASPECTS OF ECONOMIC GROWTH"(BMR). CULTURE LOC/G ACT/RES...SOC IDEA/COMP METH/COMP METH MUNICH IND 14/20 REDFIELD/R. PAGE 62 F1218
METH/CNCPT TEC/DEV ECO/UNDEV

N60
COMMITTEE ECONOMIC DEVELOPMENT,GUIDING METROPOLITAN GROWTH (PAMPHLET). USA+45 LOC/G NAT/G PROF/ORG ACT/RES PLAN...SOC/WK MUNICH. PAGE 27 F0517
GEOG INDUS HEALTH

B61
BEASLEY K.E.,STATE SUPERVISION OF MUNICIPAL DEBT IN KANSAS - A CASE STUDY. USA+45 USA-45 FINAN PROVS BUDGET TAX ADJUD ADMIN CONTROL SUPEGO MUNICH. PAGE 12 F0224
LOC/G LEGIS JURID

B61
DE GRAZIA A.,AMERICAN WELFARE. CLIENT FINAN LABOR LOC/G NAT/G NEIGH EDU/PROP GP/REL...CLASSIF CON/ANAL CHARTS BIBLIOG. PAGE 31 F0598
GIVE WEALTH SECT VOL/ASSN

B61
INTL UNION LOCAL AUTHORITIES,METROPOLIS. WOR+45 DIST/IND FINAN GIVE EDU/PROP CRIME COST HEALTH WEALTH MUNICH 20. PAGE 65 F1286
GOV/COMP LOC/G BIBLIOG

B61
LEE R.R.,ENGINEERING-ECONOMIC PLANNING MISCELLANEOUS SUBJECTS: A SELECTED BIBLIOGRAPHY (MIMEOGRAPHED). FINAN LOC/G NEIGH ADMIN CONTROL INGP/REL HABITAT...GEOG MGT SOC/WK MUNICH 20 RESOURCE/N. PAGE 77 F1509
BIBLIOG/A PLAN REGION

B61
LONGRIGG S.H.,OIL IN THE MIDDLE EAST: ITS DISCOVERY AND DEVELOPMENT. ECO/UNDEV LG/CO LOC/G TEC/DEV WEALTH...STAT TIME/SEQ 20 OIL. PAGE 82 F1599
ISLAM EXTR/IND

B61
SACKS S.,FINANCING GOVERNMENT IN A METROPOLITAN GOVERNMENT. USA+45 ECO/DEV R+D LOC/G GOV/REL ...BIBLIOG MUNICH 20 CLEVELAND. PAGE 115 F2269
FINAN PLAN BUDGET

B61
STARNER F.L.,GENERAL OBLIGATION BOND FINANCING BY LOCAL GOVERNMENTS: A SURVEY OF STATE CONTROLS. CANADA UK USA+45 CONSTN PROVS...POLICY JURID METH/COMP 20 EUROPE CALIFORNIA. PAGE 125 F2471
FINAN LOC/G GOV/REL ADJUD

L61
GERWIG R.,"PUBLIC AUTHORITIES IN THE UNITED STATES." LAW CONSTN PROVS TAX ADMIN FEDERAL MUNICH. PAGE 47 F0920
LOC/G GOV/REL PWR

S61
ANDREWS R.B.,"URBAN ECONOMICS: AN APPRAISAL OF PROGRESS." LOC/G PROB/SOLV TEC/DEV...CONCPT OBS/ENVIR METH/COMP HYPO/EXP SOC/EXP SIMUL GEN/METH METH MUNICH 20. PAGE 5 F0102
PHIL/SCI ECOMETRIC

N61
US ADVISORY COMM INTERGOV REL,STATE AND LOCAL TAXATION ON PRIVATELY OWNED PROPERTY LOCATED ON FEDERAL AREAS: PROPOSED AMENDMENT OF BUCK ACT (PAMPHLET). USA+45 ACT/RES PLAN CONTROL GOV/REL INGP/REL OWN...POLICY JURID CHARTS GP/COMP 20. PAGE 133 F2629
PROVS LOC/G NAT/G TAX

B62
GROVE J.W.,GOVERNMENT AND INDUSTRY IN BRITAIN. UK FINAN LOC/G CONSULT DELIB/GP INT/TRADE ADMIN CONTROL...BIBLIOG 20. PAGE 52 F1008
ECO/TAC INDUS NAT/G GP/REL

B62
LICHFIELD N.,COST-BENEFIT ANALYSIS IN URBAN REDEVELOPMENT. CONSTRUC LOC/G NEIGH ACT/RES PROB/SOLV TEC/DEV BUDGET TAX...DECISION STAT CHARTS SOC/EXP MUNICH 20. PAGE 80 F1558
PLAN COST GOV/REL

B62
LITTLEFIELD N.,METROPOLITAN AREA PROBLEMS AND MUNICIPAL HOME RULE. USA+45 PROVS ADMIN CONTROL GP/REL PWR. PAGE 81 F1586
LOC/G SOVEREIGN JURID LEGIS

B62
SCHALLER H.G.,PUBLIC EXPENDITURE DECISIONS IN THE URBAN COMMUNITY: PREPARED FOR RESOURCES FOR THE FUTURE, INC. INDUS SERV/IND LOC/G PUB/INST PLAN PROB/SOLV BUDGET DEMAND PRODUC...CHARTS MUNICH. PAGE 116 F2289
FINAN DECISION

B62
US ADVISORY COMN INTERGOV REL,STATE CONSTITUTIONAL AND STATUTORY RESTRICTIONS ON LOCAL TAXING POWERS. USA+45 USA-45 LAW CONSTN ACT/RES CONTROL WEALTH ...JURID CHARTS 20. PAGE 133 F2632
LOC/G PROVS GOV/REL TAX

L62
ERDMANN H.H.,"ADMINISTRATIVE LAW AND FARM ECONOMICS." USA+45 LOC/G NAT/G PLAN PROB/SOLV LOBBY ...DECISION ANTHOL 20. PAGE 38 F0744
AGRI ADMIN ADJUD POLICY

L62
WATERSTON A.,"PLANNING IN MOROCCO, ORGANIZATION AND IMPLEMENTATION. BALTIMORE: HOPKINS ECON. DEVELOP. INT. BANK FOR." ISLAM ECO/DEV AGRI DIST/IND INDUS PROC/MFG SERV/IND LOC/G EX/STRUC ECO/TAC PWR WEALTH TOT/POP TRUE/GP METH/GP TERR/GP VAL/FREE 20. PAGE 144 F2829
NAT/G PLAN MOROCCO

S62
GILL P.J.,"FUTURE TAXATION POLICY IN AN INDEPENDENT EAST AFRICA" UGANDA LOC/G ECO/TAC ADMIN EFFICIENCY INCOME PRODUC...CHARTS 20. PAGE 47 F0923
ECO/UNDEV TAX AFR COLONIAL

B63
BURRUS B.R.,ADMINSTRATIVE LAW AND LOCAL GOVERNMENT. USA+45 PROVS LEGIS LICENSE ADJUD ORD/FREE 20. PAGE 20 F0392
EX/STRUC LOC/G JURID CONSTN

B63
FRIEDRICH C.J.,MAN AND HIS GOVERNMENT: AN EMPIRICAL THEORY OF POLITICS. UNIV LOC/G NAT/G ADJUD REV INGP/REL DISCRIM PWR BIBLIOG. PAGE 44 F0867
PERSON ORD/FREE PARTIC CONTROL

B63
GORDON M.S.,THE ECONOMICS OF WELFARE POLICIES. INDUS LOC/G NAT/G LEGIS WORKER INCOME AGE/O SKILL WEALTH...METH/COMP NAT/COMP 20. PAGE 49 F0959
METH/CNCPT ECO/TAC POLICY

B63
LAIRD R.D.,SOVIET AGRICULTURAL AND PEASANT AFFAIRS. FUT STRATA LOC/G DELIB/GP ACT/RES TEC/DEV ECO/TAC EDU/PROP ATTIT RIGID/FLEX ORD/FREE SKILL WEALTH ...STAT CON/ANAL ANTHOL MUNICH WORK VAL/FREE 20. PAGE 74 F1461
COM AGRI POLICY

B63
RAFUSE R.W. JR.,STATE AND LOCAL FISCAL BEHAVIOR OVER THE POSTWAR CYCLES (DISSERTATION). USA+45 TAX PRICE ATTIT...POLICY TIME/SEQ TREND CHARTS BIBLIOG 20. PAGE 109 F2135
BUDGET LOC/G ECO/TAC PROVS

B63
US ADVISORY COMN INTERGOV REL,PERFORMANCE OF URBAN FUNCTIONS: LOCAL AND AREAWIDE. TEC/DEV PARTIC REPRESENT PWR...DECISION GOV/COMP MUNICH. PAGE 133 F2633
REGION LOC/G ECO/TAC

B63
US HOUSE,URBAN RENEWAL: HOUSE COMMITTEE ON BANKING AND CURRENCY. USA+45 FINAN LOC/G NAT/G NEIGH DELIB/GP TEC/DEV BUDGET GOV/REL COST...CHARTS MUNICH 20 CONGRESS URBAN/RNWL. PAGE 136 F2684
PLAN PROB/SOLV LEGIS

S63
ANDREWS R.B.,"ECONOMIC PLANNING FOR SMALL AREAS: THE PLANNING PROCESS." INDUS PROC/MFG PROVS PROB/SOLV TAX EQUILIB...METH/COMP HYPO/EXP METH MUNICH 20. PAGE 5 F0103
ECO/TAC PLAN LOC/G

S63
LOEWENSTEIN L.K.,"THE LOCATION OF URBAN LAND USES." USA+45 LOC/G HABITAT...STAT CHARTS MUNICH 20. PAGE 81 F1595
GEOG PLAN INDUS

B64
COMMITTEE ECONOMIC DEVELOPMENT,COMMUNITY ECONOMIC DEVELOPMENT PROGRAMS. USA+45 FINAN INDUS LG/CO PROF/ORG CREATE GP/REL MUNICH NEW/YORK VERMONT PENNSYLVAN IN ARKANSAS. PAGE 27 F0519
LOC/G LABOR PLAN

B64
FITCH L.C.,URBAN TRANSPORTATION AND PUBLIC POLICY. FINAN NAT/G LEGIS PROB/SOLV TEC/DEV PRICE COST EFFICIENCY...DECISION STAT CHARTS METH/COMP MUNICH 20 NEWYORK/C PHILADELPH LOS/ANG CHICAGO WASHING/DC. PAGE 41 F0806
DIST/IND PLAN LOC/G

B64
FRIEDEN B.J.,THE FUTURE OF OLD NEIGHBORHOODS: REBUILDING FOR A CHANGING POPULATION. CONSTRUC LOC/G NAT/G ACT/RES ECO/TAC REGION ATTIT...INT SAMP MUNICH 20 NEWYORK/C LOS/ANG HARTFORD URBAN/RNWL. PAGE 44 F0855
NEIGH PROB/SOLV PLAN BUDGET

B64
GREBLER L.,URBAN RENEWAL IN EUROPEAN COUNTRIES: ITS EMERGENCE AND POTENTIALS. EUR+WWI UK ECO/DEV LOC/G NEIGH CREATE ADMIN ATTIT...TREND NAT/COMP MUNICH 20 URBAN/RNWL. PAGE 50 F0981
PLAN CONSTRUC NAT/G

B64
MANN B.,STATE CONSTITUTIONAL RESTRICTIONS ON LOCAL BORROWING AND PROPERTY TAXING POWERS. USA+45 CONSTN PROVS CT/SYS GOV/REL PWR...DECISION JURID CHARTS 20. PAGE 84 F1654
LOC/G TAX FINAN LAW

B64
MITAU G.T.,INSOLUBLE PROBLEMS: CASE PROBLEMS ON THE FUNCTIONS OF STATE AND LOCAL GOVERNMENT. USA+45 AIR FINAN LABOR POL/PAR PROB/SOLV TAX RECEIVE CONTROL GP/REL 20 CASEBOOK ZONING. PAGE 92 F1807
ADJUD LOC/G PROVS

B64
MOAK L.L.,A MANUAL OF SUGGESTED PRACTICE FOR THE PREPARATION AND ADOPTION OF CAPITAL PROGRAMS AND
LOC/G BUDGET

CAPITAL BUDGETS BY LOCAL GOVERN. USA+45 DELIB/GP PLAN TAX GP/REL COST DECISION. PAGE 92 F1812 LEGIS PROB/SOLV

B64
WEIDENBAUM M.L.,CONGRESS AND THE FEDERAL BUDGET: FEDERAL BUDGETING AND THE RESPONSIBLE USE OF POWER. LOC/G PLAN TAX CONGRESS. PAGE 144 F2843 LEGIS EX/STRUC BUDGET ADMIN

S64
HUTCHINSON E.C.,"AMERICAN AID TO AFRICA." FUT USA+45 MARKET INT/ORG LOC/G NAT/G PUB/INST PLAN ECO/TAC ATTIT RIGID/FLEX...POLICY CONCPT TREND TERR/GP 20. PAGE 63 F1248 AFR ECO/UNDEV FOR/AID

B65
ARTEL R.,THE STRUCTURE OF THE STOCKHOLM ECONOMY. SWEDEN DIST/IND LABOR LOC/G TEC/DEV DEMAND MUNICH LOUISIANA 20. PAGE 7 F0125 ECO/DEV METH/COMP BAL/PAY

B65
BOLLENS J.C.,THE METROPOLIS: ITS PEOPLE, POLITICS, AND ECONOMIC LIFE. USA+45 PLAN PROB/SOLV PERS/REL PWR...DECISION GEOG CENSUS TREND CON/ANAL MUNICH 20 NEWYORK/C LOS/ANG SAN/FRAN CHICAGO PHILADELPH. PAGE 16 F0309 HABITAT SOC LOC/G

B65
GREER S.,URBAN RENEWAL AND AMERICAN CITIES: THE DILEMMA OF DEMOCRATIC INTERVENTION. USA+45 R+D LOC/G VOL/ASSN ACT/RES BUDGET ADMIN GOV/REL...SOC INT SAMP MUNICH 20 BOSTON CHICAGO LOS/ANG MIAMI URBAN/RNWL. PAGE 51 F0992 PROB/SOLV PLAN NAT/G

B65
MAO J.C.T.,EFFICIENCY IN PUBLIC URBAN RENEWAL EXPENDITURES THROUGH CAPITAL BUDGETING. USA+45 FINAN LOC/G NAT/G NEIGH REGION UTIL...GEOG METH/CNCPT STAT SIMUL GEN/LAWS MUNICH 20 URBAN/RNWL. PAGE 85 F1662 TEC/DEV BUDGET PROB/SOLV

B65
MARGOLIS J.,THE PUBLIC ECONOMY OF URBAN COMMUNITIES. USA+45 LEGIS PROB/SOLV TAX LOBBY CHOOSE ATTIT MUNICH. PAGE 85 F1668 LOC/G DECISION FINAN

B65
MORTON H.C.,BROOKINGS PAPERS ON PUBLIC POLICY. USA+45 WOR+45 INDUS ACADEM INT/ORG LOC/G PROVS EDU/PROP MUNICH. PAGE 94 F1840 FINAN ECO/DEV TOP/EX NAT/G

B65
MUSHKIN S.J.,PROPERTY TAXES: THE 1970 OUTLOOK (PAMPHLET). FUT USA+45 ECO/DEV MARKET PROVS PLAN ...PROBABIL STAT CENSUS PREDICT CHARTS METH 20. PAGE 95 F1872 TAX OWN FINAN LOC/G

B65
US ADVISORY COMN INTERGOV REL,METROPOLITAN SOCIAL AND ECONOMIC DISPARITIES: IMPLICATIONS FOR INTERGOVERNMENTAL RELATIONS IN CENT'L CITIES AND SUBURBS. CULTURE STRATA DIST/IND LOC/G PLAN GP/REL DISCRIM HABITAT MUNICH. PAGE 134 F2634 GOV/REL GEOG

S65
KEE W.S.,"CENTRAL CITY EXPENDITURES AND METROPOLITAN AREAS." PLAN BUDGET ECO/TAC TAX GP/REL WEALTH...CHARTS MUNICH 20. PAGE 70 F1366 LOC/G GOV/COMP NEIGH

B66
DUNCOMBE H.S.,COUNTY GOVERNMENT IN AMERICA. USA+45 FINAN ADMIN ROUTINE GOV/REL...GOV/COMP MUNICH 20. PAGE 35 F0678 LOC/G PROVS CT/SYS TOP/EX

B66
EBONY,THE NEGRO HANDBOOK. ACADEM LABOR LOC/G SECT FORCES WORKER CT/SYS CRIME DISCRIM ORD/FREE...BIOG SOC/INTEG 19/20 NEGRO CIV/RIGHTS. PAGE 36 F0692 RACE/REL EDU/PROP LAW STAT

B66
GREENE L.E.,GOVERNMENT IN TENNESSEE (2ND ED.). USA+45 DIST/IND INDUS POL/PAR EX/STRUC LEGIS PLAN BUDGET GIVE CT/SYS...MGT T 20 TENNESSEE. PAGE 51 F0989 PROVS LOC/G CONSTN ADMIN

B66
MC CONNELL J.P.,LAW AND BUSINESS: PATTERNS AND ISSUES IN COMMERCIAL LAW. USA+45 USA-45 LOC/G WORKER LICENSE CRIME REPRESENT GP/REL 20. PAGE 87 F1713 ECO/DEV JURID ADJUD MGT

B66
WALTON S.D.,AMERICAN BUSINESS AND ITS ENVIRONMENT. USA+45 LAW CONSTN FINAN MARKET LOC/G EX/STRUC CT/SYS COST PRODUC...STAT 20. PAGE 143 F2813 PRICE PROFIT

B66
WILLIAMS G.,MERTHYR POLITICS: THE MAKING OF A WORKING-CLASS TRADITION. UK CHIEF WORKER LEAD SOCISM...ANTHOL MUNICH 19/20 MERTHYR RICHARD/H. PAGE 147 F2891 LOC/G POL/PAR INDUS

S66
VENTRE F.T.,"LOCAL INITIATIVES IN URBAN INDUSTRIAL DEVELOPMENT." FINAN SERV/IND TOP/EX PLAN BUDGET RENT TAX...GP/COMP MUNICH 20. PAGE 141 F2777 ECO/TAC LOC/G INDUS

N66
US ADVISORY COMN INTERGOV REL,CATALOGS AND OTHER INFORMATION SOURCES ON FEDERAL AND STATE AID PROGRAMS: A SECTED BIBLIOGRAPHY (PAPER). USA+45 LAW LOC/G NAT/G PROVS VOL/ASSN TEC/DEV ADMIN HEALTH ...WELF/ST SOC/WK MUNICH. PAGE 134 F2635 BIBLIOG/A GOV/REL FINAN ECO/DEV

B67
AARON H.J.,FINANCING URBAN DEVELOPMENT IN MEXICO CITY: A CASE STUDY OF PROPERTY TAX, LAND USE, HOUSING, AND URBAN PLANNING. LOC/G CREATE EFFICIENCY WEALTH...CHARTS MUNICH 20 MEXIC/AMER. PAGE 2 F0030 PLAN TAX PROB/SOLV

B67
BLAIR G.S.,LEGISLATIVE BODIES IN CALIFORNIA. USA+45 LAW POL/PAR LOBBY APPORT CHOOSE REPRESENT GP/REL ...T CALIFORNIA. PAGE 15 F0293 LEGIS PROVS LOC/G ADJUD

B67
BREAK G.F.,INTERGOVERNMENTAL FISCAL RELATIONS IN THE UNITED STATES. USA+45 USA-45 DELIB/GP PLAN BUDGET TAX GOV/REL CENTRAL...TREND CHARTS MUNICH. PAGE 18 F0345 LOC/G NAT/G PROVS FINAN

B67
CAMPBELL A.K.,METROPOLITAN AMERICA* FISCAL PATTERNS AND GOVERNMENTAL SYSTEMS. PROVS PLAN COST...POLICY DECISION GOV/COMP METH/COMP BIBLIOG. PAGE 21 F0405 USA+45 NAT/G LOC/G BUDGET

B67
CHAPIN F.S. JR.,SELECTED REFERENCES ON URBAN PLANNING METHODS AND TECHNIQUES. USA+45 LAW ECO/DEV LOC/G NAT/G SCHOOL CONSULT CREATE PROB/SOLV TEC/DEV ...SOC/WK MUNICH. PAGE 23 F0454 BIBLIOG NEIGH PLAN

B67
DE TORRES J.,FINANCING LOCAL GOVERNMENT. USA+45 USA-45 NAT/G PROVS GIVE ADJUST PWR...TIME/SEQ CHARTS MUNICH 20. PAGE 31 F0606 LOC/G BUDGET TAX TREND

B67
GRIPP R.C.,PATTERNS OF SOVIET POLITICS (REV. ED.). USSR LAW ELITES LOC/G PLAN CONTROL CT/SYS CHOOSE ...POLICY BIBLIOG/A DICTIONARY 9/20. PAGE 51 F1003 COM ADJUD POL/PAR

B67
LITTLE AD, INC.,COMMUNITY RENEWAL PROGRAMMING. CULTURE LOC/G ACT/RES TASK COST ATTIT...SOC/WK MODAL STAT STAND/INT CHARTS 20 SAN/FRAN. PAGE 81 F1585 STRATA NEIGH PLAN CREATE

B67
MORRIS A.J.A.,PARLIAMENTARY DEMOCRACY IN THE NINETEENTH CENTURY. UK INDUS LOC/G NAT/G POL/PAR CONSULT LEGIS INT/TRADE ADMIN CHOOSE SUFF SOVEREIGN 19 PARLIAMENT. PAGE 93 F1835 TIME/SEQ CONSTN PARL/PROC POPULISM

B67
PRINCE C.E.,NEW JERSEY'S JEFFERSONIAN REPUBLICANS; THE GENESIS OF AN EARLY PARTY MACHINE (1789-1817). USA-45 LOC/G EDU/PROP PRESS CONTROL CHOOSE...CHARTS 18/19 NEW/JERSEY REPUBLICAN. PAGE 108 F2117 POL/PAR CONSTN ADMIN PROVS

B67
UNIVERSAL REFERENCE SYSTEM,ADMINISTRATIVE MANAGEMENT: PUBLIC AND PRIVATE BUREAUCRACY (VOLUME IV). WOR+45 WOR-45 ECO/DEV LG/CO LOC/G PUB/INST VOL/ASSN GOV/REL...COMPUT/IR GEN/METH. PAGE 133 F2616 BIBLIOG/A MGT ADMIN NAT/G

L67
"GOVERNMENT CONTROL OF LAND: PROTECTING THE I-KNOW-IT-WHENI-SEE-IT INTEREST." USA+45 LAW CONSTN DELIB/GP CT/SYS HABITAT ILLINOIS. PAGE 2 F0026 PLAN LOC/G CONTROL ADJUD

L67
JOHNSTON J.D. JR.,"CONSTITUTION OF SUBDIVISION CONTROL EXACTIONS: THE QUEST FOR A RATIONALE." USA+45 PROVS PUB/INST ADJUD CT/SYS GP/REL MUNICH. PAGE 68 F1334 PLAN CONTROL LOC/G FORCES

L67
LAMBERT J.D.,"CORPORATE POLITICAL SPENDING AND CAMPAIGN FINANCE." LAW CONSTN FINAN LABOR LG/CO LOC/G NAT/G VOL/ASSN TEC/DEV ADJUD ADMIN PARTIC. PAGE 75 F1463 USA+45 POL/PAR CHOOSE COST

S67
ADAMS E.S.,"THE EXPANDING ROLE OF BANKS IN PUBLIC AFFAIRS." USA+45 GIVE LEAD ROLE...QU 20. PAGE 2 F0036 PARTIC FINAN LOC/G ATTIT

S67
DANIEL C.,"THE REGULATION OF PRIVATE ENTERPRISES AS PUBLIC UTILITIES." WOR+45 LAW LICENSE POLICY. PAGE 30 F0577 LOC/G NAT/G CONTROL SERV/IND

S67
FERGUSON D.E.,"DETERMINING CAPACITY FOR CAPITAL EXPENDITURES." USA+45 LOC/G BUDGET TAX ADMIN CONTROL...TREND MUNICH 20. PAGE 40 F0784 FINAN PAY COST

S67
FRIEDEN B.J.,"THE CHANGING PROSPECTS FOR SOCIAL PLANNING." USA+45 PROB/SOLV RACE/REL WEALTH ...SOC/WK PREDICT MUNICH 20 NEGRO. PAGE 44 F0856 PLAN LOC/G POLICY

S67
GAUSE M.E.,"ELEMENTS OF FINANCE DEPARTMENT ORGANIZATION FOR SMALL GOVERNMENTAL UNITS." USA+45 PROB/SOLV CONTROL CENTRAL...METH MUNICH. PAGE 47 F0910 ADMIN LOC/G FINAN

S67
HANCOCK J.L.,"PLANNERS IN THE CHANGING AMERICAN CITY, 1900-1940." USA-45 CONSTRUC NAT/G POL/PAR ...SOC/WK TREND MUNICH 20. PAGE 54 F1059 — PLAN CONSULT LOC/G

S67
HILL L.W.,"FINANCING URBAN RENEWAL PROGRAMS." USA+45 ECO/DEV LOC/G EDU/PROP MUNICH 20. PAGE 60 F1171 — FINAN NAT/G WEALTH

S67
LINEBERRY R.L.,"REFORMISM AND PUBLIC POLICIES IN AMERICAN CITIES." USA+45 POL/PAR EX/STRUC LEGIS BUDGET TAX GP/REL...STAT CHARTS MUNICH. PAGE 80 F1573 — DECISION POLICY LOC/G

S67
MYERS S.,"TECHNOLOGY AND URBAN TRANSIT: THE ENORMOUS POTENTIAL OF BUS AND RAIL SYSTEMS." USA+45 FINAN LOC/G WORKER PLAN PROB/SOLV PRICE AUTOMAT MUNICH 20. PAGE 96 F1877 — R+D TEC/DEV DIST/IND ACT/RES

S67
RONY V.,"HEARTBREAK IN TENNESSEE* POOR WHITES AND THE UNIONS." LAW STRUCT CAP/ISM ADJUD GP/REL. PAGE 113 F2236 — LABOR LOC/G WORKER PWR

S67
SEIDLER G.L.,"MARXIST LEGAL THOUGHT IN POLAND." POLAND SOCIETY R+D LOC/G NAT/G ACT/RES ADJUD CT/SYS SUPEGO PWR...SOC TREND 20 MARX/KARL. PAGE 119 F2343 — MARXISM LAW CONCPT EFFICIENCY

S67
SIDDIQ M.M.,"LOCAL GOVERNMENT IN PAKISTAN." PAKISTAN PROB/SOLV TAX COLONIAL GOV/REL MUNICH 20. PAGE 121 F2395 — ADMIN LOC/G DELIB/GP BUDGET

S67
STILL J.F.,"THE FUTURE OF METROPOLITAN GOVERNMENT ORGANIZATION." USA+45 LOC/G BUDGET COST ATTIT MUNICH 20. PAGE 126 F2488 — ADMIN FINAN CONTROL

S67
WARNER K.O.,"FINANCIAL IMPLICATION OF EMPLOYEE BARGAINING IN THE PUBLIC SERVICE." CANADA USA+45 FINAN ADMIN...MGT 20. PAGE 143 F2823 — BARGAIN LABOR COST LOC/G

B95
SELIGMAN E.R.A.,ESSAYS IN TAXATION. NEW/ZEALND PRUSSIA UK USA-45 MARKET LOC/G CREATE PRICE CONTROL INCOME OWN WEALTH...GOV/COMP METH/COMP 19. PAGE 119 F2349 — TAX TARIFFS INDUS NAT/G

LOCAL GOVERNMENT....SEE LOC/G

LOCKE J. F1591

LOCKE/JOHN....JOHN LOCKE

LOCKLIN D.P. F1592

LOCKWOOD W.W. F1593

LODGE/HC....HENRY CABOT LODGE

LOEWENSTEIN L.K. F1595

LOFTUS M.L. F1596

LOG....LOGIC

B31
JEVONS W.S.,THE THEORY OF POLITICAL ECONOMY (4TH ED.; 1ST ED. 1871). WOR-45 FINAN MARKET RENT WEALTH ...LOG MATH QUANT CON/ANAL IDEA/COMP BIBLIOG METH 17/19. PAGE 67 F1318 — GEN/LAWS UTIL LABOR

B57
DOWNS A.,AN ECONOMIC THEORY OF DEMOCRACY. NAT/G EDU/PROP RISK CHOOSE PERS/REL EQUILIB...SOC METH/CNCPT LOG STYLE. PAGE 34 F0659 — DECISION RATIONAL

N61
VINER J.,THE INTELLECTUAL HISTORY OF LAISSEZ FAIRE (PAMPHLET). WOR+45 WOR-45 LAW INTELL...POLICY LING LOG 19/20. PAGE 141 F2787 — ATTIT EDU/PROP LAISSEZ ECO/TAC

S65
HUTT W.H.,"KEYNESIAN REVISIONS" SOUTH/AFR ECO/DEV FINAN NAT/G WORKER BUDGET TAX PRICE EQUILIB WEALTH 20 KEYNES/JM. PAGE 64 F1252 — ECO/TAC GEN/LAWS LOG

B25
EDGEWORTH F.Y.,PAPERS RELATING TO POLITICAL ECONOMY. MOD/EUR SOCIETY STRATA DIST/IND INDUS MARKET NAT/G ACT/RES ECO/TAC EXEC WEALTH ...METH/CNCPT MATH TREND HYPO/EXP SIMUL GEN/METH FOR/TRADE VAL/FREE LOG/LING. PAGE 36 F0702 — ECO/DEV CAP/ISM

S60
BARNETT H.J.,"RESEARCH AND DEVELOPMENT, ECONOMIC GROWTH, AND NATIONAL SECURITY." AFR USA+45 R+D CREATE ECO/TAC ATTIT DRIVE PWR...POLICY SOC METH/CNCPT QUANT STAT TIME/SEQ ORG/CHARTS LOG/LING 20. PAGE 10 F0190 — ACT/RES PLAN

S64
BEIM D.,"THE COMMUNIST BLOC AND THE FOREIGN-AID GAME." AFR WOR+45 NAT/G PLAN ROUTINE ATTIT KNOWL ORD/FREE...DECISION QUANT CONT/OBS TIME/SEQ CHARTS GAME SIMUL LOG/LING 20. PAGE 12 F0231 — COM ECO/UNDEV ECO/TAC FOR/AID

LOGIC....SEE LOG

LOGIST/MGT....LOGISTICS MANAGEMENT INSTITUTE

LONDON K. F1597

LONDON....LONDON, ENGLAND

LONG T.G. F1598

LONG/FAMLY....THE LONG FAMILY OF LOUISIANA

LONGE/FD....F.D. LONGE

LONGRIGG S.H. F1599

LOPEZ VILLAMIL H. F1600

LORWIN L.L. F1601

LOS/ANG....LOS ANGELES

B64
FITCH L.C.,URBAN TRANSPORTATION AND PUBLIC POLICY. FINAN NAT/G LEGIS PROB/SOLV TEC/DEV PRICE COST EFFICIENCY...DECISION STAT CHARTS METH/COMP MUNICH 20 NEWYORK/C PHILADELPH LOS/ANG CHICAGO WASHING/DC. PAGE 41 F0806 — DIST/IND PLAN LOC/G

B64
FRIEDEN B.J.,THE FUTURE OF OLD NEIGHBORHOODS: REBUILDING FOR A CHANGING POPULATION. CONSTRUC LOC/G NAT/G ACT/RES ECO/TAC REGION ATTIT...INT SAMP MUNICH 20 NEWYORK/C LOS/ANG HARTFORD URBAN/RNWL. PAGE 44 F0855 — NEIGH PROB/SOLV PLAN BUDGET

B65
BOLLENS J.C.,THE METROPOLIS: ITS PEOPLE, POLITICS, AND ECONOMIC LIFE. USA+45 PLAN PROB/SOLV PERS/REL PWR...DECISION GEOG CENSUS TREND CON/ANAL MUNICH 20 NEWYORK/C LOS/ANG SAN/FRAN CHICAGO PHILADELPH. PAGE 16 F0309 — HABITAT SOC LOC/G

B65
GREER S.,URBAN RENEWAL AND AMERICAN CITIES: THE DILEMMA OF DEMOCRATIC INTERVENTION. USA+45 R+D LOC/G VOL/ASSN ACT/RES BUDGET ADMIN GOV/REL...SOC INT SAMP MUNICH 20 BOSTON CHICAGO LOS/ANG MIAMI URBAN/RNWL. PAGE 51 F0992 — PROB/SOLV PLAN NAT/G

S65
BRIGHAM E.F.,"THE DETERMINANTS OF RESIDENTIAL LAND VALUES." USA+45 ECO/DEV PROB/SOLV RENT PRICE ...REGRESS STAT CHARTS GEN/METH MUNICH 20 LOS/ANG. PAGE 18 F0351 — COST INDICATOR SIMUL ECOMETRIC

LOSMAN D.L. F1602

LOUCKS W.N. F1603

LOUFTY A. F1604

LOUISIANA....LOUISIANA

B65
ARTEL R.,THE STRUCTURE OF THE STOCKHOLM ECONOMY. SWEDEN DIST/IND LABOR LOC/G TEC/DEV DEMAND MUNICH LOUISIANA 20. PAGE 7 F0125 — ECO/DEV METH/COMP BAL/PAY

LOUISVILLE....LOUISVILLE, KENTUCKY

LOUVERT/T....L'OUVERTURE TOUSSANT

LOVE....AFFECTION, FRIENDSHIP, SEX RELATIONS

S53
HANSER P.M.,"EXPLODING POPULATIONS: INTERNATIONAL AND REGIONAL ASPECTS." AFR S/ASIA ECO/TAC WEAPON BIO/SOC LOVE ORD/FREE...NEW/IDEA CENSUS TOT/POP 20. PAGE 55 F1069 — ECO/UNDEV GEOG

S59
THOMPSON W.S.,"POPULATION AND PROGRESS IN THE FAR EAST." ASIA S/ASIA DIST/IND CREATE ECO/TAC WAR LOVE SKILL WEALTH...CONT/OBS TOT/POP 20. PAGE 130 F2568 — ECO/UNDEV BIO/SOC GEOG

S65
HAYTER T.,"FRENCH AID TO AFRICA* ITS SCOPE AND ACHIEVEMENTS." CULTURE ECO/TAC INT/TRADE ADMIN REGION CENTRAL FEDERAL LOVE PWR SOVEREIGN EEC. PAGE 57 F1127 — AFR FRANCE FOR/AID COLONIAL

S67
KINGSLEY R.E.,"THE US BUSINESS IMAGE IN LATIN AMERICA." L/A+17C USA+45 NAT/G TEC/DEV CAP/ISM FOR/AID DOMIN EDU/PROP...CONCPT LING IDEA/COMP 20. PAGE 71 F1396 — ATTIT LOVE DIPLOM ECO/UNDEV

S67
THEROUX P.,"HATING THE ASIANS." TANZANIA UGANDA CONSTN INDUS NAT/G POL/PAR WORKER ECO/TAC HABITAT LOVE...POLICY GEOG 20 MIGRATION. PAGE 130 F2557 — AFR RACE/REL SOVEREIGN ATTIT

LOVEJOY W.F. F0906

LOVESTN/J....JAY LOVESTONE

S66
LANGLEY D.,"POSTSCRIPT ON THE COLONIZATION OF THE INTERNATIONAL TRADE UNION MOVEMENT" USA+45 ELITES FINAN DOMIN LEGIT ADMIN PWR...SOCIALIST 20 AFL/CIO CIA LOVESTN/J. PAGE 75 F1479 — INT/TRADE LABOR NAT/G CONTROL

LOW J.O. F2824

LOWELL A.L. F1605

LOWITH

LOWRY R.L. F0355

LOYALTY....SEE SUPEGO

LUA....LUA, OR LAWA: VILLAGE PEOPLES OF NORTHERN THAILAND

LUANDA....LUANDA, ANGOLA

LUBBOCK/TX....LUBBOCK, TEXAS

LUDWIG/BAV....LUDWIG THE BAVARIAN

LUGO-MARENCO J.J. F1606

LUMBERING....SEE EXTR/IND

LUNDBERG E. F1607

LUTHER/M....MARTIN LUTHER

LUTHULI A. F1608

LUTZ F.A. F1609,F1610,F1611,F1612

LUTZ V. F1613

LUVALE....LUVALE TRIBE, CENTRAL AFRICA

LUXEMBORG R. F1614

LUXEMBOURG....SEE ALSO APPROPRIATE TIME/SPACE/CULTURE INDEX

B62
MEADE J.E.,CASE STUDIES IN EUROPEAN ECONOMIC UNION. BELGIUM EUR+WWI LUXEMBOURG NAT/G INT/TRADE REGION ROUTINE WEALTH...METH/CNCPT STAT CHARTS ECSC TOT/POP OEEC EEC FOR/TRADE 20. PAGE 89 F1738 — INT/ORG ECO/TAC

S67
BARTLETT J.L.,"AMERICAN BOND ISSUES IN THE EUROPEAN ECONOMIC COMMUNITY." EUR+WWI LUXEMBOURG USA+45 DIPLOM CONTROL BAL/PAY EEC. PAGE 11 F0201 — LAW ECO/TAC FINAN TAX

LUZ N.V. F1615

LUZON....LUZON, PHILIPPINES

LYNCH M.C. F0759

LYND S. F1616

LYONS G.M. F1617

LYTLE C.M. F1618

M

MACAO....MACAO

MACAPAGL/D....DIOSDADO MACAPAGAL

MACARTHR/D....DOUGLAS MACARTHUR

MACARTHUR D. F1619

MACAVOY P.W. F1620,F1621

MACBEAN A.I. F1622

MACCLOSKEY M. F1623

MACDONALD R.M. F1624

MACDONALD R.S.J. F1625

MACDONALD R.W. F1626

MACESICH G. F1627

MACFARQUHAR R. F1628

MACGREGOR D.H. F1629

MACHIAVELL....NICCOLO MACHIAVELLI

MACHIAVELLISM....SEE REALPOL, MACHIAVELL

MACHLUP F. F0569,F0781,F1630,F1631,F1632,F1633

MACK R.W. F1634

MACKENZIE F. F1635

MACLEISH/A....ARCHIBALD MACLEISH

MACMAHON A.W. F1636,F1637

MACMILLAN W.M. F1743

MACMILLN/H....HAROLD MACMILLAN, PRIME MINISTER

MADAGASCAR....SEE ALSO AFR

B62
KENT R.K.,FROM MADAGASCAR TO THE MALAGASY REPUBLIC. FRANCE MADAGASCAR DIPLOM NAT/LISM ORD/FREE...MGT 18/20. PAGE 70 F1379 — COLONIAL SOVEREIGN REV POL/PAR

L62
DURAND-REVILLE L.,"LE REGIME DES INVESTISSEMENTS DANS LES ETATS AFRICAINS D'EXPRESSION FRANCAISE ET A MADAGASCAR." MADAGASCAR ECO/UNDEV CAP/ISM ECO/TAC WEALTH...SOC TREND CHARTS 20. PAGE 35 F0683 — AFR FINAN

S62
PIQUEMAL M.,"LA COOPERATION FINANCIERE ENTRE LA FRANCE ET LES ETATS AFRICAINS ET MALGACHE." ISLAM INT/ORG TOP/EX ECO/TAC...JURID CHARTS 20. PAGE 106 F2089 — AFR FINAN FRANCE MADAGASCAR

S62
RAZAFIMBAHINY J.,"L'ORGANISATION AFRICAINE ET MALGACHE DE COOPERATION ECONOMIQUE." AFR ISLAM MADAGASCAR NAT/G ACT/RES ECO/TAC ALL/VALS ...TIME/SEQ 20. PAGE 110 F2158 — INT/ORG ECO/UNDEV

S63
GANDOLFI A.,"LES ACCORDS DE COOPERATION EN MATIERE DE POLITIQUE ETRANGERE ENTRE LA FRANCE ET LES NOUVEAUX ETATS AFRICAINS ET." AFR ISLAM MADAGASCAR WOR+45 ECO/DEV INT/ORG NAT/G DELIB/GP ECO/TAC ALL/VALS...CON/ANAL 20. PAGE 46 F0894 — VOL/ASSN ECO/UNDEV DIPLOM FRANCE

MADAN G.R. F1638

MADERO/F....FRANCISCO MADERO

MADHOK B. F1639

MADISON/J....PRESIDENT JAMES MADISON

MAFIA....MAFIA

MAGALHAES S. F1640

MAGHREB....SEE ALSO ISLAM

S65
CECIL C.O.,"THE DETERMINANTS OF LIBYAN FOREIGN POLICY." AFR INTELL ECO/UNDEV EXTR/IND POL/PAR CREATE REGION SOVEREIGN CONSERVE MAGHREB NASSER/G. PAGE 22 F0431 — LIBYA DIPLOM WEALTH ISLAM

MAGNA/CART....MAGNA CARTA

MAGON/F....FLORES MAGON

MAIMONIDES....MAIMONIDES

MAINE....MAINE

MAIR L.P. F1641

MAITLAND/F....FREDERIC WILLIAM MAITLAND

MAIZELS A. F1642

MAJORIT....MAJORITARIAN

NCO
CARRINGTON C.E.,THE COMMONWEALTH IN AFRICA (PAMPHLET). UK STRUCT NAT/G COLONIAL REPRESENT GOV/REL RACE/REL NAT/LISM...MAJORIT 20 EEC NEGRO. PAGE 22 F0421
ECO/UNDEV AFR DIPLOM PLAN

B15
VEBLEN T.,IMPERIAL GERMANY AND THE INDUSTRIAL REVOLUTION. GERMANY MOD/EUR UK USA-45 NAT/G TEC/DEV CAP/ISM...MAJORIT NAT/COMP 19/20 CHINJAP. PAGE 141 F2769
ECO/DEV INDUS TECHNIC BAL/PWR

N19
HAYEK FA V.O.N.,FREEDOM AND THE ECONOMIC SYSTEM. GERMANY USSR PLAN REPRESENT TOTALISM FASCISM POPULISM...MAJORIT METH/COMP GEN/LAWS 20. PAGE 57 F1123
ORD/FREE ECO/TAC CAP/ISM SOCISM

B20
PIGOU A.C.,THE ECONOMICS OF WELFARE. UNIV INDUS WORKER ACT/RES RECEIVE INCOME NEW/LIB...MAJORIT SOC/WK. PAGE 106 F2085
ECO/TAC WEALTH FINAN CONTROL

B20
WEBB S.,INDUSTRIAL DEMOCRACY. UK PARTIC GP/REL ...SOC OBS RECORD CHARTS 18/20. PAGE 144 F2838
LABOR NAT/G VOL/ASSN MAJORIT

B23
HOBSON J.A.,INCENTIVES IN THE NEW INDUSTRIAL ORDER. USA-45 NAT/G PAY COST EFFICIENCY PRODUC WEALTH ...MAJORIT PSY SOC/WK 20. PAGE 60 F1186
INDUS LABOR INCOME OPTIMAL

B36
BELLOC H.,THE RESTORATION OF PROPERTY. UK STRATA NAT/G PROF/ORG DELIB/GP WORKER CREATE PROB/SOLV ECO/TAC PARTIC UTOPIA ORD/FREE SOCISM 20. PAGE 13 F0238
CONTROL MAJORIT CAP/ISM OWN

B38
HEIMANN E.,COMMUNISM, FASCISM, OR DEMOCRACY? WOR-45 CONSTN SOCIETY STRATA AGRI CAP/ISM MORAL ORD/FREE ...MAJORIT METH/COMP NAT/COMP 19/20. PAGE 58 F1141
SOCISM MARXISM FASCISM PLURISM

B40
WUNDERLICH F.,LABOR UNDER GERMAN DEMOCRACY, ARBITRATION 1918-1933. GERMANY NAT/G PAY REPAR ADJUD CT/SYS GP/REL...MAJORIT 20. PAGE 149 F2941
LABOR WORKER INDUS BARGAIN

B44
FABIAN SOCIETY,CAN PLANNING BE DEMOCRATIC? UK CULTURE INDUS NAT/G BUDGET ORD/FREE...GEN/LAWS ANTHOL 20. PAGE 39 F0757
PLAN MAJORIT SOCIALIST ECO/DEV

B44
MERRIAM C.E.,PUBLIC AND PRIVATE GOVERNMENT. VOL/ASSN EDU/PROP ADMIN REPRESENT EFFICIENCY PWR PLURISM...MAJORIT CONCPT. PAGE 90 F1762
NAT/G NEIGH MGT POLICY

B49
MACGREGOR D.H.,ECONOMIC THOUGHT AND POLICY. WOR-45 WORKER WAR DEMAND EFFICIENCY WEALTH LAISSEZ SOCISM ...MAJORIT BIBLIOG 19/20. PAGE 83 F1629
CONCPT POLICY ECO/TAC

S49
SHEPHARD H.A.,"DEMOCRATIC CONTROL IN A LABOR UNION." FUT CONSTN STRUCT TEC/DEV LEAD PARTIC RACE/REL CENTRAL DRIVE HABITAT RECORD. PAGE 120 F2374
LABOR MAJORIT CONTROL PWR

B52
BEVAN A.,IN PLACE OF FEAR. WOR+45 STRATA LEGIS REPRESENT OWN NEW/LIB POPULISM...CHARTS 20. PAGE 14 F0273
SOCISM SOCIALIST WEALTH MAJORIT

B53
SAYLES L.R.,THE LOCAL UNION. CONSTN CULTURE DELIB/GP PARTIC CHOOSE GP/REL INGP/REL ATTIT ROLE ...MAJORIT DECISION MGT. PAGE 116 F2284
LABOR LEAD ADJUD ROUTINE

B54
EMERSON F.D.,SHAREHOLDER DEMOCRACY: A BROADER OUTLOOK FOR CORPORATIONS. DELIB/GP EX/STRUC LEGIS ADJUD CONTROL REPRESENT INGP/REL OWN PWR...POLICY STAT RECORD. PAGE 37 F0727
LG/CO PARTIC MAJORIT TREND

B54
TAFT P.,THE STRUCTURE AND GOVERNMENT OF LABOR UNIONS. SANCTION INGP/REL ORD/FREE PWR MARXISM ...MAJORIT STAT TREND. PAGE 128 F2524
LABOR ADJUD WORKER FINAN

B56
GILBERT L.D.,DIVIDENDS AND DEMOCRACY. DELIB/GP LEGIS CAP/ISM ADJUD LOBBY OWN PWR LAISSEZ MAJORIT. PAGE 47 F0922
LG/CO INGP/REL CONTROL PARTIC

B56
LIPSET S.M.,UNION DEMOCRACY. STRUCT INDUS FACE/GP WORKER CONTROL LEAD PARTIC GP/REL ATTIT LAISSEZ ...INT QU CHARTS. PAGE 80 F1577
LABOR INGP/REL MAJORIT

L56
TAGLIACOZZO D.L.,"TRADE-UNION GOVERNMENT, ITS NATURE AND ITS PROBLEMS: A BIBLIOGRAPHICAL REVIEW, 1945-1955." STRUCT LEAD PARTIC CHOOSE ATTIT ...MAJORIT METH/CNCPT BIBLIOG. PAGE 128 F2526
CLASSIF LABOR INGP/REL GP/REL

B57
BERLE A.A. JR.,ECONOMIC POWER AND FREE SOCIETY (PAMPHLET). CLIENT CONSTN EX/STRUC ECO/TAC CONTROL PARTIC PWR WEALTH MAJORIT. PAGE 14 F0261
LG/CO CAP/ISM INGP/REL LEGIT

B58
LESTER R.A.,AS UNIONS MATURE. POL/PAR BARGAIN LEAD PARTIC GP/REL CENTRAL...MAJORIT TIME/SEQ METH/COMP. PAGE 78 F1533
LABOR INDUS POLICY MGT

B58
PALMER E.E.,THE ECONOMY AND THE DEMOCRATIC IDEAL. USA+45 USA-45 STRATA CHIEF CT/SYS ORD/FREE SOCISM ...MAJORIT CONCPT ANTHOL 18/20 PRESIDENT. PAGE 103 F2021
ECO/DEV POPULISM METH/COMP ECO/TAC

B58
SEIDMAN J.I.,DEMOCRACY IN THE LABOR MOVEMENT (PAMPHLET). LAW CONSTN STRUCT DELIB/GP WORKER ADJUD PARTIC SANCTION POLICY. PAGE 119 F2345
LABOR INGP/REL PWR MAJORIT

S58
LATTIN N.D.,"MINORITY AND DISSENTING SHAREHOLDERS' RIGHTS IN FUNDAMENTAL CHANGES." FINAN LEGIS ADJUD PARTIC ROUTINE CHOOSE REPRESENT INGP/REL TREND. PAGE 76 F1487
MAJORIT LG/CO LAW CREATE

S58
O'NEAL F.H.,"RECENT LEGISLATION AFFECTING CLOSE CORPORATIONS." LAW EX/STRUC ECO/TAC ROUTINE CHOOSE RIGID/FLEX...MAJORIT MGT TREND. PAGE 100 F1959
LG/CO LEGIS REPRESENT PARTIC

B59
WORTHY J.C.,BIG BUSINESS AND FREE MEN. LG/CO EX/STRUC EDU/PROP LEAD CHOOSE GP/REL ATTIT DRIVE ROLE ORD/FREE...MAJORIT 20. PAGE 149 F2927
ELITES LOC/G TOP/EX PARTIC

B61
BALASSA B.,THE THEORY OF ECONOMIC INTEGRATION. EUR+WWI L/A+17C MOD/EUR WOR+45 ECO/UNDEV MARKET INT/ORG NAT/G VOL/ASSN DELIB/GP PLAN CAP/ISM ECO/TAC...MAJORIT FOR/TRADE OEEC 20. PAGE 8 F0157
ECO/DEV ACT/RES INT/TRADE

B61
BARBASH J.,LABOR'S GRASS ROOTS. CONSTN NAT/G EX/STRUC LEGIS WORKER LEAD...MAJORIT BIBLIOG. PAGE 10 F0184
LABOR INGP/REL GP/REL LAW

B61
LHOSTE-LACHAUME P.,OU GIT LE DESACCORD ENTRE LIBERAUX ET SOCIALISTES. EUR+WWI USA+45 USA-45 USSR CAP/ISM EDU/PROP MARXISM...MAJORIT IDEA/COMP 20 KEYNES/JM NEW/DEAL DEPRESSION. PAGE 79 F1555
LAISSEZ SOCISM FINAN

B62
HIRSCHFIELD R.S.,THE CONSTITUTION AND THE COURT. AFR SCHOOL WAR RACE/REL EQUILIB ORD/FREE...POLICY MAJORIT DECISION JURID 18/20 PRESIDENT CIVIL/LIB SUPREME/CT CONGRESS. PAGE 60 F1175
ADJUD PWR CONSTN LAW

B63
MEYNAUD J.,PLANIFICATION ET POLITIQUE. FRANCE ITALY FINAN LABOR DELIB/GP LEGIS ADMIN EFFICIENCY ...MAJORIT DECISION 20. PAGE 90 F1773
PLAN ECO/TAC PROB/SOLV

B64
MEISEL J.,PAPERS ON THE 1962 ELECTION. CANADA PROVS SECT GP/REL CONSEN EFFICIENCY...MAJORIT 20. PAGE 89 F1751
POL/PAR RECORD CHOOSE STRATA

B64
SULTAN P.E.,THE DISENCHANTED UNIONIST. NAT/G ADJUD CONTROL SANCTION RACE/REL ANOMIE ATTIT ROLE ...METH/CNCPT INT. PAGE 127 F2512
LABOR INGP/REL CHARTS MAJORIT

B64
TAWNEY R.H.,EQUALITY. UK CULTURE STRATA ECO/TAC EDU/PROP REPRESENT OWN NEW/LIB...MAJORIT WELF/ST SOC 20. PAGE 129 F2538
WEALTH STRUCT ELITES POPULISM

B65
GRIFFIN C.E.,THE FREE SOCIETY. CONSTN SOCIETY MARKET FEDERAL RATIONAL WEALTH...MAJORIT 20 CIVIL/LIB. PAGE 51 F0999
CONCPT ORD/FREE CAP/ISM POPULISM

B67
BUSEY J.L.,NOTES ON COSTA RICAN DEMOCRACY. COSTA/RICA L/A+17C NAT/G POL/PAR LEGIS CHOOSE OWN ATTIT...BIBLIOG 20. PAGE 20 F0394
CONSTN MAJORIT SOCIETY ECO/UNDEV

B67
HALLE L.J.,THE COLD WAR AS HISTORY. AFR USSR WOR+45 ECO/TAC FOR/AID NUC/PWR WAR PEACE ORD/FREE ...MAJORIT TREND 20 KENNEDY/JF KHRUSH/N BERLIN/BLO. PAGE 54 F1048
DIPLOM BAL/PWR

B67
MENDEL A.P.,POLITICAL MEMOIRS 1905-1917 BY PAUL MILIUKOV (TRANS. BY CARL GOLDBERG). USSR AGRI DIPLOM ECO/TAC POPULISM...MAJORIT 20. PAGE 90 F1757
BIOG LEAD NAT/G CONSTN

L86
OSGOOD H.L.,"SCIENTIFIC SOCIALISM: RODBERTUS" GERMANY CAP/ISM COST WEALTH...MAJORIT BIOG IDEA/COMP 19 RODBRTUS/C. PAGE 102 F2002 SOCISM MARXISM ECO/DEV ECO/TAC

MAJORITY....BEHAVIOR OF MAJOR PARTS OF A GROUP; SEE ALSO CONSEN, MAJORIT

B57
MILLIKAN M.F.,A PROPOSAL: KEY TO AN EFFECTIVE FOREIGN POLICY. USA+45 AGRI FINAN DELIB/GP DIPLOM REPRESENT MAJORITY...NEW/IDEA CHARTS. PAGE 91 F1795 FOR/AID GIVE ECO/UNDEV PLAN

B59
LEISERSON W.,AMERICAN TRADE UNION DEMOCRACY. CONSTN STRUCT ADJUD EXEC REPRESENT GP/REL INGP/REL MAJORITY ATTIT PWR. PAGE 77 F1516 LABOR LEAD PARTIC DELIB/GP

L59
FURASH E.A.,"PROBLEMS IN REVIEW: INDUSTRIAL ESPIONAGE." WORKER ECO/TAC PERS/REL OPTIMAL AGE ATTIT KNOWL...MGT DEEP/INT DEEP/QU GP/COMP IDEA/COMP. PAGE 45 F0875 INDUS TOP/EX MAJORITY

B63
GANDHI M.K.,THE WAY TO COMMUNAL HARMONY. INDIA MAJORITY RIGID/FLEX ROLE RESPECT 20 GANDHI/M. PAGE 46 F0892 RACE/REL DISCRIM ATTIT ADJUST

S65
SELLERS C.,"THE EQUILIBRIUM CYCLE IN TWO-PARTY POLITICS." USA+45 USA-45 CULTURE R+D GP/REL MAJORITY DECISION. PAGE 119 F2351 CHOOSE TREND POL/PAR

S67
GATELL F.O.,"MONEY AND PARTY IN JACKSONIAN AMERICA* A QUANTITATIVE LOOK AT NEW YORK CITY'S MEN OF QUALITY." USA-45 STRATA SECT SUFF CONSEN MAJORITY ATTIT...CHARTS HYPO/EXP 19. PAGE 46 F0908 WEALTH POL/PAR PERSON IDEA/COMP

S67
PLOTT C.R.,"A NOTION OF EQUILIBRIUM AND ITS POSSIBILITY UNDER MAJORITY RULE." CREATE...DECISION STAT CHARTS 20. PAGE 106 F2094 SIMUL EQUILIB CHOOSE MAJORITY

MAJSTRENKO I.W. F1643

MAKINTOSH W.A. F0055

MALASSIS L. F1644

MALAWI....SEE ALSO AFR,NYASALAND

MALAYA....MALAYA

B49
PELZER K.J.,SELECTED BIBLIOGRAPHY ON THE GEOGRAPHY OF SOUTHEAST ASIA (3 VOLS., 1949-1956). PHILIPPINE CULTURE...SOC 20 MALAYA. PAGE 104 F2053 BIBLIOG S/ASIA GEOG

B60
SAKAI R.K.,STUDIES ON ASIA, 1960. ASIA CHINA/COM S/ASIA COM/IND ECO/TAC...ANTHOL 17/20 MALAYA. PAGE 115 F2270 ECO/UNDEV SOC

MALAYSIA....SEE ALSO S/ASIA

B59
SILCOCK T.H.,THE COMMONWEALTH ECONOMY IN SOUTHEAST ASIA. AFR INDIA MALAYSIA S/ASIA ECO/DEV AGRI LOC/G PLAN TARIFFS COLONIAL BAL/PAY DEMAND...BIBLIOG/A 20 GATT. PAGE 122 F2401 ECO/TAC INT/TRADE RACE/REL DIPLOM

B64
SAKAI R.K.,STUDIES ON ASIA, 1964. ASIA CHINA/COM ISRAEL MALAYSIA S/ASIA USA+45 USSR ECO/UNDEV FAM POL/PAR SECT CONSULT NAT/LISM...POLICY SOC 20 CHINJAP. PAGE 115 F2272 PWR DIPLOM

B65
ONSLOW C.,ASIAN ECONOMIC DEVELOPMENT. BURMA CEYLON INDIA MALAYSIA PAKISTAN S/ASIA AGRI INDUS MARKET PROB/SOLV CAP/ISM FOR/AID INT/TRADE DEMAND WEALTH ...POLICY ANTHOL 20. PAGE 101 F1991 ECO/UNDEV ECO/TAC PLAN NAT/G

B65
RATNAM K.J.,COMMUNALISM AND THE POLITICAL PROCESS IN MALAYA. MALAYSIA WOR+45 ECO/UNDEV PARTIC CHOOSE REPRESENT GP/REL CENTRAL ATTIT...CHARTS WORSHIP 20. PAGE 109 F2152 CONSTN GOV/REL REGION

S67
LEIFER M.,"ASTRIDE THE STRAITS OF JAHORE: THE BRITISH PRESENCE AND COMMONWEALTH RIVALRY IN SOUTHEAST ASIA." MALAYSIA UK FORCES PLAN ECO/TAC ...DECISION 20 CMN/WLTH. PAGE 77 F1515 DIPLOM NAT/LISM COLONIAL

MALCOLM/X....MALCOLM X

MALDIVE....MALDIVE ISLAND; SEE ALSO S/ASIA, COMMONWLTH

MALE/SEX....MALE SEX

MALENBAUM W. F1645

MALHERBE E.G. F1646

MALI....SEE ALSO AFR

N19
SENGHOR L.S.,AFRICAN SOCIALISM (PAMPHLET). AFR FRANCE MALI USSR ELITES ECO/UNDEV NAT/G DIPLOM DOMIN EDU/PROP ATTIT 20 NEGRO. PAGE 119 F2355 SOCISM MARXISM ORD/FREE NAT/LISM

B67
JOHNSON H.G.,ECONOMIC NATIONALISM IN OLD AND NEW STATES. CANADA CHINA/COM MALI UK DIPLOM...SIMUL GEN/LAWS 19/20 MEXIC/AMER. PAGE 68 F1328 NAT/LISM ECO/UNDEV ECO/DEV NAT/COMP

MALINOWSKI B. F1647

MALINVAUD E. F1648

MALKIN A. F1649

MALLEN B.E. F1587

MALTA....SEE ALSO APPROPRIATE TIME/SPACE/CULTURE INDEX

MALTHUS T.R. F1650

MALTHUS....THOMAS ROBERT MALTHUS

B59
LINK R.G.,ENGLISH THEORIES OF ECONOMIC FLUCTUATIONS: 1815-1848. FRANCE UK AGRI WORKER DIPLOM PRICE TASK WAR DEMAND PRODUC...POLICY BIBLIOG 18 MALTHUS MILL/JS WILSON/J. PAGE 80 F1574 IDEA/COMP ECO/DEV WEALTH EQUILIB

B63
BARNETT H.J.,SCARCITY AND GROWTH: THE ECONOMICS OF NATURAL RESOURCE AVAILABILITY. FUT WOR+45 AGRI INDUS PROB/SOLV TEC/DEV CONTROL PRODUC...SOC/WK IDEA/COMP METH/COMP SIMUL 20 RESOURCE/N MALTHUS RICARDO/D MILL/JS DARWIN/C. PAGE 10 F0191 DEMAND HABITAT CENSUS GEOG

MANAGEMENT....SEE MGT, EX/STRUC, ADMIN

MANCHESTER....MANCHESTER, ENGLAND

B60
GRAMPP W.D.,THE MANCHESTER SCHOOL OF ECONOMICS. UK LAW ECO/DEV COERCE ATTIT ORD/FREE LAISSEZ ...PHIL/SCI IDEA/COMP 19/20 MANCHESTER CORN/LAWS. PAGE 50 F0973 ECO/TAC VOL/ASSN LOBBY NAT/G

MANCHU/DYN....MANCHU DYNASTY

MANGER W. F1651

MANGLAPUS R.S. F1652

MANGONE G.J. F1653

MANGUM G.L. F0327

MANITOBA....MANITOBA, CANADA

MANN B. F1654

MANN D.E. F1655

MANN S.Z. F1656

MANNE H.G. F1657

MANNERS....SEE ETIQUET

MANNHEIM/K....KARL MANNHEIM

MANPOWER....SEE LABOR

MANSFIELD E. F1658,F1659,F1660

MANSFIELD H.C. F1661

MANTON/M....MART MANTON

MANUFACTURING INDUSTRY....SEE PROC/MFG

MAO J.C.T. F1662

MAO....MAO TSE-TUNG

B64
MILIBAND R.,THE SOCIALIST REGISTER: 1964. GERMANY/W ITALY UK LABOR POL/PAR ECO/TAC FOR/AID NUC/PWR MARXISM SOCISM

...POLICY SOCIALIST IDEA/COMP 20 MAO NASSER/G. PAGE 91 F1784 — CAP/ISM PROB/SOLV

B66 GYORGY A.,ISSUES OF WORLD COMMUNISM. ALBANIA CHINA/COM COM USSR YUGOSLAVIA STRATA AGRI INT/ORG CHIEF FORCES WORKER WAR ALL/IDEOS...GEOG 20 MAO. PAGE 52 F1018 — ECO/UNDEV REV MARXISM CON/ANAL

B66 MACFARQUHAR R.,CHINA UNDER MAO: POLITICS TAKES COMMAND. CHINA/COM COM AGRI INDUS CHIEF FORCES DIPLOM INT/TRADE EDU/PROP TASK REV ADJUST...ANTHOL 20 MAO. PAGE 83 F1628 — ECO/UNDEV TEC/DEV ECO/TAC ADMIN

B67 VAN SLYKE L.P.,ENEMIES AND FRIENDS; THE UNITED FRONT IN CHINESE COMMUNIST HISTORY. CHINA/COM SOCIETY FORCES PLAN ADJUST 20 MAO. PAGE 140 F2764 — INGP/REL MARXISM ATTIT GP/REL

B67 WILLIAMS M.,THE EAST IS RED: THE VIEW INSIDE CHINA. CHINA/COM CONSTN COERCE AGE/Y ATTIT PERSON...OBS 20 MAO. PAGE 147 F2893 — REV MARXIST GP/REL DIPLOM

S67 PERKINS D.H.,"ECONOMIC GROWTH IN CHINA AND THE CULTURAL REVOLUTION(1960APRIL 1967)" CHINA/COM FUT AGRI INDUS PLAN LEAD MARXISM...CHARTS 20 MAO. PAGE 105 F2062 — ECO/TAC CULTURE REV ECO/UNDEV

MAPS....MAPS AND ATLASES

B63 PERLO V.,MILITARISM AND INDUSTRY. USA+45 INT/TRADE EDU/PROP DETER KNOWL...CHARTS MAPS 20. PAGE 105 F2064 — CIVMIL/REL INDUS LOBBY ARMS/CONT

MARAJO....MARAJO, A BRAZILIAN ISLAND

MARANHAO....MARANHAO, BRAZIL

MARCANT/V....VITO MARCANTONIO

MARCH J.G. F0566,F0567,F0568

MARCHAL J. F1663

MARCUS E. F1664

MARCUS M.R. F1664

MARCUS S. F1665

MARCUS W. F1666

MARCUSE/H....HERBERT MARCUSE

MARGOLIS J. F1667,F1668

MARITAIN/J....JACQUES MARITAIN

MARITANO N. F1669

MARITIME....MARITIME PROVINCES

B59 LOPEZ VILLAMIL H.,A STATEMENT OF THE LAWS OF THE HONDURAS IN MATTERS AFFECTING BUSINESS (2ND ED.). HONDURAS DIST/IND EXTR/IND FINAN WORKER TAX DEATH MARRIAGE OWN MARITIME 20 MIGRATION. PAGE 82 F1600 — CONSTN INDUS LEGIS NAT/G

B61 GOODWIN C.D.W.,CANADIAN ECONOMIC THOUGHT. CANADA STRATA TEC/DEV CAP/ISM TARIFFS TAX COST EFFICIENCY WEALTH...METH/CNCPT TREND 20 MARITIME ONTARIO. PAGE 49 F0952 — INT/TRADE ECO/DEV FINAN DEMAND

MARK S.M. F1670

MARKET RESEARCH....SEE MARKET

MARKET....MARKETING SYSTEM

N INTERNATIONAL BIBLIOGRAPHY OF ECONOMICS. WOR+45 FINAN MARKET ADMIN DEMAND INCOME PRODUC...POLICY IDEA/COMP METH. PAGE 1 F0002 — BIBLIOG ECO/DEV ECO/UNDEV INT/TRADE

N ECONOMIC ABSTRACTS. WOR+45 FINAN INDUS MARKET LABOR ACT/RES INT/TRADE WRITING GP/REL...MGT 20. PAGE 1 F0005 — BIBLIOG/A EDU/PROP

N ECONOMIC LIBRARY SELECTIONS. AGRI INDUS MARKET ADMIN...STAT NAT/COMP 20. PAGE 1 F0007 — BIBLIOG/A WRITING FINAN

N SOUTH AFRICAN JOURNAL OF ECONOMICS. SOUTH/AFR FINAN — ECO/UNDEV

MARKET ACT/RES OP/RES...PHIL/SCI STAT CON/ANAL METH/COMP BIBLIOG/A 20. PAGE 1 F0009 — ACADEM INTELL R+D

N AMERICAN ECONOMIC ASSOCIATION,THE JOURNAL OF ECONOMIC ABSTRACTS. ECO/UNDEV MARKET LABOR DIPLOM ...MGT CONCPT METH 20. PAGE 5 F0086 — BIBLIOG/A R+D FINAN

B00 LIST F.,NATIONAL SYSTEM OF POLITICAL ECONOMY. ECO/DEV AGRI EXTR/IND FINAN INDUS TEC/DEV ECO/TAC ATTIT WEALTH...TREND GEN/LAWS FOR/TRADE 19. PAGE 81 F1581 — MOD/EUR MARKET

B00 MILL J.S.,PRINCIPLES OF POLITICAL ECONOMY. WOR-45 CULTURE SOCIETY STRATA ECO/DEV AGRI EXTR/IND FINAN INDUS DELIB/GP ECO/TAC WEALTH...CONCPT MATH TREND 20. PAGE 91 F1786 — MARKET INT/ORG INT/TRADE

B04 MARX K.,A CONTRIBUTION TO THE CRITIQUE OF POLITICAL ECONOMY (TRANS. FROM 2ND ED. BY N.I. STONE). UK STRATA ECO/DEV FINAN MARKET PLAN BARGAIN CAP/ISM ECO/TAC ATTIT WEALTH...METH/CNCPT BIOG 19. PAGE 86 F1687 — MARXIST NEW/IDEA MARXISM

B11 SCOTT W.D.,INFLUENCING MEN IN BUSINESS: THE PSYCHOLOGY OF ARGUMENT AND SUGGESTION. WOR-45 WORKER EDU/PROP DEMAND ATTIT PERSON 20. PAGE 118 F2336 — PSY MARKET SML/CO TOP/EX

N19 ATOMIC INDUSTRIAL FORUM,COMMENTARY ON LEGISLATION TO PERMIT PRIVATE OWNERSHIP OF SPECIAL NUCLEAR MATERIAL (PAMPHLET). USA+45 DELIB/GP LEGIS PLAN OWN ...POLICY 20 AEC CONGRESS. PAGE 7 F0134 — NUC/PWR MARKET INDUS LAW

N19 BASSIE V.L.,UNCERTAINTY IN FORECASTING AND POLICY FORMATION (PAMPHLET). UNIV MARKET ECO/TAC PRODUC ...POLICY DECISION MGT MATH CHARTS 20. PAGE 11 F0205 — ECO/DEV FINAN PREDICT PROB/SOLV

N19 KINDLEBERGER C.P.,BALANCE-OF-PAYMENTS DEFICITS AND THE INTERNATIONAL MARKET FOR LIQUIDITY (PAMPHLET). ECO/DEV NAT/G PLAN DIPLOM ECO/TAC PRODUC...POLICY STAT CHARTS. PAGE 71 F1389 — BAL/PAY INT/TRADE MARKET FINAN

N19 KRIESBERG M.,CANCELLATION OF THE RATION STAMPS (PAMPHLET). USA+45 USA-45 MARKET PROB/SOLV PRICE GOV/REL RIGID/FLEX 20 OPA. PAGE 73 F1439 — RATION DECISION ADMIN NAT/G

N19 LAWRENCE S.A.,THE BATTERY ADDITIVE CONTROVERSY (PAMPHLET). USA+45 LAW MARKET PROC/MFG R+D CAP/ISM CT/SYS GOV/REL OWN FTC CONGRESS BUR/STNDRD RITCHIE/JM. PAGE 76 F1494 — PHIL/SCI LOBBY INSPECT

N19 LUTZ F.A.,THE PROBLEM OF INTERNATIONAL LIQUIDITY AND THE MULTIPLECURRENCY STANDARD (PAMPHLET). WOR+45 MARKET INT/ORG PRICE BAL/PAY...NEW/IDEA METH/COMP BIBLIOG 20 IMF. PAGE 82 F1609 — PROB/SOLV FINAN DIPLOM ECO/TAC

N19 PALAMOUNTAIN JC J.R.,THE DOLCIN CASE AND THE FEDERAL TRADE COMMISSION (PAMPHLET). USA+45 LAW MARKET SERV/IND LG/CO NAT/G BIO/SOC 20 FTC. PAGE 103 F2018 — ADJUD PROB/SOLV EDU/PROP HEALTH

N19 PATRICK H.T.,CYCLICAL INSTABILITY AND FISCAL-MONETARY POLICY IN POST-WAR JAPAN (PAMPHLET). INDUS MARKET DIPLOM TAX PRICE BAL/PAY...TREND CHARTS EQULIB 20 CHINJAP. PAGE 104 F2036 — ECO/DEV PRODUC STAT

N19 US BUREAU OF THE CENSUS,THE PROPORTION OF THE SHIPMENTS (OR EMPLOYEES) OF EACH INDUSTRY... (PAMPHLET). USA+45 ECO/DEV EXTR/IND INDUS CONTROL PROFIT...STAT 20 CONGRESS MONOPOLY. PAGE 134 F2645 — PROC/MFG PRODUC MARKET CHARTS

N19 US CHAMBER OF COMMERCE,THE SIGNIFICANCE OF CONCENTRATION RATIOS (PAMPHLET). USA+45 FINAN INDUS ADMIN...METH/CNCPT SAMP CHARTS 20. PAGE 134 F2647 — MARKET PREDICT LG/CO CONTROL

N19 VELYAMINOV G.,AFRICA AND THE COMMON MARKET (PAMPHLET). AFR MARKET VOL/ASSN ECO/TAC COLONIAL ORD/FREE...SOCIALIST 20 THIRD/WRLD. PAGE 141 F2775 — INT/ORG INT/TRADE SOVEREIGN ECO/UNDEV

B20 MALTHUS T.R.,PRINCIPLES OF POLITICAL ECONOMY. UK AGRI INDUS MARKET NAT/G DIPLOM PRICE CONTROL BAL/PAY COST OWN PWR LAISSEZ 18/19. PAGE 84 F1650 — GEN/LAWS DEMAND WEALTH

B25 EDGEWORTH F.Y.,PAPERS RELATING TO POLITICAL ECONOMY. MOD/EUR SOCIETY STRATA DIST/IND INDUS MARKET NAT/G ACT/RES ECO/TAC EXEC WEALTH ...METH/CNCPT MATH TREND HYPO/EXP SIMUL GEN/METH FOR/TRADE VAL/FREE LOG/LING. PAGE 36 F0702 — ECO/DEV CAP/ISM

B27 WEBER M.,GENERAL ECONOMIC HISTORY. CHRIST-17C MOD/EUR STRUCT AGRI EXTR/IND FINAN INDUS MARKET FAM — ECO/DEV CAP/ISM

NAT/G PROF/ORG SECT ECO/TAC MUNICH 8/20. PAGE 144 F2839

B30
BEVERIDGE W.H.,UNEMPLOYMENT: A PROBLEM OF INDUSTRY (1909-1930). USA-45 LAW ECO/DEV MARKET DELIB/GP WAR DEMAND INCOME...POLICY STAT CHARTS 20. PAGE 14 F0274
WORKER ECO/TAC GEN/LAWS

B30
BIEL G.,TREATISE ON THE POWER AND UTILITY OF MONEY (1484). INDUS MARKET LOC/G NAT/G SECT ECO/TAC PRODUC WEALTH 15. PAGE 15 F0280
FINAN COST PRICE GEN/LAWS

B30
HAWTREY R.G.,ECONOMIC ASPECTS OF SOVEREIGNTY. UNIV WOR+45 WOR-45 ECO/DEV ECO/UNDEV AGRI COM/IND INDUS MARKET NAT/G TEC/DEV ECO/TAC EDU/PROP COERCE ATTIT KNOWL WEALTH...CONCPT CON/ANAL GEN/LAWS 20. PAGE 57 F1118
FORCES PWR SOVEREIGN WAR

B30
KEYNES J.M.,A TREATISE ON MONEY (2 VOLS.). UK USA-45 INDUS MARKET WORKER PRICE CONTROL COST OPTIMAL PROFIT WEALTH...POLICY 19/20 KEYNES/JM. PAGE 70 F1385
EQUILIB ECO/TAC FINAN GEN/LAWS

B31
JEVONS W.S.,THE THEORY OF POLITICAL ECONOMY (4TH ED.; 1ST ED. 1871). WOR-45 FINAN MARKET RENT WEALTH ...LOG MATH QUANT CON/ANAL IDEA/COMP BIBLIOG METH 17/19. PAGE 67 F1318
GEN/LAWS UTIL LABOR

B32
DICKINSON H.D.,INSTITUTIONAL REVENUE: A STUDY OF THE INFLUENCE OF SOCIAL INSTITUTIONS ON THE DISTRIBUTION OF WEALTH. SOCIETY STRATA FINAN ...NEW/IDEA IDEA/COMP 20. PAGE 33 F0632
WEALTH CONCPT METH/CNCPT MARKET

B32
THOMPSON C.D.,CONFESSIONS OF THE POWER TRUST. MARKET ACT/RES EDU/PROP CONTROL GOV/REL INCOME OWN ...MGT 20 FTC MONOPOLY. PAGE 130 F2564
LG/CO SERV/IND PWR FINAN

B34
GRAHAM F.D.,PROTECTIVE TARIFFS. FUT USA+45 WOR-45 INDUS MARKET VOL/ASSN PLAN CAP/ISM ECO/TAC PEACE ATTIT DRIVE HEALTH ORD/FREE...OBS TREND GEN/LAWS FOR/TRADE 20. PAGE 50 F0970
INT/ORG TARIFFS

B34
ROBINSON J.,THE ECONOMICS OF IMPERFECT COMPETITION. FINAN ECO/TAC PRICE COST DEMAND EQUILIB OPTIMAL WEALTH...METH MONOPOLY. PAGE 113 F2221
MARKET WORKER INDUS

B35
KEYNES J.M.,THE GENERAL THEORY OF EMPLOYMENT, INTEREST, AND MONEY. AGRI INDUS WORKER ECO/TAC DEMAND EQUILIB INCOME PRODUC PROFIT ATTIT WEALTH 20. PAGE 71 F1386
FINAN GEN/LAWS MARKET PRICE

B36
BURNS A.R.,THE DECLINE OF COMPETITION. LAW LG/CO NAT/G SML/CO LEGIS PRICE AGREE CONTROL GP/REL INCOME PRODUC...POLICY 19/20 NRA. PAGE 20 F0390
MARKET GEN/LAWS INDUS

B38
LANGE O.,ON THE ECONOMIC THEORY OF SOCIALISM. UNIV ECO/DEV FINAN INDUS INT/ORG PUB/INST ROUTINE ATTIT ALL/VALS...SOC CONCPT STAT TREND 20. PAGE 75 F1475
MARKET ECO/TAC INT/TRADE SOCISM

B38
MEADE J.E.,AN INTRODUCTION TO ECONOMIC ANALYSIS AND POLICY (AMERICAN EDITION EDITED BY C.J. HITCH). FINAN INDUS MARKET LABOR INT/TRADE CONTROL COST DEMAND INCOME...CLASSIF CHARTS T 20 KEYNES/JM MONOPOLY. PAGE 89 F1737
CONCPT PROFIT PRODUC

B40
BLAISDELL D.C.,GOVERNMENT AND AGRICULTURE; THE GROWTH OF FEDERAL FARM AID. USA-45 MARKET PLAN PROB/SOLV TEC/DEV ECO/TAC GOV/REL ADJUST ATTIT ...CHARTS 20 DEPT/AGRI. PAGE 15 F0296
NAT/G GIVE AGRI DELIB/GP

B40
CAMPBELL P.,CONSUMER REPRESENTATION IN THE NEW DEAL. AGRI INDUS MARKET EX/STRUC PLAN CAP/ISM CONTROL GP/REL DEMAND POLICY. PAGE 21 F0408
CLIENT REPRESENT NAT/G

B40
GAUS J.M.,PUBLIC ADMINISTRATION AND THE UNITED STATES DEPARTMENT OF AGRICULTURE. USA-45 STRUCT DIST/IND FINAN MARKET EX/STRUC PROB/SOLV GIVE PRODUC...POLICY GEOG CHARTS 20 DEPT/AGRI. PAGE 47 F0909
ADMIN AGRI DELIB/GP OP/RES

B44
LANDAUER C.,THEORY OF NATIONAL ECONOMIC PLANNING. USA-45 INDUS MARKET WORKER PROB/SOLV DIPLOM RATION PRICE CONTROL WAR COST 20. PAGE 75 F1465
ECO/TAC PLAN NAT/G ECO/DEV

B47
BAERWALD F.,FUNDAMENTALS OF LABOR ECONOMICS. LAW INDUS LABOR LG/CO CONTROL GP/REL INCOME TOTALISM ...MGT CHARTS GEN/LAWS BIBLIOG 20. PAGE 8 F0150
ECO/DEV WORKER MARKET

B47
HEILPERIN M.A.,THE TRADE OF NATIONS. USA+45 USA-45 WOR+45 WOR-45 CULTURE ECO/DEV NAT/G DELIB/GP EDU/PROP ATTIT DISPL ORD/FREE PWR WEALTH TOT/POP 20. PAGE 58 F1139
MARKET INT/ORG INT/TRADE PEACE

B47
LEVER E.A.,ADVERTISING AND ECONOMIC THEORY. FINAN ECO/TAC DEMAND EFFICIENCY ATTIT...MGT PSY SAMP/SIZ CHARTS 20. PAGE 79 F1539
EDU/PROP MARKET COM/IND ECO/DEV

B47
TOWLE L.W.,INTERNATIONAL TRADE AND COMMERCIAL POLICY. WOR+45 LAW ECO/DEV FINAN INDUS NAT/G ECO/TAC WEALTH...TIME/SEQ ILO 20. PAGE 131 F2582
MARKET INT/ORG INT/TRADE

B48
HOOVER E.M.,THE LOCATION OF ECONOMIC ACTIVITY. WOR+45 MARKET WORKER PROB/SOLV INT/TRADE ADMIN COST ...POLICY CHARTS T MUNICH 20. PAGE 62 F1211
HABITAT INDUS ECO/TAC GEOG

B48
ROBERTSON D.H.,MONEY. AFR ECO/DEV NAT/G DIPLOM INT/TRADE BAL/PAY INCOME WEALTH...TIME/SEQ 20 DEPRESSION. PAGE 112 F2212
FINAN MARKET COST PRICE

B48
SAMUELSON P.A.,FOUNDATIONS OF ECONOMIC ANALYSIS. MARKET RATION DEMAND UTIL...MATH METH T 20. PAGE 115 F2276
EQUILIB GEN/LAWS ECO/DEV

B48
VON HAYEK F.A.,INDIVIDUALISM AND ECONOMIC ORDER. GERMANY USA-45 USSR FINAN MARKET INT/ORG ECO/TAC INT/TRADE PRICE REPRESENT ORD/FREE...PLURIST GEN/LAWS 20. PAGE 142 F2793
SOCISM CAP/ISM POPULISM FEDERAL

B49
SHISTER J.,ECONOMICS OF THE LABOR MARKET. LOC/G NAT/G WORKER TEC/DEV BARGAIN PAY PRICE EXEC GP/REL INCOME...MGT T 20. PAGE 121 F2381
MARKET LABOR INDUS

B50
CHAMBERLIN E.,THE THEORY OF MONOPOLISTIC COMPETITION (1933). INDUS PAY GP/REL COST DEMAND EFFICIENCY OPTIMAL PRODUC WEALTH...GEN/LAWS 20. PAGE 23 F0443
MARKET PRICE ECO/TAC EQUILIB

B50
CLARK J.M.,ALTERNATIVE TO SERFDOM. SOCIETY STRATA INDUS MARKET WORKER PRICE GP/REL PROFIT BIO/SOC PWR WEALTH...GEN/LAWS 20 KEYNES/JM. PAGE 25 F0481
ORD/FREE POPULISM ECO/TAC REPRESENT

B50
HOOVER G.,TWENTIETH CENTURY ECONOMIC THOUGHT. USA+45 ECO/DEV AGRI FINAN INDUS MARKET SERV/IND LABOR NAT/G...STAT 20. PAGE 62 F1213
ECO/TAC CAP/ISM INT/TRADE

B51
CLARK C.,THE CONDITIONS OF ECONOMIC PROGRESS. EUR+WWI WOR+45 WOR-45 ECO/DEV INDUS CAP/ISM MORAL ...WELF/ST METH/CNCPT STAT TOT/POP VAL/FREE 20. PAGE 25 F0477
MARKET WEALTH

B51
DIMOCK M.E.,FREE ENTERPRISE AND THE ADMINISTRATIVE STATE. FINAN LG/CO BARGAIN BUDGET DOMIN CONTROL INGP/REL EFFICIENCY 20. PAGE 33 F0640
CAP/ISM ADMIN MGT MARKET

B51
ROEPKE W.,THE PROBLEM OF ECONOMIC ORDER. WOR+45 SOCIETY PROB/SOLV CONTROL EFFICIENCY...CON/ANAL IDEA/COMP GEN/METH 20. PAGE 113 F2231
ECO/TAC ORD/FREE MARKET PROC/MFG

B52
ALEXANDROWICZ C.H.,INTERNATIONAL ECONOMIC ORGANIZATION. WOR+45 ECO/DEV ECO/UNDEV DIST/IND FINAN MARKET PLAN ECO/TAC LEGIT DRIVE WEALTH ...POLICY CONCPT QUANT OBS TIME/SEQ GEN/LAWS WORK METH/GP EEC ILO OEEC UNESCO 20. PAGE 4 F0063
INT/ORG INT/TRADE

B52
ASHWORTH W.,A SHORT HISTORY OF THE INTERNATIONAL ECONOMY 1850-1950. WOR+45 WOR-45 AGRI FINAN INDUS MARKET LABOR ECO/TAC...CONCPT STAT HIST/WRIT FOR/TRADE ILO 19/20. PAGE 7 F0131
ECO/DEV TEC/DEV INT/TRADE

B52
AYRES C.E.,THE INDUSTRIAL ECONOMY. USA+45 FINAN MARKET NAT/G PUB/INST PLAN ECO/TAC TAX DEMAND INCOME...BIBLIOG/A 20. PAGE 8 F0146
ECO/DEV INDUS FUT PROB/SOLV

B52
DE JOUVENEL B.,THE ETHICS OF REDISTRIBUTION. UK ELITES MARKET WORKER GIVE PAY INCOME PERSON ...POLICY PSY GEN/LAWS 20. PAGE 31 F0602
WEALTH TAX SOCISM TRADIT

B52
EGLE W.P.,ECONOMIC STABILIZATION. USA+45 SOCIETY FINAN MARKET PLAN ECO/TAC DOMIN EDU/PROP LEGIT EXEC WEALTH...CONCPT METH/CNCPT TREND HYPO/EXP GEN/METH TOT/POP VAL/FREE 20. PAGE 36 F0708
NAT/G ECO/DEV CAP/ISM

B52
SURANYI-UNGER T.,COMPARATIVE ECONOMIC SYSTEMS. FINAN MARKET DIPLOM PRICE WEALTH...GEOG SOC BIBLIOG METH T 20. PAGE 128 F2517
LAISSEZ PLAN ECO/DEV IDEA/COMP

B52
WU Y.,ECONOMIC WARFARE. MARKET PLAN PROB/SOLV FOR/AID CONTROL EFFICIENCY WEALTH...METH/COMP 20. PAGE 149 F2937
ECO/TAC WAR INT/TRADE

DIPLOM

B53
MILLIKAN M.F.,INCOME STABILIZATION FOR A DEVELOPING DEMOCRACY. USA+45 ECO/DEV LABOR BUDGET ECO/TAC TAX ADMIN ADJUST PRODUC WEALTH...POLICY TREND 20. PAGE 91 F1794
ANTHOL MARKET EQUILIB EFFICIENCY

B53
NEISSER H.,NATIONAL INCOMES AND INTERNATIONAL TRADE. FRANCE GERMANY SWEDEN UK USA-45 EXTR/IND FINAN INDUS TEC/DEV PRICE BAL/PAY EQUILIB INCOME WEALTH...CHARTS METH 19 CHINJAP. PAGE 97 F1908
INT/TRADE PRODUC MARKET CON/ANAL

B53
ROBINSON E.A.G.,THE STRUCTURE OF COMPETITIVE INDUSTRY. UK ECO/DEV DIST/IND MARKET TEC/DEV DIPLOM EDU/PROP ADMIN EFFICIENCY WEALTH...MGT 19/20. PAGE 113 F2217
INDUS PRODUC WORKER OPTIMAL

B54
MITCHELL W.G.,BUSINESS CYCLES. FINAN MARKET PRICE COST EQUILIB OPTIMAL PRODUC PROFIT...IDEA/COMP GEN/LAWS 19/20. PAGE 92 F1809
INDUS TIME/SEQ METH/COMP STAT

B54
MOSK S.A.,INDUSTRIAL REVOLUTION IN MEXICO. MARKET LABOR CREATE CAP/ISM ADMIN ATTIT SOCISM...POLICY 20 MEXIC/AMER. PAGE 94 F1843
INDUS TEC/DEV ECO/UNDEV NAT/G

S54
FORM W.H.,"THE PLACE OF SOCIAL STRUCTURE IN THE DETERMINATION OF LAND USE: SOME IMPLICATIONS FOR A THEORY OF URBAN ECOLOGY" (BMR)" STRUCT...GEOG PHIL/SCI SOC MUNICH 20. PAGE 42 F0827
HABITAT MARKET ORD/FREE

B55
O'CONNOR H.,THE EMPIRE OF OIL. USA+45 DIST/IND FINAN MARKET CAP/ISM TAX CONTROL...POLICY MARXIST BIBLIOG/A 20. PAGE 100 F1955
EXTR/IND INT/TRADE CENTRAL NAT/G

B55
PEDLER F.J.,ECONOMIC GEOGRAPHY OF WEST AFRICA. GAMBIA NIGER SIER/LEONE STRATA EXTR/IND MARKET LABOR INT/TRADE DEMAND HABITAT WEALTH...CHARTS 20. PAGE 104 F2046
ECO/UNDEV GEOG PRODUC EFFICIENCY

S55
KELLY W.E.,"HOW SALES EXECUTIVES USE FACTORING TO BOOST SALES AND PROFITS TODAY." FINAN LG/CO BUDGET EFFICIENCY PROFIT...MGT PRODUCT. PAGE 70 F1372
INDUS ECO/DEV CONSULT MARKET

B56
BONNETT C.E.,HISTORY OF EMPLOYERS' ASSOCIATIONS IN THE UNITED STATES (1ST ED.). MARKET DETER GP/REL ADJUST. PAGE 16 F0316
LABOR VOL/ASSN LG/CO

B56
GREENHUT M.L.,PLANT LOCATION IN THEORY AND PRACTICE; THE ECONOMICS OF SPACE. WOR+45 WOR-45 MARKET WORKER COST DEMAND...CONCPT STAT CHARTS HYPO/EXP BIBLIOG 19/20. PAGE 51 F0991
SML/CO ECO/DEV CAP/ISM IDEA/COMP

B56
ISARD W.,LOCATION AND SPACE-ECONOMY: GENERAL THEORY RELATING TO INDUSTRIAL LOCATION, MARKET AREAS, LAND USE, TRADE... UNIV DIST/IND MARKET LG/CO SML/CO TEC/DEV GP/REL EQUILIB HABITAT...NEW/IDEA MATH CHARTS 20. PAGE 66 F1290
GEN/LAWS GEOG INDUS REGION

L56
SCHELLING T.C.,"AN ESSAY ON BARGAINING" (BMR)" OP/RES PROB/SOLV PRICE CHOOSE PWR...DECISION MODELS 20. PAGE 116 F2294
BARGAIN MARKET ECO/TAC GAME

B57
FOUSEK P.G.,FOREIGN CENTRAL BANKING: THE INSTRUMENTS OF MONETARY POLICY. WOR+45 CONTROL ...TREND CHARTS 20 MONEY. PAGE 43 F0836
FINAN ECO/TAC ECO/DEV MARKET

B57
HARRIS S.E.,INTERNATIONAL AND INTERREGIONAL ECONOMICS. AFR WOR+45 WOR-45 NAT/G TARIFFS BAL/PAY EQUILIB...POLICY CONCPT STAT CHARTS IDEA/COMP 19/20. PAGE 55 F1088
INT/TRADE ECO/DEV MARKET FINAN

B57
HARWOOD E.C.,CAUSE AND CONTROL OF THE BUSINESS CYCLE (5TH ED.). AFR USA-45 PRICE CONTROL WAR DEMAND INCOME WEALTH...TREND CHARTS 19. PAGE 56 F1107
PRODUC MARKET FINAN

B57
LENIN V.I.,THE DEVELOPMENT OF CAPITALISM IN RUSSIA. MOD/EUR USSR AGRI MARKET POL/PAR TEC/DEV...CONCPT 19/20. PAGE 78 F1521
COM INDUS CAP/ISM

B57
MASON E.S.,ECONOMIC CONCENTRATION AND THE MONOPOLY PROBLEM. USA+45 USA-45 LAW ELITES ECO/DEV LABOR RATION PRICE PWR WEALTH...CHARTS 20 MONOPOLY. PAGE 87 F1696
GP/REL LG/CO CONTROL MARKET

B57
NANIWADA H.,STAAT UND WIRTSCHAFT; GRUNDLEGUNG DER NATIONALOEKONOMIE ALS DER LOGIK DER BURGERLICHEN GESELLSCHAFT. WOR+45 WOR-45 STRATA MARKET WORKER INGP/REL DEMAND EQUILIB WEALTH...POLICY IDEA/COMP GEN/LAWS 17/20 MARX/KARL KEYNES/JM LENIN/VI. PAGE 96 F1890
ALL/IDEOS ECO/TAC SOCIETY NAT/G

B57
NEUMARK S.D.,ECONOMIC INFLUENCES ON THE SOUTH AFRICAN FRONTIER, 1652-1836. SOUTH/AFR SEA AGRI NAT/G FORCES WORKER DIPLOM INT/TRADE PRICE DEMAND PRODUC...STAT CHARTS 17/19 FRONTIER. PAGE 97 F1915
COLONIAL ECO/UNDEV ECO/TAC MARKET

B58
ATOMIC INDUSTRIAL FORUM,MANAGEMENT AND ATOMIC ENERGY. WOR+45 SEA LAW MARKET NAT/G TEC/DEV INSPECT INT/TRADE CONFER PEACE HEALTH...ANTHOL 20. PAGE 7 F0136
NUC/PWR INDUS MGT ECO/TAC

B58
BERLINER J.S.,SOVIET ECONOMIC AID: THE AID AND TRADE POLICY IN UNDERDEVELOPED COUNTRIES. AFR COM ISLAM L/A+17C S/ASIA USSR ECO/DEV DIST/IND FINAN MARKET INT/ORG ACT/RES PLAN BAL/PWR WEAPON PWR WEALTH...CHARTS FOR/TRADE 20. PAGE 14 F0263
ECO/UNDEV ECO/TAC FOR/AID

B58
COLM G.,THE ECONOMY OF THE AMERICAN PEOPLE: PROGRESS, PROBLEMS, PROSPECTS. USA+45 INDUS MARKET LABOR TEC/DEV INCOME 20. PAGE 26 F0509
WEALTH PRODUC CAP/ISM MGT

B58
DOWNIE J.,THE COMPETITIVE PROCESS. ECO/TAC PRICE EFFICIENCY OPTIMAL PRODUC WEALTH...IDEA/COMP METH/COMP 20 MONOPOLY. PAGE 34 F0658
EQUILIB MARKET INDUS ECO/DEV

B58
EHRHARD J.,LE DESTIN DU COLONIALISME. AFR FRANCE ECO/UNDEV AGRI FINAN MARKET CREATE PLAN TEC/DEV BUDGET DIPLOM PRICE 20. PAGE 36 F0710
COLONIAL FOR/AID INT/TRADE INDUS

B58
MIKESELL R.F.,FINANCING FREE WORLD TRADE WITH THE SINO-SOVIET BLOC. CHINA/COM COM USSR WOR+45 ECO/DEV AGRI DIST/IND EXTR/IND FINAN INDUS MARKET PROC/MFG NAT/G PLAN TEC/DEV ECO/TAC...CHARTS METH/GP EEC FOR/TRADE 20. PAGE 91 F1780
STAT BAL/PAY

B58
MUSGRAVE R.A.,CLASSICS IN THE THEORY OF PUBLIC FINANCE. UNIV MARKET LG/CO NAT/G CAP/ISM PRICE OPTIMAL...IDEA/COMP ANTHOL 19/20 SAY/EMIL EDGEWORTH LINDAHL/E RITSCHL/H. PAGE 95 F1870
TAX FINAN ECO/TAC GP/REL

B58
US CONGRESS JOINT ECO COMM,THE RELATIONSHIP OF PRICES TO ECONOMIC STABILITY AND GROWTH. USA+45 MARKET TAX ADJUST COST DEMAND INCOME PRODUC ...POLICY TREND CHARTS ANTHOL 20 CONGRESS. PAGE 134 F2650
ECO/DEV PLAN EQUILIB PRICE

L58
ARROW K.J.,"ON THE STABILITY OF THE COMPETITIVE EQUILIBRIUM: I." WOR+45...METH/CNCPT MATH STAT CHARTS SIMUL. PAGE 6 F0122
DECISION MARKET ECO/DEV ECO/TAC

L58
TRAGER F.N.,"A SELECTED AND ANNOTATED BIBLIOGRAPHY ON ECONOMIC DEVELOPMENT, 1953-1957." WOR+45 AGRI FINAN INDUS MARKET LABOR WORKER PLAN INT/TRADE PRODUC...CENSUS MUNICH. PAGE 131 F2583
BIBLIOG/A ECO/UNDEV ECO/DEV

S58
ARROW K.J.,"UTILITIES, ATTITUDES, CHOICES: A REVIEW NOTE." USA+45 PLAN...METH/CNCPT MATH STAT CHARTS HYPO/EXP. PAGE 6 F0121
DECISION DIST/IND MARKET CREATE

S58
ARROW K.J.,"A NOTE ON EXPECTATIONS AND STABILITY." WOR+45...METH/CNCPT MATH STAT CHARTS HYPO/EXP. PAGE 7 F0123
DECISION MARKET ECO/DEV ECO/TAC

S58
FOLDES L.,"UNCERTAINTY, PROBABILITY AND POTENTIAL SURPRISE." MARKET PROB/SOLV RISK PERSON...DECISION MGT HYPO/EXP GAME. PAGE 42 F0820
PROBABIL ADMIN ROUTINE

N58
EUROPEAN COMM ECO-SOC PROG,EUROPEAN BUSINESS CYCLE POLICY (PAMPHLET). AFR EUR+WWI MARKET WORKER DIPLOM PRICE BAL/PAY 20 EUROPE. PAGE 39 F0754
ECO/DEV FINAN ECO/TAC PROB/SOLV

B59
BLACK J.D.,ECONOMICS FOR AGRICULTURE. USA+45 EXTR/IND FAM WORKER ACT/RES PLAN PRICE EATING INCOME...CENSUS BIBLIOG 20. PAGE 15 F0291
AGRI ECO/TAC MARKET POLICY

B59
ETSCHMANN R.,DIE WAHRUNGS- UND DEVISENPOLITIK DES OSTBLOCKS UND IHRE AUSWIRKUNGEN AUF DIE WIRTSCHAFTSBEZIEHUNGEN ZWISCHEN OST U WEST. BULGARIA CZECHOSLVK HUNGARY POLAND USSR MARKET NAT/G PLAN DIPLOM...NAT/COMP 20. PAGE 39 F0753
ECO/TAC FINAN POLICY INT/TRADE

B59
HAX K.,DIE HOCHSCHULLEHRER DER WIRTSCHAFTSWISSENSCHAFTEN IN DER BUNDESREPUBLIK DEUTSCHLAND EINSCHL. WESTBERLIN, OSTERREICH. AUSTRIA GERMANY/W SWITZERLND FINAN MARKET PROF/ORG BUDGET ECO/TAC INT/TRADE PRICE COST 20. PAGE 57 F1119
BIBLIOG ACADEM INTELL

B59
HAZLEWOOD A.,THE ECONOMICS OF "UNDER-DEVELOPED" AREAS. WOR+45 DIST/IND EXTR/IND FINAN INDUS MARKET PLAN FOR/AID...GEOG 20. PAGE 57 F1129
BIBLIOG/A ECO/UNDEV AGRI INT/TRADE

B59
LEWIS J.P.,BUSINESS CONDITIONS ANALYSIS. USA+45 MARKET LABOR BUDGET TAX AUTOMAT WAR DEMAND PRODUC ...ECOMETRIC CHARTS BIBLIOG 19/20. PAGE 79 F1549
FINAN PRICE TREND

B59
MAYER H.M.,READINGS IN URBAN GEOGRAPHY. WOR+45 SOCIETY DIST/IND INDUS MARKET HABITAT...CLASSIF CENSUS CHARTS ANTHOL MUNICH 20 WATER. PAGE 87 F1706
GEOG STRUCT

B59
MEYER A.J.,MIDDLE EASTERN CAPITALISM: NINE ESSAYS. ISLAM CULTURE ECO/UNDEV INDUS MARKET NAT/G PLAN ATTIT RIGID/FLEX...STAT OBS TREND GEN/LAWS. PAGE 90 F1767
TEC/DEV ECO/TAC ANTHOL

B59
NORTON P.L.,URBAN PROBLEMS AND TECHNIQUES. AIR AGRI INDUS MARKET TEC/DEV BUDGET LEISURE ALL/VALS ...ANTHOL MUNICH 20 URBAN/RNWL. PAGE 99 F1936
PLAN LOC/G HABITAT

B59
SELIGSOHN I.J.,"USING COMPUTER SERVICES IN SMALL BUSINESS" MANAGEMENT AIDS FOR SMALL MANUFACTURERS 109 (PAMPHLET). DIST/IND MARKET PROC/MFG COST EFFICIENCY PRODUC...DECISION IDEA/COMP. PAGE 119 F2350
SML/CO COMPUTER MGT PROB/SOLV

B59
SERAPHIM H.J.,PROBLEME DER WILLENSBILDUNG UND DER WIRTSCHAFTSPOLITISCHEN FUEHRUNG. WOR+45 MARKET ACT/RES OP/RES PLAN EDU/PROP INGP/REL HABITAT PLURISM...MGT PERS/COMP METH 20. PAGE 119 F2357
POLICY DECISION PSY

B59
SHACKLE G.L.S.,ECONOMICS FOR PLEASURE. FINAN MARKET NAT/G WORKER PLAN INT/TRADE TARIFFS PAY BAL/PAY COST PRODUC 20. PAGE 120 F2361
METH/CNCPT WEALTH INCOME

B59
SHUBIK M.,STRATEGY AND MARKET STRUCTURE: COMPETITION, OLIGOPOLY, AND THE THEORY OF GAMES. ELITES STRUCT MARKET OP/RES EXEC EFFICIENCY INCOME ...MGT MATH STAT CHARTS 20. PAGE 121 F2389
ECO/DEV ECO/TAC DECISION GAME

B59
WELTON H.,THE THIRD WORLD WAR; TRADE AND INDUSTRY, THE NEW BATTLEGROUND. AFR WOR+45 ECO/DEV INDUS MARKET TASK...MGT IDEA/COMP. PAGE 145 F2855
INT/TRADE PLAN DIPLOM

L59
ARROW K.J.,"ON THE STABILITY OF THE COMPETITIVE EQUILIBRIUM: II." WOR+45...METH/CNCPT MATH STAT CHARTS HYPO/EXP. PAGE 7 F0124
DECISION MARKET ECO/DEV ECO/TAC

L59
MURPHY J.C.,"SOME IMPLICATIONS OF EUROPE'S COMMON MARKET. IN (COOK P, ECONOMIC DEVELOPMENT AND INTERNATIONAL TRADE.." EUR+WWI ECO/DEV DIST/IND INDUS NAT/G PLAN ECO/TAC INT/TRADE WEALTH...STAT TREND OEEC TOT/POP 20 EEC. PAGE 95 F1866
MARKET INT/ORG REGION

L59
SIMON H.A.,"THEORIES OF DECISION-MAKING IN ECONOMICS AND BEHAVIORAL SCIENCE" (BMR)" MARKET BARGAIN UTIL DRIVE...DECISION MGT PROBABIL HYPO/EXP SIMUL 20 BEHAVIORSM. PAGE 122 F2409
PSY GEN/LAWS PROB/SOLV

S59
ALKHIMOV V.S.,"SOVIET FOREIGN TRADE CHANNELS." COM FUT USA+45 USSR ECO/DEV MARKET CONSULT PLAN WEALTH ...MARXIST OBS CON/ANAL FOR/TRADE 20. PAGE 4 F0068
FINAN ECO/TAC DIPLOM

S59
ALLEN G.,"NATIONAL FARMERS UNION AS A PRESSURE GROUP: II." UK ECO/DEV MARKET POL/PAR DELIB/GP PROB/SOLV ECO/TAC LOBBY INCOME...POLICY METH/COMP 19/20 NAT/FARMER. PAGE 4 F0069
DIST/IND AGRI PROF/ORG TREND

S59
KINDLEBERGER C.P.,"UNITED STATES ECONOMIC FOREIGN POLICY: RESEARCH REQUIREMENTS FOR 1965." FUT USA+45 WOR+45 DIST/IND MARKET INT/ORG ECO/TAC INT/TRADE WEALTH...OBS TREND CON/ANAL GEN/LAWS FOR/TRADE VAL/FREE 20. PAGE 71 F1392
FINAN ECO/DEV FOR/AID

S59
PLAZA G.,"FOR A REGIONAL MARKET IN LATIN AMERICA." FUT L/A+17C CULTURE INDUS NAT/G ECO/TAC INT/TRADE ATTIT WEALTH...NEW/IDEA TREND OAS 20. PAGE 106 F2092
MARKET INT/ORG REGION

S59
STREETEN P.,"UNBALANCED GROWTH" UK ECO/DEV AGRI MARKET TEC/DEV CAP/ISM ECO/TAC FOR/AID INT/TRADE DEMAND ORD/FREE...CONCPT 20. PAGE 127 F2502
IDEA/COMP FINAN PRODUC EQUILIB

S59
ZAUBERMAN A.,"SOVIET BLOC ECONOMIC INTEGRATION." COM CULTURE INTELL ECO/DEV INDUS TOP/EX ACT/RES PLAN ECO/TAC INT/TRADE ROUTINE CHOOSE ATTIT ...TIME/SEQ 20. PAGE 150 F2958
MARKET INT/ORG USSR TOTALISM

C59
MINTZ S.W.,"INTERNAL MARKET SYS AS MECHANISMS OF SOCIAL ARTIC," IN V.F. RAY, INTERMED SOCIETIES, SOCIAL MOBILITY, AND COMMUNIC (BMR). UNIV STRATA GP/REL INGP/REL...GEOG SOC BIBLIOG. PAGE 92 F1804
MARKET SOCIETY ECO/UNDEV STRUCT

B60
BAYER H.,WIRTSCHAFTSPROGNOSE UND WIRTSCHAFTSGESTALTUNG. GERMANY NETHERLAND MARKET PLAN CAP/ISM DEBATE...NAT/COMP 20. PAGE 12 F0220
ECO/DEV ECO/UNDEV FINAN POLICY

B60
BIERMAN H.,THE CAPITAL BUDGETING DECISION. AFR ECO/DEV MARKET TAX PRICE RISK COST INCOME TIME 20. PAGE 15 F0282
FINAN OPTIMAL BUDGET PROFIT

B60
BRYCE M.D.,INDUSTRIAL DEVELOPMENT: A GUIDE FOR ACCELERATING ECONOMIC GROWTH. WOR+45 FINAN MARKET COST EFFICIENCY PRODUC. PAGE 20 F0378
INDUS PLAN ECO/UNDEV TEC/DEV

B60
CAMPBELL R.W.,SOVIET ECONOMIC POWER. COM USA+45 DIST/IND MARKET TOP/EX ACT/RES CAP/ISM ECO/TAC DOMIN EDU/PROP ADMIN ROUTINE DRIVE...MATH TIME/SEQ CHARTS WORK 20. PAGE 21 F0409
ECO/DEV PLAN SOCISM USSR

B60
GRIER E.,PRIVATELY DEVELOPED INTERRACIAL HOUSING: AN ANALYSIS OF EXPERIENCE. FINAN MARKET COST DISCRIM PROFIT SOC/INTEG 20. PAGE 51 F0997
RACE/REL CONSTRUC HABITAT

B60
HOFFMANN P.G.,ONE HUNDRED COUNTRIES, ONE AND ONE QUARTER BILLION PEOPLE. MARKET INT/ORG TEC/DEV CAP/ISM...GEOG CHARTS METH/COMP 20 UN. PAGE 61 F1191
FOR/AID ECO/TAC ECO/UNDEV INT/TRADE

B60
LISTER L.,EUROPE'S COAL AND STEEL COMMUNITY. FRANCE GERMANY STRUCT ECO/DEV EXTR/IND INDUS MARKET NAT/G DELIB/GP ECO/TAC INT/TRADE EDU/PROP ATTIT RIGID/FLEX ORD/FREE PWR WEALTH...CONCPT STAT TIME/SEQ CHARTS ECSC TERR/GP 20. PAGE 81 F1582
EUR+WWI INT/ORG REGION

B60
MOORE W.E.,LABOR COMMITMENT AND SOCIAL CHANGE IN DEVELOPING AREAS. SOCIETY STRATA ECO/UNDEV MARKET VOL/ASSN WORKER AUTHORIT SKILL...MGT NAT/COMP SOC/INTEG 20. PAGE 93 F1823
LABOR ORD/FREE ATTIT INDUS

B60
RAPKIN C.,THE DEMAND FOR HOUSING IN RACIALLY MIXED AREAS: A STUDY OF THE NATURE OF NEIGHBORHOOD CHANGE. USA+45 FINAN PRICE COST DRIVE...GEOG 20. PAGE 109 F2151
RACE/REL NEIGH DISCRIM MARKET

B60
ROBERTSON D.,THE CONTROL OF INDUSTRY. UK MARKET LABOR WORKER PRICE CONTROL GP/REL COST DEMAND ORD/FREE WEALTH NEW/LIB SOCISM 20. PAGE 112 F2211
INDUS FINAN NAT/G ECO/DEV

B60
ROBINSON J.,AN ESSAY ON MARXIAN ECONOMICS. USA+45 STRATA INDUS MARKET CAP/ISM...METH/COMP 19/20 MARX/KARL. PAGE 113 F2222
IDEA/COMP MARXISM ACADEM

B60
SIEGEL B.N.,AGGREGATE ECONOMICS AND PUBLIC POLICY. ECO/DEV TEC/DEV ECO/TAC TASK DEMAND EQUILIB INCOME ...CHARTS 20. PAGE 121 F2396
ECOMETRIC WEALTH PRODUC MARKET

B60
SIMOONS F.J.,NORTHWEST ETHIOPIA; PEOPLES AND ECONOMY. ETHIOPIA MARKET CREATE 20. PAGE 122 F2411
SOCIETY STRUCT AGRI INDUS

B60
STEIN E.,AMERICAN ENTERPRISE IN THE EUROPEAN COMMON MARKET: A LEGAL PROFILE. EUR+WWI FUT USA+45 SOCIETY STRUCT ECO/DEV NAT/G VOL/ASSN CONSULT PLAN TEC/DEV ECO/TAC INT/TRADE ADMIN ATTIT RIGID/FLEX PWR...MGT NEW/IDEA STAT TREND COMPUT/IR SIMUL EEC 20. PAGE 125 F2475
MARKET ADJUD INT/LAW

S60
GARNICK D.H.,"ON THE ECONOMIC FEASIBILITY OF A MIDDLE EASTERN COMMON MARKET." AFR ISLAM CULTURE INDUS NAT/G PLAN TEC/DEV ECO/TAC ADMIN ATTIT DRIVE RIGID/FLEX...PLURIST STAT TREND GEN/LAWS 20. PAGE 46 F0907
MARKET INT/TRADE

S60
NANES A.,"THE EUROPEAN COMMUNITY AND THE UNITED STATES: EVOLVING RELATIONS." EUR+WWI USA+45 WOR+45 ECO/UNDEV MARKET NAT/G DELIB/GP PLAN LEGIT ATTIT PWR WEALTH...CONCPT STAT TIME/SEQ CON/ANAL EEC METH/GP OEEC 20 EURATOM. PAGE 96 F1889
INT/ORG REGION

S60
OWEN C.F.,"US AND SOVIET RELATIONS WITH UNDERDEVELOPED COUNTRIES: LATIN AMERICA-A CASE STUDY." AFR COM L/A+17C USA+45 USSR EXTR/IND MARKET TEC/DEV DIPLOM ECO/TAC NAT/LISM ORD/FREE PWR ...TREND WORK 20. PAGE 102 F2005
ECO/UNDEV DRIVE INT/TRADE

N60
ERDMAN P.E.,COMMON MARKETS AND FREE TRADE AREAS (PAMPHLET). USA+45 MARKET INT/ORG TEC/DEV DIPLOM UTIL...CON/ANAL CHARTS BIBLIOG 20 EEC OEEC. PAGE 38 F0743
TREND PROB/SOLV INT/TRADE ECO/DEV

B61

ASCHHEIM J.,TECHNIQUES OF MONETARY CONTROL. UK USA+45 CONTROL WAR DEMAND INCOME WEALTH...TREND CHARTS 20 MONEY. PAGE 7 F0127 — FINAN MARKET BUDGET CENTRAL

B61

BALASSA B.,THE THEORY OF ECONOMIC INTEGRATION. EUR+WWI L/A+17C MOD/EUR WOR+45 ECO/UNDEV MARKET INT/ORG NAT/G VOL/ASSN DELIB/GP PLAN CAP/ISM ECO/TAC...MAJORIT FOR/TRADE OEEC 20. PAGE 8 F0157 — ECO/DEV ACT/RES INT/TRADE

B61

FELLNER W.,THE PROBLEM OF RISING PRICES. AGRI INDUS WORKER BUDGET CAP/ISM ECO/TAC INT/TRADE PAY DEMAND ...POLICY 20 EEC. PAGE 40 F0780 — PRICE MARKET ECO/DEV COST

B61

GREY A.L.,ECONOMIC ISSUES AND POLICIES; READINGS IN INTRODUCTORY ECONOMICS (2ND ED.). WOR+45 ECO/UNDEV FINAN MARKET LABOR LG/CO INT/TRADE BAL/PAY WEALTH ...ANTHOL T. PAGE 51 F0996 — ECO/TAC PROB/SOLV METH/COMP

B61

HARRIS S.E.,THE DOLLAR IN CRISIS. AFR USA+45 MARKET INT/ORG ECO/TAC PRICE CONTROL WEALTH...METH/COMP ANTHOL 20. PAGE 55 F1089 — BAL/PAY DIPLOM FINAN INT/TRADE

B61

HODGKINS J.A.,SOVIET POWER: ENERGY RESOURCES, PRODUCTION AND POTENTIALS. USSR ECO/DEV INDUS MARKET...POLICY STAT CHARTS 20 RESOURCE/N. PAGE 60 F1188 — GEOG EXTR/IND TEC/DEV

B61

KITZINGER V.W.,THE CHALLENGE OF THE COMMON MARKET. EUR+WWI ECO/DEV DIST/IND PLAN ECO/TAC INT/TRADE LEGIT ATTIT PWR WEALTH...TIME/SEQ TREND CHARTS EEC 20. PAGE 71 F1403 — MARKET INT/ORG UK

B61

MARX K.,THE COMMUNIST MANIFESTO. IN (MENDEL A. ESSENTIAL WORKS OF MARXISM, NEW YORK: BANTAM. FUT MOD/EUR CULTURE ECO/DEV ECO/UNDEV AGRI FINAN INDUS MARKET PROC/MFG LABOR POL/PAR CONSULT FORCES CREATE PLAN ADMIN ATTIT DRIVE RIGID/FLEX ORD/FREE PWR RESPECT MARX/KARL MUNICH WORK. PAGE 86 F1691 — COM NEW/IDEA CAP/ISM REV

B61

MCCRACKEN H.L.,KEYNESIAN ECONOMICS IN THE STREAM OF ECONOMIC THOUGHT. FINAN MARKET BARGAIN EFFICIENCY OPTIMAL...PHIL/SCI CONCPT IDEA/COMP BIBLIOG 18/20 KEYNES/JM. PAGE 88 F1724 — ECO/TAC DEMAND ECOMETRIC

B61

MOORE G.H.,BUSINESS CYCLE INDICATORS (TWO VOLS.). LABOR DIPLOM PRICE RISK TASK WAR PRODUC...CHARTS BIBLIOG 20. PAGE 93 F1822 — MARKET FINAN WEALTH

B61

PETCH G.A.,ECONOMIC DEVELOPMENT AND MODERN WEST AFRICA. AFR CONGO/BRAZ GHANA NIGER SIER/LEONE AGRI MARKET LABOR FOR/AID TAX COST EFFICIENCY EQUILIB PRODUC...GEOG TREND 20. PAGE 105 F2068 — ECO/UNDEV TEC/DEV EXTR/IND ECO/TAC

B61

ROEPKE W.,JENSEITS VON ANGEBOT UND NACHFRAGE (DRITTE VERAENDERTE AUFLAGE). WOR+45 MARKET TEC/DEV ECO/TAC GP/REL INGP/REL NEW/LIB...POLICY SOC IDEA/COMP PERS/COMP 20. PAGE 113 F2233 — SOCIETY STRANGE ECO/DEV STRUCT

B61

THEOBALD R.,THE CHALLENGE OF ABUNDANCE. USA+45 WOR+45 MARKET DIPLOM FOR/AID REV PRODUC UTOPIA SUPEGO...POLICY TREND BIBLIOG/A 20. PAGE 129 F2554 — WELF/ST ECO/UNDEV PROB/SOLV ECO/TAC

S61

DEUTSCH K.W.,"NATIONAL INDUSTRIALIZATION AND THE DECLINING SHARE OF THE INTERNATIONAL ECONOMIC SECTOR." EUR+WWI FUT WOR+45 WOR-45 MARKET PLAN EDU/PROP WEALTH...WELF/ST OBS TESTS 20. PAGE 32 F0624 — DIST/IND ECO/DEV INT/TRADE

S61

LANFALUSSY A.,"EUROPE'S PROGRESS: DUE TO COMMON MARKET." EUR+WWI ECO/DEV DELIB/GP PLAN ECO/TAC ROUTINE WEALTH...GEOG TREND EEC TERR/GP 20. PAGE 75 F1473 — INT/ORG MARKET

S61

NEAL A.C.,"NEW ECONOMIC POLICIES FOR THE WEST." COM EUR+WWI FUT USA+45 WOR+45 ECO/DEV ECO/UNDEV INDUS MARKET ROUTINE HEALTH ORD/FREE PWR...OLD/LIB METH/CNCPT 20. PAGE 97 F1904 — PLAN ECO/TAC

S61

VINER J.,"ECONOMIC FOREIGN POLICY ON THE NEW FRONTIER." USA+45 ECO/UNDEV AGRI FINAN INDUS MARKET INT/ORG NAT/G FOR/AID INT/TRADE ADMIN ATTIT PWR 20 KENNEDY/JF. PAGE 141 F2786 — TOP/EX ECO/TAC BAL/PAY TARIFFS

B62

BARTELS R.,THE DEVELOPMENT OF MARKETING THOUGHT. USA+45 USA-45 FINAN ECO/TAC...CONCPT TREND. PAGE 11 F0199 — ECO/DEV MARKET MGT EDU/PROP

B62

CAIRNCROSS A.K.,FACTORS IN ECONOMIC DEVELOPMENT. WOR+45 ECO/UNDEV INDUS R+D LG/CO NAT/G EX/STRUC PLAN TEC/DEV ECO/TAC ATTIT HEALTH KNOWL PWR WEALTH ...TIME/SEQ GEN/LAWS TOT/POP TRUE/GP VAL/FREE 20. PAGE 21 F0399 — MARKET ECO/DEV

B62

EINZIG P.,THE HISTORY OF FOREIGN EXCHANGE. CHRIST-17C ISLAM MEDIT-7 PRE/AMER WOR+45 ECO/DEV FINAN PLAN ECO/TAC ATTIT KNOWL WEALTH...SIMUL GEN/LAWS. PAGE 37 F0714 — MARKET TIME/SEQ INT/TRADE

B62

FERBER R.,RESEARCH METHODS IN ECONOMICS AND BUSINESS. AFR ECO/DEV FINAN MARKET LG/CO SML/CO CONSULT CONTROL COST...STAT METH/COMP 20. PAGE 40 F0783 — ACT/RES PROB/SOLV ECO/TAC MGT

B62

HUMPHREY D.D.,THE UNITED STATES AND THE COMMON MARKET. USA+45 INDUS MARKET INT/ORG PLAN EDU/PROP BAL/PAY DRIVE PWR WEALTH...TREND STERTYP FOR/TRADE EEC 20. PAGE 63 F1241 — ATTIT ECO/TAC

B62

LIPPMANN W.,WESTERN UNITY AND THE COMMON MARKET. EUR+WWI FRANCE GERMANY/W UK USA+45 ECO/DEV AGRI FINAN MARKET INT/ORG NAT/G FOR/AID AGREE WEALTH 20 EEC. PAGE 80 F1575 — DIPLOM INT/TRADE VOL/ASSN

B62

LUTZ F.A.,GELD UND WAHRUNG. AFR MARKET LABOR BUDGET 20 EUROPE. PAGE 82 F1610 — ECO/TAC FINAN DIPLOM POLICY

B62

MCCRONE G.,THE ECONOMICS OF SUBSIDING AGRICULTURE. UK ECO/DEV MARKET PLAN TARIFFS PROFIT 20 EEC. PAGE 88 F1725 — AGRI BAL/PAY INT/TRADE LABOR

B62

MEANS G.C.,THE CORPORATE REVOLUTION IN AMERICA: ECONOMIC REALITY VS. ECONOMIC THEORY. USA+45 USA-45 INDUS WORKER PLAN CAP/ISM ADMIN...IDEA/COMP 20. PAGE 89 F1742 — LG/CO MARKET CONTROL PRICE

B62

MEYER F.V.,THE TERMS OF TRADE. WOR+45 AGRI MARKET PROC/MFG DIPLOM PRICE DEMAND PRODUC 20. PAGE 90 F1769 — INT/TRADE BAL/PAY SIMUL EQUILIB

B62

MICHAELY M.,CONCENTRATION IN INTERNATIONAL TRADE. ECO/DEV ECO/UNDEV PRICE INCOME...CHARTS NAT/COMP 20. PAGE 91 F1779 — INT/TRADE MARKET FINAN GEOG

B62

MORGAN C.A.,LABOR ECONOMICS. LAW INDUS MARKET WORKER PLAN PROB/SOLV GOV/REL INCOME ROLE...T 20 DEPT/LABOR NLRB. PAGE 93 F1829 — LABOR ECO/TAC ECO/DEV CAP/ISM

B62

NATIONAL BUREAU ECONOMIC RES,THE RATE AND DIRECTION OF INVENTIVE ACTIVITY: ECONOMIC AND SOCIAL FACTORS. STRUCT INDUS MARKET R+D CREATE OP/RES TEC/DEV EFFICIENCY PRODUC RATIONAL UTIL...WELF/ST PHIL/SCI METH/CNCPT TIME. PAGE 97 F1895 — DECISION PROB/SOLV MGT

B62

PERROUX F.,L'ECONOMIE DES JEUNES NATIONS. EUR+WWI SOUTH/AFR FINAN MARKET TEC/DEV CAP/ISM FOR/AID INT/TRADE 20. PAGE 105 F2065 — INDUS ECO/UNDEV ECO/TAC DIPLOM

B62

ROBINSON M.A.,AN INTRODUCTION TO ECONOMIC REASONING. FINAN MARKET LABOR DIPLOM INT/TRADE BAL/PAY INCOME PRODUC WEALTH...POLICY MGT 20. PAGE 113 F2223 — ECO/TAC METH/CNCPT NAT/G

B62

URQUIDI V.L.,FREE TRADE AND ECONOMIC INTEGRATION IN LATIN AMERICA: THE EVOLUTION OF A COMMON MARKET POLICY. ECO/UNDEV MARKET DIPLOM BAL/PAY FEDERAL ...POLICY CHARTS 20 LAFTA. PAGE 133 F2627 — INT/TRADE REGION INT/ORG L/A+17C

B62

US BUREAU OF THE CENSUS,REPORT FOR SUBCOMMITTEE ON ANTITRUST AND MONOPOLY: CONCENTRATION RATIOS IN MANUFACTURING INDUSTRY 1958. USA+45 ECO/DEV CONTROL GOV/REL OWN PRODUC PROFIT...STAT 20 CONGRESS MONOPOLY. PAGE 134 F2646 — CHARTS PROC/MFG MARKET LG/CO

B62

VANEK J.,INTERNATIONAL TRADE - THEORY AND ECONOMIC POLICY. LABOR BAL/PWR ECO/TAC TARIFFS PRICE BAL/PAY COST DEMAND 20. PAGE 140 F2765 — INT/TRADE DIPLOM BARGAIN MARKET

S62

BOONE A.,"THE FOREIGN TRADE OF CHINA." AFR ECO/DEV ECO/UNDEV INDUS MARKET NAT/G TEC/DEV WEALTH ...POLICY STAT TREND CHARTS FOR/TRADE. PAGE 17 F0318 — ASIA ECO/TAC

S62

LIPSON H.A.,"FORMAL REASONING AND MARKETING STRATEGY." ECO/DEV PROB/SOLV PRICE ALL/VALS CONT/OBS. PAGE 81 F1578 — MARKET DECISION GAME ECO/TAC

S62

MUELLER E.,"LOCATION DECISIONS OF MANUFACTURERS." — DECISION

USA+45 MARKET ATTIT...POLICY STAT INT CHARTS 20. PAGE 94 F1852 PROC/MFG GEOG TOP/EX

S62
SCOTT J.B.,"ANGLO-SOVIET TRADE AND ITS EFFECTS ON THE COMMONWEALTH." COM FUT UK USSR WOR+45 ECO/DEV MARKET INT/ORG CONSULT WEALTH...POLICY TREND CMN/WLTH FOR/TRADE 20. PAGE 118 F2333 NAT/G ECO/TAC

C62
GREEN L.P.,"DEVELOPMENT IN AFRICA." RHODESIA SOUTH/AFR UGANDA MARKET PROC/MFG PRODUC WEALTH ...GEOG 20. PAGE 50 F0986 BIBLIOG ECO/UNDEV AFR AGRI

B63
BARBOUR V.,CAPITALISM IN AMSTERDAM IN THE 17TH CENTURY. NETHERLAND FINAN ECO/TAC...METH/COMP BIBLIOG MUNICH 16. PAGE 10 F0185 CAP/ISM INT/TRADE MARKET WEALTH

B63
BERLE A.A. JR.,THE AMERICAN ECONOMIC REPUBLIC. STRUCT FINAN MARKET LABOR NAT/G PLAN...POLICY WELF/ST DECISION. PAGE 14 F0262 CAP/ISM ECO/TAC TREND CONCPT

B63
BONINI C.P.,SIMULATION OF INFORMATION AND DECISION SYSTEMS IN THE FIRM. MARKET BUDGET DOMIN EDU/PROP ADMIN COST ATTIT HABITAT PERCEPT PWR...CONCPT PROBABIL QUANT PREDICT HYPO/EXP BIBLIOG. PAGE 16 F0313 INDUS SIMUL DECISION MGT

B63
BURTT E.J. JR.,LABOR MARKETS, UNIONS, AND GOVERNMENT POLICIES. USA+45 MARKET NAT/G DELIB/GP CREATE BARGAIN GP/REL ORD/FREE PWR...POLICY CHARTS 20 AFL/CIO. PAGE 20 F0393 LABOR ECO/DEV CONTROL WORKER

B63
CENTRO ESTUDIOS MONETARIOS LAT,COOPERACION FINANCIERA EN AMERICA LATINA. L/A+17C PLAN PROB/SOLV CONTROL REGION DEMAND...POLICY ANTHOL 20. PAGE 22 F0433 ECO/UNDEV INT/TRADE MARKET FINAN

B63
CHAMPION J.M.,CRITICAL INCIDENTS IN MANAGEMENT. MARKET LG/CO SML/CO OP/RES ADMIN CONTROL LEAD GP/REL PERS/REL COST ATTIT SUPEGO ALL/VALS...PSY PERS/TEST BIBLIOG. PAGE 23 F0445 MGT DECISION EX/STRUC INDUS

B63
COPPOCK J.,NORTH ATLANTIC POLICY - THE AGRICULTURAL GAP. EUR+WWI ELITES ECO/DEV DIST/IND MARKET PLAN WEALTH...STAT TREND GEN/LAWS OEEC TOT/POP VAL/FREE FAO 20. PAGE 27 F0535 AGRI TEC/DEV INT/TRADE

B63
COURNOT A.A.,RESEARCHES INTO THE MATHEMATICAL PRINCIPLES OF THE THEORY OF WEALTH (1838). UNIV ECO/DEV ECO/UNDEV AGRI INDUS MARKET PAY CONTROL COST INCOME 19. PAGE 28 F0544 ECOMETRIC GEN/LAWS WEALTH

B63
GOLDMAN M.I.,SOVIET MARKETING. USSR DIST/IND FINAN RATION OWN WEALTH...SOC BIBLIOG 20. PAGE 48 F0937 MARKET ECO/TAC CONTROL MARXISM

B63
GRIGSBY W.G.,HOUSING MARKETS AND PUBLIC POLICY. USA+45 FAM NEIGH PRICE DEMAND WEALTH...POLICY CHARTS BIBLIOG METH MUNICH 20. PAGE 51 F1002 MARKET RENT HABITAT PLAN

B63
KOLKO G.,THE TRIUMPH OF CONSERVATISM. USA-45 INDUS LG/CO NAT/G PWR 20 PRESIDENT CONGRESS MONOPOLY PROGRSV/M. PAGE 72 F1421 CONSERVE CAP/ISM FINAN MARKET

B63
LEE M.W.,MACROECONOMICS: FLUCTUATIONS, GROWTH AND STABILITY (3RD ED.). MARKET LABOR TEC/DEV INT/TRADE TAX PRICE WAR PRODUC...POLICY ECOMETRIC CHARTS 19/20. PAGE 77 F1505 EQUILIB TREND WEALTH

B63
LINDBERG L.,POLITICAL DYNAMICS OF EUROPEAN ECONOMIC INTEGRATION. EUR+WWI ECO/DEV INT/ORG VOL/ASSN DELIB/GP ADMIN WEALTH...DECISION EEC TERR/GP 20. PAGE 80 F1567 MARKET ECO/TAC

B63
MEEK R.L.,THE ECONOMICS OF PHYSIOCRACY. FRANCE UK AGRI FINAN WORKER CAP/ISM TAX DEMAND EQUILIB INCOME HABITAT...CHARTS ANTHOL 17. PAGE 89 F1744 PRODUC WEALTH MARKET

B63
PAN AMERICAN UNION,THE EFFECTS OF THE EUROPEAN ECONOMIC COMMUNITY ON THE LATIN AMERICAN ECONOMIES (BMR). EUR+WWI L/A+17C ECO/UNDEV AGRI INDUS MARKET REGION 20 EEC TREATY. PAGE 103 F2024 INT/TRADE INT/ORG AGREE POLICY

B63
RANGEL I.,A INFLACAO BRASILEIRA (2ND ED.). AFR BRAZIL AGRI INDUS MARKET INT/TRADE DEMAND EQUILIB ATTIT 20. PAGE 109 F2144 ECO/UNDEV FINAN PRICE TAX

B63
RICARDO D.,THE PRINCIPLES OF POLITICAL ECONOMY AND TAXATION (1817). UK INDUS MARKET ECO/TAC INT/TRADE TARIFFS PRICE COST DEMAND OPTIMAL WEALTH...CONCPT 19 INTRVN/ECO. PAGE 111 F2183 GEN/LAWS TAX LAISSEZ

B63
ROTHBARD M.N.,AMERICA'S GREAT DEPRESSION. USA-45 NAT/G ECO/TAC LAISSEZ...POLICY IDEA/COMP 20. PAGE 114 F2248 FINAN CAP/ISM MARKET GEN/LAWS

B63
SCHOECK H.,THE NEW ARGUMENT IN ECONOMICS. UK USA+45 INDUS MARKET LABOR NAT/G ECO/TAC ADMIN ROUTINE BAL/PAY PWR...POLICY BOLIV. PAGE 117 F2309 WELF/ST FOR/AID ECO/DEV ALL/IDEOS

B63
SELF P.,THE STATE AND THE FARMER. UK ECO/DEV MARKET WORKER PRICE CONTROL GP/REL...WELF/ST 20 DEPT/AGRI. PAGE 119 F2346 AGRI NAT/G ADMIN VOL/ASSN

B63
THEOBALD R.,FREE MEN AND FREE MARKETS. USA+45 USA-45 ECO/DEV NAT/G TEC/DEV DIPLOM INT/TRADE INCOME ORD/FREE WEALTH...TREND 19/20 KEYNES/JM. PAGE 130 F2556 CONCPT ECO/TAC CAP/ISM MARKET

B63
US ECON SURVEY TEAM INDONESIA,INDONESIA - PERSPECTIVE AND PROPOSALS FOR UNITED STATES ECONOMIC AID. INDONESIA AGRI MARKET TEC/DEV DIPLOM INT/TRADE EDU/PROP 20. PAGE 136 F2678 FOR/AID ECO/UNDEV PLAN INDUS

B63
VON MISES L.,HUMAN ACTION: A TREATISE ON ECONOMICS (2ND ED.). SOCIETY MARKET TAX PAY PRICE DEMAND EQUILIB RATIONAL...PSY 20. PAGE 142 F2794 PLAN DRIVE ATTIT

L63
ADERBIGDE A.,"SYMPOSIUM ON WEST AFRICA INTEGRATION." AFR EUR+WWI FUT CULTURE SOCIETY STRATA DIST/IND INDUS MARKET SERV/IND DELIB/GP PLAN TEC/DEV DOMIN EDU/PROP LEGIT COERCE ATTIT ALL/VALS ...POLICY STAT TREND CHARTS VAL/FREE. PAGE 2 F0040 FINAN ECO/TAC REGION

S63
ADAMS F.G.,"ECONOMIC CONSIDERATIONS OF AN ATLANTIC ENERGY POLICY." EUR+WWI FUT USA+45 DIST/IND EXTR/IND MARKET CONSULT LEGIS ECO/TAC WEALTH ...POLICY EEC FOR/TRADE OEEC 20. PAGE 2 F0037 ECO/DEV TEC/DEV NUC/PWR

S63
APPERT K.,"BERECHTIGE VORBEHALTE DER SCHWEIZERISCHEN ZUR INTEGRATION." EUR+WWI UK MARKET SERV/IND NAT/G PLAN RIGID/FLEX OEEC 20 EEC. PAGE 6 F0108 FINAN ATTIT SWITZERLND

S63
BARZANSKI S.,"REGIONAL UNDERDEVELOPMENT IN THE EUROPEAN ECONOMIC COMMUNITY." EUR+WWI ELITES DIST/IND MARKET VOL/ASSN CONSULT EX/STRUC ECO/TAC RIGID/FLEX WEALTH EEC OEEC 20. PAGE 11 F0202 ECO/UNDEV PLAN

S63
BEGUIN H.,"ASPECTS STRUCTURELS DU COMMERCE EXTERIEUR DES PAYS SOUS-DEVELOPPES." FUT WOR+45 STRUCT FINAN SERV/IND POL/PAR TEC/DEV PERCEPT WEALTH FOR/TRADE 20. PAGE 12 F0229 MARKET ECO/UNDEV FOR/AID

S63
DIEBOLD W. JR.,"THE NEW SITUATION OF INTERNATIONAL TRADE POLICY." EUR+WWI FRANCE FUT UK USA+45 WOR+45 DIST/IND PLAN INT/TRADE EDU/PROP PWR WEALTH ...RECORD TREND GEN/LAWS EEC TRUE/GP VAL/FREE APPLIC 20. PAGE 33 F0636 MARKET ECO/TAC

S63
HALLSTEIN W.,"THE EUROPEAN COMMUNITY AND ATLANTIC PARTNERSHIP." EUR+WWI USA+45 MARKET NAT/G VOL/ASSN DELIB/GP ARMS/CONT NUC/PWR ATTIT PWR...CONCPT STAT TIME/SEQ TREND OEEC 20 EEC. PAGE 54 F1053 INT/ORG ECO/TAC UK

S63
MATHUR P.N.,"GAINS IN ECONOMIC GROWTH FROM INTERNATIONAL TRADE." USA-45 ECO/DEV FINAN INDUS ATTIT WEALTH...MATH QUANT STAT BIOG TREND GEN/LAWS WORK 20. PAGE 87 F1704 MARKET ECO/TAC CAP/ISM INT/TRADE

S63
POLYANOV N.,"THE DOLLAR'S VENTURES IN EUROPE." EUR+WWI FRANCE USA+45 ECO/DEV MARKET POL/PAR TEC/DEV ECO/TAC EDU/PROP DRIVE PWR WEALTH...MARXIST MYTH STAT TREND EEC 20. PAGE 107 F2100 FINAN PLAN BAL/PAY CAP/ISM

S63
PRYBYLA J.,"THE QUEST FOR ECONOMIC RATIONALITY IN THE SOVIET BLOC." COM FUT WOR+45 WOR-45 DIST/IND MARKET PLAN ECO/TAC ATTIT...METH/CNCPT TOT/POP 20. PAGE 108 F2128 ECO/DEV TREND USSR

S63
REDDAWAY W.B.,"THE ECONOMICS OF UNDERDEVELOPED COUNTRIES." S/ASIA WOR+45 WOR-45 STRATA AGRI COM/IND DIST/IND MARKET PROC/MFG PLAN TEC/DEV FOR/AID BAL/PAY ATTIT DRIVE SKILL WORK FOR/TRADE 20. PAGE 110 F2165 ECO/TAC ECO/UNDEV INDIA

S63
SCHOFLING J.A.,"EFTA: THE OTHER EUROPE." ECO/DEV MARKET CONSULT ECO/TAC WEALTH...TIME/SEQ EEC OEEC 20 EFTA. PAGE 117 F2310 EUR+WWI INT/ORG REGION

S63
SHONFIELD A.,"AFTER BRUSSELS." EUR+WWI FRANCE GERMANY UK ECO/DEV DIST/IND MARKET VOL/ASSN PLAN ECO/TAC

DELIB/GP CREATE INT/TRADE ATTIT RIGID/FLEX...RECORD TREND GEN/LAWS EEC COMMUN CMN/WLTH 20. PAGE 121 F2385

S63
SHWADRAN B.,"MIDDLE EAST OIL, 1962." ISLAM USSR ECO/DEV DIST/IND INDUS PLAN BAL/PWR DISPL DRIVE ...POLICY STAT TREND GEN/LAWS TERR/GP METH/GP EEC OEEC 20 OIL. PAGE 121 F2394
MARKET ECO/TAC INT/TRADE

S63
WALKER H.,"THE INTERNATIONAL LAW OF COMMODITY AGREEMENTS." FUT WOR+45 ECO/DEV ECO/UNDEV FINAN INT/ORG NAT/G CONSULT CREATE PLAN ECO/TAC ATTIT PERCEPT...CONCPT GEN/LAWS TOT/POP GATT 20. PAGE 142 F2804
MARKET VOL/ASSN INT/LAW INT/TRADE

S63
WILES P.J.D.,"WILL CAPITALISM AND COMMUNISM SPONTANEOUSLY CONVERGE." COM FUT USA+45 ECO/DEV DIST/IND MARKET CAP/ISM ECO/TAC RIGID/FLEX WEALTH MARXISM SOCISM...MATH STAT TREND COMPUT/IR 20. PAGE 146 F2885
PLAN TEC/DEV USSR

B64
BALL R.J.,INFLATION AND THE THEORY OF MONEY. MARKET TAX PAY PRICE TASK ADJUST BAL/PAY COST INCOME PRODUC WEALTH...METH/COMP 20 KEYNES/JM MONEY. PAGE 9 F0167
EQUILIB DEMAND POLICY

B64
BARKSDALE H.C.,MARKETING: CHANGE AND EXCHANGE. USA+45 FINAN ACADEM TEC/DEV PRICE AUTOMAT WEALTH ...CHARTS 20. PAGE 10 F0187
MARKET ECO/DEV DEMAND TREND

B64
BASTIAT F.,ECONOMIC SOPHISMS (1845). FINAN MARKET INT/TRADE TAX EDU/PROP LAISSEZ. PAGE 11 F0207
TARIFFS INDUS ECO/TAC CAP/ISM

B64
BROWN E.H.P.,A COURSE IN APPLIED ECONOMICS (2ND ED.). ECO/DEV FINAN MARKET WORKER INT/TRADE RATION RENT PAY PRICE BAL/PAY...DECISION T RESOURCE/N. PAGE 19 F0368
POLICY ECO/TAC PROB/SOLV

B64
CENTRO ESTUDIOS MONETARIOS LAT,PROBLEMAS DE PAGOS EN AMERICA LATINA. L/A+17C MARKET BUDGET ECO/TAC EFFICIENCY WEALTH 20 CENTRAL/AM. PAGE 22 F0434
FINAN INT/TRADE BAL/PAY ECO/UNDEV

B64
CHANDLER A.D. JR.,GIANT ENTERPRISE: FORD, GENERAL MOTORS, AND THE AUTOMOBILE INDUSTRY; SOURCES AND READINGS. USA+45 USA-45 FINAN MARKET CREATE ADMIN ...TIME/SEQ ANTHOL 20 AUTOMOBILE. PAGE 23 F0447
LG/CO DIST/IND LABOR MGT

B64
FEI J.C.H.,DEVELOPMENT OF THE LABOR SURPLUS ECONOMY: THEORY AND POLICY. WOR+45 AGRI INDUS MARKET PROB/SOLV TEC/DEV...STAT CHARTS GEN/LAWS METH 20 THIRD/WRLD. PAGE 40 F0772
ECO/TAC POLICY WORKER ECO/UNDEV

B64
FRIEDMANN J.,REGIONAL DEVELOPMENT AND PLANNING: A READER. AGRI MARKET NAT/G ECO/TAC INCOME...GEOG STAT CENSUS CHARTS ANTHOL BIBLIOG MUNICH 20 OPEN/SPACE. PAGE 44 F0863
PLAN REGION INDUS ECO/DEV

B64
GARFIELD PJ LOVEJOY WF,PUBLIC UTILITY ECONOMICS. DIST/IND FINAN MARKET ADMIN COST DEMAND ...TECHNIC JURID MUNICH 20 MONOPOLY. PAGE 46 F0906
T ECO/TAC OWN SERV/IND

B64
HATHAWAY D.E.,PROBLEMS OF PROGRESS IN THE AGRICULTURAL ECONOMY. USA+45 USA-45 ECO/DEV NAT/G INT/TRADE PRICE DEMAND EFFICIENCY OPTIMAL 20. PAGE 57 F1112
AGRI ECO/TAC MARKET PLAN

B64
HINSHAW R.,THE EUROPEAN COMMUNITY AND AMERICAN TRADE: A STUDY IN ATLANTIC ECONOMICS AND POLICY. EUR+WWI UK USA+45 ECO/DEV ECO/UNDEV AGRI INDUS INT/ORG NAT/G ECO/TAC TARIFFS REGION...STAT CHARTS EEC 20. PAGE 60 F1174
MARKET TREND INT/TRADE

B64
KAPLAN A.D.H.,BIG ENTERPRISE IN A COMPETITIVE SYSTEM (REV. ED.). USA+45 INDUS MARKET WORKER TEC/DEV ECO/TAC PRICE ADJUD ADMIN CONTROL...MGT CHARTS 20 MONOPOLY. PAGE 69 F1351
FINAN GP/REL NAT/G LG/CO

B64
KRAUSE L.B.,THE COMMON MARKET: PROGRESS AND CONTROVERSY. EUR+WWI UK ECO/DEV REGION...ANTHOL NATO EEC. PAGE 73 F1433
DIPLOM MARKET INT/TRADE INT/ORG

B64
LANGHOFF P.,MODELS, MEASUREMENT AND MARKETING. ACT/RES COMPUTER OP/RES PLAN BUDGET...MGT PHIL/SCI METH/CNCPT STAT PROG/TEAC BIBLIOG. PAGE 75 F1478
DECISION SIMUL MARKET R+D

B64
LI C.M.,INDUSTRIAL DEVELOPMENT IN COMMUNIST CHINA. CHINA/COM ECO/DEV ECO/UNDEV AGRI FINAN INDUS MARKET LABOR NAT/G ECO/TAC INT/TRADE EXEC ALL/VALS ...POLICY RELATIV TREND WORK TOT/POP VAL/FREE 20. PAGE 79 F1556
ASIA TEC/DEV

B64
LITVAK I.A.,MARKETING: CANADA. CANADA STRATA PROC/MFG LEGIS TEC/DEV DIPLOM INT/TRADE PRICE AUTOMAT ATTIT WEALTH...ANTHOL 20. PAGE 81 F1587
ECO/TAC MARKET ECO/DEV EFFICIENCY

B64
MANSFIELD E.,MONOPOLY POWER AND ECONOMIC PERFORMANCE: AN INTRODUCTION TO A CURRENT ISSUE OF PUBLIC POLICY. ECO/DEV INDUS NAT/G PLAN CAP/ISM PRICE CONTROL LOBBY EFFICIENCY PRODUC...POLICY 20 CONGRESS KENNEDY/JF MONOPOLY. PAGE 85 F1659
LG/CO PWR ECO/TAC MARKET

B64
MEZERIK A.G.,TRADE, AID AND ECONOMIC DEVELOPMENT. WOR+45 FINAN INDUS MARKET PLAN BAL/PWR BARGAIN FOR/AID TARIFFS EDU/PROP WEALTH...GP/COMP 20 UN GATT IMF IBRD. PAGE 91 F1777
ECO/TAC ECO/DEV INT/ORG INT/TRADE

B64
ORGANIZATION AMERICAN STATES,ECONOMIC SURVEY OF LATIN AMERICA, 1962. L/A+17C AGRI DIST/IND INDUS MARKET PROC/MFG R+D PLAN TEC/DEV ECO/TAC REGION BAL/PAY ALL/VALS...CON/ANAL ORG/CHARTS GEN/METH OAS ALL/PROG 20 ALL/PROG. PAGE 102 F1998
ECO/UNDEV CHARTS

B64
RAMAZANI R.K.,THE MIDDLE EAST AND THE EUROPEAN COMMON MARKET. EUR+WWI ISLAM ECO/DEV EXTR/IND MARKET PROC/MFG INT/ORG NAT/G TEC/DEV ECO/TAC REGION DRIVE WEALTH...STAT CHARTS EEC TOT/POP 20. PAGE 109 F2141
ECO/UNDEV ATTIT INT/TRADE

B64
SANDEE J.,EUROPE'S FUTURE CONSUMPTION. EUR+WWI FUT EDU/PROP...IDEA/COMP NAT/COMP ANTHOL 20 EUROPE. PAGE 115 F2277
MARKET ECO/DEV PREDICT PRICE

B64
STONIER A.W.,EXERCISES IN ECONOMICS. FINAN INDUS TEC/DEV RENT PAY EQUILIB PRODUC PROFIT...METH/COMP T. PAGE 127 F2498
PRICE MARKET WORKER

B64
US SENATE COMM ON JUDICIARY,HEARINGS BEFORE SUBCOMMITTEE ON ANTITRUST AND MONOPOLY: ECONOMIC CONCENTRATION VOLUMES 1-5 JULY 1964-SEPT 1966. USA+45 LAW FINAN ECO/TAC ADJUD COST EFFICIENCY PRODUC...STAT CHARTS 20 CONGRESS MONOPOLY. PAGE 140 F2749
ECO/DEV CONTROL MARKET LG/CO

B64
WELLISZ S.,THE ECONOMICS OF THE SOVIET BLOC. COM USSR INDUS WORKER PLAN BUDGET INT/TRADE TAX PRICE PRODUC WEALTH MARXISM...METH/COMP 20. PAGE 145 F2854
EFFICIENCY ADMIN MARKET

B64
WILLIAMSON O.E.,THE ECONOMICS OF DISCRETIONARY BEHAVIOR: MANAGERIAL OBJECTIVES IN A THEORY OF THE FIRM. MARKET BUDGET CAP/ISM PRODUC DRIVE PERSON ...STAT CHARTS BIBLIOG METH 20. PAGE 147 F2897
EFFICIENCY MGT ECO/TAC CHOOSE

B64
YUDELMAN M.,AFRICANS ON THE LAND. RHODESIA MARKET LABOR OWN...ECOMETRIC TREND 20. PAGE 150 F2955
ECO/DEV AFR AGRI ECO/TAC

B64
ZEBOT C.A.,THE ECONOMICS OF COMPETITIVE COEXISTENCE. CHINA/COM USSR WOR+45 FINAN MARKET FOR/AID PRICE DEMAND EQUILIB WEALTH ALL/IDEOS 20. PAGE 150 F2961
TEC/DEV DIPLOM METH/COMP

B64
ZOBER M.,MARKETING MANAGEMENT. FINAN BUDGET EDU/PROP PRICE PRODUC ATTIT...POLICY TREND CHARTS METH/COMP EQULIB 20. PAGE 150 F2966
ECO/DEV MGT CONTROL MARKET

L64
ARMENGALD A.,"ECONOMIE ET COEXISTENCE." COM EUR+WWI FUT USA+45 WOR+45 ECO/DEV ECO/UNDEV FINAN INT/ORG NAT/G EXEC CHOOSE ATTIT ALL/VALS...POLICY RELATIV DECISION TREND SOC/EXP WORK 20. PAGE 6 F0113
MARKET ECO/TAC AFR CAP/ISM

L64
BHAGWATI J.,"THE PURE THEORY OF INTERNATIONAL TRADE: A SURVEY." WOR+45 ECO/DEV ECO/UNDEV FINAN MARKET PROC/MFG INT/ORG LABOR LG/CO NAT/G TEC/DEV ECO/TAC SKILL WEALTH...POLICY RELATIV MGT CONCPT NEW/IDEA MATH QUANT GEN/LAWS FOR/TRADE 20. PAGE 14 F0276
INDUS HYPO/EXP

L64
HAAS E.B.,"ECONOMICS AND DIFFERENTIAL PATTERNS OF POLITICAL INTEGRATION: PROJECTIONS ABOUT UNITY IN LATIN AMERICA." SOCIETY NAT/G DELIB/GP ACT/RES CREATE PLAN ECO/TAC REGION ROUTINE ATTIT DRIVE PWR WEALTH...CONCPT TREND CHARTS LAFTA TERR/GP 20. PAGE 52 F1020
L/A+17C INT/ORG MARKET

L64
STERN R.M.,"POLICIES FOR TRADE AND DEVELOPMENT." AFR FUT WOR+45 DIST/IND FINAN NAT/G DELIB/GP PLAN ECO/TAC ORD/FREE WEALTH...POLICY STAT TIME/SEQ CHARTS METH/GP 20. PAGE 126 F2480
MARKET ECO/UNDEV INT/TRADE

S64
GARDNER R.N.,"GATT AND THE UNITED NATIONS
INT/ORG

CONFERENCE ON TRADE AND DEVELOPMENT." USA+45 WOR+45 SOCIETY ECO/UNDEV MARKET NAT/G DELIB/GP ACT/RES PLAN ECO/TAC TARIFFS EDU/PROP ROUTINE DRIVE RIGID/FLEX WEALTH...DECISION MGT TREND UN TOT/POP 20 GATT. PAGE 46 F0905 — INT/TRADE

S64
GERBET P.,"LA MISE EN OEUVRE DU MARCHE COMMUN AGRICOLE." ECO/DEV MARKET INT/ORG NAT/G PLAN EDU/PROP NAT/LISM WEALTH...OBS EEC VAL/FREE 20. PAGE 47 F0917 — EUR+WWI AGRI REGION

S64
HERMAN L.M.,"THE ECONOMIC CONTENT OF SOVIET TRADE WITH THE WEST." WOR+45 ECO/DEV ECO/UNDEV AGRI COM/IND INDUS CAP/ISM ECO/TAC ATTIT RIGID/FLEX WEALTH...OBS TREND VAL/FREE MARX/KARL 20. PAGE 59 F1152 — COM MARKET INT/TRADE USSR

S64
HUELIN D.,"ECONOMIC INTEGRATION IN LATIN AMERICAN: PROGRESS AND PROBLEMS." L/A+17C ECO/DEV AGRI DIST/IND FINAN INDUS NAT/G VOL/ASSN CONSULT DELIB/GP EX/STRUC ACT/RES PLAN TEC/DEV ECO/TAC ROUTINE BAL/PAY WEALTH FOR/TRADE WORK TERR/GP 20. PAGE 63 F1232 — MARKET ECO/UNDEV INT/TRADE

S64
HUTCHINSON E.C.,"AMERICAN AID TO AFRICA." FUT USA+45 MARKET INT/ORG LOC/G NAT/G PUB/INST PLAN ECO/TAC ATTIT RIGID/FLEX...POLICY CONCPT TREND TERR/GP 20. PAGE 63 F1248 — AFR ECO/UNDEV FOR/AID

S64
KLEIN H.,"AMERICAN OIL COMPANIES IN LATIN AMERICA: THE BOLIVIAN EXPERIENCE." L/A+17C USA+45 USA-45 EXTR/IND LG/CO NAT/G ECO/TAC WEALTH...POLICY GEN/LAWS BOLIV TOT/POP 20 OIL. PAGE 72 F1405 — MARKET ECO/UNDEV NAT/LISM

S64
KOJIMA K.,"THE PATTERN OF INTERNATIONAL TRADE AMONG ADVANCED COUNTRIES." EUR+WWI UK USA+45 WOR+45 MARKET NAT/G ECO/TAC WEALTH...MATH STAT CON/ANAL CHARTS METH/GP EEC CHINJAP 20 CHINJAP. PAGE 72 F1419 — ECO/DEV TREND INT/TRADE

S64
PATEL S.J.,"THE ECONOMIC DISTANCE BETWEEN NATIONS: ITS ORIGIN, MEASUREMENT AND OUTLOOK." WOR+45 ECO/DEV AGRI FINAN INDUS MARKET LABOR NAT/G CONSULT TEC/DEV ECO/TAC WEALTH...POLICY RELATIV MGT TREND WORK 20. PAGE 103 F2035 — ECO/UNDEV PLAN

S64
READER D.H.,"A SURVEY OF CATEGORIES OF ECONOMIC ACTIVITIES AMONG THE PEOPLES OF AFRICA." AGRI INDUS MARKET KIN HEALTH SKILL WEALTH...GEOG METH/CNCPT CHARTS TERR/GP WORK TOT/POP VAL/FREE 20. PAGE 110 F2160 — TEC/DEV ECO/UNDEV AFR

B65
ALDERSON W.,DYNAMIC MARKETING BEHAVIOR. USA+45 FINAN CREATE TEC/DEV EDU/PROP PRICE COST 20. PAGE 3 F0057 — MGT MARKET ATTIT CAP/ISM

B65
BAERRESEN D.W.,LATIN AMERICAN TRADE PATTERNS. L/A+17C ECO/UNDEV AGRI INDUS MARKET CREATE ...NET/THEORY CHARTS LAFTA. PAGE 8 F0149 — INT/TRADE STAT REGION

B65
BAUMOL W.J.,ECONOMIC THEORY AND OPERATIONS ANALYSIS (2ND ED.). MARKET LG/CO BUDGET PRICE COST EQUILIB PRODUC...DECISION MATH CHARTS GAME 20. PAGE 12 F0219 — OP/RES ECO/DEV METH/COMP STAT

B65
BLAIR T.L.V.,AFRICA: A MARKET PROFILE. AFR COM/IND DIST/IND FINAN UTIL...DECISION CHARTS BIBLIOG 20. PAGE 15 F0295 — MARKET OP/RES ECO/UNDEV INDUS

B65
BRENNAN M.J.,PATTERNS OF MARKET BEHAVIOR. AFR USA+45 OP/RES CAP/ISM ECO/TAC INT/TRADE...CHARTS METH/COMP ANTHOL TIME 20. PAGE 18 F0346 — MARKET LABOR FINAN ECOMETRIC

B65
BRYCE M.D.,POLICIES AND METHODS FOR INDUSTRIAL DEVELOPMENT. WOR+45 FINAN MARKET CONSULT TARIFFS TAX COST. PAGE 20 F0379 — INDUS PLAN ECO/DEV TEC/DEV

B65
COLLOQUE SUR LA PLANIFICATION,LA PLANIFICATION COMME PROCESSUS DE DECISION. FRANCE SOCIETY MARKET LABOR LEGIS GP/REL EFFICIENCY INCOME ATTIT TECHRACY ...MYTH IDEA/COMP 20. PAGE 26 F0508 — PLAN ECO/TAC PROB/SOLV

B65
COX D.W.,THE PERILS OF PEACE* CONVERSION TO WHAT? FUT USA+45 ECO/DEV NAT/G ACT/RES CREATE PLAN NUC/PWR WAR DEMAND MGT. PAGE 28 F0546 — PEACE WORKER FORCES MARKET

B65
CRANE E.,MARKETING COMMUNICATION: A BEHAVIORAL APPROACH TO MEN, MESSAGES, AND MEDIA. STRATA R+D VOL/ASSN CROWD DRIVE PERSON SKILL WEALTH. PAGE 28 F0551 — EDU/PROP MARKET PERCEPT ATTIT

B65
DOWD L.P.,PRINCIPLES OF WORLD BUSINESS. SERV/IND NAT/G DIPLOM ECO/TAC TARIFFS...INT/LAW JURID 20. PAGE 34 F0657 — INT/TRADE MGT FINAN MARKET

B65
GORDON W.,THE POLITICAL ECONOMY OF LATIN AMERICA. L/A+17C FINAN MARKET PROB/SOLV TEC/DEV RECEIVE ADMIN WEALTH 20. PAGE 49 F0962 — ECO/UNDEV INT/TRADE REGION POLICY

B65
GRAMPP W.D.,ECONOMIC LIBERALISM; THE BEGINNINGS (VOL. I). USA-45 WOR-45 MARKET LABOR ATTIT WEALTH ...POLICY CONCPT BIBLIOG GREECE/ANC MERCANTLST REPUBLICAN FEDERALIST. PAGE 50 F0974 — ECO/DEV CAP/ISM IDEA/COMP ECO/TAC

B65
GRAMPP W.D.,ECONOMIC LIBERALISM; THE CLASSICAL VIEW (VOL. II). MOD/EUR SOCIETY MARKET INT/TRADE NAT/LISM WEALTH LAISSEZ...POLICY PSY CONCPT BIBLIOG 19 SMITH/ADAM HUME/D MILL/JS. PAGE 50 F0975 — ECO/DEV CAP/ISM IDEA/COMP ECO/TAC

B65
GRIFFIN C.E.,THE FREE SOCIETY. CONSTN SOCIETY MARKET FEDERAL RATIONAL WEALTH...MAJORIT 20 CIVIL/LIB. PAGE 51 F0999 — CONCPT ORD/FREE CAP/ISM POPULISM

B65
INT. BANK RECONSTR. DEVELOP.,ECONOMIC DEVELOPMENT OF KUWAIT. ISLAM KUWAIT AGRI FINAN MARKET EX/STRUC TEC/DEV ECO/TAC ADMIN WEALTH...OBS CON/ANAL CHARTS 20. PAGE 64 F1266 — INDUS NAT/G

B65
LYONS G.M.,AMERICA: PURPOSE AND POWER. UK USA+45 FINAN INDUS MARKET WORKER TEC/DEV DIPLOM AUTOMAT NUC/PWR WAR RACE/REL ORD/FREE 20 EEC CONGRESS SUPREME/CT CIV/RIGHTS. PAGE 82 F1617 — PWR PROB/SOLV ECO/DEV TASK

B65
MARCUS E.,INTERNATIONAL TRADE AND FINANCE. EFFICIENCY EQUILIB...CHARTS METH/COMP BIBLIOG METH T 20. PAGE 85 F1664 — INT/TRADE FINAN MARKET WEALTH

B65
MUSHKIN S.J.,PROPERTY TAXES: THE 1970 OUTLOOK (PAMPHLET). FUT USA+45 ECO/DEV MARKET PROVS PLAN ...PROBABIL STAT CENSUS PREDICT CHARTS METH 20. PAGE 95 F1872 — TAX OWN FINAN LOC/G

B65
ONSLOW C.,ASIAN ECONOMIC DEVELOPMENT. BURMA CEYLON INDIA MALAYSIA PAKISTAN S/ASIA AGRI INDUS MARKET PROB/SOLV CAP/ISM FOR/AID INT/TRADE DEMAND WEALTH ...POLICY ANTHOL 20. PAGE 101 F1991 — ECO/UNDEV ECO/TAC PLAN NAT/G

B65
PROCHNOW H.V.,WORLD ECONOMIC PROBLEMS AND POLICIES. INDIA ISRAEL WOR+45 AGRI LABOR PROB/SOLV FOR/AID TARIFFS CONTROL BAL/PAY NAT/LISM WEALTH...TREND CHARTS 20 CHINJAP EEC. PAGE 108 F2124 — MARKET ECO/TAC PRODUC IDEA/COMP

B65
ROSS A.M.,EMPLOYMENT POLICY AND THE LABOR MARKET. USA+45 MARKET LABOR NAT/G PROB/SOLV PAY EDU/PROP PARTIC UTIL...POLICY 20. PAGE 114 F2242 — ECO/DEV WORKER WEALTH DEMAND

B65
ROWE J.W.,PRIMARY COMMODITIES IN INTERNATIONAL TRADE. MARKET CAP/ISM ECO/TAC DEMAND...NAT/COMP 20. PAGE 114 F2253 — INT/TRADE AGRI RATION PRICE

B65
RUEFF J.,THE ROLE AND THE RULE OF GOLD: AN ARGUMENT (PAMPHLET). AFR FRANCE USA+45 WOR+45 MARKET NAT/G PLAN DIPLOM ATTIT...POLICY INT 20 DEGAULLE/C. PAGE 115 F2258 — FINAN ECO/DEV INT/TRADE BAL/PAY

B65
SCHWARTZ G.,SCIENCE IN MARKETING. OP/RES PROB/SOLV INT/TRADE PRICE CONTROL ADJUST PRODUC...CONCPT 20. PAGE 118 F2324 — PHIL/SCI TREND ECO/DEV MARKET

B65
US SENATE COMM ON JUDICIARY,ANTITRUST EXEMPTIONS FOR AGREEMENTS RELATING TO BALANCE OF PAYMENTS. FINAN ECO/TAC CONTROL WEALTH...POLICY 20 CONGRESS. PAGE 140 F2750 — BAL/PAY ADJUD MARKET INT/TRADE

B65
WISH J.R.,ECONOMIC DEVELOPMENT IN LATIN AMERICA: AN ANNOTATED BIBLIOGRAPHY. L/A+17C COM/IND MARKET R+D CREATE CAP/ISM ATTIT...STAT METH 20. PAGE 148 F2912 — BIBLIOG/A ECO/UNDEV TEC/DEV AGRI

L65
WILLIAMS S.,"NEGOTIATING INVESTMENT IN EMERGING COUNTRIES." USA+45 WOR+45 INDUS MARKET NAT/G TOP/EX TEC/DEV CAP/ISM ECO/TAC ADMIN SKILL WEALTH...POLICY RELATIV MGT WORK 20. PAGE 147 F2894 — FINAN ECO/UNDEV

L65
WIONCZEK M.,"LATIN AMERICA FREE TRADE ASSOCIATION." AGRI DIST/IND FINAN INDUS INT/ORG LABOR NAT/G TEC/DEV ECO/TAC HEALTH SKILL WEALTH...POLICY RELATIV MGT LAFTA 20. PAGE 148 F2909 — L/A+17C MARKET REGION

S65
DICKMAN A.B.,"SOUTH AFRICAN MONEY MARKET - PROGRESS AND PROBLEMS SINCE 1960." SOUTH/AFR PROB/SOLV ROLE ...PREDICT CHARTS 20. PAGE 33 F0633
FINAN PLAN MARKET

S65
MULLER A.L.,"THE ECONOMIC POSITION OF THE ASIANS IN AFRICA." AFR SOUTH/AFR ECO/UNDEV MARKET ECO/TAC GP/REL INCOME...CHARTS IND 20 MONOPOLY ASIANS. PAGE 95 F1856
WORKER RACE/REL CAP/ISM DISCRIM

B66
AMER ENTERPRISE INST FOR PUBL,INTERNATIONAL PAYMENTS PROBLEM. MARKET DIPLOM DEBATE PRICE COST INCOME 20. PAGE 4 F0082
FINAN INT/TRADE POLICY

B66
BALDWIN R.E.,ECONOMIC DEVELOPMENT AND EXPORT GROWTH: A STUDY OF NORTHERN RHODESIA, 1920-1960. AFR RHODESIA AGRI EXTR/IND FINAN MARKET LABOR WORKER ECO/TAC...CONCPT NEW/IDEA MUNICH 20. PAGE 9 F0166
ECO/UNDEV TEC/DEV INT/TRADE CAP/ISM

B66
BARAN P.A.,MONOPOLY CAPITAL; AN ESSAY ON THE AMERICAN ECONOMIC AND SOCIAL ORDER. USA+45 USA-45 ECO/UNDEV FINAN MARKET PLAN DIPLOM COLONIAL RACE/REL DEMAND MARXISM...CHARTS 20. PAGE 9 F0179
LG/CO CAP/ISM PRICE CONTROL

B66
BOYD H.W.,MARKETING MANAGEMENT: CASES FROM EMERGING COUNTRIES. BRAZIL GHANA ISRAEL WOR+45 ADMIN PERS/REL ATTIT HABITAT WEALTH...ANTHOL 20 ARGEN CASEBOOK. PAGE 17 F0332
MGT ECO/UNDEV PROB/SOLV MARKET

B66
BROWN R.T.,TRANSPORT AND THE ECONOMIC INTEGRATION OF SOUTH AMERICA. L/A+17C ECO/UNDEV NAT/G OP/RES DIPLOM INT/TRADE REGION WEALTH...ECOMETRIC GEOG STAT LAFTA TIME. PAGE 19 F0373
MARKET DIST/IND SIMUL

B66
ECKSTEIN A.,COMMUNIST CHINA'S ECONOMIC GROWTH AND FOREIGN TRADE* IMPLICATIONS FOR US POLICY. COM USA+45 USSR STRUCT INDUS MARKET DIPLOM ECO/TAC FOR/AID INT/TRADE...STAT CHARTS. PAGE 36 F0696
ASIA ECO/UNDEV CREATE PWR

B66
FELKER J.L.,SOVIET ECONOMIC CONTROVERSIES. USSR INDUS PLAN INT/TRADE GP/REL MARXISM SOCISM...POLICY 20. PAGE 40 F0778
ECO/DEV MARKET PROFIT PRICE

B66
FELLNER W.,MAINTAINING AND RESTORING BALANCE IN INTERNATIONAL PAYMENTS. ECO/UNDEV MARKET ECO/TAC PRICE INCOME WEALTH...POLICY METH/COMP 20 MONEY. PAGE 40 F0781
BAL/PAY DIPLOM FINAN INT/TRADE

B66
FRANKEL P.H.,MATTEI; OIL AND POWER POLITICS. ITALY EXTR/IND MARKET GP/REL NAT/LISM SOCISM...POLICY MGT BIOG 20 MATTEI/E. PAGE 43 F0844
LEAD NAT/G CONTROL LG/CO

B66
HALLER H.,DAS PROBLEM DER GELDWERTSTABILITAT. MARKET LABOR INCOME PRODUC...POLICY 20. PAGE 54 F1049
PRICE COST FINAN ECO/TAC

B66
INGRAM J.C.,INTERNATIONAL ECONOMIC PROBLEMS. ECO/DEV ECO/UNDEV INDUS MARKET TEC/DEV TARIFFS BAL/PAY CENTRAL...POLICY 20 EEC. PAGE 64 F1265
INT/TRADE INT/ORG FINAN

B66
JENSEN F.B.,READINGS IN INTERNATIONAL ECONOMIC RELATIONS. COM ECO/UNDEV MARKET NAT/G FOR/AID ...ANTHOL 20. PAGE 67 F1317
BAL/PAY INT/TRADE FINAN

B66
KAESTNER K.,GESAMTWIRTSCHAFTLICHE PLANUNG IN EINER GEMISCHTEN WIRTSCHAFTSORDNUNG (WIRTSCHAFTSPOLITISCHE STUDIEN 5). GERMANY/W WOR+45 WOR-45 INDUS MARKET NAT/G ACT/RES GP/REL INGP/REL PRODUC...ECOMETRIC MGT BIBLIOG 20. PAGE 68 F1346
ECO/TAC PLAN POLICY PREDICT

B66
LAMBERG R.F.,PRAG UND DIE DRITTE WELT. AFR ASIA CZECHOSLVK L/A+17C MARKET TEC/DEV ECO/TAC REV ATTIT 20 TREATY. PAGE 75 F1462
DIPLOM ECO/UNDEV INT/TRADE FOR/AID

B66
MACBEAN A.I.,EXPORT INSTABILITY AND ECONOMIC DEVELOPMENT. CHILE PAKISTAN PUERT/RICO TANZANIA UGANDA WOR+45 MARKET ECO/TAC...POLICY REGRESS CHARTS BIBLIOG TIME 20. PAGE 83 F1622
INT/TRADE ECO/UNDEV ECOMETRIC INSPECT

B66
MEERHAEGHE M.,INTERNATIONAL ECONOMIC INSTITUTIONS. EUR+WWI FINAN INDUS MARKET PLAN TARIFFS BAL/PAY EQUILIB...POLICY BIBLIOG/A 20 GATT OEEC EEC IBRD EURCOALSTL. PAGE 89 F1745
ECO/TAC ECO/DEV INT/TRADE INT/ORG

B66
NICOSIA F.N.,CONSUMER DECISION PROCESSES* MARKETING AND ADVERTISING IMPLICATIONS. DIST/IND INDUS CONSULT EDU/PROP ATTIT. PAGE 98 F1925
MARKET PROB/SOLV SERV/IND

B66
NICOSIA M.N.,CONSUMER DECISION PROCESSES: MARKETING AND ADVERTISING IMPLICATIONS. ECO/TAC ATTIT PERSON ...DECISION MGT SOC. PAGE 98 F1926
MARKET SOCIETY CREATE ACT/RES

B66
PERSALL E.S.,AN ECONOMETRIC STUDY OF FINANCIAL MARKETS. COMPUTER PROB/SOLV TEC/DEV...MATH STAT CHARTS METH/COMP BIBLIOG 20. PAGE 105 F2066
ECOMETRIC FINAN MARKET METH

B66
SCHNEIDER E.,WIRTSCHAFTSKREISLAUF UND WIRTSCHAFTSWACHSTUM. ECO/DEV MARKET...CONCPT 20 MONEY. PAGE 117 F2306
ECO/TAC FINAN INCOME COST

B66
TURNER H.A.,PRICES, WAGES, AND INCOME POLICIES IN INDUSTRIALIZED MARKET ECONOMIES. AFR WOR+45 ECO/DEV INDUS PROB/SOLV ECO/TAC CONTROL WEALTH...CHARTS 20 INTRVN/ECO. PAGE 131 F2593
PRICE PAY MARKET INCOME

B66
US DEPARTMENT OF LABOR,PRODUCTIVITY: A BIBLIOGRAPHY. ECO/DEV INDUS MARKET OP/RES AUTOMAT COST...STAT 20. PAGE 135 F2668
BIBLIOG/A PRODUC LABOR PLAN

B66
WALTON S.D.,AMERICAN BUSINESS AND ITS ENVIRONMENT. USA+45 LAW CONSTN FINAN MARKET LOC/G EX/STRUC CT/SYS COST PRODUC...STAT 20. PAGE 143 F2813
PRICE PROFIT

B66
WILCOX C.,ECONOMIES OF THE WORLD TODAY: THEIR ORGANIZATION, DEVELOPMENT, AND PERFORMANCE (2ND ED.). CHINA/COM COM INDIA NIGERIA UK WOR+45 WOR-45 INDUS MARKET PLAN ECO/TAC SOCISM...CHARTS METH/COMP 20. PAGE 146 F2878
ECO/DEV ECO/UNDEV MARXISM CAP/ISM

S66
MARKSHAK J.,"ECONOMIC PLANNING AND THE COST OF THINKING." COM MARKET EX/STRUC...DECISION GEN/LAWS. PAGE 85 F1672
ECO/UNDEV ECO/TAC PLAN ECO/DEV

B67
ANDERSON S.V.,THE NORDIC COUNCIL: A STUDY OF SCANDINAVIAN REGIONALISM. DENMARK FINLAND ICELAND NORWAY SWEDEN MARKET NAT/G VOL/ASSN CONSULT PARL/PROC ATTIT...TIME/SEQ BIBLIOG 20. PAGE 5 F0098
INT/ORG REGION DIPLOM LEGIS

B67
HAGUE D.C.,PRICE FORMATION IN VARIOUS ECONOMIES; PROCEEDINGS OF A CONFERENCE HELD BY THE INTERNATIONAL ECONOMIC ASSOCIATION. WOR+45 FINAN MARKET PLAN CONFER COST...DECISION MATH PREDICT CHARTS SIMUL 20 INTL/ECON. PAGE 53 F1037
PRICE CAP/ISM SOCISM METH/COMP

B67
HOGAN J.,THE US BALANCE OF PAYMENTS AND CAPITAL FLOWS. MARKET INT/ORG ECO/TAC PRICE CONTROL WEALTH ...METH/COMP 20 EEC. PAGE 61 F1192
BAL/PAY FINAN DIPLOM INT/TRADE

B67
KEWEN P.B.,INTERNATIONAL ECONOMICS (2ND ED.). USA+45 WOR+45 MARKET TARIFFS...BIBLIOG T 20. PAGE 70 F1384
INT/TRADE BAL/PAY FINAN EQUILIB

B67
KREININ M.E.,ALTERNATIVE COMMERCIAL POLICIES - THEIR EFFECT ON THE AMERICAN ECONOMY. USA+45 LAW ECO/DEV MARKET INT/ORG DIPLOM ECO/TAC TARIFFS PRICE DEMAND WEALTH...QUANT EEC AFTA. PAGE 73 F1437
INT/TRADE BAL/PAY NAT/G POLICY

B67
NARVER J.C.,CONGLOMERATE MERGERS AND MARKET COMPETITION. USA+45 LAW STRUCT ADMIN LEAD RISK COST PROFIT WEALTH...POLICY CHARTS BIBLIOG. PAGE 96 F1892
DEMAND LG/CO MARKET MGT

B67
ROBINSON R.D.,INTERNATIONAL MANAGEMENT. LAW MARKET LABOR PRICE CONTROL COST DEMAND OWN PRODUC WEALTH 20. PAGE 113 F2225
T OP/RES MGT DIPLOM

B67
ROSS A.M.,EMPLOYMENT, RACE, AND POVERTY. USA+45 LAW STRATA MARKET LABOR EDU/PROP ISOLAT SKILL...MGT ANTHOL 20 NEGRO. PAGE 114 F2244
RACE/REL WORKER WEALTH DISCRIM

B67
SCOTT J.C.,ANTITRUST AND TRADE REGULATION TODAY: 1967. USA+45 MARKET LG/CO DELIB/GP LEGIS CAP/ISM INT/TRADE TAX PRICE INGP/REL WEALTH 20 SUPREME/CT. PAGE 118 F2334
NAT/G INDUS CONTROL JURID

B67
US CONGRESS SENATE,SURVEY OF THE ALLIANCE FOR PROGRESS; INFLATION IN LATIN AMERICA (PAMPHLET). USA+45 MARKET INT/ORG DIPLOM INT/TRADE BAL/PAY SENATE ALL/PROG. PAGE 135 F2666
L/A+17C FINAN POLICY FOR/AID

L67
BERNHARD R.C.,"COMPETITION IN LAW AND ECONOMICS." LAW PLAN PRICE CONTROL PRODUC PROFIT...METH/CNCPT IDEA/COMP GEN/LAWS 20. PAGE 14 F0265
MARKET POLICY NAT/G CT/SYS

L67
DROBNIG U.,"CONFLICT OF LAWS AND THE EUROPEAN ECONOMIC COMMUNITY." EUR+WWI PROB/SOLV DIPLOM ...JURID EEC. PAGE 34 F0663
INT/LAW ADJUD INT/ORG

MARKET

L67
MEIER G.M.,"UNCTAD PROPOSALS FOR INTERNATIONAL ECONOMIC REFORM." WOR+45 MARKET INT/ORG TARIFFS CONFER UN GATT IMF. PAGE 89 F1749 — INT/TRADE FINAN INT/LAW ECO/UNDEV

L67
ROBERTS E.F.,"THE CASE OF THE UNWARY HOME BUYER: THE HOUSING MERCHANT DID IT." USA+45 CLIENT DIST/IND MARKET LG/CO SML/CO PROB/SOLV LEGIT COST PROFIT. PAGE 112 F2207 — ADJUD CONSTRUC OWN LAW

L67
SEABERG G.P.,"THE DRUG ABUSE PROBLEMS AND SOME PROPOSALS." UK USA+45 MARKET SANCTION CRIME ...POLICY NEW/IDEA. PAGE 119 F2339 — BIO/SOC LAW ADJUD PROB/SOLV

S67
ALBAUM G.,"INFORMATION FLOW AND DECENTRALIZED DECISION MAKING IN MARKETING." EX/STRUC COMPUTER OP/RES PROB/SOLV EFFICIENCY OPTIMAL...METH/COMP ORG/CHARTS 20. PAGE 3 F0056 — LG/CO ROUTINE KNOWL MARKET

S67
COSGROVE C.A.,"AGRICULTURE, FINANCE AND POLITICS IN THE EUROPEAN COMMUNITY." EUR+WWI DIST/IND MARKET INT/ORG VOL/ASSN DELIB/GP TEC/DEV BAL/PWR BARGAIN ECO/TAC RATION CONFER 20 EEC. PAGE 28 F0538 — ECO/DEV DIPLOM AGRI INT/TRADE

S67
DAVIS O.A.,"ON THE DISTINCTION BETWEEN PUBLIC AND PRIVATE GOODS." USA+45 COM/IND LG/CO NAT/G TV DEBATE PRICE ADMIN ROLE...MATH IDEA/COMP. PAGE 31 F0593 — MARKET OWN CONCPT

S67
HALE G.E.,"EXPANDING ENTERPRISE: GEOGRAPHICAL CURBS ON MERGERS." USA+45 MARKET LG/CO ADJUD CONTROL GP/REL 20. PAGE 53 F1041 — LAW HABITAT INDUS EX/STRUC

S67
KOTLER P.,"OPERATIONS RESEARCH IN MARKETING." USA+45 DIST/IND INDUS LG/CO CONSULT BUDGET TASK DEMAND EFFICIENCY PROFIT WEALTH DECISION. PAGE 73 F1429 — ECOMETRIC OP/RES MARKET PLAN

S67
MALKIN A.,"BUSINESS BOOKS OF 1966." INDUS LABOR OP/RES TEC/DEV CAP/ISM ECO/TAC INCOME WEALTH 20. PAGE 84 F1649 — BIBLIOG/A FINAN MARKET

S67
RICHMAN B.M.,"SOVIET MANAGEMENT IN TRANSITION." USSR FINAN MARKET EX/STRUC PLAN PROB/SOLV TEC/DEV CONTROL LEAD CENTRAL EFFICIENCY...METH/COMP 20 REFORMERS. PAGE 111 F2186 — MGT MARXISM POLICY AUTHORIT

S67
ROCKE J.R.M.,"THE BRITISH EXPORT BATTLE FOR THE CARIBBEAN" GP/REL...POLICY 20 CMN/WLTH. PAGE 113 F2229 — INT/TRADE DIPLOM MARKET ECO/TAC

S67
SCHACHTER G.,"REGIONAL DEVELOPMENT IN THE ITALIAN DUAL ECONOMY" ITALY AGRI INDUS MARKET WORKER ECO/TAC CONTROL INCOME PRODUC 20. PAGE 116 F2287 — REGION ECO/UNDEV NAT/G PROB/SOLV

S67
SCHNEIDER E.,"DIE ENTPOLITISIERUNG DES DEUTSCHEN OSTHANDELS." AFR MARKET TEC/DEV OBJECTIVE 20. PAGE 117 F2307 — ATTIT INT/TRADE ECO/TAC DIPLOM

B75
JEVONS W.S.,MONEY AND THE MECHANISM OF EXCHANGE. INDUS MARKET DIPLOM COST EQUILIB WEALTH LAISSEZ ...GEN/LAWS 19 MONEY. PAGE 67 F1319 — PRICE FINAN ECO/TAC POLICY

B95
SELIGMAN E.R.A.,ESSAYS IN TAXATION. NEW/ZEALND PRUSSIA UK USA-45 MARKET LOC/G CREATE PRICE CONTROL INCOME OWN WEALTH...GOV/COMP METH/COMP 19. PAGE 119 F2349 — TAX TARIFFS INDUS NAT/G

B98
MARSHALL A.,PRINCIPLES OF ECONOMICS. INDUS WORKER PRICE COST EQUILIB INCOME OPTIMAL PRODUC...TIME/SEQ METH RICARDO/D. PAGE 86 F1678 — WEALTH GEN/LAWS MARKET

MARKETING SYSTEM....SEE MARKET

MARKHAM J.W. F1671

MARKSHAK J. F1672

MARQUAND H.A. F1673

MARRIAGE....WEDLOCK; SEE ALSO LOVE

B55
SERRANO MOSCOSO E.,A STATEMENT OF THE LAWS OF ECUADOR IN MATTERS AFFECTING BUSINESS (2ND ED.). ECUADOR INDUS LABOR LG/CO NAT/G LEGIS TAX CONTROL MARRIAGE 20. PAGE 120 F2359 — FINAN ECO/UNDEV LAW CONSTN

B55
WRONG D.H.,AMERICAN AND CANADIAN VIEWPOINTS. CANADA USA+45 CONSTN STRATA FAM SECT WORKER ECO/TAC EDU/PROP ADJUD MARRIAGE...IDEA/COMP 20. PAGE 149 F2936 — DIPLOM ATTIT NAT/COMP CULTURE

B59
LOPEZ VILLAMIL H.,A STATEMENT OF THE LAWS OF THE HONDURAS IN MATTERS AFFECTING BUSINESS (2ND ED.). HONDURAS DIST/IND EXTR/IND FINAN WORKER TAX DEATH MARRIAGE OWN MARITIME 20 MIGRATION. PAGE 82 F1600 — CONSTN INDUS LEGIS NAT/G

B61
RUEDA B.,A STATEMENT OF THE LAWS OF COLOMBIA IN MATTERS AFFECTING BUSINESS (3RD ED.). INDUS FAM LABOR LG/CO NAT/G LEGIS TAX CONTROL MARRIAGE 20 COLOMB. PAGE 115 F2257 — FINAN ECO/UNDEV LAW CONSTN

B61
SEPULVEDA C.,A STATEMENT OF THE LAWS OF MEXICO IN MATTERS AFFECTING BUSINESS (3RD ED.). AGRI DIST/IND EXTR/IND FINAN INDUS WORKER TAX MARRIAGE OWN ORD/FREE...BIBLIOG 20 MEXIC/AMER TREATY MIGRATION MONOPOLY. PAGE 119 F2356 — CONSTN NAT/G JURID LEGIS

B62
PASTOR R.S.,A STATEMENT OF THE LAWS OF PARAGUAY IN MATTERS AFFECTING BUSINESS (2ND ED.). PARAGUAY INDUS FAM LABOR LG/CO NAT/G LEGIS TAX CONTROL MARRIAGE 20. PAGE 103 F2033 — FINAN ECO/UNDEV LAW CONSTN

B62
VACCARO J.R.,A STATEMENT OF THE LAWS OF CHILE IN MATTERS AFFECTING BUSINESS (3RD ED.). CHILE AGRI FINAN FAM LABOR ECO/TAC FOR/AID TAX ADJUD CONTROL MARRIAGE STRANGE...BIBLIOG 20. PAGE 140 F2756 — CONSTN LAW INDUS MGT

B64
TELLADO A.,A STATEMENT OF THE LAWS OF THE DOMINICAN REPUBLIC IN MATTERS AFFECTING BUSINESS (3RD ED.). DOMIN/REP AGRI DIST/IND EXTR/IND FINAN FAM WORKER ECO/TAC TAX CT/SYS MARRIAGE OWN...BIBLIOG 20 MIGRATION. PAGE 129 F2542 — CONSTN LEGIS NAT/G INDUS

B65
LUGO-MARENCO J.J.,A STATEMENT OF THE LAWS OF NICARAGUA IN MATTERS AFFECTING BUSINESS. NICARAGUA AGRI DIST/IND EXTR/IND FINAN INDUS FAM WORKER INT/TRADE TAX MARRIAGE OWN BIO/SOC 20 TREATY RESOURCE/N MIGRATION. PAGE 82 F1606 — CONSTN NAT/G LEGIS JURID

B67
BIRMINGHAM W.,A STUDY OF CONTEMPORARY GHANA VOL. I: SOME ASPECTS OF SOCIAL STRUCTURE. AFR GHANA AGRI FAM SECT PLAN EDU/PROP MARRIAGE OWN...POLICY STAT CHARTS MUNICH 20. PAGE 15 F0287 — SOCIETY STRUCT CENSUS ECO/UNDEV

MARRIS P. F1674,F1675

MARSH D.C. F1676

MARSH J.F. F1677

MARSHALL A. F1678

MARSHALL A.H. F1679

MARSHALL/A....ALFRED MARSHALL

N19
HABERLER G.,A SURVEY OF INTERNATIONAL TRADE THEORY (PAMPHLET). FINAN NAT/G COST INCOME 18/20 MONEY HUME/D MARSHALL/A. PAGE 52 F1022 — INT/TRADE BAL/PAY GEN/LAWS POLICY

B35
HICKS J.R.,THE THEORY OF WAGES. INDUS NAT/G PAY PRICE CONTROL COST EFFICIENCY WEALTH 19/20 MARSHALL/A CLARK/JB. PAGE 59 F1164 — INCOME WORKER LABOR PRODUC

B48
HICKS J.R.,VALUE AND CAPITAL. FINAN PRICE EQUILIB INCOME PRODUC WEALTH...TIME/SEQ 20 MARSHALL/A PARETO/V SAMUELSN/P. PAGE 59 F1165 — ECOMETRIC MATH DEMAND PROB/SOLV

MARSHALL/J....JOHN MARSHALL

B60
MENDELSON W.,CAPITALISM, DEMOCRACY, AND THE SUPREME COURT. USA+45 USA-45 CONSTN DIPLOM GOV/REL ATTIT ORD/FREE LAISSEZ...POLICY CHARTS PERS/COMP 18/20 SUPREME/CT MARSHALL/J HOLMES/OW TANEY/RB FIELD/JJ. PAGE 90 F1758 — JUDGE CT/SYS JURID NAT/G

MARSHL/PLN....MARSHALL PLAN

B55
OECD,MARSHALL PLAN IN TURKEY. TURKEY USA+45 COM/IND CONSTRUC SERV/IND FORCES BUDGET...STAT 20 MARSHL/PLN. PAGE 100 F1964 — FOR/AID ECO/UNDEV AGRI INDUS

B62
SCHMITT H.A.,THE PATH TO EUROPEAN UNITY. EUR+WWI USA+45 PLAN TEC/DEV DIPLOM FOR/AID CONFER...INT/LAW 20 EEC EURCOALSTL MARSHL/PLN UNIFICA. PAGE 117 F2300
INT/ORG INT/TRADE REGION ECO/DEV

B64
MASON E.S.,FOREIGN AID AND FOREIGN POLICY. USA+45 AGRI INDUS NAT/G EX/STRUC ACT/RES RIGID/FLEX ALL/VALS...POLICY GEN/LAWS MARSHL/PLN ALL/PROG CONGRESS 20. PAGE 87 F1699
ECO/UNDEV ECO/TAC FOR/AID DIPLOM

B66
ZISCHKA A.,WAR ES EIN WUNDER? GERMANY/W ECO/DEV FINAN LG/CO BARGAIN CAP/ISM FOR/AID RATION 20 MARSHL/PLN. PAGE 150 F2965
ECO/TAC INT/TRADE INDUS WAR

MARTHELOT P. F1680

MARTI/JOSE....JOSE MARTI

MARTIN D.D. F1681

MARTIN E.M. F1682

MARTIN K. F1683

MARTIN P. F1684

MARTINS A.F. F1685

MARX H.L. F1686

MARX K. F1687,F1688,F1689,F1690,F1691,F1692,F1693

MARX/KARL....KARL MARX

B39
ROBBINS L.,ECONOMIC CAUSES OF WAR. WOR-45 ECO/DEV ECO/UNDEV INT/ORG NAT/G TEC/DEV DIPLOM DOMIN COLONIAL ATTIT DRIVE PWR WEALTH...POLICY CONCPT OBS SAMP TREND CON/ANAL GEN/LAWS MARX/KARL 20. PAGE 112 F2203
COERCE ECO/TAC WAR

B50
SCHUMPETER J.A.,CAPITALISM, SOCIALISM, AND DEMOCRACY (3RD ED.). USA-45 USSR WOR+45 WOR-45 INTELL ECO/DEV ECO/UNDEV ECO/TAC WAR PRODUC ORD/FREE...MGT SOC 20 MARX/KARL. PAGE 118 F2321
SOCIALIST CAP/ISM MARXISM IDEA/COMP

S53
BIRNBAUM N.,"CONFLICTING INTERPRETATIONS OF THE RISE OF CAPITALISM: MARX AND WEBER" (BMR)" WOR-45 INTELL SOCIETY STRUCT INDUS WORKER...PHIL/SCI SOC PERS/COMP 19/20 MARX/KARL WEBER/MAX. PAGE 15 F0288
CAP/ISM IDEA/COMP ECO/DEV MARXISM

S53
LINCOLN G.,"FACTORS DETERMINING ARMS AID." COM FUT USA+45 USSR WOR+45 ECO/DEV NAT/G CONSULT PLAN TEC/DEV DIPLOM DOMIN EDU/PROP PERCEPT PWR ...DECISION CONCPT TREND MARX/KARL 20. PAGE 80 F1566
FORCES POLICY BAL/PWR FOR/AID

B54
LENIN V.I.,SELECTED WORKS (12 VOLS.). USSR INTELL SOCIETY STRATA STRUCT NAT/G POL/PAR WORKER CAP/ISM REV WAR...MARXIST PHIL/SCI 20 MARX/KARL LENIN/VI. PAGE 78 F1520
COM MARXISM

B54
MEYER A.G.,MARXISM. INTELL ECO/DEV WORKER CAP/ISM LEAD WAR ATTIT ALL/IDEOS...SOC 19/20 MARX/KARL. PAGE 90 F1766
MARXISM CONCPT ECO/TAC STRUCT

B55
MAYO H.B.,DEMOCRACY AND MARXISM. COM USSR STRATA NAT/G WORKER ECO/TAC REV MORAL...PHIL/SCI HIST/WRIT IDEA/COMP WORSHIP 20 MARX/KARL LENIN/VI STALIN/J TROTSKY/L. PAGE 87 F1708
MARXISM CAP/ISM

B57
NANIWADA H.,STAAT UND WIRTSCHAFT; GRUNDLEGUNG DER NATIONALOEKONOMIE ALS DER LOGIK DER BURGERLICHEN GESELLSCHAFT. WOR+45 WOR-45 STRATA MARKET WORKER INGP/REL DEMAND EQUILIB WEALTH...POLICY IDEA/COMP GEN/LAWS 17/20 MARX/KARL KEYNES/JM LENIN/VI. PAGE 96 F1890
ALL/IDEOS ECO/TAC SOCIETY NAT/G

B59
HENDEL S.,THE SOVIET CRUCIBLE. USSR LEAD COERCE NAT/LISM UTOPIA PWR...POLICY CONCPT ANTHOL 20 STALIN/J LENIN/VI MARX/KARL BOLSHEVIK. PAGE 58 F1147
COM MARXISM REV TOTALISM

B60
ROBINSON J.,AN ESSAY ON MARXIAN ECONOMICS. USA+45 STRATA INDUS MARKET CAP/ISM...METH/COMP 19/20 MARX/KARL. PAGE 113 F2222
IDEA/COMP MARXISM ACADEM

B61
MARX K.,THE COMMUNIST MANIFESTO. IN (MENDEL A. ESSENTIAL WORKS OF MARXISM, NEW YORK: BANTAM. FUT MOD/EUR CULTURE ECO/DEV ECO/UNDEV AGRI FINAN INDUS MARKET PROC/MFG LABOR POL/PAR CONSULT FORCES CREATE PLAN ADMIN ATTIT DRIVE RIGID/FLEX ORD/FREE PWR RESPECT MARX/KARL MUNICH WORK. PAGE 86 F1691
COM NEW/IDEA CAP/ISM REV

B63
MARX K.,THE POVERTY OF PHILOSOPHY (1847). SOCIETY STRATA INDUS WORKER OWN UTOPIA SOCISM...GEN/LAWS MARX/KARL. PAGE 86 F1692
MARXIST PRODUC

S64
HERMAN L.M.,"THE ECONOMIC CONTENT OF SOVIET TRADE WITH THE WEST." WOR+45 ECO/DEV ECO/UNDEV AGRI COM/IND INDUS CAP/ISM ECO/TAC ATTIT RIGID/FLEX WEALTH...OBS TREND VAL/FREE MARX/KARL 20. PAGE 59 F1152
COM MARKET INT/TRADE USSR

B65
COLLINS H.,KARL MARX AND THE BRITISH LABOR MOVEMENT, YEARS OF THE FIRST INTERNATIONAL. EUR+WWI MOD/EUR UK STRATA INDUS NAT/G POL/PAR SOCISM ...CONCPT 19/20 MARX/KARL. PAGE 26 F0507
MARXISM LABOR INT/ORG WORKER

B66
LENSKI G.E.,POWER AND PRIVILEGE: A THEORY OF SOCIAL STRATIFICATION. SWEDEN UK UNIV USSR CULTURE ECO/UNDEV PRIVIL PWR...PHIL/SCI CONCPT CHARTS IDEA/COMP HYPO/EXP METH MARX/KARL. PAGE 78 F1525
SOC STRATA STRUCT SOCIETY

B67
GARAUDY R.,KARL MARX: THE EVOLUTION OF HIS THOUGHT. SOCIETY...BIBLIOG 20 MARX/KARL STALIN/J. PAGE 46 F0899
MARXIST GEN/LAWS CONCPT TIME/SEQ

S67
LEONTYEV L.,"THE LENINIST PRINCIPLES OF SOCIALIST ECONOMIC MANAGEMENT." USA+45 USSR POL/PAR WORKER PLAN ECO/TAC EFFICIENCY PRODUC MARXISM...POLICY SOCIALIST MGT TREND 20 LENIN/VI MARX/KARL. PAGE 78 F1529
SOCISM CAP/ISM IDEA/COMP ECO/DEV

S67
SEIDLER G.L.,"MARXIST LEGAL THOUGHT IN POLAND." POLAND SOCIETY R+D LOC/G NAT/G ACT/RES ADJUD CT/SYS SUPEGO PWR...SOC TREND 20 MARX/KARL. PAGE 119 F2343
MARXISM LAW CONCPT EFFICIENCY

MARXISM....MARXISM, COMMUNISM; SEE ALSO MARXIST

N
BROCKWAY A.F.,AFRICAN SOCIALISM. EUR+WWI GHANA ISLAM UAR ECO/UNDEV CAP/ISM INT/TRADE COLONIAL COERCE GOV/REL DISCRIM 20 NEGRO NKRUMAH/K NASSER/G. PAGE 19 F0356
AFR SOCISM MARXISM

B02
SELIGMAN E.R.,THE ECONOMIC INTERPRETATION OF HISTORY. ECO/TAC MARXISM SOCISM...PHIL/SCI METH/CNCPT 18/20. PAGE 119 F2348
IDEA/COMP HIST/WRIT GP/REL

B04
MARX K.,A CONTRIBUTION TO THE CRITIQUE OF POLITICAL ECONOMY (TRANS. FROM 2ND ED. BY N.I. STONE). UK STRATA ECO/DEV FINAN MARKET PLAN BARGAIN CAP/ISM ECO/TAC ATTIT WEALTH...METH/CNCPT BIOG 19. PAGE 86 F1687
MARXIST NEW/IDEA MARXISM

N19
ENGELS F.,THE BRITISH LABOUR MOVEMENT (PAMPHLET). FRANCE GERMANY MOD/EUR UK USA-45 POL/PAR WORKER PAY EDU/PROP PRICE REPRESENT GP/REL 19. PAGE 37 F0730
ECO/TAC MARXISM LABOR STRATA

N19
FRANCK P.G.,AFGHANISTAN BETWEEN EAST AND WEST: THE ECONOMICS OF COMPETITIVE COEXISTENCE (PAMPHLET). AFGHANISTN USA+45 USA-45 USSR INDUS ECO/TAC INT/TRADE CONTROL NEUTRAL ORD/FREE MARXISM...GEOG 20 UN. PAGE 43 F0842
FOR/AID PLAN DIPLOM ECO/UNDEV

N19
SENGHOR L.S.,AFRICAN SOCIALISM (PAMPHLET). AFR FRANCE MALI USSR ELITES ECO/UNDEV NAT/G DIPLOM DOMIN EDU/PROP ATTIT 20 NEGRO. PAGE 119 F2355
SOCISM MARXISM ORD/FREE NAT/LISM

B28
DE MAN H.,THE PSYCHOLOGY OF SOCIALISM. EUR+WWI USSR LABOR NAT/LISM PERSON WEALTH MARXISM...METH/COMP 20. PAGE 31 F0604
WORKER ATTIT SOC SOCISM

B35
MARX K.,WAGE-LABOR AND CAPITAL -- VALUE, PRICE AND PROFIT. LABOR PAY PRICE COST INCOME OWN PROFIT WEALTH 19. PAGE 86 F1690
STRATA WORKER MARXIST MARXISM

B35
O'CONNOR H.,REVOLUTION IN SEATTLE. USA-45 STRATA WORKER GP/REL ATTIT SOCISM...OBS BIBLIOG/A 20 SEATTLE STRIKE COM/PARTY. PAGE 99 F1954
REV EDU/PROP LABOR MARXISM

B36
HUBERMAN L.,MAN'S WORLDLY GOODS: THE STORY OF THE WEALTH OF NATIONS. CHRIST-17C EUR+WWI MOD/EUR SOCIETY DOMIN REV ORD/FREE...TIME/SEQ METH/COMP. PAGE 63 F1231
WEALTH CAP/ISM MARXISM CREATE

B38
HARPER S.N.,THE GOVERNMENT OF THE SOVIET UNION. COM USSR LAW CONSTN ECO/DEV PLAN TEC/DEV DIPLOM INT/TRADE ADMIN REV NAT/LISM...POLICY 20. PAGE 55 F1085
MARXISM NAT/G LEAD POL/PAR

B38
HEIMANN E.,COMMUNISM, FASCISM, OR DEMOCRACY? WOR-45 CONSTN SOCIETY STRATA AGRI CAP/ISM MORAL ORD/FREE ...MAJORIT METH/COMP NAT/COMP 19/20. PAGE 58 F1141
SOCISM MARXISM FASCISM PLURISM

B42
SWEEZY P.M.,THE THEORY OF CAPITALIST DEVELOPMENT. FUT NAT/G COST FASCISM BIBLIOG. PAGE 128 F2519
ECO/DEV CAP/ISM MARXISM COLONIAL

B44
BIENSTOCK G.,MANAGEMENT IN RUSSIAN INDUSTRY AND AGRICULTURE. USSR CONSULT WORKER LEAD COST PROFIT ATTIT DRIVE PWR...MGT METH/COMP DICTIONARY ACCT 20. PAGE 15 F0281
ADMIN MARXISM SML/CO AGRI

B48
DURBIN E.F.M.,THE POLITICS OF DEMOCRATIC SOCIALISM; AN ESSAY ON SOCIAL POLICY. STRATA POL/PAR PLAN COERCE DRIVE PERSON PWR MARXISM...CHARTS METH/COMP. PAGE 35 F0684
SOCIALIST POPULISM POLICY SOCIETY

B48
MCCABE D.A.,LABOR AND SOCIAL ORGANIZATION. LEGIS WORKER CAP/ISM ECO/TAC PAY MARXISM SOCISM SOC/INTEG 20 INTRVN/ECO. PAGE 88 F1717
LABOR STRATA NEW/LIB

B48
WINSLOW E.M.,THE PATTERN OF IMPERIALISM; A STUDY IN THE THEORIES OF POWER. DOMIN WAR PWR MARXISM ...IDEA/COMP METH/COMP BIBLIOG 20. PAGE 147 F2906
SOCISM CAP/ISM COLONIAL ECO/TAC

B49
US DEPARTMENT OF STATE,SOVIET BIBLIOGRAPHY (PAMPHLET). CHINA/COM COM USSR LAW AGRI INT/ORG ECO/TAC EDU/PROP...POLICY GEOG IND 20. PAGE 135 F2670
BIBLIOG/A MARXISM CULTURE DIPLOM

B50
HUNT R.N.,THE THEORY AND PRACTICE OF COMMUNISM. STRUCT WORKER NAT/LISM TOTALISM...CONCPT TREND 19/20 STALIN/J EUROPE. PAGE 63 F1244
MARXISM SOCISM REV STRATA

B50
SCHUMPETER J.A.,CAPITALISM, SOCIALISM, AND DEMOCRACY (3RD ED.). USA-45 USSR WOR+45 WOR-45 INTELL ECO/DEV ECO/UNDEV ECO/TAC WAR PRODUC ORD/FREE...MGT SOC 20 MARX/KARL. PAGE 118 F2321
SOCIALIST CAP/ISM MARXISM IDEA/COMP

B51
BROGAN D.W.,THE PRICE OF REVOLUTION. FRANCE USA+45 USA-45 USSR CONSTN NAT/G DIPLOM COLONIAL NAT/LISM ORD/FREE POPULISM...CONCPT 18/20 PRE/US/AM. PAGE 19 F0359
REV METH/COMP COST MARXISM

B53
PURCELL T.V.,THE WORKER SPEAKS HIS MIND ON COMPANY AND UNION. WORKER ADJUD LEAD RACE/REL ATTIT DRIVE MARXISM...MGT CLASSIF STAT OBS INT SAMP BIBLIOG. PAGE 108 F2131
LABOR PARTIC INGP/REL HAPPINESS

S53
BIRNBAUM N.,"CONFLICTING INTERPRETATIONS OF THE RISE OF CAPITALISM: MARX AND WEBER" (BMR)" WOR-45 INTELL SOCIETY STRUCT INDUS WORKER...PHIL/SCI SOC PERS/COMP 19/20 MARX/KARL WEBER/MAX. PAGE 15 F0288
CAP/ISM IDEA/COMP ECO/DEV MARXISM

B54
LENIN V.I.,SELECTED WORKS (12 VOLS.). USSR INTELL SOCIETY STRATA STRUCT NAT/G POL/PAR WORKER CAP/ISM REV WAR...MARXIST PHIL/SCI 20 MARX/KARL LENIN/VI. PAGE 78 F1520
COM MARXISM

B54
MEYER A.G.,MARXISM. INTELL ECO/DEV WORKER CAP/ISM LEAD WAR ATTIT ALL/IDEOS...SOC 19/20 MARX/KARL. PAGE 90 F1766
MARXISM CONCPT ECO/TAC STRUCT

B54
STALEY E.,THE FUTURE OF UNDERDEVELOPED COUNTRIES: POLITICAL IMPLICATIONS OF ECONOMIC DEVELOPMENT. AFR COM FUT USA+45 SOCIETY ECO/UNDEV CREATE PLAN CAP/ISM ATTIT DRIVE MARXISM SOCISM...POLICY CONCPT CHARTS 20. PAGE 125 F2466
EDU/PROP ECO/TAC FOR/AID

B54
TAFT P.,THE STRUCTURE AND GOVERNMENT OF LABOR UNIONS. SANCTION INGP/REL ORD/FREE PWR MARXISM ...MAJORIT STAT TREND. PAGE 128 F2524
LABOR ADJUD WORKER FINAN

B55
MAYO H.B.,DEMOCRACY AND MARXISM. COM USSR STRATA NAT/G WORKER ECO/TAC REV MORAL...PHIL/SCI HIST/WRIT IDEA/COMP WORSHIP 20 MARX/KARL LENIN/VI STALIN/J TROTSKY/L. PAGE 87 F1708
MARXISM CAP/ISM

B55
UYEHARA C.H.,COMPARATIVE PLATFORMS OF JAPAN'S MAJOR PARTIES... USA+45 AGRI LEGIS WORKER CAP/ISM ORD/FREE MARXISM SOCISM...IDEA/COMP 20 CHINJAP. PAGE 140 F2755
POLICY POL/PAR DIPLOM NAT/G

B56
BARBASH J.,THE PRACTICE OF UNIONISM. ECO/TAC LEAD LOBBY GP/REL INGP/REL DRIVE MARXISM BIBLIOG. PAGE 10 F0182
LABOR REPRESENT CONTROL ADMIN

B57
BAUER P.T.,THE ECONOMICS OF UNDERDEVELOPED COUNTRIES. WOR+45 AGRI FINAN INDUS PROC/MFG WORKER CAP/ISM PAY PRICE INCOME MARXISM...METH/COMP 20 RESOURCE/N. PAGE 11 F0213
ECO/UNDEV ECO/TAC PROB/SOLV NAT/G

B57
LOUCKS W.N.,COMPARATIVE ECONOMIC SYSTEMS (5TH ED.). COM UK USSR INDUS POL/PAR PLAN CAP/ISM TOTALISM MARXISM...PHIL/SCI BIBLIOG 19/20. PAGE 82 F1603
NAT/COMP IDEA/COMP SOCISM

B57
NAUMANN R.,THEORIE UND PRAXIS DES NEOLIBERALISMUS; DAS MAERCHEN VON DER FREIEN ODER SOZIALEN MARKTWIRTSCHAFT. GERMANY/W FORCES PLAN EDU/PROP SOCISM...POLICY MARXIST IDEA/COMP BIBLIOG 18/20 ADENAUER/K. PAGE 97 F1903
MARXISM NEW/LIB ECO/TAC CAP/ISM

B58
COLE G.D.H.,COMMUNISM AND SOCIAL DEMOCRACY (VOL. IV OF "HISTORY OF SOCIAL THOUGHT"). COM GERMANY ITALY UK AGRI INT/ORG WORKER DIPLOM COLONIAL NAT/LISM ALL/IDEOS...BIBLIOG 20 LEAGUE/NAT AUST/HUNG. PAGE 26 F0502
MARXISM REV POL/PAR SOCISM

B58
SCOTT D.J.R.,RUSSIAN POLITICAL INSTITUTIONS. RUSSIA USSR CONSTN AGRI DELIB/GP PLAN EDU/PROP CONTROL CHOOSE EFFICIENCY ATTIT MARXISM...BIBLIOG/A IND 13/20. PAGE 118 F2332
NAT/G POL/PAR ADMIN DECISION

B58
TILLION G.,ALGERIA: THE REALITIES. ALGERIA FRANCE ISLAM CULTURE STRATA PROB/SOLV DOMIN REV NAT/LISM WEALTH MARXISM...GEOG 20. PAGE 130 F2573
ECO/UNDEV SOC COLONIAL DIPLOM

B59
ENGELS F.,SOCIALISM: UTOPIAN AND SCIENTIFIC (2ND ED.). SOCISM...CONCPT CON/ANAL GEN/LAWS 19 DUHRING/E. PAGE 38 F0732
MARXISM PHIL/SCI UTOPIA IDEA/COMP

B59
HENDEL S.,THE SOVIET CRUCIBLE. USSR LEAD COERCE NAT/LISM UTOPIA PWR...POLICY CONCPT ANTHOL 20 STALIN/J LENIN/VI MARX/KARL BOLSHEVIK. PAGE 58 F1147
COM MARXISM REV TOTALISM

B59
KRIPALANI J.B.,CLASS STRUGGLE. INDIA WOR+45 ECO/UNDEV LABOR CAP/ISM EDU/PROP INGP/REL ...SOCIALIST IDEA/COMP 17/20. PAGE 73 F1440
MARXISM STRATA COERCE ECO/TAC

B59
LI CHOH-MING,ECONOMIC DEVELOPMENT OF COMMUNIST CHINA. ASIA CHINA/COM AGRI FINAN TAX INCOME MARXISM ...MGT 20. PAGE 80 F1557
ECO/UNDEV INDUS ORD/FREE TEC/DEV

B59
MADHOK B.,POLITICAL TRENDS IN INDIA. INDIA PAKISTAN UK STRATA ECO/UNDEV POL/PAR LEGIS CAP/ISM DIPLOM COLONIAL CHOOSE MARXISM...SOC TREND 20 GANDHI/M NEHRU/J. PAGE 84 F1639
GEOG NAT/G

B59
MARTIN K.,WAR, HISTORY, AND HUMAN NATURE. FRANCE GERMANY INDIA UK UNIV POL/PAR COLONIAL DETER REV MARXISM PACIFISM...PSY CONCPT PREDICT LENIN/VI GANDHI/M. PAGE 86 F1683
PERSON WAR ATTIT IDEA/COMP

B59
NOVE A.,COMMUNIST ECONOMIC STRATEGY: SOVIET GROWTH AND CAPABILITIES. USSR AGRI LABOR PLAN TEC/DEV CAP/ISM INT/TRADE EFFICIENCY MARXISM 20 THIRD/WRLD. PAGE 99 F1941
FOR/AID ECO/TAC DIPLOM INDUS

B60
BILLERBECK K.,SOVIET BLOC FOREIGN AID TO UNDERDEVELOPED COUNTRIES. COM FUT USSR FINAN FORCES TEC/DEV DIPLOM INT/TRADE EDU/PROP NUC/PWR...TREND 20. PAGE 15 F0285
FOR/AID ECO/UNDEV ECO/TAC MARXISM

B60
FRANCIS R.G.,THE PREDICTIVE PROCESS. PLAN MARXISM ...DECISION SOC CONCPT NAT/COMP 19/20. PAGE 43 F0840
PREDICT PHIL/SCI TREND

B60
HUGHES R.,THE CHINESE COMMUNES; A BACKGROUND BOOK. CHINA/COM SOCIETY CONTROL ROUTINE ADJUST EFFICIENCY PRODUC 20. PAGE 63 F1234
AGRI INDUS STRUCT MARXISM

B60
MAYO H.B.,INTRODUCTION TO MARXIST THEORY. SECT WORKER POPULISM SOCISM 19/20. PAGE 87 F1709
MARXISM STRATA IDEA/COMP PHIL/SCI

B60
MC CLELLAN G.S.,INDIA. AFR CHINA/COM INDIA CONSTN ELITES STRATA AGRI POL/PAR FOR/AID ARMS/CONT REV MARXISM...CENSUS BIBLIOG 20 GANDHI/M NEHRU/J. PAGE 87 F1712
DIPLOM NAT/G SOCIETY ECO/UNDEV

B60
ROBINSON J.,AN ESSAY ON MARXIAN ECONOMICS. USA+45 STRATA INDUS MARKET CAP/ISM...METH/COMP 19/20 MARX/KARL. PAGE 113 F2222
IDEA/COMP MARXISM ACADEM

B60
ROSTOW W.W.,THE STAGES OF ECONOMIC GROWTH. UK
ECO/UNDEV

USA+45 USSR WOR+45 WOR-45 ECO/DEV PERSON MARXISM ...METH/CNCPT TIME/SEQ GEN/LAWS GEN/METH 20. PAGE 114 F2246 — NEW/IDEA CAP/ISM

B60
WENTHOLT W.,INFLATION OR SECURITY? EUR+WWI USA+45 INDUS CONSULT TEC/DEV CAP/ISM DIPLOM FOR/AID INT/TRADE MARXISM 20 EEC. PAGE 145 F2858 — ECO/DEV ECO/TAC FINAN ORD/FREE

B61
DEWITT N.,EDUCATION AND PROFESSIONAL EMPLOYMENT IN THE USSR. USSR PROF/ORG WORKER PLAN ADMIN UTIL AGE/C AGE/Y MARXISM...STAT CHARTS 20. PAGE 32 F0629 — EDU/PROP ACADEM SCHOOL INTELL

B61
HEMPSTONE S.,THE NEW AFRICA. AGRI INDUS KIN NAT/G COLONIAL MARXISM...SOC INT TREND NAT/COMP BIBLIOG/A 20. PAGE 58 F1146 — AFR ORD/FREE PERSON CULTURE

B61
HENDERSON W.O.,THE INDUSTRIAL REVOLUTION IN EUROPE. FRANCE GERMANY MOD/EUR RUSSIA WORKER PROFIT PWR MARXISM SOCISM...SOC HIST/WRIT 19 INDUS/REV. PAGE 58 F1148 — INDUS REV CAP/ISM TEC/DEV

B61
LENIN V.I.,WHAT IS TO BE DONE? (1902). RUSSIA LABOR NAT/G POL/PAR WORKER CAP/ISM ECO/TAC ADMIN PARTIC ...MARXIST IDEA/COMP GEN/LAWS 19/20. PAGE 78 F1522 — EDU/PROP PRESS MARXISM METH/COMP

B61
LETHBRIDGE H.J.,CHINA'S URBAN COMMUNES. CHINA/COM FUT ECO/UNDEV DIPLOM EDU/PROP DEMAND INCOME MARXISM ...POLICY MUNICH 20. PAGE 78 F1534 — CONTROL ECO/TAC NAT/G

B61
LHOSTE-LACHAUME P.,OU GIT LE DESACCORD ENTRE LIBERAUX ET SOCIALISTES. EUR+WWI USA+45 USA-45 USSR CAP/ISM EDU/PROP MARXISM...MAJORIT IDEA/COMP 20 KEYNES/JM NEW/DEAL DEPRESSION. PAGE 79 F1555 — LAISSEZ SOCISM FINAN

B61
LICHTHEIM G.,MARXISM. GERMANY SOCIETY WORKER CAP/ISM ECO/TAC NAT/LISM POPULISM...TIME/SEQ GOV/COMP NAT/COMP 18/20 COM/PARTY. PAGE 80 F1559 — MARXISM SOCISM IDEA/COMP CULTURE

B61
NOVE A.,THE SOVIET ECONOMY. USSR ECO/DEV FINAN NAT/G ECO/TAC PRICE ADMIN EFFICIENCY MARXISM ...TREND BIBLIOG 20. PAGE 99 F1943 — PLAN PRODUC POLICY

B61
SCHWARTZ H.,THE RED PHOENIX: RUSSIA SINCE WORLD WAR II. USA+45 WOR+45 ELITES POL/PAR TEC/DEV ECO/TAC MARXISM. PAGE 118 F2325 — DIPLOM NAT/G ECO/DEV

B61
STARK H.,SOCIAL AND ECONOMIC FRONTIERS IN LATIN AMERICA (2ND ED.). CUBA FUT CULTURE AGRI INDUS ECO/TAC PRODUC ATTIT MARXISM...NAT/COMP BIBLIOG T 20. PAGE 125 F2470 — L/A+17C SOCIETY DIPLOM ECO/UNDEV

B61
WARD B.J.,INDIA AND THE WEST. INDIA UK USA+45 INT/TRADE GIVE COLONIAL ATTIT MARXISM 19/20. PAGE 143 F2817 — PLAN ECO/UNDEV ECO/TAC FOR/AID

B62
BRUMBERG A.,RUSSIA UNDER KHRUSHCHEV. FUT USSR SOCIETY ECO/DEV AGRI PERF/ART WORKER PWR...SOC ANTHOL 20 KHRUSH/N. PAGE 20 F0377 — COM MARXISM NAT/G CHIEF

B62
ELLIOTT J.R.,THE APPEAL OF COMMUNISM IN THE UNDERDEVELOPED NATIONS. AFR USSR WOR+45 INT/ORG NAT/G DIPLOM DOMIN EDU/PROP ROUTINE ATTIT RIGID/FLEX ORD/FREE PWR WEALTH MARXISM...POLICY SOC METH/CNCPT MYTH TOT/POP METH/GP 20. PAGE 37 F0722 — COM ECO/UNDEV

B62
FRIEDRICH-EBERT-STIFTUNG,THE SOVIET BLOC AND DEVELOPING COUNTRIES. CHINA/COM COM GERMANY/E USSR WOR+45 ECO/UNDEV INT/ORG NAT/G TEC/DEV NEUTRAL PWR ...POLICY 20. PAGE 44 F0868 — MARXISM DIPLOM ECO/TAC FOR/AID

B62
KIRPICEVA I.K.,HANDBUCH DER RUSSISCHEN UND SOWJETISCHEN BIBLIOGRAPHIEN (5 VOLS.). USSR STRUCT ECO/DEV DIPLOM LEAD ATTIT 18/20. PAGE 71 F1400 — BIBLIOG/A NAT/G MARXISM COM

B62
LEVY H.V.,LIBERDADE E JUSTICA SOCIAL (2ND ED.). BRAZIL COM L/A+17C USSR INT/ORG PARTIC GP/REL WEALTH 20 UN COM/PARTY. PAGE 79 F1544 — ORD/FREE MARXISM CAP/ISM LAW

B62
WALSTON H.,AGRICULTURE UNDER COMMUNISM. CHINA/COM COM PROB/SOLV HAPPINESS RIGID/FLEX...POLICY METH/COMP 20. PAGE 143 F2811 — AGRI MARXISM PLAN CREATE

S62
IOVTCHOUK M.T.,"ON SOME THEORETICAL PRINCIPLES AND METHODS OF SOCIOLOGICAL INVESTIGATIONS (IN RUSSIAN)." FUT USA+45 STRATA R+D NAT/G POL/PAR TOP/EX ACT/RES PLAN ECO/TAC EDU/PROP ROUTINE ATTIT RIGID/FLEX MARXISM SOCISM...MARXIST METH/CNCPT OBS TREND NAT/COMP GEN/LAWS 20. PAGE 65 F1288 — COM ECO/DEV CAP/ISM USSR

B63
CERAMI C.A.,ALLIANCE BORN OF DANGER. EUR+WWI USA+45 USSR ECO/DEV INDUS VOL/ASSN ECO/TAC REGION ATTIT MARXISM ATLAN/ALL 20 NATO EEC. PAGE 22 F0437 — DIPLOM INT/ORG NAT/G POLICY

B63
CHEN N.-.R.,THE ECONOMY OF MAINLAND CHINA, 1949-1963: A BIBLIOGRAPHY OF MATERIALS IN ENGLISH. CHINA/COM ECO/UNDEV PRESS 20. PAGE 24 F0461 — BIBLIOG MARXISM NAT/G ASIA

B63
GOLDMAN M.I.,SOVIET MARKETING. USSR DIST/IND FINAN RATION OWN WEALTH...SOC BIBLIOG 20. PAGE 48 F0937 — MARKET ECO/TAC CONTROL MARXISM

B63
HYDE D.,THE PEACEFUL ASSAULT. COM UAR USSR ECO/DEV ECO/UNDEV NAT/G POL/PAR CAP/ISM PWR 20. PAGE 64 F1256 — MARXISM CONTROL ECO/TAC DIPLOM

B63
LETHBRIDGE H.J.,THE PEASANT AND THE COMMUNES. CHINA/COM COM USSR NEIGH PROB/SOLV ADJUST EFFICIENCY...POLICY METH/COMP NAT/COMP 20. PAGE 78 F1535 — MARXISM ECO/TAC AGRI WORKER

S63
FLOREA I.,"CU PRIVIRE LA OBIECTUL MATERIALISMULUI ISTORIC SI AL COMUNISMULUI STIINTIFIC SI LA RAPORTUL DINTRE ELE." EUR+WWI WOR+45 WOR-45 INTELL NAT/G POL/PAR WORKER EDU/PROP PERCEPT MARXISM ...MARXIST PHIL/SCI CONCPT TOT/POP 20. PAGE 42 F0812 — COM ATTIT TOTALISM

S63
WILES P.J.D.,"WILL CAPITALISM AND COMMUNISM SPONTANEOUSLY CONVERGE." COM FUT USA+45 ECO/DEV DIST/IND MARKET CAP/ISM ECO/TAC RIGID/FLEX WEALTH MARXISM SOCISM...MATH STAT TREND COMPUT/IR 20. PAGE 146 F2885 — PLAN TEC/DEV USSR

B64
ASH W.,MARXISM AND MORAL CONCEPTS. CAP/ISM GP/REL ORD/FREE...BIBLIOG 20. PAGE 7 F0128 — MARXISM CONCPT MORAL SOCIETY

B64
DANIELS R.V.,RUSSIA. RUSSIA USSR STRUCT NAT/LISM TOTALISM ORD/FREE WEALTH...POLICY DECISION TREND. PAGE 30 F0579 — MARXISM REV ECO/DEV DIPLOM

B64
GRIFFITH W.E.,COMMUNISM IN EUROPE (2 VOLS.). CZECHOSLVK USSR WOR+45 WOR-45 YUGOSLAVIA INGP/REL MARXISM SOCISM...ANTHOL 20 EUROPE/E. PAGE 51 F1000 — COM POL/PAR DIPLOM GOV/COMP

B64
LETICHE J.M.,A HISTORY OF RUSSIAN ECONOMIC THOUGHT: NINTH THROUGH EIGHTEENTH CENTURIES. RUSSIA FINAN SECT CAP/ISM DOMIN DEMAND EFFICIENCY OWN MARXISM ...TECHNIC ANTHOL BIBLIOG 9/18. PAGE 78 F1536 — ECO/TAC TIME/SEQ IDEA/COMP ECO/UNDEV

B64
LISKA G.,EUROPE ASCENDANT. EUR+WWI ECO/DEV FORCES INT/TRADE MARXISM 20 EEC. PAGE 81 F1579 — DIPLOM BAL/PWR TARIFFS CENTRAL

B64
MILIBAND R.,THE SOCIALIST REGISTER: 1964. GERMANY/W ITALY UK LABOR POL/PAR ECO/TAC FOR/AID NUC/PWR ...POLICY SOCIALIST IDEA/COMP 20 MAO NASSER/G. PAGE 91 F1784 — MARXISM SOCISM CAP/ISM PROB/SOLV

B64
STRONG A.L.,THE RISE OF THE CHINESE PEOPLE'S COMMUNES - AND SIX YEARS AFTER (2ND ED.). CHINA/COM AGRI INDUS FORCES WORKER PROB/SOLV EDU/PROP EFFICIENCY ISOLAT 20. PAGE 127 F2503 — NEIGH ECO/TAC MARXISM METH/COMP

B64
WELLISZ S.,THE ECONOMICS OF THE SOVIET BLOC. COM USSR INDUS WORKER PLAN BUDGET INT/TRADE TAX PRICE PRODUC WEALTH MARXISM...METH/COMP 20. PAGE 145 F2854 — EFFICIENCY ADMIN MARKET

S64
FYFE J.,"LIST OF CURRENT ACQUISITIONS OF PERIODICALS AND NEWSPAPERS DEALING WITH THE SOVIET UNION AND EAST EUROPEAN COUNTRIES." USSR WRITING GP/REL INGP/REL MARXISM 20. PAGE 45 F0879 — BIBLIOG COM EDU/PROP PRESS

S64
HORECKY P.L.,"LIBRARY OF CONGRESS PUBLICATIONS IN AID OF USSR AND EAST EUROPEAN RESEARCH." BULGARIA CZECHOSLVK POLAND USSR YUGOSLAVIA NAT/G POL/PAR DIPLOM ADMIN GOV/REL...CLASSIF 20. PAGE 62 F1214 — BIBLIOG/A COM MARXISM

C64
GOLDMAN M.I.,"COMPARATIVE ECONOMIC SYSTEMS: A READER." COM ECO/UNDEV NAT/G BUDGET CAP/ISM ADMIN TOTALISM MARXISM SOCISM...MGT ANTHOL BIBLIOG 19/20. PAGE 48 F0938 — NAT/COMP CONTROL IDEA/COMP

C64
LANDAUER C.,"CONTEMPORARY ECONOMIC SYSTEMS." COM WOR+45 ECO/UNDEV PLAN GP/REL...BIBLIOG 20. PAGE 75 F1466
CAP/ISM SOCISM MARXISM IDEA/COMP

B65
CAMPBELL J.C.,AMERICAN POLICY TOWARDS COMMUNIST EASTERN EUROPE* THE CHOICES AHEAD. AFR USA+45 ECO/DEV BAL/PWR MARXISM TREND. PAGE 21 F0406
POLAND YUGOSLAVIA DIPLOM COM

B65
COLLINS H.,KARL MARX AND THE BRITISH LABOUR MOVEMENT; YEARS OF THE FIRST INTERNATIONAL. FRANCE SWITZERLND UK CAP/ISM WAR...MARXIST IDEA/COMP BIBLIOG 19. PAGE 26 F0506
MARXISM LABOR INT/ORG REV

B65
COLLINS H.,KARL MARX AND THE BRITISH LABOR MOVEMENT, YEARS OF THE FIRST INTERNATIONAL. EUR+WWI MOD/EUR UK STRATA INDUS NAT/G POL/PAR SOCISM ...CONCPT 19/20 MARX/KARL. PAGE 26 F0507
MARXISM LABOR INT/ORG WORKER

B65
HAPGOOD D.,AFRICA: FROM INDEPENDENCE TO TOMARROW. AFR GUINEA SENEGAL CULTURE ELITES ECO/UNDEV AGRI SCHOOL FOR/AID COLONIAL MARXISM...TREND 20. PAGE 55 F1070
ECO/TAC SOCIETY NAT/G

B65
JAIN S.C.,THE STATE AND AGRICULTURE. INDIA S/ASIA ECO/UNDEV PROB/SOLV CAP/ISM MARXISM SOCISM 20. PAGE 66 F1304
NAT/G POLICY AGRI ECO/TAC

B65
JASNY H.,KHRUSHCHEV'S CROP POLICY. USSR ECO/DEV PLAN MARXISM...STAT 20 KHRUSH/N RESOURCE/N. PAGE 66 F1306
AGRI NAT/G POLICY ECO/TAC

B65
KRAUSE W.,ECONOMIC DEVELOPMENT: THE UNDERDEVELOPED WORLD AND THE AMERICAN INTEREST. USA+45 AGRI PLAN MARXISM...CHARTS 20. PAGE 73 F1434
FOR/AID ECO/UNDEV FINAN PROB/SOLV

B65
NARASIMHAN V.K.,DEMOCRACY AND MIXED ECONOMY. INDIA CONTROL...CENSUS IDEA/COMP 20. PAGE 96 F1891
CAP/ISM MARXISM ORD/FREE NEW/LIB

B65
O'BRIEN F.,CRISIS IN WORLD COMMUNISM* MARXISM IN SEARCH OF EFFICIENCY. AFR COM ECO/DEV PLAN INT/TRADE WAR ADJUST PEACE...STAT TIME/SEQ GOV/COMP NAT/COMP. PAGE 99 F1951
MARXISM USSR DRIVE EFFICIENCY

B65
ONUOHA B.,THE ELEMENTS OF AFRICAN SOCIALISM. AFR FINAN SECT TEC/DEV FOR/AID GP/REL OWN LAISSEZ MARXISM...CONCPT BIBLIOG 20. PAGE 101 F1992
SOCISM ECO/UNDEV NAT/G EX/STRUC

B65
ORG FOR ECO COOP AND DEVEL,THE MEDITERRANEAN REGIONAL PROJECT: YUGOSLAVIA; EDUCATION AND DEVELOPMENT. YUGOSLAVIA SOCIETY FINAN PROF/ORG PLAN ADMIN COST DEMAND MARXISM...STAT TREND CHARTS METH 20 OECD. PAGE 102 F1996
EDU/PROP ACADEM SCHOOL ECO/UNDEV

B65
OXENFELDT A.R.,ECONOMIC SYSTEMS IN ACTION. FRANCE USA+45 USSR CULTURE PLAN PROB/SOLV TEC/DEV INCOME PRODUC WEALTH...METH/COMP 20. PAGE 102 F2007
ECO/DEV CAP/ISM MARXISM ECO/TAC

B65
PLOSS S.I.,CONFLICT AND DECISION-MAKING IN SOVIET RUSSIA - A CASE STUDY OF AGRICULTURAL POLICY - 1953-1963. USSR DELIB/GP INGP/REL PWR MARXISM. PAGE 106 F2093
AGRI DECISION ATTIT

B65
SHAFFER H.G.,THE SOVIET SYSTEM IN THEORY AND PRACTICE: SELECTED WESTERN AND SOVIET VIEWS. USSR LAW SOCIETY CREATE FOR/AID EDU/PROP PRESS CHOOSE PEACE ORD/FREE...ANTHOL 20 STALIN/J. PAGE 120 F2362
MARXISM SOCISM IDEA/COMP

B65
WU YUAN-LI,THE ECONOMY OF COMMUNIST CHINA. CHINA/COM USSR AGRI FINAN INDUS POL/PAR WORKER PROB/SOLV INT/TRADE PRICE EATING INCOME OWN WEALTH 20. PAGE 149 F2939
ECO/TAC MARXISM PLAN EFFICIENCY

B66
BARAN P.A.,MONOPOLY CAPITAL; AN ESSAY ON THE AMERICAN ECONOMIC AND SOCIAL ORDER. USA+45 USA-45 ECO/UNDEV FINAN MARKET PLAN DIPLOM COLONIAL RACE/REL DEMAND MARXISM...CHARTS 20. PAGE 9 F0179
LG/CO CAP/ISM PRICE CONTROL

B66
BRODERSEN A.,THE SOVIET WORKER: LABOR AND GOVERNMENT IN SOVIET SOCIETY. USSR STRUCT INDUS LABOR PLAN PAY INGP/REL PRODUC...POLICY GEN/LAWS BIBLIOG 20 STALIN/J LENIN/VI BOLSHEVISM KHRUSH/N. PAGE 19 F0357
WORKER ROLE NAT/G MARXISM

B66
BROWN J.F.,THE NEW EASTERN EUROPE. ALBANIA BULGARIA HUNGARY POLAND ROMANIA CULTURE AGRI POL/PAR WAR NAT/LISM MARXISM...CHARTS BIBLIOG 20. PAGE 19 F0369
DIPLOM COM NAT/G

ECO/UNDEV

B66
DOBB M.,SOVIET ECONOMIC DEVELOPMENT SINCE 1917. USSR ECO/DEV ECO/UNDEV LABOR NAT/G TEC/DEV ECO/TAC ROUTINE PRODUC MARXISM 20. PAGE 33 F0647
PLAN INDUS WORKER

B66
FELKER J.L.,SOVIET ECONOMIC CONTROVERSIES. USSR INDUS PLAN INT/TRADE GP/REL MARXISM SOCISM...POLICY 20. PAGE 40 F0778
ECO/DEV MARKET PROFIT PRICE

B66
FORD P.,CARDINAL MORAN AND THE A. L. P. NAT/G POL/PAR SECT DELIB/GP LOBBY REV CHOOSE ORD/FREE MARXISM 19/20 AUSTRAL PROTESTANT LABOR/PAR. PAGE 42 F0825
CATHISM SOCISM LABOR SOCIETY

B66
FUSFELD D.R.,THE AGE OF THE ECONOMIST. ECO/TAC WEALTH LAISSEZ MARXISM...EPIST 18/20 KEYNES/JM. PAGE 45 F0878
PHIL/SCI CAP/ISM POLICY

B66
GYORGY A.,ISSUES OF WORLD COMMUNISM. ALBANIA CHINA/COM COM USSR YUGOSLAVIA STRATA AGRI INT/ORG CHIEF FORCES WORKER WAR ALL/IDEOS...GEOG 20 MAO. PAGE 52 F1018
ECO/UNDEV REV MARXISM CON/ANAL

B66
JACKSON G.D.,COMINTERN AND PEASANT IN EAST EUROPE 1919-1930. BULGARIA COM CZECHOSLVK EUR+WWI POLAND ROMANIA YUGOSLAVIA STRATA AGRI VOL/ASSN DIPLOM CONTROL CROWD WEALTH...POLICY NAT/COMP 20. PAGE 66 F1293
MARXISM ECO/UNDEV WORKER INT/ORG

B66
KURAKOV I.G.,SCIENCE, TECHNOLOGY AND COMMUNISM; SOME QUESTIONS OF DEVELOPMENT (TRANS. BY CARIN DEDIJER). USSR INDUS PLAN PROB/SOLV COST PRODUC ...MGT MATH CHARTS METH 20. PAGE 74 F1450
CREATE TEC/DEV MARXISM ECO/TAC

B66
LEONTIEF W.,ESSAYS IN ECONOMICS. ECO/UNDEV INDUS NAT/G CAP/ISM FOR/AID AUTOMAT MARXISM...ECOMETRIC CHARTS ANTHOL METH 20 KEYNES/JM. PAGE 78 F1528
CONCPT METH/CNCPT METH/COMP

B66
LICHTMAN R.,TOWARD COMMUNITY (PAPER). PLAN PROB/SOLV WEALTH MARXISM...HEAL CONCPT 20. PAGE 80 F1561
NEW/LIB EFFICIENCY CAP/ISM ADJUST

B66
MADAN G.R.,ECONOMIC THINKING IN INDIA. INDIA ECO/UNDEV AGRI FINAN INDUS LABOR PLAN CAP/ISM INT/TRADE MARXISM SOCISM...POLICY 1/20. PAGE 84 F1638
ECO/TAC PHIL/SCI NAT/G POL/PAR

B66
US DEPARTMENT OF STATE,RESEARCH ON THE USSR AND EASTERN EUROPE (EXTERNAL RESEARCH LIST NO 1-25). USSR LAW CULTURE SOCIETY NAT/G TEC/DEV DIPLOM EDU/PROP REGION...GEOG LING. PAGE 136 F2675
BIBLIOG/A EUR+WWI COM MARXISM

B66
US DEPARTMENT OF STATE,RESEARCH ON WESTERN EUROPE, GREAT BRITAIN, AND CANADA (EXTERNAL RESEARCH LIST NO 3-25). CANADA GERMANY/W UK LAW CULTURE NAT/G POL/PAR FORCES EDU/PROP REGION MARXISM...GEOG SOC WORSHIP 20 CMN/WLTH. PAGE 136 F2676
BIBLIOG/A EUR+WWI DIPLOM

B66
WETTER G.A.,SOVIET IDEOLOGY TODAY. USSR ECO/UNDEV SECT WORKER CAP/ISM CONTROL TASK EFFICIENCY TOTALISM DRIVE WEALTH...TREND 18/20. PAGE 145 F2864
ALL/IDEOS MARXISM REV

B66
WILCOX C.,ECONOMIES OF THE WORLD TODAY: THEIR ORGANIZATION, DEVELOPMENT, AND PERFORMANCE (2ND ED.). CHINA/COM COM INDIA NIGERIA UK WOR+45 WOR-45 INDUS MARKET PLAN ECO/TAC SOCISM...CHARTS METH/COMP 20. PAGE 146 F2878
ECO/DEV ECO/UNDEV MARXISM CAP/ISM

S66
COHEN A.,"THE TECHNOLOGY/ELITE APPROACH TO THE DEVELOPMENTAL PROCESS* PERUVIAN CASE STUDY." L/A+17C STRUCT CREATE ECO/TAC FOR/AID CIVMIL/REL MARXISM TECHRACY HYPO/EXP. PAGE 26 F0496
ECO/UNDEV ELITES PERU

S66
DUROSELLE J.B.,"THE FUTURE OF THE ATLANTIC COMMUNITY." EUR+WWI USA+45 USSR NAT/G CAP/ISM REGION DETER NUC/PWR ATTIT MARXISM...INT/LAW 20 NATO. PAGE 35 F0686
FUT DIPLOM MYTH POLICY

S66
KLEIN S.,"A SURVEY OF SINO-JAPANESE TRADE, 1950-1966" TAIWAN EDU/PROP 20 CHINJAP. PAGE 72 F1409
INT/TRADE DIPLOM MARXISM

S66
POSEN G.S.,"RECENT TRENDS IN SOVIET ECONOMIC THOUGHT." USSR ECO/DEV PLAN CONTROL CENTRAL 20. PAGE 107 F2107
ECO/TAC MARXISM INDUS PROFIT

C66
WINT G.,"ASIA: A HANDBOOK." ASIA S/ASIA INDUS LABOR SECT PRESS RACE/REL MARXISM...STAT CHARTS BIBLIOG 20. PAGE 148 F2908
ECO/UNDEV DIPLOM NAT/G SOCIETY

B67
ANDERSON C.W.,ISSUES OF POLITICAL DEVELOPMENT.
NAT/LISM

BURMA WOR+45 CULTURE TOP/EX ECO/TAC MARXISM ...CHARTS NAT/COMP 20 COLOMB CONGO/LEOP. PAGE 5 F0094 COERCE ECO/UNDEV SOCISM B67

ANDERSON T.,RUSSIAN POLITICAL THOUGHT; AN INTRODUCTION. USSR NAT/G POL/PAR CHIEF MARXISM ...TIME/SEQ BIBLIOG 9/20. PAGE 5 F0099 TREND CONSTN ATTIT B67

BARNETT A.D.,CHINA AFTER MAO. ASIA CHINA/COM CULTURE ECO/UNDEV ECO/TAC CONTROL EFFICIENCY NAT/LISM MARXISM 20. PAGE 10 F0189 POL/PAR NAT/G TEC/DEV GP/REL B67

BROMKE A.,POLAND'S POLITICS: IDEALISM VS. REALISM. COM GERMANY POLAND RUSSIA USSR POL/PAR CATHISM ...BIBLIOG 19/20. PAGE 19 F0360 NAT/G DIPLOM MARXISM B67

CEFKIN J.L.,THE BACKGROUND OF CURRENT WORLD PROBLEMS. AFR NAT/G MARXISM...T 20 UN. PAGE 22 F0432 DIPLOM NAT/LISM ECO/UNDEV B67

CHO S.S.,KOREA IN WORLD POLITICS 1940-1950; AN EVALUATION OF AMERICAN RESPONSIBILITY. KOREA USA+45 USSR CONSTN INT/ORG NAT/G FORCES FOR/AID ANOMIE SUPEGO MARXISM...DECISION BIBLIOG 20. PAGE 24 F0469 POLICY DIPLOM PROB/SOLV WAR B67

DAVIS H.B.,NATIONALISM AND SOCIALISM: MARXIST AND LABOR THEORIES OF NATIONALISM TO 1917. WOR-45 PROB/SOLV SOVEREIGN...CONCPT IDEA/COMP 19/20. PAGE 30 F0589 MARXISM ATTIT NAT/LISM SOCISM B67

DINERSTEIN H.S.,INTERVENTION AGAINST COMMUNISM (STUDIES IN INTERNATIONAL AFFAIRS NO. 1). CUBA DOMIN/REP GREECE USA+45 USSR VIETNAM OP/RES COERCE WAR 20. PAGE 33 F0643 MARXISM DIPLOM NAT/LISM B67

EBENSTEIN W.,TODAY'S ISMS: COMMUNISM, FASCISM, CAPITALISM, SOCIALISM (5TH ED.). COM WOR+45 PERCEPT PWR...SOC TREND IDEA/COMP NAT/COMP 20. PAGE 35 F0691 FASCISM MARXISM SOCISM CAP/ISM B67

EVANS R.H.,COEXISTENCE: COMMUNISM AND ITS PRACTICE IN BOLOGNA, 1945-1965. ITALY CAP/ISM ADMIN CHOOSE PEACE ORD/FREE...SOC STAT DEEP/INT SAMP CHARTS BIBLIOG MUNICH 20. PAGE 39 F0756 MARXISM CULTURE POL/PAR B67

FALL B.B.,HO CHI MINH ON REVOLUTION: SELECTED WRITINGS, 1920-66. COM VIETNAM ELITES NAT/G COERCE GUERRILLA RACE/REL MARXISM...MARXIST ANTHOL 20. PAGE 39 F0761 REV COLONIAL ECO/UNDEV S/ASIA B67

FILENE P.G.,AMERICANS AND THE SOVIET EXPERIMENT, 1917-1933. USA-45 USSR INTELL NAT/G CAP/ISM DIPLOM EDU/PROP PRESS REV SOCISM...PSY 20. PAGE 41 F0793 ATTIT RIGID/FLEX MARXISM SOCIETY B67

FONER P.S.,THE BOLSHEVIK REVOLUTION. USA-45 POL/PAR WORKER DIPLOM EDU/PROP MARXISM...STERTYP 20. PAGE 42 F0821 LABOR INTELL REV PRESS B67

GRIFFITH W.E.,SINO-SOVIET RELATIONS, 1964-1965. CHINA/COM COM USSR CHIEF 20. PAGE 51 F1001 DIPLOM PWR DOMIN MARXISM B67

HERRESHOFF D.,AMERICAN DISCIPLES OF MARX: FROM THE AGE OF JACKSON TO THE PROGRESSIVE ERA. USA-45 AGRI POL/PAR 19/20. PAGE 59 F1155 MARXISM ATTIT WORKER CONCPT B67

JHANGIANI M.A.,JANA SANGH AND SWATANTRA: A PROFILE OF THE RIGHTIST PARTIES IN INDIA. INDIA ADMIN CHOOSE MARXISM SOCISM...INT CHARTS BIBLIOG 20. PAGE 67 F1320 POL/PAR LAISSEZ NAT/LISM ATTIT B67

LISS S.B.,THE CANAL, ASPECTS OF UNITED STATES-PANAMANIAN RELATIONS. AFR FUT PANAMA DOMIN COERCE ATTIT SOVEREIGN MARXISM 20 JOHNSON/LB KENNEDY/JF. PAGE 81 F1580 DIPLOM POLICY B67

MAZOUR A.G.,SOVIET ECONOMIC DEVELOPMENT: OPERATION OUTSTRIP: 1921-1965. USSR ECO/UNDEV FINAN CHIEF WORKER PROB/SOLV CONTROL PRODUC MARXISM...CHARTS ORG/CHARTS 20 STALIN/J. PAGE 87 F1711 ECO/TAC AGRI INDUS PLAN B67

MCNELLY T.,SOURCES IN MODERN EAST ASIAN HISTORY AND POLITICS. KOREA VIETNAM CULTURE DIPLOM COLONIAL REV WAR PWR ALL/IDEOS MARXISM...ANTHOL 20 CHINJAP. PAGE 88 F1733 NAT/COMP ASIA S/ASIA SOCIETY B67

NYOMARKAY J.,CHARISMA AND FACTIONALISM IN THE NAZI PARTY. GERMANY POL/PAR LEGIT LEAD MARXISM ...NEW/IDEA METH/COMP GEN/LAWS BIBLIOG 20 HITLER/A. PAGE 99 F1949 FASCISM INGP/REL CHIEF PWR B67

OGLESBY C.,CONTAINMENT AND CHANGE. AFR COM USA+45 ECO/UNDEV TEC/DEV ECO/TAC FOR/AID INT/TRADE DOMIN GUERRILLA REV PEACE 20 STALIN/J. PAGE 101 F1983 DIPLOM BAL/PWR MARXISM CULTURE B67

ROELOFS H.M.,THE LANGUAGE OF MODERN POLITICS: AN INTRODUCTION TO THE STUDY OF GOVERNMENT. DIPLOM ADMIN MARXISM NEW/LIB...JURID CONCPT METH/COMP T 20. PAGE 113 F2230 LEAD NAT/COMP PERS/REL NAT/G B67

SCHECTER J.,THE NEW FACE OF BUDDHA: BUDDHISM AND POLITICAL POWER IN SOUTHEAST ASIA. S/ASIA NAT/G POL/PAR NAT/LISM ATTIT MARXISM...BIBLIOG 20. PAGE 116 F2292 SECT POLICY PWR LEAD B67

SHAFFER H.G.,THE COMMUNIST WORLD: MARXIST AND NON-MARXIST VIEWS. WOR+45 SOCIETY DIPLOM ECO/TAC CONTROL SOCISM...MARXIST ANTHOL BIBLIOG/A 20. PAGE 120 F2363 MARXISM NAT/COMP IDEA/COMP COM B67

SPECTOR S.D.,CHECKLIST OF ITEMS IN THE NDEA INSTITUTE LIBRARY (PAMPHLET). USA+45 NAT/G SECT EDU/PROP ATTIT ALL/IDEOS...SOC BIOG. PAGE 124 F2448 BIBLIOG/A COM MARXISM B67

TANSKY L.,US AND USSR AID TO DEVELOPING COUNTRIES. INDIA TURKEY USA+45 USSR INDUS PLAN CAP/ISM WAR PWR WEALTH MARXISM...CHARTS NAT/COMP BIBLIOG 20. PAGE 128 F2534 ECO/UNDEV FOR/AID DIPLOM ECO/TAC B67

TANSKY L.,US AND USSR AID TO DEVELOPING COUNTRIES. INDIA TURKEY UAR USA+45 USSR FINAN PLAN TEC/DEV ADMIN WEALTH...TREND METH/COMP 20. PAGE 128 F2535 FOR/AID ECO/UNDEV MARXISM CAP/ISM B67

VAN SLYKE L.P.,ENEMIES AND FRIENDS; THE UNITED FRONT IN CHINESE COMMUNIST HISTORY. CHINA/COM SOCIETY FORCES PLAN ADJUST 20 MAO. PAGE 140 F2764 INGP/REL MARXISM ATTIT GP/REL B67

ZALESKI E.,PLANNING REFORMS IN THE SOVIET UNION 1962-1966. COM USSR NAT/G CONFER CONTROL EFFICIENCY MARXISM...POLICY DECISION 20. PAGE 150 F2957 ECO/DEV PLAN ADMIN CENTRAL L67

AUSTIN D.A.,"POLITICAL CONFLICT IN AFRICA." CONSTN NAT/G CREATE ADMIN COLONIAL ORD/FREE MARXISM POPULISM SOCISM...NAT/COMP ANTHOL 20. PAGE 8 F0141 ANOMIE AFR POL/PAR L67

GREGORY A.J.,"AFRICAN SOCIALISM, SOCIALISM AND FASCISM: AN APPRAISAL." FUT LEAD REV GP/REL RACE/REL NAT/LISM ATTIT...IDEA/COMP STERTYP 20. PAGE 51 F0993 FASCISM MARXISM SOCISM AFR S67

ALEXANDER R.J.,"'THIRD FORCE' IN WORLD COMMUNISM?" CHINA/COM CUBA USSR INT/ORG DIPLOM TASK INGP/REL ATTIT PWR 20 CASTRO/F. PAGE 3 F0060 CHIEF MARXISM LEAD REV S67

ANDERSON S.S.,"SOVIET RUSSIA AND THE TWO EUROPES." AFR USSR PROB/SOLV CENTRAL SOVEREIGN 20. PAGE 5 F0097 DIPLOM POLICY MARXISM S67

AVTORKHANOV A.,"A NEW AGRARIAN REVOLUTION." COM USSR ECO/DEV PLAN TEC/DEV ADMIN CONTROL OPTIMAL WEALTH SOCISM 20 KHRUSH/N STALIN/J. PAGE 8 F0144 AGRI METH/COMP MARXISM OWN S67

CAMMETT J.M.,"COMMUNIST THEORIES OF FASCISM, 1920-35." ITALY POL/PAR PROF/ORG VOL/ASSN WORKER COLONIAL TOTALISM...SOCIALIST 20. PAGE 21 F0403 MARXISM FASCISM ATTIT S67

CATTELL D.T.,"THE FIFTIETH ANNIVERSARY: A SOVIET WATERSHED?" USSR CONSTN ECO/DEV NAT/G LEAD TOTALISM 20 KHRUSH/N. PAGE 22 F0430 MARXISM CHIEF POLICY ADJUST S67

FADDEYEV N.,"CMEA CO-OPERATION OF EQUAL NATIONS." COM R+D PLAN CAP/ISM DIPLOM FOR/AID WEALTH...POLICY MARXIST. PAGE 39 F0758 MARXISM ECO/TAC INT/ORG ECO/UNDEV S67

FEDYSHYN O.S.,"KHRUSHCHEV'S 'LEAP FORWARD': NATIONAL ASSIMILATION IN THE USSR AFTER STALIN." USSR PLAN NAT/LISM PERSON...POLICY 20 KHRUSH/N STALIN/J. PAGE 39 F0771 GP/REL INGP/REL MARXISM METH S67

FRANKEL T.,"ECONOMIC REFORM* A TENTATIVE APPRAISAL." COM USSR OP/RES BUDGET CONFER EFFICIENCY PRODUC MARXISM SOCISM...MGT 20. PAGE 43 F0847 ECO/DEV INDUS PLAN WEALTH S67

GAMARNIKOW M.,"THE NEW ROLE OF PRIVATE ENTERPRISE." ECO/DEV INDUS NAT/G SML/CO CREATE PROB/SOLV MARXISM ...POLICY TREND IDEA/COMP 20. PAGE 46 F0890 ECO/TAC ATTIT CAP/ISM COM

S67
GEISS I.,"THE GERMANS AND THE MIDDLE EAST CRISIS." GERMANY/W ISLAM ISRAEL USSR POL/PAR RACE/REL MARXISM...GP/COMP 20 JEWS. PAGE 47 F0914 ATTIT DIPLOM WAR POLICY

S67
HEILBRONER R.L.,"BUILDING NEW NATIONS." AFR STRUCT PLAN TEC/DEV ADJUST MARXISM...POLICY 20. PAGE 58 F1138 PROB/SOLV REV NAT/LISM ECO/UNDEV

S67
HUTCHINGS R.,"THE ENDING OF UNEMPLOYMENT IN THE USSR" USSR PLAN ECO/TAC PRICE INGP/REL...GEOG STAT CHARTS 20 MIGRATION. PAGE 63 F1247 WORKER AGRI INDUS MARXISM

S67
JEDLICKI W.,"THE FREE SPEECH MOVEMENT IN WARSAW." POLAND FORCES EDU/PROP LEAD ATTIT MARXISM ...IDEA/COMP 20. PAGE 67 F1310 COERCE CROWD ORD/FREE ACADEM

S67
KRAUS J.,"A MARXIST IN GHANA." GHANA ELITES CHIEF PROB/SOLV TEC/DEV DIPLOM ECO/TAC COLONIAL PARTIC PWR 20 NKRUMAH/K. PAGE 73 F1432 MARXISM PLAN ATTIT CREATE

S67
LEE R.L.,"THE PARADOX OF EQUALITY: A THREAT TO INDIVIDUAL AND SYSTEM FUNCTIONING." CHINA/COM ECO/UNDEV WORKER...SIMUL GEN/LAWS 20. PAGE 77 F1508 SOCIETY STRATA MARXISM IDEA/COMP

S67
LEONTYEV L.,"THE LENINIST PRINCIPLES OF SOCIALIST ECONOMIC MANAGEMENT." USA+45 USSR POL/PAR WORKER PLAN ECO/TAC EFFICIENCY PRODUC MARXISM...POLICY SOCIALIST MGT TREND 20 LENIN/VI MARX/KARL. PAGE 78 F1529 SOCISM CAP/ISM IDEA/COMP ECO/DEV

S67
MAJSTRENKO I.W.,"PROBLEMS CONFRONTING SOVIET AGRICULTURE." COM USSR ECO/DEV ECO/TAC EFFICIENCY OPTIMAL WEALTH MARXISM 20. PAGE 84 F1643 AGRI PROB/SOLV CENTRAL TEC/DEV

S67
MOSELY P.E.,"EASTERN EUROPE IN WORLD POWER POLITICS: WHERE DE-STALINIZATION HAS LED." ECO/UNDEV NAT/LISM 20. PAGE 94 F1842 COM NAT/G DIPLOM MARXISM

S67
ORAZEM F.,"THE NEW SOVIET PLAN FOR AGRICULTURE (1960-1970)" USSR WORKER CAP/ISM ECO/TAC PRICE OWN HABITAT MARXISM...CHARTS 20. PAGE 101 F1994 AGRI PLAN COM ECO/DEV

S67
PERKINS D.H.,"ECONOMIC GROWTH IN CHINA AND THE CULTURAL REVOLUTION(1960APRIL 1967)" CHINA/COM FUT AGRI INDUS PLAN LEAD MARXISM...CHARTS 20 MAO. PAGE 105 F2062 ECO/TAC CULTURE REV ECO/UNDEV

S67
PETRAS J.,"GUERRILLA MOVEMENTS IN LATIN AMERICA - I." GUATEMALA PERU VENEZUELA NAT/G COLONIAL LEAD ATTIT PWR...TIME/SEQ METH/COMP 20 COLOMB. PAGE 105 F2072 GUERRILLA REV L/A+17C MARXISM

S67
RAMA C.M.,"PASADO Y PRESENTE DE LA RELIGION EN AMERICA LATINA." L/A+17C ELITES SOCIETY STRATA MARXISM...STAT WORSHIP PROTESTANT. PAGE 109 F2139 SECT CATHISM STRUCT NAT/COMP

S67
RICHMAN B.M.,"CAPITALISTS & MANAGERS IN COMMUNIST CHINA." ASIA CHINA/COM ECO/UNDEV NAT/G CONSULT EX/STRUC PLAN EFFICIENCY PRODUC WEALTH MARXISM ...MGT CHARTS 20. PAGE 111 F2185 CAP/ISM INDUS

S67
RICHMAN B.M.,"SOVIET MANAGEMENT IN TRANSITION." USSR FINAN MARKET EX/STRUC PLAN PROB/SOLV TEC/DEV CONTROL LEAD CENTRAL EFFICIENCY...METH/COMP 20 REFORMERS. PAGE 111 F2186 MGT MARXISM POLICY AUTHORIT

S67
SEIDLER G.L.,"MARXIST LEGAL THOUGHT IN POLAND." POLAND SOCIETY R+D LOC/G NAT/G ACT/RES ADJUD CT/SYS SUPEGO PWR...SOC TREND 20 MARX/KARL. PAGE 119 F2343 MARXISM LAW CONCPT EFFICIENCY

S67
SPITTMANN I.,"EAST GERMANY: THE SWINGING PENDULUM." COM GERMANY/E NAT/G EFFICIENCY MARXISM 20. PAGE 125 F2458 PRODUC POL/PAR WEALTH ATTIT

S67
STOLTE S.C.,"THREE PROBLEMS FACING THE SOVIET BLOC." ASIA COM USA+45 USSR FORCES MARXISM ...IDEA/COMP METH/COMP 20 NATO WARSAW/P. PAGE 127 F2496 ECO/TAC DIPLOM INT/ORG POLICY

S67
STYCOS J.M.,"POLITICS AND POPULATION CONTROL IN LATIN AMERICA." USA+45 FAM NAT/G GP/REL AGE/C ATTIT CATHISM MARXISM...POLICY UN WHO. PAGE 127 F2509 PLAN CENSUS CONTROL L/A+17C

S67
TABORSKY E.,"THE CLASS STRUGGLE, THE PROLETARIAT, AND THE DEVELOPING NATIONS." USSR LABOR POL/PAR FOR/AID COLONIAL GP/REL 20. PAGE 128 F2521 DIPLOM MARXISM ECO/UNDEV WORKER

S67
WEISSKOPF W.A.,"THE DIALECTICS OF ABUNDANCE." UNIV CAP/ISM ATTIT MARXISM...CONCPT 20. PAGE 145 F2853 INDUS SOCIETY IDEA/COMP ALL/VALS

S67
WILES P.J.,"THE POLITICAL AND SOCIAL PREREQUISITES FOR A SOVIET-TYPE ECONOMY." COM USSR LAW CULTURE CREATE ADMIN FEEDBACK ROUTINE COST OPTIMAL TOTALISM MARXISM 20. PAGE 146 F2883 ECO/DEV PLAN EX/STRUC EFFICIENCY

N67
US CONGRESS JOINT ECO COMM,MAINLAND CHINA IN THE WORLD ECONOMY (PAMPHLET). CHINA/COM USA+45 AGRI CHIEF MARXISM CONGRESS. PAGE 135 F2661 ECO/UNDEV POLICY ECO/TAC INT/TRADE

N67
US HOUSE COMM FOREIGN AFFAIRS,COMMUNIST ACTIVITIES IN LATIN AMERICA 1967 (PAMPHLET). CUBA USA+45 DIPLOM INT/TRADE EDU/PROP COERCE GUERRILLA HOUSE/REP OAS. PAGE 137 F2696 L/A+17C MARXISM ORD/FREE ECO/TAC

N67
US SENATE COMM ON FOREIGN REL,THE RIM OF ASIA (PAMPHLET). WAR MARXISM 20. PAGE 139 F2745 ASIA PROB/SOLV SOVEREIGN POLICY

B68
NENAROKOV A.P.,RUSSIA IN THE 20TH CENTURY: THE OFFICIAL SOVIET HISTORY. USSR SOCIETY REV...AUD/VIS 20. PAGE 97 F1913 COM ADJUST MARXISM

L86
OSGOOD H.L.,"SCIENTIFIC SOCIALISM: RODBERTUS" GERMANY CAP/ISM COST WEALTH...MAJORIT BIOG IDEA/COMP 19 RODBRTUS/C. PAGE 102 F2002 SOCISM MARXISM ECO/DEV ECO/TAC

B92
ENGELS F.,THE CONDITION OF THE WORKING-CLASS IN ENGLAND (1848). UK INDUS LABOR PRICE CONTROL COST INCOME HEALTH MARXISM MUNICH 19. PAGE 38 F0733 WORKER WEALTH MARXIST CAP/ISM

MARXIST....MARXIST

N
US LIBRARY OF CONGRESS,EAST EUROPEAN ACCESSIONS INDEX. NAT/G ISOLAT ATTIT KNOWL...POLICY 20. PAGE 138 F2711 BIBLIOG COM MARXIST DIPLOM

B04
MARX K.,A CONTRIBUTION TO THE CRITIQUE OF POLITICAL ECONOMY (TRANS. FROM 2ND ED. BY N.I. STONE). UK STRATA ECO/DEV FINAN MARKET PLAN BARGAIN CAP/ISM ECO/TAC ATTIT WEALTH...METH/CNCPT BIOG 19. PAGE 86 F1687 MARXIST NEW/IDEA MARXISM

B18
MARX K.,CAPITAL. FUT MOD/EUR STRATA DIST/IND PROC/MFG TEC/DEV WEALTH...MARXIST WORK 19. PAGE 86 F1688 ECO/DEV CAP/ISM SOCISM

B19
VEBLEN T.B.,THE VESTED INTERESTS AND THE STATE OF THE INDUSTRIAL ARTS. USA-45 LAW FINAN WORKER PAY DOMIN PRICE COST SOCISM...MARXIST 19/20. PAGE 141 F2771 INDUS CAP/ISM METH/COMP WEALTH

N19
HALL G.,MAIN STREET TO WALL STREET: END THE COLD WAR (PAMPHLET). AFR USA+45 LAW STRUCT POL/PAR WORKER INT/TRADE DOMIN INCOME...POLICY 20 COM/PARTY. PAGE 53 F1046 MARXIST CAP/ISM DIPLOM NAT/G

B34
MARX K.,THE CLASS STRUGGLES IN FRANCE. FRANCE INDUS WORKER CONSERVE...TREND GEN/LAWS 19. PAGE 86 F1689 MARXIST STRATA REV INT/TRADE

B35
MARX K.,WAGE-LABOR AND CAPITAL -- VALUE, PRICE AND PROFIT. LABOR PAY PRICE COST INCOME OWN PROFIT WEALTH 19. PAGE 86 F1690 STRATA WORKER MARXIST MARXISM

B39
ENGELS F.,HERRN EUGEN DUHRING'S REVOLUTION IN SCIENCE (1878). CULTURE STRATA STRUCT FAM SECT ECO/TAC REV WAR SOCISM...MARXIST 19. PAGE 37 F0731 PWR SOCIETY WEALTH GEN/LAWS

B51
LUXEMBORG R.,THE ACCUMULATION OF CAPITAL (TRANS. BY AGNES SCHWARZSCHILD). ECO/TAC DOMIN COLONIAL ATTIT LAISSEZ 19 MONEY. PAGE 82 F1614 MARXIST INT/TRADE CAP/ISM FINAN

B54
LENIN V.I.,SELECTED WORKS (12 VOLS.). USSR INTELL SOCIETY STRATA STRUCT NAT/G POL/PAR WORKER CAP/ISM REV WAR...MARXIST PHIL/SCI 20 MARX/KARL LENIN/VI. COM MARXISM

PAGE 78 F1520

B55
O'CONNOR H.,THE EMPIRE OF OIL. USA+45 DIST/IND FINAN MARKET CAP/ISM TAX CONTROL...POLICY MARXIST BIBLIOG/A 20. PAGE 100 F1955 — EXTR/IND INT/TRADE CENTRAL NAT/G

B57
NAUMANN R.,THEORIE UND PRAXIS DES NEOLIBERALISMUS; DAS MAERCHEN VON DER FREIEN ODER SOZIALEN MARKTWIRTSCHAFT. GERMANY/W FORCES PLAN EDU/PROP SOCISM...POLICY MARXIST IDEA/COMP BIBLIOG 18/20 ADENAUER/K. PAGE 97 F1903 — MARXISM NEW/LIB ECO/TAC CAP/ISM

S59
ALKHIMOV V.S.,"SOVIET FOREIGN TRADE CHANNELS." COM FUT USA+45 USSR ECO/DEV MARKET CONSULT PLAN WEALTH ...MARXIST OBS CON/ANAL FOR/TRADE 20. PAGE 4 F0068 — FINAN ECO/TAC DIPLOM

B60
APTHEKER H.,DISARMAMENT AND THE AMERICAN ECONOMY: A SYMPOSIUM. FUT USA+45 ECO/DEV DIST/IND FINAN INDUS PROC/MFG LABOR NAT/G POL/PAR CONSULT PLAN CAP/ISM INT/TRADE PEACE ATTIT MORAL WEALTH...TREND GEN/LAWS TOT/POP 20. PAGE 6 F0110 — MARXIST ARMS/CONT

S60
HERZ J.H.,"EAST GERMANY: PROGRESS AND PROSPECTS." COM AGRI FINAN INDUS LOC/G NAT/G FORCES PLAN TEC/DEV DOMIN ADMIN COERCE DRIVE PERCEPT RIGID/FLEX MORAL ORD/FREE PWR...MARXIST PSY SOC RECORD STERTYP WORK. PAGE 59 F1158 — POL/PAR STRUCT GERMANY

B61
LENIN V.I.,WHAT IS TO BE DONE? (1902). RUSSIA LABOR NAT/G POL/PAR WORKER CAP/ISM ECO/TAC ADMIN PARTIC ...MARXIST IDEA/COMP GEN/LAWS 19/20. PAGE 78 F1522 — EDU/PROP PRESS MARXISM METH/COMP

S62
IOVTCHOUK M.T.,"ON SOME THEORETICAL PRINCIPLES AND METHODS OF SOCIOLOGICAL INVESTIGATIONS (IN RUSSIAN)." FUT USA+45 STRATA R+D NAT/G POL/PAR TOP/EX ACT/RES PLAN ECO/TAC EDU/PROP ROUTINE ATTIT RIGID/FLEX MARXISM SOCISM...MARXIST METH/CNCPT OBS TREND NAT/COMP GEN/LAWS 20. PAGE 65 F1288 — COM ECO/DEV CAP/ISM USSR

B63
MARX K.,THE POVERTY OF PHILOSOPHY (1847). SOCIETY STRATA INDUS WORKER OWN UTOPIA SOCISM...GEN/LAWS MARX/KARL. PAGE 86 F1692 — MARXIST PRODUC

S63
FLOREA I.,"CU PRIVIRE LA OBIECTUL MATERIALISMULUI ISTORIC SI AL COMUNISMULUI STIINTIFIC SI LA RAPORTUL DINTRE ELE." EUR+WWI WOR+45 WOR-45 INTELL NAT/G POL/PAR WORKER EDU/PROP PERCEPT MARXISM ...MARXIST PHIL/SCI CONCPT TOT/POP 20. PAGE 42 F0812 — COM ATTIT TOTALISM

S63
GRUSHIN B.A.,"PROBLEMS OF THE MOVEMENT OF COMMUNIST LABOR IN THE USSR." COM SOCIETY LABOR ECO/TAC EDU/PROP COERCE RIGID/FLEX ORD/FREE...POLICY MARXIST STAT QU WORK 20. PAGE 52 F1011 — ATTIT USSR

S63
POLYANOV N.,"THE DOLLAR'S VENTURES IN EUROPE." EUR+WWI FRANCE USA+45 ECO/DEV MARKET POL/PAR TEC/DEV ECO/TAC EDU/PROP DRIVE PWR WEALTH...MARXIST MYTH STAT TREND EEC 20. PAGE 107 F2100 — FINAN PLAN BAL/PAY CAP/ISM

B65
COLLINS H.,KARL MARX AND THE BRITISH LABOUR MOVEMENT; YEARS OF THE FIRST INTERNATIONAL. FRANCE SWITZERLND UK CAP/ISM WAR...MARXIST IDEA/COMP BIBLIOG 19. PAGE 26 F0506 — MARXISM LABOR INT/ORG REV

S65
RUSINOW D.I.,"YUGOSLAV DEVELOPMENT BETWEEN EAST AND WEST." AGRI VOL/ASSN PLAN CAP/ISM ECO/TAC FOR/AID INT/TRADE BAL/PAY...MARXIST EEC COMECON. PAGE 115 F2262 — YUGOSLAVIA ECO/UNDEV STAT

S66
JACOBS P.,"RE-RADICALIZING THE DE-RADICALIZED." USA+45 SOCIETY STRUCT FINAN PLAN PROB/SOLV CAP/ISM WEALTH CONSERVE NEW/LIB 20. PAGE 66 F1297 — NAT/G POLICY MARXIST ADMIN

B67
APTHEKER H.,THE NATURE OF DEMOCRACY, FREEDOM AND REVOLUTION. WOR+45 PROB/SOLV COERCE COST...CONCPT TIME/SEQ METH/COMP. PAGE 6 F0111 — REV POPULISM MARXIST ORD/FREE

B67
FALL B.B.,HO CHI MINH ON REVOLUTION: SELECTED WRITINGS, 1920-66. COM VIETNAM ELITES NAT/G COERCE GUERRILLA RACE/REL MARXISM...MARXIST ANTHOL 20. PAGE 39 F0761 — REV COLONIAL ECO/UNDEV S/ASIA

B67
GARAUDY R.,KARL MARX: THE EVOLUTION OF HIS THOUGHT. SOCIETY...BIBLIOG 20 MARX/KARL STALIN/J. PAGE 46 F0899 — MARXIST GEN/LAWS CONCPT TIME/SEQ

B67
SHAFFER H.G.,THE COMMUNIST WORLD: MARXIST AND NON-MARXIST VIEWS. WOR+45 SOCIETY DIPLOM ECO/TAC CONTROL SOCISM...MARXIST ANTHOL BIBLIOG/A 20. PAGE 120 F2363 — MARXISM NAT/COMP IDEA/COMP COM

B67
WILLIAMS M.,THE EAST IS RED: THE VIEW INSIDE CHINA. CHINA/COM CONSTN COERCE AGE/Y ATTIT PERSON...OBS 20 MAO. PAGE 147 F2893 — REV MARXIST GP/REL DIPLOM

S67
DEWHURST A.,"THE WAGE MOVEMENT IN CANADA." CANADA AGRI NAT/G PARTIC COST PRODUC PROFIT 20. PAGE 32 F0627 — WORKER MARXIST INDUS LABOR

S67
FADDEYEV N.,"CMEA CO-OPERATION OF EQUAL NATIONS." COM R+D PLAN CAP/ISM DIPLOM FOR/AID WEALTH...POLICY MARXIST. PAGE 39 F0758 — MARXISM ECO/TAC INT/ORG ECO/UNDEV

S67
GONZALEZ M.P.,"CUBA, UNA REVOLUCION EN MARCHA." CUBA L/A+17C USA+45 VIETNAM ECO/UNDEV FORCES DIPLOM DOMIN...POLICY MARXIST NAT/COMP CASTRO/F. PAGE 48 F0946 — REV NAT/G COLONIAL SOVEREIGN

S67
NUSENBAUM A.A.,"ON THE QUESTION OF TENDENCIES IN AMERICAN EDUCATION." USA+45 USSR SOCIETY SCHOOL RATIONAL 20. PAGE 99 F1946 — MARXIST IDEA/COMP GEN/LAWS EDU/PROP

B92
ENGELS F.,THE CONDITION OF THE WORKING-CLASS IN ENGLAND (1848). UK INDUS LABOR PRICE CONTROL COST INCOME HEALTH MARXISM MUNICH 19. PAGE 38 F0733 — WORKER WEALTH MARXIST CAP/ISM

B96
MARX K.,REVOLUTION AND COUNTER-REVOLUTION. GERMANY CONSTN ELITES INDUS NAT/G DIPLOM ECO/TAC WEALTH. PAGE 86 F1693 — MARXIST REV PWR STRATA

MARYLAND....MARYLAND

B30
GREEN F.M.,CONSTITUTIONAL DEVELOPMENT IN THE SOUTH ATLANTIC STATES, 1776-1860; A STUDY IN THE EVOLUTION OF DEMOCRACY. USA-45 ELITES SOCIETY STRATA ECO/DEV AGRI POL/PAR EX/STRUC LEGIS CT/SYS REGION...BIBLIOG 18/19 MARYLAND VIRGINIA GEORGIA NORTH/CAR SOUTH/CAR. PAGE 50 F0984 — CONSTN PROVS PLURISM REPRESENT

MASCHLER M. F1694

MASON E.S. F1695,F1696,F1697,F1698,F1699,F1700

MASON J.B. F1701

MASS MEDIA....SEE EDU/PROP, COM/IND

MASS. INST. TECH. F1702

MASSACHU....MASSACHUSETTS

MASTERS N.A. F2376

MATH....MATHEMATICS

B00
MILL J.S.,PRINCIPLES OF POLITICAL ECONOMY. WOR-45 CULTURE SOCIETY STRATA ECO/DEV AGRI EXTR/IND FINAN INDUS DELIB/GP ECO/TAC WEALTH...CONCPT MATH TREND 20. PAGE 91 F1786 — MARKET INT/ORG INT/TRADE

N19
BASSIE V.L.,UNCERTAINTY IN FORECASTING AND POLICY FORMATION (PAMPHLET). UNIV MARKET ECO/TAC PRODUC ...POLICY DECISION MGT MATH CHARTS 20. PAGE 11 F0205 — ECO/DEV FINAN PREDICT PROB/SOLV

N19
ROBERTSON D.,GROWTH, WAGES, MONEY (PAMPHLET). UNIV WORKER BUDGET PRICE DEMAND PRODUC WEALTH...CONCPT MATH MONEY. PAGE 112 F2210 — FINAN ECO/DEV ECO/TAC PAY

B25
EDGEWORTH F.Y.,PAPERS RELATING TO POLITICAL ECONOMY. MOD/EUR SOCIETY STRATA DIST/IND INDUS MARKET NAT/G ACT/RES ECO/TAC EXEC WEALTH ...METH/CNCPT MATH TREND HYPO/EXP SIMUL GEN/METH FOR/TRADE VAL/FREE LOG/LING. PAGE 36 F0702 — ECO/DEV CAP/ISM

B31
JEVONS W.S.,THE THEORY OF POLITICAL ECONOMY (4TH ED.; 1ST ED. 1871). WOR-45 FINAN MARKET RENT WEALTH ...LOG MATH QUANT CON/ANAL IDEA/COMP BIBLIOG METH 17/19. PAGE 67 F1318 — GEN/LAWS UTIL LABOR

B48
HICKS J.R.,VALUE AND CAPITAL. FINAN PRICE EQUILIB INCOME PRODUC WEALTH...TIME/SEQ 20 MARSHALL/A PARETO/V SAMUELSN/P. PAGE 59 F1165 — ECOMETRIC MATH DEMAND PROB/SOLV

B48
SAMUELSON P.A.,FOUNDATIONS OF ECONOMIC ANALYSIS. MARKET RATION DEMAND UTIL...MATH METH T 20. — EQUILIB GEN/LAWS

PAGE 115 F2276
ECO/DEV

B50
SURANYI-UNGER T.,PRIVATE ENTERPRISE AND GOVERNMENTAL PLANNING. STRUCT FINAN BAL/PWR HAPPINESS DRIVE NEW/LIB PLURISM...MATH QUANT STAT TREND BIBLIOG. PAGE 127 F2516
PLAN NAT/G LAISSEZ POLICY

B56
ISARD W.,LOCATION AND SPACE-ECONOMY: GENERAL THEORY RELATING TO INDUSTRIAL LOCATION, MARKET AREAS, LAND USE, TRADE... UNIV DIST/IND MARKET LG/CO SML/CO TEC/DEV GP/REL EQUILIB HABITAT...NEW/IDEA MATH CHARTS 20. PAGE 66 F1290
GEN/LAWS GEOG INDUS REGION

B57
OLIVECRONA K.,THE PROBLEM OF THE MONETARY UNIT. AFR UNIV PAY PRICE UTIL...MATH 20 MONEY SILVER. PAGE 101 F1986
FINAN ECO/TAC ECO/DEV CONCPT

B58
DUESENBERRY J.S.,BUSINESS CYCLES AND ECONOMIC GROWTH. USA+45 PROB/SOLV PAY PRICE...CONCPT MATH CHARTS IDEA/COMP 20 DEPRESSION KEYNES/JM. PAGE 34 F0672
FINAN ECO/DEV ECO/TAC INCOME

B58
THEIL H.,ECONOMIC FORECASTS AND POLICY. UNIV CAP/ISM PRICE EFFICIENCY...DECISION CONCPT STAT 20. PAGE 129 F2551
SIMUL MATH ECOMETRIC PREDICT

L58
ARROW K.J.,"ON THE STABILITY OF THE COMPETITIVE EQUILIBRIUM: I." WOR+45...METH/CNCPT MATH STAT CHARTS SIMUL. PAGE 6 F0122
DECISION MARKET ECO/DEV ECO/TAC

S58
ARROW K.J.,"UTILITIES, ATTITUDES, CHOICES: A REVIEW NOTE." USA+45 PLAN...METH/CNCPT MATH STAT CHARTS HYPO/EXP. PAGE 6 F0121
DECISION DIST/IND MARKET CREATE

S58
ARROW K.J.,"A NOTE ON EXPECTATIONS AND STABILITY." WOR+45...METH/CNCPT MATH STAT CHARTS HYPO/EXP. PAGE 7 F0123
DECISION MARKET ECO/DEV ECO/TAC

B59
HARVARD UNIVERSITY LAW SCHOOL,INTERNATIONAL PROBLEMS OF FINANCIAL PROTECTION AGAINST NUCLEAR RISK. WOR+45 NAT/G DELIB/GP PROB/SOLV DIPLOM CONTROL ATTIT...POLICY INT/LAW MATH 20. PAGE 56 F1105
NUC/PWR ADJUD INDUS FINAN

B59
KARLIN S.,MATHEMATICAL METHODS AND THEORY IN GAMES, PROGRAMMING, AND ECONOMICS. COMPUTER PLAN CONTROL TASK...MATH 20. PAGE 69 F1357
GAME METH/COMP ACT/RES DECISION

B59
SHUBIK M.,STRATEGY AND MARKET STRUCTURE: COMPETITION, OLIGOPOLY, AND THE THEORY OF GAMES. ELITES STRUCT MARKET OP/RES EXEC EFFICIENCY INCOME ...MGT MATH STAT CHARTS 20. PAGE 121 F2389
ECO/DEV ECO/TAC DECISION GAME

L59
ARROW K.J.,"ON THE STABILITY OF THE COMPETITIVE EQUILIBRIUM: II." WOR+45...METH/CNCPT MATH STAT CHARTS HYPO/EXP. PAGE 7 F0124
DECISION MARKET ECO/DEV ECO/TAC

S59
CYERT R.M.,"MODELS IN A BEHAVIORAL THEORY OF THE FIRM." ROUTINE...DECISION MGT METH/CNCPT MATH. PAGE 29 F0567
SIMUL GAME PREDICT INDUS

S59
REUBENS E.D.,"THE BASIS FOR REORIENATION OF AMERICAN FOREIGN AID POLICY." USA+45 USSR STRUCT INT/ORG CONSULT ECO/TAC ADMIN DRIVE MORAL ORD/FREE PWR WEALTH...RELATIV MATH STAT TREND GEN/LAWS VAL/FREE 20. PAGE 111 F2180
ECO/UNDEV PLAN FOR/AID DIPLOM

B60
BOULDING K.E.,LINEAR PROGRAMMING AND THE THEORY OF THE FIRM. ACT/RES PLAN...MGT MATH. PAGE 17 F0323
LG/CO NEW/IDEA COMPUTER

B60
CAMPBELL R.W.,SOVIET ECONOMIC POWER. COM USA+45 DIST/IND MARKET TOP/EX ACT/RES CAP/ISM ECO/TAC DOMIN EDU/PROP ADMIN ROUTINE DRIVE...MATH TIME/SEQ CHARTS WORK 20. PAGE 21 F0409
ECO/DEV PLAN SOCISM USSR

B60
HARBERGER A.C.,THE DEMAND FOR DURABLE GOODS. AGRI FINAN COST EQUILIB...MATH STAT TIME/SEQ TREND CON/ANAL CHARTS SIMUL ANTHOL 20. PAGE 55 F1072
ECOMETRIC DEMAND PRICE

B60
HOSELITZ B.F.,SOCIOLOGICAL ASPECTS OF ECONOMIC GROWTH. WOR+45 WOR-45 ECO/UNDEV CAP/ISM RIGID/FLEX WEALTH...MATH CHARTS. PAGE 62 F1221
ECO/DEV SOC

B60
LERNER A.P.,THE ECONOMICS OF CONTROL. USA+45 ECO/UNDEV INT/ORG ACT/RES PLAN CAP/ISM INT/TRADE ATTIT WEALTH...SOC MATH STAT GEN/LAWS INDEX 20. PAGE 78 F1530
ECO/DEV ROUTINE ECO/TAC SOCISM

L60
CHENERY H.B.,"PATTERNS OF INDUSTRIAL GROWTH." INT/TRADE DEMAND PRODUC...MATH REGRESS CHARTS SIMUL METH 20. PAGE 24 F0462
ECO/TAC ECO/DEV GP/COMP CON/ANAL

S60
FRANKEL S.H.,"ECONOMIC ASPECTS OF POLITICAL INDEPENDENCE IN AFRICA." AFR FUT SOCIETY ECO/UNDEV COM/IND FINAN LEGIS PLAN TEC/DEV CAP/ISM ECO/TAC INT/TRADE ADMIN ATTIT DRIVE RIGID/FLEX PWR WEALTH ...MGT NEW/IDEA MATH TIME/SEQ VAL/FREE 20. PAGE 43 F0846
NAT/G FOR/AID

S60
HOOVER C.B.,"NATIONAL POLICY AND RATES OF ECONOMIC GROWTH: THE US SOVIET RUSSIA AND WESTERN EUROPE." COM EUR+WWI USA+45 USSR NAT/G PLAN ECO/TAC PWR WEALTH...MATH STAT GEN/LAWS 20. PAGE 61 F1207
ECO/DEV ACT/RES

S60
NEISSER H.,"ECONOMIC IMPERALISM RECONSIDERED." WOR+45 WOR-45 ECO/DEV ECO/UNDEV DIST/IND LEGIT COLONIAL PWR WEALTH SOCISM...MYTH MATH TIME/SEQ 20. PAGE 97 F1909
ACT/RES ECO/TAC CAP/ISM INT/TRADE

B61
ACKLEY G.,MACROECONOMIC THEORY. AFR FINAN WORKER ECO/TAC PRICE COST INCOME PRODUC...MATH TREND CHARTS IDEA/COMP T KEYNES/JM. PAGE 2 F0034
SIMUL ECOMETRIC WEALTH

B61
KLEIN L.R.,AN ECONOMETRIC MODEL OF THE UNITED KINGDOM. UK PRICE COST...MATH PREDICT TREND CHARTS SIMUL METH 20. PAGE 72 F1407
ECOMETRIC COMPUTER STAT COMPUT/IR

S61
BENNION E.G.,"ECONOMETRICS FOR MANAGEMENT." USA+45 INDUS EX/STRUC ACT/RES COMPUTER UTIL...MATH STAT PREDICT METH/COMP HYPO/EXP. PAGE 13 F0248
ECOMETRIC MGT SIMUL DECISION

B62
BRANCH M.C.,THE CORPORATE PLANNING PROCESS. FINAN EX/STRUC EDU/PROP CONTROL LEAD GP/REL PERS/REL RATIONAL PERCEPT...MGT MATH PROBABIL STAT GAME. PAGE 18 F0338
PROF/ORG PLAN DECISION PERSON

B62
HOLMAN A.G.,SOME MEASURES AND INTERPRETATIONS OF EFFECTS OF US FOREIGN ENTERPRISES ON US BALANCE OF PAYMENTS. USA+45 COST INCOME WEALTH...MATH CHARTS 20. PAGE 61 F1199
BAL/PAY INT/TRADE FINAN ECO/TAC

B62
KLEIN L.R.,AN INTRODUCTION TO ECONOMETRICS. DIST/IND DEMAND PRODUC WEALTH...MATH TIME/SEQ T 20. PAGE 72 F1408
ECOMETRIC SIMUL PREDICT STAT

B62
US CONGRESS JOINT ECO COMM,INVENTORY FLUCTUATIONS AND ECONOMIC STABILIZATION. USA+45 LG/CO...MATH CHARTS CONGRESS. PAGE 134 F2652
ECO/TAC FINAN INDUS PROB/SOLV

B62
VANEK J.,THE BALANCE OF PAYMENTS, LEVEL OF ECONOMIC ACTIVITY AND THE VALUE OF CURRENCY: THEORY AND SOME RECENT EXPERIENCES. UNIV PRICE INCOME...MATH 20 KEYNES/JM. PAGE 140 F2766
BAL/PAY ECO/TAC FINAN GEN/LAWS

B63
HOLLAND E.P.,EXPERIMENTS ON A SIMULATED UNDERDEVELOPED ECONOMY: DEVELOPMENT PLANS AND BALANCE-OF-PAYMENTS POLICIES. WOR+45 ECO/UNDEV FINAN PLAN ECO/TAC...MATH STAT CHARTS SIMUL VAL/FREE. PAGE 61 F1196
AFR BAL/PAY

B63
MAIZELS A.,INDUSTRIAL GROWTH AND WORLD TRADE. FUT WOR+45 ECO/DEV FINAN INT/ORG PLAN TEC/DEV ECO/TAC WEALTH...MATH STAT CHARTS VAL/FREE 19/20. PAGE 84 F1642
INDUS ECO/UNDEV INT/TRADE

B63
MEIER G.,INTERNATIONAL TRADE AND DEVELOPMENT. FINAN BAL/PAY COST DEMAND DISCRIM EQUILIB WEALTH...POLICY ECOMETRIC MATH STAT BIBLIOG/A 20. PAGE 89 F1747
ECO/UNDEV ECO/TAC INT/TRADE IDEA/COMP

B63
MULLENBACH P.,CIVILIAN NUCLEAR POWER: ECONOMIC ISSUES AND POLICY FORMATION. AFR FINAN INT/ORG DELIB/GP ACT/RES ECO/TAC ATTIT SUPEGO HEALTH ORD/FREE PWR...POLICY CONCPT MATH STAT CHARTS VAL/FREE 20. PAGE 94 F1855
USA+45 ECO/DEV NUC/PWR

B63
US CONGRESS JOINT ECO COMM,THE UNITED STATES BALANCE OF PAYMENTS. USA+45 DELIB/GP CONFER...MATH PREDICT CHARTS 20 CONGRESS. PAGE 135 F2656
BAL/PAY ECO/TAC INT/TRADE CONSULT

L63
KUZNETS S.,"QUANTITATIVE ASPECTS OF THE ECONOMIC GROWTH OF NATIONS: DISTRIBUTION OF INCOME BY SIZE." WOR+45 FINAN ACT/RES HEALTH...MATH STAT VAL/FREE 20. PAGE 74 F1454
WEALTH ECO/TAC

S63
CLARK P.G.,"TOWARDS MORE COMPREHENSIVE PLANNING IN EAST AFRICA" AFR OP/RES ECO/TAC RATION TAX
ECO/UNDEV PLAN

EFFICIENCY INCOME...MATH TREND CHARTS 20 AFRICA/E. PAGE 25 F0484
STAT METH/COMP

S63
COLLERY A.,"A FULL EMPLOYMENT, KEYNESIAN THEORY OF INTERNATIONAL TRADE." WOR+45 ECO/DEV ACT/RES ECO/TAC ROUTINE ORD/FREE WEALTH...MATH CHARTS 20 KEYNES/JM. PAGE 26 F0504
SIMUL INT/TRADE

S63
MATHUR P.N.,"GAINS IN ECONOMIC GROWTH FROM INTERNATIONAL TRADE." USA-45 ECO/DEV FINAN INDUS ATTIT WEALTH...MATH QUANT STAT BIOG TREND GEN/LAWS WORK 20. PAGE 87 F1704
MARKET ECO/TAC CAP/ISM INT/TRADE

S63
WILES P.J.D.,"WILL CAPITALISM AND COMMUNISM SPONTANEOUSLY CONVERGE." COM FUT USA+45 ECO/DEV DIST/IND MARKET CAP/ISM ECO/TAC RIGID/FLEX WEALTH MARXISM SOCISM...MATH STAT TREND COMPUT/IR 20. PAGE 146 F2885
PLAN TEC/DEV USSR

B64
GEORGIADIS H.G.,BALANCE OF PAYMENTS EQUILIBRIUM. COST DEMAND...CONCPT MATH GEN/LAWS 20 KEYNES/JM. PAGE 47 F0916
BAL/PAY EQUILIB SIMUL INT/TRADE

B64
KEMP M.C.,THE PURE THEORY OF INTERNATIONAL TRADE. WOR+45 WOR-45 ECO/DEV ECO/UNDEV DIST/IND ECO/TAC ...MATH CON/ANAL CHARTS VAL/FREE. PAGE 70 F1374
FINAN CREATE INT/TRADE

B64
LANG A.S.,URBAN RAIL TRANSIT. OP/RES PLAN PROB/SOLV TEC/DEV AUTOMAT COST...TECHNIC MATH CON/ANAL CHARTS METH/COMP SIMUL MUNICH 20 RAILROAD PUB/TRANS. PAGE 75 F1474
DIST/IND ECOMETRIC

B64
SCHULTZ T.W.,TRANSFORMING TRADITIONAL AGRICULTURE. WOR+45 WOR-45 CULTURE STRATA FINAN ACT/RES ECO/TAC ATTIT KNOWL SKILL...MATH STAT TIME/SEQ GEN/LAWS VAL/FREE. PAGE 117 F2316
AGRI ECO/UNDEV

B64
WILLIAMSON J.G.,AMERICAN GROWTH AND THE BALANCE OF PAYMENTS, 1820-1913: A STUDY OF THE LONG SWING. EUR+WWI MOD/EUR USA+45 USA-45 ECO/DEV NAT/G ECO/TAC ROUTINE ORD/FREE WEALTH...MATH STAT TIME/SEQ CHARTS SIMUL GEN/LAWS TRUE/GP METH/GP VAL/FREE 19/20. PAGE 147 F2896
FINAN BAL/PAY

L64
BHAGWATI J.,"THE PURE THEORY OF INTERNATIONAL TRADE: A SURVEY." WOR+45 ECO/DEV ECO/UNDEV FINAN MARKET PROC/MFG INT/ORG LABOR LG/CO NAT/G TEC/DEV ECO/TAC SKILL WEALTH...POLICY RELATIV MGT CONCPT NEW/IDEA MATH QUANT GEN/LAWS FOR/TRADE 20. PAGE 14 F0276
INDUS HYPO/EXP

S64
KOJIMA K.,"THE PATTERN OF INTERNATIONAL TRADE AMONG ADVANCED COUNTRIES." EUR+WWI UK USA+45 WOR+45 MARKET NAT/G ECO/TAC WEALTH...MATH STAT CON/ANAL CHARTS METH/GP EEC CHINJAP 20 CHINJAP. PAGE 72 F1419
ECO/DEV TREND INT/TRADE

S64
RUSSETT B.M.,"INEQUALITY AND INSTABILITY: THE RELATION OF LAND TENURE TO POLITICS." WOR+45 ECO/DEV ECO/UNDEV AGRI NAT/G COERCE PWR...MATH STAT CHARTS GEN/LAWS TERR/GP TRUE/GP METH/GP VAL/FREE 20. PAGE 115 F2263
WEALTH GEOG ECO/TAC ORD/FREE

B65
BAUMOL W.J.,ECONOMIC THEORY AND OPERATIONS ANALYSIS (2ND ED.). MARKET LG/CO BUDGET PRICE COST EQUILIB PRODUC...DECISION MATH CHARTS GAME 20. PAGE 12 F0219
OP/RES ECO/DEV METH/COMP STAT

B65
DODDY F.S.,INTRODUCTION TO THE USE OF ECONOMIC INDICATORS. FINAN LABOR PLAN COST...ECOMETRIC INDICATOR MATH PREDICT CHARTS METH 20. PAGE 33 F0649
TEC/DEV STAT PRODUC PRICE

B65
KANTOROVICH L.V.,THE BEST USE OF ECONOMIC RESOURCES. USSR SOCIETY FINAN ACT/RES TEC/DEV ECO/TAC PRICE CONTROL COST DEMAND EFFICIENCY OPTIMAL...MGT STAT. PAGE 69 F1350
PLAN MATH DECISION

B65
OECD,TECHNIQUES OF ECONOMIC FORECASTING. CANADA FRANCE NETHERLAND SWEDEN UK USA+45 PROB/SOLV ROUTINE...CONCPT MATH CHARTS BIBLIOG METH 20. PAGE 100 F1974
PREDICT METH/COMP PLAN

B65
OZGA S.A.,EXPECTATIONS IN ECONOMIC THEORY. MORAL ...ECOMETRIC MATH STAT IDEA/COMP 20. PAGE 102 F2008
RISK GAME CONCPT PREDICT

B65
PINCUS J.A.,ECONOMIC AID AND INTERNATIONAL COST SHARING* A RAND CORPORATION RESEARCH STUDY. INT/ORG BUDGET CENTRAL...ECOMETRIC MATH QUANT STAT SIMUL. PAGE 106 F2088
ECO/UNDEV COST FOR/AID INT/TRADE

B65
RIGBY P.H.,CONCEPTUAL FOUNDATIONS OF BUSINESS RESEARCH. COMPUTER PROB/SOLV OPTIMAL...MGT CONCPT MATH STAT TESTS SIMUL GEN/METH. PAGE 111 F2192
PROFIT R+D INDUS DECISION

B65
VANEK J.,GENERAL EQUILIBRIUM OF INTERNATIONAL DISCRIMINATION; THE CASE OF CUSTOMS UNIONS. LABOR PROB/SOLV ECO/TAC DISCRIM INCOME...MATH CHARTS METH 20. PAGE 140 F2767
INT/TRADE TARIFFS INT/ORG EQUILIB

B66
CONFERENCE REGIONAL ACCOUNTS,REGIONAL ACCOUNTS FOR POLICY DECISIONS. PROB/SOLV CONTROL RATIONAL KNOWL ORD/FREE...POLICY DECISION MATH STAT ANTHOL 20. PAGE 27 F0523
GOV/REL REGION PLAN ECO/TAC

B66
HEISS K.P.,GAME THEORY AND HUMAN CONFLICTS (RESEARCH MEMORANDUM). UNIV ACT/RES...DECISION SOC MATH PROBABIL SIMUL 20 DEFINETT/B. PAGE 58 F1142
GAME ECOMETRIC PLAN PROB/SOLV

B66
KUENNE R.E.,THE POLARIS MISSILE STRIKE* A GENERAL ECONOMIC SYSTEMS ANALYSIS. USA+45 USSR NAT/G BAL/PWR ARMS/CONT WAR...MATH PROBABIL COMPUT/IR CHARTS HYPO/EXP SIMUL. PAGE 74 F1446
NUC/PWR FORCES DETER DIPLOM

B66
KURAKOV I.G.,SCIENCE, TECHNOLOGY AND COMMUNISM; SOME QUESTIONS OF DEVELOPMENT (TRANS. BY CARIN DEDIJER). USSR INDUS PLAN PROB/SOLV COST PRODUC ...MGT MATH CHARTS METH 20. PAGE 74 F1450
CREATE TEC/DEV MARXISM ECO/TAC

B66
LERNER E.M.,A THEORY OF FINANCIAL ANALYSIS. UNIV LG/CO COST DEMAND INCOME PROFIT...MATH STAT CHARTS SIMUL T 20. PAGE 78 F1531
CONCPT FINAN ECO/DEV OPTIMAL

B66
OHLIN G.,AID AND INDEBTEDNESS. AUSTRIA FINAN INT/ORG PLAN DIPLOM GIVE...POLICY MATH CHARTS 20. PAGE 101 F1984
FOR/AID ECO/UNDEV ADMIN WEALTH

B66
PERSALL E.S.,AN ECONOMETRIC STUDY OF FINANCIAL MARKETS. COMPUTER PROB/SOLV TEC/DEV...MATH STAT CHARTS METH/COMP BIBLIOG 20. PAGE 105 F2066
ECOMETRIC FINAN MARKET METH

B66
SASTRI K.V.S.,FEDERAL-STATE FISCAL RELATIONS IN INDIA: A STUDY OF THE FINANCE COMMISSION AND TECHNIQUES OF FINANCIAL ADJUSTMENT. INDIA PROVS DELIB/GP GOV/REL FEDERAL...MATH CHARTS 20. PAGE 116 F2283
TAX BUDGET FINAN NAT/G

B66
WESTON J.F.,THE SCOPE AND METHODOLOGY OF FINANCE. PLAN TEC/DEV CONTROL EFFICIENCY INCOME UTIL...MGT CONCPT MATH STAT TREND METH 20. PAGE 145 F2863
FINAN ECO/DEV POLICY PRICE

B67
ALLEN R.G.,MACRO-ECONOMIC THEORY: A MATHEMATICAL TREATMENT. UNIV...SIMUL T. PAGE 4 F0070
ECOMETRIC MATH EQUILIB GAME

B67
BERGMANN D KAUN B.,STRUCTURAL UNEMPLOYMENT IN THE UNITED STATES. USA+45 ECO/DEV PRICE ADMIN INGP/REL DEMAND EQUILIB WEALTH...MATH REGRESS STAT 20 NEGRO. PAGE 13 F0258
ECOMETRIC METH WORKER ECO/TAC

B67
CARNEY D.,PATTERNS AND MECHANICS OF ECONOMIC GROWTH: A GENERAL THEORETICAL APPROACH. WOR+45 OP/RES INCOME...MATH TREND CHARTS 20. PAGE 21 F0416
PLAN ECO/DEV FINAN

B67
CLEMENT M.O.,THEORETICAL ISSUES IN INTERNATIONAL ECONOMICS. WOR+45 PLAN PROB/SOLV TEC/DEV ...ECOMETRIC METH/CNCPT MATH BIBLIOG T MONEY. PAGE 25 F0489
INT/TRADE FINAN CREATE BAL/PAY

B67
HAGUE D.C.,PRICE FORMATION IN VARIOUS ECONOMIES; PROCEEDINGS OF A CONFERENCE HELD BY THE INTERNATIONAL ECONOMIC ASSOCIATION. WOR+45 FINAN MARKET PLAN CONFER COST...DECISION MATH PREDICT CHARTS SIMUL 20 INTL/ECON. PAGE 53 F1037
PRICE CAP/ISM SOCISM METH/COMP

B67
HARDT J.P.,MATHEMATICS AND COMPUTERS IN SOVIET ECONOMIC PLANNING. COM USSR OP/RES PROB/SOLV OPTIMAL...MODAL SIMUL 20. PAGE 55 F1082
PLAN TEC/DEV MATH COMPUT/IR

B67
MALINVAUD E.,ACTIVITY ANALYSIS IN THE THEORY OF GROWTH AND PLANNING. UNIV AGRI COMPUTER OP/RES REGION...CHARTS ANTHOL METH. PAGE 84 F1648
MATH GAME SIMUL

B67
PORWIT K.,CENTRAL PLANNING: EVALUATION OF VARIANTS. PRICE OPTIMAL PRODUC...DECISION MATH CHARTS SIMUL BIBLIOG MODELS 20. PAGE 107 F2106
PLAN MGT ECOMETRIC

L67
STILL C.H.,"MONETARY RECOVERY UNDER THE FAIR LABOR STANDARDS ACT." USA+45 USA-45 WORKER PAY ADJUD GOV/REL HEALTH ORD/FREE...MATH 20 NLRB. PAGE 126 F2487
LABOR CONTROL LAW FINAN

MENCHER S. F1755

MENDE T. F1756

MENDEL A.P. F1757

MENDELSON W. F1758

MENEZES A.J. F1759

MENON/KRSH....KRISHNA MENON

MENSHEVIK....MENSHEVIKS

MENTAL DISORDERS....SEE HEALTH

MENTAL HEALTH....SEE HEALTH, PSY

MENTAL INSTITUTION....SEE PUB/INST

MENZIES/RG....ROBERT G. MENZIES

MERCANTLST....MERCANTILIST ECONOMIC THEORY

B65
GRAMPP W.D.,ECONOMIC LIBERALISM; THE BEGINNINGS (VOL. I). USA-45 WOR-45 MARKET LABOR ATTIT WEALTH ...POLICY CONCPT BIBLIOG GREECE/ANC MERCANTLST REPUBLICAN FEDERALIST. PAGE 50 F0974
ECO/DEV CAP/ISM IDEA/COMP ECO/TAC

B66
HUTTENBACH R.A.,BRITISH IMPERIAL EXPERIENCE. AFR S/ASIA UK WOR-45 INT/ORG TEC/DEV...CHARTS 16/20 MERCANTLST. PAGE 64 F1253
COLONIAL TIME/SEQ INT/TRADE

B82
CUNNINGHAM W.,THE GROWTH OF ENGLISH INDUSTRY AND COMMERCE. FUT UK FINAN NAT/G CAP/ISM...POLICY 20 MERCANTLST CHRISTIAN POPE. PAGE 29 F0562
INDUS INT/TRADE SML/CO CONSERVE

B96
SCHMOLLER G.,THE MERCANTILE SYSTEM AND ITS HISTORICAL SIGNIFICANCE: ILLUSTRATED CHIEFLY FROM PRUSSIAN HISTORY (TRANS.). PRUSSIA CULTURE INDUS KIN NAT/G PROVS OP/RES ECO/TAC INT/TRADE SUPEGO PWR WEALTH MUNICH 19 MERCANTLST. PAGE 117 F2302
GEN/METH INGP/REL CONCPT

MERCIER/E....ERNEST MERCIER

MEREDITH/J....JAMES MEREDITH

MERGERS....SEE INDUS, EX/STRUC, FINAN

MERIKOSKI V. F1760

MERON T. F1761

MERRIAM C.E. F1762

MERRIAM R.E. F1763

MERTHYR....MERTHYR, WALES

B66
WILLIAMS G.,MERTHYR POLITICS: THE MAKING OF A WORKING-CLASS TRADITION. UK CHIEF WORKER LEAD SOCISM...ANTHOL MUNICH 19/20 MERTHYR RICHARD/H. PAGE 147 F2891
LOC/G POL/PAR INDUS

MERTON/R....ROBERT MERTON

MESOPOTAM....MESOPOTAMIA

MESTMACKER E.J. F1764

METH....HEAVILY EMPHASIZED METHODOLOGY OR TECHNIQUE OF STUDY

N
INTERNATIONAL BIBLIOGRAPHY OF ECONOMICS. WOR+45 FINAN MARKET ADMIN DEMAND INCOME PRODUC...POLICY IDEA/COMP METH. PAGE 1 F0002
BIBLIOG ECO/DEV ECO/UNDEV INT/TRADE

N
AMERICAN ECONOMIC ASSOCIATION,THE JOURNAL OF ECONOMIC ABSTRACTS. ECO/UNDEV MARKET LABOR DIPLOM ...MGT CONCPT METH 20. PAGE 5 F0086
BIBLIOG/A R+D FINAN

N19
HAGEN E.E.,AN ANALYTICAL MODEL OF THE TRANSITION TO ECONOMIC GROWTH (PAMPHLET). WOR+45 WOR-45 SOCIETY STRATA FINAN NAT/G CONTROL PARTIC PRODUC...PHIL/SCI BIBLIOG 17/20. PAGE 53 F1033
SIMUL ECO/DEV METH TEC/DEV

N19
INTERNATIONAL LABOUR OFFICE,EMPLOYMENT, UNEMPLOYMENT AND LABOUR FORCE STATISTICS (PAMPHLET). EUR+WWI STRATA AGRI INDUS NAT/G PROB/SOLV PAY AGE SEX...SAMP NAT/COMP METH 20 ILO. PAGE 65 F1278
WORKER LABOR STAT ECO/DEV

B31
JEVONS W.S.,THE THEORY OF POLITICAL ECONOMY (4TH ED.; 1ST ED. 1871). WOR-45 FINAN MARKET RENT WEALTH ...LOG MATH QUANT CON/ANAL IDEA/COMP BIBLIOG METH 17/19. PAGE 67 F1318
GEN/LAWS UTIL LABOR

B34
ROBINSON J.,THE ECONOMICS OF IMPERFECT COMPETITION. FINAN ECO/TAC PRICE COST DEMAND EQUILIB OPTIMAL WEALTH...METH MONOPOLY. PAGE 113 F2221
MARKET WORKER INDUS

B39
FIRTH R.,PRIMITIVE POLYNESIAN ECONOMY. SOCIETY DIST/IND SECT CHIEF CAP/ISM PRODUC WEALTH...SOC OBS METH WORSHIP 20 POLYNESIA. PAGE 41 F0802
ECO/UNDEV CULTURE AGRI ECO/TAC

B44
KAUFMANN F.,METHODOLOGY OF THE SOCIAL SCIENCES. PERSON...RELATIV PSY CONCPT LING METH 20. PAGE 69 F1363
SOC PHIL/SCI GEN/LAWS METH/CNCPT

B48
SAMUELSON P.A.,FOUNDATIONS OF ECONOMIC ANALYSIS. MARKET RATION DEMAND UTIL...MATH METH T 20. PAGE 115 F2276
EQUILIB GEN/LAWS ECO/DEV

B50
ADORNO T.W.,THE AUTHORITARIAN PERSONALITY. STRATA SECT PROB/SOLV ECO/TAC DISCRIM ATTIT SEX...SOC INT CHARTS METH 20. PAGE 3 F0044
AUTHORIT PERSON ALL/IDEOS SOCIETY

B52
SURANYI-UNGER T.,COMPARATIVE ECONOMIC SYSTEMS. FINAN MARKET DIPLOM PRICE WEALTH...GEOG SOC BIBLIOG METH T 20. PAGE 128 F2517
LAISSEZ PLAN ECO/DEV IDEA/COMP

S52
HEBERLE R.,"ON POLITICAL ECOLOGY" (BMR)" INCOME ATTIT WEALTH...GEOG METH SOC/INTEG 20. PAGE 58 F1133
HABITAT STRATA CHOOSE

S52
LEWIS V.B.,"TOWARD A THEORY OF BUDGETING" (BMR)" USA+45 NAT/G PLAN PROB/SOLV...IDEA/COMP METH 20 SUPREME/CT. PAGE 79 F1551
BUDGET CONCPT CREATE

B53
FLORENCE P.S.,THE LOGIC OF BRITISH AND AMERICAN INDUSTRY; A REALISTIC ANALYSIS OF ECONOMIC STRUCTURE AND GOVERNMENT. UK USA+45 USA-45 FINAN LABOR CAP/ISM INGP/REL EFFICIENCY...MGT CONCPT STAT CHARTS METH 20. PAGE 42 F0813
INDUS ECO/DEV NAT/G NAT/COMP

B53
NEISSER H.,NATIONAL INCOMES AND INTERNATIONAL TRADE. FRANCE GERMANY SWEDEN UK USA-45 EXTR/IND FINAN INDUS TEC/DEV PRICE BAL/PAY EQUILIB INCOME WEALTH...CHARTS METH 19 CHINJAP. PAGE 97 F1908
INT/TRADE PRODUC MARKET CON/ANAL

B54
SCHUMPETER J.A.,HISTORY OF ECONOMIC ANALYSIS. WOR-45...PHIL/SCI METH/CNCPT STAT IDEA/COMP GRECO/ROMN. PAGE 118 F2322
KNOWL GEN/LAWS METH

B55
MOHL R.V.,DIE GESCHICHTE UND LITERATUR DER STAATSWISSENSCHAFTEN (3 VOLS.). LAW NAT/G...JURID METH/COMP METH. PAGE 92 F1814
PHIL/SCI MOD/EUR

S55
DIESING P.,"NONECONOMIC DECISION-MAKING" (BMR)" PROB/SOLV GP/REL ORD/FREE...STAT METH/COMP SIMUL 20. PAGE 33 F0638
DECISION METH EFFICIENCY SOC

B56
HICKMAN C.A.,INDIVIDUALS, GROUPS, AND ECONOMIC BEHAVIOR. WORKER PAY CONTROL EXEC GP/REL INGP/REL PERSON ROLE...PSY SOC PERS/COMP METH 20. PAGE 59 F1163
MGT ADMIN ECO/TAC PLAN

B58
BROWN B.,INCOME TRENDS IN THE UNITED STATES THROUGH 1975. USA+45 NAT/G WEALTH...GEOG CENSUS PREDICT CHARTS METH 20. PAGE 19 F0366
STAT INCOME TREND TAX

B58
INTERNATIONAL ECONOMIC ASSN,ECONOMICS OF INTERNATIONAL MIGRATION. WOR+45 WOR-45 ECO/UNDEV FINAN NAT/G REGION...NAT/COMP METH 20. PAGE 65 F1275
CENSUS GEOG DIPLOM ECO/TAC

B59
FELS R.,AMERICAN BUSINESS CYCLES 1865-1897. USA+45 ECO/DEV LG/CO SML/CO PROB/SOLV TEC/DEV CAP/ISM INT/TRADE DEMAND...POLICY CHARTS METH 19 DEPRESSION. PAGE 40 F0782
FINAN INDUS TREND ECO/TAC

B59
SERAPHIM H.J.,PROBLEME DER WILLENSBILDUNG UND DER WIRTSCHAFTSPOLITISCHEN FUEHRUNG. WOR+45 MARKET ACT/RES OP/RES PLAN EDU/PROP INGP/REL HABITAT PLURISM...MGT PERS/COMP METH 20. PAGE 119 F2357
POLICY DECISION PSY

B59
WIBBERLEY G.P.,AGRICULTURE AND URBAN GROWTH. UK USA+45 ECO/DEV FINAN PROB/SOLV INT/TRADE COST ...GEOG STAT CHARTS METH/COMP HYPO/EXP METH MUNICH 20. PAGE 146 F2876
AGRI PLAN

B60
PFOUTS R.W.,THE TECHNIQUES OF URBAN ECONOMIC ANALYSIS. USA+45...ECOMETRIC CONCPT CHARTS IDEA/COMP ANTHOL MUNICH 20. PAGE 106 F2078
METH ECO/DEV METH/COMP

L60
CHENERY H.B.,"PATTERNS OF INDUSTRIAL GROWTH." INT/TRADE DEMAND PRODUC...MATH REGRESS CHARTS SIMUL METH 20. PAGE 24 F0462
ECO/TAC ECO/DEV GP/COMP CON/ANAL

S60
STOCKWELL E.G.,"THE MEASUREMENT OF ECONOMIC DEVELOPMENT." WOR+45 SOCIETY ECO/DEV ECO/UNDEV INDUS ECO/TAC HEALTH WEALTH...WELF/ST GEOG METH/CNCPT CHARTS METH METH/GP 20. PAGE 126 F2492
FAM STAT

C60
HOSELITZ B.,"THE ROLE OF CITIES IN THE ECONOMIC GROWTH OF UNDERDEVELOPED COUNTRIES" IN "SOCIOLOGICAL ASPECTS OF ECONOMIC GROWTH"(BMR). CULTURE LOC/G ACT/RES...SOC IDEA/COMP METH/COMP METH MUNICH IND 14/20 REDFIELD/R. PAGE 62 F1218
METH/CNCPT TEC/DEV ECO/UNDEV

B61
KLEIN L.R.,AN ECONOMETRIC MODEL OF THE UNITED KINGDOM. UK PRICE COST...MATH PREDICT TREND CHARTS SIMUL METH 20. PAGE 72 F1407
ECOMETRIC COMPUTER STAT COMPUT/IR

B61
SHARP W.R.,FIELD ADMINISTRATION IN THE UNITED NATION SYSTEM: THE CONDUCT OF INTERNATIONAL ECONOMIC AND SOCIAL PROGRAMS. FUT WOR+45 CONSTN SOCIETY ECO/UNDEV R+D DELIB/GP ACT/RES PLAN TEC/DEV EDU/PROP EXEC ROUTINE HEALTH WEALTH...HUM CONCPT CHARTS METH ILO UNESCO GP VAL/FREE UN 20. PAGE 120 F2369
INT/ORG CONSULT

S61
ANDREWS R.B.,"URBAN ECONOMICS: AN APPRAISAL OF PROGRESS." LOC/G PROB/SOLV TEC/DEV...CONCPT OBS/ENVIR METH/COMP HYPO/EXP SOC/EXP SIMUL GEN/METH METH MUNICH 20. PAGE 5 F0102
PHIL/SCI ECOMETRIC

S61
DALTON G.,"ECONOMIC THEORY AND PRIMITIVE SOCIETY" (BMR)" UNIV AGRI KIN TEC/DEV ECO/TAC REGION HABITAT SKILL...METH/COMP BIBLIOG. PAGE 30 F0574
ECO/UNDEV METH PHIL/SCI SOC

B62
DOUGLAS A.,INDUSTRIAL PEACEMAKING. CONSULT ACT/RES ...MGT PSY METH 20. PAGE 34 F0656
BARGAIN INDUS LABOR GP/REL

B62
GEARY R.C.,EUROPE'S FUTURE IN FIGURES. FUT GOV/REL DEMAND PRODUC...STAT CHARTS METH/COMP ANTHOL METH 20 EUROPE. PAGE 47 F0912
FINAN ECO/DEV PREDICT WEALTH

B63
GRIGSBY W.G.,HOUSING MARKETS AND PUBLIC POLICY. USA+45 FAM NEIGH PRICE DEMAND WEALTH...POLICY CHARTS BIBLIOG METH MUNICH 20. PAGE 51 F1002
MARKET RENT HABITAT PLAN

B63
MACHLUP F.,ESSAYS ON ECONOMIC SEMANTICS. UNIV ECO/DEV FINAN COST DEMAND PRODUC...POLICY STAT CHARTS BIBLIOG. PAGE 83 F1632
LING CONCPT METH

B63
OECD,FOOD AID: ITS ROLE IN ECONOMIC DEVELOPMENT. FINAN NAT/G PLAN DIPLOM GIVE TASK WEALTH ...METH/COMP METH 20. PAGE 100 F1966
ECO/UNDEV FOR/AID INT/ORG POLICY

B63
RUMMEL J.F.,RESEARCH METHODOLOGY IN BUSINESS. COMPUTER CREATE PROB/SOLV...CONT/OBS REC/INT QU/SEMANT SYS/QU SAMP CHARTS METH/COMP T 20. PAGE 115 F2260
OP/RES METH/CNCPT METH STAT

S63
ANDREWS R.B.,"ECONOMIC PLANNING FOR SMALL AREAS: THE PLANNING PROCESS." INDUS PROC/MFG PROVS PROB/SOLV TAX EQUILIB...METH/COMP HYPO/EXP METH MUNICH 20. PAGE 5 F0103
ECO/TAC PLAN LOC/G

N63
LEDERER W.,THE BALANCE ON FOREIGN TRANSACTIONS: PROBLEMS OF DEFINITION AND MEASUREMENT (PAMPHLET). USA+45 BUDGET DIPLOM ECO/TAC PRICE GOV/REL...POLICY STAT NAT/COMP METH 20. PAGE 77 F1502
FINAN BAL/PAY INT/TRADE ECO/DEV

B64
FEI J.C.H.,DEVELOPMENT OF THE LABOR SURPLUS ECONOMY: THEORY AND POLICY. WOR+45 AGRI INDUS MARKET PROB/SOLV TEC/DEV...STAT CHARTS GEN/LAWS METH 20 THIRD/WRLD. PAGE 40 F0772
ECO/TAC POLICY WORKER ECO/UNDEV

B64
HANSEN A.H.,BUSINESS CYCLES AND NATIONAL INCOME. USA+45 FINAN ECO/TAC COST OPTIMAL...POLICY METH 20 KEYNES/JM. PAGE 54 F1065
INCOME WEALTH PRODUC INDUS

B64
LINDHOLM R.W.,ECONOMIC DEVELOPMENT POLICY WITH EMPHASIS ON VIET-NAM. KOREA/S PAKISTAN VIETNAM/S AGRI INDUS CONSULT DELIB/GP FOR/AID...METH 20. PAGE 80 F1571
ECO/UNDEV TAX FINAN ECO/TAC

B64
MCNULTY J.E.,SOME ECONOMIC ASPECTS OF BUSINESS ORGANIZATION. ECO/DEV UTIL...MGT CHARTS BIBLIOG METH 20. PAGE 88 F1734
ADMIN LG/CO GEN/LAWS

B64
ODEH H.S.,THE IMPACT OF INFLATION ON THE LEVEL OF ECONOMIC ACTIVITY. AFR BRAZIL CHILE BUDGET GOV/REL COST DEMAND INCOME WEALTH...STAT METH 20 MONEY. PAGE 100 F1963
ECOMETRIC ECO/TAC ECO/UNDEV FINAN

B64
WERTHEIM W.F.,EAST-WEST PARALLELS. INDONESIA S/ASIA NAT/G SECT...TIME/SEQ METH REFORMERS S/EASTASIA. PAGE 145 F2860
SOC ECO/UNDEV CULTURE NAT/LISM

B64
WILLIAMSON O.E.,THE ECONOMICS OF DISCRETIONARY BEHAVIOR: MANAGERIAL OBJECTIVES IN A THEORY OF THE FIRM. MARKET BUDGET CAP/ISM PRODUC DRIVE PERSON ...STAT CHARTS BIBLIOG METH 20. PAGE 147 F2897
EFFICIENCY MGT ECO/TAC CHOOSE

B65
DODDY F.S.,INTRODUCTION TO THE USE OF ECONOMIC INDICATORS. FINAN LABOR PLAN COST...ECOMETRIC INDICATOR MATH PREDICT CHARTS METH 20. PAGE 33 F0649
TEC/DEV STAT PRODUC PRICE

B65
HASSON J.A.,THE ECONOMICS OF NUCLEAR POWER. INDIA UK USA+45 WOR+45 INT/ORG TEC/DEV COST...SOC STAT CHARTS 20 EURATOM. PAGE 56 F1108
NUC/PWR INDUS ECO/DEV METH

B65
KLASSEN L.H.,AREA ECONOMIC AND SOCIAL REDEVELOPMENT. ECO/UNDEV INDUS NAT/G PLAN CAP/ISM TAX...ECOMETRIC SIMUL 20. PAGE 72 F1404
OPTIMAL WORKER METH ECO/TAC

B65
MARCUS E.,INTERNATIONAL TRADE AND FINANCE. EFFICIENCY EQUILIB...CHARTS METH/COMP BIBLIOG METH T 20. PAGE 85 F1664
INT/TRADE FINAN MARKET WEALTH

B65
MUSHKIN S.J.,PROPERTY TAXES: THE 1970 OUTLOOK (PAMPHLET). FUT USA+45 ECO/DEV MARKET PROVS PLAN ...PROBABIL STAT CENSUS PREDICT CHARTS METH 20. PAGE 95 F1872
TAX OWN FINAN LOC/G

B65
OECD,THE MEDITERRANEAN REGIONAL PROJECT: PORTUGAL; EDUCATION AND DEVELOPMENT. PORTUGAL SOCIETY STRATA FINAN PROF/ORG WORKER PLAN PROB/SOLV ADMIN...POLICY STAT CHARTS METH 20 OECD. PAGE 100 F1970
EDU/PROP SCHOOL ACADEM ECO/UNDEV

B65
OECD,THE MEDITERRANEAN REGIONAL PROJECT: ITALY; EDUCATION AND DEVELOPMENT. ITALY SOCIETY STRATA FINAN NAT/G PROF/ORG WORKER PLAN PROB/SOLV ADMIN ...STAT CHARTS METH 20 OECD. PAGE 100 F1971
SCHOOL EDU/PROP ECO/UNDEV ACADEM

B65
OECD,TECHNIQUES OF ECONOMIC FORECASTING. CANADA FRANCE NETHERLAND SWEDEN UK USA+45 PROB/SOLV ROUTINE...CONCPT MATH CHARTS BIBLIOG METH 20. PAGE 100 F1974
PREDICT METH/COMP PLAN

B65
ORG FOR ECO COOP AND DEVEL,THE MEDITERRANEAN REGIONAL PROJECT: YUGOSLAVIA; EDUCATION AND DEVELOPMENT. YUGOSLAVIA SOCIETY FINAN PROF/ORG PLAN ADMIN COST DEMAND MARXISM...STAT TREND CHARTS METH 20 OECD. PAGE 102 F1996
EDU/PROP ACADEM SCHOOL ECO/UNDEV

B65
VANEK J.,GENERAL EQUILIBRIUM OF INTERNATIONAL DISCRIMINATION; THE CASE OF CUSTOMS UNIONS. LABOR PROB/SOLV ECO/TAC DISCRIM INCOME...MATH CHARTS METH 20. PAGE 140 F2767
INT/TRADE TARIFFS INT/ORG EQUILIB

B65
VON RENESSE E.A.,UNVOLLENDETE DEMOKRATIEN. AFR ISLAM S/ASIA SOCIETY ACT/RES COLONIAL...JURID CHARTS BIBLIOG METH 13/20. PAGE 142 F2795
ECO/UNDEV NAT/COMP SOVEREIGN

B65
WISH J.R.,ECONOMIC DEVELOPMENT IN LATIN AMERICA: AN ANNOTATED BIBLIOGRAPHY. L/A+17C COM/IND MARKET R+D CREATE CAP/ISM ATTIT...STAT METH 20. PAGE 148 F2912
BIBLIOG/A ECO/UNDEV TEC/DEV AGRI

N65
STUDY GP CREATE RESERVE ASSETS,REPORT TO DEPUTIES (PAMPHLET). AFR FUT PLAN CONTROL DEMAND WEALTH ...ANTHOL METH 20. PAGE 127 F2507
INT/ORG INT/TRADE FINAN BUDGET

B66
AGGARWALA R.N.,FINANCIAL COMMITTEES OF THE INDIAN PARLIAMENT: A STUDY IN PARLIAMENTARY CONTROL OVER PUBLIC EXPENDITURE. INDIA FINAN NAT/G ROLE...CHARTS METH/COMP METH 20 PARLIAMENT. PAGE 3 F0049
PARL/PROC BUDGET CONTROL DELIB/GP

B66
KURAKOV I.G.,SCIENCE, TECHNOLOGY AND COMMUNISM; SOME QUESTIONS OF DEVELOPMENT (TRANS. BY CARIN DEDIJER). USSR INDUS PLAN PROB/SOLV COST PRODUC ...MGT MATH CHARTS METH 20. PAGE 74 F1450
CREATE TEC/DEV MARXISM ECO/TAC

B66
LENSKI G.E.,POWER AND PRIVILEGE: A THEORY OF SOCIAL STRATIFICATION. SWEDEN UK UNIV USSR CULTURE ECO/UNDEV PRIVIL PWR...PHIL/SCI CONCPT CHARTS IDEA/COMP HYPO/EXP METH MARX/KARL. PAGE 78 F1525 SOC STRATA STRUCT SOCIETY

B66
LEONTIEF W.,ESSAYS IN ECONOMICS. ECO/UNDEV INDUS NAT/G CAP/ISM FOR/AID AUTOMAT MARXISM...ECOMETRIC CHARTS ANTHOL METH 20 KEYNES/JM. PAGE 78 F1528 CONCPT METH/CNCPT METH/COMP

B66
PERSALL E.S.,AN ECONOMETRIC STUDY OF FINANCIAL MARKETS. COMPUTER PROB/SOLV TEC/DEV...MATH STAT CHARTS METH/COMP BIBLIOG 20. PAGE 105 F2066 ECOMETRIC FINAN MARKET METH

B66
WESTON J.F.,THE SCOPE AND METHODOLOGY OF FINANCE. PLAN TEC/DEV CONTROL EFFICIENCY INCOME UTIL...MGT CONCPT MATH STAT TREND METH 20. PAGE 145 F2863 FINAN ECO/DEV POLICY PRICE

B67
BARANSON J.,TECHNOLOGY FOR UNDERDEVELOPED AREAS: AN ANNOTATED BIBLIOGRAPHY. FUT WOR+45 CULTURE INDUS INT/ORG CREATE PROB/SOLV INT/TRADE EDU/PROP AUTOMAT ...CONCPT METH. PAGE 10 F0181 BIBLIOG/A ECO/UNDEV TEC/DEV R+D

B67
BERGMANN D KAUN B.,STRUCTURAL UNEMPLOYMENT IN THE UNITED STATES. USA+45 ECO/DEV PRICE ADMIN INGP/REL DEMAND EQUILIB WEALTH...MATH REGRESS STAT 20 NEGRO. PAGE 13 F0258 ECOMETRIC METH WORKER ECO/TAC

B67
DE JOUVENAL B.,THE ART OF CONJECTURE. WOR+45 EFFICIENCY PERCEPT KNOWL...DECISION PHIL/SCI CONCPT METH/COMP BIBLIOG 20. PAGE 31 F0600 FUT PREDICT SIMUL METH

B67
DIEGUES M.,SOCIAL SCIENCE IN LATIN AMERICA. L/A+17C ...JURID SOC ANTHOL 20. PAGE 33 F0637 METH ACADEM EDU/PROP ACT/RES

B67
FIELD G.L.,COMPARATIVE POLITICAL DEVELOPMENT: THE PRECEDENT OF THE WEST. FRANCE GERMANY SWEDEN UK USSR STRATA STRUCT POL/PAR...METH 20. PAGE 40 F0790 NAT/COMP CONCPT ECO/DEV SOCIETY

B67
MALINVAUD E.,ACTIVITY ANALYSIS IN THE THEORY OF GROWTH AND PLANNING. UNIV AGRI COMPUTER OP/RES REGION...CHARTS ANTHOL METH. PAGE 84 F1648 MATH GAME SIMUL

B67
TUMIN M.M.,SOCIAL STRATIFICATION; THE FORMS AND FUNCTIONS OF INEQUALITY. SENIOR SANCTION WEALTH ...SOC CLASSIF METH 20. PAGE 131 F2592 STRATA DISCRIM CONCPT SOCIETY

L67
WILKINSON J.H. JR.,"THE NET OPERATING LOSS DEDUCTION AND RELATED INCOME TAX DEVICES." PROB/SOLV BUDGET PAY GOV/REL ORD/FREE...MATH CHARTS METH 20. PAGE 146 F2886 TAX FINAN LAW ADJUD

S67
EHRLICH S.,"INTERNATIONAL PRESSURE GROUPS: A CONTRIBUTION TO THE SOCIOLOGY OF INTERNATIONAL RELATIONS IN THE CAPITALIST WORLD." GP/REL...METH 20. PAGE 36 F0711 INT/ORG LOBBY DIPLOM DECISION

S67
FEDYSHYN O.S.,"KHRUSHCHEV'S 'LEAP FORWARD': NATIONAL ASSIMILATION IN THE USSR AFTER STALIN." USSR PLAN NAT/LISM PERSON...POLICY 20 KHRUSH/N STALIN/J. PAGE 39 F0771 GP/REL INGP/REL MARXISM METH

S67
GAUSE M.E.,"ELEMENTS OF FINANCE DEPARTMENT ORGANIZATION FOR SMALL GOVERNMENTAL UNITS." USA+45 PROB/SOLV CONTROL CENTRAL...METH MUNICH. PAGE 47 F0910 ADMIN LOC/G FINAN

S67
SANDMEYER R.L.,"METHODOLOGICAL ISSUES IN THE STUDY OF LABOR FORCE PARTICIPATION RATES." WOR+45 ...CLASSIF REGRESS CHARTS SIMUL. PAGE 116 F2278 METH CON/ANAL PARTIC WORKER

S67
TELLER A.,"AIR-POLLUTION ABATEMENT: ECONOMIC RATIONALITY AND REALITY." NAT/G DELIB/GP ECO/TAC GOV/REL CENTRAL EFFICIENCY HEALTH...CHARTS METH MUNICH. PAGE 129 F2543 PROB/SOLV CONTROL COST AIR

B98
MARSHALL A.,PRINCIPLES OF ECONOMICS. INDUS WORKER PRICE COST EQUILIB INCOME OPTIMAL PRODUC...TIME/SEQ METH RICARDO/D. PAGE 86 F1678 WEALTH GEN/LAWS MARKET

METH/CNCPT....METHODOLOGICAL CONCEPTS

METH/COMP....COMPARISON OF METHODS

N
SOUTH AFRICAN JOURNAL OF ECONOMICS. SOUTH/AFR FINAN MARKET ACT/RES OP/RES...PHIL/SCI STAT CON/ANAL METH/COMP BIBLIOG/A 20. PAGE 1 F0009 ECO/UNDEV ACADEM INTELL R+D

B19
VEBLEN T.B.,THE VESTED INTERESTS AND THE STATE OF THE INDUSTRIAL ARTS. USA-45 LAW FINAN WORKER PAY DOMIN PRICE COST SOCISM...MARXIST 19/20. PAGE 141 F2771 INDUS CAP/ISM METH/COMP WEALTH

N19
ARNOW K.,SELF-INSURANCE IN THE TREASURY (PAMPHLET). USA+45 LAW RIGID/FLEX...POLICY METH/COMP 20 DEPT/TREAS. PAGE 6 F0117 ADMIN PLAN EFFICIENCY NAT/G

N19
BOS H.C.,A DISCUSSION ON METHODS OF MONETARY ANALYSIS AND NORMS FOR MONETARY POLICY (PAMPHLET). BAL/PAY COST INCOME...METH/COMP 20. PAGE 17 F0319 FINAN POLICY EQUILIB SIMUL

N19
DWYER J.W.,YARDSTICKS FOR PERFORMANCE (PAMPHLET). USA+45 FINAN CONTROL...CONCPT METH/COMP MUNICH. PAGE 35 F0688 BUDGET LOC/G EFFICIENCY

N19
FREEMAN H.A.,COERCION OF STATES IN FEDERAL UNIONS (PAMPHLET). WOR-45 DIPLOM CONTROL COERCE PEACE ORD/FREE...GOV/COMP METH/COMP NAT/COMP PACIFIST 20. PAGE 43 F0850 FEDERAL WAR INT/ORG PACIFISM

N19
HAYEK FA V.O.N.,FREEDOM AND THE ECONOMIC SYSTEM. GERMANY USSR PLAN REPRESENT TOTALISM FASCISM POPULISM...MAJORIT METH/COMP GEN/LAWS 20. PAGE 57 F1123 ORD/FREE ECO/TAC CAP/ISM SOCISM

N19
LUTZ F.A.,THE PROBLEM OF INTERNATIONAL LIQUIDITY AND THE MULTIPLECURRENCY STANDARD (PAMPHLET). WOR+45 MARKET INT/ORG PRICE BAL/PAY...NEW/IDEA METH/COMP BIBLIOG 20 IMF. PAGE 82 F1609 PROB/SOLV FINAN DIPLOM ECO/TAC

N19
STALEY E.,SCIENTIFIC RESEARCH AND PROGRESS IN NEWLY DEVELOPING COUNTRIES (PAMPHLET). AFR ASIA L/A+17C CONSULT DIPLOM...METH/COMP 20. PAGE 125 F2463 ECO/UNDEV ACT/RES FOR/AID TEC/DEV

B28
DE MAN H.,THE PSYCHOLOGY OF SOCIALISM. EUR+WWI USSR LABOR NAT/LISM PERSON WEALTH MARXISM...METH/COMP 20. PAGE 31 F0604 WORKER ATTIT SOC SOCISM

B32
ROBBINS L.,AN ESSAY ON THE NATURE AND SIGNIFICANCE OF ECONOMIC SCIENCE. DEMAND EQUILIB PRODUC UTIL ...ECOMETRIC 20. PAGE 112 F2201 GEN/LAWS METH/COMP ECO/DEV

B36
HUBERMAN L.,MAN'S WORLDLY GOODS: THE STORY OF THE WEALTH OF NATIONS. CHRIST-17C EUR+WWI MOD/EUR SOCIETY DOMIN REV ORD/FREE...TIME/SEQ METH/COMP. PAGE 63 F1231 WEALTH CAP/ISM MARXISM CREATE

B37
MACKENZIE F.,PLANNED SOCIETY: YESTERDAY, TODAY, AND TOMORROW. ECO/DEV ECO/UNDEV AGRI FINAN INDUS PLAN INSPECT CONTROL ALL/IDEOS...TREND METH/COMP BIBLIOG 20 RESOURCE/N. PAGE 83 F1635 SOC CONCPT ANTHOL

B37
VON HAYEK F.A.,MONETARY NATIONALISM AND INTERNATIONAL STABILITY. WOR-45 ECO/DEV NAT/G PROB/SOLV INT/TRADE...POLICY CONCPT METH/COMP NAT/COMP 20. PAGE 142 F2792 ECO/TAC FINAN DIPLOM NAT/LISM

B38
HEIMANN E.,COMMUNISM, FASCISM, OR DEMOCRACY? WOR-45 CONSTN SOCIETY STRATA AGRI CAP/ISM MORAL ORD/FREE ...MAJORIT METH/COMP NAT/COMP 19/20. PAGE 58 F1141 SOCISM MARXISM FASCISM PLURISM

B38
LAWLEY F.E.,THE GROWTH OF COLLECTIVE ECONOMY VOL. 1: NATIONAL. EUR+WWI AGRI INDUS NAT/G BARGAIN CAP/ISM ECO/TAC WAR OPTIMAL WEALTH...GOV/COMP METH/COMP 19/20 MONOPOLY. PAGE 76 F1492 SOCISM PRICE CONTROL OWN

B39
CLARK J.M.,SOCIAL CONTROL OF BUSINESS (2ND ED.). ECO/DEV FINAN LG/CO PLAN ECO/TAC PRICE SUPEGO...T 20. PAGE 25 F0480 CAP/ISM CONTROL LAISSEZ METH/COMP

B40
HUNTER R.,REVOLUTION: WHY, HOW, WHEN? NAT/G ECO/TAC EDU/PROP COERCE ORD/FREE FASCISM POPULISM SOCISM 18/20 HITLER/A LENIN/VI. PAGE 63 F1246 REV METH/COMP LEAD CONSTN

B44
BIENSTOCK G.,MANAGEMENT IN RUSSIAN INDUSTRY AND AGRICULTURE. USSR CONSULT WORKER LEAD COST PROFIT ATTIT DRIVE PWR...MGT METH/COMP DICTIONARY ACCT 20. PAGE 15 F0281 ADMIN MARXISM SML/CO AGRI

B44
LOCKE J.,FURTHER CONSIDERATIONS CONCERNING RAISING THE VALUE OF MONEY. AFR UK NAT/G ECO/TAC INCOME WEALTH...METH/COMP GEN/LAWS 17 SILVER. PAGE 81 F1591 COST FINAN PRICE CONTROL

B48
DURBIN E.F.M.,THE POLITICS OF DEMOCRATIC SOCIALISM; SOCIALIST

AN ESSAY ON SOCIAL POLICY. STRATA POL/PAR PLAN COERCE DRIVE PERSON PWR MARXISM...CHARTS METH/COMP. PAGE 35 F0684
POPULISM POLICY SOCIETY

B48
HART A.G.,MONEY, DEBT, AND ECONOMIC ACTIVITY. AFR WORKER DIPLOM PRICE CONTROL BAL/PAY COST OWN PRODUC ...METH/COMP 20 FED/RESERV. PAGE 56 F1097
FINAN WEALTH ECO/TAC NAT/G

B48
WINSLOW E.M.,THE PATTERN OF IMPERIALISM; A STUDY IN THE THEORIES OF POWER. DOMIN WAR PWR MARXISM ...IDEA/COMP METH/COMP BIBLIOG 20. PAGE 147 F2906
SOCISM CAP/ISM COLONIAL ECO/TAC

B49
HANSEN A.H.,MONETARY THEORY AND FISCAL POLICY. CONSULT PLAN INT/TRADE BAL/PAY OPTIMAL...TREND CHARTS METH/COMP BIBLIOG T 19/20 MONEY. PAGE 54 F1063
FINAN GEN/LAWS POLICY ECO/TAC

S49
HART C.W.M.,"INDUSTRIAL RELATIONS RESEARCH AND SOCIAL THEORY." CANADA VOL/ASSN WORKER LEAD EFFICIENCY...MGT SOC METH/CNCPT METH/COMP MUNICH 20. PAGE 56 F1099
GEN/LAWS LABOR GP/REL

B50
LIPSET S.M.,AGRARIAN SOCIALISM. CANADA POL/PAR OP/RES ECO/TAC ADMIN ATTIT...TIME/SEQ NAT/COMP SOC/EXP 20 SASKATCH. PAGE 80 F1576
SOCISM AGRI METH/COMP STRUCT

B51
BROGAN D.W.,THE PRICE OF REVOLUTION. FRANCE USA+45 USA-45 USSR CONSTN NAT/G DIPLOM COLONIAL NAT/LISM ORD/FREE POPULISM...CONCPT 18/20 PRE/US/AM. PAGE 19 F0359
REV METH/COMP COST MARXISM

B51
PRINCETON U INDUSTRIAL REL SEC,COMPULSORY ARBITRATION OF UTILITY DISPUTES IN NEW JERSEY AND PENNSYLVANIA. USA+45 LEGIS WORKER ADJUD ORD/FREE ...POLICY MGT METH/COMP 20 NEW/JERSEY PENNSYLVAN. PAGE 108 F2118
BARGAIN PROVS INDUS LABOR

B52
WU Y.,ECONOMIC WARFARE. MARKET PLAN PROB/SOLV FOR/AID CONTROL EFFICIENCY WEALTH...METH/COMP 20. PAGE 149 F2937
ECO/TAC WAR INT/TRADE DIPLOM

B54
MITCHELL W.G.,BUSINESS CYCLES. FINAN MARKET PRICE COST EQUILIB OPTIMAL PRODUC PROFIT...IDEA/COMP GEN/LAWS 19/20. PAGE 92 F1809
INDUS TIME/SEQ METH/COMP STAT

B55
BERNAYS E.L.,THE ENGINEERING OF CONSENT. VOL/ASSN OP/RES ROUTINE INGP/REL ATTIT RESPECT...POLICY METH/CNCPT METH/COMP 20. PAGE 14 F0264
GP/REL PLAN ACT/RES ADJUST

B55
MOHL R.V.,DIE GESCHICHTE UND LITERATUR DER STAATSWISSENSCHAFTEN (3 VOLS.). LAW NAT/G...JURID METH/COMP METH. PAGE 92 F1814
PHIL/SCI MOD/EUR

B55
PANT Y.P.,PLANNING IN UNDERDEVELOPED ECONOMIES. INDIA NEPAL INT/TRADE COLONIAL SOVEREIGN ALL/IDEOS ...TIME/SEQ METH/COMP 20. PAGE 103 F2026
ECO/UNDEV PLAN ECO/TAC DIPLOM

S55
DIESING P.,"NONECONOMIC DECISION-MAKING" (BMR)" PROB/SOLV GP/REL ORD/FREE...STAT METH/COMP SIMUL 20. PAGE 33 F0638
DECISION METH EFFICIENCY SOC

C55
ADAMS G.P. JR.,"COMPETITIVE ECONOMIC SYSTEMS." WOR+45 WOR-45 PWR...BIBLIOG/A 20. PAGE 2 F0038
METH/COMP ECO/TAC TEC/DEV DIPLOM

B56
BROWN R.E.,CHARLES BEARD AND THE CONSTITUTION. USA-45 NAT/G ORD/FREE WEALTH...HUM TIME/SEQ METH/COMP 20 BEARD/CA. PAGE 19 F0372
CONSTN ELITES HIST/WRIT

B56
FELLNER W.,TRENDS AND CYCLES IN ECONOMIC ACTIVITY: AN INTRODUCTION TO PROBLEMS OF ECONOMIC GROWTH. USA+45 INDUS ACT/RES CAP/ISM EQUILIB...MODAL METH/COMP BIBLIOG 20. PAGE 40 F0779
ECO/TAC TREND FINAN ECO/DEV

B56
POOLE K.E.,PUBLIC FINANCE AND ECONOMIC WELFARE. STRUCT ECO/DEV LOC/G NAT/G BUDGET PAY ROUTINE COST EQUILIB WEALTH...SOC/WK METH/COMP 20. PAGE 107 F2103
FINAN TAX ORD/FREE

B57
BAUER P.T.,THE ECONOMICS OF UNDERDEVELOPED COUNTRIES. WOR+45 AGRI FINAN INDUS PROC/MFG WORKER CAP/ISM PAY PRICE INCOME MARXISM...METH/COMP 20 RESOURCE/N. PAGE 11 F0213
ECO/UNDEV ECO/TAC PROB/SOLV NAT/G

B57
BAUER P.T.,ECONOMIC ANALYSIS AND POLICY IN UNDERDEVELOPED COUNTRIES. AFR WOR+45 AGRI INT/TRADE TAX PRICE...GEN/METH BIBLIOG/A 20. PAGE 11 F0214
ECO/UNDEV METH/COMP POLICY

B57
UDY S.H. JR.,THE ORGANIZATION OF PRODUCTION IN NONINDUSTRIAL CULTURE. VOL/ASSN DELIB/GP TEC/DEV ...CHARTS BIBLIOG. PAGE 132 F2598
METH/COMP ECO/UNDEV PRODUC ADMIN

B58
DEFENSE AGAINST INFLATION. USA+45 LEGIS WORKER TAX PRICE DEMAND INCOME PRODUC...POLICY TREND METH/COMP 20 GOLD/STAND. PAGE 1 F0012
ECO/TAC EQUILIB WEALTH PROB/SOLV

B58
CHEEK G.,ECONOMIC AND SOCIAL IMPLICATIONS OF AUTOMATION: A BIBLIOGRAPHIC REVIEW (PAMPHLET). USA+45 LG/CO WORKER CREATE PLAN CONTROL ROUTINE PERS/REL EFFICIENCY PRODUC...METH/COMP 20. PAGE 24 F0459
BIBLIOG/A SOCIETY INDUS AUTOMAT

B58
DAVIS E.H.,OF THE PEOPLE, BY THE PEOPLE, FOR THE PEOPLE. INCOME WEALTH...METH/COMP MUNICH 20. PAGE 30 F0587
FINAN LOC/G TAX

B58
DOWNIE J.,THE COMPETITIVE PROCESS. ECO/TAC PRICE EFFICIENCY OPTIMAL PRODUC WEALTH...IDEA/COMP METH/COMP 20 MONOPOLY. PAGE 34 F0658
EQUILIB MARKET INDUS ECO/DEV

B58
LESTER R.A.,AS UNIONS MATURE. POL/PAR BARGAIN LEAD PARTIC GP/REL CENTRAL...MAJORIT TIME/SEQ METH/COMP. PAGE 78 F1533
LABOR INDUS POLICY MGT

B58
OGDEN F.D.,THE POLL TAX IN THE SOUTH. USA+45 USA-45 CONSTN ADJUD ADMIN PARTIC CRIME...TIME/SEQ GOV/COMP METH/COMP 18/20 SOUTH/US. PAGE 101 F1982
TAX CHOOSE RACE/REL DISCRIM

B58
PALMER E.E.,THE ECONOMY AND THE DEMOCRATIC IDEAL. USA+45 USA-45 STRATA CHIEF CT/SYS ORD/FREE SOCISM ...MAJORIT CONCPT ANTHOL 18/20 PRESIDENT. PAGE 103 F2021
ECO/DEV POPULISM METH/COMP ECO/TAC

B58
WOODS H.D.,PATTERNS OF INDUSTRIAL DISPUTE SETTLEMENT IN FIVE CANADIAN INDUSTRIES. CANADA USA+45 CONSULT ADJUD GP/REL...JURID GOV/COMP METH/COMP ANTHOL 20. PAGE 148 F2923
BARGAIN INDUS LABOR NAT/G

B59
CONTY J.M.,PSYCHOLOGIE DE LA DECISION....PSY GAME 20. PAGE 27 F0528
DECISION PROB/SOLV OP/RES METH/COMP

B59
KARLIN S.,MATHEMATICAL METHODS AND THEORY IN GAMES, PROGRAMMING, AND ECONOMICS. COMPUTER PLAN CONTROL TASK...MATH 20. PAGE 69 F1357
GAME METH/COMP ACT/RES DECISION

B59
MARTIN D.D.,MERGERS AND THE CLAYTON ACT. FINAN LEGIS GP/REL...DECISION METH/COMP BIBLIOG 20. PAGE 86 F1681
OWN ECO/TAC LG/CO POLICY

B59
ROPKE W.,INTERNATIONAL ORDER AND ECONOMIC INTEGRATION. ECO/DEV ECO/UNDEV AGRI FINAN INDUS INT/ORG WAR PEACE ORD/FREE...SOC METH/COMP 20 EEC. PAGE 114 F2238
INT/TRADE DIPLOM BAL/PAY ALL/IDEOS

B59
WAHLKE J.C.,LEGISLATIVE BEHAVIOR: A READER IN THEORY AND RESEARCH. USA+45 CONSTN ELITES POL/PAR LOBBY REPRESENT PERS/REL PERSON ROLE...IDEA/COMP METH/COMP SIMUL. PAGE 142 F2800
LEGIS CHOOSE INGP/REL ATTIT

B59
WIBBERLEY G.P.,AGRICULTURE AND URBAN GROWTH. UK USA+45 ECO/DEV FINAN PROB/SOLV INT/TRADE COST ...GEOG STAT CHARTS METH/COMP HYPO/EXP METH MUNICH 20. PAGE 146 F2876
AGRI PLAN

S59
ALLEN G.,"NATIONAL FARMERS UNION AS A PRESSURE GROUP: II." UK ECO/DEV MARKET POL/PAR DELIB/GP PROB/SOLV ECO/TAC LOBBY INCOME...POLICY METH/COMP 19/20 NAT/FARMER. PAGE 4 F0069
DIST/IND AGRI PROF/ORG TREND

B60
HOFFMANN P.G.,ONE HUNDRED COUNTRIES, ONE AND ONE QUARTER BILLION PEOPLE. MARKET INT/ORG TEC/DEV CAP/ISM...GEOG CHARTS METH/COMP 20 UN. PAGE 61 F1191
FOR/AID ECO/TAC ECO/UNDEV INT/TRADE

B60
HUGHES J.,NATIONALISED INDUSTRIES IN THE MIXED ECONOMY (PAMPHLET). FINAN PROB/SOLV CAP/ISM OWN ...SOCIALIST STAT METH/COMP 20. PAGE 63 F1233
SOCISM LG/CO GOV/REL ECO/DEV

B60
LATIFI D.,INDIA AND UNITED STATES AID. ASIA INDIA UK USA+45 AGRI FINAN INDUS COLONIAL ORD/FREE SOVEREIGN WEALTH...METH/COMP 20. PAGE 76 F1486
FOR/AID DIPLOM ECO/UNDEV

B60
PENTONY D.E.,UNITED STATES FOREIGN AID. INDIA LAOS
FOR/AID

USA+45 ECO/UNDEV INT/TRADE ADMIN PEACE ATTIT ...POLICY METH/COMP ANTHOL 20. PAGE 105 F2060
DIPLOM ECO/TAC

B60
PFOUTS R.W.,THE TECHNIQUES OF URBAN ECONOMIC ANALYSIS. USA+45...ECOMETRIC CONCPT CHARTS IDEA/COMP ANTHOL MUNICH 20. PAGE 106 F2078
METH ECO/DEV METH/COMP

B60
ROBINSON E.A.G.,ECONOMIC CONSEQUENCES OF THE SIZE OF NATIONS. AGRI INDUS DELIB/GP FOR/AID ADMIN EFFICIENCY...METH/COMP 20. PAGE 113 F2218
CONCPT INT/ORG NAT/COMP

B60
ROBINSON J.,AN ESSAY ON MARXIAN ECONOMICS. USA+45 STRATA INDUS MARKET CAP/ISM...METH/COMP 19/20 MARX/KARL. PAGE 113 F2222
IDEA/COMP MARXISM ACADEM

B60
STOLPER W.F.,GERMANY BETWEEN EAST AND WEST: THE ECONOMICS OF COMPETITIVE COEXISTENCE. AFR FUT GERMANY/E GERMANY/W WOR+45 FINAN POL/PAR BUDGET ECO/TAC FOR/AID INT/TRADE...STAT CHARTS METH/COMP 20. PAGE 126 F2495
ECO/DEV DIPLOM GOV/COMP BAL/PWR

C60
HOSELITZ B.,"THE ROLE OF CITIES IN THE ECONOMIC GROWTH OF UNDERDEVELOPED COUNTRIES" IN "SOCIOLOGICAL ASPECTS OF ECONOMIC GROWTH"(BMR). CULTURE LOC/G ACT/RES...SOC IDEA/COMP METH/COMP METH MUNICH IND 14/20 REDFIELD/R. PAGE 62 F1218
METH/CNCPT TEC/DEV ECO/UNDEV

B61
AUBREY H.G.,COEXISTENCE: ECONOMIC CHALLENGE AND RESPONSE. AFR USSR WOR+45 ACT/RES BAL/PWR CAP/ISM DIPLOM ECO/TAC FOR/AID INT/TRADE PEACE SOCISM ...METH/COMP NAT/COMP. PAGE 7 F0139
POLICY ECO/UNDEV PLAN COM

B61
CARNEY D.E.,GOVERNMENT AND ECONOMY IN BRITISH WEST AFRICA. GAMBIA GHANA NIGERIA SIER/LEONE DOMIN ADMIN GOV/REL SOVEREIGN WEALTH LAISSEZ...BIBLIOG 20 CMN/WLTH. PAGE 21 F0417
METH/COMP COLONIAL ECO/TAC ECO/UNDEV

B61
FILLOL T.R.,SOCIAL FACTORS IN ECONOMIC DEVELOPMENT: THE ARGENTINE CASE. STRUCT INDUS LABOR CREATE TEC/DEV EFFICIENCY PRODUC DRIVE...METH/CNCPT METH/COMP BIBLIOG/A 20 ARGEN. PAGE 41 F0795
ECO/UNDEV MGT PERS/REL TREND

B61
FRIEDMANN G.,THE ANATOMY OF WORK. USA+45 SOCIETY CONTROL ROUTINE DRIVE SKILL...PSY SOC STAT OBS METH/COMP PERS/COMP 20. PAGE 44 F0862
AUTOMAT WORKER INDUS PERSON

B61
GALENSON W.,TRADE UNION DEMOCRACY IN WESTERN EUROPE. ECO/DEV INDUS PROF/ORG WORKER INCOME ...METH/COMP 20. PAGE 45 F0886
LABOR GP/REL ECO/TAC EUR+WWI

B61
GREY A.L.,ECONOMIC ISSUES AND POLICIES; READINGS IN INTRODUCTORY ECONOMICS (2ND ED.). WOR+45 ECO/UNDEV FINAN MARKET LABOR LG/CO INT/TRADE BAL/PAY WEALTH ...ANTHOL T. PAGE 51 F0996
ECO/TAC PROB/SOLV METH/COMP

B61
HARRIS S.E.,THE DOLLAR IN CRISIS. AFR USA+45 MARKET INT/ORG ECO/TAC PRICE CONTROL WEALTH...METH/COMP ANTHOL 20. PAGE 55 F1089
BAL/PAY DIPLOM FINAN INT/TRADE

B61
LENIN V.I.,WHAT IS TO BE DONE? (1902). RUSSIA LABOR NAT/G POL/PAR WORKER CAP/ISM ECO/TAC ADMIN PARTIC ...MARXIST IDEA/COMP GEN/LAWS 19/20. PAGE 78 F1522
EDU/PROP PRESS MARXISM METH/COMP

B61
STARNER F.L.,GENERAL OBLIGATION BOND FINANCING BY LOCAL GOVERNMENTS: A SURVEY OF STATE CONTROLS. CANADA UK USA+45 CONSTN PROVS...POLICY JURID METH/COMP 20 EUROPE CALIFORNIA. PAGE 125 F2471
FINAN LOC/G GOV/REL ADJUD

L61
CHENERY H.B.,"COMPARATIVE ADVANTAGE AND DEVELOPMENT POLICY." FINAN INT/TRADE RATION OPTIMAL...CHARTS METH/COMP GEN/LAWS BIBLIOG 20 RESOURCE/N. PAGE 24 F0463
ECO/UNDEV ECO/TAC PLAN EFFICIENCY

S61
ANDREWS R.B.,"URBAN ECONOMICS: AN APPRAISAL OF PROGRESS." LOC/G PROB/SOLV TEC/DEV...CONCPT OBS/ENVIR METH/COMP HYPO/EXP SOC/EXP SIMUL GEN/METH METH MUNICH 20. PAGE 5 F0102
PHIL/SCI ECOMETRIC

S61
BENNION E.G.,"ECONOMETRICS FOR MANAGEMENT." USA+45 INDUS EX/STRUC ACT/RES COMPUTER UTIL...MATH STAT PREDICT METH/COMP HYPO/EXP. PAGE 13 F0248
ECOMETRIC MGT SIMUL DECISION

S61
DALTON G.,"ECONOMIC THEORY AND PRIMITIVE SOCIETY" (BMR)" UNIV AGRI KIN TEC/DEV ECO/TAC REGION HABITAT SKILL...METH/COMP BIBLIOG. PAGE 30 F0574
ECO/UNDEV METH PHIL/SCI SOC

C61
FILLOL T.R.,"SOCIAL FACTORS IN ECONOMIC DEVELOPMENT: THE ARGENTINE CASE" INDUS LABOR CREATE TEC/DEV PERS/REL EFFICIENCY PRODUC DRIVE ...METH/CNCPT METH/COMP 20 ARGEN. PAGE 41 F0794
BIBLIOG ECO/UNDEV MGT TREND

B62
FERBER R.,RESEARCH METHODS IN ECONOMICS AND BUSINESS. AFR ECO/DEV FINAN MARKET LG/CO SML/CO CONSULT CONTROL COST...STAT METH/COMP 20. PAGE 40 F0783
ACT/RES PROB/SOLV ECO/TAC MGT

B62
GALENSON W.,LABOR IN DEVELOPING COUNTRIES. BRAZIL INDONESIA ISRAEL PAKISTAN TURKEY AGRI INDUS WORKER PAY PRICE GP/REL WEALTH...MGT CHARTS METH/COMP NAT/COMP 20. PAGE 45 F0888
LABOR ECO/UNDEV BARGAIN POL/PAR

B62
GEARY R.C.,EUROPE'S FUTURE IN FIGURES. FUT GOV/REL DEMAND PRODUC...STAT CHARTS METH/COMP ANTHOL METH 20 EUROPE. PAGE 47 F0912
FINAN ECO/DEV PREDICT WEALTH

B62
HATTERY L.H.,INFORMATION RETRIEVAL MANAGEMENT. CLIENT INDUS TOP/EX COMPUTER OP/RES TEC/DEV ROUTINE COST EFFICIENCY RIGID/FLEX...METH/COMP ANTHOL 20. PAGE 57 F1113
R+D COMPUT/IR MGT CREATE

B62
LITWACK L.,THE AMERICAN LABOR MOVEMENT. USA-45 NAT/G CREATE TEC/DEV CAP/ISM ECO/TAC ADJUD AUTOMAT SKILL...TREND ANTHOL 19/20. PAGE 81 F1588
INDUS LABOR GP/REL METH/COMP

B62
MARTINS A.F.,REVOLUCAO BRANCA NO CAMPO. L/A+17C SERV/IND DEMAND EFFICIENCY PRODUC...POLICY METH/COMP. PAGE 86 F1685
AGRI ECO/UNDEV TEC/DEV NAT/COMP

B62
PRAKASH O.M.,THE THEORY AND WORKING OF STATE CORPORATIONS: WITH SPECIAL REFERENCE TO INDIA. INDIA UK USA+45 TOP/EX PRICE ADMIN EFFICIENCY...MGT METH/COMP 20 TVA. PAGE 107 F2112
LG/CO ECO/UNDEV GOV/REL SOCISM

B62
SHINOHARA M.,GROWTH AND CYCLES IN THE JAPANESE ECONOMY. INDUS LABOR TEC/DEV CAP/ISM INT/TRADE PAY COST EFFICIENCY INCOME WEALTH...METH/COMP 20 CHINJAP. PAGE 121 F2380
PRODUC ECO/DEV EQUILIB ECOMETRIC

B62
SRIVASTAVA G.L.,COLLECTIVE BARGAINING AND LABOR-MANAGEMENT RELATIONS IN INDIA. INDIA UK USA+45 INDUS LEGIS WORKER ADJUD EFFICIENCY PRODUC ...METH/COMP 20. PAGE 125 F2462
LABOR MGT BARGAIN GP/REL

B62
WALSTON H.,AGRICULTURE UNDER COMMUNISM. CHINA/COM COM PROB/SOLV HAPPINESS RIGID/FLEX...POLICY METH/COMP 20. PAGE 143 F2811
AGRI MARXISM PLAN CREATE

B62
WENDT P.F.,HOUSING POLICY - THE SEARCH FOR SOLUTIONS. GERMANY/W SWEDEN UK USA+45 OP/RES HABITAT WEALTH...SOC/WK CHARTS 20. PAGE 145 F2856
PLAN ADMIN METH/COMP NAT/G

B63
BARBOUR V.,CAPITALISM IN AMSTERDAM IN THE 17TH CENTURY. NETHERLAND FINAN ECO/TAC...METH/COMP BIBLIOG MUNICH 16. PAGE 10 F0185
CAP/ISM INT/TRADE MARKET WEALTH

B63
BARNETT H.J.,SCARCITY AND GROWTH: THE ECONOMICS OF NATURAL RESOURCE AVAILABILITY. FUT WOR+45 AGRI INDUS PROB/SOLV TEC/DEV CONTROL PRODUC...SOC/WK IDEA/COMP METH/COMP SIMUL 20 RESOURCE/N MALTHUS RICARDO/D MILL/JS DARWIN/C. PAGE 10 F0191
DEMAND HABITAT CENSUS GEOG

B63
DUE J.F.,STATE SALES TAX ADMINISTRATION. OP/RES BUDGET PAY ADMIN EXEC ROUTINE COST EFFICIENCY PROFIT...CHARTS METH/COMP 20. PAGE 34 F0671
PROVS TAX STAT GOV/COMP

B63
EL-NAGGAR S.,FOREIGN AID TO UNITED ARAB REPUBLIC. UAR USA+45 USSR AGRI FINAN INDUS FORCES EATING DEMAND...CHARTS METH/COMP 20 RESOURCE/N AID. PAGE 37 F0718
FOR/AID ECO/UNDEV RECEIVE PLAN

B63
FATEMI N.S.,THE DOLLAR CRISIS. USA+45 INDUS NAT/G LEGIS BUDGET TAX COST...CHARTS METH/COMP 20 EEC. PAGE 39 F0766
PROB/SOLV BAL/PAY FOR/AID PLAN

B63
GORDON M.S.,THE ECONOMICS OF WELFARE POLICIES. INDUS LOC/G NAT/G LEGIS WORKER INCOME AGE/O SKILL WEALTH...METH/COMP NAT/COMP 20. PAGE 49 F0959
METH/CNCPT ECO/TAC POLICY

B63
HARROD R.F.,INTERNATIONAL TRADE THEORY IN A DEVELOPING WORLD. COM WOR+45 FOR/AID REGION COST DEMAND WEALTH...POLICY 20 INTL/ECON. PAGE 56 F1095
INT/TRADE BAL/PAY ECO/UNDEV METH/COMP

B63
INTERNATIONAL ASSOCIATION RES,AFRICAN STUDIES IN INCOME AND WEALTH. AFR NAT/G PROB/SOLV DEMAND INCOME...ECOMETRIC METH/COMP 20. PAGE 64 F1270
WEALTH PLAN ECO/UNDEV BUDGET

B63
LETHBRIDGE H.J.,THE PEASANT AND THE COMMUNES. CHINA/COM COM USSR NEIGH PROB/SOLV ADJUST EFFICIENCY...POLICY METH/COMP NAT/COMP 20. PAGE 78 F1535
MARXISM ECO/TAC AGRI WORKER

B63
OECD,FOOD AID: ITS ROLE IN ECONOMIC DEVELOPMENT. FINAN NAT/G PLAN DIPLOM GIVE TASK WEALTH ...METH/COMP METH 20. PAGE 100 F1966
ECO/UNDEV FOR/AID INT/ORG POLICY

B63
ROPKE W.,ECONOMICS OF THE FREE SOCIETY. FINAN INT/TRADE BAL/PAY COST DEMAND EFFICIENCY ORD/FREE WEALTH...CON/ANAL METH/COMP T 20 KEYNES/JM. PAGE 114 F2240
SOCIETY BUDGET ECO/DEV ECO/TAC

B63
RUMMEL J.F.,RESEARCH METHODOLOGY IN BUSINESS. COMPUTER CREATE PROB/SOLV...CONT/OBS REC/INT QU/SEMANT SYS/QU SAMP CHARTS METH/COMP T 20. PAGE 115 F2260
OP/RES METH/CNCPT METH STAT

B63
SHANKS M.,THE LESSONS OF PUBLIC ENTERPRISE. UK LEGIS WORKER ECO/TAC ADMIN PARL/PROC GOV/REL ATTIT ...POLICY MGT METH/COMP NAT/COMP ANTHOL 20 PARLIAMENT. PAGE 120 F2364
SOCISM OWN NAT/G INDUS

B63
SMELSER N.J.,THE SOCIOLOGY OF ECONOMIC LIFE. UNIV CULTURE PERCEPT...PSY T 18/20. PAGE 123 F2425
SOC METH/COMP IDEA/COMP

B63
SMITH R.A.,CORPORATIONS IN CRISIS. USA+45 LG/CO EX/STRUC ECO/TAC CONTROL LEAD PERS/REL...MGT 20. PAGE 123 F2432
ELITES INDUS PROB/SOLV METH/COMP

S63
ANDREWS R.B.,"ECONOMIC PLANNING FOR SMALL AREAS: THE PLANNING PROCESS." INDUS PROC/MFG PROVS PROB/SOLV TAX EQUILIB...METH/COMP HYPO/EXP METH MUNICH 20. PAGE 5 F0103
ECO/TAC PLAN LOC/G

S63
CLARK P.G.,"TOWARDS MORE COMPREHENSIVE PLANNING IN EAST AFRICA" AFR OP/RES ECO/TAC RATION TAX EFFICIENCY INCOME...MATH TREND CHARTS 20 AFRICA/E. PAGE 25 F0484
ECO/UNDEV PLAN STAT METH/COMP

S63
REES A.,"THE EFFECTS OF UNIONS ON RESOURCE ALLOCATION." USA+45 WORKER PRICE CONTROL GP/REL ...MGT METH/COMP 20. PAGE 110 F2173
LABOR BARGAIN RATION INCOME

B64
BALL R.J.,INFLATION AND THE THEORY OF MONEY. MARKET TAX PAY PRICE TASK ADJUST BAL/PAY COST INCOME PRODUC WEALTH...METH/COMP 20 KEYNES/JM MONEY. PAGE 9 F0167
EQUILIB DEMAND POLICY

B64
BOWEN W.G.,ECONOMIC ASPECTS OF EDUCATION (NO. 104). EUR+WWI UK USA+45 PROF/ORG PLAN TEC/DEV PAY ...POLICY STAT 20. PAGE 17 F0329
EDU/PROP ACADEM FINAN METH/COMP

B64
FITCH L.C.,URBAN TRANSPORTATION AND PUBLIC POLICY. FINAN NAT/G LEGIS PROB/SOLV TEC/DEV PRICE COST EFFICIENCY...DECISION STAT CHARTS METH/COMP MUNICH 20 NEWYORK/C PHILADELPH LOS/ANG CHICAGO WASHING/DC. PAGE 41 F0806
DIST/IND PLAN LOC/G

B64
GOWDA K.V.,INTERNATIONAL CURRENCY PLANS AND EXPANSION OF WORLD TRADE. INT/ORG CREATE BUDGET CONTROL BAL/PAY WEALTH 20 KEYNES/JM. PAGE 50 F0969
INT/TRADE FINAN METH/COMP

B64
INTERNATIONAL LABOUR OFFICE,EMPLOYMENT AND ECONOMIC GROWTH. ECO/DEV ECO/UNDEV NAT/G PLAN DIPLOM INT/TRADE CONTROL INCOME PRODUC WEALTH...STAT NAT/COMP 20 ILO. PAGE 65 F1279
WORKER METH/COMP ECO/TAC OPTIMAL

B64
JACOBY N.H.,UNITED STATES MONETARY POLICY. UK USA+45 LAW NAT/G TEC/DEV TAX EQUILIB INCOME ...METH/COMP 20 FED/RESERV. PAGE 66 F1300
ECO/DEV POLICY ECO/TAC FINAN

B64
KALDOR N.,ESSAYS ON ECONOMIC POLICY (VOL. II). CHILE GERMANY INDIA FINAN...GOV/COMP METH/COMP 20 KEYNES/JM. PAGE 69 F1348
BAL/PAY INT/TRADE METH/CNCPT ECO/UNDEV

B64
KNIGHT R.,BIBLIOGRAPHY ON INCOME AND WEALTH, 1957-1960 (VOL VIII). WOR+45 ECO/DEV FINAN INT/TRADE...GOV/COMP METH/COMP. PAGE 72 F1412
BIBLIOG/A ECO/UNDEV WEALTH INCOME

B64
LANG A.S.,URBAN RAIL TRANSIT. OP/RES PLAN PROB/SOLV TEC/DEV AUTOMAT COST...TECHNIC MATH CON/ANAL CHARTS METH/COMP SIMUL MUNICH 20 RAILROAD PUB/TRANS. PAGE 75 F1474
DIST/IND ECOMETRIC

B64
MORRISSENS L.,ECONOMIC POLICY IN OUR TIME: COUNTRY STUDIES. BELGIUM EUR+WWI FRANCE GERMANY/W ITALY NETHERLAND INDUS BARGAIN BUDGET GOV/REL BAL/PAY PRODUC...CON/ANAL CHARTS COSTS 20. PAGE 94 F1839
ECO/DEV ECO/TAC METH/COMP PLAN

B64
RANIS G.,THE UNITED STATES AND THE DEVELOPING ECONOMIES. COM USA+45 AGRI FINAN TEC/DEV CAP/ISM ECO/TAC INT/TRADE...POLICY METH/COMP ANTHOL 20 AID. PAGE 109 F2145
ECO/UNDEV DIPLOM FOR/AID

B64
REDLICH F.,THE GERMAN MILITARY ENTERPRISER AND HIS WORK FORCE. CHRIST-17C GERMANY ELITES SOCIETY FINAN ECO/TAC CIVMIL/REL GP/REL INGP/REL...HIST/WRIT METH/COMP 14/17. PAGE 110 F2170
EX/STRUC FORCES PROFIT WORKER

B64
STONIER A.W.,EXERCISES IN ECONOMICS. FINAN INDUS TEC/DEV RENT PAY EQUILIB PRODUC PROFIT...METH/COMP T. PAGE 127 F2498
PRICE MARKET WORKER

B64
STRONG A.L.,THE RISE OF THE CHINESE PEOPLE'S COMMUNES - AND SIX YEARS AFTER (2ND ED.). CHINA/COM AGRI INDUS FORCES WORKER PROB/SOLV EDU/PROP EFFICIENCY ISOLAT 20. PAGE 127 F2503
NEIGH ECO/TAC MARXISM METH/COMP

B64
WELLISZ S.,THE ECONOMICS OF THE SOVIET BLOC. COM USSR INDUS WORKER PLAN BUDGET INT/TRADE TAX PRICE PRODUC WEALTH MARXISM...METH/COMP 20. PAGE 145 F2854
EFFICIENCY ADMIN MARKET

B64
ZEBOT C.A.,THE ECONOMICS OF COMPETITIVE COEXISTENCE. CHINA/COM USSR WOR+45 FINAN MARKET FOR/AID PRICE DEMAND EQUILIB WEALTH ALL/IDEOS 20. PAGE 150 F2961
TEC/DEV DIPLOM METH/COMP

B64
ZOBER M.,MARKETING MANAGEMENT. FINAN BUDGET EDU/PROP PRICE PRODUC ATTIT...POLICY TREND CHARTS METH/COMP EQULIB 20. PAGE 150 F2966
ECO/DEV MGT CONTROL MARKET

S64
NEWLYN W.T.,"MONETARY SYSTEMS AND INTEGRATION" AFR BUDGET ADMIN FEDERAL PRODUC PROFIT UTIL...CHARTS 20 AFRICA/E. PAGE 98 F1922
ECO/UNDEV REGION METH/COMP FINAN

S64
STONE P.A.,"DECISION TECHNIQUES FOR TOWN DEVELOPMENT." PLAN COST PROFIT...DECISION MGT CON/ANAL CHARTS METH/COMP BIBLIOG MUNICH 20. PAGE 127 F2497
OP/RES ADMIN PROB/SOLV

B65
ARTEL R.,THE STRUCTURE OF THE STOCKHOLM ECONOMY. SWEDEN DIST/IND LABOR LOC/G TEC/DEV DEMAND MUNICH LOUISIANA 20. PAGE 7 F0125
ECO/DEV METH/COMP BAL/PAY

B65
BALDWIN D.A.,SOFT LOANS AND AMERICAN FOREIGN POLICY: 1943-1962 (THESIS). USA+45 WOR+45 FINAN NAT/G FOR/AID BAL/PAY ATTIT...POLICY METH/COMP 20 UN CONGRESS. PAGE 9 F0161
DIPLOM ECO/TAC ECO/UNDEV

B65
BAUMOL W.J.,ECONOMIC THEORY AND OPERATIONS ANALYSIS (2ND ED.). MARKET LG/CO BUDGET PRICE COST EQUILIB PRODUC...DECISION MATH CHARTS GAME 20. PAGE 12 F0219
OP/RES ECO/DEV METH/COMP STAT

B65
BELASSA B.,ECONOMIC DEVELOPMENT AND INTEGRATION. LG/CO PROB/SOLV TEC/DEV INT/TRADE TARIFFS COST WEALTH...POLICY METH/COMP 20. PAGE 12 F0232
ECO/UNDEV ECO/TAC INT/ORG INDUS

B65
BRENNAN M.J.,PATTERNS OF MARKET BEHAVIOR. AFR USA+45 OP/RES CAP/ISM ECO/TAC INT/TRADE...CHARTS METH/COMP ANTHOL TIME 20. PAGE 18 F0346
MARKET LABOR FINAN ECOMETRIC

B65
LITTLE I.M.D.,INTERNATIONAL AID. UK WOR+45 AGRI INDUS GIVE RECEIVE COLONIAL BAL/PAY WEALTH...POLICY GOV/COMP METH/COMP 20. PAGE 81 F1584
FOR/AID DIPLOM ECO/UNDEV NAT/G

B65
MARCUS E.,INTERNATIONAL TRADE AND FINANCE. EFFICIENCY EQUILIB...CHARTS METH/COMP BIBLIOG METH T 20. PAGE 85 F1664
INT/TRADE FINAN MARKET WEALTH

B65
OECD,TECHNIQUES OF ECONOMIC FORECASTING. CANADA FRANCE NETHERLAND SWEDEN UK USA+45 PROB/SOLV ROUTINE...CONCPT MATH CHARTS BIBLIOG METH 20. PAGE 100 F1974
PREDICT METH/COMP PLAN

B65
OXENFELDT A.R.,ECONOMIC SYSTEMS IN ACTION. FRANCE USA+45 USSR CULTURE PLAN PROB/SOLV TEC/DEV INCOME PRODUC WEALTH...METH/COMP 20. PAGE 102 F2007
ECO/DEV CAP/ISM MARXISM ECO/TAC

B65
REDFORD E.S.,AMERICAN GOVERNMENT AND THE ECONOMY. FUT USA+45 USA-45 INDUS PROB/SOLV GOV/REL...POLICY DECISION METH/COMP BIBLIOG T 18/20. PAGE 110 F2168
CONSTN NAT/G

B65 SHONFIELD A.,MODERN CAPITALISM: THE CHANGING BALANCE OF PUBLIC AND PRIVATE POWER. FRANCE GERMANY/W UK USA+45 WOR+45 ECO/DEV INT/ORG NAT/G CONSULT INT/TRADE PRODUC...POLICY CONCPT METH/COMP 20. PAGE 121 F2386 — CAP/ISM CONTROL BAL/PWR CREATE

B65 STEINER G.A.,THE CREATIVE ORGANIZATION. ELITES LG/CO PLAN PROB/SOLV TEC/DEV INSPECT CAP/ISM CONTROL EXEC PERSON...METH/COMP HYPO/EXP 20. PAGE 126 F2476 — CREATE MGT ADMIN SOC

B65 US BUREAU OF THE BUDGET,THE BALANCE OF PAYMENTS STATISTICS OF THE UNITED STATES: A REVIEW AND APPRAISAL. USA+45 FINAN NAT/G PROB/SOLV DIPLOM. PAGE 134 F2644 — BAL/PAY STAT METH/COMP BUDGET

B65 WARD R.J.,INTERNATIONAL FINANCE. INT/ORG DIPLOM DEMAND INCOME...POLICY METH/COMP 20. PAGE 143 F2819 — INT/TRADE ECO/TAC FINAN BAL/PAY

S65 STEENKAMP W.F.J.,"THE PROBLEM OF WAGE REGULATION." SOUTH/AFR LAW ECO/DEV ECO/UNDEV LABOR NAT/G BARGAIN PAY INGP/REL DISCRIM WEALTH...METH/COMP 20. PAGE 125 F2473 — ECO/TAC PRICE WORKER RATION

B66 AGGARWALA R.N.,FINANCIAL COMMITTEES OF THE INDIAN PARLIAMENT: A STUDY IN PARLIAMENTARY CONTROL OVER PUBLIC EXPENDITURE. INDIA FINAN NAT/G ROLE...CHARTS METH/COMP METH 20 PARLIAMENT. PAGE 3 F0049 — PARL/PROC BUDGET CONTROL DELIB/GP

B66 FELLNER W.,MAINTAINING AND RESTORING BALANCE IN INTERNATIONAL PAYMENTS. ECO/UNDEV MARKET ECO/TAC PRICE INCOME WEALTH...POLICY METH/COMP 20 MONEY. PAGE 40 F0781 — BAL/PAY DIPLOM FINAN INT/TRADE

B66 GITTINGER J.P.,THE LITERATURE OF AGRICULTURAL PLANNING. UNIV INT/ORG CONSULT WORKER TEC/DEV ECO/TAC OPTIMAL...POLICY METH/COMP BIBLIOG/A 20. PAGE 47 F0927 — ECO/UNDEV AGRI PLAN WRITING

B66 LEONTIEF W.,ESSAYS IN ECONOMICS. ECO/UNDEV INDUS NAT/G CAP/ISM FOR/AID AUTOMAT MARXISM...ECOMETRIC CHARTS ANTHOL METH 20 KEYNES/JM. PAGE 78 F1528 — CONCPT METH/CNCPT METH/COMP

B66 O'CONNER A.M.,AN ECONOMIC GEOGRAPHY OF EAST AFRICA. AFR TANZANIA UGANDA AGRI WORKER INT/TRADE COLONIAL GOV/REL...CHARTS METH/COMP 20 AFRICA/E. PAGE 99 F1953 — ECO/UNDEV EXTR/IND GEOG HABITAT

B66 PERSALL E.S.,AN ECONOMETRIC STUDY OF FINANCIAL MARKETS. COMPUTER PROB/SOLV TEC/DEV...MATH STAT CHARTS METH/COMP BIBLIOG 20. PAGE 105 F2066 — ECOMETRIC FINAN MARKET METH

B66 ROBINSON E.A.,THE ECONOMICS OF EDUCATION. WOR+45 CULTURE ECO/UNDEV FINAN SCHOOL DIPLOM PRICE COST DEMAND...CHARTS METH/COMP 20. PAGE 112 F2216 — EDU/PROP ADJUST CONFER

B66 SHULTZ G.P.,STRATEGIES FOR THE DISPLACED WORKER. USA+45 COMPUTER TEC/DEV BARGAIN RECEIVE EDU/PROP CONFER GP/REL...MGT METH/COMP 20. PAGE 121 F2391 — ECO/DEV WORKER PLAN AUTOMAT

B66 SPULBER N.,THE STATE AND ECONOMIC DEVELOPMENT IN EASTERN EUROPE. BULGARIA COM CZECHOSLVK HUNGARY POLAND YUGOSLAVIA CULTURE PLAN CAP/ISM INT/TRADE CONTROL...POLICY CHARTS METH/COMP BIBLIOG/A 19/20. PAGE 125 F2460 — ECO/DEV ECO/UNDEV NAT/G TOTALISM

B66 THEIL H.,APPLIED ECONOMIC FORECASTING. UNIV USA+45 ELITES INTELL CONSULT PRODUC...DECISION MGT PREDICT CHARTS METH/COMP SIMUL 20. PAGE 129 F2552 — FUT OP/RES PLAN

B66 TRIFFIN R.,THE WORLD MONEY MAZE. AFR INT/ORG ECO/TAC PRICE OPTIMAL WEALTH...METH/COMP 20 EEC OEEC SILVER. PAGE 131 F2589 — BAL/PAY FINAN INT/TRADE DIPLOM

B66 WILCOX C.,ECONOMIES OF THE WORLD TODAY: THEIR ORGANIZATION, DEVELOPMENT, AND PERFORMANCE (2ND ED.). CHINA/COM COM INDIA NIGERIA UK WOR+45 WOR-45 INDUS MARKET PLAN ECO/TAC SOCISM...CHARTS METH/COMP 20. PAGE 146 F2878 — ECO/DEV ECO/UNDEV MARXISM CAP/ISM

S66 DAVIS O.A.,"A THEORY OF THE BUDGETARY PROCESS." ECO/DEV FINAN LEGIS PROB/SOLV GOV/REL...ECOMETRIC METH/CNCPT STAT CONT/OBS TREND METH/COMP SIMUL 20 CONGRESS. PAGE 30 F0592 — DECISION NAT/G BUDGET EFFICIENCY

B67 APTHEKER H.,THE NATURE OF DEMOCRACY, FREEDOM AND REVOLUTION. WOR+45 PROB/SOLV COERCE COST...CONCPT TIME/SEQ METH/COMP. PAGE 6 F0111 — REV POPULISM MARXIST ORD/FREE

B67 CAMPBELL A.K.,METROPOLITAN AMERICA* FISCAL PATTERNS AND GOVERNMENTAL SYSTEMS. PROVS PLAN COST...POLICY DECISION GOV/COMP METH/COMP BIBLIOG. PAGE 21 F0405 — USA+45 NAT/G LOC/G BUDGET

B67 DE JOUVENAL B.,THE ART OF CONJECTURE. WOR+45 EFFICIENCY PERCEPT KNOWL...DECISION PHIL/SCI CONCPT METH/COMP BIBLIOG 20. PAGE 31 F0600 — FUT PREDICT SIMUL METH

B67 GREEN C.,NEGATIVE TAXES AND THE POVERTY PROBLEM. COST EFFICIENCY INCOME NEW/LIB...METH/CNCPT CHARTS METH/COMP BIBLIOG 20. PAGE 50 F0983 — TAX RECEIVE WEALTH PLAN

B67 HAGUE D.C.,PRICE FORMATION IN VARIOUS ECONOMIES; PROCEEDINGS OF A CONFERENCE HELD BY THE INTERNATIONAL ECONOMIC ASSOCIATION. WOR+45 FINAN MARKET PLAN CONFER COST...DECISION MATH PREDICT CHARTS SIMUL 20 INTL/ECON. PAGE 53 F1037 — PRICE CAP/ISM SOCISM METH/COMP

B67 HANNAH H.W.,THE LEGAL BASE FOR UNIVERSITIES IN DEVELOPING COUNTRIES. AFR ASIA L/A+17C S/ASIA USA+45 FINAN CREATE EDU/PROP TASK EFFICIENCY ...JURID METH/COMP 20. PAGE 54 F1060 — ADMIN LAW ACADEM LEGIS

B67 HOGAN J.,THE US BALANCE OF PAYMENTS AND CAPITAL FLOWS. MARKET INT/ORG ECO/TAC PRICE CONTROL WEALTH ...METH/COMP 20 EEC. PAGE 61 F1192 — BAL/PAY FINAN DIPLOM INT/TRADE

B67 JOHNSON H.G.,ECONOMIC POLICY TOWARD LESS DEVELOPED COUNTRIES. USA+45 ECO/DEV INT/ORG PLAN CAP/ISM FOR/AID TARIFFS GIVE WEALTH...NEW/IDEA CHARTS 20 UN GATT. PAGE 67 F1327 — ECO/UNDEV ECO/TAC METH/COMP

B67 KAPLAN J.J.,CHALLENGE OF FOREIGN AID. USA+45 CONTROL BAL/PAY COST ATTIT ALL/VALS...METH/COMP 20. PAGE 69 F1352 — FOR/AID PLAN GIVE POLICY

B67 MARRIS P.,DILEMMAS OF SOCIAL REFORM: POVERTY AND COMMUNITY ACTION IN THE UNITED STATES. USA+45 NAT/G OP/RES ADMIN PARTIC EFFICIENCY WEALTH...SOC METH/COMP T MUNICH 20 REFORMERS. PAGE 85 F1674 — STRUCT PROB/SOLV COST

B67 NYOMARKAY J.,CHARISMA AND FACTIONALISM IN THE NAZI PARTY. GERMANY POL/PAR LEGIT LEAD MARXISM ...NEW/IDEA METH/COMP GEN/LAWS BIBLIOG 20 HITLER/A. PAGE 99 F1949 — FASCISM INGP/REL CHIEF PWR

B67 POWLEDGE F.,BLACK POWER WHITE RESISTANCE. USA+45 STRUCT PLAN GP/REL DISCRIM HABITAT ORD/FREE WEALTH ...METH/COMP SOC/INTEG NEGRO. PAGE 107 F2111 — RACE/REL ATTIT PWR

B67 ROBERTS B.C.,COLLECTIVE BARGAINING IN AFRICAN COUNTRIES. AFR LAW ECO/UNDEV BARGAIN GP/REL ...DECISION METH/COMP 20. PAGE 112 F2206 — LABOR MGT PLAN ECO/TAC

B67 ROELOFS H.M.,THE LANGUAGE OF MODERN POLITICS: AN INTRODUCTION TO THE STUDY OF GOVERNMENT. DIPLOM ADMIN MARXISM NEW/LIB...JURID CONCPT METH/COMP T 20. PAGE 113 F2230 — LEAD NAT/COMP PERS/REL NAT/G

B67 RUEFF J.,BALANCE OF PAYMENTS: PROPOSALS FOR RESOLVING THE CRITICAL WORLD ECONOMIC PROBLEM OF OUR TIME. USA+45 INDUS FOR/AID REPAR DEMAND OPTIMAL ...ECOMETRIC CHARTS METH/COMP 20. PAGE 115 F2259 — BAL/PAY INT/TRADE FINAN NEW/IDEA

B67 SAPARINA Y.,CYBERNETICS WITHIN US. WOR+45 EDU/PROP FEEDBACK PERCEPT HEALTH...DECISION METH/CNCPT NEW/IDEA 20. PAGE 116 F2281 — COMPUTER METH/COMP CONTROL SIMUL

B67 SYMONS L.,AGRICULTURAL GEOGRAPHY. OP/RES SKILL ...CONCPT CHARTS BIBLIOG T 20. PAGE 128 F2520 — AGRI GEOG METH/COMP OBS

B67 TANSKY L.,US AND USSR AID TO DEVELOPING COUNTRIES. INDIA TURKEY UAR USA+45 USSR FINAN PLAN TEC/DEV ADMIN WEALTH...TREND METH/COMP 20. PAGE 128 F2535 — FOR/AID ECO/UNDEV MARXISM CAP/ISM

B67 ZUPNICK E.,UNDERSTANDING THE INTERNATIONAL MONEY SYSTEM (HEADLINE SERIES, NO. 182) (PAMPHLET). ECO/DEV NAT/G DIPLOM INT/TRADE...METH/COMP 20 IMF. PAGE 151 F2971 — FINAN PLAN INT/ORG PROB/SOLV

L67 LENT G.E.,"TAX INCENTIVES FOR INVESTMENT IN DEVELOPING COUNTRIES" WOR+45 LAW INDUS PLAN BUDGET TARIFFS ADMIN...METH/COMP 20. PAGE 78 F1526 — ECO/UNDEV TAX FINAN ECO/TAC

L67
MACHLUP F.,"THEORIES OF THE FIRM* MARGINALIST, BEHAVIORALIST, MANAGERIAL." ADMIN EXEC EFFICIENCY PROFIT METH/CNCPT. PAGE 83 F1633
METH/COMP GEN/LAWS INDUS

L67
MIXON J.,"JANE JACOBS AND THE LAW - ZONING FOR DIVERSITY EXAMINED." FUT USA+45 CONSTN NEIGH PROB/SOLV CONTROL CT/SYS PARTIC ATTIT...POLICY CENSUS METH/COMP MUNICH. PAGE 92 F1810
IDEA/COMP PLAN LAW

S67
ADAMS D.W.,"MINIFUNDIA IN AGRARIAN REFORM: A COLOMBIAN EXAMPLE."...SOC CLASSIF 20 COLOMB. PAGE 2 F0035
AGRI METH/COMP OWN PRODUC

S67
ALBAUM G.,"INFORMATION FLOW AND DECENTRALIZED DECISION MAKING IN MARKETING." EX/STRUC COMPUTER OP/RES PROB/SOLV EFFICIENCY OPTIMAL...METH/COMP ORG/CHARTS 20. PAGE 3 F0056
LG/CO ROUTINE KNOWL MARKET

S67
AVTORKHANOV A.,"A NEW AGRARIAN REVOLUTION." COM USSR ECO/DEV PLAN TEC/DEV ADMIN CONTROL OPTIMAL WEALTH SOCISM 20 KHRUSH/N STALIN/J. PAGE 8 F0144
AGRI METH/COMP MARXISM OWN

S67
CLABAULT J.M.,"PRACTICALITIES IN COMPETITOR EXCHANGING PRICE INFORMATION." ECO/DEV PLAN ...CONCPT 20. PAGE 24 F0473
INDUS LAW METH/COMP

S67
FRANKLIN N.N.,"THE CONCEPT AND MEASUREMENT OF 'MINIMUM LIVING STANDARDS'." UNIV OP/RES PAY INGP/REL DEMAND INCOME DRIVE WEALTH...SOC CHARTS METH/COMP. PAGE 43 F0849
CONCPT PHIL/SCI ALL/VALS HAPPINESS

S67
GREEN C.,"SCHEMES FOR TRANSFERRING INCOME TO THE POOR." BUDGET GIVE RECEIVE DEBATE COST INCOME ...SOC/WK METH/COMP. PAGE 50 F0982
TAX WEALTH PLAN ACT/RES

S67
HILDEBRAND G.H.,"SECOND THOUGHTS ON THE NEGATIVE INCOME TAX." PLAN BUDGET ECO/TAC GIVE RECEIVE DEBATE EFFICIENCY INCOME...METH/COMP COSTS. PAGE 59 F1169
TAX WEALTH SOC/WK ACT/RES

S67
LEWIS W.A.,"THE STATUTORY LANGUAGE OF LABOR DISQUALIFICATION IN STATE EMPLOYMENT SECURITY LAWS." LABOR WORKER WORK 20. PAGE 79 F1553
METH/COMP LEGIS SOC PROVS

S67
MENCHER S.,"THE PROBLEM OF MEASURING POVERTY." UNIV USA+45 STRATA PROB/SOLV...NEW/IDEA METH/COMP 20. PAGE 89 F1755
WEALTH CENSUS STAT GEN/LAWS

S67
MERIKOSKI V.,"BASIC PROBLEMS OF UNIVERSITY ADMINISTRATION." PROVS SECT CONTROL...CLASSIF 20. PAGE 90 F1760
ACADEM ADMIN SOVEREIGN METH/COMP

S67
PAULY M.V.,"MIXED PUBLIC AND PRIVATE FINANCING OF EDUCATION." STRATA PAY RECEIVE COST INCOME OPTIMAL METH/COMP. PAGE 104 F2039
SCHOOL PLAN TAX EFFICIENCY

S67
PETRAS J.,"GUERRILLA MOVEMENTS IN LATIN AMERICA - I." GUATEMALA PERU VENEZUELA NAT/G COLONIAL LEAD ATTIT PWR...TIME/SEQ METH/COMP 20 COLOMB. PAGE 105 F2072
GUERRILLA REV L/A+17C MARXISM

S67
RICHMAN B.M.,"SOVIET MANAGEMENT IN TRANSITION." USSR FINAN MARKET EX/STRUC PLAN PROB/SOLV TEC/DEV CONTROL LEAD CENTRAL EFFICIENCY...METH/COMP 20 REFORMERS. PAGE 111 F2186
MGT MARXISM POLICY AUTHORIT

S67
SCRIPP J.,"CONTROLLING PREJUDICIAL PUBLICITY BY THE CONTEMPT POWER: THE BRITISH PRACTICE AND ITS PROSPECT IN AMERICAN LAW." UK USA+45 EDU/PROP CONTROL GP/REL ORD/FREE JURID. PAGE 119 F2338
METH/COMP LAW PRESS ADJUD

S67
STOLTE S.C.,"THREE PROBLEMS FACING THE SOVIET BLOC." ASIA COM USA+45 USSR FORCES MARXISM ...IDEA/COMP METH/COMP 20 NATO WARSAW/P. PAGE 127 F2496
ECO/TAC DIPLOM INT/ORG POLICY

S67
ZOETEWEIJ B.,"INCOME POLICIES ABROAD: AN INTERIM REPORT." NAT/G PROB/SOLV BARGAIN BUDGET PRICE RISK CENTRAL EFFICIENCY EQUILIB...MGT NAT/COMP 20. PAGE 150 F2967
METH/COMP INCOME POLICY LABOR

B91
MILL J.S.,SOCIALISM (1859). MOD/EUR AGRI INDUS NAT/G REV INCOME PRODUC ORD/FREE POPULISM SOCISM ...GOV/COMP METH/COMP 19. PAGE 91 F1787
WEALTH SOCIALIST ECO/TAC OWN

B95
SELIGMAN E.R.A.,ESSAYS IN TAXATION. NEW/ZEALND PRUSSIA UK USA-45 MARKET LOC/G CREATE PRICE CONTROL INCOME OWN WEALTH...GOV/COMP METH/COMP 19. PAGE 119 F2349
TAX TARIFFS INDUS NAT/G

METH/GP

B52
ALEXANDROWICZ C.H.,INTERNATIONAL ECONOMIC ORGANIZATION. WOR+45 ECO/DEV ECO/UNDEV DIST/IND FINAN MARKET PLAN ECO/TAC LEGIT DRIVE WEALTH ...POLICY CONCPT QUANT OBS TIME/SEQ GEN/LAWS WORK METH/GP EEC ILO OEEC UNESCO 20. PAGE 4 F0063
INT/ORG INT/TRADE

L53
NELSON J.R.,"UNITED STATES FOREIGN ECONOMIC POLICY AND THE STERLING AREA." USA-45 WOR+45 WOR-45 NAT/G ECO/TAC WEALTH...STAT TIME/SEQ TREND CHARTS METH/GP TERR/GP CMN/WLTH 20. PAGE 97 F1911
FINAN DIPLOM UK

S53
BLOUGH R.,"THE ROLE OF THE ECONOMIST IN FEDERAL POLICY MAKING." USA+45 ELITES INTELL ECO/DEV NAT/G CONSULT EX/STRUC ACT/RES PLAN INT/TRADE BAL/PAY WEALTH...POLICY METH/GP CONGRESS 20. PAGE 16 F0301
DELIB/GP ECO/TAC

B58
MIKESELL R.F.,FINANCING FREE WORLD TRADE WITH THE SINO-SOVIET BLOC. CHINA/COM COM USSR WOR+45 ECO/DEV AGRI DIST/IND EXTR/IND FINAN INDUS MARKET PROC/MFG NAT/G PLAN TEC/DEV ECO/TAC...CHARTS METH/GP EEC FOR/TRADE 20. PAGE 91 F1780
STAT BAL/PAY

S60
MURPHEY R.,"ECONOMIC CONFLICTS IN SOUTH ASIA." ASIA CULTURE INTELL ECO/TAC REGION ATTIT DRIVE KNOWL ...METH/CNCPT TIME/SEQ STERTYP TOT/POP METH/GP VAL/FREE 20. PAGE 95 F1864
S/ASIA ECO/UNDEV

S60
NANES A.,"THE EUROPEAN COMMUNITY AND THE UNITED STATES: EVOLVING RELATIONS." EUR+WWI USA+45 WOR+45 ECO/UNDEV MARKET NAT/G DELIB/GP PLAN LEGIT ATTIT PWR WEALTH...CONCPT STAT TIME/SEQ CON/ANAL EEC METH/GP OEEC 20 EURATOM. PAGE 96 F1889
INT/ORG REGION

S60
STOCKWELL E.G.,"THE MEASUREMENT OF ECONOMIC DEVELOPMENT." WOR+45 SOCIETY ECO/DEV ECO/UNDEV INDUS ECO/TAC HEALTH WEALTH...WELF/ST GEOG METH/CNCPT CHARTS METH METH/GP 20. PAGE 126 F2492
FAM STAT

S61
GALBRAITH J.K.,"A POSITIVE APPROACH TO ECONOMIC AID." FUT USA+45 INTELL NAT/G CONSULT ACT/RES DIPLOM ECO/TAC EDU/PROP ATTIT KNOWL PWR WEALTH ...SOC STERTYP MID/EX METH/GP 20. PAGE 45 F0883
ECO/UNDEV ROUTINE FOR/AID

B62
ELLIOTT J.R.,THE APPEAL OF COMMUNISM IN THE UNDERDEVELOPED NATIONS. AFR USSR WOR+45 INT/ORG NAT/G DIPLOM DOMIN EDU/PROP ROUTINE ATTIT RIGID/FLEX ORD/FREE PWR WEALTH MARXISM...POLICY SOC METH/CNCPT MYTH TOT/POP METH/GP 20. PAGE 37 F0722
COM ECO/UNDEV

L62
WATERSTON A.,"PLANNING IN MOROCCO, ORGANIZATION AND IMPLEMENTATION. BALTIMORE: HOPKINS ECON. DEVELOP. INT. BANK FOR." ISLAM ECO/DEV AGRI DIST/IND INDUS PROC/MFG SERV/IND LOC/G EX/STRUC ECO/TAC PWR WEALTH TOT/POP TRUE/GP METH/GP TERR/GP VAL/FREE 20. PAGE 144 F2829
NAT/G PLAN MOROCCO

S62
BOKOR-SZEGO H.,"LA CONVENTION DE BELGRADE ET LE REGIME DU DANUBE." COM EUR+WWI WOR+45 STRUCT POL/PAR VOL/ASSN PLAN EDU/PROP WEALTH...TIME/SEQ METH/GP COMMUN 20. PAGE 16 F0308
INT/ORG TOTALISM YUGOSLAVIA

B63
GEERTZ C.,PEDDLERS AND PRINCES: SOCIAL DEVELOPMENT AND ECONOMIC CHANGE IN TWO INDONESIAN TOWNS. S/ASIA CULTURE SOCIETY STRATA FACE/GP CREATE TEC/DEV ECO/TAC ORD/FREE WEALTH...OBS INT CENSUS CHARTS WORK TOT/POP METH/GP TERR/GP VAL/FREE 20 MUNICH. PAGE 47 F0913
ECO/UNDEV SOC ELITES INDONESIA

B63
LAGOS G.,INTERNATIONAL STRATIFICATION AND UNDERDEVELOPED COUNTRIES. L/A+17C WOR+45 PLAN ECO/TAC PWR RESPECT WEALTH...METH/CNCPT STAT CHARTS SIMUL GEN/LAWS TRUE/GP METH/GP VAL/FREE 20. PAGE 74 F1459
ECO/UNDEV STRATA

S63
BALOGH T.,"L'INFLUENCE DES INSTITUTIONS MONETAIRES ET COMMERCIALES SUR LA STRUCTURE ECONOMIQUE AFRICAIN." AFR EUR+WWI FUT USA+45 USA-45 WOR+45 SERV/IND INT/ORG NAT/G TOP/EX ROUTINE...INDEX EEC METH/GP 20. PAGE 9 F0168
FINAN

S63
DOSSER D.,"TOWARD A THEORY OF INTERNATIONAL PUBLIC FINANCE." WOR+45 ECO/DEV PLAN ECO/TAC WEALTH ...WELF/ST TREND GEN/LAWS TRUE/GP METH/GP 20. PAGE 34 F0654
FINAN INT/ORG FOR/AID

S63
MILLEN B.H.,"INTERNATIONAL TRADE AND POLITICAL INDEPENDENCE." WOR+45 ECO/DEV WEALTH...STAT CHARTS FOR/TRADE METH/GP TERR/GP VAL/FREE 20. PAGE 91 F1788
ECO/UNDEV ECO/TAC INT/TRADE

S63
SHWADRAN B.,"MIDDLE EAST OIL, 1962." ISLAM DIST/IND INDUS PLAN ATTIT DRIVE WEALTH...POLICY STAT CONT/OBS TREND CHARTS GEN/LAWS TERR/GP METH/GP 20 OIL. PAGE 121 F2393
PROC/MFG ECO/TAC ELITES REGION

S63
SHWADRAN B.,"MIDDLE EAST OIL, 1962." ISLAM USSR ECO/DEV DIST/IND INDUS PLAN BAL/PWR DISPL DRIVE ...POLICY STAT TREND GEN/LAWS TERR/GP METH/GP EEC OEEC 20 OIL. PAGE 121 F2394
MARKET ECO/TAC INT/TRADE

B64
STOESSINGER J.G.,FINANCING THE UNITED NATIONS SYSTEM. FUT WOR+45 CONSTN NAT/G VOL/ASSN DELIB/GP EX/STRUC ECO/TAC LEGIT CT/SYS PWR WEALTH...STAT TIME/SEQ TREND CHARTS TRUE/GP METH/GP TERR/GP VAL/FREE. PAGE 126 F2493
FINAN INT/ORG

B64
WILLIAMSON J.G.,AMERICAN GROWTH AND THE BALANCE OF PAYMENTS, 1820-1913: A STUDY OF THE LONG SWING. EUR+WWI MOD/EUR USA+45 USA-45 ECO/DEV NAT/G ECO/TAC ROUTINE ORD/FREE WEALTH...MATH STAT TIME/SEQ CHARTS SIMUL GEN/LAWS TRUE/GP METH/GP VAL/FREE 19/20. PAGE 147 F2896
FINAN BAL/PAY

L64
STERN R.M.,"POLICIES FOR TRADE AND DEVELOPMENT." AFR FUT WOR+45 DIST/IND FINAN NAT/G DELIB/GP PLAN ECO/TAC ORD/FREE WEALTH...POLICY STAT TIME/SEQ CHARTS METH/GP 20. PAGE 126 F2480
MARKET ECO/UNDEV INT/TRADE

S64
KOJIMA K.,"THE PATTERN OF INTERNATIONAL TRADE AMONG ADVANCED COUNTRIES." EUR+WWI UK USA+45 WOR+45 MARKET NAT/G ECO/TAC WEALTH...MATH STAT CON/ANAL CHARTS METH/GP EEC CHINJAP 20 CHINJAP. PAGE 72 F1419
ECO/DEV TREND INT/TRADE

S64
PESELT B.M.,"COMMUNIST ECONOMIC OFFENSIVE." WOR+45 SOCIETY INT/ORG PLAN ECO/TAC DOMIN EDU/PROP ATTIT PERSON PWR WEALTH...TREND CHARTS METH/GP 20. PAGE 105 F2067
COM ECO/UNDEV FOR/AID USSR

S64
RUSSETT B.M.,"INEQUALITY AND INSTABILITY: THE RELATION OF LAND TENURE TO POLITICS." WOR+45 ECO/DEV ECO/UNDEV AGRI NAT/G COERCE PWR...MATH STAT CHARTS GEN/LAWS TERR/GP TRUE/GP METH/GP VAL/FREE 20. PAGE 115 F2263
WEALTH GEOG ECO/TAC ORD/FREE

S65
SPAAK P.H.,"THE SEARCH FOR CONSENSUS: A NEW EFFORT TO BUILD EUROPE." FRANCE GERMANY ECO/DEV NAT/G CONSULT FORCES PLAN EDU/PROP REGION CONSEN ATTIT ...SOC METH/CNCPT OBS TREND EEC NATO WORK TERR/GP METH/GP 20. PAGE 124 F2447
EUR+WWI INT/ORG

METHOD, COMPARATIVE....SEE IDEA/COMP, METH/COMP

METHODOLOGY....SEE METH, PHIL/SCI, METHODOLOGICAL INDEXES, PP. XIII-XIV

METRO/COUN....METROPOLITAN COUNCIL

METROPOLITAN....SEE MUNIC

METROPOLITAN COUNCIL....SEE METRO/COUN

METTRNCH/K....PRINCE K. VON METTERNICH

METZLER L.A. F1765

MEXIC/AMER....MEXICAN-AMERICANS

B33
TANNENBAUM F.,PEACE BY REVOLUTION. ECO/UNDEV AGRI SECT WORKER DIPLOM EDU/PROP DISCRIM OWN WEALTH POPULISM 17/20 MEXIC/AMER INDIAN/AM. PAGE 128 F2532
CULTURE COLONIAL RACE/REL REV

B39
MARQUAND H.A.,ORGANIZED LABOUR IN FOUR CONTINENTS. EUR+WWI USA-45 INDUS NAT/G PAY GP/REL TOTALISM ATTIT WEALTH ALL/IDEOS...TREND NAT/COMP 20 ILO AFL/CIO EUROPE CHINJAP MEXIC/AMER. PAGE 85 F1673
LABOR WORKER CONCPT ANTHOL

B54
MOSK S.A.,INDUSTRIAL REVOLUTION IN MEXICO. MARKET LABOR CREATE CAP/ISM ADMIN ATTIT SOCISM...POLICY 20 MEXIC/AMER. PAGE 94 F1843
INDUS TEC/DEV ECO/UNDEV NAT/G

B54
WILLIAMSON H.F.,ECONOMIC DEVELOPMENT - PRINCIPLES AND PATTERNS. INDIA KOREA CULTURE ECO/DEV ECO/UNDEV TEC/DEV...CENSUS NAT/COMP FOR/TRADE 20 CHINJAP MEXIC/AMER RESOURCE/N. PAGE 147 F2895
ECO/TAC GEOG LABOR

B58
COALE A.J.,POPULATION GROWTH AND ECONOMIC DEVELOPMENT IN LOW-INCOME COUNTRIES: A CASE STUDY OF INDIA'S PROSPECTS. INDIA AGRI WORKER INCOME AGE WEALTH...CHARTS 20 MEXIC/AMER. PAGE 25 F0495
ECO/UNDEV GEOG CENSUS SEX

B58
PAYNO M.,LA REFORMA SOCIAL EN ESPANA Y MEXICO. SPAIN ECO/TAC TAX LOBBY COERCE REV OWN CATHISM 19/20 MEXIC/AMER. PAGE 104 F2043
SECT NAT/G LAW ELITES

B60
GONZALEZ NAVARRO M.,LA COLONIZACION EN MEXICO, 1877-1910. AGRI NAT/G PLAN PROB/SOLV INCOME ...POLICY JURID CENSUS 19/20 MEXIC/AMER MIGRATION. PAGE 48 F0947
ECO/UNDEV GEOG HABITAT COLONIAL

B61
MEXICO; CINCUENTA ANOS DE REVOLUCION VOL. II. L/A+17C SOCIETY LABOR RECEIVE GP/REL AGE/Y HEALTH ...SOC/WK ANTHOL MUNICH 20 MEXIC/AMER. PAGE 1 F0014
ECO/UNDEV STRUCT INDUS POL/PAR

B61
ERASMUS C.J.,MAN TAKES CONTROL: CULTURAL DEVELOPMENT AND AMERICAN AID. STRUCT OWN DRIVE PERCEPT...SOC 20 MEXIC/AMER. PAGE 38 F0741
ORD/FREE CULTURE ECO/UNDEV TEC/DEV

B61
SEPULVEDA C.,A STATEMENT OF THE LAWS OF MEXICO IN MATTERS AFFECTING BUSINESS (3RD ED.). AGRI DIST/IND EXTR/IND FINAN INDUS WORKER TAX MARRIAGE OWN ORD/FREE...BIBLIOG 20 MEXIC/AMER TREATY MIGRATION MONOPOLY. PAGE 119 F2356
CONSTN NAT/G JURID LEGIS

B63
GLADE W.P. JR.,THE POLITICAL ECONOMY OF MEXICO. FUT L/A+17C CULTURE SOCIETY AGRI INDUS DELIB/GP ACT/RES ECO/TAC ATTIT HEALTH ORD/FREE...STAT TIME/SEQ TREND MEXIC/AMER TOT/POP VAL/FREE 20. PAGE 48 F0928
FINAN ECO/UNDEV

B64
WITHERS W.,THE ECONOMIC CRISIS IN LATIN AMERICA. BRAZIL CHILE STRATA AGRI DIPLOM FOR/AID PWR SOCISM ...POLICY 20 MEXIC/AMER ARGEN ALL/PROG. PAGE 148 F2914
L/A+17C ECO/UNDEV CAP/ISM ALL/IDEOS

S65
BRANDENBURG F.,"THE RELEVANCE OF MEXICAN EXPERIENCE TO LATIN AMERICAN DEVELOPMENT." BRAZIL CHILE VENEZUELA STRUCT ECO/UNDEV AGRI CREATE ECO/TAC ...STAT RECORD MEXIC/AMER ARGEN COLOMB. PAGE 18 F0340
L/A+17C GOV/COMP

B66
INARRITU A.L.,EL PATRON CAMBIO-ORO Y SUS REFORMAS. AFR L/A+17C WOR+45 PLAN PROB/SOLV BUDGET ECO/TAC INT/TRADE EFFICIENCY ORD/FREE 20 MEXIC/AMER. PAGE 64 F1262
ECO/UNDEV FINAN DIPLOM POLICY

B67
AARON H.J.,FINANCING URBAN DEVELOPMENT IN MEXICO CITY: A CASE STUDY OF PROPERTY TAX, LAND USE, HOUSING, AND URBAN PLANNING. LOC/G CREATE EFFICIENCY WEALTH...CHARTS MUNICH 20 MEXIC/AMER. PAGE 2 F0030
PLAN TAX PROB/SOLV

B67
JOHNSON D.G.,THE STRUGGLE AGAINST WORLD HUNGER (HEADLINE SERIES, NO. 184) (PAMPHLET). PLAN TEC/DEV FOR/AID...CHARTS 20 FAO MEXIC/AMER. PAGE 67 F1322
AGRI PROB/SOLV ECO/UNDEV HEALTH

B67
JOHNSON H.G.,ECONOMIC NATIONALISM IN OLD AND NEW STATES. CANADA CHINA/COM MALI UK DIPLOM...SIMUL GEN/LAWS 19/20 MEXIC/AMER. PAGE 68 F1328
NAT/LISM ECO/UNDEV ECO/DEV NAT/COMP

S67
MILLER C.H.,"B. TRAVEN Y EL 'PROBLEMA PETROLERO'." USA-45 ECO/UNDEV INDUS TEC/DEV INT/TRADE ATTIT ORD/FREE SOVEREIGN 20 MEXIC/AMER. PAGE 91 F1791
EXTR/IND DIPLOM ECO/TAC DOMIN

MEXICO....SEE ALSO L/A+17C

MEYER A.G. F1766

MEYER A.J. F1767

MEYER F.V. F1768,F1769

MEYER J.R. F1770,F1771

MEYERS M. F1772

MEYNAUD J. F1773,F1774

MEZERIK A.G. F1775,F1776,F1777,F1778

MGT....MANAGEMENT

B
BRITISH COMMONWEALTH BUR AGRI,WORLD AGRICULTURAL ECONOMICS AND RURAL SOCIOLOGY ABSTRACTS. NAT/G OP/RES PLAN TEC/DEV LEAD PRODUC...GEOG MGT NAT/COMP 20. PAGE 18 F0354
BIBLIOG/A AGRI SOC WORKER

N
ECONOMIC ABSTRACTS. WOR+45 FINAN INDUS MARKET LABOR ACT/RES INT/TRADE WRITING GP/REL...MGT 20. PAGE 1 F0005
BIBLIOG/A EDU/PROP

N
AMERICAN ECONOMIC ASSOCIATION,THE JOURNAL OF ECONOMIC ABSTRACTS. ECO/UNDEV MARKET LABOR DIPLOM ...MGT CONCPT METH 20. PAGE 5 F0086
BIBLIOG/A R+D FINAN

N
RAND SCHOOL OF SOCIAL SCIENCE,INDEX TO LABOR ARTICLES. ECO/DEV INT/ORG LEGIS DIPLOM GP/REL ...NAT/COMP 20. PAGE 109 F2143
BIBLIOG LABOR MGT ADJUD

N
UNIVERSITY OF FLORIDA,CARIBBEAN ACQUISITIONS: MATERIALS ACQUIRED BY THE UNIVERSITY OF FLORIDA 1957-1960. L/A+17C...ART/METH GEOG MGT 20. PAGE 133 F2620
BIBLIOG ECO/UNDEV EDU/PROP JURID

N
US SUPERINTENDENT OF DOCUMENTS,LABOR (PRICE LIST 33). USA+45 LAW AGRI CONSTRUC INDUS NAT/G BARGAIN PRICE ADMIN AUTOMAT PRODUC MGT. PAGE 140 F2753
BIBLIOG/A WORKER LABOR LEGIS

N19
BASSIE V.L.,UNCERTAINTY IN FORECASTING AND POLICY FORMATION (PAMPHLET). UNIV MARKET ECO/TAC PRODUC ...POLICY DECISION MGT MATH CHARTS 20. PAGE 11 F0205
ECO/DEV FINAN PREDICT PROB/SOLV

N19
DOTSON A.,PRODUCTION PLANNING IN THE PATENT OFFICE (PAMPHLET). USA+45 DIST/IND PROB/SOLV PRODUC...MGT PHIL/SCI 20 BUR/BUDGET PATENT/OFF. PAGE 34 F0655
EFFICIENCY PLAN NAT/G ADMIN

N19
FAHRNKOPF N.,STATE AND LOCAL GOVERNMENT IN ILLINOIS (PAMPHLET). CONSTN ADMIN PARTIC CHOOSE REPRESENT GOV/REL...JURID MGT 20 ILLINOIS. PAGE 39 F0759
BIBLIOG LOC/G LEGIS CT/SYS

N19
RIDLEY C.E.,MEASURING MUNICIPAL ACTIVITIES (PAMPHLET). FINAN SERV/IND FORCES RECEIVE INGP/REL HABITAT...POLICY SOC/WK 20. PAGE 111 F2191
MGT HEALTH WEALTH LOC/G

B28
HARDMAN J.B.,AMERICAN LABOR DYNAMICS. WORKER ECO/TAC DOMIN ADJUD LEAD LOBBY PWR...POLICY MGT. PAGE 55 F1079
LABOR INGP/REL ATTIT GP/REL

B32
THOMPSON C.D.,CONFESSIONS OF THE POWER TRUST. MARKET ACT/RES EDU/PROP CONTROL GOV/REL INCOME OWN ...MGT 20 FTC MONOPOLY. PAGE 130 F2564
LG/CO SERV/IND PWR FINAN

B38
REICH N.,LABOR RELATIONS IN REPUBLICAN GERMANY. GERMANY CONSTN ECO/DEV INDUS NAT/G ADMIN CONTROL GP/REL FASCISM POPULISM 20 WEIMAR/REP. PAGE 110 F2176
WORKER MGT LABOR BARGAIN

S38
HALL R.C.,"REPRESENTATION OF BIG BUSINESS IN THE HOUSE OF COMMONS." UK ECO/DEV INDUS PROF/ORG LEGIS CAP/ISM ECO/TAC LAISSEZ...POLICY OLD/LIB PLURIST MGT 20 HOUSE/CMNS. PAGE 53 F1047
LOBBY NAT/G

B39
JENNINGS W.I.,PARLIAMENT. UK POL/PAR OP/RES BUDGET LEAD CHOOSE GP/REL...MGT 20 PARLIAMENT HOUSE/LORD HOUSE/CMNS. PAGE 67 F1315
PARL/PROC LEGIS CONSTN NAT/G

B41
DAUGHERTY C.R.,LABOR PROBLEMS IN AMERICAN INDUSTRY (5TH ED.). USA-45 SOCIETY OP/RES ECO/TAC...MGT PSY T 20. PAGE 30 F0581
LABOR INDUS GP/REL PROB/SOLV

B41
LESTER R.A.,ECONOMICS OF LABOR. UK USA-45 TEC/DEV BARGAIN PAY INGP/REL INCOME...MGT 19/20. PAGE 78 F1532
LABOR ECO/DEV INDUS WORKER

B41
MACMAHON A.W.,THE ADMINISTRATION OF FEDERAL WORK RELIEF. USA-45 EX/STRUC WORKER BUDGET EFFICIENCY ...CONT/OBS CHARTS 20 WPA. PAGE 84 F1636
ADMIN NAT/G MGT GIVE

B41
SLICHTER S.H.,UNION POLICIES AND INDUSTRIAL MANAGEMENT. USA-45 INDUS TEC/DEV PAY GP/REL INGP/REL COST EFFICIENCY PRODUC...POLICY 20. PAGE 123 F2420
BARGAIN LABOR MGT WORKER

S43
GOLDEN C.S.,"NEW PATTERNS OF DEMOCRACY." NEIGH DELIB/GP EDU/PROP EXEC PARTIC...MGT METH/CNCPT OBS TREND. PAGE 48 F0935
LABOR REPRESENT LG/CO GP/REL

B44
BIENSTOCK G.,MANAGEMENT IN RUSSIAN INDUSTRY AND AGRICULTURE. USSR CONSULT WORKER LEAD COST PROFIT ATTIT DRIVE PWR...MGT METH/COMP DICTIONARY ACCT 20. PAGE 15 F0281
ADMIN MARXISM SML/CO AGRI

B44
MERRIAM C.E.,PUBLIC AND PRIVATE GOVERNMENT. VOL/ASSN EDU/PROP ADMIN REPRESENT EFFICIENCY PWR PLURISM...MAJORIT CONCPT. PAGE 90 F1762
NAT/G NEIGH MGT POLICY

B45
MILLIS H.A.,ORGANIZED LABOR (FIRST ED.). LAW STRUCT DELIB/GP WORKER ECO/TAC ADJUD CONTROL REPRESENT INGP/REL INCOME MGT. PAGE 92 F1797
LABOR POLICY ROUTINE GP/REL

B46
HARRISON S.M.,AMERICAN FOUNDATIONS FOR SOCIAL WELFARE. OP/RES CONTROL...POLICY MGT METH/CNCPT STAT TREND BIBLIOG. PAGE 56 F1092
GIVE FINAN CLASSIF ADMIN

B47
BAERWALD F.,FUNDAMENTALS OF LABOR ECONOMICS. LAW INDUS LABOR LG/CO CONTROL GP/REL INCOME TOTALISM ...MGT CHARTS GEN/LAWS BIBLIOG 20. PAGE 8 F0150
ECO/DEV WORKER MARKET

B47
LEVER E.A.,ADVERTISING AND ECONOMIC THEORY. FINAN ECO/TAC DEMAND EFFICIENCY ATTIT...MGT PSY SAMP/SIZ CHARTS 20. PAGE 79 F1539
EDU/PROP MARKET COM/IND ECO/DEV

B47
SLICHTER S.H.,THE CHALLENGE OF INDUSTRIAL RELATIONS: TRADE UNIONS, MANAGEMENT AND THE PUBLIC INTEREST. PLAN ECO/TAC ADJUD CONTROL LEAD SANCTION GP/REL INGP/REL INCOME. PAGE 123 F2421
LABOR MGT CLIENT POLICY

B47
WARNER W.L.,THE SOCIAL SYSTEM OF THE MODERN FACTORY; THE STRIKE: AN ANALYSIS. USA-45 STRATA WORKER ECO/TAC GP/REL INGP/REL...MGT SOC CHARTS 20 YANKEE/C. PAGE 143 F2824
ROLE STRUCT LABOR PROC/MFG

B47
WHITEHEAD T.N.,LEADERSHIP IN A FREE SOCIETY; A STUDY IN HUMAN RELATIONS BASED ON AN ANALYSIS OF PRESENT-DAY INDUSTRIAL CIVILIZATION. WOR-45 STRUCT R+D LABOR LG/CO SML/CO WORKER PLAN PROB/SOLV TEC/DEV DRIVE...MGT 20. PAGE 146 F2872
INDUS LEAD ORD/FREE SOCIETY

B48
METZLER L.A.,INCOME, EMPLOYMENT, AND PUBLIC POLICY. FINAN INDUS LOC/G NAT/G TAX GIVE PAY COST PRODUC ...MGT TIME/SEQ 20. PAGE 90 F1765
INCOME WEALTH POLICY ECO/TAC

B48
WHYTE W.F.,HUMAN RELATIONS IN THE RESTAURANT INDUSTRY (1ST ED). CLIENT WORKER WAR ATTIT...MGT OBS INT. PAGE 146 F2874
INGP/REL GP/REL SERV/IND LABOR

S48
HARDIN L.M.,"REFLECTIONS ON AGRICULTURAL POLICY FORMATION IN THE UNITED STATES." LEGIS PLAN BUDGET ECO/TAC LEAD CENTRAL...MGT SOC NEW/IDEA STAT FAO. PAGE 55 F1078
AGRI POLICY ADMIN NEW/LIB

B49
SHISTER J.,ECONOMICS OF THE LABOR MARKET. LOC/G NAT/G WORKER TEC/DEV BARGAIN PAY PRICE EXEC GP/REL INCOME...MGT T 20. PAGE 121 F2381
MARKET LABOR INDUS

S49
HART C.W.M.,"INDUSTRIAL RELATIONS RESEARCH AND SOCIAL THEORY." CANADA VOL/ASSN WORKER LEAD EFFICIENCY...MGT SOC METH/CNCPT METH/COMP MUNICH 20. PAGE 56 F1099
GEN/LAWS LABOR GP/REL

S49
STEINMETZ H.,"THE PROBLEMS OF THE LANDRAT: A STUDY OF COUNTY GOVERNMENT IN THE US ZONE OF GERMANY." GERMANY/W USA+45 INDUS PLAN DIPLOM EDU/PROP CONTROL WAR GOV/REL FEDERAL WEALTH PLURISM...GOV/COMP 20 LANDRAT. PAGE 126 F2478
LOC/G COLONIAL MGT TOP/EX

B50
SCHUMPETER J.A.,CAPITALISM, SOCIALISM, AND DEMOCRACY (3RD ED.). USA-45 USSR WOR+45 WOR-45 INTELL ECO/DEV ECO/UNDEV ECO/TAC WAR PRODUC ORD/FREE...MGT SOC 20 MARX/KARL. PAGE 118 F2321
SOCIALIST CAP/ISM MARXISM IDEA/COMP

S50
DALTON M.,"CONFLICTS BETWEEN STAFF AND LINE MANAGERIAL OFFICERS" (BMR). USA+45 USA-45 ELITES LG/CO WORKER PROB/SOLV ADMIN EXEC EFFICIENCY PRODUC ...GP/COMP 20. PAGE 30 F0576
MGT ATTIT GP/REL INDUS

S50
DREYFUS S.,"THE INDUSTRIAL DESIGNER AND THE BUSINESSMAN." SERV/IND PROB/SOLV ECO/TAC COST EFFICIENCY PROFIT RATIONAL...DECISION MGT. PAGE 34 F0662
CONSULT INDUS PRODUC UTIL

B51
DIMOCK M.E.,FREE ENTERPRISE AND THE ADMINISTRATIVE STATE. FINAN LG/CO BARGAIN BUDGET DOMIN CONTROL INGP/REL EFFICIENCY 20. PAGE 33 F0640
CAP/ISM ADMIN MGT MARKET

B51
HARBISON F.H.,GOALS AND STRATEGY IN COLLECTIVE BARGAINING. WORKER BAL/PWR PARTIC DRIVE...POLICY MGT. PAGE 55 F1074
LABOR BARGAIN GP/REL ADMIN

B51
PRINCETON U INDUSTRIAL REL SEC,COMPULSORY ARBITRATION OF UTILITY DISPUTES IN NEW JERSEY AND
BARGAIN PROVS

PENNSYLVANIA. USA+45 LEGIS WORKER ADJUD ORD/FREE ...POLICY MGT METH/COMP 20 NEW/JERSEY PENNSYLVAN. PAGE 108 F2118 — INDUS LABOR

C51
HOMANS G.C.,"THE WESTERN ELECTRIC RESEARCHES" IN S. HOSLETT, ED., HUMAN FACTORS IN MANAGEMENT (BMR)" ACT/RES GP/REL HAPPINESS PRODUC DRIVE...MGT OBS 20. PAGE 61 F1202 — OP/RES EFFICIENCY SOC/EXP WORKER

S52
KLUMB S.,"EMPLOYEE DETERMINATION OF MANAGERIAL FUNCTIONS AND CHARACTERISTICS." DELIB/GP WORKER PARTIC ROUTINE INGP/REL...CLASSIF OBS QU. PAGE 72 F1410 — MGT INDUS EX/STRUC CHOOSE

B53
BOWEN H.R.,SOCIAL RESPONSIBILITIES OF THE BUSINESSMAN (FIRST EDITION). LAW FINAN ACT/RES CAP/ISM ROUTINE DRIVE PWR LAISSEZ...DECISION BIBLIOG. PAGE 17 F0326 — MGT PERSON SUPEGO MORAL

B53
FLORENCE P.S.,THE LOGIC OF BRITISH AND AMERICAN INDUSTRY; A REALISTIC ANALYSIS OF ECONOMIC STRUCTURE AND GOVERNMENT. UK USA+45 USA-45 FINAN LABOR CAP/ISM INGP/REL EFFICIENCY...MGT CONCPT STAT CHARTS METH 20. PAGE 42 F0813 — INDUS ECO/DEV NAT/G NAT/COMP

B53
PURCELL T.V.,THE WORKER SPEAKS HIS MIND ON COMPANY AND UNION. WORKER ADJUD LEAD RACE/REL ATTIT DRIVE MARXISM...MGT CLASSIF STAT OBS INT SAMP BIBLIOG. PAGE 108 F2131 — LABOR PARTIC INGP/REL HAPPINESS

B53
ROBINSON E.A.G.,THE STRUCTURE OF COMPETITIVE INDUSTRY. UK ECO/DEV DIST/IND MARKET TEC/DEV DIPLOM EDU/PROP ADMIN EFFICIENCY WEALTH...MGT 19/20. PAGE 113 F2217 — INDUS PRODUC WORKER OPTIMAL

B53
SAYLES L.R.,THE LOCAL UNION. CONSTN CULTURE DELIB/GP PARTIC CHOOSE GP/REL INGP/REL ATTIT ROLE ...MAJORIT DECISION MGT. PAGE 116 F2284 — LABOR LEAD ADJUD ROUTINE

S53
DRUCKER P.F.,"THE EMPLOYEE SOCIETY." STRUCT BAL/PWR PARTIC REPRESENT PWR...DECISION CONCPT. PAGE 34 F0666 — LABOR MGT WORKER CULTURE

S53
MCKEE J.B.,"STATUS AND POWER IN THE INDUSTRIAL COMMUNITY; A COMMENT ON DRUCKER'S THESIS." LABOR LEGIT LEAD GP/REL PWR...MGT CONCPT. PAGE 88 F1730 — SOC STRATA NEIGH PARTIC

S53
SIMON H.A.,"BIRTH OF AN ORGANIZATION: THE ECONOMIC COOPERATION ADMINISTRATION." USA+45 PROB/SOLV INGP/REL EFFICIENCY 20. PAGE 122 F2408 — ADMIN EX/STRUC EXEC MGT

B54
CHILDS M.W.,ETHICS IN A BUSINESS SOCIETY. PROF/ORG LEAD WAR GP/REL ATTIT DRIVE PERSON KNOWL MORAL PWR ...WELF/ST BIBLIOG. PAGE 24 F0466 — MGT SOCIETY

B54
RECK D.,GOVERNMENT PURCHASING AND COMPETITION. USA+45 LEGIS CAP/ISM ECO/TAC GOV/REL CENTRAL ...POLICY 20 CONGRESS. PAGE 110 F2164 — NAT/G FINAN MGT COST

C54
BERLE A.A. JR.,"THE 20TH CENTURY CAPITALIST REVOLUTION." ECO/DEV NAT/G DIPLOM PRICE CONTROL ATTIT...BIBLIOG/A 20. PAGE 14 F0260 — LG/CO CAP/ISM MGT PWR

B55
SMITHIES A.,THE BUDGETARY PROCESS IN THE UNITED STATES. AFR ECO/DEV AGRI EX/STRUC FORCES LEGIS PROB/SOLV TAX ROUTINE EFFICIENCY...MGT CONGRESS PRESIDENT. PAGE 124 F2436 — NAT/G ADMIN BUDGET GOV/REL

L55
KISER M.,"ORGANIZATION OF AMERICAN STATES." L/A+17C USA+45 ECO/UNDEV INT/ORG NAT/G PLAN TEC/DEV DIPLOM ECO/TAC INT/TRADE EDU/PROP ADMIN ALL/VALS...POLICY MGT RECORD ORG/CHARTS OAS COMMUN 20. PAGE 71 F1401 — VOL/ASSN ECO/DEV REGION

S55
BUNZEL J.H.,"THE GENERAL IDEOLOGY OF AMERICAN SMALL BUSINESS"(BMR)" USA+45 USA-45 AGRI GP/REL INGP/REL PERSON...MGT IDEA/COMP 18/20. PAGE 20 F0383 — ALL/IDEOS ATTIT SML/CO INDUS

S55
KELLY W.E.,"HOW SALES EXECUTIVES USE FACTORING TO BOOST SALES AND PROFITS TODAY." FINAN LG/CO BUDGET EFFICIENCY PROFIT...MGT PRODUCT. PAGE 70 F1372 — INDUS ECO/DEV CONSULT MARKET

B56
BURKHEAD J.,GOVERNMENT BUDGETING. ECO/DEV PROB/SOLV ECO/TAC ADMIN ROUTINE GOV/REL EFFICIENCY...DECISION MGT. PAGE 20 F0388 — BUDGET NAT/G PROVS EX/STRUC

B56
HICKMAN C.A.,INDIVIDUALS, GROUPS, AND ECONOMIC BEHAVIOR. WORKER PAY CONTROL EXEC GP/REL INGP/REL PERSON ROLE...PSY SOC PERS/COMP METH 20. PAGE 59 F1163 — MGT ADMIN ECO/TAC PLAN

S56
MARGOLIS J.,"ON MUNICIPAL LAND POLICY FOR FISCAL GAINS." USA+45 PLAN TAX COST EFFICIENCY HABITAT KNOWL...MGT MUNICH 20. PAGE 85 F1667 — BUDGET POLICY GEOG LOC/G

S56
MYERS C.A.,"LINE AND STAFF IN INDUSTRIAL RELATIONS." INDUS LABOR GP/REL PWR...MGT INT. PAGE 96 F1876 — ROLE PROB/SOLV ADMIN CONSULT

B57
BARAN P.A.,THE POLITICAL ECONOMY OF GROWTH. MOD/EUR USA+45 USA-45 TEC/DEV TAX SOCISM...MGT CONCPT GOV/COMP. PAGE 9 F0178 — CAP/ISM CONTROL ECO/UNDEV FINAN

B57
COMMITTEE ECONOMIC DEVELOPMENT,ECONOMIC DEVELOPMENT ASSISTANCE. USA+45 WOR+45 AGRI CONFER ORD/FREE ...MGT CHARTS 20. PAGE 27 F0515 — FOR/AID ECO/UNDEV FINAN PLAN

B57
MURDESHWAR A.K.,ADMINISTRATIVE PROBLEMS RELATING TO NATIONALISATION: WITH SPECIAL REFERENCE TO INDIAN STATE ENTERPRISES. CZECHOSLVK FRANCE INDIA UK USA+45 LEGIS WORKER PROB/SOLV BUDGET PRICE CONTROL ...MGT GEN/LAWS 20 PARLIAMENT. PAGE 95 F1863 — NAT/G OWN INDUS ADMIN

B57
SCHNEIDER E.V.,INDUSTRIAL SOCIOLOGY: THE SOCIAL RELATIONS OF INDUSTRY AND COMMUNITY. STRATA INDUS NAT/G NEIGH CREATE ADMIN PARTIC GP/REL RACE/REL ROLE PWR...POLICY BIBLIOG. PAGE 117 F2308 — LABOR MGT INGP/REL STRUCT

S57
ANSHEN M.,"BUSINESS, LAWYERS, AND ECONOMISTS." PROB/SOLV ECO/TAC CONFER PROFIT RIGID/FLEX OBJECTIVE...MGT GP/COMP. PAGE 6 F0106 — INDUS CONSULT ROUTINE EFFICIENCY

S57
CUNNINGHAM E.M.,"THE BUSINESS MAN AND HIS LAWYER." USA+45 LG/CO SML/CO TOP/EX CHOOSE SKILL...JURID MGT 20. PAGE 29 F0561 — CONSULT LAW DECISION SERV/IND

S57
DUBIN R.,"POWER AND UNION-MANAGEMENT RELATIONS." PROB/SOLV ADJUD ROUTINE ATTIT ORD/FREE...MGT STERTYP. PAGE 34 F0668 — PWR LABOR BARGAIN GP/REL

S57
ROURKE F.E.,"THE POLITICS OF ADMINISTRATIVE ORGANIZATION: A CASE HISTORY." USA+45 LABOR WORKER PLAN ADMIN TASK EFFICIENCY 20 DEPT/LABOR CONGRESS. PAGE 114 F2251 — POLICY ATTIT MGT GP/COMP

B58
ATOMIC INDUSTRIAL FORUM,MANAGEMENT AND ATOMIC ENERGY. WOR+45 SEA LAW MARKET NAT/G TEC/DEV INSPECT INT/TRADE CONFER PEACE HEALTH...ANTHOL 20. PAGE 7 F0136 — NUC/PWR INDUS MGT ECO/TAC

B58
BARRERE A.,POLITIQUE FINANCIERE. FRANCE BUDGET ECO/TAC TAX BAL/PAY INCOME PRODUC...MGT BIBLIOG T 20. PAGE 10 F0193 — FINAN NAT/G PLAN

B58
COLM G.,THE ECONOMY OF THE AMERICAN PEOPLE: PROGRESS, PROBLEMS, PROSPECTS. USA+45 INDUS MARKET LABOR TEC/DEV INCOME 20. PAGE 26 F0509 — WEALTH PRODUC CAP/ISM MGT

B58
CUNNINGHAM W.B.,COMPULSORY CONCILIATION AND COLLECTIVE BARGAINING. CANADA NAT/G LEGIS ADJUD CT/SYS GP/REL...MGT 20 NEW/BRUNS STRIKE CASEBOOK. PAGE 29 F0563 — POLICY BARGAIN LABOR INDUS

B58
DUBIN R.,WORKING UNION-MANAGEMENT RELATIONS. LAW PLAN ECO/TAC CHOOSE REPRESENT INGP/REL PWR...POLICY SOC BIBLIOG. PAGE 34 F0669 — LABOR MGT AUTHORIT GP/REL

B58
HENNING C.N.,INTERNATIONAL FINANCING. WOR+45 ECO/DEV INT/ORG EX/STRUC INSPECT CAP/ISM BAL/PAY COST PROFIT...MGT CHARTS T 20. PAGE 58 F1150 — FINAN DIPLOM INT/TRADE

B58
LESTER R.A.,AS UNIONS MATURE. POL/PAR BARGAIN LEAD PARTIC GP/REL CENTRAL...MAJORIT TIME/SEQ METH/COMP. PAGE 78 F1533 — LABOR INDUS POLICY MGT

B58
TANNENBAUM A.S.,PARTICIPATION IN UNION LOCALS. SOCIETY FINAN CONTROL LEAD GP/REL...BIBLIOG 20. PAGE 128 F2531 — LABOR MGT PARTIC INGP/REL

B58
WARNER A.W.,CONCEPTS AND CASES IN ECONOMIC ANALYSIS. PROB/SOLV BARGAIN CONTROL INCOME PRODUC ...ECOMETRIC MGT CONCPT CLASSIF CHARTS 20 KEYNES/JM. PAGE 143 F2820 — ECO/TAC DEMAND EQUILIB COST

L58
FORRESTER J.W.,"INDUSTRIAL DYNAMICS* A MAJOR BREAKTHROUGH FOR DECISION MAKERS." COMPUTER OP/RES ...DECISION CONCPT NEW/IDEA. PAGE 42 F0830 — INDUS ACT/RES MGT PROB/SOLV

S58
FOLDES L.,"UNCERTAINTY, PROBABILITY AND POTENTIAL SURPRISE." MARKET PROB/SOLV RISK PERSON...DECISION MGT HYPO/EXP GAME. PAGE 42 F0820 — PROBABIL ADMIN ROUTINE

S58
O'NEAL F.H.,"RECENT LEGISLATION AFFECTING CLOSE CORPORATIONS." LAW EX/STRUC ECO/TAC ROUTINE CHOOSE RIGID/FLEX...MAJORIT MGT TREND. PAGE 100 F1959 — LG/CO LEGIS REPRESENT PARTIC

B59
BONNETT C.E.,LABOR-MANAGEMENT RELATIONS. USA+45 OP/RES PROB/SOLV EDU/PROP...AUD/VIS CHARTS 20. PAGE 16 F0317 — MGT LABOR INDUS GP/REL

B59
LI CHOH-MING,ECONOMIC DEVELOPMENT OF COMMUNIST CHINA. ASIA CHINA/COM AGRI FINAN TAX INCOME MARXISM ...MGT 20. PAGE 80 F1557 — ECO/UNDEV INDUS ORD/FREE TEC/DEV

B59
MUSOLF L.D.,PUBLIC OWNERSHIP AND ACCOUNTABILITY: THE CANADIAN EXPERIENCE. CANADA REPRESENT PWR 20. PAGE 95 F1873 — MGT CONTROL INDUS

B59
SELIGSOHN I.J.,"USING COMPUTER SERVICES IN SMALL BUSINESS" MANAGEMENT AIDS FOR SMALL MANUFACTURERS 109 (PAMPHLET). DIST/IND MARKET PROC/MFG COST EFFICIENCY PRODUC...DECISION IDEA/COMP. PAGE 119 F2350 — SML/CO COMPUTER MGT PROB/SOLV

B59
SERAPHIM H.J.,PROBLEME DER WILLENSBILDUNG UND DER WIRTSCHAFTSPOLITISCHEN FUEHRUNG. WOR+45 MARKET ACT/RES OP/RES PLAN EDU/PROP INGP/REL HABITAT PLURISM...MGT PERS/COMP METH 20. PAGE 119 F2357 — POLICY DECISION PSY

B59
SHUBIK M.,STRATEGY AND MARKET STRUCTURE: COMPETITION, OLIGOPOLY, AND THE THEORY OF GAMES. ELITES STRUCT MARKET OP/RES EXEC EFFICIENCY INCOME ...MGT MATH STAT CHARTS 20. PAGE 121 F2389 — ECO/DEV ECO/TAC DECISION GAME

B59
US NATIONAL LABOR RELATIONS BD,LEGISLATIVE HISTORY OF THE LABOR-MANAGEMENT REPORTING AND DISCLOSURE ACT OF 1959 (2 VOLS.). USA+45 LEGIS...MGT CHARTS. PAGE 138 F2720 — LAW LABOR GP/REL

B59
VERNEY D.V.,PUBLIC ENTERPRISE IN SWEDEN. FUT SWEDEN UK INDUS POL/PAR LEGIS PROB/SOLV CAP/ISM INT/TRADE CONTROL SOCISM...MGT CONCPT NAT/COMP 20 SOCDEM/PAR CIVIL/SERV. PAGE 141 F2778 — ECO/DEV POLICY LG/CO NAT/G

B59
WELTON H.,THE THIRD WORLD WAR; TRADE AND INDUSTRY, THE NEW BATTLEGROUND. AFR WOR+45 ECO/DEV INDUS MARKET TASK...MGT IDEA/COMP. PAGE 145 F2855 — INT/TRADE PLAN DIPLOM

L59
FURASH E.A.,"PROBLEMS IN REVIEW: INDUSTRIAL ESPIONAGE." WORKER ECO/TAC PERS/REL OPTIMAL AGE ATTIT KNOWL...MGT DEEP/INT DEEP/QU GP/COMP IDEA/COMP. PAGE 45 F0875 — INDUS TOP/EX MAJORITY

L59
SIMON H.A.,"THEORIES OF DECISION-MAKING IN ECONOMICS AND BEHAVIORAL SCIENCE" (BMR)" MARKET BARGAIN UTIL DRIVE...DECISION MGT PROBABIL HYPO/EXP SIMUL 20 BEHAVIORSM. PAGE 122 F2409 — PSY GEN/LAWS PROB/SOLV

S59
BENDIX R.,"INDUSTRIALIZATION, IDEOLOGIES, AND SOCIAL STRUCTURE" (BMR)" UK USA-45 USSR STRUCT WORKER GP/REL EFFICIENCY...IDEA/COMP 20. PAGE 13 F0243 — INDUS ATTIT MGT ADMIN

S59
CYERT R.M.,"MODELS IN A BEHAVIORAL THEORY OF THE FIRM." ROUTINE...DECISION MGT METH/CNCPT MATH. PAGE 29 F0567 — SIMUL GAME PREDICT INDUS

S59
MILLER A.S.,"CONSTITUTIONALIZING THE CORPORATION." LABOR NAT/G WORKER PWR...POLICY MGT. PAGE 91 F1789 — CONSTN INGP/REL LG/CO CONTROL

S59
TEITSWORTH C.S.,"GROWING ROLE OF THE COMPANY ECONOMIST." USA+45 PLAN PROB/SOLV CAP/ISM ECO/TAC ADMIN ATTIT MGT. PAGE 129 F2541 — INDUS CONSULT UTIL DECISION

S59
WALLACE R.A.,"CONGRESSIONAL CONTROL OF THE BUDGET." USA+45 NAT/G CHIEF GP/REL FEDERAL OBJECTIVE...MGT CONGRESS. PAGE 143 F2807 — LEGIS EX/STRUC BUDGET CONSTN

B60
BOULDING K.E.,LINEAR PROGRAMMING AND THE THEORY OF THE FIRM. ACT/RES PLAN...MGT MATH. PAGE 17 F0323 — LG/CO NEW/IDEA COMPUTER

B60
ELKOURI F.,HOW ARBITRATION WORKS (REV. ED.). LAW INDUS BARGAIN 20. PAGE 37 F0720 — MGT LABOR ADJUD GP/REL

B60
FORBUSH D.R.,PROBLEMS OF CORPORATE POWER. CLIENT LAW ELITES ADJUD...DECISION MGT. PAGE 42 F0822 — LG/CO PWR CONTROL GP/REL

B60
FORM W.H.,INDUSTRY, LABOR, AND COMMUNITY. STRUCT NEIGH SECT BAL/PWR EDU/PROP PARTIC ATTIT ROLE PWR WEALTH...METH/CNCPT CHARTS. PAGE 42 F0828 — LABOR MGT GP/REL CONTROL

B60
KERR C.,INDUSTRIALISM AND INDUSTRIAL MAN. CULTURE SOCIETY ECO/UNDEV NAT/G ADMIN PRODUC WEALTH ...PREDICT TREND NAT/COMP 19/20. PAGE 70 F1381 — WORKER MGT ECO/DEV INDUS

B60
MOORE W.E.,LABOR COMMITMENT AND SOCIAL CHANGE IN DEVELOPING AREAS. SOCIETY STRATA ECO/UNDEV MARKET VOL/ASSN WORKER AUTHORIT SKILL...MGT NAT/COMP SOC/INTEG 20. PAGE 93 F1823 — LABOR ORD/FREE ATTIT INDUS

B60
MORRIS W.T.,ENGINEERING ECONOMY. AUTOMAT RISK RATIONAL...PROBABIL STAT CHARTS GAME SIMUL BIBLIOG T 20. PAGE 94 F1838 — OP/RES DECISION MGT PROB/SOLV

B60
SLOTKIN J.S.,FROM FIELD TO FACTORY; NEW INDUSTRIAL EMPLOYEES. HABITAT...MGT NEW/IDEA NAT/COMP BIBLIOG SOC/INTEG 20. PAGE 123 F2423 — INDUS LABOR CULTURE WORKER

B60
STEIN E.,AMERICAN ENTERPRISE IN THE EUROPEAN COMMON MARKET: A LEGAL PROFILE. EUR+WWI FUT USA+45 SOCIETY STRUCT ECO/DEV NAT/G VOL/ASSN CONSULT PLAN TEC/DEV ECO/TAC INT/TRADE ADMIN ATTIT RIGID/FLEX PWR...MGT NEW/IDEA STAT TREND COMPUT/IR SIMUL EEC 20. PAGE 125 F2475 — MARKET ADJUD INT/LAW

S60
BAUM M.,"THE CASE FOR BUSINESS CIVILIZATION." R+D CAP/ISM GIVE EDU/PROP HAPPINESS...SOC TREND. PAGE 12 F0218 — MGT CULTURE WEALTH

S60
FRANKEL S.H.,"ECONOMIC ASPECTS OF POLITICAL INDEPENDENCE IN AFRICA." AFR FUT SOCIETY ECO/UNDEV COM/IND FINAN LEGIS PLAN TEC/DEV CAP/ISM ECO/TAC INT/TRADE ADMIN ATTIT DRIVE RIGID/FLEX PWR WEALTH ...MGT NEW/IDEA MATH TIME/SEQ VAL/FREE 20. PAGE 43 F0846 — NAT/G FOR/AID

S60
MAIR L.P.,"SOCIAL CHANGE IN SOUTH AFRICA." MOD/EUR SOUTH/AFR WOR+45 ECO/UNDEV EX/STRUC TEC/DEV ATTIT DRIVE PERCEPT ORD/FREE...MGT CONCPT TIME/SEQ IND 20. PAGE 84 F1641 — AFR NAT/G REV SOVEREIGN

S60
POLLARD J.A.,"EMERGING PATTERNS OF CORPORATE GIVING." FINAN DELIB/GP PLAN EDU/PROP CENTRAL TREND. PAGE 107 F2098 — GIVE LG/CO ADMIN MGT

S60
RIVKIN A.,"AFRICAN ECONOMIC DEVELOPMENT: ADVANCED TECHNOLOGY AND THE STAGES OF GROWTH." CULTURE ECO/UNDEV AGRI COM/IND EXTR/IND PLAN ECO/TAC ATTIT DRIVE RIGID/FLEX SKILL WEALTH...MGT SOC GEN/LAWS FOR/TRADE WORK TOT/POP 20. PAGE 111 F2195 — AFR TEC/DEV FOR/AID

B61
AMERICAN MANAGEMENT ASSN,SUPERIOR-SUBORDINATE COMMUNICATION IN MANAGEMENT. STRATA FINAN INDUS SML/CO WORKER CONTROL EXEC ATTIT 20. PAGE 5 F0090 — MGT ACT/RES PERS/REL LG/CO

B61
BENOIT E.,EUROPE AT SIXES AND SEVENS: THE COMMON MARKET, THE FREE TRADE ASSOCIATION AND THE UNITED STATES. EUR+WWI FUT USA+45 INDUS CONSULT DELIB/GP EX/STRUC TOP/EX ACT/RES ECO/TAC EDU/PROP ROUTINE CHOOSE PERCEPT WEALTH...MGT TREND EEC FOR/TRADE TOT/POP 20 EFTA. PAGE 13 F0249 — FINAN ECO/DEV VOL/ASSN

B61
CARROTHERS A.W.R.,LABOR ARBITRATION IN CANADA. CANADA LAW NAT/G CONSULT LEGIS WORKER ADJUD ADMIN CT/SYS 20. PAGE 22 F0422 — LABOR MGT GP/REL BARGAIN

B61
DUKE UNIVERSITY,EXPULSION OR OPPRESSION OF BUSINESS ASSOCIATES: "SQUEEZE-OUTS" IN SMALL ENTERPRISES. LAW CONTROL PARTIC COERCE INGP/REL...POLICY RECORD INT. PAGE 35 F0674 — PWR MGT SML/CO ECO/TAC

B61
FILLOL T.R.,SOCIAL FACTORS IN ECONOMIC DEVELOPMENT: THE ARGENTINE CASE. STRUCT INDUS LABOR CREATE TEC/DEV EFFICIENCY PRODUC DRIVE...METH/CNCPT — ECO/UNDEV MGT PERS/REL

METH/COMP BIBLIOG/A 20 ARGEN. PAGE 41 F0795 TREND

B61
GORDON R.A.,BUSINESS LEADERSHIP IN THE LARGE CORPORATION. USA+45 SOCIETY EX/STRUC ADMIN CONTROL ROUTINE GP/REL PWR...MGT 20. PAGE 49 F0960 LG/CO LEAD DECISION LOBBY

B61
HART W.R.,COLLECTIVE BARGAINING IN THE FEDERAL CIVIL SERVICE. NAT/G EX/STRUC ADMIN EXEC 20. PAGE 56 F1101 INGP/REL MGT REPRESENT LABOR

B61
LEE R.R.,ENGINEERING-ECONOMIC PLANNING MISCELLANEOUS SUBJECTS: A SELECTED BIBLIOGRAPHY (MIMEOGRAPHED). FINAN LOC/G NEIGH ADMIN CONTROL INGP/REL HABITAT...GEOG MGT SOC/WK MUNICH 20 RESOURCE/N. PAGE 77 F1509 BIBLIOG/A PLAN REGION

B61
QURESHI S.,INCENTIVES IN AMERICAN EMPLOYMENT (THESIS, UNIVERSITY OF PENNSYLVANIA). DELIB/GP TOP/EX BUDGET ROUTINE SANCTION COST TECHRACY MGT. PAGE 108 F2134 SERV/IND ADMIN PAY EX/STRUC

B61
SLICHTER S.H.,ECONOMIC GROWTH IN THE UNITED STATES. FUT USA+45 USA-45 LABOR PAY INCOME PRODUC...MGT 19/20. PAGE 123 F2422 ECO/DEV TEC/DEV CAP/ISM DEMAND

S61
BENNION E.G.,"ECONOMETRICS FOR MANAGEMENT." USA+45 INDUS EX/STRUC ACT/RES COMPUTER UTIL...MATH STAT PREDICT METH/COMP HYPO/EXP. PAGE 13 F0248 ECOMETRIC MGT SIMUL DECISION

S61
CYERT R.M.,"TWO EXPERIMENTS ON BIAS AND CONFLICT IN ORGANIZATIONAL ESTIMATION." WORKER PROB/SOLV EFFICIENCY...MGT PSY STAT CHARTS. PAGE 29 F0568 LAB/EXP ROUTINE ADMIN DECISION

S61
LINDSAY F.A.,"PLANNING IN FOREIGN AFFAIRS: THE MISSING ELEMENT." FUT USA+45 ROUTINE SKILL...MGT TOT/POP 20. PAGE 80 F1572 ECO/DEV PLAN DIPLOM

S61
SHUBIK M.,"APPROACHES TO THE STUDY OF DECISION-MAKING RELEVANT TO THE FIRM." INDUS COMPUTER OP/RES ...PROBABIL STAT 20. PAGE 121 F2390 GAME DECISION MGT SIMUL

C61
FILLOL T.R.,"SOCIAL FACTORS IN ECONOMIC DEVELOPMENT: THE ARGENTINE CASE" INDUS LABOR CREATE TEC/DEV PERS/REL EFFICIENCY PRODUC DRIVE ...METH/CNCPT METH/COMP 20 ARGEN. PAGE 41 F0794 BIBLIOG ECO/UNDEV MGT TREND

B62
BARTELS R.,THE DEVELOPMENT OF MARKETING THOUGHT. USA+45 USA-45 FINAN ECO/TAC...CONCPT TREND. PAGE 11 F0199 ECO/DEV MARKET MGT EDU/PROP

B62
BRANCH M.C.,THE CORPORATE PLANNING PROCESS. FINAN EX/STRUC EDU/PROP CONTROL LEAD GP/REL PERS/REL RATIONAL PERCEPT...MGT MATH PROBABIL STAT GAME. PAGE 18 F0338 PROF/ORG PLAN DECISION PERSON

B62
COLLIER A.T.,MANAGEMENT, MEN, AND VALUES. INDUS FACE/GP EX/STRUC PLAN PROB/SOLV DEBATE SENIOR ADMIN PROFIT PERSON...PSY SOC 20. PAGE 26 F0505 MGT ATTIT PERS/REL DECISION

B62
DOUGLAS A.,INDUSTRIAL PEACEMAKING. CONSULT ACT/RES ...MGT PSY METH 20. PAGE 34 F0656 BARGAIN INDUS LABOR GP/REL

B62
FERBER R.,RESEARCH METHODS IN ECONOMICS AND BUSINESS. AFR ECO/DEV FINAN MARKET LG/CO SML/CO CONSULT CONTROL COST...STAT METH/COMP 20. PAGE 40 F0783 ACT/RES PROB/SOLV ECO/TAC MGT

B62
GALENSON W.,LABOR IN DEVELOPING COUNTRIES. BRAZIL INDONESIA ISRAEL PAKISTAN TURKEY AGRI INDUS WORKER PAY PRICE GP/REL WEALTH...MGT CHARTS METH/COMP NAT/COMP 20. PAGE 45 F0888 LABOR ECO/UNDEV BARGAIN POL/PAR

B62
GRANICK D.,THE EUROPEAN EXECUTIVE. BELGIUM FRANCE GERMANY/W UK INDUS LABOR LG/CO SML/CO EX/STRUC PLAN TEC/DEV CAP/ISM COST DEMAND...POLICY CHARTS 20. PAGE 50 F0977 MGT ECO/DEV ECO/TAC EXEC

B62
HATTERY L.H.,INFORMATION RETRIEVAL MANAGEMENT. CLIENT INDUS TOP/EX COMPUTER OP/RES TEC/DEV ROUTINE COST EFFICIENCY RIGID/FLEX...METH/COMP ANTHOL 20. PAGE 57 F1113 R+D COMPUT/IR MGT CREATE

B62
KENT R.K.,FROM MADAGASCAR TO THE MALAGASY REPUBLIC. FRANCE MADAGASCAR DIPLOM NAT/LISM ORD/FREE...MGT 18/20. PAGE 70 F1379 COLONIAL SOVEREIGN REV POL/PAR

B62
KUHN T.E.,PUBLIC ENTERPRISES, PROJECT PLANNING AND ECONOMIC DEVELOPMENT (PAMPHLET). ECO/UNDEV FINAN PLAN ADMIN EFFICIENCY OWN...MGT STAT CHARTS ANTHOL 20. PAGE 74 F1447 ECO/DEV ECO/TAC LG/CO NAT/G

B62
NATIONAL BUREAU ECONOMIC RES,THE RATE AND DIRECTION OF INVENTIVE ACTIVITY: ECONOMIC AND SOCIAL FACTORS. STRUCT INDUS MARKET R+D CREATE OP/RES TEC/DEV EFFICIENCY PRODUC RATIONAL UTIL...WELF/ST PHIL/SCI METH/CNCPT TIME. PAGE 97 F1895 DECISION PROB/SOLV MGT

B62
PRAKASH O.M.,THE THEORY AND WORKING OF STATE CORPORATIONS: WITH SPECIAL REFERENCE TO INDIA. INDIA UK USA+45 TOP/EX PRICE ADMIN EFFICIENCY...MGT METH/COMP 20 TVA. PAGE 107 F2112 LG/CO ECO/UNDEV GOV/REL SOCISM

B62
ROBINSON M.A.,AN INTRODUCTION TO ECONOMIC REASONING. FINAN MARKET LABOR DIPLOM INT/TRADE BAL/PAY INCOME PRODUC WEALTH...POLICY MGT 20. PAGE 113 F2223 ECO/TAC METH/CNCPT NAT/G

B62
SMITH G.A. JR.,POLICY FORMULATION AND ADMINISTRATION: A CASEBOOK OF TOPMANAGEMENT PROBLEMS IN BUSINESS. EX/STRUC PLAN PROB/SOLV ADMIN CONTROL EXEC LEAD ROUTINE EFFICIENCY ATTIT MGT. PAGE 123 F2430 INDUS SOC/EXP TOP/EX DECISION

B62
SRIVASTAVA G.L.,COLLECTIVE BARGAINING AND LABOR-MANAGEMENT RELATIONS IN INDIA. INDIA UK USA+45 INDUS LEGIS WORKER ADJUD EFFICIENCY PRODUC ...METH/COMP 20. PAGE 125 F2462 LABOR MGT BARGAIN GP/REL

B62
VACCARO J.R.,A STATEMENT OF THE LAWS OF CHILE IN MATTERS AFFECTING BUSINESS (3RD ED.). CHILE AGRI FINAN FAM LABOR ECO/TAC FOR/AID TAX ADJUD CONTROL MARRIAGE STRANGE...BIBLIOG 20. PAGE 140 F2756 CONSTN LAW INDUS MGT

S62
READ W.H.,"UPWARD COMMUNICATION IN INDUSTRIAL HIERARCHIES." LG/CO TOP/EX PROB/SOLV DOMIN EXEC PERS/REL ATTIT DRIVE PERCEPT...CORREL STAT CHARTS 20. PAGE 110 F2159 ADMIN INGP/REL PSY MGT

B63
BONINI C.P.,SIMULATION OF INFORMATION AND DECISION SYSTEMS IN THE FIRM. MARKET BUDGET DOMIN EDU/PROP ADMIN COST ATTIT HABITAT PERCEPT PWR...CONCPT PROBABIL QUANT PREDICT HYPO/EXP BIBLIOG. PAGE 16 F0313 INDUS SIMUL DECISION MGT

B63
BRAIBANTI R.J.D.,ADMINISTRATION AND ECONOMIC DEVELOPMENT IN INDIA. INDIA S/ASIA SOCIETY STRATA ECO/TAC PERSON WEALTH...MGT GEN/LAWS TOT/POP VAL/FREE 20. PAGE 18 F0337 ECO/UNDEV ADMIN

B63
CHAMPION J.M.,CRITICAL INCIDENTS IN MANAGEMENT. MARKET LG/CO SML/CO OP/RES ADMIN CONTROL LEAD GP/REL PERS/REL COST ATTIT SUPEGO ALL/VALS...PSY PERS/TEST BIBLIOG. PAGE 23 F0445 MGT DECISION EX/STRUC INDUS

B63
GANGULY D.S.,PUBLIC CORPORATIONS IN A NATIONAL ECONOMY. INDIA WOR+45 FINAN INDUS TOP/EX PRICE EFFICIENCY...MGT STAT CHARTS BIBLIOG 20. PAGE 46 F0897 ECO/UNDEV LG/CO SOCISM GOV/REL

B63
HAUSMAN W.H.,MANAGING ECONOMIC DEVELOPMENT IN AFRICA. AFR USA+45 LAW FINAN WORKER TEC/DEV WEALTH ...ANTHOL 20. PAGE 57 F1116 ECO/UNDEV PLAN FOR/AID MGT

B63
KAPP W.K.,HINDU CULTURE: ECONOMIC DEVELOPMENT AND ECONOMIC PLANNING IN INDIA. INDIA S/ASIA CULTURE ECO/TAC EDU/PROP ADMIN ALL/VALS...POLICY MGT TIME/SEQ TRUE/GP VAL/FREE 20. PAGE 69 F1353 SECT ECO/UNDEV

B63
MANN D.E.,THE POLITICS OF WATER IN ARIZONA. AGRI EXTR/IND PROVS ACT/RES CREATE PLAN GOV/REL COST HABITAT...MGT CHARTS 20 ARIZONA WATER. PAGE 84 F1655 POLICY ECO/TAC TEC/DEV

B63
MCDONOUGH A.M.,INFORMATION ECONOMICS AND MANAGEMENT SYSTEMS. ECO/DEV OP/RES AUTOMAT EFFICIENCY 20. PAGE 88 F1726 COMPUT/IR MGT CONCPT COMPUTER

B63
SHANKS M.,THE LESSONS OF PUBLIC ENTERPRISE. UK LEGIS WORKER ECO/TAC ADMIN PARL/PROC GOV/REL ATTIT ...POLICY MGT METH/COMP NAT/COMP ANTHOL 20 PARLIAMENT. PAGE 120 F2364 SOCISM OWN NAT/G INDUS

B63
SMITH R.A.,CORPORATIONS IN CRISIS. USA+45 LG/CO EX/STRUC ECO/TAC CONTROL LEAD PERS/REL...MGT 20. PAGE 123 F2432 ELITES INDUS PROB/SOLV METH/COMP

B63
UN SECRETARY GENERAL,PLANNING FOR ECONOMIC DEVELOPMENT. ECO/UNDEV FINAN BUDGET INT/TRADE PLAN ECO/TAC

TARIFFS TAX ADMIN 20 UN. PAGE 132 F2603 MGT NAT/COMP

L63

LIVERNASH E.R.,"THE RELATION OF POWER TO THE STRUCTURE AND PROCESS OF COLLECTIVE BARGAINING." ADJUD ORD/FREE...POLICY MGT CLASSIF GP/COMP. PAGE 81 F1589 LABOR GP/REL PWR ECO/TAC

S63

CLEMHOUT S.,"PRODUCTION FUNCTION ANALYSIS APPLIED TO THE LEONTIEF SCARCE-FACTOR PARADOX OF INTERNATIONAL TRADE." EUR+WWI USA+45 DIST/IND NAT/G PLAN TEC/DEV DIPLOM PWR WEALTH...MGT METH/CNCPT CONT/OBS CON/ANAL CHARTS SIMUL GEN/LAWS FOR/TRADE 20. PAGE 25 F0490 ECO/DEV ECO/TAC

S63

GANDILHON J.,"LA SCIENCE ET LA TECHNIQUE A L'AIDE DES REGIONS PEU DEVELOPPEES." FRANCE FUT WOR+45 ECO/DEV R+D PROF/ORG ACT/RES PLAN...MGT TOT/POP VAL/FREE 20 UN. PAGE 46 F0893 ECO/UNDEV TEC/DEV FOR/AID

S63

LEDUC G.,"L'AIDE INTERNATIONALE AU DEVELOPPEMENT." FUT WOR+45 ECO/DEV ECO/UNDEV R+D PROF/ORG TEC/DEV ECO/TAC ROUTINE ATTIT ALL/VALS...MGT TIME/SEQ FOR/TRADE TOT/POP 20. PAGE 77 F1503 FINAN PLAN FOR/AID

S63

MASON E.S.,"INTERESTS, IDEOLOGIES AND THE PROBLEM OF STABILITY AND GROWTH." EUR+WWI USA+45 DELIB/GP CREATE PLAN EXEC ROUTINE BAL/PAY ATTIT PWR...MGT CONCPT OEEC 20. PAGE 87 F1698 NAT/G ECO/DEV

S63

NADLER E.B.,"SOME ECONOMIC DISADVANTAGES OF THE ARMS RACE." AFR USA+45 INDUS R+D FORCES PLAN TEC/DEV ECO/TAC FOR/AID EDU/PROP PWR WEALTH...TREND FOR/TRADE 20. PAGE 96 F1886 ECO/DEV MGT BAL/PAY

S63

REES A.,"THE EFFECTS OF UNIONS ON RESOURCE ALLOCATION." USA+45 WORKER PRICE CONTROL GP/REL ...MGT METH/COMP 20. PAGE 110 F2173 LABOR BARGAIN RATION INCOME

S63

VINER J.,"REPORT OF THE CLAY COMMITTEE ON FOREIGN AID: A SYMPOSIUM." USA+45 WOR+45 NAT/G CONSULT PLAN BAL/PWR ATTIT WEALTH...MGT CONCPT TOT/POP 20. PAGE 142 F2788 ACT/RES ECO/TAC FOR/AID

B64

BLACKSTOCK P.W.,THE STRATEGY OF SUBVERSION. USA+45 FORCES EDU/PROP ADMIN COERCE GOV/REL...DECISION MGT 20 DEPT/DEFEN CIA DEPT/STATE. PAGE 15 F0292 ORD/FREE DIPLOM CONTROL

B64

BRIGHT J.R.,RESEARCH, DEVELOPMENT AND TECHNOLOGICAL INNOVATION. CULTURE R+D CREATE PLAN PROB/SOLV AUTOMAT RISK PERSON...DECISION CONCPT PREDICT BIBLIOG. PAGE 18 F0352 TEC/DEV NEW/IDEA INDUS MGT

B64

CHANDLER A.D. JR.,GIANT ENTERPRISE: FORD, GENERAL MOTORS, AND THE AUTOMOBILE INDUSTRY; SOURCES AND READINGS. USA+45 USA-45 FINAN MARKET CREATE ADMIN ...TIME/SEQ ANTHOL 20 AUTOMOBILE. PAGE 23 F0447 LG/CO DIST/IND LABOR MGT

B64

CHEIT E.F.,THE BUSINESS ESTABLISHMENT. FRANCE WOR+45 PROF/ORG TOP/EX PROB/SOLV CAP/ISM ADMIN SUPEGO MORAL PWR...METH/CNCPT MYTH NEW/IDEA 20. PAGE 24 F0460 PERSON EX/STRUC MGT INDUS

B64

FLORENCE P.S.,ECONOMICS AND SOCIOLOGY OF INDUSTRY; A REALISTIC ANALYSIS OF DEVELOPMENT. ECO/UNDEV LG/CO NAT/G PLAN...GEOG MGT BIBLIOG 20. PAGE 42 F0814 INDUS SOC ADMIN

B64

HAZLEWOOD A.,THE ECONOMICS OF DEVELOPMENT: AN ANNOTATED LIST OF BOOKS AND ARTICLES PUBLISHED 1958-1962. AGRI FINAN INDUS LABOR NAT/G DIPLOM INT/TRADE INCOME...MGT 20. PAGE 58 F1130 BIBLIOG/A ECO/UNDEV TEC/DEV

B64

JUCKER-FLEETWOOD E.,MONEY AND FINANCE IN AFRICA. ISLAM ECO/UNDEV SERV/IND NAT/G EX/STRUC PLAN ECO/TAC ROUTINE WEALTH...MGT TOT/POP 20. PAGE 68 F1344 AFR FINAN

B64

KAPLAN A.D.H.,BIG ENTERPRISE IN A COMPETITIVE SYSTEM (REV. ED.). USA+45 INDUS MARKET WORKER TEC/DEV ECO/TAC PRICE ADJUD ADMIN CONTROL...MGT CHARTS 20 MONOPOLY. PAGE 69 F1351 FINAN GP/REL NAT/G LG/CO

B64

LANGHOFF P.,MODELS, MEASUREMENT AND MARKETING. ACT/RES COMPUTER OP/RES PLAN BUDGET...MGT PHIL/SCI METH/CNCPT STAT PROG/TEAC BIBLIOG. PAGE 75 F1478 DECISION SIMUL MARKET R+D

B64

MARRIS R.,THE ECONOMIC THEORY OF "MANAGERIAL" CAPITALISM. USA+45 ECO/DEV LG/CO ECO/TAC DEMAND ...CHARTS BIBLIOG 20. PAGE 86 F1675 CAP/ISM MGT CONTROL OP/RES

B64

MCNULTY J.E.,SOME ECONOMIC ASPECTS OF BUSINESS ORGANIZATION. ECO/DEV UTIL...MGT CHARTS BIBLIOG METH 20. PAGE 88 F1734 ADMIN LG/CO GEN/LAWS

B64

ROBINSON R.D.,INTERNATIONAL BUSINESS POLICY. AFR INDIA L/A+17C USA+45 ELITES AGRI FOR/AID COERCE BAL/PAY...DECISION INT/LAW MGT 20. PAGE 113 F2224 ECO/TAC DIST/IND COLONIAL FINAN

B64

RUSTAMJI R.F.,THE LAW OF INDUSTRIAL DISPUTES IN INDIA. INDIA LEGIS WORKER CONTROL GP/REL...JURID MGT TIME/SEQ 20. PAGE 115 F2264 INDUS ADJUD BARGAIN LABOR

B64

STEWART C.F.,A BIBLIOGRAPHY OF INTERNATIONAL BUSINESS. WOR+45 FINAN LG/CO NAT/G PLAN ECO/TAC TARIFFS...DECISION MGT GP/COMP NAT/COMP 20 EEC. PAGE 126 F2484 BIBLIOG INT/ORG OP/RES INT/TRADE

B64

TINBERGEN J.,CENTRAL PLANNING. COM INTELL ECO/DEV ECO/UNDEV FINAN INT/ORG PROB/SOLV ECO/TAC CONTROL EXEC ROUTINE DECISION. PAGE 130 F2576 PLAN INDUS MGT CENTRAL

B64

WERNETTE J.P.,GOVERNMENT AND BUSINESS. LABOR CAP/ISM ECO/TAC INT/TRADE TAX ADMIN AUTOMAT NUC/PWR CIVMIL/REL DEMAND...MGT 20 MONOPOLY. PAGE 145 F2859 NAT/G FINAN ECO/DEV CONTROL

B64

WILLIAMSON O.E.,THE ECONOMICS OF DISCRETIONARY BEHAVIOR: MANAGERIAL OBJECTIVES IN A THEORY OF THE FIRM. MARKET BUDGET CAP/ISM PRODUC DRIVE PERSON ...STAT CHARTS BIBLIOG METH 20. PAGE 147 F2897 EFFICIENCY MGT ECO/TAC CHOOSE

B64

ZOBER M.,MARKETING MANAGEMENT. FINAN BUDGET EDU/PROP PRICE PRODUC ATTIT...POLICY TREND CHARTS METH/COMP EQULIB 20. PAGE 150 F2966 ECO/DEV MGT CONTROL MARKET

L64

BHAGWATI J.,"THE PURE THEORY OF INTERNATIONAL TRADE: A SURVEY." WOR+45 ECO/DEV ECO/UNDEV FINAN MARKET PROC/MFG INT/ORG LABOR LG/CO NAT/G TEC/DEV ECO/TAC SKILL WEALTH...POLICY RELATIV MGT CONCPT NEW/IDEA MATH QUANT GEN/LAWS FOR/TRADE 20. PAGE 14 F0276 INDUS HYPO/EXP

S64

CLELLAND D.A.,"ECONOMIC DOMINANTS AND COMMUNITY POWER: A COMPARATIVE ANALYSIS." ELITES ADJUST ATTIT WEALTH...DECISION MUNICH. PAGE 25 F0488 LEAD MGT PWR

S64

FLORINSKY M.T.,"TRENDS IN THE SOVIET ECONOMY." COM USA+45 USSR INDUS LABOR NAT/G PLAN TEC/DEV ECO/TAC ALL/VALS SOCISM...MGT METH/CNCPT STYLE CON/ANAL GEN/METH WORK 20. PAGE 42 F0817 ECO/DEV AGRI

S64

GARDNER R.N.,"GATT AND THE UNITED NATIONS CONFERENCE ON TRADE AND DEVELOPMENT." USA+45 WOR+45 SOCIETY ECO/UNDEV MARKET NAT/G DELIB/GP ACT/RES PLAN ECO/TAC TARIFFS EDU/PROP ROUTINE DRIVE RIGID/FLEX WEALTH...DECISION MGT TREND UN TOT/POP 20 GATT. PAGE 46 F0905 INT/ORG INT/TRADE

S64

PATEL S.J.,"THE ECONOMIC DISTANCE BETWEEN NATIONS: ITS ORIGIN, MEASUREMENT AND OUTLOOK." WOR+45 ECO/DEV AGRI FINAN INDUS MARKET LABOR NAT/G CONSULT TEC/DEV ECO/TAC WEALTH...POLICY RELATIV MGT TREND WORK 20. PAGE 103 F2035 ECO/UNDEV PLAN

S64

STONE P.A.,"DECISION TECHNIQUES FOR TOWN DEVELOPMENT." PLAN COST PROFIT...DECISION MGT CON/ANAL CHARTS METH/COMP BIBLIOG MUNICH 20. PAGE 127 F2497 OP/RES ADMIN PROB/SOLV

C64

GOLDMAN M.I.,"COMPARATIVE ECONOMIC SYSTEMS: A READER." COM ECO/UNDEV NAT/G BUDGET CAP/ISM ADMIN TOTALISM MARXISM SOCISM...MGT ANTHOL BIBLIOG 19/20. PAGE 48 F0938 NAT/COMP CONTROL IDEA/COMP

C64

NORGREN P.H.,"TOWARD FAIR EMPLOYMENT." USA+45 LAW STRATA LABOR NAT/G FORCES ACT/RES ADMIN ATTIT ...POLICY BIBLIOG 20 NEGRO. PAGE 98 F1932 RACE/REL DISCRIM WORKER MGT

N64

US BOARD GOVERNORS FEDL RESRV,SELECTED BIBLIOGRAPHY ON MONETARY POLICY AND MANAGEMENT OF THE PUBLIC DEBT 1947-1960 AND 1961-1963 SUPPLEMENT (PAMPH.). USA+45 PLAN...POLICY MGT OWE 20. PAGE 134 F2642 BIBLIOG FINAN NAT/G

B65

ACHTERBERG E.,BERLINER HOCHFINANZ - KAISER, FURSTEN, MILLIONARE UM 1900. GERMANY NAT/G EDU/PROP PERSON...MGT MUNICH 19/20. PAGE 2 F0033 FINAN BIOG ECO/TAC

B65

ALDERSON W.,DYNAMIC MARKETING BEHAVIOR. USA+45 FINAN CREATE TEC/DEV EDU/PROP PRICE COST 20. PAGE 3 F0057 MGT MARKET ATTIT CAP/ISM

B65

BOCK E.,GOVERNMENT REGULATION OF BUSINESS. USA+45 MGT

LAW EX/STRUC LEGIS EXEC ORD/FREE PWR...ANTHOL CONGRESS. PAGE 16 F0303
ADMIN NAT/G CONTROL

B65
COPELAND M.A.,OUR FREE ENTERPRISE ECONOMY. USA+45 INDUS LABOR ADMIN CONTROL GP/REL MGT. PAGE 27 F0533
CAP/ISM PLAN FINAN ECO/DEV

B65
COX D.W.,THE PERILS OF PEACE* CONVERSION TO WHAT? FUT USA+45 ECO/DEV NAT/G ACT/RES CREATE PLAN NUC/PWR WAR DEMAND MGT. PAGE 28 F0546
PEACE WORKER FORCES MARKET

B65
DERBER M.,PLANT UNION-MANAGEMENT RELATIONS: FROM PRACTICE TO THEORY. PROC/MFG NEIGH PROB/SOLV ORD/FREE...DECISION MGT OBS QU SAMP. PAGE 32 F0621
LG/CO LABOR GP/REL ATTIT

B65
DOWD L.P.,PRINCIPLES OF WORLD BUSINESS. SERV/IND NAT/G DIPLOM ECO/TAC TARIFFS...INT/LAW JURID 20. PAGE 34 F0657
INT/TRADE MGT FINAN MARKET

B65
FRYE R.J.,HOUSING AND URBAN RENEWAL IN ALABAMA. USA+45 NEIGH LEGIS BUDGET ADJUD ADMIN PARTIC...MGT MUNICH 20 ALABAMA URBAN/RNWL. PAGE 45 F0871
PROB/SOLV PLAN GOV/REL

B65
KANTOROVICH L.V.,THE BEST USE OF ECONOMIC RESOURCES. USSR SOCIETY FINAN ACT/RES TEC/DEV ECO/TAC PRICE CONTROL COST DEMAND EFFICIENCY OPTIMAL...MGT STAT. PAGE 69 F1350
PLAN MATH DECISION

B65
MACESICH G.,COMMERCIAL BANKING AND REGIONAL DEVELOPMENT IN THE US, 1950-1960. USA+45 NAT/G PLAN ECO/TAC DEMAND...MGT 20 FED/RESERV SOUTH/US. PAGE 83 F1627
FINAN ECO/DEV INCOME COST

B65
MOORE W.E.,THE IMPACT OF INDUSTRY. CULTURE STRUCT ORD/FREE...TREND 20. PAGE 93 F1824
INDUS MGT TEC/DEV ECO/UNDEV

B65
RIGBY P.H.,CONCEPTUAL FOUNDATIONS OF BUSINESS RESEARCH. COMPUTER PROB/SOLV OPTIMAL...MGT CONCPT MATH STAT TESTS SIMUL GEN/METH. PAGE 111 F2192
PROFIT R+D INDUS DECISION

B65
ROLFE S.E.,GOLD AND WORLD POWER. AFR UK USA+45 WOR-45 INDUS WORKER INT/TRADE DEMAND...MGT CHARTS 20. PAGE 113 F2234
BAL/PAY EQUILIB ECO/TAC DIPLOM

B65
ROSS P.,THE GOVERNMENT AS A SOURCE OF UNION POWER. USA+45 LAW ECO/DEV PROB/SOLV ECO/TAC LEAD GP/REL ...MGT 20. PAGE 114 F2245
LABOR BARGAIN POLICY NAT/G

B65
STEINER G.A.,THE CREATIVE ORGANIZATION. ELITES LG/CO PLAN PROB/SOLV TEC/DEV INSPECT CAP/ISM CONTROL EXEC PERSON...METH/COMP HYPO/EXP 20. PAGE 126 F2476
CREATE MGT ADMIN SOC

B65
VAID K.N.,STATE AND LABOR IN INDIA. INDIA INDUS WORKER PAY PRICE ADJUD CONTROL PARL/PROC GP/REL ORD/FREE 20. PAGE 140 F2757
LAW LABOR MGT NEW/LIB

B65
WATERSTON A.,DEVELOPMENT PLANNING* LESSONS OF EXPERIENCE. ECO/TAC CENTRAL...MGT QUANT BIBLIOG. PAGE 144 F2830
ECO/UNDEV CREATE PLAN ADMIN

B65
WEIL G.L.,A HANDBOOK ON THE EUROPEAN ECONOMIC COMMUNITY. BELGIUM EUR+WWI FRANCE GERMANY/W ITALY CONSTN ECO/DEV CREATE PARTIC GP/REL...DECISION MGT CHARTS 20 EEC. PAGE 144 F2846
INT/TRADE INT/ORG TEC/DEV INT/LAW

L65
WILLIAMS S.,"NEGOTIATING INVESTMENT IN EMERGING COUNTRIES." USA+45 WOR+45 INDUS MARKET NAT/G TOP/EX TEC/DEV CAP/ISM ECO/TAC ADMIN SKILL WEALTH...POLICY RELATIV MGT WORK 20. PAGE 147 F2894
FINAN ECO/UNDEV

L65
WIONCZEK M.,"LATIN AMERICA FREE TRADE ASSOCIATION." AGRI DIST/IND FINAN INDUS INT/ORG LABOR NAT/G TEC/DEV ECO/TAC HEALTH SKILL WEALTH...POLICY RELATIV MGT LAFTA 20. PAGE 148 F2909
L/A+17C MARKET REGION

S65
GRENIEWSKI H.,"INTENTION AND PERFORMANCE: A PRIMER OF CYBERNETICS OF PLANNING." EFFICIENCY OPTIMAL KNOWL SKILL...DECISION MGT EQULIB. PAGE 51 F0995
SIMUL GAME GEN/METH PLAN

S65
MALHERBE E.G.,"MANPOWER TRAINING: EDUCATIONAL REQUIREMENTS FOR ECONOMIC EXPANSION." SOUTH/AFR ECO/DEV INDUS EDU/PROP...MGT STAT CHARTS 20. PAGE 84 F1646
LABOR SKILL SCHOOL ACADEM

S65
TENDLER J.D.,"TECHNOLOGY AND ECONOMIC DEVELOPMENT* THE CASE OF HYDRO VS THERMAL POWER." CONSTRUC DIST/IND CREATE TEC/DEV INT/TRADE CENTRAL PWR SKILL WEALTH...MGT NAT/COMP ARGEN. PAGE 129 F2544
BRAZIL INDUS ECO/UNDEV

B66
ALEXANDER Y.,INTERNATIONAL TECHNICAL ASSISTANCE EXPERTS* A CASE STUDY OF THE U.N. EXPERIENCE. ECO/UNDEV CONSULT EX/STRUC CREATE PLAN DIPLOM FOR/AID TASK EFFICIENCY...ORG/CHARTS UN. PAGE 3 F0061
ECO/TAC INT/ORG ADMIN MGT

B66
BAKKE E.W.,MUTUAL SURVIVAL; THE GOAL OF UNION AND MANAGEMENT (2ND ED.). USA+45 ELITES ECO/DEV ECO/TAC CONFER ADMIN REPRESENT GP/REL INGP/REL ATTIT ...GP/COMP 20. PAGE 8 F0155
MGT LABOR BARGAIN INDUS

B66
BOYD H.W.,MARKETING MANAGEMENT: CASES FROM EMERGING COUNTRIES. BRAZIL GHANA ISRAEL WOR+45 ADMIN PERS/REL ATTIT HABITAT WEALTH...ANTHOL 20 ARGEN CASEBOOK. PAGE 17 F0332
MGT ECO/UNDEV PROB/SOLV MARKET

B66
COOK P.W. JR.,PROBLEMS OF CORPORATE POWER. WOR+45 FINAN INDUS BARGAIN GP/REL...MGT ANTHOL. PAGE 27 F0530
ADMIN LG/CO PWR ECO/TAC

B66
FRANKEL P.H.,MATTEI; OIL AND POWER POLITICS. ITALY EXTR/IND MARKET GP/REL NAT/LISM SOCISM...POLICY MGT BIOG 20 MATTEI/E. PAGE 43 F0844
LEAD NAT/G CONTROL LG/CO

B66
GOODMAN L.H.,ECONOMIC PROGRESS AND SOCIAL WELFARE. USA+45 STRATA STRUCT ECO/TAC EFFICIENCY...MGT 20. PAGE 49 F0949
SOC/WK RECEIVE GP/COMP POLICY

B66
GREENE L.E.,GOVERNMENT IN TENNESSEE (2ND ED.). USA+45 DIST/IND INDUS POL/PAR EX/STRUC LEGIS PLAN BUDGET GIVE CT/SYS...MGT T 20 TENNESSEE. PAGE 51 F0989
PROVS LOC/G CONSTN ADMIN

B66
GROSS H.,MAKE OR BUY. AFR USA+45 FINAN INDUS CREATE PRICE PRODUC 20. PAGE 51 F1006
ECO/TAC PLAN MGT COST

B66
HACKETT J.,L'ECONOMIE BRITANNIQUE: PROBLEMES ET PERSPECTIVES. FRANCE UK LABOR NAT/G EX/STRUC PROB/SOLV BAL/PAY INCOME RIGID/FLEX...MGT PHIL/SCI CHARTS MUNICH 20. PAGE 53 F1027
ECO/DEV FINAN ECO/TAC PLAN

B66
HASTINGS P.G.,THE MANAGEMENT OF BUSINESS FINANCE. ECO/DEV PLAN BUDGET CONTROL COST...DECISION CHARTS BIBLIOG T 20. PAGE 56 F1109
FINAN MGT INDUS ECO/TAC

B66
KAESTNER K.,GESAMTWIRTSCHAFTLICHE PLANUNG IN EINER GEMISCHTEN WIRTSCHAFTSORDNUNG (WIRTSCHAFTSPOLITISCHE STUDIEN 5). GERMANY/W WOR+45 WOR-45 INDUS MARKET NAT/G ACT/RES GP/REL INGP/REL PRODUC...ECOMETRIC MGT BIBLIOG 20. PAGE 68 F1346
ECO/TAC PLAN POLICY PREDICT

B66
KUPAKOV I.G.,SCIENCE, TECHNOLOGY AND COMMUNISM; SOME QUESTIONS OF DEVELOPMENT (TRANS. BY CARIN DEDIJER). USSR INDUS PLAN PROB/SOLV COST PRODUC ...MGT MATH CHARTS METH 20. PAGE 74 F1450
CREATE TEC/DEV MARXISM ECO/TAC

B66
MANGONE G.J.,UN ADMINISTRATION OF ECONOMIC AND SOCIAL PROGRAMS. CONSULT BUDGET INT/TRADE REGION 20 UN. PAGE 84 F1653
ADMIN MGT ECO/TAC DELIB/GP

B66
MANSFIELD E.,MANAGERIAL ECONOMICS AND OPERATIONS RESEARCH; A NONMATHEMATICAL INTRODUCTION. USA+45 ELITES ECO/DEV CONSULT EX/STRUC PROB/SOLV ROUTINE EFFICIENCY OPTIMAL...GAME T 20. PAGE 85 F1660
ECO/TAC OP/RES MGT COMPUTER

B66
MC CONNELL J.P.,LAW AND BUSINESS: PATTERNS AND ISSUES IN COMMERCIAL LAW. USA+45 USA-45 LOC/G WORKER LICENSE CRIME REPRESENT GP/REL 20. PAGE 87 F1713
ECO/DEV JURID ADJUD MGT

B66
NICOSIA M.N.,CONSUMER DECISION PROCESSES: MARKETING AND ADVERTISING IMPLICATIONS. ECO/TAC ATTIT PERSON ...DECISION MGT SOC. PAGE 98 F1926
MARKET SOCIETY CREATE ACT/RES

B66
SHULTZ G.P.,STRATEGIES FOR THE DISPLACED WORKER. USA+45 COMPUTER TEC/DEV BARGAIN RECEIVE EDU/PROP CONFER GP/REL...MGT METH/COMP 20. PAGE 121 F2391
ECO/DEV WORKER PLAN AUTOMAT

B66
THEIL H.,APPLIED ECONOMIC FORECASTING. UNIV USA+45 ELITES INTELL CONSULT PRODUC...DECISION MGT PREDICT
FUT OP/RES

CHARTS METH/COMP SIMUL 20. PAGE 129 F2552
PLAN

B66
US DEPARTMENT OF LABOR,TECHNOLOGICAL TRENDS IN MAJOR AMERICAN INDUSTRIES. USA+45 R+D LABOR GP/REL PRODUC...MGT BIBLIOG 20. PAGE 135 F2669
TEC/DEV INDUS TREND AUTOMAT

B66
WESTON J.F.,THE SCOPE AND METHODOLOGY OF FINANCE. PLAN TEC/DEV CONTROL EFFICIENCY INCOME UTIL...MGT CONCPT MATH STAT TREND METH 20. PAGE 145 F2863
FINAN ECO/DEV POLICY PRICE

B66
YOUNG S.,MANAGEMENT: A SYSTEMS ANALYSIS. DELIB/GP EX/STRUC ECO/TAC CONTROL EFFICIENCY...NET/THEORY 20. PAGE 150 F2952
PROB/SOLV MGT DECISION SIMUL

L66
AMERICAN ECONOMIC REVIEW,"SIXTY-THIRD LIST OF DOCTORAL DISSERTATIONS IN POLITICAL ECONOMY IN AMERICAN UNIVERSITIES AND COLLEGES." ECO/DEV AGRI FINAN LABOR WORKER PLAN BUDGET INT/TRADE ADMIN DEMAND...MGT STAT 20. PAGE 5 F0088
BIBLIOG/A CONCPT ACADEM

S66
FLEMING W.G.,"AUTHORITY, EFFICIENCY, AND ROLE STRESS: PROBLEMS IN THE DEVELOPMENT OF EAST AFRICAN BUREAUCRACIES." AFR UGANDA STRUCT PROB/SOLV ROUTINE INGP/REL ROLE...MGT SOC GP/COMP GOV/COMP 20 TANGANYIKA AFRICA/E. PAGE 41 F0810
DOMIN EFFICIENCY COLONIAL ADMIN

N66
PRINCETON U INDUSTRIAL REL SEC,RECENT MATERIAL ON COLLECTIVE BARGAINING IN GOVERNMENT (PAMPHLET NO. 130). USA+45 ECO/DEV LABOR WORKER ECO/TAC GOV/REL ...MGT 20. PAGE 108 F2120
BIBLIOG/A BARGAIN NAT/G GP/REL

B67
BEAL E.F.,THE PRACTICE OF COLLECTIVE BARGAINING (3RD ED.). USA+45 WOR+45 ECO/DEV INDUS LG/CO PROF/ORG WORKER ECO/TAC GP/REL WEALTH...JURID METH/CNCPT. PAGE 12 F0221
BARGAIN MGT LABOR ADJUD

B67
DONALD A.G.,MANAGEMENT, INFORMATION, AND SYSTEMS. WOR+45 LG/CO PROB/SOLV CONTROL FEEDBACK KNOWL MGT. PAGE 34 F0653
ROUTINE TEC/DEV CONCPT ADMIN

B67
ELDREDGE H.W.,TAMING MEGALOPOLIS; HOW TO MANAGE AN URBANIZED WORLD. WOR+45 SOCIETY ECO/DEV ECO/UNDEV NAT/G COMPUTER CREATE PARTIC EFFICIENCY WEALTH ...MGT ANTHOL MUNICH. PAGE 37 F0716
TEC/DEV PLAN PROB/SOLV

B67
ENKE S.,DEFENSE MANAGEMENT. USA+45 R+D FORCES WORKER PLAN ECO/TAC ADMIN NUC/PWR BAL/PAY UTIL WEALTH...MGT DEPT/DEFEN. PAGE 38 F0738
DECISION DELIB/GP EFFICIENCY BUDGET

B67
FARRIS M.T.,MODERN TRANSPORTATION: SELECTED READINGS. UNIV CONTROL...POLICY ANTHOL T 20. PAGE 39 F0765
DIST/IND MGT COST

B67
GOLEMBIEWSKI R.T.,ORGANIZING MEN AND POWER: PATTERNS OF BEHAVIOR AND LINESTAFF MODELS. WOR+45 EX/STRUC ACT/RES DOMIN PERS/REL...NEW/IDEA 20. PAGE 48 F0943
ADMIN CONTROL SIMUL MGT

B67
GROSS B.M.,ACTION UNDER PLANNING: THE GUIDANCE OF ECONOMIC DEVELOPMENT. STRUCT R+D NAT/G ACT/RES HABITAT...DECISION 20. PAGE 51 F1005
ECO/UNDEV PLAN ADMIN MGT

B67
KARDOUCHE G.K.,THE UAR IN DEVELOPMENT. UAR ECO/TAC INT/TRADE BAL/PAY...STAT CHARTS BIBLIOG 20. PAGE 69 F1355
FINAN MGT CAP/ISM ECO/UNDEV

B67
NARVER J.C.,CONGLOMERATE MERGERS AND MARKET COMPETITION. USA+45 LAW STRUCT ADMIN LEAD RISK COST PROFIT WEALTH...POLICY CHARTS BIBLIOG. PAGE 96 F1892
DEMAND LG/CO MARKET MGT

B67
PORWIT K.,CENTRAL PLANNING: EVALUATION OF VARIANTS. PRICE OPTIMAL PRODUC...DECISION MATH CHARTS SIMUL BIBLIOG MODELS 20. PAGE 107 F2106
PLAN MGT ECOMETRIC

B67
ROBERTS B.C.,COLLECTIVE BARGAINING IN AFRICAN COUNTRIES. AFR LAW ECO/UNDEV BARGAIN GP/REL ...DECISION METH/COMP 20. PAGE 112 F2206
LABOR MGT PLAN ECO/TAC

B67
ROBINSON R.D.,INTERNATIONAL MANAGEMENT. LAW MARKET LABOR PRICE CONTROL COST DEMAND OWN PRODUC WEALTH 20. PAGE 113 F2225
T OP/RES MGT DIPLOM

B67
ROSS A.M.,EMPLOYMENT, RACE, AND POVERTY. USA+45 LAW STRATA MARKET LABOR EDU/PROP ISOLAT SKILL...MGT ANTHOL 20 NEGRO. PAGE 114 F2244
RACE/REL WORKER WEALTH DISCRIM

B67
UNIVERSAL REFERENCE SYSTEM,ADMINISTRATIVE MANAGEMENT: PUBLIC AND PRIVATE BUREAUCRACY (VOLUME IV). WOR+45 WOR-45 ECO/DEV LG/CO LOC/G PUB/INST VOL/ASSN GOV/REL...COMPUT/IR GEN/METH. PAGE 133 F2616
BIBLIOG/A MGT ADMIN NAT/G

B67
UNIVERSAL REFERENCE SYSTEM,PUBLIC POLICY AND THE MANAGEMENT OF SCIENCE (VOLUME IX). FUT SPACE WOR+45 LAW NAT/G TEC/DEV CONTROL NUC/PWR GOV/REL ...COMPUT/IR GEN/METH. PAGE 133 F2618
BIBLIOG/A POLICY MGT PHIL/SCI

L67
GOULD W.B.,"THE STATUS OF UNAUTHORIZED AND 'WILDCAT' STRIKES UNDER THE NATIONAL LABOR RELATIONS ACT." USA+45 ACT/RES BARGAIN ECO/TAC LEGIT ADJUD ADMIN GP/REL MGT. PAGE 50 F0968
ECO/DEV INDUS LABOR POLICY

S67
ALPANDER G.G.,"ENTREPRENEURS AND PRIVATE ENTERPRISE IN TURKEY." TURKEY INDUS PROC/MFG EDU/PROP ATTIT DRIVE WEALTH...GEOG MGT SOC STAT TREND CHARTS 20. PAGE 4 F0077
ECO/UNDEV LG/CO NAT/G POLICY

S67
CHAMBERLAIN N.W.,"STRIKES IN CONTEMPORARY CONTEXT." LAW INDUS NAT/G CHIEF CONFER COST ATTIT ORD/FREE ...POLICY MGT 20. PAGE 23 F0442
LABOR BARGAIN EFFICIENCY PROB/SOLV

S67
FRANKEL T.,"ECONOMIC REFORM* A TENTATIVE APPRAISAL." COM USSR OP/RES BUDGET CONFER EFFICIENCY PRODUC MARXISM SOCISM...MGT 20. PAGE 43 F0847
ECO/DEV INDUS PLAN WEALTH

S67
JANSSEN P.,"NEA: THE RELUCTANT DRAGON." NAT/G EXEC LOBBY PARTIC SANCTION RACE/REL ROLE TREND. PAGE 66 F1305
EDU/PROP PROF/ORG MGT POLICY

S67
JENCKS C.E.,"SOCIAL STATUS OF COAL MINERS IN BRITAIN SINCE NATIONALIZATION." UK STRATA STRUCT LABOR RECEIVE GP/REL INCOME OWN ATTIT HABITAT...MGT T 20. PAGE 67 F1312
EXTR/IND WORKER CONTROL NAT/G

S67
LEONTYEV L.,"THE LENINIST PRINCIPLES OF SOCIALIST ECONOMIC MANAGEMENT." USA+45 USSR POL/PAR WORKER PLAN ECO/TAC EFFICIENCY PRODUC MARXISM...POLICY SOCIALIST MGT TREND 20 LENIN/VI MARX/KARL. PAGE 78 F1529
SOCISM CAP/ISM IDEA/COMP ECO/DEV

S67
MELTZER B.D.,"RUMINATIONS ABOUT IDEOLOGY, LAW, AND LABOR ARBITRATION." USA+45 ECO/DEV PROB/SOLV CONFER MGT. PAGE 89 F1754
JURID ADJUD LABOR CONSULT

S67
MODESITT L.E.,"THE MUTUAL FUND - A CORPORATE ANOMALY." USA+45 CONTROL...MGT 20. PAGE 92 F1813
SERV/IND FINAN ADMIN LAW

S67
MORTON J.A.,"A SYSTEMS APPROACH TO THE INNOVATION PROCESS: ITS USE IN THE BELL SYSTEM." USA+45 INTELL INDUS LG/CO CONSULT WORKER COMPUTER AUTOMAT DEMAND ...MGT CHARTS 20. PAGE 94 F1841
TEC/DEV GEN/METH R+D COM/IND

S67
RICHMAN B.M.,"CAPITALISTS & MANAGERS IN COMMUNIST CHINA." ASIA CHINA/COM ECO/UNDEV NAT/G CONSULT EX/STRUC PLAN EFFICIENCY PRODUC WEALTH MARXISM ...MGT CHARTS 20. [illegible]GE 111 F2185
CAP/ISM INDUS

S67
RICHMAN B.M.,"SOVIET MANAGEMENT IN TRANSITION." USSR FINAN MARKET EX/STRUC PLAN PROB/SOLV TEC/DEV CONTROL LEAD CENTRAL EFFICIENCY...METH/COMP 20 REFORMERS. PAGE 111 F2186
MGT MARXISM POLICY AUTHORIT

S67
WARNER K.O.,"FINANCIAL IMPLICATION OF EMPLOYEE BARGAINING IN THE PUBLIC SERVICE." CANADA USA+45 FINAN ADMIN...MGT 20. PAGE 143 F2823
BARGAIN LABOR COST LOC/G

S67
WEIL G.L.,"THE MERGER OF THE INSTITUTIONS OF THE EUROPEAN COMMUNITIES" EUR+WWI ECO/DEV INT/TRADE CONSEN PLURISM...DECISION MGT 20 EEC EURATOM ECSC TREATY. PAGE 145 F2847
ECO/TAC INT/ORG CENTRAL INT/LAW

S67
WILLIAMS C.,"REGIONAL MANAGEMENT OVERSEAS." USA+45 WOR+45 DIST/IND LG/CO EX/STRUC INT/TRADE TARIFFS ADMIN TASK CENTRAL. PAGE 147 F2889
MGT EUR+WWI ECO/DEV PLAN

S67
ZACK A.M.,"ARE STRIKES OF PUBLIC EMPLOYEES NECESSARY?" USA+45 DELIB/GP PROB/SOLV REPRESENT GP/REL MGT. PAGE 150 F2956
LABOR NAT/G WORKER BARGAIN

S67
ZOETEWEIJ B.,"INCOME POLICIES ABROAD: AN INTERIM REPORT." NAT/G PROB/SOLV BARGAIN BUDGET PRICE RISK CENTRAL EFFICIENCY EQUILIB...MGT NAT/COMP 20.
METH/COMP INCOME POLICY

PAGE 150 F2967 LABOR

N67
US CONGRESS JOINT ECO COMM,ECONOMY IN GOVERNMENT (PAMPHLET). USA+45 ECO/DEV FINAN NAT/G PLAN BUDGET SENATE. PAGE 135 F2662
ECO/TAC COST EFFICIENCY MGT

N67
US CONGRESS JT COMM ECO GOVT,BACKGROUND MATERIAL ON ECONOMY IN GOVERNMENT 1967 (PAMPHLET). WOR+45 ECO/DEV BARGAIN PRICE DEMAND OPTIMAL...STAT DEPT/DEFEN. PAGE 135 F2665
BUDGET COST MGT NAT/G

MGT/OBJECT....MANAGEMENT BY OBJECTIVES

MIAMI

B65
GREER S.,URBAN RENEWAL AND AMERICAN CITIES: THE DILEMMA OF DEMOCRATIC INTERVENTION. USA+45 R+D LOC/G VOL/ASSN ACT/RES BUDGET ADMIN GOV/REL...SOC INT SAMP MUNICH 20 BOSTON CHICAGO LOS/ANG MIAMI URBAN/RNWL. PAGE 51 F0992
PROB/SOLV PLAN NAT/G

MICH/STA/U....MICHIGAN STATE UNIVERSITY

MICH/U....UNIVERSITY OF MICHIGAN

MICHAELY M. F1779

MICHIGAN STATE UNIVERSITY....SEE MICH/STA/U

MICHIGAN....MICHIGAN

B62
US AGENCY INTERNATIONAL DEV,OPERATIONS REPORT - 1962 (PAMPHLET). AFR ASIA L/A+17C USA+45 ECO/UNDEV FINAN INT/ORG NAT/G 20 MICHIGAN. PAGE 134 F2636
FOR/AID CHARTS STAT BUDGET

MICRONESIA....MICRONESIA

MID/EAST....MIDDLE EAST

B51
US HOUSE COMM APPROPRIATIONS,MUTUAL SECURITY PROGRAM APPROPRIATIONS FOR 1952: HEARINGS BEFORE A SUBCOMMITTEE OF THE COMMITTEE ON APPROPRIATIONS. AFR KOREA L/A+17C ECO/DEV ECO/UNDEV INT/ORG INSPECT BAL/PWR DIPLOM DEBATE WAR...POLICY STAT ASIA/S 20 CONGRESS NATO MID/EAST. PAGE 136 F2686
LEGIS FORCES BUDGET FOR/AID

B63
US SENATE COMM GOVT OPERATIONS,REPORT OF A STUDY OF US FOREIGN AID IN TEN MIDDLE EASTERN AND AFRICAN COUNTRIES. AFR ISLAM USA+45 FORCES PLAN BUDGET DIPLOM TAX DETER WEALTH...STAT CHARTS 20 CONGRESS AID MID/EAST. PAGE 138 F2728
FOR/AID EFFICIENCY ECO/TAC FINAN

MID/EX ....MIDDLE EXECUTIVES; HEADS OF DEPARTMENTS

S61
GALBRAITH J.K.,"A POSITIVE APPROACH TO ECONOMIC AID." FUT USA+45 INTELL NAT/G CONSULT ACT/RES DIPLOM ECO/TAC EDU/PROP ATTIT KNOWL PWR WEALTH ...SOC STERTYP MID/EX METH/GP 20. PAGE 45 F0883
ECO/UNDEV ROUTINE FOR/AID

L62
MACHLUP F.,"PLANS FOR REFORM OF THE INTERNATIONAL MONETARY SYSTEM. PRINCETON: U. PR., 1962, 70 PP., $0.25." WOR+45 INT/ORG ECO/TAC BAL/PAY HEALTH ORD/FREE WEALTH MID/EX TERR/GP VAL/FREE APPLIC 20. PAGE 83 F1631
ECO/DEV STAT

MIDDLETOWN....MIDDLETOWN: LOCATION OF LYND STUDY

MIDWEST/US....MIDWESTERN UNITED STATES

S59
GILPATRICK T.V.,"PRICE SUPPORT POLICY AND THE MIDWEST FARM VOTE" (BMR)" NAT/G PRICE CONTROL REGION...POLICY CHARTS 440 20 MIDWEST/US CONGRESS REPUBLICAN EISNHWR/DD 20. PAGE 47 F0925
POL/PAR AGRI ATTIT CHOOSE

MIGRATION....MIGRATION; IMMIGRATION AND EMIGRATION; SEE ALSO HABITAT, GEOG

B47
ISAAC J.,ECONOMICS OF MIGRATION. MOD/EUR CULTURE STRATA STRUCT NAT/G COLONIAL WEALTH...OLD/LIB TREND TIME 19/20 EUROPE/W MIGRATION. PAGE 65 F1289
HABITAT SOC GEOG

S49
ECKLER A.R.,"IMMIGRATION AND THE LABOR FORCE." USA+45 USA-45 EXTR/IND FINAN PROC/MFG AGE/Y SKILL ...CHARTS 19/20 MIGRATION. PAGE 36 F0694
WORKER STRANGE INDUS ECO/TAC

B59
LOPEZ VILLAMIL H.,A STATEMENT OF THE LAWS OF THE HONDURAS IN MATTERS AFFECTING BUSINESS (2ND ED.). HONDURAS DIST/IND EXTR/IND FINAN WORKER TAX DEATH MARRIAGE OWN MARITIME 20 MIGRATION. PAGE 82 F1600
CONSTN INDUS LEGIS NAT/G

B59
ROCHE J.,LA COLONISATION ALLEMANDE ET LE RIO GRANDE DO SUL. BRAZIL L/A+17C NAT/G PROVS INGP/REL RACE/REL DISCRIM HABITAT...GEOG SOC/INTEG 19/20 MIGRATION. PAGE 113 F2228
ECO/UNDEV GP/REL ATTIT

B60
GONZALEZ NAVARRO M.,LA COLONIZACION EN MEXICO, 1877-1910. AGRI NAT/G PLAN PROB/SOLV INCOME ...POLICY JURID CENSUS 19/20 MEXIC/AMER MIGRATION. PAGE 48 F0947
ECO/UNDEV GEOG HABITAT COLONIAL

B61
SEPULVEDA C.,A STATEMENT OF THE LAWS OF MEXICO IN MATTERS AFFECTING BUSINESS (3RD ED.). AGRI DIST/IND EXTR/IND FINAN INDUS WORKER TAX MARRIAGE OWN ORD/FREE...BIBLIOG 20 MEXIC/AMER TREATY MIGRATION MONOPOLY. PAGE 119 F2356
CONSTN NAT/G JURID LEGIS

B62
MULLER E.,DIE HEIMATVERTRIEBENEN IN BADEN-WURTTEMBERG. GERMANY/W AGRI INDUS LABOR PROVS SOC/INTEG 20 MIGRATION. PAGE 95 F1858
GP/REL INGP/REL

B64
MORGAN H.W.,AMERICAN SOCIALISM 1900-1960. AFR USA+45 USA-45 INTELL AGRI LABOR WORKER BARGAIN ECO/TAC GP/REL RACE/REL 20 NEGRO MIGRATION. PAGE 93 F1830
SOCISM POL/PAR ECO/DEV STRATA

B64
TELLADO A.,A STATEMENT OF THE LAWS OF THE DOMINICAN REPUBLIC IN MATTERS AFFECTING BUSINESS (3RD ED.). DOMIN/REP AGRI DIST/IND EXTR/IND FINAN FAM WORKER ECO/TAC TAX CT/SYS MARRIAGE OWN...BIBLIOG 20 MIGRATION. PAGE 129 F2542
CONSTN LEGIS NAT/G INDUS

B65
HERRICK B.H.,URBAN MIGRATION AND ECONOMIC DEVELOPMENT IN CHILE. CHILE AGRI INDUS LABOR NAT/G CENTRAL PRODUC...STAT SAMP CHARTS BIBLIOG/A MUNICH 20 MIGRATION. PAGE 59 F1156
HABITAT GEOG ECO/UNDEV

B65
LUGO-MARENCO J.J.,A STATEMENT OF THE LAWS OF NICARAGUA IN MATTERS AFFECTING BUSINESS. NICARAGUA AGRI DIST/IND EXTR/IND FINAN INDUS FAM WORKER INT/TRADE TAX MARRIAGE OWN BIO/SOC 20 TREATY RESOURCE/N MIGRATION. PAGE 82 F1606
CONSTN NAT/G LEGIS JURID

B67
BAILY S.L.,LABOR, NATIONALISM, AND POLITICS IN ARGENTINA. POL/PAR TOP/EX GP/REL...BIBLIOG/A 19/20 MIGRATION PERON/JUAN ARGEN. PAGE 8 F0154
LABOR NAT/LISM

S67
HUTCHINGS R.,"THE ENDING OF UNEMPLOYMENT IN THE USSR" USSR PLAN ECO/TAC PRICE INGP/REL...GEOG STAT CHARTS 20 MIGRATION. PAGE 63 F1247
WORKER AGRI INDUS MARXISM

S67
THEROUX P.,"HATING THE ASIANS." TANZANIA UGANDA CONSTN INDUS NAT/G POL/PAR WORKER ECO/TAC HABITAT LOVE...POLICY GEOG 20 MIGRATION. PAGE 130 F2557
AFR RACE/REL SOVEREIGN ATTIT

MIKESELL R.F. F1780,F1781,F1782,F1783

MIL/ACAD....MILITARY ACADEMY

MILIBAND R. F1784

MILITARY....SEE FORCES

MILL J. F1785

MILL J.S. F1786,F1787

MILL/JAMES....JAMES MILL

MILL/JS....JOHN STUART MILL

B59
LINK R.G.,ENGLISH THEORIES OF ECONOMIC FLUCTUATIONS: 1815-1848. FRANCE UK AGRI WORKER DIPLOM PRICE TASK WAR DEMAND PRODUC...POLICY BIBLIOG 18 MALTHUS MILL/JS WILSON/J. PAGE 80 F1574
IDEA/COMP ECO/DEV WEALTH EQUILIB

B63
BARNETT H.J.,SCARCITY AND GROWTH: THE ECONOMICS OF NATURAL RESOURCE AVAILABILITY. FUT WOR+45 AGRI INDUS PROB/SOLV TEC/DEV CONTROL PRODUC...SOC/WK IDEA/COMP METH/COMP SIMUL 20 RESOURCE/N MALTHUS RICARDO/D MILL/JS DARWIN/C. PAGE 10 F0191
DEMAND HABITAT CENSUS GEOG

B65
GRAMPP W.D.,ECONOMIC LIBERALISM; THE CLASSICAL VIEW (VOL. II). MOD/EUR SOCIETY MARKET INT/TRADE NAT/LISM WEALTH LAISSEZ...POLICY PSY CONCPT BIBLIOG 19 SMITH/ADAM HUME/D MILL/JS. PAGE 50 F0975
ECO/DEV CAP/ISM IDEA/COMP ECO/TAC

MILLEN B.H. F1788

MILLER A.S. F1789,F1790

MILLER C.H. F1791

MILLER J.C. F1727

MILLER M.H. F1632

MILLER R.F. F0335

MILLER S.Q. F1106

MILLER W. F1792

MILLETT J.D. F1636,F1793

MILLIKAN M.F. F1794,F1795

MILLIKEN M. F1796

MILLIS H.A. F1797

MILLS C.W. F1798,F1799

MILLS G. F1100

MILLS/CW....C. WRIGHT MILLS

MILNE R.S. F1800

MILNER/A....ALFRED MILNER

MILTON/J....MILTON, JOHN

MINER J. F1801

MINGAY G.E. F1802

MINING....SEE EXTR/IND

MINNESOTA....MINNESOTA

N19

YLVISAKER P.N.,THE NATURAL CEMENT ISSUE (PAMPHLET). USA+45 USA-45 CONSTRUC PROVS CAP/ISM ADMIN LOBBY PERS/REL OWN RIGID/FLEX ROLE 20 MINNESOTA. PAGE 150 F2948 — POLICY NAT/G PLAN GOV/REL

MINORITY....SEE RACE/REL

MINTZ S.W. F1804

MIRANDON S. F1010

MISCEGEN....MISCEGENATION

MISSION....MISSIONARIES

MISSISSIPP....MISSISSIPPI

MISSOURI RIVER BASIN PLAN....SEE MO/BASIN

MISSOURI....MISSOURI

MIT CENTER INTERNATIONAL STU F1805,F1806

MITAU G.T. F1807

MITCHELL J.D.B. F1808

MITCHELL W.G. F1809

MIXON J. F1810

MIYASAWA K. F1811

MNR....MOVIMIENTO NACIONALISTA REVOLUCIONARIO (BOLIVIA)

MO/BASIN....MISSOURI RIVER BASIN PLAN

MOAK L.L. F1812

MOB....SEE CROWD

MOBUTU/J....JOSEPH MOBUTU

MOCHE....MOCHE, PERU

MOD/EUR....MODERN EUROPE (1700-1918); SEE ALSO APPROPRIATE NATIONS

B00

LIST F.,NATIONAL SYSTEM OF POLITICAL ECONOMY. ECO/DEV AGRI EXTR/IND FINAN INDUS TEC/DEV ECO/TAC ATTIT WEALTH...TREND GEN/LAWS FOR/TRADE 19. PAGE 81 F1581 — MOD/EUR MARKET

B12

HOBSON J.A.,THE EVOLUTION OF MODERN CAPITALISM. MOD/EUR UK STRATA ECO/DEV INDUS INCOME UTIL WEALTH ...SOC GEN/LAWS 7/20. PAGE 60 F1184 — CAP/ISM WORKER TEC/DEV TIME/SEQ

B14

DE BLOCH J.,THE FUTURE OF WAR IN ITS TECHNICAL, ECONOMIC, AND POLITICAL RELATIONS (1899). MOD/EUR TEC/DEV BUDGET INT/TRADE DETER GUERRILLA WEAPON COST PEACE 20. PAGE 31 F0596 — WAR BAL/PWR PREDICT FORCES

B15

VEBLEN T.,IMPERIAL GERMANY AND THE INDUSTRIAL REVOLUTION. GERMANY MOD/EUR UK USA-45 NAT/G TEC/DEV CAP/ISM...MAJORIT NAT/COMP 19/20 CHINJAP. PAGE 141 F2769 — ECO/DEV INDUS TECHNIC BAL/PWR

B18

MARX K.,CAPITAL. FUT MOD/EUR STRATA DIST/IND PROC/MFG TEC/DEV WEALTH...MARXIST WORK 19. PAGE 86 F1688 — ECO/DEV CAP/ISM SOCISM

N19

ENGELS F.,THE BRITISH LABOUR MOVEMENT (PAMPHLET). FRANCE GERMANY MOD/EUR UK USA-45 POL/PAR WORKER PAY EDU/PROP PRICE REPRESENT GP/REL 19. PAGE 37 F0730 — ECO/TAC MARXISM LABOR STRATA

B20

MOREL E.D.,THE BLACK MAN'S BURDEN. AFR MOD/EUR AGRI EXTR/IND PROB/SOLV INT/TRADE ADMIN CONTROL COERCE DISCRIM...POLICY 19/20 NEGRO LEAGUE/NAT. PAGE 93 F1828 — ORD/FREE CAP/ISM RACE/REL DOMIN

B21

CLAPHAN J.H.,THE ECONOMIC DEVELOPMENT OF FRANCE AND GERMANY 1815-1914. FRANCE GERMANY MOD/EUR COM/IND DIST/IND FINAN INT/TRADE EDU/PROP 19/20. PAGE 24 F0476 — ECO/UNDEV ECO/DEV AGRI INDUS

B25

EDGEWORTH F.Y.,PAPERS RELATING TO POLITICAL ECONOMY. MOD/EUR SOCIETY STRATA DIST/IND INDUS MARKET NAT/G ACT/RES ECO/TAC EXEC WEALTH ...METH/CNCPT MATH TREND HYPO/EXP SIMUL GEN/METH FOR/TRADE VAL/FREE LOG/LING. PAGE 36 F0702 — ECO/DEV CAP/ISM

B27

WEBER M.,GENERAL ECONOMIC HISTORY. CHRIST-17C MOD/EUR STRUCT AGRI EXTR/IND FINAN INDUS MARKET FAM NAT/G PROF/ORG SECT ECO/TAC MUNICH 8/20. PAGE 144 F2839 — ECO/DEV CAP/ISM

B30

FEIS H.,EUROPE, THE WORLD'S BANKER, 1871-1914. FRANCE GERMANY MOD/EUR UK WOR-45 NAT/G PLAN ECO/TAC EXEC ATTIT PWR WEALTH...CONCPT HIST/WRIT GEN/LAWS VAL/FREE 19/20. PAGE 40 F0773 — FINAN DIPLOM INT/TRADE

B36

HUBERMAN L.,MAN'S WORLDLY GOODS: THE STORY OF THE WEALTH OF NATIONS. CHRIST-17C EUR+WWI MOD/EUR SOCIETY DOMIN REV ORD/FREE...TIME/SEQ METH/COMP. PAGE 63 F1231 — WEALTH CAP/ISM MARXISM CREATE

B38

HOBSON J.A.,IMPERIALISM. MOD/EUR UK WOR-45 CULTURE ECO/UNDEV NAT/G VOL/ASSN PLAN EDU/PROP LEGIT REGION COERCE ATTIT PWR...POLICY PLURIST TIME/SEQ GEN/LAWS TERR/GP 19/20. PAGE 60 F1187 — DOMIN ECO/TAC BAL/PWR COLONIAL

B41

YOUNG G.,FEDERALISM AND FREEDOM. EUR+WWI MOD/EUR RUSSIA USA-45 WOR-45 SOCIETY STRUCT ECO/DEV INT/ORG EXEC FEDERAL ATTIT PERSON ALL/VALS...OLD/LIB CONCPT OBS TREND LEAGUE/NAT TOT/POP. PAGE 150 F2950 — NAT/G WAR

B46

CLOUGH S.B.,ECONOMIC HISTORY OF EUROPE. CHRIST-17C EUR+WWI MOD/EUR WOR-45 SOCIETY EXEC ATTIT WEALTH ...CONCPT GEN/LAWS WORK TOT/POP VAL/FREE 7/20. PAGE 25 F0493 — ECO/TAC CAP/ISM

B47

ISAAC J.,ECONOMICS OF MIGRATION. MOD/EUR CULTURE STRATA STRUCT NAT/G COLONIAL WEALTH...OLD/LIB TREND TIME 19/20 EUROPE/W MIGRATION. PAGE 65 F1289 — HABITAT SOC GEOG

B48

LAUTERBACH A.,ECONOMIC SECURITY AND INDIVIDUAL FREEDOM: CAN WE HAVE BOTH? COM EUR+WWI MOD/EUR UNIV WOR+45 CAP/ISM TOTALISM ALL/VALS...GOV/COMP BIBLIOG 20. PAGE 76 F1490 — ORD/FREE ECO/DEV DECISION INGP/REL

B54

HAYEK FA V.O.N.,CAPITALISM AND THE HISTORIANS. MOD/EUR TEC/DEV GP/REL WEALTH...HIST/WRIT ANTHOL 19. PAGE 57 F1124 — CAP/ISM LABOR STRATA ECO/TAC

B55

MOHL R.V.,DIE GESCHICHTE UND LITERATUR DER STAATSWISSENSCHAFTEN (3 VOLS.). LAW NAT/G...JURID METH/COMP METH. PAGE 92 F1814 — PHIL/SCI MOD/EUR

B56

KINDLEBERGER C.P.,THE TERMS OF TRADE: A EUROPEAN CASE-STUDY. EUR+WWI MOD/EUR ECO/DEV ECO/UNDEV AGRI INDUS BAL/PAY...METH/CNCPT STAT CONT/OBS CON/ANAL SOC/EXP SIMUL FOR/TRADE 20. PAGE 71 F1390 — PLAN ECO/TAC

B56
WOLFF R.L.,THE BALKANS IN OUR TIME. ALBANIA FUT MOD/EUR USSR YUGOSLAVIA CULTURE INT/ORG SECT DIPLOM EDU/PROP COERCE WAR ORD/FREE...CHARTS 4/20 BALKANS COMINFORM. PAGE 148 F2919
GEOG COM

B57
BARAN P.A.,THE POLITICAL ECONOMY OF GROWTH. MOD/EUR USA+45 USA-45 TEC/DEV TAX SOCISM...MGT CONCPT GOV/COMP. PAGE 9 F0178
CAP/ISM CONTROL ECO/UNDEV FINAN

B57
EHRMANN H.W.,ORGANIZED BUSINESS IN FRANCE. EUR+WWI MOD/EUR ECO/DEV VOL/ASSN LEGIT ATTIT PERCEPT PWR RESPECT...PLURIST SOC INT TOT/POP 20. PAGE 36 F0712
PROF/ORG ECO/TAC FRANCE

B57
LENIN V.I.,THE DEVELOPMENT OF CAPITALISM IN RUSSIA. MOD/EUR USSR AGRI MARKET POL/PAR TEC/DEV...CONCPT 19/20. PAGE 78 F1521
COM INDUS CAP/ISM

B58
ELLSWORTH P.T.,THE INTERNATIONAL ECONOMY. EUR+WWI MOD/EUR INT/ORG CAP/ISM FOR/AID BAL/PAY LAISSEZ 16/20. PAGE 37 F0725
INT/TRADE TARIFFS ECO/DEV

B59
AITKEN H.,THE STATE AND ECONOMIC GROWTH. COM EUR+WWI MOD/EUR S/ASIA USA+45 FINAN NAT/G DELIB/GP PLAN PWR WEALTH 20. PAGE 3 F0054
DIST/IND ECO/DEV

B60
HEILPERIN M.A.,STUDIES IN ECONOMIC NATIONALISM. EUR+WWI MOD/EUR USA+45 ECO/DEV PLAN INT/TRADE TARIFFS WAR PRODUC PROFIT 18/20 KEYNES/JM. PAGE 58 F1140
ECO/TAC NAT/G NAT/LISM POLICY

S60
MAIR L.P.,"SOCIAL CHANGE IN SOUTH AFRICA." MOD/EUR SOUTH/AFR WOR+45 ECO/UNDEV EX/STRUC TEC/DEV ATTIT DRIVE PERCEPT ORD/FREE...MGT CONCPT TIME/SEQ IND 20. PAGE 84 F1641
AFR NAT/G REV SOVEREIGN

B61
BALASSA B.,THE THEORY OF ECONOMIC INTEGRATION. EUR+WWI L/A+17C MOD/EUR WOR+45 ECO/UNDEV MARKET INT/ORG NAT/G VOL/ASSN DELIB/GP PLAN CAP/ISM ECO/TAC...MAJORIT FOR/TRADE OEEC 20. PAGE 8 F0157
ECO/DEV ACT/RES INT/TRADE

B61
HENDERSON W.O.,THE INDUSTRIAL REVOLUTION IN EUROPE. FRANCE GERMANY MOD/EUR RUSSIA WORKER PROFIT PWR MARXISM SOCISM...SOC HIST/WRIT 19 INDUS/REV. PAGE 58 F1148
INDUS REV CAP/ISM TEC/DEV

B61
MARX K.,THE COMMUNIST MANIFESTO. IN (MENDEL A. ESSENTIAL WORKS OF MARXISM, NEW YORK: BANTAM. FUT MOD/EUR CULTURE ECO/DEV ECO/UNDEV AGRI FINAN INDUS MARKET PROC/MFG LABOR POL/PAR CONSULT FORCES CREATE PLAN ADMIN ATTIT DRIVE RIGID/FLEX ORD/FREE PWR RESPECT MARX/KARL MUNICH WORK. PAGE 86 F1691
COM NEW/IDEA CAP/ISM REV

B61
WRIGHT H.M.,THE "NEW IMPERIALISM": ANALYSIS OF LATE NINETEENTH-CENTURY EXPANSION. MOD/EUR WOR-45 SOCIETY FINAN ECO/TAC INT/TRADE NAT/LISM...ANTHOL BIBLIOG/A 19. PAGE 149 F2933
HIST/WRIT IDEA/COMP COLONIAL DOMIN

B62
HENDERSON W.O.,THE GENESIS OF THE COMMON MARKET. EUR+WWI FRANCE MOD/EUR UK SEA COM/IND EXTR/IND COLONIAL DISCRIM...TIME/SEQ CHARTS BIBLIOG 18/20 EEC TREATY. PAGE 58 F1149
ECO/DEV INT/TRADE DIPLOM

B63
COSSA L.,SAGGI BIBLIOGRAFICI DI ECONOMIA POLITICA. MOD/EUR LABOR PRICE COST INCOME 18/19. PAGE 28 F0539
BIBLIOG FINAN WEALTH

B63
NEUMARK S.D.,FOREIGN TRADE AND ECONOMIC DEVELOPMENT IN AFRICA: A HISTORICAL PERSPECTIVE. EUR+WWI MOD/EUR ECO/UNDEV AGRI COM/IND EXTR/IND PROC/MFG SKILL WEALTH...CONCPT TIME/SEQ TREND SIMUL FOR/TRADE WORK TOT/POP TERR/GP VAL/FREE 19/20. PAGE 98 F1916
AFR

B63
OLSON M. JR.,THE ECONOMICS OF WARTIME SHORTAGE. FRANCE GERMANY MOD/EUR UK AGRI PROB/SOLV ADMIN DEMAND WEALTH...POLICY OLD/LIB FOR/TRADE 17/20. PAGE 101 F1990
WAR ADJUST ECO/TAC NAT/COMP

S63
FOURASTIE J.,"LES SCIENCES ECONOMIQUES ET SOCIALES EN EUROPE." EUR+WWI FUT MOD/EUR WOR+45 WOR-45 INTELL SOCIETY R+D PLAN ROUTINE ATTIT RIGID/FLEX KNOWL...OBS TREND. PAGE 43 F0833
ACT/RES CULTURE

B64
KOHNSTAMM M.,THE EUROPEAN COMMUNITY AND ITS ROLE IN THE WORLD. FUT MOD/EUR UK USA+45 ECO/DEV 20. PAGE 72 F1418
INT/ORG NAT/G REGION DIPLOM

B64
RIVKIN A.,AFRICA AND THE EUROPEAN COMMON MARKET (PAMPHLET). AFR MOD/EUR WOR+45 TEC/DEV FOR/AID TARIFFS BAL/PAY...POLICY 20 EEC. PAGE 111 F2196
INT/ORG INT/TRADE ECO/TAC ECO/UNDEV

B64
WILLIAMSON J.G.,AMERICAN GROWTH AND THE BALANCE OF PAYMENTS, 1820-1913: A STUDY OF THE LONG SWING. EUR+WWI MOD/EUR USA+45 USA-45 ECO/DEV NAT/G ECO/TAC ROUTINE ORD/FREE WEALTH...MATH STAT TIME/SEQ CHARTS SIMUL GEN/LAWS TRUE/GP METH/GP VAL/FREE 19/20. PAGE 147 F2896
FINAN BAL/PAY

B64
WRIGHT G.,RURAL REVOLUTION IN FRANCE: THE PEASANTRY IN THE TWENTIETH CENTURY. EUR+WWI MOD/EUR LAW CULTURE AGRI POL/PAR DELIB/GP LEGIS ECO/TAC EDU/PROP COERCE CHOOSE ATTIT RIGID/FLEX HEALTH ...STAT CENSUS CHARTS VAL/FREE 20. PAGE 149 F2932
PWR STRATA FRANCE REV

B65
COLLINS H.,KARL MARX AND THE BRITISH LABOR MOVEMENT, YEARS OF THE FIRST INTERNATIONAL. EUR+WWI MOD/EUR UK STRATA INDUS NAT/G POL/PAR SOCISM ...CONCPT 19/20 MARX/KARL. PAGE 26 F0507
MARXISM LABOR INT/ORG WORKER

B65
GRAMPP W.D.,ECONOMIC LIBERALISM; THE CLASSICAL VIEW (VOL. II). MOD/EUR SOCIETY MARKET INT/TRADE NAT/LISM WEALTH LAISSEZ...POLICY PSY CONCPT BIBLIOG 19 SMITH/ADAM HUME/D MILL/JS. PAGE 50 F0975
ECO/DEV CAP/ISM IDEA/COMP ECO/TAC

B65
WRIGHT L.B.,THE DREAM OF PROSPERITY IN COLONIAL AMERICA. USA-45 ECO/UNDEV AGRI EXTR/IND PARLIAMENT 17/18. PAGE 149 F2934
PROVS WEALTH MOD/EUR

B66
WECHSBERG J.,THE MERCHANT BANKERS. EUR+WWI MOD/EUR CONTROL...BIOG GP/COMP PERS/COMP 16/20. PAGE 144 F2842
FINAN PWR WEALTH FAM

B67
GUTKIND E.A.,URBAN DEVELOPMENT IN SOUTHERN EUROPE* SPAIN AND PORTUGAL. CHRIST-17C EUR+WWI MOD/EUR PORTUGAL SPAIN CULTURE AGRI...SOC SAMP/SIZ BIBLIOG MUNICH. PAGE 52 F1015
TEC/DEV ECO/DEV

B67
STEARNS P.N.,EUROPEAN SOCIETY IN UPHEAVAL* SOCIAL HISTORY SINCE 1800. EUR+WWI MOD/EUR STRATA SECT WORKER TEC/DEV WAR...WELF/ST SOC TREND BIBLIOG 19/20. PAGE 125 F2472
REGION ECO/DEV SOCIETY INDUS

S67
DEYRUP F.J.,"SOCIAL MOBILITY AS A MAJOR FACTOR IN ECONOMIC DEVELOPMENT." CHRIST-17C EUR+WWI MOD/EUR ECO/UNDEV DEMAND 20. PAGE 32 F0630
STRATA ECO/DEV INDUS WORKER

S67
SCOVILLE W.J.,"GOVERNMENT REGULATION AND GROWTH IN THE FRENCH PAPER INDUSTRY DURING THE EIGHTEENTH CENTURY." FRANCE MOD/EUR FINAN CAP/ISM TAX ADMIN CONTROL PRIVIL LAISSEZ...POLICY 18. PAGE 118 F2337
NAT/G PROC/MFG ECO/DEV INGP/REL

S67
WAITS C.R.,"CRAFT GILDS AS AN INSTITUTIONAL BARRIER TO THE INDUSTRIAL REVOLUTION." CHRIST-17C MOD/EUR ECO/UNDEV CONTROL GP/REL ATTIT 16/19. PAGE 142 F2801
TEC/DEV INDUS REV PROF/ORG

B91
MILL J.S.,SOCIALISM (1859). MOD/EUR AGRI INDUS NAT/G REV INCOME PRODUC ORD/FREE POPULISM SOCISM ...GOV/COMP METH/COMP 19. PAGE 91 F1787
WEALTH SOCIALIST ECO/TAC OWN

MODAL....MODAL TYPES, FASHIONS

B41
ESTEY J.A.,BUSINESS CYCLES: THEIR NATURE, CAUSE, AND CONTROL. NAT/G BUDGET CAP/ISM TAX PRICE CONTROL INCOME...MODAL TIME/SEQ GEN/METH T 18/20 KEYNES/JM MONEY. PAGE 38 F0749
INDUS FINAN ECO/TAC POLICY

B56
FELLNER W.,TRENDS AND CYCLES IN ECONOMIC ACTIVITY: AN INTRODUCTION TO PROBLEMS OF ECONOMIC GROWTH. USA+45 INDUS ACT/RES CAP/ISM EQUILIB...MODAL METH/COMP BIBLIOG 20. PAGE 40 F0779
ECO/TAC TREND FINAN ECO/DEV

B67
HARDT J.P.,MATHEMATICS AND COMPUTERS IN SOVIET ECONOMIC PLANNING. COM USSR OP/RES PROB/SOLV OPTIMAL...MODAL SIMUL 20. PAGE 55 F1082
PLAN TEC/DEV MATH COMPUT/IR

B67
LITTLE AD, INC.,COMMUNITY RENEWAL PROGRAMMING. CULTURE LOC/G ACT/RES TASK COST ATTIT...SOC/WK MODAL STAT STAND/INT CHARTS 20 SAN/FRAN. PAGE 81 F1585
STRATA NEIGH PLAN CREATE

MODELS....SEE SIMUL, MATH, ALSO MODELS INDEX, P. XIV

L56
SCHELLING T.C.,"AN ESSAY ON BARGAINING" (BMR)" OP/RES PROB/SOLV PRICE CHOOSE PWR...DECISION MODELS 20. PAGE 116 F2294
BARGAIN MARKET ECO/TAC GAME

B64
HART P.E.,ECONOMETRIC ANALYSIS FOR NATIONAL ECONOMIC PLANNING. INDUS OP/RES PRICE PRODUC ...SIMUL ANTHOL MODELS 20. PAGE 56 F1100
PLAN ECOMETRIC STAT

B67
PORWIT K.,CENTRAL PLANNING: EVALUATION OF VARIANTS. PRICE OPTIMAL PRODUC...DECISION MATH CHARTS SIMUL BIBLIOG MODELS 20. PAGE 107 F2106 — PLAN MGT ECOMETRIC

MODERNIZE....MODERNIZATION

MODESITT L.E. F1813

MODIGLIANI F1908

MOHL R.V. F1814

MOLTMANN G. F1815

MONACO....SEE ALSO APPROPRIATE TIME/SPACE/CULTURE INDEX

MONARCH....SEE CHIEF, KING

MONARCHY....SEE CONSERVE, CHIEF, KING

MONCRIEFF A. F1816

MONETARY POLICY....SEE FINAN, PLAN

MONEY....SEE FINAN

N19
HABERLER G.,A SURVEY OF INTERNATIONAL TRADE THEORY (PAMPHLET). FINAN NAT/G COST INCOME 18/20 MONEY HUME/D MARSHALL/A. PAGE 52 F1022 — INT/TRADE BAL/PAY GEN/LAWS POLICY

N19
ROBERTSON D.,GROWTH, WAGES, MONEY (PAMPHLET). UNIV WORKER BUDGET PRICE DEMAND PRODUC WEALTH...CONCPT MATH MONEY. PAGE 112 F2210 — FINAN ECO/DEV ECO/TAC PAY

B41
ESTEY J.A.,BUSINESS CYCLES; THEIR NATURE, CAUSE, AND CONTROL. NAT/G BUDGET CAP/ISM TAX PRICE CONTROL INCOME...MODAL TIME/SEQ GEN/METH T 18/20 KEYNES/JM MONEY. PAGE 38 F0749 — INDUS FINAN ECO/TAC POLICY

B42
WRIGHT D.M.,THE CREATION OF PURCHASING POWER. USA-45 NAT/G PRICE ADMIN WAR INCOME PRODUC...POLICY CONCPT IDEA/COMP BIBLIOG 20 MONEY. PAGE 149 F2930 — FINAN ECO/TAC ECO/DEV CREATE

B49
HANSEN A.H.,MONETARY THEORY AND FISCAL POLICY. CONSULT PLAN INT/TRADE BAL/PAY OPTIMAL...TREND CHARTS METH/COMP BIBLIOG T 19/20 MONEY. PAGE 54 F1063 — FINAN GEN/LAWS POLICY ECO/TAC

B51
LUXEMBORG R.,THE ACCUMULATION OF CAPITAL (TRANS. BY AGNES SCHWARZSCHILD). ECO/TAC DOMIN COLONIAL ATTIT LAISSEZ 19 MONEY. PAGE 82 F1614 — MARXIST INT/TRADE CAP/ISM FINAN

C52
HUME D.,"OF COMMERCE" IN D. HUME, POLITICAL DISCOURSES (1752)" UK FINAN DIPLOM WEALTH ...GEN/LAWS 18 MONEY. PAGE 63 F1238 — INDUS INT/TRADE PWR AGRI

C52
HUME D.,"OF INTEREST" IN D. HUME, POLITICAL DISCOURSES (1752)" UK INDUS WORKER DIPLOM PAY DEMAND INCOME WEALTH...GEN/LAWS 18 MONEY. PAGE 63 F1239 — PRICE COST FINAN INT/TRADE

C52
HUME D.,"OF MONEY" IN D. HUME, POLITICAL DISCOURSES (1752)" UK INDUS DIPLOM INT/TRADE...GEN/LAWS 18 MONEY. PAGE 63 F1240 — FINAN COST PRICE WEALTH

B57
FOUSEK P.G.,FOREIGN CENTRAL BANKING: THE INSTRUMENTS OF MONETARY POLICY. WOR+45 CONTROL ...TREND CHARTS 20 MONEY. PAGE 43 F0836 — FINAN ECO/TAC ECO/DEV MARKET

B57
INTL BANKING SUMMER SCHOOL,RELATIONS BETWEEN THE CENTRAL BANKS AND COMMERCIAL BANKS. EUR+WWI FRANCE GERMANY/W ITALY UK USA+45 USSR INDUS INT/ORG CAP/ISM CONTROL MONEY. PAGE 65 F1282 — FINAN NAT/G GP/REL LG/CO

B57
OLIVECRONA K.,THE PROBLEM OF THE MONETARY UNIT. AFR UNIV PAY PRICE UTIL...MATH 20 MONEY SILVER. PAGE 101 F1986 — FINAN ECO/TAC ECO/DEV CONCPT

B58
JUCKER-FLEETWOOD E.,ECONOMIC THEORY AND POLICY IN FINLAND 1914-1925. FINLAND INT/TRADE PRICE COST 20 MONEY. PAGE 68 F1343 — FINAN GEN/LAWS ECO/TAC PLAN

B58
MOULTON H.G.,CAN INFLATION BE CONTROLLED? ECO/DEV INDUS CAP/ISM RATION GOV/REL COST INCOME PEACE WEALTH...CHARTS TIME 20 KEYNES/JM MONEY. PAGE 94 F1847 — ECO/TAC CONTROL DEMAND FINAN

B60
RICHARDSON G.B.,INFORMATION AND INVESTMENT. PLAN PROB/SOLV CAP/ISM ECO/TAC KNOWL...CONCPT 20 MONEY. PAGE 111 F2184 — ECO/DEV EQUILIB FINAN PHIL/SCI

B60
ROBINSON R.I.,FINANCIAL INSTITUTIONS. USA+45 PRICE GOV/REL DEMAND WEALTH...CHARTS T 20 MONEY. PAGE 113 F2226 — FINAN ECO/TAC ECO/DEV BUDGET

B61
ASCHHEIM J.,TECHNIQUES OF MONETARY CONTROL. UK USA+45 CONTROL WAR DEMAND INCOME WEALTH...TREND CHARTS 20 MONEY. PAGE 7 F0127 — FINAN MARKET BUDGET CENTRAL

B61
HAUSER M.,DIE URSACHEN DER FRANZOSISCHEN INFLATION IN DEN JAHREN 1946-1952. AFR FRANCE INDUS NAT/G BUDGET DIPLOM ECO/TAC FOR/AID COST MONEY 20. PAGE 57 F1114 — ECO/DEV FINAN PRICE

B62
BRIEFS H.W.,PRICING POWER AND "ADMINISTRATIVE" INFLATION (PAMPHLET). AFR USA+45 PROC/MFG CONTROL EFFICIENCY MONEY. PAGE 18 F0349 — ECO/DEV PRICE POLICY EXEC

B62
JOHNSON H.G.,MONEY, TRADE AND ECONOMIC GROWTH. ECO/DEV ECO/UNDEV FINAN COST WEALTH...POLICY SOC IDEA/COMP 20 KEYNES/JM MONEY. PAGE 67 F1324 — PLAN BAL/PAY INT/TRADE ECO/TAC

B62
LUTZ F.A.,THE PROBLEM OF INTERNATIONAL ECONOMIC EQUILIBRIUM. FINAN PRODUC WEALTH 20 MONEY. PAGE 82 F1611 — DIPLOM EQUILIB BAL/PAY PROB/SOLV

B62
SHANNON I.,THE ECONOMIC FUNCTIONS OF GOLD. AFR FUT WOR+45 WOR-45 INT/ORG BUDGET INT/TRADE BAL/PAY DEMAND PEACE 20 MONEY. PAGE 120 F2366 — FINAN PRICE ECO/DEV ECO/TAC

B63
HAHN L.A.,DIE AMERIKANISCHE KONJUNKTURPOLITIK DER DOLLAR UND DIE DMARK. GERMANY/W USA+45 DIPLOM PRICE BAL/PAY COST...POLICY MONEY. PAGE 53 F1038 — FINAN BUDGET ECO/TAC LABOR

B63
INTERNATIONAL MONETARY FUND,COMPENSATORY FINANCING OF EXPORT FLUCTUATIONS (PAMPHLET). WOR+45 ECO/DEV ECO/UNDEV INT/ORG WEALTH...TREND 20 IMF MONEY. PAGE 65 F1281 — BAL/PAY FINAN BUDGET INT/TRADE

B63
US CONGRESS JOINT ECO COMM,THE UNITED STATES BALANCE OF PAYMENTS. AFR USA+45 DELIB/GP BUDGET PRICE PRODUC 20 CONGRESS MONEY. PAGE 135 F2655 — BAL/PAY INT/TRADE FINAN ECO/TAC

B64
BALL R.J.,INFLATION AND THE THEORY OF MONEY. MARKET TAX PAY PRICE TASK ADJUST BAL/PAY COST INCOME PRODUC WEALTH...METH/COMP 20 KEYNES/JM MONEY. PAGE 9 F0167 — EQUILIB DEMAND POLICY

B64
DUSCHA J.,ARMS, MONEY, AND POLITICS. USA+45 INDUS POL/PAR ECO/TAC TAX DETER NUC/PWR WAR WEAPON GOV/REL ATTIT...BIBLIOG/A 20 CONGRESS MONEY DEPT/DEFEN. PAGE 35 F0687 — NAT/G FORCES POLICY BUDGET

B64
MYINT H.,THE ECONOMICS OF THE DEVELOPING COUNTRIES. WOR+45 AGRI PLAN COST...POLICY GEOG 20 MONEY. PAGE 96 F1878 — ECO/UNDEV INT/TRADE EXTR/IND FINAN

B64
ODEH H.S.,THE IMPACT OF INFLATION ON THE LEVEL OF ECONOMIC ACTIVITY. AFR BRAZIL CHILE BUDGET GOV/REL COST DEMAND INCOME WEALTH...STAT METH 20 MONEY. PAGE 100 F1963 — ECOMETRIC ECO/TAC ECO/UNDEV FINAN

B65
SCITOVSKY T.,REQUIREMENTS OF AN INTERNATIONAL RESERVE SYSTEM. AFR ECO/TAC...PREDICT 20 SILVER MONEY. PAGE 118 F2330 — BAL/PAY FINAN EQUILIB INT/TRADE

B65
US CONGRESS JOINT ECO COMM,GUIDELINES FOR INTERNATIONAL MONETARY REFORM. USA+45 WOR+45 DELIB/GP BAL/PAY 20 CONGRESS IMF MONEY. PAGE 135 F2659 — DIPLOM FINAN PLAN INT/ORG

B66
FELLNER W.,MAINTAINING AND RESTORING BALANCE IN INTERNATIONAL PAYMENTS. ECO/UNDEV MARKET ECO/TAC PRICE INCOME WEALTH...POLICY METH/COMP 20 MONEY. PAGE 40 F0781 — BAL/PAY DIPLOM FINAN INT/TRADE

B66
SCHNEIDER E.,WIRTSCHAFTSKREISLAUF UND WIRTSCHAFTSWACHSTUM. ECO/DEV MARKET...CONCPT 20 — ECO/TAC FINAN

MONEY. PAGE 117 F2306 — INCOME COST

B66
US CONGRESS JOINT ECO COMM,NEW APPROACH TO UNITED STATES INTERNATIONAL ECONOMIC POLICY. USA+45 WOR+45 CHIEF DELIB/GP CONFER...CHARTS 20 CONGRESS MONEY. PAGE 135 F2660 — DIPLOM ECO/TAC BAL/PAY FINAN

B66
YEAGER L.B.,INTERNATIONAL MONETARY RELATIONS: THEORY, HISTORY, AND POLICY. WOR+45 WOR-45 INT/TRADE BAL/PAY...NAT/COMP 18/20 MONEY. PAGE 150 F2947 — FINAN DIPLOM ECO/TAC IDEA/COMP

B67
CLEMENT M.O.,THEORETICAL ISSUES IN INTERNATIONAL ECONOMICS. WOR+45 PLAN PROB/SOLV TEC/DEV ...ECOMETRIC METH/CNCPT MATH BIBLIOG T MONEY. PAGE 25 F0489 — INT/TRADE FINAN CREATE BAL/PAY

B75
JEVONS W.S.,MONEY AND THE MECHANISM OF EXCHANGE. INDUS MARKET DIPLOM COST EQUILIB WEALTH LAISSEZ ...GEN/LAWS 19 MONEY. PAGE 67 F1319 — PRICE FINAN ECO/TAC POLICY

MONGOLIA....SEE ALSO USSR

MONOPOLY....MONOPOLIES, OLIGOPOLIES, AND ANTI-TRUST ACTIONS

B08
LLOYD H.D.,THE SWISS DEMOCRACY. SWITZERLND INDUS NAT/G WORKER CHOOSE OWN ORD/FREE SOCISM...PLURIST 19/20 MONOPOLY. PAGE 81 F1590 — NAT/COMP GOV/COMP REPRESENT POPULISM

N19
US BUREAU OF THE CENSUS,THE PROPORTION OF THE SHIPMENTS (OR EMPLOYEES) OF EACH INDUSTRY... (PAMPHLET). USA+45 ECO/DEV EXTR/IND INDUS CONTROL PROFIT...STAT 20 CONGRESS MONOPOLY. PAGE 134 F2645 — PROC/MFG PRODUC MARKET CHARTS

B32
THOMPSON C.D.,CONFESSIONS OF THE POWER TRUST. MARKET ACT/RES EDU/PROP CONTROL GOV/REL INCOME OWN ...MGT 20 FTC MONOPOLY. PAGE 130 F2564 — LG/CO SERV/IND PWR FINAN

B34
ROBINSON J.,THE ECONOMICS OF IMPERFECT COMPETITION. FINAN ECO/TAC PRICE COST DEMAND EQUILIB OPTIMAL WEALTH...METH MONOPOLY. PAGE 113 F2221 — MARKET WORKER INDUS

B38
DAVIES E.,"NATIONAL" CAPITALISM: THE GOVERNMENT'S RECORD AS PROTECTOR OF PRIVATE MONOPOLY. UK ELITES SOCIETY STRATA POL/PAR WORKER PROB/SOLV CONTROL SOCISM 20 MONOPOLY LABOR/PAR CHAMBRLN/N. PAGE 30 F0583 — CAP/ISM NAT/G INDUS POLICY

B38
LAWLEY F.E.,THE GROWTH OF COLLECTIVE ECONOMY VOL. 1: NATIONAL. EUR+WWI AGRI INDUS NAT/G BARGAIN CAP/ISM ECO/TAC WAR OPTIMAL WEALTH...GOV/COMP METH/COMP 19/20 MONOPOLY. PAGE 76 F1492 — SOCISM PRICE CONTROL OWN

B38
LAWLEY F.E.,THE GROWTH OF COLLECTIVE ECONOMY VOL. 2: INTERNATIONAL. WOR-45 AGRI INDUS EQUILIB OPTIMAL OWN WEALTH...NAT/COMP 19/20 NAZI NEW/DEAL MONOPOLY. PAGE 76 F1493 — ECO/TAC SOCISM NAT/LISM CONTROL

B38
MEADE J.E.,AN INTRODUCTION TO ECONOMIC ANALYSIS AND POLICY (AMERICAN EDITION EDITED BY C.J. HITCH). FINAN INDUS MARKET LABOR INT/TRADE CONTROL COST DEMAND INCOME...CLASSIF CHARTS T 20 KEYNES/JM MONOPOLY. PAGE 89 F1737 — CONCPT PROFIT PRODUC

B40
TRIFFIN R.,MONOPOLISTIC COMPETITION AND GENERAL EQUILIBRIUM THEORY. DIST/IND PLAN TASK EQUILIB OPTIMAL...IDEA/COMP 20 MONOPOLY. PAGE 131 F2586 — INT/TRADE INDUS COST

B54
FRIEDMAN W.,THE PUBLIC CORPORATION: A COMPARATIVE SYMPOSIUM (UNIVERSITY OF TORONTO SCHOOL OF LAW COMPARATIVE LAW SERIES, VOL. I). AFR SWEDEN USA+45 INDUS INT/ORG NAT/G REGION CENTRAL FEDERAL...POLICY JURID IDEA/COMP NAT/COMP ANTHOL 20 MONOPOLY EUROPE. PAGE 44 F0861 — LAW SOCISM LG/CO OWN

B54
RICHTER R.,DAS KONKURRENZ PROBLEM IM OLIGOPOL. LG/CO BARGAIN PRICE COST...CONCPT 20 MONOPOLY. PAGE 111 F2188 — CONTROL GAME ECO/TAC GP/REL

B55
BERNSTEIN M.H.,REGULATING BUSINESS BY INDEPENDENT COMMISSION. USA+45 USA-45 LG/CO CHIEF LEGIS PROB/SOLV ADJUD SANCTION GP/REL ATTIT...TIME/SEQ 19/20 MONOPOLY PRESIDENT CONGRESS. PAGE 14 F0268 — DELIB/GP CONTROL CONSULT

B57
MASON E.S.,ECONOMIC CONCENTRATION AND THE MONOPOLY PROBLEM. USA+45 USA-45 LAW ELITES ECO/DEV LABOR RATION PRICE PWR WEALTH...CHARTS 20 MONOPOLY. PAGE 87 F1696 — GP/REL LG/CO CONTROL MARKET

B57
PALACIOS A.L.,PETROLEO, MONOPOLIOS, Y LATIFUNDIOS. L/A+17C EXTR/IND NAT/G TEC/DEV ECO/TAC CONTROL PRODUC 20 ARGEN MONOPOLY RESOURCE/N. PAGE 103 F2017 — ECO/UNDEV NAT/LISM INDUS AGRI

B58
DOWNIE J.,THE COMPETITIVE PROCESS. ECO/TAC PRICE EFFICIENCY OPTIMAL PRODUC WEALTH...IDEA/COMP METH/COMP 20 MONOPOLY. PAGE 34 F0658 — EQUILIB MARKET INDUS ECO/DEV

B61
SEPULVEDA C.,A STATEMENT OF THE LAWS OF MEXICO IN MATTERS AFFECTING BUSINESS (3RD ED.). AGRI DIST/IND EXTR/IND FINAN INDUS WORKER TAX MARRIAGE OWN ORD/FREE...BIBLIOG 20 MEXIC/AMER TREATY MIGRATION MONOPOLY. PAGE 119 F2356 — CONSTN NAT/G JURID LEGIS

B62
DOBB M.,CAPITALISM YESTERDAY AND TODAY. UK WORKER WAR PRODUC PROFIT 18/20 MONOPOLY. PAGE 33 F0646 — CAP/ISM TIME/SEQ CONCPT ECO/TAC

B62
US BUREAU OF THE CENSUS,REPORT FOR SUBCOMMITTEE ON ANTITRUST AND MONOPOLY: CONCENTRATION RATIOS IN MANUFACTURING INDUSTRY 1958. USA+45 ECO/DEV CONTROL GOV/REL OWN PRODUC PROFIT...STAT 20 CONGRESS MONOPOLY. PAGE 134 F2646 — CHARTS PROC/MFG MARKET LG/CO

N62
US SENATE COMM ON JUDICIARY,LEGISLATION TO STRENGTHEN PENALTIES UNDER THE ANTITRUST LAWS (PAMPHLET). USA+45 LG/CO CONFER CONTROL SANCTION ORD/FREE 20 SENATE MONOPOLY. PAGE 139 F2748 — LEAD ADJUD INDUS ECO/TAC

B63
BOWIE R.R.,GOVERNMENT REGULATION OF BUSINESS: CASES FROM THE NATIONAL REPORTER SYSTEM. USA+45 USA-45 NAT/G ECO/TAC ADJUD...ANTHOL 19/20 SUPREME/CT FTC FAIR/LABOR MONOPOLY. PAGE 17 F0331 — LAW CONTROL INDUS CT/SYS

B63
KOLKO G.,THE TRIUMPH OF CONSERVATISM. USA-45 INDUS LG/CO NAT/G PWR 20 PRESIDENT CONGRESS MONOPOLY PROGRSV/M. PAGE 72 F1421 — CONSERVE CAP/ISM FINAN MARKET

B64
GARFIELD PJ LOVEJOY WF,PUBLIC UTILITY ECONOMICS. DIST/IND FINAN MARKET ADMIN COST DEMAND ...TECHNIC JURID MUNICH 20 MONOPOLY. PAGE 46 F0906 — T ECO/TAC OWN SERV/IND

B64
KAPLAN A.D.H.,BIG ENTERPRISE IN A COMPETITIVE SYSTEM (REV. ED.). USA+45 INDUS MARKET WORKER TEC/DEV ECO/TAC PRICE ADJUD ADMIN CONTROL...MGT CHARTS 20 MONOPOLY. PAGE 69 F1351 — FINAN GP/REL NAT/G LG/CO

B64
MANSFIELD E.,MONOPOLY POWER AND ECONOMIC PERFORMANCE: AN INTRODUCTION TO A CURRENT ISSUE OF PUBLIC POLICY. ECO/DEV INDUS NAT/G PLAN CAP/ISM PRICE CONTROL LOBBY EFFICIENCY PRODUC...POLICY 20 CONGRESS KENNEDY/JF MONOPOLY. PAGE 85 F1659 — LG/CO PWR ECO/TAC MARKET

B64
US SENATE COMM ON JUDICIARY,HEARINGS BEFORE SUBCOMMITTEE ON ANTITRUST AND MONOPOLY: ECONOMIC CONCENTRATION VOLUMES 1-5 JULY 1964-SEPT 1966. USA+45 LAW FINAN ECO/TAC ADJUD COST EFFICIENCY PRODUC...STAT CHARTS 20 CONGRESS MONOPOLY. PAGE 140 F2749 — ECO/DEV CONTROL MARKET LG/CO

B64
WERNETTE J.P.,GOVERNMENT AND BUSINESS. LABOR CAP/ISM ECO/TAC INT/TRADE TAX ADMIN AUTOMAT NUC/PWR CIVMIL/REL DEMAND...MGT 20 MONOPOLY. PAGE 145 F2859 — NAT/G FINAN ECO/DEV CONTROL

B65
HABERLER G.,A SURVEY OF INTERNATIONAL TRADE THEORY. CANADA FRANCE GERMANY ECO/TAC TARIFFS AGREE COST DEMAND WEALTH...ECOMETRIC 19/20 MONOPOLY TREATY. PAGE 52 F1024 — INT/TRADE BAL/PAY DIPLOM POLICY

S65
MULLER A.L.,"THE ECONOMIC POSITION OF THE ASIANS IN AFRICA." AFR SOUTH/AFR ECO/UNDEV MARKET ECO/TAC GP/REL INCOME...CHARTS IND 20 MONOPOLY ASIANS. PAGE 95 F1856 — WORKER RACE/REL CAP/ISM DISCRIM

MONROE A.D. F1817

MONROE/DOC....MONROE DOCTRINE

MONROE/J....PRESIDENT JAMES MONROE

MONTANA....MONTANA

MONTECARLO....MONTE CARLO - OPERATIONAL RESEARCH DECISION-MAKING MODEL

MONTENEGRO C.V. F2756

MONTESQ....MONTESQUIEU, CHARLES LOUIS DE SECONDAT

MONTGOMERY J.D. F1818

MONTGOMERY R.E. F1797

MONTGOMERY....MONTGOMERY, ALABAMA

MOONEY J.D. F1820

MOONEY R.E. F1821

MOORE G.H. F1822

MOORE W.E. F1823,F1824

MORAL....RECTITUDE, MORALITY, GOODNESS (ALSO IMMORALITY)

B03
MOREL E.D.,THE BRITISH CASE IN FRENCH CONGO. CONGO/BRAZ FRANCE UK COERCE MORAL WEALTH...POLICY INT/LAW 20 CONGO/LEOP. PAGE 93 F1827
DIPLOM INT/TRADE COLONIAL AFR

B13
KROPOTKIN P.,THE CONQUEST OF BREAD. SOCIETY STRATA AGRI INDUS WORKER REV HAPPINESS INCOME PRODUC HEALTH MORAL ORD/FREE. PAGE 74 F1444
ANARCH SOCIALIST OWN AGREE

N19
DEANE H.,THE WAR IN VIETNAM (PAMPHLET). AFR CHINA/COM VIETNAM BAL/PWR DIPLOM ECO/TAC SOCISM INTERVENT INTERVENT. PAGE 31 F0610
WAR SOCIALIST MORAL CAP/ISM

B20
TAWNEY R.H.,THE ACQUISITIVE SOCIETY. STRATA WORKER PROB/SOLV CAP/ISM ECO/TAC CONTROL GP/REL OWN PRIVIL ATTIT ORD/FREE WEALTH 20. PAGE 128 F2536
INDUS SOCIETY PRODUC MORAL

B22
FOURIER C.,TRAITE DE L'ASSOCIATION DOMESTIQUE-AGRICOLE (2 VOLS.). UNIV SOCIETY INDUS ECO/TAC PERSON MORAL ANARCH. PAGE 43 F0834
VOL/ASSN AGRI UTOPIA CONCPT

B35
WADE J.,HISTORY OF THE MIDDLE AND WORKING CLASSES; WITH A POPULAR EXPOSITION OF THE ECONOMICAL AND POLITICAL PRINCIPLES.... FRANCE UK CONSTN FINAN INDUS LABOR INCOME PROFIT KNOWL MORAL ORD/FREE WEALTH...CHARTS 14/19. PAGE 142 F2797
WORKER STRATA CONCPT

B38
HEIMANN E.,COMMUNISM, FASCISM, OR DEMOCRACY? WOR-45 CONSTN SOCIETY STRATA AGRI CAP/ISM MORAL ORD/FREE ...MAJORIT METH/COMP NAT/COMP 19/20. PAGE 58 F1141
SOCISM MARXISM FASCISM PLURISM

B48
HAYEK F.A.,INDIVIDUALISM AND ECONOMIC ORDER. FINAN PLAN MORAL LAISSEZ SOCISM...POLICY DECISION PHIL/SCI HIST/WRIT. PAGE 57 F1122
RATIONAL KNOWL PERSON

B50
SOREL G.,REFLECTIONS ON VIOLENCE (1908) (TRANS. BY T.E. HULME AND J. ROTH). UNIV SOCIETY LABOR UTOPIA MORAL SOCISM...ANARCH SOCIALIST CONCPT 20. PAGE 124 F2445
COERCE REV WORKER MYTH

B51
CLARK C.,THE CONDITIONS OF ECONOMIC PROGRESS. EUR+WWI WOR+45 WOR-45 ECO/DEV INDUS CAP/ISM MORAL ...WELF/ST METH/CNCPT STAT TOT/POP VAL/FREE 20. PAGE 25 F0477
MARKET WEALTH

B53
BOULDING K.E.,THE ORGANIZATIONAL REVOLUTION. FUT CULTURE ECO/DEV LABOR PROF/ORG ECO/TAC MORAL...SOC CONCPT RECORD INT SOC/EXP 20. PAGE 17 F0321
SOCIETY TREND

B53
BOWEN H.R.,SOCIAL RESPONSIBILITIES OF THE BUSINESSMAN (FIRST EDITION). LAW FINAN ACT/RES CAP/ISM ROUTINE DRIVE PWR LAISSEZ...DECISION BIBLIOG. PAGE 17 F0326
MGT PERSON SUPEGO MORAL

B54
CHILDS M.W.,ETHICS IN A BUSINESS SOCIETY. PROF/ORG LEAD WAR GP/REL ATTIT DRIVE PERSON KNOWL MORAL PWR ...WELF/ST BIBLIOG. PAGE 24 F0466
MGT SOCIETY

B55
MAYO H.B.,DEMOCRACY AND MARXISM. COM USSR STRATA NAT/G WORKER ECO/TAC REV MORAL...PHIL/SCI HIST/WRIT IDEA/COMP WORSHIP 20 MARX/KARL LENIN/VI STALIN/J TROTSKY/L. PAGE 87 F1708
MARXISM CAP/ISM

B56
ABELS J.,THE TRUMAN SCANDALS. USA+45 USA-45 POL/PAR TAX LEGIT CT/SYS CHOOSE PRIVIL MORAL WEALTH 20 TRUMAN/HS PRESIDENT CONGRESS. PAGE 2 F0031
CRIME ADMIN CHIEF TRIBUTE

B56
FIELD G.C.,POLITICAL THEORY. POL/PAR REPRESENT MORAL SOVEREIGN...JURID IDEA/COMP. PAGE 40 F0789
CONCPT NAT/G ORD/FREE DIPLOM

S59
REUBENS E.D.,"THE BASIS FOR REORIENATION OF AMERICAN FOREIGN AID POLICY." USA+45 USSR STRUCT INT/ORG CONSULT ECO/TAC ADMIN DRIVE MORAL ORD/FREE PWR WEALTH...RELATIV MATH STAT TREND GEN/LAWS VAL/FREE 20. PAGE 111 F2180
ECO/UNDEV PLAN FOR/AID DIPLOM

B60
APTHEKER H.,DISARMAMENT AND THE AMERICAN ECONOMY: A SYMPOSIUM. FUT USA+45 ECO/DEV DIST/IND FINAN INDUS PROC/MFG LABOR NAT/G POL/PAR CONSULT PLAN CAP/ISM INT/TRADE PEACE ATTIT MORAL WEALTH...TREND GEN/LAWS TOT/POP 20. PAGE 6 F0110
MARXIST ARMS/CONT

B60
ROEPKE W.,A HUMANE ECONOMY: THE SOCIAL FRAMEWORK OF THE FREE MARKET. FUT USSR WOR+45 CULTURE SOCIETY ECO/DEV PLAN ECO/TAC ADMIN ATTIT PERSON RIGID/FLEX SUPEGO MORAL WEALTH SOCISM...POLICY OLD/LIB CONCPT TREND GEN/LAWS 20. PAGE 113 F2232
DRIVE EDU/PROP CAP/ISM

S60
HERZ J.H.,"EAST GERMANY: PROGRESS AND PROSPECTS." COM AGRI FINAN INDUS LOC/G NAT/G FORCES PLAN TEC/DEV DOMIN ADMIN COERCE DRIVE PERCEPT RIGID/FLEX MORAL ORD/FREE PWR...MARXIST PSY SOC RECORD STERTYP WORK. PAGE 59 F1158
POL/PAR STRUCT GERMANY

S61
NOVE A.,"THE SOVIET MODEL AND UNDERDEVELOPED COUNTRIES." COM FUT USSR WOR+45 CULTURE ECO/DEV POL/PAR FOR/AID EDU/PROP ADMIN MORAL WEALTH ...POLICY RECORD HIST/WRIT 20. PAGE 99 F1942
ECO/UNDEV PLAN

B62
DIMOCK M.E.,THE NEW AMERICAN POLITICAL ECONOMY: A SYNTHESIS OF POLITICS AND ECONOMICS. USA+45 FINAN LG/CO PLAN ADMIN REGION GP/REL CENTRAL MORAL 20. PAGE 33 F0642
FEDERAL ECO/TAC NAT/G PARTIC

B62
MCCLELLAN J.L.,CRIME WITHOUT PUNISHMENT. USA+45 LAW SOCIETY DELIB/GP TRIBUTE CONTROL LOBBY COERCE GP/REL ANOMIE MORAL...CRIMLGY 20 CONGRESS HOFFA/J. PAGE 88 F1718
CRIME ACT/RES LABOR PWR

B64
ASH W.,MARXISM AND MORAL CONCEPTS. CAP/ISM GP/REL ORD/FREE...BIBLIOG 20. PAGE 7 F0128
MARXISM CONCPT MORAL SOCIETY

B64
CHEIT E.F.,THE BUSINESS ESTABLISHMENT. FRANCE WOR+45 PROF/ORG TOP/EX PROB/SOLV CAP/ISM ADMIN SUPEGO MORAL PWR...METH/CNCPT MYTH NEW/IDEA 20. PAGE 24 F0460
PERSON EX/STRUC MGT INDUS

B65
OZGA S.A.,EXPECTATIONS IN ECONOMIC THEORY. MORAL ...ECOMETRIC MATH STAT IDEA/COMP 20. PAGE 102 F2008
RISK GAME CONCPT PREDICT

B67
BANFIELD E.C.,THE MORAL BASIS OF A BACKWARD SOCIETY. EUR+WWI ITALY STRATA NEIGH PARTIC INGP/REL ...SOC QU PREDICT TREND HYPO/EXP MUNICH 20. PAGE 9 F0173
MORAL WEALTH ATTIT

B67
GOODMAN P.,LIKE A CONQUERED PROVINCE: THE MORAL AMBIGUITY OF AMERICA. AFR USA+45 NAT/G PROB/SOLV EDU/PROP ADJUST EFFICIENCY 20. PAGE 49 F0950
SOCIETY TEC/DEV WAR MORAL

S67
WILSON C.E.,"AMERICAN INVESTMENT IN PORTUGUESE AFRICA: A PROBLEM OF "DEMOCRATIC" COLONIALISM." AFR ECO/UNDEV DIPLOM MORAL...IDEA/COMP 20 ANGOLA MOZAMBIQUE. PAGE 147 F2901
COLONIAL DOMIN ORD/FREE POLICY

B68
PROUDHON P.J.,SYSTEME DES CONTRADICTIONS ECONOMIQUES, OU PHILOSOPHIE DA LA MISERE (2 VOLS.) (1846). SECT WORKER GP/REL ISOLAT PRODUC IDEA/COMP. PAGE 108 F2126
SOCIETY STRATA MORAL

B76
PROUDHON P.J.,WHAT IS PROPERTY? (TRANS. BY B.R. TUCKER). SOCIETY AGRI CAP/ISM CRIME GP/REL PERSON MORAL ORD/FREE WEALTH. PAGE 108 F2127
OWN WORKER PRODUC ANARCH

MORALES C.J. F1825

MORALITY....SEE MORAL, CULTURE, ALL/VALS

MORE/THOM....SIR THOMAS MORE

MOREL E.D. F1826,F1827,F1828

MORGAN C.A. F1829

MORGAN H.W. F1830

MORGAN J.N. F1852

MORGENSTERN O. F1831,F1832

MORGENTH/H.... HANS MORGENTHAU

MORGENTHAU H.J. F1833

MORL/MINTO....MORLEY-MINTO - ERA OF BRITISH RULE IN INDIA (1905-1910)

MORLEY F. F1834

MORLEY L. F1834

MORLEY/J....JOHN MORLEY

MORMON....MORMON PEOPLE AND MORMON FAITH

MOROCCO....SEE ALSO ISLAM

B61
LAHAYE R.,LES ENTREPRISES PUBLIQUES AU MAROC. FRANCE MOROCCO LAW DIST/IND EXTR/IND FINAN CONSULT PLAN TEC/DEV ADMIN AGREE CONTROL OWN...POLICY 20. PAGE 74 F1460 — NAT/G INDUS ECO/UNDEV ECO/TAC

L62
WATERSTON A.,"PLANNING IN MOROCCO, ORGANIZATION AND IMPLEMENTATION. BALTIMORE: HOPKINS ECON. DEVELOP. INT. BANK FOR." ISLAM ECO/DEV AGRI DIST/IND INDUS PROC/MFG SERV/IND LOC/G EX/STRUC ECO/TAC PWR WEALTH TOT/POP TRUE/GP METH/GP TERR/GP VAL/FREE 20. PAGE 144 F2829 — NAT/G PLAN MOROCCO

S63
ARDANT G.,"A PLAN FOR FULL EMPLOYMENT IN THE DEVELOPING COUNTRIES." AFR FUT WOR+45 DELIB/GP ACT/RES PLAN ECO/TAC ATTIT ALL/VALS...POLICY STAT CHARTS TUNIS VAL/FREE 20. PAGE 6 F0112 — ECO/UNDEV SOCIETY MOROCCO

MORRIS A.J.A. F1835

MORRIS B.R. F1836

MORRIS M.D. F1837

MORRIS W.T. F1838

MORRIS/CW....C.W. MORRIS

MORRIS/G....G. MORRIS

MORRISSENS L. F1839

MORROW/DW....DWIGHT W. MORROW

MORSE C. F0191

MORSE D. F2821

MORTON H.C. F1840,F2223

MORTON J.A. F1841

MOSCA/G....GAETANO MOSCA

MOSCOW....MOSCOW, U.S.S.R.

MOSELY P.E. F1842

MOSK S.A. F1843

MOSKOW M.H. F1844

MOSKOWITZ M. F1845

MOSS F.M. F1846

MOSSI....MOSSI TRIBE

MOTIVATION....SEE DRIVE

MOULTON H.G. F1847

MOUNTJOY A.B. F1848

MOUSKHELY M. F1849

MOUSSA P. F1850

MOUTON J.S. F0297

MOVIES....SEE FILM

MOVIMIENTO NACIONALISTA REVOLUCIONARIO (BOLIVIA)....SEE MNR

MOWITZ R.J. F1851

MOYNI/RPRT....MOYNIHAN REPORT

MOZAMBIQUE....MOZAMBIQUE

S67
WILSON C.E.,"AMERICAN INVESTMENT IN PORTUGUESE AFRICA: A PROBLEM OF "DEMOCRATIC" COLONIALISM." AFR ECO/UNDEV DIPLOM MORAL...IDEA/COMP 20 ANGOLA MOZAMBIQUE. PAGE 147 F2901 — COLONIAL DOMIN ORD/FREE POLICY

MUCKRAKER....MUCKRAKERS

MUELLER E. F1852

MUGWUMP....MUGWUMP

MUHAMMAD A.C. F1853

MUKERJEE R. F1854

MULATTO....MULATTO

MULLANEY T.E. F1349

MULLENBACH P. F1855

MULLER A.L. F1856,F1857

MULLER E. F1858

MULTIVAR....MULTIVARIATE ANALYSIS

MULTIVARIATE ANALYSIS....SEE MULTIVAR

MUNBY D. F1859

MUND V.A. F1860

MUNDHEIM R.H. F1861

MUNIC....CITIES, TOWNS, VILLAGES

MUNICH....MUNICH, GERMANY

N
JOHNSON R.B.,FINANCING A SUBURBAN CITY. USA+45 TAX COST...SAMP/SIZ MUNICH 20 COL. PAGE 68 F1331 — FINAN PAY PROB/SOLV

N19
CHATTERS C.H.,NEW MUNICIPAL REVENUES FOR NEW MUNICIPAL EXPENDITURES (PAMPHLET). PLAN PRICE UTIL HABITAT...IDEA/COMP MUNICH 20. PAGE 23 F0457 — LOC/G BUDGET TAX

N19
DWYER J.W.,YARDSTICKS FOR PERFORMANCE (PAMPHLET). USA+45 FINAN CONTROL...CONCPT METH/COMP MUNICH. PAGE 35 F0688 — BUDGET LOC/G EFFICIENCY

N19
KRESSBACH T.W.,HE MICHIGAN CITY MANAGER IN BUDGETARY PROCEEDINGS (PAMPHLET). USA+45 PROVS DELIB/GP GP/REL SUPEGO...POLICY MUNICH. PAGE 73 F1438 — LOC/G BUDGET FINAN

N19
PEGRUM D.F.,URBAN TRANSPORT AND THE LOCATION OF INDUSTRY IN METROPOLITAN LOS ANGELES (PAMPHLET). USA+45 WORKER...GEOG CHARTS MUNICH. PAGE 104 F2049 — DIST/IND REGION INDUS

N19
STUTZ R.L.,COLLECTIVE DEALING BY UNITS OF LOCAL GOVERNMENT IN CONNECTICUT (PAMPHLET). USA+45 LOC/G PROVS...STAT MUNICH 20 CONNECTICT. PAGE 127 F2508 — VOL/ASSN LABOR WORKER

B27
WEBER M.,GENERAL ECONOMIC HISTORY. CHRIST-17C MOD/EUR STRUCT AGRI EXTR/IND FINAN INDUS MARKET FAM NAT/G PROF/ORG SECT ECO/TAC MUNICH 8/20. PAGE 144 F2839 — ECO/DEV CAP/ISM

B37
COLE W.E.,RECENT TRENDS IN RURAL PLANNING. USA-45 LAW ECO/DEV LOC/G SECT EDU/PROP CRIME LEISURE AGE/Y HABITAT...SOC/WK MUNICH 20. PAGE 26 F0503 — AGRI NEIGH PLAN ACT/RES

B48
HOOVER E.M.,THE LOCATION OF ECONOMIC ACTIVITY. WOR+45 MARKET WORKER PROB/SOLV INT/TRADE ADMIN COST ...POLICY CHARTS T MUNICH 20. PAGE 62 F1211 — HABITAT INDUS ECO/TAC GEOG

S49
HART C.W.M.,"INDUSTRIAL RELATIONS RESEARCH AND SOCIAL THEORY." CANADA VOL/ASSN WORKER LEAD EFFICIENCY...MGT SOC METH/CNCPT METH/COMP MUNICH 20. PAGE 56 F1099 — GEN/LAWS LABOR GP/REL

S51
HAWLEY A.H.,"METROPOLITAN POPULATION AND MUNICIPAL GOVERNMENT EXPENDITURES IN CENTRAL CITIES" (BMR)" USA+45 FINAN TAX...STAT CON/ANAL CHARTS MUNICH 20. PAGE 57 F1117 — GEOG LOC/G COST BUDGET

S54
FORM W.H.,"THE PLACE OF SOCIAL STRUCTURE IN THE DETERMINATION OF LAND USE: SOME IMPLICATIONS FOR A THEORY OF URBAN ECOLOGY" (BMR)" STRUCT...GEOG — HABITAT MARKET ORD/FREE

PHIL/SCI SOC MUNICH 20. PAGE 42 F0827

B55
GOMES F.A.,OPERACAO MUNICIPIO. BRAZIL L/A+17C SERV/IND LOC/G BUDGET ECO/TAC COST DEMAND...POLICY MUNICH 20. PAGE 48 F0944 ECO/UNDEV FEDERAL GOV/REL

B55
US ADVISORY COMN INTERGOV REL,THE COMMISSION ON INTERGOVERNMENTAL RELATIONS; A REPORT TO THE PRESIDENT FOR TRANSMITTAL TO THE CONGRESS. USA+45 ECO/DEV AGRI COM/IND FINAN FORCES PLAN EDU/PROP HEALTH WEALTH...STAT MUNICH 20 CIV/DEFENS. PAGE 133 F2630 GOV/REL NAT/G LOC/G PROVS

S56
MARGOLIS J.,"ON MUNICIPAL LAND POLICY FOR FISCAL GAINS." USA+45 PLAN TAX COST EFFICIENCY HABITAT KNOWL...MGT MUNICH 20. PAGE 85 F1667 BUDGET POLICY GEOG LOC/G

C56
MCKEE J.B.,"THE POWER TO DECIDE" IN M. WEINBERG AND O. SHABET, SOCIETY AND MAN." ELITES STRATA REPRESENT GP/REL ATTIT PWR MUNICH BUSINESS. PAGE 88 F1731 LABOR DECISION LEAD

B57
BOUSTEDT O.,REGIONALE STRUKTUR- UND WIRTSCHAFTSFORSCHUNG. WOR+45 WOR-45 PROVS...STAT MUNICH. PAGE 17 F0325 GEOG CONCPT NAT/COMP

B57
DRUCKER P.F.,AMERICA'S NEXT TWENTY YEARS. USA+45 DIST/IND ACADEM SCHOOL DIPLOM ECO/TAC AUTOMAT HABITAT HEALTH...SOC/WK TREND MUNICH 20 URBAN/RNWL PUB/TRANS. PAGE 34 F0667 WORKER FOR/AID CENSUS GEOG

S57
VERNON R.,"PRODUCTION AND DISTRIBUTION IN THE LARGE METROPOLIS" (BMR)" USA+45 PROC/MFG ECO/TAC HABITAT ...CENSUS TREND MUNICH 20. PAGE 141 F2779 PRODUC DIST/IND PROB/SOLV

N57
U WISCONSIN BUREAU OF GOVT,SERVICE SALES OF THE CITY OF MADISON TO METROPOLITAN COMMUNITIES AND NONRESIDENTS (PAMPHLET). DIST/IND LOC/G ADMIN ...DECISION GOV/COMP MUNICH. PAGE 132 F2597 REGION ECO/TAC PLAN

B58
CLAUNCH J.M.,THE PROBLEM OF GOVERNMENT IN METROPOLITAN AREAS. CULTURE INDUS POL/PAR PLAN REGION GP/REL...CENSUS ANTHOL MUNICH 20. PAGE 25 F0486 PROB/SOLV SOC

B58
DAVIS E.H.,OF THE PEOPLE, BY THE PEOPLE, FOR THE PEOPLE. INCOME WEALTH...METH/COMP MUNICH 20. PAGE 30 F0587 FINAN LOC/G TAX

B58
INDIAN INST OF PUBLIC ADMIN,IMPROVING CITY GOVERNMENT. INDIA ECO/UNDEV PLAN BUDGET PARTIC GP/REL MUNICH 20. PAGE 64 F1263 LOC/G PROB/SOLV ADMIN

B58
NICULESCU B.,COLONIAL PLANNING: A COMPARATIVE STUDY. AFR AGRI LOC/G NAT/G DELIB/GP COLONIAL MUNICH 20. PAGE 98 F1927 PLAN ECO/UNDEV TEC/DEV NAT/COMP

L58
TRAGER F.N.,"A SELECTED AND ANNOTATED BIBLIOGRAPHY ON ECONOMIC DEVELOPMENT, 1953-1957." WOR+45 AGRI FINAN INDUS MARKET LABOR WORKER PLAN INT/TRADE PRODUC...CENSUS MUNICH. PAGE 131 F2583 BIBLIOG/A ECO/UNDEV ECO/DEV

S58
LANE F.C.,"ECONOMIC CONSEQUENCES OF ORGANIZED VIOLENCE." FUT WOR+45 WOR-45 ECO/DEV DIST/IND SERV/IND NAT/G PROVS EX/STRUC CHOOSE ORD/FREE PWR ...TIME/SEQ GEN/LAWS MUNICH 20. PAGE 75 F1472 WEALTH COERCE

B59
MAYER H.M.,READINGS IN URBAN GEOGRAPHY. WOR+45 SOCIETY DIST/IND INDUS MARKET HABITAT...CLASSIF CENSUS CHARTS ANTHOL MUNICH 20 WATER. PAGE 87 F1706 GEOG STRUCT

B59
NORTON P.L.,URBAN PROBLEMS AND TECHNIQUES. AIR AGRI INDUS MARKET TEC/DEV BUDGET LEISURE ALL/VALS ...ANTHOL MUNICH 20 URBAN/RNWL. PAGE 99 F1936 PLAN LOC/G HABITAT

B59
WIBBERLEY G.P.,AGRICULTURE AND URBAN GROWTH. UK USA+45 ECO/DEV FINAN PROB/SOLV INT/TRADE COST ...GEOG STAT CHARTS METH/COMP HYPO/EXP METH MUNICH 20. PAGE 146 F2876 AGRI PLAN

B60
ILLINOIS U BUR COMMUNITY PLAN,PROCEEDINGS OF ILLINOIS STATEWIDE PLANNING CONFERENCE 1960. USA+45 FINAN LOC/G ACT/RES LEAD GOV/REL GP/REL WEALTH MUNICH 20 ILLINOIS. PAGE 64 F1260 PLAN DELIB/GP VOL/ASSN

B60
PENNSYLVANIA ECONOMY LEAGUE,URBAN RENEWAL IMPACT STUDY: ADMINISTRATIVE-LEGAL-FISCAL. USA+45 FINAN LOC/G NEIGH ADMIN EFFICIENCY...CENSUS CHARTS MUNICH 20 PENNSYLVAN. PAGE 105 F2059 PLAN BUDGET ADJUD

B60
PFOUTS R.W.,THE TECHNIQUES OF URBAN ECONOMIC ANALYSIS. USA+45...ECOMETRIC CONCPT CHARTS IDEA/COMP ANTHOL MUNICH 20. PAGE 106 F2078 METH ECO/DEV METH/COMP

B60
POOLEY B.J.,THE EVOLUTION OF BRITISH PLANNING LEGISLATION. UK ECO/DEV LOC/G CONSULT DELIB/GP ADMIN MUNICH 20 URBAN/RNWL. PAGE 107 F2104 PLAN LEGIS PROB/SOLV

B60
RAMA C.M.,LAS CLASES SOCIALES EN EL URUGUAY. L/A+17C URUGUAY ELITES SOCIETY STRATA INDUS ATTIT HABITAT PWR...GEOG SOC/INTEG MUNICH 20. PAGE 109 F2138 ECO/UNDEV STRUCT PARTIC

B60
SHANNON D.A.,THE GREAT DEPRESSION. USA-45 FINAN LG/CO SCHOOL SML/CO DELIB/GP RECEIVE REV EATING INCOME...ANTHOL MUNICH 20 ROOSEVLT/F CONGRESS. PAGE 120 F2365 WEALTH NAT/G AGRI INDUS

B60
US SENATE COMM ON COMMERCE,URBAN MASS TRANSPORTATION. FUT USA+45 AIR ECO/DEV FINAN LOC/G LEGIS CREATE PROB/SOLV TEC/DEV MUNICH 20 PUB/TRANS. PAGE 139 F2732 DIST/IND PLAN NAT/G LAW

B60
VERNON R.,METROPOLIS 1985. LOC/G PLAN TAX LEAD PWR MUNICH. PAGE 141 F2780 REGION ECO/TAC DECISION

C60
HOSELITZ B.,"THE ROLE OF CITIES IN THE ECONOMIC GROWTH OF UNDERDEVELOPED COUNTRIES" IN "SOCIOLOGICAL ASPECTS OF ECONOMIC GROWTH"(BMR). CULTURE LOC/G ACT/RES...SOC IDEA/COMP METH/COMP METH MUNICH IND 14/20 REDFIELD/R. PAGE 62 F1218 METH/CNCPT TEC/DEV ECO/UNDEV

N60
COMMITTEE ECONOMIC DEVELOPMENT,GUIDING METROPOLITAN GROWTH (PAMPHLET). USA+45 LOC/G NAT/G PROF/ORG ACT/RES PLAN...SOC/WK MUNICH. PAGE 27 F0517 GEOG INDUS HEALTH

B61
MEXICO; CINCUENTA ANOS DE REVOLUCION VOL. II. L/A+17C SOCIETY LABOR RECEIVE GP/REL AGE/Y HEALTH ...SOC/WK ANTHOL MUNICH 20 MEXIC/AMER. PAGE 1 F0014 ECO/UNDEV STRUCT INDUS POL/PAR

B61
BEASLEY K.E.,STATE SUPERVISION OF MUNICIPAL DEBT IN KANSAS - A CASE STUDY. USA+45 USA-45 FINAN PROVS BUDGET TAX ADJUD ADMIN CONTROL SUPEGO MUNICH. PAGE 12 F0224 LOC/G LEGIS JURID

B61
DOIG J.W.,THE POLITICS OF METROPOLITAN TRANSPORTATION. DELIB/GP WORKER DIPLOM TASK EFFICIENCY UTIL...CHARTS BIBLIOG MUNICH 20 NEW/YORK NEW/JERSEY PUB/TRANS RAILROAD. PAGE 34 F0652 PROB/SOLV STRATA DIST/IND

B61
INTL UNION LOCAL AUTHORITIES,METROPOLIS. WOR+45 DIST/IND FINAN GIVE EDU/PROP CRIME COST HEALTH WEALTH MUNICH 20. PAGE 65 F1286 GOV/COMP LOC/G BIBLIOG

B61
LEE R.R.,ENGINEERING-ECONOMIC PLANNING MISCELLANEOUS SUBJECTS: A SELECTED BIBLIOGRAPHY (MIMEOGRAPHED). FINAN LOC/G NEIGH ADMIN CONTROL INGP/REL HABITAT...GEOG MGT SOC/WK MUNICH 20 RESOURCE/N. PAGE 77 F1509 BIBLIOG/A PLAN REGION

B61
LENSKI G.,THE RELIGIOUS FACTOR: A SOCIOLOGICAL STUDY OF RELIGION'S IMPACT ON POLITICS, ECONOMICS, AND FAMILY LIFE. FAM PROF/ORG EDU/PROP ROLE CATHISM ...INT SAMP MUNICH. PAGE 78 F1524 SECT GP/REL

B61
LETHBRIDGE H.J.,CHINA'S URBAN COMMUNES. CHINA/COM FUT ECO/UNDEV DIPLOM EDU/PROP DEMAND INCOME MARXISM ...POLICY MUNICH 20. PAGE 78 F1534 CONTROL ECO/TAC NAT/G

B61
MARX K.,THE COMMUNIST MANIFESTO. IN (MENDEL A. ESSENTIAL WORKS OF MARXISM, NEW YORK: BANTAM. FUT MOD/EUR CULTURE ECO/DEV ECO/UNDEV AGRI FINAN INDUS MARKET PROC/MFG LABOR POL/PAR CONSULT FORCES CREATE PLAN ADMIN ATTIT DRIVE RIGID/FLEX ORD/FREE PWR RESPECT MARX/KARL MUNICH WORK. PAGE 86 F1691 COM NEW/IDEA CAP/ISM REV

B61
NEW JERSEY LEGISLATURE-SENATE,PUBLIC HEARINGS BEFORE COMMITTEE ON REVISION AND AMENDMENT OF LAWS ON SENATE BILL NO. 8. USA+45 FINAN PROVS WORKER ACT/RES PLAN BUDGET TAX CRIME...IDEA/COMP MUNICH 20 NEW/JERSEY URBAN/RNWL. PAGE 98 F1919 LEGIS INDUS PROB/SOLV

B61
SACKS S.,FINANCING GOVERNMENT IN A METROPOLITAN GOVERNMENT. USA+45 ECO/DEV R+D LOC/G GOV/REL ...BIBLIOG MUNICH 20 CLEVELAND. PAGE 115 F2269 FINAN PLAN BUDGET

B61
UNIVS-NATL BUR COMM ECO RES,PUBLIC FINANCES: NEEDS, SOURCES, AND UTILIZATION. USA+45 FORCES PLAN TAX CONFER PRICE FEDERAL UTIL...ANTHOL MUNICH 20. PAGE 133 F2623 NAT/G FINAN DECISION BUDGET

L61
GERWIG R.,"PUBLIC AUTHORITIES IN THE UNITED STATES." LAW CONSTN PROVS TAX ADMIN FEDERAL MUNICH. PAGE 47 F0920 LOC/G GOV/REL PWR

S61
ANDREWS R.B.,"URBAN ECONOMICS: AN APPRAISAL OF PROGRESS." LOC/G PROB/SOLV TEC/DEV...CONCPT PHIL/SCI ECOMETRIC

OBS/ENVIR METH/COMP HYPO/EXP SOC/EXP SIMUL GEN/METH METH MUNICH 20. PAGE 5 F0102

N61
US ADVISORY COMN INTERGOV REL,STATE CONSTITUTIONAL AND STATUTORY RESTRICTIONS ON LOCAL GOVERNMENT DEBT (PAMPHLET). LAW CONSTN CHOOSE PWR...DECISION MUNICH. PAGE 133 F2631
TAX PROVS GOV/REL

B62
CHAPIN F.S.,URBAN GROWTH DYNAMICS IN A REGIONAL CLUSTER OF CITIES. TEC/DEV ECO/TAC HABITAT...GEOG SOC MUNICH. PAGE 23 F0453
REGION PLAN

B62
HOOVER E.M.,ANATOMY OF A METROPOLIS. FUT USA+45 SOCIETY ECO/DEV DIST/IND INDUS WORKER ECO/TAC TAX GP/REL COST WEALTH MUNICH 20 NEWYORK/C. PAGE 62 F1212
ROUTINE TREND INCOME

B62
LICHFIELD N.,COST-BENEFIT ANALYSIS IN URBAN REDEVELOPMENT. CONSTRUC LOC/G NEIGH ACT/RES PROB/SOLV TEC/DEV BUDGET TAX...DECISION STAT CHARTS SOC/EXP MUNICH 20. PAGE 80 F1558
PLAN COST GOV/REL

B62
MOWITZ R.J.,PROFILE OF A METROPOLIS: A CASE BOOK. COM/IND CONSTRUC INDUS PUB/INST PLAN TEC/DEV LEAD GP/REL...POLICY TECHNIC WELF/ST MUNICH. PAGE 94 F1851
DECISION ADMIN

B62
SCHALLER H.G.,PUBLIC EXPENDITURE DECISIONS IN THE URBAN COMMUNITY: PREPARED FOR RESOURCES FOR THE FUTURE, INC. INDUS SERV/IND LOC/G PUB/INST PLAN PROB/SOLV BUDGET DEMAND PRODUC...CHARTS MUNICH. PAGE 116 F2289
FINAN DECISION

B63
BARBOUR V.,CAPITALISM IN AMSTERDAM IN THE 17TH CENTURY. NETHERLAND FINAN ECO/TAC...METH/COMP BIBLIOG MUNICH 16. PAGE 10 F0185
CAP/ISM INT/TRADE MARKET WEALTH

B63
GAMBLE S.D.,NORTH CHINA VILLAGES: SOCIAL, POLITICAL, AND ECONOMIC ACTIVITIES BEFORE 1933. ASIA CULTURE STRUCT FAM DOMIN EDU/PROP MUNICH WORSHIP 20. PAGE 46 F0891
AGRI LEAD FINAN

B63
GEERTZ C.,PEDDLERS AND PRINCES: SOCIAL DEVELOPMENT AND ECONOMIC CHANGE IN TWO INDONESIAN TOWNS. S/ASIA CULTURE SOCIETY STRATA FACE/GP CREATE TEC/DEV ECO/TAC ORD/FREE WEALTH...OBS INT CENSUS CHARTS WORK TOT/POP METH/GP TERR/GP VAL/FREE 20 MUNICH. PAGE 47 F0913
ECO/UNDEV SOC ELITES INDONESIA

B63
GRIGSBY W.G.,HOUSING MARKETS AND PUBLIC POLICY. USA+45 FAM NEIGH PRICE DEMAND WEALTH...POLICY CHARTS BIBLIOG METH MUNICH 20. PAGE 51 F1002
MARKET RENT HABITAT PLAN

B63
LAIRD R.D.,SOVIET AGRICULTURAL AND PEASANT AFFAIRS. FUT STRATA LOC/G DELIB/GP ACT/RES TEC/DEV ECO/TAC EDU/PROP ATTIT RIGID/FLEX ORD/FREE SKILL WEALTH ...STAT CON/ANAL ANTHOL MUNICH WORK VAL/FREE 20. PAGE 74 F1461
COM AGRI POLICY

B63
MILLER W.,REVENUE-COST RATIOS OF RURAL TOWNSHIPS WITH CHANGING LAND USES. USA+45 INDUS SERV/IND PROVS GP/REL HABITAT...CHARTS GP/COMP MUNICH 20 NEW/JERSEY. PAGE 91 F1792
TAX COST AGRI

B63
US ADVISORY COMN INTERGOV REL,PERFORMANCE OF URBAN FUNCTIONS: LOCAL AND AREAWIDE. TEC/DEV PARTIC REPRESENT PWR...DECISION GOV/COMP MUNICH. PAGE 133 F2633
REGION LOC/G ECO/TAC

B63
US HOUSE,URBAN RENEWAL: HOUSE COMMITTEE ON BANKING AND CURRENCY. USA+45 FINAN LOC/G NAT/G NEIGH DELIB/GP TEC/DEV BUDGET GOV/REL COST...CHARTS MUNICH 20 CONGRESS URBAN/RNWL. PAGE 136 F2684
PLAN PROB/SOLV LEGIS

S63
ANDREWS R.B.,"ECONOMIC PLANNING FOR SMALL AREAS: THE PLANNING PROCESS." INDUS PROC/MFG PROVS PROB/SOLV TAX EQUILIB...METH/COMP HYPO/EXP METH MUNICH 20. PAGE 5 F0103
ECO/TAC PLAN LOC/G

S63
LOEWENSTEIN L.K.,"THE LOCATION OF URBAN LAND USES." USA+45 LOC/G HABITAT...STAT CHARTS MUNICH 20. PAGE 81 F1595
GEOG PLAN INDUS

S63
STEFANIAK N.J.,"A REFINEMENT OF HAIG'S THEORY." USA+45 INDUS PROB/SOLV TEC/DEV...CONCPT CHARTS MUNICH 20 HAIG. PAGE 125 F2474
GEOG GEN/LAWS PLAN

N63
NORTH CAROLINA U INST GOVT,COSTING URBAN DEVELOPMENT AND REDEVELOPMENT (PAMPHLET). USA+45 USA-45 NEIGH PLAN TEC/DEV TAX OWN...GEOG MUNICH 20. PAGE 98 F1934
BIBLIOG COST FINAN

B64
CHINITZ B.,CITY AND SUBURB: THE ECONOMICS OF METROPOLITAN GROWTH. DIST/IND BUDGET GOV/REL DEMAND ATTIT HABITAT MUNICH PHILADELPH. PAGE 24 F0467
TEC/DEV PLAN

B64
COMMITTEE ECONOMIC DEVELOPMENT,COMMUNITY ECONOMIC DEVELOPMENT PROGRAMS. USA+45 FINAN INDUS LG/CO PROF/ORG CREATE GP/REL MUNICH NEW/YORK VERMONT PENNSYLVAN IN ARKANSAS. PAGE 27 F0519
LOC/G LABOR PLAN

B64
FITCH L.C.,URBAN TRANSPORTATION AND PUBLIC POLICY. FINAN NAT/G LEGIS PROB/SOLV TEC/DEV PRICE COST EFFICIENCY...DECISION STAT CHARTS METH/COMP MUNICH 20 NEWYORK/C PHILADELPH LOS/ANG CHICAGO WASHING/DC. PAGE 41 F0806
DIST/IND PLAN LOC/G

B64
FRIEDEN B.J.,THE FUTURE OF OLD NEIGHBORHOODS: REBUILDING FOR A CHANGING POPULATION. CONSTRUC LOC/G NAT/G ACT/RES ECO/TAC REGION ATTIT...INT SAMP MUNICH 20 NEWYORK/C LOS/ANG HARTFORD URBAN/RNWL. PAGE 44 F0855
NEIGH PROB/SOLV PLAN BUDGET

B64
FRIEDMANN J.,REGIONAL DEVELOPMENT AND PLANNING: A READER. AGRI MARKET NAT/G ECO/TAC INCOME...GEOG STAT CENSUS CHARTS ANTHOL BIBLIOG MUNICH 20 OPEN/SPACE. PAGE 44 F0863
PLAN REGION INDUS ECO/DEV

B64
GARFIELD PJ LOVEJOY WF,PUBLIC UTILITY ECONOMICS. DIST/IND FINAN MARKET ADMIN COST DEMAND ...TECHNIC JURID MUNICH 20 MONOPOLY. PAGE 46 F0906
T ECO/TAC OWN SERV/IND

B64
GREBLER L.,URBAN RENEWAL IN EUROPEAN COUNTRIES: ITS EMERGENCE AND POTENTIALS. EUR+WWI UK ECO/DEV LOC/G NEIGH CREATE ADMIN ATTIT...TREND NAT/COMP MUNICH 20 URBAN/RNWL. PAGE 50 F0981
PLAN CONSTRUC NAT/G

B64
HAAR C.M.,LAW AND LAND: ANGLO-AMERICAN PLANNING PRACTICE. UK USA+45 NAT/G TEC/DEV BUDGET CT/SYS INGP/REL EFFICIENCY OWN...JURID MUNICH 20. PAGE 52 F1019
LAW PLAN NAT/COMP

B64
LANG A.S.,URBAN RAIL TRANSIT. OP/RES PLAN PROB/SOLV TEC/DEV AUTOMAT COST...TECHNIC MATH CON/ANAL CHARTS METH/COMP SIMUL MUNICH 20 RAILROAD PUB/TRANS. PAGE 75 F1474
DIST/IND ECOMETRIC

B64
NEHEMKIS P.,LATIN AMERICA: MYTH AND REALITY. INDUS INT/ORG PROB/SOLV CAP/ISM DIPLOM REV...SOC MUNICH 20. PAGE 97 F1907
REGION MYTH L/A+17C ECO/UNDEV

B64
RESOURCES FOR THE FUTURE,URBAN AND REGIONAL STUDIES AT US UNIVERSITIES; A REPORT BASED ON A 1963 SURVEY OF URBAN AND REGIONAL RESEARCH. USA+45 SOCIETY CONSTRUC DIST/IND ACADEM NAT/G ACT/RES ECO/TAC ...CENSUS IDEA/COMP MUNICH. PAGE 111 F2179
BIBLIOG/A REGION PLAN

B64
TAEUBER I.B.,POPULATION TRENDS IN THE UNITED STATES: 1900 TO 1960. USA+45 USA-45 PROVS INCOME AGE...SOC TIME/SEQ TREND CHARTS MUNICH TIME 20 NEGRO. PAGE 128 F2522
CENSUS GEOG STRATA STRUCT

B64
TAX S.,EL CAPITALISMO DEL CENTAVO; UNA ECONOMIA INDIGENA DE GUATEMALA (2 VOLS.). GUATEMALA L/A+17C SOCIETY GP/REL DEMAND INCOME HABITAT...SOC MUNICH 20 INDIAN/AM. PAGE 129 F2539
ECO/UNDEV AGRI WEALTH COST

S64
CLELLAND D.A.,"ECONOMIC DOMINANTS AND COMMUNITY POWER: A COMPARATIVE ANALYSIS." ELITES ADJUST ATTIT WEALTH...DECISION MUNICH. PAGE 25 F0488
LEAD MGT PWR

S64
STONE P.A.,"DECISION TECHNIQUES FOR TOWN DEVELOPMENT." PLAN COST PROFIT...DECISION MGT CON/ANAL CHARTS METH/COMP BIBLIOG MUNICH 20. PAGE 127 F2497
OP/RES ADMIN PROB/SOLV

B65
ACHTERBERG E.,BERLINER HOCHFINANZ - KAISER, FURSTEN, MILLIONARE UM 1900. GERMANY NAT/G EDU/PROP PERSON...MGT MUNICH 19/20. PAGE 2 F0033
FINAN BIOG ECO/TAC

B65
ARTEL R.,THE STRUCTURE OF THE STOCKHOLM ECONOMY. SWEDEN DIST/IND LABOR LOC/G TEC/DEV DEMAND MUNICH LOUISIANA 20. PAGE 7 F0125
ECO/DEV METH/COMP BAL/PAY

B65
BEYER G.H.,HOUSING AND SOCIETY. USA+45 ECO/DEV FAM NAT/G PLAN RENT...CHARTS BIBLIOG MUNICH 20. PAGE 14 F0275
HABITAT AGE/O CONSTRUC

B65
BOLLENS J.C.,THE METROPOLIS: ITS PEOPLE, POLITICS, AND ECONOMIC LIFE. USA+45 PLAN PROB/SOLV PERS/REL PWR...DECISION GEOG CENSUS TREND CON/ANAL MUNICH 20 NEWYORK/C LOS/ANG SAN/FRAN CHICAGO PHILADELPH. PAGE 16 F0309
HABITAT SOC LOC/G

B65
DANIELSON M.N.,FEDERAL-METROPOLITAN POLITICS AND THE COMMUTER CRISIS. PROVS LEGIS EXEC LEAD PWR ...DECISION MUNICH. PAGE 30 F0580
FEDERAL GOV/REL DIST/IND

B65
DELHI INSTITUTE OF ECO GROWTH,A STUDY IN THE WORKING OF THE INTENSIVE AREA SCHEME OF THE KHADI AND VILLAGE INDUSTRIES COMMISSION. INDIA AGRI FINAN DELIB/GP ECO/TAC EFFICIENCY...QU CHARTS MUNICH 20. PAGE 32 F0614
PLAN INDUS ECO/UNDEV

B65
DUGGAR G.S.,RENEWAL OF TOWN AND VILLAGE I: A WORLD-WIDE SURVEY OF LOCAL GOVERNMENT EXPERIENCE. WOR+45 CONSTRUC INDUS CREATE BUDGET REGION GOV/REL...QU NAT/COMP MUNICH 20 URBAN/RNWL. PAGE 35 F0673
NEIGH PLAN ADMIN

B65
FRYE R.J.,HOUSING AND URBAN RENEWAL IN ALABAMA. USA+45 NEIGH LEGIS BUDGET ADJUD ADMIN PARTIC...MGT MUNICH 20 ALABAMA URBAN/RNWL. PAGE 45 F0871
PROB/SOLV PLAN GOV/REL

B65
GOODSELL C.T.,ADMINISTRATION OF A REVOLUTION. PUERT/RICO ECO/UNDEV FINAN POL/PAR PROVS LEGIS PLAN BUDGET RECEIVE ADMIN COLONIAL LEAD MUNICH 20 ROOSEVLT/F. PAGE 49 F0951
EXEC SOC

B65
GREEN J.L.,METROPOLITAN ECONOMIC REPUBLICS. USA+45 ECO/TAC INCOME...GEOG SOC CONCPT SIMUL MUNICH 20 ATLANTA. PAGE 50 F0985
SOC/WK PLAN LABOR

B65
GREER S.,URBAN RENEWAL AND AMERICAN CITIES: THE DILEMMA OF DEMOCRATIC INTERVENTION. USA+45 R+D LOC/G VOL/ASSN ACT/RES BUDGET ADMIN GOV/REL...SOC INT SAMP MUNICH 20 BOSTON CHICAGO LOS/ANG MIAMI URBAN/RNWL. PAGE 51 F0992
PROB/SOLV PLAN NAT/G

B65
HAUSER P.M.,THE STUDY OF URBANIZATION. S/ASIA ECO/DEV ECO/UNDEV NEIGH ACT/RES...GEOG MUNICH. PAGE 57 F1115
CULTURE SOC

B65
HERRICK B.H.,URBAN MIGRATION AND ECONOMIC DEVELOPMENT IN CHILE. CHILE AGRI INDUS LABOR NAT/G CENTRAL PRODUC...STAT SAMP CHARTS BIBLIOG/A MUNICH 20 MIGRATION. PAGE 59 F1156
HABITAT GEOG ECO/UNDEV

B65
MAO J.C.T.,EFFICIENCY IN PUBLIC URBAN RENEWAL EXPENDITURES THROUGH CAPITAL BUDGETING. USA+45 FINAN LOC/G NAT/G NEIGH REGION UTIL...GEOG METH/CNCPT STAT SIMUL GEN/LAWS MUNICH 20 URBAN/RNWL. PAGE 85 F1662
TEC/DEV BUDGET PROB/SOLV

B65
MARGOLIS J.,THE PUBLIC ECONOMY OF URBAN COMMUNITIES. USA+45 LEGIS PROB/SOLV TAX LOBBY CHOOSE ATTIT MUNICH. PAGE 85 F1668
LOC/G DECISION FINAN

B65
MORTON H.C.,BROOKINGS PAPERS ON PUBLIC POLICY. USA+45 WOR+45 INDUS ACADEM INT/ORG LOC/G PROVS EDU/PROP MUNICH. PAGE 94 F1840
FINAN ECO/DEV TOP/EX NAT/G

B65
RIVKIN M.D.,AREA DEVELOPMENT FOR NATIONAL GROWTH; THE TURKISH PRECEDENT. ISLAM TURKEY ACT/RES INGP/REL...POLICY CHARTS GP/COMP MUNICH 20 ATATURK/MK INONU/I. PAGE 112 F2197
ECO/UNDEV REGION ECO/TAC PLAN

B65
SIMMS R.P.,URBANIZATION IN WEST AFRICA; A REVIEW OF CURRENT LITERATURE. AFR PLAN TEC/DEV...SOC OBS NAT/COMP MUNICH 20. PAGE 122 F2405
BIBLIOG/A ECO/DEV ECO/UNDEV

B65
SMERK G.M.,URBAN TRANSPORTATION; THE FEDERAL ROLE. FUT USA+45 FINAN PROB/SOLV TEC/DEV AUTOMAT GOV/REL COST...STAT BIBLIOG MUNICH 20 PUB/TRANS. PAGE 123 F2426
PLAN DIST/IND NAT/G

B65
US ADVISORY COMN INTERGOV REL,METROPOLITAN SOCIAL AND ECONOMIC DISPARITIES: IMPLICATIONS FOR INTERGOVERNMENTAL RELATIONS IN CENT'L CITIES AND SUBURBS. CULTURE STRATA DIST/IND LOC/G PLAN GP/REL DISCRIM HABITAT MUNICH. PAGE 134 F2634
GOV/REL GEOG

B65
US OFFICE ECONOMIC OPPORTUNITY,CATALOG OF FEDERAL PROGRAMS FOR INDIVIDUAL AND COMMUNITY IMPROVEMENT. USA+45 GIVE RECEIVE ADMIN HEALTH KNOWL SKILL WEALTH ...CHARTS MUNICH. PAGE 138 F2721
BIBLIOG CLIENT ECO/TAC

B65
WILKINSON T.O.,THE URBANIZATION OF JAPANESE LABOR, 1868-1955. AGRI PROC/MFG CAP/ISM PRODUC PROFIT ...SOC CLASSIF CENSUS CHARTS MUNICH 19/20 CHINJAP. PAGE 146 F2887
LABOR INDUS GEOG

S65
BANOVETZ J.M.,"METROPOLITAN SUBSIDIES: AN APPRAISAL." LEAD GP/REL DISCRIM MUNICH. PAGE 9 F0175
REGION TAX GOV/REL

S65
BRIGHAM E.F.,"THE DETERMINANTS OF RESIDENTIAL LAND VALUES." USA+45 ECO/DEV PROB/SOLV RENT PRICE ...REGRESS STAT CHARTS GEN/METH MUNICH 20 LOS/ANG. PAGE 18 F0351
COST INDICATOR SIMUL ECOMETRIC

S65
KEE W.S.,"CENTRAL CITY EXPENDITURES AND METROPOLITAN AREAS." PLAN BUDGET ECO/TAC TAX GP/REL WEALTH...CHARTS MUNICH 20. PAGE 70 F1366
LOC/G GOV/COMP NEIGH

S65
VAN DER HORST S.T.,"THE ECONOMICS OF DECENTRALISATION OF INDUSTRY." SOUTH/AFR ECO/DEV LG/CO AUTOMAT DISCRIM...POLICY MUNICH 20. PAGE 140 F2761
PLAN INDUS CENTRAL TEC/DEV

B66
BALDWIN R.E.,ECONOMIC DEVELOPMENT AND EXPORT GROWTH: A STUDY OF NORTHERN RHODESIA, 1920-1960. AFR RHODESIA AGRI EXTR/IND FINAN MARKET LABOR WORKER ECO/TAC...CONCPT NEW/IDEA MUNICH 20. PAGE 9 F0166
ECO/UNDEV TEC/DEV INT/TRADE CAP/ISM

B66
BEQIRAJ M.,PEASANTRY IN REVOLUTION. STRATA ECO/UNDEV AGRI ROUTINE REV HABITAT RIGID/FLEX ...EPIST GEOG NEW/IDEA TREND MUNICH 20. PAGE 13 F0256
WORKER KNOWL NAT/LISM SOC

B66
DAVIES JC I.I.I.,NEIGHBORHOOD GROUPS AND URBAN RENEWAL. USA+45 PLAN LOBBY PARTIC CHOOSE RACE/REL ...POLICY DECISION SOC INT MUNICH SOC/INTEG 20 NEWYORK/C. PAGE 30 F0586
NEIGH CREATE PROB/SOLV

B66
DUNCAN O.,METROPOLIS AND REGION (PREPARED FOR RESOURCES FOR THE FUTURE INC., WASHINGTON, D.C.). FINAN INDUS ECO/TAC TAX...CHARTS GOV/COMP MUNICH. PAGE 35 F0677
REGION GEOG

B66
DUNCOMBE H.S.,COUNTY GOVERNMENT IN AMERICA. USA+45 FINAN ADMIN ROUTINE GOV/REL...GOV/COMP MUNICH 20. PAGE 35 F0678
LOC/G PROVS CT/SYS TOP/EX

B66
HACKETT J.,L'ECONOMIE BRITANNIQUE: PROBLEMES ET PERSPECTIVES. FRANCE UK LABOR NAT/G EX/STRUC PROB/SOLV BAL/PAY INCOME RIGID/FLEX...MGT PHIL/SCI CHARTS MUNICH 20. PAGE 53 F1027
ECO/DEV FINAN ECO/TAC PLAN

B66
HUNT C.L.,SOCIAL ASPECTS OF ECONOMIC DEVELOPMENT. S/ASIA AGRI FAM TEC/DEV RECEIVE EDU/PROP OWN...GEOG MUNICH 20. PAGE 63 F1243
SOC STRATA ATTIT ECO/UNDEV

B66
RAO Y.V.L.,COMMUNICATION AND DEVELOPMENT. INDIA S/ASIA SOCIETY ACT/RES EDU/PROP PARTIC ATTIT...SOC GP/COMP BIBLIOG MUNICH MUNICH 20. PAGE 109 F2149
COM/IND ECO/UNDEV OBS

B66
RAO Y.V.L.,COMMUNICATION AND DEVELOPMENT. INDIA S/ASIA SOCIETY ACT/RES EDU/PROP PARTIC ATTIT...SOC GP/COMP BIBLIOG MUNICH MUNICH 20. PAGE 109 F2149
COM/IND ECO/UNDEV OBS

B66
WILLIAMS G.,MERTHYR POLITICS: THE MAKING OF A WORKING-CLASS TRADITION. UK CHIEF WORKER LEAD SOCISM...ANTHOL MUNICH 19/20 MERTHYR RICHARD/H. PAGE 147 F2891
LOC/G POL/PAR INDUS

B66
WOODMAN H.D.,SLAVERY AND THE SOUTHERN ECONOMY: SOURCES AND READINGS. USA-45 CULTURE STRUCT AGRI ECO/TAC LEAD RACE/REL DISCRIM EFFICIENCY...CHARTS ANTHOL MUNICH 18/19 NEGRO SOUTH/US. PAGE 148 F2922
ECO/DEV STRATA WORKER UTIL

S66
VENTRE F.T.,"LOCAL INITIATIVES IN URBAN INDUSTRIAL DEVELOPMENT." FINAN SERV/IND TOP/EX PLAN BUDGET RENT TAX...GP/COMP MUNICH 20. PAGE 141 F2777
ECO/TAC LOC/G INDUS

S66
VERSLUYS J.D.N.,"SOME NOTES ON THE SOCIAL AND ECONOMIC EFFECTS OF RURAL ELECTRIFICATION IN BURMA" BURMA EDU/PROP PRODUC ORD/FREE...SOC QU MUNICH TIME 20. PAGE 141 F2782
TEC/DEV SOCIETY CREATE

N66
US ADVISORY COMN INTERGOV REL,CATALOGS AND OTHER INFORMATION SOURCES ON FEDERAL AND STATE AID PROGRAMS: A SECTED BIBLIOGRAPHY (PAPER). USA+45 LAW LOC/G NAT/G PROVS VOL/ASSN TEC/DEV ADMIN HEALTH ...WELF/ST SOC/WK MUNICH. PAGE 134 F2635
BIBLIOG/A GOV/REL FINAN ECO/DEV

B67
AARON H.J.,FINANCING URBAN DEVELOPMENT IN MEXICO CITY: A CASE STUDY OF PROPERTY TAX, LAND USE, HOUSING, AND URBAN PLANNING. LOC/G CREATE EFFICIENCY WEALTH...CHARTS MUNICH 20 MEXIC/AMER. PAGE 2 F0030
PLAN TAX PROB/SOLV

B67
BANFIELD E.C.,THE MORAL BASIS OF A BACKWARD SOCIETY. EUR+WWI ITALY STRATA NEIGH PARTIC INGP/REL ...SOC QU PREDICT TREND HYPO/EXP MUNICH 20. PAGE 9 F0173
MORAL WEALTH ATTIT

B67
BIRMINGHAM W.,A STUDY OF CONTEMPORARY GHANA VOL. I: SOME ASPECTS OF SOCIAL STRUCTURE. AFR GHANA AGRI FAM SECT PLAN EDU/PROP MARRIAGE OWN...POLICY STAT CHARTS MUNICH 20. PAGE 15 F0287
SOCIETY STRUCT CENSUS ECO/UNDEV

B67
BLAIR P.W.,THE MINISTATE DILEMMA. WOR+45 AGREE COLONIAL ORD/FREE...GEOG CHARTS MUNICH LEAGUE/NAT UN. PAGE 15 F0294
INT/ORG NAT/G CENSUS

B67
BREAK G.F.,INTERGOVERNMENTAL FISCAL RELATIONS IN THE UNITED STATES. USA+45 USA-45 DELIB/GP PLAN BUDGET TAX GOV/REL CENTRAL...TREND CHARTS MUNICH. PAGE 18 F0345
LOC/G NAT/G PROVS FINAN

B67
CHAPIN F.S. JR.,SELECTED REFERENCES ON URBAN PLANNING METHODS AND TECHNIQUES. USA+45 LAW ECO/DEV LOC/G NAT/G SCHOOL CONSULT CREATE PROB/SOLV TEC/DEV ...SOC/WK MUNICH. PAGE 23 F0454
BIBLIOG NEIGH PLAN

B67
DE TORRES J.,FINANCING LOCAL GOVERNMENT. USA+45 USA-45 NAT/G PROVS GIVE ADJUST PWR...TIME/SEQ CHARTS MUNICH 20. PAGE 31 F0606
LOC/G BUDGET TAX TREND

B67
ELDREDGE H.W.,TAMING MEGALOPOLIS; HOW TO MANAGE AN URBANIZED WORLD. WOR+45 SOCIETY ECO/DEV ECO/UNDEV NAT/G COMPUTER CREATE PARTIC EFFICIENCY WEALTH ...MGT ANTHOL MUNICH. PAGE 37 F0716
TEC/DEV PLAN PROB/SOLV

B67
ELDREDGE H.W.,TAMING MEGALOPOLIS; WHAT IT IS AND WHAT COULD BE (VOL. I). FUT USA+45 WOR+45 SOCIETY STRUCT ECO/DEV INDUS LEISURE WEALTH...ANTHOL MUNICH. PAGE 37 F0717
PROB/SOLV PLAN TEC/DEV

B67
EVANS R.H.,COEXISTENCE: COMMUNISM AND ITS PRACTICE IN BOLOGNA, 1945-1965. ITALY CAP/ISM ADMIN CHOOSE PEACE ORD/FREE...SOC STAT DEEP/INT SAMP CHARTS BIBLIOG MUNICH 20. PAGE 39 F0756
MARXISM CULTURE POL/PAR

B67
GITTELL M.,PARTICIPANTS AND PARTICIPATION: A STUDY OF SCHOOL POLICY IN NEW YORK. USA+45 EX/STRUC BUDGET PAY ATTIT...POLICY MUNICH 20 NEWYORK/C. PAGE 47 F0926
SCHOOL DECISION PARTIC ADMIN

B67
GUTKIND E.A.,URBAN DEVELOPMENT IN SOUTHERN EUROPE* SPAIN AND PORTUGAL. CHRIST-17C EUR+WWI MOD/EUR PORTUGAL SPAIN CULTURE AGRI...SOC SAMP/SIZ BIBLIOG MUNICH. PAGE 52 F1015
TEC/DEV ECO/DEV

B67
HODGKINSON R.G.,THE ORIGINS OF THE NATIONAL HEALTH SERVICE: THE MEDICAL SERVICES OF THE NEW POOR LAW, 1834-1871. UK INDUS WORKER PROB/SOLV EFFICIENCY ATTIT HEALTH WEALTH SOCISM...JURID SOC/WK MUNICH 19/20. PAGE 60 F1189
HEAL NAT/G POLICY LAW

B67
KULSKI J.E.,LAND OF URBAN PROMISE* CONTINUING THE GREAT TRADITION* A SEARCH FOR SIGNIFICANT URBAN SPACE IN URBANIZED NORTHEAST. USA+45 DIST/IND PUB/INST CONSULT CREATE TEC/DEV...SOC NEW/IDEA CHARTS BIBLIOG MUNICH. PAGE 74 F1448
PLAN PROB/SOLV ECO/DEV

B67
MARRIS P.,DILEMMAS OF SOCIAL REFORM: POVERTY AND COMMUNITY ACTION IN THE UNITED STATES. USA+45 NAT/G OP/RES ADMIN PARTIC EFFICIENCY WEALTH...SOC METH/COMP T MUNICH 20 REFORMERS. PAGE 85 F1674
STRUCT PROB/SOLV COST

B67
RIDKER R.G.,ECONOMIC COSTS OF AIR POLLUTION* STUDIES IN MEASUREMENT. R+D GP/REL KNOWL...OBS MUNICH 20. PAGE 111 F2190
OP/RES HABITAT PHIL/SCI

L67
GLAZER N.,"HOUSING PROBLEMS AND HOUSING POLICIES." USA+45 PLAN RENT ADJUST CONSEN DEMAND DISCRIM AGE ATTIT HEALTH WEALTH MUNICH NEGRO. PAGE 48 F0929
POLICY CONSTRUC CREATE HABITAT

L67
JOHNSTON J.D. JR.,"CONSTITUTION OF SUBDIVISION CONTROL EXACTIONS: THE QUEST FOR A RATIONALE." USA+45 PROVS PUB/INST ADJUD CT/SYS GP/REL MUNICH. PAGE 68 F1334
PLAN CONTROL LOC/G FORCES

L67
MIXON J.,"JANE JACOBS AND THE LAW - ZONING FOR DIVERSITY EXAMINED." FUT USA+45 CONSTN NEIGH PROB/SOLV CONTROL CT/SYS PARTIC ATTIT...POLICY CENSUS METH/COMP MUNICH. PAGE 92 F1810
IDEA/COMP PLAN LAW

L67
ZEIDBERG L.D.,"THE NASHVILLE AIR POLLUTION STUDY" (PARTS V-VII)" USA+45 PLAN AGE HEALTH...GEOG STAT CENSUS SAMP/SIZ CHARTS BIBLIOG MUNICH. PAGE 150 F2962
DEATH HABITAT AIR BIO/SOC

S67
FERGUSON D.E.,"DETERMINING CAPACITY FOR CAPITAL EXPENDITURES." USA+45 LOC/G BUDGET TAX ADMIN CONTROL...TREND MUNICH 20. PAGE 40 F0784
FINAN PAY COST

S67
FRIEDEN B.J.,"THE CHANGING PROSPECTS FOR SOCIAL PLANNING." USA+45 PROB/SOLV RACE/REL WEALTH ...SOC/WK PREDICT MUNICH 20 NEGRO. PAGE 44 F0856
PLAN LOC/G POLICY

S67
GAUSE M.E.,"ELEMENTS OF FINANCE DEPARTMENT ORGANIZATION FOR SMALL GOVERNMENTAL UNITS." USA+45 PROB/SOLV CONTROL CENTRAL...METH MUNICH. PAGE 47 F0910
ADMIN LOC/G FINAN

S67
HANCOCK J.L.,"PLANNERS IN THE CHANGING AMERICAN CITY, 1900-1940." USA-45 CONSTRUC NAT/G POL/PAR ...SOC/WK TREND MUNICH 20. PAGE 54 F1059
PLAN CONSULT LOC/G

S67
HILL L.W.,"FINANCING URBAN RENEWAL PROGRAMS." USA+45 ECO/DEV LOC/G EDU/PROP MUNICH 20. PAGE 60 F1171
FINAN NAT/G WEALTH

S67
LINEBERRY R.L.,"REFORMISM AND PUBLIC POLICIES IN AMERICAN CITIES." USA+45 POL/PAR EX/STRUC LEGIS BUDGET TAX GP/REL...STAT CHARTS MUNICH. PAGE 80 F1573
DECISION POLICY LOC/G

S67
MOONEY J.D.,"URBAN POVERTY AND LABOR FORCE PARTICIPATION." FAM DISCRIM...SOC/WK STAT CHARTS MUNICH. PAGE 93 F1820
INCOME WORKER WEALTH

S67
MYERS S.,"TECHNOLOGY AND URBAN TRANSIT: THE ENORMOUS POTENTIAL OF BUS AND RAIL SYSTEMS." USA+45 FINAN LOC/G WORKER PLAN PROB/SOLV PRICE AUTOMAT MUNICH 20. PAGE 96 F1877
R+D TEC/DEV DIST/IND ACT/RES

S67
PETRAS J.,"MINERS AND AGRARIAN RADICALISM." CHILE AGRI EXTR/IND WORKER CHOOSE ATTIT SOCISM MUNICH 20. PAGE 105 F2073
PARTIC EDU/PROP LABOR

S67
SCHWARZWELLER H.K.,"SOCIAL CLASS ORIGINS, RURAL-URBAN MIGRATION, AND ECONOMIC LIFE CHANGES." USA+45 SOCIETY STRUCT FAM NEIGH INCOME...SOC RECORD CHARTS MUNICH. PAGE 118 F2326
CLASSIF WEALTH AGRI

S67
SIDDIQ M.M.,"LOCAL GOVERNMENT IN PAKISTAN." PAKISTAN PROB/SOLV TAX COLONIAL GOV/REL MUNICH 20. PAGE 121 F2395
ADMIN LOC/G DELIB/GP BUDGET

S67
STEMPEL GH I.I.I.,"A NEW ANALYSIS OF MONOPOLY AND COMPETITION." USA+45 INDUS TV ATTIT MUNICH. PAGE 126 F2479
PRESS COM/IND GP/REL

S67
STILL J.F.,"THE FUTURE OF METROPOLITAN GOVERNMENT ORGANIZATION." USA+45 LOC/G BUDGET COST ATTIT MUNICH 20. PAGE 126 F2488
ADMIN FINAN CONTROL

S67
TELLER A.,"AIR-POLLUTION ABATEMENT: ECONOMIC RATIONALITY AND REALITY." NAT/G DELIB/GP ECO/TAC GOV/REL CENTRAL EFFICIENCY HEALTH...CHARTS METH MUNICH. PAGE 129 F2543
PROB/SOLV CONTROL COST AIR

S67
VAN KLAVEREN J.,"DIE WIRTSCHAFTLICHEN AUSWIRKUNGEN DES SCHWARZEN TODES" GERMANY PRICE DEMAND PRODUC MUNICH 14/15 DEPRESSION. PAGE 140 F2762
HEALTH AGRI GEOG

N67
NATIONAL COMN COMMUNITY HEALTH,ACTION - PLANNING FOR COMMUNITY HEALTH SERVICES (PAMPHLET). USA+45 PROF/ORG DELIB/GP BUDGET ROUTINE GP/REL ATTIT ...HEAL SOC SOC/WK CHARTS MUNICH TIME 20. PAGE 97 F1898
PLAN HEALTH ADJUST

N67
US HOUSE,MESSAGE FROM THE PRESIDENT OF THE UNITED STATES: URBAN AND RURAL POVERTY (PAMPHLET). USA+45 ACT/RES PLAN BUDGET RENT MUNICH 20 PRESIDENT. PAGE 136 F2685
NAT/G POLICY CREATE RECEIVE

B92
ENGELS F.,THE CONDITION OF THE WORKING-CLASS IN ENGLAND (1848). UK INDUS LABOR PRICE CONTROL COST INCOME HEALTH MARXISM MUNICH 19. PAGE 38 F0733
WORKER WEALTH MARXIST CAP/ISM

B96
SCHMOLLER G.,THE MERCANTILE SYSTEM AND ITS HISTORICAL SIGNIFICANCE: ILLUSTRATED CHIEFLY FROM PRUSSIAN HISTORY (TRANS.). PRUSSIA CULTURE INDUS KIN NAT/G PROVS OP/RES ECO/TAC INT/TRADE SUPEGO PWR WEALTH MUNICH 19 MERCANTLST. PAGE 117 F2302
GEN/METH INGP/REL CONCPT

B99
KROPOTKIN P.,FIELDS, FACTORIES, AND WORKSHOPS. UNIV INTELL ECO/DEV LG/CO SCHOOL SML/CO ECO/TAC PRODUC UTOPIA...NEW/IDEA MUNICH. PAGE 74 F1445
SOCIETY WORKER AGRI INDUS

MUNICIPALITIES....SEE MUNIC

MUNZI U. F1862

MURDER....MURDER, ASSASSINATION; SEE ALSO CRIME

B67
NKRUMAH K.,CHALLENGE OF THE CONGO. FORCES ECO/TAC FOR/AID REGION MURDER REPRESENT 20 CONGO/LEOP UN. PAGE 98 F1930
REV ECO/UNDEV ORD/FREE DIPLOM

MURDESHWAR A.K. F1863

MURNGIN....MURNGIN, AN AUSTRALIAN TRIBE

MURPHEY R. F1864

MURPHY G.G. F1865

MURPHY J.C. F1866,F1867

MURRAY/JC....JOHN COURTNEY MURRAY

MURTY B.S. F1868

MURUMBI J. F1869

MUSCAT....MUSCAT AND OMAN; SEE ALSO ISLAM

MUSGRAVE R.A. F1870

MUSHKIN S.J. F1871,F1872

MUSIC....MUSIC AND SONGS

MUSLIM....MUSLIM PEOPLE AND RELIGION

B60
AUSTRUY J.,STRUCTURE ECONOMIQUE ET CIVILISATION: L'EGYPTE ET LE DESTIN ECONOMIQUE DE L'ISLAM. ISLAM UAR CREATE OP/RES ECO/TAC...SOC BIBLIOG 20 MUSLIM. PAGE 8 F0142 — ECO/UNDEV CULTURE STRUCT

B66
RIZK C.,LE REGIME POLITIQUE LIBANAIS. ISLAM LEBANON STRUCT POL/PAR SECT LOBBY GP/REL 20 ARABS MUSLIM CHRISTIAN. PAGE 112 F2198 — ECO/UNDEV NAT/G CULTURE

MUSLIM/LG....MUSLIM LEAGUE

MUSOLF L.D. F1873,F1874

MUSSOLIN/B....BENITO MUSSOLINI

MUTTER C. F1128

MYERS C.A. F1073,F1075,F1876

MYERS S. F1877

MYRDAL G. F1875,F1879,F1880,F1881,F1882,F1883

MYRDAL/G....GUNNAR MYRDAL

MYSTIC....MYSTICAL

MYSTICISM....SEE MYSTISM

MYSTISM....MYSTICISM

MYTH....FICTION

B13
BEARD C.A.,AN ECONOMIC INTERPRETATION OF THE CONSTITUTION OF THE UNITED STATES. USA-45 AGRI INT/TRADE SUFF OWN ATTIT...CONCPT MYTH BIOG HIST/WRIT 18. PAGE 12 F0222 — CONSTN ECO/TAC CHOOSE

B15
JONES J.H.,THE ECONOMICS OF WAR AND CONQUEST. WOR-45 ECO/DEV NAT/G WEALTH...STAT TREND STERTYP GEN/LAWS TOT/POP 20. PAGE 68 F1338 — MYTH WAR

S21
MALINOWSKI B.,"THE PRIMITIVE ECONOMICS OF THE TROBRIAND ISLANDERS" (BMR)" CULTURE SOCIETY NAT/G CHIEF LEAD OWN...SOC MYTH WORSHIP 20 NEW/GUINEA TROBRIAND RESOURCE/N. PAGE 84 F1647 — ECO/UNDEV AGRI PRODUC STRUCT

B50
SOREL G.,REFLECTIONS ON VIOLENCE (1908) (TRANS. BY T.E. HULME AND J. ROTH). UNIV SOCIETY LABOR UTOPIA MORAL SOCISM...ANARCH SOCIALIST CONCPT 20. PAGE 124 F2445 — COERCE REV WORKER MYTH

S60
KREININ M.E.,"THE 'OUTER-SEVEN' AND EUROPEAN INTEGRATION." EUR+WWI FRANCE GERMANY ITALY UK ECO/DEV DIST/IND INT/TRADE DRIVE WEALTH...MYTH CHARTS EEC OEEC 20. PAGE 73 F1436 — ECO/TAC GEN/LAWS

S60
NEISSER H.,"ECONOMIC IMPERALISM RECONSIDERED." WOR+45 WOR-45 ECO/DEV ECO/UNDEV DIST/IND LEGIT COLONIAL PWR WEALTH SOCISM...MYTH MATH TIME/SEQ 20. PAGE 97 F1909 — ACT/RES ECO/TAC CAP/ISM INT/TRADE

B62
ARNOLD T.W.,THE FOLKLORE OF CAPITALISM. USA+45 USA-45 SOCIETY LG/CO SML/CO EX/STRUC ECO/TAC EDU/PROP ADJUST INCOME...MYTH CHARTS 20. PAGE 6 F0116 — CAP/ISM ATTIT STERTYP ECO/DEV

B62
ELLIOTT J.R.,THE APPEAL OF COMMUNISM IN THE UNDERDEVELOPED NATIONS. AFR USSR WOR+45 INT/ORG NAT/G DIPLOM DOMIN EDU/PROP ROUTINE ATTIT RIGID/FLEX ORD/FREE PWR WEALTH MARXISM...POLICY SOC METH/CNCPT MYTH TOT/POP METH/GP 20. PAGE 37 F0722 — COM ECO/UNDEV

S63
HOOVER C.B.,"ECONOMIC REFORM VERSUS ECONOMIC GROWTH IN UNDERDEVELOPED COUNTRIES." FUT WOR+45 ELITES STRATA ECO/UNDEV DIST/IND INDUS TEC/DEV CAP/ISM FOR/AID INT/TRADE ATTIT WEALTH...MYTH TREND STERTYP GEN/LAWS WORK 20. PAGE 61 F1209 — ECO/DEV ECO/TAC

S63
POLYANOV N.,"THE DOLLAR'S VENTURES IN EUROPE." EUR+WWI FRANCE USA+45 ECO/DEV MARKET POL/PAR TEC/DEV ECO/TAC EDU/PROP DRIVE PWR WEALTH...MARXIST MYTH STAT TREND EEC 20. PAGE 107 F2100 — FINAN PLAN BAL/PAY CAP/ISM

B64
CHEIT E.F.,THE BUSINESS ESTABLISHMENT. FRANCE WOR+45 PROF/ORG TOP/EX PROB/SOLV CAP/ISM ADMIN SUPEGO MORAL PWR...METH/CNCPT MYTH NEW/IDEA 20. PAGE 24 F0460 — PERSON EX/STRUC MGT INDUS

B64
NEHEMKIS P.,LATIN AMERICA: MYTH AND REALITY. INDUS INT/ORG PROB/SOLV CAP/ISM DIPLOM REV...SOC MUNICH 20. PAGE 97 F1907 — REGION MYTH L/A+17C ECO/UNDEV

B65
COLLOQUE SUR LA PLANIFICATION,LA PLANIFICATION COMME PROCESSUS DE DECISION. FRANCE SOCIETY MARKET LABOR LEGIS GP/REL EFFICIENCY INCOME ATTIT TECHRACY ...MYTH IDEA/COMP 20. PAGE 26 F0508 — PLAN ECO/TAC PROB/SOLV

S66
DUROSELLE J.B.,"THE FUTURE OF THE ATLANTIC COMMUNITY." EUR+WWI USA+45 USSR NAT/G CAP/ISM REGION DETER NUC/PWR ATTIT MARXISM...INT/LAW 20 NATO. PAGE 35 F0686 — FUT DIPLOM MYTH POLICY

B67
SCHON D.A.,TECHNOLOGY AND CHANGE* THE NEW HERACLITUS. TEC/DEV CONTROL COST DEMAND EFFICIENCY RIGID/FLEX...MYTH 20. PAGE 117 F2311 — INDUS PROB/SOLV R+D CREATE

N

NAACP....NATIONAL ASSOCIATION FOR THE ADVANCEMENT OF COLORED PEOPLE

B59
VOSE C.E.,CAUCASIANS ONLY: THE SUPREME COURT, THE NAACP, AND THE RESTRICTIVE COVENANT CASES. USA+45 LAW CONSTN LOBBY...SOC 20 NAACP SUPREME/CT NEGRO. PAGE 142 F2796 — CT/SYS RACE/REL DISCRIM

NABALOI....NABALOI TRIBE, PHILIPPINES

NADLER E.B. F1886

NAFTA....NORTH ATLANTIC FREE TRADE AREA

NAGEL P.C. F1887

NAM....NATIONAL ASSOCIATION OF MANUFACTURERS

S53
GABLE R.W.,"NAM: INFLUENTIAL LOBBY OR KISS OF DEATH?" (BMR)" USA+45 LAW INSPECT EDU/PROP ADMIN CONTROL INGP/REL EFFICIENCY PWR 20 CONGRESS NAM TAFT/HART. PAGE 45 F0880 — LOBBY LEGIS INDUS LG/CO

NAM/TIEN....NAM TIEN

NAMBOODIRIPAD E.M. F1888

NANES A. F1889

NANIWADA H. F1890

NAPOLEON/B....NAPOLEON BONAPARTE

B58
SHAW S.J.,THE FINANCIAL AND ADMINISTRATIVE ORGANIZATION AND DEVELOPMENT OF OTTOMAN EGYPT 1517-1798. UAR LOC/G FORCES BUDGET INT/TRADE TAX EATING INCOME WEALTH...CHARTS BIBLIOG 16/18 OTTOMAN NAPOLEON/B. PAGE 120 F2371 — FINAN ADMIN GOV/REL CULTURE

NARAIN D. F2148

NARASIMHAN V.K. F1891

NARAYAN/J....JAYPRAKASH NARAYAN

NARCO/ACT....UNIFORM NARCOTIC DRUG ACT

NARVER J.C. F1892

NASA....NATIONAL AERONAUTIC AND SPACE ADMINISTRATION

N67
US HOUSE COMM SCI ASTRONAUT,AUTHORIZING APPROPRIATIONS TO THE NATIONAL AERONAUTICS AND SPACE ADMINISTRATION (PAMPHLET). USA+45 NAT/G OP/RES TEC/DEV BUDGET NASA HOUSE/REP. PAGE 137 F2704
SPACE R+D PHIL/SCI NUC/PWR

NASH M. F1893,F1894

NASHVILLE....NASHVILLE, TENNESSEE

NASSER/G....GAMAL ABDUL NASSER

N
BROCKWAY A.F.,AFRICAN SOCIALISM. EUR+WWI GHANA ISLAM UAR ECO/UNDEV CAP/ISM INT/TRADE COLONIAL COERCE GOV/REL DISCRIM 20 NEGRO NKRUMAH/K NASSER/G. PAGE 19 F0356
AFR SOCISM MARXISM

B64
MILIBAND R.,THE SOCIALIST REGISTER: 1964. GERMANY/W ITALY UK LABOR POL/PAR ECO/TAC FOR/AID NUC/PWR ...POLICY SOCIALIST IDEA/COMP 20 MAO NASSER/G. PAGE 91 F1784
MARXISM SOCISM CAP/ISM PROB/SOLV

S65
CECIL C.O.,"THE DETERMINANTS OF LIBYAN FOREIGN POLICY." AFR INTELL ECO/UNDEV EXTR/IND POL/PAR CREATE REGION SOVEREIGN CONSERVE MAGHREB NASSER/G. PAGE 22 F0431
LIBYA DIPLOM WEALTH ISLAM

NAT/COMP....COMPARISON OF NATIONS

B
BRITISH COMMONWEALTH BUR AGRI,WORLD AGRICULTURAL ECONOMICS AND RURAL SOCIOLOGY ABSTRACTS. NAT/G OP/RES PLAN TEC/DEV LEAD PRODUC...GEOG MGT NAT/COMP 20. PAGE 18 F0354
BIBLIOG/A AGRI SOC WORKER

N
ECONOMIC LIBRARY SELECTIONS. AGRI INDUS MARKET ADMIN...STAT NAT/COMP 20. PAGE 1 F0007
BIBLIOG/A WRITING FINAN

N
RAND SCHOOL OF SOCIAL SCIENCE,INDEX TO LABOR ARTICLES. ECO/DEV INT/ORG LEGIS DIPLOM GP/REL ...NAT/COMP 20. PAGE 109 F2143
BIBLIOG LABOR MGT ADJUD

B08
LLOYD H.D.,THE SWISS DEMOCRACY. SWITZERLND INDUS NAT/G WORKER CHOOSE OWN ORD/FREE SOCISM...PLURIST 19/20 MONOPOLY. PAGE 81 F1590
NAT/COMP GOV/COMP REPRESENT POPULISM

B15
VEBLEN T.,IMPERIAL GERMANY AND THE INDUSTRIAL REVOLUTION. GERMANY MOD/EUR UK USA-45 NAT/G TEC/DEV CAP/ISM...MAJORIT NAT/COMP 19/20 CHINJAP. PAGE 141 F2769
ECO/DEV INDUS TECHNIC BAL/PWR

N19
FREEMAN H.A.,COERCION OF STATES IN FEDERAL UNIONS (PAMPHLET). WOR-45 DIPLOM CONTROL COERCE PEACE ORD/FREE...GOV/COMP METH/COMP NAT/COMP PACIFIST 20. PAGE 43 F0850
FEDERAL WAR INT/ORG PACIFISM

N19
INTERNATIONAL LABOUR OFFICE,EMPLOYMENT, UNEMPLOYMENT AND LABOUR FORCE STATISTICS (PAMPHLET). EUR+WWI STRATA AGRI INDUS NAT/G PROB/SOLV PAY AGE SEX...SAMP NAT/COMP METH 20 ILO. PAGE 65 F1278
WORKER LABOR STAT ECO/DEV

B23
FINER H.,REPRESENTATIVE GOVERNMENT AND A PARLIAMENT OF INDUSTRY. A STUDY OF THE GERMAN FEDERAL ECONOMIC COUNCIL. GERMANY UK CONSTN INDUS PARL/PROC ...NAT/COMP 20. PAGE 41 F0796
DELIB/GP ECO/TAC WAR REV

B24
HOLDSWORTH W.S.,A HISTORY OF ENGLISH LAW; THE COMMON LAW AND ITS RIVALS (VOL. IV). UK SEA AGRI CHIEF ADJUD CONTROL CRIME GOV/REL...INT/LAW JURID NAT/COMP 16/17 PARLIAMENT COMMON/LAW CANON/LAW ENGLSH/LAW. PAGE 61 F1195
LAW LEGIS CT/SYS CONSTN

B31
CROOK W.H.,THE GENERAL STRIKE: A STUDY OF LABOR'S TRAGIC WEAPON IN THEORY AND PRACTICE. BELGIUM FRANCE SWEDEN UK WOR-45 PROB/SOLV ECO/TAC DOMIN PWR ...POLICY TIME/SEQ NAT/COMP GEN/LAWS 19/20 STRIKE. PAGE 29 F0555
LABOR WORKER LG/CO BARGAIN

B37
VON HAYEK F.A.,MONETARY NATIONALISM AND INTERNATIONAL STABILITY. WOR-45 ECO/DEV NAT/G PROB/SOLV INT/TRADE...POLICY CONCPT METH/COMP NAT/COMP 20. PAGE 142 F2792
ECO/TAC FINAN DIPLOM NAT/LISM

B38
HEIMANN E.,COMMUNISM, FASCISM, OR DEMOCRACY? WOR-45 CONSTN SOCIETY STRATA AGRI CAP/ISM MORAL ORD/FREE ...MAJORIT METH/COMP NAT/COMP 19/20. PAGE 58 F1141
SOCISM MARXISM FASCISM PLURISM

B38
LAWLEY F.E.,THE GROWTH OF COLLECTIVE ECONOMY VOL. 2: INTERNATIONAL. WOR-45 AGRI INDUS EQUILIB OPTIMAL OWN WEALTH...NAT/COMP 19/20 NAZI NEW/DEAL MONOPOLY. PAGE 76 F1493
ECO/TAC SOCISM NAT/LISM CONTROL

B39
MARQUAND H.A.,ORGANIZED LABOUR IN FOUR CONTINENTS. EUR+WWI USA-45 INDUS NAT/G PAY GP/REL TOTALISM ATTIT WEALTH ALL/IDEOS...TREND NAT/COMP 20 ILO AFL/CIO EUROPE CHINJAP MEXIC/AMER. PAGE 85 F1673
LABOR WORKER CONCPT ANTHOL

B47
ENKE S.,INTERNATIONAL ECONOMICS. UK USA+45 USSR INT/ORG BAL/PWR BARGAIN CAP/ISM BAL/PAY...NAT/COMP 20 TREATY. PAGE 38 F0735
INT/TRADE FINAN TARIFFS ECO/TAC

B50
LIPSET S.M.,AGRARIAN SOCIALISM. CANADA POL/PAR OP/RES ECO/TAC ADMIN ATTIT...TIME/SEQ NAT/COMP SOC/EXP 20 SASKATCH. PAGE 80 F1576
SOCISM AGRI METH/COMP STRUCT

B53
BOEKE J.H.,ECONOMICS AND ECONOMIC POLICY OF DUAL SOCIETIES AS EXEMPLIFIED BY INDONESIA. INDIA INDONESIA SOCIETY CAP/ISM INT/TRADE GIVE PRICE GP/REL WEALTH SOCISM...POLICY NAT/COMP GEN/LAWS 20. PAGE 16 F0304
ECO/TAC ECO/UNDEV NAT/G CONTROL

B53
FLORENCE P.S.,THE LOGIC OF BRITISH AND AMERICAN INDUSTRY; A REALISTIC ANALYSIS OF ECONOMIC STRUCTURE AND GOVERNMENT. UK USA+45 USA-45 FINAN LABOR CAP/ISM INGP/REL EFFICIENCY...MGT CONCPT STAT CHARTS METH 20. PAGE 42 F0813
INDUS ECO/DEV NAT/G NAT/COMP

B54
FRIEDMAN W.,THE PUBLIC CORPORATION: A COMPARATIVE SYMPOSIUM (UNIVERSITY OF TORONTO SCHOOL OF LAW COMPARATIVE LAW SERIES, VOL. I). AFR SWEDEN USA+45 INDUS INT/ORG NAT/G REGION CENTRAL FEDERAL...POLICY JURID IDEA/COMP NAT/COMP ANTHOL 20 MONOPOLY EUROPE. PAGE 44 F0861
LAW SOCISM LG/CO OWN

B54
WILLIAMSON H.F.,ECONOMIC DEVELOPMENT - PRINCIPLES AND PATTERNS. INDIA KOREA CULTURE ECO/DEV ECO/UNDEV TEC/DEV...CENSUS NAT/COMP FOR/TRADE 20 CHINJAP MEXIC/AMER RESOURCE/N. PAGE 147 F2895
ECO/TAC GEOG LABOR

B55
HELANDER S.,DAS AUTARKIEPROBLEM IN DER WELTWIRTSCHAFT. PROB/SOLV BAL/PWR BARGAIN CAP/ISM ECO/TAC SOVEREIGN FOR/TRADE 20. PAGE 58 F1144
NAT/COMP COLONIAL DIPLOM

B55
UN ECONOMIC COMN ASIA & FAR E,ECONOMIC SURVEY OF ASIA AND THE FAR EAST, 1954. AFGHANISTN CEYLON INDIA PHILIPPINE S/ASIA ECO/DEV FINAN INDUS INT/TRADE PRODUC WEALTH...STAT CHARTS 20 CHINJAP. PAGE 132 F2600
ECO/UNDEV PRICE NAT/COMP ASIA

B55
WOYTINSKY W.S.,WORLD COMMERCE AND GOVERNMENTS: TRENDS AND OUTLOOK. WOR+45 FINAN POL/PAR DIPLOM ECO/TAC FOR/AID DOMIN WAR CHOOSE...CHARTS BIBLIOG 20 LEAGUE/NAT UN ILO. PAGE 149 F2929
INT/TRADE DIST/IND NAT/COMP NAT/G

B55
WRONG D.H.,AMERICAN AND CANADIAN VIEWPOINTS. CANADA USA+45 CONSTN STRATA FAM SECT WORKER ECO/TAC EDU/PROP ADJUD MARRIAGE...IDEA/COMP 20. PAGE 149 F2936
DIPLOM ATTIT NAT/COMP CULTURE

B57
BOUSTEDT O.,REGIONALE STRUKTUR- UND WIRTSCHAFTSFORSCHUNG. WOR+45 WOR-45 PROVS...STAT MUNICH. PAGE 17 F0325
GEOG CONCPT NAT/COMP

B57
LOUCKS W.N.,COMPARATIVE ECONOMIC SYSTEMS (5TH ED.). COM UK USSR INDUS POL/PAR PLAN CAP/ISM TOTALISM MARXISM...PHIL/SCI BIBLIOG 19/20. PAGE 82 F1603
NAT/COMP IDEA/COMP SOCISM

B58
AVRAMOVIC D.,POSTWAR GROWTH IN INTERNATIONAL INDEBTEDNESS. AFR WOR+45 AGRI INDUS CAP/ISM PRICE INCOME...NAT/COMP 20 SILVER. PAGE 8 F0143
INT/TRADE FINAN COST BAL/PAY

B58
INTERNATIONAL ECONOMIC ASSN,ECONOMICS OF INTERNATIONAL MIGRATION. WOR+45 WOR-45 ECO/UNDEV FINAN NAT/G REGION...NAT/COMP METH 20. PAGE 65 F1275
CENSUS GEOG DIPLOM ECO/TAC

B58
JACOBSSON P.,SOME MONETARY PROBLEMS, INTERNATIONAL AND NATIONAL. WOR+45 WOR-45 ECO/DEV FORCES WORKER PROB/SOLV DIPLOM INT/TRADE...ANTHOL 20. PAGE 66 F1299
FINAN PLAN ECO/TAC NAT/COMP

B58
NICULESCU B.,COLONIAL PLANNING: A COMPARATIVE STUDY. AFR AGRI LOC/G NAT/G DELIB/GP COLONIAL MUNICH 20. PAGE 98 F1927
PLAN ECO/UNDEV TEC/DEV

NAT/COMP

S58
LOCKWOOD W.W.,"THE SOCIALISTIC SOCIETY: INDIA AND JAPAN." INDIA ECO/DEV ECO/UNDEV INDUS NAT/G CONTROL LEAD PRODUC WEALTH 20 CHINJAP. PAGE 81 F1593
ECO/TAC NAT/COMP FINAN SOCISM

B59
ETSCHMANN R.,DIE WAHRUNGS- UND DEVISENPOLITIK DES OSTBLOCKS UND IHRE AUSWIRKUNGEN AUF DIE WIRTSCHAFTSBEZIEHUNGEN ZWISCHEN OST U WEST. BULGARIA CZECHOSLVK HUNGARY POLAND USSR MARKET NAT/G PLAN DIPLOM...NAT/COMP 20. PAGE 39 F0753
ECO/TAC FINAN POLICY INT/TRADE

B59
STERNBERG F.,THE MILITARY AND INDUSTRIAL REVOLUTION OF OUR TIME. USA+45 USSR WOR+45 WORKER COMPUTER PLAN TEC/DEV NUC/PWR GP/REL...POLICY NAT/COMP 20. PAGE 126 F2481
DIPLOM FORCES INDUS CIVMIL/REL

B59
VERNEY D.V.,PUBLIC ENTERPRISE IN SWEDEN. FUT SWEDEN UK INDUS POL/PAR LEGIS PROB/SOLV CAP/ISM INT/TRADE CONTROL SOCISM...MGT CONCPT NAT/COMP 20 SOCDEM/PAR CIVIL/SERV. PAGE 141 F2778
ECO/DEV POLICY LG/CO NAT/G

B60
BAYER H.,WIRTSCHAFTSPROGNOSE UND WIRTSCHAFTSGESTALTUNG. GERMANY NETHERLAND MARKET PLAN CAP/ISM DEBATE...NAT/COMP 20. PAGE 12 F0220
ECO/DEV ECO/UNDEV FINAN POLICY

B60
FRANCIS R.G.,THE PREDICTIVE PROCESS. PLAN MARXISM ...DECISION SOC CONCPT NAT/COMP 19/20. PAGE 43 F0840
PREDICT PHIL/SCI TREND

B60
KERR C.,INDUSTRIALISM AND INDUSTRIAL MAN. CULTURE SOCIETY ECO/UNDEV NAT/G ADMIN PRODUC WEALTH ...PREDICT TREND NAT/COMP 19/20. PAGE 70 F1381
WORKER MGT ECO/DEV INDUS

B60
MOORE W.E.,LABOR COMMITMENT AND SOCIAL CHANGE IN DEVELOPING AREAS. SOCIETY STRATA ECO/UNDEV MARKET VOL/ASSN WORKER AUTHORIT SKILL...MGT NAT/COMP SOC/INTEG 20. PAGE 93 F1823
LABOR ORD/FREE ATTIT INDUS

B60
NEALE A.D.,THE FLOW OF RESOURCES FROM RICH TO POOR. WOR+45 ECO/DEV ECO/UNDEV FINAN INDUS NAT/G PLAN EFFICIENCY WEALTH...POLICY NAT/COMP 20 RESOURCE/N. PAGE 97 F1905
FOR/AID DIPLOM METH/CNCPT

B60
OEEC,STATISTICS OF SOURCES AND USES OF FINANCE. NAT/G CAP/ISM TAX PRICE COST 20 OEEC. PAGE 101 F1978
FINAN PRODUC INCOME NAT/COMP

B60
ROBINSON E.A.G.,ECONOMIC CONSEQUENCES OF THE SIZE OF NATIONS. AGRI INDUS DELIB/GP FOR/AID ADMIN EFFICIENCY...METH/COMP 20. PAGE 113 F2218
CONCPT INT/ORG NAT/COMP

B60
SLOTKIN J.S.,FROM FIELD TO FACTORY; NEW INDUSTRIAL EMPLOYEES. HABITAT...MGT NEW/IDEA NAT/COMP BIBLIOG SOC/INTEG 20. PAGE 123 F2423
INDUS LABOR CULTURE WORKER

B60
THE ECONOMIST (LONDON),THE COMMONWEALTH AND EUROPE. EUR+WWI WOR+45 AGRI FINAN INCOME...STAT CENSUS CHARTS CMN/WLTH EEC. PAGE 129 F2550
INT/TRADE INDUS INT/ORG NAT/COMP

B61
AUBREY H.G.,COEXISTENCE: ECONOMIC CHALLENGE AND RESPONSE. AFR USSR WOR+45 ACT/RES BAL/PWR CAP/ISM DIPLOM ECO/TAC FOR/AID INT/TRADE PEACE SOCISM ...METH/COMP NAT/COMP. PAGE 7 F0139
POLICY ECO/UNDEV PLAN COM

B61
GANGULI B.N.,ECONOMIC INTEGRATION. FINAN LABOR CAP/ISM DIPLOM WEALTH...NAT/COMP 20. PAGE 46 F0895
ECO/TAC METH/CNCPT EQUILIB ECO/UNDEV

B61
HARDT J.P.,THE COLD WAR ECONOMIC GAP. AFR USA+45 USSR ECO/DEV FORCES INT/TRADE NUC/PWR PWR 20. PAGE 55 F1081
DIPLOM ECO/TAC NAT/COMP POLICY

B61
HEMPSTONE S.,THE NEW AFRICA. AGRI INDUS KIN NAT/G COLONIAL MARXISM...SOC INT TREND NAT/COMP BIBLIOG/A 20. PAGE 58 F1146
AFR ORD/FREE PERSON CULTURE

B61
LICHTHEIM G.,MARXISM. GERMANY SOCIETY WORKER CAP/ISM ECO/TAC NAT/LISM POPULISM...TIME/SEQ GOV/COMP NAT/COMP 18/20 COM/PARTY. PAGE 80 F1559
MARXISM SOCISM IDEA/COMP CULTURE

B61
OECD,STATISTICS OF BALANCE OF PAYMENTS 1950-61. WOR+45 FINAN ECO/TAC INT/TRADE DEMAND WEALTH...STAT NAT/COMP 20 OEEC OECD. PAGE 100 F1965
BAL/PAY ECO/DEV INT/ORG CHARTS

B61
STARK H.,SOCIAL AND ECONOMIC FRONTIERS IN LATIN AMERICA (2ND ED.). CUBA FUT CULTURE AGRI INDUS ECO/TAC PRODUC ATTIT MARXISM...NAT/COMP BIBLIOG T 20. PAGE 125 F2470
L/A+17C SOCIETY DIPLOM ECO/UNDEV

B61
VEIT O.,GRUNDRISS DER WAHRUNGSPOLITIK. AFR FRANCE GERMANY USSR DIPLOM INT/TRADE...NAT/COMP 19/20 SILVER. PAGE 141 F2773
FINAN POLICY ECO/TAC CAP/ISM

B62
DEBUYST F.,LAS CLASES SOCIALES EN AMERICA LATINA. L/A+17C SOCIETY STRUCT WORKER EDU/PROP RACE/REL ATTIT HABITAT ROLE...GEOG SOC NAT/COMP SOC/INTEG 20. PAGE 32 F0612
STRATA GP/REL WEALTH

B62
FATOUROS A.A.,GOVERNMENT GUARANTEES TO FOREIGN INVESTORS. WOR+45 ECO/UNDEV INDUS WORKER ADJUD ...NAT/COMP BIBLIOG TREATY. PAGE 39 F0767
NAT/G FINAN INT/TRADE ECO/DEV

B62
FRIEDMANN W.,METHODS AND POLICIES OF PRINCIPAL DONOR COUNTRIES IN PUBLIC INTERNATIONAL DEVELOPMENT FINANCING: PRELIMINARY APPRAISAL. FRANCE GERMANY/W UK USA+45 USSR WOR+45 FINAN TEC/DEV CAP/ISM DIPLOM ECO/TAC ATTIT 20 EEC. PAGE 44 F0864
INT/ORG FOR/AID NAT/COMP ADMIN

B62
GALENSON W.,LABOR IN DEVELOPING COUNTRIES. BRAZIL INDONESIA ISRAEL PAKISTAN TURKEY AGRI INDUS WORKER PAY PRICE GP/REL WEALTH...MGT CHARTS METH/COMP NAT/COMP 20. PAGE 45 F0888
LABOR ECO/UNDEV BARGAIN POL/PAR

B62
HAGUE D.C.,INFLATION. AFR ECO/DEV ECO/UNDEV LABOR BUDGET CAP/ISM INT/TRADE TARIFFS SOCISM 20. PAGE 53 F1036
FINAN NAT/COMP BARGAIN ECO/TAC

B62
MARTINS A.F.,REVOLUCAO BRANCA NO CAMPO. L/A+17C SERV/IND DEMAND EFFICIENCY PRODUC...POLICY METH/COMP. PAGE 86 F1685
AGRI ECO/UNDEV TEC/DEV NAT/COMP

B62
MICHAELY M.,CONCENTRATION IN INTERNATIONAL TRADE. ECO/DEV ECO/UNDEV PRICE INCOME...CHARTS NAT/COMP 20. PAGE 91 F1779
INT/TRADE MARKET FINAN GEOG

B62
PHELPS E.S.,THE GOAL OF ECONOMIC GROWTH: SOURCES, COSTS, BENEFITS. USA+45 USSR FINAN TAX CONTROL DEMAND WEALTH...POLICY NAT/COMP ANTHOL BIBLIOG 20. PAGE 106 F2079
ECO/TAC ECO/DEV NAT/G FUT

S62
IOVTCHOUK M.T.,"ON SOME THEORETICAL PRINCIPLES AND METHODS OF SOCIOLOGICAL INVESTIGATIONS (IN RUSSIAN)." FUT USA+45 STRATA R+D NAT/G POL/PAR TOP/EX ACT/RES PLAN ECO/TAC EDU/PROP ROUTINE ATTIT RIGID/FLEX MARXISM SOCISM...MARXIST METH/CNCPT OBS TREND NAT/COMP GEN/LAWS 20. PAGE 65 F1288
COM ECO/DEV CAP/ISM USSR

B63
AHN L.A.,FUNFZIG JAHRE ZWISCHEN INFLATION UND DEFLATION. AFR GERMANY DIPLOM PRICE...CONCPT 20. PAGE 3 F0053
FINAN CAP/ISM NAT/COMP ECO/TAC

B63
BERGSON A.,ECONOMIC TRENDS IN THE SOVIET UNION. USSR ECO/UNDEV AGRI NAT/G FORCES PLAN TEC/DEV INT/TRADE BAL/PAY...POLICY ANTHOL 20. PAGE 14 F0259
ECO/DEV NAT/COMP INDUS LABOR

B63
GANGULI B.N.,ECONOMIC CONSEQUENCES OF DISARMAMENT. EUR+WWI ECO/DEV ECO/UNDEV FORCES ACT/RES BUDGET DIPLOM INT/TRADE...STAT CHARTS NAT/COMP. PAGE 46 F0896
ECOMETRIC ARMS/CONT COST HYPO/EXP

B63
GORDON M.S.,THE ECONOMICS OF WELFARE POLICIES. INDUS LOC/G NAT/G LEGIS WORKER INCOME AGE/O SKILL WEALTH...METH/COMP NAT/COMP 20. PAGE 49 F0959
METH/CNCPT ECO/TAC POLICY

B63
LETHBRIDGE H.J.,THE PEASANT AND THE COMMUNES. CHINA/COM COM USSR NEIGH PROB/SOLV ADJUST EFFICIENCY...POLICY METH/COMP NAT/COMP 20. PAGE 78 F1535
MARXISM ECO/TAC AGRI WORKER

B63
OLSON M. JR.,THE ECONOMICS OF WARTIME SHORTAGE. FRANCE GERMANY MOD/EUR UK AGRI PROB/SOLV ADMIN DEMAND WEALTH...POLICY OLD/LIB FOR/TRADE 17/20. PAGE 101 F1990
WAR ADJUST ECO/TAC NAT/COMP

B63
SHANKS M.,THE LESSONS OF PUBLIC ENTERPRISE. UK LEGIS WORKER ECO/TAC ADMIN PARL/PROC GOV/REL ATTIT ...POLICY MGT METH/COMP NAT/COMP ANTHOL 20 PARLIAMENT. PAGE 120 F2364
SOCISM OWN NAT/G INDUS

B63
UN SECRETARY GENERAL,PLANNING FOR ECONOMIC DEVELOPMENT. ECO/UNDEV FINAN BUDGET INT/TRADE TARIFFS TAX ADMIN 20 UN. PAGE 132 F2603
PLAN ECO/TAC MGT

NAT/COMP

N63
LEDERER W.,THE BALANCE ON FOREIGN TRANSACTIONS: PROBLEMS OF DEFINITION AND MEASUREMENT (PAMPHLET). USA+45 BUDGET DIPLOM ECO/TAC PRICE GOV/REL...POLICY STAT NAT/COMP METH 20. PAGE 77 F1502
FINAN BAL/PAY INT/TRADE ECO/DEV

B64
BALOGH T.,THE ECONOMIC IMPACT OF MONETARY AND COMMERCIAL INSTITUTIONS OF A EUROPEAN ORIGIN IN AFRICA. AFR UAR INDUS FOR/AID COLONIAL CONTROL ...NAT/COMP 20. PAGE 9 F0169
TEC/DEV FINAN ECO/UNDEV ECO/TAC

B64
BROWN W.M.,THE EXTERNAL LIQUIDITY OF AN ADVANCED COUNTRY. CANADA FRANCE GERMANY/W SWEDEN UK USA+45 ECO/DEV DIPLOM PRICE...CONCPT STAT NAT/COMP 20. PAGE 20 F0376
FINAN INT/TRADE COST INCOME

B64
GREBLER L.,URBAN RENEWAL IN EUROPEAN COUNTRIES: ITS EMERGENCE AND POTENTIALS. EUR+WWI UK ECO/DEV LOC/G NEIGH CREATE ADMIN ATTIT...TREND NAT/COMP MUNICH 20 URBAN/RNWL. PAGE 50 F0981
PLAN CONSTRUC NAT/G

B64
GUTMANN P.M.,ECONOMIC GROWTH: AN AMERICAN PROBLEM. USA+45 FINAN R+D...POLICY NAT/COMP ANTHOL BIBLIOG 20. PAGE 52 F1016
WEALTH ECO/DEV CAP/ISM ORD/FREE

B64
HAAR C.M.,LAW AND LAND: ANGLO-AMERICAN PLANNING PRACTICE. UK USA+45 NAT/G TEC/DEV BUDGET CT/SYS INGP/REL EFFICIENCY OWN...JURID MUNICH 20. PAGE 52 F1019
LAW PLAN NAT/COMP

B64
HARBISON F.H.,EDUCATION, MANPOWER, AND ECONOMIC GROWTH. WOR+45 ECO/DEV ECO/UNDEV ACADEM LABOR SCHOOL WORKER UTIL...IDEA/COMP NAT/COMP. PAGE 55 F1075
PLAN TEC/DEV EDU/PROP SKILL

B64
INTERNATIONAL LABOUR OFFICE,EMPLOYMENT AND ECONOMIC GROWTH. ECO/DEV ECO/UNDEV NAT/G PLAN DIPLOM INT/TRADE CONTROL INCOME PRODUC WEALTH...STAT NAT/COMP 20 ILO. PAGE 65 F1279
WORKER METH/COMP ECO/TAC OPTIMAL

B64
LEWIN P.,THE FOREIGN TRADE OF COMMUNIST CHINA* ITS IMPACT ON THE FREE WORLD. AFR EUR+WWI L/A+17C S/ASIA ECO/UNDEV CREATE FOR/AID...STAT NET/THEORY TREND CHARTS. PAGE 79 F1546
ASIA INT/TRADE NAT/COMP USSR

B64
OECD,DEVELOPMENT ASSISTANCE EFFORTS - POLICIES OF THE MEMBERS. AGRI INDUS BUDGET...GEOG NAT/COMP 20 OECD. PAGE 100 F1967
INT/ORG FOR/AID ECO/UNDEV TEC/DEV

B64
SANDEE J.,EUROPE'S FUTURE CONSUMPTION. EUR+WWI FUT EDU/PROP...IDEA/COMP NAT/COMP ANTHOL 20 EUROPE. PAGE 115 F2277
MARKET ECO/DEV PREDICT PRICE

B64
SOLOW R.M.,THE NATURE AND SOURCES OF UNEMPLOYMENT IN THE UNITED STATES (PAMPHLET). USA+45 INDUS LABOR TEC/DEV ECO/TAC SKILL WEALTH...TREND NAT/COMP 20. PAGE 124 F2439
ECO/DEV WORKER STAT PRODUC

B64
STEWART C.F.,A BIBLIOGRAPHY OF INTERNATIONAL BUSINESS. WOR+45 FINAN LG/CO NAT/G PLAN ECO/TAC TARIFFS...DECISION MGT GP/COMP NAT/COMP 20 EEC. PAGE 126 F2484
BIBLIOG INT/ORG OP/RES INT/TRADE

B64
WHEARE K.C.,FEDERAL GOVERNMENT (4TH ED.). WOR+45 WOR-45 POL/PAR LEGIS BAL/PWR CT/SYS...POLICY JURID CONCPT GOV/COMP 17/20. PAGE 145 F2866
FEDERAL CONSTN EX/STRUC NAT/COMP

B64
WILSON T.,POLICIES FOR REGIONAL DEVELOPMENT. CANADA UK FINAN INDUS NAT/G BUDGET TAX GIVE COST ...NAT/COMP 20. PAGE 147 F2904
REGION PLAN ECO/DEV ECO/TAC

S64
NASH M.,"SOCIAL PREREQUISITES TO ECONOMIC GROWTH IN LATIN AMERICA AND SOUTHEAST ASIA." L/A+17C S/ASIA CULTURE SOCIETY ECO/UNDEV AGRI INDUS NAT/G PLAN TEC/DEV EDU/PROP ROUTINE ALL/VALS...POLICY RELATIV SOC NAT/COMP WORK TOT/POP 20. PAGE 96 F1894
ECO/DEV PERCEPT

C64
GOLDMAN M.I.,"COMPARATIVE ECONOMIC SYSTEMS: A READER." COM ECO/UNDEV NAT/G BUDGET CAP/ISM ADMIN TOTALISM MARXISM SOCISM...MGT ANTHOL BIBLIOG 19/20. PAGE 48 F0938
NAT/COMP CONTROL IDEA/COMP

B65
ALEXANDER R.J.,ORGANIZED LABOR IN LATIN AMERICA. L/A+17C INT/ORG LEGIS WORKER TEC/DEV BARGAIN INT/TRADE REV...NAT/COMP BIBLIOG 20. PAGE 3 F0059
LABOR POL/PAR ECO/UNDEV POLICY

B65
CHAO K.,THE RATE AND PATTERN OF INDUSTRIAL GROWTH IN COMMUNIST CHINA. CHINA/COM ECO/UNDEV TEC/DEV PRICE...NAT/COMP BIBLIOG 20. PAGE 23 F0452
INDUS INDEX STAT PRODUC

B65
CRABB C.V. JR.,THE ELEPHANTS AND THE GRASS* A STUDY OF NONALIGNMENT. ASIA INDIA S/ASIA USA+45 USSR BAL/PWR NEUTRAL ATTIT...TREND NAT/COMP. PAGE 28 F0549
ECO/UNDEV AFR DIPLOM CONCPT

B65
DUGGAR G.S.,RENEWAL OF TOWN AND VILLAGE I: A WORLD-WIDE SURVEY OF LOCAL GOVERNMENT EXPERIENCE. WOR+45 CONSTRUC INDUS CREATE BUDGET REGION GOV/REL...QU NAT/COMP MUNICH 20 URBAN/RNWL. PAGE 35 F0673
NEIGH PLAN ADMIN

B65
EUROPEAN FREE TRADE ASSN,REGIONAL DEVELOPMENT POLICIES IN EFTA. ECO/UNDEV INT/ORG PLAN REGION ...POLICY GEOG EFTA. PAGE 39 F0755
EUR+WWI ECO/DEV NAT/COMP INT/TRADE

B65
HARBISON F.,MANPOWER AND EDUCATION. AFR CHINA/COM IRAN L/A+17C S/ASIA TEC/DEV ADJUST OPTIMAL SKILL ...ANTHOL 20. PAGE 55 F1073
ECO/UNDEV EDU/PROP WORKER NAT/COMP

B65
HLA MYINT U.,THE ECONOMICS OF THE DEVELOPING COUNTRIES. USA+45 WOR+45 AGRI FINAN NAT/G INT/TRADE ...CLASSIF CENSUS TREND NAT/COMP SIMUL GEN/LAWS. PAGE 60 F1180
ECO/UNDEV FOR/AID GEOG

B65
THE STATE AND ECONOMIC ENTERPRISE IN JAPAN; ESSAYS IN THE POLITICAL ECONOMY OF GROWTH. AGRI INDUS DRIVE POPULISM...CHARTS NAT/COMP ANTHOL 19/20 CHINJAP. PAGE 81 F1594
ECO/UNDEV ECO/DEV CAP/ISM ECO/TAC

B65
O'BRIEN F.,CRISIS IN WORLD COMMUNISM* MARXISM IN SEARCH OF EFFICIENCY. AFR COM ECO/DEV PLAN INT/TRADE WAR ADJUST PEACE...STAT TIME/SEQ GOV/COMP NAT/COMP. PAGE 99 F1951
MARXISM USSR DRIVE EFFICIENCY

B65
O'CONNELL D.P.,INTERNATIONAL LAW (2 VOLS.). WOR+45 WOR-45 ECO/DEV ECO/UNDEV INT/ORG NAT/G AGREE ...POLICY JURID CONCPT NAT/COMP 20 TREATY. PAGE 99 F1952
INT/LAW DIPLOM CT/SYS

B65
ROWE J.W.,PRIMARY COMMODITIES IN INTERNATIONAL TRADE. MARKET CAP/ISM ECO/TAC DEMAND...NAT/COMP 20. PAGE 114 F2253
INT/TRADE AGRI RATION PRICE

B65
SABLE M.H.,PERIODICALS FOR LATIN AMERICAN ECONOMIC DEVELOPMENT, TRADE, AND FINANCE: AN ANNOTATED BIBLIOGRAPHY (A PAMPHLET). ECO/TAC PRODUC PROFIT ...STAT NAT/COMP 20 OAS. PAGE 115 F2266
BIBLIOG/A L/A+17C ECO/UNDEV INT/TRADE

B65
SIMMS R.P.,URBANIZATION IN WEST AFRICA; A REVIEW OF CURRENT LITERATURE. AFR PLAN TEC/DEV...SOC OBS NAT/COMP MUNICH 20. PAGE 122 F2405
BIBLIOG/A ECO/DEV ECO/UNDEV

B65
VON RENESSE E.A.,UNVOLLENDETE DEMOKRATIEN. AFR ISLAM S/ASIA SOCIETY ACT/RES COLONIAL...JURID CHARTS BIBLIOG METH 13/20. PAGE 142 F2795
ECO/UNDEV NAT/COMP SOVEREIGN

B65
WINT G.,ASIA: A HANDBOOK. ASIA COM INDIA USSR CULTURE INTELL NAT/G...GEOG STAT CENSUS NAT/COMP WORSHIP 20 TREATY CHINJAP. PAGE 148 F2907
DIPLOM SOC

S65
GOLDMAN M.I.,"A BALANCE SHEET OF SOVIET FOREIGN AID." USA+45 ECO/UNDEV BAL/PWR ECO/TAC RENT GIVE EDU/PROP CONTROL COST PROFIT GEN/METH. PAGE 48 F0939
USSR FOR/AID NAT/COMP EFFICIENCY

S65
KINDLEBERGER C.P.,"MASS MIGRATION, THEN AND NOW." LAW ECO/DEV ECO/UNDEV INDUS LABOR INT/TRADE FEEDBACK REGION RIGID/FLEX...SOC NAT/COMP EEC. PAGE 71 F1394
EUR+WWI USA-45 WORKER IDEA/COMP

S65
TENDLER J.D.,"TECHNOLOGY AND ECONOMIC DEVELOPMENT* THE CASE OF HYDRO VS THERMAL POWER." CONSTRUC DIST/IND CREATE TEC/DEV INT/TRADE CENTRAL PWR SKILL WEALTH...MGT NAT/COMP ARGEN. PAGE 129 F2544
BRAZIL INDUS ECO/UNDEV

S65
WHITE J.,"WEST GERMAN AID TO DEVELOPING COUNTRIES." AFR INT/ORG OP/RES GIVE CENTRAL ATTIT DRIVE...STAT NAT/COMP. PAGE 146 F2869
GERMANY FOR/AID ECO/UNDEV CAP/ISM

B66
HOLT R.T.,THE POLITICAL BASIS OF ECONOMIC DEVELOPMENT. STRATA STRUCT NAT/G DIPLOM ADMIN...SOC NAT/COMP BIBLIOG 20. PAGE 61 F1201
ECO/TAC GOV/COMP CONSTN EX/STRUC

B66
JACKSON G.D.,COMINTERN AND PEASANT IN EAST EUROPE 1919-1930. BULGARIA COM CZECHOSLVK EUR+WWI POLAND ROMANIA YUGOSLAVIA STRATA AGRI VOL/ASSN DIPLOM CONTROL CROWD WEALTH...POLICY NAT/COMP 20. PAGE 66 F1293
MARXISM ECO/UNDEV WORKER INT/ORG

B66
KUZNETS S.,MODERN ECONOMIC GROWTH. WOR+45 WOR-45
TIME/SEQ

ECO/DEV ECO/UNDEV AGRI FINAN INDUS TEC/DEV EFFICIENCY INCOME...NAT/COMP 19/20. PAGE 74 F1456
WEALTH PRODUC

B66
MASON E.S.,ECONOMIC DEVELOPMENT IN INDIA AND PAKISTAN. INDIA PAKISTAN AGRI FINAN PLAN BUDGET INT/TRADE WEALTH...POLICY STAT TREND CHARTS 20. PAGE 87 F1700
NAT/COMP ECO/UNDEV ECO/TAC FOR/AID

B66
NEVITT A.A.,THE ECONOMIC PROBLEMS OF HOUSING. WOR+45 ECO/DEV ECO/UNDEV ACT/RES PROB/SOLV ECO/TAC RENT...OBS CHARTS 20. PAGE 98 F1917
HABITAT PROC/MFG DELIB/GP NAT/COMP

B66
OECD DEVELOPMENT CENTRE,CATALOGUE OF SOCIAL AND ECONOMIC DEVELOPMENT INSTITUTES AND PROGRAMMES* RESEARCH. ACT/RES PLAN TEC/DEV EDU/PROP...SOC GP/COMP NAT/COMP. PAGE 101 F1976
ECO/UNDEV ECO/DEV R+D ACADEM

B66
THOMPSON J.H.,MODERNIZATION OF THE ARAB WORLD. FUT ISRAEL STRUCT ECO/UNDEV DIPLOM INGP/REL ATTIT ...CENSUS ANTHOL 20 ARABS. PAGE 130 F2565
ADJUST ISLAM PROB/SOLV NAT/COMP

B66
US SENATE COMM ON FOREIGN REL,HEARINGS ON S 2859 AND S 2861. USA+45 WOR+45 FORCES BUDGET CAP/ISM ADMIN DETER WEAPON TOTALISM...NAT/COMP 20 UN CONGRESS. PAGE 139 F2735
FOR/AID DIPLOM ORD/FREE ECO/UNDEV

B66
YEAGER L.B.,INTERNATIONAL MONETARY RELATIONS: THEORY, HISTORY, AND POLICY. WOR+45 WOR-45 INT/TRADE BAL/PAY...NAT/COMP 18/20 MONEY. PAGE 150 F2947
FINAN DIPLOM ECO/TAC IDEA/COMP

S66
BENOIT J.,"WORLD DEFENSE EXPENDITURES." WOR+45 WEAPON COST PRODUC. PAGE 13 F0253
FORCES STAT NAT/COMP BUDGET

B67
ANDERSON C.W.,POLITICS AND ECONOMIC CHANGE IN LATIN AMERICA. L/A+17C INDUS NAT/G OP/RES ADMIN DEMAND ...POLICY STAT CHARTS NAT/COMP 20. PAGE 5 F0093
ECO/UNDEV PROB/SOLV PLAN ECO/TAC

B67
ANDERSON C.W.,ISSUES OF POLITICAL DEVELOPMENT. BURMA WOR+45 CULTURE TOP/EX ECO/TAC MARXISM ...CHARTS NAT/COMP 20 COLOMB CONGO/LEOP. PAGE 5 F0094
NAT/LISM COERCE ECO/UNDEV SOCISM

B67
CASTILLO C.M.,GROWTH AND INTEGRATION IN CENTRAL AMERICA. L/A+17C CREATE PROB/SOLV ECO/TAC REGION PRODUC...OBS BIBLIOG 20. PAGE 22 F0429
ECO/UNDEV INT/TRADE NAT/COMP

B67
CHILCOTE R.H.,PORTUGUESE AFRICA. PORTUGAL CULTURE SOCIETY ECO/UNDEV DOMIN NAT/LISM...TREND IDEA/COMP NAT/COMP BIBLIOG 15/20. PAGE 24 F0465
AFR COLONIAL ORD/FREE PROB/SOLV

B67
EBENSTEIN W.,TODAY'S ISMS: COMMUNISM, FASCISM, CAPITALISM, SOCIALISM (5TH ED.). COM WOR+45 PERCEPT PWR...SOC TREND IDEA/COMP NAT/COMP 20. PAGE 35 F0691
FASCISM MARXISM SOCISM CAP/ISM

B67
FIELD G.L.,COMPARATIVE POLITICAL DEVELOPMENT: THE PRECEDENT OF THE WEST. FRANCE GERMANY SWEDEN UK USSR STRATA STRUCT POL/PAR...METH 20. PAGE 40 F0790
NAT/COMP CONCPT ECO/DEV SOCIETY

B67
FORDE D.,WEST AFRICAN KINGDOMS IN THE NINETEENTH CENTURY. ECO/UNDEV AGRI KIN...SOC CHARTS NAT/COMP 19. PAGE 42 F0826
AFR REGION CULTURE

B67
JOHNSON H.G.,ECONOMIC NATIONALISM IN OLD AND NEW STATES. CANADA CHINA/COM MALI UK DIPLOM...SIMUL GEN/LAWS 19/20 MEXIC/AMER. PAGE 68 F1328
NAT/LISM ECO/UNDEV ECO/DEV NAT/COMP

B67
MCNELLY T.,SOURCES IN MODERN EAST ASIAN HISTORY AND POLITICS. KOREA VIETNAM CULTURE DIPLOM COLONIAL REV WAR PWR ALL/IDEOS MARXISM...ANTHOL 20 CHINJAP. PAGE 88 F1733
NAT/COMP ASIA S/ASIA SOCIETY

B67
OVERSEAS DEVELOPMENT INSTIT,EFFECTIVE AID. WOR+45 INT/ORG TEC/DEV DIPLOM INT/TRADE ADMIN. PAGE 102 F2004
FOR/AID ECO/UNDEV ECO/TAC NAT/COMP

B67
ROELOFS H.M.,THE LANGUAGE OF MODERN POLITICS: AN INTRODUCTION TO THE STUDY OF GOVERNMENT. DIPLOM ADMIN MARXISM NEW/LIB...JURID CONCPT METH/COMP T 20. PAGE 113 F2230
LEAD NAT/COMP PERS/REL NAT/G

B67
SHAFFER H.G.,THE COMMUNIST WORLD: MARXIST AND NON-MARXIST VIEWS. WOR+45 SOCIETY DIPLOM ECO/TAC CONTROL SOCISM...MARXIST ANTHOL BIBLIOG/A 20. PAGE 120 F2363
MARXISM NAT/COMP IDEA/COMP COM

B67
SPIRO H.S.,PATTERNS OF AFRICAN DEVLOPMENT: FIVE COMPARISONS. STRUCT ECO/UNDEV NAT/G CONSERVE SOCISM ...PREDICT NAT/COMP 20 CHINJAP. PAGE 125 F2457
AFR CONSTN NAT/LISM TREND

B67
TANSKY L.,US AND USSR AID TO DEVELOPING COUNTRIES. INDIA TURKEY USA+45 USSR INDUS PLAN CAP/ISM WAR PWR WEALTH MARXISM...CHARTS NAT/COMP BIBLIOG 20. PAGE 128 F2534
ECO/UNDEV FOR/AID DIPLOM ECO/TAC

B67
THOMAN R.S.,GEOGRAPHY OF INTERNATIONAL TRADE. WOR+45 ECO/DEV ECO/UNDEV INT/ORG LG/CO PLAN BAL/PAY ...STAT CHARTS NAT/COMP 20. PAGE 130 F2559
INT/TRADE GEOG ECO/TAC DIPLOM

B67
WISEMAN H.V.,BRITAIN AND THE COMMONWEALTH. EUR+WWI FUT UK ECO/DEV POL/PAR TEC/DEV INT/TRADE LEAD ROLE SOVEREIGN...SOC TREND 20 CMN/WLTH. PAGE 148 F2911
INT/ORG DIPLOM NAT/G NAT/COMP

L67
AUSTIN D.A.,"POLITICAL CONFLICT IN AFRICA." CONSTN NAT/G CREATE ADMIN COLONIAL ORD/FREE MARXISM POPULISM SOCISM...NAT/COMP ANTHOL 20. PAGE 8 F0141
ANOMIE AFR POL/PAR

S67
ADAMS R.N.,"ETHICS AND THE SOCIAL ANTHROPOLOGIST IN LATIN AMERICA." USA+45 INTELL PROB/SOLV ECO/TAC LEAD...DECISION SOC NAT/COMP PERS/COMP. PAGE 2 F0039
L/A+17C POLICY ECO/UNDEV CONSULT

S67
GONZALEZ M.P.,"CUBA, UNA REVOLUCION EN MARCHA." CUBA L/A+17C USA+45 VIETNAM ECO/UNDEV FORCES DIPLOM DOMIN...POLICY MARXIST NAT/COMP CASTRO/F. PAGE 48 F0946
REV NAT/G COLONIAL SOVEREIGN

S67
MANGLAPUS R.S.,"ASIAN REVOLUTION AND AMERICAN IDEOLOGY." USA+45 SOCIETY CAP/ISM DIPLOM ADJUST CENTRAL...NAT/COMP 20. PAGE 84 F1652
REV POPULISM ATTIT ASIA

S67
RAMA C.M.,"PASADO Y PRESENTE DE LA RELIGION EN AMERICA LATINA." L/A+17C ELITES SOCIETY STRATA MARXISM...STAT WORSHIP PROTESTANT. PAGE 109 F2139
SECT CATHISM STRUCT NAT/COMP

S67
ZOETEWEIJ B.,"INCOME POLICIES ABROAD: AN INTERIM REPORT." NAT/G PROB/SOLV BARGAIN BUDGET PRICE RISK CENTRAL EFFICIENCY EQUILIB...MGT NAT/COMP 20. PAGE 150 F2967
METH/COMP INCOME POLICY LABOR

NAT/FARMER....NATIONAL FARMERS' ASSOCIATION

S59
ALLEN G.,"NATIONAL FARMERS UNION AS A PRESSURE GROUP: II." UK ECO/DEV MARKET POL/PAR DELIB/GP PROB/SOLV ECO/TAC LOBBY INCOME...POLICY METH/COMP 19/20 NAT/FARMER. PAGE 4 F0069
DIST/IND AGRI PROF/ORG TREND

NAT/LISM....NATIONALISM

NCO
CARRINGTON C.E.,THE COMMONWEALTH IN AFRICA (PAMPHLET). UK STRUCT NAT/G COLONIAL REPRESENT GOV/REL RACE/REL NAT/LISM...MAJORIT 20 EEC NEGRO. PAGE 22 F0421
ECO/UNDFV AFR DIPLOM PLAN

N19
JACKSON R.G.A.,THE CASE FOR AN INTERNATIONAL DEVELOPMENT AUTHORITY (PAMPHLET). WOR+45 ECO/DEV DIPLOM GIVE CONTROL GP/REL EFFICIENCY NAT/LISM SOVEREIGN 20. PAGE 66 F1295
FOR/AID INT/ORG ECO/UNDEV ADMIN

N19
SENGHOR L.S.,AFRICAN SOCIALISM (PAMPHLET). AFR FRANCE MALI USSR ELITES ECO/UNDEV NAT/G DIPLOM DOMIN EDU/PROP ATTIT 20 NEGRO. PAGE 119 F2355
SOCISM MARXISM ORD/FREE NAT/LISM

B28
DE MAN H.,THE PSYCHOLOGY OF SOCIALISM. EUR+WWI USSR LABOR NAT/LISM PERSON WEALTH MARXISM...METH/COMP 20. PAGE 31 F0604
WORKER ATTIT SOC SOCISM

B37
VON HAYEK F.A.,MONETARY NATIONALISM AND INTERNATIONAL STABILITY. WOR-45 ECO/DEV NAT/G PROB/SOLV INT/TRADE...POLICY CONCPT METH/COMP NAT/COMP 20. PAGE 142 F2792
ECO/TAC FINAN DIPLOM NAT/LISM

B38
HARPER S.N.,THE GOVERNMENT OF THE SOVIET UNION. COM USSR LAW CONSTN ECO/DEV PLAN TEC/DEV DIPLOM INT/TRADE ADMIN REV NAT/LISM...POLICY 20. PAGE 55 F1085
MARXISM NAT/G LEAD POL/PAR

B38
LAWLEY F.E.,THE GROWTH OF COLLECTIVE ECONOMY VOL. 2: INTERNATIONAL. WOR-45 AGRI INDUS EQUILIB OPTIMAL OWN WEALTH...NAT/COMP 19/20 NAZI NEW/DEAL MONOPOLY.
ECO/TAC SOCISM NAT/LISM

PAGE 76 F1493 — CONTROL

B50
HUNT R.N.,THE THEORY AND PRACTICE OF COMMUNISM. STRUCT WORKER NAT/LISM TOTALISM...CONCPT TREND 19/20 STALIN/J EUROPE. PAGE 63 F1244 — MARXISM SOCISM REV STRATA

C50
ELLSWORTH P.T.,"INTERNATIONAL ECONOMY." ECO/DEV ECO/UNDEV FINAN LABOR DIPLOM FOR/AID TARIFFS BAL/PAY EQUILIB NAT/LISM OPTIMAL...INT/LAW 20 ILO GATT. PAGE 37 F0724 — BIBLIOG INT/TRADE ECO/TAC INT/ORG

B51
BROGAN D.W.,THE PRICE OF REVOLUTION. FRANCE USA+45 USA-45 USSR CONSTN NAT/G DIPLOM COLONIAL NAT/LISM ORD/FREE POPULISM...CONCPT 18/20 PRE/US/AM. PAGE 19 F0359 — REV METH/COMP COST MARXISM

B52
SACHS E.S.,THE CHOICE BEFORE SOUTH AFRICA. SOUTH/AFR AGRI EXTR/IND PROC/MFG PROB/SOLV ORD/FREE SOVEREIGN 20 NEGRO. PAGE 115 F2267 — NAT/LISM DISCRIM RACE/REL LABOR

N56
US HOUSE COMM FOREIGN AFFAIRS,REPORT OF THE SPECIAL STUDY MISSION TO AFRICA, SOUTH AND EAST OF THE SAHARA (PAMPHLET). AFR SOUTH/AFR USA+45 STRUCT INT/TRADE PARL/PROC NAT/LISM ATTIT ALL/VALS HEALTH ...POLICY 20 CONGRESS. PAGE 136 F2691 — FOR/AID COLONIAL ECO/UNDEV DIPLOM

B57
ARON R.,L'UNIFICATION ECONOMIQUE DE L'EUROPE. EUR+WWI SWITZERLND UK INT/ORG NAT/G REGION NAT/LISM ORD/FREE PWR...CONCPT METH/CNCPT OBS TREND STERTYP GEN/LAWS EEC FOR/TRADE 20. PAGE 6 F0118 — VOL/ASSN ECO/TAC

B57
OLIVER H.M. JR.,ECONOMIC OPINION AND POLICY IN CEYLON. CEYLON FINAN POL/PAR WORKER INT/TRADE INCOME WEALTH...GEOG UNPLAN/INT BIBLIOG 20 CMN/WLTH. PAGE 101 F1987 — ECO/UNDEV NAT/LISM POLICY COLONIAL

B57
PALACIOS A.L.,PETROLEO, MONOPOLIOS, Y LATIFUNDIOS. L/A+17C EXTR/IND NAT/G TEC/DEV ECO/TAC CONTROL PRODUC 20 ARGEN MONOPOLY RESOURCE/N. PAGE 103 F2017 — ECO/UNDEV NAT/LISM INDUS AGRI

B58
COLE G.D.H.,COMMUNISM AND SOCIAL DEMOCRACY (VOL. IV OF "HISTORY OF SOCIAL THOUGHT"). COM GERMANY ITALY UK AGRI INT/ORG WORKER DIPLOM COLONIAL NAT/LISM ALL/IDEOS...BIBLIOG 20 LEAGUE/NAT AUST/HUNG. PAGE 26 F0502 — MARXISM REV POL/PAR SOCISM

B58
JENNINGS I.,PROBLEMS OF THE NEW COMMONWEALTH. AFR CEYLON INDIA PAKISTAN S/ASIA ECO/UNDEV INT/ORG LOC/G DIPLOM ECO/TAC INT/TRADE COLONIAL RACE/REL DISCRIM 20 PARLIAMENT. PAGE 67 F1314 — NAT/LISM NEUTRAL FOR/AID POL/PAR

B58
MOSKOWITZ M.,HUMAN RIGHTS AND WORLD ORDER. INT/ORG PLAN GP/REL NAT/LISM SOVEREIGN...CONCPT 20 UN TREATY CIV/RIGHTS. PAGE 94 F1845 — DIPLOM INT/LAW ORD/FREE

B58
TILLION G.,ALGERIA: THE REALITIES. ALGERIA FRANCE ISLAM CULTURE STRATA PROB/SOLV DOMIN REV NAT/LISM WEALTH MARXISM...GEOG 20. PAGE 130 F2573 — ECO/UNDEV SOC COLONIAL DIPLOM

B59
HENDEL S.,THE SOVIET CRUCIBLE. USSR LEAD COERCE NAT/LISM UTOPIA PWR...POLICY CONCPT ANTHOL 20 STALIN/J LENIN/VI MARX/KARL BOLSHEVIK. PAGE 58 F1147 — COM MARXISM REV TOTALISM

B59
WARD B.,5 IDEAS THAT CHANGE THE WORLD. WOR+45 WOR-45 SOCIETY STRUCT AGRI INDUS INT/ORG NAT/G FORCES ACT/RES ARMS/CONT TOTALISM ATTIT DRIVE GEN/LAWS. PAGE 143 F2815 — ECO/UNDEV ALL/VALS NAT/LISM COLONIAL

B59
YRARRAZAVAL E.,AMERICA LATINE EN LA GUERRA FRIA. AFR EUR+WWI L/A+17C USA+45 USSR WOR+45 INDUS INT/ORG NAT/LISM POLICY. PAGE 150 F2953 — REGION DIPLOM ECO/UNDEV INT/TRADE

B60
ARON R.,COLLOQUES DE RHEINFELDEN. AFR USA+45 USSR WOR+45 WOR-45 CULTURE ECO/UNDEV NAT/G POL/PAR DIPLOM NAT/LISM TOTALISM ATTIT DRIVE ALL/VALS ...PLURIST CONCPT STERTYP GEN/LAWS TOT/POP 20. PAGE 6 F0120 — ECO/DEV SOCIETY CAP/ISM SOCISM

B60
HEILPERIN M.A.,STUDIES IN ECONOMIC NATIONALISM. EUR+WWI MOD/EUR USA+45 ECO/DEV PLAN INT/TRADE TARIFFS WAR PRODUC PROFIT 18/20 KEYNES/JM. PAGE 58 F1140 — ECO/TAC NAT/G NAT/LISM POLICY

B60
LENCZOWSKI G.,OIL AND STATE IN THE MIDDLE EAST. FUT IRAN LAW ECO/UNDEV EXTR/IND NAT/G TOP/EX PLAN TEC/DEV ECO/TAC LEGIT ADMIN COERCE ATTIT ALL/VALS PWR...CHARTS 20. PAGE 78 F1519 — ISLAM INDUS NAT/LISM

S60
NICHOLS J.P.,"HAZARDS OF AMERICAN PRIVATE INVESTMENT IN UNDERDEVELOPED COUNTRIES." FUT L/A+17C USA+45 USA-45 EXTR/IND CONSULT BAL/PWR ECO/TAC DOMIN ADJUD ATTIT SOVEREIGN WEALTH ...HIST/WRIT TIME/SEQ TREND TERR/GP VAL/FREE 20. PAGE 98 F1924 — FINAN ECO/UNDEV CAP/ISM NAT/LISM

S60
OWEN C.F.,"US AND SOVIET RELATIONS WITH UNDERDEVELOPED COUNTRIES: LATIN AMERICA-A CASE STUDY." AFR COM L/A+17C USA+45 USSR EXTR/IND MARKET TEC/DEV DIPLOM ECO/TAC NAT/LISM ORD/FREE PWR ...TREND WORK 20. PAGE 102 F2005 — ECO/UNDEV DRIVE INT/TRADE

B61
ESTEBAN J.C.,IMPERIALISMO Y DESARROLLO ECONOMICO. L/A+17C FINAN INDUS NAT/G ECO/TAC CONTROL ROLE. PAGE 38 F0747 — ECO/UNDEV NAT/LISM DIPLOM BAL/PAY

B61
LEHMAN R.L.,AFRICA SOUTH OF THE SAHARA (PAMPHLET). DIPLOM COLONIAL NAT/LISM. PAGE 77 F1512 — BIBLIOG/A AFR CULTURE NAT/G

B61
LICHTHEIM G.,MARXISM. GERMANY SOCIETY WORKER CAP/ISM ECO/TAC NAT/LISM POPULISM...TIME/SEQ GOV/COMP NAT/COMP 18/20 COM/PARTY. PAGE 80 F1559 — MARXISM SOCISM IDEA/COMP CULTURE

B61
LUZ N.V.,A LUTA PELA INDUSTRIALIZACAO DO BRAZIL. BRAZIL L/A+17C AGRI NAT/G TEC/DEV COLONIAL 19/20. PAGE 82 F1615 — ECO/UNDEV INDUS NAT/LISM POLICY

B61
SAKAI R.K.,STUDIES ON ASIA, 1961. ASIA BURMA INDIA S/ASIA FINAN ECO/TAC NAT/LISM SOCISM...POLICY ANTHOL 19/20 CHINJAP. PAGE 115 F2271 — ECO/UNDEV SECT

B61
WRIGHT H.M.,THE "NEW IMPERIALISM": ANALYSIS OF LATE NINETEENTH-CENTURY EXPANSION. MOD/EUR WOR-45 SOCIETY FINAN ECO/TAC INT/TRADE NAT/LISM...ANTHOL BIBLIOG/A 19. PAGE 149 F2933 — HIST/WRIT IDEA/COMP COLONIAL DOMIN

B62
GREEN L.P.,DEVELOPMENT IN AFRICA. AFR CENTRL/AFR GHANA RHODESIA SOUTH/AFR AGRI PROC/MFG INT/TRADE DEMAND NAT/LISM PRODUC WEALTH...GEOG METH/CNCPT CHARTS BIBLIOG 20. PAGE 50 F0987 — CULTURE ECO/UNDEV GOV/REL TREND

B62
KENT R.K.,FROM MADAGASCAR TO THE MALAGASY REPUBLIC. FRANCE MADAGASCAR DIPLOM NAT/LISM ORD/FREE...MGT 18/20. PAGE 70 F1379 — COLONIAL SOVEREIGN REV POL/PAR

B62
RIMALOV V.V.,ECONOMIC COOPERATION BETWEEN USSR AND UNDERDEVELOPED COUNTRIES. USSR FINAN TEC/DEV INT/TRADE DOMIN EDU/PROP COLONIAL NAT/LISM DRIVE SOVEREIGN...AUD/VIS 20. PAGE 111 F2194 — FOR/AID PLAN ECO/UNDEV DIPLOM

B62
VAN RENSBURG P.,GUILTY LAND: THE HISTORY OF APARTHEID. SOUTH/AFR NAT/G POL/PAR DOMIN CHOOSE ...SOC 19/20 NEGRO. PAGE 140 F2763 — RACE/REL DISCRIM NAT/LISM POLICY

B62
WARD B.,THE RICH NATIONS AND THE POOR NATIONS. FUT WOR+45 CULTURE ECO/DEV ECO/UNDEV PLAN CAP/ISM EDU/PROP REV NAT/LISM ATTIT DRIVE SOCISM...POLICY CONCPT TIME/SEQ 20. PAGE 143 F2816 — ECO/TAC GEN/LAWS

S62
ALPERT P.,"ECONOMIC POLICIES AND PLANNING IN NEWLY INDEPENDENT AFRICA." PLAN ATTIT PWR WEALTH ...STERTYP GEN/LAWS VAL/FREE 20. PAGE 4 F0078 — AFR ECO/DEV NAT/LISM COLONIAL

S62
KRISHNA K.G.V.,"PLANNING AND ECONOMIC DEVELOPMENT" AFR UGANDA AGRI INDUS R+D BUDGET RATION TAX COLONIAL 20. PAGE 73 F1441 — ECO/UNDEV ECO/TAC NAT/LISM PLAN

B63
DEUTSCH K.W.,THE POLITICAL ROLE OF LABOR IN DEVELOPING COUNTRIES. AFR ASIA S/ASIA USA+45 WOR+45 ECO/UNDEV POL/PAR ECO/TAC EDU/PROP LEGIT COERCE ORD/FREE PWR WEALTH...OBS INT TREND VAL/FREE 20. PAGE 32 F0625 — LABOR NAT/LISM

B63
IANNI O.,INDUSTRIALIZACAO E DESENVOLVIMENTO SOCIAL NO BRASIL. BRAZIL L/A+17C STRATA STRUCT ECO/UNDEV EDU/PROP LEAD LOBBY NAT/LISM 20. PAGE 64 F1257 — WORKER GP/REL INDUS PARTIC

B63
ISSAWI C.,EGYPT IN REVOLUTION: AN ECONOMIC ANALYSIS. ISLAM STRUCT ECO/UNDEV AGRI FINAN INDUS PLAN EXEC REV NAT/LISM ATTIT RIGID/FLEX WEALTH SOCISM...STAT FOR/TRADE WORK 20. PAGE 66 F1292 — NAT/G UAR

B63
LAFEBER W.,THE NEW EMPIRE: AN INTERPRETATION OF AMERICAN EXPANSION, 1860-1898. USA-45 CONSTN NAT/LISM SOVEREIGN...TREND BIBLIOG 19/20. PAGE 74 F1457 — INDUS NAT/G DIPLOM CAP/ISM

B63
LEWIN J.,POLITICS AND LAW IN SOUTH AFRICA. SOUTH/AFR UK POL/PAR BAL/PWR ECO/TAC COLONIAL CONTROL GP/REL DISCRIM PWR 20 NEGRO. PAGE 79 F1545 NAT/LISM POLICY LAW RACE/REL

B63
LEWIS G.K.,PUERTO RICO: FREEDOM AND POWER IN THE CARIBBEAN. PUERT/RICO USA+45 CULTURE STRUCT INDUS POL/PAR WORKER EDU/PROP CATHISM 20. PAGE 79 F1548 ECO/UNDEV COLONIAL NAT/LISM GEOG

B63
MENEZES A.J.,SUBDESENVOLVIMENTO E POLITICA INTERNACIONAL. BRAZIL WOR+45 PLAN CONTROL LEAD NAT/LISM ORD/FREE 20 THIRD/WRLD. PAGE 90 F1759 ECO/UNDEV DIPLOM POLICY BAL/PWR

B63
OTERO L.M.,HONDURAS. HONDURAS SPAIN STRUCT SECT COLONIAL REV WAR ATTIT PWR...GEOG WORSHIP 16/20. PAGE 102 F2003 NAT/G SOCIETY NAT/LISM ECO/UNDEV

S63
AYAL E.B.,"VALUE SYSTEM AND ECONOMIC DEVELOPMENT IN JAPAN AND THAILAND." ASIA S/ASIA THAILAND CULTURE ECO/DEV CAP/ISM DOMIN NAT/LISM DRIVE RIGID/FLEX SOCISM...WELF/ST OBS TREND CON/ANAL GEN/LAWS TERR/GP 20 CHINJAP. PAGE 8 F0145 ECO/UNDEV ALL/VALS

S63
NYE J.,"TANGANYIKA'S SELF-HELP." TANZANIA NAT/G GIVE COST EFFICIENCY NAT/LISM 20. PAGE 99 F1948 ECO/TAC POL/PAR ECO/UNDEV WORKER

B64
CASEY R.G.,THE FUTURE OF THE COMMONWEALTH. INDIA PAKISTAN UK ECO/UNDEV INT/ORG TEC/DEV COLONIAL SUPEGO 20 EEC AUSTRAL. PAGE 22 F0425 DIPLOM SOVEREIGN NAT/LISM FOR/AID

B64
DANIELS R.V.,RUSSIA. RUSSIA USSR STRUCT NAT/LISM TOTALISM ORD/FREE WEALTH...POLICY DECISION TREND. PAGE 30 F0579 MARXISM REV ECO/DEV DIPLOM

B64
HALLOWELL J.H.,DEVELOPMENT: FOR WHAT. WOR+45 POL/PAR SECT FOR/AID INT/TRADE CT/SYS PARTIC PRODUC PLURISM. PAGE 54 F1052 ECO/UNDEV CONSTN NAT/LISM ECO/TAC

B64
LUTHULI A.,AFRICA'S FREEDOM. KIN LABOR POL/PAR SCHOOL DIPLOM NEUTRAL REGION REV NAT/LISM PWR WEALTH SOCISM SOC/INTEG 20. PAGE 82 F1608 AFR ECO/UNDEV COLONIAL

B64
MAGALHAES S.,PRATICA DA EMANCIPACAO NACIONAL. L/A+17C INDUS PLAN ECO/TAC CONTROL NAT/LISM ORD/FREE. PAGE 84 F1640 BAL/PAY ECO/UNDEV DIPLOM WEALTH

B64
MELADY T.,FACES OF AFRICA. AFR FUT ISLAM NAT/G POL/PAR SCHOOL DELIB/GP PLAN ECO/TAC EDU/PROP ATTIT ALL/VALS...CHARTS TOT/POP TERR/GP VAL/FREE 20. PAGE 89 F1752 ECO/UNDEV TREND NAT/LISM

B64
SAKAI R.K.,STUDIES ON ASIA, 1964. ASIA CHINA/COM ISRAEL MALAYSIA S/ASIA USA+45 USSR ECO/UNDEV FAM POL/PAR SECT CONSULT NAT/LISM...POLICY SOC 20 CHINJAP. PAGE 115 F2272 PWR DIPLOM

B64
WERTHEIM W.F.,EAST-WEST PARALLELS. INDONESIA S/ASIA NAT/G SECT...TIME/SEQ METH REFORMERS S/EASTASIA. PAGE 145 F2860 SOC ECO/UNDEV CULTURE NAT/LISM

L64
KORBONSKI A.,"COMECON." ASIA ECO/DEV ECO/UNDEV ECO/TAC BAL/PAY NAT/LISM FOR/TRADE 20 COMECON. PAGE 73 F1425 COM INT/ORG INT/TRADE

S64
GERBET P.,"LA MISE EN OEUVRE DU MARCHE COMMUN AGRICOLE." ECO/DEV MARKET INT/ORG NAT/G PLAN EDU/PROP NAT/LISM WEALTH...OBS EEC VAL/FREE 20. PAGE 47 F0917 EUR+WWI AGRI REGION

S64
KLEIN H.,"AMERICAN OIL COMPANIES IN LATIN AMERICA: THE BOLIVIAN EXPERIENCE." L/A+17C USA+45 USA-45 EXTR/IND LG/CO NAT/G ECO/TAC WEALTH...POLICY GEN/LAWS BOLIV TOT/POP 20 OIL. PAGE 72 F1405 MARKET ECO/UNDEV NAT/LISM

S64
PADELFORD N.J.,"THE ORGANIZATION OF AFRICAN UNITY." ECO/UNDEV INT/ORG PLAN BAL/PWR DIPLOM ECO/TAC NAT/LISM ORD/FREE PWR WEALTH...CONCPT TREND STERTYP TERR/GP VAL/FREE 20. PAGE 102 F2013 AFR VOL/ASSN REGION

B65
APTER D.E.,THE POLITICS OF MODERNIZATION. AFR L/A+17C CULTURE NAT/G POL/PAR ADMIN COLONIAL NAT/LISM ATTIT RIGID/FLEX PWR...SOC CONCPT. PAGE 6 F0109 ECO/UNDEV GEN/LAWS STRATA CREATE

B65
GRAMPP W.D.,ECONOMIC LIBERALISM; THE CLASSICAL VIEW (VOL. II). MOD/EUR SOCIETY MARKET INT/TRADE NAT/LISM WEALTH LAISSEZ...POLICY PSY CONCPT BIBLIOG 19 SMITH/ADAM HUME/D MILL/JS. PAGE 50 F0975 ECO/DEV CAP/ISM IDEA/COMP ECO/TAC

B65
GREENFIELD K.R.,ECONOMICS AND LIBERALISM IN THE RISORGIMENTO (REV. ED.). ITALY AGRI FINAN PROC/MFG PLAN INT/TRADE CONTROL PWR 19. PAGE 51 F0990 NAT/LISM PRESS POLICY

B65
JOHNSON H.G.,THE WORLD ECONOMY AT THE CROSSROADS. COM WOR-45 ECO/DEV AGRI INDUS INT/TRADE REGION NAT/LISM 20. PAGE 67 F1326 FINAN DIPLOM INT/ORG ECO/UNDEV

B65
NKRUMAH K.,NEO-COLONIALISM: THE LAST STAGE OF IMPERIALISM. AFR INT/ORG WORKER FOR/AID INT/TRADE EDU/PROP GOV/REL NAT/LISM SOVEREIGN POPULISM SOCISM ...SOCIALIST 20 THIRD/WRLD INTRVN/ECO. PAGE 98 F1929 COLONIAL DIPLOM ECO/UNDEV ECO/TAC

B65
PROCHNOW H.V.,WORLD ECONOMIC PROBLEMS AND POLICIES. INDIA ISRAEL WOR+45 AGRI LABOR PROB/SOLV FOR/AID TARIFFS CONTROL BAL/PAY NAT/LISM WEALTH...TREND CHARTS 20 CHINJAP EEC. PAGE 108 F2124 MARKET ECO/TAC PRODUC IDEA/COMP

B65
SPENCE J.E.,REPUBLIC UNDER PRESSURE: A STUDY OF SOUTH AFRICAN FOREIGN POLICY. SOUTH/AFR ADMIN COLONIAL GOV/REL RACE/REL DISCRIM NAT/LISM ATTIT ROLE...TREND 20 NEGRO. PAGE 124 F2449 DIPLOM POLICY AFR

B65
THORNTON A.P.,DOCTRINES OF IMPERIALISM. WOR+45 WOR-45 DOMIN NAT/LISM PROFIT ATTIT PERSON PWR RESPECT SOVEREIGN...CONCPT STERTYP. PAGE 130 F2571 IDEA/COMP COLONIAL DRIVE

S65
JOHNSON H.G.,"A THEORETICAL MODEL OF ECONOMIC NATIONALISM IN NEW AND DEVELOPING STATES." ELITES INDUS INT/TRADE EDU/PROP COST OPTIMAL RATIONAL PWR WEALTH SOCISM STERTYP. PAGE 67 F1325 NAT/LISM ECO/UNDEV GEN/LAWS

S65
WHITAKER A.P.,"ARGENTINA: STRUGGLE FOR RECOVERY." L/A+17C USA+45 NAT/G TOP/EX PLAN LEGIT COERCE REV RIGID/FLEX PWR WEALTH...RECORD ALL/PROG ARGEN FOR/TRADE 20. PAGE 146 F2867 POL/PAR ECO/TAC NAT/LISM

B66
AMERICAN ASSEMBLY COLUMBIA U,THE UNITED STATES AND THE PHILIPPINES. PHILIPPINE S/ASIA USA+45 USA-45 SOCIETY FORCES INT/TRADE...POLICY 20. PAGE 5 F0085 COLONIAL DIPLOM NAT/LISM

B66
BEQIRAJ M.,PEASANTRY IN REVOLUTION. STRATA ECO/UNDEV AGRI ROUTINE REV HABITAT RIGID/FLEX ...EPIST GEOG NEW/IDEA TREND MUNICH 20. PAGE 13 F0256 WORKER KNOWL NAT/LISM SOC

B66
BROWN J.F.,THE NEW EASTERN EUROPE. ALBANIA BULGARIA HUNGARY POLAND ROMANIA CULTURE AGRI POL/PAR WAR NAT/LISM MARXISM...CHARTS BIBLIOG 20. PAGE 19 F0369 DIPLOM COM NAT/G ECO/UNDEV

B66
CROWDER M.,A SHORT HISTORY OF NIGERIA. AFR NIGERIA UK ECO/UNDEV CHIEF INT/TRADE RACE/REL NAT/LISM ORD/FREE...GEOG SOC CHARTS BIBLIOG 14/20. PAGE 29 F0558 COLONIAL NAT/G CULTURE

B66
FRANKEL P.H.,MATTEI; OIL AND POWER POLITICS. ITALY EXTR/IND MARKET GP/REL NAT/LISM SOCISM...POLICY MGT BIOG 20 MATTEI/E. PAGE 43 F0844 LEAD NAT/G CONTROL LG/CO

B66
KEENLEYSIDE H.L.,INTERNATIONAL AID: A SUMMARY. AFR INDIA S/ASIA UK STRATA EXTR/IND TEC/DEV ADMIN RACE/REL DEMAND NAT/LISM WEALTH...TREND CHINJAP. PAGE 70 F1367 ECO/UNDEV FOR/AID DIPLOM TASK

B66
LONDON K.,EASTERN EUROPE IN TRANSITION. CHINA/COM USSR DOMIN COLONIAL CENTRAL RIGID/FLEX PWR...SOC ANTHOL 20. PAGE 82 F1597 SOVEREIGN COM NAT/LISM DIPLOM

S66
ROTHCHILD D.,"THE LIMITS OF FEDERALISM: AN EXAMINATION OF POLITICAL INSTITUTIONAL TRANSFER IN AFRICA." AFR CONSTN CULTURE ELITES ECO/UNDEV KIN PROB/SOLV ADMIN ORD/FREE PWR...POLICY 20. PAGE 114 F2250 FEDERAL NAT/G NAT/LISM COLONIAL

B67
ANDERSON C.W.,ISSUES OF POLITICAL DEVELOPMENT. BURMA WOR+45 CULTURE TOP/EX ECO/TAC MARXISM ...CHARTS NAT/COMP 20 COLOMB CONGO/LEOP. PAGE 5 F0094 NAT/LISM COERCE ECO/UNDEV SOCISM

B67
BAILY S.L.,LABOR, NATIONALISM, AND POLITICS IN ARGENTINA. POL/PAR TOP/EX GP/REL...BIBLIOG/A 19/20 MIGRATION PERON/JUAN ARGEN. PAGE 8 F0154 LABOR NAT/LISM

B67
BARNETT A.D.,CHINA AFTER MAO. ASIA CHINA/COM CULTURE ECO/UNDEV ECO/TAC CONTROL EFFICIENCY NAT/LISM MARXISM 20. PAGE 10 F0189 POL/PAR NAT/G TEC/DEV GP/REL

B67
CEFKIN J.L.,THE BACKGROUND OF CURRENT WORLD PROBLEMS. AFR NAT/G MARXISM...T 20 UN. PAGE 22 F0432 DIPLOM NAT/LISM ECO/UNDEV

B67
CHILCOTE R.H.,PORTUGUESE AFRICA. PORTUGAL CULTURE SOCIETY ECO/UNDEV DOMIN NAT/LISM...TREND IDEA/COMP NAT/COMP BIBLIOG 15/20. PAGE 24 F0465 AFR COLONIAL ORD/FREE PROB/SOLV

B67
DAVIS H.B.,NATIONALISM AND SOCIALISM: MARXIST AND LABOR THEORIES OF NATIONALISM TO 1917. WOR-45 PROB/SOLV SOVEREIGN...CONCPT IDEA/COMP 19/20. PAGE 30 F0589 MARXISM ATTIT NAT/LISM SOCISM

B67
DINERSTEIN H.S.,INTERVENTION AGAINST COMMUNISM (STUDIES IN INTERNATIONAL AFFAIRS NO. 1). CUBA DOMIN/REP GREECE USA+45 USSR VIETNAM OP/RES COERCE WAR 20. PAGE 33 F0643 MARXISM DIPLOM NAT/LISM

B67
JHANGIANI M.A.,JANA SANGH AND SWATANTRA: A PROFILE OF THE RIGHTIST PARTIES IN INDIA. INDIA ADMIN CHOOSE MARXISM SOCISM...INT CHARTS BIBLIOG 20. PAGE 67 F1320 POL/PAR LAISSEZ NAT/LISM ATTIT

B67
JOHNSON H.G.,ECONOMIC NATIONALISM IN OLD AND NEW STATES. CANADA CHINA/COM MALI UK DIPLOM...SIMUL GEN/LAWS 19/20 MEXIC/AMER. PAGE 68 F1328 NAT/LISM ECO/UNDEV ECO/DEV NAT/COMP

B67
MEYNAUD J.,TRADE UNIONISM IN AFRICA; A STUDY OF ITS GROWTH AND ORIENTATION (TRANS. BY ANGELA BRENCH). INT/ORG PROB/SOLV COLONIAL PWR...TIME/SEQ TREND ILO. PAGE 90 F1774 LABOR AFR NAT/LISM ORD/FREE

B67
MUHAMMAD A.C.,THE EMERGENCE OF PAKISTAN. PAKISTAN S/ASIA CONSTN ECO/UNDEV NAT/G CONTROL NAT/LISM 20. PAGE 94 F1853 DIPLOM COLONIAL SECT PROB/SOLV

B67
RAVKIN A.,THE NEW STATES OF AFRICA (HEADLINE SERIES, NO. 183((PAMPHLET). CULTURE STRUCT INDUS COLONIAL NAT/LISM...SOC 20. PAGE 109 F2153 AFR ECO/UNDEV SOCIETY ADMIN

B67
SCHECTER J.,THE NEW FACE OF BUDDHA: BUDDHISM AND POLITICAL POWER IN SOUTHEAST ASIA. S/ASIA NAT/G POL/PAR NAT/LISM ATTIT MARXISM...BIBLIOG 20. PAGE 116 F2292 SECT POLICY PWR LEAD

B67
SPIRO H.S.,PATTERNS OF AFRICAN DEVLOPMENT: FIVE COMPARISONS. STRUCT ECO/UNDEV NAT/G CONSERVE SOCISM ...PREDICT NAT/COMP 20 CHINJAP. PAGE 125 F2457 AFR CONSTN NAT/LISM TREND

B67
YAMAMURA K.,ECONOMIC POLICY IN POSTWAR JAPAN. ASIA FINAN POL/PAR DIPLOM LEAD NAT/LISM ATTIT NEW/LIB POPULISM 20 CHINJAP. PAGE 149 F2946 ECO/DEV POLICY NAT/G TEC/DEV

L67
GREGORY A.J.,"AFRICAN SOCIALISM, SOCIALISM AND FASCISM: AN APPRAISAL." FUT LEAD REV GP/REL RACE/REL NAT/LISM ATTIT...IDEA/COMP STERTYP 20. PAGE 51 F0993 FASCISM MARXISM SOCISM AFR

S67
"PROTEST AGAINST SOVIET INDUSTRIALIZATION ILLS IN LITHUANIA* A MEMORANDUM." USSR LITHUANIA NAT/G PROVS COST GEOG. PAGE 1 F0024 INDUS COLONIAL NAT/LISM PLAN

S67
APEL H.,"LES NOUVEAUX ASPECTS DE LA POLITIQUE ETRANGERE ALLEMANDE." AFR EUR+WWI GERMANY POL/PAR BAL/PWR ECO/TAC INT/TRADE NUC/PWR NAT/LISM PEACE ...POLICY 20 EEC. PAGE 6 F0107 DIPLOM INT/ORG FEDERAL

S67
FEDYSHYN O.S.,"KHRUSHCHEV'S 'LEAP FORWARD': NATIONAL ASSIMILATION IN THE USSR AFTER STALIN." USSR PLAN NAT/LISM PERSON...POLICY 20 KHRUSH/N STALIN/J. PAGE 39 F0771 GP/REL INGP/REL MARXISM METH

S67
HEILBRONER R.L.,"BUILDING NEW NATIONS." AFR STRUCT PLAN TEC/DEV ADJUST MARXISM...POLICY 20. PAGE 58 F1138 PROB/SOLV REV NAT/LISM ECO/UNDEV

S67
IBARRA J.,"EL EXPERIMENTO CUBANO." COM CUBA L/A+17C USA+45 ECO/UNDEV LEGIS INT/TRADE CONTROL REV NAT/LISM PWR 19/20 TREATY. PAGE 64 F1259 COLONIAL DIPLOM NAT/G POLICY

S67
LANGLEY L.D.,"THE DEMOCRATIC TRADITION AND MILITARY REFORM, 1878-1885." USA-45 SECT EDU/PROP CROWD EFFICIENCY NAT/LISM 19 INDIAN/AM. PAGE 75 F1480 ATTIT FORCES POPULISM

S67
LEIFER M.,"ASTRIDE THE STRAITS OF JAHORE: THE BRITISH PRESENCE AND COMMONWEALTH RIVALRY IN SOUTHEAST ASIA." MALAYSIA UK FORCES PLAN ECO/TAC ...DECISION 20 CMN/WLTH. PAGE 77 F1515 DIPLOM NAT/LISM COLONIAL

S67
MOSELY P.E.,"EASTERN EUROPE IN WORLD POWER POLITICS: WHERE DE-STALINIZATION HAS LED." ECO/UNDEV NAT/LISM 20. PAGE 94 F1842 COM NAT/G DIPLOM MARXISM

S67
POWELL D.,"THE EFFECTIVENESS OF SOVIET ANTI-RELIGIOUS PROPAGANDA." USSR NAT/G DOMIN LEGIT NAT/LISM 20. PAGE 107 F2109 EDU/PROP ATTIT SECT CONTROL

S67
WILLMANN J.,"LA COMMUNAUTE EUROPEENNE ET LA GRANDE-BRETAGNE." UK PROB/SOLV TEC/DEV CAP/ISM DIPLOM CONFER FEDERAL...POLICY 20 EEC. PAGE 147 F2898 INT/ORG DRIVE NAT/LISM INT/TRADE

N67
US HOUSE COMM FOREIGN AFFAIRS,REPORT OF SPECIAL STUDY MISSION TO THE NEAR EAST (PAMPHLET). ISRAEL USA+45 YEMEN ECO/UNDEV INT/ORG FOR/AID ARMS/CONT WAR WEAPON NAT/LISM PEACE...GEOG 20 UN HOUSE/REP. PAGE 137 F2694 ISLAM DIPLOM FORCES

NAT/SAFETY....NATIONAL SAFETY COUNCIL

NAT/SERV....COMPULSORY NATIONAL SERVICE

NAT/UNITY....NATIONAL UNITY COMMITTEE (TURKEY)

NATAL

NATIONAL AERONAUTIC AND SPACE ADMINISTRATION....SEE NASA

NATIONAL ASSOCIATION FOR THE ADVANCEMENT OF COLORED PEOPLE....SEE NAACP

NATIONAL ASSOCIATION OF MANUFACTURERS....SEE NAM

NATIONAL BELLAS HESS....SEE BELLAS/HES

NATIONAL COUNCIL OF CHURCHES....SEE NCC

NATIONAL DEBT....SEE DEBT

NATIONAL DIRECTORY (IRELAND)....SEE DIRECT/NAT

NATIONAL EDUCATION ASSOCIATION....SEE NEA

NATIONAL FARMERS' ASSOCIATION....SEE NAT/FARMER

NATIONAL GUARD....SEE NATL/GUARD

NATIONAL INSTITUTE OF HEALTH....SEE NIH

NATIONAL INSTITUTE OF PUBLIC ADMINISTRATION....SEE NIPA

NATIONAL LABOR RELATIONS BOARD....SEE NLRB

NATIONAL LIBERATION COUNCIL IN GHANA....SEE NLC

NATIONAL LIBERATION FRONT (OF SOUTH VIETNAM)....SEE NLF

NATIONAL RECOVERY ADMINISTRATION....SEE NRA

NATIONAL SAFETY COUNCIL....SEE NAT/SAFETY

NATIONAL SCIENCE FOUNDATION....SEE NSF

NATIONAL SECURITY COUNCIL....SEE NSC

NATIONAL SECURITY....SEE ORD/FREE

NATIONAL SOCIAL SCIENCE FOUNDATION....SEE NSSF

NATIONAL UNITY COMMITTEE....SEE NUC

NATIONAL WEALTH....SEE NAT/G+WEALTH

NATIONAL BUREAU ECONOMIC RES F1895

NATIONAL CENTRAL LIBRARY F1897

NATIONAL COMN COMMUNITY HEALTH F1898

NATIONAL CONF SOCIAL WELFARE F1899

NATIONAL COUN APPLIED ECO RES F1900,F1901

NATIONAL INDUSTRIAL CONF BOARD F1902

NATIONALISM....SEE NAT/LISM

NATIONALIST CHINA....SEE TAIWAN

NATIONALIZATION....SEE SOCISM

NATL/GUARD....NATIONAL GUARD

NATO....NORTH ATLANTIC TREATY ORGANIZATION; SEE ALSO VOL/ASSN, INT/ORG, FORCES, DETER

B51
US HOUSE COMM APPROPRIATIONS,MUTUAL SECURITY PROGRAM APPROPRIATIONS FOR 1952: HEARINGS BEFORE A SUBCOMMITTEE OF THE COMMITTEE ON APPROPRIATIONS. AFR KOREA L/A+17C ECO/DEV ECO/UNDEV INT/ORG INSPECT BAL/PWR DIPLOM DEBATE WAR...POLICY STAT ASIA/S 20 CONGRESS NATO MID/EAST. PAGE 136 F2686
LEGIS FORCES BUDGET FOR/AID

S57
HOAG M.W.,"ECONOMIC PROBLEMS OF ALLIANCE." AFR COM EUR+WWI WOR+45 ECO/DEV ECO/UNDEV NAT/G VOL/ASSN FORCES PLAN TEC/DEV DIPLOM COERCE ORD/FREE PWR WEALTH...DECISION GEN/LAWS NATO TERR/GP. PAGE 60 F1182
INT/ORG ECO/TAC

B59
ROBERTSON A.H.,EUROPEAN INSTITUTIONS: COOPERATION, INTEGRATION, UNIFICATION. EUR+WWI FINAN INT/ORG FORCES INT/TRADE TARIFFS 20 EEC EURATOM ECSC NATO TREATY. PAGE 112 F2208
ECO/DEV DIPLOM INDUS ECO/TAC

B60
HITCH C.J.,THE ECONOMICS OF DEFENSE IN THE NUCLEAR AGE. USA+45 WOR+45 CREATE PLAN NUC/PWR ATTIT ...CON/ANAL CHARTS HYPO/EXP NATO 20. PAGE 60 F1179
R+D FORCES

B61
MORLEY L.,THE PATCHWORK HISTORY OF FOREIGN AID. AFR KOREA/S USA+45 USSR LAW FINAN INT/ORG TEC/DEV BAL/PWR GIVE 20 NATO. PAGE 93 F1834
FOR/AID ECO/UNDEV FORCES DIPLOM

B63
BELOFF M.,THE UNITED STATES AND THE UNITY OF EUROPE. EUR+WWI UK USA+45 WOR+45 VOL/ASSN DIPLOM REGION ATTIT PWR...CONCPT EEC OEEC 20 NATO. PAGE 13 F0239
ECO/DEV INT/ORG

B63
CERAMI C.A.,ALLIANCE BORN OF DANGER. EUR+WWI USA+45 USSR ECO/DEV INDUS VOL/ASSN ECO/TAC REGION ATTIT MARXISM ATLAN/ALL 20 NATO EEC. PAGE 22 F0437
DIPLOM INT/ORG NAT/G POLICY

S63
EMERSON R.,"THE ATLANTIC COMMUNITY AND THE EMERGING COUNTRIES." FUT WOR+45 ECO/DEV ECO/UNDEV R+D NAT/G DELIB/GP BAL/PWR ECO/TAC EDU/PROP ROUTINE ORD/FREE PWR WEALTH...POLICY CONCPT TREND GEN/METH EEC 20 NATO. PAGE 37 F0729
ATTIT INT/TRADE

B64
ECONOMIDES C.P.,LE POUVOIR DE DECISION DES ORGANISATIONS INTERNATIONALES EUROPEENNES. DIPLOM DOMIN INGP/REL EFFICIENCY...INT/LAW JURID 20 NATO OEEC EEC COUNCL/EUR EURATOM. PAGE 36 F0698
INT/ORG PWR DECISION GP/COMP

B64
FREYMOND J.,WESTERN EUROPE SINCE THE WAR. COM EUR+WWI USA+45 DIPLOM...BIBLIOG 20 NATO UN EEC. PAGE 44 F0854
INT/ORG POLICY ECO/DEV ECO/TAC

B64
KRAUSE L.B.,THE COMMON MARKET: PROGRESS AND CONTROVERSY. EUR+WWI UK ECO/DEV REGION...ANTHOL NATO EEC. PAGE 73 F1433
DIPLOM MARKET INT/TRADE INT/ORG

B65
CERNY K.H.,NATO IN QUEST OF COHESION* A CONFRONTATION OF VIEWPOINTS. COM EUR+WWI USA+45 FORCES LEAD REGION DETER...ANTHOL NATO. PAGE 22 F0438
CENTRAL NUC/PWR VOL/ASSN

B65
KISSINGER H.A.,THE TROUBLED PARTNERSHIP* RE-APPRAISAL OF THE WESTERN ALLIANCE. EUR+WWI USA+45 INT/ORG NAT/G VOL/ASSN TOP/EX DIPLOM ORD/FREE PWR NATO. PAGE 71 F1402
FRANCE NUC/PWR ECO/DEV

S65
SPAAK P.H.,"THE SEARCH FOR CONSENSUS: A NEW EFFORT TO BUILD EUROPE." FRANCE GERMANY ECO/DEV NAT/G CONSULT FORCES PLAN EDU/PROP REGION CONSEN ATTIT ...SOC METH/CNCPT OBS TREND EEC NATO WORK TERR/GP METH/GP 20. PAGE 124 F2447
EUR+WWI INT/ORG

B66
BEUGEL E.V.D.,FROM MARSHALL AID TO ATLANTIC PARTNERSHIP* EUROPEAN INTEGRATION AS A CONCERN OF AMERICAN FOREIGN POLICY. USA+45 INT/ORG FORCES PERSON EEC NATO. PAGE 14 F0272
REGION DIPLOM EUR+WWI VOL/ASSN

B66
SPICER K.,A SAMARITAN STATE? AFR CANADA INDIA PAKISTAN UK USA+45 FINAN INDUS PRODUC...CHARTS 20 NATO. PAGE 124 F2455
DIPLOM FOR/AID ECO/DEV ADMIN

B66
UREN P.E.,EAST - WEST TRADE* A SYMPOSIUM. COM AGRI INT/ORG PRICE HABITAT RIGID/FLEX...GEOG INT/LAW ANTHOL NATO. PAGE 133 F2625
INT/TRADE BAL/PWR AFR CANADA

B66
US HOUSE COMM FOREIGN AFFAIRS,HEARINGS ON HR 12449 A BILL TO AMEND FURTHER THE FOREIGN ASSISTANCE ACT OF 1961. AFR ASIA L/A+17C USA+45 VIETNAM INT/ORG TEC/DEV INT/TRADE ATTIT ORD/FREE 20 UN NATO CONGRESS AID. PAGE 137 F2692
FOR/AID ECO/TAC ECO/UNDEV DIPLOM

S66
DUROSELLE J.B.,"THE FUTURE OF THE ATLANTIC COMMUNITY." EUR+WWI USA+45 USSR NAT/G CAP/ISM REGION DETER NUC/PWR ATTIT MARXISM...INT/LAW 20 NATO. PAGE 35 F0686
FUT DIPLOM MYTH POLICY

B67
MACCLOSKEY M.,PACTS FOR PEACE: UN, NATO, SEATO, CENTO, OAS. WOR+45 PLAN DIPLOM CONTROL PEACE ORD/FREE...ORG/CHARTS UN NATO SEATO OAS CENTO. PAGE 83 F1623
FORCES INT/ORG LEAD POLICY

B67
ROACH J.R.,THE UNITED STATES AND THE ATLANTIC COMMUNITY; ISSUES AND PROSPECTS. AFR WOR+45 TEC/DEV ECO/TAC COLONIAL REGION PEACE ROLE...ANTHOL NATO EEC. PAGE 112 F2199
INT/ORG POLICY ADJUST DIPLOM

S67
STOLTE S.C.,"THREE PROBLEMS FACING THE SOVIET BLOC." ASIA COM USA+45 USSR FORCES MARXISM ...IDEA/COMP METH/COMP 20 NATO WARSAW/P. PAGE 127 F2496
ECO/TAC DIPLOM INT/ORG POLICY

NATURL/LAW....NATURAL LAW

NAUMANN R. F1903

NAVAHO....NAVAHO INDIANS

NAVAL/RES....OFFICE OF NAVAL RESEARCH

N19
MORGENSTERN O.,A NEW LOOK AT ECONOMIC TIMES SERIES ANALYSIS (PAMPHLET). WEALTH...BIBLIOG 20 NSF NAVAL/RES. PAGE 93 F1831
TREND IDEA/COMP EFFICIENCY

NAVY....NAVY (ALL NATIONS)

B63
BATES J.L.,THE ORIGINS OF TEAPOT DOME: PROGRESSIVES, PARTIES, AND PETROLEUM, 1909-1921. USA-45 INDUS LG/CO POL/PAR DELIB/GP CONTROL GOV/REL CONSERVE...BIBLIOG 20 NAVY. PAGE 11 F0209
EXTR/IND CRIME NAT/G

NAYLOR T.H. F0472

NAZI....NAZI MOVEMENT (ALL NATIONS); SEE ALSO GERMANY, NAT/LISM, FASCIST

B38
LAWLEY F.E.,THE GROWTH OF COLLECTIVE ECONOMY VOL. 2: INTERNATIONAL. WOR-45 AGRI INDUS EQUILIB OPTIMAL OWN WEALTH...NAT/COMP 19/20 NAZI NEW/DEAL MONOPOLY. PAGE 76 F1493
ECO/TAC SOCISM NAT/LISM CONTROL

S39
COLE G.D.H.,"NAZI ECONOMICS: HOW DO THEY MANAGE IT?" GERMANY FORCES WORKER BUDGET INT/TRADE ROUTINE COERCE WAR 20 HITLER/A NAZI. PAGE 26 F0500
FASCISM ECO/TAC ATTIT PLAN

B47
GORDON D.L.,THE HIDDEN WEAPON: THE STORY OF ECONOMIC WARFARE. EUR+WWI USA-45 LAW FINAN INDUS NAT/G CONSULT FORCES PLAN DOMIN PWR WEALTH ...INT/LAW CONCPT OBS TOT/POP NAZI 20. PAGE 49 F0955
INT/ORG ECO/TAC INT/TRADE WAR

B59
HOOVER C.B.,THE ECONOMY, LIBERTY AND THE STATE. COM EUR+WWI USA+45 USA-45 USSR CAP/ISM EDU/PROP COERCE TOTALISM ORD/FREE...POLICY OBS INT TREND NAZI 20. PAGE 61 F1206
ECO/DEV ECO/TAC

B60
BOHM F.,REDEN UND SCHRIFTEN UBER DIE ORDNUNG EINER FREIEN GESELLSCHAFT, EINER FREIEN WIRTSCHAFT, UND UBER DIE WIEDERGUTMACH. DIPLOM CRIME ORD/FREE RESPECT FASCISM 20 NAZI. PAGE 16 F0307
ECO/TAC NEW/LIB SUPEGO REPAR

NCC....NATIONAL COUNCIL OF CHURCHES

NE/WIN....NE WIN

NEA....NATIONAL EDUCATION ASSOCIATION

NEAL A.C. F0389,F1904

NEALE A.D. F1905

NEALE R.S. F1906

NEAR EAST....SEE MEDIT-7, ISLAM

NEBRASKA....NEBRASKA

NEG/INCOME....NEGATIVE INCOME TAX

NEGRITO....NEGRITO TRIBE, PHILIPPINES

NEGRO....NEGRO

N
BROCKWAY A.F.,AFRICAN SOCIALISM. EUR+WWI GHANA ISLAM UAR ECO/UNDEV CAP/ISM INT/TRADE COLONIAL COERCE GOV/REL DISCRIM 20 NEGRO NKRUMAH/K NASSER/G. PAGE 19 F0356
AFR SOCISM MARXISM

NCO
CARRINGTON C.E.,THE COMMONWEALTH IN AFRICA (PAMPHLET). UK STRUCT NAT/G COLONIAL REPRESENT GOV/REL RACE/REL NAT/LISM...MAJORIT 20 EEC NEGRO. PAGE 22 F0421
ECO/UNDEV AFR DIPLOM PLAN

B02
MOREL E.D.,AFFAIRS OF WEST AFRICA. UK FINAN INDUS FAM KIN SECT CHIEF WORKER DIPLOM RACE/REL LITERACY HEALTH...CHARTS 18/20 AFRICA/W NEGRO. PAGE 93 F1826
COLONIAL ADMIN AFR

N19
SENGHOR L.S.,AFRICAN SOCIALISM (PAMPHLET). AFR FRANCE MALI USSR ELITES ECO/UNDEV NAT/G DIPLOM DOMIN EDU/PROP ATTIT 20 NEGRO. PAGE 119 F2355
SOCISM MARXISM ORD/FREE NAT/LISM

B20
MOREL E.D.,THE BLACK MAN'S BURDEN. AFR MOD/EUR AGRI EXTR/IND PROB/SOLV INT/TRADE ADMIN CONTROL COERCE DISCRIM...POLICY 19/20 NEGRO LEAGUE/NAT. PAGE 93 F1828
ORD/FREE CAP/ISM RACE/REL DOMIN

B48
KESSELMAN L.C.,THE SOCIAL POLITICS OF THE FEPC. INDUS WORKER EDU/PROP GP/REL RACE/REL 20 NEGRO JEWS FEPC. PAGE 70 F1382
POLICY NAT/G ADMIN DISCRIM

B52
SACHS E.S.,THE CHOICE BEFORE SOUTH AFRICA. SOUTH/AFR AGRI EXTR/IND PROC/MFG PROB/SOLV ORD/FREE SOVEREIGN 20 NEGRO. PAGE 115 F2267
NAT/LISM DISCRIM RACE/REL LABOR

S52
KORNHAUSER W.,"THE NEGRO UNION OFFICIAL: A STUDY OF SPONSORSHIP AND CONTROL" (BMR)" USA+45 CONTROL DISCRIM ROLE SUPEGO...OBS 20 NEGRO. PAGE 73 F1428
LABOR LEAD RACE/REL CHOOSE

B54
KARTUN D.,AFRICA, AFRICA: A CONTINENT RISES TO ITS FEET. AFR SOUTH/AFR UK ELITES AGRI LABOR LOC/G POL/PAR EDU/PROP CONTROL COERCE DISCRIM AGE/Y NEGRO THIRD/WRLD GOLD/COAST. PAGE 69 F1358
COLONIAL ORD/FREE PROFIT EXTR/IND

B59
VOSE C.E.,CAUCASIANS ONLY: THE SUPREME COURT, THE NAACP, AND THE RESTRICTIVE COVENANT CASES. USA+45 LAW CONSTN LOBBY...SOC 20 NAACP SUPREME/CT NEGRO. PAGE 142 F2796
CT/SYS RACE/REL DISCRIM

B61
SPOONER F.P.,SOUTH AFRICAN PREDICAMENT. FUT SOUTH/AFR INDUS POL/PAR RACE/REL INCOME...CHARTS 20 NEGRO. PAGE 125 F2459
ECO/DEV DISCRIM ECO/TAC POLICY

B62
VAN RENSBURG P.,GUILTY LAND: THE HISTORY OF APARTHEID. SOUTH/AFR NAT/G POL/PAR DOMIN CHOOSE ...SOC 19/20 NEGRO. PAGE 140 F2763
RACE/REL DISCRIM NAT/LISM POLICY

B63
ELLENDER A.J.,A REPORT ON UNITED STATES FOREIGN OPERATIONS IN AFRICA. SOUTH/AFR USA+45 STRATA EXTR/IND FORCES RACE/REL ISOLAT SOVEREIGN...CHARTS 20 NEGRO. PAGE 37 F0721
FOR/AID DIPLOM WEALTH ECO/UNDEV

B63
JACOBS P.,STATE OF UNIONS. USA+45 STRATA TOP/EX GP/REL RACE/REL DEMAND DISCRIM ATTIT PWR 20 CONGRESS NEGRO HOFFA/J. PAGE 66 F1296
LABOR ECO/TAC BARGAIN DECISION

B63
LEWIN J.,POLITICS AND LAW IN SOUTH AFRICA. SOUTH/AFR UK POL/PAR BAL/PWR ECO/TAC COLONIAL CONTROL GP/REL DISCRIM PWR 20 NEGRO. PAGE 79 F1545
NAT/LISM POLICY LAW RACE/REL

B64
HUTT W.H.,THE ECONOMICS OF THE COLOUR BAR. SOUTH/AFR EXTR/IND LABOR ADJUD NEGRO. PAGE 64 F1251
INDUS DISCRIM RACE/REL ECO/UNDEV

B64
MORGAN H.W.,AMERICAN SOCIALISM 1900-1960. AFR USA+45 USA-45 INTELL AGRI LABOR WORKER BARGAIN ECO/TAC GP/REL RACE/REL 20 NEGRO MIGRATION. PAGE 93 F1830
SOCISM POL/PAR ECO/DEV STRATA

B64
TAEUBER I.B.,POPULATION TRENDS IN THE UNITED STATES: 1900 TO 1960. USA+45 USA-45 PROVS INCOME AGE...SOC TIME/SEQ TREND CHARTS MUNICH TIME 20 NEGRO. PAGE 128 F2522
CENSUS GEOG STRATA STRUCT

C64
NORGREN P.H.,"TOWARD FAIR EMPLOYMENT." USA+45 LAW STRATA LABOR NAT/G FORCES ACT/RES ADMIN ATTIT ...POLICY BIBLIOG 20 NEGRO. PAGE 98 F1932
RACE/REL DISCRIM WORKER MGT

B65
SPENCE J.E.,REPUBLIC UNDER PRESSURE: A STUDY OF SOUTH AFRICAN FOREIGN POLICY. SOUTH/AFR ADMIN COLONIAL GOV/REL RACE/REL DISCRIM NAT/LISM ATTIT ROLE...TREND 20 NEGRO. PAGE 124 F2449
DIPLOM POLICY AFR

B66
EBONY,THE NEGRO HANDBOOK. ACADEM LABOR LOC/G SECT FORCES WORKER CT/SYS CRIME DISCRIM ORD/FREE...BIOG SOC/INTEG 19/20 NEGRO CIV/RIGHTS. PAGE 36 F0692
RACE/REL EDU/PROP LAW STAT

B66
SOVERN M.I.,LEGAL RESTRAINTS ON RACIAL DISCRIMINATION IN EMPLOYMENT. USA+45 LAW INDUS LG/CO SML/CO DELIB/GP LEGIS SANCTION 20 NLRB PRESIDENT NEGRO CIV/RIGHTS RAILROAD. PAGE 124 F2446
DISCRIM RACE/REL WORKER JURID

B66
WOODMAN H.D.,SLAVERY AND THE SOUTHERN ECONOMY: SOURCES AND READINGS. USA-45 CULTURE STRUCT AGRI ECO/TAC LEAD RACE/REL DISCRIM EFFICIENCY...CHARTS ANTHOL MUNICH 18/19 NEGRO SOUTH/US. PAGE 148 F2922
ECO/DEV STRATA WORKER UTIL

B67
BERGMANN D KAUN B.,STRUCTURAL UNEMPLOYMENT IN THE UNITED STATES. USA+45 ECO/DEV PRICE ADMIN INGP/REL DEMAND EQUILIB WEALTH...MATH REGRESS STAT 20 NEGRO. PAGE 13 F0258
ECOMETRIC METH WORKER ECO/TAC

B67
POLLACK N.,THE POPULIST MIND. USA-45 STRATA AGRI NAT/G POL/PAR LEGIS WORKER RACE/REL WEALTH...ANTHOL BIBLIOG 19 NEGRO. PAGE 107 F2097
POPULISM HIST/WRIT ATTIT INGP/REL

B67
POWLEDGE F.,BLACK POWER WHITE RESISTANCE. USA+45 STRUCT PLAN GP/REL DISCRIM HABITAT ORD/FREE WEALTH ...METH/COMP SOC/INTEG NEGRO. PAGE 107 F2111
RACE/REL ATTIT PWR

B67
ROSS A.M.,EMPLOYMENT, RACE, AND POVERTY. USA+45 LAW STRATA MARKET LABOR EDU/PROP ISOLAT SKILL...MGT ANTHOL 20 NEGRO. PAGE 114 F2244
RACE/REL WORKER WEALTH DISCRIM

I67
GLAZER N.,"HOUSING PROBLEMS AND HOUSING POLICIES." USA+45 PLAN RENT ADJUST CONSEN DEMAND DISCRIM AGE ATTIT HEALTH WEALTH MUNICH NEGRO. PAGE 48 F0929
POLICY CONSTRUC CREATE HABITAT

S67
"THE FEDERAL AGRICULTURAL STABILIZATION PROGRAM AND THE NEGRO." LAW CONSTN PLAN REPRESENT DISCRIM ORD/FREE 20 NEGRO CONGRESS. PAGE 2 F0025
AGRI CONTROL NAT/G RACE/REL

S67
BRIMMER A.F.,"EMPLOYMENT PATTERNS AND THE DILEMMA OF DESEGREGATION." USA+45 SOCIETY SKILL 20 NEGRO. PAGE 18 F0353
RACE/REL DISCRIM WORKER STRATA

S67
EDGEWORTH A.B. JR.,"CIVIL RIGHTS PLUS THREE YEARS: BANKS AND THE ANTI-DISCRIMINATION LAW" USA+45 SOCIETY DELIB/GP RACE/REL EFFICIENCY 20 NEGRO CIV/RIGHTS. PAGE 36 F0701
WORKER DISCRIM FINAN LAW

S67
FRIEDEN B.J.,"THE CHANGING PROSPECTS FOR SOCIAL PLANNING." USA+45 PROB/SOLV RACE/REL WEALTH ...SOC/WK PREDICT MUNICH 20 NEGRO. PAGE 44 F0856
PLAN LOC/G POLICY

S67
LANDES W.M.,"THE EFFECT OF STATE FAIR EMPLOYMENT LAWS ON THE ECONOMIC POSITION OF NONWHITES." USA+45 PROVS SECT LEGIS ADMIN GP/REL RACE/REL...JURID CONCPT CHARTS HYPO/EXP NEGRO. PAGE 75 F1470
DISCRIM LAW WORKER

S67
MULLER A.L.,"ECONOMIC GROWTH AND MINORITIES." USA+45 SKILL...SOC GP/COMP NEGRO. PAGE 95 F1857
INCOME WORKER ECO/DEV RACE/REL

S67
PIERPONT J.R.,"NEW STAGE IN THE LONGSHORE STRUGGLE." USA+45 SENIOR ADJUD RACE/REL...JURID 20 NEGRO. PAGE 106 F2083
LABOR DISCRIM WORKER CT/SYS

S67
WASSERMAN M.,"BEYOND TOKENISM: REVERSE INTEGRATION IN ALBANY, GEORGIA." USA+45 PLAN BUDGET EDU/PROP LEAD AGE/C AGE/Y GEORGIA NEGRO. PAGE 144 F2827
REGION RACE/REL DISCRIM SCHOOL

NEHEMKIS P. F1907

NEHRU/J....JAWAHARLAL NEHRU

B59
MADHOK B.,POLITICAL TRENDS IN INDIA. INDIA PAKISTAN UK STRATA ECO/UNDEV POL/PAR LEGIS CAP/ISM DIPLOM
GEOG NAT/G

COLONIAL CHOOSE MARXISM...SOC TREND 20 GANDHI/M NEHRU/J. PAGE 84 F1639 — VOL/ASSN

B60
MC CLELLAN G.S.,INDIA. AFR CHINA/COM INDIA CONSTN ELITES STRATA AGRI POL/PAR FOR/AID ARMS/CONT REV MARXISM...CENSUS BIBLIOG 20 GANDHI/M NEHRU/J. PAGE 87 F1712 — DIPLOM NAT/G SOCIETY ECO/UNDEV

B66
ZINKIN T.,CHALLENGES IN INDIA. INDIA PAKISTAN LAW AGRI FINAN INDUS TOP/EX TEC/DEV CONTROL ROUTINE ORD/FREE PWR 20 NEHRU/J SHASTRI/LB CIVIL/SERV. PAGE 150 F2964 — NAT/G ECO/TAC POLICY ADMIN

NEHRU/PM....PANDIT MOTILAL NEHRU

NEIGH....NEIGHBORHOOD

B29
JONES M.M.,CORPORATION CONTRIBUTIONS TO COMMUNITY WELFARE AGENCIES (PAMPHLET). DELIB/GP TAX CONTROL PARTIC RATIONAL POLICY. PAGE 68 F1339 — LG/CO GIVE NEIGH SOC/WK

B37
COLE W.E.,RECENT TRENDS IN RURAL PLANNING. USA-45 LAW ECO/DEV LOC/G SECT EDU/PROP CRIME LEISURE AGE/Y HABITAT...SOC/WK MUNICH 20. PAGE 26 F0503 — AGRI NEIGH PLAN ACT/RES

S43
GOLDEN C.S.,"NEW PATTERNS OF DEMOCRACY." NEIGH DELIB/GP EDU/PROP EXEC PARTIC...MGT METH/CNCPT OBS TREND. PAGE 48 F0935 — LABOR REPRESENT LG/CO GP/REL

B44
MERRIAM C.E.,PUBLIC AND PRIVATE GOVERNMENT. VOL/ASSN EDU/PROP ADMIN REPRESENT EFFICIENCY PWR PLURISM...MAJORIT CONCPT. PAGE 90 F1762 — NAT/G NEIGH MGT POLICY

B49
LEE A.M.,SOCIAL PROBLEMS IN AMERICA: A SOURCE BOOK. STRATA STRUCT KIN NEIGH VOL/ASSN ACT/RES LEAD CRIME AGE SEX 20. PAGE 77 F1504 — SOC SOCIETY PERSON EDU/PROP

B51
HARDMAN J.B.,THE HOUSE OF LABOR. LAW R+D NEIGH EDU/PROP LEAD ROUTINE REPRESENT GP/REL...POLICY STAT. PAGE 55 F1080 — LABOR LOBBY ADMIN PRESS

S53
MCKEE J.B.,"STATUS AND POWER IN THE INDUSTRIAL COMMUNITY; A COMMENT ON DRUCKER'S THESIS." LABOR LEGIT LEAD GP/REL PWR...MGT CONCPT. PAGE 88 F1730 — SOC STRATA NEIGH PARTIC

S54
MACK R.W.,"ECOLOGICAL PATTERNS IN AN INDUSTRIAL SHOP" (BMR)" USA+45 CULTURE SOCIETY STRATA STRUCT LABOR NEIGH GP/REL ADJUST HABITAT...SOC SOC/INTEG 20. PAGE 83 F1634 — INDUS DISCRIM WORKER

B57
SCHNEIDER E.V.,INDUSTRIAL SOCIOLOGY: THE SOCIAL RELATIONS OF INDUSTRY AND COMMUNITY. STRATA INDUS NAT/G NEIGH CREATE ADMIN PARTIC GP/REL RACE/REL ROLE PWR...POLICY BIBLIOG. PAGE 117 F2308 — LABOR MGT INGP/REL STRUCT

B60
EELLS R.S.F.,THE MEANING OF MODERN BUSINESS. LOC/G NAT/G NEIGH EX/STRUC PARTIC GP/REL INGP/REL DECISION. PAGE 36 F0706 — LG/CO REPRESENT POLICY PLAN

B60
FORM W.H.,INDUSTRY, LABOR, AND COMMUNITY. STRUCT NEIGH SECT BAL/PWR EDU/PROP PARTIC ATTIT ROLE PWR WEALTH...METH/CNCPT CHARTS. PAGE 42 F0828 — LABOR MGT GP/REL CONTROL

B60
PENNSYLVANIA ECONOMY LEAGUE,URBAN RENEWAL IMPACT STUDY: ADMINISTRATIVE-LEGAL-FISCAL. USA+45 FINAN LOC/G NEIGH ADMIN EFFICIENCY...CENSUS CHARTS MUNICH 20 PENNSYLVAN. PAGE 105 F2059 — PLAN BUDGET ADJUD

B60
RAPKIN C.,THE DEMAND FOR HOUSING IN RACIALLY MIXED AREAS: A STUDY OF THE NATURE OF NEIGHBORHOOD CHANGE. USA+45 FINAN PRICE COST DRIVE...GEOG 20. PAGE 109 F2151 — RACE/REL NEIGH DISCRIM MARKET

B60
STEVENSON A.E.,PUTTING FIRST THINGS FIRST. USA+45 INT/ORG NEIGH FOR/AID DISCRIM...ANTHOL 20. PAGE 126 F2483 — DIPLOM ECO/UNDEV ORD/FREE EDU/PROP

S60
FORM W.H.,"ORGANIZED LABOR'S IMAGE OF COMMUNITY POWER STRUCTURE." LABOR LG/CO CONTROL LEAD REPRESENT...DECISION METH/CNCPT INT QU SAMP. PAGE 42 F0829 — NEIGH PARTIC PWR GP/REL

B61
DE GRAZIA A.,AMERICAN WELFARE. CLIENT FINAN LABOR LOC/G NAT/G NEIGH EDU/PROP GP/REL...CLASSIF CON/ANAL CHARTS BIBLIOG. PAGE 31 F0598 — GIVE WEALTH SECT

B61
LEE R.R.,ENGINEERING-ECONOMIC PLANNING MISCELLANEOUS SUBJECTS: A SELECTED BIBLIOGRAPHY (MIMEOGRAPHED). FINAN LOC/G NEIGH ADMIN CONTROL INGP/REL HABITAT...GEOG MGT SOC/WK MUNICH 20 RESOURCE/N. PAGE 77 F1509 — BIBLIOG/A PLAN REGION

B62
LICHFIELD N.,COST-BENEFIT ANALYSIS IN URBAN REDEVELOPMENT. CONSTRUC LOC/G NEIGH ACT/RES PROB/SOLV TEC/DEV BUDGET TAX...DECISION STAT CHARTS SOC/EXP MUNICH 20. PAGE 80 F1558 — PLAN COST GOV/REL

B62
TIEBOUT C.M.,THE COMMUNITY ECONOMIC BASE STUDY (PAMPHLET). USA+45 ECO/TAC LEAD DEMAND HABITAT 20. PAGE 130 F2572 — NEIGH INCOME ACT/RES

B63
GRIGSBY W.G.,HOUSING MARKETS AND PUBLIC POLICY. USA+45 FAM NEIGH PRICE DEMAND WEALTH...POLICY CHARTS BIBLIOG METH MUNICH 20. PAGE 51 F1002 — MARKET RENT HABITAT PLAN

B63
LETHBRIDGE H.J.,THE PEASANT AND THE COMMUNES. CHINA/COM COM USSR NEIGH PROB/SOLV ADJUST EFFICIENCY...POLICY METH/COMP NAT/COMP 20. PAGE 78 F1535 — MARXISM ECO/TAC AGRI WORKER

B63
RILEY J.W. JR.,THE CORPORATION AND ITS PUBLICS. ESSAYS ON THE CORPORATE IMAGE. CLIENT ISOLAT AGE ATTIT...POLICY SOC METH/CNCPT INT. PAGE 111 F2193 — LG/CO CLASSIF GP/REL NEIGH

B63
US HOUSE,URBAN RENEWAL: HOUSE COMMITTEE ON BANKING AND CURRENCY. USA+45 FINAN LOC/G NAT/G NEIGH DELIB/GP TEC/DEV BUDGET GOV/REL COST...CHARTS MUNICH 20 CONGRESS URBAN/RNWL. PAGE 136 F2684 — PLAN PROB/SOLV LEGIS

N63
NORTH CAROLINA U INST GOVT,COSTING URBAN DEVELOPMENT AND REDEVELOPMENT (PAMPHLET). USA+45 USA-45 NEIGH PLAN TEC/DEV TAX OWN...GEOG MUNICH 20. PAGE 98 F1934 — BIBLIOG COST FINAN

B64
FRIEDEN B.J.,THE FUTURE OF OLD NEIGHBORHOODS: REBUILDING FOR A CHANGING POPULATION. CONSTRUC LOC/G NAT/G ACT/RES ECO/TAC REGION ATTIT...INT SAMP MUNICH 20 NEWYORK/C LOS/ANG HARTFORD URBAN/RNWL. PAGE 44 F0855 — NEIGH PROB/SOLV PLAN BUDGET

B64
GREBLER L.,URBAN RENEWAL IN EUROPEAN COUNTRIES: ITS EMERGENCE AND POTENTIALS. EUR+WWI UK ECO/DEV LOC/G NEIGH CREATE ADMIN ATTIT...TREND NAT/COMP MUNICH 20 URBAN/RNWL. PAGE 50 F0981 — PLAN CONSTRUC NAT/G

B64
STRONG A.L.,THE RISE OF THE CHINESE PEOPLE'S COMMUNES - AND SIX YEARS AFTER (2ND ED.). CHINA/COM AGRI INDUS FORCES WORKER PROB/SOLV EDU/PROP EFFICIENCY ISOLAT 20. PAGE 127 F2503 — NEIGH ECO/TAC MARXISM METH/COMP

B65
DERBER M.,PLANT UNION-MANAGEMENT RELATIONS: FROM PRACTICE TO THEORY. PROC/MFG NEIGH PROB/SOLV ORD/FREE...DECISION MGT OBS QU SAMP. PAGE 32 F0621 — LG/CO LABOR GP/REL ATTIT

B65
DUGGAR G.S.,RENEWAL OF TOWN AND VILLAGE I: A WORLD-WIDE SURVEY OF LOCAL GOVERNMENT EXPERIENCE. WOR+45 CONSTRUC INDUS CREATE BUDGET REGION GOV/REL...QU NAT/COMP MUNICH 20 URBAN/RNWL. PAGE 35 F0673 — NEIGH PLAN ADMIN

B65
FRYE R.J.,HOUSING AND URBAN RENEWAL IN ALABAMA. USA+45 NEIGH LEGIS BUDGET ADJUD ADMIN PARTIC...MGT MUNICH 20 ALABAMA URBAN/RNWL. PAGE 45 F0871 — PROB/SOLV PLAN GOV/REL

B65
HAUSER P.M.,THE STUDY OF URBANIZATION. S/ASIA ECO/DEV ECO/UNDEV NEIGH ACT/RES...GEOG MUNICH. PAGE 57 F1115 — CULTURE SOC

B65
MAO J.C.T.,EFFICIENCY IN PUBLIC URBAN RENEWAL EXPENDITURES THROUGH CAPITAL BUDGETING. USA+45 FINAN LOC/G NAT/G NEIGH REGION UTIL...GEOG METH/CNCPT STAT SIMUL GEN/LAWS MUNICH 20 URBAN/RNWL. PAGE 85 F1662 — TEC/DEV BUDGET PROB/SOLV

B65
NATIONAL CONF SOCIAL WELFARE,THE SOCIAL WELFARE FORUM, 1965. LAW CULTURE VOL/ASSN CONTROL PERS/REL ADJUST POLICY. PAGE 97 F1899 — CONSTN WEALTH ORD/FREE NEIGH

B65
PEARL A.,NEW CAREERS FOR THE POOR: THE NON-PROFESSIONAL IN HUMAN SERVICE. USA+45 SERV/IND NAT/G NEIGH WORKER EDU/PROP AUTOMAT SKILL...WELF/ST NEW/IDEA BIBLIOG SOC/INTEG 20. PAGE 104 F2044 — SOC/WK WEALTH STRATA POLICY

S65
KEE W.S.,"CENTRAL CITY EXPENDITURES AND METROPOLITAN AREAS." PLAN BUDGET ECO/TAC TAX GP/REL WEALTH...CHARTS MUNICH 20. PAGE 70 F1366 — LOC/G GOV/COMP NEIGH

B66
DAVIES JC I.I.I.,NEIGHBORHOOD GROUPS AND URBAN RENEWAL. USA+45 PLAN LOBBY PARTIC CHOOSE RACE/REL ...POLICY DECISION SOC INT MUNICH SOC/INTEG 20 NEWYORK/C. PAGE 30 F0586
NEIGH CREATE PROB/SOLV

B67
BANFIELD E.C.,THE MORAL BASIS OF A BACKWARD SOCIETY. EUR+WWI ITALY STRATA NEIGH PARTIC INGP/REL ...SOC QU PREDICT TREND HYPO/EXP MUNICH 20. PAGE 9 F0173
MORAL WEALTH ATTIT

B67
CHAPIN F.S. JR.,SELECTED REFERENCES ON URBAN PLANNING METHODS AND TECHNIQUES. USA+45 LAW ECO/DEV LOC/G NAT/G SCHOOL CONSULT CREATE PROB/SOLV TEC/DEV ...SOC/WK MUNICH. PAGE 23 F0454
BIBLIOG NEIGH PLAN

B67
LITTLE AD, INC.,COMMUNITY RENEWAL PROGRAMMING. CULTURE LOC/G ACT/RES TASK COST ATTIT...SOC/WK MODAL STAT STAND/INT CHARTS 20 SAN/FRAN. PAGE 81 F1585
STRATA NEIGH PLAN CREATE

B67
WEINBERG M.,SCHOOL INTEGRATION: A COMPREHENSIVE CLASSIFIED BIBLIOGRAPHY OF 3,100 REFERENCES. USA+45 LAW NAT/G NEIGH SECT PLAN ROUTINE AGE/C WEALTH SOC/INTEG INDIAN/AM. PAGE 145 F2849
BIBLIOG SCHOOL DISCRIM RACE/REL

L67
MIXON J.,"JANE JACOBS AND THE LAW - ZONING FOR DIVERSITY EXAMINED." FUT USA+45 CONSTN NEIGH PROB/SOLV CONTROL CT/SYS PARTIC ATTIT...POLICY CENSUS METH/COMP MUNICH. PAGE 92 F1810
IDEA/COMP PLAN LAW

S67
FOX R.G.,"FAMILY, CASTE, AND COMMERCE IN A NORTH INDIAN MARKET TOWN." INDIA STRATA AGRI FACE/GP FAM NEIGH OP/RES BARGAIN ADMIN ROUTINE WEALTH...SOC CHARTS 20. PAGE 43 F0838
CULTURE GP/REL ECO/UNDEV DIST/IND

S67
LENS S.,"WALTER REUTHER TRIES TO BUILD A FIRE." WORKER LEAD DISCRIM AGE ORD/FREE NEW/LIB SOC. PAGE 78 F1523
LABOR PARTIC NEIGH PLAN

S67
SCHWARZWELLER H.K.,"SOCIAL CLASS ORIGINS, RURAL-URBAN MIGRATION, AND ECONOMIC LIFE CHANGES." USA+45 SOCIETY STRUCT FAM NEIGH INCOME...SOC RECORD CHARTS MUNICH. PAGE 118 F2326
CLASSIF WEALTH AGRI

S67
WALLACE H.M.,"AVAILABILITY AND USEFULNESS OF SELECTED HEALTH AND SOCIOECONOMIC DATA FOR COMMUNITY PLANNING." NEIGH EFFICIENCY...CORREL STAT CENSUS CHARTS. PAGE 142 F2806
HEALTH PLAN SOC/WK HEAL

NEISSER H. F1908,F1909,F1910

NELSON J.R. F1911

NELSON R.R. F1912

NENAROKOV A.P. F1913

NEOLITHIC....NEOLITHIC PERIOD

NEPAL....SEE ALSO S/ASIA

N
US LIBRARY OF CONGRESS,SOUTHERN ASIA ACCESSIONS LIST. BURMA CEYLON INDIA NEPAL PAKISTAN S/ASIA THAILAND AGRI INDUS SCHOOL WORKER...ART/METH GEOG HEAL PHIL/SCI LING 20. PAGE 137 F2710
BIBLIOG/A SOCIETY CULTURE ECO/UNDEV

B55
PANT Y.P.,PLANNING IN UNDERDEVELOPED ECONOMIES. INDIA NEPAL INT/TRADE COLONIAL SOVEREIGN ALL/IDEOS ...TIME/SEQ METH/COMP 20. PAGE 103 F2026
ECO/UNDEV PLAN ECO/TAC DIPLOM

B66
DEBENKO E.,RESEARCH SOURCES FOR SOUTH ASIAN STUDIES IN ECONOMIC DEVELOPMENT: A SELECT BIBLIOGRAPHY OF SERIAL PUBLICATIONS. CEYLON INDIA NEPAL PAKISTAN PROB/SOLV ADMIN...POLICY 20. PAGE 32 F0611
BIBLIOG ECO/UNDEV S/ASIA PLAN

NERLOVE M. F0123

NET/THEORY....NETWORK THEORY

B64
LEWIN P.,THE FOREIGN TRADE OF COMMUNIST CHINA* ITS IMPACT ON THE FREE WORLD. AFR EUR+WWI L/A+17C S/ASIA ECO/UNDEV CREATE FOR/AID...STAT NET/THEORY TREND CHARTS. PAGE 79 F1546
ASIA INT/TRADE NAT/COMP USSR

B65
BAERRESEN D.W.,LATIN AMERICAN TRADE PATTERNS. L/A+17C ECO/UNDEV AGRI INDUS MARKET CREATE ...NET/THEORY CHARTS LAFTA. PAGE 8 F0149
INT/TRADE STAT REGION

B66
YOUNG S.,MANAGEMENT: A SYSTEMS ANALYSIS. DELIB/GP EX/STRUC ECO/TAC CONTROL EFFICIENCY...NET/THEORY 20. PAGE 150 F2952
PROB/SOLV MGT DECISION SIMUL

S66
FELD W.,"NATIONAL ECONOMIC INTEREST GROUPS AND POLICY FORMATION IN THE EEC." NAT/G POL/PAR REGION CENTRAL SOVEREIGN...INT NET/THEORY EEC. PAGE 40 F0777
LOBBY ELITES DECISION

NETH/IND....NETHERLAND EAST INDIES (PRE-INDONESIA)

NETHERLAND....NETHERLANDS; SEE ALSO APPROPRIATE TIME/SPACE/ CULTURE INDEX

B39
FURNIVALL J.S.,NETHERLANDS INDIA. INDIA NETHERLAND CULTURE INDUS NAT/G DIPLOM ADMIN WEALTH...POLICY CHARTS 17/20. PAGE 45 F0876
COLONIAL ECO/UNDEV SOVEREIGN PLURISM

B55
FLORINSKY M.T.,INTEGRATED EUROPE. EUR+WWI FRANCE ITALY NETHERLAND UK ECO/DEV INT/ORG FORCES LEGIT FEDERAL ATTIT PWR WEALTH...POLICY GEOG CONCPT GEN/LAWS TOT/POP EEC OEEC 20. PAGE 42 F0816
FUT ECO/TAC REGION

B60
BAYER H.,WIRTSCHAFTSPROGNOSE UND WIRTSCHAFTSGESTALTUNG. GERMANY NETHERLAND MARKET PLAN CAP/ISM DEBATE...NAT/COMP 20. PAGE 12 F0220
ECO/DEV ECO/UNDEV FINAN POLICY

B61
INTL BANKING SUMMER SCHOOL,TRENDS IN BANK CREDIT AND FINANCE. EUR+WWI NETHERLAND ECO/DEV PROF/ORG PLAN BUDGET 20 EEC. PAGE 65 F1283
FINAN ECO/TAC NAT/G LG/CO

B62
ROBINSON A.D.,DUTCH ORGANIZED AGRICULTURE IN INTERNATIONAL POLITICS, 1945-1960. EUR+WWI NETHERLAND STRUCT ECO/DEV NAT/G VOL/ASSN CONSULT DELIB/GP PLAN TEC/DEV INT/TRADE EDU/PROP ATTIT RIGID/FLEX ALL/VALS...NEW/IDEA TREND EEC COMMUN 20. PAGE 112 F2215
AGRI INT/ORG

B62
SELOSOEMARDJAN O.,SOCIAL CHANGES IN JOGJAKARTA. INDONESIA NETHERLAND ELITES STRATA STRUCT FAM POL/PAR CREATE DIPLOM INT/TRADE EDU/PROP ADMIN GOV/REL...SOC 20 JAVA CHINJAP. PAGE 119 F2352
ECO/UNDEV CULTURE REV COLONIAL

B63
BARBOUR V.,CAPITALISM IN AMSTERDAM IN THE 17TH CENTURY. NETHERLAND FINAN ECO/TAC...METH/COMP BIBLIOG MUNICH 16. PAGE 10 F0185
CAP/ISM INT/TRADE MARKET WEALTH

B64
MORRISSENS L.,ECONOMIC POLICY IN OUR TIME: COUNTRY STUDIES. BELGIUM EUR+WWI FRANCE GERMANY/W ITALY NETHERLAND INDUS BARGAIN BUDGET GOV/REL BAL/PAY PRODUC...CON/ANAL CHARTS COSTS 20. PAGE 94 F1839
ECO/DEV ECO/TAC METH/COMP PLAN

B65
EDELMAN M.,THE POLITICS OF WAGE-PRICE DECISIONS. GERMANY ITALY NETHERLAND UK INDUS LABOR POL/PAR PROB/SOLV BARGAIN PRICE ROUTINE BAL/PAY COST DEMAND 20. PAGE 36 F0699
GOV/COMP CONTROL ECO/TAC PLAN

B65
HICKMAN B.G.,QUANTITATIVE PLANNING OF ECONOMIC POLICY. FRANCE NETHERLAND OP/RES PRICE ROUTINE UTIL ...POLICY DECISION ECOMETRIC METH/CNCPT STAT STYLE CHINJAP. PAGE 59 F1162
PROB/SOLV PLAN QUANT

B65
OECD,TECHNIQUES OF ECONOMIC FORECASTING. CANADA FRANCE NETHERLAND SWEDEN UK USA+45 PROB/SOLV ROUTINE...CONCPT MATH CHARTS BIBLIOG METH 20. PAGE 100 F1974
PREDICT METH/COMP PLAN

N67
US HOUSE COMM SCI ASTRONAUT,GOVERNMENT, SCIENCE, AND INTERNATIONAL POLICY (PAMPHLET). INDIA NETHERLAND ECO/DEV ECO/UNDEV R+D ACADEM PLAN DIPLOM FOR/AID CONFER...PREDICT 20 CHINJAP. PAGE 137 F2705
NAT/G POLICY CREATE TEC/DEV

NETWORK THEORY....SEE NET/THEORY

NEUFIELD M.F. F1914

NEUMARK S.D. F1915,F1916

NEUSTADT I. F0286,F0287

NEUTRAL....POLITICAL NONALIGNMENT, LEGAL NEUTRALITY

N19
FRANCK P.G.,AFGHANISTAN BETWEEN EAST AND WEST: THE ECONOMICS OF COMPETITIVE COEXISTENCE (PAMPHLET). AFGHANISTN USA+45 USA-45 USSR INDUS ECO/TAC INT/TRADE CONTROL NEUTRAL ORD/FREE MARXISM...GEOG 20 UN. PAGE 43 F0842
FOR/AID PLAN DIPLOM ECO/UNDEV

B58
JENNINGS I.,PROBLEMS OF THE NEW COMMONWEALTH. AFR CEYLON INDIA PAKISTAN S/ASIA ECO/UNDEV INT/ORG LOC/G DIPLOM ECO/TAC INT/TRADE COLONIAL RACE/REL DISCRIM 20 PARLIAMENT. PAGE 67 F1314
NAT/LISM NEUTRAL FOR/AID POL/PAR

B62
FRIEDRICH-EBERT-STIFTUNG,THE SOVIET BLOC AND DEVELOPING COUNTRIES. CHINA/COM COM GERMANY/E USSR WOR+45 ECO/UNDEV INT/ORG NAT/G TEC/DEV NEUTRAL PWR ...POLICY 20. PAGE 44 F0868 — MARXISM DIPLOM ECO/TAC FOR/AID

B63
WILTZ J.E.,IN SEARCH OF PEACE: THE SENATE MUNITIONS INQUIRY, 1934-36. EUR+WWI USA-45 ELITES INDUS LG/CO LEGIS INT/TRADE LOBBY NEUTRAL ARMS/CONT...POLICY CONGRESS 20 LEAGUE/NAT PRESIDENT SENATE CONSCRIPTN. PAGE 147 F2905 — DELIB/GP PROFIT WAR WEAPON

B64
LUTHULI A.,AFRICA'S FREEDOM. KIN LABOR POL/PAR SCHOOL DIPLOM NEUTRAL REGION REV NAT/LISM PWR WEALTH SOCISM SOC/INTEG 20. PAGE 82 F1608 — AFR ECO/UNDEV COLONIAL

B65
CRABB C.V. JR.,THE ELEPHANTS AND THE GRASS* A STUDY OF NONALIGNMENT. ASIA INDIA S/ASIA USA+45 USSR BAL/PWR NEUTRAL ATTIT...TREND NAT/COMP. PAGE 28 F0549 — ECO/UNDEV AFR DIPLOM CONCPT

B65
MACDONALD R.W.,THE LEAGUE OF ARAB STATES: A STUDY IN THE DYNAMICS OF REGIONAL ORGANIZATION. ISRAEL UAR USSR FINAN INT/ORG DELIB/GP ECO/TAC AGREE NEUTRAL ORD/FREE PWR...DECISION BIBLIOG 20 TREATY UN. PAGE 83 F1626 — ISLAM REGION DIPLOM ADMIN

C65
WUORINEN J.H.,"SCANDINAVIA." DENMARK FINLAND ICELAND NORWAY SWEDEN SOCIETY AGRI POL/PAR DELIB/GP DIPLOM INT/TRADE NEUTRAL WAR...CHARTS IND TREATY 20. PAGE 149 F2942 — BIBLIOG NAT/G POLICY

S67
MEHTA A.,"INDIA* POVERTY AND CHANGE." STRATA INDUS CREATE ECO/TAC FOR/AID NEUTRAL GP/REL ADJUST INCOME ...NEW/IDEA 20. PAGE 89 F1746 — INDIA SOCIETY ECO/UNDEV TEC/DEV

NEVADA....NEVADA

NEVITT A.A. F1917,F1918

NEW LIBERALISM....SEE NEW/LIB

NEW STATES....SEE ECO/UNDEV+GEOGRAPHIC AREA+COLONIAL+ NAT/LISM

NEW YORK CITY....SEE NEWYORK/C

NEW YORK TIMES....SEE NEWY/TIMES

NEW JERSEY LEGISLATURE-SENATE F1919

NEW JERSEY STATE OF F1920

NEW/BRUNS....NEW BRUNSWICK, CANADA

B58
CUNNINGHAM W.B.,COMPULSORY CONCILIATION AND COLLECTIVE BARGAINING. CANADA NAT/G LEGIS ADJUD CT/SYS GP/REL...MGT 20 NEW/BRUNS STRIKE CASEBOOK. PAGE 29 F0563 — POLICY BARGAIN LABOR INDUS

NEW/DEAL....NEW DEAL OF F.D.R.'S ADMINISTRATION

B38
LAWLEY F.E.,THE GROWTH OF COLLECTIVE ECONOMY VOL. 2: INTERNATIONAL. WOR-45 AGRI INDUS EQUILIB OPTIMAL OWN WEALTH...NAT/COMP 19/20 NAZI NEW/DEAL MONOPOLY. PAGE 76 F1493 — ECO/TAC SOCISM NAT/LISM CONTROL

B51
OWENS R.N.,BUSINESS, ORGANIZATION, AND COMBINATION. USA+45 USA-45 LAW NAT/G LEGIS ECO/TAC CONTROL INGP/REL...JURID GP/COMP 20 NEW/DEAL. PAGE 102 F2006 — SML/CO LG/CO STRUCT GP/REL

B61
LHOSTE-LACHAUME P.,OU GIT LE DESACCORD ENTRE LIBERAUX ET SOCIALISTES. EUR+WWI USA+45 USA-45 USSR CAP/ISM EDU/PROP MARXISM...MAJORIT IDEA/COMP 20 KEYNES/JM NEW/DEAL DEPRESSION. PAGE 79 F1555 — LAISSEZ SOCISM FINAN

B66
KIRKENDALL R.S.,SOCIAL SCIENTISTS AND FARM POLITICS IN THE AGE OF ROOSEVELT. ACADEM PLAN ECO/TAC GIVE ADMIN CONTROL PRODUC...SOC 20 NEW/DEAL ROOSEVLT/F BURAGR/ECO. PAGE 71 F1399 — AGRI INTELL POLICY NAT/G

B67
COHEN M.R.,LAW AND THE SOCIAL ORDER: ESSAYS IN LEGAL PHILOSOPHY. USA-45 CONSULT WORKER ECO/TAC ATTIT WEALTH...POLICY WELF/ST SOC 20 NEW/DEAL DEPRESSION. PAGE 26 F0497 — JURID LABOR IDEA/COMP

NEW/DELHI....NEW DELHI (UNCTAD MEETING OF DEVELOPED AND UNDERDEVELOPED NATIONS IN 1968)

NEW/ECO/MN....NEW ECONOMIC MECHANISM OF HUNGARY

NEW/ECONOM....NEW ECONOMICS

NEW/ENGLND....NEW ENGLAND

B50
HARTLAND P.C.,BALANCE OF INTERREGIONAL PAYMENTS OF NEW ENGLAND. USA+45 TEC/DEV ECO/TAC LEGIT ROUTINE BAL/PAY PROFIT 20 NEW/ENGLND FED/RESERV. PAGE 56 F1102 — ECO/DEV FINAN REGION PLAN

NEW/FRONTR....NEW FRONTIER OF J.F.KENNEDY

NEW/GUINEA....NEW GUINEA

N19
ARNDT H.W.,AUSTRALIAN FOREIGN AID POLICY (PAMPHLET). ECO/UNDEV DIPLOM GIVE GOV/REL COST UTIL PWR...CHARTS 20 AUSTRAL PAPUA NEW/GUINEA. PAGE 6 F0114 — FOR/AID POLICY ECO/TAC EFFICIENCY

S21
MALINOWSKI B.,"THE PRIMITIVE ECONOMICS OF THE TROBRIAND ISLANDERS" (BMR)" CULTURE SOCIETY NAT/G CHIEF LEAD OWN...SOC MYTH WORSHIP 20 NEW/GUINEA TROBRIAND RESOURCE/N. PAGE 84 F1647 — ECO/UNDEV AGRI PRODUC STRUCT

B66
FISK E.K.,NEW GUINEA ON THE THRESHOLD; ASPECTS OF SOCIAL, POLITICAL, AND ECONOMIC DEVELOPMENT. AGRI NAT/G INT/TRADE ADMIN ADJUST LITERACY ROLE...CHARTS ANTHOL 20 NEW/GUINEA. PAGE 41 F0804 — ECO/UNDEV SOCIETY

NEW/HAMPSH....NEW HAMPSHIRE

NEW/HEBRID....NEW HEBRIDES

NEW/IDEA....NEW CONCEPT

NEW/JERSEY....NEW JERSEY

N
NEW JERSEY STATE OF,SECOND REPORT TO GOVERNOR, SENATE, ASSEMBLY BY UNIFORM COMMERCIAL CODE STUDY COMMISSION. USA+45 INDUS LOC/G NAT/G PROF/ORG CONSULT ACT/RES LEGIT CT/SYS ATTIT NEW/JERSEY. PAGE 98 F1920 — LAW FINAN CENTRAL PROVS

N19
HOGARTY R.A.,NEW JERSEY FARMERS AND MIGRANT HOUSING RULES (PAMPHLET). USA+45 LAW ELITES FACE/GP LABOR PROF/ORG LOBBY PERS/REL RIGID/FLEX ROLE 20 NEW/JERSEY. PAGE 61 F1193 — AGRI PROVS WORKER HEALTH

B51
PRINCETON U INDUSTRIAL REL SEC,COMPULSORY ARBITRATION OF UTILITY DISPUTES IN NEW JERSEY AND PENNSYLVANIA. USA+45 LEGIS WORKER ADJUD ORD/FREE ...POLICY MGT METH/COMP 20 NEW/JERSEY PENNSYLVAN. PAGE 108 F2118 — BARGAIN PROVS INDUS LABOR

B61
DOIG J.W.,THE POLITICS OF METROPOLITAN TRANSPORTATION. DELIB/GP WORKER DIPLOM TASK EFFICIENCY UTIL...CHARTS BIBLIOG MUNICH 20 NEW/YORK NEW/JERSEY PUB/TRANS RAILROAD. PAGE 34 F0652 — PROB/SOLV STRATA DIST/IND

B61
NEW JERSEY LEGISLATURE-SENATE,PUBLIC HEARINGS BEFORE COMMITTEE ON REVISION AND AMENDMENT OF LAWS ON SENATE BILL NO. 8. USA+45 FINAN PROVS WORKER ACT/RES PLAN BUDGET TAX CRIME...IDEA/COMP MUNICH 20 NEW/JERSEY URBAN/RNWL. PAGE 98 F1919 — LEGIS INDUS PROB/SOLV

B63
MILLER W.,REVENUE-COST RATIOS OF RURAL TOWNSHIPS WITH CHANGING LAND USES. USA+45 INDUS SERV/IND PROVS GP/REL HABITAT...CHARTS GP/COMP MUNICH 20 NEW/JERSEY. PAGE 91 F1792 — TAX COST AGRI

B67
LEIBY J.,CHARITY AND CORRECTION IN JERSEY; A HISTORY OF STATE WELFARE INSTITUTIONS. DELIB/GP EX/STRUC PROB/SOLV INSPECT LEAD ADJUST HEALTH ...POLICY PSY NEW/JERSEY. PAGE 77 F1514 — PROVS PUB/INST ADMIN

B67
PRINCE C.E.,NEW JERSEY'S JEFFERSONIAN REPUBLICANS; THE GENESIS OF AN EARLY PARTY MACHINE (1789-1817). USA-45 LOC/G EDU/PROP PRESS CONTROL CHOOSE...CHARTS 18/19 NEW/JERSEY REPUBLICAN. PAGE 108 F2117 — POL/PAR CONSTN ADMIN PROVS

NEW/LEFT....THE NEW LEFT

NEW/LIB....NEW LIBERALISM

B20
PIGOU A.C.,THE ECONOMICS OF WELFARE. UNIV INDUS WORKER ACT/RES RECEIVE INCOME NEW/LIB...MAJORIT SOC/WK. PAGE 106 F2085 — ECO/TAC WEALTH FINAN CONTROL

B48
MCCABE D.A.,LABOR AND SOCIAL ORGANIZATION. LEGIS WORKER CAP/ISM ECO/TAC PAY MARXISM SOCISM SOC/INTEG 20 INTRVN/ECO. PAGE 88 F1717 — LABOR STRATA NEW/LIB

S48
HARDIN L.M.,"REFLECTIONS ON AGRICULTURAL POLICY FORMATION IN THE UNITED STATES." LEGIS PLAN BUDGET — AGRI POLICY

ECO/TAC LEAD CENTRAL...MGT SOC NEW/IDEA STAT FAO. PAGE 55 F1078 — ADMIN NEW/LIB

B49

DE JOUVENEL B.,PROBLEMS OF SOCIALIST ENGLAND. AFR UK USSR BAL/PWR ECO/TAC INT/TRADE PRICE WAR BAL/PAY PEACE 20. PAGE 31 F0601 — SOCISM NEW/LIB PROB/SOLV PLAN

B50

SURANYI-UNGER T.,PRIVATE ENTERPRISE AND GOVERNMENTAL PLANNING. STRUCT FINAN BAL/PWR HAPPINESS DRIVE NEW/LIB PLURISM...MATH QUANT STAT TREND BIBLIOG. PAGE 127 F2516 — PLAN NAT/G LAISSEZ POLICY

B52

BEVAN A.,IN PLACE OF FEAR. WOR+45 STRATA LEGIS REPRESENT OWN NEW/LIB POPULISM...CHARTS 20. PAGE 14 F0273 — SOCISM SOCIALIST WEALTH MAJORIT

B57

NAUMANN R.,THEORIE UND PRAXIS DES NEOLIBERALISMUS; DAS MAERCHEN VON DER FREIEN ODER SOZIALEN MARKTWIRTSCHAFT. GERMANY/W FORCES PLAN EDU/PROP SOCISM...POLICY MARXIST IDEA/COMP BIBLIOG 18/20 ADENAUER/K. PAGE 97 F1903 — MARXISM NEW/LIB ECO/TAC CAP/ISM

B57

WATSON G.,THE UNSERVILE STATE: ESSAYS IN LIBERTY AND WELFARE. UK LEGIS RECEIVE EDU/PROP COLONIAL ...WELF/ST 20 LIB/PARTY. PAGE 144 F2833 — POL/PAR ORD/FREE CONTROL NEW/LIB

B58

CLAIRMONTE F.,LE LIBERALISME ECONOMIQUE ET LES PAYS SOUS-DEVELOPPES: ETUDES SUR L'EVOLUTION D'UNE IDEE. ASIA INDIA UK FINAN INDUS PLAN CAP/ISM ECO/TAC COLONIAL NEW/LIB...BIBLIOG 20 THIRD/WRLD. PAGE 24 F0475 — LAISSEZ ECO/UNDEV

B59

JENKINS C.,POWER AT THE TOP: A CRITICAL SURVEY OF THE NATIONALIZED INDUSTRIES. UK POL/PAR CONTROL ...WELF/ST CHARTS 20 LABOR/PAR. PAGE 67 F1313 — NAT/G OWN INDUS NEW/LIB

B59

KELF-COHEN R.,NATIONALISATION IN BRITAIN: THE END OF DOGMA. EUR+WWI UK NAT/G POL/PAR WORKER ECO/TAC PARL/PROC WEALTH SOCISM...GOV/COMP 20. PAGE 70 F1369 — NEW/LIB ECO/DEV INDUS OWN

B60

BOHM F.,REDEN UND SCHRIFTEN UBER DIE ORDNUNG EINER FREIEN GESELLSCHAFT, EINER FREIEN WIRTSCHAFT, UND UBER DIE WIEDERGUTMACH. DIPLOM CRIME ORD/FREE RESPECT FASCISM 20 NAZI. PAGE 16 F0307 — ECO/TAC NEW/LIB SUPEGO REPAR

B60

PETERSON W.C.,THE WELFARE STATE IN FRANCE. EUR+WWI FRANCE FUT STRATA PROB/SOLV TAX GIVE RECEIVE INCOME ORD/FREE PWR...CHARTS 20. PAGE 105 F2070 — NEW/LIB ECO/TAC WEALTH NAT/G

B60

ROBERTSON D.,THE CONTROL OF INDUSTRY. UK MARKET LABOR WORKER PRICE CONTROL GP/REL COST DEMAND ORD/FREE WEALTH NEW/LIB SOCISM 20. PAGE 112 F2211 — INDUS FINAN NAT/G ECO/DEV

B61

DIMOCK M.E.,BUSINESS AND GOVERNMENT (4TH ED.). AGRI FINAN OP/RES PLAN BUDGET DIPLOM LOBBY NUC/PWR NEW/LIB SOCISM...POLICY BIBLIOG 20. PAGE 33 F0641 — NAT/G INDUS LABOR ECO/TAC

B61

LIEFMANN-KEIL E.,OKONOMISCHE THEORIE DER SOZIALPOLITIK. INT/ORG LABOR WORKER COST INCOME NEW/LIB...CONCPT SOC/INTEG 20. PAGE 80 F1562 — ECO/DEV INDUS NAT/G SOC/WK

B61

ROEPKE W.,JENSEITS VON ANGEBOT UND NACHFRAGE (DRITTE VERAENDERTE AUFLAGE). WOR+45 MARKET TEC/DEV ECO/TAC GP/REL INGP/REL NEW/LIB...POLICY SOC IDEA/COMP PERS/COMP 20. PAGE 113 F2233 — SOCIETY STRANGE ECO/DEV STRUCT

B62

HARRIS S.E.,THE ECONOMICS OF THE POLITICAL PARTIES. USA+45 FINAN CHIEF ACT/RES PLAN BUDGET GP/REL INGP/REL NEW/LIB...IDEA/COMP PERS/COMP 20 EISNHWR/DD KENNEDY/JF. PAGE 56 F1090 — POLICY ECO/DEV NAT/G POL/PAR

B63

HARVEY O.L.,THE ANVIL AND THE PLOW: A HISTORY OF THE UNITED STATES DEPARTMENT OF LABOR: 1913-1963. USA+45 USA-45 NAT/G CONFER NEW/LIB 20 DEPT/LABOR. PAGE 56 F1106 — EX/STRUC REPRESENT GP/REL LABOR

B63

PELLING H.M.,A HISTORY OF BRITISH TRADE UNIONISM. UK ELITES ECO/DEV POL/PAR GP/REL PWR NEW/LIB 19/20. PAGE 104 F2051 — LABOR VOL/ASSN NAT/G

B64

HARRIS S.E.,ECONOMICS OF THE KENNEDY YEARS AND A LOOK AHEAD. USA+45 PLAN BUDGET NEW/LIB...STAT RECORD IDEA/COMP PERS/COMP INDEX 20 KENNEDY/JF EISNHWR/DD JOHNSON/LB. PAGE 56 F1091 — ECO/TAC CHIEF POLICY NAT/G

B64

MARSH D.C.,THE FUTURE OF THE WELFARE STATE. UK CONSTN NAT/G POL/PAR...POLICY WELF/ST 20. PAGE 86 F1676 — NEW/LIB ADMIN CONCPT INSPECT

B64

TAWNEY R.H.,EQUALITY. UK CULTURE STRATA ECO/TAC EDU/PROP REPRESENT OWN NEW/LIB...MAJORIT WELF/ST SOC 20. PAGE 129 F2538 — WEALTH STRUCT ELITES POPULISM

B65

COUGHLIN B.J.,CHURCH AND STATE IN SOCIAL WELFARE. USA+45 RECEIVE GP/REL ORD/FREE WEALTH NEW/LIB. PAGE 28 F0542 — CULTURE SECT VOL/ASSN GIVE

B65

MUSOLF L.D.,PROMOTING THE GENERAL WELFARE: GOVERNMENT AND THE ECONOMY. USA+45 ECO/DEV CAP/ISM DEMAND OPTIMAL 20. PAGE 95 F1874 — ECO/TAC NAT/G EX/STRUC NEW/LIB

B65

NARASIMHAN V.K.,DEMOCRACY AND MIXED ECONOMY. INDIA CONTROL...CENSUS IDEA/COMP 20. PAGE 96 F1891 — CAP/ISM MARXISM ORD/FREE NEW/LIB

B65

OFFICE OF ECONOMIC OPPORTUNITY,CATALOG OF FEDERAL PROGRAMS FOR INDIVIDUAL AND COMMUNITY IMPROVEMENT. USA+45 WEALTH NEW/LIB 20. PAGE 101 F1980 — INDEX ECO/UNDEV RECEIVE NAT/G

B65

SELIGMAN B.B.,POVERTY AS A PUBLIC ISSUE. USA+45 ECO/DEV NAT/G PAY RECEIVE PERS/REL INCOME NEW/LIB 20. PAGE 119 F2347 — LEGIS ECO/TAC STRATA DISCRIM

B65

VAID K.N.,STATE AND LABOR IN INDIA. INDIA INDUS WORKER PAY PRICE ADJUD CONTROL PARL/PROC GP/REL ORD/FREE 20. PAGE 140 F2757 — LAW LABOR MGT NEW/LIB

B65

WEIDENBAUM M.L.,CONGRESS AND THE FEDERAL BUDGET. FINAN ACT/RES DOMIN CONFER EXEC UTIL PWR NEW/LIB ...CHARTS CONGRESS. PAGE 144 F2844 — BUDGET LEGIS PLAN DECISION

C65

PEGRUM D.E.,"PUBLIC REGULATION OF BUSINESS (REV ED)" LAW CONSTN DIST/IND SERV/IND LG/CO LEGIS OWN LAISSEZ SOCISM...POLICY DECISION BIBLIOG 20. PAGE 104 F2048 — INDUS PLAN NEW/LIB PRICE

B66

ECONOMIC RESEARCH SERVICE,RESEARCH DATA ON MINORITY GROUPS: AN ANNOTATED BIBLIOGRAPHY OF ECONOMIC RESEARCH SERVICE REPORTS: 1955-1965 (PAMPHLET). USA+45 STRATA ECO/DEV AGRI SCHOOL WORKER EDU/PROP HEALTH NEW/LIB SOC. PAGE 36 F0697 — BIBLIOG/A DISCRIM WEALTH RACE/REL

B66

LEE R.A.,TRUMAN AND TAFT-HARTLEY: A QUESTION OF MANDATE. USA+45 LAW CONSTN LG/CO CONTROL LOBBY GOV/REL PEACE NEW/LIB 20 TRUMAN/HS CONGRESS. PAGE 77 F1507 — LEGIS TOP/EX ADJUD LABOR

B66

LICHTMAN R.,TOWARD COMMUNITY (PAPER). PLAN PROB/SOLV WEALTH MARXISM...HEAL CONCPT 20. PAGE 80 F1561 — NEW/LIB EFFICIENCY CAP/ISM ADJUST

S66

JACOBS P.,"RE-RADICALIZING THE DE-RADICALIZED." USA+45 SOCIETY STRUCT FINAN PLAN PROB/SOLV CAP/ISM WEALTH CONSERVE NEW/LIB 20. PAGE 66 F1297 — NAT/G POLICY MARXIST ADMIN

B67

GREEN C.,NEGATIVE TAXES AND THE POVERTY PROBLEM. COST EFFICIENCY INCOME NEW/LIB...METH/CNCPT CHARTS METH/COMP BIBLIOG 20. PAGE 50 F0983 — TAX RECEIVE WEALTH PLAN

B67

ROELOFS H.M.,THE LANGUAGE OF MODERN POLITICS: AN INTRODUCTION TO THE STUDY OF GOVERNMENT. DIPLOM ADMIN MARXISM NEW/LIB...JURID CONCPT METH/COMP T 20. PAGE 113 F2230 — LEAD NAT/COMP PERS/REL NAT/G

B67

YAMAMURA K.,ECONOMIC POLICY IN POSTWAR JAPAN. ASIA FINAN POL/PAR DIPLOM LEAD NAT/LISM ATTIT NEW/LIB POPULISM 20 CHINJAP. PAGE 149 F2946 — ECO/DEV POLICY NAT/G TEC/DEV

S67

LENS S.,"WALTER REUTHER TRIES TO BUILD A FIRE." WORKER LEAD DISCRIM AGE ORD/FREE NEW/LIB SOC. PAGE 78 F1523 — LABOR PARTIC NEIGH PLAN

NEW/MEXICO....NEW MEXICO

NEW/YORK....NEW YORK STATE

N19

HERZBERG D.G.,A BUDGET FOR NEW YORK STATE, 1956-1957 (PAMPHLET). USA+45 ADMIN GOV/REL 20 — POL/PAR PROVS

NEW/YORK HARRIMAN/A. PAGE 59 F1159 BUDGET LEGIS

S30
CRAWFORD F.G.,"THE EXECUTIVE BUDGET DECISION IN NEW YORK." LEGIS EXEC PWR NEW/YORK. PAGE 28 F0552 LEAD BUDGET PROVS PROB/SOLV

B58
RUBIN B.,PUBLIC RELATIONS AND THE STATE, A CASE STUDY OF NEW YORK STATE ADMINISTRATION, 1943-54. USA+45 USA-45 COM/IND EDU/PROP GOV/REL...CHARTS 20 NEW/YORK DEWEY/THOM. PAGE 114 F2255 INGP/REL PRESS PROVS GP/REL

B61
DOIG J.W.,THE POLITICS OF METROPOLITAN TRANSPORTATION. DELIB/GP WORKER DIPLOM TASK EFFICIENCY UTIL...CHARTS BIBLIOG MUNICH 20 NEW/YORK NEW/JERSEY PUB/TRANS RAILROAD. PAGE 34 F0652 PROB/SOLV STRATA DIST/IND

B64
COMMITTEE ECONOMIC DEVELOPMENT,COMMUNITY ECONOMIC DEVELOPMENT PROGRAMS. USA+45 FINAN INDUS LG/CO PROF/ORG CREATE GP/REL MUNICH NEW/YORK VERMONT PENNSYLVAN IN ARKANSAS. PAGE 27 F0519 LOC/G LABOR PLAN

NEW/ZEALND....NEW ZEALAND; SEE ALSO S/ASIA, COMMONWLTH

B65
CAMERON W.J.,NEW ZEALAND. NEW/ZEALND S/ASIA DIPLOM INT/TRADE WRITING COLONIAL PARL/PROC...GEOG CMN/WLTH. PAGE 21 F0402 SOCIETY GP/REL STRUCT

B66
EDWARDS C.D.,TRADE REGULATIONS OVERSEAS. IRELAND NEW/ZEALND SOUTH/AFR NAT/G CAP/ISM TARIFFS CONTROL ...POLICY JURID 20 EEC CHINJAP. PAGE 36 F0703 INT/TRADE DIPLOM INT/LAW ECO/TAC

B95
SELIGMAN E.R.A.,ESSAYS IN TAXATION. NEW/ZEALND PRUSSIA UK USA-45 MARKET LOC/G CREATE PRICE CONTROL INCOME OWN WEALTH...GOV/COMP METH/COMP 19. PAGE 119 F2349 TAX TARIFFS INDUS NAT/G

NEWARK/NJ....NEWARK, N.J.

NEWCOMER H.A. F1921

NEWFNDLND....NEWFOUNDLAND, CANADA

NEWLYN W.T. F1922,F1923

NEWMAN P.K. F1869

NEWY/TIMES....NEW YORK TIMES

NEWYORK/C ....NEW YORK CITY

B62
HOOVER E.M.,ANATOMY OF A METROPOLIS. FUT USA+45 SOCIETY ECO/DEV DIST/IND INDUS WORKER ECO/TAC TAX GP/REL COST WEALTH MUNICH 20 NEWYORK/C. PAGE 62 F1212 ROUTINE TREND INCOME

B64
FISK W.M.,ADMINISTRATIVE PROCEDURE IN A REGULATORY AGENCY: THE CAB AND THE NEW YORK-CHICAGO CASE (PAMPHLET). USA+45 DIST/IND ADMIN CONTROL LOBBY GP/REL ROLE ORD/FREE NEWYORK/C CHICAGO CAB. PAGE 41 F0805 SERV/IND ECO/DEV AIR JURID

B64
FITCH L.C.,URBAN TRANSPORTATION AND PUBLIC POLICY. FINAN NAT/G LEGIS PROB/SOLV TEC/DEV PRICE COST EFFICIENCY...DECISION STAT CHARTS METH/COMP MUNICH 20 NEWYORK/C PHILADELPH LOS/ANG CHICAGO WASHING/DC. PAGE 41 F0806 DIST/IND PLAN LOC/G

B64
FRIEDEN B.J.,THE FUTURE OF OLD NEIGHBORHOODS: REBUILDING FOR A CHANGING POPULATION. CONSTRUC LOC/G NAT/G ACT/RES ECO/TAC REGION ATTIT...INT SAMP MUNICH 20 NEWYORK/C LOS/ANG HARTFORD URBAN/RNWL. PAGE 44 F0855 NEIGH PROB/SOLV PLAN BUDGET

B65
BOLLENS J.C.,THE METROPOLIS: ITS PEOPLE, POLITICS, AND ECONOMIC LIFE. USA+45 PLAN PROB/SOLV PERS/REL PWR...DECISION GEOG CENSUS TREND CON/ANAL MUNICH 20 NEWYORK/C LOS/ANG SAN/FRAN CHICAGO PHILADELPH. PAGE 16 F0309 HABITAT SOC LOC/G

B66
DAVIES JC I.I.I.,NEIGHBORHOOD GROUPS AND URBAN RENEWAL. USA+45 PLAN LOBBY PARTIC CHOOSE RACE/REL ...POLICY DECISION SOC INT MUNICH SOC/INTEG 20 NEWYORK/C. PAGE 30 F0586 NEIGH CREATE PROB/SOLV

B67
GITTELL M.,PARTICIPANTS AND PARTICIPATION: A STUDY OF SCHOOL POLICY IN NEW YORK. USA+45 EX/STRUC BUDGET PAY ATTIT...POLICY MUNICH 20 NEWYORK/C. PAGE 47 F0926 SCHOOL DECISION PARTIC ADMIN

NICARAGUA....NICARAGUA; SEE ALSO L/A+17C

B65
LUGO-MARENCO J.J.,A STATEMENT OF THE LAWS OF NICARAGUA IN MATTERS AFFECTING BUSINESS. NICARAGUA AGRI DIST/IND EXTR/IND FINAN INDUS FAM WORKER INT/TRADE TAX MARRIAGE OWN BIO/SOC 20 TREATY RESOURCE/N MIGRATION. PAGE 82 F1606 CONSTN NAT/G LEGIS JURID

NICHOLAS/I....CZAR NICHOLAS I

NICHOLS J.P. F1924

NICHOLSON T.L. F2475

NICOLSON/A....SIR ARTHUR NICOLSON

NICOSIA F.N. F1925

NICOSIA M.N. F1926

NICULESCU B. F1927

NIEBUHR/R....REINHOLD NIEBUHR

NIEBURG/HL....H.L. NIEBURG

NIETZSCH/F....FRIEDRICH NIETZSCHE

NIGER

NCO
STOLPER W.,"SOCIAL FACTORS IN ECONOMIC PLANNING, WITH SPECIAL REFERENCE TO NIGERIA" AFR NIGER CULTURE FAM SECT RECEIVE ETIQUET ADMIN DEMAND 20. PAGE 126 F2494 ECO/UNDEV PLAN ADJUST RISK

B45
DAVIS J.,AFRICA ADVANCING. AFR CONGO/BRAZ LIBERIA NIGER INT/ORG SCHOOL DIPLOM GIVE KNOWL SKILL 20. PAGE 30 F0590 SECT COLONIAL AGRI ECO/UNDEV

B55
PEDLER F.J.,ECONOMIC GEOGRAPHY OF WEST AFRICA. GAMBIA NIGER SIER/LEONE STRATA EXTR/IND MARKET LABOR INT/TRADE DEMAND HABITAT WEALTH...CHARTS 20. PAGE 104 F2046 ECO/UNDEV GEOG PRODUC EFFICIENCY

B61
PETCH G.A.,ECONOMIC DEVELOPMENT AND MODERN WEST AFRICA. AFR CONGO/BRAZ GHANA NIGER SIER/LEONE AGRI MARKET LABOR FOR/AID TAX COST EFFICIENCY EQUILIB PRODUC...GEOG TREND 20. PAGE 105 F2068 ECO/UNDEV TEC/DEV EXTR/IND ECO/TAC

NIGERIA....SEE ALSO AFR

B59
HICKS J.R.,ESSAYS IN WORLD ECONOMICS. AFR CEYLON NIGERIA WOR+45 SOCIETY ECO/DEV ORD/FREE WEALTH ...GEN/LAWS TOT/POP 20. PAGE 59 F1166 ECO/UNDEV ECO/TAC UK

B61
CARNEY D.E.,GOVERNMENT AND ECONOMY IN BRITISH WEST AFRICA. GAMBIA GHANA NIGERIA SIER/LEONE DOMIN ADMIN GOV/REL SOVEREIGN WEALTH LAISSEZ...BIBLIOG 20 CMN/WLTH. PAGE 21 F0417 METH/COMP COLONIAL ECO/TAC ECO/UNDEV

B63
PREST A.R.,PUBLIC FINANCE IN UNDERDEVELOPED COUNTRIES. UK WOR+45 WOR-45 SOCIETY INT/ORG NAT/G LEGIS ACT/RES PLAN ECO/TAC ADMIN ROUTINE...CHARTS 20. PAGE 108 F2115 FINAN ECO/UNDEV NIGERIA

B64
THE SPECIAL COMMONWEALTH AFRICAN ASSISTANCE PLAN. AFR CANADA INDIA NIGERIA UK FINAN SCHOOL...CHARTS 20 COMMONWLTH. PAGE 1 F0019 ECO/UNDEV TREND FOR/AID ADMIN

B64
BROWN C.V.,GOVERNMENT AND BANKING IN WESTERN NIGERIA. AFR NIGERIA GOV/REL GP/REL...POLICY 20. PAGE 19 F0367 ADMIN ECO/UNDEV FINAN NAT/G

B66
CROWDER M.,A SHORT HISTORY OF NIGERIA. AFR NIGERIA UK ECO/UNDEV CHIEF INT/TRADE RACE/REL NAT/LISM ORD/FREE...GEOG SOC CHARTS BIBLIOG 14/20. PAGE 29 F0558 COLONIAL NAT/G CULTURE

B66
MOUNTJOY A.B.,INDUSTRIALIZATION AND UNDER-DEVELOPED COUNTRIES (2ND REV. ED.). CHILE GHANA INDIA NIGERIA WOR+45 SOCIETY PROB/SOLV ECO/TAC...SOC CHARTS 20 INDUS/REV. PAGE 94 F1848 ECO/UNDEV INDUS GEOG HABITAT

B66
WILCOX C.,ECONOMIES OF THE WORLD TODAY: THEIR ORGANIZATION, DEVELOPMENT, AND PERFORMANCE (2ND ED.). CHINA/COM COM INDIA NIGERIA UK WOR+45 WOR-45 INDUS MARKET PLAN ECO/TAC SOCISM...CHARTS METH/COMP 20. PAGE 146 F2878 ECO/DEV ECO/UNDEV MARXISM CAP/ISM

B67
LEWIS L.J.,SOCIETY, SCHOOLS AND PROGRESS IN EDU/PROP

NIGERIA. NIGERIA WORKER ECO/TAC ADJUST 20. PAGE 79 F1550 — ECO/UNDEV SKILL SOCIETY

NIH....NATIONAL INSTITUTE OF HEALTH

NILES J.G. F1928

NIPA....NATIONAL INSTITUTE OF PUBLIC ADMINISTRATION

NISEI....NISEI: JAPANESE AMERICANS

NIXON/RM....PRESIDENT RICHARD M. NIXON

NKRUMAH K. F1929,F1930

NKRUMAH/K....KWAME NKRUMAH

N
BROCKWAY A.F.,AFRICAN SOCIALISM. EUR+WWI GHANA ISLAM UAR ECO/UNDEV CAP/ISM INT/TRADE COLONIAL COERCE GOV/REL DISCRIM 20 NEGRO NKRUMAH/K NASSER/G. PAGE 19 F0356 — AFR SOCISM MARXISM

S67
KRAUS J.,"A MARXIST IN GHANA." GHANA ELITES CHIEF PROB/SOLV TEC/DEV DIPLOM ECO/TAC COLONIAL PARTIC PWR 20 NKRUMAH/K. PAGE 73 F1432 — MARXISM PLAN ATTIT CREATE

S67
SCOTT R.,"TRADE UNIONS IN AFRICA." AFR UGANDA USA-45 ECO/UNDEV INDUS INT/ORG POL/PAR ECO/TAC WEALTH...GP/COMP 20 NKRUMAH/K. PAGE 118 F2335 — LABOR WORKER NAT/G

NLC....NATIONAL LIBERATION COUNCIL IN GHANA

NLF....NATIONAL LIBERATION FRONT OF SOUTH VIETNAM

NLRB....NATIONAL LABOR RELATIONS BOARD

B55
BLOOM G.F.,ECONOMICS OF LABOR RELATIONS. USA+45 LAW CONSULT WORKER CAP/ISM PAY ADJUD CONTROL EFFICIENCY ORD/FREE...CHARTS 19/20 AFL/CIO NLRB DEPT/LABOR. PAGE 16 F0299 — ECO/DEV ECO/TAC LABOR GOV/REL

S60
MANN S.Z.,"POLICY FORMULATION IN THE EXECUTIVE BRANCH: THE TAFT-HARTLEY EXPERIENCE." USA+45 LABOR CHIEF INGP/REL 20 NLRB. PAGE 85 F1656 — EXEC GOV/REL EX/STRUC PROB/SOLV

S61
SCHER S.,"REGULATORY AGENCY CONTROL THROUGH APPOINTMENT: THE CASE OF THE EISENHOWER ADMINISTRATION AND THE NLRB." USA+45 EX/STRUC GOV/REL 20 NLRB. PAGE 116 F2296 — CHIEF LOBBY CONTROL TOP/EX

B62
MORGAN C.A.,LABOR ECONOMICS. LAW INDUS MARKET WORKER PLAN PROB/SOLV GOV/REL INCOME ROLE...T 20 DEPT/LABOR NLRB. PAGE 93 F1829 — LABOR ECO/TAC ECO/DEV CAP/ISM

B66
SOVERN M.I.,LEGAL RESTRAINTS ON RACIAL DISCRIMINATION IN EMPLOYMENT. USA+45 LAW INDUS LG/CO SML/CO DELIB/GP LEGIS SANCTION 20 NLRB PRESIDENT NEGRO CIV/RIGHTS RAILROAD. PAGE 124 F2446 — DISCRIM RACE/REL WORKER JURID

B67
PETRO S.,THE KINGSPORT STRIKE. USA+45 PROC/MFG NAT/G JUDGE PRESS PARTIC PERS/REL...OLD/LIB OBS INT 20 NLRB. PAGE 105 F2074 — LABOR COERCE SANCTION ALL/VALS

L67
PARKER G.P. JR.,"MONETARY RECOVERY UNDER THE FEDERAL LABOR STATUTES." USA+45 USA-45 INDUS ADJUD CT/SYS GOV/REL HEALTH ORD/FREE 20 DEPT/LABOR NLRB. PAGE 103 F2027 — LABOR CONTROL LAW FINAN

L67
STILL C.H.,"MONETARY RECOVERY UNDER THE FAIR LABOR STANDARDS ACT." USA+45 USA-45 WORKER PAY ADJUD GOV/REL HEALTH ORD/FREE...MATH 20 NLRB. PAGE 126 F2487 — LABOR CONTROL LAW FINAN

NOBILITY....SEE ELITES

NOMAD M. F1931

NOMAD/MAX....MAX NOMAD

NOMADISM....SEE GEOG

NONALIGNED NATIONS....SEE THIRD/WRLD

NON-WHITE....SEE RACE/REL

NONVIOLENT....NONVIOLENCE (CONCEPT)

NORGREN P.H. F1932

NORMS....SEE AVERAGE, ALSO APPROPRIATE VALUES AND DIMENSIONS OF GROUPS, STAT, LOG, ETC.

NORTH D.C. F1933

NORTH AFRICA....SEE AFRICA/N, ISLAM

NORTH ATLANTIC TREATY ORGANIZATION....SEE NATO

NORTH VIETNAM....SEE VIETNAM/N

NORTH CAROLINA U INST GOVT F1934

NORTH/AMER....NORTH AMERICA, EXCLUSIVE OF CENTRAL AMERICA

NORTH/CAR....NORTH CAROLINA

B30
GREEN F.M.,CONSTITUTIONAL DEVELOPMENT IN THE SOUTH ATLANTIC STATES, 1776-1860; A STUDY IN THE EVOLUTION OF DEMOCRACY. USA-45 ELITES SOCIETY STRATA ECO/DEV AGRI POL/PAR EX/STRUC LEGIS CT/SYS REGION...BIBLIOG 18/19 MARYLAND VIRGINIA GEORGIA NORTH/CAR SOUTH/CAR. PAGE 50 F0984 — CONSTN PROVS PLURISM REPRESENT

NORTH/DAK....NORTH DAKOTA

NORTH/US....NORTHERN UNITED STATES

NORTHERN RHODESIA....SEE ZAMBIA

NORTHRUP H.R. F0299

NORTHW/TER....NORTHWEST TERRITORIES, CANADA

NORTHWST/U....NORTHWESTERN UNIVERSITY

NORTON H.S. F1935

NORTON P.L. F1936

NORWAY....SEE ALSO APPROPRIATE TIME/SPACE/CULTURE INDEX

C65
WUORINEN J.H.,"SCANDINAVIA." DENMARK FINLAND ICELAND NORWAY SWEDEN SOCIETY AGRI POL/PAR DELIB/GP DIPLOM INT/TRADE NEUTRAL WAR...CHARTS IND TREATY 20. PAGE 149 F2942 — BIBLIOG NAT/G POLICY

B67
ANDERSON S.V.,THE NORDIC COUNCIL: A STUDY OF SCANDINAVIAN REGIONALISM. DENMARK FINLAND ICELAND NORWAY SWEDEN MARKET NAT/G VOL/ASSN CONSULT PARL/PROC ATTIT...TIME/SEQ BIBLIOG 20. PAGE 5 F0098 — INT/ORG REGION DIPLOM LEGIS

B67
DIXON W.,SOCIETY, SCHOOLS AND PROGRESS IN SCANDINAVIA. DENMARK NORWAY SWEDEN 20. PAGE 33 F0644 — EDU/PROP SOCIETY ADJUST PLAN

NOSSITER B.D. F1937

NOURSE E.G. F1938,F1939

NOVA/SCOT....NOVA SCOTIA, CANADA

NOVACK D.E. F1940

NOVE A. F1941,F1942,F1943

NOVOTNY/A....ANTONIN NOVOTNY

NOYES C.R. F1944

NRA....NATIONAL RECOVERY ADMINISTRATION

B36
BURNS A.R.,THE DECLINE OF COMPETITION. LAW LG/CO NAT/G SML/CO LEGIS PRICE AGREE CONTROL GP/REL INCOME PRODUC...POLICY 19/20 NRA. PAGE 20 F0390 — MARKET GEN/LAWS INDUS

NSC....NATIONAL SECURITY COUNCIL

NSF....NATIONAL SCIENCE FOUNDATION

N19
MORGENSTERN O.,A NEW LOOK AT ECONOMIC TIMES SERIES ANALYSIS (PAMPHLET). WEALTH...BIBLIOG 20 NSF NAVAL/RES. PAGE 93 F1831 — TREND IDEA/COMP EFFICIENCY

NSSF....NATIONAL SOCIAL SCIENCE FOUNDATION

NUC....NATIONAL UNITY COMMITTEE (TURKEY)

NUC/PWR....NUCLEAR POWER, INCLUDING NUCLEAR WEAPONS

N19
ATOMIC INDUSTRIAL FORUM,COMMENTARY ON LEGISLATION TO PERMIT PRIVATE OWNERSHIP OF SPECIAL NUCLEAR MATERIAL (PAMPHLET). USA+45 DELIB/GP LEGIS PLAN OWN ...POLICY 20 AEC CONGRESS. PAGE 7 F0134
NUC/PWR MARKET INDUS LAW

N19
BROWN W.M.,THE DESIGN AND PERFORMANCE OF "OPTIMUM" BLAST SHELTER PROGRAMS (PAMPHLET). USA+45 ACT/RES PLAN DEATH COST EFFICIENCY OPTIMAL...POLICY CHARTS 20. PAGE 19 F0375
HABITAT NUC/PWR WAR HEALTH

N19
MEZERIK A.G.,ECONOMIC AID FOR UNDERDEVELOPED COUNTRIES (PAMPHLET). AFR USSR WOR+45 FINAN LG/CO DELIB/GP NUC/PWR...GEOG CENSUS CHARTS 20 UN THIRD/WRLD. PAGE 90 F1775
FOR/AID ECO/UNDEV DIPLOM POLICY

B47
BALDWIN H.W.,THE PRICE OF POWER. USA+45 FORCES PLAN NUC/PWR ADJUST COST ORD/FREE...POLICY PSY BIBLIOG 20. PAGE 9 F0165
PROB/SOLV PWR POPULISM PRICE

B50
LINCOLN G.,ECONOMICS OF NATIONAL SECURITY. USA+45 ELITES COM/IND DIST/IND INDUS NAT/G VOL/ASSN DELIB/GP EX/STRUC FOR/AID EDU/PROP COERCE NUC/PWR WAR ATTIT KNOWL ORD/FREE PWR TOT/POP VAL/FREE 20. PAGE 80 F1565
FORCES ECO/TAC AFR

B56
ATOMIC INDUSTRIAL FORUM,PUBLIC RELATIONS FOR THE ATOMIC INDUSTRY. WOR+45 PLAN PROB/SOLV EDU/PROP PRESS CONFER...AUD/VIS ANTHOL 20. PAGE 7 F0135
NUC/PWR INDUS GP/REL ATTIT

B57
GOLD N.L.,REGIONAL ECONOMIC DEVELOPMENT AND NUCLEAR POWER IN INDIA. FUT INDIA FINAN FOR/AID INT/TRADE BAL/PAY EFFICIENCY OPTIMAL PRODUC WEALTH...PREDICT 20. PAGE 48 F0934
ECO/UNDEV TEC/DEV NUC/PWR INDUS

B58
ATOMIC INDUSTRIAL FORUM,MANAGEMENT AND ATOMIC ENERGY. WOR+45 SEA LAW MARKET NAT/G TEC/DEV INSPECT INT/TRADE CONFER PEACE HEALTH...ANTHOL 20. PAGE 7 F0136
NUC/PWR INDUS MGT ECO/TAC

B58
CROWE S.,THE LANDSCAPE OF POWER. UK CULTURE SERV/IND NAT/G CONSULT PARTIC NUC/PWR LEISURE...SOC EXHIBIT 20. PAGE 29 F0559
HABITAT TEC/DEV PLAN CONTROL

B58
OEEC,THE INDUSTRIAL CHALLENGE OF NUCLEAR ENERGY. EUR+WWI ECO/DEV INDUS OP/RES CONFER RISK PWR ...AUD/VIS CHARTS ANTHOL 20 OEEC. PAGE 101 F1977
NUC/PWR ACT/RES ECO/TAC INT/ORG

B58
SILOW R.A.,THE POTENTIAL CONTRIBUTION OF ATOMIC ENERGY TO DEVELOPMENT IN AGRICULTURE AND RELATED INDUSTRIES (PAMPHLET). WOR+45 R+D TEC/DEV EFFICIENCY 20 UN. PAGE 122 F2403
NUC/PWR ECO/UNDEV AGRI

B59
HARVARD UNIVERSITY LAW SCHOOL,INTERNATIONAL PROBLEMS OF FINANCIAL PROTECTION AGAINST NUCLEAR RISK. WOR+45 NAT/G DELIB/GP PROB/SOLV DIPLOM CONTROL ATTIT...POLICY INT/LAW MATH 20. PAGE 56 F1105
NUC/PWR ADJUD INDUS FINAN

B59
STERNBERG F.,THE MILITARY AND INDUSTRIAL REVOLUTION OF OUR TIME. USA+45 USSR WOR+45 WORKER COMPUTER PLAN TEC/DEV NUC/PWR GP/REL...POLICY NAT/COMP 20. PAGE 126 F2481
DIPLOM FORCES INDUS CIVMIL/REL

B59
U OF MICHIGAN LAW SCHOOL,ATOMS AND THE LAW. USA+45 PROVS WORKER PROB/SOLV DIPLOM ADMIN GOV/REL ANTHOL. PAGE 132 F2596
NUC/PWR NAT/G CONTROL LAW

B60
ATOMIC INDUSTRIAL FORUM,ATOMS FOR INDUSTRY: WORLD FORUM. WOR+45 FINAN COST UTIL...JURID ANTHOL 20. PAGE 7 F0137
NUC/PWR INDUS PLAN PROB/SOLV

B60
BILLERBECK K.,SOVIET BLOC FOREIGN AID TO UNDERDEVELOPED COUNTRIES. COM FUT USSR FINAN FORCES TEC/DEV DIPLOM INT/TRADE EDU/PROP NUC/PWR...TREND 20. PAGE 15 F0285
FOR/AID ECO/UNDEV ECO/TAC MARXISM

B60
HITCH C.J.,THE ECONOMICS OF DEFENSE IN THE NUCLEAR AGE. USA+45 WOR+45 CREATE PLAN NUC/PWR ATTIT ...CON/ANAL CHARTS HYPO/EXP NATO 20. PAGE 60 F1179
R+D FORCES

B61
DIMOCK M.E.,BUSINESS AND GOVERNMENT (4TH ED.). AGRI FINAN OP/RES PLAN BUDGET DIPLOM LOBBY NUC/PWR NEW/LIB SOCISM...POLICY BIBLIOG 20. PAGE 33 F0641
NAT/G INDUS LABOR ECO/TAC

B61
HARDT J.P.,THE COLD WAR ECONOMIC GAP. AFR USA+45 USSR ECO/DEV FORCES INT/TRADE NUC/PWR PWR 20. PAGE 55 F1081
DIPLOM ECO/TAC NAT/COMP POLICY

B62
DUPRE J.S.,SCIENCE AND THE NATION: POLICY AND POLITICS. USA+45 LAW ACADEM FORCES ADMIN CIVMIL/REL GOV/REL EFFICIENCY PEACE...TREND 20 SCI/ADVSRY. PAGE 35 F0682
R+D INDUS TEC/DEV NUC/PWR

B62
SCHILLING W.R.,STRATEGY, POLITICS, AND DEFENSE BUDGETS. AFR USA+45 CHIEF LEGIS PLAN TEC/DEV BAL/PWR BUDGET NUC/PWR WAR CIVMIL/REL GOV/REL PWR 20 EISNHWR/DD. PAGE 117 F2297
NAT/G POLICY FORCES DETER

B63
MULLENBACH P.,CIVILIAN NUCLEAR POWER: ECONOMIC ISSUES AND POLICY FORMATION. AFR FINAN INT/ORG DELIB/GP ACT/RES ECO/TAC ATTIT SUPEGO HEALTH ORD/FREE PWR...POLICY CONCPT MATH STAT CHARTS VAL/FREE 20. PAGE 94 F1855
USA+45 ECO/DEV NUC/PWR

L63
MOUSKHELY M.,"LE BLOC COMMUNISTE ET LA COMMUNAUTE ECONOMIQUE EUROPEENNE." AFR COM EUR+WWI FUT USSR WOR+45 INTELL ECO/UNDEV LABOR POL/PAR NUC/PWR RIGID/FLEX...TIME/SEQ ORG/CHARTS EEC TOT/POP 20. PAGE 94 F1849
INT/ORG ECO/DEV

S63
ADAMS F.G.,"ECONOMIC CONSIDERATIONS OF AN ATLANTIC ENERGY POLICY." EUR+WWI FUT USA+45 DIST/IND EXTR/IND MARKET CONSULT LEGIS ECO/TAC WEALTH ...POLICY EEC FOR/TRADE OEEC 20. PAGE 2 F0037
ECO/DEV TEC/DEV NUC/PWR

S63
BENOIT E.,"ECONOMIC ADJUSTMENTS TO ARMS CONTROL." FUT USA+45 NAT/G NUC/PWR WAR WEAPON 20. PAGE 13 F0251
ECO/DEV PWR ARMS/CONT

S63
ENTHOVEN A.C.,"ECONOMIC ANALYSIS IN THE DEPARTMENT OF DEFENSE." USA+45 NAT/G DELIB/GP PROB/SOLV RATION NUC/PWR WEAPON COST...DECISION 20 DEPT/DEFEN RESOURCE/N. PAGE 38 F0739
PLAN BUDGET ECO/TAC FORCES

S63
HALLSTEIN W.,"THE EUROPEAN COMMUNITY AND ATLANTIC PARTNERSHIP." EUR+WWI USA+45 MARKET NAT/G VOL/ASSN DELIB/GP ARMS/CONT NUC/PWR ATTIT PWR...CONCPT STAT TIME/SEQ TREND OEEC 20 EEC. PAGE 54 F1053
INT/ORG ECO/TAC UK

B64
DUSCHA J.,ARMS, MONEY, AND POLITICS. USA+45 INDUS POL/PAR ECO/TAC TAX DETER NUC/PWR WAR WEAPON GOV/REL ATTIT...BIBLIOG/A 20 CONGRESS MONEY DEPT/DEFEN. PAGE 35 F0687
NAT/G FORCES POLICY BUDGET

B64
FIESER M.E.,ECONOMIC POLICY AND WAR POTENTIAL. AFR WOR+45 ECO/DEV INDUS NAT/G FORCES TEC/DEV NUC/PWR CIVMIL/REL ORD/FREE 20. PAGE 40 F0791
INT/TRADE POLICY ECO/TAC DETER

B64
MILIBAND R.,THE SOCIALIST REGISTER: 1964. GERMANY/W ITALY UK LABOR POL/PAR ECO/TAC FOR/AID NUC/PWR ...POLICY SOCIALIST IDEA/COMP 20 MAO NASSER/G. PAGE 91 F1784
MARXISM SOCISM CAP/ISM PROB/SOLV

B64
WERNETTE J.P.,GOVERNMENT AND BUSINESS. LABOR CAP/ISM ECO/TAC INT/TRADE TAX ADMIN AUTOMAT NUC/PWR CIVMIL/REL DEMAND...MGT 20 MONOPOLY. PAGE 145 F2859
NAT/G FINAN ECO/DEV CONTROL

B65
PEACE RESEARCH ABSTRACTS. FUT WOR+45 R+D INT/ORG NAT/G PLAN TEC/DEV BAL/PWR DIPLOM FOR/AID NUC/PWR HEALTH. PAGE 1 F0022
BIBLIOG/A PEACE ARMS/CONT WAR

B65
BEAUFRE A.,AN INTRODUCTION TO STRATEGY, WITH PARTICULAR REFERENCE TO PROBLEMS OF DEFENSE, POLITICS, ECONOMICS IN THE NUCLEAR AGE. WOR+45 FORCES DIPLOM DETER CIVMIL/REL GP/REL...NEW/IDEA IDEA/COMP 20. PAGE 12 F0226
PLAN NUC/PWR WEAPON DECISION

B65
CERNY K.H.,NATO IN QUEST OF COHESION* A CONFRONTATION OF VIEWPOINTS. COM EUR+WWI USA+45 FORCES LEAD REGION DETER...ANTHOL NATO. PAGE 22 F0438
CENTRAL NUC/PWR VOL/ASSN

B65
COX D.W.,THE PERILS OF PEACE* CONVERSION TO WHAT? FUT USA+45 ECO/DEV NAT/G ACT/RES CREATE PLAN NUC/PWR WAR DEMAND MGT. PAGE 28 F0546
PEACE WORKER FORCES MARKET

B65
HASSON J.A.,THE ECONOMICS OF NUCLEAR POWER. INDIA UK USA+45 WOR+45 INT/ORG TEC/DEV COST...SOC STAT CHARTS 20 EURATOM. PAGE 56 F1108
NUC/PWR INDUS ECO/DEV METH

B65
KISSINGER H.A.,THE TROUBLED PARTNERSHIP* RE-APPRAISAL OF THE WESTERN ALLIANCE. EUR+WWI USA+45 INT/ORG NAT/G VOL/ASSN TOP/EX DIPLOM ORD/FREE PWR
FRANCE NUC/PWR ECO/DEV

NATO. PAGE 71 F1402

B65
LYONS G.M.,AMERICA: PURPOSE AND POWER. UK USA+45 FINAN INDUS MARKET WORKER TEC/DEV DIPLOM AUTOMAT NUC/PWR WAR RACE/REL ORD/FREE 20 EEC CONGRESS SUPREME/CT CIV/RIGHTS. PAGE 82 F1617 — PWR PROB/SOLV ECO/DEV TASK

B65
RANSOM H.H.,AN AMERICAN FOREIGN POLICY READER. USA+45 FORCES EDU/PROP COERCE NUC/PWR WAR PEACE ...DECISION 20. PAGE 109 F2146 — NAT/G DIPLOM POLICY

S65
BERREBY J.J.,"IMPERATIFS STRATEGIQUES DU PETROLE." ECO/UNDEV VOL/ASSN ECO/TAC COLONIAL NUC/PWR WAR. PAGE 14 F0270 — ISLAM EXTR/IND STAT OBS

S65
DUMONT R.,"SURPEUPLEMENT CHINOIS ET SES CONSEQUENCES." AFR ECO/UNDEV AGRI PLAN PROB/SOLV ECO/TAC FOR/AID NUC/PWR...OBS INT PREDICT. PAGE 35 F0675 — GEOG ASIA STAT

B66
FREIDEL F.,AMERICAN ISSUES IN THE TWENTIETH CENTURY. SOCIETY FINAN ECO/TAC FOR/AID CONTROL NUC/PWR WAR RACE/REL PEACE ATTIT...ANTHOL T 20 WILSON/W ROOSEVLT/F KENNEDY/JF TRUMAN/HS. PAGE 44 F0851 — DIPLOM POLICY NAT/G ORD/FREE

B66
KUENNE R.E.,THE POLARIS MISSILE STRIKE* A GENERAL ECONOMIC SYSTEMS ANALYSIS. USA+45 USSR NAT/G BAL/PWR ARMS/CONT WAR...MATH PROBABIL COMPUT/IR CHARTS HYPO/EXP SIMUL. PAGE 74 F1446 — NUC/PWR FORCES DETER DIPLOM

B66
LILLEY S.,MEN, MACHINES AND HISTORY: THE STORY OF TOOLS AND MACHINES IN RELATION TO SOCIAL PROGRESS. PREHIST SPACE STRUCT COMPUTER AUTOMAT NUC/PWR ...POLICY SOC. PAGE 80 F1564 — AGRI TEC/DEV SOCIETY

B66
US PRES COMM ECO IMPACT DEFENS,REPORT* JULY 1965. USA+45 ECO/DEV INDUS DELIB/GP FORCES OP/RES ARMS/CONT NUC/PWR WEAPON BAL/PAY...PREDICT SIMUL. PAGE 138 F2726 — ACT/RES STAT WAR BUDGET

S66
DUROSELLE J.B.,"THE FUTURE OF THE ATLANTIC COMMUNITY." EUR+WWI USA+45 USSR NAT/G CAP/ISM REGION DETER NUC/PWR ATTIT MARXISM...INT/LAW 20 NATO. PAGE 35 F0686 — FUT DIPLOM MYTH POLICY

B67
BEATON L.,THE STRUGGLE FOR PEACE. INT/ORG FORCES NUC/PWR COST PWR...POLICY TREND 20. PAGE 12 F0225 — PEACE BAL/PWR DIPLOM WAR

B67
ENKE S.,DEFENSE MANAGEMENT. USA+45 R+D FORCES WORKER PLAN ECO/TAC ADMIN NUC/PWR BAL/PAY UTIL WEALTH...MGT DEPT/DEFEN. PAGE 38 F0738 — DECISION DELIB/GP EFFICIENCY BUDGET

B67
HALLE L.J.,THE COLD WAR AS HISTORY. AFR USSR WOR+45 ECO/TAC FOR/AID NUC/PWR WAR PEACE ORD/FREE ...MAJORIT TREND 20 KENNEDY/JF KHRUSH/N BERLIN/BLO. PAGE 54 F1048 — DIPLOM BAL/PWR

B67
ORLANS H.,CONTRACTING FOR ATOMS. AFR USA+45 LAW INTELL ACADEM LG/CO NAT/G PLAN TEC/DEV CONTROL DETER...TREND 20. PAGE 102 F1999 — NUC/PWR R+D PRODUC PEACE

B67
UNIVERSAL REFERENCE SYSTEM,PUBLIC POLICY AND THE MANAGEMENT OF SCIENCE (VOLUME IX). FUT SPACE WOR+45 LAW NAT/G TEC/DEV CONTROL NUC/PWR GOV/REL ...COMPUT/IR GEN/METH. PAGE 133 F2618 — BIBLIOG/A POLICY MGT PHIL/SCI

B67
WOLF C. JR.,UNITED STATES POLICY AND THE THIRD WORLD. USA+45 WOR+45 FORCES ACT/RES BAL/PWR ECO/TAC FOR/AID DETER GUERRILLA NUC/PWR REV...CHARTS 20. PAGE 148 F2916 — DIPLOM ECO/UNDEV POLICY NAT/G

S67
APEL H.,"LES NOUVEAUX ASPECTS DE LA POLITIQUE ETRANGERE ALLEMANDE." AFR EUR+WWI GERMANY POL/PAR BAL/PWR ECO/TAC INT/TRADE NUC/PWR NAT/LISM PEACE ...POLICY 20 EEC. PAGE 6 F0107 — DIPLOM INT/ORG FEDERAL

S67
GAUSSENS J.,"THE APPLICATIONS OF NUCLEAR ENERGY - TECHNICAL, ECONOMIC AND SOCIAL ASPECTS." WOR+45 INDUS R+D ACT/RES EFFICIENCY PRODUC SKILL PREDICT. PAGE 47 F0911 — NUC/PWR TEC/DEV ECO/DEV ADJUST

N67
US HOUSE COMM SCI ASTRONAUT,AUTHORIZING APPROPRIATIONS TO THE NATIONAL AERONAUTICS AND SPACE ADMINISTRATION (PAMPHLET). USA+45 NAT/G OP/RES TEC/DEV BUDGET NASA HOUSE/REP. PAGE 137 F2704 — SPACE R+D PHIL/SCI NUC/PWR

NUCLEAR POWER....SEE NUC/PWR

NUCLEAR WAR....SEE NUC/PWR+COERCE, WAR

NUMERICAL INDICES....SEE INDEX

NUNEZ JIMENEZ A. F1945

NUREMBERG....NUREMBERG WAR TRIALS

NUSENBAUM A.A. F1946

NYANZI S. F1947

NYASALAND....SEE ALSO MALAWI

B67
WILLS A.J.,AN INTRODUCTION TO THE HISTORY OF CENTRAL AFRICA. RHODESIA ZAMBIA CULTURE SOCIETY ECO/UNDEV TEC/DEV DOMIN WAR ALL/VALS...POLICY TREND BIBLIOG T 14/20 NYASALAND. PAGE 147 F2899 — AFR COLONIAL ORD/FREE

NYATURU....NYATURU, A TRIBE OF TANGANYIKA

NYC....NEW YORK CITY

NYE J. F1948

NYOMARKAY J. F1949

O

O.E.E.C. F1950

O'BRIEN F. F1951

O'CONNELL D.P. F1952

O'CONNER A.M. F1953

O'CONNOR H. F1954,F1955,F1956

O'CONNOR T.P. F1957

O'LEARY M.K. F1958

O'NEAL F.H. F1959

OAS....ORGANIZATION OF AMERICAN STATES; SEE ALSO INT/ORG, VOL/ASSN

I55
KISER M.,"ORGANIZATION OF AMERICAN STATES." L/A+17C USA+45 ECO/UNDEV INT/ORG NAT/G PLAN TEC/DEV DIPLOM ECO/TAC INT/TRADE EDU/PROP ADMIN ALL/VALS...POLICY MGT RECORD ORG/CHARTS OAS COMMUN 20. PAGE 71 F1401 — VOL/ASSN ECO/DEV REGION

B58
BUGEDA LANZAS J.,A STATEMENT OF THE LAWS OF CUBA IN MATTERS AFFECTING BUSINESS (2ND ED. REV., ENLARGED). CUBA L/A+17C LAW FINAN FAM LEGIS ACT/RES ADMIN GP/REL...BIBLIOG 20 OAS. PAGE 20 F0382 — JURID NAT/G INDUS WORKER

B58
PAN AMERICAN UNION,REPERTORIO DE PUBLICACIONES PERIODICAS ACTUALES LATINO-AMERICANAS. CULTURE ECO/UNDEV ADMIN LEAD GOV/REL 20 OAS. PAGE 103 F2023 — BIBLIOG L/A+17C NAT/G DIPLOM

B59
GOMEZ ROBLES J.,A STATEMENT OF THE LAWS OF GUATEMALA IN MATTERS AFFECTING BUSINESS (2ND ED. REV., ENLARGED). GUATEMALA L/A+17C LAW FINAN FAM WORKER ACT/RES DIPLOM ADJUD ADMIN GP/REL 20 OAS. PAGE 48 F0945 — JURID NAT/G INDUS LEGIT

S59
PLAZA G.,"FOR A REGIONAL MARKET IN LATIN AMERICA." FUT L/A+17C CULTURE INDUS NAT/G ECO/TAC INT/TRADE ATTIT WEALTH...NEW/IDEA TREND OAS 20. PAGE 106 F2092 — MARKET INT/ORG REGION

S60
"THE EMERGING COMMON MARKETS IN LATIN AMERICA." FUT L/A+17C STRATA DIST/IND INDUS LABOR NAT/G LEGIS ECO/TAC ADMIN RIGID/FLEX HEALTH...NEW/IDEA TIME/SEQ OAS 20. PAGE 1 F0013 — FINAN ECO/UNDEV INT/TRADE

B62
ALEXANDROWICZ C.H.,WORLD ECONOMIC AGENCIES: LAW AND PRACTICE. WOR+45 DIST/IND FINAN LABOR CONSULT INT/TRADE TARIFFS REPRESENT HEALTH...JURID 20 UN GATT EEC OAS ECSC. PAGE 4 F0064 — INT/LAW INT/ORG DIPLOM ADJUD

B62
DREIER J.C.,THE ALLIANCE FOR PROGRESS. L/A+17C USA+45 CULTURE ECO/DEV ECO/UNDEV NAT/G PLAN DIPLOM PWR 20 OAS ALL/PROG. PAGE 34 F0661 — FOR/AID INT/ORG ECO/TAC POLICY

B62
URQUIDI C.W.,A STATEMENT OF THE LAWS OF BOLIVIA IN MATTERS AFFECTING BUSINESS (3RD ED. REV., ENLARGED). L/A+17C LAW FINAN FAM WORKER ACT/RES DIPLOM ADJUD ADMIN GP/REL 20 BOLIV OAS. PAGE 133 F2626 — JURID INDUS NAT/G LEGIT

B63
MANGER W.,THE ALLIANCE FOR PROGRESS: A CRITICAL APPRAISAL. FUT L/A+17C USA+45 CULTURE ECO/UNDEV ACADEM NAT/G SCHOOL PLAN FOR/AID...POLICY OAS — DIPLOM INT/ORG ECO/TAC

ALL/PROG. PAGE 84 F1651 — REGION

B64
ORGANIZATION AMERICAN STATES,ECONOMIC SURVEY OF LATIN AMERICA, 1962. L/A+17C AGRI DIST/IND INDUS MARKET PROC/MFG R+D PLAN TEC/DEV ECO/TAC REGION BAL/PAY ALL/VALS...CON/ANAL ORG/CHARTS GEN/METH OAS ALL/PROG 20 ALL/PROG. PAGE 102 F1998 — ECO/UNDEV CHARTS

B65
SABLE M.H.,PERIODICALS FOR LATIN AMERICAN ECONOMIC DEVELOPMENT, TRADE, AND FINANCE: AN ANNOTATED BIBLIOGRAPHY (A PAMPHLET). ECO/TAC PRODUC PROFIT ...STAT NAT/COMP 20 OAS. PAGE 115 F2266 — BIBLIOG/A L/A+17C ECO/UNDEV INT/TRADE

S66
JAVITS J.K.,"POLITICAL ACTION VITAL FOR LATIN AMERICAN INTEGRATION." ECO/UNDEV INT/ORG POL/PAR VOL/ASSN PLAN PROB/SOLV INT/TRADE EFFICIENCY 20 OAS LAFTA ALL/PROG. PAGE 66 F1308 — L/A+17C ECO/TAC REGION

B67
MACCLOSKEY M.,PACTS FOR PEACE: UN, NATO, SEATO, CENTO, OAS. WOR+45 PLAN DIPLOM CONTROL PEACE ORD/FREE...ORG/CHARTS UN NATO SEATO OAS CENTO. PAGE 83 F1623 — FORCES INT/ORG LEAD POLICY

L67
MACDONALD R.S.J.,"THE RESORT TO ECONOMIC COERCION BY INTERNATIONAL POLITICAL ORGANIZATIONS." CUBA ETHIOPIA RHODESIA SOUTH/AFR NAT/G FOR/AID INT/TRADE DOMIN CONTROL SANCTION...DECISION LEAGUE/NAT UN OAS 20. PAGE 83 F1625 — INT/ORG COERCE ECO/TAC DIPLOM

S67
AGUILAR M.A.,"?UNA OEA MAS FUERTE O UNA AMERICA LATINA MAS DEBIL?" L/A+17C USA+45 USA-45 ECO/UNDEV INDUS CHIEF DELIB/GP FORCES CONTROL PWR 20 OAS KENNEDY/JF JOHNSON/LB. PAGE 3 F0050 — INT/ORG DIPLOM POLICY COLONIAL

S67
FRIEDENBERG D.M.,"THE US IN LATIN AMERICA; A RECKONING OF SHAME." L/A+17C USA+45 USA-45 INT/ORG CAP/ISM FOR/AID 17/20 OAS. PAGE 44 F0857 — DIPLOM POLICY DOMIN COLONIAL

N67
US HOUSE COMM FOREIGN AFFAIRS,COMMUNIST ACTIVITIES IN LATIN AMERICA 1967 (PAMPHLET). CUBA USA+45 DIPLOM INT/TRADE EDU/PROP COERCE GUERRILLA HOUSE/REP OAS. PAGE 137 F2696 — L/A+17C MARXISM ORD/FREE ECO/TAC

OAU....ORGANIZATION FOR AFRICAN UNITY

OBAID A.H. F1669

OBERER W.E. F1960

OBERLIN....OBERLIN, OHIO

OBESITY....SEE HEALTH, EATING

OBJECTIVE....OBJECTIVE, OBJECTIVITY

B56
WEBER M.,WIRTSCHAFT UND GESELLSCHAFT (2ND VOL.). STRUCT NAT/G POL/PAR LEAD PWR OBJECTIVE IDEA/COMP. PAGE 144 F2841 — LEGIT JURID SOC

S57
ANSHEN M.,"BUSINESS, LAWYERS, AND ECONOMISTS." PROB/SOLV ECO/TAC CONFER PROFIT RIGID/FLEX OBJECTIVE...MGT GP/COMP. PAGE 6 F0106 — INDUS CONSULT ROUTINE EFFICIENCY

S58
SCHULZE R.O.,"THE ROLE OF ECONOMIC DOMINANTS IN COMMUNITY POWER STRUCTURE." ECO/TAC ROUTINE ATTIT OBJECTIVE...SOC RECORD CENSUS. PAGE 118 F2319 — SOCIETY STRUCT PROB/SOLV

S59
WALLACE R.A.,"CONGRESSIONAL CONTROL OF THE BUDGET." USA+45 NAT/G CHIEF GP/REL FEDERAL OBJECTIVE...MGT CONGRESS. PAGE 143 F2807 — LEGIS EX/STRUC BUDGET CONSTN

B60
WALLACE R.A.,CONGRESSIONAL CONTROL OF FEDERAL SPENDING. USA+45 CONSTN NAT/G OP/RES CONFER DEBATE PERS/REL UTIL RIGID/FLEX PWR OBJECTIVE...OBS CHARTS. PAGE 143 F2808 — LEGIS DELIB/GP BUDGET

B64
VON DER MEHDEN F.R.,POLITICS OF THE DEVELOPING NATIONS. WOR+45 CONSTN PROB/SOLV ORD/FREE WEALTH OBJECTIVE. PAGE 142 F2790 — ECO/UNDEV SOCIETY STRUCT

S67
SCHNEIDER E.,"DIE ENTPOLITISIERUNG DES DEUTSCHEN OSTHANDELS." AFR MARKET TEC/DEV OBJECTIVE 20. PAGE 117 F2307 — ATTIT INT/TRADE ECO/TAC DIPLOM

OBLIGATION....SEE SUPEGO

OBS....OBSERVATION; SEE ALSO DIRECT OBSERVATION METHOD INDEX, P. XIV

B02
WEBB S.,THE HISTORY OF TRADE UNIONISM. UK PARTIC ...OBS CHARTS BIBLIOG/A 15/19 CASEBOOK. PAGE 144 F2837 — LABOR VOL/ASSN GP/REL

B20
WEBB S.,INDUSTRIAL DEMOCRACY. UK PARTIC GP/REL ...SOC OBS RECORD CHARTS 18/20. PAGE 144 F2838 — LABOR NAT/G VOL/ASSN MAJORIT

B30
THOMPSON W.R.,POPULATION PROBLEMS. FUT UNIV WOR-45 STRUCT DIST/IND ACT/RES ECO/TAC BIO/SOC...CONCPT OBS TIME/SEQ TOT/POP 20. PAGE 130 F2567 — ECO/UNDEV GEOG

B34
GRAHAM F.D.,PROTECTIVE TARIFFS. FUT USA+45 WOR-45 INDUS MARKET VOL/ASSN PLAN CAP/ISM ECO/TAC PEACE ATTIT DRIVE HEALTH ORD/FREE...OBS TREND GEN/LAWS FOR/TRADE 20. PAGE 50 F0970 — INT/ORG TARIFFS

B35
O'CONNOR H.,REVOLUTION IN SEATTLE. USA-45 STRATA WORKER GP/REL ATTIT SOCISM...OBS BIBLIOG/A 20 SEATTLE STRIKE COM/PARTY. PAGE 99 F1954 — REV EDU/PROP LABOR MARXISM

B39
FIRTH R.,PRIMITIVE POLYNESIAN ECONOMY. SOCIETY DIST/IND SECT CHIEF CAP/ISM PRODUC WEALTH...SOC OBS METH WORSHIP 20 POLYNESIA. PAGE 41 F0802 — ECO/UNDEV CULTURE AGRI ECO/TAC

B39
ROBBINS L.,ECONOMIC CAUSES OF WAR. WOR-45 ECO/DEV ECO/UNDEV INT/ORG NAT/G TEC/DEV DIPLOM DOMIN COLONIAL ATTIT DRIVE PWR WEALTH...POLICY CONCPT OBS SAMP TREND CON/ANAL GEN/LAWS MARX/KARL 20. PAGE 112 F2203 — COERCE ECO/TAC WAR

B41
YOUNG G.,FEDERALISM AND FREEDOM. EUR+WWI MOD/EUR RUSSIA USA-45 WOR-45 SOCIETY STRUCT ECO/DEV INT/ORG EXEC FEDERAL ATTIT PERSON ALL/VALS...OLD/LIB CONCPT OBS TREND LEAGUE/NAT TOT/POP. PAGE 150 F2950 — NAT/G WAR

S43
GOLDEN C.S.,"NEW PATTERNS OF DEMOCRACY." NEIGH DELIB/GP EDU/PROP EXEC PARTIC...MGT METH/CNCPT OBS TREND. PAGE 48 F0935 — LABOR REPRESENT LG/CO GP/REL

B47
GORDON D.L.,THE HIDDEN WEAPON: THE STORY OF ECONOMIC WARFARE. EUR+WWI USA-45 LAW FINAN INDUS NAT/G CONSULT FORCES PLAN DOMIN PWR WEALTH ...INT/LAW CONCPT OBS TOT/POP NAZI 20. PAGE 49 F0955 — INT/ORG ECO/TAC INT/TRADE WAR

B48
WHYTE W.F.,HUMAN RELATIONS IN THE RESTAURANT INDUSTRY (1ST ED). CLIENT WORKER WAR ATTIT...MGT OBS INT. PAGE 146 F2874 — INGP/REL GP/REL SERV/IND LABOR

S50
EBY K.,"RESEARCH IN LABOR UNIONS." EDU/PROP INGP/REL PWR...METH/CNCPT OBS. PAGE 36 F0693 — RECORD QU LABOR PARTIC

C51
HOMANS G.C.,"THE WESTERN ELECTRIC RESEARCHES" IN S. HOSLETT, ED., HUMAN FACTORS IN MANAGEMENT (BMR)" ACT/RES GP/REL HAPPINESS PRODUC DRIVE...MGT OBS 20. PAGE 61 F1202 — OP/RES EFFICIENCY SOC/EXP WORKER

B52
ALEXANDROWICZ C.H.,INTERNATIONAL ECONOMIC ORGANIZATION. WOR+45 ECO/DEV ECO/UNDEV DIST/IND FINAN MARKET PLAN ECO/TAC LEGIT DRIVE WEALTH ...POLICY CONCPT QUANT OBS TIME/SEQ GEN/LAWS WORK METH/GP EEC ILO OEEC UNESCO 20. PAGE 4 F0063 — INT/ORG INT/TRADE

S52
KLUMB S.,"EMPLOYEE DETERMINATION OF MANAGERIAL FUNCTIONS AND CHARACTERISTICS." DELIB/GP WORKER PARTIC ROUTINE INGP/REL...CLASSIF OBS QU. PAGE 72 F1410 — MGT INDUS EX/STRUC CHOOSE

S52
KORNHAUSER W.,"THE NEGRO UNION OFFICIAL: A STUDY OF SPONSORSHIP AND CONTROL" (BMR)" USA+45 CONTROL DISCRIM ROLE SUPEGO...OBS 20 NEGRO. PAGE 73 F1428 — LABOR LEAD RACE/REL CHOOSE

B53
FRANKEL S.H.,THE ECONOMIC IMPACT ON UNDERDEVELOPED SOCIETIES: ESSAYS ON INTERNATIONAL INVESTMENT AND SOCIAL CHANGE. AFR WOR+45 ECO/DEV FINAN INDUS NAT/G ACT/RES TEC/DEV COLONIAL ATTIT...CONCPT OBS TREND 20. PAGE 43 F0845 — ECO/UNDEV FOR/AID INT/TRADE

B53
PURCELL T.V.,THE WORKER SPEAKS HIS MIND ON COMPANY AND UNION. WORKER ADJUD LEAD RACE/REL ATTIT DRIVE MARXISM...MGT CLASSIF STAT OBS INT SAMP BIBLIOG. PAGE 108 F2131 — LABOR PARTIC INGP/REL HAPPINESS

L54
OPLER M.E.,"SOCIAL ASPECTS OF TECHNICAL ASSISTANCE IN OPERATION." WOR+45 VOL/ASSN CREATE PLAN TEC/DEV EDU/PROP ALL/VALS...METH/CNCPT OBS RECORD TREND UN 20. PAGE 101 F1993 — INT/ORG CONSULT FOR/AID

B57
ARON R.,L'UNIFICATION ECONOMIQUE DE L'EUROPE. EUR+WWI SWITZERLND UK INT/ORG NAT/G REGION NAT/LISM ORD/FREE PWR...CONCPT METH/CNCPT OBS TREND STERTYP GEN/LAWS EEC FOR/TRADE 20. PAGE 6 F0118 VOL/ASSN ECO/TAC

B57
TRIFFIN R.,EUROPE AND THE MONEY MUDDLE. USA+45 INT/ORG NAT/G CONSULT PLAN ECO/TAC EXEC ROUTINE BAL/PAY WEALTH...METH/CNCPT OBS TREND CHARTS STERTYP GEN/METH EEC TERR/GP VAL/FREE ECSC. PAGE 131 F2587 EUR+WWI ECO/DEV REGION

B57
WARRINER D.,LAND REFORM AND DEVELOPMENT IN THE MIDDLE EAST: A STUDY OF EGYPT, SYRIA AND IRAQ. IRAQ ISLAM SYRIA UAR AGRI DIST/IND PLAN TEC/DEV DOMIN REV ATTIT WEALTH...SOC METH/CNCPT STAT OBS RECORD HIST/WRIT TREND GEN/LAWS FAO 20. PAGE 143 F2825 ECO/UNDEV CONCPT

B58
HIRSCHMAN A.O.,STRATEGY OF ECONOMIC DEVELOPMENT. WOR+45 WOR-45 CULTURE ECO/DEV NAT/G PLAN TEC/DEV INT/TRADE BAL/PAY ATTIT DRIVE RIGID/FLEX WEALTH ...CONCPT METH/CNCPT OBS CHARTS SIMUL GEN/LAWS TOT/POP VAL/FREE. PAGE 60 F1176 ECO/UNDEV ECO/TAC CAP/ISM

B59
HOOVER C.B.,THE ECONOMY, LIBERTY AND THE STATE. COM EUR+WWI USA+45 USA-45 USSR CAP/ISM EDU/PROP COERCE TOTALISM ORD/FREE...POLICY OBS INT TREND NAZI 20. PAGE 61 F1206 ECO/DEV ECO/TAC

B59
MEYER A.J.,MIDDLE EASTERN CAPITALISM: NINE ESSAYS. ISLAM CULTURE ECO/UNDEV INDUS MARKET NAT/G PLAN ATTIT RIGID/FLEX...STAT OBS TREND GEN/LAWS. PAGE 90 F1767 TEC/DEV ECO/TAC ANTHOL

S59
ALKHIMOV V.S.,"SOVIET FOREIGN TRADE CHANNELS." COM FUT USA+45 USSR ECO/DEV MARKET CONSULT PLAN WEALTH ...MARXIST OBS CON/ANAL FOR/TRADE 20. PAGE 4 F0068 FINAN ECO/TAC DIPLOM

S59
KINDLEBERGER C.P.,"UNITED STATES ECONOMIC FOREIGN POLICY: RESEARCH REQUIREMENTS FOR 1965." FUT USA+45 WOR+45 DIST/IND MARKET INT/ORG ECO/TAC INT/TRADE WEALTH...OBS TREND CON/ANAL GEN/LAWS FOR/TRADE VAL/FREE 20. PAGE 71 F1392 FINAN ECO/DEV FOR/AID

S59
SOLDATI A.,"EOCNOMIC DISINTEGRATION IN EUROPE." EUR+WWI FUT WOR+45 INDUS INT/ORG NAT/G CAP/ISM WEALTH...NEW/IDEA OBS TREND CHARTS EEC 20. PAGE 124 F2438 FINAN ECO/TAC

B60
FRANCK P.G.,AFGHANISTAN: BETWEEN EAST AND WEST. AFGHANISTN AFR USA+45 USSR ECO/UNDEV PLAN ADMIN ROUTINE ATTIT PWR...STAT OBS CHARTS TOT/POP FOR/TRADE 20. PAGE 43 F0843 ECO/TAC TREND FOR/AID

B60
WALLACE R.A.,CONGRESSIONAL CONTROL OF FEDERAL SPENDING. USA+45 CONSTN NAT/G OP/RES CONFER DEBATE PERS/REL UTIL RIGID/FLEX PWR OBJECTIVE...OBS CHARTS. PAGE 143 F2808 LEGIS DELIB/GP BUDGET

S60
ENKE S.,"THE ECONOMIES OF GOVERNMENT PAYMENTS TO LIMIT POPULATION." FUT INDIA WOR+45 CULTURE FINAN NAT/G CONSULT PLAN LEGIT CONTROL COST ATTIT RIGID/FLEX HEALTH WEALTH...STAT OBS CHARTS TOT/POP VAL/FREE 20. PAGE 38 F0736 FAM ACT/RES

S60
JAFFEE A.J.,"POPULATION TRENDS AND CONTROLS IN UNDERDEVELOPED COUNTRIES." AFR FUT ISLAM L/A+17C S/ASIA CULTURE R+D FAM ACT/RES PLAN EDU/PROP BIO/SOC RIGID/FLEX HEALTH...SOC STAT OBS CHARTS 20. PAGE 66 F1303 ECO/UNDEV GEOG

S60
MILLER A.S.,"SOME OBSERVATIONS ON THE POLITICAL ECONOMY OF POPULATION GROWTH." FUT USA+45 ECO/DEV R+D CONSULT PLAN TEC/DEV ECO/TAC ROUTINE BIO/SOC WEALTH...POLICY OBS. PAGE 91 F1790 SOCIETY GEOG

B61
EINZIG P.,A DYNAMIC THEORY OF FORWARD EXCHANGE. FUT WOR+45 WOR-45 INT/TRADE BAL/PAY WEALTH...OLD/LIB NEW/IDEA OBS TREND FOR/TRADE 20. PAGE 37 F0713 FINAN ECO/TAC

B61
FRIEDMANN G.,THE ANATOMY OF WORK. USA+45 SOCIETY CONTROL ROUTINE DRIVE SKILL...PSY SOC STAT OBS METH/COMP PERS/COMP 20. PAGE 44 F0862 AUTOMAT WORKER INDUS PERSON

B61
KOVNER M.,THE CHALLENGE OF COEXISTENCE: A STUDY OF SOVIET ECONOMIC DIPLOMACY. COM FUT ECO/DEV ECO/UNDEV PLAN EDU/PROP DETER SKILL...OBS VAL/FREE 20. PAGE 73 F1430 PWR DIPLOM USSR AFR

S61
DEUTSCH K.W.,"NATIONAL INDUSTRIALIZATION AND THE DECLINING SHARE OF THE INTERNATIONAL ECONOMIC SECTOR." EUR+WWI FUT WOR+45 WOR-45 MARKET PLAN EDU/PROP WEALTH...WELF/ST OBS TESTS 20. PAGE 32 F0624 DIST/IND ECO/DEV INT/TRADE

S62
IOVTCHOUK M.T.,"ON SOME THEORETICAL PRINCIPLES AND METHODS OF SOCIOLOGICAL INVESTIGATIONS (IN RUSSIAN)." FUT USA+45 STRATA R+D NAT/G POL/PAR TOP/EX ACT/RES PLAN ECO/TAC EDU/PROP ROUTINE ATTIT RIGID/FLEX MARXISM SOCISM...MARXIST METH/CNCPT OBS TREND NAT/COMP GEN/LAWS 20. PAGE 65 F1288 COM ECO/DEV CAP/ISM USSR

B63
BAUER R.A.,AMERICAN BUSINESS AND PUBLIC POLICY: THE POLITICS OF FOREIGN TRADE. USA+45 COM/IND LG/CO NAT/G PROF/ORG SML/CO VOL/ASSN LEGIS TOP/EX ECO/TAC EDU/PROP CHOOSE HEALTH PWR WEALTH...CONCPT METH/CNCPT OBS INT QU SAMP FOR/TRADE TRUE/GP VAL/FREE HI. PAGE 11 F0217 ECO/DEV ATTIT

B63
DEUTSCH K.W.,THE POLITICAL ROLE OF LABOR IN DEVELOPING COUNTRIES. AFR ASIA S/ASIA USA+45 WOR+45 ECO/UNDEV POL/PAR ECO/TAC EDU/PROP LEGIT COERCE ORD/FREE PWR WEALTH...OBS INT TREND VAL/FREE 20. PAGE 32 F0625 LABOR NAT/LISM

B63
GEERTZ C.,PEDDLERS AND PRINCES: SOCIAL DEVELOPMENT AND ECONOMIC CHANGE IN TWO INDONESIAN TOWNS. S/ASIA CULTURE SOCIETY STRATA FACE/GP CREATE TEC/DEV ECO/TAC ORD/FREE WEALTH...OBS INT CENSUS CHARTS WORK TOT/POP METH/GP TERR/GP VAL/FREE 20 MUNICH. PAGE 47 F0913 ECO/UNDEV SOC ELITES INDONESIA

B63
WIGHTMAN D.,TOWARD ECONOMIC CO-OPERATION IN ASIA. ASIA S/ASIA VOL/ASSN ACT/RES PLAN TEC/DEV ECO/TAC EDU/PROP RIGID/FLEX SKILL...POLICY METH/CNCPT OBS INT GEN/LAWS UN 20 ECAFE. PAGE 146 F2877 ECO/UNDEV CREATE

S63
AYAL E.B.,"VALUE SYSTEM AND ECONOMIC DEVELOPMENT IN JAPAN AND THAILAND." ASIA S/ASIA THAILAND CULTURE ECO/DEV CAP/ISM DOMIN NAT/LISM DRIVE RIGID/FLEX SOCISM...WELF/ST OBS TREND CON/ANAL GEN/LAWS TERR/GP 20 CHINJAP. PAGE 8 F0145 ECO/UNDEV ALL/VALS

S63
DELWERT J.,"L'ECONOMIE CAMBODGIENNE ET SON EVOLUTION ACTUELLE." FUT S/ASIA ECO/UNDEV ACT/RES PLAN WEALTH...CONCPT OBS TIME/SEQ TREND 20. PAGE 32 F0617 FINAN ATTIT CAMBODIA

S63
DUCROS B.,"MOBILISATION DES RESSOURCES PRODUCTIVES ET DEVELOPPEMENT." FUT INTELL SOCIETY COM/IND DIST/IND EXTR/IND FINAN INDUS ROUTINE WEALTH ...METH/CNCPT OBS 20. PAGE 34 F0670 ECO/UNDEV TEC/DEV

S63
FOURASTIE J.,"LES SCIENCES ECONOMIQUES ET SOCIALES EN EUROPE." EUR+WWI FUT MOD/EUR WOR+45 WOR-45 INTELL SOCIETY R+D PLAN ROUTINE ATTIT RIGID/FLEX KNOWL...OBS TREND. PAGE 43 F0833 ACT/RES CULTURE

S63
GERHARD H.,"COMMODITY TRADE STABILIZATION THROUGH INTERNATIONAL AGREEMENTS." WOR+45 ECO/DEV ECO/UNDEV NAT/G ROUTINE ORD/FREE...INT/LAW OBS TREND GEN/METH TOT/POP 20. PAGE 47 F0918 PLAN ECO/TAC INT/TRADE

S63
MARTHELOT P.,"PROGRES DE LA REFORME AGRAIRE." INTELL ECO/DEV R+D FOR/AID ADMIN KNOWL...OBS VAL/FREE UN 20. PAGE 86 F1680 AGRI INT/ORG

B64
SEERS D.,CUBA: THE ECONOMIC AND SOCIAL REVOLUTION. L/A+17C USSR YUGOSLAVIA STRATA AGRI INDUS SCHOOL DELIB/GP PLAN ECO/TAC DOMIN EDU/PROP ATTIT RIGID/FLEX ALL/VALS...STAT OBS TIME/SEQ WORK VAL/FREE 20. PAGE 119 F2341 ACT/RES COERCE CUBA REV

S64
GERBET P.,"LA MISE EN OEUVRE DU MARCHE COMMUN AGRICOLE." ECO/DEV MARKET INT/ORG NAT/G PLAN EDU/PROP NAT/LISM WEALTH...OBS EEC VAL/FREE 20. PAGE 47 F0917 EUR+WWI AGRI REGION

S64
HERMAN L.M.,"THE ECONOMIC CONTENT OF SOVIET TRADE WITH THE WEST." WOR+45 ECO/DEV ECO/UNDEV AGRI COM/IND INDUS CAP/ISM ECO/TAC ATTIT RIGID/FLEX WEALTH...OBS TREND VAL/FREE MARX/KARL 20. PAGE 59 F1152 COM MARKET INT/TRADE USSR

S64
MC WILLIAM M.,"THE WORLD BANK AND THE TRANSFER OF POWER IN KENYA." AFR ECO/UNDEV CONSULT ACT/RES TEC/DEV PERCEPT PWR SKILL WEALTH...CONCPT OBS TREND 20. PAGE 88 F1715 NAT/G ECO/TAC

S64
SCHMITT H.D.,"POLITICAL CONDITIONS FOR INTERNATIONAL CURRENCY REFORM." WOR+45 SOCIETY ECO/DEV PLAN ECO/TAC BAL/PAY ATTIT ORD/FREE WEALTH ...SOC CONCPT OBS TREND EEC VAL/FREE ECSC 20. PAGE 117 F2301 FINAN VOL/ASSN REGION

B65
DERBER M.,PLANT UNION-MANAGEMENT RELATIONS: FROM PRACTICE TO THEORY. PROC/MFG NEIGH PROB/SOLV ORD/FREE...DECISION MGT OBS QU SAMP. PAGE 32 F0621 LG/CO LABOR GP/REL ATTIT

B65
INT. BANK RECONSTR. DEVELOP.,ECONOMIC DEVELOPMENT OF KUWAIT. ISLAM KUWAIT AGRI FINAN MARKET EX/STRUC TEC/DEV ECO/TAC ADMIN WEALTH...OBS CON/ANAL CHARTS 20. PAGE 64 F1266
INDUS NAT/G

B65
SIMMS R.P.,URBANIZATION IN WEST AFRICA; A REVIEW OF CURRENT LITERATURE. AFR PLAN TEC/DEV...SOC OBS NAT/COMP MUNICH 20. PAGE 122 F2405
BIBLIOG/A ECO/DEV ECO/UNDEV

S65
BERREBY J.J.,"IMPERATIFS STRATEGIQUES DU PETROLE." ECO/UNDEV VOL/ASSN ECO/TAC COLONIAL NUC/PWR WAR. PAGE 14 F0270
ISLAM EXTR/IND STAT OBS

S65
DUMONT R.,"SURPEUPLEMENT CHINOIS ET SES CONSEQUENCES." AFR ECO/UNDEV AGRI PLAN PROB/SOLV ECO/TAC FOR/AID NUC/PWR...OBS INT PREDICT. PAGE 35 F0675
GEOG ASIA STAT

S65
SPAAK P.H.,"THE SEARCH FOR CONSENSUS: A NEW EFFORT TO BUILD EUROPE." FRANCE GERMANY ECO/DEV NAT/G CONSULT FORCES PLAN EDU/PROP REGION CONSEN ATTIT ...SOC METH/CNCPT OBS TREND EEC NATO WORK TERR/GP METH/GP 20. PAGE 124 F2447
EUR+WWI INT/ORG

B66
NEVITT A.A.,THE ECONOMIC PROBLEMS OF HOUSING. WOR+45 ECO/DEV ECO/UNDEV ACT/RES PROB/SOLV ECO/TAC RENT...OBS CHARTS 20. PAGE 98 F1917
HABITAT PROC/MFG DELIB/GP NAT/COMP

B66
RAO Y.V.L.,COMMUNICATION AND DEVELOPMENT. INDIA S/ASIA SOCIETY ACT/RES EDU/PROP PARTIC ATTIT...SOC GP/COMP BIBLIOG MUNICH MUNICH 20. PAGE 109 F2149
COM/IND ECO/UNDEV OBS

B66
RUBIN S.J.,THE CONSCIENCE OF THE RICH NATIONS: THE DEVELOPMENT ASSISTANCE COMMITTEE AND THE COMMON AID EFFORT. EUR+WWI USA+45 ECO/UNDEV INT/ORG NAT/G VOL/ASSN ECO/TAC INT/TRADE...OBS UN AID DEV/ASSIST IBRD OECD. PAGE 114 F2256
FOR/AID ECO/DEV CONFER CENTRAL

S66
FELD W.,"EXTERNAL RELATIONS OF THE COMMON MARKET AND GROUP LEADERSHIP ATTITUDES IN THE MEMBER STATES." COM USA+45 ELITES AGRI NAT/G ATTIT...OBS EEC GATT. PAGE 40 F0776
DIPLOM CENTRAL TARIFFS INT/TRADE

B67
BIBBY J.,ON CAPITOL HILL. POL/PAR LOBBY PARL/PROC GOV/REL PERS/REL...JURID PHIL/SCI OBS INT BIBLIOG 20 CONGRESS PRESIDENT. PAGE 15 F0278
CONFER LEGIS CREATE LEAD

B67
CASTILLO C.M.,GROWTH AND INTEGRATION IN CENTRAL AMERICA. L/A+17C CREATE PROB/SOLV ECO/TAC REGION PRODUC...OBS BIBLIOG 20. PAGE 22 F0429
ECO/UNDEV INT/TRADE NAT/COMP

B67
JACOBY N.H.,US AID TO TAIWAN. CAP/ISM DIPLOM FEEDBACK COST PRODUC...OBS INT CHARTS 20. PAGE 66 F1301
FOR/AID OP/RES ECO/TAC ECO/UNDEV

B67
PETRO S.,THE KINGSPORT STRIKE. USA+45 PROC/MFG NAT/G JUDGE PRESS PARTIC PERS/REL...OLD/LIB OBS INT 20 NLRB. PAGE 105 F2074
LABOR COERCE SANCTION ALL/VALS

B67
RIDKER R.G.,ECONOMIC COSTS OF AIR POLLUTION* STUDIES IN MEASUREMENT. R+D GP/REL KNOWL...OBS MUNICH 20. PAGE 111 F2190
OP/RES HABITAT PHIL/SCI

B67
SMITH T.L.,THE PROCESS OF RURAL DEVELOPMENT IN LATIN AMERICA (A MONOGRAPH). L/A+17C STRATA INDUS PLAN GP/REL PERS/REL RIGID/FLEX WEALTH...OBS CHARTS ORG/CHARTS ANTHOL 20 COLOMB. PAGE 123 F2434
IDEA/COMP SOC AGRI ECO/UNDEV

B67
SYMONS L.,AGRICULTURAL GEOGRAPHY. OP/RES SKILL ...CONCPT CHARTS BIBLIOG T 20. PAGE 128 F2520
AGRI GEOG METH/COMP OBS

B67
US SENATE COMM ON FOREIGN REL,HARRISON E. SALISBURY'S TRIP TO NORTH VIETNAM. CHINA/COM USA+45 VIETNAM/N PRESS TASK GUERRILLA CONSEN EFFICIENCY PEACE DRIVE...OBS SENATE. PAGE 139 F2743
DIPLOM WAR FORCES ATTIT

B67
WILLIAMS M.,THE EAST IS RED: THE VIEW INSIDE CHINA. CHINA/COM CONSTN COERCE AGE/Y ATTIT PERSON...OBS 20 MAO. PAGE 147 F2893
REV MARXIST GP/REL DIPLOM

B67
ZONDAG C.H.,THE BOLIVIAN ECONOMY 1952-65. L/A+17C TEC/DEV FOR/AID ADMIN...OBS TREND CHARTS BIBLIOG 20 BOLIV. PAGE 151 F2969
ECO/UNDEV INDUS PRODUC

OBS/ENVIR....SOCIAL MILIEU OF AND RESISTANCES TO OBSERVATIONS

S61
ANDREWS R.B.,"URBAN ECONOMICS: AN APPRAISAL OF PROGRESS." LOC/G PROB/SOLV TEC/DEV...CONCPT OBS/ENVIR METH/COMP HYPO/EXP SOC/EXP SIMUL GEN/METH METH MUNICH 20. PAGE 5 F0102
PHIL/SCI ECOMETRIC

OBSCENITY....OBSCENITY

OBSERVATION....SEE DIRECT-OBSERVATION METHOD INDEX, P. XIV

OBSOLESCENCE, PLANNED....SEE OBSOLESCNC

OBSOLESCNC....OBSOLESCENCE, PLANNED

OCCUPATION....SEE WORKER

OCEANIA....OCEANIA: AUSTRALIA, NEW ZEALAND, MALAYSIA, MELANESIA, MICRONESIA, AND POLYNESIA

OCHENG D. F1961

ODEGARD P.H. F1962

ODEGARD/P....PETER ODEGARD

ODEH H.S. F1963

ODINGA/O....OGINGA ODINGA

OECD F1964,F1965,F1966,F1967,F1968,F1969,F1970,F1971,F1972 , F1973,F1974,F1975

OECD....ORGANIZATION FOR ECONOMIC COOPERATION AND DEVELOPMENT

B61
OECD,STATISTICS OF BALANCE OF PAYMENTS 1950-61. WOR+45 FINAN ECO/TAC INT/TRADE DEMAND WEALTH...STAT NAT/COMP 20 OEEC OECD. PAGE 100 F1965
BAL/PAY ECO/DEV INT/ORG CHARTS

B64
OECD,DEVELOPMENT ASSISTANCE EFFORTS - POLICIES OF THE MEMBERS. AGRI INDUS BUDGET...GEOG NAT/COMP 20 OECD. PAGE 100 F1967
INT/ORG FOR/AID ECO/UNDEV TEC/DEV

B65
OECD,MEDITERRANEAN REGIONAL PROJECT: TURKEY; EDUCATION AND DEVELOPMENT. FUT TURKEY SOCIETY STRATA FINAN NAT/G PROF/ORG PLAN PROB/SOLV ADMIN COST...STAT CHARTS 20 OECD. PAGE 100 F1969
EDU/PROP ACADEM SCHOOL ECO/UNDEV

B65
OECD,THE MEDITERRANEAN REGIONAL PROJECT: PORTUGAL; EDUCATION AND DEVELOPMENT. PORTUGAL SOCIETY STRATA FINAN PROF/ORG WORKER PLAN PROB/SOLV ADMIN...POLICY STAT CHARTS METH 20 OECD. PAGE 100 F1970
EDU/PROP SCHOOL ACADEM ECO/UNDEV

B65
OECD,THE MEDITERRANEAN REGIONAL PROJECT: ITALY; EDUCATION AND DEVELOPMENT. ITALY SOCIETY STRATA FINAN NAT/G PROF/ORG WORKER PLAN PROB/SOLV ADMIN ...STAT CHARTS METH 20 OECD. PAGE 100 F1971
SCHOOL EDU/PROP ECO/UNDEV ACADEM

B65
OECD,THE MEDITERRANEAN REGIONAL PROJECT: GREECE; EDUCATION AND DEVELOPMENT. FUT GREECE SOCIETY AGRI FINAN NAT/G PROF/ORG WORKER PLAN PROB/SOLV ADMIN DEMAND ATTIT 20 OECD. PAGE 100 F1972
EDU/PROP SCHOOL ACADEM ECO/UNDEV

B65
OECD,THE MEDITERRANEAN REGIONAL PROJECT: SPAIN; EDUCATION AND DEVELOPMENT. FUT SPAIN STRATA FINAN NAT/G WORKER PLAN PROB/SOLV ADMIN COST...POLICY STAT CHARTS 20 OECD. PAGE 100 F1973
ECO/UNDEV EDU/PROP ACADEM SCHOOL

B65
ORG FOR ECO COOP AND DEVEL,THE MEDITERRANEAN REGIONAL PROJECT: AN EXPERIMENT IN PLANNING BY SIX COUNTRIES. FUT GREECE SPAIN TURKEY YUGOSLAVIA SOCIETY FINAN NAT/G PROF/ORG EDU/PROP ADMIN REGION COST...POLICY STAT CHARTS 20 OECD. PAGE 102 F1995
PLAN ECO/UNDEV ACADEM SCHOOL

B65
ORG FOR ECO COOP AND DEVEL,THE MEDITERRANEAN REGIONAL PROJECT: YUGOSLAVIA; EDUCATION AND DEVELOPMENT. YUGOSLAVIA SOCIETY FINAN PROF/ORG PLAN ADMIN COST DEMAND MARXISM...STAT TREND CHARTS METH 20 OECD. PAGE 102 F1996
EDU/PROP ACADEM SCHOOL ECO/UNDEV

B66
ORG FOR ECO COOP AND DEVEL,GEOGRAPHICAL DISTRIBUTION OF FINANCIAL FLOWS TO LESS DEVELOPED COUNTRIES. WOR+45 DIPLOM INT/TRADE GIVE RECEIVE REPAR REGION WEALTH...GEOG STAT CHARTS 20 OECD. PAGE 102 F1997
FINAN ECO/UNDEV INT/ORG FOR/AID

B66
RUBIN S.J.,THE CONSCIENCE OF THE RICH NATIONS: THE DEVELOPMENT ASSISTANCE COMMITTEE AND THE COMMON AID EFFORT. EUR+WWI USA+45 ECO/UNDEV INT/ORG NAT/G VOL/ASSN ECO/TAC INT/TRADE...OBS UN AID DEV/ASSIST IBRD OECD. PAGE 114 F2256
FOR/AID ECO/DEV CONFER CENTRAL

S67
LEVI M.,"LES RELATIONS ECONOMIQUES ENTRE L'EST ET L'OUEST EN EUROPE" INDUS...STAT CHARTS 20 OECD COMECON. PAGE 79 F1540 — INT/TRADE INT/ORG FINAN PRODUC

OECD DEVELOPMENT CENTRE F1976

OEEC F1977,F1978

OEEC....ORGANIZATION FOR EUROPEAN ECONOMIC COOPERATION; SEE ALSO VOL/ASSN, INT/ORG

B52
ALEXANDROWICZ C.H.,INTERNATIONAL ECONOMIC ORGANIZATION. WOR+45 ECO/DEV ECO/UNDEV DIST/IND FINAN MARKET PLAN ECO/TAC LEGIT DRIVE WEALTH ...POLICY CONCPT QUANT OBS TIME/SEQ GEN/LAWS WORK METH/GP EEC ILO OEEC UNESCO 20. PAGE 4 F0063 — INT/ORG INT/TRADE

B54
TINBERGEN J.,INTERNATIONAL ECONOMIC INTEGRATION. WOR+45 WOR-45 ECO/UNDEV NAT/G ECO/TAC BAL/PAY ...METH/CNCPT STAT TIME/SEQ GEN/METH OEEC 20. PAGE 130 F2574 — INT/ORG ECO/DEV INT/TRADE

B55
FLORINSKY M.T.,INTEGRATED EUROPE. EUR+WWI FRANCE ITALY NETHERLAND UK ECO/DEV INT/ORG FORCES LEGIT FEDERAL ATTIT PWR WEALTH...POLICY GEOG CONCPT GEN/LAWS TOT/POP EEC OEEC 20. PAGE 42 F0816 — FUT ECO/TAC REGION

S55
HALLETT D.,"THE HISTORY AND STRUCTURE OF OEEC." EUR+WWI USA+45 CONSTN INDUS INT/ORG NAT/G DELIB/GP ACT/RES PLAN ORD/FREE WEALTH...CONCPT OEEC 20 CMN/WLTH. PAGE 54 F1051 — VOL/ASSN ECO/DEV

B56
MYRDAL G.,AN INTERNATIONAL ECONOMY. EUR+WWI USA+45 WOR+45 WOR-45 NAT/G DIPLOM ECO/TAC BAL/PAY...PSY CONCPT OEEC TOT/POP 20. PAGE 96 F1879 — VOL/ASSN AFR

S56
GORDON L.,"THE ORGANIZATION FOR EUROPEAN ECONOMIC COOPERATION." EUR+WWI INDUS INT/ORG NAT/G CONSULT DELIB/GP ACT/RES CREATE PLAN TEC/DEV EDU/PROP LEGIT WEALTH OEEC 20. PAGE 49 F0956 — VOL/ASSN ECO/DEV

B58
KINDLEBERGER C.P.,INTERNATIONAL ECONOMICS. WOR+45 WOR-45 ECO/DEV ECO/UNDEV FINAN VOL/ASSN ACT/RES DIPLOM ECO/TAC LEGIT REGION ATTIT DRIVE ORD/FREE WEALTH...POLICY STAT TREND GEN/LAWS EEC ECSC OEEC 20. PAGE 71 F1391 — INT/ORG BAL/PWR TARIFFS

B58
OEEC,THE INDUSTRIAL CHALLENGE OF NUCLEAR ENERGY. EUR+WWI ECO/DEV INDUS OP/RES CONFER RISK PWR ...AUD/VIS CHARTS ANTHOL 20 OEEC. PAGE 101 F1977 — NUC/PWR ACT/RES ECO/TAC INT/ORG

B58
SCITOUSKY T.,ECONOMIC THEORY AND WESTERN EUROPEAN INTEGRATION. EUR+WWI INT/ORG ACT/RES INT/TRADE REGION BAL/PAY WEALTH...METH/CNCPT STAT CHARTS GEN/METH ECSC TOT/POP EEC OEEC 20. PAGE 118 F2328 — ECO/TAC

S58
ELKIN A.B.,"OEEC-ITS STRUCTURE AND POWERS." EUR+WWI CONSTN INDUS INT/ORG NAT/G VOL/ASSN DELIB/GP ACT/RES PLAN ORD/FREE WEALTH...CHARTS ORG/CHARTS OEEC 20. PAGE 37 F0719 — ECO/DEV EX/STRUC

B59
SANNWALD R.E.,ECONOMIC INTEGRATION: THEORETICAL ASSUMPTIONS AND CONSEQUENCES OF EUROPEAN UNIFICATION. EUR+WWI FUT FINAN INDUS VOL/ASSN ACT/RES ECO/TAC...PLURIST EEC FOR/TRADE OEEC 20. PAGE 116 F2279 — INT/ORG ECO/DEV INT/TRADE

L59
MURPHY J.C.,"SOME IMPLICATIONS OF EUROPE'S COMMON MARKET. IN (COOK P, ECONOMIC DEVELOPMENT AND INTERNATIONAL TRADE.." EUR+WWI ECO/DEV DIST/IND INDUS NAT/G PLAN ECO/TAC INT/TRADE WEALTH...STAT TREND OEEC TOT/POP 20 EEC. PAGE 95 F1866 — MARKET INT/ORG REGION

B60
OEEC,STATISTICS OF SOURCES AND USES OF FINANCE. NAT/G CAP/ISM TAX PRICE COST 20 OEEC. PAGE 101 F1978 — FINAN PRODUC INCOME NAT/COMP

S60
KREININ M.E.,"THE 'OUTER-SEVEN' AND EUROPEAN INTEGRATION." EUR+WWI FRANCE GERMANY ITALY UK ECO/DEV DIST/IND INT/TRADE DRIVE WEALTH...MYTH CHARTS EEC OEEC 20. PAGE 73 F1436 — ECO/TAC GEN/LAWS

S60
NANES A.,"THE EUROPEAN COMMUNITY AND THE UNITED STATES: EVOLVING RELATIONS." EUR+WWI USA+45 WOR+45 ECO/UNDEV MARKET NAT/G DELIB/GP PLAN LEGIT ATTIT PWR WEALTH...CONCPT STAT TIME/SEQ CON/ANAL EEC METH/GP OEEC 20 EURATOM. PAGE 96 F1889 — INT/ORG REGION

N60
ERDMAN P.E.,COMMON MARKETS AND FREE TRADE AREAS (PAMPHLET). USA+45 MARKET INT/ORG TEC/DEV DIPLOM UTIL...CON/ANAL CHARTS BIBLIOG 20 EEC OEEC. PAGE 38 F0743 — TREND PROB/SOLV INT/TRADE ECO/DEV

B61
BALASSA B.,THE THEORY OF ECONOMIC INTEGRATION. EUR+WWI L/A+17C MOD/EUR WOR+45 ECO/UNDEV MARKET INT/ORG NAT/G VOL/ASSN DELIB/GP PLAN CAP/ISM ECO/TAC...MAJORIT FOR/TRADE OEEC 20. PAGE 8 F0157 — ECO/DEV ACT/RES INT/TRADE

B61
OECD,STATISTICS OF BALANCE OF PAYMENTS 1950-61. WOR+45 FINAN ECO/TAC INT/TRADE DEMAND WEALTH...STAT NAT/COMP 20 OEEC OECD. PAGE 100 F1965 — BAL/PAY ECO/DEV INT/ORG CHARTS

B61
US CONGRESS JOINT ECO COMM,INTERNATIONAL PAYMENTS IMBALANCES AND NEED FOR STRENGTHENING INTERNATIONAL FINANCIAL ARRANGEMENTS. USA+45 WOR+45 DELIB/GP DIPLOM INT/TRADE...CHARTS 20 CONGRESS OEEC. PAGE 134 F2651 — BAL/PAY INT/ORG FINAN PROB/SOLV

S61
RAY J.,"THE EUROPEAN FREE-TRADE ASSOCIATION AND ITS IMPACT ON INDIA'S TRADE." EUR+WWI FRANCE GERMANY INDIA S/ASIA UK NAT/G VOL/ASSN PLAN INT/TRADE ROUTINE WEALTH...STAT CHARTS TERR/GP CMN/WLTH EEC FOR/TRADE OEEC 20 EFTA. PAGE 109 F2155 — ECO/DEV ECO/TAC

B62
MEADE J.E.,CASE STUDIES IN EUROPEAN ECONOMIC UNION. BELGIUM EUR+WWI LUXEMBOURG NAT/G INT/TRADE REGION ROUTINE WEALTH...METH/CNCPT STAT CHARTS ECSC TOT/POP OEEC EEC FOR/TRADE 20. PAGE 89 F1738 — INT/ORG ECO/TAC

B62
US CONGRESS JOINT ECO COMM,FACTORS AFFECTING THE UNITED STATES BALANCE OF PAYMENTS. USA+45 DELIB/GP PLAN DIPLOM FOR/AID PRODUC WEALTH...CHARTS 20 CONGRESS OEEC. PAGE 134 F2653 — BAL/PAY INT/TRADE ECO/TAC FINAN

B63
BELOFF M.,THE UNITED STATES AND THE UNITY OF EUROPE. EUR+WWI UK USA+45 WOR+45 VOL/ASSN DIPLOM REGION ATTIT PWR...CONCPT EEC OEEC 20 NATO. PAGE 13 F0239 — ECO/DEV INT/ORG

B63
COPPOCK J.,NORTH ATLANTIC POLICY - THE AGRICULTURAL GAP. EUR+WWI ELITES ECO/DEV DIST/IND MARKET PLAN WEALTH...STAT TREND GEN/LAWS OEEC TOT/POP VAL/FREE FAO 20. PAGE 27 F0535 — AGRI TEC/DEV INT/TRADE

B63
KRAVIS I.B.,DOMESTIC INTERESTS AND INTERNATIONAL OBLIGATIONS: SAFEGUARDS IN INTERNATIONAL TRADE ORGANIZATIONS. EUR+WWI USA+45 WOR+45 FINAN DELIB/GP ATTIT RIGID/FLEX HEALTH...STAT EEC VAL/FREE OEEC ECSC 20. PAGE 73 F1435 — INT/ORG ECO/TAC INT/TRADE

S63
ADAMS F.G.,"ECONOMIC CONSIDERATIONS OF AN ATLANTIC ENERGY POLICY." EUR+WWI FUT USA+45 DIST/IND EXTR/IND MARKET CONSULT LEGIS ECO/TAC WEALTH ...POLICY EEC FOR/TRADE OEEC 20. PAGE 2 F0037 — ECO/DEV TEC/DEV NUC/PWR

S63
APPERT K.,"BERECHTIGE VORBEHALTE DER SCHWEIZERISCHEN ZUR INTEGRATION." EUR+WWI UK MARKET SERV/IND NAT/G PLAN RIGID/FLEX OEEC 20 EEC. PAGE 6 F0108 — FINAN ATTIT SWITZERLND

S63
BARZANSKI S.,"REGIONAL UNDERDEVELOPMENT IN THE EUROPEAN ECONOMIC COMMUNITY." EUR+WWI ELITES DIST/IND MARKET VOL/ASSN CONSULT EX/STRUC ECO/TAC RIGID/FLEX WEALTH EEC OEEC 20. PAGE 11 F0202 — ECO/UNDEV PLAN

S63
HALLSTEIN W.,"THE EUROPEAN COMMUNITY AND ATLANTIC PARTNERSHIP." EUR+WWI USA+45 MARKET NAT/G VOL/ASSN DELIB/GP ARMS/CONT NUC/PWR ATTIT PWR...CONCPT STAT TIME/SEQ TREND OEEC 20 EEC. PAGE 54 F1053 — INT/ORG ECO/TAC UK

S63
MASON E.S.,"INTERESTS, IDEOLOGIES AND THE PROBLEM OF STABILITY AND GROWTH." EUR+WWI USA+45 DELIB/GP CREATE PLAN EXEC ROUTINE BAL/PAY ATTIT PWR...MGT CONCPT OEEC 20. PAGE 87 F1698 — NAT/G ECO/DEV

S63
SCHOFLING J.A.,"EFTA: THE OTHER EUROPE." ECO/DEV MARKET CONSULT ECO/TAC WEALTH...TIME/SEQ EEC OEEC 20 EFTA. PAGE 117 F2310 — EUR+WWI INT/ORG REGION

S63
SHWADRAN B.,"MIDDLE EAST OIL, 1962." ISLAM USSR ECO/DEV DIST/IND INDUS PLAN BAL/PWR DISPL DRIVE ...POLICY STAT TREND GEN/LAWS TERR/GP METH/GP EEC OEEC 20 OIL. PAGE 121 F2394 — MARKET ECO/TAC INT/TRADE

B64
ECONOMIDES C.P.,LE POUVOIR DE DECISION DES ORGANISATIONS INTERNATIONALES EUROPEENNES. DIPLOM DOMIN INGP/REL EFFICIENCY...INT/LAW JURID 20 NATO OEEC EEC COUNCL/EUR EURATOM. PAGE 36 F0698 — INT/ORG PWR DECISION GP/COMP

B65
CASSELL F.,GOLD OR CREDIT? THE ECONOMICS AND POLITICS OF INTERNATIONAL MONEY. AFR WOR+45 PLAN PROB/SOLV BAL/PAY SOVEREIGN WEALTH 20 OEEC. PAGE 22 F0428 — FINAN INT/ORG DIPLOM ECO/TAC

B66
MEERHAEGHE M.,INTERNATIONAL ECONOMIC INSTITUTIONS. EUR+WWI FINAN INDUS MARKET PLAN TARIFFS BAL/PAY — ECO/TAC ECO/DEV

EQUILIB...POLICY BIBLIOG/A 20 GATT OEEC EEC IBRD EURCOALSTL. PAGE 89 F1745 INT/TRADE INT/ORG

B66
TRIFFIN R.,THE WORLD MONEY MAZE. AFR INT/ORG ECO/TAC PRICE OPTIMAL WEALTH...METH/COMP 20 EEC OEEC SILVER. PAGE 131 F2589 BAL/PAY FINAN INT/TRADE DIPLOM

OEO....OFFICE OF ECONOMIC OPPORTUNITY

S65
HADDAD W.F.,"MR. SHRIVER AND THE SAVAGE POLITICS OF POVERTY" USA+45 LAW NAT/G DELIB/GP LEGIS GIVE LEAD CENTRAL PWR...SOC/WK CHARTS 20 CONGRESS POVRTY/WAR SHRIVER/S OEO. PAGE 53 F1028 WEALTH GOV/REL CONTROL TOP/EX

OEP....OFFICE OF EMERGENCY PLANNING

OFER G. F1979

OFFICE OF ECONOMIC OPPORTUNITY....SEE OEO

OFFICE OF EMERGENCY PLANNING....SEE OEP

OFFICE OF PRICE ADMINISTRATION....SEE OPA

OFFICE OF WAR INFORMATION....SEE OWI

OFFICE OF ECONOMIC OPPORTUNITY F1980

OGBURN C. F1981

OGDEN F.D. F1982

OGDEN G. F1636

OGLESBY C. F1983

OHIO....OHIO

OHLIN G. F1984,F1985

OHLIN/HECK....OHLIN-HECKSCHER THEORY OF COMMODITY TRADE

B65
FORD J.L.,THE OHLIN-HECKSCHER THEORY OF THE BASIS AND EFFECTS OF COMMODITY TRADE. WOR+45 ECO/TAC DEMAND INCOME...CONCPT GEN/METH 20 OHLIN/HECK. PAGE 42 F0824 ECOMETRIC INT/TRADE NEW/IDEA SIMUL

OHM H. F1119

OIL

B61
LONGRIGG S.H.,OIL IN THE MIDDLE EAST: ITS DISCOVERY AND DEVELOPMENT. ECO/UNDEV LG/CO LOC/G TEC/DEV WEALTH...STAT TIME/SEQ 20 OIL. PAGE 82 F1599 ISLAM EXTR/IND

S63
SHWADRAN B.,"MIDDLE EAST OIL, 1962." ISLAM DIST/IND INDUS PLAN ATTIT DRIVE WEALTH...POLICY STAT CONT/OBS TREND CHARTS GEN/LAWS TERR/GP METH/GP 20 OIL. PAGE 121 F2393 PROC/MFG ECO/TAC ELITES REGION

S63
SHWADRAN B.,"MIDDLE EAST OIL, 1962." ISLAM USSR ECO/DEV DIST/IND INDUS PLAN BAL/PWR DISPL DRIVE ...POLICY STAT TREND GEN/LAWS TERR/GP METH/GP EEC OEEC 20 OIL. PAGE 121 F2394 MARKET ECO/TAC INT/TRADE

S64
KLEIN H.,"AMERICAN OIL COMPANIES IN LATIN AMERICA: THE BOLIVIAN EXPERIENCE." L/A+17C USA+45 USA-45 EXTR/IND LG/CO NAT/G ECO/TAC WEALTH...POLICY GEN/LAWS BOLIV TOT/POP 20 OIL. PAGE 72 F1405 MARKET ECO/UNDEV NAT/LISM

OKELLO/J....JOHN OKELLO

OKINAWA....OKINAWA

OKLAHOMA....OKLAHOMA

OLAS....ORGANIZATION FOR LATIN AMERICAN SOLIDARITY

OLD LIBERAL....SEE OLD/LIB

OLD/LIB....OLD LIBERAL

S38
HALL R.C.,"REPRESENTATION OF BIG BUSINESS IN THE HOUSE OF COMMONS." UK ECO/DEV INDUS PROF/ORG LEGIS CAP/ISM ECO/TAC LAISSEZ...POLICY OLD/LIB PLURIST MGT 20 HOUSE/CMNS. PAGE 53 F1047 LOBBY NAT/G

B41
YOUNG G.,FEDERALISM AND FREEDOM. EUR+WWI MOD/EUR RUSSIA USA-45 WOR-45 SOCIETY STRUCT ECO/DEV INT/ORG EXEC FEDERAL ATTIT PERSON ALL/VALS...OLD/LIB CONCPT OBS TREND LEAGUE/NAT TOT/POP. PAGE 150 F2950 NAT/G WAR

B44
HAYEK F.A.,THE ROAD TO SERFDOM. NAT/G POL/PAR CREATE EDU/PROP ATTIT WEALTH LAISSEZ...OLD/LIB CONCPT TREND 20. PAGE 57 F1121 FUT PLAN ECO/TAC SOCISM

B47
ISAAC J.,ECONOMICS OF MIGRATION. MOD/EUR CULTURE STRATA STRUCT NAT/G COLONIAL WEALTH...OLD/LIB TREND TIME 19/20 EUROPE/W MIGRATION. PAGE 65 F1289 HABITAT SOC GEOG

B60
ROEPKE W.,A HUMANE ECONOMY: THE SOCIAL FRAMEWORK OF THE FREE MARKET. FUT USSR WOR+45 CULTURE SOCIETY ECO/DEV PLAN ECO/TAC ADMIN ATTIT PERSON RIGID/FLEX SUPEGO MORAL WEALTH SOCISM...POLICY OLD/LIB CONCPT TREND GEN/LAWS 20. PAGE 113 F2232 DRIVE EDU/PROP CAP/ISM

B60
WALLICH H.C.,THE COST OF FREEDOM: A NEW LOOK AT CAPITALISM. USA+45 SOCIETY ECO/DEV INGP/REL CONSEN LAISSEZ SOCISM...OLD/LIB IDEA/COMP. PAGE 143 F2810 CAP/ISM ORD/FREE POLICY ECO/TAC

S60
BUTLER W.F.,"ECONOMIC PROGRESS IN LATIN AMERICA." L/A+17C USA+45 ECO/UNDEV AGRI FINAN NAT/G PLAN ECO/TAC FOR/AID ADMIN WEALTH...OLD/LIB TOT/POP 20. PAGE 21 F0397 INDUS ACT/RES

S60
KELLOGG C.E.,"TRANSFER OF BASIC SKILLS OF FOOD PRODUCTION." AFR FUT S/ASIA STRATA ECO/UNDEV LABOR VOL/ASSN RIGID/FLEX...OLD/LIB SOCIALIST NEW/IDEA STAT PROJ/TEST GEN/LAWS 20. PAGE 70 F1370 AGRI PLAN

B61
EINZIG P.,A DYNAMIC THEORY OF FORWARD EXCHANGE. FUT WOR+45 WOR-45 INT/TRADE BAL/PAY WEALTH...OLD/LIB NEW/IDEA OBS TREND FOR/TRADE 20. PAGE 37 F0713 FINAN ECO/TAC

B61
FRIEDMANN W.G.,JOINT INTERNATIONAL BUSINESS VENTURES. ASIA ISLAM L/A+17C ECO/DEV DIST/IND FINAN PROC/MFG FACE/GP LG/CO NAT/G VOL/ASSN CONSULT EX/STRUC PLAN ADMIN ROUTINE WEALTH...OLD/LIB FOR/TRADE WORK 20. PAGE 44 F0865 ECO/UNDEV INT/TRADE

S61
NEAL A.C.,"NEW ECONOMIC POLICIES FOR THE WEST." COM EUR+WWI FUT USA+45 WOR+45 ECO/DEV ECO/UNDEV INDUS MARKET ROUTINE HEALTH ORD/FREE PWR...OLD/LIB METH/CNCPT 20. PAGE 97 F1904 PLAN ECO/TAC

B63
OLSON M. JR.,THE ECONOMICS OF WARTIME SHORTAGE. FRANCE GERMANY MOD/EUR UK AGRI PROB/SOLV ADMIN DEMAND WEALTH...POLICY OLD/LIB FOR/TRADE 17/20. PAGE 101 F1990 WAR ADJUST ECO/TAC NAT/COMP

B67
PETRO S.,THE KINGSPORT STRIKE. USA+45 PROC/MFG NAT/G JUDGE PRESS PARTIC PERS/REL...OLD/LIB OBS INT 20 NLRB. PAGE 105 F2074 LABOR COERCE SANCTION ALL/VALS

L67
WHITNEY S.N.,"MERGERS, CONGLOMERATES, AND OLIGOPOLIES* A WIDENING OF ANTI TRUST TARGETS." LAW NAT/G TEC/DEV CAP/ISM GP/REL PWR...OLD/LIB 20. PAGE 146 F2873 ECO/TAC INDUS JURID

B76
SMITH A.,THE WEALTH OF NATIONS. UK STRUCT WORKER DIPLOM ECO/TAC OPTIMAL DRIVE PERSON ORD/FREE ...OLD/LIB GEN/LAWS 17/18. PAGE 123 F2428 WEALTH PRODUC INDUS LAISSEZ

B96
SMITH A.,LECTURES ON JUSTICE, POLICE, REVENUE AND ARMS (1763). UK LAW FAM FORCES TARIFFS AGREE COERCE INCOME OWN WEALTH LAISSEZ...GEN/LAWS 17/18. PAGE 123 F2429 DIPLOM JURID OLD/LIB TAX

OLD/STOR....CONVENTIONAL INFORMATION-STORAGE SYSTEMS

OLIGARCHY....SEE ELITES

OLIGOPOLY....SEE MONOPOLY

OLIN/MTHSN....OLIN MATHIESON

OLIVARES....OLIVARES, HEAD OF SPAIN DURING CATALAN REV., 1640

OLIVECRONA K. F1986

OLIVER H.M. F1987

OLIVIER G. F1988

OLSON M. F1989,F1990

OMABOE E.N. F0286,F0287

OMBUDSMAN....OMBUDSMAN; DOMESTIC GRIEVANCE ORGAN

ONSLOW C. F1991

ONTARIO....ONTARIO, CANADA

B61
GOODWIN C.D.W.,CANADIAN ECONOMIC THOUGHT. CANADA STRATA TEC/DEV CAP/ISM TARIFFS TAX COST EFFICIENCY WEALTH...METH/CNCPT TREND 20 MARITIME ONTARIO. PAGE 49 F0952
INT/TRADE ECO/DEV FINAN DEMAND

ONUOHA B. F1992

OP/RES....OPERATIONS RESEARCH; SEE ALSO CREATE

B
BRITISH COMMONWEALTH BUR AGRI,WORLD AGRICULTURAL ECONOMICS AND RURAL SOCIOLOGY ABSTRACTS. NAT/G OP/RES PLAN TEC/DEV LEAD PRODUC...GEOG MGT NAT/COMP 20. PAGE 18 F0354
BIBLIOG/A AGRI SOC WORKER

N
AMERICAN ECONOMIC REVIEW. FINAN INDUS LABOR OP/RES CAP/ISM INT/TRADE TAX WEALTH...CON/ANAL CHARTS 20. PAGE 1 F0001
BIBLIOG/A USA+45 ECO/DEV NAT/G

N
SOUTH AFRICAN JOURNAL OF ECONOMICS. SOUTH/AFR FINAN MARKET ACT/RES OP/RES...PHIL/SCI STAT CON/ANAL METH/COMP BIBLIOG/A 20. PAGE 1 F0009
ECO/UNDEV ACADEM INTELL R+D

C01
LOWELL A.L.,"THE INFLUENCE OF PARTY UPON LEGISLATION IN ENGLAND AND AMERICA" IN ANNUAL REPORT OF AMER HISTORICAL ASSN." LEGIS CONTROL ...CON/ANAL CHARTS 19/20 CONGRESS PARLIAMENT. PAGE 82 F1605
PARL/PROC POL/PAR DECISION OP/RES

N19
CONGRESSIONAL QUARTERLY SERV,FEDERAL ECONOMIC POLICY 1945-1965 (PAMPHLET). USA+45 FINAN OP/RES BAL/PWR ECO/TAC TAX BAL/PAY CENTRAL COST WEALTH ...CHARTS 20. PAGE 27 F0525
NAT/G ECO/DEV BUDGET POLICY

B39
JENNINGS W.I.,PARLIAMENT. UK POL/PAR OP/RES BUDGET LEAD CHOOSE GP/REL...MGT 20 PARLIAMENT HOUSE/LORD HOUSE/CMNS. PAGE 67 F1315
PARL/PROC LEGIS CONSTN NAT/G

B40
GAUS J.M.,PUBLIC ADMINISTRATION AND THE UNITED STATES DEPARTMENT OF AGRICULTURE. USA-45 STRUCT DIST/IND FINAN MARKET EX/STRUC PROB/SOLV GIVE PRODUC...POLICY GEOG CHARTS 20 DEPT/AGRI. PAGE 47 F0909
ADMIN AGRI DELIB/GP OP/RES

B41
DAUGHERTY C.R.,LABOR PROBLEMS IN AMERICAN INDUSTRY (5TH ED.). USA-45 SOCIETY OP/RES ECO/TAC...MGT PSY T 20. PAGE 30 F0581
LABOR INDUS GP/REL PROB/SOLV

B46
HARRISON S.M.,AMERICAN FOUNDATIONS FOR SOCIAL WELFARE. OP/RES CONTROL...POLICY MGT METH/CNCPT STAT TREND BIBLIOG. PAGE 56 F1092
GIVE FINAN CLASSIF ADMIN

B50
LIPSET S.M.,AGRARIAN SOCIALISM. CANADA POL/PAR OP/RES ECO/TAC ADMIN ATTIT...TIME/SEQ NAT/COMP SOC/EXP 20 SASKATCH. PAGE 80 F1576
SOCISM AGRI METH/COMP STRUCT

B51
POOLE K.,FISCAL POLICIES AND THE AMERICAN ECONOMY. AFR ECO/DEV FINAN INDUS WORKER OP/RES INT/TRADE TAX COST INCOME PROFIT WEALTH...GP/COMP 20. PAGE 107 F2102
NAT/G POLICY ANTHOL

C51
HOMANS G.C.,"THE WESTERN ELECTRIC RESEARCHES" IN S. HOSLETT, ED., HUMAN FACTORS IN MANAGEMENT (BMR)" ACT/RES GP/REL HAPPINESS PRODUC DRIVE...MGT OBS 20. PAGE 61 F1202
OP/RES EFFICIENCY SOC/EXP WORKER

B54
WASHBURNE N.F.,INTERPRETING SOCIAL CHANGE IN AMERICA. USA+45 STRATA FAM NAT/G SECT OP/RES ECO/TAC EDU/PROP HABITAT...SOC TIME/SEQ TREND 20 BUREAUCRCY. PAGE 143 F2826
CULTURE STRUCT CREATE TEC/DEV

B55
BERNAYS E.L.,THE ENGINEERING OF CONSENT. VOL/ASSN OP/RES ROUTINE INGP/REL ATTIT RESPECT...POLICY METH/CNCPT METH/COMP 20. PAGE 14 F0264
GP/REL PLAN ACT/RES ADJUST

L56
SCHELLING T.C.,"AN ESSAY ON BARGAINING" (BMR)" OP/RES PROB/SOLV PRICE CHOOSE PWR...DECISION MODELS 20. PAGE 116 F2294
BARGAIN MARKET ECO/TAC GAME

B57
ASSN U BUREAUS BUS-ECO RES,INDEX OF PUBLICATIONS OF BUREAUS OF BUSINESS AND ECONOMIC RESEARCH 1950-56 AND YEARLY SUPPLEMENTS THROUGH 1967. FINAN OP/RES PLAN GOV/REL INCOME AGE...POLICY 20. PAGE 7 F0133
BIBLIOG ECO/DEV ECO/TAC LG/CO

B58
OEEC,THE INDUSTRIAL CHALLENGE OF NUCLEAR ENERGY. EUR+WWI ECO/DEV INDUS OP/RES CONFER RISK PWR ...AUD/VIS CHARTS ANTHOL 20 OEEC. PAGE 101 F1977
NUC/PWR ACT/RES ECO/TAC INT/ORG

L58
FORRESTER J.W.,"INDUSTRIAL DYNAMICS* A MAJOR BREAKTHROUGH FOR DECISION MAKERS." COMPUTER OP/RES ...DECISION CONCPT NEW/IDEA. PAGE 42 F0830
INDUS ACT/RES MGT PROB/SOLV

S58
MANSFIELD E.,"A STUDY OF DECISION-MAKING WITHIN THE FIRM." LG/CO WORKER INGP/REL COST EFFICIENCY PRODUC ...CHARTS 20. PAGE 85 F1658
OP/RES PROB/SOLV AUTOMAT ROUTINE

B59
BONNETT C.E.,LABOR-MANAGEMENT RELATIONS. USA+45 OP/RES PROB/SOLV EDU/PROP...AUD/VIS CHARTS 20. PAGE 16 F0317
MGT LABOR INDUS GP/REL

B59
CONTY J.M.,PSYCHOLOGIE DE LA DECISION....PSY GAME 20. PAGE 27 F0528
DECISION PROB/SOLV OP/RES METH/COMP

B59
SERAPHIM H.J.,PROBLEME DER WILLENSBILDUNG UND DER WIRTSCHAFTSPOLITISCHEN FUEHRUNG. WOR+45 MARKET ACT/RES OP/RES PLAN EDU/PROP INGP/REL HABITAT PLURISM...MGT PERS/COMP METH 20. PAGE 119 F2357
POLICY DECISION PSY

B59
SHUBIK M.,STRATEGY AND MARKET STRUCTURE: COMPETITION, OLIGOPOLY, AND THE THEORY OF GAMES. ELITES STRUCT MARKET OP/RES EXEC EFFICIENCY INCOME ...MGT MATH STAT CHARTS 20. PAGE 121 F2389
ECO/DEV ECO/TAC DECISION GAME

C59
FAINSOD M.,"GOVERNMENT AND THE AMERICAN ECONOMY." USA+45 USA-45 INDUS LABOR OP/RES PROB/SOLV ECO/TAC CONTROL...CHARTS BIBLIOG T 20. PAGE 39 F0760
CONSTN ECO/DEV CAP/ISM NAT/G

C59
KURIHARA K.L.,"THE KEYNESIAN THEORY OF ECONOMIC DEVELOPMENT." WOR+45 WOR-45 PLAN OPTIMAL PRODUC ...CONCPT BIBLIOG 20. PAGE 74 F1451
ECO/DEV ECO/UNDEV OP/RES TEC/DEV

B60
AUSTRUY J.,STRUCTURE ECONOMIQUE ET CIVILISATION: L'EGYPTE ET LE DESTIN ECONOMIQUE DE L'ISLAM. ISLAM UAR CREATE OP/RES ECO/TAC...SOC BIBLIOG 20 MUSLIM. PAGE 8 F0142
ECO/UNDEV CULTURE STRUCT

B60
BISSON A.,INSTITUTIONS FINANCIERES ET ECONOMIQUES EN FRANCE. FRANCE INDUS OP/RES TAX COST PRODUC ...CHARTS 20. PAGE 15 F0289
FINAN BUDGET PLAN

B60
FINKLE J.L.,THE PRESIDENT MAKES A DECISION: A STUDY OF DIXON-YATES. OP/RES PROB/SOLV BUDGET ADMIN GOV/REL...POLICY BIBLIOG/A 20 PRESIDENT. PAGE 41 F0799
DECISION CHIEF PWR POL/PAR

B60
MORRIS W.T.,ENGINEERING ECONOMY. AUTOMAT RISK RATIONAL...PROBABIL STAT CHARTS GAME SIMUL BIBLIOG T 20. PAGE 94 F1838
OP/RES DECISION MGT PROB/SOLV

B60
WALLACE R.A.,CONGRESSIONAL CONTROL OF FEDERAL SPENDING. USA+45 CONSTN NAT/G OP/RES CONFER DEBATE PERS/REL UTIL RIGID/FLEX PWR OBJECTIVE...OBS CHARTS. PAGE 143 F2808
LEGIS DELIB/GP BUDGET

B61
CANTERBERY E.R.,THE PRESIDENT'S COUNCIL OF ECONOMIC ADVISERS. AFR USA+45 FINAN LABOR NAT/G PLAN ADMIN OPTIMAL WEALTH 20 EISNHWR/DD PRESIDENT TRUMAN/HS KEYNES/JM. PAGE 21 F0413
ECO/TAC OP/RES EXEC CHIEF

B61
DIMOCK M.E.,BUSINESS AND GOVERNMENT (4TH ED.). AGRI FINAN OP/RES PLAN BUDGET DIPLOM LOBBY NUC/PWR NEW/LIB SOCISM...POLICY BIBLIOG 20. PAGE 33 F0641
NAT/G INDUS LABOR ECO/TAC

S61
HIRSHLEIFER J.,"THE BAYESIAN APPROACH TO STATISTICAL DECISION: AN EXPOSITION." OP/RES PROB/SOLV UTIL...PROBABIL CHARTS IDEA/COMP HYPO/EXP 20. PAGE 60 F1178
DECISION GAME SIMUL STAT

S61
SHUBIK M.,"APPROACHES TO THE STUDY OF DECISION-MAKING RELEVANT TO THE FIRM." INDUS COMPUTER OP/RES ...PROBABIL STAT 20. PAGE 121 F2390
GAME DECISION MGT SIMUL

B62
HATTERY L.H.,INFORMATION RETRIEVAL MANAGEMENT. CLIENT INDUS TOP/EX COMPUTER OP/RES TEC/DEV ROUTINE COST EFFICIENCY RIGID/FLEX...METH/COMP ANTHOL 20. PAGE 57 F1113
R+D COMPUT/IR MGT CREATE

B62
NATIONAL BUREAU ECONOMIC RES,THE RATE AND DIRECTION OF INVENTIVE ACTIVITY: ECONOMIC AND SOCIAL FACTORS. STRUCT INDUS MARKET R+D CREATE OP/RES TEC/DEV
DECISION PROB/SOLV MGT

EFFICIENCY PRODUC RATIONAL UTIL...WELF/ST PHIL/SCI METH/CNCPT TIME. PAGE 97 F1895

B62
WENDT P.F.,HOUSING POLICY - THE SEARCH FOR SOLUTIONS. GERMANY/W SWEDEN UK USA+45 OP/RES HABITAT WEALTH...SOC/WK CHARTS 20. PAGE 145 F2856
PLAN ADMIN METH/COMP NAT/G

C62
JOINT ECONOMIC COMMITTEE,"DIMENSIONS OF SOVIET ECONOMIC POWER." USSR R+D FORCES ACT/RES OP/RES TEC/DEV...GEOG STAT BIBLIOG 20. PAGE 68 F1337
ECO/DEV PLAN PRODUC LABOR

B63
BRAYBROOKE D.,A STRATEGY OF DECISION: POLICY EVALUATION AS A SOCIAL PROCESS. UNIV ELITES OP/RES DOMIN CONFER FEEDBACK CONSEN PLURISM...CONCPT CENSUS. PAGE 18 F0343
DECISION POLICY CONTROL

B63
CHAMPION J.M.,CRITICAL INCIDENTS IN MANAGEMENT. MARKET LG/CO SML/CO OP/RES ADMIN CONTROL LEAD GP/REL PERS/REL COST ATTIT SUPEGO ALL/VALS...PSY PERS/TEST BIBLIOG. PAGE 23 F0445
MGT DECISION EX/STRUC INDUS

B63
DUE J.F.,STATE SALES TAX ADMINISTRATION. OP/RES BUDGET PAY ADMIN EXEC ROUTINE COST EFFICIENCY PROFIT...CHARTS METH/COMP 20. PAGE 34 F0671
PROVS TAX STAT GOV/COMP

B63
JOHNSTON J.,ECONOMETRIC METHODS. PROB/SOLV WRITING ...REGRESS CHARTS T. PAGE 68 F1333
ECOMETRIC PHIL/SCI OP/RES STAT

B63
MARCHAL J.,EXPANSION ET RECESSION. FRANCE OP/RES PROB/SOLV ROLE ORD/FREE...TREND SIMUL 20 DEPRESSION. PAGE 85 F1663
FINAN PLAN ECO/DEV

B63
MCDONOUGH A.M.,INFORMATION ECONOMICS AND MANAGEMENT SYSTEMS. ECO/DEV OP/RES AUTOMAT EFFICIENCY 20. PAGE 88 F1726
COMPUT/IR MGT CONCPT COMPUTER

B63
RUMMEL J.F.,RESEARCH METHODOLOGY IN BUSINESS. COMPUTER CREATE PROB/SOLV...CONT/OBS REC/INT QU/SEMANT SYS/QU SAMP CHARTS METH/COMP T 20. PAGE 115 F2260
OP/RES METH/CNCPT METH STAT

S63
CLARK P.G.,"TOWARDS MORE COMPREHENSIVE PLANNING IN EAST AFRICA" AFR OP/RES ECO/TAC RATION TAX EFFICIENCY INCOME...MATH TREND CHARTS 20 AFRICA/E. PAGE 25 F0484
ECO/UNDEV PLAN STAT METH/COMP

S63
GREEN P.E.,"BAYESIAN DECISION THEORY IN PRICING STRATEGY."...STAT CHARTS. PAGE 51 F0988
OP/RES PROB/SOLV BARGAIN PRICE

B64
BLAKE R.R.,MANAGING INTERGROUP CONFLICT IN INDUSTRY. INDUS DELIB/GP EX/STRUC GP/REL PERS/REL GAME. PAGE 16 F0297
CREATE PROB/SOLV OP/RES ADJUD

B64
HAMBRIDGE G.,DYNAMICS OF DEVELOPMENT. AGRI FINAN INDUS LABOR INT/TRADE EDU/PROP ADMIN LEAD OWN HEALTH...ANTHOL BIBLIOG 20. PAGE 54 F1054
ECO/UNDEV ECO/TAC OP/RES ACT/RES

B64
HART P.E.,ECONOMETRIC ANALYSIS FOR NATIONAL ECONOMIC PLANNING. INDUS OP/RES PRICE PRODUC ...SIMUL ANTHOL MODELS 20. PAGE 56 F1100
PLAN ECOMETRIC STAT

B64
LANG A.S.,URBAN RAIL TRANSIT. OP/RES PLAN PROB/SOLV TEC/DEV AUTOMAT COST...TECHNIC MATH CON/ANAL CHARTS METH/COMP SIMUL MUNICH 20 RAILROAD PUB/TRANS. PAGE 75 F1474
DIST/IND ECOMETRIC

B64
LANGHOFF P.,MODELS, MEASUREMENT AND MARKETING. ACT/RES COMPUTER OP/RES PLAN BUDGET...MGT PHIL/SCI METH/CNCPT STAT PROG/TEAC BIBLIOG. PAGE 75 F1478
DECISION SIMUL MARKET R+D

B64
MARRIS R.,THE ECONOMIC THEORY OF "MANAGERIAL" CAPITALISM. USA+45 ECO/DEV LG/CO ECO/TAC DEMAND ...CHARTS BIBLIOG 20. PAGE 86 F1675
CAP/ISM MGT CONTROL OP/RES

B64
STEWART C.F.,A BIBLIOGRAPHY OF INTERNATIONAL BUSINESS. WOR+45 FINAN LG/CO NAT/G PLAN ECO/TAC TARIFFS...DECISION MGT GP/COMP NAT/COMP 20 EEC. PAGE 126 F2484
BIBLIOG INT/ORG OP/RES INT/TRADE

S64
STONE P.A.,"DECISION TECHNIQUES FOR TOWN DEVELOPMENT." PLAN COST PROFIT...DECISION MGT CON/ANAL CHARTS METH/COMP BIBLIOG MUNICH 20. PAGE 127 F2497
OP/RES ADMIN PROB/SOLV

B65
BAUMOL W.J.,ECONOMIC THEORY AND OPERATIONS ANALYSIS (2ND ED.). MARKET LG/CO BUDGET PRICE COST EQUILIB PRODUC...DECISION MATH CHARTS GAME 20. PAGE 12 F0219
OP/RES ECO/DEV METH/COMP STAT

B65
BLAIR T.L.V.,AFRICA: A MARKET PROFILE. AFR COM/IND DIST/IND FINAN UTIL...DECISION CHARTS BIBLIOG 20. PAGE 15 F0295
MARKET OP/RES ECO/UNDEV INDUS

B65
BRENNAN M.J.,PATTERNS OF MARKET BEHAVIOR. AFR USA+45 OP/RES CAP/ISM ECO/TAC INT/TRADE...CHARTS METH/COMP ANTHOL TIME 20. PAGE 18 F0346
MARKET LABOR FINAN ECOMETRIC

B65
GOETZ-GIREY R.,LE MOUVEMENT DES GREVES EN FRANCE. FRANCE FINAN OP/RES PROB/SOLV ECO/TAC INCOME HABITAT...STAT CHARTS 19/20. PAGE 48 F0932
LABOR WORKER GP/REL INDUS

B65
HICKMAN B.G.,QUANTITATIVE PLANNING OF ECONOMIC POLICY. FRANCE NETHERLAND OP/RES PRICE ROUTINE UTIL ...POLICY DECISION ECOMETRIC METH/CNCPT STAT STYLE CHINJAP. PAGE 59 F1162
PROB/SOLV PLAN QUANT

B65
MORRIS M.D.,THE EMERGENCE OF AN INDUSTRIAL LABOR FORCE IN INDIA: A STUDY OF THE BOMBAY COTTON MILLS, 1854-1947. INDIA WORKER OP/RES ADMIN 19/20. PAGE 94 F1837
INDUS LABOR ECO/UNDEV CAP/ISM

B65
SCHWARTZ G.,SCIENCE IN MARKETING. OP/RES PROB/SOLV INT/TRADE PRICE CONTROL ADJUST PRODUC...CONCPT 20. PAGE 118 F2324
PHIL/SCI TREND ECO/DEV MARKET

B65
THAYER F.C. JR.,AIR TRANSPORT POLICY AND NATIONAL SECURITY: A POLITICAL, ECONOMIC, AND MILITARY ANALYSIS. DIST/IND OP/RES PLAN TEC/DEV DIPLOM DETER WAR COST EFFICIENCY...POLICY BIBLIOG 20 DEPT/DEFEN FAA CAB. PAGE 129 F2548
AIR FORCES CIVMIL/REL ORD/FREE

B65
WEAVER J.N.,THE INTERNATIONAL DEVELOPMENT ASSOCIATION: A NEW APPROACH TO FOREIGN AID. USA+45 NAT/G OP/RES PLAN PROB/SOLV WEALTH...CHARTS BIBLIOG 20 UN. PAGE 144 F2836
FOR/AID INT/ORG ECO/UNDEV FINAN

S65
CHU K.,"A DYNAMIC MODEL OF THE FIRM." OP/RES PROB/SOLV...DECISION ECOMETRIC NEW/IDEA STAT GAME ORG/CHARTS SIMUL. PAGE 24 F0472
INDUS COMPUTER TEC/DEV

S65
WHITE J.,"WEST GERMAN AID TO DEVELOPING COUNTRIES." AFR INT/ORG OP/RES GIVE CENTRAL ATTIT DRIVE...STAT NAT/COMP. PAGE 146 F2869
GERMANY FOR/AID ECO/UNDEV CAP/ISM

B66
BROWN R.T.,TRANSPORT AND THE ECONOMIC INTEGRATION OF SOUTH AMERICA. L/A+17C ECO/UNDEV NAT/G OP/RES DIPLOM INT/TRADE REGION WEALTH...ECOMETRIC GEOG STAT LAFTA TIME. PAGE 19 F0373
MARKET DIST/IND SIMUL

B66
CHASE S.B. JR.,PROBLEMS IN PUBLIC EXPENDITURE ANALYSIS. DIST/IND INDUS OP/RES PLAN BUDGET RECEIVE PRICE RISK COST INCOME...CHARTS ANTHOL 20. PAGE 23 F0455
ECO/DEV FINAN NAT/G INSPECT

B66
DAVIS K.,BUSINESS AND ITS ENVIRONMENT. LAW ECO/DEV INDUS OP/RES ADMIN CONTROL ROUTINE GP/REL PROFIT POLICY. PAGE 30 F0591
EX/STRUC PROB/SOLV CAP/ISM EXEC

B66
LANSING J.B.,TRANSPORTATION AND ECONOMIC POLICY. USA+45 COST DEMAND...ECOMETRIC TREND CHARTS IDEA/COMP T 20. PAGE 76 F1481
DIST/IND OP/RES ECO/DEV UTIL

B66
MANSFIELD E.,MANAGERIAL ECONOMICS AND OPERATIONS RESEARCH; A NONMATHEMATICAL INTRODUCTION. USA+45 ELITES ECO/DEV CONSULT EX/STRUC PROB/SOLV ROUTINE EFFICIENCY OPTIMAL...GAME T 20. PAGE 85 F1660
ECO/TAC OP/RES MGT COMPUTER

B66
POLK J.,U S PRODUCTION ABROAD AND THE BALANCE OF PAYMENTS* A SURVEY OF CORPORATE INVESTMENT EXPERIENCE. USA+45 SERV/IND NAT/G OP/RES COST PROFIT ATTIT...ECOMETRIC STAT INT QU GEN/METH. PAGE 107 F2096
BAL/PAY FINAN INT/TRADE INDUS

B66
THEIL H.,APPLIED ECONOMIC FORECASTING. UNIV USA+45 ELITES INTELL CONSULT PRODUC...DECISION MGT PREDICT CHARTS METH/COMP SIMUL 20. PAGE 129 F2552
FUT OP/RES PLAN

B66
US DEPARTMENT OF LABOR,PRODUCTIVITY: A BIBLIOGRAPHY. ECO/DEV INDUS MARKET OP/RES AUTOMAT COST...STAT 20. PAGE 135 F2668
BIBLIOG/A PRODUC LABOR PLAN

B66
US PRES COMM ECO IMPACT DEFENS,REPORT* JULY 1965. USA+45 ECO/DEV INDUS DELIB/GP FORCES OP/RES ARMS/CONT NUC/PWR WEAPON BAL/PAY...PREDICT SIMUL. PAGE 138 F2726 — ACT/RES STAT WAR BUDGET

B67
ANDERSON C.W.,POLITICS AND ECONOMIC CHANGE IN LATIN AMERICA. L/A+17C INDUS NAT/G OP/RES ADMIN DEMAND ...POLICY STAT CHARTS NAT/COMP 20. PAGE 5 F0093 — ECO/UNDEV PROB/SOLV PLAN ECO/TAC

B67
CARNEY D.,PATTERNS AND MECHANICS OF ECONOMIC GROWTH: A GENERAL THEORETICAL APPROACH. WOR+45 OP/RES INCOME...MATH TREND CHARTS 20. PAGE 21 F0416 — PLAN ECO/DEV FINAN

B67
DINERSTEIN H.S.,INTERVENTION AGAINST COMMUNISM (STUDIES IN INTERNATIONAL AFFAIRS NO. 1). CUBA DOMIN/REP GREECE USA+45 USSR VIETNAM OP/RES COERCE WAR 20. PAGE 33 F0643 — MARXISM DIPLOM NAT/LISM

B67
GORZ A.,STRATEGY FOR LABOR: A RADICAL PROPOSAL (TRANS. BY MARTIN NICOLAUS AND VICTORIA ORTIZ). EUR+WWI FRANCE ITALY ECO/DEV POL/PAR OP/RES PLAN GP/REL ALL/IDEOS...SOC 20 EEC. PAGE 49 F0965 — LABOR PWR STRUCT ECO/TAC

B67
HARDT J.P.,MATHEMATICS AND COMPUTERS IN SOVIET ECONOMIC PLANNING. COM USSR OP/RES PROB/SOLV OPTIMAL...MODAL SIMUL 20. PAGE 55 F1082 — PLAN TEC/DEV MATH COMPUT/IR

B67
HUMPHREY R.A.,UNIVERSITIES...AND DEVELOPMENT ASSISTANCE ABROAD. USA+45 OP/RES ECO/TAC FOR/AID ...ANTHOL 20. PAGE 63 F1242 — ACADEM DIPLOM KNOWL ECO/UNDEV

B67
JACOBY N.H.,US AID TO TAIWAN. CAP/ISM DIPLOM FEEDBACK COST PRODUC...OBS INT CHARTS 20. PAGE 66 F1301 — FOR/AID OP/RES ECO/TAC ECO/UNDEV

B67
LINDER S.B.,TRADE AND TRADE POLICY FOR DEVELOPMENT. OP/RES DIPLOM TARIFFS UTIL WEALTH...BIBLIOG 20. PAGE 80 F1569 — ECO/UNDEV ECO/TAC TEC/DEV INT/TRADE

B67
MALINVAUD E.,ACTIVITY ANALYSIS IN THE THEORY OF GROWTH AND PLANNING. UNIV AGRI COMPUTER OP/RES REGION...CHARTS ANTHOL METH. PAGE 84 F1648 — MATH GAME SIMUL

B67
MARRIS P.,DILEMMAS OF SOCIAL REFORM: POVERTY AND COMMUNITY ACTION IN THE UNITED STATES. USA+45 NAT/G OP/RES ADMIN PARTIC EFFICIENCY WEALTH...SOC METH/COMP T MUNICH 20 REFORMERS. PAGE 85 F1674 — STRUCT PROB/SOLV COST

B67
RIDKER R.G.,ECONOMIC COSTS OF AIR POLLUTION* STUDIES IN MEASUREMENT. R+D GP/REL KNOWL...OBS MUNICH 20. PAGE 111 F2190 — OP/RES HABITAT PHIL/SCI

B67
ROBINSON R.D.,INTERNATIONAL MANAGEMENT. LAW MARKET LABOR PRICE CONTROL COST DEMAND OWN PRODUC WEALTH 20. PAGE 113 F2225 — T OP/RES MGT DIPLOM

B67
SYMONS L.,AGRICULTURAL GEOGRAPHY. OP/RES SKILL ...CONCPT CHARTS BIBLIOG T 20. PAGE 128 F2520 — AGRI GEOG METH/COMP OBS

B67
VENKATESWARAN R.J.,CABINET GOVERNMENT IN INDIA. INDIA UK SOCIETY OP/RES COLONIAL LEAD EFFICIENCY ORD/FREE 20. PAGE 141 F2776 — DELIB/GP ADMIN CONSTN NAT/G

L67
STRUVE G.M.,"THE LESS-RESTRICTIVE-ALTERNATIVE PRINCIPLE AND ECONOMIC DUE PROCESS." USA+45 ECO/DEV LABOR NAT/G CONSULT DELIB/GP OP/RES PLAN WEALTH. PAGE 127 F2505 — JURID JUDGE SANCTION CAP/ISM

S67
ALBAUM G.,"INFORMATION FLOW AND DECENTRALIZED DECISION MAKING IN MARKETING." EX/STRUC COMPUTER OP/RES PROB/SOLV EFFICIENCY OPTIMAL...METH/COMP ORG/CHARTS 20. PAGE 3 F0056 — LG/CO ROUTINE KNOWL MARKET

S67
ALLISON D.,"THE GROWTH OF IDEAS." USA+45 LG/CO ADMIN. PAGE 4 F0075 — R+D OP/RES INDUS TEC/DEV

S67
BROWN M.B.,"THE TRADE UNION QUESTION." UK INDUS OP/RES PRICE PROFIT 20. PAGE 19 F0371 — WORKER LABOR GP/REL LAW

S67
FLOYD D.,"FIFTH AMENDMENT RIGHT TO COUNSEL IN FEDERAL INCOME TAX INVESTIGATIONS." USA+45 LAW OP/RES INGP/REL. PAGE 42 F0818 — JURID CT/SYS TAX CONSULT

S67
FOX R.G.,"FAMILY, CASTE, AND COMMERCE IN A NORTH INDIAN MARKET TOWN." INDIA STRATA AGRI FACE/GP FAM NEIGH OP/RES BARGAIN ADMIN ROUTINE WEALTH...SOC CHARTS 20. PAGE 43 F0838 — CULTURE GP/REL ECO/UNDEV DIST/IND

S67
FRANKEL T.,"ECONOMIC REFORM* A TENTATIVE APPRAISAL." COM USSR OP/RES BUDGET CONFER EFFICIENCY PRODUC MARXISM SOCISM...MGT 20. PAGE 43 F0847 — ECO/DEV INDUS PLAN WEALTH

S67
FRANKLIN N.N.,"THE CONCEPT AND MEASUREMENT OF 'MINIMUM LIVING STANDARDS'." UNIV OP/RES PAY INGP/REL DEMAND INCOME DRIVE WEALTH...SOC CHARTS METH/COMP. PAGE 43 F0849 — CONCPT PHIL/SCI ALL/VALS HAPPINESS

S67
KOTLER P.,"OPERATIONS RESEARCH IN MARKETING." USA+45 DIST/IND INDUS LG/CO CONSULT BUDGET TASK DEMAND EFFICIENCY PROFIT WEALTH DECISION. PAGE 73 F1429 — ECOMETRIC OP/RES MARKET PLAN

S67
MALKIN A.,"BUSINESS BOOKS OF 1966." INDUS LABOR OP/RES TEC/DEV CAP/ISM ECO/TAC INCOME WEALTH 20. PAGE 84 F1649 — BIBLIOG/A FINAN MARKET

S67
SKOLNICK J.H.,"SOCIAL CONTROL IN THE ADVERSARY SYSTEM." USA+45 CONSULT OP/RES ADMIN CONTROL. PAGE 123 F2419 — PROB/SOLV PERS/REL ADJUD CT/SYS

N67
US HOUSE COMM SCI ASTRONAUT,AUTHORIZING APPROPRIATIONS TO THE NATIONAL AERONAUTICS AND SPACE ADMINISTRATION (PAMPHLET). USA+45 NAT/G OP/RES TEC/DEV BUDGET NASA HOUSE/REP. PAGE 137 F2704 — SPACE R+D PHIL/SCI NUC/PWR

N67
US SENATE COMM ON FOREIGN REL,ARMS SALES AND FOREIGN POLICY (PAMPHLET). FINAN FOR/AID CONTROL 20. PAGE 139 F2737 — ARMS/CONT ADMIN OP/RES DIPLOM

B96
SCHMOLLER G.,THE MERCANTILE SYSTEM AND ITS HISTORICAL SIGNIFICANCE: ILLUSTRATED CHIEFLY FROM PRUSSIAN HISTORY (TRANS.). PRUSSIA CULTURE INDUS KIN NAT/G PROVS OP/RES ECO/TAC INT/TRADE SUPEGO PWR WEALTH MUNICH 19 MERCANTLST. PAGE 117 F2302 — GEN/METH INGP/REL CONCPT

OPA....OFFICE OF PRICE ADMINISTRATION

N19
KRIESBERG M.,CANCELLATION OF THE RATION STAMPS (PAMPHLET). USA+45 USA-45 MARKET PROB/SOLV PRICE GOV/REL RIGID/FLEX 20 OPA. PAGE 73 F1439 — RATION DECISION ADMIN NAT/G

OPEN/SPACE....OPEN SPACE - TOWN AND COUNTRY PLANNING

B64
FRIEDMANN J.,REGIONAL DEVELOPMENT AND PLANNING: A READER. AGRI MARKET NAT/G ECO/TAC INCOME...GEOG STAT CENSUS CHARTS ANTHOL BIBLIOG MUNICH 20 OPEN/SPACE. PAGE 44 F0863 — PLAN REGION INDUS ECO/DEV

OPERATIONAL RESEARCH AND RELATED MANAGEMENT SCIENCE.... SEE OR/MS

OPERATIONS RESEARCH....SEE OP/RES

OPINION TESTS AND POLLS....SEE KNO/TEST

OPINIONS....SEE ATTIT

OPLER M.E. F1993

OPTIMAL....OPTIMALITY

N19
BROWN W.M.,THE DESIGN AND PERFORMANCE OF "OPTIMUM" BLAST SHELTER PROGRAMS (PAMPHLET). USA+45 ACT/RES PLAN DEATH COST EFFICIENCY OPTIMAL...POLICY CHARTS 20. PAGE 19 F0375 — HABITAT NUC/PWR WAR HEALTH

B23
HOBSON J.A.,INCENTIVES IN THE NEW INDUSTRIAL ORDER. USA-45 NAT/G PAY COST EFFICIENCY PRODUC WEALTH ...MAJORIT PSY SOC/WK 20. PAGE 60 F1186 — INDUS LABOR INCOME OPTIMAL

B30
KEYNES J.M.,A TREATISE ON MONEY (2 VOLS.). UK USA-45 INDUS MARKET WORKER PRICE CONTROL COST OPTIMAL PROFIT WEALTH...POLICY 19/20 KEYNES/JM. PAGE 70 F1385 — EQUILIB ECO/TAC FINAN GEN/LAWS

B34
ROBINSON J.,THE ECONOMICS OF IMPERFECT COMPETITION. FINAN ECO/TAC PRICE COST DEMAND EQUILIB OPTIMAL WEALTH...METH MONOPOLY. PAGE 113 F2221 — MARKET WORKER INDUS

B38
LAWLEY F.E.,THE GROWTH OF COLLECTIVE ECONOMY VOL. 1: NATIONAL. EUR+WWI AGRI INDUS NAT/G BARGAIN CAP/ISM ECO/TAC WAR OPTIMAL WEALTH...GOV/COMP METH/COMP 19/20 MONOPOLY. PAGE 76 F1492
SOCISM PRICE CONTROL OWN

B38
LAWLEY F.E.,THE GROWTH OF COLLECTIVE ECONOMY VOL. 2: INTERNATIONAL. WOR-45 AGRI INDUS EQUILIB OPTIMAL OWN WEALTH...NAT/COMP 19/20 NAZI NEW/DEAL MONOPOLY. PAGE 76 F1493
ECO/TAC SOCISM NAT/LISM CONTROL

B40
TRIFFIN R.,MONOPOLISTIC COMPETITION AND GENERAL EQUILIBRIUM THEORY. DIST/IND PLAN TASK EQUILIB OPTIMAL...IDEA/COMP 20 MONOPOLY. PAGE 131 F2586
INT/TRADE INDUS COST

B41
HANSEN A.H.,FISCAL POLICY AND BUSINESS CYCLES. UK INDUS PROB/SOLV DIPLOM INT/TRADE OPTIMAL...POLICY TIME/SEQ CHARTS 19/20. PAGE 54 F1062
FINAN PLAN ECO/TAC GOV/REL

S41
MUKERJEE R.,"POPULATION THEORY AND POLITICS (BMR)" WOR-45 NAT/G PLAN PROB/SOLV ECO/TAC INT/TRADE CONTROL WAR PEACE...CENSUS 20 BIRTH/CON RESOURCE/N. PAGE 94 F1854
GEOG OPTIMAL CONCPT

B49
HANSEN A.H.,MONETARY THEORY AND FISCAL POLICY. CONSULT PLAN INT/TRADE BAL/PAY OPTIMAL...TREND CHARTS METH/COMP BIBLIOG T 19/20 MONEY. PAGE 54 F1063
FINAN GEN/LAWS POLICY ECO/TAC

B50
CHAMBERLIN E.,THE THEORY OF MONOPOLISTIC COMPETITION (1933). INDUS PAY GP/REL COST DEMAND EFFICIENCY OPTIMAL PRODUC WEALTH...GEN/LAWS 20. PAGE 23 F0443
MARKET PRICE ECO/TAC EQUILIB

C50
ELLSWORTH P.T.,"INTERNATIONAL ECONOMY." ECO/DEV ECO/UNDEV FINAN LABOR DIPLOM FOR/AID TARIFFS BAL/PAY EQUILIB NAT/LISM OPTIMAL...INT/LAW 20 ILO GATT. PAGE 37 F0724
BIBLIOG INT/TRADE ECO/TAC INT/ORG

B51
HART A.G.,DEFENSE WITHOUT INFLATION. AFR KOREA FINAN INDUS NAT/G WORKER DIPLOM RATION TAX PRICE COST OPTIMAL 20 RESOURCE/N. PAGE 56 F1098
ECO/TAC CONTROL WAR PLAN

B53
HARROD R.,THE DOLLAR. AFR USA+45 USA-45 ECO/DEV OPTIMAL WEALTH 18/20 FED/RESERV. PAGE 56 F1093
FINAN DIPLOM BAL/PAY

B53
ROBINSON E.A.G.,THE STRUCTURE OF COMPETITIVE INDUSTRY. UK ECO/DEV DIST/IND MARKET TEC/DEV DIPLOM EDU/PROP ADMIN EFFICIENCY WEALTH...MGT 19/20. PAGE 113 F2217
INDUS PRODUC WORKER OPTIMAL

B54
MITCHELL W.G.,BUSINESS CYCLES. FINAN MARKET PRICE COST EQUILIB OPTIMAL PRODUC PROFIT...IDEA/COMP GEN/LAWS 19/20. PAGE 92 F1809
INDUS TIME/SEQ METH/COMP STAT

B57
GOLD N.L.,REGIONAL ECONOMIC DEVELOPMENT AND NUCLEAR POWER IN INDIA. FUT INDIA FINAN FOR/AID INT/TRADE BAL/PAY EFFICIENCY OPTIMAL PRODUC WEALTH...PREDICT 20. PAGE 48 F0934
ECO/UNDEV TEC/DEV NUC/PWR INDUS

B58
DOWNIE J.,THE COMPETITIVE PROCESS. ECO/TAC PRICE EFFICIENCY OPTIMAL PRODUC WEALTH...IDEA/COMP METH/COMP 20 MONOPOLY. PAGE 34 F0658
EQUILIB MARKET INDUS ECO/DEV

B58
MUSGRAVE R.A.,CLASSICS IN THE THEORY OF PUBLIC FINANCE. UNIV MARKET LG/CO NAT/G CAP/ISM PRICE OPTIMAL...IDEA/COMP ANTHOL 19/20 SAY/EMIL EDGEWORTH LINDAHL/E RITSCHL/H. PAGE 95 F1870
TAX FINAN ECO/TAC GP/REL

L59
FURASH E.A.,"PROBLEMS IN REVIEW: INDUSTRIAL ESPIONAGE." WORKER ECO/TAC PERS/REL OPTIMAL AGE ATTIT KNOWL...MGT DEEP/INT DEEP/QU GP/COMP IDEA/COMP. PAGE 45 F0875
INDUS TOP/EX MAJORITY

C59
KURIHARA K.L.,"THE KEYNESIAN THEORY OF ECONOMIC DEVELOPMENT." WOR+45 WOR-45 PLAN OPTIMAL PRODUC ...CONCPT BIBLIOG 20. PAGE 74 F1451
ECO/DEV ECO/UNDEV OP/RES TEC/DEV

B60
BIERMAN H.,THE CAPITAL BUDGETING DECISION. AFR ECO/DEV MARKET TAX PRICE RISK COST INCOME TIME 20. PAGE 15 F0282
FINAN OPTIMAL BUDGET PROFIT

B60
DIA M.,REFLEXIONS SUR L'ECONOMIE DE L'AFRIQUE NOIRE (REV. ED.). CULTURE ECO/UNDEV CREATE TEC/DEV DIPLOM INT/TRADE OPTIMAL ATTIT...POLICY 20. PAGE 32 F0631
AFR ECO/TAC SOCISM PLAN

B61
CANTERBERY E.R.,THE PRESIDENT'S COUNCIL OF ECONOMIC ADVISERS. AFR USA+45 FINAN LABOR NAT/G PLAN ADMIN OPTIMAL WEALTH 20 EISNHWR/DD PRESIDENT TRUMAN/HS KEYNES/JM. PAGE 21 F0413
ECO/TAC OP/RES EXEC CHIEF

B61
MCCRACKEN H.L.,KEYNESIAN ECONOMICS IN THE STREAM OF ECONOMIC THOUGHT. FINAN MARKET BARGAIN EFFICIENCY OPTIMAL...PHIL/SCI CONCPT IDEA/COMP BIBLIOG 18/20 KEYNES/JM. PAGE 88 F1724
ECO/TAC DEMAND ECOMETRIC

L61
CHENERY H.B.,"COMPARATIVE ADVANTAGE AND DEVELOPMENT POLICY." FINAN INT/TRADE RATION OPTIMAL...CHARTS METH/COMP GEN/LAWS BIBLIOG 20 RESOURCE/N. PAGE 24 F0463
ECO/UNDEV ECO/TAC PLAN EFFICIENCY

B62
ALTMAN G.T.,INVISIBLE BARRIER: THE OPTIMUM GROWTH CURVE. USA+45 USA-45 ECO/DEV PLAN PAY CONTROL DEMAND OPTIMAL PRODUC WEALTH...STAT CHARTS 20. PAGE 4 F0080
INDUS FINAN ECO/TAC TAX

B62
BERNSTEIN P.L.,THE PRICE OF PROSPERITY. USA+45 TAX CONTROL OPTIMAL WEALTH...PREDICT 20. PAGE 14 F0269
ECO/DEV ECO/TAC NAT/G DEMAND

B62
CONGRES ECONOMISTES LANG FRAN,MONNAIE ET EXPANSION. AFR FRANCE PROB/SOLV BUDGET CENTRAL COST OPTIMAL PRODUC WEALTH 20. PAGE 27 F0524
FINAN PLAN EUR+WWI

B63
CLARK J.J.,BUSINESS FLUCTUATIONS, GROWTH, AND ECONOMIC STABILIZATION. USA+45 FINAN INT/TRADE OPTIMAL...METH/CNCPT ANTHOL BIBLIOG 20. PAGE 25 F0479
CAP/ISM ECO/TAC EQUILIB POLICY

B63
MINER J.,SOCIAL AND ECONOMIC FACTORS IN SPENDING FOR PUBLIC EDUCATION. USA+45 FINAN SCHOOL OPTIMAL ...POLICY DECISION REGRESS PREDICT CHARTS SIMUL 20. PAGE 92 F1801
EDU/PROP NAT/G COST ACT/RES

B63
RICARDO D.,THE PRINCIPLES OF POLITICAL ECONOMY AND TAXATION (1817). UK INDUS MARKET ECO/TAC INT/TRADE TARIFFS PRICE COST DEMAND OPTIMAL WEALTH...CONCPT 19 INTRVN/ECO. PAGE 111 F2183
GEN/LAWS TAX LAISSEZ

B63
WALINSKY L.J.,PLANNING AND EXECUTION OF ECONOMIC DEVELOPMENT. PROB/SOLV TEC/DEV BUDGET COST WEALTH ...CHARTS BIBLIOG 20. PAGE 142 F2802
PLAN ECO/UNDEV ECO/TAC OPTIMAL

B64
BAUCHET P.,ECONOMIC PLANNING. FRANCE STRATA LG/CO CAP/ISM ADMIN PARL/PROC DEMAND OPTIMAL ATTIT PWR SOCISM...POLICY CHARTS 20. PAGE 11 F0212
ECO/DEV NAT/G PLAN ECO/TAC

B64
COMMISSION ON MONEY AND CREDIT,INFLATION, GROWTH, AND EMPLOYMENT. AFR USA+45 PLAN PROB/SOLV PAY PRICE EFFICIENCY PRODUC WEALTH 20. PAGE 26 F0514
WORKER ECO/TAC OPTIMAL

B64
HANSEN A.H.,BUSINESS CYCLES AND NATIONAL INCOME. USA+45 FINAN ECO/TAC COST OPTIMAL...POLICY METH 20 KEYNES/JM. PAGE 54 F1065
INCOME WEALTH PRODUC INDUS

B64
HATHAWAY D.E.,PROBLEMS OF PROGRESS IN THE AGRICULTURAL ECONOMY. USA+45 USA-45 ECO/DEV NAT/G INT/TRADE PRICE DEMAND EFFICIENCY OPTIMAL 20. PAGE 57 F1112
AGRI ECO/TAC MARKET PLAN

B64
INTERNATIONAL LABOUR OFFICE,EMPLOYMENT AND ECONOMIC GROWTH. ECO/DEV ECO/UNDEV NAT/G PLAN DIPLOM INT/TRADE CONTROL INCOME PRODUC WEALTH...STAT NAT/COMP 20 ILO. PAGE 65 F1279
WORKER METH/COMP ECO/TAC OPTIMAL

B65
HARBISON F.,MANPOWER AND EDUCATION. AFR CHINA/COM IRAN L/A+17C S/ASIA TEC/DEV ADJUST OPTIMAL SKILL ...ANTHOL 20. PAGE 55 F1073
ECO/UNDEV EDU/PROP WORKER NAT/COMP

B65
KANTOROVICH L.V.,THE BEST USE OF ECONOMIC RESOURCES. USSR SOCIETY FINAN ACT/RES TEC/DEV ECO/TAC PRICE CONTROL COST DEMAND EFFICIENCY OPTIMAL...MGT STAT. PAGE 69 F1350
PLAN MATH DECISION

B65
KLASSEN L.H.,AREA ECONOMIC AND SOCIAL REDEVELOPMENT. ECO/UNDEV INDUS NAT/G PLAN CAP/ISM TAX...ECOMETRIC SIMUL 20. PAGE 72 F1404
OPTIMAL WORKER METH ECO/TAC

B65
MUSOLF L.D.,PROMOTING THE GENERAL WELFARE: GOVERNMENT AND THE ECONOMY. USA+45 ECO/DEV CAP/ISM DEMAND OPTIMAL 20. PAGE 95 F1874
ECO/TAC NAT/G EX/STRUC NEW/LIB

B65
RIGBY P.H.,CONCEPTUAL FOUNDATIONS OF BUSINESS RESEARCH. COMPUTER PROB/SOLV OPTIMAL...MGT CONCPT MATH STAT TESTS SIMUL GEN/METH. PAGE 111 F2192
PROFIT R+D INDUS DECISION

B65
WARNER A.W.,THE IMPACT OF SCIENCE ON TECHNOLOGY. UNIV INTELL SOCIETY NAT/G ACT/RES PLAN PROB/SOLV BUDGET OPTIMAL GEN/METH. PAGE 143 F2821
DECISION TEC/DEV CREATE POLICY

S65
GRENIEWSKI H.,"INTENTION AND PERFORMANCE: A PRIMER OF CYBERNETICS OF PLANNING." EFFICIENCY OPTIMAL KNOWL SKILL...DECISION MGT EQULIB. PAGE 51 F0995
SIMUL GAME GEN/METH PLAN

S65
JOHNSON H.G.,"A THEORETICAL MODEL OF ECONOMIC NATIONALISM IN NEW AND DEVELOPING STATES." ELITES INDUS INT/TRADE EDU/PROP COST OPTIMAL RATIONAL PWR WEALTH SOCISM STERTYP. PAGE 67 F1325
NAT/LISM ECO/UNDEV GEN/LAWS

B66
GITTINGER J.P.,THE LITERATURE OF AGRICULTURAL PLANNING. UNIV INT/ORG CONSULT WORKER TEC/DEV ECO/TAC OPTIMAL...POLICY METH/COMP BIBLIOG/A 20. PAGE 47 F0927
ECO/UNDEV AGRI PLAN WRITING

B66
LERNER E.M.,A THEORY OF FINANCIAL ANALYSIS. UNIV LG/CO COST DEMAND INCOME PROFIT...MATH STAT CHARTS SIMUL T 20. PAGE 78 F1531
CONCPT FINAN ECO/DEV OPTIMAL

B66
MANSFIELD E.,MANAGERIAL ECONOMICS AND OPERATIONS RESEARCH; A NONMATHEMATICAL INTRODUCTION. USA+45 ELITES ECO/DEV CONSULT EX/STRUC PROB/SOLV ROUTINE EFFICIENCY OPTIMAL...GAME T 20. PAGE 85 F1660
ECO/TAC OP/RES MGT COMPUTER

B66
TRIFFIN R.,THE WORLD MONEY MAZE. AFR INT/ORG ECO/TAC PRICE OPTIMAL WEALTH...METH/COMP 20 EEC OEEC SILVER. PAGE 131 F2589
BAL/PAY FINAN INT/TRADE DIPLOM

B67
HARDT J.P.,MATHEMATICS AND COMPUTERS IN SOVIET ECONOMIC PLANNING. COM USSR OP/RES PROB/SOLV OPTIMAL...MODAL SIMUL 20. PAGE 55 F1082
PLAN TEC/DEV MATH COMPUT/IR

B67
PORWIT K.,CENTRAL PLANNING: EVALUATION OF VARIANTS. PRICE OPTIMAL PRODUC...DECISION MATH CHARTS SIMUL BIBLIOG MODELS 20. PAGE 107 F2106
PLAN MGT ECOMETRIC

B67
RUEFF J.,BALANCE OF PAYMENTS: PROPOSALS FOR RESOLVING THE CRITICAL WORLD ECONOMIC PROBLEM OF OUR TIME. USA+45 INDUS FOR/AID REPAR DEMAND OPTIMAL ...ECOMETRIC CHARTS METH/COMP 20. PAGE 115 F2259
BAL/PAY INT/TRADE FINAN NEW/IDEA

S67
ALBAUM G.,"INFORMATION FLOW AND DECENTRALIZED DECISION MAKING IN MARKETING." EX/STRUC COMPUTER OP/RES PROB/SOLV EFFICIENCY OPTIMAL...METH/COMP ORG/CHARTS 20. PAGE 3 F0056
LG/CO ROUTINE KNOWL MARKET

S67
AVTORKHANOV A.,"A NEW AGRARIAN REVOLUTION." COM USSR ECO/DEV PLAN TEC/DEV ADMIN CONTROL OPTIMAL WEALTH SOCISM 20 KHRUSH/N STALIN/J. PAGE 8 F0144
AGRI METH/COMP MARXISM OWN

S67
MAJSTRENKO I.W.,"PROBLEMS CONFRONTING SOVIET AGRICULTURE." COM USSR ECO/DEV ECO/TAC EFFICIENCY OPTIMAL WEALTH MARXISM 20. PAGE 84 F1643
AGRI PROB/SOLV CENTRAL TEC/DEV

S67
PAULY M.V.,"MIXED PUBLIC AND PRIVATE FINANCING OF EDUCATION." STRATA PAY RECEIVE COST INCOME OPTIMAL METH/COMP. PAGE 104 F2039
SCHOOL PLAN TAX EFFICIENCY

S67
SIMONE A.J.,"SCIENTIFIC PUBLIC POLICY, MARKET PERFORMANCE, AND SIZE OF FIRM." GP/REL COST EFFICIENCY OPTIMAL PRODUC PWR. PAGE 122 F2410
LAW INDUS NAT/G PROB/SOLV

S67
WILES P.J.,"THE POLITICAL AND SOCIAL PREREQUISITES FOR A SOVIET-TYPE ECONOMY." COM USSR LAW CULTURE CREATE ADMIN FEEDBACK ROUTINE COST OPTIMAL TOTALISM MARXISM 20. PAGE 146 F2883
ECO/DEV PLAN EX/STRUC EFFICIENCY

N67
US CONGRESS JT COMM ECO GOVT,BACKGROUND MATERIAL ON ECONOMY IN GOVERNMENT 1967 (PAMPHLET). WOR+45 ECO/DEV BARGAIN PRICE DEMAND OPTIMAL...STAT DEPT/DEFEN. PAGE 135 F2665
BUDGET COST MGT NAT/G

B76
SMITH A.,THE WEALTH OF NATIONS. UK STRUCT WORKER DIPLOM ECO/TAC OPTIMAL DRIVE PERSON ORD/FREE ...OLD/LIB GEN/LAWS 17/18. PAGE 123 F2428
WEALTH PRODUC INDUS LAISSEZ

B98
MARSHALL A.,PRINCIPLES OF ECONOMICS. INDUS WORKER PRICE COST EQUILIB INCOME OPTIMAL PRODUC...TIME/SEQ METH RICARDO/D. PAGE 86 F1678
WEALTH GEN/LAWS MARKET

OR/MS....OPERATIONAL RESEARCH AND RELATED MANAGEMENT SCIENCE

ORANGE FREE STATE....SEE ORANGE/STA

ORANGE/STA....ORANGE FREE STATE

ORAZEM F. F1994

ORD H.W. F2485

ORD/FREE....SECURITY, ORDER, RESTRAINT, LIBERTY, FREEDOM

B08
LLOYD H.D.,THE SWISS DEMOCRACY. SWITZERLND INDUS NAT/G WORKER CHOOSE OWN ORD/FREE SOCISM...PLURIST 19/20 MONOPOLY. PAGE 81 F1590
NAT/COMP GOV/COMP REPRESENT POPULISM

B12
FOUAD M.,LE REGIME DE LA PRESSE EN EGYPTE: THESE POUR LE DOCTORAT. UAR LICENSE EDU/PROP ADMIN SANCTION CRIME SUPEGO PWR...ART/METH JURID 19/20. PAGE 43 F0832
ORD/FREE LEGIS CONTROL PRESS

B13
KROPOTKIN P.,THE CONQUEST OF BREAD. SOCIETY STRATA AGRI INDUS WORKER REV HAPPINESS INCOME PRODUC HEALTH MORAL ORD/FREE. PAGE 74 F1444
ANARCH SOCIALIST OWN AGREE

B19
SUMNER W.G.,WAR AND OTHER ESSAYS. USA-45 DELIB/GP DIPLOM TARIFFS COLONIAL PEACE SOVEREIGN 20. PAGE 127 F2514
INT/TRADE ORD/FREE CAP/ISM ECO/TAC

N19
FRANCK P.G.,AFGHANISTAN BETWEEN EAST AND WEST: THE ECONOMICS OF COMPETITIVE COEXISTENCE (PAMPHLET). AFGHANISTN USA+45 USA-45 USSR INDUS ECO/TAC INT/TRADE CONTROL NEUTRAL ORD/FREE MARXISM...GEOG 20 UN. PAGE 43 F0842
FOR/AID PLAN DIPLOM ECO/UNDEV

N19
FREEMAN H.A.,COERCION OF STATES IN FEDERAL UNIONS (PAMPHLET). WOR-45 DIPLOM CONTROL COERCE PEACE ORD/FREE...GOV/COMP METH/COMP NAT/COMP PACIFIST 20. PAGE 43 F0850
FEDERAL WAR INT/ORG PACIFISM

N19
HAYEK FA V.O.N.,FREEDOM AND THE ECONOMIC SYSTEM. GERMANY USSR PLAN REPRESENT TOTALISM FASCISM POPULISM...MAJORIT METH/COMP GEN/LAWS 20. PAGE 57 F1123
ORD/FREE ECO/TAC CAP/ISM SOCISM

N19
MCCONNELL G.,THE STEEL SEIZURE OF 1952 (PAMPHLET). USA+45 FINAN INDUS PROC/MFG LG/CO EX/STRUC ADJUD CONTROL GP/REL ORD/FREE PWR 20 TRUMAN/HS PRESIDENT CONGRESS. PAGE 88 F1721
DELIB/GP LABOR PROB/SOLV NAT/G

N19
SENGHOR L.S.,AFRICAN SOCIALISM (PAMPHLET). AFR FRANCE MALI USSR ELITES ECO/UNDEV NAT/G DIPLOM DOMIN EDU/PROP ATTIT 20 NEGRO. PAGE 119 F2355
SOCISM MARXISM ORD/FREE NAT/LISM

N19
VELYAMINOV G.,AFRICA AND THE COMMON MARKET (PAMPHLET). AFR MARKET VOL/ASSN ECO/TAC COLONIAL ORD/FREE...SOCIALIST 20 THIRD/WRLD. PAGE 141 F2775
INT/ORG INT/TRADE SOVEREIGN ECO/UNDEV

B20
COX H.,ECONOMIC LIBERTY. UNIV LAW INT/TRADE RATION TARIFFS RACE/REL SOCISM POLICY. PAGE 28 F0547
NAT/G ORD/FREE ECO/TAC PERSON

B20
MOREL E.D.,THE BLACK MAN'S BURDEN. AFR MOD/EUR AGRI EXTR/IND PROB/SOLV INT/TRADE ADMIN CONTROL COERCE DISCRIM...POLICY 19/20 NEGRO LEAGUE/NAT. PAGE 93 F1828
ORD/FREE CAP/ISM RACE/REL DOMIN

B20
TAWNEY R.H.,THE ACQUISITIVE SOCIETY. STRATA WORKER PROB/SOLV CAP/ISM ECO/TAC CONTROL GP/REL OWN PRIVIL ATTIT ORD/FREE WEALTH 20. PAGE 128 F2536
INDUS SOCIETY PRODUC MORAL

B27
BELLOC H.,THE SERVILE STATE (1912) (3RD ED.). PRUSSIA UK CULTURE STRATA INDUS NAT/G ECO/TAC CONTROL LEAD SUFF DISCRIM EQUILIB ORD/FREE WEALTH 20. PAGE 12 F0237
WORKER CAP/ISM DOMIN CATH

S32
DODD E.M. JR.,"FOR WHOM ARE CORPORATE MANAGERS TRUSTEES'." SERV/IND CAP/ISM GIVE LEAD REPRESENT ORD/FREE WEALTH. PAGE 33 F0648
LG/CO ROLE NAT/G PLAN

B34
GRAHAM F.D.,PROTECTIVE TARIFFS. FUT USA+45 WOR-45 INDUS MARKET VOL/ASSN PLAN CAP/ISM ECO/TAC PEACE ATTIT DRIVE HEALTH ORD/FREE...OBS TREND GEN/LAWS FOR/TRADE 20. PAGE 50 F0970
INT/ORG TARIFFS

B35
LASKI H.J.,THE STATE IN THEORY AND PRACTICE. ELITES ECO/TAC REPRESENT ORD/FREE PWR WEALTH POPULISM ...GOV/COMP GEN/LAWS 19/20. PAGE 76 F1483
CAP/ISM COERCE NAT/G FASCISM

B35
WADE J.,HISTORY OF THE MIDDLE AND WORKING CLASSES; WITH A POPULAR EXPOSITION OF THE ECONOMICAL AND POLITICAL PRINCIPLES.... FRANCE UK CONSTN FINAN INDUS LABOR INCOME PROFIT KNOWL MORAL ORD/FREE WEALTH...CHARTS 14/19. PAGE 142 F2797
WORKER STRATA CONCPT

S35
BONNETT C.E.,"THE EVOLUTION OF BUSINESS GROUPINGS." ECO/TAC EDU/PROP PRICE LOBBY ORD/FREE. PAGE 16 F0315
VOL/ASSN GP/REL PROB/SOLV

B36
BELLOC H.,THE RESTORATION OF PROPERTY. UK STRATA NAT/G PROF/ORG DELIB/GP WORKER CREATE PROB/SOLV ECO/TAC PARTIC UTOPIA ORD/FREE SOCISM 20. PAGE 13 F0238
CONTROL MAJORIT CAP/ISM OWN

B36
HUBERMAN L.,MAN'S WORLDLY GOODS: THE STORY OF THE WEALTH OF NATIONS. CHRIST-17C EUR+WWI MOD/EUR SOCIETY DOMIN REV ORD/FREE...TIME/SEQ METH/COMP. PAGE 63 F1231
WEALTH CAP/ISM MARXISM CREATE

B38
HEIMANN E.,COMMUNISM, FASCISM, OR DEMOCRACY? WOR-45 CONSTN SOCIETY STRATA AGRI CAP/ISM MORAL ORD/FREE ...MAJORIT METH/COMP NAT/COMP 19/20. PAGE 58 F1141
SOCISM MARXISM FASCISM PLURISM

B40
BATCHELOR B.,THE NEW OUTLOOK IN BUSINESS. LAW WORKER TAX LEAD ORD/FREE...POLICY TREND. PAGE 11 F0208
LG/CO GP/REL CAP/ISM LABOR

B40
HUNTER R.,REVOLUTION: WHY, HOW, WHEN? NAT/G ECO/TAC EDU/PROP COERCE ORD/FREE FASCISM POPULISM SOCISM 18/20 HITLER/A LENIN/VI. PAGE 63 F1246
REV METH/COMP LEAD CONSTN

B40
SPENCER H.,THE MAN VS. THE STATE (1892). UK POL/PAR LEGIS TARIFFS COERCE CRIME REPRESENT PWR SOCISM ...POLICY GEN/LAWS 19/20. PAGE 124 F2450
FASCISM POPULISM LAISSEZ ORD/FREE

B42
DRUCKER P.F.,THE FUTURE OF INDUSTRIAL MAN; A CONSERVATIVE APPROACH. USA-45 LOC/G PLAN WAR CENTRAL RATIONAL TOTALISM ORD/FREE LAISSEZ ...PLURIST IDEA/COMP 19/20 HITLER/A. PAGE 34 F0664
INDUS SOCIETY REGION PROB/SOLV

B42
JACKSON M.V.,EUROPEAN POWERS AND SOUTH-EAST AFRICA: A STUDY OF INTERNATIONAL RELATIONS ON SOUTH-EAST COAST OF AFRICA, 1796-1856. AFR FRANCE PORTUGAL SOUTH/AFR UK USA-45 FORCES INT/TRADE PWR...CHARTS BIBLIOG 18/19 TREATY. PAGE 66 F1294
DOMIN POLICY ORD/FREE DIPLOM

B44
FABIAN SOCIETY,CAN PLANNING BE DEMOCRATIC? UK CULTURE INDUS NAT/G BUDGET ORD/FREE...GEN/LAWS ANTHOL 20. PAGE 39 F0757
PLAN MAJORIT SOCIALIST ECO/DEV

B45
WOOTTON B.,FREEDOM UNDER PLANNING. UNIV ROUTINE ATTIT AUTHORIT DECISION. PAGE 148 F2926
PLAN ORD/FREE ECO/TAC CONTROL

B46
ERNST M.L.,THE FIRST FREEDOM. USA-45 CONSTN PRESS PRIVIL...CHARTS IDEA/COMP BIBLIOG 20 AMEND/I. PAGE 38 F0746
EDU/PROP COM/IND ORD/FREE CONTROL

B47
BALDWIN H.W.,THE PRICE OF POWER. USA+45 FORCES PLAN NUC/PWR ADJUST COST ORD/FREE...POLICY PSY BIBLIOG 20. PAGE 9 F0165
PROB/SOLV PWR POPULISM PRICE

B47
HEILPERIN M.A.,THE TRADE OF NATIONS. USA+45 USA-45 WOR+45 WOR-45 CULTURE ECO/DEV NAT/G DELIB/GP EDU/PROP ATTIT DISPL ORD/FREE PWR WEALTH TOT/POP 20. PAGE 58 F1139
MARKET INT/ORG INT/TRADE PEACE

B47
WHITEHEAD T.N.,LEADERSHIP IN A FREE SOCIETY; A STUDY IN HUMAN RELATIONS BASED ON AN ANALYSIS OF PRESENT-DAY INDUSTRIAL CIVILIZATION. WOR-45 STRUCT R+D LABOR LG/CO SML/CO WORKER PLAN PROB/SOLV TEC/DEV DRIVE...MGT 20. PAGE 146 F2872
INDUS LEAD ORD/FREE SOCIETY

B48
LAUTERBACH A.,ECONOMIC SECURITY AND INDIVIDUAL FREEDOM: CAN WE HAVE BOTH? COM EUR+WWI MOD/EUR UNIV WOR+45 CAP/ISM TOTALISM ALL/VALS...GOV/COMP BIBLIOG 20. PAGE 76 F1490
ORD/FREE ECO/DEV DECISION INGP/REL

B48
VON HAYEK F.A.,INDIVIDUALISM AND ECONOMIC ORDER. GERMANY USA-45 USSR FINAN MARKET INT/ORG ECO/TAC INT/TRADE PRICE REPRESENT ORD/FREE...PLURIST GEN/LAWS 20. PAGE 142 F2793
SOCISM CAP/ISM POPULISM FEDERAL

S48
CLEVELAND A.S.,"NAM: SPOKESMAN FOR INDUSTRY?" LEGIS PLAN LEAD LOBBY PARTIC CONSEN INCOME ATTIT ROLE ORD/FREE POLICY. PAGE 25 F0491
VOL/ASSN CLIENT REPRESENT

INDUS

B50
CLARK J.M.,ALTERNATIVE TO SERFDOM. SOCIETY STRATA INDUS MARKET WORKER PRICE GP/REL PROFIT BIO/SOC PWR WEALTH...GEN/LAWS 20 KEYNES/JM. PAGE 25 F0481
ORD/FREE POPULISM ECO/TAC REPRESENT

B50
LINCOLN G.,ECONOMICS OF NATIONAL SECURITY. USA+45 ELITES COM/IND DIST/IND INDUS NAT/G VOL/ASSN DELIB/GP EX/STRUC FOR/AID EDU/PROP COERCE NUC/PWR WAR ATTIT KNOWL ORD/FREE PWR TOT/POP VAL/FREE 20. PAGE 80 F1565
FORCES ECO/TAC AFR

B50
MARX H.L.,THE WELFARE STATE. USA+45 USA-45 CHIEF CAP/ISM CENTRAL ORD/FREE LAISSEZ...SOC ANTHOL 20. PAGE 86 F1686
ECO/DEV INDUS WEALTH WELF/ST

B50
ORTON W.A.,THE ECONOMIC ROLE OF THE STATE. INTELL ECO/UNDEV PLAN CONTROL PWR SOVEREIGN...POLICY 17/20. PAGE 102 F2000
ECO/DEV NAT/G ECO/TAC ORD/FREE

B50
SCHUMPETER J.A.,CAPITALISM, SOCIALISM, AND DEMOCRACY (3RD ED.). USA-45 USSR WOR+45 WOR-45 INTELL ECO/DEV ECO/UNDEV ECO/TAC WAR PRODUC ORD/FREE...MGT SOC 20 MARX/KARL. PAGE 118 F2321
SOCIALIST CAP/ISM MARXISM IDEA/COMP

B51
BROGAN D.W.,THE PRICE OF REVOLUTION. FRANCE USA+45 USA-45 USSR CONSTN NAT/G DIPLOM COLONIAL NAT/LISM ORD/FREE POPULISM...CONCPT 18/20 PRE/US/AM. PAGE 19 F0359
REV METH/COMP COST MARXISM

B51
HALEVY E.,IMPERIALISM AND THE RISE OF LABOR (2ND ED.). UK NAT/G POL/PAR TOP/EX ATTIT ORD/FREE PWR 19/20 PARLIAMENT LABOR/PAR. PAGE 53 F1042
COLONIAL LABOR POLICY WAR

B51
PETERSON F.,SURVEY OF LABOR ECONOMICS (REV. ED.). STRATA ECO/DEV LABOR INSPECT BARGAIN PAY PRICE EXEC ROUTINE GP/REL ALL/VALS ORD/FREE 20 AFL/CIO DEPT/LABOR. PAGE 105 F2069
WORKER DEMAND IDEA/COMP T

B51
PRINCETON U INDUSTRIAL REL SEC,COMPULSORY ARBITRATION OF UTILITY DISPUTES IN NEW JERSEY AND PENNSYLVANIA. USA+45 LEGIS WORKER ADJUD ORD/FREE ...POLICY MGT METH/COMP 20 NEW/JERSEY PENNSYLVAN. PAGE 108 F2118
BARGAIN PROVS INDUS LABOR

B51
ROEPKE W.,THE PROBLEM OF ECONOMIC ORDER. WOR+45 SOCIETY PROB/SOLV CONTROL EFFICIENCY...CON/ANAL IDEA/COMP GEN/METH 20. PAGE 113 F2231
ECO/TAC ORD/FREE MARKET PROC/MFG

B52
SACHS E.S.,THE CHOICE BEFORE SOUTH AFRICA. SOUTH/AFR AGRI EXTR/IND PROC/MFG PROB/SOLV ORD/FREE SOVEREIGN 20 NEGRO. PAGE 115 F2267
NAT/LISM DISCRIM RACE/REL LABOR

B52
TANNENBAUM F.,A PHILOSOPHY OF LABOR. SOCIETY STRATA INDUS LG/CO AGREE ADJUST OWN ORD/FREE PWR...CONCPT 20. PAGE 128 F2533
LABOR PHIL/SCI WORKER CREATE

S53
BERNSTEIN M.H.,"POLITICAL IDEAS OF SELECTED AMERICAN BUSINESS JOURNALS (BMR)" USA+45 GP/REL ATTIT RIGID/FLEX ROLE ORD/FREE POLICY. PAGE 14 F0267
IDEA/COMP NAT/G LEAD

S53
HANSER P.M.,"EXPLODING POPULATIONS: INTERNATIONAL AND REGIONAL ASPECTS." AFR S/ASIA ECO/TAC WEAPON BIO/SOC LOVE ORD/FREE...NEW/IDEA CENSUS TOT/POP 20. PAGE 55 F1069
ECO/UNDEV GEOG

B54
HOBBS E.H.,BEHIND THE PRESIDENT - A STUDY OF EXECUTIVE OFFICE AGENCIES. USA+45 NAT/G PLAN BUDGET ECO/TAC EXEC ORD/FREE 20 BUR/BUDGET. PAGE 60 F1183
EX/STRUC DELIB/GP CONFER CONSULT

B54
KARTUN D.,AFRICA, AFRICA: A CONTINENT RISES TO ITS FEET. AFR SOUTH/AFR UK ELITES AGRI LABOR LOC/G POL/PAR EDU/PROP CONTROL COERCE DISCRIM AGE/Y NEGRO THIRD/WRLD GOLD/COAST. PAGE 69 F1358
COLONIAL ORD/FREE PROFIT EXTR/IND

B54
TAFT P.,THE STRUCTURE AND GOVERNMENT OF LABOR UNIONS. SANCTION INGP/REL ORD/FREE PWR MARXISM ...MAJORIT STAT TREND. PAGE 128 F2524
LABOR ADJUD WORKER FINAN

S54
FORM W.H.,"THE PLACE OF SOCIAL STRUCTURE IN THE DETERMINATION OF LAND USE: SOME IMPLICATIONS FOR A THEORY OF URBAN ECOLOGY" (BMR)" STRUCT...GEOG PHIL/SCI SOC MUNICH 20. PAGE 42 F0827
HABITAT MARKET ORD/FREE

B55
BLOOM G.F.,ECONOMICS OF LABOR RELATIONS. USA+45 LAW CONSULT WORKER CAP/ISM PAY ADJUD CONTROL EFFICIENCY
ECO/DEV ECO/TAC

ORD/FREE...CHARTS 19/20 AFL/CIO NLRB DEPT/LABOR. PAGE 16 F0299
LABOR GOV/REL

B55
US OFFICE OF THE PRESIDENT,REPORT TO CONGRESS ON THE MUTUAL SECURITY PROGRAM FOR THE SIX MONTHS ENDED JUNE 30, 1955. ECO/DEV INT/ORG NAT/G CREATE TEC/DEV BAL/PWR ECO/TAC AGREE DETER COST ORD/FREE 20 DEPT/STATE DEPT/DEFEN. PAGE 138 F2722
DIPLOM FORCES PLAN FOR/AID

B55
UYEHARA C.H.,COMPARATIVE PLATFORMS OF JAPAN'S MAJOR PARTIES... USA+45 AGRI LEGIS WORKER CAP/ISM ORD/FREE MARXISM SOCISM...IDEA/COMP 20 CHINJAP. PAGE 140 F2755
POLICY POL/PAR DIPLOM NAT/G

S55
DIESING P.,"NONECONOMIC DECISION-MAKING" (BMR)" PROB/SOLV GP/REL ORD/FREE...STAT METH/COMP SIMUL 20. PAGE 33 F0638
DECISION METH EFFICIENCY SOC

S55
HALLETT D.,"THE HISTORY AND STRUCTURE OF OEEC." EUR+WWI USA+45 CONSTN INDUS INT/ORG NAT/G DELIB/GP ACT/RES PLAN ORD/FREE WEALTH...CONCPT OEEC 20 CMN/WLTH. PAGE 54 F1051
VOL/ASSN ECO/DEV

B56
BROWN R.E.,CHARLES BEARD AND THE CONSTITUTION. USA-45 NAT/G ORD/FREE WEALTH...HUM TIME/SEQ METH/COMP 20 BEARD/CA. PAGE 19 F0372
CONSTN ELITES HIST/WRIT

B56
FIELD G.C.,POLITICAL THEORY. POL/PAR REPRESENT MORAL SOVEREIGN...JURID IDEA/COMP. PAGE 40 F0789
CONCPT NAT/G ORD/FREE DIPLOM

B56
POOLE K.E.,PUBLIC FINANCE AND ECONOMIC WELFARE. STRUCT ECO/DEV LOC/G NAT/G BUDGET PAY ROUTINE COST EQUILIB WEALTH...SOC/WK METH/COMP 20. PAGE 107 F2103
FINAN TAX ORD/FREE

B56
US OFFICE OF THE PRESIDENT,REPORT TO CONGRESS ON THE MUTUAL SECURITY PROGRAM FOR THE SIX MONTHS ENDED DECEMBER 31, 1955. ASIA USSR ECO/DEV ECO/UNDEV INT/ORG CREATE TEC/DEV BAL/PWR ECO/TAC AGREE DETER COST ORD/FREE 20 DEPT/STATE DEPT/DEFEN EISNHWR/DD. PAGE 138 F2723
DIPLOM FORCES PLAN FOR/AID

B56
WOLFF R.L.,THE BALKANS IN OUR TIME. ALBANIA FUT MOD/EUR USSR YUGOSLAVIA CULTURE INT/ORG SECT DIPLOM EDU/PROP COERCE WAR ORD/FREE...CHARTS 4/20 BALKANS COMINFORM. PAGE 148 F2919
GEOG COM

B57
ARON R.,L'UNIFICATION ECONOMIQUE DE L'EUROPE. EUR+WWI SWITZERLND UK INT/ORG NAT/G REGION NAT/LISM ORD/FREE PWR...CONCPT METH/CNCPT OBS TREND STERTYP GEN/LAWS EEC FOR/TRADE 20. PAGE 6 F0118
VOL/ASSN ECO/TAC

B57
CLARK J.M.,ECONOMIC INSTITUTIONS AND HUMAN WELFARE. USA+45 SOCIETY ECO/DEV NAT/G WORKER PLAN PROB/SOLV CAP/ISM CONTROL...POLICY 20. PAGE 25 F0482
ECO/TAC ORD/FREE WEALTH

B57
COMMITTEE ECONOMIC DEVELOPMENT,ECONOMIC DEVELOPMENT ASSISTANCE. USA+45 WOR+45 AGRI CONFER ORD/FREE ...MGT CHARTS 20. PAGE 27 F0515
FOR/AID ECO/UNDEV FINAN PLAN

B57
LAVES W.H.C.,UNESCO. FUT WOR+45 NAT/G CONSULT DELIB/GP TEC/DEV ECO/TAC EDU/PROP PEACE ORD/FREE ...CONCPT TIME/SEQ TREND UNESCO VAL/FREE 20. PAGE 76 F1491
INT/ORG KNOWL

B57
WATSON G.,THE UNSERVILE STATE: ESSAYS IN LIBERTY AND WELFARE. UK LEGIS RECEIVE EDU/PROP COLONIAL ...WELF/ST 20 LIB/PARTY. PAGE 144 F2833
POL/PAR ORD/FREE CONTROL NEW/LIB

S57
DUBIN R.,"POWER AND UNION-MANAGEMENT RELATIONS." PROB/SOLV ADJUD ROUTINE ATTIT ORD/FREE...MGT STERTYP. PAGE 34 F0668
PWR LABOR BARGAIN GP/REL

S57
HOAG M.W.,"ECONOMIC PROBLEMS OF ALLIANCE." AFR COM EUR+WWI WOR+45 ECO/DEV ECO/UNDEV NAT/G VOL/ASSN FORCES PLAN TEC/DEV DIPLOM COERCE ORD/FREE PWR WEALTH...DECISION GEN/LAWS NATO TERR/GP. PAGE 60 F1182
INT/ORG ECO/TAC

B58
HAMEROW T.S.,RESTORATION, REVOLUTION, REACTION: ECONOMICS AND POLITICS IN GERMANY, 1815-1871. CAP/ISM ADJUST ATTIT PWR...BIBLIOG/A 19 GER/CONFED FRANK/PARL. PAGE 54 F1055
REV ORD/FREE ECO/DEV

B58
KINDLEBERGER C.P.,INTERNATIONAL ECONOMICS. WOR+45 WOR-45 ECO/DEV ECO/UNDEV FINAN VOL/ASSN ACT/RES DIPLOM ECO/TAC LEGIT REGION ATTIT DRIVE ORD/FREE WEALTH...POLICY STAT TREND GEN/LAWS EEC ECSC OEEC 20. PAGE 71 F1391
INT/ORG BAL/PWR TARIFFS

B58
MOSKOWITZ M.,HUMAN RIGHTS AND WORLD ORDER. INT/ORG PLAN GP/REL NAT/LISM SOVEREIGN...CONCPT 20 UN TREATY CIV/RIGHTS. PAGE 94 F1845
DIPLOM INT/LAW ORD/FREE

B58
PALMER E.E.,INDUSTRIAL MAN. USA+45 PERSON ORD/FREE POPULISM...PREDICT TREND ANTHOL 20. PAGE 103 F2020
INDUS ECO/UNDEV CULTURE WEALTH

B58
PALMER E.E.,THE ECONOMY AND THE DEMOCRATIC IDEAL. USA+45 USA-45 STRATA CHIEF CT/SYS ORD/FREE SOCISM ...MAJORIT CONCPT ANTHOL 18/20 PRESIDENT. PAGE 103 F2021
ECO/DEV POPULISM METH/COMP ECO/TAC

S58
ELKIN A.B.,"OEEC-ITS STRUCTURE AND POWERS." EUR+WWI CONSTN INDUS INT/ORG NAT/G VOL/ASSN DELIB/GP ACT/RES PLAN ORD/FREE WEALTH...CHARTS ORG/CHARTS OEEC 20. PAGE 37 F0719
ECO/DEV EX/STRUC

S58
LANE F.C.,"ECONOMIC CONSEQUENCES OF ORGANIZED VIOLENCE." FUT WOR+45 WOR-45 ECO/DEV DIST/IND SERV/IND NAT/G PROVS EX/STRUC CHOOSE ORD/FREE PWR ...TIME/SEQ GEN/LAWS MUNICH 20. PAGE 75 F1472
WEALTH COERCE

B59
ARON R.,IMPERIALISM AND COLONIALISM (PAMPHLET). WOR+45 WOR-45 ECO/TAC CONTROL REV ORD/FREE 19/20. PAGE 6 F0119
COLONIAL DOMIN ECO/UNDEV DIPLOM

B59
BARBASH J.,UNIONS AND UNION LEADERSHIP. NAT/G WORKER TEC/DEV ECO/TAC PARTIC GP/REL RACE/REL ORD/FREE CLASSIF. PAGE 10 F0183
LABOR VOL/ASSN CAP/ISM LEAD

B59
DIEBOLD W. JR.,THE SCHUMAN PLAN: A STUDY IN ECONOMIC COOPERATION, 1950-1959. EUR+WWI FRANCE GERMANY USA+45 EXTR/IND CONSULT DELIB/GP PLAN DIPLOM ECO/TAC INT/TRADE ROUTINE ORD/FREE WEALTH ...METH/CNCPT STAT CONT/OBS INT TIME/SEQ ECSC 20. PAGE 33 F0635
INT/ORG REGION

B59
FERRY W.H.,THE CORPORATION AND THE ECONOMY. CLIENT LAW CONSTN LABOR NAT/G PLAN INT/TRADE PARTIC CONSEN ORD/FREE PWR POLICY. PAGE 40 F0787
LG/CO CONTROL REPRESENT

B59
HICKS J.R.,ESSAYS IN WORLD ECONOMICS. AFR CEYLON NIGERIA WOR+45 SOCIETY ECO/DEV ORD/FREE WEALTH ...GEN/LAWS TOT/POP 20. PAGE 59 F1166
ECO/UNDEV ECO/TAC UK

B59
HOOVER C.B.,THE ECONOMY, LIBERTY AND THE STATE. COM EUR+WWI USA+45 USA-45 USSR CAP/ISM EDU/PROP COERCE TOTALISM ORD/FREE...POLICY OBS INT TREND NAZI 20. PAGE 61 F1206
ECO/DEV ECO/TAC

B59
LI CHOH-MING,ECONOMIC DEVELOPMENT OF COMMUNIST CHINA. ASIA CHINA/COM AGRI FINAN TAX INCOME MARXISM ...MGT 20. PAGE 80 F1557
ECO/UNDEV INDUS ORD/FREE TEC/DEV

B59
ROPKE W.,INTERNATIONAL ORDER AND ECONOMIC INTEGRATION. ECO/DEV ECO/UNDEV AGRI FINAN INDUS INT/ORG WAR PEACE ORD/FREE...SOC METH/COMP 20 EEC. PAGE 114 F2238
INT/TRADE DIPLOM BAL/PAY ALL/IDEOS

B59
VINCENT W.S.,ROLES OF THE CITIZENS: PRINCIPLES AND PRACTICES. LOC/G POL/PAR VOL/ASSN CHOOSE ROLE ORD/FREE PWR...POLICY 20. PAGE 141 F2785
INGP/REL EDU/PROP CREATE LOBBY

B59
WORTHY J.C.,BIG BUSINESS AND FREE MEN. LG/CO EX/STRUC EDU/PROP LEAD CHOOSE GP/REL ATTIT DRIVE ROLE ORD/FREE...MAJORIT 20. PAGE 149 F2927
ELITES LOC/G TOP/EX PARTIC

L59
BEGUIN B.,"ILO AND THE TRIPARTITE SYSTEM." EUR+WWI WOR+45 WOR-45 CONSTN ECO/DEV ECO/UNDEV INDUS INT/ORG NAT/G VOL/ASSN DELIB/GP PLAN TEC/DEV LEGIT ORD/FREE WEALTH...CONCPT TIME/SEQ WORK ILO 20. PAGE 12 F0228
LABOR

S59
REUBENS E.D.,"THE BASIS FOR REORIENATION OF AMERICAN FOREIGN AID POLICY." USA+45 USSR STRUCT INT/ORG CONSULT ECO/TAC ADMIN DRIVE MORAL ORD/FREE PWR WEALTH...RELATIV MATH STAT TREND GEN/LAWS VAL/FREE 20. PAGE 111 F2180
ECO/UNDEV PLAN FOR/AID DIPLOM

S59
STREETEN P.,"UNBALANCED GROWTH" UK ECO/DEV AGRI MARKET TEC/DEV CAP/ISM ECO/TAC FOR/AID INT/TRADE DEMAND ORD/FREE...CONCPT 20. PAGE 127 F2502
IDEA/COMP FINAN PRODUC EQUILIB

S59
TIPTON J.B.,"PARTICIPATION OF THE UNITED STATES IN THE INTERNATIONAL LABOR ORGANIZATION." USA+45 LAW STRUCT ECO/DEV ECO/UNDEV INDUS TEC/DEV ECO/TAC ADMIN PERCEPT ORD/FREE SKILL...STAT HIST/WRIT
LABOR INT/ORG

GEN/METH ILO WORK 20. PAGE 131 F2577

B60
BOHM F.,REDEN UND SCHRIFTEN UBER DIE ORDNUNG EINER FREIEN GESELLSCHAFT, EINER FREIEN WIRTSCHAFT, UND UBER DIE WIEDERGUTMACH. DIPLOM CRIME ORD/FREE RESPECT FASCISM 20 NAZI. PAGE 16 F0307 ECO/TAC NEW/LIB SUPEGO REPAR

B60
FERNANDES F.,MUDANCAS SOCIAIS NO BRASIL. BRAZIL L/A+17C SOCIETY AGRI PROVS LEAD GP/REL RACE/REL ORD/FREE...SOC SOC/INTEG 20 SAO/PAULO. PAGE 40 F0786 ECO/UNDEV STRATA INDUS

B60
GRAMPP W.D.,THE MANCHESTER SCHOOL OF ECONOMICS. UK LAW ECO/DEV COERCE ATTIT ORD/FREE LAISSEZ ...PHIL/SCI IDEA/COMP 19/20 MANCHESTER CORN/LAWS. PAGE 50 F0973 ECO/TAC VOL/ASSN LOBBY NAT/G

B60
LATIFI D.,INDIA AND UNITED STATES AID. ASIA INDIA UK USA+45 AGRI FINAN INDUS COLONIAL ORD/FREE SOVEREIGN WEALTH...METH/COMP 20. PAGE 76 F1486 FOR/AID DIPLOM ECO/UNDEV

B60
LISTER L.,EUROPE'S COAL AND STEEL COMMUNITY. FRANCE GERMANY STRUCT ECO/DEV EXTR/IND INDUS MARKET NAT/G DELIB/GP ECO/TAC INT/TRADE EDU/PROP ATTIT RIGID/FLEX ORD/FREE PWR WEALTH...CONCPT STAT TIME/SEQ CHARTS ECSC TERR/GP 20. PAGE 81 F1582 EUR+WWI INT/ORG REGION

B60
MENDELSON W.,CAPITALISM, DEMOCRACY, AND THE SUPREME COURT. USA+45 USA-45 CONSTN DIPLOM GOV/REL ATTIT ORD/FREE LAISSEZ...POLICY CHARTS PERS/COMP 18/20 SUPREME/CT MARSHALL/J HOLMES/OW TANEY/RB FIELD/JJ. PAGE 90 F1758 JUDGE CT/SYS JURID NAT/G

B60
MOORE W.E.,LABOR COMMITMENT AND SOCIAL CHANGE IN DEVELOPING AREAS. SOCIETY STRATA ECO/UNDEV MARKET VOL/ASSN WORKER AUTHORIT SKILL...MGT NAT/COMP SOC/INTEG 20. PAGE 93 F1823 LABOR ORD/FREE ATTIT INDUS

B60
PETERSON W.C.,THE WELFARE STATE IN FRANCE. EUR+WWI FRANCE FUT STRATA PROB/SOLV TAX GIVE RECEIVE INCOME ORD/FREE PWR...CHARTS 20. PAGE 105 F2070 NEW/LIB ECO/TAC WEALTH NAT/G

B60
ROBERTSON D.,THE CONTROL OF INDUSTRY. UK MARKET LABOR WORKER PRICE CONTROL GP/REL COST DEMAND ORD/FREE WEALTH NEW/LIB SOCISM 20. PAGE 112 F2211 INDUS FINAN NAT/G ECO/DEV

B60
ROPKE W.,A HUMANE ECONOMY. CULTURE ECO/DEV FINAN INDUS GP/REL CENTRAL WEALTH...GEOG SOC IDEA/COMP 20 EEC. PAGE 114 F2239 ECO/TAC INT/ORG DIPLOM ORD/FREE

B60
SERAPHIM H.J.,ZUR GRUNDLEGUNG WIRTSCHAFTSPOLITISCHER KONZEPTIONEN (SCHRIFTEN DES VEREINS FUR SOZIALPOLITIK, N.F. BAND 18). GERMANY/W WOR+45 ECO/DEV DELIB/GP ACT/RES ECO/TAC INGP/REL ORD/FREE...CONCPT IDEA/COMP GEN/LAWS 20. PAGE 120 F2358 POLICY PHIL/SCI PLAN

B60
STEVENSON A.E.,PUTTING FIRST THINGS FIRST. USA+45 INT/ORG NEIGH FOR/AID DISCRIM...ANTHOL 20. PAGE 126 F2483 DIPLOM ECO/UNDEV ORD/FREE EDU/PROP

B60
THEOBALD R.,THE RICH AND THE POOR: A STUDY OF THE ECONOMICS OF RISING EXPECTATIONS. WOR+45 CONSTN ECO/DEV ECO/UNDEV INT/ORG NAT/G PLAN FOR/AID ROUTINE BAL/PAY ORD/FREE PWR WEALTH...GEOG TREND WORK FOR/TRADE 20. PAGE 129 F2553 ECO/TAC INT/TRADE

B60
WALLICH H.C.,THE COST OF FREEDOM: A NEW LOOK AT CAPITALISM. USA+45 SOCIETY ECO/DEV INGP/REL CONSEN LAISSEZ SOCISM...OLD/LIB IDEA/COMP. PAGE 143 F2810 CAP/ISM ORD/FREE POLICY ECO/TAC

B60
WENTHOLT W.,INFLATION OR SECURITY? EUR+WWI USA+45 INDUS CONSULT TEC/DEV CAP/ISM DIPLOM FOR/AID INT/TRADE MARXISM 20 EEC. PAGE 145 F2858 ECO/DEV ECO/TAC FINAN ORD/FREE

B60
WODDIS J.,AFRICA: THE ROOTS OF REVOLT. SOUTH/AFR WORKER INT/TRADE RACE/REL DISCRIM ORD/FREE 20. PAGE 148 F2915 COLONIAL SOVEREIGN WAR ECO/UNDEV

L60
SPENGLER J.J.,"ECONOMIC DEVELOPMENT: POLITICAL PRECONDITIONS AND POLITICAL CONSEQUENCE." WOR+45 STRUCT ECO/UNDEV NAT/G PLAN ECO/TAC EDU/PROP ATTIT ORD/FREE WEALTH SOCISM...SOC CONCPT TREND SIMUL GEN/METH WORK 20. PAGE 124 F2452 TEC/DEV METH/CNCPT CAP/ISM

S60
HERZ J.H.,"EAST GERMANY: PROGRESS AND PROSPECTS." COM AGRI FINAN INDUS LOC/G NAT/G FORCES PLAN TEC/DEV DOMIN ADMIN COERCE DRIVE PERCEPT RIGID/FLEX MORAL ORD/FREE PWR...MARXIST PSY SOC RECORD STERTYP WORK. PAGE 59 F1158 POL/PAR STRUCT GERMANY

S60
MAIR L.P.,"SOCIAL CHANGE IN SOUTH AFRICA." MOD/EUR SOUTH/AFR WOR+45 ECO/UNDEV EX/STRUC TEC/DEV ATTIT DRIVE PERCEPT ORD/FREE...MGT CONCPT TIME/SEQ IND 20. PAGE 84 F1641 AFR NAT/G REV SOVEREIGN

S60
OWEN C.F.,"US AND SOVIET RELATIONS WITH UNDERDEVELOPED COUNTRIES: LATIN AMERICA-A CASE STUDY." AFR COM L/A+17C USA+45 USSR EXTR/IND MARKET TEC/DEV DIPLOM ECO/TAC NAT/LISM ORD/FREE PWR ...TREND WORK 20. PAGE 102 F2005 ECO/UNDEV DRIVE INT/TRADE

B61
BONNEFOUS M.,EUROPE ET TIERS MONDE. EUR+WWI SOCIETY INT/ORG NAT/G VOL/ASSN ACT/RES TEC/DEV CAP/ISM ECO/TAC ATTIT ORD/FREE SOVEREIGN...POLICY CONCPT TREND TERR/GP COMMUN 20. PAGE 16 F0314 AFR ECO/UNDEV FOR/AID INT/TRADE

B61
BRAIBANTI R.,TRADITION, VALUES AND SOCIO-ECONOMIC DEVELOPMENT. WOR+45 ACT/RES TEC/DEV ATTIT ORD/FREE CONSERVE...POLICY SOC ANTHOL. PAGE 17 F0336 ALL/VALS ECO/UNDEV CONCPT METH/CNCPT

B61
CAMPAIGNE J.G.,CHECK-OFF: LABOR BOSSES AND WORKING MEN. LEGIS WORKER EDU/PROP DEBATE COERCE REPRESENT GP/REL ORD/FREE CONSERVE. PAGE 21 F0404 LABOR ELITES PWR CONTROL

B61
ERASMUS C.J.,MAN TAKES CONTROL: CULTURAL DEVELOPMENT AND AMERICAN AID. STRUCT OWN DRIVE PERCEPT...SOC 20 MEXIC/AMER. PAGE 38 F0741 ORD/FREE CULTURE ECO/UNDEV TEC/DEV

B61
ESTEVEZ A.,ASPECTOS ECONOMICO-FINANCIEROS DE LA CAMPANA SANMARITANA. L/A+17C SPAIN FINAN COLONIAL LEAD ROLE ORD/FREE WEALTH 19 SOUTH/AMER SAN/MARTIN. PAGE 38 F0748 ECO/UNDEV REV BUDGET NAT/G

B61
FERTIG L.,PROSPERITY THROUGH FREEDOM. COM INDUS LABOR CAP/ISM ECO/TAC PRODUC PROFIT ORD/FREE WEALTH SOCISM...METH/CNCPT 20. PAGE 40 F0788 NAT/G CONTROL POLICY

B61
HEMPSTONE S.,THE NEW AFRICA. AGRI INDUS KIN NAT/G COLONIAL MARXISM...SOC INT TREND NAT/COMP BIBLIOG/A 20. PAGE 58 F1146 AFR ORD/FREE PERSON CULTURE

B61
MARX K.,THE COMMUNIST MANIFESTO. IN (MENDEL A. ESSENTIAL WORKS OF MARXISM, NEW YORK: BANTAM. FUT MOD/EUR CULTURE ECO/DEV ECO/UNDEV AGRI FINAN INDUS MARKET PROC/MFG LABOR POL/PAR CONSULT FORCES CREATE PLAN ADMIN ATTIT DRIVE RIGID/FLEX ORD/FREE PWR RESPECT MARX/KARL MUNICH WORK. PAGE 86 F1691 COM NEW/IDEA CAP/ISM REV

B61
PERKINS D.,THE UNITED STATES AND LATIN AMERICAN. L/A+17C USA+45 USA-45 STRUCT COLONIAL REV ORD/FREE 19/20. PAGE 105 F2061 DIPLOM INT/TRADE NAT/G

B61
SCHNAPPER B.,LA POLITIQUE ET LE COMMERCE FRANCAIS DANS LE GOLFE DE GUINEE DE 1838 A 1871. FRANCE GUINEA UK SEA EXTR/IND NAT/G DELIB/GP LEGIS ADMIN ORD/FREE...POLICY GEOG CENSUS CHARTS BIBLIOG 19. PAGE 117 F2303 COLONIAL INT/TRADE DOMIN AFR

B61
SEPULVEDA C.,A STATEMENT OF THE LAWS OF MEXICO IN MATTERS AFFECTING BUSINESS (3RD ED.). AGRI DIST/IND EXTR/IND FINAN INDUS WORKER TAX MARRIAGE OWN ORD/FREE...BIBLIOG 20 MEXIC/AMER TREATY MIGRATION MONOPOLY. PAGE 119 F2356 CONSTN NAT/G JURID LEGIS

B61
US SENATE COMM ON FOREIGN RELS,INTERNATIONAL DEVELOPMENT AND SECURITY: HEARINGS ON BILL (2 VOLS.). ECO/UNDEV FINAN FORCES REV COST WEALTH ...CHARTS 20 AID PRESIDENT. PAGE 139 F2747 FOR/AID CIVMIL/REL ORD/FREE ECO/TAC

S61
DICKS-MIREAUX L.A.,"THE INTERRELATIONSHIP BETWEEN COST AND PRICE CHANGES 19461959: A STUDY OF INFLATION IN POST-WAR BRITAIN" AFR UK ECO/DEV INDUS WORKER ECO/TAC ORD/FREE WEALTH...ECOMETRIC REGRESS STAT TREND CHARTS 20. PAGE 33 F0634 PRICE PAY DEMAND

S61
NEAL A.C.,"NEW ECONOMIC POLICIES FOR THE WEST." COM EUR+WWI FUT USA+45 WOR+45 ECO/DEV ECO/UNDEV INDUS MARKET ROUTINE HEALTH ORD/FREE PWR...OLD/LIB METH/CNCPT 20. PAGE 97 F1904 PLAN ECO/TAC

B62
DE LAVALLE H.,A STATEMENT OF THE LAWS OF PERU IN MATTERS AFFECTING BUSINESS (3RD ED.). PERU WORKER INT/TRADE INCOME ORD/FREE...INT/LAW 20. PAGE 31 F0603 CONSTN JURID FINAN TAX

B62
ELLIOTT J.R.,THE APPEAL OF COMMUNISM IN THE UNDERDEVELOPED NATIONS. AFR USSR WOR+45 INT/ORG NAT/G DIPLOM DOMIN EDU/PROP ROUTINE ATTIT RIGID/FLEX ORD/FREE PWR WEALTH MARXISM...POLICY SOC METH/CNCPT MYTH TOT/POP METH/GP 20. PAGE 37 F0722 COM ECO/UNDEV

B62
FRIEDMAN M.,CAPITALISM AND FREEDOM. USA+45 FINAN LG/CO WORKER INT/TRADE RECEIVE EDU/PROP CONTROL DISCRIM INCOME WEALTH POLICY. PAGE 44 F0859
CAP/ISM ORD/FREE NAT/G ECO/DEV

B62
GWYN W.B.,DEMOCRACY AND THE COST OF POLITICS IN BRITAIN. UK BUDGET CRIME CHOOSE ORD/FREE WEALTH ...TIME/SEQ 18/20. PAGE 52 F1017
COST POL/PAR POPULISM PAY

B62
HIRSCHFIELD R.S.,THE CONSTITUTION AND THE COURT. AFR SCHOOL WAR RACE/REL EQUILIB ORD/FREE...POLICY MAJORIT DECISION JURID 18/20 PRESIDENT CIVIL/LIB SUPREME/CT CONGRESS. PAGE 60 F1175
ADJUD PWR CONSTN LAW

B62
INTERNAT CONGRESS OF JURISTS,EXECUTIVE ACTION AND THE RULE OF RULE: REPORTION PROCEEDINGS OF INT'T CONGRESS OF JURISTS,-RIO DE JANEIRO, BRAZIL. WOR+45 ACADEM CONSULT JUDGE EDU/PROP ADJUD CT/SYS INGP/REL PERSON DEPT/DEFEN. PAGE 64 F1269
JURID EXEC ORD/FREE CONTROL

B62
JORDAN A.A. JR.,FOREIGN AID AND THE DEFENSE OF SOUTHEAST ASIA. PAKISTAN VIETNAM/S FINAN PLAN BUDGET ECO/TAC DETER WAR ORD/FREE...POLICY DECISION CENSUS CHARTS BIBLIOG 20. PAGE 68 F1341
FOR/AID S/ASIA FORCES ECO/UNDEV

B62
KENT R.K.,FROM MADAGASCAR TO THE MALAGASY REPUBLIC. FRANCE MADAGASCAR DIPLOM NAT/LISM ORD/FREE...MGT 18/20. PAGE 70 F1379
COLONIAL SOVEREIGN REV POL/PAR

B62
LEVY H.V.,LIBERDADE E JUSTICA SOCIAL (2ND ED.). BRAZIL COM L/A+17C USSR INT/ORG PARTIC GP/REL WEALTH 20 UN COM/PARTY. PAGE 79 F1544
ORD/FREE MARXISM CAP/ISM LAW

B62
UNIVERSITY OF TENNESSEE,GOVERNMENT AND WORLD CRISIS. USA+45 FOR/AID ORD/FREE...ANTHOL 20 UN ALL/PROG. PAGE 133 F2622
ECO/DEV DIPLOM NAT/G INT/ORG

L62
MACHLUP F.,"PLANS FOR REFORM OF THE INTERNATIONAL MONETARY SYSTEM. PRINCETON: U. PR., 1962, 70 PP., $0.25." WOR+45 INT/ORG ECO/TAC BAL/PAY HEALTH ORD/FREE WEALTH MID/EX TERR/GP VAL/FREE APPLIC 20. PAGE 83 F1631
ECO/DEV STAT

S62
MORGENTHAU H.J.,"A POLITICAL THEORY OF FOREIGN AID." ECO/UNDEV NAT/G DELIB/GP PLAN ECO/TAC EDU/PROP EXEC ORD/FREE RESPECT WEALTH...METH/CNCPT TREND 20. PAGE 93 F1833
USA+45 PHIL/SCI FOR/AID

N62
US SENATE COMM ON JUDICIARY,LEGISLATION TO STRENGTHEN PENALTIES UNDER THE ANTITRUST LAWS (PAMPHLET). USA+45 LG/CO CONFER CONTROL SANCTION ORD/FREE 20 SENATE MONOPOLY. PAGE 139 F2748
LEAD ADJUD INDUS ECO/TAC

B63
ABSHIRE D.M.,NATIONAL SECURITY: POLITICAL, MILITARY, AND ECONOMIC STRATEGIES IN THE DECADE AHEAD. ASIA COM USA+45 WOR+45 ECO/DEV ECO/UNDEV INT/ORG DELIB/GP FORCES ECO/TAC COERCE ATTIT RIGID/FLEX HEALTH ORD/FREE PWR WEALTH...POLICY STAT CHARTS ANTHOL COLD/WAR VAL/FREE APP/SCI. PAGE 2 F0032
FUT ACT/RES BAL/PWR

B63
BURRUS B.R.,ADMINSTRATIVE LAW AND LOCAL GOVERNMENT. USA+45 PROVS LEGIS LICENSE ADJUD ORD/FREE 20. PAGE 20 F0392
EX/STRUC LOC/G JURID CONSTN

B63
BURTT E.J. JR.,LABOR MARKETS, UNIONS, AND GOVERNMENT POLICIES. USA+45 MARKET NAT/G DELIB/GP CREATE BARGAIN GP/REL ORD/FREE PWR...POLICY CHARTS 20 AFL/CIO. PAGE 20 F0393
LABOR ECO/DEV CONTROL WORKER

B63
CONF ON FUTURE OF COMMONWEALTH,THE FUTURE OF THE COMMONWEALTH. AFR UK ECO/UNDEV AGRI EDU/PROP ADMIN SOC/INTEG 20. PAGE 27 F0522
DIPLOM RACE/REL ORD/FREE TEC/DEV

B63
DE VRIES E.,SOCIAL ASPECTS OF ECONOMIC DEVELOPMENT IN LATIN AMERICA. CULTURE SOCIETY STRATA FINAN INDUS INT/ORG DELIB/GP ACT/RES ECO/TAC EDU/PROP ADMIN ATTIT SUPEGO HEALTH KNOWL ORD/FREE...SOC STAT TREND ANTHOL TOT/POP VAL/FREE. PAGE 31 F0608
L/A+17C ECO/UNDEV

B63
DEUTSCH K.W.,THE POLITICAL ROLE OF LABOR IN DEVELOPING COUNTRIES. AFR ASIA S/ASIA USA+45 WOR+45 ECO/UNDEV POL/PAR ECO/TAC EDU/PROP LEGIT COERCE ORD/FREE PWR WEALTH...OBS INT TREND VAL/FREE 20. PAGE 32 F0625
LABOR NAT/LISM

B63
FRIEDRICH C.J.,MAN AND HIS GOVERNMENT: AN EMPIRICAL THEORY OF POLITICS. UNIV LOC/G NAT/G ADJUD REV INGP/REL DISCRIM PWR BIBLIOG. PAGE 44 F0867
PERSON ORD/FREE PARTIC CONTROL

B63
GEERTZ C.,PEDDLERS AND PRINCES: SOCIAL DEVELOPMENT AND ECONOMIC CHANGE IN TWO INDONESIAN TOWNS. S/ASIA CULTURE SOCIETY STRATA FACE/GP CREATE TEC/DEV ECO/TAC ORD/FREE WEALTH...OBS INT CENSUS CHARTS WORK TOT/POP METH/GP TERR/GP VAL/FREE 20 MUNICH. PAGE 47 F0913
ECO/UNDEV SOC ELITES INDONESIA

B63
GLADE W.P. JR.,THE POLITICAL ECONOMY OF MEXICO. FUT L/A+17C CULTURE SOCIETY AGRI INDUS DELIB/GP ACT/RES ECO/TAC ATTIT HEALTH ORD/FREE...STAT TIME/SEQ TREND MEXIC/AMER TOT/POP VAL/FREE 20. PAGE 48 F0928
FINAN ECO/UNDEV

B63
HIRSCHMAN A.O.,JOURNEYS TOWARD PROGRESS: STUDIES OF ECONOMIC POLICYMAKING IN LATIN AMERICA. CHILE FUT ECO/UNDEV AGRI FINAN INDUS CONSULT DELIB/GP PLAN ATTIT HEALTH ORD/FREE WEALTH...POLICY STAT VAL/FREE COLOMB 20. PAGE 60 F1177
L/A+17C ECO/TAC BRAZIL

B63
LAIRD R.D.,SOVIET AGRICULTURAL AND PEASANT AFFAIRS. FUT STRATA LOC/G DELIB/GP ACT/RES TEC/DEV ECO/TAC EDU/PROP ATTIT RIGID/FLEX ORD/FREE SKILL WEALTH ...STAT CON/ANAL ANTHOL MUNICH WORK VAL/FREE 20. PAGE 74 F1461
COM AGRI POLICY

B63
MARCHAL J.,EXPANSION ET RECESSION. FRANCE OP/RES PROB/SOLV ROLE ORD/FREE...TREND SIMUL 20 DEPRESSION. PAGE 85 F1663
FINAN PLAN ECO/DEV

B63
MENEZES A.J.,SUBDESENVOLVIMENTO E POLITICA INTERNACIONAL. BRAZIL WOR+45 PLAN CONTROL LEAD NAT/LISM ORD/FREE 20 THIRD/WRLD. PAGE 90 F1759
ECO/UNDEV DIPLOM POLICY BAL/PWR

B63
MULLENBACH P.,CIVILIAN NUCLEAR POWER: ECONOMIC ISSUES AND POLICY FORMATION. AFR FINAN INT/ORG DELIB/GP ACT/RES ECO/TAC ATTIT SUPEGO HEALTH ORD/FREE PWR...POLICY CONCPT MATH STAT CHARTS VAL/FREE 20. PAGE 94 F1855
USA+45 ECO/DEV NUC/PWR

B63
MYRDAL G.,CHALLENGE TO AFFLUENCE. USA+45 WOR+45 FINAN INT/ORG NAT/G PLAN ECO/TAC INT/TRADE BAL/PAY ORD/FREE 20 EUROPE/W. PAGE 96 F1882
ECO/DEV WEALTH DIPLOM PRODUC

B63
REAGAN M.D.,THE MANAGED ECONOMY. USA+45 INDUS LG/CO BUDGET GP/REL ORD/FREE PWR WEALTH 20. PAGE 110 F2161
PLAN ECO/DEV NAT/G ROLE

B63
ROBBINS L.,POLITICS AND ECONOMICS. ECO/DEV FINAN BUDGET DIPLOM BAL/PAY ORD/FREE 20. PAGE 112 F2204
NAT/G ATTIT

B63
ROPKE W.,ECONOMICS OF THE FREE SOCIETY. FINAN INT/TRADE BAL/PAY COST DEMAND EFFICIENCY ORD/FREE WEALTH...CON/ANAL METH/COMP T 20 KEYNES/JM. PAGE 114 F2240
SOCIETY BUDGET ECO/DEV ECO/TAC

B63
THEOBALD R.,FREE MEN AND FREE MARKETS. USA+45 USA-45 ECO/DEV NAT/G TEC/DEV DIPLOM INT/TRADE INCOME ORD/FREE WEALTH...TREND 19/20 KEYNES/JM. PAGE 130 F2556
CONCPT ECO/TAC CAP/ISM MARKET

B63
UNITED NATIONS,THE GROWTH OF WORLD INDUSTRY, 1938-1961: NATIONAL TABLES. WOR+45 STRUCT ECO/DEV ECO/UNDEV NAT/G COST...CHARTS UN. PAGE 132 F2613
STAT INDUS PRODUC ORD/FREE

L63
LIVERNASH E.R.,"THE RELATION OF POWER TO THE STRUCTURE AND PROCESS OF COLLECTIVE BARGAINING." ADJUD ORD/FREE...POLICY MGT CLASSIF GP/COMP. PAGE 81 F1589
LABOR GP/REL PWR ECO/TAC

L63
NASH M.,"PSYCHO-CULTURAL FACTORS IN ASIAN ECONOMIC GROWTH." ASIA ISLAM S/ASIA CULTURE ECO/UNDEV DELIB/GP EDU/PROP COERCE ATTIT PERSON HEALTH KNOWL ORD/FREE...PSY SOC STAT TREND ANTHOL VAL/FREE 20. PAGE 96 F1893
SOCIETY ECO/TAC

S63
BELOFF M.,"BRITAIN, EUROPE AND THE ATLANTIC COMMUNITY." EUR+WWI ELITES NAT/G VOL/ASSN TOP/EX ATTIT ORD/FREE PWR SOVEREIGN WEALTH EEC TOT/POP VAL/FREE CMN/WLTH 20. PAGE 13 F0240
INT/ORG ECO/DEV UK

S63
COLLERY A.,"A FULL EMPLOYMENT, KEYNESIAN THEORY OF INTERNATIONAL TRADE." WOR+45 ECO/DEV ACT/RES ECO/TAC ROUTINE ORD/FREE WEALTH...MATH CHARTS 20 KEYNES/JM. PAGE 26 F0504
SIMUL INT/TRADE

S63
EMERSON R.,"THE ATLANTIC COMMUNITY AND THE EMERGING COUNTRIES." FUT WOR+45 ECO/DEV ECO/UNDEV R+D NAT/G DELIB/GP BAL/PWR ECO/TAC EDU/PROP ROUTINE ORD/FREE PWR WEALTH...POLICY CONCPT TREND GEN/METH EEC 20 NATO. PAGE 37 F0729
ATTIT INT/TRADE

S63
GERHARD H.,"COMMODITY TRADE STABILIZATION THROUGH INTERNATIONAL AGREEMENTS." WOR+45 ECO/DEV ECO/UNDEV NAT/G ROUTINE ORD/FREE...INT/LAW OBS TREND GEN/METH TOT/POP 20. PAGE 47 F0918
PLAN ECO/TAC INT/TRADE

S63
GRUSHIN B.A.,"PROBLEMS OF THE MOVEMENT OF COMMUNIST LABOR IN THE USSR." COM SOCIETY LABOR ECO/TAC EDU/PROP COERCE RIGID/FLEX ORD/FREE...POLICY MARXIST STAT QU WORK 20. PAGE 52 F1011
ATTIT USSR

N63
US COMM STRENG SEC FREE WORLD,THE SCOPE AND DISTRIBUTION OF UNITED STATES MILITARY AND ECONOMIC ASSISTANCE PROGRAMS (PAMPHLET). USA+45 PLAN BAL/PWR BUDGET DIPLOM CONTROL CIVMIL/REL ATTIT. PAGE 134 F2648
DELIB/GP POLICY FOR/AID ORD/FREE

B64
ASH W.,MARXISM AND MORAL CONCEPTS. CAP/ISM GP/REL ORD/FREE...BIBLIOG 20. PAGE 7 F0128
MARXISM CONCPT MORAL SOCIETY

B64
BLACKSTOCK P.W.,THE STRATEGY OF SUBVERSION. USA+45 FORCES EDU/PROP ADMIN COERCE GOV/REL...DECISION MGT 20 DEPT/DEFEN CIA DEPT/STATE. PAGE 15 F0292
ORD/FREE DIPLOM CONTROL

B64
CALDER R.,TWO-WAY PASSAGE. INT/ORG TEC/DEV WAR PERSON ORD/FREE 20. PAGE 21 F0400
FOR/AID ECO/UNDEV ECO/TAC DIPLOM

B64
DANIELS R.V.,RUSSIA. RUSSIA USSR STRUCT NAT/LISM TOTALISM ORD/FREE WEALTH...POLICY DECISION TREND. PAGE 30 F0579
MARXISM REV ECO/DEV DIPLOM

B64
EDWARDS E.O.,THE NATION'S ECONOMIC OBJECTIVES. INDUS WORKER BUDGET DIPLOM CONTROL ORD/FREE ...POLICY SOC METH/CNCPT ANTHOL 20. PAGE 36 F0704
NAT/G ECO/TAC

B64
FIESER M.E.,ECONOMIC POLICY AND WAR POTENTIAL. AFR WOR+45 ECO/DEV INDUS NAT/G FORCES TEC/DEV NUC/PWR CIVMIL/REL ORD/FREE 20. PAGE 40 F0791
INT/TRADE POLICY ECO/TAC DETER

B64
FISK W.M.,ADMINISTRATIVE PROCEDURE IN A REGULATORY AGENCY: THE CAB AND THE NEW YORK-CHICAGO CASE (PAMPHLET). USA+45 DIST/IND ADMIN CONTROL LOBBY GP/REL ROLE ORD/FREE NEWYORK/C CHICAGO CAB. PAGE 41 F0805
SERV/IND ECO/DEV AIR JURID

B64
GARDNER L.C.,ECONOMIC ASPECTS OF NEW DEAL DIPLOMACY. USA-45 WOR-45 LAW ECO/DEV INT/ORG NAT/G VOL/ASSN LEGIS TOP/EX EDU/PROP ORD/FREE PWR WEALTH ...POLICY TIME/SEQ VAL/FREE 20 ROOSEVLT/F. PAGE 46 F0901
ECO/TAC DIPLOM

B64
GUTMANN P.M.,ECONOMIC GROWTH: AN AMERICAN PROBLEM. USA+45 FINAN R+D...POLICY NAT/COMP ANTHOL BIBLIOG 20. PAGE 52 F1016
WEALTH ECO/DEV CAP/ISM ORD/FREE

B64
HACKER A.,THE CORPORATION TAKE-OVER. CONSTN LABOR PLAN BAL/PWR CONTROL EXEC LOBBY REPRESENT GP/REL ROLE ORD/FREE POLICY. PAGE 52 F1025
LG/CO STRUCT PWR

B64
INTL INF CTR LOCAL CREDIT,GOVERNMENT MEASURES FOR THE PROMOTION OF REGIONAL ECONOMIC DEVELOPMENT. WOR+45 ECO/UNDEV FINAN INT/ORG DIPLOM ORD/FREE ...POLICY GEOG 20. PAGE 65 F1285
FOR/AID PLAN ECO/TAC REGION

B64
MAGALHAES S.,PRATICA DA EMANCIPACAO NACIONAL. L/A+17C INDUS PLAN ECO/TAC CONTROL NAT/LISM ORD/FREE. PAGE 84 F1640
BAL/PAY ECO/UNDEV DIPLOM WEALTH

B64
MARKHAM J.W.,THE COMMON MARKET: FRIEND OR COMPETITOR. AFR EUR+WWI FUT USA+45 INT/ORG LG/CO NAT/G VOL/ASSN DELIB/GP EX/STRUC PLAN TARIFFS ORD/FREE PWR WEALTH...POLICY STAT TREND EEC VAL/FREE 20. PAGE 85 F1671
ECO/DEV ECO/TAC

B64
NOSSITER B.D.,THE MYTHMAKERS: AN ESSAY ON POWER AND WEALTH. USA+45 LG/CO NAT/G TOP/EX PROB/SOLV ADMIN GP/REL ORD/FREE 20. PAGE 99 F1937
ECO/TAC WEALTH FINAN PLAN

B64
PRESTHUS R.,MEN AT THE TOP; A STUDY IN COMMUNITY POWER. USA+45 STRUCT ACT/RES REPRESENT CONSEN ALL/VALS ORD/FREE...SAMP/SIZ 20. PAGE 108 F2116
PLURISM LG/CO PWR ADMIN

B64
RAISON T.,WHY CONSERVATIVE? UK FORCES DIPLOM ECO/TAC GIVE EDU/PROP ORD/FREE WEALTH LAISSEZ ...GOV/COMP 20 TORY/PARTY CONSRV/PAR. PAGE 109 F2137
PLURISM CONSERVE POL/PAR NAT/G

B64
RENO P.,THE ORDEAL OF BRITISH GUIANA. L/A+17C USA+45 STRUCT AGRI EXTR/IND INDUS NAT/G FOR/AID ORD/FREE...GEOG 20 GUIANA/BR INTRVN/ECO. PAGE 111 F2178
COLONIAL ECO/UNDEV SOCISM PWR

B64
VON DER MEHDEN F.R.,POLITICS OF THE DEVELOPING NATIONS. WOR+45 CONSTN PROB/SOLV ORD/FREE WEALTH OBJECTIVE. PAGE 142 F2790
ECO/UNDEV SOCIETY STRUCT

B64
WILLIAMSON J.G.,AMERICAN GROWTH AND THE BALANCE OF PAYMENTS, 1820-1913: A STUDY OF THE LONG SWING. EUR+WWI MOD/EUR USA+45 USA-45 ECO/DEV NAT/G ECO/TAC ROUTINE ORD/FREE WEALTH...MATH STAT TIME/SEQ CHARTS SIMUL GEN/LAWS TRUE/GP METH/GP VAL/FREE 19/20. PAGE 147 F2896
FINAN BAL/PAY

B64
ZOLLSCHAN G.K.,EXPLORATIONS IN SOCIAL CHANGE. SOCIETY STRATA STRUCT ECO/UNDEV EX/STRUC...PSY ANTHOL 20. PAGE 151 F2968
ORD/FREE SIMUL CONCPT CULTURE

L64
STERN R.M.,"POLICIES FOR TRADE AND DEVELOPMENT." AFR FUT WOR+45 DIST/IND FINAN NAT/G DELIB/GP PLAN ECO/TAC ORD/FREE WEALTH...POLICY STAT TIME/SEQ CHARTS METH/GP 20. PAGE 126 F2480
MARKET ECO/UNDEV INT/TRADE

S64
BEIM D.,"THE COMMUNIST BLOC AND THE FOREIGN-AID GAME." AFR WOR+45 NAT/G PLAN ROUTINE ATTIT KNOWL ORD/FREE...DECISION QUANT CONT/OBS TIME/SEQ CHARTS GAME SIMUL LOG/LING 20. PAGE 12 F0231
COM ECO/UNDEV ECO/TAC FOR/AID

S64
FINLEY D.D.,"A POLITICAL PERSPECTIVE OF ECONOMIC RELATIONS IN THE COMMUNIST CAMP." COM USSR FACE/GP NAT/G ACT/RES PLAN DOMIN COERCE ATTIT ORD/FREE WEALTH...TIME/SEQ 20. PAGE 41 F0800
VOL/ASSN ECO/TAC DIPLOM REGION

S64
PADELFORD N.J.,"THE ORGANIZATION OF AFRICAN UNITY." ECO/UNDEV INT/ORG PLAN BAL/PWR DIPLOM ECO/TAC NAT/LISM ORD/FREE PWR WEALTH...CONCPT TREND STERTYP TERR/GP VAL/FREE 20. PAGE 102 F2013
AFR VOL/ASSN REGION

S64
RUSSETT B.M.,"INEQUALITY AND INSTABILITY: THE RELATION OF LAND TENURE TO POLITICS." WOR+45 ECO/DEV ECO/UNDEV AGRI NAT/G COERCE PWR...MATH STAT CHARTS GEN/LAWS TERR/GP TRUE/GP METH/GP VAL/FREE 20. PAGE 115 F2263
WEALTH GEOG ECO/TAC ORD/FREE

S64
SALVADORI M.,"EL CAPITALISMO EN LA EUROPA DE LA POSGUERRA." AFR INT/ORG NAT/G POL/PAR PLAN ECO/TAC ATTIT ORD/FREE WEALTH...HIST/WRIT EEC 20. PAGE 115 F2275
EUR+WWI ECO/DEV CAP/ISM

S64
SCHMITT H.D.,"POLITICAL CONDITIONS FOR INTERNATIONAL CURRENCY REFORM." WOR+45 SOCIETY ECO/DEV PLAN ECO/TAC BAL/PAY ATTIT ORD/FREE WEALTH ...SOC CONCPT OBS TREND EEC VAL/FREE ECSC 20. PAGE 117 F2301
FINAN VOL/ASSN REGION

B65
BOCK E.,GOVERNMENT REGULATION OF BUSINESS. USA+45 LAW EX/STRUC LEGIS EXEC ORD/FREE PWR...ANTHOL CONGRESS. PAGE 16 F0303
MGT ADMIN NAT/G CONTROL

B65
CHANDRASEKHAR S.,AMERICAN AID AND INDIA'S ECONOMIC DEVELOPMENT. AFR CHINA/COM INDIA USA+45 GIVE EDU/PROP EATING HEALTH ORD/FREE 20 AID. PAGE 23 F0449
FOR/AID PEACE DIPLOM ECO/UNDEV

B65
COOMBS P.H.,EDUCATION AND FOREIGN AID. AFR USA+45 DIPLOM EFFICIENCY KNOWL ORD/FREE...ANTHOL 20 AID. PAGE 27 F0532
EDU/PROP FOR/AID SCHOOL ECO/UNDEV

B65
COUGHLIN B.J.,CHURCH AND STATE IN SOCIAL WELFARE. USA+45 RECEIVE GP/REL ORD/FREE WEALTH NEW/LIB. PAGE 28 F0542
CULTURE SECT VOL/ASSN GIVE

B65
DERBER M.,PLANT UNION-MANAGEMENT RELATIONS: FROM PRACTICE TO THEORY. PROC/MFG NEIGH PROB/SOLV ORD/FREE...DECISION MGT OBS QU SAMP. PAGE 32 F0621
LG/CO LABOR GP/REL ATTIT

B65
GRIFFIN C.E.,THE FREE SOCIETY. CONSTN SOCIETY MARKET FEDERAL RATIONAL WEALTH...MAJORIT 20 CIVIL/LIB. PAGE 51 F0999
CONCPT ORD/FREE CAP/ISM POPULISM

B65
IANNI O.,ESTADO E CAPITALISMO. L/A+17C FINAN TEC/DEV ECO/TAC ORD/FREE WEALTH POLICY. PAGE 64 F1258
ECO/UNDEV STRUCT INDUS NAT/G

B65
KISSINGER H.A.,THE TROUBLED PARTNERSHIP* RE-APPRAISAL OF THE WESTERN ALLIANCE. EUR+WWI USA+45
FRANCE NUC/PWR

INT/ORG NAT/G VOL/ASSN TOP/EX DIPLOM ORD/FREE PWR NATO. PAGE 71 F1402 — ECO/DEV

B65
LUTZ V.,FRENCH PLANNING. FRANCE TEC/DEV RIGID/FLEX ORD/FREE 20. PAGE 82 F1613 — PLAN ADMIN FUT

B65
LYONS G.M.,AMERICA: PURPOSE AND POWER. UK USA+45 FINAN INDUS MARKET WORKER TEC/DEV DIPLOM AUTOMAT NUC/PWR WAR RACE/REL ORD/FREE 20 EEC CONGRESS SUPREME/CT CIV/RIGHTS. PAGE 82 F1617 — PWR PROB/SOLV ECO/DEV TASK

B65
MACDONALD R.W.,THE LEAGUE OF ARAB STATES: A STUDY IN THE DYNAMICS OF REGIONAL ORGANIZATION. ISRAEL UAR USSR FINAN INT/ORG DELIB/GP ECO/TAC AGREE NEUTRAL ORD/FREE PWR...DECISION BIBLIOG 20 TREATY UN. PAGE 83 F1626 — ISLAM REGION DIPLOM ADMIN

B65
MARK S.M.,ECONOMICS IN ACTION (3RD ED.). USA+45 ECO/UNDEV AGRI INDUS FOR/AID INT/TRADE BAL/PAY COST ORD/FREE...ANTHOL 20 RESOURCE/N. PAGE 85 F1670 — POLICY ECO/TAC EFFICIENCY PRICE

B65
MOORE W.E.,THE IMPACT OF INDUSTRY. CULTURE STRUCT ORD/FREE...TREND 20. PAGE 93 F1824 — INDUS MGT TEC/DEV ECO/UNDEV

B65
NARASIMHAN V.K.,DEMOCRACY AND MIXED ECONOMY. INDIA CONTROL...CENSUS IDEA/COMP 20. PAGE 96 F1891 — CAP/ISM MARXISM ORD/FREE NEW/LIB

B65
NATIONAL CONF SOCIAL WELFARE,THE SOCIAL WELFARE FORUM, 1965. LAW CULTURE VOL/ASSN CONTROL PERS/REL ADJUST POLICY. PAGE 97 F1899 — CONSTN WEALTH ORD/FREE NEIGH

B65
SHAFFER H.G.,THE SOVIET SYSTEM IN THEORY AND PRACTICE: SELECTED WESTERN AND SOVIET VIEWS. USSR LAW SOCIETY CREATE FOR/AID EDU/PROP PRESS CHOOSE PEACE ORD/FREE...ANTHOL 20 STALIN/J. PAGE 120 F2362 — MARXISM SOCISM IDEA/COMP

B65
THAYER F.C. JR.,AIR TRANSPORT POLICY AND NATIONAL SECURITY: A POLITICAL, ECONOMIC, AND MILITARY ANALYSIS. DIST/IND OP/RES PLAN TEC/DEV DIPLOM DETER WAR COST EFFICIENCY...POLICY BIBLIOG 20 DEPT/DEFEN FAA CAB. PAGE 129 F2548 — AIR FORCES CIVMIL/REL ORD/FREE

B65
US SENATE COMM ON FOREIGN REL,HEARINGS ON THE FOREIGN ASSISTANCE PROGRAM. AFR ASIA L/A+17C USA+45 WOR+45 FORCES TEC/DEV BUDGET CONTROL WEAPON ORD/FREE 20 UN CONGRESS SEC/STATE. PAGE 139 F2734 — FOR/AID DIPLOM INT/ORG ECO/UNDEV

B65
VAID K.N.,STATE AND LABOR IN INDIA. INDIA INDUS WORKER PAY PRICE ADJUD CONTROL PARL/PROC GP/REL ORD/FREE 20. PAGE 140 F2757 — LAW LABOR MGT NEW/LIB

S65
JOHNSON L.L.,"US BUSINESS INTERESTS IN CUBA AND THE RISE OF CASTRO." L/A+17C USA+45 ECO/UNDEV INDUS NAT/G VOL/ASSN ATTIT ORD/FREE PWR WEALTH ALL/PROG. PAGE 68 F1330 — DIPLOM CUBA ECO/TAC INT/TRADE

B66
ALI S.,PLANNING, DEVELOPMENT AND CHANGE: AN ANNOTATED BIBLIOGRAPHY ON DEVELOPMENTAL ADMINISTRATION. PAKISTAN SOCIETY ORD/FREE 20. PAGE 4 F0066 — BIBLIOG/A ADMIN ECO/UNDEV PLAN

B66
BAKLANOFF E.N.,NEW PERSPECTIVES ON BRAZIL. BRAZIL SOCIETY INDUS DOMIN LEAD REV CIVMIL/REL...GEOG PSY LING ANTHOL 20. PAGE 8 F0156 — ECO/UNDEV TEC/DEV DIPLOM ORD/FREE

B66
BOWEN H.R.,AUTOMATION AND ECONOMIC PROGRESS. EUR+WWI USA+45 ECO/DEV INCOME ORD/FREE WEALTH ...POLICY ANTHOL 20. PAGE 17 F0327 — AUTOMAT TEC/DEV WORKER LEISURE

B66
CONFERENCE REGIONAL ACCOUNTS,REGIONAL ACCOUNTS FOR POLICY DECISIONS. PROB/SOLV CONTROL RATIONAL KNOWL ORD/FREE...POLICY DECISION MATH STAT ANTHOL 20. PAGE 27 F0523 — GOV/REL REGION PLAN ECO/TAC

B66
CROWDER M.,A SHORT HISTORY OF NIGERIA. AFR NIGERIA UK ECO/UNDEV CHIEF INT/TRADE RACE/REL NAT/LISM ORD/FREE...GEOG SOC CHARTS BIBLIOG 14/20. PAGE 29 F0558 — COLONIAL NAT/G CULTURE

B66
DAVIES I.,AFRICAN TRADE UNIONS. AFR ECO/UNDEV INT/ORG GP/REL ORD/FREE SOVEREIGN SOCISM 20. PAGE 30 F0585 — LABOR COLONIAL PWR INDUS

B66
EBONY,THE NEGRO HANDBOOK. ACADEM LABOR LOC/G SECT FORCES WORKER CT/SYS CRIME DISCRIM ORD/FREE...BIOG SOC/INTEG 19/20 NEGRO CIV/RIGHTS. PAGE 36 F0692 — RACE/REL EDU/PROP LAW STAT

B66
FORD P.,CARDINAL MORAN AND THE A. L. P. NAT/G POL/PAR SECT DELIB/GP LOBBY REV CHOOSE ORD/FREE MARXISM 19/20 AUSTRAL PROTESTANT LABOR/PAR. PAGE 42 F0825 — CATHISM SOCISM LABOR SOCIETY

B66
FREIDEL F.,AMERICAN ISSUES IN THE TWENTIETH CENTURY. SOCIETY FINAN ECO/TAC FOR/AID CONTROL NUC/PWR WAR RACE/REL PEACE ATTIT...ANTHOL T 20 WILSON/W ROOSEVLT/F KENNEDY/JF TRUMAN/HS. PAGE 44 F0851 — DIPLOM POLICY NAT/G ORD/FREE

B66
INARRITU A.L.,EL PATRON CAMBIO-ORO Y SUS REFORMAS. AFR L/A+17C WOR+45 PLAN PROB/SOLV BUDGET ECO/TAC INT/TRADE EFFICIENCY ORD/FREE 20 MEXIC/AMER. PAGE 64 F1262 — ECO/UNDEV FINAN DIPLOM POLICY

B66
KAREFA-SMART J.,AFRICA: PROGRESS THROUGH COOPERATION. AFR FINAN TEC/DEV DIPLOM FOR/AID EDU/PROP CONFER REGION GP/REL WEALTH...HEAL SOC/INTEG 20. PAGE 69 F1356 — ORD/FREE ECO/UNDEV VOL/ASSN PLAN

B66
MOSKOW M.H.,TEACHERS AND UNIONS. SCHOOL WORKER ADJUD LOBBY ATTIT ORD/FREE 20. PAGE 94 F1844 — EDU/PROP PROF/ORG LABOR BARGAIN

B66
NAMBOODIRIPAD E.M.,ECONOMICS AND POLITICS OF INDIA'S SOCIALIST PATTERN. INDIA STRATA AGRI INDUS NAT/G PRICE ORD/FREE SOVEREIGN 20. PAGE 96 F1888 — ECO/UNDEV PLAN SOCISM CAP/ISM

B66
PFEFFER K.H.,WELT IM UMBRUCH. SOCIETY STRUCT INDUS PROF/ORG SECT TEC/DEV PARTIC SUPEGO WORSHIP 20 CHRISTIAN. PAGE 106 F2076 — ORD/FREE STRATA CREATE

B66
SOMMERFELD R.M.,TAX REFORM AND THE ALLIANCE FOR PROGRESS. USA+45 ECO/DEV ECO/UNDEV FINAN NAT/G INCOME ORD/FREE WEALTH...STAT CHARTS 20 ALL/PROG. PAGE 124 F2442 — TAX INT/ORG L/A+17C FOR/AID

B66
US HOUSE COMM FOREIGN AFFAIRS,HEARINGS ON HR 12449 A BILL TO AMEND FURTHER THE FOREIGN ASSISTANCE ACT OF 1961. AFR ASIA L/A+17C USA+45 VIETNAM INT/ORG TEC/DEV INT/TRADE ATTIT ORD/FREE 20 UN NATO CONGRESS AID. PAGE 137 F2692 — FOR/AID ECO/TAC ECO/UNDEV DIPLOM

B66
US SENATE COMM ON FOREIGN REL,HEARINGS ON S 2859 AND S 2861. USA+45 WOR+45 FORCES BUDGET CAP/ISM ADMIN DETER WEAPON TOTALISM...NAT/COMP 20 UN CONGRESS. PAGE 139 F2735 — FOR/AID DIPLOM ORD/FREE ECO/UNDEV

B66
ZINKIN T.,CHALLENGES IN INDIA. INDIA PAKISTAN LAW AGRI FINAN INDUS TOP/EX TEC/DEV CONTROL ROUTINE ORD/FREE PWR 20 NEHRU/J SHASTRI/LB CIVIL/SERV. PAGE 150 F2964 — NAT/G ECO/TAC POLICY ADMIN

S66
ANGELL J.W.,"THE LONGER RUN PROSPECTS FOR THE US BALANCE OF PAYMENTS." USA+45 DIPLOM FOR/AID RATION ORD/FREE WEALTH...IDEA/COMP GATT. PAGE 6 F0104 — BAL/PAY ECO/TAC INT/TRADE FINAN

S66
FROMM G.,"RECENT MONETARY POLICY: AN ECONOMETRIC VIEW" USA+45 ECO/DEV INDUS PAY PRICE PRODUC ORD/FREE WEALTH...STAT 20 FED/RESERV. PAGE 45 F0869 — ECOMETRIC FINAN POLICY SIMUL

S66
ROTHCHILD D.,"THE LIMITS OF FEDERALISM: AN EXAMINATION OF POLITICAL INSTITUTIONAL TRANSFER IN AFRICA." AFR CONSTN CULTURE ELITES ECO/UNDEV KIN PROB/SOLV ADMIN ORD/FREE PWR...POLICY 20. PAGE 114 F2250 — FEDERAL NAT/G NAT/LISM COLONIAL

S66
VERSLUYS J.D.N.,"SOME NOTES ON THE SOCIAL AND ECONOMIC EFFECTS OF RURAL ELECTRIFICATION IN BURMA" BURMA EDU/PROP PRODUC ORD/FREE...SOC QU MUNICH TIME 20. PAGE 141 F2782 — TEC/DEV SOCIETY CREATE

B67
APTHEKER H.,THE NATURE OF DEMOCRACY, FREEDOM AND REVOLUTION. WOR+45 PROB/SOLV COERCE COST...CONCPT TIME/SEQ METH/COMP. PAGE 6 F0111 — REV POPULISM MARXIST ORD/FREE

B67
BARDENS D.,CHURCHILL IN PARLIAMENT. UK DIPLOM ADJUD CONTROL AUTHORIT PERSON ORD/FREE 20 CHURCHLL/W PARLIAMENT. PAGE 10 F0186 — TOP/EX LEGIS GOV/REL

B67
BLAIR P.W.,THE MINISTATE DILEMMA. WOR+45 AGREE COLONIAL ORD/FREE...GEOG CHARTS MUNICH LEAGUE/NAT UN. PAGE 15 F0294 — INT/ORG NAT/G CENSUS

B67
CHILCOTE R.H.,PORTUGUESE AFRICA. PORTUGAL CULTURE SOCIETY ECO/UNDEV DOMIN NAT/LISM...TREND IDEA/COMP NAT/COMP BIBLIOG 15/20. PAGE 24 F0465 — AFR COLONIAL ORD/FREE

PROB/SOLV

B67

DAVIS F.M.,COME AS A CONQUEROR: THE UNITED STATES ARMY'S OCCUPATION OF GERMANY: 1945-1949. EUR+WWI GERMANY USA+45 SOCIETY PLAN BAL/PWR DIPLOM FOR/AID PERS/REL DEMAND PEACE ORD/FREE 20. PAGE 30 F0588
FORCES CIVMIL/REL ECO/TAC CONTROL

B67

EVANS R.H.,COEXISTENCE: COMMUNISM AND ITS PRACTICE IN BOLOGNA, 1945-1965. ITALY CAP/ISM ADMIN CHOOSE PEACE ORD/FREE...SOC STAT DEEP/INT SAMP CHARTS BIBLIOG MUNICH 20. PAGE 39 F0756
MARXISM CULTURE POL/PAR

B67

FANON F.,TOWARD THE AFRICAN REVOLUTION. AFR FRANCE CULTURE ELITES LEAD REV GP/REL ORD/FREE SOVEREIGN 20. PAGE 39 F0762
COLONIAL DOMIN ECO/UNDEV RACE/REL

B67

HALLE L.J.,THE COLD WAR AS HISTORY. AFR USSR WOR+45 ECO/TAC FOR/AID NUC/PWR WAR PEACE ORD/FREE ...MAJORIT TREND 20 KENNEDY/JF KHRUSH/N BERLIN/BLO. PAGE 54 F1048
DIPLOM BAL/PWR

B67

KIRK R.,THE POLITICAL PRINCIPLES OF ROBERT A. TAFT. USA+45 LABOR DIPLOM ADJUD ADJUST ORD/FREE TAFT/RA. PAGE 71 F1398
POL/PAR LEAD LEGIS ATTIT

B67

MACCLOSKEY M.,PACTS FOR PEACE: UN, NATO, SEATO, CENTO, OAS. WOR+45 PLAN DIPLOM CONTROL PEACE ORD/FREE...ORG/CHARTS UN NATO SEATO OAS CENTO. PAGE 83 F1623
FORCES INT/ORG LEAD POLICY

B67

MEYNAUD J.,TRADE UNIONISM IN AFRICA; A STUDY OF ITS GROWTH AND ORIENTATION (TRANS. BY ANGELA BRENCH). INT/ORG PROB/SOLV COLONIAL PWR...TIME/SEQ TREND ILO. PAGE 90 F1774
LABOR AFR NAT/LISM ORD/FREE

B67

MURTY B.S.,PROPAGANDA AND WORLD PUBLIC ORDER. FUT WOR+45 COM/IND INT/ORG PROB/SOLV ATTIT KNOWL ORD/FREE...POLICY UN. PAGE 95 F1868
EDU/PROP DIPLOM CONTROL JURID

B67

NKRUMAH K.,CHALLENGE OF THE CONGO. FORCES ECO/TAC FOR/AID REGION MURDER REPRESENT 20 CONGO/LEOP UN. PAGE 98 F1930
REV ECO/UNDEV ORD/FREE DIPLOM

B67

PELTASON J.W.,FUNCTIONS AND POLICIES OF AMERICAN GOVERNMENT (3RD ED.). USA+45 FINAN INDUS EDU/PROP CIVMIL/REL RACE/REL ORD/FREE...ANTHOL T 20 JOHNSON/LB. PAGE 104 F2052
NAT/G GOV/REL POLICY PLAN

B67

PIKE F.B.,FREEDOM AND REFORM IN LATIN AMERICA. BRAZIL URUGUAY CONSTN CULTURE SECT DIPLOM EDU/PROP PARTIC DRIVE ALL/VALS CATHISM...GEOG ANTHOL BIBLIOG REFORMERS BOLIV. PAGE 106 F2086
L/A+17C ORD/FREE ECO/UNDEV REV

B67

POWLEDGE F.,BLACK POWER WHITE RESISTANCE. USA+45 STRUCT PLAN GP/REL DISCRIM HABITAT ORD/FREE WEALTH ...METH/COMP SOC/INTEG NEGRO. PAGE 107 F2111
RACE/REL ATTIT PWR

B67

SACKS B.,SOUTH AFRICA: AN IMPERIAL DILEMMA. SOUTH/AFR UK ECO/UNDEV KIN DOMIN DEBATE CONTROL REV DISCRIM ISOLAT...POLICY STAT BIBLIOG 20. PAGE 115 F2268
COLONIAL RACE/REL DIPLOM ORD/FREE

B67

SPICER G.W.,THE SUPREME COURT AND FUNDAMENTAL FREEDOMS (2ND ED.). USA+45 CONSTN SOCIETY ATTIT 20 SUPREME/CT. PAGE 124 F2454
CT/SYS JURID CONTROL ORD/FREE

B67

VENKATESWARAN R.J.,CABINET GOVERNMENT IN INDIA. INDIA UK SOCIETY OP/RES COLONIAL LEAD EFFICIENCY ORD/FREE 20. PAGE 141 F2776
DELIB/GP ADMIN CONSTN NAT/G

B67

WILLS A.J.,AN INTRODUCTION TO THE HISTORY OF CENTRAL AFRICA. RHODESIA ZAMBIA CULTURE SOCIETY ECO/UNDEV TEC/DEV DOMIN WAR ALL/VALS...POLICY TREND BIBLIOG T 14/20 NYASALAND. PAGE 147 F2899
AFR COLONIAL ORD/FREE

L67

AFFELDT R.J.,"THE INDEPENDENT LABOR UNION AND THE GOOD LIFE." USA+45 ADJUD CONTROL SANCTION GP/REL ORD/FREE JURID. PAGE 3 F0045
LABOR CT/SYS PWR SOVEREIGN

L67

AUSTIN D.A.,"POLITICAL CONFLICT IN AFRICA." CONSTN NAT/G CREATE ADMIN COLONIAL ORD/FREE MARXISM POPULISM SOCISM...NAT/COMP ANTHOL 20. PAGE 8 F0141
ANOMIE AFR POL/PAR

L67

BARRON J.A.,"ACCESS TO THE PRESS." USA+45 TEC/DEV PRESS TV ADJUD AUD/VIS. PAGE 10 F0196
ORD/FREE COM/IND EDU/PROP LAW

L67

DEALEY S.,"MONETARY RECOVERY UNDER FEDERAL TRANSPORTATION STATUTES." USA+45 SEA WORKER TAX PAY ADJUD DEATH GOV/REL OWN HEALTH ORD/FREE 20. PAGE 31 F0609
DIST/IND LAW CONTROL FINAN

L67

DOERFER G.L.,"THE LIMITS ON TRADE SECRET LAW IMPOSED BY FEDERAL PATENT & ANTITRUST SUPREMACY." USA+45 LAW R+D CAP/ISM LICENSE CONTROL SANCTION ORD/FREE. PAGE 33 F0651
JURID GOV/REL POLICY LEGIT

L67

HUBBARD P.H.,"MONETARY RECOVERY UNDER THE COPYRIGHT, PATENT, AND TRADEMARK ACTS." PROC/MFG TAX PAY LEGIT ADJUD GOV/REL OWN ORD/FREE 20. PAGE 62 F1228
CREATE LAW CONTROL FINAN

L67

PARKER G.P. JR.,"MONETARY RECOVERY UNDER THE FEDERAL LABOR STATUTES." USA+45 USA-45 INDUS ADJUD CT/SYS GOV/REL HEALTH ORD/FREE 20 DEPT/LABOR NLRB. PAGE 103 F2027
LABOR CONTROL LAW FINAN

L67

STILL C.H.,"MONETARY RECOVERY UNDER THE FAIR LABOR STANDARDS ACT." USA+45 USA-45 WORKER PAY ADJUD GOV/REL HEALTH ORD/FREE...MATH 20 NLRB. PAGE 126 F2487
LABOR CONTROL LAW FINAN

L67

WATKINS J.B.,"MONETARY RECOVERY UNDER FEDERAL ANTITRUST STATUTES." USA+45 PROB/SOLV ADJUD CT/SYS GOV/REL ORD/FREE 20. PAGE 144 F2831
LG/CO CONTROL LAW FINAN

L67

WILKINSON J.H. JR.,"THE NET OPERATING LOSS DEDUCTION AND RELATED INCOME TAX DEVICES." PROB/SOLV BUDGET PAY GOV/REL ORD/FREE...MATH CHARTS METH 20. PAGE 146 F2886
TAX FINAN LAW ADJUD

S67

"THE FEDERAL AGRICULTURAL STABILIZATION PROGRAM AND THE NEGRO." LAW CONSTN PLAN REPRESENT DISCRIM ORD/FREE 20 NEGRO CONGRESS. PAGE 2 F0025
AGRI CONTROL NAT/G RACE/REL

S67

"THE SIERRA CLUB, POLITICAL ACTIVITY, AND TAX EXEMPT CHARITABLE STATUS." USA+45 LAW VOL/ASSN TAX PAY ADJUD LOBBY INGP/REL HABITAT 20. PAGE 2 F0027
ELITES GOV/REL FACE/GP ORD/FREE

S67

CHAMBERLAIN N.W.,"STRIKES IN CONTEMPORARY CONTEXT." LAW INDUS NAT/G CHIEF CONFER COST ATTIT ORD/FREE ...POLICY MGT 20. PAGE 23 F0442
LABOR BARGAIN EFFICIENCY PROB/SOLV

S67

DANIEL C.,"FREEDOM, EQUITY, AND THE WAR ON POVERTY." USA+45 WORKER ECO/TAC JURID. PAGE 30 F0578
WEALTH INCOME SOCIETY ORD/FREE

S67

DRAPER A.P.,"UNIONS AND THE WAR IN VIETNAM." USA+45 CONFER ADMIN LEAD WAR ORD/FREE PACIFIST 20. PAGE 34 F0660
LABOR PACIFISM ATTIT ELITES

S67

FINER S.E.,"THE ONE-PARTY REGIMES IN AFRICA: RECONSIDERATIONS." AFR DOMIN CONSEN ORD/FREE 20. PAGE 41 F0798
ELITES POL/PAR CONSTN ECO/UNDEV

S67

FLACKS R.,"CONSCRIPTION IN A DEMOCRATIC SOCIETY." USA+45 WORKER CONTROL SUFF SUPEGO. PAGE 41 F0807
POLICY FORCES ORD/FREE CIVMIL/REL

S67

GOLDSTEIN W.,"THE SCIENCE ESTABLISHMENT AND ITS POLITICAL CONTROL." WOR+45 SOCIETY GP/REL RATIONAL ORD/FREE. PAGE 48 F0941
CREATE ADJUST CONTROL

S67

GORMAN W.,"ELLUL - A PROPHETIC VOICE." WOR+45 ELITES SOCIETY ACT/RES PLAN BAL/PWR DOMIN CONTROL PARTIC TOTALISM PWR 20. PAGE 49 F0963
CREATE ORD/FREE EX/STRUC UTOPIA

S67

HALL B.,"THE COALITION AGAINST DISHWASHERS." USA+45 POL/PAR PROB/SOLV BARGAIN LEAD CHOOSE REPRESENT GP/REL ORD/FREE PWR...POLICY 20. PAGE 53 F1044
LABOR ADMIN DOMIN WORKER

S67

JEDLICKI W.,"THE FREE SPEECH MOVEMENT IN WARSAW." POLAND FORCES EDU/PROP LEAD ATTIT MARXISM ...IDEA/COMP 20. PAGE 67 F1310
COERCE CROWD ORD/FREE ACADEM

S67

LENS S.,"WALTER REUTHER TRIES TO BUILD A FIRE." WORKER LEAD DISCRIM AGE ORD/FREE NEW/LIB SOC. PAGE 78 F1523
LABOR PARTIC NEIGH PLAN

S67

MILLER C.H.,"B. TRAVEN Y EL 'PROBLEMA PETROLERO'." USA-45 ECO/UNDEV INDUS TEC/DEV INT/TRADE ATTIT ORD/FREE SOVEREIGN 20 MEXIC/AMER. PAGE 91 F1791
EXTR/IND DIPLOM ECO/TAC

DOMIN

S67
MOLTMANN G.,"ZUR FORMULIERUNG DER AMERIKANISCHEN BESATZUNGSPOLITIK IN DEUTSCHLAND AM ENDE DES ZWEITEN WELTKRIEGES" GERMANY ECO/TAC ADMIN WAR CIVMIL/REL ORD/FREE FASCISM 20. PAGE 92 F1815 — FORCES CONTROL POLICY INDUS

S67
NILES J.G.,"CIVIL ACTIONS FOR DAMAGES UNDER THE FEDERAL CIVIL RIGHTS STATUTES." CONSTN FINAN ADJUD CT/SYS GOV/REL RACE/REL 20. PAGE 98 F1928 — DISCRIM LAW CONTROL ORD/FREE

S67
PEMBERTON J., JR.,"CONSTITUTIONAL PROBLEMS IN RESTRAINT ON THE MEDIA." CONSTN PROB/SOLV EDU/PROP CONFER CONTROL JURID. PAGE 104 F2054 — LAW PRESS ORD/FREE

S67
RAGAN S.,"THE ABA RECOMMENDATIONS: A NEWSPAPERMAN'S CRITIQUE." EDU/PROP CONTROL GP/REL...JURID ABA. PAGE 109 F2136 — LAW PRESS ADJUD ORD/FREE

S67
SCRIPP J.,"CONTROLLING PREJUDICIAL PUBLICITY BY THE CONTEMPT POWER: THE BRITISH PRACTICE AND ITS PROSPECT IN AMERICAN LAW." UK USA+45 EDU/PROP CONTROL GP/REL ORD/FREE JURID. PAGE 119 F2338 — METH/COMP LAW PRESS ADJUD

S67
SMITH W.H.T.,"THE IMPLICATIONS OF THE AMERICAN BAR ASSOCIATION ADVISORY COMMITTEE RECOMMENDATIONS FOR POLICE ADMINISTRATION." AFR ADMIN...JURID 20. PAGE 123 F2435 — EDU/PROP CONTROL GP/REL ORD/FREE

S67
WILSON C.E.,"AMERICAN INVESTMENT IN PORTUGUESE AFRICA: A PROBLEM OF "DEMOCRATIC" COLONIALISM." AFR ECO/UNDEV DIPLOM MORAL...IDEA/COMP 20 ANGOLA MOZAMBIQUE. PAGE 147 F2901 — COLONIAL DOMIN ORD/FREE POLICY

N67
US HOUSE COMM FOREIGN AFFAIRS,COMMUNIST ACTIVITIES IN LATIN AMERICA 1967 (PAMPHLET). CUBA USA+45 DIPLOM INT/TRADE EDU/PROP COERCE GUERRILLA HOUSE/REP OAS. PAGE 137 F2696 — L/A+17C MARXISM ORD/FREE ECO/TAC

N67
US SENATE COMM ON FOREIGN REL,SURVEY OF THE ALLIANCE FOR PROGRESS: THE LATIN AMERICAN MILITARY (PAMPHLET). USA+45 INT/ORG POL/PAR DIPLOM AGREE GP/REL ROLE ORD/FREE 20. PAGE 139 F2746 — L/A+17C FORCES CIVMIL/REL POLICY

B76
PROUDHON P.J.,WHAT IS PROPERTY? (TRANS. BY B.R. TUCKER). SOCIETY AGRI CAP/ISM CRIME GP/REL PERSON MORAL ORD/FREE WEALTH. PAGE 108 F2127 — OWN WORKER PRODUC ANARCH

B76
SMITH A.,THE WEALTH OF NATIONS. UK STRUCT WORKER DIPLOM ECO/TAC OPTIMAL DRIVE PERSON ORD/FREE ...OLD/LIB GEN/LAWS 17/18. PAGE 123 F2428 — WEALTH PRODUC INDUS LAISSEZ

B86
O'CONNOR T.P.,THE PARNELL MOVEMENT: WITH A SKETCH OF IRISH PARTIES FROM 1843. IRELAND UK USA-45 LEGIS WORKER ECO/TAC COERCE CRIME REV CHOOSE ORD/FREE CATHISM LAISSEZ...SOC 19/20 PARLIAMENT PARNELL/CS LAND/LEAG. PAGE 100 F1957 — LEAD DOMIN POL/PAR POLICY

B91
MILL J.S.,SOCIALISM (1859). MOD/EUR AGRI INDUS NAT/G REV INCOME PRODUC ORD/FREE POPULISM SOCISM ...GOV/COMP METH/COMP 19. PAGE 91 F1787 — WEALTH SOCIALIST ECO/TAC OWN

B92
COULANGES F D.E.,THE ORIGIN OF PROPERTY IN LAND. LAW STRATA AGRI ACADEM EDU/PROP ORD/FREE 19. PAGE 28 F0543 — OWN HIST/WRIT IDEA/COMP SOCISM

ORDER....SEE ORD/FREE

OREGON....OREGON

ORG FOR ECO COOP AND DEVEL F1995,F1996,F1997

ORG/CHARTS....ORGANIZATIONAL CHARTS, BLUEPRINTS

ORGANIZATION AMERICAN STATES F1998

ORGANIZATION FOR AFRICAN UNITY....SEE OAU

ORGANIZATION FOR ECONOMIC COOPERATION AND DEVELOPMENT.... SEE OECD

ORGANIZATION FOR EUROPEAN ECONOMIC COOPERATION....SEE OEEC

ORGANIZATION FOR LATIN AMERICAN SOLIDARITY....SEE OLAS

ORGANIZATION OF AFRICAN STATES.... SEE AFR/STATES

ORGANIZATION OF AMERICAN STATES....SEE OAS

ORGANIZATION, INTERNATIONAL....SEE INT/ORG

ORGANIZATION, LABOR....SEE LABOR

ORGANIZATION, POLITICAL....SEE POL/PAR

ORGANIZATION, PROFESSIONAL....SEE PROF/ORG

ORGANIZATION, VOLUNTARY....SEE VOL/ASSN

ORGANIZATIONAL BEHAVIOR, NONEXECUTIVE....SEE ADMIN

ORLANS H. F1999

ORTHO/GK....GREEK ORTHODOX CHURCH

ORTHO/RUSS....RUSSIAN ORTHODOX CATHOLIC

ORTHODOX EASTERN CHURCH....SEE ORTHO/GK

ORTON W.A. F2000

ORWELL/G....GEORGE ORWELL

OSBORN F. F2001

OSGOOD H.L. F2002

OSHOGBO....OSHOGBO, WEST AFRICA

OSSIPOV G. F1288

OSTRY S. F2924

OTERO L.M. F2003

OTTOMAN....OTTOMAN EMPIRE

B58
SHAW S.J.,THE FINANCIAL AND ADMINISTRATIVE ORGANIZATION AND DEVELOPMENT OF OTTOMAN EGYPT 1517-1798. UAR LOC/G FORCES BUDGET INT/TRADE TAX EATING INCOME WEALTH...CHARTS BIBLIOG 16/18 OTTOMAN NAPOLEON/B. PAGE 120 F2371 — FINAN ADMIN GOV/REL CULTURE

OUTER SPACE....SEE SPACE

OUTER/MONG....OUTER MONGOLIA

B65
HOLLER J.E.,POPULATION TRENDS AND ECONOMIC DEVELOPMENT IN THE FAR EAST (PAMPHLET). KOREA S/ASIA AGRI INDUS DELIB/GP PROB/SOLV RATIONAL ...POLICY CHARTS BIBLIOG 20 OUTER/MONG CHINJAP HONG/KONG. PAGE 61 F1197 — CENSUS TREND ECO/UNDEV ASIA

OVERSEAS DEVELOPMENT INSTITUTE....SEE OVRSEA/DEV

OVERSEAS DEVELOPMENT INSTIT F2004

OVIMBUNDU....OVIMBUNDU PEOPLES OF ANGOLA

OVRSEA/DEV....OVERSEAS DEVELOPMENT INSTITUTE

B66
HAYER T.,FRENCH AID. AFR FRANCE AGRI FINAN BUDGET ADMIN WAR PRODUC...CHARTS 18/20 THIRD/WRLD OVRSEA/DEV. PAGE 57 F1125 — TEC/DEV COLONIAL FOR/AID ECO/UNDEV

N66
BRITISH DEVELOPMENT POLICIES: 1966 (PAMPHLET). UK AGRI TARIFFS BAL/PAY...TREND CHARTS 20 OVRSEA/DEV. PAGE 1 F0023 — WEALTH DIPLOM INT/TRADE FOR/AID

OWE

N64
US BOARD GOVERNORS FEDL RESRV,SELECTED BIBLIOGRAPHY ON MONETARY POLICY AND MANAGEMENT OF THE PUBLIC DEBT 1947-1960 AND 1961-1963 SUPPLEMENT (PAMPH.). USA+45 PLAN...POLICY MGT OWE 20. PAGE 134 F2642 — BIBLIOG FINAN NAT/G

OWEN C.F. F2005

OWEN/RBT....ROBERT OWEN

OWENS R.N. F2006

OWI....OFFICE OF WAR INFORMATION

OWN....OWNERSHIP, OWNER

N
US SUPERINTENDENT OF DOCUMENTS,TARIFF AND TAXATION (PRICE LIST 37). USA+45 LAW INT/TRADE ADJUD ADMIN — BIBLIOG/A TAX

CT/SYS INCOME OWN...DECISION GATT. PAGE 140 F2754 — TARIFFS NAT/G

B08
LLOYD H.D.,THE SWISS DEMOCRACY. SWITZERLND INDUS NAT/G WORKER CHOOSE OWN ORD/FREE SOCISM...PLURIST 19/20 MONOPOLY. PAGE 81 F1590 — NAT/COMP GOV/COMP REPRESENT POPULISM

B11
SOREL G.,LES ILLUSIONS DU PROGRES (1906). UNIV SOCIETY STRATA INDUS GP/REL OWN PRODUC SOCISM 17/20. PAGE 124 F2444 — WORKER POPULISM ECO/DEV ATTIT

B13
BEARD C.A.,AN ECONOMIC INTERPRETATION OF THE CONSTITUTION OF THE UNITED STATES. USA-45 AGRI INT/TRADE SUFF OWN ATTIT...CONCPT MYTH BIOG HIST/WRIT 18. PAGE 12 F0222 — CONSTN ECO/TAC CHOOSE

B13
KROPOTKIN P.,THE CONQUEST OF BREAD. SOCIETY STRATA AGRI INDUS WORKER REV HAPPINESS INCOME PRODUC HEALTH MORAL ORD/FREE. PAGE 74 F1444 — ANARCH SOCIALIST OWN AGREE

N19
ATOMIC INDUSTRIAL FORUM,COMMENTARY ON LEGISLATION TO PERMIT PRIVATE OWNERSHIP OF SPECIAL NUCLEAR MATERIAL (PAMPHLET). USA+45 DELIB/GP LEGIS PLAN OWN ...POLICY 20 AEC CONGRESS. PAGE 7 F0134 — NUC/PWR MARKET INDUS LAW

N19
LAWRENCE S.A.,THE BATTERY ADDITIVE CONTROVERSY (PAMPHLET). USA+45 LAW MARKET PROC/MFG R+D CAP/ISM CT/SYS GOV/REL OWN FTC CONGRESS BUR/STNDRD RITCHIE/JM. PAGE 76 F1494 — PHIL/SCI LOBBY INSPECT

N19
YLVISAKER P.N.,THE NATURAL CEMENT ISSUE (PAMPHLET). USA+45 USA-45 CONSTRUC PROVS CAP/ISM ADMIN LOBBY PERS/REL OWN RIGID/FLEX ROLE 20 MINNESOTA. PAGE 150 F2948 — POLICY NAT/G PLAN GOV/REL

B20
MALTHUS T.R.,PRINCIPLES OF POLITICAL ECONOMY. UK AGRI INDUS MARKET NAT/G DIPLOM PRICE CONTROL BAL/PAY COST OWN PWR LAISSEZ 18/19. PAGE 84 F1650 — GEN/LAWS DEMAND WEALTH

B20
TAWNEY R.H.,THE ACQUISITIVE SOCIETY. STRATA WORKER PROB/SOLV CAP/ISM ECO/TAC CONTROL GP/REL OWN PRIVIL ATTIT ORD/FREE WEALTH 20. PAGE 128 F2536 — INDUS SOCIETY PRODUC MORAL

S21
MALINOWSKI B.,"THE PRIMITIVE ECONOMICS OF THE TROBRIAND ISLANDERS" (BMR)" CULTURE SOCIETY NAT/G CHIEF LEAD OWN...SOC MYTH WORSHIP 20 NEW/GUINEA TROBRIAND RESOURCE/N. PAGE 84 F1647 — ECO/UNDEV AGRI PRODUC STRUCT

B24
CLARK J.B.,THE DISTRIBUTION OF WEALTH (1899). WORKER OWN PRODUC PROFIT WEALTH LAISSEZ...IDEA/COMP GEN/LAWS. PAGE 25 F0478 — ECO/TAC INDUS LABOR INCOME

B26
TAWNEY R.H.,RELIGION AND THE RISE OF CAPITALISM. UK CULTURE NAT/G TEC/DEV OWN LAISSEZ...POLICY SOC TIME/SEQ 16/19. PAGE 129 F2537 — SECT WEALTH INDUS CAP/ISM

B32
THOMPSON C.D.,CONFESSIONS OF THE POWER TRUST. MARKET ACT/RES EDU/PROP CONTROL GOV/REL INCOME OWN ...MGT 20 FTC MONOPOLY. PAGE 130 F2564 — LG/CO SERV/IND PWR FINAN

B33
TANNENBAUM F.,PEACE BY REVOLUTION. ECO/UNDEV AGRI SECT WORKER DIPLOM EDU/PROP DISCRIM OWN WEALTH POPULISM 17/20 MEXIC/AMER INDIAN/AM. PAGE 128 F2532 — CULTURE COLONIAL RACE/REL REV

B35
MARX K.,WAGE-LABOR AND CAPITAL -- VALUE, PRICE AND PROFIT. LABOR PAY PRICE COST INCOME OWN PROFIT WEALTH 19. PAGE 86 F1690 — STRATA WORKER MARXIST MARXISM

B36
BELLOC H.,THE RESTORATION OF PROPERTY. UK STRATA NAT/G PROF/ORG DELIB/GP WORKER CREATE PROB/SOLV ECO/TAC PARTIC UTOPIA ORD/FREE SOCISM 20. PAGE 13 F0238 — CONTROL MAJORIT CAP/ISM OWN

B38
LAWLEY F.E.,THE GROWTH OF COLLECTIVE ECONOMY VOL. 1: NATIONAL. EUR+WWI AGRI INDUS NAT/G BARGAIN CAP/ISM ECO/TAC WAR OPTIMAL WEALTH...GOV/COMP METH/COMP 19/20 MONOPOLY. PAGE 76 F1492 — SOCISM PRICE CONTROL OWN

B38
LAWLEY F.E.,THE GROWTH OF COLLECTIVE ECONOMY VOL. 2: INTERNATIONAL. WOR-45 AGRI INDUS EQUILIB OPTIMAL OWN WEALTH...NAT/COMP 19/20 NAZI NEW/DEAL MONOPOLY. PAGE 76 F1493 — ECO/TAC SOCISM NAT/LISM CONTROL

B48
HART A.G.,MONEY, DEBT, AND ECONOMIC ACTIVITY. AFR WORKER DIPLOM PRICE CONTROL BAL/PAY COST OWN PRODUC ...METH/COMP 20 FED/RESERV. PAGE 56 F1097 — FINAN WEALTH ECO/TAC NAT/G

B52
BEVAN A.,IN PLACE OF FEAR. WOR+45 STRATA LEGIS REPRESENT OWN NEW/LIB POPULISM...CHARTS 20. PAGE 14 F0273 — SOCISM SOCIALIST WEALTH MAJORIT

B52
TANNENBAUM F.,A PHILOSOPHY OF LABOR. SOCIETY STRATA INDUS LG/CO AGREE ADJUST OWN ORD/FREE PWR...CONCPT 20. PAGE 128 F2533 — LABOR PHIL/SCI WORKER CREATE

B54
EMERSON F.D.,SHAREHOLDER DEMOCRACY: A BROADER OUTLOOK FOR CORPORATIONS. DELIB/GP EX/STRUC LEGIS ADJUD CONTROL REPRESENT INGP/REL OWN PWR...POLICY STAT RECORD. PAGE 37 F0727 — LG/CO PARTIC MAJORIT TREND

B54
FRIEDMAN W.,THE PUBLIC CORPORATION: A COMPARATIVE SYMPOSIUM (UNIVERSITY OF TORONTO SCHOOL OF LAW COMPARATIVE LAW SERIES, VOL. I). AFR SWEDEN USA+45 INDUS INT/ORG NAT/G REGION CENTRAL FEDERAL...POLICY JURID IDEA/COMP NAT/COMP ANTHOL 20 MONOPOLY EUROPE. PAGE 44 F0861 — LAW SOCISM LG/CO OWN

B55
GEORGE H.,PROGRESS AND POVERTY (1880). STRATA STRUCT INDUS TEC/DEV CAP/ISM EQUILIB INCOME OWN UTOPIA...WELF/ST CONCPT NEW/IDEA 19. PAGE 47 F0915 — ECO/DEV ECO/TAC TAX WEALTH

B56
GILBERT L.D.,DIVIDENDS AND DEMOCRACY. DELIB/GP LEGIS CAP/ISM ADJUD LOBBY OWN PWR LAISSEZ MAJORIT. PAGE 47 F0922 — LG/CO INGP/REL CONTROL PARTIC

B57
MURDESHWAR A.K.,ADMINISTRATIVE PROBLEMS RELATING TO NATIONALISATION: WITH SPECIAL REFERENCE TO INDIAN STATE ENTERPRISES. CZECHOSLVK FRANCE INDIA UK USA+45 LEGIS WORKER PROB/SOLV BUDGET PRICE CONTROL ...MGT GEN/LAWS 20 PARLIAMENT. PAGE 95 F1863 — NAT/G OWN INDUS ADMIN

B58
PAYNO M.,LA REFORMA SOCIAL EN ESPANA Y MEXICO. SPAIN ECO/TAC TAX LOBBY COERCE REV OWN CATHISM 19/20 MEXIC/AMER. PAGE 104 F2043 — SECT NAT/G LAW ELITES

B59
JENKINS C.,POWER AT THE TOP: A CRITICAL SURVEY OF THE NATIONALIZED INDUSTRIES. UK POL/PAR CONTROL ...WELF/ST CHARTS 20 LABOR/PAR. PAGE 67 F1313 — NAT/G OWN INDUS NEW/LIB

B59
KELF-COHEN R.,NATIONALISATION IN BRITAIN: THE END OF DOGMA. EUR+WWI UK NAT/G POL/PAR WORKER ECO/TAC PARL/PROC WEALTH SOCISM...GOV/COMP 20. PAGE 70 F1369 — NEW/LIB ECO/DEV INDUS OWN

B59
LOPEZ VILLAMIL H.,A STATEMENT OF THE LAWS OF THE HONDURAS IN MATTERS AFFECTING BUSINESS (2ND ED.). HONDURAS DIST/IND EXTR/IND FINAN WORKER TAX DEATH MARRIAGE OWN MARITIME 20 MIGRATION. PAGE 82 F1600 — CONSTN INDUS LEGIS NAT/G

B59
MARTIN D.D.,MERGERS AND THE CLAYTON ACT. FINAN LEGIS GP/REL...DECISION METH/COMP BIBLIOG 20. PAGE 86 F1681 — OWN ECO/TAC LG/CO POLICY

B59
NUNEZ JIMENEZ A.,LA LIBERACION DE LAS ISLAS. CUBA L/A+17C USA+45 LAW CHIEF PLAN DIPLOM FOR/AID OWN WEALTH 20 CASTRO/F. PAGE 99 F1945 — AGRI REV ECO/UNDEV NAT/G

B60
BHAMBHRI C.P.,PARLIAMENTARY CONTROL OVER STATE ENTERPRISE IN INDIA. INDIA DELIB/GP ADMIN CONTROL INGP/REL EFFICIENCY 20 PARLIAMENT. PAGE 14 F0277 — NAT/G OWN INDUS PARL/PROC

B60
HARBRECHT P.P.,TOWARD THE PARAPROPRIETAL SOCIETY. REPRESENT INCOME OWN PROFIT AGE/O. PAGE 55 F1076 — PWR ADMIN ELITES CONTROL

B60
HUGHES J.,NATIONALISED INDUSTRIES IN THE MIXED ECONOMY (PAMPHLET). FINAN PROB/SOLV CAP/ISM OWN ...SOCIALIST STAT METH/COMP 20. PAGE 63 F1233 — SOCISM LG/CO GOV/REL ECO/DEV

B60
ROBSON W.A.,NATIONALIZED INDUSTRY AND PUBLIC OWNERSHIP. UK ECO/DEV FINAN LABOR LG/CO POL/PAR LEGIS ACT/RES GP/REL...TREND IDEA/COMP 20. PAGE 113 F2227 — NAT/G OWN INDUS ATTIT

B60
WEINER H.E.,BRITISH LABOR AND PUBLIC OWNERSHIP. UK SERV/IND LG/CO WORKER CONTROL OWN 20. PAGE 145 F2850 — LABOR NAT/G INDUS ATTIT

B61
AGARWAL R.C.,STATE ENTERPRISE IN INDIA. FUT INDIA UK FINAN INDUS ADMIN CONTROL OWN...POLICY CHARTS — ECO/UNDEV SOCISM

BIBLIOG 20 RAILROAD. PAGE 3 F0048 GOV/REL LG/CO

B61
ALFRED H.,PUBLIC OWNERSHIP IN THE USA: GOALS AND PRIORITIES. LAW INDUS INT/TRADE ADJUD GOV/REL EFFICIENCY PEACE SOCISM...POLICY ANTHOL 20 TVA. PAGE 4 F0065 CONTROL OWN ECO/DEV ECO/TAC

B61
ERASMUS C.J.,MAN TAKES CONTROL: CULTURAL DEVELOPMENT AND AMERICAN AID. STRUCT OWN DRIVE PERCEPT...SOC 20 MEXIC/AMER. PAGE 38 F0741 ORD/FREE CULTURE ECO/UNDEV TEC/DEV

B61
HUBBARD P.J.,ORIGINS OF THE TVA: THE MUSCLE SHOALS CONTROVERSY, 1920-1932. USA-45 DELIB/GP LEGIS LEAD LOBBY GOV/REL GP/REL INGP/REL OWN PERSON...BIBLIOG 20 TVA CONGRESS WATER. PAGE 62 F1229 SEA CONTROL NAT/G INDUS

B61
LAHAYE R.,LES ENTREPRISES PUBLIQUES AU MAROC. FRANCE MOROCCO LAW DIST/IND EXTR/IND FINAN CONSULT PLAN TEC/DEV ADMIN AGREE CONTROL OWN...POLICY 20. PAGE 74 F1460 NAT/G INDUS ECO/UNDEV ECO/TAC

B61
SEPULVEDA C.,A STATEMENT OF THE LAWS OF MEXICO IN MATTERS AFFECTING BUSINESS (3RD ED.). AGRI DIST/IND EXTR/IND FINAN INDUS WORKER TAX MARRIAGE OWN ORD/FREE...BIBLIOG 20 MEXIC/AMER TREATY MIGRATION MONOPOLY. PAGE 119 F2356 CONSTN NAT/G JURID LEGIS

N61
US ADVISORY COMM INTERGOV REL,STATE AND LOCAL TAXATION ON PRIVATELY OWNED PROPERTY LOCATED ON FEDERAL AREAS: PROPOSED AMENDMENT OF BUCK ACT (PAMPHLET). USA+45 ACT/RES PLAN CONTROL GOV/REL INGP/REL OWN...POLICY JURID CHARTS GP/COMP 20. PAGE 133 F2629 PROVS LOC/G NAT/G TAX

B62
KUHN T.E.,PUBLIC ENTERPRISES, PROJECT PLANNING AND ECONOMIC DEVELOPMENT (PAMPHLET). ECO/UNDEV FINAN PLAN ADMIN EFFICIENCY OWN...MGT STAT CHARTS ANTHOL 20. PAGE 74 F1447 ECO/DEV ECO/TAC LG/CO NAT/G

B62
US BUREAU OF THE CENSUS,REPORT FOR SUBCOMMITTEE ON ANTITRUST AND MONOPOLY: CONCENTRATION RATIOS IN MANUFACTURING INDUSTRY 1958. USA+45 ECO/DEV CONTROL GOV/REL OWN PRODUC PROFIT...STAT 20 CONGRESS MONOPOLY. PAGE 134 F2646 CHARTS PROC/MFG MARKET LG/CO

B63
FURTADO C.,THE ECONOMIC GROWTH OF BRAZIL: A SURVEY FROM COLONIAL TO MODERN TIMES. L/A+17C AGRI DIST/IND EXTR/IND INDUS WORKER COLONIAL RACE/REL OWN GOV/COMP. PAGE 45 F0877 ECO/UNDEV TEC/DEV LABOR DOMIN

B63
GOLDMAN M.I.,SOVIET MARKETING. USSR DIST/IND FINAN RATION OWN WEALTH...SOC BIBLIOG 20. PAGE 48 F0937 MARKET ECO/TAC CONTROL MARXISM

B63
MARX K.,THE POVERTY OF PHILOSOPHY (1847). SOCIETY STRATA INDUS WORKER OWN UTOPIA SOCISM...GEN/LAWS MARX/KARL. PAGE 86 F1692 MARXIST PRODUC

B63
MINGAY G.E.,ENGLISH LANDED SOCIETY IN THE EIGHTEENTH CENTURY. UK ELITES STRUCT AGRI INDUS CONTROL WEALTH 18. PAGE 92 F1802 OWN STRATA PWR

B63
SHANKS M.,THE LESSONS OF PUBLIC ENTERPRISE. UK LEGIS WORKER ECO/TAC ADMIN PARL/PROC GOV/REL ATTIT ...POLICY MGT METH/COMP NAT/COMP ANTHOL 20 PARLIAMENT. PAGE 120 F2364 SOCISM OWN NAT/G INDUS

N63
NORTH CAROLINA U INST GOVT,COSTING URBAN DEVELOPMENT AND REDEVELOPMENT (PAMPHLET). USA+45 USA-45 NEIGH PLAN TEC/DEV TAX OWN...GEOG MUNICH 20. PAGE 98 F1934 BIBLIOG COST FINAN

B64
GARFIELD PJ LOVEJOY WF,PUBLIC UTILITY ECONOMICS. DIST/IND FINAN MARKET ADMIN COST DEMAND ...TECHNIC JURID MUNICH 20 MONOPOLY. PAGE 46 F0906 T ECO/TAC OWN SERV/IND

B64
HAAR C.M.,LAW AND LAND: ANGLO-AMERICAN PLANNING PRACTICE. UK USA+45 NAT/G TEC/DEV BUDGET CT/SYS INGP/REL EFFICIENCY OWN...JURID MUNICH 20. PAGE 52 F1019 LAW PLAN NAT/COMP

B64
HAMBRIDGE G.,DYNAMICS OF DEVELOPMENT. AGRI FINAN INDUS LABOR INT/TRADE EDU/PROP ADMIN LEAD OWN HEALTH...ANTHOL BIBLIOG 20. PAGE 54 F1054 ECO/UNDEV ECO/TAC OP/RES ACT/RES

B64
LETICHE J.M.,A HISTORY OF RUSSIAN ECONOMIC THOUGHT: NINTH THROUGH EIGHTEENTH CENTURIES. RUSSIA FINAN SECT CAP/ISM DOMIN DEMAND EFFICIENCY OWN MARXISM ...TECHNIC ANTHOL BIBLIOG 9/18. PAGE 78 F1536 ECO/TAC TIME/SEQ IDEA/COMP ECO/UNDEV

B64
TAWNEY R.H.,EQUALITY. UK CULTURE STRATA ECO/TAC EDU/PROP REPRESENT OWN NEW/LIB...MAJORIT WELF/ST SOC 20. PAGE 129 F2538 WEALTH STRUCT ELITES POPULISM

B64
TELLADO A.,A STATEMENT OF THE LAWS OF THE DOMINICAN REPUBLIC IN MATTERS AFFECTING BUSINESS (3RD ED.). DOMIN/REP AGRI DIST/IND EXTR/IND FINAN FAM WORKER ECO/TAC TAX CT/SYS MARRIAGE OWN...BIBLIOG 20 MIGRATION. PAGE 129 F2542 CONSTN LEGIS NAT/G INDUS

B64
US HOUSE COMM GOVT OPERATIONS,US OWNED FOREIGN CURRENCIES: HEARINGS (COMMITTEE ON GOVERNMENT OPERATIONS). INDIA ECO/DEV PLAN BUDGET TAX DEMAND EFFICIENCY 20 AID CONGRESS. PAGE 137 F2699 FINAN ECO/TAC FOR/AID OWN

B64
YUDELMAN M.,AFRICANS ON THE LAND. RHODESIA MARKET LABOR OWN...ECOMETRIC TREND 20. PAGE 150 F2955 ECO/DEV AFR AGRI ECO/TAC

B65
AMERICAN FOREST PRODUCTS INDUS,GOVERNMENT LAND ACQUISITION: A SUMMARY OF LAND ACQUISITION BY FEDERAL, STATE, AND LOCAL GOVERNMENTS UP TO 1964. USA+45 USA-45 TAX...POLICY GEOG CHARTS 20. PAGE 5 F0089 NAT/G OWN ECO/TAC GOV/REL

B65
BARRY E.E.,NATIONALISATION IN BRITISH POLITICS: THE HISTORICAL BACKGROUND. UK AGRI DIST/IND EXTR/IND LABOR LG/CO ATTIT CONSERVE SOCISM 19/20 LABOR/PAR. PAGE 10 F0198 NAT/G OWN INDUS POL/PAR

B65
LUGO-MARENCO J.J.,A STATEMENT OF THE LAWS OF NICARAGUA IN MATTERS AFFECTING BUSINESS. NICARAGUA AGRI DIST/IND EXTR/IND FINAN INDUS FAM WORKER INT/TRADE TAX MARRIAGE OWN BIO/SOC 20 TREATY RESOURCE/N MIGRATION. PAGE 82 F1606 CONSTN NAT/G LEGIS JURID

B65
MUSHKIN S.J.,PROPERTY TAXES: THE 1970 OUTLOOK (PAMPHLET). FUT USA+45 ECO/DEV MARKET PROVS PLAN ...PROBABIL STAT CENSUS PREDICT CHARTS METH 20. PAGE 95 F1872 TAX OWN FINAN LOC/G

B65
ONUOHA B.,THE ELEMENTS OF AFRICAN SOCIALISM. AFR FINAN SECT TEC/DEV FOR/AID GP/REL OWN LAISSEZ MARXISM...CONCPT BIBLIOG 20. PAGE 101 F1992 SOCISM ECO/UNDEV NAT/G EX/STRUC

B65
SHEPHERD W.G.,ECONOMIC PERFORMANCE UNDER PUBLIC OWNERSHIP: BRITISH FUEL AND POWER. UK BUDGET GP/REL ...METH/CNCPT CHARTS BIBLIOG 20. PAGE 120 F2375 PROC/MFG NAT/G OWN FINAN

B65
WARD R.,BACKGROUND MATERIAL ON ECONOMIC IMPACT OF FEDERAL PROCUREMENT - 1965: FOR JOINT ECONOMIC COMMITTEE US CONGRESS. FINAN ROUTINE WEAPON CIVMIL/REL EFFICIENCY...STAT CHARTS 20 CONGRESS. PAGE 143 F2818 ECO/DEV NAT/G OWN GOV/REL

B65
WU YUAN-LI,THE ECONOMY OF COMMUNIST CHINA. CHINA/COM USSR AGRI FINAN INDUS POL/PAR WORKER PROB/SOLV INT/TRADE PRICE EATING INCOME OWN WEALTH 20. PAGE 149 F2939 ECO/TAC MARXISM PLAN EFFICIENCY

C65
PEGRUM D.E.,"PUBLIC REGULATION OF BUSINESS (REV ED)" LAW CONSTN DIST/IND SERV/IND LG/CO LEGIS OWN LAISSEZ SOCISM...POLICY DECISION BIBLIOG 20. PAGE 104 F2048 INDUS PLAN NEW/LIB PRICE

B66
HUNT C.L.,SOCIAL ASPECTS OF ECONOMIC DEVELOPMENT. S/ASIA AGRI FAM TEC/DEV RECEIVE EDU/PROP OWN...GEOG MUNICH 20. PAGE 63 F1243 SOC STRATA ATTIT ECO/UNDEV

B66
TIVEY L.J.,NATIONALISATION IN BRITISH INDUSTRY. UK LEGIS PARL/PROC GP/REL OWN ATTIT SOCISM 20. PAGE 131 F2578 NAT/G INDUS CONTROL LG/CO

B67
BIRMINGHAM W.,A STUDY OF CONTEMPORARY GHANA VOL. I: SOME ASPECTS OF SOCIAL STRUCTURE. AFR GHANA AGRI FAM SECT PLAN EDU/PROP MARRIAGE OWN...POLICY STAT CHARTS MUNICH 20. PAGE 15 F0287 SOCIETY STRUCT CENSUS ECO/UNDEV

B67
BUSEY J.L.,NOTES ON COSTA RICAN DEMOCRACY. COSTA/RICA L/A+17C NAT/G POL/PAR LEGIS CHOOSE OWN ATTIT...BIBLIOG 20. PAGE 20 F0394 CONSTN MAJORIT SOCIETY ECO/UNDEV

B67
ROBINSON R.D.,INTERNATIONAL MANAGEMENT. LAW MARKET LABOR PRICE CONTROL COST DEMAND OWN PRODUC WEALTH 20. PAGE 113 F2225 T OP/RES MGT DIPLOM

L67
DEALEY S.,"MONETARY RECOVERY UNDER FEDERAL TRANSPORTATION STATUTES." USA+45 SEA WORKER TAX PAY ADJUD DEATH GOV/REL OWN HEALTH ORD/FREE 20. PAGE 31 DIST/IND LAW CONTROL

F0609 FINAN

L67

HUBBARD P.H.,"MONETARY RECOVERY UNDER THE COPYRIGHT, PATENT, AND TRADEMARK ACTS." PROC/MFG TAX PAY LEGIT ADJUD GOV/REL OWN ORD/FREE 20. PAGE 62 F1228
CREATE LAW CONTROL FINAN

L67

ROBERTS E.F.,"THE CASE OF THE UNWARY HOME BUYER: THE HOUSING MERCHANT DID IT." USA+45 CLIENT DIST/IND MARKET LG/CO SML/CO PROB/SOLV LEGIT COST PROFIT. PAGE 112 F2207
ADJUD CONSTRUC OWN LAW

S67

ADAMS D.W.,"MINIFUNDIA IN AGRARIAN REFORM: A COLOMBIAN EXAMPLE."...SOC CLASSIF 20 COLOMB. PAGE 2 F0035
AGRI METH/COMP OWN PRODUC

S67

AVTORKHANOV A.,"A NEW AGRARIAN REVOLUTION." COM USSR ECO/DEV PLAN TEC/DEV ADMIN CONTROL OPTIMAL WEALTH SOCISM 20 KHRUSH/N STALIN/J. PAGE 8 F0144
AGRI METH/COMP MARXISM OWN

S67

BRANCO R.,"LAND REFORM* THE ANSWER TO LATIN AMERICA'S AGRICULTURAL DEVELOPMENT?" L/A+17C NAT/G PLAN TEC/DEV BUDGET RENT EFFICIENCY 20. PAGE 18 F0339
ECO/UNDEV AGRI TAX OWN

S67

CHADWELL J.T.,"ANTITRUST ASPECTS OF DEALER LICENSING AND FRANCHISING." ACT/RES LICENSE ADJUD CONTROL OWN. PAGE 23 F0439
LAW PRIVIL INDUS

S67

DAVIS O.A.,"ON THE DISTINCTION BETWEEN PUBLIC AND PRIVATE GOODS." USA+45 COM/IND LG/CO NAT/G TV DEBATE PRICE ADMIN ROLE...MATH IDEA/COMP. PAGE 31 F0593
MARKET OWN CONCPT

S67

JENCKS C.E.,"SOCIAL STATUS OF COAL MINERS IN BRITAIN SINCE NATIONALIZATION." UK STRATA STRUCT LABOR RECEIVE GP/REL INCOME OWN ATTIT HABITAT...MGT T 20. PAGE 67 F1312
EXTR/IND WORKER CONTROL NAT/G

S67

LEFCOE G.,"CONSTRUCTION LENDING AND THE EQUITABLE LIEN." LICENSE CT/SYS OWN...STAT 20. PAGE 77 F1510
CONSTRUC RENT ADJUD

S67

MEADE J.E.,"POPULATION EXPLOSION, THE STANDARD OF LIVING AND SOCIAL CONFLICT." DIPLOM FOR/AID OWN ...PREDICT TREND 20. PAGE 89 F1739
GEOG WEALTH PRODUC INCOME

S67

ORAZEM F.,"THE NEW SOVIET PLAN FOR AGRICULTURE (1960-1970)" USSR WORKER CAP/ISM ECO/TAC PRICE OWN HABITAT MARXISM...CHARTS 20. PAGE 101 F1994
AGRI PLAN COM ECO/DEV

S67

REILLY T.J.,"FREEZING AND CONFISCATION OF CUBAN PROPERTY." CUBA USA+45 LAW DIPLOM LEGIT ADJUD CONTROL. PAGE 111 F2177
STRANGE OWN ECO/TAC

B76

PROUDHON P.J.,WHAT IS PROPERTY? (TRANS. BY B.R. TUCKER). SOCIETY AGRI CAP/ISM CRIME GP/REL PERSON MORAL ORD/FREE WEALTH. PAGE 108 F2127
OWN WORKER PRODUC ANARCH

B84

MILL J.,ELEMENTS OF POLITICAL ECONOMY. UK LAW ELITES FINAN WORKER ECO/TAC RENT OWN WEALTH ...POLICY GEN/LAWS 19. PAGE 91 F1785
TAX TARIFFS NAT/G INCOME

B91

MILL J.S.,SOCIALISM (1859). MOD/EUR AGRI INDUS NAT/G REV INCOME PRODUC ORD/FREE POPULISM SOCISM ...GOV/COMP METH/COMP 19. PAGE 91 F1787
WEALTH SOCIALIST ECO/TAC OWN

B92

COULANGES F D.E.,THE ORIGIN OF PROPERTY IN LAND. LAW STRATA AGRI ACADEM EDU/PROP ORD/FREE 19. PAGE 28 F0543
OWN HIST/WRIT IDEA/COMP SOCISM

B95

SELIGMAN E.R.A.,ESSAYS IN TAXATION. NEW/ZEALND PRUSSIA UK USA-45 MARKET LOC/G CREATE PRICE CONTROL INCOME OWN WEALTH...GOV/COMP METH/COMP 19. PAGE 119 F2349
TAX TARIFFS INDUS NAT/G

B96

SMITH A.,LECTURES ON JUSTICE, POLICE, REVENUE AND ARMS (1763). UK LAW FAM FORCES TARIFFS AGREE COERCE INCOME OWN WEALTH LAISSEZ...GEN/LAWS 17/18. PAGE 123 F2429
DIPLOM JURID OLD/LIB TAX

OXENFELDT A.R. F2007

OXFORD/GRP....OXFORD GROUP

OZGA S.A. F2008

P

PAARLBERG D. F2009

PAAUW D.S. F2010

PACIFIC/IS....PACIFIC ISLANDS: US TRUST TERRITORY OF THE PACIFIC ISLANDS - CAROLINE ISLANDS, MARSHALL ISLANDS, AND MARIANA ISLANDS

PACIFISM....SEE ALSO ARMS/CONT, PEACE

N19

FREEMAN H.A.,COERCION OF STATES IN FEDERAL UNIONS (PAMPHLET). WOR-45 DIPLOM CONTROL COERCE PEACE ORD/FREE...GOV/COMP METH/COMP NAT/COMP PACIFIST 20. PAGE 43 F0850
FEDERAL WAR INT/ORG PACIFISM

B59

MARTIN K.,WAR, HISTORY, AND HUMAN NATURE. FRANCE GERMANY INDIA UK UNIV POL/PAR COLONIAL DETER REV MARXISM PACIFISM...PSY CONCPT PREDICT LENIN/VI GANDHI/M. PAGE 86 F1683
PERSON WAR ATTIT IDEA/COMP

S67

DRAPER A.P.,"UNIONS AND THE WAR IN VIETNAM." USA+45 CONFER ADMIN LEAD WAR ORD/FREE PACIFIST 20. PAGE 34 F0660
LABOR PACIFISM ATTIT ELITES

PACIFIST....PACIFIST; SEE ALSO PEACE

N19

FREEMAN H.A.,COERCION OF STATES IN FEDERAL UNIONS (PAMPHLET). WOR-45 DIPLOM CONTROL COERCE PEACE ORD/FREE...GOV/COMP METH/COMP NAT/COMP PACIFIST 20. PAGE 43 F0850
FEDERAL WAR INT/ORG PACIFISM

S67

DRAPER A.P.,"UNIONS AND THE WAR IN VIETNAM." USA+45 CONFER ADMIN LEAD WAR ORD/FREE PACIFIST 20. PAGE 34 F0660
LABOR PACIFISM ATTIT ELITES

PACKENHAM R.A. F2011

PADELFORD N.J. F2012,F2013

PAENSON I. F2014

PAI G.A. F2015

PAILLERE M. F0683

PAIN....SEE HEALTH

PAKISTAN....SEE ALSO S/ASIA

N

US LIBRARY OF CONGRESS,SOUTHERN ASIA ACCESSIONS LIST. BURMA CEYLON INDIA NEPAL PAKISTAN S/ASIA THAILAND AGRI INDUS SCHOOL WORKER...ART/METH GEOG HEAL PHIL/SCI LING 20. PAGE 137 F2710
BIBLIOG/A SOCIETY CULTURE ECO/UNDEV

N19

MASON E.S.,THE DIPLOMACY OF ECONOMIC ASSISTANCE (PAMPHLET). INDIA PAKISTAN USA+45 ECO/UNDEV NAT/G BUDGET ATTIT...POLICY 20. PAGE 87 F1695
FOR/AID DIPLOM FINAN

B58

JENNINGS I.,PROBLEMS OF THE NEW COMMONWEALTH. AFR CEYLON INDIA PAKISTAN S/ASIA ECO/UNDEV INT/ORG LOC/G DIPLOM ECO/TAC INT/TRADE COLONIAL RACE/REL DISCRIM 20 PARLIAMENT. PAGE 67 F1314
NAT/LISM NEUTRAL FOR/AID POL/PAR

B59

MADHOK B.,POLITICAL TRENDS IN INDIA. INDIA PAKISTAN UK STRATA ECO/UNDEV POL/PAR LEGIS CAP/ISM DIPLOM COLONIAL CHOOSE MARXISM...SOC TREND 20 GANDHI/M NEHRU/J. PAGE 84 F1639
GEOG NAT/G

B62

GALENSON W.,LABOR IN DEVELOPING COUNTRIES. BRAZIL INDONESIA ISRAEL PAKISTAN TURKEY AGRI INDUS WORKER PAY PRICE GP/REL WEALTH...MGT CHARTS METH/COMP NAT/COMP 20. PAGE 45 F0888
LABOR ECO/UNDEV BARGAIN POL/PAR

B62

JORDAN A.A. JR.,FOREIGN AID AND THE DEFENSE OF SOUTHEAST ASIA. PAKISTAN VIETNAM/S FINAN PLAN BUDGET ECO/TAC DETER WAR ORD/FREE...POLICY DECISION CENSUS CHARTS BIBLIOG 20. PAGE 68 F1341
FOR/AID S/ASIA FORCES ECO/UNDEV

B62

PAKISTAN MINISTRY OF FINANCE,FOREIGN ECONOMIC AID: A REVIEW OF FOREIGN ECONOMIC AID TO PAKISTAN. EUR+WWI PAKISTAN UK USA+45 USSR ECO/UNDEV INT/ORG DELIB/GP DIPLOM ECO/TAC...CHARTS CMN/WLTH CHINJAP. PAGE 103 F2016
FOR/AID RECEIVE WEALTH FINAN

B63

HAQ M.,THE STRATEGY OF ECONOMIC PLANNING. PAKISTAN AGRI FINAN INDUS NAT/G FOR/AID TAX CONTROL REGION PRODUC...POLICY CHARTS 20. PAGE 55 F1071
ECO/TAC ECO/UNDEV PLAN PROB/SOLV

B64

AHMAD M.,THE CIVIL SERVANT IN PAKISTAN. PAKISTAN ECO/UNDEV COLONIAL INGP/REL...SOC CHARTS BIBLIOG 20 CIVIL/SERV. PAGE 3 F0051
WELF/ST ADMIN ATTIT STRATA

B64
CASEY R.G.,THE FUTURE OF THE COMMONWEALTH. INDIA PAKISTAN UK ECO/UNDEV INT/ORG TEC/DEV COLONIAL SUPEGO 20 EEC AUSTRAL. PAGE 22 F0425
DIPLOM SOVEREIGN NAT/LISM FOR/AID

B64
LINDHOLM R.W.,ECONOMIC DEVELOPMENT POLICY WITH EMPHASIS ON VIET-NAM. KOREA/S PAKISTAN VIETNAM/S AGRI INDUS CONSULT DELIB/GP FOR/AID...METH 20. PAGE 80 F1571
ECO/UNDEV TAX FINAN ECO/TAC

B65
ONSLOW C.,ASIAN ECONOMIC DEVELOPMENT. BURMA CEYLON INDIA MALAYSIA PAKISTAN S/ASIA AGRI INDUS MARKET PROB/SOLV CAP/ISM FOR/AID INT/TRADE DEMAND WEALTH ...POLICY ANTHOL 20. PAGE 101 F1991
ECO/UNDEV ECO/TAC PLAN NAT/G

B65
SCHULER E.A.,THE PAKISTAN ACADEMIES FOR RURAL DEVELOPMENT COMILLA AND PESHAWAR 1959-1964. PAKISTAN S/ASIA SOCIETY STRUCT AGRI NAT/G TEC/DEV EDU/PROP 20. PAGE 117 F2314
BIBLIOG PLAN ECO/TAC ECO/UNDEV

B65
SHARIF A.,THE BALANCE OF PAYMENTS OF PAKISTAN, 1948-1958 (THESIS, UNIVERSITY OF TORONTO). PAKISTAN FINAN INDUS FOR/AID PRICE WEALTH...TREND CHARTS 20. PAGE 120 F2368
BAL/PAY BUDGET INT/TRADE ECO/UNDEV

B66
ALI S.,PLANNING, DEVELOPMENT AND CHANGE: AN ANNOTATED BIBLIOGRAPHY ON DEVELOPMENTAL ADMINISTRATION. PAKISTAN SOCIETY ORD/FREE 20. PAGE 4 F0066
BIBLIOG/A ADMIN ECO/UNDEV PLAN

B66
DEBENKO E.,RESEARCH SOURCES FOR SOUTH ASIAN STUDIES IN ECONOMIC DEVELOPMENT: A SELECT BIBLIOGRAPHY OF SERIAL PUBLICATIONS. CEYLON INDIA NEPAL PAKISTAN PROB/SOLV ADMIN...POLICY 20. PAGE 32 F0611
BIBLIOG ECO/UNDEV S/ASIA PLAN

B66
MACBEAN A.I.,EXPORT INSTABILITY AND ECONOMIC DEVELOPMENT. CHILE PAKISTAN PUERT/RICO TANZANIA UGANDA WOR+45 MARKET ECO/TAC...POLICY REGRESS CHARTS BIBLIOG TIME 20. PAGE 83 F1622
INT/TRADE ECO/UNDEV ECOMETRIC INSPECT

B66
MASON E.S.,ECONOMIC DEVELOPMENT IN INDIA AND PAKISTAN. INDIA PAKISTAN AGRI FINAN PLAN BUDGET INT/TRADE WEALTH...POLICY STAT TREND CHARTS 20. PAGE 87 F1700
NAT/COMP ECO/UNDEV ECO/TAC FOR/AID

B66
SPICER K.,A SAMARITAN STATE? AFR CANADA INDIA PAKISTAN UK USA+45 FINAN INDUS PRODUC...CHARTS 20 NATO. PAGE 124 F2455
DIPLOM FOR/AID ECO/DEV ADMIN

B66
ZINKIN T.,CHALLENGES IN INDIA. INDIA PAKISTAN LAW AGRI FINAN INDUS TOP/EX TEC/DEV CONTROL ROUTINE ORD/FREE PWR 20 NEHRU/J SHASTRI/LB CIVIL/SERV. PAGE 150 F2964
NAT/G ECO/TAC POLICY ADMIN

B67
MUHAMMAD A.C.,THE EMERGENCE OF PAKISTAN. PAKISTAN S/ASIA CONSTN ECO/UNDEV NAT/G CONTROL NAT/LISM 20. PAGE 94 F1853
DIPLOM COLONIAL SECT PROB/SOLV

B67
US SENATE COMM ON FOREIGN REL,ARMS SALES TO NEAR EAST AND SOUTH ASIAN COUNTRIES. INDIA IRAN PAKISTAN WOR+45 PROC/MFG BAL/PWR DIPLOM...DECISION SENATE. PAGE 139 F2742
WEAPON FOR/AID FORCES POLICY

S67
SIDDIQ M.M.,"LOCAL GOVERNMENT IN PAKISTAN." PAKISTAN PROB/SOLV TAX COLONIAL GOV/REL MUNICH 20. PAGE 121 F2395
ADMIN LOC/G DELIB/GP BUDGET

PAKISTAN MINISTRY OF FINANCE F2016

PAKISTAN/E....EAST PAKISTAN

PALACIOS A.L. F2017

PALAMOUNTAIN J.C. F0760

PALAMOUNTAIN JC J.R. F2018,F2019

PALESTINE....PALESTINE (PRE-1948 ISRAEL); SEE ALSO ISRAEL

PALMER D.K. F1911

PALMER E.E. F2020,F2021

PALYI M. F2022

PAN AMERICAN UNION F2023,F2024

PANAF/FREE....PAN AFRICAN FREEDOM MOVEMENT

PANAFR/ISM....PAN-AFRICANISM

PANAMA CANAL ZONE....SEE CANAL/ZONE

PANAMA....PANAMA

B67
LISS S.B.,THE CANAL, ASPECTS OF UNITED STATES-PANAMANIAN RELATIONS. AFR FUT PANAMA DOMIN COERCE ATTIT SOVEREIGN MARXISM 20 JOHNSON/LB KENNEDY/JF. PAGE 81 F1580
DIPLOM POLICY

PANIKKAR K.M. F2025

PAN-AFRICANISM....SEE PANAFR/ISM

PANJAB, PANJABI PEOPLE....SEE PUNJAB

PANKHURST R. F0470

PANT Y.P. F2026

PAPUA....PAPUA

N19
ARNDT H.W.,AUSTRALIAN FOREIGN AID POLICY (PAMPHLET). ECO/UNDEV DIPLOM GIVE GOV/REL COST UTIL PWR...CHARTS 20 AUSTRAL PAPUA NEW/GUINEA. PAGE 6 F0114
FOR/AID POLICY ECO/TAC EFFICIENCY

PARAGUAY....SEE ALSO L/A+17C

B62
PASTOR R.S.,A STATEMENT OF THE LAWS OF PARAGUAY IN MATTERS AFFECTING BUSINESS (2ND ED.). PARAGUAY INDUS FAM LABOR LG/CO NAT/G LEGIS TAX CONTROL MARRIAGE 20. PAGE 103 F2033
FINAN ECO/UNDEV LAW CONSTN

PARETO/V....VILFREDO PARETO

B48
HICKS J.R.,VALUE AND CAPITAL. FINAN PRICE EQUILIB INCOME PRODUC WEALTH...TIME/SEQ 20 MARSHALL/A PARETO/V SAMUELSN/P. PAGE 59 F1165
ECOMETRIC MATH DEMAND PROB/SOLV

PARIS....PARIS, FRANCE

PARISH H.C. F1701

PARK/R....ROBERT PARK

PARKER G.P. F2027

PARKER/H....HENRY PARKER

PARKFOREST....PARK FOREST, ILLINOIS

PARL/PROC....PARLIAMENTARY PROCESSES; SEE ALSO LEGIS

C01
LOWELL A.L.,"THE INFLUENCE OF PARTY UPON LEGISLATION IN ENGLAND AND AMERICA" IN ANNUAL REPORT OF AMER HISTORICAL ASSN." LEGIS CONTROL ...CON/ANAL CHARTS 19/20 CONGRESS PARLIAMENT. PAGE 82 F1605
PARL/PROC POL/PAR DECISION OP/RES

N19
ADMINISTRATIVE STAFF COLLEGE,THE ACCOUNTABILITY OF GOVERNMENT DEPARTMENTS (PAMPHLET) (REV. ED.). UK CONSTN FINAN NAT/G CONSULT ADMIN INGP/REL CONSEN PRIVIL 20 PARLIAMENT. PAGE 2 F0043
PARL/PROC ELITES SANCTION PROB/SOLV

N19
MARSH J.F. JR.,THE FBI RETIREMENT BILL (PAMPHLET). USA+45 EX/STRUC WORKER PLAN PROB/SOLV BUDGET LEAD LOBBY PARL/PROC PERS/REL RIGID/FLEX...POLICY 20 FBI PRESIDENT BUR/BUDGET. PAGE 86 F1677
ADMIN NAT/G SENIOR GOV/REL

B23
FINER H.,REPRESENTATIVE GOVERNMENT AND A PARLIAMENT OF INDUSTRY. A STUDY OF THE GERMAN FEDERAL ECONOMIC COUNCIL. GERMANY UK CONSTN INDUS PARL/PROC ...NAT/COMP 20. PAGE 41 F0796
DELIB/GP ECO/TAC WAR REV

B38
LEVINSON E.,LABOR ON THE MARCH. WORKER CREATE ECO/TAC ADJUD LEAD PARL/PROC PARTIC INGP/REL SKILL POLICY. PAGE 79 F1543
LABOR INCOME NAT/G PLAN

B39
JENNINGS W.I.,PARLIAMENT. UK POL/PAR OP/RES BUDGET LEAD CHOOSE GP/REL...MGT 20 PARLIAMENT HOUSE/LORD HOUSE/CMNS. PAGE 67 F1315
PARL/PROC LEGIS CONSTN NAT/G

B39
THOMAS J.A.,THE HOUSE OF COMMONS, 1832-1901; A STUDY OF ITS ECONOMIC AND FUNCTIONAL CHARACTER. UK LAW STRATA FINAN DIPLOM CONTROL LEAD LOBBY REPRESENT WEALTH...POLICY STAT BIBLIOG 19/20
PARL/PROC LEGIS POL/PAR ECO/DEV

PARLIAMENT. PAGE 130 F2561

B48
KEIR D.L.,CASES IN CONSTITUTIONAL LAW. UK CHIEF LEGIS DIPLOM TAX PARL/PROC CRIME GOV/REL...INT/LAW JURID 17/20. PAGE 70 F1368 CONSTN LAW ADJUD CT/SYS

B52
JENNINGS W.I.,CONSTITUTIONAL LAWS OF THE COMMONWEALTH. AFR UK LAW CHIEF LEGIS TAX CT/SYS PARL/PROC GOV/REL...INT/LAW 18/20 ENGLSH/LAW COMMON/LAW. PAGE 67 F1316 CONSTN JURID ADJUD COLONIAL

S56
KNAPP D.C.,"CONGRESSIONAL CONTROL OF AGRICULTURAL CONSERVATION POLICY: A CASE STUDY OF THE APPROPRIATIONS PROCESS." DELIB/GP PLAN PROB/SOLV CONFER PARL/PROC...POLICY INT CONGRESS. PAGE 72 F1411 LEGIS AGRI BUDGET CONTROL

N56
US HOUSE COMM FOREIGN AFFAIRS,REPORT OF THE SPECIAL STUDY MISSION TO AFRICA, SOUTH AND EAST OF THE SAHARA (PAMPHLET). AFR SOUTH/AFR USA+45 STRUCT INT/TRADE PARL/PROC NAT/LISM ATTIT ALL/VALS HEALTH ...POLICY 20 CONGRESS. PAGE 136 F2691 FOR/AID COLONIAL ECO/UNDEV DIPLOM

S58
SCHUMM S.,"INTEREST REPRESENTATION IN FRANCE AND GERMANY." EUR+WWI FRANCE GERMANY INSPECT PARL/PROC REPRESENT 20 WEIMAR/REP. PAGE 118 F2320 LOBBY DELIB/GP NAT/G

B59
KELF-COHEN R.,NATIONALISATION IN BRITAIN: THE END OF DOGMA. EUR+WWI UK NAT/G POL/PAR WORKER ECO/TAC PARL/PROC WEALTH SOCISM...GOV/COMP 20. PAGE 70 F1369 NEW/LIB ECO/DEV INDUS OWN

B60
BHAMBHRI C.P.,PARLIAMENTARY CONTROL OVER STATE ENTERPRISE IN INDIA. INDIA DELIB/GP ADMIN CONTROL INGP/REL EFFICIENCY 20 PARLIAMENT. PAGE 14 F0277 NAT/G OWN INDUS PARL/PROC

B62
BROWN S.D.,STUDIES ON ASIA, 1962. ASIA BURMA INDIA ISLAM ISRAEL S/ASIA ECO/UNDEV POL/PAR SECT ECO/TAC ...ANTHOL 20 CHINJAP. PAGE 19 F0374 PWR PARL/PROC

B63
SHANKS M.,THE LESSONS OF PUBLIC ENTERPRISE. UK LEGIS WORKER ECO/TAC ADMIN PARL/PROC GOV/REL ATTIT ...POLICY MGT METH/COMP NAT/COMP ANTHOL 20 PARLIAMENT. PAGE 120 F2364 SOCISM OWN NAT/G INDUS

B64
BAUCHET P.,ECONOMIC PLANNING. FRANCE STRATA LG/CO CAP/ISM ADMIN PARL/PROC DEMAND OPTIMAL ATTIT PWR SOCISM...POLICY CHARTS 20. PAGE 11 F0212 ECO/DEV NAT/G PLAN ECO/TAC

B64
US CONGRESS JOINT ECO COMM,PRIVATE INVESTMENT IN LATIN AMERICA. L/A+17C USA+45 INT/ORG PROB/SOLV ECO/TAC ATTIT...INT 20 CONGRESS. PAGE 135 F2658 FINAN ECO/UNDEV PARL/PROC LEGIS

B64
US DEPT LABOR OFF SOLICITOR,LEGISLATIVE HISTORY OF THE LABOR-MANAGEMENT AND DISCLOSURE ACT OF 1959. DELIB/GP WORKER ADMIN LOBBY PARL/PROC SANCTION CHOOSE GOV/REL 20 CONGRESS PRESIDENT. PAGE 136 F2677 LABOR LEGIS DEBATE POLICY

L64
KOLODZIEJ E.A.,"RATIONAL CONSENT AND DEFENSE BUDGETS: THE ROLE OF CONGRESS, 1945-1962." LEGIS DIPLOM CONTROL PARL/PROC 20 CONGRESS. PAGE 72 F1423 DECISION PLAN CIVMIL/REL BUDGET

B65
CAMERON W.J.,NEW ZEALAND. NEW/ZEALND S/ASIA DIPLOM INT/TRADE WRITING COLONIAL PARL/PROC...GEOG CMN/WLTH. PAGE 21 F0402 SOCIETY GP/REL STRUCT

B65
VAID K.N.,STATE AND LABOR IN INDIA. INDIA INDUS WORKER PAY PRICE ADJUD CONTROL PARL/PROC GP/REL ORD/FREE 20. PAGE 140 F2757 LAW LABOR MGT NEW/LIB

B66
AGGARWALA R.N.,FINANCIAL COMMITTEES OF THE INDIAN PARLIAMENT: A STUDY IN PARLIAMENTARY CONTROL OVER PUBLIC EXPENDITURE. INDIA FINAN NAT/G ROLE...CHARTS METH/COMP METH 20 PARLIAMENT. PAGE 3 F0049 PARL/PROC BUDGET CONTROL DELIB/GP

B66
DILLEY M.R.,BRITISH POLICY IN KENYA COLONY (2ND ED.). AFR INDIA UK LABOR BUDGET TAX ADMIN PARL/PROC GP/REL...BIBLIOG 20 PARLIAMENT. PAGE 33 F0639 COLONIAL REPRESENT SOVEREIGN

B66
TIVEY L.J.,NATIONALISATION IN BRITISH INDUSTRY. UK LEGIS PARL/PROC GP/REL OWN ATTIT SOCISM 20. PAGE 131 F2578 NAT/G INDUS CONTROL LG/CO

B67
ANDERSON S.V.,THE NORDIC COUNCIL: A STUDY OF SCANDINAVIAN REGIONALISM. DENMARK FINLAND ICELAND NORWAY SWEDEN MARKET NAT/G VOL/ASSN CONSULT PARL/PROC ATTIT...TIME/SEQ BIBLIOG 20. PAGE 5 F0098 INT/ORG REGION DIPLOM LEGIS

B67
BIBBY J.,ON CAPITOL HILL. POL/PAR LOBBY PARL/PROC GOV/REL PERS/REL...JURID PHIL/SCI OBS INT BIBLIOG 20 CONGRESS PRESIDENT. PAGE 15 F0278 CONFER LEGIS CREATE LEAD

B67
COWLING M.,1867 DISRAELI, GLADSTONE, AND REVOLUTION; THE PASSING OF THE SECOND REFORM BILL. UK LEGIS LEAD LOBBY GP/REL INGP/REL...DECISION BIBLIOG 19 REFORMERS. PAGE 28 F0545 PARL/PROC POL/PAR ATTIT LAW

B67
MORRIS A.J.A.,PARLIAMENTARY DEMOCRACY IN THE NINETEENTH CENTURY. UK INDUS LOC/G NAT/G POL/PAR CONSULT LEGIS INT/TRADE ADMIN CHOOSE SUFF SOVEREIGN 19 PARLIAMENT. PAGE 93 F1835 TIME/SEQ CONSTN PARL/PROC POPULISM

B67
O'LEARY M.K.,THE POLITICS OF AMERICAN FOREIGN AID. USA+45 POL/PAR CHIEF BUDGET EDU/PROP LOBBY CONGRESS. PAGE 100 F1958 FOR/AID DIPLOM PARL/PROC ATTIT

S67
SHEFFTZ M.C.,"THE TRADE DISPUTES AND TRADE UNIONS ACT OF 1927: THE AFTERMATH OF THE GENERAL STRIKE." UK FINAN WORKER ADJUD LEAD PARL/PROC 20. PAGE 120 F2373 LEGIS ATTIT LABOR GP/REL

S67
WHITE W.L.,"THE TREASURY BOARD AND PARLIAMENT." CANADA CONSTN CONSULT LEGIS LEAD PARL/PROC GP/REL ...DECISION 20. PAGE 146 F2871 FINAN DELIB/GP NAT/G ADMIN

PARLIAMENTARY PROCESSES....SEE PARL/PROC

PARLIAMENT....PARLIAMENT (ALL NATIONS); SEE ALSO LEGIS

C01
LOWELL A.L.,"THE INFLUENCE OF PARTY UPON LEGISLATION IN ENGLAND AND AMERICA" IN ANNUAL REPORT OF AMER HISTORICAL ASSN." LEGIS CONTROL ...CON/ANAL CHARTS 19/20 CONGRESS PARLIAMENT. PAGE 82 F1605 PARL/PROC POL/PAR DECISION OP/RES

N19
ADMINISTRATIVE STAFF COLLEGE,THE ACCOUNTABILITY OF GOVERNMENT DEPARTMENTS (PAMPHLET) (REV. ED.). UK CONSTN FINAN NAT/G CONSULT ADMIN INGP/REL CONSEN PRIVIL 20 PARLIAMENT. PAGE 2 F0043 PARL/PROC ELITES SANCTION PROB/SOLV

B24
HOLDSWORTH W.S.,A HISTORY OF ENGLISH LAW; THE COMMON LAW AND ITS RIVALS (VOL. VI). AFR UK STRATA EX/STRUC ADJUD ADMIN CONTROL CT/SYS...JURID CONCPT GEN/LAWS 17 PARLIAMENT ENGLSH/LAW COMMON/LAW. PAGE 61 F1194 LAW CONSTN LEGIS CHIEF

B24
HOLDSWORTH W.S.,A HISTORY OF ENGLISH LAW; THE COMMON LAW AND ITS RIVALS (VOL. IV). UK SEA AGRI CHIEF ADJUD CONTROL CRIME GOV/REL...INT/LAW JURID NAT/COMP 16/17 PARLIAMENT COMMON/LAW CANON/LAW ENGLSH/LAW. PAGE 61 F1195 LAW LEGIS CT/SYS CONSTN

B39
JENNINGS W.I.,PARLIAMENT. UK POL/PAR OP/RES BUDGET LEAD CHOOSE GP/REL...MGT 20 PARLIAMENT HOUSE/LORD HOUSE/CMNS. PAGE 67 F1315 PARL/PROC LEGIS CONSTN NAT/G

B39
THOMAS J.A.,THE HOUSE OF COMMONS, 1832-1901; A STUDY OF ITS ECONOMIC AND FUNCTIONAL CHARACTER. UK LAW STRATA FINAN DIPLOM CONTROL LEAD LOBBY REPRESENT WEALTH...POLICY STAT BIBLIOG 19/20 PARLIAMENT. PAGE 130 F2561 PARL/PROC LEGIS POL/PAR ECO/DEV

S47
DAHL R.A.,"WORKERS' CONTROL OF INDUSTRY AND THE BRITISH LABOUR PARTY." UK STRATA STRUCT DELIB/GP BARGAIN CAP/ISM DEBATE CONTROL CHOOSE GP/REL ATTIT ROLE PWR 19/20 PARLIAMENT LABOR/PAR FABIAN. PAGE 29 F0570 INDUS LABOR WORKER SOCISM

B51
HALEVY E.,IMPERIALISM AND THE RISE OF LABOR (2ND ED.). UK NAT/G POL/PAR TOP/EX ATTIT ORD/FREE PWR 19/20 PARLIAMENT LABOR/PAR. PAGE 53 F1042 COLONIAL LABOR POLICY WAR

B57
MURDESHWAR A.K.,ADMINISTRATIVE PROBLEMS RELATING TO NATIONALISATION: WITH SPECIAL REFERENCE TO INDIAN STATE ENTERPRISES. CZECHOSLVK FRANCE INDIA UK USA+45 LEGIS WORKER PROB/SOLV BUDGET PRICE CONTROL ...MGT GEN/LAWS 20 PARLIAMENT. PAGE 95 F1863 NAT/G OWN INDUS ADMIN

B58
JENNINGS I.,PROBLEMS OF THE NEW COMMONWEALTH. AFR CEYLON INDIA PAKISTAN S/ASIA ECO/UNDEV INT/ORG LOC/G DIPLOM ECO/TAC INT/TRADE COLONIAL RACE/REL DISCRIM 20 PARLIAMENT. PAGE 67 F1314 NAT/LISM NEUTRAL FOR/AID POL/PAR

B60
BHAMBHRI C.P.,PARLIAMENTARY CONTROL OVER STATE ENTERPRISE IN INDIA. INDIA DELIB/GP ADMIN CONTROL INGP/REL EFFICIENCY 20 PARLIAMENT. PAGE 14 F0277 NAT/G OWN INDUS PARL/PROC

B63
SHANKS M.,THE LESSONS OF PUBLIC ENTERPRISE. UK LEGIS WORKER ECO/TAC ADMIN PARL/PROC GOV/REL ATTIT ...POLICY MGT METH/COMP NAT/COMP ANTHOL 20 PARLIAMENT. PAGE 120 F2364 — SOCISM OWN NAT/G INDUS

B65
WRIGHT L.B.,THE DREAM OF PROSPERITY IN COLONIAL AMERICA. USA-45 ECO/UNDEV AGRI EXTR/IND PARLIAMENT 17/18. PAGE 149 F2934 — PROVS WEALTH MOD/EUR

B66
AGGARWALA R.N.,FINANCIAL COMMITTEES OF THE INDIAN PARLIAMENT: A STUDY IN PARLIAMENTARY CONTROL OVER PUBLIC EXPENDITURE. INDIA FINAN NAT/G ROLE...CHARTS METH/COMP METH 20 PARLIAMENT. PAGE 3 F0049 — PARL/PROC BUDGET CONTROL DELIB/GP

B66
DILLEY M.R.,BRITISH POLICY IN KENYA COLONY (2ND ED.). AFR INDIA UK LABOR BUDGET TAX ADMIN PARL/PROC GP/REL...BIBLIOG 20 PARLIAMENT. PAGE 33 F0639 — COLONIAL REPRESENT SOVEREIGN

B67
BARDENS D.,CHURCHILL IN PARLIAMENT. UK DIPLOM ADJUD CONTROL AUTHORIT PERSON ORD/FREE 20 CHURCHLL/W PARLIAMENT. PAGE 10 F0186 — TOP/EX LEGIS GOV/REL

B67
MORRIS A.J.A.,PARLIAMENTARY DEMOCRACY IN THE NINETEENTH CENTURY. UK INDUS LOC/G NAT/G POL/PAR CONSULT LEGIS INT/TRADE ADMIN CHOOSE SUFF SOVEREIGN 19 PARLIAMENT. PAGE 93 F1835 — TIME/SEQ CONSTN PARL/PROC POPULISM

B86
O'CONNOR T.P.,THE PARNELL MOVEMENT: WITH A SKETCH OF IRISH PARTIES FROM 1843. IRELAND UK USA-45 LEGIS WORKER ECO/TAC COERCE CRIME REV CHOOSE ORD/FREE CATHISM LAISSEZ...SOC 19/20 PARLIAMENT PARNELL/CS LAND/LEAG. PAGE 100 F1957 — LEAD DOMIN POL/PAR POLICY

PARMELEE M. F2028

PARNELL/CS....CHARLES STEWART PARNELL

B86
O'CONNOR T.P.,THE PARNELL MOVEMENT: WITH A SKETCH OF IRISH PARTIES FROM 1843. IRELAND UK USA-45 LEGIS WORKER ECO/TAC COERCE CRIME REV CHOOSE ORD/FREE CATHISM LAISSEZ...SOC 19/20 PARLIAMENT PARNELL/CS LAND/LEAG. PAGE 100 F1957 — LEAD DOMIN POL/PAR POLICY

PAROLE....SEE PUB/INST, ROUTINE, CRIME

PARRIS H.W. F2029

PARSONS T. F2030,F2031

PARSONS/T....TALCOTT PARSONS

PARTH/SASS....PARTHO-SASSANIAN EMPIRE

PARTIC....PARTICIPATION; CIVIC ACTIVITY AND NONACTIVITY

B02
WEBB S.,THE HISTORY OF TRADE UNIONISM. UK PARTIC ...OBS CHARTS BIBLIOG/A 15/19 CASEBOOK. PAGE 144 F2837 — LABOR VOL/ASSN GP/REL

N19
FAHRNKOPF N.,STATE AND LOCAL GOVERNMENT IN ILLINOIS (PAMPHLET). CONSTN ADMIN PARTIC CHOOSE REPRESENT GOV/REL...JURID MGT 20 ILLINOIS. PAGE 39 F0759 — BIBLIOG LOC/G LEGIS CT/SYS

N19
HAGEN E.E.,AN ANALYTICAL MODEL OF THE TRANSITION TO ECONOMIC GROWTH (PAMPHLET). WOR+45 WOR-45 SOCIETY STRATA FINAN NAT/G CONTROL PARTIC PRODUC...PHIL/SCI BIBLIOG 17/20. PAGE 53 F1033 — SIMUL ECO/DEV METH TEC/DEV

B20
WEBB S.,INDUSTRIAL DEMOCRACY. UK PARTIC GP/REL ...SOC OBS RECORD CHARTS 18/20. PAGE 144 F2838 — LABOR NAT/G VOL/ASSN MAJORIT

B29
JONES M.M.,CORPORATION CONTRIBUTIONS TO COMMUNITY WELFARE AGENCIES (PAMPHLET). DELIB/GP TAX CONTROL PARTIC RATIONAL POLICY. PAGE 68 F1339 — LG/CO GIVE NEIGH SOC/WK

B36
BELLOC H.,THE RESTORATION OF PROPERTY. UK STRATA NAT/G PROF/ORG DELIB/GP WORKER CREATE PROB/SOLV ECO/TAC PARTIC UTOPIA ORD/FREE SOCISM 20. PAGE 13 F0238 — CONTROL MAJORIT CAP/ISM OWN

B37
BROOKS R.R.,WHEN LABOR ORGANIZES. FINAN EDU/PROP ADMIN LOBBY PARTIC REPRESENT WEALTH TREND. PAGE 19 F0364 — LABOR GP/REL POLICY

B38
LEVINSON E.,LABOR ON THE MARCH. WORKER CREATE ECO/TAC ADJUD LEAD PARL/PROC PARTIC INGP/REL SKILL POLICY. PAGE 79 F1543 — LABOR INCOME NAT/G PLAN

S43
GOLDEN C.S.,"NEW PATTERNS OF DEMOCRACY." NEIGH DELIB/GP EDU/PROP EXEC PARTIC...MGT METH/CNCPT OBS TREND. PAGE 48 F0935 — LABOR REPRESENT LG/CO GP/REL

S43
HERBERG W.,"BUREAUCRACY AND DEMOCRACY IN LABOR UNIONS." LAW CONSTN STRUCT WORKER ADMIN CONTROL PARTIC RIGID/FLEX PWR TREND. PAGE 59 F1151 — LABOR REPRESENT ROUTINE INGP/REL

S48
CLEVELAND A.S.,"NAM: SPOKESMAN FOR INDUSTRY?" LEGIS PLAN LEAD LOBBY PARTIC CONSEN INCOME ATTIT ROLE ORD/FREE POLICY. PAGE 25 F0491 — VOL/ASSN CLIENT REPRESENT INDUS

B49
SELZNICK P.,TVA AND THE GRASS ROOTS: A STUDY IN THE SOCIOLOGY OF FORMAL ORGANIZATION. USA-45 EX/STRUC PROB/SOLV CONFER PARTIC ROUTINE PWR 20 TVA. PAGE 119 F2353 — REPRESENT LOBBY CONSULT

S49
SHEPHARD H.A.,"DEMOCRATIC CONTROL IN A LABOR UNION." FUT CONSTN STRUCT TEC/DEV LEAD PARTIC RACE/REL CENTRAL DRIVE HABITAT RECORD. PAGE 120 F2374 — LABOR MAJORIT CONTROL PWR

S50
EBY K.,"RESEARCH IN LABOR UNIONS." EDU/PROP INGP/REL PWR...METH/CNCPT OBS. PAGE 36 F0693 — RECORD QU LABOR PARTIC

B51
HARBISON F.H.,GOALS AND STRATEGY IN COLLECTIVE BARGAINING. WORKER BAL/PWR PARTIC DRIVE...POLICY MGT. PAGE 55 F1074 — LABOR BARGAIN GP/REL ADMIN

L51
SUMMERS C.W.,"UNION POWERS AND WORKERS RIGHTS." WORKER PROB/SOLV ECO/TAC PARTIC INGP/REL PWR. PAGE 127 F2513 — LABOR CONSTN LAW REPRESENT

B52
GOLDSTEIN J.,THE GOVERNMENT OF BRITISH TRADE UNIONS. UK ECO/DEV EX/STRUC INGP/REL...BIBLIOG 20. PAGE 48 F0940 — LABOR PARTIC

B52
ROSE A.M.,UNION SOLIDARITY: THE INTERNAL COHESION OF A LABOR UNION. SECT GP/REL RACE/REL ATTIT ROLE HEALTH WEALTH...INT QU. PAGE 114 F2241 — LABOR INGP/REL PARTIC SUPEGO

S52
KLUMB S.,"EMPLOYEE DETERMINATION OF MANAGERIAL FUNCTIONS AND CHARACTERISTICS." DELIB/GP WORKER PARTIC ROUTINE INGP/REL...CLASSIF OBS QU. PAGE 72 F1410 — MGT INDUS EX/STRUC CHOOSE

B53
PURCELL T.V.,THE WORKER SPEAKS HIS MIND ON COMPANY AND UNION. WORKER ADJUD LEAD RACE/REL ATTIT DRIVE MARXISM...MGT CLASSIF STAT OBS INT SAMP BIBLIOG. PAGE 108 F2131 — LABOR PARTIC INGP/REL HAPPINESS

B53
SAYLES L.R.,THE LOCAL UNION. CONSTN CULTURE DELIB/GP PARTIC CHOOSE GP/REL INGP/REL ATTIT ROLE ...MAJORIT DECISION MGT. PAGE 116 F2284 — LABOR LEAD ADJUD ROUTINE

S53
DRUCKER P.F.,"THE EMPLOYEE SOCIETY." STRUCT BAL/PWR PARTIC REPRESENT PWR...DECISION CONCPT. PAGE 34 F0666 — LABOR MGT WORKER CULTURE

S53
MCKEE J.B.,"STATUS AND POWER IN THE INDUSTRIAL COMMUNITY; A COMMENT ON DRUCKER'S THESIS." LABOR LEGIT LEAD GP/REL PWR...MGT CONCPT. PAGE 88 F1730 — SOC STRATA NEIGH PARTIC

B54
EMERSON F.D.,SHAREHOLDER DEMOCRACY: A BROADER OUTLOOK FOR CORPORATIONS. DELIB/GP EX/STRUC LEGIS ADJUD CONTROL REPRESENT INGP/REL OWN PWR...POLICY STAT RECORD. PAGE 37 F0727 — LG/CO PARTIC MAJORIT TREND

B55
STILLMAN C.W.,AFRICA IN THE MODERN WORLD. AFR USA+45 WOR+45 INT/TRADE COLONIAL PARTIC REGION GOV/REL RACE/REL 20. PAGE 126 F2489 — ECO/UNDEV DIPLOM POLICY STRUCT

B56
GILBERT L.D.,DIVIDENDS AND DEMOCRACY. DELIB/GP LEGIS CAP/ISM ADJUD LOBBY OWN PWR LAISSEZ MAJORIT. PAGE 47 F0922 — LG/CO INGP/REL CONTROL PARTIC

B56
LIPSET S.M.,UNION DEMOCRACY. STRUCT INDUS FACE/GP WORKER CONTROL LEAD PARTIC GP/REL ATTIT LAISSEZ ...INT QU CHARTS. PAGE 80 F1577 — LABOR INGP/REL MAJORIT

B56
UPHOFF W.H.,UNDERSTANDING THE UNION MEMBER (PAMPHLET). STRATA R+D LEAD PARTIC...METH/CNCPT — LABOR WORKER

STAT QU. PAGE 133 F2624
ATTIT DRIVE

L56
TAGLIACOZZO D.L.,"TRADE-UNION GOVERNMENT, ITS NATURE AND ITS PROBLEMS: A BIBLIOGRAPHICAL REVIEW, 1945-1955." STRUCT LEAD PARTIC CHOOSE ATTIT ...MAJORIT METH/CNCPT BIBLIOG. PAGE 128 F2526
CLASSIF LABOR INGP/REL GP/REL

S56
TANNENBAUM A.S.,"CONTROL OF STRUCTURE AND UNION FUNCTIONS." PARTIC GP/REL INGP/REL CONSEN ATTIT PWR ...QU SAMP. PAGE 128 F2529
LABOR STRUCT CONTROL LEAD

B57
BERLE A.A. JR.,ECONOMIC POWER AND FREE SOCIETY (PAMPHLET). CLIENT CONSTN EX/STRUC ECO/TAC CONTROL PARTIC PWR WEALTH MAJORIT. PAGE 14 F0261
LG/CO CAP/ISM INGP/REL LEGIT

B57
SCHNEIDER E.V.,INDUSTRIAL SOCIOLOGY: THE SOCIAL RELATIONS OF INDUSTRY AND COMMUNITY. STRATA INDUS NAT/G NEIGH CREATE ADMIN PARTIC GP/REL RACE/REL ROLE PWR...POLICY BIBLIOG. PAGE 117 F2308
LABOR MGT INGP/REL STRUCT

S57
KAHN R.L.,"UNION PRACTICES AND MEMBER PARTICIPATION." PARTIC CHOOSE REPRESENT PERS/REL PERSON SKILL...DECISION METH/CNCPT QU. PAGE 69 F1347
INGP/REL LABOR ATTIT LEAD

S57
TANNENBAUM A.S.,"ORGANIZATIONAL CONTROL STRUCTURE: A GENERAL DESCRIPTIVE TECHNIQUE AS APPLIED TO FOUR LOCAL UNIONS." LABOR PWR...METH/CNCPT CLASSIF QU CHARTS. PAGE 128 F2530
WORKER PARTIC STRUCT CONTROL

B58
CROWE S.,THE LANDSCAPE OF POWER. UK CULTURE SERV/IND NAT/G CONSULT PARTIC NUC/PWR LEISURE...SOC EXHIBIT 20. PAGE 29 F0559
HABITAT TEC/DEV PLAN CONTROL

B58
INDIAN INST OF PUBLIC ADMIN,IMPROVING CITY GOVERNMENT. INDIA ECO/UNDEV PLAN BUDGET PARTIC GP/REL MUNICH 20. PAGE 64 F1263
LOC/G PROB/SOLV ADMIN

B58
LESTER R.A.,AS UNIONS MATURE. POL/PAR BARGAIN LEAD PARTIC GP/REL CENTRAL...MAJORIT TIME/SEQ METH/COMP. PAGE 78 F1533
LABOR INDUS POLICY MGT

B58
OGDEN F.D.,THE POLL TAX IN THE SOUTH. USA+45 USA-45 CONSTN ADJUD ADMIN PARTIC CRIME...TIME/SEQ GOV/COMP METH/COMP 18/20 SOUTH/US. PAGE 101 F1982
TAX CHOOSE RACE/REL DISCRIM

B58
SEIDMAN J.I.,DEMOCRACY IN THE LABOR MOVEMENT (PAMPHLET). LAW CONSTN STRUCT DELIB/GP WORKER ADJUD PARTIC SANCTION POLICY. PAGE 119 F2345
LABOR INGP/REL PWR MAJORIT

B58
TANNENBAUM A.S.,PARTICIPATION IN UNION LOCALS. SOCIETY FINAN CONTROL LEAD GP/REL...BIBLIOG 20. PAGE 128 F2531
LABOR MGT PARTIC INGP/REL

S58
EMERSON F.D.,"THE ROLES OF MANAGEMENT AND SHAREHOLDERS IN CORPORATE GOVERNMENT." CLIENT DELIB/GP CREATE ADMIN EXEC PARTIC PERS/REL PWR. PAGE 37 F0728
LG/CO LAW INGP/REL REPRESENT

S58
LATTIN N.D.,"MINORITY AND DISSENTING SHAREHOLDERS' RIGHTS IN FUNDAMENTAL CHANGES." FINAN LEGIS ADJUD PARTIC ROUTINE CHOOSE REPRESENT INGP/REL TREND. PAGE 76 F1487
MAJORIT LG/CO LAW CREATE

S58
O'NEAL F.H.,"RECENT LEGISLATION AFFECTING CLOSE CORPORATIONS." LAW EX/STRUC ECO/TAC ROUTINE CHOOSE RIGID/FLEX...MAJORIT MGT TREND. PAGE 100 F1959
LG/CO LEGIS REPRESENT PARTIC

B59
BARBASH J.,UNIONS AND UNION LEADERSHIP. NAT/G WORKER TEC/DEV ECO/TAC PARTIC GP/REL RACE/REL ORD/FREE CLASSIF. PAGE 10 F0183
LABOR VOL/ASSN CAP/ISM LEAD

B59
FERRY W.H.,THE CORPORATION AND THE ECONOMY. CLIENT LAW CONSTN LABOR NAT/G PLAN INT/TRADE PARTIC CONSEN ORD/FREE PWR POLICY. PAGE 40 F0787
LG/CO CONTROL REPRESENT

B59
LEISERSON W.,AMERICAN TRADE UNION DEMOCRACY. CONSTN STRUCT ADJUD EXEC REPRESENT GP/REL INGP/REL MAJORITY ATTIT PWR. PAGE 77 F1516
LABOR LEAD PARTIC DELIB/GP

B59
WORTHY J.C.,BIG BUSINESS AND FREE MEN. LG/CO EX/STRUC EDU/PROP LEAD CHOOSE GP/REL ATTIT DRIVE ROLE ORD/FREE...MAJORIT 20. PAGE 149 F2927
ELITES LOC/G TOP/EX PARTIC

L59
OBERER W.E.,"VOLUNTARY IMPARTIAL REVIEW OF LABOR: SOME REFLECTIONS." DELIB/GP LEGIS PROB/SOLV ADJUD CONTROL COERCE PWR PLURISM POLICY. PAGE 100 F1960
LABOR LAW PARTIC INGP/REL

B60
EELLS R.S.F.,THE MEANING OF MODERN BUSINESS. LOC/G NAT/G NEIGH EX/STRUC PARTIC GP/REL INGP/REL DECISION. PAGE 36 F0706
LG/CO REPRESENT POLICY PLAN

B60
FORM W.H.,INDUSTRY, LABOR, AND COMMUNITY. STRUCT NEIGH SECT BAL/PWR EDU/PROP PARTIC ATTIT ROLE PWR WEALTH...METH/CNCPT CHARTS. PAGE 42 F0828
LABOR MGT GP/REL CONTROL

B60
RAMA C.M.,LAS CLASES SOCIALES EN EL URUGUAY. L/A+17C URUGUAY ELITES SOCIETY STRATA INDUS ATTIT HABITAT PWR...GEOG SOC/INTEG MUNICH 20. PAGE 109 F2138
ECO/UNDEV STRUCT PARTIC

S60
FORM W.H.,"ORGANIZED LABOR'S IMAGE OF COMMUNITY POWER STRUCTURE." LABOR LG/CO CONTROL LEAD REPRESENT...DECISION METH/CNCPT INT QU SAMP. PAGE 42 F0829
NEIGH PARTIC PWR GP/REL

S60
SPINRAD W.,"CORRELATES OF TRADE UNION PARTICIPATION: A SUMMARY OF LITERATURE." ACT/RES PERS/REL HAPPINESS HABITAT...BIBLIOG WORK. PAGE 125 F2456
LABOR PARTIC CORREL ROLE

B61
DUKE UNIVERSITY,EXPULSION OR OPPRESSION OF BUSINESS ASSOCIATES: "SQUEEZE-OUTS" IN SMALL ENTERPRISES. LAW CONTROL PARTIC COERCE INGP/REL...POLICY RECORD INT. PAGE 35 F0674
PWR MGT SML/CO ECO/TAC

B61
LENIN V.I.,WHAT IS TO BE DONE? (1902). RUSSIA LABOR NAT/G POL/PAR WORKER CAP/ISM ECO/TAC ADMIN PARTIC ...MARXIST IDEA/COMP GEN/LAWS 19/20. PAGE 78 F1522
EDU/PROP PRESS MARXISM METH/COMP

S61
BRAFF A.J.,"WAGE-PRICE POLICIES UNDER PUBLIC PRESSURE." USA+45 EX/STRUC LOBBY REPRESENT PWR 20. PAGE 17 F0335
ATTIT PARTIC PROB/SOLV

B62
DIMOCK M.E.,THE NEW AMERICAN POLITICAL ECONOMY: A SYNTHESIS OF POLITICS AND ECONOMICS. USA+45 FINAN LG/CO PLAN ADMIN REGION GP/REL CENTRAL MORAL 20. PAGE 33 F0642
FEDERAL ECO/TAC NAT/G PARTIC

B62
GALENSON W.,TRADE UNIONS MONOGRAPH SERIES (A SERIES OF NINE TEXTS). DELIB/GP LEAD PARTIC...DECISION ORG/CHARTS. PAGE 45 F0887
LABOR INGP/REL CONSTN REPRESENT

B62
HARRINGTON M.,THE RETAIL CLERKS. ECO/TAC LEAD PARTIC CHOOSE GP/REL INGP/REL CENTRAL POLICY. PAGE 55 F1087
LABOR SERV/IND STRUCT DELIB/GP

B62
LEVY H.V.,LIBERDADE E JUSTICA SOCIAL (2ND ED.). BRAZIL COM L/A+17C USSR INT/ORG PARTIC GP/REL WEALTH 20 UN COM/PARTY. PAGE 79 F1544
ORD/FREE MARXISM CAP/ISM LAW

B63
FRIEDRICH C.J.,MAN AND HIS GOVERNMENT: AN EMPIRICAL THEORY OF POLITICS. UNIV LOC/G NAT/G ADJUD REV INGP/REL DISCRIM PWR BIBLIOG. PAGE 44 F0867
PERSON ORD/FREE PARTIC CONTROL

B63
IANNI O.,INDUSTRIALIZACAO E DESENVOLVIMENTO SOCIAL NO BRASIL. BRAZIL L/A+17C STRATA STRUCT ECO/UNDEV EDU/PROP LEAD LOBBY NAT/LISM 20. PAGE 64 F1257
WORKER GP/REL INDUS PARTIC

B63
US ADVISORY COMN INTERGOV REL,PERFORMANCE OF URBAN FUNCTIONS: LOCAL AND AREAWIDE. TEC/DEV PARTIC REPRESENT PWR...DECISION GOV/COMP MUNICH. PAGE 133 F2633
REGION LOC/G ECO/TAC

B64
HALLOWELL J.H.,DEVELOPMENT: FOR WHAT. WOR+45 POL/PAR SECT FOR/AID INT/TRADE CT/SYS PARTIC PRODUC PLURISM. PAGE 54 F1052
ECO/UNDEV CONSTN NAT/LISM ECO/TAC

S64
HOWE M.,"THE TRANSPORT ACT, 1962, AND THE CONSUMERS' CONSULTATIVE COMMITTEES." UK CONFER EXEC PWR 20. PAGE 62 F1225
PARTIC REPRESENT DELIB/GP DIST/IND

B65
FRYE R.J.,HOUSING AND URBAN RENEWAL IN ALABAMA. USA+45 NEIGH LEGIS BUDGET ADJUD ADMIN PARTIC...MGT MUNICH 20 ALABAMA URBAN/RNWL. PAGE 45 F0871
PROB/SOLV PLAN GOV/REL

B65
HADWIGER D.F.,PRESSURES AND PROTEST. NAT/G LEGIS PLAN LEAD PARTIC ROUTINE ATTIT POLICY. PAGE 53
AGRI GP/REL

F1030 — LOBBY CHOOSE

B65
RATNAM K.J.,COMMUNALISM AND THE POLITICAL PROCESS IN MALAYA. MALAYSIA WOR+45 ECO/UNDEV PARTIC CHOOSE REPRESENT GP/REL CENTRAL ATTIT...CHARTS WORSHIP 20. PAGE 109 F2152 — CONSTN GOV/REL REGION

B65
ROSS A.M.,EMPLOYMENT POLICY AND THE LABOR MARKET. USA+45 MARKET LABOR NAT/G PROB/SOLV PAY EDU/PROP PARTIC UTIL...POLICY 20. PAGE 114 F2242 — ECO/DEV WORKER WEALTH DEMAND

B65
SIMON B.,EDUCATION AND THE LABOR MOVEMENT, 1870-1920. UK SOCIETY STRATA LABOR POL/PAR SCHOOL CONTROL PARTIC SOCISM...BIBLIOG 19/20. PAGE 122 F2406 — EDU/PROP WORKER ADJUST LAW

B65
WEIL G.L.,A HANDBOOK ON THE EUROPEAN ECONOMIC COMMUNITY. BELGIUM EUR+WWI FRANCE GERMANY/W ITALY CONSTN ECO/DEV CREATE PARTIC GP/REL...DECISION MGT CHARTS 20 EEC. PAGE 144 F2846 — INT/TRADE INT/ORG TEC/DEV INT/LAW

B66
DAVIES JC I.I.I.,NEIGHBORHOOD GROUPS AND URBAN RENEWAL. USA+45 PLAN LOBBY PARTIC CHOOSE RACE/REL ...POLICY DECISION SOC INT MUNICH SOC/INTEG 20 NEWYORK/C. PAGE 30 F0586 — NEIGH CREATE PROB/SOLV

B66
HOROWITZ D.,HEMISPHERES NORTH AND SOUTH: ECONOMIC DISPARITY AMONG NATIONS. WOR+45 ECO/DEV ECO/UNDEV INT/ORG PLAN DIPLOM INT/TRADE GIVE PARTIC GP/REL ...WELF/ST 20. PAGE 62 F1215 — ECO/TAC FOR/AID STRATA WEALTH

B66
PFEFFER K.H.,WELT IM UMBRUCH. SOCIETY STRUCT INDUS PROF/ORG SECT TEC/DEV PARTIC SUPEGO WORSHIP 20 CHRISTIAN. PAGE 106 F2076 — ORD/FREE STRATA CREATE

B66
RAO Y.V.L.,COMMUNICATION AND DEVELOPMENT. INDIA S/ASIA SOCIETY ACT/RES EDU/PROP PARTIC ATTIT...SOC GP/COMP BIBLIOG MUNICH MUNICH 20. PAGE 109 F2149 — COM/IND ECO/UNDEV OBS

B67
BANFIELD E.C.,THE MORAL BASIS OF A BACKWARD SOCIETY. EUR+WWI ITALY STRATA NEIGH PARTIC INGP/REL ...SOC QU PREDICT TREND HYPO/EXP MUNICH 20. PAGE 9 F0173 — MORAL WEALTH ATTIT

B67
ELDREDGE H.W.,TAMING MEGALOPOLIS; HOW TO MANAGE AN URBANIZED WORLD. WOR+45 SOCIETY ECO/DEV ECO/UNDEV NAT/G COMPUTER CREATE PARTIC EFFICIENCY WEALTH ...MGT ANTHOL MUNICH. PAGE 37 F0716 — TEC/DEV PLAN PROB/SOLV

B67
GITTELL M.,PARTICIPANTS AND PARTICIPATION: A STUDY OF SCHOOL POLICY IN NEW YORK. USA+45 EX/STRUC BUDGET PAY ATTIT...POLICY MUNICH 20 NEWYORK/C. PAGE 47 F0926 — SCHOOL DECISION PARTIC ADMIN

B67
MARRIS P.,DILEMMAS OF SOCIAL REFORM: POVERTY AND COMMUNITY ACTION IN THE UNITED STATES. USA+45 NAT/G OP/RES ADMIN PARTIC EFFICIENCY WEALTH...SOC METH/COMP T MUNICH 20 REFORMERS. PAGE 85 F1674 — STRUCT PROB/SOLV COST

B67
PETRO S.,THE KINGSPORT STRIKE. USA+45 PROC/MFG NAT/G JUDGE PRESS PARTIC PERS/REL...OLD/LIB OBS INT 20 NLRB. PAGE 105 F2074 — LABOR COERCE SANCTION ALL/VALS

B67
PIKE F.B.,FREEDOM AND REFORM IN LATIN AMERICA. BRAZIL URUGUAY CONSTN CULTURE SECT DIPLOM EDU/PROP PARTIC DRIVE ALL/VALS CATHISM...GEOG ANTHOL BIBLIOG REFORMERS BOLIV. PAGE 106 F2086 — L/A+17C ORD/FREE ECO/UNDEV REV

B67
REHMUS C.M.,LABOR AND AMERICAN POLITICS. POL/PAR WORKER EDU/PROP PARTIC ATTIT PWR. PAGE 110 F2175 — LABOR ROLE LOBBY

B67
WOOTON G.,WORKERS, UNIONS, AND THE STATE. INDUS PROB/SOLV GP/REL DRIVE SUPEGO RESPECT...PSY SOC. PAGE 148 F2925 — PARTIC WORKER NAT/G LABOR

L67
LAMBERT J.D.,"CORPORATE POLITICAL SPENDING AND CAMPAIGN FINANCE." LAW CONSTN FINAN LABOR LG/CO LOC/G NAT/G VOL/ASSN TEC/DEV ADJUD ADMIN PARTIC. PAGE 75 F1463 — USA+45 POL/PAR CHOOSE COST

L67
MACDONALD R.M.,"COLLECTIVE BARGAINING IN THE POSTWAR PERIOD." WORKER PROB/SOLV ECO/TAC PARTIC RISK CENTRAL EFFICIENCY DRIVE WEALTH...TREND 20. PAGE 83 F1624 — LABOR INDUS BARGAIN CAP/ISM

L67
MIXON J.,"JANE JACOBS AND THE LAW - ZONING FOR DIVERSITY EXAMINED." FUT USA+45 CONSTN NEIGH PROB/SOLV CONTROL CT/SYS PARTIC ATTIT...POLICY CENSUS METH/COMP MUNICH. PAGE 92 F1810 — IDEA/COMP PLAN LAW

S67
ADAMS E.S.,"THE EXPANDING ROLE OF BANKS IN PUBLIC AFFAIRS." USA+45 GIVE LEAD ROLE...QU 20. PAGE 2 F0036 — PARTIC FINAN LOC/G ATTIT

S67
BAGDKIAN B.H.,"NEWS AS A BYPRODUCT: WHAT HAPPENS WHEN JOURNALISM IS HITCHED TO GREAT, DIVERSIFIED CORPORATIONS?" USA+45 INDUS EDU/PROP PARTIC PROFIT ATTIT. PAGE 8 F0152 — COM/IND PRESS CONTROL LG/CO

S67
BAILEY S.L.,"THE ITALIANS AND ORGANIZED LABOR IN THE UNITED STATES AND ARGENTINA: 1880-1910." ITALY USA-45 PARTIC HABITAT PWR...GEOG GP/COMP 19/20 ARGEN. PAGE 8 F0153 — LABOR LEAD WEALTH GP/REL

S67
DEWHURST A.,"THE WAGE MOVEMENT IN CANADA." CANADA AGRI NAT/G PARTIC COST PRODUC PROFIT 20. PAGE 32 F0627 — WORKER MARXIST INDUS LABOR

S67
GORMAN W.,"ELLUL - A PROPHETIC VOICE." WOR+45 ELITES SOCIETY ACT/RES PLAN BAL/PWR DOMIN CONTROL PARTIC TOTALISM PWR 20. PAGE 49 F0963 — CREATE ORD/FREE EX/STRUC UTOPIA

S67
JANSSEN P.,"NEA: THE RELUCTANT DRAGON." NAT/G EXEC LOBBY PARTIC SANCTION RACE/REL ROLE TREND. PAGE 66 F1305 — EDU/PROP PROF/ORG MGT POLICY

S67
KRAUS J.,"A MARXIST IN GHANA." GHANA ELITES CHIEF PROB/SOLV TEC/DEV DIPLOM ECO/TAC COLONIAL PARTIC PWR 20 NKRUMAH/K. PAGE 73 F1432 — MARXISM PLAN ATTIT CREATE

S67
LASLETT J.H.M.,"SOCIALISM AND THE AMERICAN LABOR MOVEMENT* SOME NEW REFLECTIONS." USA-45 VOL/ASSN LOBBY PARTIC CENTRAL ALL/VALS SOCISM...GP/COMP 20. PAGE 76 F1484 — LABOR ROUTINE ATTIT GP/REL

S67
LENS S.,"WALTER REUTHER TRIES TO BUILD A FIRE." WORKER LEAD DISCRIM AGE ORD/FREE NEW/LIB SOC. PAGE 78 F1523 — LABOR PARTIC NEIGH PLAN

S67
MUNDHEIM R.H.,"SOME THOUGHTS ON THE DUTIES AND RESPONSIBILITIES OF UNAFFILIATED DIRECTORS OF MUTUAL FUNDS." USA+45 LG/CO SML/CO CONSULT LEAD PARTIC. PAGE 95 F1861 — FINAN WEALTH ECO/TAC ADMIN

S67
NEALE R.S.,"WORKING CLASS WOMEN AND WOMEN'S SUFFRAGE." UK LAW CONSTN LABOR NAT/G DELIB/GP LEGIS WORKER PAY PARTIC CHOOSE 19 FEMALE/SEX. PAGE 97 F1906 — STRATA SEX SUFF DISCRIM

S67
PETRAS J.,"MINERS AND AGRARIAN RADICALISM." CHILE AGRI EXTR/IND WORKER CHOOSE ATTIT SOCISM MUNICH 20. PAGE 105 F2073 — PARTIC EDU/PROP LABOR

S67
PFEFFERMANN G.,"TRADE UNIONS AND POLITICS IN FRENCH WEST AFRICA DURING THE FOURTH REPUBLIC." AFR INDUS POL/PAR COLONIAL ATTIT PWR 20. PAGE 106 F2077 — PARTIC DRIVE INT/TRADE LABOR

S67
SANDMEYER R.L.,"METHODOLOGICAL ISSUES IN THE STUDY OF LABOR FORCE PARTICIPATION RATES." WOR+45 ...CLASSIF REGRESS CHARTS SIMUL. PAGE 116 F2278 — METH CON/ANAL PARTIC WORKER

B76
TAINE H.A.,THE ANCIENT REGIME. FRANCE STRATA FORCES PARTIC EQUILIB WEALTH CONSERVE POPULISM...GOV/COMP SOC/INTEG 18/19. PAGE 128 F2527 — NAT/G GOV/REL TAX REV

PARTIES, POLITICAL....SEE POL/PAR

PARTITION....PARTITIONS AND PARTITIONING - DIVISION OF AN EXISTING POLITICAL-GEOGRAPHICAL ENTITY INTO TWO OR MORE AUTONOMOUS ZONES

PASSIN H. F2032

PASSPORT....SEE LICENSE, TRAVEL

PASTOR R.S. F2033

PATAI R. F2034

PATEL S.J. F2035

PATENT....PATENT

PATENT/OFF....U.S. PATENT OFFICE

N19
DOTSON A.,PRODUCTION PLANNING IN THE PATENT OFFICE (PAMPHLET). USA+45 DIST/IND PROB/SOLV PRODUC...MGT — EFFICIENCY PLAN

PHIL/SCI 20 BUR/BUDGET PATENT/OFF. PAGE 34 F0655 — NAT/G ADMIN

PATHAN....PATHAN PEOPLE (PAKISTAN, AFGHANISTAN)

PATHET/LAO....PATHET LAO

PATRICK H.T. F2036

PATRIOTISM....SEE NAT/LISM

PATTON R. F2038

PAULING/L....LINUS PAULING

PAULLIN O. F0850

PAULY M.V. F2039

PAUNIO J.J. F2040

PAWERA J.C. F2041

PAY....EARNINGS; SEE ALSO INCOME

N

JOHNSON R.B.,FINANCING A SUBURBAN CITY. USA+45 TAX COST...SAMP/SIZ MUNICH 20 COL. PAGE 68 F1331 — FINAN PAY PROB/SOLV

B14

HOBSON J.A.,WORK AND WEALTH. CULTURE FINAN INDUS WORKER TEC/DEV ECO/TAC GIVE PAY PRICE COST PRODUC UTIL. PAGE 60 F1185 — WEALTH INCOME GEN/LAWS

B19

VEBLEN T.B.,THE VESTED INTERESTS AND THE STATE OF THE INDUSTRIAL ARTS. USA-45 LAW FINAN WORKER PAY DOMIN PRICE COST SOCISM...MARXIST 19/20. PAGE 141 F2771 — INDUS CAP/ISM METH/COMP WEALTH

N19

BUSINESS ECONOMISTS' GROUP,INCOME POLICIES (PAMPHLET). UK INDUS LABOR TOP/EX PAY COST PRODUC ...ECOMETRIC GOV/COMP SIMUL ANTHOL 20. PAGE 20 F0395 — INCOME WORKER WEALTH POLICY

N19

CARPER E.T.,LOBBYING AND THE NATURAL GAS BILL (PAMPHLET). USA+45 SERV/IND BARGAIN PAY DRIVE ROLE WEALTH 20 CONGRESS SENATE EISNHWR/DD. PAGE 22 F0418 — LOBBY ADJUD TRIBUTE NAT/G

N19

ENGELS F.,THE BRITISH LABOUR MOVEMENT (PAMPHLET). FRANCE GERMANY MOD/EUR UK USA-45 POL/PAR WORKER PAY EDU/PROP PRICE REPRESENT GP/REL 19. PAGE 37 F0730 — ECO/TAC MARXISM LABOR STRATA

N19

FIKS M.,PUBLIC ADMINISTRATION IN ISRAEL (PAMPHLET). ISRAEL SCHOOL EX/STRUC BUDGET PAY INGP/REL ...DECISION 20 CIVIL/SERV. PAGE 41 F0792 — EDU/PROP NAT/G ADMIN WORKER

N19

HABERLER G.,INFLATION; ITS CAUSES AND CURES (PAMPHLET). AFR USA+45 FINAN BUDGET PAY PRICE COST DEMAND 20. PAGE 52 F1021 — ECO/DEV BAL/PAY POLICY NAT/G

N19

INTERNATIONAL LABOUR OFFICE,EMPLOYMENT, UNEMPLOYMENT AND LABOUR FORCE STATISTICS (PAMPHLET). EUR+WWI STRATA AGRI INDUS NAT/G PROB/SOLV PAY AGE SEX...SAMP NAT/COMP METH 20 ILO. PAGE 65 F1278 — WORKER LABOR STAT ECO/DEV

N19

ROBERTSON D.,GROWTH, WAGES, MONEY (PAMPHLET). UNIV WORKER BUDGET PRICE DEMAND PRODUC WEALTH...CONCPT MATH MONEY. PAGE 112 F2210 — FINAN ECO/DEV ECO/TAC PAY

B23

HOBSON J.A.,INCENTIVES IN THE NEW INDUSTRIAL ORDER. USA-45 NAT/G PAY COST EFFICIENCY PRODUC WEALTH ...MAJORIT PSY SOC/WK 20. PAGE 60 F1186 — INDUS LABOR INCOME OPTIMAL

B35

HICKS J.R.,THE THEORY OF WAGES. INDUS NAT/G PAY PRICE CONTROL COST EFFICIENCY WEALTH 19/20 MARSHALL/A CLARK/JB. PAGE 59 F1164 — INCOME WORKER LABOR PRODUC

B35

MARX K.,WAGE-LABOR AND CAPITAL -- VALUE, PRICE AND PROFIT. LABOR PAY PRICE COST INCOME OWN PROFIT WEALTH 19. PAGE 86 F1690 — STRATA WORKER MARXIST MARXISM

B39

MARQUAND H.A.,ORGANIZED LABOUR IN FOUR CONTINENTS. EUR+WWI USA-45 INDUS NAT/G PAY GP/REL TOTALISM ATTIT WEALTH ALL/IDEOS...TREND NAT/COMP 20 ILO AFL/CIO EUROPE CHINJAP MEXIC/AMER. PAGE 85 F1673 — LABOR WORKER CONCPT ANTHOL

B40

WUNDERLICH F.,LABOR UNDER GERMAN DEMOCRACY, ARBITRATION 1918-1933. GERMANY NAT/G PAY REPAR ADJUD CT/SYS GP/REL...MAJORIT 20. PAGE 149 F2941 — LABOR WORKER INDUS BARGAIN

B41

LESTER R.A.,ECONOMICS OF LABOR. UK USA-45 TEC/DEV BARGAIN PAY INGP/REL INCOME...MGT 19/20. PAGE 78 F1532 — LABOR ECO/DEV INDUS WORKER

B41

SLICHTER S.H.,UNION POLICIES AND INDUSTRIAL MANAGEMENT. USA-45 INDUS TEC/DEV PAY GP/REL INGP/REL COST EFFICIENCY PRODUC...POLICY 20. PAGE 123 F2420 — BARGAIN LABOR MGT WORKER

C43

BENTHAM J.,"THE RATIONALE OF REWARD" IN J. BOWRING, ED., THE WORKS OF JEREMY BENTHAM (VOL. 2)" LAW WORKER CREATE INSPECT PAY ROUTINE HAPPINESS PRODUC SUPEGO WEALTH METH/CNCPT. PAGE 13 F0254 — SANCTION ECO/TAC INCOME PWR

B48

MCCABE D.A.,LABOR AND SOCIAL ORGANIZATION. LEGIS WORKER CAP/ISM ECO/TAC PAY MARXISM SOCISM SOC/INTEG 20 INTRVN/ECO. PAGE 88 F1717 — LABOR STRATA NEW/LIB

B48

METZLER L.A.,INCOME, EMPLOYMENT, AND PUBLIC POLICY. FINAN INDUS LOC/G NAT/G TAX GIVE PAY COST PRODUC ...MGT TIME/SEQ 20. PAGE 90 F1765 — INCOME WEALTH POLICY ECO/TAC

B49

SHISTER J.,ECONOMICS OF THE LABOR MARKET. LOC/G NAT/G WORKER TEC/DEV BARGAIN PAY PRICE EXEC GP/REL INCOME...MGT T 20. PAGE 121 F2381 — MARKET LABOR INDUS

B50

CHAMBERLIN E.,THE THEORY OF MONOPOLISTIC COMPETITION (1933). INDUS PAY GP/REL COST DEMAND EFFICIENCY OPTIMAL PRODUC WEALTH...GEN/LAWS 20. PAGE 23 F0443 — MARKET PRICE ECO/TAC EQUILIB

B50

SHAW E.S.,MONEY, INCOME, AND MONETARY POLICY. AFR USA-45 NAT/G DIPLOM PAY CONTROL COST INCOME PRODUC WEALTH...T 20 FED/RESERV DEPT/TREAS. PAGE 120 F2370 — FINAN ECO/TAC ECO/DEV PRICE

B51

CHANDLER L.V.,INFLATION IN THE UNITED STATES 1940-1948. AFR NAT/G BUDGET PAY PRICE CONTROL WAR INCOME PRODUC...POLICY BIBLIOG 20. PAGE 23 F0448 — ECO/TAC FINAN PROB/SOLV WEALTH

B51

PETERSON F.,SURVEY OF LABOR ECONOMICS (REV. ED.). STRATA ECO/DEV LABOR INSPECT BARGAIN PAY PRICE EXEC ROUTINE GP/REL ALL/VALS ORD/FREE 20 AFL/CIO DEPT/LABOR. PAGE 105 F2069 — WORKER DEMAND IDEA/COMP T

B52

DE JOUVENEL B.,THE ETHICS OF REDISTRIBUTION. UK ELITES MARKET WORKER GIVE PAY INCOME PERSON ...POLICY PSY GEN/LAWS 20. PAGE 31 F0602 — WEALTH TAX SOCISM TRADIT

C52

HUME D.,"OF INTEREST" IN D. HUME, POLITICAL DISCOURSES (1752)" UK INDUS WORKER DIPLOM PAY DEMAND INCOME WEALTH...GEN/LAWS 18 MONEY. PAGE 63 F1239 — PRICE COST FINAN INT/TRADE

B54

BERNSTEIN I.,ARBITRATION OF WAGES. USA+45 CONSULT PAY COST PRODUC WEALTH...CHARTS 20. PAGE 14 F0266 — DELIB/GP BARGAIN WORKER PRICE

B55

BLOOM G.F.,ECONOMICS OF LABOR RELATIONS. USA+45 LAW CONSULT WORKER CAP/ISM PAY ADJUD CONTROL EFFICIENCY ORD/FREE...CHARTS 19/20 AFL/CIO NLRB DEPT/LABOR. PAGE 16 F0299 — ECO/DEV ECO/TAC LABOR GOV/REL

B56

HICKMAN C.A.,INDIVIDUALS, GROUPS, AND ECONOMIC BEHAVIOR. WORKER PAY CONTROL EXEC GP/REL INGP/REL PERSON ROLE...PSY SOC PERS/COMP METH 20. PAGE 59 F1163 — MGT ADMIN ECO/TAC PLAN

B56

POOLE K.E.,PUBLIC FINANCE AND ECONOMIC WELFARE. STRUCT ECO/DEV LOC/G NAT/G BUDGET PAY ROUTINE COST EQUILIB WEALTH...SOC/WK METH/COMP 20. PAGE 107 F2103 — FINAN TAX ORD/FREE

B57

BAUER P.T.,THE ECONOMICS OF UNDERDEVELOPED COUNTRIES. WOR+45 AGRI FINAN INDUS PROC/MFG WORKER CAP/ISM PAY PRICE INCOME MARXISM...METH/COMP 20 RESOURCE/N. PAGE 11 F0213 — ECO/UNDEV ECO/TAC PROB/SOLV NAT/G

B57

DUNLOP J.T.,THE THEORY OF WAGE DETERMINATION; PROCEEDINGS OF CONFERENCE HELD BY INTERNATIONAL ECONOMIC ASSOCIATION. AFR ECO/DEV LABOR BARGAIN PAY CONFER...CHARTS ANTHOL 20. PAGE 35 F0679 — PRICE WORKER GEN/LAWS INCOME

B57

OLIVECRONA K.,THE PROBLEM OF THE MONETARY UNIT. AFR UNIV PAY PRICE UTIL...MATH 20 MONEY SILVER. PAGE 101 F1986 — FINAN ECO/TAC ECO/DEV CONCPT

B58
DUESENBERRY J.S.,BUSINESS CYCLES AND ECONOMIC GROWTH. USA+45 PROB/SOLV PAY PRICE...CONCPT MATH CHARTS IDEA/COMP 20 DEPRESSION KEYNES/JM. PAGE 34 F0672
FINAN ECO/DEV ECO/TAC INCOME

B59
SHACKLE G.L.S.,ECONOMICS FOR PLEASURE. FINAN MARKET NAT/G WORKER PLAN INT/TRADE TARIFFS PAY BAL/PAY COST PRODUC 20. PAGE 120 F2361
METH/CNCPT WEALTH INCOME

B60
DALE W.B.,THE FOREIGN DEFICIT OF THE UNITED STATES. ECO/TAC TARIFFS PAY PRICE CONTROL COST WEALTH POLICY. PAGE 30 F0573
BAL/PAY DIPLOM FINAN INT/TRADE

B60
KENEN P.B.,BRITISH MONETARY POLICY AND THE BALANCE OF PAYMENTS 1951-57. UK PLAN BUDGET ECO/TAC INT/TRADE PAY PRICE COST ATTIT 20. PAGE 70 F1377
BAL/PAY PROB/SOLV FINAN NAT/G

B61
FELLNER W.,THE PROBLEM OF RISING PRICES. AGRI INDUS WORKER BUDGET CAP/ISM ECO/TAC INT/TRADE PAY DEMAND ...POLICY 20 EEC. PAGE 40 F0780
PRICE MARKET ECO/DEV COST

B61
QURESHI S.,INCENTIVES IN AMERICAN EMPLOYMENT (THESIS, UNIVERSITY OF PENNSYLVANIA). DELIB/GP TOP/EX BUDGET ROUTINE SANCTION COST TECHRACY MGT. PAGE 108 F2134
SERV/IND ADMIN PAY EX/STRUC

B61
SLICHTER S.H.,ECONOMIC GROWTH IN THE UNITED STATES. FUT USA+45 USA-45 LABOR PAY INCOME PRODUC...MGT 19/20. PAGE 123 F2422
ECO/DEV TEC/DEV CAP/ISM DEMAND

S61
DICKS-MIREAUX L.A.,"THE INTERRELATIONSHIP BETWEEN COST AND PRICE CHANGES 19461959: A STUDY OF INFLATION IN POST-WAR BRITAIN" AFR UK ECO/DEV INDUS WORKER ECO/TAC ORD/FREE WEALTH...ECOMETRIC REGRESS STAT TREND CHARTS 20. PAGE 33 F0634
PRICE PAY DEMAND

B62
ALTMAN G.T.,INVISIBLE BARRIER: THE OPTIMUM GROWTH CURVE. USA+45 USA-45 ECO/DEV PLAN PAY CONTROL DEMAND OPTIMAL PRODUC WEALTH...STAT CHARTS 20. PAGE 4 F0080
INDUS FINAN ECO/TAC TAX

B62
GALENSON W.,LABOR IN DEVELOPING COUNTRIES. BRAZIL INDONESIA ISRAEL PAKISTAN TURKEY AGRI INDUS WORKER PAY PRICE GP/REL WEALTH...MGT CHARTS METH/COMP NAT/COMP 20. PAGE 45 F0888
LABOR ECO/UNDEV BARGAIN POL/PAR

B62
GWYN W.B.,DEMOCRACY AND THE COST OF POLITICS IN BRITAIN. UK BUDGET CRIME CHOOSE ORD/FREE WEALTH ...TIME/SEQ 18/20. PAGE 52 F1017
COST POL/PAR POPULISM PAY

B62
SCHNEIDER E.,MONEY, INCOME AND EMPLOYMENT. TAX PAY DEMAND...CHARTS BIBLIOG 20. PAGE 117 F2305
ECO/DEV FINAN INCOME

B62
SHINOHARA M.,GROWTH AND CYCLES IN THE JAPANESE ECONOMY. INDUS LABOR TEC/DEV CAP/ISM INT/TRADE PAY COST EFFICIENCY INCOME WEALTH...METH/COMP 20 CHINJAP. PAGE 121 F2380
PRODUC ECO/DEV EQUILIB ECOMETRIC

B62
VAIZEY J.,THE ECONOMICS OF EDUCATION. INTELL ECO/TAC PAY COST PRODUC 20. PAGE 140 F2758
ECO/DEV SCHOOL ACADEM PROFIT

B62
WOODS H.D.,LABOUR POLICY AND LABOUR ECONOMICS IN CANADA. CANADA FUT NAT/G VOL/ASSN WORKER BARGAIN ECO/TAC PAY CONFER GP/REL 20. PAGE 148 F2924
LABOR POLICY INDUS ECO/DEV

L62
BELSHAW D.G.R.,"PUBLIC INVESTMENT IN AGRICULTURE AND ECONOMIC DEVELOPMENT OF UGANDA" UGANDA AGRI INDUS R+D ECO/TAC RATION TAX PAY COLONIAL 20 WORLD/BANK. PAGE 13 F0242
ECO/UNDEV PLAN ADMIN CENTRAL

B63
CHATTERJEE I.K.,ECONOMIC DEVELOPMENT PAYMENTS DEFICIT AND PAYMENT RESTRICTION. INDIA WOR+45 FINAN INT/TRADE CONTROL BAL/PAY WEALTH...POLICY CONCPT STAT CHARTS IDEA/COMP BIBLIOG 20. PAGE 23 F0456
ECO/DEV ECO/TAC PAY GOV/REL

B63
COURNOT A.A.,RESEARCHES INTO THE MATHEMATICAL PRINCIPLES OF THE THEORY OF WEALTH (1838). UNIV ECO/DEV ECO/UNDEV AGRI INDUS MARKET PAY CONTROL COST INCOME 19. PAGE 28 F0544
ECOMETRIC GEN/LAWS WEALTH

B63
DUE J.F.,STATE SALES TAX ADMINISTRATION. OP/RES BUDGET PAY ADMIN EXEC ROUTINE COST EFFICIENCY PROFIT...CHARTS METH/COMP 20. PAGE 34 F0671
PROVS TAX STAT GOV/COMP

B63
VON MISES L.,HUMAN ACTION: A TREATISE ON ECONOMICS (2ND ED.). SOCIETY MARKET TAX PAY PRICE DEMAND EQUILIB RATIONAL...PSY 20. PAGE 142 F2794
PLAN DRIVE ATTIT

B64
BALL R.J.,INFLATION AND THE THEORY OF MONEY. MARKET TAX PAY PRICE TASK ADJUST BAL/PAY COST INCOME PRODUC WEALTH...METH/COMP 20 KEYNES/JM MONEY. PAGE 9 F0167
EQUILIB DEMAND POLICY

B64
BOWEN W.G.,ECONOMIC ASPECTS OF EDUCATION (NO. 104). EUR+WWI UK USA+45 PROF/ORG PLAN TEC/DEV PAY ...POLICY STAT 20. PAGE 17 F0329
EDU/PROP ACADEM FINAN METH/COMP

B64
BROWN E.H.P.,A COURSE IN APPLIED ECONOMICS (2ND ED.). ECO/DEV FINAN MARKET WORKER INT/TRADE RATION RENT PAY PRICE BAL/PAY...DECISION T RESOURCE/N. PAGE 19 F0368
POLICY ECO/TAC PROB/SOLV

B64
CLAIRBORN E.L.,FORECASTING THE BALANCE OF PAYMENTS: AN EVALUATION. AFR FUT UK USA+45 WOR+45 FINAN PLAN BUDGET PAY CONTROL...STAT CHARTS BIBLIOG 20. PAGE 24 F0474
PREDICT BAL/PAY ECO/DEV ECO/TAC

B64
COMMISSION ON MONEY AND CREDIT,INFLATION, GROWTH, AND EMPLOYMENT. AFR USA+45 PLAN PROB/SOLV PAY PRICE EFFICIENCY PRODUC WEALTH 20. PAGE 26 F0514
WORKER ECO/TAC OPTIMAL

B64
HAGGER A.J.,THE THEORY OF INFLATION. AFR PLAN PROB/SOLV PAY COST INCOME 20. PAGE 53 F1035
DEMAND TEC/DEV FINAN

B64
PIERSON J.H.,INSURING FULL EMPLOYMENT. USA+45 LABOR DIPLOM ECO/TAC PAY BAL/PAY 20. PAGE 106 F2084
ECO/DEV INT/TRADE POLICY WORKER

B64
STONIER A.W.,EXERCISES IN ECONOMICS. FINAN INDUS TEC/DEV RENT PAY EQUILIB PRODUC PROFIT...METH/COMP T. PAGE 127 F2498
PRICE MARKET WORKER

B65
BOWEN W.G.,UNEMPLOYMENT IN A PROSPEROUS ECONOMY. USA+45 ECO/DEV NAT/G ACT/RES PLAN PAY EDU/PROP DEMAND...POLICY IDEA/COMP ANTHOL 20. PAGE 17 F0330
WORKER ECO/TAC WEALTH PROB/SOLV

B65
ROSS A.M.,EMPLOYMENT POLICY AND THE LABOR MARKET. USA+45 MARKET LABOR NAT/G PROB/SOLV PAY EDU/PROP PARTIC UTIL...POLICY 20. PAGE 114 F2242
ECO/DEV WORKER WEALTH DEMAND

B65
SELIGMAN B.B.,POVERTY AS A PUBLIC ISSUE. USA+45 ECO/DEV NAT/G PAY RECEIVE PERS/REL INCOME NEW/LIB 20. PAGE 119 F2347
LEGIS ECO/TAC STRATA DISCRIM

B65
VAID K.N.,STATE AND LABOR IN INDIA. INDIA INDUS WORKER PAY PRICE ADJUD CONTROL PARL/PROC GP/REL ORD/FREE 20. PAGE 140 F2757
LAW LABOR MGT NEW/LIB

S65
KAUN D.E.,"THE FAIR LABOUR STANDARDS ACT: AN EVALUATION IN TERMS OF ITS STATED GOALS." SOUTH/AFR LAW LABOR BARGAIN PAY INGP/REL WEALTH 20. PAGE 69 F1364
ECO/TAC PRICE WORKER LEGIS

S65
STEENKAMP W.F.J.,"THE PROBLEM OF WAGE REGULATION." SOUTH/AFR LAW ECO/DEV ECO/UNDEV LABOR NAT/G BARGAIN PAY INGP/REL DISCRIM WEALTH...METH/COMP 20. PAGE 125 F2473
ECO/TAC PRICE WORKER RATION

B66
BEN-PORATH Y.,THE ARAB LABOR FORCE IN ISRAEL. ISLAM ISRAEL AGRI INDUS SCHOOL CAP/ISM PAY DEMAND...GEOG REGRESS STAT CHARTS 20 ARABS. PAGE 13 F0245
WORKER CENSUS GP/REL STRUCT

B66
BRODERSEN A.,THE SOVIET WORKER: LABOR AND GOVERNMENT IN SOVIET SOCIETY. USSR STRUCT INDUS LABOR PLAN PAY INGP/REL PRODUC...POLICY GEN/LAWS BIBLIOG 20 STALIN/J LENIN/VI BOLSHEVISM KHRUSH/N. PAGE 19 F0357
WORKER ROLE NAT/G MARXISM

B66
NATIONAL INDUSTRIAL CONF BOARD,GOLD AND WORLD MONETARY PROBLEMS. AFR FUT WOR+45 PROB/SOLV BUDGET INT/TRADE PAY GOV/REL...POLICY ANTHOL 20. PAGE 97 F1902
FINAN ECO/TAC PRICE BAL/PAY

B66
TURNER H.A.,PRICES, WAGES, AND INCOME POLICIES IN INDUSTRIALIZED MARKET ECONOMIES. AFR WOR+45 ECO/DEV INDUS PROB/SOLV ECO/TAC CONTROL WEALTH...CHARTS 20 INTRVN/ECO. PAGE 131 F2593
PRICE PAY MARKET INCOME

B66
US SENATE COMM GOVT OPERATIONS,INTERGOVERNMENTAL PERSONNEL ACT OF 1966. USA+45 NAT/G CONSULT DELIB/GP WORKER TEC/DEV PAY AUTOMAT UTIL 20 CONGRESS. PAGE 139 F2730
ADMIN LEGIS EFFICIENCY EDU/PROP

S66
FROMM G.,"RECENT MONETARY POLICY: AN ECONOMETRIC VIEW" USA+45 ECO/DEV INDUS PAY PRICE PRODUC ORD/FREE WEALTH...STAT 20 FED/RESERV. PAGE 45 F0869 — ECOMETRIC FINAN POLICY SIMUL

B67
GITTELL M.,PARTICIPANTS AND PARTICIPATION: A STUDY OF SCHOOL POLICY IN NEW YORK. USA+45 EX/STRUC BUDGET PAY ATTIT...POLICY MUNICH 20 NEWYORK/C. PAGE 47 F0926 — SCHOOL DECISION PARTIC ADMIN

L67
DEALEY S.,"MONETARY RECOVERY UNDER FEDERAL TRANSPORTATION STATUTES." USA+45 SEA WORKER TAX PAY ADJUD DEATH GOV/REL OWN HEALTH ORD/FREE 20. PAGE 31 F0609 — DIST/IND LAW CONTROL FINAN

L67
HUBBARD P.H.,"MONETARY RECOVERY UNDER THE COPYRIGHT, PATENT, AND TRADEMARK ACTS." PROC/MFG TAX PAY LEGIT ADJUD GOV/REL OWN ORD/FREE 20. PAGE 62 F1228 — CREATE LAW CONTROL FINAN

L67
STILL C.H.,"MONETARY RECOVERY UNDER THE FAIR LABOR STANDARDS ACT." USA+45 USA-45 WORKER PAY ADJUD GOV/REL HEALTH ORD/FREE...MATH 20 NLRB. PAGE 126 F2487 — LABOR CONTROL LAW FINAN

L67
TANDON Y.,"CONSENSUS AND AUTHORITY BEHIND UNITED NATIONS PEACEKEEPING OPERATIONS." FINAN VOL/ASSN BUDGET DIPLOM PAY DOMIN...CHARTS 20 UN. PAGE 128 F2528 — CONSEN INT/ORG PWR PEACE

L67
WILKINSON J.H. JR.,"THE NET OPERATING LOSS DEDUCTION AND RELATED INCOME TAX DEVICES." PROB/SOLV BUDGET PAY GOV/REL ORD/FREE...MATH CHARTS METH 20. PAGE 146 F2886 — TAX FINAN LAW ADJUD

S67
"THE SIERRA CLUB, POLITICAL ACTIVITY, AND TAX EXEMPT CHARITABLE STATUS." USA+45 LAW VOL/ASSN TAX PAY ADJUD LOBBY INGP/REL HABITAT 20. PAGE 2 F0027 — ELITES GOV/REL FACE/GP ORD/FREE

S67
FERGUSON D.E.,"DETERMINING CAPACITY FOR CAPITAL EXPENDITURES." USA+45 LOC/G BUDGET TAX ADMIN CONTROL...TREND MUNICH 20. PAGE 40 F0784 — FINAN PAY COST

S67
FRANKLIN N.N.,"THE CONCEPT AND MEASUREMENT OF 'MINIMUM LIVING STANDARDS'." UNIV OP/RES PAY INGP/REL DEMAND INCOME DRIVE WEALTH...SOC CHARTS METH/COMP. PAGE 43 F0849 — CONCPT PHIL/SCI ALL/VALS HAPPINESS

S67
MERON T.,"THE UN'S 'COMMON SYSTEM' OF SALARY, ALLOWANCE, AND BENEFITS: CRITICAL APPR'SAL OF COORD IN PERSONNEL MATTERS." VOL/ASSN PAY EFFICIENCY ...CHARTS 20 UN. PAGE 90 F1761 — ADMIN EX/STRUC INT/ORG BUDGET

S67
NEALE R.S.,"WORKING CLASS WOMEN AND WOMEN'S SUFFRAGE." UK LAW CONSTN LABOR NAT/G DELIB/GP LEGIS WORKER PAY PARTIC CHOOSE 19 FEMALE/SEX. PAGE 97 F1906 — STRATA SEX SUFF DISCRIM

S67
PAULY M.V.,"MIXED PUBLIC AND PRIVATE FINANCING OF EDUCATION." STRATA PAY RECEIVE COST INCOME OPTIMAL METH/COMP. PAGE 104 F2039 — SCHOOL PLAN TAX EFFICIENCY

PAYNE J.L. F2042

PAYNO M. F2043

PEACE CORPS....SEE PEACE/CORP

PEACE OF WESTPHALIA....SEE WESTPHALIA

PEACE....SEE ALSO ORD/FREE

B14
DE BLOCH J.,THE FUTURE OF WAR IN ITS TECHNICAL, ECONOMIC, AND POLITICAL RELATIONS (1899). MOD/EUR TEC/DEV BUDGET INT/TRADE DETER GUERRILLA WEAPON COST PEACE 20. PAGE 31 F0596 — WAR BAL/PWR PREDICT FORCES

B19
SUMNER W.G.,WAR AND OTHER ESSAYS. USA-45 DELIB/GP DIPLOM TARIFFS COLONIAL PEACE SOVEREIGN 20. PAGE 127 F2514 — INT/TRADE ORD/FREE CAP/ISM ECO/TAC

N19
FREEMAN H.A.,COERCION OF STATES IN FEDERAL UNIONS (PAMPHLET). WOR-45 DIPLOM CONTROL COERCE PEACE ORD/FREE...GOV/COMP METH/COMP NAT/COMP PACIFIST 20. PAGE 43 F0850 — FEDERAL WAR INT/ORG PACIFISM

B34
GRAHAM F.D.,PROTECTIVE TARIFFS. FUT USA+45 WOR-45 INDUS MARKET VOL/ASSN PLAN CAP/ISM ECO/TAC PEACE ATTIT DRIVE HEALTH ORD/FREE...OBS TREND GEN/LAWS FOR/TRADE 20. PAGE 50 F0970 — INT/ORG TARIFFS

S41
MUKERJEE R.,"POPULATION THEORY AND POLITICS (BMR)" WOR-45 NAT/G PLAN PROB/SOLV ECO/TAC INT/TRADE CONTROL WAR PEACE...CENSUS 20 BIRTH/CON RESOURCE/N. PAGE 94 F1854 — GEOG OPTIMAL CONCPT

B47
HEILPERIN M.A.,THE TRADE OF NATIONS. USA+45 USA-45 WOR+45 WOR-45 CULTURE ECO/DEV NAT/G DELIB/GP EDU/PROP ATTIT DISPL ORD/FREE PWR WEALTH TOT/POP 20. PAGE 58 F1139 — MARKET INT/ORG INT/TRADE PEACE

B47
US LIBRARY OF CONGRESS,POSTWAR PLANNING AND RECONSTRUCTION: JANUARY-MARCH 1943. WOR+45 SOCIETY INT/ORG DIPLOM...SOC PREDICT 20. PAGE 138 F2714 — BIBLIOG/A WAR PEACE PLAN

B49
DE JOUVENEL B.,PROBLEMS OF SOCIALIST ENGLAND. AFR UK USSR BAL/PWR ECO/TAC INT/TRADE PRICE WAR BAL/PAY PEACE 20. PAGE 31 F0601 — SOCISM NEW/LIB PROB/SOLV PLAN

B50
US DEPARTMENT OF STATE,POINT FOUR: COOPERATIVE PROGRAM FOR AID IN THE DEVELOPMENT OF ECONOMICALLY UNDERDEVELOPED AREAS. WOR+45 AGRI INDUS INT/ORG PLAN TEC/DEV DIPLOM EDU/PROP ADMIN PEACE PRODUC WEALTH 20 CONGRESS UN. PAGE 135 F2671 — ECO/UNDEV FOR/AID FINAN INT/TRADE

B52
GALBRAITH J.K.,AMERICAN CAPITALISM: THE CONCEPT OF COUNTERVAILING POWER. AFR FUT USA+45 FINAN PRICE CENTRAL INCOME PEACE WEALTH...POLICY DECISION 20. PAGE 45 F0881 — ECO/TAC CAP/ISM TREND NAT/G

B57
LAVES W.H.C.,UNESCO. FUT WOR+45 NAT/G CONSULT DELIB/GP TEC/DEV ECO/TAC EDU/PROP PEACE ORD/FREE ...CONCPT TIME/SEQ TREND UNESCO VAL/FREE 20. PAGE 76 F1491 — INT/ORG KNOWL

B57
SINGH D.B.,INFLATIONARY PRICE TRENDS IN INDIA SINCE 1939. AFR INDIA ECO/TAC RATION CONTROL WAR GOV/REL BAL/PAY DEMAND INCOME PEACE PRODUC...POLICY CHARTS 20. PAGE 122 F2413 — BUDGET ECO/UNDEV PRICE FINAN

B58
ATOMIC INDUSTRIAL FORUM,MANAGEMENT AND ATOMIC ENERGY. WOR+45 SEA LAW MARKET NAT/G TEC/DEV INSPECT INT/TRADE CONFER PEACE HEALTH...ANTHOL 20. PAGE 7 F0136 — NUC/PWR INDUS MGT ECO/TAC

B58
BIDWELL P.W.,RAW MATERIALS: A STUDY OF AMERICAN POLICY. USA+45 USA-45 ECO/UNDEV AGRI INDUS KIN CREATE PLAN ECO/TAC WAR PEACE ATTIT DRIVE WEALTH ...STAT CHARTS CONGRESS FOR/TRADE VAL/FREE. PAGE 15 F0279 — EXTR/IND ECO/DEV

B58
GALBRAITH J.K.,THE AFFLUENT SOCIETY. EUR+WWI FUT USA+45 USSR CULTURE SERV/IND PEACE WEALTH SOCISM ...NEW/IDEA TREND VAL/FREE 20. PAGE 45 F0882 — ATTIT ECO/TAC CAP/ISM

B58
MOULTON H.G.,CAN INFLATION BE CONTROLLED? ECO/DEV INDUS CAP/ISM RATION GOV/REL COST INCOME PEACE WEALTH...CHARTS TIME 20 KEYNES/JM MONEY. PAGE 94 F1847 — ECO/TAC CONTROL DEMAND FINAN

B59
ROPKE W.,INTERNATIONAL ORDER AND ECONOMIC INTEGRATION. ECO/DEV ECO/UNDEV AGRI FINAN INDUS INT/ORG WAR PEACE ORD/FREE...SOC METH/COMP 20 EEC. PAGE 114 F2238 — INT/TRADE DIPLOM BAL/PAY ALL/IDEOS

B60
APTHEKER H.,DISARMAMENT AND THE AMERICAN ECONOMY: A SYMPOSIUM. FUT USA+45 ECO/DEV DIST/IND FINAN INDUS PROC/MFG LABOR NAT/G POL/PAR CONSULT PLAN CAP/ISM INT/TRADE PEACE ATTIT MORAL WEALTH...TREND GEN/LAWS TOT/POP 20. PAGE 6 F0110 — MARXIST ARMS/CONT

B60
PENTONY D.E.,UNITED STATES FOREIGN AID. INDIA LAOS USA+45 ECO/UNDEV INT/TRADE ADMIN PEACE ATTIT ...POLICY METH/COMP ANTHOL 20. PAGE 105 F2060 — FOR/AID DIPLOM ECO/TAC

B61
ALFRED H.,PUBLIC OWNERSHIP IN THE USA: GOALS AND PRIORITIES. LAW INDUS INT/TRADE ADJUD GOV/REL EFFICIENCY PEACE SOCISM...POLICY ANTHOL 20 TVA. PAGE 4 F0065 — CONTROL OWN ECO/DEV ECO/TAC

B61
AUBREY H.G.,COEXISTENCE: ECONOMIC CHALLENGE AND RESPONSE. AFR USSR WOR+45 ACT/RES BAL/PWR CAP/ISM DIPLOM ECO/TAC FOR/AID INT/TRADE PEACE SOCISM ...METH/COMP NAT/COMP. PAGE 7 F0139 — POLICY ECO/UNDEV PLAN COM

B61
JAVITS B.A.,THE PEACE BY INVESTMENT CORPORATION. WOR+45 NAT/G LEGIS PROB/SOLV PERS/REL WEALTH ...POLICY 20. PAGE 66 F1307 — ECO/UNDEV DIPLOM FOR/AID PEACE

B61
PROUDHON P.J.,LA GUERRE ET LA PAIX (2 VOLS.). UNIV STRATA PROB/SOLV EQUILIB INCOME ATTIT...CONCPT 19. PAGE 108 F2125 — WAR PEACE WEALTH

B62
DUPRE J.S.,SCIENCE AND THE NATION: POLICY AND POLITICS. USA+45 LAW ACADEM FORCES ADMIN CIVMIL/REL GOV/REL EFFICIENCY PEACE...TREND 20 SCI/ADVSRY. PAGE 35 F0682
R+D INDUS TEC/DEV NUC/PWR

B62
SHANNON I.,THE ECONOMIC FUNCTIONS OF GOLD. AFR FUT WOR+45 WOR-45 INT/ORG BUDGET INT/TRADE BAL/PAY DEMAND PEACE 20 MONEY. PAGE 120 F2366
FINAN PRICE ECO/DEV ECO/TAC

B62
VIET J.,INTERNATIONAL COOPERATION AND PROGRAMMES OF ECONOMIC AND SOCIAL DEVELOPMENT. TEC/DEV FOR/AID DOMIN COLONIAL PEACE WEALTH 20 UNESCO. PAGE 141 F2784
BIBLIOG/A INT/ORG DIPLOM ECO/UNDEV

L63
OLSON M. JR.,"RAPID ECONOMIC GROWTH AS A DESTABILIZING FORCE." WOR+45 WOR-45 STRATA ECO/UNDEV FAM KIN CREATE TEC/DEV DIPLOM PEACE ATTIT PERSON RIGID/FLEX PWR RESPECT WEALTH...SOC 20. PAGE 101 F1989
SOCIETY FOR/AID

B64
LAURSEN K.,THE GERMAN INFLATION, 1918-23. EUR+WWI GERMANY/E GERMANY/W WOR-45 BUDGET TAX GOV/REL BAL/PAY DEMAND PEACE...POLICY CHARTS 20 WEIMAR/REP. PAGE 76 F1489
ECO/DEV FINAN REPAR ECO/TAC

B64
SEGAL R.,SANCTIONS AGAINST SOUTH AFRICA. AFR SOUTH/AFR NAT/G INT/TRADE RACE/REL PEACE PWR ...INT/LAW ANTHOL 20 UN. PAGE 119 F2342
SANCTION DISCRIM ECO/TAC POLICY

B64
SULLIVAN G.,THE STORY OF THE PEACE CORPS. USA+45 WOR+45 INTELL FACE/GP NAT/G SCHOOL VOL/ASSN CONSULT EX/STRUC PLAN EDU/PROP ADMIN ATTIT DRIVE ALL/VALS ...POLICY HEAL SOC CONCPT INT QU BIOG TREND SOC/EXP WORK. PAGE 127 F2511
INT/ORG ECO/UNDEV FOR/AID PEACE

B65
PEACE RESEARCH ABSTRACTS. FUT WOR+45 R+D INT/ORG NAT/G PLAN TEC/DEV BAL/PWR DIPLOM FOR/AID NUC/PWR HEALTH. PAGE 1 F0022
BIBLIOG/A PEACE ARMS/CONT WAR

B65
CHANDRASEKHAR S.,AMERICAN AID AND INDIA'S ECONOMIC DEVELOPMENT. AFR CHINA/COM INDIA USA+45 GIVE EDU/PROP EATING HEALTH ORD/FREE 20 AID. PAGE 23 F0449
FOR/AID PEACE DIPLOM ECO/UNDEV

B65
CLARK T.D.,THREE PATHS TO THE MODERN SOUTH: EDUCATION, AGRICULTURE, AND CONSERVATION. FUT USA-45 ECO/DEV ECO/TAC PEACE WEALTH...POLICY 20 SOUTH/US. PAGE 25 F0485
AGRI EDU/PROP GOV/REL REGION

B65
COX D.W.,THE PERILS OF PEACE* CONVERSION TO WHAT? FUT USA+45 ECO/DEV NAT/G ACT/RES CREATE PLAN NUC/PWR WAR DEMAND MGT. PAGE 28 F0546
PEACE WORKER FORCES MARKET

B65
O'BRIEN F.,CRISIS IN WORLD COMMUNISM* MARXISM IN SEARCH OF EFFICIENCY. AFR COM ECO/DEV PLAN INT/TRADE WAR ADJUST PEACE...STAT TIME/SEQ GOV/COMP NAT/COMP. PAGE 99 F1951
MARXISM USSR DRIVE EFFICIENCY

B65
RANSOM H.H.,AN AMERICAN FOREIGN POLICY READER. USA+45 FORCES EDU/PROP COERCE NUC/PWR WAR PEACE ...DECISION 20. PAGE 109 F2146
NAT/G DIPLOM POLICY

B65
SHAFFER H.G.,THE SOVIET SYSTEM IN THEORY AND PRACTICE: SELECTED WESTERN AND SOVIET VIEWS. USSR LAW SOCIETY CREATE FOR/AID EDU/PROP PRESS CHOOSE PEACE ORD/FREE...ANTHOL 20 STALIN/J. PAGE 120 F2362
MARXISM SOCISM IDEA/COMP

B66
BOLTON R.E.,DEFENSE AND DISARMAMENT: THE ECONOMICS OF TRANSITION. USA+45 R+D FORCES PLAN LOBBY DETER WAR COST PEACE...ANTHOL BIBLIOG 20. PAGE 16 F0310
ARMS/CONT POLICY INDUS

B66
FREIDEL F.,AMERICAN ISSUES IN THE TWENTIETH CENTURY. SOCIETY FINAN ECO/TAC FOR/AID CONTROL NUC/PWR WAR RACE/REL PEACE ATTIT...ANTHOL T 20 WILSON/W ROOSEVLT/F KENNEDY/JF TRUMAN/HS. PAGE 44 F0851
DIPLOM POLICY NAT/G ORD/FREE

B66
HEVESY P.D.,THE UNIFICATION OF THE WORLD. FUT USA+45 WOR+45 ECO/DEV ECO/UNDEV LEGIS PROB/SOLV BAL/PWR ECO/TAC INT/TRADE PEACE. PAGE 59 F1160
DIPLOM FINAN INT/ORG

B66
LEE R.A.,TRUMAN AND TAFT-HARTLEY: A QUESTION OF MANDATE. USA+45 LAW CONSTN LG/CO CONTROL LOBBY GOV/REL PEACE NEW/LIB 20 TRUMAN/HS CONGRESS. PAGE 77 F1507
LEGIS TOP/EX ADJUD LABOR

B67
BEATON L.,THE STRUGGLE FOR PEACE. INT/ORG FORCES NUC/PWR COST PWR...POLICY TREND 20. PAGE 12 F0225
PEACE BAL/PWR DIPLOM WAR

B67
DAVIS F.M.,COME AS A CONQUEROR: THE UNITED STATES ARMY'S OCCUPATION OF GERMANY: 1945-1949. EUR+WWI GERMANY USA+45 SOCIETY PLAN BAL/PWR DIPLOM FOR/AID PERS/REL DEMAND PEACE ORD/FREE 20. PAGE 30 F0588
FORCES CIVMIL/REL ECO/TAC CONTROL

B67
EVANS R.H.,COEXISTENCE: COMMUNISM AND ITS PRACTICE IN BOLOGNA, 1945-1965. ITALY CAP/ISM ADMIN CHOOSE PEACE ORD/FREE...SOC STAT DEEP/INT SAMP CHARTS BIBLIOG MUNICH 20. PAGE 39 F0756
MARXISM CULTURE POL/PAR

B67
GIAP V.N.,BIG VICTORY, GREAT TASK. VIETNAM WOR+45 FORCES PLAN DOMIN LEGIT RISK PEACE 20. PAGE 47 F0921
WAR LEAD ATTIT INSPECT

B67
HALLE L.J.,THE COLD WAR AS HISTORY. AFR USSR WOR+45 ECO/TAC FOR/AID NUC/PWR WAR PEACE ORD/FREE ...MAJORIT TREND 20 KENNEDY/JF KHRUSH/N BERLIN/BLO. PAGE 54 F1048
DIPLOM BAL/PWR

B67
MACCLOSKEY M.,PACTS FOR PEACE: UN, NATO, SEATO, CENTO, OAS. WOR+45 PLAN DIPLOM CONTROL PEACE ORD/FREE...ORG/CHARTS UN NATO SEATO OAS CENTO. PAGE 83 F1623
FORCES INT/ORG LEAD POLICY

B67
MARTIN P.,CANADA AND THE QUEST FOR PEACE. CANADA VIETNAM ECO/UNDEV PLAN FOR/AID WAR 20 UN. PAGE 86 F1684
DIPLOM PEACE INT/ORG POLICY

B67
OGLESBY C.,CONTAINMENT AND CHANGE. AFR COM USA+45 ECO/UNDEV TEC/DEV ECO/TAC FOR/AID INT/TRADE DOMIN GUERRILLA REV PEACE 20 STALIN/J. PAGE 101 F1983
DIPLOM BAL/PWR MARXISM CULTURE

B67
ORLANS H.,CONTRACTING FOR ATOMS. AFR USA+45 LAW INTELL ACADEM LG/CO NAT/G PLAN TEC/DEV CONTROL DETER...TREND 20. PAGE 102 F1999
NUC/PWR R+D PRODUC PEACE

B67
ROACH J.R.,THE UNITED STATES AND THE ATLANTIC COMMUNITY; ISSUES AND PROSPECTS. AFR WOR+45 TEC/DEV ECO/TAC COLONIAL REGION PEACE ROLE...ANTHOL NATO EEC. PAGE 112 F2199
INT/ORG POLICY ADJUST DIPLOM

B67
TOMA P.A.,THE POLITICS OF FOOD FOR PEACE; EXECUTIVE-LEGISLATIVE INTERACTION. USA+45 ECO/UNDEV POL/PAR DEBATE EXEC LOBBY CHOOSE PEACE...DECISION CHARTS. PAGE 131 F2580
FOR/AID POLICY LEGIS AGRI

B67
US SENATE COMM ON FOREIGN REL,HARRISON E. SALISBURY'S TRIP TO NORTH VIETNAM. CHINA/COM USA+45 VIETNAM/N PRESS TASK GUERRILLA CONSEN EFFICIENCY PEACE DRIVE...OBS SENATE. PAGE 139 F2743
DIPLOM WAR FORCES ATTIT

L67
TANDON Y.,"CONSENSUS AND AUTHORITY BEHIND UNITED NATIONS PEACEKEEPING OPERATIONS." FINAN VOL/ASSN BUDGET DIPLOM PAY DOMIN...CHARTS 20 UN. PAGE 128 F2528
CONSEN INT/ORG PWR PEACE

S67
APEL H.,"LES NOUVEAUX ASPECTS DE LA POLITIQUE ETRANGERE ALLEMANDE." AFR EUR+WWI GERMANY POL/PAR BAL/PWR ECO/TAC INT/TRADE NUC/PWR NAT/LISM PEACE ...POLICY 20 EEC. PAGE 6 F0107
DIPLOM INT/ORG FEDERAL

S67
CAMPBELL J.C.,"SOVIET-AMERICAN RELATIONS: CONFLICT AND COOPERATION." AFR USA+45 USSR AGREE WAR PEACE 20 KHRUSH/N KENNEDY/JF. PAGE 21 F0407
DIPLOM POLICY

S67
CROKER F.P.U.,"ECONOMIC PEACEKEEPING." UK PLAN PROB/SOLV TEC/DEV BAL/PWR DIPLOM COERCE PEACE ...POLICY DECISION 20. PAGE 28 F0553
FORCES WEAPON COST WAR

S67
ISELIN J.J.,"THE TRUMAN DOCTRINE: ITS PASSAGE THROUGH CONGRESS AND THE AFTERMATH." USA+45 ECO/UNDEV R+D INT/ORG DELIB/GP BAL/PWR REV PEACE ...POLICY UN. PAGE 66 F1291
DIPLOM COM FOR/AID AFR

S67
RONNING C.,"NANKING: 1950." ASIA CANADA CHINA/COM NAT/G PLAN ECO/TAC REV ADJUST 20. PAGE 113 F2235
DIPLOM ROLE PEACE

N67
US HOUSE COMM FOREIGN AFFAIRS,REPORT OF SPECIAL STUDY MISSION TO THE NEAR EAST (PAMPHLET). ISRAEL USA+45 YEMEN ECO/UNDEV INT/ORG FOR/AID ARMS/CONT WAR WEAPON NAT/LISM PEACE...GEOG 20 UN HOUSE/REP. PAGE 137 F2694
ISLAM DIPLOM FORCES

N67
US SENATE COMM ON FOREIGN REL,THE UNITED NATIONS AT TWENTY-ONE (PAMPHLET). WOR+45 BUDGET ADMIN SENATE UN. PAGE 139 F2738
INT/ORG DIPLOM PEACE

C83
BURKE E.,"RESOLUTIONS FOR CONCILIATION WITH AMERICA" (1775), IN E. BURKE, COLLECTED WORKS, VOL.
COLONIAL WAR

2." UK USA-45 FORCES INT/TRADE TARIFFS TAX SANCTION PEACE...POLICY 18 PRE/US/AM. PAGE 20 F0387 SOVEREIGN ECO/TAC

PEACE/CORP....PEACE CORPS

B63
GODWIN F.W.,THE HIDDEN FORCE. PUERT/RICO WOR+45 STRUCT VOL/ASSN PROB/SOLV DIPLOM CONFER...BIBLIOG 20 PEACE/CORP. PAGE 48 F0931 ECO/UNDEV WORKER SKILL ECO/TAC

PEACEFUL COEXISTENCE....SEE PEACE+COLD/WAR

PEACOCK A.T. F1870

PEARL A. F2044

PEARSON/L....LESTER PEARSON

PEASNT/WAR....PEASANT WAR (1525)

PECCEI A. F2045

PECK M.J. F1912

PEDERSEN J. F1489

PEDLER F.J. F2046

PEDLEY F.H. F2047

PEGRUM D.F. F2049

PEIRCE W.S. F2050

PELLING H.M. F2051

PELTASON J.W. F2052

PELZER K.J. F2053

PEMBERTON J., F2054

PEN I. F2055

PENN/WM....WILLIAM PENN

PENNEY N. F2056

PENNOCK J.R. F2057,F2058

PENNSYLVANIA ECONOMY LEAGUE F2059

PENNSYLVAN....PENNSYLVANIA

B51
PRINCETON U INDUSTRIAL REL SEC,COMPULSORY ARBITRATION OF UTILITY DISPUTES IN NEW JERSEY AND PENNSYLVANIA. USA+45 LEGIS WORKER ADJUD ORD/FREE ...POLICY MGT METH/COMP 20 NEW/JERSEY PENNSYLVAN. PAGE 108 F2118 BARGAIN PROVS INDUS LABOR

B60
PENNSYLVANIA ECONOMY LEAGUE,URBAN RENEWAL IMPACT STUDY: ADMINISTRATIVE-LEGAL-FISCAL. USA+45 FINAN LOC/G NEIGH ADMIN EFFICIENCY...CENSUS CHARTS MUNICH 20 PENNSYLVAN. PAGE 105 F2059 PLAN BUDGET ADJUD

B64
COMMITTEE ECONOMIC DEVELOPMENT,COMMUNITY ECONOMIC DEVELOPMENT PROGRAMS. USA+45 FINAN INDUS LG/CO PROF/ORG CREATE GP/REL MUNICH NEW/YORK VERMONT PENNSYLVAN IN ARKANSAS. PAGE 27 F0519 LOC/G LABOR PLAN

PENOLOGY....SEE CRIME

PENTAGON....PENTAGON

PENTONY D.E. F2060

PERCEPT....PERCEPTION AND COGNITION

B51
PARSONS T.,THE SOCIAL SYSTEM. UNIV INTELL SOCIETY ECO/DEV SECT PLAN PERCEPT...CONCPT METH/CNCPT. PAGE 103 F2030 DRIVE SOC

S53
LINCOLN G.,"FACTORS DETERMINING ARMS AID." COM FUT USA+45 USSR WOR+45 ECO/DEV NAT/G CONSULT PLAN TEC/DEV DIPLOM DOMIN EDU/PROP PERCEPT PWR ...DECISION CONCPT TREND MARX/KARL 20. PAGE 80 F1566 FORCES POLICY BAL/PWR FOR/AID

B57
EHRMANN H.W.,ORGANIZED BUSINESS IN FRANCE. EUR+WWI MOD/EUR ECO/DEV VOL/ASSN LEGIT ATTIT PERCEPT PWR RESPECT...PLURIST SOC INT TOT/POP 20. PAGE 36 F0712 PROF/ORG ECO/TAC FRANCE

S59
TIPTON J.B.,"PARTICIPATION OF THE UNITED STATES IN THE INTERNATIONAL LABOR ORGANIZATION." USA+45 LAW STRUCT ECO/DEV ECO/UNDEV INDUS TEC/DEV ECO/TAC ADMIN PERCEPT ORD/FREE SKILL...STAT HIST/WRIT GEN/METH ILO WORK 20. PAGE 131 F2577 LABOR INT/ORG

S60
HERZ J.H.,"EAST GERMANY: PROGRESS AND PROSPECTS." COM AGRI FINAN INDUS LOC/G NAT/G FORCES PLAN TEC/DEV DOMIN ADMIN COERCE DRIVE PERCEPT RIGID/FLEX MORAL ORD/FREE PWR...MARXIST PSY SOC RECORD STERTYP WORK. PAGE 59 F1158 POL/PAR STRUCT GERMANY

S60
MAIR L.P.,"SOCIAL CHANGE IN SOUTH AFRICA." MOD/EUR SOUTH/AFR WOR+45 ECO/UNDEV EX/STRUC TEC/DEV ATTIT DRIVE PERCEPT ORD/FREE...MGT CONCPT TIME/SEQ IND 20. PAGE 84 F1641 AFR NAT/G REV SOVEREIGN

B61
BENOIT E.,EUROPE AT SIXES AND SEVENS: THE COMMON MARKET, THE FREE TRADE ASSOCIATION AND THE UNITED STATES. EUR+WWI FUT USA+45 INDUS CONSULT DELIB/GP EX/STRUC TOP/EX ACT/RES ECO/TAC EDU/PROP ROUTINE CHOOSE PERCEPT WEALTH...MGT TREND EEC FOR/TRADE TOT/POP 20 EFTA. PAGE 13 F0249 FINAN ECO/DEV VOL/ASSN

B61
ERASMUS C.J.,MAN TAKES CONTROL: CULTURAL DEVELOPMENT AND AMERICAN AID. STRUCT OWN DRIVE PERCEPT...SOC 20 MEXIC/AMER. PAGE 38 F0741 ORD/FREE CULTURE ECO/UNDEV TEC/DEV

S61
GORDON L.,"ECONOMIC REGIONALISM RECONSIDERED." FUT USA+45 WOR+45 INDUS NAT/G TEC/DEV DIPLOM ROUTINE PERCEPT WEALTH...WELF/ST METH/CNCPT WORK 20. PAGE 49 F0957 ECO/DEV ATTIT CAP/ISM REGION

S61
HAYTES W.,"THREE VIEWS ON THE SOVIET ECONOMIC THREAT." AFR COM USA+45 USSR WOR+45 WOR-45 INDUS TEC/DEV ECO/TAC DOMIN ATTIT PERCEPT PWR FOR/TRADE 20. PAGE 57 F1128 ECO/DEV PLAN TOTALISM

B62
BRANCH M.C.,THE CORPORATE PLANNING PROCESS. FINAN EX/STRUC EDU/PROP CONTROL LEAD GP/REL PERS/REL RATIONAL PERCEPT...MGT MATH PROBABIL STAT GAME. PAGE 18 F0338 PROF/ORG PLAN DECISION PERSON

B62
SHERIF M.,INTERGROUP RELATIONS AND LEADERSHIP: APPROACHES AND RESEARCH IN INDUSTRIAL, ETHNIC, CULTURAL AND POLITICAL AREAS. CULTURE R+D LABOR DIPLOM GP/REL RACE/REL PERCEPT...PSY CONCPT. PAGE 121 F2377 LEAD REPRESENT PWR INGP/REL

S62
READ W.H.,"UPWARD COMMUNICATION IN INDUSTRIAL HIERARCHIES." LG/CO TOP/EX PROB/SOLV DOMIN EXEC PERS/REL ATTIT DRIVE PERCEPT...CORREL STAT CHARTS 20. PAGE 110 F2159 ADMIN INGP/REL PSY MGT

B63
BONINI C.P.,SIMULATION OF INFORMATION AND DECISION SYSTEMS IN THE FIRM. MARKET BUDGET DOMIN EDU/PROP ADMIN COST ATTIT HABITAT PERCEPT PWR...CONCPT PROBABIL QUANT PREDICT HYPO/EXP BIBLIOG. PAGE 16 F0313 INDUS SIMUL DECISION MGT

B63
SMELSER N.J.,THE SOCIOLOGY OF ECONOMIC LIFE. UNIV CULTURE PERCEPT...PSY T 18/20. PAGE 123 F2425 SOC METH/COMP IDEA/COMP

S63
BEGUIN H.,"ASPECTS STRUCTURELS DU COMMERCE EXTERIEUR DES PAYS SOUS-DEVELOPPES." FUT WOR+45 STRUCT FINAN SERV/IND POL/PAR TEC/DEV PERCEPT WEALTH FOR/TRADE 20. PAGE 12 F0229 MARKET ECO/UNDEV FOR/AID

S63
DE FOREST J.D.,"LOW LEVELS OF TECHNOLOGY AND ECONOMIC DEVELOPMENT PROSPECTS." WOR+45 WOR-45 CULTURE ACT/RES CREATE PLAN ECO/TAC ROUTINE PERCEPT WEALTH...METH/CNCPT GEN/LAWS 20. PAGE 31 F0597 ECO/UNDEV TEC/DEV

S63
FLOREA I.,"CU PRIVIRE LA OBIECTUL MATERIALISMULUI ISTORIC SI AL COMUNISMULUI STIINTIFIC SI LA RAPORTUL DINTRE ELE." EUR+WWI WOR+45 WOR-45 INTELL NAT/G POL/PAR WORKER EDU/PROP PERCEPT MARXISM ...MARXIST PHIL/SCI CONCPT TOT/POP 20. PAGE 42 F0812 COM ATTIT TOTALISM

S63
WALKER H.,"THE INTERNATIONAL LAW OF COMMODITY AGREEMENTS." FUT WOR+45 ECO/DEV ECO/UNDEV FINAN INT/ORG NAT/G CONSULT CREATE PLAN ECO/TAC ATTIT PERCEPT...CONCPT GEN/LAWS TOT/POP GATT 20. PAGE 142 F2804 MARKET VOL/ASSN INT/LAW INT/TRADE

S64
MC WILLIAM M.,"THE WORLD BANK AND THE TRANSFER OF POWER IN KENYA." AFR ECO/UNDEV CONSULT ACT/RES TEC/DEV PERCEPT PWR SKILL WEALTH...CONCPT OBS TREND 20. PAGE 88 F1715 NAT/G ECO/TAC

S64
NASH M.,"SOCIAL PREREQUISITES TO ECONOMIC GROWTH IN ECO/DEV
LATIN AMERICA AND SOUTHEAST ASIA." L/A+17C S/ASIA PERCEPT
CULTURE SOCIETY ECO/UNDEV AGRI INDUS NAT/G PLAN
TEC/DEV EDU/PROP ROUTINE ALL/VALS...POLICY RELATIV
SOC NAT/COMP WORK TOT/POP 20. PAGE 96 F1894

B65
ANDERSON C.A.,EDUCATION AND ECONOMIC DEVELOPMENT. ANTHOL
INDUS R+D SCHOOL TEC/DEV ECO/TAC EDU/PROP AGE ECO/DEV
HEREDITY PERCEPT SKILL 20. PAGE 5 F0092 ECO/UNDEV
WORKER

B65
CRANE E.,MARKETING COMMUNICATION: A BEHAVIORAL EDU/PROP
APPROACH TO MEN, MESSAGES, AND MEDIA. STRATA R+D MARKET
VOL/ASSN CROWD DRIVE PERSON SKILL WEALTH. PAGE 28 PERCEPT
F0551 ATTIT

B67
DE JOUVENAL B.,THE ART OF CONJECTURE. WOR+45 FUT
EFFICIENCY PERCEPT KNOWL...DECISION PHIL/SCI CONCPT PREDICT
METH/COMP BIBLIOG 20. PAGE 31 F0600 SIMUL
METH

B67
EBENSTEIN W.,TODAY'S ISMS: COMMUNISM, FASCISM, FASCISM
CAPITALISM, SOCIALISM (5TH ED.). COM WOR+45 PERCEPT MARXISM
PWR...SOC TREND IDEA/COMP NAT/COMP 20. PAGE 35 SOCISM
F0691 CAP/ISM

B67
SAPARINA Y.,CYBERNETICS WITHIN US. WOR+45 EDU/PROP COMPUTER
FEEDBACK PERCEPT HEALTH...DECISION METH/CNCPT METH/COMP
NEW/IDEA 20. PAGE 116 F2281 CONTROL
SIMUL

PERCEPTION....SEE PERCEPT

PERCY/CHAS....CHARLES PERCY

PERF/ART....PERFORMING ARTS

B62
BRUMBERG A.,RUSSIA UNDER KHRUSHCHEV. FUT USSR COM
SOCIETY ECO/DEV AGRI PERF/ART WORKER PWR...SOC MARXISM
ANTHOL 20 KHRUSH/N. PAGE 20 F0377 NAT/G
CHIEF

PERFORMING ARTS....SEE PERF/ART; ALSO ART/METH

PERKINS D. F2061

PERKINS D.H. F2062

PERLO V. F2063,F2064

PERON/JUAN....JUAN PERON

B67
BAILY S.L.,LABOR, NATIONALISM, AND POLITICS IN LABOR
ARGENTINA. POL/PAR TOP/EX GP/REL...BIBLIOG/A 19/20 NAT/LISM
MIGRATION PERON/JUAN ARGEN. PAGE 8 F0154

PERROUX F. F2065

PERS/COMP....COMPARISON OF PERSONS

S53
BIRNBAUM N.,"CONFLICTING INTERPRETATIONS OF THE CAP/ISM
RISE OF CAPITALISM: MARX AND WEBER" (BMR)" WOR-45 IDEA/COMP
INTELL SOCIETY STRUCT INDUS WORKER...PHIL/SCI SOC ECO/DEV
PERS/COMP 19/20 MARX/KARL WEBER/MAX. PAGE 15 F0288 MARXISM

B56
HICKMAN C.A.,INDIVIDUALS, GROUPS, AND ECONOMIC MGT
BEHAVIOR. WORKER PAY CONTROL EXEC GP/REL INGP/REL ADMIN
PERSON ROLE...PSY SOC PERS/COMP METH 20. PAGE 59 ECO/TAC
F1163 PLAN

B59
SERAPHIM H.J.,PROBLEME DER WILLENSBILDUNG UND DER POLICY
WIRTSCHAFTSPOLITISCHEN FUEHRUNG. WOR+45 MARKET DECISION
ACT/RES OP/RES PLAN EDU/PROP INGP/REL HABITAT PSY
PLURISM...MGT PERS/COMP METH 20. PAGE 119 F2357

B60
MENDELSON W.,CAPITALISM, DEMOCRACY, AND THE SUPREME JUDGE
COURT. USA+45 USA-45 CONSTN DIPLOM GOV/REL ATTIT CT/SYS
ORD/FREE LAISSEZ...POLICY CHARTS PERS/COMP 18/20 JURID
SUPREME/CT MARSHALL/J HOLMES/OW TANEY/RB FIELD/JJ. NAT/G
PAGE 90 F1758

B61
FRIEDMANN G.,THE ANATOMY OF WORK. USA+45 SOCIETY AUTOMAT
CONTROL ROUTINE DRIVE SKILL...PSY SOC STAT OBS WORKER
METH/COMP PERS/COMP 20. PAGE 44 F0862 INDUS
PERSON

B61
ROEPKE W.,JENSEITS VON ANGEBOT UND NACHFRAGE SOCIETY
(DRITTE VERAENDERTE AUFLAGE). WOR+45 MARKET TEC/DEV STRANGE
ECO/TAC GP/REL INGP/REL NEW/LIB...POLICY SOC ECO/DEV
IDEA/COMP PERS/COMP 20. PAGE 113 F2233 STRUCT

B62
HARRIS S.E.,THE ECONOMICS OF THE POLITICAL PARTIES. POLICY
USA+45 FINAN CHIEF ACT/RES PLAN BUDGET GP/REL ECO/DEV
INGP/REL NEW/LIB...IDEA/COMP PERS/COMP 20 NAT/G
EISNHWR/DD KENNEDY/JF. PAGE 56 F1090 POL/PAR

B64
HARRIS S.E.,ECONOMICS OF THE KENNEDY YEARS AND A ECO/TAC
LOOK AHEAD. USA+45 PLAN BUDGET NEW/LIB...STAT CHIEF
RECORD IDEA/COMP PERS/COMP INDEX 20 KENNEDY/JF POLICY
EISNHWR/DD JOHNSON/LB. PAGE 56 F1091 NAT/G

B66
WECHSBERG J.,THE MERCHANT BANKERS. EUR+WWI MOD/EUR FINAN
CONTROL...BIOG GP/COMP PERS/COMP 16/20. PAGE 144 PWR
F2842 WEALTH
FAM

S67
ADAMS R.N.,"ETHICS AND THE SOCIAL ANTHROPOLOGIST IN L/A+17C
LATIN AMERICA." USA+45 INTELL PROB/SOLV ECO/TAC POLICY
LEAD...DECISION SOC NAT/COMP PERS/COMP. PAGE 2 ECO/UNDEV
F0039 CONSULT

PERS/REL....RELATIONS BETWEEN PERSONS AND INTERPERSONAL
COMMUNICATION; SEE ALSO COMMUN

N19
HOGARTY R.A.,NEW JERSEY FARMERS AND MIGRANT HOUSING AGRI
RULES (PAMPHLET). USA+45 LAW ELITES FACE/GP LABOR PROVS
PROF/ORG LOBBY PERS/REL RIGID/FLEX ROLE 20 WORKER
NEW/JERSEY. PAGE 61 F1193 HEALTH

N19
MARSH J.F. JR.,THE FBI RETIREMENT BILL (PAMPHLET). ADMIN
USA+45 EX/STRUC WORKER PLAN PROB/SOLV BUDGET LEAD NAT/G
LOBBY PARL/PROC PERS/REL RIGID/FLEX...POLICY 20 FBI SENIOR
PRESIDENT BUR/BUDGET. PAGE 86 F1677 GOV/REL

N19
MASCHLER M.,STABLE PAYOFF CONFIGURATIONS FOR QUOTA ECOMETRIC
GAMES (PAMPHLET). PLAN PERS/REL 20. PAGE 87 F1694 GAME
COMPUTER
DECISION

N19
SILVERMAN C.,THE PRESIDENT'S ECONOMIC ADVISERS CONSULT
(PAMPHLET). USA+45 LAW ELITES ECO/DEV EX/STRUC PROB/SOLV
ADMIN LEAD GOV/REL PERS/REL ROLE...POLICY DECISION NAT/G
20 PRESIDENT CONGRESS EISNHWR/DD. PAGE 122 F2404 PLAN

N19
YLVISAKER P.N.,THE NATURAL CEMENT ISSUE (PAMPHLET). POLICY
USA+45 USA-45 CONSTRUC PROVS CAP/ISM ADMIN LOBBY NAT/G
PERS/REL OWN RIGID/FLEX ROLE 20 MINNESOTA. PAGE 150 PLAN
F2948 GOV/REL

S56
LANDAUER J.D.,"PROFESSIONAL CONSULTANTS: A NEW CONSULT
FACTOR IN REAL ESTATE." USA+45 PROB/SOLV ECO/TAC CONSTRUC
PERS/REL DEMAND EFFICIENCY DECISION. PAGE 75 F1467 CLIENT

B57
DOWNS A.,AN ECONOMIC THEORY OF DEMOCRACY. NAT/G DECISION
EDU/PROP RISK CHOOSE PERS/REL EQUILIB...SOC RATIONAL
METH/CNCPT LOG STYLE. PAGE 34 F0659

S57
KAHN R.L.,"UNION PRACTICES AND MEMBER INGP/REL
PARTICIPATION." PARTIC CHOOSE REPRESENT PERS/REL LABOR
PERSON SKILL...DECISION METH/CNCPT QU. PAGE 69 ATTIT
F1347 LEAD

B58
CHEEK G.,ECONOMIC AND SOCIAL IMPLICATIONS OF BIBLIOG/A
AUTOMATION: A BIBLIOGRAPHIC REVIEW (PAMPHLET). SOCIETY
USA+45 LG/CO WORKER CREATE PLAN CONTROL ROUTINE INDUS
PERS/REL EFFICIENCY PRODUC...METH/COMP 20. PAGE 24 AUTOMAT
F0459

S58
EMERSON F.D.,"THE ROLES OF MANAGEMENT AND LG/CO
SHAREHOLDERS IN CORPORATE GOVERNMENT." CLIENT LAW
DELIB/GP CREATE ADMIN EXEC PARTIC PERS/REL PWR. INGP/REL
PAGE 37 F0728 REPRESENT

B59
WAHLKE J.C.,LEGISLATIVE BEHAVIOR: A READER IN LEGIS
THEORY AND RESEARCH. USA+45 CONSTN ELITES POL/PAR CHOOSE
LOBBY REPRESENT PERS/REL PERSON ROLE...IDEA/COMP INGP/REL
METH/COMP SIMUL. PAGE 142 F2800 ATTIT

I59
FURASH E.A.,"PROBLEMS IN REVIEW: INDUSTRIAL INDUS
ESPIONAGE." WORKER ECO/TAC PERS/REL OPTIMAL AGE TOP/EX
ATTIT KNOWL...MGT DEEP/INT DEEP/QU GP/COMP MAJORITY
IDEA/COMP. PAGE 45 F0875

B60
SIEGEL S.,BARGAINING AND GROUP DECISION-MAKING: DECISION
EXPERIMENTS IN BILATERAL MONOPOLY. EFFICIENCY...PSY PERS/REL
CHARTS. PAGE 122 F2397 PROB/SOLV
BARGAIN

B60
WALLACE R.A.,CONGRESSIONAL CONTROL OF FEDERAL LEGIS
SPENDING. USA+45 CONSTN NAT/G OP/RES CONFER DEBATE DELIB/GP
PERS/REL UTIL RIGID/FLEX PWR OBJECTIVE...OBS BUDGET
CHARTS. PAGE 143 F2808

S60
FRENCH J.R.P. JR.,"AN EXPERIMENT ON PARTICIPATION INDUS
IN A NORWEGIAN FACTORY:INTERPERSONAL DIMENSIONS OF PLAN
DECISION-MAKING." LABOR LEAD PERS/REL EFFICIENCY RIGID/FLEX
PRODUC...DECISION SOC CHARTS SOC/EXP. PAGE 44 F0853 GP/REL

S60
SPINRAD W.,"CORRELATES OF TRADE UNION PARTICIPATION: A SUMMARY OF LITERATURE." ACT/RES PERS/REL HAPPINESS HABITAT...BIBLIOG WORK. PAGE 125 F2456
LABOR PARTIC CORREL ROLE

B61
AMERICAN MANAGEMENT ASSN,SUPERIOR-SUBORDINATE COMMUNICATION IN MANAGEMENT. STRATA FINAN INDUS SML/CO WORKER CONTROL EXEC ATTIT 20. PAGE 5 F0090
MGT ACT/RES PERS/REL LG/CO

B61
FILLOL T.R.,SOCIAL FACTORS IN ECONOMIC DEVELOPMENT: THE ARGENTINE CASE. STRUCT INDUS LABOR CREATE TEC/DEV EFFICIENCY PRODUC DRIVE...METH/CNCPT METH/COMP BIBLIOG/A 20 ARGEN. PAGE 41 F0795
ECO/UNDEV MGT PERS/REL TREND

B61
JAVITS B.A.,THE PEACE BY INVESTMENT CORPORATION. WOR+45 NAT/G LEGIS PROB/SOLV PERS/REL WEALTH ...POLICY 20. PAGE 66 F1307
ECO/UNDEV DIPLOM FOR/AID PEACE

C61
FILLOL T.R.,"SOCIAL FACTORS IN ECONOMIC DEVELOPMENT: THE ARGENTINE CASE" INDUS LABOR CREATE TEC/DEV PERS/REL EFFICIENCY PRODUC DRIVE ...METH/CNCPT METH/COMP 20 ARGEN. PAGE 41 F0794
BIBLIOG ECO/UNDEV MGT TREND

B62
BRANCH M.C.,THE CORPORATE PLANNING PROCESS. FINAN EX/STRUC EDU/PROP CONTROL LEAD GP/REL PERS/REL RATIONAL PERCEPT...MGT MATH PROBABIL STAT GAME. PAGE 18 F0338
PROF/ORG PLAN DECISION PERSON

B62
COLLIER A.T.,MANAGEMENT, MEN, AND VALUES. INDUS FACE/GP EX/STRUC PLAN PROB/SOLV DEBATE SENIOR ADMIN PROFIT PERSON...PSY SOC 20. PAGE 26 F0505
MGT ATTIT PERS/REL DECISION

S62
READ W.H.,"UPWARD COMMUNICATION IN INDUSTRIAL HIERARCHIES." LG/CO TOP/EX PROB/SOLV DOMIN EXEC PERS/REL ATTIT DRIVE PERCEPT...CORREL STAT CHARTS 20. PAGE 110 F2159
ADMIN INGP/REL PSY MGT

B63
CHAMPION J.M.,CRITICAL INCIDENTS IN MANAGEMENT. MARKET LG/CO SML/CO OP/RES ADMIN CONTROL LEAD GP/REL PERS/REL COST ATTIT SUPEGO ALL/VALS...PSY PERS/TEST BIBLIOG. PAGE 23 F0445
MGT DECISION EX/STRUC INDUS

B63
LANGE O.,ECONOMIC DEVELOPMENT, PLANNING, AND INTERNATIONAL COOPERATION. UAR WOR+45 FINAN CAP/ISM PERS/REL 20. PAGE 75 F1476
ECO/UNDEV DIPLOM INT/TRADE PLAN

B63
SMITH R.A.,CORPORATIONS IN CRISIS. USA+45 LG/CO EX/STRUC ECO/TAC CONTROL LEAD PERS/REL...MGT 20. PAGE 123 F2432
ELITES INDUS PROB/SOLV METH/COMP

B64
BLAKE R.R.,MANAGING INTERGROUP CONFLICT IN INDUSTRY. INDUS DELIB/GP EX/STRUC GP/REL PERS/REL GAME. PAGE 16 F0297
CREATE PROB/SOLV OP/RES ADJUD

S64
LEFF N.H.,"ECONOMIC DEVELOPMENT THROUGH BUREAUCRATIC CORRUPTION." ELITES NAT/G ROUTINE REPRESENT GP/REL PERS/REL. PAGE 77 F1511
ECO/UNDEV CLIENT EX/STRUC

B65
BOLLENS J.C.,THE METROPOLIS: ITS PEOPLE, POLITICS, AND ECONOMIC LIFE. USA+45 PLAN PROB/SOLV PERS/REL PWR...DECISION GEOG CENSUS TREND CON/ANAL MUNICH 20 NEWYORK/C LOS/ANG SAN/FRAN CHICAGO PHILADELPH. PAGE 16 F0309
HABITAT SOC LOC/G

B65
NATIONAL CONF SOCIAL WELFARE,THE SOCIAL WELFARE FORUM, 1965. LAW CULTURE VOL/ASSN CONTROL PERS/REL ADJUST POLICY. PAGE 97 F1899
CONSTN WEALTH ORD/FREE NEIGH

B65
SELIGMAN B.B.,POVERTY AS A PUBLIC ISSUE. USA+45 ECO/DEV NAT/G PAY RECEIVE PERS/REL INCOME NEW/LIB 20. PAGE 119 F2347
LEGIS ECO/TAC STRATA DISCRIM

S65
KUNKEL J.H.,"VALUES AND BEHAVIOR IN ECONOMIC DEVELOPMENT." INDIA PERU CULTURE STRUCT CREATE PERS/REL ATTIT PERSON...CHARTS HYPO/EXP ARGEN. PAGE 74 F1449
SIMUL ECO/UNDEV PSY STERTYP

B66
BOYD H.W.,MARKETING MANAGEMENT: CASES FROM EMERGING COUNTRIES. BRAZIL GHANA ISRAEL WOR+45 ADMIN PERS/REL ATTIT HABITAT WEALTH...ANTHOL 20 ARGEN CASEBOOK. PAGE 17 F0332
MGT ECO/UNDEV PROB/SOLV MARKET

B67
BIBBY J.,ON CAPITOL HILL. POL/PAR LOBBY PARL/PROC GOV/REL PERS/REL...JURID PHIL/SCI OBS INT BIBLIOG 20 CONGRESS PRESIDENT. PAGE 15 F0278
CONFER LEGIS CREATE LEAD

B67
DAVIS F.M.,COME AS A CONQUEROR: THE UNITED STATES ARMY'S OCCUPATION OF GERMANY: 1945-1949. EUR+WWI GERMANY USA+45 SOCIETY PLAN BAL/PWR DIPLOM FOR/AID PERS/REL DEMAND PEACE ORD/FREE 20. PAGE 30 F0588
FORCES CIVMIL/REL ECO/TAC CONTROL

B67
GOLEMBIEWSKI R.T.,ORGANIZING MEN AND POWER: PATTERNS OF BEHAVIOR AND LINESTAFF MODELS. WOR+45 EX/STRUC ACT/RES DOMIN PERS/REL...NEW/IDEA 20. PAGE 48 F0943
ADMIN CONTROL SIMUL MGT

B67
PETRO S.,THE KINGSPORT STRIKE. USA+45 PROC/MFG NAT/G JUDGE PRESS PARTIC PERS/REL...OLD/LIB OBS INT 20 NLRB. PAGE 105 F2074
LABOR COERCE SANCTION ALL/VALS

B67
ROELOFS H.M.,THE LANGUAGE OF MODERN POLITICS: AN INTRODUCTION TO THE STUDY OF GOVERNMENT. DIPLOM ADMIN MARXISM NEW/LIB...JURID CONCPT METH/COMP T 20. PAGE 113 F2230
LEAD NAT/COMP PERS/REL NAT/G

B67
SMITH T.L.,THE PROCESS OF RURAL DEVELOPMENT IN LATIN AMERICA (A MONOGRAPH). L/A+17C STRATA INDUS PLAN GP/REL PERS/REL RIGID/FLEX WEALTH...OBS CHARTS ORG/CHARTS ANTHOL 20 COLOMB. PAGE 123 F2434
IDEA/COMP SOC AGRI ECO/UNDEV

B67
SPURRIER R.B.,THE OVERPOPULATED SOCIETY. WORKER EATING PERS/REL DEMAND EQUILIB ILLEGIT INCOME HABITAT 20. PAGE 125 F2461
BIO/SOC FOR/AID DRIVE RECEIVE

S67
BRAUCHER R.,"RECLAMATION OF GOODS FROM A FRAUDULENT BUYER." USA+45 CLIENT FINAN CT/SYS PERS/REL COST WEALTH. PAGE 18 F0341
LAW ADJUD GOV/REL INT/TRADE

S67
KELLY F.K.,"A PROPOSAL FOR AN ANNUAL REPORT ON THE STATE OF MANKIND." FUT INTELL COM/IND INT/ORG CREATE PROB/SOLV PERS/REL...CONCPT 20 UN. PAGE 70 F1371
SOCIETY UNIV ATTIT NEW/IDEA

S67
LEMIEUX V.,"LA DIMENSION POLITIQUE DE L'ACTION RATIONNELLE." CONTROL GP/REL PERS/REL...DECISION NEW/IDEA GAME 20. PAGE 77 F1518
GEN/LAWS RATIONAL PWR

S67
SKOLNICK J.H.,"SOCIAL CONTROL IN THE ADVERSARY SYSTEM." USA+45 CONSULT OP/RES ADMIN CONTROL. PAGE 123 F2419
PROB/SOLV PERS/REL ADJUD CT/SYS

PERS/TEST....PERSONALITY TESTS

B56
WHYTE W.H. JR.,THE ORGANIZATION MAN. CULTURE FINAN VOL/ASSN DOMIN EDU/PROP EXEC DISPL HABITAT ROLE ...PERS/TEST STERTYP. PAGE 146 F2875
ADMIN LG/CO PERSON CONSEN

B63
CHAMPION J.M.,CRITICAL INCIDENTS IN MANAGEMENT. MARKET LG/CO SML/CO OP/RES ADMIN CONTROL LEAD GP/REL PERS/REL COST ATTIT SUPEGO ALL/VALS...PSY PERS/TEST BIBLIOG. PAGE 23 F0445
MGT DECISION EX/STRUC INDUS

PERSALL E.S. F2066

PERSIA....PERSIA: ANCIENT IRAN

PERSON....PERSONALITY AND HUMAN NATURE

N
DEUTSCHE BUCHEREI,DEUTSCHES BUCHERVERZEICHNIS. GERMANY LAW CULTURE POL/PAR ADMIN LEAD ATTIT PERSON ...SOC 20. PAGE 32 F0626
BIBLIOG NAT/G DIPLOM ECO/DEV

B11
SCOTT W.D.,INFLUENCING MEN IN BUSINESS: THE PSYCHOLOGY OF ARGUMENT AND SUGGESTION. WOR-45 WORKER EDU/PROP DEMAND ATTIT PERSON 20. PAGE 118 F2336
PSY MARKET SML/CO TOP/EX

B14
VEBLEN T.,THE INSTINCT OF WORKMANSHIP. UNIV SOCIETY ECO/DEV ECO/UNDEV CREATE TEC/DEV ECO/TAC EDU/PROP ROUTINE PERSON...HUM CONCPT TIME/SEQ GEN/LAWS. PAGE 140 F2768
DRIVE SKILL

B20
COX H.,ECONOMIC LIBERTY. UNIV LAW INT/TRADE RATION TARIFFS RACE/REL SOCISM POLICY. PAGE 28 F0547
NAT/G ORD/FREE ECO/TAC PERSON

B22
FOURIER C.,TRAITE DE L'ASSOCIATION DOMESTIQUE-AGRICOLE (2 VOLS.). UNIV SOCIETY INDUS ECO/TAC PERSON MORAL ANARCH. PAGE 43 F0834
VOL/ASSN AGRI UTOPIA CONCPT

B22
VON ENGELIN O.D.,INHERITING THE EARTH, THE
INGP/REL

GEOGRAPHICAL FACTOR IN NATIONAL DEVELOPMENT. WOR-45 CULTURE DIPLOM BIO/SOC HABITAT PERSON...PSY SOC CONCPT IDEA/COMP. PAGE 142 F2791
GEOG SOCIETY ROLE

B28
DE MAN H.,THE PSYCHOLOGY OF SOCIALISM. EUR+WWI USSR LABOR NAT/LISM PERSON WEALTH MARXISM...METH/COMP 20. PAGE 31 F0604
WORKER ATTIT SOC SOCISM

B41
YOUNG G.,FEDERALISM AND FREEDOM. EUR+WWI MOD/EUR RUSSIA USA-45 WOR-45 SOCIETY STRUCT ECO/DEV INT/ORG EXEC FEDERAL ATTIT PERSON ALL/VALS...OLD/LIB CONCPT OBS TREND LEAGUE/NAT TOT/POP. PAGE 150 F2950
NAT/G WAR

B44
KAUFMANN F.,METHODOLOGY OF THE SOCIAL SCIENCES. PERSON...RELATIV PSY CONCPT LING METH 20. PAGE 69 F1363
SOC PHIL/SCI GEN/LAWS METH/CNCPT

B48
DURBIN E.F.M.,THE POLITICS OF DEMOCRATIC SOCIALISM; AN ESSAY ON SOCIAL POLICY. STRATA POL/PAR PLAN COERCE DRIVE PERSON PWR MARXISM...CHARTS METH/COMP. PAGE 35 F0684
SOCIALIST POPULISM POLICY SOCIETY

B48
HAYEK F.A.,INDIVIDUALISM AND ECONOMIC ORDER. FINAN PLAN MORAL LAISSEZ SOCISM...POLICY DECISION PHIL/SCI HIST/WRIT. PAGE 57 F1122
RATIONAL KNOWL PERSON

B49
LEE A.M.,SOCIAL PROBLEMS IN AMERICA: A SOURCE BOOK. STRATA STRUCT KIN NEIGH VOL/ASSN ACT/RES LEAD CRIME AGE SEX 20. PAGE 77 F1504
SOC SOCIETY PERSON EDU/PROP

B50
ADORNO T.W.,THE AUTHORITARIAN PERSONALITY. STRATA SECT PROB/SOLV ECO/TAC DISCRIM ATTIT SEX...SOC INT CHARTS METH 20. PAGE 3 F0044
AUTHORIT PERSON ALL/IDEOS SOCIETY

B51
HARROD R.F.,THE LIFE OF JOHN MAYNARD KEYNES. UK INTELL FAM CAP/ISM DIPLOM ECO/TAC WAR ATTIT PERSON ROLE 20 KEYNES/JM WWI. PAGE 56 F1094
BIOG FINAN GEN/LAWS

B52
DE JOUVENEL B.,THE ETHICS OF REDISTRIBUTION. UK ELITES MARKET WORKER GIVE PAY INCOME PERSON ...POLICY PSY GEN/LAWS 20. PAGE 31 F0602
WEALTH TAX SOCISM TRADIT

B53
BOWEN H.R.,SOCIAL RESPONSIBILITIES OF THE BUSINESSMAN (FIRST EDITION). LAW FINAN ACT/RES CAP/ISM ROUTINE DRIVE PWR LAISSEZ...DECISION BIBLIOG. PAGE 17 F0326
MGT PERSON SUPEGO MORAL

B53
WOYTINSKY W.S.,WORLD POPULATION AND PRODUCTION: TRENDS AND OUTLOOK. FUT WOR+45 WOR-45 CULTURE SOCIETY ECO/DEV AGRI INDUS TEC/DEV EDU/PROP SKILL WEALTH...SOC TREND. PAGE 149 F2928
ECO/UNDEV METH/CNCPT GEOG PERSON

B54
CHILDS M.W.,ETHICS IN A BUSINESS SOCIETY. PROF/ORG LEAD WAR GP/REL ATTIT DRIVE PERSON KNOWL MORAL PWR ...WELF/ST BIBLIOG. PAGE 24 F0466
MGT SOCIETY

B54
POTTER D.M.,PEOPLE OF PLENTY: ECONOMIC ABUNDANCE AND THE AMERICAN CHARACTER. USA+45 USA-45 ECO/DEV ATTIT PERSON...PSY SOC CONCPT TREND GEN/METH TOT/POP 20. PAGE 107 F2108
CULTURE WEALTH

S55
BUNZEL J.H.,"THE GENERAL IDEOLOGY OF AMERICAN SMALL BUSINESS"(BMR)" USA+45 USA-45 AGRI GP/REL INGP/REL PERSON...MGT IDEA/COMP 18/20. PAGE 20 F0383
ALL/IDEOS ATTIT SML/CO INDUS

B56
HICKMAN C.A.,INDIVIDUALS, GROUPS, AND ECONOMIC BEHAVIOR. WORKER PAY CONTROL EXEC GP/REL INGP/REL PERSON ROLE...PSY SOC PERS/COMP METH 20. PAGE 59 F1163
MGT ADMIN ECO/TAC PLAN

B56
WHYTE W.H. JR.,THE ORGANIZATION MAN. CULTURE FINAN VOL/ASSN DOMIN EDU/PROP EXEC DISPL HABITAT ROLE ...PERS/TEST STERTYP. PAGE 146 F2875
ADMIN LG/CO PERSON CONSEN

S57
KAHN R.L.,"UNION PRACTICES AND MEMBER PARTICIPATION." PARTIC CHOOSE REPRESENT PERS/REL PERSON SKILL...DECISION METH/CNCPT QU. PAGE 69 F1347
INGP/REL LABOR ATTIT LEAD

B58
PALMER E.E.,INDUSTRIAL MAN. USA+45 PERSON ORD/FREE POPULISM...PREDICT TREND ANTHOL 20. PAGE 103 F2020
INDUS ECO/UNDEV CULTURE WEALTH

S58
FOLDES L.,"UNCERTAINTY, PROBABILITY AND POTENTIAL SURPRISE." MARKET PROB/SOLV RISK PERSON...DECISION MGT HYPO/EXP GAME. PAGE 42 F0820
PROBABIL ADMIN ROUTINE

B59
ALLEN R.L.,SOVIET INFLUENCE IN LATIN AMERICA. ECO/UNDEV FINAN PROC/MFG NAT/G TEC/DEV EDU/PROP EXEC ROUTINE ATTIT DRIVE PERSON ALL/VALS PWR...STAT CHARTS WORK FOR/TRADE 20. PAGE 4 F0071
L/A+17C ECO/TAC INT/TRADE USSR

B59
MARTIN K.,WAR, HISTORY, AND HUMAN NATURE. FRANCE GERMANY INDIA UK UNIV POL/PAR COLONIAL DETER REV MARXISM PACIFISM...PSY CONCPT PREDICT LENIN/VI GANDHI/M. PAGE 86 F1683
PERSON WAR ATTIT IDEA/COMP

B59
WAHLKE J.C.,LEGISLATIVE BEHAVIOR: A READER IN THEORY AND RESEARCH. USA+45 CONSTN ELITES POL/PAR LOBBY REPRESENT PERS/REL PERSON ROLE...IDEA/COMP METH/COMP SIMUL. PAGE 142 F2800
LEGIS CHOOSE INGP/REL ATTIT

B60
MARSHALL A.H.,FINANCIAL ADMINISTRATION IN LOCAL GOVERNMENT. UK DELIB/GP CONFER COST INCOME PERSON ...JURID 20. PAGE 86 F1679
FINAN LOC/G BUDGET ADMIN

B60
ROEPKE W.,A HUMANE ECONOMY: THE SOCIAL FRAMEWORK OF THE FREE MARKET. FUT USSR WOR+45 CULTURE SOCIETY ECO/DEV PLAN ECO/TAC ADMIN ATTIT PERSON RIGID/FLEX SUPEGO MORAL WEALTH SOCISM...POLICY OLD/LIB CONCPT TREND GEN/LAWS 20. PAGE 113 F2232
DRIVE EDU/PROP CAP/ISM

B60
ROSTOW W.W.,THE STAGES OF ECONOMIC GROWTH. UK USA+45 USSR WOR+45 WOR-45 ECO/DEV PERSON MARXISM ...METH/CNCPT TIME/SEQ GEN/LAWS GEN/METH 20. PAGE 114 F2246
ECO/UNDEV NEW/IDEA CAP/ISM

B61
FRIEDMANN G.,THE ANATOMY OF WORK. USA+45 SOCIETY CONTROL ROUTINE DRIVE SKILL...PSY SOC STAT OBS METH/COMP PERS/COMP 20. PAGE 44 F0862
AUTOMAT WORKER INDUS PERSON

B61
HEMPSTONE S.,THE NEW AFRICA. AGRI INDUS KIN NAT/G COLONIAL MARXISM...SOC INT TREND NAT/COMP BIBLIOG/A 20. PAGE 58 F1146
AFR ORD/FREE PERSON CULTURE

B61
HUBBARD P.J.,ORIGINS OF THE TVA: THE MUSCLE SHOALS CONTROVERSY, 1920-1932. USA-45 DELIB/GP LEGIS LEAD LOBBY GOV/REL GP/REL INGP/REL OWN PERSON...BIBLIOG 20 TVA CONGRESS WATER. PAGE 62 F1229
SEA CONTROL NAT/G INDUS

B61
KATKOFF U.,SOVIET ECONOMY 1940-1965. COM WOR+45 WOR-45 INTELL NAT/G POL/PAR TOP/EX ATTIT PWR ...POLICY TIME/SEQ VAL/FREE 20. PAGE 69 F1360
AGRI PERSON TOTALISM USSR

B62
BRANCH M.C.,THE CORPORATE PLANNING PROCESS. FINAN EX/STRUC EDU/PROP CONTROL LEAD GP/REL PERS/REL RATIONAL PERCEPT...MGT MATH PROBABIL STAT GAME. PAGE 18 F0338
PROF/ORG PLAN DECISION PERSON

B62
COLLIER A.T.,MANAGEMENT, MEN, AND VALUES. INDUS FACE/GP EX/STRUC PLAN PROB/SOLV DEBATE SENIOR ADMIN PROFIT PERSON...PSY SOC 20. PAGE 26 F0505
MGT ATTIT PERS/REL DECISION

B62
INTERNAT CONGRESS OF JURISTS,EXECUTIVE ACTION AND THE RULE OF RULE: REPORTION PROCEEDINGS OF INT'T CONGRESS OF JURISTS,-RIO DE JANEIRO, BRAZIL. WOR+45 ACADEM CONSULT JUDGE EDU/PROP ADJUD CT/SYS INGP/REL PERSON DEPT/DEFEN. PAGE 64 F1269
JURID EXEC ORD/FREE CONTROL

B63
BRAIBANTI R.J.D.,ADMINISTRATION AND ECONOMIC DEVELOPMENT IN INDIA. INDIA S/ASIA SOCIETY STRATA ECO/TAC PERSON WEALTH...MGT GEN/LAWS TOT/POP VAL/FREE 20. PAGE 18 F0337
ECO/UNDEV ADMIN

B63
FRIEDRICH C.J.,MAN AND HIS GOVERNMENT: AN EMPIRICAL THEORY OF POLITICS. UNIV LOC/G NAT/G ADJUD REV INGP/REL DISCRIM PWR BIBLIOG. PAGE 44 F0867
PERSON ORD/FREE PARTIC CONTROL

L63
NASH M.,"PSYCHO-CULTURAL FACTORS IN ASIAN ECONOMIC GROWTH." ASIA ISLAM S/ASIA CULTURE ECO/UNDEV DELIB/GP EDU/PROP COERCE ATTIT PERSON HEALTH KNOWL ORD/FREE...PSY SOC STAT TREND ANTHOL VAL/FREE 20. PAGE 96 F1893
SOCIETY ECO/TAC

L63
OLSON M. JR.,"RAPID ECONOMIC GROWTH AS A DESTABILIZING FORCE." WOR+45 WOR-45 STRATA ECO/UNDEV FAM KIN CREATE TEC/DEV DIPLOM PEACE ATTIT PERSON RIGID/FLEX PWR RESPECT WEALTH...SOC 20. PAGE 101 F1989
SOCIETY FOR/AID

B64
BRIGHT J.R.,RESEARCH, DEVELOPMENT AND TECHNOLOGICAL INNOVATION. CULTURE R+D CREATE PLAN PROB/SOLV AUTOMAT RISK PERSON...DECISION CONCPT PREDICT BIBLIOG. PAGE 18 F0352
TEC/DEV NEW/IDEA INDUS MGT

B64
CALDER R.,TWO-WAY PASSAGE. INT/ORG TEC/DEV WAR PERSON ORD/FREE 20. RAGE 21 F0400
FOR/AID ECO/UNDEV ECO/TAC

DIPLOM

B64
CHEIT E.F.,THE BUSINESS ESTABLISHMENT. FRANCE WOR+45 PROF/ORG TOP/EX PROB/SOLV CAP/ISM ADMIN SUPEGO MORAL PWR...METH/CNCPT MYTH NEW/IDEA 20. PAGE 24 F0460
PERSON EX/STRUC MGT INDUS

B64
WILLIAMSON O.E.,THE ECONOMICS OF DISCRETIONARY BEHAVIOR: MANAGERIAL OBJECTIVES IN A THEORY OF THE FIRM. MARKET BUDGET CAP/ISM PRODUC DRIVE PERSON ...STAT CHARTS BIBLIOG METH 20. PAGE 147 F2897
EFFICIENCY MGT ECO/TAC CHOOSE

S64
PESELT B.M.,"COMMUNIST ECONOMIC OFFENSIVE." WOR+45 SOCIETY INT/ORG PLAN ECO/TAC DOMIN EDU/PROP ATTIT PERSON PWR WEALTH...TREND CHARTS METH/GP 20. PAGE 105 F2067
COM ECO/UNDEV FOR/AID USSR

B65
ACHTERBERG E.,BERLINER HOCHFINANZ - KAISER, FURSTEN, MILLIONARE UM 1900. GERMANY NAT/G EDU/PROP PERSON...MGT MUNICH 19/20. PAGE 2 F0033
FINAN BIOG ECO/TAC

B65
CRANE E.,MARKETING COMMUNICATION: A BEHAVIORAL APPROACH TO MEN, MESSAGES, AND MEDIA. STRATA R+D VOL/ASSN CROWD DRIVE PERSON SKILL WEALTH. PAGE 28 F0551
EDU/PROP MARKET PERCEPT ATTIT

B65
SCHECHTER A.,THE BUSINESSMAN IN GOVERNMENT (THESIS, COLUMBIA UNIVERSITY). USA+45 CONFER GP/REL PERSON ...QU 20 PRESIDENT TRUMAN/HS CABINET. PAGE 116 F2291
INDUS NAT/G EX/STRUC DELIB/GP

B65
STEINER G.A.,THE CREATIVE ORGANIZATION. ELITES LG/CO PLAN PROB/SOLV TEC/DEV INSPECT CAP/ISM CONTROL EXEC PERSON...METH/COMP HYPO/EXP 20. PAGE 126 F2476
CREATE MGT ADMIN SOC

B65
THORNTON A.P.,DOCTRINES OF IMPERIALISM. WOR+45 WOR-45 DOMIN NAT/LISM PROFIT ATTIT PERSON PWR RESPECT SOVEREIGN...CONCPT STERTYP. PAGE 130 F2571
IDEA/COMP COLONIAL DRIVE

L65
HAGE J.,"AN AXIOMATIC THEORY OF ORGANIZATIONS" USA+45 STRUCT LABOR PRODUC DRIVE PERSON RIGID/FLEX 20 WEBER/MAX. PAGE 53 F1032
GP/REL EFFICIENCY PROF/ORG ATTIT

S65
KUNKEL J.H.,"VALUES AND BEHAVIOR IN ECONOMIC DEVELOPMENT." INDIA PERU CULTURE STRUCT CREATE PERS/REL ATTIT PERSON...CHARTS HYPO/EXP ARGEN. PAGE 74 F1449
SIMUL ECO/UNDEV PSY STERTYP

B66
BEUGEL E.V.D.,FROM MARSHALL AID TO ATLANTIC PARTNERSHIP* EUROPEAN INTEGRATION AS A CONCERN OF AMERICAN FOREIGN POLICY. USA+45 INT/ORG FORCES PERSON EEC NATO. PAGE 14 F0272
REGION DIPLOM EUR+WWI VOL/ASSN

B66
NICOSIA M.N.,CONSUMER DECISION PROCESSES: MARKETING AND ADVERTISING IMPLICATIONS. ECO/TAC ATTIT PERSON ...DECISION MGT SOC. PAGE 98 F1926
MARKET SOCIETY CREATE ACT/RES

B67
BARDENS D.,CHURCHILL IN PARLIAMENT. UK DIPLOM ADJUD CONTROL AUTHORIT PERSON ORD/FREE 20 CHURCHLL/W PARLIAMENT. PAGE 10 F0186
TOP/EX LEGIS GOV/REL

B67
WILLIAMS M.,THE EAST IS RED: THE VIEW INSIDE CHINA. CHINA/COM CONSTN COERCE AGE/Y ATTIT PERSON...OBS 20 MAO. PAGE 147 F2893
REV MARXIST GP/REL DIPLOM

S67
FEDYSHYN O.S.,"KHRUSHCHEV'S 'LEAP FORWARD': NATIONAL ASSIMILATION IN THE USSR AFTER STALIN." USSR PLAN NAT/LISM PERSON...POLICY 20 KHRUSH/N STALIN/J. PAGE 39 F0771
GP/REL INGP/REL MARXISM METH

S67
GATELL F.O.,"MONEY AND PARTY IN JACKSONIAN AMERICA* A QUANTITATIVE LOOK AT NEW YORK CITY'S MEN OF QUALITY." USA-45 STRATA SECT SUFF CONSEN MAJORITY ATTIT...CHARTS HYPO/EXP 19. PAGE 46 F0908
WEALTH POL/PAR PERSON IDEA/COMP

S67
GOSALVEZ R.B.,"PERFIL DEL GENERAL VINCENTE ROJO." SPAIN DIPLOM CIVMIL/REL EFFICIENCY PERSON SKILL 20 BOLIV. PAGE 49 F0966
WAR FORCES ELITES BIOG

B76
FOURIER C.,SOCIAL DESTINIES, IN A. BRISBANE, GENERAL INTRODUCTION TO SOCIAL SCIENCE. UNIV AGRI INDUS SECT PRODUC...PHIL/SCI CONCPT. PAGE 43 F0835
UTOPIA SOCIETY PERSON VOL/ASSN

B76
PROUDHON P.J.,WHAT IS PROPERTY? (TRANS. BY B.R. TUCKER). SOCIETY AGRI CAP/ISM CRIME GP/REL PERSON MORAL ORD/FREE WEALTH. PAGE 108 F2127
OWN WORKER PRODUC ANARCH

B76
SMITH A.,THE WEALTH OF NATIONS. UK STRUCT WORKER DIPLOM ECO/TAC OPTIMAL DRIVE PERSON ORD/FREE ...OLD/LIB GEN/LAWS 17/18. PAGE 123 F2428
WEALTH PRODUC INDUS LAISSEZ

PERSONAL RELATIONS....SEE PERS/REL

PERSONALITY....SEE PERSON, ALSO PERSONALITY INDEX, P. XIII

PERSONALITY TESTS....SEE PERS/TEST

PERSUASION....SEE LOBBY, EDU/PROP

PERU....SEE ALSO L/A+17C

B62
DE LAVALLE H.,A STATEMENT OF THE LAWS OF PERU IN MATTERS AFFECTING BUSINESS (3RD ED.). PERU WORKER INT/TRADE INCOME ORD/FREE...INT/LAW 20. PAGE 31 F0603
CONSTN JURID FINAN TAX

B65
PAYNE J.L.,LABOR AND POLITICS IN PERU; THE SYSTEM OF POLITICAL BARGAINING. PERU CONSTN VOL/ASSN EX/STRUC LEAD PWR...CHARTS 20. PAGE 104 F2042
LABOR POL/PAR BARGAIN GP/REL

S65
KUNKEL J.H.,"VALUES AND BEHAVIOR IN ECONOMIC DEVELOPMENT." INDIA PERU CULTURE STRUCT CREATE PERS/REL ATTIT PERSON...CHARTS HYPO/EXP ARGEN. PAGE 74 F1449
SIMUL ECO/UNDEV PSY STERTYP

S66
COHEN A.,"THE TECHNOLOGY/ELITE APPROACH TO THE DEVELOPMENTAL PROCESS* PERUVIAN CASE STUDY." L/A+17C STRUCT CREATE ECO/TAC FOR/AID CIVMIL/REL MARXISM TECHRACY HYPO/EXP. PAGE 26 F0496
ECO/UNDEV ELITES PERU

S67
PETRAS J.,"GUERRILLA MOVEMENTS IN LATIN AMERICA - I." GUATEMALA PERU VENEZUELA NAT/G COLONIAL LEAD ATTIT PWR...TIME/SEQ METH/COMP 20 COLOMB. PAGE 105 F2072
GUERRILLA REV L/A+17C MARXISM

PESELT B.M. F2067

PETAIN/HP....H.P. PETAIN

PETCH G.A. F2068

PETERS E. F2113

PETERS....PETERS V. NEW YORK

PETERSON F. F2069

PETERSON W.C. F2070

PETRAS J. F2071,F2072,F2073

PETRO S. F2074

PETROVICH M.B. F2075

PFEFFER K.H. F2076

PFEFFERMANN G. F2077

PFISTER R.L. F0489

PFOUTS R.W. F2078

PHALLE T.D. F0766

PHELPS E.S. F2079,F2080,F2081

PHIL/SCI....SCIENTIFIC METHOD AND PHILOSOPHY OF SCIENCE

N
SOUTH AFRICAN JOURNAL OF ECONOMICS. SOUTH/AFR FINAN MARKET ACT/RES OP/RES...PHIL/SCI STAT CON/ANAL METH/COMP BIBLIOG/A 20. PAGE 1 F0009
ECO/UNDEV ACADEM INTELL R+D

N
SCIENTIFIC COUNCIL FOR AFRICA,INVENTORY OF ECONOMIC STUDIES CONCERNING AFRICA SOUTH OF THE SAHARA. AFR ...PHIL/SCI 20. PAGE 118 F2327
BIBLIOG/A GEOG ECO/UNDEV

N
US LIBRARY OF CONGRESS,SOUTHERN ASIA ACCESSIONS LIST. BURMA CEYLON INDIA NEPAL PAKISTAN S/ASIA THAILAND AGRI INDUS SCHOOL WORKER...ART/METH GEOG HEAL PHIL/SCI LING 20. PAGE 137 F2710
BIBLIOG/A SOCIETY CULTURE ECO/UNDEV

B02
SELIGMAN E.R.,THE ECONOMIC INTERPRETATION OF HISTORY. ECO/TAC MARXISM SOCISM...PHIL/SCI METH/CNCPT 18/20. PAGE 119 F2348
IDEA/COMP HIST/WRIT GP/REL

N19
DOTSON A.,PRODUCTION PLANNING IN THE PATENT OFFICE (PAMPHLET). USA+45 DIST/IND PROB/SOLV PRODUC...MGT PHIL/SCI 20 BUR/BUDGET PATENT/OFF. PAGE 34 F0655
EFFICIENCY PLAN NAT/G ADMIN

N19
HAGEN E.E.,AN ANALYTICAL MODEL OF THE TRANSITION TO ECONOMIC GROWTH (PAMPHLET). WOR+45 WOR-45 SOCIETY STRATA FINAN NAT/G CONTROL PARTIC PRODUC...PHIL/SCI BIBLIOG 17/20. PAGE 53 F1033 — SIMUL ECO/DEV METH TEC/DEV

N19
LAWRENCE S.A.,THE BATTERY ADDITIVE CONTROVERSY (PAMPHLET). USA+45 LAW MARKET PROC/MFG R+D CAP/ISM CT/SYS GOV/REL OWN FTC CONGRESS BUR/STNDRD RITCHIE/JM. PAGE 76 F1494 — PHIL/SCI LOBBY INSPECT

B44
KAUFMANN F.,METHODOLOGY OF THE SOCIAL SCIENCES. PERSON...RELATIV PSY CONCPT LING METH 20. PAGE 69 F1363 — SOC PHIL/SCI GEN/LAWS METH/CNCPT

B47
WEBER M.,THE THEORY OF SOCIAL AND ECONOMIC ORGANIZATION. STRUCT LABOR POL/PAR ECO/TAC LEGIT PRODUC BIOG. PAGE 144 F2840 — ECO/DEV SOC PHIL/SCI LEAD

B48
HAYEK F.A.,INDIVIDUALISM AND ECONOMIC ORDER. FINAN PLAN MORAL LAISSEZ SOCISM...POLICY DECISION PHIL/SCI HIST/WRIT. PAGE 57 F1122 — RATIONAL KNOWL PERSON

B52
TANNENBAUM F.,A PHILOSOPHY OF LABOR. SOCIETY STRATA INDUS LG/CO AGREE ADJUST OWN ORD/FREE PWR...CONCPT 20. PAGE 128 F2533 — LABOR PHIL/SCI WORKER CREATE

B53
DAHL R.A.,POLITICS, ECONOMICS AND WELFARE: PLANNING AND POLITICOECONOMIC SYSTEMS RESOLVED INTO BASIC SOCIAL PROCESSES. WOR+45 WOR-45 ECO/DEV ECO/UNDEV R+D CREATE PLAN TEC/DEV EDU/PROP HEALTH WEALTH ...SOC SELF/OBS TREND CHARTS GEN/METH 20. PAGE 29 F0571 — ECO/TAC PHIL/SCI

S53
BIRNBAUM N.,"CONFLICTING INTERPRETATIONS OF THE RISE OF CAPITALISM: MARX AND WEBER" (BMR)" WOR-45 INTELL SOCIETY STRUCT INDUS WORKER...PHIL/SCI SOC PERS/COMP 19/20 MARX/KARL WEBER/MAX. PAGE 15 F0288 — CAP/ISM IDEA/COMP ECO/DEV MARXISM

B54
LENIN V.I.,SELECTED WORKS (12 VOLS.). USSR INTELL SOCIETY STRATA STRUCT NAT/G POL/PAR WORKER CAP/ISM REV WAR...MARXIST PHIL/SCI 20 MARX/KARL LENIN/VI. PAGE 78 F1520 — COM MARXISM

B54
SCHUMPETER J.A.,HISTORY OF ECONOMIC ANALYSIS. WOR-45...PHIL/SCI METH/CNCPT STAT IDEA/COMP GRECO/ROMN. PAGE 118 F2322 — KNOWL GEN/LAWS METH

S54
FORM W.H.,"THE PLACE OF SOCIAL STRUCTURE IN THE DETERMINATION OF LAND USE: SOME IMPLICATIONS FOR A THEORY OF URBAN ECOLOGY" (BMR)" STRUCT...GEOG PHIL/SCI SOC MUNICH 20. PAGE 42 F0827 — HABITAT MARKET ORD/FREE

B55
BOULDING K.E.,ECONOMIC ANALYSIS (3RD ED.). USA+45 PLAN ECO/TAC COST DEMAND INCOME...POLICY STAT CHARTS SIMUL T. PAGE 17 F0322 — PHIL/SCI ECO/DEV CAP/ISM

B55
MAYO H.B.,DEMOCRACY AND MARXISM. COM USSR STRATA NAT/G WORKER ECO/TAC REV MORAL...PHIL/SCI HIST/WRIT IDEA/COMP WORSHIP 20 MARX/KARL LENIN/VI STALIN/J TROTSKY/L. PAGE 87 F1708 — MARXISM CAP/ISM

B55
MOHL R.V.,DIE GESCHICHTE UND LITERATUR DER STAATSWISSENSCHAFTEN (3 VOLS.). LAW NAT/G...JURID METH/COMP METH. PAGE 92 F1814 — PHIL/SCI MOD/EUR

B56
PARSONS T.,ECONOMY AND SOCIETY: A STUDY IN THE INTEGRATION OF ECONOMIC AND SOCIAL THEORY. UNIV ACT/RES...SOC CHARTS IDEA/COMP BIBLIOG/A. PAGE 103 F2031 — STRUCT METH/CNCPT UTIL PHIL/SCI

B57
LOUCKS W.N.,COMPARATIVE ECONOMIC SYSTEMS (5TH ED.). COM UK USSR INDUS POL/PAR PLAN CAP/ISM TOTALISM MARXISM...PHIL/SCI BIBLIOG 19/20. PAGE 82 F1603 — NAT/COMP IDEA/COMP SOCISM

B59
ENGELS F.,SOCIALISM: UTOPIAN AND SCIENTIFIC (2ND ED.). SOCISM...CONCPT CON/ANAL GEN/LAWS 19 DUHRING/E. PAGE 38 F0732 — MARXISM PHIL/SCI UTOPIA IDEA/COMP

B60
FRANCIS R.G.,THE PREDICTIVE PROCESS. PLAN MARXISM ...DECISION SOC CONCPT NAT/COMP 19/20. PAGE 43 F0840 — PREDICT PHIL/SCI TREND

B60
GRAMPP W.D.,THE MANCHESTER SCHOOL OF ECONOMICS. UK LAW ECO/DEV COERCE ATTIT ORD/FREE LAISSEZ ...PHIL/SCI IDEA/COMP 19/20 MANCHESTER CORN/LAWS. PAGE 50 F0973 — ECO/TAC VOL/ASSN LOBBY NAT/G

B60
MAYO H.B.,INTRODUCTION TO MARXIST THEORY. SECT WORKER POPULISM SOCISM 19/20. PAGE 87 F1709 — MARXISM STRATA IDEA/COMP PHIL/SCI

B60
RICHARDSON G.B.,INFORMATION AND INVESTMENT. PLAN PROB/SOLV CAP/ISM ECO/TAC KNOWL...CONCPT 20 MONEY. PAGE 111 F2184 — ECO/DEV EQUILIB FINAN PHIL/SCI

B60
SERAPHIM H.J.,ZUR GRUNDLEGUNG WIRTSCHAFTSPOLITISCHER KONZEPTIONEN (SCHRIFTEN DES VEREINS FUR SOZIALPOLITIK, N.F. BAND 18). GERMANY/W WOR+45 ECO/DEV DELIB/GP ACT/RES ECO/TAC INGP/REL ORD/FREE...CONCPT IDEA/COMP GEN/LAWS 20. PAGE 120 F2358 — POLICY PHIL/SCI PLAN

B61
MCCRACKEN H.L.,KEYNESIAN ECONOMICS IN THE STREAM OF ECONOMIC THOUGHT. FINAN MARKET BARGAIN EFFICIENCY OPTIMAL...PHIL/SCI CONCPT IDEA/COMP BIBLIOG 18/20 KEYNES/JM. PAGE 88 F1724 — ECO/TAC DEMAND ECOMETRIC

S61
ANDREWS R.B.,"URBAN ECONOMICS: AN APPRAISAL OF PROGRESS." LOC/G PROB/SOLV TEC/DEV...CONCPT OBS/ENVIR METH/COMP HYPO/EXP SOC/EXP SIMUL GEN/METH METH MUNICH 20. PAGE 5 F0102 — PHIL/SCI ECOMETRIC

S61
DALTON G.,"ECONOMIC THEORY AND PRIMITIVE SOCIETY" (BMR)" UNIV AGRI KIN TEC/DEV ECO/TAC REGION HABITAT SKILL...METH/COMP BIBLIOG. PAGE 30 F0574 — ECO/UNDEV METH PHIL/SCI SOC

B62
NATIONAL BUREAU ECONOMIC RES,THE RATE AND DIRECTION OF INVENTIVE ACTIVITY: ECONOMIC AND SOCIAL FACTORS. STRUCT INDUS MARKET R+D CREATE OP/RES TEC/DEV EFFICIENCY PRODUC RATIONAL UTIL...WELF/ST PHIL/SCI METH/CNCPT TIME. PAGE 97 F1895 — DECISION PROB/SOLV MGT

S62
MORGENTHAU H.J.,"A POLITICAL THEORY OF FOREIGN AID." ECO/UNDEV NAT/G DELIB/GP PLAN ECO/TAC EDU/PROP EXEC ORD/FREE RESPECT WEALTH...METH/CNCPT TREND 20. PAGE 93 F1833 — USA+45 PHIL/SCI FOR/AID

B63
ENKE S.,ECONOMICS FOR DEVELOPMENT. AGRI TEC/DEV CAP/ISM DIPLOM ECO/TAC TAX ATTIT DRIVE HABITAT WEALTH...GOV/COMP BIBLIOG 20. PAGE 38 F0737 — ECO/UNDEV PHIL/SCI CON/ANAL

B63
JOHNSTON J.,ECONOMETRIC METHODS. PROB/SOLV WRITING ...REGRESS CHARTS T. PAGE 68 F1333 — ECOMETRIC PHIL/SCI OP/RES STAT

B63
KAPP W.K.,SOCIAL COSTS OF BUSINESS ENTERPRISE. WOR+45 LABOR TEC/DEV CAP/ISM HABITAT...PHIL/SCI NEW/IDEA CON/ANAL 20. PAGE 69 F1354 — COST SOCIETY INDUS RIGID/FLEX

S63
FLOREA I.,"CU PRIVIRE LA OBIECTUL MATERIALISMULUI ISTORIC SI AL COMUNISMULUI STIINTIFIC SI LA RAPORTUL DINTRE ELE." EUR+WWI WOR+45 WOR-45 INTELL NAT/G POL/PAR WORKER EDU/PROP PERCEPT MARXISM ...MARXIST PHIL/SCI CONCPT TOT/POP 20. PAGE 42 F0812 — COM ATTIT TOTALISM

B64
LANGHOFF P.,MODELS, MEASUREMENT AND MARKETING. ACT/RES COMPUTER OP/RES PLAN BUDGET...MGT PHIL/SCI METH/CNCPT STAT PROG/TEAC BIBLIOG. PAGE 75 F1478 — DECISION SIMUL MARKET R+D

B64
LEKACHMAN R.,KEYNES' GENERAL THEORY: REPORTS OF THREE DECADES. FINAN ATTIT...POLICY 20 KEYNES/JM. PAGE 77 F1517 — PHIL/SCI GEN/METH IDEA/COMP

B65
SCHWARTZ G.,SCIENCE IN MARKETING. OP/RES PROB/SOLV INT/TRADE PRICE CONTROL ADJUST PRODUC...CONCPT 20. PAGE 118 F2324 — PHIL/SCI TREND ECO/DEV MARKET

B66
FUSFELD D.R.,THE AGE OF THE ECONOMIST. ECO/TAC WEALTH LAISSEZ MARXISM...EPIST 18/20 KEYNES/JM. PAGE 45 F0878 — PHIL/SCI CAP/ISM POLICY

B66
HACKETT J.,L'ECONOMIE BRITANNIQUE: PROBLEMES ET PERSPECTIVES. FRANCE UK LABOR NAT/G EX/STRUC PROB/SOLV BAL/PAY INCOME RIGID/FLEX...MGT PHIL/SCI CHARTS MUNICH 20. PAGE 53 F1027 — ECO/DEV FINAN ECO/TAC PLAN

B66
HOROWITZ I.L.,THREE WORLDS OF DEVELOPMENT. COM USA+45 STRUCT ECO/DEV PLAN PROB/SOLV TEC/DEV CIVMIL/REL...PHIL/SCI IDEA/COMP 20. PAGE 62 F1216 — ECO/UNDEV BAL/PWR POL/PAR REV

B66
LENSKI G.E.,POWER AND PRIVILEGE: A THEORY OF SOCIAL STRATIFICATION. SWEDEN UK UNIV USSR CULTURE ECO/UNDEV PRIVIL PWR...PHIL/SCI CONCPT CHARTS IDEA/COMP HYPO/EXP METH MARX/KARL. PAGE 78 F1525 — SOC STRATA STRUCT SOCIETY

B66
MADAN G.R.,ECONOMIC THINKING IN INDIA. INDIA ECO/UNDEV AGRI FINAN INDUS LABOR PLAN CAP/ISM INT/TRADE MARXISM SOCISM...POLICY 1/20. PAGE 84 — ECO/TAC PHIL/SCI NAT/G

F1638 POL/PAR

B66
PEIRCE W.S.,SELECTIVE MANPOWER POLICIES AND THE TRADE-OFF BETWEEN RISING PRICES AND UNEMPLOYMENT (DISSERTATION). ECO/DEV WORKER ACT/RES...PHIL/SCI 20. PAGE 104 F2050
PRICE LABOR POLICY ECO/TAC

B67
BIBBY J.,ON CAPITOL HILL. POL/PAR LOBBY PARL/PROC GOV/REL PERS/REL...JURID PHIL/SCI OBS INT BIBLIOG 20 CONGRESS PRESIDENT. PAGE 15 F0278
CONFER LEGIS CREATE LEAD

B67
DE JOUVENAL B.,THE ART OF CONJECTURE. WOR+45 EFFICIENCY PERCEPT KNOWL...DECISION PHIL/SCI CONCPT METH/COMP BIBLIOG 20. PAGE 31 F0600
FUT PREDICT SIMUL METH

B67
NELSON R.R.,TECHNOLOGY, ECONOMIC GROWTH, AND PUBLIC POLICY. USA+45 PLAN GP/REL UTIL KNOWL...POLICY PHIL/SCI CHARTS BIBLIOG 20. PAGE 97 F1912
R+D CONSULT CREATE ACT/RES

B67
RIDKER R.G.,ECONOMIC COSTS OF AIR POLLUTION* STUDIES IN MEASUREMENT. R+D GP/REL KNOWL...OBS MUNICH 20. PAGE 111 F2190
OP/RES HABITAT PHIL/SCI

B67
UNIVERSAL REFERENCE SYSTEM,PUBLIC POLICY AND THE MANAGEMENT OF SCIENCE (VOLUME IX). FUT SPACE WOR+45 LAW NAT/G TEC/DEV CONTROL NUC/PWR GOV/REL ...COMPUT/IR GEN/METH. PAGE 133 F2618
BIBLIOG/A POLICY MGT PHIL/SCI

S67
FRANKLIN N.N.,"THE CONCEPT AND MEASUREMENT OF 'MINIMUM LIVING STANDARDS'." UNIV OP/RES PAY INGP/REL DEMAND INCOME DRIVE WEALTH...SOC CHARTS METH/COMP. PAGE 43 F0849
CONCPT PHIL/SCI ALL/VALS HAPPINESS

S67
LEVIN T.,"PSYCHOANALYSIS AND SOCIAL CHANGE." SOCIETY ANOMIE DRIVE PWR 20. PAGE 79 F1541
PSY PHIL/SCI ADJUST WEALTH

N67
US HOUSE COMM SCI ASTRONAUT,AUTHORIZING APPROPRIATIONS TO THE NATIONAL AERONAUTICS AND SPACE ADMINISTRATION (PAMPHLET). USA+45 NAT/G OP/RES TEC/DEV BUDGET NASA HOUSE/REP. PAGE 137 F2704
SPACE R+D PHIL/SCI NUC/PWR

B76
FOURIER C.,SOCIAL DESTINIES, IN A. BRISBANE, GENERAL INTRODUCTION TO SOCIAL SCIENCE. UNIV AGRI INDUS SECT PRODUC...PHIL/SCI CONCPT. PAGE 43 F0835
UTOPIA SOCIETY PERSON VOL/ASSN

PHILADELPH....PHILADELPHIA, PENNSYLVANIA

B64
CHINITZ B.,CITY AND SUBURB: THE ECONOMICS OF METROPOLITAN GROWTH. DIST/IND BUDGET GOV/REL DEMAND ATTIT HABITAT MUNICH PHILADELPH. PAGE 24 F0467
TEC/DEV PLAN

B64
FITCH L.C.,URBAN TRANSPORTATION AND PUBLIC POLICY. FINAN NAT/G LEGIS PROB/SOLV TEC/DEV PRICE COST EFFICIENCY...DECISION STAT CHARTS METH/COMP MUNICH 20 NEWYORK/C PHILADELPH LOS/ANG CHICAGO WASHING/DC. PAGE 41 F0806
DIST/IND PLAN LOC/G

B65
BOLLENS J.C.,THE METROPOLIS: ITS PEOPLE, POLITICS, AND ECONOMIC LIFE. USA+45 PLAN PROB/SOLV PERS/REL PWR...DECISION GEOG CENSUS TREND CON/ANAL MUNICH 20 NEWYORK/C LOS/ANG SAN/FRAN CHICAGO PHILADELPH. PAGE 16 F0309
HABITAT SOC LOC/G

PHILANTHROPY....SEE GIVE+WEALTH

PHILIP A. F1673

PHILIP/J....JOHN PHILIP

PHILIPPINE....PHILIPPINES; SEE ALSO S/ASIA

B49
PELZER K.J.,SELECTED BIBLIOGRAPHY ON THE GEOGRAPHY OF SOUTHEAST ASIA (3 VOLS., 1949-1956). PHILIPPINE CULTURE...SOC 20 MALAYA. PAGE 104 F2053
BIBLIOG S/ASIA GEOG

B55
UN ECONOMIC COMN ASIA & FAR E,ECONOMIC SURVEY OF ASIA AND THE FAR EAST, 1954. AFGHANISTN CEYLON INDIA PHILIPPINE S/ASIA ECO/DEV FINAN INDUS INT/TRADE PRODUC WEALTH...STAT CHARTS 20 CHINJAP. PAGE 132 F2600
ECO/UNDEV PRICE NAT/COMP ASIA

L59
WURFEL D.,"FOREIGN AID AND SOCIAL REFORM IN POLITICAL DEVELOPMENT" (BMR)" PHILIPPINE USA+45 WOR+45 SOCIETY POL/PAR ACT/RES TEC/DEV DIPLOM 20. PAGE 149 F2943
FOR/AID PROB/SOLV ECO/TAC ECO/UNDEV

B63
STIFEL L.D.,THE TEXTILE INDUSTRY - A CASE STUDY OF INDUSTRIAL DEVELOPMENT IN THE PHILIPPINES (PAPER). PHILIPPINE WORKER CAP/ISM INT/TRADE TARIFFS RECEIVE PRICE ADMIN COST EFFICIENCY WEALTH...BIBLIOG 20. PAGE 126 F2486
S/ASIA ECO/UNDEV PROC/MFG NAT/G

B66
AMERICAN ASSEMBLY COLUMBIA U,THE UNITED STATES AND THE PHILIPPINES. PHILIPPINE S/ASIA USA+45 USA-45 SOCIETY FORCES INT/TRADE...POLICY 20. PAGE 5 F0085
COLONIAL DIPLOM NAT/LISM

B67
CHANDRASEKHAR S.,PROBLEMS OF ECONOMIC DEVELOPMENT. AFR INDIA PHILIPPINE UAR WOR+45 INDUS...GEOG SOC ANTHOL BIBLIOG 20 CHINJAP. PAGE 23 F0450
ECO/UNDEV PLAN AGRI PROB/SOLV

PHILLIP/IV....PHILLIP IV OF SPAIN

PHILLIPS C. F2082

PHILLIPS/F....F. PHILLIPS - POLICE CHIEF, N.Y.C.

PHILOSOPHR....PHILOSOPHER

PHILOSOPHY....SEE GEN/LAWS. PHILOSOPHY OF SCIENCE....SEE PHIL/SCI

PHILOSOPHY OF SCIENCE....SEE PHIL/SCI

PHOTOGRAPHS....SEE AUD/VIS

PHS....PUBLIC HEALTH SERVICE

PIERCE/F....PRESIDENT FRANKLIN PIERCE

PIERPONT J.R. F2083

PIERSON J.H. F2084

PIGOU A.C. F2085

PIGOU/AC....ARTHUR CECIL PIGOU

PIKE F.B. F2086

PINCUS J. F2087

PINCUS J.A. F2088

PINCUS/J....JOHN PINCUS

PIQUEMAL M. F2089

PIQUET H.S. F2090

PITCHER G.M. F2091

PITTSBURGH....PITTSBURGH, PENNSYLVANIA

PLAN....PLANNING

B
BRITISH COMMONWEALTH BUR AGRI,WORLD AGRICULTURAL ECONOMICS AND RURAL SOCIOLOGY ABSTRACTS. NAT/G OP/RES PLAN TEC/DEV LEAD PRODUC...GEOG MGT NAT/COMP 20. PAGE 18 F0354
BIBLIOG/A AGRI SOC WORKER

N
UNESCO,INTERNATIONAL BIBLIOGRAPHY OF ECONOMICS (VOLUMES 1-8). WOR+45 AGRI INDUS LABOR PLAN TEC/DEV 20. PAGE 132 F2607
BIBLIOG ECO/DEV ECO/UNDEV

NCO
CARRINGTON C.E.,THE COMMONWEALTH IN AFRICA (PAMPHLET). UK STRUCT NAT/G COLONIAL REPRESENT GOV/REL RACE/REL NAT/LISM...MAJORIT 20 EEC NEGRO. PAGE 22 F0421
ECO/UNDEV AFR DIPLOM PLAN

NCO
STOLPER W.,"SOCIAL FACTORS IN ECONOMIC PLANNING, WITH SPECIAL REFERENCE TO NIGERIA" AFR NIGER CULTURE FAM SECT RECEIVE ETIQUET ADMIN DEMAND 20. PAGE 126 F2494
ECO/UNDEV PLAN ADJUST RISK

B04
MARX K.,A CONTRIBUTION TO THE CRITIQUE OF POLITICAL ECONOMY (TRANS. FROM 2ND ED. BY N.I. STONE). UK STRATA ECO/DEV FINAN MARKET PLAN BARGAIN CAP/ISM ECO/TAC ATTIT WEALTH...METH/CNCPT BIOG 19. PAGE 86 F1687
MARXIST NEW/IDEA MARXISM

N19
ANDERSON J.,THE ORGANIZATION OF ECONOMIC STUDIES IN RELATION TO THE PROBLEMS OF GOVERNMENT (PAMPHLET). UK FINAN INDUS DELIB/GP PLAN PROB/SOLV ADMIN 20. PAGE 5 F0095
ECO/TAC ACT/RES NAT/G CENTRAL

N19
ARNOW K.,SELF-INSURANCE IN THE TREASURY (PAMPHLET). USA+45 LAW RIGID/FLEX...POLICY METH/COMP 20 DEPT/TREAS. PAGE 6 F0117
ADMIN PLAN EFFICIENCY NAT/G

N19
ATOMIC INDUSTRIAL FORUM,COMMENTARY ON LEGISLATION TO PERMIT PRIVATE OWNERSHIP OF SPECIAL NUCLEAR MATERIAL (PAMPHLET). USA+45 DELIB/GP LEGIS PLAN OWN ...POLICY 20 AEC CONGRESS. PAGE 7 F0134
NUC/PWR MARKET INDUS LAW

N19
BROWN W.M.,THE DESIGN AND PERFORMANCE OF "OPTIMUM" BLAST SHELTER PROGRAMS (PAMPHLET). USA+45 ACT/RES PLAN DEATH COST EFFICIENCY OPTIMAL...POLICY CHARTS 20. PAGE 19 F0375
HABITAT NUC/PWR WAR HEALTH

N19
CHATTERS C.H.,NEW MUNICIPAL REVENUES FOR NEW MUNICIPAL EXPENDITURES (PAMPHLET). PLAN PRICE UTIL HABITAT...IDEA/COMP MUNICH 20. PAGE 23 F0457
LOC/G BUDGET TAX

N19
DOTSON A.,PRODUCTION PLANNING IN THE PATENT OFFICE (PAMPHLET). USA+45 DIST/IND PROB/SOLV PRODUC...MGT PHIL/SCI 20 BUR/BUDGET PATENT/OFF. PAGE 34 F0655
EFFICIENCY PLAN NAT/G ADMIN

N19
EAST KENTUCKY REGIONAL PLAN,PROGRAM 60: A DECADE OF ACTION FOR PROGRESS IN EASTERN KENTUCKY (PAMPHLET). USA+45 AGRI CONSTRUC INDUS CONSULT ACT/RES PROB/SOLV EDU/PROP GOV/REL HEALTH KENTUCKY. PAGE 35 F0689
REGION ADMIN PLAN ECO/UNDEV

N19
EAST KENTUCKY REGIONAL PLAN,PROGRAM 60 REPORT: ACTION FOR PORGRESS IN EASTERN KENTUCKY (PAMPHLET). USA+45 CONSTRUC INDUS ACT/RES PROB/SOLV EDU/PROP ADMIN GOV/REL KENTUCKY. PAGE 35 F0690
REGION PLAN ECO/UNDEV CONSULT

N19
FRANCK P.G.,AFGHANISTAN BETWEEN EAST AND WEST: THE ECONOMICS OF COMPETITIVE COEXISTENCE (PAMPHLET). AFGHANISTN USA+45 USA-45 USSR INDUS ECO/TAC INT/TRADE CONTROL NEUTRAL ORD/FREE MARXISM...GEOG 20 UN. PAGE 43 F0842
FOR/AID PLAN DIPLOM ECO/UNDEV

N19
HACKETT J.,ECONOMIC PLANNING IN FRANCE; ITS RELATION TO THE POLICIES OF THE DEVELOPED COUNTRIES OF WESTERN EUROPE (PAMPHLET). EUR+WWI FRANCE ECO/DEV PROB/SOLV CONTROL...POLICY 20 EUROPE/W. PAGE 52 F1026
ECO/TAC NAT/G PLAN INSPECT

N19
HAYEK FA V.O.N.,FREEDOM AND THE ECONOMIC SYSTEM. GERMANY USSR PLAN REPRESENT TOTALISM FASCISM POPULISM...MAJORIT METH/COMP GEN/LAWS 20. PAGE 57 F1123
ORD/FREE ECO/TAC CAP/ISM SOCISM

N19
HUBERMAN L.,SOCIALISM IS THE ONLY ANSWER (PAMPHLET). CREATE ECO/TAC EDU/PROP CONTROL ...SOCIALIST GEN/LAWS ANTHOL 20. PAGE 62 F1230
SOCISM ECO/DEV CAP/ISM PLAN

N19
KINDLEBERGER C.P.,BALANCE-OF-PAYMENTS DEFICITS AND THE INTERNATIONAL MARKET FOR LIQUIDITY (PAMPHLET). ECO/DEV NAT/G PLAN DIPLOM ECO/TAC PRODUC...POLICY STAT CHARTS. PAGE 71 F1389
BAL/PAY INT/TRADE MARKET FINAN

N19
LANGE O.R.,"DISARMAMENT ECONOMIC GROWTH AND INTERNATIONAL CO-OPERATION" (PAMPHLET). WOR+45 DIST/IND PLAN INT/TRADE GIVE TASK DETER WEALTH SOCISM 18/19 BOLIVAR/S. PAGE 75 F1477
ARMS/CONT DIPLOM ECO/DEV ECO/UNDEV

N19
MARCUS W.,US PRIVATE INVESTMENT AND ECONOMIC AID IN UNDERDEVELOPED COUNTRIES (PAMPHLET). USA+45 LG/CO NAT/G CAP/ISM EDU/PROP 20. PAGE 85 F1666
FOR/AID ECO/UNDEV FINAN PLAN

N19
MARSH J.F. JR.,THE FBI RETIREMENT BILL (PAMPHLET). USA+45 EX/STRUC WORKER PLAN PROB/SOLV BUDGET LEAD LOBBY PARL/PROC PERS/REL RIGID/FLEX...POLICY 20 FBI PRESIDENT BUR/BUDGET. PAGE 86 F1677
ADMIN NAT/G SENIOR GOV/REL

N19
MASCHLER M.,STABLE PAYOFF CONFIGURATIONS FOR QUOTA GAMES (PAMPHLET). PLAN PERS/REL 20. PAGE 87 F1694
ECOMETRIC GAME COMPUTER DECISION

N19
SAPIR H.M.,JAPAN, CHINA, AND THE WEST (PAMPHLET). AFR ASIA CHINA/COM PROB/SOLV GOV/REL 20 CHINJAP. PAGE 116 F2282
ECO/UNDEV INT/TRADE DECISION PLAN

N19
SILVERMAN C.,THE PRESIDENT'S ECONOMIC ADVISERS (PAMPHLET). USA+45 LAW ELITES ECO/DEV EX/STRUC ADMIN LEAD GOV/REL PERS/REL ROLE...POLICY DECISION 20 PRESIDENT CONGRESS EISNHWR/DD. PAGE 122 F2404
CONSULT PROB/SOLV NAT/G PLAN

N19
STEUBER F.A.,THE CONTRIBUTION OF SWITZERLAND TO THE ECONOMIC AND SOCIAL DEVELOPMENT OF LOW-INCOME COUNTRIES (PAMPHLET). SWITZERLND FINAN NAT/G VOL/ASSN INT/TRADE DRIVE...CHARTS 20. PAGE 126 F2482
FOR/AID ECO/UNDEV PLAN DIPLOM

N19
WILSON T.,FINANCIAL ASSISTANCE WITH REGIONAL DEVELOPMENT (PAMPHLET). CANADA INDUS NAT/G PLAN TAX CONTROL COST EFFICIENCY...POLICY CHARTS 20. PAGE 147 F2902
FINAN ECO/TAC REGION GOV/REL

N19
YLVISAKER P.N.,THE NATURAL CEMENT ISSUE (PAMPHLET). USA+45 USA-45 CONSTRUC PROVS CAP/ISM ADMIN LOBBY PERS/REL OWN RIGID/FLEX ROLE 20 MINNESOTA. PAGE 150 F2948
POLICY NAT/G PLAN GOV/REL

B26
MCPHEE A.,THE ECONOMIC REVOLUTION IN BRITISH WEST AFRICA. AFR UK CULTURE DIST/IND FINAN INDUS PLAN GP/REL RACE/REL 20 AFRICA/W. PAGE 88 F1735
ECO/UNDEV INT/TRADE COLONIAL GEOG

B28
CROS L.,AFRIQUE FRANCAISE POUR TOUS. EUR+WWI FRANCE PLAN TEC/DEV ATTIT 20. PAGE 29 F0556
COLONIAL DOMIN ECO/TAC AFR

B28
TRUE A.C.,A HISTORY OF AGRICULTURAL EXTENSION WORK IN THE UNITED STATES, 1785-1923. USA-45 LAW SCHOOL WAR ADJUST...CHARTS BIBLIOG 18/20 SMITH/LEVR COUNTY/AGT. PAGE 131 F2591
EDU/PROP AGRI VOL/ASSN PLAN

B30
FEIS H.,EUROPE, THE WORLD'S BANKER, 1871-1914. FRANCE GERMANY MOD/EUR UK WOR-45 NAT/G PLAN ECO/TAC EXEC ATTIT PWR WEALTH...CONCPT HIST/WRIT GEN/LAWS VAL/FREE 19/20. PAGE 40 F0773
FINAN DIPLOM INT/TRADE

B32
WRIGHT Q.,GOLD AND MONETARY STABILIZATION. FUT USA-45 WOR-45 INTELL ECO/DEV INT/ORG NAT/G CONSULT PLAN ECO/TAC ADMIN ATTIT WEALTH...CONCPT TREND 20. PAGE 149 F2935
FINAN POLICY

S32
DODD E.M. JR.,"FOR WHOM ARE CORPORATE MANAGERS TRUSTEES'." SERV/IND CAP/ISM GIVE LEAD REPRESENT ORD/FREE WEALTH. PAGE 33 F0648
LG/CO ROLE NAT/G PLAN

B34
GRAHAM F.D.,PROTECTIVE TARIFFS. FUT USA+45 WOR-45 INDUS MARKET VOL/ASSN PLAN CAP/ISM ECO/TAC PEACE ATTIT DRIVE HEALTH ORD/FREE...OBS TREND GEN/LAWS FOR/TRADE 20. PAGE 50 F0970
INT/ORG TARIFFS

B37
COLE W.E.,RECENT TRENDS IN RURAL PLANNING. USA-45 LAW ECO/DEV LOC/G SECT EDU/PROP CRIME LEISURE AGE/Y HABITAT...SOC/WK MUNICH 20. PAGE 26 F0503
AGRI NEIGH PLAN ACT/RES

B37
MACKENZIE F.,PLANNED SOCIETY: YESTERDAY, TODAY, AND TOMORROW. ECO/DEV ECO/UNDEV AGRI FINAN INDUS PLAN INSPECT CONTROL ALL/IDEOS...TREND METH/COMP BIBLIOG 20 RESOURCE/N. PAGE 83 F1635
SOC CONCPT ANTHOL

B37
ROBBINS L.,ECONOMIC PLANNING AND INTERNATIONAL ORDER. WOR-45 SOCIETY FINAN INDUS NAT/G ECO/TAC ROUTINE WEALTH...SOC TIME/SEQ GEN/METH WORK 20 KEYNES/JM. PAGE 112 F2202
INT/ORG PLAN INT/TRADE

B38
HARPER S.N.,THE GOVERNMENT OF THE SOVIET UNION. COM USSR LAW CONSTN ECO/DEV PLAN TEC/DEV DIPLOM INT/TRADE ADMIN REV NAT/LISM...POLICY 20. PAGE 55 F1085
MARXISM NAT/G LEAD POL/PAR

B38
HOBSON J.A.,IMPERIALISM. MOD/EUR UK WOR-45 CULTURE ECO/UNDEV NAT/G VOL/ASSN PLAN EDU/PROP LEGIT REGION COERCE ATTIT PWR...POLICY PLURIST TIME/SEQ GEN/LAWS TERR/GP 19/20. PAGE 60 F1187
DOMIN ECO/TAC BAL/PWR COLONIAL

B38
LEVINSON E.,LABOR ON THE MARCH. WORKER CREATE ECO/TAC ADJUD LEAD PARL/PROC PARTIC INGP/REL SKILL POLICY. PAGE 79 F1543
LABOR INCOME NAT/G PLAN

B39
CLARK J.M.,SOCIAL CONTROL OF BUSINESS (2ND ED.). ECO/DEV FINAN LG/CO PLAN ECO/TAC PRICE SUPEGO...T 20. PAGE 25 F0480
CAP/ISM CONTROL LAISSEZ METH/COMP

S39
COLE G.D.H.,"NAZI ECONOMICS: HOW DO THEY MANAGE IT?" GERMANY FORCES WORKER BUDGET INT/TRADE ROUTINE COERCE WAR 20 HITLER/A NAZI. PAGE 26 F0500
FASCISM ECO/TAC ATTIT PLAN

B40
BLAISDELL D.C.,GOVERNMENT AND AGRICULTURE; THE GROWTH OF FEDERAL FARM AID. USA-45 MARKET PLAN PROB/SOLV TEC/DEV ECO/TAC GOV/REL ADJUST ATTIT ...CHARTS 20 DEPT/AGRI. PAGE 15 F0296
NAT/G GIVE AGRI DELIB/GP

B40
CAMPBELL P.,CONSUMER REPRESENTATION IN THE NEW DEAL. AGRI INDUS MARKET EX/STRUC PLAN CAP/ISM CONTROL GP/REL DEMAND POLICY. PAGE 21 F0408
CLIENT REPRESENT NAT/G

B40
FULLER G.H.,LIST OF REFERENCES ON PRIORITIES (MIMEOGRAPHED PAPER). WOR-45 NAT/G RATION 20. PAGE 45 F0874
BIBLIOG/A WAR ECO/TAC PLAN

B40
HELLMAN F.S.,THE NEW DEAL: SELECTED LIST OF REFERENCES. USA-45 FINAN LABOR EX/STRUC CREATE INT/TRADE ADMIN CT/SYS 20 SUPREME/CT. PAGE 58 F1145
BIBLIOG/A ECO/TAC PLAN POLICY

B40
SIKES E.R.,CONTEMPORARY ECONOMIC SYSTEMS: THEIR ANALYSIS AND SOCIAL BACKGROUND. GERMANY ITALY USSR AGRI INDUS PLAN CAP/ISM ROUTINE TOTALISM FASCISM ...POLICY CON/ANAL BIBLIOG 20. PAGE 122 F2400
COM SOCISM CONCPT

B40
TRIFFIN R.,MONOPOLISTIC COMPETITION AND GENERAL EQUILIBRIUM THEORY. DIST/IND PLAN TASK EQUILIB OPTIMAL...IDEA/COMP 20 MONOPOLY. PAGE 131 F2586
INT/TRADE INDUS COST

B41
HANSEN A.H.,FISCAL POLICY AND BUSINESS CYCLES. UK INDUS PROB/SOLV DIPLOM INT/TRADE OPTIMAL...POLICY TIME/SEQ CHARTS 19/20. PAGE 54 F1062
FINAN PLAN ECO/TAC GOV/REL

S41
MUKERJEE R.,"POPULATION THEORY AND POLITICS (BMR)" WOR-45 NAT/G PLAN PROB/SOLV ECO/TAC INT/TRADE CONTROL WAR PEACE...CENSUS 20 BIRTH/CON RESOURCE/N. PAGE 94 F1854
GEOG OPTIMAL CONCPT

B42
DRUCKER P.F.,THE FUTURE OF INDUSTRIAL MAN; A CONSERVATIVE APPROACH. USA-45 LOC/G PLAN WAR CENTRAL RATIONAL TOTALISM ORD/FREE LAISSEZ ...PLURIST IDEA/COMP 19/20 HITLER/A. PAGE 34 F0664
INDUS SOCIETY REGION PROB/SOLV

B42
US LIBRARY OF CONGRESS,ECONOMICS OF WAR (APRIL 1941-MARCH 1942). WOR-45 FINAN INDUS LOC/G NAT/G PLAN BUDGET RATION COST DEMAND...POLICY 20. PAGE 138 F2712
BIBLIOG/A INT/TRADE ECO/TAC WAR

B43
BRADY R.A.,BUSINESS AS A SYSTEM OF POWER. EX/STRUC PLAN ECO/TAC CONTROL GP/REL PWR...TREND GP/COMP. PAGE 17 F0334
VOL/ASSN LOBBY POLICY

B44
FABIAN SOCIETY,CAN PLANNING BE DEMOCRATIC? UK CULTURE INDUS NAT/G BUDGET ORD/FREE...GEN/LAWS ANTHOL 20. PAGE 39 F0757
PLAN MAJORIT SOCIALIST ECO/DEV

B44
HAYEK F.A.,THE ROAD TO SERFDOM. NAT/G POL/PAR CREATE EDU/PROP ATTIT WEALTH LAISSEZ...OLD/LIB CONCPT TREND 20. PAGE 57 F1121
FUT PLAN ECO/TAC SOCISM

B44
LANDAUER C.,THEORY OF NATIONAL ECONOMIC PLANNING. USA-45 INDUS MARKET WORKER PROB/SOLV DIPLOM RATION PRICE CONTROL WAR COST 20. PAGE 75 F1465
ECO/TAC PLAN NAT/G ECO/DEV

B45
WOOTTON B.,FREEDOM UNDER PLANNING. UNIV ROUTINE ATTIT AUTHORIT DECISION. PAGE 148 F2926
PLAN ORD/FREE ECO/TAC CONTROL

B47
BALDWIN H.W.,THE PRICE OF POWER. USA+45 FORCES PLAN NUC/PWR ADJUST COST ORD/FREE...POLICY PSY BIBLIOG 20. PAGE 9 F0165
PROB/SOLV PWR POPULISM PRICE

B47
GORDON D.L.,THE HIDDEN WEAPON: THE STORY OF ECONOMIC WARFARE. EUR+WWI USA-45 LAW FINAN INDUS NAT/G CONSULT FORCES PLAN DOMIN PWR WEALTH ...INT/LAW CONCPT OBS TOT/POP NAZI 20. PAGE 49 F0955
INT/ORG ECO/TAC INT/TRADE WAR

B47
MILLETT J.D.,THE PROCESS AND ORGANIZATION OF GOVERNMENT PLANNING. USA+45 DELIB/GP ACT/RES LEAD LOBBY TASK...POLICY GEOG TIME 20 RESOURCE/N. PAGE 91 F1793
ADMIN NAT/G PLAN CONSULT

B47
SLICHTER S.H.,THE CHALLENGE OF INDUSTRIAL RELATIONS: TRADE UNIONS, MANAGEMENT AND THE PUBLIC INTEREST. PLAN ECO/TAC ADJUD CONTROL LEAD SANCTION GP/REL INGP/REL INCOME. PAGE 123 F2421
LABOR MGT CLIENT POLICY

B47
US LIBRARY OF CONGRESS,POSTWAR PLANNING AND RECONSTRUCTION: JANUARY-MARCH 1943. WOR+45 SOCIETY INT/ORG DIPLOM...SOC PREDICT 20. PAGE 138 F2714
BIBLIOG/A WAR PEACE PLAN

B47
WHITEHEAD T.N.,LEADERSHIP IN A FREE SOCIETY; A STUDY IN HUMAN RELATIONS BASED ON AN ANALYSIS OF PRESENT-DAY INDUSTRIAL CIVILIZATION. WOR-45 STRUCT R+D LABOR LG/CO SML/CO WORKER PLAN PROB/SOLV TEC/DEV DRIVE...MGT 20. PAGE 146 F2872
INDUS LEAD ORD/FREE SOCIETY

B48
DURBIN E.F.M.,THE POLITICS OF DEMOCRATIC SOCIALISM; AN ESSAY ON SOCIAL POLICY. STRATA POL/PAR PLAN COERCE DRIVE PERSON PWR MARXISM...CHARTS METH/COMP. PAGE 35 F0684
SOCIALIST POPULISM POLICY SOCIETY

B48
GRAHAM F.D.,THE THEORY OF INTERNATIONAL VALUES. FUT WOR+45 WOR-45 ECO/DEV FINAN INT/ORG PLAN TEC/DEV CAP/ISM DIPLOM ECO/TAC TARIFFS ROUTINE BAL/PAY DRIVE PWR WEALTH SOCISM...POLICY STAT HYPO/EXP GEN/LAWS 20. PAGE 50 F0971
NEW/IDEA INT/TRADE

B48
HAYEK F.A.,INDIVIDUALISM AND ECONOMIC ORDER. FINAN PLAN MORAL LAISSEZ SOCISM...POLICY DECISION PHIL/SCI HIST/WRIT. PAGE 57 F1122
RATIONAL KNOWL PERSON

B48
MILLS C.W.,THE NEW MEN OF POWER. ELITES INTELL STRUCT WORKER ANOMIE ATTIT PWR POLICY. PAGE 92 F1799
LABOR LEAD PLAN

B48
TAYLOR P.E.,THE ECONOMICS OF PUBLIC FINANCE. USA+45 USA-45 ECO/DEV WORKER PLAN BUDGET WAR INCOME WEALTH ...CONCPT STAT BIBLIOG 20. PAGE 129 F2540
FINAN POLICY NAT/G TAX

S48
CLEVELAND A.S.,"NAM: SPOKESMAN FOR INDUSTRY?" LEGIS PLAN LEAD LOBBY PARTIC CONSEN INCOME ATTIT ROLE ORD/FREE POLICY. PAGE 25 F0491
VOL/ASSN CLIENT REPRESENT INDUS

S48
HARDIN L.M.,"REFLECTIONS ON AGRICULTURAL POLICY FORMATION IN THE UNITED STATES." LEGIS PLAN BUDGET ECO/TAC LEAD CENTRAL...MGT SOC NEW/IDEA STAT FAO. PAGE 55 F1078
AGRI POLICY ADMIN NEW/LIB

B49
DE JOUVENEL B.,PROBLEMS OF SOCIALIST ENGLAND. AFR UK USSR BAL/PWR ECO/TAC INT/TRADE PRICE WAR BAL/PAY PEACE 20. PAGE 31 F0601
SOCISM NEW/LIB PROB/SOLV PLAN

B49
HANSEN A.H.,MONETARY THEORY AND FISCAL POLICY. CONSULT PLAN INT/TRADE BAL/PAY OPTIMAL...TREND CHARTS METH/COMP BIBLIOG T 19/20 MONEY. PAGE 54 F1063
FINAN GEN/LAWS POLICY ECO/TAC

B49
PARMELEE M.,GEO-ECONOMIC REGIONAL AND WORLD FEDERATION. FUT WOR+45 WOR-45 SOCIETY VOL/ASSN PLAN ...METH/CNCPT SIMUL GEN/METH TERR/GP TOT/POP 20. PAGE 103 F2028
INT/ORG GEOG REGION

S49
BANFIELD E.C.,"CONGRESS AND THE BUDGET: A PLANNER'S CRITICISM" USA+45 NAT/G PLAN LOBBY. PAGE 9 F0172
LEGIS BUDGET EXEC POLICY

S49
STEINMETZ H.,"THE PROBLEMS OF THE LANDRAT: A STUDY OF COUNTY GOVERNMENT IN THE US ZONE OF GERMANY." GERMANY/W USA+45 INDUS PLAN DIPLOM EDU/PROP CONTROL WAR GOV/REL FEDERAL WEALTH PLURISM...GOV/COMP 20 LANDRAT. PAGE 126 F2478
LOC/G COLONIAL MGT TOP/EX

B50
HARTLAND P.C.,BALANCE OF INTERREGIONAL PAYMENTS OF NEW ENGLAND. USA+45 TEC/DEV ECO/TAC LEGIT ROUTINE BAL/PAY PROFIT 20 NEW/ENGLND FED/RESERV. PAGE 56 F1102
ECO/DEV FINAN REGION PLAN

B50
KOENIG L.W.,THE SALE OF THE TANKERS. USA+45 SEA DIST/IND POL/PAR DIPLOM ADMIN CIVMIL/REL ATTIT ...DECISION 20 PRESIDENT DEPT/STATE. PAGE 72 F1414
NAT/G POLICY PLAN GOV/REL

B50
ORTON W.A.,THE ECONOMIC ROLE OF THE STATE. INTELL ECO/UNDEV PLAN CONTROL PWR SOVEREIGN...POLICY 17/20. PAGE 102 F2000
ECO/DEV NAT/G ECO/TAC ORD/FREE

B50
SURANYI-UNGER T.,PRIVATE ENTERPRISE AND GOVERNMENTAL PLANNING. STRUCT FINAN BAL/PWR HAPPINESS DRIVE NEW/LIB PLURISM...MATH QUANT STAT TREND BIBLIOG. PAGE 127 F2516
PLAN NAT/G LAISSEZ POLICY

B50
US DEPARTMENT OF STATE,POINT FOUR: COOPERATIVE PROGRAM FOR AID IN THE DEVELOPMENT OF ECONOMICALLY UNDERDEVELOPED AREAS. WOR+45 AGRI INDUS INT/ORG PLAN TEC/DEV DIPLOM EDU/PROP ADMIN PEACE PRODUC WEALTH 20 CONGRESS UN. PAGE 135 F2671
ECO/UNDEV FOR/AID FINAN INT/TRADE

B51
HART A.G.,DEFENSE WITHOUT INFLATION. AFR KOREA FINAN INDUS NAT/G WORKER DIPLOM RATION TAX PRICE COST OPTIMAL 20 RESOURCE/N. PAGE 56 F1098
ECO/TAC CONTROL WAR PLAN

B51
PARSONS T.,THE SOCIAL SYSTEM. UNIV INTELL SOCIETY ECO/DEV SECT PLAN PERCEPT...CONCPT METH/CNCPT. PAGE 103 F2030
DRIVE SOC

B51
US DEPARTMENT OF STATE,POINT FOUR, NEAR EAST AND AFRICA, A SELECTED BIBLIOGRAPHY OF STUDIES ON ECONOMICALLY UNDERDEVELOPED COUNTRIES. AGRI COM/IND FINAN INDUS PLAN INT/TRADE...SOC TREND 20. PAGE 135 F2672
BIBLIOG/A AFR S/ASIA ISLAM

ALEXANDROWICZ C.H.,INTERNATIONAL ECONOMIC ORGANIZATION. WOR+45 ECO/DEV ECO/UNDEV DIST/IND FINAN MARKET PLAN ECO/TAC LEGIT DRIVE WEALTH ...POLICY CONCPT QUANT OBS TIME/SEQ GEN/LAWS WORK METH/GP EEC ILO OEEC UNESCO 20. PAGE 4 F0063 — B52 INT/ORG INT/TRADE

AYRES C.E.,THE INDUSTRIAL ECONOMY. USA+45 FINAN MARKET NAT/G PUB/INST PLAN ECO/TAC TAX DEMAND INCOME...BIBLIOG/A 20. PAGE 8 F0146 — B52 ECO/DEV INDUS FUT PROB/SOLV

EGLE W.P.,ECONOMIC STABILIZATION. USA+45 SOCIETY FINAN MARKET PLAN ECO/TAC DOMIN EDU/PROP LEGIT EXEC WEALTH...CONCPT METH/CNCPT TREND HYPO/EXP GEN/METH TOT/POP VAL/FREE 20. PAGE 36 F0708 — B52 NAT/G ECO/DEV CAP/ISM

EGLE W.P.,ECONOMIC STABILIZATION: OBJECTIVES, RULES, AND MECHANISMS. UNIV FINAN PROB/SOLV CAP/ISM ECO/TAC CONTROL...IDEA/COMP 20. PAGE 36 F0709 — B52 EQUILIB PLAN NAT/G ECO/DEV

HOSELITZ B.F.,THE PROGRESS OF UNDERDEVELOPED AREAS. AFR FUT WOR+45 WOR-45 ECO/DEV ECO/TAC INT/TRADE WEALTH...SOC TREND GEN/LAWS TOT/POP VAL/FREE FOR/TRADE 20. PAGE 62 F1219 — B52 ECO/UNDEV PLAN FOR/AID

SECRETARIAT COUNCIL OF EUROPE,THE STRASBOURG PLAN. EUR+WWI CONSULT PLAN ECO/TAC TARIFFS DEBATE REGION 20 COUNCL/EUR STRASBOURG. PAGE 119 F2340 — B52 INT/ORG ECO/DEV INT/TRADE DIPLOM

SURANYI-UNGER T.,COMPARATIVE ECONOMIC SYSTEMS. FINAN MARKET DIPLOM PRICE WEALTH...GEOG SOC BIBLIOG METH T 20. PAGE 128 F2517 — B52 LAISSEZ PLAN ECO/DEV IDEA/COMP

WU Y.,ECONOMIC WARFARE. MARKET PLAN PROB/SOLV FOR/AID CONTROL EFFICIENCY WEALTH...METH/COMP 20. PAGE 149 F2937 — B52 ECO/TAC WAR INT/TRADE DIPLOM

HUTH A.G.,"COMMUNICATION AND ECONOMIC DEVELOPMENT." FUT WOR+45 CULTURE SOCIETY INT/ORG PLAN TEC/DEV EDU/PROP DRIVE KNOWL WEALTH...POLICY CONCPT RECORD STERTYP GEN/LAWS COMMUN TOT/POP UNESCO 20 UN CMN/WLTH. PAGE 64 F1250 — L52 ECO/UNDEV

LEWIS V.B.,"TOWARD A THEORY OF BUDGETING" (BMR)" USA+45 NAT/G PLAN PROB/SOLV...IDEA/COMP METH 20 SUPREME/CT. PAGE 79 F1551 — S52 BUDGET CONCPT CREATE

DAHL R.A.,POLITICS, ECONOMICS AND WELFARE: PLANNING AND POLITICOECONOMIC SYSTEMS RESOLVED INTO BASIC SOCIAL PROCESSES. WOR+45 WOR-45 ECO/DEV ECO/UNDEV R+D CREATE PLAN TEC/DEV EDU/PROP HEALTH WEALTH ...SOC SELF/OBS TREND CHARTS GEN/METH 20. PAGE 29 F0571 — B53 ECO/TAC PHIL/SCI

BLOUGH R.,"THE ROLE OF THE ECONOMIST IN FEDERAL POLICY MAKING." USA+45 ELITES INTELL ECO/DEV NAT/G CONSULT EX/STRUC ACT/RES PLAN INT/TRADE BAL/PAY WEALTH...POLICY METH/GP CONGRESS 20. PAGE 16 F0301 — S53 DELIB/GP ECO/TAC

LINCOLN G.,"FACTORS DETERMINING ARMS AID." COM FUT USA+45 USSR WOR+45 ECO/DEV NAT/G CONSULT PLAN TEC/DEV DIPLOM DOMIN EDU/PROP PERCEPT PWR ...DECISION CONCPT TREND MARX/KARL 20. PAGE 80 F1566 — S53 FORCES POLICY BAL/PWR FOR/AID

HOBBS E.H.,BEHIND THE PRESIDENT - A STUDY OF EXECUTIVE OFFICE AGENCIES. USA+45 NAT/G PLAN BUDGET ECO/TAC EXEC ORD/FREE 20 BUR/BUDGET. PAGE 60 F1183 — B54 EX/STRUC DELIB/GP CONFER CONSULT

STALEY E.,THE FUTURE OF UNDERDEVELOPED COUNTRIES: POLITICAL IMPLICATIONS OF ECONOMIC DEVELOPMENT. AFR COM FUT USA+45 SOCIETY ECO/UNDEV CREATE PLAN CAP/ISM ATTIT DRIVE MARXISM SOCISM...POLICY CONCPT CHARTS 20. PAGE 125 F2466 — B54 EDU/PROP ECO/TAC FOR/AID

OPLER M.E.,"SOCIAL ASPECTS OF TECHNICAL ASSISTANCE IN OPERATION." WOR+45 VOL/ASSN CREATE PLAN TEC/DEV EDU/PROP ALL/VALS...METH/CNCPT OBS RECORD TREND UN 20. PAGE 101 F1993 — L54 INT/ORG CONSULT FOR/AID

BERNAYS E.L.,THE ENGINEERING OF CONSENT. VOL/ASSN OP/RES ROUTINE INGP/REL ATTIT RESPECT...POLICY METH/CNCPT METH/COMP 20. PAGE 14 F0264 — B55 GP/REL PLAN ACT/RES ADJUST

BOULDING K.E.,ECONOMIC ANALYSIS (3RD ED.). USA+45 PLAN ECO/TAC COST DEMAND INCOME...POLICY STAT CHARTS SIMUL T. PAGE 17 F0322 — B55 PHIL/SCI ECO/DEV CAP/ISM

JOHR W.A.,THE ROLE OF THE ECONOMIST AS OFFICIAL ADVISER. WOR+45 INTELL ECO/DEV NAT/G PLAN GP/REL ROLE...DECISION PREDICT IDEA/COMP. PAGE 68 F1336 — B55 CONSULT ECO/TAC POLICY INGP/REL

PANT Y.P.,PLANNING IN UNDERDEVELOPED ECONOMIES. INDIA NEPAL INT/TRADE COLONIAL SOVEREIGN ALL/IDEOS ...TIME/SEQ METH/COMP 20. PAGE 103 F2026 — B55 ECO/UNDEV PLAN ECO/TAC DIPLOM

RUSTOW D.A.,THE POLITICS OF COMPROMISE. SWEDEN LABOR EX/STRUC LEGIS PLAN REPRESENT SOCISM...SOC 19/20. PAGE 115 F2265 — B55 POL/PAR NAT/G POLICY ECO/TAC

US ADVISORY COMN INTERGOV REL,THE COMMISSION ON INTERGOVERNMENTAL RELATIONS; A REPORT TO THE PRESIDENT FOR TRANSMITTAL TO THE CONGRESS. USA+45 ECO/DEV AGRI COM/IND FINAN FORCES PLAN EDU/PROP HEALTH WEALTH...STAT MUNICH 20 CIV/DEFENS. PAGE 133 F2630 — B55 GOV/REL NAT/G LOC/G PROVS

US OFFICE OF THE PRESIDENT,REPORT TO CONGRESS ON THE MUTUAL SECURITY PROGRAM FOR THE SIX MONTHS ENDED JUNE 30, 1955. ECO/DEV INT/ORG NAT/G CREATE TEC/DEV BAL/PWR ECO/TAC AGREE DETER COST ORD/FREE 20 DEPT/STATE DEPT/DEFEN. PAGE 138 F2722 — B55 DIPLOM FORCES PLAN FOR/AID

KISER M.,"ORGANIZATION OF AMERICAN STATES." L/A+17C USA+45 ECO/UNDEV INT/ORG NAT/G PLAN TEC/DEV DIPLOM ECO/TAC INT/TRADE EDU/PROP ADMIN ALL/VALS...POLICY MGT RECORD ORG/CHARTS OAS COMMUN 20. PAGE 71 F1401 — L55 VOL/ASSN ECO/DEV REGION

HALLETT D.,"THE HISTORY AND STRUCTURE OF OEEC." EUR+WWI USA+45 CONSTN INDUS INT/ORG NAT/G DELIB/GP ACT/RES PLAN ORD/FREE WEALTH...CONCPT OEEC 20 CMN/WLTH. PAGE 54 F1051 — S55 VOL/ASSN ECO/DEV

ATOMIC INDUSTRIAL FORUM,PUBLIC RELATIONS FOR THE ATOMIC INDUSTRY. WOR+45 PLAN PROB/SOLV EDU/PROP PRESS CONFER...AUD/VIS ANTHOL 20. PAGE 7 F0135 — B56 NUC/PWR INDUS GP/REL ATTIT

BELL P.W.,THE STERLING AREA IN THE POSTWAR WORLD. EUR+WWI FUT S/ASIA UK ECO/DEV PLAN DIPLOM WEALTH ...STAT RECORD CHARTS GEN/LAWS FOR/TRADE TOT/POP 20. PAGE 12 F0235 — B56 FINAN ECO/TAC

GARDNER R.N.,STERLING-DOLLAR DIPLOMACY. EUR+WWI USA+45 INT/ORG NAT/G PLAN INT/TRADE EDU/PROP ADMIN KNOWL PWR WEALTH...POLICY SOC METH/CNCPT STAT CHARTS SIMUL GEN/LAWS 20. PAGE 46 F0902 — B56 ECO/DEV DIPLOM

HICKMAN C.A.,INDIVIDUALS, GROUPS, AND ECONOMIC BEHAVIOR. WORKER PAY CONTROL EXEC GP/REL INGP/REL PERSON ROLE...PSY SOC PERS/COMP METH 20. PAGE 59 F1163 — B56 MGT ADMIN ECO/TAC PLAN

KINDLEBERGER C.P.,THE TERMS OF TRADE: A EUROPEAN CASE-STUDY. EUR+WWI MOD/EUR ECO/DEV ECO/UNDEV AGRI INDUS BAL/PAY...METH/CNCPT STAT CONT/OBS CON/ANAL SOC/EXP SIMUL FOR/TRADE 20. PAGE 71 F1390 — B56 PLAN ECO/TAC

KNORR K.E.,RUBLE DIPLOMACY: CHALLENGE TO AMERICAN FOREIGN AID(PAMPHLET). AFR CHINA/COM USA+45 USSR PLAN TEC/DEV CAP/ISM INT/TRADE DOMIN EDU/PROP CONTROL LEAD 20. PAGE 72 F1413 — B56 ECO/UNDEV COM DIPLOM FOR/AID

KOHLER E.L.,ACCOUNTING IN THE FEDERAL GOVERNMENT. USA+45 LOC/G PLAN TAX CONTROL COST 20. PAGE 72 F1416 — B56 BUDGET AFR NAT/G FINAN

US OFFICE OF THE PRESIDENT,REPORT TO CONGRESS ON THE MUTUAL SECURITY PROGRAM FOR THE SIX MONTHS ENDED DECEMBER 31, 1955. ASIA USSR ECO/DEV ECO/UNDEV INT/ORG CREATE TEC/DEV BAL/PWR ECO/TAC AGREE DETER COST ORD/FREE 20 DEPT/STATE DEPT/DEFEN EISNHWR/DD. PAGE 138 F2723 — B56 DIPLOM FORCES PLAN FOR/AID

GORDON L.,"THE ORGANIZATION FOR EUROPEAN ECONOMIC COOPERATION." EUR+WWI INDUS INT/ORG NAT/G CONSULT DELIB/GP ACT/RES CREATE PLAN TEC/DEV EDU/PROP LEGIT WEALTH OEEC 20. PAGE 49 F0956 — S56 VOL/ASSN ECO/DEV

KNAPP D.C.,"CONGRESSIONAL CONTROL OF AGRICULTURAL CONSERVATION POLICY: A CASE STUDY OF THE APPROPRIATIONS PROCESS." DELIB/GP PLAN PROB/SOLV CONFER PARL/PROC...POLICY INT CONGRESS. PAGE 72 F1411 — S56 LEGIS AGRI BUDGET CONTROL

MARGOLIS J.,"ON MUNICIPAL LAND POLICY FOR FISCAL GAINS." USA+45 PLAN TAX COST EFFICIENCY HABITAT KNOWL...MGT MUNICH 20. PAGE 85 F1667 — S56 BUDGET POLICY GEOG LOC/G

ASHER R.E.,THE UNITED NATIONS AND ECONOMIC AND — B57 INT/ORG

SOCIAL COOPERATION. ECO/UNDEV COM/IND DIST/IND FINAN PLAN PROB/SOLV INT/TRADE TASK WEALTH...SOC 20 UN. PAGE 7 F0129
DIPLOM FOR/AID

B57
ASSN U BUREAUS BUS-ECO RES,INDEX OF PUBLICATIONS OF BUREAUS OF BUSINESS AND ECONOMIC RESEARCH 1950-56 AND YEARLY SUPPLEMENTS THROUGH 1967. FINAN OP/RES PLAN GOV/REL INCOME AGE...POLICY 20. PAGE 7 F0133
BIBLIOG ECO/DEV ECO/TAC LG/CO

B57
CLARK J.M.,ECONOMIC INSTITUTIONS AND HUMAN WELFARE. USA+45 SOCIETY ECO/DEV NAT/G WORKER PLAN PROB/SOLV CAP/ISM CONTROL...POLICY 20. PAGE 25 F0482
ECO/TAC ORD/FREE WEALTH

B57
COMMITTEE ECONOMIC DEVELOPMENT,ECONOMIC DEVELOPMENT ASSISTANCE. USA+45 WOR+45 AGRI CONFER ORD/FREE ...MGT CHARTS 20. PAGE 27 F0515
FOR/AID ECO/UNDEV FINAN PLAN

B57
HUTTON D.G.,INFLATION AND SOCIETY. AFR FINAN PLAN COST DEMAND EQUILIB...CONCPT 20. PAGE 64 F1254
ECO/DEV POLICY NAT/G ECO/TAC

B57
LOUCKS W.N.,COMPARATIVE ECONOMIC SYSTEMS (5TH ED.). COM UK USSR INDUS POL/PAR PLAN CAP/ISM TOTALISM MARXISM...PHIL/SCI BIBLIOG 19/20. PAGE 82 F1603
NAT/COMP IDEA/COMP SOCISM

B57
LUNDBERG E.,BUSINESS CYCLES AND ECONOMIC POLICY (TRANS. BY J. POTTER). SWEDEN ECO/DEV FINAN DELIB/GP PLAN PRICE CONTROL BAL/PAY 20 INTRVN/ECO. PAGE 82 F1607
ECO/TAC INDUS INT/TRADE BUDGET

B57
MEIER G.M.,ECONOMIC DEVELOPMENT: THEORY, HISTORY, AND POLICY. WOR+45 WOR-45 ECO/DEV ECO/UNDEV PLAN CAP/ISM BAL/PAY ATTIT PWR WEALTH SOCISM...CHARTS TOT/POP FOR/TRADE 20. PAGE 89 F1748
ECO/TAC GEN/LAWS

B57
MILLIKAN M.F.,A PROPOSAL: KEY TO AN EFFECTIVE FOREIGN POLICY. USA+45 AGRI FINAN DELIB/GP DIPLOM REPRESENT MAJORITY...NEW/IDEA CHARTS. PAGE 91 F1795
FOR/AID GIVE ECO/UNDEV PLAN

B57
NAUMANN R.,THEORIE UND PRAXIS DES NEOLIBERALISMUS; DAS MAERCHEN VON DER FREIEN ODER SOZIALEN MARKTWIRTSCHAFT. GERMANY/W FORCES PLAN EDU/PROP SOCISM...POLICY MARXIST IDEA/COMP BIBLIOG 18/20 ADENAUER/K. PAGE 97 F1903
MARXISM NEW/LIB ECO/TAC CAP/ISM

B57
THOMAS R.G.,OUR MODERN BANKING AND MONETARY SYSTEM (3RD ED.). AFR USA+45 USA-45 ACT/RES PLAN PROB/SOLV INT/TRADE PRICE WAR BAL/PAY INCOME...POLICY METH/CNCPT 20 DEPRESSION. PAGE 130 F2563
FINAN SERV/IND ECO/TAC

B57
TRIFFIN R.,EUROPE AND THE MONEY MUDDLE. USA+45 INT/ORG NAT/G CONSULT PLAN ECO/TAC EXEC ROUTINE BAL/PAY WEALTH...METH/CNCPT OBS TREND CHARTS STERTYP GEN/METH EEC TERR/GP VAL/FREE ECSC. PAGE 131 F2587
EUR+WWI ECO/DEV REGION

B57
WARRINER D.,LAND REFORM AND DEVELOPMENT IN THE MIDDLE EAST: A STUDY OF EGYPT, SYRIA AND IRAQ. IRAQ ISLAM SYRIA UAR AGRI DIST/IND PLAN TEC/DEV DOMIN REV ATTIT WEALTH...SOC METH/CNCPT STAT OBS RECORD HIST/WRIT TREND GEN/LAWS FAO 20. PAGE 143 F2825
ECO/UNDEV CONCPT

S57
DETAMBEL M.H.,"PROBABILITY AND WORK AS DETERMINERS OF MULTICHOICE BEHAVIOR." PLAN TASK EFFICIENCY ...DECISION GAME. PAGE 32 F0622
HYPO/EXP PROB/SOLV GEN/LAWS PROBABIL

S57
HOAG M.W.,"ECONOMIC PROBLEMS OF ALLIANCE." AFR COM EUR+WWI WOR+45 ECO/DEV ECO/UNDEV NAT/G VOL/ASSN FORCES PLAN TEC/DEV DIPLOM COERCE ORD/FREE PWR WEALTH...DECISION GEN/LAWS NATO TERR/GP. PAGE 60 F1182
INT/ORG ECO/TAC

S57
LEWIS E.G.,"PARLIAMENTARY CONTROL OF NATIONALIZED INDUSTRY IN FRANCE." FRANCE NAT/G DELIB/GP ACT/RES PLAN PROB/SOLV ECO/TAC DOMIN CENTRAL. PAGE 79 F1547
PWR LEGIS INDUS CONTROL

S57
ROURKE F.E.,"THE POLITICS OF ADMINISTRATIVE ORGANIZATION: A CASE HISTORY." USA+45 LABOR WORKER PLAN ADMIN TASK EFFICIENCY 20 DEPT/LABOR CONGRESS. PAGE 114 F2251
POLICY ATTIT MGT GP/COMP

N57
U WISCONSIN BUREAU OF GOVT,SERVICE SALES OF THE CITY OF MADISON TO METROPOLITAN COMMUNITIES AND NONRESIDENTS (PAMPHLET). DIST/IND LOC/G ADMIN ...DECISION GOV/COMP MUNICH. PAGE 132 F2597
REGION ECO/TAC PLAN

B58
BARRERE A.,POLITIQUE FINANCIERE. FRANCE BUDGET ECO/TAC TAX BAL/PAY INCOME PRODUC...MGT BIBLIOG T 20. PAGE 10 F0193
FINAN NAT/G PLAN

B58
BERLINER J.S.,SOVIET ECONOMIC AID: THE AID AND TRADE POLICY IN UNDERDEVELOPED COUNTRIES. AFR COM ISLAM L/A+17C S/ASIA USSR ECO/DEV DIST/IND FINAN MARKET INT/ORG ACT/RES PLAN BAL/PWR WEAPON PWR WEALTH...CHARTS FOR/TRADE 20. PAGE 14 F0263
ECO/UNDEV ECO/TAC FOR/AID

B58
BIDWELL P.W.,RAW MATERIALS: A STUDY OF AMERICAN POLICY. USA+45 USA-45 ECO/UNDEV AGRI INDUS KIN CREATE PLAN ECO/TAC WAR PEACE ATTIT DRIVE WEALTH ...STAT CHARTS CONGRESS FOR/TRADE VAL/FREE. PAGE 15 F0279
EXTR/IND ECO/DEV

B58
CHAMBERLIN E.H.,LABOR UNIONS AND PUBLIC POLICY. PLAN BARGAIN SANCTION INGP/REL JURID. PAGE 23 F0444
LABOR WEALTH PWR NAT/G

B58
CHEEK G.,ECONOMIC AND SOCIAL IMPLICATIONS OF AUTOMATION: A BIBLIOGRAPHIC REVIEW (PAMPHLET). USA+45 LG/CO WORKER CREATE PLAN CONTROL ROUTINE PERS/REL EFFICIENCY PRODUC...METH/COMP 20. PAGE 24 F0459
BIBLIOG/A SOCIETY INDUS AUTOMAT

B58
CLAIRMONTE F.,LE LIBERALISME ECONOMIQUE ET LES PAYS SOUS-DEVELOPPES: ETUDES SUR L'EVOLUTION D'UNE IDEE. ASIA INDIA UK FINAN INDUS PLAN CAP/ISM ECO/TAC COLONIAL NEW/LIB...BIBLIOG 20 THIRD/WRLD. PAGE 24 F0475
LAISSEZ ECO/UNDEV

B58
CLAUNCH J.M.,THE PROBLEM OF GOVERNMENT IN METROPOLITAN AREAS. CULTURE INDUS POL/PAR PLAN REGION GP/REL...CENSUS ANTHOL MUNICH 20. PAGE 25 F0486
PROB/SOLV SOC

B58
CROWE S.,THE LANDSCAPE OF POWER. UK CULTURE SERV/IND NAT/G CONSULT PARTIC NUC/PWR LEISURE...SOC EXHIBIT 20. PAGE 29 F0559
HABITAT TEC/DEV PLAN CONTROL

B58
DUBIN R.,WORKING UNION-MANAGEMENT RELATIONS. LAW PLAN ECO/TAC CHOOSE REPRESENT INGP/REL PWR...POLICY SOC BIBLIOG. PAGE 34 F0669
LABOR MGT AUTHORIT GP/REL

B58
EHRHARD J.,LE DESTIN DU COLONIALISME. AFR FRANCE ECO/UNDEV AGRI FINAN MARKET CREATE PLAN TEC/DEV BUDGET DIPLOM PRICE 20. PAGE 36 F0710
COLONIAL FOR/AID INT/TRADE INDUS

B58
HANCE W.A.,AFRICAN ECONOMIC DEVELOPMENT. AGRI DIST/IND INDUS R+D ACT/RES PLAN CAP/ISM FOR/AID ...GOV/COMP BIBLIOG 20. PAGE 54 F1058
AFR ECO/UNDEV PROB/SOLV TEC/DEV

B58
HIRSCHMAN A.O.,STRATEGY OF ECONOMIC DEVELOPMENT. WOR+45 WOR-45 CULTURE ECO/DEV NAT/G PLAN TEC/DEV INT/TRADE BAL/PAY ATTIT DRIVE RIGID/FLEX WEALTH ...CONCPT METH/CNCPT OBS CHARTS SIMUL GEN/LAWS TOT/POP VAL/FREE. PAGE 60 F1176
ECO/UNDEV ECO/TAC CAP/ISM

B58
INDIAN INST OF PUBLIC ADMIN,IMPROVING CITY GOVERNMENT. INDIA ECO/UNDEV PLAN BUDGET PARTIC GP/REL MUNICH 20. PAGE 64 F1263
LOC/G PROB/SOLV ADMIN

B58
JACOBSSON P.,SOME MONETARY PROBLEMS, INTERNATIONAL AND NATIONAL. WOR+45 WOR-45 ECO/DEV FORCES WORKER PROB/SOLV DIPLOM INT/TRADE...ANTHOL 20. PAGE 66 F1299
FINAN PLAN ECO/TAC NAT/COMP

B58
JUCKER-FLEETWOOD E.,ECONOMIC THEORY AND POLICY IN FINLAND 1914-1925. FINLAND INT/TRADE PRICE COST 20 MONEY. PAGE 68 F1343
FINAN GEN/LAWS ECO/TAC PLAN

B58
MIKESELL R.F.,FINANCING FREE WORLD TRADE WITH THE SINO-SOVIET BLOC. CHINA/COM COM USSR WOR+45 ECO/DEV AGRI DIST/IND EXTR/IND FINAN INDUS MARKET PROC/MFG NAT/G PLAN TEC/DEV ECO/TAC...CHARTS METH/GP EEC FOR/TRADE 20. PAGE 91 F1780
STAT BAL/PAY

B58
MOSKOWITZ M.,HUMAN RIGHTS AND WORLD ORDER. INT/ORG PLAN GP/REL NAT/LISM SOVEREIGN...CONCPT 20 UN TREATY CIV/RIGHTS. PAGE 94 F1845
DIPLOM INT/LAW ORD/FREE

B58
MYRDAL G.,RICH LANDS AND POOR: THE ROAD TO WORLD PROSPERITY. FUT WOR+45 WOR-45 ECO/DEV ECO/UNDEV INT/ORG PLAN ECO/TAC REGION...GEOG TIME/SEQ GEN/LAWS TOT/POP 20. PAGE 96 F1880
WEALTH TREND FOR/AID INT/TRADE

B58
NICULESCU B.,COLONIAL PLANNING: A COMPARATIVE STUDY. AFR AGRI LOC/G NAT/G DELIB/GP COLONIAL MUNICH 20. PAGE 98 F1927
PLAN ECO/UNDEV TEC/DEV NAT/COMP

B58
POLLOCK F.,AUTOMATION: A STUDY OF ITS ECONOMIC AND SOCIAL CONSEQUENCES. FUT USA+45 USA-45 SOCIETY ECO/DEV LABOR ACT/RES PLAN ECO/TAC AUTOMAT ROUTINE
TEC/DEV SOC CAP/ISM

ALL/VALS...STAT TREND COMPUT/IR CHARTS SOC/EXP WORK 20. PAGE 107 F2099

B58
ROBERTS B.C.,NATIONAL WAGES POLICY IN WAR AND PEACE. EUR+WWI GERMANY S/ASIA SWEDEN UK USA+45 USA-45 STRATA ECO/DEV LABOR NAT/G DELIB/GP PLAN INT/TRADE WEALTH...STAT TREND CHARTS 20. PAGE 112 F2205
CREATE ECO/TAC

B58
SCOTT D.J.R.,RUSSIAN POLITICAL INSTITUTIONS. RUSSIA USSR CONSTN AGRI DELIB/GP PLAN EDU/PROP CONTROL CHOOSE EFFICIENCY ATTIT MARXISM...BIBLIOG/A IND 13/20. PAGE 118 F2332
NAT/G POL/PAR ADMIN DECISION

B58
US CONGRESS JOINT ECO COMM,THE RELATIONSHIP OF PRICES TO ECONOMIC STABILITY AND GROWTH. USA+45 MARKET TAX ADJUST COST DEMAND INCOME PRODUC ...POLICY TREND CHARTS ANTHOL 20 CONGRESS. PAGE 134 F2650
ECO/DEV PLAN EQUILIB PRICE

L58
MASON E.S.,"ECONOMIC PLANNING IN UNDERDEVELOPED AREAS." FUT WOR+45 PLAN TEC/DEV EDU/PROP ATTIT RIGID/FLEX KNOWL...SOC CONCPT GEN/LAWS TOT/POP 20. PAGE 87 F1697
NAT/G ECO/UNDEV

L58
TRAGER F.N.,"A SELECTED AND ANNOTATED BIBLIOGRAPHY ON ECONOMIC DEVELOPMENT, 1953-1957." WOR+45 AGRI FINAN INDUS MARKET LABOR WORKER PLAN INT/TRADE PRODUC...CENSUS MUNICH. PAGE 131 F2583
BIBLIOG/A ECO/UNDEV ECO/DEV

S58
ARROW K.J.,"UTILITIES, ATTITUDES, CHOICES: A REVIEW NOTE." USA+45 PLAN...METH/CNCPT MATH STAT CHARTS HYPO/EXP. PAGE 6 F0121
DECISION DIST/IND MARKET CREATE

S58
ELKIN A.B.,"OEEC-ITS STRUCTURE AND POWERS." EUR+WWI CONSTN INDUS INT/ORG NAT/G VOL/ASSN DELIB/GP ACT/RES PLAN ORD/FREE WEALTH...CHARTS ORG/CHARTS OEEC 20. PAGE 37 F0719
ECO/DEV EX/STRUC

S58
JOHNSON D.G.,"GOVERNMENT AND AGRICULTURE: IS AGRICULTURE A SPECIAL CASE?" PLAN ECO/TAC LOBBY WEALTH POLICY. PAGE 67 F1321
INDUS GP/REL INCOME NAT/G

B59
AITKEN H.,THE STATE AND ECONOMIC GROWTH. COM EUR+WWI MOD/EUR S/ASIA USA+45 FINAN NAT/G DELIB/GP PLAN PWR WEALTH 20. PAGE 3 F0054
DIST/IND ECO/DEV

B59
BAUER P.T.,UNITED STATES AID AND INDIAN ECONOMIC DEVELOPMENT. INDIA STRATA FINAN PLAN BUDGET DIPLOM INGP/REL EFFICIENCY SOCISM 20 AID. PAGE 11 F0215
FOR/AID ECO/UNDEV ECO/TAC POLICY

B59
BLACK J.D.,ECONOMICS FOR AGRICULTURE. USA+45 EXTR/IND FAM WORKER ACT/RES PLAN PRICE EATING INCOME...CENSUS BIBLIOG 20. PAGE 15 F0291
AGRI ECO/TAC MARKET POLICY

B59
CHECCHI V.,HONDURAS: A PROBLEM IN ECONOMIC DEVELOPMENT. HONDURAS AGRI FINAN INDUS LABOR WORKER INT/TRADE EDU/PROP PRICE HEALTH...GEOG CHARTS BIBLIOG 20. PAGE 24 F0458
ECO/UNDEV ECO/TAC PROB/SOLV PLAN

B59
CUCCORESE H.J.,HISTORIA DE LA CONVERSION DEL PAPEL MONEDA EN BUENOS AIRES, 1861-1867. AFR LAW LOC/G NAT/G ATTIT...POLICY BIBLIOG 19 ARGEN BUENOS/AIR. PAGE 29 F0560
FINAN PLAN LEGIS

B59
DIEBOLD W. JR.,THE SCHUMAN PLAN: A STUDY IN ECONOMIC COOPERATION, 1950-1959. EUR+WWI FRANCE GERMANY USA+45 EXTR/IND CONSULT DELIB/GP PLAN DIPLOM ECO/TAC INT/TRADE ROUTINE ORD/FREE WEALTH ...METH/CNCPT STAT CONT/OBS INT TIME/SEQ ECSC 20. PAGE 33 F0635
INT/ORG REGION

B59
ETSCHMANN R.,DIE WAHRUNGS- UND DEVISENPOLITIK DES OSTBLOCKS UND IHRE AUSWIRKUNGEN AUF DIE WIRTSCHAFTSBEZIEHUNGEN ZWISCHEN OST U WEST. BULGARIA CZECHOSLVK HUNGARY POLAND USSR MARKET NAT/G PLAN DIPLOM...NAT/COMP 20. PAGE 39 F0753
ECO/TAC FINAN POLICY INT/TRADE

B59
FERRY W.H.,THE CORPORATION AND THE ECONOMY. CLIENT LAW CONSTN LABOR NAT/G PLAN INT/TRADE PARTIC CONSEN ORD/FREE PWR POLICY. PAGE 40 F0787
LG/CO CONTROL REPRESENT

B59
GUDIN E.,INFLACAO (2ND ED.). INDUS NAT/G PLAN ECO/TAC CONTROL COST 20. PAGE 52 F1012
ECO/UNDEV INT/TRADE BAL/PAY FINAN

B59
HAZLEWOOD A.,THE ECONOMICS OF "UNDER-DEVELOPED" AREAS. WOR+45 DIST/IND EXTR/IND FINAN INDUS MARKET PLAN FOR/AID...GEOG 20. PAGE 57 F1129
BIBLIOG/A ECO/UNDEV AGRI INT/TRADE

B59
KARLIN S.,MATHEMATICAL METHODS AND THEORY IN GAMES, PROGRAMMING, AND ECONOMICS. COMPUTER PLAN CONTROL TASK...MATH 20. PAGE 69 F1357
GAME METH/COMP ACT/RES DECISION

B59
MEYER A.J.,MIDDLE EASTERN CAPITALISM: NINE ESSAYS. ISLAM CULTURE ECO/UNDEV INDUS MARKET NAT/G PLAN ATTIT RIGID/FLEX...STAT OBS TREND GEN/LAWS. PAGE 90 F1767
TEC/DEV ECO/TAC ANTHOL

B59
NORTON P.L.,URBAN PROBLEMS AND TECHNIQUES. AIR AGRI INDUS MARKET TEC/DEV BUDGET LEISURE ALL/VALS ...ANTHOL MUNICH 20 URBAN/RNWL. PAGE 99 F1936
PLAN LOC/G HABITAT

B59
NOVE A.,COMMUNIST ECONOMIC STRATEGY: SOVIET GROWTH AND CAPABILITIES. USSR AGRI LABOR PLAN TEC/DEV CAP/ISM INT/TRADE EFFICIENCY MARXISM 20 THIRD/WRLD. PAGE 99 F1941
FOR/AID ECO/TAC DIPLOM INDUS

B59
NUNEZ JIMENEZ A.,LA LIBERACION DE LAS ISLAS. CUBA L/A+17C USA+45 LAW CHIEF PLAN DIPLOM FOR/AID OWN WEALTH 20 CASTRO/F. PAGE 99 F1945
AGRI REV ECO/UNDEV NAT/G

B59
OGBURN C.,ECONOMIC PLAN AND ACTION. USA+45 FINAN LABOR DIPLOM ECO/TAC FOR/AID 20. PAGE 101 F1981
ECO/DEV INT/TRADE PLAN BAL/PAY

B59
RAMANADHAM V.V.,PROBLEMS OF PUBLIC ENTERPRISE: THOUGHTS ON BRITISH EXPERIENCE. UK FINAN INDUS PLAN PRICE CENTRAL...POLICY 20. PAGE 109 F2140
SOCISM LG/CO ECO/DEV GOV/REL

B59
SERAPHIM H.J.,PROBLEME DER WILLENSBILDUNG UND DER WIRTSCHAFTSPOLITISCHEN FUEHRUNG. WOR+45 MARKET ACT/RES OP/RES PLAN EDU/PROP INGP/REL HABITAT PLURISM...MGT PERS/COMP METH 20. PAGE 119 F2357
POLICY DECISION PSY

B59
SHACKLE G.L.S.,ECONOMICS FOR PLEASURE. FINAN MARKET NAT/G WORKER PLAN INT/TRADE TARIFFS PAY BAL/PAY COST PRODUC 20. PAGE 120 F2361
METH/CNCPT WEALTH INCOME

B59
SILCOCK T.H.,THE COMMONWEALTH ECONOMY IN SOUTHEAST ASIA. AFR INDIA MALAYSIA S/ASIA ECO/DEV AGRI LOC/G PLAN TARIFFS COLONIAL BAL/PAY DEMAND...BIBLIOG/A 20 GATT. PAGE 122 F2401
ECO/TAC INT/TRADE RACE/REL DIPLOM

B59
STANFORD U, BOARD OF TRUSTEES,THE ALLOCATION OF ECONOMIC RESOURCES. WORKER PLAN BUDGET ECO/TAC TAX RECEIVE COST PRODUC...POLICY IDEA/COMP SIMUL ANTHOL 20. PAGE 125 F2468
INCOME PRICE FINAN

B59
STERNBERG F.,THE MILITARY AND INDUSTRIAL REVOLUTION OF OUR TIME. USA+45 USSR WOR+45 WORKER COMPUTER PLAN TEC/DEV NUC/PWR GP/REL...POLICY NAT/COMP 20. PAGE 126 F2481
DIPLOM FORCES INDUS CIVMIL/REL

B59
US GENERAL ACCOUNTING OFFICE,EXAM OF ECONOMIC AND TECHNICAL ASSISTANCE PROGRAM FOR INDIA INT'NAT'L COOP ADMIN REPORT TO CONGRESS 1955-1958. INDIA USA+45 ECO/UNDEV FINAN PLAN DIPLOM COST UTIL WEALTH ...CHARTS 20 CONGRESS AID. PAGE 136 F2679
FOR/AID EFFICIENCY ECO/TAC TEC/DEV

B59
US HOUSE COMM GOVT OPERATIONS,UNITED STATES AID OPERATIONS IN LAOS. LAOS USA+45 PLAN INSPECT HOUSE/REP. PAGE 137 F2697
FOR/AID ADMIN FORCES ECO/UNDEV

B59
WELTON H.,THE THIRD WORLD WAR; TRADE AND INDUSTRY, THE NEW BATTLEGROUND. AFR WOR+45 ECO/DEV INDUS MARKET TASK...MGT IDEA/COMP. PAGE 145 F2855
INT/TRADE PLAN DIPLOM

B59
WENTHOLT W.,SOME COMMENTS ON THE LIQUIDATION OF THE EUROPEAN PAYMENT UNION AND RELATED PROBLEMS (PAMPHLET). AFR WOR+45 PLAN BUDGET PRICE CONTROL 20 EEC. PAGE 145 F2857
FINAN ECO/DEV INT/ORG ECO/TAC

B59
WIBBERLEY G.P.,AGRICULTURE AND URBAN GROWTH. UK USA+45 ECO/DEV FINAN PROB/SOLV INT/TRADE COST ...GEOG STAT CHARTS METH/COMP HYPO/EXP METH MUNICH 20. PAGE 146 F2876
AGRI PLAN

L59
BEGUIN B.,"ILO AND THE TRIPARTITE SYSTEM." EUR+WWI WOR+45 WOR-45 CONSTN ECO/DEV ECO/UNDEV INDUS INT/ORG NAT/G VOL/ASSN DELIB/GP PLAN TEC/DEV LEGIT ORD/FREE WEALTH...CONCPT TIME/SEQ WORK ILO 20. PAGE 12 F0228
LABOR

L59
MURPHY J.C.,"SOME IMPLICATIONS OF EUROPE'S COMMON MARKET. IN (COOK P, ECONOMIC DEVELOPMENT AND INTERNATIONAL TRADE,." EUR+WWI ECO/DEV DIST/IND INDUS NAT/G PLAN ECO/TAC INT/TRADE WEALTH...STAT TREND OEEC TOT/POP 20 EEC. PAGE 95 F1866
MARKET INT/ORG REGION

S59
ALKHIMOV V.S.,"SOVIET FOREIGN TRADE CHANNELS." COM FUT USA+45 USSR ECO/DEV MARKET CONSULT PLAN WEALTH ...MARXIST OBS CON/ANAL FOR/TRADE 20. PAGE 4 F0068
FINAN ECO/TAC DIPLOM

S59
DUNNING J.H.,"NON-PECUNIARY ELEMENTS AND BUSINESS BEHAVIOUR." PLAN PROB/SOLV COST...METH/CNCPT CLASSIF QUANT STAT. PAGE 35 F0681
DECISION DRIVE PRODUC PRICE

S59
REUBENS E.D.,"THE BASIS FOR REORIENATION OF AMERICAN FOREIGN AID POLICY." USA+45 USSR STRUCT INT/ORG CONSULT ECO/TAC ADMIN DRIVE MORAL ORD/FREE PWR WEALTH...RELATIV MATH STAT TREND GEN/LAWS VAL/FREE 20. PAGE 111 F2180
ECO/UNDEV PLAN FOR/AID DIPLOM

S59
STINCHCOMBE A.L.,"BUREAUCRATIC AND CRAFT ADMINISTRATION OF PRODUCTION: A COMPARATIVE STUDY" (BMR)" USA+45 STRUCT EX/STRUC ECO/TAC GP/REL ...CLASSIF GP/COMP IDEA/COMP GEN/LAWS 20 WEBER/MAX. PAGE 126 F2490
CONSTRUC PROC/MFG ADMIN PLAN

S59
TEITSWORTH C.S.,"GROWING ROLE OF THE COMPANY ECONOMIST." USA+45 PLAN PROB/SOLV CAP/ISM ECO/TAC ADMIN ATTIT MGT. PAGE 129 F2541
INDUS CONSULT UTIL DECISION

S59
ZAUBERMAN A.,"SOVIET BLOC ECONOMIC INTEGRATION." COM CULTURE INTELL ECO/DEV INDUS TOP/EX ACT/RES PLAN ECO/TAC INT/TRADE ROUTINE CHOOSE ATTIT ...TIME/SEQ 20. PAGE 150 F2958
MARKET INT/ORG USSR TOTALISM

C59
KURIHARA K.L.,"THE KEYNESIAN THEORY OF ECONOMIC DEVELOPMENT." WOR+45 WOR-45 PLAN OPTIMAL PRODUC ...CONCPT BIBLIOG 20. PAGE 74 F1451
ECO/DEV ECO/UNDEV OP/RES TEC/DEV

B60
ALLEN R.L.,SOVIET ECONOMIC WARFARE. USSR FINAN INDUS NAT/G PLAN TEC/DEV FOR/AID DETER WEALTH ...TREND GEN/LAWS FOR/TRADE 20. PAGE 4 F0072
COM ECO/TAC

B60
APTHEKER H.,DISARMAMENT AND THE AMERICAN ECONOMY: A SYMPOSIUM. FUT USA+45 ECO/DEV DIST/IND FINAN INDUS PROC/MFG LABOR NAT/G POL/PAR CONSULT PLAN CAP/ISM INT/TRADE PEACE ATTIT MORAL WEALTH...TREND GEN/LAWS TOT/POP 20. PAGE 6 F0110
MARXIST ARMS/CONT

B60
ATOMIC INDUSTRIAL FORUM,ATOMS FOR INDUSTRY: WORLD FORUM. WOR+45 FINAN COST UTIL...JURID ANTHOL 20. PAGE 7 F0137
NUC/PWR INDUS PLAN PROB/SOLV

B60
BAYER H.,WIRTSCHAFTSPROGNOSE UND WIRTSCHAFTSGESTALTUNG. GERMANY NETHERLAND MARKET PLAN CAP/ISM DEBATE...NAT/COMP 20. PAGE 12 F0220
ECO/DEV ECO/UNDEV FINAN POLICY

B60
BISSON A.,INSTITUTIONS FINANCIERES ET ECONOMIQUES EN FRANCE. FRANCE INDUS OP/RES TAX COST PRODUC ...CHARTS 20. PAGE 15 F0289
FINAN BUDGET PLAN

B60
BLACK E.R.,THE DIPLOMACY OF ECONOMIC DEVELOPMENT. WOR+45 CONSULT PLAN TEC/DEV DIPLOM ECO/TAC FOR/AID ...CONCPT TREND 20. PAGE 15 F0290
ECO/UNDEV ACT/RES

B60
BOULDING K.E.,LINEAR PROGRAMMING AND THE THEORY OF THE FIRM. ACT/RES PLAN...MGT MATH. PAGE 17 F0323
LG/CO NEW/IDEA COMPUTER

B60
BRYCE M.D.,INDUSTRIAL DEVELOPMENT: A GUIDE FOR ACCELERATING ECONOMIC GROWTH. WOR+45 FINAN MARKET COST EFFICIENCY PRODUC. PAGE 20 F0378
INDUS PLAN ECO/UNDEV TEC/DEV

B60
CAMPBELL R.W.,SOVIET ECONOMIC POWER. COM USA+45 DIST/IND MARKET TOP/EX ACT/RES CAP/ISM ECO/TAC DOMIN EDU/PROP ADMIN ROUTINE DRIVE...MATH TIME/SEQ CHARTS WORK 20. PAGE 21 F0409
ECO/DEV PLAN SOCISM USSR

B60
DIA M.,REFLEXIONS SUR L'ECONOMIE DE L'AFRIQUE NOIRE (REV. ED.). CULTURE ECO/UNDEV CREATE TEC/DEV DIPLOM INT/TRADE OPTIMAL ATTIT...POLICY 20. PAGE 32 F0631
AFR ECO/TAC SOCISM PLAN

B60
EELLS R.S.F.,THE MEANING OF MODERN BUSINESS. LOC/G NAT/G NEIGH EX/STRUC PARTIC GP/REL INGP/REL DECISION. PAGE 36 F0706
LG/CO REPRESENT POLICY PLAN

B60
FIRESTONE J.M.,FEDERAL RECEIPTS AND EXPENDITURES DURING BUSINESS CYCLES, 1879-1958. USA+45 USA-45 INDUS PLAN ECO/TAC TAX WAR COST...CHARTS 19/20. PAGE 41 F0801
FINAN INCOME BUDGET NAT/G

B60
FRANCIS R.G.,THE PREDICTIVE PROCESS. PLAN MARXISM ...DECISION SOC CONCPT NAT/COMP 19/20. PAGE 43 F0840
PREDICT PHIL/SCI TREND

B60
FRANCK P.G.,AFGHANISTAN: BETWEEN EAST AND WEST. AFGHANISTN AFR USA+45 USSR ECO/UNDEV PLAN ADMIN ROUTINE ATTIT PWR...STAT OBS CHARTS TOT/POP FOR/TRADE 20. PAGE 43 F0843
ECO/TAC TREND FOR/AID

B60
GARBARINO J.W.,HEALTH PLANS AND COLLECTIVE BARGAINING. USA+45 LABOR BARGAIN GP/REL WEALTH ...WELF/ST CHARTS 20 DEPT/HEW SAN/FRAN. PAGE 46 F0900
HEAL PLAN FINAN SERV/IND

B60
GILMORE D.R.,DEVELOPING THE "LITTLE" ECONOMIES. USA+45 FINAN LG/CO PROF/ORG VOL/ASSN CREATE ADMIN. PAGE 47 F0924
ECO/TAC LOC/G PROVS PLAN

B60
GONZALEZ NAVARRO M.,LA COLONIZACION EN MEXICO, 1877-1910. AGRI NAT/G PLAN PROB/SOLV INCOME ...POLICY JURID CENSUS 19/20 MEXIC/AMER MIGRATION. PAGE 48 F0947
ECO/UNDEV GEOG HABITAT COLONIAL

B60
GRANICK D.,THE RED EXECUTIVE. COM USA+45 SOCIETY ECO/DEV INDUS NAT/G POL/PAR EX/STRUC PLAN ECO/TAC EDU/PROP ADMIN EXEC ATTIT DRIVE...GP/COMP 20. PAGE 50 F0976
PWR STRATA USSR ELITES

B60
HEILPERIN M.A.,STUDIES IN ECONOMIC NATIONALISM. EUR+WWI MOD/EUR USA+45 ECO/DEV PLAN INT/TRADE TARIFFS WAR PRODUC PROFIT 18/20 KEYNES/JM. PAGE 58 F1140
ECO/TAC NAT/G NAT/LISM POLICY

B60
HITCH C.J.,THE ECONOMICS OF DEFENSE IN THE NUCLEAR AGE. USA+45 WOR+45 CREATE PLAN NUC/PWR ATTIT ...CON/ANAL CHARTS HYPO/EXP NATO 20. PAGE 60 F1179
R+D FORCES

B60
HOSELITZ B.F.,THEORIES OF ECONOMIC GROWTH. UK WOR+45 WOR-45 ECO/UNDEV PLAN INT/TRADE KNOWL ...CONCPT METH/CNCPT TIME/SEQ GEN/LAWS TOT/POP. PAGE 62 F1220
ECO/DEV INTELL

B60
ILLINOIS U BUR COMMUNITY PLAN,PROCEEDINGS OF ILLINOIS STATEWIDE PLANNING CONFERENCE 1960. USA+45 FINAN LOC/G ACT/RES LEAD GOV/REL GP/REL WEALTH MUNICH 20 ILLINOIS. PAGE 64 F1260
PLAN DELIB/GP VOL/ASSN

B60
KENEN P.B.,GIANT AMONG NATIONS: PROBLEMS IN UNITED STATES FOREIGN ECONOMIC POLICY. AFR USA+45 FINAN DIPLOM TARIFFS BAL/PAY WEALTH 20. PAGE 70 F1376
FOR/AID ECO/UNDEV INT/TRADE PLAN

B60
KENEN P.B.,BRITISH MONETARY POLICY AND THE BALANCE OF PAYMENTS 1951-57. UK PLAN BUDGET ECO/TAC INT/TRADE PAY PRICE COST ATTIT 20. PAGE 70 F1377
BAL/PAY PROB/SOLV FINAN NAT/G

B60
KILLOUGH H.B.,INTERNATIONAL ECONOMICS. PLAN PROB/SOLV FOR/AID TARIFFS CONTROL BAL/PAY...POLICY CHARTS T 20. PAGE 71 F1388
CONCPT ECO/UNDEV INT/ORG INT/TRADE

B60
LENCZOWSKI G.,OIL AND STATE IN THE MIDDLE EAST. FUT IRAN LAW ECO/UNDEV EXTR/IND NAT/G TOP/EX PLAN TEC/DEV ECO/TAC LEGIT ADMIN COERCE ATTIT ALL/VALS PWR...CHARTS 20. PAGE 78 F1519
ISLAM INDUS NAT/LISM

B60
LERNER A.P.,THE ECONOMICS OF CONTROL. USA+45 ECO/UNDEV INT/ORG ACT/RES PLAN CAP/ISM INT/TRADE ATTIT WEALTH...SOC MATH STAT GEN/LAWS INDEX 20. PAGE 78 F1530
ECO/DEV ROUTINE ECO/TAC SOCISM

B60
MYRDAL G.,BEYOND THE WELFARE STATE: ECONOMIC PLANNING AND ITS IMPLICATIONS. EUR+WWI FUT USA+45 USSR ECO/DEV ECO/UNDEV TEC/DEV SKILL WEALTH...PSY TREND FOR/TRADE 20. PAGE 96 F1881
PLAN ECO/TAC CAP/ISM

B60
NEALE A.D.,THE FLOW OF RESOURCES FROM RICH TO POOR. WOR+45 ECO/DEV ECO/UNDEV FINAN INDUS NAT/G PLAN EFFICIENCY WEALTH...POLICY NAT/COMP 20 RESOURCE/N. PAGE 97 F1905
FOR/AID DIPLOM METH/CNCPT

B60
PENNSYLVANIA ECONOMY LEAGUE,URBAN RENEWAL IMPACT STUDY: ADMINISTRATIVE-LEGAL-FISCAL. USA+45 FINAN LOC/G NEIGH ADMIN EFFICIENCY...CENSUS CHARTS MUNICH 20 PENNSYLVAN. PAGE 105 F2059
PLAN BUDGET ADJUD

B60
POOLEY B.J.,THE EVOLUTION OF BRITISH PLANNING LEGISLATION. UK ECO/DEV LOC/G CONSULT DELIB/GP ADMIN MUNICH 20 URBAN/RNWL. PAGE 107 F2104
PLAN LEGIS PROB/SOLV

B60
RAO V.K.R.,INTERNATIONAL AID FOR ECONOMIC DEVELOPMENT - POSSIBILITIES AND LIMITATIONS. FINAN PLAN TEC/DEV ADMIN TASK EFFICIENCY...POLICY SOC METH/CNCPT CHARTS 20 UN. PAGE 109 F2147
FOR/AID DIPLOM INT/ORG ECO/UNDEV

B60
RICHARDSON G.B.,INFORMATION AND INVESTMENT. PLAN
ECO/DEV

PROB/SOLV CAP/ISM ECO/TAC KNOWL...CONCPT 20 MONEY. PAGE 111 F2184 EQUILIB FINAN PHIL/SCI

B60
ROEPKE W.,A HUMANE ECONOMY: THE SOCIAL FRAMEWORK OF THE FREE MARKET. FUT USSR WOR+45 CULTURE SOCIETY ECO/DEV PLAN ECO/TAC ADMIN ATTIT PERSON RIGID/FLEX SUPEGO MORAL WEALTH SOCISM...POLICY OLD/LIB CONCPT TREND GEN/LAWS 20. PAGE 113 F2232 DRIVE EDU/PROP CAP/ISM

B60
SANTHANAM K.,UNION-STATE RELATIONS IN INDIA. INDIA FINAN PROVS PLAN ECO/TAC...LING 20. PAGE 116 F2280 FEDERAL GOV/REL CONSTN POLICY

B60
SERAPHIM H.J.,ZUR GRUNDLEGUNG WIRTSCHAFTSPOLITISCHER KONZEPTIONEN (SCHRIFTEN DES VEREINS FUR SOZIALPOLITIK, N.F. BAND 18). GERMANY/W WOR+45 ECO/DEV DELIB/GP ACT/RES ECO/TAC INGP/REL ORD/FREE...CONCPT IDEA/COMP GEN/LAWS 20. PAGE 120 F2358 POLICY PHIL/SCI PLAN

B60
SHONFIELD A.,THE ATTACK ON WORLD POVERTY. WOR+45 ECO/DEV ECO/UNDEV FINAN VOL/ASSN PLAN EDU/PROP DRIVE KNOWL WEALTH...CONT/OBS STAND/INT ORG/CHARTS TOT/POP UNESCO 20. PAGE 121 F2383 INT/ORG ECO/TAC FOR/AID INT/TRADE

B60
STANFORD RESEARCH INSTITUTE,AFRICAN DEVELOPMENT: A TEST FOR INTERNATIONAL COOPERATION. AFR USA+45 WOR+45 FINAN INT/ORG PLAN PROB/SOLV ECO/TAC INT/TRADE ADMIN...CHARTS 20. PAGE 125 F2467 FOR/AID ECO/UNDEV ATTIT DIPLOM

B60
STEIN E.,AMERICAN ENTERPRISE IN THE EUROPEAN COMMON MARKET: A LEGAL PROFILE. EUR+WWI FUT USA+45 SOCIETY STRUCT ECO/DEV NAT/G VOL/ASSN CONSULT PLAN TEC/DEV ECO/TAC INT/TRADE ADMIN ATTIT RIGID/FLEX PWR...MGT NEW/IDEA STAT TREND COMPUT/IR SIMUL EEC 20. PAGE 125 F2475 MARKET ADJUD INT/LAW

B60
THEOBALD R.,THE RICH AND THE POOR: A STUDY OF THE ECONOMICS OF RISING EXPECTATIONS. WOR+45 CONSTN ECO/DEV ECO/UNDEV INT/ORG NAT/G PLAN FOR/AID ROUTINE BAL/PAY ORD/FREE PWR WEALTH...GEOG TREND WORK FOR/TRADE 20. PAGE 129 F2553 ECO/TAC INT/TRADE

B60
US GENERAL ACCOUNTING OFFICE,EXAMINATION OF ECONOMIC AND TECHNICAL ASSISTANCE PROGRAM FOR GUATEMALA. GUATEMALA L/A+17C USA+45 FINAN INDUS PLAN...POLICY STAT CHARTS 20 DEPT/STATE. PAGE 136 F2680 FOR/AID ECO/UNDEV TEC/DEV NAT/G

B60
US HOUSE COMM GOVT OPERATIONS,OPERATIONS OF THE DEVELOPMENT LOAN FUND: HEARINGS (COMMITTEE ON GOVERNMENT OPERATIONS). USA+45 PLAN BUDGET DIPLOM GOV/REL COST...CHARTS 20 CONGRESS DEPT/STATE AID. PAGE 137 F2698 FINAN FOR/AID ECO/TAC EFFICIENCY

B60
US SENATE COMM ON COMMERCE,URBAN MASS TRANSPORTATION. FUT USA+45 AIR ECO/DEV FINAN LOC/G LEGIS CREATE PROB/SOLV TEC/DEV MUNICH 20 PUB/TRANS. PAGE 139 F2732 DIST/IND PLAN NAT/G LAW

B60
VERNON R.,METROPOLIS 1985. LOC/G PLAN TAX LEAD PWR MUNICH. PAGE 141 F2780 REGION ECO/TAC DECISION

B60
WATSON D.S.,ECONOMIC POLICY: BUSINESS AND GOVERNMENT. USA+45 FINAN LABOR PLAN BUDGET INT/TRADE GP/REL WEALTH LAISSEZ...CHARTS T. PAGE 144 F2832 ECO/TAC NAT/G POLICY ECO/DEV

L60
SPENGLER J.J.,"ECONOMIC DEVELOPMENT: POLITICAL PRECONDITIONS AND POLITICAL CONSEQUENCE." WOR+45 STRUCT ECO/UNDEV NAT/G PLAN ECO/TAC EDU/PROP ATTIT ORD/FREE WEALTH SOCISM...SOC CONCPT TREND SIMUL GEN/METH WORK 20. PAGE 124 F2452 TEC/DEV METH/CNCPT CAP/ISM

S60
BARNETT H.J.,"RESEARCH AND DEVELOPMENT, ECONOMIC GROWTH, AND NATIONAL SECURITY." AFR USA+45 R+D CREATE ECO/TAC ATTIT DRIVE PWR...POLICY SOC METH/CNCPT QUANT STAT TIME/SEQ ORG/CHARTS LOG/LING 20. PAGE 10 F0190 ACT/RES PLAN

S60
BECKER A.S.,"COMPARISIONS OF UNITED STATES AND USSR NATIONAL OUTPUT: SOME RULES OF THE GAME." COM USA+45 ECO/DEV AGRI DIST/IND INDUS R+D CONSULT PLAN ECO/TAC RIGID/FLEX KNOWL...METH/CNCPT CHARTS 20. PAGE 12 F0227 STAT USSR

S60
BERG E.J.,"ECONOMIC BASIS OF POLITICAL CHOICE IN FRENCH WEST AFRICA." FRANCE ECO/UNDEV AGRI INDUS NAT/G PLAN LEGIT COLONIAL REGION ATTIT PWR WEALTH ...CONCPT FOR/TRADE 20. PAGE 13 F0257 AFR ECO/TAC

S60
BUTLER W.F.,"ECONOMIC PROGRESS IN LATIN AMERICA." L/A+17C USA+45 ECO/UNDEV AGRI FINAN NAT/G PLAN ECO/TAC FOR/AID ADMIN WEALTH...OLD/LIB TOT/POP 20. PAGE 21 F0397 INDUS ACT/RES

S60
ENKE S.,"THE ECONOMIES OF GOVERNMENT PAYMENTS TO LIMIT POPULATION." FUT INDIA WOR+45 CULTURE FINAN NAT/G CONSULT PLAN LEGIT CONTROL COST ATTIT RIGID/FLEX HEALTH WEALTH...STAT OBS CHARTS TOT/POP VAL/FREE 20. PAGE 38 F0736 FAM ACT/RES

S60
FRANKEL S.H.,"ECONOMIC ASPECTS OF POLITICAL INDEPENDENCE IN AFRICA." AFR FUT SOCIETY ECO/UNDEV COM/IND FINAN LEGIS PLAN TEC/DEV CAP/ISM ECO/TAC INT/TRADE ADMIN ATTIT DRIVE RIGID/FLEX PWR WEALTH ...MGT NEW/IDEA MATH TIME/SEQ VAL/FREE 20. PAGE 43 F0846 NAT/G FOR/AID

S60
FRENCH J.R.P. JR.,"AN EXPERIMENT ON PARTICIPATION IN A NORWEGIAN FACTORY:INTERPERSONAL DIMENSIONS OF DECISION-MAKING." LABOR LEAD PERS/REL EFFICIENCY PRODUC...DECISION SOC CHARTS SOC/EXP. PAGE 44 F0853 INDUS PLAN RIGID/FLEX GP/REL

S60
GARNICK D.H.,"ON THE ECONOMIC FEASIBILITY OF A MIDDLE EASTERN COMMON MARKET." AFR ISLAM CULTURE INDUS NAT/G PLAN TEC/DEV ECO/TAC ADMIN ATTIT DRIVE RIGID/FLEX...PLURIST STAT TREND GEN/LAWS 20. PAGE 46 F0907 MARKET INT/TRADE

S60
GROSSMAN G.,"SOVIET GROWTH: ROUTINE, INERTIA, AND PRESSURE." COM STRATA NAT/G DELIB/GP PLAN TEC/DEV ECO/TAC EDU/PROP ADMIN ROUTINE DRIVE WEALTH 20. PAGE 52 F1007 POL/PAR ECO/DEV AFR USSR

S60
HERRERA F.,"THE INTER-AMERICAN DEVELOPMENT BANK." USA+45 ECO/UNDEV INT/ORG CONSULT DELIB/GP PLAN ECO/TAC INT/TRADE ROUTINE WEALTH...STAT TERR/GP 20. PAGE 59 F1153 L/A+17C FINAN FOR/AID REGION

S60
HERZ J.H.,"EAST GERMANY: PROGRESS AND PROSPECTS." COM AGRI FINAN INDUS LOC/G NAT/G FORCES PLAN TEC/DEV DOMIN ADMIN COERCE DRIVE PERCEPT RIGID/FLEX MORAL ORD/FREE PWR...MARXIST PSY SOC RECORD STERTYP WORK. PAGE 59 F1158 POL/PAR STRUCT GERMANY

S60
HOOVER C.B.,"NATIONAL POLICY AND RATES OF ECONOMIC GROWTH: THE US SOVIET RUSSIA AND WESTERN EUROPE." COM EUR+WWI USA+45 USSR NAT/G PLAN ECO/TAC PWR WEALTH...MATH STAT GEN/LAWS 20. PAGE 61 F1207 ECO/DEV ACT/RES

S60
JAFFEE A.J.,"POPULATION TRENDS AND CONTROLS IN UNDERDEVELOPED COUNTRIES." AFR FUT ISLAM L/A+17C S/ASIA CULTURE R+D FAM ACT/RES PLAN EDU/PROP BIO/SOC RIGID/FLEX HEALTH...SOC STAT OBS CHARTS 20. PAGE 66 F1303 ECO/UNDEV GEOG

S60
KELLOGG C.E.,"TRANSFER OF BASIC SKILLS OF FOOD PRODUCTION." AFR FUT S/ASIA STRATA ECO/UNDEV LABOR VOL/ASSN RIGID/FLEX...OLD/LIB SOCIALIST NEW/IDEA STAT PROJ/TEST GEN/LAWS 20. PAGE 70 F1370 AGRI PLAN

S60
MARTIN E.M.,"NEW TRENDS IN UNITED STATES ECONOMIC FOREIGN POLICY." USA+45 INTELL DELIB/GP FOR/AID INT/TRADE ROUTINE BAL/PAY...RELATIV TRUE/GP 20. PAGE 86 F1682 NAT/G PLAN DIPLOM

S60
MIKESELL R.F.,"AMERICA'S ECONOMIC RESPONSIBILITY AS A GREAT POWER." COM FUT USA+45 USSR WOR+45 INT/ORG PLAN ECO/TAC FOR/AID EDU/PROP CHOOSE WEALTH ...POLICY 20. PAGE 91 F1781 ECO/UNDEV BAL/PWR CAP/ISM

S60
MILLER A.S.,"SOME OBSERVATIONS ON THE POLITICAL ECONOMY OF POPULATION GROWTH." FUT USA+45 ECO/DEV R+D CONSULT PLAN TEC/DEV ECO/TAC ROUTINE BIO/SOC WEALTH...POLICY OBS. PAGE 91 F1790 SOCIETY GEOG

S60
NANES A.,"THE EUROPEAN COMMUNITY AND THE UNITED STATES: EVOLVING RELATIONS." EUR+WWI USA+45 WOR+45 ECO/UNDEV MARKET NAT/G DELIB/GP PLAN LEGIT ATTIT PWR WEALTH...CONCPT STAT TIME/SEQ CON/ANAL EEC METH/GP OEEC 20 EURATOM. PAGE 96 F1889 INT/ORG REGION

S60
POLLARD J.A.,"EMERGING PATTERNS OF CORPORATE GIVING." FINAN DELIB/GP PLAN EDU/PROP CENTRAL TREND. PAGE 107 F2098 GIVE LG/CO ADMIN MGT

S60
PYE L.W.,"SOVIET AND AMERICAN STYLES IN FOREIGN AID." COM USA+45 USSR WOR+45 NAT/G PLAN ECO/TAC ROUTINE RIGID/FLEX...POLICY CONCPT TREND GEN/LAWS TOT/POP 20. PAGE 108 F2132 ECO/UNDEV ATTIT FOR/AID

S60
RICHTER J.H.,"TOWARDS AN INTERNATIONAL POLICY ON AGRICULTURAL TRADE." EUR+WWI USA+45 ECO/DEV NAT/G PLAN ECO/TAC ATTIT PWR WEALTH...CONCPT GEN/LAWS 20. PAGE 111 F2187 AGRI INT/ORG

S60
RIVKIN A.,"AFRICAN ECONOMIC DEVELOPMENT: ADVANCED AFR

TECHNOLOGY AND THE STAGES OF GROWTH." CULTURE ECO/UNDEV AGRI COM/IND EXTR/IND PLAN ECO/TAC ATTIT DRIVE RIGID/FLEX SKILL WEALTH...MGT SOC GEN/LAWS FOR/TRADE WORK TOT/POP 20. PAGE 111 F2195 TEC/DEV FOR/AID

N60

COMMITTEE ECONOMIC DEVELOPMENT,GUIDING METROPOLITAN GROWTH (PAMPHLET). USA+45 LOC/G NAT/G PROF/ORG ACT/RES PLAN...SOC/WK MUNICH. PAGE 27 F0517 GEOG INDUS HEALTH

B61

ASHER R.E.,GRANTS, LOANS, AND LOCAL CURRENCIES; THEIR ROLE IN FOREIGN AID. AFR USA+45 ECO/UNDEV INT/ORG ACT/RES PLAN ECO/TAC GIVE CONTROL WEALTH 20. PAGE 7 F0130 FOR/AID FINAN NAT/G BUDGET

B61

AUBREY H.G.,COEXISTENCE: ECONOMIC CHALLENGE AND RESPONSE. AFR USSR WOR+45 ACT/RES BAL/PWR CAP/ISM DIPLOM ECO/TAC FOR/AID INT/TRADE PEACE SOCISM ...METH/COMP NAT/COMP. PAGE 7 F0139 POLICY ECO/UNDEV PLAN COM

B61

BALASSA B.,THE THEORY OF ECONOMIC INTEGRATION. EUR+WWI L/A+17C MOD/EUR WOR+45 ECO/UNDEV MARKET INT/ORG NAT/G VOL/ASSN DELIB/GP PLAN CAP/ISM ECO/TAC...MAJORIT FOR/TRADE OEEC 20. PAGE 8 F0157 ECO/DEV ACT/RES INT/TRADE

B61

BAUER P.T.,INDIAN ECONOMIC POLICY AND DEVELOPMENT. INDIA STRATA AGRI FINAN POL/PAR BUDGET FOR/AID GOV/REL EFFICIENCY...CENSUS 20. PAGE 11 F0216 ECO/UNDEV ECO/TAC POLICY PLAN

B61

BREWIS T.N.,CANADIAN ECONOMIC POLICY. AFR CANADA BUDGET CAP/ISM INT/TRADE RATION TARIFFS TAX PRICE CONTROL ROUTINE FEDERAL INCOME PRODUC 20. PAGE 18 F0348 ECO/DEV ECO/TAC NAT/G PLAN

B61

CANTERBERY E.R.,THE PRESIDENT'S COUNCIL OF ECONOMIC ADVISERS. AFR USA+45 FINAN LABOR NAT/G PLAN ADMIN OPTIMAL WEALTH 20 EISNHWR/DD PRESIDENT TRUMAN/HS KEYNES/JM. PAGE 21 F0413 ECO/TAC OP/RES EXEC CHIEF

B61

DEWITT N.,EDUCATION AND PROFESSIONAL EMPLOYMENT IN THE USSR. USSR PROF/ORG WORKER PLAN ADMIN UTIL AGE/C AGE/Y MARXISM...STAT CHARTS 20. PAGE 32 F0629 EDU/PROP ACADEM SCHOOL INTELL

B61

DIMOCK M.E.,BUSINESS AND GOVERNMENT (4TH ED.). AGRI FINAN OP/RES PLAN BUDGET DIPLOM LOBBY NUC/PWR NEW/LIB SOCISM...POLICY BIBLIOG 20. PAGE 33 F0641 NAT/G INDUS LABOR ECO/TAC

B61

ELLIS H.S.,ECONOMIC DEVELOPMENT FOR LATIN AMERICA. L/A+17C AGRI FINAN INDUS FOR/AID GP/REL BAL/PAY DEMAND...ANTHOL 20 INTL/ECON. PAGE 37 F0723 ECO/UNDEV ECO/TAC PLAN INT/TRADE

B61

FEARN H.,AN AFRICAN ECONOMY. AFR EUR+WWI PLAN COLONIAL WEALTH...CONT/OBS TREND EEC VAL/FREE 20. PAGE 39 F0770 ECO/UNDEV

B61

FRIEDMANN W.G.,JOINT INTERNATIONAL BUSINESS VENTURES. ASIA ISLAM L/A+17C ECO/DEV DIST/IND FINAN PROC/MFG FACE/GP LG/CO NAT/G VOL/ASSN CONSULT EX/STRUC PLAN ADMIN ROUTINE WEALTH...OLD/LIB FOR/TRADE WORK 20. PAGE 44 F0865 ECO/UNDEV INT/TRADE

B61

HICKS U.K.,FEDERALISM AND ECONOMIC GROWTH IN UNDERDEVELOPED COUNTRIES. WOR+45 WOR-45 FINAN NAT/G PLAN BUDGET DIPLOM INT/TRADE DEMAND WEALTH...ANTHOL 20. PAGE 59 F1167 ECO/UNDEV ECO/TAC FEDERAL CONSTN

B61

HORVATH B.,THE CHARACTERISTICS OF YUGOSLAV ECONOMIC DEVELOPMENT. COM ECO/UNDEV AGRI INDUS PLAN CAP/ISM ECO/TAC ROUTINE WEALTH...SOCIALIST STAT CHARTS STERTYP WORK 20. PAGE 62 F1217 ACT/RES YUGOSLAVIA

B61

INDUSTRIAL COUN SOC-ECO STU,THE SWEDISH ECONOMY AND THE UNDERDEVELOPED COUNTRIES. SWEDEN INDUS DELIB/GP TEC/DEV INT/TRADE EDU/PROP COLONIAL DRIVE...CHARTS 20. PAGE 64 F1264 FOR/AID ECO/UNDEV PLAN FINAN

B61

INTL BANKING SUMMER SCHOOL,TRENDS IN BANK CREDIT AND FINANCE. EUR+WWI NETHERLAND ECO/DEV PROF/ORG PLAN BUDGET 20 EEC. PAGE 65 F1283 FINAN ECO/TAC NAT/G LG/CO

B61

KITZINGER V.W.,THE CHALLENGE OF THE COMMON MARKET. EUR+WWI ECO/DEV DIST/IND PLAN ECO/TAC INT/TRADE LEGIT ATTIT PWR WEALTH...TIME/SEQ TREND CHARTS EEC 20. PAGE 71 F1403 MARKET INT/ORG UK

B61

KOVNER M.,THE CHALLENGE OF COEXISTENCE: A STUDY OF SOVIET ECONOMIC DIPLOMACY. COM FUT ECO/DEV ECO/UNDEV PLAN EDU/PROP DETER SKILL...OBS VAL/FREE 20. PAGE 73 F1430 PWR DIPLOM USSR AFR

B61

LAHAYE R.,LES ENTREPRISES PUBLIQUES AU MAROC. FRANCE MOROCCO LAW DIST/IND EXTR/IND FINAN CONSULT PLAN TEC/DEV ADMIN AGREE CONTROL OWN...POLICY 20. PAGE 74 F1460 NAT/G INDUS ECO/UNDEV ECO/TAC

B61

LEE R.R.,ENGINEERING-ECONOMIC PLANNING MISCELLANEOUS SUBJECTS: A SELECTED BIBLIOGRAPHY (MIMEOGRAPHED). FINAN LOC/G NEIGH ADMIN CONTROL INGP/REL HABITAT...GEOG MGT SOC/WK MUNICH 20 RESOURCE/N. PAGE 77 F1509 BIBLIOG/A PLAN REGION

B61

MACMAHON A.W.,DELEGATION AND AUTONOMY. INDIA STRUCT LEGIS BARGAIN BUDGET ECO/TAC LEGIT EXEC REPRESENT GOV/REL CENTRAL DEMAND EFFICIENCY PRODUC. PAGE 84 F1637 ADMIN PLAN FEDERAL

B61

MARX K.,THE COMMUNIST MANIFESTO. IN (MENDEL A. ESSENTIAL WORKS OF MARXISM, NEW YORK: BANTAM. FUT MOD/EUR CULTURE ECO/DEV ECO/UNDEV AGRI FINAN INDUS MARKET PROC/MFG LABOR POL/PAR CONSULT FORCES CREATE PLAN ADMIN ATTIT DRIVE RIGID/FLEX ORD/FREE PWR RESPECT MARX/KARL MUNICH WORK. PAGE 86 F1691 COM NEW/IDEA CAP/ISM REV

B61

MAYNE A.,DESIGNING AND ADMINISTERING A REGIONAL ECONOMIC DEVELOPMENT PLAN WITH SPECIFIC REFERENCE TO PUERTO RICO (PAMPHLET). PUERT/RICO SOCIETY NAT/G DELIB/GP REGION...DECISION 20. PAGE 87 F1707 ECO/UNDEV PLAN CREATE ADMIN

B61

MEZERIK A.G.,ECONOMIC DEVELOPMENT AIDS FOR UNDERDEVELOPED COUNTRIES. WOR+45 FINAN LEGIS PROB/SOLV TEC/DEV DIPLOM FOR/AID GIVE TASK WAR 20 UN. PAGE 91 F1776 ECO/UNDEV INT/ORG WEALTH PLAN

B61

NEW JERSEY LEGISLATURE-SENATE,PUBLIC HEARINGS BEFORE COMMITTEE ON REVISION AND AMENDMENT OF LAWS ON SENATE BILL NO. 8. USA+45 FINAN PROVS WORKER ACT/RES PLAN BUDGET TAX CRIME...IDEA/COMP MUNICH 20 NEW/JERSEY URBAN/RNWL. PAGE 98 F1919 LEGIS INDUS PROB/SOLV

B61

NOVE A.,THE SOVIET ECONOMY. USSR ECO/DEV FINAN NAT/G ECO/TAC PRICE ADMIN EFFICIENCY MARXISM ...TREND BIBLIOG 20. PAGE 99 F1943 PLAN PRODUC POLICY

B61

SACKS S.,FINANCING GOVERNMENT IN A METROPOLITAN GOVERNMENT. USA+45 ECO/DEV R+D LOC/G GOV/REL ...BIBLIOG MUNICH 20 CLEVELAND. PAGE 115 F2269 FINAN PLAN BUDGET

B61

SHARP W.R.,FIELD ADMINISTRATION IN THE UNITED NATION SYSTEM: THE CONDUCT OF INTERNATIONAL ECONOMIC AND SOCIAL PROGRAMS. FUT WOR+45 CONSTN SOCIETY ECO/UNDEV R+D DELIB/GP ACT/RES PLAN TEC/DEV EDU/PROP EXEC ROUTINE HEALTH WEALTH...HUM CONCPT CHARTS METH ILO UNESCO GP VAL/FREE UN 20. PAGE 120 F2369 INT/ORG CONSULT

B61

SHONFIELD A.,ECONOMIC GROWTH AND INFLATION; A STUDY OF INDIAN PLANNING. AFR INDIA AGRI INDUS TEC/DEV CONTROL DEMAND UTIL 20. PAGE 121 F2384 ECO/UNDEV PRICE PLAN BUDGET

B61

STOCKING G.W.,WORKABLE COMPETITION AND ANTITRUST POLICY. USA+45 NAT/G CONSULT PLAN PRICE GOV/REL COST DEMAND PROFIT...POLICY 20. PAGE 126 F2491 LG/CO INDUS ECO/TAC CONTROL

B61

UNIVS-NATL BUR COMM ECO RES,PUBLIC FINANCES: NEEDS, SOURCES, AND UTILIZATION. USA+45 FORCES PLAN TAX CONFER PRICE FEDERAL UTIL...ANTHOL MUNICH 20. PAGE 133 F2623 NAT/G FINAN DECISION BUDGET

B61

WAGLE S.S.,TECHNIQUE OF PLANNING FOR ACCELERATED ECONOMIC GROWTH OF UNDERDEVELOPED COUNTRIES. WOR+45 ACT/RES PROB/SOLV RATION BAL/PAY DEMAND INCOME 20. PAGE 142 F2798 ECO/UNDEV PLAN INDUS ECO/TAC

B61

WARD B.J.,INDIA AND THE WEST. INDIA UK USA+45 INT/TRADE GIVE COLONIAL ATTIT MARXISM 19/20. PAGE 143 F2817 PLAN ECO/UNDEV ECO/TAC FOR/AID

B61

WILSON T.,INFLATION. FINAN PLAN CAP/ISM PRICE CONTROL...CHARTS 20. PAGE 147 F2903 ECO/DEV ECO/TAC POLICY COST

L61

CHENERY H.B.,"COMPARATIVE ADVANTAGE AND DEVELOPMENT POLICY." FINAN INT/TRADE RATION OPTIMAL...CHARTS METH/COMP GEN/LAWS BIBLIOG 20 RESOURCE/N. PAGE 24 F0463 ECO/UNDEV ECO/TAC PLAN EFFICIENCY

L61

JOHNSTON B.F.,"THE ROLE OF AGRICULTURE IN ECONOMIC DEVELOPMENT." FINAN PRODUC ROLE BIBLIOG. PAGE 68 F1332 AGRI ECO/UNDEV PLAN INDUS

S61

BARALL M.,"THE UNITED STATES GOVERNMENT RESPONDS." L/A+17C USA+45 SOCIETY NAT/G CREATE PLAN DIPLOM ECO/TAC ATTIT DRIVE RIGID/FLEX KNOWL SKILL WEALTH ECO/UNDEV ACT/RES FOR/AID

...METH/CNCPT TIME/SEQ GEN/METH 20. PAGE 9 F0176

S61
BENOIT E.,"THE PROPENSITY TO REDUCE THE NATIONAL DEBT OUT OF DEFENSE SAVINGS." FUT USA+45 SOCIETY R+D PLAN...WELF/ST SOC REC/INT STERTYP TOT/POP 20. PAGE 13 F0250
WEALTH ECO/TAC

S61
DEUTSCH K.W.,"NATIONAL INDUSTRIALIZATION AND THE DECLINING SHARE OF THE INTERNATIONAL ECONOMIC SECTOR." EUR+WWI FUT WOR+45 WOR-45 MARKET PLAN EDU/PROP WEALTH...WELF/ST OBS TESTS 20. PAGE 32 F0624
DIST/IND ECO/DEV INT/TRADE

S61
HAYTES W.,"THREE VIEWS ON THE SOVIET ECONOMIC THREAT." AFR COM USA+45 USA-45 USSR WOR+45 WOR-45 INDUS TEC/DEV ECO/TAC DOMIN ATTIT PERCEPT PWR FOR/TRADE 20. PAGE 57 F1128
ECO/DEV PLAN TOTALISM

S61
HEILBRONER R.L.,"DYNAMICS OF FOREIGN AID: PROBLEMS OF UNDERDEVELOPED NATIONS PLAGUE ASSISTANCE PROGRAM." FUT USA+45 WOR+45 STRATA NAT/G PLAN TEC/DEV ATTIT DRIVE WEALTH WORK 20. PAGE 58 F1135
ECO/UNDEV ECO/TAC FOR/AID

S61
LANFALUSSY A.,"EUROPE'S PROGRESS: DUE TO COMMON MARKET." EUR+WWI ECO/DEV DELIB/GP PLAN ECO/TAC ROUTINE WEALTH...GEOG TREND EEC TERR/GP 20. PAGE 75 F1473
INT/ORG MARKET

S61
LINDSAY F.A.,"PLANNING IN FOREIGN AFFAIRS: THE MISSING ELEMENT." FUT USA+45 ROUTINE SKILL...MGT TOT/POP 20. PAGE 80 F1572
ECO/DEV PLAN DIPLOM

S61
NEAL A.C.,"NEW ECONOMIC POLICIES FOR THE WEST." COM EUR+WWI FUT USA+45 WOR+45 ECO/DEV ECO/UNDEV INDUS MARKET ROUTINE HEALTH ORD/FREE PWR...OLD/LIB METH/CNCPT 20. PAGE 97 F1904
PLAN ECO/TAC

S61
NOVE A.,"THE SOVIET MODEL AND UNDERDEVELOPED COUNTRIES." COM FUT USSR WOR+45 CULTURE ECO/DEV POL/PAR FOR/AID EDU/PROP ADMIN MORAL WEALTH ...POLICY RECORD HIST/WRIT 20. PAGE 99 F1942
ECO/UNDEV PLAN

S61
RAY J.,"THE EUROPEAN FREE-TRADE ASSOCIATION AND ITS IMPACT ON INDIA'S TRADE." EUR+WWI FRANCE GERMANY INDIA S/ASIA UK NAT/G VOL/ASSN PLAN INT/TRADE ROUTINE WEALTH...STAT CHARTS TERR/GP CMN/WLTH EEC FOR/TRADE OEEC 20 EFTA. PAGE 109 F2155
ECO/DEV ECO/TAC

S61
VALLET R.,"IRAN: KEY TO THE MIDDLE EAST." COM IRAQ ISLAM KUWAIT LEBANON SAUDI/ARAB TURKEY ELITES SOCIETY INDUS PROC/MFG POL/PAR TOP/EX PLAN BAL/PWR DIPLOM ECO/TAC ALL/VALS...TREND FOR/TRADE CENTO 20. PAGE 140 F2760
NAT/G ECO/UNDEV IRAN

S61
VERNON R.,"A TRADE POLICY FOR THE 1960'S." COM FUT USA+45 WOR+45 ECO/DEV ECO/UNDEV FINAN TOP/EX ACT/RES...WELF/ST METH/CNCPT CONT/OBS TOT/POP 20. PAGE 141 F2781
PLAN INT/TRADE

S61
WILDAVSKY A.,"POLITICAL IMPLICATIONS OF BUDGETARY REFORM." AFR NAT/G POL/PAR DELIB/GP EX/STRUC ATTIT PWR CONGRESS. PAGE 146 F2881
BUDGET PLAN LEGIS

N61
US ADVISORY COMM INTERGOV REL,STATE AND LOCAL TAXATION ON PRIVATELY OWNED PROPERTY LOCATED ON FEDERAL AREAS: PROPOSED AMENDMENT OF BUCK ACT (PAMPHLET). USA+45 ACT/RES PLAN CONTROL GOV/REL INGP/REL OWN...POLICY JURID CHARTS GP/COMP 20. PAGE 133 F2629
PROVS LOC/G NAT/G TAX

B62
ROUND TABLE ON EUROPE'S ROLE IN LATIN AMERICAN DEVELOPMENT. EUR+WWI L/A+17C PLAN BAL/PAY UTIL ROLE WEALTH...CHARTS ANTHOL 20 UN INT/AM/DEV. PAGE 1 F0017
ECO/UNDEV FINAN TEC/DEV FOR/AID

B62
ALTMAN G.T.,INVISIBLE BARRIER: THE OPTIMUM GROWTH CURVE. USA+45 USA-45 ECO/DEV PLAN PAY CONTROL DEMAND OPTIMAL PRODUC WEALTH...STAT CHARTS 20. PAGE 4 F0080
INDUS FINAN ECO/TAC TAX

B62
BRANCH M.C.,THE CORPORATE PLANNING PROCESS. FINAN EX/STRUC EDU/PROP CONTROL LEAD GP/REL PERS/REL RATIONAL PERCEPT...MGT MATH PROBABIL STAT GAME. PAGE 18 F0338
PROF/ORG PLAN DECISION PERSON

B62
BUREAU OF NATIONAL AFFAIRS,FEDERAL-STATE REGULATION OF WELFARE FUNDS (REV. ED.). USA+45 LAW LEGIS DEBATE AGE/O 20 CONGRESS. PAGE 20 F0386
WELF/ST WEALTH PLAN SOC/WK

B62
CAIRNCROSS A.K.,FACTORS IN ECONOMIC DEVELOPMENT. WOR+45 ECO/UNDEV INDUS R+D LG/CO NAT/G EX/STRUC PLAN TEC/DEV ECO/TAC ATTIT HEALTH KNOWL PWR WEALTH ...TIME/SEQ GEN/LAWS TOT/POP TRUE/GP VAL/FREE 20. PAGE 21 F0399
MARKET ECO/DEV

B62
CHANDLER A.D.,STRATEGY AND STRUCTURE: CHAPTERS IN THE HISTORY OF THE INDUSTRIAL ENTERPRISE. USA+45 USA-45 ECO/DEV EX/STRUC ECO/TAC EXEC...DECISION 20. PAGE 23 F0446
LG/CO PLAN ADMIN FINAN

B62
CHAPIN F.S.,URBAN GROWTH DYNAMICS IN A REGIONAL CLUSTER OF CITIES. TEC/DEV ECO/TAC HABITAT...GEOG SOC MUNICH. PAGE 23 F0453
REGION PLAN

B62
COLLIER A.T.,MANAGEMENT, MEN, AND VALUES. INDUS FACE/GP EX/STRUC PLAN PROB/SOLV DEBATE SENIOR ADMIN PROFIT PERSON...PSY SOC 20. PAGE 26 F0505
MGT ATTIT PERS/REL DECISION

B62
CONGRES ECONOMISTES LANG FRAN,MONNAIE ET EXPANSION. AFR FRANCE PROB/SOLV BUDGET CENTRAL COST OPTIMAL PRODUC WEALTH 20. PAGE 27 F0524
FINAN PLAN EUR+WWI

B62
DIMOCK M.E.,THE NEW AMERICAN POLITICAL ECONOMY: A SYNTHESIS OF POLITICS AND ECONOMICS. USA+45 FINAN LG/CO PLAN ADMIN REGION GP/REL CENTRAL MORAL 20. PAGE 33 F0642
FEDERAL ECO/TAC NAT/G PARTIC

B62
DREIER J.C.,THE ALLIANCE FOR PROGRESS. L/A+17C USA+45 CULTURE ECO/DEV ECO/UNDEV NAT/G PLAN DIPLOM PWR 20 OAS ALL/PROG. PAGE 34 F0661
FOR/AID INT/ORG ECO/TAC POLICY

B62
EINZIG P.,THE HISTORY OF FOREIGN EXCHANGE. CHRIST-17C ISLAM MEDIT-7 PRE/AMER WOR+45 ECO/DEV FINAN PLAN ECO/TAC ATTIT KNOWL WEALTH...SIMUL GEN/LAWS. PAGE 37 F0714
MARKET TIME/SEQ INT/TRADE

B62
GRANICK D.,THE EUROPEAN EXECUTIVE. BELGIUM FRANCE GERMANY/W UK INDUS LABOR LG/CO SML/CO EX/STRUC PLAN TEC/DEV CAP/ISM COST DEMAND...POLICY CHARTS 20. PAGE 50 F0977
MGT ECO/DEV ECO/TAC EXEC

B62
HARRIS S.E.,THE ECONOMICS OF THE POLITICAL PARTIES. USA+45 FINAN CHIEF ACT/RES PLAN BUDGET GP/REL INGP/REL NEW/LIB...IDEA/COMP PERS/COMP 20 EISNHWR/DD KENNEDY/JF. PAGE 56 F1090
POLICY ECO/DEV NAT/G POL/PAR

B62
HOOVER C.B.,ECONOMIC SYSTEMS OF THE COMMONWEALTH. AFR CANADA INDIA UK ECO/DEV ECO/UNDEV AGRI INDUS TEC/DEV TARIFFS PRICE BAL/PAY DEMAND...SIMUL 20 AUSTRAL. PAGE 61 F1208
CAP/ISM SOCISM ECO/TAC PLAN

B62
HUHNE L.H.,FINANCING ECONOMIC DEVELOPMENT THROUGH NATIONAL AND INTERNATIONAL ORGANIZATIONS (THESIS; U OF WIS.). USA+45 INT/ORG PLAN GIVE GOV/REL WEALTH 20. PAGE 63 F1235
RATION FINAN FOR/AID ECO/UNDEV

B62
HUMPHREY D.D.,THE UNITED STATES AND THE COMMON MARKET. USA+45 INDUS MARKET INT/ORG PLAN EDU/PROP BAL/PAY DRIVE PWR WEALTH...TREND STERTYP FOR/TRADE EEC 20. PAGE 63 F1241
ATTIT ECO/TAC

B62
JOHNSON H.G.,MONEY, TRADE AND ECONOMIC GROWTH. ECO/DEV ECO/UNDEV FINAN COST WEALTH...POLICY SOC IDEA/COMP 20 KEYNES/JM MONEY. PAGE 67 F1324
PLAN BAL/PAY INT/TRADE ECO/TAC

B62
JORDAN A.A. JR.,FOREIGN AID AND THE DEFENSE OF SOUTHEAST ASIA. PAKISTAN VIETNAM/S FINAN PLAN BUDGET ECO/TAC DETER WAR ORD/FREE...POLICY DECISION CENSUS CHARTS BIBLIOG 20. PAGE 68 F1341
FOR/AID S/ASIA FORCES ECO/UNDEV

B62
KUHN T.E.,PUBLIC ENTERPRISES, PROJECT PLANNING AND ECONOMIC DEVELOPMENT (PAMPHLET). ECO/UNDEV FINAN PLAN ADMIN EFFICIENCY OWN...MGT STAT CHARTS ANTHOL 20. PAGE 74 F1447
ECO/DEV ECO/TAC LG/CO NAT/G

B62
LICHFIELD N.,COST-BENEFIT ANALYSIS IN URBAN REDEVELOPMENT. CONSTRUC LOC/G NEIGH ACT/RES PROB/SOLV TEC/DEV BUDGET TAX...DECISION STAT CHARTS SOC/EXP MUNICH 20. PAGE 80 F1558
PLAN COST GOV/REL

B62
MCCRONE G.,THE ECONOMICS OF SUBSIDING AGRICULTURE. UK ECO/DEV MARKET PLAN TARIFFS PROFIT 20 EEC. PAGE 88 F1725
AGRI BAL/PAY INT/TRADE LABOR

B62
MEANS G.C.,PRICING POWER AND THE PUBLIC INTEREST. PLAN PROB/SOLV COST EFFICIENCY PROFIT RIGID/FLEX WEALTH. PAGE 89 F1741
LG/CO EX/STRUC PRICE ECO/TAC

B62
MEANS G.C.,THE CORPORATE REVOLUTION IN AMERICA: ECONOMIC REALITY VS. ECONOMIC THEORY. USA+45 USA-45 INDUS WORKER PLAN CAP/ISM ADMIN...IDEA/COMP 20. PAGE 89 F1742
LG/CO MARKET CONTROL PRICE

B62
MORGAN C.A.,LABOR ECONOMICS. LAW INDUS MARKET WORKER PLAN PROB/SOLV GOV/REL INCOME ROLE...T 20
LABOR ECO/TAC

DEPT/LABOR NLRB. PAGE 93 F1829 ECO/DEV CAP/ISM

B62
MOUSSA P.,THE UNDERPRIVILEGED NATIONS. FINAN INT/ORG PLAN PROB/SOLV CAP/ISM GIVE TASK WEALTH ...POLICY SOC IND 20. PAGE 94 F1850 ECO/UNDEV NAT/G DIPLOM FOR/AID

B62
MOWITZ R.J.,PROFILE OF A METROPOLIS: A CASE BOOK. COM/IND CONSTRUC INDUS PUB/INST PLAN TEC/DEV LEAD GP/REL...POLICY TECHNIC WELF/ST MUNICH. PAGE 94 F1851 DECISION ADMIN

B62
RIMALOV V.V.,ECONOMIC COOPERATION BETWEEN USSR AND UNDERDEVELOPED COUNTRIES. USSR FINAN TEC/DEV INT/TRADE DOMIN EDU/PROP COLONIAL NAT/LISM DRIVE SOVEREIGN...AUD/VIS 20. PAGE 111 F2194 FOR/AID PLAN ECO/UNDEV DIPLOM

B62
ROBERTSON B.C.,REGIONAL DEVELOPMENT IN THE EUROPEAN ECONOMIC COMMUNITY. EUR+WWI FRANCE FUT ITALY UK ECO/UNDEV WORKER ACT/RES PROB/SOLV TEC/DEV ECO/TAC INT/TRADE EEC. PAGE 112 F2209 PLAN ECO/DEV INT/ORG REGION

B62
ROBINSON A.D.,DUTCH ORGANIZED AGRICULTURE IN INTERNATIONAL POLITICS, 1945-1960. EUR+WWI NETHERLAND STRUCT ECO/DEV NAT/G VOL/ASSN CONSULT DELIB/GP PLAN TEC/DEV INT/TRADE EDU/PROP ATTIT RIGID/FLEX ALL/VALS...NEW/IDEA TREND EEC COMMUN 20. PAGE 112 F2215 AGRI INT/ORG

B62
SCHALLER H.G.,PUBLIC EXPENDITURE DECISIONS IN THE URBAN COMMUNITY: PREPARED FOR RESOURCES FOR THE FUTURE, INC. INDUS SERV/IND LOC/G PUB/INST PLAN PROB/SOLV BUDGET DEMAND PRODUC...CHARTS MUNICH. PAGE 116 F2289 FINAN DECISION

B62
SCHILLING W.R.,STRATEGY, POLITICS, AND DEFENSE BUDGETS. AFR USA+45 CHIEF LEGIS PLAN TEC/DEV BAL/PWR BUDGET NUC/PWR WAR CIVMIL/REL GOV/REL PWR 20 EISNHWR/DD. PAGE 117 F2297 NAT/G POLICY FORCES DETER

B62
SCHMITT H.A.,THE PATH TO EUROPEAN UNITY. EUR+WWI USA+45 PLAN TEC/DEV DIPLOM FOR/AID CONFER...INT/LAW 20 EEC EURCOALSTL MARSHL/PLN UNIFICA. PAGE 117 F2300 INT/ORG INT/TRADE REGION ECO/DEV

B62
SEN S.R.,THE STRATEGY FOR AGRICULTURAL DEVELOPMENT AND OTHER ESSAYS ON ECONOMIC POLICY AND PLANNING. INDIA FINAN ACT/RES TEC/DEV CAP/ISM PRICE...STAT 20. PAGE 119 F2354 ECO/UNDEV PLAN AGRI POLICY

B62
SMITH G.A. JR.,POLICY FORMULATION AND ADMINISTRATION: A CASEBOOK OF TOPMANAGEMENT PROBLEMS IN BUSINESS. EX/STRUC PLAN PROB/SOLV ADMIN CONTROL EXEC LEAD ROUTINE EFFICIENCY ATTIT MGT. PAGE 123 F2430 INDUS SOC/EXP TOP/EX DECISION

B62
THEOBALD R.,NATIONAL DEVELOPMENT EFFORTS (PAMPHLET). WOR+45 AGRI BUDGET FOR/AID INT/TRADE TAX 20. PAGE 129 F2555 ECO/UNDEV PLAN BAL/PAY WEALTH

B62
UNECA LIBRARY,BOOKS ON AFRICA IN THE UNECA LIBRARY. WOR+45 AGRI INT/ORG NAT/G PLAN WRITING REGION...SOC STAT UN. PAGE 132 F2605 BIBLIOG AFR ECO/UNDEV TEC/DEV

B62
UNECA LIBRARY,NEW ACQUISITIONS IN THE UNECA LIBRARY. LAW NAT/G PLAN PROB/SOLV TEC/DEV ADMIN REGION...GEOG SOC 20 UN. PAGE 132 F2606 BIBLIOG AFR ECO/UNDEV INT/ORG

B62
US CONGRESS JOINT ECO COMM,FACTORS AFFECTING THE UNITED STATES BALANCE OF PAYMENTS. USA+45 DELIB/GP PLAN DIPLOM FOR/AID PRODUC WEALTH...CHARTS 20 CONGRESS OEEC. PAGE 134 F2653 BAL/PAY INT/TRADE ECO/TAC FINAN

B62
WALSTON H.,AGRICULTURE UNDER COMMUNISM. CHINA/COM COM PROB/SOLV HAPPINESS RIGID/FLEX...POLICY METH/COMP 20. PAGE 143 F2811 AGRI MARXISM PLAN CREATE

B62
WARD B.,THE RICH NATIONS AND THE POOR NATIONS. FUT WOR+45 CULTURE ECO/DEV ECO/UNDEV PLAN CAP/ISM EDU/PROP REV NAT/LISM ATTIT DRIVE SOCISM...POLICY CONCPT TIME/SEQ 20. PAGE 143 F2816 ECO/TAC GEN/LAWS

B62
WENDT P.F.,HOUSING POLICY - THE SEARCH FOR SOLUTIONS. GERMANY/W SWEDEN UK USA+45 OP/RES HABITAT WEALTH...SOC/WK CHARTS 20. PAGE 145 F2856 PLAN ADMIN METH/COMP NAT/G

L62
BELSHAW D.G.R.,"PUBLIC INVESTMENT IN AGRICULTURE AND ECONOMIC DEVELOPMENT OF UGANDA" UGANDA AGRI INDUS R+D ECO/TAC RATION TAX PAY COLONIAL 20 WORLD/BANK. PAGE 13 F0242 ECO/UNDEV PLAN ADMIN CENTRAL

L62
ERDMANN H.H.,"ADMINISTRATIVE LAW AND FARM ECONOMICS." USA+45 LOC/G NAT/G PLAN PROB/SOLV LOBBY ...DECISION ANTHOL 20. PAGE 38 F0744 AGRI ADMIN ADJUD POLICY

L62
GALBRAITH J.K.,"ECONOMIC DEVELOPMENT IN PERSPECTIVE." CAP/ISM ECO/TAC ROUTINE ATTIT WEALTH ...TREND CHARTS SOC/EXP WORK TERR/GP 20. PAGE 45 F0884 ECO/UNDEV PLAN

L62
WATERSTON A.,"PLANNING IN MOROCCO, ORGANIZATION AND IMPLEMENTATION. BALTIMORE: HOPKINS ECON. DEVELOP. INT. BANK FOR." ISLAM ECO/DEV AGRI DIST/IND INDUS PROC/MFG SERV/IND LOC/G EX/STRUC ECO/TAC PWR WEALTH TOT/POP TRUE/GP METH/GP TERR/GP VAL/FREE 20. PAGE 144 F2829 NAT/G PLAN MOROCCO

S62
ALPERT P.,"ECONOMIC POLICIES AND PLANNING IN NEWLY INDEPENDENT AFRICA." PLAN ATTIT PWR WEALTH ...STERTYP GEN/LAWS VAL/FREE 20. PAGE 4 F0078 AFR ECO/DEV NAT/LISM COLONIAL

S62
BOKOR-SZEGO H.,"LA CONVENTION DE BELGRADE ET LE REGIME DU DANUBE." COM EUR+WWI WOR+45 STRUCT POL/PAR VOL/ASSN PLAN EDU/PROP WEALTH...TIME/SEQ METH/GP COMMUN 20. PAGE 16 F0308 INT/ORG TOTALISM YUGOSLAVIA

S62
IOVTCHOUK M.T.,"ON SOME THEORETICAL PRINCIPLES AND METHODS OF SOCIOLOGICAL INVESTIGATIONS (IN RUSSIAN)." FUT USA+45 STRATA R+D NAT/G POL/PAR TOP/EX ACT/RES PLAN ECO/TAC EDU/PROP ROUTINE ATTIT RIGID/FLEX MARXISM SOCISM...MARXIST METH/CNCPT OBS TREND NAT/COMP GEN/LAWS 20. PAGE 65 F1288 COM ECO/DEV CAP/ISM USSR

S62
KRISHNA K.G.V.,"PLANNING AND ECONOMIC DEVELOPMENT" AFR UGANDA AGRI INDUS R+D BUDGET RATION TAX COLONIAL 20. PAGE 73 F1441 ECO/UNDEV ECO/TAC NAT/LISM PLAN

S62
MILLIKEN M.,"NEW AND OLD CRITERIA FOR AID." WOR+45 ECO/DEV ECO/UNDEV ACT/RES PLAN ATTIT KNOWL...TREND CON/ANAL SIMUL GEN/METH TERR/GP 20. PAGE 92 F1796 USA+45 ECO/TAC FOR/AID

S62
MORGENTHAU H.J.,"A POLITICAL THEORY OF FOREIGN AID." ECO/UNDEV NAT/G DELIB/GP PLAN ECO/TAC EDU/PROP EXEC ORD/FREE RESPECT WEALTH...METH/CNCPT TREND 20. PAGE 93 F1833 USA+45 PHIL/SCI FOR/AID

S62
ZAUBERMAN A.,"SOVIET AND CHINESE STRATEGY FOR ECONOMIC GROWTH." ASIA CHINA/COM COM USSR STRATA VOL/ASSN PLAN ATTIT PWR...METH/CNCPT GEN/LAWS WORK TERR/GP 20. PAGE 150 F2959 ECO/DEV EDU/PROP

C62
JOINT ECONOMIC COMMITTEE,"DIMENSIONS OF SOVIET ECONOMIC POWER." USSR R+D FORCES ACT/RES OP/RES TEC/DEV...GEOG STAT BIBLIOG 20. PAGE 68 F1337 ECO/DEV PLAN PRODUC LABOR

B63
BERGSON A.,ECONOMIC TRENDS IN THE SOVIET UNION. USSR ECO/UNDEV AGRI NAT/G FORCES PLAN TEC/DEV INT/TRADE BAL/PAY...POLICY ANTHOL 20. PAGE 14 F0259 ECO/DEV NAT/COMP INDUS LABOR

B63
BERLE A.A. JR.,THE AMERICAN ECONOMIC REPUBLIC. STRUCT FINAN MARKET LABOR NAT/G PLAN...POLICY WELF/ST DECISION. PAGE 14 F0262 CAP/ISM ECO/TAC TREND CONCPT

B63
BROUDE H.W.,STEEL DECISIONS AND THE NATIONAL ECONOMY. USA+45 LG/CO PLAN ADMIN COST DECISION. PAGE 19 F0365 PROC/MFG NAT/G CONTROL ECO/TAC

B63
BURNS T.G.,DEVELOPMENT BANKING BIBLIOGRAPHY (PAPER). WOR+45 SML/CO VOL/ASSN PLAN BUDGET. PAGE 20 F0391 BIBLIOG/A ECO/DEV FINAN ECO/UNDEV

B63
CENTRO ESTUDIOS MONETARIOS LAT,COOPERACION FINANCIERA EN AMERICA LATINA. L/A+17C PLAN PROB/SOLV CONTROL REGION DEMAND...POLICY ANTHOL 20. PAGE 22 F0433 ECO/UNDEV INT/TRADE MARKET FINAN

B63
CENTRO PARA EL DESARROLLO,LA ALIANZA PARA EL PROGRESO Y EL DESARROLLO SOCIAL DE AMERICA LATINA. L/A+17C INT/ORG DIPLOM ECO/TAC INT/TRADE ATTIT 20 ALL/PROG. PAGE 22 F0435 ECO/UNDEV FOR/AID PLAN REGION

B63
COLUMBIA U SCHOOL OF LAW,PUBLIC INTERNATIONAL DEVELOPMENT FINANCING IN SENEGAL. SENEGAL FINAN DELIB/GP GIVE EFFICIENCY...CHARTS GOV/COMP ANTHOL 20. PAGE 26 F0511 FOR/AID PLAN RECEIVE ECO/UNDEV

B63
COPPOCK J.,NORTH ATLANTIC POLICY - THE AGRICULTURAL GAP. EUR+WWI ELITES ECO/DEV DIST/IND MARKET PLAN AGRI TEC/DEV

WEALTH...STAT TREND GEN/LAWS OEEC TOT/POP VAL/FREE FAO 20. PAGE 27 F0535
INT/TRADE

B63
EL-NAGGAR S.,FOREIGN AID TO UNITED ARAB REPUBLIC. UAR USA+45 USSR AGRI FINAN INDUS FORCES EATING DEMAND...CHARTS METH/COMP 20 RESOURCE/N AID. PAGE 37 F0718
FOR/AID ECO/UNDEV RECEIVE PLAN

B63
ERHARD L.,THE ECONOMICS OF SUCCESS. GERMANY/W WOR+45 LABOR CHIEF TAX REGION COST DEMAND ANTHOL. PAGE 38 F0745
ECO/DEV INT/TRADE PLAN DIPLOM

B63
FATEMI N.S.,THE DOLLAR CRISIS. USA+45 INDUS NAT/G LEGIS BUDGET TAX COST...CHARTS METH/COMP 20 EEC. PAGE 39 F0766
PROB/SOLV BAL/PAY FOR/AID PLAN

B63
FLORES E.,LAND REFORM AND THE ALLIANCE FOR PROGRESS (PAMPHLET). L/A+17C USA+45 STRUCT ECO/UNDEV NAT/G WORKER CREATE PLAN ECO/TAC COERCE REV 20 ALL/PROG. PAGE 42 F0815
AGRI INT/ORG DIPLOM POLICY

B63
FOX S.,ECONOMIC CONTROL AND FREE ENTERPRISE. PLAN BUDGET INT/TRADE TAX...TREND 20. PAGE 43 F0839
CONTROL FINAN ECO/TAC

B63
FRIEDMAN M.,INFLATION: CAUSES AND CURES. AFR INDIA ECO/DEV ECO/TAC INT/TRADE RATION PRICE DEMAND ...POLICY 20. PAGE 44 F0860
ECO/UNDEV PLAN FINAN EQUILIB

B63
GORDON L.,A NEW DEAL FOR LATIN AMERICA. L/A+17C USA+45 CULTURE NAT/G TEC/DEV DIPLOM FOR/AID REGION TASK...POLICY 20 ALL/PROG DEPT/STATE. PAGE 49 F0958
ECO/UNDEV ECO/TAC INT/ORG PLAN

B63
GRIGSBY W.G.,HOUSING MARKETS AND PUBLIC POLICY. USA+45 FAM NEIGH PRICE DEMAND WEALTH...POLICY CHARTS BIBLIOG METH MUNICH 20. PAGE 51 F1002
MARKET RENT HABITAT PLAN

B63
HAQ M.,THE STRATEGY OF ECONOMIC PLANNING. PAKISTAN AGRI FINAN INDUS NAT/G FOR/AID TAX CONTROL REGION PRODUC...POLICY CHARTS 20. PAGE 55 F1071
ECO/TAC ECO/UNDEV PLAN PROB/SOLV

B63
HAUSMAN W.H.,MANAGING ECONOMIC DEVELOPMENT IN AFRICA. AFR USA+45 LAW FINAN WORKER TEC/DEV WEALTH ...ANTHOL 20. PAGE 57 F1116
ECO/UNDEV PLAN FOR/AID MGT

B63
HIRSCHMAN A.O.,JOURNEYS TOWARD PROGRESS: STUDIES OF ECONOMIC POLICYMAKING IN LATIN AMERICA. CHILE FUT ECO/UNDEV AGRI FINAN INDUS CONSULT DELIB/GP PLAN ATTIT HEALTH ORD/FREE WEALTH...POLICY STAT VAL/FREE COLOMB 20. PAGE 60 F1177
L/A+17C ECO/TAC BRAZIL

B63
HOLLAND E.P.,EXPERIMENTS ON A SIMULATED UNDERDEVELOPED ECONOMY: DEVELOPMENT PLANS AND BALANCE-OF-PAYMENTS POLICIES. WOR+45 ECO/UNDEV FINAN PLAN ECO/TAC...MATH STAT CHARTS SIMUL VAL/FREE. PAGE 61 F1196
AFR BAL/PAY

B63
HUNTER A.,THE ECONOMICS OF AUSTRALIAN INDUSTRY. DIST/IND EXTR/IND FINAN PROC/MFG SERV/IND ACT/RES PLAN TARIFFS GP/REL INGP/REL 20 AUSTRAL. PAGE 63 F1245
INDUS ECO/DEV HABITAT GP/COMP

B63
INTERAMERICAN ECO AND SOC COUN,THE ALLIANCE FOR PROGRESS: ITS FIRST YEAR: 1961-1962. AGRI SCHOOL PLAN TEC/DEV INT/TRADE TAX GIVE ADMIN WEALTH...SOC 20 ALL/PROG SOUTH/AMER. PAGE 64 F1267
INT/ORG PROB/SOLV ECO/TAC L/A+17C

B63
INTERNATIONAL ASSOCIATION RES,AFRICAN STUDIES IN INCOME AND WEALTH. AFR NAT/G PROB/SOLV DEMAND INCOME...ECOMETRIC METH/COMP 20. PAGE 64 F1270
WEALTH PLAN ECO/UNDEV BUDGET

B63
ISSAWI C.,EGYPT IN REVOLUTION: AN ECONOMIC ANALYSIS. ISLAM STRUCT ECO/UNDEV AGRI FINAN INDUS PLAN EXEC REV NAT/LISM ATTIT RIGID/FLEX WEALTH SOCISM...STAT FOR/TRADE WORK 20. PAGE 66 F1292
NAT/G UAR

B63
KATZ S.M.,A SELECTED LIST OF US READINGS ON DEVELOPMENT. AGRI COM/IND DIST/IND INDUS LABOR PLAN FOR/AID EDU/PROP HEALTH...POLICY SOC/WK 20. PAGE 69 F1361
BIBLIOG/A ECO/UNDEV TEC/DEV ACT/RES

B63
LAGOS G.,INTERNATIONAL STRATIFICATION AND UNDERDEVELOPED COUNTRIES. L/A+17C WOR+45 PLAN ECO/TAC PWR RESPECT WEALTH...METH/CNCPT STAT CHARTS SIMUL GEN/LAWS TRUE/GP METH/GP VAL/FREE 20. PAGE 74 F1459
ECO/UNDEV STRATA

B63
LANGE O.,ECONOMIC DEVELOPMENT, PLANNING, AND INTERNATIONAL COOPERATION. UAR WOR+45 FINAN CAP/ISM PERS/REL 20. PAGE 75 F1476
ECO/UNDEV DIPLOM INT/TRADE PLAN

B63
LARY M.B.,PROBLEMS OF THE UNITED STATES AS WORLD TRADER AND BANKER. USA+45 NAT/G PLAN DIPLOM FOR/AID ...TREND CHARTS. PAGE 76 F1482
ECO/DEV FINAN BAL/PAY INT/TRADE

B63
MAIZELS A.,INDUSTRIAL GROWTH AND WORLD TRADE. FUT WOR+45 ECO/DEV FINAN INT/ORG PLAN TEC/DEV ECO/TAC WEALTH...MATH STAT CHARTS VAL/FREE 19/20. PAGE 84 F1642
INDUS ECO/UNDEV INT/TRADE

B63
MANGER W.,THE ALLIANCE FOR PROGRESS: A CRITICAL APPRAISAL. FUT L/A+17C USA+45 CULTURE ECO/UNDEV ACADEM NAT/G SCHOOL PLAN FOR/AID...POLICY OAS ALL/PROG. PAGE 84 F1651
DIPLOM INT/ORG ECO/TAC REGION

B63
MANN D.E.,THE POLITICS OF WATER IN ARIZONA. AGRI EXTR/IND PROVS ACT/RES CREATE PLAN GOV/REL COST HABITAT...MGT CHARTS 20 ARIZONA WATER. PAGE 84 F1655
POLICY ECO/TAC TEC/DEV

B63
MARCHAL J.,EXPANSION ET RECESSION. FRANCE OP/RES PROB/SOLV ROLE ORD/FREE...TREND SIMUL 20 DEPRESSION. PAGE 85 F1663
FINAN PLAN ECO/DEV

B63
MARITANO N.,AN ALLIANCE FOR PROGRESS. FUT L/A+17C USA+45 CULTURE ECO/UNDEV NAT/G PLAN CONTROL ...POLICY ALL/PROG. PAGE 85 F1669
DIPLOM INT/ORG ECO/TAC FOR/AID

B63
MENEZES A.J.,SUBDESENVOLVIMENTO E POLITICA INTERNACIONAL. BRAZIL WOR+45 PLAN CONTROL LEAD NAT/LISM ORD/FREE 20 THIRD/WRLD. PAGE 90 F1759
ECO/UNDEV DIPLOM POLICY BAL/PWR

B63
MEYNAUD J.,PLANIFICATION ET POLITIQUE. FRANCE ITALY FINAN LABOR DELIB/GP LEGIS ADMIN EFFICIENCY ...MAJORIT DECISION 20. PAGE 90 F1773
PLAN ECO/TAC PROB/SOLV

B63
MYRDAL G.,CHALLENGE TO AFFLUENCE. USA+45 WOR+45 FINAN INT/ORG NAT/G PLAN ECO/TAC INT/TRADE BAL/PAY ORD/FREE 20 EUROPE/W. PAGE 96 F1882
ECO/DEV WEALTH DIPLOM PRODUC

B63
OECD,FOOD AID: ITS ROLE IN ECONOMIC DEVELOPMENT. FINAN NAT/G PLAN DIPLOM GIVE TASK WEALTH ...METH/COMP METH 20. PAGE 100 F1966
ECO/UNDEV FOR/AID INT/ORG POLICY

B63
PREST A.R.,PUBLIC FINANCE IN UNDERDEVELOPED COUNTRIES. UK WOR+45 WOR-45 SOCIETY INT/ORG NAT/G LEGIS ACT/RES PLAN ECO/TAC ADMIN ROUTINE...CHARTS 20. PAGE 108 F2115
FINAN ECO/UNDEV NIGERIA

B63
PRYOR F.L.,THE COMMUNIST FOREIGN TRADE SYSTEM. COM CZECHOSLVK GERMANY YUGOSLAVIA LAW ECO/DEV DIST/IND POL/PAR PLAN DOMIN TOTALISM DRIVE RIGID/FLEX WEALTH ...STAT STAND/INT CHARTS FOR/TRADE 20. PAGE 108 F2130
ATTIT ECO/TAC

B63
REAGAN M.D.,THE MANAGED ECONOMY. USA+45 INDUS LG/CO BUDGET GP/REL ORD/FREE PWR WEALTH 20. PAGE 110 F2161
PLAN ECO/DEV NAT/G ROLE

B63
TREVES G.,GOVERNMENT ORGANIZATION FOR ECONOMIC DEVELOPMENT (PAMPHLET). WOR+45 LAW BUDGET ECO/TAC GOV/REL...DECISION 20. PAGE 131 F2585
ECO/DEV ECO/UNDEV PLAN POLICY

B63
UN SECRETARY GENERAL,PLANNING FOR ECONOMIC DEVELOPMENT. ECO/UNDEV FINAN BUDGET INT/TRADE TARIFFS TAX ADMIN 20 UN. PAGE 132 F2603
PLAN ECO/TAC MGT NAT/COMP

B63
US ECON SURVEY TEAM INDONESIA,INDONESIA - PERSPECTIVE AND PROPOSALS FOR UNITED STATES ECONOMIC AID. INDONESIA AGRI MARKET TEC/DEV DIPLOM INT/TRADE EDU/PROP 20. PAGE 136 F2678
FOR/AID ECO/UNDEV PLAN INDUS

B63
US GOVERNMENT,REPORT TO INTER-AMERICAN ECONOMIC AND SOCIAL COUNCIL AT SECOND ANNUAL MEETING. L/A+17C USA+45 VOL/ASSN TEC/DEV DIPLOM TAX EATING EFFICIENCY HEALTH...STAT CHARTS 20 AID. PAGE 136 F2682
ECO/TAC FOR/AID FINAN PLAN

B63
US HOUSE,URBAN RENEWAL: HOUSE COMMITTEE ON BANKING AND CURRENCY. USA+45 FINAN LOC/G NAT/G NEIGH DELIB/GP TEC/DEV BUDGET GOV/REL COST...CHARTS MUNICH 20 CONGRESS URBAN/RNWL. PAGE 136 F2684
PLAN PROB/SOLV LEGIS

B63
US HOUSE COMM BANKING-CURR,RECENT CHANGES IN MONETARY POLICY AND BALANCE OF PAYMENTS PROBLEMS.
BAL/PAY FINAN

USA+45 DELIB/GP PLAN DIPLOM...CHARTS 20 CONGRESS. PAGE 136 F2688 — ECO/TAC POLICY

B63
US SENATE COMM GOVT OPERATIONS,REPORT OF A STUDY OF US FOREIGN AID IN TEN MIDDLE EASTERN AND AFRICAN COUNTRIES. AFR ISLAM USA+45 FORCES PLAN BUDGET DIPLOM TAX DETER WEALTH...STAT CHARTS 20 CONGRESS AID MID/EAST. PAGE 138 F2728 — FOR/AID EFFICIENCY ECO/TAC FINAN

B63
VELEZ GARCIA J.,DEVALUACION 1962; HISTORIA DOCUMENTAL DE UN PROCESO ECONOMICO. AFR L/A+17C USA+45 FINAN FOR/AID PRODUC WEALTH...POLICY STAT CHARTS ANTHOL 20 COLOMB. PAGE 141 F2774 — ECO/UNDEV ECO/TAC PLAN NAT/G

B63
VON MISES L.,HUMAN ACTION: A TREATISE ON ECONOMICS (2ND ED.). SOCIETY MARKET TAX PAY PRICE DEMAND EQUILIB RATIONAL...PSY 20. PAGE 142 F2794 — PLAN DRIVE ATTIT

B63
WALINSKY L.J.,PLANNING AND EXECUTION OF ECONOMIC DEVELOPMENT. PROB/SOLV TEC/DEV BUDGET COST WEALTH ...CHARTS BIBLIOG 20. PAGE 142 F2802 — PLAN ECO/UNDEV ECO/TAC OPTIMAL

B63
WALKER F.V.,GROWTH, EMPLOYMENT, AND THE PRICE LEVEL. USA+45 NAT/G PLAN ECO/TAC DEMAND EFFICIENCY CHARTS. PAGE 142 F2803 — ECO/DEV FINAN PRICE WORKER

B63
WIGHTMAN D.,TOWARD ECONOMIC CO-OPERATION IN ASIA. ASIA S/ASIA VOL/ASSN ACT/RES PLAN TEC/DEV ECO/TAC EDU/PROP RIGID/FLEX SKILL...POLICY METH/CNCPT OBS INT GEN/LAWS UN 20 ECAFE. PAGE 146 F2877 — ECO/UNDEV CREATE

L63
ADERBIGDE A.,"SYMPOSIUM ON WEST AFRICA INTEGRATION." AFR EUR+WWI FUT CULTURE SOCIETY STRATA DIST/IND INDUS MARKET SERV/IND DELIB/GP PLAN TEC/DEV DOMIN EDU/PROP LEGIT COERCE ATTIT ALL/VALS ...POLICY STAT TREND CHARTS VAL/FREE. PAGE 2 F0040 — FINAN ECO/TAC REGION

L63
MCKERSIE R.B.,"NONPROFESSIONAL HOSPITAL WORKERS AND A UNION ORGANIZING DRIVE." PLAN GP/REL RACE/REL ATTIT DRIVE...CORREL STAT INT GP/COMP. PAGE 88 F1732 — VOL/ASSN HEALTH INGP/REL LABOR

L63
PADELFORD N.J.,"FINANCIAL CRISIS AND THE UNITED NATIONS." FUT USSR WOR+45 LAW CONSTN FINAN INT/ORG DELIB/GP FORCES PLAN BUDGET DIPLOM COST WEALTH ...STAT CHARTS UN CONGO 20. PAGE 102 F2012 — CREATE ECO/TAC

S63
ANDREWS R.B.,"ECONOMIC PLANNING FOR SMALL AREAS: THE PLANNING PROCESS." INDUS PROC/MFG PROVS PROB/SOLV TAX EQUILIB...METH/COMP HYPO/EXP METH MUNICH 20. PAGE 5 F0103 — ECO/TAC PLAN LOC/G

S63
APPERT K.,"BERECHTIGE VORBEHALTE DER SCHWEIZERISCHEN ZUR INTEGRATION." EUR+WWI UK MARKET SERV/IND NAT/G PLAN RIGID/FLEX OEEC 20 EEC. PAGE 6 F0108 — FINAN ATTIT SWITZERLND

S63
ARDANT G.,"A PLAN FOR FULL EMPLOYMENT IN THE DEVELOPING COUNTRIES." AFR FUT WOR+45 DELIB/GP ACT/RES PLAN ECO/TAC ATTIT ALL/VALS...POLICY STAT CHARTS TUNIS VAL/FREE 20. PAGE 6 F0112 — ECO/UNDEV SOCIETY MOROCCO

S63
BARANSON J.,"ECONOMIC AND SOCIAL CONSIDERATIONS IN ADAPTING TECHNOLOGIES FOR DEVELOPING COUNTRIES." WOR+45 PLAN WEALTH...TECHNIC SOC 20. PAGE 10 F0180 — ECO/UNDEV TEC/DEV

S63
BARTHELEMY G.,"LE NOUVEAU FRANC (CFA) ET LA BANQUE CENTRALE DES ETATS DE L'AFRIQUE DE L'OUEST." FUT STRUCT INT/ORG PLAN ATTIT ALL/VALS FOR/TRADE 20. PAGE 11 F0200 — AFR FINAN

S63
BARZANSKI S.,"REGIONAL UNDERDEVELOPMENT IN THE EUROPEAN ECONOMIC COMMUNITY." EUR+WWI ELITES DIST/IND MARKET VOL/ASSN CONSULT EX/STRUC ECO/TAC RIGID/FLEX WEALTH EEC OEEC 20. PAGE 11 F0202 — ECO/UNDEV PLAN

S63
CLARK P.G.,"TOWARDS MORE COMPREHENSIVE PLANNING IN EAST AFRICA" AFR OP/RES ECO/TAC RATION TAX EFFICIENCY INCOME...MATH TREND CHARTS 20 AFRICA/E. PAGE 25 F0484 — ECO/UNDEV PLAN STAT METH/COMP

S63
CLEMHOUT S.,"PRODUCTION FUNCTION ANALYSIS APPLIED TO THE LEONTIEF SCARCE-FACTOR PARADOX OF INTERNATIONAL TRADE." EUR+WWI USA+45 DIST/IND NAT/G PLAN TEC/DEV DIPLOM PWR WEALTH...MGT METH/CNCPT CONT/OBS CON/ANAL CHARTS SIMUL GEN/LAWS FOR/TRADE 20. PAGE 25 F0490 — ECO/DEV ECO/TAC

S63
DE FOREST J.D.,"LOW LEVELS OF TECHNOLOGY AND ECONOMIC DEVELOPMENT PROSPECTS." WOR+45 WOR-45 CULTURE ACT/RES CREATE PLAN ECO/TAC ROUTINE PERCEPT WEALTH...METH/CNCPT GEN/LAWS 20. PAGE 31 F0597 — ECO/UNDEV TEC/DEV

S63
DELWERT J.,"L'ECONOMIE CAMBODGIENNE ET SON EVOLUTION ACTUELLE." FUT S/ASIA ECO/UNDEV ACT/RES PLAN WEALTH...CONCPT OBS TIME/SEQ TREND 20. PAGE 32 F0617 — FINAN ATTIT CAMBODIA

S63
DIEBOLD W. JR.,"THE NEW SITUATION OF INTERNATIONAL TRADE POLICY." EUR+WWI FRANCE FUT UK USA+45 WOR+45 DIST/IND PLAN INT/TRADE EDU/PROP PWR WEALTH ...RECORD TREND GEN/LAWS EEC TRUE/GP VAL/FREE APPLIC 20. PAGE 33 F0636 — MARKET ECO/TAC

S63
DOSSER D.,"TOWARD A THEORY OF INTERNATIONAL PUBLIC FINANCE." WOR+45 ECO/DEV PLAN ECO/TAC WEALTH ...WELF/ST TREND GEN/LAWS TRUE/GP METH/GP 20. PAGE 34 F0654 — FINAN INT/ORG FOR/AID

S63
ENTHOVEN A.C.,"ECONOMIC ANALYSIS IN THE DEPARTMENT OF DEFENSE." USA+45 NAT/G DELIB/GP PROB/SOLV RATION NUC/PWR WEAPON COST...DECISION 20 DEPT/DEFEN RESOURCE/N. PAGE 38 F0739 — PLAN BUDGET ECO/TAC FORCES

S63
ETHERINGTON D.M.,"LAND RESETTLEMENT IN KENYA; POLICY AND PRACTICE" AFR TEC/DEV ECO/TAC FOR/AID TAX PRODUC...CHARTS 20. PAGE 39 F0752 — ECO/UNDEV AGRI WORKER PLAN

S63
FOURASTIE J.,"LES SCIENCES ECONOMIQUES ET SOCIALES EN EUROPE." EUR+WWI FUT MOD/EUR WOR+45 WOR-45 INTELL SOCIETY R+D PLAN ROUTINE ATTIT RIGID/FLEX KNOWL...OBS TREND. PAGE 43 F0833 — ACT/RES CULTURE

S63
GANDILHON J.,"LA SCIENCE ET LA TECHNIQUE A L'AIDE DES REGIONS PEU DEVELOPPEES." FRANCE FUT WOR+45 ECO/DEV R+D PROF/ORG ACT/RES PLAN...MGT TOT/POP VAL/FREE 20 UN. PAGE 46 F0893 — ECO/UNDEV TEC/DEV FOR/AID

S63
GERHARD H.,"COMMODITY TRADE STABILIZATION THROUGH INTERNATIONAL AGREEMENTS." WOR+45 ECO/DEV ECO/UNDEV NAT/G ROUTINE ORD/FREE...INT/LAW OBS TREND GEN/METH TOT/POP 20. PAGE 47 F0918 — PLAN ECO/TAC INT/TRADE

S63
GORDON B.,"ECONOMIC IMPEDIMENTS TO REGIONALISM IN SOUTH EAST ASIA." BURMA FUT S/ASIA THAILAND USA+45 AGRI INDUS R+D NAT/G PLAN ECO/TAC WEALTH...STAT CONT/OBS 20. PAGE 49 F0954 — VOL/ASSN ECO/UNDEV INT/TRADE REGION

S63
LEDUC G.,"L'AIDE INTERNATIONALE AU DEVELOPPEMENT." FUT WOR+45 ECO/DEV ECO/UNDEV R+D PROF/ORG TEC/DEV ECO/TAC ROUTINE ATTIT ALL/VALS...MGT TIME/SEQ FOR/TRADE TOT/POP 20. PAGE 77 F1503 — FINAN PLAN FOR/AID

S63
LOEWENSTEIN L.K.,"THE LOCATION OF URBAN LAND USES." USA+45 LOC/G HABITAT...STAT CHARTS MUNICH 20. PAGE 81 F1595 — GEOG PLAN INDUS

S63
MASON E.S.,"INTERESTS, IDEOLOGIES AND THE PROBLEM OF STABILITY AND GROWTH." EUR+WWI USA+45 DELIB/GP CREATE PLAN EXEC ROUTINE BAL/PAY ATTIT PWR...MGT CONCPT OEEC 20. PAGE 87 F1698 — NAT/G ECO/DEV

S63
NADLER E.B.,"SOME ECONOMIC DISADVANTAGES OF THE ARMS RACE." AFR USA+45 INDUS R+D FORCES PLAN TEC/DEV ECO/TAC FOR/AID EDU/PROP PWR WEALTH...TREND FOR/TRADE 20. PAGE 96 F1886 — ECO/DEV MGT BAL/PAY

S63
POLYANOV N.,"THE DOLLAR'S VENTURES IN EUROPE." EUR+WWI FRANCE USA+45 ECO/DEV MARKET POL/PAR TEC/DEV ECO/TAC EDU/PROP DRIVE PWR WEALTH...MARXIST MYTH STAT TREND EEC 20. PAGE 107 F2100 — FINAN PLAN BAL/PAY CAP/ISM

S63
POPPINO R.E.,"IMBALANCE IN BRAZIL." L/A+17C NAT/G TOP/EX PLAN DIPLOM LEGIT DRIVE WEALTH...CON/ANAL FOR/TRADE LAFTA 20. PAGE 107 F2105 — POL/PAR ECO/TAC BRAZIL

S63
PRYBYLA J.,"THE QUEST FOR ECONOMIC RATIONALITY IN THE SOVIET BLOC." COM FUT WOR+45 WOR-45 DIST/IND MARKET PLAN ECO/TAC ATTIT...METH/CNCPT TOT/POP 20. PAGE 108 F2128 — ECO/DEV TREND USSR

S63
REDDAWAY W.B.,"THE ECONOMICS OF UNDERDEVELOPED COUNTRIES." S/ASIA WOR+45 WOR-45 STRATA AGRI COM/IND DIST/IND MARKET PROC/MFG PLAN TEC/DEV FOR/AID BAL/PAY ATTIT DRIVE SKILL WORK FOR/TRADE 20. PAGE 110 F2165 — ECO/TAC ECO/UNDEV INDIA

S63
SCHURMANN F.,"ECONOMIC POLICY AND POLITICAL POWER IN COMMUNIST CHINA." ASIA CHINA/COM USSR SOCIETY ECO/UNDEV AGRI INDUS CREATE ADMIN ROUTINE ATTIT DRIVE RIGID/FLEX PWR WEALTH...HIST/WRIT TREND CHARTS WORK 20. PAGE 118 F2323 — PLAN ECO/TAC

S63
SHONFIELD A.,"AFTER BRUSSELS." EUR+WWI FRANCE GERMANY UK ECO/DEV DIST/IND MARKET VOL/ASSN DELIB/GP CREATE INT/TRADE ATTIT RIGID/FLEX...RECORD TREND GEN/LAWS EEC COMMUN CMN/WLTH 20. PAGE 121 F2385 — PLAN ECO/TAC

S63
SHWADRAN B.,"MIDDLE EAST OIL, 1962." ISLAM DIST/IND INDUS PLAN ATTIT DRIVE WEALTH...POLICY STAT CONT/OBS TREND CHARTS GEN/LAWS TERR/GP METH/GP 20 OIL. PAGE 121 F2393 — PROC/MFG ECO/TAC ELITES REGION

S63
SHWADRAN B.,"MIDDLE EAST OIL, 1962." ISLAM USSR ECO/DEV DIST/IND INDUS PLAN BAL/PWR DISPL DRIVE ...POLICY STAT TREND GEN/LAWS TERR/GP METH/GP EEC OEEC 20 OIL. PAGE 121 F2394 — MARKET ECO/TAC INT/TRADE

S63
STEFANIAK N.J.,"A REFINEMENT OF HAIG'S THEORY." USA+45 INDUS PROB/SOLV TEC/DEV...CONCPT CHARTS MUNICH 20 HAIG. PAGE 125 F2474 — GEOG GEN/LAWS PLAN

S63
VINER J.,"REPORT OF THE CLAY COMMITTEE ON FOREIGN AID: A SYMPOSIUM." USA+45 WOR+45 NAT/G CONSULT PLAN BAL/PWR ATTIT WEALTH...MGT CONCPT TOT/POP 20. PAGE 142 F2788 — ACT/RES ECO/TAC FOR/AID

S63
WALKER H.,"THE INTERNATIONAL LAW OF COMMODITY AGREEMENTS." FUT WOR+45 ECO/DEV ECO/UNDEV FINAN INT/ORG NAT/G CONSULT CREATE PLAN ECO/TAC ATTIT PERCEPT...CONCPT GEN/LAWS TOT/POP GATT 20. PAGE 142 F2804 — MARKET VOL/ASSN INT/LAW INT/TRADE

S63
WILES P.J.D.,"WILL CAPITALISM AND COMMUNISM SPONTANEOUSLY CONVERGE." COM FUT USA+45 ECO/DEV DIST/IND MARKET CAP/ISM ECO/TAC RIGID/FLEX WEALTH MARXISM SOCISM...MATH STAT TREND COMPUT/IR 20. PAGE 146 F2885 — PLAN TEC/DEV USSR

N63
COMM ON FEDERAL TAX POLICY,FINANCING AMERICA'S FUTURE: TAXES, ECONOMIC STABILITY AND GROWTH (PAMPHLET). USA+45 LG/CO SML/CO DELIB/GP INCOME ...CHARTS 20. PAGE 26 F0513 — TAX NAT/G EQUILIB PLAN

N63
COMMITTEE ECONOMIC DEVELOPMENT,TAXES AND TRADE: 20 YEARS OF CED POLICY (PAMPHLET). USA+45 ECO/DEV PLAN BUDGET LEAD...POLICY KENNEDY/JF PRESIDENT. PAGE 27 F0518 — FINAN ECO/TAC NAT/G DELIB/GP

N63
NORTH CAROLINA U INST GOVT,COSTING URBAN DEVELOPMENT AND REDEVELOPMENT (PAMPHLET). USA+45 USA-45 NEIGH PLAN TEC/DEV TAX OWN...GEOG MUNICH 20. PAGE 98 F1934 — BIBLIOG COST FINAN

N63
US AGENCY INTERNATIONAL DEV,PRINCIPLES OF FOREIGN ECONOMIC ASSISTANCE (PAMPHLET). USA+45 FINAN GP/REL BAL/PAY EFFICIENCY 20 AID. PAGE 134 F2638 — FOR/AID PLAN ECO/UNDEV ATTIT

N63
US COMM STRENG SEC FREE WORLD,THE SCOPE AND DISTRIBUTION OF UNITED STATES MILITARY AND ECONOMIC ASSISTANCE PROGRAMS (PAMPHLET). USA+45 PLAN BAL/PWR BUDGET DIPLOM CONTROL CIVMIL/REL ATTIT. PAGE 134 F2648 — DELIB/GP POLICY FOR/AID ORD/FREE

B64
INTERNATIONAL MONETARY ARRANGEMENTS: THE PROBLEM OF CHOICE. PLAN PROB/SOLV INT/TRADE ADJUST COST EQUILIB 20. PAGE 1 F0020 — POLICY DIPLOM FINAN ECO/DEV

B64
BALASSA B.,TRADE PROSPECTS FOR DEVELOPING COUNTRIES. WOR+45 ECO/DEV AGRI EXTR/IND INDUS CREATE PLAN PRICE...ECOMETRIC CLASSIF TIME/SEQ GEN/METH. PAGE 8 F0158 — INT/TRADE ECO/UNDEV TREND STAT

B64
BALASSA B.,CHANGING PATTERNS IN FOREIGN TRADE AND PAYMENTS. AFR USA+45 USA-45 ECO/DEV NAT/G PLAN BAL/PWR...POLICY ANTHOL BIBLIOG 20. PAGE 8 F0159 — ECO/TAC INT/TRADE BAL/PAY WEALTH

B64
BASTIAT F.,ECONOMIC HARMONIES (1850). STRATA STRUCT ECO/DEV BUDGET TAX PRICE LOBBY COST. PAGE 11 F0206 — ECO/TAC PLAN INT/TRADE LAISSEZ

B64
BAUCHET P.,ECONOMIC PLANNING. FRANCE STRATA LG/CO CAP/ISM ADMIN PARL/PROC DEMAND OPTIMAL ATTIT PWR SOCISM...POLICY CHARTS 20. PAGE 11 F0212 — ECO/DEV NAT/G PLAN ECO/TAC

B64
BERRILL K.,ECONOMIC DEVELOPMENT WITH SPECIAL REFERENCE TO EAST ASIA. ASIA INDIA S/ASIA AGRI INDUS LABOR DELIB/GP PLAN INT/TRADE COST PRODUC 20 CHINJAP. PAGE 14 F0271 — FINAN ECO/UNDEV INT/ORG CAP/ISM

B64
BOGEN J.I.,FINANCIAL HANDBOOK (4TH ED.). UNIV LAW PLAN TAX RISK 20. PAGE 16 F0306 — FINAN DICTIONARY

B64
BOWEN W.G.,ECONOMIC ASPECTS OF EDUCATION (NO. 104). EUR+WWI UK USA+45 PROF/ORG PLAN TEC/DEV PAY ...POLICY STAT 20. PAGE 17 F0329 — EDU/PROP ACADEM FINAN METH/COMP

B64
BRIGHT J.R.,RESEARCH, DEVELOPMENT AND TECHNOLOGICAL INNOVATION. CULTURE R+D CREATE PLAN PROB/SOLV AUTOMAT RISK PERSON...DECISION CONCPT PREDICT BIBLIOG. PAGE 18 F0352 — TEC/DEV NEW/IDEA INDUS MGT

B64
CEPEDE M.,POPULATION AND FOOD. USA+45 STRUCT ECO/UNDEV FAM PLAN TEC/DEV FOR/AID CONTROL...CATH SOC TREND 19/20. PAGE 22 F0436 — FUT GEOG AGRI CENSUS

B64
CHINITZ B.,CITY AND SUBURB: THE ECONOMICS OF METROPOLITAN GROWTH. DIST/IND BUDGET GOV/REL DEMAND ATTIT HABITAT MUNICH PHILADELPH. PAGE 24 F0467 — TEC/DEV PLAN

B64
CLAIRBORN E.L.,FORECASTING THE BALANCE OF PAYMENTS: AN EVALUATION. AFR FUT UK USA+45 WOR+45 FINAN PLAN BUDGET PAY CONTROL...STAT CHARTS BIBLIOG 20. PAGE 24 F0474 — PREDICT BAL/PAY ECO/DEV ECO/TAC

B64
COLSTON RESEARCH SOCIETY,ECONOMETRIC ANALYSIS FOR NATIONAL ECONOMIC PLANNING (PROCEEDINGS OF SIXTEENTH SYMPOSIUM OF COLSTON RESEARCH SOCIETY). UK USA+45 FINAN FAM LABOR NAT/G PLAN PRICE ...METH/CNCPT TREND CHARTS TIME 20. PAGE 26 F0510 — ECOMETRIC DELIB/GP ECO/TAC PROB/SOLV

B64
COLUMBIA U SCHOOL OF LAW,PUBLIC INTERNATIONAL DEVELOPMENT FINANCING IN INDIA. GERMANY/W INDIA UK USA+45 INDUS PLAN TEC/DEV DIPLOM ECO/TAC GIVE ADMIN UTIL ATTIT 20. PAGE 26 F0512 — ECO/UNDEV FINAN FOR/AID INT/ORG

B64
COMMISSION ON MONEY AND CREDIT,INFLATION, GROWTH, AND EMPLOYMENT. AFR USA+45 PLAN PROB/SOLV PAY PRICE EFFICIENCY PRODUC WEALTH 20. PAGE 26 F0514 — WORKER ECO/TAC OPTIMAL

B64
COMMITTEE ECONOMIC DEVELOPMENT,COMMUNITY ECONOMIC DEVELOPMENT PROGRAMS. USA+45 FINAN INDUS LG/CO PROF/ORG CREATE GP/REL MUNICH NEW/YORK VERMONT PENNSYLVAN IN ARKANSAS. PAGE 27 F0519 — LOC/G LABOR PLAN

B64
COMPOS R.O.,A MOEDA, O GOVERNO E O TEMPO. AFR BRAZIL WOR+45 FINAN TEC/DEV FOR/AID REGION DEMAND ...ANTHOL 20. PAGE 27 F0520 — ECO/UNDEV PLAN DIPLOM INT/TRADE

B64
EINZIG P.,MONETARY POLICY: ENDS AND MEANS. AFR UK INDUS WORKER PLAN DIPLOM PRICE BAL/PAY COST WEALTH ...DECISION TIME/SEQ 20. PAGE 37 F0715 — FINAN POLICY ECO/TAC BUDGET

B64
FITCH L.C.,URBAN TRANSPORTATION AND PUBLIC POLICY. FINAN NAT/G LEGIS PROB/SOLV TEC/DEV PRICE COST EFFICIENCY...DECISION STAT CHARTS METH/COMP MUNICH 20 NEWYORK/C PHILADELPH LOS/ANG CHICAGO WASHING/DC. PAGE 41 F0806 — DIST/IND PLAN LOC/G

B64
FLORENCE P.S.,ECONOMICS AND SOCIOLOGY OF INDUSTRY; A REALISTIC ANALYSIS OF DEVELOPMENT. ECO/UNDEV LG/CO NAT/G PLAN...GEOG MGT BIBLIOG 20. PAGE 42 F0814 — INDUS SOC ADMIN

B64
FRIEDEN B.J.,THE FUTURE OF OLD NEIGHBORHOODS: REBUILDING FOR A CHANGING POPULATION. CONSTRUC LOC/G NAT/G ACT/RES ECO/TAC REGION ATTIT...INT SAMP MUNICH 20 NEWYORK/C LOS/ANG HARTFORD URBAN/RNWL. PAGE 44 F0855 — NEIGH PROB/SOLV PLAN BUDGET

B64
FRIEDMANN J.,REGIONAL DEVELOPMENT AND PLANNING: A READER. AGRI MARKET NAT/G ECO/TAC INCOME...GEOG STAT CENSUS CHARTS ANTHOL BIBLIOG MUNICH 20 OPEN/SPACE. PAGE 44 F0863 — PLAN REGION INDUS ECO/DEV

B64
GREBLER L.,URBAN RENEWAL IN EUROPEAN COUNTRIES: ITS EMERGENCE AND POTENTIALS. EUR+WWI UK ECO/DEV LOC/G NEIGH CREATE ADMIN ATTIT...TREND NAT/COMP MUNICH 20 URBAN/RNWL. PAGE 50 F0981 — PLAN CONSTRUC NAT/G

B64
HAAR C.M.,LAW AND LAND: ANGLO-AMERICAN PLANNING PRACTICE. UK USA+45 NAT/G TEC/DEV BUDGET CT/SYS INGP/REL EFFICIENCY OWN...JURID MUNICH 20. PAGE 52 F1019 — LAW PLAN NAT/COMP

B64
HACKER A.,THE CORPORATION TAKE-OVER. CONSTN LABOR PLAN BAL/PWR CONTROL EXEC LOBBY REPRESENT GP/REL ROLE ORD/FREE POLICY. PAGE 52 F1025 — LG/CO STRUCT PWR

B64
HAGGER A.J.,THE THEORY OF INFLATION. AFR PLAN PROB/SOLV PAY COST INCOME 20. PAGE 53 F1035 — DEMAND TEC/DEV FINAN

B64
HARBISON F.H.,EDUCATION, MANPOWER, AND ECONOMIC GROWTH. WOR+45 ECO/DEV ECO/UNDEV ACADEM LABOR SCHOOL WORKER UTIL...IDEA/COMP NAT/COMP. PAGE 55 F1075 — PLAN TEC/DEV EDU/PROP SKILL

B64
HARRIS S.E.,ECONOMICS OF THE KENNEDY YEARS AND A — ECO/TAC

LOOK AHEAD. USA+45 PLAN BUDGET NEW/LIB...STAT RECORD IDEA/COMP PERS/COMP INDEX 20 KENNEDY/JF EISNHWR/DD JOHNSON/LB. PAGE 56 F1091
CHIEF POLICY NAT/G

B64
HART P.E.,ECONOMETRIC ANALYSIS FOR NATIONAL ECONOMIC PLANNING. INDUS OP/RES PRICE PRODUC ...SIMUL ANTHOL MODELS 20. PAGE 56 F1100
PLAN ECOMETRIC STAT

B64
HATHAWAY D.E.,PROBLEMS OF PROGRESS IN THE AGRICULTURAL ECONOMY. USA+45 USA-45 ECO/DEV NAT/G INT/TRADE PRICE DEMAND EFFICIENCY OPTIMAL 20. PAGE 57 F1112
AGRI ECO/TAC MARKET PLAN

B64
HERSKOVITS M.J.,ECONOMIC TRANSITION IN AFRICA. FUT INT/ORG NAT/G WORKER PROB/SOLV TEC/DEV INT/TRADE EQUILIB INCOME...ANTHOL 20. PAGE 59 F1157
AFR ECO/UNDEV PLAN ADMIN

B64
INTERNATIONAL LABOUR OFFICE,EMPLOYMENT AND ECONOMIC GROWTH. ECO/DEV ECO/UNDEV NAT/G PLAN DIPLOM INT/TRADE CONTROL INCOME PRODUC WEALTH...STAT NAT/COMP 20 ILO. PAGE 65 F1279
WORKER METH/COMP ECO/TAC OPTIMAL

B64
INTL INF CTR LOCAL CREDIT,GOVERNMENT MEASURES FOR THE PROMOTION OF REGIONAL ECONOMIC DEVELOPMENT. WOR+45 ECO/UNDEV FINAN INT/ORG DIPLOM ORD/FREE ...POLICY GEOG 20. PAGE 65 F1285
FOR/AID PLAN ECO/TAC REGION

B64
JUCKER-FLEETWOOD E.,MONEY AND FINANCE IN AFRICA. ISLAM ECO/UNDEV SERV/IND NAT/G EX/STRUC PLAN ECO/TAC ROUTINE WEALTH...MGT TOT/POP 20. PAGE 68 F1344
AFR FINAN

B64
LANG A.S.,URBAN RAIL TRANSIT. OP/RES PLAN PROB/SOLV TEC/DEV AUTOMAT COST...TECHNIC MATH CON/ANAL CHARTS METH/COMP SIMUL MUNICH 20 RAILROAD PUB/TRANS. PAGE 75 F1474
DIST/IND ECOMETRIC

B64
LANGHOFF P.,MODELS, MEASUREMENT AND MARKETING. ACT/RES COMPUTER OP/RES PLAN BUDGET...MGT PHIL/SCI METH/CNCPT STAT PROG/TEAC BIBLIOG. PAGE 75 F1478
DECISION SIMUL MARKET R+D

B64
MAGALHAES S.,PRATICA DA EMANCIPACAO NACIONAL. L/A+17C INDUS PLAN ECO/TAC CONTROL NAT/LISM ORD/FREE. PAGE 84 F1640
BAL/PAY ECO/UNDEV DIPLOM WEALTH

B64
MANSFIELD E.,MONOPOLY POWER AND ECONOMIC PERFORMANCE: AN INTRODUCTION TO A CURRENT ISSUE OF PUBLIC POLICY. ECO/DEV INDUS NAT/G PLAN CAP/ISM PRICE CONTROL LOBBY EFFICIENCY PRODUC...POLICY 20 CONGRESS KENNEDY/JF MONOPOLY. PAGE 85 F1659
LG/CO PWR ECO/TAC MARKET

B64
MARKHAM J.W.,THE COMMON MARKET: FRIEND OR COMPETITOR. AFR EUR+WWI FUT USA+45 INT/ORG LG/CO NAT/G VOL/ASSN DELIB/GP EX/STRUC PLAN TARIFFS ORD/FREE PWR WEALTH...POLICY STAT TREND EEC VAL/FREE 20. PAGE 85 F1671
ECO/DEV ECO/TAC

B64
MELADY T.,FACES OF AFRICA. AFR FUT ISLAM NAT/G POL/PAR SCHOOL DELIB/GP PLAN ECO/TAC EDU/PROP ATTIT ALL/VALS...CHARTS TOT/POP TERR/GP VAL/FREE 20. PAGE 89 F1752
ECO/UNDEV TREND NAT/LISM

B64
MEZERIK A.G.,TRADE, AID AND ECONOMIC DEVELOPMENT. WOR+45 FINAN INDUS MARKET PLAN BAL/PWR BARGAIN FOR/AID TARIFFS EDU/PROP WEALTH...GP/COMP 20 UN GATT IMF IBRD. PAGE 91 F1777
ECO/TAC ECO/DEV INT/ORG INT/TRADE

B64
MOAK L.L.,A MANUAL OF SUGGESTED PRACTICE FOR THE PREPARATION AND ADOPTION OF CAPITAL PROGRAMS AND CAPITAL BUDGETS BY LOCAL GOVERN. USA+45 DELIB/GP PLAN TAX GP/REL COST DECISION. PAGE 92 F1812
LOC/G BUDGET LEGIS PROB/SOLV

B64
MORRISSENS L.,ECONOMIC POLICY IN OUR TIME: COUNTRY STUDIES. BELGIUM EUR+WWI FRANCE GERMANY/W ITALY NETHERLAND INDUS BARGAIN BUDGET GOV/REL BAL/PAY PRODUC...CON/ANAL CHARTS COSTS 20. PAGE 94 F1839
ECO/DEV ECO/TAC METH/COMP PLAN

B64
MYINT H.,THE ECONOMICS OF THE DEVELOPING COUNTRIES. WOR+45 AGRI PLAN COST...POLICY GEOG 20 MONEY. PAGE 96 F1878
ECO/UNDEV INT/TRADE EXTR/IND FINAN

B64
NATIONAL COUN APPLIED ECO RES,A STRATEGY FOR THE FOURTH PLAN. INDIA DIST/IND EXTR/IND SERV/IND ECO/TAC RATION EDU/PROP EATING HEALTH...CHARTS 20. PAGE 97 F1900
ECO/UNDEV PLAN AGRI WORKER

B64
NOSSITER B.D.,THE MYTHMAKERS: AN ESSAY ON POWER AND WEALTH. USA+45 LG/CO NAT/G TOP/EX PROB/SOLV ADMIN GP/REL ORD/FREE 20. PAGE 99 F1937
ECO/TAC WEALTH FINAN PLAN

B64
ORGANIZATION AMERICAN STATES,ECONOMIC SURVEY OF LATIN AMERICA, 1962. L/A+17C AGRI DIST/IND INDUS MARKET PROC/MFG R+D PLAN TEC/DEV ECO/TAC REGION BAL/PAY ALL/VALS...CON/ANAL ORG/CHARTS GEN/METH OAS ALL/PROG 20 ALL/PROG. PAGE 102 F1998
ECO/UNDEV CHARTS

B64
PAWERA J.C.,ALGERIA'S INFRASTRUCTURE. ALGERIA PLAN WEALTH...METH/CNCPT 20. PAGE 104 F2041
ECO/UNDEV INDUS TEC/DEV COM/IND

B64
POWELSON J.P.,LATIN AMERICA: TODAY'S ECONOMIC AND SOCIAL REVOLUTION. L/A+17C INTELL SOCIETY STRUCT AGRI INDUS NAT/G DIPLOM ECO/TAC REV...POLICY 20. PAGE 107 F2110
ECO/UNDEV WEALTH ADJUST PLAN

B64
RESOURCES FOR THE FUTURE,URBAN AND REGIONAL STUDIES AT US UNIVERSITIES; A REPORT BASED ON A 1963 SURVEY OF URBAN AND REGIONAL RESEARCH. USA+45 SOCIETY CONSTRUC DIST/IND ACADEM NAT/G ACT/RES ECO/TAC ...CENSUS IDEA/COMP MUNICH. PAGE 111 F2179
BIBLIOG/A REGION PLAN

B64
REUSS H.S.,THE CRITICAL DECADE - AN ECONOMIC POLICY FOR AMERICA AND THE FREE WORLD. AFR USA+45 FINAN POL/PAR WORKER PLAN DIPLOM ECO/TAC TARIFFS BAL/PAY ...POLICY 20 CONGRESS. PAGE 111 F2181
FOR/AID INT/TRADE LABOR LEGIS

B64
ROBINSON E.A.G.,ECONOMIC DEVELOPMENT FOR AFRICA SOUTH OF THE SAHARA. AFR AGRI INDUS LABOR BUDGET INT/TRADE PRICE...POLICY GEOG ANTHOL 20. PAGE 113 F2219
ECO/UNDEV ECO/TAC ACT/RES PLAN

B64
SEERS D.,CUBA: THE ECONOMIC AND SOCIAL REVOLUTION. L/A+17C USSR YUGOSLAVIA STRATA AGRI INDUS SCHOOL DELIB/GP PLAN ECO/TAC DOMIN EDU/PROP ATTIT RIGID/FLEX ALL/VALS...STAT OBS TIME/SEQ WORK VAL/FREE 20. PAGE 119 F2341
ACT/RES COERCE CUBA REV

B64
STEWART C.F.,A BIBLIOGRAPHY OF INTERNATIONAL BUSINESS. WOR+45 FINAN LG/CO NAT/G PLAN ECO/TAC TARIFFS...DECISION MGT GP/COMP NAT/COMP 20 EEC. PAGE 126 F2484
BIBLIOG INT/ORG OP/RES INT/TRADE

B64
SULLIVAN G.,THE STORY OF THE PEACE CORPS. USA+45 WOR+45 INTELL FACE/GP NAT/G SCHOOL VOL/ASSN CONSULT EX/STRUC PLAN EDU/PROP ADMIN ATTIT DRIVE ALL/VALS ...POLICY HEAL SOC CONCPT INT QU BIOG TREND SOC/EXP WORK. PAGE 127 F2511
INT/ORG ECO/UNDEV FOR/AID PEACE

B64
THAILAND NATIONAL ECO DEV,THE NATIONAL ECONOMIC DEVELOPMENT PLAN: 1961-66: SECOND PHASE 1964-66. THAILAND AGRI FINAN BUDGET EFFICIENCY INCOME...STAT CHARTS 20. PAGE 129 F2547
ECO/UNDEV ECO/TAC PLAN NAT/G

B64
TINBERGEN J.,CENTRAL PLANNING. COM INTELL ECO/DEV ECO/UNDEV FINAN INT/ORG PROB/SOLV ECO/TAC CONTROL EXEC ROUTINE DECISION. PAGE 130 F2576
PLAN INDUS MGT CENTRAL

B64
US HOUSE COMM GOVT OPERATIONS,US OWNED FOREIGN CURRENCIES: HEARINGS (COMMITTEE ON GOVERNMENT OPERATIONS). INDIA ECO/DEV PLAN BUDGET TAX DEMAND EFFICIENCY 20 AID CONGRESS. PAGE 137 F2699
FINAN ECO/TAC FOR/AID OWN

B64
WEIDENBAUM M.L.,CONGRESS AND THE FEDERAL BUDGET: FEDERAL BUDGETING AND THE RESPONSIBLE USE OF POWER. LOC/G PLAN TAX CONGRESS. PAGE 144 F2843
LEGIS EX/STRUC BUDGET ADMIN

B64
WELLISZ S.,THE ECONOMICS OF THE SOVIET BLOC. COM USSR INDUS WORKER PLAN BUDGET INT/TRADE TAX PRICE PRODUC WEALTH MARXISM...METH/COMP 20. PAGE 145 F2854
EFFICIENCY ADMIN MARKET

B64
WILSON T.,POLICIES FOR REGIONAL DEVELOPMENT. CANADA UK FINAN INDUS NAT/G BUDGET TAX GIVE COST ...NAT/COMP 20. PAGE 147 F2904
REGION PLAN ECO/DEV ECO/TAC

L64
CARNEGIE ENDOWMENT INT. PEACE,"ECONOMIC AND SOCIAL QUESTION (ISSUES BEFORE THE NINETEENTH GENERAL ASSEMBLY)." WOR+45 ECO/DEV ECO/UNDEV INDUS R+D DELIB/GP CREATE PLAN TEC/DEV ECO/TAC FOR/AID BAL/PAY...RECORD UN 20. PAGE 21 F0414
INT/ORG INT/TRADE

L64
HAAS E.B.,"ECONOMICS AND DIFFERENTIAL PATTERNS OF POLITICAL INTEGRATION: PROJECTIONS ABOUT UNITY IN LATIN AMERICA." SOCIETY NAT/G DELIB/GP ACT/RES CREATE PLAN ECO/TAC REGION ROUTINE ATTIT DRIVE PWR WEALTH...CONCPT TREND CHARTS LAFTA TERR/GP 20. PAGE 52 F1020
L/A+17C INT/ORG MARKET

L64
KOLODZIEJ E.A.,"RATIONAL CONSENT AND DEFENSE BUDGETS: THE ROLE OF CONGRESS, 1945-1962." LEGIS DIPLOM CONTROL PARL/PROC 20 CONGRESS. PAGE 72 F1423
DECISION PLAN CIVMIL/REL BUDGET

L64
STERN R.M.,"POLICIES FOR TRADE AND DEVELOPMENT." AFR FUT WOR+45 DIST/IND FINAN NAT/G DELIB/GP PLAN ECO/TAC ORD/FREE WEALTH...POLICY STAT TIME/SEQ CHARTS METH/GP 20. PAGE 126 F2480
MARKET ECO/UNDEV INT/TRADE

S64
BEIM D.,"THE COMMUNIST BLOC AND THE FOREIGN-AID GAME." AFR WOR+45 NAT/G PLAN ROUTINE ATTIT KNOWL ORD/FREE...DECISION QUANT CONT/OBS TIME/SEQ CHARTS GAME SIMUL LOG/LING 20. PAGE 12 F0231
COM ECO/UNDEV ECO/TAC FOR/AID

S64
FINLEY D.D.,"A POLITICAL PERSPECTIVE OF ECONOMIC RELATIONS IN THE COMMUNIST CAMP." COM USSR FACE/GP NAT/G ACT/RES PLAN DOMIN COERCE ATTIT ORD/FREE WEALTH...TIME/SEQ 20. PAGE 41 F0800
VOL/ASSN ECO/TAC DIPLOM REGION

S64
FLORINSKY M.T.,"TRENDS IN THE SOVIET ECONOMY." COM USA+45 USSR INDUS LABOR NAT/G PLAN TEC/DEV ECO/TAC ALL/VALS SOCISM...MGT METH/CNCPT STYLE CON/ANAL GEN/METH WORK 20. PAGE 42 F0817
ECO/DEV AGRI

S64
GARDNER R.N.,"GATT AND THE UNITED NATIONS CONFERENCE ON TRADE AND DEVELOPMENT." USA+45 WOR+45 SOCIETY ECO/UNDEV MARKET NAT/G DELIB/GP ACT/RES PLAN ECO/TAC TARIFFS EDU/PROP ROUTINE DRIVE RIGID/FLEX WEALTH...DECISION MGT TREND UN TOT/POP 20 GATT. PAGE 46 F0905
INT/ORG INT/TRADE

S64
GERBET P.,"LA MISE EN OEUVRE DU MARCHE COMMUN AGRICOLE." ECO/DEV MARKET INT/ORG NAT/G PLAN EDU/PROP NAT/LISM WEALTH...OBS EEC VAL/FREE 20. PAGE 47 F0917
EUR+WWI AGRI REGION

S64
HUELIN D.,"ECONOMIC INTEGRATION IN LATIN AMERICAN: PROGRESS AND PROBLEMS." L/A+17C ECO/DEV AGRI DIST/IND FINAN INDUS NAT/G VOL/ASSN CONSULT DELIB/GP EX/STRUC ACT/RES PLAN TEC/DEV ECO/TAC ROUTINE BAL/PAY WEALTH FOR/TRADE WORK TERR/GP 20. PAGE 63 F1232
MARKET ECO/UNDEV INT/TRADE

S64
HUTCHINSON E.C.,"AMERICAN AID TO AFRICA." FUT USA+45 MARKET INT/ORG LOC/G NAT/G PUB/INST PLAN ECO/TAC ATTIT RIGID/FLEX...POLICY CONCPT TREND TERR/GP 20. PAGE 63 F1248
AFR ECO/UNDEV FOR/AID

S64
NASH M.,"SOCIAL PREREQUISITES TO ECONOMIC GROWTH IN LATIN AMERICA AND SOUTHEAST ASIA." L/A+17C S/ASIA CULTURE SOCIETY ECO/UNDEV AGRI INDUS NAT/G PLAN TEC/DEV EDU/PROP ROUTINE ALL/VALS...POLICY RELATIV SOC NAT/COMP WORK TOT/POP 20. PAGE 96 F1894
ECO/DEV PERCEPT

S64
NEISSER H.,"THE EXTERNAL EQUILIBRIUM OF THE UNITED STATES ECONOMY." FUT USA+45 NAT/G ACT/RES PLAN ECO/TAC ATTIT WEALTH...METH/CNCPT GEN/METH VAL/FREE FOR/TRADE 20. PAGE 97 F1910
FINAN ECO/DEV BAL/PAY INT/TRADE

S64
PADELFORD N.J.,"THE ORGANIZATION OF AFRICAN UNITY." ECO/UNDEV INT/ORG PLAN BAL/PWR DIPLOM ECO/TAC NAT/LISM ORD/FREE PWR WEALTH...CONCPT TREND STERTYP TERR/GP VAL/FREE 20. PAGE 102 F2013
AFR VOL/ASSN REGION

S64
PATEL S.J.,"THE ECONOMIC DISTANCE BETWEEN NATIONS: ITS ORIGIN, MEASUREMENT AND OUTLOOK." WOR+45 ECO/DEV AGRI FINAN INDUS MARKET LABOR NAT/G CONSULT TEC/DEV ECO/TAC WEALTH...POLICY RELATIV MGT TREND WORK 20. PAGE 103 F2035
ECO/UNDEV PLAN

S64
PESELT B.M.,"COMMUNIST ECONOMIC OFFENSIVE." WOR+45 SOCIETY INT/ORG PLAN ECO/TAC DOMIN EDU/PROP ATTIT PERSON PWR WEALTH...TREND CHARTS METH/GP 20. PAGE 105 F2067
COM ECO/UNDEV FOR/AID USSR

S64
SALVADORI M.,"EL CAPITALISMO EN LA EUROPA DE LA POSGUERRA." AFR INT/ORG NAT/G POL/PAR PLAN ECO/TAC ATTIT ORD/FREE WEALTH...HIST/WRIT EEC 20. PAGE 115 F2275
EUR+WWI ECO/DEV CAP/ISM

S64
SCHMITT H.D.,"POLITICAL CONDITIONS FOR INTERNATIONAL CURRENCY REFORM." WOR+45 SOCIETY ECO/DEV PLAN ECO/TAC BAL/PAY ATTIT ORD/FREE WEALTH ...SOC CONCPT OBS TREND EEC VAL/FREE ECSC 20. PAGE 117 F2301
FINAN VOL/ASSN REGION

S64
STONE P.A.,"DECISION TECHNIQUES FOR TOWN DEVELOPMENT." PLAN COST PROFIT...DECISION MGT CON/ANAL CHARTS METH/COMP BIBLIOG MUNICH 20. PAGE 127 F2497
OP/RES ADMIN PROB/SOLV

S64
WU Y.,"CHINA'S ECONOMY AND ITS PROSPECTS." ASIA CHINA/COM FUT USSR AGRI INDUS PLAN ECO/TAC LEGIT WEALTH...STAT CON/ANAL CHARTS GEN/LAWS FOR/TRADE 20. PAGE 149 F2938
ECO/DEV

C64
LANDAUER C.,"CONTEMPORARY ECONOMIC SYSTEMS." COM WOR+45 ECO/UNDEV PLAN GP/REL...BIBLIOG 20. PAGE 75 F1466
CAP/ISM SOCISM MARXISM IDEA/COMP

C64
LOUFTY A.,"LA PLANIFICATION DE L'ECONOMIE." FRANCE USSR FINAN INDUS BUDGET INCOME PRODUC...BIBLIOG 20. PAGE 82 F1604
PLAN ECO/UNDEV ECO/DEV

N64
GREAT BRITAIN CENTRAL OFF INF,THE COLOMBO PLAN (PAMPHLET). AFR ASIA S/ASIA USA+45 VOL/ASSN ...CHARTS 20 RESOURCE/N. PAGE 50 F0980
FOR/AID PLAN INT/ORG ECO/UNDEV

N64
KENYA MINISTRY ECO PLAN DEV,AFRICAN SOCIALISM AND ITS APPLICATION TO PLANNING IN KENYA (PAMPHLET). AFR AGRI INDUS WORKER TAX COLONIAL WEALTH 20. PAGE 70 F1380
NAT/G SOCISM PLAN ECO/UNDEV

N64
US BOARD GOVERNORS FEDL RESRV,SELECTED BIBLIOGRAPHY ON MONETARY POLICY AND MANAGEMENT OF THE PUBLIC DEBT 1947-1960 AND 1961-1963 SUPPLEMENT (PAMPH.). USA+45 PLAN...POLICY MGT OWE 20. PAGE 134 F2642
BIBLIOG FINAN NAT/G

B65
ANALYSIS AND ASSESSMENT OF THE ECONOMIC EFFECTS: PUBLIC LAW 480 TITLE I PROGRAM TURKEY. INDIA TURKEY USA+45 AGRI NAT/G PLAN BUDGET DIPLOM COST EFFICIENCY...CHARTS 20. PAGE 1 F0021
ECO/TAC FOR/AID FINAN ECO/UNDEV

B65
PEACE RESEARCH ABSTRACTS. FUT WOR+45 R+D INT/ORG NAT/G PLAN TEC/DEV BAL/PWR DIPLOM FOR/AID NUC/PWR HEALTH. PAGE 1 F0022
BIBLIOG/A PEACE ARMS/CONT WAR

B65
AMERICAN ECONOMIC ASSOCIATION,INDEX OF ECONOMIC JOURNALS 1886-1965 (7 VOLS.). UK USA+45 USA-45 AGRI FINAN PLAN ECO/TAC INT/TRADE ADMIN...STAT CENSUS 19/20. PAGE 5 F0087
BIBLIOG WRITING INDUS

B65
BARRERE A.,ECONOMIE ET INSTITUTIONS FINANCIERES (VOL. I). AFR FRANCE PLAN...BIBLIOG T 20. PAGE 10 F0194
ECO/DEV BUDGET NAT/G FINAN

B65
BEAUFRE A.,AN INTRODUCTION TO STRATEGY, WITH PARTICULAR REFERENCE TO PROBLEMS OF DEFENSE, POLITICS, ECONOMICS IN THE NUCLEAR AGE. WOR+45 FORCES DIPLOM DETER CIVMIL/REL GP/REL...NEW/IDEA IDEA/COMP 20. PAGE 12 F0226
PLAN NUC/PWR WEAPON DECISION

B65
BEYER G.H.,HOUSING AND SOCIETY. USA+45 ECO/DEV FAM NAT/G PLAN RENT...CHARTS BIBLIOG MUNICH 20. PAGE 14 F0275
HABITAT AGE/O CONSTRUC

B65
BOLLENS J.C.,THE METROPOLIS: ITS PEOPLE, POLITICS, AND ECONOMIC LIFE. USA+45 PLAN PROB/SOLV PERS/REL PWR...DECISION GEOG CENSUS TREND CON/ANAL MUNICH 20 NEWYORK/C LOS/ANG SAN/FRAN CHICAGO PHILADELPH. PAGE 16 F0309
HABITAT SOC LOC/G

B65
BOWEN W.G.,UNEMPLOYMENT IN A PROSPEROUS ECONOMY. USA+45 ECO/DEV NAT/G ACT/RES PLAN PAY EDU/PROP DEMAND...POLICY IDEA/COMP ANTHOL 20. PAGE 17 F0330
WORKER ECO/TAC WEALTH PROB/SOLV

B65
BRYCE M.D.,POLICIES AND METHODS FOR INDUSTRIAL DEVELOPMENT. WOR+45 FINAN MARKET CONSULT TARIFFS TAX COST. PAGE 20 F0379
INDUS PLAN ECO/DEV TEC/DEV

B65
CASSELL F.,GOLD OR CREDIT? THE ECONOMICS AND POLITICS OF INTERNATIONAL MONEY. AFR WOR+45 PLAN PROB/SOLV BAL/PAY SOVEREIGN WEALTH 20 OEEC. PAGE 22 F0428
FINAN INT/ORG DIPLOM ECO/TAC

B65
COLLOQUE SUR LA PLANIFICATION,LA PLANIFICATION COMME PROCESSUS DE DECISION. FRANCE SOCIETY MARKET LABOR LEGIS GP/REL EFFICIENCY INCOME ATTIT TECHRACY ...MYTH IDEA/COMP 20. PAGE 26 F0508
PLAN ECO/TAC PROB/SOLV

B65
COPELAND M.A.,OUR FREE ENTERPRISE ECONOMY. USA+45 INDUS LABOR ADMIN CONTROL GP/REL MGT. PAGE 27 F0533
CAP/ISM PLAN FINAN ECO/DEV

B65
COX D.W.,THE PERILS OF PEACE* CONVERSION TO WHAT? FUT USA+45 ECO/DEV NAT/G ACT/RES CREATE PLAN NUC/PWR WAR DEMAND MGT. PAGE 28 F0546
PEACE WORKER FORCES MARKET

B65
DELHI INSTITUTE OF ECO GROWTH,A STUDY IN THE WORKING OF THE INTENSIVE AREA SCHEME OF THE KHADI AND VILLAGE INDUSTRIES COMMISSION. INDIA AGRI FINAN DELIB/GP ECO/TAC EFFICIENCY...QU CHARTS MUNICH 20. PAGE 32 F0614
PLAN INDUS ECO/UNDEV

B65
DEMAS W.G.,THE ECONOMICS OF DEVELOPMENT IN SMALL COUNTRIES WITH SPECIAL REFERENCE TO THE CARIBBEAN. WOR+45 BAL/PAY DEMAND EFFICIENCY PRODUC...GEOG
ECO/UNDEV PLAN WEALTH

CARIBBEAN. PAGE 32 F0618
INT/TRADE
B65

DODDY F.S.,INTRODUCTION TO THE USE OF ECONOMIC INDICATORS. FINAN LABOR PLAN COST...ECOMETRIC INDICATOR MATH PREDICT CHARTS METH 20. PAGE 33 F0649
TEC/DEV STAT PRODUC PRICE
B65

DUGGAR G.S.,RENEWAL OF TOWN AND VILLAGE I: A WORLD-WIDE SURVEY OF LOCAL GOVERNMENT EXPERIENCE. WOR+45 CONSTRUC INDUS CREATE BUDGET REGION GOV/REL...QU NAT/COMP MUNICH 20 URBAN/RNWL. PAGE 35 F0673
NEIGH PLAN ADMIN
B65

EDELMAN M.,THE POLITICS OF WAGE-PRICE DECISIONS. GERMANY ITALY NETHERLAND UK INDUS LABOR POL/PAR PROB/SOLV BARGAIN PRICE ROUTINE BAL/PAY COST DEMAND 20. PAGE 36 F0699
GOV/COMP CONTROL ECO/TAC PLAN
B65

EUROPEAN FREE TRADE ASSN,REGIONAL DEVELOPMENT POLICIES IN EFTA. ECO/UNDEV INT/ORG PLAN REGION ...POLICY GEOG EFTA. PAGE 39 F0755
EUR+WWI ECO/DEV NAT/COMP INT/TRADE
B65

FARER T.J.,FINANCING AFRICAN DEVELOPMENT. AFR ECO/TAC FOR/AID SOCISM 20. PAGE 39 F0764
ECO/UNDEV FINAN CAP/ISM PLAN
B65

FLASH E.S. JR.,ECONOMIC ADVICE AND PRESIDENTIAL LEADERSHIP: THE COUNCIL OF ECONOMIC ADVISORS. USA+45 NAT/G EX/STRUC LEGIS TOP/EX ACT/RES ADMIN PRESIDENT CONGRESS. PAGE 41 F0808
PLAN CONSULT CHIEF
B65

FRIEDLANDER S.L.,LABOR MIGRATION AND ECONOMIC GROWTH: A CASE STUDY OF PUERTO RICO. PUERT/RICO AGRI WORKER PLAN PROB/SOLV...ECOMETRIC STAT PREDICT CHARTS HYPO/EXP SIMUL 20. PAGE 44 F0858
CENSUS GEOG ECO/UNDEV WEALTH
B65

FRYE R.J.,HOUSING AND URBAN RENEWAL IN ALABAMA. USA+45 NEIGH LEGIS BUDGET ADJUD ADMIN PARTIC...MGT MUNICH 20 ALABAMA URBAN/RNWL. PAGE 45 F0871
PROB/SOLV PLAN GOV/REL
B65

GOODSELL C.T.,ADMINISTRATION OF A REVOLUTION. PUERT/RICO ECO/UNDEV FINAN POL/PAR PROVS LEGIS PLAN BUDGET RECEIVE ADMIN COLONIAL LEAD MUNICH 20 ROOSEVLT/F. PAGE 49 F0951
EXEC SOC
B65

GREEN J.L.,METROPOLITAN ECONOMIC REPUBLICS. USA+45 ECO/TAC INCOME...GEOG SOC CONCPT SIMUL MUNICH 20 ATLANTA. PAGE 50 F0985
SOC/WK PLAN LABOR
B65

GREENFIELD K.R.,ECONOMICS AND LIBERALISM IN THE RISORGIMENTO (REV. ED.). ITALY AGRI FINAN PROC/MFG PLAN INT/TRADE CONTROL PWR 19. PAGE 51 F0990
NAT/LISM PRESS POLICY
B65

GREER S.,URBAN RENEWAL AND AMERICAN CITIES: THE DILEMMA OF DEMOCRATIC INTERVENTION. USA+45 R+D LOC/G VOL/ASSN ACT/RES BUDGET ADMIN GOV/REL...SOC INT SAMP MUNICH 20 BOSTON CHICAGO LOS/ANG MIAMI URBAN/RNWL. PAGE 51 F0992
PROB/SOLV PLAN NAT/G
B65

HADWIGER D.F.,PRESSURES AND PROTEST. NAT/G LEGIS PLAN LEAD PARTIC ROUTINE ATTIT POLICY. PAGE 53 F1030
AGRI GP/REL LOBBY CHOOSE
B65

HICKMAN B.G.,QUANTITATIVE PLANNING OF ECONOMIC POLICY. FRANCE NETHERLAND OP/RES PRICE ROUTINE UTIL ...POLICY DECISION ECOMETRIC METH/CNCPT STAT STYLE CHINJAP. PAGE 59 F1162
PROB/SOLV PLAN QUANT
B65

HONDURAS CONSEJO NAC DE ECO,PLAN NACIONAL DE DESARROLLO ECONOMICO Y SOCIAL DE HONDURAS 1965-69. HONDURAS AGRI INDUS BAL/PAY INCOME 20. PAGE 61 F1203
ECO/UNDEV NAT/G PLAN POLICY
B65

INTERAMERICAN ECO AND SOC COUN,THE ALLIANCE FOR PROGRESS: ITS THIRD YEAR 1963-1964. FUT L/A+17C WOR+45 ECO/DEV INT/ORG PLAN CONTROL ADJUST...STAT ANTHOL SOC/INTEG 20 ALL/PROG. PAGE 64 F1268
ECO/UNDEV ECO/TAC FINAN FOR/AID
B65

JASNY H.,KHRUSHCHEV'S CROP POLICY. USSR ECO/DEV PLAN MARXISM...STAT 20 KHRUSH/N RESOURCE/N. PAGE 66 F1306
AGRI NAT/G POLICY ECO/TAC
B65

KANTOROVICH L.V.,THE BEST USE OF ECONOMIC RESOURCES. USSR SOCIETY FINAN ACT/RES TEC/DEV ECO/TAC PRICE CONTROL COST DEMAND EFFICIENCY OPTIMAL...MGT STAT. PAGE 69 F1350
PLAN MATH DECISION
B65

KASER M.,COMECON* INTEGRATION PROBLEMS OF THE PLANNED ECONOMIES. INT/ORG TEC/DEV INT/TRADE PRICE ADMIN ADJUST CENTRAL...STAT TIME/SEQ ORG/CHARTS COMECON. PAGE 69 F1359
PLAN ECO/DEV COM REGION
B65

KLASSEN L.H.,AREA ECONOMIC AND SOCIAL REDEVELOPMENT. ECO/UNDEV INDUS NAT/G PLAN CAP/ISM TAX...ECOMETRIC SIMUL 20. PAGE 72 F1404
OPTIMAL WORKER METH ECO/TAC
B65

KLEIN J.J.,MONEY AND THE ECONOMY. USA+45 NAT/G DIPLOM CONTROL...POLICY T 20 FED/RESERV. PAGE 72 F1406
FINAN PLAN WEALTH BAL/PAY
B65

KRAUSE W.,ECONOMIC DEVELOPMENT: THE UNDERDEVELOPED WORLD AND THE AMERICAN INTEREST. USA+45 AGRI PLAN MARXISM...CHARTS 20. PAGE 73 F1434
FOR/AID ECO/UNDEV FINAN PROB/SOLV
B65

LEYS C.T.,FEDERATION IN EAST AFRICA. LAW AGRI DIST/IND FINAN INT/ORG LABOR INT/TRADE CONFER ADMIN CONTROL GP/REL...ANTHOL 20 AFRICA/E. PAGE 79 F1554
FEDERAL REGION ECO/UNDEV PLAN
B65

LUTZ V.,FRENCH PLANNING. FRANCE TEC/DEV RIGID/FLEX ORD/FREE 20. PAGE 82 F1613
PLAN ADMIN FUT
B65

MACESICH G.,COMMERCIAL BANKING AND REGIONAL DEVELOPMENT IN THE US, 1950-1960. USA+45 NAT/G PLAN ECO/TAC DEMAND...MGT 20 FED/RESERV SOUTH/US. PAGE 83 F1627
FINAN ECO/DEV INCOME COST
B65

MEAGHER R.F.,PUBLIC INTERNATIONAL DEVELOPMENT FINANCING IN SUDAN. SUDAN FINAN DELIB/GP GIVE ...CHARTS GOV/COMP 20. PAGE 89 F1740
FOR/AID PLAN RECEIVE ECO/UNDEV
B65

MONCRIEFF A.,SECOND THOUGHTS ON AID. WOR+45 ECO/UNDEV AGRI FINAN VOL/ASSN PLAN TEC/DEV GIVE EDU/PROP ROLE WEALTH 20. PAGE 93 F1816
FOR/AID ECO/TAC INT/ORG IDEA/COMP
B65

MUSHKIN S.J.,PROPERTY TAXES: THE 1970 OUTLOOK (PAMPHLET). FUT USA+45 ECO/DEV MARKET PROVS PLAN ...PROBABIL STAT CENSUS PREDICT CHARTS METH 20. PAGE 95 F1872
TAX OWN FINAN LOC/G
B65

NATIONAL CENTRAL LIBRARY,LATIN AMERICAN ECONOMIC AND SOCIAL SERIALS. UK SOCIETY NAT/G PLAN PROB/SOLV ...SOC 20. PAGE 97 F1897
BIBLIOG INT/TRADE ECO/UNDEV L/A+17C
B65

O'BRIEN F.,CRISIS IN WORLD COMMUNISM* MARXISM IN SEARCH OF EFFICIENCY. AFR COM ECO/DEV PLAN INT/TRADE WAR ADJUST PEACE...STAT TIME/SEQ GOV/COMP NAT/COMP. PAGE 99 F1951
MARXISM USSR DRIVE EFFICIENCY
B65

OECD,MEDITERRANEAN REGIONAL PROJECT: TURKEY; EDUCATION AND DEVELOPMENT. FUT TURKEY SOCIETY STRATA FINAN NAT/G PROF/ORG PLAN PROB/SOLV ADMIN COST...STAT CHARTS 20 OECD. PAGE 100 F1969
EDU/PROP ACADEM SCHOOL ECO/UNDEV
B65

OECD,THE MEDITERRANEAN REGIONAL PROJECT: PORTUGAL; EDUCATION AND DEVELOPMENT. PORTUGAL SOCIETY STRATA FINAN PROF/ORG WORKER PLAN PROB/SOLV ADMIN...POLICY STAT CHARTS METH 20 OECD. PAGE 100 F1970
EDU/PROP SCHOOL ACADEM ECO/UNDEV
B65

OECD,THE MEDITERRANEAN REGIONAL PROJECT: ITALY; EDUCATION AND DEVELOPMENT. ITALY SOCIETY STRATA FINAN NAT/G PROF/ORG WORKER PLAN PROB/SOLV ADMIN ...STAT CHARTS METH 20 OECD. PAGE 100 F1971
SCHOOL EDU/PROP ECO/UNDEV ACADEM
B65

OECD,THE MEDITERRANEAN REGIONAL PROJECT: GREECE; EDUCATION AND DEVELOPMENT. FUT GREECE SOCIETY AGRI FINAN NAT/G PROF/ORG WORKER PLAN PROB/SOLV ADMIN DEMAND ATTIT 20 OECD. PAGE 100 F1972
EDU/PROP SCHOOL ACADEM ECO/UNDEV
B65

OECD,THE MEDITERRANEAN REGIONAL PROJECT: SPAIN; EDUCATION AND DEVELOPMENT. FUT SPAIN STRATA FINAN NAT/G WORKER PLAN PROB/SOLV ADMIN COST...POLICY STAT CHARTS 20 OECD. PAGE 100 F1973
ECO/UNDEV EDU/PROP ACADEM SCHOOL
B65

OECD,TECHNIQUES OF ECONOMIC FORECASTING. CANADA FRANCE NETHERLAND SWEDEN UK USA+45 PROB/SOLV ROUTINE...CONCPT MATH CHARTS BIBLIOG METH 20. PAGE 100 F1974
PREDICT METH/COMP PLAN
B65

ONSLOW C.,ASIAN ECONOMIC DEVELOPMENT. BURMA CEYLON INDIA MALAYSIA PAKISTAN S/ASIA AGRI INDUS MARKET PROB/SOLV CAP/ISM FOR/AID INT/TRADE DEMAND WEALTH ...POLICY ANTHOL 20. PAGE 101 F1991
ECO/UNDEV ECO/TAC PLAN NAT/G
B65

ORG FOR ECO COOP AND DEVEL,THE MEDITERRANEAN REGIONAL PROJECT: AN EXPERIMENT IN PLANNING BY SIX COUNTRIES. FUT GREECE SPAIN TURKEY YUGOSLAVIA SOCIETY FINAN NAT/G PROF/ORG EDU/PROP ADMIN REGION COST...POLICY STAT CHARTS 20 OECD. PAGE 102 F1995
PLAN ECO/UNDEV ACADEM SCHOOL
B65

ORG FOR ECO COOP AND DEVEL,THE MEDITERRANEAN REGIONAL PROJECT: YUGOSLAVIA; EDUCATION AND
EDU/PROP ACADEM

DEVELOPMENT. YUGOSLAVIA SOCIETY FINAN PROF/ORG PLAN ADMIN COST DEMAND MARXISM...STAT TREND CHARTS METH 20 OECD. PAGE 102 F1996 — SCHOOL ECO/UNDEV

B65
OXENFELDT A.R.,ECONOMIC SYSTEMS IN ACTION. FRANCE USA+45 USSR CULTURE PLAN PROB/SOLV TEC/DEV INCOME PRODUC WEALTH...METH/COMP 20. PAGE 102 F2007 — ECO/DEV CAP/ISM MARXISM ECO/TAC

B65
PARRIS H.W.,GOVERNMENT AND THE RAILWAYS IN NINETEENTH-CENTURY BRITAIN. UK DELIB/GP CONTROL LEAD CENTRAL 19 RAILROAD. PAGE 103 F2029 — DIST/IND NAT/G PLAN GP/REL

B65
PHELPS E.S.,PRIVATE WANTS AND PUBLIC NEEDS - AN INTRODUCTION TO A CURRENT ISSUE OF PUBLIC POLICY (REV. ED.). USA+45 PLAN CAP/ISM INGP/REL ROLE ...DECISION TIME/SEQ 20. PAGE 106 F2081 — NAT/G POLICY DEMAND

B65
RIVKIN M.D.,AREA DEVELOPMENT FOR NATIONAL GROWTH; THE TURKISH PRECEDENT. ISLAM TURKEY ACT/RES INGP/REL...POLICY CHARTS GP/COMP MUNICH 20 ATATURK/MK INONU/I. PAGE 112 F2197 — ECO/UNDEV REGION ECO/TAC PLAN

B65
RUEFF J.,THE ROLE AND THE RULE OF GOLD: AN ARGUMENT (PAMPHLET). AFR FRANCE USA+45 WOR+45 MARKET NAT/G PLAN DIPLOM ATTIT...POLICY INT 20 DEGAULLE/C. PAGE 115 F2258 — FINAN ECO/DEV INT/TRADE BAL/PAY

B65
SCHULER E.A.,THE PAKISTAN ACADEMIES FOR RURAL DEVELOPMENT COMILLA AND PESHAWAR 1959-1964. PAKISTAN S/ASIA SOCIETY STRUCT AGRI NAT/G TEC/DEV EDU/PROP 20. PAGE 117 F2314 — BIBLIOG PLAN ECO/TAC ECO/UNDEV

B65
SIMMS R.P.,URBANIZATION IN WEST AFRICA; A REVIEW OF CURRENT LITERATURE. AFR PLAN TEC/DEV...SOC OBS NAT/COMP MUNICH 20. PAGE 122 F2405 — BIBLIOG/A ECO/DEV ECO/UNDEV

B65
SINHA M.R.,THE ECONOMICS OF MANPOWER PLANNING. FUT HUNGARY NAT/G CONTROL...POLICY GEOG ANTHOL 20 CHINJAP. PAGE 122 F2415 — ECO/UNDEV PLAN WORKER ECO/TAC

B65
SMERK G.M.,URBAN TRANSPORTATION; THE FEDERAL ROLE. FUT USA+45 FINAN PROB/SOLV TEC/DEV AUTOMAT GOV/REL COST...STAT BIBLIOG MUNICH 20 PUB/TRANS. PAGE 123 F2426 — PLAN DIST/IND NAT/G

B65
STEINER G.A.,THE CREATIVE ORGANIZATION. ELITES LG/CO PLAN PROB/SOLV TEC/DEV INSPECT CAP/ISM CONTROL EXEC PERSON...METH/COMP HYPO/EXP 20. PAGE 126 F2476 — CREATE MGT ADMIN SOC

B65
THAYER F.C. JR.,AIR TRANSPORT POLICY AND NATIONAL SECURITY: A POLITICAL, ECONOMIC, AND MILITARY ANALYSIS. DIST/IND OP/RES PLAN TEC/DEV DIPLOM DETER WAR COST EFFICIENCY...POLICY BIBLIOG 20 DEPT/DEFEN FAA CAB. PAGE 129 F2548 — AIR FORCES CIVMIL/REL ORD/FREE

B65
US ADVISORY COMN INTERGOV REL,METROPOLITAN SOCIAL AND ECONOMIC DISPARITIES: IMPLICATIONS FOR INTERGOVERNMENTAL RELATIONS IN CENT'L CITIES AND SUBURBS. CULTURE STRATA DIST/IND LOC/G PLAN GP/REL DISCRIM HABITAT MUNICH. PAGE 134 F2634 — GOV/REL GEOG

B65
US BUREAU EDUC CULTURAL AFF,RESOURCES SURVEY FOR LATIN AMERICAN COUNTRIES. L/A+17C USA+45 CULTURE INDUS INT/ORG SECT PLAN EDU/PROP POLICY. PAGE 134 F2643 — NAT/G ECO/UNDEV FOR/AID DIPLOM

B65
US CONGRESS JOINT ECO COMM,GUIDELINES FOR INTERNATIONAL MONETARY REFORM. USA+45 WOR+45 DELIB/GP BAL/PAY 20 CONGRESS IMF MONEY. PAGE 135 F2659 — DIPLOM FINAN PLAN INT/ORG

B65
WARNER A.W.,THE IMPACT OF SCIENCE ON TECHNOLOGY. UNIV INTELL SOCIETY NAT/G ACT/RES PLAN PROB/SOLV BUDGET OPTIMAL GEN/METH. PAGE 143 F2821 — DECISION TEC/DEV CREATE POLICY

B65
WATERSTON A.,DEVELOPMENT PLANNING* LESSONS OF EXPERIENCE. ECO/TAC CENTRAL...MGT QUANT BIBLIOG. PAGE 144 F2830 — ECO/UNDEV CREATE PLAN ADMIN

B65
WEAVER J.N.,THE INTERNATIONAL DEVELOPMENT ASSOCIATION: A NEW APPROACH TO FOREIGN AID. USA+45 NAT/G OP/RES PLAN PROB/SOLV WEALTH...CHARTS BIBLIOG 20 UN. PAGE 144 F2836 — FOR/AID INT/ORG ECO/UNDEV FINAN

B65
WEIDENBAUM M.L.,CONGRESS AND THE FEDERAL BUDGET. FINAN ACT/RES DOMIN CONFER EXEC UTIL PWR NEW/LIB ...CHARTS CONGRESS. PAGE 144 F2844 — BUDGET LEGIS PLAN DECISION

B65
WHITE J.,GERMAN AID. GERMANY/W FINAN PLAN TEC/DEV INT/TRADE ADMIN ATTIT...POLICY 20. PAGE 146 F2870 — FOR/AID ECO/UNDEV DIPLOM ECO/TAC

B65
WU YUAN-LI,THE ECONOMY OF COMMUNIST CHINA. CHINA/COM USSR AGRI FINAN INDUS POL/PAR WORKER PROB/SOLV INT/TRADE PRICE EATING INCOME OWN WEALTH 20. PAGE 149 F2939 — ECO/TAC MARXISM PLAN EFFICIENCY

L65
DAANE J.D.,"THE EVOLVING INTERNATIONAL MONETARY MECHANISM." VOL/ASSN CREATE PLAN FOR/AID INT/TRADE CONFER BAL/PAY...RECORD PREDICT IMF. PAGE 29 F0569 — INT/ORG ECO/TAC TREND GP/COMP

L65
LETICHE J.M.,"EUROPEAN INTEGRATION: AN AMERICAN VIEW." EUR+WWI FRANCE WOR+45 ECO/DEV DIST/IND EXTR/IND NAT/G DELIB/GP TOP/EX PLAN ECO/TAC ATTIT ...STAT CON/ANAL CHARTS EEC 20. PAGE 78 F1537 — INDUS AGRI

L65
LOFTUS M.L.,"INTERNATIONAL MONETARY FUND, 1962-1965: A SELECTED BIBLIOGRAPHY." WOR+45 PLAN BUDGET INCOME PROFIT WEALTH. PAGE 81 F1596 — BIBLIOG FINAN INT/TRADE INT/ORG

S65
CAMPOLONGO A.,"EUROPEAN INVESTMENT BANK* ACTIVITY AND PROSPECTS." FUT ECO/UNDEV FINAN PLAN DIPLOM ...STAT EEC LOAN EIB. PAGE 21 F0410 — ECO/TAC PREDICT

S65
DICKMAN A.B.,"SOUTH AFRICAN MONEY MARKET - PROGRESS AND PROBLEMS SINCE 1960." SOUTH/AFR PROB/SOLV ROLE ...PREDICT CHARTS 20. PAGE 33 F0633 — FINAN PLAN MARKET

S65
DUMONT R.,"SURPEUPLEMENT CHINOIS ET SES CONSEQUENCES." AFR ECO/UNDEV AGRI PLAN PROB/SOLV ECO/TAC FOR/AID NUC/PWR...OBS INT PREDICT. PAGE 35 F0675 — GEOG ASIA STAT

S65
GRENIEWSKI H.,"INTENTION AND PERFORMANCE: A PRIMER OF CYBERNETICS OF PLANNING." EFFICIENCY OPTIMAL KNOWL SKILL...DECISION MGT EQULIB. PAGE 51 F0995 — SIMUL GAME GEN/METH PLAN

S65
KEE W.S.,"CENTRAL CITY EXPENDITURES AND METROPOLITAN AREAS." PLAN BUDGET ECO/TAC TAX GP/REL WEALTH...CHARTS MUNICH 20. PAGE 70 F1366 — LOC/G GOV/COMP NEIGH

S65
LECLERCQ H.,"ECONOMIC RESEARCH AND DEVELOPMENT IN TROPICAL AFRICA." ECO/UNDEV INT/ORG CREATE PLAN UN. PAGE 77 F1500 — AFR R+D ACADEM ECO/TAC

S65
RUSINOW D.I.,"YUGOSLAV DEVELOPMENT BETWEEN EAST AND WEST." AGRI VOL/ASSN PLAN CAP/ISM ECO/TAC FOR/AID INT/TRADE BAL/PAY...MARXIST EEC COMECON. PAGE 115 F2262 — YUGOSLAVIA ECO/UNDEV STAT

S65
SCHROEDER G.,"LABOR PLANNING IN THE USSR." COM USSR ECO/DEV INDUS SCHOOL PRODUC WEALTH...PREDICT TIME/SEQ TREND TIME 20. PAGE 117 F2313 — WORKER PLAN CENSUS

S65
SPAAK P.H.,"THE SEARCH FOR CONSENSUS: A NEW EFFORT TO BUILD EUROPE." FRANCE GERMANY ECO/DEV NAT/G CONSULT FORCES PLAN EDU/PROP REGION CONSEN ATTIT ...SOC METH/CNCPT OBS TREND EEC NATO WORK TERR/GP METH/GP 20. PAGE 124 F2447 — EUR+WWI INT/ORG

S65
VAN DER HORST S.T.,"THE ECONOMICS OF DECENTRALISATION OF INDUSTRY." SOUTH/AFR ECO/DEV LG/CO AUTOMAT DISCRIM...POLICY MUNICH 20. PAGE 140 F2761 — PLAN INDUS CENTRAL TEC/DEV

S65
WHITAKER A.P.,"ARGENTINA: STRUGGLE FOR RECOVERY." L/A+17C USA+45 NAT/G TOP/EX PLAN LEGIT COERCE REV RIGID/FLEX PWR WEALTH...RECORD ALL/PROG ARGEN FOR/TRADE 20. PAGE 146 F2867 — POL/PAR ECO/TAC NAT/LISM

C65
PEGRUM D.E.,"PUBLIC REGULATION OF BUSINESS (REV ED)" LAW CONSTN DIST/IND SERV/IND LG/CO LEGIS OWN LAISSEZ SOCISM...POLICY DECISION BIBLIOG 20. PAGE 104 F2048 — INDUS PLAN NEW/LIB PRICE

N65
STUDY GP CREATE RESERVE ASSETS,REPORT TO DEPUTIES (PAMPHLET). AFR FUT PLAN CONTROL DEMAND WEALTH ...ANTHOL METH 20. PAGE 127 F2507 — INT/ORG INT/TRADE FINAN BUDGET

B66
ALEXANDER Y.,INTERNATIONAL TECHNICAL ASSISTANCE EXPERTS* A CASE STUDY OF THE U.N. EXPERIENCE. ECO/UNDEV CONSULT EX/STRUC CREATE PLAN DIPLOM FOR/AID TASK EFFICIENCY...ORG/CHARTS UN. PAGE 3 F0061 — ECO/TAC INT/ORG ADMIN MGT

B66
ALEXANDER Y.,INTERNATIONAL TECHNICAL ASSISTANCE EXPERTS: A CASE STUDY OF THE U.N. EXPERIENCE. USA+45 WOR+45 WORKER CREATE PLAN PROB/SOLV ECO/TAC FOR/AID GIVE EDU/PROP...CHARTS BIBLIOG 20 UN. — SKILL INT/ORG TEC/DEV CONSULT

PAGE 3 F0062

B66
ALI S.,PLANNING, DEVELOPMENT AND CHANGE: AN ANNOTATED BIBLIOGRAPHY ON DEVELOPMENTAL ADMINISTRATION. PAKISTAN SOCIETY ORD/FREE 20. PAGE 4 F0066 — BIBLIOG/A ADMIN ECO/UNDEV PLAN

B66
AMER ENTERPRISE INST PUB POL,SIGNIFICANT ISSUES IN ECONOMIC AID TO DEVELOPING COUNTRIES. FINAN INT/ORG NAT/G PLAN PROB/SOLV GIVE TASK WEALTH...DECISION 20. PAGE 4 F0083 — ECO/UNDEV FOR/AID DIPLOM POLICY

B66
BARAN P.A.,MONOPOLY CAPITAL; AN ESSAY ON THE AMERICAN ECONOMIC AND SOCIAL ORDER. USA+45 USA-45 ECO/UNDEV FINAN MARKET PLAN DIPLOM COLONIAL RACE/REL DEMAND MARXISM...CHARTS 20. PAGE 9 F0179 — LG/CO CAP/ISM PRICE CONTROL

B66
BIRMINGHAM W.,A STUDY OF CONTEMPORARY GHANA VOL I: THE ECONOMY OF GHANA. AFR GHANA PLAN...POLICY STAT CHARTS ANTHOL BIBLIOG 20. PAGE 15 F0286 — ECO/UNDEV ECO/TAC NAT/G PRODUC

B66
BOLTON R.E.,DEFENSE AND DISARMAMENT: THE ECONOMICS OF TRANSITION. USA+45 R+D FORCES PLAN LOBBY DETER WAR COST PEACE...ANTHOL BIBLIOG 20. PAGE 16 F0310 — ARMS/CONT POLICY INDUS

B66
BRODERSEN A.,THE SOVIET WORKER: LABOR AND GOVERNMENT IN SOVIET SOCIETY. USSR STRUCT INDUS LABOR PLAN PAY INGP/REL PRODUC...POLICY GEN/LAWS BIBLIOG 20 STALIN/J LENIN/VI BOLSHEVISM KHRUSH/N. PAGE 19 F0357 — WORKER ROLE NAT/G MARXISM

B66
BROEKMEIJER M.W.J.,FICTION AND TRUTH ABOUT THE "DECADE OF DEVELOPMENT" WOR+45 AGRI FINAN INDUS NAT/G TEC/DEV DIPLOM EDU/PROP LEAD SKILL 20 THIRD/WRLD. PAGE 19 F0358 — FOR/AID POLICY ECO/UNDEV PLAN

B66
CHASE S.B. JR.,PROBLEMS IN PUBLIC EXPENDITURE ANALYSIS. DIST/IND INDUS OP/RES PLAN BUDGET RECEIVE PRICE RISK COST INCOME...CHARTS ANTHOL 20. PAGE 23 F0455 — ECO/DEV FINAN NAT/G INSPECT

B66
COLE A.B.,SOCIALIST PARTIES IN POSTWAR JAPAN. STRATA AGRI LABOR PLAN DIPLOM ECO/TAC AGREE LEAD CHOOSE ATTIT...CHARTS 20 CHINJAP SOC/DEMPAR. PAGE 26 F0499 — POL/PAR POLICY SOCISM NAT/G

B66
CONFERENCE REGIONAL ACCOUNTS,REGIONAL ACCOUNTS FOR POLICY DECISIONS. PROB/SOLV CONTROL RATIONAL KNOWL ORD/FREE...POLICY DECISION MATH STAT ANTHOL 20. PAGE 27 F0523 — GOV/REL REGION PLAN ECO/TAC

B66
CURRIE L.,ACCELERATING DEVELOPMENT: THE NECESSITY AND MEANS. COLOMBIA USA+45 INDUS DIPLOM EFFICIENCY WEALTH...METH/CNCPT NEW/IDEA 20. PAGE 29 F0564 — PLAN ECO/UNDEV FOR/AID TEC/DEV

B66
DAVIES JC I.I.I.,NEIGHBORHOOD GROUPS AND URBAN RENEWAL. USA+45 PLAN LOBBY PARTIC CHOOSE RACE/REL ...POLICY DECISION SOC INT MUNICH SOC/INTEG 20 NEWYORK/C. PAGE 30 F0586 — NEIGH CREATE PROB/SOLV

B66
DEBENKO E.,RESEARCH SOURCES FOR SOUTH ASIAN STUDIES IN ECONOMIC DEVELOPMENT: A SELECT BIBLIOGRAPHY OF SERIAL PUBLICATIONS. CEYLON INDIA NEPAL PAKISTAN PROB/SOLV ADMIN...POLICY 20. PAGE 32 F0611 — BIBLIOG ECO/UNDEV S/ASIA PLAN

B66
DOBB M.,SOVIET ECONOMIC DEVELOPMENT SINCE 1917. USSR ECO/DEV ECO/UNDEV LABOR NAT/G TEC/DEV ECO/TAC ROUTINE PRODUC MARXISM 20. PAGE 33 F0647 — PLAN INDUS WORKER

B66
FELKER J.L.,SOVIET ECONOMIC CONTROVERSIES. USSR INDUS PLAN INT/TRADE GP/REL MARXISM SOCISM...POLICY 20. PAGE 40 F0778 — ECO/DEV MARKET PROFIT PRICE

B66
FOX K.A.,THE THEORY OF QUANTITATIVE ECONOMIC POLICY WITH APPLICATIONS TO ECONOMIC GROWTH AND STABILIZATION. ECO/DEV AGRI NAT/G PLAN ADMIN RISK ...DECISION IDEA/COMP SIMUL T. PAGE 43 F0837 — ECO/TAC ECOMETRIC EQUILIB GEN/LAWS

B66
FRIEDMANN W.G.,INTERNATIONAL FINANCIAL AID. USA+45 ECO/DEV ECO/UNDEV NAT/G VOL/ASSN EX/STRUC PLAN RENT GIVE BAL/PAY PWR...GEOG INT/LAW STAT TREND UN EEC COMECON. PAGE 44 F0866 — INT/ORG FOR/AID TEC/DEV ECO/TAC

B66
GITTINGER J.P.,THE LITERATURE OF AGRICULTURAL PLANNING. UNIV INT/ORG CONSULT WORKER TEC/DEV ECO/TAC OPTIMAL...POLICY METH/COMP BIBLIOG/A 20. PAGE 47 F0927 — ECO/UNDEV AGRI PLAN WRITING

B66
GORDON R.A.,PROSPERITY AND UNEMPLOYMENT. USA+45 PLAN ECO/TAC ADJUST DEMAND ALL/VALS...POLICY DECISION TREND CHARTS ANTHOL 20. PAGE 49 F0961 — WORKER INDUS ECO/DEV WEALTH

B66
GREENE L.E.,GOVERNMENT IN TENNESSEE (2ND ED.). USA+45 DIST/IND INDUS POL/PAR EX/STRUC LEGIS PLAN BUDGET GIVE CT/SYS...MGT T 20 TENNESSEE. PAGE 51 F0989 — PROVS LOC/G CONSTN ADMIN

B66
GROSS H.,MAKE OR BUY. AFR USA+45 FINAN INDUS CREATE PRICE PRODUC 20. PAGE 51 F1006 — ECO/TAC PLAN MGT COST

B66
HACKETT J.,L'ECONOMIE BRITANNIQUE: PROBLEMES ET PERSPECTIVES. FRANCE UK LABOR NAT/G EX/STRUC PROB/SOLV BAL/PAY INCOME RIGID/FLEX...MGT PHIL/SCI CHARTS MUNICH 20. PAGE 53 F1027 — ECO/DEV FINAN ECO/TAC PLAN

B66
HARLOW J.S.,FRENCH ECONOMIC PLANNING: A CHALLENGE TO REASON. EUR+WWI FRANCE PROB/SOLV 20 EUROPE. PAGE 55 F1084 — ECO/TAC PLAN STRUCT

B66
HASTINGS P.G.,THE MANAGEMENT OF BUSINESS FINANCE. ECO/DEV PLAN BUDGET CONTROL COST...DECISION CHARTS BIBLIOG T 20. PAGE 56 F1109 — FINAN MGT INDUS ECO/TAC

B66
HEISS K.P.,GAME THEORY AND HUMAN CONFLICTS (RESEARCH MEMORANDUM). UNIV ACT/RES...DECISION SOC MATH PROBABIL SIMUL 20 DEFINETT/B. PAGE 58 F1142 — GAME ECOMETRIC PLAN PROB/SOLV

B66
HO YHI-MIN,AGRICULTURAL DEVELOPMENT OF TAIWAN: 1903-1960. FINAN WORKER EDU/PROP...STAT CHARTS BIBLIOG 20. PAGE 60 F1181 — ECO/UNDEV AGRI PRODUC PLAN

B66
HOROWITZ D.,HEMISPHERES NORTH AND SOUTH: ECONOMIC DISPARITY AMONG NATIONS. WOR+45 ECO/DEV ECO/UNDEV INT/ORG PLAN DIPLOM INT/TRADE GIVE PARTIC GP/REL ...WELF/ST 20. PAGE 62 F1215 — ECO/TAC FOR/AID STRATA WEALTH

B66
HOROWITZ I.L.,THREE WORLDS OF DEVELOPMENT. COM USA+45 STRUCT ECO/DEV PLAN PROB/SOLV TEC/DEV CIVMIL/REL...PHIL/SCI IDEA/COMP 20. PAGE 62 F1216 — ECO/UNDEV BAL/PWR POL/PAR REV

B66
INARRITU A.L.,EL PATRON CAMBIO-ORO Y SUS REFORMAS. AFR L/A+17C WOR+45 PLAN PROB/SOLV BUDGET ECO/TAC INT/TRADE EFFICIENCY ORD/FREE 20 MEXIC/AMER. PAGE 64 F1262 — ECO/UNDEV FINAN DIPLOM POLICY

B66
KAESTNER K.,GESAMTWIRTSCHAFTLICHE PLANUNG IN EINER GEMISCHTEN WIRTSCHAFTSORDNUNG (WIRTSCHAFTSPOLITISCHE STUDIEN 5). GERMANY/W WOR+45 WOR-45 INDUS MARKET NAT/G ACT/RES GP/REL INGP/REL PRODUC...ECOMETRIC MGT BIBLIOG 20. PAGE 68 F1346 — ECO/TAC PLAN POLICY PREDICT

B66
KAREFA-SMART J.,AFRICA: PROGRESS THROUGH COOPERATION. AFR FINAN TEC/DEV DIPLOM FOR/AID EDU/PROP CONFER REGION GP/REL WEALTH...HEAL SOC/INTEG 20. PAGE 69 F1356 — ORD/FREE ECO/UNDEV VOL/ASSN PLAN

B66
KIRDAR U.,THE STRUCTURE OF UNITED NATIONS ECONOMIC AID TO UNDERDEVELOPED COUNTRIES. AGRI FINAN INDUS NAT/G EX/STRUC PLAN GIVE TASK...POLICY 20 UN. PAGE 71 F1397 — INT/ORG FOR/AID ECO/UNDEV ADMIN

B66
KIRKENDALL R.S.,SOCIAL SCIENTISTS AND FARM POLITICS IN THE AGE OF ROOSEVELT. ACADEM PLAN ECO/TAC GIVE ADMIN CONTROL PRODUC...SOC 20 NEW/DEAL ROOSEVLT/F BURAGR/ECO. PAGE 71 F1399 — AGRI INTELL POLICY NAT/G

B66
KOMIYA R.,POSTWAR ECONOMIC GROWTH IN JAPAN. ELITES NAT/G EX/STRUC TEC/DEV BUDGET DIPLOM CONTROL BAL/PAY PRODUC...BIBLIOG 20 CHINJAP. PAGE 73 F1424 — ECO/DEV POLICY PLAN ADJUST

B66
KURAKOV I.G.,SCIENCE, TECHNOLOGY AND COMMUNISM; SOME QUESTIONS OF DEVELOPMENT (TRANS. BY CARIN DEDIJER). USSR INDUS PLAN PROB/SOLV COST PRODUC ...MGT MATH CHARTS METH 20. PAGE 74 F1450 — CREATE TEC/DEV MARXISM ECO/TAC

B66
LEAGUE OF WOMEN VOTERS OF US,FOREIGN AID AT THE CROSSROADS. USA+45 WOR+45 DELIB/GP PROB/SOLV DIPLOM INT/TRADE RECEIVE BAL/PAY...CHARTS 20 UN ALL/PROG. PAGE 76 F1498 — FOR/AID GIVE ECO/UNDEV PLAN

B66
LECHT L.,GOAL, PRIORITIES, AND DOLLARS: THE NEXT DECADE. SPACE USA+45 SOCIETY AGRI BUDGET FOR/AID ...HEAL SOC/WK STAT CHARTS 20 URBAN/RNWL PUB/TRANS. PAGE 76 F1499 — IDEA/COMP POLICY CONSEN PLAN

B66
LEWIS W.A.,DEVELOPMENT PLANNING; THE ESSENTIALS OF ECONOMIC POLICY. USA+45 FINAN INDUS NAT/G WORKER FOR/AID INT/TRADE ADMIN ROUTINE WEALTH...CONCPT STAT. PAGE 79 F1552 — PLAN ECO/DEV POLICY CREATE

B66
LICHTMAN R.,TOWARD COMMUNITY (PAPER). PLAN PROB/SOLV WEALTH MARXISM...HEAL CONCPT 20. PAGE 80 F1561
NEW/LIB EFFICIENCY CAP/ISM ADJUST

B66
MADAN G.R.,ECONOMIC THINKING IN INDIA. INDIA ECO/UNDEV AGRI FINAN INDUS LABOR PLAN CAP/ISM INT/TRADE MARXISM SOCISM...POLICY 1/20. PAGE 84 F1638
ECO/TAC PHIL/SCI NAT/G POL/PAR

B66
MALASSIS L.,ECONOMIC DEVELOPMENT AND THE PROGRAMMING OF RURAL EDUCATION. CONSULT PROB/SOLV LITERACY KNOWL...CHARTS GEN/METH 20. PAGE 84 F1644
AGRI ECO/UNDEV SCHOOL PLAN

B66
MASON E.S.,ECONOMIC DEVELOPMENT IN INDIA AND PAKISTAN. INDIA PAKISTAN AGRI FINAN PLAN BUDGET INT/TRADE WEALTH...POLICY STAT TREND CHARTS 20. PAGE 87 F1700
NAT/COMP ECO/UNDEV ECO/TAC FOR/AID

B66
MEERHAEGHE M.,INTERNATIONAL ECONOMIC INSTITUTIONS. EUR+WWI FINAN INDUS MARKET PLAN TARIFFS BAL/PAY EQUILIB...POLICY BIBLIOG/A 20 GATT OEEC EEC IBRD EURCOALSTL. PAGE 89 F1745
ECO/TAC ECO/DEV INT/TRADE INT/ORG

B66
MUNBY D.,ECONOMIC GROWTH IN WORLD PERSPECTIVE. AFR WOR+45 SOCIETY INDUS PLAN TEC/DEV ECO/TAC FOR/AID INT/TRADE COST CATHISM...ANTHOL 20 EUROPE/W CHURCH/STA. PAGE 95 F1859
SECT ECO/UNDEV ECO/DEV

B66
MURPHY G.G.,SOVIET MONGOLIA: A STUDY OF THE OLDEST POLITICAL SATELLITE. USSR STRATA STRUCT COST INCOME ATTIT SOCISM 20. PAGE 95 F1865
DIPLOM ECO/TAC PLAN DOMIN

B66
NAMBOODIRIPAD E.M.,ECONOMICS AND POLITICS OF INDIA'S SOCIALIST PATTERN. INDIA STRATA AGRI INDUS NAT/G PRICE ORD/FREE SOVEREIGN 20. PAGE 96 F1888
ECO/UNDEV PLAN SOCISM CAP/ISM

B66
NATIONAL COUN APPLIED ECO RES,DEVELOPMENT WITHOUT AID. INDIA FINAN TEC/DEV EFFICIENCY...ANTHOL 20. PAGE 97 F1901
FOR/AID PLAN SOVEREIGN ECO/UNDEV

B66
NEVITT A.A.,HOUSING, TAXATION AND SUBSIDIES; A STUDY OF HOUSING IN THE UNITED KINGDOM. UK FINAN GIVE CONTROL COST INCOME...CHARTS 20. PAGE 98 F1918
PLAN TAX HABITAT RENT

B66
OECD DEVELOPMENT CENTRE,CATALOGUE OF SOCIAL AND ECONOMIC DEVELOPMENT INSTITUTES AND PROGRAMMES* RESEARCH. ACT/RES PLAN TEC/DEV EDU/PROP...SOC GP/COMP NAT/COMP. PAGE 101 F1976
ECO/UNDEV ECO/DEV R+D ACADEM

B66
OHLIN G.,AID AND INDEBTEDNESS. AUSTRIA FINAN INT/ORG PLAN DIPLOM GIVE...POLICY MATH CHARTS 20. PAGE 101 F1984
FOR/AID ECO/UNDEV ADMIN WEALTH

B66
OHLIN G.,FOREIGN AID POLICIES RECONSIDERED. ECO/DEV ECO/UNDEV VOL/ASSN CONSULT PLAN CONTROL ATTIT ...CONCPT CHARTS BIBLIOG 20. PAGE 101 F1985
FOR/AID DIPLOM GIVE

B66
RUPPENTHAL K.M.,TRANSPORTATION AND TOMORROW. FUT SPACE USA+45 SEA AIR FORCES TEC/DEV INT/TRADE ...ANTHOL 20 RAILROAD. PAGE 115 F2261
DIST/IND PLAN CIVMIL/REL PREDICT

B66
SHULTZ G.P.,STRATEGIES FOR THE DISPLACED WORKER. USA+45 COMPUTER TEC/DEV BARGAIN RECEIVE EDU/PROP CONFER GP/REL...MGT METH/COMP 20. PAGE 121 F2391
ECO/DEV WORKER PLAN AUTOMAT

B66
SINGH L.P.,THE POLITICS OF ECONOMIC COOPERATION IN ASIA; A STUDY OF ASIAN INTERNATIONAL ORGANIZATIONS. ASIA INT/ORG ACT/RES PLAN GP/REL...POLICY GP/COMP BIBLIOG 20 UN SEATO. PAGE 122 F2414
ECO/UNDEV ECO/TAC REGION DIPLOM

B66
SMITH H.E.,READINGS IN ECONOMIC DEVELOPMENT AND ADMINISTRATION IN TANZANIA. TANZANIA FINAN INDUS LABOR NAT/G PLAN PROB/SOLV INT/TRADE COLONIAL REGION...ANTHOL BIBLIOG 20 AFRICA/E. PAGE 123 F2431
TEC/DEV ADMIN GOV/REL

B66
SPULBER N.,THE STATE AND ECONOMIC DEVELOPMENT IN EASTERN EUROPE. BULGARIA COM CZECHOSLVK HUNGARY POLAND YUGOSLAVIA CULTURE PLAN CAP/ISM INT/TRADE CONTROL...POLICY CHARTS METH/COMP BIBLIOG/A 19/20. PAGE 125 F2460
ECO/DEV ECO/UNDEV NAT/G TOTALISM

B66
THEIL H.,APPLIED ECONOMIC FORECASTING. UNIV USA+45 ELITES INTELL CONSULT PRODUC...DECISION MGT PREDICT CHARTS METH/COMP SIMUL 20. PAGE 129 F2552
FUT OP/RES PLAN

B66
US DEPARTMENT OF LABOR,PRODUCTIVITY: A BIBLIOGRAPHY. ECO/DEV INDUS MARKET OP/RES AUTOMAT COST...STAT 20. PAGE 135 F2668
BIBLIOG/A PRODUC LABOR PLAN

B66
US SENATE COMM GOVT OPERATIONS,HEARINGS BEFORE SUBCOMMITTEE ON FOREIGN AID EXPENDITURES: POPULATION CRISIS VOLUMES 1-5 JUNE-SEPT 1965. STRATA ECO/UNDEV PLAN TEC/DEV EDU/PROP ATTIT HEALTH ...GEOG CHARTS 20 CONGRESS BIRTH/CON CASEBOOK. PAGE 138 F2729
ECO/DEV CENSUS FAM CONTROL

B66
WESTON J.F.,THE SCOPE AND METHODOLOGY OF FINANCE. PLAN TEC/DEV CONTROL EFFICIENCY INCOME UTIL...MGT CONCPT MATH STAT TREND METH 20. PAGE 145 F2863
FINAN ECO/DEV POLICY PRICE

B66
WILCOX C.,ECONOMIES OF THE WORLD TODAY: THEIR ORGANIZATION, DEVELOPMENT, AND PERFORMANCE (2ND ED.). CHINA/COM COM INDIA NIGERIA UK WOR+45 WOR-45 INDUS MARKET PLAN ECO/TAC SOCISM...CHARTS METH/COMP 20. PAGE 146 F2878
ECO/DEV ECO/UNDEV MARXISM CAP/ISM

L66
AFRICAN BIBLIOGRAPHIC CENTER,"AFRICAN ECONOMIC AFFAIRS: A SELECT BIBLIOGRAPHICAL SURVEY, 1965-1966." AFR FINAN INDUS INT/ORG LABOR PLAN BUDGET DIPLOM INT/TRADE ADMIN EFFICIENCY WEALTH 20. PAGE 3 F0046
BIBLIOG ECO/UNDEV TEC/DEV FOR/AID

L66
AFRICAN BIBLIOGRAPHIC CENTER,"AFRICAN ECONOMIC AFFAIRS: A SELECT BIBLIOGRAPHICAL SURVEY, 1965-1966; SUPPLEMENTS NUMBERS 1-3." AFR FINAN INDUS LABOR PLAN BUDGET CAP/ISM DIPLOM INT/TRADE ADMIN...GEOG 20. PAGE 3 F0047
BIBLIOG/A ECO/UNDEV FOR/AID TEC/DEV

L66
AMERICAN ECONOMIC REVIEW,"SIXTY-THIRD LIST OF DOCTORAL DISSERTATIONS IN POLITICAL ECONOMY IN AMERICAN UNIVERSITIES AND COLLEGES." ECO/DEV AGRI FINAN LABOR WORKER PLAN BUDGET INT/TRADE ADMIN DEMAND...MGT STAT 20. PAGE 5 F0088
BIBLIOG/A CONCPT ACADEM

S66
JACOBS P.,"RE-RADICALIZING THE DE-RADICALIZED." USA+45 SOCIETY STRUCT FINAN PLAN PROB/SOLV CAP/ISM WEALTH CONSERVE NEW/LIB 20. PAGE 66 F1297
NAT/G POLICY MARXIST ADMIN

S66
JAVITS J.K.,"POLITICAL ACTION VITAL FOR LATIN AMERICAN INTEGRATION." ECO/UNDEV INT/ORG POL/PAR VOL/ASSN PLAN PROB/SOLV INT/TRADE EFFICIENCY 20 OAS LAFTA ALL/PROG. PAGE 66 F1308
L/A+17C ECO/TAC REGION

S66
LINDBLOOM C.E.,"HAS INDIA AN ECONOMIC FUTURE?" FUT INDIA NAT/G PROB/SOLV...POLICY 20. PAGE 80 F1568
AGRI PRODUC PLAN ECO/UNDEV

S66
MALENBAUM W.,"GOVERNMENT, ENTREPRENEURSHIP, AND ECONOMIC GROWTH IN POOR LANDS." ELITES ECO/UNDEV INDUS CREATE DRIVE. PAGE 84 F1645
ECO/TAC PLAN CONSERVE NAT/G

S66
MARKSHAK J.,"ECONOMIC PLANNING AND THE COST OF THINKING." COM MARKET EX/STRUC...DECISION GEN/LAWS. PAGE 85 F1672
ECO/UNDEV ECO/TAC PLAN ECO/DEV

S66
POSEN G.S.,"RECENT TRENDS IN SOVIET ECONOMIC THOUGHT." USSR ECO/DEV PLAN CONTROL CENTRAL 20. PAGE 107 F2107
ECO/TAC MARXISM INDUS PROFIT

S66
VENTRE F.T.,"LOCAL INITIATIVES IN URBAN INDUSTRIAL DEVELOPMENT." FINAN SERV/IND TOP/EX PLAN BUDGET RENT TAX...GP/COMP MUNICH 20. PAGE 141 F2777
ECO/TAC LOC/G INDUS

N66
EOMMITTEE ECONOMIC DEVELOPMENT,THE DOLLAR AND THE WORLD MONETARY SYSTEM: A STATEMENT ON NATIONAL POLICY (PAMPHLET). AFR USA+45 NAT/G PLAN PROB/SOLV BUDGET ECO/TAC FOR/AID INCOME...POLICY 20 EUROPE. PAGE 38 F0740
FINAN BAL/PAY DIPLOM ECO/DEV

N66
OECD,THE BALANCE OF PAYMENTS ADJUSTMENT PROCESS (PAMPHLET). EUR+WWI ECO/DEV FINAN CONSULT PLAN PROB/SOLV BUDGET CAP/ISM INT/TRADE PRICE CONTROL EQUILIB 20. PAGE 101 F1975
BAL/PAY ECO/TAC DIPLOM INT/ORG

N66
PRINCETON U INDUSTRIAL REL SEC,PUBLIC PROGRAMS TO CREATE JOBS (PAMPHLET NO. 125). USA+45 ECO/DEV INDUS PLAN ECO/TAC AGE/Y 20. PAGE 108 F2119
BIBLIOG/A NAT/G POLICY WORKER

N66
PRINCETON U INDUSTRIAL REL SEC,THE ROLE OF THE PUBLIC EMPLOYMENT SERVICE (PAMPHLET NO. 129). USA+45 ECO/DEV PLAN ECO/TAC GOV/REL 20. PAGE 108 F2121
BIBLIOG/A NAT/G POLICY LABOR

B67
AARON H.J.,FINANCING URBAN DEVELOPMENT IN MEXICO
PLAN

CITY: A CASE STUDY OF PROPERTY TAX, LAND USE, HOUSING, AND URBAN PLANNING. LOC/G CREATE EFFICIENCY WEALTH...CHARTS MUNICH 20 MEXIC/AMER. PAGE 2 F0030
TAX PROB/SOLV

B67
ANDERSON C.W.,POLITICS AND ECONOMIC CHANGE IN LATIN AMERICA. L/A+17C INDUS NAT/G OP/RES ADMIN DEMAND ...POLICY STAT CHARTS NAT/COMP 20. PAGE 5 F0093
ECO/UNDEV PROB/SOLV PLAN ECO/TAC

B67
BADGLEY R.F.,DOCTORS' STRIKE; MEDICAL CARE AND CONFLICT IN SASKATCHEWAN. CANADA NAT/G PROF/ORG GP/REL ADJUST ATTIT...HEAL SOC 20. PAGE 8 F0148
HEALTH PLAN LABOR BARGAIN

B67
BALDWIN G.B.,PLANNING AND DEVELOPMENT IN IRAN. IRAN AGRI INDUS CONSULT WORKER EDU/PROP BAL/PAY...CHARTS 20. PAGE 9 F0164
PLAN ECO/UNDEV ADMIN PROB/SOLV

B67
BIRMINGHAM W.,A STUDY OF CONTEMPORARY GHANA VOL. I: SOME ASPECTS OF SOCIAL STRUCTURE. AFR GHANA AGRI FAM SECT PLAN EDU/PROP MARRIAGE OWN...POLICY STAT CHARTS MUNICH 20. PAGE 15 F0287
SOCIETY STRUCT CENSUS ECO/UNDEV

B67
BLAUG M.,ECONOMICS OF EDUCATION: A SELECTED ANNOTATED BIBLIOGRAPHY. EUR+WWI INTELL ECO/DEV ECO/UNDEV ACADEM INT/ORG NAT/G CREATE ADMIN EFFICIENCY ROLE PREDICT. PAGE 16 F0298
BIBLIOG/A EDU/PROP FINAN PLAN

B67
BREAK G.F.,INTERGOVERNMENTAL FISCAL RELATIONS IN THE UNITED STATES. USA+45 USA-45 DELIB/GP PLAN BUDGET TAX GOV/REL CENTRAL...TREND CHARTS MUNICH. PAGE 18 F0345
LOC/G NAT/G PROVS FINAN

B67
BRIEFS H.W.,REGAINING BALANCE IN A HIGH EMPLOYMENT ECONOMY: UNRESOLVED ISSUES FOR 1967 AND BEYOND. USA+45 NAT/G PLAN PROB/SOLV FOR/AID...CHARTS 20. PAGE 18 F0350
ECO/DEV FINAN BAL/PAY BUDGET

B67
CAMPBELL A.K.,METROPOLITAN AMERICA* FISCAL PATTERNS AND GOVERNMENTAL SYSTEMS. PROVS PLAN COST...POLICY DECISION GOV/COMP METH/COMP BIBLIOG. PAGE 21 F0405
USA+45 NAT/G LOC/G BUDGET

B67
CARNEY D.,PATTERNS AND MECHANICS OF ECONOMIC GROWTH: A GENERAL THEORETICAL APPROACH. WOR+45 OP/RES INCOME...MATH TREND CHARTS 20. PAGE 21 F0416
PLAN ECO/DEV FINAN

B67
CHANDRASEKHAR S.,PROBLEMS OF ECONOMIC DEVELOPMENT. AFR INDIA PHILIPPINE UAR WOR+45 INDUS...GEOG SOC ANTHOL BIBLIOG 20 CHINJAP. PAGE 23 F0450
ECO/UNDEV PLAN AGRI PROB/SOLV

B67
CHAPIN F.S. JR.,SELECTED REFERENCES ON URBAN PLANNING METHODS AND TECHNIQUES. USA+45 LAW ECO/DEV LOC/G NAT/G SCHOOL CONSULT CREATE PROB/SOLV TEC/DEV ...SOC/WK MUNICH. PAGE 23 F0454
BIBLIOG NEIGH PLAN

B67
CLEMENT M.O.,THEORETICAL ISSUES IN INTERNATIONAL ECONOMICS. WOR+45 PLAN PROB/SOLV TEC/DEV ...ECOMETRIC METH/CNCPT MATH BIBLIOG T MONEY. PAGE 25 F0489
INT/TRADE FINAN CREATE BAL/PAY

B67
COTTAM R.W.,COMPETITIVE INTERFERENCE AND TWENTIETH CENTURY DIPLOMACY. IRAN ACT/RES CREATE PLAN ECO/TAC EFFICIENCY ATTIT...DECISION NEW/IDEA TREND 20 CIA. PAGE 28 F0541
DIPLOM DOMIN GAME

B67
DAVIS F.M.,COME AS A CONQUEROR: THE UNITED STATES ARMY'S OCCUPATION OF GERMANY: 1945-1949. EUR+WWI GERMANY USA+45 SOCIETY PLAN BAL/PWR DIPLOM FOR/AID PERS/REL DEMAND PEACE ORD/FREE 20. PAGE 30 F0588
FORCES CIVMIL/REL ECO/TAC CONTROL

B67
DIXON W.,SOCIETY, SCHOOLS AND PROGRESS IN SCANDINAVIA. DENMARK NORWAY SWEDEN 20. PAGE 33 F0644
EDU/PROP SOCIETY ADJUST PLAN

B67
ELDREDGE H.W.,TAMING MEGALOPOLIS; HOW TO MANAGE AN URBANIZED WORLD. WOR+45 SOCIETY ECO/DEV ECO/UNDEV NAT/G COMPUTER CREATE PARTIC EFFICIENCY WEALTH ...MGT ANTHOL MUNICH. PAGE 37 F0716
TEC/DEV PLAN PROB/SOLV

B67
ELDREDGE H.W.,TAMING MEGALOPOLIS; WHAT IT IS AND WHAT COULD BE (VOL. I). FUT USA+45 WOR+45 SOCIETY STRUCT ECO/DEV INDUS LEISURE WEALTH...ANTHOL MUNICH. PAGE 37 F0717
PROB/SOLV PLAN TEC/DEV

B67
ENKE S.,DEFENSE MANAGEMENT. USA+45 R+D FORCES WORKER PLAN ECO/TAC ADMIN NUC/PWR BAL/PAY UTIL WEALTH...MGT DEPT/DEFEN. PAGE 38 F0738
DECISION DELIB/GP EFFICIENCY BUDGET

B67
GIAP V.N.,BIG VICTORY, GREAT TASK. VIETNAM WOR+45 FORCES PLAN DOMIN LEGIT RISK PEACE 20. PAGE 47 F0921
WAR LEAD ATTIT INSPECT

B67
GORZ A.,STRATEGY FOR LABOR: A RADICAL PROPOSAL (TRANS. BY MARTIN NICOLAUS AND VICTORIA ORTIZ). EUR+WWI FRANCE ITALY ECO/DEV POL/PAR OP/RES PLAN GP/REL ALL/IDEOS...SOC 20 EEC. PAGE 49 F0965
LABOR PWR STRUCT ECO/TAC

B67
GREEN C.,NEGATIVE TAXES AND THE POVERTY PROBLEM. COST EFFICIENCY INCOME NEW/LIB...METH/CNCPT CHARTS METH/COMP BIBLIOG 20. PAGE 50 F0983
TAX RECEIVE WEALTH PLAN

B67
GRIPP R.C.,PATTERNS OF SOVIET POLITICS (REV. ED.). USSR LAW ELITES LOC/G PLAN CONTROL CT/SYS CHOOSE ...POLICY BIBLIOG/A DICTIONARY 9/20. PAGE 51 F1003
COM ADJUD POL/PAR

B67
GROSS B.M.,ACTION UNDER PLANNING: THE GUIDANCE OF ECONOMIC DEVELOPMENT. STRUCT R+D NAT/G ACT/RES HABITAT...DECISION 20. PAGE 51 F1005
ECO/UNDEV PLAN ADMIN MGT

B67
HAGUE D.C.,PRICE FORMATION IN VARIOUS ECONOMIES; PROCEEDINGS OF A CONFERENCE HELD BY THE INTERNATIONAL ECONOMIC ASSOCIATION. WOR+45 FINAN MARKET PLAN CONFER COST...DECISION MATH PREDICT CHARTS SIMUL 20 INTL/ECON. PAGE 53 F1037
PRICE CAP/ISM SOCISM METH/COMP

B67
HARDT J.P.,MATHEMATICS AND COMPUTERS IN SOVIET ECONOMIC PLANNING. COM USSR OP/RES PROB/SOLV OPTIMAL...MODAL SIMUL 20. PAGE 55 F1082
PLAN TEC/DEV MATH COMPUT/IR

B67
JOHNSON D.G.,THE STRUGGLE AGAINST WORLD HUNGER (HEADLINE SERIES, NO. 184) (PAMPHLET). PLAN TEC/DEV FOR/AID...CHARTS 20 FAO MEXIC/AMER. PAGE 67 F1322
AGRI PROB/SOLV ECO/UNDEV HEALTH

B67
JOHNSON H.G.,ECONOMIC POLICY TOWARD LESS DEVELOPED COUNTRIES. USA+45 ECO/DEV INT/ORG PLAN CAP/ISM FOR/AID TARIFFS GIVE WEALTH...NEW/IDEA CHARTS 20 UN GATT. PAGE 67 F1327
ECO/UNDEV ECO/TAC METH/COMP

B67
KAPLAN J.J.,CHALLENGE OF FOREIGN AID. USA+45 CONTROL BAL/PAY COST ATTIT ALL/VALS...METH/COMP 20. PAGE 69 F1352
FOR/AID PLAN GIVE POLICY

B67
KULSKI J.E.,LAND OF URBAN PROMISE* CONTINUING THE GREAT TRADITION* A SEARCH FOR SIGNIFICANT URBAN SPACE IN URBANIZED NORTHEAST. USA+45 DIST/IND PUB/INST CONSULT CREATE TEC/DEV...SOC NEW/IDEA CHARTS BIBLIOG MUNICH. PAGE 74 F1448
PLAN PROB/SOLV ECO/DEV

B67
LITTLE AD, INC.,COMMUNITY RENEWAL PROGRAMMING. CULTURE LOC/G ACT/RES TASK COST ATTIT...SOC/WK MODAL STAT STAND/INT CHARTS 20 SAN/FRAN. PAGE 81 F1585
STRATA NEIGH PLAN CREATE

B67
MACCLOSKEY M.,PACTS FOR PEACE: UN, NATO, SEATO, CENTO, OAS. WOR+45 PLAN DIPLOM CONTROL PEACE ORD/FREE...ORG/CHARTS UN NATO SEATO OAS CENTO. PAGE 83 F1623
FORCES INT/ORG LEAD POLICY

B67
MARTIN P.,CANADA AND THE QUEST FOR PEACE. CANADA VIETNAM ECO/UNDEV PLAN FOR/AID WAR 20 UN. PAGE 86 F1684
DIPLOM PEACE INT/ORG POLICY

B67
MAZOUR A.G.,SOVIET ECONOMIC DEVELOPMENT: OPERATION OUTSTRIP: 1921-1965. USSR ECO/UNDEV FINAN CHIEF WORKER PROB/SOLV CONTROL PRODUC MARXISM...CHARTS ORG/CHARTS 20 STALIN/J. PAGE 87 F1711
ECO/TAC AGRI INDUS PLAN

B67
NELSON R.R.,TECHNOLOGY, ECONOMIC GROWTH, AND PUBLIC POLICY. USA+45 PLAN GP/REL UTIL KNOWL...POLICY PHIL/SCI CHARTS BIBLIOG 20. PAGE 97 F1912
R+D CONSULT CREATE ACT/RES

B67
ORLANS H.,CONTRACTING FOR ATOMS. AFR USA+45 LAW INTELL ACADEM LG/CO NAT/G PLAN TEC/DEV CONTROL DETER...TREND 20. PAGE 102 F1999
NUC/PWR R+D PRODUC PEACE

B67
PELTASON J.W.,FUNCTIONS AND POLICIES OF AMERICAN GOVERNMENT (3RD ED.). USA+45 FINAN INDUS EDU/PROP CIVMIL/REL RACE/REL ORD/FREE...ANTHOL T 20 JOHNSON/LB. PAGE 104 F2052
NAT/G GOV/REL POLICY PLAN

B67
PORWIT K.,CENTRAL PLANNING: EVALUATION OF VARIANTS. PRICE OPTIMAL PRODUC...DECISION MATH CHARTS SIMUL BIBLIOG MODELS 20. PAGE 107 F2106
PLAN MGT ECOMETRIC

B67
POWLEDGE F.,BLACK POWER WHITE RESISTANCE. USA+45 STRUCT PLAN GP/REL DISCRIM HABITAT ORD/FREE WEALTH ...METH/COMP SOC/INTEG NEGRO. PAGE 107 F2111
RACE/REL ATTIT PWR

B67
ROBERTS B.C.,COLLECTIVE BARGAINING IN AFRICAN COUNTRIES. AFR LAW ECO/UNDEV BARGAIN GP/REL ...DECISION METH/COMP 20. PAGE 112 F2206
LABOR MGT PLAN ECO/TAC

B67
ROBINSON E.A.G.,ECONOMIC PLANNING IN THE UNITED KINGDOM. UK WORKER PLAN PROB/SOLV BAL/PAY 20. PAGE 113 F2220
ECO/DEV INDUS PRODUC BUDGET

B67
SMITH T.L.,THE PROCESS OF RURAL DEVELOPMENT IN LATIN AMERICA (A MONOGRAPH). L/A+17C STRATA INDUS PLAN GP/REL PERS/REL RIGID/FLEX WEALTH...OBS CHARTS ORG/CHARTS ANTHOL 20 COLOMB. PAGE 123 F2434
IDEA/COMP SOC AGRI ECO/UNDEV

B67
TANSKY L.,US AND USSR AID TO DEVELOPING COUNTRIES. INDIA TURKEY USA+45 USSR INDUS PLAN CAP/ISM WAR PWR WEALTH MARXISM...CHARTS NAT/COMP BIBLIOG 20. PAGE 128 F2534
ECO/UNDEV FOR/AID DIPLOM ECO/TAC

B67
TANSKY L.,US AND USSR AID TO DEVELOPING COUNTRIES. INDIA TURKEY UAR USA+45 USSR FINAN PLAN TEC/DEV ADMIN WEALTH...TREND METH/COMP 20. PAGE 128 F2535
FOR/AID ECO/UNDEV MARXISM CAP/ISM

B67
THOMAN R.S.,GEOGRAPHY OF INTERNATIONAL TRADE. WOR+45 ECO/DEV ECO/UNDEV INT/ORG LG/CO PLAN BAL/PAY ...STAT CHARTS NAT/COMP 20. PAGE 130 F2559
INT/TRADE GEOG ECO/TAC DIPLOM

B67
US CONGRESS JOINT ECO COMM,REPORT ON JANUARY 1967 ECONOMIC REPORT OF THE PRESIDENT. FINAN LABOR NAT/G LEGIS BUDGET INT/TRADE COST DEMAND INCOME PRODUC ...POLICY IDEA/COMP 20 CONGRESS. PAGE 135 F2663
CHIEF ECO/TAC PLAN DELIB/GP

B67
US CONGRESS JOINT ECO COMM,AN ECONOMIC PROFILE OF MAINLAND CHINA, VOLUMES I AND II. CHINA/COM AGRI DIST/IND FINAN INDUS LABOR FORCES ACT/RES PLAN INT/TRADE INGP/REL BAL/PAY 20 CONGRESS. PAGE 135 F2664
ECO/UNDEV WEALTH ECO/TAC DELIB/GP

B67
US SENATE COMM ON FOREIGN REL,LATIN AMERICAN SUMMIT CONFERENCE. L/A+17C USA+45 FINAN PLAN SENATE ALL/PROG. PAGE 139 F2740
FOR/AID BUDGET DIPLOM INT/ORG

B67
VAN SLYKE L.P.,ENEMIES AND FRIENDS; THE UNITED FRONT IN CHINESE COMMUNIST HISTORY. CHINA/COM SOCIETY FORCES PLAN ADJUST 20 MAO. PAGE 140 F2764
INGP/REL MARXISM ATTIT GP/REL

B67
WEINBERG M.,SCHOOL INTEGRATION: A COMPREHENSIVE CLASSIFIED BIBLIOGRAPHY OF 3,100 REFERENCES. USA+45 LAW NAT/G NEIGH SECT PLAN ROUTINE AGE/C WEALTH SOC/INTEG INDIAN/AM. PAGE 145 F2849
BIBLIOG SCHOOL DISCRIM RACE/REL

B67
YOUNG J.M.,THE BRAZILIAN REVOLUTION OF 1930 AND THE AFTERMATH. BRAZIL COLONIAL PWR...BIBLIOG/A 16/20. PAGE 150 F2951
PLAN CHIEF FORCES REV

B67
ZALESKI E.,PLANNING REFORMS IN THE SOVIET UNION 1962-1966. COM USSR NAT/G CONFER CONTROL EFFICIENCY MARXISM...POLICY DECISION 20. PAGE 150 F2957
ECO/DEV PLAN ADMIN CENTRAL

B67
ZUPNICK E.,UNDERSTANDING THE INTERNATIONAL MONEY SYSTEM (HEADLINE SERIES, NO. 182) (PAMPHLET). ECO/DEV NAT/G DIPLOM INT/TRADE...METH/COMP 20 IMF. PAGE 151 F2971
FINAN PLAN INT/ORG PROB/SOLV

L67
"GOVERNMENT CONTROL OF LAND: PROTECTING THE I-KNOW-IT-WHENI-SEE-IT INTEREST." USA+45 LAW CONSTN DELIB/GP CT/SYS HABITAT ILLINOIS. PAGE 2 F0026
PLAN LOC/G CONTROL ADJUD

L67
BERNHARD R.C.,"COMPETITION IN LAW AND ECONOMICS." LAW PLAN PRICE CONTROL PRODUC PROFIT...METH/CNCPT IDEA/COMP GEN/LAWS 20. PAGE 14 F0265
MARKET POLICY NAT/G CT/SYS

L67
GLAZER N.,"HOUSING PROBLEMS AND HOUSING POLICIES." USA+45 PLAN RENT ADJUST CONSEN DEMAND DISCRIM AGE ATTIT HEALTH WEALTH MUNICH NEGRO. PAGE 48 F0929
POLICY CONSTRUC CREATE HABITAT

L67
JOHNSTON J.D. JR.,"CONSTITUTION OF SUBDIVISION CONTROL EXACTIONS: THE QUEST FOR A RATIONALE." USA+45 PROVS PUB/INST ADJUD CT/SYS GP/REL MUNICH. PAGE 68 F1334
PLAN CONTROL LOC/G FORCES

L67
LENT G.E.,"TAX INCENTIVES FOR INVESTMENT IN DEVELOPING COUNTRIES" WOR+45 LAW INDUS PLAN BUDGET TARIFFS ADMIN...METH/COMP 20. PAGE 78 F1526
ECO/UNDEV TAX FINAN ECO/TAC

L67
MIXON J.,"JANE JACOBS AND THE LAW - ZONING FOR DIVERSITY EXAMINED." FUT USA+45 CONSTN NEIGH PROB/SOLV CONTROL CT/SYS PARTIC ATTIT...POLICY CENSUS METH/COMP MUNICH. PAGE 92 F1810
IDEA/COMP PLAN LAW

L67
STRUVE G.M.,"THE LESS-RESTRICTIVE-ALTERNATIVE PRINCIPLE AND ECONOMIC DUE PROCESS." USA+45 ECO/DEV LABOR NAT/G CONSULT DELIB/GP OP/RES PLAN WEALTH. PAGE 127 F2505
JURID JUDGE SANCTION CAP/ISM

L67
TRAVERS H. JR.,"AN EXAMINATION OF THE CAB'S MERGER POLICY." USA+45 USA-45 LAW NAT/G LEGIS PLAN ADMIN ...DECISION 20 CONGRESS. PAGE 131 F2584
ADJUD LG/CO POLICY DIST/IND

L67
ZEIDBERG L.D.,"THE NASHVILLE AIR POLLUTION STUDY" (PARTS V-VII)" USA+45 PLAN AGE HEALTH...GEOG STAT CENSUS SAMP/SIZ CHARTS BIBLIOG MUNICH. PAGE 150 F2962
DEATH HABITAT AIR BIO/SOC

S67
"PROTEST AGAINST SOVIET INDUSTRIALIZATION ILLS IN LITHUANIA* A MEMORANDUM." USSR LITHUANIA NAT/G PROVS COST GEOG. PAGE 1 F0024
INDUS COLONIAL NAT/LISM PLAN

S67
"THE FEDERAL AGRICULTURAL STABILIZATION PROGRAM AND THE NEGRO." LAW CONSTN PLAN REPRESENT DISCRIM ORD/FREE 20 NEGRO CONGRESS. PAGE 2 F0025
AGRI CONTROL NAT/G RACE/REL

S67
AVTORKHANOV A.,"A NEW AGRARIAN REVOLUTION." COM USSR ECO/DEV PLAN TEC/DEV ADMIN CONTROL OPTIMAL WEALTH SOCISM 20 KHRUSH/N STALIN/J. PAGE 8 F0144
AGRI METH/COMP MARXISM OWN

S67
BARAN P.,"THE FUTURE COMPUTER UTILITY." USA+45 NAT/G PLAN CONTROL COST...POLICY 20. PAGE 9 F0177
COMPUTER UTIL FUT TEC/DEV

S67
BENN W.,"TECHNOLOGY HAS AN INEXORABLE EFFECT." FUT UK ECO/DEV INT/ORG CONSULT PLAN EDU/PROP ADMIN LEAD GP/REL PRODUC...INT 20 EEC. PAGE 13 F0246
R+D LG/CO TEC/DEV INDUS

S67
BRANCO R.,"LAND REFORM* THE ANSWER TO LATIN AMERICA'S AGRICULTURAL DEVELOPMENT?" L/A+17C NAT/G PLAN TEC/DEV BUDGET RENT EFFICIENCY 20. PAGE 18 F0339
ECO/UNDEV AGRI TAX OWN

S67
CLABAULT J.M.,"PRACTICALITIES IN COMPETITOR EXCHANGING PRICE INFORMATION." ECO/DEV PLAN ...CONCPT 20. PAGE 24 F0473
INDUS LAW METH/COMP

S67
CROKER F.P.U.,"ECONOMIC PEACEKEEPING." UK PLAN PROB/SOLV TEC/DEV BAL/PWR DIPLOM COERCE PEACE ...POLICY DECISION 20. PAGE 28 F0553
FORCES WEAPON COST WAR

S67
FADDEYEV N.,"CMEA CO-OPERATION OF EQUAL NATIONS." COM R+D PLAN CAP/ISM DIPLOM FOR/AID WEALTH...POLICY MARXIST. PAGE 39 F0758
MARXISM ECO/TAC INT/ORG ECO/UNDEV

S67
FEDYSHYN O.S.,"KHRUSHCHEV'S 'LEAP FORWARD': NATIONAL ASSIMILATION IN THE USSR AFTER STALIN." USSR PLAN NAT/LISM PERSON...POLICY 20 KHRUSH/N STALIN/J. PAGE 39 F0771
GP/REL INGP/REL MARXISM METH

S67
FRANKEL T.,"ECONOMIC REFORM* A TENTATIVE APPRAISAL." COM USSR OP/RES BUDGET CONFER EFFICIENCY PRODUC MARXISM SOCISM...MGT 20. PAGE 43 F0847
ECO/DEV INDUS PLAN WEALTH

S67
FRIEDEN B.J.,"THE CHANGING PROSPECTS FOR SOCIAL PLANNING." USA+45 PROB/SOLV RACE/REL WEALTH ...SOC/WK PREDICT MUNICH 20 NEGRO. PAGE 44 F0856
PLAN LOC/G POLICY

S67
GORMAN W.,"ELLUL - A PROPHETIC VOICE." WOR+45 ELITES SOCIETY ACT/RES PLAN BAL/PWR DOMIN CONTROL PARTIC TOTALISM PWR 20. PAGE 49 F0963
CREATE ORD/FREE EX/STRUC UTOPIA

S67
GREEN C.,"SCHEMES FOR TRANSFERRING INCOME TO THE POOR." BUDGET GIVE RECEIVE DEBATE COST INCOME ...SOC/WK METH/COMP. PAGE 50 F0982
TAX WEALTH PLAN ACT/RES

S67
GREGORY R.,"THE MINISTER'S LINE: OR, THE M4 COMES TO BERKSHIRE. PART I." UK CONSTN DIST/IND LEGIS TOP/EX PLAN ADJUD...GEOG 20. PAGE 51 F0994
DECISION CONSTRUC NAT/G DELIB/GP

S67
HADDOCK G.B.,"CORPORATE GROWTH AS AFFECTED BY THE FEDERAL ANTITRUST LAWS" ECO/DEV NAT/G PLAN TEC/DEV
INDUS JURID

CAP/ISM ECO/TAC 20. PAGE 53 F1029 — ADJUD

S67
HANCOCK J.L.,"PLANNERS IN THE CHANGING AMERICAN CITY, 1900-1940." USA-45 CONSTRUC NAT/G POL/PAR ...SOC/WK TREND MUNICH 20. PAGE 54 F1059 — PLAN CONSULT LOC/G

S67
HEILBRONER R.L.,"BUILDING NEW NATIONS." AFR STRUCT PLAN TEC/DEV ADJUST MARXISM...POLICY 20. PAGE 58 F1138 — PROB/SOLV REV NAT/LISM ECO/UNDEV

S67
HILDEBRAND G.H.,"SECOND THOUGHTS ON THE NEGATIVE INCOME TAX." PLAN BUDGET ECO/TAC GIVE RECEIVE DEBATE EFFICIENCY INCOME...METH/COMP COSTS. PAGE 59 F1169 — TAX WEALTH SOC/WK ACT/RES

S67
HUTCHINGS R.,"THE ENDING OF UNEMPLOYMENT IN THE USSR" USSR PLAN ECO/TAC PRICE INGP/REL...GEOG STAT CHARTS 20 MIGRATION. PAGE 63 F1247 — WORKER AGRI INDUS MARXISM

S67
KOTLER P.,"OPERATIONS RESEARCH IN MARKETING." USA+45 DIST/IND INDUS LG/CO CONSULT BUDGET TASK DEMAND EFFICIENCY PROFIT WEALTH DECISION. PAGE 73 F1429 — ECOMETRIC OP/RES MARKET PLAN

S67
KRAUS J.,"A MARXIST IN GHANA." GHANA ELITES CHIEF PROB/SOLV TEC/DEV DIPLOM ECO/TAC COLONIAL PARTIC PWR 20 NKRUMAH/K. PAGE 73 F1432 — MARXISM PLAN ATTIT CREATE

S67
LEIFER M.,"ASTRIDE THE STRAITS OF JAHORE: THE BRITISH PRESENCE AND COMMONWEALTH RIVALRY IN SOUTHEAST ASIA." MALAYSIA UK FORCES PLAN ECO/TAC ...DECISION 20 CMN/WLTH. PAGE 77 F1515 — DIPLOM NAT/LISM COLONIAL

S67
LENS S.,"WALTER REUTHER TRIES TO BUILD A FIRE." WORKER LEAD DISCRIM AGE ORD/FREE NEW/LIB SOC. PAGE 78 F1523 — LABOR PARTIC NEIGH PLAN

S67
LEONTYEV L.,"THE LENINIST PRINCIPLES OF SOCIALIST ECONOMIC MANAGEMENT." USA+45 USSR POL/PAR WORKER PLAN ECO/TAC EFFICIENCY PRODUC MARXISM...POLICY SOCIALIST MGT TREND 20 LENIN/VI MARX/KARL. PAGE 78 F1529 — SOCISM CAP/ISM IDEA/COMP ECO/DEV

S67
MCCOLL R.W.,"A POLITICAL GEOGRAPHY OF REVOLUTION: CHINA, VIETNAM, AND THAILAND." ASIA THAILAND VIETNAM FORCES CONTROL 20. PAGE 88 F1720 — REV GEOG PLAN DECISION

S67
MYERS S.,"TECHNOLOGY AND URBAN TRANSIT: THE ENORMOUS POTENTIAL OF BUS AND RAIL SYSTEMS." USA+45 FINAN LOC/G WORKER PLAN PROB/SOLV PRICE AUTOMAT MUNICH 20. PAGE 96 F1877 — R+D TEC/DEV DIST/IND ACT/RES

S67
OLIVIER G.,"ASPECTS JURIDIQUES DE L'ADOPTION DU TRAITE CECA A LA CRISE CHARBONNIERE (SUITE ET FIN)" LAW DIST/IND PLAN DIPLOM RATION PRICE ADMIN COST DEMAND...POLICY CON/ANAL ECSC TREATY. PAGE 101 F1988 — INT/TRADE INT/ORG EXTR/IND CONSTN

S67
ORAZEM F.,"THE NEW SOVIET PLAN FOR AGRICULTURE (1960-1970)" USSR WORKER CAP/ISM ECO/TAC PRICE OWN HABITAT MARXISM...CHARTS 20. PAGE 101 F1994 — AGRI PLAN COM ECO/DEV

S67
PAI G.A.,"TAXATION AND PLANNING IN INDIA: A BIRDS-EYE VIEW." INDIA ELITES NAT/G LEGIS BUDGET CONTROL LOBBY INCOME...STAT CHARTS 20. PAGE 102 F2015 — TAX PLAN WEALTH STRATA

S67
PAULY M.V.,"MIXED PUBLIC AND PRIVATE FINANCING OF EDUCATION." STRATA PAY RECEIVE COST INCOME OPTIMAL METH/COMP. PAGE 104 F2039 — SCHOOL PLAN TAX EFFICIENCY

S67
PERKINS D.H.,"ECONOMIC GROWTH IN CHINA AND THE CULTURAL REVOLUTION(1960APRIL 1967)" CHINA/COM FUT AGRI INDUS PLAN LEAD MARXISM...CHARTS 20 MAO. PAGE 105 F2062 — ECO/TAC CULTURE REV ECO/UNDEV

S67
PRATT R.C.,"THE ADMINISTRATION OF ECONOMIC PLANNING IN A NEWLY INDEPEND ENT STATE* THE TANZANIAN EXPERIENCE 1963-1966." AFR TANZANIA ECO/UNDEV PLAN CONTROL ROUTINE TASK EFFICIENCY 20. PAGE 107 F2114 — NAT/G DELIB/GP ADMIN TEC/DEV

S67
RICHMAN B.M.,"CAPITALISTS & MANAGERS IN COMMUNIST CHINA." ASIA CHINA/COM ECO/UNDEV NAT/G CONSULT EX/STRUC PLAN EFFICIENCY PRODUC WEALTH MARXISM ...MGT CHARTS 20. PAGE 111 F2185 — CAP/ISM INDUS

S67
RICHMAN B.M.,"SOVIET MANAGEMENT IN TRANSITION." USSR FINAN MARKET EX/STRUC PLAN PROB/SOLV TEC/DEV CONTROL LEAD CENTRAL EFFICIENCY...METH/COMP 20 REFORMERS. PAGE 111 F2186 — MGT MARXISM POLICY AUTHORIT

S67
RONNING C.,"NANKING: 1950." ASIA CANADA CHINA/COM NAT/G PLAN ECO/TAC REV ADJUST 20. PAGE 113 F2235 — DIPLOM ROLE PEACE

S67
STYCOS J.M.,"POLITICS AND POPULATION CONTROL IN LATIN AMERICA." USA+45 FAM NAT/G GP/REL AGE/C ATTIT CATHISM MARXISM...POLICY UN WHO. PAGE 127 F2509 — PLAN CENSUS CONTROL L/A+17C

S67
THORKELSON H.,"FOOD STAMPS AND HUNGER IN AMERICA." USA+45 LAW DELIB/GP ADMIN COST DEMAND POLICY. PAGE 130 F2570 — WEALTH RECEIVE EATING PLAN

S67
WALLACE H.M.,"AVAILABILITY AND USEFULNESS OF SELECTED HEALTH AND SOCIOECONOMIC DATA FOR COMMUNITY PLANNING." NEIGH EFFICIENCY...CORREL STAT CENSUS CHARTS. PAGE 142 F2806 — HEALTH PLAN SOC/WK HEAL

S67
WASSERMAN M.,"BEYOND TOKENISM: REVERSE INTEGRATION IN ALBANY, GEORGIA." USA+45 PLAN BUDGET EDU/PROP LEAD AGE/C AGE/Y GEORGIA NEGRO. PAGE 144 F2827 — REGION RACE/REL DISCRIM SCHOOL

S67
WILES P.J.,"THE POLITICAL AND SOCIAL PREREQUISITES FOR A SOVIET-TYPE ECONOMY." COM USSR LAW CULTURE CREATE ADMIN FEEDBACK ROUTINE COST OPTIMAL TOTALISM MARXISM 20. PAGE 146 F2883 — ECO/DEV PLAN EX/STRUC EFFICIENCY

S67
WILLIAMS C.,"REGIONAL MANAGEMENT OVERSEAS." USA+45 WOR+45 DIST/IND LG/CO EX/STRUC INT/TRADE TARIFFS ADMIN TASK CENTRAL. PAGE 147 F2889 — MGT EUR+WWI ECO/DEV PLAN

S67
WOLFE T.W.,"SOVIET MILITARY POLICY AT THE FIFTY YEAR MARK." USSR VIETNAM WOR+45 RATION AGREE WAR WEAPON CIVMIL/REL TREATY. PAGE 148 F2917 — FORCES POLICY TIME/SEQ PLAN

S67
WOLFSON M.,"GOVERNMENT'S ROLE IN TOURISM DEVELOPMENT." WOR+45 ECO/DEV ECO/UNDEV FINAN BUDGET DIPLOM EDU/PROP. PAGE 148 F2920 — SERV/IND NAT/G CONTROL PLAN

N67
NATIONAL COMN COMMUNITY HEALTH,ACTION - PLANNING FOR COMMUNITY HEALTH SERVICES (PAMPHLET). USA+45 PROF/ORG DELIB/GP BUDGET ROUTINE GP/REL ATTIT ...HEAL SOC SOC/WK CHARTS MUNICH TIME 20. PAGE 97 F1898 — PLAN HEALTH ADJUST

N67
US CONGRESS JOINT ECO COMM,ECONOMY IN GOVERNMENT (PAMPHLET). USA+45 ECO/DEV FINAN NAT/G PLAN BUDGET SENATE. PAGE 135 F2662 — ECO/TAC COST EFFICIENCY MGT

N67
US HOUSE,MESSAGE FROM THE PRESIDENT OF THE UNITED STATES: URBAN AND RURAL POVERTY (PAMPHLET). USA+45 ACT/RES PLAN BUDGET RENT MUNICH 20 PRESIDENT. PAGE 136 F2685 — NAT/G POLICY CREATE RECEIVE

N67
US HOUSE COMM ON COMMERCE,PARTNERSHIP FOR HEALTH AMENDMENTS FOR 1967 (PAMPHLET). PUB/INST DELIB/GP PROB/SOLV BUDGET EFFICIENCY 20 CONGRESS. PAGE 137 F2701 — HEAL PLAN NAT/G JURID

N67
US HOUSE COMM SCI ASTRONAUT,GOVERNMENT, SCIENCE, AND INTERNATIONAL POLICY (PAMPHLET). INDIA NETHERLAND ECO/DEV ECO/UNDEV R+D ACADEM PLAN DIPLOM FOR/AID CONFER...PREDICT 20 CHINJAP. PAGE 137 F2705 — NAT/G POLICY CREATE TEC/DEV

N67
US SENATE COMM ON FOREIGN REL,WAR OR PEACE IN THE MIDDLE EAST (PAMPHLET). GREECE ISLAM ISRAEL JORDAN UAR CHIEF PROB/SOLV FOR/AID WAR PWR 20 SENATE. PAGE 139 F2739 — DIPLOM FORCES PLAN

PLAN/UNIT....PLANNED UNIT DEVELOPMENT

PLATO....PLATO

PLAZA G. F2092

PLEKHNV/GV....G.V. PLEKHANOV

PLOSS S.I. F2093

PLOTT C.R. F2094

PLUNKITT/G....G.W. PLUNKITT, TAMMANY BOSS

PLURALISM....SEE PLURISM, PLURIST

PLURISM....PLURALISM, SOCIO-POLITICAL ORDER OF AUTONOMOUS GROUPS

B30
GREEN F.M.,CONSTITUTIONAL DEVELOPMENT IN THE SOUTH ATLANTIC STATES, 1776-1860; A STUDY IN THE EVOLUTION OF DEMOCRACY. USA-45 ELITES SOCIETY STRATA ECO/DEV AGRI POL/PAR EX/STRUC LEGIS CT/SYS REGION...BIBLIOG 18/19 MARYLAND VIRGINIA GEORGIA NORTH/CAR SOUTH/CAR. PAGE 50 F0984
CONSTN PROVS PLURISM REPRESENT

B38
HEIMANN E.,COMMUNISM, FASCISM, OR DEMOCRACY? WOR-45 CONSTN SOCIETY STRATA AGRI CAP/ISM MORAL ORD/FREE ...MAJORIT METH/COMP NAT/COMP 19/20. PAGE 58 F1141
SOCISM MARXISM FASCISM PLURISM

B39
FURNIVALL J.S.,NETHERLANDS INDIA. INDIA NETHERLAND CULTURE INDUS NAT/G DIPLOM ADMIN WEALTH...POLICY CHARTS 17/20. PAGE 45 F0876
COLONIAL ECO/UNDEV SOVEREIGN PLURISM

B44
MERRIAM C.E.,PUBLIC AND PRIVATE GOVERNMENT. VOL/ASSN EDU/PROP ADMIN REPRESENT EFFICIENCY PWR PLURISM...MAJORIT CONCPT. PAGE 90 F1762
NAT/G NEIGH MGT POLICY

S49
STEINMETZ H.,"THE PROBLEMS OF THE LANDRAT: A STUDY OF COUNTY GOVERNMENT IN THE US ZONE OF GERMANY." GERMANY/W USA+45 INDUS PLAN DIPLOM EDU/PROP CONTROL WAR GOV/REL FEDERAL WEALTH PLURISM...GOV/COMP 20 LANDRAT. PAGE 126 F2478
LOC/G COLONIAL MGT TOP/EX

B50
SURANYI-UNGER T.,PRIVATE ENTERPRISE AND GOVERNMENTAL PLANNING. STRUCT FINAN BAL/PWR HAPPINESS DRIVE NEW/LIB PLURISM...MATH QUANT STAT TREND BIBLIOG. PAGE 127 F2516
PLAN NAT/G LAISSEZ POLICY

B58
FINER S.E.,PRIVATE INDUSTRY AND POLITICAL POWER (PAMPHLET). UK INDUS CONTROL LOBBY PWR. PAGE 41 F0797
PLURISM REPRESENT EX/STRUC

B59
SERAPHIM H.J.,PROBLEME DER WILLENSBILDUNG UND DER WIRTSCHAFTSPOLITISCHEN FUEHRUNG. WOR+45 MARKET ACT/RES OP/RES PLAN EDU/PROP INGP/REL HABITAT PLURISM...MGT PERS/COMP METH 20. PAGE 119 F2357
POLICY DECISION PSY

L59
OBERER W.E.,"VOLUNTARY IMPARTIAL REVIEW OF LABOR: SOME REFLECTIONS." DELIB/GP LEGIS PROB/SOLV ADJUD CONTROL COERCE PWR PLURISM POLICY. PAGE 100 F1960
LABOR LAW PARTIC INGP/REL

S59
SEIDMAN H.,"THE GOVERNMENT CORPORATION IN THE UNITED STATES." USA+45 LEGIS ADMIN PLURISM 20. PAGE 119 F2344
CONTROL GOV/REL EX/STRUC EXEC

B63
BRAYBROOKE D.,A STRATEGY OF DECISION: POLICY EVALUATION AS A SOCIAL PROCESS. UNIV ELITES OP/RES DOMIN CONFER FEEDBACK CONSEN PLURISM...CONCPT CENSUS. PAGE 18 F0343
DECISION POLICY CONTROL

B64
HALLOWELL J.H.,DEVELOPMENT: FOR WHAT. WOR+45 POL/PAR SECT FOR/AID INT/TRADE CT/SYS PARTIC PRODUC PLURISM. PAGE 54 F1052
ECO/UNDEV CONSTN NAT/LISM ECO/TAC

B64
PRESTHUS R.,MEN AT THE TOP; A STUDY IN COMMUNITY POWER. USA+45 STRUCT ACT/RES REPRESENT CONSEN ALL/VALS ORD/FREE...SAMP/SIZ 20. PAGE 108 F2116
PLURISM LG/CO PWR ADMIN

B64
RAISON T.,WHY CONSERVATIVE? UK FORCES DIPLOM ECO/TAC GIVE EDU/PROP ORD/FREE WEALTH LAISSEZ ...GOV/COMP 20 TORY/PARTY CONSRV/PAR. PAGE 109 F2137
PLURISM CONSERVE POL/PAR NAT/G

S67
WEIL G.L.,"THE MERGER OF THE INSTITUTIONS OF THE EUROPEAN COMMUNITIES" EUR+WWI ECO/DEV INT/TRADE CONSEN PLURISM...DECISION MGT 20 EEC EURATOM ECSC TREATY. PAGE 145 F2847
ECO/TAC INT/ORG CENTRAL INT/LAW

PLURIST....PLURALIST

B08
LLOYD H.D.,THE SWISS DEMOCRACY. SWITZERLND INDUS NAT/G WORKER CHOOSE OWN ORD/FREE SOCISM...PLURIST 19/20 MONOPOLY. PAGE 81 F1590
NAT/COMP GOV/COMP REPRESENT POPULISM

B38
HOBSON J.A.,IMPERIALISM. MOD/EUR UK WOR-45 CULTURE ECO/UNDEV NAT/G VOL/ASSN PLAN EDU/PROP LEGIT REGION COERCE ATTIT PWR...POLICY PLURIST TIME/SEQ GEN/LAWS TERR/GP 19/20. PAGE 60 F1187
DOMIN ECO/TAC BAL/PWR COLONIAL

S38
HALL R.C.,"REPRESENTATION OF BIG BUSINESS IN THE HOUSE OF COMMONS." UK ECO/DEV INDUS PROF/ORG LEGIS CAP/ISM ECO/TAC LAISSEZ...POLICY OLD/LIB PLURIST MGT 20 HOUSE/CMNS. PAGE 53 F1047
LOBBY NAT/G

B42
DRUCKER P.F.,THE FUTURE OF INDUSTRIAL MAN; A CONSERVATIVE APPROACH. USA-45 LOC/G PLAN WAR CENTRAL RATIONAL TOTALISM ORD/FREE LAISSEZ ...PLURIST IDEA/COMP 19/20 HITLER/A. PAGE 34 F0664
INDUS SOCIETY REGION PROB/SOLV

B48
VON HAYEK F.A.,INDIVIDUALISM AND ECONOMIC ORDER. GERMANY USA-45 USSR FINAN MARKET INT/ORG ECO/TAC INT/TRADE PRICE REPRESENT ORD/FREE...PLURIST GEN/LAWS 20. PAGE 142 F2793
SOCISM CAP/ISM POPULISM FEDERAL

B57
EHRMANN H.W.,ORGANIZED BUSINESS IN FRANCE. EUR+WWI MOD/EUR ECO/DEV VOL/ASSN LEGIT ATTIT PERCEPT PWR RESPECT...PLURIST SOC INT TOT/POP 20. PAGE 36 F0712
PROF/ORG ECO/TAC FRANCE

B59
SANNWALD R.E.,ECONOMIC INTEGRATION: THEORETICAL ASSUMPTIONS AND CONSEQUENCES OF EUROPEAN UNIFICATION. EUR+WWI FUT FINAN INDUS VOL/ASSN ACT/RES ECO/TAC...PLURIST EEC FOR/TRADE OEEC 20. PAGE 116 F2279
INT/ORG ECO/DEV INT/TRADE

B60
ARON R.,COLLOQUES DE RHEINFELDEN. AFR USA+45 USSR WOR+45 WOR-45 CULTURE ECO/UNDEV NAT/G POL/PAR DIPLOM NAT/LISM TOTALISM ATTIT DRIVE ALL/VALS ...PLURIST CONCPT STERTYP GEN/LAWS TOT/POP 20. PAGE 6 F0120
ECO/DEV SOCIETY CAP/ISM SOCISM

S60
GARNICK D.H.,"ON THE ECONOMIC FEASIBILITY OF A MIDDLE EASTERN COMMON MARKET." AFR ISLAM CULTURE INDUS NAT/G PLAN TEC/DEV ECO/TAC ADMIN ATTIT DRIVE RIGID/FLEX...PLURIST STAT TREND GEN/LAWS 20. PAGE 46 F0907
MARKET INT/TRADE

POL....POLITICAL AND POWER PROCESS

POL/PAR....POLITICAL PARTIES

N
DEUTSCHE BUCHEREI,DEUTSCHES BUCHERVERZEICHNIS. GERMANY LAW CULTURE POL/PAR ADMIN LEAD ATTIT PERSON ...SOC 20. PAGE 32 F0626
BIBLIOG NAT/G DIPLOM ECO/DEV

C01
LOWELL A.L.,"THE INFLUENCE OF PARTY UPON LEGISLATION IN ENGLAND AND AMERICA" IN ANNUAL REPORT OF AMER HISTORICAL ASSN." LEGIS CONTROL ...CON/ANAL CHARTS 19/20 CONGRESS PARLIAMENT. PAGE 82 F1605
PARL/PROC POL/PAR DECISION OP/RES

N19
ENGELS F.,THE BRITISH LABOUR MOVEMENT (PAMPHLET). FRANCE GERMANY MOD/EUR UK USA-45 POL/PAR WORKER PAY EDU/PROP PRICE REPRESENT GP/REL 19. PAGE 37 F0730
ECO/TAC MARXISM LABOR STRATA

N19
HALL G.,MAIN STREET TO WALL STREET: END THE COLD WAR (PAMPHLET). AFR USA+45 LAW STRUCT POL/PAR WORKER INT/TRADE DOMIN INCOME...POLICY 20 COM/PARTY. PAGE 53 F1046
MARXIST CAP/ISM DIPLOM NAT/G

N19
HERZBERG D.G.,A BUDGET FOR NEW YORK STATE, 1956-1957 (PAMPHLET). USA+45 ADMIN GOV/REL 20 NEW/YORK HARRIMAN/A. PAGE 59 F1159
POL/PAR PROVS BUDGET LEGIS

B20
BUCK S.J.,THE AGRARIAN CRUSADE: A CHRONICLE OF THE FARMER IN POLITICS. USA-45 INDUS PROB/SOLV PWR WEALTH...GEOG CENSUS 19/20 GREENBACK GRANGE SILVER. PAGE 20 F0381
AGRI POPULISM VOL/ASSN POL/PAR

B27
SIEGFRIED A.,AMERICA COMES OF AGE: A FRENCH ANALYSIS (TRANS. BY H.H. HEMMING AND DORIS HEMMING). FRANCE UK POL/PAR WORKER TEC/DEV DIPLOM REGION RACE/REL ADJUST PRODUC HEREDITY...TIME/SEQ GP/COMP SOC/INTEG 20 DEMOCRAT REPUBLICAN KKK. PAGE 122 F2398
USA-45 CULTURE ECO/DEV SOC

B30
GREEN F.M.,CONSTITUTIONAL DEVELOPMENT IN THE SOUTH ATLANTIC STATES, 1776-1860; A STUDY IN THE EVOLUTION OF DEMOCRACY. USA-45 ELITES SOCIETY STRATA ECO/DEV AGRI POL/PAR EX/STRUC LEGIS CT/SYS REGION...BIBLIOG 18/19 MARYLAND VIRGINIA GEORGIA NORTH/CAR SOUTH/CAR. PAGE 50 F0984
CONSTN PROVS PLURISM REPRESENT

B38
DAVIES E.,"NATIONAL" CAPITALISM: THE GOVERNMENT'S RECORD AS PROTECTOR OF PRIVATE MONOPOLY. UK ELITES SOCIETY STRATA POL/PAR WORKER PROB/SOLV CONTROL SOCISM 20 MONOPOLY LABOR/PAR CHAMBRLN/N. PAGE 30 F0583
CAP/ISM NAT/G INDUS POLICY

B38
HARPER S.N.,THE GOVERNMENT OF THE SOVIET UNION. COM USSR LAW CONSTN ECO/DEV PLAN TEC/DEV DIPLOM INT/TRADE ADMIN REV NAT/LISM...POLICY 20. PAGE 55 F1085
MARXISM NAT/G LEAD POL/PAR

B39
JENNINGS W.I.,PARLIAMENT. UK POL/PAR OP/RES BUDGET LEAD CHOOSE GP/REL...MGT 20 PARLIAMENT HOUSE/LORD
PARL/PROC LEGIS

HOUSE/CMNS. PAGE 67 F1315 CONSTN NAT/G

B39
THOMAS J.A.,THE HOUSE OF COMMONS, 1832-1901; A STUDY OF ITS ECONOMIC AND FUNCTIONAL CHARACTER. UK LAW STRATA FINAN DIPLOM CONTROL LEAD LOBBY REPRESENT WEALTH...POLICY STAT BIBLIOG 19/20 PARLIAMENT. PAGE 130 F2561 PARL/PROC LEGIS POL/PAR ECO/DEV

B40
SPENCER H.,THE MAN VS. THE STATE (1892). UK POL/PAR LEGIS TARIFFS COERCE CRIME REPRESENT PWR SOCISM ...POLICY GEN/LAWS 19/20. PAGE 124 F2450 FASCISM POPULISM LAISSEZ ORD/FREE

B43
WILMERDING L. JR.,THE SPENDING POWER: A HISTORY OF THE EFFORTS OF CONGRESS TO CONTROL EXPENDITURES. USA-45 POL/PAR DELIB/GP EX/STRUC TOP/EX TARIFFS ADMIN GOV/REL...TIME/SEQ SENATE HOUSE/REP. PAGE 147 F2900 LEGIS BUDGET CONTROL

B44
HAYEK F.A.,THE ROAD TO SERFDOM. NAT/G POL/PAR CREATE EDU/PROP ATTIT WEALTH LAISSEZ...OLD/LIB CONCPT TREND 20. PAGE 57 F1121 FUT PLAN ECO/TAC SOCISM

B44
MCFADYEAN A.,GOVERNMENT AND INDUSTRY (PAMPHLET). UK INDUS CONTROL REPRESENT 20. PAGE 88 F1728 POL/PAR SOCISM

B47
WEBER M.,THE THEORY OF SOCIAL AND ECONOMIC ORGANIZATION. STRUCT LABOR POL/PAR ECO/TAC LEGIT PRODUC BIOG. PAGE 144 F2840 ECO/DEV SOC PHIL/SCI LEAD

B48
DURBIN E.F.M.,THE POLITICS OF DEMOCRATIC SOCIALISM; AN ESSAY ON SOCIAL POLICY. STRATA POL/PAR PLAN COERCE DRIVE PERSON PWR MARXISM...CHARTS METH/COMP. PAGE 35 F0684 SOCIALIST POPULISM POLICY SOCIETY

B50
KOENIG L.W.,THE SALE OF THE TANKERS. USA+45 SEA DIST/IND POL/PAR DIPLOM ADMIN CIVMIL/REL ATTIT ...DECISION 20 PRESIDENT DEPT/STATE. PAGE 72 F1414 NAT/G POLICY PLAN GOV/REL

B50
LIPSET S.M.,AGRARIAN SOCIALISM. CANADA POL/PAR OP/RES ECO/TAC ADMIN ATTIT...TIME/SEQ NAT/COMP SOC/EXP 20 SASKATCH. PAGE 80 F1576 SOCISM AGRI METH/COMP STRUCT

B51
HALEVY E.,IMPERIALISM AND THE RISE OF LABOR (2ND ED.). UK NAT/G POL/PAR TOP/EX ATTIT ORD/FREE PWR 19/20 PARLIAMENT LABOR/PAR. PAGE 53 F1042 COLONIAL LABOR POLICY WAR

B51
US LIBRARY OF CONGRESS,EAST EUROPEAN ACCESSIONS LIST (VOL. I). POL/PAR DIPLOM ADMIN LEAD 20. PAGE 138 F2715 BIBLIOG/A COM SOCIETY NAT/G

B54
KARTUN D.,AFRICA, AFRICA: A CONTINENT RISES TO ITS FEET. AFR SOUTH/AFR UK ELITES AGRI LABOR LOC/G POL/PAR EDU/PROP CONTROL COERCE DISCRIM AGE/Y NEGRO THIRD/WRLD GOLD/COAST. PAGE 69 F1358 COLONIAL ORD/FREE PROFIT EXTR/IND

B54
LENIN V.I.,SELECTED WORKS (12 VOLS.). USSR INTELL SOCIETY STRATA STRUCT NAT/G POL/PAR WORKER CAP/ISM REV WAR...MARXIST PHIL/SCI 20 MARX/KARL LENIN/VI. PAGE 78 F1520 COM MARXISM

B54
REYNOLDS P.A.,BRITISH FOREIGN POLICY IN THE INTER-WAR YEARS. CZECHOSLVK GERMANY POLAND UK USA-45 POL/PAR FORCES ECO/TAC ARMS/CONT WAR ATTIT 20. PAGE 111 F2182 DIPLOM POLICY NAT/G

B55
RUSTOW D.A.,THE POLITICS OF COMPROMISE. SWEDEN LABOR EX/STRUC LEGIS PLAN REPRESENT SOCISM...SOC 19/20. PAGE 115 F2265 POL/PAR NAT/G POLICY ECO/TAC

B55
UYEHARA C.H.,COMPARATIVE PLATFORMS OF JAPAN'S MAJOR PARTIES... USA+45 AGRI LEGIS WORKER CAP/ISM ORD/FREE MARXISM SOCISM...IDEA/COMP 20 CHINJAP. PAGE 140 F2755 POLICY POL/PAR DIPLOM NAT/G

B55
WOYTINSKY W.S.,WORLD COMMERCE AND GOVERNMENTS: TRENDS AND OUTLOOK. WOR+45 FINAN POL/PAR DIPLOM ECO/TAC FOR/AID DOMIN WAR CHOOSE...CHARTS BIBLIOG 20 LEAGUE/NAT UN ILO. PAGE 149 F2929 INT/TRADE DIST/IND NAT/COMP NAT/G

B56
ABELS J.,THE TRUMAN SCANDALS. USA+45 USA-45 POL/PAR TAX LEGIT CT/SYS CHOOSE PRIVIL MORAL WEALTH 20 TRUMAN/HS PRESIDENT CONGRESS. PAGE 2 F0031 CRIME ADMIN CHIEF TRIBUTE

B56
FIELD G.C.,POLITICAL THEORY. POL/PAR REPRESENT MORAL SOVEREIGN...JURID IDEA/COMP. PAGE 40 F0789 CONCPT NAT/G ORD/FREE DIPLOM

B56
WEBER M.,WIRTSCHAFT UND GESELLSCHAFT (2ND VOL.). STRUCT NAT/G POL/PAR LEAD PWR OBJECTIVE IDEA/COMP. PAGE 144 F2841 LEGIT JURID SOC

L56
PENNOCK J.R.,"PARTY AND CONSTITUENCY IN POSTWAR AGRICULTURAL PRICE SUPPORT LEGISLATION." USA+45 LEGIS DEBATE LOBBY RIGID/FLEX. PAGE 105 F2057 POL/PAR REPRESENT AGRI CHOOSE

B57
LENIN V.I.,THE DEVELOPMENT OF CAPITALISM IN RUSSIA. MOD/EUR USSR AGRI MARKET POL/PAR TEC/DEV...CONCPT 19/20. PAGE 78 F1521 COM INDUS CAP/ISM

B57
LOUCKS W.N.,COMPARATIVE ECONOMIC SYSTEMS (5TH ED.). COM UK USSR INDUS POL/PAR PLAN CAP/ISM TOTALISM MARXISM...PHIL/SCI BIBLIOG 19/20. PAGE 82 F1603 NAT/COMP IDEA/COMP SOCISM

B57
OLIVER H.M. JR.,ECONOMIC OPINION AND POLICY IN CEYLON. CEYLON FINAN POL/PAR WORKER INT/TRADE INCOME WEALTH...GEOG UNPLAN/INT BIBLIOG 20 CMN/WLTH. PAGE 101 F1987 ECO/UNDEV NAT/LISM POLICY COLONIAL

B57
ROBERTSON H.M.,SOUTH AFRICA, ECONOMIC AND POLITICAL ASPECTS. SOUTH/AFR CONSTN CULTURE POL/PAR LEGIS DIPLOM DOMIN COLONIAL...SOC BIBLIOG 19/20. PAGE 112 F2214 RACE/REL ECO/UNDEV ECO/TAC DISCRIM

B57
WATSON G.,THE UNSERVILE STATE: ESSAYS IN LIBERTY AND WELFARE. UK LEGIS RECEIVE EDU/PROP COLONIAL ...WELF/ST 20 LIB/PARTY. PAGE 144 F2833 POL/PAR ORD/FREE CONTROL NEW/LIB

B58
CLAUNCH J.M.,THE PROBLEM OF GOVERNMENT IN METROPOLITAN AREAS. CULTURE INDUS POL/PAR PLAN REGION GP/REL...CENSUS ANTHOL MUNICH 20. PAGE 25 F0486 PROB/SOLV SOC

B58
COLE G.D.H.,COMMUNISM AND SOCIAL DEMOCRACY (VOL. IV OF "HISTORY OF SOCIAL THOUGHT"). COM GERMANY ITALY UK AGRI INT/ORG WORKER DIPLOM COLONIAL NAT/LISM ALL/IDEOS...BIBLIOG 20 LEAGUE/NAT AUST/HUNG. PAGE 26 F0502 MARXISM REV POL/PAR SOCISM

B58
JENNINGS I.,PROBLEMS OF THE NEW COMMONWEALTH. AFR CEYLON INDIA PAKISTAN S/ASIA ECO/UNDEV INT/ORG LOC/G DIPLOM ECO/TAC INT/TRADE COLONIAL RACE/REL DISCRIM 20 PARLIAMENT. PAGE 67 F1314 NAT/LISM NEUTRAL FOR/AID POL/PAR

B58
LESTER R.A.,AS UNIONS MATURE. POL/PAR BARGAIN LEAD PARTIC GP/REL CENTRAL...MAJORIT TIME/SEQ METH/COMP. PAGE 78 F1533 LABOR INDUS POLICY MGT

B58
SCOTT D.J.R.,RUSSIAN POLITICAL INSTITUTIONS. RUSSIA USSR CONSTN AGRI DELIB/GP PLAN EDU/PROP CONTROL CHOOSE EFFICIENCY ATTIT MARXISM...BIBLIOG/A IND 13/20. PAGE 118 F2332 NAT/G POL/PAR ADMIN DECISION

B59
JENKINS C.,POWER AT THE TOP: A CRITICAL SURVEY OF THE NATIONALIZED INDUSTRIES. UK POL/PAR CONTROL ...WELF/ST CHARTS 20 LABOR/PAR. PAGE 67 F1313 NAT/G OWN INDUS NEW/LIB

B59
KELF-COHEN R.,NATIONALISATION IN BRITAIN: THE END OF DOGMA. EUR+WWI UK NAT/G POL/PAR WORKER ECO/TAC PARL/PROC WEALTH SOCISM...GOV/COMP 20. PAGE 70 F1369 NEW/LIB ECO/DEV INDUS OWN

B59
MADHOK B.,POLITICAL TRENDS IN INDIA. INDIA PAKISTAN UK STRATA ECO/UNDEV POL/PAR LEGIS CAP/ISM DIPLOM COLONIAL CHOOSE MARXISM...SOC TREND 20 GANDHI/M NEHRU/J. PAGE 84 F1639 GEOG NAT/G

B59
MARTIN K.,WAR, HISTORY, AND HUMAN NATURE. FRANCE GERMANY INDIA UK UNIV POL/PAR COLONIAL DETER REV MARXISM PACIFISM...PSY CONCPT PREDICT LENIN/VI GANDHI/M. PAGE 86 F1683 PERSON WAR ATTIT IDEA/COMP

B59
PANIKKAR K.M.,THE AFRO-ASIAN STATES AND THEIR PROBLEMS. COM CULTURE KIN POL/PAR SECT DIPLOM EDU/PROP COLONIAL SOVEREIGN...TECHNIC GOV/COMP 20. PAGE 103 F2025 AFR S/ASIA ECO/UNDEV

B59
VERNEY D.V.,PUBLIC ENTERPRISE IN SWEDEN. FUT SWEDEN UK INDUS POL/PAR LEGIS PROB/SOLV CAP/ISM INT/TRADE CONTROL SOCISM...MGT CONCPT NAT/COMP 20 SOCDEM/PAR CIVIL/SERV. PAGE 141 F2778 ECO/DEV POLICY LG/CO NAT/G

B59
VINCENT W.S.,ROLES OF THE CITIZENS: PRINCIPLES AND PRACTICES. LOC/G POL/PAR VOL/ASSN CHOOSE ROLE ORD/FREE PWR...POLICY 20. PAGE 141 F2785 INGP/REL EDU/PROP CREATE LOBBY

B59
WAHLKE J.C.,LEGISLATIVE BEHAVIOR: A READER IN LEGIS

THEORY AND RESEARCH. USA+45 CONSTN ELITES POL/PAR LOBBY REPRESENT PERS/REL PERSON ROLE...IDEA/COMP METH/COMP SIMUL. PAGE 142 F2800
CHOOSE INGP/REL ATTIT

L59
WURFEL D.,"FOREIGN AID AND SOCIAL REFORM IN POLITICAL DEVELOPMENT" (BMR)" PHILIPPINE USA+45 WOR+45 SOCIETY POL/PAR ACT/RES TEC/DEV DIPLOM 20. PAGE 149 F2943
FOR/AID PROB/SOLV ECO/TAC ECO/UNDEV

S59
ALLEN G.,"NATIONAL FARMERS UNION AS A PRESSURE GROUP: II." UK ECO/DEV MARKET POL/PAR DELIB/GP PROB/SOLV ECO/TAC LOBBY INCOME...POLICY METH/COMP 19/20 NAT/FARMER. PAGE 4 F0069
DIST/IND AGRI PROF/ORG TREND

S59
GILPATRICK T.V.,"PRICE SUPPORT POLICY AND THE MIDWEST FARM VOTE" (BMR)" NAT/G PRICE CONTROL REGION...POLICY CHARTS 440 20 MIDWEST/US CONGRESS REPUBLICAN EISNHWR/DD 20. PAGE 47 F0925
POL/PAR AGRI ATTIT CHOOSE

B60
APTHEKER H.,DISARMAMENT AND THE AMERICAN ECONOMY: A SYMPOSIUM. FUT USA+45 ECO/DEV DIST/IND FINAN INDUS PROC/MFG LABOR NAT/G POL/PAR CONSULT PLAN CAP/ISM INT/TRADE PEACE ATTIT MORAL WEALTH...TREND GEN/LAWS TOT/POP 20. PAGE 6 F0110
MARXIST ARMS/CONT

B60
ARON R.,COLLOQUES DE RHEINFELDEN. AFR USA+45 USSR WOR+45 WOR-45 CULTURE ECO/UNDEV NAT/G POL/PAR DIPLOM NAT/LISM TOTALISM ATTIT DRIVE ALL/VALS ...PLURIST CONCPT STERTYP GEN/LAWS TOT/POP 20. PAGE 6 F0120
ECO/DEV SOCIETY CAP/ISM SOCISM

B60
FINKLE J.L.,THE PRESIDENT MAKES A DECISION: A STUDY OF DIXON-YATES. OP/RES PROB/SOLV BUDGET ADMIN GOV/REL...POLICY BIBLIOG/A 20 PRESIDENT. PAGE 41 F0799
DECISION CHIEF PWR POL/PAR

B60
GRANICK D.,THE RED EXECUTIVE. COM USA+45 SOCIETY ECO/DEV INDUS NAT/G POL/PAR EX/STRUC PLAN ECO/TAC EDU/PROP ADMIN EXEC ATTIT DRIVE...GP/COMP 20. PAGE 50 F0976
PWR STRATA USSR ELITES

B60
MC CLELLAN G.S.,INDIA. AFR CHINA/COM INDIA CONSTN ELITES STRATA AGRI POL/PAR FOR/AID ARMS/CONT REV MARXISM...CENSUS BIBLIOG 20 GANDHI/M NEHRU/J. PAGE 87 F1712
DIPLOM NAT/G SOCIETY ECO/UNDEV

B60
ROBSON W.A.,NATIONALIZED INDUSTRY AND PUBLIC OWNERSHIP. UK ECO/DEV FINAN LABOR LG/CO POL/PAR LEGIS ACT/RES GP/REL...TREND IDEA/COMP 20. PAGE 113 F2227
NAT/G OWN INDUS ATTIT

B60
STOLPER W.F.,GERMANY BETWEEN EAST AND WEST: THE ECONOMICS OF COMPETITIVE COEXISTENCE. AFR FUT GERMANY/E GERMANY/W WOR+45 FINAN POL/PAR BUDGET ECO/TAC FOR/AID INT/TRADE...STAT CHARTS METH/COMP 20. PAGE 126 F2495
ECO/DEV DIPLOM GOV/COMP BAL/PWR

S60
GROSSMAN G.,"SOVIET GROWTH: ROUTINE, INERTIA, AND PRESSURE." COM STRATA NAT/G DELIB/GP PLAN TEC/DEV ECO/TAC EDU/PROP ADMIN ROUTINE DRIVE WEALTH 20. PAGE 52 F1007
POL/PAR ECO/DEV AFR USSR

S60
HERZ J.H.,"EAST GERMANY: PROGRESS AND PROSPECTS." COM AGRI FINAN INDUS LOC/G NAT/G FORCES PLAN TEC/DEV DOMIN ADMIN COERCE DRIVE PERCEPT RIGID/FLEX MORAL ORD/FREE PWR...MARXIST PSY SOC RECORD STERTYP WORK. PAGE 59 F1158
POL/PAR STRUCT GERMANY

B61
MEXICO; CINCUENTA ANOS DE REVOLUCION VOL. II. L/A+17C SOCIETY LABOR RECEIVE GP/REL AGE/Y HEALTH ...SOC/WK ANTHOL MUNICH 20 MEXIC/AMER. PAGE 1 F0014
ECO/UNDEV STRUCT INDUS POL/PAR

B61
BAUER P.T.,INDIAN ECONOMIC POLICY AND DEVELOPMENT. INDIA STRATA AGRI FINAN POL/PAR BUDGET FOR/AID GOV/REL EFFICIENCY...CENSUS 20. PAGE 11 F0216
ECO/UNDEV ECO/TAC POLICY PLAN

B61
KATKOFF U.,SOVIET ECONOMY 1940-1965. COM WOR+45 WOR-45 INTELL NAT/G POL/PAR TOP/EX ATTIT PWR ...POLICY TIME/SEQ VAL/FREE 20. PAGE 69 F1360
AGRI PERSON TOTALISM USSR

B61
LENIN V.I.,WHAT IS TO BE DONE? (1902). RUSSIA LABOR NAT/G POL/PAR WORKER CAP/ISM ECO/TAC ADMIN PARTIC ...MARXIST IDEA/COMP GEN/LAWS 19/20. PAGE 78 F1522
EDU/PROP PRESS MARXISM METH/COMP

B61
MARX K.,THE COMMUNIST MANIFESTO. IN (MENDEL A. ESSENTIAL WORKS OF MARXISM, NEW YORK: BANTAM. FUT MOD/EUR CULTURE ECO/DEV ECO/UNDEV AGRI FINAN INDUS MARKET PROC/MFG LABOR POL/PAR CONSULT FORCES CREATE PLAN ADMIN ATTIT DRIVE RIGID/FLEX ORD/FREE PWR RESPECT MARX/KARL MUNICH WORK. PAGE 86 F1691
COM NEW/IDEA CAP/ISM REV

B61
SCHWARTZ H.,THE RED PHOENIX: RUSSIA SINCE WORLD WAR II. USA+45 WOR+45 ELITES POL/PAR TEC/DEV ECO/TAC MARXISM. PAGE 118 F2325
DIPLOM NAT/G ECO/DEV

B61
SPOONER F.P.,SOUTH AFRICAN PREDICAMENT. FUT SOUTH/AFR INDUS POL/PAR RACE/REL INCOME...CHARTS 20 NEGRO. PAGE 125 F2459
ECO/DEV DISCRIM ECO/TAC POLICY

S61
NOVE A.,"THE SOVIET MODEL AND UNDERDEVELOPED COUNTRIES." COM FUT USSR WOR+45 CULTURE ECO/DEV POL/PAR FOR/AID EDU/PROP ADMIN MORAL WEALTH ...POLICY RECORD HIST/WRIT 20. PAGE 99 F1942
ECO/UNDEV PLAN

S61
VALLET R.,"IRAN: KEY TO THE MIDDLE EAST." COM IRAQ ISLAM KUWAIT LEBANON SAUDI/ARAB TURKEY ELITES SOCIETY INDUS PROC/MFG POL/PAR TOP/EX PLAN BAL/PWR DIPLOM ECO/TAC ALL/VALS...TREND FOR/TRADE CENTO 20. PAGE 140 F2760
NAT/G ECO/UNDEV IRAN

S61
WILDAVSKY A.,"POLITICAL IMPLICATIONS OF BUDGETARY REFORM." AFR NAT/G POL/PAR DELIB/GP EX/STRUC ATTIT PWR CONGRESS. PAGE 146 F2881
BUDGET PLAN LEGIS

B62
BROWN S.D.,STUDIES ON ASIA, 1962. ASIA BURMA INDIA ISLAM ISRAEL S/ASIA ECO/UNDEV POL/PAR SECT ECO/TAC ...ANTHOL 20 CHINJAP. PAGE 19 F0374
PWR PARL/PROC

B62
GALENSON W.,LABOR IN DEVELOPING COUNTRIES. BRAZIL INDONESIA ISRAEL PAKISTAN TURKEY AGRI INDUS WORKER PAY PRICE GP/REL WEALTH...MGT CHARTS METH/COMP NAT/COMP 20. PAGE 45 F0888
LABOR ECO/UNDEV BARGAIN POL/PAR

B62
GWYN W.B.,DEMOCRACY AND THE COST OF POLITICS IN BRITAIN. UK BUDGET CRIME CHOOSE ORD/FREE WEALTH ...TIME/SEQ 18/20. PAGE 52 F1017
COST POL/PAR POPULISM PAY

B62
HARRIS S.E.,THE ECONOMICS OF THE POLITICAL PARTIES. USA+45 FINAN CHIEF ACT/RES PLAN BUDGET GP/REL INGP/REL NEW/LIB...IDEA/COMP PERS/COMP 20 EISNHWR/DD KENNEDY/JF. PAGE 56 F1090
POLICY ECO/DEV NAT/G POL/PAR

B62
KENT R.K.,FROM MADAGASCAR TO THE MALAGASY REPUBLIC. FRANCE MADAGASCAR DIPLOM NAT/LISM ORD/FREE...MGT 18/20. PAGE 70 F1379
COLONIAL SOVEREIGN REV POL/PAR

B62
SELOSOEMARDJAN O.,SOCIAL CHANGES IN JOGJAKARTA. INDONESIA NETHERLAND ELITES STRATA STRUCT FAM POL/PAR CREATE DIPLOM INT/TRADE EDU/PROP ADMIN GOV/REL...SOC 20 JAVA CHINJAP. PAGE 119 F2352
ECO/UNDEV CULTURE REV COLONIAL

B62
VAN RENSBURG P.,GUILTY LAND: THE HISTORY OF APARTHEID. SOUTH/AFR NAT/G POL/PAR DOMIN CHOOSE ...SOC 19/20 NEGRO. PAGE 140 F2763
RACE/REL DISCRIM NAT/LISM POLICY

S62
BOKOR-SZEGO H.,"LA CONVENTION DE BELGRADE ET LE REGIME DU DANUBE." COM EUR+WWI WOR+45 STRUCT POL/PAR VOL/ASSN PLAN EDU/PROP WEALTH...TIME/SEQ METH/GP COMMUN 20. PAGE 16 F0308
INT/ORG TOTALISM YUGOSLAVIA

S62
IOVTCHOUK M.T.,"ON SOME THEORETICAL PRINCIPLES AND METHODS OF SOCIOLOGICAL INVESTIGATIONS (IN RUSSIAN)." FUT USA+45 STRATA R+D NAT/G POL/PAR TOP/EX ACT/RES PLAN ECO/TAC EDU/PROP ROUTINE ATTIT RIGID/FLEX MARXISM SOCISM...MARXIST METH/CNCPT OBS TREND NAT/COMP GEN/LAWS 20. PAGE 65 F1288
COM ECO/DEV CAP/ISM USSR

B63
BATES J.L.,THE ORIGINS OF TEAPOT DOME: PROGRESSIVES, PARTIES, AND PETROLEUM, 1909-1921. USA-45 INDUS LG/CO POL/PAR DELIB/GP CONTROL GOV/REL CONSERVE...BIBLIOG 20 NAVY. PAGE 11 F0209
EXTR/IND CRIME NAT/G

B63
DEUTSCH K.W.,THE POLITICAL ROLE OF LABOR IN DEVELOPING COUNTRIES. AFR ASIA S/ASIA USA+45 WOR+45 ECO/UNDEV POL/PAR ECO/TAC EDU/PROP LEGIT COERCE ORD/FREE PWR WEALTH...OBS INT TREND VAL/FREE 20. PAGE 32 F0625
LABOR NAT/LISM

B63
HYDE D.,THE PEACEFUL ASSAULT. COM UAR USSR ECO/DEV ECO/UNDEV NAT/G POL/PAR CAP/ISM PWR 20. PAGE 64 F1256
MARXISM CONTROL ECO/TAC DIPLOM

B63
LEWIN J.,POLITICS AND LAW IN SOUTH AFRICA. SOUTH/AFR UK POL/PAR BAL/PWR ECO/TAC COLONIAL CONTROL GP/REL DISCRIM PWR 20 NEGRO. PAGE 79 F1545
NAT/LISM POLICY LAW RACE/REL

B63
LEWIS G.K.,PUERTO RICO: FREEDOM AND POWER IN THE CARIBBEAN. PUERT/RICO USA+45 CULTURE STRUCT INDUS POL/PAR WORKER EDU/PROP CATHISM 20. PAGE 79 F1548
ECO/UNDEV COLONIAL NAT/LISM GEOG

B63
PELLING H.M.,A HISTORY OF BRITISH TRADE UNIONISM.
LABOR

UK ELITES ECO/DEV POL/PAR GP/REL PWR NEW/LIB 19/20. PAGE 104 F2051 VOL/ASSN NAT/G

B63
PRYOR F.L.,THE COMMUNIST FOREIGN TRADE SYSTEM. COM CZECHOSLVK GERMANY YUGOSLAVIA LAW ECO/DEV DIST/IND POL/PAR PLAN DOMIN TOTALISM DRIVE RIGID/FLEX WEALTH ...STAT STAND/INT CHARTS FOR/TRADE 20. PAGE 108 F2130 ATTIT ECO/TAC

L63
MOUSKHELY M.,"LE BLOC COMMUNISTE ET LA COMMUNAUTE ECONOMIQUE EUROPEENNE." AFR COM EUR+WWI FUT USSR WOR+45 INTELL ECO/UNDEV LABOR POL/PAR NUC/PWR RIGID/FLEX...TIME/SEQ ORG/CHARTS EEC TOT/POP 20. PAGE 94 F1849 INT/ORG ECO/DEV

S63
BEGUIN H.,"ASPECTS STRUCTURELS DU COMMERCE EXTERIEUR DES PAYS SOUS-DEVELOPPES." FUT WOR+45 STRUCT FINAN SERV/IND POL/PAR TEC/DEV PERCEPT WEALTH FOR/TRADE 20. PAGE 12 F0229 MARKET ECO/UNDEV FOR/AID

S63
FLOREA I.,"CU PRIVIRE LA OBIECTUL MATERIALISMULUI ISTORIC SI AL COMUNISMULUI STIINTIFIC SI LA RAPORTUL DINTRE ELE." EUR+WWI WOR+45 WOR-45 INTELL NAT/G POL/PAR WORKER EDU/PROP PERCEPT MARXISM ...MARXIST PHIL/SCI CONCPT TOT/POP 20. PAGE 42 F0812 COM ATTIT TOTALISM

S63
HINDLEY D.,"FOREIGN AID TO INDONESIA AND ITS POLITICAL IMPLICATIONS." INDONESIA POL/PAR ATTIT SOVEREIGN...CHARTS 20. PAGE 60 F1173 FOR/AID NAT/G WEALTH ECO/TAC

S63
NYE J.,"TANGANYIKA'S SELF-HELP." TANZANIA NAT/G GIVE COST EFFICIENCY NAT/LISM 20. PAGE 99 F1948 ECO/TAC POL/PAR ECO/UNDEV WORKER

S63
POLYANOV N.,"THE DOLLAR'S VENTURES IN EUROPE." EUR+WWI FRANCE USA+45 ECO/DEV MARKET POL/PAR TEC/DEV ECO/TAC EDU/PROP DRIVE PWR WEALTH...MARXIST MYTH STAT TREND EEC 20. PAGE 107 F2100 FINAN PLAN BAL/PAY CAP/ISM

S63
POPPINO R.E.,"IMBALANCE IN BRAZIL." L/A+17C NAT/G TOP/EX PLAN DIPLOM LEGIT DRIVE WEALTH...CON/ANAL FOR/TRADE LAFTA 20. PAGE 107 F2105 POL/PAR ECO/TAC BRAZIL

S63
RAMERIE L.,"TENSION AU SEIN DU COMECON: LE CAS ROUMAIN." COM EUR+WWI USSR WOR+45 ECO/DEV DIST/IND NAT/G POL/PAR VOL/ASSN EDU/PROP TOTALISM ATTIT WEALTH...TIME/SEQ 20 COMECON. PAGE 109 F2142 INT/ORG ECO/TAC INT/TRADE ROMANIA

B64
DUSCHA J.,ARMS, MONEY, AND POLITICS. USA+45 INDUS POL/PAR ECO/TAC TAX DETER NUC/PWR WAR WEAPON GOV/REL ATTIT...BIBLIOG/A 20 CONGRESS MONEY DEPT/DEFEN. PAGE 35 F0687 NAT/G FORCES POLICY BUDGET

B64
GRIFFITH W.E.,COMMUNISM IN EUROPE (2 VOLS.). CZECHOSLVK USSR WOR+45 WOR-45 YUGOSLAVIA INGP/REL MARXISM SOCISM...ANTHOL 20 EUROPE/E. PAGE 51 F1000 COM POL/PAR DIPLOM GOV/COMP

B64
HALLOWELL J.H.,DEVELOPMENT: FOR WHAT. WOR+45 POL/PAR SECT FOR/AID INT/TRADE CT/SYS PARTIC PRODUC PLURISM. PAGE 54 F1052 ECO/UNDEV CONSTN NAT/LISM ECO/TAC

B64
IMAZ J.L.,LOS QUE MANDAN. INDUS LABOR NAT/G POL/PAR PROVS SECT CHIEF TOP/EX CONTROL 20 ARGEN. PAGE 64 F1261 LEAD FORCES ELITES ATTIT

B64
LUTHULI A.,AFRICA'S FREEDOM. KIN LABOR POL/PAR SCHOOL DIPLOM NEUTRAL REGION REV NAT/LISM PWR WEALTH SOCISM SOC/INTEG 20. PAGE 82 F1608 AFR ECO/UNDEV COLONIAL

B64
MARSH D.C.,THE FUTURE OF THE WELFARE STATE. UK CONSTN NAT/G POL/PAR...POLICY WELF/ST 20. PAGE 86 F1676 NEW/LIB ADMIN CONCPT INSPECT

B64
MEISEL J.,PAPERS ON THE 1962 ELECTION. CANADA PROVS SECT GP/REL CONSEN EFFICIENCY...MAJORIT 20. PAGE 89 F1751 POL/PAR RECORD CHOOSE STRATA

B64
MELADY T.,FACES OF AFRICA. AFR FUT ISLAM NAT/G POL/PAR SCHOOL DELIB/GP PLAN ECO/TAC EDU/PROP ATTIT ALL/VALS...CHARTS TOT/POP TERR/GP VAL/FREE 20. PAGE 89 F1752 ECO/UNDEV TREND NAT/LISM

B64
MILIBAND R.,THE SOCIALIST REGISTER: 1964. GERMANY/W ITALY UK LABOR POL/PAR ECO/TAC FOR/AID NUC/PWR ...POLICY SOCIALIST IDEA/COMP 20 MAO NASSER/G. PAGE 91 F1784 MARXISM SOCISM CAP/ISM PROB/SOLV

B64
MITAU G.T.,INSOLUBLE PROBLEMS: CASE PROBLEMS ON THE FUNCTIONS OF STATE AND LOCAL GOVERNMENT. USA+45 AIR FINAN LABOR POL/PAR PROB/SOLV TAX RECEIVE CONTROL GP/REL 20 CASEBOOK ZONING. PAGE 92 F1807 ADJUD LOC/G PROVS

B64
MORGAN H.W.,AMERICAN SOCIALISM 1900-1960. AFR USA+45 USA-45 INTELL AGRI LABOR WORKER BARGAIN ECO/TAC GP/REL RACE/REL 20 NEGRO MIGRATION. PAGE 93 F1830 SOCISM POL/PAR ECO/DEV STRATA

B64
PENNOCK J.R.,SELF-GOVERNMENT IN MODERNIZING NATIONS. AFR COM USA+45 ECO/DEV POL/PAR PROB/SOLV DIPLOM ECO/TAC COLONIAL REV POPULISM SOCISM 20. PAGE 105 F2058 ECO/UNDEV POLICY SOVEREIGN NAT/G

B64
RAISON T.,WHY CONSERVATIVE? UK FORCES DIPLOM ECO/TAC GIVE EDU/PROP ORD/FREE WEALTH LAISSEZ ...GOV/COMP 20 TORY/PARTY CONSRV/PAR. PAGE 109 F2137 PLURISM CONSERVE POL/PAR NAT/G

B64
REUSS H.S.,THE CRITICAL DECADE - AN ECONOMIC POLICY FOR AMERICA AND THE FREE WORLD. AFR USA+45 FINAN POL/PAR WORKER PLAN DIPLOM ECO/TAC TARIFFS BAL/PAY ...POLICY 20 CONGRESS. PAGE 111 F2181 FOR/AID INT/TRADE LABOR LEGIS

B64
SAKAI R.K.,STUDIES ON ASIA, 1964. ASIA CHINA/COM ISRAEL MALAYSIA S/ASIA USA+45 USSR ECO/UNDEV FAM POL/PAR SECT CONSULT NAT/LISM...POLICY SOC 20 CHINJAP. PAGE 115 F2272 PWR DIPLOM

B64
WHEARE K.C.,FEDERAL GOVERNMENT (4TH ED.). WOR+45 WOR-45 POL/PAR LEGIS BAL/PWR CT/SYS...POLICY JURID CONCPT GOV/COMP 17/20. PAGE 145 F2866 FEDERAL CONSTN EX/STRUC NAT/COMP

B64
WRIGHT G.,RURAL REVOLUTION IN FRANCE: THE PEASANTRY IN THE TWENTIETH CENTURY. EUR+WWI MOD/EUR LAW CULTURE AGRI POL/PAR DELIB/GP LEGIS ECO/TAC EDU/PROP COERCE CHOOSE ATTIT RIGID/FLEX HEALTH ...STAT CENSUS CHARTS VAL/FREE 20. PAGE 149 F2932 PWR STRATA FRANCE REV

S64
HORECKY P.L.,"LIBRARY OF CONGRESS PUBLICATIONS IN AID OF USSR AND EAST EUROPEAN RESEARCH." BULGARIA CZECHOSLVK POLAND USSR YUGOSLAVIA NAT/G POL/PAR DIPLOM ADMIN GOV/REL...CLASSIF 20. PAGE 62 F1214 BIBLIOG/A COM MARXISM

S64
SALVADORI M.,"EL CAPITALISMO EN LA EUROPA DE LA POSGUERRA." AFR INT/ORG NAT/G POL/PAR PLAN ECO/TAC ATTIT ORD/FREE WEALTH...HIST/WRIT EEC 20. PAGE 115 F2275 EUR+WWI ECO/DEV CAP/ISM

B65
ALEXANDER R.J.,ORGANIZED LABOR IN LATIN AMERICA. L/A+17C INT/ORG LEGIS WORKER TEC/DEV BARGAIN INT/TRADE REV...NAT/COMP BIBLIOG 20. PAGE 3 F0059 LABOR POL/PAR ECO/UNDEV POLICY

B65
APTER D.E.,THE POLITICS OF MODERNIZATION. AFR L/A+17C CULTURE NAT/G POL/PAR ADMIN COLONIAL NAT/LISM ATTIT RIGID/FLEX PWR...SOC CONCPT. PAGE 6 F0109 ECO/UNDEV GEN/LAWS STRATA CREATE

B65
BARRY E.E.,NATIONALISATION IN BRITISH POLITICS: THE HISTORICAL BACKGROUND. UK AGRI DIST/IND EXTR/IND LABOR LG/CO ATTIT CONSERVE SOCISM 19/20 LABOR/PAR. PAGE 10 F0198 NAT/G OWN INDUS POL/PAR

B65
COLLINS H.,KARL MARX AND THE BRITISH LABOR MOVEMENT, YEARS OF THE FIRST INTERNATIONAL. EUR+WWI MOD/EUR UK STRATA INDUS NAT/G POL/PAR SOCISM ...CONCPT 19/20 MARX/KARL. PAGE 26 F0507 MARXISM LABOR INT/ORG WORKER

B65
EDELMAN M.,THE POLITICS OF WAGE-PRICE DECISIONS. GERMANY ITALY NETHERLAND UK INDUS LABOR POL/PAR PROB/SOLV BARGAIN PRICE ROUTINE BAL/PAY COST DEMAND 20. PAGE 36 F0699 GOV/COMP CONTROL ECO/TAC PLAN

B65
GOODSELL C.T.,ADMINISTRATION OF A REVOLUTION. PUERT/RICO ECO/UNDEV FINAN POL/PAR PROVS LEGIS PLAN BUDGET RECEIVE ADMIN COLONIAL LEAD MUNICH 20 ROOSEVLT/F. PAGE 49 F0951 EXEC SOC

B65
PAYNE J.L.,LABOR AND POLITICS IN PERU; THE SYSTEM OF POLITICAL BARGAINING. PERU CONSTN VOL/ASSN EX/STRUC LEAD PWR...CHARTS 20. PAGE 104 F2042 LABOR POL/PAR BARGAIN GP/REL

B65
SIMON B.,EDUCATION AND THE LABOR MOVEMENT, 1870-1920. UK SOCIETY STRATA LABOR POL/PAR SCHOOL CONTROL PARTIC SOCISM...BIBLIOG 19/20. PAGE 122 F2406 EDU/PROP WORKER ADJUST LAW

B65
WU YUAN-LI,THE ECONOMY OF COMMUNIST CHINA. CHINA/COM USSR AGRI FINAN INDUS POL/PAR WORKER PROB/SOLV INT/TRADE PRICE EATING INCOME OWN WEALTH 20. PAGE 149 F2939 ECO/TAC MARXISM PLAN EFFICIENCY

S65
CECIL C.O.,"THE DETERMINANTS OF LIBYAN FOREIGN LIBYA

POLICY." AFR INTELL ECO/UNDEV EXTR/IND POL/PAR CREATE REGION SOVEREIGN CONSERVE MAGHREB NASSER/G. PAGE 22 F0431
DIPLOM WEALTH ISLAM

S65
SELLERS C.,"THE EQUILIBRIUM CYCLE IN TWO-PARTY POLITICS." USA+45 USA-45 CULTURE R+D GP/REL MAJORITY DECISION. PAGE 119 F2351
CHOOSE TREND POL/PAR

S65
WHITAKER A.P.,"ARGENTINA: STRUGGLE FOR RECOVERY." L/A+17C USA+45 NAT/G TOP/EX PLAN LEGIT COERCE REV RIGID/FLEX PWR WEALTH...RECORD ALL/PROG ARGEN FOR/TRADE 20. PAGE 146 F2867
POL/PAR ECO/TAC NAT/LISM

C65
WUORINEN J.H.,"SCANDINAVIA." DENMARK FINLAND ICELAND NORWAY SWEDEN SOCIETY AGRI POL/PAR DELIB/GP DIPLOM INT/TRADE NEUTRAL WAR...CHARTS IND TREATY 20. PAGE 149 F2942
BIBLIOG NAT/G POLICY

B66
BROWN J.F.,THE NEW EASTERN EUROPE. ALBANIA BULGARIA HUNGARY POLAND ROMANIA CULTURE AGRI POL/PAR WAR NAT/LISM MARXISM...CHARTS BIBLIOG 20. PAGE 19 F0369
DIPLOM COM NAT/G ECO/UNDEV

B66
COLE A.B.,SOCIALIST PARTIES IN POSTWAR JAPAN. STRATA AGRI LABOR PLAN DIPLOM ECO/TAC AGREE LEAD CHOOSE ATTIT...CHARTS 20 CHINJAP SOC/DEMPAR. PAGE 26 F0499
POL/PAR POLICY SOCISM NAT/G

B66
FORD P.,CARDINAL MORAN AND THE A. L. P. NAT/G POL/PAR SECT DELIB/GP LOBBY REV CHOOSE ORD/FREE MARXISM 19/20 AUSTRAL PROTESTANT LABOR/PAR. PAGE 42 F0825
CATHISM SOCISM LABOR SOCIETY

B66
GREENE L.E.,GOVERNMENT IN TENNESSEE (2ND ED.). USA+45 DIST/IND INDUS POL/PAR EX/STRUC LEGIS PLAN BUDGET GIVE CT/SYS...MGT T 20 TENNESSEE. PAGE 51 F0989
PROVS LOC/G CONSTN ADMIN

B66
HOROWITZ I.L.,THREE WORLDS OF DEVELOPMENT. COM USA+45 STRUCT ECO/DEV PLAN PROB/SOLV TEC/DEV CIVMIL/REL...PHIL/SCI IDEA/COMP 20. PAGE 62 F1216
ECO/UNDEV BAL/PWR POL/PAR REV

B66
MADAN G.R.,ECONOMIC THINKING IN INDIA. INDIA ECO/UNDEV AGRI FINAN INDUS LABOR PLAN CAP/ISM INT/TRADE MARXISM SOCISM...POLICY 1/20. PAGE 84 F1638
ECO/TAC PHIL/SCI NAT/G POL/PAR

B66
RIZK C.,LE REGIME POLITIQUE LIBANAIS. ISLAM LEBANON STRUCT POL/PAR SECT LOBBY GP/REL 20 ARABS MUSLIM CHRISTIAN. PAGE 112 F2198
ECO/UNDEV NAT/G CULTURE

B66
ROSS A.M.,INDUSTRIAL RELATIONS AND ECONOMIC DEVELOPMENT. POL/PAR LEGIS WORKER BARGAIN PRICE EXEC LOBBY INCOME PWR...DECISION ANTHOL BIBLIOG 20. PAGE 114 F2243
ECO/UNDEV LABOR NAT/G GP/REL

B66
US DEPARTMENT OF STATE,RESEARCH ON WESTERN EUROPE, GREAT BRITAIN, AND CANADA (EXTERNAL RESEARCH LIST NO 3-25). CANADA GERMANY/W UK LAW CULTURE NAT/G POL/PAR FORCES EDU/PROP REGION MARXISM...GEOG SOC WORSHIP 20 CMN/WLTH. PAGE 136 F2676
BIBLIOG/A EUR+WWI DIPLOM

B66
WILLIAMS G.,MERTHYR POLITICS: THE MAKING OF A WORKING-CLASS TRADITION. UK CHIEF WORKER LEAD SOCISM...ANTHOL MUNICH 19/20 MERTHYR RICHARD/H. PAGE 147 F2891
LOC/G POL/PAR INDUS

S66
FELD W.,"NATIONAL ECONOMIC INTEREST GROUPS AND POLICY FORMATION IN THE EEC." NAT/G POL/PAR REGION CENTRAL SOVEREIGN...INT NET/THEORY EEC. PAGE 40 F0777
LOBBY ELITES DECISION

S66
JAVITS J.K.,"POLITICAL ACTION VITAL FOR LATIN AMERICAN INTEGRATION." ECO/UNDEV INT/ORG POL/PAR VOL/ASSN PLAN PROB/SOLV INT/TRADE EFFICIENCY 20 OAS LAFTA ALL/PROG. PAGE 66 F1308
L/A+17C ECO/TAC REGION

B67
ANDERSON T.,RUSSIAN POLITICAL THOUGHT; AN INTRODUCTION. USSR NAT/G POL/PAR CHIEF MARXISM ...TIME/SEQ BIBLIOG 9/20. PAGE 5 F0099
TREND CONSTN ATTIT

B67
BAILY S.L.,LABOR, NATIONALISM, AND POLITICS IN ARGENTINA. POL/PAR TOP/EX GP/REL...BIBLIOG/A 19/20 MIGRATION PERON/JUAN ARGEN. PAGE 8 F0154
LABOR NAT/LISM

B67
BARNETT A.D.,CHINA AFTER MAO. ASIA CHINA/COM CULTURE ECO/UNDEV ECO/TAC CONTROL EFFICIENCY NAT/LISM MARXISM 20. PAGE 10 F0189
POL/PAR NAT/G TEC/DEV GP/REL

B67
BIBBY J.,ON CAPITOL HILL. POL/PAR LOBBY PARL/PROC GOV/REL PERS/REL...JURID PHIL/SCI OBS INT BIBLIOG 20 CONGRESS PRESIDENT. PAGE 15 F0278
CONFER LEGIS CREATE LEAD

B67
BLAIR G.S.,LEGISLATIVE BODIES IN CALIFORNIA. USA+45 LAW POL/PAR LOBBY APPORT CHOOSE REPRESENT GP/REL ...T CALIFORNIA. PAGE 15 F0293
LEGIS PROVS LOC/G ADJUD

B67
BROMKE A.,POLAND'S POLITICS: IDEALISM VS. REALISM. COM GERMANY POLAND RUSSIA USSR POL/PAR CATHISM ...BIBLIOG 19/20. PAGE 19 F0360
NAT/G DIPLOM MARXISM

B67
BURDEN H.T.,THE NUREMBERG PARTY RALLIES 1923-39. GERMANY POL/PAR SECT CREATE DOMIN WAR ATTIT ...AUD/VIS FILM 20. PAGE 20 F0384
EDU/PROP CONTROL CROWD TOTALISM

B67
BUSEY J.L.,NOTES ON COSTA RICAN DEMOCRACY. COSTA/RICA L/A+17C NAT/G POL/PAR LEGIS CHOOSE OWN ATTIT...BIBLIOG 20. PAGE 20 F0394
CONSTN MAJORIT SOCIETY ECO/UNDEV

B67
COWLING M.,1867 DISRAELI, GLADSTONE, AND REVOLUTION; THE PASSING OF THE SECOND REFORM BILL. UK LEGIS LEAD LOBBY GP/REL INGP/REL...DECISION BIBLIOG 19 REFORMERS. PAGE 28 F0545
PARL/PROC POL/PAR ATTIT LAW

B67
EVANS R.H.,COEXISTENCE: COMMUNISM AND ITS PRACTICE IN BOLOGNA, 1945-1965. ITALY CAP/ISM ADMIN CHOOSE PEACE ORD/FREE...SOC STAT DEEP/INT SAMP CHARTS BIBLIOG MUNICH 20. PAGE 39 F0756
MARXISM CULTURE POL/PAR

B67
FIELD G.L.,COMPARATIVE POLITICAL DEVELOPMENT: THE PRECEDENT OF THE WEST. FRANCE GERMANY SWEDEN UK USSR STRATA STRUCT POL/PAR...METH 20. PAGE 40 F0790
NAT/COMP CONCPT ECO/DEV SOCIETY

B67
FONER P.S.,THE BOLSHEVIK REVOLUTION. USA-45 POL/PAR WORKER DIPLOM EDU/PROP MARXISM...STERTYP 20. PAGE 42 F0821
LABOR INTELL REV PRESS

B67
GOODMAN J.S.,THE DEMOCRATS AND LABOR IN RHODE ISLAND 9152-1962; CHANGES IN THE OLD ALLIANCE. USA+45 EDU/PROP LEAD GP/REL ROLE RHODE/ISL DEMOCRAT. PAGE 49 F0948
LABOR LOBBY POL/PAR LEGIS

B67
GORZ A.,STRATEGY FOR LABOR: A RADICAL PROPOSAL (TRANS. BY MARTIN NICOLAUS AND VICTORIA ORTIZ). EUR+WWI FRANCE ITALY ECO/DEV POL/PAR OP/RES PLAN GP/REL ALL/IDEOS...SOC 20 EEC. PAGE 49 F0965
LABOR PWR STRUCT ECO/TAC

B67
GRIPP R.C.,PATTERNS OF SOVIET POLITICS (REV. ED.). USSR LAW ELITES LOC/G PLAN CONTROL CT/SYS CHOOSE ...POLICY BIBLIOG/A DICTIONARY 9/20. PAGE 51 F1003
COM ADJUD POL/PAR

B67
HANRIEDER W.F.,WEST GERMAN FOREIGN POLICY 1949-1963: INTERNATIONAL PRESSURE AND DOMESTIC RESPONSE. EUR+WWI GERMANY/W POL/PAR LOBBY CONSEN 20. PAGE 54 F1061
DIPLOM POLICY NAT/G ATTIT

B67
HERRESHOFF D.,AMERICAN DISCIPLES OF MARX: FROM THE AGE OF JACKSON TO THE PROGRESSIVE ERA. USA-45 AGRI POL/PAR 19/20. PAGE 59 F1155
MARXISM ATTIT WORKER CONCPT

B67
JHANGIANI M.A.,JANA SANGH AND SWATANTRA: A PROFILE OF THE RIGHTIST PARTIES IN INDIA. INDIA ADMIN CHOOSE MARXISM SOCISM...INT CHARTS BIBLIOG 20. PAGE 67 F1320
POL/PAR LAISSEZ NAT/LISM ATTIT

B67
KIRK R.,THE POLITICAL PRINCIPLES OF ROBERT A. TAFT. USA+45 LABOR DIPLOM ADJUD ADJUST ORD/FREE TAFT/RA. PAGE 71 F1398
POL/PAR LEAD LEGIS ATTIT

B67
MORRIS A.J.A.,PARLIAMENTARY DEMOCRACY IN THE NINETEENTH CENTURY. UK INDUS LOC/G NAT/G POL/PAR CONSULT LEGIS INT/TRADE ADMIN CHOOSE SUFF SOVEREIGN 19 PARLIAMENT. PAGE 93 F1835
TIME/SEQ CONSTN PARL/PROC POPULISM

B67
NYOMARKAY J.,CHARISMA AND FACTIONALISM IN THE NAZI PARTY. GERMANY POL/PAR LEGIT LEAD MARXISM ...NEW/IDEA METH/COMP GEN/LAWS BIBLIOG 20 HITLER/A. PAGE 99 F1949
FASCISM INGP/REL CHIEF PWR

B67
O'LEARY M.K.,THE POLITICS OF AMERICAN FOREIGN AID. USA+45 POL/PAR CHIEF BUDGET EDU/PROP LOBBY CONGRESS. PAGE 100 F1958
FOR/AID DIPLOM PARL/PROC ATTIT

B67
POLLACK N.,THE POPULIST MIND. USA-45 STRATA AGRI NAT/G POL/PAR LEGIS WORKER RACE/REL WEALTH...ANTHOL BIBLIOG 19 NEGRO. PAGE 107 F2097
POPULISM HIST/WRIT ATTIT INGP/REL

B67
PRINCE C.E.,NEW JERSEY'S JEFFERSONIAN REPUBLICANS; THE GENESIS OF AN EARLY PARTY MACHINE (1789-1817).
POL/PAR CONSTN

USA-45 LOC/G EDU/PROP PRESS CONTROL CHOOSE...CHARTS 18/19 NEW/JERSEY REPUBLICAN. PAGE 108 F2117 ADMIN PROVS

B67
REHMUS C.M.,LABOR AND AMERICAN POLITICS. POL/PAR WORKER EDU/PROP PARTIC ATTIT PWR. PAGE 110 F2175 LABOR ROLE LOBBY

B67
SCHECTER J.,THE NEW FACE OF BUDDHA: BUDDHISM AND POLITICAL POWER IN SOUTHEAST ASIA. S/ASIA NAT/G POL/PAR NAT/LISM ATTIT MARXISM...BIBLIOG 20. PAGE 116 F2292 SECT POLICY PWR LEAD

B67
TOMA P.A.,THE POLITICS OF FOOD FOR PEACE; EXECUTIVE-LEGISLATIVE INTERACTION. USA+45 ECO/UNDEV POL/PAR DEBATE EXEC LOBBY CHOOSE PEACE...DECISION CHARTS. PAGE 131 F2580 FOR/AID POLICY LEGIS AGRI

B67
WILLIAMS E.J.,LATIN AMERICAN CHRISTIAN DEMOCRATIC PARTIES. L/A+17C FAM LABOR FORCES...CATH TREND BIBLIOG 20. PAGE 147 F2890 POL/PAR GP/COMP CATHISM ALL/VALS

B67
WISEMAN H.V.,BRITAIN AND THE COMMONWEALTH. EUR+WWI FUT UK ECO/DEV POL/PAR TEC/DEV INT/TRADE LEAD ROLE SOVEREIGN...SOC TREND 20 CMN/WLTH. PAGE 148 F2911 INT/ORG DIPLOM NAT/G NAT/COMP

B67
YAMAMURA K.,ECONOMIC POLICY IN POSTWAR JAPAN. ASIA FINAN POL/PAR DIPLOM LEAD NAT/LISM ATTIT NEW/LIB POPULISM 20 CHINJAP. PAGE 149 F2946 ECO/DEV POLICY NAT/G TEC/DEV

L67
AUSTIN D.A.,"POLITICAL CONFLICT IN AFRICA." CONSTN NAT/G CREATE ADMIN COLONIAL ORD/FREE MARXISM POPULISM SOCISM...NAT/COMP ANTHOL 20. PAGE 8 F0141 ANOMIE AFR POL/PAR

L67
LAMBERT J.D.,"CORPORATE POLITICAL SPENDING AND CAMPAIGN FINANCE." LAW CONSTN FINAN LABOR LG/CO LOC/G NAT/G VOL/ASSN TEC/DEV ADJUD ADMIN PARTIC. PAGE 75 F1463 USA+45 POL/PAR CHOOSE COST

L67
SCALAPINO R.A.,"A SURVEY OF ASIA IN 1966." ASIA S/ASIA CONSTN SOCIETY POL/PAR CHIEF WAR...ANTHOL 20. PAGE 116 F2285 DIPLOM

S67
APEL H.,"LES NOUVEAUX ASPECTS DE LA POLITIQUE ETRANGERE ALLEMANDE." AFR EUR+WWI GERMANY POL/PAR BAL/PWR ECO/TAC INT/TRADE NUC/PWR NAT/LISM PEACE ...POLICY 20 EEC. PAGE 6 F0107 DIPLOM INT/ORG FEDERAL

S67
BUTT R.,"THE COMMON MARKET AND CONSERVATIVE POLITICS, 1961-2." UK CHIEF DIPLOM ECO/TAC INT/TRADE CONFER DEBATE REGION ATTIT...POLICY 20 EEC. PAGE 21 F0398 EUR+WWI INT/ORG POL/PAR

S67
CAMMETT J.M.,"COMMUNIST THEORIES OF FASCISM, 1920-35." ITALY POL/PAR PROF/ORG VOL/ASSN WORKER COLONIAL TOTALISM...SOCIALIST 20. PAGE 21 F0403 MARXISM FASCISM ATTIT

S67
FINER S.E.,"THE ONE-PARTY REGIMES IN AFRICA: RECONSIDERATIONS." AFR DOMIN CONSEN ORD/FREE 20. PAGE 41 F0798 ELITES POL/PAR CONSTN ECO/UNDEV

S67
GATELL F.O.,"MONEY AND PARTY IN JACKSONIAN AMERICA* A QUANTITATIVE LOOK AT NEW YORK CITY'S MEN OF QUALITY." USA-45 STRATA SECT SUFF CONSEN MAJORITY ATTIT...CHARTS HYPO/EXP 19. PAGE 46 F0908 WEALTH POL/PAR PERSON IDEA/COMP

S67
GEISS I.,"THE GERMANS AND THE MIDDLE EAST CRISIS." GERMANY/W ISLAM ISRAEL USSR POL/PAR RACE/REL MARXISM...GP/COMP 20 JEWS. PAGE 47 F0914 ATTIT DIPLOM WAR POLICY

S67
GRAHAM R.,"BRAZIL'S DILEMMA." BRAZIL FUT L/A+17C NAT/G CHIEF PROB/SOLV ECO/TAC PWR 20. PAGE 50 F0972 ECO/UNDEV CONSTN POL/PAR POLICY

S67
GUPTA S.,"FOREIGN POLICY IN THE 1967 MANIFESTOS." ASIA COM INDIA USA+45 FORCES FOR/AID TAX ATTIT ...DECISION 20. PAGE 52 F1013 IDEA/COMP POL/PAR POLICY DIPLOM

S67
HALL B.,"THE COALITION AGAINST DISHWASHERS." USA+45 POL/PAR PROB/SOLV BARGAIN LEAD CHOOSE REPRESENT GP/REL ORD/FREE PWR...POLICY 20. PAGE 53 F1044 LABOR ADMIN DOMIN WORKER

S67
HANCOCK J.L.,"PLANNERS IN THE CHANGING AMERICAN CITY, 1900-1940." USA-45 CONSTRUC NAT/G POL/PAR ...SOC/WK TREND MUNICH 20. PAGE 54 F1059 PLAN CONSULT LOC/G

S67
HEATH D.B.,"BOLIVIA UNDER BARRIENTOS." L/A+17C NAT/G CHIEF DIPLOM ECO/TAC...POLICY 20 BOLIV. PAGE 58 F1132 ECO/UNDEV POL/PAR REV

CONSTN

S67
LEONTYEV L.,"THE LENINIST PRINCIPLES OF SOCIALIST ECONOMIC MANAGEMENT." USA+45 USSR POL/PAR WORKER PLAN ECO/TAC EFFICIENCY PRODUC MARXISM...POLICY SOCIALIST MGT TREND 20 LENIN/VI MARX/KARL. PAGE 78 F1529 SOCISM CAP/ISM IDEA/COMP ECO/DEV

S67
LINEBERRY R.L.,"REFORMISM AND PUBLIC POLICIES IN AMERICAN CITIES." USA+45 POL/PAR EX/STRUC LEGIS BUDGET TAX GP/REL...STAT CHARTS MUNICH. PAGE 80 F1573 DECISION POLICY LOC/G

S67
PFEFFERMANN G.,"TRADE UNIONS AND POLITICS IN FRENCH WEST AFRICA DURING THE FOURTH REPUBLIC." AFR INDUS POL/PAR COLONIAL ATTIT PWR 20. PAGE 106 F2077 PARTIC DRIVE INT/TRADE LABOR

S67
RAZA M.A.,"EMERGING TRENDS IN PUBLIC LABOR POLICIES AND UNION - GOVERN MENT RELATIONS IN ASIA AND AFRICA." LAW NAT/G POL/PAR COLONIAL COERCE GP/REL ATTIT 20. PAGE 110 F2157 LABOR CONTROL TREND

S67
SCOTT R.,"TRADE UNIONS IN AFRICA." AFR UGANDA USA-45 ECO/UNDEV INDUS INT/ORG POL/PAR ECO/TAC WEALTH...GP/COMP 20 NKRUMAH/K. PAGE 118 F2335 LABOR WORKER NAT/G

S67
SHERWOOD W.B.,"THE RISE OF THE JUSTICE PARTY IN TURKEY." FUT TURKEY LEAD ATTIT 20. PAGE 121 F2378 POL/PAR ECO/UNDEV STRUCT SOCIETY

S67
SIPPEL D.,"INDIENS UNSICHERE ZUKUNFT." INDIA CULTURE ACADEM POL/PAR LEGIS COLONIAL CHOOSE SOVEREIGN...JURID 20. PAGE 122 F2416 SOCIETY STRUCT ECO/UNDEV NAT/G

S67
SPITTMANN I.,"EAST GERMANY: THE SWINGING PENDULUM." COM GERMANY/E NAT/G EFFICIENCY MARXISM 20. PAGE 125 F2458 PRODUC POL/PAR WEALTH ATTIT

S67
TABORSKY E.,"THE CLASS STRUGGLE, THE PROLETARIAT, AND THE DEVELOPING NATIONS." USSR LABOR POL/PAR FOR/AID COLONIAL GP/REL 20. PAGE 128 F2521 DIPLOM MARXISM ECO/UNDEV WORKER

S67
THEROUX P.,"HATING THE ASIANS." TANZANIA UGANDA CONSTN INDUS NAT/G POL/PAR WORKER ECO/TAC HABITAT LOVE...POLICY GEOG 20 MIGRATION. PAGE 130 F2557 AFR RACE/REL SOVEREIGN ATTIT

N67
US SENATE COMM ON FOREIGN REL,SURVEY OF THE ALLIANCE FOR PROGRESS: THE LATIN AMERICAN MILITARY (PAMPHLET). USA+45 INT/ORG POL/PAR DIPLOM AGREE GP/REL ROLE ORD/FREE 20. PAGE 139 F2746 L/A+17C FORCES CIVMIL/REL POLICY

B86
O'CONNOR T.P.,THE PARNELL MOVEMENT: WITH A SKETCH OF IRISH PARTIES FROM 1843. IRELAND UK USA-45 LEGIS WORKER ECO/TAC COERCE CRIME REV CHOOSE ORD/FREE CATHISM LAISSEZ...SOC 19/20 PARLIAMENT PARNELL/CS LAND/LEAG. PAGE 100 F1957 LEAD DOMIN POL/PAR POLICY

POLAK J.J. F0569

POLAND....SEE ALSO COM

B54
REYNOLDS P.A.,BRITISH FOREIGN POLICY IN THE INTER-WAR YEARS. CZECHOSLVK GERMANY POLAND UK USA-45 POL/PAR FORCES ECO/TAC ARMS/CONT WAR ATTIT 20. PAGE 111 F2182 DIPLOM POLICY NAT/G

B59
ETSCHMANN R.,DIE WAHRUNGS- UND DEVISENPOLITIK DES OSTBLOCKS UND IHRE AUSWIRKUNGEN AUF DIE WIRTSCHAFTSBEZIEHUNGEN ZWISCHEN OST U WEST. BULGARIA CZECHOSLVK HUNGARY POLAND USSR MARKET NAT/G PLAN DIPLOM...NAT/COMP 20. PAGE 39 F0753 ECO/TAC FINAN POLICY INT/TRADE

S64
HORECKY P.L.,"LIBRARY OF CONGRESS PUBLICATIONS IN AID OF USSR AND EAST EUROPEAN RESEARCH." BULGARIA CZECHOSLVK POLAND USSR YUGOSLAVIA NAT/G POL/PAR DIPLOM ADMIN GOV/REL...CLASSIF 20. PAGE 62 F1214 BIBLIOG/A COM MARXISM

B65
CAMPBELL J.C.,AMERICAN POLICY TOWARDS COMMUNIST EASTERN EUROPE* THE CHOICES AHEAD. AFR USA+45 ECO/DEV BAL/PWR MARXISM TREND. PAGE 21 F0406 POLAND YUGOSLAVIA DIPLOM COM

B66
BROWN J.F.,THE NEW EASTERN EUROPE. ALBANIA BULGARIA HUNGARY POLAND ROMANIA CULTURE AGRI POL/PAR WAR NAT/LISM MARXISM...CHARTS BIBLIOG 20. PAGE 19 F0369 DIPLOM COM NAT/G ECO/UNDEV

B66
JACKSON G.D.,COMINTERN AND PEASANT IN EAST EUROPE 1919-1930. BULGARIA COM CZECHOSLVK EUR+WWI POLAND MARXISM ECO/UNDEV

ROMANIA YUGOSLAVIA STRATA AGRI VOL/ASSN DIPLOM CONTROL CROWD WEALTH...POLICY NAT/COMP 20. PAGE 66 F1293
WORKER INT/ORG

B66
SPULBER N.,THE STATE AND ECONOMIC DEVELOPMENT IN EASTERN EUROPE. BULGARIA COM CZECHOSLVK HUNGARY POLAND YUGOSLAVIA CULTURE PLAN CAP/ISM INT/TRADE CONTROL...POLICY CHARTS METH/COMP BIBLIOG/A 19/20. PAGE 125 F2460
ECO/DEV ECO/UNDEV NAT/G TOTALISM

B67
BROMKE A.,POLAND'S POLITICS: IDEALISM VS. REALISM. COM GERMANY POLAND RUSSIA USSR POL/PAR CATHISM ...BIBLIOG 19/20. PAGE 19 F0360
NAT/G DIPLOM MARXISM

S67
JEDLICKI W.,"THE FREE SPEECH MOVEMENT IN WARSAW." POLAND FORCES EDU/PROP LEAD ATTIT MARXISM ...IDEA/COMP 20. PAGE 67 F1310
COERCE CROWD ORD/FREE ACADEM

S67
SEIDLER G.L.,"MARXIST LEGAL THOUGHT IN POLAND." POLAND SOCIETY R+D LOC/G NAT/G ACT/RES ADJUD CT/SYS SUPEGO PWR...SOC TREND 20 MARX/KARL. PAGE 119 F2343
MARXISM LAW CONCPT EFFICIENCY

POLARIS J. F2095

POLICE....SEE FORCES

POLICY....ETHICS OF PUBLIC POLICIES

POLIT/ACTN....POLITICAL ACTION COMMITTEE

POLITBURO....POLITBURO (U.S.S.R.)

POLITICAL BEHAVIOR....SEE POL

POLITICAL FINANCING....SEE POL+FINAN

POLITICAL MACHINE....SEE POL+ADMIN

POLITICAL MOVEMENT....SEE IDEOLOGICAL TOPIC INDEX

POLITICAL ORGANIZATION....SEE POL/PAR

POLITICAL PROCESS....SEE LEGIS, POL

POLITICAL SCIENCE....SEE POL

POLITICAL SYSTEMS....SEE IDEOLOGICAL TOPIC INDEX

POLITICAL SYSTEMS THEORY....SEE GEN/LAWS+NET/THEORY+POL

POLITICAL THEORY....SEE IDEOLOGICAL TOPIC INDEX

POLITICS....SEE POL

POLK J. F2096

POLK/JAMES....PRESIDENT JAMES POLK

POLLACK N. F0851,F2097

POLLACK/N....NORMAN POLLACK

POLLARD J.A. F2098

POLLOCK F. F2099

POLLUTION....AIR OR WATER POLLUTION

POLYANOV N. F2100

POLYNESIA....POLYNESIA

B39
FIRTH R.,PRIMITIVE POLYNESIAN ECONOMY. SOCIETY DIST/IND SECT CHIEF CAP/ISM PRODUC WEALTH...SOC OBS METH WORSHIP 20 POLYNESIA. PAGE 41 F0802
ECO/UNDEV CULTURE AGRI ECO/TAC

PONCET J. F2101

POOL I. F0217

POOLE K. F2102

POOLE K.E. F2103

POOLEY B.J. F2104

POONA....POONA, INDIA

POPE....POPE

B82
CUNNINGHAM W.,THE GROWTH OF ENGLISH INDUSTRY AND COMMERCE. FUT UK FINAN NAT/G CAP/ISM...POLICY 20 MERCANTLST CHRISTIAN POPE. PAGE 29 F0562
INDUS INT/TRADE SML/CO CONSERVE

POPPER/K....KARL POPPER

POPPINO R.E. F2105

POPULATION....SEE GEOG, CENSUS

POPULISM....MAJORITARIANISM

B08
LLOYD H.D.,THE SWISS DEMOCRACY. SWITZERLND INDUS NAT/G WORKER CHOOSE OWN ORD/FREE SOCISM...PLURIST 19/20 MONOPOLY. PAGE 81 F1590
NAT/COMP GOV/COMP REPRESENT POPULISM

B11
SOREL G.,LES ILLUSIONS DU PROGRES (1906). UNIV SOCIETY STRATA INDUS GP/REL OWN PRODUC SOCISM 17/20. PAGE 124 F2444
WORKER POPULISM ECO/DEV ATTIT

N19
HAYEK FA V.O.N.,FREEDOM AND THE ECONOMIC SYSTEM. GERMANY USSR PLAN REPRESENT TOTALISM FASCISM POPULISM...MAJORIT METH/COMP GEN/LAWS 20. PAGE 57 F1123
ORD/FREE ECO/TAC CAP/ISM SOCISM

B20
BUCK S.J.,THE AGRARIAN CRUSADE: A CHRONICLE OF THE FARMER IN POLITICS. USA-45 INDUS PROB/SOLV PWR WEALTH...GEOG CENSUS 19/20 GREENBACK GRANGE SILVER. PAGE 20 F0381
AGRI POPULISM VOL/ASSN POL/PAR

B33
TANNENBAUM F.,PEACE BY REVOLUTION. ECO/UNDEV AGRI SECT WORKER DIPLOM EDU/PROP DISCRIM OWN WEALTH POPULISM 17/20 MEXIC/AMER INDIAN/AM. PAGE 128 F2532
CULTURE COLONIAL RACE/REL REV

B35
LASKI H.J.,THE STATE IN THEORY AND PRACTICE. ELITES ECO/TAC REPRESENT ORD/FREE PWR WEALTH POPULISM ...GOV/COMP GEN/LAWS 19/20. PAGE 76 F1483
CAP/ISM COERCE NAT/G FASCISM

B38
REICH N.,LABOR RELATIONS IN REPUBLICAN GERMANY. GERMANY CONSTN ECO/DEV INDUS NAT/G ADMIN CONTROL GP/REL FASCISM POPULISM 20 WEIMAR/REP. PAGE 110 F2176
WORKER MGT LABOR BARGAIN

B40
HUNTER R.,REVOLUTION: WHY, HOW, WHEN? NAT/G ECO/TAC EDU/PROP COERCE ORD/FREE FASCISM POPULISM SOCISM 18/20 HITLER/A LENIN/VI. PAGE 63 F1246
REV METH/COMP LEAD CONSTN

B40
SPENCER H.,THE MAN VS. THE STATE (1892). UK POL/PAR LEGIS TARIFFS COERCE CRIME REPRESENT PWR SOCISM ...POLICY GEN/LAWS 19/20. PAGE 124 F2450
FASCISM POPULISM LAISSEZ ORD/FREE

B47
BALDWIN H.W.,THE PRICE OF POWER. USA+45 FORCES PLAN NUC/PWR ADJUST COST ORD/FREE...POLICY PSY BIBLIOG 20. PAGE 9 F0165
PROB/SOLV PWR POPULISM PRICE

B48
DURBIN E.F.M.,THE POLITICS OF DEMOCRATIC SOCIALISM; AN ESSAY ON SOCIAL POLICY. STRATA POL/PAR PLAN COERCE DRIVE PERSON PWR MARXISM...CHARTS METH/COMP. PAGE 35 F0684
SOCIALIST POPULISM POLICY SOCIETY

B48
VON HAYEK F.A.,INDIVIDUALISM AND ECONOMIC ORDER. GERMANY USA-45 USSR FINAN MARKET INT/ORG ECO/TAC INT/TRADE PRICE REPRESENT ORD/FREE...PLURIST GEN/LAWS 20. PAGE 142 F2793
SOCISM CAP/ISM POPULISM FEDERAL

B50
CLARK J.M.,ALTERNATIVE TO SERFDOM. SOCIETY STRATA INDUS MARKET WORKER PRICE GP/REL PROFIT BIO/SOC PWR WEALTH...GEN/LAWS 20 KEYNES/JM. PAGE 25 F0481
ORD/FREE POPULISM ECO/TAC REPRESENT

B51
BROGAN D.W.,THE PRICE OF REVOLUTION. FRANCE USA+45 USA-45 USSR CONSTN NAT/G DIPLOM COLONIAL NAT/LISM ORD/FREE POPULISM...CONCPT 18/20 PRE/US/AM. PAGE 19 F0359
REV METH/COMP COST MARXISM

B52
BEVAN A.,IN PLACE OF FEAR. WOR+45 STRATA LEGIS REPRESENT OWN NEW/LIB POPULISM...CHARTS 20. PAGE 14 F0273
SOCISM SOCIALIST WEALTH MAJORIT

B58
PALMER E.E.,INDUSTRIAL MAN. USA+45 PERSON ORD/FREE POPULISM...PREDICT TREND ANTHOL 20. PAGE 103 F2020
INDUS ECO/UNDEV CULTURE WEALTH

B58
PALMER E.E.,THE ECONOMY AND THE DEMOCRATIC IDEAL. USA+45 USA-45 STRATA CHIEF CT/SYS ORD/FREE SOCISM ...MAJORIT CONCPT ANTHOL 18/20 PRESIDENT. PAGE 103
ECO/DEV POPULISM METH/COMP

F2021 ECO/TAC

B60
MAYO H.B.,INTRODUCTION TO MARXIST THEORY. SECT WORKER POPULISM SOCISM 19/20. PAGE 87 F1709
MARXISM STRATA IDEA/COMP PHIL/SCI

B61
LICHTHEIM G.,MARXISM. GERMANY SOCIETY WORKER CAP/ISM ECO/TAC NAT/LISM POPULISM...TIME/SEQ GOV/COMP NAT/COMP 18/20 COM/PARTY. PAGE 80 F1559
MARXISM SOCISM IDEA/COMP CULTURE

B62
GWYN W.B.,DEMOCRACY AND THE COST OF POLITICS IN BRITAIN. UK BUDGET CRIME CHOOSE ORD/FREE WEALTH ...TIME/SEQ 18/20. PAGE 52 F1017
COST POL/PAR POPULISM PAY

B64
PENNOCK J.R.,SELF-GOVERNMENT IN MODERNIZING NATIONS. AFR COM USA+45 ECO/DEV POL/PAR PROB/SOLV DIPLOM ECO/TAC COLONIAL REV POPULISM SOCISM 20. PAGE 105 F2058
ECO/UNDEV POLICY SOVEREIGN NAT/G

B64
TAWNEY R.H.,EQUALITY. UK CULTURE STRATA ECO/TAC EDU/PROP REPRESENT OWN NEW/LIB...MAJORIT WELF/ST SOC 20. PAGE 129 F2538
WEALTH STRUCT ELITES POPULISM

B65
GRIFFIN C.E.,THE FREE SOCIETY. CONSTN SOCIETY MARKET FEDERAL RATIONAL WEALTH...MAJORIT 20 CIVIL/LIB. PAGE 51 F0999
CONCPT ORD/FREE CAP/ISM POPULISM

B65
THE STATE AND ECONOMIC ENTERPRISE IN JAPAN; ESSAYS IN THE POLITICAL ECONOMY OF GROWTH. AGRI INDUS DRIVE POPULISM...CHARTS NAT/COMP ANTHOL 19/20 CHINJAP. PAGE 81 F1594
ECO/UNDEV ECO/DEV CAP/ISM ECO/TAC

B65
NKRUMAH K.,NEO-COLONIALISM: THE LAST STAGE OF IMPERIALISM. AFR INT/ORG WORKER FOR/AID INT/TRADE EDU/PROP GOV/REL NAT/LISM SOVEREIGN POPULISM SOCISM ...SOCIALIST 20 THIRD/WRLD INTRVN/ECO. PAGE 98 F1929
COLONIAL DIPLOM ECO/UNDEV ECO/TAC

B67
APTHEKER H.,THE NATURE OF DEMOCRACY, FREEDOM AND REVOLUTION. WOR+45 PROB/SOLV COERCE COST...CONCPT TIME/SEQ METH/COMP. PAGE 6 F0111
REV POPULISM MARXIST ORD/FREE

B67
MENDEL A.P.,POLITICAL MEMOIRS 1905-1917 BY PAUL MILIUKOV (TRANS. BY CARL GOLDBERG). USSR AGRI DIPLOM ECO/TAC POPULISM...MAJORIT 20. PAGE 90 F1757
BIOG LEAD NAT/G CONSTN

B67
MORRIS A.J.A.,PARLIAMENTARY DEMOCRACY IN THE NINETEENTH CENTURY. UK INDUS LOC/G NAT/G POL/PAR CONSULT LEGIS INT/TRADE ADMIN CHOOSE SUFF SOVEREIGN 19 PARLIAMENT. PAGE 93 F1835
TIME/SEQ CONSTN PARL/PROC POPULISM

B67
POLLACK N.,THE POPULIST MIND. USA-45 STRATA AGRI NAT/G POL/PAR LEGIS WORKER RACE/REL WEALTH...ANTHOL BIBLIOG 19 NEGRO. PAGE 107 F2097
POPULISM HIST/WRIT ATTIT INGP/REL

B67
YAMAMURA K.,ECONOMIC POLICY IN POSTWAR JAPAN. ASIA FINAN POL/PAR DIPLOM LEAD NAT/LISM ATTIT NEW/LIB POPULISM 20 CHINJAP. PAGE 149 F2946
ECO/DEV POLICY NAT/G TEC/DEV

L67
AUSTIN D.A.,"POLITICAL CONFLICT IN AFRICA." CONSTN NAT/G CREATE ADMIN COLONIAL ORD/FREE MARXISM POPULISM SOCISM...NAT/COMP ANTHOL 20. PAGE 8 F0141
ANOMIE AFR POL/PAR

S67
LANGLEY L.D.,"THE DEMOCRATIC TRADITION AND MILITARY REFORM, 1878-1885." USA-45 SECT EDU/PROP CROWD EFFICIENCY NAT/LISM 19 INDIAN/AM. PAGE 75 F1480
ATTIT FORCES POPULISM

S67
MANGLAPUS R.S.,"ASIAN REVOLUTION AND AMERICAN IDEOLOGY." USA+45 SOCIETY CAP/ISM DIPLOM ADJUST CENTRAL...NAT/COMP 20. PAGE 84 F1652
REV POPULISM ATTIT ASIA

S67
SOLT L.F.,"PURITANISM, CAPITALISM, DEMOCRACY, AND THE NEW SCIENCE." NAT/G GP/REL CONSERVE...IDEA/COMP GEN/LAWS. PAGE 124 F2440
SECT CAP/ISM RATIONAL POPULISM

B76
TAINE H.A.,THE ANCIENT REGIME. FRANCE STRATA FORCES PARTIC EQUILIB WEALTH CONSERVE POPULISM...GOV/COMP SOC/INTEG 18/19. PAGE 128 F2527
NAT/G GOV/REL TAX REV

B91
MILL J.S.,SOCIALISM (1859). MOD/EUR AGRI INDUS NAT/G REV INCOME PRODUC ORD/FREE POPULISM SOCISM ...GOV/COMP METH/COMP 19. PAGE 91 F1787
WEALTH SOCIALIST ECO/TAC OWN

PORTUGAL....SEE ALSO APPROPRIATE TIME/SPACE/CULTURE INDEX

B42
JACKSON M.V.,EUROPEAN POWERS AND SOUTH-EAST AFRICA: A STUDY OF INTERNATIONAL RELATIONS ON SOUTH-EAST COAST OF AFRICA, 1796-1856. AFR FRANCE PORTUGAL SOUTH/AFR UK USA-45 FORCES INT/TRADE PWR...CHARTS BIBLIOG 18/19 TREATY. PAGE 66 F1294
DOMIN POLICY ORD/FREE DIPLOM

B44
INTL CHAMBER OF COMMERCE,TERMS COMMONLY USED IN DISTRIBUTION AND ADVERTISING. PORTUGAL SPAIN UK WOR-45 SERV/IND 20. PAGE 65 F1284
DICTIONARY EDU/PROP DIST/IND INT/TRADE

B65
OECD,THE MEDITERRANEAN REGIONAL PROJECT: PORTUGAL; EDUCATION AND DEVELOPMENT. PORTUGAL SOCIETY STRATA FINAN PROF/ORG WORKER PLAN PROB/SOLV ADMIN...POLICY STAT CHARTS METH 20 OECD. PAGE 100 F1970
EDU/PROP SCHOOL ACADEM ECO/UNDEV

S65
MUNZI U.,"THE EUROPEAN SOCIAL FUND IN THE DEVELOPMENT OF THE MEDITERRANEAN REGIONS OF THE EEC." FUT GREECE ITALY PORTUGAL SPAIN TURKEY WORKER TEC/DEV ECO/TAC REGION...STAT EEC. PAGE 95 F1862
ECO/UNDEV PREDICT RECORD

B67
CHILCOTE R.H.,PORTUGUESE AFRICA. PORTUGAL CULTURE SOCIETY ECO/UNDEV DOMIN NAT/LISM...TREND IDEA/COMP NAT/COMP BIBLIOG 15/20. PAGE 24 F0465
AFR COLONIAL ORD/FREE PROB/SOLV

B67
GUTKIND E.A.,URBAN DEVELOPMENT IN SOUTHERN EUROPE* SPAIN AND PORTUGAL. CHRIST-17C EUR+WWI MOD/EUR PORTUGAL SPAIN CULTURE AGRI...SOC SAMP/SIZ BIBLIOG MUNICH. PAGE 52 F1015
TEC/DEV ECO/DEV

PORWIT K. F2106

POSEN G.S. F2107

POSTAL/SYS....POSTAL SYSTEMS

POSTOFFICE....POST OFFICE DEPARTMENT

POTSDAM....POTSDAM

POTTER D.M. F2108

POUND/ROS....ROSCOE POUND

POVERTY....SEE WEALTH, INCOME

POVRTY/WAR....WAR ON POVERTY; SEE ALSO JOHNSON/LB

B65
FERMAN L.A.,POVERTY IN AMERICA: A BOOK OF READINGS. USA+45 CULTURE ECO/DEV PROB/SOLV ALL/VALS...POLICY ANTHOL BIBLIOG 20 POVRTY/WAR. PAGE 40 F0785
WEALTH TEC/DEV CONCPT RECEIVE

B65
SHOSTAK A.B.,NEW PERSPECTIVES ON POVERTY. USA+45 SCHOOL WORKER INGP/REL RACE/REL AGE/C AGE/Y ATTIT HEALTH...ANTHOL BIBLIOG 20 JOHNSON/LB POVRTY/WAR. PAGE 121 F2388
WEALTH NAT/G RECEIVE INCOME

S65
HADDAD W.F.,"MR. SHRIVER AND THE SAVAGE POLITICS OF POVERTY" USA+45 LAW NAT/G DELIB/GP LEGIS GIVE LEAD CENTRAL PWR...SOC/WK CHARTS 20 CONGRESS POVRTY/WAR SHRIVER/S OEO. PAGE 53 F1028
WEALTH GOV/REL CONTROL TOP/EX

POWELL D. F2109

POWELL/AC....ADAM CLAYTON POWELL

POWELSON J.P. F2110

POWER....SEE PWR

POWLEDGE F. F2111

PPBS....PLANNING-PROGRAMMING-BUDGETING SYSTEM

PRAGMATICS....SEE LOG

PRAKASH O.M. F2112

PRASOW P. F2113

PRATT R.C. F2114

PRE/AMER....PRE-EUROPEAN AMERICAS

B62
EINZIG P.,THE HISTORY OF FOREIGN EXCHANGE. CHRIST-17C ISLAM MEDIT-7 PRE/AMER WOR+45 ECO/DEV FINAN PLAN ECO/TAC ATTIT KNOWL WEALTH...SIMUL
MARKET TIME/SEQ INT/TRADE

GEN/LAWS. PAGE 37 F0714

PRE/US/AM....PRE-1776 UNITED STATES (THE COLONIES)

B51
BROGAN D.W.,THE PRICE OF REVOLUTION. FRANCE USA+45 USA-45 USSR CONSTN NAT/G DIPLOM COLONIAL NAT/LISM ORD/FREE POPULISM...CONCPT 18/20 PRE/US/AM. PAGE 19 F0359
REV METH/COMP COST MARXISM

C83
BURKE E.,"RESOLUTIONS FOR CONCILIATION WITH AMERICA" (1775), IN E. BURKE, COLLECTED WORKS, VOL. 2." UK USA-45 FORCES INT/TRADE TARIFFS TAX SANCTION PEACE...POLICY 18 PRE/US/AM. PAGE 20 F0387
COLONIAL WAR SOVEREIGN ECO/TAC

PREDICT....PREDICTION OF FUTURE EVENTS, SEE ALSO FUT

B14
DE BLOCH J.,THE FUTURE OF WAR IN ITS TECHNICAL, ECONOMIC, AND POLITICAL RELATIONS (1899). MOD/EUR TEC/DEV BUDGET INT/TRADE DETER GUERRILLA WEAPON COST PEACE 20. PAGE 31 F0596
WAR BAL/PWR PREDICT FORCES

N19
BASCH A.,THE FUTURE OF FOREIGN LENDING FOR DEVELOPMENT (PAMPHLET). WOR+45 ECO/UNDEV FINAN INT/ORG ECO/TAC ATTIT...PREDICT 20. PAGE 11 F0203
FOR/AID ECO/DEV DIPLOM GIVE

N19
BASSIE V.L.,UNCERTAINTY IN FORECASTING AND POLICY FORMATION (PAMPHLET). UNIV MARKET ECO/TAC PRODUC ...POLICY DECISION MGT MATH CHARTS 20. PAGE 11 F0205
ECO/DEV FINAN PREDICT PROB/SOLV

N19
MUSHKIN S.J.,LOCAL SCHOOL EXPENDITURES: 1970 PROJECTIONS (PAMPHLET). FUT USA+45 CONSTRUC FINAN PROVS EDU/PROP COST...GEOG CENSUS PREDICT CHARTS SIMUL 20. PAGE 95 F1871
LOC/G SCHOOL BUDGET

N19
US CHAMBER OF COMMERCE,THE SIGNIFICANCE OF CONCENTRATION RATIOS (PAMPHLET). USA+45 FINAN INDUS ADMIN...METH/CNCPT SAMP CHARTS 20. PAGE 134 F2647
MARKET PREDICT LG/CO CONTROL

B47
US LIBRARY OF CONGRESS,POSTWAR PLANNING AND RECONSTRUCTION: JANUARY-MARCH 1943. WOR+45 SOCIETY INT/ORG DIPLOM...SOC PREDICT 20. PAGE 138 F2714
BIBLIOG/A WAR PEACE PLAN

B55
JOHR W.A.,THE ROLE OF THE ECONOMIST AS OFFICIAL ADVISER. WOR+45 INTELL ECO/DEV NAT/G PLAN GP/REL ROLE...DECISION PREDICT IDEA/COMP. PAGE 68 F1336
CONSULT ECO/TAC POLICY INGP/REL

B57
GOLD N.L.,REGIONAL ECONOMIC DEVELOPMENT AND NUCLEAR POWER IN INDIA. FUT INDIA FINAN FOR/AID INT/TRADE BAL/PAY EFFICIENCY OPTIMAL PRODUC WEALTH...PREDICT 20. PAGE 48 F0934
ECO/UNDEV TEC/DEV NUC/PWR INDUS

B58
BROWN B.,INCOME TRENDS IN THE UNITED STATES THROUGH 1975. USA+45 NAT/G WEALTH...GEOG CENSUS PREDICT CHARTS METH 20. PAGE 19 F0366
STAT INCOME TREND TAX

B58
PALMER E.E.,INDUSTRIAL MAN. USA+45 PERSON ORD/FREE POPULISM...PREDICT TREND ANTHOL 20. PAGE 103 F2020
INDUS ECO/UNDEV CULTURE WEALTH

B58
THEIL H.,ECONOMIC FORECASTS AND POLICY. UNIV CAP/ISM PRICE EFFICIENCY...DECISION CONCPT STAT 20. PAGE 129 F2551
SIMUL MATH ECOMETRIC PREDICT

B59
MARTIN K.,WAR, HISTORY, AND HUMAN NATURE. FRANCE GERMANY INDIA UK UNIV POL/PAR COLONIAL DETER REV MARXISM PACIFISM...PSY CONCPT PREDICT LENIN/VI GANDHI/M. PAGE 86 F1683
PERSON WAR ATTIT IDEA/COMP

S59
CYERT R.M.,"MODELS IN A BEHAVIORAL THEORY OF THE FIRM." ROUTINE...DECISION MGT METH/CNCPT MATH. PAGE 29 F0567
SIMUL GAME PREDICT INDUS

B60
FRANCIS R.G.,THE PREDICTIVE PROCESS. PLAN MARXISM ...DECISION SOC CONCPT NAT/COMP 19/20. PAGE 43 F0840
PREDICT PHIL/SCI TREND

B60
KERR C.,INDUSTRIALISM AND INDUSTRIAL MAN. CULTURE SOCIETY ECO/UNDEV NAT/G ADMIN PRODUC WEALTH ...PREDICT TREND NAT/COMP 19/20. PAGE 70 F1381
WORKER MGT ECO/DEV INDUS

B61
KLEIN L.R.,AN ECONOMETRIC MODEL OF THE UNITED KINGDOM. UK PRICE COST...MATH PREDICT TREND CHARTS SIMUL METH 20. PAGE 72 F1407
ECOMETRIC COMPUTER STAT COMPUT/IR

S61
BENNION E.G.,"ECONOMETRICS FOR MANAGEMENT." USA+45 INDUS EX/STRUC ACT/RES COMPUTER UTIL...MATH STAT PREDICT METH/COMP HYPO/EXP. PAGE 13 F0248
ECOMETRIC MGT SIMUL DECISION

B62
BERNSTEIN P.L.,THE PRICE OF PROSPERITY. USA+45 TAX CONTROL OPTIMAL WEALTH...PREDICT 20. PAGE 14 F0269
ECO/DEV ECO/TAC NAT/G DEMAND

B62
GEARY R.C.,EUROPE'S FUTURE IN FIGURES. FUT GOV/REL DEMAND PRODUC...STAT CHARTS METH/COMP ANTHOL METH 20 EUROPE. PAGE 47 F0912
FINAN ECO/DEV PREDICT WEALTH

B62
KLEIN L.R.,AN INTRODUCTION TO ECONOMETRICS. DIST/IND DEMAND PRODUC WEALTH...MATH TIME/SEQ T 20. PAGE 72 F1408
ECOMETRIC SIMUL PREDICT STAT

B63
BONINI C.P.,SIMULATION OF INFORMATION AND DECISION SYSTEMS IN THE FIRM. MARKET BUDGET DOMIN EDU/PROP ADMIN COST ATTIT HABITAT PERCEPT PWR...CONCPT PROBABIL QUANT PREDICT HYPO/EXP BIBLIOG. PAGE 16 F0313
INDUS SIMUL DECISION MGT

B63
MINER J.,SOCIAL AND ECONOMIC FACTORS IN SPENDING FOR PUBLIC EDUCATION. USA+45 FINAN SCHOOL OPTIMAL ...POLICY DECISION REGRESS PREDICT CHARTS SIMUL 20. PAGE 92 F1801
EDU/PROP NAT/G COST ACT/RES

B63
UN FAO,BIBLIOGRAPHY ON THE ANALYSIS AND PROJECTION OF DEMAND AND PRODUCTION, 1963. WOR+45 ECO/DEV ECO/UNDEV...PREDICT TREND 20. PAGE 132 F2601
BIBLIOG/A AGRI INDUS

B63
US CONGRESS JOINT ECO COMM,THE UNITED STATES BALANCE OF PAYMENTS. USA+45 DELIB/GP CONFER...MATH PREDICT CHARTS 20 CONGRESS. PAGE 135 F2656
BAL/PAY ECO/TAC INT/TRADE CONSULT

B64
BRIGHT J.R.,RESEARCH, DEVELOPMENT AND TECHNOLOGICAL INNOVATION. CULTURE R+D CREATE PLAN PROB/SOLV AUTOMAT RISK PERSON...DECISION CONCPT PREDICT BIBLIOG. PAGE 18 F0352
TEC/DEV NEW/IDEA INDUS MGT

B64
CLAIRBORN E.L.,FORECASTING THE BALANCE OF PAYMENTS: AN EVALUATION. AFR FUT UK USA+45 WOR+45 FINAN PLAN BUDGET PAY CONTROL...STAT CHARTS BIBLIOG 20. PAGE 24 F0474
PREDICT BAL/PAY ECO/DEV ECO/TAC

B64
JUSTER F.T.,ANTICIPATIONS AND PURCHASES; AN ANALYSIS OF CONSUMER BEHAVIOR. PROB/SOLV RISK COST PRODUC DRIVE...STAT STYLE SAMP CON/ANAL CHARTS HYPO/EXP GAME SIMUL. PAGE 68 F1345
PROBABIL DECISION PREDICT DEMAND

B64
MEYER J.R.,INVESTMENT DECISIONS, ECONOMIC FORECASTING, AND PUBLIC POLICY. ECO/DEV ECO/TAC ...DECISION REGRESS TIME/SEQ CHARTS GP/COMP SIMUL 20. PAGE 90 F1771
FINAN PROB/SOLV PREDICT LG/CO

B64
SANDEE J.,EUROPE'S FUTURE CONSUMPTION. EUR+WWI FUT EDU/PROP...IDEA/COMP NAT/COMP ANTHOL 20 EUROPE. PAGE 115 F2277
MARKET ECO/DEV PREDICT PRICE

B65
DODDY F.S.,INTRODUCTION TO THE USE OF ECONOMIC INDICATORS. FINAN LABOR PLAN COST...ECOMETRIC INDICATOR MATH PREDICT CHARTS METH 20. PAGE 33 F0649
TEC/DEV STAT PRODUC PRICE

B65
FLEMING R.W.,THE LABOR ARBITRATION PROCESS. USA+45 LAW BARGAIN ADJUD ROUTINE SANCTION COST...PREDICT CHARTS TIME 20. PAGE 41 F0809
GP/REL LABOR CONSULT DELIB/GP

B65
FRIEDLANDER S.L.,LABOR MIGRATION AND ECONOMIC GROWTH: A CASE STUDY OF PUERTO RICO. PUERT/RICO AGRI WORKER PLAN PROB/SOLV...ECOMETRIC STAT PREDICT CHARTS HYPO/EXP SIMUL 20. PAGE 44 F0858
CENSUS GEOG ECO/UNDEV WEALTH

B65
MUSHKIN S.J.,PROPERTY TAXES: THE 1970 OUTLOOK (PAMPHLET). FUT USA+45 ECO/DEV MARKET PROVS PLAN ...PROBABIL STAT CENSUS PREDICT CHARTS METH 20. PAGE 95 F1872
TAX OWN FINAN LOC/G

B65
OECD,TECHNIQUES OF ECONOMIC FORECASTING. CANADA FRANCE NETHERLAND SWEDEN UK USA+45 PROB/SOLV ROUTINE...CONCPT MATH CHARTS BIBLIOG METH 20. PAGE 100 F1974
PREDICT METH/COMP PLAN

B65
OZGA S.A.,EXPECTATIONS IN ECONOMIC THEORY. MORAL ...ECOMETRIC MATH STAT IDEA/COMP 20. PAGE 102 F2008
RISK GAME CONCPT PREDICT

B65
SCITOVSKY T.,REQUIREMENTS OF AN INTERNATIONAL RESERVE SYSTEM. AFR ECO/TAC...PREDICT 20 SILVER MONEY. PAGE 118 F2330
BAL/PAY FINAN EQUILIB INT/TRADE

L65
DAANE J.D.,"THE EVOLVING INTERNATIONAL MONETARY MECHANISM." VOL/ASSN CREATE PLAN FOR/AID INT/TRADE CONFER BAL/PAY...RECORD PREDICT IMF. PAGE 29 F0569
INT/ORG ECO/TAC TREND GP/COMP

S65
CAMPOLONGO A.,"EUROPEAN INVESTMENT BANK* ACTIVITY AND PROSPECTS." FUT ECO/UNDEV FINAN PLAN DIPLOM ...STAT EEC LOAN EIB. PAGE 21 F0410
ECO/TAC PREDICT

S65
DICKMAN A.B.,"SOUTH AFRICAN MONEY MARKET - PROGRESS AND PROBLEMS SINCE 1960." SOUTH/AFR PROB/SOLV ROLE ...PREDICT CHARTS 20. PAGE 33 F0633
FINAN PLAN MARKET

S65
DUMONT R.,"SURPEUPLEMENT CHINOIS ET SES CONSEQUENCES." AFR ECO/UNDEV AGRI PLAN PROB/SOLV ECO/TAC FOR/AID NUC/PWR...OBS INT PREDICT. PAGE 35 F0675
GEOG ASIA STAT

S65
MUNZI U.,"THE EUROPEAN SOCIAL FUND IN THE DEVELOPMENT OF THE MEDITERRANEAN REGIONS OF THE EEC." FUT GREECE ITALY PORTUGAL SPAIN TURKEY WORKER TEC/DEV ECO/TAC REGION...STAT EEC. PAGE 95 F1862
ECO/UNDEV PREDICT RECORD

S65
SCHROEDER G.,"LABOR PLANNING IN THE USSR." COM USSR ECO/DEV INDUS SCHOOL PRODUC WEALTH...PREDICT TIME/SEQ TREND TIME 20. PAGE 117 F2313
WORKER PLAN CENSUS

B66
HAYS P.R.,LABOR ARBITRATION: A DISSENTING VIEW. USA+45 LAW DELIB/GP BARGAIN ADJUD...PREDICT 20. PAGE 57 F1126
GP/REL LABOR CONSULT CT/SYS

B66
KAESTNER K.,GESAMTWIRTSCHAFTLICHE PLANUNG IN EINER GEMISCHTEN WIRTSCHAFTSORDNUNG (WIRTSCHAFTSPOLITISCHE STUDIEN 5). GERMANY/W WOR+45 WOR-45 INDUS MARKET NAT/G ACT/RES GP/REL INGP/REL PRODUC...ECOMETRIC MGT BIBLIOG 20. PAGE 68 F1346
ECO/TAC PLAN POLICY PREDICT

B66
RUPPENTHAL K.M.,TRANSPORTATION AND TOMORROW. FUT SPACE USA+45 SEA AIR FORCES TEC/DEV INT/TRADE ...ANTHOL 20 RAILROAD. PAGE 115 F2261
DIST/IND PLAN CIVMIL/REL PREDICT

B66
THEIL H.,APPLIED ECONOMIC FORECASTING. UNIV USA+45 ELITES INTELL CONSULT PRODUC...DECISION MGT PREDICT CHARTS METH/COMP SIMUL 20. PAGE 129 F2552
FUT OP/RES PLAN

B66
US PRES COMM ECO IMPACT DEFENS,REPORT* JULY 1965. USA+45 ECO/DEV INDUS DELIB/GP FORCES OP/RES ARMS/CONT NUC/PWR WEAPON BAL/PAY...PREDICT SIMUL. PAGE 138 F2726
ACT/RES STAT WAR BUDGET

S66
LAURENS H.,"LES PAYS OCCIDENTAUX ET LE MARCHE CHINOIS." EUR+WWI FUT S/ASIA AGRI INDUS VOL/ASSN ECO/TAC BAL/PAY...RECORD PREDICT TREATY. PAGE 76 F1488
ASIA INT/TRADE TREND STAT

B67
BANFIELD E.C.,THE MORAL BASIS OF A BACKWARD SOCIETY. EUR+WWI ITALY STRATA NEIGH PARTIC INGP/REL ...SOC QU PREDICT TREND HYPO/EXP MUNICH 20. PAGE 9 F0173
MORAL WEALTH ATTIT

B67
BLAUG M.,ECONOMICS OF EDUCATION: A SELECTED ANNOTATED BIBLIOGRAPHY. EUR+WWI INTELL ECO/DEV ECO/UNDEV ACADEM INT/ORG NAT/G CREATE ADMIN EFFICIENCY ROLE PREDICT. PAGE 16 F0298
BIBLIOG/A EDU/PROP FINAN PLAN

B67
DE JOUVENAL B.,THE ART OF CONJECTURE. WOR+45 EFFICIENCY PERCEPT KNOWL...DECISION PHIL/SCI CONCPT METH/COMP BIBLIOG 20. PAGE 31 F0600
FUT PREDICT SIMUL METH

B67
HAGUE D.C.,PRICE FORMATION IN VARIOUS ECONOMIES; PROCEEDINGS OF A CONFERENCE HELD BY THE INTERNATIONAL ECONOMIC ASSOCIATION. WOR+45 FINAN MARKET PLAN CONFER COST...DECISION MATH PREDICT CHARTS SIMUL 20 INTL/ECON. PAGE 53 F1037
PRICE CAP/ISM SOCISM METH/COMP

B67
KANNER L.,THE NEW YORK TIMES WORLD ECONOMIC REVIEW AND FORECAST: 1967. WOR+45 ECO/DEV ECO/UNDEV TEC/DEV...STAT PREDICT CHARTS 20. PAGE 69 F1349
INDUS FINAN TREND ECO/TAC

B67
SPIRO H.S.,PATTERNS OF AFRICAN DEVLOPMENT: FIVE COMPARISONS. STRUCT ECO/UNDEV NAT/G CONSERVE SOCISM ...PREDICT NAT/COMP 20 CHINJAP. PAGE 125 F2457
AFR CONSTN NAT/LISM TREND

S67
FRIEDEN B.J.,"THE CHANGING PROSPECTS FOR SOCIAL PLANNING." USA+45 PROB/SOLV RACE/REL WEALTH ...SOC/WK PREDICT MUNICH 20 NEGRO. PAGE 44 F0856
PLAN LOC/G POLICY

S67
GAUSSENS J.,"THE APPLICATIONS OF NUCLEAR ENERGY - TECHNICAL, ECONOMIC AND SOCIAL ASPECTS." WOR+45 INDUS R+D ACT/RES EFFICIENCY PRODUC SKILL PREDICT. PAGE 47 F0911
NUC/PWR TEC/DEV ECO/DEV ADJUST

S67
MEADE J.E.,"POPULATION EXPLOSION, THE STANDARD OF LIVING AND SOCIAL CONFLICT." DIPLOM FOR/AID OWN ...PREDICT TREND 20. PAGE 89 F1739
GEOG WEALTH PRODUC INCOME

S67
WALKER R.L.,"THE WEST AND THE 'NEW ASIA'." CHINA/COM ECO/UNDEV DIPLOM...PREDICT 20. PAGE 142 F2805
ASIA INT/TRADE COLONIAL REGION

N67
US HOUSE COMM SCI ASTRONAUT,GOVERNMENT, SCIENCE, AND INTERNATIONAL POLICY (PAMPHLET). INDIA NETHERLAND ECO/DEV ECO/UNDEV R+D ACADEM PLAN DIPLOM FOR/AID CONFER...PREDICT 20 CHINJAP. PAGE 137 F2705
NAT/G POLICY CREATE TEC/DEV

PREDICTION....SEE PREDICT, FUT

PREFECT....PREFECTS AND PREFECTORALISM

PREHIST....PREHISTORIC SOCIETY, PRIOR TO 3000 B.C.

B63
STUCKI C.W.,AMERICAN DOCTORAL DISSERTATIONS ON ASIA 1933-62 (A PAPER). PREHIST INDUS NAT/G GOV/REL ALL/IDEOS...ART/METH GEOG SOC LING 20. PAGE 127 F2506
BIBLIOG ASIA SOCIETY S/ASIA

B66
LILLEY S.,MEN, MACHINES AND HISTORY: THE STORY OF TOOLS AND MACHINES IN RELATION TO SOCIAL PROGRESS. PREHIST SPACE STRUCT COMPUTER AUTOMAT NUC/PWR ...POLICY SOC. PAGE 80 F1564
AGRI TEC/DEV SOCIETY

PREHISTORIC SOCIETY....SEE PREHIST

PREJUDICE....SEE DISCRIM

PRENTICE E.S. F0743

PRESIDENT....PRESIDENCY (ALL NATIONS); SEE ALSO CHIEF

N19
MARSH J.F. JR.,THE FBI RETIREMENT BILL (PAMPHLET). USA+45 EX/STRUC WORKER PLAN PROB/SOLV BUDGET LEAD LOBBY PARL/PROC PERS/REL RIGID/FLEX...POLICY 20 FBI PRESIDENT BUR/BUDGET. PAGE 86 F1677
ADMIN NAT/G SENIOR GOV/REL

N19
MCCONNELL G.,THE STEEL SEIZURE OF 1952 (PAMPHLET). USA+45 FINAN INDUS PROC/MFG LG/CO EX/STRUC ADJUD CONTROL GP/REL ORD/FREE PWR 20 TRUMAN/HS PRESIDENT CONGRESS. PAGE 88 F1721
DELIB/GP LABOR PROB/SOLV NAT/G

N19
SILVERMAN C.,THE PRESIDENT'S ECONOMIC ADVISERS (PAMPHLET). USA+45 LAW ELITES ECO/DEV EX/STRUC ADMIN LEAD GOV/REL PERS/REL ROLE...POLICY DECISION 20 PRESIDENT CONGRESS EISNHWR/DD. PAGE 122 F2404
CONSULT PROB/SOLV NAT/G PLAN

S48
NOURSE E.G.,"THE ROLE OF THE COUNCIL OF ECONOMIC ADVISERS." USA+45 DELIB/GP...DECISION PRESIDENT. PAGE 99 F1938
EX/STRUC CHIEF PROB/SOLV

B50
KOENIG L.W.,THE SALE OF THE TANKERS. USA+45 SEA DIST/IND POL/PAR DIPLOM ADMIN CIVMIL/REL ATTIT ...DECISION 20 PRESIDENT DEPT/STATE. PAGE 72 F1414
NAT/G POLICY PLAN GOV/REL

B55
BERNSTEIN M.H.,REGULATING BUSINESS BY INDEPENDENT COMMISSION. USA+45 USA-45 LG/CO CHIEF LEGIS PROB/SOLV ADJUD SANCTION GP/REL ATTIT...TIME/SEQ 19/20 MONOPOLY PRESIDENT CONGRESS. PAGE 14 F0268
DELIB/GP CONTROL CONSULT

B55
SMITHIES A.,THE BUDGETARY PROCESS IN THE UNITED STATES. AFR ECO/DEV AGRI EX/STRUC FORCES LEGIS PROB/SOLV TAX ROUTINE EFFICIENCY...MGT CONGRESS PRESIDENT. PAGE 124 F2436
NAT/G ADMIN BUDGET GOV/REL

B56
ABELS J.,THE TRUMAN SCANDALS. USA+45 USA-45 POL/PAR TAX LEGIT CT/SYS CHOOSE PRIVIL MORAL WEALTH 20 TRUMAN/HS PRESIDENT CONGRESS. PAGE 2 F0031
CRIME ADMIN CHIEF TRIBUTE

S56
BONILLA F.,"WHEN IS PETITION 'PRESSURE?'" (BMR)" USA+45 ELITES INDUS LABOR CHIEF EDU/PROP LEGIT ATTIT...INT CHARTS 20 CONGRESS PRESIDENT EISNHWR/DD. PAGE 16 F0312
LEGIS EX/STRUC INT/TRADE TARIFFS

S56
TYLER G.,"THE PRESIDENCY AND LABOR." USA+45 USA-45 NAT/G LOBBY GOV/REL PWR 20 PRESIDENT. PAGE 131 F2595
LABOR REPRESENT CHIEF

B58
PALMER E.E.,THE ECONOMY AND THE DEMOCRATIC IDEAL. USA+45 USA-45 STRATA CHIEF CT/SYS ORD/FREE SOCISM ...MAJORIT CONCPT ANTHOL 18/20 PRESIDENT. PAGE 103 F2021
ECO/DEV POPULISM METH/COMP ECO/TAC

B60
CARPER E.T.,THE DEFENSE APPROPRIATIONS RIDER (PAMPHLET). USA+45 CONSTN CHIEF DELIB/GP LEGIS BUDGET LOBBY CIVMIL/REL...POLICY 20 CONGRESS EISNHWR/DD DEPT/DEFEN PRESIDENT BOSTON. PAGE 22 F0419
GOV/REL ADJUD LAW CONTROL

B60
FINKLE J.L.,THE PRESIDENT MAKES A DECISION: A STUDY OF DIXON-YATES. OP/RES PROB/SOLV BUDGET ADMIN GOV/REL...POLICY BIBLIOG/A 20 PRESIDENT. PAGE 41 F0799
DECISION CHIEF PWR POL/PAR

B61
CANTERBERY E.R.,THE PRESIDENT'S COUNCIL OF ECONOMIC ADVISERS. AFR USA+45 FINAN LABOR NAT/G PLAN ADMIN OPTIMAL WEALTH 20 EISNHWR/DD PRESIDENT TRUMAN/HS KEYNES/JM. PAGE 21 F0413
ECO/TAC OP/RES EXEC CHIEF

B61
US SENATE COMM ON FOREIGN RELS,INTERNATIONAL DEVELOPMENT AND SECURITY: HEARINGS ON BILL (2 VOLS.). ECO/UNDEV FINAN FORCES REV COST WEALTH ...CHARTS 20 AID PRESIDENT. PAGE 139 F2747
FOR/AID CIVMIL/REL ORD/FREE ECO/TAC

B62
HIRSCHFIELD R.S.,THE CONSTITUTION AND THE COURT. AFR SCHOOL WAR RACE/REL EQUILIB ORD/FREE...POLICY MAJORIT DECISION JURID 18/20 PRESIDENT CIVIL/LIB SUPREME/CT CONGRESS. PAGE 60 F1175
ADJUD PWR CONSTN LAW

B63
KOLKO G.,THE TRIUMPH OF CONSERVATISM. USA-45 INDUS LG/CO NAT/G PWR 20 PRESIDENT CONGRESS MONOPOLY PROGRSV/M. PAGE 72 F1421
CONSERVE CAP/ISM FINAN MARKET

B63
MCCONNELL G.,STEEL AND THE PRESIDENCY, 1962. USA+45 INDUS PROB/SOLV CONFER ROLE...POLICY 20 PRESIDENT. PAGE 88 F1722
PWR CHIEF REPRESENT DOMIN

B63
WILTZ J.E.,IN SEARCH OF PEACE: THE SENATE MUNITIONS INQUIRY, 1934-36. EUR+WWI USA-45 ELITES INDUS LG/CO LEGIS INT/TRADE LOBBY NEUTRAL ARMS/CONT...POLICY CONGRESS 20 LEAGUE/NAT PRESIDENT SENATE CONSCRIPTN. PAGE 147 F2905
DELIB/GP PROFIT WAR WEAPON

N63
COMMITTEE ECONOMIC DEVELOPMENT,TAXES AND TRADE: 20 YEARS OF CED POLICY (PAMPHLET). USA+45 ECO/DEV PLAN BUDGET LEAD...POLICY KENNEDY/JF PRESIDENT. PAGE 27 F0518
FINAN ECO/TAC NAT/G DELIB/GP

B64
US DEPT LABOR OFF SOLICITOR,LEGISLATIVE HISTORY OF THE LABOR-MANAGEMENT AND DISCLOSURE ACT OF 1959. DELIB/GP WORKER ADMIN LOBBY PARL/PROC SANCTION CHOOSE GOV/REL 20 CONGRESS PRESIDENT. PAGE 136 F2677
LABOR LEGIS DEBATE POLICY

B64
US HOUSE COMM BANKING-CURR,INTERNATIONAL DEVELOPMENT ASSOCIATION ACT AMENDMENT. CHINA/COM USA+45 USSR FINAN FORCES LEGIS DIPLOM CONFER EFFICIENCY...CHARTS GOV/COMP 20 PRESIDENT CONGRESS INTL/DEV. PAGE 136 F2689
BAL/PAY FOR/AID RECORD ECO/TAC

B65
FLASH E.S. JR.,ECONOMIC ADVICE AND PRESIDENTIAL LEADERSHIP: THE COUNCIL OF ECONOMIC ADVISORS. USA+45 NAT/G EX/STRUC LEGIS TOP/EX ACT/RES ADMIN PRESIDENT CONGRESS. PAGE 41 F0808
PLAN CONSULT CHIEF

B65
SCHECHTER A.,THE BUSINESSMAN IN GOVERNMENT (THESIS, COLUMBIA UNIVERSITY). USA+45 CONFER GP/REL PERSON ...QU 20 PRESIDENT TRUMAN/HS CABINET. PAGE 116 F2291
INDUS NAT/G EX/STRUC DELIB/GP

B66
CONGRESSIONAL QUARTERLY SERV,FEDERAL ECONOMIC POLICY 1945-1965. USA+45 FINAN NAT/G CHIEF CONSULT TAX...CHARTS 20 PRESIDENT DEBT. PAGE 27 F0526
ECO/TAC BUDGET LEGIS

B66
SHULTZ G.P.,GUIDELINES, INFORMAL CONTROLS, AND THE MARKET PLACE: POLICY CHOICES IN A FULL EMPLOYMENT ECONOMY. UK ECO/DEV LABOR INT/TRADE CONFER GOV/REL BAL/PAY DEMAND INCOME...POLICY ANTHOL 20 PRESIDENT. PAGE 121 F2392
ECO/TAC CONTROL FINAN RATION

B66
SOVERN M.I.,LEGAL RESTRAINTS ON RACIAL DISCRIMINATION IN EMPLOYMENT. USA+45 LAW INDUS LG/CO SML/CO DELIB/GP LEGIS SANCTION 20 NLRB PRESIDENT NEGRO CIV/RIGHTS RAILROAD. PAGE 124 F2446
DISCRIM RACE/REL WORKER JURID

B67
BIBBY J.,ON CAPITOL HILL. POL/PAR LOBBY PARL/PROC GOV/REL PERS/REL...JURID PHIL/SCI OBS INT BIBLIOG 20 CONGRESS PRESIDENT. PAGE 15 F0278
CONFER LEGIS CREATE LEAD

B67
MEYERS M.,SOURCES OF THE AMERICAN REPUBLIC; A DOCUMENTARY HISTORY OF POLITICS, SOCIETY, AND THOUGHT (VOL. I, REV. ED.). USA-45 CULTURE STRUCT NAT/G LEGIS LEAD ATTIT...JURID SOC ANTHOL 17/19 PRESIDENT. PAGE 90 F1772
COLONIAL REV WAR

B67
NORTON H.S.,NATIONAL TRANSPORTATION POLICY: FORMATION AND IMPLEMENTATION. USA+45 USA-45 DELIB/GP LEAD...DECISION TIME/SEQ 19/20 PRESIDENT CONGRESS. PAGE 98 F1935
POLICY DIST/IND NAT/G PROB/SOLV

B67
THOMAS M.J.,PRESIDENTIAL STATEMENTS ON EDUCATION: EXCERPTS FROM INAUGURAL AND STATE OF THE UNION MESSAGES 1789-1967. USA+45 USA-45 NAT/G BUDGET ...IDEA/COMP 18/20 PRESIDENT. PAGE 130 F2562
EDU/PROP TOP/EX LEGIS SCHOOL

N67
US HOUSE,MESSAGE FROM THE PRESIDENT OF THE UNITED STATES: URBAN AND PURAL POVERTY (PAMPHLET). USA+45 ACT/RES PLAN BUDGET RENT MUNICH 20 PRESIDENT. PAGE 136 F2685
NAT/G POLICY CREATE RECEIVE

PRESS....PRESS, OPERATIONS OF ALL PRINTED MEDIA, EXCEPT FILM AND TV (Q.V.), JOURNALISM; SEE ALSO COM/IND

N
LONDON TIMES OFFICIAL INDEX. UK LAW ECO/DEV NAT/G DIPLOM LEAD ATTIT 20. PAGE 1 F0006
BIBLIOG INDEX PRESS WRITING

N
UNESCO,SOUTH ASIA SOCIAL SCIENCES ABSTRACTS. BURMA CEYLON INDIA S/ASIA PRESS...PSY 20. PAGE 132 F2608
BIBLIOG/A SOC

B12
FOUAD M.,LE REGIME DE LA PRESSE EN EGYPTE: THESE POUR LE DOCTORAT. UAR LICENSE EDU/PROP ADMIN SANCTION CRIME SUPEGO PWR...ART/METH JURID 19/20. PAGE 43 F0832
ORD/FREE LEGIS CONTROL PRESS

S41
BRITT S.H.,"CONFORMITY OF LABOR NEWSPAPERS WITH RESPECT TO THE AFL-CIO CONFLICT." BAL/PWR CONSEN ATTIT. PAGE 18 F0355
LABOR PRESS DOMIN GP/REL

B46
ERNST M.L.,THE FIRST FREEDOM. USA-45 CONSTN PRESS PRIVIL...CHARTS IDEA/COMP BIBLIOG 20 AMEND/I. PAGE 38 F0746
EDU/PROP COM/IND ORD/FREE CONTROL

B51
HARDMAN J.B.,THE HOUSE OF LABOR. LAW R+D NEIGH EDU/PROP LEAD ROUTINE REPRESENT GP/REL...POLICY STAT. PAGE 55 F1080
LABOR LOBBY ADMIN PRESS

B56
ATOMIC INDUSTRIAL FORUM,PUBLIC RELATIONS FOR THE ATOMIC INDUSTRY. WOR+45 PLAN PROB/SOLV EDU/PROP PRESS CONFER...AUD/VIS ANTHOL 20. PAGE 7 F0135
NUC/PWR INDUS GP/REL ATTIT

B56
US LIBRARY OF CONGRESS,UNITED STATES DIRECT ECONOMIC AID TO FOREIGN COUNTRIES: A COLLECTION OF EXCERPTS AND A BIBLIOGRAPHY (PAMPHLET). USA+45 PRESS DEBATE...ANTHOL BIBLIOG/A CONGRESS. PAGE 138 F2716
FOR/AID POLICY DIPLOM ECO/UNDEV

B58
MOONEY R.E.,INFLATION AND RECESSION? AFR USA+45 LABOR LG/CO PRESS LEAD...IDEA/COMP ANTHOL 20. PAGE 93 F1821
PRICE ECO/TAC NAT/G PRODUC

B58
RUBIN B.,PUBLIC RELATIONS AND THE STATE, A CASE STUDY OF NEW YORK STATE ADMINISTRATION, 1943-54. USA+45 USA-45 COM/IND EDU/PROP GOV/REL...CHARTS 20 NEW/YORK DEWEY/THOM. PAGE 114 F2255
INGP/REL PRESS PROVS GP/REL

B59
BROMWICH L.,UNION CONSTITUTIONS. CONSTN EX/STRUC PRESS ADJUD CONTROL CHOOSE REPRESENT PWR SAMP. PAGE 19 F0361
LABOR ROUTINE INGP/REL RACE/REL

B61
LENIN V.I.,WHAT IS TO BE DONE? (1902). RUSSIA LABOR NAT/G POL/PAR WORKER CAP/ISM ECO/TAC ADMIN PARTIC ...MARXIST IDEA/COMP GEN/LAWS 19/20. PAGE 78 F1522
EDU/PROP PRESS MARXISM METH/COMP

B62
BOGARDUS J.,OUTLINE FOR THE COURSE IN BUSINESS AND ECONOMICS LITERATURE (REV. ED; PAMPHLET). USA+45 FINAN INDUS NAT/G VOL/ASSN PRESS WRITING INDEX. PAGE 16 F0305
BIBLIOG/A STAT

B63
CHEN N.-R.,THE ECONOMY OF MAINLAND CHINA, 1949-1963: A BIBLIOGRAPHY OF MATERIALS IN ENGLISH. CHINA/COM ECO/UNDEV PRESS 20. PAGE 24 F0461
BIBLIOG MARXISM NAT/G ASIA

B64
BEARDSLEY R.K.,STUDIES ON ECONOMIC LIFE IN JAPAN (OCCASIONAL PAPERS NO. 8). INDUS FAM HABITAT...GEOG GOV/COMP 20 CHINJAP. PAGE 12 F0223
WEALTH PRESS PRODUC

INCOME

S64
FYFE J.,"LIST OF CURRENT ACQUISITIONS OF PERIODICALS AND NEWSPAPERS DEALING WITH THE SOVIET UNION AND EAST EUROPEAN COUNTRIES." USSR WRITING GP/REL INGP/REL MARXISM 20. PAGE 45 F0879
BIBLIOG COM EDU/PROP PRESS

B65
GREENFIELD K.R.,ECONOMICS AND LIBERALISM IN THE RISORGIMENTO (REV. ED.). ITALY AGRI FINAN PROC/MFG PLAN INT/TRADE CONTROL PWR 19. PAGE 51 F0990
NAT/LISM PRESS POLICY

B65
SHAFFER H.G.,THE SOVIET SYSTEM IN THEORY AND PRACTICE: SELECTED WESTERN AND SOVIET VIEWS. USSR LAW SOCIETY CREATE FOR/AID EDU/PROP PRESS CHOOSE PEACE ORD/FREE...ANTHOL 20 STALIN/J. PAGE 120 F2362
MARXISM SOCISM IDEA/COMP

B65
WISCONSIN HISTORICAL SOCIETY,LABOR PAPERS ON MICROFILM: A COMBINED LIST. USA+45 USA-45 WORKER 20. PAGE 148 F2910
BIBLIOG LABOR PRESS

B66
GOODWIN C.D.W.,ECONOMIC INQUIRY IN AUSTRALIA. ECO/DEV ECO/UNDEV ACADEM INT/TRADE RENT TARIFFS TAX PRESS GOV/REL SOCISM 18/20 AUSTRAL. PAGE 49 F0953
ECO/TAC IDEA/COMP BUDGET COLONIAL

C66
WINT G.,"ASIA: A HANDBOOK." ASIA S/ASIA INDUS LABOR SECT PRESS RACE/REL MARXISM...STAT CHARTS BIBLIOG 20. PAGE 148 F2908
ECO/UNDEV DIPLOM NAT/G SOCIETY

B67
FILENE P.G.,AMERICANS AND THE SOVIET EXPERIMENT, 1917-1933. USA-45 USSR INTELL NAT/G CAP/ISM DIPLOM EDU/PROP PRESS REV SOCISM...PSY 20. PAGE 41 F0793
ATTIT RIGID/FLEX MARXISM SOCIETY

B67
FONER P.S.,THE BOLSHEVIK REVOLUTION. USA-45 POL/PAR WORKER DIPLOM EDU/PROP MARXISM...STERTYP 20. PAGE 42 F0821
LABOR INTELL REV PRESS

B67
PETRO S.,THE KINGSPORT STRIKE. USA+45 PROC/MFG NAT/G JUDGE PRESS PARTIC PERS/REL...OLD/LIB OBS INT 20 NLRB. PAGE 105 F2074
LABOR COERCE SANCTION ALL/VALS

B67
PRINCE C.E.,NEW JERSEY'S JEFFERSONIAN REPUBLICANS; THE GENESIS OF AN EARLY PARTY MACHINE (1789-1817). USA-45 LOC/G EDU/PROP PRESS CONTROL CHOOSE...CHARTS 18/19 NEW/JERSEY REPUBLICAN. PAGE 108 F2117
POL/PAR CONSTN ADMIN PROVS

B67
US SENATE COMM ON FOREIGN REL,HARRISON E. SALISBURY'S TRIP TO NORTH VIETNAM. CHINA/COM USA+45 VIETNAM/N PRESS TASK GUERRILLA CONSEN EFFICIENCY PEACE DRIVE...OBS SENATE. PAGE 139 F2743
DIPLOM WAR FORCES ATTIT

L67
BARRON J.A.,"ACCESS TO THE PRESS." USA+45 TEC/DEV PRESS TV ADJUD AUD/VIS. PAGE 10 F0196
ORD/FREE COM/IND EDU/PROP LAW

S67
BAGDKIAN B.H.,"NEWS AS A BYPRODUCT: WHAT HAPPENS WHEN JOURNALISM IS HITCHED TO GREAT, DIVERSIFIED CORPORATIONS?" USA+45 INDUS EDU/PROP PARTIC PROFIT ATTIT. PAGE 8 F0152
COM/IND PRESS CONTROL LG/CO

S67
PEMBERTON J., JR.,"CONSTITUTIONAL PROBLEMS IN RESTRAINT ON THE MEDIA." CONSTN PROB/SOLV EDU/PROP CONFER CONTROL JURID. PAGE 104 F2054
LAW PRESS ORD/FREE

S67
RAGAN S.,"THE ABA RECOMMENDATIONS: A NEWSPAPERMAN'S CRITIQUE." EDU/PROP CONTROL GP/REL...JURID ABA. PAGE 109 F2136
LAW PRESS ADJUD ORD/FREE

S67
SCRIPP J.,"CONTROLLING PREJUDICIAL PUBLICITY BY THE CONTEMPT POWER: THE BRITISH PRACTICE AND ITS PROSPECT IN AMERICAN LAW." UK USA+45 EDU/PROP CONTROL GP/REL ORD/FREE JURID. PAGE 119 F2338
METH/COMP LAW PRESS ADJUD

S67
STEMPEL GH I.I.I.,"A NEW ANALYSIS OF MONOPOLY AND COMPETITION." USA+45 INDUS TV ATTIT MUNICH. PAGE 126 F2479
PRESS COM/IND GP/REL

PRESSURE GROUPS....SEE LOBBY

PREST A.R. F2115

PRESTHUS R. F2116

PRICE F.W. F1512

PRICE CONTROL....SEE PRICE, COST, PLAN, RATION

PRICE....SEE ALSO COST

N
US SUPERINTENDENT OF DOCUMENTS,LABOR (PRICE LIST 33). USA+45 LAW AGRI CONSTRUC INDUS NAT/G BARGAIN PRICE ADMIN AUTOMAT PRODUC MGT. PAGE 140 F2753
BIBLIOG/A WORKER LABOR LEGIS

LCA
GODFREY E.M.,"THE ECONOMICS OF AN AFRICAN UNIVERSITY." AFR SCHOOL PRICE EFFICIENCY INCOME WEALTH...ECOMETRIC CHARTS 20. PAGE 48 F0930
ACADEM ECO/TAC COST EDU/PROP

B04
VEBLEN T.B.,THE THEORY OF BUSINESS ENTERPRISE. USA-45 FINAN WORKER ECO/TAC PRICE GP/REL COST ...POLICY 19/20. PAGE 141 F2770
TEC/DEV GEN/LAWS SOCIETY WEALTH

B13
DAVENPORT H.J.,THE ECONOMICS OF ENTERPRISE. UNIV FINAN SML/CO RENT COST WEALTH GEN/LAWS. PAGE 30 F0582
CAP/ISM PRICE ECO/TAC LG/CO

B14
HOBSON J.A.,WORK AND WEALTH. CULTURE FINAN INDUS WORKER TEC/DEV ECO/TAC GIVE PAY PRICE COST PRODUC UTIL. PAGE 60 F1185
WEALTH INCOME GEN/LAWS

B19
VEBLEN T.B.,THE VESTED INTERESTS AND THE STATE OF THE INDUSTRIAL ARTS. USA-45 LAW FINAN WORKER PAY DOMIN PRICE COST SOCISM...MARXIST 19/20. PAGE 141 F2771
INDUS CAP/ISM METH/COMP WEALTH

N19
CHATTERS C.H.,NEW MUNICIPAL REVENUES FOR NEW MUNICIPAL EXPENDITURES (PAMPHLET). PLAN PRICE UTIL HABITAT...IDEA/COMP MUNICH 20. PAGE 23 F0457
LOC/G BUDGET TAX

N19
ENGELS F.,THE BRITISH LABOUR MOVEMENT (PAMPHLET). FRANCE GERMANY MOD/EUR UK USA-45 POL/PAR WORKER PAY EDU/PROP PRICE REPRESENT GP/REL 19. PAGE 37 F0730
ECO/TAC MARXISM LABOR STRATA

N19
HABERLER G.,INFLATION; ITS CAUSES AND CURES (PAMPHLET). AFR USA+45 FINAN BUDGET PAY PRICE COST DEMAND 20. PAGE 52 F1021
ECO/DEV BAL/PAY POLICY NAT/G

N19
HANSEN B.,INFLATION PROBLEMS IN SMALL COUNTRIES (PAMPHLET). AFR UNIV FOR/AID CONTROL BAL/PAY DEMAND PRODUC 20. PAGE 54 F1066
PRICE FINAN ECO/UNDEV ECO/TAC

N19
KRIESBERG M.,CANCELLATION OF THE RATION STAMPS (PAMPHLET). USA+45 USA-45 MARKET PROB/SOLV PRICE GOV/REL RIGID/FLEX 20 OPA. PAGE 73 F1439
RATION DECISION ADMIN NAT/G

N19
LUTZ F.A.,THE PROBLEM OF INTERNATIONAL LIQUIDITY AND THE MULTIPLECURRENCY STANDARD (PAMPHLET). WOR+45 MARKET INT/ORG PRICE BAL/PAY...NEW/IDEA METH/COMP BIBLIOG 20 IMF. PAGE 82 F1609
PROB/SOLV FINAN DIPLOM ECO/TAC

N19
PATRICK H.T.,CYCLICAL INSTABILITY AND FISCAL-MONETARY POLICY IN POST-WAR JAPAN (PAMPHLET). INDUS MARKET DIPLOM TAX PRICE BAL/PAY...TREND CHARTS EQULIB 20 CHINJAP. PAGE 104 F2036
ECO/DEV PRODUC STAT

N19
ROBERTSON D.,GROWTH, WAGES, MONEY (PAMPHLET). UNIV WORKER BUDGET PRICE DEMAND PRODUC WEALTH...CONCPT MATH MONEY. PAGE 112 F2210
FINAN ECO/DEV ECO/TAC PAY

B20
MALTHUS T.R.,PRINCIPLES OF POLITICAL ECONOMY. UK AGRI INDUS MARKET NAT/G DIPLOM PRICE CONTROL BAL/PAY COST OWN PWR LAISSEZ 18/19. PAGE 84 F1650
GEN/LAWS DEMAND WEALTH

B30
BIEL G.,TREATISE ON THE POWER AND UTILITY OF MONEY (1484). INDUS MARKET LOC/G NAT/G SECT ECO/TAC PRODUC WEALTH 15. PAGE 15 F0280
FINAN COST PRICE GEN/LAWS

B30
KEYNES J.M.,A TREATISE ON MONEY (2 VOLS.). UK USA-45 INDUS MARKET WORKER PRICE CONTROL COST OPTIMAL PROFIT WEALTH...POLICY 19/20 KEYNES/JM. PAGE 70 F1385
EQUILIB ECO/TAC FINAN GEN/LAWS

B34
ROBINSON J.,THE ECONOMICS OF IMPERFECT COMPETITION. FINAN ECO/TAC PRICE COST DEMAND EQUILIB OPTIMAL WEALTH...METH MONOPOLY. PAGE 113 F2221
MARKET WORKER INDUS

B35
HICKS J.R.,THE THEORY OF WAGES. INDUS NAT/G PAY PRICE CONTROL COST EFFICIENCY WEALTH 19/20 MARSHALL/A CLARK/JB. PAGE 59 F1164
INCOME WORKER LABOR PRODUC

B35
KEYNES J.M.,THE GENERAL THEORY OF EMPLOYMENT, INTEREST, AND MONEY. AGRI INDUS WORKER ECO/TAC DEMAND EQUILIB INCOME PRODUC PROFIT ATTIT WEALTH 20. PAGE 71 F1386
FINAN GEN/LAWS MARKET PRICE

B35
MARX K.,WAGE-LABOR AND CAPITAL -- VALUE, PRICE AND PROFIT. LABOR PAY PRICE COST INCOME OWN PROFIT WEALTH 19. PAGE 86 F1690
STRATA WORKER MARXIST MARXISM

S35
BONNETT C.E.,"THE EVOLUTION OF BUSINESS GROUPINGS." ECO/TAC EDU/PROP PRICE LOBBY ORD/FREE. PAGE 16 F0315
VOL/ASSN GP/REL PROB/SOLV

B36
BURNS A.R.,THE DECLINE OF COMPETITION. LAW LG/CO NAT/G SML/CO LEGIS PRICE AGREE CONTROL GP/REL INCOME PRODUC...POLICY 19/20 NRA. PAGE 20 F0390
MARKET GEN/LAWS INDUS

B37
BRESCIANI-TURRONI C,THE ECONOMICS OF INFLATION: A STUDY OF CURRENCY DEPRECIATION IN POST-WAR GERMANY. AFR GERMANY FINAN INT/TRADE PRICE TOTALISM...POLICY TIME/SEQ CHARTS GEN/LAWS 20 HITLER/A. PAGE 18 F0347
ECO/TAC WEALTH SOCIETY

B38
LAWLEY F.E.,THE GROWTH OF COLLECTIVE ECONOMY VOL. 1: NATIONAL. EUR+WWI AGRI INDUS NAT/G BARGAIN CAP/ISM ECO/TAC WAR OPTIMAL WEALTH...GOV/COMP METH/COMP 19/20 MONOPOLY. PAGE 76 F1492
SOCISM PRICE CONTROL OWN

B39
CLARK J.M.,SOCIAL CONTROL OF BUSINESS (2ND ED.). ECO/DEV FINAN LG/CO PLAN ECO/TAC PRICE SUPEGO...T 20. PAGE 25 F0480
CAP/ISM CONTROL LAISSEZ METH/COMP

B41
ESTEY J.A.,BUSINESS CYCLES; THEIR NATURE, CAUSE, AND CONTROL. NAT/G BUDGET CAP/ISM TAX PRICE CONTROL INCOME...MODAL TIME/SEQ GEN/METH T 18/20 KEYNES/JM MONEY. PAGE 38 F0749
INDUS FINAN ECO/TAC POLICY

B42
US LIBRARY OF CONGRESS,THE WAR PRODUCTION PROGRAM: SELECTED DOCUMENTATION ON THE ECONOMICS OF WAR (PAMPHLET). USA-45 ECO/DEV AGRI FINAN NAT/G ECO/TAC RATION PRICE EFFICIENCY 20. PAGE 138 F2713
BIBLIOG/A WAR PRODUC INDUS

B42
WRIGHT D.M.,THE CREATION OF PURCHASING POWER. USA-45 NAT/G PRICE ADMIN WAR INCOME PRODUC...POLICY CONCPT IDEA/COMP BIBLIOG 20 MONEY. PAGE 149 F2930
FINAN ECO/TAC ECO/DEV CREATE

B44
LANDAUER C.,THEORY OF NATIONAL ECONOMIC PLANNING. USA-45 INDUS MARKET WORKER PROB/SOLV DIPLOM RATION PRICE CONTROL WAR COST 20. PAGE 75 F1465
ECO/TAC PLAN NAT/G ECO/DEV

B44
LOCKE J.,FURTHER CONSIDERATIONS CONCERNING RAISING THE VALUE OF MONEY. AFR UK NAT/G ECO/TAC INCOME WEALTH...METH/COMP GEN/LAWS 17 SILVER. PAGE 81 F1591
COST FINAN PRICE CONTROL

B46
DRUCKER P.F.,CONCEPT OF CORPORATION. LAW LABOR WORKER PRICE CONTROL LEAD GP/REL POLICY. PAGE 34 F0665
LG/CO CENTRAL INGP/REL

B47
BALDWIN H.W.,THE PRICE OF POWER. USA+45 FORCES PLAN NUC/PWR ADJUST COST ORD/FREE...POLICY PSY BIBLIOG 20. PAGE 9 F0165
PROB/SOLV PWR POPULISM PRICE

B48
HART A.G.,MONEY, DEBT, AND ECONOMIC ACTIVITY. AFR WORKER DIPLOM PRICE CONTROL BAL/PAY COST OWN PRODUC ...METH/COMP 20 FED/RESERV. PAGE 56 F1097
FINAN WEALTH ECO/TAC NAT/G

B48
HICKS J.R.,VALUE AND CAPITAL. FINAN PRICE EQUILIB INCOME PRODUC WEALTH...TIME/SEQ 20 MARSHALL/A PARETO/V SAMUELSN/P. PAGE 59 F1165
ECOMETRIC MATH DEMAND PROB/SOLV

B48
ROBERTSON D.H.,MONEY. AFR ECO/DEV NAT/G DIPLOM INT/TRADE BAL/PAY INCOME WEALTH...TIME/SEQ 20 DEPRESSION. PAGE 112 F2212
FINAN MARKET COST PRICE

B48
VON HAYEK F.A.,INDIVIDUALISM AND ECONOMIC ORDER. GERMANY USA-45 USSR FINAN MARKET INT/ORG ECO/TAC INT/TRADE PRICE REPRESENT ORD/FREE...PLURIST GEN/LAWS 20. PAGE 142 F2793
SOCISM CAP/ISM POPULISM FEDERAL

B49
DE JOUVENEL B.,PROBLEMS OF SOCIALIST ENGLAND. AFR UK USSR BAL/PWR ECO/TAC INT/TRADE PRICE WAR BAL/PAY PEACE 20. PAGE 31 F0601
SOCISM NEW/LIB PROB/SOLV PLAN

B49
SHISTER J.,ECONOMICS OF THE LABOR MARKET. LOC/G NAT/G WORKER TEC/DEV BARGAIN PAY PRICE EXEC GP/REL INCOME...MGT T 20. PAGE 121 F2381
MARKET LABOR INDUS

B50
CHAMBERLIN E.,THE THEORY OF MONOPOLISTIC COMPETITION (1933). INDUS PAY GP/REL COST DEMAND EFFICIENCY OPTIMAL PRODUC WEALTH...GEN/LAWS 20. PAGE 23 F0443
MARKET PRICE ECO/TAC EQUILIB

B50
CLARK J.M.,ALTERNATIVE TO SERFDOM. SOCIETY STRATA INDUS MARKET WORKER PRICE GP/REL PROFIT BIO/SOC PWR WEALTH...GEN/LAWS 20 KEYNES/JM. PAGE 25 F0481
ORD/FREE POPULISM ECO/TAC REPRESENT

B50
SHAW E.S.,MONEY, INCOME, AND MONETARY POLICY. AFR USA-45 NAT/G DIPLOM PAY CONTROL COST INCOME PRODUC WEALTH...T 20 FED/RESERV DEPT/TREAS. PAGE 120 F2370
FINAN ECO/TAC ECO/DEV PRICE

B51
CHANDLER L.V.,INFLATION IN THE UNITED STATES 1940-1948. AFR NAT/G BUDGET PAY PRICE CONTROL WAR INCOME PRODUC...POLICY BIBLIOG 20. PAGE 23 F0448
ECO/TAC FINAN PROB/SOLV WEALTH

B51
HANSEN B.,A STUDY IN THE THEORY OF INFLATION. WOR-45 FINAN WAR DEMAND...CHARTS 20. PAGE 54 F1067
PRICE ECO/TAC EQUILIB PRODUC

B51
HART A.G.,DEFENSE WITHOUT INFLATION. AFR KOREA FINAN INDUS NAT/G WORKER DIPLOM RATION TAX PRICE COST OPTIMAL 20 RESOURCE/N. PAGE 56 F1098
ECO/TAC CONTROL WAR PLAN

B51
PETERSON F.,SURVEY OF LABOR ECONOMICS (REV. ED.). STRATA ECO/DEV LABOR INSPECT BARGAIN PAY PRICE EXEC ROUTINE GP/REL ALL/VALS ORD/FREE 20 AFL/CIO DEPT/LABOR. PAGE 105 F2069
WORKER DEMAND IDEA/COMP T

B52
GALBRAITH J.K.,AMERICAN CAPITALISM: THE CONCEPT OF COUNTERVAILING POWER. AFR FUT USA+45 FINAN PRICE CENTRAL INCOME PEACE WEALTH...POLICY DECISION 20. PAGE 45 F0881
ECO/TAC CAP/ISM TREND NAT/G

B52
SURANYI-UNGER T.,COMPARATIVE ECONOMIC SYSTEMS. FINAN MARKET DIPLOM PRICE WEALTH...GEOG SOC BIBLIOG METH T 20. PAGE 128 F2517
LAISSEZ PLAN ECO/DEV IDEA/COMP

C52
HUME D.,"OF THE BALANCE OF TRADE" IN D. HUME, POLITICAL DISCOURSES (1752)" UK FINAN NAT/G TARIFFS PRICE PWR LAISSEZ...POLICY GEN/LAWS 18. PAGE 63 F1237
BAL/PAY INT/TRADE DIPLOM WEALTH

C52
HUME D.,"OF INTEREST" IN D. HUME, POLITICAL DISCOURSES (1752)" UK INDUS WORKER DIPLOM PAY DEMAND INCOME WEALTH...GEN/LAWS 18 MONEY. PAGE 63 F1239
PRICE COST FINAN INT/TRADE

C52
HUME D.,"OF MONEY" IN D. HUME, POLITICAL DISCOURSES (1752)" UK INDUS DIPLOM INT/TRADE...GEN/LAWS 18 MONEY. PAGE 63 F1240
FINAN COST PRICE WEALTH

B53
BOEKE J.H.,ECONOMICS AND ECONOMIC POLICY OF DUAL SOCIETIES AS EXEMPLIFIED BY INDONESIA. INDIA INDONESIA SOCIETY CAP/ISM INT/TRADE GIVE PRICE GP/REL WEALTH SOCISM...POLICY NAT/COMP GEN/LAWS 20. PAGE 16 F0304
ECO/TAC ECO/UNDEV NAT/G CONTROL

B53
BURNS A.E.,MODERN ECONOMICS. UNIV ECO/DEV INT/TRADE PRICE INCOME WEALTH...POLICY CHARTS T 20 KEYNES/JM. PAGE 20 F0389
NAT/G ECO/TAC FINAN

B53
DAHL R.A.,POLITICS, ECONOMICS, AND WELFARE. TEC/DEV BARGAIN ECO/TAC RECEIVE PRICE CONTROL LEAD INGP/REL ...POLICY GEN/LAWS. PAGE 29 F0572
SOCIETY GIVE

B53
NEISSER H.,NATIONAL INCOMES AND INTERNATIONAL TRADE. FRANCE GERMANY SWEDEN UK USA-45 EXTR/IND FINAN INDUS TEC/DEV PRICE BAL/PAY EQUILIB INCOME WEALTH...CHARTS METH 19 CHINJAP. PAGE 97 F1908
INT/TRADE PRODUC MARKET CON/ANAL

B54
BERNSTEIN I.,ARBITRATION OF WAGES. USA+45 CONSULT PAY COST PRODUC WEALTH...CHARTS 20. PAGE 14 F0266
DELIB/GP BARGAIN WORKER PRICE

B54
MITCHELL W.G.,BUSINESS CYCLES. FINAN MARKET PRICE COST EQUILIB OPTIMAL PRODUC PROFIT...IDEA/COMP GEN/LAWS 19/20. PAGE 92 F1809
INDUS TIME/SEQ METH/COMP STAT

B54
RICHTER R.,DAS KONKURRENZ PROBLEM IM OLIGOPOL. LG/CO BARGAIN PRICE COST...CONCPT 20 MONOPOLY. PAGE 111 F2188
CONTROL GAME ECO/TAC GP/REL

C54
BERLE A.A. JR.,"THE 20TH CENTURY CAPITALIST REVOLUTION." ECO/DEV NAT/G DIPLOM PRICE CONTROL ATTIT...BIBLIOG/A 20. PAGE 14 F0260
LG/CO CAP/ISM MGT PWR

B55
UN ECONOMIC COMN ASIA & FAR E,ECONOMIC SURVEY OF
ECO/UNDEV

ASIA AND THE FAR EAST, 1954. AFGHANISTN CEYLON INDIA PHILIPPINE S/ASIA ECO/DEV FINAN INDUS INT/TRADE PRODUC WEALTH...STAT CHARTS 20 CHINJAP. PAGE 132 F2600 — PRICE NAT/COMP ASIA

L56

SCHELLING T.C.,"AN ESSAY ON BARGAINING" (BMR)" OP/RES PROB/SOLV PRICE CHOOSE PWR...DECISION MODELS 20. PAGE 116 F2294 — BARGAIN MARKET ECO/TAC GAME

B57

BAUER P.T.,THE ECONOMICS OF UNDERDEVELOPED COUNTRIES. WOR+45 AGRI FINAN INDUS PROC/MFG WORKER CAP/ISM PAY PRICE INCOME MARXISM...METH/COMP 20 RESOURCE/N. PAGE 11 F0213 — ECO/UNDEV ECO/TAC PROB/SOLV NAT/G

B57

BAUER P.T.,ECONOMIC ANALYSIS AND POLICY IN UNDERDEVELOPED COUNTRIES. AFR WOR+45 AGRI INT/TRADE TAX PRICE...GEN/METH BIBLIOG/A 20. PAGE 11 F0214 — ECO/UNDEV METH/COMP POLICY

B57

DAY A.C.L.,OUTLINE OF MONETARY ECONOMICS. AFR WOR-45 INT/ORG WORKER DIPLOM BAL/PAY COST INCOME WEALTH...TIME/SEQ SIMUL 20. PAGE 31 F0594 — FINAN NAT/G EQUILIB PRICE

B57

DUNLOP J.T.,THE THEORY OF WAGE DETERMINATION; PROCEEDINGS OF CONFERENCE HELD BY INTERNATIONAL ECONOMIC ASSOCIATION. AFR ECO/DEV LABOR BARGAIN PAY CONFER...CHARTS ANTHOL 20. PAGE 35 F0679 — PRICE WORKER GEN/LAWS INCOME

B57

HARWOOD E.C.,CAUSE AND CONTROL OF THE BUSINESS CYCLE (5TH ED.). AFR USA-45 PRICE CONTROL WAR DEMAND INCOME WEALTH...TREND CHARTS 19. PAGE 56 F1107 — PRODUC MARKET FINAN

B57

LUNDBERG E.,BUSINESS CYCLES AND ECONOMIC POLICY (TRANS. BY J. POTTER). SWEDEN ECO/DEV FINAN DELIB/GP PLAN PRICE CONTROL BAL/PAY 20 INTRVN/ECO. PAGE 82 F1607 — ECO/TAC INDUS INT/TRADE BUDGET

B57

MASON E.S.,ECONOMIC CONCENTRATION AND THE MONOPOLY PROBLEM. USA+45 USA-45 LAW ELITES ECO/DEV LABOR RATION PRICE PWR WEALTH...CHARTS 20 MONOPOLY. PAGE 87 F1696 — GP/REL LG/CO CONTROL MARKET

B57

MURDESHWAR A.K.,ADMINISTRATIVE PROBLEMS RELATING TO NATIONALISATION: WITH SPECIAL REFERENCE TO INDIAN STATE ENTERPRISES. CZECHOSLVK FRANCE INDIA UK USA+45 LEGIS WORKER PROB/SOLV BUDGET PRICE CONTROL ...MGT GEN/LAWS 20 PARLIAMENT. PAGE 95 F1863 — NAT/G OWN INDUS ADMIN

B57

NEUMARK S.D.,ECONOMIC INFLUENCES ON THE SOUTH AFRICAN FRONTIER, 1652-1836. SOUTH/AFR SEA AGRI NAT/G FORCES WORKER DIPLOM INT/TRADE PRICE DEMAND PRODUC...STAT CHARTS 17/19 FRONTIER. PAGE 97 F1915 — COLONIAL ECO/UNDEV ECO/TAC MARKET

B57

OLIVECRONA K.,THE PROBLEM OF THE MONETARY UNIT. AFR UNIV PAY PRICE UTIL...MATH 20 MONEY SILVER. PAGE 101 F1986 — FINAN ECO/TAC ECO/DEV CONCPT

B57

SINGH D.B.,INFLATIONARY PRICE TRENDS IN INDIA SINCE 1939. AFR INDIA ECO/TAC RATION CONTROL WAR GOV/REL BAL/PAY DEMAND INCOME PEACE PRODUC...POLICY CHARTS 20. PAGE 122 F2413 — BUDGET ECO/UNDEV PRICE FINAN

B57

THOMAS R.G.,OUR MODERN BANKING AND MONETARY SYSTEM (3RD ED.). AFR USA+45 USA-45 ACT/RES PLAN PROB/SOLV INT/TRADE PRICE WAR BAL/PAY INCOME...POLICY METH/CNCPT 20 DEPRESSION. PAGE 130 F2563 — FINAN SERV/IND ECO/TAC

B58

DEFENSE AGAINST INFLATION. USA+45 LEGIS WORKER TAX PRICE DEMAND INCOME PRODUC...POLICY TREND METH/COMP 20 GOLD/STAND. PAGE 1 F0012 — ECO/TAC EQUILIB WEALTH PROB/SOLV

B58

AVRAMOVIC D.,POSTWAR GROWTH IN INTERNATIONAL INDEBTEDNESS. AFR WOR+45 AGRI INDUS CAP/ISM PRICE INCOME...NAT/COMP 20 SILVER. PAGE 8 F0143 — INT/TRADE FINAN COST BAL/PAY

B58

CHANG C.,THE INFLATIONARY SPIRAL: THE EXPERIENCE IN CHINA 1939-50. CHINA/COM BUDGET INT/TRADE PRICE ADMIN CONTROL WAR DEMAND...POLICY CHARTS 20. PAGE 23 F0451 — FINAN ECO/TAC BAL/PAY GOV/REL

B58

DOWNIE J.,THE COMPETITIVE PROCESS. ECO/TAC PRICE EFFICIENCY OPTIMAL PRODUC WEALTH...IDEA/COMP METH/COMP 20 MONOPOLY. PAGE 34 F0658 — EQUILIB MARKET INDUS ECO/DEV

B58

DUESENBERRY J.S.,BUSINESS CYCLES AND ECONOMIC GROWTH. USA+45 PROB/SOLV PAY PRICE...CONCPT MATH CHARTS IDEA/COMP 20 DEPRESSION KEYNES/JM. PAGE 34 F0672 — FINAN ECO/DEV ECO/TAC INCOME

B58

EHRHARD J.,LE DESTIN DU COLONIALISME. AFR FRANCE ECO/UNDEV AGRI FINAN MARKET CREATE PLAN TEC/DEV BUDGET DIPLOM PRICE 20. PAGE 36 F0710 — COLONIAL FOR/AID INT/TRADE INDUS

B58

JUCKER-FLEETWOOD E.,ECONOMIC THEORY AND POLICY IN FINLAND 1914-1925. FINLAND INT/TRADE PRICE COST 20 MONEY. PAGE 68 F1343 — FINAN GEN/LAWS ECO/TAC PLAN

B58

MOONEY R.E.,INFLATION AND RECESSION? AFR USA+45 LABOR LG/CO PRESS LEAD...IDEA/COMP ANTHOL 20. PAGE 93 F1821 — PRICE ECO/TAC NAT/G PRODUC

B58

MUSGRAVE R.A.,CLASSICS IN THE THEORY OF PUBLIC FINANCE. UNIV MARKET LG/CO NAT/G CAP/ISM PRICE OPTIMAL...IDEA/COMP ANTHOL 19/20 SAY/EMIL EDGEWORTH LINDAHL/E RITSCHL/H. PAGE 95 F1870 — TAX FINAN ECO/TAC GP/REL

B58

THEIL H.,ECONOMIC FORECASTS AND POLICY. UNIV CAP/ISM PRICE EFFICIENCY...DECISION CONCPT STAT 20. PAGE 129 F2551 — SIMUL MATH ECOMETRIC PREDICT

B58

US CONGRESS JOINT ECO COMM,THE RELATIONSHIP OF PRICES TO ECONOMIC STABILITY AND GROWTH. USA+45 MARKET TAX ADJUST COST DEMAND INCOME PRODUC ...POLICY TREND CHARTS ANTHOL 20 CONGRESS. PAGE 134 F2650 — ECO/DEV PLAN EQUILIB PRICE

L58

CYERT R.M.,"THE ROLE OF EXPECTATIONS IN BUSINESS DECISION-MAKING." PROB/SOLV PRICE RIGID/FLEX. PAGE 29 F0566 — LG/CO DECISION ROUTINE EXEC

N58

EUROPEAN COMM ECO-SOC PROG,EUROPEAN BUSINESS CYCLE POLICY (PAMPHLET). AFR EUR+WWI MARKET WORKER DIPLOM PRICE BAL/PAY 20 EUROPE. PAGE 39 F0754 — ECO/DEV FINAN ECO/TAC PROB/SOLV

B59

BLACK J.D.,ECONOMICS FOR AGRICULTURE. USA+45 EXTR/IND FAM WORKER ACT/RES PLAN PRICE EATING INCOME...CENSUS BIBLIOG 20. PAGE 15 F0291 — AGRI ECO/TAC MARKET POLICY

B59

CHECCHI V.,HONDURAS: A PROBLEM IN ECONOMIC DEVELOPMENT. HONDURAS AGRI FINAN INDUS LABOR WORKER INT/TRADE EDU/PROP PRICE HEALTH...GEOG CHARTS BIBLIOG 20. PAGE 24 F0458 — ECO/UNDEV ECO/TAC PROB/SOLV PLAN

B59

HARTOG F.,EUROPEAN TRADE CYCLE POLICY. WORKER TAX PRICE WAR CENTRAL DEMAND...TREND CHARTS 20 UN. PAGE 56 F1103 — EQUILIB EUR+WWI INT/TRADE

B59

HAX K.,DIE HOCHSCHULLEHRER DER WIRTSCHAFTSWISSENSCHAFTEN IN DER BUNDESREPUBLIK DEUTSCHLAND EINSCHL. WESTBERLIN, OSTERREICH. AUSTRIA GERMANY/W SWITZERLND FINAN MARKET PROF/ORG BUDGET ECO/TAC INT/TRADE PRICE COST 20. PAGE 57 F1119 — BIBLIOG ACADEM INTELL

B59

LEWIS J.P.,BUSINESS CONDITIONS ANALYSIS. USA+45 MARKET LABOR BUDGET TAX AUTOMAT WAR DEMAND PRODUC ...ECOMETRIC CHARTS BIBLIOG 19/20. PAGE 79 F1549 — FINAN PRICE TREND

B59

LINK R.G.,ENGLISH THEORIES OF ECONOMIC FLUCTUATIONS: 1815-1848. FRANCE UK AGRI WORKER DIPLOM PRICE TASK WAR DEMAND PRODUC...POLICY BIBLIOG 18 MALTHUS MILL/JS WILSON/J. PAGE 80 F1574 — IDEA/COMP ECO/DEV WEALTH EQUILIB

B59

MATTHEWS R.C.O.,THE BUSINESS CYCLE. AFR LABOR INT/TRADE TAX PRICE RISK ADJUST WEALTH...POLICY ECOMETRIC CHARTS SIMUL TIME 20. PAGE 87 F1705 — FINAN DEMAND TASK

B59

RAMANADHAM V.V.,PROBLEMS OF PUBLIC ENTERPRISE: THOUGHTS ON BRITISH EXPERIENCE. UK FINAN INDUS PLAN PRICE CENTRAL...POLICY 20. PAGE 109 F2140 — SOCISM LG/CO ECO/DEV GOV/REL

B59

STANFORD U, BOARD OF TRUSTEES,THE ALLOCATION OF ECONOMIC RESOURCES. WORKER PLAN BUDGET ECO/TAC TAX RECEIVE COST PRODUC...POLICY IDEA/COMP SIMUL ANTHOL 20. PAGE 125 F2468 — INCOME PRICE FINAN

B59

STOVEL J.A.,CANADA IN THE WORLD ECONOMY. CANADA PRICE DEMAND...STAT CHARTS BIBLIOG 20 VINER/J. PAGE 127 F2499 — INT/TRADE BAL/PAY FINAN ECO/TAC

B59

WENTHOLT W.,SOME COMMENTS ON THE LIQUIDATION OF THE EUROPEAN PAYMENT UNION AND RELATED PROBLEMS (PAMPHLET). AFR WOR+45 PLAN BUDGET PRICE CONTROL 20 EEC. PAGE 145 F2857 — FINAN ECO/DEV INT/ORG ECO/TAC

S59

DUNNING J.H.,"NON-PECUNIARY ELEMENTS AND BUSINESS BEHAVIOUR." PLAN PROB/SOLV COST...METH/CNCPT — DECISION DRIVE

CLASSIF QUANT STAT. PAGE 35 F0681 — PRODUC PRICE

S59
GILPATRICK T.V.,"PRICE SUPPORT POLICY AND THE MIDWEST FARM VOTE" (BMR)" NAT/G PRICE CONTROL REGION...POLICY CHARTS 440 20 MIDWEST/US CONGRESS REPUBLICAN EISNHWR/DD 20. PAGE 47 F0925 — POL/PAR AGRI ATTIT CHOOSE

S59
REES A.,"DO UNIONS CAUSE INFLATION?" CONTROL 20. PAGE 110 F2171 — LABOR ECO/TAC PRICE WORKER

B60
BIERMAN H.,THE CAPITAL BUDGETING DECISION. AFR ECO/DEV MARKET TAX PRICE RISK COST INCOME TIME 20. PAGE 15 F0282 — FINAN OPTIMAL BUDGET PROFIT

B60
DALE W.B.,THE FOREIGN DEFICIT OF THE UNITED STATES. ECO/TAC TARIFFS PAY PRICE CONTROL COST WEALTH POLICY. PAGE 30 F0573 — BAL/PAY DIPLOM FINAN INT/TRADE

B60
HARBERGER A.C.,THE DEMAND FOR DURABLE GOODS. AGRI FINAN COST EQUILIB...MATH STAT TIME/SEQ TREND CON/ANAL CHARTS SIMUL ANTHOL 20. PAGE 55 F1072 — ECOMETRIC DEMAND PRICE

B60
KENEN P.B.,BRITISH MONETARY POLICY AND THE BALANCE OF PAYMENTS 1951-57. UK PLAN BUDGET ECO/TAC INT/TRADE PAY PRICE COST ATTIT 20. PAGE 70 F1377 — BAL/PAY PROB/SOLV FINAN NAT/G

B60
OEEC,STATISTICS OF SOURCES AND USES OF FINANCE. NAT/G CAP/ISM TAX PRICE COST 20 OEEC. PAGE 101 F1978 — FINAN PRODUC INCOME NAT/COMP

B60
RAPKIN C.,THE DEMAND FOR HOUSING IN RACIALLY MIXED AREAS: A STUDY OF THE NATURE OF NEIGHBORHOOD CHANGE. USA+45 FINAN PRICE COST DRIVE...GEOG 20. PAGE 109 F2151 — RACE/REL NEIGH DISCRIM MARKET

B60
ROBERTSON D.,THE CONTROL OF INDUSTRY. UK MARKET LABOR WORKER PRICE CONTROL GP/REL COST DEMAND ORD/FREE WEALTH NEW/LIB SOCISM 20. PAGE 112 F2211 — INDUS FINAN NAT/G ECO/DEV

B60
ROBINSON R.I.,FINANCIAL INSTITUTIONS. USA+45 PRICE GOV/REL DEMAND WEALTH...CHARTS T 20 MONEY. PAGE 113 F2226 — FINAN ECO/TAC ECO/DEV BUDGET

B60
SILK L.S.,THE RESEARCH REVOLUTION. USA+45 FINAN CAP/ISM ECO/TAC PRICE EQUILIB PRODUC...STAT TREND CHARTS. PAGE 122 F2402 — ECO/DEV R+D TEC/DEV PROB/SOLV

B61
ACKLEY G.,MACROECONOMIC THEORY. AFR FINAN WORKER ECO/TAC PRICE COST INCOME PRODUC...MATH TREND CHARTS IDEA/COMP T KEYNES/JM. PAGE 2 F0034 — SIMUL ECOMETRIC WEALTH

B61
BREWIS T.N.,CANADIAN ECONOMIC POLICY. AFR CANADA BUDGET CAP/ISM INT/TRADE RATION TARIFFS TAX PRICE CONTROL ROUTINE FEDERAL INCOME PRODUC 20. PAGE 18 F0348 — ECO/DEV ECO/TAC NAT/G PLAN

B61
BUSSCHAU W.J.,GOLD AND INTERNATIONAL LIQUIDITY. AFR WOR+45 PRICE EQUILIB WEALTH...CHARTS 20. PAGE 20 F0396 — FINAN DIPLOM PROB/SOLV

B61
CLARK J.M.,COMPETITION AS A DYNAMIC PROCESS. ECO/DEV EXTR/IND INDUS LG/CO TEC/DEV ECO/TAC PRICE EQUILIB PRODUC...NEW/IDEA CAP 20. PAGE 25 F0483 — WEALTH GP/REL FINAN PROFIT

B61
FELLNER W.,THE PROBLEM OF RISING PRICES. AGRI INDUS WORKER BUDGET CAP/ISM ECO/TAC INT/TRADE PAY DEMAND ...POLICY 20 EEC. PAGE 40 F0780 — PRICE MARKET ECO/DEV COST

B61
GURTOO D.H.N.,INDIA'S BALANCE OF PAYMENTS (1920-1960). INDIA FINAN DIPLOM FOR/AID INT/TRADE PRICE COLONIAL...CHARTS BIBLIOG 20. PAGE 52 F1014 — BAL/PAY STAT ECO/TAC ECO/UNDEV

B61
HARRIS S.E.,THE DOLLAR IN CRISIS. AFR USA+45 MARKET INT/ORG ECO/TAC PRICE CONTROL WEALTH...METH/COMP ANTHOL 20. PAGE 55 F1089 — BAL/PAY DIPLOM FINAN INT/TRADE

B61
HAUSER M.,DIE URSACHEN DER FRANZOSISCHEN INFLATION IN DEN JAHREN 1946-1952. AFR FRANCE INDUS NAT/G BUDGET DIPLOM ECO/TAC FOR/AID COST MONEY 20. PAGE 57 F1114 — ECO/DEV FINAN PRICE

B61
HOLMANS A.E.,UNITED STATES FISCAL POLICY 1945-1959. AFR USA+45 USA-45 ECO/DEV TAX PRICE WAR...BIBLIOG 20 DEMOCRAT REPUBLICAN. PAGE 61 F1200 — POLICY BUDGET NAT/G ECO/TAC

B61
KLEIN L.R.,AN ECONOMETRIC MODEL OF THE UNITED KINGDOM. UK PRICE COST...MATH PREDICT TREND CHARTS SIMUL METH 20. PAGE 72 F1407 — ECOMETRIC COMPUTER STAT COMPUT/IR

B61
LAMFALUSSY A.,INVESTMENT AND GROWTH IN MATURE ECONOMIES. BELGIUM EUR+WWI LABOR PRICE PRODUC PROFIT...STAT CONT/OBS CHARTS 20. PAGE 75 F1464 — FINAN INDUS ECO/DEV CAP/ISM

B61
MOORE G.H.,BUSINESS CYCLE INDICATORS (TWO VOLS.). LABOR DIPLOM PRICE RISK TASK WAR PRODUC...CHARTS BIBLIOG 20. PAGE 93 F1822 — MARKET FINAN WEALTH

B61
NORTH D.C.,THE ECONOMIC GROWTH OF THE UNITED STATES 1790-1860. USA-45 INDUS TEC/DEV CAP/ISM ECO/TAC PRICE COST DEMAND LAISSEZ...ECOMETRIC STAT TREND 19. PAGE 98 F1933 — AGRI ECO/UNDEV

B61
NOVE A.,THE SOVIET ECONOMY. USSR ECO/DEV FINAN NAT/G ECO/TAC PRICE ADMIN EFFICIENCY MARXISM ...TREND BIBLIOG 20. PAGE 99 F1943 — PLAN PRODUC POLICY

B61
PAUNIO J.J.,A STUDY IN THE THEORY OF OPEN INFLATION. AFR FINAN CAP/ISM PRICE DEMAND INCOME ...CHARTS BIBLIOG 20. PAGE 104 F2040 — ACT/RES ECO/DEV ECO/TAC COST

B61
SHONFIELD A.,ECONOMIC GROWTH AND INFLATION; A STUDY OF INDIAN PLANNING. AFR INDIA AGRI INDUS TEC/DEV CONTROL DEMAND UTIL 20. PAGE 121 F2384 — ECO/UNDEV PRICE PLAN BUDGET

B61
STOCKING G.W.,WORKABLE COMPETITION AND ANTITRUST POLICY. USA+45 NAT/G CONSULT PLAN PRICE GOV/REL COST DEMAND PROFIT...POLICY 20. PAGE 126 F2491 — LG/CO INDUS ECO/TAC CONTROL

B61
TRIFFIN R.,GOLD AND THE DOLLAR CRISIS: THE FUTURE OF CONVERTIBILITY. AFR USA+45 USA-45 INT/ORG PROB/SOLV BUDGET INT/TRADE PRICE...STAT CHARTS 19/20. PAGE 131 F2588 — FINAN ECO/DEV ECO/TAC BAL/PAY

B61
UNIVS-NATL BUR COMM ECO RES,PUBLIC FINANCES: NEEDS, SOURCES, AND UTILIZATION. USA+45 FORCES PLAN TAX CONFER PRICE FEDERAL UTIL...ANTHOL MUNICH 20. PAGE 133 F2623 — NAT/G FINAN DECISION BUDGET

B61
WILSON T.,INFLATION. FINAN PLAN CAP/ISM PRICE CONTROL...CHARTS 20. PAGE 147 F2903 — ECO/DEV ECO/TAC POLICY COST

S61
DICKS-MIREAUX L.A.,"THE INTERRELATIONSHIP BETWEEN COST AND PRICE CHANGES 19461959: A STUDY OF INFLATION IN POST-WAR BRITAIN" AFR UK ECO/DEV INDUS WORKER ECO/TAC ORD/FREE WEALTH...ECOMETRIC REGRESS STAT TREND CHARTS 20. PAGE 33 F0634 — PRICE PAY DEMAND

B62
BACKMAN J.,THE ECONOMICS OF THE ELECTRICAL MACHINERY INDUSTRY. USA+45 PROC/MFG LABOR WORKER INT/TRADE TV PRICE COST...CHARTS 19/20. PAGE 8 F0147 — PRODUC TEC/DEV TREND

B62
BRIEFS H.W.,PRICING POWER AND "ADMINISTRATIVE" INFLATION (PAMPHLET). AFR USA+45 PROC/MFG CONTROL EFFICIENCY MONEY. PAGE 18 F0349 — ECO/DEV PRICE POLICY EXEC

B62
DENISON E.F.,THE SOURCES OF ECONOMIC GROWTH IN THE UNITED STATES AND THE ALTERNATIVES BEFORE US. AGRI INDUS SCHOOL TEC/DEV CAP/ISM ECO/TAC PRICE COST WEALTH...STAT TREND CHARTS 20. PAGE 32 F0620 — ECO/DEV WORKER PRODUC

B62
GALENSON W.,LABOR IN DEVELOPING COUNTRIES. BRAZIL INDONESIA ISRAEL PAKISTAN TURKEY AGRI INDUS WORKER PAY PRICE GP/REL WEALTH...MGT CHARTS METH/COMP NAT/COMP 20. PAGE 45 F0888 — LABOR ECO/UNDEV BARGAIN POL/PAR

B62
HOOVER C.B.,ECONOMIC SYSTEMS OF THE COMMONWEALTH. AFR CANADA INDIA UK ECO/DEV ECO/UNDEV AGRI INDUS TEC/DEV TARIFFS PRICE BAL/PAY DEMAND...SIMUL 20 AUSTRAL. PAGE 61 F1208 — CAP/ISM SOCISM ECO/TAC PLAN

B62
MEANS G.C.,PRICING POWER AND THE PUBLIC INTEREST. PLAN PROB/SOLV COST EFFICIENCY PROFIT RIGID/FLEX WEALTH. PAGE 89 F1741 — LG/CO EX/STRUC PRICE ECO/TAC

B62
MEANS G.C.,THE CORPORATE REVOLUTION IN AMERICA: ECONOMIC REALITY VS. ECONOMIC THEORY. USA+45 USA-45 INDUS WORKER PLAN CAP/ISM ADMIN...IDEA/COMP 20. — LG/CO MARKET CONTROL

PAGE 89 F1742 PRICE

B62
MEYER F.V.,THE TERMS OF TRADE. WOR+45 AGRI MARKET PROC/MFG DIPLOM PRICE DEMAND PRODUC 20. PAGE 90 F1769
INT/TRADE BAL/PAY SIMUL EQUILIB

B62
MICHAELY M.,CONCENTRATION IN INTERNATIONAL TRADE. ECO/DEV ECO/UNDEV PRICE INCOME...CHARTS NAT/COMP 20. PAGE 91 F1779
INT/TRADE MARKET FINAN GEOG

B62
PRAKASH O.M.,THE THEORY AND WORKING OF STATE CORPORATIONS: WITH SPECIAL REFERENCE TO INDIA. INDIA UK USA+45 TOP/EX PRICE ADMIN EFFICIENCY...MGT METH/COMP 20 TVA. PAGE 107 F2112
LG/CO ECO/UNDEV GOV/REL SOCISM

B62
REES A.,THE ECONOMICS OF TRADE UNIONS. FUT ECO/DEV INDUS BARGAIN CAP/ISM PRICE SENIOR CONTROL GP/REL COST...TREND 20 AFL/CIO. PAGE 110 F2172
LABOR WORKER ECO/TAC

B62
SEN S.R.,THE STRATEGY FOR AGRICULTURAL DEVELOPMENT AND OTHER ESSAYS ON ECONOMIC POLICY AND PLANNING. INDIA FINAN ACT/RES TEC/DEV CAP/ISM PRICE...STAT 20. PAGE 119 F2354
ECO/UNDEV PLAN AGRI POLICY

B62
SHANNON I.,THE ECONOMIC FUNCTIONS OF GOLD. AFR FUT WOR+45 WOR-45 INT/ORG BUDGET INT/TRADE BAL/PAY DEMAND PEACE 20 MONEY. PAGE 120 F2366
FINAN PRICE ECO/DEV ECO/TAC

B62
VANEK J.,INTERNATIONAL TRADE - THEORY AND ECONOMIC POLICY. LABOR BAL/PWR ECO/TAC TARIFFS PRICE BAL/PAY COST DEMAND 20. PAGE 140 F2765
INT/TRADE DIPLOM BARGAIN MARKET

B62
VANEK J.,THE BALANCE OF PAYMENTS, LEVEL OF ECONOMIC ACTIVITY AND THE VALUE OF CURRENCY: THEORY AND SOME RECENT EXPERIENCES. UNIV PRICE INCOME...MATH 20 KEYNES/JM. PAGE 140 F2766
BAL/PAY ECO/TAC FINAN GEN/LAWS

S62
LIPSON H.A.,"FORMAL REASONING AND MARKETING STRATEGY." ECO/DEV PROB/SOLV PRICE ALL/VALS CONT/OBS. PAGE 81 F1578
MARKET DECISION GAME ECO/TAC

N62
BANK INTERNATIONAL SETTLEMENTS,AUSTRIA: MONETARY AND ECONOMIC SITUATION 1952-61 (PAMPHLET). AUSTRIA WORKER BUDGET INT/TRADE PRICE BAL/PAY DEMAND EFFICIENCY INCOME PRODUC...STAT 20 SILVER. PAGE 9 F0174
FINAN ECO/DEV CHARTS WEALTH

B63
AHN L.A.,FUNFZIG JAHRE ZWISCHEN INFLATION UND DEFLATION. AFR GERMANY DIPLOM PRICE...CONCPT 20. PAGE 3 F0053
FINAN CAP/ISM NAT/COMP ECO/TAC

B63
ALPERT P.,ECONOMIC DEVELOPMENT. WOR+45 FINAN TEC/DEV ECO/TAC PRICE GOV/REL HABITAT...GEOG BIBLIOG T 20 THIRD/WRLD. PAGE 4 F0079
ECO/DEV ECO/UNDEV INT/TRADE FOR/AID

B63
BANERJI A.K.,INDIA'S BALANCE OF PAYMENTS. INDIA NAT/G PRICE BAL/PAY COST INCOME 20. PAGE 9 F0171
INT/TRADE DIPLOM FINAN BUDGET

B63
COSSA L.,SAGGI BIBLIOGRAFICI DI ECONOMIA POLITICA. MOD/EUR LABOR PRICE COST INCOME 18/19. PAGE 28 F0539
BIBLIOG FINAN WEALTH

B63
FRIEDMAN M.,INFLATION: CAUSES AND CURES. AFR INDIA ECO/DEV ECO/TAC INT/TRADE RATION PRICE DEMAND ...POLICY 20. PAGE 44 F0860
ECO/UNDEV PLAN FINAN EQUILIB

B63
GANGULY D.S.,PUBLIC CORPORATIONS IN A NATIONAL ECONOMY. INDIA WOR+45 FINAN INDUS TOP/EX PRICE EFFICIENCY...MGT STAT CHARTS BIBLIOG 20. PAGE 46 F0897
ECO/UNDEV LG/CO SOCISM GOV/REL

B63
GRIGSBY W.G.,HOUSING MARKETS AND PUBLIC POLICY. USA+45 FAM NEIGH PRICE DEMAND WEALTH...POLICY CHARTS BIBLIOG METH MUNICH 20. PAGE 51 F1002
MARKET RENT HABITAT PLAN

B63
HAHN L.A.,DIE AMERIKANISCHE KONJUNKTURPOLITIK DER DOLLAR UND DIE DMARK. GERMANY/W USA+45 DIPLOM PRICE BAL/PAY COST...POLICY MONEY. PAGE 53 F1038
FINAN BUDGET ECO/TAC LABOR

B63
HOOPES R.,THE STEEL CRISIS. USA+45 INDUS ECO/TAC EDU/PROP PRICE CONTROL ATTIT...POLICY 20 KENNEDY/JF. PAGE 61 F1205
PROC/MFG NAT/G RATION CHIEF

B63
LEE M.W.,MACROECONOMICS: FLUCTUATIONS, GROWTH AND STABILITY (3RD ED.). MARKET LABOR TEC/DEV INT/TRADE TAX PRICE WAR PRODUC...POLICY ECOMETRIC CHARTS 19/20. PAGE 77 F1505
EQUILIB TREND WEALTH

B63
RAFUSE R.W. JR.,STATE AND LOCAL FISCAL BEHAVIOR OVER THE POSTWAR CYCLES (DISSERTATION). USA+45 TAX PRICE ATTIT...POLICY TIME/SEQ TREND CHARTS BIBLIOG 20. PAGE 109 F2135
BUDGET LOC/G ECO/TAC PROVS

B63
RANGEL I.,A INFLACAO BRASILEIRA (2ND ED.). AFR BRAZIL AGRI INDUS MARKET INT/TRADE DEMAND EQUILIB ATTIT 20. PAGE 109 F2144
ECO/UNDEV FINAN PRICE TAX

B63
RICARDO D.,THE PRINCIPLES OF POLITICAL ECONOMY AND TAXATION (1817). UK INDUS MARKET ECO/TAC INT/TRADE TARIFFS PRICE COST DEMAND OPTIMAL WEALTH...CONCPT 19 INTRVN/ECO. PAGE 111 F2183
GEN/LAWS TAX LAISSEZ

B63
SELF P.,THE STATE AND THE FARMER. UK ECO/DEV MARKET WORKER PRICE CONTROL GP/REL...WELF/ST 20 DEPT/AGRI. PAGE 119 F2346
AGRI NAT/G ADMIN VOL/ASSN

B63
STIFEL L.D.,THE TEXTILE INDUSTRY - A CASE STUDY OF INDUSTRIAL DEVELOPMENT IN THE PHILIPPINES (PAPER). PHILIPPINE WORKER CAP/ISM INT/TRADE TARIFFS RECEIVE PRICE ADMIN COST EFFICIENCY WEALTH...BIBLIOG 20. PAGE 126 F2486
S/ASIA ECO/UNDEV PROC/MFG NAT/G

B63
US BD GOVERNORS FEDL RESRV,THE FEDERAL RESERVE AND THE TREASURY. USA+45 WORKER PROB/SOLV PRICE COST DEMAND WEALTH...STAT INT CHARTS 20 FED/RESERV DEPT/TREAS. PAGE 134 F2641
FINAN GOV/REL CONTROL BUDGET

B63
US CONGRESS JOINT ECO COMM,THE UNITED STATES BALANCE OF PAYMENTS. AFR USA+45 DELIB/GP BUDGET PRICE PRODUC 20 CONGRESS MONEY. PAGE 135 F2655
BAL/PAY INT/TRADE FINAN ECO/TAC

B63
VON MISES L.,HUMAN ACTION: A TREATISE ON ECONOMICS (2ND ED.). SOCIETY MARKET TAX PAY PRICE DEMAND EQUILIB RATIONAL...PSY 20. PAGE 142 F2794
PLAN DRIVE ATTIT

B63
WALKER F.V.,GROWTH, EMPLOYMENT, AND THE PRICE LEVEL. USA+45 NAT/G PLAN ECO/TAC DEMAND EFFICIENCY CHARTS. PAGE 142 F2803
ECO/DEV FINAN PRICE WORKER

S63
GREEN P.E.,"BAYESIAN DECISION THEORY IN PRICING STRATEGY."...STAT CHARTS. PAGE 51 F0988
OP/RES PROB/SOLV BARGAIN PRICE

S63
REES A.,"THE EFFECTS OF UNIONS ON RESOURCE ALLOCATION." USA+45 WORKER PRICE CONTROL GP/REL ...MGT METH/COMP 20. PAGE 110 F2173
LABOR BARGAIN RATION INCOME

N63
LEDERER W.,THE BALANCE ON FOREIGN TRANSACTIONS: PROBLEMS OF DEFINITION AND MEASUREMENT (PAMPHLET). USA+45 BUDGET DIPLOM ECO/TAC PRICE GOV/REL...POLICY STAT NAT/COMP METH 20. PAGE 77 F1502
FINAN BAL/PAY INT/TRADE ECO/DEV

B64
BALASSA B.,TRADE PROSPECTS FOR DEVELOPING COUNTRIES. WOR+45 ECO/DEV AGRI EXTR/IND INDUS CREATE PLAN PRICE...ECOMETRIC CLASSIF TIME/SEQ GEN/METH. PAGE 8 F0158
INT/TRADE ECO/UNDEV TREND STAT

B64
BALL R.J.,INFLATION AND THE THEORY OF MONEY. MARKET TAX PAY PRICE TASK ADJUST BAL/PAY COST INCOME PRODUC WEALTH...METH/COMP 20 KEYNES/JM MONEY. PAGE 9 F0167
EQUILIB DEMAND POLICY

B64
BARKSDALE H.C.,MARKETING: CHANGE AND EXCHANGE. USA+45 FINAN ACADEM TEC/DEV PRICE AUTOMAT WEALTH ...CHARTS 20. PAGE 10 F0187
MARKET ECO/DEV DEMAND TREND

B64
BASTIAT F.,ECONOMIC HARMONIES (1850). STRATA STRUCT ECO/DEV BUDGET TAX PRICE LOBBY COST. PAGE 11 F0206
ECO/TAC PLAN INT/TRADE LAISSEZ

B64
BOARMAN P.M.,GERMANY'S ECONOMIC DILEMMA - INFLATION AND THE BALANCE OF PAYMENTS. AFR GERMANY/W LABOR CAP/ISM PRICE BAL/PAY COST INCOME 20. PAGE 16 F0302
ECO/DEV FINAN INT/TRADE BUDGET

B64
BROWN E.H.P.,A COURSE IN APPLIED ECONOMICS (2ND ED.). ECO/DEV FINAN MARKET WORKER INT/TRADE RATION RENT PAY PRICE BAL/PAY...DECISION T RESOURCE/N. PAGE 19 F0368
POLICY ECO/TAC PROB/SOLV

B64
BROWN W.M.,THE EXTERNAL LIQUIDITY OF AN ADVANCED COUNTRY. CANADA FRANCE GERMANY/W SWEDEN UK USA+45 ECO/DEV DIPLOM PRICE...CONCPT STAT NAT/COMP 20. PAGE 20 F0376
FINAN INT/TRADE COST INCOME

B64
COLSTON RESEARCH SOCIETY,ECONOMETRIC ANALYSIS FOR NATIONAL ECONOMIC PLANNING (PROCEEDINGS OF SIXTEENTH SYMPOSIUM OF COLSTON RESEARCH SOCIETY). UK USA+45 FINAN FAM LABOR NAT/G PLAN PRICE ...METH/CNCPT TREND CHARTS TIME 20. PAGE 26 F0510
ECOMETRIC DELIB/GP ECO/TAC PROB/SOLV

B64
COMMISSION ON MONEY AND CREDIT,INFLATION, GROWTH, AND EMPLOYMENT. AFR USA+45 PLAN PROB/SOLV PAY PRICE EFFICIENCY PRODUC WEALTH 20. PAGE 26 F0514
WORKER ECO/TAC OPTIMAL

B64
EINZIG P.,MONETARY POLICY: ENDS AND MEANS. AFR UK INDUS WORKER PLAN DIPLOM PRICE BAL/PAY COST WEALTH ...DECISION TIME/SEQ 20. PAGE 37 F0715
FINAN POLICY ECO/TAC BUDGET

B64
FITCH L.C.,URBAN TRANSPORTATION AND PUBLIC POLICY. FINAN NAT/G LEGIS PROB/SOLV TEC/DEV PRICE COST EFFICIENCY...DECISION STAT CHARTS METH/COMP MUNICH 20 NEWYORK/C PHILADELPH LOS/ANG CHICAGO WASHING/DC. PAGE 41 F0806
DIST/IND PLAN LOC/G

B64
HANSEN B.,INTERNATIONAL LIQUIDITY. USA+45 INT/ORG ECO/TAC PRICE CONTROL WEALTH...POLICY 20. PAGE 54 F1068
BAL/PAY INT/TRADE DIPLOM FINAN

B64
HART P.E.,ECONOMETRIC ANALYSIS FOR NATIONAL ECONOMIC PLANNING. INDUS OP/RES PRICE PRODUC ...SIMUL ANTHOL MODELS 20. PAGE 56 F1100
PLAN ECOMETRIC STAT

B64
HATHAWAY D.E.,PROBLEMS OF PROGRESS IN THE AGRICULTURAL ECONOMY. USA+45 USA-45 ECO/DEV NAT/G INT/TRADE PRICE DEMAND EFFICIENCY OPTIMAL 20. PAGE 57 F1112
AGRI ECO/TAC MARKET PLAN

B64
KAPLAN A.D.H.,BIG ENTERPRISE IN A COMPETITIVE SYSTEM (REV. ED.). USA+45 INDUS MARKET WORKER TEC/DEV ECO/TAC PRICE ADJUD ADMIN CONTROL...MGT CHARTS 20 MONOPOLY. PAGE 69 F1351
FINAN GP/REL NAT/G LG/CO

B64
KUZNETS S.,POSTWAR ECONOMIC GROWTH: FOUR LECTURES. WOR+45 INDUS NAT/G WORKER TEC/DEV ECO/TAC RATION TARIFFS PRICE BAL/PAY COST DEMAND 20. PAGE 74 F1455
ECO/DEV ECO/UNDEV TREND FINAN

B64
LITVAK I.A.,MARKETING: CANADA. CANADA STRATA PROC/MFG LEGIS TEC/DEV DIPLOM INT/TRADE PRICE AUTOMAT ATTIT WEALTH...ANTHOL 20. PAGE 81 F1587
ECO/TAC MARKET ECO/DEV EFFICIENCY

B64
MANSFIELD E.,MONOPOLY POWER AND ECONOMIC PERFORMANCE: AN INTRODUCTION TO A CURRENT ISSUE OF PUBLIC POLICY. ECO/DEV INDUS NAT/G PLAN CAP/ISM PRICE CONTROL LOBBY EFFICIENCY PRODUC...POLICY 20 CONGRESS KENNEDY/JF MONOPOLY. PAGE 85 F1659
LG/CO PWR ECO/TAC MARKET

B64
MAZA ZAVALA D.F.,VENEZUELA; UNA ECONOMIA DEPENDIENTE. L/A+17C VENEZUELA FINAN INDUS ...ECOMETRIC STAT TREND 20. PAGE 87 F1710
ECO/UNDEV BAL/PAY INT/TRADE PRICE

B64
ROBINSON E.A.G.,ECONOMIC DEVELOPMENT FOR AFRICA SOUTH OF THE SAHARA. AFR AGRI INDUS LABOR BUDGET INT/TRADE PRICE...POLICY GEOG ANTHOL 20. PAGE 113 F2219
ECO/UNDEV ECO/TAC ACT/RES PLAN

B64
SANDEE J.,EUROPE'S FUTURE CONSUMPTION. EUR+WWI FUT EDU/PROP...IDEA/COMP NAT/COMP ANTHOL 20 EUROPE. PAGE 115 F2277
MARKET ECO/DEV PREDICT PRICE

B64
SHANNON I.,INTERNATIONAL LIQUIDITY. AFR FUT USA+45 WOR+45 ECO/TAC PRICE DEMAND WEALTH...CONCPT 20. PAGE 120 F2367
FINAN DIPLOM BAL/PAY ECO/DEV

B64
STONIER A.W.,EXERCISES IN ECONOMICS. FINAN INDUS TEC/DEV RENT PAY EQUILIB PRODUC PROFIT...METH/COMP T. PAGE 127 F2498
PRICE MARKET WORKER

B64
URQUIDI V.L.,THE CHALLENGE OF DEVELOPMENT IN LATIN AMERICA. L/A+17C FINAN INT/ORG TEC/DEV DIPLOM INT/TRADE PRICE REGION PRODUC...CHARTS 20 ALL/PROG. PAGE 133 F2628
ECO/UNDEV ECO/TAC NAT/G TREND

B64
WELLISZ S.,THE ECONOMICS OF THE SOVIET BLOC. COM USSR INDUS WORKER PLAN BUDGET INT/TRADE TAX PRICE PRODUC WEALTH MARXISM...METH/COMP 20. PAGE 145 F2854
EFFICIENCY ADMIN MARKET

B64
ZEBOT C.A.,THE ECONOMICS OF COMPETITIVE COEXISTENCE. CHINA/COM USSR WOR+45 FINAN MARKET FOR/AID PRICE DEMAND EQUILIB WEALTH ALL/IDEOS 20. PAGE 150 F2961
TEC/DEV DIPLOM METH/COMP

B64
ZOBER M.,MARKETING MANAGEMENT. FINAN BUDGET EDU/PROP PRICE PRODUC ATTIT...POLICY TREND CHARTS METH/COMP EQULIB 20. PAGE 150 F2966
ECO/DEV MGT CONTROL MARKET

B65
ALDERSON W.,DYNAMIC MARKETING BEHAVIOR. USA+45 FINAN CREATE TEC/DEV EDU/PROP PRICE COST 20. PAGE 3 F0057
MGT MARKET ATTIT CAP/ISM

B65
ALLEN W.R.,INTERNATIONAL TRADE THEORY: HUME TO OHLIN. FINAN LABOR TARIFFS TAX PRICE DEMAND PRODUC PROFIT...ANTHOL 18/20. PAGE 4 F0074
INT/TRADE WEALTH METH/CNCPT

B65
BAUMOL W.J.,ECONOMIC THEORY AND OPERATIONS ANALYSIS (2ND ED.). MARKET LG/CO BUDGET PRICE COST EQUILIB PRODUC...DECISION MATH CHARTS GAME 20. PAGE 12 F0219
OP/RES ECO/DEV METH/COMP STAT

B65
CHAO K.,THE RATE AND PATTERN OF INDUSTRIAL GROWTH IN COMMUNIST CHINA. CHINA/COM ECO/UNDEV TEC/DEV PRICE...NAT/COMP BIBLIOG 20. PAGE 23 F0452
INDUS INDEX STAT PRODUC

B65
DODDY F.S.,INTRODUCTION TO THE USE OF ECONOMIC INDICATORS. FINAN LABOR PLAN COST...ECOMETRIC INDICATOR MATH PREDICT CHARTS METH 20. PAGE 33 F0649
TEC/DEV STAT PRODUC PRICE

B65
EDELMAN M.,THE POLITICS OF WAGE-PRICE DECISIONS. GERMANY ITALY NETHERLAND UK INDUS LABOR POL/PAR PROB/SOLV BARGAIN PRICE ROUTINE BAL/PAY COST DEMAND 20. PAGE 36 F0699
GOV/COMP CONTROL ECO/TAC PLAN

B65
HAEFELE E.T.,GOVERNMENT CONTROLS ON TRANSPORT. AFR RHODESIA TANZANIA DIPLOM ECO/TAC TARIFFS PRICE ADJUD CONTROL REGION EFFICIENCY...POLICY 20 CONGO. PAGE 53 F1031
ECO/UNDEV DIST/IND FINAN NAT/G

B65
HICKMAN B.G.,QUANTITATIVE PLANNING OF ECONOMIC POLICY. FRANCE NETHERLAND OP/RES PRICE ROUTINE UTIL ...POLICY DECISION ECOMETRIC METH/CNCPT STAT STYLE CHINJAP. PAGE 59 F1162
PROB/SOLV PLAN QUANT

B65
KANTOROVICH L.V.,THE BEST USE OF ECONOMIC RESOURCES. USSR SOCIETY FINAN ACT/RES TEC/DEV ECO/TAC PRICE CONTROL COST DEMAND EFFICIENCY OPTIMAL...MGT STAT. PAGE 69 F1350
PLAN MATH DECISION

B65
KASER M.,COMECON* INTEGRATION PROBLEMS OF THE PLANNED ECONOMIES. INT/ORG TEC/DEV INT/TRADE PRICE ADMIN ADJUST CENTRAL...STAT TIME/SEQ ORG/CHARTS COMECON. PAGE 69 F1359
PLAN ECO/DEV COM REGION

B65
MACAVOY P.W.,THE ECONOMIC EFFECTS OF REGULATION: THE TRUNK-LINE RAILROAD CARTELS AND THE INTERSTATE COMMERCE COMMISSION BEFORE 1900. USA-45 PRICE PROFIT...STAT CHARTS BIBLIOG 19 RAILROAD. PAGE 83 F1620
ECO/TAC DIST/IND PROF/ORG RATION

B65
MARK S.M.,ECONOMICS IN ACTION (3RD ED.). USA+45 ECO/UNDEV AGRI INDUS FOR/AID INT/TRADE BAL/PAY COST ORD/FREE...ANTHOL 20 RESOURCE/N. PAGE 85 F1670
POLICY ECO/TAC EFFICIENCY PRICE

B65
MUND V.A.,GOVERNMENT AND BUSINESS (4TH ED.). USA+45 INDUS LG/CO SML/CO LEGIS INT/TRADE LICENSE PRICE ADJUD. PAGE 95 F1860
NAT/G ECO/TAC BUDGET CONTROL

B65
ROWE J.W.,PRIMARY COMMODITIES IN INTERNATIONAL TRADE. MARKET CAP/ISM ECO/TAC DEMAND...NAT/COMP 20. PAGE 114 F2253
INT/TRADE AGRI RATION PRICE

B65
SCHWARTZ G.,SCIENCE IN MARKETING. OP/RES PROB/SOLV INT/TRADE PRICE CONTROL ADJUST PRODUC...CONCPT 20. PAGE 118 F2324
PHIL/SCI TREND ECO/DEV MARKET

B65
SHARIF A.,THE BALANCE OF PAYMENTS OF PAKISTAN, 1948-1958 (THESIS, UNIVERSITY OF TORONTO). PAKISTAN FINAN INDUS FOR/AID PRICE WEALTH...TREND CHARTS 20. PAGE 120 F2368
BAL/PAY BUDGET INT/TRADE ECO/UNDEV

B65
TEW B.,WEALTH AND INCOME. UK BUDGET INT/TRADE PRICE BAL/PAY DEMAND...CHARTS GOV/COMP 20 AUSTRAL. PAGE 129 F2546
FINAN ECO/DEV WEALTH INCOME

B65
VAID K.N.,STATE AND LABOR IN INDIA. INDIA INDUS WORKER PAY PRICE ADJUD CONTROL PARL/PROC GP/REL ORD/FREE 20. PAGE 140 F2757
LAW LABOR MGT NEW/LIB

B65
WU YUAN-LI,THE ECONOMY OF COMMUNIST CHINA. CHINA/COM USSR AGRI FINAN INDUS POL/PAR WORKER PROB/SOLV INT/TRADE PRICE EATING INCOME OWN WEALTH 20. PAGE 149 F2939
ECO/TAC MARXISM PLAN EFFICIENCY

B65
YOUNG A.N.,CHINA'S WARTIME FINANCE AND INFLATION. ASIA AGRI INDUS NAT/G ECO/TAC CONFER PRICE WAR COST 20. PAGE 150 F2949
FINAN FOR/AID TAX BUDGET

B65
ZAWADZKI K.K.F.,THE ECONOMICS OF INFLATIONARY PROCESSES. FINAN INT/TRADE PRICE CONTROL DEMAND EQUILIB PROFIT 20. PAGE 150 F2960
ECO/DEV COST ECO/TAC CAP/ISM

S65
BRIGHAM E.F.,"THE DETERMINANTS OF RESIDENTIAL LAND VALUES." USA+45 ECO/DEV PROB/SOLV RENT PRICE ...REGRESS STAT CHARTS GEN/METH MUNICH 20 LOS/ANG. PAGE 18 F0351
COST INDICATOR SIMUL ECOMETRIC

S65
HUTT W.H.,"KEYNESIAN REVISIONS" SOUTH/AFR ECO/DEV FINAN NAT/G WORKER BUDGET TAX PRICE EQUILIB WEALTH 20 KEYNES/JM. PAGE 64 F1252
ECO/TAC GEN/LAWS LOG

S65
KAUN D.E.,"THE FAIR LABOUR STANDARDS ACT: AN EVALUATION IN TERMS OF ITS STATED GOALS." SOUTH/AFR LAW LABOR BARGAIN PAY INGP/REL WEALTH 20. PAGE 69 F1364
ECO/TAC PRICE WORKER LEGIS

S65
STEENKAMP W.F.J.,"THE PROBLEM OF WAGE REGULATION." SOUTH/AFR LAW ECO/DEV ECO/UNDEV LABOR NAT/G BARGAIN PAY INGP/REL DISCRIM WEALTH...METH/COMP 20. PAGE 125 F2473
ECO/TAC PRICE WORKER RATION

C65
PEGRUM D.E.,"PUBLIC REGULATION OF BUSINESS (REV ED)" LAW CONSTN DIST/IND SERV/IND LG/CO LEGIS OWN LAISSEZ SOCISM...POLICY DECISION BIBLIOG 20. PAGE 104 F2048
INDUS PLAN NEW/LIB PRICE

B66
ALIBER R.Z.,THE FUTURE OF THE DOLLAR AS AN INTERNATIONAL CURRENCY. AFR USA+45 USA-45 ECO/DEV PRICE COST INCOME...POLICY 20. PAGE 4 F0067
FINAN DIPLOM INT/ORG INT/TRADE

B66
AMER ENTERPRISE INST FOR PUBL,INTERNATIONAL PAYMENTS PROBLEM. MARKET DIPLOM DEBATE PRICE COST INCOME 20. PAGE 4 F0082
FINAN INT/TRADE POLICY

B66
BARAN P.A.,MONOPOLY CAPITAL; AN ESSAY ON THE AMERICAN ECONOMIC AND SOCIAL ORDER. USA+45 USA-45 ECO/UNDEV FINAN MARKET PLAN DIPLOM COLONIAL RACE/REL DEMAND MARXISM...CHARTS 20. PAGE 9 F0179
LG/CO CAP/ISM PRICE CONTROL

B66
CHASE S.B. JR.,PROBLEMS IN PUBLIC EXPENDITURE ANALYSIS. DIST/IND INDUS OP/RES PLAN BUDGET RECEIVE PRICE RISK COST INCOME...CHARTS ANTHOL 20. PAGE 23 F0455
ECO/DEV FINAN NAT/G INSPECT

B66
FELKER J.L.,SOVIET ECONOMIC CONTROVERSIES. USSR INDUS PLAN INT/TRADE GP/REL MARXISM SOCISM...POLICY 20. PAGE 40 F0778
ECO/DEV MARKET PROFIT PRICE

B66
FELLNER W.,MAINTAINING AND RESTORING BALANCE IN INTERNATIONAL PAYMENTS. ECO/UNDEV MARKET ECO/TAC PRICE INCOME WEALTH...POLICY METH/COMP 20 MONEY. PAGE 40 F0781
BAL/PAY DIPLOM FINAN INT/TRADE

B66
GROSS H.,MAKE OR BUY. AFR USA+45 FINAN INDUS CREATE PRICE PRODUC 20. PAGE 51 F1006
ECO/TAC PLAN MGT COST

B66
HAINES W.W.,MONEY PRICES AND POLICY. WOR+45 ECO/DEV BUDGET CONTROL INCOME...POLICY STAT CHARTS BIBLIOG T 20. PAGE 53 F1039
PRICE FINAN ECO/TAC GOV/REL

B66
HALLER H.,DAS PROBLEM DER GELDWERTSTABILITAT. MARKET LABOR INCOME PRODUC...POLICY 20. PAGE 54 F1049
PRICE COST FINAN ECO/TAC

B66
LEE M.W.,TOWARD ECONOMIC STABILITY. USA+45 BUDGET TAX PRICE EQUILIB INCOME. PAGE 77 F1506
ECO/TAC CONTROL POLICY NAT/G

B66
NAMBOODIRIPAD E.M.,ECONOMICS AND POLITICS OF INDIA'S SOCIALIST PATTERN. INDIA STRATA AGRI INDUS NAT/G PRICE ORD/FREE SOVEREIGN 20. PAGE 96 F1888
ECO/UNDEV PLAN SOCISM CAP/ISM

B66
NATIONAL INDUSTRIAL CONF BOARD,GOLD AND WORLD MONETARY PROBLEMS. AFR FUT WOR+45 PROB/SOLV BUDGET INT/TRADE PAY GOV/REL...POLICY ANTHOL 20. PAGE 97 F1902
FINAN ECO/TAC PRICE BAL/PAY

B66
PEIRCE W.S.,SELECTIVE MANPOWER POLICIES AND THE TRADE-OFF BETWEEN RISING PRICES AND UNEMPLOYMENT (DISSERTATION). ECO/DEV WORKER ACT/RES...PHIL/SCI 20. PAGE 104 F2050
PRICE LABOR POLICY ECO/TAC

B66
ROBINSON E.A.,THE ECONOMICS OF EDUCATION. WOR+45 CULTURE ECO/UNDEV FINAN SCHOOL DIPLOM PRICE COST DEMAND...CHARTS METH/COMP 20. PAGE 112 F2216
EDU/PROP ADJUST CONFER

B66
ROSS A.M.,INDUSTRIAL RELATIONS AND ECONOMIC DEVELOPMENT. POL/PAR LEGIS WORKER BARGAIN PRICE EXEC LOBBY INCOME PWR...DECISION ANTHOL BIBLIOG 20. PAGE 114 F2243
ECO/UNDEV LABOR NAT/G GP/REL

B66
TRIFFIN R.,THE WORLD MONEY MAZE. AFR INT/ORG ECO/TAC PRICE OPTIMAL WEALTH...METH/COMP 20 EEC OEEC SILVER. PAGE 131 F2589
BAL/PAY FINAN INT/TRADE DIPLOM

B66
TRIFFIN R.,THE BALANCE OF PAYMENTS AND THE FOREIGN INVESTMENT POSITION OF THE UNITED STATES. AFR USA+45 INT/ORG INT/TRADE PRICE CONTROL...POLICY 20. PAGE 131 F2590
BAL/PAY DIPLOM FINAN ECO/TAC

B66
TURNER H.A.,PRICES, WAGES, AND INCOME POLICIES IN INDUSTRIALIZED MARKET ECONOMIES. AFR WOR+45 ECO/DEV INDUS PROB/SOLV ECO/TAC CONTROL WEALTH...CHARTS 20 INTRVN/ECO. PAGE 131 F2593
PRICE PAY MARKET INCOME

B66
UREN P.E.,EAST - WEST TRADE* A SYMPOSIUM. COM AGRI INT/ORG PRICE HABITAT RIGID/FLEX...GEOG INT/LAW ANTHOL NATO. PAGE 133 F2625
INT/TRADE BAL/PWR AFR CANADA

B66
WALTON S.D.,AMERICAN BUSINESS AND ITS ENVIRONMENT. USA+45 LAW CONSTN FINAN MARKET LOC/G EX/STRUC CT/SYS COST PRODUC...STAT 20. PAGE 143 F2813
PRICE PROFIT

B66
WESTON J.F.,THE SCOPE AND METHODOLOGY OF FINANCE. PLAN TEC/DEV CONTROL EFFICIENCY INCOME UTIL...MGT CONCPT MATH STAT TREND METH 20. PAGE 145 F2863
FINAN ECO/DEV POLICY PRICE

S66
FROMM G.,"RECENT MONETARY POLICY: AN ECONOMETRIC VIEW" USA+45 ECO/DEV INDUS PAY PRICE PRODUC ORD/FREE WEALTH...STAT 20 FED/RESERV. PAGE 45 F0869
ECOMETRIC FINAN POLICY SIMUL

N66
OECD,THE BALANCE OF PAYMENTS ADJUSTMENT PROCESS (PAMPHLET). EUR+WWI ECO/DEV FINAN CONSULT PLAN PROB/SOLV BUDGET CAP/ISM INT/TRADE PRICE CONTROL EQUILIB 20. PAGE 101 F1975
BAL/PAY ECO/TAC DIPLOM INT/ORG

B67
ALEXANDER G.J.,HONESTY AND COMPETITION: FALSE-ADVERTISING LAW AND POLICY UNDER FTC ADMINISTRATION. USA+45 INDUS NAT/G PRICE GP/REL 20 FTC. PAGE 3 F0058
EDU/PROP SERV/IND CONTROL DELIB/GP

B67
BERGMANN D KAUN B.,STRUCTURAL UNEMPLOYMENT IN THE UNITED STATES. USA+45 ECO/DEV PRICE ADMIN INGP/REL DEMAND EQUILIB WEALTH...MATH REGRESS STAT 20 NEGRO. PAGE 13 F0258
ECOMETRIC METH WORKER ECO/TAC

B67
HAGUE D.C.,PRICE FORMATION IN VARIOUS ECONOMIES; PROCEEDINGS OF A CONFERENCE HELD BY THE INTERNATIONAL ECONOMIC ASSOCIATION. WOR+45 FINAN MARKET PLAN CONFER COST...DECISION MATH PREDICT CHARTS SIMUL 20 INTL/ECON. PAGE 53 F1037
PRICE CAP/ISM SOCISM METH/COMP

B67
HOGAN J.,THE US BALANCE OF PAYMENTS AND CAPITAL FLOWS. MARKET INT/ORG ECO/TAC PRICE CONTROL WEALTH ...METH/COMP 20 EEC. PAGE 61 F1192
BAL/PAY FINAN DIPLOM INT/TRADE

B67
KREININ M.E.,ALTERNATIVE COMMERCIAL POLICIES - THEIR EFFECT ON THE AMERICAN ECONOMY. USA+45 LAW ECO/DEV MARKET INT/ORG DIPLOM ECO/TAC TARIFFS PRICE DEMAND WEALTH...QUANT EEC AFTA. PAGE 73 F1437
INT/TRADE BAL/PAY NAT/G POLICY

B67
MACAVOY P.W.,REGULATION OF TRANSPORT INNOVATION. ACT/RES ADJUD COST DEMAND...POLICY CHARTS 20. PAGE 83 F1621
DIST/IND CONTROL PRICE PROFIT

B67
PORWIT K.,CENTRAL PLANNING: EVALUATION OF VARIANTS. PRICE OPTIMAL PRODUC...DECISION MATH CHARTS SIMUL BIBLIOG MODELS 20. PAGE 107 F2106
PLAN MGT ECOMETRIC

B67
ROBINSON R.D.,INTERNATIONAL MANAGEMENT. LAW MARKET LABOR PRICE CONTROL COST DEMAND OWN PRODUC WEALTH 20. PAGE 113 F2225
T OP/RES MGT DIPLOM

B67
SCOTT J.C.,ANTITRUST AND TRADE REGULATION TODAY: 1967. USA+45 MARKET LG/CO DELIB/GP LEGIS CAP/ISM INT/TRADE TAX PRICE INGP/REL WEALTH 20 SUPREME/CT. PAGE 118 F2334
NAT/G INDUS CONTROL JURID

L67
BERNHARD R.C.,"COMPETITION IN LAW AND ECONOMICS." LAW PLAN PRICE CONTROL PRODUC PROFIT...METH/CNCPT IDEA/COMP GEN/LAWS 20. PAGE 14 F0265
MARKET POLICY NAT/G CT/SYS

S67
BROWN M.B.,"THE TRADE UNION QUESTION." UK INDUS OP/RES PRICE PROFIT 20. PAGE 19 F0371
WORKER LABOR GP/REL LAW

S67
DAVIS O.A.,"ON THE DISTINCTION BETWEEN PUBLIC AND PRIVATE GOODS." USA+45 COM/IND LG/CO NAT/G TV DEBATE PRICE ADMIN ROLE...MATH IDEA/COMP. PAGE 31 F0593
MARKET OWN CONCPT

S67
DEMUTH J.,"GE: PROFILE OF A CORPORATION." USA+45 USA-45 LABOR ACT/RES RATION EDU/PROP ADJUD CT/SYS FASCISM 20. PAGE 32 F0619
LG/CO CONSERVE PRICE

S67
HUTCHINGS R.,"THE ENDING OF UNEMPLOYMENT IN THE USSR" USSR PLAN ECO/TAC PRICE INGP/REL...GEOG STAT CHARTS 20 MIGRATION. PAGE 63 F1247
WORKER AGRI INDUS MARXISM

S67
KENNY L.M.,"THE AFTERMATH OF DEFEAT IN EGYPT." ISLAM ISRAEL UAR UK USA+45 USSR INDUS FORCES ECO/TAC PRICE COERCE WEAPON COST ATTIT. PAGE 70 F1378
WAR ECO/UNDEV DIPLOM POLICY

S67
MYERS S.,"TECHNOLOGY AND URBAN TRANSIT: THE ENORMOUS POTENTIAL OF BUS AND RAIL SYSTEMS." USA+45 FINAN LOC/G WORKER PLAN PROB/SOLV PRICE AUTOMAT MUNICH 20. PAGE 96 F1877
R+D TEC/DEV DIST/IND ACT/RES

S67
OLIVIER G.,"ASPECTS JURIDIQUES DE L'ADOPTION DU TRAITE CECA A LA CRISE CHARBONNIERE (SUITE ET FIN)" LAW DIST/IND PLAN DIPLOM RATION PRICE ADMIN COST DEMAND...POLICY CON/ANAL ECSC TREATY. PAGE 101 F1988
INT/TRADE INT/ORG EXTR/IND CONSTN

S67
ORAZEM F.,"THE NEW SOVIET PLAN FOR AGRICULTURE (1960-1970)" USSR WORKER CAP/ISM ECO/TAC PRICE OWN HABITAT MARXISM...CHARTS 20. PAGE 101 F1994
AGRI PLAN COM ECO/DEV

S67
SMALL A.H.,"THE EFFECT OF TARIFF REDUCTIONS ON US IMPORT VOLUME." USA+45 INT/ORG NAT/G DIPLOM CONFER DEMAND...POLICY INT/LAW STAT CHARTS GATT EEC. PAGE 123 F2424
TARIFFS INT/TRADE PRICE ECO/TAC

S67
VAN KLAVEREN J.,"DIE WIRTSCHAFTLICHEN AUSWIRKUNGEN DES SCHWARZEN TODES" GERMANY PRICE DEMAND PRODUC MUNICH 14/15 DEPRESSION. PAGE 140 F2762
HEALTH AGRI GEOG

S67
ZOETEWEIJ B.,"INCOME POLICIES ABROAD: AN INTERIM REPORT." NAT/G PROB/SOLV BARGAIN BUDGET PRICE RISK CENTRAL EFFICIENCY EQUILIB...MGT NAT/COMP 20. PAGE 150 F2967
METH/COMP INCOME POLICY LABOR

N67
US CONGRESS JT COMM ECO GOVT,BACKGROUND MATERIAL ON ECONOMY IN GOVERNMENT 1967 (PAMPHLET). WOR+45 ECO/DEV BARGAIN PRICE DEMAND OPTIMAL...STAT DEPT/DEFEN. PAGE 135 F2665
BUDGET COST MGT NAT/G

B75
JEVONS W.S.,MONEY AND THE MECHANISM OF EXCHANGE. INDUS MARKET DIPLOM COST EQUILIB WEALTH LAISSEZ ...GEN/LAWS 19 MONEY. PAGE 67 F1319
PRICE FINAN ECO/TAC POLICY

B92
ENGELS F.,THE CONDITION OF THE WORKING-CLASS IN ENGLAND (1848). UK INDUS LABOR PRICE CONTROL COST INCOME HEALTH MARXISM MUNICH 19. PAGE 38 F0733
WORKER WEALTH MARXIST CAP/ISM

B95
SELIGMAN E.R.A.,ESSAYS IN TAXATION. NEW/ZEALND PRUSSIA UK USA-45 MARKET LOC/G CREATE PRICE CONTROL INCOME OWN WEALTH...GOV/COMP METH/COMP 19. PAGE 119 F2349
TAX TARIFFS INDUS NAT/G

B98
MARSHALL A.,PRINCIPLES OF ECONOMICS. INDUS WORKER PRICE COST EQUILIB INCOME OPTIMAL PRODUC...TIME/SEQ METH RICARDO/D. PAGE 86 F1678
WEALTH GEN/LAWS MARKET

PRICING....SEE PRICE

PRIMARIES....ELECTORAL PRIMARIES

PRIME/MIN....PRIME MINISTER

PRINCE C.E. F2117

PRINCETN/U....PRINCETON UNIVERSITY

PRINCETON U INDUSTRIAL REL SEC F2118,F2119,F2120,F2121

PRISON....PRISONS; SEE ALSO PUB/INST

PRITCHETT C.H. F2122

PRIVACY....PRIVACY AND ITS INVASION

PRIVIL....PRIVILEGED, AS CONDITION

N19
ADMINISTRATIVE STAFF COLLEGE,THE ACCOUNTABILITY OF GOVERNMENT DEPARTMENTS (PAMPHLET) (REV. ED.). UK CONSTN FINAN NAT/G CONSULT ADMIN INGP/REL CONSEN PRIVIL 20 PARLIAMENT. PAGE 2 F0043
PARL/PROC ELITES SANCTION PROB/SOLV

B20
TAWNEY R.H.,THE ACQUISITIVE SOCIETY. STRATA WORKER PROB/SOLV CAP/ISM ECO/TAC CONTROL GP/REL OWN PRIVIL ATTIT ORD/FREE WEALTH 20. PAGE 128 F2536
INDUS SOCIETY PRODUC MORAL

B46
ERNST M.L.,THE FIRST FREEDOM. USA-45 CONSTN PRESS PRIVIL...CHARTS IDEA/COMP BIBLIOG 20 AMEND/I. PAGE 38 F0746
EDU/PROP COM/IND ORD/FREE CONTROL

B56
ABELS J.,THE TRUMAN SCANDALS. USA+45 USA-45 POL/PAR TAX LEGIT CT/SYS CHOOSE PRIVIL MORAL WEALTH 20 TRUMAN/HS PRESIDENT CONGRESS. PAGE 2 F0031
CRIME ADMIN CHIEF TRIBUTE

L57
SURREY S.S.,"THE CONGRESS AND THE TAX LOBBYIST - HOW SPECIAL TAX PROVISIONS GET ENACTED." LOBBY REPRESENT PRIVIL CONGRESS. PAGE 128 F2518
LEGIS TAX EX/STRUC ROLE

B66
LENSKI G.E.,POWER AND PRIVILEGE: A THEORY OF SOCIAL STRATIFICATION. SWEDEN UK UNIV USSR CULTURE ECO/UNDEV PRIVIL PWR...PHIL/SCI CONCPT CHARTS IDEA/COMP HYPO/EXP METH MARX/KARL. PAGE 78 F1525
SOC STRATA STRUCT SOCIETY

S67
AMERASINGHE C.F.,"SOME LEGAL PROBLEMS OF STATE TRADING IN SOUTHEAST ASIA." PROB/SOLV ADJUD CONTROL CT/SYS GP/REL 20. PAGE 5 F0084
INT/TRADE NAT/G INT/LAW PRIVIL

S67
CHADWELL J.T.,"ANTITRUST ASPECTS OF DEALER LICENSING AND FRANCHISING." ACT/RES LICENSE ADJUD CONTROL OWN. PAGE 23 F0439
LAW PRIVIL INDUS

S67
CRAIG A.,"ARGENTINA: THE LATEST REVOLUTION." ELITES NAT/G CHIEF FORCES ECO/TAC CIVMIL/REL GOV/REL EQUILIB PRIVIL 20 ARGEN. PAGE 28 F0550
ECO/UNDEV FINAN ATTIT REV

S67
SCOVILLE W.J.,"GOVERNMENT REGULATION AND GROWTH IN THE FRENCH PAPER INDUSTRY DURING THE EIGHTEENTH CENTURY." FRANCE MOD/EUR FINAN CAP/ISM TAX ADMIN CONTROL PRIVIL LAISSEZ...POLICY 18. PAGE 118 F2337
NAT/G PROC/MFG ECO/DEV INGP/REL

PRIVILEGE....SEE PRIVIL

PROB/SOLV....PROBLEM SOLVING

N
JOHNSON R.B.,FINANCING A SUBURBAN CITY. USA+45 TAX COST...SAMP/SIZ MUNICH 20 COL. PAGE 68 F1331
FINAN PAY PROB/SOLV

N
US LIBRARY OF CONGRESS,SELECTED AND ANNOTATED BIBLIOGRAPHY ON INDUSTRIAL PROBLEMS AND POLICIES IN WARTIME (PAMPHLET). WOR-45 CONSTRUC NAT/G PROB/SOLV COST DEMAND PRODUC 20. PAGE 137 F2707
BIBLIOG/A ECO/DEV INDUS WAR

N19
ADMINISTRATIVE STAFF COLLEGE,THE ACCOUNTABILITY OF GOVERNMENT DEPARTMENTS (PAMPHLET) (REV. ED.). UK CONSTN FINAN NAT/G CONSULT ADMIN INGP/REL CONSEN PRIVIL 20 PARLIAMENT. PAGE 2 F0043
PARL/PROC ELITES SANCTION PROB/SOLV

N19
ANDERSON J.,THE ORGANIZATION OF ECONOMIC STUDIES IN RELATION TO THE PROBLEMS OF GOVERNMENT (PAMPHLET). UK FINAN INDUS DELIB/GP PLAN PROB/SOLV ADMIN 20. PAGE 5 F0095
ECO/TAC ACT/RES NAT/G CENTRAL

N19
BASSIE V.L.,UNCERTAINTY IN FORECASTING AND POLICY FORMATION (PAMPHLET). UNIV MARKET ECO/TAC PRODUC ...POLICY DECISION MGT MATH CHARTS 20. PAGE 11 F0205
ECO/DEV FINAN PREDICT PROB/SOLV

N19
DOTSON A.,PRODUCTION PLANNING IN THE PATENT OFFICE (PAMPHLET). USA+45 DIST/IND PROB/SOLV PRODUC...MGT PHIL/SCI 20 BUR/BUDGET PATENT/OFF. PAGE 34 F0655 EFFICIENCY PLAN NAT/G ADMIN

N19
EAST KENTUCKY REGIONAL PLAN,PROGRAM 60: A DECADE OF ACTION FOR PROGRESS IN EASTERN KENTUCKY (PAMPHLET). USA+45 AGRI CONSTRUC INDUS CONSULT ACT/RES PROB/SOLV EDU/PROP GOV/REL HEALTH KENTUCKY. PAGE 35 F0689 REGION ADMIN PLAN ECO/UNDEV

N19
EAST KENTUCKY REGIONAL PLAN,PROGRAM 60 REPORT: ACTION FOR PORGRESS IN EASTERN KENTUCKY (PAMPHLET). USA+45 CONSTRUC INDUS ACT/RES PROB/SOLV EDU/PROP ADMIN GOV/REL KENTUCKY. PAGE 35 F0690 REGION PLAN ECO/UNDEV CONSULT

N19
HACKETT J.,ECONOMIC PLANNING IN FRANCE; ITS RELATION TO THE POLICIES OF THE DEVELOPED COUNTRIES OF WESTERN EUROPE (PAMPHLET). EUR+WWI FRANCE ECO/DEV PROB/SOLV CONTROL...POLICY 20 EUROPE/W. PAGE 52 F1026 ECO/TAC NAT/G PLAN INSPECT

N19
INTERNATIONAL LABOUR OFFICE,EMPLOYMENT, UNEMPLOYMENT AND LABOUR FORCE STATISTICS (PAMPHLET). EUR+WWI STRATA AGRI INDUS NAT/G PROB/SOLV PAY AGE SEX...SAMP NAT/COMP METH 20 ILO. PAGE 65 F1278 WORKER LABOR STAT ECO/DEV

N19
KRIESBERG M.,CANCELLATION OF THE RATION STAMPS (PAMPHLET). USA+45 USA-45 MARKET PROB/SOLV PRICE GOV/REL RIGID/FLEX 20 OPA. PAGE 73 F1439 RATION DECISION ADMIN NAT/G

N19
LUTZ F.A.,THE PROBLEM OF INTERNATIONAL LIQUIDITY AND THE MULTIPLECURRENCY STANDARD (PAMPHLET). WOR+45 MARKET INT/ORG PRICE BAL/PAY...NEW/IDEA METH/COMP BIBLIOG 20 IMF. PAGE 82 F1609 PROB/SOLV FINAN DIPLOM ECO/TAC

N19
MARSH J.F. JR.,THE FBI RETIREMENT BILL (PAMPHLET). USA+45 EX/STRUC WORKER PLAN PROB/SOLV BUDGET LEAD LOBBY PARL/PROC PERS/REL RIGID/FLEX...POLICY 20 FBI PRESIDENT BUR/BUDGET. PAGE 86 F1677 ADMIN NAT/G SENIOR GOV/REL

N19
MCCONNELL G.,THE STEEL SEIZURE OF 1952 (PAMPHLET). USA+45 FINAN INDUS PROC/MFG LG/CO EX/STRUC ADJUD CONTROL GP/REL ORD/FREE PWR 20 TRUMAN/HS PRESIDENT CONGRESS. PAGE 88 F1721 DELIB/GP LABOR PROB/SOLV NAT/G

N19
PALAMOUNTAIN JC J.R.,THE DOLCIN CASE AND THE FEDERAL TRADE COMMISSION (PAMPHLET). USA+45 LAW MARKET SERV/IND LG/CO NAT/G BIO/SOC 20 FTC. PAGE 103 F2018 ADJUD PROB/SOLV EDU/PROP HEALTH

N19
SAPIR H.M.,JAPAN, CHINA, AND THE WEST (PAMPHLET). AFR ASIA CHINA/COM PROB/SOLV GOV/REL 20 CHINJAP. PAGE 116 F2282 ECO/UNDEV INT/TRADE DECISION PLAN

N19
SILVERMAN C.,THE PRESIDENT'S ECONOMIC ADVISERS (PAMPHLET). USA+45 LAW ELITES ECO/DEV EX/STRUC ADMIN LEAD GOV/REL PERS/REL ROLE...POLICY DECISION 20 PRESIDENT CONGRESS EISNHWR/DD. PAGE 122 F2404 CONSULT PROB/SOLV NAT/G PLAN

B20
BUCK S.J.,THE AGRARIAN CRUSADE: A CHRONICLE OF THE FARMER IN POLITICS. USA-45 INDUS PROB/SOLV PWR WEALTH...GEOG CENSUS 19/20 GREENBACK GRANGE SILVER. PAGE 20 F0381 AGRI POPULISM VOL/ASSN POL/PAR

B20
MOREL E.D.,THE BLACK MAN'S BURDEN. AFR MOD/EUR AGRI EXTR/IND PROB/SOLV INT/TRADE ADMIN CONTROL COERCE DISCRIM...POLICY 19/20 NEGRO LEAGUE/NAT. PAGE 93 F1828 ORD/FREE CAP/ISM RACE/REL DOMIN

B20
TAWNEY R.H.,THE ACQUISITIVE SOCIETY. STRATA WORKER PROB/SOLV CAP/ISM ECO/TAC CONTROL GP/REL OWN PRIVIL ATTIT ORD/FREE WEALTH 20. PAGE 128 F2536 INDUS SOCIETY PRODUC MORAL

B28
FRANKFURTER F.,THE BUSINESS OF THE SUPREME COURT; A STUDY IN THE FEDERAL JUDICIAL SYSTEM. USA-45 CONSTN EX/STRUC PROB/SOLV GP/REL ATTIT PWR...POLICY JURID 18/20 SUPREME/CT CONGRESS. PAGE 43 F0848 CT/SYS ADJUD LAW FEDERAL

S30
CRAWFORD F.G.,"THE EXECUTIVE BUDGET DECISION IN NEW YORK." LEGIS EXEC PWR NEW/YORK. PAGE 28 F0552 LEAD BUDGET PROVS PROB/SOLV

B31
CROOK W.H.,THE GENERAL STRIKE: A STUDY OF LABOR'S TRAGIC WEAPON IN THEORY AND PRACTICE. BELGIUM FRANCE SWEDEN UK WOR-45 PROB/SOLV ECO/TAC DOMIN PWR ...POLICY TIME/SEQ NAT/COMP GEN/LAWS 19/20 STRIKE. PAGE 29 F0555 LABOR WORKER LG/CO BARGAIN

B31
LORWIN L.L.,ADVISORY ECONOMIC COUNCILS. EUR+WWI FRANCE GERMANY PROB/SOLV INGP/REL...CLASSIF GP/COMP. PAGE 82 F1601 CONSULT DELIB/GP ECO/TAC NAT/G

S35
BONNETT C.E.,"THE EVOLUTION OF BUSINESS GROUPINGS." ECO/TAC EDU/PROP PRICE LOBBY ORD/FREE. PAGE 16 F0315 VOL/ASSN GP/REL PROB/SOLV

B36
BELLOC H.,THE RESTORATION OF PROPERTY. UK STRATA NAT/G PROF/ORG DELIB/GP WORKER CREATE PROB/SOLV ECO/TAC PARTIC UTOPIA ORD/FREE SOCISM 20. PAGE 13 F0238 CONTROL MAJORIT CAP/ISM OWN

B37
DALTON J.E.,SUGAR: A CASE STUDY OF GOVERNMENT CONTROL. USA-45 AGRI PROC/MFG LG/CO LEGIS PROB/SOLV ECO/TAC GP/REL...CHARTS 19/20. PAGE 30 F0575 CONTROL NAT/G INDUS POLICY

B37
VON HAYEK F.A.,MONETARY NATIONALISM AND INTERNATIONAL STABILITY. WOR-45 ECO/DEV NAT/G PROB/SOLV INT/TRADE...POLICY CONCPT METH/COMP NAT/COMP 20. PAGE 142 F2792 ECO/TAC FINAN DIPLOM NAT/LISM

B38
DAVIES E.,"NATIONAL" CAPITALISM: THE GOVERNMENT'S RECORD AS PROTECTOR OF PRIVATE MONOPOLY. UK ELITES SOCIETY STRATA POL/PAR WORKER PROB/SOLV CONTROL SOCISM 20 MONOPOLY LABOR/PAR CHAMBRLN/N. PAGE 30 F0583 CAP/ISM NAT/G INDUS POLICY

B40
BLAISDELL D.C.,GOVERNMENT AND AGRICULTURE; THE GROWTH OF FEDERAL FARM AID. USA-45 MARKET PLAN PROB/SOLV TEC/DEV ECO/TAC GOV/REL ADJUST ATTIT ...CHARTS 20 DEPT/AGRI. PAGE 15 F0296 NAT/G GIVE AGRI DELIB/GP

B40
GAUS J.M.,PUBLIC ADMINISTRATION AND THE UNITED STATES DEPARTMENT OF AGRICULTURE. USA-45 STRUCT DIST/IND FINAN MARKET EX/STRUC PROB/SOLV GIVE PRODUC...POLICY GEOG CHARTS 20 DEPT/AGRI. PAGE 47 F0909 ADMIN AGRI DELIB/GP OP/RES

B41
DAUGHERTY C.R.,LABOR PROBLEMS IN AMERICAN INDUSTRY (5TH ED.). USA-45 SOCIETY OP/RES ECO/TAC...MGT PSY T 20. PAGE 30 F0581 LABOR INDUS GP/REL PROB/SOLV

B41
HANSEN A.H.,FISCAL POLICY AND BUSINESS CYCLES. UK INDUS PROB/SOLV DIPLOM INT/TRADE OPTIMAL...POLICY TIME/SEQ CHARTS 19/20. PAGE 54 F1062 FINAN PLAN ECO/TAC GOV/REL

S41
MUKERJEE R.,"POPULATION THEORY AND POLITICS (BMR)" WOR-45 NAT/G PLAN PROB/SOLV ECO/TAC INT/TRADE CONTROL WAR PEACE...CENSUS 20 BIRTH/CON RESOURCE/N. PAGE 94 F1854 GEOG OPTIMAL CONCPT

B42
DRUCKER P.F.,THE FUTURE OF INDUSTRIAL MAN; A CONSERVATIVE APPROACH. USA-45 LOC/G PLAN WAR CENTRAL RATIONAL TOTALISM ORD/FREE LAISSEZ ...PLURIST IDEA/COMP 19/20 HITLER/A. PAGE 34 F0664 INDUS SOCIETY REGION PROB/SOLV

B44
LANDAUER C.,THEORY OF NATIONAL ECONOMIC PLANNING. USA-45 INDUS MARKET WORKER PROB/SOLV DIPLOM RATION PRICE CONTROL WAR COST 20. PAGE 75 F1465 ECO/TAC PLAN NAT/G ECO/DEV

B46
DAVIES E.,NATIONAL ENTERPRISE: THE DEVELOPMENT OF THE PUBLIC CORPORATION. UK LG/CO EX/STRUC WORKER PROB/SOLV COST ATTIT SOCISM 20. PAGE 30 F0584 ADMIN NAT/G CONTROL INDUS

B47
BALDWIN H.W.,THE PRICE OF POWER. USA+45 FORCES PLAN NUC/PWR ADJUST COST ORD/FREE...POLICY PSY BIBLIOG 20. PAGE 9 F0165 PROB/SOLV PWR POPULISM PRICE

B47
WHITEHEAD T.N.,LEADERSHIP IN A FREE SOCIETY; A STUDY IN HUMAN RELATIONS BASED ON AN ANALYSIS OF PRESENT-DAY INDUSTRIAL CIVILIZATION. WOR-45 STRUCT R+D LABOR LG/CO SML/CO WORKER PLAN PROB/SOLV TEC/DEV DRIVE...MGT 20. PAGE 146 F2872 INDUS LEAD ORD/FREE SOCIETY

B48
HICKS J.R.,VALUE AND CAPITAL. FINAN PRICE EQUILIB INCOME PRODUC WEALTH...TIME/SEQ 20 MARSHALL/A PARETO/V SAMUELSN/P. PAGE 59 F1165 ECOMETRIC MATH DEMAND PROB/SOLV

B48
HOOVER E.M.,THE LOCATION OF ECONOMIC ACTIVITY. WOR+45 MARKET WORKER PROB/SOLV INT/TRADE ADMIN COST ...POLICY CHARTS T MUNICH 20. PAGE 62 F1211 HABITAT INDUS ECO/TAC GEOG

S48
NOURSE E.G.,"THE ROLE OF THE COUNCIL OF ECONOMIC ADVISERS." USA+45 DELIB/GP...DECISION PRESIDENT. PAGE 99 F1938 EX/STRUC CHIEF PROB/SOLV

B49
DE JOUVENEL B.,PROBLEMS OF SOCIALIST ENGLAND. AFR SOCISM

UK USSR BAL/PWR ECO/TAC INT/TRADE PRICE WAR BAL/PAY PEACE 20. PAGE 31 F0601 — NEW/LIB PROB/SOLV PLAN

B49
SELZNICK P.,TVA AND THE GRASS ROOTS: A STUDY IN THE SOCIOLOGY OF FORMAL ORGANIZATION. USA-45 EX/STRUC PROB/SOLV CONFER PARTIC ROUTINE PWR 20 TVA. PAGE 119 F2353 — REPRESENT LOBBY CONSULT

B50
ADORNO T.W.,THE AUTHORITARIAN PERSONALITY. STRATA SECT PROB/SOLV ECO/TAC DISCRIM ATTIT SEX...SOC INT CHARTS METH 20. PAGE 3 F0044 — AUTHORIT PERSON ALL/IDEOS SOCIETY

S50
DALTON M.,"CONFLICTS BETWEEN STAFF AND LINE MANAGERIAL OFFICERS" (BMR). USA+45 USA-45 ELITES LG/CO WORKER PROB/SOLV ADMIN EXEC EFFICIENCY PRODUC ...GP/COMP 20. PAGE 30 F0576 — MGT ATTIT GP/REL INDUS

S50
DREYFUS S.,"THE INDUSTRIAL DESIGNER AND THE BUSINESSMAN." SERV/IND PROB/SOLV ECO/TAC COST EFFICIENCY PROFIT RATIONAL...DECISION MGT. PAGE 34 F0662 — CONSULT INDUS PRODUC UTIL

B51
CHANDLER L.V.,INFLATION IN THE UNITED STATES 1940-1948. AFR NAT/G BUDGET PAY PRICE CONTROL WAR INCOME PRODUC...POLICY BIBLIOG 20. PAGE 23 F0448 — ECO/TAC FINAN PROB/SOLV WEALTH

B51
ROEPKE W.,THE PROBLEM OF ECONOMIC ORDER. WOR+45 SOCIETY PROB/SOLV CONTROL EFFICIENCY...CON/ANAL IDEA/COMP GEN/METH 20. PAGE 113 F2231 — ECO/TAC ORD/FREE MARKET PROC/MFG

L51
SUMMERS C.W.,"UNION POWERS AND WORKERS RIGHTS." WORKER PROB/SOLV ECO/TAC PARTIC INGP/REL PWR. PAGE 127 F2513 — LABOR CONSTN LAW REPRESENT

B52
AYRES C.E.,THE INDUSTRIAL ECONOMY. USA+45 FINAN MARKET NAT/G PUB/INST PLAN ECO/TAC TAX DEMAND INCOME...BIBLIOG/A 20. PAGE 8 F0146 — ECO/DEV INDUS FUT PROB/SOLV

B52
EGLE W.P.,ECONOMIC STABILIZATION: OBJECTIVES, RULES, AND MECHANISMS. UNIV FINAN PROB/SOLV CAP/ISM ECO/TAC CONTROL...IDEA/COMP 20. PAGE 36 F0709 — EQUILIB PLAN NAT/G ECO/DEV

B52
SACHS E.S.,THE CHOICE BEFORE SOUTH AFRICA. SOUTH/AFR AGRI EXTR/IND PROC/MFG PROB/SOLV ORD/FREE SOVEREIGN 20 NEGRO. PAGE 115 F2267 — NAT/LISM DISCRIM RACE/REL LABOR

B52
WU Y.,ECONOMIC WARFARE. MARKET PLAN PROB/SOLV FOR/AID CONTROL EFFICIENCY WEALTH...METH/COMP 20. PAGE 149 F2937 — ECO/TAC WAR INT/TRADE DIPLOM

S52
LEWIS V.B.,"TOWARD A THEORY OF BUDGETING" (BMR)" USA+45 NAT/G PLAN PROB/SOLV...IDEA/COMP METH 20 SUPREME/CT. PAGE 79 F1551 — BUDGET CONCPT CREATE

S53
SIMON H.A.,"BIRTH OF AN ORGANIZATION: THE ECONOMIC COOPERATION ADMINISTRATION." USA+45 PROB/SOLV INGP/REL EFFICIENCY 20. PAGE 122 F2408 — ADMIN EX/STRUC EXEC MGT

B54
BATTEN T.R.,PROBLEMS OF AFRICAN DEVELOPMENT (2ND ED.). AFR LAW SOCIETY SCHOOL ECO/TAC TAX...GEOG HEAL SOC 20. PAGE 11 F0211 — ECO/UNDEV AGRI LOC/G PROB/SOLV

B55
BERNSTEIN M.H.,REGULATING BUSINESS BY INDEPENDENT COMMISSION. USA+45 USA-45 LG/CO CHIEF LEGIS PROB/SOLV ADJUD SANCTION GP/REL ATTIT...TIME/SEQ 19/20 MONOPOLY PRESIDENT CONGRESS. PAGE 14 F0268 — DELIB/GP CONTROL CONSULT

B55
FOGARTY M.P.,ECONOMIC CONTROL. FUT UK ECO/DEV FINAN CONSULT INT/TRADE...CHARTS BIBLIOG/A 20. PAGE 42 F0819 — ECO/TAC NAT/G CONTROL PROB/SOLV

B55
HELANDER S.,DAS AUTARKIEPROBLEM IN DER WELTWIRTSCHAFT. PROB/SOLV BAL/PWR BARGAIN CAP/ISM ECO/TAC SOVEREIGN FOR/TRADE 20. PAGE 58 F1144 — NAT/COMP COLONIAL DIPLOM

B55
SMITHIES A.,THE BUDGETARY PROCESS IN THE UNITED STATES. AFR ECO/DEV AGRI EX/STRUC FORCES LEGIS PROB/SOLV TAX ROUTINE EFFICIENCY...MGT CONGRESS PRESIDENT. PAGE 124 F2436 — NAT/G ADMIN BUDGET GOV/REL

S55
DIESING P.,"NONECONOMIC DECISION-MAKING" (BMR)" PROB/SOLV GP/REL ORD/FREE...STAT METH/COMP SIMUL 20. PAGE 33 F0638 — DECISION METH EFFICIENCY SOC

B56
ATOMIC INDUSTRIAL FORUM,PUBLIC RELATIONS FOR THE ATOMIC INDUSTRY. WOR+45 PLAN PROB/SOLV EDU/PROP PRESS CONFER...AUD/VIS ANTHOL 20. PAGE 7 F0135 — NUC/PWR INDUS GP/REL ATTIT

B56
BURKHEAD J.,GOVERNMENT BUDGETING. ECO/DEV PROB/SOLV ECO/TAC ADMIN ROUTINE GOV/REL EFFICIENCY...DECISION MGT. PAGE 20 F0388 — BUDGET NAT/G PROVS EX/STRUC

B56
REDFORD E.S.,PUBLIC ADMINISTRATION AND POLICY FORMATION: STUDIES IN OIL, GAS, BANKING, RIVER DEVELOPMENT AND CORPORATE INVESTIGATIONS. USA+45 CLIENT NAT/G ADMIN LOBBY REPRESENT GOV/REL INGP/REL 20. PAGE 110 F2167 — EX/STRUC PROB/SOLV CONTROL EXEC

L56
SCHELLING T.C.,"AN ESSAY ON BARGAINING" (BMR)" OP/RES PROB/SOLV PRICE CHOOSE PWR...DECISION MODELS 20. PAGE 116 F2294 — BARGAIN MARKET ECO/TAC GAME

S56
KNAPP D.C.,"CONGRESSIONAL CONTROL OF AGRICULTURAL CONSERVATION POLICY: A CASE STUDY OF THE APPROPRIATIONS PROCESS." DELIB/GP PLAN PROB/SOLV CONFER PARL/PROC...POLICY INT CONGRESS. PAGE 72 F1411 — LEGIS AGRI BUDGET CONTROL

S56
LANDAUER J.D.,"PROFESSIONAL CONSULTANTS: A NEW FACTOR IN REAL ESTATE." USA+45 PROB/SOLV ECO/TAC PERS/REL DEMAND EFFICIENCY DECISION. PAGE 75 F1467 — CONSULT CONSTRUC CLIENT

S56
MYERS C.A.,"LINE AND STAFF IN INDUSTRIAL RELATIONS." INDUS LABOR GP/REL PWR...MGT INT. PAGE 96 F1876 — ROLE PROB/SOLV ADMIN CONSULT

B57
ASHER R.E.,THE UNITED NATIONS AND ECONOMIC AND SOCIAL COOPERATION. ECO/UNDEV COM/IND DIST/IND FINAN PLAN PROB/SOLV INT/TRADE TASK WEALTH...SOC 20 UN. PAGE 7 F0129 — INT/ORG DIPLOM FOR/AID

B57
BAUER P.T.,THE ECONOMICS OF UNDERDEVELOPED COUNTRIES. WOR+45 AGRI FINAN INDUS PROC/MFG WORKER CAP/ISM PAY PRICE INCOME MARXISM...METH/COMP 20 RESOURCE/N. PAGE 11 F0213 — ECO/UNDEV ECO/TAC PROB/SOLV NAT/G

B57
CLARK J.M.,ECONOMIC INSTITUTIONS AND HUMAN WELFARE. USA+45 SOCIETY ECO/DEV NAT/G WORKER PLAN PROB/SOLV CAP/ISM CONTROL...POLICY 20. PAGE 25 F0482 — ECO/TAC ORD/FREE WEALTH

B57
HALD M.,A SELECTED BIBLIOGRAPHY ON ECONOMIC DEVELOPMENT AND FOREIGN AID. INT/ORG PROB/SOLV ...SOC 20. PAGE 53 F1040 — BIBLIOG ECO/UNDEV TEC/DEV FOR/AID

B57
MURDESHWAR A.K.,ADMINISTRATIVE PROBLEMS RELATING TO NATIONALISATION: WITH SPECIAL REFERENCE TO INDIAN STATE ENTERPRISES. CZECHOSLVK FRANCE INDIA UK USA+45 LEGIS WORKER PROB/SOLV BUDGET PRICE CONTROL ...MGT GEN/LAWS 20 PARLIAMENT. PAGE 95 F1863 — NAT/G OWN INDUS ADMIN

B57
THOMAS R.G.,OUR MODERN BANKING AND MONETARY SYSTEM (3RD ED.). AFR USA+45 USA-45 ACT/RES PLAN PROB/SOLV INT/TRADE PRICE WAR BAL/PAY INCOME...POLICY METH/CNCPT 20 DEPRESSION. PAGE 130 F2563 — FINAN SERV/IND ECO/TAC

S57
ANSHEN M.,"BUSINESS, LAWYERS, AND ECONOMISTS." PROB/SOLV ECO/TAC CONFER PROFIT RIGID/FLEX OBJECTIVE...MGT GP/COMP. PAGE 6 F0106 — INDUS CONSULT ROUTINE EFFICIENCY

S57
DETAMBEL M.H.,"PROBABILITY AND WORK AS DETERMINERS OF MULTICHOICE BEHAVIOR." PLAN TASK EFFICIENCY ...DECISION GAME. PAGE 32 F0622 — HYPO/EXP PROB/SOLV GEN/LAWS PROBABIL

S57
DUBIN R.,"POWER AND UNION-MANAGEMENT RELATIONS." PROB/SOLV ADJUD ROUTINE ATTIT ORD/FREE...MGT STERTYP. PAGE 34 F0668 — PWR LABOR BARGAIN GP/REL

S57
LEWIS E.G.,"PARLIAMENTARY CONTROL OF NATIONALIZED INDUSTRY IN FRANCE." FRANCE NAT/G DELIB/GP ACT/RES PLAN PROB/SOLV ECO/TAC DOMIN CENTRAL. PAGE 79 F1547 — PWR LEGIS INDUS CONTROL

S57
VERNON R.,"PRODUCTION AND DISTRIBUTION IN THE LARGE METROPOLIS" (BMR)" USA+45 PROC/MFG ECO/TAC HABITAT ...CENSUS TREND MUNICH 20. PAGE 141 F2779 — PRODUC DIST/IND PROB/SOLV

B58
DEFENSE AGAINST INFLATION. USA+45 LEGIS WORKER TAX PRICE DEMAND INCOME PRODUC...POLICY TREND METH/COMP 20 GOLD/STAND. PAGE 1 F0012 — ECO/TAC EQUILIB WEALTH PROB/SOLV

B58
CLAUNCH J.M.,THE PROBLEM OF GOVERNMENT IN METROPOLITAN AREAS. CULTURE INDUS POL/PAR PLAN REGION GP/REL...CENSUS ANTHOL MUNICH 20. PAGE 25 F0486 PROB/SOLV SOC

B58
DUESENBERRY J.S.,BUSINESS CYCLES AND ECONOMIC GROWTH. USA+45 PROB/SOLV PAY PRICE...CONCPT MATH CHARTS IDEA/COMP 20 DEPRESSION KEYNES/JM. PAGE 34 F0672 FINAN ECO/DEV ECO/TAC INCOME

B58
HANCE W.A.,AFRICAN ECONOMIC DEVELOPMENT. AGRI DIST/IND INDUS R+D ACT/RES PLAN CAP/ISM FOR/AID ...GOV/COMP BIBLIOG 20. PAGE 54 F1058 AFR ECO/UNDEV PROB/SOLV TEC/DEV

B58
INDIAN INST OF PUBLIC ADMIN,IMPROVING CITY GOVERNMENT. INDIA ECO/UNDEV PLAN BUDGET PARTIC GP/REL MUNICH 20. PAGE 64 F1263 LOC/G PROB/SOLV ADMIN

B58
JACOBSSON P.,SOME MONETARY PROBLEMS, INTERNATIONAL AND NATIONAL. WOR+45 WOR-45 ECO/DEV FORCES WORKER PROB/SOLV DIPLOM INT/TRADE...ANTHOL 20. PAGE 66 F1299 FINAN PLAN ECO/TAC NAT/COMP

B58
TILLION G.,ALGERIA: THE REALITIES. ALGERIA FRANCE ISLAM CULTURE STRATA PROB/SOLV DOMIN REV NAT/LISM WEALTH MARXISM...GEOG 20. PAGE 130 F2573 ECO/UNDEV SOC COLONIAL DIPLOM

B58
WARNER A.W.,CONCEPTS AND CASES IN ECONOMIC ANALYSIS. PROB/SOLV BARGAIN CONTROL INCOME PRODUC ...ECOMETRIC MGT CONCPT CLASSIF CHARTS 20 KEYNES/JM. PAGE 143 F2820 ECO/TAC DEMAND EQUILIB COST

L58
CYERT R.M.,"THE ROLE OF EXPECTATIONS IN BUSINESS DECISION-MAKING." PROB/SOLV PRICE RIGID/FLEX. PAGE 29 F0566 LG/CO DECISION ROUTINE EXEC

L58
FORRESTER J.W.,"INDUSTRIAL DYNAMICS* A MAJOR BREAKTHROUGH FOR DECISION MAKERS." COMPUTER OP/RES ...DECISION CONCPT NEW/IDEA. PAGE 42 F0830 INDUS ACT/RES MGT PROB/SOLV

S58
FOLDES L.,"UNCERTAINTY, PROBABILITY AND POTENTIAL SURPRISE." MARKET PROB/SOLV RISK PERSON...DECISION MGT HYPO/EXP GAME. PAGE 42 F0820 PROBABIL ADMIN ROUTINE

S58
MANSFIELD E.,"A STUDY OF DECISION-MAKING WITHIN THE FIRM." LG/CO WORKER INGP/REL COST EFFICIENCY PRODUC ...CHARTS 20. PAGE 85 F1658 OP/RES PROB/SOLV AUTOMAT ROUTINE

S58
SCHULZE R.O.,"THE ROLE OF ECONOMIC DOMINANTS IN COMMUNITY POWER STRUCTURE." ECO/TAC ROUTINE ATTIT OBJECTIVE...SOC RECORD CENSUS. PAGE 118 F2319 SOCIETY STRUCT PROB/SOLV

N58
EUROPEAN COMM ECO-SOC PROG,EUROPEAN BUSINESS CYCLE POLICY (PAMPHLET). AFR EUR+WWI MARKET WORKER DIPLOM PRICE BAL/PAY 20 EUROPE. PAGE 39 F0754 ECO/DEV FINAN ECO/TAC PROB/SOLV

B59
BONNETT C.E.,LABOR-MANAGEMENT RELATIONS. USA+45 OP/RES PROB/SOLV EDU/PROP...AUD/VIS CHARTS 20. PAGE 16 F0317 MGT LABOR INDUS GP/REL

B59
CHECCHI V.,HONDURAS: A PROBLEM IN ECONOMIC DEVELOPMENT. HONDURAS AGRI FINAN INDUS LABOR WORKER INT/TRADE EDU/PROP PRICE HEALTH...GEOG CHARTS BIBLIOG 20. PAGE 24 F0458 ECO/UNDEV ECO/TAC PROB/SOLV PLAN

B59
CONTY J.M.,PSYCHOLOGIE DE LA DECISION....PSY GAME 20. PAGE 27 F0528 DECISION PROB/SOLV OP/RES METH/COMP

B59
FELS R.,AMERICAN BUSINESS CYCLES 1865-1897. USA+45 ECO/DEV LG/CO SML/CO PROB/SOLV TEC/DEV CAP/ISM INT/TRADE DEMAND...POLICY CHARTS METH 19 DEPRESSION. PAGE 40 F0782 FINAN INDUS TREND ECO/TAC

B59
HARVARD UNIVERSITY LAW SCHOOL,INTERNATIONAL PROBLEMS OF FINANCIAL PROTECTION AGAINST NUCLEAR RISK. WOR+45 NAT/G DELIB/GP PROB/SOLV DIPLOM CONTROL ATTIT...POLICY INT/LAW MATH 20. PAGE 56 F1105 NUC/PWR ADJUD INDUS FINAN

B59
SELIGSOHN I.J.,"USING COMPUTER SERVICES IN SMALL BUSINESS" MANAGEMENT AIDS FOR SMALL MANUFACTURERS 109 (PAMPHLET). DIST/IND MARKET PROC/MFG COST EFFICIENCY PRODUC...DECISION IDEA/COMP. PAGE 119 F2350 SML/CO COMPUTER MGT PROB/SOLV

B59
THE BROOKINGS INSTITUTION,ECONOMICS AND THE POLICY MAKER. USA+45 CREATE...ANTHOL 20. PAGE 129 F2549 ELITES ECO/TAC PROB/SOLV ECO/DEV

B59
U OF MICHIGAN LAW SCHOOL,ATOMS AND THE LAW. USA+45 PROVS WORKER PROB/SOLV DIPLOM ADMIN GOV/REL ANTHOL. PAGE 132 F2596 NUC/PWR NAT/G CONTROL LAW

B59
VERNEY D.V.,PUBLIC ENTERPRISE IN SWEDEN. FUT SWEDEN UK INDUS POL/PAR LEGIS PROB/SOLV CAP/ISM INT/TRADE CONTROL SOCISM...MGT CONCPT NAT/COMP 20 SOCDEM/PAR CIVIL/SERV. PAGE 141 F2778 ECO/DEV POLICY LG/CO NAT/G

B59
WIBBERLEY G.P.,AGRICULTURE AND URBAN GROWTH. UK USA+45 ECO/DEV FINAN PROB/SOLV INT/TRADE COST ...GEOG STAT CHARTS METH/COMP HYPO/EXP METH MUNICH 20. PAGE 146 F2876 AGRI PLAN

L59
OBERER W.E.,"VOLUNTARY IMPARTIAL REVIEW OF LABOR: SOME REFLECTIONS." DELIB/GP LEGIS PROB/SOLV ADJUD CONTROL COERCE PWR PLURISM POLICY. PAGE 100 F1960 LABOR LAW PARTIC INGP/REL

L59
SIMON H.A.,"THEORIES OF DECISION-MAKING IN ECONOMICS AND BEHAVIORAL SCIENCE" (BMR)" MARKET BARGAIN UTIL DRIVE...DECISION MGT PROBABIL HYPO/EXP SIMUL 20 BEHAVIORSM. PAGE 122 F2409 PSY GEN/LAWS PROB/SOLV

L59
WURFEL D.,"FOREIGN AID AND SOCIAL REFORM IN POLITICAL DEVELOPMENT" (BMR)" PHILIPPINE USA+45 WOR+45 SOCIETY POL/PAR ACT/RES TEC/DEV DIPLOM 20. PAGE 149 F2943 FOR/AID PROB/SOLV ECO/TAC ECO/UNDEV

S59
ALLEN G.,"NATIONAL FARMERS UNION AS A PRESSURE GROUP: II." UK ECO/DEV MARKET POL/PAR DELIB/GP PROB/SOLV ECO/TAC LOBBY INCOME...POLICY METH/COMP 19/20 NAT/FARMER. PAGE 4 F0069 DIST/IND AGRI PROF/ORG TREND

S59
DUNNING J.H.,"NON-PECUNIARY ELEMENTS AND BUSINESS BEHAVIOUR." PLAN PROB/SOLV COST...METH/CNCPT CLASSIF QUANT STAT. PAGE 35 F0681 DECISION DRIVE PRODUC PRICE

S59
HARING J.E.,"UTILITY THEORY, DECISION THEORY, AND PROFIT MAXIMIZATION." PROB/SOLV GAMBLE UTIL ...DECISION CHARTS IDEA/COMP HYPO/EXP SIMUL GEN/METH. PAGE 55 F1083 PROBABIL RISK GAME

S59
TEITSWORTH C.S.,"GROWING ROLE OF THE COMPANY ECONOMIST." USA+45 PLAN PROB/SOLV CAP/ISM ECO/TAC ADMIN ATTIT MGT. PAGE 129 F2541 INDUS CONSULT UTIL DECISION

C59
FAINSOD M.,"GOVERNMENT AND THE AMERICAN ECONOMY." USA+45 USA-45 INDUS LABOR OP/RES PROB/SOLV ECO/TAC CONTROL...CHARTS BIBLIOG T 20. PAGE 39 F0760 CONSTN ECO/DEV CAP/ISM NAT/G

N59
CHAMBER OF COMMERCE OF USA,ECONOMIC LESSONS OF POSTWAR RECESSIONS (PAMPHLET). AFR USA+45 LAW LEGIS WORKER TAX...CHARTS 20 CONGRESS FED/RESERV. PAGE 23 F0440 ECO/DEV PROB/SOLV FINAN ECO/TAC

B60
ATOMIC INDUSTRIAL FORUM,ATOMS FOR INDUSTRY: WORLD FORUM. WOR+45 FINAN COST UTIL...JURID ANTHOL 20. PAGE 7 F0137 NUC/PWR INDUS PLAN PROB/SOLV

B60
FINKLE J.L.,THE PRESIDENT MAKES A DECISION: A STUDY OF DIXON-YATES. OP/RES PROB/SOLV BUDGET ADMIN GOV/REL...POLICY BIBLIOG/A 20 PRESIDENT. PAGE 41 F0799 DECISION CHIEF PWR POL/PAR

B60
GONZALEZ NAVARRO M.,LA COLONIZACION EN MEXICO, 1877-1910. AGRI NAT/G PLAN PROB/SOLV INCOME ...POLICY JURID CENSUS 19/20 MEXIC/AMER MIGRATION. PAGE 48 F0947 ECO/UNDEV GEOG HABITAT COLONIAL

B60
HUGHES J.,NATIONALISED INDUSTRIES IN THE MIXED ECONOMY (PAMPHLET). FINAN PROB/SOLV CAP/ISM OWN ...SOCIALIST STAT METH/COMP 20. PAGE 63 F1233 SOCISM LG/CO GOV/REL ECO/DEV

B60
KENEN P.B.,BRITISH MONETARY POLICY AND THE BALANCE OF PAYMENTS 1951-57. UK PLAN BUDGET ECO/TAC INT/TRADE PAY PRICE COST ATTIT 20. PAGE 70 F1377 BAL/PAY PROB/SOLV FINAN NAT/G

B60
KILLOUGH H.B.,INTERNATIONAL ECONOMICS. PLAN PROB/SOLV FOR/AID TARIFFS CONTROL BAL/PAY...POLICY CHARTS T 20. PAGE 71 F1388 CONCPT ECO/UNDEV INT/ORG INT/TRADE

B60
MORRIS W.T.,ENGINEERING ECONOMY. AUTOMAT RISK RATIONAL...PROBABIL STAT CHARTS GAME SIMUL BIBLIOG OP/RES DECISION

T 20. PAGE 94 F1838 MGT
PROB/SOLV
B60

PETERSON W.C.,THE WELFARE STATE IN FRANCE. EUR+WWI NEW/LIB
FRANCE FUT STRATA PROB/SOLV TAX GIVE RECEIVE INCOME ECO/TAC
ORD/FREE PWR...CHARTS 20. PAGE 105 F2070 WEALTH
NAT/G
B60

POOLEY B.J.,THE EVOLUTION OF BRITISH PLANNING PLAN
LEGISLATION. UK ECO/DEV LOC/G CONSULT DELIB/GP LEGIS
ADMIN MUNICH 20 URBAN/RNWL. PAGE 107 F2104 PROB/SOLV
B60

RICHARDSON G.B.,INFORMATION AND INVESTMENT. PLAN ECO/DEV
PROB/SOLV CAP/ISM ECO/TAC KNOWL...CONCPT 20 MONEY. EQUILIB
PAGE 111 F2184 FINAN
PHIL/SCI
B60

SIEGEL S.,BARGAINING AND GROUP DECISION-MAKING: DECISION
EXPERIMENTS IN BILATERAL MONOPOLY. EFFICIENCY...PSY PERS/REL
CHARTS. PAGE 122 F2397 PROB/SOLV
BARGAIN
B60

SILK L.S.,THE RESEARCH REVOLUTION. USA+45 FINAN ECO/DEV
CAP/ISM ECO/TAC PRICE EQUILIB PRODUC...STAT TREND R+D
CHARTS. PAGE 122 F2402 TEC/DEV
PROB/SOLV
B60

STANFORD RESEARCH INSTITUTE,AFRICAN DEVELOPMENT: A FOR/AID
TEST FOR INTERNATIONAL COOPERATION. AFR USA+45 ECO/UNDEV
WOR+45 FINAN INT/ORG PLAN PROB/SOLV ECO/TAC ATTIT
INT/TRADE ADMIN...CHARTS 20. PAGE 125 F2467 DIPLOM
B60

THOMPSON V.A.,THE REGULATORY PROCESS IN OPA EX/STRUC
RATIONING. USA-45 CLIENT PROB/SOLV ADMIN LOBBY GOV/REL
REPRESENT 20. PAGE 130 F2566 INGP/REL
B60

US SENATE COMM ON COMMERCE,URBAN MASS DIST/IND
TRANSPORTATION. FUT USA+45 AIR ECO/DEV FINAN LOC/G PLAN
LEGIS CREATE PROB/SOLV TEC/DEV MUNICH 20 PUB/TRANS. NAT/G
PAGE 139 F2732 LAW
S60

MANN S.Z.,"POLICY FORMULATION IN THE EXECUTIVE EXEC
BRANCH: THE TAFT-HARTLEY EXPERIENCE." USA+45 LABOR GOV/REL
CHIEF INGP/REL 20 NLRB. PAGE 85 F1656 EX/STRUC
PROB/SOLV
N60

ERDMAN P.E.,COMMON MARKETS AND FREE TRADE AREAS TREND
(PAMPHLET). USA+45 MARKET INT/ORG TEC/DEV DIPLOM PROB/SOLV
UTIL...CON/ANAL CHARTS BIBLIOG 20 EEC OEEC. PAGE 38 INT/TRADE
F0743 ECO/DEV
B61

BUSSCHAU W.J.,GOLD AND INTERNATIONAL LIQUIDITY. AFR FINAN
WOR+45 PRICE EQUILIB WEALTH...CHARTS 20. PAGE 20 DIPLOM
F0396 PROB/SOLV
B61

DELEFORTRIE-SOU N.,LES DIRIGEANTS DE L'INDUSTRIE INDUS
FRANCAISE. FRANCE CULTURE ELITES PROB/SOLV STRATA
...DECISION STAT CHARTS 20. PAGE 32 F0613 TOP/EX
LEAD
B61

DOIG J.W.,THE POLITICS OF METROPOLITAN PROB/SOLV
TRANSPORTATION. DELIB/GP WORKER DIPLOM TASK STRATA
EFFICIENCY UTIL...CHARTS BIBLIOG MUNICH 20 NEW/YORK DIST/IND
NEW/JERSEY PUB/TRANS RAILROAD. PAGE 34 F0652
B61

GREY A.L.,ECONOMIC ISSUES AND POLICIES; READINGS IN ECO/TAC
INTRODUCTORY ECONOMICS (2ND ED.). WOR+45 ECO/UNDEV PROB/SOLV
FINAN MARKET LABOR LG/CO INT/TRADE BAL/PAY WEALTH METH/COMP
...ANTHOL T. PAGE 51 F0996
B61

JAVITS B.A.,THE PEACE BY INVESTMENT CORPORATION. ECO/UNDEV
WOR+45 NAT/G LEGIS PROB/SOLV PERS/REL WEALTH DIPLOM
...POLICY 20. PAGE 66 F1307 FOR/AID
PEACE
B61

MEZERIK A.G.,ECONOMIC DEVELOPMENT AIDS FOR ECO/UNDEV
UNDERDEVELOPED COUNTRIES. WOR+45 FINAN LEGIS INT/ORG
PROB/SOLV TEC/DEV DIPLOM FOR/AID GIVE TASK WAR 20 WEALTH
UN. PAGE 91 F1776 PLAN
B61

NEW JERSEY LEGISLATURE-SENATE,PUBLIC HEARINGS LEGIS
BEFORE COMMITTEE ON REVISION AND AMENDMENT OF LAWS INDUS
ON SENATE BILL NO. 8. USA+45 FINAN PROVS WORKER PROB/SOLV
ACT/RES PLAN BUDGET TAX CRIME...IDEA/COMP MUNICH 20
NEW/JERSEY URBAN/RNWL. PAGE 98 F1919
B61

PROUDHON P.J.,LA GUERRE ET LA PAIX (2 VOLS.). UNIV WAR
STRATA PROB/SOLV EQUILIB INCOME ATTIT...CONCPT 19. PEACE
PAGE 108 F2125 WEALTH
B61

THEOBALD R.,THE CHALLENGE OF ABUNDANCE. USA+45 WELF/ST
WOR+45 MARKET DIPLOM FOR/AID REV PRODUC UTOPIA ECO/UNDEV
SUPEGO...POLICY TREND BIBLIOG/A 20. PAGE 129 F2554 PROB/SOLV
ECO/TAC
B61

TRIFFIN R.,GOLD AND THE DOLLAR CRISIS: THE FUTURE FINAN
OF CONVERTIBILITY. AFR USA+45 USA-45 INT/ORG ECO/DEV
PROB/SOLV BUDGET INT/TRADE PRICE...STAT CHARTS ECO/TAC
19/20. PAGE 131 F2588 BAL/PAY
B61

US CONGRESS JOINT ECO COMM,INTERNATIONAL PAYMENTS BAL/PAY
IMBALANCES AND NEED FOR STRENGTHENING INTERNATIONAL INT/ORG
FINANCIAL ARRANGEMENTS. USA+45 WOR+45 DELIB/GP FINAN
DIPLOM INT/TRADE...CHARTS 20 CONGRESS OEEC. PROB/SOLV
PAGE 134 F2651
B61

WAGLE S.S.,TECHNIQUE OF PLANNING FOR ACCELERATED ECO/UNDEV
ECONOMIC GROWTH OF UNDERDEVELOPED COUNTRIES. WOR+45 PLAN
ACT/RES PROB/SOLV RATION BAL/PAY DEMAND INCOME 20. INDUS
PAGE 142 F2798 ECO/TAC
S61

ANDREWS R.B.,"URBAN ECONOMICS: AN APPRAISAL OF PHIL/SCI
PROGRESS." LOC/G PROB/SOLV TEC/DEV...CONCPT ECOMETRIC
OBS/ENVIR METH/COMP HYPO/EXP SOC/EXP SIMUL GEN/METH
METH MUNICH 20. PAGE 5 F0102
S61

BRAFF A.J.,"WAGE-PRICE POLICIES UNDER PUBLIC ATTIT
PRESSURE." USA+45 EX/STRUC LOBBY REPRESENT PWR 20. PARTIC
PAGE 17 F0335 PROB/SOLV
S61

CYERT R.M.,"TWO EXPERIMENTS ON BIAS AND CONFLICT IN LAB/EXP
ORGANIZATIONAL ESTIMATION." WORKER PROB/SOLV ROUTINE
EFFICIENCY...MGT PSY STAT CHARTS. PAGE 29 F0568 ADMIN
DECISION
S61

HIRSHLEIFER J.,"THE BAYESIAN APPROACH TO DECISION
STATISTICAL DECISION: AN EXPOSITION." OP/RES GAME
PROB/SOLV UTIL...PROBABIL CHARTS IDEA/COMP HYPO/EXP SIMUL
20. PAGE 60 F1178 STAT
S61

HOSELITZ B.F.,"ECONOMIC DEVELOPMENT AND POLITICAL ECO/UNDEV
STABILITY IN INDIA" INDIA NAT/G GP/REL...POLICY 20. GEN/LAWS
PAGE 62 F1222 PROB/SOLV
S61

NYANZI S.,"THE EAST AFRICAN MARKET: FOR BETTER OF ECO/TAC
FOR WORSE." AFR TANZANIA UGANDA PROB/SOLV TARIFFS ECO/UNDEV
TAX BAL/PAY. PAGE 99 F1947 INT/ORG
INT/TRADE
B62

BROOKINGS INSTITUTION,DEVELOPMENT OF THE EMERGING ECO/UNDEV
COUNTRIES; AN AGENDA FOR RESEARCH. WOR+45 AGRI R+D
TEC/DEV FOR/AID EDU/PROP ADJUST HABITAT KNOWL...PSY SOCIETY
SOC ANTHOL 20 THIRD/WRLD. PAGE 19 F0362 PROB/SOLV
B62

COLLIER A.T.,MANAGEMENT, MEN, AND VALUES. INDUS MGT
FACE/GP EX/STRUC PLAN PROB/SOLV DEBATE SENIOR ADMIN ATTIT
PROFIT PERSON...PSY SOC 20. PAGE 26 F0505 PERS/REL
DECISION
B62

CONGRES ECONOMISTES LANG FRAN,MONNAIE ET EXPANSION. FINAN
AFR FRANCE PROB/SOLV BUDGET CENTRAL COST OPTIMAL PLAN
PRODUC WEALTH 20. PAGE 27 F0524 EUR+WWI
B62

FERBER R.,RESEARCH METHODS IN ECONOMICS AND ACT/RES
BUSINESS. AFR ECO/DEV FINAN MARKET LG/CO SML/CO PROB/SOLV
CONSULT CONTROL COST...STAT METH/COMP 20. PAGE 40 ECO/TAC
F0783 MGT
B62

LEVENSTEIN A.,WHY PEOPLE WORK; CHANGING INCENTIVES DRIVE
IN A TROUBLED WORLD. USA+45 SOCIETY PROB/SOLV WORKER
TEC/DEV EDU/PROP ADJUST...CENSUS BIBLIOG 20. ECO/DEV
PAGE 79 F1538 ANOMIE
B62

LICHFIELD N.,COST-BENEFIT ANALYSIS IN URBAN PLAN
REDEVELOPMENT. CONSTRUC LOC/G NEIGH ACT/RES COST
PROB/SOLV TEC/DEV BUDGET TAX...DECISION STAT CHARTS GOV/REL
SOC/EXP MUNICH 20. PAGE 80 F1558
B62

LUTZ F.A.,THE PROBLEM OF INTERNATIONAL ECONOMIC DIPLOM
EQUILIBRIUM. FINAN PRODUC WEALTH 20 MONEY. PAGE 82 EQUILIB
F1611 BAL/PAY
PROB/SOLV
B62

MEANS G.C.,PRICING POWER AND THE PUBLIC INTEREST. LG/CO
PLAN PROB/SOLV COST EFFICIENCY PROFIT RIGID/FLEX EX/STRUC
WEALTH. PAGE 89 F1741 PRICE
ECO/TAC
B62

MORGAN C.A.,LABOR ECONOMICS. LAW INDUS MARKET LABOR
WORKER PLAN PROB/SOLV GOV/REL INCOME ROLE...T 20 ECO/TAC
DEPT/LABOR NLRB. PAGE 93 F1829 ECO/DEV
CAP/ISM
B62

MOUSSA P.,THE UNDERPRIVILEGED NATIONS. FINAN ECO/UNDEV
INT/ORG PLAN PROB/SOLV CAP/ISM GIVE TASK WEALTH NAT/G
...POLICY SOC IND 20. PAGE 94 F1850 DIPLOM
FOR/AID
B62

NATIONAL BUREAU ECONOMIC RES,THE RATE AND DIRECTION DECISION
OF INVENTIVE ACTIVITY: ECONOMIC AND SOCIAL FACTORS. PROB/SOLV
STRUCT INDUS MARKET R+D CREATE OP/RES TEC/DEV MGT
EFFICIENCY PRODUC RATIONAL UTIL...WELF/ST PHIL/SCI

METH/CNCPT TIME. PAGE 97 F1895

B62
ROBERTSON B.C.,REGIONAL DEVELOPMENT IN THE EUROPEAN ECONOMIC COMMUNITY. EUR+WWI FRANCE FUT ITALY UK ECO/UNDEV WORKER ACT/RES PROB/SOLV TEC/DEV ECO/TAC INT/TRADE EEC. PAGE 112 F2209
PLAN ECO/DEV INT/ORG REGION

B62
SCHALLER H.G.,PUBLIC EXPENDITURE DECISIONS IN THE URBAN COMMUNITY: PREPARED FOR RESOURCES FOR THE FUTURE, INC. INDUS SERV/IND LOC/G PUB/INST PLAN PROB/SOLV BUDGET DEMAND PRODUC...CHARTS MUNICH. PAGE 116 F2289
FINAN DECISION

B62
SMITH G.A. JR.,POLICY FORMULATION AND ADMINISTRATION: A CASEBOOK OF TOPMANAGEMENT PROBLEMS IN BUSINESS. EX/STRUC PLAN PROB/SOLV ADMIN CONTROL EXEC LEAD ROUTINE EFFICIENCY ATTIT MGT. PAGE 123 F2430
INDUS SOC/EXP TOP/EX DECISION

B62
UNECA LIBRARY,NEW ACQUISITIONS IN THE UNECA LIBRARY. LAW NAT/G PLAN PROB/SOLV TEC/DEV ADMIN REGION...GEOG SOC 20 UN. PAGE 132 F2606
BIBLIOG AFR ECO/UNDEV INT/ORG

B62
US CONGRESS JOINT ECO COMM,INVENTORY FLUCTUATIONS AND ECONOMIC STABILIZATION. USA+45 LG/CO...MATH CHARTS CONGRESS. PAGE 134 F2652
ECO/TAC FINAN INDUS PROB/SOLV

B62
US CONGRESS JOINT ECO COMM,ECONOMIC DEVELOPMENTS IN SOUTH AMERICA. USA+45 SOCIETY FINAN NAT/G PROB/SOLV TEC/DEV INT/TRADE TAX EFFICIENCY PRODUC ATTIT ...POLICY 20 ALL/PROG CONGRESS SOUTH/AMER. PAGE 135 F2654
L/A+17C ECO/UNDEV FOR/AID DIPLOM

B62
WALSTON H.,AGRICULTURE UNDER COMMUNISM. CHINA/COM COM PROB/SOLV HAPPINESS RIGID/FLEX...POLICY METH/COMP 20. PAGE 143 F2811
AGRI MARXISM PLAN CREATE

L62
"BIBLIOGRAPHY ON EDUCATION AND ECONOMIC AND SOCIAL DEVELOPMENT (AMERICAN SOURCES)" L/A+17C ECO/UNDEV PROB/SOLV...SOC 20. PAGE 1 F0015
BIBLIOG/A ACADEM EDU/PROP INTELL

L62
ERDMANN H.H.,"ADMINISTRATIVE LAW AND FARM ECONOMICS." USA+45 LOC/G NAT/G PLAN PROB/SOLV LOBBY ...DECISION ANTHOL 20. PAGE 38 F0744
AGRI ADMIN ADJUD POLICY

S62
LIPSON H.A.,"FORMAL REASONING AND MARKETING STRATEGY." ECO/DEV PROB/SOLV PRICE ALL/VALS CONT/OBS. PAGE 81 F1578
MARKET DECISION GAME ECO/TAC

S62
READ W.H.,"UPWARD COMMUNICATION IN INDUSTRIAL HIERARCHIES." LG/CO TOP/EX PROB/SOLV DOMIN EXEC PERS/REL ATTIT DRIVE PERCEPT...CORREL STAT CHARTS 20. PAGE 110 F2159
ADMIN INGP/REL PSY MGT

B63
BARNETT H.J.,SCARCITY AND GROWTH: THE ECONOMICS OF NATURAL RESOURCE AVAILABILITY. FUT WOR+45 AGRI INDUS PROB/SOLV TEC/DEV CONTROL PRODUC...SOC/WK IDEA/COMP METH/COMP SIMUL 20 RESOURCE/N MALTHUS RICARDO/D MILL/JS DARWIN/C. PAGE 10 F0191
DEMAND HABITAT CENSUS GEOG

B63
CENTRO ESTUDIOS MONETARIOS LAT,COOPERACION FINANCIERA EN AMERICA LATINA. L/A+17C PLAN PROB/SOLV CONTROL REGION DEMAND...POLICY ANTHOL 20. PAGE 22 F0433
ECO/UNDEV INT/TRADE MARKET FINAN

B63
FATEMI N.S.,THE DOLLAR CRISIS. USA+45 INDUS NAT/G LEGIS BUDGET TAX COST...CHARTS METH/COMP 20 EEC. PAGE 39 F0766
PROB/SOLV BAL/PAY FOR/AID PLAN

B63
GODWIN F.W.,THE HIDDEN FORCE. PUERT/RICO WOR+45 STRUCT VOL/ASSN PROB/SOLV DIPLOM CONFER...BIBLIOG 20 PEACE/CORP. PAGE 48 F0931
ECO/UNDEV WORKER SKILL ECO/TAC

B63
HAQ M.,THE STRATEGY OF ECONOMIC PLANNING. PAKISTAN AGRI FINAN INDUS NAT/G FOR/AID TAX CONTROL REGION PRODUC...POLICY CHARTS 20. PAGE 55 F1071
ECO/TAC ECO/UNDEV PLAN PROB/SOLV

B63
HATHAWAY D.A.,GOVERNMENT AND AGRICULTURE: PUBLIC POLICY IN A DEMOCRATIC SOCIETY. USA+45 LEGIS ADMIN EXEC LOBBY REPRESENT PWR 20. PAGE 57 F1111
AGRI GOV/REL PROB/SOLV EX/STRUC

B63
INTERAMERICAN ECO AND SOC COUN,THE ALLIANCE FOR PROGRESS: ITS FIRST YEAR: 1961-1962. AGRI SCHOOL PLAN TEC/DEV INT/TRADE TAX GIVE ADMIN WEALTH...SOC 20 ALL/PROG SOUTH/AMER. PAGE 64 F1267
INT/ORG PROB/SOLV ECO/TAC L/A+17C

B63
INTERNATIONAL ASSOCIATION RES,AFRICAN STUDIES IN INCOME AND WEALTH. AFR NAT/G PROB/SOLV DEMAND INCOME...ECOMETRIC METH/COMP 20. PAGE 64 F1270
WEALTH PLAN ECO/UNDEV BUDGET

B63
JOHNSTON J.,ECONOMETRIC METHODS. PROB/SOLV WRITING ...REGRESS CHARTS T. PAGE 68 F1333
ECOMETRIC PHIL/SCI OP/RES STAT

B63
LETHBRIDGE H.J.,THE PEASANT AND THE COMMUNES. CHINA/COM COM USSR NEIGH PROB/SOLV ADJUST EFFICIENCY...POLICY METH/COMP NAT/COMP 20. PAGE 78 F1535
MARXISM ECO/TAC AGRI WORKER

B63
MARCHAL J.,EXPANSION ET RECESSION. FRANCE OP/RES PROB/SOLV ROLE ORD/FREE...TREND SIMUL 20 DEPRESSION. PAGE 85 F1663
FINAN PLAN ECO/DEV

B63
MCCONNELL G.,STEEL AND THE PRESIDENCY, 1962. USA+45 INDUS PROB/SOLV CONFER ROLE...POLICY 20 PRESIDENT. PAGE 88 F1722
PWR CHIEF REPRESENT DOMIN

B63
MEYNAUD J.,PLANIFICATION ET POLITIQUE. FRANCE ITALY FINAN LABOR DELIB/GP LEGIS ADMIN EFFICIENCY ...MAJORIT DECISION 20. PAGE 90 F1773
PLAN ECO/TAC PROB/SOLV

B63
OLSON M. JR.,THE ECONOMICS OF WARTIME SHORTAGE. FRANCE GERMANY MOD/EUR UK AGRI PROB/SOLV ADMIN DEMAND WEALTH...POLICY OLD/LIB FOR/TRADE 17/20. PAGE 101 F1990
WAR ADJUST ECO/TAC NAT/COMP

B63
PRITCHETT C.H.,THE THIRD BRANCH OF GOVERNMENT. USA+45 USA-45 CONSTN SOCIETY INDUS SECT LEGIS JUDGE PROB/SOLV GOV/REL 20 SUPREME/CT CHURCH/STA. PAGE 108 F2122
JURID NAT/G ADJUD CT/SYS

B63
RAO V.K.R.,FOREIGN AID AND INDIA'S ECONOMIC DEVELOPMENT. INDIA INT/ORG PROB/SOLV TEC/DEV ECO/TAC CONTROL WEALTH...TREND 20. PAGE 109 F2148
FOR/AID ECO/UNDEV RECEIVE DIPLOM

B63
RUMMEL J.F.,RESEARCH METHODOLOGY IN BUSINESS. COMPUTER CREATE PROB/SOLV...CONT/OBS REC/INT QU/SEMANT SYS/QU SAMP CHARTS METH/COMP T 20. PAGE 115 F2260
OP/RES METH/CNCPT METH STAT

B63
SMITH R.A.,CORPORATIONS IN CRISIS. USA+45 LG/CO EX/STRUC ECO/TAC CONTROL LEAD PERS/REL...MGT 20. PAGE 123 F2432
ELITES INDUS PROB/SOLV METH/COMP

B63
US BD GOVERNORS FEDL RESRV,THE FEDERAL RESERVE AND THE TREASURY. USA+45 WORKER PROB/SOLV PRICE COST DEMAND WEALTH...STAT INT CHARTS 20 FED/RESERV DEPT/TREAS. PAGE 134 F2641
FINAN GOV/REL CONTROL BUDGET

B63
US CONGRESS JOINT ECO COMM,OUTLOOK FOR UNITED STATES BALANCE OF PAYMENTS. AFR USA+45 ECO/DEV NAT/G FORCES DIPLOM FOR/AID COST EFFICIENCY ...POLICY CONGRESS EEC. PAGE 135 F2657
BAL/PAY FINAN INT/TRADE PROB/SOLV

B63
US HOUSE,URBAN RENEWAL: HOUSE COMMITTEE ON BANKING AND CURRENCY. USA+45 FINAN LOC/G NAT/G NEIGH DELIB/GP TEC/DEV BUDGET GOV/REL COST...CHARTS MUNICH 20 CONGRESS URBAN/RNWL. PAGE 136 F2684
PLAN PROB/SOLV LEGIS

B63
WALINSKY L.J.,PLANNING AND EXECUTION OF ECONOMIC DEVELOPMENT. PROB/SOLV TEC/DEV BUDGET COST WEALTH ...CHARTS BIBLIOG 20. PAGE 142 F2802
PLAN ECO/UNDEV ECO/TAC OPTIMAL

L63
MEYER J.R.,"REGIONAL ECONOMICS: A SURVEY." INTELL ACADEM CREATE...IDEA/COMP BIBLIOG. PAGE 90 F1770
REGION ECO/TAC GEN/LAWS PROB/SOLV

S63
ANDREWS R.B.,"ECONOMIC PLANNING FOR SMALL AREAS: THE PLANNING PROCESS." INDUS PROC/MFG PROVS PROB/SOLV TAX EQUILIB...METH/COMP HYPO/EXP METH MUNICH 20. PAGE 5 F0103
ECO/TAC PLAN LOC/G

S63
ENTHOVEN A.C.,"ECONOMIC ANALYSIS IN THE DEPARTMENT OF DEFENSE." USA+45 NAT/G DELIB/GP PROB/SOLV RATION NUC/PWR WEAPON COST...DECISION 20 DEPT/DEFEN RESOURCE/N. PAGE 38 F0739
PLAN BUDGET ECO/TAC FORCES

S63
GREEN P.E.,"BAYESIAN DECISION THEORY IN PRICING STRATEGY."...STAT CHARTS. PAGE 51 F0988
OP/RES PROB/SOLV BARGAIN PRICE

S63
STEFANIAK N.J.,"A REFINEMENT OF HAIG'S THEORY." USA+45 INDUS PROB/SOLV TEC/DEV...CONCPT CHARTS
GEOG GEN/LAWS

MUNICH 20 HAIG. PAGE 125 F2474
PLAN

B64
INTERNATIONAL MONETARY ARRANGEMENTS: THE PROBLEM OF CHOICE. PLAN PROB/SOLV INT/TRADE ADJUST COST EQUILIB 20. PAGE 1 F0020
POLICY DIPLOM FINAN ECO/DEV

B64
BLAKE R.R.,MANAGING INTERGROUP CONFLICT IN INDUSTRY. INDUS DELIB/GP EX/STRUC GP/REL PERS/REL GAME. PAGE 16 F0297
CREATE PROB/SOLV OP/RES ADJUD

B64
BRIGHT J.R.,RESEARCH, DEVELOPMENT AND TECHNOLOGICAL INNOVATION. CULTURE R+D CREATE PLAN PROB/SOLV AUTOMAT RISK PERSON...DECISION CONCPT PREDICT BIBLIOG. PAGE 18 F0352
TEC/DEV NEW/IDEA INDUS MGT

B64
BROWN E.H.P.,A COURSE IN APPLIED ECONOMICS (2ND ED.). ECO/DEV FINAN MARKET WORKER INT/TRADE RATION RENT PAY PRICE BAL/PAY...DECISION T RESOURCE/N. PAGE 19 F0368
POLICY ECO/TAC PROB/SOLV

B64
CHEIT E.F.,THE BUSINESS ESTABLISHMENT. FRANCE WOR+45 PROF/ORG TOP/EX PROB/SOLV CAP/ISM ADMIN SUPEGO MORAL PWR...METH/CNCPT MYTH NEW/IDEA 20. PAGE 24 F0460
PERSON EX/STRUC MGT INDUS

B64
COLSTON RESEARCH SOCIETY,ECONOMETRIC ANALYSIS FOR NATIONAL ECONOMIC PLANNING (PROCEEDINGS OF SIXTEENTH SYMPOSIUM OF COLSTON RESEARCH SOCIETY). UK USA+45 FINAN FAM LABOR NAT/G PLAN PRICE ...METH/CNCPT TREND CHARTS TIME 20. PAGE 26 F0510
ECOMETRIC DELIB/GP ECO/TAC PROB/SOLV

B64
COMMISSION ON MONEY AND CREDIT,INFLATION, GROWTH, AND EMPLOYMENT. AFR USA+45 PLAN PROB/SOLV PAY PRICE EFFICIENCY PRODUC WEALTH 20. PAGE 26 F0514
WORKER ECO/TAC OPTIMAL

B64
FEI J.C.H.,DEVELOPMENT OF THE LABOR SURPLUS ECONOMY: THEORY AND POLICY. WOR+45 AGRI INDUS MARKET PROB/SOLV TEC/DEV...STAT CHARTS GEN/LAWS METH 20 THIRD/WRLD. PAGE 40 F0772
ECO/TAC POLICY WORKER ECO/UNDEV

B64
FITCH L.C.,URBAN TRANSPORTATION AND PUBLIC POLICY. FINAN NAT/G LEGIS PROB/SOLV TEC/DEV PRICE COST EFFICIENCY...DECISION STAT CHARTS METH/COMP MUNICH 20 NEWYORK/C PHILADELPH LOS/ANG CHICAGO WASHING/DC. PAGE 41 F0806
DIST/IND PLAN LOC/G

B64
FRIEDEN B.J.,THE FUTURE OF OLD NEIGHBORHOODS: REBUILDING FOR A CHANGING POPULATION. CONSTRUC LOC/G NAT/G ACT/RES ECO/TAC REGION ATTIT...INT SAMP MUNICH 20 NEWYORK/C LOS/ANG HARTFORD URBAN/RNWL. PAGE 44 F0855
NEIGH PROB/SOLV PLAN BUDGET

B64
HAGGER A.J.,THE THEORY OF INFLATION. AFR PLAN PROB/SOLV PAY COST INCOME 20. PAGE 53 F1035
DEMAND TEC/DEV FINAN

B64
HERSKOVITS M.J.,ECONOMIC TRANSITION IN AFRICA. FUT INT/ORG NAT/G WORKER PROB/SOLV TEC/DEV INT/TRADE EQUILIB INCOME...ANTHOL 20. PAGE 59 F1157
AFR ECO/UNDEV PLAN ADMIN

B64
JUSTER F.T.,ANTICIPATIONS AND PURCHASES; AN ANALYSIS OF CONSUMER BEHAVIOR. PROB/SOLV RISK COST PRODUC DRIVE...STAT STYLE SAMP CON/ANAL CHARTS HYPO/EXP GAME SIMUL. PAGE 68 F1345
PROBABIL DECISION PREDICT DEMAND

B64
LANG A.S.,URBAN RAIL TRANSIT. OP/RES PLAN PROB/SOLV TEC/DEV AUTOMAT COST...TECHNIC MATH CON/ANAL CHARTS METH/COMP SIMUL MUNICH 20 RAILROAD PUB/TRANS. PAGE 75 F1474
DIST/IND ECOMETRIC

B64
MEYER J.R.,INVESTMENT DECISIONS, ECONOMIC FORECASTING, AND PUBLIC POLICY. ECO/DEV ECO/TAC ...DECISION REGRESS TIME/SEQ CHARTS GP/COMP SIMUL 20. PAGE 90 F1771
FINAN PROB/SOLV PREDICT LG/CO

B64
MILIBAND R.,THE SOCIALIST REGISTER: 1964. GERMANY/W ITALY UK LABOR POL/PAR ECO/TAC FOR/AID NUC/PWR ...POLICY SOCIALIST IDEA/COMP 20 MAO NASSER/G. PAGE 91 F1784
MARXISM SOCISM CAP/ISM PROB/SOLV

B64
MITAU G.T.,INSOLUBLE PROBLEMS: CASE PROBLEMS ON THE FUNCTIONS OF STATE AND LOCAL GOVERNMENT. USA+45 AIR FINAN LABOR POL/PAR PROB/SOLV TAX RECEIVE CONTROL GP/REL 20 CASEBOOK ZONING. PAGE 92 F1807
ADJUD LOC/G PROVS

B64
MOAK L.L.,A MANUAL OF SUGGESTED PRACTICE FOR THE PREPARATION AND ADOPTION OF CAPITAL PROGRAMS AND CAPITAL BUDGETS BY LOCAL GOVERN. USA+45 DELIB/GP PLAN TAX GP/REL COST DECISION. PAGE 92 F1812
LOC/G BUDGET LEGIS PROB/SOLV

B64
NEHEMKIS P.,LATIN AMERICA: MYTH AND REALITY. INDUS INT/ORG PROB/SOLV CAP/ISM DIPLOM REV...SOC MUNICH 20. PAGE 97 F1907
REGION MYTH L/A+17C

ECO/UNDEV

B64
NOSSITER B.D.,THE MYTHMAKERS: AN ESSAY ON POWER AND WEALTH. USA+45 LG/CO NAT/G TOP/EX PROB/SOLV ADMIN GP/REL ORD/FREE 20. PAGE 99 F1937
ECO/TAC WEALTH FINAN PLAN

B64
PAARLBERG D.,AMERICAN FARM POLICY: A CASE STUDY IN CENTRALIZED DECISION-MAKING. USA+45 NAT/G LEGIS LOBBY REPRESENT GOV/REL PWR LAISSEZ 20. PAGE 102 F2009
PROB/SOLV EX/STRUC AGRI

B64
PENNOCK J.R.,SELF-GOVERNMENT IN MODERNIZING NATIONS. AFR COM USA+45 ECO/DEV POL/PAR PROB/SOLV DIPLOM ECO/TAC COLONIAL REV POPULISM SOCISM 20. PAGE 105 F2058
ECO/UNDEV POLICY SOVEREIGN NAT/G

B64
STRONG A.L.,THE RISE OF THE CHINESE PEOPLE'S COMMUNES - AND SIX YEARS AFTER (2ND ED.). CHINA/COM AGRI INDUS FORCES WORKER PROB/SOLV EDU/PROP EFFICIENCY ISOLAT 20. PAGE 127 F2503
NEIGH ECO/TAC MARXISM METH/COMP

B64
TINBERGEN J.,CENTRAL PLANNING. COM INTELL ECO/DEV ECO/UNDEV FINAN INT/ORG PROB/SOLV ECO/TAC CONTROL EXEC ROUTINE DECISION. PAGE 130 F2576
PLAN INDUS MGT CENTRAL

B64
US CONGRESS JOINT ECO COMM,PRIVATE INVESTMENT IN LATIN AMERICA. L/A+17C USA+45 INT/ORG PROB/SOLV ECO/TAC ATTIT...INT 20 CONGRESS. PAGE 135 F2658
FINAN ECO/UNDEV PARL/PROC LEGIS

B64
VON DER MEHDEN F.R.,POLITICS OF THE DEVELOPING NATIONS. WOR+45 CONSTN PROB/SOLV ORD/FREE WEALTH OBJECTIVE. PAGE 142 F2790
ECO/UNDEV SOCIETY STRUCT

S64
STONE P.A.,"DECISION TECHNIQUES FOR TOWN DEVELOPMENT." PLAN COST PROFIT...DECISION MGT CON/ANAL CHARTS METH/COMP BIBLIOG MUNICH 20. PAGE 127 F2497
OP/RES ADMIN PROB/SOLV

B65
BELASSA B.,ECONOMIC DEVELOPMENT AND INTEGRATION. LG/CO PROB/SOLV TEC/DEV INT/TRADE TARIFFS COST WEALTH...POLICY METH/COMP 20. PAGE 12 F0232
ECO/UNDEV ECO/TAC INT/ORG INDUS

B65
BOLLENS J.C.,THE METROPOLIS: ITS PEOPLE, POLITICS, AND ECONOMIC LIFE. USA+45 PLAN PROB/SOLV PERS/REL PWR...DECISION GEOG CENSUS TREND CON/ANAL MUNICH 20 NEWYORK/C LOS/ANG SAN/FRAN CHICAGO PHILADELPH. PAGE 16 F0309
HABITAT SOC LOC/G

B65
BOWEN W.G.,UNEMPLOYMENT IN A PROSPEROUS ECONOMY. USA+45 ECO/DEV NAT/G ACT/RES PLAN PAY EDU/PROP DEMAND...POLICY IDEA/COMP ANTHOL 20. PAGE 17 F0330
WORKER ECO/TAC WEALTH PROB/SOLV

B65
CASSELL F.,GOLD OR CREDIT? THE ECONOMICS AND POLITICS OF INTERNATIONAL MONEY. AFR WOR+45 PLAN PROB/SOLV BAL/PAY SOVEREIGN WEALTH 20 OEEC. PAGE 22 F0428
FINAN INT/ORG DIPLOM ECO/TAC

B65
COLLOQUE SUR LA PLANIFICATION,LA PLANIFICATION COMME PROCESSUS DE DECISION. FRANCE SOCIETY MARKET LABOR LEGIS GP/REL EFFICIENCY INCOME ATTIT TECHRACY ...MYTH IDEA/COMP 20. PAGE 26 F0508
PLAN ECO/TAC PROB/SOLV

B65
DERBER M.,PLANT UNION-MANAGEMENT RELATIONS: FROM PRACTICE TO THEORY. PROC/MFG NEIGH PROB/SOLV ORD/FREE...DECISION MGT OBS QU SAMP. PAGE 32 F0621
LG/CO LABOR GP/REL ATTIT

B65
EDELMAN M.,THE POLITICS OF WAGE-PRICE DECISIONS. GERMANY ITALY NETHERLAND UK INDUS LABOR POL/PAR PROB/SOLV BARGAIN PRICE ROUTINE BAL/PAY COST DEMAND 20. PAGE 36 F0699
GOV/COMP CONTROL ECO/TAC PLAN

B65
FERMAN L.A.,POVERTY IN AMERICA: A BOOK OF READINGS. USA+45 CULTURE ECO/DEV PROB/SOLV ALL/VALS...POLICY ANTHOL BIBLIOG 20 POVRTY/WAR. PAGE 40 F0785
WEALTH TEC/DEV CONCPT RECEIVE

B65
FRIEDLANDER S.L.,LABOR MIGRATION AND ECONOMIC GROWTH: A CASE STUDY OF PUERTO RICO. PUERT/RICO AGRI WORKER PLAN PROB/SOLV...ECOMETRIC STAT PREDICT CHARTS HYPO/EXP SIMUL 20. PAGE 44 F0858
CENSUS GEOG ECO/UNDEV WEALTH

B65
FRYE R.J.,HOUSING AND URBAN RENEWAL IN ALABAMA. USA+45 NEIGH LEGIS BUDGET ADJUD ADMIN PARTIC...MGT MUNICH 20 ALABAMA URBAN/RNWL. PAGE 45 F0871
PROB/SOLV PLAN GOV/REL

B65
GOETZ-GIREY R.,LE MOUVEMENT DES GREVES EN FRANCE. FRANCE FINAN OP/RES PROB/SOLV ECO/TAC INCOME HABITAT...STAT CHARTS 19/20. PAGE 48 F0932
LABOR WORKER GP/REL INDUS

GORDON W.,THE POLITICAL ECONOMY OF LATIN AMERICA. L/A+17C FINAN MARKET PROB/SOLV TEC/DEV RECEIVE ADMIN WEALTH 20. PAGE 49 F0962
B65 ECO/UNDEV INT/TRADE REGION POLICY

GREER S.,URBAN RENEWAL AND AMERICAN CITIES: THE DILEMMA OF DEMOCRATIC INTERVENTION. USA+45 R+D LOC/G VOL/ASSN ACT/RES BUDGET ADMIN GOV/REL...SOC INT SAMP MUNICH 20 BOSTON CHICAGO LOS/ANG MIAMI URBAN/RNWL. PAGE 51 F0992
B65 PROB/SOLV PLAN NAT/G

HICKMAN B.G.,QUANTITATIVE PLANNING OF ECONOMIC POLICY. FRANCE NETHERLAND OP/RES PRICE ROUTINE UTIL ...POLICY DECISION ECOMETRIC METH/CNCPT STAT STYLE CHINJAP. PAGE 59 F1162
B65 PROB/SOLV PLAN QUANT

HOLLER J.E.,POPULATION TRENDS AND ECONOMIC DEVELOPMENT IN THE FAR EAST (PAMPHLET). KOREA S/ASIA AGRI INDUS DELIB/GP PROB/SOLV RATIONAL ...POLICY CHARTS BIBLIOG 20 OUTER/MONG CHINJAP HONG/KONG. PAGE 61 F1197
B65 CENSUS TREND ECO/UNDEV ASIA

JAIN S.C.,THE STATE AND AGRICULTURE. INDIA S/ASIA ECO/UNDEV PROB/SOLV CAP/ISM MARXISM SOCISM 20. PAGE 66 F1304
B65 NAT/G POLICY AGRI ECO/TAC

KRAUSE W.,ECONOMIC DEVELOPMENT: THE UNDERDEVELOPED WORLD AND THE AMERICAN INTEREST. USA+45 AGRI PLAN MARXISM...CHARTS 20. PAGE 73 F1434
B65 FOR/AID ECO/UNDEV FINAN PROB/SOLV

LAZARUS S.,RESOLVING BUSINESS DISPUTES: THE POTENTIAL OF COMMERCIAL ARBITRATION. USA+45 INDUS LG/CO ACT/RES PROB/SOLV EDU/PROP CONSEN UTIL ...TREND 20. PAGE 76 F1496
B65 FINAN DELIB/GP CONSULT ADJUD

LYONS G.M.,AMERICA: PURPOSE AND POWER. UK USA+45 FINAN INDUS MARKET WORKER TEC/DEV DIPLOM AUTOMAT NUC/PWR WAR RACE/REL ORD/FREE 20 EEC CONGRESS SUPREME/CT CIV/RIGHTS. PAGE 82 F1617
B65 PWR PROB/SOLV ECO/DEV TASK

MAO J.C.T.,EFFICIENCY IN PUBLIC URBAN RENEWAL EXPENDITURES THROUGH CAPITAL BUDGETING. USA+45 FINAN LOC/G NAT/G NEIGH REGION UTIL...GEOG METH/CNCPT STAT SIMUL GEN/LAWS MUNICH 20 URBAN/RNWL. PAGE 85 F1662
B65 TEC/DEV BUDGET PROB/SOLV

MARGOLIS J.,THE PUBLIC ECONOMY OF URBAN COMMUNITIES. USA+45 LEGIS PROB/SOLV TAX LOBBY CHOOSE ATTIT MUNICH. PAGE 85 F1668
B65 LOC/G DECISION FINAN

NATIONAL CENTRAL LIBRARY,LATIN AMERICAN ECONOMIC AND SOCIAL SERIALS. UK SOCIETY NAT/G PLAN PROB/SOLV ...SOC 20. PAGE 97 F1897
B65 BIBLIOG INT/TRADE ECO/UNDEV L/A+17C

OECD,MEDITERRANEAN REGIONAL PROJECT: TURKEY; EDUCATION AND DEVELOPMENT. FUT TURKEY SOCIETY STRATA FINAN NAT/G PROF/ORG PLAN PROB/SOLV ADMIN COST...STAT CHARTS 20 OECD. PAGE 100 F1969
B65 EDU/PROP ACADEM SCHOOL ECO/UNDEV

OECD,THE MEDITERRANEAN REGIONAL PROJECT: PORTUGAL; EDUCATION AND DEVELOPMENT. PORTUGAL SOCIETY STRATA FINAN PROF/ORG WORKER PLAN PROB/SOLV ADMIN...POLICY STAT CHARTS METH 20 OECD. PAGE 100 F1970
B65 EDU/PROP SCHOOL ACADEM ECO/UNDEV

OECD,THE MEDITERRANEAN REGIONAL PROJECT: ITALY; EDUCATION AND DEVELOPMENT. ITALY SOCIETY STRATA FINAN NAT/G PROF/ORG WORKER PLAN PROB/SOLV ADMIN ...STAT CHARTS METH 20 OECD. PAGE 100 F1971
B65 SCHOOL EDU/PROP ECO/UNDEV ACADEM

OECD,THE MEDITERRANEAN REGIONAL PROJECT: GREECE; EDUCATION AND DEVELOPMENT. FUT GREECE SOCIETY AGRI FINAN NAT/G PROF/ORG WORKER PLAN PROB/SOLV ADMIN DEMAND ATTIT 20 OECD. PAGE 100 F1972
B65 EDU/PROP SCHOOL ACADEM ECO/UNDEV

OECD,THE MEDITERRANEAN REGIONAL PROJECT: SPAIN; EDUCATION AND DEVELOPMENT. FUT SPAIN STRATA FINAN NAT/G WORKER PLAN PROB/SOLV ADMIN COST...POLICY STAT CHARTS 20 OECD. PAGE 100 F1973
B65 ECO/UNDEV EDU/PROP ACADEM SCHOOL

OECD,TECHNIQUES OF ECONOMIC FORECASTING. CANADA FRANCE NETHERLAND SWEDEN UK USA+45 PROB/SOLV ROUTINE...CONCPT MATH CHARTS BIBLIOG METH 20. PAGE 100 F1974
B65 PREDICT METH/COMP PLAN

ONSLOW C.,ASIAN ECONOMIC DEVELOPMENT. BURMA CEYLON INDIA MALAYSIA PAKISTAN S/ASIA AGRI INDUS MARKET PROB/SOLV CAP/ISM FOR/AID INT/TRADE DEMAND WEALTH ...POLICY ANTHOL 20. PAGE 101 F1991
B65 ECO/UNDEV ECO/TAC PLAN NAT/G

OXENFELDT A.R.,ECONOMIC SYSTEMS IN ACTION. FRANCE USA+45 USSR CULTURE PLAN PROB/SOLV TEC/DEV INCOME PRODUC WEALTH...METH/COMP 20. PAGE 102 F2007
B65 ECO/DEV CAP/ISM MARXISM ECO/TAC

PROCHNOW H.V.,WORLD ECONOMIC PROBLEMS AND POLICIES. INDIA ISRAEL WOR+45 AGRI LABOR PROB/SOLV FOR/AID TARIFFS CONTROL BAL/PAY NAT/LISM WEALTH...TREND CHARTS 20 CHINJAP EEC. PAGE 108 F2124
B65 MARKET ECO/TAC PRODUC IDEA/COMP

REDFORD E.S.,AMERICAN GOVERNMENT AND THE ECONOMY. FUT USA+45 USA-45 INDUS PROB/SOLV GOV/REL...POLICY DECISION METH/COMP BIBLIOG T 18/20. PAGE 110 F2168
B65 CONSTN NAT/G

RIGBY P.H.,CONCEPTUAL FOUNDATIONS OF BUSINESS RESEARCH. COMPUTER PROB/SOLV OPTIMAL...MGT CONCPT MATH STAT TESTS SIMUL GEN/METH. PAGE 111 F2192
B65 PROFIT R+D INDUS DECISION

ROSS A.M.,EMPLOYMENT POLICY AND THE LABOR MARKET. USA+45 MARKET LABOR NAT/G PROB/SOLV PAY EDU/PROP PARTIC UTIL...POLICY 20. PAGE 114 F2242
B65 ECO/DEV WORKER WEALTH DEMAND

ROSS P.,THE GOVERNMENT AS A SOURCE OF UNION POWER. USA+45 LAW ECO/DEV PROB/SOLV ECO/TAC LEAD GP/REL ...MGT 20. PAGE 114 F2245
B65 LABOR BARGAIN POLICY NAT/G

SCHWARTZ G.,SCIENCE IN MARKETING. OP/RES PROB/SOLV INT/TRADE PRICE CONTROL ADJUST PRODUC...CONCPT 20. PAGE 118 F2324
B65 PHIL/SCI TREND ECO/DEV MARKET

SMERK G.M.,URBAN TRANSPORTATION; THE FEDERAL ROLE. FUT USA+45 FINAN PROB/SOLV TEC/DEV AUTOMAT GOV/REL COST...STAT BIBLIOG MUNICH 20 PUB/TRANS. PAGE 123 F2426
B65 PLAN DIST/IND NAT/G

STEINER G.A.,THE CREATIVE ORGANIZATION. ELITES LG/CO PLAN PROB/SOLV TEC/DEV INSPECT CAP/ISM CONTROL EXEC PERSON...METH/COMP HYPO/EXP 20. PAGE 126 F2476
B65 CREATE MGT ADMIN SOC

US BUREAU OF THE BUDGET,THE BALANCE OF PAYMENTS STATISTICS OF THE UNITED STATES: A REVIEW AND APPRAISAL. USA+45 FINAN NAT/G PROB/SOLV DIPLOM. PAGE 134 F2644
B65 BAL/PAY STAT METH/COMP BUDGET

US HOUSE COMM BANKING-CURR,INTERNATIONAL TRAVEL IN RELATION TO THE BALANCE OF PAYMENTS DEFICIT. USA+45 DELIB/GP...CHARTS 20 CONGRESS TRAVEL. PAGE 136 F2690
B65 BAL/PAY ECO/TAC SERV/IND PROB/SOLV

VANEK J.,GENERAL EQUILIBRIUM OF INTERNATIONAL DISCRIMINATION; THE CASE OF CUSTOMS UNIONS. LABOR PROB/SOLV ECO/TAC DISCRIM INCOME...MATH CHARTS METH 20. PAGE 140 F2767
B65 INT/TRADE TARIFFS INT/ORG EQUILIB

WALTON R.E.,A BEHAVIORAL THEORY OF LABOR NEGOTIATIONS: AN ANALYSIS OF A SOCIAL INTERACTION SYSTEM. USA+45 FINAN PROB/SOLV ECO/TAC GP/REL INGP/REL...DECISION BIBLIOG. PAGE 143 F2812
B65 SOC LABOR BARGAIN ADMIN

WARNER A.W.,THE IMPACT OF SCIENCE ON TECHNOLOGY. UNIV INTELL SOCIETY NAT/G ACT/RES PLAN PROB/SOLV BUDGET OPTIMAL GEN/METH. PAGE 143 F2821
B65 DECISION TEC/DEV CREATE POLICY

WEAVER J.N.,THE INTERNATIONAL DEVELOPMENT ASSOCIATION: A NEW APPROACH TO FOREIGN AID. USA+45 NAT/G OP/RES PLAN PROB/SOLV WEALTH...CHARTS BIBLIOG 20 UN. PAGE 144 F2836
B65 FOR/AID INT/ORG ECO/UNDEV FINAN

WU YUAN-LI,THE ECONOMY OF COMMUNIST CHINA. CHINA/COM USSR AGRI FINAN INDUS POL/PAR WORKER PROB/SOLV INT/TRADE PRICE EATING INCOME OWN WEALTH 20. PAGE 149 F2939
B65 ECO/TAC MARXISM PLAN EFFICIENCY

BRIGHAM E.F.,"THE DETERMINANTS OF RESIDENTIAL LAND VALUES." USA+45 ECO/DEV PROB/SOLV RENT PRICE ...REGRESS STAT CHARTS GEN/METH MUNICH 20 LOS/ANG. PAGE 18 F0351
S65 COST INDICATOR SIMUL ECOMETRIC

CHU K.,"A DYNAMIC MODEL OF THE FIRM." OP/RES PROB/SOLV...DECISION ECOMETRIC NEW/IDEA STAT GAME ORG/CHARTS SIMUL. PAGE 24 F0472
S65 INDUS COMPUTER TEC/DEV

DICKMAN A.B.,"SOUTH AFRICAN MONEY MARKET - PROGRESS AND PROBLEMS SINCE 1960." SOUTH/AFR PROB/SOLV ROLE ...PREDICT CHARTS 20. PAGE 33 F0633
S65 FINAN PLAN MARKET

DUMONT R.,"SURPEUPLEMENT CHINOIS ET SES CONSEQUENCES." AFR ECO/UNDEV AGRI PLAN PROB/SOLV ECO/TAC FOR/AID NUC/PWR...OBS INT PREDICT. PAGE 35 F0675
S65 GEOG ASIA STAT

WILDAVSKY A.,"TVA AND POWER POLITICS." USA+45 CLIENT PROB/SOLV EXEC GOV/REL 20. PAGE 146 F2882
S65 PWR EX/STRUC

LOBBY

B66
ALEXANDER Y.,INTERNATIONAL TECHNICAL ASSISTANCE EXPERTS: A CASE STUDY OF THE U.N. EXPERIENCE. USA+45 WOR+45 WORKER CREATE PLAN PROB/SOLV ECO/TAC FOR/AID GIVE EDU/PROP...CHARTS BIBLIOG 20 UN. PAGE 3 F0062
SKILL INT/ORG TEC/DEV CONSULT

B66
AMER ENTERPRISE INST PUB POL,SIGNIFICANT ISSUES IN ECONOMIC AID TO DEVELOPING COUNTRIES. FINAN INT/ORG NAT/G PLAN PROB/SOLV GIVE TASK WEALTH...DECISION 20. PAGE 4 F0083
ECO/UNDEV FOR/AID DIPLOM POLICY

B66
ANDRESKI S.,PARASITISM AND SUBVERSION* THE CASE OF LATIN AMERICA. CULTURE ECO/UNDEV LABOR NAT/G SECT PROB/SOLV RACE/REL TOTALISM ATTIT WEALTH ALL/IDEOS. PAGE 5 F0100
L/A+17C GOV/COMP STRATA REV

B66
BOYD H.W.,MARKETING MANAGEMENT: CASES FROM EMERGING COUNTRIES. BRAZIL GHANA ISRAEL WOR+45 ADMIN PERS/REL ATTIT HABITAT WEALTH...ANTHOL 20 ARGEN CASEBOOK. PAGE 17 F0332
MGT ECO/UNDEV PROB/SOLV MARKET

B66
CONFERENCE REGIONAL ACCOUNTS,REGIONAL ACCOUNTS FOR POLICY DECISIONS. PROB/SOLV CONTROL RATIONAL KNOWL ORD/FREE...POLICY DECISION MATH STAT ANTHOL 20. PAGE 27 F0523
GOV/REL REGION PLAN ECO/TAC

B66
DAVIES JC I.I.I.,NEIGHBORHOOD GROUPS AND URBAN RENEWAL. USA+45 PLAN LOBBY PARTIC CHOOSE RACE/REL ...POLICY DECISION SOC INT MUNICH SOC/INTEG 20 NEWYORK/C. PAGE 30 F0586
NEIGH CREATE PROB/SOLV

B66
DAVIS K.,BUSINESS AND ITS ENVIRONMENT. LAW ECO/DEV INDUS OP/RES ADMIN CONTROL ROUTINE GP/REL PROFIT POLICY. PAGE 30 F0591
EX/STRUC PROB/SOLV CAP/ISM EXEC

B66
DEBENKO E.,RESEARCH SOURCES FOR SOUTH ASIAN STUDIES IN ECONOMIC DEVELOPMENT: A SELECT BIBLIOGRAPHY OF SERIAL PUBLICATIONS. CEYLON INDIA NEPAL PAKISTAN PROB/SOLV ADMIN...POLICY 20. PAGE 32 F0611
BIBLIOG ECO/UNDEV S/ASIA PLAN

B66
HACKETT J.,L'ECONOMIE BRITANNIQUE: PROBLEMES ET PERSPECTIVES. FRANCE UK LABOR NAT/G EX/STRUC PROB/SOLV BAL/PAY INCOME RIGID/FLEX...MGT PHIL/SCI CHARTS MUNICH 20. PAGE 53 F1027
ECO/DEV FINAN ECO/TAC PLAN

B66
HARLOW J.S.,FRENCH ECONOMIC PLANNING: A CHALLENGE TO REASON. EUR+WWI FRANCE PROB/SOLV 20 EUROPE. PAGE 55 F1084
ECO/TAC PLAN STRUCT

B66
HEISS K.P.,GAME THEORY AND HUMAN CONFLICTS (RESEARCH MEMORANDUM). UNIV ACT/RES...DECISION SOC MATH PROBABIL SIMUL 20 DEFINETT/B. PAGE 58 F1142
GAME ECOMETRIC PLAN PROB/SOLV

B66
HEVESY P.D.,THE UNIFICATION OF THE WORLD. FUT USA+45 WOR+45 ECO/DEV ECO/UNDEV LEGIS PROB/SOLV BAL/PWR ECO/TAC INT/TRADE PEACE. PAGE 59 F1160
DIPLOM FINAN INT/ORG

B66
HOROWITZ I.L.,THREE WORLDS OF DEVELOPMENT. COM USA+45 STRUCT ECO/DEV PLAN PROB/SOLV TEC/DEV CIVMIL/REL...PHIL/SCI IDEA/COMP 20. PAGE 62 F1216
ECO/UNDEV BAL/PWR POL/PAR REV

B66
INARRITU A.L.,EL PATRON CAMBIO-ORO Y SUS REFORMAS. AFR L/A+17C WOR+45 PLAN PROB/SOLV BUDGET ECO/TAC INT/TRADE EFFICIENCY ORD/FREE 20 MEXIC/AMER. PAGE 64 F1262
ECO/UNDEV FINAN DIPLOM POLICY

B66
INTERNATIONAL ECO POLICY ASSN,THE UNITED STATES BALANCE OF PAYMENTS. INT/ORG NAT/G PROB/SOLV BUDGET DIPLOM INT/TRADE WEALTH 20. PAGE 65 F1274
BAL/PAY ECO/TAC POLICY FINAN

B66
KURAKOV I.G.,SCIENCE, TECHNOLOGY AND COMMUNISM; SOME QUESTIONS OF DEVELOPMENT (TRANS. BY CARIN DEDIJER). USSR INDUS PLAN PROB/SOLV COST PRODUC ...MGT MATH CHARTS METH 20. PAGE 74 F1450
CREATE TEC/DEV MARXISM ECO/TAC

B66
LEAGUE OF WOMEN VOTERS OF US,FOREIGN AID AT THE CROSSROADS. USA+45 WOR+45 DELIB/GP PROB/SOLV DIPLOM INT/TRADE RECEIVE BAL/PAY...CHARTS 20 UN ALL/PROG. PAGE 76 F1498
FOR/AID GIVE ECO/UNDEV PLAN

B66
LICHTMAN R.,TOWARD COMMUNITY (PAPER). PLAN PROB/SOLV WEALTH MARXISM...HEAL CONCPT 20. PAGE 80 F1561
NEW/LIB EFFICIENCY CAP/ISM ADJUST

B66
MALASSIS L.,ECONOMIC DEVELOPMENT AND THE PROGRAMMING OF RURAL EDUCATION. CONSULT PROB/SOLV LITERACY KNOWL...CHARTS GEN/METH 20. PAGE 84 F1644
AGRI ECO/UNDEV SCHOOL PLAN

B66
MANSFIELD E.,MANAGERIAL ECONOMICS AND OPERATIONS RESEARCH; A NONMATHEMATICAL INTRODUCTION. USA+45 ELITES ECO/DEV CONSULT EX/STRUC PROB/SOLV ROUTINE EFFICIENCY OPTIMAL...GAME T 20. PAGE 85 F1660
ECO/TAC OP/RES MGT COMPUTER

B66
MOUNTJOY A.B.,INDUSTRIALIZATION AND UNDER-DEVELOPED COUNTRIES (2ND REV. ED.). CHILE GHANA INDIA NIGERIA WOR+45 SOCIETY PROB/SOLV ECO/TAC...SOC CHARTS 20 INDUS/REV. PAGE 94 F1848
ECO/UNDEV INDUS GEOG HABITAT

B66
NATIONAL INDUSTRIAL CONF BOARD,GOLD AND WORLD MONETARY PROBLEMS. AFR FUT WOR+45 PROB/SOLV BUDGET INT/TRADE PAY GOV/REL...POLICY ANTHOL 20. PAGE 97 F1902
FINAN ECO/TAC PRICE BAL/PAY

B66
NEVITT A.A.,THE ECONOMIC PROBLEMS OF HOUSING. WOR+45 ECO/DEV ECO/UNDEV ACT/RES PROB/SOLV ECO/TAC RENT...OBS CHARTS 20. PAGE 98 F1917
HABITAT PROC/MFG DELIB/GP NAT/COMP

B66
NICOSIA F.N.,CONSUMER DECISION PROCESSES* MARKETING AND ADVERTISING IMPLICATIONS. DIST/IND INDUS CONSULT EDU/PROP ATTIT. PAGE 98 F1925
MARKET PROB/SOLV SERV/IND

B66
PERSALL E.S.,AN ECONOMETRIC STUDY OF FINANCIAL MARKETS. COMPUTER PROB/SOLV TEC/DEV...MATH STAT CHARTS METH/COMP BIBLIOG 20. PAGE 105 F2066
ECOMETRIC FINAN MARKET METH

B66
PIQUET H.S.,THE US BALANCE OF PAYMENTS AND INTERNATIONAL MONETARY RESERVES. AFR USA+45 PROB/SOLV INT/TRADE GOV/REL EQUILIB...POLICY STAT CHARTS 20. PAGE 106 F2090
BAL/PAY DIPLOM FINAN ECO/TAC

B66
REDFORD E.S.,THE ROLE OF GOVERNMENT IN THE AMERICAN ECONOMY. USA+45 USA-45 FINAN INDUS LG/CO PROB/SOLV ADMIN INGP/REL INCOME PRODUC 18/20. PAGE 110 F2169
NAT/G ECO/DEV CAP/ISM ECO/TAC

B66
SEWELL J.P.,FUNCTIONALISM AND WORLD POLITICS* A STUDY BASED ON UNITED NATIONS PROGRAMS FINANCING ECONOMICAL DEVELOPMENT. ECO/UNDEV FINAN PROB/SOLV DIPLOM ECO/TAC FEEDBACK REGION ADJUST ATTIT UN IBRD INTL/FINAN INTL/DEV UNSF. PAGE 120 F2360
TASK INT/ORG IDEA/COMP GEN/LAWS

B66
SMITH H.E.,READINGS IN ECONOMIC DEVELOPMENT AND ADMINISTRATION IN TANZANIA. TANZANIA FINAN INDUS LABOR NAT/G PLAN PROB/SOLV INT/TRADE COLONIAL REGION...ANTHOL BIBLIOG 20 AFRICA/E. PAGE 123 F2431
TEC/DEV ADMIN GOV/REL

B66
THOMPSON J.H.,MODERNIZATION OF THE ARAB WORLD. FUT ISRAEL STRUCT ECO/UNDEV DIPLOM INGP/REL ATTIT ...CENSUS ANTHOL 20 ARABS. PAGE 130 F2565
ADJUST ISLAM PROB/SOLV NAT/COMP

B66
TURNER H.A.,PRICES, WAGES, AND INCOME POLICIES IN INDUSTRIALIZED MARKET ECONOMIES. AFR WOR+45 ECO/DEV INDUS PROB/SOLV ECO/TAC CONTROL WEALTH...CHARTS 20 INTRVN/ECO. PAGE 131 F2593
PRICE PAY MARKET INCOME

B66
YOUNG S.,MANAGEMENT: A SYSTEMS ANALYSIS. DELIB/GP EX/STRUC ECO/TAC CONTROL EFFICIENCY...NET/THEORY 20. PAGE 150 F2952
PROB/SOLV MGT DECISION SIMUL

S66
DAVIS O.A.,"A THEORY OF THE BUDGETARY PROCESS." ECO/DEV FINAN LEGIS PROB/SOLV GOV/REL...ECOMETRIC METH/CNCPT STAT CONT/OBS TREND METH/COMP SIMUL 20 CONGRESS. PAGE 30 F0592
DECISION NAT/G BUDGET EFFICIENCY

S66
FLEMING W.G.,"AUTHORITY, EFFICIENCY, AND ROLE STRESS: PROBLEMS IN THE DEVELOPMENT OF EAST AFRICAN BUREAUCRACIES." AFR UGANDA STRUCT PROB/SOLV ROUTINE INGP/REL ROLE...MGT SOC GP/COMP GOV/COMP 20 TANGANYIKA AFRICA/E. PAGE 41 F0810
DOMIN EFFICIENCY COLONIAL ADMIN

S66
JACOBS P.,"RE-RADICALIZING THE DE-RADICALIZED." USA+45 SOCIETY STRUCT FINAN PLAN PROB/SOLV CAP/ISM WEALTH CONSERVE NEW/LIB 20. PAGE 66 F1297
NAT/G POLICY MARXIST ADMIN

S66
JAVITS J.K.,"POLITICAL ACTION VITAL FOR LATIN AMERICAN INTEGRATION." ECO/UNDEV INT/ORG POL/PAR VOL/ASSN PLAN PROB/SOLV INT/TRADE EFFICIENCY 20 OAS LAFTA ALL/PROG. PAGE 66 F1308
L/A+17C ECO/TAC REGION

S66
LINDBLOOM C.E.,"HAS INDIA AN ECONOMIC FUTURE?" FUT INDIA NAT/G PROB/SOLV...POLICY 20. PAGE 80 F1568
AGRI PRODUC PLAN ECO/UNDEV

S66
ROTHCHILD D.,"THE LIMITS OF FEDERALISM: AN EXAMINATION OF POLITICAL INSTITUTIONAL TRANSFER IN AFRICA." AFR CONSTN CULTURE ELITES ECO/UNDEV KIN PROB/SOLV ADMIN ORD/FREE PWR...POLICY 20. PAGE 114
FEDERAL NAT/G NAT/LISM COLONIAL

F2250

N66

EOMMITTEE ECONOMIC DEVELOPMENT,THE DOLLAR AND THE WORLD MONETARY SYSTEM: A STATEMENT ON NATIONAL POLICY (PAMPHLET). AFR USA+45 NAT/G PLAN PROB/SOLV BUDGET ECO/TAC FOR/AID INCOME...POLICY 20 EUROPE. PAGE 38 F0740
FINAN
BAL/PAY
DIPLOM
ECO/DEV

N66

OECD,THE BALANCE OF PAYMENTS ADJUSTMENT PROCESS (PAMPHLET). EUR+WWI ECO/DEV FINAN CONSULT PLAN PROB/SOLV BUDGET CAP/ISM INT/TRADE PRICE CONTROL EQUILIB 20. PAGE 101 F1975
BAL/PAY
ECO/TAC
DIPLOM
INT/ORG

B67

AARON H.J.,FINANCING URBAN DEVELOPMENT IN MEXICO CITY: A CASE STUDY OF PROPERTY TAX, LAND USE, HOUSING, AND URBAN PLANNING. LOC/G CREATE EFFICIENCY WEALTH...CHARTS MUNICH 20 MEXIC/AMER. PAGE 2 F0030
PLAN
TAX
PROB/SOLV

B67

ANDERSON C.W.,POLITICS AND ECONOMIC CHANGE IN LATIN AMERICA. L/A+17C INDUS NAT/G OP/RES ADMIN DEMAND ...POLICY STAT CHARTS NAT/COMP 20. PAGE 5 F0093
ECO/UNDEV
PROB/SOLV
PLAN
ECO/TAC

B67

APTHEKER H.,THE NATURE OF DEMOCRACY, FREEDOM AND REVOLUTION. WOR+45 PROB/SOLV COERCE COST...CONCPT TIME/SEQ METH/COMP. PAGE 6 F0111
REV
POPULISM
MARXIST
ORD/FREE

B67

BALDWIN G.B.,PLANNING AND DEVELOPMENT IN IRAN. IRAN AGRI INDUS CONSULT WORKER EDU/PROP BAL/PAY...CHARTS 20. PAGE 9 F0164
PLAN
ECO/UNDEV
ADMIN
PROB/SOLV

B67

BARANSON J.,TECHNOLOGY FOR UNDERDEVELOPED AREAS: AN ANNOTATED BIBLIOGRAPHY. FUT WOR+45 CULTURE INDUS INT/ORG CREATE PROB/SOLV INT/TRADE EDU/PROP AUTOMAT ...CONCPT METH. PAGE 10 F0181
BIBLIOG/A
ECO/UNDEV
TEC/DEV
R+D

B67

BRIEFS H.W.,REGAINING BALANCE IN A HIGH EMPLOYMENT ECONOMY: UNRESOLVED ISSUES FOR 1967 AND BEYOND. USA+45 NAT/G PLAN PROB/SOLV FOR/AID...CHARTS 20. PAGE 18 F0350
ECO/DEV
FINAN
BAL/PAY
BUDGET

B67

CASTILLO C.M.,GROWTH AND INTEGRATION IN CENTRAL AMERICA. L/A+17C CREATE PROB/SOLV ECO/TAC REGION PRODUC...OBS BIBLIOG 20. PAGE 22 F0429
ECO/UNDEV
INT/TRADE
NAT/COMP

B67

CHANDRASEKHAR S.,PROBLEMS OF ECONOMIC DEVELOPMENT. AFR INDIA PHILIPPINE UAR WOR+45 INDUS...GEOG SOC ANTHOL BIBLIOG 20 CHINJAP. PAGE 23 F0450
ECO/UNDEV
PLAN
AGRI
PROB/SOLV

B67

CHAPIN F.S. JR.,SELECTED REFERENCES ON URBAN PLANNING METHODS AND TECHNIQUES. USA+45 LAW ECO/DEV LOC/G NAT/G SCHOOL CONSULT CREATE PROB/SOLV TEC/DEV ...SOC/WK MUNICH. PAGE 23 F0454
BIBLIOG
NEIGH
PLAN

B67

CHILCOTE R.H.,PORTUGUESE AFRICA. PORTUGAL CULTURE SOCIETY ECO/UNDEV DOMIN NAT/LISM...TREND IDEA/COMP NAT/COMP BIBLIOG 15/20. PAGE 24 F0465
AFR
COLONIAL
ORD/FREE
PROB/SOLV

B67

CHO S.S.,KOREA IN WORLD POLITICS 1940-1950; AN EVALUATION OF AMERICAN RESPONSIBILITY. KOREA USA+45 USSR CONSTN INT/ORG NAT/G FORCES FOR/AID ANOMIE SUPEGO MARXISM...DECISION BIBLIOG 20. PAGE 24 F0469
POLICY
DIPLOM
PROB/SOLV
WAR

B67

CLEGERN W.M.,BRITISH HONDURAS: COLONIAL DEAD END, 1859-1900. HONDURAS AGRI FINAN PROB/SOLV INT/TRADE PWR WEALTH...BIBLIOG/A 19. PAGE 25 F0487
COLONIAL
POLICY
ECO/UNDEV
DOMIN

B67

CLEMENT M.O.,THEORETICAL ISSUES IN INTERNATIONAL ECONOMICS. WOR+45 PLAN PROB/SOLV TEC/DEV ...ECOMETRIC METH/CNCPT MATH BIBLIOG T MONEY. PAGE 25 F0489
INT/TRADE
FINAN
CREATE
BAL/PAY

B67

DAVIS H.B.,NATIONALISM AND SOCIALISM: MARXIST AND LABOR THEORIES OF NATIONALISM TO 1917. WOR-45 PROB/SOLV SOVEREIGN...CONCPT IDEA/COMP 19/20. PAGE 30 F0589
MARXISM
ATTIT
NAT/LISM
SOCISM

B67

DONALD A.G.,MANAGEMENT, INFORMATION, AND SYSTEMS. WOR+45 LG/CO PROB/SOLV CONTROL FEEDBACK KNOWL MGT. PAGE 34 F0653
ROUTINE
TEC/DEV
CONCPT
ADMIN

B67

EGGERT G.G.,RAILROAD LABOR DISPUTES. USA+45 USA-45 ELITES DIST/IND DELIB/GP FORCES JUDGE WORKER PROB/SOLV DOMIN PWR...POLICY 20. PAGE 36 F0707
GP/REL
NAT/G
LABOR
BARGAIN

B67

ELDREDGE H.W.,TAMING MEGALOPOLIS; HOW TO MANAGE AN URBANIZED WORLD. WOR+45 SOCIETY ECO/DEV ECO/UNDEV NAT/G COMPUTER CREATE PARTIC EFFICIENCY WEALTH ...MGT ANTHOL MUNICH. PAGE 37 F0716
TEC/DEV
PLAN
PROB/SOLV

B67

ELDREDGE H.W.,TAMING MEGALOPOLIS; WHAT IT IS AND WHAT COULD BE (VOL. I). FUT USA+45 WOR+45 SOCIETY STRUCT ECO/DEV INDUS LEISURE WEALTH...ANTHOL MUNICH. PAGE 37 F0717
PROB/SOLV
PLAN
TEC/DEV

B67

GOLDMAN M.,CONTROLLING POLLUTION: THE ECONOMICS OF A CLEANER AMERICA. USA+45 SOCIETY PROB/SOLV CONTROL COST ANTHOL. PAGE 48 F0936
HEALTH
ECO/DEV
NAT/G
FINAN

B67

GOODMAN P.,LIKE A CONQUERED PROVINCE: THE MORAL AMBIGUITY OF AMERICA. AFR USA+45 NAT/G PROB/SOLV EDU/PROP ADJUST EFFICIENCY 20. PAGE 49 F0950
SOCIETY
TEC/DEV
WAR
MORAL

B67

HARDT J.P.,MATHEMATICS AND COMPUTERS IN SOVIET ECONOMIC PLANNING. COM USSR OP/RES PROB/SOLV OPTIMAL...MODAL SIMUL 20. PAGE 55 F1082
PLAN
TEC/DEV
MATH
COMPUT/IR

B67

HODGKINSON R.G.,THE ORIGINS OF THE NATIONAL HEALTH SERVICE: THE MEDICAL SERVICES OF THE NEW POOR LAW, 1834-1871. UK INDUS WORKER PROB/SOLV EFFICIENCY ATTIT HEALTH WEALTH SOCISM...JURID SOC/WK MUNICH 19/20. PAGE 60 F1189
HEAL
NAT/G
POLICY
LAW

B67

JOHNSON D.G.,THE STRUGGLE AGAINST WORLD HUNGER (HEADLINE SERIES, NO. 184) (PAMPHLET). PLAN TEC/DEV FOR/AID...CHARTS 20 FAO MEXIC/AMER. PAGE 67 F1322
AGRI
PROB/SOLV
ECO/UNDEV
HEALTH

B67

KULSKI J.E.,LAND OF URBAN PROMISE* CONTINUING THE GREAT TRADITION* A SEARCH FOR SIGNIFICANT URBAN SPACE IN URBANIZED NORTHEAST. USA+45 DIST/IND PUB/INST CONSULT CREATE TEC/DEV...SOC NEW/IDEA CHARTS BIBLIOG MUNICH. PAGE 74 F1448
PLAN
PROB/SOLV
ECO/DEV

B67

LEIBY J.,CHARITY AND CORRECTION IN JERSEY; A HISTORY OF STATE WELFARE INSTITUTIONS. DELIB/GP EX/STRUC PROB/SOLV INSPECT LEAD ADJUST HEALTH ...POLICY PSY NEW/JERSEY. PAGE 77 F1514
PROVS
PUB/INST
ADMIN

B67

LYND S.,RECONSTRUCTION. USA-45 PROB/SOLV RACE/REL ...IDEA/COMP ANTHOL 19. PAGE 82 F1616
SUFF
ECO/TAC
ADJUST

B67

LYTLE C.M.,THE WARREN COURT AND ITS CRITICS. USA+45 NAT/G PROVS FORCES LOBBY RACE/REL DISCRIM SOVEREIGN 20 SUPREME/CT WARRN/EARL. PAGE 83 F1618
CT/SYS
ADJUD
PROB/SOLV
ATTIT

B67

MARRIS P.,DILEMMAS OF SOCIAL REFORM: POVERTY AND COMMUNITY ACTION IN THE UNITED STATES. USA+45 NAT/G OP/RES ADMIN PARTIC EFFICIENCY WEALTH...SOC METH/COMP T MUNICH 20 REFORMERS. PAGE 85 F1674
STRUCT
PROB/SOLV
COST

B67

MAZOUR A.G.,SOVIET ECONOMIC DEVELOPMENT: OPERATION OUTSTRIP: 1921-1965. USSR ECO/UNDEV FINAN CHIEF WORKER PROB/SOLV CONTROL PRODUC MARXISM...CHARTS ORG/CHARTS 20 STALIN/J. PAGE 87 F1711
ECO/TAC
AGRI
INDUS
PLAN

B67

MCDOUGAL M.S.,THE INTERPRETATION OF AGREEMENTS AND WORLD PUBLIC ORDER: PRINCIPLES OF CONTENT AND PROCEDURE. WOR+45 CONSTN PROB/SOLV TEC/DEV ...CON/ANAL TREATY. PAGE 88 F1727
INT/LAW
STRUCT
ECO/UNDEV
DIPLOM

B67

MEYNAUD J.,TRADE UNIONISM IN AFRICA; A STUDY OF ITS GROWTH AND ORIENTATION (TRANS. BY ANGELA BRENCH). INT/ORG PROB/SOLV COLONIAL PWR...TIME/SEQ TREND ILO. PAGE 90 F1774
LABOR
AFR
NAT/LISM
ORD/FREE

B67

MOSS F.M.,THE WATER CRISIS. PROB/SOLV CONTROL ...POLICY NEW/IDEA. PAGE 94 F1846
GEOG
ACT/RES
PRODUC
WEALTH

B67

MUHAMMAD A.C.,THE EMERGENCE OF PAKISTAN. PAKISTAN S/ASIA CONSTN ECO/UNDEV NAT/G CONTROL NAT/LISM 20. PAGE 94 F1853
DIPLOM
COLONIAL
SECT
PROB/SOLV

B67

MURTY B.S.,PROPAGANDA AND WORLD PUBLIC ORDER. FUT WOR+45 COM/IND INT/ORG PROB/SOLV ATTIT KNOWL ORD/FREE...POLICY UN. PAGE 95 F1868
EDU/PROP
DIPLOM
CONTROL
JURID

B67

NORTON H.S.,NATIONAL TRANSPORTATION POLICY: FORMATION AND IMPLEMENTATION. USA+45 USA-45 DELIB/GP LEAD...DECISION TIME/SEQ 19/20 PRESIDENT CONGRESS. PAGE 98 F1935
POLICY
DIST/IND
NAT/G
PROB/SOLV

B67

ROBINSON E.A.G.,ECONOMIC PLANNING IN THE UNITED KINGDOM. UK WORKER PLAN PROB/SOLV BAL/PAY 20. PAGE 113 F2220
ECO/DEV
INDUS
PRODUC

BUDGET

B67
SCHON D.A.,TECHNOLOGY AND CHANGE* THE NEW HERACLITUS. TEC/DEV CONTROL COST DEMAND EFFICIENCY RIGID/FLEX...MYTH 20. PAGE 117 F2311 — INDUS PROB/SOLV R+D CREATE

B67
WOOTON G.,WORKERS, UNIONS, AND THE STATE. INDUS PROB/SOLV GP/REL DRIVE SUPEGO RESPECT...PSY SOC. PAGE 148 F2925 — PARTIC WORKER NAT/G LABOR

B67
ZUPNICK E.,UNDERSTANDING THE INTERNATIONAL MONEY SYSTEM (HEADLINE SERIES, NO. 182) (PAMPHLET). ECO/DEV NAT/G DIPLOM INT/TRADE...METH/COMP 20 IMF. PAGE 151 F2971 — FINAN PLAN INT/ORG PROB/SOLV

L67
DROBNIG U.,"CONFLICT OF LAWS AND THE EUROPEAN ECONOMIC COMMUNITY." EUR+WWI PROB/SOLV DIPLOM ...JURID EEC. PAGE 34 F0663 — INT/LAW ADJUD INT/ORG MARKET

L67
MACDONALD R.M.,"COLLECTIVE BARGAINING IN THE POSTWAR PERIOD." WORKER PROB/SOLV ECO/TAC PARTIC RISK CENTRAL EFFICIENCY DRIVE WEALTH...TREND 20. PAGE 83 F1624 — LABOR INDUS BARGAIN CAP/ISM

L67
MIXON J.,"JANE JACOBS AND THE LAW - ZONING FOR DIVERSITY EXAMINED." FUT USA+45 CONSTN NEIGH PROB/SOLV CONTROL CT/SYS PARTIC ATTIT...POLICY CENSUS METH/COMP MUNICH. PAGE 92 F1810 — IDEA/COMP PLAN LAW

L67
ROBERTS E.F.,"THE CASE OF THE UNWARY HOME BUYER: THE HOUSING MERCHANT DID IT." USA+45 CLIENT DIST/IND MARKET LG/CO SML/CO PROB/SOLV LEGIT COST PROFIT. PAGE 112 F2207 — ADJUD CONSTRUC OWN LAW

L67
SCHNEIDER C.W.,"REFORM OF THE FEDERAL SECURITIES LAWS." FUT USA+45 LAW FINAN INDUS DELIB/GP ACT/RES PROB/SOLV GP/REL. PAGE 117 F2304 — NAT/G LG/CO ADMIN CONTROL

L67
SEABERG G.P.,"THE DRUG ABUSE PROBLEMS AND SOME PROPOSALS." UK USA+45 MARKET SANCTION CRIME ...POLICY NEW/IDEA. PAGE 119 F2339 — BIO/SOC LAW ADJUD PROB/SOLV

L67
WATKINS J.B.,"MONETARY RECOVERY UNDER FEDERAL ANTITRUST STATUTES." USA+45 PROB/SOLV ADJUD CT/SYS GOV/REL ORD/FREE 20. PAGE 144 F2831 — LG/CO CONTROL LAW FINAN

L67
WILKINSON J.H. JR.,"THE NET OPERATING LOSS DEDUCTION AND RELATED INCOME TAX DEVICES." PROB/SOLV BUDGET PAY GOV/REL ORD/FREE...MATH CHARTS METH 20. PAGE 146 F2886 — TAX FINAN LAW ADJUD

S67
"ANTITRUST VENUE: TRANSACTING BUSINESS UNDER THE CLAYTON ACT." USA+45 DIST/IND PROB/SOLV ECO/TAC ADJUD CT/SYS 20. PAGE 2 F0028 — LAW LG/CO CONTROL NAT/G

S67
ADAMS R.N.,"ETHICS AND THE SOCIAL ANTHROPOLOGIST IN LATIN AMERICA." USA+45 INTELL PROB/SOLV ECO/TAC LEAD...DECISION SOC NAT/COMP PERS/COMP. PAGE 2 F0039 — L/A+17C POLICY ECO/UNDEV CONSULT

S67
ALBAUM G.,"INFORMATION FLOW AND DECENTRALIZED DECISION MAKING IN MARKETING." EX/STRUC COMPUTER OP/RES PROB/SOLV EFFICIENCY OPTIMAL...METH/COMP ORG/CHARTS 20. PAGE 3 F0056 — LG/CO ROUTINE KNOWL MARKET

S67
AMERASINGHE C.F.,"SOME LEGAL PROBLEMS OF STATE TRADING IN SOUTHEAST ASIA." PROB/SOLV ADJUD CONTROL CT/SYS GP/REL 20. PAGE 5 F0084 — INT/TRADE NAT/G INT/LAW PRIVIL

S67
ANDERSON S.S.,"SOVIET RUSSIA AND THE TWO EUROPES." AFR USSR PROB/SOLV CENTRAL SOVEREIGN 20. PAGE 5 F0097 — DIPLOM POLICY MARXISM

S67
BELL D.E.,"THE QUALITY OF AID." USA+45 R+D DIPLOM GP/REL. PAGE 12 F0234 — POLICY FOR/AID PROB/SOLV INSPECT

S67
CHAMBERLAIN N.W.,"STRIKES IN CONTEMPORARY CONTEXT." LAW INDUS NAT/G CHIEF CONFER COST ATTIT ORD/FREE ...POLICY MGT 20. PAGE 23 F0442 — LABOR BARGAIN EFFICIENCY PROB/SOLV

S67
CROKER F.P.U.,"ECONOMIC PEACEKEEPING." UK PLAN PROB/SOLV TEC/DEV BAL/PWR DIPLOM COERCE PEACE ...POLICY DECISION 20. PAGE 28 F0553 — FORCES WEAPON COST WAR

S67
FRIEDEN B.J.,"THE CHANGING PROSPECTS FOR SOCIAL PLANNING." USA+45 PROB/SOLV RACE/REL WEALTH ...SOC/WK PREDICT MUNICH 20 NEGRO. PAGE 44 F0856 — PLAN LOC/G POLICY

S67
FUCHS V.R.,"REDEFINING POVERTY AND REDISTRIBUTING INCOME." USA+45 NAT/G ECO/TAC GIVE COST...NEW/IDEA CHARTS. PAGE 45 F0873 — WEALTH INCOME STRATA PROB/SOLV

S67
GAMARNIKOW M.,"THE NEW ROLE OF PRIVATE ENTERPRISE." ECO/DEV INDUS NAT/G SML/CO CREATE PROB/SOLV MARXISM ...POLICY TREND IDEA/COMP 20. PAGE 46 F0890 — ECO/TAC ATTIT CAP/ISM COM

S67
GAUSE M.E.,"ELEMENTS OF FINANCE DEPARTMENT ORGANIZATION FOR SMALL GOVERNMENTAL UNITS." USA+45 PROB/SOLV CONTROL CENTRAL...METH MUNICH. PAGE 47 F0910 — ADMIN LOC/G FINAN

S67
GRAHAM R.,"BRAZIL'S DILEMMA." BRAZIL FUT L/A+17C NAT/G CHIEF PROB/SOLV ECO/TAC PWR 20. PAGE 50 F0972 — ECO/UNDEV CONSTN POL/PAR POLICY

S67
GRUN C.,"DEUX ETUDES ALLEMANDES SUR LES PREJUGES NATIONAUX ET LES MOYENS DE LES COMBATTRE." FRANCE GERMANY DIST/IND PROB/SOLV GP/REL AGE/Y RIGID/FLEX ...PSY STAT INT SAMP. PAGE 52 F1010 — ATTIT REGION DISCRIM STERTYP

S67
HALL B.,"THE PAINTER'S UNION: A PARTIAL VICTORY." USA+45 PROB/SOLV LEGIT ADMIN REPRESENT 20. PAGE 53 F1043 — LABOR CHIEF CHOOSE CRIME

S67
HALL B.,"THE COALITION AGAINST DISHWASHERS." USA+45 POL/PAR PROB/SOLV BARGAIN LEAD CHOOSE REPRESENT GP/REL ORD/FREE PWR...POLICY 20. PAGE 53 F1044 — LABOR ADMIN DOMIN WORKER

S67
HEILBRONER R.L.,"BUILDING NEW NATIONS." AFR STRUCT PLAN TEC/DEV ADJUST MARXISM...POLICY 20. PAGE 58 F1138 — PROB/SOLV REV NAT/LISM ECO/UNDEV

S67
HILTON G.W.,"FEDERAL PARTICIPATION IN THE SUPERSONIC TRANSPORT PROGRAM." USA+45 LEGIS PROB/SOLV BUDGET ATTIT 20. PAGE 60 F1172 — DIST/IND TEC/DEV FINAN NAT/G

S67
JOHNSON L.B.,"BULLETS DO NOT DISCRIMINATE-LANDLORDS DO." PROB/SOLV EXEC LOBBY DEMAND...REALPOL SOC 20. PAGE 68 F1329 — NAT/G DISCRIM POLICY

S67
KELLY F.K.,"A PROPOSAL FOR AN ANNUAL REPORT ON THE STATE OF MANKIND." FUT INTELL COM/IND INT/ORG CREATE PROB/SOLV PERS/REL...CONCPT 20 UN. PAGE 70 F1371 — SOCIETY UNIV ATTIT NEW/IDEA

S67
KRAUS J.,"A MARXIST IN GHANA." GHANA ELITES CHIEF PROB/SOLV TEC/DEV DIPLOM ECO/TAC COLONIAL PARTIC PWR 20 NKRUMAH/K. PAGE 73 F1432 — MARXISM PLAN ATTIT CREATE

S67
LEDEBUR L.C.,"THE PROBLEM OF SOCIAL COST." STRUCT PROB/SOLV...CHARTS GEN/LAWS. PAGE 77 F1501 — COST INCOME SOCIETY ECO/TAC

S67
MAJSTRENKO I.W.,"PROBLEMS CONFRONTING SOVIET AGRICULTURE." COM USSR ECO/DEV ECO/TAC EFFICIENCY OPTIMAL WEALTH MARXISM 20. PAGE 84 F1643 — AGRI PROB/SOLV CENTRAL TEC/DEV

S67
MELTZER B.D.,"RUMINATIONS ABOUT IDEOLOGY, LAW, AND LABOR ARBITRATION." USA+45 ECO/DEV PROB/SOLV CONFER MGT. PAGE 89 F1754 — JURID ADJUD LABOR CONSULT

S67
MENCHER S.,"THE PROBLEM OF MEASURING POVERTY." UNIV USA+45 STRATA PROB/SOLV...NEW/IDEA METH/COMP 20. PAGE 89 F1755 — WEALTH CENSUS STAT GEN/LAWS

S67
MYERS S.,"TECHNOLOGY AND URBAN TRANSIT: THE ENORMOUS POTENTIAL OF BUS AND RAIL SYSTEMS." USA+45 FINAN LOC/G WORKER PLAN PROB/SOLV PRICE AUTOMAT MUNICH 20. PAGE 96 F1877 — R+D TEC/DEV DIST/IND ACT/RES

S67
PEMBERTON J., JR.,"CONSTITUTIONAL PROBLEMS IN RESTRAINT ON THE MEDIA." CONSTN PROB/SOLV EDU/PROP CONFER CONTROL JURID. PAGE 104 F2054 — LAW PRESS ORD/FREE

S67
RICHMAN B.M.,"SOVIET MANAGEMENT IN TRANSITION." USSR FINAN MARKET EX/STRUC PLAN PROB/SOLV TEC/DEV CONTROL LEAD CENTRAL EFFICIENCY...METH/COMP 20 — MGT MARXISM POLICY

REFORMERS. PAGE 111 F2186 AUTHORIT

S67
SCHACHTER G.,"REGIONAL DEVELOPMENT IN THE ITALIAN DUAL ECONOMY" ITALY AGRI INDUS MARKET WORKER ECO/TAC CONTROL INCOME PRODUC 20. PAGE 116 F2287
REGION ECO/UNDEV NAT/G PROB/SOLV

S67
SCHELLING T.C.,"ECONOMICS AND CRIMINAL ENTERPRISE." LAW FORCES BARGAIN ECO/TAC CONTROL GAMBLE ROUTINE ADJUST DEMAND INCOME PROFIT CRIMLGY. PAGE 116 F2295
CRIME PROB/SOLV CONCPT

S67
SIDDIQ M.M.,"LOCAL GOVERNMENT IN PAKISTAN." PAKISTAN PROB/SOLV TAX COLONIAL GOV/REL MUNICH 20. PAGE 121 F2395
ADMIN LOC/G DELIB/GP BUDGET

S67
SIMONE A.J.,"SCIENTIFIC PUBLIC POLICY, MARKET PERFORMANCE, AND SIZE OF FIRM." GP/REL COST EFFICIENCY OPTIMAL PRODUC PWR. PAGE 122 F2410
LAW INDUS NAT/G PROB/SOLV

S67
SKOLNICK J.H.,"SOCIAL CONTROL IN THE ADVERSARY SYSTEM." USA+45 CONSULT OP/RES ADMIN CONTROL. PAGE 123 F2419
PROB/SOLV PERS/REL ADJUD CT/SYS

S67
STRANGE S.,"DEBTS, DEFAULTERS AND DEVELOPMENT." WOR+45 PROB/SOLV FOR/AID INT/TRADE. PAGE 127 F2500
NAT/G FINAN ECO/UNDEV

S67
TELLER A.,"AIR-POLLUTION ABATEMENT: ECONOMIC RATIONALITY AND REALITY." NAT/G DELIB/GP ECO/TAC GOV/REL CENTRAL EFFICIENCY HEALTH...CHARTS METH MUNICH. PAGE 129 F2543
PROB/SOLV CONTROL COST AIR

S67
WILLMANN J.,"LA COMMUNAUTE EUROPEENNE ET LA GRANDE-BRETAGNE." UK PROB/SOLV TEC/DEV CAP/ISM DIPLOM CONFER FEDERAL...POLICY 20 EEC. PAGE 147 F2898
INT/ORG DRIVE NAT/LISM INT/TRADE

S67
ZACK A.M.,"ARE STRIKES OF PUBLIC EMPLOYEES NECESSARY?" USA+45 DELIB/GP PROB/SOLV REPRESENT GP/REL MGT. PAGE 150 F2956
LABOR NAT/G WORKER BARGAIN

S67
ZOETEWEIJ B.,"INCOME POLICIES ABROAD: AN INTERIM REPORT." NAT/G PROB/SOLV BARGAIN BUDGET PRICE RISK CENTRAL EFFICIENCY EQUILIB...MGT NAT/COMP 20. PAGE 150 F2967
METH/COMP INCOME POLICY LABOR

N67
US HOUSE COMM ON COMMERCE,PARTNERSHIP FOR HEALTH AMENDMENTS FOR 1967 (PAMPHLET). PUB/INST DELIB/GP PROB/SOLV BUDGET EFFICIENCY 20 CONGRESS. PAGE 137 F2701
HEAL PLAN NAT/G JURID

N67
US SENATE COMM ON FOREIGN REL,WAR OR PEACE IN THE MIDDLE EAST (PAMPHLET). GREECE ISLAM ISRAEL JORDAN UAR CHIEF PROB/SOLV FOR/AID WAR PWR 20 SENATE. PAGE 139 F2739
DIPLOM FORCES PLAN

N67
US SENATE COMM ON FOREIGN REL,THE RIM OF ASIA (PAMPHLET). WAR MARXISM 20. PAGE 139 F2745
ASIA PROB/SOLV SOVEREIGN POLICY

PROBABIL....PROBABILITY; SEE ALSO GAMBLE

S57
DETAMBEL M.H.,"PROBABILITY AND WORK AS DETERMINERS OF MULTICHOICE BEHAVIOR." PLAN TASK EFFICIENCY ...DECISION GAME. PAGE 32 F0622
HYPO/EXP PROB/SOLV GEN/LAWS PROBABIL

S58
FOLDES L.,"UNCERTAINTY, PROBABILITY AND POTENTIAL SURPRISE." MARKET PROB/SOLV RISK PERSON...DECISION MGT HYPO/EXP GAME. PAGE 42 F0820
PROBABIL ADMIN ROUTINE

L59
SIMON H.A.,"THEORIES OF DECISION-MAKING IN ECONOMICS AND BEHAVIORAL SCIENCE" (BMR)" MARKET BARGAIN UTIL DRIVE...DECISION MGT PROBABIL HYPO/EXP SIMUL 20 BEHAVIORSM. PAGE 122 F2409
PSY GEN/LAWS PROB/SOLV

S59
HARING J.E.,"UTILITY THEORY, DECISION THEORY, AND PROFIT MAXIMIZATION." PROB/SOLV GAMBLE UTIL ...DECISION CHARTS IDEA/COMP HYPO/EXP SIMUL GEN/METH. PAGE 55 F1083
PROBABIL RISK GAME

B60
MORRIS W.T.,ENGINEERING ECONOMY. AUTOMAT RISK RATIONAL...PROBABIL STAT CHARTS GAME SIMUL BIBLIOG T 20. PAGE 94 F1838
OP/RES DECISION MGT PROB/SOLV

S61
HIRSHLEIFER J.,"THE BAYESIAN APPROACH TO STATISTICAL DECISION: AN EXPOSITION." OP/RES PROB/SOLV UTIL...PROBABIL CHARTS IDEA/COMP HYPO/EXP 20. PAGE 60 F1178
DECISION GAME SIMUL STAT

S61
SHUBIK M.,"APPROACHES TO THE STUDY OF DECISION-MAKING RELEVANT TO THE FIRM." INDUS COMPUTER OP/RES ...PROBABIL STAT 20. PAGE 121 F2390
GAME DECISION MGT SIMUL

B62
BRANCH M.C.,THE CORPORATE PLANNING PROCESS. FINAN EX/STRUC EDU/PROP CONTROL LEAD GP/REL PERS/REL RATIONAL PERCEPT...MGT MATH PROBABIL STAT GAME. PAGE 18 F0338
PROF/ORG PLAN DECISION PERSON

B63
BONINI C.P.,SIMULATION OF INFORMATION AND DECISION SYSTEMS IN THE FIRM. MARKET BUDGET DOMIN EDU/PROP ADMIN COST ATTIT HABITAT PERCEPT PWR...CONCPT PROBABIL QUANT PREDICT HYPO/EXP BIBLIOG. PAGE 16 F0313
INDUS SIMUL DECISION MGT

B64
JUSTER F.T.,ANTICIPATIONS AND PURCHASES; AN ANALYSIS OF CONSUMER BEHAVIOR. PROB/SOLV RISK COST PRODUC DRIVE...STAT STYLE SAMP CON/ANAL CHARTS HYPO/EXP GAME SIMUL. PAGE 68 F1345
PROBABIL DECISION PREDICT DEMAND

B65
MUSHKIN S.J.,PROPERTY TAXES: THE 1970 OUTLOOK (PAMPHLET). FUT USA+45 ECO/DEV MARKET PROVS PLAN ...PROBABIL STAT CENSUS PREDICT CHARTS METH 20. PAGE 95 F1872
TAX OWN FINAN LOC/G

B66
HEISS K.P.,GAME THEORY AND HUMAN CONFLICTS (RESEARCH MEMORANDUM). UNIV ACT/RES...DECISION SOC MATH PROBABIL SIMUL 20 DEFINETT/B. PAGE 58 F1142
GAME ECOMETRIC PLAN PROB/SOLV

B66
KUENNE R.E.,THE POLARIS MISSILE STRIKE* A GENERAL ECONOMIC SYSTEMS ANALYSIS. USA+45 USSR NAT/G BAL/PWR ARMS/CONT WAR...MATH PROBABIL COMPUT/IR CHARTS HYPO/EXP SIMUL. PAGE 74 F1446
NUC/PWR FORCES DETER DIPLOM

PROBABILITY....SEE PROBABIL

PROBERT J.R. F2123

PROBLEM SOLVING....SEE PROB/SOLV

PROC/MFG....PROCESSING OR MANUFACTURING INDUSTRIES

B18
MARX K.,CAPITAL. FUT MOD/EUR STRATA DIST/IND PROC/MFG TEC/DEV WEALTH...MARXIST WORK 19. PAGE 86 F1688
ECO/DEV CAP/ISM SOCISM

N19
LAWRENCE S.A.,THE BATTERY ADDITIVE CONTROVERSY (PAMPHLET). USA+45 LAW MARKET PROC/MFG R+D CAP/ISM CT/SYS GOV/REL OWN FTC CONGRESS BUR/STNDRD RITCHIE/JM. PAGE 76 F1494
PHIL/SCI LOBBY INSPECT

N19
MCCONNELL G.,THE STEEL SEIZURE OF 1952 (PAMPHLET). USA+45 FINAN INDUS PROC/MFG LG/CO EX/STRUC ADJUD CONTROL GP/REL ORD/FREE PWR 20 TRUMAN/HS PRESIDENT CONGRESS. PAGE 88 F1721
DELIB/GP LABOR PROB/SOLV NAT/G

N19
US BUREAU OF THE CENSUS,THE PROPORTION OF THE SHIPMENTS (OR EMPLOYEES) OF EACH INDUSTRY... (PAMPHLET). USA+45 ECO/DEV EXTR/IND INDUS CONTROL PROFIT...STAT 20 CONGRESS MONOPOLY. PAGE 134 F2645
PROC/MFG PRODUC MARKET CHARTS

B37
DALTON J.E.,SUGAR: A CASE STUDY OF GOVERNMENT CONTROL. USA-45 AGRI PROC/MFG LG/CO LEGIS PROB/SOLV ECO/TAC GP/REL...CHARTS 19/20. PAGE 30 F0575
CONTROL NAT/G INDUS POLICY

B47
WARNER W.L.,THE SOCIAL SYSTEM OF THE MODERN FACTORY; THE STRIKE: AN ANALYSIS. USA-45 STRATA WORKER ECO/TAC GP/REL INGP/REL...MGT SOC CHARTS 20 YANKEE/C. PAGE 143 F2824
ROLE STRUCT LABOR PROC/MFG

S49
ECKLER A.R.,"IMMIGRATION AND THE LABOR FORCE." USA+45 USA-45 EXTR/IND FINAN PROC/MFG AGE/Y SKILL ...CHARTS 19/20 MIGRATION. PAGE 36 F0694
WORKER STRANGE INDUS ECO/TAC

B51
ROEPKE W.,THE PROBLEM OF ECONOMIC ORDER. WOR+45 SOCIETY PROB/SOLV CONTROL EFFICIENCY...CON/ANAL IDEA/COMP GEN/METH 20. PAGE 113 F2231
ECO/TAC ORD/FREE MARKET PROC/MFG

B52
SACHS E.S.,THE CHOICE BEFORE SOUTH AFRICA. SOUTH/AFR AGRI EXTR/IND PROC/MFG PROB/SOLV ORD/FREE SOVEREIGN 20 NEGRO. PAGE 115 F2267
NAT/LISM DISCRIM RACE/REL LABOR

B57
BAUER P.T.,THE ECONOMICS OF UNDERDEVELOPED COUNTRIES. WOR+45 AGRI FINAN INDUS PROC/MFG WORKER CAP/ISM PAY PRICE INCOME MARXISM...METH/COMP 20 RESOURCE/N. PAGE 11 F0213
ECO/UNDEV ECO/TAC PROB/SOLV NAT/G

S57
VERNON R.,"PRODUCTION AND DISTRIBUTION IN THE LARGE PRODUC

METROPOLIS" (BMR)" USA+45 PROC/MFG ECO/TAC HABITAT ...CENSUS TREND MUNICH 20. PAGE 141 F2779 DIST/IND PROB/SOLV

B58
MIKESELL R.F.,FINANCING FREE WORLD TRADE WITH THE SINO-SOVIET BLOC. CHINA/COM COM USSR WOR+45 ECO/DEV AGRI DIST/IND EXTR/IND FINAN INDUS MARKET PROC/MFG NAT/G PLAN TEC/DEV ECO/TAC...CHARTS METH/GP EEC FOR/TRADE 20. PAGE 91 F1780 STAT BAL/PAY

B59
ALLEN R.L.,SOVIET INFLUENCE IN LATIN AMERICA. ECO/UNDEV FINAN PROC/MFG NAT/G TEC/DEV EDU/PROP EXEC ROUTINE ATTIT DRIVE PERSON ALL/VALS PWR...STAT CHARTS WORK FOR/TRADE 20. PAGE 4 F0071 L/A+17C ECO/TAC INT/TRADE USSR

B59
SELIGSOHN I.J.,"USING COMPUTER SERVICES IN SMALL BUSINESS" MANAGEMENT AIDS FOR SMALL MANUFACTURERS 109 (PAMPHLET). DIST/IND MARKET PROC/MFG COST EFFICIENCY PRODUC...DECISION IDEA/COMP. PAGE 119 F2350 SML/CO COMPUTER MGT PROB/SOLV

S59
STINCHCOMBE A.L.,"BUREAUCRATIC AND CRAFT ADMINISTRATION OF PRODUCTION: A COMPARATIVE STUDY" (BMR)" USA+45 STRUCT EX/STRUC ECO/TAC GP/REL ...CLASSIF GP/COMP IDEA/COMP GEN/LAWS 20 WEBER/MAX. PAGE 126 F2490 CONSTRUC PROC/MFG ADMIN PLAN

B60
APTHEKER H.,DISARMAMENT AND THE AMERICAN ECONOMY: A SYMPOSIUM. FUT USA+45 ECO/DEV DIST/IND FINAN INDUS PROC/MFG LABOR NAT/G POL/PAR CONSULT PLAN CAP/ISM INT/TRADE PEACE ATTIT MORAL WEALTH...TREND GEN/LAWS TOT/POP 20. PAGE 6 F0110 MARXIST ARMS/CONT

B61
FRIEDMANN W.G.,JOINT INTERNATIONAL BUSINESS VENTURES. ASIA ISLAM L/A+17C ECO/DEV DIST/IND FINAN PROC/MFG FACE/GP LG/CO NAT/G VOL/ASSN CONSULT EX/STRUC PLAN ADMIN ROUTINE WEALTH...OLD/LIB FOR/TRADE WORK 20. PAGE 44 F0865 ECO/UNDEV INT/TRADE

B61
MARX K.,THE COMMUNIST MANIFESTO. IN (MENDEL A. ESSENTIAL WORKS OF MARXISM, NEW YORK: BANTAM. FUT MOD/EUR CULTURE ECO/DEV ECO/UNDEV AGRI FINAN INDUS MARKET PROC/MFG LABOR POL/PAR CONSULT FORCES CREATE PLAN ADMIN ATTIT DRIVE RIGID/FLEX ORD/FREE PWR RESPECT MARX/KARL MUNICH WORK. PAGE 86 F1691 COM NEW/IDEA CAP/ISM REV

S61
VALLET R.,"IRAN: KEY TO THE MIDDLE EAST." COM IRAQ ISLAM KUWAIT LEBANON SAUDI/ARAB TURKEY ELITES SOCIETY INDUS PROC/MFG POL/PAR TOP/EX PLAN BAL/PWR DIPLOM ECO/TAC ALL/VALS...TREND FOR/TRADE CENTO 20. PAGE 140 F2760 NAT/G ECO/UNDEV IRAN

B62
BACKMAN J.,THE ECONOMICS OF THE ELECTRICAL MACHINERY INDUSTRY. USA+45 PROC/MFG LABOR WORKER INT/TRADE TV PRICE COST...CHARTS 19/20. PAGE 8 F0147 PRODUC TEC/DEV TREND

B62
BRIEFS H.W.,PRICING POWER AND "ADMINISTRATIVE" INFLATION (PAMPHLET). AFR USA+45 PROC/MFG CONTROL EFFICIENCY MONEY. PAGE 18 F0349 ECO/DEV PRICE POLICY EXEC

B62
GORT M.,DIVERSIFICATION AND INTEGRATION IN AMERICAN INDUSTRY. CLIENT DIST/IND PROC/MFG SERV/IND LG/CO CONTROL DEMAND PWR...METH/CNCPT STAT TREND CON/ANAL GP/COMP. PAGE 49 F0964 CONCPT GP/REL CLASSIF

B62
GREEN L.P.,DEVELOPMENT IN AFRICA. AFR CENTRL/AFR GHANA RHODESIA SOUTH/AFR AGRI PROC/MFG INT/TRADE DEMAND NAT/LISM PRODUC WEALTH...GEOG METH/CNCPT CHARTS BIBLIOG 20. PAGE 50 F0987 CULTURE ECO/UNDEV GOV/REL TREND

B62
MEYER F.V.,THE TERMS OF TRADE. WOR+45 AGRI MARKET PROC/MFG DIPLOM PRICE DEMAND PRODUC 20. PAGE 90 F1769 INT/TRADE BAL/PAY SIMUL EQUILIB

B62
US BUREAU OF THE CENSUS,REPORT FOR SUBCOMMITTEE ON ANTITRUST AND MONOPOLY: CONCENTRATION RATIOS IN MANUFACTURING INDUSTRY 1958. USA+45 ECO/DEV CONTROL GOV/REL OWN PRODUC PROFIT...STAT 20 CONGRESS MONOPOLY. PAGE 134 F2646 CHARTS PROC/MFG MARKET LG/CO

L62
WATERSTON A.,"PLANNING IN MOROCCO, ORGANIZATION AND IMPLEMENTATION. BALTIMORE: HOPKINS ECON. DEVELOP. INT. BANK FOR." ISLAM ECO/DEV AGRI DIST/IND INDUS PROC/MFG SERV/IND LOC/G EX/STRUC ECO/TAC PWR WEALTH TOT/POP TRUE/GP METH/GP TERR/GP VAL/FREE 20. PAGE 144 F2829 NAT/G PLAN MOROCCO

S62
MUELLER E.,"LOCATION DECISIONS OF MANUFACTURERS." USA+45 MARKET ATTIT...POLICY STAT INT CHARTS 20. PAGE 94 F1852 DECISION PROC/MFG GEOG TOP/EX

C62
GREEN L.P.,"DEVELOPMENT IN AFRICA." RHODESIA SOUTH/AFR UGANDA MARKET PROC/MFG PRODUC WEALTH ...GEOG 20. PAGE 50 F0986 BIBLIOG ECO/UNDEV AFR AGRI

B63
BROUDE H.W.,STEEL DECISIONS AND THE NATIONAL ECONOMY. USA+45 LG/CO PLAN ADMIN COST DECISION. PAGE 19 F0365 PROC/MFG NAT/G CONTROL ECO/TAC

B63
HOOPES R.,THE STEEL CRISIS. USA+45 INDUS ECO/TAC EDU/PROP PRICE CONTROL ATTIT...POLICY 20 KENNEDY/JF. PAGE 61 F1205 PROC/MFG NAT/G RATION CHIEF

B63
HUNTER A.,THE ECONOMICS OF AUSTRALIAN INDUSTRY. DIST/IND EXTR/IND FINAN PROC/MFG SERV/IND ACT/RES PLAN TARIFFS GP/REL INGP/REL 20 AUSTRAL. PAGE 63 F1245 INDUS ECO/DEV HABITAT GP/COMP

B63
NEUMARK S.D.,FOREIGN TRADE AND ECONOMIC DEVELOPMENT IN AFRICA: A HISTORICAL PERSPECTIVE. EUR+WWI MOD/EUR ECO/UNDEV AGRI COM/IND EXTR/IND PROC/MFG SKILL WEALTH...CONCPT TIME/SEQ TREND SIMUL FOR/TRADE WORK TOT/POP TERR/GP VAL/FREE 19/20. PAGE 98 F1916 AFR

B63
STIFEL L.D.,THE TEXTILE INDUSTRY - A CASE STUDY OF INDUSTRIAL DEVELOPMENT IN THE PHILIPPINES (PAPER). PHILIPPINE WORKER CAP/ISM INT/TRADE TARIFFS RECEIVE PRICE ADMIN COST EFFICIENCY WEALTH...BIBLIOG 20. PAGE 126 F2486 S/ASIA ECO/UNDEV PROC/MFG NAT/G

S63
ANDREWS R.B.,"ECONOMIC PLANNING FOR SMALL AREAS: THE PLANNING PROCESS." INDUS PROC/MFG PROVS PROB/SOLV TAX EQUILIB...METH/COMP HYPO/EXP METH MUNICH 20. PAGE 5 F0103 ECO/TAC PLAN LOC/G

S63
GALENSON W.,"ECONOMIC DEVELOPMENT AND THE SECTORAL EXPANSION OF EMPLOYMENT, INT." FUT WOR+45 ECO/UNDEV DIST/IND PROC/MFG SERV/IND ACT/RES HEALTH SKILL WEALTH...STAT TIME/SEQ VAL/FREE 20. PAGE 46 F0889 INDUS ECO/TAC

S63
PAAUW D.S.,"ECONOMIC PROGRESS IN SOUTHEAST ASIA." S/ASIA AGRI INDUS PROC/MFG ACT/RES ECO/TAC...CHARTS VAL/FREE 20. PAGE 102 F2010 ECO/UNDEV STAT

S63
REDDAWAY W.B.,"THE ECONOMICS OF UNDERDEVELOPED COUNTRIES." S/ASIA WOR+45 WOR-45 STRATA AGRI COM/IND DIST/IND MARKET PROC/MFG PLAN TEC/DEV FOR/AID BAL/PAY ATTIT DRIVE SKILL WORK FOR/TRADE 20. PAGE 110 F2165 ECO/TAC ECO/UNDEV INDIA

S63
SHWADRAN B.,"MIDDLE EAST OIL, 1962." ISLAM DIST/IND INDUS PLAN ATTIT DRIVE WEALTH...POLICY STAT CONT/OBS TREND CHARTS GEN/LAWS TERR/GP METH/GP 20 OIL. PAGE 121 F2393 PROC/MFG ECO/TAC ELITES REGION

B64
LITVAK I.A.,MARKETING: CANADA. CANADA STRATA PROC/MFG LEGIS TEC/DEV DIPLOM INT/TRADE PRICE AUTOMAT ATTIT WEALTH...ANTHOL 20. PAGE 81 F1587 ECO/TAC MARKET ECO/DEV EFFICIENCY

B64
ORGANIZATION AMERICAN STATES,ECONOMIC SURVEY OF LATIN AMERICA, 1962. L/A+17C AGRI DIST/IND INDUS MARKET PROC/MFG R+D PLAN TEC/DEV ECO/TAC REGION BAL/PAY ALL/VALS...CON/ANAL ORG/CHARTS GEN/METH OAS ALL/PROG 20 ALL/PROG. PAGE 102 F1998 ECO/UNDEV CHARTS

B64
RAMAZANI R.K.,THE MIDDLE EAST AND THE EUROPEAN COMMON MARKET. EUR+WWI ISLAM ECO/DEV EXTR/IND MARKET PROC/MFG INT/ORG NAT/G TEC/DEV ECO/TAC REGION DRIVE WEALTH...STAT CHARTS EEC TOT/POP 20. PAGE 109 F2141 ECO/UNDEV ATTIT INT/TRADE

L64
BHAGWATI J.,"THE PURE THEORY OF INTERNATIONAL TRADE: A SURVEY." WOR+45 ECO/DEV ECO/UNDEV FINAN MARKET PROC/MFG INT/ORG LABOR LG/CO NAT/G TEC/DEV ECO/TAC SKILL WEALTH...POLICY RELATIV MGT CONCPT NEW/IDEA MATH QUANT GEN/LAWS FOR/TRADE 20. PAGE 14 F0276 INDUS HYPO/EXP

B65
DERBER M.,PLANT UNION-MANAGEMENT RELATIONS: FROM PRACTICE TO THEORY. PROC/MFG NEIGH PROB/SOLV ORD/FREE...DECISION MGT OBS QU SAMP. PAGE 32 F0621 LG/CO LABOR GP/REL ATTIT

B65
GREENFIELD K.R.,ECONOMICS AND LIBERALISM IN THE RISORGIMENTO (REV. ED.). ITALY AGRI FINAN PROC/MFG PLAN INT/TRADE CONTROL PWR 19. PAGE 51 F0990 NAT/LISM PRESS POLICY

B65
MURUMBI J.,PROBLEMS OF ECONOMIC DEVELOPMENT IN EAST AFRICA. FINAN INDUS WORKER TEC/DEV INT/TRADE TAX DEMAND EFFICIENCY PRODUC SOCISM...TREND CHARTS 20 AFRICA/E. PAGE 95 F1869 AGRI ECO/TAC ECO/UNDEV PROC/MFG

B65
SHEPHERD W.G.,ECONOMIC PERFORMANCE UNDER PUBLIC OWNERSHIP: BRITISH FUEL AND POWER. UK BUDGET GP/REL PROC/MFG NAT/G

...METH/CNCPT CHARTS BIBLIOG 20. PAGE 120 F2375
OWN FINAN

B65
WILKINSON T.O.,THE URBANIZATION OF JAPANESE LABOR, 1868-1955. AGRI PROC/MFG CAP/ISM PRODUC PROFIT ...SOC CLASSIF CENSUS CHARTS MUNICH 19/20 CHINJAP. PAGE 146 F2887
LABOR INDUS GEOG

B66
NEVITT A.A.,THE ECONOMIC PROBLEMS OF HOUSING. WOR+45 ECO/DEV ECO/UNDEV ACT/RES PROB/SOLV ECO/TAC RENT...OBS CHARTS 20. PAGE 98 F1917
HABITAT PROC/MFG DELIB/GP NAT/COMP

B67
PETRO S.,THE KINGSPORT STRIKE. USA+45 PROC/MFG NAT/G JUDGE PRESS PARTIC PERS/REL...OLD/LIB OBS INT 20 NLRB. PAGE 105 F2074
LABOR COERCE SANCTION ALL/VALS

B67
US SENATE COMM ON FOREIGN REL,ARMS SALES TO NEAR EAST AND SOUTH ASIAN COUNTRIES. INDIA IRAN PAKISTAN WOR+45 PROC/MFG BAL/PWR DIPLOM...DECISION SENATE. PAGE 139 F2742
WEAPON FOR/AID FORCES POLICY

L67
HUBBARD P.H.,"MONETARY RECOVERY UNDER THE COPYRIGHT, PATENT, AND TRADEMARK ACTS." PROC/MFG TAX PAY LEGIT ADJUD GOV/REL OWN ORD/FREE 20. PAGE 62 F1228
CREATE LAW CONTROL FINAN

S67
ALPANDER G.G.,"ENTREPRENEURS AND PRIVATE ENTERPRISE IN TURKEY." TURKEY INDUS PROC/MFG EDU/PROP ATTIT DRIVE WEALTH...GEOG MGT SOC STAT TREND CHARTS 20. PAGE 4 F0077
ECO/UNDEV LG/CO NAT/G POLICY

S67
BARRO S.,"ECONOMIC IMPACT OF SPACE EXPENDITURES: SOME BROAD ISSUES DEALING WITH COSTS AND BENEFITS." USA+45 PROC/MFG R+D LG/CO CONSULT COST PRODUC 20. PAGE 10 F0195
SPACE FINAN ECO/TAC NAT/G

S67
ROY E.V.,"AN INTERPRETATION OF NORTHERN THAI PEASANT ECONOMY." THAILAND CLIENT CULTURE AGRI PROC/MFG FACE/GP DEMAND INCOME 20. PAGE 114 F2254
STRUCT STRATA ECO/UNDEV INGP/REL

S67
SCOVILLE W.J.,"GOVERNMENT REGULATION AND GROWTH IN THE FRENCH PAPER INDUSTRY DURING THE EIGHTEENTH CENTURY." FRANCE MOD/EUR FINAN CAP/ISM TAX ADMIN CONTROL PRIVIL LAISSEZ...POLICY 18. PAGE 118 F2337
NAT/G PROC/MFG ECO/DEV INGP/REL

PROCEDURAL SYSTEMS....SEE ROUTINE, ALSO PROCESSES AND PRACTICES INDEX

PROCESSING OR MANUFACTURING INDUSTRY....SEE PROC/MFG

PROCHNOW H.V. F2124

PRODUC....PRODUCTIVITY; SEE ALSO PLAN

B
BRITISH COMMONWEALTH BUR AGRI,WORLD AGRICULTURAL ECONOMICS AND RURAL SOCIOLOGY ABSTRACTS. NAT/G OP/RES PLAN TEC/DEV LEAD PRODUC...GEOG MGT NAT/COMP 20. PAGE 18 F0354
BIBLIOG/A AGRI SOC WORKER

N
INTERNATIONAL BIBLIOGRAPHY OF ECONOMICS. WOR+45 FINAN MARKET ADMIN DEMAND INCOME PRODUC...POLICY IDEA/COMP METH. PAGE 1 F0002
BIBLIOG ECO/DEV ECO/UNDEV INT/TRADE

N
US LIBRARY OF CONGRESS,SELECTED AND ANNOTATED BIBLIOGRAPHY ON AGRICULTURAL PROBLEMS AND POLICIES IN A WARTIME ECONOMY (PAMPHLET). R+D WORKER PRODUC 20. PAGE 137 F2706
BIBLIOG/A WAR AGRI EXTR/IND

N
US LIBRARY OF CONGRESS,SELECTED AND ANNOTATED BIBLIOGRAPHY ON INDUSTRIAL PROBLEMS AND POLICIES IN WARTIME (PAMPHLET). WOR-45 CONSTRUC NAT/G PROB/SOLV COST DEMAND PRODUC 20. PAGE 137 F2707
BIBLIOG/A ECO/DEV INDUS WAR

N
US LIBRARY OF CONGRESS,SELECTED AND ANNOTATED BIBLIOGRAPHY ON LABOR PROBLEMS AND POLICIES IN A WARTIME ECONOMY (PAMPHLET). USA-45 INDUS LEGIS GP/REL DISCRIM PRODUC...SOC 20. PAGE 137 F2708
BIBLIOG/A WAR LABOR WORKER

N
US LIBRARY OF CONGRESS,SELECTED AND ANNOTATED BIBLIOGRAPHY ON RAW MATERIALS IN A WARTIME ECONOMY (PAMPHLET). WOR-45 NAT/G DEMAND PRODUC 20. PAGE 137 F2709
BIBLIOG/A ECO/DEV EXTR/IND WAR

N
US SUPERINTENDENT OF DOCUMENTS,LABOR (PRICE LIST 33). USA+45 LAW AGRI CONSTRUC INDUS NAT/G BARGAIN PRICE ADMIN AUTOMAT PRODUC MGT. PAGE 140 F2753
BIBLIOG/A WORKER LABOR LEGIS

B11
SOREL G.,LES ILLUSIONS DU PROGRES (1906). UNIV SOCIETY STRATA INDUS GP/REL OWN PRODUC SOCISM 17/20. PAGE 124 F2444
WORKER POPULISM ECO/DEV ATTIT

B13
KROPOTKIN P.,THE CONQUEST OF BREAD. SOCIETY STRATA AGRI INDUS WORKER REV HAPPINESS INCOME PRODUC HEALTH MORAL ORD/FREE. PAGE 74 F1444
ANARCH SOCIALIST OWN AGREE

B14
HOBSON J.A.,WORK AND WEALTH. CULTURE FINAN INDUS WORKER TEC/DEV ECO/TAC GIVE PAY PRICE COST PRODUC UTIL. PAGE 60 F1185
WEALTH INCOME GEN/LAWS

N19
BASSIE V.L.,UNCERTAINTY IN FORECASTING AND POLICY FORMATION (PAMPHLET). UNIV MARKET ECO/TAC PRODUC ...POLICY DECISION MGT MATH CHARTS 20. PAGE 11 F0205
ECO/DEV FINAN PREDICT PROB/SOLV

N19
BUSINESS ECONOMISTS' GROUP,INCOME POLICIES (PAMPHLET). UK INDUS LABOR TOP/EX PAY COST PRODUC ...ECOMETRIC GOV/COMP SIMUL ANTHOL 20. PAGE 20 F0395
INCOME WORKER WEALTH POLICY

N19
DOTSON A.,PRODUCTION PLANNING IN THE PATENT OFFICE (PAMPHLET). USA+45 DIST/IND PROB/SOLV PRODUC...MGT PHIL/SCI 20 BUR/BUDGET PATENT/OFF. PAGE 34 F0655
EFFICIENCY PLAN NAT/G ADMIN

N19
HAGEN E.E.,AN ANALYTICAL MODEL OF THE TRANSITION TO ECONOMIC GROWTH (PAMPHLET). WOR+45 WOR-45 SOCIETY STRATA FINAN NAT/G CONTROL PARTIC PRODUC...PHIL/SCI BIBLIOG 17/20. PAGE 53 F1033
SIMUL ECO/DEV METH TEC/DEV

N19
HANSEN B.,INFLATION PROBLEMS IN SMALL COUNTRIES (PAMPHLET). AFR UNIV FOR/AID CONTROL BAL/PAY DEMAND PRODUC 20. PAGE 54 F1066
PRICE FINAN ECO/UNDEV ECO/TAC

N19
HATANAKA M.,A SPECTRAL ANALYSIS OF BUSINESS CYCLE INDICATORS: LEAD-LAG IN TERMS OF ALL TIME POINTS (PAMPHLET). UNIV WORKER EFFICIENCY...REGRESS STAT CHARTS TIME 20. PAGE 56 F1110
ECOMETRIC ADJUST PRODUC CON/ANAL

N19
KINDLEBERGER C.P.,BALANCE-OF-PAYMENTS DEFICITS AND THE INTERNATIONAL MARKET FOR LIQUIDITY (PAMPHLET). ECO/DEV NAT/G PLAN DIPLOM ECO/TAC PRODUC...POLICY STAT CHARTS. PAGE 71 F1389
BAL/PAY INT/TRADE MARKET FINAN

N19
PATRICK H.T.,CYCLICAL INSTABILITY AND FISCAL-MONETARY POLICY IN POST-WAR JAPAN (PAMPHLET). INDUS MARKET DIPLOM TAX PRICE BAL/PAY...TREND CHARTS EQULIB 20 CHINJAP. PAGE 104 F2036
ECO/DEV PRODUC STAT

N19
ROBERTSON D.,GROWTH, WAGES, MONEY (PAMPHLET). UNIV WORKER BUDGET PRICE DEMAND PRODUC WEALTH...CONCPT MATH MONEY. PAGE 112 F2210
FINAN ECO/DEV ECO/TAC PAY

N19
US BUREAU OF THE CENSUS,THE PROPORTION OF THE SHIPMENTS (OR EMPLOYEES) OF EACH INDUSTRY... (PAMPHLET). USA+45 ECO/DEV EXTR/IND INDUS CONTROL PROFIT...STAT 20 CONGRESS MONOPOLY. PAGE 134 F2645
PROC/MFG PRODUC MARKET CHARTS

B20
TAWNEY R.H.,THE ACQUISITIVE SOCIETY. STRATA WORKER PROB/SOLV CAP/ISM ECO/TAC CONTROL GP/REL OWN PRIVIL ATTIT ORD/FREE WEALTH 20. PAGE 128 F2536
INDUS SOCIETY PRODUC MORAL

S21
MALINOWSKI B.,"THE PRIMITIVE ECONOMICS OF THE TROBRIAND ISLANDERS" (BMR)" CULTURE SOCIETY NAT/G CHIEF LEAD OWN...SOC MYTH WORSHIP 20 NEW/GUINEA TROBRIAND RESOURCE/N. PAGE 84 F1647
ECO/UNDEV AGRI PRODUC STRUCT

B23
HOBSON J.A.,INCENTIVES IN THE NEW INDUSTRIAL ORDER. USA-45 NAT/G PAY COST EFFICIENCY PRODUC WEALTH ...MAJORIT PSY SOC/WK 20. PAGE 60 F1186
INDUS LABOR INCOME OPTIMAL

B24
CLARK J.B.,THE DISTRIBUTION OF WEALTH (1899). WORKER OWN PRODUC PROFIT WEALTH LAISSEZ...IDEA/COMP GEN/LAWS. PAGE 25 F0478
ECO/TAC INDUS LABOR INCOME

B27
SIEGFRIED A.,AMERICA COMES OF AGE: A FRENCH ANALYSIS (TRANS. BY H.H. HEMMING AND DORIS HEMMING). FRANCE UK POL/PAR WORKER TEC/DEV DIPLOM REGION RACE/REL ADJUST PRODUC HEREDITY...TIME/SEQ GP/COMP SOC/INTEG 20 DEMOCRAT REPUBLICAN KKK. PAGE 122 F2398
USA-45 CULTURE ECO/DEV SOC

B29
DE MAN H.,JOY IN WORK. STRATA ECO/DEV ECO/TAC PRODUC ANOMIE ROLE SOCISM...IDEA/COMP 20. PAGE 31 F0605
SOC WORKER HAPPINESS RESPECT

B30
BIEL G.,TREATISE ON THE POWER AND UTILITY OF MONEY (1484). INDUS MARKET LOC/G NAT/G SECT ECO/TAC PRODUC WEALTH 15. PAGE 15 F0280
FINAN COST PRICE

GEN/LAWS

B32
ROBBINS L.,AN ESSAY ON THE NATURE AND SIGNIFICANCE OF ECONOMIC SCIENCE. DEMAND EQUILIB PRODUC UTIL ...ECOMETRIC 20. PAGE 112 F2201
GEN/LAWS METH/COMP ECO/DEV

B35
HICKS J.R.,THE THEORY OF WAGES. INDUS NAT/G PAY PRICE CONTROL COST EFFICIENCY WEALTH 19/20 MARSHALL/A CLARK/JB. PAGE 59 F1164
INCOME WORKER LABOR PRODUC

B35
KEYNES J.M.,THE GENERAL THEORY OF EMPLOYMENT, INTEREST, AND MONEY. AGRI INDUS WORKER ECO/TAC DEMAND EQUILIB INCOME PRODUC PROFIT ATTIT WEALTH 20. PAGE 71 F1386
FINAN GEN/LAWS MARKET PRICE

B36
BURNS A.R.,THE DECLINE OF COMPETITION. LAW LG/CO NAT/G SML/CO LEGIS PRICE AGREE CONTROL GP/REL INCOME PRODUC...POLICY 19/20 NRA. PAGE 20 F0390
MARKET GEN/LAWS INDUS

B38
MEADE J.E.,AN INTRODUCTION TO ECONOMIC ANALYSIS AND POLICY (AMERICAN EDITION EDITED BY C.J. HITCH). FINAN INDUS MARKET LABOR INT/TRADE CONTROL COST DEMAND INCOME...CLASSIF CHARTS T 20 KEYNES/JM MONOPOLY. PAGE 89 F1737
CONCPT PROFIT PRODUC

B39
FIRTH R.,PRIMITIVE POLYNESIAN ECONOMY. SOCIETY DIST/IND SECT CHIEF CAP/ISM PRODUC WEALTH...SOC OBS METH WORSHIP 20 POLYNESIA. PAGE 41 F0802
ECO/UNDEV CULTURE AGRI ECO/TAC

B40
GAUS J.M.,PUBLIC ADMINISTRATION AND THE UNITED STATES DEPARTMENT OF AGRICULTURE. USA-45 STRUCT DIST/IND FINAN MARKET EX/STRUC PROB/SOLV GIVE PRODUC...POLICY GEOG CHARTS 20 DEPT/AGRI. PAGE 47 F0909
ADMIN AGRI DELIB/GP OP/RES

B41
HAYEK F.A.,THE PURE THEORY OF CAPITAL. UNIV ECO/DEV ECO/TAC COST EQUILIB PROFIT WEALTH...SIMUL GEN/LAWS BIBLIOG INDEX TIME 20. PAGE 57 F1120
CAP/ISM METH/CNCPT PRODUC FINAN

B41
SLICHTER S.H.,UNION POLICIES AND INDUSTRIAL MANAGEMENT. USA-45 INDUS TEC/DEV PAY GP/REL INGP/REL COST EFFICIENCY PRODUC...POLICY 20. PAGE 123 F2420
BARGAIN LABOR MGT WORKER

B42
US LIBRARY OF CONGRESS,THE WAR PRODUCTION PROGRAM: SELECTED DOCUMENTATION ON THE ECONOMICS OF WAR (PAMPHLET). USA-45 ECO/DEV AGRI FINAN NAT/G ECO/TAC RATION PRICE EFFICIENCY 20. PAGE 138 F2713
BIBLIOG/A WAR PRODUC INDUS

B42
VEBLEN T.B.,THE THEORY OF THE LEISURE CLASS. USA-45 SOCIETY STRATA STRUCT NAT/G SECT WORKER CREATE EDU/PROP ATTIT...SOC GEN/LAWS 19. PAGE 141 F2772
WEALTH ELITES LEISURE PRODUC

B42
WRIGHT D.M.,THE CREATION OF PURCHASING POWER. USA-45 NAT/G PRICE ADMIN WAR INCOME PRODUC...POLICY CONCPT IDEA/COMP BIBLIOG 20 MONEY. PAGE 149 F2930
FINAN ECO/TAC ECO/DEV CREATE

C43
BENTHAM J.,"THE RATIONALE OF REWARD" IN J. BOWRING, ED., THE WORKS OF JEREMY BENTHAM (VOL. 2)" LAW WORKER CREATE INSPECT PAY ROUTINE HAPPINESS PRODUC SUPEGO WEALTH METH/CNCPT. PAGE 13 F0254
SANCTION ECO/TAC INCOME PWR

B47
WEBER M.,THE THEORY OF SOCIAL AND ECONOMIC ORGANIZATION. STRUCT LABOR POL/PAR ECO/TAC LEGIT PRODUC BIOG. PAGE 144 F2840
ECO/DEV SOC PHIL/SCI LEAD

B48
HART A.G.,MONEY, DEBT, AND ECONOMIC ACTIVITY. AFR WORKER DIPLOM PRICE CONTROL BAL/PAY COST OWN PRODUC ...METH/COMP 20 FED/RESERV. PAGE 56 F1097
FINAN WEALTH ECO/TAC NAT/G

B48
HICKS J.R.,VALUE AND CAPITAL. FINAN PRICE EQUILIB INCOME PRODUC WEALTH...TIME/SEQ 20 MARSHALL/A PARETO/V SAMUELSN/P. PAGE 59 F1165
ECOMETRIC MATH DEMAND PROB/SOLV

B48
METZLER L.A.,INCOME, EMPLOYMENT, AND PUBLIC POLICY. FINAN INDUS LOC/G NAT/G TAX GIVE PAY COST PRODUC ...MGT TIME/SEQ 20. PAGE 90 F1765
INCOME WEALTH POLICY ECO/TAC

B48
NOYES C.R.,ECONOMIC MAN IN RELATION TO HIS NATURAL ENVIRONMENT (2 VOLS.). UNIV COST DEMAND EFFICIENCY HAPPINESS INCOME PRODUC PROFIT HEREDITY...CHARTS BIBLIOG. PAGE 99 F1944
HABITAT METH/CNCPT GEN/METH

B48
WHITE C.L.,HUMAN GEOGRAPHY: AN ECOLOGICAL STUDY OF GEOGRAPHY. UNIV SEA CULTURE AGRI EXTR/IND RACE/REL PRODUC...CHARTS HYPO/EXP SIMUL GEN/LAWS T. PAGE 146 F2868
SOC HABITAT GEOG SOCIETY

B50
CHAMBERLIN E.,THE THEORY OF MONOPOLISTIC COMPETITION (1933). INDUS PAY GP/REL COST DEMAND EFFICIENCY OPTIMAL PRODUC WEALTH...GEN/LAWS 20. PAGE 23 F0443
MARKET PRICE ECO/TAC EQUILIB

B50
SCHUMPETER J.A.,CAPITALISM, SOCIALISM, AND DEMOCRACY (3RD ED.). USA-45 USSR WOR+45 WOR-45 INTELL ECO/DEV ECO/UNDEV ECO/TAC WAR PRODUC ORD/FREE...MGT SOC 20 MARX/KARL. PAGE 118 F2321
SOCIALIST CAP/ISM MARXISM IDEA/COMP

B50
SHAW E.S.,MONEY, INCOME, AND MONETARY POLICY. AFR USA-45 NAT/G DIPLOM PAY CONTROL COST INCOME PRODUC WEALTH...T 20 FED/RESERV DEPT/TREAS. PAGE 120 F2370
FINAN ECO/TAC ECO/DEV PRICE

B50
US DEPARTMENT OF STATE,POINT FOUR: COOPERATIVE PROGRAM FOR AID IN THE DEVELOPMENT OF ECONOMICALLY UNDERDEVELOPED AREAS. WOR+45 AGRI INDUS INT/ORG PLAN TEC/DEV DIPLOM EDU/PROP ADMIN PEACE PRODUC WEALTH 20 CONGRESS UN. PAGE 135 F2671
ECO/UNDEV FOR/AID FINAN INT/TRADE

S50
DALTON M.,"CONFLICTS BETWEEN STAFF AND LINE MANAGERIAL OFFICERS" (BMR). USA+45 USA-45 ELITES LG/CO WORKER PROB/SOLV ADMIN EXEC EFFICIENCY PRODUC ...GP/COMP 20. PAGE 30 F0576
MGT ATTIT GP/REL INDUS

S50
DREYFUS S.,"THE INDUSTRIAL DESIGNER AND THE BUSINESSMAN." SERV/IND PROB/SOLV ECO/TAC COST EFFICIENCY PROFIT RATIONAL...DECISION MGT. PAGE 34 F0662
CONSULT INDUS PRODUC UTIL

B51
CHANDLER L.V.,INFLATION IN THE UNITED STATES 1940-1948. AFR NAT/G BUDGET PAY PRICE CONTROL WAR INCOME PRODUC...POLICY BIBLIOG 20. PAGE 23 F0448
ECO/TAC FINAN PROB/SOLV WEALTH

B51
HANSEN B.,A STUDY IN THE THEORY OF INFLATION. WOR-45 FINAN WAR DEMAND...CHARTS 20. PAGE 54 F1067
PRICE ECO/TAC EQUILIB PRODUC

C51
HOMANS G.C.,"THE WESTERN ELECTRIC RESEARCHES" IN S. HOSLETT, ED., HUMAN FACTORS IN MANAGEMENT (BMR)" ACT/RES GP/REL HAPPINESS PRODUC DRIVE...MGT OBS 20. PAGE 61 F1202
OP/RES EFFICIENCY SOC/EXP WORKER

B53
MILLIKAN M.F.,INCOME STABILIZATION FOR A DEVELOPING DEMOCRACY. USA+45 ECO/DEV LABOR BUDGET ECO/TAC TAX ADMIN ADJUST PRODUC WEALTH...POLICY TREND 20. PAGE 91 F1794
ANTHOL MARKET EQUILIB EFFICIENCY

B53
NEISSER H.,NATIONAL INCOMES AND INTERNATIONAL TRADE. FRANCE GERMANY SWEDEN UK USA-45 EXTR/IND FINAN INDUS TEC/DEV PRICE BAL/PAY EQUILIB INCOME WEALTH...CHARTS METH 19 CHINJAP. PAGE 97 F1908
INT/TRADE PRODUC MARKET CON/ANAL

B53
ROBINSON E.A.G.,THE STRUCTURE OF COMPETITIVE INDUSTRY. UK ECO/DEV DIST/IND MARKET TEC/DEV DIPLOM EDU/PROP ADMIN EFFICIENCY WEALTH...MGT 19/20. PAGE 113 F2217
INDUS PRODUC WORKER OPTIMAL

B54
BERNSTEIN I.,ARBITRATION OF WAGES. USA+45 CONSULT PAY COST PRODUC WEALTH...CHARTS 20. PAGE 14 F0266
DELIB/GP BARGAIN WORKER PRICE

B54
MEYER F.V.,INFLATION AND CAPITAL. AFR UK WOR+45 BUDGET GOV/REL INCOME PRODUC PROFIT WEALTH...CONCPT CHARTS 20. PAGE 90 F1768
ECO/DEV FINAN ECO/TAC DEMAND

B54
MITCHELL W.G.,BUSINESS CYCLES. FINAN MARKET PRICE COST EQUILIB OPTIMAL PRODUC PROFIT...IDEA/COMP GEN/LAWS 19/20. PAGE 92 F1809
INDUS TIME/SEQ METH/COMP STAT

B55
PEDLER F.J.,ECONOMIC GEOGRAPHY OF WEST AFRICA. GAMBIA NIGER SIER/LEONE STRATA EXTR/IND MARKET LABOR INT/TRADE DEMAND HABITAT WEALTH...CHARTS 20. PAGE 104 F2046
ECO/UNDEV GEOG PRODUC EFFICIENCY

B55
UN ECONOMIC COMN ASIA & FAR E,ECONOMIC SURVEY OF ASIA AND THE FAR EAST, 1954. AFGHANISTN CEYLON INDIA PHILIPPINE S/ASIA ECO/DEV FINAN INDUS INT/TRADE PRODUC WEALTH...STAT CHARTS 20 CHINJAP. PAGE 132 F2600
ECO/UNDEV PRICE NAT/COMP ASIA

B57
GOLD N.L.,REGIONAL ECONOMIC DEVELOPMENT AND NUCLEAR POWER IN INDIA. FUT INDIA FINAN FOR/AID INT/TRADE BAL/PAY EFFICIENCY OPTIMAL PRODUC WEALTH...PREDICT 20. PAGE 48 F0934
ECO/UNDEV TEC/DEV NUC/PWR INDUS

B57
HARWOOD E.C.,CAUSE AND CONTROL OF THE BUSINESS CYCLE (5TH ED.). AFR USA-45 PRICE CONTROL WAR DEMAND INCOME WEALTH...TREND CHARTS 19. PAGE 56
PRODUC MARKET FINAN

F1107

B57
LEIBENSTEIN H.,ECONOMIC BACKWARDNESS AND ECONOMIC GROWTH. WOR+45 SOCIETY AGRI INDUS TEC/DEV CAP/ISM FOR/AID COST DEMAND WEALTH...CHARTS IDEA/COMP 20. PAGE 77 F1513
ECO/UNDEV ECO/TAC PRODUC POLICY

B57
NEUMARK S.D.,ECONOMIC INFLUENCES ON THE SOUTH AFRICAN FRONTIER, 1652-1836. SOUTH/AFR SEA AGRI NAT/G FORCES WORKER DIPLOM INT/TRADE PRICE DEMAND PRODUC...STAT CHARTS 17/19 FRONTIER. PAGE 97 F1915
COLONIAL ECO/UNDEV ECO/TAC MARKET

B57
PALACIOS A.L.,PETROLEO, MONOPOLIOS, Y LATIFUNDIOS. L/A+17C EXTR/IND NAT/G TEC/DEV ECO/TAC CONTROL PRODUC 20 ARGEN MONOPOLY RESOURCE/N. PAGE 103 F2017
ECO/UNDEV NAT/LISM INDUS AGRI

B57
SINGH D.B.,INFLATIONARY PRICE TRENDS IN INDIA SINCE 1939. AFR INDIA ECO/TAC RATION CONTROL WAR GOV/REL BAL/PAY DEMAND INCOME PEACE PRODUC...POLICY CHARTS 20. PAGE 122 F2413
BUDGET ECO/UNDEV PRICE FINAN

B57
UDY S.H. JR.,THE ORGANIZATION OF PRODUCTION IN NONINDUSTRIAL CULTURE. VOL/ASSN DELIB/GP TEC/DEV ...CHARTS BIBLIOG. PAGE 132 F2598
METH/COMP ECO/UNDEV PRODUC ADMIN

S57
VERNON R.,"PRODUCTION AND DISTRIBUTION IN THE LARGE METROPOLIS" (BMR)" USA+45 PROC/MFG ECO/TAC HABITAT ...CENSUS TREND MUNICH 20. PAGE 141 F2779
PRODUC DIST/IND PROB/SOLV

B58
DEFENSE AGAINST INFLATION. USA+45 LEGIS WORKER TAX PRICE DEMAND INCOME PRODUC...POLICY TREND METH/COMP 20 GOLD/STAND. PAGE 1 F0012
ECO/TAC EQUILIB WEALTH PROB/SOLV

B58
BARRERE A.,POLITIQUE FINANCIERE. FRANCE BUDGET ECO/TAC TAX BAL/PAY INCOME PRODUC...MGT BIBLIOG T 20. PAGE 10 F0193
FINAN NAT/G PLAN

B58
CHEEK G.,ECONOMIC AND SOCIAL IMPLICATIONS OF AUTOMATION: A BIBLIOGRAPHIC REVIEW (PAMPHLET). USA+45 LG/CO WORKER CREATE PLAN CONTROL ROUTINE PERS/REL EFFICIENCY PRODUC...METH/COMP 20. PAGE 24 F0459
BIBLIOG/A SOCIETY INDUS AUTOMAT

B58
COLM G.,THE ECONOMY OF THE AMERICAN PEOPLE: PROGRESS, PROBLEMS, PROSPECTS. USA+45 INDUS MARKET LABOR TEC/DEV INCOME 20. PAGE 26 F0509
WEALTH PRODUC CAP/ISM MGT

B58
DOWNIE J.,THE COMPETITIVE PROCESS. ECO/TAC PRICE EFFICIENCY OPTIMAL PRODUC WEALTH...IDEA/COMP METH/COMP 20 MONOPOLY. PAGE 34 F0658
EQUILIB MARKET INDUS ECO/DEV

B58
MOONEY R.E.,INFLATION AND RECESSION? AFR USA+45 LABOR LG/CO PRESS LEAD...IDEA/COMP ANTHOL 20. PAGE 93 F1821
PRICE ECO/TAC NAT/G PRODUC

B58
PALYI M.,MANAGED MONEY AT THE CROSSROADS: THE EUROPEAN EXPERIENCE. AFR WOR+45 WOR-45 TEC/DEV DIPLOM INT/TRADE DEMAND WEALTH...CHARTS BIBLIOG 19/20 EUROPE SILVER. PAGE 103 F2022
FINAN ECO/TAC ECO/DEV PRODUC

B58
US CONGRESS JOINT ECO COMM,THE RELATIONSHIP OF PRICES TO ECONOMIC STABILITY AND GROWTH. USA+45 MARKET TAX ADJUST COST DEMAND INCOME PRODUC ...POLICY TREND CHARTS ANTHOL 20 CONGRESS. PAGE 134 F2650
ECO/DEV PLAN EQUILIB PRICE

B58
WARNER A.W.,CONCEPTS AND CASES IN ECONOMIC ANALYSIS. PROB/SOLV BARGAIN CONTROL INCOME PRODUC ...ECOMETRIC MGT CONCPT CLASSIF CHARTS 20 KEYNES/JM. PAGE 143 F2820
ECO/TAC DEMAND EQUILIB COST

L58
TRAGER F.N.,"A SELECTED AND ANNOTATED BIBLIOGRAPHY ON ECONOMIC DEVELOPMENT, 1953-1957." WOR+45 AGRI FINAN INDUS MARKET LABOR WORKER PLAN INT/TRADE PRODUC...CENSUS MUNICH. PAGE 131 F2583
BIBLIOG/A ECO/UNDEV ECO/DEV

S58
LOCKWOOD W.W.,"THE SOCIALISTIC SOCIETY: INDIA AND JAPAN." INDIA ECO/DEV ECO/UNDEV INDUS NAT/G CONTROL LEAD PRODUC WEALTH 20 CHINJAP. PAGE 81 F1593
ECO/TAC NAT/COMP FINAN SOCISM

S58
MANSFIELD E.,"A STUDY OF DECISION-MAKING WITHIN THE FIRM." LG/CO WORKER INGP/REL COST EFFICIENCY PRODUC ...CHARTS 20. PAGE 85 F1658
OP/RES PROB/SOLV AUTOMAT ROUTINE

B59
LEWIS J.P.,BUSINESS CONDITIONS ANALYSIS. USA+45 MARKET LABOR BUDGET TAX AUTOMAT WAR DEMAND PRODUC ...ECOMETRIC CHARTS BIBLIOG 19/20. PAGE 79 F1549
FINAN PRICE TREND

B59
LINK R.G.,ENGLISH THEORIES OF ECONOMIC FLUCTUATIONS: 1815-1848. FRANCE UK AGRI WORKER DIPLOM PRICE TASK WAR DEMAND PRODUC...POLICY BIBLIOG 18 MALTHUS MILL/JS WILSON/J. PAGE 80 F1574
IDEA/COMP ECO/DEV WEALTH EQUILIB

B59
SELIGSOHN I.J.,"USING COMPUTER SERVICES IN SMALL BUSINESS" MANAGEMENT AIDS FOR SMALL MANUFACTURERS 109 (PAMPHLET). DIST/IND MARKET PROC/MFG COST EFFICIENCY PRODUC...DECISION IDEA/COMP. PAGE 119 F2350
SML/CO COMPUTER MGT PROB/SOLV

B59
SHACKLE G.L.S.,ECONOMICS FOR PLEASURE. FINAN MARKET NAT/G WORKER PLAN INT/TRADE TARIFFS PAY BAL/PAY COST PRODUC 20. PAGE 120 F2361
METH/CNCPT WEALTH INCOME

B59
STANFORD U, BOARD OF TRUSTEES,THE ALLOCATION OF ECONOMIC RESOURCES. WORKER PLAN BUDGET ECO/TAC TAX RECEIVE COST PRODUC...POLICY IDEA/COMP SIMUL ANTHOL 20. PAGE 125 F2468
INCOME PRICE FINAN

S59
DUNNING J.H.,"NON-PECUNIARY ELEMENTS AND BUSINESS BEHAVIOUR." PLAN PROB/SOLV COST...METH/CNCPT CLASSIF QUANT STAT. PAGE 35 F0681
DECISION DRIVE PRODUC PRICE

S59
STREETEN P.,"UNBALANCED GROWTH" UK ECO/DEV AGRI MARKET TEC/DEV CAP/ISM ECO/TAC FOR/AID INT/TRADE DEMAND ORD/FREE...CONCPT 20. PAGE 127 F2502
IDEA/COMP FINAN PRODUC EQUILIB

C59
KURIHARA K.L.,"THE KEYNESIAN THEORY OF ECONOMIC DEVELOPMENT." WOR+45 WOR-45 PLAN OPTIMAL PRODUC ...CONCPT BIBLIOG 20. PAGE 74 F1451
ECO/DEV ECO/UNDEV OP/RES TEC/DEV

B60
BELLAN R.C.,PRINCIPLES OF ECONOMICS AND THE CANADIAN ECONOMY (2ND ED.). CANADA UK USA+45 LABOR WORKER CAP/ISM INT/TRADE RISK BAL/PAY EQUILIB ALL/IDEOS 20. PAGE 12 F0236
ECO/DEV PRODUC WEALTH FINAN

B60
BISSON A.,INSTITUTIONS FINANCIERES ET ECONOMIQUES EN FRANCE. FRANCE INDUS OP/RES TAX COST PRODUC ...CHARTS 20. PAGE 15 F0289
FINAN BUDGET PLAN

B60
BRYCE M.D.,INDUSTRIAL DEVELOPMENT: A GUIDE FOR ACCELERATING ECONOMIC GROWTH. WOR+45 FINAN MARKET COST EFFICIENCY PRODUC. PAGE 20 F0378
INDUS PLAN ECO/UNDEV TEC/DEV

B60
HEILPERIN M.A.,STUDIES IN ECONOMIC NATIONALISM. EUR+WWI MOD/EUR USA+45 ECO/DEV PLAN INT/TRADE TARIFFS WAR PRODUC PROFIT 18/20 KEYNES/JM. PAGE 58 F1140
ECO/TAC NAT/G NAT/LISM POLICY

B60
HUGHES R.,THE CHINESE COMMUNES; A BACKGROUND BOOK. CHINA/COM SOCIETY CONTROL ROUTINE ADJUST EFFICIENCY PRODUC 20. PAGE 63 F1234
AGRI INDUS STRUCT MARXISM

B60
KERR C.,INDUSTRIALISM AND INDUSTRIAL MAN. CULTURE SOCIETY ECO/UNDEV NAT/G ADMIN PRODUC WEALTH ...PREDICT TREND NAT/COMP 19/20. PAGE 70 F1381
WORKER MGT ECO/DEV INDUS

B60
OEEC,STATISTICS OF SOURCES AND USES OF FINANCE. NAT/G CAP/ISM TAX PRICE COST 20 OEEC. PAGE 101 F1978
FINAN PRODUC INCOME NAT/COMP

B60
SIEGEL B.N.,AGGREGATE ECONOMICS AND PUBLIC POLICY. ECO/DEV TEC/DEV ECO/TAC TASK DEMAND EQUILIB INCOME ...CHARTS 20. PAGE 121 F2396
ECOMETRIC WEALTH PRODUC MARKET

B60
SILK L.S.,THE RESEARCH REVOLUTION. USA+45 FINAN CAP/ISM ECO/TAC PRICE EQUILIB PRODUC...STAT TREND CHARTS. PAGE 122 F2402
ECO/DEV R+D TEC/DEV PROB/SOLV

B60
US OPERATIONS MISSION - TURKEY,SOME POSSIBILITIES FOR ACCELERATING TURKEY'S ECONOMIC GROWTH. TURKEY USA+45 AGRI FINAN INDUS NAT/G ACT/RES BUDGET COST ...CHARTS 20. PAGE 138 F2724
ECO/UNDEV ECO/TAC FOR/AID PRODUC

L60
CHENERY H.B.,"PATTERNS OF INDUSTRIAL GROWTH." INT/TRADE DEMAND PRODUC...MATH REGRESS CHARTS SIMUL METH 20. PAGE 24 F0462
ECO/TAC ECO/DEV GP/COMP CON/ANAL

S60
FRENCH J.R.P. JR.,"AN EXPERIMENT ON PARTICIPATION IN A NORWEGIAN FACTORY:INTERPERSONAL DIMENSIONS OF DECISION-MAKING." LABOR LEAD PERS/REL EFFICIENCY PRODUC...DECISION SOC CHARTS SOC/EXP. PAGE 44 F0853
INDUS PLAN RIGID/FLEX GP/REL

B61
ACKLEY G.,MACROECONOMIC THEORY. AFR FINAN WORKER
SIMUL

ECO/TAC PRICE COST INCOME PRODUC...MATH TREND CHARTS IDEA/COMP T KEYNES/JM. PAGE 2 F0034
ECOMETRIC WEALTH
B61

BREWIS T.N.,CANADIAN ECONOMIC POLICY. AFR CANADA BUDGET CAP/ISM INT/TRADE RATION TARIFFS TAX PRICE CONTROL ROUTINE FEDERAL INCOME PRODUC 20. PAGE 18 F0348
ECO/DEV ECO/TAC NAT/G PLAN
B61

CLARK J.M.,COMPETITION AS A DYNAMIC PROCESS. ECO/DEV EXTR/IND INDUS LG/CO TEC/DEV ECO/TAC PRICE EQUILIB PRODUC...NEW/IDEA CAP 20. PAGE 25 F0483
WEALTH GP/REL FINAN PROFIT
B61

FERTIG L.,PROSPERITY THROUGH FREEDOM. COM INDUS LABOR CAP/ISM ECO/TAC PRODUC PROFIT ORD/FREE WEALTH SOCISM...METH/CNCPT 20. PAGE 40 F0788
NAT/G CONTROL POLICY
B61

FILLOL T.R.,SOCIAL FACTORS IN ECONOMIC DEVELOPMENT: THE ARGENTINE CASE. STRUCT INDUS LABOR CREATE TEC/DEV EFFICIENCY PRODUC DRIVE...METH/CNCPT METH/COMP BIBLIOG/A 20 ARGEN. PAGE 41 F0795
ECO/UNDEV MGT PERS/REL TREND
B61

KELSO L.O.,THE NEW CAPITALISTS: A PROPOSAL TO FREE ECONOMIC GROWTH FROM THE SLAVERY OF SAVINGS. UNIV USA+45 ECO/DEV CAP/ISM PRODUC WEALTH SOCISM ...NEW/IDEA 20. PAGE 70 F1373
ECO/TAC WORKER FINAN GEN/LAWS
B61

LAMFALUSSY A.,INVESTMENT AND GROWTH IN MATURE ECONOMIES. BELGIUM EUR+WWI LABOR PRICE PRODUC PROFIT...STAT CONT/OBS CHARTS 20. PAGE 75 F1464
FINAN INDUS ECO/DEV CAP/ISM
B61

MACMAHON A.W.,DELEGATION AND AUTONOMY. INDIA STRUCT LEGIS BARGAIN BUDGET ECO/TAC LEGIT EXEC REPRESENT GOV/REL CENTRAL DEMAND EFFICIENCY PRODUC. PAGE 84 F1637
ADMIN PLAN FEDERAL
B61

MOORE G.H.,BUSINESS CYCLE INDICATORS (TWO VOLS.). LABOR DIPLOM PRICE RISK TASK WAR PRODUC...CHARTS BIBLIOG 20. PAGE 93 F1822
MARKET FINAN WEALTH
B61

NOVE A.,THE SOVIET ECONOMY. USSR ECO/DEV FINAN NAT/G ECO/TAC PRICE ADMIN EFFICIENCY MARXISM ...TREND BIBLIOG 20. PAGE 99 F1943
PLAN PRODUC POLICY
B61

PETCH G.A.,ECONOMIC DEVELOPMENT AND MODERN WEST AFRICA. AFR CONGO/BRAZ GHANA NIGER SIER/LEONE AGRI MARKET LABOR FOR/AID TAX COST EFFICIENCY EQUILIB PRODUC...GEOG TREND 20. PAGE 105 F2068
ECO/UNDEV TEC/DEV EXTR/IND ECO/TAC
B61

SLICHTER S.H.,ECONOMIC GROWTH IN THE UNITED STATES. FUT USA+45 USA-45 LABOR PAY INCOME PRODUC...MGT 19/20. PAGE 123 F2422
ECO/DEV TEC/DEV CAP/ISM DEMAND
B61

STARK H.,SOCIAL AND ECONOMIC FRONTIERS IN LATIN AMERICA (2ND ED.). CUBA FUT CULTURE AGRI INDUS ECO/TAC PRODUC ATTIT MARXISM...NAT/COMP BIBLIOG T 20. PAGE 125 F2470
L/A+17C SOCIETY DIPLOM ECO/UNDEV
B61

THEOBALD R.,THE CHALLENGE OF ABUNDANCE. USA+45 WOR+45 MARKET DIPLOM FOR/AID REV PRODUC UTOPIA SUPEGO...POLICY TREND BIBLIOG/A 20. PAGE 129 F2554
WELF/ST ECO/UNDEV PROB/SOLV ECO/TAC
L61

JOHNSTON B.F.,"THE ROLE OF AGRICULTURE IN ECONOMIC DEVELOPMENT." FINAN PRODUC ROLE BIBLIOG. PAGE 68 F1332
AGRI ECO/UNDEV PLAN INDUS
C61

FILLOL T.R.,"SOCIAL FACTORS IN ECONOMIC DEVELOPMENT: THE ARGENTINE CASE" INDUS LABOR CREATE TEC/DEV PERS/REL EFFICIENCY PRODUC DRIVE ...METH/CNCPT METH/COMP 20 ARGEN. PAGE 41 F0794
BIBLIOG ECO/UNDEV MGT TREND
B62

ALTMAN G.T.,INVISIBLE BARRIER: THE OPTIMUM GROWTH CURVE. USA+45 USA-45 ECO/DEV PLAN PAY CONTROL DEMAND OPTIMAL PRODUC WEALTH...STAT CHARTS 20. PAGE 4 F0080
INDUS FINAN ECO/TAC TAX
B62

BACKMAN J.,THE ECONOMICS OF THE ELECTRICAL MACHINERY INDUSTRY. USA+45 PROC/MFG LABOR WORKER INT/TRADE TV PRICE COST...CHARTS 19/20. PAGE 8 F0147
PRODUC TEC/DEV TREND
B62

CHRISTENSON C.L.,ECONOMIC REDEVELOPMENT IN BITUMINOUS COAL: THE SPECIAL CASE OF TECHNOLOGICAL ADVANCE IN US COAL MINES 1930-1960. USA+45 USA-45 ECO/TAC AUTOMAT INCOME PRODUC...CHARTS 20. PAGE 24 F0471
EXTR/IND LABOR TEC/DEV ECO/DEV
B62

CONGRES ECONOMISTES LANG FRAN,MONNAIE ET EXPANSION. AFR FRANCE PROB/SOLV BUDGET CENTRAL COST OPTIMAL PRODUC WEALTH 20. PAGE 27 F0524
FINAN PLAN EUR+WWI
B62

DENISON E.F.,THE SOURCES OF ECONOMIC GROWTH IN THE UNITED STATES AND THE ALTERNATIVES BEFORE US. AGRI INDUS SCHOOL TEC/DEV CAP/ISM ECO/TAC PRICE COST WEALTH...STAT TREND CHARTS 20. PAGE 32 F0620
ECO/DEV WORKER PRODUC
B62

DOBB M.,CAPITALISM YESTERDAY AND TODAY. UK WORKER WAR PRODUC PROFIT 18/20 MONOPOLY. PAGE 33 F0646
CAP/ISM TIME/SEQ CONCPT ECO/TAC
B62

FAO,FOOD AND AGRICULTURE ORGANIZATION AFRICAN SURVEY. AFR CONGO/BRAZ GHANA STRATA AGRI INT/ORG TEC/DEV FOR/AID INT/TRADE RACE/REL DEMAND EFFICIENCY PRODUC...GEOG 20 UN CONGO/LEOP. PAGE 39 F0763
ECO/TAC WEALTH EXTR/IND ECO/UNDEV
B62

GEARY R.C.,EUROPE'S FUTURE IN FIGURES. FUT GOV/REL DEMAND PRODUC...STAT CHARTS METH/COMP ANTHOL METH 20 EUROPE. PAGE 47 F0912
FINAN ECO/DEV PREDICT WEALTH
B62

GREEN L.P.,DEVELOPMENT IN AFRICA. AFR CENTRL/AFR GHANA RHODESIA SOUTH/AFR AGRI PROC/MFG INT/TRADE DEMAND NAT/LISM PRODUC WEALTH...GEOG METH/CNCPT CHARTS BIBLIOG 20. PAGE 50 F0987
CULTURE ECO/UNDEV GOV/REL TREND
B62

INTNTL COTTON ADVISORY COMMITT,GOVERNMENT REGULATIONS ON COTTON, 1962 (PAMPHLET). WOR+45 RATION PRODUC...CHARTS 20. PAGE 65 F1287
ECO/TAC LAW CONTROL AGRI
B62

KLEIN L.R.,AN INTRODUCTION TO ECONOMETRICS. DIST/IND DEMAND PRODUC WEALTH...MATH TIME/SEQ T 20. PAGE 72 F1408
ECOMETRIC SIMUL PREDICT STAT
B62

LUTZ F.A.,THE PROBLEM OF INTERNATIONAL ECONOMIC EQUILIBRIUM. FINAN PRODUC WEALTH 20 MONEY. PAGE 82 F1611
DIPLOM EQUILIB BAL/PAY PROB/SOLV
B62

MARTINS A.F.,REVOLUCAO BRANCA NO CAMPO. L/A+17C SERV/IND DEMAND EFFICIENCY PRODUC...POLICY METH/COMP. PAGE 86 F1685
AGRI ECO/UNDEV TEC/DEV NAT/COMP
B62

MEYER F.V.,THE TERMS OF TRADE. WOR+45 AGRI MARKET PROC/MFG DIPLOM PRICE DEMAND PRODUC 20. PAGE 90 F1769
INT/TRADE BAL/PAY SIMUL EQUILIB
B62

NATIONAL BUREAU ECONOMIC RES,THE RATE AND DIRECTION OF INVENTIVE ACTIVITY: ECONOMIC AND SOCIAL FACTORS. STRUCT INDUS MARKET R+D CREATE OP/RES TEC/DEV EFFICIENCY PRODUC RATIONAL UTIL...WELF/ST PHIL/SCI METH/CNCPT TIME. PAGE 97 F1895
DECISION PROB/SOLV MGT
B62

ROBINSON M.A.,AN INTRODUCTION TO ECONOMIC REASONING. FINAN MARKET LABOR DIPLOM INT/TRADE BAL/PAY INCOME PRODUC WEALTH...POLICY MGT 20. PAGE 113 F2223
ECO/TAC METH/CNCPT NAT/G
B62

SCHALLER H.G.,PUBLIC EXPENDITURE DECISIONS IN THE URBAN COMMUNITY: PREPARED FOR RESOURCES FOR THE FUTURE, INC. INDUS SERV/IND LOC/G PUB/INST PLAN PROB/SOLV BUDGET DEMAND PRODUC...CHARTS MUNICH. PAGE 116 F2289
FINAN DECISION
B62

SHINOHARA M.,GROWTH AND CYCLES IN THE JAPANESE ECONOMY. INDUS LABOR TEC/DEV CAP/ISM INT/TRADE PAY COST EFFICIENCY INCOME WEALTH...METH/COMP 20 CHINJAP. PAGE 121 F2380
PRODUC ECO/DEV EQUILIB ECOMETRIC
B62

SIEVERS A.M.,REVOLUTION, EVOLUTION AND THE ECONOMIC ORDER. INDUS LABOR TAX CONTROL REV WAR DEMAND PRODUC WEALTH...IDEA/COMP 19/20 KEYNES/JM. PAGE 122 F2399
EFFICIENCY ALL/IDEOS ECO/DEV WELF/ST
B62

SRIVASTAVA G.L.,COLLECTIVE BARGAINING AND LABOR-MANAGEMENT RELATIONS IN INDIA. INDIA UK USA+45 INDUS LEGIS WORKER ADJUD EFFICIENCY PRODUC ...METH/COMP 20. PAGE 125 F2462
LABOR MGT BARGAIN GP/REL
B62

US BUREAU OF THE CENSUS,REPORT FOR SUBCOMMITTEE ON ANTITRUST AND MONOPOLY: CONCENTRATION RATIOS IN MANUFACTURING INDUSTRY 1958. USA+45 ECO/DEV CONTROL GOV/REL OWN PRODUC PROFIT...STAT 20 CONGRESS MONOPOLY. PAGE 134 F2646
CHARTS PROC/MFG MARKET LG/CO
B62

US CONGRESS JOINT ECO COMM,FACTORS AFFECTING THE UNITED STATES BALANCE OF PAYMENTS. USA+45 DELIB/GP PLAN DIPLOM FOR/AID PRODUC WEALTH...CHARTS 20 CONGRESS OEEC. PAGE 134 F2653
BAL/PAY INT/TRADE ECO/TAC FINAN
B62

US CONGRESS JOINT ECO COMM,ECONOMIC DEVELOPMENTS IN SOUTH AMERICA. USA+45 SOCIETY FINAN NAT/G PROB/SOLV TEC/DEV INT/TRADE TAX EFFICIENCY PRODUC ATTIT
L/A+17C ECO/UNDEV FOR/AID

...POLICY 20 ALL/PROG CONGRESS SOUTH/AMER. PAGE 135 DIPLOM F2654

B62
VAIZEY J.,THE ECONOMICS OF EDUCATION. INTELL ECO/TAC PAY COST PRODUC 20. PAGE 140 F2758
ECO/DEV SCHOOL ACADEM PROFIT

B62
ZOOK P.D.,FOREIGN TRADE AND HUMAN CAPITAL. L/A+17C USA+45 FINAN DIPLOM ECO/TAC PRODUC...POLICY 20. PAGE 151 F2970
INT/TRADE ECO/UNDEV FOR/AID BAL/PAY

L62
SCHULTZ T.W.,"INVESTMENT IN HUMAN BEINGS." ECO/DEV ECO/TAC CONFER COST INCOME PRODUC HEALTH...GEOG ANTHOL. PAGE 117 F2315
FINAN WORKER EDU/PROP SKILL

S62
GILL P.J.,"FUTURE TAXATION POLICY IN AN INDEPENDENT EAST AFRICA" UGANDA LOC/G ECO/TAC ADMIN EFFICIENCY INCOME PRODUC...CHARTS 20. PAGE 47 F0923
ECO/UNDEV TAX AFR COLONIAL

C62
GREEN L.P.,"DEVELOPMENT IN AFRICA." RHODESIA SOUTH/AFR UGANDA MARKET PROC/MFG PRODUC WEALTH ...GEOG 20. PAGE 50 F0986
BIBLIOG ECO/UNDEV AFR AGRI

C62
JOINT ECONOMIC COMMITTEE,"DIMENSIONS OF SOVIET ECONOMIC POWER." USSR R+D FORCES ACT/RES OP/RES TEC/DEV...GEOG STAT BIBLIOG 20. PAGE 68 F1337
ECO/DEV PLAN PRODUC LABOR

N62
BANK INTERNATIONAL SETTLEMENTS,AUSTRIA: MONETARY AND ECONOMIC SITUATION 1952-61 (PAMPHLET). AUSTRIA WORKER BUDGET INT/TRADE PRICE BAL/PAY DEMAND EFFICIENCY INCOME PRODUC...STAT 20 SILVER. PAGE 9 F0174
FINAN ECO/DEV CHARTS WEALTH

B63
BARNETT H.J.,SCARCITY AND GROWTH: THE ECONOMICS OF NATURAL RESOURCE AVAILABILITY. FUT WOR+45 AGRI INDUS PROB/SOLV TEC/DEV CONTROL PRODUC...SOC/WK IDEA/COMP METH/COMP SIMUL 20 RESOURCE/N MALTHUS RICARDO/D MILL/JS DARWIN/C. PAGE 10 F0191
DEMAND HABITAT CENSUS GEOG

B63
HAQ M.,THE STRATEGY OF ECONOMIC PLANNING. PAKISTAN AGRI FINAN INDUS NAT/G FOR/AID TAX CONTROL REGION PRODUC...POLICY CHARTS 20. PAGE 55 F1071
ECO/TAC ECO/UNDEV PLAN PROB/SOLV

B63
LEE M.W.,MACROECONOMICS: FLUCTUATIONS, GROWTH AND STABILITY (3RD ED.). MARKET LABOR TEC/DEV INT/TRADE TAX PRICE WAR PRODUC...POLICY ECOMETRIC CHARTS 19/20. PAGE 77 F1505
EQUILIB TREND WEALTH

B63
LUTZ F.A.,DAS PROBLEM DES INTERNATIONALEN WIRTSCHAFTLICHEN GLEICHGEWICHTS. DIPLOM INT/TRADE COST INCOME 20. PAGE 82 F1612
FINAN CAP/ISM ECO/TAC PRODUC

B63
MACHLUP F.,ESSAYS ON ECONOMIC SEMANTICS. UNIV ECO/DEV FINAN COST DEMAND PRODUC...POLICY STAT CHARTS BIBLIOG. PAGE 83 F1632
LING CONCPT METH

B63
MARX K.,THE POVERTY OF PHILOSOPHY (1847). SOCIETY STRATA INDUS WORKER OWN UTOPIA SOCISM...GEN/LAWS MARX/KARL. PAGE 86 F1692
MARXIST PRODUC

B63
MEEK R.L.,THE ECONOMICS OF PHYSIOCRACY. FRANCE UK AGRI FINAN WORKER CAP/ISM TAX DEMAND EQUILIB INCOME HABITAT...CHARTS ANTHOL 17. PAGE 89 F1744
PRODUC WEALTH MARKET

B63
MYRDAL G.,CHALLENGE TO AFFLUENCE. USA+45 WOR+45 FINAN INT/ORG NAT/G PLAN ECO/TAC INT/TRADE BAL/PAY ORD/FREE 20 EUROPE/W. PAGE 96 F1882
ECO/DEV WEALTH DIPLOM PRODUC

B63
PAENSON I.,SYSTEMATIC GLOSSARY ENGLISH, FRENCH, SPANISH, RUSSIAN OF SELECTED ECONOMIC AND SOCIAL TERMS. WOR+45 FINAN LABOR INT/TRADE DEMAND PRODUC 20. PAGE 102 F2014
DICTIONARY SOC LING

B63
SALENT W.S.,THE UNITED STATES BALANCE OF PAYMENTS IN 1968. EUR+WWI UK USA+45 AGRI R+D LABOR FORCES PRODUC...GEOG CONCPT CHARTS 20 CHINJAP EEC. PAGE 115 F2274
BAL/PAY DEMAND FINAN INT/TRADE

B63
UNITED NATIONS,THE GROWTH OF WORLD INDUSTRY, 1938-1961: NATIONAL TABLES. WOR+45 STRUCT ECO/DEV ECO/UNDEV NAT/G COST...CHARTS UN. PAGE 132 F2613
STAT INDUS PRODUC ORD/FREE

B63
US CONGRESS JOINT ECO COMM,THE UNITED STATES BALANCE OF PAYMENTS. AFR USA+45 DELIB/GP BUDGET PRICE PRODUC 20 CONGRESS MONEY. PAGE 135 F2655
BAL/PAY INT/TRADE FINAN ECO/TAC

B63
VELEZ GARCIA J.,DEVALUACION 1962; HISTORIA DOCUMENTAL DE UN PROCESO ECONOMICO. AFR L/A+17C USA+45 FINAN FOR/AID PRODUC WEALTH...POLICY STAT CHARTS ANTHOL 20 COLOMB. PAGE 141 F2774
ECO/UNDEV ECO/TAC PLAN NAT/G

S63
ETHERINGTON D.M.,"LAND RESETTLEMENT IN KENYA; POLICY AND PRACTICE" AFR TEC/DEV ECO/TAC FOR/AID TAX PRODUC...CHARTS 20. PAGE 39 F0752
ECO/UNDEV AGRI WORKER PLAN

B64
BALL R.J.,INFLATION AND THE THEORY OF MONEY. MARKET TAX PAY PRICE TASK ADJUST BAL/PAY COST INCOME PRODUC WEALTH...METH/COMP 20 KEYNES/JM MONEY. PAGE 9 F0167
EQUILIB DEMAND POLICY

B64
BEARDSLEY R.K.,STUDIES ON ECONOMIC LIFE IN JAPAN (OCCASIONAL PAPERS NO. 8). INDUS FAM HABITAT...GEOG GOV/COMP 20 CHINJAP. PAGE 12 F0223
WEALTH PRESS PRODUC INCOME

B64
BERRILL K.,ECONOMIC DEVELOPMENT WITH SPECIAL REFERENCE TO EAST ASIA. ASIA INDIA S/ASIA AGRI INDUS LABOR DELIB/GP PLAN INT/TRADE COST PRODUC 20 CHINJAP. PAGE 14 F0271
FINAN ECO/UNDEV INT/ORG CAP/ISM

B64
COMMISSION ON MONEY AND CREDIT,INFLATION, GROWTH, AND EMPLOYMENT. AFR USA+45 PLAN PROB/SOLV PAY PRICE EFFICIENCY PRODUC WEALTH 20. PAGE 26 F0514
WORKER ECO/TAC OPTIMAL

B64
HALLOWELL J.H.,DEVELOPMENT: FOR WHAT. WOR+45 POL/PAR SECT FOR/AID INT/TRADE CT/SYS PARTIC PRODUC PLURISM. PAGE 54 F1052
ECO/UNDEV CONSTN NAT/LISM ECO/TAC

B64
HANSEN A.H.,BUSINESS CYCLES AND NATIONAL INCOME. USA+45 FINAN ECO/TAC COST OPTIMAL...POLICY METH 20 KEYNES/JM. PAGE 54 F1065
INCOME WEALTH PRODUC INDUS

B64
HART P.E.,ECONOMETRIC ANALYSIS FOR NATIONAL ECONOMIC PLANNING. INDUS OP/RES PRICE PRODUC ...SIMUL ANTHOL MODELS 20. PAGE 56 F1100
PLAN ECOMETRIC STAT

B64
HOLLEY I.B. JR.,US ARMY IN WORLD WAR II: SPECIAL STUDIES: BUYING AIRCRAFT: MATERIEL PROCUREMENT FOR THE ARMY AIR FORCES. USA+45 USA-45 BUDGET WEAPON GOV/REL PRODUC 20. PAGE 61 F1198
FORCES COST DIST/IND CIVMIL/REL

B64
INTERNATIONAL LABOUR OFFICE,EMPLOYMENT AND ECONOMIC GROWTH. ECO/DEV ECO/UNDEV NAT/G PLAN DIPLOM INT/TRADE CONTROL INCOME PRODUC WEALTH...STAT NAT/COMP 20 ILO. PAGE 65 F1279
WORKER METH/COMP ECO/TAC OPTIMAL

B64
JUSTER F.T.,ANTICIPATIONS AND PURCHASES; AN ANALYSIS OF CONSUMER BEHAVIOR. PROB/SOLV RISK COST PRODUC DRIVE...STAT STYLE SAMP CON/ANAL CHARTS HYPO/EXP GAME SIMUL. PAGE 68 F1345
PROBABIL DECISION PREDICT DEMAND

B64
MANSFIELD E.,MONOPOLY POWER AND ECONOMIC PERFORMANCE: AN INTRODUCTION TO A CURRENT ISSUE OF PUBLIC POLICY. ECO/DEV INDUS NAT/G PLAN CAP/ISM PRICE CONTROL LOBBY EFFICIENCY PRODUC...POLICY 20 CONGRESS KENNEDY/JF MONOPOLY. PAGE 85 F1659
LG/CO PWR ECO/TAC MARKET

B64
MORRISSENS L.,ECONOMIC POLICY IN OUR TIME: COUNTRY STUDIES. BELGIUM EUR+WWI FRANCE GERMANY/W ITALY NETHERLAND INDUS BARGAIN BUDGET GOV/REL BAL/PAY PRODUC...CON/ANAL CHARTS COSTS 20. PAGE 94 F1839
ECO/DEV ECO/TAC METH/COMP PLAN

B64
NOVACK D.E.,DEVELOPMENT AND SOCIETY; THE DYNAMICS OF ECONOMIC CHANGE. WOR+45 STRATA STRUCT ECO/TAC CONTROL CROWD REV GP/REL ADJUST PRODUC WEALTH PSY. PAGE 99 F1940
SOCIETY CULTURE SOC ECO/UNDEV

B64
SOLOW R.M.,THE NATURE AND SOURCES OF UNEMPLOYMENT IN THE UNITED STATES (PAMPHLET). USA+45 INDUS LABOR TEC/DEV ECO/TAC SKILL WEALTH...TREND NAT/COMP 20. PAGE 124 F2439
ECO/DEV WORKER STAT PRODUC

B64
STONIER A.W.,EXERCISES IN ECONOMICS. FINAN INDUS TEC/DEV RENT PAY EQUILIB PRODUC PROFIT...METH/COMP T. PAGE 127 F2498
PRICE MARKET WORKER

B64
URQUIDI V.L.,THE CHALLENGE OF DEVELOPMENT IN LATIN AMERICA. L/A+17C FINAN INT/ORG TEC/DEV DIPLOM INT/TRADE PRICE REGION PRODUC...CHARTS 20 ALL/PROG. PAGE 133 F2628
ECO/UNDEV ECO/TAC NAT/G TREND

B64
US SENATE COMM ON JUDICIARY,HEARINGS BEFORE SUBCOMMITTEE ON ANTITRUST AND MONOPOLY: ECONOMIC CONCENTRATION VOLUMES 1-5 JULY 1964-SEPT 1966. USA+45 LAW FINAN ECO/TAC ADJUD COST EFFICIENCY PRODUC...STAT CHARTS 20 CONGRESS MONOPOLY. PAGE 140 F2749
ECO/DEV CONTROL MARKET LG/CO

B64
WELLISZ S.,THE ECONOMICS OF THE SOVIET BLOC. COM USSR INDUS WORKER PLAN BUDGET INT/TRADE TAX PRICE PRODUC WEALTH MARXISM...METH/COMP 20. PAGE 145 F2854
EFFICIENCY ADMIN MARKET

B64
WILLIAMSON O.E.,THE ECONOMICS OF DISCRETIONARY BEHAVIOR: MANAGERIAL OBJECTIVES IN A THEORY OF THE FIRM. MARKET BUDGET CAP/ISM PRODUC DRIVE PERSON ...STAT CHARTS BIBLIOG METH 20. PAGE 147 F2897
EFFICIENCY MGT ECO/TAC CHOOSE

B64
ZOBER M.,MARKETING MANAGEMENT. FINAN BUDGET EDU/PROP PRICE PRODUC ATTIT...POLICY TREND CHARTS METH/COMP EQULIB 20. PAGE 150 F2966
ECO/DEV MGT CONTROL MARKET

S64
NEWLYN W.T.,"MONETARY SYSTEMS AND INTEGRATION" AFR BUDGET ADMIN FEDERAL PRODUC PROFIT UTIL...CHARTS 20 AFRICA/E. PAGE 98 F1922
ECO/UNDEV REGION METH/COMP FINAN

C64
LOUFTY A.,"LA PLANIFICATION DE L'ECONOMIE." FRANCE USSR FINAN INDUS BUDGET INCOME PRODUC...BIBLIOG 20. PAGE 82 F1604
PLAN ECO/UNDEV ECO/DEV

B65
ALLEN W.R.,INTERNATIONAL TRADE THEORY: HUME TO OHLIN. FINAN LABOR TARIFFS TAX PRICE DEMAND PRODUC PROFIT...ANTHOL 18/20. PAGE 4 F0074
INT/TRADE WEALTH METH/CNCPT

B65
BAUMOL W.J.,ECONOMIC THEORY AND OPERATIONS ANALYSIS (2ND ED.). MARKET LG/CO BUDGET PRICE COST EQUILIB PRODUC...DECISION MATH CHARTS GAME 20. PAGE 12 F0219
OP/RES ECO/DEV METH/COMP STAT

B65
CHAO K.,THE RATE AND PATTERN OF INDUSTRIAL GROWTH IN COMMUNIST CHINA. CHINA/COM ECO/UNDEV TEC/DEV PRICE...NAT/COMP BIBLIOG 20. PAGE 23 F0452
INDUS INDEX STAT PRODUC

B65
DEMAS W.G.,THE ECONOMICS OF DEVELOPMENT IN SMALL COUNTRIES WITH SPECIAL REFERENCE TO THE CARIBBEAN. WOR+45 BAL/PAY DEMAND EFFICIENCY PRODUC...GEOG CARIBBEAN. PAGE 32 F0618
ECO/UNDEV PLAN WEALTH INT/TRADE

B65
DODDY F.S.,INTRODUCTION TO THE USE OF ECONOMIC INDICATORS. FINAN LABOR PLAN COST...ECOMETRIC INDICATOR MATH PREDICT CHARTS METH 20. PAGE 33 F0649
TEC/DEV STAT PRODUC PRICE

B65
HERRICK B.H.,URBAN MIGRATION AND ECONOMIC DEVELOPMENT IN CHILE. CHILE AGRI INDUS LABOR NAT/G CENTRAL PRODUC...STAT SAMP CHARTS BIBLIOG/A MUNICH 20 MIGRATION. PAGE 59 F1156
HABITAT GEOG ECO/UNDEV

B65
MCCOLL G.D.,THE AUSTRALIAN BALANCE OF PAYMENTS. UK USA+45 AGRI WORKER DIPLOM EQUILIB PRODUC...STAT TREND CHARTS BIBLIOG/A 20 AUSTRAL. PAGE 88 F1719
ECO/DEV BAL/PAY INT/TRADE COST

B65
MURUMBI J.,PROBLEMS OF ECONOMIC DEVELOPMENT IN EAST AFRICA. FINAN INDUS WORKER TEC/DEV INT/TRADE TAX DEMAND EFFICIENCY PRODUC SOCISM...TREND CHARTS 20 AFRICA/E. PAGE 95 F1869
AGRI ECO/TAC ECO/UNDEV PROC/MFG

B65
OXENFELDT A.R.,ECONOMIC SYSTEMS IN ACTION. FRANCE USA+45 USSR CULTURE PLAN PROB/SOLV TEC/DEV INCOME PRODUC WEALTH...METH/COMP 20. PAGE 102 F2007
ECO/DEV CAP/ISM MARXISM ECO/TAC

B65
PROCHNOW H.V.,WORLD ECONOMIC PROBLEMS AND POLICIES. INDIA ISRAEL WOR+45 AGRI LABOR PROB/SOLV FOR/AID TARIFFS CONTROL BAL/PAY NAT/LISM WEALTH...TREND CHARTS 20 CHINJAP EEC. PAGE 108 F2124
MARKET ECO/TAC PRODUC IDEA/COMP

B65
SABLE M.H.,PERIODICALS FOR LATIN AMERICAN ECONOMIC DEVELOPMENT, TRADE, AND FINANCE: AN ANNOTATED BIBLIOGRAPHY (A PAMPHLET). ECO/TAC PRODUC PROFIT ...STAT NAT/COMP 20 OAS. PAGE 115 F2266
BIBLIOG/A L/A+17C ECO/UNDEV INT/TRADE

B65
SCHWARTZ G.,SCIENCE IN MARKETING. OP/RES PROB/SOLV INT/TRADE PRICE CONTROL ADJUST PRODUC...CONCPT 20. PAGE 118 F2324
PHIL/SCI TREND ECO/DEV MARKET

B65
SHONFIELD A.,MODERN CAPITALISM: THE CHANGING BALANCE OF PUBLIC AND PRIVATE POWER. FRANCE GERMANY/W UK USA+45 WOR+45 ECO/DEV INT/ORG NAT/G CONSULT INT/TRADE PRODUC...POLICY CONCPT METH/COMP 20. PAGE 121 F2386
CAP/ISM CONTROL BAL/PWR CREATE

B65
WILKINSON T.O.,THE URBANIZATION OF JAPANESE LABOR, 1868-1955. AGRI PROC/MFG CAP/ISM PRODUC PROFIT ...SOC CLASSIF CENSUS CHARTS MUNICH 19/20 CHINJAP. PAGE 146 F2887
LABOR INDUS GEOG

L65
HAGE J.,"AN AXIOMATIC THEORY OF ORGANIZATIONS" USA+45 STRUCT LABOR PRODUC DRIVE PERSON RIGID/FLEX 20 WEBER/MAX. PAGE 53 F1032
GP/REL EFFICIENCY PROF/ORG ATTIT

S65
SCHROEDER G.,"LABOR PLANNING IN THE USSR." COM USSR ECO/DEV INDUS SCHOOL PRODUC WEALTH...PREDICT TIME/SEQ TREND TIME 20. PAGE 117 F2313
WORKER PLAN CENSUS

B66
BIRMINGHAM W.,A STUDY OF CONTEMPORARY GHANA VOL I: THE ECONOMY OF GHANA. AFR GHANA PLAN...POLICY STAT CHARTS ANTHOL BIBLIOG 20. PAGE 15 F0286
ECO/UNDEV ECO/TAC NAT/G PRODUC

B66
BRODERSEN A.,THE SOVIET WORKER: LABOR AND GOVERNMENT IN SOVIET SOCIETY. USSR STRUCT INDUS LABOR PLAN PAY INGP/REL PRODUC...POLICY GEN/LAWS BIBLIOG 20 STALIN/J LENIN/VI BOLSHEVISM KHRUSH/N. PAGE 19 F0357
WORKER ROLE NAT/G MARXISM

B66
DOBB M.,SOVIET ECONOMIC DEVELOPMENT SINCE 1917. USSR ECO/DEV ECO/UNDEV LABOR NAT/G TEC/DEV ECO/TAC ROUTINE PRODUC MARXISM 20. PAGE 33 F0647
PLAN INDUS WORKER

B66
GROSS H.,MAKE OR BUY. AFR USA+45 FINAN INDUS CREATE PRICE PRODUC 20. PAGE 51 F1006
ECO/TAC PLAN MGT COST

B66
HALLER H.,DAS PROBLEM DER GELDWERTSTABILITAT. MARKET LABOR INCOME PRODUC...POLICY 20. PAGE 54 F1049
PRICE COST FINAN ECO/TAC

B66
HAYER T.,FRENCH AID. AFR FRANCE AGRI FINAN BUDGET ADMIN WAR PRODUC...CHARTS 18/20 THIRD/WRLD OVRSEA/DEV. PAGE 57 F1125
TEC/DEV COLONIAL FOR/AID ECO/UNDEV

B66
HO YHI-MIN,AGRICULTURAL DEVELOPMENT OF TAIWAN: 1903-1960. FINAN WORKER EDU/PROP...STAT CHARTS BIBLIOG 20. PAGE 60 F1181
ECO/UNDEV AGRI PRODUC PLAN

B66
KAESTNER K.,GESAMTWIRTSCHAFTLICHE PLANUNG IN EINER GEMISCHTEN WIRTSCHAFTSORDNUNG (WIRTSCHAFTSPOLITISCHE STUDIEN 5). GERMANY/W WOR+45 WOR-45 INDUS MARKET NAT/G ACT/RES GP/REL INGP/REL PRODUC...ECOMETRIC MGT BIBLIOG 20. PAGE 68 F1346
ECO/TAC PLAN POLICY PREDICT

B66
KIRKENDALL R.S.,SOCIAL SCIENTISTS AND FARM POLITICS IN THE AGE OF ROOSEVELT. ACADEM PLAN ECO/TAC GIVE ADMIN CONTROL PRODUC...SOC 20 NEW/DEAL ROOSEVLT/F BURAGR/ECO. PAGE 71 F1399
AGRI INTELL POLICY NAT/G

B66
KOMIYA R.,POSTWAR ECONOMIC GROWTH IN JAPAN. ELITES NAT/G EX/STRUC TEC/DEV BUDGET DIPLOM CONTROL BAL/PAY PRODUC...BIBLIOG 20 CHINJAP. PAGE 73 F1424
ECO/DEV POLICY PLAN ADJUST

B66
KURAKOV I.G.,SCIENCE, TECHNOLOGY AND COMMUNISM; SOME QUESTIONS OF DEVELOPMENT (TRANS. BY CARIN DEDIJER). USSR INDUS PLAN PROB/SOLV COST PRODUC ...MGT MATH CHARTS METH 20. PAGE 74 F1450
CREATE TEC/DEV MARXISM ECO/TAC

B66
KUZNETS S.,MODERN ECONOMIC GROWTH. WOR+45 WOR-45 ECO/DEV ECO/UNDEV AGRI FINAN INDUS TEC/DEV EFFICIENCY INCOME...NAT/COMP 19/20. PAGE 74 F1456
TIME/SEQ WEALTH PRODUC

B66
REDFORD E.S.,THE ROLE OF GOVERNMENT IN THE AMERICAN ECONOMY. USA+45 USA-45 FINAN INDUS LG/CO PROB/SOLV ADMIN INGP/REL INCOME PRODUC 18/20. PAGE 110 F2169
NAT/G ECO/DEV CAP/ISM ECO/TAC

B66
SPICER K.,A SAMARITAN STATE? AFR CANADA INDIA PAKISTAN UK USA+45 FINAN INDUS PRODUC...CHARTS 20 NATO. PAGE 124 F2455
DIPLOM FOR/AID ECO/DEV ADMIN

B66
THEIL H.,APPLIED ECONOMIC FORECASTING. UNIV USA+45 ELITES INTELL CONSULT PRODUC...DECISION MGT PREDICT CHARTS METH/COMP SIMUL 20. PAGE 129 F2552
FUT OP/RES PLAN

B66
US DEPARTMENT OF LABOR,PRODUCTIVITY: A BIBLIOGRAPHY. ECO/DEV INDUS MARKET OP/RES AUTOMAT COST...STAT 20. PAGE 135 F2668
BIBLIOG/A PRODUC LABOR PLAN

B66
US DEPARTMENT OF LABOR,TECHNOLOGICAL TRENDS IN MAJOR AMERICAN INDUSTRIES. USA+45 R+D LABOR GP/REL PRODUC...MGT BIBLIOG 20. PAGE 135 F2669
TEC/DEV INDUS TREND AUTOMAT

B66
WALTON S.D.,AMERICAN BUSINESS AND ITS ENVIRONMENT. USA+45 LAW CONSTN FINAN MARKET LOC/G EX/STRUC CT/SYS COST PRODUC...STAT 20. PAGE 143 F2813
PRICE PROFIT

L66
CHENERY H.B.,"FOREIGN ASSISTANCE AND ECONOMIC DEVELOPMENT" FUT WOR+45 NAT/G DIPLOM GIVE PRODUC ...METH/CNCPT CHARTS 20. PAGE 24 F0464
FOR/AID EFFICIENCY ECO/UNDEV TEC/DEV

S66
BENOIT J.,"WORLD DEFENSE EXPENDITURES." WOR+45 WEAPON COST PRODUC. PAGE 13 F0253
FORCES STAT NAT/COMP BUDGET

S66
FROMM G.,"RECENT MONETARY POLICY: AN ECONOMETRIC VIEW" USA+45 ECO/DEV INDUS PAY PRICE PRODUC ORD/FREE WEALTH...STAT 20 FED/RESERV. PAGE 45 F0869
ECOMETRIC FINAN POLICY SIMUL

S66
LINDBLOOM C.E.,"HAS INDIA AN ECONOMIC FUTURE?" FUT INDIA NAT/G PROB/SOLV...POLICY 20. PAGE 80 F1568
AGRI PRODUC PLAN ECO/UNDEV

S66
VERSLUYS J.D.N.,"SOME NOTES ON THE SOCIAL AND ECONOMIC EFFECTS OF RURAL ELECTRIFICATION IN BURMA" BURMA EDU/PROP PRODUC ORD/FREE...SOC QU MUNICH TIME 20. PAGE 141 F2782
TEC/DEV SOCIETY CREATE

B67
ALNASRAWI A.,FINANCING ECONOMIC DEVELOPMENT IN IRAQ. IRAQ INDUS CAP/ISM COST PRODUC...STAT CHARTS BIBLIOG 20. PAGE 4 F0076
ECO/UNDEV EXTR/IND TEC/DEV INT/TRADE

B67
CASTILLO C.M.,GROWTH AND INTEGRATION IN CENTRAL AMERICA. L/A+17C CREATE PROB/SOLV ECO/TAC REGION PRODUC...OBS BIBLIOG 20. PAGE 22 F0429
ECO/UNDEV INT/TRADE NAT/COMP

B67
ELSNER H.,THE TECHNOCRATS, PROPHETS OF AUTOMATION. SOCIETY INDUS VOL/ASSN COST INCOME ATTIT 20. PAGE 37 F0726
AUTOMAT TECHRACY PRODUC HIST/WRIT

B67
JACOBY N.H.,US AID TO TAIWAN. CAP/ISM DIPLOM FEEDBACK COST PRODUC...OBS INT CHARTS 20. PAGE 66 F1301
FOR/AID OP/RES ECO/TAC ECO/UNDEV

B67
MAZOUR A.G.,SOVIET ECONOMIC DEVELOPMENT: OPERATION OUTSTRIP: 1921-1965. USSR ECO/UNDEV FINAN CHIEF WORKER PROB/SOLV CONTROL PRODUC MARXISM...CHARTS ORG/CHARTS 20 STALIN/J. PAGE 87 F1711
ECO/TAC AGRI INDUS PLAN

B67
MOSS F.M.,THE WATER CRISIS. PROB/SOLV CONTROL ...POLICY NEW/IDEA. PAGE 94 F1846
GEOG ACT/RES PRODUC WEALTH

B67
OFER G.,THE SERVICE INDUSTRIES IN A DEVELOPING ECONOMY: ISRAEL AS A CASE STUDY. ISRAEL ECO/TAC INT/TRADE PRODUC WEALTH SOCISM...TIME/SEQ TREND CHARTS 20. PAGE 101 F1979
DIPLOM ECO/DEV SERV/IND

B67
ORLANS H.,CONTRACTING FOR ATOMS. AFR USA+45 LAW INTELL ACADEM LG/CO NAT/G PLAN TEC/DEV CONTROL DETER...TREND 20. PAGE 102 F1999
NUC/PWR R+D PRODUC PEACE

B67
PORWIT K.,CENTRAL PLANNING: EVALUATION OF VARIANTS. PRICE OPTIMAL PRODUC...DECISION MATH CHARTS SIMUL BIBLIOG MODELS 20. PAGE 107 F2106
PLAN MGT ECOMETRIC

B67
ROBINSON E.A.G.,ECONOMIC PLANNING IN THE UNITED KINGDOM. UK WORKER PLAN PROB/SOLV BAL/PAY 20. PAGE 113 F2220
ECO/DEV INDUS PRODUC BUDGET

B67
ROBINSON R.D.,INTERNATIONAL MANAGEMENT. LAW MARKET LABOR PRICE CONTROL COST DEMAND OWN PRODUC WEALTH 20. PAGE 113 F2225
T OP/RES MGT DIPLOM

B67
US CONGRESS JOINT ECO COMM,REPORT ON JANUARY 1967 ECONOMIC REPORT OF THE PRESIDENT. FINAN LABOR NAT/G LEGIS BUDGET INT/TRADE COST DEMAND INCOME PRODUC ...POLICY IDEA/COMP 20 CONGRESS. PAGE 135 F2663
CHIEF ECO/TAC PLAN DELIB/GP

B67
ZONDAG C.H.,THE BOLIVIAN ECONOMY 1952-65. L/A+17C TEC/DEV FOR/AID ADMIN...OBS TREND CHARTS BIBLIOG 20 BOLIV. PAGE 151 F2969
ECO/UNDEV INDUS PRODUC

L67
BERNHARD R.C.,"COMPETITION IN LAW AND ECONOMICS." LAW PLAN PRICE CONTROL PRODUC PROFIT...METH/CNCPT IDEA/COMP GEN/LAWS 20. PAGE 14 F0265
MARKET POLICY NAT/G CT/SYS

S67
ADAMS D.W.,"MINIFUNDIA IN AGRARIAN REFORM: A COLOMBIAN EXAMPLE."...SOC CLASSIF 20 COLOMB. PAGE 2 F0035
AGRI METH/COMP OWN

PRODUC

S67
AUBERT DE LA RUE P.,"PERSPECTIVES ECONOMIQUES ENTRE LES ETATS-UNIS ET L'EUROPE." FUT INDUS R+D INT/ORG ACT/RES ECO/TAC AGREE BAL/PAY PRODUC...CHARTS 20 EEC GATT WORLD/BANK. PAGE 7 F0138
INT/TRADE ECO/DEV FINAN TARIFFS

S67
BARRO S.,"ECONOMIC IMPACT OF SPACE EXPENDITURES: SOME BROAD ISSUES DEALING WITH COSTS AND BENEFITS." USA+45 PROC/MFG R+D LG/CO CONSULT COST PRODUC 20. PAGE 10 F0195
SPACE FINAN ECO/TAC NAT/G

S67
BENN W.,"TECHNOLOGY HAS AN INEXORABLE EFFECT." FUT UK ECO/DEV INT/ORG CONSULT PLAN EDU/PROP ADMIN LEAD GP/REL PRODUC...INT 20 EEC. PAGE 13 F0246
R+D LG/CO TEC/DEV INDUS

S67
BENNETT J.T.,"POLITICAL IMPLICATIONS OF ECONOMIC CHANGE: SOUTH VIETNAM." VIETNAM/S INGP/REL INCOME ATTIT 20 AID. PAGE 13 F0247
ECO/UNDEV INDUS AGRI PRODUC

S67
DEWHURST A.,"THE WAGE MOVEMENT IN CANADA." CANADA AGRI NAT/G PARTIC COST PRODUC PROFIT 20. PAGE 32 F0627
WORKER MARXIST INDUS LABOR

S67
FRANKEL T.,"ECONOMIC REFORM* A TENTATIVE APPRAISAL." COM USSR OP/RES BUDGET CONFER EFFICIENCY PRODUC MARXISM SOCISM...MGT 20. PAGE 43 F0847
ECO/DEV INDUS PLAN WEALTH

S67
GAUSSENS J.,"THE APPLICATIONS OF NUCLEAR ENERGY - TECHNICAL, ECONOMIC AND SOCIAL ASPECTS." WOR+45 INDUS R+D ACT/RES EFFICIENCY PRODUC SKILL PREDICT. PAGE 47 F0911
NUC/PWR TEC/DEV ECO/DEV ADJUST

S67
LAZUTKIN Y.,"SOCIALISM AND SPARE TIME." ECO/DEV WORKER CREATE TEC/DEV ROUTINE TIME. PAGE 76 F1497
LEISURE PRODUC SOCISM SOCIALIST

S67
LEONTYEV L.,"THE LENINIST PRINCIPLES OF SOCIALIST ECONOMIC MANAGEMENT." USA+45 USSR POL/PAR WORKER PLAN ECO/TAC EFFICIENCY PRODUC MARXISM...POLICY SOCIALIST MGT TREND 20 LENIN/VI MARX/KARL. PAGE 78 F1529
SOCISM CAP/ISM IDEA/COMP ECO/DEV

S67
LEVI M.,"LES RELATIONS ECONOMIQUES ENTRE L'EST ET L'OUEST EN EUROPE" INDUS...STAT CHARTS 20 OECD COMECON. PAGE 79 F1540
INT/TRADE INT/ORG FINAN PRODUC

S67
MEADE J.E.,"POPULATION EXPLOSION, THE STANDARD OF LIVING AND SOCIAL CONFLICT." DIPLOM FOR/AID OWN ...PREDICT TREND 20. PAGE 89 F1739
GEOG WEALTH PRODUC INCOME

S67
MYRDAL G.,"ECONOMIC DEVELOPMENT IN THE BACKWARD COUNTRIES." INT/ORG TEC/DEV CAP/ISM DIPLOM INT/TRADE PRODUC WEALTH 20. PAGE 96 F1883
ECO/UNDEV INDUS NAT/G ECO/TAC

S67
NOURSE E.G.,"EARLY FLOWERING OF THE EMPLOYMENT ACT" USA+45 LABOR CONSULT DELIB/GP LEGIS BUDGET GOV/REL PRODUC WEALTH 20 INTRVN/ECO. PAGE 99 F1939
NAT/G WORKER ECO/TAC CONTROL

S67
RICHMAN B.M.,"CAPITALISTS & MANAGERS IN COMMUNIST CHINA." ASIA CHINA/COM ECO/UNDEV NAT/G CONSULT EX/STRUC PLAN EFFICIENCY PRODUC WEALTH MARXISM ...MGT CHARTS 20. PAGE 111 F2185
CAP/ISM INDUS

S67
SCHACHTER G.,"REGIONAL DEVELOPMENT IN THE ITALIAN DUAL ECONOMY" ITALY AGRI INDUS MARKET WORKER ECO/TAC CONTROL INCOME PRODUC 20. PAGE 116 F2287
REGION ECO/UNDEV NAT/G PROB/SOLV

S67
SIMONE A.J.,"SCIENTIFIC PUBLIC POLICY, MARKET PERFORMANCE, AND SIZE OF FIRM." GP/REL COST EFFICIENCY OPTIMAL PRODUC PWR. PAGE 122 F2410
LAW INDUS NAT/G PROB/SOLV

S67
SPITTMANN I.,"EAST GERMANY: THE SWINGING PENDULUM." COM GERMANY/E NAT/G EFFICIENCY MARXISM 20. PAGE 125 F2458
PRODUC POL/PAR WEALTH ATTIT

S67
VAN KLAVEREN J.,"DIE WIRTSCHAFTLICHEN AUSWIRKUNGEN DES SCHWARZEN TODES" GERMANY PRICE DEMAND PRODUC MUNICH 14/15 DEPRESSION. PAGE 140 F2762
HEALTH AGRI GEOG

B68
PROUDHON P.J.,SYSTEME DES CONTRADICTIONS ECONOMIQUES, OU PHILOSOPHIE DA LA MISERE (2 VOLS.) (1846). SECT WORKER GP/REL ISOLAT PRODUC IDEA/COMP. PAGE 108 F2126
SOCIETY STRATA MORAL

B76
FOURIER C.,SOCIAL DESTINIES, IN A. BRISBANE, GENERAL INTRODUCTION TO SOCIAL SCIENCE. UNIV AGRI INDUS SECT PRODUC...PHIL/SCI CONCPT. PAGE 43 F0835
UTOPIA SOCIETY PERSON VOL/ASSN

B76
PROUDHON P.J.,WHAT IS PROPERTY? (TRANS. BY B.R. TUCKER). SOCIETY AGRI CAP/ISM CRIME GP/REL PERSON MORAL ORD/FREE WEALTH. PAGE 108 F2127
OWN WORKER PRODUC ANARCH

B76
SMITH A.,THE WEALTH OF NATIONS. UK STRUCT WORKER DIPLOM ECO/TAC OPTIMAL DRIVE PERSON ORD/FREE ...OLD/LIB GEN/LAWS 17/18. PAGE 123 F2428
WEALTH PRODUC INDUS LAISSEZ

B91
MILL J.S.,SOCIALISM (1859). MOD/EUR AGRI INDUS NAT/G REV INCOME PRODUC ORD/FREE POPULISM SOCISM ...GOV/COMP METH/COMP 19. PAGE 91 F1787
WEALTH SOCIALIST ECO/TAC OWN

B98
MARSHALL A.,PRINCIPLES OF ECONOMICS. INDUS WORKER PRICE COST EQUILIB INCOME OPTIMAL PRODUC...TIME/SEQ METH RICARDO/D. PAGE 86 F1678
WEALTH GEN/LAWS MARKET

B99
KROPOTKIN P.,FIELDS, FACTORIES, AND WORKSHOPS. UNIV INTELL ECO/DEV LG/CO SCHOOL SML/CO ECO/TAC PRODUC UTOPIA...NEW/IDEA MUNICH. PAGE 74 F1445
SOCIETY WORKER AGRI INDUS

S55
KELLY W.E.,"HOW SALES EXECUTIVES USE FACTORING TO BOOST SALES AND PROFITS TODAY." FINAN LG/CO BUDGET EFFICIENCY PROFIT...MGT PRODUCT. PAGE 70 F1372
INDUS ECO/DEV CONSULT MARKET

PRODUCTIVITY....SEE PRODUC

PROF/ORG....PROFESSIONAL ORGANIZATIONS

N
NEW JERSEY STATE OF,SECOND REPORT TO GOVERNOR, SENATE, ASSEMBLY BY UNIFORM COMMERCIAL CODE STUDY COMMISSION. USA+45 INDUS LOC/G NAT/G PROF/ORG CONSULT ACT/RES LEGIT CT/SYS ATTIT NEW/JERSEY. PAGE 98 F1920
LAW FINAN CENTRAL PROVS

N19
HOGARTY R.A.,NEW JERSEY FARMERS AND MIGRANT HOUSING RULES (PAMPHLET). USA+45 LAW ELITES FACE/GP LABOR PROF/ORG LOBBY PERS/REL RIGID/FLEX ROLE 20 NEW/JERSEY. PAGE 61 F1193
AGRI PROVS WORKER HEALTH

B27
WEBER M.,GENERAL ECONOMIC HISTORY. CHRIST-17C MOD/EUR STRUCT AGRI EXTR/IND FINAN INDUS MARKET FAM NAT/G PROF/ORG SECT ECO/TAC MUNICH 8/20. PAGE 144 F2839
ECO/DEV CAP/ISM

B36
BELLOC H.,THE RESTORATION OF PROPERTY. UK STRATA NAT/G PROF/ORG DELIB/GP WORKER CREATE PROB/SOLV ECO/TAC PARTIC UTOPIA ORD/FREE SOCISM 20. PAGE 13 F0238
CONTROL MAJORIT CAP/ISM OWN

S38
HALL R.C.,"REPRESENTATION OF BIG BUSINESS IN THE HOUSE OF COMMONS." UK ECO/DEV INDUS PROF/ORG LEGIS CAP/ISM ECO/TAC LAISSEZ...POLICY OLD/LIB PLURIST MGT 20 HOUSE/CMNS. PAGE 53 F1047
LOBBY NAT/G

B39
STALEY E.,WORLD ECONOMY IN TRANSITION. WOR-45 SOCIETY INT/ORG PROF/ORG ECO/TAC ATTIT WEALTH ...METH/CNCPT TREND GEN/LAWS 20. PAGE 125 F2465
TEC/DEV INT/TRADE

L42
GRANT J.A.C.,"THE GUILD RETURNS TO AMERICA." CHRIST-17C USA-45 LEGIS LICENSE ADJUD CONTROL GP/REL. PAGE 50 F0978
PROF/ORG JURID LABOR PWR

B52
HARDIN C.M.,THE POLITICS OF AGRICULTURE. USA+45 NAT/G PROF/ORG LEGIS LOBBY 20 DEPT/AGRI. PAGE 55 F1077
AGRI POLICY ECO/TAC GOV/REL

B53
BOULDING K.E.,THE ORGANIZATIONAL REVOLUTION. FUT CULTURE ECO/DEV LABOR PROF/ORG ECO/TAC MORAL...SOC CONCPT RECORD INT SOC/EXP 20. PAGE 17 F0321
SOCIETY TREND

B54
CHILDS M.W.,ETHICS IN A BUSINESS SOCIETY. PROF/ORG LEAD WAR GP/REL ATTIT DRIVE PERSON KNOWL MORAL PWR ...WELF/ST BIBLIOG. PAGE 24 F0466
MGT SOCIETY

B57
EHRMANN H.W.,ORGANIZED BUSINESS IN FRANCE. EUR+WWI MOD/EUR ECO/DEV VOL/ASSN LEGIT ATTIT PERCEPT PWR RESPECT...PLURIST SOC INT TOT/POP 20. PAGE 36 F0712
PROF/ORG ECO/TAC FRANCE

B59
HAX K.,DIE HOCHSCHULLEHRER DER WIRTSCHAFTSWISSENSCHAFTEN IN DER BUNDESREPUBLIK DEUTSCHLAND EINSCHL. WESTBERLIN, OSTERREICH. AUSTRIA GERMANY/W SWITZERLND FINAN MARKET PROF/ORG BUDGET ECO/TAC INT/TRADE PRICE COST 20. PAGE 57 F1119
BIBLIOG ACADEM INTELL

S59
ALLEN G.,"NATIONAL FARMERS UNION AS A PRESSURE GROUP: II." UK ECO/DEV MARKET POL/PAR DELIB/GP PROB/SOLV ECO/TAC LOBBY INCOME...POLICY METH/COMP 19/20 NAT/FARMER. PAGE 4 F0069
DIST/IND AGRI PROF/ORG TREND

B60
GILMORE D.R.,DEVELOPING THE "LITTLE" ECONOMIES. USA+45 FINAN LG/CO PROF/ORG VOL/ASSN CREATE ADMIN. PAGE 47 F0924
ECO/TAC LOC/G PROVS PLAN

N60
COMMITTEE ECONOMIC DEVELOPMENT,GUIDING METROPOLITAN GROWTH (PAMPHLET). USA+45 LOC/G NAT/G PROF/ORG ACT/RES PLAN...SOC/WK MUNICH. PAGE 27 F0517
GEOG INDUS HEALTH

B61
DEWITT N.,EDUCATION AND PROFESSIONAL EMPLOYMENT IN THE USSR. USSR PROF/ORG WORKER PLAN ADMIN UTIL AGE/C AGE/Y MARXISM...STAT CHARTS 20. PAGE 32 F0629
EDU/PROP ACADEM SCHOOL INTELL

B61
GALENSON W.,TRADE UNION DEMOCRACY IN WESTERN EUROPE. ECO/DEV INDUS PROF/ORG WORKER INCOME ...METH/COMP 20. PAGE 45 F0886
LABOR GP/REL ECO/TAC EUR+WWI

B61
INTL BANKING SUMMER SCHOOL,TRENDS IN BANK CREDIT AND FINANCE. EUR+WWI NETHERLAND ECO/DEV PROF/ORG PLAN BUDGET 20 EEC. PAGE 65 F1283
FINAN ECO/TAC NAT/G LG/CO

B61
LENSKI G.,THE RELIGIOUS FACTOR: A SOCIOLOGICAL STUDY OF RELIGION'S IMPACT ON POLITICS, ECONOMICS, AND FAMILY LIFE. FAM PROF/ORG EDU/PROP ROLE CATHISM ...INT SAMP MUNICH. PAGE 78 F1524
SECT GP/REL

B62
BRANCH M.C.,THE CORPORATE PLANNING PROCESS. FINAN EX/STRUC EDU/PROP CONTROL LEAD GP/REL PERS/REL RATIONAL PERCEPT...MGT MATH PROBABIL STAT GAME. PAGE 18 F0338
PROF/ORG PLAN DECISION PERSON

L62
"HIGHER EDUCATION AND ECONOMIC AND SOCIAL DEVELOPMENT IN LATIN AMERICA: A BIBLIOGRAPHY." L/A+17C SOCIETY ECO/UNDEV PROF/ORG DIPLOM CONFER ...SOC 20. PAGE 1 F0016
BIBLIOG/A ACADEM INTELL EDU/PROP

B63
BAUER R.A.,AMERICAN BUSINESS AND PUBLIC POLICY: THE POLITICS OF FOREIGN TRADE. USA+45 COM/IND LG/CO NAT/G PROF/ORG SML/CO VOL/ASSN LEGIS TOP/EX ECO/TAC EDU/PROP CHOOSE HEALTH PWR WEALTH...CONCPT METH/CNCPT OBS INT QU SAMP FOR/TRADE TRUE/GP VAL/FREE HI. PAGE 11 F0217
ECO/DEV ATTIT

S63
GANDILHON J.,"LA SCIENCE ET LA TECHNIQUE A L'AIDE DES REGIONS PEU DEVELOPPEES." FRANCE FUT WOR+45 ECO/DEV R+D PROF/ORG ACT/RES PLAN...MGT TOT/POP VAL/FREE 20 UN. PAGE 46 F0893
ECO/UNDEV TEC/DEV FOR/AID

S63
LEDUC G.,"L'AIDE INTERNATIONALE AU DEVELOPPEMENT." FUT WOR+45 ECO/DEV ECO/UNDEV R+D PROF/ORG TEC/DEV ECO/TAC ROUTINE ATTIT ALL/VALS...MGT TIME/SEQ FOR/TRADE TOT/POP 20. PAGE 77 F1503
FINAN PLAN FOR/AID

B64
BOWEN W.G.,ECONOMIC ASPECTS OF EDUCATION (NO. 104). EUR+WWI UK USA+45 PROF/ORG PLAN TEC/DEV PAY ...POLICY STAT 20. PAGE 17 F0329
EDU/PROP ACADEM FINAN METH/COMP

B64
CHEIT E.F.,THE BUSINESS ESTABLISHMENT. FRANCE WOR+45 PROF/ORG TOP/EX PROB/SOLV CAP/ISM ADMIN SUPEGO MORAL PWR...METH/CNCPT MYTH NEW/IDEA 20. PAGE 24 F0460
PERSON EX/STRUC MGT INDUS

B64
COMMITTEE ECONOMIC DEVELOPMENT,COMMUNITY ECONOMIC DEVELOPMENT PROGRAMS. USA+45 FINAN INDUS LG/CO PROF/ORG CREATE GP/REL MUNICH NEW/YORK VERMONT PENNSYLVAN IN ARKANSAS. PAGE 27 F0519
LOC/G LABOR PLAN

B65
BRADLEY J.F.,THE ROLE OF TRADE ASSOCIATIONS AND PROFESSIONAL BUSINESS SOCIETIES IN AMERICA. USA+45 USA-45 STRUCT CONSULT DELIB/GP CREATE LOBBY GP/REL 20. PAGE 17 F0333
ECO/DEV PROF/ORG VOL/ASSN SOCIETY

B65
MACAVOY P.W.,THE ECONOMIC EFFECTS OF REGULATION: THE TRUNK-LINE RAILROAD CARTELS AND THE INTERSTATE COMMERCE COMMISSION BEFORE 1900. USA-45 PRICE PROFIT...STAT CHARTS BIBLIOG 19 RAILROAD. PAGE 83 F1620
ECO/TAC DIST/IND PROF/ORG RATION

B65
OECD,MEDITERRANEAN REGIONAL PROJECT: TURKEY; EDUCATION AND DEVELOPMENT. FUT TURKEY SOCIETY STRATA FINAN NAT/G PROF/ORG PLAN PROB/SOLV ADMIN
EDU/PROP ACADEM SCHOOL

COST...STAT CHARTS 20 OECD. PAGE 100 F1969 — ECO/UNDEV

B65
OECD,THE MEDITERRANEAN REGIONAL PROJECT: PORTUGAL; EDUCATION AND DEVELOPMENT. PORTUGAL SOCIETY STRATA FINAN PROF/ORG WORKER PLAN PROB/SOLV ADMIN...POLICY STAT CHARTS METH 20 OECD. PAGE 100 F1970 — EDU/PROP SCHOOL ACADEM ECO/UNDEV

B65
OECD,THE MEDITERRANEAN REGIONAL PROJECT: ITALY; EDUCATION AND DEVELOPMENT. ITALY SOCIETY STRATA FINAN NAT/G PROF/ORG WORKER PLAN PROB/SOLV ADMIN ...STAT CHARTS METH 20 OECD. PAGE 100 F1971 — SCHOOL EDU/PROP ECO/UNDEV ACADEM

B65
OECD,THE MEDITERRANEAN REGIONAL PROJECT: GREECE; EDUCATION AND DEVELOPMENT. FUT GREECE SOCIETY AGRI FINAN NAT/G PROF/ORG WORKER PLAN PROB/SOLV ADMIN DEMAND ATTIT 20 OECD. PAGE 100 F1972 — EDU/PROP SCHOOL ACADEM ECO/UNDEV

B65
ORG FOR ECO COOP AND DEVEL,THE MEDITERRANEAN REGIONAL PROJECT: AN EXPERIMENT IN PLANNING BY SIX COUNTRIES. FUT GREECE SPAIN TURKEY YUGOSLAVIA SOCIETY FINAN NAT/G PROF/ORG EDU/PROP ADMIN REGION COST...POLICY STAT CHARTS 20 OECD. PAGE 102 F1995 — PLAN ECO/UNDEV ACADEM SCHOOL

B65
ORG FOR ECO COOP AND DEVEL,THE MEDITERRANEAN REGIONAL PROJECT: YUGOSLAVIA; EDUCATION AND DEVELOPMENT. YUGOSLAVIA SOCIETY FINAN PROF/ORG PLAN ADMIN COST DEMAND MARXISM...STAT TREND CHARTS METH 20 OECD. PAGE 102 F1996 — EDU/PROP ACADEM SCHOOL ECO/UNDEV

L65
HAGE J.,"AN AXIOMATIC THEORY OF ORGANIZATIONS" USA+45 STRUCT LABOR PRODUC DRIVE PERSON RIGID/FLEX 20 WEBER/MAX. PAGE 53 F1032 — GP/REL EFFICIENCY PROF/ORG ATTIT

B66
MOSKOW M.H.,TEACHERS AND UNIONS. SCHOOL WORKER ADJUD LOBBY ATTIT ORD/FREE 20. PAGE 94 F1844 — EDU/PROP PROF/ORG LABOR BARGAIN

B66
PFEFFER K.H.,WELT IM UMBRUCH. SOCIETY STRUCT INDUS PROF/ORG SECT TEC/DEV PARTIC SUPEGO WORSHIP 20 CHRISTIAN. PAGE 106 F2076 — ORD/FREE STRATA CREATE

B67
BADGLEY R.F.,DOCTORS' STRIKE; MEDICAL CARE AND CONFLICT IN SASKATCHEWAN. CANADA NAT/G PROF/ORG GP/REL ADJUST ATTIT...HEAL SOC 20. PAGE 8 F0148 — HEALTH PLAN LABOR BARGAIN

B67
BEAL E.F.,THE PRACTICE OF COLLECTIVE BARGAINING (3RD ED.). USA+45 WOR+45 ECO/DEV INDUS LG/CO PROF/ORG WORKER ECO/TAC GP/REL WEALTH...JURID METH/CNCPT. PAGE 12 F0221 — BARGAIN MGT LABOR ADJUD

S67
CAMMETT J.M.,"COMMUNIST THEORIES OF FASCISM, 1920-35." ITALY POL/PAR PROF/ORG VOL/ASSN WORKER COLONIAL TOTALISM...SOCIALIST 20. PAGE 21 F0403 — MARXISM FASCISM ATTIT

S67
JANSSEN P.,"NEA: THE RELUCTANT DRAGON." NAT/G EXEC LOBBY PARTIC SANCTION RACE/REL ROLE TREND. PAGE 66 F1305 — EDU/PROP PROF/ORG MGT POLICY

S67
SHISTER J.,"THE DIRECTION OF UNIONISM 1947-1967: THRUST OF DRIFT?" INDUS CENTRAL EFFICIENCY INCOME ATTIT SOCISM...POLICY TREND 20 AFL/CIO. PAGE 121 F2382 — LABOR PROF/ORG LEAD LAW

S67
WAITS C.R.,"CRAFT GILDS AS AN INSTITUTIONAL BARRIER TO THE INDUSTRIAL REVOLUTION." CHRIST-17C MOD/EUR ECO/UNDEV CONTROL GP/REL ATTIT 16/19. PAGE 142 F2801 — TEC/DEV INDUS REV PROF/ORG

N67
NATIONAL COMN COMMUNITY HEALTH,ACTION - PLANNING FOR COMMUNITY HEALTH SERVICES (PAMPHLET). USA+45 PROF/ORG DELIB/GP BUDGET ROUTINE GP/REL ATTIT ...HEAL SOC SOC/WK CHARTS MUNICH TIME 20. PAGE 97 F1898 — PLAN HEALTH ADJUST

PROFESSIONAL ORGANIZATION....SEE PROF/ORG

PROFIT....

N19
MIYASAWA K.,AN ECONOMIC SURVIVAL GAME (PAMPHLET). COST DEMAND EQUILIB INCOME PROFIT 20. PAGE 92 F1811 — ECOMETRIC GAME ECO/TAC DECISION

N19
US BUREAU OF THE CENSUS,THE PROPORTION OF THE SHIPMENTS (OR EMPLOYEES) OF EACH INDUSTRY... (PAMPHLET). USA+45 ECO/DEV EXTR/IND INDUS CONTROL PROFIT...STAT 20 CONGRESS MONOPOLY. PAGE 134 F2645 — PROC/MFG PRODUC MARKET CHARTS

B24
CLARK J.B.,THE DISTRIBUTION OF WEALTH (1899). WORKER OWN PRODUC PROFIT WEALTH LAISSEZ...IDEA/COMP GEN/LAWS. PAGE 25 F0478 — ECO/TAC INDUS LABOR INCOME

B30
KEYNES J.M.,A TREATISE ON MONEY (2 VOLS.). UK USA-45 INDUS MARKET WORKER PRICE CONTROL COST OPTIMAL PROFIT WEALTH...POLICY 19/20 KEYNES/JM. PAGE 70 F1385 — EQUILIB ECO/TAC FINAN GEN/LAWS

B35
KEYNES J.M.,THE GENERAL THEORY OF EMPLOYMENT, INTEREST, AND MONEY. AGRI INDUS WORKER ECO/TAC DEMAND EQUILIB INCOME PRODUC PROFIT ATTIT WEALTH 20. PAGE 71 F1386 — FINAN GEN/LAWS MARKET PRICE

B35
MARX K.,WAGE-LABOR AND CAPITAL -- VALUE, PRICE AND PROFIT. LABOR PAY PRICE COST INCOME OWN PROFIT WEALTH 19. PAGE 86 F1690 — STRATA WORKER MARXIST MARXISM

B35
WADE J.,HISTORY OF THE MIDDLE AND WORKING CLASSES; WITH A POPULAR EXPOSITION OF THE ECONOMICAL AND POLITICAL PRINCIPLES.... FRANCE UK CONSTN FINAN INDUS LABOR INCOME PROFIT KNOWL MORAL ORD/FREE WEALTH...CHARTS 14/19. PAGE 142 F2797 — WORKER STRATA CONCPT

B38
MEADE J.E.,AN INTRODUCTION TO ECONOMIC ANALYSIS AND POLICY (AMERICAN EDITION EDITED BY C.J. HITCH). FINAN INDUS MARKET LABOR INT/TRADE CONTROL COST DEMAND INCOME...CLASSIF CHARTS T 20 KEYNES/JM MONOPOLY. PAGE 89 F1737 — CONCPT PROFIT PRODUC

B41
HAYEK F.A.,THE PURE THEORY OF CAPITAL. UNIV ECO/DEV ECO/TAC COST EQUILIB PROFIT WEALTH...SIMUL GEN/LAWS BIBLIOG INDEX TIME 20. PAGE 57 F1120 — CAP/ISM METH/CNCPT PRODUC FINAN

B44
BIENSTOCK G.,MANAGEMENT IN RUSSIAN INDUSTRY AND AGRICULTURE. USSR CONSULT WORKER LEAD COST PROFIT ATTIT DRIVE PWR...MGT METH/COMP DICTIONARY ACCT 20. PAGE 15 F0281 — ADMIN MARXISM SML/CO AGRI

B48
NOYES C.R.,ECONOMIC MAN IN RELATION TO HIS NATURAL ENVIRONMENT (2 VOLS.). UNIV COST DEMAND EFFICIENCY HAPPINESS INCOME PRODUC PROFIT HEREDITY...CHARTS BIBLIOG. PAGE 99 F1944 — HABITAT METH/CNCPT GEN/METH

B50
CLARK J.M.,ALTERNATIVE TO SERFDOM. SOCIETY STRATA INDUS MARKET WORKER PRICE GP/REL PROFIT BIO/SOC PWR WEALTH...GEN/LAWS 20 KEYNES/JM. PAGE 25 F0481 — ORD/FREE POPULISM ECO/TAC REPRESENT

B50
HARTLAND P.C.,BALANCE OF INTERREGIONAL PAYMENTS OF NEW ENGLAND. USA+45 TEC/DEV ECO/TAC LEGIT ROUTINE BAL/PAY PROFIT 20 NEW/ENGLND FED/RESERV. PAGE 56 F1102 — ECO/DEV FINAN REGION PLAN

S50
DREYFUS S.,"THE INDUSTRIAL DESIGNER AND THE BUSINESSMAN." SERV/IND PROB/SOLV ECO/TAC COST EFFICIENCY PROFIT RATIONAL...DECISION MGT. PAGE 34 F0662 — CONSULT INDUS PRODUC UTIL

B51
COOKE C.A.,CORPORATION TRUST AND COMPANY: AN ESSAY IN LEGAL HISTORY. UK STRUCT LEGIS CAP/ISM GP/REL PROFIT 13/20 COMPNY/ACT. PAGE 27 F0531 — LG/CO FINAN ECO/TAC JURID

B51
POOLE K.,FISCAL POLICIES AND THE AMERICAN ECONOMY. AFR ECO/DEV FINAN INDUS WORKER OP/RES INT/TRADE TAX COST INCOME PROFIT WEALTH...GP/COMP 20. PAGE 107 F2102 — NAT/G POLICY ANTHOL

B54
KARTUN D.,AFRICA, AFRICA: A CONTINENT RISES TO ITS FEET. AFR SOUTH/AFR UK ELITES AGRI LABOR LOC/G POL/PAR EDU/PROP CONTROL COERCE DISCRIM AGE/Y NEGRO THIRD/WRLD GOLD/COAST. PAGE 69 F1358 — COLONIAL ORD/FREE PROFIT EXTR/IND

B54
MEYER F.V.,INFLATION AND CAPITAL. AFR UK WOR+45 BUDGET GOV/REL INCOME PRODUC PROFIT WEALTH...CONCPT CHARTS 20. PAGE 90 F1768 — ECO/DEV FINAN ECO/TAC DEMAND

B54
MITCHELL W.G.,BUSINESS CYCLES. FINAN MARKET PRICE COST EQUILIB OPTIMAL PRODUC PROFIT...IDEA/COMP GEN/LAWS 19/20. PAGE 92 F1809 — INDUS TIME/SEQ METH/COMP STAT

S55
KELLY W.E.,"HOW SALES EXECUTIVES USE FACTORING TO BOOST SALES AND PROFITS TODAY." FINAN LG/CO BUDGET EFFICIENCY PROFIT...MGT PRODUCT. PAGE 70 F1372 — INDUS ECO/DEV CONSULT MARKET

S57
ANSHEN M.,"BUSINESS, LAWYERS, AND ECONOMISTS." PROB/SOLV ECO/TAC CONFER PROFIT RIGID/FLEX OBJECTIVE...MGT GP/COMP. PAGE 6 F0106 — INDUS CONSULT ROUTINE EFFICIENCY

B58
HENNING C.N.,INTERNATIONAL FINANCING. WOR+45 ECO/DEV INT/ORG EX/STRUC INSPECT CAP/ISM BAL/PAY — FINAN DIPLOM

COST PROFIT...MGT CHARTS T 20. PAGE 58 F1150 — INT/TRADE

B60
BIERMAN H.,THE CAPITAL BUDGETING DECISION. AFR ECO/DEV MARKET TAX PRICE RISK COST INCOME TIME 20. PAGE 15 F0282 — FINAN OPTIMAL BUDGET PROFIT

B60
GRIER E.,PRIVATELY DEVELOPED INTERRACIAL HOUSING: AN ANALYSIS OF EXPERIENCE. FINAN MARKET COST DISCRIM PROFIT SOC/INTEG 20. PAGE 51 F0997 — RACE/REL CONSTRUC HABITAT

B60
HARBRECHT P.P.,TOWARD THE PARAPROPRIETAL SOCIETY. REPRESENT INCOME OWN PROFIT AGE/O. PAGE 55 F1076 — PWR ADMIN ELITES CONTROL

B60
HEILPERIN M.A.,STUDIES IN ECONOMIC NATIONALISM. EUR+WWI MOD/EUR USA+45 ECO/DEV PLAN INT/TRADE TARIFFS WAR PRODUC PROFIT 18/20 KEYNES/JM. PAGE 58 F1140 — ECO/TAC NAT/G NAT/LISM POLICY

B61
CLARK J.M.,COMPETITION AS A DYNAMIC PROCESS. ECO/DEV EXTR/IND INDUS LG/CO TEC/DEV ECO/TAC PRICE EQUILIB PRODUC...NEW/IDEA CAP 20. PAGE 25 F0483 — WEALTH GP/REL FINAN PROFIT

B61
FERTIG L.,PROSPERITY THROUGH FREEDOM. COM INDUS LABOR CAP/ISM ECO/TAC PRODUC PROFIT ORD/FREE WEALTH SOCISM...METH/CNCPT 20. PAGE 40 F0788 — NAT/G CONTROL POLICY

B61
HENDERSON W.O.,THE INDUSTRIAL REVOLUTION IN EUROPE. FRANCE GERMANY MOD/EUR RUSSIA WORKER PROFIT PWR MARXISM SOCISM...SOC HIST/WRIT 19 INDUS/REV. PAGE 58 F1148 — INDUS REV CAP/ISM TEC/DEV

B61
LAMFALUSSY A.,INVESTMENT AND GROWTH IN MATURE ECONOMIES. BELGIUM EUR+WWI LABOR PRICE PRODUC PROFIT...STAT CONT/OBS CHARTS 20. PAGE 75 F1464 — FINAN INDUS ECO/DEV CAP/ISM

B61
STOCKING G.W.,WORKABLE COMPETITION AND ANTITRUST POLICY. USA+45 NAT/G CONSULT PLAN PRICE GOV/REL COST DEMAND PROFIT...POLICY 20. PAGE 126 F2491 — LG/CO INDUS ECO/TAC CONTROL

B62
COLLIER A.T.,MANAGEMENT, MEN, AND VALUES. INDUS FACE/GP EX/STRUC PLAN PROB/SOLV DEBATE SENIOR ADMIN PROFIT PERSON...PSY SOC 20. PAGE 26 F0505 — MGT ATTIT PERS/REL DECISION

B62
DOBB M.,CAPITALISM YESTERDAY AND TODAY. UK WORKER WAR PRODUC PROFIT 18/20 MONOPOLY. PAGE 33 F0646 — CAP/ISM TIME/SEQ CONCPT ECO/TAC

B62
MCCRONE G.,THE ECONOMICS OF SUBSIDING AGRICULTURE. UK ECO/DEV MARKET PLAN TARIFFS PROFIT 20 EEC. PAGE 88 F1725 — AGRI BAL/PAY INT/TRADE LABOR

B62
MEANS G.C.,PRICING POWER AND THE PUBLIC INTEREST. PLAN PROB/SOLV COST EFFICIENCY PROFIT RIGID/FLEX WEALTH. PAGE 89 F1741 — LG/CO EX/STRUC PRICE ECO/TAC

B62
US BUREAU OF THE CENSUS,REPORT FOR SUBCOMMITTEE ON ANTITRUST AND MONOPOLY: CONCENTRATION RATIOS IN MANUFACTURING INDUSTRY 1958. USA+45 ECO/DEV CONTROL GOV/REL OWN PRODUC PROFIT...STAT 20 CONGRESS MONOPOLY. PAGE 134 F2646 — CHARTS PROC/MFG MARKET LG/CO

B62
VAIZEY J.,THE ECONOMICS OF EDUCATION. INTELL ECO/TAC PAY COST PRODUC 20. PAGE 140 F2758 — ECO/DEV SCHOOL ACADEM PROFIT

B63
DUE J.F.,STATE SALES TAX ADMINISTRATION. OP/RES BUDGET PAY ADMIN EXEC ROUTINE COST EFFICIENCY PROFIT...CHARTS METH/COMP 20. PAGE 34 F0671 — PROVS TAX STAT GOV/COMP

B63
WILTZ J.E.,IN SEARCH OF PEACE: THE SENATE MUNITIONS INQUIRY, 1934-36. EUR+WWI USA-45 ELITES INDUS LG/CO LEGIS INT/TRADE LOBBY NEUTRAL ARMS/CONT...POLICY CONGRESS 20 LEAGUE/NAT PRESIDENT SENATE CONSCRIPTN. PAGE 147 F2905 — DELIB/GP PROFIT WAR WEAPON

B64
NEWCOMER H.A.,INTERNATIONAL AIDS TO OVERSEAS INVESTMENTS AND TRADE. ECO/UNDEV TARIFFS PROFIT ...BIBLIOG 20 GATT UN. PAGE 98 F1921 — INT/TRADE FINAN DIPLOM FOR/AID

B64
REDLICH F.,THE GERMAN MILITARY ENTERPRISER AND HIS WORK FORCE. CHRIST-17C GERMANY ELITES SOCIETY FINAN ECO/TAC CIVMIL/REL GP/REL INGP/REL...HIST/WRIT METH/COMP 14/17. PAGE 110 F2170 — EX/STRUC FORCES PROFIT WORKER

B64
STONIER A.W.,EXERCISES IN ECONOMICS. FINAN INDUS TEC/DEV RENT PAY EQUILIB PRODUC PROFIT...METH/COMP T. PAGE 127 F2498 — PRICE MARKET WORKER

S64
NEWLYN W.T.,"MONETARY SYSTEMS AND INTEGRATION" AFR BUDGET ADMIN FEDERAL PRODUC PROFIT UTIL...CHARTS 20 AFRICA/E. PAGE 98 F1922 — ECO/UNDEV REGION METH/COMP FINAN

S64
STONE P.A.,"DECISION TECHNIQUES FOR TOWN DEVELOPMENT." PLAN COST PROFIT...DECISION MGT CON/ANAL CHARTS METH/COMP BIBLIOG MUNICH 20. PAGE 127 F2497 — OP/RES ADMIN PROB/SOLV

B65
ALLEN W.R.,INTERNATIONAL TRADE THEORY: HUME TO OHLIN. FINAN LABOR TARIFFS TAX PRICE DEMAND PRODUC PROFIT...ANTHOL 18/20. PAGE 4 F0074 — INT/TRADE WEALTH METH/CNCPT

B65
MACAVOY P.W.,THE ECONOMIC EFFECTS OF REGULATION: THE TRUNK-LINE RAILROAD CARTELS AND THE INTERSTATE COMMERCE COMMISSION BEFORE 1900. USA-45 PRICE PROFIT...STAT CHARTS BIBLIOG 19 RAILROAD. PAGE 83 F1620 — ECO/TAC DIST/IND PROF/ORG RATION

B65
RIGBY P.H.,CONCEPTUAL FOUNDATIONS OF BUSINESS RESEARCH. COMPUTER PROB/SOLV OPTIMAL...MGT CONCPT MATH STAT TESTS SIMUL GEN/METH. PAGE 111 F2192 — PROFIT R+D INDUS DECISION

B65
SABLE M.H.,PERIODICALS FOR LATIN AMERICAN ECONOMIC DEVELOPMENT, TRADE, AND FINANCE: AN ANNOTATED BIBLIOGRAPHY (A PAMPHLET). ECO/TAC PRODUC PROFIT ...STAT NAT/COMP 20 OAS. PAGE 115 F2266 — BIBLIOG/A L/A+17C ECO/UNDEV INT/TRADE

B65
THORNTON A.P.,DOCTRINES OF IMPERIALISM. WOR+45 WOR-45 DOMIN NAT/LISM PROFIT ATTIT PERSON PWR RESPECT SOVEREIGN...CONCPT STERTYP. PAGE 130 F2571 — IDEA/COMP COLONIAL DRIVE

B65
TYBOUT R.A.,ECONOMICS OF RESEARCH AND DEVELOPMENT. ECO/DEV ECO/UNDEV INDUS PROFIT DECISION. PAGE 131 F2594 — R+D FORCES ADMIN DIPLOM

B65
WILKINSON T.O.,THE URBANIZATION OF JAPANESE LABOR, 1868-1955. AGRI PROC/MFG CAP/ISM PRODUC PROFIT ...SOC CLASSIF CENSUS CHARTS MUNICH 19/20 CHINJAP. PAGE 146 F2887 — LABOR INDUS GEOG

B65
ZAWADZKI K.K.F.,THE ECONOMICS OF INFLATIONARY PROCESSES. FINAN INT/TRADE PRICE CONTROL DEMAND EQUILIB PROFIT 20. PAGE 150 F2960 — ECO/DEV COST ECO/TAC CAP/ISM

L65
LOFTUS M.L.,"INTERNATIONAL MONETARY FUND, 1962-1965: A SELECTED BIBLIOGRAPHY." WOR+45 PLAN BUDGET INCOME PROFIT WEALTH. PAGE 81 F1596 — BIBLIOG FINAN INT/TRADE INT/ORG

S65
GOLDMAN M.I.,"A BALANCE SHEET OF SOVIET FOREIGN AID." USA+45 ECO/UNDEV BAL/PWR ECO/TAC RENT GIVE EDU/PROP CONTROL COST PROFIT GEN/METH. PAGE 48 F0939 — USSR FOR/AID NAT/COMP EFFICIENCY

B66
DAVIS K.,BUSINESS AND ITS ENVIRONMENT. LAW ECO/DEV INDUS OP/RES ADMIN CONTROL ROUTINE GP/REL PROFIT POLICY. PAGE 30 F0591 — EX/STRUC PROB/SOLV CAP/ISM EXEC

B66
FELKER J.L.,SOVIET ECONOMIC CONTROVERSIES. USSR INDUS PLAN INT/TRADE GP/REL MARXISM SOCISM...POLICY 20. PAGE 40 F0778 — ECO/DEV MARKET PROFIT PRICE

B66
LANDERS D.S.,RISE OF CAPITALISM. LABOR AUTOMAT GP/REL CENTRAL COST PROFIT...SOC CONCPT ANTHOL 19/20. PAGE 75 F1469 — CAP/ISM INDUS AGRI

B66
LERNER E.M.,A THEORY OF FINANCIAL ANALYSIS. UNIV LG/CO COST DEMAND INCOME PROFIT...MATH STAT CHARTS SIMUL T 20. PAGE 78 F1531 — CONCPT FINAN ECO/DEV OPTIMAL

B66
POLK J.,U S PRODUCTION ABROAD AND THE BALANCE OF PAYMENTS* A SURVEY OF CORPORATE INVESTMENT EXPERIENCE. USA+45 SERV/IND NAT/G OP/RES COST PROFIT ATTIT...ECOMETRIC STAT INT QU GEN/METH. PAGE 107 F2096 — BAL/PAY FINAN INT/TRADE INDUS

B66
WALTON S.D.,AMERICAN BUSINESS AND ITS ENVIRONMENT. USA+45 LAW CONSTN FINAN MARKET LOC/G EX/STRUC CT/SYS COST PRODUC...STAT 20. PAGE 143 F2813 — PRICE PROFIT

S66
POSEN G.S.,"RECENT TRENDS IN SOVIET ECONOMIC THOUGHT." USSR ECO/DEV PLAN CONTROL CENTRAL 20. PAGE 107 F2107 — ECO/TAC MARXISM INDUS

PROFIT

B67
MACAVOY P.W.,REGULATION OF TRANSPORT INNOVATION. ACT/RES ADJUD COST DEMAND...POLICY CHARTS 20. PAGE 83 F1621
DIST/IND CONTROL PRICE PROFIT

B67
NARVER J.C.,CONGLOMERATE MERGERS AND MARKET COMPETITION. USA+45 LAW STRUCT ADMIN LEAD RISK COST PROFIT WEALTH...POLICY CHARTS BIBLIOG. PAGE 96 F1892
DEMAND LG/CO MARKET MGT

L67
BERNHARD R.C.,"COMPETITION IN LAW AND ECONOMICS." LAW PLAN PRICE CONTROL PRODUC PROFIT...METH/CNCPT IDEA/COMP GEN/LAWS 20. PAGE 14 F0265
MARKET POLICY NAT/G CT/SYS

L67
MACHLUP F.,"THEORIES OF THE FIRM* MARGINALIST, BEHAVIORALIST, MANAGERIAL." ADMIN EXEC EFFICIENCY PROFIT METH/CNCPT. PAGE 83 F1633
METH/COMP GEN/LAWS INDUS

L67
ROBERTS E.F.,"THE CASE OF THE UNWARY HOME BUYER: THE HOUSING MERCHANT DID IT." USA+45 CLIENT DIST/IND MARKET LG/CO SML/CO PROB/SOLV LEGIT COST PROFIT. PAGE 112 F2207
ADJUD CONSTRUC OWN LAW

S67
BAGDKIAN B.H.,"NEWS AS A BYPRODUCT: WHAT HAPPENS WHEN JOURNALISM IS HITCHED TO GREAT, DIVERSIFIED CORPORATIONS?" USA+45 INDUS EDU/PROP PARTIC PROFIT ATTIT. PAGE 8 F0152
COM/IND PRESS CONTROL LG/CO

S67
BROWN M.B.,"THE TRADE UNION QUESTION." UK INDUS OP/RES PRICE PROFIT 20. PAGE 19 F0371
WORKER LABOR GP/REL LAW

S67
DEWHURST A.,"THE WAGE MOVEMENT IN CANADA." CANADA AGRI NAT/G PARTIC COST PRODUC PROFIT 20. PAGE 32 F0627
WORKER MARXIST INDUS LABOR

S67
KOTLER P.,"OPERATIONS RESEARCH IN MARKETING." USA+45 DIST/IND INDUS LG/CO CONSULT BUDGET TASK DEMAND EFFICIENCY PROFIT WEALTH DECISION. PAGE 73 F1429
ECOMETRIC OP/RES MARKET PLAN

S67
SCHELLING T.C.,"ECONOMICS AND CRIMINAL ENTERPRISE." LAW FORCES BARGAIN ECO/TAC CONTROL GAMBLE ROUTINE ADJUST DEMAND INCOME PROFIT CRIMLGY. PAGE 116 F2295
CRIME PROB/SOLV CONCPT

PROFUMO/J....JOHN PROFUMO, THE PROFUMO AFFAIR

PROG/TEAC....PROGRAMMED INSTRUCTION

B64
LANGHOFF P.,MODELS, MEASUREMENT AND MARKETING. ACT/RES COMPUTER OP/RES PLAN BUDGET...MGT PHIL/SCI METH/CNCPT STAT PROG/TEAC BIBLIOG. PAGE 75 F1478
DECISION SIMUL MARKET R+D

B66
BALDWIN D.A.,FOREIGN AID AND AMERICAN FOREIGN POLICY; A DOCUMENTARY ANALYSIS. USA+45 ECO/UNDEV ADMIN...ECOMETRIC STAT STYLE CHARTS PROG/TEAC GEN/LAWS ANTHOL. PAGE 9 F0162
FOR/AID DIPLOM IDEA/COMP

PROGRAMMED INSTRUCTION....SEE PROG/TEAC

PROGRAMMING....SEE COMPUTER

PROGRSV/M....PROGRESSIVE MOVEMENT (ALL NATIONS)

B63
KOLKO G.,THE TRIUMPH OF CONSERVATISM. USA-45 INDUS LG/CO NAT/G PWR 20 PRESIDENT CONGRESS MONOPOLY PROGRSV/M. PAGE 72 F1421
CONSERVE CAP/ISM FINAN MARKET

PROJ/TEST....PROJECTIVE TESTS

S60
KELLOGG C.E.,"TRANSFER OF BASIC SKILLS OF FOOD PRODUCTION." AFR FUT S/ASIA STRATA ECO/UNDEV LABOR VOL/ASSN RIGID/FLEX...OLD/LIB SOCIALIST NEW/IDEA STAT PROJ/TEST GEN/LAWS 20. PAGE 70 F1370
AGRI PLAN

PROJECTION....SEE DISPL

PROPAGANDA....SEE EDU/PROP

PROPERTY/TX....PROPERTY TAX

PROSTITUTN....SEE ALSO SEX + CRIME

PROTECTNSM....PROTECTIONISM

PROTEST....SEE COERCE

PROTESTANT....PROTESTANTS, PROTESTANTISM

B66
FORD P.,CARDINAL MORAN AND THE A. L. P. NAT/G POL/PAR SECT DELIB/GP LOBBY REV CHOOSE ORD/FREE MARXISM 19/20 AUSTRAL PROTESTANT LABOR/PAR. PAGE 42 F0825
CATHISM SOCISM LABOR SOCIETY

S67
RAMA C.M.,"PASADO Y PRESENTE DE LA RELIGION EN AMERICA LATINA." L/A+17C ELITES SOCIETY STRATA MARXISM...STAT WORSHIP PROTESTANT. PAGE 109 F2139
SECT CATHISM STRUCT NAT/COMP

PROUDHON P.J. F2125,F2126,F2127

PROUDHON/P....PIERRE JOSEPH PROUDHON

PROVS....STATE AND PROVINCES

N
NEW JERSEY STATE OF,SECOND REPORT TO GOVERNOR, SENATE, ASSEMBLY BY UNIFORM COMMERCIAL CODE STUDY COMMISSION. USA+45 INDUS LOC/G NAT/G PROF/ORG CONSULT ACT/RES LEGIT CT/SYS ATTIT NEW/JERSEY. PAGE 98 F1920
LAW FINAN CENTRAL PROVS

N
US SUPERINTENDENT OF DOCUMENTS,CENSUS PUBLICATIONS (PRICE LIST 70). AGRI CONSTRUC DIST/IND FINAN LOC/G NAT/G PROVS INT/TRADE APPORT INCOME. PAGE 140 F2751
BIBLIOG/A CENSUS STAT USA+45

N
US SUPERINTENDENT OF DOCUMENTS,INTERSTATE COMMERCE (PRICE LIST 59). USA+45 LAW LOC/G NAT/G LEGIS TARIFFS TAX ADMIN CONTROL HEALTH DECISION. PAGE 140 F2752
BIBLIOG/A DIST/IND GOV/REL PROVS

N19
HERZBERG D.G.,A BUDGET FOR NEW YORK STATE, 1956-1957 (PAMPHLET). USA+45 ADMIN GOV/REL 20 NEW/YORK HARRIMAN/A. PAGE 59 F1159
POL/PAR PROVS BUDGET LEGIS

N19
HOGARTY R.A.,NEW JERSEY FARMERS AND MIGRANT HOUSING RULES (PAMPHLET). USA+45 LAW ELITES FACE/GP LABOR PROF/ORG LOBBY PERS/REL RIGID/FLEX ROLE 20 NEW/JERSEY. PAGE 61 F1193
AGRI PROVS WORKER HEALTH

N19
KRESSBACH T.W.,HE MICHIGAN CITY MANAGER IN BUDGETARY PROCEEDINGS (PAMPHLET). USA+45 PROVS DELIB/GP GP/REL SUPEGO...POLICY MUNICH. PAGE 73 F1438
LOC/G BUDGET FINAN

N19
MUSHKIN S.J.,LOCAL SCHOOL EXPENDITURES: 1970 PROJECTIONS (PAMPHLET). FUT USA+45 CONSTRUC FINAN PROVS EDU/PROP COST...GEOG CENSUS PREDICT CHARTS SIMUL 20. PAGE 95 F1871
LOC/G SCHOOL BUDGET

N19
STUTZ R.L.,COLLECTIVE DEALING BY UNITS OF LOCAL GOVERNMENT IN CONNECTICUT (PAMPHLET). USA+45 LOC/G PROVS...STAT MUNICH 20 CONNECTICT. PAGE 127 F2508
VOL/ASSN LABOR WORKER

N19
YLVISAKER P.N.,THE NATURAL CEMENT ISSUE (PAMPHLET). USA+45 USA-45 CONSTRUC PROVS CAP/ISM ADMIN LOBBY PERS/REL OWN RIGID/FLEX ROLE 20 MINNESOTA. PAGE 150 F2948
POLICY NAT/G PLAN GOV/REL

B25
MATHEWS J.M.,AMERICAN STATE GOVERNMENT. USA-45 LOC/G CHIEF EX/STRUC LEGIS ADJUD CONTROL CT/SYS ROUTINE GOV/REL PWR 20 GOVERNOR. PAGE 87 F1703
PROVS ADMIN FEDERAL CONSTN

B25
WILLIAMS B.,THE SELBORNE MEMORANDUM. AFR FUT SOUTH/AFR UK NAT/G BUDGET DIPLOM REGION GOV/REL SOVEREIGN...POLICY CHARTS 20 UNIFICA SELBORNE/W. PAGE 147 F2888
COLONIAL PROVS

B30
GREEN F.M.,CONSTITUTIONAL DEVELOPMENT IN THE SOUTH ATLANTIC STATES, 1776-1860; A STUDY IN THE EVOLUTION OF DEMOCRACY. USA-45 ELITES SOCIETY STRATA ECO/DEV AGRI POL/PAR EX/STRUC LEGIS CT/SYS REGION...BIBLIOG 18/19 MARYLAND VIRGINIA GEORGIA NORTH/CAR SOUTH/CAR. PAGE 50 F0984
CONSTN PROVS PLURISM REPRESENT

S30
CRAWFORD F.G.,"THE EXECUTIVE BUDGET DECISION IN NEW YORK." LEGIS EXEC PWR NEW/YORK. PAGE 28 F0552
LEAD BUDGET PROVS PROB/SOLV

B51
PRINCETON U INDUSTRIAL REL SEC,COMPULSORY ARBITRATION OF UTILITY DISPUTES IN NEW JERSEY AND PENNSYLVANIA. USA+45 LEGIS WORKER ADJUD ORD/FREE ...POLICY MGT METH/COMP 20 NEW/JERSEY PENNSYLVAN. PAGE 108 F2118
BARGAIN PROVS INDUS LABOR

B55
US ADVISORY COMN INTERGOV REL,THE COMMISSION ON INTERGOVERNMENTAL RELATIONS; A REPORT TO THE PRESIDENT FOR TRANSMITTAL TO THE CONGRESS. USA+45 ECO/DEV AGRI COM/IND FINAN FORCES PLAN EDU/PROP HEALTH WEALTH...STAT MUNICH 20 CIV/DEFENS. PAGE 133 F2630
GOV/REL NAT/G LOC/G PROVS

B56
BURKHEAD J.,GOVERNMENT BUDGETING. ECO/DEV PROB/SOLV ECO/TAC ADMIN ROUTINE GOV/REL EFFICIENCY...DECISION MGT. PAGE 20 F0388
BUDGET NAT/G PROVS EX/STRUC

B57
BOUSTEDT O.,REGIONALE STRUKTUR- UND WIRTSCHAFTSFORSCHUNG. WOR+45 WOR-45 PROVS...STAT MUNICH. PAGE 17 F0325
GEOG CONCPT NAT/COMP

B58
RUBIN B.,PUBLIC RELATIONS AND THE STATE, A CASE STUDY OF NEW YORK STATE ADMINISTRATION, 1943-54. USA+45 USA-45 COM/IND EDU/PROP GOV/REL...CHARTS 20 NEW/YORK DEWEY/THOM. PAGE 114 F2255
INGP/REL PRESS PROVS GP/REL

S58
LANE F.C.,"ECONOMIC CONSEQUENCES OF ORGANIZED VIOLENCE." FUT WOR+45 WOR-45 ECO/DEV DIST/IND SERV/IND NAT/G PROVS EX/STRUC CHOOSE ORD/FREE PWR ...TIME/SEQ GEN/LAWS MUNICH 20. PAGE 75 F1472
WEALTH COERCE

B59
ROCHE J.,LA COLONISATION ALLEMANDE ET LE RIO GRANDE DO SUL. BRAZIL L/A+17C NAT/G PROVS INGP/REL RACE/REL DISCRIM HABITAT...GEOG SOC/INTEG 19/20 MIGRATION. PAGE 113 F2228
ECO/UNDEV GP/REL ATTIT

B59
U OF MICHIGAN LAW SCHOOL,ATOMS AND THE LAW. USA+45 PROVS WORKER PROB/SOLV DIPLOM ADMIN GOV/REL ANTHOL. PAGE 132 F2596
NUC/PWR NAT/G CONTROL LAW

S59
CLONER A.,"THE CALIFORNIA LEGISLATOR AND THE PROBLEM OF COMPENSATION." USA+45 WORKER REPRESENT. PAGE 25 F0492
INCOME PROVS LEGIS SUPEGO

B60
FERNANDES F.,MUDANCAS SOCIAIS NO BRASIL. BRAZIL L/A+17C SOCIETY AGRI PROVS LEAD GP/REL RACE/REL ORD/FREE...SOC SOC/INTEG 20 SAO/PAULO. PAGE 40 F0786
ECO/UNDEV STRATA INDUS

B60
FRYE R.J.,GOVERNMENT AND LABOR: THE ALABAMA PROGRAM. USA+45 INDUS R+D LABOR WORKER BUDGET EFFICIENCY AGE/Y HEALTH...CHARTS 20 ALABAMA. PAGE 45 F0870
ADMIN LEGIS LOC/G PROVS

B60
GILMORE D.R.,DEVELOPING THE "LITTLE" ECONOMIES. USA+45 FINAN LG/CO PROF/ORG VOL/ASSN CREATE ADMIN. PAGE 47 F0924
ECO/TAC LOC/G PROVS PLAN

B60
SANTHANAM K.,UNION-STATE RELATIONS IN INDIA. INDIA FINAN PROVS PLAN ECO/TAC...LING 20. PAGE 116 F2280
FEDERAL GOV/REL CONSTN POLICY

B61
BEASLEY K.E.,STATE SUPERVISION OF MUNICIPAL DEBT IN KANSAS - A CASE STUDY. USA+45 USA-45 FINAN PROVS BUDGET TAX ADJUD ADMIN CONTROL SUPEGO MUNICH. PAGE 12 F0224
LOC/G LEGIS JURID

B61
NEW JERSEY LEGISLATURE-SENATE,PUBLIC HEARINGS BEFORE COMMITTEE ON REVISION AND AMENDMENT OF LAWS ON SENATE BILL NO. 8. USA+45 FINAN PROVS WORKER ACT/RES PLAN BUDGET TAX CRIME...IDEA/COMP MUNICH 20 NEW/JERSEY URBAN/RNWL. PAGE 98 F1919
LEGIS INDUS PROB/SOLV

B61
STARNER F.L.,GENERAL OBLIGATION BOND FINANCING BY LOCAL GOVERNMENTS: A SURVEY OF STATE CONTROLS. CANADA UK USA+45 CONSTN PROVS...POLICY JURID METH/COMP 20 EUROPE CALIFORNIA. PAGE 125 F2471
FINAN LOC/G GOV/REL ADJUD

L61
GERWIG R.,"PUBLIC AUTHORITIES IN THE UNITED STATES." LAW CONSTN PROVS TAX ADMIN FEDERAL MUNICH. PAGE 47 F0920
LOC/G GOV/REL PWR

N61
US ADVISORY COMM INTERGOV REL,STATE AND LOCAL TAXATION ON PRIVATELY OWNED PROPERTY LOCATED ON FEDERAL AREAS: PROPOSED AMENDMENT OF BUCK ACT (PAMPHLET). USA+45 ACT/RES PLAN CONTROL GOV/REL INGP/REL OWN...POLICY JURID CHARTS GP/COMP 20. PAGE 133 F2629
PROVS LOC/G NAT/G TAX

N61
US ADVISORY COMN INTERGOV REL,STATE CONSTITUTIONAL AND STATUTORY RESTRICTIONS ON LOCAL GOVERNMENT DEBT (PAMPHLET). LAW CONSTN CHOOSE PWR...DECISION MUNICH. PAGE 133 F2631
TAX PROVS GOV/REL

B62
CARPER E.T.,ILLINOIS GOES TO CONGRESS FOR ARMY LAND. USA+45 LAW EXTR/IND PROVS REGION CIVMIL/REL GOV/REL FEDERAL ATTIT 20 ILLINOIS SENATE CONGRESS DIRKSEN/E DOUGLAS/P. PAGE 22 F0420
ADMIN LOBBY GEOG LEGIS

B62
LITTLEFIELD N.,METROPOLITAN AREA PROBLEMS AND MUNICIPAL HOME RULE. USA+45 PROVS ADMIN CONTROL GP/REL PWR. PAGE 81 F1586
LOC/G SOVEREIGN JURID LEGIS

B62
MULLER E.,DIE HEIMATVERTRIEBENEN IN BADEN-WURTTEMBERG. GERMANY/W AGRI INDUS LABOR PROVS SOC/INTEG 20 MIGRATION. PAGE 95 F1858
GP/REL INGP/REL

B62
SIRUGO F.,L'ECONOMIA DEGLI STAT' ITALIANI PRIMA DELL' UNIFICAZIONE (10 VOLS.). ITALY...TIME/SEQ 18/19. PAGE 122 F2417
BIBLIOG PROVS NAT/G

B62
US ADVISORY COMN INTERGOV REL,STATE CONSTITUTIONAL AND STATUTORY RESTRICTIONS ON LOCAL TAXING POWERS. USA+45 USA-45 LAW CONSTN ACT/RES CONTROL WEALTH ...JURID CHARTS 20. PAGE 133 F2632
LOC/G PROVS GOV/REL TAX

B63
BURRUS B.R.,ADMINSTRATIVE LAW AND LOCAL GOVERNMENT. USA+45 PROVS LEGIS LICENSE ADJUD ORD/FREE 20. PAGE 20 F0392
EX/STRUC LOC/G JURID CONSTN

B63
DUE J.F.,STATE SALES TAX ADMINISTRATION. OP/RES BUDGET PAY ADMIN EXEC ROUTINE COST EFFICIENCY PROFIT...CHARTS METH/COMP 20. PAGE 34 F0671
PROVS TAX STAT GOV/COMP

B63
MANN D.E.,THE POLITICS OF WATER IN ARIZONA. AGRI EXTR/IND PROVS ACT/RES CREATE PLAN GOV/REL COST HABITAT...MGT CHARTS 20 ARIZONA WATER. PAGE 84 F1655
POLICY ECO/TAC TEC/DEV

B63
MILLER W.,REVENUE-COST RATIOS OF RURAL TOWNSHIPS WITH CHANGING LAND USES. USA+45 INDUS SERV/IND PROVS GP/REL HABITAT...CHARTS GP/COMP MUNICH 20 NEW/JERSEY. PAGE 91 F1792
TAX COST AGRI

B63
RAFUSE R.W. JR.,STATE AND LOCAL FISCAL BEHAVIOR OVER THE POSTWAR CYCLES (DISSERTATION). USA+45 TAX PRICE ATTIT...POLICY TIME/SEQ TREND CHARTS BIBLIOG 20. PAGE 109 F2135
BUDGET LOC/G ECO/TAC PROVS

S63
ANDREWS R.B.,"ECONOMIC PLANNING FOR SMALL AREAS: THE PLANNING PROCESS." INDUS PROC/MFG PROVS PROB/SOLV TAX EQUILIB...METH/COMP HYPO/EXP METH MUNICH 20. PAGE 5 F0103
ECO/TAC PLAN LOC/G

B64
IMAZ J.L.,LOS QUE MANDAN. INDUS LABOR NAT/G POL/PAR PROVS SECT CHIEF TOP/EX CONTROL 20 ARGEN. PAGE 64 F1261
LEAD FORCES ELITES ATTIT

B64
MANN B.,STATE CONSTITUTIONAL RESTRICTIONS ON LOCAL BORROWING AND PROPERTY TAXING POWERS. USA+45 CONSTN PROVS CT/SYS GOV/REL PWR...DECISION JURID CHARTS 20. PAGE 84 F1654
LOC/G TAX FINAN LAW

B64
MEISEL J.,PAPERS ON THE 1962 ELECTION. CANADA PROVS SECT GP/REL CONSEN EFFICIENCY...MAJORIT 20. PAGE 89 F1751
POL/PAR RECORD CHOOSE STRATA

B64
MITAU G.T.,INSOLUBLE PROBLEMS: CASE PROBLEMS ON THE FUNCTIONS OF STATE AND LOCAL GOVERNMENT. USA+45 AIR FINAN LABOR POL/PAR PROB/SOLV TAX RECEIVE CONTROL GP/REL 20 CASEBOOK ZONING. PAGE 92 F1807
ADJUD LOC/G PROVS

B64
TAEUBER I.B.,POPULATION TRENDS IN THE UNITED STATES: 1900 TO 1960. USA+45 USA-45 PROVS INCOME AGE...SOC TIME/SEQ TREND CHARTS MUNICH TIME 20 NEGRO. PAGE 128 F2522
CENSUS GEOG STRATA STRUCT

S64
DOE J.F.,"TROPICAL AFRICAN CONTRIBUTIONS TO FEDERAL FINANCE." AFR NAT/G PROVS CENTRAL RIGID/FLEX PWR WEALTH...STAT VAL/FREE 20 CMN/WLTH. PAGE 33 F0650
FINAN ECO/TAC

B65
COLBERG M.R.,HUMAN CAPITAL IN SOUTHERN DEVELOPMENT. USA+45 AGRI ACADEM LABOR SCHOOL WORKER CAP/ISM DISCRIM. PAGE 26 F0498
PROVS RACE/REL GP/REL

B65
DANIELSON M.N.,FEDERAL-METROPOLITAN POLITICS AND THE COMMUTER CRISIS. PROVS LEGIS EXEC LEAD PWR ...DECISION MUNICH. PAGE 30 F0580
FEDERAL GOV/REL DIST/IND

B65
GOODSELL C.T.,ADMINISTRATION OF A REVOLUTION. PUERT/RICO ECO/UNDEV FINAN POL/PAR PROVS LEGIS PLAN BUDGET RECEIVE ADMIN COLONIAL LEAD MUNICH 20 ROOSEVLT/F. PAGE 49 F0951
EXEC SOC

B65
MORTON H.C.,BROOKINGS PAPERS ON PUBLIC POLICY. USA+45 WOR+45 INDUS ACADEM INT/ORG LOC/G PROVS EDU/PROP MUNICH. PAGE 94 F1840
FINAN ECO/DEV TOP/EX

NAT/G

B65
MUSHKIN S.J.,PROPERTY TAXES: THE 1970 OUTLOOK (PAMPHLET). FUT USA+45 ECO/DEV MARKET PROVS PLAN ...PROBABIL STAT CENSUS PREDICT CHARTS METH 20. PAGE 95 F1872
TAX OWN FINAN LOC/G

B65
WRIGHT L.B.,THE DREAM OF PROSPERITY IN COLONIAL AMERICA. USA-45 ECO/UNDEV AGRI EXTR/IND PARLIAMENT 17/18. PAGE 149 F2934
PROVS WEALTH MOD/EUR

B66
DUNCOMBE H.S.,COUNTY GOVERNMENT IN AMERICA. USA+45 FINAN ADMIN ROUTINE GOV/REL...GOV/COMP MUNICH 20. PAGE 35 F0678
LOC/G PROVS CT/SYS TOP/EX

B66
GREENE L.E.,GOVERNMENT IN TENNESSEE (2ND ED.). USA+45 DIST/IND INDUS POL/PAR EX/STRUC LEGIS PLAN BUDGET GIVE CT/SYS...MGT T 20 TENNESSEE. PAGE 51 F0989
PROVS LOC/G CONSTN ADMIN

B66
HOWE R.W.,BLACK AFRICA: FROM PRE-HISTORY TO THE EVE OF THE COLONIAL ERA. ECO/UNDEV KIN PROVS SECT INT/TRADE EDU/PROP COLONIAL...BIBLIOG WORSHIP. PAGE 62 F1226
AFR CULTURE SOC

B66
SASTRI K.V.S.,FEDERAL-STATE FISCAL RELATIONS IN INDIA: A STUDY OF THE FINANCE COMMISSION AND TECHNIQUES OF FINANCIAL ADJUSTMENT. INDIA PROVS DELIB/GP GOV/REL FEDERAL...MATH CHARTS 20. PAGE 116 F2283
TAX BUDGET FINAN NAT/G

N66
US ADVISORY COMN INTERGOV REL,CATALOGS AND OTHER INFORMATION SOURCES ON FEDERAL AND STATE AID PROGRAMS: A SECTED BIBLIOGRAPHY (PAPER). USA+45 LAW LOC/G NAT/G PROVS VOL/ASSN TEC/DEV ADMIN HEALTH ...WELF/ST SOC/WK MUNICH. PAGE 134 F2635
BIBLIOG/A GOV/REL FINAN ECO/DEV

B67
BLAIR G.S.,LEGISLATIVE BODIES IN CALIFORNIA. USA+45 LAW POL/PAR LOBBY APPORT CHOOSE REPRESENT GP/REL ...T CALIFORNIA. PAGE 15 F0293
LEGIS PROVS LOC/G ADJUD

B67
BREAK G.F.,INTERGOVERNMENTAL FISCAL RELATIONS IN THE UNITED STATES. USA+45 USA-45 DELIB/GP PLAN BUDGET TAX GOV/REL CENTRAL...TREND CHARTS MUNICH. PAGE 18 F0345
LOC/G NAT/G PROVS FINAN

B67
BUREAU NATIONAL AFFAIRS,LABOR RELATIONS REFERENCE MANUAL VOL. 63. USA+45 CONSTN ECO/DEV PROVS WORKER DEBATE INGP/REL...DECISION 20. PAGE 20 F0385
LABOR ADJUD CT/SYS NAT/G

B67
CAMPBELL A.K.,METROPOLITAN AMERICA* FISCAL PATTERNS AND GOVERNMENTAL SYSTEMS. PROVS PLAN COST...POLICY DECISION GOV/COMP METH/COMP BIBLIOG. PAGE 21 F0405
USA+45 NAT/G LOC/G BUDGET

B67
DE TORRES J.,FINANCING LOCAL GOVERNMENT. USA+45 USA-45 NAT/G PROVS GIVE ADJUST PWR...TIME/SEQ CHARTS MUNICH 20. PAGE 31 F0606
LOC/G BUDGET TAX TREND

B67
LEIBY J.,CHARITY AND CORRECTION IN JERSEY; A HISTORY OF STATE WELFARE INSTITUTIONS. DELIB/GP EX/STRUC PROB/SOLV INSPECT LEAD ADJUST HEALTH ...POLICY PSY NEW/JERSEY. PAGE 77 F1514
PROVS PUB/INST ADMIN

B67
LYTLE C.M.,THE WARREN COURT AND ITS CRITICS. USA+45 NAT/G PROVS FORCES LOBBY RACE/REL DISCRIM SOVEREIGN 20 SUPREME/CT WARRN/EARL. PAGE 83 F1618
CT/SYS ADJUD PROB/SOLV ATTIT

B67
PRINCE C.E.,NEW JERSEY'S JEFFERSONIAN REPUBLICANS; THE GENESIS OF AN EARLY PARTY MACHINE (1789-1817). USA-45 LOC/G EDU/PROP PRESS CONTROL CHOOSE...CHARTS 18/19 NEW/JERSEY REPUBLICAN. PAGE 108 F2117
POL/PAR CONSTN ADMIN PROVS

L67
COSTANZA J.F.,"WHOLESOME NEUTRALITY: LAW AND EDUCATION." USA+45 GIVE EDU/PROP ADJUD CONTROL GP/REL...DECISION JURID. PAGE 28 F0540
SECT PROVS ACADEM

L67
JOHNSTON J.D. JR.,"CONSTITUTION OF SUBDIVISION CONTROL EXACTIONS: THE QUEST FOR A RATIONALE." USA+45 PROVS PUB/INST ADJUD CT/SYS GP/REL MUNICH. PAGE 68 F1334
PLAN CONTROL LOC/G FORCES

L67
MCALLISTER J.T. JR.,"THE POSSIBILITIES FOR DIPLOMACY IN SOUTHEAST ASIA." LAOS VIETNAM INT/ORG NAT/G PROVS BAL/PWR DOMIN AGREE COLONIAL WAR PWR 17/20 TREATY. PAGE 88 F1716
DIPLOM S/ASIA

S67
"PROTEST AGAINST SOVIET INDUSTRIALIZATION ILLS IN LITHUANIA* A MEMORANDUM." USSR LITHUANIA NAT/G PROVS COST GEOG. PAGE 1 F0024
INDUS COLONIAL NAT/LISM PLAN

S67
"IMPORT-EXPORT CLAUSE: A BLANKET PROHIBITION MISAPPLIED." USA+45 INT/TRADE ADJUD INCOME PWR 20. PAGE 2 F0029
CONSTN TAX PROVS LAW

S67
EDWARDS N.,"EDUCATION IN THE FEDERAL-STATE STRUCTURE OF GOVERNMENT." USA+45 SECT CONTROL GOV/REL RACE/REL DISCRIM FEDERAL ROLE PWR SOVEREIGN. PAGE 36 F0705
EDU/PROP NAT/G PROVS POLICY

S67
LANDES W.M.,"THE EFFECT OF STATE FAIR EMPLOYMENT LAWS ON THE ECONOMIC POSITION OF NONWHITES." USA+45 PROVS SECT LEGIS ADMIN GP/REL RACE/REL...JURID CONCPT CHARTS HYPO/EXP NEGRO. PAGE 75 F1470
DISCRIM LAW WORKER

S67
LEWIS W.A.,"THE STATUTORY LANGUAGE OF LABOR DISQUALIFICATION IN STATE EMPLOYMENT SECURITY LAWS." LABOR WORKER WORK 20. PAGE 79 F1553
METH/COMP LEGIS SOC PROVS

S67
MERIKOSKI V.,"BASIC PROBLEMS OF UNIVERSITY ADMINISTRATION." PROVS SECT CONTROL...CLASSIF 20. PAGE 90 F1760
ACADEM ADMIN SOVEREIGN METH/COMP

B96
SCHMOLLER G.,THE MERCANTILE SYSTEM AND ITS HISTORICAL SIGNIFICANCE: ILLUSTRATED CHIEFLY FROM PRUSSIAN HISTORY (TRANS.). PRUSSIA CULTURE INDUS KIN NAT/G PROVS OP/RES ECO/TAC INT/TRADE SUPEGO PWR WEALTH MUNICH 19 MERCANTLST. PAGE 117 F2302
GEN/METH INGP/REL CONCPT

PRUITT/DG....DEAN G. PRUITT

PRUSSIA....PRUSSIA

B27
BELLOC H.,THE SERVILE STATE (1912) (3RD ED.). PRUSSIA UK CULTURE STRATA INDUS NAT/G ECO/TAC CONTROL LEAD SUFF DISCRIM EQUILIB ORD/FREE WEALTH 20. PAGE 12 F0237
WORKER CAP/ISM DOMIN CATH

B95
SELIGMAN E.R.A.,ESSAYS IN TAXATION. NEW/ZEALND PRUSSIA UK USA-45 MARKET LOC/G CREATE PRICE CONTROL INCOME OWN WEALTH...GOV/COMP METH/COMP 19. PAGE 119 F2349
TAX TARIFFS INDUS NAT/G

B96
SCHMOLLER G.,THE MERCANTILE SYSTEM AND ITS HISTORICAL SIGNIFICANCE: ILLUSTRATED CHIEFLY FROM PRUSSIAN HISTORY (TRANS.). PRUSSIA CULTURE INDUS KIN NAT/G PROVS OP/RES ECO/TAC INT/TRADE SUPEGO PWR WEALTH MUNICH 19 MERCANTLST. PAGE 117 F2302
GEN/METH INGP/REL CONCPT

PRYBYLA J. F2128

PRYOR F.L. F2129,F2130

PSY....PSYCHOLOGY

N
UNESCO,SOUTH ASIA SOCIAL SCIENCES ABSTRACTS. BURMA CEYLON INDIA S/ASIA PRESS...PSY 20. PAGE 132 F2608
BIBLIOG/A SOC

B11
SCOTT W.D.,INFLUENCING MEN IN BUSINESS: THE PSYCHOLOGY OF ARGUMENT AND SUGGESTION. WOR-45 WORKER EDU/PROP DEMAND ATTIT PERSON 20. PAGE 118 F2336
PSY MARKET SML/CO TOP/EX

B22
VON ENGELIN O.D.,INHERITING THE EARTH, THE GEOGRAPHICAL FACTOR IN NATIONAL DEVELOPMENT. WOR-45 CULTURE DIPLOM BIO/SOC HABITAT PERSON...PSY SOC CONCPT IDEA/COMP. PAGE 142 F2791
INGP/REL GEOG SOCIETY ROLE

B23
HOBSON J.A.,INCENTIVES IN THE NEW INDUSTRIAL ORDER. USA-45 NAT/G PAY COST EFFICIENCY PRODUC WEALTH ...MAJORIT PSY SOC/WK 20. PAGE 60 F1186
INDUS LABOR INCOME OPTIMAL

B41
DAUGHERTY C.R.,LABOR PROBLEMS IN AMERICAN INDUSTRY (5TH ED.). USA-45 SOCIETY OP/RES ECO/TAC...MGT PSY T 20. PAGE 30 F0581
LABOR INDUS GP/REL PROB/SOLV

B44
KAUFMANN F.,METHODOLOGY OF THE SOCIAL SCIENCES. PERSON...RELATIV PSY CONCPT LING METH 20. PAGE 69 F1363
SOC PHIL/SCI GEN/LAWS METH/CNCPT

B47
BALDWIN H.W.,THE PRICE OF POWER. USA+45 FORCES PLAN NUC/PWR ADJUST COST ORD/FREE...POLICY PSY BIBLIOG 20. PAGE 9 F0165
PROB/SOLV PWR POPULISM PRICE

B47
LEVER E.A.,ADVERTISING AND ECONOMIC THEORY. FINAN ECO/TAC DEMAND EFFICIENCY ATTIT...MGT PSY SAMP/SIZ CHARTS 20. PAGE 79 F1539
EDU/PROP MARKET COM/IND

ECO/DEV
B52

DE JOUVENEL B.,THE ETHICS OF REDISTRIBUTION. UK ELITES MARKET WORKER GIVE PAY INCOME PERSON ...POLICY PSY GEN/LAWS 20. PAGE 31 F0602 WEALTH TAX SOCISM TRADIT
B54

POTTER D.M.,PEOPLE OF PLENTY: ECONOMIC ABUNDANCE AND THE AMERICAN CHARACTER. USA+45 USA-45 ECO/DEV ATTIT PERSON...PSY SOC CONCPT TREND GEN/METH TOT/POP 20. PAGE 107 F2108 CULTURE WEALTH
B56

HICKMAN C.A.,INDIVIDUALS, GROUPS, AND ECONOMIC BEHAVIOR. WORKER PAY CONTROL EXEC GP/REL INGP/REL PERSON ROLE...PSY SOC PERS/COMP METH 20. PAGE 59 F1163 MGT ADMIN ECO/TAC PLAN
B56

MYRDAL G.,AN INTERNATIONAL ECONOMY. EUR+WWI USA+45 WOR+45 WOR-45 NAT/G DIPLOM ECO/TAC BAL/PAY...PSY CONCPT OEEC TOT/POP 20. PAGE 96 F1879 VOL/ASSN AFR
B56

US DEPARTMENT OF STATE,ECONOMIC PROBLEMS OF UNDERDEVELOPED AREAS (PAMPHLET). AFR ASIA ISLAM L/A+17C AGRI FINAN INDUS INT/ORG LABOR INT/TRADE ...PSY SOC 20. PAGE 136 F2673 BIBLIOG ECO/UNDEV TEC/DEV R+D
B59

CONTY J.M.,PSYCHOLOGIE DE LA DECISION....PSY GAME 20. PAGE 27 F0528 DECISION PROB/SOLV OP/RES METH/COMP
B59

MARTIN K.,WAR, HISTORY, AND HUMAN NATURE. FRANCE GERMANY INDIA UK UNIV POL/PAR COLONIAL DETER REV MARXISM PACIFISM...PSY CONCPT PREDICT LENIN/VI GANDHI/M. PAGE 86 F1683 PERSON WAR ATTIT IDEA/COMP
B59

SERAPHIM H.J.,PROBLEME DER WILLENSBILDUNG UND DER WIRTSCHAFTSPOLITISCHEN FUEHRUNG. WOR+45 MARKET ACT/RES OP/RES PLAN EDU/PROP INGP/REL HABITAT PLURISM...MGT PERS/COMP METH 20. PAGE 119 F2357 POLICY DECISION PSY
L59

SIMON H.A.,"THEORIES OF DECISION-MAKING IN ECONOMICS AND BEHAVIORAL SCIENCE" (BMR)" MARKET BARGAIN UTIL DRIVE...DECISION MGT PROBABIL HYPO/EXP SIMUL 20 BEHAVIORSM. PAGE 122 F2409 PSY GEN/LAWS PROB/SOLV
B60

MYRDAL G.,BEYOND THE WELFARE STATE: ECONOMIC PLANNING AND ITS IMPLICATIONS. EUR+WWI FUT USA+45 USSR ECO/DEV ECO/UNDEV TEC/DEV SKILL WEALTH...PSY TREND FOR/TRADE 20. PAGE 96 F1881 PLAN ECO/TAC CAP/ISM
B60

SIEGEL S.,BARGAINING AND GROUP DECISION-MAKING: EXPERIMENTS IN BILATERAL MONOPOLY. EFFICIENCY...PSY CHARTS. PAGE 122 F2397 DECISION PERS/REL PROB/SOLV BARGAIN
S60

HERZ J.H.,"EAST GERMANY: PROGRESS AND PROSPECTS." COM AGRI FINAN INDUS LOC/G NAT/G FORCES PLAN TEC/DEV DOMIN ADMIN COERCE DRIVE PERCEPT RIGID/FLEX MORAL ORD/FREE PWR...MARXIST PSY SOC RECORD STERTYP WORK. PAGE 59 F1158 POL/PAR STRUCT GERMANY
B61

FRIEDMANN G.,THE ANATOMY OF WORK. USA+45 SOCIETY CONTROL ROUTINE DRIVE SKILL...PSY SOC STAT OBS METH/COMP PERS/COMP 20. PAGE 44 F0862 AUTOMAT WORKER INDUS PERSON
S61

CYERT R.M.,"TWO EXPERIMENTS ON BIAS AND CONFLICT IN ORGANIZATIONAL ESTIMATION." WORKER PROB/SOLV EFFICIENCY...MGT PSY STAT CHARTS. PAGE 29 F0568 LAB/EXP ROUTINE ADMIN DECISION
B62

BROOKINGS INSTITUTION,DEVELOPMENT OF THE EMERGING COUNTRIES; AN AGENDA FOR RESEARCH. WOR+45 AGRI TEC/DEV FOR/AID EDU/PROP ADJUST HABITAT KNOWL...PSY SOC ANTHOL 20 THIRD/WRLD. PAGE 19 F0362 ECO/UNDEV R+D SOCIETY PROB/SOLV
B62

COLLIER A.T.,MANAGEMENT, MEN, AND VALUES. INDUS FACE/GP EX/STRUC PLAN PROB/SOLV DEBATE SENIOR ADMIN PROFIT PERSON...PSY SOC 20. PAGE 26 F0505 MGT ATTIT PERS/REL DECISION
B62

DOUGLAS A.,INDUSTRIAL PEACEMAKING. CONSULT ACT/RES ...MGT PSY METH 20. PAGE 34 F0656 BARGAIN INDUS LABOR GP/REL
B62

SHERIF M.,INTERGROUP RELATIONS AND LEADERSHIP: APPROACHES AND RESEARCH IN INDUSTRIAL, ETHNIC, CULTURAL AND POLITICAL AREAS. CULTURE R+D LABOR DIPLOM GP/REL RACE/REL PERCEPT...PSY CONCPT. PAGE 121 F2377 LEAD REPRESENT PWR INGP/REL
S62

READ W.H.,"UPWARD COMMUNICATION IN INDUSTRIAL HIERARCHIES." LG/CO TOP/EX PROB/SOLV DOMIN EXEC PERS/REL ATTIT DRIVE PERCEPT...CORREL STAT CHARTS 20. PAGE 110 F2159 ADMIN INGP/REL PSY MGT
B63

CHAMPION J.M.,CRITICAL INCIDENTS IN MANAGEMENT. MARKET LG/CO SML/CO OP/RES ADMIN CONTROL LEAD GP/REL PERS/REL COST ATTIT SUPEGO ALL/VALS...PSY PERS/TEST BIBLIOG. PAGE 23 F0445 MGT DECISION EX/STRUC INDUS
B63

SMELSER N.J.,THE SOCIOLOGY OF ECONOMIC LIFE. UNIV CULTURE PERCEPT...PSY T 18/20. PAGE 123 F2425 SOC METH/COMP IDEA/COMP
B63

VON MISES L.,HUMAN ACTION: A TREATISE ON ECONOMICS (2ND ED.). SOCIETY MARKET TAX PAY PRICE DEMAND EQUILIB RATIONAL...PSY 20. PAGE 142 F2794 PLAN DRIVE ATTIT
L63

NASH M.,"PSYCHO-CULTURAL FACTORS IN ASIAN ECONOMIC GROWTH." ASIA ISLAM S/ASIA CULTURE ECO/UNDEV DELIB/GP EDU/PROP COERCE ATTIT PERSON HEALTH KNOWL ORD/FREE...PSY SOC STAT TREND ANTHOL VAL/FREE 20. PAGE 96 F1893 SOCIETY ECO/TAC
B64

NOVACK D.E.,DEVELOPMENT AND SOCIETY; THE DYNAMICS OF ECONOMIC CHANGE. WOR+45 STRATA STRUCT ECO/TAC CONTROL CROWD REV GP/REL ADJUST PRODUC WEALTH PSY. PAGE 99 F1940 SOCIETY CULTURE SOC ECO/UNDEV
B64

ZOLLSCHAN G.K.,EXPLORATIONS IN SOCIAL CHANGE. SOCIETY STRATA STRUCT ECO/UNDEV EX/STRUC...PSY ANTHOL 20. PAGE 151 F2968 ORD/FREE SIMUL CONCPT CULTURE
B65

GRAMPP W.D.,ECONOMIC LIBERALISM; THE CLASSICAL VIEW (VOL. II). MOD/EUR SOCIETY MARKET INT/TRADE NAT/LISM WEALTH LAISSEZ...POLICY PSY CONCPT BIBLIOG 19 SMITH/ADAM HUME/D MILL/JS. PAGE 50 F0975 ECO/DEV CAP/ISM IDEA/COMP ECO/TAC
L65

HAMMOND A.,"COMPREHENSIVE VERSUS INCREMENTAL BUDGETING IN THE DEPARTMENT OF AGRICULTURE" USA+45 GP/REL ATTIT...PSY INT 20 DEPT/AGRI. PAGE 54 F1057 TOP/EX EX/STRUC AGRI BUDGET
S65

KUNKEL J.H.,"VALUES AND BEHAVIOR IN ECONOMIC DEVELOPMENT." INDIA PERU CULTURE STRUCT CREATE PERS/REL ATTIT PERSON...CHARTS HYPO/EXP ARGEN. PAGE 74 F1449 SIMUL ECO/UNDEV PSY STERTYP
B66

BAKLANOFF E.N.,NEW PERSPECTIVES ON BRAZIL. BRAZIL SOCIETY INDUS DOMIN LEAD REV CIVMIL/REL...GEOG PSY LING ANTHOL 20. PAGE 8 F0156 ECO/UNDEV TEC/DEV DIPLOM ORD/FREE
B66

SOCIAL SCIENCE RESEARCH COUN,BIBLIOGRAPHY OF RESEARCH IN THE SOCIAL SCIENCES IN AUSTRALIA 1957-1960. LAW R+D DIPLOM 20 AUSTRAL. PAGE 124 F2437 BIBLIOG SOC PSY
B67

FILENE P.G.,AMERICANS AND THE SOVIET EXPERIMENT, 1917-1933. USA-45 USSR INTELL NAT/G CAP/ISM DIPLOM EDU/PROP PRESS REV SOCISM...PSY 20. PAGE 41 F0793 ATTIT RIGID/FLEX MARXISM SOCIETY
B67

LEIBY J.,CHARITY AND CORRECTION IN JERSEY; A HISTORY OF STATE WELFARE INSTITUTIONS. DELIB/GP EX/STRUC PROB/SOLV INSPECT LEAD ADJUST HEALTH ...POLICY PSY NEW/JERSEY. PAGE 77 F1514 PROVS PUB/INST ADMIN
B67

WOOTON G.,WORKERS, UNIONS, AND THE STATE. INDUS PROB/SOLV GP/REL DRIVE SUPEGO RESPECT...PSY SOC. PAGE 148 F2925 PARTIC WORKER NAT/G LABOR
S67

GRUN C.,"DEUX ETUDES ALLEMANDES SUR LES PREJUGES NATIONAUX ET LES MOYENS DE LES COMBATTRE." FRANCE GERMANY DIST/IND PROB/SOLV GP/REL AGE/Y RIGID/FLEX ...PSY STAT INT SAMP. PAGE 52 F1010 ATTIT REGION DISCRIM STERTYP
S67

LEVIN T.,"PSYCHOANALYSIS AND SOCIAL CHANGE." SOCIETY ANOMIE DRIVE PWR 20. PAGE 79 F1541 PSY PHIL/SCI ADJUST WEALTH
N67

US HOUSE COMM GOVT OPERATIONS,FEDERALLY FINANCED SOCIAL RESEARCH, EXPENDITURES, STATUS, AND OBJECTIVES (PAMPHLET). WOR+45 CREATE LEAD GP/REL ATTIT...GEOG PSY SOC. PAGE 137 F2700 ACT/RES NAT/G GIVE BUDGET

PSY/WAR....PSYCHOLOGICAL WARFARE; SEE ALSO PSY + EDU/PROP + WAR

PSYCHIATRY....SEE PSY

PSYCHOANALYSIS....SEE BIOG, PSY

PSYCHO-DRAMA....SEE SELF/OBS

PSYCHOLOGICAL WARFARE....SEE PSY+EDU/PROP+WAR

PSYCHOLOGY....SEE PSY

PUB/INST....MENTAL, CORRECTIONAL, AND OTHER HABITATIONAL INSTITUTIONS

B37
UNION OF SOUTH AFRICA,REPORT CONCERNING ADMINISTRATION OF SOUTH WEST AFRICA (6 VOLS.). SOUTH/AFR INDUS PUB/INST FORCES LEGIS BUDGET DIPLOM EDU/PROP ADJUD CT/SYS...GEOG CHARTS 20 AFRICA/SW LEAGUE/NAT. PAGE 132 F2610 — NAT/G ADMIN COLONIAL CONSTN

B38
LANGE O.,ON THE ECONOMIC THEORY OF SOCIALISM. UNIV ECO/DEV FINAN INDUS INT/ORG PUB/INST ROUTINE ATTIT ALL/VALS...SOC CONCPT STAT TREND 20. PAGE 75 F1475 — MARKET ECO/TAC INT/TRADE SOCISM

B52
AYRES C.E.,THE INDUSTRIAL ECONOMY. USA+45 FINAN MARKET NAT/G PUB/INST PLAN ECO/TAC TAX DEMAND INCOME...BIBLIOG/A 20. PAGE 8 F0146 — ECO/DEV INDUS FUT PROB/SOLV

B62
MOWITZ R.J.,PROFILE OF A METROPOLIS: A CASE BOOK. COM/IND CONSTRUC INDUS PUB/INST PLAN TEC/DEV LEAD GP/REL...POLICY TECHNIC WELF/ST MUNICH. PAGE 94 F1851 — DECISION ADMIN

B62
SCHALLER H.G.,PUBLIC EXPENDITURE DECISIONS IN THE URBAN COMMUNITY: PREPARED FOR RESOURCES FOR THE FUTURE, INC. INDUS SERV/IND LOC/G PUB/INST PLAN PROB/SOLV BUDGET DEMAND PRODUC...CHARTS MUNICH. PAGE 116 F2289 — FINAN DECISION

S64
HUTCHINSON E.C.,"AMERICAN AID TO AFRICA." FUT USA+45 MARKET INT/ORG LOC/G NAT/G PUB/INST PLAN ECO/TAC ATTIT RIGID/FLEX...POLICY CONCPT TREND TERR/GP 20. PAGE 63 F1248 — AFR ECO/UNDEV FOR/AID

B65
CONLEY R.W.,THE ECONOMICS OF VOCATIONAL REHABILITATION. USA+45 VOL/ASSN CREATE EDU/PROP COST EFFICIENCY SOC/INTEG 20. PAGE 27 F0527 — PUB/INST HEALTH GIVE GP/REL

B67
KULSKI J.E.,LAND OF URBAN PROMISE* CONTINUING THE GREAT TRADITION* A SEARCH FOR SIGNIFICANT URBAN SPACE IN URBANIZED NORTHEAST. USA+45 DIST/IND PUB/INST CONSULT CREATE TEC/DEV...SOC NEW/IDEA CHARTS BIBLIOG MUNICH. PAGE 74 F1448 — PLAN PROB/SOLV ECO/DEV

B67
LEIBY J.,CHARITY AND CORRECTION IN JERSEY; A HISTORY OF STATE WELFARE INSTITUTIONS. DELIB/GP EX/STRUC PROB/SOLV INSPECT LEAD ADJUST HEALTH ...POLICY PSY NEW/JERSEY. PAGE 77 F1514 — PROVS PUB/INST ADMIN

B67
UNIVERSAL REFERENCE SYSTEM,ADMINISTRATIVE MANAGEMENT: PUBLIC AND PRIVATE BUREAUCRACY (VOLUME IV). WOR+45 WOR-45 ECO/DEV LG/CO LOC/G PUB/INST VOL/ASSN GOV/REL...COMPUT/IR GEN/METH. PAGE 133 F2616 — BIBLIOG/A MGT ADMIN NAT/G

L67
JOHNSTON J.D. JR.,"CONSTITUTION OF SUBDIVISION CONTROL EXACTIONS: THE QUEST FOR A RATIONALE." USA+45 PROVS PUB/INST ADJUD CT/SYS GP/REL MUNICH. PAGE 68 F1334 — PLAN CONTROL LOC/G FORCES

N67
US HOUSE COMM ON COMMERCE,PARTNERSHIP FOR HEALTH AMENDMENTS FOR 1967 (PAMPHLET). PUB/INST DELIB/GP PROB/SOLV BUDGET EFFICIENCY 20 CONGRESS. PAGE 137 F2701 — HEAL PLAN NAT/G JURID

PUB/TRANS....PUBLIC TRANSPORTATION

B54
LOCKLIN D.P.,ECONOMICS OF TRANSPORTATION (4TH ED.). USA+45 USA-45 SEA AIR LAW FINAN LG/CO EX/STRUC ADMIN CONTROL...STAT CHARTS 19/20 RAILROAD PUB/TRANS. PAGE 81 F1592 — ECO/DEV DIST/IND ECO/TAC TEC/DEV

B57
DRUCKER P.F.,AMERICA'S NEXT TWENTY YEARS. USA+45 DIST/IND ACADEM SCHOOL DIPLOM ECO/TAC AUTOMAT HABITAT HEALTH...SOC/WK TREND MUNICH 20 URBAN/RNWL PUB/TRANS. PAGE 34 F0667 — WORKER FOR/AID CENSUS GEOG

B60
US SENATE COMM ON COMMERCE,URBAN MASS TRANSPORTATION. FUT USA+45 AIR ECO/DEV FINAN LOC/G LEGIS CREATE PROB/SOLV TEC/DEV MUNICH 20 PUB/TRANS. PAGE 139 F2732 — DIST/IND PLAN NAT/G LAW

B61
DOIG J.W.,THE POLITICS OF METROPOLITAN TRANSPORTATION. DELIB/GP WORKER DIPLOM TASK EFFICIENCY UTIL...CHARTS BIBLIOG MUNICH 20 NEW/YORK NEW/JERSEY PUB/TRANS RAILROAD. PAGE 34 F0652 — PROB/SOLV STRATA DIST/IND

B64
LANG A.S.,URBAN RAIL TRANSIT. OP/RES PLAN PROB/SOLV TEC/DEV AUTOMAT COST...TECHNIC MATH CON/ANAL CHARTS METH/COMP SIMUL MUNICH 20 RAILROAD PUB/TRANS. PAGE 75 F1474 — DIST/IND ECOMETRIC

B65
SMERK G.M.,URBAN TRANSPORTATION; THE FEDERAL ROLE. FUT USA+45 FINAN PROB/SOLV TEC/DEV AUTOMAT GOV/REL COST...STAT BIBLIOG MUNICH 20 PUB/TRANS. PAGE 123 F2426 — PLAN DIST/IND NAT/G

B66
LECHT L.,GOAL, PRIORITIES, AND DOLLARS: THE NEXT DECADE. SPACE USA+45 SOCIETY AGRI BUDGET FOR/AID ...HEAL SOC/WK STAT CHARTS 20 URBAN/RNWL PUB/TRANS. PAGE 76 F1499 — IDEA/COMP POLICY CONSEN PLAN

PUBL/WORKS....PUBLIC WORKS

PUBLIC ADMINISTRATION....SEE ADMIN, NAT/G

PUBLIC HEALTH SERVICE....SEE PHS

PUBLIC OPINION....SEE ATTIT

PUBLIC POLICY....SEE NAT/G+PLAN

PUBLIC RELATIONS....SEE NAT/G+RELATIONS INDEX

PUBLIC/EDU....PUBLIC EDUCATION ASSOCIATION

PUBLIC/REL....PUBLIC RELATIONS; SEE ALSO NAT/G + RELATIONS INDEX

PUBLIC/USE....PUBLIC USE

PUEBLO....PUEBLO INCIDENT; SEE ALSO KOREA/N

PUERT/RICN....PUERTO RICAN

PUERT/RICO....PUERTO RICO; SEE ALSO L/A+17C

B61
MAYNE A.,DESIGNING AND ADMINISTERING A REGIONAL ECONOMIC DEVELOPMENT PLAN WITH SPECIFIC REFERENCE TO PUERTO RICO (PAMPHLET). PUERT/RICO SOCIETY NAT/G DELIB/GP REGION...DECISION 20. PAGE 87 F1707 — ECO/UNDEV PLAN CREATE ADMIN

B63
GODWIN F.W.,THE HIDDEN FORCE. PUERT/RICO WOR+45 STRUCT VOL/ASSN PROB/SOLV DIPLOM CONFER...BIBLIOG 20 PEACE/CORP. PAGE 48 F0931 — ECO/UNDEV WORKER SKILL ECO/TAC

B63
LEWIS G.K.,PUERTO RICO: FREEDOM AND POWER IN THE CARIBBEAN. PUERT/RICO USA+45 CULTURE STRUCT INDUS POL/PAR WORKER EDU/PROP CATHISM 20. PAGE 79 F1548 — ECO/UNDEV COLONIAL NAT/LISM GEOG

B65
FRIEDLANDER S.L.,LABOR MIGRATION AND ECONOMIC GROWTH: A CASE STUDY OF PUERTO RICO. PUERT/RICO AGRI WORKER PLAN PROB/SOLV...ECOMETRIC STAT PREDICT CHARTS HYPO/EXP SIMUL 20. PAGE 44 F0858 — CENSUS GEOG ECO/UNDEV WEALTH

B65
GOODSELL C.T.,ADMINISTRATION OF A REVOLUTION. PUERT/RICO ECO/UNDEV FINAN POL/PAR PROVS LEGIS PLAN BUDGET RECEIVE ADMIN COLONIAL LEAD MUNICH 20 ROOSEVLT/F. PAGE 49 F0951 — EXEC SOC

B66
MACBEAN A.I.,EXPORT INSTABILITY AND ECONOMIC DEVELOPMENT. CHILE PAKISTAN PUERT/RICO TANZANIA UGANDA WOR+45 MARKET ECO/TAC...POLICY REGRESS CHARTS BIBLIOG TIME 20. PAGE 83 F1622 — INT/TRADE ECO/UNDEV ECOMETRIC INSPECT

PUERTO RICANS....SEE PUERTO RICO

PULLMAN....PULLMAN, ILLINOIS

PUNISHMENT....SEE ADJUD, LAW, LEGIT, SANCTION

PUNJAB....THE PUNJAB AND ITS PEOPLES

PUNTA/ESTE....PUNTA DEL ESTE

PURCELL T.V. F2131

PURGE....PURGES

PURHAM/M....MARGERY PURHAM

PURITAN....PURITANS

PURSELL G.W.E. F1431

PWR....POWER, PARTICIPATION IN DECISION-MAKING

B12
FOUAD M.,LE REGIME DE LA PRESSE EN EGYPTE: THESE — ORD/FREE

POUR LE DOCTORAT. UAR LICENSE EDU/PROP ADMIN SANCTION CRIME SUPEGO PWR...ART/METH JURID 19/20. PAGE 43 F0832
LEGIS CONTROL PRESS

N19
ARNDT H.W.,AUSTRALIAN FOREIGN AID POLICY (PAMPHLET). ECO/UNDEV DIPLOM GIVE GOV/REL COST UTIL PWR...CHARTS 20 AUSTRAL PAPUA NEW/GUINEA. PAGE 6 F0114
FOR/AID POLICY ECO/TAC EFFICIENCY

N19
MCCONNELL G.,THE STEEL SEIZURE OF 1952 (PAMPHLET). USA+45 FINAN INDUS PROC/MFG LG/CO EX/STRUC ADJUD CONTROL GP/REL ORD/FREE PWR 20 TRUMAN/HS PRESIDENT CONGRESS. PAGE 88 F1721
DELIB/GP LABOR PROB/SOLV NAT/G

B20
BUCK S.J.,THE AGRARIAN CRUSADE: A CHRONICLE OF THE FARMER IN POLITICS. USA-45 INDUS PROB/SOLV PWR WEALTH...GEOG CENSUS 19/20 GREENBACK GRANGE SILVER. PAGE 20 F0381
AGRI POPULISM VOL/ASSN POL/PAR

B20
MALTHUS T.R.,PRINCIPLES OF POLITICAL ECONOMY. UK AGRI INDUS MARKET NAT/G DIPLOM PRICE CONTROL BAL/PAY COST OWN PWR LAISSEZ 18/19. PAGE 84 F1650
GEN/LAWS DEMAND WEALTH

B25
MATHEWS J.M.,AMERICAN STATE GOVERNMENT. USA-45 LOC/G CHIEF EX/STRUC LEGIS ADJUD CONTROL CT/SYS ROUTINE GOV/REL PWR 20 GOVERNOR. PAGE 87 F1703
PROVS ADMIN FEDERAL CONSTN

B28
FRANKFURTER F.,THE BUSINESS OF THE SUPREME COURT; A STUDY IN THE FEDERAL JUDICIAL SYSTEM. USA-45 CONSTN EX/STRUC PROB/SOLV GP/REL ATTIT PWR...POLICY JURID 18/20 SUPREME/CT CONGRESS. PAGE 43 F0848
CT/SYS ADJUD LAW FEDERAL

B28
HARDMAN J.B.,AMERICAN LABOR DYNAMICS. WORKER ECO/TAC DOMIN ADJUD LEAD LOBBY PWR...POLICY MGT. PAGE 55 F1079
LABOR INGP/REL ATTIT GP/REL

B30
FEIS H.,EUROPE, THE WORLD'S BANKER, 1871-1914. FRANCE GERMANY MOD/EUR UK WOR-45 NAT/G PLAN ECO/TAC EXEC ATTIT PWR WEALTH...CONCPT HIST/WRIT GEN/LAWS VAL/FREE 19/20. PAGE 40 F0773
FINAN DIPLOM INT/TRADE

B30
HAWTREY R.G.,ECONOMIC ASPECTS OF SOVEREIGNTY. UNIV WOR+45 WOR-45 ECO/DEV ECO/UNDEV AGRI COM/IND INDUS MARKET NAT/G TEC/DEV ECO/TAC EDU/PROP COERCE ATTIT KNOWL WEALTH...CONCPT CON/ANAL GEN/LAWS 20. PAGE 57 F1118
FORCES PWR SOVEREIGN WAR

S30
CRAWFORD F.G.,"THE EXECUTIVE BUDGET DECISION IN NEW YORK." LEGIS EXEC PWR NEW/YORK. PAGE 28 F0552
LEAD BUDGET PROVS PROB/SOLV

B31
CROOK W.H.,THE GENERAL STRIKE: A STUDY OF LABOR'S TRAGIC WEAPON IN THEORY AND PRACTICE. BELGIUM FRANCE SWEDEN UK WOR-45 PROB/SOLV ECO/TAC DOMIN PWR ...POLICY TIME/SEQ NAT/COMP GEN/LAWS 19/20 STRIKE. PAGE 29 F0555
LABOR WORKER LG/CO BARGAIN

B32
THOMPSON C.D.,CONFESSIONS OF THE POWER TRUST. MARKET ACT/RES EDU/PROP CONTROL GOV/REL INCOME OWN ...MGT 20 FTC MONOPOLY. PAGE 130 F2564
LG/CO SERV/IND PWR FINAN

B35
LASKI H.J.,THE STATE IN THEORY AND PRACTICE. ELITES ECO/TAC REPRESENT ORD/FREE PWR WEALTH POPULISM ...GOV/COMP GEN/LAWS 19/20. PAGE 76 F1483
CAP/ISM COERCE NAT/G FASCISM

B35
SCHATTSCHNEIDER E.E.,POLITICS, PRESSURES AND THE TARIFF: A STUDY OF FREE PRIVATE ENTERPRISE IN PRESSURE POLITICS IN TARIFF REVISION 1929-1930. NAT/G BARGAIN ECO/TAC ROUTINE REPRESENT GOV/REL GP/REL PWR POLICY. PAGE 116 F2290
LOBBY LEGIS TARIFFS

B37
HAMILTON W.H.,THE POWER TO GOVERN. ECO/DEV FINAN INDUS ECO/TAC INT/TRADE TARIFFS TAX CONTROL CT/SYS WAR COST PWR 18/20 SUPREME/CT. PAGE 54 F1056
LING CONSTN NAT/G POLICY

B38
HOBSON J.A.,IMPERIALISM. MOD/EUR UK WOR-45 CULTURE ECO/UNDEV NAT/G VOL/ASSN PLAN EDU/PROP LEGIT REGION COERCE ATTIT PWR...POLICY PLURIST TIME/SEQ GEN/LAWS TERR/GP 19/20. PAGE 60 F1187
DOMIN ECO/TAC BAL/PWR COLONIAL

B39
ENGELS F.,HERRN EUGEN DUHRING'S REVOLUTION IN SCIENCE (1878). CULTURE STRATA STRUCT FAM SECT ECO/TAC REV WAR SOCISM...MARXIST 19. PAGE 37 F0731
PWR SOCIETY WEALTH GEN/LAWS

B39
ROBBINS L.,ECONOMIC CAUSES OF WAR. WOR-45 ECO/DEV ECO/UNDEV INT/ORG NAT/G TEC/DEV DIPLOM DOMIN COLONIAL ATTIT DRIVE PWR WEALTH...POLICY CONCPT OBS SAMP TREND CON/ANAL GEN/LAWS MARX/KARL 20. PAGE 112 F2203
COERCE ECO/TAC WAR

B40
SPENCER H.,THE MAN VS. THE STATE (1892). UK POL/PAR LEGIS TARIFFS COERCE CRIME REPRESENT PWR SOCISM ...POLICY GEN/LAWS 19/20. PAGE 124 F2450
FASCISM POPULISM LAISSEZ ORD/FREE

S41
LASSWELL H.D.,"THE GARRISON STATE" (BMR)" FUT WOR+45 ELITES INTELL FORCES ECO/TAC DOMIN EDU/PROP COERCE INGP/REL 20. PAGE 76 F1485
NAT/G DIPLOM PWR CIVMIL/REL

B42
JACKSON M.V.,EUROPEAN POWERS AND SOUTH-EAST AFRICA: A STUDY OF INTERNATIONAL RELATIONS ON SOUTH-EAST COAST OF AFRICA, 1796-1856. AFR FRANCE PORTUGAL SOUTH/AFR UK USA-45 FORCES INT/TRADE PWR...CHARTS BIBLIOG 18/19 TREATY. PAGE 66 F1294
DOMIN POLICY ORD/FREE DIPLOM

L42
GRANT J.A.C.,"THE GUILD RETURNS TO AMERICA." CHRIST-17C USA-45 LEGIS LICENSE ADJUD CONTROL GP/REL. PAGE 50 F0978
PROF/ORG JURID LABOR PWR

B43
BRADY R.A.,BUSINESS AS A SYSTEM OF POWER. EX/STRUC PLAN ECO/TAC CONTROL GP/REL PWR...TREND GP/COMP. PAGE 17 F0334
VOL/ASSN LOBBY POLICY

S43
HERBERG W.,"BUREAUCRACY AND DEMOCRACY IN LABOR UNIONS." LAW CONSTN STRUCT WORKER ADMIN CONTROL PARTIC RIGID/FLEX PWR TREND. PAGE 59 F1151
LABOR REPRESENT ROUTINE INGP/REL

C43
BENTHAM J.,"THE RATIONALE OF REWARD" IN J. BOWRING, ED., THE WORKS OF JEREMY BENTHAM (VOL. 2)" LAW WORKER CREATE INSPECT PAY ROUTINE HAPPINESS PRODUC SUPEGO WEALTH METH/CNCPT. PAGE 13 F0254
SANCTION ECO/TAC INCOME PWR

B44
BIENSTOCK G.,MANAGEMENT IN RUSSIAN INDUSTRY AND AGRICULTURE. USSR CONSULT WORKER LEAD COST PROFIT ATTIT DRIVE PWR...MGT METH/COMP DICTIONARY ACCT 20. PAGE 15 F0281
ADMIN MARXISM SML/CO AGRI

B44
MERRIAM C.E.,PUBLIC AND PRIVATE GOVERNMENT. VOL/ASSN EDU/PROP ADMIN REPRESENT EFFICIENCY PWR PLURISM...MAJORIT CONCPT. PAGE 90 F1762
NAT/G NEIGH MGT POLICY

B47
BALDWIN H.W.,THE PRICE OF POWER. USA+45 FORCES PLAN NUC/PWR ADJUST COST ORD/FREE...POLICY PSY BIBLIOG 20. PAGE 9 F0165
PROB/SOLV PWR POPULISM PRICE

B47
GORDON D.L.,THE HIDDEN WEAPON: THE STORY OF ECONOMIC WARFARE. EUR+WWI USA-45 LAW FINAN INDUS NAT/G CONSULT FORCES PLAN DOMIN PWR WEALTH ...INT/LAW CONCPT OBS TOT/POP NAZI 20. PAGE 49 F0955
INT/ORG ECO/TAC INT/TRADE WAR

B47
HEILPERIN M.A.,THE TRADE OF NATIONS. USA+45 USA-45 WOR+45 WOR-45 CULTURE ECO/DEV NAT/G DELIB/GP EDU/PROP ATTIT DISPL ORD/FREE PWR WEALTH TOT/POP 20. PAGE 58 F1139
MARKET INT/ORG INT/TRADE PEACE

S47
DAHL R.A.,"WORKERS' CONTROL OF INDUSTRY AND THE BRITISH LABOUR PARTY." UK STRATA STRUCT DELIB/GP BARGAIN CAP/ISM DEBATE CONTROL CHOOSE GP/REL ATTIT ROLE PWR 19/20 PARLIAMENT LABOR/PAR FABIAN. PAGE 29 F0570
INDUS LABOR WORKER SOCISM

B48
CLYDE P.H.,THE FAR EAST: A HISTORY OF THE IMPACT OF THE WEST ON EASTERN ASIA. CHINA/COM CULTURE INT/TRADE DOMIN COLONIAL WAR PWR...CHARTS BIBLIOG 19/20 CHINJAP. PAGE 25 F0494
DIPLOM ASIA

B48
DURBIN E.F.M.,THE POLITICS OF DEMOCRATIC SOCIALISM; AN ESSAY ON SOCIAL POLICY. STRATA POL/PAR PLAN COERCE DRIVE PERSON PWR MARXISM...CHARTS METH/COMP. PAGE 35 F0684
SOCIALIST POPULISM POLICY SOCIETY

B48
GRAHAM F.D.,THE THEORY OF INTERNATIONAL VALUES. FUT WOR+45 WOR-45 ECO/DEV FINAN INT/ORG PLAN TEC/DEV CAP/ISM DIPLOM ECO/TAC TARIFFS ROUTINE BAL/PAY DRIVE PWR WEALTH SOCISM...POLICY STAT HYPO/EXP GEN/LAWS 20. PAGE 50 F0971
NEW/IDEA INT/TRADE

B48
MILLS C.W.,THE NEW MEN OF POWER. ELITES INTELL STRUCT WORKER ANOMIE ATTIT PWR POLICY. PAGE 92 F1799
LABOR LEAD PLAN

B48
WINSLOW E.M.,THE PATTERN OF IMPERIALISM; A STUDY IN THE THEORIES OF POWER. DOMIN WAR PWR MARXISM ...IDEA/COMP METH/COMP BIBLIOG 20. PAGE 147 F2906
SOCISM CAP/ISM COLONIAL ECO/TAC

B49
SELZNICK P.,TVA AND THE GRASS ROOTS: A STUDY IN THE SOCIOLOGY OF FORMAL ORGANIZATION. USA-45 EX/STRUC PROB/SOLV CONFER PARTIC ROUTINE PWR 20 TVA.
REPRESENT LOBBY CONSULT

PAGE 119 F2353

S49
SHEPHARD H.A.,"DEMOCRATIC CONTROL IN A LABOR UNION." FUT CONSTN STRUCT TEC/DEV LEAD PARTIC RACE/REL CENTRAL DRIVE HABITAT RECORD. PAGE 120 F2374
LABOR MAJORIT CONTROL PWR

B50
CLARK J.M.,ALTERNATIVE TO SERFDOM. SOCIETY STRATA INDUS MARKET WORKER PRICE GP/REL PROFIT BIO/SOC PWR WEALTH...GEN/LAWS 20 KEYNES/JM. PAGE 25 F0481
ORD/FREE POPULISM ECO/TAC REPRESENT

B50
HUTCHISON K.,THE DECLINE AND FALL OF BRITISH CAPITALISM. UK ELITES STRATA ECO/DEV LABOR WORKER CONTROL WAR PWR...BIBLIOG/A 19/20. PAGE 63 F1249
CAP/ISM SOCISM LAISSEZ DOMIN

B50
LINCOLN G.,ECONOMICS OF NATIONAL SECURITY. USA+45 ELITES COM/IND DIST/IND INDUS NAT/G VOL/ASSN DELIB/GP EX/STRUC FOR/AID EDU/PROP COERCE NUC/PWR WAR ATTIT KNOWL ORD/FREE PWR TOT/POP VAL/FREE 20. PAGE 80 F1565
FORCES ECO/TAC AFR

B50
ORTON W.A.,THE ECONOMIC ROLE OF THE STATE. INTELL ECO/UNDEV PLAN CONTROL PWR SOVEREIGN...POLICY 17/20. PAGE 102 F2000
ECO/DEV NAT/G ECO/TAC ORD/FREE

S50
EBY K.,"RESEARCH IN LABOR UNIONS." EDU/PROP INGP/REL PWR...METH/CNCPT OBS. PAGE 36 F0693
RECORD QU LABOR PARTIC

B51
HALEVY E.,IMPERIALISM AND THE RISE OF LABOR (2ND ED.). UK NAT/G POL/PAR TOP/EX ATTIT ORD/FREE PWR 19/20 PARLIAMENT LABOR/PAR. PAGE 53 F1042
COLONIAL LABOR POLICY WAR

L51
SUMMERS C.W.,"UNION POWERS AND WORKERS RIGHTS." WORKER PROB/SOLV ECO/TAC PARTIC INGP/REL PWR. PAGE 127 F2513
LABOR CONSTN LAW REPRESENT

B52
MACHLUP F.,THE POLITICAL ECONOMY OF MONOPOLY: BUSINESS, LABOR AND GOVERNMENT POLICIES. USA+45 USA-45 ECO/DEV LABOR NAT/G CAP/ISM PWR...POLICY CHARTS T 20. PAGE 83 F1630
ECO/TAC DOMIN LG/CO CONTROL

B52
TANNENBAUM F.,A PHILOSOPHY OF LABOR. SOCIETY STRATA INDUS LG/CO AGREE ADJUST OWN ORD/FREE PWR...CONCPT 20. PAGE 128 F2533
LABOR PHIL/SCI WORKER CREATE

C52
HUME D.,"OF THE BALANCE OF TRADE" IN D. HUME, POLITICAL DISCOURSES (1752)" UK FINAN NAT/G TARIFFS PRICE PWR LAISSEZ...POLICY GEN/LAWS 18. PAGE 63 F1237
BAL/PAY INT/TRADE DIPLOM WEALTH

C52
HUME D.,"OF COMMERCE" IN D. HUME, POLITICAL DISCOURSES (1752)" UK FINAN DIPLOM WEALTH ...GEN/LAWS 18 MONEY. PAGE 63 F1238
INDUS INT/TRADE PWR AGRI

B53
BOWEN H.R.,SOCIAL RESPONSIBILITIES OF THE BUSINESSMAN (FIRST EDITION). LAW FINAN ACT/RES CAP/ISM ROUTINE DRIVE PWR LAISSEZ...DECISION BIBLIOG. PAGE 17 F0326
MGT PERSON SUPEGO MORAL

B53
MENDE T.,WORLD POWER IN THE BALANCE. FUT USA+45 USSR WOR-45 ECO/DEV ECO/TAC INT/TRADE EDU/PROP UTOPIA ATTIT...HUM CONCPT TREND TOT/POP 20. PAGE 90 F1756
WOR+45 PWR BAL/PWR AFR

S53
DRUCKER P.F.,"THE EMPLOYEE SOCIETY." STRUCT BAL/PWR PARTIC REPRESENT PWR...DECISION CONCPT. PAGE 34 F0666
LABOR MGT WORKER CULTURE

S53
GABLE R.W.,"NAM: INFLUENTIAL LOBBY OR KISS OF DEATH?" (BMR)" USA+45 LAW INSPECT EDU/PROP ADMIN CONTROL INGP/REL EFFICIENCY PWR 20 CONGRESS NAM TAFT/HART. PAGE 45 F0880
LOBBY LEGIS INDUS LG/CO

S53
LINCOLN G.,"FACTORS DETERMINING ARMS AID." COM FUT USA+45 USSR WOR+45 ECO/DEV NAT/G CONSULT PLAN TEC/DEV DIPLOM DOMIN EDU/PROP PERCEPT PWR ...DECISION CONCPT TREND MARX/KARL 20. PAGE 80 F1566
FORCES POLICY BAL/PWR FOR/AID

S53
MCKEE J.B.,"STATUS AND POWER IN THE INDUSTRIAL COMMUNITY; A COMMENT ON DRUCKER'S THESIS." LABOR LEGIT LEAD GP/REL PWR...MGT CONCPT. PAGE 88 F1730
SOC STRATA NEIGH PARTIC

B54
CHILDS M.W.,ETHICS IN A BUSINESS SOCIETY. PROF/ORG LEAD WAR GP/REL ATTIT DRIVE PERSON KNOWL MORAL PWR ...WELF/ST BIBLIOG. PAGE 24 F0466
MGT SOCIETY

B54
EMERSON F.D.,SHAREHOLDER DEMOCRACY: A BROADER OUTLOOK FOR CORPORATIONS. DELIB/GP EX/STRUC LEGIS ADJUD CONTROL REPRESENT INGP/REL OWN PWR...POLICY STAT RECORD. PAGE 37 F0727
LG/CO PARTIC MAJORIT TREND

B54
TAFT P.,THE STRUCTURE AND GOVERNMENT OF LABOR UNIONS. SANCTION INGP/REL ORD/FREE PWR MARXISM ...MAJORIT STAT TREND. PAGE 128 F2524
LABOR ADJUD WORKER FINAN

S54
EDELMAN M.J.,"LABOR'S INFLUENCE IN FOREIGN POLICY." NAT/G EXEC PWR 20. PAGE 36 F0700
LOBBY REPRESENT EX/STRUC LABOR

C54
BERLE A.A. JR.,"THE 20TH CENTURY CAPITALIST REVOLUTION." ECO/DEV NAT/G DIPLOM PRICE CONTROL ATTIT...BIBLIOG/A 20. PAGE 14 F0260
LG/CO CAP/ISM MGT PWR

B55
BUCHANAN N.S.,APPROACHES TO ECONOMIC DEVELOPMENT. FUT USA+45 WOR+45 STRATA ECO/DEV INT/ORG NAT/G TEC/DEV DIPLOM FOR/AID ATTIT KNOWL PWR WEALTH ...RELATIV METH/CNCPT SELF/OBS TREND CON/ANAL STERTYP GEN/LAWS FOR/TRADE COMMUN 20. PAGE 20 F0380
ECO/UNDEV ECO/TAC INT/TRADE

B55
FLORINSKY M.T.,INTEGRATED EUROPE. EUR+WWI FRANCE ITALY NETHERLAND UK ECO/DEV INT/ORG FORCES LEGIT FEDERAL ATTIT PWR WEALTH...POLICY GEOG CONCPT GEN/LAWS TOT/POP EEC OEEC 20. PAGE 42 F0816
FUT ECO/TAC REGION

C55
ADAMS G.P. JR.,"COMPETITIVE ECONOMIC SYSTEMS." WOR+45 WOR-45 PWR...BIBLIOG/A 20. PAGE 2 F0038
METH/COMP ECO/TAC TEC/DEV DIPLOM

B56
GARDNER R.N.,STERLING-DOLLAR DIPLOMACY. EUR+WWI USA+45 INT/ORG NAT/G PLAN INT/TRADE EDU/PROP ADMIN KNOWL PWR WEALTH...POLICY SOC METH/CNCPT STAT CHARTS SIMUL GEN/LAWS 20. PAGE 46 F0902
ECO/DEV DIPLOM

B56
GILBERT L.D.,DIVIDENDS AND DEMOCRACY. DELIB/GP LEGIS CAP/ISM ADJUD LOBBY OWN PWR LAISSEZ MAJORIT. PAGE 47 F0922
LG/CO INGP/REL CONTROL PARTIC

B56
WEBER M.,WIRTSCHAFT UND GESELLSCHAFT (2ND VOL.). STRUCT NAT/G POL/PAR LEAD PWR OBJECTIVE IDEA/COMP. PAGE 144 F2841
LEGIT JURID SOC

L56
SCHELLING T.C.,"AN ESSAY ON BARGAINING" (BMR)" OP/RES PROB/SOLV PRICE CHOOSE PWR...DECISION MODELS 20. PAGE 116 F2294
BARGAIN MARKET ECO/TAC GAME

S56
MILNE R.S.,"CONTROL OF GOVERNMENT CORPORATIONS IN THE UNITED STATES." USA+45 NAT/G CHIEF LEGIS BUDGET 20 GENACCOUNT. PAGE 92 F1800
CONTROL EX/STRUC GOV/REL PWR

S56
MYERS C.A.,"LINE AND STAFF IN INDUSTRIAL RELATIONS." INDUS LABOR GP/REL PWR...MGT INT. PAGE 96 F1876
ROLE PROB/SOLV ADMIN CONSULT

S56
TANNENBAUM A.S.,"CONTROL OF STRUCTURE AND UNION FUNCTIONS." PARTIC GP/REL INGP/REL CONSEN ATTIT PWR ...QU SAMP. PAGE 128 F2529
LABOR STRUCT CONTROL LEAD

S56
TYLER G.,"THE PRESIDENCY AND LABOR." USA+45 USA-45 NAT/G LOBBY GOV/REL PWR 20 PRESIDENT. PAGE 131 F2595
LABOR REPRESENT CHIEF

C56
MCKEE J.B.,"THE POWER TO DECIDE" IN M. WEINBERG AND O. SHABET, SOCIETY AND MAN." ELITES STRATA REPRESENT GP/REL ATTIT PWR MUNICH BUSINESS. PAGE 88 F1731
LABOR DECISION LEAD

B57
ARON R.,L'UNIFICATION ECONOMIQUE DE L'EUROPE. EUR+WWI SWITZERLND UK INT/ORG NAT/G REGION NAT/LISM ORD/FREE PWR...CONCPT METH/CNCPT OBS TREND STERTYP GEN/LAWS EEC FOR/TRADE 20. PAGE 6 F0118
VOL/ASSN ECO/TAC

B57
BERLE A.A. JR.,ECONOMIC POWER AND FREE SOCIETY (PAMPHLET). CLIENT CONSTN EX/STRUC ECO/TAC CONTROL PARTIC PWR WEALTH MAJORIT. PAGE 14 F0261
LG/CO CAP/ISM INGP/REL LEGIT

B57
EHRMANN H.W.,ORGANIZED BUSINESS IN FRANCE. EUR+WWI MOD/EUR ECO/DEV VOL/ASSN LEGIT ATTIT PERCEPT PWR RESPECT...PLURIST SOC INT TOT/POP 20. PAGE 36 F0712
PROF/ORG ECO/TAC FRANCE

B57
MASON E.S.,ECONOMIC CONCENTRATION AND THE MONOPOLY
GP/REL

PROBLEM. USA+45 USA-45 LAW ELITES ECO/DEV LABOR RATION PRICE PWR WEALTH...CHARTS 20 MONOPOLY. PAGE 87 F1696
LG/CO CONTROL MARKET

B57
MEIER G.M.,ECONOMIC DEVELOPMENT: THEORY, HISTORY, AND POLICY. WOR+45 WOR-45 ECO/DEV ECO/UNDEV PLAN CAP/ISM BAL/PAY ATTIT PWR WEALTH SOCISM...CHARTS TOT/POP FOR/TRADE 20. PAGE 89 F1748
ECO/TAC GEN/LAWS

B57
SCHNEIDER E.V.,INDUSTRIAL SOCIOLOGY: THE SOCIAL RELATIONS OF INDUSTRY AND COMMUNITY. STRATA INDUS NAT/G NEIGH CREATE ADMIN PARTIC GP/REL RACE/REL ROLE PWR...POLICY BIBLIOG. PAGE 117 F2308
LABOR MGT INGP/REL STRUCT

S57
DUBIN R.,"POWER AND UNION-MANAGEMENT RELATIONS." PROB/SOLV ADJUD ROUTINE ATTIT ORD/FREE...MGT STERTYP. PAGE 34 F0668
PWR LABOR BARGAIN GP/REL

S57
HOAG M.W.,"ECONOMIC PROBLEMS OF ALLIANCE." AFR COM EUR+WWI WOR+45 ECO/DEV ECO/UNDEV NAT/G VOL/ASSN FORCES PLAN TEC/DEV DIPLOM COERCE ORD/FREE PWR WEALTH...DECISION GEN/LAWS NATO TERR/GP. PAGE 60 F1182
INT/ORG ECO/TAC

S57
LEWIS E.G.,"PARLIAMENTARY CONTROL OF NATIONALIZED INDUSTRY IN FRANCE." FRANCE NAT/G DELIB/GP ACT/RES PLAN PROB/SOLV ECO/TAC DOMIN CENTRAL. PAGE 79 F1547
PWR LEGIS INDUS CONTROL

S57
TANNENBAUM A.S.,"ORGANIZATIONAL CONTROL STRUCTURE: A GENERAL DESCRIPTIVE TECHNIQUE AS APPLIED TO FOUR LOCAL UNIONS." LABOR PWR...METH/CNCPT CLASSIF QU CHARTS. PAGE 128 F2530
WORKER PARTIC STRUCT CONTROL

B58
BERLINER J.S.,SOVIET ECONOMIC AID: THE AID AND TRADE POLICY IN UNDERDEVELOPED COUNTRIES. AFR COM ISLAM L/A+17C S/ASIA USSR ECO/DEV DIST/IND FINAN MARKET INT/ORG ACT/RES PLAN BAL/PWR WEAPON PWR WEALTH...CHARTS FOR/TRADE 20. PAGE 14 F0263
ECO/UNDEV ECO/TAC FOR/AID

B58
CHAMBERLIN E.H.,LABOR UNIONS AND PUBLIC POLICY. PLAN BARGAIN SANCTION INGP/REL JURID. PAGE 23 F0444
LABOR WEALTH PWR NAT/G

B58
DUBIN R.,WORKING UNION-MANAGEMENT RELATIONS. LAW PLAN ECO/TAC CHOOSE REPRESENT INGP/REL PWR...POLICY SOC BIBLIOG. PAGE 34 F0669
LABOR MGT AUTHORIT GP/REL

B58
FINER S.E.,PRIVATE INDUSTRY AND POLITICAL POWER (PAMPHLET). UK INDUS CONTROL LOBBY PWR. PAGE 41 F0797
PLURISM REPRESENT EX/STRUC

B58
HAMEROW T.S.,RESTORATION, REVOLUTION, REACTION: ECONOMICS AND POLITICS IN GERMANY, 1815-1871. CAP/ISM ADJUST ATTIT PWR...BIBLIOG/A 19 GER/CONFED FRANK/PARL. PAGE 54 F1055
REV ORD/FREE ECO/DEV

B58
OEEC,THE INDUSTRIAL CHALLENGE OF NUCLEAR ENERGY. EUR+WWI ECO/DEV INDUS OP/RES CONFER RISK PWR ...AUD/VIS CHARTS ANTHOL 20 OEEC. PAGE 101 F1977
NUC/PWR ACT/RES ECO/TAC INT/ORG

B58
SEIDMAN J.I.,DEMOCRACY IN THE LABOR MOVEMENT (PAMPHLET). LAW CONSTN STRUCT DELIB/GP WORKER ADJUD PARTIC SANCTION POLICY. PAGE 119 F2345
LABOR INGP/REL PWR MAJORIT

S58
EMERSON F.D.,"THE ROLES OF MANAGEMENT AND SHAREHOLDERS IN CORPORATE GOVERNMENT." CLIENT DELIB/GP CREATE ADMIN EXEC PARTIC PERS/REL PWR. PAGE 37 F0728
LG/CO LAW INGP/REL REPRESENT

S58
LANE F.C.,"ECONOMIC CONSEQUENCES OF ORGANIZED VIOLENCE." FUT WOR+45 WOR-45 ECO/DEV DIST/IND SERV/IND NAT/G PROVS EX/STRUC CHOOSE ORD/FREE PWR ...TIME/SEQ GEN/LAWS MUNICH 20. PAGE 75 F1472
WEALTH COERCE

B59
AITKEN H.,THE STATE AND ECONOMIC GROWTH. COM EUR+WWI MOD/EUR S/ASIA USA+45 FINAN NAT/G DELIB/GP PLAN PWR WEALTH 20. PAGE 3 F0054
DIST/IND ECO/DEV

B59
ALLEN R.L.,SOVIET INFLUENCE IN LATIN AMERICA. ECO/UNDEV FINAN PROC/MFG NAT/G TEC/DEV EDU/PROP EXEC ROUTINE ATTIT DRIVE PERSON ALL/VALS PWR...STAT CHARTS WORK FOR/TRADE 20. PAGE 4 F0071
L/A+17C ECO/TAC INT/TRADE USSR

B59
BROMWICH L.,UNION CONSTITUTIONS. CONSTN EX/STRUC PRESS ADJUD CONTROL CHOOSE REPRESENT PWR SAMP. PAGE 19 F0361
LABOR ROUTINE INGP/REL RACE/REL

B59
FERRY W.H.,THE CORPORATION AND THE ECONOMY. CLIENT LAW CONSTN LABOR NAT/G PLAN INT/TRADE PARTIC CONSEN ORD/FREE PWR POLICY. PAGE 40 F0787
LG/CO CONTROL REPRESENT

B59
HENDEL S.,THE SOVIET CRUCIBLE. USSR LEAD COERCE NAT/LISM UTOPIA PWR...POLICY CONCPT ANTHOL 20 STALIN/J LENIN/VI MARX/KARL BOLSHEVIK. PAGE 58 F1147
COM MARXISM REV TOTALISM

B59
LEISERSON W.,AMERICAN TRADE UNION DEMOCRACY. CONSTN STRUCT ADJUD EXEC REPRESENT GP/REL INGP/REL MAJORITY ATTIT PWR. PAGE 77 F1516
LABOR LEAD PARTIC DELIB/GP

B59
MUSOLF L.D.,PUBLIC OWNERSHIP AND ACCOUNTABILITY: THE CANADIAN EXPERIENCE. CANADA REPRESENT PWR 20. PAGE 95 F1873
MGT CONTROL INDUS

B59
VINCENT W.S.,ROLES OF THE CITIZENS: PRINCIPLES AND PRACTICES. LOC/G POL/PAR VOL/ASSN CHOOSE ROLE ORD/FREE PWR...POLICY 20. PAGE 141 F2785
INGP/REL EDU/PROP CREATE LOBBY

B59
WUERTHNER J.J.,THE BUSINESSMAN'S GUIDE TO PRACTICAL POLITICS. USA+45 PWR 20. PAGE 149 F2940
LOBBY CHOOSE REPRESENT

L59
OBERER W.E.,"VOLUNTARY IMPARTIAL REVIEW OF LABOR: SOME REFLECTIONS." DELIB/GP LEGIS PROB/SOLV ADJUD CONTROL COERCE PWR PLURISM POLICY. PAGE 100 F1960
LABOR LAW PARTIC INGP/REL

S59
MILLER A.S.,"CONSTITUTIONALIZING THE CORPORATION." LABOR NAT/G WORKER PWR...POLICY MGT. PAGE 91 F1789
CONSTN INGP/REL LG/CO CONTROL

S59
REUBENS E.D.,"THE BASIS FOR REORIENATION OF AMERICAN FOREIGN AID POLICY." USA+45 USSR STRUCT INT/ORG CONSULT ECO/TAC ADMIN DRIVE MORAL ORD/FREE PWR WEALTH...RELATIV MATH STAT TREND GEN/LAWS VAL/FREE 20. PAGE 111 F2180
ECO/UNDEV PLAN FOR/AID DIPLOM

B60
FINKLE J.L.,THE PRESIDENT MAKES A DECISION: A STUDY OF DIXON-YATES. OP/RES PROB/SOLV BUDGET ADMIN GOV/REL...POLICY BIBLIOG/A 20 PRESIDENT. PAGE 41 F0799
DECISION CHIEF PWR POL/PAR

B60
FORBUSH D.R.,PROBLEMS OF CORPORATE POWER. CLIENT LAW ELITES ADJUD...DECISION MGT. PAGE 42 F0822
LG/CO PWR CONTROL GP/REL

B60
FORM W.H.,INDUSTRY, LABOR, AND COMMUNITY. STRUCT NEIGH SECT BAL/PWR EDU/PROP PARTIC ATTIT ROLE PWR WEALTH...METH/CNCPT CHARTS. PAGE 42 F0828
LABOR MGT GP/REL CONTROL

B60
FRANCK P.G.,AFGHANISTAN: BETWEEN EAST AND WEST. AFGHANISTN AFR USA+45 USSR ECO/UNDEV PLAN ADMIN ROUTINE ATTIT PWR...STAT OBS CHARTS TOT/POP FOR/TRADE 20. PAGE 43 F0843
ECO/TAC TREND FOR/AID

B60
GRANICK D.,THE RED EXECUTIVE. COM USA+45 SOCIETY ECO/DEV INDUS NAT/G POL/PAR EX/STRUC PLAN ECO/TAC EDU/PROP ADMIN EXEC ATTIT DRIVE...GP/COMP 20. PAGE 50 F0976
PWR STRATA USSR ELITES

B60
HARBRECHT P.P.,TOWARD THE PARAPROPRIETAL SOCIETY. REPRESENT INCOME OWN PROFIT AGE/O. PAGE 55 F1076
PWR ADMIN ELITES CONTROL

B60
KRISTENSEN T.,THE ECONOMIC WORLD BALANCE. FUT WOR+45 CULTURE ECO/DEV BAL/PWR INT/TRADE REGION PWR WEALTH...STAT TREND CHARTS 20. PAGE 73 F1442
ECO/UNDEV ECO/TAC FOR/AID

B60
LENCZOWSKI G.,OIL AND STATE IN THE MIDDLE EAST. FUT IRAN LAW ECO/UNDEV EXTR/IND NAT/G TOP/EX PLAN TEC/DEV ECO/TAC LEGIT ADMIN COERCE ATTIT ALL/VALS PWR...CHARTS 20. PAGE 78 F1519
ISLAM INDUS NAT/LISM

B60
LISTER L.,EUROPE'S COAL AND STEEL COMMUNITY. FRANCE GERMANY STRUCT ECO/DEV EXTR/IND INDUS MARKET NAT/G DELIB/GP ECO/TAC INT/TRADE EDU/PROP ATTIT RIGID/FLEX ORD/FREE PWR WEALTH...CONCPT STAT TIME/SEQ CHARTS ECSC TERR/GP 20. PAGE 81 F1582
EUR+WWI INT/ORG REGION

B60
PETERSON W.C.,THE WELFARE STATE IN FRANCE. EUR+WWI FRANCE FUT STRATA PROB/SOLV TAX GIVE RECEIVE INCOME ORD/FREE PWR...CHARTS 20. PAGE 105 F2070
NEW/LIB ECO/TAC WEALTH NAT/G

B60
RAMA C.M.,LAS CLASES SOCIALES EN EL URUGUAY. L/A+17C URUGUAY ELITES SOCIETY STRATA INDUS ATTIT HABITAT PWR...GEOG SOC/INTEG MUNICH 20. PAGE 109 F2138
ECO/UNDEV STRUCT PARTIC

B60
STEIN E.,AMERICAN ENTERPRISE IN THE EUROPEAN COMMON MARKET: A LEGAL PROFILE. EUR+WWI FUT USA+45 SOCIETY STRUCT ECO/DEV NAT/G VOL/ASSN CONSULT PLAN TEC/DEV ECO/TAC INT/TRADE ADMIN ATTIT RIGID/FLEX PWR...MGT NEW/IDEA STAT TREND COMPUT/IR SIMUL EEC 20. PAGE 125 F2475
MARKET ADJUD INT/LAW

B60
THEOBALD R.,THE RICH AND THE POOR: A STUDY OF THE ECONOMICS OF RISING EXPECTATIONS. WOR+45 CONSTN ECO/DEV ECO/UNDEV INT/ORG NAT/G PLAN FOR/AID ROUTINE BAL/PAY ORD/FREE PWR WEALTH...GEOG TREND WORK FOR/TRADE 20. PAGE 129 F2553
ECO/TAC INT/TRADE

B60
VERNON R.,METROPOLIS 1985. LOC/G PLAN TAX LEAD PWR MUNICH. PAGE 141 F2780
REGION ECO/TAC DECISION

B60
WALLACE R.A.,CONGRESSIONAL CONTROL OF FEDERAL SPENDING. USA+45 CONSTN NAT/G OP/RES CONFER DEBATE PERS/REL UTIL RIGID/FLEX PWR OBJECTIVE...OBS CHARTS. PAGE 143 F2808
LEGIS DELIB/GP BUDGET

S60
BARNETT H.J.,"RESEARCH AND DEVELOPMENT, ECONOMIC GROWTH, AND NATIONAL SECURITY." AFR USA+45 R+D CREATE ECO/TAC ATTIT DRIVE PWR...POLICY SOC METH/CNCPT QUANT STAT TIME/SEQ ORG/CHARTS LOG/LING 20. PAGE 10 F0190
ACT/RES PLAN

S60
BERG E.J.,"ECONOMIC BASIS OF POLITICAL CHOICE IN FRENCH WEST AFRICA." FRANCE ECO/UNDEV AGRI INDUS NAT/G PLAN LEGIT COLONIAL REGION ATTIT PWR WEALTH ...CONCPT FOR/TRADE 20. PAGE 13 F0257
AFR ECO/TAC

S60
FORM W.H.,"ORGANIZED LABOR'S IMAGE OF COMMUNITY POWER STRUCTURE." LABOR LG/CO CONTROL LEAD REPRESENT...DECISION METH/CNCPT INT QU SAMP. PAGE 42 F0829
NEIGH PARTIC PWR GP/REL

S60
FRANKEL S.H.,"ECONOMIC ASPECTS OF POLITICAL INDEPENDENCE IN AFRICA." AFR FUT SOCIETY ECO/UNDEV COM/IND FINAN LEGIS PLAN TEC/DEV CAP/ISM ECO/TAC INT/TRADE ADMIN ATTIT DRIVE RIGID/FLEX PWR WEALTH ...MGT NEW/IDEA MATH TIME/SEQ VAL/FREE 20. PAGE 43 F0846
NAT/G FOR/AID

S60
HERZ J.H.,"EAST GERMANY: PROGRESS AND PROSPECTS." COM AGRI FINAN INDUS LOC/G NAT/G FORCES PLAN TEC/DEV DOMIN ADMIN COERCE DRIVE PERCEPT RIGID/FLEX MORAL ORD/FREE PWR...MARXIST PSY SOC RECORD STERTYP WORK. PAGE 59 F1158
POL/PAR STRUCT GERMANY

S60
HOOVER C.B.,"NATIONAL POLICY AND RATES OF ECONOMIC GROWTH: THE US SOVIET RUSSIA AND WESTERN EUROPE." COM EUR+WWI USA+45 USSR NAT/G PLAN ECO/TAC PWR WEALTH...MATH STAT GEN/LAWS 20. PAGE 61 F1207
ECO/DEV ACT/RES

S60
NANES A.,"THE EUROPEAN COMMUNITY AND THE UNITED STATES: EVOLVING RELATIONS." EUR+WWI USA+45 WOR+45 ECO/UNDEV MARKET NAT/G DELIB/GP PLAN LEGIT ATTIT PWR WEALTH...CONCPT STAT TIME/SEQ CON/ANAL EEC METH/GP OEEC 20 EURATOM. PAGE 96 F1889
INT/ORG REGION

S60
NEISSER H.,"ECONOMIC IMPERALISM RECONSIDERED." WOR+45 WOR-45 ECO/DEV ECO/UNDEV DIST/IND LEGIT COLONIAL PWR WEALTH SOCISM...MYTH MATH TIME/SEQ 20. PAGE 97 F1909
ACT/RES ECO/TAC CAP/ISM INT/TRADE

S60
OWEN C.F.,"US AND SOVIET RELATIONS WITH UNDERDEVELOPED COUNTRIES: LATIN AMERICA-A CASE STUDY." AFR COM L/A+17C USA+45 USSR EXTR/IND MARKET TEC/DEV DIPLOM ECO/TAC NAT/LISM ORD/FREE PWR ...TREND WORK 20. PAGE 102 F2005
ECO/UNDEV DRIVE INT/TRADE

S60
RICHTER J.H.,"TOWARDS AN INTERNATIONAL POLICY ON AGRICULTURAL TRADE." EUR+WWI USA+45 ECO/DEV NAT/G PLAN ECO/TAC ATTIT PWR WEALTH...CONCPT GEN/LAWS 20. PAGE 111 F2187
AGRI INT/ORG

B61
BARRASH J.,LABOR'S GRASS ROOTS; A STUDY OF THE LOCAL UNION. STRATA BARGAIN LEAD REPRESENT DEMAND ATTIT PWR. PAGE 10 F0192
LABOR USA+45 INGP/REL EXEC

B61
CAMPAIGNE J.G.,CHECK-OFF: LABOR BOSSES AND WORKING MEN. LEGIS WORKER EDU/PROP DEBATE COERCE REPRESENT GP/REL ORD/FREE CONSERVE. PAGE 21 F0404
LABOR ELITES PWR CONTROL

B61
DUKE UNIVERSITY,EXPULSION OR OPPRESSION OF BUSINESS ASSOCIATES: "SQUEEZE-OUTS" IN SMALL ENTERPRISES. LAW CONTROL PARTIC COERCE INGP/REL...POLICY RECORD INT. PAGE 35 F0674
PWR MGT SML/CO ECO/TAC

B61
ENGLER R.,THE POLITICS OF OIL. USA+45 CLIENT ELITES DOMIN EDU/PROP EXEC PWR 20. PAGE 38 F0734
LOBBY REPRESENT POLICY

B61
GORDON R.A.,BUSINESS LEADERSHIP IN THE LARGE CORPORATION. USA+45 SOCIETY EX/STRUC ADMIN CONTROL ROUTINE GP/REL PWR...MGT 20. PAGE 49 F0960
LG/CO LEAD DECISION LOBBY

B61
HARDT J.P.,THE COLD WAR ECONOMIC GAP. AFR USA+45 USSR ECO/DEV FORCES INT/TRADE NUC/PWR PWR 20. PAGE 55 F1081
DIPLOM ECO/TAC NAT/COMP POLICY

B61
HENDERSON W.O.,THE INDUSTRIAL REVOLUTION IN EUROPE. FRANCE GERMANY MOD/EUR RUSSIA WORKER PROFIT PWR MARXISM SOCISM...SOC HIST/WRIT 19 INDUS/REV. PAGE 58 F1148
INDUS REV CAP/ISM TEC/DEV

B61
KATKOFF U.,SOVIET ECONOMY 1940-1965. COM WOR+45 WOR-45 INTELL NAT/G POL/PAR TOP/EX ATTIT PWR ...POLICY TIME/SEQ VAL/FREE 20. PAGE 69 F1360
AGRI PERSON TOTALISM USSR

B61
KITZINGER V.W.,THE CHALLENGE OF THE COMMON MARKET. EUR+WWI ECO/DEV DIST/IND PLAN ECO/TAC INT/TRADE LEGIT ATTIT PWR WEALTH...TIME/SEQ TREND CHARTS EEC 20. PAGE 71 F1403
MARKET INT/ORG UK

B61
KOVNER M.,THE CHALLENGE OF COEXISTENCE: A STUDY OF SOVIET ECONOMIC DIPLOMACY. COM FUT ECO/DEV ECO/UNDEV PLAN EDU/PROP DETER SKILL...OBS VAL/FREE 20. PAGE 73 F1430
PWR DIPLOM USSR AFR

B61
MARX K.,THE COMMUNIST MANIFESTO. IN (MENDEL A. ESSENTIAL WORKS OF MARXISM, NEW YORK: BANTAM. FUT MOD/EUR CULTURE ECO/DEV ECO/UNDEV AGRI FINAN INDUS MARKET PROC/MFG LABOR POL/PAR CONSULT FORCES CREATE PLAN ADMIN ATTIT DRIVE RIGID/FLEX ORD/FREE PWR RESPECT MARX/KARL MUNICH WORK. PAGE 86 F1691
COM NEW/IDEA CAP/ISM REV

L61
GERWIG R.,"PUBLIC AUTHORITIES IN THE UNITED STATES." LAW CONSTN PROVS TAX ADMIN FEDERAL MUNICH. PAGE 47 F0920
LOC/G GOV/REL PWR

S61
BRAFF A.J.,"WAGE-PRICE POLICIES UNDER PUBLIC PRESSURE." USA+45 EX/STRUC LOBBY REPRESENT PWR 20. PAGE 17 F0335
ATTIT PARTIC PROB/SOLV

S61
DELLA PORT G.,"PROBLEMI E PROSPETTIVE DI COESISTENZA FRA ORIENTE ED OCCIDENTE, (PART 3)." COM FUT WOR+45 NAT/G BAL/PWR FOR/AID BAL/PAY PWR WEALTH...SOC CONCPT GEN/LAWS 20. PAGE 32 F0616
AFR INT/TRADE

S61
GALBRAITH J.K.,"A POSITIVE APPROACH TO ECONOMIC AID." FUT USA+45 INTELL NAT/G CONSULT ACT/RES DIPLOM ECO/TAC EDU/PROP ATTIT KNOWL PWR WEALTH ...SOC STERTYP MID/EX METH/GP 20. PAGE 45 F0883
ECO/UNDEV ROUTINE FOR/AID

S61
HAYTES W.,"THREE VIEWS ON THE SOVIET ECONOMIC THREAT." AFR COM USA+45 USA-45 USSR WOR+45 WOR-45 INDUS TEC/DEV ECO/TAC DOMIN ATTIT PERCEPT PWR FOR/TRADE 20. PAGE 57 F1128
ECO/DEV PLAN TOTALISM

S61
NEAL A.C.,"NEW ECONOMIC POLICIES FOR THE WEST." COM EUR+WWI FUT USA+45 WOR+45 ECO/DEV ECO/UNDEV INDUS MARKET ROUTINE HEALTH ORD/FREE PWR...OLD/LIB METH/CNCPT 20. PAGE 97 F1904
PLAN ECO/TAC

S61
REAGAN M.O.,"THE POLITICAL STRUCTURE OF THE FEDERAL RESERVE SYSTEM." USA+45 FINAN NAT/G ADMIN 20. PAGE 110 F2163
PWR EX/STRUC EXEC LEAD

S61
VINER J.,"ECONOMIC FOREIGN POLICY ON THE NEW FRONTIER." USA+45 ECO/UNDEV AGRI FINAN INDUS MARKET INT/ORG NAT/G FOR/AID INT/TRADE ADMIN ATTIT PWR 20 KENNEDY/JF. PAGE 141 F2786
TOP/EX ECO/TAC BAL/PAY TARIFFS

S61
WILDAVSKY A.,"POLITICAL IMPLICATIONS OF BUDGETARY REFORM." AFR NAT/G POL/PAR DELIB/GP EX/STRUC ATTIT PWR CONGRESS. PAGE 146 F2881
BUDGET PLAN LEGIS

N61
US ADVISORY COMN INTERGOV REL,STATE CONSTITUTIONAL AND STATUTORY RESTRICTIONS ON LOCAL GOVERNMENT DEBT (PAMPHLET). LAW CONSTN CHOOSE PWR...DECISION MUNICH. PAGE 133 F2631
TAX PROVS GOV/REL

B62
ARNOLD H.J.P.,AID FOR DEVELOPING COUNTRIES. COM EUR+WWI USA+45 USSR WOR+45 EDU/PROP ATTIT DRIVE PWR WEALTH...TREND CHARTS STERTYP NAT/ 20. PAGE 6 F0115
ECO/UNDEV ECO/TAC FOR/AID

B62
BROWN S.D.,STUDIES ON ASIA, 1962. ASIA BURMA INDIA ISLAM ISRAEL S/ASIA ECO/UNDEV POL/PAR SECT ECO/TAC ...ANTHOL 20 CHINJAP. PAGE 19 F0374
PWR PARL/PROC

B62
BRUMBERG A.,RUSSIA UNDER KHRUSHCHEV. FUT USSR SOCIETY ECO/DEV AGRI PERF/ART WORKER PWR...SOC
COM MARXISM

ANTHOL 20 KHRUSH/N. PAGE 20 F0377
NAT/G CHIEF

B62
CAIRNCROSS A.K.,FACTORS IN ECONOMIC DEVELOPMENT. WOR+45 ECO/UNDEV INDUS R+D LG/CO NAT/G EX/STRUC PLAN TEC/DEV ECO/TAC ATTIT HEALTH KNOWL PWR WEALTH ...TIME/SEQ GEN/LAWS TOT/POP TRUE/GP VAL/FREE 20. PAGE 21 F0399
MARKET ECO/DEV

B62
COX O.C.,CAPITALISM AND AMERICAN LEADERSHIP. WOR+45 WOR-45 STRATA INDUS SECT INT/TRADE EXEC INGP/REL RACE/REL RATIONAL PWR WEALTH. PAGE 28 F0548
CAP/ISM LEAD ECO/DEV SOCIETY

B62
DREIER J.C.,THE ALLIANCE FOR PROGRESS. L/A+17C USA+45 CULTURE ECO/DEV ECO/UNDEV NAT/G PLAN DIPLOM PWR 20 OAS ALL/PROG. PAGE 34 F0661
FOR/AID INT/ORG ECO/TAC POLICY

B62
ELLIOTT J.R.,THE APPEAL OF COMMUNISM IN THE UNDERDEVELOPED NATIONS. AFR USSR WOR+45 INT/ORG NAT/G DIPLOM DOMIN EDU/PROP ROUTINE ATTIT RIGID/FLEX ORD/FREE PWR WEALTH MARXISM...POLICY SOC METH/CNCPT MYTH TOT/POP METH/GP 20. PAGE 37 F0722
COM ECO/UNDEV

B62
FRIEDRICH-EBERT-STIFTUNG,THE SOVIET BLOC AND DEVELOPING COUNTRIES. CHINA/COM COM GERMANY/E USSR WOR+45 ECO/UNDEV INT/ORG NAT/G TEC/DEV NEUTRAL PWR ...POLICY 20. PAGE 44 F0868
MARXISM DIPLOM ECO/TAC FOR/AID

B62
GORT M.,DIVERSIFICATION AND INTEGRATION IN AMERICAN INDUSTRY. CLIENT DIST/IND PROC/MFG SERV/IND LG/CO CONTROL DEMAND PWR...METH/CNCPT STAT TREND CON/ANAL GP/COMP. PAGE 49 F0964
CONCPT GP/REL CLASSIF

B62
HIRSCHFIELD R.S.,THE CONSTITUTION AND THE COURT. AFR SCHOOL WAR RACE/REL EQUILIB ORD/FREE...POLICY MAJORIT DECISION JURID 18/20 PRESIDENT CIVIL/LIB SUPREME/CT CONGRESS. PAGE 60 F1175
ADJUD PWR CONSTN LAW

B62
HUMPHREY D.D.,THE UNITED STATES AND THE COMMON MARKET. USA+45 INDUS MARKET INT/ORG PLAN EDU/PROP BAL/PAY DRIVE PWR WEALTH...TREND STERTYP FOR/TRADE EEC 20. PAGE 63 F1241
ATTIT ECO/TAC

B62
KOLKO G.,WEALTH AND POWER IN AMERICA. USA+45 SOCIETY STRATA LG/CO ECO/TAC TAX PWR...SOC BIBLIOG 20 DEPRESSION. PAGE 72 F1420
STRUCT INCOME ECO/DEV WEALTH

B62
LITTLEFIELD N.,METROPOLITAN AREA PROBLEMS AND MUNICIPAL HOME RULE. USA+45 PROVS ADMIN CONTROL GP/REL PWR. PAGE 81 F1586
LOC/G SOVEREIGN JURID LEGIS

B62
MCCLELLAN J.L.,CRIME WITHOUT PUNISHMENT. USA+45 LAW SOCIETY DELIB/GP TRIBUTE CONTROL LOBBY COERCE GP/REL ANOMIE MORAL...CRIMLGY 20 CONGRESS HOFFA/J. PAGE 88 F1718
CRIME ACT/RES LABOR PWR

B62
SCHILLING W.R.,STRATEGY, POLITICS, AND DEFENSE BUDGETS. AFR USA+45 CHIEF LEGIS PLAN TEC/DEV BAL/PWR BUDGET NUC/PWR WAR CIVMIL/REL GOV/REL PWR 20 EISNHWR/DD. PAGE 117 F2297
NAT/G POLICY FORCES DETER

B62
SHERIF M.,INTERGROUP RELATIONS AND LEADERSHIP: APPROACHES AND RESEARCH IN INDUSTRIAL, ETHNIC, CULTURAL AND POLITICAL AREAS. CULTURE R+D LABOR DIPLOM GP/REL RACE/REL PERCEPT...PSY CONCPT. PAGE 121 F2377
LEAD REPRESENT PWR INGP/REL

L62
WATERSTON A.,"PLANNING IN MOROCCO, ORGANIZATION AND IMPLEMENTATION. BALTIMORE: HOPKINS ECON. DEVELOP. INT. BANK FOR." ISLAM ECO/DEV AGRI DIST/IND INDUS PROC/MFG SERV/IND LOC/G EX/STRUC ECO/TAC PWR WEALTH TOT/POP TRUE/GP METH/GP TERR/GP VAL/FREE 20. PAGE 144 F2829
NAT/G PLAN MOROCCO

S62
ALPERT P.,"ECONOMIC POLICIES AND PLANNING IN NEWLY INDEPENDENT AFRICA." PLAN ATTIT PWR WEALTH ...STERTYP GEN/LAWS VAL/FREE 20. PAGE 4 F0078
AFR ECO/DEV NAT/LISM COLONIAL

S62
ZAUBERMAN A.,"SOVIET AND CHINESE STRATEGY FOR ECONOMIC GROWTH." ASIA CHINA/COM COM USSR STRATA VOL/ASSN PLAN ATTIT PWR...METH/CNCPT GEN/LAWS WORK TERR/GP 20. PAGE 150 F2959
ECO/DEV EDU/PROP

B63
ABSHIRE D.M.,NATIONAL SECURITY: POLITICAL, MILITARY, AND ECONOMIC STRATEGIES IN THE DECADE AHEAD. ASIA COM USA+45 WOR+45 ECO/DEV ECO/UNDEV INT/ORG DELIB/GP FORCES ECO/TAC COERCE ATTIT RIGID/FLEX HEALTH ORD/FREE PWR WEALTH...POLICY STAT CHARTS ANTHOL COLD/WAR VAL/FREE APP/SCI. PAGE 2 F0032
FUT ACT/RES BAL/PWR

B63
BAUER R.A.,AMERICAN BUSINESS AND PUBLIC POLICY: THE POLITICS OF FOREIGN TRADE. USA+45 COM/IND LG/CO NAT/G PROF/ORG SML/CO VOL/ASSN LEGIS TOP/EX ECO/TAC EDU/PROP CHOOSE HEALTH PWR WEALTH...CONCPT METH/CNCPT OBS INT QU SAMP FOR/TRADE TRUE/GP VAL/FREE HI. PAGE 11 F0217
ECO/DEV ATTIT

B63
BELOFF M.,THE UNITED STATES AND THE UNITY OF EUROPE. EUR+WWI UK USA+45 WOR+45 VOL/ASSN DIPLOM REGION ATTIT PWR...CONCPT EEC OEEC 20 NATO. PAGE 13 F0239
ECO/DEV INT/ORG

B63
BONINI C.P.,SIMULATION OF INFORMATION AND DECISION SYSTEMS IN THE FIRM. MARKET BUDGET DOMIN EDU/PROP ADMIN COST ATTIT HABITAT PERCEPT PWR...CONCPT PROBABIL QUANT PREDICT HYPO/EXP BIBLIOG. PAGE 16 F0313
INDUS SIMUL DECISION MGT

B63
BURTT E.J. JR.,LABOR MARKETS, UNIONS, AND GOVERNMENT POLICIES. USA+45 MARKET NAT/G DELIB/GP CREATE BARGAIN GP/REL ORD/FREE PWR...POLICY CHARTS 20 AFL/CIO. PAGE 20 F0393
LABOR ECO/DEV CONTROL WORKER

B63
CHAMBERLAIN E.H.,THE ECONOMIC ANALYSIS OF LABOR UNION POWER (PAMPHLET). WORKER ECO/TAC DOMIN COERCE GP/REL DRIVE WEALTH POLICY. PAGE 23 F0441
LABOR PWR CONTROL

B63
CORLEY R.N.,THE LEGAL ENVIRONMENT OF BUSINESS. CONSTN LEGIS TAX ADMIN CT/SYS DISCRIM ATTIT PWR ...TREND 18/20. PAGE 28 F0537
NAT/G INDUS JURID DECISION

B63
DEUTSCH K.W.,THE POLITICAL ROLE OF LABOR IN DEVELOPING COUNTRIES. AFR ASIA S/ASIA USA+45 WOR+45 ECO/UNDEV POL/PAR ECO/TAC EDU/PROP LEGIT COERCE ORD/FREE PWR WEALTH...OBS INT TREND VAL/FREE 20. PAGE 32 F0625
LABOR NAT/LISM

B63
FRIEDRICH C.J.,MAN AND HIS GOVERNMENT: AN EMPIRICAL THEORY OF POLITICS. UNIV LOC/G NAT/G ADJUD REV INGP/REL DISCRIM PWR BIBLIOG. PAGE 44 F0867
PERSON ORD/FREE PARTIC CONTROL

B63
HATHAWAY D.A.,GOVERNMENT AND AGRICULTURE: PUBLIC POLICY IN A DEMOCRATIC SOCIETY. USA+45 LEGIS ADMIN EXEC LOBBY REPRESENT PWR 20. PAGE 57 F1111
AGRI GOV/REL PROB/SOLV EX/STRUC

B63
HYDE D.,THE PEACEFUL ASSAULT. COM UAR USSR ECO/DEV ECO/UNDEV NAT/G POL/PAR CAP/ISM PWR 20. PAGE 64 F1256
MARXISM CONTROL ECO/TAC DIPLOM

B63
JACOBS P.,STATE OF UNIONS. USA+45 STRATA TOP/EX GP/REL RACE/REL DEMAND DISCRIM ATTIT PWR 20 CONGRESS NEGRO HOFFA/J. PAGE 66 F1296
LABOR ECO/TAC BARGAIN DECISION

B63
KOLKO G.,THE TRIUMPH OF CONSERVATISM. USA-45 INDUS LG/CO NAT/G PWR 20 PRESIDENT CONGRESS MONOPOLY PROGRSV/M. PAGE 72 F1421
CONSERVE CAP/ISM FINAN MARKET

B63
LAGOS G.,INTERNATIONAL STRATIFICATION AND UNDERDEVELOPED COUNTRIES. L/A+17C WOR+45 PLAN ECO/TAC PWR RESPECT WEALTH...METH/CNCPT STAT CHARTS SIMUL GEN/LAWS TRUE/GP METH/GP VAL/FREE 20. PAGE 74 F1459
ECO/UNDEV STRATA

B63
LEWIN J.,POLITICS AND LAW IN SOUTH AFRICA. SOUTH/AFR UK POL/PAR BAL/PWR ECO/TAC COLONIAL CONTROL GP/REL DISCRIM PWR 20 NEGRO. PAGE 79 F1545
NAT/LISM POLICY LAW RACE/REL

B63
MCCONNELL G.,STEEL AND THE PRESIDENCY, 1962. USA+45 INDUS PROB/SOLV CONFER ROLE...POLICY 20 PRESIDENT. PAGE 88 F1722
PWR CHIEF REPRESENT DOMIN

B63
MINGAY G.E.,ENGLISH LANDED SOCIETY IN THE EIGHTEENTH CENTURY. UK ELITES STRUCT AGRI INDUS CONTROL WEALTH 18. PAGE 92 F1802
OWN STRATA PWR

B63
MULLENBACH P.,CIVILIAN NUCLEAR POWER: ECONOMIC ISSUES AND POLICY FORMATION. AFR FINAN INT/ORG DELIB/GP ACT/RES ECO/TAC ATTIT SUPEGO HEALTH ORD/FREE PWR...POLICY CONCPT MATH STAT CHARTS VAL/FREE 20. PAGE 94 F1855
USA+45 ECO/DEV NUC/PWR

B63
OTERO L.M.,HONDURAS. HONDURAS SPAIN STRUCT SECT COLONIAL REV WAR ATTIT PWR...GEOG WORSHIP 16/20. PAGE 102 F2003
NAT/G SOCIETY NAT/LISM ECO/UNDEV

B63
PELLING H.M.,A HISTORY OF BRITISH TRADE UNIONISM.
LABOR

UK ELITES ECO/DEV POL/PAR GP/REL PWR NEW/LIB 19/20. PAGE 104 F2051
VOL/ASSN NAT/G

B63
REAGAN M.D.,THE MANAGED ECONOMY. USA+45 INDUS LG/CO BUDGET GP/REL ORD/FREE PWR WEALTH 20. PAGE 110 F2161
PLAN ECO/DEV NAT/G ROLE

B63
SCHOECK H.,THE NEW ARGUMENT IN ECONOMICS. UK USA+45 INDUS MARKET LABOR NAT/G ECO/TAC ADMIN ROUTINE BAL/PAY PWR...POLICY BOLIV. PAGE 117 F2309
WELF/ST FOR/AID ECO/DEV ALL/IDEOS

B63
US ADVISORY COMN INTERGOV REL,PERFORMANCE OF URBAN FUNCTIONS: LOCAL AND AREAWIDE. TEC/DEV PARTIC REPRESENT PWR...DECISION GOV/COMP MUNICH. PAGE 133 F2633
REGION LOC/G ECO/TAC

L63
LIVERNASH E.R.,"THE RELATION OF POWER TO THE STRUCTURE AND PROCESS OF COLLECTIVE BARGAINING." ADJUD ORD/FREE...POLICY MGT CLASSIF GP/COMP. PAGE 81 F1589
LABOR GP/REL PWR ECO/TAC

L63
OLSON M. JR.,"RAPID ECONOMIC GROWTH AS A DESTABILIZING FORCE." WOR+45 WOR-45 STRATA ECO/UNDEV FAM KIN CREATE TEC/DEV DIPLOM PEACE ATTIT PERSON RIGID/FLEX PWR RESPECT WEALTH...SOC 20. PAGE 101 F1989
SOCIETY FOR/AID

S63
BELOFF M.,"BRITAIN, EUROPE AND THE ATLANTIC COMMUNITY." EUR+WWI ELITES NAT/G VOL/ASSN TOP/EX ATTIT ORD/FREE PWR SOVEREIGN WEALTH EEC TOT/POP VAL/FREE CMN/WLTH 20. PAGE 13 F0240
INT/ORG ECO/DEV UK

S63
BENOIT E.,"ECONOMIC ADJUSTMENTS TO ARMS CONTROL." FUT USA+45 NAT/G NUC/PWR WAR WEAPON 20. PAGE 13 F0251
ECO/DEV PWR ARMS/CONT

S63
BILL J.A.,"THE SOCIAL AND ECONOMIC FOUNDATIONS OF POWER IN CONTEMPORARY IRAN." ISLAM CULTURE NAT/G ECO/TAC DOMIN COERCE ATTIT PWR WEALTH...TREND VAL/FREE 20. PAGE 15 F0284
SOCIETY STRATA IRAN

S63
CLEMHOUT S.,"PRODUCTION FUNCTION ANALYSIS APPLIED TO THE LEONTIEF SCARCE-FACTOR PARADOX OF INTERNATIONAL TRADE." EUR+WWI USA+45 DIST/IND NAT/G PLAN TEC/DEV DIPLOM PWR WEALTH...MGT METH/CNCPT CONT/OBS CON/ANAL CHARTS SIMUL GEN/LAWS FOR/TRADE 20. PAGE 25 F0490
ECO/DEV ECO/TAC

S63
DIEBOLD W. JR.,"THE NEW SITUATION OF INTERNATIONAL TRADE POLICY." EUR+WWI FRANCE FUT UK USA+45 WOR+45 DIST/IND PLAN INT/TRADE EDU/PROP PWR WEALTH ...RECORD TREND GEN/LAWS EEC TRUE/GP VAL/FREE APPLIC 20. PAGE 33 F0636
MARKET ECO/TAC

S63
EMERSON R.,"THE ATLANTIC COMMUNITY AND THE EMERGING COUNTRIES." FUT WOR+45 ECO/DEV ECO/UNDEV R+D NAT/G DELIB/GP BAL/PWR ECO/TAC EDU/PROP ROUTINE ORD/FREE PWR WEALTH...POLICY CONCPT TREND GEN/METH EEC 20 NATO. PAGE 37 F0729
ATTIT INT/TRADE

S63
HALLSTEIN W.,"THE EUROPEAN COMMUNITY AND ATLANTIC PARTNERSHIP." EUR+WWI USA+45 MARKET NAT/G VOL/ASSN DELIB/GP ARMS/CONT NUC/PWR ATTIT PWR...CONCPT STAT TIME/SEQ TREND OEEC 20 EEC. PAGE 54 F1053
INT/ORG ECO/TAC UK

S63
MASON E.S.,"INTERESTS, IDEOLOGIES AND THE PROBLEM OF STABILITY AND GROWTH." EUR+WWI USA+45 DELIB/GP CREATE PLAN EXEC ROUTINE BAL/PAY ATTIT PWR...MGT CONCPT OEEC 20. PAGE 87 F1698
NAT/G ECO/DEV

S63
MONROE A.D.,"BRITAIN AND THE EUROPEAN COMMUNITY." EUR+WWI FRANCE NAT/G DELIB/GP TOP/EX ECO/TAC DOMIN PWR...POLICY RECORD GEN/LAWS EEC EFTA 20 EFTA CMN/WLTH. PAGE 93 F1817
VOL/ASSN ATTIT UK

S63
NADLER E.B.,"SOME ECONOMIC DISADVANTAGES OF THE ARMS RACE." AFR USA+45 INDUS R+D FORCES PLAN TEC/DEV ECO/TAC FOR/AID EDU/PROP PWR WEALTH...TREND FOR/TRADE 20. PAGE 96 F1886
ECO/DEV MGT BAL/PAY

S63
POLYANOV N.,"THE DOLLAR'S VENTURES IN EUROPE." EUR+WWI FRANCE USA+45 ECO/DEV MARKET POL/PAR TEC/DEV ECO/TAC EDU/PROP DRIVE PWR WEALTH...MARXIST MYTH STAT TREND EEC 20. PAGE 107 F2100
FINAN PLAN BAL/PAY CAP/ISM

S63
SCHURMANN F.,"ECONOMIC POLICY AND POLITICAL POWER IN COMMUNIST CHINA." ASIA CHINA/COM USSR SOCIETY ECO/UNDEV AGRI INDUS CREATE ADMIN ROUTINE ATTIT DRIVE RIGID/FLEX PWR WEALTH...HIST/WRIT TREND CHARTS WORK 20. PAGE 118 F2323
PLAN ECO/TAC

S63
TENNYSON L.B.,"THE USA IN ATLANTIC COMMUNITY." EUR+WWI FRANCE UK USA+45 ECO/UNDEV VOL/ASSN DELIB/GP TOP/EX DIPLOM DOMIN PWR...POLICY CONCPT TREND GEN/LAWS EEC 20. PAGE 129 F2545
ATTIT ECO/TAC BAL/PWR

S63
WOLFERS A.,"INTEGRATION IN THE WEST: THE CONFLICT OF PERSPECTIVES." AFR EUR+WWI USA+45 ECO/DEV INT/ORG DELIB/GP CREATE TEC/DEV DIPLOM ATTIT PWR ...CONCPT HIST/WRIT TREND GEN/LAWS EEC 20. PAGE 148 F2918
RIGID/FLEX ECO/TAC

B64
BAUCHET P.,ECONOMIC PLANNING. FRANCE STRATA LG/CO CAP/ISM ADMIN PARL/PROC DEMAND OPTIMAL ATTIT PWR SOCISM...POLICY CHARTS 20. PAGE 11 F0212
ECO/DEV NAT/G PLAN ECO/TAC

B64
CHEIT E.F.,THE BUSINESS ESTABLISHMENT. FRANCE WOR+45 PROF/ORG TOP/EX PROB/SOLV CAP/ISM ADMIN SUPEGO MORAL PWR...METH/CNCPT MYTH NEW/IDEA 20. PAGE 24 F0460
PERSON EX/STRUC MGT INDUS

B64
ECONOMIDES C.P.,LE POUVOIR DE DECISION DES ORGANISATIONS INTERNATIONALES EUROPEENNES. DIPLOM DOMIN INGP/REL EFFICIENCY...INT/LAW JURID 20 NATO OEEC EEC COUNCL/EUR EURATOM. PAGE 36 F0698
INT/ORG PWR DECISION GP/COMP

B64
GARDNER L.C.,ECONOMIC ASPECTS OF NEW DEAL DIPLOMACY. USA-45 WOR-45 LAW ECO/DEV INT/ORG NAT/G VOL/ASSN LEGIS TOP/EX EDU/PROP ORD/FREE PWR WEALTH ...POLICY TIME/SEQ VAL/FREE 20 ROOSEVLT/F. PAGE 46 F0901
ECO/TAC DIPLOM

B64
HACKER A.,THE CORPORATION TAKE-OVER. CONSTN LABOR PLAN BAL/PWR CONTROL EXEC LOBBY REPRESENT GP/REL ROLE ORD/FREE POLICY. PAGE 52 F1025
LG/CO STRUCT PWR

B64
HEKHUIS D.J.,INTERNATIONAL STABILITY: MILITARY, ECONOMIC AND POLITICAL DIMENSIONS. FUT WOR+45 LAW ECO/UNDEV INT/ORG NAT/G VOL/ASSN FORCES ACT/RES BAL/PWR PWR WEALTH...STAT UN 20. PAGE 58 F1143
TEC/DEV DETER REGION

B64
LUTHULI A.,AFRICA'S FREEDOM. KIN LABOR POL/PAR SCHOOL DIPLOM NEUTRAL REGION REV NAT/LISM PWR WEALTH SOCISM SOC/INTEG 20. PAGE 82 F1608
AFR ECO/UNDEV COLONIAL

B64
MANN B.,STATE CONSTITUTIONAL RESTRICTIONS ON LOCAL BORROWING AND PROPERTY TAXING POWERS. USA+45 CONSTN PROVS CT/SYS GOV/REL PWR...DECISION JURID CHARTS 20. PAGE 84 F1654
LOC/G TAX FINAN LAW

B64
MANSFIELD E.,MONOPOLY POWER AND ECONOMIC PERFORMANCE: AN INTRODUCTION TO A CURRENT ISSUE OF PUBLIC POLICY. ECO/DEV INDUS NAT/G PLAN CAP/ISM PRICE CONTROL LOBBY EFFICIENCY PRODUC...POLICY 20 CONGRESS KENNEDY/JF MONOPOLY. PAGE 85 F1659
LG/CO PWR ECO/TAC MARKET

B64
MARKHAM J.W.,THE COMMON MARKET: FRIEND OR COMPETITOR. AFR EUR+WWI FUT USA+45 INT/ORG LG/CO NAT/G VOL/ASSN DELIB/GP EX/STRUC PLAN TARIFFS ORD/FREE PWR WEALTH...POLICY STAT TREND EEC VAL/FREE 20. PAGE 85 F1671
ECO/DEV ECO/TAC

B64
PAARLBERG D.,AMERICAN FARM POLICY: A CASE STUDY IN CENTRALIZED DECISION-MAKING. USA+45 NAT/G LEGIS LOBBY REPRESENT GOV/REL PWR LAISSEZ 20. PAGE 102 F2009
PROB/SOLV EX/STRUC AGRI

B64
PRESTHUS R.,MEN AT THE TOP; A STUDY IN COMMUNITY POWER. USA+45 STRUCT ACT/RES REPRESENT CONSEN ALL/VALS ORD/FREE...SAMP/SIZ 20. PAGE 108 F2116
PLURISM LG/CO PWR ADMIN

B64
RENO P.,THE ORDEAL OF BRITISH GUIANA. L/A+17C USA+45 STRUCT AGRI EXTR/IND INDUS NAT/G FOR/AID ORD/FREE...GEOG 20 GUIANA/BR INTRVN/ECO. PAGE 111 F2178
COLONIAL ECO/UNDEV SOCISM PWR

B64
SAKAI R.K.,STUDIES ON ASIA, 1964. ASIA CHINA/COM ISRAEL MALAYSIA S/ASIA USA+45 USSR ECO/UNDEV FAM POL/PAR SECT CONSULT NAT/LISM...POLICY SOC 20 CHINJAP. PAGE 115 F2272
PWR DIPLOM

B64
SEGAL R.,SANCTIONS AGAINST SOUTH AFRICA. AFR SOUTH/AFR NAT/G INT/TRADE RACE/REL PEACE PWR ...INT/LAW ANTHOL 20 UN. PAGE 119 F2342
SANCTION DISCRIM ECO/TAC POLICY

B64
STOESSINGER J.G.,FINANCING THE UNITED NATIONS SYSTEM. FUT WOR+45 CONSTN NAT/G VOL/ASSN DELIB/GP EX/STRUC ECO/TAC LEGIT CT/SYS PWR WEALTH...STAT TIME/SEQ TREND CHARTS TRUE/GP METH/GP TERR/GP VAL/FREE. PAGE 126 F2493
FINAN INT/ORG

B64
WITHERS W.,THE ECONOMIC CRISIS IN LATIN AMERICA. BRAZIL CHILE STRATA AGRI DIPLOM FOR/AID PWR SOCISM ...POLICY 20 MEXIC/AMER ARGEN ALL/PROG. PAGE 148 F2914
L/A+17C ECO/UNDEV CAP/ISM ALL/IDEOS

B64
WRIGHT G.,RURAL REVOLUTION IN FRANCE: THE PEASANTRY PWR

IN THE TWENTIETH CENTURY. EUR+WWI MOD/EUR LAW CULTURE AGRI POL/PAR DELIB/GP LEGIS ECO/TAC EDU/PROP COERCE CHOOSE ATTIT RIGID/FLEX HEALTH ...STAT CENSUS CHARTS VAL/FREE 20. PAGE 149 F2932
STRATA FRANCE REV

L64
HAAS E.B.,"ECONOMICS AND DIFFERENTIAL PATTERNS OF POLITICAL INTEGRATION: PROJECTIONS ABOUT UNITY IN LATIN AMERICA." SOCIETY NAT/G DELIB/GP ACT/RES CREATE PLAN ECO/TAC REGION ROUTINE ATTIT DRIVE PWR WEALTH...CONCPT TREND CHARTS LAFTA TERR/GP 20. PAGE 52 F1020
L/A+17C INT/ORG MARKET

S64
CLELLAND D.A.,"ECONOMIC DOMINANTS AND COMMUNITY POWER: A COMPARATIVE ANALYSIS." ELITES ADJUST ATTIT WEALTH...DECISION MUNICH. PAGE 25 F0488
LEAD MGT PWR

S64
DOE J.F.,"TROPICAL AFRICAN CONTRIBUTIONS TO FEDERAL FINANCE." AFR NAT/G PROVS CENTRAL RIGID/FLEX PWR WEALTH...STAT VAL/FREE 20 CMN/WLTH. PAGE 33 F0650
FINAN ECO/TAC

S64
HOOVER C.B.,"THE ROLE OF THE NATURAL AND DEVELOPED RESOURCES OF THE NATION STATES." FUT WOR+45 ECO/DEV ECO/UNDEV NAT/G PWR RESPECT SKILL WEALTH...POLICY GEOG TIME/SEQ TREND RESOURCE/N VAL/FREE 20. PAGE 62 F1210
EXTR/IND DOMIN

S64
HOWE M.,"THE TRANSPORT ACT, 1962, AND THE CONSUMERS' CONSULTATIVE COMMITTEES." UK CONFER EXEC PWR 20. PAGE 62 F1225
PARTIC REPRESENT DELIB/GP DIST/IND

S64
MC WILLIAM M.,"THE WORLD BANK AND THE TRANSFER OF POWER IN KENYA." AFR ECO/UNDEV CONSULT ACT/RES TEC/DEV PERCEPT PWR SKILL WEALTH...CONCPT OBS TREND 20. PAGE 88 F1715
NAT/G ECO/TAC

S64
PADELFORD N.J.,"THE ORGANIZATION OF AFRICAN UNITY." ECO/UNDEV INT/ORG PLAN BAL/PWR DIPLOM ECO/TAC NAT/LISM ORD/FREE PWR WEALTH...CONCPT TREND STERTYP TERR/GP VAL/FREE 20. PAGE 102 F2013
AFR VOL/ASSN REGION

S64
PESELT B.M.,"COMMUNIST ECONOMIC OFFENSIVE." WOR+45 SOCIETY INT/ORG PLAN ECO/TAC DOMIN EDU/PROP ATTIT PERSON PWR WEALTH...TREND CHARTS METH/GP 20. PAGE 105 F2067
COM ECO/UNDEV FOR/AID USSR

S64
POLARIS J.,"THE SINO-SOVIET DISPUTE: ITS ECONOMIC IMPACT ON CHINA." ASIA CHINA/COM COM WOR+45 NAT/G ATTIT PWR WEALTH...STAT TREND FOR/TRADE 20. PAGE 107 F2095
ECO/UNDEV ECO/TAC

S64
RUSSETT B.M.,"INEQUALITY AND INSTABILITY: THE RELATION OF LAND TENURE TO POLITICS." WOR+45 ECO/DEV ECO/UNDEV AGRI NAT/G COERCE PWR...MATH STAT CHARTS GEN/LAWS TERR/GP TRUE/GP METH/GP VAL/FREE 20. PAGE 115 F2263
WEALTH GEOG ECO/TAC ORD/FREE

B65
APTER D.E.,THE POLITICS OF MODERNIZATION. AFR L/A+17C CULTURE NAT/G POL/PAR ADMIN COLONIAL NAT/LISM ATTIT RIGID/FLEX PWR...SOC CONCPT. PAGE 6 F0109
ECO/UNDEV GEN/LAWS STRATA CREATE

B65
BOCK E.,GOVERNMENT REGULATION OF BUSINESS. USA+45 LAW EX/STRUC LEGIS EXEC ORD/FREE PWR...ANTHOL CONGRESS. PAGE 16 F0303
MGT ADMIN NAT/G CONTROL

B65
BOLLENS J.C.,THE METROPOLIS: ITS PEOPLE, POLITICS, AND ECONOMIC LIFE. USA+45 PLAN PROB/SOLV PERS/REL PWR...DECISION GEOG CENSUS TREND CON/ANAL MUNICH 20 NEWYORK/C LOS/ANG SAN/FRAN CHICAGO PHILADELPH. PAGE 16 F0309
HABITAT SOC LOC/G

B65
DANIELSON M.N.,FEDERAL-METROPOLITAN POLITICS AND THE COMMUTER CRISIS. PROVS LEGIS EXEC LEAD PWR ...DECISION MUNICH. PAGE 30 F0580
FEDERAL GOV/REL DIST/IND

B65
GREENFIELD K.R.,ECONOMICS AND LIBERALISM IN THE RISORGIMENTO (REV. ED.). ITALY AGRI FINAN PROC/MFG PLAN INT/TRADE CONTROL PWR 19. PAGE 51 F0990
NAT/LISM PRESS POLICY

B65
KISSINGER H.A.,THE TROUBLED PARTNERSHIP* RE-APPRAISAL OF THE WESTERN ALLIANCE. EUR+WWI USA+45 INT/ORG NAT/G VOL/ASSN TOP/EX DIPLOM ORD/FREE PWR NATO. PAGE 71 F1402
FRANCE NUC/PWR ECO/DEV

B65
LYONS G.M.,AMERICA: PURPOSE AND POWER. UK USA+45 FINAN INDUS MARKET WORKER TEC/DEV DIPLOM AUTOMAT NUC/PWR WAR RACE/REL ORD/FREE 20 EEC CONGRESS SUPREME/CT CIV/RIGHTS. PAGE 82 F1617
PWR PROB/SOLV ECO/DEV TASK

B65
MACDONALD R.W.,THE LEAGUE OF ARAB STATES: A STUDY IN THE DYNAMICS OF REGIONAL ORGANIZATION. ISRAEL UAR USSR FINAN INT/ORG DELIB/GP ECO/TAC AGREE NEUTRAL ORD/FREE PWR...DECISION BIBLIOG 20 TREATY UN. PAGE 83 F1626
ISLAM REGION DIPLOM ADMIN

B65
PAYNE J.L.,LABOR AND POLITICS IN PERU; THE SYSTEM OF POLITICAL BARGAINING. PERU CONSTN VOL/ASSN EX/STRUC LEAD PWR...CHARTS 20. PAGE 104 F2042
LABOR POL/PAR BARGAIN GP/REL

B65
PLOSS S.I.,CONFLICT AND DECISION-MAKING IN SOVIET RUSSIA - A CASE STUDY OF AGRICULTURAL POLICY - 1953-1963. USSR DELIB/GP INGP/REL PWR MARXISM. PAGE 106 F2093
AGRI DECISION ATTIT

B65
THORNTON A.P.,DOCTRINES OF IMPERIALISM. WOR+45 WOR-45 DOMIN NAT/LISM PROFIT ATTIT PERSON PWR RESPECT SOVEREIGN...CONCPT STERTYP. PAGE 130 F2571
IDEA/COMP COLONIAL DRIVE

B65
WEIDENBAUM M.L.,CONGRESS AND THE FEDERAL BUDGET. FINAN ACT/RES DOMIN CONFER EXEC UTIL PWR NEW/LIB ...CHARTS CONGRESS. PAGE 144 F2844
BUDGET LEGIS PLAN DECISION

S65
HADDAD W.F.,"MR. SHRIVER AND THE SAVAGE POLITICS OF POVERTY" USA+45 LAW NAT/G DELIB/GP LEGIS GIVE LEAD CENTRAL PWR...SOC/WK CHARTS 20 CONGRESS POVRTY/WAR SHRIVER/S OEO. PAGE 53 F1028
WEALTH GOV/REL CONTROL TOP/EX

S65
HAYTER T.,"FRENCH AID TO AFRICA* ITS SCOPE AND ACHIEVEMENTS." CULTURE ECO/TAC INT/TRADE ADMIN REGION CENTRAL FEDERAL LOVE PWR SOVEREIGN EEC. PAGE 57 F1127
AFR FRANCE FOR/AID COLONIAL

S65
JOHNSON H.G.,"A THEORETICAL MODEL OF ECONOMIC NATIONALISM IN NEW AND DEVELOPING STATES." ELITES INDUS INT/TRADE EDU/PROP COST OPTIMAL RATIONAL PWR WEALTH SOCISM STERTYP. PAGE 67 F1325
NAT/LISM ECO/UNDEV GEN/LAWS

S65
JOHNSON L.L.,"US BUSINESS INTERESTS IN CUBA AND THE RISE OF CASTRO." L/A+17C USA+45 ECO/UNDEV INDUS NAT/G VOL/ASSN ATTIT ORD/FREE PWR WEALTH ALL/PROG. PAGE 68 F1330
DIPLOM CUBA ECO/TAC INT/TRADE

S65
TENDLER J.D.,"TECHNOLOGY AND ECONOMIC DEVELOPMENT* THE CASE OF HYDRO VS THERMAL POWER." CONSTRUC DIST/IND CREATE TEC/DEV INT/TRADE CENTRAL PWR SKILL WEALTH...MGT NAT/COMP ARGEN. PAGE 129 F2544
BRAZIL INDUS ECO/UNDEV

S65
WHITAKER A.P.,"ARGENTINA: STRUGGLE FOR RECOVERY." L/A+17C USA+45 NAT/G TOP/EX PLAN LEGIT COERCE REV RIGID/FLEX PWR WEALTH...RECORD ALL/PROG ARGEN FOR/TRADE 20. PAGE 146 F2867
POL/PAR ECO/TAC NAT/LISM

S65
WILDAVSKY A.,"TVA AND POWER POLITICS." USA+45 CLIENT PROB/SOLV EXEC GOV/REL 20. PAGE 146 F2882
PWR EX/STRUC LOBBY

C65
MANSFIELD H.C.,"THE CONGRESS AND ECONOMIC POLICY" IN C. TRUMAN ED., THE CONGRESS AND AMERICA'S FUTURE." USA+45 USA-45 CONSTN NAT/G BUDGET ADMIN CONTROL EXEC LOBBY. PAGE 85 F1661
POLICY ECO/TAC PWR LEGIS

B66
ANDERSON J.E.,POLITICS AND THE ECONOMY. NAT/G LOBBY PWR 20. PAGE 5 F0096
REPRESENT EX/STRUC CONTROL

B66
COOK P.W. JR.,PROBLEMS OF CORPORATE POWER. WOR+45 FINAN INDUS BARGAIN GP/REL...MGT ANTHOL. PAGE 27 F0530
ADMIN LG/CO PWR ECO/TAC

B66
DAVIES I.,AFRICAN TRADE UNIONS. AFR ECO/UNDEV INT/ORG GP/REL ORD/FREE SOVEREIGN SOCISM 20. PAGE 30 F0585
LABOR COLONIAL PWR INDUS

B66
ECKSTEIN A.,COMMUNIST CHINA'S ECONOMIC GROWTH AND FOREIGN TRADE* IMPLICATIONS FOR US POLICY. COM USA+45 USSR STRUCT INDUS MARKET DIPLOM ECO/TAC FOR/AID INT/TRADE...STAT CHARTS. PAGE 36 F0696
ASIA ECO/UNDEV CREATE PWR

B66
FRIEDMANN W.G.,INTERNATIONAL FINANCIAL AID. USA+45 ECO/DEV ECO/UNDEV NAT/G VOL/ASSN EX/STRUC PLAN RENT GIVE BAL/PAY PWR...GEOG INT/LAW STAT TREND UN EEC COMECON. PAGE 44 F0866
INT/ORG FOR/AID TEC/DEV ECO/TAC

B66
LENSKI G.E.,POWER AND PRIVILEGE: A THEORY OF SOCIAL STRATIFICATION. SWEDEN UK UNIV USSR CULTURE ECO/UNDEV PRIVIL PWR...PHIL/SCI CONCPT CHARTS IDEA/COMP HYPO/EXP METH MARX/KARL. PAGE 78 F1525
SOC STRATA STRUCT SOCIETY

B66
LONDON K.,EASTERN EUROPE IN TRANSITION. CHINA/COM USSR DOMIN COLONIAL CENTRAL RIGID/FLEX PWR...SOC ANTHOL 20. PAGE 82 F1597
SOVEREIGN COM NAT/LISM DIPLOM

B66
ODEGARD P.H.,POLITICAL POWER AND SOCIAL CHANGE. UNIV NAT/G CREATE ALL/IDEOS...POLICY GEOG SOC CENSUS TREND. PAGE 100 F1962
PWR TEC/DEV IDEA/COMP

B66
RAPHAEL J.S.,GOVERNMENTAL REGULATION OF BUSINESS. USA+45 LAW CONSTN TAX ADJUD ADMIN EFFICIENCY PWR 20. PAGE 109 F2150
LG/CO GOV/REL CONTROL ECO/DEV

B66
RAYBACK J.G.,A HISTORY OF AMERICAN LABOR. USA+45 USA-45 ECO/DEV LEGIS COLONIAL WAR INGP/REL PWR WEALTH 17/20. PAGE 110 F2156
LABOR LOBBY ECO/UNDEV NAT/G

B66
ROSS A.M.,INDUSTRIAL RELATIONS AND ECONOMIC DEVELOPMENT. POL/PAR LEGIS WORKER BARGAIN PRICE EXEC LOBBY INCOME PWR...DECISION ANTHOL BIBLIOG 20. PAGE 114 F2243
ECO/UNDEV LABOR NAT/G GP/REL

B66
WECHSBERG J.,THE MERCHANT BANKERS. EUR+WWI MOD/EUR CONTROL...BIOG GP/COMP PERS/COMP 16/20. PAGE 144 F2842
FINAN PWR WEALTH FAM

B66
ZINKIN T.,CHALLENGES IN INDIA. INDIA PAKISTAN LAW AGRI FINAN INDUS TOP/EX TEC/DEV CONTROL ROUTINE ORD/FREE PWR 20 NEHRU/J SHASTRI/LB CIVIL/SERV. PAGE 150 F2964
NAT/G ECO/TAC POLICY ADMIN

S66
LANGLEY D.,"POSTSCRIPT ON THE COLONIZATION OF THE INTERNATIONAL TRADE UNION MOVEMENT" USA+45 ELITES FINAN DOMIN LEGIT ADMIN PWR...SOCIALIST 20 AFL/CIO CIA LOVESTN/J. PAGE 75 F1479
INT/TRADE LABOR NAT/G CONTROL

S66
ROTHCHILD D.,"THE LIMITS OF FEDERALISM: AN EXAMINATION OF POLITICAL INSTITUTIONAL TRANSFER IN AFRICA." AFR CONSTN CULTURE ELITES ECO/UNDEV KIN PROB/SOLV ADMIN ORD/FREE PWR...POLICY 20. PAGE 114 F2250
FEDERAL NAT/G NAT/LISM COLONIAL

B67
BEATON L.,THE STRUGGLE FOR PEACE. INT/ORG FORCES NUC/PWR COST PWR...POLICY TREND 20. PAGE 12 F0225
PEACE BAL/PWR DIPLOM WAR

B67
CLEGERN W.M.,BRITISH HONDURAS: COLONIAL DEAD END, 1859-1900. HONDURAS AGRI FINAN PROB/SOLV INT/TRADE PWR WEALTH...BIBLIOG/A 19. PAGE 25 F0487
COLONIAL POLICY ECO/UNDEV DOMIN

B67
DE TORRES J.,FINANCING LOCAL GOVERNMENT. USA+45 USA-45 NAT/G PROVS GIVE ADJUST PWR...TIME/SEQ CHARTS MUNICH 20. PAGE 31 F0606
LOC/G BUDGET TAX TREND

B67
EBENSTEIN W.,TODAY'S ISMS: COMMUNISM, FASCISM, CAPITALISM, SOCIALISM (5TH ED.). COM WOR+45 PERCEPT PWR...SOC TREND IDEA/COMP NAT/COMP 20. PAGE 35 F0691
FASCISM MARXISM SOCISM CAP/ISM

B67
EGGERT G.G.,RAILROAD LABOR DISPUTES. USA+45 USA-45 ELITES DIST/IND DELIB/GP FORCES JUDGE WORKER PROB/SOLV DOMIN PWR...POLICY 20. PAGE 36 F0707
GP/REL NAT/G LABOR BARGAIN

B67
GORZ A.,STRATEGY FOR LABOR: A RADICAL PROPOSAL (TRANS. BY MARTIN NICOLAUS AND VICTORIA ORTIZ). EUR+WWI FRANCE ITALY ECO/DEV POL/PAR OP/RES PLAN GP/REL ALL/IDEOS...SOC 20 EEC. PAGE 49 F0965
LABOR PWR STRUCT ECO/TAC

B67
GRIFFITH W.E.,SINO-SOVIET RELATIONS, 1964-1965. CHINA/COM COM USSR CHIEF 20. PAGE 51 F1001
DIPLOM PWR DOMIN MARXISM

B67
HEILBRONER R.L.,THE LIMITS OF AMERICAN CAPITALISM. FUT ECO/DEV INDUS LG/CO EX/STRUC LEAD PWR TECHRACY 20. PAGE 58 F1137
ELITES CREATE TEC/DEV CAP/ISM

B67
MCNELLY T.,SOURCES IN MODERN EAST ASIAN HISTORY AND POLITICS. KOREA VIETNAM CULTURE DIPLOM COLONIAL REV WAR PWR ALL/IDEOS MARXISM...ANTHOL 20 CHINJAP. PAGE 88 F1733
NAT/COMP ASIA S/ASIA SOCIETY

B67
MEYNAUD J.,TRADE UNIONISM IN AFRICA; A STUDY OF ITS GROWTH AND ORIENTATION (TRANS. BY ANGELA BRENCH). INT/ORG PROB/SOLV COLONIAL PWR...TIME/SEQ TREND ILO. PAGE 90 F1774
LABOR AFR NAT/LISM ORD/FREE

B67
NYOMARKAY J.,CHARISMA AND FACTIONALISM IN THE NAZI PARTY. GERMANY POL/PAR LEGIT LEAD MARXISM ...NEW/IDEA METH/COMP GEN/LAWS BIBLIOG 20 HITLER/A. PAGE 99 F1949
FASCISM INGP/REL CHIEF PWR

B67
POWLEDGE F.,BLACK POWER WHITE RESISTANCE. USA+45 STRUCT PLAN GP/REL DISCRIM HABITAT ORD/FREE WEALTH ...METH/COMP SOC/INTEG NEGRO. PAGE 107 F2111
RACE/REL ATTIT PWR

B67
REHMUS C.M.,LABOR AND AMERICAN POLITICS. POL/PAR WORKER EDU/PROP PARTIC ATTIT PWR. PAGE 110 F2175
LABOR ROLE LOBBY

B67
SCHECTER J.,THE NEW FACE OF BUDDHA: BUDDHISM AND POLITICAL POWER IN SOUTHEAST ASIA. S/ASIA NAT/G POL/PAR NAT/LISM ATTIT MARXISM...BIBLIOG 20. PAGE 116 F2292
SECT POLICY PWR LEAD

B67
TANSKY L.,US AND USSR AID TO DEVELOPING COUNTRIES. INDIA TURKEY USA+45 USSR INDUS PLAN CAP/ISM WAR PWR WEALTH MARXISM...CHARTS NAT/COMP BIBLIOG 20. PAGE 128 F2534
ECO/UNDEV FOR/AID DIPLOM ECO/TAC

B67
WESSON R.G.,THE IMPERIAL ORDER. WOR-45 STRUCT SECT DOMIN ADMIN COLONIAL LEAD CONSERVE...CONCPT BIBLIOG 20. PAGE 145 F2861
PWR CHIEF CONTROL SOCIETY

B67
YOUNG J.M.,THE BRAZILIAN REVOLUTION OF 1930 AND THE AFTERMATH. BRAZIL COLONIAL PWR...BIBLIOG/A 16/20. PAGE 150 F2951
PLAN CHIEF FORCES REV

L67
AFFELDT R.J.,"THE INDEPENDENT LABOR UNION AND THE GOOD LIFE." USA+45 ADJUD CONTROL SANCTION GP/REL ORD/FREE JURID. PAGE 3 F0045
LABOR CT/SYS PWR SOVEREIGN

L67
MCALLISTER J.T. JR.,"THE POSSIBILITIES FOR DIPLOMACY IN SOUTHEAST ASIA." LAOS VIETNAM INT/ORG NAT/G PROVS BAL/PWR DOMIN AGREE COLONIAL WAR PWR 17/20 TREATY. PAGE 88 F1716
DIPLOM S/ASIA

L67
TANDON Y.,"CONSENSUS AND AUTHORITY BEHIND UNITED NATIONS PEACEKEEPING OPERATIONS." FINAN VOL/ASSN BUDGET DIPLOM PAY DOMIN...CHARTS 20 UN. PAGE 128 F2528
CONSEN INT/ORG PWR PEACE

L67
WHITNEY S.N.,"MERGERS, CONGLOMERATES, AND OLIGOPOLIES* A WIDENING OF ANTI TRUST TARGETS." LAW NAT/G TEC/DEV CAP/ISM GP/REL PWR...OLD/LIB 20. PAGE 146 F2873
ECO/TAC INDUS JURID

S67
"IMPORT-EXPORT CLAUSE: A BLANKET PROHIBITION MISAPPLIED." USA+45 INT/TRADE ADJUD INCOME PWR 20. PAGE 2 F0029
CONSTN TAX PROVS LAW

S67
AGUILAR M.A.,"?UNA OEA MAS FUERTE O UNA AMERICA LATINA MAS DEBIL?" L/A+17C USA+45 USA-45 ECO/UNDEV INDUS CHIEF DELIB/GP FORCES CONTROL PWR 20 OAS KENNEDY/JF JOHNSON/LB. PAGE 3 F0050
INT/ORG DIPLOM POLICY COLONIAL

S67
ALEXANDER R.J.,"'THIRD FORCE' IN WORLD COMMUNISM?" CHINA/COM CUBA USSR INT/ORG DIPLOM TASK INGP/REL ATTIT PWR 20 CASTRO/F. PAGE 3 F0060
CHIEF MARXISM LEAD REV

S67
ALVES V.,"FOREIGN CAPITAL IN BRAZIL." BRAZIL USA+45 CAP/ISM DIPLOM ECO/TAC INT/TRADE CONTROL PWR ...POLICY 20. PAGE 4 F0081
ECO/UNDEV FINAN SOCIALIST SOCISM

S67
BAILEY S.L.,"THE ITALIANS AND ORGANIZED LABOR IN THE UNITED STATES AND ARGENTINA: 1880-1910." ITALY USA-45 PARTIC HABITAT PWR...GEOG GP/COMP 19/20 ARGEN. PAGE 8 F0153
LABOR LEAD WEALTH GP/REL

S67
EDWARDS N.,"EDUCATION IN THE FEDERAL-STATE STRUCTURE OF GOVERNMENT." USA+45 SECT CONTROL GOV/REL RACE/REL DISCRIM FEDERAL ROLE PWR SOVEREIGN. PAGE 36 F0705
EDU/PROP NAT/G PROVS POLICY

S67
GORMAN W.,"ELLUL - A PROPHETIC VOICE." WOR+45 ELITES SOCIETY ACT/RES PLAN BAL/PWR DOMIN CONTROL PARTIC TOTALISM PWR 20. PAGE 49 F0963
CREATE ORD/FREE EX/STRUC UTOPIA

S67
GRAHAM R.,"BRAZIL'S DILEMMA." BRAZIL FUT L/A+17C NAT/G CHIEF PROB/SOLV ECO/TAC PWR 20. PAGE 50 F0972
ECO/UNDEV CONSTN POL/PAR POLICY

S67
HALL B.,"THE COALITION AGAINST DISHWASHERS." USA+45 POL/PAR PROB/SOLV BARGAIN LEAD CHOOSE REPRESENT GP/REL ORD/FREE PWR...POLICY 20. PAGE 53 F1044
LABOR ADMIN DOMIN WORKER

S67
IBARRA J.,"EL EXPERIMENTO CUBANO." COM CUBA L/A+17C USA+45 ECO/UNDEV LEGIS INT/TRADE CONTROL REV NAT/LISM PWR 19/20 TREATY. PAGE 64 F1259
COLONIAL DIPLOM NAT/G POLICY

S67
KOHN W.S.G.,"THE SOVEREIGNTY OF LIECHTENSTEIN."
SOVEREIGN

LIECHTENST SWITZERLND USSR CONSTN DEBATE WAR CONSERVE 18/20 UN. PAGE 72 F1417
NAT/G PWR DIPLOM

S67
KRAUS J.,"A MARXIST IN GHANA." GHANA ELITES CHIEF PROB/SOLV TEC/DEV DIPLOM ECO/TAC COLONIAL PARTIC PWR 20 NKRUMAH/K. PAGE 73 F1432
MARXISM PLAN ATTIT CREATE

S67
LEMIEUX V.,"LA DIMENSION POLITIQUE DE L'ACTION RATIONNELLE." CONTROL GP/REL PERS/REL...DECISION NEW/IDEA GAME 20. PAGE 77 F1518
GEN/LAWS RATIONAL PWR

S67
LEVIN T.,"PSYCHOANALYSIS AND SOCIAL CHANGE." SOCIETY ANOMIE DRIVE PWR 20. PAGE 79 F1541
PSY PHIL/SCI ADJUST WEALTH

S67
LOSMAN D.L.,"FOREIGN AID, SOCIALISM AND THE EMERGING COUNTRIES" WOR+45 ADMIN CONTROL PWR 20. PAGE 82 F1602
ECO/UNDEV FOR/AID SOC

S67
PETRAS J.,"GUERRILLA MOVEMENTS IN LATIN AMERICA - I." GUATEMALA PERU VENEZUELA NAT/G COLONIAL LEAD ATTIT PWR...TIME/SEQ METH/COMP 20 COLOMB. PAGE 105 F2072
GUERRILLA REV L/A+17C MARXISM

S67
PFEFFERMANN G.,"TRADE UNIONS AND POLITICS IN FRENCH WEST AFRICA DURING THE FOURTH REPUBLIC." AFR INDUS POL/PAR COLONIAL ATTIT PWR 20. PAGE 106 F2077
PARTIC DRIVE INT/TRADE LABOR

S67
RONY V.,"HEARTBREAK IN TENNESSEE* POOR WHITES AND THE UNIONS." LAW STRUCT CAP/ISM ADJUD GP/REL. PAGE 113 F2236
LABOR LOC/G WORKER PWR

S67
SEIDLER G.L.,"MARXIST LEGAL THOUGHT IN POLAND." POLAND SOCIETY R+D LOC/G NAT/G ACT/RES ADJUD CT/SYS SUPEGO PWR...SOC TREND 20 MARX/KARL. PAGE 119 F2343
MARXISM LAW CONCPT EFFICIENCY

S67
SIMONE A.J.,"SCIENTIFIC PUBLIC POLICY, MARKET PERFORMANCE, AND SIZE OF FIRM." GP/REL COST EFFICIENCY OPTIMAL PRODUC PWR. PAGE 122 F2410
LAW INDUS NAT/G PROB/SOLV

N67
US SENATE COMM ON FOREIGN REL,WAR OR PEACE IN THE MIDDLE EAST (PAMPHLET). GREECE ISLAM ISRAEL JORDAN UAR CHIEF PROB/SOLV FOR/AID WAR PWR 20 SENATE. PAGE 139 F2739
DIPLOM FORCES PLAN

B96
MARX K.,REVOLUTION AND COUNTER-REVOLUTION. GERMANY CONSTN ELITES INDUS NAT/G DIPLOM ECO/TAC WEALTH. PAGE 86 F1693
MARXIST REV PWR STRATA

B96
SCHMOLLER G.,THE MERCANTILE SYSTEM AND ITS HISTORICAL SIGNIFICANCE: ILLUSTRATED CHIEFLY FROM PRUSSIAN HISTORY (TRANS.). PRUSSIA CULTURE INDUS KIN NAT/G PROVS OP/RES ECO/TAC INT/TRADE SUPEGO PWR WEALTH MUNICH 19 MERCANTLST. PAGE 117 F2302
GEN/METH INGP/REL CONCPT

PYE L.W. F2132,F2133

Q

QU....QUESTIONNAIRES; SEE ALSO QUESTIONNAIRES INDEX, P. XIV

S45
MILLS C.W.,"THE TRADE UNION LEADER: A COLLECTIVE PORTRAIT." EX/STRUC TOP/EX INGP/REL...QU CON/ANAL CHARTS. PAGE 92 F1798
LABOR LEAD STAT STRATA

S50
EBY K.,"RESEARCH IN LABOR UNIONS." EDU/PROP INGP/REL PWR...METH/CNCPT OBS. PAGE 36 F0693
RECORD QU LABOR PARTIC

B52
ROSE A.M.,UNION SOLIDARITY: THE INTERNAL COHESION OF A LABOR UNION. SECT GP/REL RACE/REL ATTIT ROLE HEALTH WEALTH...INT QU. PAGE 114 F2241
LABOR INGP/REL PARTIC SUPEGO

S52
KLUMB S.,"EMPLOYEE DETERMINATION OF MANAGERIAL FUNCTIONS AND CHARACTERISTICS." DELIB/GP WORKER PARTIC ROUTINE INGP/REL...CLASSIF OBS QU. PAGE 72 F1410
MGT INDUS EX/STRUC CHOOSE

B56
LIPSET S.M.,UNION DEMOCRACY. STRUCT INDUS FACE/GP WORKER CONTROL LEAD PARTIC GP/REL ATTIT LAISSEZ ...INT QU CHARTS. PAGE 80 F1577
LABOR INGP/REL MAJORIT

B56
UPHOFF W.H.,UNDERSTANDING THE UNION MEMBER (PAMPHLET). STRATA R+D LEAD PARTIC...METH/CNCPT STAT QU. PAGE 133 F2624
LABOR WORKER ATTIT DRIVE

S56
TANNENBAUM A.S.,"CONTROL OF STRUCTURE AND UNION FUNCTIONS." PARTIC GP/REL INGP/REL CONSEN ATTIT PWR ...QU SAMP. PAGE 128 F2529
LABOR STRUCT CONTROL LEAD

S57
KAHN R.L.,"UNION PRACTICES AND MEMBER PARTICIPATION." PARTIC CHOOSE REPRESENT PERS/REL PERSON SKILL...DECISION METH/CNCPT QU. PAGE 69 F1347
INGP/REL LABOR ATTIT LEAD

S57
TANNENBAUM A.S.,"ORGANIZATIONAL CONTROL STRUCTURE: A GENERAL DESCRIPTIVE TECHNIQUE AS APPLIED TO FOUR LOCAL UNIONS." LABOR PWR...METH/CNCPT CLASSIF QU CHARTS. PAGE 128 F2530
WORKER PARTIC STRUCT CONTROL

S59
SHEPPARD H.L.,"THE POLITICAL ATTITUDES AND PREFERENCES OF UNION MEMBERS: THE CASE OF THE DETROIT AUTO WORKERS." LOBBY CHOOSE ROLE...CLASSIF QU SAMP TREND. PAGE 120 F2376
LABOR ATTIT WORKER

S60
FORM W.H.,"ORGANIZED LABOR'S IMAGE OF COMMUNITY POWER STRUCTURE." LABOR LG/CO CONTROL LEAD REPRESENT...DECISION METH/CNCPT INT QU SAMP. PAGE 42 F0829
NEIGH PARTIC PWR GP/REL

B62
KAUTSKY J.H.,POLITICAL CHANGE IN UNDERDEVELOPED COUNTRIES: NATIONALISM AND COMMUNISM. WOR+45 AGRI TEC/DEV EDU/PROP ATTIT...POLICY METH/CNCPT STYLE INT QU CENSUS TREND SOC/EXP GEN/LAWS 20. PAGE 69 F1365
ECO/UNDEV SOCIETY CAP/ISM REV

B63
BAUER R.A.,AMERICAN BUSINESS AND PUBLIC POLICY: THE POLITICS OF FOREIGN TRADE. USA+45 COM/IND LG/CO NAT/G PROF/ORG SML/CO VOL/ASSN LEGIS TOP/EX ECO/TAC EDU/PROP CHOOSE HEALTH PWR WEALTH...CONCPT METH/CNCPT OBS INT QU SAMP FOR/TRADE TRUE/GP VAL/FREE HI. PAGE 11 F0217
ECO/DEV ATTIT

S63
GRUSHIN B.A.,"PROBLEMS OF THE MOVEMENT OF COMMUNIST LABOR IN THE USSR." COM SOCIETY LABOR ECO/TAC EDU/PROP COERCE RIGID/FLEX ORD/FREE...POLICY MARXIST STAT QU WORK 20. PAGE 52 F1011
ATTIT USSR

B64
SULLIVAN G.,THE STORY OF THE PEACE CORPS. USA+45 WOR+45 INTELL FACE/GP NAT/G SCHOOL VOL/ASSN CONSULT EX/STRUC PLAN EDU/PROP ADMIN ATTIT DRIVE ALL/VALS ...POLICY HEAL SOC CONCPT INT QU BIOG TREND SOC/EXP WORK. PAGE 127 F2511
INT/ORG ECO/UNDEV FOR/AID PEACE

B65
DELHI INSTITUTE OF ECO GROWTH,A STUDY IN THE WORKING OF THE INTENSIVE AREA SCHEME OF THE KHADI AND VILLAGE INDUSTRIES COMMISSION. INDIA AGRI FINAN DELIB/GP ECO/TAC EFFICIENCY...QU CHARTS MUNICH 20. PAGE 32 F0614
PLAN INDUS ECO/UNDEV

B65
DERBER M.,PLANT UNION-MANAGEMENT RELATIONS: FROM PRACTICE TO THEORY. PROC/MFG NEIGH PROB/SOLV ORD/FREE...DECISION MGT OBS QU SAMP. PAGE 32 F0621
LG/CO LABOR GP/REL ATTIT

B65
DUGGAR G.S.,RENEWAL OF TOWN AND VILLAGE I: A WORLD-WIDE SURVEY OF LOCAL GOVERNMENT EXPERIENCE. WOR+45 CONSTRUC INDUS CREATE BUDGET REGION GOV/REL...QU NAT/COMP MUNICH 20 URBAN/RNWL. PAGE 35 F0673
NEIGH PLAN ADMIN

B65
SCHECHTER A.,THE BUSINESSMAN IN GOVERNMENT (THESIS, COLUMBIA UNIVERSITY). USA+45 CONFER GP/REL PERSON ...QU 20 PRESIDENT TRUMAN/HS CABINET. PAGE 116 F2291
INDUS NAT/G EX/STRUC DELIB/GP

B66
POLK J.,U S PRODUCTION ABROAD AND THE BALANCE OF PAYMENTS* A SURVEY OF CORPORATE INVESTMENT EXPERIENCE. USA+45 SERV/IND NAT/G OP/RES COST PROFIT ATTIT...ECOMETRIC STAT INT QU GEN/METH. PAGE 107 F2096
BAL/PAY FINAN INT/TRADE INDUS

S66
VERSLUYS J.D.N.,"SOME NOTES ON THE SOCIAL AND ECONOMIC EFFECTS OF RURAL ELECTRIFICATION IN BURMA" BURMA EDU/PROP PRODUC ORD/FREE...SOC QU MUNICH TIME 20. PAGE 141 F2782
TEC/DEV SOCIETY CREATE

B67
BANFIELD E.C.,THE MORAL BASIS OF A BACKWARD SOCIETY. EUR+WWI ITALY STRATA NEIGH PARTIC INGP/REL ...SOC QU PREDICT TREND HYPO/EXP MUNICH 20. PAGE 9 F0173
MORAL WEALTH ATTIT

S67
ADAMS E.S.,"THE EXPANDING ROLE OF BANKS IN PUBLIC AFFAIRS." USA+45 GIVE LEAD ROLE...QU 20. PAGE 2 F0036
PARTIC FINAN LOC/G ATTIT

QU/SEMANT....SEMANTIC AND SOCIAL PROBLEMS OF QUESTIONNAIRES

B63
RUMMEL J.F.,RESEARCH METHODOLOGY IN BUSINESS.
OP/RES

COMPUTER CREATE PROB/SOLV...CONT/OBS REC/INT QU/SEMANT SYS/QU SAMP CHARTS METH/COMP T 20. PAGE 115 F2260 — METH/CNCPT METH STAT

QUAKER....QUAKER

QUANT....QUANTIFICATION

B31
JEVONS W.S.,THE THEORY OF POLITICAL ECONOMY (4TH ED.; 1ST ED. 1871). WOR-45 FINAN MARKET RENT WEALTH ...LOG MATH QUANT CON/ANAL IDEA/COMP BIBLIOG METH 17/19. PAGE 67 F1318 — GEN/LAWS UTIL LABOR

B50
SURANYI-UNGER T.,PRIVATE ENTERPRISE AND GOVERNMENTAL PLANNING. STRUCT FINAN BAL/PWR HAPPINESS DRIVE NEW/LIB PLURISM...MATH QUANT STAT TREND BIBLIOG. PAGE 127 F2516 — PLAN NAT/G LAISSEZ POLICY

B52
ALEXANDROWICZ C.H.,INTERNATIONAL ECONOMIC ORGANIZATION. WOR+45 ECO/DEV ECO/UNDEV DIST/IND FINAN MARKET PLAN ECO/TAC LEGIT DRIVE WEALTH ...POLICY CONCPT QUANT OBS TIME/SEQ GEN/LAWS WORK METH/GP EEC ILO OEEC UNESCO 20. PAGE 4 F0063 — INT/ORG INT/TRADE

S59
DUNNING J.H.,"NON-PECUNIARY ELEMENTS AND BUSINESS BEHAVIOUR." PLAN PROB/SOLV COST...METH/CNCPT CLASSIF QUANT STAT. PAGE 35 F0681 — DECISION DRIVE PRODUC PRICE

S60
BARNETT H.J.,"RESEARCH AND DEVELOPMENT, ECONOMIC GROWTH, AND NATIONAL SECURITY." AFR USA+45 R+D CREATE ECO/TAC ATTIT DRIVE PWR...POLICY SOC METH/CNCPT QUANT STAT TIME/SEQ ORG/CHARTS LOG/LING 20. PAGE 10 F0190 — ACT/RES PLAN

B62
GERSCHENKRON A.,ECONOMIC BACKWARDNESS IN HISTORICAL PERSPECTIVE. WOR+45 WOR-45 ECO/DEV ECO/UNDEV INDUS NAT/G LEGIT DRIVE...WELF/ST DECISION QUANT TREND CHARTS 20. PAGE 47 F0919 — TEC/DEV USSR

S62
BIERMAN H.,"PROBABILITY, STATISTICAL DECISION THEORY, AND ACCOUNTING." ACADEM TASK EFFICIENCY ...METH/CNCPT GEN/METH 20. PAGE 15 F0283 — FINAN QUANT DECISION STAT

B63
BONINI C.P.,SIMULATION OF INFORMATION AND DECISION SYSTEMS IN THE FIRM. MARKET BUDGET DOMIN EDU/PROP ADMIN COST ATTIT HABITAT PERCEPT PWR...CONCPT PROBABIL QUANT PREDICT HYPO/EXP BIBLIOG. PAGE 16 F0313 — INDUS SIMUL DECISION MGT

S63
MATHUR P.N.,"GAINS IN ECONOMIC GROWTH FROM INTERNATIONAL TRADE." USA-45 ECO/DEV FINAN INDUS ATTIT WEALTH...MATH QUANT STAT BIOG TREND GEN/LAWS WORK 20. PAGE 87 F1704 — MARKET ECO/TAC CAP/ISM INT/TRADE

L64
BHAGWATI J.,"THE PURE THEORY OF INTERNATIONAL TRADE: A SURVEY." WOR+45 ECO/DEV ECO/UNDEV FINAN MARKET PROC/MFG INT/ORG LABOR LG/CO NAT/G TEC/DEV ECO/TAC SKILL WEALTH...POLICY RELATIV MGT CONCPT NEW/IDEA MATH QUANT GEN/LAWS FOR/TRADE 20. PAGE 14 F0276 — INDUS HYPO/EXP

S64
BEIM D.,"THE COMMUNIST BLOC AND THE FOREIGN-AID GAME." AFR WOR+45 NAT/G PLAN ROUTINE ATTIT KNOWL ORD/FREE...DECISION QUANT CONT/OBS TIME/SEQ CHARTS GAME SIMUL LOG/LING 20. PAGE 12 F0231 — COM ECO/UNDEV ECO/TAC FOR/AID

B65
HICKMAN B.G.,QUANTITATIVE PLANNING OF ECONOMIC POLICY. FRANCE NETHERLAND OP/RES PRICE ROUTINE UTIL ...POLICY DECISION ECOMETRIC METH/CNCPT STAT STYLE CHINJAP. PAGE 59 F1162 — PROB/SOLV PLAN QUANT

B65
PINCUS J.A.,ECONOMIC AID AND INTERNATIONAL COST SHARING* A RAND CORPORATION RESEARCH STUDY. INT/ORG BUDGET CENTRAL...ECOMETRIC MATH QUANT STAT SIMUL. PAGE 106 F2088 — ECO/UNDEV COST FOR/AID INT/TRADE

B65
WATERSTON A.,DEVELOPMENT PLANNING* LESSONS OF EXPERIENCE. ECO/TAC CENTRAL...MGT QUANT BIBLIOG. PAGE 144 F2830 — ECO/UNDEV CREATE PLAN ADMIN

B67
KREININ M.E.,ALTERNATIVE COMMERCIAL POLICIES - THEIR EFFECT ON THE AMERICAN ECONOMY. USA+45 LAW ECO/DEV MARKET INT/ORG DIPLOM ECO/TAC TARIFFS PRICE DEMAND WEALTH...QUANT EEC AFTA. PAGE 73 F1437 — INT/TRADE BAL/PAY NAT/G POLICY

QUANTIFICATION....SEE QUANT

QUANTITATIVE CONTENT ANALYSIS....SEE CON/ANAL

QUEBEC....QUEBEC, CANADA

QUESTIONNAIRES....SEE QU

QURESHI S. F2134

R

R+D....RESEARCH AND DEVELOPMENT GROUP

N
SOUTH AFRICAN JOURNAL OF ECONOMICS. SOUTH/AFR FINAN MARKET ACT/RES OP/RES...PHIL/SCI STAT CON/ANAL METH/COMP BIBLIOG/A 20. PAGE 1 F0009 — ECO/UNDEV ACADEM INTELL R+D

N
AMERICAN ECONOMIC ASSOCIATION,THE JOURNAL OF ECONOMIC ABSTRACTS. ECO/UNDEV MARKET LABOR DIPLOM ...MGT CONCPT METH 20. PAGE 5 F0086 — BIBLIOG/A R+D FINAN

N
US LIBRARY OF CONGRESS,SELECTED AND ANNOTATED BIBLIOGRAPHY ON AGRICULTURAL PROBLEMS AND POLICIES IN A WARTIME ECONOMY (PAMPHLET). R+D WORKER PRODUC 20. PAGE 137 F2706 — BIBLIOG/A WAR AGRI EXTR/IND

N19
LAWRENCE S.A.,THE BATTERY ADDITIVE CONTROVERSY (PAMPHLET). USA+45 LAW MARKET PROC/MFG R+D CAP/ISM CT/SYS GOV/REL OWN FTC CONGRESS BUR/STNDRD RITCHIE/JM. PAGE 76 F1494 — PHIL/SCI LOBBY INSPECT

B47
WHITEHEAD T.N.,LEADERSHIP IN A FREE SOCIETY; A STUDY IN HUMAN RELATIONS BASED ON AN ANALYSIS OF PRESENT-DAY INDUSTRIAL CIVILIZATION. WOR-45 STRUCT R+D LABOR LG/CO SML/CO WORKER PLAN PROB/SOLV TEC/DEV DRIVE...MGT 20. PAGE 146 F2872 — INDUS LEAD ORD/FREE SOCIETY

B51
HARDMAN J.B.,THE HOUSE OF LABOR. LAW R+D NEIGH EDU/PROP LEAD ROUTINE REPRESENT GP/REL...POLICY STAT. PAGE 55 F1080 — LABOR LOBBY ADMIN PRESS

B53
DAHL R.A.,POLITICS, ECONOMICS AND WELFARE: PLANNING AND POLITICOECONOMIC SYSTEMS RESOLVED INTO BASIC SOCIAL PROCESSES. WOR+45 WOR-45 ECO/DEV ECO/UNDEV R+D CREATE PLAN TEC/DEV EDU/PROP HEALTH WEALTH ...SOC SELF/OBS TREND CHARTS GEN/METH 20. PAGE 29 F0571 — ECO/TAC PHIL/SCI

B56
UN HEADQUARTERS LIBRARY,BIBLIOGRAPHY OF INDUSTRIALIZATION IN UNDERDEVELOPED COUNTRIES (BIBLIOGRAPHICAL SERIES NO. 6). WOR+45 R+D ACADEM INT/ORG NAT/G. PAGE 132 F2602 — BIBLIOG ECO/UNDEV TEC/DEV

B56
UNITED NATIONS,BIBLIOGRAPHY ON INDUSTRIALIZATION IN UNDER-DEVELOPED COUNTRIES. WOR+45 R+D INT/ORG NAT/G FOR/AID ADMIN LEAD 20 UN. PAGE 132 F2612 — BIBLIOG ECO/UNDEV INDUS TEC/DEV

B56
UPHOFF W.H.,UNDERSTANDING THE UNION MEMBER (PAMPHLET). STRATA R+D LEAD PARTIC...METH/CNCPT STAT QU. PAGE 133 F2624 — LABOR WORKER ATTIT DRIVE

B56
US DEPARTMENT OF STATE,ECONOMIC PROBLEMS OF UNDERDEVELOPED AREAS (PAMPHLET). AFR ASIA ISLAM L/A+17C AGRI FINAN INDUS INT/ORG LABOR INT/TRADE ...PSY SOC 20. PAGE 136 F2673 — BIBLIOG ECO/UNDEV TEC/DEV R+D

L57
MASS. INST. TECH.,"THE CENTER FOR INTERNATIONAL STUDIES." AFR ASIA COM EUR+WWI ISLAM L/A+17C S/ASIA USA+45 USA-45 DIST/IND CONSULT FORCES ACT/RES TEC/DEV DIPLOM REV ATTIT WEALTH...CONCPT FOR/TRADE 20. PAGE 87 F1702 — R+D ECO/UNDEV

B58
HANCE W.A.,AFRICAN ECONOMIC DEVELOPMENT. AGRI DIST/IND INDUS R+D ACT/RES PLAN CAP/ISM FOR/AID ...GOV/COMP BIBLIOG 20. PAGE 54 F1058 — AFR ECO/UNDEV PROB/SOLV TEC/DEV

B58
SILOW R.A.,THE POTENTIAL CONTRIBUTION OF ATOMIC ENERGY TO DEVELOPMENT IN AGRICULTURE AND RELATED INDUSTRIES (PAMPHLET). WOR+45 R+D TEC/DEV EFFICIENCY 20 UN. PAGE 122 F2403 — NUC/PWR ECO/UNDEV AGRI

B60
FRYE R.J.,GOVERNMENT AND LABOR: THE ALABAMA PROGRAM. USA+45 INDUS R+D LABOR WORKER BUDGET EFFICIENCY AGE/Y HEALTH...CHARTS 20 ALABAMA. PAGE 45 F0870 — ADMIN LEGIS LOC/G PROVS

B60
HITCH C.J.,THE ECONOMICS OF DEFENSE IN THE NUCLEAR AGE. USA+45 WOR+45 CREATE PLAN NUC/PWR ATTIT ...CON/ANAL CHARTS HYPO/EXP NATO 20. PAGE 60 F1179 — R+D FORCES

B60
SILK L.S.,THE RESEARCH REVOLUTION. USA+45 FINAN CAP/ISM ECO/TAC PRICE EQUILIB PRODUC...STAT TREND CHARTS. PAGE 122 F2402 — ECO/DEV R+D TEC/DEV PROB/SOLV

S60
BARNETT H.J.,"RESEARCH AND DEVELOPMENT, ECONOMIC GROWTH, AND NATIONAL SECURITY." AFR USA+45 R+D CREATE ECO/TAC ATTIT DRIVE PWR...POLICY SOC METH/CNCPT QUANT STAT TIME/SEQ ORG/CHARTS LOG/LING — ACT/RES PLAN

20. PAGE 10 F0190

S60
BAUM M.,"THE CASE FOR BUSINESS CIVILIZATION." R+D CAP/ISM GIVE EDU/PROP HAPPINESS...SOC TREND. PAGE 12 F0218
MGT CULTURE WEALTH

S60
BECKER A.S.,"COMPARISIONS OF UNITED STATES AND USSR NATIONAL OUTPUT: SOME RULES OF THE GAME." COM USA+45 ECO/DEV AGRI DIST/IND INDUS R+D CONSULT PLAN ECO/TAC RIGID/FLEX KNOWL...METH/CNCPT CHARTS 20. PAGE 12 F0227
STAT USSR

S60
JAFFEE A.J.,"POPULATION TRENDS AND CONTROLS IN UNDERDEVELOPED COUNTRIES." AFR FUT ISLAM L/A+17C S/ASIA CULTURE R+D FAM ACT/RES PLAN EDU/PROP BIO/SOC RIGID/FLEX HEALTH...SOC STAT OBS CHARTS 20. PAGE 66 F1303
ECO/UNDEV GEOG

S60
MILLER A.S.,"SOME OBSERVATIONS ON THE POLITICAL ECONOMY OF POPULATION GROWTH." FUT USA+45 ECO/DEV R+D CONSULT PLAN TEC/DEV ECO/TAC ROUTINE BIO/SOC WEALTH...POLICY OBS. PAGE 91 F1790
SOCIETY GEOG

B61
LANDSKROY W.A.,OFFICIAL SERIAL PUBLICATIONS RELATING TO ECONOMIC DEVELOPMENT IN AFRICA SOUTH OF THE SAHARA (PAMPHLET). AFR UK R+D ACT/RES 20 UN. PAGE 75 F1471
BIBLIOG ECO/UNDEV COLONIAL INT/ORG

B61
SACKS S.,FINANCING GOVERNMENT IN A METROPOLITAN GOVERNMENT. USA+45 ECO/DEV R+D LOC/G GOV/REL ...BIBLIOG MUNICH 20 CLEVELAND. PAGE 115 F2269
FINAN PLAN BUDGET

B61
SHARP W.R.,FIELD ADMINISTRATION IN THE UNITED NATION SYSTEM: THE CONDUCT OF INTERNATIONAL ECONOMIC AND SOCIAL PROGRAMS. FUT WOR+45 CONSTN SOCIETY ECO/UNDEV R+D DELIB/GP ACT/RES PLAN TEC/DEV EDU/PROP EXEC ROUTINE HEALTH WEALTH...HUM CONCPT CHARTS METH ILO UNESCO GP VAL/FREE UN 20. PAGE 120 F2369
INT/ORG CONSULT

S61
BENOIT E.,"THE PROPENSITY TO REDUCE THE NATIONAL DEBT OUT OF DEFENSE SAVINGS." FUT USA+45 SOCIETY R+D PLAN...WELF/ST SOC REC/INT STERTYP TOT/POP 20. PAGE 13 F0250
WEALTH ECO/TAC

B62
BROOKINGS INSTITUTION,DEVELOPMENT OF THE EMERGING COUNTRIES; AN AGENDA FOR RESEARCH. WOR+45 AGRI TEC/DEV FOR/AID EDU/PROP ADJUST HABITAT KNOWL...PSY SOC ANTHOL 20 THIRD/WRLD. PAGE 19 F0362
ECO/UNDEV R+D SOCIETY PROB/SOLV

B62
CAIRNCROSS A.K.,FACTORS IN ECONOMIC DEVELOPMENT. WOR+45 ECO/UNDEV INDUS R+D LG/CO NAT/G EX/STRUC PLAN TEC/DEV ECO/TAC ATTIT HEALTH KNOWL PWR WEALTH ...TIME/SEQ GEN/LAWS TOT/POP TRUE/GP VAL/FREE 20. PAGE 21 F0399
MARKET ECO/DEV

B62
DUPRE J.S.,SCIENCE AND THE NATION: POLICY AND POLITICS. USA+45 LAW ACADEM FORCES ADMIN CIVMIL/REL GOV/REL EFFICIENCY PEACE...TREND 20 SCI/ADVSRY. PAGE 35 F0682
R+D INDUS TEC/DEV NUC/PWR

B62
HATTERY L.H.,INFORMATION RETRIEVAL MANAGEMENT. CLIENT INDUS TOP/EX COMPUTER OP/RES TEC/DEV ROUTINE COST EFFICIENCY RIGID/FLEX...METH/COMP ANTHOL 20. PAGE 57 F1113
R+D COMPUT/IR MGT CREATE

B62
NATIONAL BUREAU ECONOMIC RES,THE RATE AND DIRECTION OF INVENTIVE ACTIVITY: ECONOMIC AND SOCIAL FACTORS. STRUCT INDUS MARKET R+D CREATE OP/RES TEC/DEV EFFICIENCY PRODUC RATIONAL UTIL...WELF/ST PHIL/SCI METH/CNCPT TIME. PAGE 97 F1895
DECISION PROB/SOLV MGT

B62
SHERIF M.,INTERGROUP RELATIONS AND LEADERSHIP: APPROACHES AND RESEARCH IN INDUSTRIAL, ETHNIC, CULTURAL AND POLITICAL AREAS. CULTURE R+D LABOR DIPLOM GP/REL RACE/REL PERCEPT...PSY CONCPT. PAGE 121 F2377
LEAD REPRESENT PWR INGP/REL

L62
BELSHAW D.G.R.,"PUBLIC INVESTMENT IN AGRICULTURE AND ECONOMIC DEVELOPMENT OF UGANDA" UGANDA AGRI INDUS R+D ECO/TAC RATION TAX PAY COLONIAL 20 WORLD/BANK. PAGE 13 F0242
ECO/UNDEV PLAN ADMIN CENTRAL

S62
IOVTCHOUK M.T.,"ON SOME THEORETICAL PRINCIPLES AND METHODS OF SOCIOLOGICAL INVESTIGATIONS (IN RUSSIAN)." FUT USA+45 STRATA R+D NAT/G POL/PAR TOP/EX ACT/RES PLAN ECO/TAC EDU/PROP ROUTINE ATTIT RIGID/FLEX MARXISM SOCISM...MARXIST METH/CNCPT OBS TREND NAT/COMP GEN/LAWS 20. PAGE 65 F1288
COM ECO/DEV CAP/ISM USSR

S62
KRISHNA K.G.V.,"PLANNING AND ECONOMIC DEVELOPMENT" AFR UGANDA AGRI INDUS R+D BUDGET RATION TAX COLONIAL 20. PAGE 73 F1441
ECO/UNDEV ECO/TAC NAT/LISM PLAN

C62
JOINT ECONOMIC COMMITTEE,"DIMENSIONS OF SOVIET ECONOMIC POWER." USSR R+D FORCES ACT/RES OP/RES TEC/DEV...GEOG STAT BIBLIOG 20. PAGE 68 F1337
ECO/DEV PLAN PRODUC LABOR

B63
GRUBEL H.G.,WORLD MONETARY REFORM: PLANS AND ISSUES. FUT WOR+45 ECO/DEV ECO/UNDEV R+D DELIB/GP CREATE ECO/TAC ATTIT RIGID/FLEX WEALTH...STAT ANTHOL VAL/FREE 20. PAGE 52 F1009
FINAN INT/ORG BAL/PAY INT/TRADE

B63
SALENT W.S.,THE UNITED STATES BALANCE OF PAYMENTS IN 1968. EUR+WWI UK USA+45 AGRI R+D LABOR FORCES PRODUC...GEOG CONCPT CHARTS 20 CHINJAP EEC. PAGE 115 F2274
BAL/PAY DEMAND FINAN INT/TRADE

S63
EMERSON R.,"THE ATLANTIC COMMUNITY AND THE EMERGING COUNTRIES." FUT WOR+45 ECO/DEV ECO/UNDEV R+D NAT/G DELIB/GP BAL/PWR ECO/TAC EDU/PROP ROUTINE ORD/FREE PWR WEALTH...POLICY CONCPT TREND GEN/METH EEC 20 NATO. PAGE 37 F0729
ATTIT INT/TRADE

S63
FOURASTIE J.,"LES SCIENCES ECONOMIQUES ET SOCIALES EN EUROPE." EUR+WWI FUT MOD/EUR WOR+45 WOR-45 INTELL SOCIETY R+D PLAN ROUTINE ATTIT RIGID/FLEX KNOWL...OBS TREND. PAGE 43 F0833
ACT/RES CULTURE

S63
GANDILHON J.,"LA SCIENCE ET LA TECHNIQUE A L'AIDE DES REGIONS PEU DEVELOPPEES." FRANCE FUT WOR+45 ECO/DEV R+D PROF/ORG ACT/RES PLAN...MGT TOT/POP VAL/FREE 20 UN. PAGE 46 F0893
ECO/UNDEV TEC/DEV FOR/AID

S63
GORDON B.,"ECONOMIC IMPEDIMENTS TO REGIONALISM IN SOUTH EAST ASIA." BURMA FUT S/ASIA THAILAND USA+45 AGRI INDUS R+D NAT/G PLAN ECO/TAC WEALTH...STAT CONT/OBS 20. PAGE 49 F0954
VOL/ASSN ECO/UNDEV INT/TRADE REGION

S63
LEDUC G.,"L'AIDE INTERNATIONALE AU DEVELOPPEMENT." FUT WOR+45 ECO/DEV ECO/UNDEV R+D PROF/ORG TEC/DEV ECO/TAC ROUTINE ATTIT ALL/VALS...MGT TIME/SEQ FOR/TRADE TOT/POP 20. PAGE 77 F1503
FINAN PLAN FOR/AID

S63
MARTHELOT P.,"PROGRES DE LA REFORME AGRAIRE." INTELL ECO/DEV R+D FOR/AID ADMIN KNOWL...OBS VAL/FREE UN 20. PAGE 86 F1680
AGRI INT/ORG

S63
NADLER E.B.,"SOME ECONOMIC DISADVANTAGES OF THE ARMS RACE." AFR USA+45 INDUS R+D FORCES PLAN TEC/DEV ECO/TAC FOR/AID EDU/PROP PWR WEALTH...TREND FOR/TRADE 20. PAGE 96 F1886
ECO/DEV MGT BAL/PAY

B64
BRIGHT J.R.,RESEARCH, DEVELOPMENT AND TECHNOLOGICAL INNOVATION. CULTURE R+D CREATE PLAN PROB/SOLV AUTOMAT RISK PERSON...DECISION CONCPT PREDICT BIBLIOG. PAGE 18 F0352
TEC/DEV NEW/IDEA INDUS MGT

B64
GUTMANN P.M.,ECONOMIC GROWTH: AN AMERICAN PROBLEM. USA+45 FINAN R+D...POLICY NAT/COMP ANTHOL BIBLIOG 20. PAGE 52 F1016
WEALTH ECO/DEV CAP/ISM ORD/FREE

B64
LANGHOFF P.,MODELS, MEASUREMENT AND MARKETING. ACT/RES COMPUTER OP/RES PLAN BUDGET...MGT PHIL/SCI METH/CNCPT STAT PROG/TEAC BIBLIOG. PAGE 75 F1478
DECISION SIMUL MARKET R+D

B64
ORGANIZATION AMERICAN STATES,ECONOMIC SURVEY OF LATIN AMERICA, 1962. L/A+17C AGRI DIST/IND INDUS MARKET PROC/MFG R+D PLAN TEC/DEV ECO/TAC REGION BAL/PAY ALL/VALS...CON/ANAL ORG/CHARTS GEN/METH OAS ALL/PROG 20 ALL/PROG. PAGE 102 F1998
ECO/UNDEV CHARTS

L64
CARNEGIE ENDOWMENT INT. PEACE,"ECONOMIC AND SOCIAL QUESTION (ISSUES BEFORE THE NINETEENTH GENERAL ASSEMBLY)." WOR+45 ECO/DEV ECO/UNDEV INDUS R+D DELIB/GP CREATE PLAN TEC/DEV ECO/TAC FOR/AID BAL/PAY...RECORD UN 20. PAGE 21 F0414
INT/ORG INT/TRADE

B65
PEACE RESEARCH ABSTRACTS. FUT WOR+45 R+D INT/ORG NAT/G PLAN TEC/DEV BAL/PWR DIPLOM FOR/AID NUC/PWR HEALTH. PAGE 1 F0022
BIBLIOG/A PEACE ARMS/CONT WAR

B65
ANDERSON C.A.,EDUCATION AND ECONOMIC DEVELOPMENT. INDUS R+D SCHOOL TEC/DEV ECO/TAC EDU/PROP AGE HEREDITY PERCEPT SKILL 20. PAGE 5 F0092
ANTHOL ECO/DEV ECO/UNDEV WORKER

B65
CRANE E.,MARKETING COMMUNICATION: A BEHAVIORAL APPROACH TO MEN, MESSAGES, AND MEDIA. STRATA R+D VOL/ASSN CROWD DRIVE PERSON SKILL WEALTH. PAGE 28 F0551
EDU/PROP MARKET PERCEPT ATTIT

B65
GREER S.,URBAN RENEWAL AND AMERICAN CITIES: THE DILEMMA OF DEMOCRATIC INTERVENTION. USA+45 R+D LOC/G VOL/ASSN ACT/RES BUDGET ADMIN GOV/REL...SOC INT SAMP MUNICH 20 BOSTON CHICAGO LOS/ANG MIAMI URBAN/RNWL. PAGE 51 F0992
PROB/SOLV PLAN NAT/G

B65
REAGAN M.D.,POLITICS, ECONOMICS, AND THE GENERAL WELFARE. USA+45 INDUS ECO/TAC TAX WEALTH...POLICY IDEA/COMP ANTHOL 20. PAGE 110 F2162
NAT/G ECO/DEV R+D ACADEM

B65
RIGBY P.H.,CONCEPTUAL FOUNDATIONS OF BUSINESS RESEARCH. COMPUTER PROB/SOLV OPTIMAL...MGT CONCPT MATH STAT TESTS SIMUL GEN/METH. PAGE 111 F2192
PROFIT R+D INDUS DECISION

B65
TYBOUT R.A.,ECONOMICS OF RESEARCH AND DEVELOPMENT. ECO/DEV ECO/UNDEV INDUS PROFIT DECISION. PAGE 131 F2594
R+D FORCES ADMIN DIPLOM

B65
WISH J.R.,ECONOMIC DEVELOPMENT IN LATIN AMERICA: AN ANNOTATED BIBLIOGRAPHY. L/A+17C COM/IND MARKET R+D CREATE CAP/ISM ATTIT...STAT METH 20. PAGE 148 F2912
BIBLIOG/A ECO/UNDEV TEC/DEV AGRI

S65
LECLERCQ H.,"ECONOMIC RESEARCH AND DEVELOPMENT IN TROPICAL AFRICA." ECO/UNDEV INT/ORG CREATE PLAN UN. PAGE 77 F1500
AFR R+D ACADEM ECO/TAC

S65
SELLERS C.,"THE EQUILIBRIUM CYCLE IN TWO-PARTY POLITICS." USA+45 USA-45 CULTURE R+D GP/REL MAJORITY DECISION. PAGE 119 F2351
CHOOSE TREND POL/PAR

B66
BOLTON R.E.,DEFENSE AND DISARMAMENT: THE ECONOMICS OF TRANSITION. USA+45 R+D FORCES PLAN LOBBY DETER WAR COST PEACE...ANTHOL BIBLIOG 20. PAGE 16 F0310
ARMS/CONT POLICY INDUS

B66
OECD DEVELOPMENT CENTRE,CATALOGUE OF SOCIAL AND ECONOMIC DEVELOPMENT INSTITUTES AND PROGRAMMES* RESEARCH. ACT/RES PLAN TEC/DEV EDU/PROP...SOC GP/COMP NAT/COMP. PAGE 101 F1976
ECO/UNDEV ECO/DEV R+D ACADEM

B66
SOCIAL SCIENCE RESEARCH COUN,BIBLIOGRAPHY OF RESEARCH IN THE SOCIAL SCIENCES IN AUSTRALIA 1957-1960. LAW R+D DIPLOM 20 AUSTRAL. PAGE 124 F2437
BIBLIOG SOC PSY

B66
US DEPARTMENT OF LABOR,TECHNOLOGICAL TRENDS IN MAJOR AMERICAN INDUSTRIES. USA+45 R+D LABOR GP/REL PRODUC...MGT BIBLIOG 20. PAGE 135 F2669
TEC/DEV INDUS TREND AUTOMAT

L66
PACKENHAM R.A.,"POLITICAL-DEVELOPMENT DOCTRINES IN THE AMERICAN FOREIGN AID PROGRAM." STRUCT R+D CREATE DIPLOM AID. PAGE 102 F2011
FOR/AID ECO/UNDEV GEN/LAWS

B67
BARANSON J.,TECHNOLOGY FOR UNDERDEVELOPED AREAS: AN ANNOTATED BIBLIOGRAPHY. FUT WOR+45 CULTURE INDUS INT/ORG CREATE PROB/SOLV INT/TRADE EDU/PROP AUTOMAT ...CONCPT METH. PAGE 10 F0181
BIBLIOG/A ECO/UNDEV TEC/DEV R+D

B67
ENKE S.,DEFENSE MANAGEMENT. USA+45 R+D FORCES WORKER PLAN ECO/TAC ADMIN NUC/PWR BAL/PAY UTIL WEALTH...MGT DEPT/DEFEN. PAGE 38 F0738
DECISION DELIB/GP EFFICIENCY BUDGET

B67
GROSS B.M.,ACTION UNDER PLANNING: THE GUIDANCE OF ECONOMIC DEVELOPMENT. STRUCT R+D NAT/G ACT/RES HABITAT...DECISION 20. PAGE 51 F1005
ECO/UNDEV PLAN ADMIN MGT

B67
NELSON R.R.,TECHNOLOGY, ECONOMIC GROWTH, AND PUBLIC POLICY. USA+45 PLAN GP/REL UTIL KNOWL...POLICY PHIL/SCI CHARTS BIBLIOG 20. PAGE 97 F1912
R+D CONSULT CREATE ACT/RES

B67
ORLANS H.,CONTRACTING FOR ATOMS. AFR USA+45 LAW INTELL ACADEM LG/CO NAT/G PLAN TEC/DEV CONTROL DETER...TREND 20. PAGE 102 F1999
NUC/PWR R+D PRODUC PEACE

B67
RIDKER R.G.,ECONOMIC COSTS OF AIR POLLUTION* STUDIES IN MEASUREMENT. R+D GP/REL KNOWL...OBS MUNICH 20. PAGE 111 F2190
OP/RES HABITAT PHIL/SCI

B67
SCHON D.A.,TECHNOLOGY AND CHANGE* THE NEW HERACLITUS. TEC/DEV CONTROL COST DEMAND EFFICIENCY RIGID/FLEX...MYTH 20. PAGE 117 F2311
INDUS PROB/SOLV R+D CREATE

L67
DOERFER G.L.,"THE LIMITS ON TRADE SECRET LAW IMPOSED BY FEDERAL PATENT & ANTITRUST SUPREMACY." USA+45 LAW R+D CAP/ISM LICENSE CONTROL SANCTION ORD/FREE. PAGE 33 F0651
JURID GOV/REL POLICY LEGIT

S67
ALLISON D.,"THE GROWTH OF IDEAS." USA+45 LG/CO ADMIN. PAGE 4 F0075
R+D OP/RES INDUS TEC/DEV

S67
AUBERT DE LA RUE P.,"PERSPECTIVES ECONOMIQUES ENTRE LES ETATS-UNIS ET L'EUROPE." FUT INDUS R+D INT/ORG ACT/RES ECO/TAC AGREE BAL/PAY PRODUC...CHARTS 20 EEC GATT WORLD/BANK. PAGE 7 F0138
INT/TRADE ECO/DEV FINAN TARIFFS

S67
BARRO S.,"ECONOMIC IMPACT OF SPACE EXPENDITURES: SOME BROAD ISSUES DEALING WITH COSTS AND BENEFITS." USA+45 PROC/MFG R+D LG/CO CONSULT COST PRODUC 20. PAGE 10 F0195
SPACE FINAN ECO/TAC NAT/G

S67
BELL D.E.,"THE QUALITY OF AID." USA+45 R+D DIPLOM GP/REL. PAGE 12 F0234
POLICY FOR/AID PROB/SOLV INSPECT

S67
BENN W.,"TECHNOLOGY HAS AN INEXORABLE EFFECT." FUT UK ECO/DEV INT/ORG CONSULT PLAN EDU/PROP ADMIN LEAD GP/REL PRODUC...INT 20 EEC. PAGE 13 F0246
R+D LG/CO TEC/DEV INDUS

S67
FADDEYEV N.,"CMEA CO-OPERATION OF EQUAL NATIONS." COM R+D PLAN CAP/ISM DIPLOM FOR/AID WEALTH...POLICY MARXIST. PAGE 39 F0758
MARXISM ECO/TAC INT/ORG ECO/UNDEV

S67
GAUSSENS J.,"THE APPLICATIONS OF NUCLEAR ENERGY - TECHNICAL, ECONOMIC AND SOCIAL ASPECTS." WOR+45 INDUS R+D ACT/RES EFFICIENCY PRODUC SKILL PREDICT. PAGE 47 F0911
NUC/PWR TEC/DEV ECO/DEV ADJUST

S67
ISELIN J.J.,"THE TRUMAN DOCTRINE: ITS PASSAGE THROUGH CONGRESS AND THE AFTERMATH." USA+45 ECO/UNDEV R+D INT/ORG DELIB/GP BAL/PWR REV PEACE ...POLICY UN. PAGE 66 F1291
DIPLOM COM FOR/AID AFR

S67
MORTON J.A.,"A SYSTEMS APPROACH TO THE INNOVATION PROCESS: ITS USE IN THE BELL SYSTEM." USA+45 INTELL INDUS LG/CO CONSULT WORKER COMPUTER AUTOMAT DEMAND ...MGT CHARTS 20. PAGE 94 F1841
TEC/DEV GEN/METH R+D COM/IND

S67
MYERS S.,"TECHNOLOGY AND URBAN TRANSIT: THE ENORMOUS POTENTIAL OF BUS AND RAIL SYSTEMS." USA+45 FINAN LOC/G WORKER PLAN PROB/SOLV PRICE AUTOMAT MUNICH 20. PAGE 96 F1877
R+D TEC/DEV DIST/IND ACT/RES

S67
SEIDLER G.L.,"MARXIST LEGAL THOUGHT IN POLAND." POLAND SOCIETY R+D LOC/G NAT/G ACT/RES ADJUD CT/SYS SUPEGO PWR...SOC TREND 20 MARX/KARL. PAGE 119 F2343
MARXISM LAW CONCPT EFFICIENCY

N67
US HOUSE COMM SCI ASTRONAUT,AUTHORIZING APPROPRIATIONS TO THE NATIONAL AERONAUTICS AND SPACE ADMINISTRATION (PAMPHLET). USA+45 NAT/G OP/RES TEC/DEV BUDGET NASA HOUSE/REP. PAGE 137 F2704
SPACE R+D PHIL/SCI NUC/PWR

N67
US HOUSE COMM SCI ASTRONAUT,GOVERNMENT, SCIENCE, AND INTERNATIONAL POLICY (PAMPHLET). INDIA NETHERLAND ECO/DEV ECO/UNDEV R+D ACADEM PLAN DIPLOM FOR/AID CONFER...PREDICT 20 CHINJAP. PAGE 137 F2705
NAT/G POLICY CREATE TEC/DEV

RACE....SEE RACE/REL, KIN

RACE/REL....RACE RELATIONS; SEE ALSO DISCRIM, ISOLAT, KIN

NC0
CARRINGTON C.E.,THE COMMONWEALTH IN AFRICA (PAMPHLET). UK STRUCT NAT/G COLONIAL REPRESENT GOV/REL RACE/REL NAT/LISM...MAJORIT 20 EEC NEGRO. PAGE 22 F0421
ECO/UNDEV AFR DIPLOM PLAN

B02
MOREL E.D.,AFFAIRS OF WEST AFRICA. UK FINAN INDUS FAM KIN SECT CHIEF WORKER DIPLOM RACE/REL LITERACY HEALTH...CHARTS 18/20 AFRICA/W NEGRO. PAGE 93 F1826
COLONIAL ADMIN AFR

B20
COX H.,ECONOMIC LIBERTY. UNIV LAW INT/TRADE RATION TARIFFS RACE/REL SOCISM POLICY. PAGE 28 F0547
NAT/G ORD/FREE ECO/TAC PERSON

B20
MOREL E.D.,THE BLACK MAN'S BURDEN. AFR MOD/EUR AGRI EXTR/IND PROB/SOLV INT/TRADE ADMIN CONTROL COERCE DISCRIM...POLICY 19/20 NEGRO LEAGUE/NAT. PAGE 93 F1828
ORD/FREE CAP/ISM RACE/REL DOMIN

B26
MCPHEE A.,THE ECONOMIC REVOLUTION IN BRITISH WEST AFRICA. AFR UK CULTURE DIST/IND FINAN INDUS PLAN GP/REL RACE/REL 20 AFRICA/W. PAGE 88 F1735
ECO/UNDEV INT/TRADE COLONIAL GEOG

B27
SIEGFRIED A.,AMERICA COMES OF AGE: A FRENCH ANALYSIS (TRANS. BY H.H. HEMMING AND DORIS HEMMING). FRANCE UK POL/PAR WORKER TEC/DEV DIPLOM REGION RACE/REL ADJUST PRODUC HEREDITY...TIME/SEQ GP/COMP SOC/INTEG 20 DEMOCRAT REPUBLICAN KKK.
USA-45 CULTURE ECO/DEV SOC

PAGE 122 F2398

B33
TANNENBAUM F.,PEACE BY REVOLUTION. ECO/UNDEV AGRI SECT WORKER DIPLOM EDU/PROP DISCRIM OWN WEALTH POPULISM 17/20 MEXIC/AMER INDIAN/AM. PAGE 128 F2532
CULTURE COLONIAL RACE/REL REV

B38
CARVALHO C.M.,GEOGRAPHIA HUMANA; POLITICA E ECONOMICA (3RD ED.). BRAZIL CULTURE AGRI INDUS DIPLOM COLONIAL GP/REL RACE/REL...LING 20 RESOURCE/N. PAGE 22 F0424
GEOG HABITAT

B48
KESSELMAN L.C.,THE SOCIAL POLITICS OF THE FEPC. INDUS WORKER EDU/PROP GP/REL RACE/REL 20 NEGRO JEWS FEPC. PAGE 70 F1382
POLICY NAT/G ADMIN DISCRIM

B48
WHITE C.L.,HUMAN GEOGRAPHY: AN ECOLOGICAL STUDY OF GEOGRAPHY. UNIV SEA CULTURE AGRI EXTR/IND RACE/REL PRODUC...CHARTS HYPO/EXP SIMUL GEN/LAWS T. PAGE 146 F2868
SOC HABITAT GEOG SOCIETY

S49
SHEPHARD H.A.,"DEMOCRATIC CONTROL IN A LABOR UNION." FUT CONSTN STRUCT TEC/DEV LEAD PARTIC RACE/REL CENTRAL DRIVE HABITAT RECORD. PAGE 120 F2374
LABOR MAJORIT CONTROL PWR

B52
ROSE A.M.,UNION SOLIDARITY: THE INTERNAL COHESION OF A LABOR UNION. SECT GP/REL RACE/REL ATTIT ROLE HEALTH WEALTH...INT QU. PAGE 114 F2241
LABOR INGP/REL PARTIC SUPEGO

B52
SACHS E.S.,THE CHOICE BEFORE SOUTH AFRICA. SOUTH/AFR AGRI EXTR/IND PROC/MFG PROB/SOLV ORD/FREE SOVEREIGN 20 NEGRO. PAGE 115 F2267
NAT/LISM DISCRIM RACE/REL LABOR

S52
KORNHAUSER W.,"THE NEGRO UNION OFFICIAL: A STUDY OF SPONSORSHIP AND CONTROL" (BMR)" USA+45 CONTROL DISCRIM ROLE SUPEGO...OBS 20 NEGRO. PAGE 73 F1428
LABOR LEAD RACE/REL CHOOSE

B53
PURCELL T.V.,THE WORKER SPEAKS HIS MIND ON COMPANY AND UNION. WORKER ADJUD LEAD RACE/REL ATTIT DRIVE MARXISM...MGT CLASSIF STAT OBS INT SAMP BIBLIOG. PAGE 108 F2131
LABOR PARTIC INGP/REL HAPPINESS

B55
STILLMAN C.W.,AFRICA IN THE MODERN WORLD. AFR USA+45 WOR+45 INT/TRADE COLONIAL PARTIC REGION GOV/REL RACE/REL 20. PAGE 126 F2489
ECO/UNDEV DIPLOM POLICY STRUCT

B57
ROBERTSON H.M.,SOUTH AFRICA, ECONOMIC AND POLITICAL ASPECTS. SOUTH/AFR CONSTN CULTURE POL/PAR LEGIS DIPLOM DOMIN COLONIAL...SOC BIBLIOG 19/20. PAGE 112 F2214
RACE/REL ECO/UNDEV ECO/TAC DISCRIM

B57
SCHNEIDER E.V.,INDUSTRIAL SOCIOLOGY: THE SOCIAL RELATIONS OF INDUSTRY AND COMMUNITY. STRATA INDUS NAT/G NEIGH CREATE ADMIN PARTIC GP/REL RACE/REL ROLE PWR...POLICY BIBLIOG. PAGE 117 F2308
LABOR MGT INGP/REL STRUCT

B58
JENNINGS I.,PROBLEMS OF THE NEW COMMONWEALTH. AFR CEYLON INDIA PAKISTAN S/ASIA ECO/UNDEV INT/ORG LOC/G DIPLOM ECO/TAC INT/TRADE COLONIAL RACE/REL DISCRIM 20 PARLIAMENT. PAGE 67 F1314
NAT/LISM NEUTRAL FOR/AID POL/PAR

B58
OGDEN F.D.,THE POLL TAX IN THE SOUTH. USA+45 USA-45 CONSTN ADJUD ADMIN PARTIC CRIME...TIME/SEQ GOV/COMP METH/COMP 18/20 SOUTH/US. PAGE 101 F1982
TAX CHOOSE RACE/REL DISCRIM

B59
BARBASH J.,UNIONS AND UNION LEADERSHIP. NAT/G WORKER TEC/DEV ECO/TAC PARTIC GP/REL RACE/REL ORD/FREE CLASSIF. PAGE 10 F0183
LABOR VOL/ASSN CAP/ISM LEAD

B59
BROMWICH L.,UNION CONSTITUTIONS. CONSTN EX/STRUC PRESS ADJUD CONTROL CHOOSE REPRESENT PWR SAMP. PAGE 19 F0361
LABOR ROUTINE INGP/REL RACE/REL

B59
ROCHE J.,LA COLONISATION ALLEMANDE ET LE RIO GRANDE DO SUL. BRAZIL L/A+17C NAT/G PROVS INGP/REL RACE/REL DISCRIM HABITAT...GEOG SOC/INTEG 19/20 MIGRATION. PAGE 113 F2228
ECO/UNDEV GP/REL ATTIT

B59
SILCOCK T.H.,THE COMMONWEALTH ECONOMY IN SOUTHEAST ASIA. AFR INDIA MALAYSIA S/ASIA ECO/DEV AGRI LOC/G PLAN TARIFFS COLONIAL BAL/PAY DEMAND...BIBLIOG/A 20 GATT. PAGE 122 F2401
ECO/TAC INT/TRADE RACE/REL DIPLOM

B59
VOSE C.E.,CAUCASIANS ONLY: THE SUPREME COURT, THE NAACP, AND THE RESTRICTIVE COVENANT CASES. USA+45 LAW CONSTN LOBBY...SOC 20 NAACP SUPREME/CT NEGRO. PAGE 142 F2796
CT/SYS RACE/REL DISCRIM

B60
ASPREMONT-LYNDEN H.,RAPPORT SUR L'ADMINISTRATION BELGE DU RUANDA-URUNDI PENDANT L'ANNEE 1959. BELGIUM RWANDA AGRI INDUS DIPLOM ECO/TAC INT/TRADE DOMIN ADMIN RACE/REL...GEOG CENSUS 20 UN. PAGE 7 F0132
AFR COLONIAL ECO/UNDEV INT/ORG

B60
FERNANDES F.,MUDANCAS SOCIAIS NO BRASIL. BRAZIL L/A+17C SOCIETY AGRI PROVS LEAD GP/REL RACE/REL ORD/FREE...SOC SOC/INTEG 20 SAO/PAULO. PAGE 40 F0786
ECO/UNDEV STRATA INDUS

B60
GRIER E.,PRIVATELY DEVELOPED INTERRACIAL HOUSING: AN ANALYSIS OF EXPERIENCE. FINAN MARKET COST DISCRIM PROFIT SOC/INTEG 20. PAGE 51 F0997
RACE/REL CONSTRUC HABITAT

B60
RAPKIN C.,THE DEMAND FOR HOUSING IN RACIALLY MIXED AREAS: A STUDY OF THE NATURE OF NEIGHBORHOOD CHANGE. USA+45 FINAN PRICE COST DRIVE...GEOG 20. PAGE 109 F2151
RACE/REL NEIGH DISCRIM MARKET

B60
WODDIS J.,AFRICA: THE ROOTS OF REVOLT. SOUTH/AFR WORKER INT/TRADE RACE/REL DISCRIM ORD/FREE 20. PAGE 148 F2915
COLONIAL SOVEREIGN WAR ECO/UNDEV

B61
SPOONER F.P.,SOUTH AFRICAN PREDICAMENT. FUT SOUTH/AFR INDUS POL/PAR RACE/REL INCOME...CHARTS 20 NEGRO. PAGE 125 F2459
ECO/DEV DISCRIM ECO/TAC POLICY

B62
COX O.C.,CAPITALISM AND AMERICAN LEADERSHIP. WOR+45 WOR-45 STRATA INDUS SECT INT/TRADE EXEC INGP/REL RACE/REL RATIONAL PWR WEALTH. PAGE 28 F0548
CAP/ISM LEAD ECO/DEV SOCIETY

B62
DEBUYST F.,LAS CLASES SOCIALES EN AMERICA LATINA. L/A+17C SOCIETY STRUCT WORKER EDU/PROP RACE/REL ATTIT HABITAT ROLE...GEOG SOC NAT/COMP SOC/INTEG 20. PAGE 32 F0612
STRATA GP/REL WEALTH

B62
FAO,FOOD AND AGRICULTURE ORGANIZATION AFRICAN SURVEY. AFR CONGO/BRAZ GHANA STRATA AGRI INT/ORG TEC/DEV FOR/AID INT/TRADE RACE/REL DEMAND EFFICIENCY PRODUC...GEOG 20 UN CONGO/LEOP. PAGE 39 F0763
ECO/TAC WEALTH EXTR/IND ECO/UNDEV

B62
HARRINGTON M.,THE OTHER AMERICA: POVERTY IN THE UNITED STATES. WORKER CREATE REPRESENT RACE/REL AGE/O DRIVE POLICY. PAGE 55 F1086
WEALTH WELF/ST INCOME CULTURE

B62
HIRSCHFIELD R.S.,THE CONSTITUTION AND THE COURT. AFR SCHOOL WAR RACE/REL EQUILIB ORD/FREE...POLICY MAJORIT DECISION JURID 18/20 PRESIDENT CIVIL/LIB SUPREME/CT CONGRESS. PAGE 60 F1175
ADJUD PWR CONSTN LAW

B62
SHERIF M.,INTERGROUP RELATIONS AND LEADERSHIP: APPROACHES AND RESEARCH IN INDUSTRIAL, ETHNIC, CULTURAL AND POLITICAL AREAS. CULTURE R+D LABOR DIPLOM GP/REL RACE/REL PERCEPT...PSY CONCPT. PAGE 121 F2377
LEAD REPRESENT PWR INGP/REL

B62
VAN RENSBURG P.,GUILTY LAND: THE HISTORY OF APARTHEID. SOUTH/AFR NAT/G POL/PAR DOMIN CHOOSE ...SOC 19/20 NEGRO. PAGE 140 F2763
RACE/REL DISCRIM NAT/LISM POLICY

B63
CONF ON FUTURE OF COMMONWEALTH,THE FUTURE OF THE COMMONWEALTH. AFR UK ECO/UNDEV AGRI EDU/PROP ADMIN SOC/INTEG 20. PAGE 27 F0522
DIPLOM RACE/REL ORD/FREE TEC/DEV

B63
ELLENDER A.J.,A REPORT ON UNITED STATES FOREIGN OPERATIONS IN AFRICA. SOUTH/AFR USA+45 STRATA EXTR/IND FORCES RACE/REL ISOLAT SOVEREIGN...CHARTS 20 NEGRO. PAGE 37 F0721
FOR/AID DIPLOM WEALTH ECO/UNDEV

B63
FURTADO C.,THE ECONOMIC GROWTH OF BRAZIL: A SURVEY FROM COLONIAL TO MODERN TIMES. L/A+17C AGRI DIST/IND EXTR/IND INDUS WORKER COLONIAL RACE/REL OWN GOV/COMP. PAGE 45 F0877
ECO/UNDEV TEC/DEV LABOR DOMIN

B63
GANDHI M.K.,THE WAY TO COMMUNAL HARMONY. INDIA MAJORITY RIGID/FLEX ROLE RESPECT 20 GANDHI/M. PAGE 46 F0892
RACE/REL DISCRIM ATTIT ADJUST

B63
JACOBS P.,STATE OF UNIONS. USA+45 STRATA TOP/EX GP/REL RACE/REL DEMAND DISCRIM ATTIT PWR 20 CONGRESS NEGRO HOFFA/J. PAGE 66 F1296
LABOR ECO/TAC BARGAIN DECISION

B63
LEWIN J.,POLITICS AND LAW IN SOUTH AFRICA. SOUTH/AFR UK POL/PAR BAL/PWR ECO/TAC COLONIAL CONTROL GP/REL DISCRIM PWR 20 NEGRO. PAGE 79 F1545
NAT/LISM POLICY LAW

RACE/REL

L63
MCKERSIE R.B.,"NONPROFESSIONAL HOSPITAL WORKERS AND A UNION ORGANIZING DRIVE." PLAN GP/REL RACE/REL ATTIT DRIVE...CORREL STAT INT GP/COMP. PAGE 88 F1732
VOL/ASSN HEALTH INGP/REL LABOR

B64
HUTT W.H.,THE ECONOMICS OF THE COLOUR BAR. SOUTH/AFR EXTR/IND LABOR ADJUD NEGRO. PAGE 64 F1251
INDUS DISCRIM RACE/REL ECO/UNDEV

B64
MORGAN H.W.,AMERICAN SOCIALISM 1900-1960. AFR USA+45 USA-45 INTELL AGRI LABOR WORKER BARGAIN ECO/TAC GP/REL RACE/REL 20 NEGRO MIGRATION. PAGE 93 F1830
SOCISM POL/PAR ECO/DEV STRATA

B64
SEGAL R.,SANCTIONS AGAINST SOUTH AFRICA. AFR SOUTH/AFR NAT/G INT/TRADE RACE/REL PEACE PWR ...INT/LAW ANTHOL 20 UN. PAGE 119 F2342
SANCTION DISCRIM ECO/TAC POLICY

B64
SULTAN P.E.,THE DISENCHANTED UNIONIST. NAT/G ADJUD CONTROL SANCTION RACE/REL ANOMIE ATTIT ROLE ...METH/CNCPT INT. PAGE 127 F2512
LABOR INGP/REL CHARTS MAJORIT

C64
NORGREN P.H.,"TOWARD FAIR EMPLOYMENT." USA+45 LAW STRATA LABOR NAT/G FORCES ACT/RES ADMIN ATTIT ...POLICY BIBLIOG 20 NEGRO. PAGE 98 F1932
RACE/REL DISCRIM WORKER MGT

B65
COLBERG M.R.,HUMAN CAPITAL IN SOUTHERN DEVELOPMENT. USA+45 AGRI ACADEM LABOR SCHOOL WORKER CAP/ISM DISCRIM. PAGE 26 F0498
PROVS RACE/REL GP/REL

B65
LYONS G.M.,AMERICA: PURPOSE AND POWER. UK USA+45 FINAN INDUS MARKET WORKER TEC/DEV DIPLOM AUTOMAT NUC/PWR WAR RACE/REL ORD/FREE 20 EEC CONGRESS SUPREME/CT CIV/RIGHTS. PAGE 82 F1617
PWR PROB/SOLV ECO/DEV TASK

B65
SHOSTAK A.B.,NEW PERSPECTIVES ON POVERTY. USA+45 SCHOOL WORKER INGP/REL RACE/REL AGE/C AGE/Y ATTIT HEALTH...ANTHOL BIBLIOG 20 JOHNSON/LB POVRTY/WAR. PAGE 121 F2388
WEALTH NAT/G RECEIVE INCOME

B65
SPENCE J.E.,REPUBLIC UNDER PRESSURE: A STUDY OF SOUTH AFRICAN FOREIGN POLICY. SOUTH/AFR ADMIN COLONIAL GOV/REL RACE/REL DISCRIM NAT/LISM ATTIT ROLE...TREND 20 NEGRO. PAGE 124 F2449
DIPLOM POLICY AFR

S65
MULLER A.L.,"THE ECONOMIC POSITION OF THE ASIANS IN AFRICA." AFR SOUTH/AFR ECO/UNDEV MARKET ECO/TAC GP/REL INCOME...CHARTS IND 20 MONOPOLY ASIANS. PAGE 95 F1856
WORKER RACE/REL CAP/ISM DISCRIM

B66
ANDRESKI S.,PARASITISM AND SUBVERSION* THE CASE OF LATIN AMERICA. CULTURE ECO/UNDEV LABOR NAT/G SECT PROB/SOLV RACE/REL TOTALISM ATTIT WEALTH ALL/IDEOS. PAGE 5 F0100
L/A+17C GOV/COMP STRATA REV

B66
BARAN P.A.,MONOPOLY CAPITAL; AN ESSAY ON THE AMERICAN ECONOMIC AND SOCIAL ORDER. USA+45 USA-45 ECO/UNDEV FINAN MARKET PLAN DIPLOM COLONIAL RACE/REL DEMAND MARXISM...CHARTS 20. PAGE 9 F0179
LG/CO CAP/ISM PRICE CONTROL

B66
CROWDER M.,A SHORT HISTORY OF NIGERIA. AFR NIGERIA UK ECO/UNDEV CHIEF INT/TRADE RACE/REL NAT/LISM ORD/FREE...GEOG SOC CHARTS BIBLIOG 14/20. PAGE 29 F0558
COLONIAL NAT/G CULTURE

B66
DAVIES JC I.I.I.,NEIGHBORHOOD GROUPS AND URBAN RENEWAL. USA+45 PLAN LOBBY PARTIC CHOOSE RACE/REL ...POLICY DECISION SOC INT MUNICH SOC/INTEG 20 NEWYORK/C. PAGE 30 F0586
NEIGH CREATE PROB/SOLV

B66
EBONY,THE NEGRO HANDBOOK. ACADEM LABOR LOC/G SECT FORCES WORKER CT/SYS CRIME DISCRIM ORD/FREE...BIOG SOC/INTEG 19/20 NEGRO CIV/RIGHTS. PAGE 36 F0692
RACE/REL EDU/PROP LAW STAT

B66
ECONOMIC RESEARCH SERVICE,RESEARCH DATA ON MINORITY GROUPS: AN ANNOTATED BIBLIOGRAPHY OF ECONOMIC RESEARCH SERVICE REPORTS: 1955-1965 (PAMPHLET). USA+45 STRATA ECO/DEV AGRI SCHOOL WORKER EDU/PROP HEALTH NEW/LIB SOC. PAGE 36 F0697
BIBLIOG/A DISCRIM WEALTH RACE/REL

B66
FREIDEL F.,AMERICAN ISSUES IN THE TWENTIETH CENTURY. SOCIETY FINAN ECO/TAC FOR/AID CONTROL NUC/PWR WAR RACE/REL PEACE ATTIT...ANTHOL T 20 WILSON/W ROOSEVLT/F KENNEDY/JF TRUMAN/HS. PAGE 44 F0851
DIPLOM POLICY NAT/G ORD/FREE

B66
KEENLEYSIDE H.L.,INTERNATIONAL AID: A SUMMARY. AFR INDIA S/ASIA UK STRATA EXTR/IND TEC/DEV ADMIN RACE/REL DEMAND NAT/LISM WEALTH...TREND CHINJAP. PAGE 70 F1367
ECO/UNDEV FOR/AID DIPLOM TASK

B66
SOVERN M.I.,LEGAL RESTRAINTS ON RACIAL DISCRIMINATION IN EMPLOYMENT. USA+45 LAW INDUS LG/CO SML/CO DELIB/GP LEGIS SANCTION 20 NLRB PRESIDENT NEGRO CIV/RIGHTS RAILROAD. PAGE 124 F2446
DISCRIM RACE/REL WORKER JURID

B66
WOODMAN H.D.,SLAVERY AND THE SOUTHERN ECONOMY: SOURCES AND READINGS. USA-45 CULTURE STRUCT AGRI ECO/TAC LEAD RACE/REL DISCRIM EFFICIENCY...CHARTS ANTHOL MUNICH 18/19 NEGRO SOUTH/US. PAGE 148 F2922
ECO/DEV STRATA WORKER UTIL

C66
WINT G.,"ASIA: A HANDBOOK." ASIA S/ASIA INDUS LABOR SECT PRESS RACE/REL MARXISM...STAT CHARTS BIBLIOG 20. PAGE 148 F2908
ECO/UNDEV DIPLOM NAT/G SOCIETY

B67
FALL B.B.,HO CHI MINH ON REVOLUTION: SELECTED WRITINGS, 1920-66. COM VIETNAM ELITES NAT/G COERCE GUERRILLA RACE/REL MARXISM...MARXIST ANTHOL 20. PAGE 39 F0761
REV COLONIAL ECO/UNDEV S/ASIA

B67
FANON F.,TOWARD THE AFRICAN REVOLUTION. AFR FRANCE CULTURE ELITES LEAD REV GP/REL ORD/FREE SOVEREIGN 20. PAGE 39 F0762
COLONIAL DOMIN ECO/UNDEV RACE/REL

B67
LYND S.,RECONSTRUCTION. USA-45 PROB/SOLV RACE/REL ...IDEA/COMP ANTHOL 19. PAGE 82 F1616
SUFF ECO/TAC ADJUST

B67
LYTLE C.M.,THE WARREN COURT AND ITS CRITICS. USA+45 NAT/G PROVS FORCES LOBBY RACE/REL DISCRIM SOVEREIGN 20 SUPREME/CT WARRN/EARL. PAGE 83 F1618
CT/SYS ADJUD PROB/SOLV ATTIT

B67
PELTASON J.W.,FUNCTIONS AND POLICIES OF AMERICAN GOVERNMENT (3RD ED.). USA+45 FINAN INDUS EDU/PROP CIVMIL/REL RACE/REL ORD/FREE...ANTHOL T 20 JOHNSON/LB. PAGE 104 F2052
NAT/G GOV/REL POLICY PLAN

B67
POLLACK N.,THE POPULIST MIND. USA-45 STRATA AGRI NAT/G POL/PAR LEGIS WORKER RACE/REL WEALTH...ANTHOL BIBLIOG 19 NEGRO. PAGE 107 F2097
POPULISM HIST/WRIT ATTIT INGP/REL

B67
POWLEDGE F.,BLACK POWER WHITE RESISTANCE. USA+45 STRUCT PLAN GP/REL DISCRIM HABITAT ORD/FREE WEALTH ...METH/COMP SOC/INTEG NEGRO. PAGE 107 F2111
RACE/REL ATTIT PWR

B67
ROSS A.M.,EMPLOYMENT, RACE, AND POVERTY. USA+45 LAW STRATA MARKET LABOR EDU/PROP ISOLAT SKILL...MGT ANTHOL 20 NEGRO. PAGE 114 F2244
RACE/REL WORKER WEALTH DISCRIM

B67
SACKS B.,SOUTH AFRICA: AN IMPERIAL DILEMMA. SOUTH/AFR UK ECO/UNDEV KIN DOMIN DEBATE CONTROL REV DISCRIM ISOLAT...POLICY STAT BIBLIOG 20. PAGE 115 F2268
COLONIAL RACE/REL DIPLOM ORD/FREE

B67
WEINBERG M.,SCHOOL INTEGRATION: A COMPREHENSIVE CLASSIFIED BIBLIOGRAPHY OF 3,100 REFERENCES. USA+45 LAW NAT/G NEIGH SECT PLAN ROUTINE AGE/C WEALTH SOC/INTEG INDIAN/AM. PAGE 145 F2849
BIBLIOG SCHOOL DISCRIM RACE/REL

L67
GREGORY A.J.,"AFRICAN SOCIALISM, SOCIALISM AND FASCISM: AN APPRAISAL." FUT LEAD REV GP/REL RACE/REL NAT/LISM ATTIT...IDEA/COMP STERTYP 20. PAGE 51 F0993
FASCISM MARXISM SOCISM AFR

S67
"THE FEDERAL AGRICULTURAL STABILIZATION PROGRAM AND THE NEGRO." LAW CONSTN PLAN REPRESENT DISCRIM ORD/FREE 20 NEGRO CONGRESS. PAGE 2 F0025
AGRI CONTROL NAT/G RACE/REL

S67
BRIMMER A.F.,"EMPLOYMENT PATTERNS AND THE DILEMMA OF DESEGREGATION." USA+45 SOCIETY SKILL 20 NEGRO. PAGE 18 F0353
RACE/REL DISCRIM WORKER STRATA

S67
EDGEWORTH A.B. JR.,"CIVIL RIGHTS PLUS THREE YEARS: BANKS AND THE ANTI-DISCRIMINATION LAW" USA+45 SOCIETY DELIB/GP RACE/REL EFFICIENCY 20 NEGRO CIV/RIGHTS. PAGE 36 F0701
WORKER DISCRIM FINAN LAW

S67
EDWARDS N.,"EDUCATION IN THE FEDERAL-STATE STRUCTURE OF GOVERNMENT." USA+45 SECT CONTROL GOV/REL RACE/REL DISCRIM FEDERAL ROLE PWR SOVEREIGN. PAGE 36 F0705
EDU/PROP NAT/G PROVS POLICY

S67
FRIEDEN B.J.,"THE CHANGING PROSPECTS FOR SOCIAL PLANNING." USA+45 PROB/SOLV RACE/REL WEALTH ...SOC/WK PREDICT MUNICH 20 NEGRO. PAGE 44 F0856
PLAN LOC/G POLICY

S67
GEISS I.,"THE GERMANS AND THE MIDDLE EAST CRISIS." GERMANY/W ISLAM ISRAEL USSR POL/PAR RACE/REL
ATTIT DIPLOM

MARXISM...GP/COMP 20 JEWS. PAGE 47 F0914 WAR POLICY

S67
JANSSEN P.,"NEA: THE RELUCTANT DRAGON." NAT/G EXEC LOBBY PARTIC SANCTION RACE/REL ROLE TREND. PAGE 66 F1305 EDU/PROP PROF/ORG MGT POLICY

S67
LANDES W.M.,"THE EFFECT OF STATE FAIR EMPLOYMENT LAWS ON THE ECONOMIC POSITION OF NONWHITES." USA+45 PROVS SECT LEGIS ADMIN GP/REL RACE/REL...JURID CONCPT CHARTS HYPO/EXP NEGRO. PAGE 75 F1470 DISCRIM LAW WORKER

S67
MULLER A.L.,"ECONOMIC GROWTH AND MINORITIES." USA+45 SKILL...SOC GP/COMP NEGRO. PAGE 95 F1857 INCOME WORKER ECO/DEV RACE/REL

S67
NILES J.G.,"CIVIL ACTIONS FOR DAMAGES UNDER THE FEDERAL CIVIL RIGHTS STATUTES." CONSTN FINAN ADJUD CT/SYS GOV/REL RACE/REL 20. PAGE 98 F1928 DISCRIM LAW CONTROL ORD/FREE

S67
PIERPONT J.R.,"NEW STAGE IN THE LONGSHORE STRUGGLE." USA+45 SENIOR ADJUD RACE/REL...JURID 20 NEGRO. PAGE 106 F2083 LABOR DISCRIM WORKER CT/SYS

S67
THEROUX P.,"HATING THE ASIANS." TANZANIA UGANDA CONSTN INDUS NAT/G POL/PAR WORKER ECO/TAC HABITAT LOVE...POLICY GEOG 20 MIGRATION. PAGE 130 F2557 AFR RACE/REL SOVEREIGN ATTIT

S67
WASSERMAN M.,"BEYOND TOKENISM: REVERSE INTEGRATION IN ALBANY, GEORGIA." USA+45 PLAN BUDGET EDU/PROP LEAD AGE/C AGE/Y GEORGIA NEGRO. PAGE 144 F2827 REGION RACE/REL DISCRIM SCHOOL

RAF....ROYAL AIR FORCE

RAFUSE R.W. F2135

RAGAN S. F2136

RAHMAN/TA....TUNKU ABDUL RAHMAN

RAILROAD....RAILROADS AND RAILWAY SYSTEMS

B54
LOCKLIN D.P.,ECONOMICS OF TRANSPORTATION (4TH ED.). USA+45 USA-45 SEA AIR LAW FINAN LG/CO EX/STRUC ADMIN CONTROL...STAT CHARTS 19/20 RAILROAD PUB/TRANS. PAGE 81 F1592 ECO/DEV DIST/IND ECO/TAC TEC/DEV

B61
AGARWAL R.C.,STATE ENTERPRISE IN INDIA. FUT INDIA UK FINAN INDUS ADMIN CONTROL OWN...POLICY CHARTS BIBLIOG 20 RAILROAD. PAGE 3 F0048 ECO/UNDEV SOCISM GOV/REL LG/CO

B61
DOIG J.W.,THE POLITICS OF METROPOLITAN TRANSPORTATION. DELIB/GP WORKER DIPLOM TASK EFFICIENCY UTIL...CHARTS BIBLIOG MUNICH 20 NEW/YORK NEW/JERSEY PUB/TRANS RAILROAD. PAGE 34 F0652 PROB/SOLV STRATA DIST/IND

B64
LANG A.S.,URBAN RAIL TRANSIT. OP/RES PLAN PROB/SOLV TEC/DEV AUTOMAT COST...TECHNIC MATH CON/ANAL CHARTS METH/COMP SIMUL MUNICH 20 RAILROAD PUB/TRANS. PAGE 75 F1474 DIST/IND ECOMETRIC

B65
MACAVOY P.W.,THE ECONOMIC EFFECTS OF REGULATION: THE TRUNK-LINE RAILROAD CARTELS AND THE INTERSTATE COMMERCE COMMISSION BEFORE 1900. USA-45 PRICE PROFIT...STAT CHARTS BIBLIOG 19 RAILROAD. PAGE 83 F1620 ECO/TAC DIST/IND PROF/ORG RATION

B65
PARRIS H.W.,GOVERNMENT AND THE RAILWAYS IN NINETEENTH-CENTURY BRITAIN. UK DELIB/GP CONTROL LEAD CENTRAL 19 RAILROAD. PAGE 103 F2029 DIST/IND NAT/G PLAN GP/REL

B66
RUPPENTHAL K.M.,TRANSPORTATION AND TOMORROW. FUT SPACE USA+45 SEA AIR FORCES TEC/DEV INT/TRADE ...ANTHOL 20 RAILROAD. PAGE 115 F2261 DIST/IND PLAN CIVMIL/REL PREDICT

B66
SOVERN M.I.,LEGAL RESTRAINTS ON RACIAL DISCRIMINATION IN EMPLOYMENT. USA+45 LAW INDUS LG/CO SML/CO DELIB/GP LEGIS SANCTION 20 NLRB PRESIDENT NEGRO CIV/RIGHTS RAILROAD. PAGE 124 F2446 DISCRIM RACE/REL WORKER JURID

B66
US SENATE COMM LABOR-PUB WELF,AMEND THE RAILWAY LABOR ACT. USA+45 CONSTN CONSULT DELIB/GP ADJUD CONGRESS RAILROAD. PAGE 139 F2731 GP/REL LABOR DIST/IND LAW

RAISON T. F2137

RAJARATAM/S....S. RAJARATAM

RAJASTHAN....RAJASTHAN

RAMA C.M. F2138,F2139

RAMANADHAM V.V. F2140

RAMAZANI R.K. F2141

RAMERIE L. F2142

RAND SCHOOL OF SOCIAL SCIENCE F2143

RANDOMNESS....SEE PROB/SOLV

RANGEL I. F2144

RANIS G. F0772,F2145

RANKE/L....LEOPOLD VON RANKE

RANKING SYSTEMS....SEE SENIOR

RANKOVIC/A....ALEXANDER RANKOVIC, YUGOSLAVIAOS FORMER VICE PRESIDENT

RANSOM H.H. F2146

RANZ H. F0325

RAO V.K.R. F2147,F2148

RAO Y.V.L. F2149

RAPHAEL J.S. F2150

RAPKIN C. F2151

RATION....RATIONING

B03
GRIFFIN A.P.C.,LISTS PUBLISHED 1902-03: GOVERNMENT OWNERSHIP OF RAILROADS (PAMPHLET). USA-45 LAW NAT/G RATION GOV/REL CENTRAL SOCISM...POLICY 19/20. PAGE 51 F0998 BIBLIOG DIST/IND CONTROL ADJUD

N19
KRIESBERG M.,CANCELLATION OF THE RATION STAMPS (PAMPHLET). USA+45 USA-45 MARKET PROB/SOLV PRICE GOV/REL RIGID/FLEX 20 OPA. PAGE 73 F1439 RATION DECISION ADMIN NAT/G

B20
COX H.,ECONOMIC LIBERTY. UNIV LAW INT/TRADE RATION TARIFFS RACE/REL SOCISM POLICY. PAGE 28 F0547 NAT/G ORD/FREE ECO/TAC PERSON

B40
FULLER G.H.,LIST OF REFERENCES ON PRIORITIES (MIMEOGRAPHED PAPER). WOR-45 NAT/G RATION 20. PAGE 45 F0874 BIBLIOG/A WAR ECO/TAC PLAN

B42
US LIBRARY OF CONGRESS,ECONOMICS OF WAR (APRIL 1941-MARCH 1942). WOR-45 FINAN INDUS LOC/G NAT/G PLAN BUDGET RATION COST DEMAND...POLICY 20. PAGE 138 F2712 BIBLIOG/A INT/TRADE ECO/TAC WAR

B42
US LIBRARY OF CONGRESS,THE WAR PRODUCTION PROGRAM: SELECTED DOCUMENTATION ON THE ECONOMICS OF WAR (PAMPHLET). USA-45 ECO/DEV AGRI FINAN NAT/G ECO/TAC RATION PRICE EFFICIENCY 20. PAGE 138 F2713 BIBLIOG/A WAR PRODUC INDUS

B44
LANDAUER C.,THEORY OF NATIONAL ECONOMIC PLANNING. USA-45 INDUS MARKET WORKER PROB/SOLV DIPLOM RATION PRICE CONTROL WAR COST 20. PAGE 75 F1465 ECO/TAC PLAN NAT/G ECO/DEV

B48
SAMUELSON P.A.,FOUNDATIONS OF ECONOMIC ANALYSIS. MARKET RATION DEMAND UTIL...MATH METH T 20. PAGE 115 F2276 EQUILIB GEN/LAWS ECO/DEV

B51
HART A.G.,DEFENSE WITHOUT INFLATION. AFR KOREA FINAN INDUS NAT/G WORKER DIPLOM RATION TAX PRICE COST OPTIMAL 20 RESOURCE/N. PAGE 56 F1098 ECO/TAC CONTROL WAR PLAN

S56
SPENGLER J.J.,"POPULATION THREATENS PROSPERITY" (BMR)" WOR+45 SOCIETY FINAN RATION COST INCOME ...SOC CHARTS 20 RESOURCE/N. PAGE 124 F2451 CENSUS GEOG WEALTH TREND

B57
MASON E.S.,ECONOMIC CONCENTRATION AND THE MONOPOLY PROBLEM. USA+45 USA-45 LAW ELITES ECO/DEV LABOR RATION PRICE PWR WEALTH...CHARTS 20 MONOPOLY. PAGE 87 F1696 GP/REL LG/CO CONTROL MARKET

B57
SINGH D.B.,INFLATIONARY PRICE TRENDS IN INDIA SINCE 1939. AFR INDIA ECO/TAC RATION CONTROL WAR GOV/REL BAL/PAY DEMAND INCOME PEACE PRODUC...POLICY CHARTS 20. PAGE 122 F2413
BUDGET ECO/UNDEV PRICE FINAN

B58
MOULTON H.G.,CAN INFLATION BE CONTROLLED? ECO/DEV INDUS CAP/ISM RATION GOV/REL COST INCOME PEACE WEALTH...CHARTS TIME 20 KEYNES/JM MONEY. PAGE 94 F1847
ECO/TAC CONTROL DEMAND FINAN

B60
CROSSER P.K.,STATE CAPITALISM IN THE ECONOMY OF THE UNITED STATES. USA+45 USA-45 AGRI FINAN INDUS LABOR WORKER RATION CONTROL GOV/REL DEMAND...NEW/IDEA 20. PAGE 29 F0557
CAP/ISM ECO/DEV ECO/TAC NAT/G

B61
BREWIS T.N.,CANADIAN ECONOMIC POLICY. AFR CANADA BUDGET CAP/ISM INT/TRADE RATION TARIFFS TAX PRICE CONTROL ROUTINE FEDERAL INCOME PRODUC 20. PAGE 18 F0348
ECO/DEV ECO/TAC NAT/G PLAN

B61
WAGLE S.S.,TECHNIQUE OF PLANNING FOR ACCELERATED ECONOMIC GROWTH OF UNDERDEVELOPED COUNTRIES. WOR+45 ACT/RES PROB/SOLV RATION BAL/PAY DEMAND INCOME 20. PAGE 142 F2798
ECO/UNDEV PLAN INDUS ECO/TAC

L61
CHENERY H.B.,"COMPARATIVE ADVANTAGE AND DEVELOPMENT POLICY." FINAN INT/TRADE RATION OPTIMAL...CHARTS METH/COMP GEN/LAWS BIBLIOG 20 RESOURCE/N. PAGE 24 F0463
ECO/UNDEV ECO/TAC PLAN EFFICIENCY

B62
HUHNE L.H.,FINANCING ECONOMIC DEVELOPMENT THROUGH NATIONAL AND INTERNATIONAL ORGANIZATIONS (THESIS; U OF WIS.). USA+45 INT/ORG PLAN GIVE GOV/REL WEALTH 20. PAGE 63 F1235
RATION FINAN FOR/AID ECO/UNDEV

B62
INTNTL COTTON ADVISORY COMMITT,GOVERNMENT REGULATIONS ON COTTON, 1962 (PAMPHLET). WOR+45 RATION PRODUC...CHARTS 20. PAGE 65 F1287
ECO/TAC LAW CONTROL AGRI

L62
BELSHAW D.G.R.,"PUBLIC INVESTMENT IN AGRICULTURE AND ECONOMIC DEVELOPMENT OF UGANDA" UGANDA AGRI INDUS R+D ECO/TAC RATION TAX PAY COLONIAL 20 WORLD/BANK. PAGE 13 F0242
ECO/UNDEV PLAN ADMIN CENTRAL

S62
KRISHNA K.G.V.,"PLANNING AND ECONOMIC DEVELOPMENT" AFR UGANDA AGRI INDUS R+D BUDGET RATION TAX COLONIAL 20. PAGE 73 F1441
ECO/DEV ECO/TAC NAT/LISM PLAN

B63
FRIEDMAN M.,INFLATION: CAUSES AND CURES. AFR INDIA ECO/DEV ECO/TAC INT/TRADE RATION PRICE DEMAND ...POLICY 20. PAGE 44 F0860
ECO/UNDEV PLAN FINAN EQUILIB

B63
GOLDMAN M.I.,SOVIET MARKETING. USSR DIST/IND FINAN RATION OWN WEALTH...SOC BIBLIOG 20. PAGE 48 F0937
MARKET ECO/TAC CONTROL MARXISM

B63
HOOPES R.,THE STEEL CRISIS. USA+45 INDUS ECO/TAC EDU/PROP PRICE CONTROL ATTIT...POLICY 20 KENNEDY/JF. PAGE 61 F1205
PROC/MFG NAT/G RATION CHIEF

S63
CARTER A.G.T.,"THE BALANCE OF PAYMENTS OF EAST AFRICA" AFR ECO/TAC FOR/AID RATION TARIFFS TAX ADMIN...STAT 20 AFRICA/E. PAGE 22 F0423
BUDGET ECO/UNDEV BAL/PAY INT/TRADE

S63
CLARK P.G.,"TOWARDS MORE COMPREHENSIVE PLANNING IN EAST AFRICA" AFR OP/RES ECO/TAC RATION TAX EFFICIENCY INCOME...MATH TREND CHARTS 20 AFRICA/E. PAGE 25 F0484
ECO/UNDEV PLAN STAT METH/COMP

S63
ENTHOVEN A.C.,"ECONOMIC ANALYSIS IN THE DEPARTMENT OF DEFENSE." USA+45 NAT/G DELIB/GP PROB/SOLV RATION NUC/PWR WEAPON COST...DECISION 20 DEPT/DEFEN RESOURCE/N. PAGE 38 F0739
PLAN BUDGET ECO/TAC FORCES

S63
REES A.,"THE EFFECTS OF UNIONS ON RESOURCE ALLOCATION." USA+45 WORKER PRICE CONTROL GP/REL ...MGT METH/COMP 20. PAGE 110 F2173
LABOR BARGAIN RATION INCOME

B64
BROWN E.H.P.,A COURSE IN APPLIED ECONOMICS (2ND ED.). ECO/DEV FINAN MARKET WORKER INT/TRADE RATION RENT PAY PRICE BAL/PAY...DECISION T RESOURCE/N. PAGE 19 F0368
POLICY ECO/TAC PROB/SOLV

B64
KUZNETS S.,POSTWAR ECONOMIC GROWTH: FOUR LECTURES. WOR+45 INDUS NAT/G WORKER TEC/DEV ECO/TAC RATION TARIFFS PRICE BAL/PAY COST DEMAND 20. PAGE 74 F1455
ECO/DEV ECO/UNDEV TREND FINAN

B64
NATIONAL COUN APPLIED ECO RES,A STRATEGY FOR THE FOURTH PLAN. INDIA DIST/IND EXTR/IND SERV/IND ECO/TAC RATION EDU/PROP EATING HEALTH...CHARTS 20. PAGE 97 F1900
ECO/UNDEV PLAN AGRI WORKER

B65
MACAVOY P.W.,THE ECONOMIC EFFECTS OF REGULATION: THE TRUNK-LINE RAILROAD CARTELS AND THE INTERSTATE COMMERCE COMMISSION BEFORE 1900. USA-45 PRICE PROFIT...STAT CHARTS BIBLIOG 19 RAILROAD. PAGE 83 F1620
ECO/TAC DIST/IND PROF/ORG RATION

B65
ROWE J.W.,PRIMARY COMMODITIES IN INTERNATIONAL TRADE. MARKET CAP/ISM ECO/TAC DEMAND...NAT/COMP 20. PAGE 114 F2253
INT/TRADE AGRI RATION PRICE

B65
SCHULTZ T.W.,ECONOMIC CRISES IN WORLD AGRICULTURE. ASIA INDIA USSR ECO/DEV ECO/UNDEV INDUS VOL/ASSN CAP/ISM RATION COLONIAL 20. PAGE 117 F2317
AGRI ECO/TAC INCOME WORKER

S65
STEENKAMP W.F.J.,"THE PROBLEM OF WAGE REGULATION." SOUTH/AFR LAW ECO/DEV ECO/UNDEV LABOR NAT/G BARGAIN PAY INGP/REL DISCRIM WEALTH...METH/COMP 20. PAGE 125 F2473
ECO/TAC PRICE WORKER RATION

B66
SHULTZ G.P.,GUIDELINES, INFORMAL CONTROLS, AND THE MARKET PLACE: POLICY CHOICES IN A FULL EMPLOYMENT ECONOMY. UK ECO/DEV LABOR INT/TRADE CONFER GOV/REL BAL/PAY DEMAND INCOME...POLICY ANTHOL 20 PRESIDENT. PAGE 121 F2392
ECO/TAC CONTROL FINAN RATION

B66
US HOUSE COMM BANKING CURRENCY,HEARINGS BEFORE HOUSE COMMITTEE ON BANKING AND CURRENCY: SALE OF SBA LOAN POOL PARTICIPATIONS. USA+45 LAW LEGIS ECO/TAC RATION 20 CONGRESS. PAGE 136 F2687
FINAN SML/CO ADJUD GOV/REL

B66
ZISCHKA A.,WAR ES EIN WUNDER? GERMANY/W ECO/DEV FINAN LG/CO BARGAIN CAP/ISM FOR/AID RATION 20 MARSHL/PLN. PAGE 150 F2965
ECO/TAC INT/TRADE INDUS WAR

S66
ANGELL J.W.,"THE LONGER RUN PROSPECTS FOR THE US BALANCE OF PAYMENTS." USA+45 DIPLOM FOR/AID RATION ORD/FREE WEALTH...IDEA/COMP GATT. PAGE 6 F0104
BAL/PAY ECO/TAC INT/TRADE FINAN

S67
COSGROVE C.A.,"AGRICULTURE, FINANCE AND POLITICS IN THE EUROPEAN COMMUNITY." EUR+WWI DIST/IND MARKET INT/ORG VOL/ASSN DELIB/GP TEC/DEV BAL/PWR BARGAIN ECO/TAC RATION CONFER 20 EEC. PAGE 28 F0538
ECO/DEV DIPLOM AGRI INT/TRADE

S67
DEMUTH J.,"GE: PROFILE OF A CORPORATION." USA+45 USA-45 LABOR ACT/RES RATION EDU/PROP ADJUD CT/SYS FASCISM 20. PAGE 32 F0619
LG/CO CONSERVE PRICE

S67
OLIVIER G.,"ASPECTS JURIDIQUES DE L'ADOPTION DU TRAITE CECA A LA CRISE CHARBONNIERE (SUITE ET FIN)" LAW DIST/IND PLAN DIPLOM RATION PRICE ADMIN COST DEMAND...POLICY CON/ANAL ECSC TREATY. PAGE 101 F1988
INT/TRADE INT/ORG EXTR/IND CONSTN

S67
WOLFE T.W.,"SOVIET MILITARY POLICY AT THE FIFTY YEAR MARK." USSR VIETNAM WOR+45 RATION AGREE WAR WEAPON CIVMIL/REL TREATY. PAGE 148 F2917
FORCES POLICY TIME/SEQ PLAN

RATIONAL....RATIONALITY

B29
JONES M.M.,CORPORATION CONTRIBUTIONS TO COMMUNITY WELFARE AGENCIES (PAMPHLET). DELIB/GP TAX CONTROL PARTIC RATIONAL POLICY. PAGE 68 F1339
LG/CO GIVE NEIGH SOC/WK

B42
DRUCKER P.F.,THE FUTURE OF INDUSTRIAL MAN; A CONSERVATIVE APPROACH. USA-45 LOC/G PLAN WAR CENTRAL RATIONAL TOTALISM ORD/FREE LAISSEZ ...PLURIST IDEA/COMP 19/20 HITLER/A. PAGE 34 F0664
INDUS SOCIETY REGION PROB/SOLV

B48
HAYEK F.A.,INDIVIDUALISM AND ECONOMIC ORDER. FINAN PLAN MORAL LAISSEZ SOCISM...POLICY DECISION PHIL/SCI HIST/WRIT. PAGE 57 F1122
RATIONAL KNOWL PERSON

S50
DREYFUS S.,"THE INDUSTRIAL DESIGNER AND THE BUSINESSMAN." SERV/IND PROB/SOLV ECO/TAC COST EFFICIENCY PROFIT RATIONAL...DECISION MGT. PAGE 34 F0662
CONSULT INDUS PRODUC UTIL

B57
DOWNS A.,AN ECONOMIC THEORY OF DEMOCRACY. NAT/G EDU/PROP RISK CHOOSE PERS/REL EQUILIB...SOC METH/CNCPT LOG STYLE. PAGE 34 F0659
DECISION RATIONAL

B60
MORRIS W.T.,ENGINEERING ECONOMY. AUTOMAT RISK RATIONAL...PROBABIL STAT CHARTS GAME SIMUL BIBLIOG
OP/RES DECISION

T 20. PAGE 94 F1838 MGT PROB/SOLV

B62
BRANCH M.C.,THE CORPORATE PLANNING PROCESS. FINAN EX/STRUC EDU/PROP CONTROL LEAD GP/REL PERS/REL RATIONAL PERCEPT...MGT MATH PROBABIL STAT GAME. PAGE 18 F0338 PROF/ORG PLAN DECISION PERSON

B62
COX O.C.,CAPITALISM AND AMERICAN LEADERSHIP. WOR+45 WOR-45 STRATA INDUS SECT INT/TRADE EXEC INGP/REL RACE/REL RATIONAL PWR WEALTH. PAGE 28 F0548 CAP/ISM LEAD ECO/DEV SOCIETY

B62
NATIONAL BUREAU ECONOMIC RES,THE RATE AND DIRECTION OF INVENTIVE ACTIVITY: ECONOMIC AND SOCIAL FACTORS. STRUCT INDUS MARKET R+D CREATE OP/RES TEC/DEV EFFICIENCY PRODUC RATIONAL UTIL...WELF/ST PHIL/SCI METH/CNCPT TIME. PAGE 97 F1895 DECISION PROB/SOLV MGT

B63
VON MISES L.,HUMAN ACTION: A TREATISE ON ECONOMICS (2ND ED.). SOCIETY MARKET TAX PAY PRICE DEMAND EQUILIB RATIONAL...PSY 20. PAGE 142 F2794 PLAN DRIVE ATTIT

B65
GRIFFIN C.E.,THE FREE SOCIETY. CONSTN SOCIETY MARKET FEDERAL RATIONAL WEALTH...MAJORIT 20 CIVIL/LIB. PAGE 51 F0999 CONCPT ORD/FREE CAP/ISM POPULISM

B65
HOLLER J.E.,POPULATION TRENDS AND ECONOMIC DEVELOPMENT IN THE FAR EAST (PAMPHLET). KOREA S/ASIA AGRI INDUS DELIB/GP PROB/SOLV RATIONAL ...POLICY CHARTS BIBLIOG 20 OUTER/MONG CHINJAP HONG/KONG. PAGE 61 F1197 CENSUS TREND ECO/UNDEV ASIA

S65
JOHNSON H.G.,"A THEORETICAL MODEL OF ECONOMIC NATIONALISM IN NEW AND DEVELOPING STATES." ELITES INDUS INT/TRADE EDU/PROP COST OPTIMAL RATIONAL PWR WEALTH SOCISM STERTYP. PAGE 67 F1325 NAT/LISM ECO/UNDEV GEN/LAWS

B66
CONFERENCE REGIONAL ACCOUNTS,REGIONAL ACCOUNTS FOR POLICY DECISIONS. PROB/SOLV CONTROL RATIONAL KNOWL ORD/FREE...POLICY DECISION MATH STAT ANTHOL 20. PAGE 27 F0523 GOV/REL REGION PLAN ECO/TAC

S67
GOLDSTEIN W.,"THE SCIENCE ESTABLISHMENT AND ITS POLITICAL CONTROL." WOR+45 SOCIETY GP/REL RATIONAL ORD/FREE. PAGE 48 F0941 CREATE ADJUST CONTROL

S67
LEMIEUX V.,"LA DIMENSION POLITIQUE DE L'ACTION RATIONNELLE." CONTROL GP/REL PERS/REL...DECISION NEW/IDEA GAME 20. PAGE 77 F1518 GEN/LAWS RATIONAL PWR

S67
NUSENBAUM A.A.,"ON THE QUESTION OF TENDENCIES IN AMERICAN EDUCATION." USA+45 USSR SOCIETY SCHOOL RATIONAL 20. PAGE 99 F1946 MARXIST IDEA/COMP GEN/LAWS EDU/PROP

S67
SOLT L.F.,"PURITANISM, CAPITALISM, DEMOCRACY, AND THE NEW SCIENCE." NAT/G GP/REL CONSERVE...IDEA/COMP GEN/LAWS. PAGE 124 F2440 SECT CAP/ISM RATIONAL POPULISM

RATNAM K.J. F2152

RAVKIN A. F2153

RAY D.D. F2154

RAY J. F2155

RAYBACK J.G. F2156

RAZA M.A. F2157

RAZAFIMBAHINY J. F2158

READ W.H. F2159

READER D.H. F2160

REAGAN M.D. F2161,F2162,F2163

REAGAN/RON....RONALD REAGAN

REALPOL....REALPOLITIK, PRACTICAL POLITICS

S67
JOHNSON L.B.,"BULLETS DO NOT DISCRIMINATE-LANDLORDS DO." PROB/SOLV EXEC LOBBY DEMAND...REALPOL SOC 20. PAGE 68 F1329 NAT/G DISCRIM POLICY

REALPOLITIK....SEE REALPOL

REC/INT....RECORDING OF INTERVIEWS

S61
BENOIT E.,"THE PROPENSITY TO REDUCE THE NATIONAL DEBT OUT OF DEFENSE SAVINGS." FUT USA+45 SOCIETY R+D PLAN...WELF/ST SOC REC/INT STERTYP TOT/POP 20. PAGE 13 F0250 WEALTH ECO/TAC

B62
HEILBRONER R.L.,THE MAKING OF ECONOMIC SOCIETY. FUT WOR-45 SOCIETY STRATA ECO/DEV ECO/UNDEV ECO/TAC LEGIT ROUTINE...SOC RECORD REC/INT KNO/TEST CENSUS STERTYP GEN/LAWS. PAGE 58 F1136 CAP/ISM SOCISM

B63
RUMMEL J.F.,RESEARCH METHODOLOGY IN BUSINESS. COMPUTER CREATE PROB/SOLV...CONT/OBS REC/INT QU/SEMANT SYS/QU SAMP CHARTS METH/COMP T 20. PAGE 115 F2260 OP/RES METH/CNCPT METH STAT

RECALL....RECALL PROCEDURE

RECEIVE....RECEIVING (IN WELFARE SENSE)

NCO
STOLPER W.,"SOCIAL FACTORS IN ECONOMIC PLANNING, WITH SPECIAL REFERENCE TO NIGERIA" AFR NIGER CULTURE FAM SECT RECEIVE ETIQUET ADMIN DEMAND 20. PAGE 126 F2494 ECO/UNDEV PLAN ADJUST RISK

N19
RIDLEY C.E.,MEASURING MUNICIPAL ACTIVITIES (PAMPHLET). FINAN SERV/IND FORCES RECEIVE INGP/REL HABITAT...POLICY SOC/WK 20. PAGE 111 F2191 MGT HEALTH WEALTH LOC/G

B20
PIGOU A.C.,THE ECONOMICS OF WELFARE. UNIV INDUS WORKER ACT/RES RECEIVE INCOME NEW/LIB...MAJORIT SOC/WK. PAGE 106 F2085 ECO/TAC WEALTH FINAN CONTROL

B53
DAHL R.A.,POLITICS, ECONOMICS, AND WELFARE. TEC/DEV BARGAIN ECO/TAC RECEIVE PRICE CONTROL LEAD INGP/REL ...POLICY GEN/LAWS. PAGE 29 F0572 SOCIETY GIVE

B57
WATSON G.,THE UNSERVILE STATE: ESSAYS IN LIBERTY AND WELFARE. UK LEGIS RECEIVE EDU/PROP COLONIAL ...WELF/ST 20 LIB/PARTY. PAGE 144 F2833 POL/PAR ORD/FREE CONTROL NEW/LIB

B59
STANFORD U, BOARD OF TRUSTEES,THE ALLOCATION OF ECONOMIC RESOURCES. WORKER PLAN BUDGET ECO/TAC TAX RECEIVE COST PRODUC...POLICY IDEA/COMP SIMUL ANTHOL 20. PAGE 125 F2468 INCOME PRICE FINAN

B60
PETERSON W.C.,THE WELFARE STATE IN FRANCE. EUR+WWI FRANCE FUT STRATA PROB/SOLV TAX GIVE RECEIVE INCOME ORD/FREE PWR...CHARTS 20. PAGE 105 F2070 NEW/LIB ECO/TAC WEALTH NAT/G

B60
SHANNON D.A.,THE GREAT DEPRESSION. USA-45 FINAN LG/CO SCHOOL SML/CO DELIB/GP RECEIVE REV EATING INCOME...ANTHOL MUNICH 20 ROOSEVLT/F CONGRESS. PAGE 120 F2365 WEALTH NAT/G AGRI INDUS

B61
MEXICO; CINCUENTA ANOS DE REVOLUCION VOL. II. L/A+17C SOCIETY LABOR RECEIVE GP/REL AGE/Y HEALTH ...SOC/WK ANTHOL MUNICH 20 MEXIC/AMER. PAGE 1 F0014 ECO/UNDEV STRUCT INDUS POL/PAR

B62
FRIEDMAN M.,CAPITALISM AND FREEDOM. USA+45 FINAN LG/CO WORKER INT/TRADE RECEIVE EDU/PROP CONTROL DISCRIM INCOME WEALTH POLICY. PAGE 44 F0859 CAP/ISM ORD/FREE NAT/G ECO/DEV

B62
PAKISTAN MINISTRY OF FINANCE,FOREIGN ECONOMIC AID: A REVIEW OF FOREIGN ECONOMIC AID TO PAKISTAN. EUR+WWI PAKISTAN UK USA+45 USSR ECO/UNDEV INT/ORG DELIB/GP DIPLOM ECO/TAC...CHARTS CMN/WLTH CHINJAP. PAGE 103 F2016 FOR/AID RECEIVE WEALTH FINAN

B63
COLUMBIA U SCHOOL OF LAW,PUBLIC INTERNATIONAL DEVELOPMENT FINANCING IN SENEGAL. SENEGAL FINAN DELIB/GP GIVE EFFICIENCY...CHARTS GOV/COMP ANTHOL 20. PAGE 26 F0511 FOR/AID PLAN RECEIVE ECO/UNDEV

B63
EL-NAGGAR S.,FOREIGN AID TO UNITED ARAB REPUBLIC. UAR USA+45 USSR AGRI FINAN INDUS FORCES EATING DEMAND...CHARTS METH/COMP 20 RESOURCE/N AID. PAGE 37 F0718 FOR/AID ECO/UNDEV RECEIVE PLAN

B63
RAO V.K.R.,FOREIGN AID AND INDIA'S ECONOMIC DEVELOPMENT. INDIA INT/ORG PROB/SOLV TEC/DEV ECO/TAC CONTROL WEALTH...TREND 20. PAGE 109 F2148 FOR/AID ECO/UNDEV RECEIVE DIPLOM

B63
STIFEL L.D.,THE TEXTILE INDUSTRY - A CASE STUDY OF INDUSTRIAL DEVELOPMENT IN THE PHILIPPINES (PAPER). PHILIPPINE WORKER CAP/ISM INT/TRADE TARIFFS RECEIVE PRICE ADMIN COST EFFICIENCY WEALTH...BIBLIOG 20. PAGE 126 F2486 S/ASIA ECO/UNDEV PROC/MFG NAT/G

B64
MC GOVERN G.S.,WAR AGAINST WANT. USA+45 AGRI DIPLOM INT/TRADE GIVE RECEIVE DEMAND HEALTH 20 KENNEDY/JF FOOD/PEACE. PAGE 87 F1714 FOR/AID ECO/DEV POLICY EATING

B64
MITAU G.T.,INSOLUBLE PROBLEMS: CASE PROBLEMS ON THE FUNCTIONS OF STATE AND LOCAL GOVERNMENT. USA+45 AIR FINAN LABOR POL/PAR PROB/SOLV TAX RECEIVE CONTROL GP/REL 20 CASEBOOK ZONING. PAGE 92 F1807 ADJUD LOC/G PROVS

B65
COUGHLIN B.J.,CHURCH AND STATE IN SOCIAL WELFARE. USA+45 RECEIVE GP/REL ORD/FREE WEALTH NEW/LIB. PAGE 28 F0542 CULTURE SECT VOL/ASSN GIVE

B65
FERMAN L.A.,POVERTY IN AMERICA: A BOOK OF READINGS. USA+45 CULTURE ECO/DEV PROB/SOLV ALL/VALS...POLICY ANTHOL BIBLIOG 20 POVRTY/WAR. PAGE 40 F0785 WEALTH TEC/DEV CONCPT RECEIVE

B65
GOODSELL C.T.,ADMINISTRATION OF A REVOLUTION. PUERT/RICO ECO/UNDEV FINAN POL/PAR PROVS LEGIS PLAN BUDGET RECEIVE ADMIN COLONIAL LEAD MUNICH 20 ROOSEVLT/F. PAGE 49 F0951 EXEC SOC

B65
GORDON W.,THE POLITICAL ECONOMY OF LATIN AMERICA. L/A+17C FINAN MARKET PROB/SOLV TEC/DEV RECEIVE ADMIN WEALTH 20. PAGE 49 F0962 ECO/UNDEV INT/TRADE REGION POLICY

B65
LITTLE I.M.D.,INTERNATIONAL AID. UK WOR+45 AGRI INDUS GIVE RECEIVE COLONIAL BAL/PAY WEALTH...POLICY GOV/COMP METH/COMP 20. PAGE 81 F1584 FOR/AID DIPLOM ECO/UNDEV NAT/G

B65
MEAGHER R.F.,PUBLIC INTERNATIONAL DEVELOPMENT FINANCING IN SUDAN. SUDAN FINAN DELIB/GP GIVE ...CHARTS GOV/COMP 20. PAGE 89 F1740 FOR/AID PLAN RECEIVE ECO/UNDEV

B65
OFFICE OF ECONOMIC OPPORTUNITY,CATALOG OF FEDERAL PROGRAMS FOR INDIVIDUAL AND COMMUNITY IMPROVEMENT. USA+45 WEALTH NEW/LIB 20. PAGE 101 F1980 INDEX ECO/UNDEV RECEIVE NAT/G

B65
SELIGMAN B.B.,POVERTY AS A PUBLIC ISSUE. USA+45 ECO/DEV NAT/G PAY RECEIVE PERS/REL INCOME NEW/LIB 20. PAGE 119 F2347 LEGIS ECO/TAC STRATA DISCRIM

B65
SHOSTAK A.B.,NEW PERSPECTIVES ON POVERTY. USA+45 SCHOOL WORKER INGP/REL RACE/REL AGE/C AGE/Y ATTIT HEALTH...ANTHOL BIBLIOG 20 JOHNSON/LB POVRTY/WAR. PAGE 121 F2388 WEALTH NAT/G RECEIVE INCOME

B65
US OFFICE ECONOMIC OPPORTUNITY,CATALOG OF FEDERAL PROGRAMS FOR INDIVIDUAL AND COMMUNITY IMPROVEMENT. USA+45 GIVE RECEIVE ADMIN HEALTH KNOWL SKILL WEALTH ...CHARTS MUNICH. PAGE 138 F2721 BIBLIOG CLIENT ECO/TAC

B65
WEISBROD B.A.,THE ECONOMICS OF POVERTY: AN AMERICAN PARADOX. USA+45 NAT/G WORKER TASK INGP/REL DISCRIM POLICY. PAGE 145 F2852 ECO/DEV WEALTH RECEIVE STRATA

B66
CHASE S.B. JR.,PROBLEMS IN PUBLIC EXPENDITURE ANALYSIS. DIST/IND INDUS OP/RES PLAN BUDGET RECEIVE PRICE RISK COST INCOME...CHARTS ANTHOL 20. PAGE 23 F0455 ECO/DEV FINAN NAT/G INSPECT

B66
GOODMAN L.H.,ECONOMIC PROGRESS AND SOCIAL WELFARE. USA+45 STRATA STRUCT ECO/TAC EFFICIENCY...MGT 20. PAGE 49 F0949 SOC/WK RECEIVE GP/COMP POLICY

B66
HUNT C.L.,SOCIAL ASPECTS OF ECONOMIC DEVELOPMENT. S/ASIA AGRI FAM TEC/DEV RECEIVE EDU/PROP OWN...GEOG MUNICH 20. PAGE 63 F1243 SOC STRATA ATTIT ECO/UNDEV

B66
LEAGUE OF WOMEN VOTERS OF US,FOREIGN AID AT THE CROSSROADS. USA+45 WOR+45 DELIB/GP PROB/SOLV DIPLOM INT/TRADE RECEIVE BAL/PAY...CHARTS 20 UN ALL/PROG. PAGE 76 F1498 FOR/AID GIVE ECO/UNDEV PLAN

B66
ORG FOR ECO COOP AND DEVEL,GEOGRAPHICAL DISTRIBUTION OF FINANCIAL FLOWS TO LESS DEVELOPED COUNTRIES. WOR+45 DIPLOM INT/TRADE GIVE RECEIVE REPAR REGION WEALTH...GEOG STAT CHARTS 20 OECD. PAGE 102 F1997 FINAN ECO/UNDEV INT/ORG FOR/AID

B66
SHULTZ G.P.,STRATEGIES FOR THE DISPLACED WORKER. USA+45 COMPUTER TEC/DEV BARGAIN RECEIVE EDU/PROP CONFER GP/REL...MGT METH/COMP 20. PAGE 121 F2391 ECO/DEV WORKER PLAN AUTOMAT

B67
GREEN C.,NEGATIVE TAXES AND THE POVERTY PROBLEM. COST EFFICIENCY INCOME NEW/LIB...METH/CNCPT CHARTS METH/COMP BIBLIOG 20. PAGE 50 F0983 TAX RECEIVE WEALTH PLAN

B67
SPURRIER R.B.,THE OVERPOPULATED SOCIETY. WORKER EATING PERS/REL DEMAND EQUILIB ILLEGIT INCOME HABITAT 20. PAGE 125 F2461 BIO/SOC FOR/AID DRIVE RECEIVE

S67
GREEN C.,"SCHEMES FOR TRANSFERRING INCOME TO THE POOR." BUDGET GIVE RECEIVE DEBATE COST INCOME ...SOC/WK METH/COMP. PAGE 50 F0982 TAX WEALTH PLAN ACT/RES

S67
HILDEBRAND G.H.,"SECOND THOUGHTS ON THE NEGATIVE INCOME TAX." PLAN BUDGET ECO/TAC GIVE RECEIVE DEBATE EFFICIENCY INCOME...METH/COMP COSTS. PAGE 59 F1169 TAX WEALTH SOC/WK ACT/RES

S67
JENCKS C.E.,"SOCIAL STATUS OF COAL MINERS IN BRITAIN SINCE NATIONALIZATION." UK STRATA STRUCT LABOR RECEIVE GP/REL INCOME OWN ATTIT HABITAT...MGT T 20. PAGE 67 F1312 EXTR/IND WORKER CONTROL NAT/G

S67
PAULY M.V.,"MIXED PUBLIC AND PRIVATE FINANCING OF EDUCATION." STRATA PAY RECEIVE COST INCOME OPTIMAL METH/COMP. PAGE 104 F2039 SCHOOL PLAN TAX EFFICIENCY

S67
THORKELSON H.,"FOOD STAMPS AND HUNGER IN AMERICA." USA+45 LAW DELIB/GP ADMIN COST DEMAND POLICY. PAGE 130 F2570 WEALTH RECEIVE EATING PLAN

N67
US HOUSE,MESSAGE FROM THE PRESIDENT OF THE UNITED STATES: URBAN AND RURAL POVERTY (PAMPHLET). USA+45 ACT/RES PLAN BUDGET RENT MUNICH 20 PRESIDENT. PAGE 136 F2685 NAT/G POLICY CREATE RECEIVE

RECIFE....RECIFE, BRAZIL

RECIPROCITY....SEE SANCTION

RECK D. F2164

RECORD....RECORDING OF DIRECT OBSERVATIONS

B20
WEBB S.,INDUSTRIAL DEMOCRACY. UK PARTIC GP/REL ...SOC OBS RECORD CHARTS 18/20. PAGE 144 F2838 LABOR NAT/G VOL/ASSN MAJORIT

S49
SHEPHARD H.A.,"DEMOCRATIC CONTROL IN A LABOR UNION." FUT CONSTN STRUCT TEC/DEV LEAD PARTIC RACE/REL CENTRAL DRIVE HABITAT RECORD. PAGE 120 F2374 LABOR MAJORIT CONTROL PWR

S50
EBY K.,"RESEARCH IN LABOR UNIONS." EDU/PROP INGP/REL PWR...METH/CNCPT OBS. PAGE 36 F0693 RECORD QU LABOR PARTIC

L52
HUTH A.G.,"COMMUNICATION AND ECONOMIC DEVELOPMENT." FUT WOR+45 CULTURE SOCIETY INT/ORG PLAN TEC/DEV EDU/PROP DRIVE KNOWL WEALTH...POLICY CONCPT RECORD STERTYP GEN/LAWS COMMUN TOT/POP UNESCO 20 UN CMN/WLTH. PAGE 64 F1250 ECO/UNDEV

B53
BOULDING K.E.,THE ORGANIZATIONAL REVOLUTION. FUT CULTURE ECO/DEV LABOR PROF/ORG ECO/TAC MORAL...SOC CONCPT RECORD INT SOC/EXP 20. PAGE 17 F0321 SOCIETY TREND

B54
EMERSON F.D.,SHAREHOLDER DEMOCRACY: A BROADER OUTLOOK FOR CORPORATIONS. DELIB/GP EX/STRUC LEGIS ADJUD CONTROL REPRESENT INGP/REL OWN PWR...POLICY STAT RECORD. PAGE 37 F0727 LG/CO PARTIC MAJORIT TREND

L54
OPLER M.E.,"SOCIAL ASPECTS OF TECHNICAL ASSISTANCE IN OPERATION." WOR+45 VOL/ASSN CREATE PLAN TEC/DEV EDU/PROP ALL/VALS...METH/CNCPT OBS RECORD TREND UN 20. PAGE 101 F1993 INT/ORG CONSULT FOR/AID

I55
KISER M.,"ORGANIZATION OF AMERICAN STATES." L/A+17C USA+45 ECO/UNDEV INT/ORG NAT/G PLAN TEC/DEV DIPLOM ECO/TAC INT/TRADE EDU/PROP ADMIN ALL/VALS...POLICY MGT RECORD ORG/CHARTS OAS COMMUN 20. PAGE 71 F1401 VOL/ASSN ECO/DEV REGION

B56
BELL P.W.,THE STERLING AREA IN THE POSTWAR WORLD. EUR+WWI FUT S/ASIA UK ECO/DEV PLAN DIPLOM WEALTH ...STAT RECORD CHARTS GEN/LAWS FOR/TRADE TOT/POP 20. PAGE 12 F0235 FINAN ECO/TAC

B57
WARRINER D.,LAND REFORM AND DEVELOPMENT IN THE MIDDLE EAST: A STUDY OF EGYPT, SYRIA AND IRAQ. IRAQ ISLAM SYRIA UAR AGRI DIST/IND PLAN TEC/DEV DOMIN REV ATTIT WEALTH...SOC METH/CNCPT STAT OBS RECORD HIST/WRIT TREND GEN/LAWS FAO 20. PAGE 143 F2825
ECO/UNDEV CONCPT

S58
SCHULZE R.O.,"THE ROLE OF ECONOMIC DOMINANTS IN COMMUNITY POWER STRUCTURE." ECO/TAC ROUTINE ATTIT OBJECTIVE...SOC RECORD CENSUS. PAGE 118 F2319
SOCIETY STRUCT PROB/SOLV

S59
HOFFMAN P.,"OPERATION BREAKTHROUGH." AFR S/ASIA STRUCT INDUS CONSULT TEC/DEV ATTIT RIGID/FLEX SKILL WEALTH...TECHNIC CONCPT STYLE RECORD CHARTS ORG/CHARTS GEN/METH VAL/FREE 20. PAGE 61 F1190
ECO/UNDEV EDU/PROP FOR/AID

S60
DUNN J.M.,"AMERICAN DEPENDENCE ON MATERIALS IMPORTS: THE WORLD-WIDE RESOURCE BASE." USA+45 WOR+45 NAT/G ATTIT WEALTH...RECORD TIME/SEQ CHARTS FOR/TRADE 20. PAGE 35 F0680
ACT/RES ECO/TAC

S60
HERZ J.H.,"EAST GERMANY: PROGRESS AND PROSPECTS." COM AGRI FINAN INDUS LOC/G NAT/G FORCES PLAN TEC/DEV DOMIN ADMIN COERCE DRIVE PERCEPT RIGID/FLEX MORAL ORD/FREE PWR...MARXIST PSY SOC RECORD STERTYP WORK. PAGE 59 F1158
POL/PAR STRUCT GERMANY

B61
DE VRIES E.,MAN IN RAPID SOCIAL CHANGE. WOR+45 SOCIETY ECO/DEV ECO/UNDEV AGRI INDUS FAM SECT TEC/DEV ATTIT...RECORD 20 CHRISTIAN. PAGE 31 F0607
CULTURE ALL/VALS SOC TASK

B61
DUKE UNIVERSITY,EXPULSION OR OPPRESSION OF BUSINESS ASSOCIATES: "SQUEEZE-OUTS" IN SMALL ENTERPRISES. LAW CONTROL PARTIC COERCE INGP/REL...POLICY RECORD INT. PAGE 35 F0674
PWR MGT SML/CO ECO/TAC

S61
NOVE A.,"THE SOVIET MODEL AND UNDERDEVELOPED COUNTRIES." COM FUT USSR WOR+45 CULTURE ECO/DEV POL/PAR FOR/AID EDU/PROP ADMIN MORAL WEALTH ...POLICY RECORD HIST/WRIT 20. PAGE 99 F1942
ECO/UNDEV PLAN

B62
HEILBRONER R.L.,THE MAKING OF ECONOMIC SOCIETY. FUT WOR-45 SOCIETY STRATA ECO/DEV ECO/UNDEV ECO/TAC LEGIT ROUTINE...SOC RECORD REC/INT KNO/TEST CENSUS STERTYP GEN/LAWS. PAGE 58 F1136
CAP/ISM SOCISM

B63
INTERNATIONAL BANK RECONST DEV,THE WORLD BANK GROUP IN ASIA. ASIA S/ASIA INDUS TEC/DEV ECO/TAC...RECORD 20 IBRD WORLD/BANK. PAGE 65 F1273
INT/ORG DIPLOM ECO/UNDEV FINAN

S63
DIEBOLD W. JR.,"THE NEW SITUATION OF INTERNATIONAL TRADE POLICY." EUR+WWI FRANCE FUT UK USA+45 WOR+45 DIST/IND PLAN INT/TRADE EDU/PROP PWR WEALTH ...RECORD TREND GEN/LAWS EEC TRUE/GP VAL/FREE APPLIC 20. PAGE 33 F0636
MARKET ECO/TAC

S63
MONROE A.D.,"BRITAIN AND THE EUROPEAN COMMUNITY." EUR+WWI FRANCE NAT/G DELIB/GP TOP/EX ECO/TAC DOMIN PWR...POLICY RECORD GEN/LAWS EEC EFTA 20 EFTA CMN/WLTH. PAGE 93 F1817
VOL/ASSN ATTIT UK

S63
SHONFIELD A.,"AFTER BRUSSELS." EUR+WWI FRANCE GERMANY UK ECO/DEV DIST/IND MARKET VOL/ASSN DELIB/GP CREATE INT/TRADE ATTIT RIGID/FLEX...RECORD TREND GEN/LAWS EEC COMMUN CMN/WLTH 20. PAGE 121 F2385
PLAN ECO/TAC

B64
HARRIS S.E.,ECONOMICS OF THE KENNEDY YEARS AND A LOOK AHEAD. USA+45 PLAN BUDGET NEW/LIB...STAT RECORD IDEA/COMP PERS/COMP INDEX 20 KENNEDY/JF EISNHWR/DD JOHNSON/LB. PAGE 56 F1091
ECO/TAC CHIEF POLICY NAT/G

B64
MEISEL J.,PAPERS ON THE 1962 ELECTION. CANADA PROVS SECT GP/REL CONSEN EFFICIENCY...MAJORIT 20. PAGE 89 F1751
POL/PAR RECORD CHOOSE STRATA

B64
US HOUSE COMM BANKING-CURR,INTERNATIONAL DEVELOPMENT ASSOCIATION ACT AMENDMENT. CHINA/COM USA+45 USSR FINAN FORCES LEGIS DIPLOM CONFER EFFICIENCY...CHARTS GOV/COMP 20 PRESIDENT CONGRESS INTL/DEV. PAGE 136 F2689
BAL/PAY FOR/AID RECORD ECO/TAC

L64
CARNEGIE ENDOWMENT INT. PEACE,"ECONOMIC AND SOCIAL QUESTION (ISSUES BEFORE THE NINETEENTH GENERAL ASSEMBLY)." WOR+45 ECO/DEV ECO/UNDEV INDUS R+D DELIB/GP CREATE PLAN TEC/DEV ECO/TAC FOR/AID BAL/PAY...RECORD UN 20. PAGE 21 F0414
INT/ORG INT/TRADE

S64
CARNEGIE ENDOWMENT INT. PEACE,"ADMINISTRATION AND BUDGET (ISSUES BEFORE THE NINETEENTH GENERAL ASSEMBLY)." WOR+45 FINAN BUDGET ECO/TAC ROUTINE COST...STAT RECORD UN. PAGE 21 F0415
INT/ORG ADMIN

L65
DAANE J.D.,"THE EVOLVING INTERNATIONAL MONETARY MECHANISM." VOL/ASSN CREATE PLAN FOR/AID INT/TRADE CONFER BAL/PAY...RECORD PREDICT IMF. PAGE 29 F0569
INT/ORG ECO/TAC TREND GP/COMP

S65
BRANDENBURG F.,"THE RELEVANCE OF MEXICAN EXPERIENCE TO LATIN AMERICAN DEVELOPMENT." BRAZIL CHILE VENEZUELA STRUCT ECO/UNDEV AGRI CREATE ECO/TAC ...STAT RECORD MEXIC/AMER ARGEN COLOMB. PAGE 18 F0340
L/A+17C GOV/COMP

S65
MUNZI U.,"THE EUROPEAN SOCIAL FUND IN THE DEVELOPMENT OF THE MEDITERRANEAN REGIONS OF THE EEC." FUT GREECE ITALY PORTUGAL SPAIN TURKEY WORKER TEC/DEV ECO/TAC REGION...STAT EEC. PAGE 95 F1862
ECO/UNDEV PREDICT RECORD

S65
SOPER T.,"THE EEC AND AID TO AFRICA." FRANCE UK ECO/UNDEV INT/TRADE TARIFFS REGION ROUTINE CENTRAL DISCRIM...DECISION RECORD EEC. PAGE 124 F2443
AFR FOR/AID COLONIAL

S65
WHITAKER A.P.,"ARGENTINA: STRUGGLE FOR RECOVERY." L/A+17C USA+45 NAT/G TOP/EX PLAN LEGIT COERCE REV RIGID/FLEX PWR WEALTH...RECORD ALL/PROG ARGEN FOR/TRADE 20. PAGE 146 F2867
POL/PAR ECO/TAC NAT/LISM

S66
LAURENS H.,"LES PAYS OCCIDENTAUX ET LE MARCHE CHINOIS." EUR+WWI FUT S/ASIA AGRI INDUS VOL/ASSN ECO/TAC BAL/PAY...RECORD PREDICT TREATY. PAGE 76 F1488
ASIA INT/TRADE TREND STAT

S67
SCHWARZWELLER H.K.,"SOCIAL CLASS ORIGINS, RURAL-URBAN MIGRATION, AND ECONOMIC LIFE CHANGES." USA+45 SOCIETY STRUCT FAM NEIGH INCOME...SOC RECORD CHARTS MUNICH. PAGE 118 F2326
CLASSIF WEALTH AGRI

RECORDING OF INTERVIEWS....SEE REC/INT

RECTITUDE....SEE MORAL

RED/GUARD....RED GUARD

REDDAWAY W.B. F2165

REDFIELD/R....ROBERT REDFIELD

C60
HOSELITZ B.,"THE ROLE OF CITIES IN THE ECONOMIC GROWTH OF UNDERDEVELOPED COUNTRIES" IN "SOCIOLOGICAL ASPECTS OF ECONOMIC GROWTH"(BMR). CULTURE LOC/G ACT/RES...SOC IDEA/COMP METH/COMP METH MUNICH IND 14/20 REDFIELD/R. PAGE 62 F1218
METH/CNCPT TEC/DEV ECO/UNDEV

REDFORD E.S. F2166,F2167,F2168,F2169

REDLICH F. F2170

REED/STAN....JUSTICE STANLEY REED

REES A. F2171,F2172,F2173

REFERENDUM....REFERENDUM; SEE ALSO PARTIC

REFORMERS....REFORMERS

B14
LEVINE L.,SYNDICALISM IN FRANCE (2ND ED.). FRANCE LAW SOCIETY ECO/DEV NAT/G ECO/TAC LEAD ATTIT ...POLICY CONCPT STAT BIBLIOG 18/20 REFORMERS. PAGE 79 F1542
LABOR INDUS SOCISM REV

B64
WERTHEIM W.F.,EAST-WEST PARALLELS. INDONESIA S/ASIA NAT/G SECT...TIME/SEQ METH REFORMERS S/EASTASIA. PAGE 145 F2860
SOC ECO/UNDEV CULTURE NAT/LISM

B67
COWLING M.,1867 DISRAELI, GLADSTONE, AND REVOLUTION; THE PASSING OF THE SECOND REFORM BILL. UK LEGIS LEAD LOBBY GP/REL INGP/REL...DECISION BIBLIOG 19 REFORMERS. PAGE 28 F0545
PARL/PROC POL/PAR ATTIT LAW

B67
MARRIS P.,DILEMMAS OF SOCIAL REFORM: POVERTY AND COMMUNITY ACTION IN THE UNITED STATES. USA+45 NAT/G OP/RES ADMIN PARTIC EFFICIENCY WEALTH...SOC METH/COMP T MUNICH 20 REFORMERS. PAGE 85 F1674
STRUCT PROB/SOLV COST

B67
PIKE F.B.,FREEDOM AND REFORM IN LATIN AMERICA. BRAZIL URUGUAY CONSTN CULTURE SECT DIPLOM EDU/PROP PARTIC DRIVE ALL/VALS CATHISM...GEOG ANTHOL BIBLIOG REFORMERS BOLIV. PAGE 106 F2086
L/A+17C ORD/FREE ECO/UNDEV REV

S67
RICHMAN B.M.,"SOVIET MANAGEMENT IN TRANSITION." USSR FINAN MARKET EX/STRUC PLAN PROB/SOLV TEC/DEV CONTROL LEAD CENTRAL EFFICIENCY...METH/COMP 20
MGT MARXISM POLICY

REFORMERS. PAGE 111 F2186 AUTHORIT

REGION....REGIONALISM

N19
EAST KENTUCKY REGIONAL PLAN,PROGRAM 60: A DECADE OF ACTION FOR PROGRESS IN EASTERN KENTUCKY (PAMPHLET). USA+45 AGRI CONSTRUC INDUS CONSULT ACT/RES PROB/SOLV EDU/PROP GOV/REL HEALTH KENTUCKY. PAGE 35 F0689
REGION ADMIN PLAN ECO/UNDEV

N19
EAST KENTUCKY REGIONAL PLAN,PROGRAM 60 REPORT: ACTION FOR PORGRESS IN EASTERN KENTUCKY (PAMPHLET). USA+45 CONSTRUC INDUS ACT/RES PROB/SOLV EDU/PROP ADMIN GOV/REL KENTUCKY. PAGE 35 F0690
REGION PLAN ECO/UNDEV CONSULT

N19
PEGRUM D.F.,URBAN TRANSPORT AND THE LOCATION OF INDUSTRY IN METROPOLITAN LOS ANGELES (PAMPHLET). USA+45 WORKER...GEOG CHARTS MUNICH. PAGE 104 F2049
DIST/IND REGION INDUS

N19
WILSON T.,FINANCIAL ASSISTANCE WITH REGIONAL DEVELOPMENT (PAMPHLET). CANADA INDUS NAT/G PLAN TAX CONTROL COST EFFICIENCY...POLICY CHARTS 20. PAGE 147 F2902
FINAN ECO/TAC REGION GOV/REL

B25
WILLIAMS B.,THE SELBORNE MEMORANDUM. AFR FUT SOUTH/AFR UK NAT/G BUDGET DIPLOM REGION GOV/REL SOVEREIGN...POLICY CHARTS 20 UNIFICA SELBORNE/W. PAGE 147 F2888
COLONIAL PROVS

B27
SIEGFRIED A.,AMERICA COMES OF AGE: A FRENCH ANALYSIS (TRANS. BY H.H. HEMMING AND DORIS HEMMING). FRANCE UK POL/PAR WORKER TEC/DEV DIPLOM REGION RACE/REL ADJUST PRODUC HEREDITY...TIME/SEQ GP/COMP SOC/INTEG 20 DEMOCRAT REPUBLICAN KKK. PAGE 122 F2398
USA-45 CULTURE ECO/DEV SOC

B30
GREEN F.M.,CONSTITUTIONAL DEVELOPMENT IN THE SOUTH ATLANTIC STATES, 1776-1860; A STUDY IN THE EVOLUTION OF DEMOCRACY. USA-45 ELITES SOCIETY STRATA ECO/DEV AGRI POL/PAR EX/STRUC LEGIS CT/SYS REGION...BIBLIOG 18/19 MARYLAND VIRGINIA GEORGIA NORTH/CAR SOUTH/CAR. PAGE 50 F0984
CONSTN PROVS PLURISM REPRESENT

B38
HOBSON J.A.,IMPERIALISM. MOD/EUR UK WOR-45 CULTURE ECO/UNDEV NAT/G VOL/ASSN PLAN EDU/PROP LEGIT REGION COERCE ATTIT PWR...POLICY PLURIST TIME/SEQ GEN/LAWS TERR/GP 19/20. PAGE 60 F1187
DOMIN ECO/TAC BAL/PWR COLONIAL

B42
DRUCKER P.F.,THE FUTURE OF INDUSTRIAL MAN; A CONSERVATIVE APPROACH. USA-45 LOC/G PLAN WAR CENTRAL RATIONAL TOTALISM ORD/FREE LAISSEZ ...PLURIST IDEA/COMP 19/20 HITLER/A. PAGE 34 F0664
INDUS SOCIETY REGION PROB/SOLV

B49
PARMELEE M.,GEO-ECONOMIC REGIONAL AND WORLD FEDERATION. FUT WOR+45 WOR-45 SOCIETY VOL/ASSN PLAN ...METH/CNCPT SIMUL GEN/METH TERR/GP TOT/POP 20. PAGE 103 F2028
INT/ORG GEOG REGION

B50
HARTLAND P.C.,BALANCE OF INTERREGIONAL PAYMENTS OF NEW ENGLAND. USA+45 TEC/DEV ECO/TAC LEGIT ROUTINE BAL/PAY PROFIT 20 NEW/ENGLND FED/RESERV. PAGE 56 F1102
ECO/DEV FINAN REGION PLAN

B52
SECRETARIAT COUNCIL OF EUROPE,THE STRASBOURG PLAN. EUR+WWI CONSULT PLAN ECO/TAC TARIFFS DEBATE REGION 20 COUNCL/EUR STRASBOURG. PAGE 119 F2340
INT/ORG ECO/DEV INT/TRADE DIPLOM

B54
FRIEDMAN W.,THE PUBLIC CORPORATION: A COMPARATIVE SYMPOSIUM (UNIVERSITY OF TORONTO SCHOOL OF LAW COMPARATIVE LAW SERIES, VOL. I). AFR SWEDEN USA+45 INDUS INT/ORG NAT/G REGION CENTRAL FEDERAL...POLICY JURID IDEA/COMP NAT/COMP ANTHOL 20 MONOPOLY EUROPE. PAGE 44 F0861
LAW SOCISM LG/CO OWN

B55
FLORINSKY M.T.,INTEGRATED EUROPE. EUR+WWI FRANCE ITALY NETHERLAND UK ECO/DEV INT/ORG FORCES LEGIT FEDERAL ATTIT PWR WEALTH...POLICY GEOG CONCPT GEN/LAWS TOT/POP EEC OEEC 20. PAGE 42 F0816
FUT ECO/TAC REGION

B55
STILLMAN C.W.,AFRICA IN THE MODERN WORLD. AFR USA+45 WOR+45 INT/TRADE COLONIAL PARTIC REGION GOV/REL RACE/REL 20. PAGE 126 F2489
ECO/UNDEV DIPLOM POLICY STRUCT

L55
KISER M.,"ORGANIZATION OF AMERICAN STATES." L/A+17C USA+45 ECO/UNDEV INT/ORG NAT/G PLAN TEC/DEV DIPLOM ECO/TAC INT/TRADE EDU/PROP ADMIN ALL/VALS...POLICY MGT RECORD ORG/CHARTS OAS COMMUN 20. PAGE 71 F1401
VOL/ASSN ECO/DEV REGION

B56
ISARD W.,LOCATION AND SPACE-ECONOMY: GENERAL THEORY RELATING TO INDUSTRIAL LOCATION, MARKET AREAS, LAND USE, TRADE... UNIV DIST/IND MARKET LG/CO SML/CO TEC/DEV GP/REL EQUILIB HABITAT...NEW/IDEA MATH CHARTS 20. PAGE 66 F1290
GEN/LAWS GEOG INDUS REGION

B57
ARON R.,L'UNIFICATION ECONOMIQUE DE L'EUROPE. EUR+WWI SWITZERLND UK INT/ORG NAT/G REGION NAT/LISM ORD/FREE PWR...CONCPT METH/CNCPT OBS TREND STERTYP GEN/LAWS EEC FOR/TRADE 20. PAGE 6 F0118
VOL/ASSN ECO/TAC

B57
TRIFFIN R.,EUROPE AND THE MONEY MUDDLE. USA+45 INT/ORG NAT/G CONSULT PLAN ECO/TAC EXEC ROUTINE BAL/PAY WEALTH...METH/CNCPT OBS TREND CHARTS STERTYP GEN/METH EEC TERR/GP VAL/FREE ECSC. PAGE 131 F2587
EUR+WWI ECO/DEV REGION

N57
U WISCONSIN BUREAU OF GOVT,SERVICE SALES OF THE CITY OF MADISON TO METROPOLITAN COMMUNITIES AND NONRESIDENTS (PAMPHLET). DIST/IND LOC/G ADMIN ...DECISION GOV/COMP MUNICH. PAGE 132 F2597
REGION ECO/TAC PLAN

B58
CLAUNCH J.M.,THE PROBLEM OF GOVERNMENT IN METROPOLITAN AREAS. CULTURE INDUS POL/PAR PLAN REGION GP/REL...CENSUS ANTHOL MUNICH 20. PAGE 25 F0486
PROB/SOLV SOC

B58
INTERNATIONAL ECONOMIC ASSN,ECONOMICS OF INTERNATIONAL MIGRATION. WOR+45 WOR-45 ECO/UNDEV FINAN NAT/G REGION...NAT/COMP METH 20. PAGE 65 F1275
CENSUS GEOG DIPLOM ECO/TAC

B58
KINDLEBERGER C.P.,INTERNATIONAL ECONOMICS. WOR+45 WOR-45 ECO/DEV ECO/UNDEV FINAN VOL/ASSN ACT/RES DIPLOM ECO/TAC LEGIT REGION ATTIT DRIVE ORD/FREE WEALTH...POLICY STAT TREND GEN/LAWS EEC ECSC OEEC 20. PAGE 71 F1391
INT/ORG BAL/PWR TARIFFS

B58
MYRDAL G.,RICH LANDS AND POOR: THE ROAD TO WORLD PROSPERITY. FUT WOR+45 WOR-45 ECO/DEV ECO/UNDEV INT/ORG PLAN ECO/TAC REGION...GEOG TIME/SEQ GEN/LAWS TOT/POP 20. PAGE 96 F1880
WEALTH TREND FOR/AID INT/TRADE

B58
SCITOUSKY T.,ECONOMIC THEORY AND WESTERN EUROPEAN INTEGRATION. EUR+WWI INT/ORG ACT/RES INT/TRADE REGION BAL/PAY WEALTH...METH/CNCPT STAT CHARTS GEN/METH ECSC TOT/POP EEC OEEC 20. PAGE 118 F2328
ECO/TAC

B59
DIEBOLD W. JR.,THE SCHUMAN PLAN: A STUDY IN ECONOMIC COOPERATION, 1950-1959. EUR+WWI FRANCE GERMANY USA+45 EXTR/IND CONSULT DELIB/GP PLAN DIPLOM ECO/TAC INT/TRADE ROUTINE ORD/FREE WEALTH ...METH/CNCPT STAT CONT/OBS INT TIME/SEQ ECSC 20. PAGE 33 F0635
INT/ORG REGION

B59
YRARRAZAVAL E.,AMERICA LATINE EN LA GUERRA FRIA. AFR EUR+WWI L/A+17C USA+45 USSR WOR+45 INDUS INT/ORG NAT/LISM POLICY. PAGE 150 F2953
REGION DIPLOM ECO/UNDEV INT/TRADE

L59
MURPHY J.C.,"SOME IMPLICATIONS OF EUROPE'S COMMON MARKET. IN (COOK P, ECONOMIC DEVELOPMENT AND INTERNATIONAL TRADE.." EUR+WWI ECO/DEV DIST/IND INDUS NAT/G PLAN ECO/TAC INT/TRADE WEALTH...STAT TREND OEEC TOT/POP 20 EEC. PAGE 95 F1866
MARKET INT/ORG REGION

S59
GILPATRICK T.V.,"PRICE SUPPORT POLICY AND THE MIDWEST FARM VOTE" (BMR)" NAT/G PRICE CONTROL REGION...POLICY CHARTS 440 20 MIDWEST/US CONGRESS REPUBLICAN EISNHWR/DD 20. PAGE 47 F0925
POL/PAR AGRI ATTIT CHOOSE

S59
PLAZA G.,"FOR A REGIONAL MARKET IN LATIN AMERICA." FUT L/A+17C CULTURE INDUS NAT/G ECO/TAC INT/TRADE ATTIT WEALTH...NEW/IDEA TREND OAS 20. PAGE 106 F2092
MARKET INT/ORG REGION

B60
KRISTENSEN T.,THE ECONOMIC WORLD BALANCE. FUT WOR+45 CULTURE ECO/DEV BAL/PWR INT/TRADE REGION PWR WEALTH...STAT TREND CHARTS 20. PAGE 73 F1442
ECO/UNDEV ECO/TAC FOR/AID

B60
LISTER L.,EUROPE'S COAL AND STEEL COMMUNITY. FRANCE GERMANY STRUCT ECO/DEV EXTR/IND INDUS MARKET NAT/G DELIB/GP ECO/TAC INT/TRADE EDU/PROP ATTIT RIGID/FLEX ORD/FREE PWR WEALTH...CONCPT STAT TIME/SEQ CHARTS ECSC TERR/GP 20. PAGE 81 F1582
EUR+WWI INT/ORG REGION

B60
THORBECKE E.,THE TENDENCY TOWARDS REGIONALIZATION IN INTERNATIONAL TRADE, 1928-1956. WOR+45 WOR-45 ECO/DEV FINAN ECO/TAC WEALTH...GEOG CHARTS TOT/POP FOR/TRADE 20. PAGE 130 F2569
STAT BAL/PAY REGION

B60
VERNON R.,METROPOLIS 1985. LOC/G PLAN TAX LEAD PWR MUNICH. PAGE 141 F2780
REGION ECO/TAC DECISION

S60
BERG E.J.,"ECONOMIC BASIS OF POLITICAL CHOICE IN FRENCH WEST AFRICA." FRANCE ECO/UNDEV AGRI INDUS NAT/G PLAN LEGIT COLONIAL REGION ATTIT PWR WEALTH ...CONCPT FOR/TRADE 20. PAGE 13 F0257
AFR ECO/TAC

S60
HERRERA F.,"THE INTER-AMERICAN DEVELOPMENT BANK." L/A+17C

USA+45 ECO/UNDEV INT/ORG CONSULT DELIB/GP PLAN FINAN
ECO/TAC INT/TRADE ROUTINE WEALTH...STAT TERR/GP 20. FOR/AID
PAGE 59 F1153 REGION

S60
MORALES C.J.,"TRADE AND ECONOMIC INTEGRATION IN FINAN
LATIN AMERICA." FUT L/A+17C LAW STRATA ECO/UNDEV INT/TRADE
DIST/IND INDUS LABOR NAT/G LEGIS ECO/TAC ADMIN REGION
RIGID/FLEX WEALTH...CONCPT NEW/IDEA CONT/OBS
TIME/SEQ WORK 20. PAGE 93 F1825

S60
MURPHEY R.,"ECONOMIC CONFLICTS IN SOUTH ASIA." ASIA S/ASIA
CULTURE INTELL ECO/TAC REGION ATTIT DRIVE KNOWL ECO/UNDEV
...METH/CNCPT TIME/SEQ STERTYP TOT/POP METH/GP
VAL/FREE 20. PAGE 95 F1864

S60
NANES A.,"THE EUROPEAN COMMUNITY AND THE UNITED INT/ORG
STATES: EVOLVING RELATIONS." EUR+WWI USA+45 WOR+45 REGION
ECO/UNDEV MARKET NAT/G DELIB/GP PLAN LEGIT ATTIT
PWR WEALTH...CONCPT STAT TIME/SEQ CON/ANAL EEC
METH/GP OEEC 20 EURATOM. PAGE 96 F1889

B61
LEE R.R.,ENGINEERING-ECONOMIC PLANNING BIBLIOG/A
MISCELLANEOUS SUBJECTS: A SELECTED BIBLIOGRAPHY PLAN
(MIMEOGRAPHED). FINAN LOC/G NEIGH ADMIN CONTROL REGION
INGP/REL HABITAT...GEOG MGT SOC/WK MUNICH 20
RESOURCE/N. PAGE 77 F1509

B61
MAYNE A.,DESIGNING AND ADMINISTERING A REGIONAL ECO/UNDEV
ECONOMIC DEVELOPMENT PLAN WITH SPECIFIC REFERENCE PLAN
TO PUERTO RICO (PAMPHLET). PUERT/RICO SOCIETY NAT/G CREATE
DELIB/GP REGION...DECISION 20. PAGE 87 F1707 ADMIN

S61
DALTON G.,"ECONOMIC THEORY AND PRIMITIVE SOCIETY" ECO/UNDEV
(BMR)" UNIV AGRI KIN TEC/DEV ECO/TAC REGION HABITAT METH
SKILL...METH/COMP BIBLIOG. PAGE 30 F0574 PHIL/SCI
SOC

S61
GORDON L.,"ECONOMIC REGIONALISM RECONSIDERED." FUT ECO/DEV
USA+45 WOR+45 INDUS NAT/G TEC/DEV DIPLOM ROUTINE ATTIT
PERCEPT WEALTH...WELF/ST METH/CNCPT WORK 20. CAP/ISM
PAGE 49 F0957 REGION

B62
CARPER E.T.,ILLINOIS GOES TO CONGRESS FOR ARMY ADMIN
LAND. USA+45 LAW EXTR/IND PROVS REGION CIVMIL/REL LOBBY
GOV/REL FEDERAL ATTIT 20 ILLINOIS SENATE CONGRESS GEOG
DIRKSEN/E DOUGLAS/P. PAGE 22 F0420 LEGIS

B62
CHAPIN F.S.,URBAN GROWTH DYNAMICS IN A REGIONAL REGION
CLUSTER OF CITIES. TEC/DEV ECO/TAC HABITAT...GEOG PLAN
SOC MUNICH. PAGE 23 F0453

B62
DIMOCK M.E.,THE NEW AMERICAN POLITICAL ECONOMY: A FEDERAL
SYNTHESIS OF POLITICS AND ECONOMICS. USA+45 FINAN ECO/TAC
LG/CO PLAN ADMIN REGION GP/REL CENTRAL MORAL 20. NAT/G
PAGE 33 F0642 PARTIC

B62
MEADE J.E.,CASE STUDIES IN EUROPEAN ECONOMIC UNION. INT/ORG
BELGIUM EUR+WWI LUXEMBOURG NAT/G INT/TRADE REGION ECO/TAC
ROUTINE WEALTH...METH/CNCPT STAT CHARTS ECSC
TOT/POP OEEC EEC FOR/TRADE 20. PAGE 89 F1738

B62
ROBERTSON B.C.,REGIONAL DEVELOPMENT IN THE EUROPEAN PLAN
ECONOMIC COMMUNITY. EUR+WWI FRANCE FUT ITALY UK ECO/DEV
ECO/UNDEV WORKER ACT/RES PROB/SOLV TEC/DEV ECO/TAC INT/ORG
INT/TRADE EEC. PAGE 112 F2209 REGION

B62
SCHMITT H.A.,THE PATH TO EUROPEAN UNITY. EUR+WWI INT/ORG
USA+45 PLAN TEC/DEV DIPLOM FOR/AID CONFER...INT/LAW INT/TRADE
20 EEC EURCOALSTL MARSHL/PLN UNIFICA. PAGE 117 REGION
F2300 ECO/DEV

B62
UNECA LIBRARY,BOOKS ON AFRICA IN THE UNECA BIBLIOG
LIBRARY. WOR+45 AGRI INT/ORG NAT/G PLAN WRITING AFR
REGION...SOC STAT UN. PAGE 132 F2605 ECO/UNDEV
TEC/DEV

B62
UNECA LIBRARY,NEW ACQUISITIONS IN THE UNECA BIBLIOG
LIBRARY. LAW NAT/G PLAN PROB/SOLV TEC/DEV ADMIN AFR
REGION...GEOG SOC 20 UN. PAGE 132 F2606 ECO/UNDEV
INT/ORG

B62
URQUIDI V.L.,FREE TRADE AND ECONOMIC INTEGRATION IN INT/TRADE
LATIN AMERICA: THE EVOLUTION OF A COMMON MARKET REGION
POLICY. ECO/UNDEV MARKET DIPLOM BAL/PAY FEDERAL INT/ORG
...POLICY CHARTS 20 LAFTA. PAGE 133 F2627 L/A+17C

B63
BELOFF M.,THE UNITED STATES AND THE UNITY OF ECO/DEV
EUROPE. EUR+WWI UK USA+45 WOR+45 VOL/ASSN DIPLOM INT/ORG
REGION ATTIT PWR...CONCPT EEC OEEC 20 NATO. PAGE 13
F0239

B63
CENTRO ESTUDIOS MONETARIOS LAT,COOPERACION ECO/UNDEV
FINANCIERA EN AMERICA LATINA. L/A+17C PLAN INT/TRADE
PROB/SOLV CONTROL REGION DEMAND...POLICY ANTHOL 20. MARKET
PAGE 22 F0433 FINAN

B63
CENTRO PARA EL DESARROLLO,LA ALIANZA PARA EL ECO/UNDEV
PROGRESO Y EL DESARROLLO SOCIAL DE AMERICA LATINA. FOR/AID
L/A+17C INT/ORG DIPLOM ECO/TAC INT/TRADE ATTIT 20 PLAN
ALL/PROG. PAGE 22 F0435 REGION

B63
CERAMI C.A.,ALLIANCE BORN OF DANGER. EUR+WWI USA+45 DIPLOM
USSR ECO/DEV INDUS VOL/ASSN ECO/TAC REGION ATTIT INT/ORG
MARXISM ATLAN/ALL 20 NATO EEC. PAGE 22 F0437 NAT/G
POLICY

B63
ERHARD L.,THE ECONOMICS OF SUCCESS. GERMANY/W ECO/DEV
WOR+45 LABOR CHIEF TAX REGION COST DEMAND ANTHOL. INT/TRADE
PAGE 38 F0745 PLAN
DIPLOM

B63
GORDON L.,A NEW DEAL FOR LATIN AMERICA. L/A+17C ECO/UNDEV
USA+45 CULTURE NAT/G TEC/DEV DIPLOM FOR/AID REGION ECO/TAC
TASK...POLICY 20 ALL/PROG DEPT/STATE. PAGE 49 F0958 INT/ORG
PLAN

B63
HAQ M.,THE STRATEGY OF ECONOMIC PLANNING. PAKISTAN ECO/TAC
AGRI FINAN INDUS NAT/G FOR/AID TAX CONTROL REGION ECO/UNDEV
PRODUC...POLICY CHARTS 20. PAGE 55 F1071 PLAN
PROB/SOLV

B63
HARROD R.F.,INTERNATIONAL TRADE THEORY IN A INT/TRADE
DEVELOPING WORLD. COM WOR+45 FOR/AID REGION COST BAL/PAY
DEMAND WEALTH...POLICY 20 INTL/ECON. PAGE 56 F1095 ECO/UNDEV
METH/COMP

B63
MANGER W.,THE ALLIANCE FOR PROGRESS: A CRITICAL DIPLOM
APPRAISAL. FUT L/A+17C USA+45 CULTURE ECO/UNDEV INT/ORG
ACADEM NAT/G SCHOOL PLAN FOR/AID...POLICY OAS ECO/TAC
ALL/PROG. PAGE 84 F1651 REGION

B63
PAN AMERICAN UNION,THE EFFECTS OF THE EUROPEAN INT/TRADE
ECONOMIC COMMUNITY ON THE LATIN AMERICAN ECONOMIES INT/ORG
(BMR). EUR+WWI L/A+17C ECO/UNDEV AGRI INDUS MARKET AGREE
REGION 20 EEC TREATY. PAGE 103 F2024 POLICY

B63
US ADVISORY COMN INTERGOV REL,PERFORMANCE OF URBAN REGION
FUNCTIONS: LOCAL AND AREAWIDE. TEC/DEV PARTIC LOC/G
REPRESENT PWR...DECISION GOV/COMP MUNICH. PAGE 133 ECO/TAC
F2633

L63
ADERBIGDE A.,"SYMPOSIUM ON WEST AFRICA FINAN
INTEGRATION." AFR EUR+WWI FUT CULTURE SOCIETY ECO/TAC
STRATA DIST/IND INDUS MARKET SERV/IND DELIB/GP PLAN REGION
TEC/DEV DOMIN EDU/PROP LEGIT COERCE ATTIT ALL/VALS
...POLICY STAT TREND CHARTS VAL/FREE. PAGE 2 F0040

L63
MEYER J.R.,"REGIONAL ECONOMICS: A SURVEY." INTELL REGION
ACADEM CREATE...IDEA/COMP BIBLIOG. PAGE 90 F1770 ECO/TAC
GEN/LAWS
PROB/SOLV

S63
GORDON B.,"ECONOMIC IMPEDIMENTS TO REGIONALISM IN VOL/ASSN
SOUTH EAST ASIA." BURMA FUT S/ASIA THAILAND USA+45 ECO/UNDEV
AGRI INDUS R+D NAT/G PLAN ECO/TAC WEALTH...STAT INT/TRADE
CONT/OBS 20. PAGE 49 F0954 REGION

S63
SCHOFLING J.A.,"EFTA: THE OTHER EUROPE." ECO/DEV EUR+WWI
MARKET CONSULT ECO/TAC WEALTH...TIME/SEQ EEC OEEC INT/ORG
20 EFTA. PAGE 117 F2310 REGION

S63
SHWADRAN B.,"MIDDLE EAST OIL, 1962." ISLAM DIST/IND PROC/MFG
INDUS PLAN ATTIT DRIVE WEALTH...POLICY STAT ECO/TAC
CONT/OBS TREND CHARTS GEN/LAWS TERR/GP METH/GP 20 ELITES
OIL. PAGE 121 F2393 REGION

B64
COMPOS R.O.,A MOEDA, O GOVERNO E O TEMPO. AFR ECO/UNDEV
BRAZIL WOR+45 FINAN TEC/DEV FOR/AID REGION DEMAND PLAN
...ANTHOL 20. PAGE 27 F0520 DIPLOM
INT/TRADE

B64
FRIEDEN B.J.,THE FUTURE OF OLD NEIGHBORHOODS: NEIGH
REBUILDING FOR A CHANGING POPULATION. CONSTRUC PROB/SOLV
LOC/G NAT/G ACT/RES ECO/TAC REGION ATTIT...INT SAMP PLAN
MUNICH 20 NEWYORK/C LOS/ANG HARTFORD URBAN/RNWL. BUDGET
PAGE 44 F0855

B64
FRIEDMANN J.,REGIONAL DEVELOPMENT AND PLANNING: A PLAN
READER. AGRI MARKET NAT/G ECO/TAC INCOME...GEOG REGION
STAT CENSUS CHARTS ANTHOL BIBLIOG MUNICH 20 INDUS
OPEN/SPACE. PAGE 44 F0863 ECO/DEV

B64
HEKHUIS D.J.,INTERNATIONAL STABILITY: MILITARY, TEC/DEV
ECONOMIC AND POLITICAL DIMENSIONS. FUT WOR+45 LAW DETER
ECO/UNDEV INT/ORG NAT/G VOL/ASSN FORCES ACT/RES REGION
BAL/PWR PWR WEALTH...STAT UN 20. PAGE 58 F1143

B64
HINSHAW R.,THE EUROPEAN COMMUNITY AND AMERICAN MARKET
TRADE: A STUDY IN ATLANTIC ECONOMICS AND POLICY. TREND
EUR+WWI UK USA+45 ECO/DEV ECO/UNDEV AGRI INDUS INT/TRADE
INT/ORG NAT/G ECO/TAC TARIFFS REGION...STAT CHARTS

EEC 20. PAGE 60 F1174

B64
INTL INF CTR LOCAL CREDIT,GOVERNMENT MEASURES FOR THE PROMOTION OF REGIONAL ECONOMIC DEVELOPMENT. WOR+45 ECO/UNDEV FINAN INT/ORG DIPLOM ORD/FREE ...POLICY GEOG 20. PAGE 65 F1285
FOR/AID PLAN ECO/TAC REGION

B64
KOHNSTAMM M.,THE EUROPEAN COMMUNITY AND ITS ROLE IN THE WORLD. FUT MOD/EUR UK USA+45 ECO/DEV 20. PAGE 72 F1418
INT/ORG NAT/G REGION DIPLOM

B64
KRAUSE L.B.,THE COMMON MARKET: PROGRESS AND CONTROVERSY. EUR+WWI UK ECO/DEV REGION...ANTHOL NATO EEC. PAGE 73 F1433
DIPLOM MARKET INT/TRADE INT/ORG

B64
LUTHULI A.,AFRICA'S FREEDOM. KIN LABOR POL/PAR SCHOOL DIPLOM NEUTRAL REGION REV NAT/LISM PWR WEALTH SOCISM SOC/INTEG 20. PAGE 82 F1608
AFR ECO/UNDEV COLONIAL

B64
NEHEMKIS P.,LATIN AMERICA: MYTH AND REALITY. INDUS INT/ORG PROB/SOLV CAP/ISM DIPLOM REV...SOC MUNICH 20. PAGE 97 F1907
REGION MYTH L/A+17C ECO/UNDEV

B64
ORGANIZATION AMERICAN STATES,ECONOMIC SURVEY OF LATIN AMERICA, 1962. L/A+17C AGRI DIST/IND INDUS MARKET PROC/MFG R+D PLAN TEC/DEV ECO/TAC REGION BAL/PAY ALL/VALS...CON/ANAL ORG/CHARTS GEN/METH OAS ALL/PROG 20 ALL/PROG. PAGE 102 F1998
ECO/UNDEV CHARTS

B64
RAMAZANI R.K.,THE MIDDLE EAST AND THE EUROPEAN COMMON MARKET. EUR+WWI ISLAM ECO/DEV EXTR/IND MARKET PROC/MFG INT/ORG NAT/G TEC/DEV ECO/TAC REGION DRIVE WEALTH...STAT CHARTS EEC TOT/POP 20. PAGE 109 F2141
ECO/UNDEV ATTIT INT/TRADE

B64
RESOURCES FOR THE FUTURE,URBAN AND REGIONAL STUDIES AT US UNIVERSITIES; A REPORT BASED ON A 1963 SURVEY OF URBAN AND REGIONAL RESEARCH. USA+45 SOCIETY CONSTRUC DIST/IND ACADEM NAT/G ACT/RES ECO/TAC ...CENSUS IDEA/COMP MUNICH. PAGE 111 F2179
BIBLIOG/A REGION PLAN

B64
URQUIDI V.L.,THE CHALLENGE OF DEVELOPMENT IN LATIN AMERICA. L/A+17C FINAN INT/ORG TEC/DEV DIPLOM INT/TRADE PRICE REGION PRODUC...CHARTS 20 ALL/PROG. PAGE 133 F2628
ECO/UNDEV ECO/TAC NAT/G TREND

B64
WILSON T.,POLICIES FOR REGIONAL DEVELOPMENT. CANADA UK FINAN INDUS NAT/G BUDGET TAX GIVE COST ...NAT/COMP 20. PAGE 147 F2904
REGION PLAN ECO/DEV ECO/TAC

L64
HAAS E.B.,"ECONOMICS AND DIFFERENTIAL PATTERNS OF POLITICAL INTEGRATION: PROJECTIONS ABOUT UNITY IN LATIN AMERICA." SOCIETY NAT/G DELIB/GP ACT/RES CREATE PLAN ECO/TAC REGION ROUTINE ATTIT DRIVE PWR WEALTH...CONCPT TREND CHARTS LAFTA TERR/GP 20. PAGE 52 F1020
L/A+17C INT/ORG MARKET

S64
FINLEY D.D.,"A POLITICAL PERSPECTIVE OF ECONOMIC RELATIONS IN THE COMMUNIST CAMP." COM USSR FACE/GP NAT/G ACT/RES PLAN DOMIN COERCE ATTIT ORD/FREE WEALTH...TIME/SEQ 20. PAGE 41 F0800
VOL/ASSN ECO/TAC DIPLOM REGION

S64
GERBET P.,"LA MISE EN OEUVRE DU MARCHE COMMUN AGRICOLE." ECO/DEV MARKET INT/ORG NAT/G PLAN EDU/PROP NAT/LISM WEALTH...OBS EEC VAL/FREE 20. PAGE 47 F0917
EUR+WWI AGRI REGION

S64
NEWLYN W.T.,"MONETARY SYSTEMS AND INTEGRATION" AFR BUDGET ADMIN FEDERAL PRODUC PROFIT UTIL...CHARTS 20 AFRICA/E. PAGE 98 F1922
ECO/UNDEV REGION METH/COMP FINAN

S64
PADELFORD N.J.,"THE ORGANIZATION OF AFRICAN UNITY." ECO/UNDEV INT/ORG PLAN BAL/PWR DIPLOM ECO/TAC NAT/LISM ORD/FREE PWR WEALTH...CONCPT TREND STERTYP TERR/GP VAL/FREE 20. PAGE 102 F2013
AFR VOL/ASSN REGION

S64
ROTHCHILD D.,"EAST AFRICAN FEDERATION." AFR TANZANIA UGANDA INDUS REGION 20. PAGE 114 F2249
INT/ORG DIPLOM ECO/UNDEV ECO/TAC

S64
SCHMITT H.O.,"POLITICAL CONDITIONS FOR INTERNATIONAL CURRENCY REFORM." WOR+45 SOCIETY ECO/DEV PLAN ECO/TAC BAL/PAY ATTIT ORD/FREE WEALTH ...SOC CONCPT OBS TREND EEC VAL/FREE ECSC 20. PAGE 117 F2301
FINAN VOL/ASSN REGION

B65
BAERRESEN D.W.,LATIN AMERICAN TRADE PATTERNS. L/A+17C ECO/UNDEV AGRI INDUS MARKET CREATE ...NET/THEORY CHARTS LAFTA. PAGE 8 F0149
INT/TRADE STAT REGION

B65
CERNY K.H.,NATO IN QUEST OF COHESION* A CONFRONTATION OF VIEWPOINTS. COM EUR+WWI USA+45 FORCES LEAD REGION DETER...ANTHOL NATO. PAGE 22 F0438
CENTRAL NUC/PWR VOL/ASSN

B65
CLARK T.D.,THREE PATHS TO THE MODERN SOUTH: EDUCATION, AGRICULTURE, AND CONSERVATION. FUT USA-45 ECO/DEV ECO/TAC PEACE WEALTH...POLICY 20 SOUTH/US. PAGE 25 F0485
AGRI EDU/PROP GOV/REL REGION

B65
DUGGAR G.S.,RENEWAL OF TOWN AND VILLAGE I: A WORLD-WIDE SURVEY OF LOCAL GOVERNMENT EXPERIENCE. WOR+45 CONSTRUC INDUS CREATE BUDGET REGION GOV/REL...QU NAT/COMP MUNICH 20 URBAN/RNWL. PAGE 35 F0673
NEIGH PLAN ADMIN

B65
EUROPEAN FREE TRADE ASSN,REGIONAL DEVELOPMENT POLICIES IN EFTA. ECO/UNDEV INT/ORG PLAN REGION ...POLICY GEOG EFTA. PAGE 39 F0755
EUR+WWI ECO/DEV NAT/COMP INT/TRADE

B65
GORDON W.,THE POLITICAL ECONOMY OF LATIN AMERICA. L/A+17C FINAN MARKET PROB/SOLV TEC/DEV RECEIVE ADMIN WEALTH 20. PAGE 49 F0962
ECO/UNDEV INT/TRADE REGION POLICY

B65
HAEFELE E.T.,GOVERNMENT CONTROLS ON TRANSPORT. AFR RHODESIA TANZANIA DIPLOM ECO/TAC TARIFFS PRICE ADJUD CONTROL REGION EFFICIENCY...POLICY 20 CONGO. PAGE 53 F1031
ECO/UNDEV DIST/IND FINAN NAT/G

B65
JOHNSON H.G.,THE WORLD ECONOMY AT THE CROSSROADS. COM WOR-45 ECO/DEV AGRI INDUS INT/TRADE REGION NAT/LISM 20. PAGE 67 F1326
FINAN DIPLOM INT/ORG ECO/UNDEV

B65
KASER M.,COMECON* INTEGRATION PROBLEMS OF THE PLANNED ECONOMIES. INT/ORG TEC/DEV INT/TRADE PRICE ADMIN ADJUST CENTRAL...STAT TIME/SEQ ORG/CHARTS COMECON. PAGE 69 F1359
PLAN ECO/DEV COM REGION

B65
LEYS C.T.,FEDERATION IN EAST AFRICA. LAW AGRI DIST/IND FINAN INT/ORG LABOR INT/TRADE CONFER ADMIN CONTROL GP/REL...ANTHOL 20 AFRICA/E. PAGE 79 F1554
FEDERAL REGION ECO/UNDEV PLAN

B65
MACDONALD R.W.,THE LEAGUE OF ARAB STATES: A STUDY IN THE DYNAMICS OF REGIONAL ORGANIZATION. ISRAEL UAR USSR FINAN INT/ORG DELIB/GP ECO/TAC AGREE NEUTRAL ORD/FREE PWR...DECISION BIBLIOG 20 TREATY UN. PAGE 83 F1626
ISLAM REGION DIPLOM ADMIN

B65
MAO J.C.T.,EFFICIENCY IN PUBLIC URBAN RENEWAL EXPENDITURES THROUGH CAPITAL BUDGETING. USA+45 FINAN LOC/G NAT/G NEIGH REGION UTIL...GEOG METH/CNCPT STAT SIMUL GEN/LAWS MUNICH 20 URBAN/RNWL. PAGE 85 F1662
TEC/DEV BUDGET PROB/SOLV

B65
ORG FOR ECO COOP AND DEVEL,THE MEDITERRANEAN REGIONAL PROJECT: AN EXPERIMENT IN PLANNING BY SIX COUNTRIES. FUT GREECE SPAIN TURKEY YUGOSLAVIA SOCIETY FINAN NAT/G PROF/ORG EDU/PROP ADMIN REGION COST...POLICY STAT CHARTS 20 OECD. PAGE 102 F1995
PLAN ECO/UNDEV ACADEM SCHOOL

B65
RATNAM K.J.,COMMUNALISM AND THE POLITICAL PROCESS IN MALAYA. MALAYSIA WOR+45 ECO/UNDEV PARTIC CHOOSE REPRESENT GP/REL CENTRAL ATTIT...CHARTS WORSHIP 20. PAGE 109 F2152
CONSTN GOV/REL REGION

B65
RIVKIN M.D.,AREA DEVELOPMENT FOR NATIONAL GROWTH; THE TURKISH PRECEDENT. ISLAM TURKEY ACT/RES INGP/REL...POLICY CHARTS GP/COMP MUNICH 20 ATATURK/MK INONU/I. PAGE 112 F2197
ECO/UNDEV REGION ECO/TAC PLAN

B65
WEILER J.,L'ECONOMIE INTERNATIONALE DEPUIS 1950. WOR+45 DIPLOM TARIFFS CONFER...POLICY TREATY. PAGE 145 F2848
FINAN INT/TRADE REGION FOR/AID

B65
WURFEL S.W.,FOREIGN ENTERPRISE IN COLOMBIA. FINAN LABOR NAT/G ECO/TAC TAX REGION 20 COLOMB. PAGE 149 F2944
ECO/UNDEV INT/TRADE JURID CAP/ISM

L65
WIONCZEK M.,"LATIN AMERICA FREE TRADE ASSOCIATION." AGRI DIST/IND FINAN INDUS INT/ORG LABOR NAT/G TEC/DEV ECO/TAC HEALTH SKILL WEALTH...POLICY RELATIV MGT LAFTA 20. PAGE 148 F2909
L/A+17C MARKET REGION

S65
BANOVETZ J.M.,"METROPOLITAN SUBSIDIES: AN APPRAISAL." LEAD GP/REL DISCRIM MUNICH. PAGE 9 F0175
REGION TAX GOV/REL

S65
CECIL C.O.,"THE DETERMINANTS OF LIBYAN FOREIGN POLICY." AFR INTELL ECO/UNDEV EXTR/IND POL/PAR CREATE REGION SOVEREIGN CONSERVE MAGHREB NASSER/G.
LIBYA DIPLOM WEALTH

PAGE 22 F0431 ISLAM

S65

HAYTER T.,"FRENCH AID TO AFRICA* ITS SCOPE AND ACHIEVEMENTS." CULTURE ECO/TAC INT/TRADE ADMIN REGION CENTRAL FEDERAL LOVE PWR SOVEREIGN EEC. PAGE 57 F1127
AFR FRANCE FOR/AID COLONIAL

S65

KINDLEBERGER C.P.,"MASS MIGRATION, THEN AND NOW." LAW ECO/DEV ECO/UNDEV INDUS LABOR INT/TRADE FEEDBACK REGION RIGID/FLEX...SOC NAT/COMP EEC. PAGE 71 F1394
EUR+WWI USA-45 WORKER IDEA/COMP

S65

MUNZI U.,"THE EUROPEAN SOCIAL FUND IN THE DEVELOPMENT OF THE MEDITERRANEAN REGIONS OF THE EEC." FUT GREECE ITALY PORTUGAL SPAIN TURKEY WORKER TEC/DEV ECO/TAC REGION...STAT EEC. PAGE 95 F1862
ECO/UNDEV PREDICT RECORD

S65

SOPER T.,"THE EEC AND AID TO AFRICA." FRANCE UK ECO/UNDEV INT/TRADE TARIFFS REGION ROUTINE CENTRAL DISCRIM...DECISION RECORD EEC. PAGE 124 F2443
AFR FOR/AID COLONIAL

S65

SPAAK P.H.,"THE SEARCH FOR CONSENSUS: A NEW EFFORT TO BUILD EUROPE." FRANCE GERMANY ECO/DEV NAT/G CONSULT FORCES PLAN EDU/PROP REGION CONSEN ATTIT ...SOC METH/CNCPT OBS TREND EEC NATO WORK TERR/GP METH/GP 20. PAGE 124 F2447
EUR+WWI INT/ORG

B66

BEUGEL E.V.D.,FROM MARSHALL AID TO ATLANTIC PARTNERSHIP* EUROPEAN INTEGRATION AS A CONCERN OF AMERICAN FOREIGN POLICY. USA+45 INT/ORG FORCES PERSON EEC NATO. PAGE 14 F0272
REGION DIPLOM EUR+WWI VOL/ASSN

B66

BROWN R.T.,TRANSPORT AND THE ECONOMIC INTEGRATION OF SOUTH AMERICA. L/A+17C ECO/UNDEV NAT/G OP/RES DIPLOM INT/TRADE REGION WEALTH...ECOMETRIC GEOG STAT LAFTA TIME. PAGE 19 F0373
MARKET DIST/IND SIMUL

B66

CONFERENCE REGIONAL ACCOUNTS,REGIONAL ACCOUNTS FOR POLICY DECISIONS. PROB/SOLV CONTROL RATIONAL KNOWL ORD/FREE...POLICY DECISION MATH STAT ANTHOL 20. PAGE 27 F0523
GOV/REL REGION PLAN ECO/TAC

B66

DUNCAN O.,METROPOLIS AND REGION (PREPARED FOR RESOURCES FOR THE FUTURE INC., WASHINGTON, D.C.). FINAN INDUS ECO/TAC TAX...CHARTS GOV/COMP MUNICH. PAGE 35 F0677
REGION GEOG

B66

KAREFA-SMART J.,AFRICA: PROGRESS THROUGH COOPERATION. AFR FINAN TEC/DEV DIPLOM FOR/AID EDU/PROP CONFER REGION GP/REL WEALTH...HEAL SOC/INTEG 20. PAGE 69 F1356
ORD/FREE ECO/UNDEV VOL/ASSN PLAN

B66

MANGONE G.J.,UN ADMINISTRATION OF ECONOMIC AND AOCIAL PROGRAMS. CONSULT BUDGET INT/TRADE REGION 20 UN. PAGE 84 F1653
ADMIN MGT ECO/TAC DELIB/GP

B66

ORG FOR ECO COOP AND DEVEL,GEOGRAPHICAL DISTRIBUTION OF FINANCIAL FLOWS TO LESS DEVELOPED COUNTRIES. WOR+45 DIPLOM INT/TRADE GIVE RECEIVE REPAR REGION WEALTH...GEOG STAT CHARTS 20 OECD. PAGE 102 F1997
FINAN ECO/UNDEV INT/ORG FOR/AID

B66

SEWELL J.P.,FUNCTIONALISM AND WORLD POLITICS* A STUDY BASED ON UNITED NATIONS PROGRAMS FINANCING ECONOMICAL DEVELOPMENT. ECO/UNDEV FINAN PROB/SOLV DIPLOM ECO/TAC FEEDBACK REGION ADJUST ATTIT UN IBRD INTL/FINAN INTL/DEV UNSF. PAGE 120 F2360
TASK INT/ORG IDEA/COMP GEN/LAWS

B66

SINGH L.P.,THE POLITICS OF ECONOMIC COOPERATION IN ASIA; A STUDY OF ASIAN INTERNATIONAL ORGANIZATIONS. ASIA INT/ORG ACT/RES PLAN GP/REL...POLICY GP/COMP BIBLIOG 20 UN SEATO. PAGE 122 F2414
ECO/UNDEV ECO/TAC REGION DIPLOM

B66

SMITH H.E.,READINGS IN ECONOMIC DEVELOPMENT AND ADMINISTRATION IN TANZANIA. TANZANIA FINAN INDUS LABOR NAT/G PLAN PROB/SOLV INT/TRADE COLONIAL REGION...ANTHOL BIBLIOG 20 AFRICA/E. PAGE 123 F2431
TEC/DEV ADMIN GOV/REL

B66

US DEPARTMENT OF STATE,RESEARCH ON THE USSR AND EASTERN EUROPE (EXTERNAL RESEARCH LIST NO 1-25). USSR LAW CULTURE SOCIETY NAT/G TEC/DEV DIPLOM EDU/PROP REGION...GEOG LING. PAGE 136 F2675
BIBLIOG/A EUR+WWI COM MARXISM

B66

US DEPARTMENT OF STATE,RESEARCH ON WESTERN EUROPE, GREAT BRITAIN, AND CANADA (EXTERNAL RESEARCH LIST NO 3-25). CANADA GERMANY/W UK LAW CULTURE NAT/G POL/PAR FORCES EDU/PROP REGION MARXISM...GEOG SOC WORSHIP 20 CMN/WLTH. PAGE 136 F2676
BIBLIOG/A EUR+WWI DIPLOM

S66

DUROSELLE J.B.,"THE FUTURE OF THE ATLANTIC COMMUNITY." EUR+WWI USA+45 USSR NAT/G CAP/ISM REGION DETER NUC/PWR ATTIT MARXISM...INT/LAW 20 NATO. PAGE 35 F0686
FUT DIPLOM MYTH POLICY

S66

FELD W.,"NATIONAL ECONOMIC INTEREST GROUPS AND POLICY FORMATION IN THE EEC." NAT/G POL/PAR REGION CENTRAL SOVEREIGN...INT NET/THEORY EEC. PAGE 40 F0777
LOBBY ELITES DECISION

S66

JAVITS J.K.,"POLITICAL ACTION VITAL FOR LATIN AMERICAN INTEGRATION." ECO/UNDEV INT/ORG POL/PAR VOL/ASSN PLAN PROB/SOLV INT/TRADE EFFICIENCY 20 OAS LAFTA ALL/PROG. PAGE 66 F1308
L/A+17C ECO/TAC REGION

B67

ANDERSON S.V.,THE NORDIC COUNCIL: A STUDY OF SCANDINAVIAN REGIONALISM. DENMARK FINLAND ICELAND NORWAY SWEDEN MARKET NAT/G VOL/ASSN CONSULT PARL/PROC ATTIT...TIME/SEQ BIBLIOG 20. PAGE 5 F0098
INT/ORG REGION DIPLOM LEGIS

B67

CASTILLO C.M.,GROWTH AND INTEGRATION IN CENTRAL AMERICA. L/A+17C CREATE PROB/SOLV ECO/TAC REGION PRODUC...OBS BIBLIOG 20. PAGE 22 F0429
ECO/UNDEV INT/TRADE NAT/COMP

B67

FORDE D.,WEST AFRICAN KINGDOMS IN THE NINETEENTH CENTURY. ECO/UNDEV AGRI KIN...SOC CHARTS NAT/COMP 19. PAGE 42 F0826
AFR REGION CULTURE

B67

MALINVAUD E.,ACTIVITY ANALYSIS IN THE THEORY OF GROWTH AND PLANNING. UNIV AGRI COMPUTER OP/RES REGION...CHARTS ANTHOL METH. PAGE 84 F1648
MATH GAME SIMUL

B67

NKRUMAH K.,CHALLENGE OF THE CONGO. FORCES ECO/TAC FOR/AID REGION MURDER REPRESENT 20 CONGO/LEOP UN. PAGE 98 F1930
REV ECO/UNDEV ORD/FREE DIPLOM

B67

ROACH J.R.,THE UNITED STATES AND THE ATLANTIC COMMUNITY; ISSUES AND PROSPECTS. AFR WOR+45 TEC/DEV ECO/TAC COLONIAL REGION PEACE ROLE...ANTHOL NATO EEC. PAGE 112 F2199
INT/ORG POLICY ADJUST DIPLOM

B67

STEARNS P.N.,EUROPEAN SOCIETY IN UPHEAVAL* SOCIAL HISTORY SINCE 1800. EUR+WWI MOD/EUR STRATA SECT WORKER TEC/DEV WAR...WELF/ST SOC TREND BIBLIOG 19/20. PAGE 125 F2472
REGION ECO/DEV SOCIETY INDUS

L67

HOSHII I.,"JAPAN'S STAKE IN ASIA." ASIA S/ASIA CAP/ISM ECO/TAC ROLE...GEOG 20 CHINJAP. PAGE 62 F1224
DIPLOM REGION NAT/G INT/ORG

S67

BUTT R.,"THE COMMON MARKET AND CONSERVATIVE POLITICS, 1961-2." UK CHIEF DIPLOM ECO/TAC INT/TRADE CONFER DEBATE REGION ATTIT...POLICY 20 EEC. PAGE 21 F0398
EUR+WWI INT/ORG POL/PAR

S67

GRUN C.,"DEUX ETUDES ALLEMANDES SUR LES PREJUGES NATIONAUX ET LES MOYENS DE LES COMBATTRE." FRANCE GERMANY DIST/IND PROB/SOLV GP/REL AGE/Y RIGID/FLEX ...PSY STAT INT SAMP. PAGE 52 F1010
ATTIT REGION DISCRIM STERTYP

S67

HERRERA F.,"EUROPEAN PARTICIPATION IN THE LATIN AMERICAN REGIONAL INTEGRATION" EUR+WWI L/A+17C GP/REL INGP/REL 20. PAGE 59 F1154
DIPLOM REGION INT/ORG FINAN

S67

PECCEI A.,"DEVELOPED-UNDERDEVELOPED AND EAST-WEST RELATIONS." ECO/UNDEV TEC/DEV DIPLOM LEAD EFFICIENCY GEOG. PAGE 104 F2045
FOR/AID TREND REGION ECO/DEV

S67

SCHACHTER G.,"REGIONAL DEVELOPMENT IN THE ITALIAN DUAL ECONOMY" ITALY AGRI INDUS MARKET WORKER ECO/TAC CONTROL INCOME PRODUC 20. PAGE 116 F2287
REGION ECO/UNDEV NAT/G PROB/SOLV

S67

WALKER R.L.,"THE WEST AND THE 'NEW ASIA'." CHINA/COM ECO/UNDEV DIPLOM...PREDICT 20. PAGE 142 F2805
ASIA INT/TRADE COLONIAL REGION

S67

WASSERMAN M.,"BEYOND TOKENISM: REVERSE INTEGRATION IN ALBANY, GEORGIA." USA+45 PLAN BUDGET EDU/PROP LEAD AGE/C AGE/Y GEORGIA NEGRO. PAGE 144 F2827
REGION RACE/REL DISCRIM SCHOOL

REGRESS....REGRESSION ANALYSIS; SEE ALSO CON/ANAL

N19

HATANAKA M.,A SPECTRAL ANALYSIS OF BUSINESS CYCLE INDICATORS: LEAD-LAG IN TERMS OF ALL TIME POINTS (PAMPHLET). UNIV WORKER EFFICIENCY...REGRESS STAT CHARTS TIME 20. PAGE 56 F1110
ECOMETRIC ADJUST PRODUC CON/ANAL

L60

CHENERY H.B.,"PATTERNS OF INDUSTRIAL GROWTH." INT/TRADE DEMAND PRODUC...MATH REGRESS CHARTS SIMUL METH 20. PAGE 24 F0462
ECO/TAC ECO/DEV GP/COMP CON/ANAL

S61

DICKS-MIREAUX L.A.,"THE INTERRELATIONSHIP BETWEEN COST AND PRICE CHANGES 19461959: A STUDY OF
PRICE PAY

INFLATION IN POST-WAR BRITAIN" AFR UK ECO/DEV INDUS WORKER ECO/TAC ORD/FREE WEALTH...ECOMETRIC REGRESS STAT TREND CHARTS 20. PAGE 33 F0634 DEMAND

B63
JOHNSTON J.,ECONOMETRIC METHODS. PROB/SOLV WRITING ...REGRESS CHARTS T. PAGE 68 F1333 ECOMETRIC PHIL/SCI OP/RES STAT

B63
MINER J.,SOCIAL AND ECONOMIC FACTORS IN SPENDING FOR PUBLIC EDUCATION. USA+45 FINAN SCHOOL OPTIMAL ...POLICY DECISION REGRESS PREDICT CHARTS SIMUL 20. PAGE 92 F1801 EDU/PROP NAT/G COST ACT/RES

B64
MEYER J.R.,INVESTMENT DECISIONS, ECONOMIC FORECASTING, AND PUBLIC POLICY. ECO/DEV ECO/TAC ...DECISION REGRESS TIME/SEQ CHARTS GP/COMP SIMUL 20. PAGE 90 F1771 FINAN PROB/SOLV PREDICT LG/CO

S65
BRIGHAM E.F.,"THE DETERMINANTS OF RESIDENTIAL LAND VALUES." USA+45 ECO/DEV PROB/SOLV RENT PRICE ...REGRESS STAT CHARTS GEN/METH MUNICH 20 LOS/ANG. PAGE 18 F0351 COST INDICATOR SIMUL ECOMETRIC

B66
BEN-PORATH Y.,THE ARAB LABOR FORCE IN ISRAEL. ISLAM ISRAEL AGRI INDUS SCHOOL CAP/ISM PAY DEMAND...GEOG REGRESS STAT CHARTS 20 ARABS. PAGE 13 F0245 WORKER CENSUS GP/REL STRUCT

B66
MACBEAN A.I.,EXPORT INSTABILITY AND ECONOMIC DEVELOPMENT. CHILE PAKISTAN PUERT/RICO TANZANIA UGANDA WOR+45 MARKET ECO/TAC...POLICY REGRESS CHARTS BIBLIOG TIME 20. PAGE 83 F1622 INT/TRADE ECO/UNDEV ECOMETRIC INSPECT

B67
BERGMANN D KAUN B.,STRUCTURAL UNEMPLOYMENT IN THE UNITED STATES. USA+45 ECO/DEV PRICE ADMIN INGP/REL DEMAND EQUILIB WEALTH...MATH REGRESS STAT 20 NEGRO. PAGE 13 F0258 ECOMETRIC METH WORKER ECO/TAC

S67
SANDMEYER R.L.,"METHODOLOGICAL ISSUES IN THE STUDY OF LABOR FORCE PARTICIPATION RATES." WOR+45 ...CLASSIF REGRESS CHARTS SIMUL. PAGE 116 F2278 METH CON/ANAL PARTIC WORKER

REGRESSION ANALYSIS....SEE REGRESS

REHABILITN....REHABILITATION

REHMUS C.M. F2175

REICH N. F2176

REILLY T.J. F2177

REIN M. F1674

REISCHAUER R.D. F2565

RELATIONS AMONG GROUPS....SEE GP/REL

RELATISM....RELATIVISM

RELATIV....RELATIVITY

B44
KAUFMANN F.,METHODOLOGY OF THE SOCIAL SCIENCES. PERSON...RELATIV PSY CONCPT LING METH 20. PAGE 69 F1363 SOC PHIL/SCI GEN/LAWS METH/CNCPT

B55
BUCHANAN N.S.,APPROACHES TO ECONOMIC DEVELOPMENT. FUT USA+45 WOR+45 STRATA ECO/DEV INT/ORG NAT/G TEC/DEV DIPLOM FOR/AID ATTIT KNOWL PWR WEALTH ...RELATIV METH/CNCPT SELF/OBS TREND CON/ANAL STERTYP GEN/LAWS FOR/TRADE COMMUN 20. PAGE 20 F0380 ECO/UNDEV ECO/TAC INT/TRADE

S59
REUBENS E.D.,"THE BASIS FOR REORIENATION OF AMERICAN FOREIGN AID POLICY." USA+45 USSR STRUCT INT/ORG CONSULT ECO/TAC ADMIN DRIVE MORAL ORD/FREE PWR WEALTH...RELATIV MATH STAT TREND GEN/LAWS VAL/FREE 20. PAGE 111 F2180 ECO/UNDEV PLAN FOR/AID DIPLOM

S60
MARTIN E.M.,"NEW TRENDS IN UNITED STATES ECONOMIC FOREIGN POLICY." USA+45 INTELL DELIB/GP FOR/AID INT/TRADE ROUTINE BAL/PAY...RELATIV TRUE/GP 20. PAGE 86 F1682 NAT/G PLAN DIPLOM

B64
LI C.M.,INDUSTRIAL DEVELOPMENT IN COMMUNIST CHINA. CHINA/COM ECO/DEV ECO/UNDEV AGRI FINAN INDUS MARKET LABOR NAT/G ECO/TAC INT/TRADE EXEC ALL/VALS ...POLICY RELATIV TREND WORK TOT/POP VAL/FREE 20. PAGE 79 F1556 ASIA TEC/DEV

L64
ARMENGALD A.,"ECONOMIE ET COEXISTENCE." COM EUR+WWI FUT USA+45 WOR+45 ECO/DEV ECO/UNDEV FINAN INT/ORG NAT/G EXEC CHOOSE ATTIT ALL/VALS...POLICY RELATIV DECISION TREND SOC/EXP WORK 20. PAGE 6 F0113 MARKET ECO/TAC AFR CAP/ISM

L64
BHAGWATI J.,"THE PURE THEORY OF INTERNATIONAL TRADE: A SURVEY." WOR+45 ECO/DEV ECO/UNDEV FINAN MARKET PROC/MFG INT/ORG LABOR LG/CO NAT/G TEC/DEV ECO/TAC SKILL WEALTH...POLICY RELATIV MGT CONCPT NEW/IDEA MATH QUANT GEN/LAWS FOR/TRADE 20. PAGE 14 F0276 INDUS HYPO/EXP

S64
NASH M.,"SOCIAL PREREQUISITES TO ECONOMIC GROWTH IN LATIN AMERICA AND SOUTHEAST ASIA." L/A+17C S/ASIA CULTURE SOCIETY ECO/UNDEV AGRI INDUS NAT/G PLAN TEC/DEV EDU/PROP ROUTINE ALL/VALS...POLICY RELATIV SOC NAT/COMP WORK TOT/POP 20. PAGE 96 F1894 ECO/DEV PERCEPT

S64
PATEL S.J.,"THE ECONOMIC DISTANCE BETWEEN NATIONS: ITS ORIGIN, MEASUREMENT AND OUTLOOK." WOR+45 ECO/DEV AGRI FINAN INDUS MARKET LABOR NAT/G CONSULT TEC/DEV ECO/TAC WEALTH...POLICY RELATIV MGT TREND WORK 20. PAGE 103 F2035 ECO/UNDEV PLAN

L65
WILLIAMS S.,"NEGOTIATING INVESTMENT IN EMERGING COUNTRIES." USA+45 WOR+45 INDUS MARKET NAT/G TOP/EX TEC/DEV CAP/ISM ECO/TAC ADMIN SKILL WEALTH...POLICY RELATIV MGT WORK 20. PAGE 147 F2894 FINAN ECO/UNDEV

L65
WIONCZEK M.,"LATIN AMERICA FREE TRADE ASSOCIATION." AGRI DIST/IND FINAN INDUS INT/ORG LABOR NAT/G TEC/DEV ECO/TAC HEALTH SKILL WEALTH...POLICY RELATIV MGT LAFTA 20. PAGE 148 F2909 L/A+17C MARKET REGION

RELATIVISM....SEE RELATISM, RELATIV

RELATIVITY....SEE RELATIV

RELIGION....SEE SECT, WORSHIP

RELIGIOUS GROUP....SEE SECT

RENAISSAN....RENAISSANCE

RENNER G.T. F2868

RENO P. F2178

RENT....RENTING

B13
DAVENPORT H.J.,THE ECONOMICS OF ENTERPRISE. UNIV FINAN SML/CO RENT COST WEALTH GEN/LAWS. PAGE 30 F0582 CAP/ISM PRICE ECO/TAC LG/CO

B31
JEVONS W.S.,THE THEORY OF POLITICAL ECONOMY (4TH ED.; 1ST ED. 1871). WOR-45 FINAN MARKET RENT WEALTH ...LOG MATH QUANT CON/ANAL IDEA/COMP BIBLIOG METH 17/19. PAGE 67 F1318 GEN/LAWS UTIL LABOR

B63
GRIGSBY W.G.,HOUSING MARKETS AND PUBLIC POLICY. USA+45 FAM NEIGH PRICE DEMAND WEALTH...POLICY CHARTS BIBLIOG METH MUNICH 20. PAGE 51 F1002 MARKET RENT HABITAT PLAN

B64
BROWN E.H.P.,A COURSE IN APPLIED ECONOMICS (2ND ED.). ECO/DEV FINAN MARKET WORKER INT/TRADE RATION RENT PAY PRICE BAL/PAY...DECISION T RESOURCE/N. PAGE 19 F0368 POLICY ECO/TAC PROB/SOLV

B64
STONIER A.W.,EXERCISES IN ECONOMICS. FINAN INDUS TEC/DEV RENT PAY EQUILIB PRODUC PROFIT...METH/COMP T. PAGE 127 F2498 PRICE MARKET WORKER

B65
BEYER G.H.,HOUSING AND SOCIETY. USA+45 ECO/DEV FAM NAT/G PLAN RENT...CHARTS BIBLIOG MUNICH 20. PAGE 14 F0275 HABITAT AGE/O CONSTRUC

S65
BALDWIN D.A.,"THE INTERNATIONAL BANK IN POLITICAL PERSPECTIVE" USA+45 TEC/DEV FOR/AID RENT GIVE COST ...IDEA/COMP GAME IBRD. PAGE 9 F0160 FINAN INT/ORG

S65
BRIGHAM E.F.,"THE DETERMINANTS OF RESIDENTIAL LAND VALUES." USA+45 ECO/DEV PROB/SOLV RENT PRICE ...REGRESS STAT CHARTS GEN/METH MUNICH 20 LOS/ANG. PAGE 18 F0351 COST INDICATOR SIMUL ECOMETRIC

S65
GOLDMAN M.I.,"A BALANCE SHEET OF SOVIET FOREIGN AID." USA+45 ECO/UNDEV BAL/PWR ECO/TAC RENT GIVE EDU/PROP CONTROL COST PROFIT GEN/METH. PAGE 48 F0939 USSR FOR/AID NAT/COMP EFFICIENCY

B66
FRIEDMANN W.G.,INTERNATIONAL FINANCIAL AID. USA+45 ECO/DEV ECO/UNDEV NAT/G VOL/ASSN EX/STRUC PLAN RENT INT/ORG FOR/AID

GIVE BAL/PAY PWR...GEOG INT/LAW STAT TREND UN EEC COMECON. PAGE 44 F0866 TEC/DEV ECO/TAC

B66
GOODWIN C.D.W.,ECONOMIC INQUIRY IN AUSTRALIA. ECO/DEV ECO/UNDEV ACADEM INT/TRADE RENT TARIFFS TAX PRESS GOV/REL SOCISM 18/20 AUSTRAL. PAGE 49 F0953 ECO/TAC IDEA/COMP BUDGET COLONIAL

B66
NEVITT A.A.,THE ECONOMIC PROBLEMS OF HOUSING. WOR+45 ECO/DEV ECO/UNDEV ACT/RES PROB/SOLV ECO/TAC RENT...OBS CHARTS 20. PAGE 98 F1917 HABITAT PROC/MFG DELIB/GP NAT/COMP

B66
NEVITT A.A.,HOUSING, TAXATION AND SUBSIDIES; A STUDY OF HOUSING IN THE UNITED KINGDOM. UK FINAN GIVE CONTROL COST INCOME...CHARTS 20. PAGE 98 F1918 PLAN TAX HABITAT RENT

S66
VENTRE F.T.,"LOCAL INITIATIVES IN URBAN INDUSTRIAL DEVELOPMENT." FINAN SERV/IND TOP/EX PLAN BUDGET RENT TAX...GP/COMP MUNICH 20. PAGE 141 F2777 ECO/TAC LOC/G INDUS

L67
GLAZER N.,"HOUSING PROBLEMS AND HOUSING POLICIES." USA+45 PLAN RENT ADJUST CONSEN DEMAND DISCRIM AGE ATTIT HEALTH WEALTH MUNICH NEGRO. PAGE 48 F0929 POLICY CONSTRUC CREATE HABITAT

S67
BRANCO R.,"LAND REFORM* THE ANSWER TO LATIN AMERICA'S AGRICULTURAL DEVELOPMENT?" L/A+17C NAT/G PLAN TEC/DEV BUDGET RENT EFFICIENCY 20. PAGE 18 F0339 ECO/UNDEV AGRI TAX OWN

S67
LEFCOE G.,"CONSTRUCTION LENDING AND THE EQUITABLE LIEN." LICENSE CT/SYS OWN...STAT 20. PAGE 77 F1510 CONSTRUC RENT ADJUD

N67
US HOUSE,MESSAGE FROM THE PRESIDENT OF THE UNITED STATES: URBAN AND RURAL POVERTY (PAMPHLET). USA+45 ACT/RES PLAN BUDGET RENT MUNICH 20 PRESIDENT. PAGE 136 F2685 NAT/G POLICY CREATE RECEIVE

B84
MILL J.,ELEMENTS OF POLITICAL ECONOMY. UK LAW ELITES FINAN WORKER ECO/TAC RENT OWN WEALTH ...POLICY GEN/LAWS 19. PAGE 91 F1785 TAX TARIFFS NAT/G INCOME

REP/CONVEN....REPUBLICAN (PARTY - U.S.) NATIONAL CONVENTION

REPAR....REPARATIONS; SEE ALSO DIPLOM, SANCTION

B28
CASSEL G.,FOREIGN INVESTMENTS. GERMANY UK USA-45 WOR-45 ECO/DEV NAT/G VOL/ASSN CAP/ISM REPAR ATTIT WEALTH...METH/CNCPT STAT SIMUL STERTYP ANTHOL FOR/TRADE TOT/POP VAL/FREE 20. PAGE 22 F0426 FINAN ECO/TAC BAL/PAY

B40
WUNDERLICH F.,LABOR UNDER GERMAN DEMOCRACY, ARBITRATION 1918-1933. GERMANY NAT/G PAY REPAR ADJUD CT/SYS GP/REL...MAJORIT 20. PAGE 149 F2941 LABOR WORKER INDUS BARGAIN

B50
FEIS H.,THE DIPLOMACY OF THE DOLLAR: FIRST ERA 1919-32. EUR+WWI USA-45 FOR/AID REPAR ATTIT ...POLICY 20. PAGE 40 F0774 FINAN NAT/G DIPLOM ECO/TAC

B60
BOHM F.,REDEN UND SCHRIFTEN UBER DIE ORDNUNG EINER FREIEN GESELLSCHAFT, EINER FREIEN WIRTSCHAFT, UND UBER DIE WIEDERGUTMACH. DIPLOM CRIME ORD/FREE RESPECT FASCISM 20 NAZI. PAGE 16 F0307 ECO/TAC NEW/LIB SUPEGO REPAR

B64
LAURSEN K.,THE GERMAN INFLATION, 1918-23. EUR+WWI GERMANY/E GERMANY/W WOR-45 BUDGET TAX GOV/REL BAL/PAY DEMAND PEACE...POLICY CHARTS 20 WEIMAR/REP. PAGE 76 F1489 ECO/DEV FINAN REPAR ECO/TAC

B66
ORG FOR ECO COOP AND DEVEL,GEOGRAPHICAL DISTRIBUTION OF FINANCIAL FLOWS TO LESS DEVELOPED COUNTRIES. WOR+45 DIPLOM INT/TRADE GIVE RECEIVE REPAR REGION WEALTH...GEOG STAT CHARTS 20 OECD. PAGE 102 F1997 FINAN ECO/UNDEV INT/ORG FOR/AID

B67
RUEFF J.,BALANCE OF PAYMENTS: PROPOSALS FOR RESOLVING THE CRITICAL WORLD ECONOMIC PROBLEM OF OUR TIME. USA+45 INDUS FOR/AID REPAR DEMAND OPTIMAL ...ECOMETRIC CHARTS METH/COMP 20. PAGE 115 F2259 BAL/PAY INT/TRADE FINAN NEW/IDEA

REPARATIONS....SEE REPAR

REPRESENT....REPRESENTATION; SEE ALSO LEGIS

NCO
CARRINGTON C.E.,THE COMMONWEALTH IN AFRICA (PAMPHLET). UK STRUCT NAT/G COLONIAL REPRESENT GOV/REL RACE/REL NAT/LISM...MAJORIT 20 EEC NEGRO. PAGE 22 F0421 ECO/UNDEV AFR DIPLOM PLAN

B08
LLOYD H.D.,THE SWISS DEMOCRACY. SWITZERLND INDUS NAT/G WORKER CHOOSE OWN ORD/FREE SOCISM...PLURIST 19/20 MONOPOLY. PAGE 81 F1590 NAT/COMP GOV/COMP REPRESENT POPULISM

N19
ENGELS F.,THE BRITISH LABOUR MOVEMENT (PAMPHLET). FRANCE GERMANY MOD/EUR UK USA-45 POL/PAR WORKER PAY EDU/PROP PRICE REPRESENT GP/REL 19. PAGE 37 F0730 ECO/TAC MARXISM LABOR STRATA

N19
FAHRNKOPF N.,STATE AND LOCAL GOVERNMENT IN ILLINOIS (PAMPHLET). CONSTN ADMIN PARTIC CHOOSE REPRESENT GOV/REL...JURID MGT 20 ILLINOIS. PAGE 39 F0759 BIBLIOG LOC/G LEGIS CT/SYS

N19
HAYEK FA V.O.N.,FREEDOM AND THE ECONOMIC SYSTEM. GERMANY USSR PLAN REPRESENT TOTALISM FASCISM POPULISM...MAJORIT METH/COMP GEN/LAWS 20. PAGE 57 F1123 ORD/FREE ECO/TAC CAP/ISM SOCISM

B30
GREEN F.M.,CONSTITUTIONAL DEVELOPMENT IN THE SOUTH ATLANTIC STATES, 1776-1860; A STUDY IN THE EVOLUTION OF DEMOCRACY. USA-45 ELITES SOCIETY STRATA ECO/DEV AGRI POL/PAR EX/STRUC LEGIS CT/SYS REGION...BIBLIOG 18/19 MARYLAND VIRGINIA GEORGIA NORTH/CAR SOUTH/CAR. PAGE 50 F0984 CONSTN PROVS PLURISM REPRESENT

S32
DODD E.M. JR.,"FOR WHOM ARE CORPORATE MANAGERS TRUSTEES'." SERV/IND CAP/ISM GIVE LEAD REPRESENT ORD/FREE WEALTH. PAGE 33 F0648 LG/CO ROLE NAT/G PLAN

B35
LASKI H.J.,THE STATE IN THEORY AND PRACTICE. ELITES ECO/TAC REPRESENT ORD/FREE PWR WEALTH POPULISM ...GOV/COMP GEN/LAWS 19/20. PAGE 76 F1483 CAP/ISM COERCE NAT/G FASCISM

B35
SCHATTSCHNEIDER E.E.,POLITICS, PRESSURES AND THE TARIFF: A STUDY OF FREE PRIVATE ENTERPRISE IN PRESSURE POLITICS IN TARIFF REVISION 1929-1930. NAT/G BARGAIN ECO/TAC ROUTINE REPRESENT GOV/REL GP/REL PWR POLICY. PAGE 116 F2290 LOBBY LEGIS TARIFFS

B37
BROOKS R.R.,WHEN LABOR ORGANIZES. FINAN EDU/PROP ADMIN LOBBY PARTIC REPRESENT WEALTH TREND. PAGE 19 F0364 LABOR GP/REL POLICY

B39
THOMAS J.A.,THE HOUSE OF COMMONS, 1832-1901; A STUDY OF ITS ECONOMIC AND FUNCTIONAL CHARACTER. UK LAW STRATA FINAN DIPLOM CONTROL LEAD LOBBY REPRESENT WEALTH...POLICY STAT BIBLIOG 19/20 PARLIAMENT. PAGE 130 F2561 PARL/PROC LEGIS POL/PAR ECO/DEV

B40
CAMPBELL P.,CONSUMER REPRESENTATION IN THE NEW DEAL. AGRI INDUS MARKET EX/STRUC PLAN CAP/ISM CONTROL GP/REL DEMAND POLICY. PAGE 21 F0408 CLIENT REPRESENT NAT/G

B40
SPENCER H.,THE MAN VS. THE STATE (1892). UK POL/PAR LEGIS TARIFFS COERCE CRIME REPRESENT PWR SOCISM ...POLICY GEN/LAWS 19/20. PAGE 124 F2450 FASCISM POPULISM LAISSEZ ORD/FREE

S43
GOLDEN C.S.,"NEW PATTERNS OF DEMOCRACY." NEIGH DELIB/GP EDU/PROP EXEC PARTIC...MGT METH/CNCPT OBS TREND. PAGE 48 F0935 LABOR REPRESENT LG/CO GP/REL

S43
HERBERG W.,"BUREAUCRACY AND DEMOCRACY IN LABOR UNIONS." LAW CONSTN STRUCT WORKER ADMIN CONTROL PARTIC RIGID/FLEX PWR TREND. PAGE 59 F1151 LABOR REPRESENT ROUTINE INGP/REL

B44
MCFADYEAN A.,GOVERNMENT AND INDUSTRY (PAMPHLET). UK INDUS CONTROL REPRESENT 20. PAGE 88 F1728 POL/PAR SOCISM

B44
MERRIAM C.E.,PUBLIC AND PRIVATE GOVERNMENT. VOL/ASSN EDU/PROP ADMIN REPRESENT EFFICIENCY PWR PLURISM...MAJORIT CONCPT. PAGE 90 F1762 NAT/G NEIGH MGT POLICY

B45
MILLIS H.A.,ORGANIZED LABOR (FIRST ED.). LAW STRUCT DELIB/GP WORKER ECO/TAC ADJUD CONTROL REPRESENT INGP/REL INCOME MGT. PAGE 92 F1797 LABOR POLICY ROUTINE GP/REL

B48
SPERO S.D.,GOVERNMENT AS EMPLOYER. USA+45 NAT/G EX/STRUC ADMIN CONTROL EXEC 20. PAGE 124 F2453 SOVEREIGN INGP/REL REPRESENT CONFER

B48
VON HAYEK F.A.,INDIVIDUALISM AND ECONOMIC ORDER. GERMANY USA-45 USSR FINAN MARKET INT/ORG ECO/TAC INT/TRADE PRICE REPRESENT ORD/FREE...PLURIST GEN/LAWS 20. PAGE 142 F2793 SOCISM CAP/ISM POPULISM FEDERAL

S48
CLEVELAND A.S.,"NAM: SPOKESMAN FOR INDUSTRY?" LEGIS PLAN LEAD LOBBY PARTIC CONSEN INCOME ATTIT ROLE ORD/FREE POLICY. PAGE 25 F0491
VOL/ASSN CLIENT REPRESENT INDUS

B49
SELZNICK P.,TVA AND THE GRASS ROOTS: A STUDY IN THE SOCIOLOGY OF FORMAL ORGANIZATION. USA-45 EX/STRUC PROB/SOLV CONFER PARTIC ROUTINE PWR 20 TVA. PAGE 119 F2353
REPRESENT LOBBY CONSULT

B50
CLARK J.M.,ALTERNATIVE TO SERFDOM. SOCIETY STRATA INDUS MARKET WORKER PRICE GP/REL PROFIT BIO/SOC PWR WEALTH...GEN/LAWS 20 KEYNES/JM. PAGE 25 F0481
ORD/FREE POPULISM ECO/TAC REPRESENT

B51
HARDMAN J.B.,THE HOUSE OF LABOR. LAW R+D NEIGH EDU/PROP LEAD ROUTINE REPRESENT GP/REL...POLICY STAT. PAGE 55 F1080
LABOR LOBBY ADMIN PRESS

L51
SUMMERS C.W.,"UNION POWERS AND WORKERS RIGHTS." WORKER PROB/SOLV ECO/TAC PARTIC INGP/REL PWR. PAGE 127 F2513
LABOR CONSTN LAW REPRESENT

B52
BEVAN A.,IN PLACE OF FEAR. WOR+45 STRATA LEGIS REPRESENT OWN NEW/LIB POPULISM...CHARTS 20. PAGE 14 F0273
SOCISM SOCIALIST WEALTH MAJORIT

S53
DRUCKER P.F.,"THE EMPLOYEE SOCIETY." STRUCT BAL/PWR PARTIC REPRESENT PWR...DECISION CONCPT. PAGE 34 F0666
LABOR MGT WORKER CULTURE

S53
LAWTON F.J.,"LEGISLATIVE-EXECUTIVE RELATIONS IN BUDGETING AS VIEWED BY THE EXECUTIVE." NAT/G LEGIS ADMIN REPRESENT EFFICIENCY 20. PAGE 76 F1495
BUDGET EX/STRUC EXEC CONTROL

B54
EMERSON F.D.,SHAREHOLDER DEMOCRACY: A BROADER OUTLOOK FOR CORPORATIONS. DELIB/GP EX/STRUC LEGIS ADJUD CONTROL REPRESENT INGP/REL OWN PWR...POLICY STAT RECORD. PAGE 37 F0727
LG/CO PARTIC MAJORIT TREND

S54
EDELMAN M.J.,"LABOR'S INFLUENCE IN FOREIGN POLICY." NAT/G EXEC PWR 20. PAGE 36 F0700
LOBBY REPRESENT EX/STRUC LABOR

B55
RUSTOW D.A.,THE POLITICS OF COMPROMISE. SWEDEN LABOR EX/STRUC LEGIS PLAN REPRESENT SOCISM...SOC 19/20. PAGE 115 F2265
POL/PAR NAT/G POLICY ECO/TAC

B56
BARBASH J.,THE PRACTICE OF UNIONISM. ECO/TAC LEAD LOBBY GP/REL INGP/REL DRIVE MARXISM BIBLIOG. PAGE 10 F0182
LABOR REPRESENT CONTROL ADMIN

B56
FIELD G.C.,POLITICAL THEORY. POL/PAR REPRESENT MORAL SOVEREIGN...JURID IDEA/COMP. PAGE 40 F0789
CONCPT NAT/G ORD/FREE DIPLOM

B56
REDFORD E.S.,PUBLIC ADMINISTRATION AND POLICY FORMATION: STUDIES IN OIL, GAS, BANKING, RIVER DEVELOPMENT AND CORPORATE INVESTIGATIONS. USA+45 CLIENT NAT/G ADMIN LOBBY REPRESENT GOV/REL INGP/REL 20. PAGE 110 F2167
EX/STRUC PROB/SOLV CONTROL EXEC

L56
PENNOCK J.R.,"PARTY AND CONSTITUENCY IN POSTWAR AGRICULTURAL PRICE SUPPORT LEGISLATION." USA+45 LEGIS DEBATE LOBBY RIGID/FLEX. PAGE 105 F2057
POL/PAR REPRESENT AGRI CHOOSE

S56
TYLER G.,"THE PRESIDENCY AND LABOR." USA+45 USA-45 NAT/G LOBBY GOV/REL PWR 20 PRESIDENT. PAGE 131 F2595
LABOR REPRESENT CHIEF

C56
MCKEE J.B.,"THE POWER TO DECIDE" IN M. WEINBERG AND O. SHABET, SOCIETY AND MAN." ELITES STRATA REPRESENT GP/REL ATTIT PWR MUNICH BUSINESS. PAGE 88 F1731
LABOR DECISION LEAD

B57
MILLIKAN M.F.,A PROPOSAL: KEY TO AN EFFECTIVE FOREIGN POLICY. USA+45 AGRI FINAN DELIB/GP DIPLOM REPRESENT MAJORITY...NEW/IDEA CHARTS. PAGE 91 F1795
FOR/AID GIVE ECO/UNDEV PLAN

L57
SURREY S.S.,"THE CONGRESS AND THE TAX LOBBYIST - HOW SPECIAL TAX PROVISIONS GET ENACTED." LOBBY REPRESENT PRIVIL CONGRESS. PAGE 128 F2518
LEGIS TAX EX/STRUC ROLE

S57
KAHN R.L.,"UNION PRACTICES AND MEMBER PARTICIPATION." PARTIC CHOOSE REPRESENT PERS/REL PERSON SKILL...DECISION METH/CNCPT QU. PAGE 69 F1347
INGP/REL LABOR ATTIT LEAD

B58
DUBIN R.,WORKING UNION-MANAGEMENT RELATIONS. LAW PLAN ECO/TAC CHOOSE REPRESENT INGP/REL PWR...POLICY SOC BIBLIOG. PAGE 34 F0669
LABOR MGT AUTHORIT GP/REL

B58
FINER S.E.,PRIVATE INDUSTRY AND POLITICAL POWER (PAMPHLET). UK INDUS CONTROL LOBBY PWR. PAGE 41 F0797
PLURISM REPRESENT EX/STRUC

S58
EMERSON F.D.,"THE ROLES OF MANAGEMENT AND SHAREHOLDERS IN CORPORATE GOVERNMENT." CLIENT DELIB/GP CREATE ADMIN EXEC PARTIC PERS/REL PWR. PAGE 37 F0728
LG/CO LAW INGP/REL REPRESENT

S58
LATTIN N.D.,"MINORITY AND DISSENTING SHAREHOLDERS' RIGHTS IN FUNDAMENTAL CHANGES." FINAN LEGIS ADJUD PARTIC ROUTINE CHOOSE REPRESENT INGP/REL TREND. PAGE 76 F1487
MAJORIT LG/CO LAW CREATE

S58
O'NEAL F.H.,"RECENT LEGISLATION AFFECTING CLOSE CORPORATIONS." LAW EX/STRUC ECO/TAC ROUTINE CHOOSE RIGID/FLEX...MAJORIT MGT TREND. PAGE 100 F1959
LG/CO LEGIS REPRESENT PARTIC

S58
SCHUMM S.,"INTEREST REPRESENTATION IN FRANCE AND GERMANY." EUR+WWI FRANCE GERMANY INSPECT PARL/PROC REPRESENT 20 WEIMAR/REP. PAGE 118 F2320
LOBBY DELIB/GP NAT/G

B59
BROMWICH L.,UNION CONSTITUTIONS. CONSTN EX/STRUC PRESS ADJUD CONTROL CHOOSE REPRESENT PWR SAMP. PAGE 19 F0361
LABOR ROUTINE INGP/REL RACE/REL

B59
FERRY W.H.,THE CORPORATION AND THE ECONOMY. CLIENT LAW CONSTN LABOR NAT/G PLAN INT/TRADE PARTIC CONSEN ORD/FREE PWR POLICY. PAGE 40 F0787
LG/CO CONTROL REPRESENT

B59
LEISERSON W.,AMERICAN TRADE UNION DEMOCRACY. CONSTN STRUCT ADJUD EXEC REPRESENT GP/REL INGP/REL MAJORITY ATTIT PWR. PAGE 77 F1516
LABOR LEAD PARTIC DELIB/GP

B59
MUSOLF L.D.,PUBLIC OWNERSHIP AND ACCOUNTABILITY: THE CANADIAN EXPERIENCE. CANADA REPRESENT PWR 20. PAGE 95 F1873
MGT CONTROL INDUS

B59
WAHLKE J.C.,LEGISLATIVE BEHAVIOR: A READER IN THEORY AND RESEARCH. USA+45 CONSTN ELITES POL/PAR LOBBY REPRESENT PERS/REL PERSON ROLE...IDEA/COMP METH/COMP SIMUL. PAGE 142 F2800
LEGIS CHOOSE INGP/REL ATTIT

B59
WUERTHNER J.J.,THE BUSINESSMAN'S GUIDE TO PRACTICAL POLITICS. USA+45 PWR 20. PAGE 149 F2940
LOBBY CHOOSE REPRESENT

S59
CLONER A.,"THE CALIFORNIA LEGISLATOR AND THE PROBLEM OF COMPENSATION." USA+45 WORKER REPRESENT. PAGE 25 F0492
INCOME PROVS LEGIS SUPEGO

S59
SCHEEHAN D.,"PUBLIC AND PRIVATE GROUPS AS IDENTIFIED IN THE FIELD OF TRADE REGULATIONS." USA+45 ADMIN REPRESENT GOV/REL. PAGE 116 F2293
LAW CONTROL ADJUD LOBBY

S59
SHEENAN D.,"PUBLIC CORPORATIONS AND PUBLIC ACTION." UK ADMIN CONTROL REPRESENT SOCISM 20. PAGE 120 F2372
ECO/DEV EFFICIENCY EX/STRUC EXEC

S59
STREAT R.,"GOVERNMENT CONSULTATION WITH INDUSTRY." UK 20. PAGE 127 F2501
REPRESENT ADMIN EX/STRUC INDUS

B60
EELLS R.S.F.,THE MEANING OF MODERN BUSINESS. LOC/G NAT/G NEIGH EX/STRUC PARTIC GP/REL INGP/REL DECISION. PAGE 36 F0706
LG/CO REPRESENT POLICY PLAN

B60
HARBRECHT P.P.,TOWARD THE PARAPROPRIETAL SOCIETY. REPRESENT INCOME OWN PROFIT AGE/O. PAGE 55 F1076
PWR ADMIN ELITES CONTROL

B60
THOMPSON V.A.,THE REGULATORY PROCESS IN OPA RATIONING. USA-45 CLIENT PROB/SOLV ADMIN LOBBY REPRESENT 20. PAGE 130 F2566
EX/STRUC GOV/REL INGP/REL

L60
FUCHS R.F.,"FAIRNESS AND EFFECTIVENESS IN
EFFICIENCY

ADMINISTRATIVE AGENCY ORGANIZATION AND PROCEDURES." USA+45 ADJUD ADMIN REPRESENT. PAGE 45 F0872 — EX/STRUC EXEC POLICY

S60
FORM W.H.,"ORGANIZED LABOR'S IMAGE OF COMMUNITY POWER STRUCTURE." LABOR LG/CO CONTROL LEAD REPRESENT...DECISION METH/CNCPT INT QU SAMP. PAGE 42 F0829 — NEIGH PARTIC PWR GP/REL

B61
BARRASH J.,LABOR'S GRASS ROOTS; A STUDY OF THE LOCAL UNION. STRATA BARGAIN LEAD REPRESENT DEMAND ATTIT PWR. PAGE 10 F0192 — LABOR USA+45 INGP/REL EXEC

B61
CAMPAIGNE J.G.,CHECK-OFF: LABOR BOSSES AND WORKING MEN. LEGIS WORKER EDU/PROP DEBATE COERCE REPRESENT GP/REL ORD/FREE CONSERVE. PAGE 21 F0404 — LABOR ELITES PWR CONTROL

B61
ENGLER R.,THE POLITICS OF OIL. USA+45 CLIENT ELITES DOMIN EDU/PROP EXEC PWR 20. PAGE 38 F0734 — LOBBY REPRESENT POLICY

B61
HART W.R.,COLLECTIVE BARGAINING IN THE FEDERAL CIVIL SERVICE. NAT/G EX/STRUC ADMIN EXEC 20. PAGE 56 F1101 — INGP/REL MGT REPRESENT LABOR

B61
MACMAHON A.W.,DELEGATION AND AUTONOMY. INDIA STRUCT LEGIS BARGAIN BUDGET ECO/TAC LEGIT EXEC REPRESENT GOV/REL CENTRAL DEMAND EFFICIENCY PRODUC. PAGE 84 F1637 — ADMIN PLAN FEDERAL

B61
ZEIGLER H.,THE POLITICS OF SMALL BUSINESS. USA+45 EX/STRUC ADMIN 20. PAGE 150 F2963 — LOBBY REPRESENT EXEC VOL/ASSN

S61
BRAFF A.J.,"WAGE-PRICE POLICIES UNDER PUBLIC PRESSURE." USA+45 EX/STRUC LOBBY REPRESENT PWR 20. PAGE 17 F0335 — ATTIT PARTIC PROB/SOLV

B62
ALEXANDROWICZ C.H.,WORLD ECONOMIC AGENCIES: LAW AND PRACTICE. WOR+45 DIST/IND FINAN LABOR CONSULT INT/TRADE TARIFFS REPRESENT HEALTH...JURID 20 UN GATT EEC OAS ECSC. PAGE 4 F0064 — INT/LAW INT/ORG DIPLOM ADJUD

B62
GALENSON W.,TRADE UNIONS MONOGRAPH SERIES (A SERIES OF NINE TEXTS). DELIB/GP LEAD PARTIC...DECISION ORG/CHARTS. PAGE 45 F0887 — LABOR INGP/REL CONSTN REPRESENT

B62
HARRINGTON M.,THE OTHER AMERICA: POVERTY IN THE UNITED STATES. WORKER CREATE REPRESENT RACE/REL AGE/O DRIVE POLICY. PAGE 55 F1086 — WEALTH WELF/ST INCOME CULTURE

B62
SHERIF M.,INTERGROUP RELATIONS AND LEADERSHIP: APPROACHES AND RESEARCH IN INDUSTRIAL, ETHNIC, CULTURAL AND POLITICAL AREAS. CULTURE R+D LABOR DIPLOM GP/REL RACE/REL PERCEPT...PSY CONCPT. PAGE 121 F2377 — LEAD REPRESENT PWR INGP/REL

B63
HARVEY O.L.,THE ANVIL AND THE PLOW: A HISTORY OF THE UNITED STATES DEPARTMENT OF LABOR: 1913-1963. USA+45 USA-45 NAT/G CONFER NEW/LIB 20 DEPT/LABOR. PAGE 56 F1106 — EX/STRUC REPRESENT GP/REL LABOR

B63
HATHAWAY D.A.,GOVERNMENT AND AGRICULTURE: PUBLIC POLICY IN A DEMOCRATIC SOCIETY. USA+45 LEGIS ADMIN EXEC LOBBY REPRESENT PWR 20. PAGE 57 F1111 — AGRI GOV/REL PROB/SOLV EX/STRUC

B63
MCCONNELL G.,STEEL AND THE PRESIDENCY, 1962. USA+45 INDUS PROB/SOLV CONFER ROLE...POLICY 20 PRESIDENT. PAGE 88 F1722 — PWR CHIEF REPRESENT DOMIN

B63
US ADVISORY COMN INTERGOV REL,PERFORMANCE OF URBAN FUNCTIONS: LOCAL AND AREAWIDE. TEC/DEV PARTIC REPRESENT PWR...DECISION GOV/COMP MUNICH. PAGE 133 F2633 — REGION LOC/G ECO/TAC

B64
HACKER A.,THE CORPORATION TAKE-OVER. CONSTN LABOR PLAN BAL/PWR CONTROL EXEC LOBBY REPRESENT GP/REL ROLE ORD/FREE POLICY. PAGE 52 F1025 — LG/CO STRUCT PWR

B64
PAARLBERG D.,AMERICAN FARM POLICY: A CASE STUDY IN CENTRALIZED DECISION-MAKING. USA+45 NAT/G LEGIS LOBBY REPRESENT GOV/REL PWR LAISSEZ 20. PAGE 102 F2009 — PROB/SOLV EX/STRUC AGRI

B64
PRESTHUS R.,MEN AT THE TOP; A STUDY IN COMMUNITY POWER. USA+45 STRUCT ACT/RES REPRESENT CONSEN ALL/VALS ORD/FREE...SAMP/SIZ 20. PAGE 108 F2116 — PLURISM LG/CO PWR ADMIN

B64
TAWNEY R.H.,EQUALITY. UK CULTURE STRATA ECO/TAC EDU/PROP REPRESENT OWN NEW/LIB...MAJORIT WELF/ST SOC 20. PAGE 129 F2538 — WEALTH STRUCT ELITES POPULISM

S64
HOWE M.,"THE TRANSPORT ACT, 1962, AND THE CONSUMERS' CONSULTATIVE COMMITTEES." UK CONFER EXEC PWR 20. PAGE 62 F1225 — PARTIC REPRESENT DELIB/GP DIST/IND

S64
LEFF N.H.,"ECONOMIC DEVELOPMENT THROUGH BUREAUCRATIC CORRUPTION." ELITES NAT/G ROUTINE REPRESENT GP/REL PERS/REL. PAGE 77 F1511 — ECO/UNDEV CLIENT EX/STRUC

B65
RATNAM K.J.,COMMUNALISM AND THE POLITICAL PROCESS IN MALAYA. MALAYSIA WOR+45 ECO/UNDEV PARTIC CHOOSE REPRESENT GP/REL CENTRAL ATTIT...CHARTS WORSHIP 20. PAGE 109 F2152 — CONSTN GOV/REL REGION

S65
LONG T.G.,"THE ADMINISTRATIVE PROCESS: AGONIZING REAPPRAISAL IN THE FTC." NAT/G REPRESENT 20 FTC. PAGE 82 F1598 — ADJUD LOBBY ADMIN EX/STRUC

B66
ANDERSON J.E.,POLITICS AND THE ECONOMY. NAT/G LOBBY PWR 20. PAGE 5 F0096 — REPRESENT EX/STRUC CONTROL

B66
BAKKE E.W.,MUTUAL SURVIVAL; THE GOAL OF UNION AND MANAGEMENT (2ND ED.). USA+45 ELITES ECO/DEV ECO/TAC CONFER ADMIN REPRESENT GP/REL INGP/REL ATTIT ...GP/COMP 20. PAGE 8 F0155 — MGT LABOR BARGAIN INDUS

B66
DILLEY M.R.,BRITISH POLICY IN KENYA COLONY (2ND ED.). AFR INDIA UK LABOR BUDGET TAX ADMIN PARL/PROC GP/REL...BIBLIOG 20 PARLIAMENT. PAGE 33 F0639 — COLONIAL REPRESENT SOVEREIGN

B66
MC CONNELL J.P.,LAW AND BUSINESS: PATTERNS AND ISSUES IN COMMERCIAL LAW. USA+45 USA-45 LOC/G WORKER LICENSE CRIME REPRESENT GP/REL 20. PAGE 87 F1713 — ECO/DEV JURID ADJUD MGT

B67
BLAIR G.S.,LEGISLATIVE BODIES IN CALIFORNIA. USA+45 LAW POL/PAR LOBBY APPORT CHOOSE REPRESENT GP/REL ...T CALIFORNIA. PAGE 15 F0293 — LEGIS PROVS LOC/G ADJUD

B67
NKRUMAH K.,CHALLENGE OF THE CONGO. FORCES ECO/TAC FOR/AID REGION MURDER REPRESENT 20 CONGO/LEOP UN. PAGE 98 F1930 — REV ECO/UNDEV ORD/FREE DIPLOM

S67
"THE FEDERAL AGRICULTURAL STABILIZATION PROGRAM AND THE NEGRO." LAW CONSTN PLAN REPRESENT DISCRIM ORD/FREE 20 NEGRO CONGRESS. PAGE 2 F0025 — AGRI CONTROL NAT/G RACE/REL

S67
HALL B.,"THE PAINTER'S UNION: A PARTIAL VICTORY." USA+45 PROB/SOLV LEGIT ADMIN REPRESENT 20. PAGE 53 F1043 — LABOR CHIEF CHOOSE CRIME

S67
HALL B.,"THE COALITION AGAINST DISHWASHERS." USA+45 POL/PAR PROB/SOLV BARGAIN LEAD CHOOSE REPRESENT GP/REL ORD/FREE PWR...POLICY 20. PAGE 53 F1044 — LABOR ADMIN DOMIN WORKER

S67
ZACK A.M.,"ARE STRIKES OF PUBLIC EMPLOYEES NECESSARY?" USA+45 DELIB/GP PROB/SOLV REPRESENT GP/REL MGT. PAGE 150 F2956 — LABOR NAT/G WORKER BARGAIN

REPUBLICAN....REPUBLICAN PARTY (ALL NATIONS)

B27
SIEGFRIED A.,AMERICA COMES OF AGE: A FRENCH ANALYSIS (TRANS. BY H.H. HEMMING AND DORIS HEMMING). FRANCE UK POL/PAR WORKER TEC/DEV DIPLOM REGION RACE/REL ADJUST PRODUC HEREDITY...TIME/SEQ GP/COMP SOC/INTEG 20 DEMOCRAT REPUBLICAN KKK. PAGE 122 F2398 — USA-45 CULTURE ECO/DEV SOC

S59
GILPATRICK T.V.,"PRICE SUPPORT POLICY AND THE MIDWEST FARM VOTE" (BMR)" NAT/G PRICE CONTROL REGION...POLICY CHARTS 440 20 MIDWEST/US CONGRESS REPUBLICAN EISNHWR/DD 20. PAGE 47 F0925 — POL/PAR AGRI ATTIT CHOOSE

B61
HOLMANS A.E.,UNITED STATES FISCAL POLICY 1945-1959. AFR USA+45 USA-45 ECO/DEV TAX PRICE WAR...BIBLIOG 20 DEMOCRAT REPUBLICAN. PAGE 61 F1200 — POLICY BUDGET NAT/G ECO/TAC

B65
GRAMPP W.D.,ECONOMIC LIBERALISM; THE BEGINNINGS — ECO/DEV

(VOL. I). USA-45 WOR-45 MARKET LABOR ATTIT WEALTH ...POLICY CONCPT BIBLIOG GREECE/ANC MERCANTLST REPUBLICAN FEDERALIST. PAGE 50 F0974 — CAP/ISM IDEA/COMP ECO/TAC

B67
PRINCE C.E.,NEW JERSEY'S JEFFERSONIAN REPUBLICANS; THE GENESIS OF AN EARLY PARTY MACHINE (1789-1817). USA-45 LOC/G EDU/PROP PRESS CONTROL CHOOSE...CHARTS 18/19 NEW/JERSEY REPUBLICAN. PAGE 108 F2117 — POL/PAR CONSTN ADMIN PROVS

RESEARCH....SEE ACT/RES, OP/RES, R+D, CREATE

RESEARCH AND DEVELOPMENT GROUP....SEE R+D

RESERVE SYSTEM, FEDERAL....SEE FED/RESERV

RESIST/INT....SOCIAL RESISTANCE TO INTERVIEWS

RESOURCE/N....NATURAL RESOURCES

S21
MALINOWSKI B.,"THE PRIMITIVE ECONOMICS OF THE TROBRIAND ISLANDERS" (BMR)" CULTURE SOCIETY NAT/G CHIEF LEAD OWN...SOC MYTH WORSHIP 20 NEW/GUINEA TROBRIAND RESOURCE/N. PAGE 84 F1647 — ECO/UNDEV AGRI PRODUC STRUCT

B37
MACKENZIE F.,PLANNED SOCIETY: YESTERDAY, TODAY, AND TOMORROW. ECO/DEV ECO/UNDEV AGRI FINAN INDUS PLAN INSPECT CONTROL ALL/IDEOS...TREND METH/COMP BIBLIOG 20 RESOURCE/N. PAGE 83 F1635 — SOC CONCPT ANTHOL

B38
CARVALHO C.M.,GEOGRAPHIA HUMANA; POLITICA E ECONOMICA (3RD ED.). BRAZIL CULTURE AGRI INDUS DIPLOM COLONIAL GP/REL RACE/REL...LING 20 RESOURCE/N. PAGE 22 F0424 — GEOG HABITAT

S41
MUKERJEE R.,"POPULATION THEORY AND POLITICS (BMR)" WOR-45 NAT/G PLAN PROB/SOLV ECO/TAC INT/TRADE CONTROL WAR PEACE...CENSUS 20 BIRTH/CON RESOURCE/N. PAGE 94 F1854 — GEOG OPTIMAL CONCPT

B47
MILLETT J.D.,THE PROCESS AND ORGANIZATION OF GOVERNMENT PLANNING. USA+45 DELIB/GP ACT/RES LEAD LOBBY TASK...POLICY GEOG TIME 20 RESOURCE/N. PAGE 91 F1793 — ADMIN NAT/G PLAN CONSULT

B48
OSBORN F.,OUR PLUNDERED PLANET. UNIV DEATH WAR ...BIBLIOG RESOURCE/N. PAGE 102 F2001 — HABITAT GEOG ADJUST AGRI

B51
HART A.G.,DEFENSE WITHOUT INFLATION. AFR KOREA FINAN INDUS NAT/G WORKER DIPLOM RATION TAX PRICE COST OPTIMAL 20 RESOURCE/N. PAGE 56 F1098 — ECO/TAC CONTROL WAR PLAN

B54
WILLIAMSON H.F.,ECONOMIC DEVELOPMENT - PRINCIPLES AND PATTERNS. INDIA KOREA CULTURE ECO/DEV ECO/UNDEV TEC/DEV...CENSUS NAT/COMP FOR/TRADE 20 CHINJAP MEXIC/AMER RESOURCE/N. PAGE 147 F2895 — ECO/TAC GEOG LABOR

S56
SPENGLER J.J.,"POPULATION THREATENS PROSPERITY" (BMR)" WOR+45 SOCIETY FINAN RATION COST INCOME ...SOC CHARTS 20 RESOURCE/N. PAGE 124 F2451 — CENSUS GEOG WEALTH TREND

B57
BAUER P.T.,THE ECONOMICS OF UNDERDEVELOPED COUNTRIES. WOR+45 AGRI FINAN INDUS PROC/MFG WORKER CAP/ISM PAY PRICE INCOME MARXISM...METH/COMP 20 RESOURCE/N. PAGE 11 F0213 — ECO/UNDEV ECO/TAC PROB/SOLV NAT/G

B57
PALACIOS A.L.,PETROLEO, MONOPOLIOS, Y LATIFUNDIOS. L/A+17C EXTR/IND NAT/G TEC/DEV ECO/TAC CONTROL PRODUC 20 ARGEN MONOPOLY RESOURCE/N. PAGE 103 F2017 — ECO/UNDEV NAT/LISM INDUS AGRI

B60
NEALE A.D.,THE FLOW OF RESOURCES FROM RICH TO POOR. WOR+45 ECO/DEV ECO/UNDEV FINAN INDUS NAT/G PLAN EFFICIENCY WEALTH...POLICY NAT/COMP 20 RESOURCE/N. PAGE 97 F1905 — FOR/AID DIPLOM METH/CNCPT

B61
HODGKINS J.A.,SOVIET POWER: ENERGY RESOURCES, PRODUCTION AND POTENTIALS. USSR ECO/DEV INDUS MARKET...POLICY STAT CHARTS 20 RESOURCE/N. PAGE 60 F1188 — GEOG EXTR/IND TEC/DEV

B61
LEE R.R.,ENGINEERING-ECONOMIC PLANNING MISCELLANEOUS SUBJECTS: A SELECTED BIBLIOGRAPHY (MIMEOGRAPHED). FINAN LOC/G NEIGH ADMIN CONTROL INGP/REL HABITAT...GEOG MGT SOC/WK MUNICH 20 RESOURCE/N. PAGE 77 F1509 — BIBLIOG/A PLAN REGION

L61
CHENERY H.B.,"COMPARATIVE ADVANTAGE AND DEVELOPMENT POLICY." FINAN INT/TRADE RATION OPTIMAL...CHARTS METH/COMP GEN/LAWS BIBLIOG 20 RESOURCE/N. PAGE 24 F0463 — ECO/UNDEV ECO/TAC PLAN EFFICIENCY

B63
BARNETT H.J.,SCARCITY AND GROWTH: THE ECONOMICS OF NATURAL RESOURCE AVAILABILITY. FUT WOR+45 AGRI INDUS PROB/SOLV TEC/DEV CONTROL PRODUC...SOC/WK IDEA/COMP METH/COMP SIMUL 20 RESOURCE/N MALTHUS RICARDO/D MILL/JS DARWIN/C. PAGE 10 F0191 — DEMAND HABITAT CENSUS GEOG

B63
EL-NAGGAR S.,FOREIGN AID TO UNITED ARAB REPUBLIC. UAR USA+45 USSR AGRI FINAN INDUS FORCES EATING DEMAND...CHARTS METH/COMP 20 RESOURCE/N AID. PAGE 37 F0718 — FOR/AID ECO/UNDEV RECEIVE PLAN

S63
ENTHOVEN A.C.,"ECONOMIC ANALYSIS IN THE DEPARTMENT OF DEFENSE." USA+45 NAT/G DELIB/GP PROB/SOLV RATION NUC/PWR WEAPON COST...DECISION 20 DEPT/DEFEN RESOURCE/N. PAGE 38 F0739 — PLAN BUDGET ECO/TAC FORCES

B64
BROWN E.H.P.,A COURSE IN APPLIED ECONOMICS (2ND ED.). ECO/DEV FINAN MARKET WORKER INT/TRADE RATION RENT PAY PRICE BAL/PAY...DECISION T RESOURCE/N. PAGE 19 F0368 — POLICY ECO/TAC PROB/SOLV

S64
HOOVER C.B.,"THE ROLE OF THE NATURAL AND DEVELOPED RESOURCES OF THE NATION STATES." FUT WOR+45 ECO/DEV ECO/UNDEV NAT/G PWR RESPECT SKILL WEALTH...POLICY GEOG TIME/SEQ TREND RESOURCE/N VAL/FREE 20. PAGE 62 F1210 — EXTR/IND DOMIN

N64
GREAT BRITAIN CENTRAL OFF INF,THE COLOMBO PLAN (PAMPHLET). AFR ASIA S/ASIA USA+45 VOL/ASSN ...CHARTS 20 RESOURCE/N. PAGE 50 F0980 — FOR/AID PLAN INT/ORG ECO/UNDEV

B65
JASNY H.,KHRUSHCHEV'S CROP POLICY. USSR ECO/DEV PLAN MARXISM...STAT 20 KHRUSH/N RESOURCE/N. PAGE 66 F1306 — AGRI NAT/G POLICY ECO/TAC

B65
LUGO-MARENCO J.J.,A STATEMENT OF THE LAWS OF NICARAGUA IN MATTERS AFFECTING BUSINESS. NICARAGUA AGRI DIST/IND EXTR/IND FINAN INDUS FAM WORKER INT/TRADE TAX MARRIAGE OWN BIO/SOC 20 TREATY RESOURCE/N MIGRATION. PAGE 82 F1606 — CONSTN NAT/G LEGIS JURID

B65
MARK S.M.,ECONOMICS IN ACTION (3RD ED.). USA+45 ECO/UNDEV AGRI INDUS FOR/AID INT/TRADE BAL/PAY COST ORD/FREE...ANTHOL 20 RESOURCE/N. PAGE 85 F1670 — POLICY ECO/TAC EFFICIENCY PRICE

RESOURCES FOR THE FUTURE F2179

RESPECT....RESPECT, SOCIAL CLASS, STRATIFICATION (CONTEMPT)

B29
DE MAN H.,JOY IN WORK. STRATA ECO/DEV ECO/TAC PRODUC ANOMIE ROLE SOCISM...IDEA/COMP 20. PAGE 31 F0605 — SOC WORKER HAPPINESS RESPECT

B55
BERNAYS E.L.,THE ENGINEERING OF CONSENT. VOL/ASSN OP/RES ROUTINE INGP/REL ATTIT RESPECT...POLICY METH/CNCPT METH/COMP 20. PAGE 14 F0264 — GP/REL PLAN ACT/RES ADJUST

B57
EHRMANN H.W.,ORGANIZED BUSINESS IN FRANCE. EUR+WWI MOD/EUR ECO/DEV VOL/ASSN LEGIT ATTIT PERCEPT PWR RESPECT...PLURIST SOC INT TOT/POP 20. PAGE 36 F0712 — PROF/ORG ECO/TAC FRANCE

B60
BOHM F.,REDEN UND SCHRIFTEN UBER DIE ORDNUNG EINER FREIEN GESELLSCHAFT, EINER FREIEN WIRTSCHAFT, UND UBER DIE WIEDERGUTMACH. DIPLOM CRIME ORD/FREE RESPECT FASCISM 20 NAZI. PAGE 16 F0307 — ECO/TAC NEW/LIB SUPEGO REPAR

B61
MARX K.,THE COMMUNIST MANIFESTO. IN (MENDEL A. ESSENTIAL WORKS OF MARXISM, NEW YORK: BANTAM. FUT MOD/EUR CULTURE ECO/DEV ECO/UNDEV AGRI FINAN INDUS MARKET PROC/MFG LABOR POL/PAR CONSULT FORCES CREATE PLAN ADMIN ATTIT DRIVE RIGID/FLEX ORD/FREE PWR RESPECT MARX/KARL MUNICH WORK. PAGE 86 F1691 — COM NEW/IDEA CAP/ISM REV

S62
MORGENTHAU H.J.,"A POLITICAL THEORY OF FOREIGN AID." ECO/UNDEV NAT/G DELIB/GP PLAN ECO/TAC EDU/PROP EXEC ORD/FREE RESPECT WEALTH...METH/CNCPT TREND 20. PAGE 93 F1833 — USA+45 PHIL/SCI FOR/AID

B63
GANDHI M.K.,THE WAY TO COMMUNAL HARMONY. INDIA MAJORITY RIGID/FLEX ROLE RESPECT 20 GANDHI/M. PAGE 46 F0892 — RACE/REL DISCRIM ATTIT ADJUST

B63
LAGOS G.,INTERNATIONAL STRATIFICATION AND UNDERDEVELOPED COUNTRIES. L/A+17C WOR+45 PLAN ECO/TAC PWR RESPECT WEALTH...METH/CNCPT STAT CHARTS SIMUL GEN/LAWS TRUE/GP METH/GP VAL/FREE 20. PAGE 74 F1459 — ECO/UNDEV STRATA

L63
OLSON M. JR.,"RAPID ECONOMIC GROWTH AS A DESTABILIZING FORCE." WOR+45 WOR-45 STRATA ECO/UNDEV FAM KIN CREATE TEC/DEV DIPLOM PEACE ATTIT PERSON RIGID/FLEX PWR RESPECT WEALTH...SOC 20. PAGE 101 F1989 — SOCIETY FOR/AID

S64
HOOVER C.B.,"THE ROLE OF THE NATURAL AND DEVELOPED RESOURCES OF THE NATION STATES." FUT WOR+45 ECO/DEV ECO/UNDEV NAT/G PWR RESPECT SKILL WEALTH...POLICY GEOG TIME/SEQ TREND RESOURCE/N VAL/FREE 20. PAGE 62 F1210 — EXTR/IND DOMIN

B65
THORNTON A.P.,DOCTRINES OF IMPERIALISM. WOR+45 WOR-45 DOMIN NAT/LISM PROFIT ATTIT PERSON PWR RESPECT SOVEREIGN...CONCPT STERTYP. PAGE 130 F2571 — IDEA/COMP COLONIAL DRIVE

B67
WOOTON G.,WORKERS, UNIONS, AND THE STATE. INDUS PROB/SOLV GP/REL DRIVE SUPEGO RESPECT...PSY SOC. PAGE 148 F2925 — PARTIC WORKER NAT/G LABOR

RESPONSIBILITY....SEE SUPEGO, RESPECT

RESPONSIVENESS....SEE RIGID/FLEX

RESTRAINT....SEE ORD/FREE

RETAILING....SEE MARKET

RETIREMENT....SEE SENIOR, ADMIN

REUBENS E.D. F2180

REUSS H.S. F2181

REUTHER/W....WALTER REUTHER

REV....REVOLUTION; SEE ALSO WAR

B13
KROPOTKIN P.,THE CONQUEST OF BREAD. SOCIETY STRATA AGRI INDUS WORKER REV HAPPINESS INCOME PRODUC HEALTH MORAL ORD/FREE. PAGE 74 F1444 — ANARCH SOCIALIST OWN AGREE

B14
LEVINE L.,SYNDICALISM IN FRANCE (2ND ED.). FRANCE LAW SOCIETY ECO/DEV NAT/G ECO/TAC LEAD ATTIT ...POLICY CONCPT STAT BIBLIOG 18/20 REFORMERS. PAGE 79 F1542 — LABOR INDUS SOCISM REV

B23
FINER H.,REPRESENTATIVE GOVERNMENT AND A PARLIAMENT OF INDUSTRY. A STUDY OF THE GERMAN FEDERAL ECONOMIC COUNCIL. GERMANY UK CONSTN INDUS PARL/PROC ...NAT/COMP 20. PAGE 41 F0796 — DELIB/GP ECO/TAC WAR REV

B33
TANNENBAUM F.,PEACE BY REVOLUTION. ECO/UNDEV AGRI SECT WORKER DIPLOM EDU/PROP DISCRIM OWN WEALTH POPULISM 17/20 MEXIC/AMER INDIAN/AM. PAGE 128 F2532 — CULTURE COLONIAL RACE/REL REV

B34
MARX K.,THE CLASS STRUGGLES IN FRANCE. FRANCE INDUS WORKER CONSERVE...TREND GEN/LAWS 19. PAGE 86 F1689 — MARXIST STRATA REV INT/TRADE

B35
O'CONNOR H.,REVOLUTION IN SEATTLE. USA-45 STRATA WORKER GP/REL ATTIT SOCISM...OBS BIBLIOG/A 20 SEATTLE STRIKE COM/PARTY. PAGE 99 F1954 — REV EDU/PROP LABOR MARXISM

B36
HUBERMAN L.,MAN'S WORLDLY GOODS: THE STORY OF THE WEALTH OF NATIONS. CHRIST-17C EUR+WWI MOD/EUR SOCIETY DOMIN REV ORD/FREE...TIME/SEQ METH/COMP. PAGE 63 F1231 — WEALTH CAP/ISM MARXISM CREATE

B38
HARPER S.N.,THE GOVERNMENT OF THE SOVIET UNION. COM USSR LAW CONSTN ECO/DEV PLAN TEC/DEV DIPLOM INT/TRADE ADMIN REV NAT/LISM...POLICY 20. PAGE 55 F1085 — MARXISM NAT/G LEAD POL/PAR

B39
ENGELS F.,HERRN EUGEN DUHRING'S REVOLUTION IN SCIENCE (1878). CULTURE STRATA STRUCT FAM SECT ECO/TAC REV WAR SOCISM...MARXIST 19. PAGE 37 F0731 — PWR SOCIETY WEALTH GEN/LAWS

B40
HUNTER R.,REVOLUTION: WHY, HOW, WHEN? NAT/G ECO/TAC EDU/PROP COERCE ORD/FREE FASCISM POPULISM SOCISM 18/20 HITLER/A LENIN/VI. PAGE 63 F1246 — REV METH/COMP LEAD CONSTN

B50
HUNT R.N.,THE THEORY AND PRACTICE OF COMMUNISM. STRUCT WORKER NAT/LISM TOTALISM...CONCPT TREND 19/20 STALIN/J EUROPE. PAGE 63 F1244 — MARXISM SOCISM REV STRATA

B50
SOREL G.,REFLECTIONS ON VIOLENCE (1908) (TRANS. BY T.E. HULME AND J. ROTH). UNIV SOCIETY LABOR UTOPIA MORAL SOCISM...ANARCH SOCIALIST CONCPT 20. PAGE 124 F2445 — COERCE REV WORKER MYTH

B51
BROGAN D.W.,THE PRICE OF REVOLUTION. FRANCE USA+45 USA-45 USSR CONSTN NAT/G DIPLOM COLONIAL NAT/LISM ORD/FREE POPULISM...CONCPT 18/20 PRE/US/AM. PAGE 19 F0359 — REV METH/COMP COST MARXISM

B54
LENIN V.I.,SELECTED WORKS (12 VOLS.). USSR INTELL SOCIETY STRATA STRUCT NAT/G POL/PAR WORKER CAP/ISM REV WAR...MARXIST PHIL/SCI 20 MARX/KARL LENIN/VI. PAGE 78 F1520 — COM MARXISM

B55
MAYO H.B.,DEMOCRACY AND MARXISM. COM USSR STRATA NAT/G WORKER ECO/TAC REV MORAL...PHIL/SCI HIST/WRIT IDEA/COMP WORSHIP 20 MARX/KARL LENIN/VI STALIN/J TROTSKY/L. PAGE 87 F1708 — MARXISM CAP/ISM

B57
WARRINER D.,LAND REFORM AND DEVELOPMENT IN THE MIDDLE EAST: A STUDY OF EGYPT, SYRIA AND IRAQ. IRAQ ISLAM SYRIA UAR AGRI DIST/IND PLAN TEC/DEV DOMIN REV ATTIT WEALTH...SOC METH/CNCPT STAT OBS RECORD HIST/WRIT TREND GEN/LAWS FAO 20. PAGE 143 F2825 — ECO/UNDEV CONCPT

L57
MASS. INST. TECH.,"THE CENTER FOR INTERNATIONAL STUDIES." AFR ASIA COM EUR+WWI ISLAM L/A+17C S/ASIA USA+45 USA-45 DIST/IND CONSULT FORCES ACT/RES TEC/DEV DIPLOM REV ATTIT WEALTH...CONCPT FOR/TRADE 20. PAGE 87 F1702 — R+D ECO/UNDEV

B58
COLE G.D.H.,COMMUNISM AND SOCIAL DEMOCRACY (VOL. IV OF "HISTORY OF SOCIAL THOUGHT"). COM GERMANY ITALY UK AGRI INT/ORG WORKER DIPLOM COLONIAL NAT/LISM ALL/IDEOS...BIBLIOG 20 LEAGUE/NAT AUST/HUNG. PAGE 26 F0502 — MARXISM REV POL/PAR SOCISM

B58
HAMEROW T.S.,RESTORATION, REVOLUTION, REACTION: ECONOMICS AND POLITICS IN GERMANY, 1815-1871. CAP/ISM ADJUST ATTIT PWR...BIBLIOG/A 19 GER/CONFED FRANK/PARL. PAGE 54 F1055 — REV ORD/FREE ECO/DEV

B58
PAYNO M.,LA REFORMA SOCIAL EN ESPANA Y MEXICO. SPAIN ECO/TAC TAX LOBBY COERCE REV OWN CATHISM 19/20 MEXIC/AMER. PAGE 104 F2043 — SECT NAT/G LAW ELITES

B58
TILLION G.,ALGERIA: THE REALITIES. ALGERIA FRANCE ISLAM CULTURE STRATA PROB/SOLV DOMIN REV NAT/LISM WEALTH MARXISM...GEOG 20. PAGE 130 F2573 — ECO/UNDEV SOC COLONIAL DIPLOM

B59
ARON R.,IMPERIALISM AND COLONIALISM (PAMPHLET). WOR+45 WOR-45 ECO/TAC CONTROL REV ORD/FREE 19/20. PAGE 6 F0119 — COLONIAL DOMIN ECO/UNDEV DIPLOM

B59
HENDEL S.,THE SOVIET CRUCIBLE. USSR LEAD COERCE NAT/LISM UTOPIA PWR...POLICY CONCPT ANTHOL 20 STALIN/J LENIN/VI MARX/KARL BOLSHEVIK. PAGE 58 F1147 — COM MARXISM REV TOTALISM

B59
MARTIN K.,WAR, HISTORY, AND HUMAN NATURE. FRANCE GERMANY INDIA UK UNIV POL/PAR COLONIAL DETER REV MARXISM PACIFISM...PSY CONCPT PREDICT LENIN/VI GANDHI/M. PAGE 86 F1683 — PERSON WAR ATTIT IDEA/COMP

B59
NUNEZ JIMENEZ A.,LA LIBERACION DE LAS ISLAS. CUBA L/A+17C USA+45 LAW CHIEF PLAN DIPLOM FOR/AID OWN WEALTH 20 CASTRO/F. PAGE 99 F1945 — AGRI REV ECO/UNDEV NAT/G

B60
MC CLELLAN G.S.,INDIA. AFR CHINA/COM INDIA CONSTN ELITES STRATA AGRI POL/PAR FOR/AID ARMS/CONT REV MARXISM...CENSUS BIBLIOG 20 GANDHI/M NEHRU/J. PAGE 87 F1712 — DIPLOM NAT/G SOCIETY ECO/UNDEV

B60
SHANNON D.A.,THE GREAT DEPRESSION. USA-45 FINAN LG/CO SCHOOL SML/CO DELIB/GP RECEIVE REV EATING INCOME...ANTHOL MUNICH 20 ROOSEVLT/F CONGRESS. PAGE 120 F2365 — WEALTH NAT/G AGRI INDUS

S60
MAIR L.P.,"SOCIAL CHANGE IN SOUTH AFRICA." MOD/EUR SOUTH/AFR WOR+45 ECO/UNDEV EX/STRUC TEC/DEV ATTIT DRIVE PERCEPT ORD/FREE...MGT CONCPT TIME/SEQ IND 20. PAGE 84 F1641 — AFR NAT/G REV SOVEREIGN

B61
ESTEVEZ A.,ASPECTOS ECONOMICO-FINANCIEROS DE LA CAMPANA SANMARITANA. L/A+17C SPAIN FINAN COLONIAL LEAD ROLE ORD/FREE WEALTH 19 SOUTH/AMER SAN/MARTIN. PAGE 38 F0748 — ECO/UNDEV REV BUDGET NAT/G

B61
HENDERSON W.O.,THE INDUSTRIAL REVOLUTION IN EUROPE. FRANCE GERMANY MOD/EUR RUSSIA WORKER PROFIT PWR — INDUS REV

MARXISM SOCISM...SOC HIST/WRIT 19 INDUS/REV. PAGE 58 F1148
CAP/ISM TEC/DEV

B61
MARX K.,THE COMMUNIST MANIFESTO. IN (MENDEL A. ESSENTIAL WORKS OF MARXISM, NEW YORK: BANTAM. FUT MOD/EUR CULTURE ECO/DEV ECO/UNDEV AGRI FINAN INDUS MARKET PROC/MFG LABOR POL/PAR CONSULT FORCES CREATE PLAN ADMIN ATTIT DRIVE RIGID/FLEX ORD/FREE PWR RESPECT MARX/KARL MUNICH WORK. PAGE 86 F1691
COM NEW/IDEA CAP/ISM REV

B61
PERKINS D.,THE UNITED STATES AND LATIN AMERICAN. L/A+17C USA+45 USA-45 STRUCT COLONIAL REV ORD/FREE 19/20. PAGE 105 F2061
DIPLOM INT/TRADE NAT/G

B61
THEOBALD R.,THE CHALLENGE OF ABUNDANCE. USA+45 WOR+45 MARKET DIPLOM FOR/AID REV PRODUC UTOPIA SUPEGO...POLICY TREND BIBLIOG/A 20. PAGE 129 F2554
WELF/ST ECO/UNDEV PROB/SOLV ECO/TAC

B61
US SENATE COMM ON FOREIGN RELS,INTERNATIONAL DEVELOPMENT AND SECURITY: HEARINGS ON BILL (2 VOLS.). ECO/UNDEV FINAN FORCES REV COST WEALTH ...CHARTS 20 AID PRESIDENT. PAGE 139 F2747
FOR/AID CIVMIL/REL ORD/FREE ECO/TAC

B62
KAUTSKY J.H.,POLITICAL CHANGE IN UNDERDEVELOPED COUNTRIES: NATIONALISM AND COMMUNISM. WOR+45 AGRI TEC/DEV EDU/PROP ATTIT...POLICY METH/CNCPT STYLE INT QU CENSUS TREND SOC/EXP GEN/LAWS 20. PAGE 69 F1365
ECO/UNDEV SOCIETY CAP/ISM REV

B62
KENT R.K.,FROM MADAGASCAR TO THE MALAGASY REPUBLIC. FRANCE MADAGASCAR DIPLOM NAT/LISM ORD/FREE...MGT 18/20. PAGE 70 F1379
COLONIAL SOVEREIGN REV POL/PAR

B62
SELOSOEMARDJAN O.,SOCIAL CHANGES IN JOGJAKARTA. INDONESIA NETHERLAND ELITES STRATA STRUCT FAM POL/PAR CREATE DIPLOM INT/TRADE EDU/PROP ADMIN GOV/REL...SOC 20 JAVA CHINJAP. PAGE 119 F2352
ECO/UNDEV CULTURE REV COLONIAL

B62
SIEVERS A.M.,REVOLUTION, EVOLUTION AND THE ECONOMIC ORDER. INDUS LABOR TAX CONTROL REV WAR DEMAND PRODUC WEALTH...IDEA/COMP 19/20 KEYNES/JM. PAGE 122 F2399
EFFICIENCY ALL/IDEOS ECO/DEV WELF/ST

B62
WARD B.,THE RICH NATIONS AND THE POOR NATIONS. FUT WOR+45 CULTURE ECO/DEV ECO/UNDEV PLAN CAP/ISM EDU/PROP REV NAT/LISM ATTIT DRIVE SOCISM...POLICY CONCPT TIME/SEQ 20. PAGE 143 F2816
ECO/TAC GEN/LAWS

B63
FLORES E.,LAND REFORM AND THE ALLIANCE FOR PROGRESS (PAMPHLET). L/A+17C USA+45 STRUCT ECO/UNDEV NAT/G WORKER CREATE PLAN ECO/TAC COERCE REV 20 ALL/PROG. PAGE 42 F0815
AGRI INT/ORG DIPLOM POLICY

B63
FRIEDRICH C.J.,MAN AND HIS GOVERNMENT: AN EMPIRICAL THEORY OF POLITICS. UNIV LOC/G NAT/G ADJUD REV INGP/REL DISCRIM PWR BIBLIOG. PAGE 44 F0867
PERSON ORD/FREE PARTIC CONTROL

B63
ISSAWI C.,EGYPT IN REVOLUTION: AN ECONOMIC ANALYSIS. ISLAM STRUCT ECO/UNDEV AGRI FINAN INDUS PLAN EXEC REV NAT/LISM ATTIT RIGID/FLEX WEALTH SOCISM...STAT FOR/TRADE WORK 20. PAGE 66 F1292
NAT/G UAR

B63
OTERO L.M.,HONDURAS. HONDURAS SPAIN STRUCT SECT COLONIAL REV WAR ATTIT PWR...GEOG WORSHIP 16/20. PAGE 102 F2003
NAT/G SOCIETY NAT/LISM ECO/UNDEV

B64
DANIELS R.V.,RUSSIA. RUSSIA USSR STRUCT NAT/LISM TOTALISM ORD/FREE WEALTH...POLICY DECISION TREND. PAGE 30 F0579
MARXISM REV ECO/DEV DIPLOM

B64
LUTHULI A.,AFRICA'S FREEDOM. KIN LABOR POL/PAR SCHOOL DIPLOM NEUTRAL REGION REV NAT/LISM PWR WEALTH SOCISM SOC/INTEG 20. PAGE 82 F1608
AFR ECO/UNDEV COLONIAL

B64
NEHEMKIS P.,LATIN AMERICA: MYTH AND REALITY. INDUS INT/ORG PROB/SOLV CAP/ISM DIPLOM REV...SOC MUNICH 20. PAGE 97 F1907
REGION MYTH L/A+17C ECO/UNDEV

B64
NOVACK D.E.,DEVELOPMENT AND SOCIETY; THE DYNAMICS OF ECONOMIC CHANGE. WOR+45 STRATA STRUCT ECO/TAC CONTROL CROWD REV GP/REL ADJUST PRODUC WEALTH PSY. PAGE 99 F1940
SOCIETY CULTURE SOC ECO/UNDEV

B64
PENNOCK J.R.,SELF-GOVERNMENT IN MODERNIZING NATIONS. AFR COM USA+45 ECO/DEV POL/PAR PROB/SOLV DIPLOM ECO/TAC COLONIAL REV POPULISM SOCISM 20. PAGE 105 F2058
ECO/UNDEV POLICY SOVEREIGN NAT/G

B64
POWELSON J.P.,LATIN AMERICA: TODAY'S ECONOMIC AND SOCIAL REVOLUTION. L/A+17C INTELL SOCIETY STRUCT AGRI INDUS NAT/G DIPLOM ECO/TAC REV...POLICY 20. PAGE 107 F2110
ECO/UNDEV WEALTH ADJUST PLAN

B64
SEERS D.,CUBA: THE ECONOMIC AND SOCIAL REVOLUTION. L/A+17C USSR YUGOSLAVIA STRATA AGRI INDUS SCHOOL DELIB/GP PLAN ECO/TAC DOMIN EDU/PROP ATTIT RIGID/FLEX ALL/VALS...STAT OBS TIME/SEQ WORK VAL/FREE 20. PAGE 119 F2341
ACT/RES COERCE CUBA REV

B64
WRIGHT G.,RURAL REVOLUTION IN FRANCE: THE PEASANTRY IN THE TWENTIETH CENTURY. EUR+WWI MOD/EUR LAW CULTURE AGRI POL/PAR DELIB/GP LEGIS ECO/TAC EDU/PROP COERCE CHOOSE ATTIT RIGID/FLEX HEALTH ...STAT CENSUS CHARTS VAL/FREE 20. PAGE 149 F2932
PWR STRATA FRANCE REV

B65
ALEXANDER R.J.,ORGANIZED LABOR IN LATIN AMERICA. L/A+17C INT/ORG LEGIS WORKER TEC/DEV BARGAIN INT/TRADE REV...NAT/COMP BIBLIOG 20. PAGE 3 F0059
LABOR POL/PAR ECO/UNDEV POLICY

B65
COLLINS H.,KARL MARX AND THE BRITISH LABOUR MOVEMENT; YEARS OF THE FIRST INTERNATIONAL. FRANCE SWITZERLND UK CAP/ISM WAR...MARXIST IDEA/COMP BIBLIOG 19. PAGE 26 F0506
MARXISM LABOR INT/ORG REV

S65
WHITAKER A.P.,"ARGENTINA: STRUGGLE FOR RECOVERY." L/A+17C USA+45 NAT/G TOP/EX PLAN LEGIT COERCE REV RIGID/FLEX PWR WEALTH...RECORD ALL/PROG ARGEN FOR/TRADE 20. PAGE 146 F2867
POL/PAR ECO/TAC NAT/LISM

B66
ANDRESKI S.,PARASITISM AND SUBVERSION* THE CASE OF LATIN AMERICA. CULTURE ECO/UNDEV LABOR NAT/G SECT PROB/SOLV RACE/REL TOTALISM ATTIT WEALTH ALL/IDEOS. PAGE 5 F0100
L/A+17C GOV/COMP STRATA REV

B66
BAKLANOFF E.N.,NEW PERSPECTIVES ON BRAZIL. BRAZIL SOCIETY INDUS DOMIN LEAD REV CIVMIL/REL...GEOG PSY LING ANTHOL 20. PAGE 8 F0156
ECO/UNDEV TEC/DEV DIPLOM ORD/FREE

B66
BEQIRAJ M.,PEASANTRY IN REVOLUTION. STRATA ECO/UNDEV AGRI ROUTINE REV HABITAT RIGID/FLEX ...EPIST GEOG NEW/IDEA TREND MUNICH 20. PAGE 13 F0256
WORKER KNOWL NAT/LISM SOC

B66
FORD P.,CARDINAL MORAN AND THE A. L. P. NAT/G POL/PAR SECT DELIB/GP LOBBY REV CHOOSE ORD/FREE MARXISM 19/20 AUSTRAL PROTESTANT LABOR/PAR. PAGE 42 F0825
CATHISM SOCISM LABOR SOCIETY

B66
GYORGY A.,ISSUES OF WORLD COMMUNISM. ALBANIA CHINA/COM COM USSR YUGOSLAVIA STRATA AGRI INT/ORG CHIEF FORCES WORKER WAR ALL/IDEOS...GEOG 20 MAO. PAGE 52 F1018
ECO/UNDEV REV MARXISM CON/ANAL

B66
HOROWITZ I.L.,THREE WORLDS OF DEVELOPMENT. COM USA+45 STRUCT ECO/DEV PLAN PROB/SOLV TEC/DEV CIVMIL/REL...PHIL/SCI IDEA/COMP 20. PAGE 62 F1216
ECO/UNDEV BAL/PWR POL/PAR REV

B66
LAMBERG R.F.,PRAG UND DIE DRITTE WELT. AFR ASIA CZECHOSLVK L/A+17C MARKET TEC/DEV ECO/TAC REV ATTIT 20 TREATY. PAGE 75 F1462
DIPLOM ECO/UNDEV INT/TRADE FOR/AID

B66
MACFARQUHAR R.,CHINA UNDER MAO: POLITICS TAKES COMMAND. CHINA/COM COM AGRI INDUS CHIEF FORCES DIPLOM INT/TRADE EDU/PROP TASK REV ADJUST...ANTHOL 20 MAO. PAGE 83 F1628
ECO/UNDEV TEC/DEV ECO/TAC ADMIN

B66
WETTER G.A.,SOVIET IDEOLOGY TODAY. USSR ECO/UNDEV SECT WORKER CAP/ISM CONTROL TASK EFFICIENCY TOTALISM DRIVE WEALTH...TREND 18/20. PAGE 145 F2864
ALL/IDEOS MARXISM REV

B67
APTHEKER H.,THE NATURE OF DEMOCRACY, FREEDOM AND REVOLUTION. WOR+45 PROB/SOLV COERCE COST...CONCPT TIME/SEQ METH/COMP. PAGE 6 F0111
REV POPULISM MARXIST ORD/FREE

B67
BARROW T.C.,TRADE AND EMPIRE: THE BRITISH CUSTOMS SERVICE IN COLONIAL AMERICA, 1660-1775. UK USA-45 ECO/UNDEV NAT/G ECO/TAC DOMIN REV 17/18. PAGE 10 F0197
COLONIAL TARIFFS ADMIN EX/STRUC

B67
FALL B.B.,HO CHI MINH ON REVOLUTION: SELECTED WRITINGS, 1920-66. COM VIETNAM ELITES NAT/G COERCE GUERRILLA RACE/REL MARXISM...MARXIST ANTHOL 20. PAGE 39 F0761
REV COLONIAL ECO/UNDEV S/ASIA

B67
FANON F.,TOWARD THE AFRICAN REVOLUTION. AFR FRANCE CULTURE ELITES LEAD REV GP/REL ORD/FREE SOVEREIGN 20. PAGE 39 F0762
COLONIAL DOMIN ECO/UNDEV RACE/REL

B67
FILENE P.G.,AMERICANS AND THE SOVIET EXPERIMENT, 1917-1933. USA-45 USSR INTELL NAT/G CAP/ISM DIPLOM
ATTIT RIGID/FLEX

EDU/PROP PRESS REV SOCISM...PSY 20. PAGE 41 F0793 MARXISM SOCIETY

B67
FONER P.S.,THE BOLSHEVIK REVOLUTION. USA-45 POL/PAR WORKER DIPLOM EDU/PROP MARXISM...STERTYP 20. PAGE 42 F0821 LABOR INTELL REV PRESS

B67
MCNELLY T.,SOURCES IN MODERN EAST ASIAN HISTORY AND POLITICS. KOREA VIETNAM CULTURE DIPLOM COLONIAL REV WAR PWR ALL/IDEOS MARXISM...ANTHOL 20 CHINJAP. PAGE 88 F1733 NAT/COMP ASIA S/ASIA SOCIETY

B67
MEYERS M.,SOURCES OF THE AMERICAN REPUBLIC; A DOCUMENTARY HISTORY OF POLITICS, SOCIETY, AND THOUGHT (VOL. I, REV. ED.). USA-45 CULTURE STRUCT NAT/G LEGIS LEAD ATTIT...JURID SOC ANTHOL 17/19 PRESIDENT. PAGE 90 F1772 COLONIAL REV WAR

B67
NKRUMAH K.,CHALLENGE OF THE CONGO. FORCES ECO/TAC FOR/AID REGION MURDER REPRESENT 20 CONGO/LEOP UN. PAGE 98 F1930 REV ECO/UNDEV ORD/FREE DIPLOM

B67
OGLESBY C.,CONTAINMENT AND CHANGE. AFR COM USA+45 ECO/UNDEV TEC/DEV ECO/TAC FOR/AID INT/TRADE DOMIN GUERRILLA REV PEACE 20 STALIN/J. PAGE 101 F1983 DIPLOM BAL/PWR MARXISM CULTURE

B67
PIKE F.B.,FREEDOM AND REFORM IN LATIN AMERICA. BRAZIL URUGUAY CONSTN CULTURE SECT DIPLOM EDU/PROP PARTIC DRIVE ALL/VALS CATHISM...GEOG ANTHOL BIBLIOG REFORMERS BOLIV. PAGE 106 F2086 L/A+17C ORD/FREE ECO/UNDEV REV

B67
SACKS B.,SOUTH AFRICA: AN IMPERIAL DILEMMA. SOUTH/AFR UK ECO/UNDEV KIN DOMIN DEBATE CONTROL REV DISCRIM ISOLAT...POLICY STAT BIBLIOG 20. PAGE 115 F2268 COLONIAL RACE/REL DIPLOM ORD/FREE

B67
WILLIAMS M.,THE EAST IS RED: THE VIEW INSIDE CHINA. CHINA/COM CONSTN COERCE AGE/Y ATTIT PERSON...OBS 20 MAO. PAGE 147 F2893 REV MARXIST GP/REL DIPLOM

B67
WOLF C. JR.,UNITED STATES POLICY AND THE THIRD WORLD. USA+45 WOR+45 FORCES ACT/RES BAL/PWR ECO/TAC FOR/AID DETER GUERRILLA NUC/PWR REV...CHARTS 20. PAGE 148 F2916 DIPLOM ECO/UNDEV POLICY NAT/G

B67
YOUNG J.M.,THE BRAZILIAN REVOLUTION OF 1930 AND THE AFTERMATH. BRAZIL COLONIAL PWR...BIBLIOG/A 16/20. PAGE 150 F2951 PLAN CHIEF FORCES REV

L67
GREGORY A.J.,"AFRICAN SOCIALISM, SOCIALISM AND FASCISM: AN APPRAISAL." FUT LEAD REV GP/REL RACE/REL NAT/LISM ATTIT...IDEA/COMP STERTYP 20. PAGE 51 F0993 FASCISM MARXISM SOCISM AFR

S67
ALEXANDER R.J.,"'THIRD FORCE' IN WORLD COMMUNISM?" CHINA/COM CUBA USSR INT/ORG DIPLOM TASK INGP/REL ATTIT PWR 20 CASTRO/F. PAGE 3 F0060 CHIEF MARXISM LEAD REV

S67
BASOV V.,"THE DEVELOPMENT OF PUBLIC EDUCATION AND THE BUDGET." USSR NAT/G CONTROL REV COST AGE...STAT 20. PAGE 11 F0204 BUDGET GIVE EDU/PROP SCHOOL

S67
CRAIG A.,"ARGENTINA: THE LATEST REVOLUTION." ELITES NAT/G CHIEF FORCES ECO/TAC CIVMIL/REL GOV/REL EQUILIB PRIVIL 20 ARGEN. PAGE 28 F0550 ECO/UNDEV FINAN ATTIT REV

S67
GONZALEZ M.P.,"CUBA, UNA REVOLUCION EN MARCHA." CUBA L/A+17C USA+45 VIETNAM ECO/UNDEV FORCES DIPLOM DOMIN...POLICY MARXIST NAT/COMP CASTRO/F. PAGE 48 F0946 REV NAT/G COLONIAL SOVEREIGN

S67
HEATH D.B.,"BOLIVIA UNDER BARRIENTOS." L/A+17C NAT/G CHIEF DIPLOM ECO/TAC...POLICY 20 BOLIV. PAGE 58 F1132 ECO/UNDEV POL/PAR REV CONSTN

S67
HEILBRONER R.L.,"BUILDING NEW NATIONS." AFR STRUCT PLAN TEC/DEV ADJUST MARXISM...POLICY 20. PAGE 58 F1138 PROB/SOLV REV NAT/LISM ECO/UNDEV

S67
IBARRA J.,"EL EXPERIMENTO CUBANO." COM CUBA L/A+17C USA+45 ECO/UNDEV LEGIS INT/TRADE CONTROL REV NAT/LISM PWR 19/20 TREATY. PAGE 64 F1259 COLONIAL DIPLOM NAT/G POLICY

S67
ISELIN J.J.,"THE TRUMAN DOCTRINE: ITS PASSAGE THROUGH CONGRESS AND THE AFTERMATH." USA+45 ECO/UNDEV R+D INT/ORG DELIB/GP BAL/PWR REV PEACE ...POLICY UN. PAGE 66 F1291 DIPLOM COM FOR/AID AFR

S67
MANGLAPUS R.S.,"ASIAN REVOLUTION AND AMERICAN IDEOLOGY." USA+45 SOCIETY CAP/ISM DIPLOM ADJUST CENTRAL...NAT/COMP 20. PAGE 84 F1652 REV POPULISM ATTIT ASIA

S67
MCCOLL R.W.,"A POLITICAL GEOGRAPHY OF REVOLUTION: CHINA, VIETNAM, AND THAILAND." ASIA THAILAND VIETNAM FORCES CONTROL 20. PAGE 88 F1720 REV GEOG PLAN DECISION

S67
PERKINS D.H.,"ECONOMIC GROWTH IN CHINA AND THE CULTURAL REVOLUTION(1960APRIL 1967)" CHINA/COM FUT AGRI INDUS PLAN LEAD MARXISM...CHARTS 20 MAO. PAGE 105 F2062 ECO/TAC CULTURE REV ECO/UNDEV

S67
PETRAS J.,"U.S. HEGEMONY AND LATIN AMERICAN RULING CLASSES." L/A+17C USA+45 ECO/UNDEV FOR/AID REV SOC. PAGE 105 F2071 NAT/G ATTIT DIPLOM POLICY

S67
PETRAS J.,"GUERRILLA MOVEMENTS IN LATIN AMERICA - I." GUATEMALA PERU VENEZUELA NAT/G COLONIAL LEAD ATTIT PWR...TIME/SEQ METH/COMP 20 COLOMB. PAGE 105 F2072 GUERRILLA REV L/A+17C MARXISM

S67
RONNING C.,"NANKING: 1950." ASIA CANADA CHINA/COM NAT/G PLAN ECO/TAC REV ADJUST 20. PAGE 113 F2235 DIPLOM ROLE PEACE

S67
WAITS C.R.,"CRAFT GILDS AS AN INSTITUTIONAL BARRIER TO THE INDUSTRIAL REVOLUTION." CHRIST-17C MOD/EUR ECO/UNDEV CONTROL GP/REL ATTIT 16/19. PAGE 142 F2801 TEC/DEV INDUS REV PROF/ORG

B68
NENAROKOV A.P.,RUSSIA IN THE 20TH CENTURY: THE OFFICIAL SOVIET HISTORY. USSR SOCIETY REV...AUD/VIS 20. PAGE 97 F1913 COM ADJUST MARXISM

B76
TAINE H.A.,THE ANCIENT REGIME. FRANCE STRATA FORCES PARTIC EQUILIB WEALTH CONSERVE POPULISM...GOV/COMP SOC/INTEG 18/19. PAGE 128 F2527 NAT/G GOV/REL TAX REV

B86
O'CONNOR T.P.,THE PARNELL MOVEMENT: WITH A SKETCH OF IRISH PARTIES FROM 1843. IRELAND UK USA-45 LEGIS WORKER ECO/TAC COERCE CRIME REV CHOOSE ORD/FREE CATHISM LAISSEZ...SOC 19/20 PARLIAMENT PARNELL/CS LAND/LEAG. PAGE 100 F1957 LEAD DOMIN POL/PAR POLICY

B91
MILL J.S.,SOCIALISM (1859). MOD/EUR AGRI INDUS NAT/G REV INCOME PRODUC ORD/FREE POPULISM SOCISM ...GOV/COMP METH/COMP 19. PAGE 91 F1787 WEALTH SOCIALIST ECO/TAC OWN

B96
MARX K.,REVOLUTION AND COUNTER-REVOLUTION. GERMANY CONSTN ELITES INDUS NAT/G DIPLOM ECO/TAC WEALTH. PAGE 86 F1693 MARXIST REV PWR STRATA

REVOLUTION....SEE REV

REWARD....SEE SANCTION

REYNOLDS P.A. F2182

RHODE/ISL....RHODE ISLAND

B67
GOODMAN J.S.,THE DEMOCRATS AND LABOR IN RHODE ISLAND 9152-1962; CHANGES IN THE OLD ALLIANCE. USA+45 EDU/PROP LEAD GP/REL ROLE RHODE/ISL DEMOCRAT. PAGE 49 F0948 LABOR LOBBY POL/PAR LEGIS

RHODES R.S. F0439

RHODES/C....CECIL RHODES

RHODESIA....SEE ALSO AFR

B62
GREEN L.P.,DEVELOPMENT IN AFRICA. AFR CENTRL/AFR GHANA RHODESIA SOUTH/AFR AGRI PROC/MFG INT/TRADE DEMAND NAT/LISM PRODUC WEALTH...GEOG METH/CNCPT CHARTS BIBLIOG 20. PAGE 50 F0987 CULTURE ECO/UNDEV GOV/REL TREND

C62
GREEN L.P.,"DEVELOPMENT IN AFRICA." RHODESIA SOUTH/AFR UGANDA MARKET PROC/MFG PRODUC WEALTH ...GEOG 20. PAGE 50 F0986 BIBLIOG ECO/UNDEV AFR AGRI

B64
YUDELMAN M.,AFRICANS ON THE LAND. RHODESIA MARKET LABOR OWN...ECOMETRIC TREND 20. PAGE 150 F2955 ECO/DEV AFR AGRI

ECO/TAC

B65

HAEFELE E.T.,GOVERNMENT CONTROLS ON TRANSPORT. AFR RHODESIA TANZANIA DIPLOM ECO/TAC TARIFFS PRICE ADJUD CONTROL REGION EFFICIENCY...POLICY 20 CONGO. PAGE 53 F1031 — ECO/UNDEV DIST/IND FINAN NAT/G

B66

BALDWIN R.E.,ECONOMIC DEVELOPMENT AND EXPORT GROWTH: A STUDY OF NORTHERN RHODESIA, 1920-1960. AFR RHODESIA AGRI EXTR/IND FINAN MARKET LABOR WORKER ECO/TAC...CONCPT NEW/IDEA MUNICH 20. PAGE 9 F0166 — ECO/UNDEV TEC/DEV INT/TRADE CAP/ISM

B67

WILLS A.J.,AN INTRODUCTION TO THE HISTORY OF CENTRAL AFRICA. RHODESIA ZAMBIA CULTURE SOCIETY ECO/UNDEV TEC/DEV DOMIN WAR ALL/VALS...POLICY TREND BIBLIOG T 14/20 NYASALAND. PAGE 147 F2899 — AFR COLONIAL ORD/FREE

L67

MACDONALD R.S.J.,"THE RESORT TO ECONOMIC COERCION BY INTERNATIONAL POLITICAL ORGANIZATIONS." CUBA ETHIOPIA RHODESIA SOUTH/AFR NAT/G FOR/AID INT/TRADE DOMIN CONTROL SANCTION...DECISION LEAGUE/NAT UN OAS 20. PAGE 83 F1625 — INT/ORG COERCE ECO/TAC DIPLOM

RICARDO D. F2183

RICARDO/D....DAVID RICARDO

B63

BARNETT H.J.,SCARCITY AND GROWTH: THE ECONOMICS OF NATURAL RESOURCE AVAILABILITY. FUT WOR+45 AGRI INDUS PROB/SOLV TEC/DEV CONTROL PRODUC...SOC/WK IDEA/COMP METH/COMP SIMUL 20 RESOURCE/N MALTHUS RICARDO/D MILL/JS DARWIN/C. PAGE 10 F0191 — DEMAND HABITAT CENSUS GEOG

B98

MARSHALL A.,PRINCIPLES OF ECONOMICS. INDUS WORKER PRICE COST EQUILIB INCOME OPTIMAL PRODUC...TIME/SEQ METH RICARDO/D. PAGE 86 F1678 — WEALTH GEN/LAWS MARKET

RICHARD/H....HENRY RICHARD (WELSH POLITICIAN - 19TH CENTURY)

B66

WILLIAMS G.,MERTHYR POLITICS: THE MAKING OF A WORKING-CLASS TRADITION. UK CHIEF WORKER LEAD SOCISM...ANTHOL MUNICH 19/20 MERTHYR RICHARD/H. PAGE 147 F2891 — LOC/G POL/PAR INDUS

RICHARDSON G.B. F2184

RICHMAN B.M. F2185,F2186

RICHTER J.H. F2187

RICHTER R. F2188

RIDAH A. F2189

RIDKER R.G. F2190

RIDLEY C.E. F2191

RIESMAN/D....DAVID RIESMAN

RIESSMAN F. F2044

RIGBY P.H. F2192

RIGGS/FRED....FRED W. RIGGS

RIGHTS/MAN....RIGHTS OF MAN

RIGID/FLEX....DEGREE OF RESPONSIVENESS TO NEW IDEAS, METHODS, AND PEOPLE

N19

ARNOW K.,SELF-INSURANCE IN THE TREASURY (PAMPHLET). USA+45 LAW RIGID/FLEX...POLICY METH/COMP 20 DEPT/TREAS. PAGE 6 F0117 — ADMIN PLAN EFFICIENCY NAT/G

N19

HOGARTY R.A.,NEW JERSEY FARMERS AND MIGRANT HOUSING RULES (PAMPHLET). USA+45 LAW ELITES FACE/GP LABOR PROF/ORG LOBBY PERS/REL RIGID/FLEX ROLE 20 NEW/JERSEY. PAGE 61 F1193 — AGRI PROVS WORKER HEALTH

N19

KRIESBERG M.,CANCELLATION OF THE RATION STAMPS (PAMPHLET). USA+45 USA-45 MARKET PROB/SOLV PRICE GOV/REL RIGID/FLEX 20 OPA. PAGE 73 F1439 — RATION DECISION ADMIN NAT/G

N19

MARSH J.F. JR.,THE FBI RETIREMENT BILL (PAMPHLET). USA+45 EX/STRUC WORKER PLAN PROB/SOLV BUDGET LEAD LOBBY PARL/PROC PERS/REL RIGID/FLEX...POLICY 20 FBI PRESIDENT BUR/BUDGET. PAGE 86 F1677 — ADMIN NAT/G SENIOR GOV/REL

N19

YLVISAKER P.N.,THE NATURAL CEMENT ISSUE (PAMPHLET). USA+45 USA-45 CONSTRUC PROVS CAP/ISM ADMIN LOBBY PERS/REL OWN RIGID/FLEX ROLE 20 MINNESOTA. PAGE 150 F2948 — POLICY NAT/G PLAN GOV/REL

S43

HERBERG W.,"BUREAUCRACY AND DEMOCRACY IN LABOR UNIONS." LAW CONSTN STRUCT WORKER ADMIN CONTROL PARTIC RIGID/FLEX PWR TREND. PAGE 59 F1151 — LABOR REPRESENT ROUTINE INGP/REL

S53

BERNSTEIN M.H.,"POLITICAL IDEAS OF SELECTED AMERICAN BUSINESS JOURNALS (BMR)" USA+45 GP/REL ATTIT RIGID/FLEX ROLE ORD/FREE POLICY. PAGE 14 F0267 — IDEA/COMP NAT/G LEAD

L56

PENNOCK J.R.,"PARTY AND CONSTITUENCY IN POSTWAR AGRICULTURAL PRICE SUPPORT LEGISLATION." USA+45 LEGIS DEBATE LOBBY RIGID/FLEX. PAGE 105 F2057 — POL/PAR REPRESENT AGRI CHOOSE

S57

ANSHEN M.,"BUSINESS, LAWYERS, AND ECONOMISTS." PROB/SOLV ECO/TAC CONFER PROFIT RIGID/FLEX OBJECTIVE...MGT GP/COMP. PAGE 6 F0106 — INDUS CONSULT ROUTINE EFFICIENCY

B58

HIRSCHMAN A.O.,STRATEGY OF ECONOMIC DEVELOPMENT. WOR+45 WOR-45 CULTURE ECO/DEV NAT/G PLAN TEC/DEV INT/TRADE BAL/PAY ATTIT DRIVE RIGID/FLEX WEALTH ...CONCPT METH/CNCPT OBS CHARTS SIMUL GEN/LAWS TOT/POP VAL/FREE. PAGE 60 F1176 — ECO/UNDEV ECO/TAC CAP/ISM

L58

CYERT R.M.,"THE ROLE OF EXPECTATIONS IN BUSINESS DECISION-MAKING." PROB/SOLV PRICE RIGID/FLEX. PAGE 29 F0566 — LG/CO DECISION ROUTINE EXEC

L58

MASON E.S.,"ECONOMIC PLANNING IN UNDERDEVELOPED AREAS." FUT WOR+45 PLAN TEC/DEV EDU/PROP ATTIT RIGID/FLEX KNOWL...SOC CONCPT GEN/LAWS TOT/POP 20. PAGE 87 F1697 — NAT/G ECO/UNDEV

S58

O'NEAL F.H.,"RECENT LEGISLATION AFFECTING CLOSE CORPORATIONS." LAW EX/STRUC ECO/TAC ROUTINE CHOOSE RIGID/FLEX...MAJORIT MGT TREND. PAGE 100 F1959 — LG/CO LEGIS REPRESENT PARTIC

B59

MEYER A.J.,MIDDLE EASTERN CAPITALISM: NINE ESSAYS. ISLAM CULTURE ECO/UNDEV INDUS MARKET NAT/G PLAN ATTIT RIGID/FLEX...STAT OBS TREND GEN/LAWS. PAGE 90 F1767 — TEC/DEV ECO/TAC ANTHOL

S59

HOFFMAN P.,"OPERATION BREAKTHROUGH." AFR S/ASIA STRUCT INDUS CONSULT TEC/DEV ATTIT RIGID/FLEX SKILL WEALTH...TECHNIC CONCPT STYLE RECORD CHARTS ORG/CHARTS GEN/METH VAL/FREE 20. PAGE 61 F1190 — ECO/UNDEV EDU/PROP FOR/AID

B60

HOSELITZ B.F.,SOCIOLOGICAL ASPECTS OF ECONOMIC GROWTH. WOR+45 WOR-45 ECO/UNDEV CAP/ISM RIGID/FLEX WEALTH...MATH CHARTS. PAGE 62 F1221 — ECO/DEV SOC

B60

LISTER L.,EUROPE'S COAL AND STEEL COMMUNITY. FRANCE GERMANY STRUCT ECO/DEV EXTR/IND INDUS MARKET NAT/G DELIB/GP ECO/TAC INT/TRADE EDU/PROP ATTIT RIGID/FLEX ORD/FREE PWR WEALTH...CONCPT STAT TIME/SEQ CHARTS ECSC TERR/GP 20. PAGE 81 F1582 — EUR+WWI INT/ORG REGION

B60

ROEPKE W.,A HUMANE ECONOMY: THE SOCIAL FRAMEWORK OF THE FREE MARKET. FUT USSR WOR+45 CULTURE SOCIETY ECO/DEV PLAN ECO/TAC ADMIN ATTIT PERSON RIGID/FLEX SUPEGO MORAL WEALTH SOCISM...POLICY OLD/LIB CONCPT TREND GEN/LAWS 20. PAGE 113 F2232 — DRIVE EDU/PROP CAP/ISM

B60

STEIN E.,AMERICAN ENTERPRISE IN THE EUROPEAN COMMON MARKET: A LEGAL PROFILE. EUR+WWI FUT USA+45 SOCIETY STRUCT ECO/DEV NAT/G VOL/ASSN CONSULT PLAN TEC/DEV ECO/TAC INT/TRADE ADMIN ATTIT RIGID/FLEX PWR...MGT NEW/IDEA STAT TREND COMPUT/IR SIMUL EEC 20. PAGE 125 F2475 — MARKET ADJUD INT/LAW

B60

WALLACE R.A.,CONGRESSIONAL CONTROL OF FEDERAL SPENDING. USA+45 CONSTN NAT/G OP/RES CONFER DEBATE PERS/REL UTIL RIGID/FLEX PWR OBJECTIVE...OBS CHARTS. PAGE 143 F2808 — LEGIS DELIB/GP BUDGET

S60

"THE EMERGING COMMON MARKETS IN LATIN AMERICA." FUT L/A+17C STRATA DIST/IND INDUS LABOR NAT/G LEGIS ECO/TAC ADMIN RIGID/FLEX HEALTH...NEW/IDEA TIME/SEQ OAS 20. PAGE 1 F0013 — FINAN ECO/UNDEV INT/TRADE

S60

BECKER A.S.,"COMPARISIONS OF UNITED STATES AND USSR NATIONAL OUTPUT: SOME RULES OF THE GAME." COM USA+45 ECO/DEV AGRI DIST/IND INDUS R+D CONSULT PLAN ECO/TAC RIGID/FLEX KNOWL...METH/CNCPT CHARTS 20. PAGE 12 F0227 — STAT USSR

S60

ENKE S.,"THE ECONOMIES OF GOVERNMENT PAYMENTS TO LIMIT POPULATION." FUT INDIA WOR+45 CULTURE FINAN — FAM ACT/RES

S63
SCHURMANN F.,"ECONOMIC POLICY AND POLITICAL POWER IN COMMUNIST CHINA." ASIA CHINA/COM USSR SOCIETY ECO/UNDEV AGRI INDUS CREATE ADMIN ROUTINE ATTIT DRIVE RIGID/FLEX PWR WEALTH...HIST/WRIT TREND CHARTS WORK 20. PAGE 118 F2323
PLAN ECO/TAC

S63
SHONFIELD A.,"AFTER BRUSSELS." EUR+WWI FRANCE GERMANY UK ECO/DEV DIST/IND MARKET VOL/ASSN DELIB/GP CREATE INT/TRADE ATTIT RIGID/FLEX...RECORD TREND GEN/LAWS EEC COMMUN CMN/WLTH 20. PAGE 121 F2385
PLAN ECO/TAC

S63
WILES P.J.D.,"WILL CAPITALISM AND COMMUNISM SPONTANEOUSLY CONVERGE." COM FUT USA+45 ECO/DEV DIST/IND MARKET CAP/ISM ECO/TAC RIGID/FLEX WEALTH MARXISM SOCISM...MATH STAT TREND COMPUT/IR 20. PAGE 146 F2885
PLAN TEC/DEV USSR

S63
WOLFERS A.,"INTEGRATION IN THE WEST: THE CONFLICT OF PERSPECTIVES." AFR EUR+WWI USA+45 ECO/DEV INT/ORG DELIB/GP CREATE TEC/DEV DIPLOM ATTIT PWR ...CONCPT HIST/WRIT TREND GEN/LAWS EEC 20. PAGE 148 F2918
RIGID/FLEX ECO/TAC

B64
MASON E.S.,FOREIGN AID AND FOREIGN POLICY. USA+45 AGRI INDUS NAT/G EX/STRUC ACT/RES RIGID/FLEX ALL/VALS...POLICY GEN/LAWS MARSHL/PLN ALL/PROG CONGRESS 20. PAGE 87 F1699
ECO/UNDEV ECO/TAC FOR/AID DIPLOM

B64
SEERS D.,CUBA: THE ECONOMIC AND SOCIAL REVOLUTION. L/A+17C USSR YUGOSLAVIA STRATA AGRI INDUS SCHOOL DELIB/GP PLAN ECO/TAC DOMIN EDU/PROP ATTIT RIGID/FLEX ALL/VALS...STAT OBS TIME/SEQ WORK VAL/FREE 20. PAGE 119 F2341
ACT/RES COERCE CUBA REV

B64
WRIGHT G.,RURAL REVOLUTION IN FRANCE: THE PEASANTRY IN THE TWENTIETH CENTURY. EUR+WWI MOD/EUR LAW CULTURE AGRI POL/PAR DELIB/GP LEGIS ECO/TAC EDU/PROP COERCE CHOOSE ATTIT RIGID/FLEX HEALTH ...STAT CENSUS CHARTS VAL/FREE 20. PAGE 149 F2932
PWR STRATA FRANCE REV

S64
DOE J.F.,"TROPICAL AFRICAN CONTRIBUTIONS TO FEDERAL FINANCE." AFR NAT/G PROVS CENTRAL RIGID/FLEX PWR WEALTH...STAT VAL/FREE 20 CMN/WLTH. PAGE 33 F0650
FINAN ECO/TAC

S64
GARDNER R.N.,"GATT AND THE UNITED NATIONS CONFERENCE ON TRADE AND DEVELOPMENT." USA+45 WOR+45 SOCIETY ECO/UNDEV MARKET NAT/G DELIB/GP ACT/RES PLAN ECO/TAC TARIFFS EDU/PROP ROUTINE DRIVE RIGID/FLEX WEALTH...DECISION MGT TREND UN TOT/POP 20 GATT. PAGE 46 F0905
INT/ORG INT/TRADE

S64
HERMAN L.M.,"THE ECONOMIC CONTENT OF SOVIET TRADE WITH THE WEST." WOR+45 ECO/DEV ECO/UNDEV AGRI COM/IND INDUS CAP/ISM ECO/TAC ATTIT RIGID/FLEX WEALTH...OBS TREND VAL/FREE MARX/KARL 20. PAGE 59 F1152
COM MARKET INT/TRADE USSR

S64
HUTCHINSON E.C.,"AMERICAN AID TO AFRICA." FUT USA+45 MARKET INT/ORG LOC/G NAT/G PUB/INST PLAN ECO/TAC ATTIT RIGID/FLEX...POLICY CONCPT TREND TERR/GP 20. PAGE 63 F1248
AFR ECO/UNDEV FOR/AID

B65
APTER D.E.,THE POLITICS OF MODERNIZATION. AFR L/A+17C CULTURE NAT/G POL/PAR ADMIN COLONIAL NAT/LISM ATTIT RIGID/FLEX PWR...SOC CONCPT. PAGE 6 F0109
ECO/UNDEV GEN/LAWS STRATA CREATE

B65
LUTZ V.,FRENCH PLANNING. FRANCE TEC/DEV RIGID/FLEX ORD/FREE 20. PAGE 82 F1613
PLAN ADMIN FUT

L65
HAGE J.,"AN AXIOMATIC THEORY OF ORGANIZATIONS" USA+45 STRUCT LABOR PRODUC DRIVE PERSON RIGID/FLEX 20 WEBER/MAX. PAGE 53 F1032
GP/REL EFFICIENCY PROF/ORG ATTIT

S65
KINDLEBERGER C.P.,"MASS MIGRATION, THEN AND NOW." LAW ECO/DEV ECO/UNDEV INDUS LABOR INT/TRADE FEEDBACK REGION RIGID/FLEX...SOC NAT/COMP EEC. PAGE 71 F1394
EUR+WWI USA-45 WORKER IDEA/COMP

S65
KORBONSKI A.,"USA POLICY IN EAST EUROPE." COM EUR+WWI GERMANY USA+45 CULTURE ECO/UNDEV EDU/PROP RIGID/FLEX WEALTH FOR/TRADE 20. PAGE 73 F1426
ACT/RES ECO/TAC FOR/AID

S65
WHITAKER A.P.,"ARGENTINA: STRUGGLE FOR RECOVERY." L/A+17C USA+45 NAT/G TOP/EX PLAN LEGIT COERCE REV RIGID/FLEX PWR WEALTH...RECORD ALL/PROG ARGEN FOR/TRADE 20. PAGE 146 F2867
POL/PAR ECO/TAC NAT/LISM

B66
BEQIRAJ M.,PEASANTRY IN REVOLUTION. STRATA ECO/UNDEV AGRI ROUTINE REV HABITAT RIGID/FLEX ...EPIST GEOG NEW/IDEA TREND MUNICH 20. PAGE 13 F0256
WORKER KNOWL NAT/LISM SOC

B66
HACKETT J.,L'ECONOMIE BRITANNIQUE: PROBLEMES ET PERSPECTIVES. FRANCE UK LABOR NAT/G EX/STRUC PROB/SOLV BAL/PAY INCOME RIGID/FLEX...MGT PHIL/SCI CHARTS MUNICH 20. PAGE 53 F1027
ECO/DEV FINAN ECO/TAC PLAN

B66
LONDON K.,EASTERN EUROPE IN TRANSITION. CHINA/COM USSR DOMIN COLONIAL CENTRAL RIGID/FLEX PWR...SOC ANTHOL 20. PAGE 82 F1597
SOVEREIGN COM NAT/LISM DIPLOM

B66
UREN P.E.,EAST - WEST TRADE* A SYMPOSIUM. COM AGRI INT/ORG PRICE HABITAT RIGID/FLEX...GEOG INT/LAW ANTHOL NATO. PAGE 133 F2625
INT/TRADE BAL/PWR AFR CANADA

B67
FILENE P.G.,AMERICANS AND THE SOVIET EXPERIMENT, 1917-1933. USA-45 USSR INTELL NAT/G CAP/ISM DIPLOM EDU/PROP PRESS REV SOCISM...PSY 20. PAGE 41 F0793
ATTIT RIGID/FLEX MARXISM SOCIETY

B67
SCHON D.A.,TECHNOLOGY AND CHANGE* THE NEW HERACLITUS. TEC/DEV CONTROL COST DEMAND EFFICIENCY RIGID/FLEX...MYTH 20. PAGE 117 F2311
INDUS PROB/SOLV R+D CREATE

B67
SMITH T.L.,THE PROCESS OF RURAL DEVELOPMENT IN LATIN AMERICA (A MONOGRAPH). L/A+17C STRATA INDUS PLAN GP/REL PERS/REL RIGID/FLEX WEALTH...OBS CHARTS ORG/CHARTS ANTHOL 20 COLOMB. PAGE 123 F2434
IDEA/COMP SOC AGRI ECO/UNDEV

S67
GRUN C.,"DEUX ETUDES ALLEMANDES SUR LES PREJUGES NATIONAUX ET LES MOYENS DE LES COMBATTRE." FRANCE GERMANY DIST/IND PROB/SOLV GP/REL AGE/Y RIGID/FLEX ...PSY STAT INT SAMP. PAGE 52 F1010
ATTIT REGION DISCRIM STERTYP

RILEY J.W. F2193

RIMALOV V.V. F2194

RIO/PACT....RIO PACT

RIOT....RIOTS; SEE ALSO CROWD

RISK....SEE ALSO GAMBLE

NCO
STOLPER W.,"SOCIAL FACTORS IN ECONOMIC PLANNING, WITH SPECIAL REFERENCE TO NIGERIA" AFR NIGER CULTURE FAM SECT RECEIVE ETIQUET ADMIN DEMAND 20. PAGE 126 F2494
ECO/UNDEV PLAN ADJUST RISK

B57
DOWNS A.,AN ECONOMIC THEORY OF DEMOCRACY. NAT/G EDU/PROP RISK CHOOSE PERS/REL EQUILIB...SOC METH/CNCPT LOG STYLE. PAGE 34 F0659
DECISION RATIONAL

B58
OEEC,THE INDUSTRIAL CHALLENGE OF NUCLEAR ENERGY. EUR+WWI ECO/DEV INDUS OP/RES CONFER RISK PWR ...AUD/VIS CHARTS ANTHOL 20 OEEC. PAGE 101 F1977
NUC/PWR ACT/RES ECO/TAC INT/ORG

S58
FOLDES L.,"UNCERTAINTY, PROBABILITY AND POTENTIAL SURPRISE." MARKET PROB/SOLV RISK PERSON...DECISION MGT HYPO/EXP GAME. PAGE 42 F0820
PROBABIL ADMIN ROUTINE

B59
MATTHEWS R.C.O.,THE BUSINESS CYCLE. AFR LABOR INT/TRADE TAX PRICE RISK ADJUST WEALTH...POLICY ECOMETRIC CHARTS SIMUL TIME 20. PAGE 87 F1705
FINAN DEMAND TASK

S59
HARING J.E.,"UTILITY THEORY, DECISION THEORY, AND PROFIT MAXIMIZATION." PROB/SOLV GAMBLE UTIL ...DECISION CHARTS IDEA/COMP HYPO/EXP SIMUL GEN/METH. PAGE 55 F1083
PROBABIL RISK GAME

B60
BELLAN R.C.,PRINCIPLES OF ECONOMICS AND THE CANADIAN ECONOMY (2ND ED.). CANADA UK USA+45 LABOR WORKER CAP/ISM INT/TRADE RISK BAL/PAY EQUILIB ALL/IDEOS 20. PAGE 12 F0236
ECO/DEV PRODUC WEALTH FINAN

B60
BIERMAN H.,THE CAPITAL BUDGETING DECISION. AFR ECO/DEV MARKET TAX PRICE RISK COST INCOME TIME 20. PAGE 15 F0282
FINAN OPTIMAL BUDGET PROFIT

B60
MORRIS W.T.,ENGINEERING ECONOMY. AUTOMAT RISK RATIONAL...PROBABIL STAT CHARTS GAME SIMUL BIBLIOG T 20. PAGE 94 F1838
OP/RES DECISION MGT PROB/SOLV

B61
MOORE G.H.,BUSINESS CYCLE INDICATORS (TWO VOLS.). LABOR DIPLOM PRICE RISK TASK WAR PRODUC...CHARTS BIBLIOG 20. PAGE 93 F1822
MARKET FINAN WEALTH

B64
BOGEN J.I.,FINANCIAL HANDBOOK (4TH ED.). UNIV LAW PLAN TAX RISK 20. PAGE 16 F0306
FINAN DICTIONARY

B64
BRIGHT J.R.,RESEARCH, DEVELOPMENT AND TECHNOLOGICAL INNOVATION. CULTURE R+D CREATE PLAN PROB/SOLV AUTOMAT RISK PERSON...DECISION CONCPT PREDICT BIBLIOG. PAGE 18 F0352 TEC/DEV NEW/IDEA INDUS MGT

B64
JUSTER F.T.,ANTICIPATIONS AND PURCHASES; AN ANALYSIS OF CONSUMER BEHAVIOR. PROB/SOLV RISK COST PRODUC DRIVE...STAT STYLE SAMP CON/ANAL CHARTS HYPO/EXP GAME SIMUL. PAGE 68 F1345 PROBABIL DECISION PREDICT DEMAND

B65
OZGA S.A.,EXPECTATIONS IN ECONOMIC THEORY. MORAL ...ECOMETRIC MATH STAT IDEA/COMP 20. PAGE 102 F2008 RISK GAME CONCPT PREDICT

B66
CHASE S.B. JR.,PROBLEMS IN PUBLIC EXPENDITURE ANALYSIS. DIST/IND INDUS OP/RES PLAN BUDGET RECEIVE PRICE RISK COST INCOME...CHARTS ANTHOL 20. PAGE 23 F0455 ECO/DEV FINAN NAT/G INSPECT

B66
FOX K.A.,THE THEORY OF QUANTITATIVE ECONOMIC POLICY WITH APPLICATIONS TO ECONOMIC GROWTH AND STABILIZATION. ECO/DEV AGRI NAT/G PLAN ADMIN RISK ...DECISION IDEA/COMP SIMUL T. PAGE 43 F0837 ECO/TAC ECOMETRIC EQUILIB GEN/LAWS

B67
GIAP V.N.,BIG VICTORY, GREAT TASK. VIETNAM WOR+45 FORCES PLAN DOMIN LEGIT RISK PEACE 20. PAGE 47 F0921 WAR LEAD ATTIT INSPECT

B67
NARVER J.C.,CONGLOMERATE MERGERS AND MARKET COMPETITION. USA+45 LAW STRUCT ADMIN LEAD RISK COST PROFIT WEALTH...POLICY CHARTS BIBLIOG. PAGE 96 F1892 DEMAND LG/CO MARKET MGT

L67
MACDONALD R.M.,"COLLECTIVE BARGAINING IN THE POSTWAR PERIOD." WORKER PROB/SOLV ECO/TAC PARTIC RISK CENTRAL EFFICIENCY DRIVE WEALTH...TREND 20. PAGE 83 F1624 LABOR INDUS BARGAIN CAP/ISM

S67
GRAYSON D.K.,"RISK ALLOCATIONS UNDER THE PERMITS AND RESPONSIBILITIES CLAUSE OF THE STANDARD GOVERNMENT CONSTRUCTION CONTRACT." USA+45 LAW WORKER. PAGE 50 F0979 CONSTRUC CONTROL RISK NAT/G

S67
ZOETEWEIJ B.,"INCOME POLICIES ABROAD: AN INTERIM REPORT." NAT/G PROB/SOLV BARGAIN BUDGET PRICE RISK CENTRAL EFFICIENCY EQUILIB...MGT NAT/COMP 20. PAGE 150 F2967 METH/COMP INCOME POLICY LABOR

RITCHIE/JM....JESS M. RITCHIE

N19
LAWRENCE S.A.,THE BATTERY ADDITIVE CONTROVERSY (PAMPHLET). USA+45 LAW MARKET PROC/MFG R+D CAP/ISM CT/SYS GOV/REL OWN FTC CONGRESS BUR/STNDRD RITCHIE/JM. PAGE 76 F1494 PHIL/SCI LOBBY INSPECT

RITSCHL/H....HANS RITSCHL

B58
MUSGRAVE R.A.,CLASSICS IN THE THEORY OF PUBLIC FINANCE. UNIV MARKET LG/CO NAT/G CAP/ISM PRICE OPTIMAL...IDEA/COMP ANTHOL 19/20 SAY/EMIL EDGEWORTH LINDAHL/E RITSCHL/H. PAGE 95 F1870 TAX FINAN ECO/TAC GP/REL

RITUAL....RITUALS AND SYMBOLIC CEREMONIES; SEE ALSO WORSHIP, SECT

RIVKIN A. F2195,F2196

RIVKIN M.D. F2197

RIZK C. F2198

RKFDV....REICHSKOMMISSARIAT FUR DIE FESTIGUNG DEUTSCHEN VOLKSTUMS

RKO....R.K.O.

ROACH J.R. F2199

ROBBINS J.J. F2200

ROBBINS L. F2201,F2202,F2203,F2204

ROBERTS B.C. F2205,F2206

ROBERTS E.F. F2207

ROBERTSON A.H. F2208

ROBERTSON B.C. F2209

ROBERTSON D. F2210,F2211

ROBERTSON D.H. F2212

ROBERTSON D.J. F2213

ROBERTSON H.M. F2214

ROBESPR/M....MAXIMILIAN FRANCOIS ROBESPIERRE

ROBINSN/JH....JAMES HARVEY ROBINSON

ROBINSON A.D. F2215

ROBINSON E.A. F2216

ROBINSON E.A.G. F2217,F2218,F2219,F2220

ROBINSON J. F2221,F2222

ROBINSON M.A. F2223

ROBINSON R.D. F2224,F2225

ROBINSON R.I. F2226

ROBINSON/H....HENRY ROBINSON

ROBSON P. F1554

ROBSON W.A. F2227

ROCHE J. F2228

ROCKE J.R.M. F2229

ROCKEFELLER E.S. F2334

RODBRTUS/C....CARL RODBERTUS

L86
OSGOOD H.L.,"SCIENTIFIC SOCIALISM: RODBERTUS" GERMANY CAP/ISM COST WEALTH...MAJORIT BIOG IDEA/COMP 19 RODBRTUS/C. PAGE 102 F2002 SOCISM MARXISM ECO/DEV ECO/TAC

ROELOFS H.M. F2230

ROEPKE W. F2231,F2232,F2233

ROGGEVEEN V.J. F1509

ROLE....ROLE, REFERENCE GROUP, CROSS-PRESSURES

N19
BLOOMFIELD A.,MONETARY POLICY UNDER THE INTERNATIONAL GOLD STANDARD: 18801914 (PAMPHLET). AFR USA-45 DIPLOM CONTROL...POLICY 19. PAGE 16 F0300 FINAN ROLE EFFICIENCY

N19
CARPER E.T.,LOBBYING AND THE NATURAL GAS BILL (PAMPHLET). USA+45 SERV/IND BARGAIN PAY DRIVE ROLE WEALTH 20 CONGRESS SENATE EISNHWR/DD. PAGE 22 F0418 LOBBY ADJUD TRIBUTE NAT/G

N19
HOGARTY R.A.,NEW JERSEY FARMERS AND MIGRANT HOUSING RULES (PAMPHLET). USA+45 LAW ELITES FACE/GP LABOR PROF/ORG LOBBY PERS/REL RIGID/FLEX ROLE 20 NEW/JERSEY. PAGE 61 F1193 AGRI PROVS WORKER HEALTH

N19
SILVERMAN C.,THE PRESIDENT'S ECONOMIC ADVISERS (PAMPHLET). USA+45 LAW ELITES ECO/DEV EX/STRUC ADMIN LEAD GOV/REL PERS/REL ROLE...POLICY DECISION 20 PRESIDENT CONGRESS EISNHWR/DD. PAGE 122 F2404 CONSULT PROB/SOLV NAT/G PLAN

N19
YLVISAKER P.N.,THE NATURAL CEMENT ISSUE (PAMPHLET). USA+45 USA-45 CONSTRUC PROVS CAP/ISM ADMIN LOBBY PERS/REL OWN RIGID/FLEX ROLE 20 MINNESOTA. PAGE 150 F2948 POLICY NAT/G PLAN GOV/REL

B22
VON ENGELIN O.D.,INHERITING THE EARTH, THE GEOGRAPHICAL FACTOR IN NATIONAL DEVELOPMENT. WOR-45 CULTURE DIPLOM BIO/SOC HABITAT PERSON...PSY SOC CONCPT IDEA/COMP. PAGE 142 F2791 INGP/REL GEOG SOCIETY ROLE

B29
DE MAN H.,JOY IN WORK. STRATA ECO/DEV ECO/TAC PRODUC ANOMIE ROLE SOCISM...IDEA/COMP 20. PAGE 31 F0605 SOC WORKER HAPPINESS RESPECT

S32
DODD E.M. JR.,"FOR WHOM ARE CORPORATE MANAGERS TRUSTEES'." SERV/IND CAP/ISM GIVE LEAD REPRESENT ORD/FREE WEALTH. PAGE 33 F0648 LG/CO ROLE NAT/G PLAN

B47
WARNER W.L.,THE SOCIAL SYSTEM OF THE MODERN FACTORY; THE STRIKE: AN ANALYSIS. USA-45 STRATA WORKER ECO/TAC GP/REL INGP/REL...MGT SOC CHARTS 20 ROLE STRUCT LABOR

YANKEE/C. PAGE 143 F2824 PROC/MFG

S47

DAHL R.A.,"WORKERS' CONTROL OF INDUSTRY AND THE BRITISH LABOUR PARTY." UK STRATA STRUCT DELIB/GP BARGAIN CAP/ISM DEBATE CONTROL CHOOSE GP/REL ATTIT ROLE PWR 19/20 PARLIAMENT LABOR/PAR FABIAN. PAGE 29 F0570 INDUS LABOR WORKER SOCISM

S48

CLEVELAND A.S.,"NAM: SPOKESMAN FOR INDUSTRY?" LEGIS PLAN LEAD LOBBY PARTIC CONSEN INCOME ATTIT ROLE ORD/FREE POLICY. PAGE 25 F0491 VOL/ASSN CLIENT REPRESENT INDUS

B51

HARROD R.F.,THE LIFE OF JOHN MAYNARD KEYNES. UK INTELL FAM CAP/ISM DIPLOM ECO/TAC WAR ATTIT PERSON ROLE 20 KEYNES/JM WWI. PAGE 56 F1094 BIOG FINAN GEN/LAWS

B52

ROSE A.M.,UNION SOLIDARITY: THE INTERNAL COHESION OF A LABOR UNION. SECT GP/REL RACE/REL ATTIT ROLE HEALTH WEALTH...INT QU. PAGE 114 F2241 LABOR INGP/REL PARTIC SUPEGO

S52

KORNHAUSER W.,"THE NEGRO UNION OFFICIAL: A STUDY OF SPONSORSHIP AND CONTROL" (BMR)" USA+45 CONTROL DISCRIM ROLE SUPEGO...OBS 20 NEGRO. PAGE 73 F1428 LABOR LEAD RACE/REL CHOOSE

B53

SAYLES L.R.,THE LOCAL UNION. CONSTN CULTURE DELIB/GP PARTIC CHOOSE GP/REL INGP/REL ATTIT ROLE ...MAJORIT DECISION MGT. PAGE 116 F2284 LABOR LEAD ADJUD ROUTINE

S53

BERNSTEIN M.H.,"POLITICAL IDEAS OF SELECTED AMERICAN BUSINESS JOURNALS (BMR)" USA+45 GP/REL ATTIT RIGID/FLEX ROLE ORD/FREE POLICY. PAGE 14 F0267 IDEA/COMP NAT/G LEAD

B55

JOHR W.A.,THE ROLE OF THE ECONOMIST AS OFFICIAL ADVISER. WOR+45 INTELL ECO/DEV NAT/G PLAN GP/REL ROLE...DECISION PREDICT IDEA/COMP. PAGE 68 F1336 CONSULT ECO/TAC POLICY INGP/REL

B56

HICKMAN C.A.,INDIVIDUALS, GROUPS, AND ECONOMIC BEHAVIOR. WORKER PAY CONTROL EXEC GP/REL INGP/REL PERSON ROLE...PSY SOC PERS/COMP METH 20. PAGE 59 F1163 MGT ADMIN ECO/TAC PLAN

B56

WHYTE W.H. JR.,THE ORGANIZATION MAN. CULTURE FINAN VOL/ASSN DOMIN EDU/PROP EXEC DISPL HABITAT ROLE ...PERS/TEST STERTYP. PAGE 146 F2875 ADMIN LG/CO PERSON CONSEN

S56

MYERS C.A.,"LINE AND STAFF IN INDUSTRIAL RELATIONS." INDUS LABOR GP/REL PWR...MGT INT. PAGE 96 F1876 ROLE PROB/SOLV ADMIN CONSULT

B57

SCHNEIDER E.V.,INDUSTRIAL SOCIOLOGY: THE SOCIAL RELATIONS OF INDUSTRY AND COMMUNITY. STRATA INDUS NAT/G NEIGH CREATE ADMIN PARTIC GP/REL RACE/REL ROLE PWR...POLICY BIBLIOG. PAGE 117 F2308 LABOR MGT INGP/REL STRUCT

L57

SURREY S.S.,"THE CONGRESS AND THE TAX LOBBYIST - HOW SPECIAL TAX PROVISIONS GET ENACTED." LOBBY REPRESENT PRIVIL CONGRESS. PAGE 128 F2518 LEGIS TAX EX/STRUC ROLE

B58

TAFT P.,CORRUPTION AND RACKETEERING IN THE LABOR MOVEMENT (PAMPHLET). ADMIN SANCTION CENTRAL ROLE WEALTH...POLICY CLASSIF. PAGE 128 F2525 LABOR INGP/REL GP/REL CRIME

B59

VINCENT W.S.,ROLES OF THE CITIZENS: PRINCIPLES AND PRACTICES. LOC/G POL/PAR VOL/ASSN CHOOSE ROLE ORD/FREE PWR...POLICY 20. PAGE 141 F2785 INGP/REL EDU/PROP CREATE LOBBY

B59

WAHLKE J.C.,LEGISLATIVE BEHAVIOR: A READER IN THEORY AND RESEARCH. USA+45 CONSTN ELITES POL/PAR LOBBY REPRESENT PERS/REL PERSON ROLE...IDEA/COMP METH/COMP SIMUL. PAGE 142 F2800 LEGIS CHOOSE INGP/REL ATTIT

B59

WORTHY J.C.,BIG BUSINESS AND FREE MEN. LG/CO EX/STRUC EDU/PROP LEAD CHOOSE GP/REL ATTIT DRIVE ROLE ORD/FREE...MAJORIT 20. PAGE 149 F2927 ELITES LOC/G TOP/EX PARTIC

S59

SHEPPARD H.L.,"THE POLITICAL ATTITUDES AND PREFERENCES OF UNION MEMBERS: THE CASE OF THE DETROIT AUTO WORKERS." LOBBY CHOOSE ROLE...CLASSIF QU SAMP TREND. PAGE 120 F2376 LABOR ATTIT WORKER

B60

FORM W.H.,INDUSTRY, LABOR, AND COMMUNITY. STRUCT NEIGH SECT BAL/PWR EDU/PROP PARTIC ATTIT ROLE PWR WEALTH...METH/CNCPT CHARTS. PAGE 42 F0828 LABOR MGT GP/REL CONTROL

S60

SPINRAD W.,"CORRELATES OF TRADE UNION PARTICIPATION: A SUMMARY OF LITERATURE." ACT/RES PERS/REL HAPPINESS HABITAT...BIBLIOG WORK. PAGE 125 F2456 LABOR PARTIC CORREL ROLE

B61

ESTEBAN J.C.,IMPERIALISMO Y DESARROLLO ECONOMICO. L/A+17C FINAN INDUS NAT/G ECO/TAC CONTROL ROLE. PAGE 38 F0747 ECO/UNDEV NAT/LISM DIPLOM BAL/PAY

B61

ESTEVEZ A.,ASPECTOS ECONOMICO-FINANCIEROS DE LA CAMPANA SANMARITANA. L/A+17C SPAIN FINAN COLONIAL LEAD ROLE ORD/FREE WEALTH 19 SOUTH/AMER SAN/MARTIN. PAGE 38 F0748 ECO/UNDEV REV BUDGET NAT/G

B61

LENSKI G.,THE RELIGIOUS FACTOR: A SOCIOLOGICAL STUDY OF RELIGION'S IMPACT ON POLITICS, ECONOMICS, AND FAMILY LIFE. FAM PROF/ORG EDU/PROP ROLE CATHISM ...INT SAMP MUNICH. PAGE 78 F1524 SECT GP/REL

L61

JOHNSTON B.F.,"THE ROLE OF AGRICULTURE IN ECONOMIC DEVELOPMENT." FINAN PRODUC ROLE BIBLIOG. PAGE 68 F1332 AGRI ECO/UNDEV PLAN INDUS

B62

ROUND TABLE ON EUROPE'S ROLE IN LATIN AMERICAN DEVELOPMENT. EUR+WWI L/A+17C PLAN BAL/PAY UTIL ROLE WEALTH...CHARTS ANTHOL 20 UN INT/AM/DEV. PAGE 1 F0017 ECO/UNDEV FINAN TEC/DEV FOR/AID

B62

DEBUYST F.,LAS CLASES SOCIALES EN AMERICA LATINA. L/A+17C SOCIETY STRUCT WORKER EDU/PROP RACE/REL ATTIT HABITAT ROLE...GEOG SOC NAT/COMP SOC/INTEG 20. PAGE 32 F0612 STRATA GP/REL WEALTH

B62

MORGAN C.A.,LABOR ECONOMICS. LAW INDUS MARKET WORKER PLAN PROB/SOLV GOV/REL INCOME ROLE...T 20 DEPT/LABOR NLRB. PAGE 93 F1829 LABOR ECO/TAC ECO/DEV CAP/ISM

B62

PONCET J.,LA COLONISATION ET L'AGRICULTURE EUROPEENNES EN TUNISIE DEPUIS 1881. FRANCE WORKER TEC/DEV ECO/TAC CONTROL EFFICIENCY ROLE WEALTH 19/20 TUNIS. PAGE 107 F2101 ECO/UNDEV AGRI COLONIAL FINAN

B63

GANDHI M.K.,THE WAY TO COMMUNAL HARMONY. INDIA MAJORITY RIGID/FLEX ROLE RESPECT 20 GANDHI/M. PAGE 46 F0892 RACE/REL DISCRIM ATTIT ADJUST

B63

MARCHAL J.,EXPANSION ET RECESSION. FRANCE OP/RES PROB/SOLV ROLE ORD/FREE...TREND SIMUL 20 DEPRESSION. PAGE 85 F1663 FINAN PLAN ECO/DEV

B63

MCCONNELL G.,STEEL AND THE PRESIDENCY, 1962. USA+45 INDUS PROB/SOLV CONFER ROLE...POLICY 20 PRESIDENT. PAGE 88 F1722 PWR CHIEF REPRESENT DOMIN

B63

REAGAN M.D.,THE MANAGED ECONOMY. USA+45 INDUS LG/CO BUDGET GP/REL ORD/FREE PWR WEALTH 20. PAGE 110 F2161 PLAN ECO/DEV NAT/G ROLE

B64

FISK W.M.,ADMINISTRATIVE PROCEDURE IN A REGULATORY AGENCY: THE CAB AND THE NEW YORK-CHICAGO CASE (PAMPHLET). USA+45 DIST/IND ADMIN CONTROL LOBBY GP/REL ROLE ORD/FREE NEWYORK/C CHICAGO CAB. PAGE 41 F0805 SERV/IND ECO/DEV AIR JURID

B64

HACKER A.,THE CORPORATION TAKE-OVER. CONSTN LABOR PLAN BAL/PWR CONTROL EXEC LOBBY REPRESENT GP/REL ROLE ORD/FREE POLICY. PAGE 52 F1025 LG/CO STRUCT PWR

B64

SULTAN P.E.,THE DISENCHANTED UNIONIST. NAT/G ADJUD CONTROL SANCTION RACE/REL ANOMIE ATTIT ROLE ...METH/CNCPT INT. PAGE 127 F2512 LABOR INGP/REL CHARTS MAJORIT

B65

MONCRIEFF A.,SECOND THOUGHTS ON AID. WOR+45 ECO/UNDEV AGRI FINAN VOL/ASSN PLAN TEC/DEV GIVE EDU/PROP ROLE WEALTH 20. PAGE 93 F1816 FOR/AID ECO/TAC INT/ORG IDEA/COMP

B65

PHELPS E.S.,PRIVATE WANTS AND PUBLIC NEEDS - AN INTRODUCTION TO A CURRENT ISSUE OF PUBLIC POLICY (REV. ED.). USA+45 PLAN CAP/ISM INGP/REL ROLE ...DECISION TIME/SEQ 20. PAGE 106 F2081 NAT/G POLICY DEMAND

B65

SPENCE J.E.,REPUBLIC UNDER PRESSURE: A STUDY OF SOUTH AFRICAN FOREIGN POLICY. SOUTH/AFR ADMIN COLONIAL GOV/REL RACE/REL DISCRIM NAT/LISM ATTIT ROLE...TREND 20 NEGRO. PAGE 124 F2449 DIPLOM POLICY AFR

S65

DICKMAN A.B.,"SOUTH AFRICAN MONEY MARKET - PROGRESS FINAN

AND PROBLEMS SINCE 1960." SOUTH/AFR PROB/SOLV ROLE PLAN
...PREDICT CHARTS 20. PAGE 33 F0633 MARKET

B66
AGGARWALA R.N.,FINANCIAL COMMITTEES OF THE INDIAN PARL/PROC
PARLIAMENT: A STUDY IN PARLIAMENTARY CONTROL OVER BUDGET
PUBLIC EXPENDITURE. INDIA FINAN NAT/G ROLE...CHARTS CONTROL
METH/COMP METH 20 PARLIAMENT. PAGE 3 F0049 DELIB/GP

B66
BRODERSEN A.,THE SOVIET WORKER: LABOR AND WORKER
GOVERNMENT IN SOVIET SOCIETY. USSR STRUCT INDUS ROLE
LABOR PLAN PAY INGP/REL PRODUC...POLICY GEN/LAWS NAT/G
BIBLIOG 20 STALIN/J LENIN/VI BOLSHEVISM KHRUSH/N. MARXISM
PAGE 19 F0357

B66
FISK E.K.,NEW GUINEA ON THE THRESHOLD; ASPECTS OF ECO/UNDEV
SOCIAL, POLITICAL, AND ECONOMIC DEVELOPMENT. AGRI SOCIETY
NAT/G INT/TRADE ADMIN ADJUST LITERACY ROLE...CHARTS
ANTHOL 20 NEW/GUINEA. PAGE 41 F0804

S66
FLEMING W.G.,"AUTHORITY, EFFICIENCY, AND ROLE DOMIN
STRESS: PROBLEMS IN THE DEVELOPMENT OF EAST AFRICAN EFFICIENCY
BUREAUCRACIES." AFR UGANDA STRUCT PROB/SOLV ROUTINE COLONIAL
INGP/REL ROLE...MGT SOC GP/COMP GOV/COMP 20 ADMIN
TANGANYIKA AFRICA/E. PAGE 41 F0810

B67
BLAUG M.,ECONOMICS OF EDUCATION: A SELECTED BIBLIOG/A
ANNOTATED BIBLIOGRAPHY. EUR+WWI INTELL ECO/DEV EDU/PROP
ECO/UNDEV ACADEM INT/ORG NAT/G CREATE ADMIN FINAN
EFFICIENCY ROLE PREDICT. PAGE 16 F0298 PLAN

B67
GOODMAN J.S.,THE DEMOCRATS AND LABOR IN RHODE LABOR
ISLAND 9152-1962; CHANGES IN THE OLD ALLIANCE. LOBBY
USA+45 EDU/PROP LEAD GP/REL ROLE RHODE/ISL POL/PAR
DEMOCRAT. PAGE 49 F0948 LEGIS

B67
REHMUS C.M.,LABOR AND AMERICAN POLITICS. POL/PAR LABOR
WORKER EDU/PROP PARTIC ATTIT PWR. PAGE 110 F2175 ROLE
LOBBY

B67
ROACH J.R.,THE UNITED STATES AND THE ATLANTIC INT/ORG
COMMUNITY; ISSUES AND PROSPECTS. AFR WOR+45 TEC/DEV POLICY
ECO/TAC COLONIAL REGION PEACE ROLE...ANTHOL NATO ADJUST
EEC. PAGE 112 F2199 DIPLOM

B67
WISEMAN H.V.,BRITAIN AND THE COMMONWEALTH. EUR+WWI INT/ORG
FUT UK ECO/DEV POL/PAR TEC/DEV INT/TRADE LEAD ROLE DIPLOM
SOVEREIGN...SOC TREND 20 CMN/WLTH. PAGE 148 F2911 NAT/G
NAT/COMP

L67
HOSHII I.,"JAPAN'S STAKE IN ASIA." ASIA S/ASIA DIPLOM
CAP/ISM ECO/TAC ROLE...GEOG 20 CHINJAP. PAGE 62 REGION
F1224 NAT/G
INT/ORG

S67
ADAMS E.S.,"THE EXPANDING ROLE OF BANKS IN PUBLIC PARTIC
AFFAIRS." USA+45 GIVE LEAD ROLE...QU 20. PAGE 2 FINAN
F0036 LOC/G
ATTIT

S67
DAVIS O.A.,"ON THE DISTINCTION BETWEEN PUBLIC AND MARKET
PRIVATE GOODS." USA+45 COM/IND LG/CO NAT/G TV OWN
DEBATE PRICE ADMIN ROLE...MATH IDEA/COMP. PAGE 31 CONCPT
F0593

S67
EDWARDS N.,"EDUCATION IN THE FEDERAL-STATE EDU/PROP
STRUCTURE OF GOVERNMENT." USA+45 SECT CONTROL NAT/G
GOV/REL RACE/REL DISCRIM FEDERAL ROLE PWR PROVS
SOVEREIGN. PAGE 36 F0705 POLICY

S67
JANSSEN P.,"NEA: THE RELUCTANT DRAGON." NAT/G EXEC EDU/PROP
LOBBY PARTIC SANCTION RACE/REL ROLE TREND. PAGE 66 PROF/ORG
F1305 MGT
POLICY

S67
MITCHELL J.D.B.,"THE CONSTITUTIONAL IMPLICATIONS OF CONSTN
JUDICIAL CONTROL OF THE ADMINISTRATION IN THE CT/SYS
UNITED KINGDOM." UK LAW ADJUD ADMIN GOV/REL ROLE CONTROL
...GP/COMP 20. PAGE 92 F1808 EX/STRUC

S67
PRASOW P.,"THE DEVELOPMENT OF JUDICIAL ARBITRATION LABOR
IN LABOR-MANAGEMENT DISPUTES." LAW INDUS WORKER BARGAIN
GP/REL ROLE...HIST/WRIT 20. PAGE 107 F2113 ADJUD
TREND

S67
RONNING C.,"NANKING: 1950." ASIA CANADA CHINA/COM DIPLOM
NAT/G PLAN ECO/TAC REV ADJUST 20. PAGE 113 F2235 ROLE
PEACE

N67
US SENATE COMM ON FOREIGN REL,SURVEY OF THE L/A+17C
ALLIANCE FOR PROGRESS: THE LATIN AMERICAN MILITARY FORCES
(PAMPHLET). USA+45 INT/ORG POL/PAR DIPLOM AGREE CIVMIL/REL
GP/REL ROLE ORD/FREE 20. PAGE 139 F2746 POLICY

ROLFE S.E. F2234

ROMAN CATHOLIC....SEE CATH, CATHISM

ROMAN/EMP....ROMAN EMPIRE

ROMAN/LAW....ROMAN LAW

ROMAN/REP....ROMAN REPUBLIC

ROMANIA....SEE ALSO COM

S63
RAMERIE L.,"TENSION AU SEIN DU COMECON: LE CAS INT/ORG
ROUMAIN." COM EUR+WWI USSR WOR+45 ECO/DEV DIST/IND ECO/TAC
NAT/G POL/PAR VOL/ASSN EDU/PROP TOTALISM ATTIT INT/TRADE
WEALTH...TIME/SEQ 20 COMECON. PAGE 109 F2142 ROMANIA

B66
BROWN J.F.,THE NEW EASTERN EUROPE. ALBANIA BULGARIA DIPLOM
HUNGARY POLAND ROMANIA CULTURE AGRI POL/PAR WAR COM
NAT/LISM MARXISM...CHARTS BIBLIOG 20. PAGE 19 F0369 NAT/G
ECO/UNDEV

B66
JACKSON G.D.,COMINTERN AND PEASANT IN EAST EUROPE MARXISM
1919-1930. BULGARIA COM CZECHOSLVK EUR+WWI POLAND ECO/UNDEV
ROMANIA YUGOSLAVIA STRATA AGRI VOL/ASSN DIPLOM WORKER
CONTROL CROWD WEALTH...POLICY NAT/COMP 20. PAGE 66 INT/ORG
F1293

ROME....ROME

ROME/ANC....ANCIENT ROME; SEE ALSO ROM/REP, ROM/EMP

ROMNEY/GEO....GEORGE ROMNEY

RONNING C. F2235

RONY V. F2236

ROOSA R.V. F2237

ROOSEVLT/F....PRESIDENT FRANKLIN D. ROOSEVELT

B60
SHANNON D.A.,THE GREAT DEPRESSION. USA-45 FINAN WEALTH
LG/CO SCHOOL SML/CO DELIB/GP RECEIVE REV EATING NAT/G
INCOME...ANTHOL MUNICH 20 ROOSEVLT/F CONGRESS. AGRI
PAGE 120 F2365 INDUS

B64
GARDNER L.C.,ECONOMIC ASPECTS OF NEW DEAL ECO/TAC
DIPLOMACY. USA-45 WOR-45 LAW ECO/DEV INT/ORG NAT/G DIPLOM
VOL/ASSN LEGIS TOP/EX EDU/PROP ORD/FREE PWR WEALTH
...POLICY TIME/SEQ VAL/FREE 20 ROOSEVLT/F. PAGE 46
F0901

B65
GOODSELL C.T.,ADMINISTRATION OF A REVOLUTION. EXEC
PUERT/RICO ECO/UNDEV FINAN POL/PAR PROVS LEGIS PLAN SOC
BUDGET RECEIVE ADMIN COLONIAL LEAD MUNICH 20
ROOSEVLT/F. PAGE 49 F0951

B66
FREIDEL F.,AMERICAN ISSUES IN THE TWENTIETH DIPLOM
CENTURY. SOCIETY FINAN ECO/TAC FOR/AID CONTROL POLICY
NUC/PWR WAR RACE/REL PEACE ATTIT...ANTHOL T 20 NAT/G
WILSON/W ROOSEVLT/F KENNEDY/JF TRUMAN/HS. PAGE 44 ORD/FREE
F0851

B66
KIRKENDALL R.S.,SOCIAL SCIENTISTS AND FARM POLITICS AGRI
IN THE AGE OF ROOSEVELT. ACADEM PLAN ECO/TAC GIVE INTELL
ADMIN CONTROL PRODUC...SOC 20 NEW/DEAL ROOSEVLT/F POLICY
BURAGR/ECO. PAGE 71 F1399 NAT/G

ROOSEVLT/T....PRESIDENT THEODORE ROOSEVELT

ROPKE W. F2238,F2239,F2240

ROSE A.M. F2241

ROSS A.M. F2242,F2243,F2244

ROSS P. F2245

ROSS/EH....EDWARD H. ROSS

ROSSMOOR....ROSSMOOR LEISURE WORLD, SEAL BEACH, CAL.

ROSTOW E.V. F0331

ROSTOW W.W. F1795,F2246

ROTHBARD M.N. F2247,F2248

ROTHCHILD D. F2249,F2250

ROTHWELL K.J. F0489

ROURKE F.E. F2251

ROUSSEAU J.J. F2252

ROUSSEAU/J....JEAN JACQUES ROUSSEAU

ROUTINE....PROCEDURAL AND WORK SYSTEMS

B14
VEBLEN T.,THE INSTINCT OF WORKMANSHIP. UNIV SOCIETY ECO/DEV ECO/UNDEV CREATE TEC/DEV ECO/TAC EDU/PROP ROUTINE PERSON...HUM CONCPT TIME/SEQ GEN/LAWS. PAGE 140 F2768
DRIVE SKILL

B25
MATHEWS J.M.,AMERICAN STATE GOVERNMENT. USA-45 LOC/G CHIEF EX/STRUC LEGIS ADJUD CONTROL CT/SYS ROUTINE GOV/REL PWR 20 GOVERNOR. PAGE 87 F1703
PROVS ADMIN FEDERAL CONSTN

B35
SCHATTSCHNEIDER E.E.,POLITICS, PRESSURES AND THE TARIFF: A STUDY OF FREE PRIVATE ENTERPRISE IN PRESSURE POLITICS IN TARIFF REVISION 1929-1930. NAT/G BARGAIN ECO/TAC ROUTINE REPRESENT GOV/REL GP/REL PWR POLICY. PAGE 116 F2290
LOBBY LEGIS TARIFFS

B37
ROBBINS L.,ECONOMIC PLANNING AND INTERNATIONAL ORDER. WOR-45 SOCIETY FINAN INDUS NAT/G ECO/TAC ROUTINE WEALTH...SOC TIME/SEQ GEN/METH WORK 20 KEYNES/JM. PAGE 112 F2202
INT/ORG PLAN INT/TRADE

B38
LANGE O.,ON THE ECONOMIC THEORY OF SOCIALISM. UNIV ECO/DEV FINAN INDUS INT/ORG PUB/INST ROUTINE ATTIT ALL/VALS...SOC CONCPT STAT TREND 20. PAGE 75 F1475
MARKET ECO/TAC INT/TRADE SOCISM

S39
COLE G.D.H.,"NAZI ECONOMICS: HOW DO THEY MANAGE IT?" GERMANY FORCES WORKER BUDGET INT/TRADE ROUTINE COERCE WAR 20 HITLER/A NAZI. PAGE 26 F0500
FASCISM ECO/TAC ATTIT PLAN

B40
SIKES E.R.,CONTEMPORARY ECONOMIC SYSTEMS: THEIR ANALYSIS AND SOCIAL BACKGROUND. GERMANY ITALY USSR AGRI INDUS PLAN CAP/ISM ROUTINE TOTALISM FASCISM ...POLICY CON/ANAL BIBLIOG 20. PAGE 122 F2400
COM SOCISM CONCPT

S43
HERBERG W.,"BUREAUCRACY AND DEMOCRACY IN LABOR UNIONS." LAW CONSTN STRUCT WORKER ADMIN CONTROL PARTIC RIGID/FLEX PWR TREND. PAGE 59 F1151
LABOR REPRESENT ROUTINE INGP/REL

C43
BENTHAM J.,"THE RATIONALE OF REWARD" IN J. BOWRING, ED., THE WORKS OF JEREMY BENTHAM (VOL. 2)" LAW WORKER CREATE INSPECT PAY ROUTINE HAPPINESS PRODUC SUPEGO WEALTH METH/CNCPT. PAGE 13 F0254
SANCTION ECO/TAC INCOME PWR

B45
MILLIS H.A.,ORGANIZED LABOR (FIRST ED.). LAW STRUCT DELIB/GP WORKER ECO/TAC ADJUD CONTROL REPRESENT INGP/REL INCOME MGT. PAGE 92 F1797
LABOR POLICY ROUTINE GP/REL

B45
WOOTTON B.,FREEDOM UNDER PLANNING. UNIV ROUTINE ATTIT AUTHORIT DECISION. PAGE 148 F2926
PLAN ORD/FREE ECO/TAC CONTROL

B48
GRAHAM F.D.,THE THEORY OF INTERNATIONAL VALUES. FUT WOR+45 WOR-45 ECO/DEV FINAN INT/ORG PLAN TEC/DEV CAP/ISM DIPLOM ECO/TAC TARIFFS ROUTINE BAL/PAY DRIVE PWR WEALTH SOCISM...POLICY STAT HYPO/EXP GEN/LAWS 20. PAGE 50 F0971
NEW/IDEA INT/TRADE

B49
SELZNICK P.,TVA AND THE GRASS ROOTS: A STUDY IN THE SOCIOLOGY OF FORMAL ORGANIZATION. USA-45 EX/STRUC PROB/SOLV CONFER PARTIC ROUTINE PWR 20 TVA. PAGE 119 F2353
REPRESENT LOBBY CONSULT

B50
HARTLAND P.C.,BALANCE OF INTERREGIONAL PAYMENTS OF NEW ENGLAND. USA+45 TEC/DEV ECO/TAC LEGIT ROUTINE BAL/PAY PROFIT 20 NEW/ENGLND FED/RESERV. PAGE 56 F1102
ECO/DEV FINAN REGION PLAN

B51
HARDMAN J.B.,THE HOUSE OF LABOR. LAW R+D NEIGH EDU/PROP LEAD ROUTINE REPRESENT GP/REL...POLICY STAT. PAGE 55 F1080
LABOR LOBBY ADMIN PRESS

B51
PETERSON F.,SURVEY OF LABOR ECONOMICS (REV. ED.). STRATA ECO/DEV LABOR INSPECT BARGAIN PAY PRICE EXEC ROUTINE GP/REL ALL/VALS ORD/FREE 20 AFL/CIO DEPT/LABOR. PAGE 105 F2069
WORKER DEMAND IDEA/COMP T

B52
REDFORD E.S.,ADMINISTRATION OF NATIONAL ECONOMIC CONTROL. ECO/DEV DELIB/GP ADJUD CONTROL EQUILIB 20. PAGE 110 F2166
ADMIN ROUTINE GOV/REL LOBBY

S52
KLUMB S.,"EMPLOYEE DETERMINATION OF MANAGERIAL FUNCTIONS AND CHARACTERISTICS." DELIB/GP WORKER PARTIC ROUTINE INGP/REL...CLASSIF OBS QU. PAGE 72 F1410
MGT INDUS EX/STRUC CHOOSE

B53
BOWEN H.R.,SOCIAL RESPONSIBILITIES OF THE BUSINESSMAN (FIRST EDITION). LAW FINAN ACT/RES CAP/ISM ROUTINE DRIVE PWR LAISSEZ...DECISION BIBLIOG. PAGE 17 F0326
MGT PERSON SUPEGO MORAL

B53
SAYLES L.R.,THE LOCAL UNION. CONSTN CULTURE DELIB/GP PARTIC CHOOSE GP/REL INGP/REL ATTIT ROLE ...MAJORIT DECISION MGT. PAGE 116 F2284
LABOR LEAD ADJUD ROUTINE

B55
BERNAYS E.L.,THE ENGINEERING OF CONSENT. VOL/ASSN OP/RES ROUTINE INGP/REL ATTIT RESPECT...POLICY METH/CNCPT METH/COMP 20. PAGE 14 F0264
GP/REL PLAN ACT/RES ADJUST

B55
BRAUN K.,LABOR DISPUTES AND THEIR SETTLEMENT. ECO/TAC ROUTINE TASK GP/REL...DECISION GEN/LAWS. PAGE 18 F0342
INDUS LABOR BARGAIN ADJUD

B55
SMITHIES A.,THE BUDGETARY PROCESS IN THE UNITED STATES. AFR ECO/DEV AGRI EX/STRUC FORCES LEGIS PROB/SOLV TAX ROUTINE EFFICIENCY...MGT CONGRESS PRESIDENT. PAGE 124 F2436
NAT/G ADMIN BUDGET GOV/REL

B56
BURKHEAD J.,GOVERNMENT BUDGETING. ECO/DEV PROB/SOLV ECO/TAC ADMIN ROUTINE GOV/REL EFFICIENCY...DECISION MGT. PAGE 20 F0388
BUDGET NAT/G PROVS EX/STRUC

B56
POOLE K.E.,PUBLIC FINANCE AND ECONOMIC WELFARE. STRUCT ECO/DEV LOC/G NAT/G BUDGET PAY ROUTINE COST EQUILIB WEALTH...SOC/WK METH/COMP 20. PAGE 107 F2103
FINAN TAX ORD/FREE

B57
TRIFFIN R.,EUROPE AND THE MONEY MUDDLE. USA+45 INT/ORG NAT/G CONSULT PLAN ECO/TAC EXEC ROUTINE BAL/PAY WEALTH...METH/CNCPT OBS TREND CHARTS STERTYP GEN/METH EEC TERR/GP VAL/FREE ECSC. PAGE 131 F2587
EUR+WWI ECO/DEV REGION

S57
ANSHEN M.,"BUSINESS, LAWYERS, AND ECONOMISTS." PROB/SOLV ECO/TAC CONFER PROFIT RIGID/FLEX OBJECTIVE...MGT GP/COMP. PAGE 6 F0106
INDUS CONSULT ROUTINE EFFICIENCY

S57
DUBIN R.,"POWER AND UNION-MANAGEMENT RELATIONS." PROB/SOLV ADJUD ROUTINE ATTIT ORD/FREE...MGT STERTYP. PAGE 34 F0668
PWR LABOR BARGAIN GP/REL

B58
CHEEK G.,ECONOMIC AND SOCIAL IMPLICATIONS OF AUTOMATION: A BIBLIOGRAPHIC REVIEW (PAMPHLET). USA+45 LG/CO WORKER CREATE PLAN CONTROL ROUTINE PERS/REL EFFICIENCY PRODUC...METH/COMP 20. PAGE 24 F0459
BIBLIOG/A SOCIETY INDUS AUTOMAT

B58
POLLOCK F.,AUTOMATION: A STUDY OF ITS ECONOMIC AND SOCIAL CONSEQUENCES. FUT USA+45 USA-45 SOCIETY ECO/DEV LABOR ACT/RES PLAN ECO/TAC AUTOMAT ROUTINE ALL/VALS...STAT TREND COMPUT/IR CHARTS SOC/EXP WORK 20. PAGE 107 F2099
TEC/DEV SOC CAP/ISM

L58
CYERT R.M.,"THE ROLE OF EXPECTATIONS IN BUSINESS DECISION-MAKING." PROB/SOLV PRICE RIGID/FLEX. PAGE 29 F0566
LG/CO DECISION ROUTINE EXEC

S58
FOLDES L.,"UNCERTAINTY, PROBABILITY AND POTENTIAL SURPRISE." MARKET PROB/SOLV RISK PERSON...DECISION MGT HYPO/EXP GAME. PAGE 42 F0820
PROBABIL ADMIN ROUTINE

S58
LATTIN N.D.,"MINORITY AND DISSENTING SHAREHOLDERS' RIGHTS IN FUNDAMENTAL CHANGES." FINAN LEGIS ADJUD PARTIC ROUTINE CHOOSE REPRESENT INGP/REL TREND. PAGE 76 F1487
MAJORIT LG/CO LAW CREATE

S58
MANSFIELD E.,"A STUDY OF DECISION-MAKING WITHIN THE FIRM." LG/CO WORKER INGP/REL COST EFFICIENCY PRODUC ...CHARTS 20. PAGE 85 F1658
OP/RES PROB/SOLV AUTOMAT ROUTINE

S58
O'NEAL F.H.,"RECENT LEGISLATION AFFECTING CLOSE CORPORATIONS." LAW EX/STRUC ECO/TAC ROUTINE CHOOSE RIGID/FLEX...MAJORIT MGT TREND. PAGE 100 F1959
LG/CO LEGIS REPRESENT PARTIC

S58
SCHULZE R.O.,"THE ROLE OF ECONOMIC DOMINANTS IN COMMUNITY POWER STRUCTURE." ECO/TAC ROUTINE ATTIT OBJECTIVE...SOC RECORD CENSUS. PAGE 118 F2319
SOCIETY STRUCT PROB/SOLV

B59
ALLEN R.L.,SOVIET INFLUENCE IN LATIN AMERICA. ECO/UNDEV FINAN PROC/MFG NAT/G TEC/DEV EDU/PROP EXEC ROUTINE ATTIT DRIVE PERSON ALL/VALS PWR...STAT CHARTS WORK FOR/TRADE 20. PAGE 4 F0071
L/A+17C ECO/TAC INT/TRADE USSR

B59
BROMWICH L.,UNION CONSTITUTIONS. CONSTN EX/STRUC
LABOR

PRESS ADJUD CONTROL CHOOSE REPRESENT PWR SAMP. PAGE 19 F0361
ROUTINE INGP/REL RACE/REL

B59
DIEBOLD W. JR.,THE SCHUMAN PLAN: A STUDY IN ECONOMIC COOPERATION, 1950-1959. EUR+WWI FRANCE GERMANY USA+45 EXTR/IND CONSULT DELIB/GP PLAN DIPLOM ECO/TAC INT/TRADE ROUTINE ORD/FREE WEALTH ...METH/CNCPT STAT CONT/OBS INT TIME/SEQ ECSC 20. PAGE 33 F0635
INT/ORG REGION

S59
CYERT R.M.,"MODELS IN A BEHAVIORAL THEORY OF THE FIRM." ROUTINE...DECISION MGT METH/CNCPT MATH. PAGE 29 F0567
SIMUL GAME PREDICT INDUS

S59
ZAUBERMAN A.,"SOVIET BLOC ECONOMIC INTEGRATION." COM CULTURE INTELL ECO/DEV INDUS TOP/EX ACT/RES PLAN ECO/TAC INT/TRADE ROUTINE CHOOSE ATTIT ...TIME/SEQ 20. PAGE 150 F2958
MARKET INT/ORG USSR TOTALISM

B60
BAERWALD F.,ECONOMIC SYSTEM ANALYSIS: CONCEPTS AND PERSPECTIVES. USA+45 ECO/DEV NAT/G COMPUTER EQUILIB INCOME ATTIT...DECISION CONCPT IDEA/COMP. PAGE 8 F0151
ACT/RES ECO/TAC ROUTINE FINAN

B60
CAMPBELL R.W.,SOVIET ECONOMIC POWER. COM USA+45 DIST/IND MARKET TOP/EX ACT/RES CAP/ISM ECO/TAC DOMIN EDU/PROP ADMIN ROUTINE DRIVE...MATH TIME/SEQ CHARTS WORK 20. PAGE 21 F0409
ECO/DEV PLAN SOCISM USSR

B60
FRANCK P.G.,AFGHANISTAN: BETWEEN EAST AND WEST. AFGHANISTN AFR USA+45 USSR ECO/UNDEV PLAN ADMIN ROUTINE ATTIT PWR...STAT OBS CHARTS TOT/POP FOR/TRADE 20. PAGE 43 F0843
ECO/TAC TREND FOR/AID

B60
HUGHES R.,THE CHINESE COMMUNES; A BACKGROUND BOOK. CHINA/COM SOCIETY CONTROL ROUTINE ADJUST EFFICIENCY PRODUC 20. PAGE 63 F1234
AGRI INDUS STRUCT MARXISM

B60
LERNER A.P.,THE ECONOMICS OF CONTROL. USA+45 ECO/UNDEV INT/ORG ACT/RES PLAN CAP/ISM INT/TRADE ATTIT WEALTH...SOC MATH STAT GEN/LAWS INDEX 20. PAGE 78 F1530
ECO/DEV ROUTINE ECO/TAC SOCISM

B60
THEOBALD R.,THE RICH AND THE POOR: A STUDY OF THE ECONOMICS OF RISING EXPECTATIONS. WOR+45 CONSTN ECO/DEV ECO/UNDEV INT/ORG NAT/G PLAN FOR/AID ROUTINE BAL/PAY ORD/FREE PWR WEALTH...GEOG TREND WORK FOR/TRADE 20. PAGE 129 F2553
ECO/TAC INT/TRADE

S60
GROSSMAN G.,"SOVIET GROWTH: ROUTINE, INERTIA, AND PRESSURE." COM STRATA NAT/G DELIB/GP PLAN TEC/DEV ECO/TAC EDU/PROP ADMIN ROUTINE DRIVE WEALTH 20. PAGE 52 F1007
POL/PAR ECO/DEV AFR USSR

S60
HERRERA F.,"THE INTER-AMERICAN DEVELOPMENT BANK." USA+45 ECO/UNDEV INT/ORG CONSULT DELIB/GP PLAN ECO/TAC INT/TRADE ROUTINE WEALTH...STAT TERR/GP 20. PAGE 59 F1153
L/A+17C FINAN FOR/AID REGION

S60
MARTIN E.M.,"NEW TRENDS IN UNITED STATES ECONOMIC FOREIGN POLICY." USA+45 INTELL DELIB/GP FOR/AID INT/TRADE ROUTINE BAL/PAY...RELATIV TRUE/GP 20. PAGE 86 F1682
NAT/G PLAN DIPLOM

S60
MILLER A.S.,"SOME OBSERVATIONS ON THE POLITICAL ECONOMY OF POPULATION GROWTH." FUT USA+45 ECO/DEV R+D CONSULT PLAN TEC/DEV ECO/TAC ROUTINE BIO/SOC WEALTH...POLICY OBS. PAGE 91 F1790
SOCIETY GEOG

S60
PYE L.W.,"SOVIET AND AMERICAN STYLES IN FOREIGN AID." COM USA+45 USSR WOR+45 NAT/G PLAN ECO/TAC ROUTINE RIGID/FLEX...POLICY CONCPT TREND GEN/LAWS TOT/POP 20. PAGE 108 F2132
ECO/UNDEV ATTIT FOR/AID

B61
BENOIT E.,EUROPE AT SIXES AND SEVENS: THE COMMON MARKET, THE FREE TRADE ASSOCIATION AND THE UNITED STATES. EUR+WWI FUT USA+45 INDUS CONSULT DELIB/GP EX/STRUC TOP/EX ACT/RES ECO/TAC EDU/PROP ROUTINE CHOOSE PERCEPT WEALTH...MGT TREND EEC FOR/TRADE TOT/POP 20 EFTA. PAGE 13 F0249
FINAN ECO/DEV VOL/ASSN

B61
BREWIS T.N.,CANADIAN ECONOMIC POLICY. AFR CANADA BUDGET CAP/ISM INT/TRADE RATION TARIFFS TAX PRICE CONTROL ROUTINE FEDERAL INCOME PRODUC 20. PAGE 18 F0348
ECO/DEV ECO/TAC NAT/G PLAN

B61
FRIEDMANN G.,THE ANATOMY OF WORK. USA+45 SOCIETY CONTROL ROUTINE DRIVE SKILL...PSY SOC STAT OBS METH/COMP PERS/COMP 20. PAGE 44 F0862
AUTOMAT WORKER INDUS PERSON

B61
FRIEDMANN W.G.,JOINT INTERNATIONAL BUSINESS VENTURES. ASIA ISLAM L/A+17C ECO/DEV DIST/IND FINAN PROC/MFG FACE/GP LG/CO NAT/G VOL/ASSN CONSULT EX/STRUC PLAN ADMIN ROUTINE WEALTH...OLD/LIB FOR/TRADE WORK 20. PAGE 44 F0865
ECO/UNDEV INT/TRADE

B61
GARDNER R.N.,LEGAL-ECONOMIC PROBLEMS OF INTERNATIONAL TRADE. FUT WOR+45 INTELL ECO/DEV EX/STRUC INT/TRADE ROUTINE ATTIT WEALTH...GEN/LAWS ANTHOL FOR/TRADE 20. PAGE 46 F0904
FINAN ACT/RES

B61
GORDON R.A.,BUSINESS LEADERSHIP IN THE LARGE CORPORATION. USA+45 SOCIETY EX/STRUC ADMIN CONTROL ROUTINE GP/REL PWR...MGT 20. PAGE 49 F0960
LG/CO LEAD DECISION LOBBY

B61
HORVATH B.,THE CHARACTERISTICS OF YUGOSLAV ECONOMIC DEVELOPMENT. COM ECO/UNDEV AGRI INDUS PLAN CAP/ISM ECO/TAC ROUTINE WEALTH...SOCIALIST STAT CHARTS STERTYP WORK 20. PAGE 62 F1217
ACT/RES YUGOSLAVIA

B61
QURESHI S.,INCENTIVES IN AMERICAN EMPLOYMENT (THESIS, UNIVERSITY OF PENNSYLVANIA). DELIB/GP TOP/EX BUDGET ROUTINE SANCTION COST TECHRACY MGT. PAGE 108 F2134
SERV/IND ADMIN PAY EX/STRUC

B61
SHARP W.R.,FIELD ADMINISTRATION IN THE UNITED NATION SYSTEM: THE CONDUCT OF INTERNATIONAL ECONOMIC AND SOCIAL PROGRAMS. FUT WOR+45 CONSTN SOCIETY ECO/UNDEV R+D DELIB/GP ACT/RES PLAN TEC/DEV EDU/PROP EXEC ROUTINE HEALTH WEALTH...HUM CONCPT CHARTS METH ILO UNESCO GP VAL/FREE UN 20. PAGE 120 F2369
INT/ORG CONSULT

S61
CYERT R.M.,"TWO EXPERIMENTS ON BIAS AND CONFLICT IN ORGANIZATIONAL ESTIMATION." WORKER PROB/SOLV EFFICIENCY...MGT PSY STAT CHARTS. PAGE 29 F0568
LAB/EXP ROUTINE ADMIN DECISION

S61
GALBRAITH J.K.,"A POSITIVE APPROACH TO ECONOMIC AID." FUT USA+45 INTELL NAT/G CONSULT ACT/RES DIPLOM ECO/TAC EDU/PROP ATTIT KNOWL PWR WEALTH ...SOC STERTYP MID/EX METH/GP 20. PAGE 45 F0883
ECO/UNDEV ROUTINE FOR/AID

S61
GORDON L.,"ECONOMIC REGIONALISM RECONSIDERED." FUT USA+45 WOR+45 INDUS NAT/G TEC/DEV DIPLOM ROUTINE PERCEPT WEALTH...WELF/ST METH/CNCPT WORK 20. PAGE 49 F0957
ECO/DEV ATTIT CAP/ISM REGION

S61
LANFALUSSY A.,"EUROPE'S PROGRESS: DUE TO COMMON MARKET." EUR+WWI ECO/DEV DELIB/GP PLAN ECO/TAC ROUTINE WEALTH...GEOG TREND EEC TERR/GP 20. PAGE 75 F1473
INT/ORG MARKET

S61
LINDSAY F.A.,"PLANNING IN FOREIGN AFFAIRS: THE MISSING ELEMENT." FUT USA+45 ROUTINE SKILL...MGT TOT/POP 20. PAGE 80 F1572
ECO/DEV PLAN DIPLOM

S61
NEAL A.C.,"NEW ECONOMIC POLICIES FOR THE WEST." COM EUR+WWI FUT USA+45 WOR+45 ECO/DEV ECO/UNDEV INDUS MARKET ROUTINE HEALTH ORD/FREE PWR...OLD/LIB METH/CNCPT 20. PAGE 97 F1904
PLAN ECO/TAC

S61
RAY J.,"THE EUROPEAN FREE-TRADE ASSOCIATION AND ITS IMPACT ON INDIA'S TRADE." EUR+WWI FRANCE GERMANY INDIA S/ASIA UK NAT/G VOL/ASSN PLAN INT/TRADE ROUTINE WEALTH...STAT CHARTS TERR/GP CMN/WLTH EEC FOR/TRADE OEEC 20 EFTA. PAGE 109 F2155
ECO/DEV ECO/TAC

B62
ELLIOTT J.R.,THE APPEAL OF COMMUNISM IN THE UNDERDEVELOPED NATIONS. AFR USSR WOR+45 INT/ORG NAT/G DIPLOM DOMIN EDU/PROP ROUTINE ATTIT RIGID/FLEX ORD/FREE PWR WEALTH MARXISM...POLICY SOC METH/CNCPT MYTH TOT/POP METH/GP 20. PAGE 37 F0722
COM ECO/UNDEV

B62
HATTERY L.H.,INFORMATION RETRIEVAL MANAGEMENT. CLIENT INDUS TOP/EX COMPUTER OP/RES TEC/DEV ROUTINE COST EFFICIENCY RIGID/FLEX...METH/COMP ANTHOL 20. PAGE 57 F1113
R+D COMPUT/IR MGT CREATE

B62
HEILBRONER R.L.,THE MAKING OF ECONOMIC SOCIETY. FUT WOR-45 SOCIETY STRATA ECO/DEV ECO/UNDEV ECO/TAC LEGIT ROUTINE...SOC RECORD REC/INT KNO/TEST CENSUS STERTYP GEN/LAWS. PAGE 58 F1136
CAP/ISM SOCISM

B62
HOOVER E.M.,ANATOMY OF A METROPOLIS. FUT USA+45 SOCIETY ECO/DEV DIST/IND INDUS WORKER ECO/TAC TAX GP/REL COST WEALTH MUNICH 20 NEWYORK/C. PAGE 62 F1212
ROUTINE TREND INCOME

B62
MEADE J.E.,CASE STUDIES IN EUROPEAN ECONOMIC UNION. BELGIUM EUR+WWI LUXEMBOURG NAT/G INT/TRADE REGION ROUTINE WEALTH...METH/CNCPT STAT CHARTS ECSC TOT/POP OEEC EEC FOR/TRADE 20. PAGE 89 F1738
INT/ORG ECO/TAC

B62
SMITH G.A. JR.,POLICY FORMULATION AND ADMINISTRATION: A CASEBOOK OF TOPMANAGEMENT PROBLEMS IN BUSINESS. EX/STRUC PLAN PROB/SOLV ADMIN
INDUS SOC/EXP TOP/EX

CONTROL EXEC LEAD ROUTINE EFFICIENCY ATTIT MGT. PAGE 123 F2430 — DECISION

L62
GALBRAITH J.K.,"ECONOMIC DEVELOPMENT IN PERSPECTIVE." CAP/ISM ECO/TAC ROUTINE ATTIT WEALTH ...TREND CHARTS SOC/EXP WORK TERR/GP 20. PAGE 45 F0884 — ECO/UNDEV PLAN

S62
IOVTCHOUK M.T.,"ON SOME THEORETICAL PRINCIPLES AND METHODS OF SOCIOLOGICAL INVESTIGATIONS (IN RUSSIAN)." FUT USA+45 STRATA R+D NAT/G POL/PAR TOP/EX ACT/RES PLAN ECO/TAC EDU/PROP ROUTINE ATTIT RIGID/FLEX MARXISM SOCISM...MARXIST METH/CNCPT OBS TREND NAT/COMP GEN/LAWS 20. PAGE 65 F1288 — COM ECO/DEV CAP/ISM USSR

S62
PYE L.W.,"THE POLITICAL IMPULSES AND FANTASIES BEHIND FOREIGN AID." FUT USA+45 ECO/UNDEV DIPLOM ECO/TAC ROUTINE DRIVE KNOWL...SOC METH/CNCPT NEW/IDEA TREND HYPO/EXP STERTYP GEN/METH 20. PAGE 108 F2133 — ACT/RES ATTIT FOR/AID

B63
DUE J.F.,STATE SALES TAX ADMINISTRATION. OP/RES BUDGET PAY ADMIN EXEC ROUTINE COST EFFICIENCY PROFIT...CHARTS METH/COMP 20. PAGE 34 F0671 — PROVS TAX STAT GOV/COMP

B63
PREST A.R.,PUBLIC FINANCE IN UNDERDEVELOPED COUNTRIES. UK WOR+45 WOR-45 SOCIETY INT/ORG NAT/G LEGIS ACT/RES PLAN ECO/TAC ADMIN ROUTINE...CHARTS 20. PAGE 108 F2115 — FINAN ECO/UNDEV NIGERIA

B63
SCHOECK H.,THE NEW ARGUMENT IN ECONOMICS. UK USA+45 INDUS MARKET LABOR NAT/G ECO/TAC ADMIN ROUTINE BAL/PAY PWR...POLICY BOLIV. PAGE 117 F2309 — WELF/ST FOR/AID ECO/DEV ALL/IDEOS

S63
BALOGH T.,"L'INFLUENCE DES INSTITUTIONS MONETAIRES ET COMMERCIALES SUR LA STRUCTURE ECONOMIQUE AFRICAIN." AFR EUR+WWI FUT USA+45 USA-45 WOR+45 SERV/IND INT/ORG NAT/G TOP/EX ROUTINE...INDEX EEC METH/GP 20. PAGE 9 F0168 — FINAN

S63
COLLERY A.,"A FULL EMPLOYMENT, KEYNESIAN THEORY OF INTERNATIONAL TRADE." WOR+45 ECO/DEV ACT/RES ECO/TAC ROUTINE ORD/FREE WEALTH...MATH CHARTS 20 KEYNES/JM. PAGE 26 F0504 — SIMUL INT/TRADE

S63
DE FOREST J.D.,"LOW LEVELS OF TECHNOLOGY AND ECONOMIC DEVELOPMENT PROSPECTS." WOR+45 WOR-45 CULTURE ACT/RES CREATE PLAN ECO/TAC ROUTINE PERCEPT WEALTH...METH/CNCPT GEN/LAWS 20. PAGE 31 F0597 — ECO/UNDEV TEC/DEV

S63
DUCROS B.,"MOBILISATION DES RESSOURCES PRODUCTIVES ET DEVELOPPEMENT." FUT INTELL SOCIETY COM/IND DIST/IND EXTR/IND FINAN INDUS ROUTINE WEALTH ...METH/CNCPT OBS 20. PAGE 34 F0670 — ECO/UNDEV TEC/DEV

S63
EMERSON R.,"THE ATLANTIC COMMUNITY AND THE EMERGING COUNTRIES." FUT WOR+45 ECO/DEV ECO/UNDEV R+D NAT/G DELIB/GP BAL/PWR ECO/TAC EDU/PROP ROUTINE ORD/FREE PWR WEALTH...POLICY CONCPT TREND GEN/METH EEC 20 NATO. PAGE 37 F0729 — ATTIT INT/TRADE

S63
FOURASTIE J.,"LES SCIENCES ECONOMIQUES ET SOCIALES EN EUROPE." EUR+WWI FUT MOD/EUR WOR+45 WOR-45 INTELL SOCIETY R+D PLAN ROUTINE ATTIT RIGID/FLEX KNOWL...OBS TREND. PAGE 43 F0833 — ACT/RES CULTURE

S63
GERHARD H.,"COMMODITY TRADE STABILIZATION THROUGH INTERNATIONAL AGREEMENTS." WOR+45 ECO/DEV ECO/UNDEV NAT/G ROUTINE ORD/FREE...INT/LAW OBS TREND GEN/METH TOT/POP 20. PAGE 47 F0918 — PLAN ECO/TAC INT/TRADE

S63
LEDUC G.,"L'AIDE INTERNATIONALE AU DEVELOPPEMENT." FUT WOR+45 ECO/DEV ECO/UNDEV R+D PROF/ORG TEC/DEV ECO/TAC ROUTINE ATTIT ALL/VALS...MGT TIME/SEQ FOR/TRADE TOT/POP 20. PAGE 77 F1503 — FINAN PLAN FOR/AID

S63
MASON E.S.,"INTERESTS, IDEOLOGIES AND THE PROBLEM OF STABILITY AND GROWTH." EUR+WWI USA+45 DELIB/GP CREATE PLAN EXEC ROUTINE BAL/PAY ATTIT PWR...MGT CONCPT OEEC 20. PAGE 87 F1698 — NAT/G ECO/DEV

S63
SCHURMANN F.,"ECONOMIC POLICY AND POLITICAL POWER IN COMMUNIST CHINA." ASIA CHINA/COM USSR SOCIETY ECO/UNDEV AGRI INDUS CREATE ADMIN ROUTINE ATTIT DRIVE RIGID/FLEX PWR WEALTH...HIST/WRIT TREND CHARTS WORK 20. PAGE 118 F2323 — PLAN ECO/TAC

B64
BOURGOIGNIE G.E.,JEUNE AFRIQUE MOBILISABLE; LES PROBLEMES DE LA JEUNESSE DESOEUVREE EN AFRIQUE NOIRE. INT/ORG VOL/ASSN ECO/TAC ROUTINE UTIL ATTIT 20. PAGE 17 F0324 — AGE/Y AFR CREATE ECO/UNDEV

B64
JUCKER-FLEETWOOD E.,MONEY AND FINANCE IN AFRICA. ISLAM ECO/UNDEV SERV/IND NAT/G EX/STRUC PLAN ECO/TAC ROUTINE WEALTH...MGT TOT/POP 20. PAGE 68 F1344 — AFR FINAN

B64
TINBERGEN J.,CENTRAL PLANNING. COM INTELL ECO/DEV ECO/UNDEV FINAN INT/ORG PROB/SOLV ECO/TAC CONTROL EXEC ROUTINE DECISION. PAGE 130 F2576 — PLAN INDUS MGT CENTRAL

B64
WILLIAMSON J.G.,AMERICAN GROWTH AND THE BALANCE OF PAYMENTS, 1820-1913: A STUDY OF THE LONG SWING. EUR+WWI MOD/EUR USA+45 USA-45 ECO/DEV NAT/G ECO/TAC ROUTINE ORD/FREE WEALTH...MATH STAT TIME/SEQ CHARTS SIMUL GEN/LAWS TRUE/GP METH/GP VAL/FREE 19/20. PAGE 147 F2896 — FINAN BAL/PAY

L64
HAAS E.B.,"ECONOMICS AND DIFFERENTIAL PATTERNS OF POLITICAL INTEGRATION: PROJECTIONS ABOUT UNITY IN LATIN AMERICA." SOCIETY NAT/G DELIB/GP ACT/RES CREATE PLAN ECO/TAC REGION ROUTINE ATTIT DRIVE PWR WEALTH...CONCPT TREND CHARTS LAFTA TERR/GP 20. PAGE 52 F1020 — L/A+17C INT/ORG MARKET

S64
BEIM D.,"THE COMMUNIST BLOC AND THE FOREIGN-AID GAME." AFR WOR+45 NAT/G PLAN ROUTINE ATTIT KNOWL ORD/FREE...DECISION QUANT CONT/OBS TIME/SEQ CHARTS GAME SIMUL LOG/LING 20. PAGE 12 F0231 — COM ECO/UNDEV ECO/TAC FOR/AID

S64
CARNEGIE ENDOWMENT INT. PEACE,"ADMINISTRATION AND BUDGET (ISSUES BEFORE THE NINETEENTH GENERAL ASSEMBLY)." WOR+45 FINAN BUDGET ECO/TAC ROUTINE COST...STAT RECORD UN. PAGE 21 F0415 — INT/ORG ADMIN

S64
GARDNER R.N.,"GATT AND THE UNITED NATIONS CONFERENCE ON TRADE AND DEVELOPMENT." USA+45 WOR+45 SOCIETY ECO/UNDEV MARKET NAT/G DELIB/GP ACT/RES PLAN ECO/TAC TARIFFS EDU/PROP ROUTINE DRIVE RIGID/FLEX WEALTH...DECISION MGT TREND UN TOT/POP 20 GATT. PAGE 46 F0905 — INT/ORG INT/TRADE

S64
HUELIN D.,"ECONOMIC INTEGRATION IN LATIN AMERICAN: PROGRESS AND PROBLEMS." L/A+17C ECO/DEV AGRI DIST/IND FINAN INDUS NAT/G VOL/ASSN CONSULT DELIB/GP EX/STRUC ACT/RES PLAN TEC/DEV ECO/TAC ROUTINE BAL/PAY WEALTH FOR/TRADE WORK TERR/GP 20. PAGE 63 F1232 — MARKET ECO/UNDEV INT/TRADE

S64
LEFF N.H.,"ECONOMIC DEVELOPMENT THROUGH BUREAUCRATIC CORRUPTION." ELITES NAT/G ROUTINE REPRESENT GP/REL PERS/REL. PAGE 77 F1511 — ECO/UNDEV CLIENT EX/STRUC

S64
NASH M.,"SOCIAL PREREQUISITES TO ECONOMIC GROWTH IN LATIN AMERICA AND SOUTHEAST ASIA." L/A+17C S/ASIA CULTURE SOCIETY ECO/UNDEV AGRI INDUS NAT/G PLAN TEC/DEV EDU/PROP ROUTINE ALL/VALS...POLICY RELATIV SOC NAT/COMP WORK TOT/POP 20. PAGE 96 F1894 — ECO/DEV PERCEPT

B65
EDELMAN M.,THE POLITICS OF WAGE-PRICE DECISIONS. GERMANY ITALY NETHERLAND UK INDUS LABOR POL/PAR PROB/SOLV BARGAIN PRICE ROUTINE BAL/PAY COST DEMAND 20. PAGE 36 F0699 — GOV/COMP CONTROL ECO/TAC PLAN

B65
FLEMING R.W.,THE LABOR ARBITRATION PROCESS. USA+45 LAW BARGAIN ADJUD ROUTINE SANCTION COST...PREDICT CHARTS TIME 20. PAGE 41 F0809 — GP/REL LABOR CONSULT DELIB/GP

B65
HADWIGER D.F.,PRESSURES AND PROTEST. NAT/G LEGIS PLAN LEAD PARTIC ROUTINE ATTIT POLICY. PAGE 53 F1030 — AGRI GP/REL LOBBY CHOOSE

B65
HICKMAN B.G.,QUANTITATIVE PLANNING OF ECONOMIC POLICY. FRANCE NETHERLAND OP/RES PRICE ROUTINE UTIL ...POLICY DECISION ECOMETRIC METH/CNCPT STAT STYLE CHINJAP. PAGE 59 F1162 — PROB/SOLV PLAN QUANT

B65
OECD,TECHNIQUES OF ECONOMIC FORECASTING. CANADA FRANCE NETHERLAND SWEDEN UK USA+45 PROB/SOLV ROUTINE...CONCPT MATH CHARTS BIBLIOG METH 20. PAGE 100 F1974 — PREDICT METH/COMP PLAN

B65
SCOTT A.M.,THE REVOLUTION IN STATECRAFT: INFORMAL PENETRATION. WOR+45 WOR-45 CULTURE INT/ORG FORCES ECO/TAC ROUTINE...BIBLIOG 20. PAGE 118 F2331 — DIPLOM EDU/PROP FOR/AID

B65
WARD R.,BACKGROUND MATERIAL ON ECONOMIC IMPACT OF FEDERAL PROCUREMENT - 1965: FOR JOINT ECONOMIC COMMITTEE US CONGRESS. FINAN ROUTINE WEAPON CIVMIL/REL EFFICIENCY...STAT CHARTS 20 CONGRESS. PAGE 143 F2818 — ECO/DEV NAT/G OWN GOV/REL

L65
FORTE W.E.,"THE FOOD AND DRUG ADMINISTRATION, THE FEDERAL TRADE COMMISSION AND THE DECEPTIVE PACKAGING." ROUTINE...JURID 20 FTC. PAGE 43 F0831 — CONTROL HEALTH ADJUD INDUS

S

N
US LIBRARY OF CONGRESS,SOUTHERN ASIA ACCESSIONS LIST. BURMA CEYLON INDIA NEPAL PAKISTAN S/ASIA THAILAND AGRI INDUS SCHOOL WORKER...ART/METH GEOG HEAL PHIL/SCI LING 20. PAGE 137 F2710
BIBLIOG/A SOCIETY CULTURE ECO/UNDEV

B49
PELZER K.J.,SELECTED BIBLIOGRAPHY ON THE GEOGRAPHY OF SOUTHEAST ASIA (3 VOLS., 1949-1956). PHILIPPINE CULTURE...SOC 20 MALAYA. PAGE 104 F2053
BIBLIOG S/ASIA GEOG

B51
US DEPARTMENT OF STATE,POINT FOUR, NEAR EAST AND AFRICA, A SELECTED BIBLIOGRAPHY OF STUDIES ON ECONOMICALLY UNDERDEVELOPED COUNTRIES. AGRI COM/IND FINAN INDUS PLAN INT/TRADE...SOC TREND 20. PAGE 135 F2672
BIBLIOG/A AFR S/ASIA ISLAM

B51
US HOUSE COMM APPROPRIATIONS,MUTUAL SECURITY PROGRAM APPROPRIATIONS FOR 1952: HEARINGS BEFORE A SUBCOMMITTEE OF THE COMMITTEE ON APPROPRIATIONS. AFR KOREA L/A+17C ECO/DEV ECO/UNDEV INT/ORG INSPECT BAL/PWR DIPLOM DEBATE WAR...POLICY STAT ASIA/S 20 CONGRESS NATO MID/EAST. PAGE 136 F2686
LEGIS FORCES BUDGET FOR/AID

B53
MIT CENTER INTERNATIONAL STU,BIBLIOGRAPHY OF THE ECONOMIC AND POLITICAL DEVELOPMENT OF INDONESIA. INDONESIA STRUCT NAT/G COLONIAL LEAD...STAT 20. PAGE 92 F1805
BIBLIOG ECO/UNDEV TEC/DEV S/ASIA

S53
HANSER P.M.,"EXPLODING POPULATIONS: INTERNATIONAL AND REGIONAL ASPECTS." AFR S/ASIA ECO/TAC WEAPON BIO/SOC LOVE ORD/FREE...NEW/IDEA CENSUS TOT/POP 20. PAGE 55 F1069
ECO/UNDEV GEOG

B55
UN ECONOMIC COMN ASIA & FAR E,ECONOMIC SURVEY OF ASIA AND THE FAR EAST, 1954. AFGHANISTN CEYLON INDIA PHILIPPINE S/ASIA ECO/DEV FINAN INDUS INT/TRADE PRODUC WEALTH...STAT CHARTS 20 CHINJAP. PAGE 132 F2600
ECO/UNDEV PRICE NAT/COMP ASIA

B56
BELL P.W.,THE STERLING AREA IN THE POSTWAR WORLD. EUR+WWI FUT S/ASIA UK ECO/DEV PLAN DIPLOM WEALTH ...STAT RECORD CHARTS GEN/LAWS FOR/TRADE TOT/POP 20. PAGE 12 F0235
FINAN ECO/TAC

L57
MASS. INST. TECH.,"THE CENTER FOR INTERNATIONAL STUDIES." AFR ASIA COM EUR+WWI ISLAM L/A+17C S/ASIA USA+45 USA-45 DIST/IND CONSULT FORCES ACT/RES TEC/DEV DIPLOM REV ATTIT WEALTH...CONCPT FOR/TRADE 20. PAGE 87 F1702
R+D ECO/UNDEV

B58
BERLINER J.S.,SOVIET ECONOMIC AID: THE AID AND TRADE POLICY IN UNDERDEVELOPED COUNTRIES. AFR COM ISLAM L/A+17C S/ASIA USSR ECO/DEV DIST/IND FINAN MARKET INT/ORG ACT/RES PLAN BAL/PWR WEAPON PWR WEALTH...CHARTS FOR/TRADE 20. PAGE 14 F0263
ECO/UNDEV ECO/TAC FOR/AID

B58
JENNINGS I.,PROBLEMS OF THE NEW COMMONWEALTH. AFR CEYLON INDIA PAKISTAN S/ASIA ECO/UNDEV INT/ORG LOC/G DIPLOM ECO/TAC INT/TRADE COLONIAL RACE/REL DISCRIM 20 PARLIAMENT. PAGE 67 F1314
NAT/LISM NEUTRAL FOR/AID POL/PAR

B58
MASON J.B.,THAILAND BIBLIOGRAPHY. S/ASIA THAILAND CULTURE EDU/PROP ADMIN...GEOG SOC LING 20. PAGE 87 F1701
BIBLIOG/A ECO/UNDEV DIPLOM NAT/G

B58
ROBERTS B.C.,NATIONAL WAGES POLICY IN WAR AND PEACE. EUR+WWI GERMANY S/ASIA SWEDEN UK USA+45 USA-45 STRATA ECO/DEV LABOR NAT/G DELIB/GP PLAN INT/TRADE WEALTH...STAT TREND CHARTS 20. PAGE 112 F2205
CREATE ECO/TAC

B58
UNIVERSITY OF LONDON,THE FAR EAST AND SOUTH-EAST ASIA: A CUMULATED LIST OF PERIODICAL ARTICLES, MAY 1956-APRIL 1957. ASIA S/ASIA LAW ADMIN...LING 20. PAGE 133 F2621
BIBLIOG SOC

B59
AITKEN H.,THE STATE AND ECONOMIC GROWTH. COM EUR+WWI MOD/EUR S/ASIA USA+45 FINAN NAT/G DELIB/GP PLAN PWR WEALTH 20. PAGE 3 F0054
DIST/IND ECO/DEV

B59
PANIKKAR K.M.,THE AFRO-ASIAN STATES AND THEIR PROBLEMS. COM CULTURE KIN POL/PAR SECT DIPLOM EDU/PROP COLONIAL SOVEREIGN...TECHNIC GOV/COMP 20. PAGE 103 F2025
AFR S/ASIA ECO/UNDEV

B59
SILCOCK T.H.,THE COMMONWEALTH ECONOMY IN SOUTHEAST ASIA. AFR INDIA MALAYSIA S/ASIA ECO/DEV AGRI LOC/G PLAN TARIFFS COLONIAL BAL/PAY DEMAND...BIBLIOG/A 20 GATT. PAGE 122 F2401
ECO/TAC INT/TRADE RACE/REL DIPLOM

S59
HOFFMAN P.,"OPERATION BREAKTHROUGH." AFR S/ASIA STRUCT INDUS CONSULT TEC/DEV ATTIT RIGID/FLEX SKILL WEALTH...TECHNIC CONCPT STYLE RECORD CHARTS ORG/CHARTS GEN/METH VAL/FREE 20. PAGE 61 F1190
ECO/UNDEV EDU/PROP FOR/AID

S59
THOMPSON W.S.,"POPULATION AND PROGRESS IN THE FAR EAST." ASIA S/ASIA DIST/IND CREATE ECO/TAC WAR LOVE SKILL WEALTH...CONT/OBS TOT/POP 20. PAGE 130 F2568
ECO/UNDEV BIO/SOC GEOG

B60
SAKAI R.K.,STUDIES ON ASIA, 1960. ASIA CHINA/COM S/ASIA COM/IND ECO/TAC...ANTHOL 17/20 MALAYA. PAGE 115 F2270
ECO/UNDEV SOC

B60
UNESCO,SOUTHERN ASIA SOCIAL SCIENCE BIBLIOGRAPHY (WITH ANNOTATIONS AND ABSTRACTS), 1959 (PAMPHLET). S/ASIA...SOC 20. PAGE 132 F2609
BIBLIOG/A ECO/UNDEV TEC/DEV INDUS

S60
JAFFEE A.J.,"POPULATION TRENDS AND CONTROLS IN UNDERDEVELOPED COUNTRIES." AFR FUT ISLAM L/A+17C S/ASIA CULTURE R+D FAM ACT/RES PLAN EDU/PROP BIO/SOC RIGID/FLEX HEALTH...SOC STAT OBS CHARTS 20. PAGE 66 F1303
ECO/UNDEV GEOG

S60
KELLOGG C.E.,"TRANSFER OF BASIC SKILLS OF FOOD PRODUCTION." AFR FUT S/ASIA STRATA ECO/UNDEV LABOR VOL/ASSN RIGID/FLEX...OLD/LIB SOCIALIST NEW/IDEA STAT PROJ/TEST GEN/LAWS 20. PAGE 70 F1370
AGRI PLAN

S60
MURPHEY R.,"ECONOMIC CONFLICTS IN SOUTH ASIA." ASIA CULTURE INTELL ECO/TAC REGION ATTIT DRIVE KNOWL ...METH/CNCPT TIME/SEQ STERTYP TOT/POP METH/GP VAL/FREE 20. PAGE 95 F1864
S/ASIA ECO/UNDEV

B61
SAKAI R.K.,STUDIES ON ASIA, 1961. ASIA BURMA INDIA S/ASIA FINAN ECO/TAC NAT/LISM SOCISM...POLICY ANTHOL 19/20 CHINJAP. PAGE 115 F2271
ECO/UNDEV SECT

S61
RAY J.,"THE EUROPEAN FREE-TRADE ASSOCIATION AND ITS IMPACT ON INDIA'S TRADE." EUR+WWI FRANCE GERMANY INDIA S/ASIA UK NAT/G VOL/ASSN PLAN INT/TRADE ROUTINE WEALTH...STAT CHARTS TERR/GP CMN/WLTH EEC FOR/TRADE OEEC 20 EFTA. PAGE 109 F2155
ECO/DEV ECO/TAC

B62
BROWN S.D.,STUDIES ON ASIA, 1962. ASIA BURMA INDIA ISLAM ISRAEL S/ASIA ECO/UNDEV POL/PAR SECT ECO/TAC ...ANTHOL 20 CHINJAP. PAGE 19 F0374
PWR PARL/PROC

B62
GOLDWIN R.A.,WHY FOREIGN AID? - TWO MESSAGES BY PRESIDENT KENNEDY AND ESSAYS. S/ASIA USA+45 ECO/UNDEV 20 KENNEDY/JF THIRD/WRLD. PAGE 48 F0942
DIPLOM FOR/AID POLICY

B62
INTERNATIONAL BANK RECONST DEV,THE WORLD BANK AND IDA IN ASIA. ASIA S/ASIA COM/IND DIST/IND...CHARTS 20. PAGE 65 F1272
FINAN ECO/UNDEV AGRI INDUS

B62
JORDAN A.A. JR.,FOREIGN AID AND THE DEFENSE OF SOUTHEAST ASIA. PAKISTAN VIETNAM/S FINAN PLAN BUDGET ECO/TAC DETER WAR ORD/FREE...POLICY DECISION CENSUS CHARTS BIBLIOG 20. PAGE 68 F1341
FOR/AID S/ASIA FORCES ECO/UNDEV

B63
BRAIBANTI R.J.D.,ADMINISTRATION AND ECONOMIC DEVELOPMENT IN INDIA. INDIA S/ASIA SOCIETY STRATA ECO/TAC PERSON WEALTH...MGT GEN/LAWS TOT/POP VAL/FREE 20. PAGE 18 F0337
ECO/UNDEV ADMIN

B63
DEUTSCH K.W.,THE POLITICAL ROLE OF LABOR IN DEVELOPING COUNTRIES. AFR ASIA S/ASIA USA+45 WOR+45 ECO/UNDEV POL/PAR ECO/TAC EDU/PROP LEGIT COERCE ORD/FREE PWR WEALTH...OBS INT TREND VAL/FREE 20. PAGE 32 F0625
LABOR NAT/LISM

B63
GEERTZ C.,PEDDLERS AND PRINCES: SOCIAL DEVELOPMENT AND ECONOMIC CHANGE IN TWO INDONESIAN TOWNS. S/ASIA CULTURE SOCIETY STRATA FACE/GP CREATE TEC/DEV ECO/TAC ORD/FREE WEALTH...OBS INT CENSUS CHARTS WORK TOT/POP METH/GP TERR/GP VAL/FREE 20 MUNICH. PAGE 47 F0913
ECO/UNDEV SOC ELITES INDONESIA

B63
INTERNATIONAL BANK RECONST DEV,THE WORLD BANK GROUP IN ASIA. ASIA S/ASIA INDUS TEC/DEV ECO/TAC...RECORD 20 IBRD WORLD/BANK. PAGE 65 F1273
INT/ORG DIPLOM ECO/UNDEV FINAN

B63
KAPP W.K.,HINDU CULTURE: ECONOMIC DEVELOPMENT AND ECONOMIC PLANNING IN INDIA. INDIA S/ASIA CULTURE ECO/TAC EDU/PROP ADMIN ALL/VALS...POLICY MGT TIME/SEQ TRUE/GP VAL/FREE 20. PAGE 69 F1353
SECT ECO/UNDEV

B63
STIFEL L.D.,THE TEXTILE INDUSTRY - A CASE STUDY OF INDUSTRIAL DEVELOPMENT IN THE PHILIPPINES (PAPER). PHILIPPINE WORKER CAP/ISM INT/TRADE TARIFFS RECEIVE PRICE ADMIN COST EFFICIENCY WEALTH...BIBLIOG 20. PAGE 126 F2486
S/ASIA ECO/UNDEV PROC/MFG NAT/G

B63
STUCKI C.W.,AMERICAN DOCTORAL DISSERTATIONS ON ASIA 1933-62 (A PAPER). PREHIST INDUS NAT/G GOV/REL ALL/IDEOS...ART/METH GEOG SOC LING 20. PAGE 127 F2506
BIBLIOG ASIA SOCIETY S/ASIA

B63
WIGHTMAN D.,TOWARD ECONOMIC CO-OPERATION IN ASIA. ASIA S/ASIA VOL/ASSN ACT/RES PLAN TEC/DEV ECO/TAC EDU/PROP RIGID/FLEX SKILL...POLICY METH/CNCPT OBS INT GEN/LAWS UN 20 ECAFE. PAGE 146 F2877 — ECO/UNDEV CREATE

L63
NASH M.,"PSYCHO-CULTURAL FACTORS IN ASIAN ECONOMIC GROWTH." ASIA ISLAM S/ASIA CULTURE ECO/UNDEV DELIB/GP EDU/PROP COERCE ATTIT PERSON HEALTH KNOWL ORD/FREE...PSY SOC STAT TREND ANTHOL VAL/FREE 20. PAGE 96 F1893 — SOCIETY ECO/TAC

S63
AYAL E.B.,"VALUE SYSTEM AND ECONOMIC DEVELOPMENT IN JAPAN AND THAILAND." ASIA S/ASIA THAILAND CULTURE ECO/DEV CAP/ISM DOMIN NAT/LISM DRIVE RIGID/FLEX SOCISM...WELF/ST OBS TREND CON/ANAL GEN/LAWS TERR/GP 20 CHINJAP. PAGE 8 F0145 — ECO/UNDEV ALL/VALS

S63
DELWERT J.,"L'ECONOMIE CAMBODGIENNE ET SON EVOLUTION ACTUELLE." FUT S/ASIA ECO/UNDEV ACT/RES PLAN WEALTH...CONCPT OBS TIME/SEQ TREND 20. PAGE 32 F0617 — FINAN ATTIT CAMBODIA

S63
GORDON B.,"ECONOMIC IMPEDIMENTS TO REGIONALISM IN SOUTH EAST ASIA." BURMA FUT S/ASIA THAILAND USA+45 AGRI INDUS R+D NAT/G PLAN ECO/TAC WEALTH...STAT CONT/OBS 20. PAGE 49 F0954 — VOL/ASSN ECO/UNDEV INT/TRADE REGION

S63
PAAUW D.S.,"ECONOMIC PROGRESS IN SOUTHEAST ASIA." S/ASIA AGRI INDUS PROC/MFG ACT/RES ECO/TAC...CHARTS VAL/FREE 20. PAGE 102 F2010 — ECO/UNDEV STAT

S63
REDDAWAY W.B.,"THE ECONOMICS OF UNDERDEVELOPED COUNTRIES." S/ASIA WOR+45 WOR-45 STRATA AGRI COM/IND DIST/IND MARKET PROC/MFG PLAN TEC/DEV FOR/AID BAL/PAY ATTIT DRIVE SKILL WORK FOR/TRADE 20. PAGE 110 F2165 — ECO/TAC ECO/UNDEV INDIA

B64
BERRILL K.,ECONOMIC DEVELOPMENT WITH SPECIAL REFERENCE TO EAST ASIA. ASIA INDIA S/ASIA AGRI INDUS LABOR DELIB/GP PLAN INT/TRADE COST PRODUC 20 CHINJAP. PAGE 14 F0271 — FINAN ECO/UNDEV INT/ORG CAP/ISM

B64
ESTHUS R.A.,FROM ENMITY TO ALLIANCE: US AUSTRALIAN RELATIONS. S/ASIA DIST/IND VOL/ASSN FORCES ATTIT 20 AUSTRAL TREATY CMN/WLTH. PAGE 39 F0751 — DIPLOM WAR INT/TRADE FOR/AID

B64
LAFONT P.B.,BIBLIOGRAPHIE DU LAOS. LAOS S/ASIA EDU/PROP...GEOG 20. PAGE 74 F1458 — BIBLIOG LAW SOC

B64
LEWIN P.,THE FOREIGN TRADE OF COMMUNIST CHINA* ITS IMPACT ON THE FREE WORLD. AFR EUR+WWI L/A+17C S/ASIA ECO/UNDEV CREATE FOR/AID...STAT NET/THEORY TREND CHARTS. PAGE 79 F1546 — ASIA INT/TRADE NAT/COMP USSR

B64
SAKAI R.K.,STUDIES ON ASIA, 1964. ASIA CHINA/COM ISRAEL MALAYSIA S/ASIA USA+45 USSR ECO/UNDEV FAM POL/PAR SECT CONSULT NAT/LISM...POLICY SOC 20 CHINJAP. PAGE 115 F2272 — PWR DIPLOM

B64
US LIBRARY OF CONGRESS,SOUTHEAST ASIA. CULTURE ...SOC STAT 20. PAGE 138 F2718 — BIBLIOG/A S/ASIA ECO/UNDEV NAT/G

B64
WERTHEIM W.F.,EAST-WEST PARALLELS. INDONESIA S/ASIA NAT/G SECT...TIME/SEQ METH REFORMERS S/EASTASIA. PAGE 145 F2860 — SOC ECO/UNDEV CULTURE NAT/LISM

S64
NASH M.,"SOCIAL PREREQUISITES TO ECONOMIC GROWTH IN LATIN AMERICA AND SOUTHEAST ASIA." L/A+17C S/ASIA CULTURE SOCIETY ECO/UNDEV AGRI INDUS NAT/G PLAN TEC/DEV EDU/PROP ROUTINE ALL/VALS...POLICY RELATIV SOC NAT/COMP WORK TOT/POP 20. PAGE 96 F1894 — ECO/DEV PERCEPT

N64
GREAT BRITAIN CENTRAL OFF INF,THE COLOMBO PLAN (PAMPHLET). AFR ASIA S/ASIA USA+45 VOL/ASSN ...CHARTS 20 RESOURCE/N. PAGE 50 F0980 — FOR/AID PLAN INT/ORG ECO/UNDEV

B65
CAMERON W.J.,NEW ZEALAND. NEW/ZEALND S/ASIA DIPLOM INT/TRADE WRITING COLONIAL PARL/PROC...GEOG CMN/WLTH. PAGE 21 F0402 — SOCIETY GP/REL STRUCT

B65
CRABB C.V. JR.,THE ELEPHANTS AND THE GRASS* A STUDY OF NONALIGNMENT. ASIA INDIA S/ASIA USA+45 USSR BAL/PWR NEUTRAL ATTIT...TREND NAT/COMP. PAGE 28 F0549 — ECO/UNDEV AFR DIPLOM CONCPT

B65
HARBISON F.,MANPOWER AND EDUCATION. AFR CHINA/COM IRAN L/A+17C S/ASIA TEC/DEV ADJUST OPTIMAL SKILL ...ANTHOL 20. PAGE 55 F1073 — ECO/UNDEV EDU/PROP WORKER NAT/COMP

B65
HAUSER P.M.,THE STUDY OF URBANIZATION. S/ASIA ECO/DEV ECO/UNDEV NEIGH ACT/RES...GEOG MUNICH. PAGE 57 F1115 — CULTURE SOC

B65
HOLLER J.E.,POPULATION TRENDS AND ECONOMIC DEVELOPMENT IN THE FAR EAST (PAMPHLET). KOREA S/ASIA AGRI INDUS DELIB/GP PROB/SOLV RATIONAL ...POLICY CHARTS BIBLIOG 20 OUTER/MONG CHINJAP HONG/KONG. PAGE 61 F1197 — CENSUS TREND ECO/UNDEV ASIA

B65
JAIN S.C.,THE STATE AND AGRICULTURE. INDIA S/ASIA ECO/UNDEV PROB/SOLV CAP/ISM MARXISM SOCISM 20. PAGE 66 F1304 — NAT/G POLICY AGRI ECO/TAC

B65
ONSLOW C.,ASIAN ECONOMIC DEVELOPMENT. BURMA CEYLON INDIA MALAYSIA PAKISTAN S/ASIA AGRI INDUS MARKET PROB/SOLV CAP/ISM FOR/AID INT/TRADE DEMAND WEALTH ...POLICY ANTHOL 20. PAGE 101 F1991 — ECO/UNDEV ECO/TAC PLAN NAT/G

B65
SCHULER E.A.,THE PAKISTAN ACADEMIES FOR RURAL DEVELOPMENT COMILLA AND PESHAWAR 1959-1964. PAKISTAN S/ASIA SOCIETY STRUCT AGRI NAT/G TEC/DEV EDU/PROP 20. PAGE 117 F2314 — BIBLIOG PLAN ECO/TAC ECO/UNDEV

B65
VON RENESSE E.A.,UNVOLLENDETE DEMOKRATIEN. AFR ISLAM S/ASIA SOCIETY ACT/RES COLONIAL...JURID CHARTS BIBLIOG METH 13/20. PAGE 142 F2795 — ECO/UNDEV NAT/COMP SOVEREIGN

S65
KAUFMAN R.H.,"THE ASIAN GOLD TRADE." ASIA LAOS THAILAND UK CHARTS. PAGE 69 F1362 — S/ASIA FINAN STAT INT/TRADE

B66
AMERICAN ASSEMBLY COLUMBIA U,THE UNITED STATES AND THE PHILIPPINES. PHILIPPINE S/ASIA USA+45 USA-45 SOCIETY FORCES INT/TRADE...POLICY 20. PAGE 5 F0085 — COLONIAL DIPLOM NAT/LISM

B66
DEBENKO E.,RESEARCH SOURCES FOR SOUTH ASIAN STUDIES IN ECONOMIC DEVELOPMENT: A SELECT BIBLIOGRAPHY OF SERIAL PUBLICATIONS. CEYLON INDIA NEPAL PAKISTAN PROB/SOLV ADMIN...POLICY 20. PAGE 32 F0611 — BIBLIOG ECO/UNDEV S/ASIA PLAN

B66
HUNT C.L.,SOCIAL ASPECTS OF ECONOMIC DEVELOPMENT. S/ASIA AGRI FAM TEC/DEV RECEIVE EDU/PROP OWN...GEOG MUNICH 20. PAGE 63 F1243 — SOC STRATA ATTIT ECO/UNDEV

B66
HUTTENBACH R.A.,BRITISH IMPERIAL EXPERIENCE. AFR S/ASIA UK WOR-45 INT/ORG TEC/DEV...CHARTS 16/20 MERCANTLST. PAGE 64 F1253 — COLONIAL TIME/SEQ INT/TRADE

B66
KEENLEYSIDE H.L.,INTERNATIONAL AID: A SUMMARY. AFR INDIA S/ASIA UK STRATA EXTR/IND TEC/DEV ADMIN RACE/REL DEMAND NAT/LISM WEALTH...TREND CHINJAP. PAGE 70 F1367 — ECO/UNDEV FOR/AID DIPLOM TASK

B66
RAO Y.V.L.,COMMUNICATION AND DEVELOPMENT. INDIA S/ASIA SOCIETY ACT/RES EDU/PROP PARTIC ATTIT...SOC GP/COMP BIBLIOG MUNICH MUNICH 20. PAGE 109 F2149 — COM/IND ECO/UNDEV OBS

B66
US SENATE COMM ON FOREIGN REL,ASIAN DEVELOPMENT BANK ACT. USA+45 LAW DIPLOM...CHARTS 20 BLACK/EUG S/EASTASIA. PAGE 139 F2736 — FOR/AID FINAN ECO/UNDEV S/ASIA

S66
LAURENS H.,"LES PAYS OCCIDENTAUX ET LE MARCHE CHINOIS." EUR+WWI FUT S/ASIA AGRI INDUS VOL/ASSN ECO/TAC BAL/PAY...RECORD PREDICT TREATY. PAGE 76 F1488 — ASIA INT/TRADE TREND STAT

C66
WINT G.,"ASIA: A HANDBOOK." ASIA S/ASIA INDUS LABOR SECT PRESS RACE/REL MARXISM...STAT CHARTS BIBLIOG 20. PAGE 148 F2908 — ECO/UNDEV DIPLOM NAT/G SOCIETY

B67
FALL B.B.,HO CHI MINH ON REVOLUTION: SELECTED WRITINGS, 1920-66. COM VIETNAM ELITES NAT/G COERCE GUERRILLA RACE/REL MARXISM...MARXIST ANTHOL 20. PAGE 39 F0761 — REV COLONIAL ECO/UNDEV S/ASIA

B67
HANNAH H.W.,THE LEGAL BASE FOR UNIVERSITIES IN DEVELOPING COUNTRIES. AFR ASIA L/A+17C S/ASIA USA+45 FINAN CREATE EDU/PROP TASK EFFICIENCY ...JURID METH/COMP 20. PAGE 54 F1060 — ADMIN LAW ACADEM LEGIS

B67
MCNELLY T.,SOURCES IN MODERN EAST ASIAN HISTORY AND POLITICS. KOREA VIETNAM CULTURE DIPLOM COLONIAL REV WAR PWR ALL/IDEOS MARXISM...ANTHOL 20 CHINJAP. PAGE 88 F1733 — NAT/COMP ASIA S/ASIA SOCIETY

B67
MUHAMMAD A.C.,THE EMERGENCE OF PAKISTAN. PAKISTAN S/ASIA CONSTN ECO/UNDEV NAT/G CONTROL NAT/LISM 20. PAGE 94 F1853 — DIPLOM COLONIAL SECT PROB/SOLV

B67
SCHECTER J.,THE NEW FACE OF BUDDHA: BUDDHISM AND POLITICAL POWER IN SOUTHEAST ASIA. S/ASIA NAT/G POL/PAR NAT/LISM ATTIT MARXISM...BIBLIOG 20. PAGE 116 F2292
SECT POLICY PWR LEAD

B67
US AGENCY INTERNATIONAL DEV,PROPOSED FOREIGN AID PROGRAM FOR 1968: SUMMARY PRESENTATION TO THE CONGRESS. AFR S/ASIA USA+45 AGRI TEC/DEV DIPLOM ECO/TAC BAL/PAY COST HEALTH KNOWL SKILL 20 AID CONGRESS ALL/PROG. PAGE 134 F2640
ECO/UNDEV BUDGET FOR/AID STAT

B67
WATT A.,THE EVOLUTION OF AUSTRALIAN FOREIGN POLICY 1938-65. ASIA S/ASIA USA+45 USA-45 INT/ORG NAT/G FORCES FOR/AID TREATY 20 AUSTRAL. PAGE 144 F2834
DIPLOM WAR

B67
WILCOX W.A.,ASIA AND UNITED STATES POLICY. CHINA/COM USA+45. PAGE 146 F2879
ASIA S/ASIA DIPLOM POLICY

L67
HOSHII I.,"JAPAN'S STAKE IN ASIA." ASIA S/ASIA CAP/ISM ECO/TAC ROLE...GEOG 20 CHINJAP. PAGE 62 F1224
DIPLOM REGION NAT/G INT/ORG

L67
MCALLISTER J.T. JR.,"THE POSSIBILITIES FOR DIPLOMACY IN SOUTHEAST ASIA." LAOS VIETNAM INT/ORG NAT/G PROVS BAL/PWR DOMIN AGREE COLONIAL WAR PWR 17/20 TREATY. PAGE 88 F1716
DIPLOM S/ASIA

L67
SCALAPINO R.A.,"A SURVEY OF ASIA IN 1966." ASIA S/ASIA CONSTN SOCIETY POL/PAR CHIEF WAR...ANTHOL 20. PAGE 116 F2285
DIPLOM

S/EASTASIA....SOUTHEAST ASIA: CAMBODIA, LAOS, NORTH AND SOUTH VIETNAM, AND THAILAND

B64
WERTHEIM W.F.,EAST-WEST PARALLELS. INDONESIA S/ASIA NAT/G SECT...TIME/SEQ METH REFORMERS S/EASTASIA. PAGE 145 F2860
SOC ECO/UNDEV CULTURE NAT/LISM

B66
US SENATE COMM ON FOREIGN REL,ASIAN DEVELOPMENT BANK ACT. USA+45 LAW DIPLOM...CHARTS 20 BLACK/EUG S/EASTASIA. PAGE 139 F2736
FOR/AID FINAN ECO/UNDEV S/ASIA

SABAH....SABAH, MALAYSIA

SABBATINO....SABBATINO CASE

SABLE M.H. F2266

SACHS E.S. F2267

SACKS B. F2268

SACKS S. F0405,F2269

SAINT/PIER....JACQUES SAINT-PIERRE

SAINTSIMON....COMTE DE SAINT-SIMON

SAKAI R.K. F2270,F2271,F2272

SALANT W.S. F2273

SALARY....SEE WORKER, WEALTH, ROUTINE

SALAZAR/A....ANTONIO DE OLIVERA SALAZAR

SALENT W.S. F2274

SALERA V. F0735

SALIENCE....SALIENCE

SALINGER/P....PIERRE SALINGER

SALO....SALO REPUBLIC

SALOMA J.S. F2844

SALOMA JS I.I.I. F2843

SALVADORI M. F2275

SAMBURU....SAMBURU TRIBE OF EAST AFRICA

SAMP....SAMPLE SURVEY

N19
INTERNATIONAL LABOUR OFFICE,EMPLOYMENT, UNEMPLOYMENT AND LABOUR FORCE STATISTICS (PAMPHLET). EUR+WWI STRATA AGRI INDUS NAT/G PROB/SOLV PAY AGE SEX...SAMP NAT/COMP METH 20 ILO. PAGE 65 F1278
WORKER LABOR STAT ECO/DEV

N19
US CHAMBER OF COMMERCE,THE SIGNIFICANCE OF CONCENTRATION RATIOS (PAMPHLET). USA+45 FINAN INDUS ADMIN...METH/CNCPT SAMP CHARTS 20. PAGE 134 F2647
MARKET PREDICT LG/CO CONTROL

B39
ROBBINS L.,ECONOMIC CAUSES OF WAR. WOR-45 ECO/DEV ECO/UNDEV INT/ORG NAT/G TEC/DEV DIPLOM DOMIN COLONIAL ATTIT DRIVE PWR WEALTH...POLICY CONCPT OBS SAMP TREND CON/ANAL GEN/LAWS MARX/KARL 20. PAGE 112 F2203
COERCE ECO/TAC WAR

B53
PURCELL T.V.,THE WORKER SPEAKS HIS MIND ON COMPANY AND UNION. WORKER ADJUD LEAD RACE/REL ATTIT DRIVE MARXISM...MGT CLASSIF STAT OBS INT SAMP BIBLIOG. PAGE 108 F2131
LABOR PARTIC INGP/REL HAPPINESS

B56
YUAN TUNG-LI,ECONOMIC AND SOCIAL DEVELOPMENT OF MODERN CHINA: A BIBLIOGRAPHIC GUIDE. COM/IND FINAN FAM LABOR SECT CRIME INCOME...STAT SAMP CON/ANAL. PAGE 150 F2954
BIBLIOG ASIA ECO/UNDEV SOC

S56
TANNENBAUM A.S.,"CONTROL OF STRUCTURE AND UNION FUNCTIONS." PARTIC GP/REL INGP/REL CONSEN ATTIT PWR ...QU SAMP. PAGE 128 F2529
LABOR STRUCT CONTROL LEAD

B59
BROMWICH L.,UNION CONSTITUTIONS. CONSTN EX/STRUC PRESS ADJUD CONTROL CHOOSE REPRESENT PWR SAMP. PAGE 19 F0361
LABOR ROUTINE INGP/REL RACE/REL

S59
SHEPPARD H.L.,"THE POLITICAL ATTITUDES AND PREFERENCES OF UNION MEMBERS: THE CASE OF THE DETROIT AUTO WORKERS." LOBBY CHOOSE ROLE...CLASSIF QU SAMP TREND. PAGE 120 F2376
LABOR ATTIT WORKER

S60
FORM W.H.,"ORGANIZED LABOR'S IMAGE OF COMMUNITY POWER STRUCTURE." LABOR LG/CO CONTROL LEAD REPRESENT...DECISION METH/CNCPT INT QU SAMP. PAGE 42 F0829
NEIGH PARTIC PWR GP/REL

B61
LENSKI G.,THE RELIGIOUS FACTOR: A SOCIOLOGICAL STUDY OF RELIGION'S IMPACT ON POLITICS, ECONOMICS, AND FAMILY LIFE. FAM PROF/ORG EDU/PROP ROLE CATHISM ...INT SAMP MUNICH. PAGE 78 F1524
SECT GP/REL

B63
BAUER R.A.,AMERICAN BUSINESS AND PUBLIC POLICY: THE POLITICS OF FOREIGN TRADE. USA+45 COM/IND LG/CO NAT/G PROF/ORG SML/CO VOL/ASSN LEGIS TOP/EX ECO/TAC EDU/PROP CHOOSE HEALTH PWR WEALTH...CONCPT METH/CNCPT OBS INT QU SAMP FOR/TRADE TRUE/GP VAL/FREE HI. PAGE 11 F0217
ECO/DEV ATTIT

B63
RUMMEL J.F.,RESEARCH METHODOLOGY IN BUSINESS. COMPUTER CREATE PROB/SOLV...CONT/OBS REC/INT QU/SEMANT SYS/QU SAMP CHARTS METH/COMP T 20. PAGE 115 F2260
OP/RES METH/CNCPT METH STAT

B64
FRIEDEN B.J.,THE FUTURE OF OLD NEIGHBORHOODS: REBUILDING FOR A CHANGING POPULATION. CONSTRUC LOC/G NAT/G ACT/RES ECO/TAC REGION ATTIT...INT SAMP MUNICH 20 NEWYORK/C LOS/ANG HARTFORD URBAN/RNWL. PAGE 44 F0855
NEIGH PROB/SOLV PLAN BUDGET

B64
JUSTER F.T.,ANTICIPATIONS AND PURCHASES; AN ANALYSIS OF CONSUMER BEHAVIOR. PROB/SOLV RISK COST PRODUC DRIVE...STAT STYLE SAMP CON/ANAL CHARTS HYPO/EXP GAME SIMUL. PAGE 68 F1345
PROBABIL DECISION PREDICT DEMAND

B65
DERBER M.,PLANT UNION-MANAGEMENT RELATIONS: FROM PRACTICE TO THEORY. PROC/MFG NEIGH PROB/SOLV ORD/FREE...DECISION MGT OBS QU SAMP. PAGE 32 F0621
LG/CO LABOR GP/REL ATTIT

B65
GREER S.,URBAN RENEWAL AND AMERICAN CITIES: THE DILEMMA OF DEMOCRATIC INTERVENTION. USA+45 R+D LOC/G VOL/ASSN ACT/RES BUDGET ADMIN GOV/REL...SOC INT SAMP MUNICH 20 BOSTON CHICAGO LOS/ANG MIAMI URBAN/RNWL. PAGE 51 F0992
PROB/SOLV PLAN NAT/G

B65
HERRICK B.H.,URBAN MIGRATION AND ECONOMIC DEVELOPMENT IN CHILE. CHILE AGRI INDUS LABOR NAT/G CENTRAL PRODUC...STAT SAMP CHARTS BIBLIOG/A MUNICH 20 MIGRATION. PAGE 59 F1156
HABITAT GEOG ECO/UNDEV

B67
EVANS R.H.,COEXISTENCE: COMMUNISM AND ITS PRACTICE IN BOLOGNA, 1945-1965. ITALY CAP/ISM ADMIN CHOOSE
MARXISM CULTURE

PEACE ORD/FREE...SOC STAT DEEP/INT SAMP CHARTS BIBLIOG MUNICH 20. PAGE 39 F0756 — POL/PAR

S67
GRUN C.,"DEUX ETUDES ALLEMANDES SUR LES PREJUGES NATIONAUX ET LES MOYENS DE LES COMBATTRE." FRANCE GERMANY DIST/IND PROB/SOLV GP/REL AGE/Y RIGID/FLEX ...PSY STAT INT SAMP. PAGE 52 F1010 — ATTIT REGION DISCRIM STERTYP

SAMP/SIZ....SIZES AND TECHNIQUES OF SAMPLING

N
JOHNSON R.B.,FINANCING A SUBURBAN CITY. USA+45 TAX COST...SAMP/SIZ MUNICH 20 COL. PAGE 68 F1331 — FINAN PAY PROB/SOLV

B47
LEVER E.A.,ADVERTISING AND ECONOMIC THEORY. FINAN ECO/TAC DEMAND EFFICIENCY ATTIT...MGT PSY SAMP/SIZ CHARTS 20. PAGE 79 F1539 — EDU/PROP MARKET COM/IND ECO/DEV

S58
THOMAS D.S.,"AGE AND ECONOMIC DIFFERENTIALS IN INTERSTATE MIGRATION." SEX...GEOG SAMP/SIZ TREND CON/ANAL CHARTS BIBLIOG. PAGE 130 F2560 — AGE WEALTH HABITAT CENSUS

B64
PRESTHUS R.,MEN AT THE TOP; A STUDY IN COMMUNITY POWER. USA+45 STRUCT ACT/RES REPRESENT CONSEN ALL/VALS ORD/FREE...SAMP/SIZ 20. PAGE 108 F2116 — PLURISM LG/CO PWR ADMIN

B67
GUTKIND E.A.,URBAN DEVELOPMENT IN SOUTHERN EUROPE* SPAIN AND PORTUGAL. CHRIST-17C EUR+WWI MOD/EUR PORTUGAL SPAIN CULTURE AGRI...SOC SAMP/SIZ BIBLIOG MUNICH. PAGE 52 F1015 — TEC/DEV ECO/DEV

L67
ZEIDBERG L.D.,"THE NASHVILLE AIR POLLUTION STUDY" (PARTS V-VII)" USA+45 PLAN AGE HEALTH...GEOG STAT CENSUS SAMP/SIZ CHARTS BIBLIOG MUNICH. PAGE 150 F2962 — DEATH HABITAT AIR BIO/SOC

SAMPLE....SEE SAMP

SAMPLE AND SAMPLING....SEE UNIVERSES AND SAMPLING INDEX, P. XIV

SAMUELSN/P....PAUL SAMUELSON

B48
HICKS J.R.,VALUE AND CAPITAL. FINAN PRICE EQUILIB INCOME PRODUC WEALTH...TIME/SEQ 20 MARSHALL/A PARETO/V SAMUELSN/P. PAGE 59 F1165 — ECOMETRIC MATH DEMAND PROB/SOLV

SAMUELSON P.A. F2276

SAN/FRAN....SAN FRANCISCO

B60
GARBARINO J.W.,HEALTH PLANS AND COLLECTIVE BARGAINING. USA+45 LABOR BARGAIN GP/REL WEALTH ...WELF/ST CHARTS 20 DEPT/HEW SAN/FRAN. PAGE 46 F0900 — HEAL PLAN FINAN SERV/IND

B65
BOLLENS J.C.,THE METROPOLIS: ITS PEOPLE, POLITICS, AND ECONOMIC LIFE. USA+45 PLAN PROB/SOLV PERS/REL PWR...DECISION GEOG CENSUS TREND CON/ANAL MUNICH 20 NEWYORK/C LOS/ANG SAN/FRAN CHICAGO PHILADELPH. PAGE 16 F0309 — HABITAT SOC LOC/G

B67
LITTLE AD, INC.,COMMUNITY RENEWAL PROGRAMMING. CULTURE LOC/G ACT/RES TASK COST ATTIT...SOC/WK MODAL STAT STAND/INT CHARTS 20 SAN/FRAN. PAGE 81 F1585 — STRATA NEIGH PLAN CREATE

SAN/MARINO....SAN MARINO

SAN/MARTIN....JOSE DE SAN MARTIN

B61
ESTEVEZ A.,ASPECTOS ECONOMICO-FINANCIEROS DE LA CAMPANA SANMARITANA. L/A+17C SPAIN FINAN COLONIAL LEAD ROLE ORD/FREE WEALTH 19 SOUTH/AMER SAN/MARTIN. PAGE 38 F0748 — ECO/UNDEV REV BUDGET NAT/G

SAN/QUENTN....SAN QUENTIN PRISON

SANCTION....SANCTION OF LAW AND SEMI-LEGAL PRIVATE ASSOCIATIONS AND SOCIAL GROUPS

B12
FOUAD M.,LE REGIME DE LA PRESSE EN EGYPTE: THESE POUR LE DOCTORAT. UAR LICENSE EDU/PROP ADMIN SANCTION CRIME SUPEGO PWR...ART/METH JURID 19/20. PAGE 43 F0832 — ORD/FREE LEGIS CONTROL PRESS

N19
ADMINISTRATIVE STAFF COLLEGE,THE ACCOUNTABILITY OF GOVERNMENT DEPARTMENTS (PAMPHLET) (REV. ED.). UK CONSTN FINAN NAT/G CONSULT ADMIN INGP/REL CONSEN PRIVIL 20 PARLIAMENT. PAGE 2 F0043 — PARL/PROC ELITES SANCTION PROB/SOLV

C43
BENTHAM J.,"THE RATIONALE OF REWARD" IN J. BOWRING, ED., THE WORKS OF JEREMY BENTHAM (VOL. 2)" LAW WORKER CREATE INSPECT PAY ROUTINE HAPPINESS PRODUC SUPEGO WEALTH METH/CNCPT. PAGE 13 F0254 — SANCTION ECO/TAC INCOME PWR

B47
SLICHTER S.H.,THE CHALLENGE OF INDUSTRIAL RELATIONS: TRADE UNIONS, MANAGEMENT AND THE PUBLIC INTEREST. PLAN ECO/TAC ADJUD CONTROL LEAD SANCTION GP/REL INGP/REL INCOME. PAGE 123 F2421 — LABOR MGT CLIENT POLICY

B54
TAFT P.,THE STRUCTURE AND GOVERNMENT OF LABOR UNIONS. SANCTION INGP/REL ORD/FREE PWR MARXISM ...MAJORIT STAT TREND. PAGE 128 F2524 — LABOR ADJUD WORKER FINAN

B55
BERNSTEIN M.H.,REGULATING BUSINESS BY INDEPENDENT COMMISSION. USA+45 USA-45 LG/CO CHIEF LEGIS PROB/SOLV ADJUD SANCTION GP/REL ATTIT...TIME/SEQ 19/20 MONOPOLY PRESIDENT CONGRESS. PAGE 14 F0268 — DELIB/GP CONTROL CONSULT

B58
CHAMBERLIN E.H.,LABOR UNIONS AND PUBLIC POLICY. PLAN BARGAIN SANCTION INGP/REL JURID. PAGE 23 F0444 — LABOR WEALTH PWR NAT/G

B58
SEIDMAN J.I.,DEMOCRACY IN THE LABOR MOVEMENT (PAMPHLET). LAW CONSTN STRUCT DELIB/GP WORKER ADJUD PARTIC SANCTION POLICY. PAGE 119 F2345 — LABOR INGP/REL PWR MAJORIT

B58
TAFT P.,CORRUPTION AND RACKETEERING IN THE LABOR MOVEMENT (PAMPHLET). ADMIN SANCTION CENTRAL ROLE WEALTH...POLICY CLASSIF. PAGE 128 F2525 — LABOR INGP/REL GP/REL CRIME

B61
QURESHI S.,INCENTIVES IN AMERICAN EMPLOYMENT (THESIS, UNIVERSITY OF PENNSYLVANIA). DELIB/GP TOP/EX BUDGET ROUTINE SANCTION COST TECHRACY MGT. PAGE 108 F2134 — SERV/IND ADMIN PAY EX/STRUC

N62
US SENATE COMM ON JUDICIARY,LEGISLATION TO STRENGTHEN PENALTIES UNDER THE ANTITRUST LAWS (PAMPHLET). USA+45 LG/CO CONFER CONTROL SANCTION ORD/FREE 20 SENATE MONOPOLY. PAGE 139 F2748 — LEAD ADJUD INDUS ECO/TAC

B64
SEGAL R.,SANCTIONS AGAINST SOUTH AFRICA. AFR SOUTH/AFR NAT/G INT/TRADE RACE/REL PEACE PWR ...INT/LAW ANTHOL 20 UN. PAGE 119 F2342 — SANCTION DISCRIM ECO/TAC POLICY

B64
SULTAN P.E.,THE DISENCHANTED UNIONIST. NAT/G ADJUD CONTROL SANCTION RACE/REL ANOMIE ATTIT ROLE ...METH/CNCPT INT. PAGE 127 F2512 — LABOR INGP/REL CHARTS MAJORIT

B64
US DEPT LABOR OFF SOLICITOR,LEGISLATIVE HISTORY OF THE LABOR-MANAGEMENT AND DISCLOSURE ACT OF 1959. DELIB/GP WORKER ADMIN LOBBY PARL/PROC SANCTION CHOOSE GOV/REL 20 CONGRESS PRESIDENT. PAGE 136 F2677 — LABOR LEGIS DEBATE POLICY

S64
N,"QUASI-LEGISLATIVE ARBITRATION AGREEMENTS." LAW LG/CO ECO/TAC SANCTION ATTIT POLICY. PAGE 96 F1885 — ADJUD ADJUST LABOR GP/REL

B65
FLEMING R.W.,THE LABOR ARBITRATION PROCESS. USA+45 LAW BARGAIN ADJUD ROUTINE SANCTION COST...PREDICT CHARTS TIME 20. PAGE 41 F0809 — GP/REL LABOR CONSULT DELIB/GP

B66
SOVERN M.I.,LEGAL RESTRAINTS ON RACIAL DISCRIMINATION IN EMPLOYMENT. USA+45 LAW INDUS LG/CO SML/CO DELIB/GP LEGIS SANCTION 20 NLRB PRESIDENT NEGRO CIV/RIGHTS RAILROAD. PAGE 124 F2446 — DISCRIM RACE/REL WORKER JURID

B67
DUN J.L.,THE ESSENCE OF CHINESE CIVILIZATION. ASIA FAM NAT/G TEC/DEV ADMIN SANCTION WAR HABITAT ...ANTHOL WORSHIP. PAGE 35 F0676 — CULTURE SOCIETY

B67
PETRO S.,THE KINGSPORT STRIKE. USA+45 PROC/MFG NAT/G JUDGE PRESS PARTIC PERS/REL...OLD/LIB OBS INT 20 NLRB. PAGE 105 F2074 — LABOR COERCE SANCTION ALL/VALS

B67
SCHAEFER W.V.,THE SUSPECT AND SOCIETY: CRIMINAL PROCEDURE AND CONVERGING CONSTITUTIONAL DOCTRINES. USA+45 TEC/DEV LOBBY ROUTINE SANCTION...INT 20. PAGE 116 F2288 — CRIME FORCES CONSTN JURID

B67
TUMIN M.M.,SOCIAL STRATIFICATION; THE FORMS AND FUNCTIONS OF INEQUALITY. SENIOR SANCTION WEALTH ...SOC CLASSIF METH 20. PAGE 131 F2592 — STRATA DISCRIM CONCPT SOCIETY

L67
AFFELDT R.J.,"THE INDEPENDENT LABOR UNION AND THE GOOD LIFE." USA+45 ADJUD CONTROL SANCTION GP/REL ORD/FREE JURID. PAGE 3 F0045 — LABOR CT/SYS PWR SOVEREIGN

L67
DOERFER G.L.,"THE LIMITS ON TRADE SECRET LAW IMPOSED BY FEDERAL PATENT & ANTITRUST SUPREMACY." USA+45 LAW R+D CAP/ISM LICENSE CONTROL SANCTION ORD/FREE. PAGE 33 F0651 — JURID GOV/REL POLICY LEGIT

L67
JACOBY S.B.,"THE 89TH CONGRESS AND GOVERNMENT LITIGATION." USA+45 ADMIN COST...JURID 20 CONGRESS. PAGE 66 F1302 — LAW NAT/G ADJUD SANCTION

L67
MACDONALD R.S.J.,"THE RESORT TO ECONOMIC COERCION BY INTERNATIONAL POLITICAL ORGANIZATIONS." CUBA ETHIOPIA RHODESIA SOUTH/AFR NAT/G FOR/AID INT/TRADE DOMIN CONTROL SANCTION...DECISION LEAGUE/NAT UN OAS 20. PAGE 83 F1625 — INT/ORG COERCE ECO/TAC DIPLOM

L67
MANNE H.G.,"OUR TWO CORPORATION SYSTEMS* LAW AND ECONOMICS." LAW CONTROL SANCTION GP/REL...JURID 20. PAGE 85 F1657 — INDUS ELITES CAP/ISM ADMIN

L67
SEABERG G.P.,"THE DRUG ABUSE PROBLEMS AND SOME PROPOSALS." UK USA+45 MARKET SANCTION CRIME ...POLICY NEW/IDEA. PAGE 119 F2339 — BIO/SOC LAW ADJUD PROB/SOLV

L67
STRUVE G.M.,"THE LESS-RESTRICTIVE-ALTERNATIVE PRINCIPLE AND ECONOMIC DUE PROCESS." USA+45 ECO/DEV LABOR NAT/G CONSULT DELIB/GP OP/RES PLAN WEALTH. PAGE 127 F2505 — JURID JUDGE SANCTION CAP/ISM

S67
JANSSEN P.,"NEA: THE RELUCTANT DRAGON." NAT/G EXEC LOBBY PARTIC SANCTION RACE/REL ROLE TREND. PAGE 66 F1305 — EDU/PROP PROF/ORG MGT POLICY

C83
BURKE E.,"RESOLUTIONS FOR CONCILIATION WITH AMERICA" (1775), IN E. BURKE, COLLECTED WORKS, VOL. 2." UK USA-45 FORCES INT/TRADE TARIFFS TAX SANCTION PEACE...POLICY 18 PRE/US/AM. PAGE 20 F0387 — COLONIAL WAR SOVEREIGN ECO/TAC

SANDEE J. F2277

SANDMEYER R.L. F2278

SANFORD S.A. F0682

SANNWALD R.E. F2279

SANTAYAN/G....GEORGE SANTAYANA

SANTHANAM K. F2280

SAO/PAULO....SAO PAULO, BRAZIL

B60
FERNANDES F.,MUDANCAS SOCIAIS NO BRASIL. BRAZIL L/A+17C SOCIETY AGRI PROVS LEAD GP/REL RACE/REL ORD/FREE...SOC SOC/INTEG 20 SAO/PAULO. PAGE 40 F0786 — ECO/UNDEV STRATA INDUS

SAPARINA Y. F2281

SAPIR H.M. F2282

SAPIR/EDW....EDWARD SAPIR

SARAWAK....SARAWAK, MALAYSIA

SARTRE/J....JEAN-PAUL SARTRE

SARVODAYA....SARVODAYA - GANDHIAN SOCIALIST POLITICAL IDEAL OF UNIVERSAL MATERIAL AND SPIRITUAL WELFARE; SEE ALSO GANDHI/M

SASKATCH....SASKATCHEWAN, CANADA

B50
LIPSET S.M.,AGRARIAN SOCIALISM. CANADA POL/PAR OP/RES ECO/TAC ADMIN ATTIT...TIME/SEQ NAT/COMP SOC/EXP 20 SASKATCH. PAGE 80 F1576 — SOCISM AGRI METH/COMP STRUCT

SASKATCHEWAN, CANADA...SEE SASKATCH

SASTRI K.V.S. F2283

SATELLITE....SPACE SATELLITES

SATISFACTION....SEE HAPPINESS

SAUDI/ARAB....SAUDI ARABIA; SEE ALSO ISLAM

S61
VALLET R.,"IRAN: KEY TO THE MIDDLE EAST." COM IRAQ ISLAM KUWAIT LEBANON SAUDI/ARAB TURKEY ELITES SOCIETY INDUS PROC/MFG POL/PAR TOP/EX PLAN BAL/PWR DIPLOM ECO/TAC ALL/VALS...TREND FOR/TRADE CENTO 20. PAGE 140 F2760 — NAT/G ECO/UNDEV IRAN

SAUER W.L. F0828,F0829

SAVILLE J. F1784

SAX/JOSEPH....JOSEPH SAX

SAY/EMIL....EMIL SAY

B58
MUSGRAVE R.A.,CLASSICS IN THE THEORY OF PUBLIC FINANCE. UNIV MARKET LG/CO NAT/G CAP/ISM PRICE OPTIMAL...IDEA/COMP ANTHOL 19/20 SAY/EMIL EDGEWORTH LINDAHL/E RITSCHL/H. PAGE 95 F1870 — TAX FINAN ECO/TAC GP/REL

SAYLES L.R. F2284

SBA....SMALL BUSINESS ADMINISTRATION

SCALAPINO R.A. F2285

SCALES....SEE TESTS AND SCALES INDEX, P. XIV

SCAMMEL W.M. F2286

SCANDINAV....SCANDINAVIAN COUNTRIES

SCANLON/H....HUGH SCANLON

SCHACHTER G. F2287

SCHAEFER W.V. F2288

SCHAFFER M. F1510

SCHALLER H.G. F2289

SCHATTSCHNEIDER E.E. F2290

SCHECHTER A. F2291

SCHECTER J. F2292

SCHEEHAN D. F2293

SCHELLING T.C. F2294,F2295

SCHER S. F2296

SCHEURER/K....AUGUSTE SCHEURER-KESTNER

SCHILLING W.R. F2297

SCHINDLR/P....PAULINE SCHINDLER

SCHIZO....SCHIZOPHRENIA

SCHLEIFFER H. F2299

SCHMANDT H.J. F0309

SCHMIDT W.E. F0230

SCHMITT H.A. F2300

SCHMITT H.D. F2301

SCHMITTER P.C. F1020

SCHMOLLER G. F2302

SCHNAPPER B. F2303

SCHNEIDER C.W. F2304

SCHNEIDER E. F2305,F2306,F2307

SCHNEIDER E.V. F2308

SCHNORE L.F. F1115

SCHOECK H. F2309

SCHOFLING J.A. F2310

SCHOLASTIC....SCHOLASTICISM (MEDIEVAL)

SCHON D.A. F2311

SCHOOL....SCHOOLS, EXCEPT UNIVERSITIES

N
TEXTBOOKS IN PRINT. WOR+45 WOR-45 LAW DIPLOM ALL/VALS ALL/IDEOS...SOC T 19/20. PAGE 1 F0003
BIBLIOG SCHOOL KNOWL

N
US LIBRARY OF CONGRESS,SOUTHERN ASIA ACCESSIONS LIST. BURMA CEYLON INDIA NEPAL PAKISTAN S/ASIA THAILAND AGRI INDUS SCHOOL WORKER...ART/METH GEOG HEAL PHIL/SCI LING 20. PAGE 137 F2710
BIBLIOG/A SOCIETY CULTURE ECO/UNDEV

LCA
GODFREY E.M.,"THE ECONOMICS OF AN AFRICAN UNIVERSITY." AFR SCHOOL PRICE EFFICIENCY INCOME WEALTH...ECOMETRIC CHARTS 20. PAGE 48 F0930
ACADEM ECO/TAC COST EDU/PROP

N19
FIKS M.,PUBLIC ADMINISTRATION IN ISRAEL (PAMPHLET). ISRAEL SCHOOL EX/STRUC BUDGET PAY INGP/REL ...DECISION 20 CIVIL/SERV. PAGE 41 F0792
EDU/PROP NAT/G ADMIN WORKER

N19
MUSHKIN S.J.,LOCAL SCHOOL EXPENDITURES: 1970 PROJECTIONS (PAMPHLET). FUT USA+45 CONSTRUC FINAN PROVS EDU/PROP COST...GEOG CENSUS PREDICT CHARTS SIMUL 20. PAGE 95 F1871
LOC/G SCHOOL BUDGET

B28
TRUE A.C.,A HISTORY OF AGRICULTURAL EXTENSION WORK IN THE UNITED STATES, 1785-1923. USA-45 LAW SCHOOL WAR ADJUST...CHARTS BIBLIOG 18/20 SMITH/LEVR COUNTY/AGT. PAGE 131 F2591
EDU/PROP AGRI VOL/ASSN PLAN

B45
DAVIS J.,AFRICA ADVANCING. AFR CONGO/BRAZ LIBERIA NIGER INT/ORG SCHOOL DIPLOM GIVE KNOWL SKILL 20. PAGE 30 F0590
SECT COLONIAL AGRI ECO/UNDEV

B54
BATTEN T.R.,PROBLEMS OF AFRICAN DEVELOPMENT (2ND ED.). AFR LAW SOCIETY SCHOOL ECO/TAC TAX...GEOG HEAL SOC 20. PAGE 11 F0211
ECO/UNDEV AGRI LOC/G PROB/SOLV

B57
DRUCKER P.F.,AMERICA'S NEXT TWENTY YEARS. USA+45 DIST/IND ACADEM SCHOOL DIPLOM ECO/TAC AUTOMAT HABITAT HEALTH...SOC/WK TREND MUNICH 20 URBAN/RNWL PUB/TRANS. PAGE 34 F0667
WORKER FOR/AID CENSUS GEOG

B60
SHANNON D.A.,THE GREAT DEPRESSION. USA-45 FINAN LG/CO SCHOOL SML/CO DELIB/GP RECEIVE REV EATING INCOME...ANTHOL MUNICH 20 ROOSEVLT/F CONGRESS. PAGE 120 F2365
WEALTH NAT/G AGRI INDUS

B61
DEWITT N.,EDUCATION AND PROFESSIONAL EMPLOYMENT IN THE USSR. USSR PROF/ORG WORKER PLAN ADMIN UTIL AGE/C AGE/Y MARXISM...STAT CHARTS 20. PAGE 32 F0629
EDU/PROP ACADEM SCHOOL INTELL

B62
DENISON E.F.,THE SOURCES OF ECONOMIC GROWTH IN THE UNITED STATES AND THE ALTERNATIVES BEFORE US. AGRI INDUS SCHOOL TEC/DEV CAP/ISM ECO/TAC PRICE COST WEALTH...STAT TREND CHARTS 20. PAGE 32 F0620
ECO/DEV WORKER PRODUC

B62
HIRSCHFIELD R.S.,THE CONSTITUTION AND THE COURT. AFR SCHOOL WAR RACE/REL EQUILIB ORD/FREE...POLICY MAJORIT DECISION JURID 18/20 PRESIDENT CIVIL/LIB SUPREME/CT CONGRESS. PAGE 60 F1175
ADJUD PWR CONSTN LAW

B62
VAIZEY J.,THE ECONOMICS OF EDUCATION. INTELL ECO/TAC PAY COST PRODUC 20. PAGE 140 F2758
ECO/DEV SCHOOL ACADEM PROFIT

S62
ADISESHIAN M.,"EDUCATION AND DEVELOPMENT." FUT WOR+45 SOCIETY ACT/RES INT/TRADE EDU/PROP KNOWL SKILL WEALTH...POLICY CONCPT CONT/OBS CENSUS CHARTS TOT/POP VAL/FREE APPLIC FAO FOR/TRADE 20. PAGE 2 F0041
SCHOOL ECO/UNDEV

B63
BRITISH AID. UK AGRI DIST/IND INDUS SCHOOL TEC/DEV INT/TRADE COLONIAL DEMAND...TREND CHARTS 20. PAGE 1 F0018
FOR/AID ECO/UNDEV NAT/G FINAN

B63
INTERAMERICAN ECO AND SOC COUN,THE ALLIANCE FOR PROGRESS: ITS FIRST YEAR: 1961-1962. AGRI SCHOOL PLAN TEC/DEV INT/TRADE TAX GIVE ADMIN WEALTH...SOC 20 ALL/PROG SOUTH/AMER. PAGE 64 F1267
INT/ORG PROB/SOLV ECO/TAC L/A+17C

B63
MANGER W.,THE ALLIANCE FOR PROGRESS: A CRITICAL APPRAISAL. FUT L/A+17C USA+45 CULTURE ECO/UNDEV ACADEM NAT/G SCHOOL PLAN FOR/AID...POLICY OAS ALL/PROG. PAGE 84 F1651
DIPLOM INT/ORG ECO/TAC REGION

B63
MINER J.,SOCIAL AND ECONOMIC FACTORS IN SPENDING FOR PUBLIC EDUCATION. USA+45 FINAN SCHOOL OPTIMAL ...POLICY DECISION REGRESS PREDICT CHARTS SIMUL 20. PAGE 92 F1801
EDU/PROP NAT/G COST ACT/RES

B63
WAGLEY C.,INTRODUCTION TO BRAZIL. BRAZIL L/A+17C FAM KIN SCHOOL SECT ATTIT WEALTH...GEOG SOC. PAGE 142 F2799
ECO/UNDEV ELITES HABITAT STRATA

L63
RIDAH A.,"LE NEO-DESTOUR DEPUIS L'INDEPENDANCE." FUT ISLAM WOR+45 ECO/UNDEV INT/ORG SCHOOL DELIB/GP TOP/EX ACT/RES EDU/PROP LEGIT ATTIT ALL/VALS 20 TUNIS. PAGE 111 F2189
NAT/G CONSTN

B64
THE SPECIAL COMMONWEALTH AFRICAN ASSISTANCE PLAN. AFR CANADA INDIA NIGERIA UK FINAN SCHOOL...CHARTS 20 COMMONWLTH. PAGE 1 F0019
ECO/UNDEV TREND FOR/AID ADMIN

B64
HARBISON F.H.,EDUCATION, MANPOWER, AND ECONOMIC GROWTH. WOR+45 ECO/DEV ECO/UNDEV ACADEM LABOR SCHOOL WORKER UTIL...IDEA/COMP NAT/COMP. PAGE 55 F1075
PLAN TEC/DEV EDU/PROP SKILL

B64
LUTHULI A.,AFRICA'S FREEDOM. KIN LABOR POL/PAR SCHOOL DIPLOM NEUTRAL REGION REV NAT/LISM PWR WEALTH SOCISM SOC/INTEG 20. PAGE 82 F1608
AFR ECO/UNDEV COLONIAL

B64
MELADY T.,FACES OF AFRICA. AFR FUT ISLAM NAT/G POL/PAR SCHOOL DELIB/GP PLAN ECO/TAC EDU/PROP ATTIT ALL/VALS...CHARTS TOT/POP TERR/GP VAL/FREE 20. PAGE 89 F1752
ECO/UNDEV TREND NAT/LISM

B64
SEERS D.,CUBA: THE ECONOMIC AND SOCIAL REVOLUTION. L/A+17C USSR YUGOSLAVIA STRATA AGRI INDUS SCHOOL DELIB/GP PLAN ECO/TAC DOMIN EDU/PROP ATTIT RIGID/FLEX ALL/VALS...STAT OBS TIME/SEQ WORK VAL/FREE 20. PAGE 119 F2341
ACT/RES COERCE CUBA REV

B64
SULLIVAN G.,THE STORY OF THE PEACE CORPS. USA+45 WOR+45 INTELL FACE/GP NAT/G SCHOOL VOL/ASSN CONSULT EX/STRUC PLAN EDU/PROP ADMIN ATTIT DRIVE ALL/VALS ...POLICY HEAL SOC CONCPT INT QU BIOG TREND SOC/EXP WORK. PAGE 127 F2511
INT/ORG ECO/UNDEV FOR/AID PEACE

B65
ANDERSON C.A.,EDUCATION AND ECONOMIC DEVELOPMENT. INDUS R+D SCHOOL TEC/DEV ECO/TAC EDU/PROP AGE HEREDITY PERCEPT SKILL 20. PAGE 5 F0092
ANTHOL ECO/DEV ECO/UNDEV WORKER

B65
COLBERG M.R.,HUMAN CAPITAL IN SOUTHERN DEVELOPMENT. USA+45 AGRI ACADEM LABOR SCHOOL WORKER CAP/ISM DISCRIM. PAGE 26 F0498
PROVS RACE/REL GP/REL

B65
COOMBS P.H.,EDUCATION AND FOREIGN AID. AFR USA+45 DIPLOM EFFICIENCY KNOWL ORD/FREE...ANTHOL 20 AID. PAGE 27 F0532
EDU/PROP FOR/AID SCHOOL ECO/UNDEV

B65
HAPGOOD D.,AFRICA: FROM INDEPENDENCE TO TOMARROW. AFR GUINEA SENEGAL CULTURE ELITES ECO/UNDEV AGRI SCHOOL FOR/AID COLONIAL MARXISM...TREND 20. PAGE 55 F1070
ECO/TAC SOCIETY NAT/G

B65
OECD,MEDITERRANEAN REGIONAL PROJECT: TURKEY; EDUCATION AND DEVELOPMENT. FUT TURKEY SOCIETY STRATA FINAN NAT/G PROF/ORG PLAN PROB/SOLV ADMIN COST...STAT CHARTS 20 OECD. PAGE 100 F1969
EDU/PROP ACADEM SCHOOL ECO/UNDEV

B65
OECD,THE MEDITERRANEAN REGIONAL PROJECT: PORTUGAL; EDUCATION AND DEVELOPMENT. PORTUGAL SOCIETY STRATA FINAN PROF/ORG WORKER PLAN PROB/SOLV ADMIN...POLICY STAT CHARTS METH 20 OECD. PAGE 100 F1970
EDU/PROP SCHOOL ACADEM ECO/UNDEV

B65
OECD,THE MEDITERRANEAN REGIONAL PROJECT: ITALY; EDUCATION AND DEVELOPMENT. ITALY SOCIETY STRATA FINAN NAT/G PROF/ORG WORKER PLAN PROB/SOLV ADMIN ...STAT CHARTS METH 20 OECD. PAGE 100 F1971
SCHOOL EDU/PROP ECO/UNDEV ACADEM

B65
OECD,THE MEDITERRANEAN REGIONAL PROJECT: GREECE; EDUCATION AND DEVELOPMENT. FUT GREECE SOCIETY AGRI FINAN NAT/G PROF/ORG WORKER PLAN PROB/SOLV ADMIN DEMAND ATTIT 20 OECD. PAGE 100 F1972
EDU/PROP SCHOOL ACADEM ECO/UNDEV

B65
OECD,THE MEDITERRANEAN REGIONAL PROJECT: SPAIN; EDUCATION AND DEVELOPMENT. FUT SPAIN STRATA FINAN NAT/G WORKER PLAN PROB/SOLV ADMIN COST...POLICY STAT CHARTS 20 OECD. PAGE 100 F1973
ECO/UNDEV EDU/PROP ACADEM SCHOOL

B65
ORG FOR ECO COOP AND DEVEL,THE MEDITERRANEAN REGIONAL PROJECT: AN EXPERIMENT IN PLANNING BY SIX COUNTRIES. FUT GREECE SPAIN TURKEY YUGOSLAVIA SOCIETY FINAN NAT/G PROF/ORG EDU/PROP ADMIN REGION COST...POLICY STAT CHARTS 20 OECD. PAGE 102 F1995 — PLAN ECO/UNDEV ACADEM SCHOOL

B65
ORG FOR ECO COOP AND DEVEL,THE MEDITERRANEAN REGIONAL PROJECT: YUGOSLAVIA; EDUCATION AND DEVELOPMENT. YUGOSLAVIA SOCIETY FINAN PROF/ORG PLAN ADMIN COST DEMAND MARXISM...STAT TREND CHARTS METH 20 OECD. PAGE 102 F1996 — EDU/PROP ACADEM SCHOOL ECO/UNDEV

B65
SHOSTAK A.B.,NEW PERSPECTIVES ON POVERTY. USA+45 SCHOOL WORKER INGP/REL RACE/REL AGE/C AGE/Y ATTIT HEALTH...ANTHOL BIBLIOG 20 JOHNSON/LB POVRTY/WAR. PAGE 121 F2388 — WEALTH NAT/G RECEIVE INCOME

B65
SIMON B.,EDUCATION AND THE LABOR MOVEMENT, 1870-1920. UK SOCIETY STRATA LABOR POL/PAR SCHOOL CONTROL PARTIC SOCISM...BIBLIOG 19/20. PAGE 122 F2406 — EDU/PROP WORKER ADJUST LAW

S65
MALHERBE E.G.,"MANPOWER TRAINING: EDUCATIONAL REQUIREMENTS FOR ECONOMIC EXPANSION." SOUTH/AFR ECO/DEV INDUS EDU/PROP...MGT STAT CHARTS 20. PAGE 84 F1646 — LABOR SKILL SCHOOL ACADEM

S65
SCHROEDER G.,"LABOR PLANNING IN THE USSR." COM USSR ECO/DEV INDUS SCHOOL PRODUC WEALTH...PREDICT TIME/SEQ TREND TIME 20. PAGE 117 F2313 — WORKER PLAN CENSUS

B66
BEN-PORATH Y.,THE ARAB LABOR FORCE IN ISRAEL. ISLAM ISRAEL AGRI INDUS SCHOOL CAP/ISM PAY DEMAND...GEOG REGRESS STAT CHARTS 20 ARABS. PAGE 13 F0245 — WORKER CENSUS GP/REL STRUCT

B66
ECONOMIC RESEARCH SERVICE,RESEARCH DATA ON MINORITY GROUPS: AN ANNOTATED BIBLIOGRAPHY OF ECONOMIC RESEARCH SERVICE REPORTS: 1955-1965 (PAMPHLET). USA+45 STRATA ECO/DEV AGRI SCHOOL WORKER EDU/PROP HEALTH NEW/LIB SOC. PAGE 36 F0697 — BIBLIOG/A DISCRIM WEALTH RACE/REL

B66
MALASSIS L.,ECONOMIC DEVELOPMENT AND THE PROGRAMMING OF RURAL EDUCATION. CONSULT PROB/SOLV LITERACY KNOWL...CHARTS GEN/METH 20. PAGE 84 F1644 — AGRI ECO/UNDEV SCHOOL PLAN

B66
MOSKOW M.H.,TEACHERS AND UNIONS. SCHOOL WORKER ADJUD LOBBY ATTIT ORD/FREE 20. PAGE 94 F1844 — EDU/PROP PROF/ORG LABOR BARGAIN

B66
ROBINSON E.A.,THE ECONOMICS OF EDUCATION. WOR+45 CULTURE ECO/UNDEV FINAN SCHOOL DIPLOM PRICE COST DEMAND...CHARTS METH/COMP 20. PAGE 112 F2216 — EDU/PROP ADJUST CONFER

B67
CHAPIN F.S. JR.,SELECTED REFERENCES ON URBAN PLANNING METHODS AND TECHNIQUES. USA+45 LAW ECO/DEV LOC/G NAT/G SCHOOL CONSULT CREATE PROB/SOLV TEC/DEV ...SOC/WK MUNICH. PAGE 23 F0454 — BIBLIOG NEIGH PLAN

B67
GITTELL M.,PARTICIPANTS AND PARTICIPATION: A STUDY OF SCHOOL POLICY IN NEW YORK. USA+45 EX/STRUC BUDGET PAY ATTIT...POLICY MUNICH 20 NEWYORK/C. PAGE 47 F0926 — SCHOOL DECISION PARTIC ADMIN

B67
THOMAS M.J.,PRESIDENTIAL STATEMENTS ON EDUCATION: EXCERPTS FROM INAUGURAL AND STATE OF THE UNION MESSAGES 1789-1967. USA+45 USA-45 NAT/G BUDGET ...IDEA/COMP 18/20 PRESIDENT. PAGE 130 F2562 — EDU/PROP TOP/EX LEGIS SCHOOL

B67
WEINBERG M.,SCHOOL INTEGRATION: A COMPREHENSIVE CLASSIFIED BIBLIOGRAPHY OF 3,100 REFERENCES. USA+45 LAW NAT/G NEIGH SECT PLAN ROUTINE AGE/C WEALTH SOC/INTEG INDIAN/AM. PAGE 145 F2849 — BIBLIOG SCHOOL DISCRIM RACE/REL

S67
BASOV V.,"THE DEVELOPMENT OF PUBLIC EDUCATION AND THE BUDGET." USSR NAT/G CONTROL REV COST AGE...STAT 20. PAGE 11 F0204 — BUDGET GIVE EDU/PROP SCHOOL

S67
NUSENBAUM A.A.,"ON THE QUESTION OF TENDENCIES IN AMERICAN EDUCATION." USA+45 USSR SOCIETY SCHOOL RATIONAL 20. PAGE 99 F1946 — MARXIST IDEA/COMP GEN/LAWS EDU/PROP

S67
PAULY M.V.,"MIXED PUBLIC AND PRIVATE FINANCING OF EDUCATION." STRATA PAY RECEIVE COST INCOME OPTIMAL METH/COMP. PAGE 104 F2039 — SCHOOL PLAN TAX EFFICIENCY

S67
WASSERMAN M.,"BEYOND TOKENISM: REVERSE INTEGRATION IN ALBANY, GEORGIA." USA+45 PLAN BUDGET EDU/PROP LEAD AGE/C AGE/Y GEORGIA NEGRO. PAGE 144 F2827 — REGION RACE/REL DISCRIM SCHOOL

B99
KROPOTKIN P.,FIELDS, FACTORIES, AND WORKSHOPS. UNIV INTELL ECO/DEV LG/CO SCHOOL SML/CO ECO/TAC PRODUC UTOPIA...NEW/IDEA MUNICH. PAGE 74 F1445 — SOCIETY WORKER AGRI INDUS

SCHROEDER G. F2313

SCHULER E.A. F2314

SCHULMAN S. F0035

SCHULTZ T.W. F2315,F2316,F2317

SCHULTZ W.J. F2318

SCHULZE R.O. F2319

SCHUMCHR/K....KURT SCHUMACHER

SCHUMM S. F2320

SCHUMPETER J.A. F2321,F2322

SCHUMPTR/J....JOSEPH SCHUMPETER

SCHURMANN F. F2323

SCHWARTZ G. F2324

SCHWARTZ H. F2325

SCHWARZ S.M. F0281

SCHWARZWELLER H.K. F2326

SCHWINN....ARNOLD, SCHWINN + COMPANY

SCI/ADVSRY....SCIENCE ADVISORY COMMISSION

B62
DUPRE J.S.,SCIENCE AND THE NATION: POLICY AND POLITICS. USA+45 LAW ACADEM FORCES ADMIN CIVMIL/REL GOV/REL EFFICIENCY PEACE...TREND 20 SCI/ADVSRY. PAGE 35 F0682 — R+D INDUS TEC/DEV NUC/PWR

SCIENCE....SEE PHIL/SCI, CREATE

SCIENCE ADVISORY COMMISSION....SEE SCI/ADVSRY

SCIENTIFIC COUNCIL FOR AFRICA F2327

SCIENTIFIC METHOD....SEE PHIL/SCI

SCITOVSKY T. F2328,F2329,F2330

SCOT/YARD....SCOTLAND YARD - LONDON POLICE HEADQUARTERS AND DETECTIVE BUREAU

SCOTLAND....SCOTLAND

SCOTT A. F0348

SCOTT A.M. F2331

SCOTT D.J.R. F2332

SCOTT J.B. F2333

SCOTT J.C. F2334

SCOTT R. F2335

SCOTT W.D. F2336

SCOTT W.R. F0677

SCOVILLE W.J. F2337

SCREENING AND SELECTION....SEE CHOOSE, SAMP

SCRIPP J. F2338

SDR....SPECIAL DRAWING RIGHTS

SDS....STUDENTS FOR A DEMOCRATIC SOCIETY

SEA....LOCALE OF SUBJECT ACTIVITY IS AQUATIC

N19
US MARITIME ADMINISTRATION,CONTRIBUTION OF FEDERAL AID PROGRAMS TO THE OCEANBORNE FOREIGN TRADE OF THE UNITED STATES: 1959-62 (PAMPHLET). USA+45 SEA FINAN NAT/G BUDGET...POLICY 20. PAGE 138 F2719 — INT/TRADE ECO/TAC DIST/IND GIVE

B24
HOLDSWORTH W.S.,A HISTORY OF ENGLISH LAW; THE COMMON LAW AND ITS RIVALS (VOL. IV). UK SEA AGRI CHIEF ADJUD CONTROL CRIME GOV/REL...INT/LAW JURID NAT/COMP 16/17 PARLIAMENT COMMON/LAW CANON/LAW ENGLSH/LAW. PAGE 61 F1195
LAW LEGIS CT/SYS CONSTN

B48
WHITE C.L.,HUMAN GEOGRAPHY: AN ECOLOGICAL STUDY OF GEOGRAPHY. UNIV SEA CULTURE AGRI EXTR/IND RACE/REL PRODUC...CHARTS HYPO/EXP SIMUL GEN/LAWS T. PAGE 146 F2868
SOC HABITAT GEOG SOCIETY

B50
KOENIG L.W.,THE SALE OF THE TANKERS. USA+45 SEA DIST/IND POL/PAR DIPLOM ADMIN CIVMIL/REL ATTIT ...DECISION 20 PRESIDENT DEPT/STATE. PAGE 72 F1414
NAT/G POLICY PLAN GOV/REL

B54
LOCKLIN D.P.,ECONOMICS OF TRANSPORTATION (4TH ED.). USA+45 USA-45 SEA AIR LAW FINAN LG/CO EX/STRUC ADMIN CONTROL...STAT CHARTS 19/20 RAILROAD PUB/TRANS. PAGE 81 F1592
ECO/DEV DIST/IND ECO/TAC TEC/DEV

B57
NEUMARK S.D.,ECONOMIC INFLUENCES ON THE SOUTH AFRICAN FRONTIER, 1652-1836. SOUTH/AFR SEA AGRI NAT/G FORCES WORKER DIPLOM INT/TRADE PRICE DEMAND PRODUC...STAT CHARTS 17/19 FRONTIER. PAGE 97 F1915
COLONIAL ECO/UNDEV ECO/TAC MARKET

B58
ATOMIC INDUSTRIAL FORUM,MANAGEMENT AND ATOMIC ENERGY. WOR+45 SEA LAW MARKET NAT/G TEC/DEV INSPECT INT/TRADE CONFER PEACE HEALTH...ANTHOL 20. PAGE 7 F0136
NUC/PWR INDUS MGT ECO/TAC

B61
HUBBARD P.J.,ORIGINS OF THE TVA: THE MUSCLE SHOALS CONTROVERSY, 1920-1932. USA-45 DELIB/GP LEGIS LEAD LOBBY GOV/REL GP/REL INGP/REL OWN PERSON...BIBLIOG 20 TVA CONGRESS WATER. PAGE 62 F1229
SEA CONTROL NAT/G INDUS

B61
SCHNAPPER B.,LA POLITIQUE ET LE COMMERCE FRANCAIS DANS LE GOLFE DE GUINEE DE 1838 A 1871. FRANCE GUINEA UK SEA EXTR/IND NAT/G DELIB/GP LEGIS ADMIN ORD/FREE...POLICY GEOG CENSUS CHARTS BIBLIOG 19. PAGE 117 F2303
COLONIAL INT/TRADE DOMIN AFR

B62
HENDERSON W.O.,THE GENESIS OF THE COMMON MARKET. EUR+WWI FRANCE MOD/EUR UK SEA COM/IND EXTR/IND COLONIAL DISCRIM...TIME/SEQ CHARTS BIBLIOG 18/20 EEC TREATY. PAGE 58 F1149
ECO/DEV INT/TRADE DIPLOM

B66
RUPPENTHAL K.M.,TRANSPORTATION AND TOMORROW. FUT SPACE USA+45 SEA AIR FORCES TEC/DEV INT/TRADE ...ANTHOL 20 RAILROAD. PAGE 115 F2261
DIST/IND PLAN CIVMIL/REL PREDICT

L67
DEALEY S.,"MONETARY RECOVERY UNDER FEDERAL TRANSPORTATION STATUTES." USA+45 SEA WORKER TAX PAY ADJUD DEATH GOV/REL OWN HEALTH ORD/FREE 20. PAGE 31 F0609
DIST/IND LAW CONTROL FINAN

SEABERG G.P. F2339

SEARCH FOR EDUCATION, ELEVATION, AND KNOWLEDGE....SEE SEEK

SEATO....SOUTH EAST ASIA TREATY ORGANIZATION; SEE ALSO INT/ORG, VOL/ASSN, FORCES, DETER

B66
SINGH L.P.,THE POLITICS OF ECONOMIC COOPERATION IN ASIA; A STUDY OF ASIAN INTERNATIONAL ORGANIZATIONS. ASIA INT/ORG ACT/RES PLAN GP/REL...POLICY GP/COMP BIBLIOG 20 UN SEATO. PAGE 122 F2414
ECO/UNDEV ECO/TAC REGION DIPLOM

B67
MACCLOSKEY M.,PACTS FOR PEACE: UN, NATO, SEATO, CENTO, OAS. WOR+45 PLAN DIPLOM CONTROL PEACE ORD/FREE...ORG/CHARTS UN NATO SEATO OAS CENTO. PAGE 83 F1623
FORCES INT/ORG LEAD POLICY

SEATTLE....SEATTLE, WASHINGTON

B35
O'CONNOR H.,REVOLUTION IN SEATTLE. USA-45 STRATA WORKER GP/REL ATTIT SOCISM...OBS BIBLIOG/A 20 SEATTLE STRIKE COM/PARTY. PAGE 99 F1954
REV EDU/PROP LABOR MARXISM

SEC/EXCHNG....SECURITY EXCHANGE COMMISSION

SEC/REFORM....SECOND REFORM ACT OF 1867 (U.K.)

SEC/STATE....U.S. SECRETARY OF STATE

B65
US SENATE COMM ON FOREIGN REL,HEARINGS ON THE FOREIGN ASSISTANCE PROGRAM. AFR ASIA L/A+17C USA+45 WOR+45 FORCES TEC/DEV BUDGET CONTROL WEAPON ORD/FREE 20 UN CONGRESS SEC/STATE. PAGE 139 F2734
FOR/AID DIPLOM INT/ORG ECO/UNDEV

SECOND REFORM ACT OF 1867 (U.K.)....SEE SEC/REFORM

SECRETARIAT COUNCIL OF EUROPE F2340

SECRETARY OF STATE (U.S.)....SEE SEC/STATE

SECT....CHURCH, SECT, RELIGIOUS GROUP

NCO
STOLPER W.,"SOCIAL FACTORS IN ECONOMIC PLANNING, WITH SPECIAL REFERENCE TO NIGERIA" AFR NIGER CULTURE FAM SECT RECEIVE ETIQUET ADMIN DEMAND 20. PAGE 126 F2494
ECO/UNDEV PLAN ADJUST RISK

B02
MOREL E.D.,AFFAIRS OF WEST AFRICA. UK FINAN INDUS FAM KIN SECT CHIEF WORKER DIPLOM RACE/REL LITERACY HEALTH...CHARTS 18/20 AFRICA/W NEGRO. PAGE 93 F1826
COLONIAL ADMIN AFR

B26
TAWNEY R.H.,RELIGION AND THE RISE OF CAPITALISM. UK CULTURE NAT/G TEC/DEV OWN LAISSEZ...POLICY SOC TIME/SEQ 16/19. PAGE 129 F2537
SECT WEALTH INDUS CAP/ISM

B27
WEBER M.,GENERAL ECONOMIC HISTORY. CHRIST-17C MOD/EUR STRUCT AGRI EXTR/IND FINAN INDUS MARKET FAM NAT/G PROF/ORG SECT ECO/TAC MUNICH 8/20. PAGE 144 F2839
ECO/DEV CAP/ISM

B30
BIEL G.,TREATISE ON THE POWER AND UTILITY OF MONEY (1484). INDUS MARKET LOC/G NAT/G SECT ECO/TAC PRODUC WEALTH 15. PAGE 15 F0280
FINAN COST PRICE GEN/LAWS

B33
TANNENBAUM F.,PEACE BY REVOLUTION. ECO/UNDEV AGRI SECT WORKER DIPLOM EDU/PROP DISCRIM OWN WEALTH POPULISM 17/20 MEXIC/AMER INDIAN/AM. PAGE 128 F2532
CULTURE COLONIAL RACE/REL REV

B37
COLE W.E.,RECENT TRENDS IN RURAL PLANNING. USA-45 LAW ECO/DEV LOC/G SECT EDU/PROP CRIME LEISURE AGE/Y HABITAT...SOC/WK MUNICH 20. PAGE 26 F0503
AGRI NEIGH PLAN ACT/RES

B39
ENGELS F.,HERRN EUGEN DUHRING'S REVOLUTION IN SCIENCE (1878). CULTURE STRATA STRUCT FAM SECT ECO/TAC REV WAR SOCISM...MARXIST 19. PAGE 37 F0731
PWR SOCIETY WEALTH GEN/LAWS

B39
FIRTH R.,PRIMITIVE POLYNESIAN ECONOMY. SOCIETY DIST/IND SECT CHIEF CAP/ISM PRODUC WEALTH...SOC OBS METH WORSHIP 20 POLYNESIA. PAGE 41 F0802
ECO/UNDEV CULTURE AGRI ECO/TAC

B42
VEBLEN T.B.,THE THEORY OF THE LEISURE CLASS. USA-45 SOCIETY STRATA STRUCT NAT/G SECT WORKER CREATE EDU/PROP ATTIT...SOC GEN/LAWS 19. PAGE 141 F2772
WEALTH ELITES LEISURE PRODUC

B45
DAVIS J.,AFRICA ADVANCING. AFR CONGO/BRAZ LIBERIA NIGER INT/ORG SCHOOL DIPLOM GIVE KNOWL SKILL 20. PAGE 30 F0590
SECT COLONIAL AGRI ECO/UNDEV

B50
ADORNO T.W.,THE AUTHORITARIAN PERSONALITY. STRATA SECT PROB/SOLV ECO/TAC DISCRIM ATTIT SEX...SOC INT CHARTS METH 20. PAGE 3 F0044
AUTHORIT PERSON ALL/IDEOS SOCIETY

B51
PARSONS T.,THE SOCIAL SYSTEM. UNIV INTELL SOCIETY ECO/DEV SECT PLAN PERCEPT...CONCPT METH/CNCPT. PAGE 103 F2030
DRIVE SOC

B52
ROSE A.M.,UNION SOLIDARITY: THE INTERNAL COHESION OF A LABOR UNION. SECT GP/REL RACE/REL ATTIT ROLE HEALTH WEALTH...INT QU. PAGE 114 F2241
LABOR INGP/REL PARTIC SUPEGO

B54
WASHBURNE N.F.,INTERPRETING SOCIAL CHANGE IN AMERICA. USA+45 STRATA FAM NAT/G SECT OP/RES ECO/TAC EDU/PROP HABITAT...SOC TIME/SEQ TREND 20 BUREAUCRCY. PAGE 143 F2826
CULTURE STRUCT CREATE TEC/DEV

B55
WRONG D.H.,AMERICAN AND CANADIAN VIEWPOINTS. CANADA USA+45 CONSTN STRATA FAM SECT WORKER ECO/TAC EDU/PROP ADJUD MARRIAGE...IDEA/COMP 20. PAGE 149 F2936
DIPLOM ATTIT NAT/COMP CULTURE

B56
WOLFF R.L.,THE BALKANS IN OUR TIME. ALBANIA FUT MOD/EUR USSR YUGOSLAVIA CULTURE INT/ORG SECT DIPLOM EDU/PROP COERCE WAR ORD/FREE...CHARTS 4/20 BALKANS COMINFORM. PAGE 148 F2919
GEOG COM

B56
YUAN TUNG-LI,ECONOMIC AND SOCIAL DEVELOPMENT OF MODERN CHINA: A BIBLIOGRAPHIC GUIDE. COM/IND FINAN FAM LABOR SECT CRIME INCOME...STAT SAMP CON/ANAL. PAGE 150 F2954
BIBLIOG ASIA ECO/UNDEV SOC

B57
WEIGERT H.W.,PRINCIPLES OF POLITICAL GEOGRAPHY. WOR+45 ECO/DEV ECO/UNDEV SECT ECO/TAC COLONIAL HABITAT...CHARTS T 20. PAGE 144 F2845
GEOG CULTURE

B58
PAYNO M.,LA REFORMA SOCIAL EN ESPANA Y MEXICO. SPAIN ECO/TAC TAX LOBBY COERCE REV OWN CATHISM 19/20 MEXIC/AMER. PAGE 104 F2043
SECT NAT/G LAW ELITES

B59
PANIKKAR K.M.,THE AFRO-ASIAN STATES AND THEIR PROBLEMS. COM CULTURE KIN POL/PAR SECT DIPLOM EDU/PROP COLONIAL SOVEREIGN...TECHNIC GOV/COMP 20. PAGE 103 F2025
AFR S/ASIA ECO/UNDEV

B60
FORM W.H.,INDUSTRY, LABOR, AND COMMUNITY. STRUCT NEIGH SECT BAL/PWR EDU/PROP PARTIC ATTIT ROLE PWR WEALTH...METH/CNCPT CHARTS. PAGE 42 F0828
LABOR MGT GP/REL CONTROL

B60
MAYO H.B.,INTRODUCTION TO MARXIST THEORY. SECT WORKER POPULISM SOCISM 19/20. PAGE 87 F1709
MARXISM STRATA IDEA/COMP PHIL/SCI

B61
DE GRAZIA A.,AMERICAN WELFARE. CLIENT FINAN LABOR LOC/G NAT/G NEIGH EDU/PROP GP/REL...CLASSIF CON/ANAL CHARTS BIBLIOG. PAGE 31 F0598
GIVE WEALTH SECT VOL/ASSN

B61
DE VRIES E.,MAN IN RAPID SOCIAL CHANGE. WOR+45 SOCIETY ECO/DEV ECO/UNDEV AGRI INDUS FAM SECT TEC/DEV ATTIT...RECORD 20 CHRISTIAN. PAGE 31 F0607
CULTURE ALL/VALS SOC TASK

B61
LENSKI G.,THE RELIGIOUS FACTOR: A SOCIOLOGICAL STUDY OF RELIGION'S IMPACT ON POLITICS, ECONOMICS, AND FAMILY LIFE. FAM PROF/ORG EDU/PROP ROLE CATHISM ...INT SAMP MUNICH. PAGE 78 F1524
SECT GP/REL

B61
SAKAI R.K.,STUDIES ON ASIA, 1961. ASIA BURMA INDIA S/ASIA FINAN ECO/TAC NAT/LISM SOCISM...POLICY ANTHOL 19/20 CHINJAP. PAGE 115 F2271
ECO/UNDEV SECT

B62
BROWN S.D.,STUDIES ON ASIA, 1962. ASIA BURMA INDIA ISLAM ISRAEL S/ASIA ECO/UNDEV POL/PAR SECT ECO/TAC ...ANTHOL 20 CHINJAP. PAGE 19 F0374
PWR PARL/PROC

B62
COX O.C.,CAPITALISM AND AMERICAN LEADERSHIP. WOR+45 WOR-45 STRATA INDUS SECT INT/TRADE EXEC INGP/REL RACE/REL RATIONAL PWR WEALTH. PAGE 28 F0548
CAP/ISM LEAD ECO/DEV SOCIETY

B62
US LIBRARY OF CONGRESS,A LIST OF AMERICAN DOCTORAL DISSERTATIONS ON AFRICA. SOCIETY SECT DIPLOM EDU/PROP ADMIN...GEOG 19/20. PAGE 138 F2717
BIBLIOG AFR ACADEM CULTURE

B63
CHOJNACKI S.,REGISTER ON CURRENT RESEARCH ON ETHIOPIA AND THE HORN OF AFRICA. ETHIOPIA LAW CULTURE AGRI SECT EDU/PROP ADMIN...GEOG HEAL LING 20. PAGE 24 F0470
BIBLIOG ACT/RES INTELL ACADEM

B63
KAPP W.K.,HINDU CULTURE: ECONOMIC DEVELOPMENT AND ECONOMIC PLANNING IN INDIA. INDIA S/ASIA CULTURE ECO/TAC EDU/PROP ADMIN ALL/VALS...POLICY MGT TIME/SEQ TRUE/GP VAL/FREE 20. PAGE 69 F1353
SECT ECO/UNDEV

B63
OTERO L.M.,HONDURAS. HONDURAS SPAIN STRUCT SECT COLONIAL REV WAR ATTIT PWR...GEOG WORSHIP 16/20. PAGE 102 F2003
NAT/G SOCIETY NAT/LISM ECO/UNDEV

B63
PRITCHETT C.H.,THE THIRD BRANCH OF GOVERNMENT. USA+45 USA-45 CONSTN SOCIETY INDUS SECT LEGIS JUDGE PROB/SOLV GOV/REL 20 SUPREME/CT CHURCH/STA. PAGE 108 F2122
JURID NAT/G ADJUD CT/SYS

B63
WAGLEY C.,INTRODUCTION TO BRAZIL. BRAZIL L/A+17C FAM KIN SCHOOL SECT ATTIT WEALTH...GEOG SOC. PAGE 142 F2799
ECO/UNDEV ELITES HABITAT STRATA

B64
HALLOWELL J.H.,DEVELOPMENT: FOR WHAT. WOR+45 POL/PAR SECT FOR/AID INT/TRADE CT/SYS PARTIC PRODUC PLURISM. PAGE 54 F1052
ECO/UNDEV CONSTN NAT/LISM ECO/TAC

B64
IMAZ J.L.,LOS QUE MANDAN. INDUS LABOR NAT/G POL/PAR PROVS SECT CHIEF TOP/EX CONTROL 20 ARGEN. PAGE 64 F1261
LEAD FORCES ELITES ATTIT

B64
LETICHE J.M.,A HISTORY OF RUSSIAN ECONOMIC THOUGHT: NINTH THROUGH EIGHTEENTH CENTURIES. RUSSIA FINAN SECT CAP/ISM DOMIN DEMAND EFFICIENCY OWN MARXISM ...TECHNIC ANTHOL BIBLIOG 9/18. PAGE 78 F1536
ECO/TAC TIME/SEQ IDEA/COMP ECO/UNDEV

B64
MEISEL J.,PAPERS ON THE 1962 ELECTION. CANADA PROVS SECT GP/REL CONSEN EFFICIENCY...MAJORIT 20. PAGE 89 F1751
POL/PAR RECORD CHOOSE STRATA

B64
SAKAI R.K.,STUDIES ON ASIA, 1964. ASIA CHINA/COM ISRAEL MALAYSIA S/ASIA USA+45 USSR ECO/UNDEV FAM POL/PAR SECT CONSULT NAT/LISM...POLICY SOC 20 CHINJAP. PAGE 115 F2272
PWR DIPLOM

B64
WERTHEIM W.F.,EAST-WEST PARALLELS. INDONESIA S/ASIA NAT/G SECT...TIME/SEQ METH REFORMERS S/EASTASIA. PAGE 145 F2860
SOC ECO/UNDEV CULTURE NAT/LISM

B65
COUGHLIN B.J.,CHURCH AND STATE IN SOCIAL WELFARE. USA+45 RECEIVE GP/REL ORD/FREE WEALTH NEW/LIB. PAGE 28 F0542
CULTURE SECT VOL/ASSN GIVE

B65
ONUOHA B.,THE ELEMENTS OF AFRICAN SOCIALISM. AFR FINAN SECT TEC/DEV FOR/AID GP/REL OWN LAISSEZ MARXISM...CONCPT BIBLIOG 20. PAGE 101 F1992
SOCISM ECO/UNDEV NAT/G EX/STRUC

B65
US BUREAU EDUC CULTURAL AFF,RESOURCES SURVEY FOR LATIN AMERICAN COUNTRIES. L/A+17C USA+45 CULTURE INDUS INT/ORG SECT PLAN EDU/PROP POLICY. PAGE 134 F2643
NAT/G ECO/UNDEV FOR/AID DIPLOM

B66
ANDRESKI S.,PARASITISM AND SUBVERSION* THE CASE OF LATIN AMERICA. CULTURE ECO/UNDEV LABOR NAT/G SECT PROB/SOLV RACE/REL TOTALISM ATTIT WEALTH ALL/IDEOS. PAGE 5 F0100
L/A+17C GOV/COMP STRATA REV

B66
EBONY,THE NEGRO HANDBOOK. ACADEM LABOR LOC/G SECT FORCES WORKER CT/SYS CRIME DISCRIM ORD/FREE...BIOG SOC/INTEG 19/20 NEGRO CIV/RIGHTS. PAGE 36 F0692
RACE/REL EDU/PROP LAW STAT

B66
FORD P.,CARDINAL MORAN AND THE A. L. P. NAT/G POL/PAR SECT DELIB/GP LOBBY REV CHOOSE ORD/FREE MARXISM 19/20 AUSTRAL PROTESTANT LABOR/PAR. PAGE 42 F0825
CATHISM SOCISM LABOR SOCIETY

B66
HOWE R.W.,BLACK AFRICA: FROM PRE-HISTORY TO THE EVE OF THE COLONIAL ERA. ECO/UNDEV KIN PROVS SECT INT/TRADE EDU/PROP COLONIAL...BIBLIOG WORSHIP. PAGE 62 F1226
AFR CULTURE SOC

B66
MUNBY D.,ECONOMIC GROWTH IN WORLD PERSPECTIVE. AFR WOR+45 SOCIETY INDUS PLAN TEC/DEV ECO/TAC FOR/AID INT/TRADE COST CATHISM...ANTHOL 20 EUROPE/W CHURCH/STA. PAGE 95 F1859
SECT ECO/UNDEV ECO/DEV

B66
PFEFFER K.H.,WELT IM UMBRUCH. SOCIETY STRUCT INDUS PROF/ORG SECT TEC/DEV PARTIC SUPEGO WORSHIP 20 CHRISTIAN. PAGE 106 F2076
ORD/FREE STRATA CREATE

B66
RIZK C.,LE REGIME POLITIQUE LIBANAIS. ISLAM LEBANON STRUCT POL/PAR SECT LOBBY GP/REL 20 ARABS MUSLIM CHRISTIAN. PAGE 112 F2198
ECO/UNDEV NAT/G CULTURE

B66
WETTER G.A.,SOVIET IDEOLOGY TODAY. USSR ECO/UNDEV SECT WORKER CAP/ISM CONTROL TASK EFFICIENCY TOTALISM DRIVE WEALTH...TREND 18/20. PAGE 145 F2864
ALL/IDEOS MARXISM REV

C66
WINT G.,"ASIA: A HANDBOOK." ASIA S/ASIA INDUS LABOR SECT PRESS RACE/REL MARXISM...STAT CHARTS BIBLIOG 20. PAGE 148 F2908
ECO/UNDEV DIPLOM NAT/G SOCIETY

B67
BIRMINGHAM W.,A STUDY OF CONTEMPORARY GHANA VOL. I: SOME ASPECTS OF SOCIAL STRUCTURE. AFR GHANA AGRI FAM SECT PLAN EDU/PROP MARRIAGE OWN...POLICY STAT CHARTS MUNICH 20. PAGE 15 F0287
SOCIETY STRUCT CENSUS ECO/UNDEV

B67
BURDEN H.T.,THE NUREMBERG PARTY RALLIES 1923-39. GERMANY POL/PAR SECT CREATE DOMIN WAR ATTIT ...AUD/VIS FILM 20. PAGE 20 F0384
EDU/PROP CONTROL CROWD TOTALISM

B67
LANDEN R.G.,OMAN SINCE 1856: DISRUPTIVE MODERNIZATION IN A TRADITIONAL ARAB SOCIETY. UK DIST/IND EXTR/IND SECT DIPLOM INT/TRADE...SOC LING CHARTS BIBLIOG 19/20. PAGE 75 F1468
ISLAM CULTURE ECO/UNDEV NAT/G

B67
MUHAMMAD A.C.,THE EMERGENCE OF PAKISTAN. PAKISTAN S/ASIA CONSTN ECO/UNDEV NAT/G CONTROL NAT/LISM 20. PAGE 94 F1853
DIPLOM COLONIAL SECT PROB/SOLV

B67
PIKE F.B.,FREEDOM AND REFORM IN LATIN AMERICA. BRAZIL URUGUAY CONSTN CULTURE SECT DIPLOM EDU/PROP
L/A+17C ORD/FREE

PARTIC DRIVE ALL/VALS CATHISM...GEOG ANTHOL BIBLIOG ECO/UNDEV
REFORMERS BOLIV. PAGE 106 F2086 REV

B67
SCHECTER J.,THE NEW FACE OF BUDDHA: BUDDHISM AND SECT
POLITICAL POWER IN SOUTHEAST ASIA. S/ASIA NAT/G POLICY
POL/PAR NAT/LISM ATTIT MARXISM...BIBLIOG 20. PWR
PAGE 116 F2292 LEAD

B67
SPECTOR S.D.,CHECKLIST OF ITEMS IN THE NDEA BIBLIOG/A
INSTITUTE LIBRARY (PAMPHLET). USA+45 NAT/G SECT COM
EDU/PROP ATTIT ALL/IDEOS...SOC BIOG. PAGE 124 F2448 MARXISM

B67
STEARNS P.N.,EUROPEAN SOCIETY IN UPHEAVAL* SOCIAL REGION
HISTORY SINCE 1800. EUR+WWI MOD/EUR STRATA SECT ECO/DEV
WORKER TEC/DEV WAR...WELF/ST SOC TREND BIBLIOG SOCIETY
19/20. PAGE 125 F2472 INDUS

B67
WEINBERG M.,SCHOOL INTEGRATION: A COMPREHENSIVE BIBLIOG
CLASSIFIED BIBLIOGRAPHY OF 3,100 REFERENCES. USA+45 SCHOOL
LAW NAT/G NEIGH SECT PLAN ROUTINE AGE/C WEALTH DISCRIM
SOC/INTEG INDIAN/AM. PAGE 145 F2849 RACE/REL

B67
WESSON R.G.,THE IMPERIAL ORDER. WOR-45 STRUCT SECT PWR
DOMIN ADMIN COLONIAL LEAD CONSERVE...CONCPT BIBLIOG CHIEF
20. PAGE 145 F2861 CONTROL
SOCIETY

L67
COSTANZA J.F.,"WHOLESOME NEUTRALITY: LAW AND SECT
EDUCATION." USA+45 GIVE EDU/PROP ADJUD CONTROL PROVS
GP/REL...DECISION JURID. PAGE 28 F0540 ACADEM

S67
EDWARDS N.,"EDUCATION IN THE FEDERAL-STATE EDU/PROP
STRUCTURE OF GOVERNMENT." USA+45 SECT CONTROL NAT/G
GOV/REL RACE/REL DISCRIM FEDERAL ROLE PWR PROVS
SOVEREIGN. PAGE 36 F0705 POLICY

S67
GATELL F.O.,"MONEY AND PARTY IN JACKSONIAN AMERICA* WEALTH
A QUANTITATIVE LOOK AT NEW YORK CITY'S MEN OF POL/PAR
QUALITY." USA-45 STRATA SECT SUFF CONSEN MAJORITY PERSON
ATTIT...CHARTS HYPO/EXP 19. PAGE 46 F0908 IDEA/COMP

S67
LANDES W.M.,"THE EFFECT OF STATE FAIR EMPLOYMENT DISCRIM
LAWS ON THE ECONOMIC POSITION OF NONWHITES." USA+45 LAW
PROVS SECT LEGIS ADMIN GP/REL RACE/REL...JURID WORKER
CONCPT CHARTS HYPO/EXP NEGRO. PAGE 75 F1470

S67
LANGLEY L.D.,"THE DEMOCRATIC TRADITION AND MILITARY ATTIT
REFORM, 1878-1885." USA-45 SECT EDU/PROP CROWD FORCES
EFFICIENCY NAT/LISM 19 INDIAN/AM. PAGE 75 F1480 POPULISM

S67
MERIKOSKI V.,"BASIC PROBLEMS OF UNIVERSITY ACADEM
ADMINISTRATION." PROVS SECT CONTROL...CLASSIF 20. ADMIN
PAGE 90 F1760 SOVEREIGN
METH/COMP

S67
POWELL D.,"THE EFFECTIVENESS OF SOVIET ANTI- EDU/PROP
RELIGIOUS PROPAGANDA." USSR NAT/G DOMIN LEGIT ATTIT
NAT/LISM 20. PAGE 107 F2109 SECT
CONTROL

S67
RAMA C.M.,"PASADO Y PRESENTE DE LA RELIGION EN SECT
AMERICA LATINA." L/A+17C ELITES SOCIETY STRATA CATHISM
MARXISM...STAT WORSHIP PROTESTANT. PAGE 109 F2139 STRUCT
NAT/COMP

S67
SOLT L.F.,"PURITANISM, CAPITALISM, DEMOCRACY, AND SECT
THE NEW SCIENCE." NAT/G GP/REL CONSERVE...IDEA/COMP CAP/ISM
GEN/LAWS. PAGE 124 F2440 RATIONAL
POPULISM

B68
PROUDHON P.J.,SYSTEME DES CONTRADICTIONS SOCIETY
ECONOMIQUES, OU PHILOSOPHIE DA LA MISERE (2 VOLS.) STRATA
(1846). SECT WORKER GP/REL ISOLAT PRODUC IDEA/COMP. MORAL
PAGE 108 F2126

B76
FOURIER C.,SOCIAL DESTINIES, IN A. BRISBANE, UTOPIA
GENERAL INTRODUCTION TO SOCIAL SCIENCE. UNIV AGRI SOCIETY
INDUS SECT PRODUC...PHIL/SCI CONCPT. PAGE 43 F0835 PERSON
VOL/ASSN

SECUR/COUN....UNITED NATIONS SECURITY COUNCIL

SECUR/PROG....SECURITY PROGRAM

SECURITIES....SEE FINAN

SECURITY....SEE ORD/FREE

SECURITY COUNCIL....SEE UN+DELIB/GP+PWR

SEDITION....SEDITION

SEEK....SEARCH FOR EDUCATION, ELEVATION, AND KNOWLEDGE

SEERS D. F2341

SEGAL R. F2342

SEGREGATION....SEE NEGRO, SOUTH/US, RACE/REL, SOC/INTEG,
CIV/RIGHTS, DISCRIM, MISCEGEN, ISOLAT, SCHOOL,
STRANGE, ANOMIE

SEIDLER G.L. F2343

SEIDMAN H. F2344

SEIDMAN J.I. F2345

SELASSIE/H....HAILE SELASSIE

SELBORNE/W....WILLIAM SELBORNE

B25
WILLIAMS B.,THE SELBORNE MEMORANDUM. AFR FUT COLONIAL
SOUTH/AFR UK NAT/G BUDGET DIPLOM REGION GOV/REL PROVS
SOVEREIGN...POLICY CHARTS 20 UNIFICA SELBORNE/W.
PAGE 147 F2888

SELEC/SERV....SELECTIVE SERVICE

SELF P. F2346

SELF/OBS....SELF/OBSERVATION

B53
DAHL R.A.,POLITICS, ECONOMICS AND WELFARE: PLANNING ECO/TAC
AND POLITICOECONOMIC SYSTEMS RESOLVED INTO BASIC PHIL/SCI
SOCIAL PROCESSES. WOR+45 WOR-45 ECO/DEV ECO/UNDEV
R+D CREATE PLAN TEC/DEV EDU/PROP HEALTH WEALTH
...SOC SELF/OBS TREND CHARTS GEN/METH 20. PAGE 29
F0571

B55
BUCHANAN N.S.,APPROACHES TO ECONOMIC DEVELOPMENT. ECO/UNDEV
FUT USA+45 WOR+45 STRATA ECO/DEV INT/ORG NAT/G ECO/TAC
TEC/DEV DIPLOM FOR/AID ATTIT KNOWL PWR WEALTH INT/TRADE
...RELATIV METH/CNCPT SELF/OBS TREND CON/ANAL
STERTYP GEN/LAWS FOR/TRADE COMMUN 20. PAGE 20 F0380

SELIGMAN B.B. F2347

SELIGMAN E.R. F2348

SELIGMAN E.R.A. F2349

SELIGSOHN I.J. F2350

SELLERS C. F2351

SELOSOEMARDJAN O. F2352

SELZNICK P. F2353

SEMANTICS...SEE LOG

SEN S.R. F2354

SEN/SPACE....UNITED STATES SENATE SPECIAL COMMITTEE ON
SPACE ASTRONAUTICS

SENATE SPECIAL COMMITTEE ON SPACE ASTRONAUTICS....SEE
SEN/SPACE

SENATE....SENATE (ALL NATIONS); SEE ALSO CONGRESS, LEGIS

N19
CARPER E.T.,LOBBYING AND THE NATURAL GAS BILL LOBBY
(PAMPHLET). USA+45 SERV/IND BARGAIN PAY DRIVE ROLE ADJUD
WEALTH 20 CONGRESS SENATE EISNHWR/DD. PAGE 22 F0418 TRIBUTE
NAT/G

B43
WILMERDING L. JR.,THE SPENDING POWER: A HISTORY OF LEGIS
THE EFFORTS OF CONGRESS TO CONTROL EXPENDITURES. BUDGET
USA-45 POL/PAR DELIB/GP EX/STRUC TOP/EX TARIFFS CONTROL
ADMIN GOV/REL...TIME/SEQ SENATE HOUSE/REP. PAGE 147
F2900

B62
CARPER E.T.,ILLINOIS GOES TO CONGRESS FOR ARMY ADMIN
LAND. USA+45 LAW EXTR/IND PROVS REGION CIVMIL/REL LOBBY
GOV/REL FEDERAL ATTIT 20 ILLINOIS SENATE CONGRESS GEOG
DIRKSEN/E DOUGLAS/P. PAGE 22 F0420 LEGIS

N62
US SENATE COMM ON JUDICIARY,LEGISLATION TO LEAD
STRENGTHEN PENALTIES UNDER THE ANTITRUST LAWS ADJUD
(PAMPHLET). USA+45 LG/CO CONFER CONTROL SANCTION INDUS
ORD/FREE 20 SENATE MONOPOLY. PAGE 139 F2748 ECO/TAC

B63
WILTZ J.E.,IN SEARCH OF PEACE: THE SENATE MUNITIONS DELIB/GP
INQUIRY, 1934-36. EUR+WWI USA-45 ELITES INDUS LG/CO PROFIT

LEGIS INT/TRADE LOBBY NEUTRAL ARMS/CONT...POLICY CONGRESS 20 LEAGUE/NAT PRESIDENT SENATE CONSCRIPTN. PAGE 147 F2905 — WAR WEAPON

B67
US CONGRESS SENATE,SURVEY OF THE ALLIANCE FOR PROGRESS; INFLATION IN LATIN AMERICA (PAMPHLET). USA+45 MARKET INT/ORG DIPLOM INT/TRADE BAL/PAY SENATE ALL/PROG. PAGE 135 F2666 — L/A+17C FINAN POLICY FOR/AID

B67
US SENATE COMM ON FOREIGN REL,LATIN AMERICAN SUMMIT CONFERENCE. L/A+17C USA+45 FINAN PLAN SENATE ALL/PROG. PAGE 139 F2740 — FOR/AID BUDGET DIPLOM INT/ORG

B67
US SENATE COMM ON FOREIGN REL,INTER-AMERICAN DEVELOPMENT BANK ACT AMENDMENT. L/A+17C USA+45 DELIB/GP DIPLOM FOR/AID BAL/PAY...CHARTS SENATE. PAGE 139 F2741 — LAW FINAN INT/ORG ECO/UNDEV

B67
US SENATE COMM ON FOREIGN REL,ARMS SALES TO NEAR EAST AND SOUTH ASIAN COUNTRIES. INDIA IRAN PAKISTAN WOR+45 PROC/MFG BAL/PWR DIPLOM...DECISION SENATE. PAGE 139 F2742 — WEAPON FOR/AID FORCES POLICY

B67
US SENATE COMM ON FOREIGN REL,HARRISON E. SALISBURY'S TRIP TO NORTH VIETNAM. CHINA/COM USA+45 VIETNAM/N PRESS TASK GUERRILLA CONSEN EFFICIENCY PEACE DRIVE...OBS SENATE. PAGE 139 F2743 — DIPLOM WAR FORCES ATTIT

B67
US SENATE COMM ON FOREIGN REL,FOREIGN ASSISTANCE ACT OF 1967. VIETNAM WOR+45 DELIB/GP CONFER CONTROL WAR WEAPON BAL/PAY...CENSUS CHARTS SENATE. PAGE 139 F2744 — FOR/AID LAW DIPLOM POLICY

N67
US CONGRESS JOINT ECO COMM,ECONOMY IN GOVERNMENT (PAMPHLET). USA+45 ECO/DEV FINAN NAT/G PLAN BUDGET SENATE. PAGE 135 F2662 — ECO/TAC COST EFFICIENCY MGT

N67
US SENATE COMM ON FOREIGN REL,THE UNITED NATIONS AT TWENTY-ONE (PAMPHLET). WOR+45 BUDGET ADMIN SENATE UN. PAGE 139 F2738 — INT/ORG DIPLOM PEACE

N67
US SENATE COMM ON FOREIGN REL,WAR OR PEACE IN THE MIDDLE EAST (PAMPHLET). GREECE ISLAM ISRAEL JORDAN UAR CHIEF PROB/SOLV FOR/AID WAR PWR 20 SENATE. PAGE 139 F2739 — DIPLOM FORCES PLAN

SENEGAL....SEE ALSO AFR

B63
COLUMBIA U SCHOOL OF LAW,PUBLIC INTERNATIONAL DEVELOPMENT FINANCING IN SENEGAL. SENEGAL FINAN DELIB/GP GIVE EFFICIENCY...CHARTS GOV/COMP ANTHOL 20. PAGE 26 F0511 — FOR/AID PLAN RECEIVE ECO/UNDEV

B65
HAPGOOD D.,AFRICA: FROM INDEPENDENCE TO TOMARROW. AFR GUINEA SENEGAL CULTURE ELITES ECO/UNDEV AGRI SCHOOL FOR/AID COLONIAL MARXISM...TREND 20. PAGE 55 F1070 — ECO/TAC SOCIETY NAT/G

SENGHOR L.S. F2355

SENGUPTA J.K. F0837

SENIOR....SENIORITY; SEE ALSO ADMIN, ROUTINE

N19
MARSH J.F. JR.,THE FBI RETIREMENT BILL (PAMPHLET). USA+45 EX/STRUC WORKER PLAN PROB/SOLV BUDGET LEAD LOBBY PARL/PROC PERS/REL RIGID/FLEX...POLICY 20 FBI PRESIDENT BUR/BUDGET. PAGE 86 F1677 — ADMIN NAT/G SENIOR GOV/REL

B62
COLLIER A.T.,MANAGEMENT, MEN, AND VALUES. INDUS FACE/GP EX/STRUC PLAN PROB/SOLV DEBATE SENIOR ADMIN PROFIT PERSON...PSY SOC 20. PAGE 26 F0505 — MGT ATTIT PERS/REL DECISION

B62
REES A.,THE ECONOMICS OF TRADE UNIONS. FUT ECO/DEV INDUS BARGAIN CAP/ISM PRICE SENIOR CONTROL GP/REL COST...TREND 20 AFL/CIO. PAGE 110 F2172 — LABOR WORKER ECO/TAC

B67
TUMIN M.M.,SOCIAL STRATIFICATION; THE FORMS AND FUNCTIONS OF INEQUALITY. SENIOR SANCTION WEALTH ...SOC CLASSIF METH 20. PAGE 131 F2592 — STRATA DISCRIM CONCPT SOCIETY

S67
PIERPONT J.R.,"NEW STAGE IN THE LONGSHORE STRUGGLE." USA+45 SENIOR ADJUD RACE/REL...JURID 20 NEGRO. PAGE 106 F2083 — LABOR DISCRIM WORKER CT/SYS

SEPARATION....SEE ISOLAT, DISCRIM, RACE/REL

SEPULVEDA C. F2356

SERAPHIM H.J. F2357,F2358

SERBIA....SERBIA

SERRANO MOSCOSO E. F2359

SERV/IND....SERVICE INDUSTRY

N19
CARPER E.T.,LOBBYING AND THE NATURAL GAS BILL (PAMPHLET). USA+45 SERV/IND BARGAIN PAY DRIVE ROLE WEALTH 20 CONGRESS SENATE EISNHWR/DD. PAGE 22 F0418 — LOBBY ADJUD TRIBUTE NAT/G

N19
PALAMOUNTAIN JC J.R.,THE DOLCIN CASE AND THE FEDERAL TRADE COMMISSION (PAMPHLET). USA+45 LAW MARKET SERV/IND LG/CO NAT/G BIO/SOC 20 FTC. PAGE 103 F2018 — ADJUD PROB/SOLV EDU/PROP HEALTH

N19
RIDLEY C.E.,MEASURING MUNICIPAL ACTIVITIES (PAMPHLET). FINAN SERV/IND FORCES RECEIVE INGP/REL HABITAT...POLICY SOC/WK 20. PAGE 111 F2191 — MGT HEALTH WEALTH LOC/G

B32
THOMPSON C.D.,CONFESSIONS OF THE POWER TRUST. MARKET ACT/RES EDU/PROP CONTROL GOV/REL INCOME OWN ...MGT 20 FTC MONOPOLY. PAGE 130 F2564 — LG/CO SERV/IND PWR FINAN

S32
DODD E.M. JR.,"FOR WHOM ARE CORPORATE MANAGERS TRUSTEES'." SERV/IND CAP/ISM GIVE LEAD REPRESENT ORD/FREE WEALTH. PAGE 33 F0648 — LG/CO ROLE NAT/G PLAN

B44
INTL CHAMBER OF COMMERCE,TERMS COMMONLY USED IN DISTRIBUTION AND ADVERTISING. PORTUGAL SPAIN UK WOR-45 SERV/IND 20. PAGE 65 F1284 — DICTIONARY EDU/PROP DIST/IND INT/TRADE

B48
WHYTE W.F.,HUMAN RELATIONS IN THE RESTAURANT INDUSTRY (1ST ED). CLIENT WORKER WAR ATTIT...MGT OBS INT. PAGE 146 F2874 — INGP/REL GP/REL SERV/IND LABOR

B50
HOOVER G.,TWENTIETH CENTURY ECONOMIC THOUGHT. USA+45 ECO/DEV AGRI FINAN INDUS MARKET SERV/IND LABOR NAT/G...STAT 20. PAGE 62 F1213 — ECO/TAC CAP/ISM INT/TRADE

S50
DREYFUS S.,"THE INDUSTRIAL DESIGNER AND THE BUSINESSMAN." SERV/IND PROB/SOLV ECO/TAC COST EFFICIENCY PROFIT RATIONAL...DECISION MGT. PAGE 34 F0662 — CONSULT INDUS PRODUC UTIL

S54
SCITOVSKY T.,"TWO CONCEPTS OF EXTERNAL ECONOMIES." ECO/DEV IDEA/COMP. PAGE 118 F2329 — SERV/IND GEN/LAWS INDUS EQUILIB

B55
GOMES F.A.,OPERACAO MUNICIPIO. BRAZIL L/A+17C SERV/IND LOC/G BUDGET ECO/TAC COST DEMAND...POLICY MUNICH 20. PAGE 48 F0944 — ECO/UNDEV FEDERAL GOV/REL

B55
OECD,MARSHALL PLAN IN TURKEY. TURKEY USA+45 COM/IND CONSTRUC SERV/IND FORCES BUDGET...STAT 20 MARSHL/PLN. PAGE 100 F1964 — FOR/AID ECO/UNDEV AGRI INDUS

B57
THOMAS R.G.,OUR MODERN BANKING AND MONETARY SYSTEM (3RD ED.). AFR USA+45 USA-45 ACT/RES PLAN PROB/SOLV INT/TRADE PRICE WAR BAL/PAY INCOME...POLICY METH/CNCPT 20 DEPRESSION. PAGE 130 F2563 — FINAN SERV/IND ECO/TAC

S57
CUNNINGHAM E.M.,"THE BUSINESS MAN AND HIS LAWYER." USA+45 LG/CO SML/CO TOP/EX CHOOSE SKILL...JURID MGT 20. PAGE 29 F0561 — CONSULT LAW DECISION SERV/IND

B58
CROWE S.,THE LANDSCAPE OF POWER. UK CULTURE SERV/IND NAT/G CONSULT PARTIC NUC/PWR LEISURE...SOC EXHIBIT 20. PAGE 29 F0559 — HABITAT TEC/DEV PLAN CONTROL

B58
GALBRAITH J.K.,THE AFFLUENT SOCIETY. EUR+WWI FUT USA+45 USSR CULTURE SERV/IND PEACE WEALTH SOCISM ...NEW/IDEA TREND VAL/FREE 20. PAGE 45 F0882 — ATTIT ECO/TAC CAP/ISM

S58
LANE F.C.,"ECONOMIC CONSEQUENCES OF ORGANIZED VIOLENCE." FUT WOR+45 WOR-45 ECO/DEV DIST/IND SERV/IND NAT/G PROVS EX/STRUC CHOOSE ORD/FREE PWR ...TIME/SEQ GEN/LAWS MUNICH 20. PAGE 75 F1472 — WEALTH COERCE

B60
GARBARINO J.W.,HEALTH PLANS AND COLLECTIVE BARGAINING. USA+45 LABOR BARGAIN GP/REL WEALTH ...WELF/ST CHARTS 20 DEPT/HEW SAN/FRAN. PAGE 46 F0900 — HEAL PLAN FINAN SERV/IND

B60
WEINER H.E.,BRITISH LABOR AND PUBLIC OWNERSHIP. UK LABOR
SERV/IND LG/CO WORKER CONTROL OWN 20. PAGE 145 NAT/G
F2850 INDUS
ATTIT

B61
QURESHI S.,INCENTIVES IN AMERICAN EMPLOYMENT SERV/IND
(THESIS, UNIVERSITY OF PENNSYLVANIA). DELIB/GP ADMIN
TOP/EX BUDGET ROUTINE SANCTION COST TECHRACY MGT. PAY
PAGE 108 F2134 EX/STRUC

B62
GORT M.,DIVERSIFICATION AND INTEGRATION IN AMERICAN CONCPT
INDUSTRY. CLIENT DIST/IND PROC/MFG SERV/IND LG/CO GP/REL
CONTROL DEMAND PWR...METH/CNCPT STAT TREND CON/ANAL CLASSIF
GP/COMP. PAGE 49 F0964

B62
HARRINGTON M.,THE RETAIL CLERKS. ECO/TAC LEAD LABOR
PARTIC CHOOSE GP/REL INGP/REL CENTRAL POLICY. SERV/IND
PAGE 55 F1087 STRUCT
DELIB/GP

B62
MARTINS A.F.,REVOLUCAO BRANCA NO CAMPO. L/A+17C AGRI
SERV/IND DEMAND EFFICIENCY PRODUC...POLICY ECO/UNDEV
METH/COMP. PAGE 86 F1685 TEC/DEV
NAT/COMP

B62
SCHALLER H.G.,PUBLIC EXPENDITURE DECISIONS IN THE FINAN
URBAN COMMUNITY: PREPARED FOR RESOURCES FOR THE DECISION
FUTURE, INC. INDUS SERV/IND LOC/G PUB/INST PLAN
PROB/SOLV BUDGET DEMAND PRODUC...CHARTS MUNICH.
PAGE 116 F2289

L62
WATERSTON A.,"PLANNING IN MOROCCO, ORGANIZATION AND NAT/G
IMPLEMENTATION. BALTIMORE: HOPKINS ECON. DEVELOP. PLAN
INT. BANK FOR." ISLAM ECO/DEV AGRI DIST/IND INDUS MOROCCO
PROC/MFG SERV/IND LOC/G EX/STRUC ECO/TAC PWR WEALTH
TOT/POP TRUE/GP METH/GP TERR/GP VAL/FREE 20.
PAGE 144 F2829

B63
HUNTER A.,THE ECONOMICS OF AUSTRALIAN INDUSTRY. INDUS
DIST/IND EXTR/IND FINAN PROC/MFG SERV/IND ACT/RES ECO/DEV
PLAN TARIFFS GP/REL INGP/REL 20 AUSTRAL. PAGE 63 HABITAT
F1245 GP/COMP

B63
MILLER W.,REVENUE-COST RATIOS OF RURAL TOWNSHIPS TAX
WITH CHANGING LAND USES. USA+45 INDUS SERV/IND COST
PROVS GP/REL HABITAT...CHARTS GP/COMP MUNICH 20 AGRI
NEW/JERSEY. PAGE 91 F1792

L63
ADERBIGDE A.,"SYMPOSIUM ON WEST AFRICA FINAN
INTEGRATION." AFR EUR+WWI FUT CULTURE SOCIETY ECO/TAC
STRATA DIST/IND INDUS MARKET SERV/IND DELIB/GP PLAN REGION
TEC/DEV DOMIN EDU/PROP LEGIT COERCE ATTIT ALL/VALS
...POLICY STAT TREND CHARTS VAL/FREE. PAGE 2 F0040

S63
APPERT K.,"BERECHTIGE VORBEHALTE DER FINAN
SCHWEIZERISCHEN ZUR INTEGRATION." EUR+WWI UK MARKET ATTIT
SERV/IND NAT/G PLAN RIGID/FLEX OEEC 20 EEC. PAGE 6 SWITZERLND
F0108

S63
BALOGH T.,"L'INFLUENCE DES INSTITUTIONS MONETAIRES FINAN
ET COMMERCIALES SUR LA STRUCTURE ECONOMIQUE
AFRICAIN." AFR EUR+WWI FUT USA+45 USA-45 WOR+45
SERV/IND INT/ORG NAT/G TOP/EX ROUTINE...INDEX EEC
METH/GP 20. PAGE 9 F0168

S63
BEGUIN H.,"ASPECTS STRUCTURELS DU COMMERCE MARKET
EXTERIEUR DES PAYS SOUS-DEVELOPPES." FUT WOR+45 ECO/UNDEV
STRUCT FINAN SERV/IND POL/PAR TEC/DEV PERCEPT FOR/AID
WEALTH FOR/TRADE 20. PAGE 12 F0229

S63
GALENSON W.,"ECONOMIC DEVELOPMENT AND THE SECTORAL INDUS
EXPANSION OF EMPLOYMENT, INT." FUT WOR+45 ECO/UNDEV ECO/TAC
DIST/IND PROC/MFG SERV/IND ACT/RES HEALTH SKILL
WEALTH...STAT TIME/SEQ VAL/FREE 20. PAGE 46 F0889

B64
FISK W.M.,ADMINISTRATIVE PROCEDURE IN A REGULATORY SERV/IND
AGENCY: THE CAB AND THE NEW YORK-CHICAGO CASE ECO/DEV
(PAMPHLET). USA+45 DIST/IND ADMIN CONTROL LOBBY AIR
GP/REL ROLE ORD/FREE NEWYORK/C CHICAGO CAB. PAGE 41 JURID
F0805

B64
GARFIELD PJ LOVEJOY WF,PUBLIC UTILITY T
ECONOMICS. DIST/IND FINAN MARKET ADMIN COST DEMAND ECO/TAC
...TECHNIC JURID MUNICH 20 MONOPOLY. PAGE 46 F0906 OWN
SERV/IND

B64
JUCKER-FLEETWOOD E.,MONEY AND FINANCE IN AFRICA. AFR
ISLAM ECO/UNDEV SERV/IND NAT/G EX/STRUC PLAN FINAN
ECO/TAC ROUTINE WEALTH...MGT TOT/POP 20. PAGE 68
F1344

B64
NATIONAL COUN APPLIED ECO RES,A STRATEGY FOR THE ECO/UNDEV
FOURTH PLAN. INDIA DIST/IND EXTR/IND SERV/IND PLAN
ECO/TAC RATION EDU/PROP EATING HEALTH...CHARTS 20. AGRI
PAGE 97 F1900 WORKER

B65
DOWD L.P.,PRINCIPLES OF WORLD BUSINESS. SERV/IND INT/TRADE
NAT/G DIPLOM ECO/TAC TARIFFS...INT/LAW JURID 20. MGT
PAGE 34 F0657 FINAN
MARKET

B65
PEARL A.,NEW CAREERS FOR THE POOR: THE NON- SOC/WK
PROFESSIONAL IN HUMAN SERVICE. USA+45 SERV/IND WEALTH
NAT/G NEIGH WORKER EDU/PROP AUTOMAT SKILL...WELF/ST STRATA
NEW/IDEA BIBLIOG SOC/INTEG 20. PAGE 104 F2044 POLICY

B65
US HOUSE COMM BANKING-CURR,INTERNATIONAL TRAVEL IN BAL/PAY
RELATION TO THE BALANCE OF PAYMENTS DEFICIT. USA+45 ECO/TAC
DELIB/GP...CHARTS 20 CONGRESS TRAVEL. PAGE 136 SERV/IND
F2690 PROB/SOLV

C65
PEGRUM D.E.,"PUBLIC REGULATION OF BUSINESS (REV INDUS
ED)" LAW CONSTN DIST/IND SERV/IND LG/CO LEGIS OWN PLAN
LAISSEZ SOCISM...POLICY DECISION BIBLIOG 20. NEW/LIB
PAGE 104 F2048 PRICE

B66
NICOSIA F.N.,CONSUMER DECISION PROCESSES* MARKETING MARKET
AND ADVERTISING IMPLICATIONS. DIST/IND INDUS PROB/SOLV
CONSULT EDU/PROP ATTIT. PAGE 98 F1925 SERV/IND

B66
POLK J.,U S PRODUCTION ABROAD AND THE BALANCE OF BAL/PAY
PAYMENTS* A SURVEY OF CORPORATE INVESTMENT FINAN
EXPERIENCE. USA+45 SERV/IND NAT/G OP/RES COST INT/TRADE
PROFIT ATTIT...ECOMETRIC STAT INT QU GEN/METH. INDUS
PAGE 107 F2096

S66
VENTRE F.T.,"LOCAL INITIATIVES IN URBAN INDUSTRIAL ECO/TAC
DEVELOPMENT." FINAN SERV/IND TOP/EX PLAN BUDGET LOC/G
RENT TAX...GP/COMP MUNICH 20. PAGE 141 F2777 INDUS

B67
ALEXANDER G.J.,HONESTY AND COMPETITION: FALSE- EDU/PROP
ADVERTISING LAW AND POLICY UNDER FTC SERV/IND
ADMINISTRATION. USA+45 INDUS NAT/G PRICE GP/REL 20 CONTROL
FTC. PAGE 3 F0058 DELIB/GP

B67
OFER G.,THE SERVICE INDUSTRIES IN A DEVELOPING DIPLOM
ECONOMY: ISRAEL AS A CASE STUDY. ISRAEL ECO/TAC ECO/DEV
INT/TRADE PRODUC WEALTH SOCISM...TIME/SEQ TREND SERV/IND
CHARTS 20. PAGE 101 F1979

L67
BONFIELD A.E.,"THE SUBSTANCE OF AMERICAN FAIR LAW
EMPLOYMENT PRACTICES LEGISLA TION II - EMPLOYMENT WORKER
AGENCIES, LABOR ORGANIZATIONS, ETC." ACT/RES LABOR
DISCRIM EFFICIENCY. PAGE 16 F0311 SERV/IND

S67
DANIEL C.,"THE REGULATION OF PRIVATE ENTERPRISES AS LOC/G
PUBLIC UTILITIES." WOR+45 LAW LICENSE POLICY. NAT/G
PAGE 30 F0577 CONTROL
SERV/IND

S67
MODESITT L.E.,"THE MUTUAL FUND - A CORPORATE SERV/IND
ANOMALY." USA+45 CONTROL...MGT 20. PAGE 92 F1813 FINAN
ADMIN
LAW

S67
WOLFSON M.,"GOVERNMENT'S ROLE IN TOURISM SERV/IND
DEVELOPMENT." WOR+45 ECO/DEV ECO/UNDEV FINAN BUDGET NAT/G
DIPLOM EDU/PROP. PAGE 148 F2920 CONTROL
PLAN

SERVAN/JJ....JEAN JACQUES SERVAN-SCHREIBER

SERVICE INDUSTRY....SEE SERV/IND

SET THEORY....SEE CLASSIF

SEVENTHDAY....SEVENTH DAY ADVENTISTS

SEWELL J.P. F2360

SEX DIFFERENCES....SEE SEX

SEX....SEE ALSO BIO/SOC

N19
INTERNATIONAL LABOUR OFFICE,EMPLOYMENT, WORKER
UNEMPLOYMENT AND LABOUR FORCE STATISTICS LABOR
(PAMPHLET). EUR+WWI STRATA AGRI INDUS NAT/G STAT
PROB/SOLV PAY AGE SEX...SAMP NAT/COMP METH 20 ILO. ECO/DEV
PAGE 65 F1278

B49
LEE A.M.,SOCIAL PROBLEMS IN AMERICA: A SOURCE BOOK. SOC
STRATA STRUCT KIN NEIGH VOL/ASSN ACT/RES LEAD CRIME SOCIETY
AGE SEX 20. PAGE 77 F1504 PERSON
EDU/PROP

B50
ADORNO T.W.,THE AUTHORITARIAN PERSONALITY. STRATA AUTHORIT
SECT PROB/SOLV ECO/TAC DISCRIM ATTIT SEX...SOC INT PERSON
CHARTS METH 20. PAGE 3 F0044 ALL/IDEOS

SOCIETY

B58
COALE A.J.,POPULATION GROWTH AND ECONOMIC DEVELOPMENT IN LOW-INCOME COUNTRIES: A CASE STUDY OF INDIA'S PROSPECTS. INDIA AGRI WORKER INCOME AGE WEALTH...CHARTS 20 MEXIC/AMER. PAGE 25 F0495 — ECO/UNDEV GEOG CENSUS SEX

S58
THOMAS D.S.,"AGE AND ECONOMIC DIFFERENTIALS IN INTERSTATE MIGRATION." SEX...GEOG SAMP/SIZ TREND CON/ANAL CHARTS BIBLIOG. PAGE 130 F2560 — AGE WEALTH HABITAT CENSUS

S67
NEALE R.S.,"WORKING CLASS WOMEN AND WOMEN'S SUFFRAGE." UK LAW CONSTN LABOR NAT/G DELIB/GP LEGIS WORKER PAY PARTIC CHOOSE 19 FEMALE/SEX. PAGE 97 F1906 — STRATA SEX SUFF DISCRIM

SEXUAL BEHAVIOR....SEE SEX, PERSON

SHACK W.A. F0470

SHACKLE G.L.S. F2361

SHAFFER H.G. F2362,F2363

SHANGHAI....SHANGHAI

SHANKS M. F2364

SHANNON D.A. F2365

SHANNON I. F2366,F2367

SHARIF A. F2368

SHARP W.R. F2369

SHASTRI/LB....LAL BAHADUR SHASTRI

B66
ZINKIN T.,CHALLENGES IN INDIA. INDIA PAKISTAN LAW AGRI FINAN INDUS TOP/EX TEC/DEV CONTROL ROUTINE ORD/FREE PWR 20 NEHRU/J SHASTRI/LB CIVIL/SERV. PAGE 150 F2964 — NAT/G ECO/TAC POLICY ADMIN

SHAULL R. F1983

SHAW E.S. F2370

SHAW S.J. F2371

SHEENAN D. F2372

SHEFFTZ M.C. F2373

SHEPARD H.A. F0297,F2374

SHEPHERD W.G. F2375

SHEPPARD H.L. F2376

SHEPPARD/S....SAMUEL SHEPPARD

SHERIF M. F2377

SHERMN/ACT....SHERMAN ANTI-TRUST ACT; SEE ALSO MONOPOLY

SHERWOOD W.B. F2378

SHINOHARA M. F2380

SHIPMAN S.S. F0306

SHISTER J. F2381,F2382

SHONFIELD A. F2383,F2384,F2385,F2386

SHORTE F.C. F2387

SHOSTAK A.B. F2388

SHOUP/C....C. SHOUP

SHRIVER/S....SARGENT SHRIVER

S65
HADDAD W.F.,"MR. SHRIVER AND THE SAVAGE POLITICS OF POVERTY" USA+45 LAW NAT/G DELIB/GP LEGIS GIVE LEAD CENTRAL PWR...SOC/WK CHARTS 20 CONGRESS POVRTY/WAR SHRIVER/S OEO. PAGE 53 F1028 — WEALTH GOV/REL CONTROL TOP/EX

SHUBIK M. F2389,F2390

SHULTZ G.P. F2391,F2392

SHWADRAN B. F2393,F2394

SIBERIA....SIBERIA

SIBRON....SIBRON V. NEW YORK

SICILY....SICILY

SICKNESS....SEE HEALTH

SIDDIQ M.M. F2395

SIDGWICK/H....HENRY SIDGWICK

SIEGEL B.N. F2396

SIEGEL S. F2397

SIEGFRIED A. F2398

SIER/LEONE....SIERRA LEONE; SEE ALSO AFR

B55
PEDLER F.J.,ECONOMIC GEOGRAPHY OF WEST AFRICA. GAMBIA NIGER SIER/LEONE STRATA EXTR/IND MARKET LABOR INT/TRADE DEMAND HABITAT WEALTH...CHARTS 20. PAGE 104 F2046 — ECO/UNDEV GEOG PRODUC EFFICIENCY

B61
CARNEY D.E.,GOVERNMENT AND ECONOMY IN BRITISH WEST AFRICA. GAMBIA GHANA NIGERIA SIER/LEONE DOMIN ADMIN GOV/REL SOVEREIGN WEALTH LAISSEZ...BIBLIOG 20 CMN/WLTH. PAGE 21 F0417 — METH/COMP COLONIAL ECO/TAC ECO/UNDEV

B61
PETCH G.A.,ECONOMIC DEVELOPMENT AND MODERN WEST AFRICA. AFR CONGO/BRAZ GHANA NIGER SIER/LEONE AGRI MARKET LABOR FOR/AID TAX COST EFFICIENCY EQUILIB PRODUC...GEOG TREND 20. PAGE 105 F2068 — ECO/UNDEV TEC/DEV EXTR/IND ECO/TAC

SIEVERS A.M. F2399

SIHANOUK....NORODOM SIHANOUK

SIKES E.R. F2400

SIKKIM....SEE ALSO S/ASIA

SILCOCK T.H. F2401

SILK L.S. F2402

SILOW R.A. F2403

SILVER....SILVER STANDARD AND POLICIES RELATING TO SILVER

B20
BUCK S.J.,THE AGRARIAN CRUSADE: A CHRONICLE OF THE FARMER IN POLITICS. USA-45 INDUS PROB/SOLV PWR WEALTH...GEOG CENSUS 19/20 GREENBACK GRANGE SILVER. PAGE 20 F0381 — AGRI POPULISM VOL/ASSN POL/PAR

B44
LOCKE J.,FURTHER CONSIDERATIONS CONCERNING RAISING THE VALUE OF MONEY. AFR UK NAT/G ECO/TAC INCOME WEALTH...METH/COMP GEN/LAWS 17 SILVER. PAGE 81 F1591 — COST FINAN PRICE CONTROL

B57
OLIVECRONA K.,THE PROBLEM OF THE MONETARY UNIT. AFR UNIV PAY PRICE UTIL...MATH 20 MONEY SILVER. PAGE 101 F1986 — FINAN ECO/TAC ECO/DEV CONCPT

B58
AVRAMOVIC D.,POSTWAR GROWTH IN INTERNATIONAL INDEBTEDNESS. AFR WOR+45 AGRI INDUS CAP/ISM PRICE INCOME...NAT/COMP 20 SILVER. PAGE 8 F0143 — INT/TRADE FINAN COST BAL/PAY

B58
PALYI M.,MANAGED MONEY AT THE CROSSROADS: THE EUROPEAN EXPERIENCE. AFR WOR+45 WOR-45 TEC/DEV DIPLOM INT/TRADE DEMAND WEALTH...CHARTS BIBLIOG 19/20 EUROPE SILVER. PAGE 103 F2022 — FINAN ECO/TAC ECO/DEV PRODUC

B61
VEIT O.,GRUNDRISS DER WAHRUNGSPOLITIK. AFR FRANCE GERMANY USSR DIPLOM INT/TRADE...NAT/COMP 19/20 SILVER. PAGE 141 F2773 — FINAN POLICY ECO/TAC CAP/ISM

N62
BANK INTERNATIONAL SETTLEMENTS,AUSTRIA: MONETARY AND ECONOMIC SITUATION 1952-61 (PAMPHLET). AUSTRIA WORKER BUDGET INT/TRADE PRICE BAL/PAY DEMAND EFFICIENCY INCOME PRODUC...STAT 20 SILVER. PAGE 9 F0174 — FINAN ECO/DEV CHARTS WEALTH

B65
SCITOVSKY T.,REQUIREMENTS OF AN INTERNATIONAL RESERVE SYSTEM. AFR ECO/TAC...PREDICT 20 SILVER MONEY. PAGE 118 F2330 — BAL/PAY FINAN EQUILIB

INT/TRADE

B66
CONAN A.R.,THE PROBLEM OF STERLING. UK WOR+45 BUDGET ECO/TAC...POLICY STAT CHARTS 20 SILVER. PAGE 27 F0521
FINAN ECO/DEV BAL/PAY DIPLOM

B66
TRIFFIN R.,THE WORLD MONEY MAZE. AFR INT/ORG ECO/TAC PRICE OPTIMAL WEALTH...METH/COMP 20 EEC OEEC SILVER. PAGE 131 F2589
BAL/PAY FINAN INT/TRADE DIPLOM

SILVERMAN C. F2404

SIMMEL/G....GEORG SIMMEL

SIMMONS G.B. F2484

SIMMS R.P. F2405

SIMON B. F2406

SIMON H.A. F2191,F2408,F2409

SIMONE A.J. F2410

SIMOONS F.J. F2411

SIMPSON....SIMPSON V. UNION OIL COMPANY

SIMUL....SCIENTIFIC MODELS

N19
BOS H.C.,A DISCUSSION ON METHODS OF MONETARY ANALYSIS AND NORMS FOR MONETARY POLICY (PAMPHLET). BAL/PAY COST INCOME...METH/COMP 20. PAGE 17 F0319
FINAN POLICY EQUILIB SIMUL

N19
BUSINESS ECONOMISTS' GROUP,INCOME POLICIES (PAMPHLET). UK INDUS LABOR TOP/EX PAY COST PRODUC ...ECOMETRIC GOV/COMP SIMUL ANTHOL 20. PAGE 20 F0395
INCOME WORKER WEALTH POLICY

N19
HAGEN E.E.,AN ANALYTICAL MODEL OF THE TRANSITION TO ECONOMIC GROWTH (PAMPHLET). WOR+45 WOR-45 SOCIETY STRATA FINAN NAT/G CONTROL PARTIC PRODUC...PHIL/SCI BIBLIOG 17/20. PAGE 53 F1033
SIMUL ECO/DEV METH TEC/DEV

N19
MUSHKIN S.J.,LOCAL SCHOOL EXPENDITURES: 1970 PROJECTIONS (PAMPHLET). FUT USA+45 CONSTRUC FINAN PROVS EDU/PROP COST...GEOG CENSUS PREDICT CHARTS SIMUL 20. PAGE 95 F1871
LOC/G SCHOOL BUDGET

B25
EDGEWORTH F.Y.,PAPERS RELATING TO POLITICAL ECONOMY. MOD/EUR SOCIETY STRATA DIST/IND INDUS MARKET NAT/G ACT/RES ECO/TAC EXEC WEALTH ...METH/CNCPT MATH TREND HYPO/EXP SIMUL GEN/METH FOR/TRADE VAL/FREE LOG/LING. PAGE 36 F0702
ECO/DEV CAP/ISM

B28
CASSEL G.,FOREIGN INVESTMENTS. GERMANY UK USA-45 WOR-45 ECO/DEV NAT/G VOL/ASSN CAP/ISM REPAR ATTIT WEALTH...METH/CNCPT STAT SIMUL STERTYP ANTHOL FOR/TRADE TOT/POP VAL/FREE 20. PAGE 22 F0426
FINAN ECO/TAC BAL/PAY

B41
HAYEK F.A.,THE PURE THEORY OF CAPITAL. UNIV ECO/DEV ECO/TAC COST EQUILIB PROFIT WEALTH...SIMUL GEN/LAWS BIBLIOG INDEX TIME 20. PAGE 57 F1120
CAP/ISM METH/CNCPT PRODUC FINAN

B48
WHITE C.L.,HUMAN GEOGRAPHY: AN ECOLOGICAL STUDY OF GEOGRAPHY. UNIV SEA CULTURE AGRI EXTR/IND RACE/REL PRODUC...CHARTS HYPO/EXP SIMUL GEN/LAWS T. PAGE 146 F2868
SOC HABITAT GEOG SOCIETY

B49
PARMELEE M.,GEO-ECONOMIC REGIONAL AND WORLD FEDERATION. FUT WOR+45 WOR-45 SOCIETY VOL/ASSN PLAN ...METH/CNCPT SIMUL GEN/METH TERR/GP TOT/POP 20. PAGE 103 F2028
INT/ORG GEOG REGION

B55
BOULDING K.E.,ECONOMIC ANALYSIS (3RD ED.). USA+45 PLAN ECO/TAC COST DEMAND INCOME...POLICY STAT CHARTS SIMUL T. PAGE 17 F0322
PHIL/SCI ECO/DEV CAP/ISM

S55
DIESING P.,"NONECONOMIC DECISION-MAKING" (BMR)" PROB/SOLV GP/REL ORD/FREE...STAT METH/COMP SIMUL 20. PAGE 33 F0638
DECISION METH EFFICIENCY SOC

B56
GARDNER R.N.,STERLING-DOLLAR DIPLOMACY. EUR+WWI USA+45 INT/ORG NAT/G PLAN INT/TRADE EDU/PROP ADMIN KNOWL PWR WEALTH...POLICY SOC METH/CNCPT STAT CHARTS SIMUL GEN/LAWS 20. PAGE 46 F0902
ECO/DEV DIPLOM

B56
KINDLEBERGER C.P.,THE TERMS OF TRADE: A EUROPEAN CASE-STUDY. EUR+WWI MOD/EUR ECO/DEV ECO/UNDEV AGRI INDUS BAL/PAY...METH/CNCPT STAT CONT/OBS CON/ANAL SOC/EXP SIMUL FOR/TRADE 20. PAGE 71 F1390
PLAN ECO/TAC

S56
HARSANYI J.C.,"APPROACHES TO THE BARGAINING PROBLEM BEFORE AND AFTER THE THEORY OF GAMES."...DECISION CON/ANAL SIMUL GEN/LAWS. PAGE 56 F1096
NEW/IDEA GAME IDEA/COMP

B57
DAY A.C.L.,OUTLINE OF MONETARY ECONOMICS. AFR WOR-45 INT/ORG WORKER DIPLOM BAL/PAY COST INCOME WEALTH...TIME/SEQ SIMUL 20. PAGE 31 F0594
FINAN NAT/G EQUILIB PRICE

B58
HIRSCHMAN A.O.,STRATEGY OF ECONOMIC DEVELOPMENT. WOR+45 WOR-45 CULTURE ECO/DEV NAT/G PLAN TEC/DEV INT/TRADE BAL/PAY ATTIT DRIVE RIGID/FLEX WEALTH ...CONCPT METH/CNCPT OBS CHARTS SIMUL GEN/LAWS TOT/POP VAL/FREE. PAGE 60 F1176
ECO/UNDEV ECO/TAC CAP/ISM

B58
THEIL H.,ECONOMIC FORECASTS AND POLICY. UNIV CAP/ISM PRICE EFFICIENCY...DECISION CONCPT STAT 20. PAGE 129 F2551
SIMUL MATH ECOMETRIC PREDICT

L58
ARROW K.J.,"ON THE STABILITY OF THE COMPETITIVE EQUILIBRIUM: I." WOR+45...METH/CNCPT MATH STAT CHARTS SIMUL. PAGE 6 F0122
DECISION MARKET ECO/DEV ECO/TAC

B59
MATTHEWS R.C.O.,THE BUSINESS CYCLE. AFR LABOR INT/TRADE TAX PRICE RISK ADJUST WEALTH...POLICY ECOMETRIC CHARTS SIMUL TIME 20. PAGE 87 F1705
FINAN DEMAND TASK

B59
STANFORD U, BOARD OF TRUSTEES,THE ALLOCATION OF ECONOMIC RESOURCES. WORKER PLAN BUDGET ECO/TAC TAX RECEIVE COST PRODUC...POLICY IDEA/COMP SIMUL ANTHOL 20. PAGE 125 F2468
INCOME PRICE FINAN

B59
WAHLKE J.C.,LEGISLATIVE BEHAVIOR: A READER IN THEORY AND RESEARCH. USA+45 CONSTN ELITES POL/PAR LOBBY REPRESENT PERS/REL PERSON ROLE...IDEA/COMP METH/COMP SIMUL. PAGE 142 F2800
LEGIS CHOOSE INGP/REL ATTIT

L59
SIMON H.A.,"THEORIES OF DECISION-MAKING IN ECONOMICS AND BEHAVIORAL SCIENCE" (BMR)" MARKET BARGAIN UTIL DRIVE...DECISION MGT PROBABIL HYPO/EXP SIMUL 20 BEHAVIORSM. PAGE 122 F2409
PSY GEN/LAWS PROB/SOLV

S59
CYERT R.M.,"MODELS IN A BEHAVIORAL THEORY OF THE FIRM." ROUTINE...DECISION MGT METH/CNCPT MATH. PAGE 29 F0567
SIMUL GAME PREDICT INDUS

S59
HARING J.E.,"UTILITY THEORY, DECISION THEORY, AND PROFIT MAXIMIZATION." PROB/SOLV GAMBLE UTIL ...DECISION CHARTS IDEA/COMP HYPO/EXP SIMUL GEN/METH. PAGE 55 F1083
PROBABIL RISK GAME

B60
HARBERGER A.C.,THE DEMAND FOR DURABLE GOODS. AGRI FINAN COST EQUILIB...MATH STAT TIME/SEQ TREND CON/ANAL CHARTS SIMUL ANTHOL 20. PAGE 55 F1072
ECOMETRIC DEMAND PRICE

B60
MORRIS W.T.,ENGINEERING ECONOMY. AUTOMAT RISK RATIONAL...PROBABIL STAT CHARTS GAME SIMUL BIBLIOG T 20. PAGE 94 F1838
OP/RES DECISION MGT PROB/SOLV

B60
STEIN E.,AMERICAN ENTERPRISE IN THE EUROPEAN COMMON MARKET: A LEGAL PROFILE. EUR+WWI FUT USA+45 SOCIETY STRUCT ECO/DEV NAT/G VOL/ASSN CONSULT PLAN TEC/DEV ECO/TAC INT/TRADE ADMIN ATTIT RIGID/FLEX PWR...MGT NEW/IDEA STAT TREND COMPUT/IR SIMUL EEC 20. PAGE 125 F2475
MARKET ADJUD INT/LAW

L60
CHENERY H.B.,"PATTERNS OF INDUSTRIAL GROWTH." INT/TRADE DEMAND PRODUC...MATH REGRESS CHARTS SIMUL METH 20. PAGE 24 F0462
ECO/TAC ECO/DEV GP/COMP CON/ANAL

L60
SPENGLER J.J.,"ECONOMIC DEVELOPMENT: POLITICAL PRECONDITIONS AND POLITICAL CONSEQUENCE." WOR+45 STRUCT ECO/UNDEV NAT/G PLAN ECO/TAC EDU/PROP ATTIT ORD/FREE WEALTH SOCISM...SOC CONCPT TREND SIMUL GEN/METH WORK 20. PAGE 124 F2452
TEC/DEV METH/CNCPT CAP/ISM

B61
ACKLEY G.,MACROECONOMIC THEORY. AFR FINAN WORKER ECO/TAC PRICE COST INCOME PRODUC...MATH TREND CHARTS IDEA/COMP T KEYNES/JM. PAGE 2 F0034
SIMUL ECOMETRIC WEALTH

B61
KLEIN L.R.,AN ECONOMETRIC MODEL OF THE UNITED KINGDOM. UK PRICE COST...MATH PREDICT TREND CHARTS SIMUL METH 20. PAGE 72 F1407
ECOMETRIC COMPUTER STAT COMPUT/IR

S61
ANDREWS R.B.,"URBAN ECONOMICS: AN APPRAISAL OF PROGRESS." LOC/G PROB/SOLV TEC/DEV...CONCPT OBS/ENVIR METH/COMP HYPO/EXP SOC/EXP SIMUL GEN/METH METH MUNICH 20. PAGE 5 F0102
PHIL/SCI ECOMETRIC

S61
BENNION E.G.,"ECONOMETRICS FOR MANAGEMENT." USA+45 INDUS EX/STRUC ACT/RES COMPUTER UTIL...MATH STAT PREDICT METH/COMP HYPO/EXP. PAGE 13 F0248
ECOMETRIC MGT SIMUL DECISION

S61
HIRSHLEIFER J.,"THE BAYESIAN APPROACH TO STATISTICAL DECISION: AN EXPOSITION." OP/RES PROB/SOLV UTIL...PROBABIL CHARTS IDEA/COMP HYPO/EXP 20. PAGE 60 F1178
DECISION GAME SIMUL STAT

S61
SHUBIK M.,"APPROACHES TO THE STUDY OF DECISION-MAKING RELEVANT TO THE FIRM." INDUS COMPUTER OP/RES ...PROBABIL STAT 20. PAGE 121 F2390
GAME DECISION MGT SIMUL

B62
EINZIG P.,THE HISTORY OF FOREIGN EXCHANGE. CHRIST-17C ISLAM MEDIT-7 PRE/AMER WOR+45 ECO/DEV FINAN PLAN ECO/TAC ATTIT KNOWL WEALTH...SIMUL GEN/LAWS. PAGE 37 F0714
MARKET TIME/SEQ INT/TRADE

B62
HOOVER C.B.,ECONOMIC SYSTEMS OF THE COMMONWEALTH. AFR CANADA INDIA UK ECO/DEV ECO/UNDEV AGRI INDUS TEC/DEV TARIFFS PRICE BAL/PAY DEMAND...SIMUL 20 AUSTRAL. PAGE 61 F1208
CAP/ISM SOCISM ECO/TAC PLAN

B62
KLEIN L.R.,AN INTRODUCTION TO ECONOMETRICS. DIST/IND DEMAND PRODUC WEALTH...MATH TIME/SEQ T 20. PAGE 72 F1408
ECOMETRIC SIMUL PREDICT STAT

B62
MEYER F.V.,THE TERMS OF TRADE. WOR+45 AGRI MARKET PROC/MFG DIPLOM PRICE DEMAND PRODUC 20. PAGE 90 F1769
INT/TRADE BAL/PAY SIMUL EQUILIB

B62
WRIGHT D.M.,THE KEYNESIAN SYSTEM. WOR+45 WOR-45 LABOR NAT/G CONTROL COST DEMAND EFFICIENCY...POLICY CONCPT CHARTS SIMUL 20 KEYNES/JM. PAGE 149 F2931
INCOME ECO/DEV FINAN ECO/TAC

S62
MILLIKEN M.,"NEW AND OLD CRITERIA FOR AID." WOR+45 ECO/DEV ECO/UNDEV ACT/RES PLAN ATTIT KNOWL...TREND CON/ANAL SIMUL GEN/METH TERR/GP 20. PAGE 92 F1796
USA+45 ECO/TAC FOR/AID

B63
BARNETT H.J.,SCARCITY AND GROWTH: THE ECONOMICS OF NATURAL RESOURCE AVAILABILITY. FUT WOR+45 AGRI INDUS PROB/SOLV TEC/DEV CONTROL PRODUC...SOC/WK IDEA/COMP METH/COMP SIMUL 20 RESOURCE/N MALTHUS RICARDO/D MILL/JS DARWIN/C. PAGE 10 F0191
DEMAND HABITAT CENSUS GEOG

B63
BONINI C.P.,SIMULATION OF INFORMATION AND DECISION SYSTEMS IN THE FIRM. MARKET BUDGET DOMIN EDU/PROP ADMIN COST ATTIT HABITAT PERCEPT PWR...CONCPT PROBABIL QUANT PREDICT HYPO/EXP BIBLIOG. PAGE 16 F0313
INDUS SIMUL DECISION MGT

B63
HOLLAND E.P.,EXPERIMENTS ON A SIMULATED UNDERDEVELOPED ECONOMY: DEVELOPMENT PLANS AND BALANCE-OF-PAYMENTS POLICIES. WOR+45 ECO/UNDEV FINAN PLAN ECO/TAC...MATH STAT CHARTS SIMUL VAL/FREE. PAGE 61 F1196
AFR BAL/PAY

B63
LAGOS G.,INTERNATIONAL STRATIFICATION AND UNDERDEVELOPED COUNTRIES. L/A+17C WOR+45 PLAN ECO/TAC PWR RESPECT WEALTH...METH/CNCPT STAT CHARTS SIMUL GEN/LAWS TRUE/GP METH/GP VAL/FREE 20. PAGE 74 F1459
ECO/UNDEV STRATA

B63
MARCHAL J.,EXPANSION ET RECESSION. FRANCE OP/RES PROB/SOLV ROLE ORD/FREE...TREND SIMUL 20 DEPRESSION. PAGE 85 F1663
FINAN PLAN ECO/DEV

B63
MINER J.,SOCIAL AND ECONOMIC FACTORS IN SPENDING FOR PUBLIC EDUCATION. USA+45 FINAN SCHOOL OPTIMAL ...POLICY DECISION REGRESS PREDICT CHARTS SIMUL 20. PAGE 92 F1801
EDU/PROP NAT/G COST ACT/RES

B63
NEUMARK S.D.,FOREIGN TRADE AND ECONOMIC DEVELOPMENT IN AFRICA: A HISTORICAL PERSPECTIVE. EUR+WWI MOD/EUR ECO/UNDEV AGRI COM/IND EXTR/IND PROC/MFG SKILL WEALTH...CONCPT TIME/SEQ TREND SIMUL FOR/TRADE WORK TOT/POP TERR/GP VAL/FREE 19/20. PAGE 98 F1916
AFR

B63
SALANT W.S.,THE UNITED STATES BALANCE OF PAYMENTS IN 1968. USA+45 ECO/DEV ECO/UNDEV INT/ORG DELIB/GP ECO/TAC...POLICY STAT SIMUL 20. PAGE 115 F2273
FUT FINAN BAL/PAY

S63
CLEMHOUT S.,"PRODUCTION FUNCTION ANALYSIS APPLIED TO THE LEONTIEF SCARCE-FACTOR PARADOX OF INTERNATIONAL TRADE." EUR+WWI USA+45 DIST/IND NAT/G PLAN TEC/DEV DIPLOM PWR WEALTH...MGT METH/CNCPT CONT/OBS CON/ANAL CHARTS SIMUL GEN/LAWS FOR/TRADE 20. PAGE 25 F0490
ECO/DEV ECO/TAC

S63
COLLERY A.,"A FULL EMPLOYMENT, KEYNESIAN THEORY OF INTERNATIONAL TRADE." WOR+45 ECO/DEV ACT/RES ECO/TAC ROUTINE ORD/FREE WEALTH...MATH CHARTS 20 KEYNES/JM. PAGE 26 F0504
SIMUL INT/TRADE

B64
GEORGIADIS H.G.,BALANCE OF PAYMENTS EQUILIBRIUM. COST DEMAND...CONCPT MATH GEN/LAWS 20 KEYNES/JM. PAGE 47 F0916
BAL/PAY EQUILIB SIMUL INT/TRADE

B64
HART P.E.,ECONOMETRIC ANALYSIS FOR NATIONAL ECONOMIC PLANNING. INDUS OP/RES PRICE PRODUC ...SIMUL ANTHOL MODELS 20. PAGE 56 F1100
PLAN ECOMETRIC STAT

B64
JUSTER F.T.,ANTICIPATIONS AND PURCHASES; AN ANALYSIS OF CONSUMER BEHAVIOR. PROB/SOLV RISK COST PRODUC DRIVE...STAT STYLE SAMP CON/ANAL CHARTS HYPO/EXP GAME SIMUL. PAGE 68 F1345
PROBABIL DECISION PREDICT DEMAND

B64
LANG A.S.,URBAN RAIL TRANSIT. OP/RES PLAN PROB/SOLV TEC/DEV AUTOMAT COST...TECHNIC MATH CON/ANAL CHARTS METH/COMP SIMUL MUNICH 20 RAILROAD PUB/TRANS. PAGE 75 F1474
DIST/IND ECOMETRIC

B64
LANGHOFF P.,MODELS, MEASUREMENT AND MARKETING. ACT/RES COMPUTER OP/RES PLAN BUDGET...MGT PHIL/SCI METH/CNCPT STAT PROG/TEAC BIBLIOG. PAGE 75 F1478
DECISION SIMUL MARKET R+D

B64
MEYER J.R.,INVESTMENT DECISIONS, ECONOMIC FORECASTING, AND PUBLIC POLICY. ECO/DEV ECO/TAC ...DECISION REGRESS TIME/SEQ CHARTS GP/COMP SIMUL 20. PAGE 90 F1771
FINAN PROB/SOLV PREDICT LG/CO

B64
WILLIAMSON J.G.,AMERICAN GROWTH AND THE BALANCE OF PAYMENTS, 1820-1913: A STUDY OF THE LONG SWING. EUR+WWI MOD/EUR USA+45 USA-45 ECO/DEV NAT/G ECO/TAC ROUTINE ORD/FREE WEALTH...MATH STAT TIME/SEQ CHARTS SIMUL GEN/LAWS TRUE/GP METH/GP VAL/FREE 19/20. PAGE 147 F2896
FINAN BAL/PAY

B64
ZOLLSCHAN G.K.,EXPLORATIONS IN SOCIAL CHANGE. SOCIETY STRATA STRUCT ECO/UNDEV EX/STRUC...PSY ANTHOL 20. PAGE 151 F2968
ORD/FREE SIMUL CONCPT CULTURE

S64
BEIM D.,"THE COMMUNIST BLOC AND THE FOREIGN-AID GAME." AFR WOR+45 NAT/G PLAN ROUTINE ATTIT KNOWL ORD/FREE...DECISION QUANT CONT/OBS TIME/SEQ CHARTS GAME SIMUL LOG/LING 20. PAGE 12 F0231
COM ECO/UNDEV ECO/TAC FOR/AID

B65
FORD J.L.,THE OHLIN-HECKSCHER THEORY OF THE BASIS AND EFFECTS OF COMMODITY TRADE. WOR+45 ECO/TAC DEMAND INCOME...CONCPT GEN/METH 20 OHLIN/HECK. PAGE 42 F0824
ECOMETRIC INT/TRADE NEW/IDEA SIMUL

B65
FRIEDLANDER S.L.,LABOR MIGRATION AND ECONOMIC GROWTH: A CASE STUDY OF PUERTO RICO. PUERT/RICO AGRI WORKER PLAN PROB/SOLV...ECOMETRIC STAT PREDICT CHARTS HYPO/EXP SIMUL 20. PAGE 44 F0858
CENSUS GEOG ECO/UNDEV WEALTH

B65
GREEN J.L.,METROPOLITAN ECONOMIC REPUBLICS. USA+45 ECO/TAC INCOME...GEOG SOC CONCPT SIMUL MUNICH 20 ATLANTA. PAGE 50 F0985
SOC/WK PLAN LABOR

B65
HLA MYINT U.,THE ECONOMICS OF THE DEVELOPING COUNTRIES. USA+45 WOR+45 AGRI FINAN NAT/G INT/TRADE ...CLASSIF CENSUS TREND NAT/COMP SIMUL GEN/LAWS. PAGE 60 F1180
ECO/UNDEV FOR/AID GEOG

B65
KLASSEN L.H.,AREA ECONOMIC AND SOCIAL REDEVELOPMENT. ECO/UNDEV INDUS NAT/G PLAN CAP/ISM TAX...ECOMETRIC SIMUL 20. PAGE 72 F1404
OPTIMAL WORKER METH ECO/TAC

B65
MAO J.C.T.,EFFICIENCY IN PUBLIC URBAN RENEWAL EXPENDITURES THROUGH CAPITAL BUDGETING. USA+45 FINAN LOC/G NAT/G NEIGH REGION UTIL...GEOG METH/CNCPT STAT SIMUL GEN/LAWS MUNICH 20 URBAN/RNWL. PAGE 85 F1662
TEC/DEV BUDGET PROB/SOLV

B65
PINCUS J.A.,ECONOMIC AID AND INTERNATIONAL COST SHARING* A RAND CORPORATION RESEARCH STUDY. INT/ORG BUDGET CENTRAL...ECOMETRIC MATH QUANT STAT SIMUL. PAGE 106 F2088
ECO/UNDEV COST FOR/AID INT/TRADE

B65
RIGBY P.H.,CONCEPTUAL FOUNDATIONS OF BUSINESS RESEARCH. COMPUTER PROB/SOLV OPTIMAL...MGT CONCPT MATH STAT TESTS SIMUL GEN/METH. PAGE 111 F2192
PROFIT R+D INDUS DECISION

S65
BRIGHAM E.F.,"THE DETERMINANTS OF RESIDENTIAL LAND VALUES." USA+45 ECO/DEV PROB/SOLV RENT PRICE ...REGRESS STAT CHARTS GEN/METH MUNICH 20 LOS/ANG. PAGE 18 F0351
COST INDICATOR SIMUL ECOMETRIC

S65
CHU K.,"A DYNAMIC MODEL OF THE FIRM." OP/RES PROB/SOLV...DECISION ECOMETRIC NEW/IDEA STAT GAME ORG/CHARTS SIMUL. PAGE 24 F0472
INDUS COMPUTER TEC/DEV

S65
GRENIEWSKI H.,"INTENTION AND PERFORMANCE: A PRIMER OF CYBERNETICS OF PLANNING." EFFICIENCY OPTIMAL KNOWL SKILL...DECISION MGT EQULIB. PAGE 51 F0995
SIMUL GAME GEN/METH PLAN

S65
KUNKEL J.H.,"VALUES AND BEHAVIOR IN ECONOMIC DEVELOPMENT." INDIA PERU CULTURE STRUCT CREATE PERS/REL ATTIT PERSON...CHARTS HYPO/EXP ARGEN. PAGE 74 F1449
SIMUL ECO/UNDEV PSY STERTYP

B66
BROWN R.T.,TRANSPORT AND THE ECONOMIC INTEGRATION OF SOUTH AMERICA. L/A+17C ECO/UNDEV NAT/G OP/RES DIPLOM INT/TRADE REGION WEALTH...ECOMETRIC GEOG STAT LAFTA TIME. PAGE 19 F0373
MARKET DIST/IND SIMUL

B66
FOX K.A.,THE THEORY OF QUANTITATIVE ECONOMIC POLICY WITH APPLICATIONS TO ECONOMIC GROWTH AND STABILIZATION. ECO/DEV AGRI NAT/G PLAN ADMIN RISK ...DECISION IDEA/COMP SIMUL T. PAGE 43 F0837
ECO/TAC ECOMETRIC EQUILIB GEN/LAWS

B66
HEISS K.P.,GAME THEORY AND HUMAN CONFLICTS (RESEARCH MEMORANDUM). UNIV ACT/RES...DECISION SOC MATH PROBABIL SIMUL 20 DEFINETT/B. PAGE 58 F1142
GAME ECOMETRIC PLAN PROB/SOLV

B66
KUENNE R.E.,THE POLARIS MISSILE STRIKE* A GENERAL ECONOMIC SYSTEMS ANALYSIS. USA+45 USSR NAT/G BAL/PWR ARMS/CONT WAR...MATH PROBABIL COMPUT/IR CHARTS HYPO/EXP SIMUL. PAGE 74 F1446
NUC/PWR FORCES DETER DIPLOM

B66
LERNER E.M.,A THEORY OF FINANCIAL ANALYSIS. UNIV LG/CO COST DEMAND INCOME PROFIT...MATH STAT CHARTS SIMUL T 20. PAGE 78 F1531
CONCPT FINAN ECO/DEV OPTIMAL

B66
THEIL H.,APPLIED ECONOMIC FORECASTING. UNIV USA+45 ELITES INTELL CONSULT PRODUC...DECISION MGT PREDICT CHARTS METH/COMP SIMUL 20. PAGE 129 F2552
FUT OP/RES PLAN

B66
US PRES COMM ECO IMPACT DEFENS,REPORT* JULY 1965. USA+45 ECO/DEV INDUS DELIB/GP FORCES OP/RES ARMS/CONT NUC/PWR WEAPON BAL/PAY...PREDICT SIMUL. PAGE 138 F2726
ACT/RES STAT WAR BUDGET

B66
YOUNG S.,MANAGEMENT: A SYSTEMS ANALYSIS. DELIB/GP EX/STRUC ECO/TAC CONTROL EFFICIENCY...NET/THEORY 20. PAGE 150 F2952
PROB/SOLV MGT DECISION SIMUL

S66
DAVIS O.A.,"A THEORY OF THE BUDGETARY PROCESS." ECO/DEV FINAN LEGIS PROB/SOLV GOV/REL...ECOMETRIC METH/CNCPT STAT CONT/OBS TREND METH/COMP SIMUL 20 CONGRESS. PAGE 30 F0592
DECISION NAT/G BUDGET EFFICIENCY

S66
FROMM G.,"RECENT MONETARY POLICY: AN ECONOMETRIC VIEW" USA+45 ECO/DEV INDUS PAY PRICE PRODUC ORD/FREE WEALTH...STAT 20 FED/RESERV. PAGE 45 F0869
ECOMETRIC FINAN POLICY SIMUL

B67
ALLEN R.G.,MACRO-ECONOMIC THEORY. A MATHEMATICAL TREATMENT. UNIV...SIMUL T. PAGE 4 F0070
ECOMETRIC MATH EQUILIB GAME

B67
DE JOUVENAL B.,THE ART OF CONJECTURE. WOR+45 EFFICIENCY PERCEPT KNOWL...DECISION PHIL/SCI CONCPT METH/COMP BIBLIOG 20. PAGE 31 F0600
FUT PREDICT SIMUL METH

B67
GOLEMBIEWSKI R.T.,ORGANIZING MEN AND POWER: PATTERNS OF BEHAVIOR AND LINESTAFF MODELS. WOR+45 EX/STRUC ACT/RES DOMIN PERS/REL...NEW/IDEA 20. PAGE 48 F0943
ADMIN CONTROL SIMUL MGT

B67
HAGUE D.C.,PRICE FORMATION IN VARIOUS ECONOMIES; PROCEEDINGS OF A CONFERENCE HELD BY THE INTERNATIONAL ECONOMIC ASSOCIATION. WOR+45 FINAN MARKET PLAN CONFER COST...DECISION MATH PREDICT CHARTS SIMUL 20 INTL/ECON. PAGE 53 F1037
PRICE CAP/ISM SOCISM METH/COMP

B67
HARDT J.P.,MATHEMATICS AND COMPUTERS IN SOVIET ECONOMIC PLANNING. COM USSR OP/RES PROB/SOLV OPTIMAL...MODAL SIMUL 20. PAGE 55 F1082
PLAN TEC/DEV MATH COMPUT/IR

B67
JOHNSON H.G.,ECONOMIC NATIONALISM IN OLD AND NEW STATES. CANADA CHINA/COM MALI UK DIPLOM...SIMUL GEN/LAWS 19/20 MEXIC/AMER. PAGE 68 F1328
NAT/LISM ECO/UNDEV ECO/DEV NAT/COMP

B67
MALINVAUD E.,ACTIVITY ANALYSIS IN THE THEORY OF GROWTH AND PLANNING. UNIV AGRI COMPUTER OP/RES REGION...CHARTS ANTHOL METH. PAGE 84 F1648
MATH GAME SIMUL

B67
PORWIT K.,CENTRAL PLANNING: EVALUATION OF VARIANTS. PRICE OPTIMAL PRODUC...DECISION MATH CHARTS SIMUL BIBLIOG MODELS 20. PAGE 107 F2106
PLAN MGT ECOMETRIC

B67
SAPARINA Y.,CYBERNETICS WITHIN US. WOR+45 EDU/PROP FEEDBACK PERCEPT HEALTH...DECISION METH/CNCPT NEW/IDEA 20. PAGE 116 F2281
COMPUTER METH/COMP CONTROL SIMUL

S67
LEE R.L.,"THE PARADOX OF EQUALITY: A THREAT TO INDIVIDUAL AND SYSTEM FUNCTIONING." CHINA/COM ECO/UNDEV WORKER...SIMUL GEN/LAWS 20. PAGE 77 F1508
SOCIETY STRATA MARXISM IDEA/COMP

S67
PLOTT C.R.,"A NOTION OF EQUILIBRIUM AND ITS POSSIBILITY UNDER MAJORITY RULE." CREATE...DECISION STAT CHARTS 20. PAGE 106 F2094
SIMUL EQUILIB CHOOSE MAJORITY

S67
SANDMEYER R.L.,"METHODOLOGICAL ISSUES IN THE STUDY OF LABOR FORCE PARTICIPATION RATES." WOR+45 ...CLASSIF REGRESS CHARTS SIMUL. PAGE 116 F2278
METH CON/ANAL PARTIC WORKER

SIMULATION....SEE SIMUL, MODELS INDEX

SINAI....SINAI

SIND....SIND - REGION OF PAKISTAN

SINGAPORE....SINGAPORE; SEE ALSO MALAYSIA

SINGER H.W. F1336,F2412

SINGH D.B. F2413

SINGH L.P. F2414

SINHA M.R. F2415

SINO/SOV....SINO-SOVIET RELATIONSHIPS

SINYAVSK/A....ANDREY SINYAVSKY

SIPPEL D. F2416

SIRS....SALARY INFORMATION RETRIEVAL SYSTEM

SIRUGO F. F2417

SKILL....DEXTERITY

B14
VEBLEN T.,THE INSTINCT OF WORKMANSHIP. UNIV SOCIETY ECO/DEV ECO/UNDEV CREATE TEC/DEV ECO/TAC EDU/PROP ROUTINE PERSON...HUM CONCPT TIME/SEQ GEN/LAWS. PAGE 140 F2768
DRIVE SKILL

B38
LEVINSON E.,LABOR ON THE MARCH. WORKER CREATE ECO/TAC ADJUD LEAD PARL/PROC PARTIC INGP/REL SKILL POLICY. PAGE 79 F1543
LABOR INCOME NAT/G PLAN

S43
HUZAR E.,"CONGRESS AND THE ARMY: APPROPRIATIONS." USA-45 CONFER CONTROL ATTIT SUPEGO SKILL CONGRESS. PAGE 64 F1255
LEGIS FORCES BUDGET DELIB/GP

B45
DAVIS J.,AFRICA ADVANCING. AFR CONGO/BRAZ LIBERIA NIGER INT/ORG SCHOOL DIPLOM GIVE KNOWL SKILL 20. PAGE 30 F0590
SECT COLONIAL AGRI ECO/UNDEV

S49
ECKLER A.R.,"IMMIGRATION AND THE LABOR FORCE." USA+45 USA-45 EXTR/IND FINAN PROC/MFG AGE/Y SKILL ...CHARTS 19/20 MIGRATION. PAGE 36 F0694
WORKER STRANGE INDUS ECO/TAC

S52
CHINOY E.,"THE TRADITION OF OPPORTUNITY AND THE ASPIRATIONS OF AUTOMOBILE WORKERS" (BMR)" STRATA ACT/RES ALL/VALS SKILL...INT 20. PAGE 24 F0468
WORKER ECO/DEV DRIVE INDUS

B53
WOYTINSKY W.S.,WORLD POPULATION AND PRODUCTION: TRENDS AND OUTLOOK. FUT WOR+45 WOR-45 CULTURE SOCIETY ECO/DEV AGRI INDUS TEC/DEV EDU/PROP SKILL WEALTH...SOC TREND. PAGE 149 F2928
ECO/UNDEV METH/CNCPT GEOG PERSON

S57
CUNNINGHAM E.M.,"THE BUSINESS MAN AND HIS LAWYER." USA+45 LG/CO SML/CO TOP/EX CHOOSE SKILL...JURID MGT 20. PAGE 29 F0561
CONSULT LAW DECISION

SERV/IND

S57
KAHN R.L.,"UNION PRACTICES AND MEMBER PARTICIPATION." PARTIC CHOOSE REPRESENT PERS/REL PERSON SKILL...DECISION METH/CNCPT QU. PAGE 69 F1347
INGP/REL LABOR ATTIT LEAD

S59
HOFFMAN P.,"OPERATION BREAKTHROUGH." AFR S/ASIA STRUCT INDUS CONSULT TEC/DEV ATTIT RIGID/FLEX SKILL WEALTH...TECHNIC CONCPT STYLE RECORD CHARTS ORG/CHARTS GEN/METH VAL/FREE 20. PAGE 61 F1190
ECO/UNDEV EDU/PROP FOR/AID

S59
THOMPSON W.S.,"POPULATION AND PROGRESS IN THE FAR EAST." ASIA S/ASIA DIST/IND CREATE ECO/TAC WAR LOVE SKILL WEALTH...CONT/OBS TOT/POP 20. PAGE 130 F2568
ECO/UNDEV BIO/SOC GEOG

S59
TIPTON J.B.,"PARTICIPATION OF THE UNITED STATES IN THE INTERNATIONAL LABOR ORGANIZATION." USA+45 LAW STRUCT ECO/DEV ECO/UNDEV INDUS TEC/DEV ECO/TAC ADMIN PERCEPT ORD/FREE SKILL...STAT HIST/WRIT GEN/METH ILO WORK 20. PAGE 131 F2577
LABOR INT/ORG

B60
MOORE W.E.,LABOR COMMITMENT AND SOCIAL CHANGE IN DEVELOPING AREAS. SOCIETY STRATA ECO/UNDEV MARKET VOL/ASSN WORKER AUTHORIT SKILL...MGT NAT/COMP SOC/INTEG 20. PAGE 93 F1823
LABOR ORD/FREE ATTIT INDUS

B60
MYRDAL G.,BEYOND THE WELFARE STATE: ECONOMIC PLANNING AND ITS IMPLICATIONS. EUR+WWI FUT USA+45 USSR ECO/DEV ECO/UNDEV TEC/DEV SKILL WEALTH...PSY TREND FOR/TRADE 20. PAGE 96 F1881
PLAN ECO/TAC CAP/ISM

S60
RIVKIN A.,"AFRICAN ECONOMIC DEVELOPMENT: ADVANCED TECHNOLOGY AND THE STAGES OF GROWTH." CULTURE ECO/UNDEV AGRI COM/IND EXTR/IND PLAN ECO/TAC ATTIT DRIVE RIGID/FLEX SKILL WEALTH...MGT SOC GEN/LAWS FOR/TRADE WORK TOT/POP 20. PAGE 111 F2195
AFR TEC/DEV FOR/AID

B61
FRIEDMANN G.,THE ANATOMY OF WORK. USA+45 SOCIETY CONTROL ROUTINE DRIVE SKILL...PSY SOC STAT OBS METH/COMP PERS/COMP 20. PAGE 44 F0862
AUTOMAT WORKER INDUS PERSON

B61
KOVNER M.,THE CHALLENGE OF COEXISTENCE: A STUDY OF SOVIET ECONOMIC DIPLOMACY. COM FUT ECO/DEV ECO/UNDEV PLAN EDU/PROP DETER SKILL...OBS VAL/FREE 20. PAGE 73 F1430
PWR DIPLOM USSR AFR

S61
BARALL M.,"THE UNITED STATES GOVERNMENT RESPONDS." L/A+17C USA+45 SOCIETY NAT/G CREATE PLAN DIPLOM ECO/TAC ATTIT DRIVE RIGID/FLEX KNOWL SKILL WEALTH ...METH/CNCPT TIME/SEQ GEN/METH 20. PAGE 9 F0176
ECO/UNDEV ACT/RES FOR/AID

S61
DALTON G.,"ECONOMIC THEORY AND PRIMITIVE SOCIETY" (BMR)" UNIV AGRI KIN TEC/DEV ECO/TAC REGION HABITAT SKILL...METH/COMP BIBLIOG. PAGE 30 F0574
ECO/UNDEV METH PHIL/SCI SOC

S61
LINDSAY F.A.,"PLANNING IN FOREIGN AFFAIRS: THE MISSING ELEMENT." FUT USA+45 ROUTINE SKILL...MGT TOT/POP 20. PAGE 80 F1572
ECO/DEV PLAN DIPLOM

B62
LITWACK L.,THE AMERICAN LABOR MOVEMENT. USA-45 NAT/G CREATE TEC/DEV CAP/ISM ECO/TAC ADJUD AUTOMAT SKILL...TREND ANTHOL 19/20. PAGE 81 F1588
INDUS LABOR GP/REL METH/COMP

L62
SCHULTZ T.W.,"INVESTMENT IN HUMAN BEINGS." ECO/DEV ECO/TAC CONFER COST INCOME PRODUC HEALTH...GEOG ANTHOL. PAGE 117 F2315
FINAN WORKER EDU/PROP SKILL

S62
ADISESHIAN M.,"EDUCATION AND DEVELOPMENT." FUT WOR+45 SOCIETY ACT/RES INT/TRADE EDU/PROP KNOWL SKILL WEALTH...POLICY CONCPT CONT/OBS CENSUS CHARTS TOT/POP VAL/FREE APPLIC FAO FOR/TRADE 20. PAGE 2 F0041
SCHOOL ECO/UNDEV

B63
GODWIN F.W.,THE HIDDEN FORCE. PUERT/RICO WOR+45 STRUCT VOL/ASSN PROB/SOLV DIPLOM CONFER...BIBLIOG 20 PEACE/CORP. PAGE 48 F0931
ECO/UNDEV WORKER SKILL ECO/TAC

B63
GORDON M.S.,THE ECONOMICS OF WELFARE POLICIES. INDUS LOC/G NAT/G LEGIS WORKER INCOME AGE/O SKILL WEALTH...METH/COMP NAT/COMP 20. PAGE 49 F0959
METH/CNCPT ECO/TAC POLICY

B63
LAIRD R.D.,SOVIET AGRICULTURAL AND PEASANT AFFAIRS. FUT STRATA LOC/G DELIB/GP ACT/RES TEC/DEV ECO/TAC EDU/PROP ATTIT RIGID/FLEX ORD/FREE SKILL WEALTH ...STAT CON/ANAL ANTHOL MUNICH WORK VAL/FREE 20. PAGE 74 F1461
COM AGRI POLICY

B63
NEUMARK S.D.,FOREIGN TRADE AND ECONOMIC DEVELOPMENT IN AFRICA: A HISTORICAL PERSPECTIVE. EUR+WWI MOD/EUR ECO/UNDEV AGRI COM/IND EXTR/IND PROC/MFG SKILL WEALTH...CONCPT TIME/SEQ TREND SIMUL FOR/TRADE WORK TOT/POP TERR/GP VAL/FREE 19/20. PAGE 98 F1916
AFR

B63
WIGHTMAN D.,TOWARD ECONOMIC CO-OPERATION IN ASIA. ASIA S/ASIA VOL/ASSN ACT/RES PLAN TEC/DEV ECO/TAC EDU/PROP RIGID/FLEX SKILL...POLICY METH/CNCPT OBS INT GEN/LAWS UN 20 ECAFE. PAGE 146 F2877
ECO/UNDEV CREATE

S63
GALENSON W.,"ECONOMIC DEVELOPMENT AND THE SECTORAL EXPANSION OF EMPLOYMENT, INT." FUT WOR+45 ECO/UNDEV DIST/IND PROC/MFG SERV/IND ACT/RES HEALTH SKILL WEALTH...STAT TIME/SEQ VAL/FREE 20. PAGE 46 F0889
INDUS ECO/TAC

S63
REDDAWAY W.B.,"THE ECONOMICS OF UNDERDEVELOPED COUNTRIES." S/ASIA WOR+45 WOR-45 STRATA AGRI COM/IND DIST/IND MARKET PROC/MFG PLAN TEC/DEV FOR/AID BAL/PAY ATTIT DRIVE SKILL WORK FOR/TRADE 20. PAGE 110 F2165
ECO/TAC ECO/UNDEV INDIA

B64
HARBISON F.H.,EDUCATION, MANPOWER, AND ECONOMIC GROWTH. WOR+45 ECO/DEV ECO/UNDEV ACADEM LABOR SCHOOL WORKER UTIL...IDEA/COMP NAT/COMP. PAGE 55 F1075
PLAN TEC/DEV EDU/PROP SKILL

B64
SCHULTZ T.W.,TRANSFORMING TRADITIONAL AGRICULTURE. WOR+45 WOR-45 CULTURE STRATA FINAN ACT/RES ECO/TAC ATTIT KNOWL SKILL...MATH STAT TIME/SEQ GEN/LAWS VAL/FREE. PAGE 117 F2316
AGRI ECO/UNDEV

B64
SOLOW R.M.,THE NATURE AND SOURCES OF UNEMPLOYMENT IN THE UNITED STATES (PAMPHLET). USA+45 INDUS LABOR TEC/DEV ECO/TAC SKILL WEALTH...TREND NAT/COMP 20. PAGE 124 F2439
ECO/DEV WORKER STAT PRODUC

L64
BHAGWATI J.,"THE PURE THEORY OF INTERNATIONAL TRADE: A SURVEY." WOR+45 ECO/DEV ECO/UNDEV FINAN MARKET PROC/MFG INT/ORG LABOR LG/CO NAT/G TEC/DEV ECO/TAC SKILL WEALTH...POLICY RELATIV MGT CONCPT NEW/IDEA MATH QUANT GEN/LAWS FOR/TRADE 20. PAGE 14 F0276
INDUS HYPO/EXP

S64
HOOVER C.B.,"THE ROLE OF THE NATURAL AND DEVELOPED RESOURCES OF THE NATION STATES." FUT WOR+45 ECO/DEV ECO/UNDEV NAT/G PWR RESPECT SKILL WEALTH...POLICY GEOG TIME/SEQ TREND RESOURCE/N VAL/FREE 20. PAGE 62 F1210
EXTR/IND DOMIN

S64
MC WILLIAM M.,"THE WORLD BANK AND THE TRANSFER OF POWER IN KENYA." AFR ECO/UNDEV CONSULT ACT/RES TEC/DEV PERCEPT PWR SKILL WEALTH...CONCPT OBS TREND 20. PAGE 88 F1715
NAT/G ECO/TAC

S64
READER D.H.,"A SURVEY OF CATEGORIES OF ECONOMIC ACTIVITIES AMONG THE PEOPLES OF AFRICA." AGRI INDUS MARKET KIN HEALTH SKILL WEALTH...GEOG METH/CNCPT CHARTS TERR/GP WORK TOT/POP VAL/FREE 20. PAGE 110 F2160
TEC/DEV ECO/UNDEV AFR

B65
ANDERSON C.A.,EDUCATION AND ECONOMIC DEVELOPMENT. INDUS R+D SCHOOL TEC/DEV ECO/TAC EDU/PROP AGE HEREDITY PERCEPT SKILL 20. PAGE 5 F0092
ANTHOL ECO/DEV ECO/UNDEV WORKER

B65
CRANE E.,MARKETING COMMUNICATION: A BEHAVIORAL APPROACH TO MEN, MESSAGES, AND MEDIA. STRATA R+D VOL/ASSN CROWD DRIVE PERSON SKILL WEALTH. PAGE 28 F0551
EDU/PROP MARKET PERCEPT ATTIT

B65
HARBISON F.,MANPOWER AND EDUCATION. AFR CHINA/COM IRAN L/A+17C S/ASIA TEC/DEV ADJUST OPTIMAL SKILL ...ANTHOL 20. PAGE 55 F1073
ECO/UNDEV EDU/PROP WORKER NAT/COMP

B65
PEARL A.,NEW CAREERS FOR THE POOR: THE NON-PROFESSIONAL IN HUMAN SERVICE. USA+45 SERV/IND NAT/G NEIGH WORKER EDU/PROP AUTOMAT SKILL...WELF/ST NEW/IDEA BIBLIOG SOC/INTEG 20. PAGE 104 F2044
SOC/WK WEALTH STRATA POLICY

B65
US OFFICE ECONOMIC OPPORTUNITY,CATALOG OF FEDERAL PROGRAMS FOR INDIVIDUAL AND COMMUNITY IMPROVEMENT. USA+45 GIVE RECEIVE ADMIN HEALTH KNOWL SKILL WEALTH ...CHARTS MUNICH. PAGE 138 F2721
BIBLIOG CLIENT ECO/TAC

L65
WILLIAMS S.,"NEGOTIATING INVESTMENT IN EMERGING COUNTRIES." USA+45 WOR+45 INDUS MARKET NAT/G TOP/EX TEC/DEV CAP/ISM ECO/TAC ADMIN SKILL WEALTH...POLICY RELATIV MGT WORK 20. PAGE 147 F2894
FINAN ECO/UNDEV

L65
WIONCZEK M.,"LATIN AMERICA FREE TRADE ASSOCIATION." AGRI DIST/IND FINAN INDUS INT/ORG LABOR NAT/G TEC/DEV ECO/TAC HEALTH SKILL WEALTH...POLICY RELATIV MGT LAFTA 20. PAGE 148 F2909
L/A+17C MARKET REGION

S65
GRENIEWSKI H.,"INTENTION AND PERFORMANCE: A PRIMER OF CYBERNETICS OF PLANNING." EFFICIENCY OPTIMAL
SIMUL GAME

KNOWL SKILL...DECISION MGT EQULIB. PAGE 51 F0995 GEN/METH PLAN

S65
MALHERBE E.G.,"MANPOWER TRAINING: EDUCATIONAL REQUIREMENTS FOR ECONOMIC EXPANSION." SOUTH/AFR ECO/DEV INDUS EDU/PROP...MGT STAT CHARTS 20. PAGE 84 F1646 LABOR SKILL SCHOOL ACADEM

S65
TENDLER J.D.,"TECHNOLOGY AND ECONOMIC DEVELOPMENT* THE CASE OF HYDRO VS THERMAL POWER." CONSTRUC DIST/IND CREATE TEC/DEV INT/TRADE CENTRAL PWR SKILL WEALTH...MGT NAT/COMP ARGEN. PAGE 129 F2544 BRAZIL INDUS ECO/UNDEV

B66
ALEXANDER Y.,INTERNATIONAL TECHNICAL ASSISTANCE EXPERTS: A CASE STUDY OF THE U.N. EXPERIENCE. USA+45 WOR+45 WORKER CREATE PLAN PROB/SOLV ECO/TAC FOR/AID GIVE EDU/PROP...CHARTS BIBLIOG 20 UN. PAGE 3 F0062 SKILL INT/ORG TEC/DEV CONSULT

B66
BROEKMEIJER M.W.J.,FICTION AND TRUTH ABOUT THE "DECADE OF DEVELOPMENT" WOR+45 AGRI FINAN INDUS NAT/G TEC/DEV DIPLOM EDU/PROP LEAD SKILL 20 THIRD/WRLD. PAGE 19 F0358 FOR/AID POLICY ECO/UNDEV PLAN

B67
KRANZBERG M.,TECHNOLOGY IN WESTERN CIVILIZATION VOLUME ONE. UNIV INDUS SKILL. PAGE 73 F1431 TEC/DEV ACT/RES AUTOMAT POLICY

B67
LEWIS L.J.,SOCIETY, SCHOOLS AND PROGRESS IN NIGERIA. NIGERIA WORKER ECO/TAC ADJUST 20. PAGE 79 F1550 EDU/PROP ECO/UNDEV SKILL SOCIETY

B67
ROSS A.M.,EMPLOYMENT, RACE, AND POVERTY. USA+45 LAW STRATA MARKET LABOR EDU/PROP ISOLAT SKILL...MGT ANTHOL 20 NEGRO. PAGE 114 F2244 RACE/REL WORKER WEALTH DISCRIM

B67
SYMONS L.,AGRICULTURAL GEOGRAPHY. OP/RES SKILL ...CONCPT CHARTS BIBLIOG T 20. PAGE 128 F2520 AGRI GEOG METH/COMP OBS

B67
US AGENCY INTERNATIONAL DEV,PROPOSED FOREIGN AID PROGRAM FOR 1968: SUMMARY PRESENTATION TO THE CONGRESS. AFR S/ASIA USA+45 AGRI TEC/DEV DIPLOM ECO/TAC BAL/PAY COST HEALTH KNOWL SKILL 20 AID CONGRESS ALL/PROG. PAGE 134 F2640 ECO/UNDEV BUDGET FOR/AID STAT

S67
BRIMMER A.F.,"EMPLOYMENT PATTERNS AND THE DILEMMA OF DESEGREGATION." USA+45 SOCIETY SKILL 20 NEGRO. PAGE 18 F0353 RACE/REL DISCRIM WORKER STRATA

S67
GAUSSENS J.,"THE APPLICATIONS OF NUCLEAR ENERGY - TECHNICAL, ECONOMIC AND SOCIAL ASPECTS." WOR+45 INDUS R+D ACT/RES EFFICIENCY PRODUC SKILL PREDICT. PAGE 47 F0911 NUC/PWR TEC/DEV ECO/DEV ADJUST

S67
GOSALVEZ R.B.,"PERFIL DEL GENERAL VINCENTE ROJO." SPAIN DIPLOM CIVMIL/REL EFFICIENCY PERSON SKILL 20 BOLIV. PAGE 49 F0966 WAR FORCES ELITES BIOG

S67
MULLER A.L.,"ECONOMIC GROWTH AND MINORITIES." USA+45 SKILL...SOC GP/COMP NEGRO. PAGE 95 F1857 INCOME WORKER ECO/DEV RACE/REL

SKILTON R.M. F2418

SKOLNICK J.H. F2419

SLAV/MACED....SLAVO-MACEDONIANS

SLAVERY....SEE ORD/FREE, DOMIN

SLAVS....SLAVS - PERTAINING TO THE SLAVIC PEOPLE AND SLAVOPHILISM

SLEEP....SLEEPING AND FATIGUE

SLICHTER S.H. F2420,F2421,F2422

SLOSS J. F1621

SLOTKIN J.S. F2423

SLUMS....SLUMS

SMALL A.H. F2424

SMELSER N.J. F2031,F2425

SMERK G.M. F2426

SMET G. F2427

SMIDT S. F0282

SMITH A. F2428,F2429

SMITH G.A. F2430

SMITH H.E. F2431

SMITH R.A. F2432

SMITH R.M. F2433

SMITH T.L. F2434

SMITH W.H.T. F2435

SMITH/ACT....SMITH ACT

SMITH/ADAM....ADAM SMITH

B65
GRAMPP W.D.,ECONOMIC LIBERALISM; THE CLASSICAL VIEW (VOL. II). MOD/EUR SOCIETY MARKET INT/TRADE NAT/LISM WEALTH LAISSEZ...POLICY PSY CONCPT BIBLIOG 19 SMITH/ADAM HUME/D MILL/JS. PAGE 50 F0975 ECO/DEV CAP/ISM IDEA/COMP ECO/TAC

B88
BENTHAM J.,DEFENCE OF USURY (1787). UK LAW NAT/G TEC/DEV ECO/TAC CONTROL ATTIT...CONCPT IDEA/COMP 18 SMITH/ADAM. PAGE 13 F0255 TAX FINAN ECO/DEV POLICY

SMITH/ALF....ALFRED E. SMITH

SMITH/IAN....IAN SMITH

SMITH/JOS....JOSEPH SMITH

SMITH/LEVR....SMITH-LEVER ACT

B28
TRUE A.C.,A HISTORY OF AGRICULTURAL EXTENSION WORK IN THE UNITED STATES, 1785-1923. USA-45 LAW SCHOOL WAR ADJUST...CHARTS BIBLIOG 18/20 SMITH/LEVR COUNTY/AGT. PAGE 131 F2591 EDU/PROP AGRI VOL/ASSN PLAN

SMITHIES A. F2436

SML/CO....SMALL COMPANY

B11
SCOTT W.D.,INFLUENCING MEN IN BUSINESS: THE PSYCHOLOGY OF ARGUMENT AND SUGGESTION. WOR-45 WORKER EDU/PROP DEMAND ATTIT PERSON 20. PAGE 118 F2336 PSY MARKET SML/CO TOP/EX

B13
DAVENPORT H.J.,THE ECONOMICS OF ENTERPRISE. UNIV FINAN SML/CO RENT COST WEALTH GEN/LAWS. PAGE 30 F0582 CAP/ISM PRICE ECO/TAC LG/CO

B36
BURNS A.R.,THE DECLINE OF COMPETITION. LAW LG/CO NAT/G SML/CO LEGIS PRICE AGREE CONTROL GP/REL INCOME PRODUC...POLICY 19/20 NRA. PAGE 20 F0390 MARKET GEN/LAWS INDUS

B44
BIENSTOCK G.,MANAGEMENT IN RUSSIAN INDUSTRY AND AGRICULTURE. USSR CONSULT WORKER LEAD COST PROFIT ATTIT DRIVE PWR...MGT METH/COMP DICTIONARY ACCT 20. PAGE 15 F0281 ADMIN MARXISM SML/CO AGRI

B47
WHITEHEAD T.N.,LEADERSHIP IN A FREE SOCIETY; A STUDY IN HUMAN RELATIONS BASED ON AN ANALYSIS OF PRESENT-DAY INDUSTRIAL CIVILIZATION. WOR-45 STRUCT R+D LABOR LG/CO SML/CO WORKER PLAN PROB/SOLV TEC/DEV DRIVE...MGT 20. PAGE 146 F2872 INDUS LEAD ORD/FREE SOCIETY

B51
OWENS R.N.,BUSINESS, ORGANIZATION, AND COMBINATION. USA+45 USA-45 LAW NAT/G LEGIS ECO/TAC CONTROL INGP/REL...JURID GP/COMP 20 NEW/DEAL. PAGE 102 F2006 SML/CO LG/CO STRUCT GP/REL

B52
ANDREWS F.E.,CORPORATION GIVING. LAW TAX EDU/PROP ADMIN...POLICY STAT CHARTS. PAGE 5 F0101 LG/CO GIVE SML/CO FINAN

B55
PALAMOUNTAIN JC J.R.,THE POLITICS OF DISTRIBUTION. USA+45 LG/CO SML/CO BAL/PWR CONTROL EQUILIB 20. PAGE 103 F2019 DIST/IND ECO/TAC CAP/ISM GP/REL

S55
BUNZEL J.H.,"THE GENERAL IDEOLOGY OF AMERICAN SMALL BUSINESS"(BMR)" USA+45 USA-45 AGRI GP/REL INGP/REL ALL/IDEOS ATTIT

PERSON...MGT IDEA/COMP 18/20. PAGE 20 F0383 SML/CO INDUS

B56
GREENHUT M.L.,PLANT LOCATION IN THEORY AND PRACTICE: THE ECONOMICS OF SPACE. WOR+45 WOR-45 MARKET WORKER COST DEMAND...CONCPT STAT CHARTS HYPO/EXP BIBLIOG 19/20. PAGE 51 F0991 SML/CO ECO/DEV CAP/ISM IDEA/COMP

B56
ISARD W.,LOCATION AND SPACE-ECONOMY: GENERAL THEORY RELATING TO INDUSTRIAL LOCATION, MARKET AREAS, LAND USE, TRADE... UNIV DIST/IND MARKET LG/CO SML/CO TEC/DEV GP/REL EQUILIB HABITAT...NEW/IDEA MATH CHARTS 20. PAGE 66 F1290 GEN/LAWS GEOG INDUS REGION

S57
CUNNINGHAM E.M.,"THE BUSINESS MAN AND HIS LAWYER." USA+45 LG/CO SML/CO TOP/EX CHOOSE SKILL...JURID MGT 20. PAGE 29 F0561 CONSULT LAW DECISION SERV/IND

B58
COOK P.L.,EFFECTS OF MERGERS: SIX STUDIES. USA+45 ECO/DEV LABOR LG/CO SML/CO VOL/ASSN ADMIN EFFICIENCY 20 CASEBOOK. PAGE 27 F0529 INDUS FINAN EX/STRUC GP/REL

B58
MCIVOR R.C.,CANADIAN MONETARY, BANKING, AND FISCAL DEVELOPMENT. CANADA INDUS LG/CO NAT/G SML/CO CONTROL WAR...GEN/LAWS BIBLIOG 17/20. PAGE 88 F1729 ECO/TAC FINAN ECO/DEV WEALTH

B59
FELS R.,AMERICAN BUSINESS CYCLES 1865-1897. USA+45 ECO/DEV LG/CO SML/CO PROB/SOLV TEC/DEV CAP/ISM INT/TRADE DEMAND...POLICY CHARTS METH 19 DEPRESSION. PAGE 40 F0782 FINAN INDUS TREND ECO/TAC

B59
SELIGSOHN I.J.,"USING COMPUTER SERVICES IN SMALL BUSINESS" MANAGEMENT AIDS FOR SMALL MANUFACTURERS 109 (PAMPHLET). DIST/IND MARKET PROC/MFG COST EFFICIENCY PRODUC...DECISION IDEA/COMP. PAGE 119 F2350 SML/CO COMPUTER MGT PROB/SOLV

B60
RAY D.D.,ACCOUNTING AND BUSINESS FLUCTUATIONS. LG/CO SML/CO FEEDBACK DEMAND...CHARTS IDEA/COMP BIBLIOG 20. PAGE 109 F2154 FINAN AFR CONTROL

B60
SHANNON D.A.,THE GREAT DEPRESSION. USA-45 FINAN LG/CO SCHOOL SML/CO DELIB/GP RECEIVE REV EATING INCOME...ANTHOL MUNICH 20 ROOSEVLT/F CONGRESS. PAGE 120 F2365 WEALTH NAT/G AGRI INDUS

B61
AMERICAN MANAGEMENT ASSN,SUPERIOR-SUBORDINATE COMMUNICATION IN MANAGEMENT. STRATA FINAN INDUS SML/CO WORKER CONTROL EXEC ATTIT 20. PAGE 5 F0090 MGT ACT/RES PERS/REL LG/CO

B61
DUKE UNIVERSITY,EXPULSION OR OPPRESSION OF BUSINESS ASSOCIATES: "SQUEEZE-OUTS" IN SMALL ENTERPRISES. LAW CONTROL PARTIC COERCE INGP/REL...POLICY RECORD INT. PAGE 35 F0674 PWR MGT SML/CO ECO/TAC

B62
ARNOLD T.W.,THE FOLKLORE OF CAPITALISM. USA+45 USA-45 SOCIETY LG/CO SML/CO EX/STRUC ECO/TAC EDU/PROP ADJUST INCOME...MYTH CHARTS 20. PAGE 6 F0116 CAP/ISM ATTIT STERTYP ECO/DEV

B62
FERBER R.,RESEARCH METHODS IN ECONOMICS AND BUSINESS. AFR ECO/DEV FINAN MARKET LG/CO SML/CO CONSULT CONTROL COST...STAT METH/COMP 20. PAGE 40 F0783 ACT/RES PROB/SOLV ECO/TAC MGT

B62
GRANICK D.,THE EUROPEAN EXECUTIVE. BELGIUM FRANCE GERMANY/W UK INDUS LABOR LG/CO SML/CO EX/STRUC PLAN TEC/DEV CAP/ISM COST DEMAND...POLICY CHARTS 20. PAGE 50 F0977 MGT ECO/DEV ECO/TAC EXEC

B63
BAUER R.A.,AMERICAN BUSINESS AND PUBLIC POLICY: THE POLITICS OF FOREIGN TRADE. USA+45 COM/IND LG/CO NAT/G PROF/ORG SML/CO VOL/ASSN LEGIS TOP/EX ECO/TAC EDU/PROP CHOOSE HEALTH PWR WEALTH...CONCPT METH/CNCPT OBS INT QU SAMP FOR/TRADE TRUE/GP VAL/FREE HI. PAGE 11 F0217 ECO/DEV ATTIT

B63
BURNS T.G.,DEVELOPMENT BANKING BIBLIOGRAPHY (PAPER). WOR+45 SML/CO VOL/ASSN PLAN BUDGET. PAGE 20 F0391 BIBLIOG/A ECO/DEV FINAN ECO/UNDEV

B63
CHAMPION J.M.,CRITICAL INCIDENTS IN MANAGEMENT. MARKET LG/CO SML/CO OP/RES ADMIN CONTROL LEAD GP/REL PERS/REL COST ATTIT SUPEGO ALL/VALS...PSY PERS/TEST BIBLIOG. PAGE 23 F0445 MGT DECISION EX/STRUC INDUS

N63
COMM ON FEDERAL TAX POLICY,FINANCING AMERICA'S FUTURE: TAXES, ECONOMIC STABILITY AND GROWTH (PAMPHLET). USA+45 LG/CO SML/CO DELIB/GP INCOME ...CHARTS 20. PAGE 26 F0513 TAX NAT/G EQUILIB PLAN

S64
WOOD N.,"THE FAMILY FIRM - BASE OF JAPAN'S GROWING ECONOMY." ECO/DEV ECO/UNDEV ECO/TAC WEALTH...POLICY TRADIT BIOG TREND 20 CHINJAP. PAGE 148 F2921 ASIA SML/CO FAM

B65
BREAK G.F.,FEDERAL LENDING AND ECONOMIC STABILITY. USA+45 ECO/DEV LG/CO SML/CO EQUILIB...CHARTS 20. PAGE 18 F0344 BUDGET FINAN NAT/G ECO/TAC

B65
MUND V.A.,GOVERNMENT AND BUSINESS (4TH ED.). USA+45 INDUS LG/CO SML/CO LEGIS INT/TRADE LICENSE PRICE ADJUD. PAGE 95 F1860 NAT/G ECO/TAC BUDGET CONTROL

B66
SOVERN M.I.,LEGAL RESTRAINTS ON RACIAL DISCRIMINATION IN EMPLOYMENT. USA+45 LAW INDUS LG/CO SML/CO DELIB/GP LEGIS SANCTION 20 NLRB PRESIDENT NEGRO CIV/RIGHTS RAILROAD. PAGE 124 F2446 DISCRIM RACE/REL WORKER JURID

B66
US HOUSE COMM BANKING CURRENCY,HEARINGS BEFORE HOUSE COMMITTEE ON BANKING AND CURRENCY: SALE OF SBA LOAN POOL PARTICIPATIONS. USA+45 LAW LEGIS ECO/TAC RATION 20 CONGRESS. PAGE 136 F2687 FINAN SML/CO ADJUD GOV/REL

L67
ROBERTS E.F.,"THE CASE OF THE UNWARY HOME BUYER: THE HOUSING MERCHANT DID IT." USA+45 CLIENT DIST/IND MARKET LG/CO SML/CO PROB/SOLV LEGIT COST PROFIT. PAGE 112 F2207 ADJUD CONSTRUC OWN LAW

S67
BOSHER J.F.,"GOVERNMENT AND PRIVATE INTERESTS IN NEW FRANCE." CANADA FRANCE INDUS LG/CO SML/CO CAP/ISM INT/TRADE COLONIAL GP/REL...HIST/WRIT 17/18. PAGE 17 F0320 NAT/G FINAN ADMIN CONTROL

S67
GAMARNIKOW M.,"THE NEW ROLE OF PRIVATE ENTERPRISE." ECO/DEV INDUS NAT/G SML/CO CREATE PROB/SOLV MARXISM ...POLICY TREND IDEA/COMP 20. PAGE 46 F0890 ECO/TAC ATTIT CAP/ISM COM

S67
MUNDHEIM R.H.,"SOME THOUGHTS ON THE DUTIES AND RESPONSIBILITIES OF UNAFFILIATED DIRECTORS OF MUTUAL FUNDS." USA+45 LG/CO SML/CO CONSULT LEAD PARTIC. PAGE 95 F1861 FINAN WEALTH ECO/TAC ADMIN

B82
CUNNINGHAM W.,THE GROWTH OF ENGLISH INDUSTRY AND COMMERCE. FUT UK FINAN NAT/G CAP/ISM...POLICY 20 MERCANTLST CHRISTIAN POPE. PAGE 29 F0562 INDUS INT/TRADE SML/CO CONSERVE

B99
KROPOTKIN P.,FIELDS, FACTORIES, AND WORKSHOPS. UNIV INTELL ECO/DEV LG/CO SCHOOL SML/CO ECO/TAC PRODUC UTOPIA...NEW/IDEA MUNICH. PAGE 74 F1445 SOCIETY WORKER AGRI INDUS

SMUTS/JAN....JAN CHRISTIAN SMUTS

SNCC....STUDENT NONVIOLENT COORDINATING COMMITTEE; SEE ALSO STUDNT/PWR

SNYDER G.H. F2297

SOBERMAN R.M. F1474

SOC....SOCIOLOGY

B
BRITISH COMMONWEALTH BUR AGRI,WORLD AGRICULTURAL ECONOMICS AND RURAL SOCIOLOGY ABSTRACTS. NAT/G OP/RES PLAN TEC/DEV LEAD PRODUC...GEOG MGT NAT/COMP 20. PAGE 18 F0354 BIBLIOG/A AGRI SOC WORKER

N
TEXTBOOKS IN PRINT. WOR+45 WOR-45 LAW DIPLOM ALL/VALS ALL/IDEOS...SOC T 19/20. PAGE 1 F0003 BIBLIOG SCHOOL KNOWL

N
DOCUMENTATION ECONOMIQUE: REVUE BIBLIOGRAPHIQUE DE SYNTHESE. WOR+45 COM/IND FINAN BUDGET DIPLOM...GEOG 20. PAGE 1 F0004 BIBLIOG/A SOC

N
DEUTSCHE BUCHEREI,DEUTSCHES BUCHERVERZEICHNIS. GERMANY LAW CULTURE POL/PAR ADMIN LEAD ATTIT PERSON ...SOC 20. PAGE 32 F0626 BIBLIOG NAT/G DIPLOM ECO/DEV

N
UNESCO,SOUTH ASIA SOCIAL SCIENCES ABSTRACTS. BURMA CEYLON INDIA S/ASIA PRESS...PSY 20. PAGE 132 F2608 BIBLIOG/A SOC

N
UNITED NATIONS,OFFICIAL RECORDS OF THE ECONOMIC AND SOCIAL COUNCIL OF THE UNITED NATIONS. WOR+45 DIPLOM INT/TRADE CONFER...SOC SOC/WK 20 UN UNESCO. PAGE 132 F2611 INT/ORG DELIB/GP WRITING

N
US LIBRARY OF CONGRESS,SELECTED AND ANNOTATED BIBLIOGRAPHY ON LABOR PROBLEMS AND POLICIES IN A WARTIME ECONOMY (PAMPHLET). USA-45 INDUS LEGIS BIBLIOG/A WAR LABOR

GP/REL DISCRIM PRODUC...SOC 20. PAGE 137 F2708 WORKER

B12
HOBSON J.A.,THE EVOLUTION OF MODERN CAPITALISM. MOD/EUR UK STRATA ECO/DEV INDUS INCOME UTIL WEALTH ...SOC GEN/LAWS 7/20. PAGE 60 F1184
CAP/ISM WORKER TEC/DEV TIME/SEQ

B20
WEBB S.,INDUSTRIAL DEMOCRACY. UK PARTIC GP/REL ...SOC OBS RECORD CHARTS 18/20. PAGE 144 F2838
LABOR NAT/G VOL/ASSN MAJORIT

S21
MALINOWSKI B.,"THE PRIMITIVE ECONOMICS OF THE TROBRIAND ISLANDERS" (BMR)" CULTURE SOCIETY NAT/G CHIEF LEAD OWN...SOC MYTH WORSHIP 20 NEW/GUINEA TROBRIAND RESOURCE/N. PAGE 84 F1647
ECO/UNDEV AGRI PRODUC STRUCT

B22
VON ENGELIN O.D.,INHERITING THE EARTH, THE GEOGRAPHICAL FACTOR IN NATIONAL DEVELOPMENT. WOR-45 CULTURE DIPLOM BIO/SOC HABITAT PERSON...PSY SOC CONCPT IDEA/COMP. PAGE 142 F2791
INGP/REL GEOG SOCIETY ROLE

B26
TAWNEY R.H.,RELIGION AND THE RISE OF CAPITALISM. UK CULTURE NAT/G TEC/DEV OWN LAISSEZ...POLICY SOC TIME/SEQ 16/19. PAGE 129 F2537
SECT WEALTH INDUS CAP/ISM

B27
SIEGFRIED A.,AMERICA COMES OF AGE: A FRENCH ANALYSIS (TRANS. BY H.H. HEMMING AND DORIS HEMMING). FRANCE UK POL/PAR WORKER TEC/DEV DIPLOM REGION RACE/REL ADJUST PRODUC HEREDITY...TIME/SEQ GP/COMP SOC/INTEG 20 DEMOCRAT REPUBLICAN KKK. PAGE 122 F2398
USA-45 CULTURE ECO/DEV SOC

B28
DE MAN H.,THE PSYCHOLOGY OF SOCIALISM. EUR+WWI USSR LABOR NAT/LISM PERSON WEALTH MARXISM...METH/COMP 20. PAGE 31 F0604
WORKER ATTIT SOC SOCISM

B29
DE MAN H.,JOY IN WORK. STRATA ECO/DEV ECO/TAC PRODUC ANOMIE ROLE SOCISM...IDEA/COMP 20. PAGE 31 F0605
SOC WORKER HAPPINESS RESPECT

B37
MACKENZIE F.,PLANNED SOCIETY: YESTERDAY, TODAY, AND TOMORROW. ECO/DEV ECO/UNDEV AGRI FINAN INDUS PLAN INSPECT CONTROL ALL/IDEOS...TREND METH/COMP BIBLIOG 20 RESOURCE/N. PAGE 83 F1635
SOC CONCPT ANTHOL

B37
ROBBINS L.,ECONOMIC PLANNING AND INTERNATIONAL ORDER. WOR-45 SOCIETY FINAN INDUS NAT/G ECO/TAC ROUTINE WEALTH...SOC TIME/SEQ GEN/METH WORK 20 KEYNES/JM. PAGE 112 F2202
INT/ORG PLAN INT/TRADE

B38
LANGE O.,ON THE ECONOMIC THEORY OF SOCIALISM. UNIV ECO/DEV FINAN INDUS INT/ORG PUB/INST ROUTINE ATTIT ALL/VALS...SOC CONCPT STAT TREND 20. PAGE 75 F1475
MARKET ECO/TAC INT/TRADE SOCISM

B39
FIRTH R.,PRIMITIVE POLYNESIAN ECONOMY. SOCIETY DIST/IND SECT CHIEF CAP/ISM PRODUC WEALTH...SOC OBS METH WORSHIP 20 POLYNESIA. PAGE 41 F0802
ECO/UNDEV CULTURE AGRI ECO/TAC

B40
MEEK C.K.,EUROPE AND WEST AFRICA. AFR EUR+WWI EXTR/IND DIPLOM INT/TRADE EDU/PROP GP/REL...SOC 20. PAGE 89 F1743
CULTURE TEC/DEV ECO/UNDEV COLONIAL

B42
VEBLEN T.B.,THE THEORY OF THE LEISURE CLASS. USA-45 SOCIETY STRATA STRUCT NAT/G SECT WORKER CREATE EDU/PROP ATTIT...SOC GEN/LAWS 19. PAGE 141 F2772
WEALTH ELITES LEISURE PRODUC

B44
KAUFMANN F.,METHODOLOGY OF THE SOCIAL SCIENCES. PERSON...RELATIV PSY CONCPT LING METH 20. PAGE 69 F1363
SOC PHIL/SCI GEN/LAWS METH/CNCPT

B47
BOWEN R.H.,GERMAN THEORIES OF THE CORPORATIVE STATE, WITH SPECIAL REFERENCES TO THE PERIOD 1870-1919. GERMANY INDUS LG/CO CATHISM SOCISM...SOC 18/20. PAGE 17 F0328
IDEA/COMP CENTRAL NAT/G POLICY

B47
ISAAC J.,ECONOMICS OF MIGRATION. MOD/EUR CULTURE STRATA STRUCT NAT/G COLONIAL WEALTH...OLD/LIB TREND TIME 19/20 EUROPE/W MIGRATION. PAGE 65 F1289
HABITAT SOC GEOG

B47
US LIBRARY OF CONGRESS,POSTWAR PLANNING AND RECONSTRUCTION: JANUARY-MARCH 1943. WOR+45 SOCIETY INT/ORG DIPLOM...SOC PREDICT 20. PAGE 138 F2714
BIBLIOG/A WAR PEACE PLAN

B47
WARNER W.L.,THE SOCIAL SYSTEM OF THE MODERN FACTORY; THE STRIKE: AN ANALYSIS. USA-45 STRATA WORKER ECO/TAC GP/REL INGP/REL...MGT SOC CHARTS 20 YANKEE/C. PAGE 143 F2824
ROLE STRUCT LABOR PROC/MFG

B47
WEBER M.,THE THEORY OF SOCIAL AND ECONOMIC ORGANIZATION. STRUCT LABOR POL/PAR ECO/TAC LEGIT PRODUC BIOG. PAGE 144 F2840
ECO/DEV SOC PHIL/SCI LEAD

B48
WHITE C.L.,HUMAN GEOGRAPHY: AN ECOLOGICAL STUDY OF GEOGRAPHY. UNIV SEA CULTURE AGRI EXTR/IND RACE/REL PRODUC...CHARTS HYPO/EXP SIMUL GEN/LAWS T. PAGE 146 F2868
SOC HABITAT GEOG SOCIETY

S48
HARDIN L.M.,"REFLECTIONS ON AGRICULTURAL POLICY FORMATION IN THE UNITED STATES." LEGIS PLAN BUDGET ECO/TAC LEAD CENTRAL...MGT SOC NEW/IDEA STAT FAO. PAGE 55 F1078
AGRI POLICY ADMIN NEW/LIB

B49
LEE A.M.,SOCIAL PROBLEMS IN AMERICA: A SOURCE BOOK. STRATA STRUCT KIN NEIGH VOL/ASSN ACT/RES LEAD CRIME AGE SEX 20. PAGE 77 F1504
SOC SOCIETY PERSON EDU/PROP

B49
PELZER K.J.,SELECTED BIBLIOGRAPHY ON THE GEOGRAPHY OF SOUTHEAST ASIA (3 VOLS., 1949-1956). PHILIPPINE CULTURE...SOC 20 MALAYA. PAGE 104 F2053
BIBLIOG S/ASIA GEOG

S49
HART C.W.M.,"INDUSTRIAL RELATIONS RESEARCH AND SOCIAL THEORY." CANADA VOL/ASSN WORKER LEAD EFFICIENCY...MGT SOC METH/CNCPT METH/COMP MUNICH 20. PAGE 56 F1099
GEN/LAWS LABOR GP/REL

B50
ADORNO T.W.,THE AUTHORITARIAN PERSONALITY. STRATA SECT PROB/SOLV ECO/TAC DISCRIM ATTIT SEX...SOC INT CHARTS METH 20. PAGE 3 F0044
AUTHORIT PERSON ALL/IDEOS SOCIETY

B50
MARX H.L.,THE WELFARE STATE. USA+45 USA-45 CHIEF CAP/ISM CENTRAL ORD/FREE LAISSEZ...SOC ANTHOL 20. PAGE 86 F1686
ECO/DEV INDUS WEALTH WELF/ST

B50
SCHUMPETER J.A.,CAPITALISM, SOCIALISM, AND DEMOCRACY (3RD ED.). USA-45 USSR WOR+45 WOR-45 INTELL ECO/DEV ECO/UNDEV ECO/TAC WAR PRODUC ORD/FREE...MGT SOC 20 MARX/KARL. PAGE 118 F2321
SOCIALIST CAP/ISM MARXISM IDEA/COMP

B51
PARSONS T.,THE SOCIAL SYSTEM. UNIV INTELL SOCIETY ECO/DEV SECT PLAN PERCEPT...CONCPT METH/CNCPT. PAGE 103 F2030
DRIVE SOC

B51
US DEPARTMENT OF STATE,POINT FOUR, NEAR EAST AND AFRICA, A SELECTED BIBLIOGRAPHY OF STUDIES ON ECONOMICALLY UNDERDEVELOPED COUNTRIES. AGRI COM/IND FINAN INDUS PLAN INT/TRADE...SOC TREND 20. PAGE 135 F2672
BIBLIOG/A AFR S/ASIA ISLAM

B52
HOSELITZ B.F.,THE PROGRESS OF UNDERDEVELOPED AREAS. AFR FUT WOR+45 WOR-45 ECO/DEV ECO/TAC INT/TRADE WEALTH...SOC TREND GEN/LAWS TOT/POP VAL/FREE FOR/TRADE 20. PAGE 62 F1219
ECO/UNDEV PLAN FOR/AID

B52
SURANYI-UNGER T.,COMPARATIVE ECONOMIC SYSTEMS. FINAN MARKET DIPLOM PRICE WEALTH...GEOG SOC BIBLIOG METH T 20. PAGE 128 F2517
LAISSEZ PLAN ECO/DEV IDEA/COMP

B53
BOULDING K.E.,THE ORGANIZATIONAL REVOLUTION. FUT CULTURE ECO/DEV LABOR PROF/ORG ECO/TAC MORAL...SOC CONCPT RECORD INT SOC/EXP 20. PAGE 17 F0321
SOCIETY TREND

B53
DAHL R.A.,POLITICS, ECONOMICS AND WELFARE: PLANNING AND POLITICOECONOMIC SYSTEMS RESOLVED INTO BASIC SOCIAL PROCESSES. WOR+45 WOR-45 ECO/DEV ECO/UNDEV R+D CREATE PLAN TEC/DEV EDU/PROP HEALTH WEALTH ...SOC SELF/OBS TREND CHARTS GEN/METH 20. PAGE 29 F0571
ECO/TAC PHIL/SCI

B53
WOYTINSKY W.S.,WORLD POPULATION AND PRODUCTION: TRENDS AND OUTLOOK. FUT WOR+45 WOR-45 CULTURE SOCIETY ECO/DEV AGRI INDUS TEC/DEV EDU/PROP SKILL WEALTH...SOC TREND. PAGE 149 F2928
ECO/UNDEV METH/CNCPT GEOG PERSON

S53
BIRNBAUM N.,"CONFLICTING INTERPRETATIONS OF THE RISE OF CAPITALISM: MARX AND WEBER" (BMR)" WOR-45 INTELL SOCIETY STRUCT INDUS WORKER...PHIL/SCI SOC PERS/COMP 19/20 MARX/KARL WEBER/MAX. PAGE 15 F0288
CAP/ISM IDEA/COMP ECO/DEV MARXISM

S53
MCKEE J.B.,"STATUS AND POWER IN THE INDUSTRIAL COMMUNITY; A COMMENT ON DRUCKER'S THESIS." LABOR LEGIT LEAD GP/REL PWR...MGT CONCPT. PAGE 88 F1730
SOC STRATA NEIGH PARTIC

B54
BATTEN T.R.,PROBLEMS OF AFRICAN DEVELOPMENT (2ND ED.). AFR LAW SOCIETY SCHOOL ECO/TAC TAX...GEOG HEAL SOC 20. PAGE 11 F0211
ECO/UNDEV AGRI LOC/G PROB/SOLV

B54
MEYER A.G.,MARXISM. INTELL ECO/DEV WORKER CAP/ISM LEAD WAR ATTIT ALL/IDEOS...SOC 19/20 MARX/KARL. PAGE 90 F1766
MARXISM CONCPT ECO/TAC STRUCT

B54
POTTER D.M.,PEOPLE OF PLENTY: ECONOMIC ABUNDANCE AND THE AMERICAN CHARACTER. USA+45 USA-45 ECO/DEV ATTIT PERSON...PSY SOC CONCPT TREND GEN/METH TOT/POP 20. PAGE 107 F2108
CULTURE WEALTH

B54
WASHBURNE N.F.,INTERPRETING SOCIAL CHANGE IN AMERICA. USA+45 STRATA FAM NAT/G SECT OP/RES ECO/TAC EDU/PROP HABITAT...SOC TIME/SEQ TREND 20 BUREAUCRCY. PAGE 143 F2826
CULTURE STRUCT CREATE TEC/DEV

S54
FORM W.H.,"THE PLACE OF SOCIAL STRUCTURE IN THE DETERMINATION OF LAND USE: SOME IMPLICATIONS FOR A THEORY OF URBAN ECOLOGY" (BMR)" STRUCT...GEOG PHIL/SCI SOC MUNICH 20. PAGE 42 F0827
HABITAT MARKET ORD/FREE

S54
MACK R.W.,"ECOLOGICAL PATTERNS IN AN INDUSTRIAL SHOP" (BMR)" USA+45 CULTURE SOCIETY STRATA STRUCT LABOR NEIGH GP/REL ADJUST HABITAT...SOC SOC/INTEG 20. PAGE 83 F1634
INDUS DISCRIM WORKER

B55
RUSTOW D.A.,THE POLITICS OF COMPROMISE. SWEDEN LABOR EX/STRUC LEGIS PLAN REPRESENT SOCISM...SOC 19/20. PAGE 115 F2265
POL/PAR NAT/G POLICY ECO/TAC

S55
DIESING P.,"NONECONOMIC DECISION-MAKING" (BMR)" PROB/SOLV GP/REL ORD/FREE...STAT METH/COMP SIMUL 20. PAGE 33 F0638
DECISION METH EFFICIENCY SOC

B56
HISTORICAL ABSTRACTS. NAT/G CREATE DIPLOM ATTIT ...SOC DICTIONARY INDEX 18/20. PAGE 1 F0011
WOR-45 COMPUT/IR BIBLIOG/A

B56
GARDNER R.N.,STERLING-DOLLAR DIPLOMACY. EUR+WWI USA+45 INT/ORG NAT/G PLAN INT/TRADE EDU/PROP ADMIN KNOWL PWR WEALTH...POLICY SOC METH/CNCPT STAT CHARTS SIMUL GEN/LAWS 20. PAGE 46 F0902
ECO/DEV DIPLOM

B56
HICKMAN C.A.,INDIVIDUALS, GROUPS, AND ECONOMIC BEHAVIOR. WORKER PAY CONTROL EXEC GP/REL INGP/REL PERSON ROLE...PSY SOC PERS/COMP METH 20. PAGE 59 F1163
MGT ADMIN ECO/TAC PLAN

B56
JUAN T.L.,ECONOMIC AND SOCIAL DEVELOPMENT OF MODERN CHINA: A BIBLIOGRAPHICAL GUIDE. ASIA AGRI COM/IND DIST/IND FINAN INDUS DIPLOM...STAT 20. PAGE 68 F1342
BIBLIOG SOC

B56
PARSONS T.,ECONOMY AND SOCIETY: A STUDY IN THE INTEGRATION OF ECONOMIC AND SOCIAL THEORY. UNIV ACT/RES...SOC CHARTS IDEA/COMP BIBLIOG/A. PAGE 103 F2031
STRUCT METH/CNCPT UTIL PHIL/SCI

B56
UNIVERSITY OF CHICAGO,BIBLIOGRAPHY OF UKRAINE (PAMPHLET). USSR...SOC 20. PAGE 133 F2619
BIBLIOG/A COM

B56
US DEPARTMENT OF STATE,ECONOMIC PROBLEMS OF UNDERDEVELOPED AREAS (PAMPHLET). AFR ASIA ISLAM L/A+17C AGRI FINAN INDUS INT/ORG LABOR INT/TRADE ...PSY SOC 20. PAGE 136 F2673
BIBLIOG ECO/UNDEV TEC/DEV R+D

B56
WEBER M.,WIRTSCHAFT UND GESELLSCHAFT (2ND VOL.). STRUCT NAT/G POL/PAR LEAD PWR OBJECTIVE IDEA/COMP. PAGE 144 F2841
LEGIT JURID SOC

B56
YABUKI K.,JAPAN BIBLIOGRAPHIC ANNUAL, 1956: THE LATEST LIST OF OLD AND NEW BOOKS ON JAPAN IN ENGLISH. EDU/PROP...LING 20 CHINJAP. PAGE 149 F2945
BIBLIOG SOC

B56
YUAN TUNG-LI,ECONOMIC AND SOCIAL DEVELOPMENT OF MODERN CHINA: A BIBLIOGRAPHIC GUIDE. COM/IND FINAN FAM LABOR SECT CRIME INCOME...STAT SAMP CON/ANAL. PAGE 150 F2954
BIBLIOG ASIA ECO/UNDEV SOC

S56
SPENGLER J.J.,"POPULATION THREATENS PROSPERITY" (BMR)" WOR+45 SOCIETY FINAN RATION COST INCOME ...SOC CHARTS 20 RESOURCE/N. PAGE 124 F2451
CENSUS GEOG WEALTH TREND

B57
ASHER R.E.,THE UNITED NATIONS AND ECONOMIC AND SOCIAL COOPERATION. ECO/UNDEV COM/IND DIST/IND FINAN PLAN PROB/SOLV INT/TRADE TASK WEALTH...SOC 20 UN. PAGE 7 F0129
INT/ORG DIPLOM FOR/AID

B57
DOWNS A.,AN ECONOMIC THEORY OF DEMOCRACY. NAT/G EDU/PROP RISK CHOOSE PERS/REL EQUILIB...SOC METH/CNCPT LOG STYLE. PAGE 34 F0659
DECISION RATIONAL

B57
EHRMANN H.W.,ORGANIZED BUSINESS IN FRANCE. EUR+WWI MOD/EUR ECO/DEV VOL/ASSN LEGIT ATTIT PERCEPT PWR RESPECT...PLURIST SOC INT TOT/POP 20. PAGE 36 F0712
PROF/ORG ECO/TAC FRANCE

B57
HALD M.,A SELECTED BIBLIOGRAPHY ON ECONOMIC DEVELOPMENT AND FOREIGN AID. INT/ORG PROB/SOLV ...SOC 20. PAGE 53 F1040
BIBLIOG ECO/UNDEV TEC/DEV FOR/AID

B57
PATAI R.,JORDAN, LEBANON AND SYRIA: AN ANNOTATED BIBLIOGRAPHY. ISLAM JORDAN LEBANON SYRIA...GEOG 20. PAGE 103 F2034
BIBLIOG/A SOC

B57
ROBERTSON H.M.,SOUTH AFRICA, ECONOMIC AND POLITICAL ASPECTS. SOUTH/AFR CONSTN CULTURE POL/PAR LEGIS DIPLOM DOMIN COLONIAL...SOC BIBLIOG 19/20. PAGE 112 F2214
RACE/REL ECO/UNDEV ECO/TAC DISCRIM

B57
WARRINER D.,LAND REFORM AND DEVELOPMENT IN THE MIDDLE EAST: A STUDY OF EGYPT, SYRIA AND IRAQ. IRAQ ISLAM SYRIA UAR AGRI DIST/IND PLAN TEC/DEV DOMIN REV ATTIT WEALTH...SOC METH/CNCPT STAT OBS RECORD HIST/WRIT TREND GEN/LAWS FAO 20. PAGE 143 F2825
ECO/UNDEV CONCPT

B58
CLAUNCH J.M.,THE PROBLEM OF GOVERNMENT IN METROPOLITAN AREAS. CULTURE INDUS POL/PAR PLAN REGION GP/REL...CENSUS ANTHOL MUNICH 20. PAGE 25 F0486
PROB/SOLV SOC

B58
CROWE S.,THE LANDSCAPE OF POWER. UK CULTURE SERV/IND NAT/G CONSULT PARTIC NUC/PWR LEISURE...SOC EXHIBIT 20. PAGE 29 F0559
HABITAT TEC/DEV PLAN CONTROL

B58
DUBIN R.,WORKING UNION-MANAGEMENT RELATIONS. LAW PLAN ECO/TAC CHOOSE REPRESENT INGP/REL PWR...POLICY SOC BIBLIOG. PAGE 34 F0669
LABOR MGT AUTHORIT GP/REL

B58
MASON J.B.,THAILAND BIBLIOGRAPHY. S/ASIA THAILAND CULTURE EDU/PROP ADMIN...GEOG SOC LING 20. PAGE 87 F1701
BIBLIOG/A ECO/UNDEV DIPLOM NAT/G

B58
POLLOCK F.,AUTOMATION: A STUDY OF ITS ECONOMIC AND SOCIAL CONSEQUENCES. FUT USA+45 USA-45 SOCIETY ECO/DEV LABOR ACT/RES PLAN ECO/TAC AUTOMAT ROUTINE ALL/VALS...STAT TREND COMPUT/IR CHARTS SOC/EXP WORK 20. PAGE 107 F2099
TEC/DEV SOC CAP/ISM

B58
TILLION G.,ALGERIA: THE REALITIES. ALGERIA FRANCE ISLAM CULTURE STRATA PROB/SOLV DOMIN REV NAT/LISM WEALTH MARXISM...GEOG 20. PAGE 130 F2573
ECO/UNDEV SOC COLONIAL DIPLOM

B58
UNIVERSITY OF LONDON,THE FAR EAST AND SOUTH-EAST ASIA: A CUMULATED LIST OF PERIODICAL ARTICLES, MAY 1956-APRIL 1957. ASIA S/ASIA LAW ADMIN...LING 20. PAGE 133 F2621
BIBLIOG SOC

L58
MASON E.S.,"ECONOMIC PLANNING IN UNDERDEVELOPED AREAS." FUT WOR+45 PLAN TEC/DEV EDU/PROP ATTIT RIGID/FLEX KNOWL...SOC CONCPT GEN/LAWS TOT/POP 20. PAGE 87 F1697
NAT/G ECO/UNDEV

S58
SCHULZE R.O.,"THE ROLE OF ECONOMIC DOMINANTS IN COMMUNITY POWER STRUCTURE." ECO/TAC ROUTINE ATTIT OBJECTIVE...SOC RECORD CENSUS. PAGE 118 F2319
SOCIETY STRUCT PROB/SOLV

B59
MADHOK B.,POLITICAL TRENDS IN INDIA. INDIA PAKISTAN UK STRATA ECO/UNDEV POL/PAR LEGIS CAP/ISM DIPLOM COLONIAL CHOOSE MARXISM...SOC TREND 20 GANDHI/M NEHRU/J. PAGE 84 F1639
GEOG NAT/G

B59
ROPKE W.,INTERNATIONAL ORDER AND ECONOMIC INTEGRATION. ECO/DEV ECO/UNDEV AGRI FINAN INDUS INT/ORG WAR PEACE ORD/FREE...SOC METH/COMP 20 EEC. PAGE 114 F2238
INT/TRADE DIPLOM BAL/PAY ALL/IDEOS

B59
VOSE C.E.,CAUCASIANS ONLY: THE SUPREME COURT, THE NAACP, AND THE RESTRICTIVE COVENANT CASES. USA+45 LAW CONSTN LOBBY...SOC 20 NAACP SUPREME/CT NEGRO. PAGE 142 F2796
CT/SYS RACE/REL DISCRIM

C59
MINTZ S.W.,"INTERNAL MARKET SYS AS MECHANISMS OF SOCIAL ARTIC," IN V.F. RAY, INTERMED SOCIETIES, SOCIAL MOBILITY, AND COMMUNIC (BMR). UNIV STRATA GP/REL INGP/REL...GEOG SOC BIBLIOG. PAGE 92 F1804
MARKET SOCIETY ECO/UNDEV STRUCT

B60
ANGERS F.A.,ESSAI SUR LA CENTRALISATION: ANALYSE DES PRINCIPES ET PERSPECTIVES CANADIENNES. CANADA ECO/TAC CONTROL...SOC IDEA/COMP BIBLIOG 20. PAGE 6 F0105
CENTRAL ADMIN

B60
AUSTRUY J.,STRUCTURE ECONOMIQUE ET CIVILISATION: L'EGYPTE ET LE DESTIN ECONOMIQUE DE L'ISLAM. ISLAM UAR CREATE OP/RES ECO/TAC...SOC BIBLIOG 20 MUSLIM.
ECO/UNDEV CULTURE STRUCT

PAGE 8 F0142

B60
FERNANDES F.,MUDANCAS SOCIAIS NO BRASIL. BRAZIL L/A+17C SOCIETY AGRI PROVS LEAD GP/REL RACE/REL ORD/FREE...SOC SOC/INTEG 20 SAO/PAULO. PAGE 40 F0786
ECO/UNDEV STRATA INDUS

B60
FRANCIS R.G.,THE PREDICTIVE PROCESS. PLAN MARXISM ...DECISION SOC CONCPT NAT/COMP 19/20. PAGE 43 F0840
PREDICT PHIL/SCI TREND

B60
HOSELITZ B.F.,SOCIOLOGICAL ASPECTS OF ECONOMIC GROWTH. WOR+45 WOR-45 ECO/UNDEV CAP/ISM RIGID/FLEX WEALTH...MATH CHARTS. PAGE 62 F1221
ECO/DEV SOC

B60
LERNER A.P.,THE ECONOMICS OF CONTROL. USA+45 ECO/UNDEV INT/ORG ACT/RES PLAN CAP/ISM INT/TRADE ATTIT WEALTH...SOC MATH STAT GEN/LAWS INDEX 20. PAGE 78 F1530
ECO/DEV ROUTINE ECO/TAC SOCISM

B60
PITCHER G.M.,BIBLIOGRAPHY OF GHANA. AFR GHANA NAT/G 20. PAGE 106 F2091
BIBLIOG/A SOC

B60
RAO V.K.R.,INTERNATIONAL AID FOR ECONOMIC DEVELOPMENT - POSSIBILITIES AND LIMITATIONS. FINAN PLAN TEC/DEV ADMIN TASK EFFICIENCY...POLICY SOC METH/CNCPT CHARTS 20 UN. PAGE 109 F2147
FOR/AID DIPLOM INT/ORG ECO/UNDEV

B60
ROPKE W.,A HUMANE ECONOMY. CULTURE ECO/DEV FINAN INDUS GP/REL CENTRAL WEALTH...GEOG SOC IDEA/COMP 20 EEC. PAGE 114 F2239
ECO/TAC INT/ORG DIPLOM ORD/FREE

B60
SAKAI R.K.,STUDIES ON ASIA, 1960. ASIA CHINA/COM S/ASIA COM/IND ECO/TAC...ANTHOL 17/20 MALAYA. PAGE 115 F2270
ECO/UNDEV SOC

B60
UNESCO,SOUTHERN ASIA SOCIAL SCIENCE BIBLIOGRAPHY (WITH ANNOTATIONS AND ABSTRACTS), 1959 (PAMPHLET). S/ASIA...SOC 20. PAGE 132 F2609
BIBLIOG/A ECO/UNDEV TEC/DEV INDUS

L60
SPENGLER J.J.,"ECONOMIC DEVELOPMENT: POLITICAL PRECONDITIONS AND POLITICAL CONSEQUENCE." WOR+45 STRUCT ECO/UNDEV NAT/G PLAN ECO/TAC EDU/PROP ATTIT ORD/FREE WEALTH SOCISM...SOC CONCPT TREND SIMUL GEN/METH WORK 20. PAGE 124 F2452
TEC/DEV METH/CNCPT CAP/ISM

S60
BARNETT H.J.,"RESEARCH AND DEVELOPMENT, ECONOMIC GROWTH, AND NATIONAL SECURITY." AFR USA+45 R+D CREATE ECO/TAC ATTIT DRIVE PWR...POLICY SOC METH/CNCPT QUANT STAT TIME/SEQ ORG/CHARTS LOG/LING 20. PAGE 10 F0190
ACT/RES PLAN

S60
BAUM M.,"THE CASE FOR BUSINESS CIVILIZATION." R+D CAP/ISM GIVE EDU/PROP HAPPINESS...SOC TREND. PAGE 12 F0218
MGT CULTURE WEALTH

S60
FRENCH J.R.P. JR.,"AN EXPERIMENT ON PARTICIPATION IN A NORWEGIAN FACTORY:INTERPERSONAL DIMENSIONS OF DECISION-MAKING." LABOR LEAD PERS/REL EFFICIENCY PRODUC...DECISION SOC CHARTS SOC/EXP. PAGE 44 F0853
INDUS PLAN RIGID/FLEX GP/REL

S60
HERZ J.H.,"EAST GERMANY: PROGRESS AND PROSPECTS." COM AGRI FINAN INDUS LOC/G NAT/G FORCES PLAN TEC/DEV DOMIN ADMIN COERCE DRIVE PERCEPT RIGID/FLEX MORAL ORD/FREE PWR...MARXIST PSY SOC RECORD STERTYP WORK. PAGE 59 F1158
POL/PAR STRUCT GERMANY

S60
JAFFEE A.J.,"POPULATION TRENDS AND CONTROLS IN UNDERDEVELOPED COUNTRIES." AFR FUT ISLAM L/A+17C S/ASIA CULTURE R+D FAM ACT/RES PLAN EDU/PROP BIO/SOC RIGID/FLEX HEALTH...SOC STAT OBS CHARTS 20. PAGE 66 F1303
ECO/UNDEV GEOG

S60
RIVKIN A.,"AFRICAN ECONOMIC DEVELOPMENT: ADVANCED TECHNOLOGY AND THE STAGES OF GROWTH." CULTURE ECO/UNDEV AGRI COM/IND EXTR/IND PLAN ECO/TAC ATTIT DRIVE RIGID/FLEX SKILL WEALTH...MGT SOC GEN/LAWS FOR/TRADE WORK TOT/POP 20. PAGE 111 F2195
AFR TEC/DEV FOR/AID

C60
HOSELITZ B.,"THE ROLE OF CITIES IN THE ECONOMIC GROWTH OF UNDERDEVELOPED COUNTRIES" IN "SOCIOLOGICAL ASPECTS OF ECONOMIC GROWTH"(BMR). CULTURE LOC/G ACT/RES...SOC IDEA/COMP METH/COMP METH MUNICH IND 14/20 REDFIELD/R. PAGE 62 F1218
METH/CNCPT TEC/DEV ECO/UNDEV

B61
BRAIBANTI R.,TRADITION, VALUES AND SOCIO-ECONOMIC DEVELOPMENT. WOR+45 ACT/RES TEC/DEV ATTIT ORD/FREE CONSERVE...POLICY SOC ANTHOL. PAGE 17 F0336
ALL/VALS ECO/UNDEV CONCPT METH/CNCPT

B61
DE VRIES E.,MAN IN RAPID SOCIAL CHANGE. WOR+45 SOCIETY ECO/DEV ECO/UNDEV AGRI INDUS FAM SECT TEC/DEV ATTIT...RECORD 20 CHRISTIAN. PAGE 31 F0607
CULTURE ALL/VALS SOC TASK

B61
DETHINE P.,BIBLIOGRAPHIE DES ASPECTS ECONOMIQUES ET SOCIAUX DE L'INDUSTRIALISATION EN AFRIQUE. AFR FINAN LABOR FOR/AID...SOC 20. PAGE 32 F0623
BIBLIOG/A ECO/UNDEV INDUS TEC/DEV

B61
ERASMUS C.J.,MAN TAKES CONTROL: CULTURAL DEVELOPMENT AND AMERICAN AID. STRUCT OWN DRIVE PERCEPT...SOC 20 MEXIC/AMER. PAGE 38 F0741
ORD/FREE CULTURE ECO/UNDEV TEC/DEV

B61
FLINN M.W.,AN ECONOMIC AND SOCIAL HISTORY OF BRITAIN, 1066-1939. UK LAW STRATA STRUCT AGRI DIST/IND INDUS WORKER INT/TRADE WAR...CENSUS 11/20. PAGE 42 F0811
SOCIETY SOC

B61
FRIEDMANN G.,THE ANATOMY OF WORK. USA+45 SOCIETY CONTROL ROUTINE DRIVE SKILL...PSY SOC STAT OBS METH/COMP PERS/COMP 20. PAGE 44 F0862
AUTOMAT WORKER INDUS PERSON

B61
HEMPSTONE S.,THE NEW AFRICA. AGRI INDUS KIN NAT/G COLONIAL MARXISM...SOC INT TREND NAT/COMP BIBLIOG/A 20. PAGE 58 F1146
AFR ORD/FREE PERSON CULTURE

B61
HENDERSON W.O.,THE INDUSTRIAL REVOLUTION IN EUROPE. FRANCE GERMANY MOD/EUR RUSSIA WORKER PROFIT PWR MARXISM SOCISM...SOC HIST/WRIT 19 INDUS/REV. PAGE 58 F1148
INDUS REV CAP/ISM TEC/DEV

B61
ROEPKE W.,JENSEITS VON ANGEBOT UND NACHFRAGE (DRITTE VERAENDERTE AUFLAGE). WOR+45 MARKET TEC/DEV ECO/TAC GP/REL INGP/REL NEW/LIB...POLICY SOC IDEA/COMP PERS/COMP 20. PAGE 113 F2233
SOCIETY STRANGE ECO/DEV STRUCT

S61
BENOIT E.,"THE PROPENSITY TO REDUCE THE NATIONAL DEBT OUT OF DEFENSE SAVINGS." FUT USA+45 SOCIETY R+D PLAN...WELF/ST SOC REC/INT STERTYP TOT/POP 20. PAGE 13 F0250
WEALTH ECO/TAC

S61
DALTON G.,"ECONOMIC THEORY AND PRIMITIVE SOCIETY" (BMR)" UNIV AGRI KIN TEC/DEV ECO/TAC REGION HABITAT SKILL...METH/COMP BIBLIOG. PAGE 30 F0574
ECO/UNDEV METH PHIL/SCI SOC

S61
DELLA PORT G.,"PROBLEMI E PROSPETTIVE DI COESISTENZA FRA ORIENTE ED OCCIDENTE, (PART 3)." COM FUT WOR+45 NAT/G BAL/PWR FOR/AID BAL/PAY PWR WEALTH...SOC CONCPT GEN/LAWS 20. PAGE 32 F0616
AFR INT/TRADE

S61
GALBRAITH J.K.,"A POSITIVE APPROACH TO ECONOMIC AID." FUT USA+45 INTELL NAT/G CONSULT ACT/RES DIPLOM ECO/TAC EDU/PROP ATTIT KNOWL PWR WEALTH ...SOC STERTYP MID/EX METH/GP 20. PAGE 45 F0883
ECO/UNDEV ROUTINE FOR/AID

B62
BROOKINGS INSTITUTION,DEVELOPMENT OF THE EMERGING COUNTRIES; AN AGENDA FOR RESEARCH. WOR+45 AGRI TEC/DEV FOR/AID EDU/PROP ADJUST HABITAT KNOWL...PSY SOC ANTHOL 20 THIRD/WRLD. PAGE 19 F0362
ECO/UNDEV R+D SOCIETY PROB/SOLV

B62
BRUMBERG A.,RUSSIA UNDER KHRUSHCHEV. FUT USSR SOCIETY ECO/DEV AGRI PERF/ART WORKER PWR...SOC ANTHOL 20 KHRUSH/N. PAGE 20 F0377
COM MARXISM NAT/G CHIEF

B62
CHAPIN F.S.,URBAN GROWTH DYNAMICS IN A REGIONAL CLUSTER OF CITIES. TEC/DEV ECO/TAC HABITAT...GEOG SOC MUNICH. PAGE 23 F0453
REGION PLAN

B62
COLLIER A.T.,MANAGEMENT, MEN, AND VALUES. INDUS FACE/GP EX/STRUC PLAN PROB/SOLV DEBATE SENIOR ADMIN PROFIT PERSON...PSY SOC 20. PAGE 26 F0505
MGT ATTIT PERS/REL DECISION

B62
DE GRAZIA S.,OF TIME, WORK, AND LEISURE. USA+45 ECO/DEV WORKER HAPPINESS UTOPIA ALL/VALS...SOC NEW/IDEA TIME. PAGE 31 F0599
CULTURE LEISURE CONCPT

B62
DEBUYST F.,LAS CLASES SOCIALES EN AMERICA LATINA. L/A+17C SOCIETY STRUCT WORKER EDU/PROP RACE/REL ATTIT HABITAT ROLE...GEOG SOC NAT/COMP SOC/INTEG 20. PAGE 32 F0612
STRATA GP/REL WEALTH

B62
ELLIOTT J.R.,THE APPEAL OF COMMUNISM IN THE UNDERDEVELOPED NATIONS. AFR USSR WOR+45 INT/ORG NAT/G DIPLOM DOMIN EDU/PROP ROUTINE ATTIT RIGID/FLEX ORD/FREE PWR WEALTH MARXISM...POLICY SOC METH/CNCPT MYTH TOT/POP METH/GP 20. PAGE 37 F0722
COM ECO/UNDEV

B62
HEILBRONER R.L.,THE MAKING OF ECONOMIC SOCIETY. FUT WOR-45 SOCIETY STRATA ECO/DEV ECO/UNDEV ECO/TAC LEGIT ROUTINE...SOC RECORD REC/INT KNO/TEST CENSUS STERTYP GEN/LAWS. PAGE 58 F1136
CAP/ISM SOCISM

B62
JOHNSON H.G.,MONEY, TRADE AND ECONOMIC GROWTH.
PLAN

ECO/DEV ECO/UNDEV FINAN COST WEALTH...POLICY SOC IDEA/COMP 20 KEYNES/JM MONEY. PAGE 67 F1324
BAL/PAY INT/TRADE ECO/TAC

B62
KOLKO G.,WEALTH AND POWER IN AMERICA. USA+45 SOCIETY STRATA LG/CO ECO/TAC TAX PWR...SOC BIBLIOG 20 DEPRESSION. PAGE 72 F1420
STRUCT INCOME ECO/DEV WEALTH

B62
MOUSSA P.,THE UNDERPRIVILEGED NATIONS. FINAN INT/ORG PLAN PROB/SOLV CAP/ISM GIVE TASK WEALTH ...POLICY SOC IND 20. PAGE 94 F1850
ECO/UNDEV NAT/G DIPLOM FOR/AID

B62
SELOSOEMARDJAN O.,SOCIAL CHANGES IN JOGJAKARTA. INDONESIA NETHERLAND ELITES STRATA STRUCT FAM POL/PAR CREATE DIPLOM INT/TRADE EDU/PROP ADMIN GOV/REL...SOC 20 JAVA CHINJAP. PAGE 119 F2352
ECO/UNDEV CULTURE REV COLONIAL

B62
UNECA LIBRARY,BOOKS ON AFRICA IN THE UNECA LIBRARY. WOR+45 AGRI INT/ORG NAT/G PLAN WRITING REGION...SOC STAT UN. PAGE 132 F2605
BIBLIOG AFR ECO/UNDEV TEC/DEV

B62
UNECA LIBRARY,NEW ACQUISITIONS IN THE UNECA LIBRARY. LAW NAT/G PLAN PROB/SOLV TEC/DEV ADMIN REGION...GEOG SOC 20 UN. PAGE 132 F2606
BIBLIOG AFR ECO/UNDEV INT/ORG

B62
VAN RENSBURG P.,GUILTY LAND: THE HISTORY OF APARTHEID. SOUTH/AFR NAT/G POL/PAR DOMIN CHOOSE ...SOC 19/20 NEGRO. PAGE 140 F2763
RACE/REL DISCRIM NAT/LISM POLICY

L62
"BIBLIOGRAPHY ON EDUCATION AND ECONOMIC AND SOCIAL DEVELOPMENT (AMERICAN SOURCES)" L/A+17C ECO/UNDEV PROB/SOLV...SOC 20. PAGE 1 F0015
BIBLIOG/A ACADEM EDU/PROP INTELL

L62
"HIGHER EDUCATION AND ECONOMIC AND SOCIAL DEVELOPMENT IN LATIN AMERICA: A BIBLIOGRAPHY." L/A+17C SOCIETY ECO/UNDEV PROF/ORG DIPLOM CONFER ...SOC 20. PAGE 1 F0016
BIBLIOG/A ACADEM INTELL EDU/PROP

L62
DURAND-REVILLE L.,"LE REGIME DES INVESTISSEMENTS DANS LES ETATS AFRICAINS D'EXPRESSION FRANCAISE ET A MADAGASCAR." MADAGASCAR ECO/UNDEV CAP/ISM ECO/TAC WEALTH...SOC TREND CHARTS 20. PAGE 35 F0683
AFR FINAN

S62
PYE L.W.,"THE POLITICAL IMPULSES AND FANTASIES BEHIND FOREIGN AID." FUT USA+45 ECO/UNDEV DIPLOM ECO/TAC ROUTINE DRIVE KNOWL...SOC METH/CNCPT NEW/IDEA TREND HYPO/EXP STERTYP GEN/METH 20. PAGE 108 F2133
ACT/RES ATTIT FOR/AID

B63
DE VRIES E.,SOCIAL ASPECTS OF ECONOMIC DEVELOPMENT IN LATIN AMERICA. CULTURE SOCIETY STRATA FINAN INDUS INT/ORG DELIB/GP ACT/RES ECO/TAC EDU/PROP ADMIN ATTIT SUPEGO HEALTH KNOWL ORD/FREE...SOC STAT TREND ANTHOL TOT/POP VAL/FREE. PAGE 31 F0608
L/A+17C ECO/UNDEV

B63
GEERTZ C.,PEDDLERS AND PRINCES: SOCIAL DEVELOPMENT AND ECONOMIC CHANGE IN TWO INDONESIAN TOWNS. S/ASIA CULTURE SOCIETY STRATA FACE/GP CREATE TEC/DEV ECO/TAC ORD/FREE WEALTH...OBS INT CENSUS CHARTS WORK TOT/POP METH/GP TERR/GP VAL/FREE 20 MUNICH. PAGE 47 F0913
ECO/UNDEV SOC ELITES INDONESIA

B63
GOLDMAN M.I.,SOVIET MARKETING. USSR DIST/IND FINAN RATION OWN WEALTH...SOC BIBLIOG 20. PAGE 48 F0937
MARKET ECO/TAC CONTROL MARXISM

B63
INTERAMERICAN ECO AND SOC COUN,THE ALLIANCE FOR PROGRESS: ITS FIRST YEAR: 1961-1962. AGRI SCHOOL PLAN TEC/DEV INT/TRADE TAX GIVE ADMIN WEALTH...SOC 20 ALL/PROG SOUTH/AMER. PAGE 64 F1267
INT/ORG PROB/SOLV ECO/TAC L/A+17C

B63
NOMAD M.,POLITICAL HERETICS: FROM PLATO TO MAO TSE-TUNG. UNIV INGP/REL...SOC IDEA/COMP. PAGE 98 F1931
SOCIETY UTOPIA ALL/IDEOS CONCPT

B63
PAENSON I.,SYSTEMATIC GLOSSARY ENGLISH, FRENCH, SPANISH, RUSSIAN OF SELECTED ECONOMIC AND SOCIAL TERMS. WOR+45 FINAN LABOR INT/TRADE DEMAND PRODUC 20. PAGE 102 F2014
DICTIONARY SOC LING

B63
RILEY J.W. JR.,THE CORPORATION AND ITS PUBLICS. ESSAYS ON THE CORPORATE IMAGE. CLIENT ISOLAT AGE ATTIT...POLICY SOC METH/CNCPT INT. PAGE 111 F2193
LG/CO CLASSIF GP/REL NEIGH

B63
SMELSER N.J.,THE SOCIOLOGY OF ECONOMIC LIFE. UNIV CULTURE PERCEPT...PSY T 18/20. PAGE 123 F2425
SOC METH/COMP IDEA/COMP

B63
STUCKI C.W.,AMERICAN DOCTORAL DISSERTATIONS ON ASIA 1933-62 (A PAPER). PREHIST INDUS NAT/G GOV/REL ALL/IDEOS...ART/METH GEOG SOC LING 20. PAGE 127 F2506
BIBLIOG ASIA SOCIETY S/ASIA

B63
WAGLEY C.,INTRODUCTION TO BRAZIL. BRAZIL L/A+17C FAM KIN SCHOOL SECT ATTIT WEALTH...GEOG SOC. PAGE 142 F2799
ECO/UNDEV ELITES HABITAT STRATA

L63
NASH M.,"PSYCHO-CULTURAL FACTORS IN ASIAN ECONOMIC GROWTH." ASIA ISLAM S/ASIA CULTURE ECO/UNDEV DELIB/GP EDU/PROP COERCE ATTIT PERSON HEALTH KNOWL ORD/FREE...PSY SOC STAT TREND ANTHOL VAL/FREE 20. PAGE 96 F1893
SOCIETY ECO/TAC

L63
OLSON M. JR.,"RAPID ECONOMIC GROWTH AS A DESTABILIZING FORCE." WOR+45 WOR-45 STRATA ECO/UNDEV FAM KIN CREATE TEC/DEV DIPLOM PEACE ATTIT PERSON RIGID/FLEX PWR RESPECT WEALTH...SOC 20. PAGE 101 F1989
SOCIETY FOR/AID

S63
BARANSON J.,"ECONOMIC AND SOCIAL CONSIDERATIONS IN ADAPTING TECHNOLOGIES FOR DEVELOPING COUNTRIES." WOR+45 PLAN WEALTH...TECHNIC SOC 20. PAGE 10 F0180
ECO/UNDEV TEC/DEV

B64
AHMAD M.,THE CIVIL SERVANT IN PAKISTAN. PAKISTAN ECO/UNDEV COLONIAL INGP/REL...SOC CHARTS BIBLIOG 20 CIVIL/SERV. PAGE 3 F0051
WELF/ST ADMIN ATTIT STRATA

B64
CEPEDE M.,POPULATION AND FOOD. USA+45 STRUCT ECO/UNDEV FAM PLAN TEC/DEV FOR/AID CONTROL...CATH SOC TREND 19/20. PAGE 22 F0436
FUT GEOG AGRI CENSUS

B64
DE BARY W.T.,APPROACHES TO ASIAN CIVILIZATIONS. INDIA ISLAM USA+45 CULTURE ACADEM...SOC ANTHOL 20 CHINJAP ARABS. PAGE 31 F0595
ASIA EDU/PROP SOCIETY

B64
EDWARDS E.O.,THE NATION'S ECONOMIC OBJECTIVES. INDUS WORKER BUDGET DIPLOM CONTROL ORD/FREE ...POLICY SOC METH/CNCPT ANTHOL 20. PAGE 36 F0704
NAT/G ECO/TAC

B64
FEIS H.,FOREIGN AID AND FOREIGN POLICY. USA+45 WOR+45 NAT/G VOL/ASSN ACT/RES TEC/DEV ATTIT HEALTH WEALTH...SOC GEN/LAWS 20. PAGE 40 F0775
ECO/UNDEV ECO/TAC FOR/AID DIPLOM

B64
FIRTH R.,CAPITAL, SAVING AND CREDIT IN PEASANT SOCIETIES. WOR+45 WOR-45 FAM ACT/RES ECO/TAC HEALTH ...SOC CONCPT STAT CHARTS ANTHOL CARIBBEAN VAL/FREE 20. PAGE 41 F0803
AGRI FINAN

B64
FLORENCE P.S.,ECONOMICS AND SOCIOLOGY OF INDUSTRY; A REALISTIC ANALYSIS OF DEVELOPMENT. ECO/UNDEV LG/CO NAT/G PLAN...GEOG MGT BIBLIOG 20. PAGE 42 F0814
INDUS SOC ADMIN

B64
LAFONT P.B.,BIBLIOGRAPHIE DU LAOS. LAOS S/ASIA EDU/PROP...GEOG 20. PAGE 74 F1458
BIBLIOG LAW SOC

B64
NEHEMKIS P.,LATIN AMERICA: MYTH AND REALITY. INDUS INT/ORG PROB/SOLV CAP/ISM DIPLOM REV...SOC MUNICH 20. PAGE 97 F1907
REGION MYTH L/A+17C ECO/UNDEV

B64
NOVACK D.E.,DEVELOPMENT AND SOCIETY; THE DYNAMICS OF ECONOMIC CHANGE. WOR+45 STRATA STRUCT ECO/TAC CONTROL CROWD REV GP/REL ADJUST PRODUC WEALTH PSY. PAGE 99 F1940
SOCIETY CULTURE SOC ECO/UNDEV

B64
SAKAI R.K.,STUDIES ON ASIA, 1964. ASIA CHINA/COM ISRAEL MALAYSIA S/ASIA USA+45 USSR ECO/UNDEV FAM POL/PAR SECT CONSULT NAT/LISM...POLICY SOC 20 CHINJAP. PAGE 115 F2272
PWR DIPLOM

B64
SULLIVAN G.,THE STORY OF THE PEACE CORPS. USA+45 WOR+45 INTELL FACE/GP NAT/G SCHOOL VOL/ASSN CONSULT EX/STRUC PLAN EDU/PROP ADMIN ATTIT DRIVE ALL/VALS ...POLICY HEAL SOC CONCPT INT QU BIOG TREND SOC/EXP WORK. PAGE 127 F2511
INT/ORG ECO/UNDEV FOR/AID PEACE

B64
TAEUBER I.B.,POPULATION TRENDS IN THE UNITED STATES: 1900 TO 1960. USA+45 USA-45 PROVS INCOME AGE...SOC TIME/SEQ TREND CHARTS MUNICH TIME 20 NEGRO. PAGE 128 F2522
CENSUS GEOG STRATA STRUCT

B64
TAWNEY R.H.,EQUALITY. UK CULTURE STRATA ECO/TAC EDU/PROP REPRESENT OWN NEW/LIB...MAJORIT WELF/ST SOC 20. PAGE 129 F2538
WEALTH STRUCT ELITES POPULISM

B64
TAX S.,EL CAPITALISMO DEL CENTAVO; UNA ECONOMIA
ECO/UNDEV

INDIGENA DE GUATEMALA (2 VOLS.). GUATEMALA L/A+17C SOCIETY GP/REL DEMAND INCOME HABITAT...SOC MUNICH 20 INDIAN/AM. PAGE 129 F2539 AGRI WEALTH COST B64

US LIBRARY OF CONGRESS,SOUTHEAST ASIA. CULTURE ...SOC STAT 20. PAGE 138 F2718 BIBLIOG/A S/ASIA ECO/UNDEV NAT/G B64

WERTHEIM W.F.,EAST-WEST PARALLELS. INDONESIA S/ASIA NAT/G SECT...TIME/SEQ METH REFORMERS S/EASTASIA. PAGE 145 F2860 SOC ECO/UNDEV CULTURE NAT/LISM S64

NASH M.,"SOCIAL PREREQUISITES TO ECONOMIC GROWTH IN LATIN AMERICA AND SOUTHEAST ASIA." L/A+17C S/ASIA CULTURE SOCIETY ECO/UNDEV AGRI INDUS NAT/G PLAN TEC/DEV EDU/PROP ROUTINE ALL/VALS...POLICY RELATIV SOC NAT/COMP WORK TOT/POP 20. PAGE 96 F1894 ECO/DEV PERCEPT S64

SCHMITT H.D.,"POLITICAL CONDITIONS FOR INTERNATIONAL CURRENCY REFORM." WOR+45 SOCIETY ECO/DEV PLAN ECO/TAC BAL/PAY ATTIT ORD/FREE WEALTH ...SOC CONCPT OBS TREND EEC VAL/FREE ECSC 20. PAGE 117 F2301 FINAN VOL/ASSN REGION S64

TOBIN J.,"ECONOMIC GROWTH AS AN OBJECTIVE OF GOVERNMENT POLICY." FUT WOR+45 FINAN WORKER BUDGET INCOME...SOC 20. PAGE 131 F2579 ECO/DEV POLICY ECO/TAC IDEA/COMP B65

APTER D.E.,THE POLITICS OF MODERNIZATION. AFR L/A+17C CULTURE NAT/G POL/PAR ADMIN COLONIAL NAT/LISM ATTIT RIGID/FLEX PWR...SOC CONCPT. PAGE 6 F0109 ECO/UNDEV GEN/LAWS STRATA CREATE B65

BOLLENS J.C.,THE METROPOLIS: ITS PEOPLE, POLITICS, AND ECONOMIC LIFE. USA+45 PLAN PROB/SOLV PERS/REL PWR...DECISION GEOG CENSUS TREND CON/ANAL MUNICH 20 NEWYORK/C LOS/ANG SAN/FRAN CHICAGO PHILADELPH. PAGE 16 F0309 HABITAT SOC LOC/G B65

GOODSELL C.T.,ADMINISTRATION OF A REVOLUTION. PUERT/RICO ECO/UNDEV FINAN POL/PAR PROVS LEGIS PLAN BUDGET RECEIVE ADMIN COLONIAL LEAD MUNICH 20 ROOSEVLT/F. PAGE 49 F0951 EXEC SOC B65

GREEN J.L.,METROPOLITAN ECONOMIC REPUBLICS. USA+45 ECO/TAC INCOME...GEOG SOC CONCPT SIMUL MUNICH 20 ATLANTA. PAGE 50 F0985 SOC/WK PLAN LABOR B65

GREER S.,URBAN RENEWAL AND AMERICAN CITIES: THE DILEMMA OF DEMOCRATIC INTERVENTION. USA+45 R+D LOC/G VOL/ASSN ACT/RES BUDGET ADMIN GOV/REL...SOC INT SAMP MUNICH 20 BOSTON CHICAGO LOS/ANG MIAMI URBAN/RNWL. PAGE 51 F0992 PROB/SOLV PLAN NAT/G B65

HASSON J.A.,THE ECONOMICS OF NUCLEAR POWER. INDIA UK USA+45 WOR+45 INT/ORG TEC/DEV COST...SOC STAT CHARTS 20 EURATOM. PAGE 56 F1108 NUC/PWR INDUS ECO/DEV METH B65

HAUSER P.M.,THE STUDY OF URBANIZATION. S/ASIA ECO/DEV ECO/UNDEV NEIGH ACT/RES...GEOG MUNICH. PAGE 57 F1115 CULTURE SOC B65

NATIONAL CENTRAL LIBRARY,LATIN AMERICAN ECONOMIC AND SOCIAL SERIALS. UK SOCIETY NAT/G PLAN PROB/SOLV ...SOC 20. PAGE 97 F1897 BIBLIOG INT/TRADE ECO/UNDEV L/A+17C B65

SIMMS R.P.,URBANIZATION IN WEST AFRICA; A REVIEW OF CURRENT LITERATURE. AFR PLAN TEC/DEV...SOC OBS NAT/COMP MUNICH 20. PAGE 122 F2405 BIBLIOG/A ECO/DEV ECO/UNDEV B65

STEINER G.A.,THE CREATIVE ORGANIZATION. ELITES LG/CO PLAN PROB/SOLV TEC/DEV INSPECT CAP/ISM CONTROL EXEC PERSON...METH/COMP HYPO/EXP 20. PAGE 126 F2476 CREATE MGT ADMIN SOC B65

WALTON R.E.,A BEHAVIORAL THEORY OF LABOR NEGOTIATIONS: AN ANALYSIS OF A SOCIAL INTERACTION SYSTEM. USA+45 FINAN PROB/SOLV ECO/TAC GP/REL INGP/REL...DECISION BIBLIOG. PAGE 143 F2812 SOC LABOR BARGAIN ADMIN B65

WILKINSON T.O.,THE URBANIZATION OF JAPANESE LABOR, 1868-1955. AGRI PROC/MFG CAP/ISM PRODUC PROFIT ...SOC CLASSIF CENSUS CHARTS MUNICH 19/20 CHINJAP. PAGE 146 F2887 LABOR INDUS GEOG B65

WINT G.,ASIA: A HANDBOOK. ASIA COM INDIA USSR CULTURE INTELL NAT/G...GEOG STAT CENSUS NAT/COMP WORSHIP 20 TREATY CHINJAP. PAGE 148 F2907 DIPLOM SOC S65

KINDLEBERGER C.P.,"MASS MIGRATION, THEN AND NOW." LAW ECO/DEV ECO/UNDEV INDUS LABOR INT/TRADE FEEDBACK REGION RIGID/FLEX...SOC NAT/COMP EEC. PAGE 71 F1394 EUR+WWI USA-45 WORKER IDEA/COMP S65

SPAAK P.H.,"THE SEARCH FOR CONSENSUS: A NEW EFFORT TO BUILD EUROPE." FRANCE GERMANY ECO/DEV NAT/G CONSULT FORCES PLAN EDU/PROP REGION CONSEN ATTIT ...SOC METH/CNCPT OBS TREND EEC NATO WORK TERR/GP METH/GP 20. PAGE 124 F2447 EUR+WWI INT/ORG B66

BEQIRAJ M.,PEASANTRY IN REVOLUTION. STRATA ECO/UNDEV AGRI ROUTINE REV HABITAT RIGID/FLEX ...EPIST GEOG NEW/IDEA TREND MUNICH 20. PAGE 13 F0256 WORKER KNOWL NAT/LISM SOC B66

CANNING HOUSE LIBRARY,AUTHOR AND SUBJECT CATALOGUES OF THE CANNING HOUSE LIBRARY (5 VOLS.). UK CULTURE LEAD...SOC 19/20. PAGE 21 F0411 BIBLIOG L/A+17C NAT/G DIPLOM B66

CROWDER M.,A SHORT HISTORY OF NIGERIA. AFR NIGERIA UK ECO/UNDEV CHIEF INT/TRADE RACE/REL NAT/LISM ORD/FREE...GEOG SOC CHARTS BIBLIOG 14/20. PAGE 29 F0558 COLONIAL NAT/G CULTURE B66

DAVIES JC I.I.I.,NEIGHBORHOOD GROUPS AND URBAN RENEWAL. USA+45 PLAN LOBBY PARTIC CHOOSE RACE/REL ...POLICY DECISION SOC INT MUNICH SOC/INTEG 20 NEWYORK/C. PAGE 30 F0586 NEIGH CREATE PROB/SOLV B66

ECONOMIC RESEARCH SERVICE,RESEARCH DATA ON MINORITY GROUPS: AN ANNOTATED BIBLIOGRAPHY OF ECONOMIC RESEARCH SERVICE REPORTS: 1955-1965 (PAMPHLET). USA+45 STRATA ECO/DEV AGRI SCHOOL WORKER EDU/PROP HEALTH NEW/LIB SOC. PAGE 36 F0697 BIBLIOG/A DISCRIM WEALTH RACE/REL B66

FRANCK L.R.,LA POLITIQUE ECONOMIQUE DES ETATS-UNIS. USA+45 USA-45 FINAN INDUS CONTROL CROWD GOV/REL GP/REL...POLICY SOC CHARTS 18/20. PAGE 43 F0841 NAT/G INT/TRADE GEOG B66

HEISS K.P.,GAME THEORY AND HUMAN CONFLICTS (RESEARCH MEMORANDUM). UNIV ACT/RES...DECISION SOC MATH PROBABIL SIMUL 20 DEFINETT/B. PAGE 58 F1142 GAME ECOMETRIC PLAN PROB/SOLV B66

HOLT R.T.,THE POLITICAL BASIS OF ECONOMIC DEVELOPMENT. STRATA STRUCT NAT/G DIPLOM ADMIN...SOC NAT/COMP BIBLIOG 20. PAGE 61 F1201 ECO/TAC GOV/COMP CONSTN EX/STRUC B66

HOWE R.W.,BLACK AFRICA: FROM PRE-HISTORY TO THE EVE OF THE COLONIAL ERA. ECO/UNDEV KIN PROVS SECT INT/TRADE EDU/PROP COLONIAL...BIBLIOG WORSHIP. PAGE 62 F1226 AFR CULTURE SOC B66

HUNT C.L.,SOCIAL ASPECTS OF ECONOMIC DEVELOPMENT. S/ASIA AGRI FAM TEC/DEV RECEIVE EDU/PROP OWN...GEOG MUNICH 20. PAGE 63 F1243 SOC STRATA ATTIT ECO/UNDEV B66

KIRKENDALL R.S.,SOCIAL SCIENTISTS AND FARM POLITICS IN THE AGE OF ROOSEVELT. ACADEM PLAN ECO/TAC GIVE ADMIN CONTROL PRODUC...SOC 20 NEW/DEAL ROOSEVLT/F BURAGR/ECO. PAGE 71 F1399 AGRI INTELL POLICY NAT/G B66

LANDERS D.S.,RISE OF CAPITALISM. LABOR AUTOMAT GP/REL CENTRAL COST PROFIT...SOC CONCPT ANTHOL 19/20. PAGE 75 F1469 CAP/ISM INDUS AGRI B66

LENSKI G.E.,POWER AND PRIVILEGE: A THEORY OF SOCIAL STRATIFICATION. SWEDEN UK UNIV USSR CULTURE ECO/UNDEV PRIVIL PWR...PHIL/SCI CONCPT CHARTS IDEA/COMP HYPO/EXP METH MARX/KARL. PAGE 78 F1525 SOC STRATA STRUCT SOCIETY B66

LILLEY S.,MEN, MACHINES AND HISTORY: THE STORY OF TOOLS AND MACHINES IN RELATION TO SOCIAL PROGRESS. PREHIST SPACE STRUCT COMPUTER AUTOMAT NUC/PWR ...POLICY SOC. PAGE 80 F1564 AGRI TEC/DEV SOCIETY B66

LONDON K.,EASTERN EUROPE IN TRANSITION. CHINA/COM USSR DOMIN COLONIAL CENTRAL RIGID/FLEX PWR...SOC ANTHOL 20. PAGE 82 F1597 SOVEREIGN COM NAT/LISM DIPLOM B66

MOUNTJOY A.B.,INDUSTRIALIZATION AND UNDER-DEVELOPED COUNTRIES (2ND REV. ED.). CHILE GHANA INDIA NIGERIA WOR+45 SOCIETY PROB/SOLV ECO/TAC...SOC CHARTS 20 INDUS/REV. PAGE 94 F1848 ECO/UNDEV INDUS GEOG HABITAT B66

NICOSIA M.N.,CONSUMER DECISION PROCESSES: MARKETING AND ADVERTISING IMPLICATIONS. ECO/TAC ATTIT PERSON ...DECISION MGT SOC. PAGE 98 F1926 MARKET SOCIETY CREATE ACT/RES B66

ODEGARD P.H.,POLITICAL POWER AND SOCIAL CHANGE. UNIV NAT/G CREATE ALL/IDEOS...POLICY GEOG SOC CENSUS TREND. PAGE 100 F1962 PWR TEC/DEV IDEA/COMP

B66
OECD DEVELOPMENT CENTRE,CATALOGUE OF SOCIAL AND ECONOMIC DEVELOPMENT INSTITUTES AND PROGRAMMES* RESEARCH. ACT/RES PLAN TEC/DEV EDU/PROP...SOC GP/COMP NAT/COMP. PAGE 101 F1976
ECO/UNDEV ECO/DEV R+D ACADEM

B66
RAO Y.V.L.,COMMUNICATION AND DEVELOPMENT. INDIA S/ASIA SOCIETY ACT/RES EDU/PROP PARTIC ATTIT...SOC GP/COMP BIBLIOG MUNICH MUNICH 20. PAGE 109 F2149
COM/IND ECO/UNDEV OBS

B66
SOCIAL SCIENCE RESEARCH COUN,BIBLIOGRAPHY OF RESEARCH IN THE SOCIAL SCIENCES IN AUSTRALIA 1957-1960. LAW R+D DIPLOM 20 AUSTRAL. PAGE 124 F2437
BIBLIOG SOC PSY

B66
THIESENHUSEN W.C.,CHILE'S EXPERIMENTS IN AGRARIAN REFORM. CHILE STRUCT NAT/G ACT/RES ECO/TAC GOV/REL COST SOCISM...TREND CHARTS SOC/EXP 20. PAGE 130 F2558
AGRI ECO/UNDEV SOC TEC/DEV

B66
US DEPARTMENT OF STATE,RESEARCH ON WESTERN EUROPE, GREAT BRITAIN, AND CANADA (EXTERNAL RESEARCH LIST NO 3-25). CANADA GERMANY/W UK LAW CULTURE NAT/G POL/PAR FORCES EDU/PROP REGION MARXISM...GEOG SOC WORSHIP 20 CMN/WLTH. PAGE 136 F2676
BIBLIOG/A EUR+WWI DIPLOM

S66
FLEMING W.G.,"AUTHORITY, EFFICIENCY, AND ROLE STRESS: PROBLEMS IN THE DEVELOPMENT OF EAST AFRICAN BUREAUCRACIES." AFR UGANDA STRUCT PROB/SOLV ROUTINE INGP/REL ROLE...MGT SOC GP/COMP GOV/COMP 20 TANGANYIKA AFRICA/E. PAGE 41 F0810
DOMIN EFFICIENCY COLONIAL ADMIN

S66
SHORTE F.C.,"THE APPLICATION OF DEVELOPMENT HYPOTHESES IN MIDDLE EASTERN STUDIES." STRUCT AGRI CREATE DEMAND...GEOG STAT CON/ANAL CHARTS. PAGE 121 F2387
ECO/UNDEV ISLAM SOC HYPO/EXP

S66
VERSLUYS J.D.N.,"SOME NOTES ON THE SOCIAL AND ECONOMIC EFFECTS OF RURAL ELECTRIFICATION IN BURMA" BURMA EDU/PROP PRODUC ORD/FREE...SOC QU MUNICH TIME 20. PAGE 141 F2782
TEC/DEV SOCIETY CREATE

B67
BADGLEY R.F.,DOCTORS' STRIKE; MEDICAL CARE AND CONFLICT IN SASKATCHEWAN. CANADA NAT/G PROF/ORG GP/REL ADJUST ATTIT...HEAL SOC 20. PAGE 8 F0148
HEALTH PLAN LABOR BARGAIN

B67
BANFIELD E.C.,THE MORAL BASIS OF A BACKWARD SOCIETY. EUR+WWI ITALY STRATA NEIGH PARTIC INGP/REL ...SOC QU PREDICT TREND HYPO/EXP MUNICH 20. PAGE 9 F0173
MORAL WEALTH ATTIT

B67
CHANDRASEKHAR S.,PROBLEMS OF ECONOMIC DEVELOPMENT. AFR INDIA PHILIPPINE UAR WOR+45 INDUS...GEOG SOC ANTHOL BIBLIOG 20 CHINJAP. PAGE 23 F0450
ECO/UNDEV PLAN AGRI PROB/SOLV

B67
COHEN M.R.,LAW AND THE SOCIAL ORDER: ESSAYS IN LEGAL PHILOSOPHY. USA-45 CONSULT WORKER ECO/TAC ATTIT WEALTH...POLICY WELF/ST SOC 20 NEW/DEAL DEPRESSION. PAGE 26 F0497
JURID LABOR IDEA/COMP

B67
DIEGUES M.,SOCIAL SCIENCE IN LATIN AMERICA. L/A+17C ...JURID SOC ANTHOL 20. PAGE 33 F0637
METH ACADEM EDU/PROP ACT/RES

B67
EBENSTEIN W.,TODAY'S ISMS: COMMUNISM, FASCISM, CAPITALISM, SOCIALISM (5TH ED.). COM WOR+45 PERCEPT PWR...SOC TREND IDEA/COMP NAT/COMP 20. PAGE 35 F0691
FASCISM MARXISM SOCISM CAP/ISM

B67
EVANS R.H.,COEXISTENCE: COMMUNISM AND ITS PRACTICE IN BOLOGNA, 1945-1965. ITALY CAP/ISM ADMIN CHOOSE PEACE ORD/FREE...SOC STAT DEEP/INT SAMP CHARTS BIBLIOG MUNICH 20. PAGE 39 F0756
MARXISM CULTURE POL/PAR

B67
FORDE D.,WEST AFRICAN KINGDOMS IN THE NINETEENTH CENTURY. ECO/UNDEV AGRI KIN...SOC CHARTS NAT/COMP 19. PAGE 42 F0826
AFR REGION CULTURE

B67
GORZ A.,STRATEGY FOR LABOR: A RADICAL PROPOSAL (TRANS. BY MARTIN NICOLAUS AND VICTORIA ORTIZ). EUR+WWI FRANCE ITALY ECO/DEV POL/PAR OP/RES PLAN GP/REL ALL/IDEOS...SOC 20 EEC. PAGE 49 F0965
LABOR PWR STRUCT ECO/TAC

B67
GUTKIND E.A.,URBAN DEVELOPMENT IN SOUTHERN EUROPE* SPAIN AND PORTUGAL. CHRIST-17C EUR+WWI MOD/EUR PORTUGAL SPAIN CULTURE AGRI...SOC SAMP/SIZ BIBLIOG MUNICH. PAGE 52 F1015
TEC/DEV ECO/DEV

B67
KULSKI J.E.,LAND OF URBAN PROMISE* CONTINUING THE GREAT TRADITION* A SEARCH FOR SIGNIFICANT URBAN SPACE IN URBANIZED NORTHEAST. USA+45 DIST/IND PUB/INST CONSULT CREATE TEC/DEV...SOC NEW/IDEA CHARTS BIBLIOG MUNICH. PAGE 74 F1448
PLAN PROB/SOLV ECO/DEV

B67
LANDEN R.G.,OMAN SINCE 1856: DISRUPTIVE MODERNIZATION IN A TRADITIONAL ARAB SOCIETY. UK DIST/IND EXTR/IND SECT DIPLOM INT/TRADE...SOC LING CHARTS BIBLIOG 19/20. PAGE 75 F1468
ISLAM CULTURE ECO/UNDEV NAT/G

B67
MARRIS P.,DILEMMAS OF SOCIAL REFORM: POVERTY AND COMMUNITY ACTION IN THE UNITED STATES. USA+45 NAT/G OP/RES ADMIN PARTIC EFFICIENCY WEALTH...SOC METH/COMP T MUNICH 20 REFORMERS. PAGE 85 F1674
STRUCT PROB/SOLV COST

B67
MEYERS M.,SOURCES OF THE AMERICAN REPUBLIC; A DOCUMENTARY HISTORY OF POLITICS, SOCIETY, AND THOUGHT (VOL. I, REV. ED.). USA-45 CULTURE STRUCT NAT/G LEGIS LEAD ATTIT...JURID SOC ANTHOL 17/19 PRESIDENT. PAGE 90 F1772
COLONIAL REV WAR

B67
MONTGOMERY J.D.,FOREIGN AID IN INTERNATIONAL POLITICS. USA+45 USA-45 WOR+45 ECO/TAC EFFICIENCY ...SOC TREND CHARTS BIBLIOG/A 20 AID. PAGE 93 F1818
DIPLOM FOR/AID

B67
RAVKIN A.,THE NEW STATES OF AFRICA (HEADLINE SERIES, NO. 183((PAMPHLET). CULTURE STRUCT INDUS COLONIAL NAT/LISM...SOC 20. PAGE 109 F2153
AFR ECO/UNDEV SOCIETY ADMIN

B67
SMITH T.L.,THE PROCESS OF RURAL DEVELOPMENT IN LATIN AMERICA (A MONOGRAPH). L/A+17C STRATA INDUS PLAN GP/REL PERS/REL RIGID/FLEX WEALTH...OBS CHARTS ORG/CHARTS ANTHOL 20 COLOMB. PAGE 123 F2434
IDEA/COMP SOC AGRI ECO/UNDEV

B67
SPECTOR S.D.,CHECKLIST OF ITEMS IN THE NDEA INSTITUTE LIBRARY (PAMPHLET). USA+45 NAT/G SECT EDU/PROP ATTIT ALL/IDEOS...SOC BIOG. PAGE 124 F2448
BIBLIOG/A COM MARXISM

B67
STEARNS P.N.,EUROPEAN SOCIETY IN UPHEAVAL* SOCIAL HISTORY SINCE 1800. EUR+WWI MOD/EUR STRATA SECT WORKER TEC/DEV WAR...WELF/ST SOC TREND BIBLIOG 19/20. PAGE 125 F2472
REGION ECO/DEV SOCIETY INDUS

B67
TUMIN M.M.,SOCIAL STRATIFICATION; THE FORMS AND FUNCTIONS OF INEQUALITY. SENIOR SANCTION WEALTH ...SOC CLASSIF METH 20. PAGE 131 F2592
STRATA DISCRIM CONCPT SOCIETY

B67
UNIVERSAL REFERENCE SYSTEM,BIBLIOGRAPHY OF BIBLIOGRAPHIES IN POLITICAL SCIENCE, GOVERNMENT, AND PUBLIC POLICY (VOLUME III). WOR+45 WOR-45 LAW ADMIN...SOC CON/ANAL COMPUT/IR GEN/METH. PAGE 133 F2615
BIBLIOG/A NAT/G DIPLOM POLICY

B67
WALLBANK T.W.,CIVILIZATION PAST AND PRESENT (3RD ED.). FUT WOR+45 WOR-45 SOCIETY...SOC CONCPT TIME/SEQ CHARTS BIBLIOG T. PAGE 143 F2809
CULTURE STRUCT TREND

B67
WISEMAN H.V.,BRITAIN AND THE COMMONWEALTH. EUR+WWI FUT UK ECO/DEV POL/PAR TEC/DEV INT/TRADE LEAD ROLE SOVEREIGN...SOC TREND 20 CMN/WLTH. PAGE 148 F2911
INT/ORG DIPLOM NAT/G NAT/COMP

B67
WOOTON G.,WORKERS, UNIONS, AND THE STATE. INDUS PROB/SOLV GP/REL DRIVE SUPEGO RESPECT...PSY SOC. PAGE 148 F2925
PARTIC WORKER NAT/G LABOR

S67
ADAMS D.W.,"MINIFUNDIA IN AGRARIAN REFORM: A COLOMBIAN EXAMPLE."...SOC CLASSIF 20 COLOMB. PAGE 2 F0035
AGRI METH/COMP OWN PRODUC

S67
ADAMS R.N.,"ETHICS AND THE SOCIAL ANTHROPOLOGIST IN LATIN AMERICA." USA+45 INTELL PROB/SOLV ECO/TAC LEAD...DECISION SOC NAT/COMP PERS/COMP. PAGE 2 F0039
L/A+17C POLICY ECO/UNDEV CONSULT

S67
ALPANDER G.G.,"ENTREPRENEURS AND PRIVATE ENTERPRISE IN TURKEY." TURKEY INDUS PROC/MFG EDU/PROP ATTIT DRIVE WEALTH...GEOG MGT SOC STAT TREND CHARTS 20. PAGE 4 F0077
ECO/UNDEV LG/CO NAT/G POLICY

S67
FOX R.G.,"FAMILY, CASTE, AND COMMERCE IN A NORTH INDIAN MARKET TOWN." INDIA STRATA AGRI FACE/GP FAM NEIGH OP/RES BARGAIN ADMIN ROUTINE WEALTH...SOC CHARTS 20. PAGE 43 F0838
CULTURE GP/REL ECO/UNDEV DIST/IND

S67
FRANKLIN N.N.,"THE CONCEPT AND MEASUREMENT OF 'MINIMUM LIVING STANDARDS'." UNIV OP/RES PAY INGP/REL DEMAND INCOME DRIVE WEALTH...SOC CHARTS METH/COMP. PAGE 43 F0849
CONCPT PHIL/SCI ALL/VALS HAPPINESS

S67
JOHNSON L.B.,"BULLETS DO NOT DISCRIMINATE-LANDLORDS DO." PROB/SOLV EXEC LOBBY DEMAND...REALPOL SOC 20. PAGE 68 F1329
NAT/G DISCRIM POLICY

S67
LENS S.,"WALTER REUTHER TRIES TO BUILD A FIRE." WORKER LEAD DISCRIM AGE ORD/FREE NEW/LIB SOC.
LABOR PARTIC

PAGE 78 F1523 NEIGH PLAN

S67
LEWIS W.A.,"THE STATUTORY LANGUAGE OF LABOR DISQUALIFICATION IN STATE EMPLOYMENT SECURITY LAWS." LABOR WORKER WORK 20. PAGE 79 F1553 METH/COMP LEGIS SOC PROVS

S67
LOSMAN D.L.,"FOREIGN AID, SOCIALISM AND THE EMERGING COUNTRIES" WOR+45 ADMIN CONTROL PWR 20. PAGE 82 F1602 ECO/UNDEV FOR/AID SOC

S67
MULLER A.L.,"ECONOMIC GROWTH AND MINORITIES." USA+45 SKILL...SOC GP/COMP NEGRO. PAGE 95 F1857 INCOME WORKER ECO/DEV RACE/REL

S67
PETRAS J.,"U.S. HEGEMONY AND LATIN AMERICAN RULING CLASSES." L/A+17C USA+45 ECO/UNDEV FOR/AID REV SOC. PAGE 105 F2071 NAT/G ATTIT DIPLOM POLICY

S67
SCHWARZWELLER H.K.,"SOCIAL CLASS ORIGINS, RURAL-URBAN MIGRATION, AND ECONOMIC LIFE CHANGES." USA+45 SOCIETY STRUCT FAM NEIGH INCOME...SOC RECORD CHARTS MUNICH. PAGE 118 F2326 CLASSIF WEALTH AGRI

S67
SEIDLER G.L.,"MARXIST LEGAL THOUGHT IN POLAND." POLAND SOCIETY R+D LOC/G NAT/G ACT/RES ADJUD CT/SYS SUPEGO PWR...SOC TREND 20 MARX/KARL. PAGE 119 F2343 MARXISM LAW CONCPT EFFICIENCY

N67
NATIONAL COMN COMMUNITY HEALTH,ACTION - PLANNING FOR COMMUNITY HEALTH SERVICES (PAMPHLET). USA+45 PROF/ORG DELIB/GP BUDGET ROUTINE GP/REL ATTIT ...HEAL SOC SOC/WK CHARTS MUNICH TIME 20. PAGE 97 F1898 PLAN HEALTH ADJUST

N67
US HOUSE COMM GOVT OPERATIONS,FEDERALLY FINANCED SOCIAL RESEARCH, EXPENDITURES, STATUS, AND OBJECTIVES (PAMPHLET). WOR+45 CREATE LEAD GP/REL ATTIT...GEOG PSY SOC. PAGE 137 F2700 ACT/RES NAT/G GIVE BUDGET

B86
O'CONNOR T.P.,THE PARNELL MOVEMENT: WITH A SKETCH OF IRISH PARTIES FROM 1843. IRELAND UK USA-45 LEGIS WORKER ECO/TAC COERCE CRIME REV CHOOSE ORD/FREE CATHISM LAISSEZ...SOC 19/20 PARLIAMENT PARNELL/CS LAND/LEAG. PAGE 100 F1957 LEAD DOMIN POL/PAR POLICY

SOC/DEMPAR....SOCIAL DEMOCRATIC PARTY (USE WITH SPECIFIC NATION); SEE ALSO SOCDEM/PAR

B66
COLE A.B.,SOCIALIST PARTIES IN POSTWAR JAPAN. STRATA AGRI LABOR PLAN DIPLOM ECO/TAC AGREE LEAD CHOOSE ATTIT...CHARTS 20 CHINJAP SOC/DEMPAR. PAGE 26 F0499 POL/PAR POLICY SOCISM NAT/G

SOC/EXP...."SOCIAL" EXPERIMENTATION UNDER UNCONTROLLED CONDITIONS

B50
LIPSET S.M.,AGRARIAN SOCIALISM. CANADA POL/PAR OP/RES ECO/TAC ADMIN ATTIT...TIME/SEQ NAT/COMP SOC/EXP 20 SASKATCH. PAGE 80 F1576 SOCISM AGRI METH/COMP STRUCT

C51
HOMANS G.C.,"THE WESTERN ELECTRIC RESEARCHES" IN S. HOSLETT, ED., HUMAN FACTORS IN MANAGEMENT (BMR)" ACT/RES GP/REL HAPPINESS PRODUC DRIVE...MGT OBS 20. PAGE 61 F1202 OP/RES EFFICIENCY SOC/EXP WORKER

B53
BOULDING K.E.,THE ORGANIZATIONAL REVOLUTION. FUT CULTURE ECO/DEV LABOR PROF/ORG ECO/TAC MORAL...SOC CONCPT RECORD INT SOC/EXP 20. PAGE 17 F0321 SOCIETY TREND

B56
KINDLEBERGER C.P.,THE TERMS OF TRADE: A EUROPEAN CASE-STUDY. EUR+WWI MOD/EUR ECO/DEV ECO/UNDEV AGRI INDUS BAL/PAY...METH/CNCPT STAT CONT/OBS CON/ANAL SOC/EXP SIMUL FOR/TRADE 20. PAGE 71 F1390 PLAN ECO/TAC

B58
POLLOCK F.,AUTOMATION: A STUDY OF ITS ECONOMIC AND SOCIAL CONSEQUENCES. FUT USA+45 USA-45 SOCIETY ECO/DEV LABOR ACT/RES PLAN ECO/TAC AUTOMAT ROUTINE ALL/VALS...STAT TREND COMPUT/IR CHARTS SOC/EXP WORK 20. PAGE 107 F2099 TEC/DEV SOC CAP/ISM

S60
FRENCH J.R.P. JR.,"AN EXPERIMENT ON PARTICIPATION IN A NORWEGIAN FACTORY:INTERPERSONAL DIMENSIONS OF DECISION-MAKING." LABOR LEAD PERS/REL EFFICIENCY PRODUC...DECISION SOC CHARTS SOC/EXP. PAGE 44 F0853 INDUS PLAN RIGID/FLEX GP/REL

S61
ANDREWS R.B.,"URBAN ECONOMICS: AN APPRAISAL OF PROGRESS." LOC/G PROB/SOLV TEC/DEV...CONCPT OBS/ENVIR METH/COMP HYPO/EXP SOC/EXP SIMUL GEN/METH METH MUNICH 20. PAGE 5 F0102 PHIL/SCI ECOMETRIC

B62
KAUTSKY J.H.,POLITICAL CHANGE IN UNDERDEVELOPED COUNTRIES: NATIONALISM AND COMMUNISM. WOR+45 AGRI TEC/DEV EDU/PROP ATTIT...POLICY METH/CNCPT STYLE INT QU CENSUS TREND SOC/EXP GEN/LAWS 20. PAGE 69 F1365 ECO/UNDEV SOCIETY CAP/ISM REV

B62
LICHFIELD N.,COST-BENEFIT ANALYSIS IN URBAN REDEVELOPMENT. CONSTRUC LOC/G NEIGH ACT/RES PROB/SOLV TEC/DEV BUDGET TAX...DECISION STAT CHARTS SOC/EXP MUNICH 20. PAGE 80 F1558 PLAN COST GOV/REL

B62
SMITH G.A. JR.,POLICY FORMULATION AND ADMINISTRATION: A CASEBOOK OF TOPMANAGEMENT PROBLEMS IN BUSINESS. EX/STRUC PLAN PROB/SOLV ADMIN CONTROL EXEC LEAD ROUTINE EFFICIENCY ATTIT MGT. PAGE 123 F2430 INDUS SOC/EXP TOP/EX DECISION

L62
GALBRAITH J.K.,"ECONOMIC DEVELOPMENT IN PERSPECTIVE." CAP/ISM ECO/TAC ROUTINE ATTIT WEALTH ...TREND CHARTS SOC/EXP WORK TERR/GP 20. PAGE 45 F0884 ECO/UNDEV PLAN

B64
SULLIVAN G.,THE STORY OF THE PEACE CORPS. USA+45 WOR+45 INTELL FACE/GP NAT/G SCHOOL VOL/ASSN CONSULT EX/STRUC PLAN EDU/PROP ADMIN ATTIT DRIVE ALL/VALS ...POLICY HEAL SOC CONCPT INT QU BIOG TREND SOC/EXP WORK. PAGE 127 F2511 INT/ORG ECO/UNDEV FOR/AID PEACE

L64
ARMENGALD A.,"ECONOMIE ET COEXISTENCE." COM EUR+WWI FUT USA+45 WOR+45 ECO/DEV ECO/UNDEV FINAN INT/ORG NAT/G EXEC CHOOSE ATTIT ALL/VALS...POLICY RELATIV DECISION TREND SOC/EXP WORK 20. PAGE 6 F0113 MARKET ECO/TAC AFR CAP/ISM

B66
THIESENHUSEN W.C.,CHILE'S EXPERIMENTS IN AGRARIAN REFORM. CHILE STRUCT NAT/G ACT/RES ECO/TAC GOV/REL COST SOCISM...TREND CHARTS SOC/EXP 20. PAGE 130 F2558 AGRI ECO/UNDEV SOC TEC/DEV

SOC/INTEG....SOCIAL INTEGRATION; SEE ALSO CONSEN, RACE/REL

B27
SIEGFRIED A.,AMERICA COMES OF AGE: A FRENCH ANALYSIS (TRANS. BY H.H. HEMMING AND DORIS HEMMING). FRANCE UK POL/PAR WORKER TEC/DEV DIPLOM REGION RACE/REL ADJUST PRODUC HEREDITY...TIME/SEQ GP/COMP SOC/INTEG 20 DEMOCRAT REPUBLICAN KKK. PAGE 122 F2398 USA-45 CULTURE ECO/DEV SOC

B48
MCCABE D.A.,LABOR AND SOCIAL ORGANIZATION. LEGIS WORKER CAP/ISM ECO/TAC PAY MARXISM SOCISM SOC/INTEG 20 INTRVN/ECO. PAGE 88 F1717 LABOR STRATA NEW/LIB

S52
HEBERLE R.,"ON POLITICAL ECOLOGY" (BMR)" INCOME ATTIT WEALTH...GEOG METH SOC/INTEG 20. PAGE 58 F1133 HABITAT STRATA CHOOSE

S54
MACK R.W.,"ECOLOGICAL PATTERNS IN AN INDUSTRIAL SHOP" (BMR)" USA+45 CULTURE SOCIETY STRATA STRUCT LABOR NEIGH GP/REL ADJUST HABITAT...SOC SOC/INTEG 20. PAGE 83 F1634 INDUS DISCRIM WORKER

B59
KOLLAI H.R.,DIE EINGLIEDERUNG DER VERTRIEBENEN UND ZUWANDERER IN NIEDERSACHSEN. GERMANY/W SOCIETY STRATA STRUCT LABOR SOC/INTEG 20. PAGE 72 F1422 GP/REL INGP/REL

B59
ROCHE J.,LA COLONISATION ALLEMANDE ET LE RIO GRANDE DO SUL. BRAZIL L/A+17C NAT/G PROVS INGP/REL RACE/REL DISCRIM HABITAT...GEOG SOC/INTEG 19/20 MIGRATION. PAGE 113 F2228 ECO/UNDEV GP/REL ATTIT

B60
FERNANDES F.,MUDANCAS SOCIAIS NO BRASIL. BRAZIL L/A+17C SOCIETY AGRI PROVS LEAD GP/REL RACE/REL ORD/FREE...SOC SOC/INTEG 20 SAO/PAULO. PAGE 40 F0786 ECO/UNDEV STRATA INDUS

B60
GRIER E.,PRIVATELY DEVELOPED INTERRACIAL HOUSING: AN ANALYSIS OF EXPERIENCE. FINAN MARKET COST DISCRIM PROFIT SOC/INTEG 20. PAGE 51 F0997 RACE/REL CONSTRUC HABITAT

B60
MOORE W.E.,LABOR COMMITMENT AND SOCIAL CHANGE IN DEVELOPING AREAS. SOCIETY STRATA ECO/UNDEV MARKET VOL/ASSN WORKER AUTHORIT SKILL...MGT NAT/COMP SOC/INTEG 20. PAGE 93 F1823 LABOR ORD/FREE ATTIT INDUS

B60
RAMA C.M.,LAS CLASES SOCIALES EN EL URUGUAY. L/A+17C URUGUAY ELITES SOCIETY STRATA INDUS ATTIT HABITAT PWR...GEOG SOC/INTEG MUNICH 20. PAGE 109 F2138 ECO/UNDEV STRUCT PARTIC

B60
SLOTKIN J.S.,FROM FIELD TO FACTORY; NEW INDUSTRIAL EMPLOYEES. HABITAT...MGT NEW/IDEA NAT/COMP BIBLIOG SOC/INTEG 20. PAGE 123 F2423 INDUS LABOR CULTURE WORKER

B61
LIEFMANN-KEIL E.,OKONOMISCHE THEORIE DER ECO/DEV

SOZIALPOLITIK. INT/ORG LABOR WORKER COST INCOME NEW/LIB...CONCPT SOC/INTEG 20. PAGE 80 F1562
INDUS NAT/G SOC/WK

B62
DEBUYST F.,LAS CLASES SOCIALES EN AMERICA LATINA. L/A+17C SOCIETY STRUCT WORKER EDU/PROP RACE/REL ATTIT HABITAT ROLE...GEOG SOC NAT/COMP SOC/INTEG 20. PAGE 32 F0612
STRATA GP/REL WEALTH

B62
MULLER E.,DIE HEIMATVERTRIEBENEN IN BADEN-WURTTEMBERG. GERMANY/W AGRI INDUS LABOR PROVS SOC/INTEG 20 MIGRATION. PAGE 95 F1858
GP/REL INGP/REL

B63
CONF ON FUTURE OF COMMONWEALTH,THE FUTURE OF THE COMMONWEALTH. AFR UK ECO/UNDEV AGRI EDU/PROP ADMIN SOC/INTEG 20. PAGE 27 F0522
DIPLOM RACE/REL ORD/FREE TEC/DEV

B64
LUTHULI A.,AFRICA'S FREEDOM. KIN LABOR POL/PAR SCHOOL DIPLOM NEUTRAL REGION REV NAT/LISM PWR WEALTH SOCISM SOC/INTEG 20. PAGE 82 F1608
AFR ECO/UNDEV COLONIAL

B65
CONLEY R.W.,THE ECONOMICS OF VOCATIONAL REHABILITATION. USA+45 VOL/ASSN CREATE EDU/PROP COST EFFICIENCY SOC/INTEG 20. PAGE 27 F0527
PUB/INST HEALTH GIVE GP/REL

B65
INTERAMERICAN ECO AND SOC COUN,THE ALLIANCE FOR PROGRESS: ITS THIRD YEAR 1963-1964. FUT L/A+17C WOR+45 ECO/DEV INT/ORG PLAN CONTROL ADJUST...STAT ANTHOL SOC/INTEG 20 ALL/PROG. PAGE 64 F1268
ECO/UNDEV ECO/TAC FINAN FOR/AID

B65
PEARL A.,NEW CAREERS FOR THE POOR: THE NON-PROFESSIONAL IN HUMAN SERVICE. USA+45 SERV/IND NAT/G NEIGH WORKER EDU/PROP AUTOMAT SKILL...WELF/ST NEW/IDEA BIBLIOG SOC/INTEG 20. PAGE 104 F2044
SOC/WK WEALTH STRATA POLICY

B66
DAVIES JC I.I.I.,NEIGHBORHOOD GROUPS AND URBAN RENEWAL. USA+45 PLAN LOBBY PARTIC CHOOSE RACE/REL ...POLICY DECISION SOC INT MUNICH SOC/INTEG 20 NEWYORK/C. PAGE 30 F0586
NEIGH CREATE PROB/SOLV

B66
EBONY,THE NEGRO HANDBOOK. ACADEM LABOR LOC/G SECT FORCES WORKER CT/SYS CRIME DISCRIM ORD/FREE...BIOG SOC/INTEG 19/20 NEGRO CIV/RIGHTS. PAGE 36 F0692
RACE/REL EDU/PROP LAW STAT

B66
KAREFA-SMART J.,AFRICA: PROGRESS THROUGH COOPERATION. AFR FINAN TEC/DEV DIPLOM FOR/AID EDU/PROP CONFER REGION GP/REL WEALTH...HEAL SOC/INTEG 20. PAGE 69 F1356
ORD/FREE ECO/UNDEV VOL/ASSN PLAN

B67
POWLEDGE F.,BLACK POWER WHITE RESISTANCE. USA+45 STRUCT PLAN GP/REL DISCRIM HABITAT ORD/FREE WEALTH ...METH/COMP SOC/INTEG NEGRO. PAGE 107 F2111
RACE/REL ATTIT PWR

B67
WEINBERG M.,SCHOOL INTEGRATION: A COMPREHENSIVE CLASSIFIED BIBLIOGRAPHY OF 3,100 REFERENCES. USA+45 LAW NAT/G NEIGH SECT PLAN ROUTINE AGE/C WEALTH SOC/INTEG INDIAN/AM. PAGE 145 F2849
BIBLIOG SCHOOL DISCRIM RACE/REL

B76
TAINE H.A.,THE ANCIENT REGIME. FRANCE STRATA FORCES PARTIC EQUILIB WEALTH CONSERVE POPULISM...GOV/COMP SOC/INTEG 18/19. PAGE 128 F2527
NAT/G GOV/REL TAX REV

SOC/PAR....SOCIALIST PARTY (USE WITH SPECIFIC NATION)

SOC/REVPAR....SOCIALIST REVOLUTIONARY PARTY (USE WITH SPECIFIC NATION)

SOC/SECUR....SOCIAL SECURITY

SOC/WK....SOCIAL WORK, SOCIAL SERVICE ORGANIZATION

N
UNITED NATIONS,OFFICIAL RECORDS OF THE ECONOMIC AND SOCIAL COUNCIL OF THE UNITED NATIONS. WOR+45 DIPLOM INT/TRADE CONFER...SOC SOC/WK 20 UN UNESCO. PAGE 132 F2611
INT/ORG DELIB/GP WRITING

N19
RIDLEY C.E.,MEASURING MUNICIPAL ACTIVITIES (PAMPHLET). FINAN SERV/IND FORCES RECEIVE INGP/REL HABITAT...POLICY SOC/WK 20. PAGE 111 F2191
MGT HEALTH WEALTH LOC/G

B20
PIGOU A.C.,THE ECONOMICS OF WELFARE. UNIV INDUS WORKER ACT/RES RECEIVE INCOME NEW/LIB...MAJORIT SOC/WK. PAGE 106 F2085
ECO/TAC WEALTH FINAN CONTROL

B23
HOBSON J.A.,INCENTIVES IN THE NEW INDUSTRIAL ORDER. USA-45 NAT/G PAY COST EFFICIENCY PRODUC WEALTH ...MAJORIT PSY SOC/WK 20. PAGE 60 F1186
INDUS LABOR INCOME OPTIMAL

B29
JONES M.M.,CORPORATION CONTRIBUTIONS TO COMMUNITY WELFARE AGENCIES (PAMPHLET). DELIB/GP TAX CONTROL PARTIC RATIONAL POLICY. PAGE 68 F1339
LG/CO GIVE NEIGH SOC/WK

B37
COLE W.E.,RECENT TRENDS IN RURAL PLANNING. USA-45 LAW ECO/DEV LOC/G SECT EDU/PROP CRIME LEISURE AGE/Y HABITAT...SOC/WK MUNICH 20. PAGE 26 F0503
AGRI NEIGH PLAN ACT/RES

B51
LEONARD L.L.,INTERNATIONAL ORGANIZATION. WOR+45 WOR-45 EX/STRUC FORCES LEGIS ECO/TAC INT/TRADE COLONIAL ARMS/CONT...SOC/WK GOV/COMP BIBLIOG. PAGE 78 F1527
NAT/G DIPLOM INT/ORG DELIB/GP

B56
POOLE K.E.,PUBLIC FINANCE AND ECONOMIC WELFARE. STRUCT ECO/DEV LOC/G NAT/G BUDGET PAY ROUTINE COST EQUILIB WEALTH...SOC/WK METH/COMP 20. PAGE 107 F2103
FINAN TAX ORD/FREE

B57
DRUCKER P.F.,AMERICA'S NEXT TWENTY YEARS. USA+45 DIST/IND ACADEM SCHOOL DIPLOM ECO/TAC AUTOMAT HABITAT HEALTH...SOC/WK TREND MUNICH 20 URBAN/RNWL PUB/TRANS. PAGE 34 F0667
WORKER FOR/AID CENSUS GEOG

N60
COMMITTEE ECONOMIC DEVELOPMENT,GUIDING METROPOLITAN GROWTH (PAMPHLET). USA+45 LOC/G NAT/G PROF/ORG ACT/RES PLAN...SOC/WK MUNICH. PAGE 27 F0517
GEOG INDUS HEALTH

B61
MEXICO; CINCUENTA ANOS DE REVOLUCION VOL. II. L/A+17C SOCIETY LABOR RECEIVE GP/REL AGE/Y HEALTH ...SOC/WK ANTHOL MUNICH 20 MEXIC/AMER. PAGE 1 F0014
ECO/UNDEV STRUCT INDUS POL/PAR

B61
LEE R.R.,ENGINEERING-ECONOMIC PLANNING MISCELLANEOUS SUBJECTS: A SELECTED BIBLIOGRAPHY (MIMEOGRAPHED). FINAN LOC/G NEIGH ADMIN CONTROL INGP/REL HABITAT...GEOG MGT SOC/WK MUNICH 20 RESOURCE/N. PAGE 77 F1509
BIBLIOG/A PLAN REGION

B61
LIEFMANN-KEIL E.,OKONOMISCHE THEORIE DER SOZIALPOLITIK. INT/ORG LABOR WORKER COST INCOME NEW/LIB...CONCPT SOC/INTEG 20. PAGE 80 F1562
ECO/DEV INDUS NAT/G SOC/WK

B62
BUREAU OF NATIONAL AFFAIRS,FEDERAL-STATE REGULATION OF WELFARE FUNDS (REV. ED.). USA+45 LAW LEGIS DEBATE AGE/O 20 CONGRESS. PAGE 20 F0386
WELF/ST WEALTH PLAN SOC/WK

B62
WENDT P.F.,HOUSING POLICY - THE SEARCH FOR SOLUTIONS. GERMANY/W SWEDEN UK USA+45 OP/RES HABITAT WEALTH...SOC/WK CHARTS 20. PAGE 145 F2856
PLAN ADMIN METH/COMP NAT/G

B63
BARNETT H.J.,SCARCITY AND GROWTH: THE ECONOMICS OF NATURAL RESOURCE AVAILABILITY. FUT WOR+45 AGRI INDUS PROB/SOLV TEC/DEV CONTROL PRODUC...SOC/WK IDEA/COMP METH/COMP SIMUL 20 RESOURCE/N MALTHUS RICARDO/D MILL/JS DARWIN/C. PAGE 10 F0191
DEMAND HABITAT CENSUS GEOG

B63
KATZ S.M.,A SELECTED LIST OF US READINGS ON DEVELOPMENT. AGRI COM/IND DIST/IND INDUS LABOR PLAN FOR/AID EDU/PROP HEALTH...POLICY SOC/WK 20. PAGE 69 F1361
BIBLIOG/A ECO/UNDEV TEC/DEV ACT/RES

B65
GREEN J.L.,METROPOLITAN ECONOMIC REPUBLICS. USA+45 ECO/TAC INCOME...GEOG SOC CONCPT SIMUL MUNICH 20 ATLANTA. PAGE 50 F0985
SOC/WK PLAN LABOR

B65
PEARL A.,NEW CAREERS FOR THE POOR: THE NON-PROFESSIONAL IN HUMAN SERVICE. USA+45 SERV/IND NAT/G NEIGH WORKER EDU/PROP AUTOMAT SKILL...WELF/ST NEW/IDEA BIBLIOG SOC/INTEG 20. PAGE 104 F2044
SOC/WK WEALTH STRATA POLICY

S65
HADDAD W.F.,"MR. SHRIVER AND THE SAVAGE POLITICS OF POVERTY" USA+45 LAW NAT/G DELIB/GP LEGIS GIVE LEAD CENTRAL PWR...SOC/WK CHARTS 20 CONGRESS POVRTY/WAR SHRIVER/S OEO. PAGE 53 F1028
WEALTH GOV/REL CONTROL TOP/EX

B66
GOODMAN L.H.,ECONOMIC PROGRESS AND SOCIAL WELFARE. USA+45 STRATA STRUCT ECO/TAC EFFICIENCY...MGT 20. PAGE 49 F0949
SOC/WK RECEIVE GP/COMP POLICY

B66
LECHT L.,GOAL, PRIORITIES, AND DOLLARS: THE NEXT DECADE. SPACE USA+45 SOCIETY AGRI BUDGET FOR/AID ...HEAL SOC/WK STAT CHARTS 20 URBAN/RNWL PUB/TRANS. PAGE 76 F1499
IDEA/COMP POLICY CONSEN PLAN

N66
US ADVISORY COMN INTERGOV REL,CATALOGS AND OTHER INFORMATION SOURCES ON FEDERAL AND STATE AID PROGRAMS: A SECTED BIBLIOGRAPHY (PAPER). USA+45 LAW LOC/G NAT/G PROVS VOL/ASSN TEC/DEV ADMIN HEALTH ...WELF/ST SOC/WK MUNICH. PAGE 134 F2635
BIBLIOG/A GOV/REL FINAN ECO/DEV

B67
CHAPIN F.S. JR.,SELECTED REFERENCES ON URBAN PLANNING METHODS AND TECHNIQUES. USA+45 LAW ECO/DEV LOC/G NAT/G SCHOOL CONSULT CREATE PROB/SOLV TEC/DEV ...SOC/WK MUNICH. PAGE 23 F0454
BIBLIOG NEIGH PLAN

B67
HODGKINSON R.G.,THE ORIGINS OF THE NATIONAL HEALTH SERVICE: THE MEDICAL SERVICES OF THE NEW POOR LAW, 1834-1871. UK INDUS WORKER PROB/SOLV EFFICIENCY ATTIT HEALTH WEALTH SOCISM...JURID SOC/WK MUNICH 19/20. PAGE 60 F1189
HEAL NAT/G POLICY LAW

B67
LITTLE AD, INC.,COMMUNITY RENEWAL PROGRAMMING. CULTURE LOC/G ACT/RES TASK COST ATTIT...SOC/WK MODAL STAT STAND/INT CHARTS 20 SAN/FRAN. PAGE 81 F1585
STRATA NEIGH PLAN CREATE

B67
PEDLEY F.H.,EDUCATION AND SOCIAL WORK. USA+45 INTELL TEC/DEV. PAGE 104 F2047
GP/REL EDU/PROP SOC/WK EFFICIENCY

B67
ULMAN L.,CHALLENGES TO COLLECTIVE BARGAINING. ECO/TAC DISCRIM EQUILIB ATTIT...JURID SOC/WK. PAGE 132 F2599
LABOR BARGAIN ADJUD POLICY

S67
FRIEDEN B.J.,"THE CHANGING PROSPECTS FOR SOCIAL PLANNING." USA+45 PROB/SOLV RACE/REL WEALTH ...SOC/WK PREDICT MUNICH 20 NEGRO. PAGE 44 F0856
PLAN LOC/G POLICY

S67
GREEN C.,"SCHEMES FOR TRANSFERRING INCOME TO THE POOR." BUDGET GIVE RECEIVE DEBATE COST INCOME ...SOC/WK METH/COMP. PAGE 50 F0982
TAX WEALTH PLAN ACT/RES

S67
HANCOCK J.L.,"PLANNERS IN THE CHANGING AMERICAN CITY, 1900-1940." USA-45 CONSTRUC NAT/G POL/PAR ...SOC/WK TREND MUNICH 20. PAGE 54 F1059
PLAN CONSULT LOC/G

S67
HILDEBRAND G.H.,"SECOND THOUGHTS ON THE NEGATIVE INCOME TAX." PLAN BUDGET ECO/TAC GIVE RECEIVE DEBATE EFFICIENCY INCOME...METH/COMP COSTS. PAGE 59 F1169
TAX WEALTH SOC/WK ACT/RES

S67
MOONEY J.D.,"URBAN POVERTY AND LABOR FORCE PARTICIPATION." FAM DISCRIM...SOC/WK STAT CHARTS MUNICH. PAGE 93 F1820
INCOME WORKER WEALTH

S67
WALLACE H.M.,"AVAILABILITY AND USEFULNESS OF SELECTED HEALTH AND SOCIOECONOMIC DATA FOR COMMUNITY PLANNING." NEIGH EFFICIENCY...CORREL STAT CENSUS CHARTS. PAGE 142 F2806
HEALTH PLAN SOC/WK HEAL

N67
NATIONAL COMN COMMUNITY HEALTH,ACTION - PLANNING FOR COMMUNITY HEALTH SERVICES (PAMPHLET). USA+45 PROF/ORG DELIB/GP BUDGET ROUTINE GP/REL ATTIT ...HEAL SOC SOC/WK CHARTS MUNICH TIME 20. PAGE 97 F1898
PLAN HEALTH ADJUST

SOCDEM/PAR....SOCIAL DEMOCRATIC PARTY; SEE ALSO SOC/DEMPAR

B59
VERNEY D.V.,PUBLIC ENTERPRISE IN SWEDEN. FUT SWEDEN UK INDUS POL/PAR LEGIS PROB/SOLV CAP/ISM INT/TRADE CONTROL SOCISM...MGT CONCPT NAT/COMP 20 SOCDEM/PAR CIVIL/SERV. PAGE 141 F2778
ECO/DEV POLICY LG/CO NAT/G

SOCIAL ANALYSIS....SEE SOC

SOCIAL DEMOCRATIC PARTY (ALL NATIONS)....SEE SOC/DEMPAR

SOCIAL CLASS....SEE STRATA

SOCIAL INSTITUTIONS....SEE INSTITUTIONAL INDEX

SOCIAL MOBILITY....SEE STRATA

SOCIAL PSYCHOLOGY (GROUPS)....SEE SOC

SOCIAL PSYCHOLOGY (INDIVIDUALS)....SEE PSY

SOCIAL STRUCTURE....SEE STRUCT

SOCIAL WORK....SEE SOC/WK

SOCIAL STRUCTURE....SEE STRUCT, STRATA

SOCIAL SCIENCE RESEARCH COUN F2437

SOCIALISM....SEE SOCISM, SOCIALIST

SOCIALIST....NON-COMMUNIST SOCIALIST; SEE ALSO SOCISM

B13
KROPOTKIN P.,THE CONQUEST OF BREAD. SOCIETY STRATA AGRI INDUS WORKER REV HAPPINESS INCOME PRODUC HEALTH MORAL ORD/FREE. PAGE 74 F1444
ANARCH SOCIALIST OWN AGREE

N19
DEANE H.,THE WAR IN VIETNAM (PAMPHLET). AFR CHINA/COM VIETNAM BAL/PWR DIPLOM ECO/TAC SOCISM INTERVENT INTERVENT. PAGE 31 F0610
WAR SOCIALIST MORAL CAP/ISM

N19
HUBERMAN L.,SOCIALISM IS THE ONLY ANSWER (PAMPHLET). CREATE ECO/TAC EDU/PROP CONTROL ...SOCIALIST GEN/LAWS ANTHOL 20. PAGE 62 F1230
SOCISM ECO/DEV CAP/ISM PLAN

N19
VELYAMINOV G.,AFRICA AND THE COMMON MARKET (PAMPHLET). AFR MARKET VOL/ASSN ECO/TAC COLONIAL ORD/FREE...SOCIALIST 20 THIRD/WRLD. PAGE 141 F2775
INT/ORG INT/TRADE SOVEREIGN ECO/UNDEV

B44
FABIAN SOCIETY,CAN PLANNING BE DEMOCRATIC? UK CULTURE INDUS NAT/G BUDGET ORD/FREE...GEN/LAWS ANTHOL 20. PAGE 39 F0757
PLAN MAJORIT SOCIALIST ECO/DEV

B48
DURBIN E.F.M.,THE POLITICS OF DEMOCRATIC SOCIALISM; AN ESSAY ON SOCIAL POLICY. STRATA POL/PAR PLAN COERCE DRIVE PERSON PWR MARXISM...CHARTS METH/COMP. PAGE 35 F0684
SOCIALIST POPULISM POLICY SOCIETY

B50
SCHUMPETER J.A.,CAPITALISM, SOCIALISM, AND DEMOCRACY (3RD ED.). USA-45 USSR WOR+45 WOR-45 INTELL ECO/DEV ECO/UNDEV ECO/TAC WAR PRODUC ORD/FREE...MGT SOC 20 MARX/KARL. PAGE 118 F2321
SOCIALIST CAP/ISM MARXISM IDEA/COMP

B50
SOREL G.,REFLECTIONS ON VIOLENCE (1908) (TRANS. BY T.E. HULME AND J. ROTH). UNIV SOCIETY LABOR UTOPIA MORAL SOCISM...ANARCH SOCIALIST CONCPT 20. PAGE 124 F2445
COERCE REV WORKER MYTH

B52
BEVAN A.,IN PLACE OF FEAR. WOR+45 STRATA LEGIS REPRESENT OWN NEW/LIB POPULISM...CHARTS 20. PAGE 14 F0273
SOCISM SOCIALIST WEALTH MAJORIT

B59
KRIPALANI J.B.,CLASS STRUGGLE. INDIA WOR+45 ECO/UNDEV LABOR CAP/ISM EDU/PROP INGP/REL ...SOCIALIST IDEA/COMP 17/20. PAGE 73 F1440
MARXISM STRATA COERCE ECO/TAC

B60
HUGHES J.,NATIONALISED INDUSTRIES IN THE MIXED ECONOMY (PAMPHLET). FINAN PROB/SOLV CAP/ISM OWN ...SOCIALIST STAT METH/COMP 20. PAGE 63 F1233
SOCISM LG/CO GOV/REL ECO/DEV

S60
KELLOGG C.E.,"TRANSFER OF BASIC SKILLS OF FOOD PRODUCTION." AFR FUT S/ASIA STRATA ECO/UNDEV LABOR VOL/ASSN RIGID/FLEX...OLD/LIB SOCIALIST NEW/IDEA STAT PROJ/TEST GEN/LAWS 20. PAGE 70 F1370
AGRI PLAN

B61
HORVATH B.,THE CHARACTERISTICS OF YUGOSLAV ECONOMIC DEVELOPMENT. COM ECO/UNDEV AGRI INDUS PLAN CAP/ISM ECO/TAC ROUTINE WEALTH...SOCIALIST STAT CHARTS STERTYP WORK 20. PAGE 62 F1217
ACT/RES YUGOSLAVIA

B61
PERLO V.,EL IMPERIALISMO NORTHEAMERICANO. USA+45 USA-45 FINAN CAP/ISM DIPLOM DOMIN CONTROL DISCRIM 19/20. PAGE 105 F2063
SOCIALIST ECO/DEV INT/TRADE ECO/TAC

B64
MILIBAND R.,THE SOCIALIST REGISTER: 1964. GERMANY/W ITALY UK LABOR POL/PAR ECO/TAC FOR/AID NUC/PWR ...POLICY SOCIALIST IDEA/COMP 20 MAO NASSER/G. PAGE 91 F1784
MARXISM SOCISM CAP/ISM PROB/SOLV

B65
NKRUMAH K.,NEO-COLONIALISM: THE LAST STAGE OF IMPERIALISM. AFR INT/ORG WORKER FOR/AID INT/TRADE EDU/PROP GOV/REL NAT/LISM SOVEREIGN POPULISM SOCISM ...SOCIALIST 20 THIRD/WRLD INTRVN/ECO. PAGE 98 F1929
COLONIAL DIPLOM ECO/UNDEV ECO/TAC

S66
LANGLEY D.,"POSTSCRIPT ON THE COLONIZATION OF THE INTERNATIONAL TRADE UNION MOVEMENT" USA+45 ELITES FINAN DOMIN LEGIT ADMIN PWR...SOCIALIST 20 AFL/CIO CIA LOVESTN/J. PAGE 75 F1479
INT/TRADE LABOR NAT/G CONTROL

S67
ALVES V.,"FOREIGN CAPITAL IN BRAZIL." BRAZIL USA+45 CAP/ISM DIPLOM ECO/TAC INT/TRADE CONTROL PWR ...POLICY 20. PAGE 4 F0081
ECO/UNDEV FINAN SOCIALIST SOCISM

S67
CAMMETT J.M.,"COMMUNIST THEORIES OF FASCISM, 1920-35." ITALY POL/PAR PROF/ORG VOL/ASSN WORKER COLONIAL TOTALISM...SOCIALIST 20. PAGE 21 F0403
MARXISM FASCISM ATTIT

S67
LAZUTKIN Y.,"SOCIALISM AND SPARE TIME." ECO/DEV WORKER CREATE TEC/DEV ROUTINE TIME. PAGE 76 F1497
LEISURE PRODUC SOCISM SOCIALIST

S67
LEONTYEV L.,"THE LENINIST PRINCIPLES OF SOCIALIST ECONOMIC MANAGEMENT." USA+45 USSR POL/PAR WORKER PLAN ECO/TAC EFFICIENCY PRODUC MARXISM...POLICY SOCIALIST MGT TREND 20 LENIN/VI MARX/KARL. PAGE 78 F1529
SOCISM CAP/ISM IDEA/COMP ECO/DEV

B91
MILL J.S.,SOCIALISM (1859). MOD/EUR AGRI INDUS NAT/G REV INCOME PRODUC ORD/FREE POPULISM SOCISM ...GOV/COMP METH/COMP 19. PAGE 91 F1787
WEALTH SOCIALIST ECO/TAC OWN

SOCIALIZATION....SEE ADJUST

SOCIETY....SOCIETY AS A WHOLE

SOCIOLOGY....SEE SOC

SOCIOLOGY OF KNOWLEDGE....SEE EPIST

SOCISM....SOCIALISM; SEE ALSO SOCIALIST

N
BROCKWAY A.F.,AFRICAN SOCIALISM. EUR+WWI GHANA ISLAM UAR ECO/UNDEV CAP/ISM INT/TRADE COLONIAL COERCE GOV/REL DISCRIM 20 NEGRO NKRUMAH/K NASSER/G. PAGE 19 F0356
AFR SOCISM MARXISM

B02
SELIGMAN E.R.,THE ECONOMIC INTERPRETATION OF HISTORY. ECO/TAC MARXISM SOCISM...PHIL/SCI METH/CNCPT 18/20. PAGE 119 F2348
IDEA/COMP HIST/WRIT GP/REL

B03
GRIFFIN A.P.C.,LISTS PUBLISHED 1902-03: GOVERNMENT OWNERSHIP OF RAILROADS (PAMPHLET). USA-45 LAW NAT/G RATION GOV/REL CENTRAL SOCISM...POLICY 19/20. PAGE 51 F0998
BIBLIOG DIST/IND CONTROL ADJUD

B08
LLOYD H.D.,THE SWISS DEMOCRACY. SWITZERLND INDUS NAT/G WORKER CHOOSE OWN ORD/FREE SOCISM...PLURIST 19/20 MONOPOLY. PAGE 81 F1590
NAT/COMP GOV/COMP REPRESENT POPULISM

B11
SOREL G.,LES ILLUSIONS DU PROGRES (1906). UNIV SOCIETY STRATA INDUS GP/REL OWN PRODUC SOCISM 17/20. PAGE 124 F2444
WORKER POPULISM ECO/DEV ATTIT

B14
LEVINE L.,SYNDICALISM IN FRANCE (2ND ED.). FRANCE LAW SOCIETY ECO/DEV NAT/G ECO/TAC LEAD ATTIT ...POLICY CONCPT STAT BIBLIOG 18/20 REFORMERS. PAGE 79 F1542
LABOR INDUS SOCISM REV

B18
MARX K.,CAPITAL. FUT MOD/EUR STRATA DIST/IND PROC/MFG TEC/DEV WEALTH...MARXIST WORK 19. PAGE 86 F1688
ECO/DEV CAP/ISM SOCISM

B19
VEBLEN T.B.,THE VESTED INTERESTS AND THE STATE OF THE INDUSTRIAL ARTS. USA-45 LAW FINAN WORKER PAY DOMIN PRICE COST SOCISM...MARXIST 19/20. PAGE 141 F2771
INDUS CAP/ISM METH/COMP WEALTH

N19
DEANE H.,THE WAR IN VIETNAM (PAMPHLET). AFR CHINA/COM VIETNAM BAL/PWR DIPLOM ECO/TAC SOCISM INTERVENT INTERVENT. PAGE 31 F0610
WAR SOCIALIST MORAL CAP/ISM

N19
HAYEK FA V.O.N.,FREEDOM AND THE ECONOMIC SYSTEM. GERMANY USSR PLAN REPRESENT TOTALISM FASCISM POPULISM...MAJORIT METH/COMP GEN/LAWS 20. PAGE 57 F1123
ORD/FREE ECO/TAC CAP/ISM SOCISM

N19
HUBERMAN L.,SOCIALISM IS THE ONLY ANSWER (PAMPHLET). CREATE ECO/TAC EDU/PROP CONTROL ...SOCIALIST GEN/LAWS ANTHOL 20. PAGE 62 F1230
SOCISM ECO/DEV CAP/ISM PLAN

N19
LANGE O.R.,"DISARMAMENT ECONOMIC GROWTH AND INTERNATIONAL CO-OPERATION" (PAMPHLET). WOR+45 DIST/IND PLAN INT/TRADE GIVE TASK DETER WEALTH SOCISM 18/19 BOLIVAR/S. PAGE 75 F1477
ARMS/CONT DIPLOM ECO/DEV ECO/UNDEV

N19
SENGHOR L.S.,AFRICAN SOCIALISM (PAMPHLET). AFR FRANCE MALI USSR ELITES ECO/UNDEV NAT/G DIPLOM DOMIN EDU/PROP ATTIT 20 NEGRO. PAGE 119 F2355
SOCISM MARXISM ORD/FREE NAT/LISM

B20
COX H.,ECONOMIC LIBERTY. UNIV LAW INT/TRADE RATION TARIFFS RACE/REL SOCISM POLICY. PAGE 28 F0547
NAT/G ORD/FREE ECO/TAC

PERSON

B28
DE MAN H.,THE PSYCHOLOGY OF SOCIALISM. EUR+WWI USSR LABOR NAT/LISM PERSON WEALTH MARXISM...METH/COMP 20. PAGE 31 F0604
WORKER ATTIT SOC SOCISM

B29
DE MAN H.,JOY IN WORK. STRATA ECO/DEV ECO/TAC PRODUC ANOMIE ROLE SOCISM...IDEA/COMP 20. PAGE 31 F0605
SOC WORKER HAPPINESS RESPECT

B35
O'CONNOR H.,REVOLUTION IN SEATTLE. USA-45 STRATA WORKER GP/REL ATTIT SOCISM...OBS BIBLIOG/A 20 SEATTLE STRIKE COM/PARTY. PAGE 99 F1954
REV EDU/PROP LABOR MARXISM

B36
BELLOC H.,THE RESTORATION OF PROPERTY. UK STRATA NAT/G PROF/ORG DELIB/GP WORKER CREATE PROB/SOLV ECO/TAC PARTIC UTOPIA ORD/FREE SOCISM 20. PAGE 13 F0238
CONTROL MAJORIT CAP/ISM OWN

B38
DAVIES E.,"NATIONAL" CAPITALISM: THE GOVERNMENT'S RECORD AS PROTECTOR OF PRIVATE MONOPOLY. UK ELITES SOCIETY STRATA POL/PAR WORKER PROB/SOLV CONTROL SOCISM 20 MONOPOLY LABOR/PAR CHAMBRLN/N. PAGE 30 F0583
CAP/ISM NAT/G INDUS POLICY

B38
HEIMANN E.,COMMUNISM, FASCISM, OR DEMOCRACY? WOR-45 CONSTN SOCIETY STRATA AGRI CAP/ISM MORAL ORD/FREE ...MAJORIT METH/COMP NAT/COMP 19/20. PAGE 58 F1141
SOCISM MARXISM FASCISM PLURISM

B38
LANGE O.,ON THE ECONOMIC THEORY OF SOCIALISM. UNIV ECO/DEV FINAN INDUS INT/ORG PUB/INST ROUTINE ATTIT ALL/VALS...SOC CONCPT STAT TREND 20. PAGE 75 F1475
MARKET ECO/TAC INT/TRADE SOCISM

B38
LAWLEY F.E.,THE GROWTH OF COLLECTIVE ECONOMY VOL. 1: NATIONAL. EUR+WWI AGRI INDUS NAT/G BARGAIN CAP/ISM ECO/TAC WAR OPTIMAL WEALTH...GOV/COMP METH/COMP 19/20 MONOPOLY. PAGE 76 F1492
SOCISM PRICE CONTROL OWN

B38
LAWLEY F.E.,THE GROWTH OF COLLECTIVE ECONOMY VOL. 2: INTERNATIONAL. WOR-45 AGRI INDUS EQUILIB OPTIMAL OWN WEALTH...NAT/COMP 19/20 NAZI NEW/DEAL MONOPOLY. PAGE 76 F1493
ECO/TAC SOCISM NAT/LISM CONTROL

B39
ENGELS F.,HERRN EUGEN DUHRING'S REVOLUTION IN SCIENCE (1878). CULTURE STRATA STRUCT FAM SECT ECO/TAC REV WAR SOCISM...MARXIST 19. PAGE 37 F0731
PWR SOCIETY WEALTH GEN/LAWS

B40
HUNTER R.,REVOLUTION: WHY, HOW, WHEN? NAT/G ECO/TAC EDU/PROP COERCE ORD/FREE FASCISM POPULISM SOCISM 18/20 HITLER/A LENIN/VI. PAGE 63 F1246
REV METH/COMP LEAD CONSTN

B40
SIKES E.R.,CONTEMPORARY ECONOMIC SYSTEMS: THEIR ANALYSIS AND SOCIAL BACKGROUND. GERMANY ITALY USSR AGRI INDUS PLAN CAP/ISM ROUTINE TOTALISM FASCISM ...POLICY CON/ANAL BIBLIOG 20. PAGE 122 F2400
COM SOCISM CONCPT

B40
SPENCER H.,THE MAN VS. THE STATE (1892). UK POL/PAR LEGIS TARIFFS COERCE CRIME REPRESENT PWR SOCISM ...POLICY GEN/LAWS 19/20. PAGE 124 F2450
FASCISM POPULISM LAISSEZ ORD/FREE

B44
HAYEK F.A.,THE ROAD TO SERFDOM. NAT/G POL/PAR CREATE EDU/PROP ATTIT WEALTH LAISSEZ...OLD/LIB CONCPT TREND 20. PAGE 57 F1121
FUT PLAN ECO/TAC SOCISM

B44
MCFADYEAN A.,GOVERNMENT AND INDUSTRY (PAMPHLET). UK INDUS CONTROL REPRESENT 20. PAGE 88 F1728
POL/PAR SOCISM

B46
DAVIES E.,NATIONAL ENTERPRISE: THE DEVELOPMENT OF THE PUBLIC CORPORATION. UK LG/CO EX/STRUC WORKER PROB/SOLV COST ATTIT SOCISM 20. PAGE 30 F0584
ADMIN NAT/G CONTROL INDUS

B47
BOWEN R.H.,GERMAN THEORIES OF THE CORPORATIVE STATE, WITH SPECIAL REFERENCES TO THE PERIOD 1870-1919. GERMANY INDUS LG/CO CATHISM SOCISM...SOC 18/20. PAGE 17 F0328
IDEA/COMP CENTRAL NAT/G POLICY

S47
DAHL R.A.,"WORKERS' CONTROL OF INDUSTRY AND THE BRITISH LABOUR PARTY." UK STRATA STRUCT DELIB/GP BARGAIN CAP/ISM DEBATE CONTROL CHOOSE GP/REL ATTIT ROLE PWR 19/20 PARLIAMENT LABOR/PAR FABIAN. PAGE 29 F0570
INDUS LABOR WORKER SOCISM

B48
GRAHAM F.D.,THE THEORY OF INTERNATIONAL VALUES. FUT WOR+45 WOR-45 ECO/DEV FINAN INT/ORG PLAN TEC/DEV CAP/ISM DIPLOM ECO/TAC TARIFFS ROUTINE BAL/PAY DRIVE PWR WEALTH SOCISM...POLICY STAT HYPO/EXP
NEW/IDEA INT/TRADE

GEN/LAWS 20. PAGE 50 F0971

B48
HAYEK F.A.,INDIVIDUALISM AND ECONOMIC ORDER. FINAN PLAN MORAL LAISSEZ SOCISM...POLICY DECISION PHIL/SCI HIST/WRIT. PAGE 57 F1122
RATIONAL KNOWL PERSON

B48
MCCABE D.A.,LABOR AND SOCIAL ORGANIZATION. LEGIS WORKER CAP/ISM ECO/TAC PAY MARXISM SOCISM SOC/INTEG 20 INTRVN/ECO. PAGE 88 F1717
LABOR STRATA NEW/LIB

B48
VON HAYEK F.A.,INDIVIDUALISM AND ECONOMIC ORDER. GERMANY USA-45 USSR FINAN MARKET INT/ORG ECO/TAC INT/TRADE PRICE REPRESENT ORD/FREE...PLURIST GEN/LAWS 20. PAGE 142 F2793
SOCISM CAP/ISM POPULISM FEDERAL

B48
WINSLOW E.M.,THE PATTERN OF IMPERIALISM; A STUDY IN THE THEORIES OF POWER. DOMIN WAR PWR MARXISM ...IDEA/COMP METH/COMP BIBLIOG 20. PAGE 147 F2906
SOCISM CAP/ISM COLONIAL ECO/TAC

B49
DE JOUVENEL B.,PROBLEMS OF SOCIALIST ENGLAND. AFR UK USSR BAL/PWR ECO/TAC INT/TRADE PRICE WAR BAL/PAY PEACE 20. PAGE 31 F0601
SOCISM NEW/LIB PROB/SOLV PLAN

B49
MACGREGOR D.H.,ECONOMIC THOUGHT AND POLICY. WOR-45 WORKER WAR DEMAND EFFICIENCY WEALTH LAISSEZ SOCISM ...MAJORIT BIBLIOG 19/20. PAGE 83 F1629
CONCPT POLICY ECO/TAC

B50
HUNT R.N.,THE THEORY AND PRACTICE OF COMMUNISM. STRUCT WORKER NAT/LISM TOTALISM...CONCPT TREND 19/20 STALIN/J EUROPE. PAGE 63 F1244
MARXISM SOCISM REV STRATA

B50
HUTCHISON K.,THE DECLINE AND FALL OF BRITISH CAPITALISM. UK ELITES STRATA ECO/DEV LABOR WORKER CONTROL WAR PWR...BIBLIOG/A 19/20. PAGE 63 F1249
CAP/ISM SOCISM LAISSEZ DOMIN

B50
LIPSET S.M.,AGRARIAN SOCIALISM. CANADA POL/PAR OP/RES ECO/TAC ADMIN ATTIT...TIME/SEQ NAT/COMP SOC/EXP 20 SASKATCH. PAGE 80 F1576
SOCISM AGRI METH/COMP STRUCT

B50
SOREL G.,REFLECTIONS ON VIOLENCE (1908) (TRANS. BY T.E. HULME AND J. ROTH). UNIV SOCIETY LABOR UTOPIA MORAL SOCISM...ANARCH SOCIALIST CONCPT 20. PAGE 124 F2445
COERCE REV WORKER MYTH

B52
BEVAN A.,IN PLACE OF FEAR. WOR+45 STRATA LEGIS REPRESENT OWN NEW/LIB POPULISM...CHARTS 20. PAGE 14 F0273
SOCISM SOCIALIST WEALTH MAJORIT

B52
DE JOUVENEL B.,THE ETHICS OF REDISTRIBUTION. UK ELITES MARKET WORKER GIVE PAY INCOME PERSON ...POLICY PSY GEN/LAWS 20. PAGE 31 F0602
WEALTH TAX SOCISM TRADIT

B52
MACARTHUR D.,REVITALIZING A NATION. ASIA COM FUT KOREA WOR+45 NAT/G FOR/AID TAX GIVE WAR ATTIT SOCISM 20 CHINJAP EUROPE. PAGE 83 F1619
LEAD FORCES TOP/EX POLICY

B53
BOEKE J.H.,ECONOMICS AND ECONOMIC POLICY OF DUAL SOCIETIES AS EXEMPLIFIED BY INDONESIA. INDIA INDONESIA SOCIETY CAP/ISM INT/TRADE GIVE PRICE GP/REL WEALTH SOCISM...POLICY NAT/COMP GEN/LAWS 20. PAGE 16 F0304
ECO/TAC ECO/UNDEV NAT/G CONTROL

B54
FRIEDMAN W.,THE PUBLIC CORPORATION: A COMPARATIVE SYMPOSIUM (UNIVERSITY OF TORONTO SCHOOL OF LAW COMPARATIVE LAW SERIES, VOL. I). AFR SWEDEN USA+45 INDUS INT/ORG NAT/G REGION CENTRAL FEDERAL...POLICY JURID IDEA/COMP NAT/COMP ANTHOL 20 MONOPOLY EUROPE. PAGE 44 F0861
LAW SOCISM LG/CO OWN

B54
MOSK S.A.,INDUSTRIAL REVOLUTION IN MEXICO. MARKET LABOR CREATE CAP/ISM ADMIN ATTIT SOCISM...POLICY 20 MEXIC/AMER. PAGE 94 F1843
INDUS TEC/DEV ECO/UNDEV NAT/G

B54
STALEY E.,THE FUTURE OF UNDERDEVELOPED COUNTRIES: POLITICAL IMPLICATIONS OF ECONOMIC DEVELOPMENT. AFR COM FUT USA+45 SOCIETY ECO/UNDEV CREATE PLAN CAP/ISM ATTIT DRIVE MARXISM SOCISM...POLICY CONCPT CHARTS 20. PAGE 125 F2466
EDU/PROP ECO/TAC FOR/AID

B55
RUSTOW D.A.,THE POLITICS OF COMPROMISE. SWEDEN LABOR EX/STRUC LEGIS PLAN REPRESENT SOCISM...SOC 19/20. PAGE 115 F2265
POL/PAR NAT/G POLICY ECO/TAC

B55
UYEHARA C.H.,COMPARATIVE PLATFORMS OF JAPAN'S MAJOR PARTIES... USA+45 AGRI LEGIS WORKER CAP/ISM ORD/FREE MARXISM SOCISM...IDEA/COMP 20 CHINJAP. PAGE 140 F2755
POLICY POL/PAR DIPLOM NAT/G

B57
BARAN P.A.,THE POLITICAL ECONOMY OF GROWTH. MOD/EUR USA+45 USA-45 TEC/DEV TAX SOCISM...MGT CONCPT GOV/COMP. PAGE 9 F0178
CAP/ISM CONTROL ECO/UNDEV FINAN

B57
LOUCKS W.N.,COMPARATIVE ECONOMIC SYSTEMS (5TH ED.). COM UK USSR INDUS POL/PAR PLAN CAP/ISM TOTALISM MARXISM...PHIL/SCI BIBLIOG 19/20. PAGE 82 F1603
NAT/COMP IDEA/COMP SOCISM

B57
MEIER G.M.,ECONOMIC DEVELOPMENT: THEORY, HISTORY, AND POLICY. WOR+45 WOR-45 ECO/DEV ECO/UNDEV PLAN CAP/ISM BAL/PAY ATTIT PWR WEALTH SOCISM...CHARTS TOT/POP FOR/TRADE 20. PAGE 89 F1748
ECO/TAC GEN/LAWS

B57
NAUMANN R.,THEORIE UND PRAXIS DES NEOLIBERALISMUS; DAS MAERCHEN VON DER FREIEN ODER SOZIALEN MARKTWIRTSCHAFT. GERMANY/W FORCES PLAN EDU/PROP SOCISM...POLICY MARXIST IDEA/COMP BIBLIOG 18/20 ADENAUER/K. PAGE 97 F1903
MARXISM NEW/LIB ECO/TAC CAP/ISM

B58
COLE G.D.H.,COMMUNISM AND SOCIAL DEMOCRACY (VOL. IV OF "HISTORY OF SOCIAL THOUGHT"). COM GERMANY ITALY UK AGRI INT/ORG WORKER DIPLOM COLONIAL NAT/LISM ALL/IDEOS...BIBLIOG 20 LEAGUE/NAT AUST/HUNG. PAGE 26 F0502
MARXISM REV POL/PAR SOCISM

B58
GALBRAITH J.K.,THE AFFLUENT SOCIETY. EUR+WWI FUT USA+45 USSR CULTURE SERV/IND PEACE WEALTH SOCISM ...NEW/IDEA TREND VAL/FREE 20. PAGE 45 F0882
ATTIT ECO/TAC CAP/ISM

B58
PALMER E.E.,THE ECONOMY AND THE DEMOCRATIC IDEAL. USA+45 USA-45 STRATA CHIEF CT/SYS ORD/FREE SOCISM ...MAJORIT CONCPT ANTHOL 18/20 PRESIDENT. PAGE 103 F2021
ECO/DEV POPULISM METH/COMP ECO/TAC

S58
LOCKWOOD W.W.,"THE SOCIALISTIC SOCIETY: INDIA AND JAPAN." INDIA ECO/DEV ECO/UNDEV INDUS NAT/G CONTROL LEAD PRODUC WEALTH 20 CHINJAP. PAGE 81 F1593
ECO/TAC NAT/COMP FINAN SOCISM

B59
BAUER P.T.,UNITED STATES AID AND INDIAN ECONOMIC DEVELOPMENT. INDIA STRATA FINAN PLAN BUDGET DIPLOM INGP/REL EFFICIENCY SOCISM 20 AID. PAGE 11 F0215
FOR/AID ECO/UNDEV ECO/TAC POLICY

B59
ENGELS F.,SOCIALISM: UTOPIAN AND SCIENTIFIC (2ND ED.). SOCISM...CONCPT CON/ANAL GEN/LAWS 19 DUHRING/E. PAGE 38 F0732
MARXISM PHIL/SCI UTOPIA IDEA/COMP

B59
KELF-COHEN R.,NATIONALISATION IN BRITAIN: THE END OF DOGMA. EUR+WWI UK NAT/G POL/PAR WORKER ECO/TAC PARL/PROC WEALTH SOCISM...GOV/COMP 20. PAGE 70 F1369
NEW/LIB ECO/DEV INDUS OWN

B59
RAMANADHAM V.V.,PROBLEMS OF PUBLIC ENTERPRISE: THOUGHTS ON BRITISH EXPERIENCE. UK FINAN INDUS PLAN PRICE CENTRAL...POLICY 20. PAGE 109 F2140
SOCISM LG/CO ECO/DEV GOV/REL

B59
VERNEY D.V.,PUBLIC ENTERPRISE IN SWEDEN. FUT SWEDEN UK INDUS POL/PAR LEGIS PROB/SOLV CAP/ISM INT/TRADE CONTROL SOCISM...MGT CONCPT NAT/COMP 20 SOCDEM/PAR CIVIL/SERV. PAGE 141 F2778
ECO/DEV POLICY LG/CO NAT/G

S59
SHEENAN D.,"PUBLIC CORPORATIONS AND PUBLIC ACTION." UK ADMIN CONTROL REPRESENT SOCISM 20. PAGE 120 F2372
ECO/DEV EFFICIENCY EX/STRUC EXEC

B60
ARON R.,COLLOQUES DE RHEINFELDEN. AFR USA+45 USSR WOR+45 WOR-45 CULTURE ECO/UNDEV NAT/G POL/PAR DIPLOM NAT/LISM TOTALISM ATTIT DRIVE ALL/VALS ...PLURIST CONCPT STERTYP GEN/LAWS TOT/POP 20. PAGE 6 F0120
ECO/DEV SOCIETY CAP/ISM SOCISM

B60
CAMPBELL R.W.,SOVIET ECONOMIC POWER. COM USA+45 DIST/IND MARKET TOP/EX ACT/RES CAP/ISM ECO/TAC DOMIN EDU/PROP ADMIN ROUTINE DRIVE...MATH TIME/SEQ CHARTS WORK 20. PAGE 21 F0409
ECO/DEV PLAN SOCISM USSR

B60
DIA M.,REFLEXIONS SUR L'ECONOMIE DE L'AFRIQUE NOIRE (REV. ED.). CULTURE ECO/UNDEV CREATE TEC/DEV DIPLOM INT/TRADE OPTIMAL ATTIT...POLICY 20. PAGE 32 F0631
AFR ECO/TAC SOCISM PLAN

B60
HUGHES J.,NATIONALISED INDUSTRIES IN THE MIXED ECONOMY (PAMPHLET). FINAN PROB/SOLV CAP/ISM OWN ...SOCIALIST STAT METH/COMP 20. PAGE 63 F1233
SOCISM LG/CO GOV/REL ECO/DEV

B60
LERNER A.P.,THE ECONOMICS OF CONTROL. USA+45 ECO/UNDEV INT/ORG ACT/RES PLAN CAP/ISM INT/TRADE ATTIT WEALTH...SOC MATH STAT GEN/LAWS INDEX 20.
ECO/DEV ROUTINE ECO/TAC

PAGE 78 F1530 — SOCISM

B60
MAYO H.B.,INTRODUCTION TO MARXIST THEORY. SECT WORKER POPULISM SOCISM 19/20. PAGE 87 F1709
MARXISM STRATA IDEA/COMP PHIL/SCI

B60
ROBERTSON D.,THE CONTROL OF INDUSTRY. UK MARKET LABOR WORKER PRICE CONTROL GP/REL COST DEMAND ORD/FREE WEALTH NEW/LIB SOCISM 20. PAGE 112 F2211
INDUS FINAN NAT/G ECO/DEV

B60
ROEPKE W.,A HUMANE ECONOMY: THE SOCIAL FRAMEWORK OF THE FREE MARKET. FUT USSR WOR+45 CULTURE SOCIETY ECO/DEV PLAN ECO/TAC ADMIN ATTIT PERSON RIGID/FLEX SUPEGO MORAL WEALTH SOCISM...POLICY OLD/LIB CONCPT TREND GEN/LAWS 20. PAGE 113 F2232
DRIVE EDU/PROP CAP/ISM

B60
WALLICH H.C.,THE COST OF FREEDOM: A NEW LOOK AT CAPITALISM. USA+45 SOCIETY ECO/DEV INGP/REL CONSEN LAISSEZ SOCISM...OLD/LIB IDEA/COMP. PAGE 143 F2810
CAP/ISM ORD/FREE POLICY ECO/TAC

L60
SPENGLER J.J.,"ECONOMIC DEVELOPMENT: POLITICAL PRECONDITIONS AND POLITICAL CONSEQUENCE." WOR+45 STRUCT ECO/UNDEV NAT/G PLAN ECO/TAC EDU/PROP ATTIT ORD/FREE WEALTH SOCISM...SOC CONCPT TREND SIMUL GEN/METH WORK 20. PAGE 124 F2452
TEC/DEV METH/CNCPT CAP/ISM

S60
NEISSER H.,"ECONOMIC IMPERALISM RECONSIDERED." WOR+45 WOR-45 ECO/DEV ECO/UNDEV DIST/IND LEGIT COLONIAL PWR WEALTH SOCISM...MYTH MATH TIME/SEQ 20. PAGE 97 F1909
ACT/RES ECO/TAC CAP/ISM INT/TRADE

B61
AGARWAL R.C.,STATE ENTERPRISE IN INDIA. FUT INDIA UK FINAN INDUS ADMIN CONTROL OWN...POLICY CHARTS BIBLIOG 20 RAILROAD. PAGE 3 F0048
ECO/UNDEV SOCISM GOV/REL LG/CO

B61
ALFRED H.,PUBLIC OWNERSHIP IN THE USA: GOALS AND PRIORITIES. LAW INDUS INT/TRADE ADJUD GOV/REL EFFICIENCY PEACE SOCISM...POLICY ANTHOL 20 TVA. PAGE 4 F0065
CONTROL OWN ECO/DEV ECO/TAC

B61
AUBREY H.G.,COEXISTENCE: ECONOMIC CHALLENGE AND RESPONSE. AFR USSR WOR+45 ACT/RES BAL/PWR CAP/ISM DIPLOM ECO/TAC FOR/AID INT/TRADE PEACE SOCISM ...METH/COMP NAT/COMP. PAGE 7 F0139
POLICY ECO/UNDEV PLAN COM

B61
DIMOCK M.E.,BUSINESS AND GOVERNMENT (4TH ED.). AGRI FINAN OP/RES PLAN BUDGET DIPLOM LOBBY NUC/PWR NEW/LIB SOCISM...POLICY BIBLIOG 20. PAGE 33 F0641
NAT/G INDUS LABOR ECO/TAC

B61
FERTIG L.,PROSPERITY THROUGH FREEDOM. COM INDUS LABOR CAP/ISM ECO/TAC PRODUC PROFIT ORD/FREE WEALTH SOCISM...METH/CNCPT 20. PAGE 40 F0788
NAT/G CONTROL POLICY

B61
HENDERSON W.O.,THE INDUSTRIAL REVOLUTION IN EUROPE. FRANCE GERMANY MOD/EUR RUSSIA WORKER PROFIT PWR MARXISM SOCISM...SOC HIST/WRIT 19 INDUS/REV. PAGE 58 F1148
INDUS REV CAP/ISM TEC/DEV

B61
KELSO L.O.,THE NEW CAPITALISTS: A PROPOSAL TO FREE ECONOMIC GROWTH FROM THE SLAVERY OF SAVINGS. UNIV USA+45 ECO/DEV CAP/ISM PRODUC WEALTH SOCISM ...NEW/IDEA 20. PAGE 70 F1373
ECO/TAC WORKER FINAN GEN/LAWS

B61
LHOSTE-LACHAUME P.,OU GIT LE DESACCORD ENTRE LIBERAUX ET SOCIALISTES. EUR+WWI USA+45 USA-45 USSR CAP/ISM EDU/PROP MARXISM...MAJORIT IDEA/COMP 20 KEYNES/JM NEW/DEAL DEPRESSION. PAGE 79 F1555
LAISSEZ SOCISM FINAN

B61
LICHTHEIM G.,MARXISM. GERMANY SOCIETY WORKER CAP/ISM ECO/TAC NAT/LISM POPULISM...TIME/SEQ GOV/COMP NAT/COMP 18/20 COM/PARTY. PAGE 80 F1559
MARXISM SOCISM IDEA/COMP CULTURE

B61
SAKAI R.K.,STUDIES ON ASIA, 1961. ASIA BURMA INDIA S/ASIA FINAN ECO/TAC NAT/LISM SOCISM...POLICY ANTHOL 19/20 CHINJAP. PAGE 115 F2271
ECO/UNDEV SECT

B62
HAGUE D.C.,INFLATION. AFR ECO/DEV ECO/UNDEV LABOR BUDGET CAP/ISM INT/TRADE TARIFFS SOCISM 20. PAGE 53 F1036
FINAN NAT/COMP BARGAIN ECO/TAC

B62
HEILBRONER R.L.,THE MAKING OF ECONOMIC SOCIETY. FUT WOR-45 SOCIETY STRATA ECO/DEV ECO/UNDEV ECO/TAC LEGIT ROUTINE...SOC RECORD REC/INT KNO/TEST CENSUS STERTYP GEN/LAWS. PAGE 58 F1136
CAP/ISM SOCISM

B62
HOOVER C.B.,ECONOMIC SYSTEMS OF THE COMMONWEALTH. AFR CANADA INDIA UK ECO/DEV ECO/UNDEV AGRI INDUS TEC/DEV TARIFFS PRICE BAL/PAY DEMAND...SIMUL 20 AUSTRAL. PAGE 61 F1208
CAP/ISM SOCISM ECO/TAC PLAN

B62
O'CONNOR H.,WORLD CRISES IN OIL (BMR). ISLAM L/A+17C INDUS LG/CO INT/TRADE 20. PAGE 100 F1956
EXTR/IND DIPLOM ECO/UNDEV SOCISM

B62
PRAKASH O.M.,THE THEORY AND WORKING OF STATE CORPORATIONS: WITH SPECIAL REFERENCE TO INDIA. INDIA UK USA+45 TOP/EX PRICE ADMIN EFFICIENCY...MGT METH/COMP 20 TVA. PAGE 107 F2112
LG/CO ECO/UNDEV GOV/REL SOCISM

B62
WARD B.,THE RICH NATIONS AND THE POOR NATIONS. FUT WOR+45 CULTURE ECO/DEV ECO/UNDEV PLAN CAP/ISM EDU/PROP REV NAT/LISM ATTIT DRIVE SOCISM...POLICY CONCPT TIME/SEQ 20. PAGE 143 F2816
ECO/TAC GEN/LAWS

S62
IOVTCHOUK M.T.,"ON SOME THEORETICAL PRINCIPLES AND METHODS OF SOCIOLOGICAL INVESTIGATIONS (IN RUSSIAN)." FUT USA+45 STRATA R+D NAT/G POL/PAR TOP/EX ACT/RES PLAN ECO/TAC EDU/PROP ROUTINE ATTIT RIGID/FLEX MARXISM SOCISM...MARXIST METH/CNCPT OBS TREND NAT/COMP GEN/LAWS 20. PAGE 65 F1288
COM ECO/DEV CAP/ISM USSR

B63
GANGULY D.S.,PUBLIC CORPORATIONS IN A NATIONAL ECONOMY. INDIA WOR+45 FINAN INDUS TOP/EX PRICE EFFICIENCY...MGT STAT CHARTS BIBLIOG 20. PAGE 46 F0897
ECO/UNDEV LG/CO SOCISM GOV/REL

B63
ISSAWI C.,EGYPT IN REVOLUTION: AN ECONOMIC ANALYSIS. ISLAM STRUCT ECO/UNDEV AGRI FINAN INDUS PLAN EXEC REV NAT/LISM ATTIT RIGID/FLEX WEALTH SOCISM...STAT FOR/TRADE WORK 20. PAGE 66 F1292
NAT/G UAR

B63
MARX K.,THE POVERTY OF PHILOSOPHY (1847). SOCIETY STRATA INDUS WORKER OWN UTOPIA SOCISM...GEN/LAWS MARX/KARL. PAGE 86 F1692
MARXIST PRODUC

B63
SHANKS M.,THE LESSONS OF PUBLIC ENTERPRISE. UK LEGIS WORKER ECO/TAC ADMIN PARL/PROC GOV/REL ATTIT ...POLICY MGT METH/COMP NAT/COMP ANTHOL 20 PARLIAMENT. PAGE 120 F2364
SOCISM OWN NAT/G INDUS

S63
AYAL E.B.,"VALUE SYSTEM AND ECONOMIC DEVELOPMENT IN JAPAN AND THAILAND." ASIA S/ASIA THAILAND CULTURE ECO/DEV CAP/ISM DOMIN NAT/LISM DRIVE RIGID/FLEX SOCISM...WELF/ST OBS TREND CON/ANAL GEN/LAWS TERR/GP 20 CHINJAP. PAGE 8 F0145
ECO/UNDEV ALL/VALS

S63
WILES P.J.D.,"WILL CAPITALISM AND COMMUNISM SPONTANEOUSLY CONVERGE." COM FUT USA+45 ECO/DEV DIST/IND MARKET CAP/ISM ECO/TAC RIGID/FLEX WEALTH MARXISM SOCISM...MATH STAT TREND COMPUT/IR 20. PAGE 146 F2885
PLAN TEC/DEV USSR

B64
BAUCHET P.,ECONOMIC PLANNING. FRANCE STRATA LG/CO CAP/ISM ADMIN PARL/PROC DEMAND OPTIMAL ATTIT PWR SOCISM...POLICY CHARTS 20. PAGE 11 F0212
ECO/DEV NAT/G PLAN ECO/TAC

B64
GRIFFITH W.E.,COMMUNISM IN EUROPE (2 VOLS.). CZECHOSLVK USSR WOR+45 WOR-45 YUGOSLAVIA INGP/REL MARXISM SOCISM...ANTHOL 20 EUROPE/E. PAGE 51 F1000
COM POL/PAR DIPLOM GOV/COMP

B64
LUTHULI A.,AFRICA'S FREEDOM. KIN LABOR POL/PAR SCHOOL DIPLOM NEUTRAL REGION REV NAT/LISM PWR WEALTH SOCISM SOC/INTEG 20. PAGE 82 F1608
AFR ECO/UNDEV COLONIAL

B64
MILIBAND R.,THE SOCIALIST REGISTER: 1964. GERMANY/W ITALY UK LABOR POL/PAR ECO/TAC FOR/AID NUC/PWR ...POLICY SOCIALIST IDEA/COMP 20 MAO NASSER/G. PAGE 91 F1784
MARXISM SOCISM CAP/ISM PROB/SOLV

B64
MORGAN H.W.,AMERICAN SOCIALISM 1900-1960. AFR USA+45 USA-45 INTELL AGRI LABOR WORKER BARGAIN ECO/TAC GP/REL RACE/REL 20 NEGRO MIGRATION. PAGE 93 F1830
SOCISM POL/PAR ECO/DEV STRATA

B64
PENNOCK J.R.,SELF-GOVERNMENT IN MODERNIZING NATIONS. AFR COM USA+45 ECO/DEV POL/PAR PROB/SOLV DIPLOM ECO/TAC COLONIAL REV POPULISM SOCISM 20. PAGE 105 F2058
ECO/UNDEV POLICY SOVEREIGN NAT/G

B64
RENO P.,THE ORDEAL OF BRITISH GUIANA. L/A+17C USA+45 STRUCT AGRI EXTR/IND INDUS NAT/G FOR/AID ORD/FREE...GEOG 20 GUIANA/BR INTRVN/ECO. PAGE 111 F2178
COLONIAL ECO/UNDEV SOCISM PWR

B64
WITHERS W.,THE ECONOMIC CRISIS IN LATIN AMERICA. BRAZIL CHILE STRATA AGRI DIPLOM FOR/AID PWR SOCISM ...POLICY 20 MEXIC/AMER ARGEN ALL/PROG. PAGE 148 F2914
L/A+17C ECO/UNDEV CAP/ISM ALL/IDEOS

S64
FLORINSKY M.T.,"TRENDS IN THE SOVIET ECONOMY." COM USA+45 USSR INDUS LABOR NAT/G PLAN TEC/DEV ECO/TAC ALL/VALS SOCISM...MGT METH/CNCPT STYLE CON/ANAL
ECO/DEV AGRI

GEN/METH WORK 20. PAGE 42 F0817

C64
GOLDMAN M.I.,"COMPARATIVE ECONOMIC SYSTEMS: A READER." COM ECO/UNDEV NAT/G BUDGET CAP/ISM ADMIN TOTALISM MARXISM SOCISM...MGT ANTHOL BIBLIOG 19/20. PAGE 48 F0938
NAT/COMP CONTROL IDEA/COMP

C64
LANDAUER C.,"CONTEMPORARY ECONOMIC SYSTEMS." COM WOR+45 ECO/UNDEV PLAN GP/REL...BIBLIOG 20. PAGE 75 F1466
CAP/ISM SOCISM MARXISM IDEA/COMP

N64
KENYA MINISTRY ECO PLAN DEV,AFRICAN SOCIALISM AND ITS APPLICATION TO PLANNING IN KENYA (PAMPHLET). AFR AGRI INDUS WORKER TAX COLONIAL WEALTH 20. PAGE 70 F1380
NAT/G SOCISM PLAN ECO/UNDEV

B65
BARRY E.E.,NATIONALISATION IN BRITISH POLITICS: THE HISTORICAL BACKGROUND. UK AGRI DIST/IND EXTR/IND LABOR LG/CO ATTIT CONSERVE SOCISM 19/20 LABOR/PAR. PAGE 10 F0198
NAT/G OWN INDUS POL/PAR

B65
COLLINS H.,KARL MARX AND THE BRITISH LABOR MOVEMENT, YEARS OF THE FIRST INTERNATIONAL. EUR+WWI MOD/EUR UK STRATA INDUS NAT/G POL/PAR SOCISM ...CONCPT 19/20 MARX/KARL. PAGE 26 F0507
MARXISM LABOR INT/ORG WORKER

B65
FARER T.J.,FINANCING AFRICAN DEVELOPMENT. AFR ECO/TAC FOR/AID SOCISM 20. PAGE 39 F0764
ECO/UNDEV FINAN CAP/ISM PLAN

B65
JAIN S.C.,THE STATE AND AGRICULTURE. INDIA S/ASIA ECO/UNDEV PROB/SOLV CAP/ISM MARXISM SOCISM 20. PAGE 66 F1304
NAT/G POLICY AGRI ECO/TAC

B65
MURUMBI J.,PROBLEMS OF ECONOMIC DEVELOPMENT IN EAST AFRICA. FINAN INDUS WORKER TEC/DEV INT/TRADE TAX DEMAND EFFICIENCY PRODUC SOCISM...TREND CHARTS 20 AFRICA/E. PAGE 95 F1869
AGRI ECO/TAC ECO/UNDEV PROC/MFG

B65
NKRUMAH K.,NEO-COLONIALISM: THE LAST STAGE OF IMPERIALISM. AFR INT/ORG WORKER FOR/AID INT/TRADE EDU/PROP GOV/REL NAT/LISM SOVEREIGN POPULISM SOCISM ...SOCIALIST 20 THIRD/WRLD INTRVN/ECO. PAGE 98 F1929
COLONIAL DIPLOM ECO/UNDEV ECO/TAC

B65
ONUOHA B.,THE ELEMENTS OF AFRICAN SOCIALISM. AFR FINAN SECT TEC/DEV FOR/AID GP/REL OWN LAISSEZ MARXISM...CONCPT BIBLIOG 20. PAGE 101 F1992
SOCISM ECO/UNDEV NAT/G EX/STRUC

B65
SHAFFER H.G.,THE SOVIET SYSTEM IN THEORY AND PRACTICE: SELECTED WESTERN AND SOVIET VIEWS. USSR LAW SOCIETY CREATE FOR/AID EDU/PROP PRESS CHOOSE PEACE ORD/FREE...ANTHOL 20 STALIN/J. PAGE 120 F2362
MARXISM SOCISM IDEA/COMP

B65
SIMON B.,EDUCATION AND THE LABOR MOVEMENT, 1870-1920. UK SOCIETY STRATA LABOR POL/PAR SCHOOL CONTROL PARTIC SOCISM...BIBLIOG 19/20. PAGE 122 F2406
EDU/PROP WORKER ADJUST LAW

S65
JOHNSON H.G.,"A THEORETICAL MODEL OF ECONOMIC NATIONALISM IN NEW AND DEVELOPING STATES." ELITES INDUS INT/TRADE EDU/PROP COST OPTIMAL RATIONAL PWR WEALTH SOCISM STERTYP. PAGE 67 F1325
NAT/LISM ECO/UNDEV GEN/LAWS

C65
PEGRUM D.E.,"PUBLIC REGULATION OF BUSINESS (REV ED)" LAW CONSTN DIST/IND SERV/IND LG/CO LEGIS OWN LAISSEZ SOCISM...POLICY DECISION BIBLIOG 20. PAGE 104 F2048
INDUS PLAN NEW/LIB PRICE

B66
COLE A.B.,SOCIALIST PARTIES IN POSTWAR JAPAN. STRATA AGRI LABOR PLAN DIPLOM ECO/TAC AGREE LEAD CHOOSE ATTIT...CHARTS 20 CHINJAP SOC/DEMPAR. PAGE 26 F0499
POL/PAR POLICY SOCISM NAT/G

B66
DAVIES I.,AFRICAN TRADE UNIONS. AFR ECO/UNDEV INT/ORG GP/REL ORD/FREE SOVEREIGN SOCISM 20. PAGE 30 F0585
LABOR COLONIAL PWR INDUS

B66
FELKER J.L.,SOVIET ECONOMIC CONTROVERSIES. USSR INDUS PLAN INT/TRADE GP/REL MARXISM SOCISM...POLICY 20. PAGE 40 F0778
ECO/DEV MARKET PROFIT PRICE

B66
FORD P.,CARDINAL MORAN AND THE A. L. P. NAT/G POL/PAR SECT DELIB/GP LOBBY REV CHOOSE ORD/FREE MARXISM 19/20 AUSTRAL PROTESTANT LABOR/PAR. PAGE 42 F0825
CATHISM SOCISM LABOR SOCIETY

B66
FRANKEL P.H.,MATTEI; OIL AND POWER POLITICS. ITALY EXTR/IND MARKET GP/REL NAT/LISM SOCISM...POLICY MGT BIOG 20 MATTEI/E. PAGE 43 F0844
LEAD NAT/G CONTROL LG/CO

B66
GOODWIN C.D.W.,ECONOMIC INQUIRY IN AUSTRALIA. ECO/DEV ECO/UNDEV ACADEM INT/TRADE RENT TARIFFS TAX PRESS GOV/REL SOCISM 18/20 AUSTRAL. PAGE 49 F0953
ECO/TAC IDEA/COMP BUDGET COLONIAL

B66
MADAN G.R.,ECONOMIC THINKING IN INDIA. INDIA ECO/UNDEV AGRI FINAN INDUS LABOR PLAN CAP/ISM INT/TRADE MARXISM SOCISM...POLICY 1/20. PAGE 84 F1638
ECO/TAC PHIL/SCI NAT/G POL/PAR

B66
MURPHY G.G.,SOVIET MONGOLIA: A STUDY OF THE OLDEST POLITICAL SATELLITE. USSR STRATA STRUCT COST INCOME ATTIT SOCISM 20. PAGE 95 F1865
DIPLOM ECO/TAC PLAN DOMIN

B66
NAMBOODIRIPAD E.M.,ECONOMICS AND POLITICS OF INDIA'S SOCIALIST PATTERN. INDIA STRATA AGRI INDUS NAT/G PRICE ORD/FREE SOVEREIGN 20. PAGE 96 F1888
ECO/UNDEV PLAN SOCISM CAP/ISM

B66
THIESENHUSEN W.C.,CHILE'S EXPERIMENTS IN AGRARIAN REFORM. CHILE STRUCT NAT/G ACT/RES ECO/TAC GOV/REL COST SOCISM...TREND CHARTS SOC/EXP 20. PAGE 130 F2558
AGRI ECO/UNDEV SOC TEC/DEV

B66
TIVEY L.J.,NATIONALISATION IN BRITISH INDUSTRY. UK LEGIS PARL/PROC GP/REL OWN ATTIT SOCISM 20. PAGE 131 F2578
NAT/G INDUS CONTROL LG/CO

B66
WILCOX C.,ECONOMIES OF THE WORLD TODAY: THEIR ORGANIZATION, DEVELOPMENT, AND PERFORMANCE (2ND ED.). CHINA/COM COM INDIA NIGERIA UK WOR+45 WOR-45 INDUS MARKET PLAN ECO/TAC SOCISM...CHARTS METH/COMP 20. PAGE 146 F2878
ECO/DEV ECO/UNDEV MARXISM CAP/ISM

B66
WILLIAMS G.,MERTHYR POLITICS: THE MAKING OF A WORKING-CLASS TRADITION. UK CHIEF WORKER LEAD SOCISM...ANTHOL MUNICH 19/20 MERTHYR RICHARD/H. PAGE 147 F2891
LOC/G POL/PAR INDUS

B67
ANDERSON C.W.,ISSUES OF POLITICAL DEVELOPMENT. BURMA WOR+45 CULTURE TOP/EX ECO/TAC MARXISM ...CHARTS NAT/COMP 20 COLOMB CONGO/LEOP. PAGE 5 F0094
NAT/LISM COERCE ECO/UNDEV SOCISM

B67
DAVIS H.B.,NATIONALISM AND SOCIALISM: MARXIST AND LABOR THEORIES OF NATIONALISM TO 1917. WOR-45 PROB/SOLV SOVEREIGN...CONCPT IDEA/COMP 19/20. PAGE 30 F0589
MARXISM ATTIT NAT/LISM SOCISM

B67
EBENSTEIN W.,TODAY'S ISMS: COMMUNISM, FASCISM, CAPITALISM, SOCIALISM (5TH ED.). COM WOR+45 PERCEPT PWR...SOC TREND IDEA/COMP NAT/COMP 20. PAGE 35 F0691
FASCISM MARXISM SOCISM CAP/ISM

B67
FILENE P.G.,AMERICANS AND THE SOVIET EXPERIMENT, 1917-1933. USA-45 USSR INTELL NAT/G CAP/ISM DIPLOM EDU/PROP PRESS REV SOCISM...PSY 20. PAGE 41 F0793
ATTIT RIGID/FLEX MARXISM SOCIETY

B67
HAGUE D.C.,PRICE FORMATION IN VARIOUS ECONOMIES; PROCEEDINGS OF A CONFERENCE HELD BY THE INTERNATIONAL ECONOMIC ASSOCIATION. WOR+45 FINAN MARKET PLAN CONFER COST...DECISION MATH PREDICT CHARTS SIMUL 20 INTL/ECON. PAGE 53 F1037
PRICE CAP/ISM SOCISM METH/COMP

B67
HODGKINSON R.G.,THE ORIGINS OF THE NATIONAL HEALTH SERVICE: THE MEDICAL SERVICES OF THE NEW POOR LAW, 1834-1871. UK INDUS WORKER PROB/SOLV EFFICIENCY ATTIT HEALTH WEALTH SOCISM...JURID SOC/WK MUNICH 19/20. PAGE 60 F1189
HEAL NAT/G POLICY LAW

B67
JHANGIANI M.A.,JANA SANGH AND SWATANTRA: A PROFILE OF THE RIGHTIST PARTIES IN INDIA. INDIA ADMIN CHOOSE MARXISM SOCISM...INT CHARTS BIBLIOG 20. PAGE 67 F1320
POL/PAR LAISSEZ NAT/LISM ATTIT

B67
OFER G.,THE SERVICE INDUSTRIES IN A DEVELOPING ECONOMY: ISRAEL AS A CASE STUDY. ISRAEL ECO/TAC INT/TRADE PRODUC WEALTH SOCISM...TIME/SEQ TREND CHARTS 20. PAGE 101 F1979
DIPLOM ECO/DEV SERV/IND

B67
SHAFFER H.G.,THE COMMUNIST WORLD: MARXIST AND NON-MARXIST VIEWS. WOR+45 SOCIETY DIPLOM ECO/TAC CONTROL SOCISM...MARXIST ANTHOL BIBLIOG/A 20. PAGE 120 F2363
MARXISM NAT/COMP IDEA/COMP COM

B67
SPIRO H.S.,PATTERNS OF AFRICAN DEVLOPMENT: FIVE COMPARISONS. STRUCT ECO/UNDEV NAT/G CONSERVE SOCISM ...PREDICT NAT/COMP 20 CHINJAP. PAGE 125 F2457
AFR CONSTN NAT/LISM TREND

L67
AUSTIN D.A.,"POLITICAL CONFLICT IN AFRICA." CONSTN
ANOMIE

NAT/G CREATE ADMIN COLONIAL ORD/FREE MARXISM AFR
POPULISM SOCISM...NAT/COMP ANTHOL 20. PAGE 8 F0141 POL/PAR

L67
GREGORY A.J.,"AFRICAN SOCIALISM, SOCIALISM AND FASCISM
FASCISM: AN APPRAISAL." FUT LEAD REV GP/REL MARXISM
RACE/REL NAT/LISM ATTIT...IDEA/COMP STERTYP 20. SOCISM
PAGE 51 F0993 AFR

S67
ALVES V.,"FOREIGN CAPITAL IN BRAZIL." BRAZIL USA+45 ECO/UNDEV
CAP/ISM DIPLOM ECO/TAC INT/TRADE CONTROL PWR FINAN
...POLICY 20. PAGE 4 F0081 SOCIALIST
SOCISM

S67
AVTORKHANOV A.,"A NEW AGRARIAN REVOLUTION." COM AGRI
USSR ECO/DEV PLAN TEC/DEV ADMIN CONTROL OPTIMAL METH/COMP
WEALTH SOCISM 20 KHRUSH/N STALIN/J. PAGE 8 F0144 MARXISM
OWN

S67
FRANKEL T.,"ECONOMIC REFORM* A TENTATIVE ECO/DEV
APPRAISAL." COM USSR OP/RES BUDGET CONFER INDUS
EFFICIENCY PRODUC MARXISM SOCISM...MGT 20. PAGE 43 PLAN
F0847 WEALTH

S67
JENCKS C.E.,"COAL MINERS IN BRITAIN SINCE EXTR/IND
NATIONALIZATION." UK LABOR GP/REL ADJUST SOCISM WORKER
...INT 20. PAGE 67 F1311 STRATA
ATTIT

S67
LASLETT J.H.M.,"SOCIALISM AND THE AMERICAN LABOR LABOR
MOVEMENT* SOME NEW REFLECTIONS." USA-45 VOL/ASSN ROUTINE
LOBBY PARTIC CENTRAL ALL/VALS SOCISM...GP/COMP 20. ATTIT
PAGE 76 F1484 GP/REL

S67
LAZUTKIN Y.,"SOCIALISM AND SPARE TIME." ECO/DEV LEISURE
WORKER CREATE TEC/DEV ROUTINE TIME. PAGE 76 F1497 PRODUC
SOCISM
SOCIALIST

S67
LEONTYEV L.,"THE LENINIST PRINCIPLES OF SOCIALIST SOCISM
ECONOMIC MANAGEMENT." USA+45 USSR POL/PAR WORKER CAP/ISM
PLAN ECO/TAC EFFICIENCY PRODUC MARXISM...POLICY IDEA/COMP
SOCIALIST MGT TREND 20 LENIN/VI MARX/KARL. PAGE 78 ECO/DEV
F1529

S67
PETRAS J.,"MINERS AND AGRARIAN RADICALISM." CHILE PARTIC
AGRI EXTR/IND WORKER CHOOSE ATTIT SOCISM MUNICH 20. EDU/PROP
PAGE 105 F2073 LABOR

S67
SHISTER J.,"THE DIRECTION OF UNIONISM 1947-1967: LABOR
THRUST OF DRIFT?" INDUS CENTRAL EFFICIENCY INCOME PROF/ORG
ATTIT SOCISM...POLICY TREND 20 AFL/CIO. PAGE 121 LEAD
F2382 LAW

L86
OSGOOD H.L.,"SCIENTIFIC SOCIALISM: RODBERTUS" SOCISM
GERMANY CAP/ISM COST WEALTH...MAJORIT BIOG MARXISM
IDEA/COMP 19 RODBRTUS/C. PAGE 102 F2002 ECO/DEV
ECO/TAC

B91
MILL J.S.,SOCIALISM (1859). MOD/EUR AGRI INDUS WEALTH
NAT/G REV INCOME PRODUC ORD/FREE POPULISM SOCISM SOCIALIST
...GOV/COMP METH/COMP 19. PAGE 91 F1787 ECO/TAC
OWN

B92
COULANGES F D.E.,THE ORIGIN OF PROPERTY IN LAND. OWN
LAW STRATA AGRI ACADEM EDU/PROP ORD/FREE 19. HIST/WRIT
PAGE 28 F0543 IDEA/COMP
SOCISM

SOCRATES....SOCRATES

SOLDATI A. F2438

SOLOMONS....THE SOLOMON ISLANDS

SOLOW R.M. F2439

SOLT L.F. F2440

SOMALIA....SOMALIA; SEE ALSO AFR

SOMMERFELD R.M. F2442

SONGAI....SONGAI EMPIRES (AFRICA)

SOPER T. F2443

SOREL G. F2444,F2445

SOREL/G....GEORGES SOREL

SOUPHANGOU....PRINCE SOUPHANGOU-VONG (LEADER OF PATHET LAO)

SOUTH ARABIA....SEE ARABIA/SOU

SOUTH KOREA....SEE KOREA/S

SOUTH VIETNAM....SEE VIETNAM/S

SOUTH/AFR....UNION OF SOUTH AFRICA

N
SOUTH AFRICAN JOURNAL OF ECONOMICS. SOUTH/AFR FINAN ECO/UNDEV
MARKET ACT/RES OP/RES...PHIL/SCI STAT CON/ANAL ACADEM
METH/COMP BIBLIOG/A 20. PAGE 1 F0009 INTELL
R+D

B25
WILLIAMS B.,THE SELBORNE MEMORANDUM. AFR FUT COLONIAL
SOUTH/AFR UK NAT/G BUDGET DIPLOM REGION GOV/REL PROVS
SOVEREIGN...POLICY CHARTS 20 UNIFICA SELBORNE/W.
PAGE 147 F2888

B37
UNION OF SOUTH AFRICA,REPORT CONCERNING NAT/G
ADMINISTRATION OF SOUTH WEST AFRICA (6 VOLS.). ADMIN
SOUTH/AFR INDUS PUB/INST FORCES LEGIS BUDGET DIPLOM COLONIAL
EDU/PROP ADJUD CT/SYS...GEOG CHARTS 20 AFRICA/SW CONSTN
LEAGUE/NAT. PAGE 132 F2610

B42
JACKSON M.V.,EUROPEAN POWERS AND SOUTH-EAST AFRICA: DOMIN
A STUDY OF INTERNATIONAL RELATIONS ON SOUTH-EAST POLICY
COAST OF AFRICA, 1796-1856. AFR FRANCE PORTUGAL ORD/FREE
SOUTH/AFR UK USA-45 FORCES INT/TRADE PWR...CHARTS DIPLOM
BIBLIOG 18/19 TREATY. PAGE 66 F1294

B52
SACHS E.S.,THE CHOICE BEFORE SOUTH AFRICA. NAT/LISM
SOUTH/AFR AGRI EXTR/IND PROC/MFG PROB/SOLV ORD/FREE DISCRIM
SOVEREIGN 20 NEGRO. PAGE 115 F2267 RACE/REL
LABOR

B54
KARTUN D.,AFRICA, AFRICA: A CONTINENT RISES TO ITS COLONIAL
FEET. AFR SOUTH/AFR UK ELITES AGRI LABOR LOC/G ORD/FREE
POL/PAR EDU/PROP CONTROL COERCE DISCRIM AGE/Y NEGRO PROFIT
THIRD/WRLD GOLD/COAST. PAGE 69 F1358 EXTR/IND

N56
US HOUSE COMM FOREIGN AFFAIRS,REPORT OF THE SPECIAL FOR/AID
STUDY MISSION TO AFRICA, SOUTH AND EAST OF THE COLONIAL
SAHARA (PAMPHLET). AFR SOUTH/AFR USA+45 STRUCT ECO/UNDEV
INT/TRADE PARL/PROC NAT/LISM ATTIT ALL/VALS HEALTH DIPLOM
...POLICY 20 CONGRESS. PAGE 136 F2691

B57
NEUMARK S.D.,ECONOMIC INFLUENCES ON THE SOUTH COLONIAL
AFRICAN FRONTIER, 1652-1836. SOUTH/AFR SEA AGRI ECO/UNDEV
NAT/G FORCES WORKER DIPLOM INT/TRADE PRICE DEMAND ECO/TAC
PRODUC...STAT CHARTS 17/19 FRONTIER. PAGE 97 F1915 MARKET

B57
ROBERTSON H.M.,SOUTH AFRICA, ECONOMIC AND POLITICAL RACE/REL
ASPECTS. SOUTH/AFR CONSTN CULTURE POL/PAR LEGIS ECO/UNDEV
DIPLOM DOMIN COLONIAL...SOC BIBLIOG 19/20. PAGE 112 ECO/TAC
F2214 DISCRIM

B60
WODDIS J.,AFRICA: THE ROOTS OF REVOLT. SOUTH/AFR COLONIAL
WORKER INT/TRADE RACE/REL DISCRIM ORD/FREE 20. SOVEREIGN
PAGE 148 F2915 WAR
ECO/UNDEV

S60
MAIR L.P.,"SOCIAL CHANGE IN SOUTH AFRICA." MOD/EUR AFR
SOUTH/AFR WOR+45 ECO/UNDEV EX/STRUC TEC/DEV ATTIT NAT/G
DRIVE PERCEPT ORD/FREE...MGT CONCPT TIME/SEQ IND REV
20. PAGE 84 F1641 SOVEREIGN

B61
SPOONER F.P.,SOUTH AFRICAN PREDICAMENT. FUT ECO/DEV
SOUTH/AFR INDUS POL/PAR RACE/REL INCOME...CHARTS 20 DISCRIM
NEGRO. PAGE 125 F2459 ECO/TAC
POLICY

B62
GREEN L.P.,DEVELOPMENT IN AFRICA. AFR CENTRL/AFR CULTURE
GHANA RHODESIA SOUTH/AFR AGRI PROC/MFG INT/TRADE ECO/UNDEV
DEMAND NAT/LISM PRODUC WEALTH...GEOG METH/CNCPT GOV/REL
CHARTS BIBLIOG 20. PAGE 50 F0987 TREND

B62
PERROUX F.,L'ECONOMIE DES JEUNES NATIONS. EUR+WWI INDUS
SOUTH/AFR FINAN MARKET TEC/DEV CAP/ISM FOR/AID ECO/UNDEV
INT/TRADE 20. PAGE 105 F2065 ECO/TAC
DIPLOM

B62
VAN RENSBURG P.,GUILTY LAND: THE HISTORY OF RACE/REL
APARTHEID. SOUTH/AFR NAT/G POL/PAR DOMIN CHOOSE DISCRIM
...SOC 19/20 NEGRO. PAGE 140 F2763 NAT/LISM
POLICY

C62
GREEN L.P.,"DEVELOPMENT IN AFRICA." RHODESIA BIBLIOG
SOUTH/AFR UGANDA MARKET PROC/MFG PRODUC WEALTH ECO/UNDEV
...GEOG 20. PAGE 50 F0986 AFR
AGRI

B63
ELLENDER A.J.,A REPORT ON UNITED STATES FOREIGN FOR/AID
OPERATIONS IN AFRICA. SOUTH/AFR USA+45 STRATA DIPLOM
EXTR/IND FORCES RACE/REL ISOLAT SOVEREIGN...CHARTS WEALTH
20 NEGRO. PAGE 37 F0721 ECO/UNDEV

B63
LEWIN J.,POLITICS AND LAW IN SOUTH AFRICA. SOUTH/AFR UK POL/PAR BAL/PWR ECO/TAC COLONIAL CONTROL GP/REL DISCRIM PWR 20 NEGRO. PAGE 79 F1545
NAT/LISM POLICY LAW RACE/REL

B64
HUTT W.H.,THE ECONOMICS OF THE COLOUR BAR. SOUTH/AFR EXTR/IND LABOR ADJUD NEGRO. PAGE 64 F1251
INDUS DISCRIM RACE/REL ECO/UNDEV

B64
SEGAL R.,SANCTIONS AGAINST SOUTH AFRICA. AFR SOUTH/AFR NAT/G INT/TRADE RACE/REL PEACE PWR ...INT/LAW ANTHOL 20 UN. PAGE 119 F2342
SANCTION DISCRIM ECO/TAC POLICY

B65
SPENCE J.E.,REPUBLIC UNDER PRESSURE: A STUDY OF SOUTH AFRICAN FOREIGN POLICY. SOUTH/AFR ADMIN COLONIAL GOV/REL RACE/REL DISCRIM NAT/LISM ATTIT ROLE...TREND 20 NEGRO. PAGE 124 F2449
DIPLOM POLICY AFR

S65
DICKMAN A.B.,"SOUTH AFRICAN MONEY MARKET - PROGRESS AND PROBLEMS SINCE 1960." SOUTH/AFR PROB/SOLV ROLE ...PREDICT CHARTS 20. PAGE 33 F0633
FINAN PLAN MARKET

S65
HUTT W.H.,"KEYNESIAN REVISIONS" SOUTH/AFR ECO/DEV FINAN NAT/G WORKER BUDGET TAX PRICE EQUILIB WEALTH 20 KEYNES/JM. PAGE 64 F1252
ECO/TAC GEN/LAWS LOG

S65
KAUN D.E.,"THE FAIR LABOUR STANDARDS ACT: AN EVALUATION IN TERMS OF ITS STATED GOALS." SOUTH/AFR LAW LABOR BARGAIN PAY INGP/REL WEALTH 20. PAGE 69 F1364
ECO/TAC PRICE WORKER LEGIS

S65
MALHERBE E.G.,"MANPOWER TRAINING: EDUCATIONAL REQUIREMENTS FOR ECONOMIC EXPANSION." SOUTH/AFR ECO/DEV INDUS EDU/PROP...MGT STAT CHARTS 20. PAGE 84 F1646
LABOR SKILL SCHOOL ACADEM

S65
MULLER A.L.,"THE ECONOMIC POSITION OF THE ASIANS IN AFRICA." AFR SOUTH/AFR ECO/UNDEV MARKET ECO/TAC GP/REL INCOME...CHARTS IND 20 MONOPOLY ASIANS. PAGE 95 F1856
WORKER RACE/REL CAP/ISM DISCRIM

S65
STEENKAMP W.F.J.,"THE PROBLEM OF WAGE REGULATION." SOUTH/AFR LAW ECO/DEV ECO/UNDEV LABOR NAT/G BARGAIN PAY INGP/REL DISCRIM WEALTH...METH/COMP 20. PAGE 125 F2473
ECO/TAC PRICE WORKER RATION

S65
VAN DER HORST S.T.,"THE ECONOMICS OF DECENTRALISATION OF INDUSTRY." SOUTH/AFR ECO/DEV LG/CO AUTOMAT DISCRIM...POLICY MUNICH 20. PAGE 140 F2761
PLAN INDUS CENTRAL TEC/DEV

B66
EDWARDS C.D.,TRADE REGULATIONS OVERSEAS. IRELAND NEW/ZEALND SOUTH/AFR NAT/G CAP/ISM TARIFFS CONTROL ...POLICY JURID 20 EEC CHINJAP. PAGE 36 F0703
INT/TRADE DIPLOM INT/LAW ECO/TAC

B67
SACKS B.,SOUTH AFRICA: AN IMPERIAL DILEMMA. SOUTH/AFR UK ECO/UNDEV KIN DOMIN DEBATE CONTROL REV DISCRIM ISOLAT...POLICY STAT BIBLIOG 20. PAGE 115 F2268
COLONIAL RACE/REL DIPLOM ORD/FREE

L67
MACDONALD R.S.J.,"THE RESORT TO ECONOMIC COERCION BY INTERNATIONAL POLITICAL ORGANIZATIONS." CUBA ETHIOPIA RHODESIA SOUTH/AFR NAT/G FOR/AID INT/TRADE DOMIN CONTROL SANCTION...DECISION LEAGUE/NAT UN OAS 20. PAGE 83 F1625
INT/ORG COERCE ECO/TAC DIPLOM

SOUTH/AMER....SOUTH AMERICA

B61
ESTEVEZ A.,ASPECTOS ECONOMICO-FINANCIEROS DE LA CAMPANA SANMARITANA. L/A+17C SPAIN FINAN COLONIAL LEAD ROLE ORD/FREE WEALTH 19 SOUTH/AMER SAN/MARTIN. PAGE 38 F0748
ECO/UNDEV REV BUDGET NAT/G

B62
US CONGRESS JOINT ECO COMM,ECONOMIC DEVELOPMENTS IN SOUTH AMERICA. USA+45 SOCIETY FINAN NAT/G PROB/SOLV TEC/DEV INT/TRADE TAX EFFICIENCY PRODUC ATTIT ...POLICY 20 ALL/PROG CONGRESS SOUTH/AMER. PAGE 135 F2654
L/A+17C ECO/UNDEV FOR/AID DIPLOM

B63
INTERAMERICAN ECO AND SOC COUN,THE ALLIANCE FOR PROGRESS: ITS FIRST YEAR: 1961-1962. AGRI SCHOOL PLAN TEC/DEV INT/TRADE TAX GIVE ADMIN WEALTH...SOC 20 ALL/PROG SOUTH/AMER. PAGE 64 F1267
INT/ORG PROB/SOLV ECO/TAC L/A+17C

SOUTH/CAR....SOUTH CAROLINA

B30
GREEN F.M.,CONSTITUTIONAL DEVELOPMENT IN THE SOUTH ATLANTIC STATES, 1776-1860; A STUDY IN THE EVOLUTION OF DEMOCRACY. USA-45 ELITES SOCIETY STRATA ECO/DEV AGRI POL/PAR EX/STRUC LEGIS CT/SYS REGION...BIBLIOG 18/19 MARYLAND VIRGINIA GEORGIA NORTH/CAR SOUTH/CAR. PAGE 50 F0984
CONSTN PROVS PLURISM REPRESENT

SOUTH/DAK....SOUTH DAKOTA

SOUTH/US....SOUTH (UNITED STATES)

B58
OGDEN F.D.,THE POLL TAX IN THE SOUTH. USA+45 USA-45 CONSTN ADJUD ADMIN PARTIC CRIME...TIME/SEQ GOV/COMP METH/COMP 18/20 SOUTH/US. PAGE 101 F1982
TAX CHOOSE RACE/REL DISCRIM

B65
CLARK T.D.,THREE PATHS TO THE MODERN SOUTH: EDUCATION, AGRICULTURE, AND CONSERVATION. FUT USA-45 ECO/DEV ECO/TAC PEACE WEALTH...POLICY 20 SOUTH/US. PAGE 25 F0485
AGRI EDU/PROP GOV/REL REGION

B65
MACESICH G.,COMMERCIAL BANKING AND REGIONAL DEVELOPMENT IN THE US, 1950-1960. USA+45 NAT/G PLAN ECO/TAC DEMAND...MGT 20 FED/RESERV SOUTH/US. PAGE 83 F1627
FINAN ECO/DEV INCOME COST

B66
WOODMAN H.D.,SLAVERY AND THE SOUTHERN ECONOMY: SOURCES AND READINGS. USA-45 CULTURE STRUCT AGRI ECO/TAC LEAD RACE/REL DISCRIM EFFICIENCY...CHARTS ANTHOL MUNICH 18/19 NEGRO SOUTH/US. PAGE 148 F2922
ECO/DEV STRATA WORKER UTIL

SOUTHEAST ASIA....SEE S/EASTASIA, S/ASIA

SOUTHEAST ASIA TREATY ORGANIZATION....SEE SEATO

SOUTHERN RHODESIA....SEE RHODESIA, COMMONWLTH

SOVEREIGN....SOVEREIGNTY

B19
SUMNER W.G.,WAR AND OTHER ESSAYS. USA-45 DELIB/GP DIPLOM TARIFFS COLONIAL PEACE SOVEREIGN 20. PAGE 127 F2514
INT/TRADE ORD/FREE CAP/ISM ECO/TAC

N19
JACKSON R.G.A.,THE CASE FOR AN INTERNATIONAL DEVELOPMENT AUTHORITY (PAMPHLET). WOR+45 ECO/DEV DIPLOM GIVE CONTROL GP/REL EFFICIENCY NAT/LISM SOVEREIGN 20. PAGE 66 F1295
FOR/AID INT/ORG ECO/UNDEV ADMIN

N19
VELYAMINOV G.,AFRICA AND THE COMMON MARKET (PAMPHLET). AFR MARKET VOL/ASSN ECO/TAC COLONIAL ORD/FREE...SOCIALIST 20 THIRD/WRLD. PAGE 141 F2775
INT/ORG INT/TRADE SOVEREIGN ECO/UNDEV

B25
WILLIAMS B.,THE SELBORNE MEMORANDUM. AFR FUT SOUTH/AFR UK NAT/G BUDGET DIPLOM REGION GOV/REL SOVEREIGN...POLICY CHARTS 20 UNIFICA SELBORNE/W. PAGE 147 F2888
COLONIAL PROVS

B30
HAWTREY R.G.,ECONOMIC ASPECTS OF SOVEREIGNTY. UNIV WOR+45 WOR-45 ECO/DEV ECO/UNDEV AGRI COM/IND INDUS MARKET NAT/G TEC/DEV ECO/TAC EDU/PROP COERCE ATTIT KNOWL WEALTH...CONCPT CON/ANAL GEN/LAWS 20. PAGE 57 F1118
FORCES PWR SOVEREIGN WAR

B39
FURNIVALL J.S.,NETHERLANDS INDIA. INDIA NETHERLAND CULTURE INDUS NAT/G DIPLOM ADMIN WEALTH...POLICY CHARTS 17/20. PAGE 45 F0876
COLONIAL ECO/UNDEV SOVEREIGN PLURISM

B48
SPERO S.D.,GOVERNMENT AS EMPLOYER. USA+45 NAT/G EX/STRUC ADMIN CONTROL EXEC 20. PAGE 124 F2453
SOVEREIGN INGP/REL REPRESENT CONFER

B50
ORTON W.A.,THE ECONOMIC ROLE OF THE STATE. INTELL ECO/UNDEV PLAN CONTROL PWR SOVEREIGN...POLICY 17/20. PAGE 102 F2000
ECO/DEV NAT/G ECO/TAC ORD/FREE

B52
SACHS E.S.,THE CHOICE BEFORE SOUTH AFRICA. SOUTH/AFR AGRI EXTR/IND PROC/MFG PROB/SOLV ORD/FREE SOVEREIGN 20 NEGRO. PAGE 115 F2267
NAT/LISM DISCRIM RACE/REL LABOR

B55
HELANDER S.,DAS AUTARKIEPROBLEM IN DER WELTWIRTSCHAFT. PROB/SOLV BAL/PWR BARGAIN CAP/ISM ECO/TAC SOVEREIGN FOR/TRADE 20. PAGE 58 F1144
NAT/COMP COLONIAL DIPLOM

B55
PANT Y.P.,PLANNING IN UNDERDEVELOPED ECONOMIES. INDIA NEPAL INT/TRADE COLONIAL SOVEREIGN ALL/IDEOS ...TIME/SEQ METH/COMP 20. PAGE 103 F2026
ECO/UNDEV PLAN ECO/TAC DIPLOM

B56
FIELD G.C.,POLITICAL THEORY. POL/PAR REPRESENT MORAL SOVEREIGN...JURID IDEA/COMP. PAGE 40 F0789
CONCPT NAT/G ORD/FREE DIPLOM

B58
MOSKOWITZ M.,HUMAN RIGHTS AND WORLD ORDER. INT/ORG PLAN GP/REL NAT/LISM SOVEREIGN...CONCPT 20 UN TREATY CIV/RIGHTS. PAGE 94 F1845
DIPLOM INT/LAW ORD/FREE

B59
PANIKKAR K.M.,THE AFRO-ASIAN STATES AND THEIR PROBLEMS. COM CULTURE KIN POL/PAR SECT DIPLOM EDU/PROP COLONIAL SOVEREIGN...TECHNIC GOV/COMP 20. PAGE 103 F2025
AFR S/ASIA ECO/UNDEV

B60
HEYSE T.,PROBLEMS FONCIERS ET REGIME DES TERRES (ASPECTS ECONOMIQUES, JURIDIQUES ET SOCIAUX). AFR CONGO/BRAZ INT/ORG DIPLOM SOVEREIGN...GEOG TREATY 20. PAGE 59 F1161
BIBLIOG AGRI ECO/UNDEV LEGIS

B60
LATIFI D.,INDIA AND UNITED STATES AID. ASIA INDIA UK USA+45 AGRI FINAN INDUS COLONIAL ORD/FREE SOVEREIGN WEALTH...METH/COMP 20. PAGE 76 F1486
FOR/AID DIPLOM ECO/UNDEV

B60
WHEARE K.C.,THE CONSTITUTIONAL STRUCTURE OF THE COMMONWEALTH. UK EX/STRUC DIPLOM DOMIN ADMIN COLONIAL CONTROL LEAD INGP/REL SUPEGO 20 CMN/WLTH. PAGE 145 F2865
CONSTN INT/ORG VOL/ASSN SOVEREIGN

B60
WODDIS J.,AFRICA: THE ROOTS OF REVOLT. SOUTH/AFR WORKER INT/TRADE RACE/REL DISCRIM ORD/FREE 20. PAGE 148 F2915
COLONIAL SOVEREIGN WAR ECO/UNDEV

S60
MAIR L.P.,"SOCIAL CHANGE IN SOUTH AFRICA." MOD/EUR SOUTH/AFR WOR+45 ECO/UNDEV EX/STRUC TEC/DEV ATTIT DRIVE PERCEPT ORD/FREE...MGT CONCPT TIME/SEQ IND 20. PAGE 84 F1641
AFR NAT/G REV SOVEREIGN

S60
NICHOLS J.P.,"HAZARDS OF AMERICAN PRIVATE INVESTMENT IN UNDERDEVELOPED COUNTRIES." FUT L/A+17C USA+45 USA-45 EXTR/IND CONSULT BAL/PWR ECO/TAC DOMIN ADJUD ATTIT SOVEREIGN WEALTH ...HIST/WRIT TIME/SEQ TREND TERR/GP VAL/FREE 20. PAGE 98 F1924
FINAN ECO/UNDEV CAP/ISM NAT/LISM

B61
BONNEFOUS M.,EUROPE ET TIERS MONDE. EUR+WWI SOCIETY INT/ORG NAT/G VOL/ASSN ACT/RES TEC/DEV CAP/ISM ECO/TAC ATTIT ORD/FREE SOVEREIGN...POLICY CONCPT TREND TERR/GP COMMUN 20. PAGE 16 F0314
AFR ECO/UNDEV FOR/AID INT/TRADE

B61
CARNEY D.E.,GOVERNMENT AND ECONOMY IN BRITISH WEST AFRICA. GAMBIA GHANA NIGERIA SIER/LEONE DOMIN ADMIN GOV/REL SOVEREIGN WEALTH LAISSEZ...BIBLIOG 20 CMN/WLTH. PAGE 21 F0417
METH/COMP COLONIAL ECO/TAC ECO/UNDEV

S61
OCHENG D.,"ECONOMIC FORCES AND UGANDA'S FOREIGN POLICY." AFR UGANDA INT/TRADE TARIFFS INCOME SOVEREIGN WEALTH 20 EACM EEC TANGANYIKA. PAGE 100 F1961
ECO/TAC DIPLOM ECO/UNDEV INT/ORG

B62
KENT R.K.,FROM MADAGASCAR TO THE MALAGASY REPUBLIC. FRANCE MADAGASCAR DIPLOM NAT/LISM ORD/FREE...MGT 18/20. PAGE 70 F1379
COLONIAL SOVEREIGN REV POL/PAR

B62
LITTLEFIELD N.,METROPOLITAN AREA PROBLEMS AND MUNICIPAL HOME RULE. USA+45 PROVS ADMIN CONTROL GP/REL PWR. PAGE 81 F1586
LOC/G SOVEREIGN JURID LEGIS

B62
RIMALOV V.V.,ECONOMIC COOPERATION BETWEEN USSR AND UNDERDEVELOPED COUNTRIES. USSR FINAN TEC/DEV INT/TRADE DOMIN EDU/PROP COLONIAL NAT/LISM DRIVE SOVEREIGN...AUD/VIS 20. PAGE 111 F2194
FOR/AID PLAN ECO/UNDEV DIPLOM

B63
ELLENDER A.J.,A REPORT ON UNITED STATES FOREIGN OPERATIONS IN AFRICA. SOUTH/AFR USA+45 STRATA EXTR/IND FORCES RACE/REL ISOLAT SOVEREIGN...CHARTS 20 NEGRO. PAGE 37 F0721
FOR/AID DIPLOM WEALTH ECO/UNDEV

B63
LAFEBER W.,THE NEW EMPIRE: AN INTERPRETATION OF AMERICAN EXPANSION, 1860-1898. USA-45 CONSTN NAT/LISM SOVEREIGN...TREND BIBLIOG 19/20. PAGE 74 F1457
INDUS NAT/G DIPLOM CAP/ISM

S63
BELOFF M.,"BRITAIN, EUROPE AND THE ATLANTIC COMMUNITY." EUR+WWI ELITES NAT/G VOL/ASSN TOP/EX ATTIT ORD/FREE PWR SOVEREIGN WEALTH EEC TOT/POP VAL/FREE CMN/WLTH 20. PAGE 13 F0240
INT/ORG ECO/DEV UK

S63
HINDLEY D.,"FOREIGN AID TO INDONESIA AND ITS POLITICAL IMPLICATIONS." INDONESIA POL/PAR ATTIT SOVEREIGN...CHARTS 20. PAGE 60 F1173
FOR/AID NAT/G WEALTH ECO/TAC

B64
CASEY R.G.,THE FUTURE OF THE COMMONWEALTH. INDIA PAKISTAN UK ECO/UNDEV INT/ORG TEC/DEV COLONIAL SUPEGO 20 EEC AUSTRAL. PAGE 22 F0425
DIPLOM SOVEREIGN NAT/LISM FOR/AID

B64
PENNOCK J.R.,SELF-GOVERNMENT IN MODERNIZING NATIONS. AFR COM USA+45 ECO/DEV POL/PAR PROB/SOLV DIPLOM ECO/TAC COLONIAL REV POPULISM SOCISM 20. PAGE 105 F2058
ECO/UNDEV POLICY SOVEREIGN NAT/G

B65
CASSELL F.,GOLD OR CREDIT? THE ECONOMICS AND POLITICS OF INTERNATIONAL MONEY. AFR WOR+45 PLAN PROB/SOLV BAL/PAY SOVEREIGN WEALTH 20 OEEC. PAGE 22 F0428
FINAN INT/ORG DIPLOM ECO/TAC

B65
JOHNSTONE A.,UNITED STATES DIRECT INVESTMENT IN FRANCE: AN INVESTIGATION OF THE FRENCH CHARGES. FRANCE USA+45 ECO/DEV INDUS LG/CO NAT/G ECO/TAC CONTROL WEALTH...BIBLIOG 20 INTERVENT. PAGE 68 F1335
FINAN DIPLOM POLICY SOVEREIGN

B65
NKRUMAH K.,NEO-COLONIALISM: THE LAST STAGE OF IMPERIALISM. AFR INT/ORG WORKER FOR/AID INT/TRADE EDU/PROP GOV/REL NAT/LISM SOVEREIGN POPULISM SOCISM ...SOCIALIST 20 THIRD/WRLD INTRVN/ECO. PAGE 98 F1929
COLONIAL DIPLOM ECO/UNDEV ECO/TAC

B65
THORNTON A.P.,DOCTRINES OF IMPERIALISM. WOR+45 WOR-45 DOMIN NAT/LISM PROFIT ATTIT PERSON PWR RESPECT SOVEREIGN...CONCPT STERTYP. PAGE 130 F2571
IDEA/COMP COLONIAL DRIVE

B65
VON RENESSE E.A.,UNVOLLENDETE DEMOKRATIEN. AFR ISLAM S/ASIA SOCIETY ACT/RES COLONIAL...JURID CHARTS BIBLIOG METH 13/20. PAGE 142 F2795
ECO/UNDEV NAT/COMP SOVEREIGN

S65
CECIL C.O.,"THE DETERMINANTS OF LIBYAN FOREIGN POLICY." AFR INTELL ECO/UNDEV EXTR/IND POL/PAR CREATE REGION SOVEREIGN CONSERVE MAGHREB NASSER/G. PAGE 22 F0431
LIBYA DIPLOM WEALTH ISLAM

S65
HAYTER T.,"FRENCH AID TO AFRICA* ITS SCOPE AND ACHIEVEMENTS." CULTURE ECO/TAC INT/TRADE ADMIN REGION CENTRAL FEDERAL LOVE PWR SOVEREIGN EEC. PAGE 57 F1127
AFR FRANCE FOR/AID COLONIAL

B66
DAVIES I.,AFRICAN TRADE UNIONS. AFR ECO/UNDEV INT/ORG GP/REL ORD/FREE SOVEREIGN SOCISM 20. PAGE 30 F0585
LABOR COLONIAL PWR INDUS

B66
DILLEY M.R.,BRITISH POLICY IN KENYA COLONY (2ND ED.). AFR INDIA UK LABOR BUDGET TAX ADMIN PARL/PROC GP/REL...BIBLIOG 20 PARLIAMENT. PAGE 33 F0639
COLONIAL REPRESENT SOVEREIGN

B66
LONDON K.,EASTERN EUROPE IN TRANSITION. CHINA/COM USSR DOMIN COLONIAL CENTRAL RIGID/FLEX PWR...SOC ANTHOL 20. PAGE 82 F1597
SOVEREIGN COM NAT/LISM DIPLOM

B66
NAMBOODIRIPAD E.M.,ECONOMICS AND POLITICS OF INDIA'S SOCIALIST PATTERN. INDIA STRATA AGRI INDUS NAT/G PRICE ORD/FREE SOVEREIGN 20. PAGE 96 F1888
ECO/UNDEV PLAN SOCISM CAP/ISM

B66
NATIONAL COUN APPLIED ECO RES,DEVELOPMENT WITHOUT AID. INDIA FINAN TEC/DEV EFFICIENCY...ANTHOL 20. PAGE 97 F1901
FOR/AID PLAN SOVEREIGN ECO/UNDEV

S66
FELD W.,"NATIONAL ECONOMIC INTEREST GROUPS AND POLICY FORMATION IN THE EEC." NAT/G POL/PAR REGION CENTRAL SOVEREIGN...INT NET/THEORY EEC. PAGE 40 F0777
LOBBY ELITES DECISION

B67
DAVIS H.B.,NATIONALISM AND SOCIALISM: MARXIST AND LABOR THEORIES OF NATIONALISM TO 1917. WOR-45 PROB/SOLV SOVEREIGN...CONCPT IDEA/COMP 19/20. PAGE 30 F0589
MARXISM ATTIT NAT/LISM SOCISM

B67
FANON F.,TOWARD THE AFRICAN REVOLUTION. AFR FRANCE CULTURE ELITES LEAD REV GP/REL ORD/FREE SOVEREIGN 20. PAGE 39 F0762
COLONIAL DOMIN ECO/UNDEV RACE/REL

B67
LISS S.B.,THE CANAL, ASPECTS OF UNITED STATES-PANAMANIAN RELATIONS. AFR FUT PANAMA DOMIN COERCE ATTIT SOVEREIGN MARXISM 20 JOHNSON/LB KENNEDY/JF. PAGE 81 F1580
DIPLOM POLICY

B67
LYTLE C.M.,THE WARREN COURT AND ITS CRITICS. USA+45 NAT/G PROVS FORCES LOBBY RACE/REL DISCRIM SOVEREIGN 20 SUPREME/CT WARRN/EARL. PAGE 83 F1618
CT/SYS ADJUD PROB/SOLV ATTIT

B67
MORRIS A.J.A.,PARLIAMENTARY DEMOCRACY IN THE NINETEENTH CENTURY. UK INDUS LOC/G NAT/G POL/PAR CONSULT LEGIS INT/TRADE ADMIN CHOOSE SUFF SOVEREIGN 19 PARLIAMENT. PAGE 93 F1835
TIME/SEQ CONSTN PARL/PROC POPULISM

B67
WISEMAN H.V.,BRITAIN AND THE COMMONWEALTH. EUR+WWI
INT/ORG

FUT UK ECO/DEV POL/PAR TEC/DEV INT/TRADE LEAD ROLE SOVEREIGN...SOC TREND 20 CMN/WLTH. PAGE 148 F2911
DIPLOM NAT/G NAT/COMP

L67
AFFELDT R.J.,"THE INDEPENDENT LABOR UNION AND THE GOOD LIFE." USA+45 ADJUD CONTROL SANCTION GP/REL ORD/FREE JURID. PAGE 3 F0045
LABOR CT/SYS PWR SOVEREIGN

S67
ANDERSON S.S.,"SOVIET RUSSIA AND THE TWO EUROPES." AFR USSR PROB/SOLV CENTRAL SOVEREIGN 20. PAGE 5 F0097
DIPLOM POLICY MARXISM

S67
EDWARDS N.,"EDUCATION IN THE FEDERAL-STATE STRUCTURE OF GOVERNMENT." USA+45 SECT CONTROL GOV/REL RACE/REL DISCRIM FEDERAL ROLE PWR SOVEREIGN. PAGE 36 F0705
EDU/PROP NAT/G PROVS POLICY

S67
GONZALEZ M.P.,"CUBA, UNA REVOLUCION EN MARCHA." CUBA L/A+17C USA+45 VIETNAM ECO/UNDEV FORCES DIPLOM DOMIN...POLICY MARXIST NAT/COMP CASTRO/F. PAGE 48 F0946
REV NAT/G COLONIAL SOVEREIGN

S67
HILDEBRAND J.R.,"THE CENTRAL AMERICAN COMMON MARKET: ECONOMIC AND POLITICAL INTEGRATION." L/A+17C USA+45 ECO/DEV ECO/UNDEV AGRI SOVEREIGN. PAGE 59 F1170
DIPLOM ECO/TAC INT/TRADE INT/ORG

S67
KOHN W.S.G.,"THE SOVEREIGNTY OF LIECHTENSTEIN." LIECHTENST SWITZERLND USSR CONSTN DEBATE WAR CONSERVE 18/20 UN. PAGE 72 F1417
SOVEREIGN NAT/G PWR DIPLOM

S67
MERIKOSKI V.,"BASIC PROBLEMS OF UNIVERSITY ADMINISTRATION." PROVS SECT CONTROL...CLASSIF 20. PAGE 90 F1760
ACADEM ADMIN SOVEREIGN METH/COMP

S67
MILLER C.H.,"B. TRAVEN Y EL 'PROBLEMA PETROLERO'." USA-45 ECO/UNDEV INDUS TEC/DEV INT/TRADE ATTIT ORD/FREE SOVEREIGN 20 MEXIC/AMER. PAGE 91 F1791
EXTR/IND DIPLOM ECO/TAC DOMIN

S67
SIPPEL D.,"INDIENS UNSICHERE ZUKUNFT." INDIA CULTURE ACADEM POL/PAR LEGIS COLONIAL CHOOSE SOVEREIGN...JURID 20. PAGE 122 F2416
SOCIETY STRUCT ECO/UNDEV NAT/G

S67
THEROUX P.,"HATING THE ASIANS." TANZANIA UGANDA CONSTN INDUS NAT/G POL/PAR WORKER ECO/TAC HABITAT LOVE...POLICY GEOG 20 MIGRATION. PAGE 130 F2557
AFR RACE/REL SOVEREIGN ATTIT

N67
US SENATE COMM ON FOREIGN REL,THE RIM OF ASIA (PAMPHLET). WAR MARXISM 20. PAGE 139 F2745
ASIA PROB/SOLV SOVEREIGN POLICY

C83
BURKE E.,"RESOLUTIONS FOR CONCILIATION WITH AMERICA" (1775), IN E. BURKE, COLLECTED WORKS, VOL. 2." UK USA-45 FORCES INT/TRADE TARIFFS TAX SANCTION PEACE...POLICY 18 PRE/US/AM. PAGE 20 F0387
COLONIAL WAR SOVEREIGN ECO/TAC

SOVEREIGNTY....SEE SOVEREIGN

SOVERN M.I. F2446

SOVIET UNION....SEE USSR

SPAAK P.H. F2447

SPACE....OUTER SPACE, SPACE LAW

B65
MELMANS S.,OUR DEPLETED SOCIETY. AFR SPACE USA+45 ECO/DEV FORCES BUDGET ECO/TAC ADMIN WEAPON EFFICIENCY 20. PAGE 89 F1753
CIVMIL/REL INDUS EDU/PROP CONTROL

B66
LECHT L.,GOAL, PRIORITIES, AND DOLLARS: THE NEXT DECADE. SPACE USA+45 SOCIETY AGRI BUDGET FOR/AID ...HEAL SOC/WK STAT CHARTS 20 URBAN/RNWL PUB/TRANS. PAGE 76 F1499
IDEA/COMP POLICY CONSEN PLAN

B66
LILLEY S.,MEN, MACHINES AND HISTORY: THE STORY OF TOOLS AND MACHINES IN RELATION TO SOCIAL PROGRESS. PREHIST SPACE STRUCT COMPUTER AUTOMAT NUC/PWR ...POLICY SOC. PAGE 80 F1564
AGRI TEC/DEV SOCIETY

B66
RUPPENTHAL K.M.,TRANSPORTATION AND TOMORROW. FUT SPACE USA+45 SEA AIR FORCES TEC/DEV INT/TRADE ...ANTHOL 20 RAILROAD. PAGE 115 F2261
DIST/IND PLAN CIVMIL/REL PREDICT

B67
UNIVERSAL REFERENCE SYSTEM,PUBLIC POLICY AND THE MANAGEMENT OF SCIENCE (VOLUME IX). FUT SPACE WOR+45 LAW NAT/G TEC/DEV CONTROL NUC/PWR GOV/REL ...COMPUT/IR GEN/METH. PAGE 133 F2618
BIBLIOG/A POLICY MGT PHIL/SCI

S67
BARRO S.,"ECONOMIC IMPACT OF SPACE EXPENDITURES: SOME BROAD ISSUES DEALING WITH COSTS AND BENEFITS." USA+45 PROC/MFG R+D LG/CO CONSULT COST PRODUC 20. PAGE 10 F0195
SPACE FINAN ECO/TAC NAT/G

N67
US HOUSE COMM SCI ASTRONAUT,AUTHORIZING APPROPRIATIONS TO THE NATIONAL AERONAUTICS AND SPACE ADMINISTRATION (PAMPHLET). USA+45 NAT/G OP/RES TEC/DEV BUDGET NASA HOUSE/REP. PAGE 137 F2704
SPACE R+D PHIL/SCI NUC/PWR

SPAIN....SPAIN

B44
INTL CHAMBER OF COMMERCE,TERMS COMMONLY USED IN DISTRIBUTION AND ADVERTISING. PORTUGAL SPAIN UK WOR-45 SERV/IND 20. PAGE 65 F1284
DICTIONARY EDU/PROP DIST/IND INT/TRADE

B58
PAYNO M.,LA REFORMA SOCIAL EN ESPANA Y MEXICO. SPAIN ECO/TAC TAX LOBBY COERCE REV OWN CATHISM 19/20 MEXIC/AMER. PAGE 104 F2043
SECT NAT/G LAW ELITES

B61
ESTEVEZ A.,ASPECTOS ECONOMICO-FINANCIEROS DE LA CAMPANA SANMARITANA. L/A+17C SPAIN FINAN COLONIAL LEAD ROLE ORD/FREE WEALTH 19 SOUTH/AMER SAN/MARTIN. PAGE 38 F0748
ECO/UNDEV REV BUDGET NAT/G

B63
OTERO L.M.,HONDURAS. HONDURAS SPAIN STRUCT SECT COLONIAL REV WAR ATTIT PWR...GEOG WORSHIP 16/20. PAGE 102 F2003
NAT/G SOCIETY NAT/LISM ECO/UNDEV

B65
OECD,THE MEDITERRANEAN REGIONAL PROJECT: SPAIN; EDUCATION AND DEVELOPMENT. FUT SPAIN STRATA FINAN NAT/G WORKER PLAN PROB/SOLV ADMIN COST...POLICY STAT CHARTS 20 OECD. PAGE 100 F1973
ECO/UNDEV EDU/PROP ACADEM SCHOOL

B65
ORG FOR ECO COOP AND DEVEL,THE MEDITERRANEAN REGIONAL PROJECT: AN EXPERIMENT IN PLANNING BY SIX COUNTRIES. FUT GREECE SPAIN TURKEY YUGOSLAVIA SOCIETY FINAN NAT/G PROF/ORG EDU/PROP ADMIN REGION COST...POLICY STAT CHARTS 20 OECD. PAGE 102 F1995
PLAN ECO/UNDEV ACADEM SCHOOL

S65
MUNZI U.,"THE EUROPEAN SOCIAL FUND IN THE DEVELOPMENT OF THE MEDITERRANEAN REGIONS OF THE EEC." FUT GREECE ITALY PORTUGAL SPAIN TURKEY WORKER TEC/DEV ECO/TAC REGION...STAT EEC. PAGE 95 F1862
ECO/UNDEV PREDICT RECORD

B67
GUTKIND E.A.,URBAN DEVELOPMENT IN SOUTHERN EUROPE* SPAIN AND PORTUGAL. CHRIST-17C EUR+WWI MOD/EUR PORTUGAL SPAIN CULTURE AGRI...SOC SAMP/SIZ BIBLIOG MUNICH. PAGE 52 F1015
TEC/DEV ECO/DEV

S67
GOSALVEZ R.B.,"PERFIL DEL GENERAL VINCENTE ROJO." SPAIN DIPLOM CIVMIL/REL EFFICIENCY PERSON SKILL 20 BOLIV. PAGE 49 F0966
WAR FORCES ELITES BIOG

SPAN/AMER....SPANISH-AMERICAN CULTURE

SPEAKER OF THE HOUSE....SEE CONGRESS, HOUSE/REP, LEGIS, PARLIAMENT

SPEAR/BRWN....SPEARMAN BROWN PREDICTION FORMULA

SPECIAL DRAWING RIGHTS....SEE SDR

SPECIALIZATION....SEE TASK, SKILL

SPECTOR S.D. F2448

SPECULATION....SEE GAMBLE, RISK

SPENCE J.E. F2449

SPENCER H. F2450

SPENCER/H....HERBERT SPENCER

SPENGLER J.J. F0336,F0337,F2451,F2452

SPENGLER/O....OSWALD SPENGLER

SPERO S.D. F2453

SPICER G.W. F2454

SPICER K. F2455

SPINOZA/B....BARUCH (OR BENEDICT) SPINOZA

SPINRAD W. F2456

SPIRO H.S. F2457

SPITTMANN I. F2458

SPIVEY W.A. F0323

SPOCK/B....BENJAMIN SPOCK

SPOONER F.P. F2459

SPORTS....SPORTS AND ATHLETIC COMPETITIONS

SPULBER N. F2460

SPURRIER R.B. F2461

SRAFFA/P....PIERO SRAFFA

SRIVASTAVA G.L. F2462

SST....SUPERSONIC TRANSPORT

ST/LOUIS....ST. LOUIS, MO.

ST/PAUL....SAINT PAUL, MINNESOTA

STAGES....SEE TIME/SEQ

STALEY E. F2463,F2464,F2465,F2466

STALIN/J....JOSEPH STALIN

B50
HUNT R.N.,THE THEORY AND PRACTICE OF COMMUNISM. STRUCT WORKER NAT/LISM TOTALISM...CONCPT TREND 19/20 STALIN/J EUROPE. PAGE 63 F1244 — MARXISM SOCISM REV STRATA

B55
MAYO H.B.,DEMOCRACY AND MARXISM. COM USSR STRATA NAT/G WORKER ECO/TAC REV MORAL...PHIL/SCI HIST/WRIT IDEA/COMP WORSHIP 20 MARX/KARL LENIN/VI STALIN/J TROTSKY/L. PAGE 87 F1708 — MARXISM CAP/ISM

B59
HENDEL S.,THE SOVIET CRUCIBLE. USSR LEAD COERCE NAT/LISM UTOPIA PWR...POLICY CONCPT ANTHOL 20 STALIN/J LENIN/VI MARX/KARL BOLSHEVIK. PAGE 58 F1147 — COM MARXISM REV TOTALISM

B65
SHAFFER H.G.,THE SOVIET SYSTEM IN THEORY AND PRACTICE: SELECTED WESTERN AND SOVIET VIEWS. USSR LAW SOCIETY CREATE FOR/AID EDU/PROP PRESS CHOOSE PEACE ORD/FREE...ANTHOL 20 STALIN/J. PAGE 120 F2362 — MARXISM SOCISM IDEA/COMP

B66
BRODERSEN A.,THE SOVIET WORKER: LABOR AND GOVERNMENT IN SOVIET SOCIETY. USSR STRUCT INDUS LABOR PLAN PAY INGP/REL PRODUC...POLICY GEN/LAWS BIBLIOG 20 STALIN/J LENIN/VI BOLSHEVISM KHRUSH/N. PAGE 19 F0357 — WORKER ROLE NAT/G MARXISM

B67
GARAUDY R.,KARL MARX: THE EVOLUTION OF HIS THOUGHT. SOCIETY...BIBLIOG 20 MARX/KARL STALIN/J. PAGE 46 F0899 — MARXIST GEN/LAWS CONCPT TIME/SEQ

B67
MAZOUR A.G.,SOVIET ECONOMIC DEVELOPMENT: OPERATION OUTSTRIP: 1921-1965. USSR ECO/UNDEV FINAN CHIEF WORKER PROB/SOLV CONTROL PRODUC MARXISM...CHARTS ORG/CHARTS 20 STALIN/J. PAGE 87 F1711 — ECO/TAC AGRI INDUS PLAN

B67
OGLESBY C.,CONTAINMENT AND CHANGE. AFR COM USA+45 ECO/UNDEV TEC/DEV ECO/TAC FOR/AID INT/TRADE DOMIN GUERRILLA REV PEACE 20 STALIN/J. PAGE 101 F1983 — DIPLOM BAL/PWR MARXISM CULTURE

S67
AVTORKHANOV A.,"A NEW AGRARIAN REVOLUTION." COM USSR ECO/DEV PLAN TEC/DEV ADMIN CONTROL OPTIMAL WEALTH SOCISM 20 KHRUSH/N STALIN/J. PAGE 8 F0144 — AGRI METH/COMP MARXISM OWN

S67
FEDYSHYN O.S.,"KHRUSHCHEV'S 'LEAP FORWARD': NATIONAL ASSIMILATION IN THE USSR AFTER STALIN." USSR PLAN NAT/LISM PERSON...POLICY 20 KHRUSH/N STALIN/J. PAGE 39 F0771 — GP/REL INGP/REL MARXISM METH

STAMMLER/R....RUDOLF STAMMLER

STAND/INT....STANDARDIZED INTERVIEWS

B60
SHONFIELD A.,THE ATTACK ON WORLD POVERTY. WOR+45 ECO/DEV ECO/UNDEV FINAN VOL/ASSN PLAN EDU/PROP DRIVE KNOWL WEALTH...CONT/OBS STAND/INT ORG/CHARTS TOT/POP UNESCO 20. PAGE 121 F2383 — INT/ORG ECO/TAC FOR/AID INT/TRADE

B63
PRYOR F.L.,THE COMMUNIST FOREIGN TRADE SYSTEM. COM CZECHOSLVK GERMANY YUGOSLAVIA LAW ECO/DEV DIST/IND POL/PAR PLAN DOMIN TOTALISM DRIVE RIGID/FLEX WEALTH ...STAT STAND/INT CHARTS FOR/TRADE 20. PAGE 108 F2130 — ATTIT ECO/TAC

B67
LITTLE AD, INC.,COMMUNITY RENEWAL PROGRAMMING. CULTURE LOC/G ACT/RES TASK COST ATTIT...SOC/WK MODAL STAT STAND/INT CHARTS 20 SAN/FRAN. PAGE 81 F1585 — STRATA NEIGH PLAN CREATE

STANDARDIZED INTERVIEWS....SEE STAND/INT

STANFORD RESEARCH INSTITUTE F2467

STANFORD U, BOARD OF TRUSTEES F2468

STANFORD/U....STANFORD UNIVERSITY

STANKIEW/W....W.J. STANKIEWICZ

STANKIEWICZ, W.J.....SEE STANKIEW/W

STANLEY C.J. F2469

STAR/CARR....STAR-CARR, A PREHISTORIC SOCIETY

STARBUCK W.H. F0568

STARK H. F2470

STARNER F.L. F2471

STAT....STATISTICS; SEE ALSO ACCT

N
ECONOMIC LIBRARY SELECTIONS. AGRI INDUS MARKET ADMIN...STAT NAT/COMP 20. PAGE 1 F0007 — BIBLIOG/A WRITING FINAN

N
THE MIDDLE EAST AND NORTH AFRICA. AFR ISLAM CULTURE ECO/UNDEV AGRI NAT/G TEC/DEV FOR/AID INT/TRADE EDU/PROP...CHARTS 20. PAGE 1 F0008 — INDEX INDUS FINAN STAT

N
SOUTH AFRICAN JOURNAL OF ECONOMICS. SOUTH/AFR FINAN MARKET ACT/RES OP/RES...PHIL/SCI STAT CON/ANAL METH/COMP BIBLIOG/A 20. PAGE 1 F0009 — ECO/UNDEV ACADEM INTELL R+D

N
MINISTRY OF OVERSEAS DEVELOPME,TECHNICAL CO-OPERATION -- A BIBLIOGRAPHY. UK LAW SOCIETY DIPLOM ECO/TAC FOR/AID...STAT 20 CMN/WLTH. PAGE 92 F1803 — BIBLIOG TEC/DEV ECO/DEV NAT/G

N
US SUPERINTENDENT OF DOCUMENTS,CENSUS PUBLICATIONS (PRICE LIST 70). AGRI CONSTRUC DIST/IND FINAN LOC/G NAT/G PROVS INT/TRADE APPORT INCOME. PAGE 140 F2751 — BIBLIOG/A CENSUS STAT USA+45

B14
LEVINE L.,SYNDICALISM IN FRANCE (2ND ED.). FRANCE LAW SOCIETY ECO/DEV NAT/G ECO/TAC LEAD ATTIT ...POLICY CONCPT STAT BIBLIOG 18/20 REFORMERS. PAGE 79 F1542 — LABOR INDUS SOCISM REV

B15
JONES J.H.,THE ECONOMICS OF WAR AND CONQUEST. WOR-45 ECO/DEV NAT/G WEALTH...STAT TREND STERTYP GEN/LAWS TOT/POP 20. PAGE 68 F1338 — MYTH WAR

N19
HATANAKA M.,A SPECTRAL ANALYSIS OF BUSINESS CYCLE INDICATORS: LEAD-LAG IN TERMS OF ALL TIME POINTS (PAMPHLET). UNIV WORKER EFFICIENCY...REGRESS STAT CHARTS TIME 20. PAGE 56 F1110 — ECOMETRIC ADJUST PRODUC CON/ANAL

N19
INTERNATIONAL LABOUR OFFICE,EMPLOYMENT, UNEMPLOYMENT AND LABOUR FORCE STATISTICS (PAMPHLET). EUR+WWI STRATA AGRI INDUS NAT/G PROB/SOLV PAY AGE SEX...SAMP NAT/COMP METH 20 ILO. PAGE 65 F1278 — WORKER LABOR STAT ECO/DEV

N19
KINDLEBERGER C.P.,BALANCE-OF-PAYMENTS DEFICITS AND THE INTERNATIONAL MARKET FOR LIQUIDITY (PAMPHLET). ECO/DEV NAT/G PLAN DIPLOM ECO/TAC PRODUC...POLICY STAT CHARTS. PAGE 71 F1389 — BAL/PAY INT/TRADE MARKET FINAN

N19
PATRICK H.T.,CYCLICAL INSTABILITY AND FISCAL-MONETARY POLICY IN POST-WAR JAPAN (PAMPHLET). INDUS MARKET DIPLOM TAX PRICE BAL/PAY...TREND CHARTS EQULIB 20 CHINJAP. PAGE 104 F2036 — ECO/DEV PRODUC STAT

N19
STUTZ R.L.,COLLECTIVE DEALING BY UNITS OF LOCAL GOVERNMENT IN CONNECTICUT (PAMPHLET). USA+45 LOC/G PROVS...STAT MUNICH 20 CONNECTICT. PAGE 127 F2508 — VOL/ASSN LABOR WORKER

N19
US BUREAU OF THE CENSUS,THE PROPORTION OF THE — PROC/MFG

SHIPMENTS (OR EMPLOYEES) OF EACH INDUSTRY... (PAMPHLET). USA+45 ECO/DEV EXTR/IND INDUS CONTROL PROFIT...STAT 20 CONGRESS MONOPOLY. PAGE 134 F2645
PRODUC MARKET CHARTS

B28

CASSEL G.,FOREIGN INVESTMENTS. GERMANY UK USA-45 WOR-45 ECO/DEV NAT/G VOL/ASSN CAP/ISM REPAR ATTIT WEALTH...METH/CNCPT STAT SIMUL STERTYP ANTHOL FOR/TRADE TOT/POP VAL/FREE 20. PAGE 22 F0426
FINAN ECO/TAC BAL/PAY

B30

BEVERIDGE W.H.,UNEMPLOYMENT: A PROBLEM OF INDUSTRY (1909-1930). USA-45 LAW ECO/DEV MARKET DELIB/GP WAR DEMAND INCOME...POLICY STAT CHARTS 20. PAGE 14 F0274
WORKER ECO/TAC GEN/LAWS

B38

LANGE O.,ON THE ECONOMIC THEORY OF SOCIALISM. UNIV ECO/DEV FINAN INDUS INT/ORG PUB/INST ROUTINE ATTIT ALL/VALS...SOC CONCPT STAT TREND 20. PAGE 75 F1475
MARKET ECO/TAC INT/TRADE SOCISM

B39

THOMAS J.A.,THE HOUSE OF COMMONS, 1832-1901; A STUDY OF ITS ECONOMIC AND FUNCTIONAL CHARACTER. UK LAW STRATA FINAN DIPLOM CONTROL LEAD LOBBY REPRESENT WEALTH...POLICY STAT BIBLIOG 19/20 PARLIAMENT. PAGE 130 F2561
PARL/PROC LEGIS POL/PAR ECO/DEV

S45

MILLS C.W.,"THE TRADE UNION LEADER: A COLLECTIVE PORTRAIT." EX/STRUC TOP/EX INGP/REL...QU CON/ANAL CHARTS. PAGE 92 F1798
LABOR LEAD STAT STRATA

B46

HARRISON S.M.,AMERICAN FOUNDATIONS FOR SOCIAL WELFARE. OP/RES CONTROL...POLICY MGT METH/CNCPT STAT TREND BIBLIOG. PAGE 56 F1092
GIVE FINAN CLASSIF ADMIN

B48

GRAHAM F.D.,THE THEORY OF INTERNATIONAL VALUES. FUT WOR+45 WOR-45 ECO/DEV FINAN INT/ORG PLAN TEC/DEV CAP/ISM DIPLOM ECO/TAC TARIFFS ROUTINE BAL/PAY DRIVE PWR WEALTH SOCISM...POLICY STAT HYPO/EXP GEN/LAWS 20. PAGE 50 F0971
NEW/IDEA INT/TRADE

B48

TAYLOR P.E.,THE ECONOMICS OF PUBLIC FINANCE. USA+45 USA-45 ECO/DEV WORKER PLAN BUDGET WAR INCOME WEALTH ...CONCPT STAT BIBLIOG 20. PAGE 129 F2540
FINAN POLICY NAT/G TAX

S48

HARDIN L.M.,"REFLECTIONS ON AGRICULTURAL POLICY FORMATION IN THE UNITED STATES." LEGIS PLAN BUDGET ECO/TAC LEAD CENTRAL...MGT SOC NEW/IDEA STAT FAO. PAGE 55 F1078
AGRI POLICY ADMIN NEW/LIB

B50

HOOVER G.,TWENTIETH CENTURY ECONOMIC THOUGHT. USA+45 ECO/DEV AGRI FINAN INDUS MARKET SERV/IND LABOR NAT/G...STAT 20. PAGE 62 F1213
ECO/TAC CAP/ISM INT/TRADE

B50

SURANYI-UNGER T.,PRIVATE ENTERPRISE AND GOVERNMENTAL PLANNING. STRUCT FINAN BAL/PWR HAPPINESS DRIVE NEW/LIB PLURISM...MATH QUANT STAT TREND BIBLIOG. PAGE 127 F2516
PLAN NAT/G LAISSEZ POLICY

B51

CLARK C.,THE CONDITIONS OF ECONOMIC PROGRESS. EUR+WWI WOR+45 WOR-45 ECO/DEV INDUS CAP/ISM MORAL ...WELF/ST METH/CNCPT STAT TOT/POP VAL/FREE 20. PAGE 25 F0477
MARKET WEALTH

B51

HARDMAN J.B.,THE HOUSE OF LABOR. LAW R+D NEIGH EDU/PROP LEAD ROUTINE REPRESENT GP/REL...POLICY STAT. PAGE 55 F1080
LABOR LOBBY ADMIN PRESS

B51

US HOUSE COMM APPROPRIATIONS,MUTUAL SECURITY PROGRAM APPROPRIATIONS FOR 1952: HEARINGS BEFORE A SUBCOMMITTEE OF THE COMMITTEE ON APPROPRIATIONS. AFR KOREA L/A+17C ECO/DEV ECO/UNDEV INT/ORG INSPECT BAL/PWR DIPLOM DEBATE WAR...POLICY STAT ASIA/S 20 CONGRESS NATO MID/EAST. PAGE 136 F2686
LEGIS FORCES BUDGET FOR/AID

S51

HAWLEY A.H.,"METROPOLITAN POPULATION AND MUNICIPAL GOVERNMENT EXPENDITURES IN CENTRAL CITIES" (BMR)" USA+45 FINAN TAX...STAT CON/ANAL CHARTS MUNICH 20. PAGE 57 F1117
GEOG LOC/G COST BUDGET

B52

ANDREWS F.E.,CORPORATION GIVING. LAW TAX EDU/PROP ADMIN...POLICY STAT CHARTS. PAGE 5 F0101
LG/CO GIVE SML/CO FINAN

B52

ASHWORTH W.,A SHORT HISTORY OF THE INTERNATIONAL ECONOMY 1850-1950. WOR+45 WOR-45 AGRI FINAN INDUS MARKET LABOR ECO/TAC...CONCPT STAT HIST/WRIT FOR/TRADE ILO 19/20. PAGE 7 F0131
ECO/DEV TEC/DEV INT/TRADE

B53

FLORENCE P.S.,THE LOGIC OF BRITISH AND AMERICAN INDUSTRY; A REALISTIC ANALYSIS OF ECONOMIC STRUCTURE AND GOVERNMENT. UK USA+45 USA-45 FINAN LABOR CAP/ISM INGP/REL EFFICIENCY...MGT CONCPT STAT CHARTS METH 20. PAGE 42 F0813
INDUS ECO/DEV NAT/G NAT/COMP

B53

MIT CENTER INTERNATIONAL STU,BIBLIOGRAPHY OF THE ECONOMIC AND POLITICAL DEVELOPMENT OF INDONESIA. INDONESIA STRUCT NAT/G COLONIAL LEAD...STAT 20. PAGE 92 F1805
BIBLIOG ECO/UNDEV TEC/DEV S/ASIA

B53

PURCELL T.V.,THE WORKER SPEAKS HIS MIND ON COMPANY AND UNION. WORKER ADJUD LEAD RACE/REL ATTIT DRIVE MARXISM...MGT CLASSIF STAT OBS INT SAMP BIBLIOG. PAGE 108 F2131
LABOR PARTIC INGP/REL HAPPINESS

L53

NELSON J.R.,"UNITED STATES FOREIGN ECONOMIC POLICY AND THE STERLING AREA." USA+45 WOR+45 NAT/G ECO/TAC WEALTH...STAT TIME/SEQ TREND CHARTS METH/GP TERR/GP CMN/WLTH 20. PAGE 97 F1911
FINAN DIPLOM UK

B54

EMERSON F.D.,SHAREHOLDER DEMOCRACY: A BROADER OUTLOOK FOR CORPORATIONS. DELIB/GP EX/STRUC LEGIS ADJUD CONTROL REPRESENT INGP/REL OWN PWR...POLICY STAT RECORD. PAGE 37 F0727
LG/CO PARTIC MAJORIT TREND

B54

LOCKLIN D.P.,ECONOMICS OF TRANSPORTATION (4TH ED.). USA+45 USA-45 SEA AIR LAW FINAN LG/CO EX/STRUC ADMIN CONTROL...STAT CHARTS 19/20 RAILROAD PUB/TRANS. PAGE 81 F1592
ECO/DEV DIST/IND ECO/TAC TEC/DEV

B54

MITCHELL W.G.,BUSINESS CYCLES. FINAN MARKET PRICE COST EQUILIB OPTIMAL PRODUC PROFIT...IDEA/COMP GEN/LAWS 19/20. PAGE 92 F1809
INDUS TIME/SEQ METH/COMP STAT

B54

O.E.E.C.,PRIVATE UNITED STATES INVESTMENT IN EUROPE AND THE OVERSEAS TERRITORIES. EUR+WWI WOR+45 ECO/DEV ECO/UNDEV INT/ORG NAT/G VOL/ASSN ECO/TAC ATTIT WEALTH...GEOG STAT SYS/QU CHARTS VAL/FREE 20. PAGE 99 F1950
USA+45 FINAN BAL/PAY FOR/AID

B54

SCHUMPETER J.A.,HISTORY OF ECONOMIC ANALYSIS. WOR-45...PHIL/SCI METH/CNCPT STAT IDEA/COMP GRECO/ROMN. PAGE 118 F2322
KNOWL GEN/LAWS METH

B54

TAFT P.,THE STRUCTURE AND GOVERNMENT OF LABOR UNIONS. SANCTION INGP/REL ORD/FREE PWR MARXISM ...MAJORIT STAT TREND. PAGE 128 F2524
LABOR ADJUD WORKER FINAN

B54

TINBERGEN J.,INTERNATIONAL ECONOMIC INTEGRATION. WOR+45 WOR-45 ECO/UNDEV NAT/G ECO/TAC BAL/PAY ...METH/CNCPT STAT TIME/SEQ GEN/METH OEEC 20. PAGE 130 F2574
INT/ORG ECO/DEV INT/TRADE

B55

BOULDING K.E.,ECONOMIC ANALYSIS (3RD ED.). USA+45 PLAN ECO/TAC COST DEMAND INCOME...POLICY STAT CHARTS SIMUL T. PAGE 17 F0322
PHIL/SCI ECO/DEV CAP/ISM

B55

OECD,MARSHALL PLAN IN TURKEY. TURKEY USA+45 COM/IND CONSTRUC SERV/IND FORCES BUDGET...STAT 20 MARSHL/PLN. PAGE 100 F1964
FOR/AID ECO/UNDEV AGRI INDUS

B55

UN ECONOMIC COMN ASIA & FAR E,ECONOMIC SURVEY OF ASIA AND THE FAR EAST, 1954. AFGHANISTN CEYLON INDIA PHILIPPINE S/ASIA ECO/DEV FINAN INDUS INT/TRADE PRODUC WEALTH...STAT CHARTS 20 CHINJAP. PAGE 132 F2600
ECO/UNDEV PRICE NAT/COMP ASIA

B55

US ADVISORY COMN INTERGOV REL,THE COMMISSION ON INTERGOVERNMENTAL RELATIONS; A REPORT TO THE PRESIDENT FOR TRANSMITTAL TO THE CONGRESS. USA+45 ECO/DEV AGRI COM/IND FINAN FORCES PLAN EDU/PROP HEALTH WEALTH...STAT MUNICH 20 CIV/DEFENS. PAGE 133 F2630
GOV/REL NAT/G LOC/G PROVS

S55

DIESING P.,"NONECONOMIC DECISION-MAKING" (BMR)" PROB/SOLV GP/REL ORD/FREE...STAT METH/COMP SIMUL 20. PAGE 33 F0638
DECISION METH EFFICIENCY SOC

B56

BELL P.W.,THE STERLING AREA IN THE POSTWAR WORLD. EUR+WWI FUT S/ASIA UK ECO/DEV PLAN DIPLOM WEALTH ...STAT RECORD CHARTS GEN/LAWS FOR/TRADE TOT/POP 20. PAGE 12 F0235
FINAN ECO/TAC

B56

GARDNER R.N.,STERLING-DOLLAR DIPLOMACY. EUR+WWI USA+45 INT/ORG NAT/G PLAN INT/TRADE EDU/PROP ADMIN KNOWL PWR WEALTH...POLICY SOC METH/CNCPT STAT CHARTS SIMUL GEN/LAWS 20. PAGE 46 F0902
ECO/DEV DIPLOM

B56

GREENHUT M.L.,PLANT LOCATION IN THEORY AND PRACTICE; THE ECONOMICS OF SPACE. WOR+45 WOR-45 MARKET WORKER COST DEMAND...CONCPT STAT CHARTS HYPO/EXP BIBLIOG 19/20. PAGE 51 F0991
SML/CO ECO/DEV CAP/ISM IDEA/COMP

B56

JUAN T.L.,ECONOMIC AND SOCIAL DEVELOPMENT OF MODERN CHINA: A BIBLIOGRAPHICAL GUIDE. ASIA AGRI COM/IND
BIBLIOG SOC

DIST/IND FINAN INDUS DIPLOM...STAT 20. PAGE 68 F1342 — ECO/TAC

B56
KINDLEBERGER C.P.,THE TERMS OF TRADE: A EUROPEAN CASE-STUDY. EUR+WWI MOD/EUR ECO/DEV ECO/UNDEV AGRI INDUS BAL/PAY...METH/CNCPT STAT CONT/OBS CON/ANAL SOC/EXP SIMUL FOR/TRADE 20. PAGE 71 F1390 — PLAN ECO/TAC

B56
UPHOFF W.H.,UNDERSTANDING THE UNION MEMBER (PAMPHLET). STRATA R+D LEAD PARTIC...METH/CNCPT STAT QU. PAGE 133 F2624 — LABOR WORKER ATTIT DRIVE

B56
YUAN TUNG-LI,ECONOMIC AND SOCIAL DEVELOPMENT OF MODERN CHINA: A BIBLIOGRAPHIC GUIDE. COM/IND FINAN FAM LABOR SECT CRIME INCOME...STAT SAMP CON/ANAL. PAGE 150 F2954 — BIBLIOG ASIA ECO/UNDEV SOC

B57
BOUSTEDT O.,REGIONALE STRUKTUR- UND WIRTSCHAFTSFORSCHUNG. WOR+45 WOR-45 PROVS...STAT MUNICH. PAGE 17 F0325 — GEOG CONCPT NAT/COMP

B57
HARRIS S.E.,INTERNATIONAL AND INTERREGIONAL ECONOMICS. AFR WOR+45 WOR-45 NAT/G TARIFFS BAL/PAY EQUILIB...POLICY CONCPT STAT CHARTS IDEA/COMP 19/20. PAGE 55 F1088 — INT/TRADE ECO/DEV MARKET FINAN

B57
NEUMARK S.D.,ECONOMIC INFLUENCES ON THE SOUTH AFRICAN FRONTIER, 1652-1836. SOUTH/AFR SEA AGRI NAT/G FORCES WORKER DIPLOM INT/TRADE PRICE DEMAND PRODUC...STAT CHARTS 17/19 FRONTIER. PAGE 97 F1915 — COLONIAL ECO/UNDEV ECO/TAC MARKET

B57
WARRINER D.,LAND REFORM AND DEVELOPMENT IN THE MIDDLE EAST: A STUDY OF EGYPT, SYRIA AND IRAQ. IRAQ ISLAM SYRIA UAR AGRI DIST/IND PLAN TEC/DEV DOMIN REV ATTIT WEALTH...SOC METH/CNCPT STAT OBS RECORD HIST/WRIT TREND GEN/LAWS FAO 20. PAGE 143 F2825 — ECO/UNDEV CONCPT

B58
BANCROFT G.,THE AMERICAN LABOR FORCE: ITS GROWTH AND CHANGING COMPOSITION. FUT USA+45 USA-45 ECO/DEV INDUS WORKER...GEOG CHARTS 19/20. PAGE 9 F0170 — LABOR STAT TREND CENSUS

B58
BIDWELL P.W.,RAW MATERIALS: A STUDY OF AMERICAN POLICY. USA+45 USA-45 ECO/UNDEV AGRI INDUS KIN CREATE PLAN ECO/TAC WAR PEACE ATTIT DRIVE WEALTH ...STAT CHARTS CONGRESS FOR/TRADE VAL/FREE. PAGE 15 F0279 — EXTR/IND ECO/DEV

B58
BROWN B.,INCOME TRENDS IN THE UNITED STATES THROUGH 1975. USA+45 NAT/G WEALTH...GEOG CENSUS PREDICT CHARTS METH 20. PAGE 19 F0366 — STAT INCOME TREND TAX

B58
KINDLEBERGER C.P.,INTERNATIONAL ECONOMICS. WOR+45 WOR-45 ECO/DEV ECO/UNDEV FINAN VOL/ASSN ACT/RES DIPLOM ECO/TAC LEGIT REGION ATTIT DRIVE ORD/FREE WEALTH...POLICY STAT TREND GEN/LAWS EEC ECSC OEEC 20. PAGE 71 F1391 — INT/ORG BAL/PWR TARIFFS

B58
MIKESELL R.F.,FINANCING FREE WORLD TRADE WITH THE SINO-SOVIET BLOC. CHINA/COM COM USSR WOR+45 ECO/DEV AGRI DIST/IND EXTR/IND FINAN INDUS MARKET PROC/MFG NAT/G PLAN TEC/DEV ECO/TAC...CHARTS METH/GP EEC FOR/TRADE 20. PAGE 91 F1780 — STAT BAL/PAY

B58
POLLOCK F.,AUTOMATION: A STUDY OF ITS ECONOMIC AND SOCIAL CONSEQUENCES. FUT USA+45 USA-45 SOCIETY ECO/DEV LABOR ACT/RES PLAN ECO/TAC AUTOMAT ROUTINE ALL/VALS...STAT TREND COMPUT/IR CHARTS SOC/EXP WORK 20. PAGE 107 F2099 — TEC/DEV SOC CAP/ISM

B58
ROBERTS B.C.,NATIONAL WAGES POLICY IN WAR AND PEACE. EUR+WWI GERMANY S/ASIA SWEDEN UK USA+45 USA-45 STRATA ECO/DEV LABOR NAT/G DELIB/GP PLAN INT/TRADE WEALTH...STAT TREND CHARTS 20. PAGE 112 F2205 — CREATE ECO/TAC

B58
SCITOUSKY T.,ECONOMIC THEORY AND WESTERN EUROPEAN INTEGRATION. EUR+WWI INT/ORG ACT/RES INT/TRADE REGION BAL/PAY WEALTH...METH/CNCPT STAT CHARTS GEN/METH ECSC TOT/POP EEC OEEC 20. PAGE 118 F2328 — ECO/TAC

B58
THEIL H.,ECONOMIC FORECASTS AND POLICY. UNIV CAP/ISM PRICE EFFICIENCY...DECISION CONCPT STAT 20. PAGE 129 F2551 — SIMUL MATH ECOMETRIC PREDICT

B58
US OPERATIONS MISSION TO VIET,BUILDING ECONOMIC STRENGTH (PAMPHLET). USA+45 VIETNAM/S INDUS TEC/DEV BUDGET ADMIN EATING HEALTH...STAT 20. PAGE 138 F2725 — FOR/AID ECO/UNDEV AGRI EDU/PROP

L58
ARROW K.J.,"ON THE STABILITY OF THE COMPETITIVE EQUILIBRIUM: I." WOR+45...METH/CNCPT MATH STAT CHARTS SIMUL. PAGE 6 F0122 — DECISION MARKET ECO/DEV ECO/TAC

S58
ARROW K.J.,"UTILITIES, ATTITUDES, CHOICES: A REVIEW NOTE." USA+45 PLAN...METH/CNCPT MATH STAT CHARTS HYPO/EXP. PAGE 6 F0121 — DECISION DIST/IND MARKET CREATE

S58
ARROW K.J.,"A NOTE ON EXPECTATIONS AND STABILITY." WOR+45...METH/CNCPT MATH STAT CHARTS HYPO/EXP. PAGE 7 F0123 — DECISION MARKET ECO/DEV ECO/TAC

B59
ALLEN R.L.,SOVIET INFLUENCE IN LATIN AMERICA. ECO/UNDEV FINAN PROC/MFG NAT/G TEC/DEV EDU/PROP EXEC ROUTINE ATTIT DRIVE PERSON ALL/VALS PWR...STAT CHARTS WORK FOR/TRADE 20. PAGE 4 F0071 — L/A+17C ECO/TAC INT/TRADE USSR

B59
DIEBOLD W. JR.,THE SCHUMAN PLAN: A STUDY IN ECONOMIC COOPERATION, 1950-1959. EUR+WWI FRANCE GERMANY USA+45 EXTR/IND CONSULT DELIB/GP PLAN DIPLOM ECO/TAC INT/TRADE ROUTINE ORD/FREE WEALTH ...METH/CNCPT STAT CONT/OBS INT TIME/SEQ ECSC 20. PAGE 33 F0635 — INT/ORG REGION

B59
MEYER A.J.,MIDDLE EASTERN CAPITALISM: NINE ESSAYS. ISLAM CULTURE ECO/UNDEV INDUS MARKET NAT/G PLAN ATTIT RIGID/FLEX...STAT OBS TREND GEN/LAWS. PAGE 90 F1767 — TEC/DEV ECO/TAC ANTHOL

B59
MORGENSTERN O.,INTERNATIONAL FINANCIAL TRANSACTIONS AND BUSINESS CYCLES. FRANCE GERMANY UK USA+45 USA-45 WOR+45 WOR-45 ECO/DEV ECO/TAC WEALTH ...CONCPT STAT CON/ANAL CHARTS 19/20. PAGE 93 F1832 — FINAN TIME/SEQ INT/TRADE

B59
SHUBIK M.,STRATEGY AND MARKET STRUCTURE: COMPETITION, OLIGOPOLY, AND THE THEORY OF GAMES. ELITES STRUCT MARKET OP/RES EXEC EFFICIENCY INCOME ...MGT MATH STAT CHARTS 20. PAGE 121 F2389 — ECO/DEV ECO/TAC DECISION GAME

B59
STOVEL J.A.,CANADA IN THE WORLD ECONOMY. CANADA PRICE DEMAND...STAT CHARTS BIBLIOG 20 VINER/J. PAGE 127 F2499 — INT/TRADE BAL/PAY FINAN ECO/TAC

B59
WIBBERLEY G.P.,AGRICULTURE AND URBAN GROWTH. UK USA+45 ECO/DEV FINAN PROB/SOLV INT/TRADE COST ...GEOG STAT CHARTS METH/COMP HYPO/EXP METH MUNICH 20. PAGE 146 F2876 — AGRI PLAN

L59
ARROW K.J.,"ON THE STABILITY OF THE COMPETITIVE EQUILIBRIUM: II." WOR+45...METH/CNCPT MATH STAT CHARTS HYPO/EXP. PAGE 7 F0124 — DECISION MARKET ECO/DEV ECO/TAC

L59
MURPHY J.C.,"SOME IMPLICATIONS OF EUROPE'S COMMON MARKET. IN (COOK P, ECONOMIC DEVELOPMENT AND INTERNATIONAL TRADE.," EUR+WWI ECO/DEV DIST/IND INDUS NAT/G PLAN ECO/TAC INT/TRADE WEALTH...STAT TREND OEEC TOT/POP 20 EEC. PAGE 95 F1866 — MARKET INT/ORG REGION

S59
DUNNING J.H.,"NON-PECUNIARY ELEMENTS AND BUSINESS BEHAVIOUR." PLAN PROB/SOLV COST...METH/CNCPT CLASSIF QUANT STAT. PAGE 35 F0681 — DECISION DRIVE PRODUC PRICE

S59
REUBENS E.D.,"THE BASIS FOR REORIENATION OF AMERICAN FOREIGN AID POLICY." USA+45 USSR STRUCT INT/ORG CONSULT ECO/TAC ADMIN DRIVE MORAL ORD/FREE PWR WEALTH...RELATIV MATH STAT TREND GEN/LAWS VAL/FREE 20. PAGE 111 F2180 — ECO/UNDEV PLAN FOR/AID DIPLOM

S59
TIPTON J.B.,"PARTICIPATION OF THE UNITED STATES IN THE INTERNATIONAL LABOR ORGANIZATION." USA+45 LAW STRUCT ECO/DEV ECO/UNDEV INDUS TEC/DEV ECO/TAC ADMIN PERCEPT ORD/FREE SKILL...STAT HIST/WRIT GEN/METH ILO WORK 20. PAGE 131 F2577 — LABOR INT/ORG

B60
AMERICAN U BEIRUT ECO RES INST,A SELECTED AND ANNOTATED BIBLIOGRAPHY OF ECONOMIC LITERATURE ON THE ARABIC SPEAKING COUNTRIES OF THE MIDDLE EAST. ISLAM AGRI COM/IND DIST/IND FINAN INDUS LABOR ...GEOG 20. PAGE 5 F0091 — BIBLIOG/A ECO/UNDEV STAT

B60
BATOR F.M.,QUESTION OF GOVERNMENT SPENDING. USA+45 DIST/IND FINAN BAL/PAY...STAT CENSUS CHARTS CONGRESS 20. PAGE 11 F0210 — ECO/DEV

B60
COMMITTEE ECONOMIC DEVELOPMENT,NATIONAL OBJECTIVES AND THE BALANCE OF PAYMENTS PROBLEM: A STATEMENT ON NATIONAL POLICY. USA+45 WOR+45 DIST/IND FINAN INDUS LABOR NAT/G DELIB/GP ACT/RES FOR/AID INT/TRADE ...STAT CHARTS FOR/TRADE 20. PAGE 27 F0516 — ECO/DEV ECO/TAC BAL/PAY

B60
FRANCK P.G.,AFGHANISTAN: BETWEEN EAST AND WEST. AFGHANISTN AFR USA+45 USSR ECO/UNDEV PLAN ADMIN ROUTINE ATTIT PWR...STAT OBS CHARTS TOT/POP — ECO/TAC TREND FOR/AID

FOR/TRADE 20. PAGE 43 F0843

B60

HARBERGER A.C.,THE DEMAND FOR DURABLE GOODS. AGRI FINAN COST EQUILIB...MATH STAT TIME/SEQ TREND CON/ANAL CHARTS SIMUL ANTHOL 20. PAGE 55 F1072
ECOMETRIC DEMAND PRICE

B60

HUGHES J.,NATIONALISED INDUSTRIES IN THE MIXED ECONOMY (PAMPHLET). FINAN PROB/SOLV CAP/ISM OWN ...SOCIALIST STAT METH/COMP 20. PAGE 63 F1233
SOCISM LG/CO GOV/REL ECO/DEV

B60

KRISTENSEN T.,THE ECONOMIC WORLD BALANCE. FUT WOR+45 CULTURE ECO/DEV BAL/PWR INT/TRADE REGION PWR WEALTH...STAT TREND CHARTS 20. PAGE 73 F1442
ECO/UNDEV ECO/TAC FOR/AID

B60

LERNER A.P.,THE ECONOMICS OF CONTROL. USA+45 ECO/UNDEV INT/ORG ACT/RES PLAN CAP/ISM INT/TRADE ATTIT WEALTH...SOC MATH STAT GEN/LAWS INDEX 20. PAGE 78 F1530
ECO/DEV ROUTINE ECO/TAC SOCISM

B60

LISTER L.,EUROPE'S COAL AND STEEL COMMUNITY. FRANCE GERMANY STRUCT ECO/DEV EXTR/IND INDUS MARKET NAT/G DELIB/GP ECO/TAC INT/TRADE EDU/PROP ATTIT RIGID/FLEX ORD/FREE PWR WEALTH...CONCPT STAT TIME/SEQ CHARTS ECSC TERR/GP 20. PAGE 81 F1582
EUR+WWI INT/ORG REGION

B60

MORRIS W.T.,ENGINEERING ECONOMY. AUTOMAT RISK RATIONAL...PROBABIL STAT CHARTS GAME SIMUL BIBLIOG T 20. PAGE 94 F1838
OP/RES DECISION MGT PROB/SOLV

B60

SILK L.S.,THE RESEARCH REVOLUTION. USA+45 FINAN CAP/ISM ECO/TAC PRICE EQUILIB PRODUC...STAT TREND CHARTS. PAGE 122 F2402
ECO/DEV R+D TEC/DEV PROB/SOLV

B60

STEIN E.,AMERICAN ENTERPRISE IN THE EUROPEAN COMMON MARKET: A LEGAL PROFILE. EUR+WWI FUT USA+45 SOCIETY STRUCT ECO/DEV NAT/G VOL/ASSN CONSULT PLAN TEC/DEV ECO/TAC INT/TRADE ADMIN ATTIT RIGID/FLEX PWR...MGT NEW/IDEA STAT TREND COMPUT/IR SIMUL EEC 20. PAGE 125 F2475
MARKET ADJUD INT/LAW

B60

STOLPER W.F.,GERMANY BETWEEN EAST AND WEST: THE ECONOMICS OF COMPETITIVE COEXISTENCE. AFR FUT GERMANY/E GERMANY/W WOR+45 FINAN POL/PAR BUDGET ECO/TAC FOR/AID INT/TRADE...STAT CHARTS METH/COMP 20. PAGE 126 F2495
ECO/DEV DIPLOM GOV/COMP BAL/PWR

B60

THE ECONOMIST (LONDON),THE COMMONWEALTH AND EUROPE. EUR+WWI WOR+45 AGRI FINAN INCOME...STAT CENSUS CHARTS CMN/WLTH EEC. PAGE 129 F2550
INT/TRADE INDUS INT/ORG NAT/COMP

B60

THORBECKE E.,THE TENDENCY TOWARDS REGIONALIZATION IN INTERNATIONAL TRADE, 1928-1956. WOR+45 WOR-45 ECO/DEV FINAN ECO/TAC WEALTH...GEOG CHARTS TOT/POP FOR/TRADE 20. PAGE 130 F2569
STAT BAL/PAY REGION

B60

US GENERAL ACCOUNTING OFFICE,EXAMINATION OF ECONOMIC AND TECHNICAL ASSISTANCE PROGRAM FOR GUATEMALA. GUATEMALA L/A+17C USA+45 FINAN INDUS PLAN...POLICY STAT CHARTS 20 DEPT/STATE. PAGE 136 F2680
FOR/AID ECO/UNDEV TEC/DEV NAT/G

S60

BARNETT H.J.,"RESEARCH AND DEVELOPMENT, ECONOMIC GROWTH, AND NATIONAL SECURITY." AFR USA+45 R+D CREATE ECO/TAC ATTIT DRIVE PWR...POLICY SOC METH/CNCPT QUANT STAT TIME/SEQ ORG/CHARTS LOG/LING 20. PAGE 10 F0190
ACT/RES PLAN

S60

BECKER A.S.,"COMPARISIONS OF UNITED STATES AND USSR NATIONAL OUTPUT: SOME RULES OF THE GAME." COM USA+45 ECO/DEV AGRI DIST/IND INDUS R+D CONSULT PLAN ECO/TAC RIGID/FLEX KNOWL...METH/CNCPT CHARTS 20. PAGE 12 F0227
STAT USSR

S60

ENKE S.,"THE ECONOMIES OF GOVERNMENT PAYMENTS TO LIMIT POPULATION." FUT INDIA WOR+45 CULTURE FINAN NAT/G CONSULT PLAN LEGIT CONTROL COST ATTIT RIGID/FLEX HEALTH WEALTH...STAT OBS CHARTS TOT/POP VAL/FREE 20. PAGE 38 F0736
FAM ACT/RES

S60

GARNICK D.H.,"ON THE ECONOMIC FEASIBILITY OF A MIDDLE EASTERN COMMON MARKET." AFR ISLAM CULTURE INDUS NAT/G PLAN TEC/DEV ECO/TAC ADMIN ATTIT DRIVE RIGID/FLEX...PLURIST STAT TREND GEN/LAWS 20. PAGE 46 F0907
MARKET INT/TRADE

S60

HERRERA F.,"THE INTER-AMERICAN DEVELOPMENT BANK." USA+45 ECO/UNDEV INT/ORG CONSULT DELIB/GP PLAN ECO/TAC INT/TRADE ROUTINE WEALTH...STAT TERR/GP 20. PAGE 59 F1153
L/A+17C FINAN FOR/AID REGION

S60

HOOVER C.B.,"NATIONAL POLICY AND RATES OF ECONOMIC GROWTH: THE US SOVIET RUSSIA AND WESTERN EUROPE." COM EUR+WWI USA+45 USSR NAT/G PLAN ECO/TAC PWR WEALTH...MATH STAT GEN/LAWS 20. PAGE 61 F1207
ECO/DEV ACT/RES

S60

JAFFEE A.J.,"POPULATION TRENDS AND CONTROLS IN UNDERDEVELOPED COUNTRIES." AFR FUT ISLAM L/A+17C S/ASIA CULTURE R+D FAM ACT/RES PLAN EDU/PROP BIO/SOC RIGID/FLEX HEALTH...SOC STAT OBS CHARTS 20. PAGE 66 F1303
ECO/UNDEV GEOG

S60

KELLOGG C.E.,"TRANSFER OF BASIC SKILLS OF FOOD PRODUCTION." AFR FUT S/ASIA STRATA ECO/UNDEV LABOR VOL/ASSN RIGID/FLEX...OLD/LIB SOCIALIST NEW/IDEA STAT PROJ/TEST GEN/LAWS 20. PAGE 70 F1370
AGRI PLAN

S60

NANES A.,"THE EUROPEAN COMMUNITY AND THE UNITED STATES: EVOLVING RELATIONS." EUR+WWI USA+45 WOR+45 ECO/UNDEV MARKET NAT/G DELIB/GP PLAN LEGIT ATTIT PWR WEALTH...CONCPT STAT TIME/SEQ CON/ANAL EEC METH/GP OEEC 20 EURATOM. PAGE 96 F1889
INT/ORG REGION

S60

STOCKWELL E.G.,"THE MEASUREMENT OF ECONOMIC DEVELOPMENT." WOR+45 SOCIETY ECO/DEV ECO/UNDEV INDUS ECO/TAC HEALTH WEALTH...WELF/ST GEOG METH/CNCPT CHARTS METH METH/GP 20. PAGE 126 F2492
FAM STAT

B61

DELEFORTRIE-SOU N.,LES DIRIGEANTS DE L'INDUSTRIE FRANCAISE. FRANCE CULTURE ELITES PROB/SOLV ...DECISION STAT CHARTS 20. PAGE 32 F0613
INDUS STRATA TOP/EX LEAD

B61

DEWITT N.,EDUCATION AND PROFESSIONAL EMPLOYMENT IN THE USSR. USSR PROF/ORG WORKER PLAN ADMIN UTIL AGE/C AGE/Y MARXISM...STAT CHARTS 20. PAGE 32 F0629
EDU/PROP ACADEM SCHOOL INTELL

B61

FRIEDMANN G.,THE ANATOMY OF WORK. USA+45 SOCIETY CONTROL ROUTINE DRIVE SKILL...PSY SOC STAT OBS METH/COMP PERS/COMP 20. PAGE 44 F0862
AUTOMAT WORKER INDUS PERSON

B61

GURTOO D.H.N.,INDIA'S BALANCE OF PAYMENTS (1920-1960). INDIA FINAN DIPLOM FOR/AID INT/TRADE PRICE COLONIAL...CHARTS BIBLIOG 20. PAGE 52 F1014
BAL/PAY STAT ECO/TAC ECO/UNDEV

B61

HODGKINS J.A.,SOVIET POWER: ENERGY RESOURCES, PRODUCTION AND POTENTIALS. USSR ECO/DEV INDUS MARKET...POLICY STAT CHARTS 20 RESOURCE/N. PAGE 60 F1188
GEOG EXTR/IND TEC/DEV

B61

HORVATH B.,THE CHARACTERISTICS OF YUGOSLAV ECONOMIC DEVELOPMENT. COM ECO/UNDEV AGRI INDUS PLAN CAP/ISM ECO/TAC ROUTINE WEALTH...SOCIALIST STAT CHARTS STERTYP WORK 20. PAGE 62 F1217
ACT/RES YUGOSLAVIA

B61

KLEIN L.R.,AN ECONOMETRIC MODEL OF THE UNITED KINGDOM. UK PRICE COST...MATH PREDICT TREND CHARTS SIMUL METH 20. PAGE 72 F1407
ECOMETRIC COMPUTER STAT COMPUT/IR

B61

LAMFALUSSY A.,INVESTMENT AND GROWTH IN MATURE ECONOMIES. BELGIUM EUR+WWI LABOR PRICE PRODUC PROFIT...STAT CONT/OBS CHARTS 20. PAGE 75 F1464
FINAN INDUS ECO/DEV CAP/ISM

B61

LONGRIGG S.H.,OIL IN THE MIDDLE EAST: ITS DISCOVERY AND DEVELOPMENT. ECO/UNDEV LG/CO LOC/G TEC/DEV WEALTH...STAT TIME/SEQ 20 OIL. PAGE 82 F1599
ISLAM EXTR/IND

B61

NORTH D.C.,THE ECONOMIC GROWTH OF THE UNITED STATES 1790-1860. USA-45 INDUS TEC/DEV CAP/ISM ECO/TAC PRICE COST DEMAND LAISSEZ...ECOMETRIC STAT TREND 19. PAGE 98 F1933
AGRI ECO/UNDEV

B61

OECD,STATISTICS OF BALANCE OF PAYMENTS 1950-61. WOR+45 FINAN ECO/TAC INT/TRADE DEMAND WEALTH...STAT NAT/COMP 20 OEEC OECD. PAGE 100 F1965
BAL/PAY ECO/DEV INT/ORG CHARTS

B61

TRIFFIN R.,GOLD AND THE DOLLAR CRISIS: THE FUTURE OF CONVERTIBILITY. AFR USA+45 USA-45 INT/ORG PROB/SOLV BUDGET INT/TRADE PRICE...STAT CHARTS 19/20. PAGE 131 F2588
FINAN ECO/DEV ECO/TAC BAL/PAY

B61

WEISBROD B.A.,ECONOMICS OF PUBLIC HEALTH. USA+45 INGP/REL HABITAT...POLICY STAT COSTS 20. PAGE 145 F2851
SOCIETY HEALTH NEW/IDEA ECO/DEV

B61

WESTON J.F.,THE ROLE OF MERGERS IN THE GROWTH OF LARGE FIRMS. USA+45 USA-45 LEGIS CONTROL...CONCPT STAT CHARTS 19/20. PAGE 145 F2862
LG/CO CENTRAL INDUS FINAN

S61

BENNION E.G.,"ECONOMETRICS FOR MANAGEMENT." USA+45 INDUS EX/STRUC ACT/RES COMPUTER UTIL...MATH STAT
ECOMETRIC MGT

PREDICT METH/COMP HYPO/EXP. PAGE 13 F0248 — SIMUL DECISION

S61 — CYERT R.M.,"TWO EXPERIMENTS ON BIAS AND CONFLICT IN ORGANIZATIONAL ESTIMATION." WORKER PROB/SOLV EFFICIENCY...MGT PSY STAT CHARTS. PAGE 29 F0568 — LAB/EXP ROUTINE ADMIN DECISION

S61 — DICKS-MIREAUX L.A.,"THE INTERRELATIONSHIP BETWEEN COST AND PRICE CHANGES 19461959: A STUDY OF INFLATION IN POST-WAR BRITAIN" AFR UK ECO/DEV INDUS WORKER ECO/TAC ORD/FREE WEALTH...ECOMETRIC REGRESS STAT TREND CHARTS 20. PAGE 33 F0634 — PRICE PAY DEMAND

S61 — HIRSHLEIFER J.,"THE BAYESIAN APPROACH TO STATISTICAL DECISION: AN EXPOSITION." OP/RES PROB/SOLV UTIL...PROBABIL CHARTS IDEA/COMP HYPO/EXP 20. PAGE 60 F1178 — DECISION GAME SIMUL STAT

S61 — RAY J.,"THE EUROPEAN FREE-TRADE ASSOCIATION AND ITS IMPACT ON INDIA'S TRADE." EUR+WWI FRANCE GERMANY INDIA S/ASIA UK NAT/G VOL/ASSN PLAN INT/TRADE ROUTINE WEALTH...STAT CHARTS TERR/GP CMN/WLTH EEC FOR/TRADE OEEC 20 EFTA. PAGE 109 F2155 — ECO/DEV ECO/TAC

S61 — SHUBIK M.,"APPROACHES TO THE STUDY OF DECISION-MAKING RELEVANT TO THE FIRM." INDUS COMPUTER OP/RES ...PROBABIL STAT 20. PAGE 121 F2390 — GAME DECISION MGT SIMUL

B62 — ALTMAN G.T.,INVISIBLE BARRIER: THE OPTIMUM GROWTH CURVE. USA+45 USA-45 ECO/DEV PLAN PAY CONTROL DEMAND OPTIMAL PRODUC WEALTH...STAT CHARTS 20. PAGE 4 F0080 — INDUS FINAN ECO/TAC TAX

B62 — BOGARDUS J.,OUTLINE FOR THE COURSE IN BUSINESS AND ECONOMICS LITERATURE (REV. ED; PAMPHLET). USA+45 FINAN INDUS NAT/G VOL/ASSN PRESS WRITING INDEX. PAGE 16 F0305 — BIBLIOG/A STAT

B62 — BRANCH M.C.,THE CORPORATE PLANNING PROCESS. FINAN EX/STRUC EDU/PROP CONTROL LEAD GP/REL PERS/REL RATIONAL PERCEPT...MGT MATH PROBABIL STAT GAME. PAGE 18 F0338 — PROF/ORG PLAN DECISION PERSON

B62 — COPPOCK J.D.,INTERNATIONAL ECONOMIC INSTABILITY: THE EXPERIENCE AFTER WORLD WAR II. WOR+45 FINAN CAP/ISM CONTROL EFFICIENCY...CHARTS 20. PAGE 28 F0536 — ECO/TAC ECOMETRIC INT/TRADE STAT

B62 — DENISON E.F.,THE SOURCES OF ECONOMIC GROWTH IN THE UNITED STATES AND THE ALTERNATIVES BEFORE US. AGRI INDUS SCHOOL TEC/DEV CAP/ISM ECO/TAC PRICE COST WEALTH...STAT TREND CHARTS 20. PAGE 32 F0620 — ECO/DEV WORKER PRODUC

B62 — FERBER R.,RESEARCH METHODS IN ECONOMICS AND BUSINESS. AFR ECO/DEV FINAN MARKET LG/CO SML/CO CONSULT CONTROL COST...STAT METH/COMP 20. PAGE 40 F0783 — ACT/RES PROB/SOLV ECO/TAC MGT

B62 — FORD A.G.,THE GOLD STANDARD 1880-1914: BRITAIN AND ARGENTINA. AFR UK ECO/UNDEV INT/TRADE ADMIN GOV/REL DEMAND EFFICIENCY...STAT CHARTS 19/20 ARGEN. PAGE 42 F0823 — FINAN ECO/TAC BUDGET BAL/PAY

B62 — GEARY R.C.,EUROPE'S FUTURE IN FIGURES. FUT GOV/REL DEMAND PRODUC...STAT CHARTS METH/COMP ANTHOL METH 20 EUROPE. PAGE 47 F0912 — FINAN ECO/DEV PREDICT WEALTH

B62 — GORT M.,DIVERSIFICATION AND INTEGRATION IN AMERICAN INDUSTRY. CLIENT DIST/IND PROC/MFG SERV/IND LG/CO CONTROL DEMAND PWR...METH/CNCPT STAT TREND CON/ANAL GP/COMP. PAGE 49 F0964 — CONCPT GP/REL CLASSIF

B62 — KLEIN L.R.,AN INTRODUCTION TO ECONOMETRICS. DIST/IND DEMAND PRODUC WEALTH...MATH TIME/SEQ T 20. PAGE 72 F1408 — ECOMETRIC SIMUL PREDICT STAT

B62 — KUHN T.E.,PUBLIC ENTERPRISES, PROJECT PLANNING AND ECONOMIC DEVELOPMENT (PAMPHLET). ECO/UNDEV FINAN PLAN ADMIN EFFICIENCY OWN...MGT STAT CHARTS ANTHOL 20. PAGE 74 F1447 — ECO/DEV ECO/TAC LG/CO NAT/G

B62 — LICHFIELD N.,COST-BENEFIT ANALYSIS IN URBAN REDEVELOPMENT. CONSTRUC LOC/G NEIGH ACT/RES PROB/SOLV TEC/DEV BUDGET TAX...DECISION STAT CHARTS SOC/EXP MUNICH 20. PAGE 80 F1558 — PLAN COST GOV/REL

B62 — MEADE J.E.,CASE STUDIES IN EUROPEAN ECONOMIC UNION. BELGIUM EUR+WWI LUXEMBOURG NAT/G INT/TRADE REGION ROUTINE WEALTH...METH/CNCPT STAT CHARTS ECSC TOT/POP OEEC EEC FOR/TRADE 20. PAGE 89 F1738 — INT/ORG ECO/TAC

B62 — SEN S.R.,THE STRATEGY FOR AGRICULTURAL DEVELOPMENT AND OTHER ESSAYS ON ECONOMIC POLICY AND PLANNING. INDIA FINAN ACT/RES TEC/DEV CAP/ISM PRICE...STAT 20. PAGE 119 F2354 — ECO/UNDEV PLAN AGRI POLICY

B62 — UNECA LIBRARY,BOOKS ON AFRICA IN THE UNECA LIBRARY. WOR+45 AGRI INT/ORG NAT/G PLAN WRITING REGION...SOC STAT UN. PAGE 132 F2605 — BIBLIOG AFR ECO/UNDEV TEC/DEV

B62 — US AGENCY INTERNATIONAL DEV,OPERATIONS REPORT - 1962 (PAMPHLET). AFR ASIA L/A+17C USA+45 ECO/UNDEV FINAN INT/ORG NAT/G 20 MICHIGAN. PAGE 134 F2636 — FOR/AID CHARTS STAT BUDGET

B62 — US BUREAU OF THE CENSUS,REPORT FOR SUBCOMMITTEE ON ANTITRUST AND MONOPOLY: CONCENTRATION RATIOS IN MANUFACTURING INDUSTRY 1958. USA+45 ECO/DEV CONTROL GOV/REL OWN PRODUC PROFIT...STAT 20 CONGRESS MONOPOLY. PAGE 134 F2646 — CHARTS PROC/MFG MARKET LG/CO

L62 — MACHLUP F.,"PLANS FOR REFORM OF THE INTERNATIONAL MONETARY SYSTEM. PRINCETON: U. PR., 1962, 70 PP., $0.25." WOR+45 INT/ORG ECO/TAC BAL/PAY HEALTH ORD/FREE WEALTH MID/EX TERR/GP VAL/FREE APPLIC 20. PAGE 83 F1631 — ECO/DEV STAT

S62 — BIERMAN H.,"PROBABILITY, STATISTICAL DECISION THEORY, AND ACCOUNTING." ACADEM TASK EFFICIENCY ...METH/CNCPT GEN/METH 20. PAGE 15 F0283 — FINAN QUANT DECISION STAT

S62 — BOONE A.,"THE FOREIGN TRADE OF CHINA." AFR ECO/DEV ECO/UNDEV INDUS MARKET NAT/G TEC/DEV WEALTH ...POLICY STAT TREND CHARTS FOR/TRADE. PAGE 17 F0318 — ASIA ECO/TAC

S62 — MUELLER E.,"LOCATION DECISIONS OF MANUFACTURERS." USA+45 MARKET ATTIT...POLICY STAT INT CHARTS 20. PAGE 94 F1852 — DECISION PROC/MFG GEOG TOP/EX

S62 — READ W.H.,"UPWARD COMMUNICATION IN INDUSTRIAL HIERARCHIES." LG/CO TOP/EX PROB/SOLV DOMIN EXEC PERS/REL ATTIT DRIVE PERCEPT...CORREL STAT CHARTS 20. PAGE 110 F2159 — ADMIN INGP/REL PSY MGT

C62 — JOINT ECONOMIC COMMITTEE,"DIMENSIONS OF SOVIET ECONOMIC POWER." USSR R+D FORCES ACT/RES OP/RES TEC/DEV...GEOG STAT BIBLIOG 20. PAGE 68 F1337 — ECO/DEV PLAN PRODUC LABOR

N62 — BANK INTERNATIONAL SETTLEMENTS,AUSTRIA: MONETARY AND ECONOMIC SITUATION 1952-61 (PAMPHLET). AUSTRIA WORKER BUDGET INT/TRADE PRICE BAL/PAY DEMAND EFFICIENCY INCOME PRODUC...STAT 20 SILVER. PAGE 9 F0174 — FINAN ECO/DEV CHARTS WEALTH

B63 — ABSHIRE D.M.,NATIONAL SECURITY: POLITICAL, MILITARY, AND ECONOMIC STRATEGIES IN THE DECADE AHEAD. ASIA COM USA+45 WOR+45 ECO/DEV ECO/UNDEV INT/ORG DELIB/GP FORCES ECO/TAC COERCE ATTIT RIGID/FLEX HEALTH ORD/FREE PWR WEALTH...POLICY STAT CHARTS ANTHOL COLD/WAR VAL/FREE APP/SCI. PAGE 2 F0032 — FUT ACT/RES BAL/PWR

B63 — BENOIT E.,DISARMAMENT AND THE ECONOMY. USA+45 NAT/G ACT/RES ECO/TAC BAL/PAY...STAT CON/ANAL GEN/LAWS 20. PAGE 13 F0252 — ECO/DEV ARMS/CONT

B63 — CHATTERJEE I.K.,ECONOMIC DEVELOPMENT PAYMENTS DEFICIT AND PAYMENT RESTRICTION. INDIA WOR+45 FINAN INT/TRADE CONTROL BAL/PAY WEALTH...POLICY CONCPT STAT CHARTS IDEA/COMP BIBLIOG 20. PAGE 23 F0456 — ECO/DEV ECO/TAC PAY GOV/REL

B63 — COPPOCK J.,NORTH ATLANTIC POLICY - THE AGRICULTURAL GAP. EUR+WWI ELITES ECO/DEV DIST/IND MARKET PLAN WEALTH...STAT TREND GEN/LAWS OEEC TOT/POP VAL/FREE FAO 20. PAGE 27 F0535 — AGRI TEC/DEV INT/TRADE

B63 — DE VRIES E.,SOCIAL ASPECTS OF ECONOMIC DEVELOPMENT IN LATIN AMERICA. CULTURE SOCIETY STRATA FINAN INDUS INT/ORG DELIB/GP ACT/RES ECO/TAC EDU/PROP ADMIN ATTIT SUPEGO HEALTH KNOWL ORD/FREE...SOC STAT TREND ANTHOL TOT/POP VAL/FREE. PAGE 31 F0608 — L/A+17C ECO/UNDEV

B63 — DUE J.F.,STATE SALES TAX ADMINISTRATION. OP/RES BUDGET PAY ADMIN EXEC ROUTINE COST EFFICIENCY PROFIT...CHARTS METH/COMP 20. PAGE 34 F0671 — PROVS TAX STAT GOV/COMP

B63 — GANGULI B.N.,ECONOMIC CONSEQUENCES OF DISARMAMENT. EUR+WWI ECO/DEV ECO/UNDEV FORCES ACT/RES BUDGET DIPLOM INT/TRADE...STAT CHARTS NAT/COMP. PAGE 46 F0896 — ECOMETRIC ARMS/CONT COST HYPO/EXP

B63 — GANGULY D.S.,PUBLIC CORPORATIONS IN A NATIONAL — ECO/UNDEV

ECONOMY. INDIA WOR+45 FINAN INDUS TOP/EX PRICE EFFICIENCY...MGT STAT CHARTS BIBLIOG 20. PAGE 46 F0897 — LG/CO SOCISM GOV/REL

B63
GLADE W.P. JR.,THE POLITICAL ECONOMY OF MEXICO. FUT L/A+17C CULTURE SOCIETY AGRI INDUS DELIB/GP ACT/RES ECO/TAC ATTIT HEALTH ORD/FREE...STAT TIME/SEQ TREND MEXIC/AMER TOT/POP VAL/FREE 20. PAGE 48 F0928 — FINAN ECO/UNDEV

B63
GRUBEL H.G.,WORLD MONETARY REFORM: PLANS AND ISSUES. FUT WOR+45 ECO/DEV ECO/UNDEV R+D DELIB/GP CREATE ECO/TAC ATTIT RIGID/FLEX WEALTH...STAT ANTHOL VAL/FREE 20. PAGE 52 F1009 — FINAN INT/ORG BAL/PAY INT/TRADE

B63
HIRSCHMAN A.O.,JOURNEYS TOWARD PROGRESS: STUDIES OF ECONOMIC POLICYMAKING IN LATIN AMERICA. CHILE FUT ECO/UNDEV AGRI FINAN INDUS CONSULT DELIB/GP PLAN ATTIT HEALTH ORD/FREE WEALTH...POLICY STAT VAL/FREE COLOMB 20. PAGE 60 F1177 — L/A+17C ECO/TAC BRAZIL

B63
HOLLAND E.P.,EXPERIMENTS ON A SIMULATED UNDERDEVELOPED ECONOMY: DEVELOPMENT PLANS AND BALANCE-OF-PAYMENTS POLICIES. WOR+45 ECO/UNDEV FINAN PLAN ECO/TAC...MATH STAT CHARTS SIMUL VAL/FREE. PAGE 61 F1196 — AFR BAL/PAY

B63
ISSAWI C.,EGYPT IN REVOLUTION: AN ECONOMIC ANALYSIS. ISLAM STRUCT ECO/UNDEV AGRI FINAN INDUS PLAN EXEC REV NAT/LISM ATTIT RIGID/FLEX WEALTH SOCISM...STAT FOR/TRADE WORK 20. PAGE 66 F1292 — NAT/G UAR

B63
JOHNSTON J.,ECONOMETRIC METHODS. PROB/SOLV WRITING ...REGRESS CHARTS T. PAGE 68 F1333 — ECOMETRIC PHIL/SCI OP/RES STAT

B63
KRAVIS I.B.,DOMESTIC INTERESTS AND INTERNATIONAL OBLIGATIONS: SAFEGUARDS IN INTERNATIONAL TRADE ORGANIZATIONS. EUR+WWI USA+45 WOR+45 FINAN DELIB/GP ATTIT RIGID/FLEX HEALTH...STAT EEC VAL/FREE OEEC ECSC 20. PAGE 73 F1435 — INT/ORG ECO/TAC INT/TRADE

B63
LAGOS G.,INTERNATIONAL STRATIFICATION AND UNDERDEVELOPED COUNTRIES. L/A+17C WOR+45 PLAN ECO/TAC PWR RESPECT WEALTH...METH/CNCPT STAT CHARTS SIMUL GEN/LAWS TRUE/GP METH/GP VAL/FREE 20. PAGE 74 F1459 — ECO/UNDEV STRATA

B63
LAIRD R.D.,SOVIET AGRICULTURAL AND PEASANT AFFAIRS. FUT STRATA LOC/G DELIB/GP ACT/RES TEC/DEV ECO/TAC EDU/PROP ATTIT RIGID/FLEX ORD/FREE SKILL WEALTH ...STAT CON/ANAL ANTHOL MUNICH WORK VAL/FREE 20. PAGE 74 F1461 — COM AGRI POLICY

B63
MACHLUP F.,ESSAYS ON ECONOMIC SEMANTICS. UNIV ECO/DEV FINAN COST DEMAND PRODUC...POLICY STAT CHARTS BIBLIOG. PAGE 83 F1632 — LING CONCPT METH

B63
MAIZELS A.,INDUSTRIAL GROWTH AND WORLD TRADE. FUT WOR+45 ECO/DEV FINAN INT/ORG PLAN TEC/DEV ECO/TAC WEALTH...MATH STAT CHARTS VAL/FREE 19/20. PAGE 84 F1642 — INDUS ECO/UNDEV INT/TRADE

B63
MEIER G.,INTERNATIONAL TRADE AND DEVELOPMENT. FINAN BAL/PAY COST DEMAND DISCRIM EQUILIB WEALTH...POLICY ECOMETRIC MATH STAT BIBLIOG/A 20. PAGE 89 F1747 — ECO/UNDEV ECO/TAC INT/TRADE IDEA/COMP

B63
MULLENBACH P.,CIVILIAN NUCLEAR POWER: ECONOMIC ISSUES AND POLICY FORMATION. AFR FINAN INT/ORG DELIB/GP ACT/RES ECO/TAC ATTIT SUPEGO HEALTH ORD/FREE PWR...POLICY CONCPT MATH STAT CHARTS VAL/FREE 20. PAGE 94 F1855 — USA+45 ECO/DEV NUC/PWR

B63
PRYOR F.L.,THE COMMUNIST FOREIGN TRADE SYSTEM. COM CZECHOSLVK GERMANY YUGOSLAVIA LAW ECO/DEV DIST/IND POL/PAR PLAN DOMIN TOTALISM DRIVE RIGID/FLEX WEALTH ...STAT STAND/INT CHARTS FOR/TRADE 20. PAGE 108 F2130 — ATTIT ECO/TAC

B63
RUMMEL J.F.,RESEARCH METHODOLOGY IN BUSINESS. COMPUTER CREATE PROB/SOLV...CONT/OBS REC/INT QU/SEMANT SYS/QU SAMP CHARTS METH/COMP T 20. PAGE 115 F2260 — OP/RES METH/CNCPT METH STAT

B63
SALANT W.S.,THE UNITED STATES BALANCE OF PAYMENTS IN 1968. USA+45 ECO/DEV ECO/UNDEV INT/ORG DELIB/GP ECO/TAC...POLICY STAT SIMUL 20. PAGE 115 F2273 — FUT FINAN BAL/PAY

B63
UNITED NATIONS,THE GROWTH OF WORLD INDUSTRY, 1938-1961: NATIONAL TABLES. WOR+45 STRUCT ECO/DEV ECO/UNDEV NAT/G COST...CHARTS UN. PAGE 132 F2613 — STAT INDUS PRODUC ORD/FREE

B63
US AGENCY INTERNATIONAL DEV,OPERATIONS REPORT - 1963. AFR ASIA L/A+17C USA+45 ECO/UNDEV FINAN INT/ORG NAT/G. PAGE 134 F2637 — FOR/AID CHARTS STAT BUDGET

B63
US BD GOVERNORS FEDL RESRV,THE FEDERAL RESERVE AND THE TREASURY. USA+45 WORKER PROB/SOLV PRICE COST DEMAND WEALTH...STAT INT CHARTS 20 FED/RESERV DEPT/TREAS. PAGE 134 F2641 — FINAN GOV/REL CONTROL BUDGET

B63
US GOVERNMENT,REPORT TO INTER-AMERICAN ECONOMIC AND SOCIAL COUNCIL AT SECOND ANNUAL MEETING. L/A+17C USA+45 VOL/ASSN TEC/DEV DIPLOM TAX EATING EFFICIENCY HEALTH...STAT CHARTS 20 AID. PAGE 136 F2682 — ECO/TAC FOR/AID FINAN PLAN

B63
US SENATE COMM GOVT OPERATIONS,REPORT OF A STUDY OF US FOREIGN AID IN TEN MIDDLE EASTERN AND AFRICAN COUNTRIES. AFR ISLAM USA+45 FORCES PLAN BUDGET DIPLOM TAX DETER WEALTH...STAT CHARTS 20 CONGRESS AID MID/EAST. PAGE 138 F2728 — FOR/AID EFFICIENCY ECO/TAC FINAN

B63
VELEZ GARCIA J.,DEVALUACION 1962; HISTORIA DOCUMENTAL DE UN PROCESO ECONOMICO. AFR L/A+17C USA+45 FINAN FOR/AID PRODUC WEALTH...POLICY STAT CHARTS ANTHOL 20 COLOMB. PAGE 141 F2774 — ECO/UNDEV ECO/TAC PLAN NAT/G

L63
ADERBIGDE A.,"SYMPOSIUM ON WEST AFRICA INTEGRATION." AFR EUR+WWI FUT CULTURE SOCIETY STRATA DIST/IND INDUS MARKET SERV/IND DELIB/GP PLAN TEC/DEV DOMIN EDU/PROP LEGIT COERCE ATTIT ALL/VALS ...POLICY STAT TREND CHARTS VAL/FREE. PAGE 2 F0040 — FINAN ECO/TAC REGION

L63
KUZNETS S.,"QUANTITATIVE ASPECTS OF THE ECONOMIC GROWTH OF NATIONS: DISTRIBUTION OF INCOME BY SIZE." WOR+45 FINAN ACT/RES HEALTH...MATH STAT VAL/FREE 20. PAGE 74 F1454 — WEALTH ECO/TAC

L63
MCKERSIE R.B.,"NONPROFESSIONAL HOSPITAL WORKERS AND A UNION ORGANIZING DRIVE." PLAN GP/REL RACE/REL ATTIT DRIVE...CORREL STAT INT GP/COMP. PAGE 88 F1732 — VOL/ASSN HEALTH INGP/REL LABOR

L63
NASH M.,"PSYCHO-CULTURAL FACTORS IN ASIAN ECONOMIC GROWTH." ASIA ISLAM S/ASIA CULTURE ECO/UNDEV DELIB/GP EDU/PROP COERCE ATTIT PERSON HEALTH KNOWL ORD/FREE...PSY SOC STAT TREND ANTHOL VAL/FREE 20. PAGE 96 F1893 — SOCIETY ECO/TAC

L63
PADELFORD N.J.,"FINANCIAL CRISIS AND THE UNITED NATIONS." FUT USSR WOR+45 LAW CONSTN FINAN INT/ORG DELIB/GP FORCES PLAN BUDGET DIPLOM COST WEALTH ...STAT CHARTS UN CONGO 20. PAGE 102 F2012 — CREATE ECO/TAC

S63
ARDANT G.,"A PLAN FOR FULL EMPLOYMENT IN THE DEVELOPING COUNTRIES." AFR FUT WOR+45 DELIB/GP ACT/RES PLAN ECO/TAC ATTIT ALL/VALS...POLICY STAT CHARTS TUNIS VAL/FREE 20. PAGE 6 F0112 — ECO/UNDEV SOCIETY MOROCCO

S63
CARTER A.G.T.,"THE BALANCE OF PAYMENTS OF EAST AFRICA" AFR ECO/TAC FOR/AID RATION TARIFFS TAX ADMIN...STAT 20 AFRICA/E. PAGE 22 F0423 — BUDGET ECO/UNDEV BAL/PAY INT/TRADE

S63
CLARK P.G.,"TOWARDS MORE COMPREHENSIVE PLANNING IN EAST AFRICA" AFR OP/RES ECO/TAC RATION TAX EFFICIENCY INCOME...MATH TREND CHARTS 20 AFRICA/E. PAGE 25 F0484 — ECO/UNDEV PLAN STAT METH/COMP

S63
GALENSON W.,"ECONOMIC DEVELOPMENT AND THE SECTORAL EXPANSION OF EMPLOYMENT, INT." FUT WOR+45 ECO/UNDEV DIST/IND PROC/MFG SERV/IND ACT/RES HEALTH SKILL WEALTH...STAT TIME/SEQ VAL/FREE 20. PAGE 46 F0889 — INDUS ECO/TAC

S63
GORDON B.,"ECONOMIC IMPEDIMENTS TO REGIONALISM IN SOUTH EAST ASIA." BURMA FUT S/ASIA THAILAND USA+45 AGRI INDUS R+D NAT/G PLAN ECO/TAC WEALTH...STAT CONT/OBS 20. PAGE 49 F0954 — VOL/ASSN ECO/UNDEV INT/TRADE REGION

S63
GREEN P.E.,"BAYESIAN DECISION THEORY IN PRICING STRATEGY."...STAT CHARTS. PAGE 51 F0988 — OP/RES PROB/SOLV BARGAIN PRICE

S63
GRUSHIN B.A.,"PROBLEMS OF THE MOVEMENT OF COMMUNIST LABOR IN THE USSR." COM SOCIETY LABOR ECO/TAC EDU/PROP COERCE RIGID/FLEX ORD/FREE...POLICY MARXIST STAT QU WORK 20. PAGE 52 F1011 — ATTIT USSR

S63
HALLSTEIN W.,"THE EUROPEAN COMMUNITY AND ATLANTIC PARTNERSHIP." EUR+WWI USA+45 MARKET NAT/G VOL/ASSN DELIB/GP ARMS/CONT NUC/PWR ATTIT PWR...CONCPT STAT TIME/SEQ TREND OEEC 20 EEC. PAGE 54 F1053 — INT/ORG ECO/TAC UK

S63
LOEWENSTEIN L.K.,"THE LOCATION OF URBAN LAND USES." USA+45 LOC/G HABITAT...STAT CHARTS MUNICH 20. PAGE 81 F1595 — GEOG PLAN INDUS

S63
MATHUR P.N.,"GAINS IN ECONOMIC GROWTH FROM INTERNATIONAL TRADE." USA-45 ECO/DEV FINAN INDUS ATTIT WEALTH...MATH QUANT STAT BIOG TREND GEN/LAWS WORK 20. PAGE 87 F1704 MARKET ECO/TAC CAP/ISM INT/TRADE

S63
MILLEN B.H.,"INTERNATIONAL TRADE AND POLITICAL INDEPENDENCE." WOR+45 ECO/DEV WEALTH...STAT CHARTS FOR/TRADE METH/GP TERR/GP VAL/FREE 20. PAGE 91 F1788 ECO/UNDEV ECO/TAC INT/TRADE

S63
PAAUW D.S.,"ECONOMIC PROGRESS IN SOUTHEAST ASIA." S/ASIA AGRI INDUS PROC/MFG ACT/RES ECO/TAC...CHARTS VAL/FREE 20. PAGE 102 F2010 ECO/UNDEV STAT

S63
PINCUS J.,"THE COST OF FOREIGN AID." WOR+45 ECO/DEV FINAN NAT/G VOL/ASSN CREATE ECO/TAC EDU/PROP WEALTH ...METH/CNCPT STAT CHARTS HYPO/EXP TOT/POP VAL/FREE 20. PAGE 106 F2087 USA+45 ECO/UNDEV FOR/AID

S63
POLYANOV N.,"THE DOLLAR'S VENTURES IN EUROPE." EUR+WWI FRANCE USA+45 ECO/DEV MARKET POL/PAR TEC/DEV ECO/TAC EDU/PROP DRIVE PWR WEALTH...MARXIST MYTH STAT TREND EEC 20. PAGE 107 F2100 FINAN PLAN BAL/PAY CAP/ISM

S63
SHWADRAN B.,"MIDDLE EAST OIL, 1962." ISLAM DIST/IND INDUS PLAN ATTIT DRIVE WEALTH...POLICY STAT CONT/OBS TREND CHARTS GEN/LAWS TERR/GP METH/GP 20 OIL. PAGE 121 F2393 PROC/MFG ECO/TAC ELITES REGION

S63
SHWADRAN B.,"MIDDLE EAST OIL, 1962." ISLAM USSR ECO/DEV DIST/IND INDUS PLAN BAL/PWR DISPL DRIVE ...POLICY STAT TREND GEN/LAWS TERR/GP METH/GP EEC OEEC 20 OIL. PAGE 121 F2394 MARKET ECO/TAC INT/TRADE

S63
WILES P.J.D.,"WILL CAPITALISM AND COMMUNISM SPONTANEOUSLY CONVERGE." COM FUT USA+45 ECO/DEV DIST/IND MARKET CAP/ISM ECO/TAC RIGID/FLEX WEALTH MARXISM SOCISM...MATH STAT TREND COMPUT/IR 20. PAGE 146 F2885 PLAN TEC/DEV USSR

N63
LEDERER W.,THE BALANCE ON FOREIGN TRANSACTIONS: PROBLEMS OF DEFINITION AND MEASUREMENT (PAMPHLET). USA+45 BUDGET DIPLOM ECO/TAC PRICE GOV/REL...POLICY STAT NAT/COMP METH 20. PAGE 77 F1502 FINAN BAL/PAY INT/TRADE ECO/DEV

B64
BALASSA B.,TRADE PROSPECTS FOR DEVELOPING COUNTRIES. WOR+45 ECO/DEV AGRI EXTR/IND INDUS CREATE PLAN PRICE...ECOMETRIC CLASSIF TIME/SEQ GEN/METH. PAGE 8 F0158 INT/TRADE ECO/UNDEV TREND STAT

B64
BOWEN W.G.,ECONOMIC ASPECTS OF EDUCATION (NO. 104). EUR+WWI UK USA+45 PROF/ORG PLAN TEC/DEV PAY ...POLICY STAT 20. PAGE 17 F0329 EDU/PROP ACADEM FINAN METH/COMP

B64
BROWN W.M.,THE EXTERNAL LIQUIDITY OF AN ADVANCED COUNTRY. CANADA FRANCE GERMANY/W SWEDEN UK USA+45 ECO/DEV DIPLOM PRICE...CONCPT STAT NAT/COMP 20. PAGE 20 F0376 FINAN INT/TRADE COST INCOME

B64
CLAIRBORN E.L.,FORECASTING THE BALANCE OF PAYMENTS: AN EVALUATION. AFR FUT UK USA+45 WOR+45 FINAN PLAN BUDGET PAY CONTROL...STAT CHARTS BIBLIOG 20. PAGE 24 F0474 PREDICT BAL/PAY ECO/DEV ECO/TAC

B64
FEI J.C.H.,DEVELOPMENT OF THE LABOR SURPLUS ECONOMY: THEORY AND POLICY. WOR+45 AGRI INDUS MARKET PROB/SOLV TEC/DEV...STAT CHARTS GEN/LAWS METH 20 THIRD/WRLD. PAGE 40 F0772 ECO/TAC POLICY WORKER ECO/UNDEV

B64
FIRTH R.,CAPITAL, SAVING AND CREDIT IN PEASANT SOCIETIES. WOR+45 WOR-45 FAM ACT/RES ECO/TAC HEALTH ...SOC CONCPT STAT CHARTS ANTHOL CARIBBEAN VAL/FREE 20. PAGE 41 F0803 AGRI FINAN

B64
FITCH L.C.,URBAN TRANSPORTATION AND PUBLIC POLICY. FINAN NAT/G LEGIS PROB/SOLV TEC/DEV PRICE COST EFFICIENCY...DECISION STAT CHARTS METH/COMP MUNICH 20 NEWYORK/C PHILADELPH LOS/ANG CHICAGO WASHING/DC. PAGE 41 F0806 DIST/IND PLAN LOC/G

B64
FRIEDMANN J.,REGIONAL DEVELOPMENT AND PLANNING: A READER. AGRI MARKET NAT/G ECO/TAC INCOME...GEOG STAT CENSUS CHARTS ANTHOL BIBLIOG MUNICH 20 OPEN/SPACE. PAGE 44 F0863 PLAN REGION INDUS ECO/DEV

B64
HARRIS S.E.,ECONOMICS OF THE KENNEDY YEARS AND A LOOK AHEAD. USA+45 PLAN BUDGET NEW/LIB...STAT RECORD IDEA/COMP PERS/COMP INDEX 20 KENNEDY/JF EISNHWR/DD JOHNSON/LB. PAGE 56 F1091 ECO/TAC CHIEF POLICY NAT/G

B64
HART P.E.,ECONOMETRIC ANALYSIS FOR NATIONAL ECONOMIC PLANNING. INDUS OP/RES PRICE PRODUC ...SIMUL ANTHOL MODELS 20. PAGE 56 F1100 PLAN ECOMETRIC STAT

B64
HEKHUIS D.J.,INTERNATIONAL STABILITY: MILITARY, ECONOMIC AND POLITICAL DIMENSIONS. FUT WOR+45 LAW ECO/UNDEV INT/ORG NAT/G VOL/ASSN FORCES ACT/RES BAL/PWR PWR WEALTH...STAT UN 20. PAGE 58 F1143 TEC/DEV DETER REGION

B64
HINSHAW R.,THE EUROPEAN COMMUNITY AND AMERICAN TRADE: A STUDY IN ATLANTIC ECONOMICS AND POLICY. EUR+WWI UK USA+45 ECO/DEV ECO/UNDEV AGRI INDUS INT/ORG NAT/G ECO/TAC TARIFFS REGION...STAT CHARTS EEC 20. PAGE 60 F1174 MARKET TREND INT/TRADE

B64
INTERNATIONAL LABOUR OFFICE,EMPLOYMENT AND ECONOMIC GROWTH. ECO/DEV ECO/UNDEV NAT/G PLAN DIPLOM INT/TRADE CONTROL INCOME PRODUC WEALTH...STAT NAT/COMP 20 ILO. PAGE 65 F1279 WORKER METH/COMP ECO/TAC OPTIMAL

B64
JUSTER F.T.,ANTICIPATIONS AND PURCHASES; AN ANALYSIS OF CONSUMER BEHAVIOR. PROB/SOLV RISK COST PRODUC DRIVE...STAT STYLE SAMP CON/ANAL CHARTS HYPO/EXP GAME SIMUL. PAGE 68 F1345 PROBABIL DECISION PREDICT DEMAND

B64
LANGHOFF P.,MODELS, MEASUREMENT AND MARKETING. ACT/RES COMPUTER OP/RES PLAN BUDGET...MGT PHIL/SCI METH/CNCPT STAT PROG/TEAC BIBLIOG. PAGE 75 F1478 DECISION SIMUL MARKET R+D

B64
LEWIN P.,THE FOREIGN TRADE OF COMMUNIST CHINA* ITS IMPACT ON THE FREE WORLD. AFR EUR+WWI L/A+17C S/ASIA ECO/UNDEV CREATE FOR/AID...STAT NET/THEORY TREND CHARTS. PAGE 79 F1546 ASIA INT/TRADE NAT/COMP USSR

B64
MARKHAM J.W.,THE COMMON MARKET: FRIEND OR COMPETITOR. AFR EUR+WWI FUT USA+45 INT/ORG LG/CO NAT/G VOL/ASSN DELIB/GP EX/STRUC PLAN TARIFFS ORD/FREE PWR WEALTH...POLICY STAT TREND EEC VAL/FREE 20. PAGE 85 F1671 ECO/DEV ECO/TAC

B64
MAZA ZAVALA D.F.,VENEZUELA; UNA ECONOMIA DEPENDIENTE. L/A+17C VENEZUELA FINAN INDUS ...ECOMETRIC STAT TREND 20. PAGE 87 F1710 ECO/UNDEV BAL/PAY INT/TRADE PRICE

B64
ODEH H.S.,THE IMPACT OF INFLATION ON THE LEVEL OF ECONOMIC ACTIVITY. AFR BRAZIL CHILE BUDGET GOV/REL COST DEMAND INCOME WEALTH...STAT METH 20 MONEY. PAGE 100 F1963 ECOMETRIC ECO/TAC ECO/UNDEV FINAN

B64
OECD,THE FLOW OF FINANCIAL RESOURCES TO LESS DEVELOPED COUNTRIES 1956-1963. WOR+45 FINAN CAP/ISM ...POLICY STAT 20. PAGE 100 F1968 FOR/AID BUDGET INT/ORG ECO/UNDEV

B64
RAMAZANI R.K.,THE MIDDLE EAST AND THE EUROPEAN COMMON MARKET. EUR+WWI ISLAM ECO/DEV EXTR/IND MARKET PROC/MFG INT/ORG NAT/G TEC/DEV ECO/TAC REGION DRIVE WEALTH...STAT CHARTS EEC TOT/POP 20. PAGE 109 F2141 ECO/UNDEV ATTIT INT/TRADE

B64
SCHULTZ T.W.,TRANSFORMING TRADITIONAL AGRICULTURE. WOR+45 WOR-45 CULTURE STRATA FINAN ACT/RES ECO/TAC ATTIT KNOWL SKILL...MATH STAT TIME/SEQ GEN/LAWS VAL/FREE. PAGE 117 F2316 AGRI ECO/UNDEV

B64
SEERS D.,CUBA: THE ECONOMIC AND SOCIAL REVOLUTION. L/A+17C USSR YUGOSLAVIA STRATA AGRI INDUS SCHOOL DELIB/GP PLAN ECO/TAC DOMIN EDU/PROP ATTIT RIGID/FLEX ALL/VALS...STAT OBS TIME/SEQ WORK VAL/FREE 20. PAGE 119 F2341 ACT/RES COERCE CUBA REV

B64
SINGER H.W.,INTERNATIONAL DEVELOPMENT: GROWTH AND CHANGE. AFR BRAZIL L/A+17C WOR+45 CULTURE AGRI INDUS NAT/G ACT/RES ECO/TAC EDU/PROP WEALTH...GEOG CONCPT METH/CNCPT STAT HYPO/EXP WORK TOT/POP 20. PAGE 122 F2412 FINAN ECO/UNDEV FOR/AID INT/TRADE

B64
SOLOW R.M.,THE NATURE AND SOURCES OF UNEMPLOYMENT IN THE UNITED STATES (PAMPHLET). USA+45 INDUS LABOR TEC/DEV ECO/TAC SKILL WEALTH...TREND NAT/COMP 20. PAGE 124 F2439 ECO/DEV WORKER STAT PRODUC

B64
STOESSINGER J.G.,FINANCING THE UNITED NATIONS SYSTEM. FUT WOR+45 CONSTN NAT/G VOL/ASSN DELIB/GP EX/STRUC ECO/TAC LEGIT CT/SYS PWR WEALTH...STAT TIME/SEQ TREND CHARTS TRUE/GP METH/GP TERR/GP VAL/FREE. PAGE 126 F2493 FINAN INT/ORG

B64
THAILAND NATIONAL ECO DEV,THE NATIONAL ECONOMIC DEVELOPMENT PLAN: 1961-66: SECOND PHASE 1964-66. THAILAND AGRI FINAN BUDGET EFFICIENCY INCOME...STAT CHARTS 20. PAGE 129 F2547 ECO/UNDEV ECO/TAC PLAN NAT/G

B64
US AGENCY INTERNATIONAL DEV,A.I.D. PROJECTS IN FISCAL YEAR 1963: BY COUNTRY AND FIELD OF ACTIVITY. USA+45 ECO/UNDEV ECO/TAC EDU/PROP GOV/REL...CHARTS 20 AID. PAGE 134 F2639 FINAN FOR/AID COST STAT

B64
US LIBRARY OF CONGRESS,SOUTHEAST ASIA. CULTURE ...SOC STAT 20. PAGE 138 F2718 BIBLIOG/A S/ASIA ECO/UNDEV NAT/G

B64
US SENATE COMM ON JUDICIARY,HEARINGS BEFORE SUBCOMMITTEE ON ANTITRUST AND MONOPOLY: ECONOMIC CONCENTRATION VOLUMES 1-5 JULY 1964-SEPT 1966. USA+45 LAW FINAN ECO/TAC ADJUD COST EFFICIENCY PRODUC...STAT CHARTS 20 CONGRESS MONOPOLY. PAGE 140 F2749 ECO/DEV CONTROL MARKET LG/CO

B64
WILLIAMSON J.G.,AMERICAN GROWTH AND THE BALANCE OF PAYMENTS, 1820-1913: A STUDY OF THE LONG SWING. EUR+WWI MOD/EUR USA+45 USA-45 ECO/DEV NAT/G ECO/TAC ROUTINE ORD/FREE WEALTH...MATH STAT TIME/SEQ CHARTS SIMUL GEN/LAWS TRUE/GP METH/GP VAL/FREE 19/20. PAGE 147 F2896 FINAN BAL/PAY

B64
WILLIAMSON O.E.,THE ECONOMICS OF DISCRETIONARY BEHAVIOR: MANAGERIAL OBJECTIVES IN A THEORY OF THE FIRM. MARKET BUDGET CAP/ISM PRODUC DRIVE PERSON ...STAT CHARTS BIBLIOG METH 20. PAGE 147 F2897 EFFICIENCY MGT ECO/TAC CHOOSE

B64
WRIGHT G.,RURAL REVOLUTION IN FRANCE: THE PEASANTRY IN THE TWENTIETH CENTURY. EUR+WWI MOD/EUR LAW CULTURE AGRI POL/PAR DELIB/GP LEGIS ECO/TAC EDU/PROP COERCE CHOOSE ATTIT RIGID/FLEX HEALTH ...STAT CENSUS CHARTS VAL/FREE 20. PAGE 149 F2932 PWR STRATA FRANCE REV

L64
STERN R.M.,"POLICIES FOR TRADE AND DEVELOPMENT." AFR FUT WOR+45 DIST/IND FINAN NAT/G DELIB/GP PLAN ECO/TAC ORD/FREE WEALTH...POLICY STAT TIME/SEQ CHARTS METH/GP 20. PAGE 126 F2480 MARKET ECO/UNDEV INT/TRADE

S64
CARNEGIE ENDOWMENT INT. PEACE,"ADMINISTRATION AND BUDGET (ISSUES BEFORE THE NINETEENTH GENERAL ASSEMBLY)." WOR+45 FINAN BUDGET ECO/TAC ROUTINE COST...STAT RECORD UN. PAGE 21 F0415 INT/ORG ADMIN

S64
DOE J.F.,"TROPICAL AFRICAN CONTRIBUTIONS TO FEDERAL FINANCE." AFR NAT/G PROVS CENTRAL RIGID/FLEX PWR WEALTH...STAT VAL/FREE 20 CMN/WLTH. PAGE 33 F0650 FINAN ECO/TAC

S64
KOJIMA K.,"THE PATTERN OF INTERNATIONAL TRADE AMONG ADVANCED COUNTRIES." EUR+WWI UK USA+45 WOR+45 MARKET NAT/G ECO/TAC WEALTH...MATH STAT CON/ANAL CHARTS METH/GP EEC CHINJAP 20 CHINJAP. PAGE 72 F1419 ECO/DEV TREND INT/TRADE

S64
POLARIS J.,"THE SINO-SOVIET DISPUTE: ITS ECONOMIC IMPACT ON CHINA." ASIA CHINA/COM COM WOR+45 NAT/G ATTIT PWR WEALTH...STAT TREND FOR/TRADE 20. PAGE 107 F2095 ECO/UNDEV ECO/TAC

S64
RUSSETT B.M.,"INEQUALITY AND INSTABILITY: THE RELATION OF LAND TENURE TO POLITICS." WOR+45 ECO/DEV ECO/UNDEV AGRI NAT/G COERCE PWR...MATH STAT CHARTS GEN/LAWS TERR/GP TRUE/GP METH/GP VAL/FREE 20. PAGE 115 F2263 WEALTH GEOG ECO/TAC ORD/FREE

S64
WU Y.,"CHINA'S ECONOMY AND ITS PROSPECTS." ASIA CHINA/COM FUT USSR AGRI INDUS PLAN ECO/TAC LEGIT WEALTH...STAT CON/ANAL CHARTS GEN/LAWS FOR/TRADE 20. PAGE 149 F2938 ECO/DEV

B65
AMERICAN ECONOMIC ASSOCIATION,INDEX OF ECONOMIC JOURNALS 1886-1965 (7 VOLS.). UK USA+45 USA-45 AGRI FINAN PLAN ECO/TAC INT/TRADE ADMIN...STAT CENSUS 19/20. PAGE 5 F0087 BIBLIOG WRITING INDUS

B65
BAERRESEN D.W.,LATIN AMERICAN TRADE PATTERNS. L/A+17C ECO/UNDEV AGRI INDUS MARKET CREATE ...NET/THEORY CHARTS LAFTA. PAGE 8 F0149 INT/TRADE STAT REGION

B65
BAUMOL W.J.,ECONOMIC THEORY AND OPERATIONS ANALYSIS (2ND ED.). MARKET LG/CO BUDGET PRICE COST EQUILIB PRODUC...DECISION MATH CHARTS GAME 20. PAGE 12 F0219 OP/RES ECO/DEV METH/COMP STAT

B65
CHAO K.,THE RATE AND PATTERN OF INDUSTRIAL GROWTH IN COMMUNIST CHINA. CHINA/COM ECO/UNDEV TEC/DEV PRICE...NAT/COMP BIBLIOG 20. PAGE 23 F0452 INDUS INDEX STAT PRODUC

B65
DODDY F.S.,INTRODUCTION TO THE USE OF ECONOMIC INDICATORS. FINAN LABOR PLAN COST...ECOMETRIC INDICATOR MATH PREDICT CHARTS METH 20. PAGE 33 F0649 TEC/DEV STAT PRODUC PRICE

B65
FRIEDLANDER S.L.,LABOR MIGRATION AND ECONOMIC GROWTH: A CASE STUDY OF PUERTO RICO. PUERT/RICO AGRI WORKER PLAN PROB/SOLV...ECOMETRIC STAT PREDICT CHARTS HYPO/EXP SIMUL 20. PAGE 44 F0858 CENSUS GEOG ECO/UNDEV WEALTH

B65
GOETZ-GIREY R.,LE MOUVEMENT DES GREVES EN FRANCE. FRANCE FINAN OP/RES PROB/SOLV ECO/TAC INCOME HABITAT...STAT CHARTS 19/20. PAGE 48 F0932 LABOR WORKER GP/REL INDUS

B65
HASSON J.A.,THE ECONOMICS OF NUCLEAR POWER. INDIA UK USA+45 WOR+45 INT/ORG TEC/DEV COST...SOC STAT CHARTS 20 EURATOM. PAGE 56 F1108 NUC/PWR INDUS ECO/DEV METH

B65
HERRICK B.H.,URBAN MIGRATION AND ECONOMIC DEVELOPMENT IN CHILE. CHILE AGRI INDUS LABOR NAT/G CENTRAL PRODUC...STAT SAMP CHARTS BIBLIOG/A MUNICH 20 MIGRATION. PAGE 59 F1156 HABITAT GEOG ECO/UNDEV

B65
HICKMAN B.G.,QUANTITATIVE PLANNING OF ECONOMIC POLICY. FRANCE NETHERLAND OP/RES PRICE ROUTINE UTIL ...POLICY DECISION ECOMETRIC METH/CNCPT STAT STYLE CHINJAP. PAGE 59 F1162 PROB/SOLV PLAN QUANT

B65
HOSELITZ B.F.,ECONOMICS AND THE IDEA OF MANKIND. UNIV ECO/DEV ECO/UNDEV DIST/IND INDUS INT/ORG NAT/G ACT/RES ECO/TAC WEALTH...CONCPT STAT. PAGE 62 F1223 CREATE INT/TRADE

B65
INTERAMERICAN ECO AND SOC COUN,THE ALLIANCE FOR PROGRESS: ITS THIRD YEAR 1963-1964. FUT L/A+17C WOR+45 ECO/DEV INT/ORG PLAN CONTROL ADJUST...STAT ANTHOL SOC/INTEG 20 ALL/PROG. PAGE 64 F1268 ECO/UNDEV ECO/TAC FINAN FOR/AID

B65
JASNY H.,KHRUSHCHEV'S CROP POLICY. USSR ECO/DEV PLAN MARXISM...STAT 20 KHRUSH/N RESOURCE/N. PAGE 66 F1306 AGRI NAT/G POLICY ECO/TAC

B65
KANTOROVICH L.V.,THE BEST USE OF ECONOMIC RESOURCES. USSR SOCIETY FINAN ACT/RES TEC/DEV ECO/TAC PRICE CONTROL COST DEMAND EFFICIENCY OPTIMAL...MGT STAT. PAGE 69 F1350 PLAN MATH DECISION

B65
KASER M.,COMECON* INTEGRATION PROBLEMS OF THE PLANNED ECONOMIES. INT/ORG TEC/DEV INT/TRADE PRICE ADMIN ADJUST CENTRAL...STAT TIME/SEQ ORG/CHARTS COMECON. PAGE 69 F1359 PLAN ECO/DEV COM REGION

B65
MACAVOY P.W.,THE ECONOMIC EFFECTS OF REGULATION: THE TRUNK-LINE RAILROAD CARTELS AND THE INTERSTATE COMMERCE COMMISSION BEFORE 1900. USA-45 PRICE PROFIT...STAT CHARTS BIBLIOG 19 RAILROAD. PAGE 83 F1620 ECO/TAC DIST/IND PROF/ORG RATION

B65
MAO J.C.T.,EFFICIENCY IN PUBLIC URBAN RENEWAL EXPENDITURES THROUGH CAPITAL BUDGETING. USA+45 FINAN LOC/G NAT/G NEIGH REGION UTIL...GEOG METH/CNCPT STAT SIMUL GEN/LAWS MUNICH 20 URBAN/RNWL. PAGE 85 F1662 TEC/DEV BUDGET PROB/SOLV

B65
MCCOLL G.D.,THE AUSTRALIAN BALANCE OF PAYMENTS. UK USA+45 AGRI WORKER DIPLOM EQUILIB PRODUC...STAT TREND CHARTS BIBLIOG/A 20 AUSTRAL. PAGE 88 F1719 ECO/DEV BAL/PAY INT/TRADE COST

B65
MUSHKIN S.J.,PROPERTY TAXES: THE 1970 OUTLOOK (PAMPHLET). FUT USA+45 ECO/DEV MARKET PROVS PLAN ...PROBABIL STAT CENSUS PREDICT CHARTS METH 20. PAGE 95 F1872 TAX OWN FINAN LOC/G

B65
O'BRIEN F.,CRISIS IN WORLD COMMUNISM* MARXISM IN SEARCH OF EFFICIENCY. AFR COM ECO/DEV PLAN INT/TRADE WAR ADJUST PEACE...STAT TIME/SEQ GOV/COMP NAT/COMP. PAGE 99 F1951 MARXISM USSR DRIVE EFFICIENCY

B65
OECD,MEDITERRANEAN REGIONAL PROJECT: TURKEY; EDUCATION AND DEVELOPMENT. FUT TURKEY SOCIETY STRATA FINAN NAT/G PROF/ORG PLAN PROB/SOLV ADMIN COST...STAT CHARTS 20 OECD. PAGE 100 F1969 EDU/PROP ACADEM SCHOOL ECO/UNDEV

B65
OECD,THE MEDITERRANEAN REGIONAL PROJECT: PORTUGAL; EDUCATION AND DEVELOPMENT. PORTUGAL SOCIETY STRATA FINAN PROF/ORG WORKER PLAN PROB/SOLV ADMIN...POLICY STAT CHARTS METH 20 OECD. PAGE 100 F1970 EDU/PROP SCHOOL ACADEM ECO/UNDEV

B65
OECD,THE MEDITERRANEAN REGIONAL PROJECT: ITALY; EDUCATION AND DEVELOPMENT. ITALY SOCIETY STRATA FINAN NAT/G PROF/ORG WORKER PLAN PROB/SOLV ADMIN ...STAT CHARTS METH 20 OECD. PAGE 100 F1971 SCHOOL EDU/PROP ECO/UNDEV ACADEM

B65
OECD,THE MEDITERRANEAN REGIONAL PROJECT: SPAIN; EDUCATION AND DEVELOPMENT. FUT SPAIN STRATA FINAN NAT/G WORKER PLAN PROB/SOLV ADMIN COST...POLICY STAT CHARTS 20 OECD. PAGE 100 F1973 ECO/UNDEV EDU/PROP ACADEM SCHOOL

B65
ORG FOR ECO COOP AND DEVEL,THE MEDITERRANEAN REGIONAL PROJECT: AN EXPERIMENT IN PLANNING BY SIX COUNTRIES. FUT GREECE SPAIN TURKEY YUGOSLAVIA SOCIETY FINAN NAT/G PROF/ORG EDU/PROP ADMIN REGION PLAN ECO/UNDEV ACADEM SCHOOL

COST...POLICY STAT CHARTS 20 OECD. PAGE 102 F1995

B65
ORG FOR ECO COOP AND DEVEL,THE MEDITERRANEAN REGIONAL PROJECT: YUGOSLAVIA; EDUCATION AND DEVELOPMENT. YUGOSLAVIA SOCIETY FINAN PROF/ORG PLAN ADMIN COST DEMAND MARXISM...STAT TREND CHARTS METH 20 OECD. PAGE 102 F1996
EDU/PROP ACADEM SCHOOL ECO/UNDEV

B65
OZGA S.A.,EXPECTATIONS IN ECONOMIC THEORY. MORAL ...ECOMETRIC MATH STAT IDEA/COMP 20. PAGE 102 F2008
RISK GAME CONCPT PREDICT

B65
PINCUS J.A.,ECONOMIC AID AND INTERNATIONAL COST SHARING* A RAND CORPORATION RESEARCH STUDY. INT/ORG BUDGET CENTRAL...ECOMETRIC MATH QUANT STAT SIMUL. PAGE 106 F2088
ECO/UNDEV COST FOR/AID INT/TRADE

B65
RIGBY P.H.,CONCEPTUAL FOUNDATIONS OF BUSINESS RESEARCH. COMPUTER PROB/SOLV OPTIMAL...MGT CONCPT MATH STAT TESTS SIMUL GEN/METH. PAGE 111 F2192
PROFIT R+D INDUS DECISION

B65
SABLE M.H.,PERIODICALS FOR LATIN AMERICAN ECONOMIC DEVELOPMENT, TRADE, AND FINANCE: AN ANNOTATED BIBLIOGRAPHY (A PAMPHLET). ECO/TAC PRODUC PROFIT ...STAT NAT/COMP 20 OAS. PAGE 115 F2266
BIBLIOG/A L/A+17C ECO/UNDEV INT/TRADE

B65
SMERK G.M.,URBAN TRANSPORTATION; THE FEDERAL ROLE. FUT USA+45 FINAN PROB/SOLV TEC/DEV AUTOMAT GOV/REL COST...STAT BIBLIOG MUNICH 20 PUB/TRANS. PAGE 123 F2426
PLAN DIST/IND NAT/G

B65
US BUREAU OF THE BUDGET,THE BALANCE OF PAYMENTS STATISTICS OF THE UNITED STATES: A REVIEW AND APPRAISAL. USA+45 FINAN NAT/G PROB/SOLV DIPLOM. PAGE 134 F2644
BAL/PAY STAT METH/COMP BUDGET

B65
WARD R.,BACKGROUND MATERIAL ON ECONOMIC IMPACT OF FEDERAL PROCUREMENT - 1965: FOR JOINT ECONOMIC COMMITTEE US CONGRESS. FINAN ROUTINE WEAPON CIVMIL/REL EFFICIENCY...STAT CHARTS 20 CONGRESS. PAGE 143 F2818
ECO/DEV NAT/G OWN GOV/REL

B65
WINT G.,ASIA: A HANDBOOK. ASIA COM INDIA USSR CULTURE INTELL NAT/G...GEOG STAT CENSUS NAT/COMP WORSHIP 20 TREATY CHINJAP. PAGE 148 F2907
DIPLOM SOC

B65
WISH J.R.,ECONOMIC DEVELOPMENT IN LATIN AMERICA: AN ANNOTATED BIBLIOGRAPHY. L/A+17C COM/IND MARKET R+D CREATE CAP/ISM ATTIT...STAT METH 20. PAGE 148 F2912
BIBLIOG/A ECO/UNDEV TEC/DEV AGRI

L65
LETICHE J.M.,"EUROPEAN INTEGRATION: AN AMERICAN VIEW." EUR+WWI FRANCE WOR+45 ECO/DEV DIST/IND EXTR/IND NAT/G DELIB/GP TOP/EX PLAN ECO/TAC ATTIT ...STAT CON/ANAL CHARTS EEC 20. PAGE 78 F1537
INDUS AGRI

S65
BERREBY J.J.,"IMPERATIFS STRATEGIQUES DU PETROLE." ECO/UNDEV VOL/ASSN ECO/TAC COLONIAL NUC/PWR WAR. PAGE 14 F0270
ISLAM EXTR/IND STAT OBS

S65
BRANDENBURG F.,"THE RELEVANCE OF MEXICAN EXPERIENCE TO LATIN AMERICAN DEVELOPMENT." BRAZIL CHILE VENEZUELA STRUCT ECO/UNDEV AGRI CREATE ECO/TAC ...STAT RECORD MEXIC/AMER ARGEN COLOMB. PAGE 18 F0340
L/A+17C GOV/COMP

S65
BRIGHAM E.F.,"THE DETERMINANTS OF RESIDENTIAL LAND VALUES." USA+45 ECO/DEV PROB/SOLV RENT PRICE ...REGRESS STAT CHARTS GEN/METH MUNICH 20 LOS/ANG. PAGE 18 F0351
COST INDICATOR SIMUL ECOMETRIC

S65
CAMPOLONGO A.,"EUROPEAN INVESTMENT BANK* ACTIVITY AND PROSPECTS." FUT ECO/UNDEV FINAN PLAN DIPLOM ...STAT EEC LOAN EIB. PAGE 21 F0410
ECO/TAC PREDICT

S65
CHU K.,"A DYNAMIC MODEL OF THE FIRM." OP/RES PROB/SOLV...DECISION ECOMETRIC NEW/IDEA STAT GAME ORG/CHARTS SIMUL. PAGE 24 F0472
INDUS COMPUTER TEC/DEV

S65
DUMONT R.,"SURPEUPLEMENT CHINOIS ET SES CONSEQUENCES." AFR ECO/UNDEV AGRI PLAN PROB/SOLV ECO/TAC FOR/AID NUC/PWR...OBS INT PREDICT. PAGE 35 F0675
GEOG ASIA STAT

S65
KAUFMAN R.H.,"THE ASIAN GOLD TRADE." ASIA LAOS THAILAND UK CHARTS. PAGE 69 F1362
S/ASIA FINAN STAT INT/TRADE

S65
MALHERBE E.G.,"MANPOWER TRAINING: EDUCATIONAL REQUIREMENTS FOR ECONOMIC EXPANSION." SOUTH/AFR ECO/DEV INDUS EDU/PROP...MGT STAT CHARTS 20. PAGE 84 F1646
LABOR SKILL SCHOOL ACADEM

S65
MUNZI U.,"THE EUROPEAN SOCIAL FUND IN THE DEVELOPMENT OF THE MEDITERRANEAN REGIONS OF THE EEC." FUT GREECE ITALY PORTUGAL SPAIN TURKEY WORKER TEC/DEV ECO/TAC REGION...STAT EEC. PAGE 95 F1862
ECO/UNDEV PREDICT RECORD

S65
RUSINOW D.I.,"YUGOSLAV DEVELOPMENT BETWEEN EAST AND WEST." AGRI VOL/ASSN PLAN CAP/ISM ECO/TAC FOR/AID INT/TRADE BAL/PAY...MARXIST EEC COMECON. PAGE 115 F2262
YUGOSLAVIA ECO/UNDEV STAT

S65
WHITE J.,"WEST GERMAN AID TO DEVELOPING COUNTRIES." AFR INT/ORG OP/RES GIVE CENTRAL ATTIT DRIVE...STAT NAT/COMP. PAGE 146 F2869
GERMANY FOR/AID ECO/UNDEV CAP/ISM

B66
BALDWIN D.A.,FOREIGN AID AND AMERICAN FOREIGN POLICY; A DOCUMENTARY ANALYSIS. USA+45 ECO/UNDEV ADMIN...ECOMETRIC STAT STYLE CHARTS PROG/TEAC GEN/LAWS ANTHOL. PAGE 9 F0162
FOR/AID DIPLOM IDEA/COMP

B66
BEN-PORATH Y.,THE ARAB LABOR FORCE IN ISRAEL. ISLAM ISRAEL AGRI INDUS SCHOOL CAP/ISM PAY DEMAND...GEOG REGRESS STAT CHARTS 20 ARABS. PAGE 13 F0245
WORKER CENSUS GP/REL STRUCT

B66
BIRMINGHAM W.,A STUDY OF CONTEMPORARY GHANA VOL I: THE ECONOMY OF GHANA. AFR GHANA PLAN...POLICY STAT CHARTS ANTHOL BIBLIOG 20. PAGE 15 F0286
ECO/UNDEV ECO/TAC NAT/G PRODUC

B66
BROWN R.T.,TRANSPORT AND THE ECONOMIC INTEGRATION OF SOUTH AMERICA. L/A+17C ECO/UNDEV NAT/G OP/RES DIPLOM INT/TRADE REGION WEALTH...ECOMETRIC GEOG STAT LAFTA TIME. PAGE 19 F0373
MARKET DIST/IND SIMUL

B66
CONAN A.R.,THE PROBLEM OF STERLING. UK WOR+45 BUDGET ECO/TAC...POLICY STAT CHARTS 20 SILVER. PAGE 27 F0521
FINAN ECO/DEV BAL/PAY DIPLOM

B66
CONFERENCE REGIONAL ACCOUNTS,REGIONAL ACCOUNTS FOR POLICY DECISIONS. PROB/SOLV CONTROL RATIONAL KNOWL ORD/FREE...POLICY DECISION MATH STAT ANTHOL 20. PAGE 27 F0523
GOV/REL REGION PLAN ECO/TAC

B66
EBONY,THE NEGRO HANDBOOK. ACADEM LABOR LOC/G SECT FORCES WORKER CT/SYS CRIME DISCRIM ORD/FREE...BIOG SOC/INTEG 19/20 NEGRO CIV/RIGHTS. PAGE 36 F0692
RACE/REL EDU/PROP LAW STAT

B66
ECKSTEIN A.,COMMUNIST CHINA'S ECONOMIC GROWTH AND FOREIGN TRADE* IMPLICATIONS FOR US POLICY. COM USA+45 USSR STRUCT INDUS MARKET DIPLOM ECO/TAC FOR/AID INT/TRADE...STAT CHARTS. PAGE 36 F0696
ASIA ECO/UNDEV CREATE PWR

B66
FRIEDMANN W.G.,INTERNATIONAL FINANCIAL AID. USA+45 ECO/DEV ECO/UNDEV NAT/G VOL/ASSN EX/STRUC PLAN RENT GIVE BAL/PAY PWR...GEOG INT/LAW STAT TREND UN EEC COMECON. PAGE 44 F0866
INT/ORG FOR/AID TEC/DEV ECO/TAC

B66
GOULD J.M.,THE TECHNICAL ELITE. INDUS LABOR TECHRACY...POLICY DECISION STAT CHARTS 20. PAGE 49 F0967
ECO/DEV TEC/DEV ELITES TECHNIC

B66
HAINES W.W.,MONEY PRICES AND POLICY. WOR+45 ECO/DEV BUDGET CONTROL INCOME...POLICY STAT CHARTS BIBLIOG T 20. PAGE 53 F1039
PRICE FINAN ECO/TAC GOV/REL

B66
HO YHI-MIN,AGRICULTURAL DEVELOPMENT OF TAIWAN: 1903-1960. FINAN WORKER EDU/PROP...STAT CHARTS BIBLIOG 20. PAGE 60 F1181
ECO/UNDEV AGRI PRODUC PLAN

B66
LECHT L.,GOAL, PRIORITIES, AND DOLLARS: THE NEXT DECADE. SPACE USA+45 SOCIETY AGRI BUDGET FOR/AID ...HEAL SOC/WK STAT CHARTS 20 URBAN/RNWL PUB/TRANS. PAGE 76 F1499
IDEA/COMP POLICY CONSEN PLAN

B66
LERNER E.M.,A THEORY OF FINANCIAL ANALYSIS. UNIV LG/CO COST DEMAND INCOME PROFIT...MATH STAT CHARTS SIMUL T 20. PAGE 78 F1531
CONCPT FINAN ECO/DEV OPTIMAL

B66
LEWIS W.A.,DEVELOPMENT PLANNING; THE ESSENTIALS OF ECONOMIC POLICY. USA+45 FINAN INDUS NAT/G WORKER FOR/AID INT/TRADE ADMIN ROUTINE WEALTH...CONCPT STAT. PAGE 79 F1552
PLAN ECO/DEV POLICY CREATE

B66
MASON E.S.,ECONOMIC DEVELOPMENT IN INDIA AND PAKISTAN. INDIA PAKISTAN AGRI FINAN PLAN BUDGET INT/TRADE WEALTH...POLICY STAT TREND CHARTS 20. PAGE 87 F1700
NAT/COMP ECO/UNDEV ECO/TAC FOR/AID

B66
ORG FOR ECO COOP AND DEVEL,GEOGRAPHICAL DISTRIBUTION OF FINANCIAL FLOWS TO LESS DEVELOPED COUNTRIES. WOR+45 DIPLOM INT/TRADE GIVE RECEIVE REPAR REGION WEALTH...GEOG STAT CHARTS 20 OECD. PAGE 102 F1997
FINAN ECO/UNDEV INT/ORG FOR/AID

B66
PERSALL E.S.,AN ECONOMETRIC STUDY OF FINANCIAL MARKETS. COMPUTER PROB/SOLV TEC/DEV...MATH STAT CHARTS METH/COMP BIBLIOG 20. PAGE 105 F2066
ECOMETRIC FINAN MARKET METH

B66
PIQUET H.S.,THE US BALANCE OF PAYMENTS AND INTERNATIONAL MONETARY RESERVES. AFR USA+45 PROB/SOLV INT/TRADE GOV/REL EQUILIB...POLICY STAT CHARTS 20. PAGE 106 F2090
BAL/PAY DIPLOM FINAN ECO/TAC

B66
POLK J.,U S PRODUCTION ABROAD AND THE BALANCE OF PAYMENTS* A SURVEY OF CORPORATE INVESTMENT EXPERIENCE. USA+45 SERV/IND NAT/G OP/RES COST PROFIT ATTIT...ECOMETRIC STAT INT QU GEN/METH. PAGE 107 F2096
BAL/PAY FINAN INT/TRADE INDUS

B66
SOMMERFELD R.M.,TAX REFORM AND THE ALLIANCE FOR PROGRESS. USA+45 ECO/DEV ECO/UNDEV FINAN NAT/G INCOME ORD/FREE WEALTH...STAT CHARTS 20 ALL/PROG. PAGE 124 F2442
TAX INT/ORG L/A+17C FOR/AID

B66
UN STATISTICAL OFFICE,STATISTICAL YEARBOOK (17TH ED.). WOR+45 AGRI...GEOG CHARTS 20. PAGE 132 F2604
STAT INDEX SOCIETY INDUS

B66
UNITED NATIONS,YEARBOOK OF INTERNATIONAL TRADE STATISTICS, 1964 (15TH ISSUE). WOR+45 ECO/DEV ECO/UNDEV UN. PAGE 132 F2614
STAT INT/TRADE DIPLOM CHARTS

B66
US DEPARTMENT OF LABOR,PRODUCTIVITY: A BIBLIOGRAPHY. ECO/DEV INDUS MARKET OP/RES AUTOMAT COST...STAT 20. PAGE 135 F2668
BIBLIOG/A PRODUC LABOR PLAN

B66
US PRES COMM ECO IMPACT DEFENS,REPORT* JULY 1965. USA+45 ECO/DEV INDUS DELIB/GP FORCES OP/RES ARMS/CONT NUC/PWR WEAPON BAL/PAY...PREDICT SIMUL. PAGE 138 F2726
ACT/RES STAT WAR BUDGET

B66
WALTON S.D.,AMERICAN BUSINESS AND ITS ENVIRONMENT. USA+45 LAW CONSTN FINAN MARKET LOC/G EX/STRUC CT/SYS COST PRODUC...STAT 20. PAGE 143 F2813
PRICE PROFIT

B66
WESTON J.F.,THE SCOPE AND METHODOLOGY OF FINANCE. PLAN TEC/DEV CONTROL EFFICIENCY INCOME UTIL...MGT CONCPT MATH STAT TREND METH 20. PAGE 145 F2863
FINAN ECO/DEV POLICY PRICE

L66
AMERICAN ECONOMIC REVIEW,"SIXTY-THIRD LIST OF DOCTORAL DISSERTATIONS IN POLITICAL ECONOMY IN AMERICAN UNIVERSITIES AND COLLEGES." ECO/DEV AGRI FINAN LABOR WORKER PLAN BUDGET INT/TRADE ADMIN DEMAND...MGT STAT 20. PAGE 5 F0088
BIBLIOG/A CONCPT ACADEM

S66
BENOIT J.,"WORLD DEFENSE EXPENDITURES." WOR+45 WEAPON COST PRODUC. PAGE 13 F0253
FORCES STAT NAT/COMP BUDGET

S66
DAVIS O.A.,"A THEORY OF THE BUDGETARY PROCESS." ECO/DEV FINAN LEGIS PROB/SOLV GOV/REL...ECOMETRIC METH/CNCPT STAT CONT/OBS TREND METH/COMP SIMUL 20 CONGRESS. PAGE 30 F0592
DECISION NAT/G BUDGET EFFICIENCY

S66
FROMM G.,"RECENT MONETARY POLICY: AN ECONOMETRIC VIEW" USA+45 ECO/DEV INDUS PAY PRICE PRODUC ORD/FREE WEALTH...STAT 20 FED/RESERV. PAGE 45 F0869
ECOMETRIC FINAN POLICY SIMUL

S66
LAURENS H.,"LES PAYS OCCIDENTAUX ET LE MARCHE CHINOIS." EUR+WWI FUT S/ASIA AGRI INDUS VOL/ASSN ECO/TAC BAL/PAY...RECORD PREDICT TREATY. PAGE 76 F1488
ASIA INT/TRADE TREND STAT

S66
SHORTE F.C.,"THE APPLICATION OF DEVELOPMENT HYPOTHESES IN MIDDLE EASTERN STUDIES." STRUCT AGRI CREATE DEMAND...GEOG STAT CON/ANAL CHARTS. PAGE 121 F2387
ECO/UNDEV ISLAM SOC HYPO/EXP

C66
WINT G.,"ASIA: A HANDBOOK." ASIA S/ASIA INDUS LABOR SECT PRESS RACE/REL MARXISM...STAT CHARTS BIBLIOG 20. PAGE 148 F2908
ECO/UNDEV DIPLOM NAT/G SOCIETY

B67
ALNASRAWI A.,FINANCING ECONOMIC DEVELOPMENT IN IRAQ. IRAQ INDUS CAP/ISM COST PRODUC...STAT CHARTS BIBLIOG 20. PAGE 4 F0076
ECO/UNDEV EXTR/IND TEC/DEV

INT/TRADE

B67
ANDERSON C.W.,POLITICS AND ECONOMIC CHANGE IN LATIN AMERICA. L/A+17C INDUS NAT/G OP/RES ADMIN DEMAND ...POLICY STAT CHARTS NAT/COMP 20. PAGE 5 F0093
ECO/UNDEV PROB/SOLV PLAN ECO/TAC

B67
BERGMANN D KAUN B.,STRUCTURAL UNEMPLOYMENT IN THE UNITED STATES. USA+45 ECO/DEV PRICE ADMIN INGP/REL DEMAND EQUILIB WEALTH...MATH REGRESS STAT 20 NEGRO. PAGE 13 F0258
ECOMETRIC METH WORKER ECO/TAC

B67
BIRMINGHAM W.,A STUDY OF CONTEMPORARY GHANA VOL. I: SOME ASPECTS OF SOCIAL STRUCTURE. AFR GHANA AGRI FAM SECT PLAN EDU/PROP MARRIAGE OWN...POLICY STAT CHARTS MUNICH 20. PAGE 15 F0287
SOCIETY STRUCT CENSUS ECO/UNDEV

B67
EVANS R.H.,COEXISTENCE: COMMUNISM AND ITS PRACTICE IN BOLOGNA, 1945-1965. ITALY CAP/ISM ADMIN CHOOSE PEACE ORD/FREE...SOC STAT DEEP/INT SAMP CHARTS BIBLIOG MUNICH 20. PAGE 39 F0756
MARXISM CULTURE POL/PAR

B67
KANNER L.,THE NEW YORK TIMES WORLD ECONOMIC REVIEW AND FORECAST: 1967. WOR+45 ECO/DEV ECO/UNDEV TEC/DEV...STAT PREDICT CHARTS 20. PAGE 69 F1349
INDUS FINAN TREND ECO/TAC

B67
KARDOUCHE G.K.,THE UAR IN DEVELOPMENT. UAR ECO/TAC INT/TRADE BAL/PAY...STAT CHARTS BIBLIOG 20. PAGE 69 F1355
FINAN MGT CAP/ISM ECO/UNDEV

B67
LITTLE AD, INC.,COMMUNITY RENEWAL PROGRAMMING. CULTURE LOC/G ACT/RES TASK COST ATTIT...SOC/WK MODAL STAT STAND/INT CHARTS 20 SAN/FRAN. PAGE 81 F1585
STRATA NEIGH PLAN CREATE

B67
SACKS B.,SOUTH AFRICA: AN IMPERIAL DILEMMA. SOUTH/AFR UK ECO/UNDEV KIN DOMIN DEBATE CONTROL REV DISCRIM ISOLAT...POLICY STAT BIBLIOG 20. PAGE 115 F2268
COLONIAL RACE/REL DIPLOM ORD/FREE

B67
THOMAN R.S.,GEOGRAPHY OF INTERNATIONAL TRADE. WOR+45 ECO/DEV ECO/UNDEV INT/ORG LG/CO PLAN BAL/PAY ...STAT CHARTS NAT/COMP 20. PAGE 130 F2559
INT/TRADE GEOG ECO/TAC DIPLOM

B67
US AGENCY INTERNATIONAL DEV,PROPOSED FOREIGN AID PROGRAM FOR 1968: SUMMARY PRESENTATION TO THE CONGRESS. AFR S/ASIA USA+45 AGRI TEC/DEV DIPLOM ECO/TAC BAL/PAY COST HEALTH KNOWL SKILL 20 AID CONGRESS ALL/PROG. PAGE 134 F2640
ECO/UNDEV BUDGET FOR/AID STAT

L67
ZEIDBERG L.D.,"THE NASHVILLE AIR POLLUTION STUDY" (PARTS V-VII)" USA+45 PLAN AGE HEALTH...GEOG STAT CENSUS SAMP/SIZ CHARTS BIBLIOG MUNICH. PAGE 150 F2962
DEATH HABITAT AIR BIO/SOC

S67
ALPANDER G.G.,"ENTREPRENEURS AND PRIVATE ENTERPRISE IN TURKEY." TURKEY INDUS PROC/MFG EDU/PROP ATTIT DRIVE WEALTH...GEOG MGT SOC STAT TREND CHARTS 20. PAGE 4 F0077
ECO/UNDEV LG/CO NAT/G POLICY

S67
BASOV V.,"THE DEVELOPMENT OF PUBLIC EDUCATION AND THE BUDGET." USSR NAT/G CONTROL REV COST AGE...STAT 20. PAGE 11 F0204
BUDGET GIVE EDU/PROP SCHOOL

S67
GRUN C.,"DEUX ETUDES ALLEMANDES SUR LES PREJUGES NATIONAUX ET LES MOYENS DE LES COMBATTRE." FRANCE GERMANY DIST/IND PROB/SOLV GP/REL AGE/Y RIGID/FLEX ...PSY STAT INT SAMP. PAGE 52 F1010
ATTIT REGION DISCRIM STERTYP

S67
HUTCHINGS R.,"THE ENDING OF UNEMPLOYMENT IN THE USSR" USSR PLAN ECO/TAC PRICE INGP/REL...GEOG STAT CHARTS 20 MIGRATION. PAGE 63 F1247
WORKER AGRI INDUS MARXISM

S67
LEFCOE G.,"CONSTRUCTION LENDING AND THE EQUITABLE LIEN." LICENSE CT/SYS OWN...STAT 20. PAGE 77 F1510
CONSTRUC RENT ADJUD

S67
LEVI M.,"LES RELATIONS ECONOMIQUES ENTRE L'EST ET L'OUEST EN EUROPE" INDUS...STAT CHARTS 20 OECD COMECON. PAGE 79 F1540
INT/TRADE INT/ORG FINAN PRODUC

S67
LINEBERRY R.L.,"REFORMISM AND PUBLIC POLICIES IN AMERICAN CITIES." USA+45 POL/PAR EX/STRUC LEGIS BUDGET TAX GP/REL...STAT CHARTS MUNICH. PAGE 80 F1573
DECISION POLICY LOC/G

S67
MENCHER S.,"THE PROBLEM OF MEASURING POVERTY." UNIV USA+45 STRATA PROB/SOLV...NEW/IDEA METH/COMP 20. PAGE 89 F1755
WEALTH CENSUS STAT GEN/LAWS

S67
MOONEY J.D.,"URBAN POVERTY AND LABOR FORCE PARTICIPATION." FAM DISCRIM...SOC/WK STAT CHARTS MUNICH. PAGE 93 F1820
INCOME WORKER WEALTH

S67
PAI G.A.,"TAXATION AND PLANNING IN INDIA: A BIRDS-EYE VIEW." INDIA ELITES NAT/G LEGIS BUDGET CONTROL LOBBY INCOME...STAT CHARTS 20. PAGE 102 F2015
TAX PLAN WEALTH STRATA

S67
PLOTT C.R.,"A NOTION OF EQUILIBRIUM AND ITS POSSIBILITY UNDER MAJORITY RULE." CREATE...DECISION STAT CHARTS 20. PAGE 106 F2094
SIMUL EQUILIB CHOOSE MAJORITY

S67
RAMA C.M.,"PASADO Y PRESENTE DE LA RELIGION EN AMERICA LATINA." L/A+17C ELITES SOCIETY STRATA MARXISM...STAT WORSHIP PROTESTANT. PAGE 109 F2139
SECT CATHISM STRUCT NAT/COMP

S67
SMALL A.H.,"THE EFFECT OF TARIFF REDUCTIONS ON US IMPORT VOLUME." USA+45 INT/ORG NAT/G DIPLOM CONFER DEMAND...POLICY INT/LAW STAT CHARTS GATT EEC. PAGE 123 F2424
TARIFFS INT/TRADE PRICE ECO/TAC

S67
WALLACE H.M.,"AVAILABILITY AND USEFULNESS OF SELECTED HEALTH AND SOCIOECONOMIC DATA FOR COMMUNITY PLANNING." NEIGH EFFICIENCY...CORREL STAT CENSUS CHARTS. PAGE 142 F2806
HEALTH PLAN SOC/WK HEAL

N67
US CONGRESS JT COMM ECO GOVT,BACKGROUND MATERIAL ON ECONOMY IN GOVERNMENT 1967 (PAMPHLET). WOR+45 ECO/DEV BARGAIN PRICE DEMAND OPTIMAL...STAT DEPT/DEFEN. PAGE 135 F2665
BUDGET COST MGT NAT/G

S86
SMITH R.M.,"THE NATIONAL BUREAU OF LABOR AND INDUSTRIAL DEPRESSIONS" USA-45 DELIB/GP BARGAIN CONTROL COST INCOME WEALTH...STAT 19 DEPRESSION. PAGE 123 F2433
LABOR INDUS FINAN GOV/REL

STATE GOVERNMENT....SEE PROVS

STATE DEPARTMENT....SEE DEPT/STATE

STATISTICS....SEE STAT, ALSO LOGIC, MATHEMATICS, AND LANGUAGE INDEX, P. XIV

STEARNS P.N. F2472

STEENKAMP W.F.J. F2473

STEFANIAK N.J. F2474

STEIN E. F2475

STEIN H.A. F0391

STEINBERG E.B. F1031

STEINER G.A. F2476

STEINHEIMER R.L. F2477

STEINMETZ H. F2478

STEMPEL GH I.I.I. F2479

STEREOTYPE....SEE STERTYP

STERN R.M. F2480

STERN/GANG....STERN GANG (PALESTINE)

STERNBERG F. F2481

STEROTYPE....SEE STERTYP

STERTYP....STEREOTYPE

B15
JONES J.H.,THE ECONOMICS OF WAR AND CONQUEST. WOR-45 ECO/DEV NAT/G WEALTH...STAT TREND STERTYP GEN/LAWS TOT/POP 20. PAGE 68 F1338
MYTH WAR

B28
CASSEL G.,FOREIGN INVESTMENTS. GERMANY UK USA-45 WOR-45 ECO/DEV NAT/G VOL/ASSN CAP/ISM REPAR ATTIT WEALTH...METH/CNCPT STAT SIMUL STERTYP ANTHOL FOR/TRADE TOT/POP VAL/FREE 20. PAGE 22 F0426
FINAN ECO/TAC BAL/PAY

L52
HUTH A.G.,"COMMUNICATION AND ECONOMIC DEVELOPMENT." FUT WOR+45 CULTURE SOCIETY INT/ORG PLAN TEC/DEV EDU/PROP DRIVE KNOWL WEALTH...POLICY CONCPT RECORD STERTYP GEN/LAWS COMMUN TOT/POP UNESCO 20 UN CMN/WLTH. PAGE 64 F1250
ECO/UNDEV

B55
BUCHANAN N.S.,APPROACHES TO ECONOMIC DEVELOPMENT. FUT USA+45 WOR+45 STRATA ECO/DEV INT/ORG NAT/G TEC/DEV DIPLOM FOR/AID ATTIT KNOWL PWR WEALTH ...RELATIV METH/CNCPT SELF/OBS TREND CON/ANAL STERTYP GEN/LAWS FOR/TRADE COMMUN 20. PAGE 20 F0380
ECO/UNDEV ECO/TAC INT/TRADE

B56
WHYTE W.H. JR.,THE ORGANIZATION MAN. CULTURE FINAN VOL/ASSN DOMIN EDU/PROP EXEC DISPL HABITAT ROLE ...PERS/TEST STERTYP. PAGE 146 F2875
ADMIN LG/CO PERSON CONSEN

B57
ARON R.,L'UNIFICATION ECONOMIQUE DE L'EUROPE. EUR+WWI SWITZERLND UK INT/ORG NAT/G REGION NAT/LISM ORD/FREE PWR...CONCPT METH/CNCPT OBS TREND STERTYP GEN/LAWS EEC FOR/TRADE 20. PAGE 6 F0118
VOL/ASSN ECO/TAC

B57
TRIFFIN R.,EUROPE AND THE MONEY MUDDLE. USA+45 INT/ORG NAT/G CONSULT PLAN ECO/TAC EXEC ROUTINE BAL/PAY WEALTH...METH/CNCPT OBS TREND CHARTS STERTYP GEN/METH EEC TERR/GP VAL/FREE ECSC. PAGE 131 F2587
EUR+WWI ECO/DEV REGION

S57
DUBIN R.,"POWER AND UNION-MANAGEMENT RELATIONS." PROB/SOLV ADJUD ROUTINE ATTIT ORD/FREE...MGT STERTYP. PAGE 34 F0668
PWR LABOR BARGAIN GP/REL

B60
ARON R.,COLLOQUES DE RHEINFELDEN. AFR USA+45 USSR WOR+45 WOR-45 CULTURE ECO/UNDEV NAT/G POL/PAR DIPLOM NAT/LISM TOTALISM ATTIT DRIVE ALL/VALS ...PLURIST CONCPT STERTYP GEN/LAWS TOT/POP 20. PAGE 6 F0120
ECO/DEV SOCIETY CAP/ISM SOCISM

S60
HERZ J.H.,"EAST GERMANY: PROGRESS AND PROSPECTS." COM AGRI FINAN INDUS LOC/G NAT/G FORCES PLAN TEC/DEV DOMIN ADMIN COERCE DRIVE PERCEPT RIGID/FLEX MORAL ORD/FREE PWR...MARXIST PSY SOC RECORD STERTYP WORK. PAGE 59 F1158
POL/PAR STRUCT GERMANY

S60
MURPHEY R.,"ECONOMIC CONFLICTS IN SOUTH ASIA." ASIA CULTURE INTELL ECO/TAC REGION ATTIT DRIVE KNOWL ...METH/CNCPT TIME/SEQ STERTYP TOT/POP METH/GP VAL/FREE 20. PAGE 95 F1864
S/ASIA ECO/UNDEV

B61
HORVATH B.,THE CHARACTERISTICS OF YUGOSLAV ECONOMIC DEVELOPMENT. COM ECO/UNDEV AGRI INDUS PLAN CAP/ISM ECO/TAC ROUTINE WEALTH...SOCIALIST STAT CHARTS STERTYP WORK 20. PAGE 62 F1217
ACT/RES YUGOSLAVIA

S61
BENOIT E.,"THE PROPENSITY TO REDUCE THE NATIONAL DEBT OUT OF DEFENSE SAVINGS." FUT USA+45 SOCIETY R+D PLAN...WELF/ST SOC REC/INT STERTYP TOT/POP 20. PAGE 13 F0250
WEALTH ECO/TAC

S61
GALBRAITH J.K.,"A POSITIVE APPROACH TO ECONOMIC AID." FUT USA+45 INTELL NAT/G CONSULT ACT/RES DIPLOM ECO/TAC EDU/PROP ATTIT KNOWL PWR WEALTH ...SOC STERTYP MID/EX METH/GP 20. PAGE 45 F0883
ECO/UNDEV ROUTINE FOR/AID

B62
ARNOLD H.J.P.,AID FOR DEVELOPING COUNTRIES. COM EUR+WWI USA+45 USSR WOR+45 EDU/PROP ATTIT DRIVE PWR WEALTH...TREND CHARTS STERTYP NAT/ 20. PAGE 6 F0115
ECO/UNDEV ECO/TAC FOR/AID

B62
ARNOLD T.W.,THE FOLKLORE OF CAPITALISM. USA+45 USA-45 SOCIETY LG/CO SML/CO EX/STRUC ECO/TAC EDU/PROP ADJUST INCOME...MYTH CHARTS 20. PAGE 6 F0116
CAP/ISM ATTIT STERTYP ECO/DEV

B62
HEILBRONER R.L.,THE MAKING OF ECONOMIC SOCIETY. FUT WOR-45 SOCIETY STRATA ECO/DEV ECO/UNDEV ECO/TAC LEGIT ROUTINE...SOC RECORD REC/INT KNO/TEST CENSUS STERTYP GEN/LAWS. PAGE 58 F1136
CAP/ISM SOCISM

B62
HUMPHREY D.D.,THE UNITED STATES AND THE COMMON MARKET. USA+45 INDUS MARKET INT/ORG PLAN EDU/PROP BAL/PAY DRIVE PWR WEALTH...TREND STERTYP FOR/TRADE EEC 20. PAGE 63 F1241
ATTIT ECO/TAC

L62
PRYOR F.L.,"FOREIGN TRADE IN THE COMMUNIST BLOC." COM ECO/DEV VOL/ASSN...METH/CNCPT GEN/LAWS FOR/TRADE TERR/GP 20. PAGE 108 F2129
ECO/TAC STERTYP USSR

S62
ALPERT P.,"ECONOMIC POLICIES AND PLANNING IN NEWLY INDEPENDENT AFRICA." PLAN ATTIT PWR WEALTH ...STERTYP GEN/LAWS VAL/FREE 20. PAGE 4 F0078
AFR ECO/DEV NAT/LISM COLONIAL

S62
PYE L.W.,"THE POLITICAL IMPULSES AND FANTASIES BEHIND FOREIGN AID." FUT USA+45 ECO/UNDEV DIPLOM ECO/TAC ROUTINE DRIVE KNOWL...SOC METH/CNCPT NEW/IDEA TREND HYPO/EXP STERTYP GEN/METH 20. PAGE 108 F2133
ACT/RES ATTIT FOR/AID

S63
HOOVER C.B.,"ECONOMIC REFORM VERSUS ECONOMIC GROWTH IN UNDERDEVELOPED COUNTRIES." FUT WOR+45 ELITES STRATA ECO/UNDEV DIST/IND INDUS TEC/DEV CAP/ISM FOR/AID INT/TRADE ATTIT WEALTH...MYTH TREND STERTYP
ECO/DEV ECO/TAC

GEN/LAWS WORK 20. PAGE 61 F1209

S64
PADELFORD N.J.,"THE ORGANIZATION OF AFRICAN UNITY." ECO/UNDEV INT/ORG PLAN BAL/PWR DIPLOM ECO/TAC NAT/LISM ORD/FREE PWR WEALTH...CONCPT TREND STERTYP TERR/GP VAL/FREE 20. PAGE 102 F2013 — AFR VOL/ASSN REGION

B65
THORNTON A.P.,DOCTRINES OF IMPERIALISM. WOR+45 WOR-45 DOMIN NAT/LISM PROFIT ATTIT PERSON PWR RESPECT SOVEREIGN...CONCPT STERTYP. PAGE 130 F2571 — IDEA/COMP COLONIAL DRIVE

S65
JOHNSON H.G.,"A THEORETICAL MODEL OF ECONOMIC NATIONALISM IN NEW AND DEVELOPING STATES." ELITES INDUS INT/TRADE EDU/PROP COST OPTIMAL RATIONAL PWR WEALTH SOCISM STERTYP. PAGE 67 F1325 — NAT/LISM ECO/UNDEV GEN/LAWS

S65
KUNKEL J.H.,"VALUES AND BEHAVIOR IN ECONOMIC DEVELOPMENT." INDIA PERU CULTURE STRUCT CREATE PERS/REL ATTIT PERSON...CHARTS HYPO/EXP ARGEN. PAGE 74 F1449 — SIMUL ECO/UNDEV PSY STERTYP

B67
FONER P.S.,THE BOLSHEVIK REVOLUTION. USA-45 POL/PAR WORKER DIPLOM EDU/PROP MARXISM...STERTYP 20. PAGE 42 F0821 — LABOR INTELL REV PRESS

L67
GREGORY A.J.,"AFRICAN SOCIALISM, SOCIALISM AND FASCISM: AN APPRAISAL." FUT LEAD REV GP/REL RACE/REL NAT/LISM ATTIT...IDEA/COMP STERTYP 20. PAGE 51 F0993 — FASCISM MARXISM SOCISM AFR

S67
GRUN C.,"DEUX ETUDES ALLEMANDES SUR LES PREJUGES NATIONAUX ET LES MOYENS DE LES COMBATTRE." FRANCE GERMANY DIST/IND PROB/SOLV GP/REL AGE/Y RIGID/FLEX ...PSY STAT INT SAMP. PAGE 52 F1010 — ATTIT REGION DISCRIM STERTYP

STEUBER F.A. F2482

STEVENSN/A....ADLAI STEVENSON

STEVENSON A.E. F2483

STEWARD/JH....JULIAN H. STEWARD

STEWART C.F. F2484

STEWART I.G. F2485

STIFEL L.D. F2486

STILL C.H. F2487

STILL J.F. F2488

STILLMAN C.W. F2489

STIMSON/HL....HENRY L. STIMSON

STINCHCOMBE A.L. F2490

STOCHASTIC PROCESSES....SEE PROB/SOLV, MODELS INDEX

STOCKHOLM....STOCKHOLM

STOCKING G.W. F2491

STOCKWELL E.G. F2492

STOESSINGER J.G. F2493

STOHLER J. F2279

STOKES/CB....CARL B. STOKES

STOL....SHORT TAKE-OFF AND LANDING AIRCRAFT

STOLPER W. F2494

STOLPER W.F. F2495

STOLTE S.C. F2496

STOLUROW L.M. F0622

STONE P.A. F2497

STONE/HF....HARLAN FISKE STONE

STONE/IF....I.F. STONE

STONIER A.W. F2498

STORING H.J. F2346

STORING/HJ....H.J. STORING

STOVEL J.A. F2499

STRANGE S. F2500

STRANGE....ESTRANGEMENT, ALIENATION, IMPERSONALITY

S49
ECKLER A.R.,"IMMIGRATION AND THE LABOR FORCE." USA+45 USA-45 EXTR/IND FINAN PROC/MFG AGE/Y SKILL ...CHARTS 19/20 MIGRATION. PAGE 36 F0694 — WORKER STRANGE INDUS ECO/TAC

B61
ROEPKE W.,JENSEITS VON ANGEBOT UND NACHFRAGE (DRITTE VERAENDERTE AUFLAGE). WOR+45 MARKET TEC/DEV ECO/TAC GP/REL INGP/REL NEW/LIB...POLICY SOC IDEA/COMP PERS/COMP 20. PAGE 113 F2233 — SOCIETY STRANGE ECO/DEV STRUCT

B62
VACCARO J.R.,A STATEMENT OF THE LAWS OF CHILE IN MATTERS AFFECTING BUSINESS (3RD ED.). CHILE AGRI FINAN FAM LABOR ECO/TAC FOR/AID TAX ADJUD CONTROL MARRIAGE STRANGE...BIBLIOG 20. PAGE 140 F2756 — CONSTN LAW INDUS MGT

S67
REILLY T.J.,"FREEZING AND CONFISCATION OF CUBAN PROPERTY." CUBA USA+45 LAW DIPLOM LEGIT ADJUD CONTROL. PAGE 111 F2177 — STRANGE OWN ECO/TAC

STRASBOURG....STRASBOURG PLAN

B52
SECRETARIAT COUNCIL OF EUROPE,THE STRASBOURG PLAN. EUR+WWI CONSULT PLAN ECO/TAC TARIFFS DEBATE REGION 20 COUNCL/EUR STRASBOURG. PAGE 119 F2340 — INT/ORG ECO/DEV INT/TRADE DIPLOM

STRATA....SOCIAL STRATA, CLASS DIVISION

B00
MILL J.S.,PRINCIPLES OF POLITICAL ECONOMY. WOR-45 CULTURE SOCIETY STRATA ECO/DEV AGRI EXTR/IND FINAN INDUS DELIB/GP ECO/TAC WEALTH...CONCPT MATH TREND 20. PAGE 91 F1786 — MARKET INT/ORG INT/TRADE

B04
MARX K.,A CONTRIBUTION TO THE CRITIQUE OF POLITICAL ECONOMY (TRANS. FROM 2ND ED. BY N.I. STONE). UK STRATA ECO/DEV FINAN MARKET PLAN BARGAIN CAP/ISM ECO/TAC ATTIT WEALTH...METH/CNCPT BIOG 19. PAGE 86 F1687 — MARXIST NEW/IDEA MARXISM

B11
SOREL G.,LES ILLUSIONS DU PROGRES (1906). UNIV SOCIETY STRATA INDUS GP/REL OWN PRODUC SOCISM 17/20. PAGE 124 F2444 — WORKER POPULISM ECO/DEV ATTIT

B12
HOBSON J.A.,THE EVOLUTION OF MODERN CAPITALISM. MOD/EUR UK STRATA ECO/DEV INDUS INCOME UTIL WEALTH ...SOC GEN/LAWS 7/20. PAGE 60 F1184 — CAP/ISM WORKER TEC/DEV TIME/SEQ

B13
KROPOTKIN P.,THE CONQUEST OF BREAD. SOCIETY STRATA AGRI INDUS WORKER REV HAPPINESS INCOME PRODUC HEALTH MORAL ORD/FREE. PAGE 74 F1444 — ANARCH SOCIALIST OWN AGREE

B18
MARX K.,CAPITAL. FUT MOD/EUR STRATA DIST/IND PROC/MFG TEC/DEV WEALTH...MARXIST WORK 19. PAGE 86 F1688 — ECO/DEV CAP/ISM SOCISM

N19
ENGELS F.,THE BRITISH LABOUR MOVEMENT (PAMPHLET). FRANCE GERMANY MOD/EUR UK USA-45 POL/PAR WORKER PAY EDU/PROP PRICE REPRESENT GP/REL 19. PAGE 37 F0730 — ECO/TAC MARXISM LABOR STRATA

N19
HAGEN E.E.,AN ANALYTICAL MODEL OF THE TRANSITION TO ECONOMIC GROWTH (PAMPHLET). WOR+45 WOR-45 SOCIETY STRATA FINAN NAT/G CONTROL PARTIC PRODUC...PHIL/SCI BIBLIOG 17/20. PAGE 53 F1033 — SIMUL ECO/DEV METH TEC/DEV

N19
INTERNATIONAL LABOUR OFFICE,EMPLOYMENT, UNEMPLOYMENT AND LABOUR FORCE STATISTICS (PAMPHLET). EUR+WWI STRATA AGRI INDUS NAT/G PROB/SOLV PAY AGE SEX...SAMP NAT/COMP METH 20 ILO. PAGE 65 F1278 — WORKER LABOR STAT ECO/DEV

B20
TAWNEY R.H.,THE ACQUISITIVE SOCIETY. STRATA WORKER PROB/SOLV CAP/ISM ECO/TAC CONTROL GP/REL OWN PRIVIL ATTIT ORD/FREE WEALTH 20. PAGE 128 F2536 — INDUS SOCIETY PRODUC MORAL

B24
HOLDSWORTH W.S.,A HISTORY OF ENGLISH LAW; THE COMMON LAW AND ITS RIVALS (VOL. VI). AFR UK STRATA EX/STRUC ADJUD ADMIN CONTROL CT/SYS...JURID CONCPT GEN/LAWS 17 PARLIAMENT ENGLSH/LAW COMMON/LAW. PAGE 61 F1194 — LAW CONSTN LEGIS CHIEF

B25
EDGEWORTH F.Y.,PAPERS RELATING TO POLITICAL ECONOMY. MOD/EUR SOCIETY STRATA DIST/IND INDUS — ECO/DEV CAP/ISM

MARKET NAT/G ACT/RES ECO/TAC EXEC WEALTH ...METH/CNCPT MATH TREND HYPO/EXP SIMUL GEN/METH FOR/TRADE VAL/FREE LOG/LING. PAGE 36 F0702

B27
BELLOC H.,THE SERVILE STATE (1912) (3RD ED.). PRUSSIA UK CULTURE STRATA INDUS NAT/G ECO/TAC CONTROL LEAD SUFF DISCRIM EQUILIB ORD/FREE WEALTH 20. PAGE 12 F0237
WORKER CAP/ISM DOMIN CATH

B29
DE MAN H.,JOY IN WORK. STRATA ECO/DEV ECO/TAC PRODUC ANOMIE ROLE SOCISM...IDEA/COMP 20. PAGE 31 F0605
SOC WORKER HAPPINESS RESPECT

B30
GREEN F.M.,CONSTITUTIONAL DEVELOPMENT IN THE SOUTH ATLANTIC STATES, 1776-1860; A STUDY IN THE EVOLUTION OF DEMOCRACY. USA-45 ELITES SOCIETY STRATA ECO/DEV AGRI POL/PAR EX/STRUC LEGIS CT/SYS REGION...BIBLIOG 18/19 MARYLAND VIRGINIA GEORGIA NORTH/CAR SOUTH/CAR. PAGE 50 F0984
CONSTN PROVS PLURISM REPRESENT

B32
DICKINSON H.D.,INSTITUTIONAL REVENUE: A STUDY OF THE INFLUENCE OF SOCIAL INSTITUTIONS ON THE DISTRIBUTION OF WEALTH. SOCIETY STRATA FINAN ...NEW/IDEA IDEA/COMP 20. PAGE 33 F0632
WEALTH CONCPT METH/CNCPT MARKET

B34
MARX K.,THE CLASS STRUGGLES IN FRANCE. FRANCE INDUS WORKER CONSERVE...TREND GEN/LAWS 19. PAGE 86 F1689
MARXIST STRATA REV INT/TRADE

B35
MARX K.,WAGE-LABOR AND CAPITAL -- VALUE, PRICE AND PROFIT. LABOR PAY PRICE COST INCOME OWN PROFIT WEALTH 19. PAGE 86 F1690
STRATA WORKER MARXIST MARXISM

B35
O'CONNOR H.,REVOLUTION IN SEATTLE. USA-45 STRATA WORKER GP/REL ATTIT SOCISM...OBS BIBLIOG/A 20 SEATTLE STRIKE COM/PARTY. PAGE 99 F1954
REV EDU/PROP LABOR MARXISM

B35
WADE J.,HISTORY OF THE MIDDLE AND WORKING CLASSES; WITH A POPULAR EXPOSITION OF THE ECONOMICAL AND POLITICAL PRINCIPLES.... FRANCE UK CONSTN FINAN INDUS LABOR INCOME PROFIT KNOWL MORAL ORD/FREE WEALTH...CHARTS 14/19. PAGE 142 F2797
WORKER STRATA CONCPT

B36
BELLOC H.,THE RESTORATION OF PROPERTY. UK STRATA NAT/G PROF/ORG DELIB/GP WORKER CREATE PROB/SOLV ECO/TAC PARTIC UTOPIA ORD/FREE SOCISM 20. PAGE 13 F0238
CONTROL MAJORIT CAP/ISM OWN

B38
DAVIES E.,"NATIONAL" CAPITALISM: THE GOVERNMENT'S RECORD AS PROTECTOR OF PRIVATE MONOPOLY. UK ELITES SOCIETY STRATA POL/PAR WORKER PROB/SOLV CONTROL SOCISM 20 MONOPOLY LABOR/PAR CHAMBRLN/N. PAGE 30 F0583
CAP/ISM NAT/G INDUS POLICY

B38
HEIMANN E.,COMMUNISM, FASCISM, OR DEMOCRACY? WOR-45 CONSTN SOCIETY STRATA AGRI CAP/ISM MORAL ORD/FREE ...MAJORIT METH/COMP NAT/COMP 19/20. PAGE 58 F1141
SOCISM MARXISM FASCISM PLURISM

B39
ENGELS F.,HERRN EUGEN DUHRING'S REVOLUTION IN SCIENCE (1878). CULTURE STRATA STRUCT FAM SECT ECO/TAC REV WAR SOCISM...MARXIST 19. PAGE 37 F0731
PWR SOCIETY WEALTH GEN/LAWS

B39
THOMAS J.A.,THE HOUSE OF COMMONS, 1832-1901; A STUDY OF ITS ECONOMIC AND FUNCTIONAL CHARACTER. UK LAW STRATA FINAN DIPLOM CONTROL LEAD LOBBY REPRESENT WEALTH...POLICY STAT BIBLIOG 19/20 PARLIAMENT. PAGE 130 F2561
PARL/PROC LEGIS POL/PAR ECO/DEV

B42
VEBLEN T.B.,THE THEORY OF THE LEISURE CLASS. USA-45 SOCIETY STRATA STRUCT NAT/G SECT WORKER CREATE EDU/PROP ATTIT...SOC GEN/LAWS 19. PAGE 141 F2772
WEALTH ELITES LEISURE PRODUC

S45
MILLS C.W.,"THE TRADE UNION LEADER: A COLLECTIVE PORTRAIT." EX/STRUC TOP/EX INGP/REL...QU CON/ANAL CHARTS. PAGE 92 F1798
LABOR LEAD STAT STRATA

B47
ISAAC J.,ECONOMICS OF MIGRATION. MOD/EUR CULTURE STRATA STRUCT NAT/G COLONIAL WEALTH...OLD/LIB TREND TIME 19/20 EUROPE/W MIGRATION. PAGE 65 F1289
HABITAT SOC GEOG

B47
WARNER W.L.,THE SOCIAL SYSTEM OF THE MODERN FACTORY; THE STRIKE: AN ANALYSIS. USA-45 STRATA WORKER ECO/TAC GP/REL INGP/REL...MGT SOC CHARTS 20 YANKEE/C. PAGE 143 F2824
ROLE STRUCT LABOR PROC/MFG

S47
DAHL R.A.,"WORKERS' CONTROL OF INDUSTRY AND THE BRITISH LABOUR PARTY." UK STRATA STRUCT DELIB/GP BARGAIN CAP/ISM DEBATE CONTROL CHOOSE GP/REL ATTIT
INDUS LABOR WORKER

ROLE PWR 19/20 PARLIAMENT LABOR/PAR FABIAN. PAGE 29 F0570
SOCISM

B48
DURBIN E.F.M.,THE POLITICS OF DEMOCRATIC SOCIALISM; AN ESSAY ON SOCIAL POLICY. STRATA POL/PAR PLAN COERCE DRIVE PERSON PWR MARXISM...CHARTS METH/COMP. PAGE 35 F0684
SOCIALIST POPULISM POLICY SOCIETY

B48
MCCABE D.A.,LABOR AND SOCIAL ORGANIZATION. LEGIS WORKER CAP/ISM ECO/TAC PAY MARXISM SOCISM SOC/INTEG 20 INTRVN/ECO. PAGE 88 F1717
LABOR STRATA NEW/LIB

B49
LEE A.M.,SOCIAL PROBLEMS IN AMERICA: A SOURCE BOOK. STRATA STRUCT KIN NEIGH VOL/ASSN ACT/RES LEAD CRIME AGE SEX 20. PAGE 77 F1504
SOC SOCIETY PERSON EDU/PROP

B50
ADORNO T.W.,THE AUTHORITARIAN PERSONALITY. STRATA SECT PROB/SOLV ECO/TAC DISCRIM ATTIT SEX...SOC INT CHARTS METH 20. PAGE 3 F0044
AUTHORIT PERSON ALL/IDEOS SOCIETY

B50
CLARK J.M.,ALTERNATIVE TO SERFDOM. SOCIETY STRATA INDUS MARKET WORKER PRICE GP/REL PROFIT BIO/SOC PWR WEALTH...GEN/LAWS 20 KEYNES/JM. PAGE 25 F0481
ORD/FREE POPULISM ECO/TAC REPRESENT

B50
HUNT R.N.,THE THEORY AND PRACTICE OF COMMUNISM. STRUCT WORKER NAT/LISM TOTALISM...CONCPT TREND 19/20 STALIN/J EUROPE. PAGE 63 F1244
MARXISM SOCISM REV STRATA

B50
HUTCHISON K.,THE DECLINE AND FALL OF BRITISH CAPITALISM. UK ELITES STRATA ECO/DEV LABOR WORKER CONTROL WAR PWR...BIBLIOG/A 19/20. PAGE 63 F1249
CAP/ISM SOCISM LAISSEZ DOMIN

C50
ROUSSEAU J.J.,"A DISCOURSE ON POLITICAL ECONOMY" (1755) IN THE SOCIAL CONTRACT AND DISCOURSES." UNIV SOCIETY STRATA STRUCT CONSEN EQUILIB HAPPINESS UTOPIA HEALTH WEALTH...POLICY WELF/ST. PAGE 114 F2252
NAT/G ECO/TAC TAX GEN/LAWS

B51
PETERSON F.,SURVEY OF LABOR ECONOMICS (REV. ED.). STRATA ECO/DEV LABOR INSPECT BARGAIN PAY PRICE EXEC ROUTINE GP/REL ALL/VALS ORD/FREE 20 AFL/CIO DEPT/LABOR. PAGE 105 F2069
WORKER DEMAND IDEA/COMP T

B52
BEVAN A.,IN PLACE OF FEAR. WOR+45 STRATA LEGIS REPRESENT OWN NEW/LIB POPULISM...CHARTS 20. PAGE 14 F0273
SOCISM SOCIALIST WEALTH MAJORIT

B52
TANNENBAUM F.,A PHILOSOPHY OF LABOR. SOCIETY STRATA INDUS LG/CO AGREE ADJUST OWN ORD/FREE PWR...CONCPT 20. PAGE 128 F2533
LABOR PHIL/SCI WORKER CREATE

S52
CHINOY E.,"THE TRADITION OF OPPORTUNITY AND THE ASPIRATIONS OF AUTOMOBILE WORKERS" (BMR)" STRATA ACT/RES ALL/VALS SKILL...INT 20. PAGE 24 F0468
WORKER ECO/DEV DRIVE INDUS

S52
HEBERLE R.,"ON POLITICAL ECOLOGY" (BMR)" INCOME ATTIT WEALTH...GEOG METH SOC/INTEG 20. PAGE 58 F1133
HABITAT STRATA CHOOSE

S53
MCKEE J.B.,"STATUS AND POWER IN THE INDUSTRIAL COMMUNITY; A COMMENT ON DRUCKER'S THESIS." LABOR LEGIT LEAD GP/REL PWR...MGT CONCPT. PAGE 88 F1730
SOC STRATA NEIGH PARTIC

B54
HAYEK FA V.O.N.,CAPITALISM AND THE HISTORIANS. MOD/EUR TEC/DEV GP/REL WEALTH...HIST/WRIT ANTHOL 19. PAGE 57 F1124
CAP/ISM LABOR STRATA ECO/TAC

B54
LENIN V.I.,SELECTED WORKS (12 VOLS.). USSR INTELL SOCIETY STRATA STRUCT NAT/G POL/PAR WORKER CAP/ISM REV WAR...MARXIST PHIL/SCI 20 MARX/KARL LENIN/VI. PAGE 78 F1520
COM MARXISM

B54
WASHBURNE N.F.,INTERPRETING SOCIAL CHANGE IN AMERICA. USA+45 STRATA FAM NAT/G SECT OP/RES ECO/TAC EDU/PROP HABITAT...SOC TIME/SEQ TREND 20 BUREAUCRCY. PAGE 143 F2826
CULTURE STRUCT CREATE TEC/DEV

S54
MACK R.W.,"ECOLOGICAL PATTERNS IN AN INDUSTRIAL SHOP" (BMR)" USA+45 CULTURE SOCIETY STRATA STRUCT LABOR NEIGH GP/REL ADJUST HABITAT...SOC SOC/INTEG 20. PAGE 83 F1634
INDUS DISCRIM WORKER

B55
BUCHANAN N.S.,APPROACHES TO ECONOMIC DEVELOPMENT. FUT USA+45 WOR+45 STRATA ECO/DEV INT/ORG NAT/G TEC/DEV DIPLOM FOR/AID ATTIT KNOWL PWR WEALTH ...RELATIV METH/CNCPT SELF/OBS TREND CON/ANAL
ECO/UNDEV ECO/TAC INT/TRADE

STERTYP GEN/LAWS FOR/TRADE COMMUN 20. PAGE 20 F0380

B55
COLE G.D.H.,STUDIES IN CLASS STRUCTURE. UK NAT/G WORKER TEC/DEV EDU/PROP...CLASSIF CHARTS 20. PAGE 26 F0501
STRUCT STRATA ELITES CONCPT

B55
GEORGE H.,PROGRESS AND POVERTY (1880). STRATA STRUCT INDUS TEC/DEV CAP/ISM EQUILIB INCOME OWN UTOPIA...WELF/ST CONCPT NEW/IDEA 19. PAGE 47 F0915
ECO/DEV ECO/TAC TAX WEALTH

B55
MAYO H.B.,DEMOCRACY AND MARXISM. COM USSR STRATA NAT/G WORKER ECO/TAC REV MORAL...PHIL/SCI HIST/WRIT IDEA/COMP WORSHIP 20 MARX/KARL LENIN/VI STALIN/J TROTSKY/L. PAGE 87 F1708
MARXISM CAP/ISM

B55
PEDLER F.J.,ECONOMIC GEOGRAPHY OF WEST AFRICA. GAMBIA NIGER SIER/LEONE STRATA EXTR/IND MARKET LABOR INT/TRADE DEMAND HABITAT WEALTH...CHARTS 20. PAGE 104 F2046
ECO/UNDEV GEOG PRODUC EFFICIENCY

B55
WRONG D.H.,AMERICAN AND CANADIAN VIEWPOINTS. CANADA USA+45 CONSTN STRATA FAM SECT WORKER ECO/TAC EDU/PROP ADJUD MARRIAGE...IDEA/COMP 20. PAGE 149 F2936
DIPLOM ATTIT NAT/COMP CULTURE

B56
UPHOFF W.H.,UNDERSTANDING THE UNION MEMBER (PAMPHLET). STRATA R+D LEAD PARTIC...METH/CNCPT STAT QU. PAGE 133 F2624
LABOR WORKER ATTIT DRIVE

C56
MCKEE J.B.,"THE POWER TO DECIDE" IN M. WEINBERG AND O. SHABET, SOCIETY AND MAN." ELITES STRATA REPRESENT GP/REL ATTIT PWR MUNICH BUSINESS. PAGE 88 F1731
LABOR DECISION LEAD

B57
NANIWADA H.,STAAT UND WIRTSCHAFT; GRUNDLEGUNG DER NATIONALOEKONOMIE ALS DER LOGIK DER BURGERLICHEN GESELLSCHAFT. WOR+45 WOR-45 STRATA MARKET WORKER INGP/REL DEMAND EQUILIB WEALTH...POLICY IDEA/COMP GEN/LAWS 17/20 MARX/KARL KEYNES/JM LENIN/VI. PAGE 96 F1890
ALL/IDEOS ECO/TAC SOCIETY NAT/G

B57
SCHNEIDER E.V.,INDUSTRIAL SOCIOLOGY: THE SOCIAL RELATIONS OF INDUSTRY AND COMMUNITY. STRATA INDUS NAT/G NEIGH CREATE ADMIN PARTIC GP/REL RACE/REL ROLE PWR...POLICY BIBLIOG. PAGE 117 F2308
LABOR MGT INGP/REL STRUCT

B58
PALMER E.E.,THE ECONOMY AND THE DEMOCRATIC IDEAL. USA+45 USA-45 STRATA CHIEF CT/SYS ORD/FREE SOCISM ...MAJORIT CONCPT ANTHOL 18/20 PRESIDENT. PAGE 103 F2021
ECO/DEV POPULISM METH/COMP ECO/TAC

B58
ROBERTS B.C.,NATIONAL WAGES POLICY IN WAR AND PEACE. EUR+WWI GERMANY S/ASIA SWEDEN UK USA+45 USA-45 STRATA ECO/DEV LABOR NAT/G DELIB/GP PLAN INT/TRADE WEALTH...STAT TREND CHARTS 20. PAGE 112 F2205
CREATE ECO/TAC

B58
TILLION G.,ALGERIA: THE REALITIES. ALGERIA FRANCE ISLAM CULTURE STRATA PROB/SOLV DOMIN REV NAT/LISM WEALTH MARXISM...GEOG 20. PAGE 130 F2573
ECO/UNDEV SOC COLONIAL DIPLOM

B59
BAUER P.T.,UNITED STATES AID AND INDIAN ECONOMIC DEVELOPMENT. INDIA STRATA FINAN PLAN BUDGET DIPLOM INGP/REL EFFICIENCY SOCISM 20 AID. PAGE 11 F0215
FOR/AID ECO/UNDEV ECO/TAC POLICY

B59
KOLLAI H.R.,DIE EINGLIEDERUNG DER VERTRIEBENEN UND ZUWANDERER IN NIEDERSACHSEN. GERMANY/W SOCIETY STRATA STRUCT LABOR SOC/INTEG 20. PAGE 72 F1422
GP/REL INGP/REL

B59
KRIPALANI J.B.,CLASS STRUGGLE. INDIA WOR+45 ECO/UNDEV LABOR CAP/ISM EDU/PROP INGP/REL ...SOCIALIST IDEA/COMP 17/20. PAGE 73 F1440
MARXISM STRATA COERCE ECO/TAC

B59
MADHOK B.,POLITICAL TRENDS IN INDIA. INDIA PAKISTAN UK STRATA ECO/UNDEV POL/PAR LEGIS CAP/ISM DIPLOM COLONIAL CHOOSE MARXISM...SOC TREND 20 GANDHI/M NEHRU/J. PAGE 84 F1639
GEOG NAT/G

C59
MINTZ S.W.,"INTERNAL MARKET SYS AS MECHANISMS OF SOCIAL ARTIC," IN V.F. RAY, INTERMED SOCIETIES, SOCIAL MOBILITY, AND COMMUNIC (BMR). UNIV STRATA GP/REL INGP/REL...GEOG SOC BIBLIOG. PAGE 92 F1804
MARKET SOCIETY ECO/UNDEV STRUCT

B60
FERNANDES F.,MUDANCAS SOCIAIS NO BRASIL. BRAZIL L/A+17C SOCIETY AGRI PROVS LEAD GP/REL RACE/REL ORD/FREE...SOC SOC/INTEG 20 SAO/PAULO. PAGE 40 F0786
ECO/UNDEV STRATA INDUS

B60
GRANICK D.,THE RED EXECUTIVE. COM USA+45 SOCIETY ECO/DEV INDUS NAT/G POL/PAR EX/STRUC PLAN ECO/TAC EDU/PROP ADMIN EXEC ATTIT DRIVE...GP/COMP 20. PAGE 50 F0976
PWR STRATA USSR ELITES

B60
MAYO H.B.,INTRODUCTION TO MARXIST THEORY. SECT WORKER POPULISM SOCISM 19/20. PAGE 87 F1709
MARXISM STRATA IDEA/COMP PHIL/SCI

B60
MC CLELLAN G.S.,INDIA. AFR CHINA/COM INDIA CONSTN ELITES STRATA AGRI POL/PAR FOR/AID ARMS/CONT REV MARXISM...CENSUS BIBLIOG 20 GANDHI/M NEHRU/J. PAGE 87 F1712
DIPLOM NAT/G SOCIETY ECO/UNDEV

B60
MOORE W.E.,LABOR COMMITMENT AND SOCIAL CHANGE IN DEVELOPING AREAS. SOCIETY STRATA ECO/UNDEV MARKET VOL/ASSN WORKER AUTHORIT SKILL...MGT NAT/COMP SOC/INTEG 20. PAGE 93 F1823
LABOR ORD/FREE ATTIT INDUS

B60
PETERSON W.C.,THE WELFARE STATE IN FRANCE. EUR+WWI FRANCE FUT STRATA PROB/SOLV TAX GIVE RECEIVE INCOME ORD/FREE PWR...CHARTS 20. PAGE 105 F2070
NEW/LIB ECO/TAC WEALTH NAT/G

B60
RAMA C.M.,LAS CLASES SOCIALES EN EL URUGUAY. L/A+17C URUGUAY ELITES SOCIETY STRATA INDUS ATTIT HABITAT PWR...GEOG SOC/INTEG MUNICH 20. PAGE 109 F2138
ECO/UNDEV STRUCT PARTIC

B60
ROBINSON J.,AN ESSAY ON MARXIAN ECONOMICS. USA+45 STRATA INDUS MARKET CAP/ISM...METH/COMP 19/20 MARX/KARL. PAGE 113 F2222
IDEA/COMP MARXISM ACADEM

S60
"THE EMERGING COMMON MARKETS IN LATIN AMERICA." FUT L/A+17C STRATA DIST/IND INDUS LABOR NAT/G LEGIS ECO/TAC ADMIN RIGID/FLEX HEALTH...NEW/IDEA TIME/SEQ OAS 20. PAGE 1 F0013
FINAN ECO/UNDEV INT/TRADE

S60
GROSSMAN G.,"SOVIET GROWTH: ROUTINE, INERTIA, AND PRESSURE." COM STRATA NAT/G DELIB/GP PLAN TEC/DEV ECO/TAC EDU/PROP ADMIN ROUTINE DRIVE WEALTH 20. PAGE 52 F1007
POL/PAR ECO/DEV AFR USSR

S60
KELLOGG C.E.,"TRANSFER OF BASIC SKILLS OF FOOD PRODUCTION." AFR FUT S/ASIA STRATA ECO/UNDEV LABOR VOL/ASSN RIGID/FLEX...OLD/LIB SOCIALIST NEW/IDEA STAT PROJ/TEST GEN/LAWS 20. PAGE 70 F1370
AGRI PLAN

S60
MORALES C.J.,"TRADE AND ECONOMIC INTEGRATION IN LATIN AMERICA." FUT L/A+17C LAW STRATA ECO/UNDEV DIST/IND INDUS LABOR NAT/G LEGIS ECO/TAC ADMIN RIGID/FLEX WEALTH...CONCPT NEW/IDEA CONT/OBS TIME/SEQ WORK 20. PAGE 93 F1825
FINAN INT/TRADE REGION

B61
AMERICAN MANAGEMENT ASSN,SUPERIOR-SUBORDINATE COMMUNICATION IN MANAGEMENT. STRATA FINAN INDUS SML/CO WORKER CONTROL EXEC ATTIT 20. PAGE 5 F0090
MGT ACT/RES PERS/REL LG/CO

B61
BARRASH J.,LABOR'S GRASS ROOTS; A STUDY OF THE LOCAL UNION. STRATA BARGAIN LEAD REPRESENT DEMAND ATTIT PWR. PAGE 10 F0192
LABOR USA+45 INGP/REL EXEC

B61
BAUER P.T.,INDIAN ECONOMIC POLICY AND DEVELOPMENT. INDIA STRATA AGRI FINAN POL/PAR BUDGET FOR/AID GOV/REL EFFICIENCY...CENSUS 20. PAGE 11 F0216
ECO/UNDEV ECO/TAC POLICY PLAN

B61
DELEFORTRIE-SOU N.,LES DIRIGEANTS DE L'INDUSTRIE FRANCAISE. FRANCE CULTURE ELITES PROB/SOLV ...DECISION STAT CHARTS 20. PAGE 32 F0613
INDUS STRATA TOP/EX LEAD

B61
DOIG J.W.,THE POLITICS OF METROPOLITAN TRANSPORTATION. DELIB/GP WORKER DIPLOM TASK EFFICIENCY UTIL...CHARTS BIBLIOG MUNICH 20 NEW/YORK NEW/JERSEY PUB/TRANS RAILROAD. PAGE 34 F0652
PROB/SOLV STRATA DIST/IND

B61
FLINN M.W.,AN ECONOMIC AND SOCIAL HISTORY OF BRITAIN, 1066-1939. UK LAW STRATA STRUCT AGRI DIST/IND INDUS WORKER INT/TRADE WAR...CENSUS 11/20. PAGE 42 F0811
SOCIETY SOC

B61
GOODWIN C.D.W.,CANADIAN ECONOMIC THOUGHT. CANADA STRATA TEC/DEV CAP/ISM TARIFFS TAX COST EFFICIENCY WEALTH...METH/CNCPT TREND 20 MARITIME ONTARIO. PAGE 49 F0952
INT/TRADE ECO/DEV FINAN DEMAND

B61
PROUDHON P.J.,LA GUERRE ET LA PAIX (2 VOLS.). UNIV STRATA PROB/SOLV EQUILIB INCOME ATTIT...CONCPT 19. PAGE 108 F2125
WAR PEACE WEALTH

B61
STROUD G.S.,LABOR HISTORY IN THE UNITED STATES: A GENERAL BIBLIOGRAPHY. USA+45 USA-45 STRATA VOL/ASSN AUTOMAT GP/REL INGP/REL ATTIT HEALTH 18/20. PAGE 127 F2504
BIBLIOG WORKER LABOR

S61
HEILBRONER R.L.,"DYNAMICS OF FOREIGN AID: PROBLEMS OF UNDERDEVELOPED NATIONS PLAGUE ASSISTANCE PROGRAM." FUT USA+45 WOR+45 STRATA NAT/G PLAN TEC/DEV ATTIT DRIVE WEALTH WORK 20. PAGE 58 F1135 ECO/UNDEV ECO/TAC FOR/AID

B62
COX O.C.,CAPITALISM AND AMERICAN LEADERSHIP. WOR+45 WOR-45 STRATA INDUS SECT INT/TRADE EXEC INGP/REL RACE/REL RATIONAL PWR WEALTH. PAGE 28 F0548 CAP/ISM LEAD ECO/DEV SOCIETY

B62
DEBUYST F.,LAS CLASES SOCIALES EN AMERICA LATINA. L/A+17C SOCIETY STRUCT WORKER EDU/PROP RACE/REL ATTIT HABITAT ROLE...GEOG SOC NAT/COMP SOC/INTEG 20. PAGE 32 F0612 STRATA GP/REL WEALTH

B62
FAO,FOOD AND AGRICULTURE ORGANIZATION AFRICAN SURVEY. AFR CONGO/BRAZ GHANA STRATA AGRI INT/ORG TEC/DEV FOR/AID INT/TRADE RACE/REL DEMAND EFFICIENCY PRODUC...GEOG 20 UN CONGO/LEOP. PAGE 39 F0763 ECO/TAC WEALTH EXTR/IND ECO/UNDEV

B62
HEILBRONER R.L.,THE MAKING OF ECONOMIC SOCIETY. FUT WOR-45 SOCIETY STRATA ECO/DEV ECO/UNDEV ECO/TAC LEGIT ROUTINE...SOC RECORD REC/INT KNO/TEST CENSUS STERTYP GEN/LAWS. PAGE 58 F1136 CAP/ISM SOCISM

B62
KOLKO G.,WEALTH AND POWER IN AMERICA. USA+45 SOCIETY STRATA LG/CO ECO/TAC TAX PWR...SOC BIBLIOG 20 DEPRESSION. PAGE 72 F1420 STRUCT INCOME ECO/DEV WEALTH

B62
SELOSOEMARDJAN O.,SOCIAL CHANGES IN JOGJAKARTA. INDONESIA NETHERLAND ELITES STRATA STRUCT FAM POL/PAR CREATE DIPLOM INT/TRADE EDU/PROP ADMIN GOV/REL...SOC 20 JAVA CHINJAP. PAGE 119 F2352 ECO/UNDEV CULTURE REV COLONIAL

S62
IOVTCHOUK M.T.,"ON SOME THEORETICAL PRINCIPLES AND METHODS OF SOCIOLOGICAL INVESTIGATIONS (IN RUSSIAN)." FUT USA+45 STRATA R+D NAT/G POL/PAR TOP/EX ACT/RES PLAN ECO/TAC EDU/PROP ROUTINE ATTIT RIGID/FLEX MARXISM SOCISM...MARXIST METH/CNCPT OBS TREND NAT/COMP GEN/LAWS 20. PAGE 65 F1288 COM ECO/DEV CAP/ISM USSR

S62
ZAUBERMAN A.,"SOVIET AND CHINESE STRATEGY FOR ECONOMIC GROWTH." ASIA CHINA/COM COM USSR STRATA VOL/ASSN PLAN ATTIT PWR...METH/CNCPT GEN/LAWS WORK TERR/GP 20. PAGE 150 F2959 ECO/DEV EDU/PROP

B63
BRAIBANTI R.J.D.,ADMINISTRATION AND ECONOMIC DEVELOPMENT IN INDIA. INDIA S/ASIA SOCIETY STRATA ECO/TAC PERSON WEALTH...MGT GEN/LAWS TOT/POP VAL/FREE 20. PAGE 18 F0337 ECO/UNDEV ADMIN

B63
DE VRIES E.,SOCIAL ASPECTS OF ECONOMIC DEVELOPMENT IN LATIN AMERICA. CULTURE SOCIETY STRATA FINAN INDUS INT/ORG DELIB/GP ACT/RES ECO/TAC EDU/PROP ADMIN ATTIT SUPEGO HEALTH KNOWL ORD/FREE...SOC STAT TREND ANTHOL TOT/POP VAL/FREE. PAGE 31 F0608 L/A+17C ECO/UNDEV

B63
ELLENDER A.J.,A REPORT ON UNITED STATES FOREIGN OPERATIONS IN AFRICA. SOUTH/AFR USA+45 STRATA EXTR/IND FORCES RACE/REL ISOLAT SOVEREIGN...CHARTS 20 NEGRO. PAGE 37 F0721 FOR/AID DIPLOM WEALTH ECO/UNDEV

B63
GEERTZ C.,PEDDLERS AND PRINCES: SOCIAL DEVELOPMENT AND ECONOMIC CHANGE IN TWO INDONESIAN TOWNS. S/ASIA CULTURE SOCIETY STRATA FACE/GP CREATE TEC/DEV ECO/TAC ORD/FREE WEALTH...OBS INT CENSUS CHARTS WORK TOT/POP METH/GP TERR/GP VAL/FREE 20 MUNICH. PAGE 47 F0913 ECO/UNDEV SOC ELITES INDONESIA

B63
IANNI O.,INDUSTRIALIZACAO E DESENVOLVIMENTO SOCIAL NO BRASIL. BRAZIL L/A+17C STRATA STRUCT ECO/UNDEV EDU/PROP LEAD LOBBY NAT/LISM 20. PAGE 64 F1257 WORKER GP/REL INDUS PARTIC

B63
JACOBS P.,STATE OF UNIONS. USA+45 STRATA TOP/EX GP/REL RACE/REL DEMAND DISCRIM ATTIT PWR 20 CONGRESS NEGRO HOFFA/J. PAGE 66 F1296 LABOR ECO/TAC BARGAIN DECISION

B63
LAGOS G.,INTERNATIONAL STRATIFICATION AND UNDERDEVELOPED COUNTRIES. L/A+17C WOR+45 PLAN ECO/TAC PWR RESPECT WEALTH...METH/CNCPT STAT CHARTS SIMUL GEN/LAWS TRUE/GP METH/GP VAL/FREE 20. PAGE 74 F1459 ECO/UNDEV STRATA

B63
LAIRD R.D.,SOVIET AGRICULTURAL AND PEASANT AFFAIRS. FUT STRATA LOC/G DELIB/GP ACT/RES TEC/DEV ECO/TAC EDU/PROP ATTIT RIGID/FLEX ORD/FREE SKILL WEALTH ...STAT CON/ANAL ANTHOL MUNICH WORK VAL/FREE 20. PAGE 74 F1461 COM AGRI POLICY

B63
MARX K.,THE POVERTY OF PHILOSOPHY (1847). SOCIETY STRATA INDUS WORKER OWN UTOPIA SOCISM...GEN/LAWS MARX/KARL. PAGE 86 F1692 MARXIST PRODUC

B63
MINGAY G.E.,ENGLISH LANDED SOCIETY IN THE EIGHTEENTH CENTURY. UK ELITES STRUCT AGRI INDUS CONTROL WEALTH 18. PAGE 92 F1802 OWN STRATA PWR

B63
WAGLEY C.,INTRODUCTION TO BRAZIL. BRAZIL L/A+17C FAM KIN SCHOOL SECT ATTIT WEALTH...GEOG SOC. PAGE 142 F2799 ECO/UNDEV ELITES HABITAT STRATA

L63
ADERBIGDE A.,"SYMPOSIUM ON WEST AFRICA INTEGRATION." AFR EUR+WWI FUT CULTURE SOCIETY STRATA DIST/IND INDUS MARKET SERV/IND DELIB/GP PLAN TEC/DEV DOMIN EDU/PROP LEGIT COERCE ATTIT ALL/VALS ...POLICY STAT TREND CHARTS VAL/FREE. PAGE 2 F0040 FINAN ECO/TAC REGION

L63
OLSON M. JR.,"RAPID ECONOMIC GROWTH AS A DESTABILIZING FORCE." WOR+45 WOR-45 STRATA ECO/UNDEV FAM KIN CREATE TEC/DEV DIPLOM PEACE ATTIT PERSON RIGID/FLEX PWR RESPECT WEALTH...SOC 20. PAGE 101 F1989 SOCIETY FOR/AID

S63
BILL J.A.,"THE SOCIAL AND ECONOMIC FOUNDATIONS OF POWER IN CONTEMPORARY IRAN." ISLAM CULTURE NAT/G ECO/TAC DOMIN COERCE ATTIT PWR WEALTH...TREND VAL/FREE 20. PAGE 15 F0284 SOCIETY STRATA IRAN

S63
HOOVER C.B.,"ECONOMIC REFORM VERSUS ECONOMIC GROWTH IN UNDERDEVELOPED COUNTRIES." FUT WOR+45 ELITES STRATA ECO/UNDEV DIST/IND INDUS TEC/DEV CAP/ISM FOR/AID INT/TRADE ATTIT WEALTH...MYTH TREND STERTYP GEN/LAWS WORK 20. PAGE 61 F1209 ECO/DEV ECO/TAC

S63
REDDAWAY W.B.,"THE ECONOMICS OF UNDERDEVELOPED COUNTRIES." S/ASIA WOR+45 WOR-45 STRATA AGRI COM/IND DIST/IND MARKET PROC/MFG PLAN TEC/DEV FOR/AID BAL/PAY ATTIT DRIVE SKILL WORK FOR/TRADE 20. PAGE 110 F2165 ECO/TAC ECO/UNDEV INDIA

B64
AHMAD M.,THE CIVIL SERVANT IN PAKISTAN. PAKISTAN ECO/UNDEV COLONIAL INGP/REL...SOC CHARTS BIBLIOG 20 CIVIL/SERV. PAGE 3 F0051 WELF/ST ADMIN ATTIT STRATA

B64
BASTIAT F.,ECONOMIC HARMONIES (1850). STRATA STRUCT ECO/DEV BUDGET TAX PRICE LOBBY COST. PAGE 11 F0206 ECO/TAC PLAN INT/TRADE LAISSEZ

B64
BAUCHET P.,ECONOMIC PLANNING. FRANCE STRATA LG/CO CAP/ISM ADMIN PARL/PROC DEMAND OPTIMAL ATTIT PWR SOCISM...POLICY CHARTS 20. PAGE 11 F0212 ECO/DEV NAT/G PLAN ECO/TAC

B64
LITVAK I.A.,MARKETING: CANADA. CANADA STRATA PROC/MFG LEGIS TEC/DEV DIPLOM INT/TRADE PRICE AUTOMAT ATTIT WEALTH...ANTHOL 20. PAGE 81 F1587 ECO/TAC MARKET ECO/DEV EFFICIENCY

B64
MEISEL J.,PAPERS ON THE 1962 ELECTION. CANADA PROVS SECT GP/REL CONSEN EFFICIENCY...MAJORIT 20. PAGE 89 F1751 POL/PAR RECORD CHOOSE STRATA

B64
MORGAN H.W.,AMERICAN SOCIALISM 1900-1960. AFR USA+45 USA-45 INTELL AGRI LABOR WORKER BARGAIN ECO/TAC GP/REL RACE/REL 20 NEGRO MIGRATION. PAGE 93 F1830 SOCISM POL/PAR ECO/DEV STRATA

B64
NOVACK D.E.,DEVELOPMENT AND SOCIETY; THE DYNAMICS OF ECONOMIC CHANGE. WOR+45 STRATA STRUCT ECO/TAC CONTROL CROWD REV GP/REL ADJUST PRODUC WEALTH PSY. PAGE 99 F1940 SOCIETY CULTURE SOC ECO/UNDEV

B64
SCHULTZ T.W.,TRANSFORMING TRADITIONAL AGRICULTURE. WOR+45 WOR-45 CULTURE STRATA FINAN ACT/RES ECO/TAC ATTIT KNOWL SKILL...MATH STAT TIME/SEQ GEN/LAWS VAL/FREE. PAGE 117 F2316 AGRI ECO/UNDEV

B64
SEERS D.,CUBA: THE ECONOMIC AND SOCIAL REVOLUTION. L/A+17C USSR YUGOSLAVIA STRATA AGRI INDUS SCHOOL DELIB/GP PLAN ECO/TAC DOMIN EDU/PROP ATTIT RIGID/FLEX ALL/VALS...STAT OBS TIME/SEQ WORK VAL/FREE 20. PAGE 119 F2341 ACT/RES COERCE CUBA REV

B64
TAEUBER I.B.,POPULATION TRENDS IN THE UNITED STATES: 1900 TO 1960. USA+45 USA-45 PROVS INCOME AGE...SOC TIME/SEQ TREND CHARTS MUNICH TIME 20 NEGRO. PAGE 128 F2522 CENSUS GEOG STRATA STRUCT

B64
TAWNEY R.H.,EQUALITY. UK CULTURE STRATA ECO/TAC EDU/PROP REPRESENT OWN NEW/LIB...MAJORIT WELF/ST SOC 20. PAGE 129 F2538 WEALTH STRUCT ELITES POPULISM

B64
WITHERS W.,THE ECONOMIC CRISIS IN LATIN AMERICA. L/A+17C
BRAZIL CHILE STRATA AGRI DIPLOM FOR/AID PWR SOCISM ECO/UNDEV
...POLICY 20 MEXIC/AMER ARGEN ALL/PROG. PAGE 148 CAP/ISM
F2914 ALL/IDEOS

B64
WRIGHT G.,RURAL REVOLUTION IN FRANCE: THE PEASANTRY PWR
IN THE TWENTIETH CENTURY. EUR+WWI MOD/EUR LAW STRATA
CULTURE AGRI POL/PAR DELIB/GP LEGIS ECO/TAC FRANCE
EDU/PROP COERCE CHOOSE ATTIT RIGID/FLEX HEALTH REV
...STAT CENSUS CHARTS VAL/FREE 20. PAGE 149 F2932

B64
ZOLLSCHAN G.K.,EXPLORATIONS IN SOCIAL CHANGE. ORD/FREE
SOCIETY STRATA STRUCT ECO/UNDEV EX/STRUC...PSY SIMUL
ANTHOL 20. PAGE 151 F2968 CONCPT
CULTURE

C64
NORGREN P.H.,"TOWARD FAIR EMPLOYMENT." USA+45 LAW RACE/REL
STRATA LABOR NAT/G FORCES ACT/RES ADMIN ATTIT DISCRIM
...POLICY BIBLIOG 20 NEGRO. PAGE 98 F1932 WORKER
MGT

B65
APTER D.E.,THE POLITICS OF MODERNIZATION. AFR ECO/UNDEV
L/A+17C CULTURE NAT/G POL/PAR ADMIN COLONIAL GEN/LAWS
NAT/LISM ATTIT RIGID/FLEX PWR...SOC CONCPT. PAGE 6 STRATA
F0109 CREATE

B65
COLLINS H.,KARL MARX AND THE BRITISH LABOR MARXISM
MOVEMENT, YEARS OF THE FIRST INTERNATIONAL. EUR+WWI LABOR
MOD/EUR UK STRATA INDUS NAT/G POL/PAR SOCISM INT/ORG
...CONCPT 19/20 MARX/KARL. PAGE 26 F0507 WORKER

B65
CRANE E.,MARKETING COMMUNICATION: A BEHAVIORAL EDU/PROP
APPROACH TO MEN, MESSAGES, AND MEDIA. STRATA R+D MARKET
VOL/ASSN CROWD DRIVE PERSON SKILL WEALTH. PAGE 28 PERCEPT
F0551 ATTIT

B65
OECD,MEDITERRANEAN REGIONAL PROJECT: TURKEY; EDU/PROP
EDUCATION AND DEVELOPMENT. FUT TURKEY SOCIETY ACADEM
STRATA FINAN NAT/G PROF/ORG PLAN PROB/SOLV ADMIN SCHOOL
COST...STAT CHARTS 20 OECD. PAGE 100 F1969 ECO/UNDEV

B65
OECD,THE MEDITERRANEAN REGIONAL PROJECT: PORTUGAL; EDU/PROP
EDUCATION AND DEVELOPMENT. PORTUGAL SOCIETY STRATA SCHOOL
FINAN PROF/ORG WORKER PLAN PROB/SOLV ADMIN...POLICY ACADEM
STAT CHARTS METH 20 OECD. PAGE 100 F1970 ECO/UNDEV

B65
OECD,THE MEDITERRANEAN REGIONAL PROJECT: ITALY; SCHOOL
EDUCATION AND DEVELOPMENT. ITALY SOCIETY STRATA EDU/PROP
FINAN NAT/G PROF/ORG WORKER PLAN PROB/SOLV ADMIN ECO/UNDEV
...STAT CHARTS METH 20 OECD. PAGE 100 F1971 ACADEM

B65
OECD,THE MEDITERRANEAN REGIONAL PROJECT: SPAIN; ECO/UNDEV
EDUCATION AND DEVELOPMENT. FUT SPAIN STRATA FINAN EDU/PROP
NAT/G WORKER PLAN PROB/SOLV ADMIN COST...POLICY ACADEM
STAT CHARTS 20 OECD. PAGE 100 F1973 SCHOOL

B65
PEARL A.,NEW CAREERS FOR THE POOR: THE NON- SOC/WK
PROFESSIONAL IN HUMAN SERVICE. USA+45 SERV/IND WEALTH
NAT/G NEIGH WORKER EDU/PROP AUTOMAT SKILL...WELF/ST STRATA
NEW/IDEA BIBLIOG SOC/INTEG 20. PAGE 104 F2044 POLICY

B65
SELIGMAN B.B.,POVERTY AS A PUBLIC ISSUE. USA+45 LEGIS
ECO/DEV NAT/G PAY RECEIVE PERS/REL INCOME NEW/LIB ECO/TAC
20. PAGE 119 F2347 STRATA
DISCRIM

B65
SIMON B.,EDUCATION AND THE LABOR MOVEMENT, EDU/PROP
1870-1920. UK SOCIETY STRATA LABOR POL/PAR SCHOOL WORKER
CONTROL PARTIC SOCISM...BIBLIOG 19/20. PAGE 122 ADJUST
F2406 LAW

B65
US ADVISORY COMN INTERGOV REL,METROPOLITAN SOCIAL GOV/REL
AND ECONOMIC DISPARITIES: IMPLICATIONS FOR GEOG
INTERGOVERNMENTAL RELATIONS IN CENT'L CITIES AND
SUBURBS. CULTURE STRATA DIST/IND LOC/G PLAN GP/REL
DISCRIM HABITAT MUNICH. PAGE 134 F2634

B65
WEISBROD B.A.,THE ECONOMICS OF POVERTY: AN AMERICAN ECO/DEV
PARADOX. USA+45 NAT/G WORKER TASK INGP/REL DISCRIM WEALTH
POLICY. PAGE 145 F2852 RECEIVE
STRATA

B66
ANDRESKI S.,PARASITISM AND SUBVERSION* THE CASE OF L/A+17C
LATIN AMERICA. CULTURE ECO/UNDEV LABOR NAT/G SECT GOV/COMP
PROB/SOLV RACE/REL TOTALISM ATTIT WEALTH ALL/IDEOS. STRATA
PAGE 5 F0100 REV

B66
BEQIRAJ M.,PEASANTRY IN REVOLUTION. STRATA WORKER
ECO/UNDEV AGRI ROUTINE REV HABITAT RIGID/FLEX KNOWL
...EPIST GEOG NEW/IDEA TREND MUNICH 20. PAGE 13 NAT/LISM
F0256 SOC

B66
COLE A.B.,SOCIALIST PARTIES IN POSTWAR JAPAN. POL/PAR
STRATA AGRI LABOR PLAN DIPLOM ECO/TAC AGREE LEAD POLICY
CHOOSE ATTIT...CHARTS 20 CHINJAP SOC/DEMPAR. SOCISM
PAGE 26 F0499 NAT/G

B66
ECONOMIC RESEARCH SERVICE,RESEARCH DATA ON MINORITY BIBLIOG/A
GROUPS: AN ANNOTATED BIBLIOGRAPHY OF ECONOMIC DISCRIM
RESEARCH SERVICE REPORTS: 1955-1965 (PAMPHLET). WEALTH
USA+45 STRATA ECO/DEV AGRI SCHOOL WORKER EDU/PROP RACE/REL
HEALTH NEW/LIB SOC. PAGE 36 F0697

B66
GOODMAN L.H.,ECONOMIC PROGRESS AND SOCIAL WELFARE. SOC/WK
USA+45 STRATA STRUCT ECO/TAC EFFICIENCY...MGT 20. RECEIVE
PAGE 49 F0949 GP/COMP
POLICY

B66
GYORGY A.,ISSUES OF WORLD COMMUNISM. ALBANIA ECO/UNDEV
CHINA/COM COM USSR YUGOSLAVIA STRATA AGRI INT/ORG REV
CHIEF FORCES WORKER WAR ALL/IDEOS...GEOG 20 MAO. MARXISM
PAGE 52 F1018 CON/ANAL

B66
HOLT R.T.,THE POLITICAL BASIS OF ECONOMIC ECO/TAC
DEVELOPMENT. STRATA STRUCT NAT/G DIPLOM ADMIN...SOC GOV/COMP
NAT/COMP BIBLIOG 20. PAGE 61 F1201 CONSTN
EX/STRUC

B66
HOROWITZ D.,HEMISPHERES NORTH AND SOUTH: ECONOMIC ECO/TAC
DISPARITY AMONG NATIONS. WOR+45 ECO/DEV ECO/UNDEV FOR/AID
INT/ORG PLAN DIPLOM INT/TRADE GIVE PARTIC GP/REL STRATA
...WELF/ST 20. PAGE 62 F1215 WEALTH

B66
HUNT C.L.,SOCIAL ASPECTS OF ECONOMIC DEVELOPMENT. SOC
S/ASIA AGRI FAM TEC/DEV RECEIVE EDU/PROP OWN...GEOG STRATA
MUNICH 20. PAGE 63 F1243 ATTIT
ECO/UNDEV

B66
JACKSON G.D.,COMINTERN AND PEASANT IN EAST EUROPE MARXISM
1919-1930. BULGARIA COM CZECHOSLVK EUR+WWI POLAND ECO/UNDEV
ROMANIA YUGOSLAVIA STRATA AGRI VOL/ASSN DIPLOM WORKER
CONTROL CROWD WEALTH...POLICY NAT/COMP 20. PAGE 66 INT/ORG
F1293

B66
KEENLEYSIDE H.L.,INTERNATIONAL AID: A SUMMARY. AFR ECO/UNDEV
INDIA S/ASIA UK STRATA EXTR/IND TEC/DEV ADMIN FOR/AID
RACE/REL DEMAND NAT/LISM WEALTH...TREND CHINJAP. DIPLOM
PAGE 70 F1367 TASK

B66
KOH S.J.,STAGES OF INDUSTRIAL DEVELOPMENT IN ASIA. INDUS
ASIA INDIA KOREA STRATA STRUCT NAT/G INT/TRADE ECO/UNDEV
...CHARTS 19/20 CHINJAP. PAGE 72 F1415 ECO/DEV
LABOR

B66
LENSKI G.E.,POWER AND PRIVILEGE: A THEORY OF SOCIAL SOC
STRATIFICATION. SWEDEN UK UNIV USSR CULTURE STRATA
ECO/UNDEV PRIVIL PWR...PHIL/SCI CONCPT CHARTS STRUCT
IDEA/COMP HYPO/EXP METH MARX/KARL. PAGE 78 F1525 SOCIETY

B66
MURPHY G.G.,SOVIET MONGOLIA: A STUDY OF THE OLDEST DIPLOM
POLITICAL SATELLITE. USSR STRATA STRUCT COST INCOME ECO/TAC
ATTIT SOCISM 20. PAGE 95 F1865 PLAN
DOMIN

B66
NAMBOODIRIPAD E.M.,ECONOMICS AND POLITICS OF ECO/UNDEV
INDIA'S SOCIALIST PATTERN. INDIA STRATA AGRI INDUS PLAN
NAT/G PRICE ORD/FREE SOVEREIGN 20. PAGE 98 F1888 SOCISM
CAP/ISM

B66
PFEFFER K.H.,WELT IM UMBRUCH. SOCIETY STRUCT INDUS ORD/FREE
PROF/ORG SECT TEC/DEV PARTIC SUPEGO WORSHIP 20 STRATA
CHRISTIAN. PAGE 106 F2076 CREATE

B66
US SENATE COMM GOVT OPERATIONS,HEARINGS BEFORE ECO/DEV
SUBCOMMITTEE ON FOREIGN AID EXPENDITURES: CENSUS
POPULATION CRISIS VOLUMES 1-5 JUNE-SEPT 1965. FAM
STRATA ECO/UNDEV PLAN TEC/DEV EDU/PROP ATTIT HEALTH CONTROL
...GEOG CHARTS 20 CONGRESS BIRTH/CON CASEBOOK.
PAGE 138 F2729

B66
WOODMAN H.D.,SLAVERY AND THE SOUTHERN ECONOMY: ECO/DEV
SOURCES AND READINGS. USA-45 CULTURE STRUCT AGRI STRATA
ECO/TAC LEAD RACE/REL DISCRIM EFFICIENCY...CHARTS WORKER
ANTHOL MUNICH 18/19 NEGRO SOUTH/US. PAGE 148 F2922 UTIL

B67
BANFIELD E.C.,THE MORAL BASIS OF A BACKWARD MORAL
SOCIETY. EUR+WWI ITALY STRATA NEIGH PARTIC INGP/REL WEALTH
...SOC QU PREDICT TREND HYPO/EXP MUNICH 20. PAGE 9 ATTIT
F0173

B67
FIELD G.L.,COMPARATIVE POLITICAL DEVELOPMENT: THE NAT/COMP
PRECEDENT OF THE WEST. FRANCE GERMANY SWEDEN UK CONCPT
USSR STRATA STRUCT POL/PAR...METH 20. PAGE 40 F0790 ECO/DEV
SOCIETY

B67
LITTLE AD, INC.,COMMUNITY RENEWAL PROGRAMMING. STRATA
CULTURE LOC/G ACT/RES TASK COST ATTIT...SOC/WK NEIGH
MODAL STAT STAND/INT CHARTS 20 SAN/FRAN. PAGE 81 PLAN
F1585 CREATE

B67
POLLACK N.,THE POPULIST MIND. USA-45 STRATA AGRI POPULISM

NAT/G POL/PAR LEGIS WORKER RACE/REL WEALTH...ANTHOL BIBLIOG 19 NEGRO. PAGE 107 F2097 — HIST/WRIT ATTIT INGP/REL

B67
ROSS A.M.,EMPLOYMENT, RACE, AND POVERTY. USA+45 LAW STRATA MARKET LABOR EDU/PROP ISOLAT SKILL...MGT ANTHOL 20 NEGRO. PAGE 114 F2244 — RACE/REL WORKER WEALTH DISCRIM

B67
SMITH T.L.,THE PROCESS OF RURAL DEVELOPMENT IN LATIN AMERICA (A MONOGRAPH). L/A+17C STRATA INDUS PLAN GP/REL PERS/REL RIGID/FLEX WEALTH...OBS CHARTS ORG/CHARTS ANTHOL 20 COLOMB. PAGE 123 F2434 — IDEA/COMP SOC AGRI ECO/UNDEV

B67
STEARNS P.N.,EUROPEAN SOCIETY IN UPHEAVAL* SOCIAL HISTORY SINCE 1800. EUR+WWI MOD/EUR STRATA SECT WORKER TEC/DEV WAR...WELF/ST SOC TREND BIBLIOG 19/20. PAGE 125 F2472 — REGION ECO/DEV SOCIETY INDUS

B67
TUMIN M.M.,SOCIAL STRATIFICATION; THE FORMS AND FUNCTIONS OF INEQUALITY. SENIOR SANCTION WEALTH ...SOC CLASSIF METH 20. PAGE 131 F2592 — STRATA DISCRIM CONCPT SOCIETY

S67
BRIMMER A.F.,"EMPLOYMENT PATTERNS AND THE DILEMMA OF DESEGREGATION." USA+45 SOCIETY SKILL 20 NEGRO. PAGE 18 F0353 — RACE/REL DISCRIM WORKER STRATA

S67
DEYRUP F.J.,"SOCIAL MOBILITY AS A MAJOR FACTOR IN ECONOMIC DEVELOPMENT." CHRIST-17C EUR+WWI MOD/EUR ECO/UNDEV DEMAND 20. PAGE 32 F0630 — STRATA ECO/DEV INDUS WORKER

S67
FOX R.G.,"FAMILY, CASTE, AND COMMERCE IN A NORTH INDIAN MARKET TOWN." INDIA STRATA AGRI FACE/GP FAM NEIGH OP/RES BARGAIN ADMIN ROUTINE WEALTH...SOC CHARTS 20. PAGE 43 F0838 — CULTURE GP/REL ECO/UNDEV DIST/IND

S67
FUCHS V.R.,"REDEFINING POVERTY AND REDISTRIBUTING INCOME." USA+45 NAT/G ECO/TAC GIVE COST...NEW/IDEA CHARTS. PAGE 45 F0873 — WEALTH INCOME STRATA PROB/SOLV

S67
GATELL F.O.,"MONEY AND PARTY IN JACKSONIAN AMERICA* A QUANTITATIVE LOOK AT NEW YORK CITY'S MEN OF QUALITY." USA-45 STRATA SECT SUFF CONSEN MAJORITY ATTIT...CHARTS HYPO/EXP 19. PAGE 46 F0908 — WEALTH POL/PAR PERSON IDEA/COMP

S67
JENCKS C.E.,"COAL MINERS IN BRITAIN SINCE NATIONALIZATION." UK LABOR GP/REL ADJUST SOCISM ...INT 20. PAGE 67 F1311 — EXTR/IND WORKER STRATA ATTIT

S67
JENCKS C.E.,"SOCIAL STATUS OF COAL MINERS IN BRITAIN SINCE NATIONALIZATION." UK STRATA STRUCT LABOR RECEIVE GP/REL INCOME OWN ATTIT HABITAT...MGT T 20. PAGE 67 F1312 — EXTR/IND WORKER CONTROL NAT/G

S67
LEE R.L.,"THE PARADOX OF EQUALITY: A THREAT TO INDIVIDUAL AND SYSTEM FUNCTIONING." CHINA/COM ECO/UNDEV WORKER...SIMUL GEN/LAWS 20. PAGE 77 F1508 — SOCIETY STRATA MARXISM IDEA/COMP

S67
MEHTA A.,"INDIA* POVERTY AND CHANGE." STRATA INDUS CREATE ECO/TAC FOR/AID NEUTRAL GP/REL ADJUST INCOME ...NEW/IDEA 20. PAGE 89 F1746 — INDIA SOCIETY ECO/UNDEV TEC/DEV

S67
MENCHER S.,"THE PROBLEM OF MEASURING POVERTY." UNIV USA+45 STRATA PROB/SOLV...NEW/IDEA METH/COMP 20. PAGE 89 F1755 — WEALTH CENSUS STAT GEN/LAWS

S67
NEALE R.S.,"WORKING CLASS WOMEN AND WOMEN'S SUFFRAGE." UK LAW CONSTN LABOR NAT/G DELIB/GP LEGIS WORKER PAY PARTIC CHOOSE 19 FEMALE/SEX. PAGE 97 F1906 — STRATA SEX SUFF DISCRIM

S67
PAI G.A.,"TAXATION AND PLANNING IN INDIA: A BIRDS-EYE VIEW." INDIA ELITES NAT/G LEGIS BUDGET CONTROL LOBBY INCOME...STAT CHARTS 20. PAGE 102 F2015 — TAX PLAN WEALTH STRATA

S67
PAULY M.V.,"MIXED PUBLIC AND PRIVATE FINANCING OF EDUCATION." STRATA PAY RECEIVE COST INCOME OPTIMAL METH/COMP. PAGE 104 F2039 — SCHOOL PLAN TAX EFFICIENCY

S67
RAMA C.M.,"PASADO Y PRESENTE DE LA RELIGION EN AMERICA LATINA." L/A+17C ELITES SOCIETY STRATA MARXISM...STAT WORSHIP PROTESTANT. PAGE 109 F2139 — SECT CATHISM STRUCT NAT/COMP

S67
ROY E.V.,"AN INTERPRETATION OF NORTHERN THAI PEASANT ECONOMY." THAILAND CLIENT CULTURE AGRI PROC/MFG FACE/GP DEMAND INCOME 20. PAGE 114 F2254 — STRUCT STRATA ECO/UNDEV INGP/REL

B68
PROUDHON P.J.,SYSTEME DES CONTRADICTIONS ECONOMIQUES, OU PHILOSOPHIE DA LA MISERE (2 VOLS.) (1846). SECT WORKER GP/REL ISOLAT PRODUC IDEA/COMP. PAGE 108 F2126 — SOCIETY STRATA MORAL

B76
TAINE H.A.,THE ANCIENT REGIME. FRANCE STRATA FORCES PARTIC EQUILIB WEALTH CONSERVE POPULISM...GOV/COMP SOC/INTEG 18/19. PAGE 128 F2527 — NAT/G GOV/REL TAX REV

B92
COULANGES F D.E.,THE ORIGIN OF PROPERTY IN LAND. LAW STRATA AGRI ACADEM EDU/PROP ORD/FREE 19. PAGE 28 F0543 — OWN HIST/WRIT IDEA/COMP SOCISM

B96
MARX K.,REVOLUTION AND COUNTER-REVOLUTION. GERMANY CONSTN ELITES INDUS NAT/G DIPLOM ECO/TAC WEALTH. PAGE 86 F1693 — MARXIST REV PWR STRATA

STRATEGY....SEE PLAN, DECISION

STRATIFICATION....SEE STRATA

STRAUSS G. F2284

STREAT R. F2501

STREETEN P. F2502

STRESEMANN, GUSTAV....SEE STRESEMN/G

STRESEMN/G....GUSTAV STRESEMANN

STRESS....SEE PERSON, DRIVE

STRICK J.C. F2871

STRIKE....STRIKE OF WORKERS; SEE ALSO LABOR, GP/REL, FINAN

B31
CROOK W.H.,THE GENERAL STRIKE: A STUDY OF LABOR'S TRAGIC WEAPON IN THEORY AND PRACTICE. BELGIUM FRANCE SWEDEN UK WOR-45 PROB/SOLV ECO/TAC DOMIN PWR ...POLICY TIME/SEQ NAT/COMP GEN/LAWS 19/20 STRIKE. PAGE 29 F0555 — LABOR WORKER LG/CO BARGAIN

B35
O'CONNOR H.,REVOLUTION IN SEATTLE. USA-45 STRATA WORKER GP/REL ATTIT SOCISM...OBS BIBLIOG/A 20 SEATTLE STRIKE COM/PARTY. PAGE 99 F1954 — REV EDU/PROP LABOR MARXISM

B58
CUNNINGHAM W.B.,COMPULSORY CONCILIATION AND COLLECTIVE BARGAINING. CANADA NAT/G LEGIS ADJUD CT/SYS GP/REL...MGT 20 NEW/BRUNS STRIKE CASEBOOK. PAGE 29 F0563 — POLICY BARGAIN LABOR INDUS

STRONG A.L. F2503

STROUD G.S. F2504

STROUT A.M. F0464

STRUC/FUNC....STRUCTURAL-FUNCTIONAL THEORY

STRUCT...SOCIAL STRUCTURE

NC0
CARRINGTON C.E.,THE COMMONWEALTH IN AFRICA (PAMPHLET). UK STRUCT NAT/G COLONIAL REPRESENT GOV/REL RACE/REL NAT/LISM...MAJORIT 20 EEC NEGRO. PAGE 22 F0421 — ECO/UNDEV AFR DIPLOM PLAN

N19
HALL G.,MAIN STREET TO WALL STREET: END THE COLD WAR (PAMPHLET). AFR USA+45 LAW STRUCT POL/PAR WORKER INT/TRADE DOMIN INCOME...POLICY 20 COM/PARTY. PAGE 53 F1046 — MARXIST CAP/ISM DIPLOM NAT/G

S21
MALINOWSKI B.,"THE PRIMITIVE ECONOMICS OF THE TROBRIAND ISLANDERS" (BMR)" CULTURE SOCIETY NAT/G CHIEF LEAD OWN...SOC MYTH WORSHIP 20 NEW/GUINEA TROBRIAND RESOURCE/N. PAGE 84 F1647 — ECO/UNDEV AGRI PRODUC STRUCT

B27
WEBER M.,GENERAL ECONOMIC HISTORY. CHRIST-17C MOD/EUR STRUCT AGRI EXTR/IND FINAN INDUS MARKET FAM NAT/G PROF/ORG SECT ECO/TAC MUNICH 8/20. PAGE 144 F2839 — ECO/DEV CAP/ISM

B30
THOMPSON W.R.,POPULATION PROBLEMS. FUT UNIV WOR-45 STRUCT DIST/IND ACT/RES ECO/TAC BIO/SOC...CONCPT OBS TIME/SEQ TOT/POP 20. PAGE 130 F2567 — ECO/UNDEV GEOG

B39
ENGELS F.,HERRN EUGEN DUHRING'S REVOLUTION IN PWR
SCIENCE (1878). CULTURE STRATA STRUCT FAM SECT SOCIETY
ECO/TAC REV WAR SOCISM...MARXIST 19. PAGE 37 F0731 WEALTH
GEN/LAWS

B40
GAUS J.M.,PUBLIC ADMINISTRATION AND THE UNITED ADMIN
STATES DEPARTMENT OF AGRICULTURE. USA-45 STRUCT AGRI
DIST/IND FINAN MARKET EX/STRUC PROB/SOLV GIVE DELIB/GP
PRODUC...POLICY GEOG CHARTS 20 DEPT/AGRI. PAGE 47 OP/RES
F0909

B41
YOUNG G.,FEDERALISM AND FREEDOM. EUR+WWI MOD/EUR NAT/G
RUSSIA USA-45 SOCIETY STRUCT ECO/DEV INT/ORG WAR
EXEC FEDERAL ATTIT PERSON ALL/VALS...OLD/LIB CONCPT
OBS TREND LEAGUE/NAT TOT/POP. PAGE 150 F2950

B42
VEBLEN T.B.,THE THEORY OF THE LEISURE CLASS. USA-45 WEALTH
SOCIETY STRATA STRUCT NAT/G SECT WORKER CREATE ELITES
EDU/PROP ATTIT...SOC GEN/LAWS 19. PAGE 141 F2772 LEISURE
PRODUC

S43
HERBERG W.,"BUREAUCRACY AND DEMOCRACY IN LABOR LABOR
UNIONS." LAW CONSTN STRUCT WORKER ADMIN CONTROL REPRESENT
PARTIC RIGID/FLEX PWR TREND. PAGE 59 F1151 ROUTINE
INGP/REL

B45
MILLIS H.A.,ORGANIZED LABOR (FIRST ED.). LAW STRUCT LABOR
DELIB/GP WORKER ECO/TAC ADJUD CONTROL REPRESENT POLICY
INGP/REL INCOME MGT. PAGE 92 F1797 ROUTINE
GP/REL

B47
ISAAC J.,ECONOMICS OF MIGRATION. MOD/EUR CULTURE HABITAT
STRATA STRUCT NAT/G COLONIAL WEALTH...OLD/LIB TREND SOC
TIME 19/20 EUROPE/W MIGRATION. PAGE 65 F1289 GEOG

B47
WARNER W.L.,THE SOCIAL SYSTEM OF THE MODERN ROLE
FACTORY; THE STRIKE: AN ANALYSIS. USA-45 STRATA STRUCT
WORKER ECO/TAC GP/REL INGP/REL...MGT SOC CHARTS 20 LABOR
YANKEE/C. PAGE 143 F2824 PROC/MFG

B47
WEBER M.,THE THEORY OF SOCIAL AND ECONOMIC ECO/DEV
ORGANIZATION. STRUCT LABOR POL/PAR ECO/TAC LEGIT SOC
PRODUC BIOG. PAGE 144 F2840 PHIL/SCI
LEAD

B47
WHITEHEAD T.N.,LEADERSHIP IN A FREE SOCIETY; A INDUS
STUDY IN HUMAN RELATIONS BASED ON AN ANALYSIS OF LEAD
PRESENT-DAY INDUSTRIAL CIVILIZATION. WOR-45 STRUCT ORD/FREE
R+D LABOR LG/CO SML/CO WORKER PLAN PROB/SOLV SOCIETY
TEC/DEV DRIVE...MGT 20. PAGE 146 F2872

S47
DAHL R.A.,"WORKERS' CONTROL OF INDUSTRY AND THE INDUS
BRITISH LABOUR PARTY." UK STRATA STRUCT DELIB/GP LABOR
BARGAIN CAP/ISM DEBATE CONTROL CHOOSE GP/REL ATTIT WORKER
ROLE PWR 19/20 PARLIAMENT LABOR/PAR FABIAN. PAGE 29 SOCISM
F0570

B48
KILE O.M.,THE FARM BUREAU MOVEMENT: THE FARM BUREAU AGRI
THROUGH THREE DECADES. NAT/G LEGIS LEAD LOBBY STRUCT
GP/REL INCOME POLICY. PAGE 71 F1387 VOL/ASSN
DOMIN

B48
MILLS C.W.,THE NEW MEN OF POWER. ELITES INTELL LABOR
STRUCT WORKER ANOMIE ATTIT PWR POLICY. PAGE 92 LEAD
F1799 PLAN

B49
LEE A.M.,SOCIAL PROBLEMS IN AMERICA: A SOURCE BOOK. SOC
STRATA STRUCT KIN NEIGH VOL/ASSN ACT/RES LEAD CRIME SOCIETY
AGE SEX 20. PAGE 77 F1504 PERSON
EDU/PROP

S49
SHEPHARD H.A.,"DEMOCRATIC CONTROL IN A LABOR LABOR
UNION." FUT CONSTN STRUCT TEC/DEV LEAD PARTIC MAJORIT
RACE/REL CENTRAL DRIVE HABITAT RECORD. PAGE 120 CONTROL
F2374 PWR

B50
HUNT R.N.,THE THEORY AND PRACTICE OF COMMUNISM. MARXISM
STRUCT WORKER NAT/LISM TOTALISM...CONCPT TREND SOCISM
19/20 STALIN/J EUROPE. PAGE 63 F1244 REV
STRATA

B50
LIPSET S.M.,AGRARIAN SOCIALISM. CANADA POL/PAR SOCISM
OP/RES ECO/TAC ADMIN ATTIT...TIME/SEQ NAT/COMP AGRI
SOC/EXP 20 SASKATCH. PAGE 80 F1576 METH/COMP
STRUCT

B50
SURANYI-UNGER T.,PRIVATE ENTERPRISE AND PLAN
GOVERNMENTAL PLANNING. STRUCT FINAN BAL/PWR NAT/G
HAPPINESS DRIVE NEW/LIB PLURISM...MATH QUANT STAT LAISSEZ
TREND BIBLIOG. PAGE 127 F2516 POLICY

C50
ROUSSEAU J.J.,"A DISCOURSE ON POLITICAL ECONOMY" NAT/G
(1755) IN THE SOCIAL CONTRACT AND DISCOURSES." UNIV ECO/TAC
SOCIETY STRATA STRUCT CONSEN EQUILIB HAPPINESS TAX
UTOPIA HEALTH WEALTH...POLICY WELF/ST. PAGE 114 GEN/LAWS
F2252

B51
COOKE C.A.,CORPORATION TRUST AND COMPANY: AN ESSAY LG/CO
IN LEGAL HISTORY. UK STRUCT LEGIS CAP/ISM GP/REL FINAN
PROFIT 13/20 COMPNY/ACT. PAGE 27 F0531 ECO/TAC
JURID

B51
OWENS R.N.,BUSINESS, ORGANIZATION, AND COMBINATION. SML/CO
USA+45 USA-45 LAW NAT/G LEGIS ECO/TAC CONTROL LG/CO
INGP/REL...JURID GP/COMP 20 NEW/DEAL. PAGE 102 STRUCT
F2006 GP/REL

B53
MIT CENTER INTERNATIONAL STU,BIBLIOGRAPHY OF THE BIBLIOG
ECONOMIC AND POLITICAL DEVELOPMENT OF INDONESIA. ECO/UNDEV
INDONESIA STRUCT NAT/G COLONIAL LEAD...STAT 20. TEC/DEV
PAGE 92 F1805 S/ASIA

S53
BIRNBAUM N.,"CONFLICTING INTERPRETATIONS OF THE CAP/ISM
RISE OF CAPITALISM: MARX AND WEBER" (BMR)" WOR-45 IDEA/COMP
INTELL SOCIETY STRUCT INDUS WORKER...PHIL/SCI SOC ECO/DEV
PERS/COMP 19/20 MARX/KARL WEBER/MAX. PAGE 15 F0288 MARXISM

S53
DRUCKER P.F.,"THE EMPLOYEE SOCIETY." STRUCT BAL/PWR LABOR
PARTIC REPRESENT PWR...DECISION CONCPT. PAGE 34 MGT
F0666 WORKER
CULTURE

B54
LENIN V.I.,SELECTED WORKS (12 VOLS.). USSR INTELL COM
SOCIETY STRATA STRUCT NAT/G POL/PAR WORKER CAP/ISM MARXISM
REV WAR...MARXIST PHIL/SCI 20 MARX/KARL LENIN/VI.
PAGE 78 F1520

B54
MEYER A.G.,MARXISM. INTELL ECO/DEV WORKER CAP/ISM MARXISM
LEAD WAR ATTIT ALL/IDEOS...SOC 19/20 MARX/KARL. CONCPT
PAGE 90 F1766 ECO/TAC
STRUCT

B54
WASHBURNE N.F.,INTERPRETING SOCIAL CHANGE IN CULTURE
AMERICA. USA+45 STRATA FAM NAT/G SECT OP/RES STRUCT
ECO/TAC EDU/PROP HABITAT...SOC TIME/SEQ TREND 20 CREATE
BUREAUCRCY. PAGE 143 F2826 TEC/DEV

S54
FORM W.H.,"THE PLACE OF SOCIAL STRUCTURE IN THE HABITAT
DETERMINATION OF LAND USE: SOME IMPLICATIONS FOR A MARKET
THEORY OF URBAN ECOLOGY" (BMR)" STRUCT...GEOG ORD/FREE
PHIL/SCI SOC MUNICH 20. PAGE 42 F0827

S54
MACK R.W.,"ECOLOGICAL PATTERNS IN AN INDUSTRIAL INDUS
SHOP" (BMR)" USA+45 CULTURE SOCIETY STRATA STRUCT DISCRIM
LABOR NEIGH GP/REL ADJUST HABITAT...SOC SOC/INTEG WORKER
20. PAGE 83 F1634

B55
COLE G.D.H.,STUDIES IN CLASS STRUCTURE. UK NAT/G STRUCT
WORKER TEC/DEV EDU/PROP...CLASSIF CHARTS 20. STRATA
PAGE 26 F0501 ELITES
CONCPT

B55
GEORGE H.,PROGRESS AND POVERTY (1880). STRATA ECO/DEV
STRUCT INDUS TEC/DEV CAP/ISM EQUILIB INCOME OWN ECO/TAC
UTOPIA...WELF/ST CONCPT NEW/IDEA 19. PAGE 47 F0915 TAX
WEALTH

B55
STILLMAN C.W.,AFRICA IN THE MODERN WORLD. AFR ECO/UNDEV
USA+45 WOR+45 INT/TRADE COLONIAL PARTIC REGION DIPLOM
GOV/REL RACE/REL 20. PAGE 126 F2489 POLICY
STRUCT

B56
LIPSET S.M.,UNION DEMOCRACY. STRUCT INDUS FACE/GP LABOR
WORKER CONTROL LEAD PARTIC GP/REL ATTIT LAISSEZ INGP/REL
...INT QU CHARTS. PAGE 80 F1577 MAJORIT

B56
PARSONS T.,ECONOMY AND SOCIETY: A STUDY IN THE STRUCT
INTEGRATION OF ECONOMIC AND SOCIAL THEORY. UNIV METH/CNCPT
ACT/RES...SOC CHARTS IDEA/COMP BIBLIOG/A. PAGE 103 UTIL
F2031 PHIL/SCI

B56
POOLE K.E.,PUBLIC FINANCE AND ECONOMIC WELFARE. FINAN
STRUCT ECO/DEV LOC/G NAT/G BUDGET PAY ROUTINE COST TAX
EQUILIB WEALTH...SOC/WK METH/COMP 20. PAGE 107 ORD/FREE
F2103

B56
WEBER M.,WIRTSCHAFT UND GESELLSCHAFT (2ND VOL.). LEGIT
STRUCT NAT/G POL/PAR LEAD PWR OBJECTIVE IDEA/COMP. JURID
PAGE 144 F2841 SOC

L56
TAGLIACOZZO D.L.,"TRADE-UNION GOVERNMENT, ITS CLASSIF
NATURE AND ITS PROBLEMS: A BIBLIOGRAPHICAL REVIEW, LABOR
1945-1955." STRUCT LEAD PARTIC CHOOSE ATTIT INGP/REL
...MAJORIT METH/CNCPT BIBLIOG. PAGE 128 F2526 GP/REL

S56
TANNENBAUM A.S.,"CONTROL OF STRUCTURE AND UNION LABOR
FUNCTIONS." PARTIC GP/REL INGP/REL CONSEN ATTIT PWR STRUCT
...QU SAMP. PAGE 128 F2529 CONTROL
LEAD

N56
US HOUSE COMM FOREIGN AFFAIRS,REPORT OF THE SPECIAL FOR/AID

STUDY MISSION TO AFRICA, SOUTH AND EAST OF THE SAHARA (PAMPHLET). AFR SOUTH/AFR USA+45 STRUCT INT/TRADE PARL/PROC NAT/LISM ATTIT ALL/VALS HEALTH ...POLICY 20 CONGRESS. PAGE 136 F2691
COLONIAL ECO/UNDEV DIPLOM

B57
SCHNEIDER E.V.,INDUSTRIAL SOCIOLOGY: THE SOCIAL RELATIONS OF INDUSTRY AND COMMUNITY. STRATA INDUS NAT/G NEIGH CREATE ADMIN PARTIC GP/REL RACE/REL ROLE PWR...POLICY BIBLIOG. PAGE 117 F2308
LABOR MGT INGP/REL STRUCT

S57
TANNENBAUM A.S.,"ORGANIZATIONAL CONTROL STRUCTURE: A GENERAL DESCRIPTIVE TECHNIQUE AS APPLIED TO FOUR LOCAL UNIONS." LABOR PWR...METH/CNCPT CLASSIF QU CHARTS. PAGE 128 F2530
WORKER PARTIC STRUCT CONTROL

B58
SEIDMAN J.I.,DEMOCRACY IN THE LABOR MOVEMENT (PAMPHLET). LAW CONSTN STRUCT DELIB/GP WORKER ADJUD PARTIC SANCTION POLICY. PAGE 119 F2345
LABOR INGP/REL PWR MAJORIT

S58
SCHULZE R.O.,"THE ROLE OF ECONOMIC DOMINANTS IN COMMUNITY POWER STRUCTURE." ECO/TAC ROUTINE ATTIT OBJECTIVE...SOC RECORD CENSUS. PAGE 118 F2319
SOCIETY STRUCT PROB/SOLV

B59
KOLLAI H.R.,DIE EINGLIEDERUNG DER VERTRIEBENEN UND ZUWANDERER IN NIEDERSACHSEN. GERMANY/W SOCIETY STRATA STRUCT LABOR SOC/INTEG 20. PAGE 72 F1422
GP/REL INGP/REL

B59
LEISERSON W.,AMERICAN TRADE UNION DEMOCRACY. CONSTN STRUCT ADJUD EXEC REPRESENT GP/REL INGP/REL MAJORITY ATTIT PWR. PAGE 77 F1516
LABOR LEAD PARTIC DELIB/GP

B59
MAYER H.M.,READINGS IN URBAN GEOGRAPHY. WOR+45 SOCIETY DIST/IND INDUS MARKET HABITAT...CLASSIF CENSUS CHARTS ANTHOL MUNICH 20 WATER. PAGE 87 F1706
GEOG STRUCT

B59
SHUBIK M.,STRATEGY AND MARKET STRUCTURE: COMPETITION, OLIGOPOLY, AND THE THEORY OF GAMES. ELITES STRUCT MARKET OP/RES EXEC EFFICIENCY INCOME ...MGT MATH STAT CHARTS 20. PAGE 121 F2389
ECO/DEV ECO/TAC DECISION GAME

B59
WARD B.,5 IDEAS THAT CHANGE THE WORLD. WOR+45 WOR-45 SOCIETY STRUCT AGRI INDUS INT/ORG NAT/G FORCES ACT/RES ARMS/CONT TOTALISM ATTIT DRIVE GEN/LAWS. PAGE 143 F2815
ECO/UNDEV ALL/VALS NAT/LISM COLONIAL

S59
BENDIX R.,"INDUSTRIALIZATION, IDEOLOGIES, AND SOCIAL STRUCTURE" (BMR)" UK USA-45 USSR STRUCT WORKER GP/REL EFFICIENCY...IDEA/COMP 20. PAGE 13 F0243
INDUS ATTIT MGT ADMIN

S59
HOFFMAN P.,"OPERATION BREAKTHROUGH." AFR S/ASIA STRUCT INDUS CONSULT TEC/DEV ATTIT RIGID/FLEX SKILL WEALTH...TECHNIC CONCPT STYLE RECORD CHARTS ORG/CHARTS GEN/METH VAL/FREE 20. PAGE 61 F1190
ECO/UNDEV EDU/PROP FOR/AID

S59
REUBENS E.D.,"THE BASIS FOR REORIENATION OF AMERICAN FOREIGN AID POLICY." USA+45 USSR STRUCT INT/ORG CONSULT ECO/TAC ADMIN DRIVE MORAL ORD/FREE PWR WEALTH...RELATIV MATH STAT TREND GEN/LAWS VAL/FREE 20. PAGE 111 F2180
ECO/UNDEV PLAN FOR/AID DIPLOM

S59
STINCHCOMBE A.L.,"BUREAUCRATIC AND CRAFT ADMINISTRATION OF PRODUCTION: A COMPARATIVE STUDY" (BMR)" USA+45 STRUCT EX/STRUC ECO/TAC GP/REL ...CLASSIF GP/COMP IDEA/COMP GEN/LAWS 20 WEBER/MAX. PAGE 126 F2490
CONSTRUC PROC/MFG ADMIN PLAN

S59
TIPTON J.B.,"PARTICIPATION OF THE UNITED STATES IN THE INTERNATIONAL LABOR ORGANIZATION." USA+45 LAW STRUCT ECO/DEV ECO/UNDEV INDUS TEC/DEV ECO/TAC ADMIN PERCEPT ORD/FREE SKILL...STAT HIST/WRIT GEN/METH ILO WORK 20. PAGE 131 F2577
LABOR INT/ORG

C59
MINTZ S.W.,"INTERNAL MARKET SYS AS MECHANISMS OF SOCIAL ARTIC." IN V.F. RAY, INTERMED SOCIETIES, SOCIAL MOBILITY, AND COMMUNIC (BMR). UNIV STRATA GP/REL INGP/REL...GEOG SOC BIBLIOG. PAGE 92 F1804
MARKET SOCIETY ECO/UNDEV STRUCT

B60
AUSTRUY J.,STRUCTURE ECONOMIQUE ET CIVILISATION: L'EGYPTE ET LE DESTIN ECONOMIQUE DE L'ISLAM. ISLAM UAR CREATE OP/RES ECO/TAC...SOC BIBLIOG 20 MUSLIM. PAGE 8 F0142
ECO/UNDEV CULTURE STRUCT

B60
FORM W.H.,INDUSTRY, LABOR, AND COMMUNITY. STRUCT NEIGH SECT BAL/PWR EDU/PROP PARTIC ATTIT ROLE PWR WEALTH...METH/CNCPT CHARTS. PAGE 42 F0828
LABOR MGT GP/REL CONTROL

B60
HUGHES R.,THE CHINESE COMMUNES; A BACKGROUND BOOK. CHINA/COM SOCIETY CONTROL ROUTINE ADJUST EFFICIENCY PRODUC 20. PAGE 63 F1234
AGRI INDUS STRUCT MARXISM

B60
LISTER L.,EUROPE'S COAL AND STEEL COMMUNITY. FRANCE GERMANY STRUCT ECO/DEV EXTR/IND INDUS MARKET NAT/G DELIB/GP ECO/TAC INT/TRADE EDU/PROP ATTIT RIGID/FLEX ORD/FREE PWR WEALTH...CONCPT STAT TIME/SEQ CHARTS ECSC TERR/GP 20. PAGE 81 F1582
EUR+WWI INT/ORG REGION

B60
RAMA C.M.,LAS CLASES SOCIALES EN EL URUGUAY. L/A+17C URUGUAY ELITES SOCIETY STRATA INDUS ATTIT HABITAT PWR...GEOG SOC/INTEG MUNICH 20. PAGE 109 F2138
ECO/UNDEV STRUCT PARTIC

B60
SIMOONS F.J.,NORTHWEST ETHIOPIA; PEOPLES AND ECONOMY. ETHIOPIA MARKET CREATE 20. PAGE 122 F2411
SOCIETY STRUCT AGRI INDUS

B60
STEIN E.,AMERICAN ENTERPRISE IN THE EUROPEAN COMMON MARKET: A LEGAL PROFILE. EUR+WWI FUT USA+45 SOCIETY STRUCT ECO/DEV NAT/G VOL/ASSN CONSULT PLAN TEC/DEV ECO/TAC INT/TRADE ADMIN ATTIT RIGID/FLEX PWR...MGT NEW/IDEA STAT TREND COMPUT/IR SIMUL EEC 20. PAGE 125 F2475
MARKET ADJUD INT/LAW

L60
SPENGLER J.J.,"ECONOMIC DEVELOPMENT: POLITICAL PRECONDITIONS AND POLITICAL CONSEQUENCE." WOR+45 STRUCT ECO/UNDEV NAT/G PLAN ECO/TAC EDU/PROP ATTIT ORD/FREE WEALTH SOCISM...SOC CONCPT TREND SIMUL GEN/METH WORK 20. PAGE 124 F2452
TEC/DEV METH/CNCPT CAP/ISM

S60
HERZ J.H.,"EAST GERMANY: PROGRESS AND PROSPECTS." COM AGRI FINAN INDUS LOC/G NAT/G FORCES PLAN TEC/DEV DOMIN ADMIN COERCE DRIVE PERCEPT RIGID/FLEX MORAL ORD/FREE PWR...MARXIST PSY SOC RECORD STERTYP WORK. PAGE 59 F1158
POL/PAR STRUCT GERMANY

S60
JACOBSON H.K.,"THE USSR AND ILO." AFR COM STRUCT ECO/DEV ECO/UNDEV CONSULT DELIB/GP ECO/TAC ILO WORK 20. PAGE 66 F1298
INT/ORG LABOR USSR

B61
MEXICO; CINCUENTA ANOS DE REVOLUCION VOL. II. L/A+17C SOCIETY LABOR RECEIVE GP/REL AGE/Y HEALTH ...SOC/WK ANTHOL MUNICH 20 MEXIC/AMER. PAGE 1 F0014
ECO/UNDEV STRUCT INDUS POL/PAR

B61
ERASMUS C.J.,MAN TAKES CONTROL: CULTURAL DEVELOPMENT AND AMERICAN AID. STRUCT OWN DRIVE PERCEPT...SOC 20 MEXIC/AMER. PAGE 38 F0741
ORD/FREE CULTURE ECO/UNDEV TEC/DEV

B61
FILLOL T.R.,SOCIAL FACTORS IN ECONOMIC DEVELOPMENT: THE ARGENTINE CASE. STRUCT INDUS LABOR CREATE TEC/DEV EFFICIENCY PRODUC DRIVE...METH/CNCPT METH/COMP BIBLIOG/A 20 ARGEN. PAGE 41 F0795
ECO/UNDEV MGT PERS/REL TREND

B61
FLINN M.W.,AN ECONOMIC AND SOCIAL HISTORY OF BRITAIN, 1066-1939. UK LAW STRATA STRUCT AGRI DIST/IND INDUS WORKER INT/TRADE WAR...CENSUS 11/20. PAGE 42 F0811
SOCIETY SOC

B61
MACMAHON A.W.,DELEGATION AND AUTONOMY. INDIA STRUCT LEGIS BARGAIN BUDGET ECO/TAC LEGIT EXEC REPRESENT GOV/REL CENTRAL DEMAND EFFICIENCY PRODUC. PAGE 84 F1637
ADMIN PLAN FEDERAL

B61
PERKINS D.,THE UNITED STATES AND LATIN AMERICAN. L/A+17C USA+45 USA-45 STRUCT COLONIAL REV ORD/FREE 19/20. PAGE 105 F2061
DIPLOM INT/TRADE NAT/G

B61
ROEPKE W.,JENSEITS VON ANGEBOT UND NACHFRAGE (DRITTE VERAENDERTE AUFLAGE). WOR+45 MARKET TEC/DEV ECO/TAC GP/REL INGP/REL NEW/LIB...POLICY SOC IDEA/COMP PERS/COMP 20. PAGE 113 F2233
SOCIETY STRANGE ECO/DEV STRUCT

B62
DEBUYST F.,LAS CLASES SOCIALES EN AMERICA LATINA. L/A+17C SOCIETY STRUCT WORKER EDU/PROP RACE/REL ATTIT HABITAT ROLE...GEOG SOC NAT/COMP SOC/INTEG 20. PAGE 32 F0612
STRATA GP/REL WEALTH

B62
HARRINGTON M.,THE RETAIL CLERKS. ECO/TAC LEAD PARTIC CHOOSE GP/REL INGP/REL CENTRAL POLICY. PAGE 55 F1087
LABOR SERV/IND STRUCT DELIB/GP

B62
KIRPICEVA I.K.,HANDBUCH DER RUSSISCHEN UND SOWJETISCHEN BIBLIOGRAPHIEN (5 VOLS.). USSR STRUCT ECO/DEV DIPLOM LEAD ATTIT 18/20. PAGE 71 F1400
BIBLIOG/A NAT/G MARXISM COM

B62
KOLKO G.,WEALTH AND POWER IN AMERICA. USA+45 SOCIETY STRATA LG/CO ECO/TAC TAX PWR...SOC BIBLIOG 20 DEPRESSION. PAGE 72 F1420
STRUCT INCOME ECO/DEV WEALTH

B62
NATIONAL BUREAU ECONOMIC RES,THE RATE AND DIRECTION OF INVENTIVE ACTIVITY: ECONOMIC AND SOCIAL FACTORS. STRUCT INDUS MARKET R+D CREATE OP/RES TEC/DEV EFFICIENCY PRODUC RATIONAL UTIL...WELF/ST PHIL/SCI
DECISION PROB/SOLV MGT

METH/CNCPT TIME. PAGE 97 F1895

B62
ROBINSON A.D.,DUTCH ORGANIZED AGRICULTURE IN INTERNATIONAL POLITICS, 1945-1960. EUR+WWI NETHERLAND STRUCT ECO/DEV NAT/G VOL/ASSN CONSULT DELIB/GP PLAN TEC/DEV INT/TRADE EDU/PROP ATTIT RIGID/FLEX ALL/VALS...NEW/IDEA TREND EEC COMMUN 20. PAGE 112 F2215
AGRI INT/ORG

B62
SELOSOEMARDJAN O.,SOCIAL CHANGES IN JOGJAKARTA. INDONESIA NETHERLAND ELITES STRATA STRUCT FAM POL/PAR CREATE DIPLOM INT/TRADE EDU/PROP ADMIN GOV/REL...SOC 20 JAVA CHINJAP. PAGE 119 F2352
ECO/UNDEV CULTURE REV COLONIAL

S62
BOKOR-SZEGO H.,"LA CONVENTION DE BELGRADE ET LE REGIME DU DANUBE." COM EUR+WWI WOR+45 STRUCT POL/PAR VOL/ASSN PLAN EDU/PROP WEALTH...TIME/SEQ METH/GP COMMUN 20. PAGE 16 F0308
INT/ORG TOTALISM YUGOSLAVIA

B63
BERLE A.A. JR.,THE AMERICAN ECONOMIC REPUBLIC. STRUCT FINAN MARKET LABOR NAT/G PLAN...POLICY WELF/ST DECISION. PAGE 14 F0262
CAP/ISM ECO/TAC TREND CONCPT

B63
FLORES E.,LAND REFORM AND THE ALLIANCE FOR PROGRESS (PAMPHLET). L/A+17C USA+45 STRUCT ECO/UNDEV NAT/G WORKER CREATE PLAN ECO/TAC COERCE REV 20 ALL/PROG. PAGE 42 F0815
AGRI INT/ORG DIPLOM POLICY

B63
GAMBLE S.D.,NORTH CHINA VILLAGES: SOCIAL, POLITICAL, AND ECONOMIC ACTIVITIES BEFORE 1933. ASIA CULTURE STRUCT FAM DOMIN EDU/PROP MUNICH WORSHIP 20. PAGE 46 F0891
AGRI LEAD FINAN

B63
GODWIN F.W.,THE HIDDEN FORCE. PUERT/RICO WOR+45 STRUCT VOL/ASSN PROB/SOLV DIPLOM CONFER...BIBLIOG 20 PEACE/CORP. PAGE 48 F0931
ECO/UNDEV WORKER SKILL ECO/TAC

B63
IANNI O.,INDUSTRIALIZACAO E DESENVOLVIMENTO SOCIAL NO BRASIL. BRAZIL L/A+17C STRATA STRUCT ECO/UNDEV EDU/PROP LEAD LOBBY NAT/LISM 20. PAGE 64 F1257
WORKER GP/REL INDUS PARTIC

B63
ISSAWI C.,EGYPT IN REVOLUTION: AN ECONOMIC ANALYSIS. ISLAM STRUCT ECO/UNDEV AGRI FINAN INDUS PLAN EXEC REV NAT/LISM ATTIT RIGID/FLEX WEALTH SOCISM...STAT FOR/TRADE WORK 20. PAGE 66 F1292
NAT/G UAR

B63
LEWIS G.K.,PUERTO RICO: FREEDOM AND POWER IN THE CARIBBEAN. PUERT/RICO USA+45 CULTURE STRUCT INDUS POL/PAR WORKER EDU/PROP CATHISM 20. PAGE 79 F1548
ECO/UNDEV COLONIAL NAT/LISM GEOG

B63
MINGAY G.E.,ENGLISH LANDED SOCIETY IN THE EIGHTEENTH CENTURY. UK ELITES STRUCT AGRI INDUS CONTROL WEALTH 18. PAGE 92 F1802
OWN STRATA PWR

B63
OTERO L.M.,HONDURAS. HONDURAS SPAIN STRUCT SECT COLONIAL REV WAR ATTIT PWR...GEOG WORSHIP 16/20. PAGE 102 F2003
NAT/G SOCIETY NAT/LISM ECO/UNDEV

B63
UNITED NATIONS,THE GROWTH OF WORLD INDUSTRY, 1938-1961: NATIONAL TABLES. WOR+45 STRUCT ECO/DEV ECO/UNDEV NAT/G COST...CHARTS UN. PAGE 132 F2613
STAT INDUS PRODUC ORD/FREE

S63
BARTHELEMY G.,"LE NOUVEAU FRANC (CFA) ET LA BANQUE CENTRALE DES ETATS DE L'AFRIQUE DE L'OUEST." FUT STRUCT INT/ORG PLAN ATTIT ALL/VALS FOR/TRADE 20. PAGE 11 F0200
AFR FINAN

S63
BEGUIN H.,"ASPECTS STRUCTURELS DU COMMERCE EXTERIEUR DES PAYS SOUS-DEVELOPPES." FUT WOR+45 STRUCT FINAN SERV/IND POL/PAR TEC/DEV PERCEPT WEALTH FOR/TRADE 20. PAGE 12 F0229
MARKET ECO/UNDEV FOR/AID

B64
BASTIAT F.,ECONOMIC HARMONIES (1850). STRATA STRUCT ECO/DEV BUDGET TAX PRICE LOBBY COST. PAGE 11 F0206
ECO/TAC PLAN INT/TRADE LAISSEZ

B64
CEPEDE M.,POPULATION AND FOOD. USA+45 STRUCT ECO/UNDEV FAM PLAN TEC/DEV FOR/AID CONTROL...CATH SOC TREND 19/20. PAGE 22 F0436
FUT GEOG AGRI CENSUS

B64
DANIELS R.V.,RUSSIA. RUSSIA USSR STRUCT NAT/LISM TOTALISM ORD/FREE WEALTH...POLICY DECISION TREND. PAGE 30 F0579
MARXISM REV ECO/DEV DIPLOM

B64
HACKER A.,THE CORPORATION TAKE-OVER. CONSTN LABOR PLAN BAL/PWR CONTROL EXEC LOBBY REPRESENT GP/REL ROLE ORD/FREE POLICY. PAGE 52 F1025
LG/CO STRUCT PWR

B64
NOVACK D.E.,DEVELOPMENT AND SOCIETY; THE DYNAMICS OF ECONOMIC CHANGE. WOR+45 STRATA STRUCT ECO/TAC CONTROL CROWD REV GP/REL ADJUST PRODUC WEALTH PSY. PAGE 99 F1940
SOCIETY CULTURE SOC ECO/UNDEV

B64
POWELSON J.P.,LATIN AMERICA: TODAY'S ECONOMIC AND SOCIAL REVOLUTION. L/A+17C INTELL SOCIETY STRUCT AGRI INDUS NAT/G DIPLOM ECO/TAC REV...POLICY 20. PAGE 107 F2110
ECO/UNDEV WEALTH ADJUST PLAN

B64
PRESTHUS R.,MEN AT THE TOP; A STUDY IN COMMUNITY POWER. USA+45 STRUCT ACT/RES REPRESENT CONSEN ALL/VALS ORD/FREE...SAMP/SIZ 20. PAGE 108 F2116
PLURISM LG/CO PWR ADMIN

B64
RENO P.,THE ORDEAL OF BRITISH GUIANA. L/A+17C USA+45 STRUCT AGRI EXTR/IND INDUS NAT/G FOR/AID ORD/FREE...GEOG 20 GUIANA/BR INTRVN/ECO. PAGE 111 F2178
COLONIAL ECO/UNDEV SOCISM PWR

B64
TAEUBER I.B.,POPULATION TRENDS IN THE UNITED STATES: 1900 TO 1960. USA+45 USA-45 PROVS INCOME AGE...SOC TIME/SEQ TREND CHARTS MUNICH TIME 20 NEGRO. PAGE 128 F2522
CENSUS GEOG STRATA STRUCT

B64
TAWNEY R.H.,EQUALITY. UK CULTURE STRATA ECO/TAC EDU/PROP REPRESENT OWN NEW/LIB...MAJORIT WELF/ST SOC 20. PAGE 129 F2538
WEALTH STRUCT ELITES POPULISM

B64
VON DER MEHDEN F.R.,POLITICS OF THE DEVELOPING NATIONS. WOR+45 CONSTN PROB/SOLV ORD/FREE WEALTH OBJECTIVE. PAGE 142 F2790
ECO/UNDEV SOCIETY STRUCT

B64
ZOLLSCHAN G.K.,EXPLORATIONS IN SOCIAL CHANGE. SOCIETY STRATA STRUCT ECO/UNDEV EX/STRUC...PSY ANTHOL 20. PAGE 151 F2968
ORD/FREE SIMUL CONCPT CULTURE

B65
BRADLEY J.F.,THE ROLE OF TRADE ASSOCIATIONS AND PROFESSIONAL BUSINESS SOCIETIES IN AMERICA. USA+45 USA-45 STRUCT CONSULT DELIB/GP CREATE LOBBY GP/REL 20. PAGE 17 F0333
ECO/DEV PROF/ORG VOL/ASSN SOCIETY

B65
CAMERON W.J.,NEW ZEALAND. NEW/ZEALND S/ASIA DIPLOM INT/TRADE WRITING COLONIAL PARL/PROC...GEOG CMN/WLTH. PAGE 21 F0402
SOCIETY GP/REL STRUCT

B65
IANNI O.,ESTADO E CAPITALISMO. L/A+17C FINAN TEC/DEV ECO/TAC ORD/FREE WEALTH POLICY. PAGE 64 F1258
ECO/UNDEV STRUCT INDUS NAT/G

B65
MOORE W.E.,THE IMPACT OF INDUSTRY. CULTURE STRUCT ORD/FREE...TREND 20. PAGE 93 F1824
INDUS MGT TEC/DEV ECO/UNDEV

B65
SCHULER E.A.,THE PAKISTAN ACADEMIES FOR RURAL DEVELOPMENT COMILLA AND PESHAWAR 1959-1964. PAKISTAN S/ASIA SOCIETY STRUCT AGRI NAT/G TEC/DEV EDU/PROP 20. PAGE 117 F2314
BIBLIOG PLAN ECO/TAC ECO/UNDEV

L65
HAGE J.,"AN AXIOMATIC THEORY OF ORGANIZATIONS" USA+45 STRUCT LABOR PRODUC DRIVE PERSON RIGID/FLEX 20 WEBER/MAX. PAGE 53 F1032
GP/REL EFFICIENCY PROF/ORG ATTIT

S65
BRANDENBURG F.,"THE RELEVANCE OF MEXICAN EXPERIENCE TO LATIN AMERICAN DEVELOPMENT." BRAZIL CHILE VENEZUELA STRUCT ECO/UNDEV AGRI CREATE ECO/TAC ...STAT RECORD MEXIC/AMER ARGEN COLOMB. PAGE 18 F0340
L/A+17C GOV/COMP

S65
KUNKEL J.H.,"VALUES AND BEHAVIOR IN ECONOMIC DEVELOPMENT." INDIA PERU CULTURE STRUCT CREATE PERS/REL ATTIT PERSON...CHARTS HYPO/EXP ARGEN. PAGE 74 F1449
SIMUL ECO/UNDEV PSY STERTYP

B66
BEN-PORATH Y.,THE ARAB LABOR FORCE IN ISRAEL. ISLAM ISRAEL AGRI INDUS SCHOOL CAP/ISM PAY DEMAND...GEOG REGRESS STAT CHARTS 20 ARABS. PAGE 13 F0245
WORKER CENSUS GP/REL STRUCT

B66
BRODERSEN A.,THE SOVIET WORKER: LABOR AND GOVERNMENT IN SOVIET SOCIETY. USSR STRUCT INDUS LABOR PLAN PAY INGP/REL PRODUC...POLICY GEN/LAWS BIBLIOG 20 STALIN/J LENIN/VI BOLSHEVISM KHRUSH/N. PAGE 19 F0357
WORKER ROLE NAT/G MARXISM

B66
ECKSTEIN A.,COMMUNIST CHINA'S ECONOMIC GROWTH AND FOREIGN TRADE* IMPLICATIONS FOR US POLICY. COM USA+45 USSR STRUCT INDUS MARKET DIPLOM ECO/TAC FOR/AID INT/TRADE...STAT CHARTS. PAGE 36 F0696
ASIA ECO/UNDEV CREATE PWR

B66
GOODMAN L.H.,ECONOMIC PROGRESS AND SOCIAL WELFARE. USA+45 STRATA STRUCT ECO/TAC EFFICIENCY...MGT 20. PAGE 49 F0949
SOC/WK RECEIVE GP/COMP POLICY

B66
HARLOW J.S.,FRENCH ECONOMIC PLANNING: A CHALLENGE TO REASON. EUR+WWI FRANCE PROB/SOLV 20 EUROPE. PAGE 55 F1084
ECO/TAC PLAN STRUCT

B66
HOLT R.T.,THE POLITICAL BASIS OF ECONOMIC DEVELOPMENT. STRATA STRUCT NAT/G DIPLOM ADMIN...SOC NAT/COMP BIBLIOG 20. PAGE 61 F1201
ECO/TAC GOV/COMP CONSTN EX/STRUC

B66
HOROWITZ I.L.,THREE WORLDS OF DEVELOPMENT. COM USA+45 STRUCT ECO/DEV PLAN PROB/SOLV TEC/DEV CIVMIL/REL...PHIL/SCI IDEA/COMP 20. PAGE 62 F1216
ECO/UNDEV BAL/PWR POL/PAR REV

B66
KOH S.J.,STAGES OF INDUSTRIAL DEVELOPMENT IN ASIA. ASIA INDIA KOREA STRATA STRUCT NAT/G INT/TRADE ...CHARTS 19/20 CHINJAP. PAGE 72 F1415
INDUS ECO/UNDEV ECO/DEV LABOR

B66
LENSKI G.E.,POWER AND PRIVILEGE: A THEORY OF SOCIAL STRATIFICATION. SWEDEN UK UNIV USSR CULTURE ECO/UNDEV PRIVIL PWR...PHIL/SCI CONCPT CHARTS IDEA/COMP HYPO/EXP METH MARX/KARL. PAGE 78 F1525
SOC STRATA STRUCT SOCIETY

B66
LILLEY S.,MEN, MACHINES AND HISTORY: THE STORY OF TOOLS AND MACHINES IN RELATION TO SOCIAL PROGRESS. PREHIST SPACE STRUCT COMPUTER AUTOMAT NUC/PWR ...POLICY SOC. PAGE 80 F1564
AGRI TEC/DEV SOCIETY

B66
MURPHY G.G.,SOVIET MONGOLIA: A STUDY OF THE OLDEST POLITICAL SATELLITE. USSR STRATA STRUCT COST INCOME ATTIT SOCISM 20. PAGE 95 F1865
DIPLOM ECO/TAC PLAN DOMIN

B66
PFEFFER K.H.,WELT IM UMBRUCH. SOCIETY STRUCT INDUS PROF/ORG SECT TEC/DEV PARTIC SUPEGO WORSHIP 20 CHRISTIAN. PAGE 106 F2076
ORD/FREE STRATA CREATE

B66
RIZK C.,LE REGIME POLITIQUE LIBANAIS. ISLAM LEBANON STRUCT POL/PAR SECT LOBBY GP/REL 20 ARABS MUSLIM CHRISTIAN. PAGE 112 F2198
ECO/UNDEV NAT/G CULTURE

B66
THIESENHUSEN W.C.,CHILE'S EXPERIMENTS IN AGRARIAN REFORM. CHILE STRUCT NAT/G ACT/RES ECO/TAC GOV/REL COST SOCISM...TREND CHARTS SOC/EXP 20. PAGE 130 F2558
AGRI ECO/UNDEV SOC TEC/DEV

B66
THOMPSON J.H.,MODERNIZATION OF THE ARAB WORLD. FUT ISRAEL STRUCT ECO/UNDEV DIPLOM INGP/REL ATTIT ...CENSUS ANTHOL 20 ARABS. PAGE 130 F2565
ADJUST ISLAM PROB/SOLV NAT/COMP

B66
WOODMAN H.D.,SLAVERY AND THE SOUTHERN ECONOMY: SOURCES AND READINGS. USA-45 CULTURE STRUCT AGRI ECO/TAC LEAD RACE/REL DISCRIM EFFICIENCY...CHARTS ANTHOL MUNICH 18/19 NEGRO SOUTH/US. PAGE 148 F2922
ECO/DEV STRATA WORKER UTIL

L66
PACKENHAM R.A.,"POLITICAL-DEVELOPMENT DOCTRINES IN THE AMERICAN FOREIGN AID PROGRAM." STRUCT R+D CREATE DIPLOM AID. PAGE 102 F2011
FOR/AID ECO/UNDEV GEN/LAWS

S66
COHEN A.,"THE TECHNOLOGY/ELITE APPROACH TO THE DEVELOPMENTAL PROCESS* PERUVIAN CASE STUDY." L/A+17C STRUCT CREATE ECO/TAC FOR/AID CIVMIL/REL MARXISM TECHRACY HYPO/EXP. PAGE 26 F0496
ECO/UNDEV ELITES PERU

S66
FLEMING W.G.,"AUTHORITY, EFFICIENCY, AND ROLE STRESS: PROBLEMS IN THE DEVELOPMENT OF EAST AFRICAN BUREAUCRACIES." AFR UGANDA STRUCT PROB/SOLV ROUTINE INGP/REL ROLE...MGT SOC GP/COMP GOV/COMP 20 TANGANYIKA AFRICA/E. PAGE 41 F0810
DOMIN EFFICIENCY COLONIAL ADMIN

S66
JACOBS P.,"RE-RADICALIZING THE DE-RADICALIZED." USA+45 SOCIETY STRUCT FINAN PLAN PROB/SOLV CAP/ISM WEALTH CONSERVE NEW/LIB 20. PAGE 66 F1297
NAT/G POLICY MARXIST ADMIN

S66
SHORTE F.C.,"THE APPLICATION OF DEVELOPMENT HYPOTHESES IN MIDDLE EASTERN STUDIES." STRUCT AGRI CREATE DEMAND...GEOG STAT CON/ANAL CHARTS. PAGE 121 F2387
ECO/UNDEV ISLAM SOC HYPO/EXP

B67
BIRMINGHAM W.,A STUDY OF CONTEMPORARY GHANA VOL. I: SOME ASPECTS OF SOCIAL STRUCTURE. AFR GHANA AGRI FAM SECT PLAN EDU/PROP MARRIAGE OWN...POLICY STAT CHARTS MUNICH 20. PAGE 15 F0287
SOCIETY STRUCT CENSUS ECO/UNDEV

B67
ELDREDGE H.W.,TAMING MEGALOPOLIS; WHAT IT IS AND WHAT COULD BE (VOL. I). FUT USA+45 WOR+45 SOCIETY STRUCT ECO/DEV INDUS LEISURE WEALTH...ANTHOL MUNICH. PAGE 37 F0717
PROB/SOLV PLAN TEC/DEV

B67
FIELD G.L.,COMPARATIVE POLITICAL DEVELOPMENT: THE PRECEDENT OF THE WEST. FRANCE GERMANY SWEDEN UK USSR STRATA STRUCT POL/PAR...METH 20. PAGE 40 F0790
NAT/COMP CONCPT ECO/DEV SOCIETY

B67
GORZ A.,STRATEGY FOR LABOR: A RADICAL PROPOSAL (TRANS. BY MARTIN NICOLAUS AND VICTORIA ORTIZ). EUR+WWI FRANCE ITALY ECO/DEV POL/PAR OP/RES PLAN GP/REL ALL/IDEOS...SOC 20 EEC. PAGE 49 F0965
LABOR PWR STRUCT ECO/TAC

B67
GROSS B.M.,ACTION UNDER PLANNING: THE GUIDANCE OF ECONOMIC DEVELOPMENT. STRUCT R+D NAT/G ACT/RES HABITAT...DECISION 20. PAGE 51 F1005
ECO/UNDEV PLAN ADMIN MGT

B67
MARRIS P.,DILEMMAS OF SOCIAL REFORM: POVERTY AND COMMUNITY ACTION IN THE UNITED STATES. USA+45 NAT/G OP/RES ADMIN PARTIC EFFICIENCY WEALTH...SOC METH/COMP T MUNICH 20 REFORMERS. PAGE 85 F1674
STRUCT PROB/SOLV COST

B67
MCDOUGAL M.S.,THE INTERPRETATION OF AGREEMENTS AND WORLD PUBLIC ORDER: PRINCIPLES OF CONTENT AND PROCEDURE. WOR+45 CONSTN PROB/SOLV TEC/DEV ...CON/ANAL TREATY. PAGE 88 F1727
INT/LAW STRUCT ECO/UNDEV DIPLOM

B67
MEYERS M.,SOURCES OF THE AMERICAN REPUBLIC; A DOCUMENTARY HISTORY OF POLITICS, SOCIETY, AND THOUGHT (VOL. I, REV. ED.). USA-45 CULTURE STRUCT NAT/G LEGIS LEAD ATTIT...JURID SOC ANTHOL 17/19 PRESIDENT. PAGE 90 F1772
COLONIAL REV WAR

B67
NARVER J.C.,CONGLOMERATE MERGERS AND MARKET COMPETITION. USA+45 LAW STRUCT ADMIN LEAD RISK COST PROFIT WEALTH...POLICY CHARTS BIBLIOG. PAGE 96 F1892
DEMAND LG/CO MARKET MGT

B67
POWLEDGE F.,BLACK POWER WHITE RESISTANCE. USA+45 STRUCT PLAN GP/REL DISCRIM HABITAT ORD/FREE WEALTH ...METH/COMP SOC/INTEG NEGRO. PAGE 107 F2111
RACE/REL ATTIT PWR

B67
RAVKIN A.,THE NEW STATES OF AFRICA (HEADLINE SERIES, NO. 183((PAMPHLET). CULTURE STRUCT INDUS COLONIAL NAT/LISM...SOC 20. PAGE 109 F2153
AFR ECO/UNDEV SOCIETY ADMIN

B67
SPIRO H.S.,PATTERNS OF AFRICAN DEVLOPMENT: FIVE COMPARISONS. STRUCT ECO/UNDEV NAT/G CONSERVE SOCISM ...PREDICT NAT/COMP 20 CHINJAP. PAGE 125 F2457
AFR CONSTN NAT/LISM TREND

B67
WALLBANK T.W.,CIVILIZATION PAST AND PRESENT (3RD ED.). FUT WOR+45 WOR-45 SOCIETY...SOC CONCPT TIME/SEQ CHARTS BIBLIOG T. PAGE 143 F2809
CULTURE STRUCT TREND

B67
WESSON R.G.,THE IMPERIAL ORDER. WOR-45 STRUCT SECT DOMIN ADMIN COLONIAL LEAD CONSERVE...CONCPT BIBLIOG 20. PAGE 145 F2861
PWR CHIEF CONTROL SOCIETY

S67
HEILBRONER R.L.,"BUILDING NEW NATIONS." AFR STRUCT PLAN TEC/DEV ADJUST MARXISM...POLICY 20. PAGE 58 F1138
PROB/SOLV REV NAT/LISM ECO/UNDEV

S67
JENCKS C.E.,"SOCIAL STATUS OF COAL MINERS IN BRITAIN SINCE NATIONALIZATION." UK STRATA STRUCT LABOR RECEIVE GP/REL INCOME OWN ATTIT HABITAT...MGT T 20. PAGE 67 F1312
EXTR/IND WORKER CONTROL NAT/G

S67
LEDEBUR L.C.,"THE PROBLEM OF SOCIAL COST." STRUCT PROB/SOLV...CHARTS GEN/LAWS. PAGE 77 F1501
COST INCOME SOCIETY ECO/TAC

S67
RAMA C.M.,"PASADO Y PRESENTE DE LA RELIGION EN AMERICA LATINA." L/A+17C ELITES SOCIETY STRATA MARXISM...STAT WORSHIP PROTESTANT. PAGE 109 F2139
SECT CATHISM STRUCT NAT/COMP

S67
RONY V.,"HEARTBREAK IN TENNESSEE* POOR WHITES AND THE UNIONS." LAW STRUCT CAP/ISM ADJUD GP/REL. PAGE 113 F2236
LABOR LOC/G WORKER PWR

S67
ROY E.V.,"AN INTERPRETATION OF NORTHERN THAI PEASANT ECONOMY." THAILAND CLIENT CULTURE AGRI PROC/MFG FACE/GP DEMAND INCOME 20. PAGE 114 F2254
STRUCT STRATA ECO/UNDEV INGP/REL

S67
SCHWARZWELLER H.K.,"SOCIAL CLASS ORIGINS, RURAL-URBAN MIGRATION, AND ECONOMIC LIFE CHANGES." USA+45 SOCIETY STRUCT FAM NEIGH INCOME...SOC RECORD CHARTS MUNICH. PAGE 118 F2326
CLASSIF WEALTH AGRI

S67
SHERWOOD W.B.,"THE RISE OF THE JUSTICE PARTY IN TURKEY." FUT TURKEY LEAD ATTIT 20. PAGE 121 F2378
POL/PAR
ECO/UNDEV
STRUCT
SOCIETY

S67
SIPPEL D.,"INDIENS UNSICHERE ZUKUNFT." INDIA CULTURE ACADEM POL/PAR LEGIS COLONIAL CHOOSE SOVEREIGN...JURID 20. PAGE 122 F2416
SOCIETY
STRUCT
ECO/UNDEV
NAT/G

B76
SMITH A.,THE WEALTH OF NATIONS. UK STRUCT WORKER DIPLOM ECO/TAC OPTIMAL DRIVE PERSON ORD/FREE ...OLD/LIB GEN/LAWS 17/18. PAGE 123 F2428
WEALTH
PRODUC
INDUS
LAISSEZ

STRUVE G.M. F2505

STRUVE/P....PETER STRUVE

STUART DYNASTY....SEE STUART/DYN

STUART/DYN....THE STUART DYNASTY

STUCKI C.W. F2506

STUDENT NONVIOLENT COORDINATING COMMITTEE....SEE SNCC, STUDNT/PWR

STUDENTS FOR A DEMOCRATIC SOCIETY....SEE SDS

STUDNT/PWR....STUDENT POWER: STUDENT PROTESTS AND PROTEST MOVEMENTS

STUDY GP CREATE RESERVE ASSETS F2507

STUTZ R.L. F2508

STYCOS J.M. F2509

STYLE....STYLES OF SCIENTIFIC COMMUNICATION

B57
DOWNS A.,AN ECONOMIC THEORY OF DEMOCRACY. NAT/G EDU/PROP RISK CHOOSE PERS/REL EQUILIB...SOC METH/CNCPT LOG STYLE. PAGE 34 F0659
DECISION
RATIONAL

S59
HOFFMAN P.,"OPERATION BREAKTHROUGH." AFR S/ASIA STRUCT INDUS CONSULT TEC/DEV ATTIT RIGID/FLEX SKILL WEALTH...TECHNIC CONCPT STYLE RECORD CHARTS ORG/CHARTS GEN/METH VAL/FREE 20. PAGE 61 F1190
ECO/UNDEV
EDU/PROP
FOR/AID

B62
KAUTSKY J.H.,POLITICAL CHANGE IN UNDERDEVELOPED COUNTRIES: NATIONALISM AND COMMUNISM. WOR+45 AGRI TEC/DEV EDU/PROP ATTIT...POLICY METH/CNCPT STYLE INT QU CENSUS TREND SOC/EXP GEN/LAWS 20. PAGE 69 F1365
ECO/UNDEV
SOCIETY
CAP/ISM
REV

B64
JUSTER F.T.,ANTICIPATIONS AND PURCHASES; AN ANALYSIS OF CONSUMER BEHAVIOR. PROB/SOLV RISK COST PRODUC DRIVE...STAT STYLE SAMP CON/ANAL CHARTS HYPO/EXP GAME SIMUL. PAGE 68 F1345
PROBABIL
DECISION
PREDICT
DEMAND

S64
FLORINSKY M.T.,"TRENDS IN THE SOVIET ECONOMY." COM USA+45 USSR INDUS LABOR NAT/G PLAN TEC/DEV ECO/TAC ALL/VALS SOCISM...MGT METH/CNCPT STYLE CON/ANAL GEN/METH WORK 20. PAGE 42 F0817
ECO/DEV
AGRI

B65
HICKMAN B.G.,QUANTITATIVE PLANNING OF ECONOMIC POLICY. FRANCE NETHERLAND OP/RES PRICE ROUTINE UTIL ...POLICY DECISION ECOMETRIC METH/CNCPT STAT STYLE CHINJAP. PAGE 59 F1162
PROB/SOLV
PLAN
QUANT

B66
BALDWIN D.A.,FOREIGN AID AND AMERICAN FOREIGN POLICY; A DOCUMENTARY ANALYSIS. USA+45 ECO/UNDEV ADMIN...ECOMETRIC STAT STYLE CHARTS PROG/TEAC GEN/LAWS ANTHOL. PAGE 9 F0162
FOR/AID
DIPLOM
IDEA/COMP

SUAREZ/F....FRANCISCO SUAREZ

SUBMARINE....SUBMARINES AND SUBMARINE WARFARE

SUBSIDIES....SEE FINAN

SUBURBS....SUBURBS

SUBVERT....SUBVERSION

SUCCESSION....SUCCESSION (POLITICAL)

SUDAN....SEE ALSO AFR

B65
MEAGHER R.F.,PUBLIC INTERNATIONAL DEVELOPMENT FINANCING IN SUDAN. SUDAN FINAN DELIB/GP GIVE ...CHARTS GOV/COMP 20. PAGE 89 F1740
FOR/AID
PLAN
RECEIVE
ECO/UNDEV

SUDETENLND....SUDETENLAND

SUEZ CRISIS....SEE NAT/LISM+COERCE, ALSO INDIVIDUAL NATIONS, SUEZ

SUEZ....SUEZ CANAL

B56
WATT D.C.,BRITAIN AND THE SUEZ CANAL. COM UAR UK ...INT/LAW 20 SUEZ TREATY. PAGE 144 F2835
DIPLOM
INT/TRADE
DIST/IND
NAT/G

SUFF....SUFFRAGE; SEE ALSO CHOOSE

B13
BEARD C.A.,AN ECONOMIC INTERPRETATION OF THE CONSTITUTION OF THE UNITED STATES. USA-45 AGRI INT/TRADE SUFF OWN ATTIT...CONCPT MYTH BIOG HIST/WRIT 18. PAGE 12 F0222
CONSTN
ECO/TAC
CHOOSE

B27
BELLOC H.,THE SERVILE STATE (1912) (3RD ED.). PRUSSIA UK CULTURE STRATA INDUS NAT/G ECO/TAC CONTROL LEAD SUFF DISCRIM EQUILIB ORD/FREE WEALTH 20. PAGE 12 F0237
WORKER
CAP/ISM
DOMIN
CATH

B67
LYND S.,RECONSTRUCTION. USA-45 PROB/SOLV RACE/REL ...IDEA/COMP ANTHOL 19. PAGE 82 F1616
SUFF
ECO/TAC
ADJUST

B67
MORRIS A.J.A.,PARLIAMENTARY DEMOCRACY IN THE NINETEENTH CENTURY. UK INDUS LOC/G NAT/G POL/PAR CONSULT LEGIS INT/TRADE ADMIN CHOOSE SUFF SOVEREIGN 19 PARLIAMENT. PAGE 93 F1835
TIME/SEQ
CONSTN
PARL/PROC
POPULISM

S67
FLACKS R.,"CONSCRIPTION IN A DEMOCRATIC SOCIETY." USA+45 WORKER CONTROL SUFF SUPEGO. PAGE 41 F0807
POLICY
FORCES
ORD/FREE
CIVMIL/REL

S67
GATELL F.O.,"MONEY AND PARTY IN JACKSONIAN AMERICA* A QUANTITATIVE LOOK AT NEW YORK CITY'S MEN OF QUALITY." USA-45 STRATA SECT SUFF CONSEN MAJORITY ATTIT...CHARTS HYPO/EXP 19. PAGE 46 F0908
WEALTH
POL/PAR
PERSON
IDEA/COMP

S67
NEALE R.S.,"WORKING CLASS WOMEN AND WOMEN'S SUFFRAGE." UK LAW CONSTN LABOR NAT/G DELIB/GP LEGIS WORKER PAY PARTIC CHOOSE 19 FEMALE/SEX. PAGE 97 F1906
STRATA
SEX
SUFF
DISCRIM

SUFFRAGE....SEE SUFF

SUFRIN S.C. F2510

SUICIDE....SUICIDE AND RELATED SELF-DESTRUCTIVENESS

SUKARNO/A....ACHMED SUKARNO

SULLIVAN G. F2511

SULTAN P.E. F2512

SUMATRA....SUMATRA

SUMER....SUMER, A PRE- OR EARLY HISTORIC SOCIETY

SUMMERS C.W. F2513

SUMNER W.G. F2514

SUN/YAT....SUN YAT SEN

SUPEGO....CONSCIENCE, SUPEREGO, RESPONSIBILITY

B12
FOUAD M.,LE REGIME DE LA PRESSE EN EGYPTE: THESE POUR LE DOCTORAT. UAR LICENSE EDU/PROP ADMIN SANCTION CRIME SUPEGO PWR...ART/METH JURID 19/20. PAGE 43 F0832
ORD/FREE
LEGIS
CONTROL
PRESS

N19
KRESSBACH T.W.,HE MICHIGAN CITY MANAGER IN BUDGETARY PROCEEDINGS (PAMPHLET). USA+45 PROVS DELIB/GP GP/REL SUPEGO...POLICY MUNICH. PAGE 73 F1438
LOC/G
BUDGET
FINAN

B39
CLARK J.M.,SOCIAL CONTROL OF BUSINESS (2ND ED.). ECO/DEV FINAN LG/CO PLAN ECO/TAC PRICE SUPEGO...T 20. PAGE 25 F0480
CAP/ISM
CONTROL
LAISSEZ
METH/COMP

S43
HUZAR E.,"CONGRESS AND THE ARMY: APPROPRIATIONS." USA-45 CONFER CONTROL ATTIT SUPEGO SKILL CONGRESS.
LEGIS
FORCES

PAGE 64 F1255 BUDGET
DELIB/GP

C43
BENTHAM J.,"THE RATIONALE OF REWARD" IN J. BOWRING, ED., THE WORKS OF JEREMY BENTHAM (VOL. 2)" LAW WORKER CREATE INSPECT PAY ROUTINE HAPPINESS PRODUC SUPEGO WEALTH METH/CNCPT. PAGE 13 F0254
SANCTION ECO/TAC INCOME PWR

B52
ROSE A.M.,UNION SOLIDARITY: THE INTERNAL COHESION OF A LABOR UNION. SECT GP/REL RACE/REL ATTIT ROLE HEALTH WEALTH...INT QU. PAGE 114 F2241
LABOR INGP/REL PARTIC SUPEGO

S52
KORNHAUSER W.,"THE NEGRO UNION OFFICIAL: A STUDY OF SPONSORSHIP AND CONTROL" (BMR)" USA+45 CONTROL DISCRIM ROLE SUPEGO...OBS 20 NEGRO. PAGE 73 F1428
LABOR LEAD RACE/REL CHOOSE

B53
BOWEN H.R.,SOCIAL RESPONSIBILITIES OF THE BUSINESSMAN (FIRST EDITION). LAW FINAN ACT/RES CAP/ISM ROUTINE DRIVE PWR LAISSEZ...DECISION BIBLIOG. PAGE 17 F0326
MGT PERSON SUPEGO MORAL

S59
CLONER A.,"THE CALIFORNIA LEGISLATOR AND THE PROBLEM OF COMPENSATION." USA+45 WORKER REPRESENT. PAGE 25 F0492
INCOME PROVS LEGIS SUPEGO

B60
BOHM F.,REDEN UND SCHRIFTEN UBER DIE ORDNUNG EINER FREIEN GESELLSCHAFT, EINER FREIEN WIRTSCHAFT, UND UBER DIE WIEDERGUTMACH. DIPLOM CRIME ORD/FREE RESPECT FASCISM 20 NAZI. PAGE 16 F0307
ECO/TAC NEW/LIB SUPEGO REPAR

B60
ROEPKE W.,A HUMANE ECONOMY: THE SOCIAL FRAMEWORK OF THE FREE MARKET. FUT USSR WOR+45 CULTURE SOCIETY ECO/DEV PLAN ECO/TAC ADMIN ATTIT PERSON RIGID/FLEX SUPEGO MORAL WEALTH SOCISM...POLICY OLD/LIB CONCPT TREND GEN/LAWS 20. PAGE 113 F2232
DRIVE EDU/PROP CAP/ISM

B60
WHEARE K.C.,THE CONSTITUTIONAL STRUCTURE OF THE COMMONWEALTH. UK EX/STRUC DIPLOM DOMIN ADMIN COLONIAL CONTROL LEAD INGP/REL SUPEGO 20 CMN/WLTH. PAGE 145 F2865
CONSTN INT/ORG VOL/ASSN SOVEREIGN

B61
BEASLEY K.E.,STATE SUPERVISION OF MUNICIPAL DEBT IN KANSAS - A CASE STUDY. USA+45 USA-45 FINAN PROVS BUDGET TAX ADJUD ADMIN CONTROL SUPEGO MUNICH. PAGE 12 F0224
LOC/G LEGIS JURID

B61
THEOBALD R.,THE CHALLENGE OF ABUNDANCE. USA+45 WOR+45 MARKET DIPLOM FOR/AID REV PRODUC UTOPIA SUPEGO...POLICY TREND BIBLIOG/A 20. PAGE 129 F2554
WELF/ST ECO/UNDEV PROB/SOLV ECO/TAC

B63
CHAMPION J.M.,CRITICAL INCIDENTS IN MANAGEMENT. MARKET LG/CO SML/CO OP/RES ADMIN CONTROL LEAD GP/REL PERS/REL COST ATTIT SUPEGO ALL/VALS...PSY PERS/TEST BIBLIOG. PAGE 23 F0445
MGT DECISION EX/STRUC INDUS

B63
DE VRIES E.,SOCIAL ASPECTS OF ECONOMIC DEVELOPMENT IN LATIN AMERICA. CULTURE SOCIETY STRATA FINAN INDUS INT/ORG DELIB/GP ACT/RES ECO/TAC EDU/PROP ADMIN ATTIT SUPEGO HEALTH KNOWL ORD/FREE...SOC STAT TREND ANTHOL TOT/POP VAL/FREE. PAGE 31 F0608
L/A+17C ECO/UNDEV

B63
MULLENBACH P.,CIVILIAN NUCLEAR POWER: ECONOMIC ISSUES AND POLICY FORMATION. AFR FINAN INT/ORG DELIB/GP ACT/RES ECO/TAC ATTIT SUPEGO HEALTH ORD/FREE PWR...POLICY CONCPT MATH STAT CHARTS VAL/FREE 20. PAGE 94 F1855
USA+45 ECO/DEV NUC/PWR

B64
CASEY R.G.,THE FUTURE OF THE COMMONWEALTH. INDIA PAKISTAN UK ECO/UNDEV INT/ORG TEC/DEV COLONIAL SUPEGO 20 EEC AUSTRAL. PAGE 22 F0425
DIPLOM SOVEREIGN NAT/LISM FOR/AID

B64
CHEIT E.F.,THE BUSINESS ESTABLISHMENT. FRANCE WOR+45 PROF/ORG TOP/EX PROB/SOLV CAP/ISM ADMIN SUPEGO MORAL PWR...METH/CNCPT MYTH NEW/IDEA 20. PAGE 24 F0460
PERSON EX/STRUC MGT INDUS

B66
PFEFFER K.H.,WELT IM UMBRUCH. SOCIETY STRUCT INDUS PROF/ORG SECT TEC/DEV PARTIC SUPEGO WORSHIP 20 CHRISTIAN. PAGE 106 F2076
ORD/FREE STRATA CREATE

B67
CHO S.S.,KOREA IN WORLD POLITICS 1940-1950; AN EVALUATION OF AMERICAN RESPONSIBILITY. KOREA USA+45 USSR CONSTN INT/ORG NAT/G FORCES FOR/AID ANOMIE SUPEGO MARXISM...DECISION BIBLIOG 20. PAGE 24 F0469
POLICY DIPLOM PROB/SOLV WAR

B67
WOOTON G.,WORKERS, UNIONS, AND THE STATE. INDUS PROB/SOLV GP/REL DRIVE SUPEGO RESPECT...PSY SOC. PAGE 148 F2925
PARTIC WORKER NAT/G LABOR

S67
FLACKS R.,"CONSCRIPTION IN A DEMOCRATIC SOCIETY." USA+45 WORKER CONTROL SUFF SUPEGO. PAGE 41 F0807
POLICY FORCES ORD/FREE CIVMIL/REL

S67
SEIDLER G.L.,"MARXIST LEGAL THOUGHT IN POLAND." POLAND SOCIETY R+D LOC/G NAT/G ACT/RES ADJUD CT/SYS SUPEGO PWR...SOC TREND 20 MARX/KARL. PAGE 119 F2343
MARXISM LAW CONCPT EFFICIENCY

B96
SCHMOLLER G.,THE MERCANTILE SYSTEM AND ITS HISTORICAL SIGNIFICANCE: ILLUSTRATED CHIEFLY FROM PRUSSIAN HISTORY (TRANS.). PRUSSIA CULTURE INDUS KIN NAT/G PROVS OP/RES ECO/TAC INT/TRADE SUPEGO PWR WEALTH MUNICH 19 MERCANTLST. PAGE 117 F2302
GEN/METH INGP/REL CONCPT

SUPERSONIC TRANSPORT....SEE SST

SUPERVISION....SEE EXEC, CONTROL, LEAD, TASK

SUPREME/CT....SUPREME COURT (ALL NATIONS)

B28
FRANKFURTER F.,THE BUSINESS OF THE SUPREME COURT; A STUDY IN THE FEDERAL JUDICIAL SYSTEM. USA-45 CONSTN EX/STRUC PROB/SOLV GP/REL ATTIT PWR...POLICY JURID 18/20 SUPREME/CT CONGRESS. PAGE 43 F0848
CT/SYS ADJUD LAW FEDERAL

B37
HAMILTON W.H.,THE POWER TO GOVERN. ECO/DEV FINAN INDUS ECO/TAC INT/TRADE TARIFFS TAX CONTROL CT/SYS WAR COST PWR 18/20 SUPREME/CT. PAGE 54 F1056
LING CONSTN NAT/G POLICY

B40
HELLMAN F.S.,THE NEW DEAL: SELECTED LIST OF REFERENCES. USA-45 FINAN LABOR EX/STRUC CREATE INT/TRADE ADMIN CT/SYS 20 SUPREME/CT. PAGE 58 F1145
BIBLIOG/A ECO/TAC PLAN POLICY

S52
LEWIS V.B.,"TOWARD A THEORY OF BUDGETING" (BMR)" USA+45 NAT/G PLAN PROB/SOLV...IDEA/COMP METH 20 SUPREME/CT. PAGE 79 F1551
BUDGET CONCPT CREATE

B59
VOSE C.E.,CAUCASIANS ONLY: THE SUPREME COURT, THE NAACP, AND THE RESTRICTIVE COVENANT CASES. USA+45 LAW CONSTN LOBBY...SOC 20 NAACP SUPREME/CT NEGRO. PAGE 142 F2796
CT/SYS RACE/REL DISCRIM

B60
MENDELSON W.,CAPITALISM, DEMOCRACY, AND THE SUPREME COURT. USA+45 USA-45 CONSTN DIPLOM GOV/REL ATTIT ORD/FREE LAISSEZ...POLICY CHARTS PERS/COMP 18/20 SUPREME/CT MARSHALL/J HOLMES/OW TANEY/RB FIELD/JJ. PAGE 90 F1758
JUDGE CT/SYS JURID NAT/G

B62
HIRSCHFIELD R.S.,THE CONSTITUTION AND THE COURT. AFR SCHOOL WAR RACE/REL EQUILIB ORD/FREE...POLICY MAJORIT DECISION JURID 18/20 PRESIDENT CIVIL/LIB SUPREME/CT CONGRESS. PAGE 60 F1175
ADJUD PWR CONSTN LAW

B63
BOWIE R.R.,GOVERNMENT REGULATION OF BUSINESS: CASES FROM THE NATIONAL REPORTER SYSTEM. USA+45 USA-45 NAT/G ECO/TAC ADJUD...ANTHOL 19/20 SUPREME/CT FTC FAIR/LABOR MONOPOLY. PAGE 17 F0331
LAW CONTROL INDUS CT/SYS

B63
PRITCHETT C.H.,THE THIRD BRANCH OF GOVERNMENT. USA+45 USA-45 CONSTN SOCIETY INDUS SECT LEGIS JUDGE PROB/SOLV GOV/REL 20 SUPREME/CT CHURCH/STA. PAGE 108 F2122
JURID NAT/G ADJUD CT/SYS

B65
LYONS G.M.,AMERICA: PURPOSE AND POWER. UK USA+45 FINAN INDUS MARKET WORKER TEC/DEV DIPLOM AUTOMAT NUC/PWR WAR RACE/REL ORD/FREE 20 EEC CONGRESS SUPREME/CT CIV/RIGHTS. PAGE 82 F1617
PWR PROB/SOLV ECO/DEV TASK

B67
LYTLE C.M.,THE WARREN COURT AND ITS CRITICS. USA+45 NAT/G PROVS FORCES LOBBY RACE/REL DISCRIM SOVEREIGN 20 SUPREME/CT WARRN/EARL. PAGE 83 F1618
CT/SYS ADJUD PROB/SOLV ATTIT

B67
MARCUS S.,COMPETITION AND THE LAW. USA+45 INDUS LG/CO NAT/G CONSERVE LAISSEZ...BIBLIOG 20 FTC SUPREME/CT. PAGE 85 F1665
LAW ECO/DEV FINAN JURID

B67
SCOTT J.C.,ANTITRUST AND TRADE REGULATION TODAY: 1967. USA+45 MARKET LG/CO DELIB/GP LEGIS CAP/ISM INT/TRADE TAX PRICE INGP/REL WEALTH 20 SUPREME/CT. PAGE 118 F2334
NAT/G INDUS CONTROL JURID

B67
SPICER G.W.,THE SUPREME COURT AND FUNDAMENTAL FREEDOMS (2ND ED.). USA+45 CONSTN SOCIETY ATTIT 20 SUPREME/CT. PAGE 124 F2454
CT/SYS JURID CONTROL ORD/FREE

L67
VIA J.W. JR.,"ANTITRUST AND THE AMENDED BANK MERGER AND HOLDING COMPANY ACTS: THE SEARCH FOR STANDARDS." USA+45 CONTROL GP/REL WEALTH SUPREME/CT. PAGE 141 F2783
FINAN CT/SYS LAW EX/STRUC

SURANYI-UNGER T. F2516,F2517

SURPLUS....SEE DEMAND,PLAN

SURREY S.S. F2518

SURVEY ANALYSIS....SEE SAMP/SIZ

SWATANTRA....SWATANTRA - COALITION RIGHT-WING PARTY IN INDIA

SWEDEN....SEE ALSO APPROPRIATE TIME/SPACE/CULTURE INDEX

B31
CROOK W.H.,THE GENERAL STRIKE: A STUDY OF LABOR'S TRAGIC WEAPON IN THEORY AND PRACTICE. BELGIUM FRANCE SWEDEN UK WOR-45 PROB/SOLV ECO/TAC DOMIN PWR ...POLICY TIME/SEQ NAT/COMP GEN/LAWS 19/20 STRIKE. PAGE 29 F0555 — LABOR WORKER LG/CO BARGAIN

B42
ROBBINS J.J.,THE GOVERNMENT OF LABOR RELATIONS IN SWEDEN. SWEDEN LAW CONSTN ADJUD CT/SYS GP/REL ...JURID 20. PAGE 112 F2200 — NAT/G BARGAIN LABOR INDUS

B53
NEISSER H.,NATIONAL INCOMES AND INTERNATIONAL TRADE. FRANCE GERMANY SWEDEN UK USA-45 EXTR/IND FINAN INDUS TEC/DEV PRICE BAL/PAY EQUILIB INCOME WEALTH...CHARTS METH 19 CHINJAP. PAGE 97 F1908 — INT/TRADE PRODUC MARKET CON/ANAL

B54
FRIEDMAN W.,THE PUBLIC CORPORATION: A COMPARATIVE SYMPOSIUM (UNIVERSITY OF TORONTO SCHOOL OF LAW COMPARATIVE LAW SERIES, VOL. I). AFR SWEDEN USA+45 INDUS INT/ORG NAT/G REGION CENTRAL FEDERAL...POLICY JURID IDEA/COMP NAT/COMP ANTHOL 20 MONOPOLY EUROPE. PAGE 44 F0861 — LAW SOCISM LG/CO OWN

B55
RUSTOW D.A.,THE POLITICS OF COMPROMISE. SWEDEN LABOR EX/STRUC LEGIS PLAN REPRESENT SOCISM...SOC 19/20. PAGE 115 F2265 — POL/PAR NAT/G POLICY ECO/TAC

B57
LUNDBERG E.,BUSINESS CYCLES AND ECONOMIC POLICY (TRANS. BY J. POTTER). SWEDEN ECO/DEV FINAN DELIB/GP PLAN PRICE CONTROL BAL/PAY 20 INTRVN/ECO. PAGE 82 F1607 — ECO/TAC INDUS INT/TRADE BUDGET

B58
ROBERTS B.C.,NATIONAL WAGES POLICY IN WAR AND PEACE. EUR+WWI GERMANY S/ASIA SWEDEN UK USA+45 USA-45 STRATA ECO/DEV LABOR NAT/G DELIB/GP PLAN INT/TRADE WEALTH...STAT TREND CHARTS 20. PAGE 112 F2205 — CREATE ECO/TAC

B59
VERNEY D.V.,PUBLIC ENTERPRISE IN SWEDEN. FUT SWEDEN UK INDUS POL/PAR LEGIS PROB/SOLV CAP/ISM INT/TRADE CONTROL SOCISM...MGT CONCPT NAT/COMP 20 SOCDEM/PAR CIVIL/SERV. PAGE 141 F2778 — ECO/DEV POLICY LG/CO NAT/G

B61
INDUSTRIAL COUN SOC-ECO STU,THE SWEDISH ECONOMY AND THE UNDERDEVELOPED COUNTRIES. SWEDEN INDUS DELIB/GP TEC/DEV INT/TRADE EDU/PROP COLONIAL DRIVE...CHARTS 20. PAGE 64 F1264 — FOR/AID ECO/UNDEV PLAN FINAN

B62
WENDT P.F.,HOUSING POLICY - THE SEARCH FOR SOLUTIONS. GERMANY/W SWEDEN UK USA+45 OP/RES HABITAT WEALTH...SOC/WK CHARTS 20. PAGE 145 F2856 — PLAN ADMIN METH/COMP NAT/G

B64
BROWN W.M.,THE EXTERNAL LIQUIDITY OF AN ADVANCED COUNTRY. CANADA FRANCE GERMANY/W SWEDEN UK USA+45 ECO/DEV DIPLOM PRICE...CONCPT STAT NAT/COMP 20. PAGE 20 F0376 — FINAN INT/TRADE COST INCOME

B65
ARTEL R.,THE STRUCTURE OF THE STOCKHOLM ECONOMY. SWEDEN DIST/IND LABOR LOC/G TEC/DEV DEMAND MUNICH LOUISIANA 20. PAGE 7 F0125 — ECO/DEV METH/COMP BAL/PAY

B65
OECD,TECHNIQUES OF ECONOMIC FORECASTING. CANADA FRANCE NETHERLAND SWEDEN UK USA+45 PROB/SOLV ROUTINE...CONCPT MATH CHARTS BIBLIOG METH 20. PAGE 100 F1974 — PREDICT METH/COMP PLAN

C65
WUORINEN J.H.,"SCANDINAVIA." DENMARK FINLAND ICELAND NORWAY SWEDEN SOCIETY AGRI POL/PAR DELIB/GP DIPLOM INT/TRADE NEUTRAL WAR...CHARTS IND TREATY 20. PAGE 149 F2942 — BIBLIOG NAT/G POLICY

B66
LENSKI G.E.,POWER AND PRIVILEGE: A THEORY OF SOCIAL STRATIFICATION. SWEDEN UK UNIV USSR CULTURE ECO/UNDEV PRIVIL PWR...PHIL/SCI CONCPT CHARTS IDEA/COMP HYPO/EXP METH MARX/KARL. PAGE 78 F1525 — SOC STRATA STRUCT SOCIETY

B67
ANDERSON S.V.,THE NORDIC COUNCIL: A STUDY OF SCANDINAVIAN REGIONALISM. DENMARK FINLAND ICELAND NORWAY SWEDEN MARKET NAT/G VOL/ASSN CONSULT PARL/PROC ATTIT...TIME/SEQ BIBLIOG 20. PAGE 5 F0098 — INT/ORG REGION DIPLOM LEGIS

B67
DIXON W.,SOCIETY, SCHOOLS AND PROGRESS IN SCANDINAVIA. DENMARK NORWAY SWEDEN 20. PAGE 33 F0644 — EDU/PROP SOCIETY ADJUST PLAN

B67
FIELD G.L.,COMPARATIVE POLITICAL DEVELOPMENT: THE PRECEDENT OF THE WEST. FRANCE GERMANY SWEDEN UK USSR STRATA STRUCT POL/PAR...METH 20. PAGE 40 F0790 — NAT/COMP CONCPT ECO/DEV SOCIETY

SWEEZY P.M. F0179,F1230,F2519

SWITZERLND....SWITZERLAND; SEE ALSO APPROPRIATE TIME/SPACE/ CULTURE INDEX

B08
LLOYD H.D.,THE SWISS DEMOCRACY. SWITZERLND INDUS NAT/G WORKER CHOOSE OWN ORD/FREE SOCISM...PLURIST 19/20 MONOPOLY. PAGE 81 F1590 — NAT/COMP GOV/COMP REPRESENT POPULISM

N19
STEUBER F.A.,THE CONTRIBUTION OF SWITZERLAND TO THE ECONOMIC AND SOCIAL DEVELOPMENT OF LOW-INCOME COUNTRIES (PAMPHLET). SWITZERLND FINAN NAT/G VOL/ASSN INT/TRADE DRIVE...CHARTS 20. PAGE 126 F2482 — FOR/AID ECO/UNDEV PLAN DIPLOM

B57
ARON R.,L'UNIFICATION ECONOMIQUE DE L'EUROPE. EUR+WWI SWITZERLND UK INT/ORG NAT/G REGION NAT/LISM ORD/FREE PWR...CONCPT METH/CNCPT OBS TREND STERTYP GEN/LAWS EEC FOR/TRADE 20. PAGE 6 F0118 — VOL/ASSN ECO/TAC

B59
HAX K.,DIE HOCHSCHULLEHRER DER WIRTSCHAFTSWISSENSCHAFTEN IN DER BUNDESREPUBLIK DEUTSCHLAND EINSCHL. WESTBERLIN, OSTERREICH. AUSTRIA GERMANY/W SWITZERLND FINAN MARKET PROF/ORG BUDGET ECO/TAC INT/TRADE PRICE COST 20. PAGE 57 F1119 — BIBLIOG ACADEM INTELL

S63
APPERT K.,"BERECHTIGE VORBEHALTE DER SCHWEIZERISCHEN ZUR INTEGRATION." EUR+WWI UK MARKET SERV/IND NAT/G PLAN RIGID/FLEX OEEC 20 EEC. PAGE 6 F0108 — FINAN ATTIT SWITZERLND

B65
COLLINS H.,KARL MARX AND THE BRITISH LABOUR MOVEMENT; YEARS OF THE FIRST INTERNATIONAL. FRANCE SWITZERLND UK CAP/ISM WAR...MARXIST IDEA/COMP BIBLIOG 19. PAGE 26 F0506 — MARXISM LABOR INT/ORG REV

S67
KOHN W.S.G.,"THE SOVEREIGNTY OF LIECHTENSTEIN." LIECHTENST SWITZERLND USSR CONSTN DEBATE WAR CONSERVE 18/20 UN. PAGE 72 F1417 — SOVEREIGN NAT/G PWR DIPLOM

SYMONS L. F2520

SYNANON....SYNANON: COMMUNITY OF FORMER DRUG ADDICTS AND CRIMINALS

SYNTAX....SEE LOG

SYRIA....SEE ALSO UAR

B57
PATAI R.,JORDAN, LEBANON AND SYRIA: AN ANNOTATED BIBLIOGRAPHY. ISLAM JORDAN LEBANON SYRIA...GEOG 20. PAGE 103 F2034 — BIBLIOG/A SOC

B57
WARRINER D.,LAND REFORM AND DEVELOPMENT IN THE MIDDLE EAST: A STUDY OF EGYPT, SYRIA AND IRAQ. IRAQ ISLAM SYRIA UAR AGRI DIST/IND PLAN TEC/DEV DOMIN REV ATTIT WEALTH...SOC METH/CNCPT STAT OBS RECORD HIST/WRIT TREND GEN/LAWS FAO 20. PAGE 143 F2825 — ECO/UNDEV CONCPT

SYS/QU....SYSTEMATIZING AND ANALYZING QUESTIONNAIRES

B54
O.E.E.C.,PRIVATE UNITED STATES INVESTMENT IN EUROPE AND THE OVERSEAS TERRITORIES. EUR+WWI WOR+45 ECO/DEV ECO/UNDEV INT/ORG NAT/G VOL/ASSN ECO/TAC ATTIT WEALTH...GEOG STAT SYS/QU CHARTS VAL/FREE 20. PAGE 99 F1950 — USA+45 FINAN BAL/PAY FOR/AID

B63
RUMMEL J.F.,RESEARCH METHODOLOGY IN BUSINESS. COMPUTER CREATE PROB/SOLV...CONT/OBS REC/INT QU/SEMANT SYS/QU SAMP CHARTS METH/COMP T 20. PAGE 115 F2260 — OP/RES METH/CNCPT METH STAT

SYSTEMS....SEE ROUTINE, COMPUTER

SZASZ/T....THOMAS SZASZ

T

T....TEXTBOOK

N
TEXTBOOKS IN PRINT. WOR+45 WOR-45 LAW DIPLOM ALL/VALS ALL/IDEOS...SOC T 19/20. PAGE 1 F0003
BIBLIOG SCHOOL KNOWL

B38
MEADE J.E.,AN INTRODUCTION TO ECONOMIC ANALYSIS AND POLICY (AMERICAN EDITION EDITED BY C.J. HITCH). FINAN INDUS MARKET LABOR INT/TRADE CONTROL COST DEMAND INCOME...CLASSIF CHARTS T 20 KEYNES/JM MONOPOLY. PAGE 89 F1737
CONCPT PROFIT PRODUC

B39
CLARK J.M.,SOCIAL CONTROL OF BUSINESS (2ND ED.). ECO/DEV FINAN LG/CO PLAN ECO/TAC PRICE SUPEGO...T 20. PAGE 25 F0480
CAP/ISM CONTROL LAISSEZ METH/COMP

B41
DAUGHERTY C.R.,LABOR PROBLEMS IN AMERICAN INDUSTRY (5TH ED.). USA-45 SOCIETY OP/RES ECO/TAC...MGT PSY T 20. PAGE 30 F0581
LABOR INDUS GP/REL PROB/SOLV

B41
ESTEY J.A.,BUSINESS CYCLES; THEIR NATURE, CAUSE, AND CONTROL. NAT/G BUDGET CAP/ISM TAX PRICE CONTROL INCOME...MODAL TIME/SEQ GEN/METH T 18/20 KEYNES/JM MONEY. PAGE 38 F0749
INDUS FINAN ECO/TAC POLICY

B48
HOOVER E.M.,THE LOCATION OF ECONOMIC ACTIVITY. WOR+45 MARKET WORKER PROB/SOLV INT/TRADE ADMIN COST ...POLICY CHARTS T MUNICH 20. PAGE 62 F1211
HABITAT INDUS ECO/TAC GEOG

B48
SAMUELSON P.A.,FOUNDATIONS OF ECONOMIC ANALYSIS. MARKET RATION DEMAND UTIL...MATH METH T 20. PAGE 115 F2276
EQUILIB GEN/LAWS ECO/DEV

B48
WHITE C.L.,HUMAN GEOGRAPHY: AN ECOLOGICAL STUDY OF GEOGRAPHY. UNIV SEA CULTURE AGRI EXTR/IND RACE/REL PRODUC...CHARTS HYPO/EXP SIMUL GEN/LAWS T. PAGE 146 F2868
SOC HABITAT GEOG SOCIETY

B49
HANSEN A.H.,MONETARY THEORY AND FISCAL POLICY. CONSULT PLAN INT/TRADE BAL/PAY OPTIMAL...TREND CHARTS METH/COMP BIBLIOG T 19/20 MONEY. PAGE 54 F1063
FINAN GEN/LAWS POLICY ECO/TAC

B49
SHISTER J.,ECONOMICS OF THE LABOR MARKET. LOC/G NAT/G WORKER TEC/DEV BARGAIN PAY PRICE EXEC GP/REL INCOME...MGT T 20. PAGE 121 F2381
MARKET LABOR INDUS

B50
SHAW E.S.,MONEY, INCOME, AND MONETARY POLICY. AFR USA-45 NAT/G DIPLOM PAY CONTROL COST INCOME PRODUC WEALTH...T 20 FED/RESERV DEPT/TREAS. PAGE 120 F2370
FINAN ECO/TAC ECO/DEV PRICE

B51
PETERSON F.,SURVEY OF LABOR ECONOMICS (REV. ED.). STRATA ECO/DEV LABOR INSPECT BARGAIN PAY PRICE EXEC ROUTINE GP/REL ALL/VALS ORD/FREE 20 AFL/CIO DEPT/LABOR. PAGE 105 F2069
WORKER DEMAND IDEA/COMP T

B52
MACHLUP F.,THE POLITICAL ECONOMY OF MONOPOLY: BUSINESS, LABOR AND GOVERNMENT POLICIES. USA+45 USA-45 ECO/DEV LABOR NAT/G CAP/ISM PWR...POLICY CHARTS T 20. PAGE 83 F1630
ECO/TAC DOMIN LG/CO CONTROL

B52
SURANYI-UNGER T.,COMPARATIVE ECONOMIC SYSTEMS. FINAN MARKET DIPLOM PRICE WEALTH...GEOG SOC BIBLIOG METH T 20. PAGE 128 F2517
LAISSEZ PLAN ECO/DEV IDEA/COMP

B53
BURNS A.E.,MODERN ECONOMICS. UNIV ECO/DEV INT/TRADE PRICE INCOME WEALTH...POLICY CHARTS T 20 KEYNES/JM. PAGE 20 F0389
NAT/G ECO/TAC FINAN

B55
BOULDING K.E.,ECONOMIC ANALYSIS (3RD ED.). USA+45 PLAN ECO/TAC COST DEMAND INCOME...POLICY STAT CHARTS SIMUL T. PAGE 17 F0322
PHIL/SCI ECO/DEV CAP/ISM

B57
BEHRMAN J.N.,INTERNATIONAL ECONOMICS: THEORY, PRACTICE, POLICY. AGRI INDUS NAT/G TARIFFS CONTROL BAL/PAY...POLICY METH/CNCPT T 19/20. PAGE 12 F0230
INT/TRADE FINAN DIPLOM FOR/AID

B57
WEIGERT H.W.,PRINCIPLES OF POLITICAL GEOGRAPHY. WOR+45 ECO/DEV ECO/UNDEV SECT ECO/TAC COLONIAL HABITAT...CHARTS T 20. PAGE 144 F2845
GEOG CULTURE

B58
BARRERE A.,POLITIQUE FINANCIERE. FRANCE BUDGET ECO/TAC TAX BAL/PAY INCOME PRODUC...MGT BIBLIOG T 20. PAGE 10 F0193
FINAN NAT/G PLAN

B58
HENNING C.N.,INTERNATIONAL FINANCING. WOR+45 ECO/DEV INT/ORG EX/STRUC INSPECT CAP/ISM BAL/PAY COST PROFIT...MGT CHARTS T 20. PAGE 58 F1150
FINAN DIPLOM INT/TRADE

C59
FAINSOD M.,"GOVERNMENT AND THE AMERICAN ECONOMY." USA+45 USA-45 INDUS LABOR OP/RES PROB/SOLV ECO/TAC CONTROL...CHARTS BIBLIOG T 20. PAGE 39 F0760
CONSTN ECO/DEV CAP/ISM NAT/G

B60
KILLOUGH H.B.,INTERNATIONAL ECONOMICS. PLAN PROB/SOLV FOR/AID TARIFFS CONTROL BAL/PAY...POLICY CHARTS T 20. PAGE 71 F1388
CONCPT ECO/UNDEV INT/ORG INT/TRADE

B60
MORRIS W.T.,ENGINEERING ECONOMY. AUTOMAT RISK RATIONAL...PROBABIL STAT CHARTS GAME SIMUL BIBLIOG T 20. PAGE 94 F1838
OP/RES DECISION MGT PROB/SOLV

B60
ROBINSON R.I.,FINANCIAL INSTITUTIONS. USA+45 PRICE GOV/REL DEMAND WEALTH...CHARTS T 20 MONEY. PAGE 113 F2226
FINAN ECO/TAC ECO/DEV BUDGET

B60
WATSON D.S.,ECONOMIC POLICY: BUSINESS AND GOVERNMENT. USA+45 FINAN LABOR PLAN BUDGET INT/TRADE GP/REL WEALTH LAISSEZ...CHARTS T. PAGE 144 F2832
ECO/TAC NAT/G POLICY ECO/DEV

C60
FAULKNER H.U.,"AMERICAN ECONOMIC HISTORY (8TH ED.)" USA+45 USA-45 FINAN...CHARTS BIBLIOG/A T 17/20. PAGE 39 F0769
AGRI INDUS ECO/DEV CAP/ISM

B61
ACKLEY G.,MACROECONOMIC THEORY. AFR FINAN WORKER ECO/TAC PRICE COST INCOME PRODUC...MATH TREND CHARTS IDEA/COMP T KEYNES/JM. PAGE 2 F0034
SIMUL ECOMETRIC WEALTH

B61
GREY A.L.,ECONOMIC ISSUES AND POLICIES; READINGS IN INTRODUCTORY ECONOMICS (2ND ED.). WOR+45 ECO/UNDEV FINAN MARKET LABOR LG/CO INT/TRADE BAL/PAY WEALTH ...ANTHOL T. PAGE 51 F0996
ECO/TAC PROB/SOLV METH/COMP

B61
STARK H.,SOCIAL AND ECONOMIC FRONTIERS IN LATIN AMERICA (2ND ED.). CUBA FUT CULTURE AGRI INDUS ECO/TAC PRODUC ATTIT MARXISM...NAT/COMP BIBLIOG T 20. PAGE 125 F2470
L/A+17C SOCIETY DIPLOM ECO/UNDEV

B62
KLEIN L.R.,AN INTRODUCTION TO ECONOMETRICS. DIST/IND DEMAND PRODUC WEALTH...MATH TIME/SEQ T 20. PAGE 72 F1408
ECOMETRIC SIMUL PREDICT STAT

B62
MORGAN C.A.,LABOR ECONOMICS. LAW INDUS MARKET WORKER PLAN PROB/SOLV GOV/REL INCOME ROLE...T 20 DEPT/LABOR NLRB. PAGE 93 F1829
LABOR ECO/TAC ECO/DEV CAP/ISM

B63
ALPERT P.,ECONOMIC DEVELOPMENT. WOR+45 FINAN TEC/DEV ECO/TAC PRICE GOV/REL HABITAT...GEOG BIBLIOG T 20 THIRD/WRLD. PAGE 4 F0079
ECO/DEV ECO/UNDEV INT/TRADE FOR/AID

B63
JOHNSTON J.,ECONOMETRIC METHODS. PROB/SOLV WRITING ...REGRESS CHARTS T. PAGE 68 F1333
ECOMETRIC PHIL/SCI OP/RES STAT

B63
ROPKE W.,ECONOMICS OF THE FREE SOCIETY. FINAN INT/TRADE BAL/PAY COST DEMAND EFFICIENCY ORD/FREE WEALTH...CON/ANAL METH/COMP T 20 KEYNES/JM. PAGE 114 F2240
SOCIETY BUDGET ECO/DEV ECO/TAC

B63
RUMMEL J.F.,RESEARCH METHODOLOGY IN BUSINESS. COMPUTER CREATE PROB/SOLV...CONT/OBS REC/INT QU/SEMANT SYS/QU SAMP CHARTS METH/COMP T 20. PAGE 115 F2260
OP/RES METH/CNCPT METH STAT

B63
SMELSER N.J.,THE SOCIOLOGY OF ECONOMIC LIFE. UNIV CULTURE PERCEPT...PSY T 18/20. PAGE 123 F2425
SOC METH/COMP IDEA/COMP

B64
BROWN E.H.P.,A COURSE IN APPLIED ECONOMICS (2ND ED.). ECO/DEV FINAN MARKET WORKER INT/TRADE RATION RENT PAY PRICE BAL/PAY...DECISION T RESOURCE/N. PAGE 19 F0368
POLICY ECO/TAC PROB/SOLV

B64
GARFIELD PJ LOVEJOY WF,PUBLIC UTILITY ECONOMICS. DIST/IND FINAN MARKET ADMIN COST DEMAND ...TECHNIC JURID MUNICH 20 MONOPOLY. PAGE 46 F0906
T ECO/TAC OWN SERV/IND

B64
STONIER A.W.,EXERCISES IN ECONOMICS. FINAN INDUS TEC/DEV RENT PAY EQUILIB PRODUC PROFIT...METH/COMP T. PAGE 127 F2498
PRICE MARKET WORKER

B65
BARRERE A.,ECONOMIE ET INSTITUTIONS FINANCIERES (VOL. I). AFR FRANCE PLAN...BIBLIOG T 20. PAGE 10 F0194
ECO/DEV BUDGET NAT/G FINAN

B65
KLEIN J.J.,MONEY AND THE ECONOMY. USA+45 NAT/G
FINAN

DIPLOM CONTROL...POLICY T 20 FED/RESERV. PAGE 72 F1406
PLAN WEALTH BAL/PAY

B65
MARCUS E.,INTERNATIONAL TRADE AND FINANCE. EFFICIENCY EQUILIB...CHARTS METH/COMP BIBLIOG METH T 20. PAGE 85 F1664
INT/TRADE FINAN MARKET WEALTH

B65
REDFORD E.S.,AMERICAN GOVERNMENT AND THE ECONOMY. FUT USA+45 USA-45 INDUS PROB/SOLV GOV/REL...POLICY DECISION METH/COMP BIBLIOG T 18/20. PAGE 110 F2168
CONSTN NAT/G

B66
FOX K.A.,THE THEORY OF QUANTITATIVE ECONOMIC POLICY WITH APPLICATIONS TO ECONOMIC GROWTH AND STABILIZATION. ECO/DEV AGRI NAT/G PLAN ADMIN RISK ...DECISION IDEA/COMP SIMUL T. PAGE 43 F0837
ECO/TAC ECOMETRIC EQUILIB GEN/LAWS

B66
FREIDEL F.,AMERICAN ISSUES IN THE TWENTIETH CENTURY. SOCIETY FINAN ECO/TAC FOR/AID CONTROL NUC/PWR WAR RACE/REL PEACE ATTIT...ANTHOL T 20 WILSON/W ROOSEVLT/F KENNEDY/JF TRUMAN/HS. PAGE 44 F0851
DIPLOM POLICY NAT/G ORD/FREE

B66
GREENE L.E.,GOVERNMENT IN TENNESSEE (2ND ED.). USA+45 DIST/IND INDUS POL/PAR EX/STRUC LEGIS PLAN BUDGET GIVE CT/SYS...MGT T 20 TENNESSEE. PAGE 51 F0989
PROVS LOC/G CONSTN ADMIN

B66
HAINES W.W.,MONEY PRICES AND POLICY. WOR+45 ECO/DEV BUDGET CONTROL INCOME...POLICY STAT CHARTS BIBLIOG T 20. PAGE 53 F1039
PRICE FINAN ECO/TAC GOV/REL

B66
HASTINGS P.G.,THE MANAGEMENT OF BUSINESS FINANCE. ECO/DEV PLAN BUDGET CONTROL COST...DECISION CHARTS BIBLIOG T 20. PAGE 56 F1109
FINAN MGT INDUS ECO/TAC

B66
LANSING J.B.,TRANSPORTATION AND ECONOMIC POLICY. USA+45 COST DEMAND...ECOMETRIC TREND CHARTS IDEA/COMP T 20. PAGE 76 F1481
DIST/IND OP/RES ECO/DEV UTIL

B66
LERNER E.M.,A THEORY OF FINANCIAL ANALYSIS. UNIV LG/CO COST DEMAND INCOME PROFIT...MATH STAT CHARTS SIMUL T 20. PAGE 78 F1531
CONCPT FINAN ECO/DEV OPTIMAL

B66
MANSFIELD E.,MANAGERIAL ECONOMICS AND OPERATIONS RESEARCH; A NONMATHEMATICAL INTRODUCTION. USA+45 ELITES ECO/DEV CONSULT EX/STRUC PROB/SOLV ROUTINE EFFICIENCY OPTIMAL...GAME T 20. PAGE 85 F1660
ECO/TAC OP/RES MGT COMPUTER

B67
ALLEN R.G.,MACRO-ECONOMIC THEORY: A MATHEMATICAL TREATMENT. UNIV...SIMUL T. PAGE 4 F0070
ECOMETRIC MATH EQUILIB GAME

B67
BLAIR G.S.,LEGISLATIVE BODIES IN CALIFORNIA. USA+45 LAW POL/PAR LOBBY APPORT CHOOSE REPRESENT GP/REL ...T CALIFORNIA. PAGE 15 F0293
LEGIS PROVS LOC/G ADJUD

B67
CEFKIN J.L.,THE BACKGROUND OF CURRENT WORLD PROBLEMS. AFR NAT/G MARXISM...T 20 UN. PAGE 22 F0432
DIPLOM NAT/LISM ECO/UNDEV

B67
CLEMENT M.O.,THEORETICAL ISSUES IN INTERNATIONAL ECONOMICS. WOR+45 PLAN PROB/SOLV TEC/DEV ...ECOMETRIC METH/CNCPT MATH BIBLIOG T MONEY. PAGE 25 F0489
INT/TRADE FINAN CREATE BAL/PAY

B67
ESTEY M.,THE UNIONS: STRUCTURE, DEVELOPMENT, AND MANAGEMENT. FUT USA+45 ADJUD CONTROL INGP/REL DRIVE ...DECISION T 20 AFL/CIO. PAGE 38 F0750
LABOR EX/STRUC ADMIN GOV/REL

B67
FARRIS M.T.,MODERN TRANSPORTATION: SELECTED READINGS. UNIV CONTROL...POLICY ANTHOL T 20. PAGE 39 F0765
DIST/IND MGT COST

B67
KEWEN P.B.,INTERNATIONAL ECONOMICS (2ND ED.). USA+45 WOR+45 MARKET TARIFFS...BIBLIOG T 20. PAGE 70 F1384
INT/TRADE BAL/PAY FINAN EQUILIB

B67
MARRIS P.,DILEMMAS OF SOCIAL REFORM: POVERTY AND COMMUNITY ACTION IN THE UNITED STATES. USA+45 NAT/G OP/RES ADMIN PARTIC EFFICIENCY WEALTH...SOC METH/COMP T MUNICH 20 REFORMERS. PAGE 85 F1674
STRUCT PROB/SOLV COST

B67
PELTASON J.W.,FUNCTIONS AND POLICIES OF AMERICAN GOVERNMENT (3RD ED.). USA+45 FINAN INDUS EDU/PROP CIVMIL/REL RACE/REL ORD/FREE...ANTHOL T 20 JOHNSON/LB. PAGE 104 F2052
NAT/G GOV/REL POLICY PLAN

B67
ROBINSON R.D.,INTERNATIONAL MANAGEMENT. LAW MARKET LABOR PRICE CONTROL COST DEMAND OWN PRODUC WEALTH 20. PAGE 113 F2225
T OP/RES MGT DIPLOM

B67
ROELOFS H.M.,THE LANGUAGE OF MODERN POLITICS: AN INTRODUCTION TO THE STUDY OF GOVERNMENT. DIPLOM ADMIN MARXISM NEW/LIB...JURID CONCPT METH/COMP T 20. PAGE 113 F2230
LEAD NAT/COMP PERS/REL NAT/G

B67
SYMONS L.,AGRICULTURAL GEOGRAPHY. OP/RES SKILL ...CONCPT CHARTS BIBLIOG T 20. PAGE 128 F2520
AGRI GEOG METH/COMP OBS

B67
WALLBANK T.W.,CIVILIZATION PAST AND PRESENT (3RD ED.). FUT WOR+45 WOR-45 SOCIETY...SOC CONCPT TIME/SEQ CHARTS BIBLIOG T. PAGE 143 F2809
CULTURE STRUCT TREND

B67
WILLS A.J.,AN INTRODUCTION TO THE HISTORY OF CENTRAL AFRICA. RHODESIA ZAMBIA CULTURE SOCIETY ECO/UNDEV TEC/DEV DOMIN WAR ALL/VALS...POLICY TREND BIBLIOG T 14/20 NYASALAND. PAGE 147 F2899
AFR COLONIAL ORD/FREE

S67
JENCKS C.E.,"SOCIAL STATUS OF COAL MINERS IN BRITAIN SINCE NATIONALIZATION." UK STRATA STRUCT LABOR RECEIVE GP/REL INCOME OWN ATTIT HABITAT...MGT T 20. PAGE 67 F1312
EXTR/IND WORKER CONTROL NAT/G

TABOOS....SEE CULTURE

TABORSKY E. F2521

TAEUBER I.B. F2522

TAFT P. F2524,F2525

TAFT/HART....TAFT-HARTLEY ACT

S53
GABLE R.W.,"NAM: INFLUENTIAL LOBBY OR KISS OF DEATH?" (BMR)" USA+45 LAW INSPECT EDU/PROP ADMIN CONTROL INGP/REL EFFICIENCY PWR 20 CONGRESS NAM TAFT/HART. PAGE 45 F0880
LOBBY LEGIS INDUS LG/CO

TAFT/RA....ROBERT A. TAFT

B67
KIRK R.,THE POLITICAL PRINCIPLES OF ROBERT A. TAFT. USA+45 LABOR DIPLOM ADJUD ADJUST ORD/FREE TAFT/RA. PAGE 71 F1398
POL/PAR LEAD LEGIS ATTIT

TAFT/WH....PRESIDENT WILLIAM HOWARD TAFT

TAGLIACOZZO D.L. F2526

TAHITI....TAHITI

TAINE H.A. F2527

TAIWAN....TAIWAN AND REPUBLIC OF CHINA

S66
KLEIN S.,"A SURVEY OF SINO-JAPANESE TRADE, 1950-1966" TAIWAN EDU/PROP 20 CHINJAP. PAGE 72 F1409
INT/TRADE DIPLOM MARXISM

TALBOTT R.B. F1030

TAMMANY....TAMMANY HALL

TANDON Y. F2528

TANEY/RB....ROGER B. TANEY

B60
MENDELSON W.,CAPITALISM, DEMOCRACY, AND THE SUPREME COURT. USA+45 USA-45 CONSTN DIPLOM GOV/REL ATTIT ORD/FREE LAISSEZ...POLICY CHARTS PERS/COMP 18/20 SUPREME/CT MARSHALL/J HOLMES/OW TANEY/RB FIELD/JJ. PAGE 90 F1758
JUDGE CT/SYS JURID NAT/G

TANGANYIKA....SEE ALSO TANZANIA

S61
OCHENG D.,"ECONOMIC FORCES AND UGANDA'S FOREIGN POLICY." AFR UGANDA INT/TRADE TARIFFS INCOME SOVEREIGN WEALTH 20 EACM EEC TANGANYIKA. PAGE 100 F1961
ECO/TAC DIPLOM ECO/UNDFV INT/ORG

S66
FLEMING W.G.,"AUTHORITY, EFFICIENCY, AND ROLF STRESS: PROBLEMS IN THE DEVELOPMENT OF EAST AFRICAN BUREAUCRACIES." AFR UGANDA STRUCT PROB/SOLV ROUTINE INGP/REL ROLE...MGT SOC GP/COMP GOV/COMP 20
DOMIN EFFICIENCY COLONIAL ADMIN

TANGANYIKA AFRICA/E. PAGE 41 F0810

TANNENBAUM A.S. F1347,F2529,F2530,F2531

TANNENBAUM F. F2532,F2533

TANSKY L. F2534,F2535

TANZANIA....TANZANIA; SEE ALSO AFR, TANGANYIKA

S61
NYANZI S.,"THE EAST AFRICAN MARKET: FOR BETTER OF FOR WORSE." AFR TANZANIA UGANDA PROB/SOLV TARIFFS TAX BAL/PAY. PAGE 99 F1947
ECO/TAC ECO/UNDEV INT/ORG INT/TRADE

S63
NYE J.,"TANGANYIKA'S SELF-HELP." TANZANIA NAT/G GIVE COST EFFICIENCY NAT/LISM 20. PAGE 99 F1948
ECO/TAC POL/PAR ECO/UNDEV WORKER

S64
ROTHCHILD D.,"EAST AFRICAN FEDERATION." AFR TANZANIA UGANDA INDUS REGION 20. PAGE 114 F2249
INT/ORG DIPLOM ECO/UNDEV ECO/TAC

B65
HAEFELE E.T.,GOVERNMENT CONTROLS ON TRANSPORT. AFR RHODESIA TANZANIA DIPLOM ECO/TAC TARIFFS PRICE ADJUD CONTROL REGION EFFICIENCY...POLICY 20 CONGO. PAGE 53 F1031
ECO/UNDEV DIST/IND FINAN NAT/G

B66
MACBEAN A.I.,EXPORT INSTABILITY AND ECONOMIC DEVELOPMENT. CHILE PAKISTAN PUERT/RICO TANZANIA UGANDA WOR+45 MARKET ECO/TAC...POLICY REGRESS CHARTS BIBLIOG TIME 20. PAGE 83 F1622
INT/TRADE ECO/UNDEV ECOMETRIC INSPECT

B66
O'CONNER A.M.,AN ECONOMIC GEOGRAPHY OF EAST AFRICA. AFR TANZANIA UGANDA AGRI WORKER INT/TRADE COLONIAL GOV/REL...CHARTS METH/COMP 20 AFRICA/E. PAGE 99 F1953
ECO/UNDEV EXTR/IND GEOG HABITAT

B66
SMITH H.E.,READINGS IN ECONOMIC DEVELOPMENT AND ADMINISTRATION IN TANZANIA. TANZANIA FINAN INDUS LABOR NAT/G PLAN PROB/SOLV INT/TRADE COLONIAL REGION...ANTHOL BIBLIOG 20 AFRICA/E. PAGE 123 F2431
TEC/DEV ADMIN GOV/REL

S66
NEWLYN W.T.,"MONEY MARKETS IN EAST AFRICA." AFR TANZANIA UGANDA UK DIPLOM CENTRAL 20. PAGE 98 F1923
FINAN WEALTH BAL/PAY ECO/UNDEV

S67
PRATT R.C.,"THE ADMINISTRATION OF ECONOMIC PLANNING IN A NEWLY INDEPEND ENT STATE* THE TANZANIAN EXPERIENCE 1963-1966." AFR TANZANIA ECO/UNDEV PLAN CONTROL ROUTINE TASK EFFICIENCY 20. PAGE 107 F2114
NAT/G DELIB/GP ADMIN TEC/DEV

S67
THEROUX P.,"HATING THE ASIANS." TANZANIA UGANDA CONSTN INDUS NAT/G POL/PAR WORKER ECO/TAC HABITAT LOVE...POLICY GEOG 20 MIGRATION. PAGE 130 F2557
AFR RACE/REL SOVEREIGN ATTIT

TARIFFS....SEE ALSO INT/TRADE, GATT

N
US SUPERINTENDENT OF DOCUMENTS,INTERSTATE COMMERCE (PRICE LIST 59). USA+45 LAW LOC/G NAT/G LEGIS TARIFFS TAX ADMIN CONTROL HEALTH DECISION. PAGE 140 F2752
BIBLIOG/A DIST/IND GOV/REL PROVS

N
US SUPERINTENDENT OF DOCUMENTS,TARIFF AND TAXATION (PRICE LIST 37). USA+45 LAW INT/TRADE ADJUD ADMIN CT/SYS INCOME OWN...DECISION GATT. PAGE 140 F2754
BIBLIOG/A TAX TARIFFS NAT/G

B19
SUMNER W.G.,WAR AND OTHER ESSAYS. USA-45 DELIB/GP DIPLOM TARIFFS COLONIAL PEACE SOVEREIGN 20. PAGE 127 F2514
INT/TRADE ORD/FREE CAP/ISM ECO/TAC

B20
COX H.,ECONOMIC LIBERTY. UNIV LAW INT/TRADE RATION TARIFFS RACE/REL SOCISM POLICY. PAGE 28 F0547
NAT/G ORD/FREE ECO/TAC PERSON

B34
GRAHAM F.D.,PROTECTIVE TARIFFS. FUT USA+45 WOR-45 INDUS MARKET VOL/ASSN PLAN CAP/ISM ECO/TAC PEACE ATTIT DRIVE HEALTH ORD/FREE...OBS TREND GEN/LAWS FOR/TRADE 20. PAGE 50 F0970
INT/ORG TARIFFS

B35
SCHATTSCHNEIDER E.E.,POLITICS, PRESSURES AND THE TARIFF: A STUDY OF FREE PRIVATE ENTERPRISE IN PRESSURE POLITICS IN TARIFF REVISION 1929-1930. NAT/G BARGAIN ECO/TAC ROUTINE REPRESENT GOV/REL GP/REL PWR POLICY. PAGE 116 F2290
LOBBY LEGIS TARIFFS

B37
HAMILTON W.H.,THE POWER TO GOVERN. ECO/DEV FINAN INDUS ECO/TAC INT/TRADE TARIFFS TAX CONTROL CT/SYS WAR COST PWR 18/20 SUPREME/CT. PAGE 54 F1056
LING CONSTN NAT/G POLICY

B40
SPENCER H.,THE MAN VS. THE STATE (1892). UK POL/PAR LEGIS TARIFFS COERCE CRIME REPRESENT PWR SOCISM ...POLICY GEN/LAWS 19/20. PAGE 124 F2450
FASCISM POPULISM LAISSEZ ORD/FREE

B43
WILMERDING L. JR.,THE SPENDING POWER: A HISTORY OF THE EFFORTS OF CONGRESS TO CONTROL EXPENDITURES. USA-45 POL/PAR DELIB/GP EX/STRUC TOP/EX TARIFFS ADMIN GOV/REL...TIME/SEQ SENATE HOUSE/REP. PAGE 147 F2900
LEGIS BUDGET CONTROL

B47
ENKE S.,INTERNATIONAL ECONOMICS. UK USA+45 USSR INT/ORG BAL/PWR BARGAIN CAP/ISM BAL/PAY...NAT/COMP 20 TREATY. PAGE 38 F0735
INT/TRADE FINAN TARIFFS ECO/TAC

B48
GRAHAM F.D.,THE THEORY OF INTERNATIONAL VALUES. FUT WOR+45 WOR-45 ECO/DEV FINAN INT/ORG PLAN TEC/DEV CAP/ISM DIPLOM ECO/TAC TARIFFS ROUTINE BAL/PAY DRIVE PWR WEALTH SOCISM...POLICY STAT HYPO/EXP GEN/LAWS 20. PAGE 50 F0971
NEW/IDEA INT/TRADE

C50
ELLSWORTH P.T.,"INTERNATIONAL ECONOMY." ECO/DEV ECO/UNDEV FINAN LABOR DIPLOM FOR/AID TARIFFS BAL/PAY EQUILIB NAT/LISM OPTIMAL...INT/LAW 20 ILO GATT. PAGE 37 F0724
BIBLIOG INT/TRADE ECO/TAC INT/ORG

B52
SECRETARIAT COUNCIL OF EUROPE,THE STRASBOURG PLAN. EUR+WWI CONSULT PLAN ECO/TAC TARIFFS DEBATE REGION 20 COUNCL/EUR STRASBOURG. PAGE 119 F2340
INT/ORG ECO/DEV INT/TRADE DIPLOM

C52
HUME D.,"OF THE BALANCE OF TRADE" IN D. HUME, POLITICAL DISCOURSES (1752)" UK FINAN NAT/G TARIFFS PRICE PWR LAISSEZ...POLICY GEN/LAWS 18. PAGE 63 F1237
BAL/PAY INT/TRADE DIPLOM WEALTH

S56
BONILLA F.,"WHEN IS PETITION 'PRESSURE?'" (BMR)" USA+45 ELITES INDUS LABOR CHIEF EDU/PROP LEGIT ATTIT...INT CHARTS 20 CONGRESS PRESIDENT EISNHWR/DD. PAGE 16 F0312
LEGIS EX/STRUC INT/TRADE TARIFFS

B57
BEHRMAN J.N.,INTERNATIONAL ECONOMICS: THEORY, PRACTICE, POLICY. AGRI INDUS NAT/G TARIFFS CONTROL BAL/PAY...POLICY METH/CNCPT T 19/20. PAGE 12 F0230
INT/TRADE FINAN DIPLOM FOR/AID

B57
HARRIS S.E.,INTERNATIONAL AND INTERREGIONAL ECONOMICS. AFR WOR+45 WOR-45 NAT/G TARIFFS BAL/PAY EQUILIB...POLICY CONCPT STAT CHARTS IDEA/COMP 19/20. PAGE 55 F1088
INT/TRADE ECO/DEV MARKET FINAN

B58
ELLSWORTH P.T.,THE INTERNATIONAL ECONOMY. EUR+WWI MOD/EUR INT/ORG CAP/ISM FOR/AID BAL/PAY LAISSEZ 16/20. PAGE 37 F0725
INT/TRADE TARIFFS ECO/DEV

B58
JOHNSON H.G.,INTERNATIONAL TRADE AND ECONOMIC GROWTH. WOR+45 BUDGET CAP/ISM ECO/TAC TARIFFS BAL/PAY 20. PAGE 67 F1323
INT/TRADE BAL/PWR BARGAIN DIPLOM

B58
KINDLEBERGER C.P.,INTERNATIONAL ECONOMICS. WOR+45 WOR-45 ECO/DEV ECO/UNDEV FINAN VOL/ASSN ACT/RES DIPLOM ECO/TAC LEGIT REGION ATTIT DRIVE ORD/FREE WEALTH...POLICY STAT TREND GEN/LAWS EEC ECSC OEEC 20. PAGE 71 F1391
INT/ORG BAL/PWR TARIFFS

B59
ROBERTSON A.H.,EUROPEAN INSTITUTIONS: COOPERATION, INTEGRATION, UNIFICATION. EUR+WWI FINAN INT/ORG FORCES INT/TRADE TARIFFS 20 EEC EURATOM ECSC NATO TREATY. PAGE 112 F2208
ECO/DEV DIPLOM INDUS ECO/TAC

B59
SHACKLE G.L.S.,ECONOMICS FOR PLEASURE. FINAN MARKET NAT/G WORKER PLAN INT/TRADE TARIFFS PAY BAL/PAY COST PRODUC 20. PAGE 120 F2361
METH/CNCPT WEALTH INCOME

B59
SILCOCK T.H.,THE COMMONWEALTH ECONOMY IN SOUTHEAST ASIA. AFR INDIA MALAYSIA S/ASIA ECO/DEV AGRI LOC/G PLAN TARIFFS COLONIAL BAL/PAY DEMAND...BIBLIOG/A 20 GATT. PAGE 122 F2401
ECO/TAC INT/TRADE RACE/REL DIPLOM

B60
DALE W.B.,THE FOREIGN DEFICIT OF THE UNITED STATES. ECO/TAC TARIFFS PAY PRICE CONTROL COST WEALTH POLICY. PAGE 30 F0573
BAL/PAY DIPLOM FINAN INT/TRADE

B60
HEILPERIN M.A.,STUDIES IN ECONOMIC NATIONALISM. EUR+WWI MOD/EUR USA+45 ECO/DEV PLAN INT/TRADE TARIFFS WAR PRODUC PROFIT 18/20 KEYNES/JM. PAGE 58 F1140
ECO/TAC NAT/G NAT/LISM POLICY

B60
KENEN P.B.,GIANT AMONG NATIONS: PROBLEMS IN UNITED STATES FOREIGN ECONOMIC POLICY. AFR USA+45 FINAN DIPLOM TARIFFS BAL/PAY WEALTH 20. PAGE 70 F1376
FOR/AID ECO/UNDEV INT/TRADE PLAN

B60
KILLOUGH H.B.,INTERNATIONAL ECONOMICS. PLAN PROB/SOLV FOR/AID TARIFFS CONTROL BAL/PAY...POLICY CHARTS T 20. PAGE 71 F1388
CONCPT ECO/UNDEV INT/ORG INT/TRADE

B61
BREWIS T.N.,CANADIAN ECONOMIC POLICY. AFR CANADA BUDGET CAP/ISM INT/TRADE RATION TARIFFS TAX PRICE CONTROL ROUTINE FEDERAL INCOME PRODUC 20. PAGE 18 F0348
ECO/DEV ECO/TAC NAT/G PLAN

B61
GOODWIN C.D.W.,CANADIAN ECONOMIC THOUGHT. CANADA STRATA TEC/DEV CAP/ISM TARIFFS TAX COST EFFICIENCY WEALTH...METH/CNCPT TREND 20 MARITIME ONTARIO. PAGE 49 F0952
INT/TRADE ECO/DEV FINAN DEMAND

S61
NYANZI S.,"THE EAST AFRICAN MARKET: FOR BETTER OF FOR WORSE." AFR TANZANIA UGANDA PROB/SOLV TARIFFS TAX BAL/PAY. PAGE 99 F1947
ECO/TAC ECO/UNDEV INT/ORG INT/TRADE

S61
OCHENG D.,"ECONOMIC FORCES AND UGANDA'S FOREIGN POLICY." AFR UGANDA INT/TRADE TARIFFS INCOME SOVEREIGN WEALTH 20 EACM EEC TANGANYIKA. PAGE 100 F1961
ECO/TAC DIPLOM ECO/UNDEV INT/ORG

S61
VINER J.,"ECONOMIC FOREIGN POLICY ON THE NEW FRONTIER." USA+45 ECO/UNDEV AGRI FINAN INDUS MARKET INT/ORG NAT/G FOR/AID INT/TRADE ADMIN ATTIT PWR 20 KENNEDY/JF. PAGE 141 F2786
TOP/EX ECO/TAC BAL/PAY TARIFFS

B62
ALEXANDROWICZ C.H.,WORLD ECONOMIC AGENCIES: LAW AND PRACTICE. WOR+45 DIST/IND FINAN LABOR CONSULT INT/TRADE TARIFFS REPRESENT HEALTH...JURID 20 UN GATT EEC OAS ECSC. PAGE 4 F0064
INT/LAW INT/ORG DIPLOM ADJUD

B62
HAGUE D.C.,INFLATION. AFR ECO/DEV ECO/UNDEV LABOR BUDGET CAP/ISM INT/TRADE TARIFFS SOCISM 20. PAGE 53 F1036
FINAN NAT/COMP BARGAIN ECO/TAC

B62
HOOVER C.B.,ECONOMIC SYSTEMS OF THE COMMONWEALTH. AFR CANADA INDIA UK ECO/DEV ECO/UNDEV AGRI INDUS TEC/DEV TARIFFS PRICE BAL/PAY DEMAND...SIMUL 20 AUSTRAL. PAGE 61 F1208
CAP/ISM SOCISM ECO/TAC PLAN

B62
MCCRONE G.,THE ECONOMICS OF SUBSIDING AGRICULTURE. UK ECO/DEV MARKET PLAN TARIFFS PROFIT 20 EEC. PAGE 88 F1725
AGRI BAL/PAY INT/TRADE LABOR

B62
ROTHBARD M.N.,THE PANIC OF 1819; REACTIONS AND POLICIES. AFR USA-45 LAW FINAN BUDGET TARIFFS DEMAND 19 DEPRESSION. PAGE 114 F2247
ECO/UNDEV POLICY ATTIT ECO/TAC

B62
VANEK J.,INTERNATIONAL TRADE - THEORY AND ECONOMIC POLICY. LABOR BAL/PWR ECO/TAC TARIFFS PRICE BAL/PAY COST DEMAND 20. PAGE 140 F2765
INT/TRADE DIPLOM BARGAIN MARKET

S62
MEAD W.,"SOME POLITICAL-ECONOMIC ISSUES DETERMINING USA TARIFF POLICY." USA+45 USA-45 ECO/DEV NAT/G TARIFFS ATTIT...TIME/SEQ TREND CHARTS 19/20. PAGE 89 F1736
ECO/TAC METH/CNCPT BAL/PAY

B63
HUNTER A.,THE ECONOMICS OF AUSTRALIAN INDUSTRY. DIST/IND EXTR/IND FINAN PROC/MFG SERV/IND ACT/RES PLAN TARIFFS GP/REL INGP/REL 20 AUSTRAL. PAGE 63 F1245
INDUS ECO/DEV HABITAT GP/COMP

B63
RICARDO D.,THE PRINCIPLES OF POLITICAL ECONOMY AND TAXATION (1817). UK INDUS MARKET ECO/TAC INT/TRADE TARIFFS PRICE COST DEMAND OPTIMAL WEALTH...CONCPT 19 INTRVN/ECO. PAGE 111 F2183
GEN/LAWS TAX LAISSEZ

B63
STIFEL L.D.,THE TEXTILE INDUSTRY - A CASE STUDY OF INDUSTRIAL DEVELOPMENT IN THE PHILIPPINES (PAPER). PHILIPPINE WORKER CAP/ISM INT/TRADE TARIFFS RECEIVE PRICE ADMIN COST EFFICIENCY WEALTH...BIBLIOG 20. PAGE 126 F2486
S/ASIA ECO/UNDEV PROC/MFG NAT/G

B63
UN SECRETARY GENERAL,PLANNING FOR ECONOMIC DEVELOPMENT. ECO/UNDEV FINAN BUDGET INT/TRADE TARIFFS TAX ADMIN 20 UN. PAGE 132 F2603
PLAN ECO/TAC MGT NAT/COMP

S63
CARTER A.G.T.,"THE BALANCE OF PAYMENTS OF EAST AFRICA" AFR ECO/TAC FOR/AID RATION TARIFFS TAX ADMIN...STAT 20 AFRICA/E. PAGE 22 F0423
BUDGET ECO/UNDEV BAL/PAY INT/TRADE

B64
BASTIAT F.,ECONOMIC SOPHISMS (1845). FINAN MARKET INT/TRADE TAX EDU/PROP LAISSEZ. PAGE 11 F0207
TARIFFS INDUS ECO/TAC CAP/ISM

B64
HINSHAW R.,THE EUROPEAN COMMUNITY AND AMERICAN TRADE: A STUDY IN ATLANTIC ECONOMICS AND POLICY. EUR+WWI UK USA+45 ECO/DEV ECO/UNDEV AGRI INDUS INT/ORG NAT/G ECO/TAC TARIFFS REGION...STAT CHARTS EEC 20. PAGE 60 F1174
MARKET TREND INT/TRADE

B64
KUZNETS S.,POSTWAR ECONOMIC GROWTH: FOUR LECTURES. WOR+45 INDUS NAT/G WORKER TEC/DEV ECO/TAC RATION TARIFFS PRICE BAL/PAY COST DEMAND 20. PAGE 74 F1455
ECO/DEV ECO/UNDEV TREND FINAN

B64
LISKA G.,EUROPE ASCENDANT. EUR+WWI ECO/DEV FORCES INT/TRADE MARXISM 20 EEC. PAGE 81 F1579
DIPLOM BAL/PWR TARIFFS CENTRAL

B64
MARKHAM J.W.,THE COMMON MARKET: FRIEND OR COMPETITOR. AFR EUR+WWI FUT USA+45 INT/ORG LG/CO NAT/G VOL/ASSN DELIB/GP EX/STRUC PLAN TARIFFS ORD/FREE PWR WEALTH...POLICY STAT TREND EEC VAL/FREE 20. PAGE 85 F1671
ECO/DEV ECO/TAC

B64
MEZERIK A.G.,TRADE, AID AND ECONOMIC DEVELOPMENT. WOR+45 FINAN INDUS MARKET PLAN BAL/PWR BARGAIN FOR/AID TARIFFS EDU/PROP WEALTH...GP/COMP 20 UN GATT IMF IBRD. PAGE 91 F1777
ECO/TAC ECO/DEV INT/ORG INT/TRADE

B64
NEWCOMER H.A.,INTERNATIONAL AIDS TO OVERSEAS INVESTMENTS AND TRADE. ECO/UNDEV TARIFFS PROFIT ...BIBLIOG 20 GATT UN. PAGE 98 F1921
INT/TRADE FINAN DIPLOM FOR/AID

B64
REUSS H.S.,THE CRITICAL DECADE - AN ECONOMIC POLICY FOR AMERICA AND THE FREE WORLD. AFR USA+45 FINAN POL/PAR WORKER PLAN DIPLOM ECO/TAC TARIFFS BAL/PAY ...POLICY 20 CONGRESS. PAGE 111 F2181
FOR/AID INT/TRADE LABOR LEGIS

B64
RIVKIN A.,AFRICA AND THE EUROPEAN COMMON MARKET (PAMPHLET). AFR MOD/EUR WOR+45 TEC/DEV FOR/AID TARIFFS BAL/PAY...POLICY 20 EEC. PAGE 111 F2196
INT/ORG INT/TRADE ECO/TAC ECO/UNDEV

B64
STEWART C.F.,A BIBLIOGRAPHY OF INTERNATIONAL BUSINESS. WOR+45 FINAN LG/CO NAT/G PLAN ECO/TAC TARIFFS...DECISION MGT GP/COMP NAT/COMP 20 EEC. PAGE 126 F2484
BIBLIOG INT/ORG OP/RES INT/TRADE

S64
GARDNER R.N.,"GATT AND THE UNITED NATIONS CONFERENCE ON TRADE AND DEVELOPMENT." USA+45 WOR+45 SOCIETY ECO/UNDEV MARKET NAT/G DELIB/GP ACT/RES PLAN ECO/TAC TARIFFS EDU/PROP ROUTINE DRIVE RIGID/FLEX WEALTH...DECISION MGT TREND UN TOT/POP 20 GATT. PAGE 46 F0905
INT/ORG INT/TRADE

B65
ALLEN W.R.,INTERNATIONAL TRADE THEORY: HUME TO OHLIN. FINAN LABOR TARIFFS TAX PRICE DEMAND PRODUC PROFIT...ANTHOL 18/20. PAGE 4 F0074
INT/TRADE WEALTH METH/CNCPT

B65
BELASSA B.,ECONOMIC DEVELOPMENT AND INTEGRATION. LG/CO PROB/SOLV TEC/DEV INT/TRADE TARIFFS COST WEALTH...POLICY METH/COMP 20. PAGE 12 F0232
ECO/UNDEV ECO/TAC INT/ORG INDUS

B65
BRYCE M.D.,POLICIES AND METHODS FOR INDUSTRIAL DEVELOPMENT. WOR+45 FINAN MARKET CONSULT TARIFFS TAX COST. PAGE 20 F0379
INDUS PLAN ECO/DEV TEC/DEV

B65
DOWD L.P.,PRINCIPLES OF WORLD BUSINESS. SERV/IND NAT/G DIPLOM ECO/TAC TARIFFS...INT/LAW JURID 20. PAGE 34 F0657
INT/TRADE MGT FINAN MARKET

B65
HABERLER G.,A SURVEY OF INTERNATIONAL TRADE THEORY. CANADA FRANCE GERMANY ECO/TAC TARIFFS AGREE COST DEMAND WEALTH...ECOMETRIC 19/20 MONOPOLY TREATY. PAGE 52 F1024
INT/TRADE BAL/PAY DIPLOM POLICY

B65
HAEFELE E.T.,GOVERNMENT CONTROLS ON TRANSPORT. AFR RHODESIA TANZANIA DIPLOM ECO/TAC TARIFFS PRICE ADJUD CONTROL REGION EFFICIENCY...POLICY 20 CONGO. PAGE 53 F1031
ECO/UNDEV DIST/IND FINAN NAT/G

B65
PROCHNOW H.V.,WORLD ECONOMIC PROBLEMS AND POLICIES. INDIA ISRAEL WOR+45 AGRI LABOR PROB/SOLV FOR/AID TARIFFS CONTROL BAL/PAY NAT/LISM WEALTH...TREND CHARTS 20 CHINJAP EEC. PAGE 108 F2124
MARKET ECO/TAC PRODUC IDEA/COMP

B65
VANEK J.,GENERAL EQUILIBRIUM OF INTERNATIONAL DISCRIMINATION; THE CASE OF CUSTOMS UNIONS. LABOR
INT/TRADE TARIFFS

PROB/SOLV ECO/TAC DISCRIM INCOME...MATH CHARTS METH 20. PAGE 140 F2767
INT/ORG EQUILIB

B65
WEILER J.,L'ECONOMIE INTERNATIONALE DEPUIS 1950. WOR+45 DIPLOM TARIFFS CONFER...POLICY TREATY. PAGE 145 F2848
FINAN INT/TRADE REGION FOR/AID

S65
SOPER T.,"THE EEC AND AID TO AFRICA." FRANCE UK ECO/UNDEV INT/TRADE TARIFFS REGION ROUTINE CENTRAL DISCRIM...DECISION RECORD EEC. PAGE 124 F2443
AFR FOR/AID COLONIAL

B66
EDWARDS C.D.,TRADE REGULATIONS OVERSEAS. IRELAND NEW/ZEALND SOUTH/AFR NAT/G CAP/ISM TARIFFS CONTROL ...POLICY JURID 20 EEC CHINJAP. PAGE 36 F0703
INT/TRADE DIPLOM INT/LAW ECO/TAC

B66
GOODWIN C.D.W.,ECONOMIC INQUIRY IN AUSTRALIA. ECO/DEV ECO/UNDEV ACADEM INT/TRADE RENT TARIFFS TAX PRESS GOV/REL SOCISM 18/20 AUSTRAL. PAGE 49 F0953
ECO/TAC IDEA/COMP BUDGET COLONIAL

B66
INGRAM J.C.,INTERNATIONAL ECONOMIC PROBLEMS. ECO/DEV ECO/UNDEV INDUS MARKET TEC/DEV TARIFFS BAL/PAY CENTRAL...POLICY 20 EEC. PAGE 64 F1265
INT/TRADE INT/ORG FINAN

B66
MEERHAEGHE M.,INTERNATIONAL ECONOMIC INSTITUTIONS. EUR+WWI FINAN INDUS MARKET PLAN TARIFFS BAL/PAY EQUILIB...POLICY BIBLIOG/A 20 GATT OEEC EEC IBRD EURCOALSTL. PAGE 89 F1745
ECO/TAC ECO/DEV INT/TRADE INT/ORG

S66
FELD W.,"EXTERNAL RELATIONS OF THE COMMON MARKET AND GROUP LEADERSHIP ATTITUDES IN THE MEMBER STATES." COM USA+45 ELITES AGRI NAT/G ATTIT...OBS EEC GATT. PAGE 40 F0776
DIPLOM CENTRAL TARIFFS INT/TRADE

N66
BRITISH DEVELOPMENT POLICIES: 1966 (PAMPHLET). UK AGRI TARIFFS BAL/PAY...TREND CHARTS 20 OVRSEA/DEV. PAGE 1 F0023
WEALTH DIPLOM INT/TRADE FOR/AID

B67
BARROW T.C.,TRADE AND EMPIRE: THE BRITISH CUSTOMS SERVICE IN COLONIAL AMERICA, 1660-1775. UK USA-45 ECO/UNDEV NAT/G ECO/TAC DOMIN REV 17/18. PAGE 10 F0197
COLONIAL TARIFFS ADMIN EX/STRUC

B67
JOHNSON H.G.,ECONOMIC POLICY TOWARD LESS DEVELOPED COUNTRIES. USA+45 ECO/DEV INT/ORG PLAN CAP/ISM FOR/AID TARIFFS GIVE WEALTH...NEW/IDEA CHARTS 20 UN GATT. PAGE 67 F1327
ECO/UNDEV ECO/TAC METH/COMP

B67
KEWEN P.B.,INTERNATIONAL ECONOMICS (2ND ED.). USA+45 WOR+45 MARKET TARIFFS...BIBLIOG T 20. PAGE 70 F1384
INT/TRADE BAL/PAY FINAN EQUILIB

B67
KREININ M.E.,ALTERNATIVE COMMERCIAL POLICIES - THEIR EFFECT ON THE AMERICAN ECONOMY. USA+45 LAW ECO/DEV MARKET INT/ORG DIPLOM ECO/TAC TARIFFS PRICE DEMAND WEALTH...QUANT EEC AFTA. PAGE 73 F1437
INT/TRADE BAL/PAY NAT/G POLICY

B67
LINDER S.B.,TRADE AND TRADE POLICY FOR DEVELOPMENT. OP/RES DIPLOM TARIFFS UTIL WEALTH...BIBLIOG 20. PAGE 80 F1569
ECO/UNDEV ECO/TAC TEC/DEV INT/TRADE

L67
LENT G.E.,"TAX INCENTIVES FOR INVESTMENT IN DEVELOPING COUNTRIES" WOR+45 LAW INDUS PLAN BUDGET TARIFFS ADMIN...METH/COMP 20. PAGE 78 F1526
ECO/UNDEV TAX FINAN ECO/TAC

L67
MEIER G.M.,"UNCTAD PROPOSALS FOR INTERNATIONAL ECONOMIC REFORM." WOR+45 MARKET INT/ORG TARIFFS CONFER UN GATT IMF. PAGE 89 F1749
INT/TRADE FINAN INT/LAW ECO/UNDEV

L67
MESTMACKER E.J.,"STATE TRADING MONOPOLIES IN THE EUROPEAN ECONOMIC COMMUNITY. DIPLOM ECO/TAC ADJUD CONTROL DISCRIM 20 EEC. PAGE 90 F1764
INT/TRADE INT/ORG LAW TARIFFS

S67
AUBERT DE LA RUE P.,"PERSPECTIVES ECONOMIQUES ENTRE LES ETATS-UNIS ET L'EUROPE." FUT INDUS R+D INT/ORG ACT/RES ECO/TAC AGREE BAL/PAY PRODUC...CHARTS 20 EEC GATT WORLD/BANK. PAGE 7 F0138
INT/TRADE ECO/DEV FINAN TARIFFS

S67
SMALL A.H.,"THE EFFECT OF TARIFF REDUCTIONS ON US IMPORT VOLUME." USA+45 INT/ORG NAT/G DIPLOM CONFER DEMAND...POLICY INT/LAW STAT CHARTS GATT EEC. PAGE 123 F2424
TARIFFS INT/TRADE PRICE ECO/TAC

S67
WILLIAMS C.,"REGIONAL MANAGEMENT OVERSEAS." USA+45 WOR+45 DIST/IND LG/CO EX/STRUC INT/TRADE TARIFFS ADMIN TASK CENTRAL. PAGE 147 F2889
MGT EUR+WWI ECO/DEV PLAN

C83
BURKE E.,"RESOLUTIONS FOR CONCILIATION WITH AMERICA" (1775), IN E. BURKE, COLLECTED WORKS, VOL. 2." UK USA-45 FORCES INT/TRADE TARIFFS TAX SANCTION PEACE...POLICY 18 PRE/US/AM. PAGE 20 F0387
COLONIAL WAR SOVEREIGN ECO/TAC

B84
MILL J.,ELEMENTS OF POLITICAL ECONOMY. UK LAW ELITES FINAN WORKER ECO/TAC RENT OWN WEALTH ...POLICY GEN/LAWS 19. PAGE 91 F1785
TAX TARIFFS NAT/G INCOME

B95
SELIGMAN E.R.A.,ESSAYS IN TAXATION. NEW/ZEALND PRUSSIA UK USA-45 MARKET LOC/G CREATE PRICE CONTROL INCOME OWN WEALTH...GOV/COMP METH/COMP 19. PAGE 119 F2349
TAX TARIFFS INDUS NAT/G

B96
SMITH A.,LECTURES ON JUSTICE, POLICE, REVENUE AND ARMS (1763). UK LAW FAM FORCES TARIFFS AGREE COERCE INCOME OWN WEALTH LAISSEZ...GEN/LAWS 17/18. PAGE 123 F2429
DIPLOM JURID OLD/LIB TAX

TARTARS....TARTARS

TASK....SPECIFIC SELF-ASSIGNED OR OTHER ASSIGNED OPERATIONS

N19
LANGE O.R.,"DISARMAMENT ECONOMIC GROWTH AND INTERNATIONAL CO-OPERATION" (PAMPHLET). WOR+45 DIST/IND PLAN INT/TRADE GIVE TASK DETER WEALTH SOCISM 18/19 BOLIVAR/S. PAGE 75 F1477
ARMS/CONT DIPLOM ECO/DEV ECO/UNDEV

B40
TRIFFIN R.,MONOPOLISTIC COMPETITION AND GENERAL EQUILIBRIUM THEORY. DIST/IND PLAN TASK EQUILIB OPTIMAL...IDEA/COMP 20 MONOPOLY. PAGE 131 F2586
INT/TRADE INDUS COST

B47
MILLETT J.D.,THE PROCESS AND ORGANIZATION OF GOVERNMENT PLANNING. USA+45 DELIB/GP ACT/RES LEAD LOBBY TASK...POLICY GEOG TIME 20 RESOURCE/N. PAGE 91 F1793
ADMIN NAT/G PLAN CONSULT

S52
PHILLIPS C.,"THE HIGH COST OF OUR LOW-PAID CONGRESS" (NYT MAG. 2/24/52)" USA+45 FINAN WRITING TASK TIME CONGRESS. PAGE 106 F2082
LEGIS INCOME COST EFFICIENCY

B55
BRAUN K.,LABOR DISPUTES AND THEIR SETTLEMENT. ECO/TAC ROUTINE TASK GP/REL...DECISION GEN/LAWS. PAGE 18 F0342
INDUS LABOR BARGAIN ADJUD

B57
ASHER R.E.,THE UNITED NATIONS AND ECONOMIC AND SOCIAL COOPERATION. ECO/UNDEV COM/IND DIST/IND FINAN PLAN PROB/SOLV INT/TRADE TASK WEALTH...SOC 20 UN. PAGE 7 F0129
INT/ORG DIPLOM FOR/AID

S57
DETAMBEL M.H.,"PROBABILITY AND WORK AS DETERMINERS OF MULTICHOICE BEHAVIOR." PLAN TASK EFFICIENCY ...DECISION GAME. PAGE 32 F0622
HYPO/EXP PROB/SOLV GEN/LAWS PROBABIL

S57
ROURKE F.E.,"THE POLITICS OF ADMINISTRATIVE ORGANIZATION: A CASE HISTORY." USA+45 LABOR WORKER PLAN ADMIN TASK EFFICIENCY 20 DEPT/LABOR CONGRESS. PAGE 114 F2251
POLICY ATTIT MGT GP/COMP

B59
KARLIN S.,MATHEMATICAL METHODS AND THEORY IN GAMES, PROGRAMMING, AND ECONOMICS. COMPUTER PLAN CONTROL TASK...MATH 20. PAGE 69 F1357
GAME METH/COMP ACT/RES DECISION

B59
LINK R.G.,ENGLISH THEORIES OF ECONOMIC FLUCTUATIONS: 1815-1848. FRANCE UK AGRI WORKER DIPLOM PRICE TASK WAR DEMAND PRODUC...POLICY BIBLIOG 18 MALTHUS MILL/JS WILSON/J. PAGE 80 F1574
IDEA/COMP ECO/DEV WEALTH EQUILIB

B59
MATTHEWS R.C.O.,THE BUSINESS CYCLE. AFR LABOR INT/TRADE TAX PRICE RISK ADJUST WEALTH...POLICY ECOMETRIC CHARTS SIMUL TIME 20. PAGE 87 F1705
FINAN DEMAND TASK

B59
WELTON H.,THE THIRD WORLD WAR; TRADE AND INDUSTRY, THE NEW BATTLEGROUND. AFR WOR+45 ECO/DEV INDUS MARKET TASK...MGT IDEA/COMP. PAGE 145 F2855
INT/TRADE PLAN DIPLOM

B60
RAO V.K.R.,INTERNATIONAL AID FOR ECONOMIC DEVELOPMENT - POSSIBILITIES AND LIMITATIONS. FINAN PLAN TEC/DEV ADMIN TASK EFFICIENCY...POLICY SOC METH/CNCPT CHARTS 20 UN. PAGE 109 F2147
FOR/AID DIPLOM INT/ORG ECO/UNDEV

B60
SIEGEL B.N.,AGGREGATE ECONOMICS AND PUBLIC POLICY. ECO/DEV TEC/DEV ECO/TAC TASK DEMAND EQUILIB INCOME ...CHARTS 20. PAGE 121 F2396
ECOMETRIC WEALTH PRODUC MARKET

B61
DE VRIES E.,MAN IN RAPID SOCIAL CHANGE. WOR+45 SOCIETY ECO/DEV ECO/UNDEV AGRI INDUS FAM SECT TEC/DEV ATTIT...RECORD 20 CHRISTIAN. PAGE 31 F0607
CULTURE ALL/VALS SOC

TASK

B61
DOIG J.W.,THE POLITICS OF METROPOLITAN TRANSPORTATION. DELIB/GP WORKER DIPLOM TASK EFFICIENCY UTIL...CHARTS BIBLIOG MUNICH 20 NEW/YORK NEW/JERSEY PUB/TRANS RAILROAD. PAGE 34 F0652
PROB/SOLV STRATA DIST/IND

B61
MEZERIK A.G.,ECONOMIC DEVELOPMENT AIDS FOR UNDERDEVELOPED COUNTRIES. WOR+45 FINAN LEGIS PROB/SOLV TEC/DEV DIPLOM FOR/AID GIVE TASK WAR 20 UN. PAGE 91 F1776
ECO/UNDEV INT/ORG WEALTH PLAN

B61
MOORE G.H.,BUSINESS CYCLE INDICATORS (TWO VOLS.). LABOR DIPLOM PRICE RISK TASK WAR PRODUC...CHARTS BIBLIOG 20. PAGE 93 F1822
MARKET FINAN WEALTH

B62
MOUSSA P.,THE UNDERPRIVILEGED NATIONS. FINAN INT/ORG PLAN PROB/SOLV CAP/ISM GIVE TASK WEALTH ...POLICY SOC IND 20. PAGE 94 F1850
ECO/UNDEV NAT/G DIPLOM FOR/AID

S62
BIERMAN H.,"PROBABILITY, STATISTICAL DECISION THEORY, AND ACCOUNTING." ACADEM TASK EFFICIENCY ...METH/CNCPT GEN/METH 20. PAGE 15 F0283
FINAN QUANT DECISION STAT

B63
GORDON L.,A NEW DEAL FOR LATIN AMERICA. L/A+17C USA+45 CULTURE NAT/G TEC/DEV DIPLOM FOR/AID REGION TASK...POLICY 20 ALL/PROG DEPT/STATE. PAGE 49 F0958
ECO/UNDEV ECO/TAC INT/ORG PLAN

B63
OECD,FOOD AID: ITS ROLE IN ECONOMIC DEVELOPMENT. FINAN NAT/G PLAN DIPLOM GIVE TASK WEALTH ...METH/COMP METH 20. PAGE 100 F1966
ECO/UNDEV FOR/AID INT/ORG POLICY

B64
BALL R.J.,INFLATION AND THE THEORY OF MONEY. MARKET TAX PAY PRICE TASK ADJUST BAL/PAY COST INCOME PRODUC WEALTH...METH/COMP 20 KEYNES/JM MONEY. PAGE 9 F0167
EQUILIB DEMAND POLICY

B65
LYONS G.M.,AMERICA: PURPOSE AND POWER. UK USA+45 FINAN INDUS MARKET WORKER TEC/DEV DIPLOM AUTOMAT NUC/PWR WAR RACE/REL ORD/FREE 20 EEC CONGRESS SUPREME/CT CIV/RIGHTS. PAGE 82 F1617
PWR PROB/SOLV ECO/DEV TASK

B65
WEISBROD B.A.,THE ECONOMICS OF POVERTY: AN AMERICAN PARADOX. USA+45 NAT/G WORKER TASK INGP/REL DISCRIM POLICY. PAGE 145 F2852
ECO/DEV WEALTH RECEIVE STRATA

B66
ALEXANDER Y.,INTERNATIONAL TECHNICAL ASSISTANCE EXPERTS* A CASE STUDY OF THE U.N. EXPERIENCE. ECO/UNDEV CONSULT EX/STRUC CREATE PLAN DIPLOM FOR/AID TASK EFFICIENCY...ORG/CHARTS UN. PAGE 3 F0061
ECO/TAC INT/ORG ADMIN MGT

B66
AMER ENTERPRISE INST PUB POL,SIGNIFICANT ISSUES IN ECONOMIC AID TO DEVELOPING COUNTRIES. FINAN INT/ORG NAT/G PLAN PROB/SOLV GIVE TASK WEALTH...DECISION 20. PAGE 4 F0083
ECO/UNDEV FOR/AID DIPLOM POLICY

B66
KEENLEYSIDE H.L.,INTERNATIONAL AID: A SUMMARY. AFR INDIA S/ASIA UK STRATA EXTR/IND TEC/DEV ADMIN RACE/REL DEMAND NAT/LISM WEALTH...TREND CHINJAP. PAGE 70 F1367
ECO/UNDEV FOR/AID DIPLOM TASK

B66
KIRDAR U.,THE STRUCTURE OF UNITED NATIONS ECONOMIC AID TO UNDERDEVELOPED COUNTRIES. AGRI FINAN INDUS NAT/G EX/STRUC PLAN GIVE TASK...POLICY 20 UN. PAGE 71 F1397
INT/ORG FOR/AID ECO/UNDEV ADMIN

B66
MACFARQUHAR R.,CHINA UNDER MAO: POLITICS TAKES COMMAND. CHINA/COM COM AGRI INDUS CHIEF FORCES DIPLOM INT/TRADE EDU/PROP TASK REV ADJUST...ANTHOL 20 MAO. PAGE 83 F1628
ECO/UNDEV TEC/DEV ECO/TAC ADMIN

B66
SEWELL J.P.,FUNCTIONALISM AND WORLD POLITICS* A STUDY BASED ON UNITED NATIONS PROGRAMS FINANCING ECONOMICAL DEVELOPMENT. ECO/UNDEV FINAN PROB/SOLV DIPLOM ECO/TAC FEEDBACK REGION ADJUST ATTIT UN IBRD INTL/FINAN INTL/DEV UNSF. PAGE 120 F2360
TASK INT/ORG IDEA/COMP GEN/LAWS

B66
WETTER G.A.,SOVIET IDEOLOGY TODAY. USSR ECO/UNDEV SECT WORKER CAP/ISM CONTROL TASK EFFICIENCY TOTALISM DRIVE WEALTH...TREND 18/20. PAGE 145 F2864
ALL/IDEOS MARXISM REV

B67
HANNAH H.W.,THE LEGAL BASE FOR UNIVERSITIES IN DEVELOPING COUNTRIES. AFR ASIA L/A+17C S/ASIA USA+45 FINAN CREATE EDU/PROP TASK EFFICIENCY ...JURID METH/COMP 20. PAGE 54 F1060
ADMIN LAW ACADEM LEGIS

B67
LITTLE AD, INC.,COMMUNITY RENEWAL PROGRAMMING. CULTURE LOC/G ACT/RES TASK COST ATTIT...SOC/WK MODAL STAT STAND/INT CHARTS 20 SAN/FRAN. PAGE 81 F1585
STRATA NEIGH PLAN CREATE

B67
US SENATE COMM ON FOREIGN REL,HARRISON E. SALISBURY'S TRIP TO NORTH VIETNAM. CHINA/COM USA+45 VIETNAM/N PRESS TASK GUERRILLA CONSEN EFFICIENCY PEACE DRIVE...OBS SENATE. PAGE 139 F2743
DIPLOM WAR FORCES ATTIT

S67
ALEXANDER R.J.,"'THIRD FORCE' IN WORLD COMMUNISM?" CHINA/COM CUBA USSR INT/ORG DIPLOM TASK INGP/REL ATTIT PWR 20 CASTRO/F. PAGE 3 F0060
CHIEF MARXISM LEAD REV

S67
KOTLER P.,"OPERATIONS RESEARCH IN MARKETING." USA+45 DIST/IND INDUS LG/CO CONSULT BUDGET TASK DEMAND EFFICIENCY PROFIT WEALTH DECISION. PAGE 73 F1429
ECOMETRIC OP/RES MARKET PLAN

S67
PRATT R.C.,"THE ADMINISTRATION OF ECONOMIC PLANNING IN A NEWLY INDEPEND ENT STATE* THE TANZANIAN EXPERIENCE 1963-1966." AFR TANZANIA ECO/UNDEV PLAN CONTROL ROUTINE TASK EFFICIENCY 20. PAGE 107 F2114
NAT/G DELIB/GP ADMIN TEC/DEV

S67
WILLIAMS C.,"REGIONAL MANAGEMENT OVERSEAS." USA+45 WOR+45 DIST/IND LG/CO EX/STRUC INT/TRADE TARIFFS ADMIN TASK CENTRAL. PAGE 147 F2889
MGT EUR+WWI ECO/DEV PLAN

TATE J.H. F0366

TAWNEY R.H. F2536,F2537,F2538

TAX S. F2539

TAX....TAXING, TAXATION

N
JOHNSON R.B.,FINANCING A SUBURBAN CITY. USA+45 TAX COST...SAMP/SIZ MUNICH 20 COL. PAGE 68 F1331
FINAN PAY PROB/SOLV

N
AMERICAN ECONOMIC REVIEW. FINAN INDUS LABOR OP/RES CAP/ISM INT/TRADE TAX WEALTH...CON/ANAL CHARTS 20. PAGE 1 F0001
BIBLIOG/A USA+45 ECO/DEV NAT/G

N
US SUPERINTENDENT OF DOCUMENTS,INTERSTATE COMMERCE (PRICE LIST 59). USA+45 LAW LOC/G NAT/G LEGIS TARIFFS TAX ADMIN CONTROL HEALTH DECISION. PAGE 140 F2752
BIBLIOG/A DIST/IND GOV/REL PROVS

N
US SUPERINTENDENT OF DOCUMENTS,TARIFF AND TAXATION (PRICE LIST 37). USA+45 LAW INT/TRADE ADJUD ADMIN CT/SYS INCOME OWN...DECISION GATT. PAGE 140 F2754
BIBLIOG/A TAX TARIFFS NAT/G

N19
CHATTERS C.H.,NEW MUNICIPAL REVENUES FOR NEW MUNICIPAL EXPENDITURES (PAMPHLET). PLAN PRICE UTIL HABITAT...IDEA/COMP MUNICH 20. PAGE 23 F0457
LOC/G BUDGET TAX

N19
CONGRESSIONAL QUARTERLY SERV,FEDERAL ECONOMIC POLICY 1945-1965 (PAMPHLET). USA+45 FINAN OP/RES BAL/PWR ECO/TAC TAX BAL/PAY CENTRAL COST WEALTH ...CHARTS 20. PAGE 27 F0525
NAT/G ECO/DEV BUDGET POLICY

N19
PATRICK H.T.,CYCLICAL INSTABILITY AND FISCAL-MONETARY POLICY IN POST-WAR JAPAN (PAMPHLET). INDUS MARKET DIPLOM TAX PRICE BAL/PAY...TREND CHARTS EQUILIB 20 CHINJAP. PAGE 104 F2036
ECO/DEV PRODUC STAT

N19
WILSON T.,FINANCIAL ASSISTANCE WITH REGIONAL DEVELOPMENT (PAMPHLET). CANADA INDUS NAT/G PLAN TAX CONTROL COST EFFICIENCY...POLICY CHARTS 20. PAGE 147 F2902
FINAN ECO/TAC REGION GOV/REL

B29
JONES M.M.,CORPORATION CONTRIBUTIONS TO COMMUNITY WELFARE AGENCIES (PAMPHLET). DELIB/GP TAX CONTROL PARTIC RATIONAL POLICY. PAGE 68 F1339
LG/CO GIVE NEIGH SOC/WK

B37
HAMILTON W.H.,THE POWER TO GOVERN. ECO/DEV FINAN INDUS ECO/TAC INT/TRADE TARIFFS TAX CONTROL CT/SYS WAR COST PWR 18/20 SUPREME/CT. PAGE 54 F1056
LING CONSTN NAT/G POLICY

B40
BATCHELOR B.,THE NEW OUTLOOK IN BUSINESS. LAW WORKER TAX LEAD ORD/FREE...POLICY TREND. PAGE 11 F0208
LG/CO GP/REL CAP/ISM LABOR

B41
ESTEY J.A.,BUSINESS CYCLES; THEIR NATURE, CAUSE, AND CONTROL. NAT/G BUDGET CAP/ISM TAX PRICE CONTROL INCOME...MODAL TIME/SEQ GEN/METH T 18/20 KEYNES/JM MONEY. PAGE 38 F0749
INDUS FINAN ECO/TAC POLICY

B48
KEIR D.L.,CASES IN CONSTITUTIONAL LAW. UK CHIEF LEGIS DIPLOM TAX PARL/PROC CRIME GOV/REL...INT/LAW JURID 17/20. PAGE 70 F1368
CONSTN LAW ADJUD

CT/SYS

B48

METZLER L.A.,INCOME, EMPLOYMENT, AND PUBLIC POLICY. FINAN INDUS LOC/G NAT/G TAX GIVE PAY COST PRODUC ...MGT TIME/SEQ 20. PAGE 90 F1765
INCOME WEALTH POLICY ECO/TAC

B48

TAYLOR P.E.,THE ECONOMICS OF PUBLIC FINANCE. USA+45 USA-45 ECO/DEV WORKER PLAN BUDGET WAR INCOME WEALTH ...CONCPT STAT BIBLIOG 20. PAGE 129 F2540
FINAN POLICY NAT/G TAX

B49

SCHULTZ W.J.,AMERICAN PUBLIC FINANCE. USA+45 ECO/TAC TAX ADMIN GOV/REL GP/REL INCOME 20. PAGE 117 F2318
FINAN POLICY ECO/DEV NAT/G

C50

ROUSSEAU J.J.,"A DISCOURSE ON POLITICAL ECONOMY" (1755) IN THE SOCIAL CONTRACT AND DISCOURSES." UNIV SOCIETY STRATA STRUCT CONSEN EQUILIB HAPPINESS UTOPIA HEALTH WEALTH...POLICY WELF/ST. PAGE 114 F2252
NAT/G ECO/TAC TAX GEN/LAWS

B51

HART A.G.,DEFENSE WITHOUT INFLATION. AFR KOREA FINAN INDUS NAT/G WORKER DIPLOM RATION TAX PRICE COST OPTIMAL 20 RESOURCE/N. PAGE 56 F1098
ECO/TAC CONTROL WAR PLAN

B51

POOLE K.,FISCAL POLICIES AND THE AMERICAN ECONOMY. AFR ECO/DEV FINAN INDUS WORKER OP/RES INT/TRADE TAX COST INCOME PROFIT WEALTH...GP/COMP 20. PAGE 107 F2102
NAT/G POLICY ANTHOL

S51

HAWLEY A.H.,"METROPOLITAN POPULATION AND MUNICIPAL GOVERNMENT EXPENDITURES IN CENTRAL CITIES" (BMR)" USA+45 FINAN TAX...STAT CON/ANAL CHARTS MUNICH 20. PAGE 57 F1117
GEOG LOC/G COST BUDGET

B52

ANDREWS F.E.,CORPORATION GIVING. LAW TAX EDU/PROP ADMIN...POLICY STAT CHARTS. PAGE 5 F0101
LG/CO GIVE SML/CO FINAN

B52

AYRES C.E.,THE INDUSTRIAL ECONOMY. USA+45 FINAN MARKET NAT/G PUB/INST PLAN ECO/TAC TAX DEMAND INCOME...BIBLIOG/A 20. PAGE 8 F0146
ECO/DEV INDUS FUT PROB/SOLV

B52

DE JOUVENEL B.,THE ETHICS OF REDISTRIBUTION. UK ELITES MARKET WORKER GIVE PAY INCOME PERSON ...POLICY PSY GEN/LAWS 20. PAGE 31 F0602
WEALTH TAX SOCISM TRADIT

B52

JENNINGS W.I.,CONSTITUTIONAL LAWS OF THE COMMONWEALTH. AFR UK LAW CHIEF LEGIS TAX CT/SYS PARL/PROC GOV/REL...INT/LAW 18/20 ENGLSH/LAW COMMON/LAW. PAGE 67 F1316
CONSTN JURID ADJUD COLONIAL

B52

MACARTHUR D.,REVITALIZING A NATION. ASIA COM FUT KOREA WOR+45 NAT/G FOR/AID TAX GIVE WAR ATTIT SOCISM 20 CHINJAP EUROPE. PAGE 83 F1619
LEAD FORCES TOP/EX POLICY

C52

HUME D.,"OF TAXES" IN D. HUME, POLITICAL DISCOURSES (1752)" UK NAT/G COST INCOME LAISSEZ...GEN/LAWS 18. PAGE 63 F1236
TAX FINAN WEALTH POLICY

B53

MILLIKAN M.F.,INCOME STABILIZATION FOR A DEVELOPING DEMOCRACY. USA+45 ECO/DEV LABOR BUDGET ECO/TAC TAX ADMIN ADJUST PRODUC WEALTH...POLICY TREND 20. PAGE 91 F1794
ANTHOL MARKET EQUILIB EFFICIENCY

B53

WILLIAMS J.H.,ECONOMIC STABILITY IN A CHANGING WORLD. FRANCE USA+45 USSR AGRI WORKER BUDGET INT/TRADE TAX WAR BAL/PAY COST EFFICIENCY ALL/IDEOS EQULIB 20 KEYNES/JM. PAGE 147 F2892
POLICY FINAN ECO/TAC WEALTH

B54

BATTEN T.R.,PROBLEMS OF AFRICAN DEVELOPMENT (2ND ED.). AFR LAW SOCIETY SCHOOL ECO/TAC TAX...GEOG HEAL SOC 20. PAGE 11 F0211
ECO/UNDEV AGRI LOC/G PROB/SOLV

B55

GEORGE H.,PROGRESS AND POVERTY (1880). STRATA STRUCT INDUS TEC/DEV CAP/ISM EQUILIB INCOME OWN UTOPIA...WELF/ST CONCPT NEW/IDEA 19. PAGE 47 F0915
ECO/DEV ECO/TAC TAX WEALTH

B55

O'CONNOR H.,THE EMPIRE OF OIL. USA+45 DIST/IND FINAN MARKET CAP/ISM TAX CONTROL...POLICY MARXIST BIBLIOG/A 20. PAGE 100 F1955
EXTR/IND INT/TRADE CENTRAL NAT/G

B55

SERRANO MOSCOSO E.,A STATEMENT OF THE LAWS OF ECUADOR IN MATTERS AFFECTING BUSINESS (2ND ED.). ECUADOR INDUS LABOR LG/CO NAT/G LEGIS TAX CONTROL MARRIAGE 20. PAGE 120 F2359
FINAN ECO/UNDEV LAW CONSTN

B55

SMITHIES A.,THE BUDGETARY PROCESS IN THE UNITED STATES. AFR ECO/DEV AGRI EX/STRUC FORCES LEGIS PROB/SOLV TAX ROUTINE EFFICIENCY...MGT CONGRESS PRESIDENT. PAGE 124 F2436
NAT/G ADMIN BUDGET GOV/REL

B56

ABELS J.,THE TRUMAN SCANDALS. USA+45 USA-45 POL/PAR TAX LEGIT CT/SYS CHOOSE PRIVIL MORAL WEALTH 20 TRUMAN/HS PRESIDENT CONGRESS. PAGE 2 F0031
CRIME ADMIN CHIEF TRIBUTE

B56

KOHLER E.L.,ACCOUNTING IN THE FEDERAL GOVERNMENT. USA+45 LOC/G PLAN TAX CONTROL COST 20. PAGE 72 F1416
BUDGET AFR NAT/G FINAN

B56

POOLE K.E.,PUBLIC FINANCE AND ECONOMIC WELFARE. STRUCT ECO/DEV LOC/G NAT/G BUDGET PAY ROUTINE COST EQUILIB WEALTH...SOC/WK METH/COMP 20. PAGE 107 F2103
FINAN TAX ORD/FREE

B56

VAKIL C.N.,PLANNING FOR AN EXPANDING ECONOMY. INDIA TAX COST 20. PAGE 140 F2759
TEC/DEV LABOR BUDGET CAP/ISM

S56

MARGOLIS J.,"ON MUNICIPAL LAND POLICY FOR FISCAL GAINS." USA+45 PLAN TAX COST EFFICIENCY HABITAT KNOWL...MGT MUNICH 20. PAGE 85 F1667
BUDGET POLICY GEOG LOC/G

B57

BARAN P.A.,THE POLITICAL ECONOMY OF GROWTH. MOD/EUR USA+45 USA-45 TEC/DEV TAX SOCISM...MGT CONCPT GOV/COMP. PAGE 9 F0178
CAP/ISM CONTROL ECO/UNDEV FINAN

B57

BAUER P.T.,ECONOMIC ANALYSIS AND POLICY IN UNDERDEVELOPED COUNTRIES. AFR WOR+45 AGRI INT/TRADE TAX PRICE...GEN/METH BIBLIOG/A 20. PAGE 11 F0214
ECO/UNDEV METH/COMP POLICY

L57

SURREY S.S.,"THE CONGRESS AND THE TAX LOBBYIST - HOW SPECIAL TAX PROVISIONS GET ENACTED." LOBBY REPRESENT PRIVIL CONGRESS. PAGE 128 F2518
LEGIS TAX EX/STRUC ROLE

B58

DEFENSE AGAINST INFLATION. USA+45 LEGIS WORKER TAX PRICE DEMAND INCOME PRODUC...POLICY TREND METH/COMP 20 GOLD/STAND. PAGE 1 F0012
ECO/TAC EQUILIB WEALTH PROB/SOLV

B58

BARRERE A.,POLITIQUE FINANCIERE. FRANCE BUDGET ECO/TAC TAX BAL/PAY INCOME PRODUC...MGT BIBLIOG T 20. PAGE 10 F0193
FINAN NAT/G PLAN

B58

BROWN B.,INCOME TRENDS IN THE UNITED STATES THROUGH 1975. USA+45 NAT/G WEALTH...GEOG CENSUS PREDICT CHARTS METH 20. PAGE 19 F0366
STAT INCOME TREND TAX

B58

DAVIS E.H.,OF THE PEOPLE, BY THE PEOPLE, FOR THE PEOPLE. INCOME WEALTH...METH/COMP MUNICH 20. PAGE 30 F0587
FINAN LOC/G TAX

B58

MUSGRAVE R.A.,CLASSICS IN THE THEORY OF PUBLIC FINANCE. UNIV MARKET LG/CO NAT/G CAP/ISM PRICE OPTIMAL...IDEA/COMP ANTHOL 19/20 SAY/EMIL EDGEWORTH LINDAHL/E RITSCHL/H. PAGE 95 F1870
TAX FINAN ECO/TAC GP/REL

B58

OGDEN F.D.,THE POLL TAX IN THE SOUTH. USA+45 USA-45 CONSTN ADJUD ADMIN PARTIC CRIME...TIME/SEQ GOV/COMP METH/COMP 18/20 SOUTH/US. PAGE 101 F1982
TAX CHOOSE RACE/REL DISCRIM

B58

PAYNO M.,LA REFORMA SOCIAL EN ESPANA Y MEXICO. SPAIN ECO/TAC TAX LOBBY COERCE REV OWN CATHISM 19/20 MEXIC/AMER. PAGE 104 F2043
SECT NAT/G LAW ELITES

B58

SHAW S.J.,THE FINANCIAL AND ADMINISTRATIVE ORGANIZATION AND DEVELOPMENT OF OTTOMAN EGYPT 1517-1798. UAR LOC/G FORCES BUDGET INT/TRADE TAX EATING INCOME WEALTH...CHARTS BIBLIOG 16/18 OTTOMAN NAPOLEON/B. PAGE 120 F2371
FINAN ADMIN GOV/REL CULTURE

B58

US CONGRESS JOINT ECO COMM,THE RELATIONSHIP OF PRICES TO ECONOMIC STABILITY AND GROWTH. USA+45 MARKET TAX ADJUST COST DEMAND INCOME PRODUC ...POLICY TREND CHARTS ANTHOL 20 CONGRESS. PAGE 134 F2650
ECO/DEV PLAN EQUILIB PRICE

B59

HARTOG F.,EUROPEAN TRADE CYCLE POLICY. WORKER TAX PRICE WAR CENTRAL DEMAND...TREND CHARTS 20 UN. PAGE 56 F1103
EQUILIB EUR+WWI INT/TRADE

B59

LEWIS J.P.,BUSINESS CONDITIONS ANALYSIS. USA+45
FINAN

MARKET LABOR BUDGET TAX AUTOMAT WAR DEMAND PRODUC ...ECOMETRIC CHARTS BIBLIOG 19/20. PAGE 79 F1549
PRICE TREND

B59
LI CHOH-MING,ECONOMIC DEVELOPMENT OF COMMUNIST CHINA. ASIA CHINA/COM AGRI FINAN TAX INCOME MARXISM ...MGT 20. PAGE 80 F1557
ECO/UNDEV INDUS ORD/FREE TEC/DEV

B59
LOPEZ VILLAMIL H.,A STATEMENT OF THE LAWS OF THE HONDURAS IN MATTERS AFFECTING BUSINESS (2ND ED.). HONDURAS DIST/IND EXTR/IND FINAN WORKER TAX DEATH MARRIAGE OWN MARITIME 20 MIGRATION. PAGE 82 F1600
CONSTN INDUS LEGIS NAT/G

B59
MATTHEWS R.C.O.,THE BUSINESS CYCLE. AFR LABOR INT/TRADE TAX PRICE RISK ADJUST WEALTH...POLICY ECOMETRIC CHARTS SIMUL TIME 20. PAGE 87 F1705
FINAN DEMAND TASK

B59
STANFORD U, BOARD OF TRUSTEES,THE ALLOCATION OF ECONOMIC RESOURCES. WORKER PLAN BUDGET ECO/TAC TAX RECEIVE COST PRODUC...POLICY IDEA/COMP SIMUL ANTHOL 20. PAGE 125 F2468
INCOME PRICE FINAN

N59
CHAMBER OF COMMERCE OF USA,ECONOMIC LESSONS OF POSTWAR RECESSIONS (PAMPHLET). AFR USA+45 LAW LEGIS WORKER TAX...CHARTS 20 CONGRESS FED/RESERV. PAGE 23 F0440
ECO/DEV PROB/SOLV FINAN ECO/TAC

B60
BIERMAN H.,THE CAPITAL BUDGETING DECISION. AFR ECO/DEV MARKET TAX PRICE RISK COST INCOME TIME 20. PAGE 15 F0282
FINAN OPTIMAL BUDGET PROFIT

B60
BISSON A.,INSTITUTIONS FINANCIERES ET ECONOMIQUES EN FRANCE. FRANCE INDUS OP/RES TAX COST PRODUC ...CHARTS 20. PAGE 15 F0289
FINAN BUDGET PLAN

B60
FIRESTONE J.M.,FEDERAL RECEIPTS AND EXPENDITURES DURING BUSINESS CYCLES, 1879-1958. USA+45 USA-45 INDUS PLAN ECO/TAC TAX WAR COST...CHARTS 19/20. PAGE 41 F0801
FINAN INCOME BUDGET NAT/G

B60
HALL C.A. JR.,FISCAL POLICY FOR STABLE GROWTH. USA+45 FINAN TEC/DEV TAX COST DEMAND INCOME ...BIBLIOG 20. PAGE 53 F1045
ECO/TAC BUDGET NAT/G POLICY

B60
OEEC,STATISTICS OF SOURCES AND USES OF FINANCE. NAT/G CAP/ISM TAX PRICE COST 20 OEEC. PAGE 101 F1978
FINAN PRODUC INCOME NAT/COMP

B60
PETERSON W.C.,THE WELFARE STATE IN FRANCE. EUR+WWI FRANCE FUT STRATA PROB/SOLV TAX GIVE RECEIVE INCOME ORD/FREE PWR...CHARTS 20. PAGE 105 F2070
NEW/LIB ECO/TAC WEALTH NAT/G

B60
VERNON R.,METROPOLIS 1985. LOC/G PLAN TAX LEAD PWR MUNICH. PAGE 141 F2780
REGION ECO/TAC DECISION

B61
BEASLEY K.E.,STATE SUPERVISION OF MUNICIPAL DEBT IN KANSAS - A CASE STUDY. USA+45 USA-45 FINAN PROVS BUDGET TAX ADJUD ADMIN CONTROL SUPEGO MUNICH. PAGE 12 F0224
LOC/G LEGIS JURID

B61
BREWIS T.N.,CANADIAN ECONOMIC POLICY. AFR CANADA BUDGET CAP/ISM INT/TRADE RATION TARIFFS TAX PRICE CONTROL ROUTINE FEDERAL INCOME PRODUC 20. PAGE 18 F0348
ECO/DEV ECO/TAC NAT/G PLAN

B61
GOODWIN C.D.W.,CANADIAN ECONOMIC THOUGHT. CANADA STRATA TEC/DEV CAP/ISM TARIFFS TAX COST EFFICIENCY WEALTH...METH/CNCPT TREND 20 MARITIME ONTARIO. PAGE 49 F0952
INT/TRADE ECO/DEV FINAN DEMAND

B61
HOLMANS A.E.,UNITED STATES FISCAL POLICY 1945-1959. AFR USA+45 USA-45 ECO/DEV TAX PRICE WAR...BIBLIOG 20 DEMOCRAT REPUBLICAN. PAGE 61 F1200
POLICY BUDGET NAT/G ECO/TAC

B61
INTERNATIONAL BANK RECONST DEV,THE WORLD BANK IN AFRICA: SUMMARY OF ACTIVITIES. AGRI COM/IND DIST/IND EXTR/IND INDUS TAX COST...CHARTS 20. PAGE 65 F1271
FINAN ECO/UNDEV INT/ORG AFR

B61
NEW JERSEY LEGISLATURE-SENATE,PUBLIC HEARINGS BEFORE COMMITTEE ON REVISION AND AMENDMENT OF LAWS ON SENATE BILL NO. 8. USA+45 FINAN PROVS WORKER ACT/RES PLAN BUDGET TAX CRIME...IDEA/COMP MUNICH 20 NEW/JERSEY URBAN/RNWL. PAGE 98 F1919
LEGIS INDUS PROB/SOLV

B61
PETCH G.A.,ECONOMIC DEVELOPMENT AND MODERN WEST AFRICA. AFR CONGO/BRAZ GHANA NIGER SIER/LEONE AGRI MARKET LABOR FOR/AID TAX COST EFFICIENCY EQUILIB PRODUC...GEOG TREND 20. PAGE 105 F2068
ECO/UNDEV TEC/DEV EXTR/IND ECO/TAC

B61
RUEDA B.,A STATEMENT OF THE LAWS OF COLOMBIA IN MATTERS AFFECTING BUSINESS (3RD ED.). INDUS FAM LABOR LG/CO NAT/G LEGIS TAX CONTROL MARRIAGE 20 COLOMB. PAGE 115 F2257
FINAN ECO/UNDEV LAW CONSTN

B61
SEPULVEDA C.,A STATEMENT OF THE LAWS OF MEXICO IN MATTERS AFFECTING BUSINESS (3RD ED.). AGRI DIST/IND EXTR/IND FINAN INDUS WORKER TAX MARRIAGE OWN ORD/FREE...BIBLIOG 20 MEXIC/AMER TREATY MIGRATION MONOPOLY. PAGE 119 F2356
CONSTN NAT/G JURID LEGIS

B61
STANLEY C.J.,LATE CH'ING FINANCE: HU KUANG-YUNG AS AN INNOVATOR. ASIA NAT/G FORCES BUDGET TAX WAR GOV/REL COST...POLICY BIOG CHARTS BIBLIOG 19. PAGE 125 F2469
FINAN ECO/TAC CIVMIL/REL ADMIN

B61
UNIVS-NATL BUR COMM ECO RES,PUBLIC FINANCES: NEEDS, SOURCES, AND UTILIZATION. USA+45 FORCES PLAN TAX CONFER PRICE FEDERAL UTIL...ANTHOL MUNICH 20. PAGE 133 F2623
NAT/G FINAN DECISION BUDGET

L61
GERWIG R.,"PUBLIC AUTHORITIES IN THE UNITED STATES." LAW CONSTN PROVS TAX ADMIN FEDERAL MUNICH. PAGE 47 F0920
LOC/G GOV/REL PWR

S61
NYANZI S.,"THE EAST AFRICAN MARKET: FOR BETTER OF FOR WORSE." AFR TANZANIA UGANDA PROB/SOLV TARIFFS TAX BAL/PAY. PAGE 99 F1947
ECO/TAC ECO/UNDEV INT/ORG INT/TRADE

N61
US ADVISORY COMM INTERGOV REL,STATE AND LOCAL TAXATION ON PRIVATELY OWNED PROPERTY LOCATED ON FEDERAL AREAS: PROPOSED AMENDMENT OF BUCK ACT (PAMPHLET). USA+45 ACT/RES PLAN CONTROL GOV/REL INGP/REL OWN...POLICY JURID CHARTS GP/COMP 20. PAGE 133 F2629
PROVS LOC/G NAT/G TAX

N61
US ADVISORY COMN INTERGOV REL,STATE CONSTITUTIONAL AND STATUTORY RESTRICTIONS ON LOCAL GOVERNMENT DEBT (PAMPHLET). LAW CONSTN CHOOSE PWR...DECISION MUNICH. PAGE 133 F2631
TAX PROVS GOV/REL

B62
ALTMAN G.T.,INVISIBLE BARRIER: THE OPTIMUM GROWTH CURVE. USA+45 USA-45 ECO/DEV PLAN PAY CONTROL DEMAND OPTIMAL PRODUC WEALTH...STAT CHARTS 20. PAGE 4 F0080
INDUS FINAN ECO/TAC TAX

B62
BERNSTEIN P.L.,THE PRICE OF PROSPERITY. USA+45 TAX CONTROL OPTIMAL WEALTH...PREDICT 20. PAGE 14 F0269
ECO/DEV ECO/TAC NAT/G DEMAND

B62
DE LAVALLE H.,A STATEMENT OF THE LAWS OF PERU IN MATTERS AFFECTING BUSINESS (3RD ED.). PERU WORKER INT/TRADE INCOME ORD/FREE...INT/LAW 20. PAGE 31 F0603
CONSTN JURID FINAN TAX

B62
HOOVER E.M.,ANATOMY OF A METROPOLIS. FUT USA+45 SOCIETY ECO/DEV DIST/IND INDUS WORKER ECO/TAC TAX GP/REL COST WEALTH MUNICH 20 NEWYORK/C. PAGE 62 F1212
ROUTINE TREND INCOME

B62
KOLKO G.,WEALTH AND POWER IN AMERICA. USA+45 SOCIETY STRATA LG/CO ECO/TAC TAX PWR...SOC BIBLIOG 20 DEPRESSION. PAGE 72 F1420
STRUCT INCOME ECO/DEV WEALTH

B62
LICHFIELD N.,COST-BENEFIT ANALYSIS IN URBAN REDEVELOPMENT. CONSTRUC LOC/G NEIGH ACT/RES PROB/SOLV TEC/DEV BUDGET TAX...DECISION STAT CHARTS SOC/EXP MUNICH 20. PAGE 80 F1558
PLAN COST GOV/REL

B62
PASTOR R.S.,A STATEMENT OF THE LAWS OF PARAGUAY IN MATTERS AFFECTING BUSINESS (2ND ED.). PARAGUAY INDUS FAM LABOR LG/CO NAT/G LEGIS TAX CONTROL MARRIAGE 20. PAGE 103 F2033
FINAN ECO/UNDEV LAW CONSTN

B62
PHELPS E.S.,THE GOAL OF ECONOMIC GROWTH: SOURCES, COSTS, BENEFITS. USA+45 USSR FINAN TAX CONTROL DEMAND WEALTH...POLICY NAT/COMP ANTHOL BIBLIOG 20. PAGE 106 F2079
ECO/TAC ECO/DEV NAT/G FUT

B62
SCHNEIDER E.,MONEY, INCOME AND EMPLOYMENT. TAX PAY DEMAND...CHARTS BIBLIOG 20. PAGE 117 F2305
ECO/DEV FINAN INCOME

B62
SIEVERS A.M.,REVOLUTION, EVOLUTION AND THE ECONOMIC ORDER. INDUS LABOR TAX CONTROL REV WAR DEMAND PRODUC WEALTH...IDEA/COMP 19/20 KEYNES/JM. PAGE 122 F2399
EFFICIENCY ALL/IDEOS ECO/DEV WELF/ST

B62
THEOBALD R.,NATIONAL DEVELOPMENT EFFORTS (PAMPHLET). WOR+45 AGRI BUDGET FOR/AID INT/TRADE TAX 20. PAGE 129 F2555
ECO/UNDEV PLAN BAL/PAY WEALTH

B62
US ADVISORY COMN INTERGOV REL,STATE CONSTITUTIONAL AND STATUTORY RESTRICTIONS ON LOCAL TAXING POWERS. USA+45 USA-45 LAW CONSTN ACT/RES CONTROL WEALTH ...JURID CHARTS 20. PAGE 133 F2632 LOC/G PROVS GOV/REL TAX

B62
US CONGRESS,LEGISLATIVE HISTORY OF UNITED STATES TAX CONVENTIONS(VOL. 1). USA+45 USA-45 DELIB/GP WEALTH...CHARTS 20 CONGRESS. PAGE 134 F2649 TAX LEGIS LAW DIPLOM

B62
US CONGRESS JOINT ECO COMM,ECONOMIC DEVELOPMENTS IN SOUTH AMERICA. USA+45 SOCIETY FINAN NAT/G PROB/SOLV TEC/DEV INT/TRADE TAX EFFICIENCY PRODUC ATTIT ...POLICY 20 ALL/PROG CONGRESS SOUTH/AMER. PAGE 135 F2654 L/A+17C ECO/UNDEV FOR/AID DIPLOM

B62
VACCARO J.R.,A STATEMENT OF THE LAWS OF CHILE IN MATTERS AFFECTING BUSINESS (3RD ED.). CHILE AGRI FINAN FAM LABOR ECO/TAC FOR/AID TAX ADJUD CONTROL MARRIAGE STRANGE...BIBLIOG 20. PAGE 140 F2756 CONSTN LAW INDUS MGT

L62
BELSHAW D.G.R.,"PUBLIC INVESTMENT IN AGRICULTURE AND ECONOMIC DEVELOPMENT OF UGANDA" UGANDA AGRI INDUS R+D ECO/TAC RATION TAX PAY COLONIAL 20 WORLD/BANK. PAGE 13 F0242 ECO/UNDEV PLAN ADMIN CENTRAL

S62
GILL P.J.,"FUTURE TAXATION POLICY IN AN INDEPENDENT EAST AFRICA" UGANDA LOC/G ECO/TAC ADMIN EFFICIENCY INCOME PRODUC...CHARTS 20. PAGE 47 F0923 ECO/UNDEV TAX AFR COLONIAL

S62
KRISHNA K.G.V.,"PLANNING AND ECONOMIC DEVELOPMENT" AFR UGANDA AGRI INDUS R+D BUDGET RATION TAX COLONIAL 20. PAGE 73 F1441 ECO/UNDEV ECO/TAC NAT/LISM PLAN

B63
CORLEY R.N.,THE LEGAL ENVIRONMENT OF BUSINESS. CONSTN LEGIS TAX ADMIN CT/SYS DISCRIM ATTIT PWR ...TREND 18/20. PAGE 28 F0537 NAT/G INDUS JURID DECISION

B63
DUE J.F.,STATE SALES TAX ADMINISTRATION. OP/RES BUDGET PAY ADMIN EXEC ROUTINE COST EFFICIENCY PROFIT...CHARTS METH/COMP 20. PAGE 34 F0671 PROVS TAX STAT GOV/COMP

B63
ENKE S.,ECONOMICS FOR DEVELOPMENT. AGRI TEC/DEV CAP/ISM DIPLOM ECO/TAC TAX ATTIT DRIVE HABITAT WEALTH...GOV/COMP BIBLIOG 20. PAGE 38 F0737 ECO/UNDEV PHIL/SCI CON/ANAL

B63
ERHARD L.,THE ECONOMICS OF SUCCESS. GERMANY/W WOR+45 LABOR CHIEF TAX REGION COST DEMAND ANTHOL. PAGE 38 F0745 ECO/DEV INT/TRADE PLAN DIPLOM

B63
FATEMI N.S.,THE DOLLAR CRISIS. USA+45 INDUS NAT/G LEGIS BUDGET TAX COST...CHARTS METH/COMP 20 EEC. PAGE 39 F0766 PROB/SOLV BAL/PAY FOR/AID PLAN

B63
FOX S.,ECONOMIC CONTROL AND FREE ENTERPRISE. PLAN BUDGET INT/TRADE TAX...TREND 20. PAGE 43 F0839 CONTROL FINAN ECO/TAC

B63
HAQ M.,THE STRATEGY OF ECONOMIC PLANNING. PAKISTAN AGRI FINAN INDUS NAT/G FOR/AID TAX CONTROL REGION PRODUC...POLICY CHARTS 20. PAGE 55 F1071 ECO/TAC ECO/UNDEV PLAN PROB/SOLV

B63
INTERAMERICAN ECO AND SOC COUN,THE ALLIANCE FOR PROGRESS: ITS FIRST YEAR: 1961-1962. AGRI SCHOOL PLAN TEC/DEV INT/TRADE TAX GIVE ADMIN WEALTH...SOC 20 ALL/PROG SOUTH/AMER. PAGE 64 F1267 INT/ORG PROB/SOLV ECO/TAC L/A+17C

B63
LEE M.W.,MACROECONOMICS: FLUCTUATIONS, GROWTH AND STABILITY (3RD ED.). MARKET LABOR TEC/DEV INT/TRADE TAX PRICE WAR PRODUC...POLICY ECOMETRIC CHARTS 19/20. PAGE 77 F1505 EQUILIB TREND WEALTH

B63
MEEK R.L.,THE ECONOMICS OF PHYSIOCRACY. FRANCE UK AGRI FINAN WORKER CAP/ISM TAX DEMAND EQUILIB INCOME HABITAT...CHARTS ANTHOL 17. PAGE 89 F1744 PRODUC WEALTH MARKET

B63
MILLER W.,REVENUE-COST RATIOS OF RURAL TOWNSHIPS WITH CHANGING LAND USES. USA+45 INDUS SERV/IND PROVS GP/REL HABITAT...CHARTS GP/COMP MUNICH 20 NEW/JERSEY. PAGE 91 F1792 TAX COST AGRI

B63
RAFUSE R.W. JR.,STATE AND LOCAL FISCAL BEHAVIOR OVER THE POSTWAR CYCLES (DISSERTATION). USA+45 TAX PRICE ATTIT...POLICY TIME/SEQ TREND CHARTS BIBLIOG 20. PAGE 109 F2135 BUDGET LOC/G ECO/TAC PROVS

B63
RANGEL I.,A INFLACAO BRASILEIRA (2ND ED.). AFR BRAZIL AGRI INDUS MARKET INT/TRADE DEMAND EQUILIB ATTIT 20. PAGE 109 F2144 ECO/UNDEV FINAN PRICE TAX

B63
RICARDO D.,THE PRINCIPLES OF POLITICAL ECONOMY AND TAXATION (1817). UK INDUS MARKET ECO/TAC INT/TRADE TARIFFS PRICE COST DEMAND OPTIMAL WEALTH...CONCPT 19 INTRVN/ECO. PAGE 111 F2183 GEN/LAWS TAX LAISSEZ

B63
UN SECRETARY GENERAL,PLANNING FOR ECONOMIC DEVELOPMENT. ECO/UNDEV FINAN BUDGET INT/TRADE TARIFFS TAX ADMIN 20 UN. PAGE 132 F2603 PLAN ECO/TAC MGT NAT/COMP

B63
US GOVERNMENT,REPORT TO INTER-AMERICAN ECONOMIC AND SOCIAL COUNCIL AT SECOND ANNUAL MEETING. L/A+17C USA+45 VOL/ASSN TEC/DEV DIPLOM TAX EATING EFFICIENCY HEALTH...STAT CHARTS 20 AID. PAGE 136 F2682 ECO/TAC FOR/AID FINAN PLAN

B63
US SENATE COMM GOVT OPERATIONS,REPORT OF A STUDY OF US FOREIGN AID IN TEN MIDDLE EASTERN AND AFRICAN COUNTRIES. AFR ISLAM USA+45 FORCES PLAN BUDGET DIPLOM TAX DETER WEALTH...STAT CHARTS 20 CONGRESS AID MID/EAST. PAGE 138 F2728 FOR/AID EFFICIENCY ECO/TAC FINAN

B63
VON MISES L.,HUMAN ACTION: A TREATISE ON ECONOMICS (2ND ED.). SOCIETY MARKET TAX PAY PRICE DEMAND EQUILIB RATIONAL...PSY 20. PAGE 142 F2794 PLAN DRIVE ATTIT

S63
ANDREWS R.B.,"ECONOMIC PLANNING FOR SMALL AREAS: THE PLANNING PROCESS." INDUS PROC/MFG PROVS PROB/SOLV TAX EQUILIB...METH/COMP HYPO/EXP METH MUNICH 20. PAGE 5 F0103 ECO/TAC PLAN LOC/G

S63
CARTER A.G.T.,"THE BALANCE OF PAYMENTS OF EAST AFRICA" AFR ECO/TAC FOR/AID RATION TARIFFS TAX ADMIN...STAT 20 AFRICA/E. PAGE 22 F0423 BUDGET ECO/UNDEV BAL/PAY INT/TRADE

S63
CLARK P.G.,"TOWARDS MORE COMPREHENSIVE PLANNING IN EAST AFRICA" AFR OP/RES ECO/TAC RATION TAX EFFICIENCY INCOME...MATH TREND CHARTS 20 AFRICA/E. PAGE 25 F0484 ECO/UNDEV PLAN STAT METH/COMP

S63
ETHERINGTON D.M.,"LAND RESETTLEMENT IN KENYA; POLICY AND PRACTICE" AFR TEC/DEV ECO/TAC FOR/AID TAX PRODUC...CHARTS 20. PAGE 39 F0752 ECO/UNDEV AGRI WORKER PLAN

N63
COMM ON FEDERAL TAX POLICY,FINANCING AMERICA'S FUTURE: TAXES, ECONOMIC STABILITY AND GROWTH (PAMPHLET). USA+45 LG/CO SML/CO DELIB/GP INCOME ...CHARTS 20. PAGE 26 F0513 TAX NAT/G EQUILIB PLAN

N63
NORTH CAROLINA U INST GOVT,COSTING URBAN DEVELOPMENT AND REDEVELOPMENT (PAMPHLET). USA+45 USA-45 NEIGH PLAN TEC/DEV TAX OWN...GEOG MUNICH 20. PAGE 98 F1934 BIBLIOG COST FINAN

B64
BALL R.J.,INFLATION AND THE THEORY OF MONEY. MARKET TAX PAY PRICE TASK ADJUST BAL/PAY COST INCOME PRODUC WEALTH...METH/COMP 20 KEYNES/JM MONEY. PAGE 9 F0167 EQUILIB DEMAND POLICY

B64
BASTIAT F.,ECONOMIC HARMONIES (1850). STRATA STRUCT ECO/DEV BUDGET TAX PRICE LOBBY COST. PAGE 11 F0206 ECO/TAC PLAN INT/TRADE LAISSEZ

B64
BASTIAT F.,ECONOMIC SOPHISMS (1845). FINAN MARKET INT/TRADE TAX EDU/PROP LAISSEZ. PAGE 11 F0207 TARIFFS INDUS ECO/TAC CAP/ISM

B64
BOGEN J.I.,FINANCIAL HANDBOOK (4TH ED.). UNIV LAW PLAN TAX RISK 20. PAGE 16 F0306 FINAN DICTIONARY

B64
DUSCHA J.,ARMS, MONEY, AND POLITICS. USA+45 INDUS POL/PAR ECO/TAC TAX DETER NUC/PWR WAR WEAPON GOV/REL ATTIT...BIBLIOG/A 20 CONGRESS MONEY DEPT/DEFEN. PAGE 35 F0687 NAT/G FORCES POLICY BUDGET

B64
JACOBY N.H.,UNITED STATES MONETARY POLICY. UK USA+45 LAW NAT/G TEC/DEV TAX EQUILIB INCOME ...METH/COMP 20 FED/RESERV. PAGE 66 F1300 ECO/DEV POLICY ECO/TAC FINAN

B64
LAURSEN K.,THE GERMAN INFLATION, 1918-23. EUR+WWI GERMANY/E GERMANY/W WOR-45 BUDGET TAX GOV/REL BAL/PAY DEMAND PEACE...POLICY CHARTS 20 WEIMAR/REP. PAGE 76 F1489 ECO/DEV FINAN REPAR ECO/TAC

B64
LINDHOLM R.W.,ECONOMIC DEVELOPMENT POLICY WITH EMPHASIS ON VIET-NAM. KOREA/S PAKISTAN VIETNAM/S AGRI INDUS CONSULT DELIB/GP FOR/AID...METH 20. PAGE 80 F1571 ECO/UNDEV TAX FINAN ECO/TAC

B64
MANN B.,STATE CONSTITUTIONAL RESTRICTIONS ON LOCAL BORROWING AND PROPERTY TAXING POWERS. USA+45 CONSTN PROVS CT/SYS GOV/REL PWR...DECISION JURID CHARTS 20. PAGE 84 F1654
LOC/G TAX FINAN LAW

B64
MITAU G.T.,INSOLUBLE PROBLEMS: CASE PROBLEMS ON THE FUNCTIONS OF STATE AND LOCAL GOVERNMENT. USA+45 AIR FINAN LABOR POL/PAR PROB/SOLV TAX RECEIVE CONTROL GP/REL 20 CASEBOOK ZONING. PAGE 92 F1807
ADJUD LOC/G PROVS

B64
MOAK L.L.,A MANUAL OF SUGGESTED PRACTICE FOR THE PREPARATION AND ADOPTION OF CAPITAL PROGRAMS AND CAPITAL BUDGETS BY LOCAL GOVERN. USA+45 DELIB/GP PLAN TAX GP/REL COST DECISION. PAGE 92 F1812
LOC/G BUDGET LEGIS PROB/SOLV

B64
TELLADO A.,A STATEMENT OF THE LAWS OF THE DOMINICAN REPUBLIC IN MATTERS AFFECTING BUSINESS (3RD ED.). DOMIN/REP AGRI DIST/IND EXTR/IND FINAN FAM WORKER ECO/TAC TAX CT/SYS MARRIAGE OWN...BIBLIOG 20 MIGRATION. PAGE 129 F2542
CONSTN LEGIS NAT/G INDUS

B64
US HOUSE COMM GOVT OPERATIONS,US OWNED FOREIGN CURRENCIES: HEARINGS (COMMITTEE ON GOVERNMENT OPERATIONS). INDIA ECO/DEV PLAN BUDGET TAX DEMAND EFFICIENCY 20 AID CONGRESS. PAGE 137 F2699
FINAN ECO/TAC FOR/AID OWN

B64
WEIDENBAUM M.L.,CONGRESS AND THE FEDERAL BUDGET: FEDERAL BUDGETING AND THE RESPONSIBLE USE OF POWER. LOC/G PLAN TAX CONGRESS. PAGE 144 F2843
LEGIS EX/STRUC BUDGET ADMIN

B64
WELLISZ S.,THE ECONOMICS OF THE SOVIET BLOC. COM USSR INDUS WORKER PLAN BUDGET INT/TRADE TAX PRICE PRODUC WEALTH MARXISM...METH/COMP 20. PAGE 145 F2854
EFFICIENCY ADMIN MARKET

B64
WERNETTE J.P.,GOVERNMENT AND BUSINESS. LABOR CAP/ISM ECO/TAC INT/TRADE TAX ADMIN AUTOMAT NUC/PWR CIVMIL/REL DEMAND...MGT 20 MONOPOLY. PAGE 145 F2859
NAT/G FINAN ECO/DEV CONTROL

B64
WILSON T.,POLICIES FOR REGIONAL DEVELOPMENT. CANADA UK FINAN INDUS NAT/G BUDGET TAX GIVE COST ...NAT/COMP 20. PAGE 147 F2904
REGION PLAN ECO/DEV ECO/TAC

N64
KENYA MINISTRY ECO PLAN DEV,AFRICAN SOCIALISM AND ITS APPLICATION TO PLANNING IN KENYA (PAMPHLET). AFR AGRI INDUS WORKER TAX COLONIAL WEALTH 20. PAGE 70 F1380
NAT/G SOCISM PLAN ECO/UNDEV

B65
ALLEN W.R.,INTERNATIONAL TRADE THEORY: HUME TO OHLIN. FINAN LABOR TARIFFS TAX PRICE DEMAND PRODUC PROFIT...ANTHOL 18/20. PAGE 4 F0074
INT/TRADE WEALTH METH/CNCPT

B65
AMERICAN FOREST PRODUCTS INDUS,GOVERNMENT LAND ACQUISITION: A SUMMARY OF LAND ACQUISITION BY FEDERAL, STATE, AND LOCAL GOVERNMENTS UP TO 1964. USA+45 USA-45 TAX...POLICY GEOG CHARTS 20. PAGE 5 F0089
NAT/G OWN ECO/TAC GOV/REL

B65
BROOKINGS INSTITUTION,BROOKINGS PAPERS ON PUBLIC POLICY. USA+45 ECO/UNDEV LEGIS CAP/ISM ECO/TAC TAX EDU/PROP CONTROL APPORT 20. PAGE 19 F0363
DIPLOM FOR/AID POLICY FINAN

B65
BRYCE M.D.,POLICIES AND METHODS FOR INDUSTRIAL DEVELOPMENT. WOR+45 FINAN MARKET CONSULT TARIFFS TAX COST. PAGE 20 F0379
INDUS PLAN ECO/DEV TEC/DEV

B65
KLASSEN L.H.,AREA ECONOMIC AND SOCIAL REDEVELOPMENT. ECO/UNDEV INDUS NAT/G PLAN CAP/ISM TAX...ECOMETRIC SIMUL 20. PAGE 72 F1404
OPTIMAL WORKER METH ECO/TAC

B65
LUGO-MARENCO J.J.,A STATEMENT OF THE LAWS OF NICARAGUA IN MATTERS AFFECTING BUSINESS. NICARAGUA AGRI DIST/IND EXTR/IND FINAN INDUS FAM WORKER INT/TRADE TAX MARRIAGE OWN BIO/SOC 20 TREATY RESOURCE/N MIGRATION. PAGE 82 F1606
CONSTN NAT/G LEGIS JURID

B65
MARGOLIS J.,THE PUBLIC ECONOMY OF URBAN COMMUNITIES. USA+45 LEGIS PROB/SOLV TAX LOBBY CHOOSE ATTIT MUNICH. PAGE 85 F1668
LOC/G DECISION FINAN

B65
MURUMBI J.,PROBLEMS OF ECONOMIC DEVELOPMENT IN EAST AFRICA. FINAN INDUS WORKER TEC/DEV INT/TRADE TAX DEMAND EFFICIENCY PRODUC SOCISM...TREND CHARTS 20 AFRICA/E. PAGE 95 F1869
AGRI ECO/TAC ECO/UNDEV PROC/MFG

B65
MUSHKIN S.J.,PROPERTY TAXES: THE 1970 OUTLOOK (PAMPHLET). FUT USA+45 ECO/DEV MARKET PROVS PLAN ...PROBABIL STAT CENSUS PREDICT CHARTS METH 20. PAGE 95 F1872
TAX OWN FINAN LOC/G

B65
PHELPS E.S.,FISCAL NEUTRALITY TOWARD ECONOMIC GROWTH. FINAN NAT/G BUDGET CAP/ISM CONTROL INCOME 20. PAGE 106 F2080
ECO/DEV POLICY ECO/TAC TAX

B65
REAGAN M.D.,POLITICS, ECONOMICS, AND THE GENERAL WELFARE. USA+45 INDUS ECO/TAC TAX WEALTH...POLICY IDEA/COMP ANTHOL 20. PAGE 110 F2162
NAT/G ECO/DEV R+D ACADEM

B65
WURFEL S.W.,FOREIGN ENTERPRISE IN COLOMBIA. FINAN LABOR NAT/G ECO/TAC TAX REGION 20 COLOMB. PAGE 149 F2944
ECO/UNDEV INT/TRADE JURID CAP/ISM

B65
YOUNG A.N.,CHINA'S WARTIME FINANCE AND INFLATION. ASIA AGRI INDUS NAT/G ECO/TAC CONFER PRICE WAR COST 20. PAGE 150 F2949
FINAN FOR/AID TAX BUDGET

S65
BANOVETZ J.M.,"METROPOLITAN SUBSIDIES: AN APPRAISAL." LEAD GP/REL DISCRIM MUNICH. PAGE 9 F0175
REGION TAX GOV/REL

S65
HUTT W.H.,"KEYNESIAN REVISIONS" SOUTH/AFR ECO/DEV FINAN NAT/G WORKER BUDGET TAX PRICE EQUILIB WEALTH 20 KEYNES/JM. PAGE 64 F1252
ECO/TAC GEN/LAWS LOG

S65
KEE W.S.,"CENTRAL CITY EXPENDITURES AND METROPOLITAN AREAS." PLAN BUDGET ECO/TAC TAX GP/REL WEALTH...CHARTS MUNICH 20. PAGE 70 F1366
LOC/G GOV/COMP NEIGH

B66
CONGRESSIONAL QUARTERLY SERV,FEDERAL ECONOMIC POLICY 1945-1965. USA+45 FINAN NAT/G CHIEF CONSULT TAX...CHARTS 20 PRESIDENT DEBT. PAGE 27 F0526
ECO/TAC BUDGET LEGIS

B66
DILLEY M.R.,BRITISH POLICY IN KENYA COLONY (2ND ED.). AFR INDIA UK LABOR BUDGET TAX ADMIN PARL/PROC GP/REL...BIBLIOG 20 PARLIAMENT. PAGE 33 F0639
COLONIAL REPRESENT SOVEREIGN

B66
DUNCAN O.,METROPOLIS AND REGION (PREPARED FOR RESOURCES FOR THE FUTURE INC., WASHINGTON, D.C.). FINAN INDUS ECO/TAC TAX...CHARTS GOV/COMP MUNICH. PAGE 35 F0677
REGION GEOG

B66
GOODWIN C.D.W.,ECONOMIC INQUIRY IN AUSTRALIA. ECO/DEV ECO/UNDEV ACADEM INT/TRADE RENT TARIFFS TAX PRESS GOV/REL SOCISM 18/20 AUSTRAL. PAGE 49 F0953
ECO/TAC IDEA/COMP BUDGET COLONIAL

B66
KROOSS H.E.,AMERICAN ECONOMIC DEVELOPMENT (2ND ED.). USA+45 USA-45 AGRI INDUS LABOR WORKER INT/TRADE TAX WAR...CHARTS 18/20. PAGE 73 F1443
ECO/TAC NAT/G CAP/ISM ECO/DEV

B66
LEE M.W.,TOWARD ECONOMIC STABILITY. USA+45 BUDGET TAX PRICE EQUILIB INCOME. PAGE 77 F1506
ECO/TAC CONTROL POLICY NAT/G

B66
NEVITT A.A.,HOUSING, TAXATION AND SUBSIDIES; A STUDY OF HOUSING IN THE UNITED KINGDOM. UK FINAN GIVE CONTROL COST INCOME...CHARTS 20. PAGE 98 F1918
PLAN TAX HABITAT RENT

B66
RAPHAEL J.S.,GOVERNMENTAL REGULATION OF BUSINESS. USA+45 LAW CONSTN TAX ADJUD ADMIN EFFICIENCY PWR 20. PAGE 109 F2150
LG/CO GOV/REL CONTROL ECO/DEV

B66
ROBERTSON D.J.,THE BRITISH BALANCE OF PAYMENTS. UK WOR+45 INDUS BUDGET TAX ADJUST...CHARTS ANTHOL 20. PAGE 112 F2213
FINAN BAL/PAY ECO/DEV INT/TRADE

B66
SASTRI K.V.S.,FEDERAL-STATE FISCAL RELATIONS IN INDIA: A STUDY OF THE FINANCE COMMISSION AND TECHNIQUES OF FINANCIAL ADJUSTMENT. INDIA PROVS DELIB/GP GOV/REL FEDERAL...MATH CHARTS 20. PAGE 116 F2283
TAX BUDGET FINAN NAT/G

B66
SOMMERFELD R.M.,TAX REFORM AND THE ALLIANCE FOR PROGRESS. USA+45 ECO/DEV ECO/UNDEV FINAN NAT/G INCOME ORD/FREE WEALTH...STAT CHARTS 20 ALL/PROG. PAGE 124 F2442
TAX INT/ORG L/A+17C FOR/AID

S66
VENTRE F.T.,"LOCAL INITIATIVES IN URBAN INDUSTRIAL DEVELOPMENT." FINAN SERV/IND TOP/EX PLAN BUDGET RENT TAX...GP/COMP MUNICH 20. PAGE 141 F2777
ECO/TAC LOC/G INDUS

B67
AARON H.J.,FINANCING URBAN DEVELOPMENT IN MEXICO CITY: A CASE STUDY OF PROPERTY TAX, LAND USE, HOUSING, AND URBAN PLANNING. LOC/G CREATE EFFICIENCY WEALTH...CHARTS MUNICH 20 MEXIC/AMER. PAGE 2 F0030
PLAN TAX PROB/SOLV

B67
BREAK G.F.,INTERGOVERNMENTAL FISCAL RELATIONS IN THE UNITED STATES. USA+45 USA-45 DELIB/GP PLAN BUDGET TAX GOV/REL CENTRAL...TREND CHARTS MUNICH. PAGE 18 F0345
LOC/G NAT/G PROVS FINAN

B67
DE TORRES J.,FINANCING LOCAL GOVERNMENT. USA+45 USA-45 NAT/G PROVS GIVE ADJUST PWR...TIME/SEQ CHARTS MUNICH 20. PAGE 31 F0606
LOC/G BUDGET TAX TREND

B67
GREEN C.,NEGATIVE TAXES AND THE POVERTY PROBLEM. COST EFFICIENCY INCOME NEW/LIB...METH/CNCPT CHARTS METH/COMP BIBLIOG 20. PAGE 50 F0983
TAX RECEIVE WEALTH PLAN

B67
SCOTT J.C.,ANTITRUST AND TRADE REGULATION TODAY: 1967. USA+45 MARKET LG/CO DELIB/GP LEGIS CAP/ISM INT/TRADE TAX PRICE INGP/REL WEALTH 20 SUPREME/CT. PAGE 118 F2334
NAT/G INDUS CONTROL JURID

L67
DEALEY S.,"MONETARY RECOVERY UNDER FEDERAL TRANSPORTATION STATUTES." USA+45 SEA WORKER TAX PAY ADJUD DEATH GOV/REL OWN HEALTH ORD/FREE 20. PAGE 31 F0609
DIST/IND LAW CONTROL FINAN

L67
HUBBARD P.H.,"MONETARY RECOVERY UNDER THE COPYRIGHT, PATENT, AND TRADEMARK ACTS." PROC/MFG TAX PAY LEGIT ADJUD GOV/REL OWN ORD/FREE 20. PAGE 62 F1228
CREATE LAW CONTROL FINAN

L67
LENT G.E.,"TAX INCENTIVES FOR INVESTMENT IN DEVELOPING COUNTRIES" WOR+45 LAW INDUS PLAN BUDGET TARIFFS ADMIN...METH/COMP 20. PAGE 78 F1526
ECO/UNDEV TAX FINAN ECO/TAC

L67
WILKINSON J.H. JR.,"THE NET OPERATING LOSS DEDUCTION AND RELATED INCOME TAX DEVICES." PROB/SOLV BUDGET PAY GOV/REL ORD/FREE...MATH CHARTS METH 20. PAGE 146 F2886
TAX FINAN LAW ADJUD

S67
"THE SIERRA CLUB, POLITICAL ACTIVITY, AND TAX EXEMPT CHARITABLE STATUS." USA+45 LAW VOL/ASSN TAX PAY ADJUD LOBBY INGP/REL HABITAT 20. PAGE 2 F0027
ELITES GOV/REL FACE/GP ORD/FREE

S67
"IMPORT-EXPORT CLAUSE: A BLANKET PROHIBITION MISAPPLIED." USA+45 INT/TRADE ADJUD INCOME PWR 20. PAGE 2 F0029
CONSTN TAX PROVS LAW

S67
BARTLETT J.L.,"AMERICAN BOND ISSUES IN THE EUROPEAN ECONOMIC COMMUNITY." EUR+WWI LUXEMBOURG USA+45 DIPLOM CONTROL BAL/PAY EEC. PAGE 11 F0201
LAW ECO/TAC FINAN TAX

S67
BRANCO R.,"LAND REFORM* THE ANSWER TO LATIN AMERICA'S AGRICULTURAL DEVELOPMENT?" L/A+17C NAT/G PLAN TEC/DEV BUDGET RENT EFFICIENCY 20. PAGE 18 F0339
ECO/UNDEV AGRI TAX OWN

S67
FERGUSON D.E.,"DETERMINING CAPACITY FOR CAPITAL EXPENDITURES." USA+45 LOC/G BUDGET TAX ADMIN CONTROL...TREND MUNICH 20. PAGE 40 F0784
FINAN PAY COST

S67
FLOYD D.,"FIFTH AMENDMENT RIGHT TO COUNSEL IN FEDERAL INCOME TAX INVESTIGATIONS." USA+45 LAW OP/RES INGP/REL. PAGE 42 F0818
JURID CT/SYS TAX CONSULT

S67
GREEN C.,"SCHEMES FOR TRANSFERRING INCOME TO THE POOR." BUDGET GIVE RECEIVE DEBATE COST INCOME ...SOC/WK METH/COMP. PAGE 50 F0982
TAX WEALTH PLAN ACT/RES

S67
GUPTA S.,"FOREIGN POLICY IN THE 1967 MANIFESTOS." ASIA COM INDIA USA+45 FORCES FOR/AID TAX ATTIT ...DECISION 20. PAGE 52 F1013
IDEA/COMP POL/PAR POLICY DIPLOM

S67
HILDEBRAND G.H.,"SECOND THOUGHTS ON THE NEGATIVE INCOME TAX." PLAN BUDGET ECO/TAC GIVE RECEIVE DEBATE EFFICIENCY INCOME...METH/COMP COSTS. PAGE 59 F1169
TAX WEALTH SOC/WK ACT/RES

S67
LINEBERRY R.L.,"REFORMISM AND PUBLIC POLICIES IN AMERICAN CITIES." USA+45 POL/PAR EX/STRUC LEGIS BUDGET TAX GP/REL...STAT CHARTS MUNICH. PAGE 80 F1573
DECISION POLICY LOC/G

S67
PAI G.A.,"TAXATION AND PLANNING IN INDIA: A BIRDS-EYE VIEW." INDIA ELITES NAT/G LEGIS BUDGET CONTROL LOBBY INCOME...STAT CHARTS 20. PAGE 102 F2015
TAX PLAN WEALTH STRATA

S67
PAULY M.V.,"MIXED PUBLIC AND PRIVATE FINANCING OF EDUCATION." STRATA PAY RECEIVE COST INCOME OPTIMAL METH/COMP. PAGE 104 F2039
SCHOOL PLAN TAX EFFICIENCY

S67
SCOVILLE W.J.,"GOVERNMENT REGULATION AND GROWTH IN THE FRENCH PAPER INDUSTRY DURING THE EIGHTEENTH CENTURY." FRANCE MOD/EUR FINAN CAP/ISM TAX ADMIN CONTROL PRIVIL LAISSEZ...POLICY 18. PAGE 118 F2337
NAT/G PROC/MFG ECO/DEV INGP/REL

S67
SIDDIQ M.M.,"LOCAL GOVERNMENT IN PAKISTAN." PAKISTAN PROB/SOLV TAX COLONIAL GOV/REL MUNICH 20. PAGE 121 F2395
ADMIN LOC/G DELIB/GP BUDGET

B76
TAINE H.A.,THE ANCIENT REGIME. FRANCE STRATA FORCES PARTIC EQUILIB WEALTH CONSERVE POPULISM...GOV/COMP SOC/INTEG 18/19. PAGE 128 F2527
NAT/G GOV/REL TAX REV

C83
BURKE E.,"RESOLUTIONS FOR CONCILIATION WITH AMERICA" (1775), IN E. BURKE, COLLECTED WORKS, VOL. 2." UK USA-45 FORCES INT/TRADE TARIFFS TAX SANCTION PEACE...POLICY 18 PRE/US/AM. PAGE 20 F0387
COLONIAL WAR SOVEREIGN ECO/TAC

B84
MILL J.,ELEMENTS OF POLITICAL ECONOMY. UK LAW ELITES FINAN WORKER ECO/TAC RENT OWN WEALTH ...POLICY GEN/LAWS 19. PAGE 91 F1785
TAX TARIFFS NAT/G INCOME

B88
BENTHAM J.,DEFENCE OF USURY (1787). UK LAW NAT/G TEC/DEV ECO/TAC CONTROL ATTIT...CONCPT IDEA/COMP 18 SMITH/ADAM. PAGE 13 F0255
TAX FINAN ECO/DEV POLICY

B95
SELIGMAN E.R.A.,ESSAYS IN TAXATION. NEW/ZEALND PRUSSIA UK USA-45 MARKET LOC/G CREATE PRICE CONTROL INCOME OWN WEALTH...GOV/COMP METH/COMP 19. PAGE 119 F2349
TAX TARIFFS INDUS NAT/G

B96
SMITH A.,LECTURES ON JUSTICE, POLICE, REVENUE AND ARMS (1763). UK LAW FAM FORCES TARIFFS AGREE COERCE INCOME OWN WEALTH LAISSEZ...GEN/LAWS 17/18. PAGE 123 F2429
DIPLOM JURID OLD/LIB TAX

TAYLOR A.M. F2809

TAYLOR F.Y. F1475

TAYLOR P.E. F2540

TAYLOR/AJP....A.J.P. TAYLOR

TAYLOR/Z....PRESIDENT ZACHARY TAYLOR

TCHAD....SEE CHAD

TEC/DEV....DEVELOPMENT OF TECHNIQUES

B
BRITISH COMMONWEALTH BUR AGRI,WORLD AGRICULTURAL ECONOMICS AND RURAL SOCIOLOGY ABSTRACTS. NAT/G OP/RES PLAN TEC/DEV LEAD PRODUC...GEOG MGT NAT/COMP 20. PAGE 18 F0354
BIBLIOG/A AGRI SOC WORKER

N
THE MIDDLE EAST AND NORTH AFRICA. AFR ISLAM CULTURE ECO/UNDEV AGRI NAT/G TEC/DEV FOR/AID INT/TRADE EDU/PROP...CHARTS 20. PAGE 1 F0008
INDEX INDUS FINAN STAT

N
MINISTRY OF OVERSEAS DEVELOPME,TECHNICAL CO-OPERATION -- A BIBLIOGRAPHY. UK LAW SOCIETY DIPLOM ECO/TAC FOR/AID...STAT 20 CMN/WLTH. PAGE 92 F1803
BIBLIOG TEC/DEV ECO/DEV NAT/G

N
UNESCO,INTERNATIONAL BIBLIOGRAPHY OF ECONOMICS (VOLUMES 1-8). WOR+45 AGRI INDUS LABOR PLAN TEC/DEV 20. PAGE 132 F2607
BIBLIOG ECO/DEV ECO/UNDEV

B00
LIST F.,NATIONAL SYSTEM OF POLITICAL ECONOMY. ECO/DEV AGRI EXTR/IND FINAN INDUS TEC/DEV ECO/TAC ATTIT WEALTH...TREND GEN/LAWS FOR/TRADE 19. PAGE 81 F1581
MOD/EUR MARKET

B04
VEBLEN T.B.,THE THEORY OF BUSINESS ENTERPRISE. USA-45 FINAN WORKER ECO/TAC PRICE GP/REL COST ...POLICY 19/20. PAGE 141 F2770
TEC/DEV GEN/LAWS SOCIETY WEALTH

B12
HOBSON J.A.,THE EVOLUTION OF MODERN CAPITALISM. MOD/EUR UK STRATA ECO/DEV INDUS INCOME UTIL WEALTH ...SOC GEN/LAWS 7/20. PAGE 60 F1184
CAP/ISM WORKER TEC/DEV TIME/SEQ

B14
DE BLOCH J.,THE FUTURE OF WAR IN ITS TECHNICAL, ECONOMIC, AND POLITICAL RELATIONS (1899). MOD/EUR TEC/DEV BUDGET INT/TRADE DETER GUERRILLA WEAPON
WAR BAL/PWR PREDICT

COST PEACE 20. PAGE 31 F0596 — FORCES

B14
HOBSON J.A.,WORK AND WEALTH. CULTURE FINAN INDUS WORKER TEC/DEV ECO/TAC GIVE PAY PRICE COST PRODUC UTIL. PAGE 60 F1185 — WEALTH INCOME GEN/LAWS

B14
VEBLEN T.,THE INSTINCT OF WORKMANSHIP. UNIV SOCIETY ECO/DEV ECO/UNDEV CREATE TEC/DEV ECO/TAC EDU/PROP ROUTINE PERSON...HUM CONCPT TIME/SEQ GEN/LAWS. PAGE 140 F2768 — DRIVE SKILL

B15
VEBLEN T.,IMPERIAL GERMANY AND THE INDUSTRIAL REVOLUTION. GERMANY MOD/EUR UK USA-45 NAT/G TEC/DEV CAP/ISM...MAJORIT NAT/COMP 19/20 CHINJAP. PAGE 141 F2769 — ECO/DEV INDUS TECHNIC BAL/PWR

B18
MARX K.,CAPITAL. FUT MOD/EUR STRATA DIST/IND PROC/MFG TEC/DEV WEALTH...MARXIST WORK 19. PAGE 86 F1688 — ECO/DEV CAP/ISM SOCISM

N19
HAGEN E.E.,AN ANALYTICAL MODEL OF THE TRANSITION TO ECONOMIC GROWTH (PAMPHLET). WOR+45 WOR-45 SOCIETY STRATA FINAN NAT/G CONTROL PARTIC PRODUC...PHIL/SCI BIBLIOG 17/20. PAGE 53 F1033 — SIMUL ECO/DEV METH TEC/DEV

N19
STALEY E.,SCIENTIFIC RESEARCH AND PROGRESS IN NEWLY DEVELOPING COUNTRIES (PAMPHLET). AFR ASIA L/A+17C CONSULT DIPLOM...METH/COMP 20. PAGE 125 F2463 — ECO/UNDEV ACT/RES FOR/AID TEC/DEV

B26
TAWNEY R.H.,RELIGION AND THE RISE OF CAPITALISM. UK CULTURE NAT/G TEC/DEV OWN LAISSEZ...POLICY SOC TIME/SEQ 16/19. PAGE 129 F2537 — SECT WEALTH INDUS CAP/ISM

B27
SIEGFRIED A.,AMERICA COMES OF AGE: A FRENCH ANALYSIS (TRANS. BY H.H. HEMMING AND DORIS HEMMING). FRANCE UK POL/PAR WORKER TEC/DEV DIPLOM REGION RACE/REL ADJUST PRODUC HEREDITY...TIME/SEQ GP/COMP SOC/INTEG 20 DEMOCRAT REPUBLICAN KKK. PAGE 122 F2398 — USA-45 CULTURE ECO/DEV SOC

B28
CROS L.,AFRIQUE FRANCAISE POUR TOUS. EUR+WWI FRANCE PLAN TEC/DEV ATTIT 20. PAGE 29 F0556 — COLONIAL DOMIN ECO/TAC AFR

B30
HAWTREY R.G.,ECONOMIC ASPECTS OF SOVEREIGNTY. UNIV WOR+45 WOR-45 ECO/DEV ECO/UNDEV AGRI COM/IND INDUS MARKET NAT/G TEC/DEV ECO/TAC EDU/PROP COERCE ATTIT KNOWL WEALTH...CONCPT CON/ANAL GEN/LAWS 20. PAGE 57 F1118 — FORCES PWR SOVEREIGN WAR

B38
HARPER S.N.,THE GOVERNMENT OF THE SOVIET UNION. COM USSR LAW CONSTN ECO/DEV PLAN TEC/DEV DIPLOM INT/TRADE ADMIN REV NAT/LISM...POLICY 20. PAGE 55 F1085 — MARXISM NAT/G LEAD POL/PAR

B39
ROBBINS L.,ECONOMIC CAUSES OF WAR. WOR-45 ECO/DEV ECO/UNDEV INT/ORG NAT/G TEC/DEV DIPLOM DOMIN COLONIAL ATTIT DRIVE PWR WEALTH...POLICY CONCPT OBS SAMP TREND CON/ANAL GEN/LAWS MARX/KARL 20. PAGE 112 F2203 — COERCE ECO/TAC WAR

B39
STALEY E.,WORLD ECONOMY IN TRANSITION. WOR-45 SOCIETY INT/ORG PROF/ORG ECO/TAC ATTIT WEALTH ...METH/CNCPT TREND GEN/LAWS 20. PAGE 125 F2465 — TEC/DEV INT/TRADE

B40
BLAISDELL D.C.,GOVERNMENT AND AGRICULTURE; THE GROWTH OF FEDERAL FARM AID. USA-45 MARKET PLAN PROB/SOLV TEC/DEV ECO/TAC GOV/REL ADJUST ATTIT ...CHARTS 20 DEPT/AGRI. PAGE 15 F0296 — NAT/G GIVE AGRI DELIB/GP

B40
MEEK C.K.,EUROPE AND WEST AFRICA. AFR EUR+WWI EXTR/IND DIPLOM INT/TRADE EDU/PROP GP/REL...SOC 20. PAGE 89 F1743 — CULTURE TEC/DEV ECO/UNDEV COLONIAL

B41
LESTER R.A.,ECONOMICS OF LABOR. UK USA-45 TEC/DEV BARGAIN PAY INGP/REL INCOME...MGT 19/20. PAGE 78 F1532 — LABOR ECO/DEV INDUS WORKER

B41
SLICHTER S.H.,UNION POLICIES AND INDUSTRIAL MANAGEMENT. USA-45 INDUS TEC/DEV PAY GP/REL INGP/REL COST EFFICIENCY PRODUC...POLICY 20. PAGE 123 F2420 — BARGAIN LABOR MGT WORKER

B47
WHITEHEAD T.N.,LEADERSHIP IN A FREE SOCIETY; A STUDY IN HUMAN RELATIONS BASED ON AN ANALYSIS OF PRESENT-DAY INDUSTRIAL CIVILIZATION. WOR-45 STRUCT R+D LABOR LG/CO SML/CO WORKER PLAN PROB/SOLV TEC/DEV DRIVE...MGT 20. PAGE 146 F2872 — INDUS LEAD ORD/FREE SOCIETY

B48
GRAHAM F.D.,THE THEORY OF INTERNATIONAL VALUES. FUT WOR+45 WOR-45 ECO/DEV FINAN INT/ORG PLAN TEC/DEV CAP/ISM DIPLOM ECO/TAC TARIFFS ROUTINE BAL/PAY DRIVE PWR WEALTH SOCISM...POLICY STAT HYPO/EXP GEN/LAWS 20. PAGE 50 F0971 — NEW/IDEA INT/TRADE

B49
SHISTER J.,ECONOMICS OF THE LABOR MARKET. LOC/G NAT/G WORKER TEC/DEV BARGAIN PAY PRICE EXEC GP/REL INCOME...MGT T 20. PAGE 121 F2381 — MARKET LABOR INDUS

S49
SHEPHARD H.A.,"DEMOCRATIC CONTROL IN A LABOR UNION." FUT CONSTN STRUCT TEC/DEV LEAD PARTIC RACE/REL CENTRAL DRIVE HABITAT RECORD. PAGE 120 F2374 — LABOR MAJORIT CONTROL PWR

B50
HARTLAND P.C.,BALANCE OF INTERREGIONAL PAYMENTS OF NEW ENGLAND. USA+45 TEC/DEV ECO/TAC LEGIT ROUTINE BAL/PAY PROFIT 20 NEW/ENGLND FED/RESERV. PAGE 56 F1102 — ECO/DEV FINAN REGION PLAN

B50
US DEPARTMENT OF STATE,POINT FOUR: COOPERATIVE PROGRAM FOR AID IN THE DEVELOPMENT OF ECONOMICALLY UNDERDEVELOPED AREAS. WOR+45 AGRI INDUS INT/ORG PLAN TEC/DEV DIPLOM EDU/PROP ADMIN PEACE PRODUC WEALTH 20 CONGRESS UN. PAGE 135 F2671 — ECO/UNDEV FOR/AID FINAN INT/TRADE

B52
ASHWORTH W.,A SHORT HISTORY OF THE INTERNATIONAL ECONOMY 1850-1950. WOR+45 WOR-45 AGRI FINAN INDUS MARKET LABOR ECO/TAC...CONCPT STAT HIST/WRIT FOR/TRADE ILO 19/20. PAGE 7 F0131 — ECO/DEV TEC/DEV INT/TRADE

L52
HUTH A.G.,"COMMUNICATION AND ECONOMIC DEVELOPMENT." FUT WOR+45 CULTURE SOCIETY INT/ORG PLAN TEC/DEV EDU/PROP DRIVE KNOWL WEALTH...POLICY CONCPT RECORD STERTYP GEN/LAWS COMMUN TOT/POP UNESCO 20 UN CMN/WLTH. PAGE 64 F1250 — ECO/UNDEV

B53
DAHL R.A.,POLITICS, ECONOMICS AND WELFARE: PLANNING AND POLITICOECONOMIC SYSTEMS RESOLVED INTO BASIC SOCIAL PROCESSES. WOR+45 WOR-45 ECO/DEV ECO/UNDEV R+D CREATE PLAN TEC/DEV EDU/PROP HEALTH WEALTH ...SOC SELF/OBS TREND CHARTS GEN/METH 20. PAGE 29 F0571 — ECO/TAC PHIL/SCI

B53
DAHL R.A.,POLITICS, ECONOMICS, AND WELFARE. TEC/DEV BARGAIN ECO/TAC RECEIVE PRICE CONTROL LEAD INGP/REL ...POLICY GEN/LAWS. PAGE 29 F0572 — SOCIETY GIVE

B53
FRANKEL S.H.,THE ECONOMIC IMPACT ON UNDERDEVELOPED SOCIETIES: ESSAYS ON INTERNATIONAL INVESTMENT AND SOCIAL CHANGE. AFR WOR+45 ECO/DEV FINAN INDUS NAT/G ACT/RES TEC/DEV COLONIAL ATTIT...CONCPT OBS TREND 20. PAGE 43 F0845 — ECO/UNDEV FOR/AID INT/TRADE

B53
MIT CENTER INTERNATIONAL STU,BIBLIOGRAPHY OF THE ECONOMIC AND POLITICAL DEVELOPMENT OF INDONESIA. INDONESIA STRUCT NAT/G COLONIAL LEAD...STAT 20. PAGE 92 F1805 — BIBLIOG ECO/UNDEV TEC/DEV S/ASIA

B53
NEISSER H.,NATIONAL INCOMES AND INTERNATIONAL TRADE. FRANCE GERMANY SWEDEN UK USA-45 EXTR/IND FINAN INDUS TEC/DEV PRICE BAL/PAY EQUILIB INCOME WEALTH...CHARTS METH 19 CHINJAP. PAGE 97 F1908 — INT/TRADE PRODUC MARKET CON/ANAL

B53
ROBINSON E.A.G.,THE STRUCTURE OF COMPETITIVE INDUSTRY. UK ECO/DEV DIST/IND MARKET TEC/DEV DIPLOM EDU/PROP ADMIN EFFICIENCY WEALTH...MGT 19/20. PAGE 113 F2217 — INDUS PRODUC WORKER OPTIMAL

B53
WOYTINSKY W.S.,WORLD POPULATION AND PRODUCTION: TRENDS AND OUTLOOK. FUT WOR+45 WOR-45 CULTURE SOCIETY ECO/DEV AGRI INDUS TEC/DEV EDU/PROP SKILL WEALTH...SOC TREND. PAGE 149 F2928 — ECO/UNDEV METH/CNCPT GEOG PERSON

S53
LINCOLN G.,"FACTORS DETERMINING ARMS AID." COM FUT USA+45 USSR WOR+45 ECO/DEV NAT/G CONSULT PLAN TEC/DEV DIPLOM DOMIN EDU/PROP PERCEPT PWR ...DECISION CONCPT TREND MARX/KARL 20. PAGE 80 F1566 — FORCES POLICY BAL/PWR FOR/AID

B54
HAYEK FA V.O.N.,CAPITALISM AND THE HISTORIANS. MOD/EUR TEC/DEV GP/REL WEALTH...HIST/WRIT ANTHOL 19. PAGE 57 F1124 — CAP/ISM LABOR STRATA ECO/TAC

B54
LOCKLIN D.P.,ECONOMICS OF TRANSPORTATION (4TH ED.). USA+45 USA-45 SEA AIR LAW FINAN LG/CO EX/STRUC ADMIN CONTROL...STAT CHARTS 19/20 RAILROAD PUB/TRANS. PAGE 81 F1592 — ECO/DEV DIST/IND ECO/TAC TEC/DEV

B54
MOSK S.A.,INDUSTRIAL REVOLUTION IN MEXICO. MARKET LABOR CREATE CAP/ISM ADMIN ATTIT SOCISM...POLICY 20 MEXIC/AMER. PAGE 94 F1843 — INDUS TEC/DEV ECO/UNDEV NAT/G

B54
WASHBURNE N.F.,INTERPRETING SOCIAL CHANGE IN AMERICA. USA+45 STRATA FAM NAT/G SECT OP/RES ECO/TAC EDU/PROP HABITAT...SOC TIME/SEQ TREND 20 — CULTURE STRUCT CREATE

BUREAUCRCY. PAGE 143 F2826 — TEC/DEV

B54
WILLIAMSON H.F.,ECONOMIC DEVELOPMENT - PRINCIPLES AND PATTERNS. INDIA KOREA CULTURE ECO/DEV ECO/UNDEV TEC/DEV...CENSUS NAT/COMP FOR/TRADE 20 CHINJAP MEXIC/AMER RESOURCE/N. PAGE 147 F2895 — ECO/TAC GEOG LABOR

L54
OPLER M.E.,"SOCIAL ASPECTS OF TECHNICAL ASSISTANCE IN OPERATION." WOR+45 VOL/ASSN CREATE PLAN TEC/DEV EDU/PROP ALL/VALS...METH/CNCPT OBS RECORD TREND UN 20. PAGE 101 F1993 — INT/ORG CONSULT FOR/AID

B55
BUCHANAN N.S.,APPROACHES TO ECONOMIC DEVELOPMENT. FUT USA+45 WOR+45 STRATA ECO/DEV INT/ORG NAT/G TEC/DEV DIPLOM FOR/AID ATTIT KNOWL PWR WEALTH ...RELATIV METH/CNCPT SELF/OBS TREND CON/ANAL STERTYP GEN/LAWS FOR/TRADE COMMUN 20. PAGE 20 F0380 — ECO/UNDEV ECO/TAC INT/TRADE

B55
COLE G.D.H.,STUDIES IN CLASS STRUCTURE. UK NAT/G WORKER TEC/DEV EDU/PROP...CLASSIF CHARTS 20. PAGE 26 F0501 — STRUCT STRATA ELITES CONCPT

B55
GEORGE H.,PROGRESS AND POVERTY (1880). STRATA STRUCT INDUS TEC/DEV CAP/ISM EQUILIB INCOME OWN UTOPIA...WELF/ST CONCPT NEW/IDEA 19. PAGE 47 F0915 — ECO/DEV ECO/TAC TAX WEALTH

B55
JONES T.B.,A BIBLIOGRAPHY ON SOUTH AMERICAN ECONOMIC AFFAIRS: ARTICLES IN NINETEENTH CENTURY PERIODICALS (PAMPHLET). AGRI COM/IND DIST/IND EXTR/IND FINAN INDUS LABOR NAT/G 19. PAGE 68 F1340 — BIBLIOG ECO/UNDEV L/A+17C TEC/DEV

B55
US OFFICE OF THE PRESIDENT,REPORT TO CONGRESS ON THE MUTUAL SECURITY PROGRAM FOR THE SIX MONTHS ENDED JUNE 30, 1955. ECO/DEV INT/ORG NAT/G CREATE TEC/DEV BAL/PWR ECO/TAC AGREE DETER COST ORD/FREE 20 DEPT/STATE DEPT/DEFEN. PAGE 138 F2722 — DIPLOM FORCES PLAN FOR/AID

L55
KISER M.,"ORGANIZATION OF AMERICAN STATES." L/A+17C USA+45 ECO/UNDEV INT/ORG NAT/G PLAN TEC/DEV DIPLOM ECO/TAC INT/TRADE EDU/PROP ADMIN ALL/VALS...POLICY MGT RECORD ORG/CHARTS OAS COMMUN 20. PAGE 71 F1401 — VOL/ASSN ECO/DEV REGION

C55
ADAMS G.P. JR.,"COMPETITIVE ECONOMIC SYSTEMS." WOR+45 WOR-45 PWR...BIBLIOG/A 20. PAGE 2 F0038 — METH/COMP ECO/TAC TEC/DEV DIPLOM

B56
ISARD W.,LOCATION AND SPACE-ECONOMY: GENERAL THEORY RELATING TO INDUSTRIAL LOCATION, MARKET AREAS, LAND USE, TRADE... UNIV DIST/IND MARKET LG/CO SML/CO TEC/DEV GP/REL EQUILIB HABITAT...NEW/IDEA MATH CHARTS 20. PAGE 66 F1290 — GEN/LAWS GEOG INDUS REGION

B56
KNORR K.E.,RUBLE DIPLOMACY: CHALLENGE TO AMERICAN FOREIGN AID(PAMPHLET). AFR CHINA/COM USA+45 USSR PLAN TEC/DEV CAP/ISM INT/TRADE DOMIN EDU/PROP CONTROL LEAD 20. PAGE 72 F1413 — ECO/UNDEV COM DIPLOM FOR/AID

B56
UN HEADQUARTERS LIBRARY,BIBLIOGRAPHY OF INDUSTRIALIZATION IN UNDERDEVELOPED COUNTRIES (BIBLIOGRAPHICAL SERIES NO. 6). WOR+45 R+D ACADEM INT/ORG NAT/G. PAGE 132 F2602 — BIBLIOG ECO/UNDEV TEC/DEV

B56
UNITED NATIONS,BIBLIOGRAPHY ON INDUSTRIALIZATION IN UNDER-DEVELOPED COUNTRIES. WOR+45 R+D INT/ORG NAT/G FOR/AID ADMIN LEAD 20 UN. PAGE 132 F2612 — BIBLIOG ECO/UNDEV INDUS TEC/DEV

B56
US DEPARTMENT OF STATE,ECONOMIC PROBLEMS OF UNDERDEVELOPED AREAS (PAMPHLET). AFR ASIA ISLAM L/A+17C AGRI FINAN INDUS INT/ORG LABOR INT/TRADE ...PSY SOC 20. PAGE 136 F2673 — BIBLIOG ECO/UNDEV TEC/DEV R+D

B56
US OFFICE OF THE PRESIDENT,REPORT TO CONGRESS ON THE MUTUAL SECURITY PROGRAM FOR THE SIX MONTHS ENDED DECEMBER 31, 1955. ASIA USSR ECO/DEV ECO/UNDEV INT/ORG CREATE TEC/DEV BAL/PWR ECO/TAC AGREE DETER COST ORD/FREE 20 DEPT/STATE DEPT/DEFEN EISNHWR/DD. PAGE 138 F2723 — DIPLOM FORCES PLAN FOR/AID

B56
VAKIL C.N.,PLANNING FOR AN EXPANDING ECONOMY. INDIA TAX COST 20. PAGE 140 F2759 — TEC/DEV LABOR BUDGET CAP/ISM

S56
GORDON L.,"THE ORGANIZATION FOR EUROPEAN ECONOMIC COOPERATION." EUR+WWI INDUS INT/ORG NAT/G CONSULT DELIB/GP ACT/RES CREATE PLAN TEC/DEV EDU/PROP LEGIT WEALTH OEEC 20. PAGE 49 F0956 — VOL/ASSN ECO/DEV

B57
BARAN P.A.,THE POLITICAL ECONOMY OF GROWTH. MOD/EUR USA+45 USA-45 TEC/DEV TAX SOCISM...MGT CONCPT GOV/COMP. PAGE 9 F0178 — CAP/ISM CONTROL ECO/UNDEV FINAN

B57
GOLD N.L.,REGIONAL ECONOMIC DEVELOPMENT AND NUCLEAR POWER IN INDIA. FUT INDIA FINAN FOR/AID INT/TRADE BAL/PAY EFFICIENCY OPTIMAL PRODUC WEALTH...PREDICT 20. PAGE 48 F0934 — ECO/UNDEV TEC/DEV NUC/PWR INDUS

B57
HALD M.,A SELECTED BIBLIOGRAPHY ON ECONOMIC DEVELOPMENT AND FOREIGN AID. INT/ORG PROB/SOLV ...SOC 20. PAGE 53 F1040 — BIBLIOG ECO/UNDEV TEC/DEV FOR/AID

B57
LAVES W.H.C.,UNESCO. FUT WOR+45 NAT/G CONSULT DELIB/GP TEC/DEV ECO/TAC EDU/PROP PEACE ORD/FREE ...CONCPT TIME/SEQ TREND UNESCO VAL/FREE 20. PAGE 76 F1491 — INT/ORG KNOWL

B57
LEIBENSTEIN H.,ECONOMIC BACKWARDNESS AND ECONOMIC GROWTH. WOR+45 SOCIETY AGRI INDUS TEC/DEV CAP/ISM FOR/AID COST DEMAND WEALTH...CHARTS IDEA/COMP 20. PAGE 77 F1513 — ECO/UNDEV ECO/TAC PRODUC POLICY

B57
LENIN V.I.,THE DEVELOPMENT OF CAPITALISM IN RUSSIA. MOD/EUR USSR AGRI MARKET POL/PAR TEC/DEV...CONCPT 19/20. PAGE 78 F1521 — COM INDUS CAP/ISM

B57
PALACIOS A.L.,PETROLEO, MONOPOLIOS, Y LATIFUNDIOS. L/A+17C EXTR/IND NAT/G TEC/DEV ECO/TAC CONTROL PRODUC 20 ARGEN MONOPOLY RESOURCE/N. PAGE 103 F2017 — ECO/UNDEV NAT/LISM INDUS AGRI

B57
UDY S.H. JR.,THE ORGANIZATION OF PRODUCTION IN NONINDUSTRIAL CULTURE. VOL/ASSN DELIB/GP TEC/DEV ...CHARTS BIBLIOG. PAGE 132 F2598 — METH/COMP ECO/UNDEV PRODUC ADMIN

B57
WARRINER D.,LAND REFORM AND DEVELOPMENT IN THE MIDDLE EAST: A STUDY OF EGYPT, SYRIA AND IRAQ. IRAQ ISLAM SYRIA UAR AGRI DIST/IND PLAN TEC/DEV DOMIN REV ATTIT WEALTH...SOC METH/CNCPT STAT OBS RECORD HIST/WRIT TREND GEN/LAWS FAO 20. PAGE 143 F2825 — ECO/UNDEV CONCPT

L57
MASS. INST. TECH.,"THE CENTER FOR INTERNATIONAL STUDIES." AFR ASIA COM EUR+WWI ISLAM L/A+17C S/ASIA USA+45 USA-45 DIST/IND CONSULT FORCES ACT/RES TEC/DEV DIPLOM REV ATTIT WEALTH...CONCPT FOR/TRADE 20. PAGE 87 F1702 — R+D ECO/UNDEV

S57
HOAG M.W.,"ECONOMIC PROBLEMS OF ALLIANCE." AFR COM EUR+WWI WOR+45 ECO/DEV ECO/UNDEV NAT/G VOL/ASSN FORCES PLAN TEC/DEV DIPLOM COERCE ORD/FREE PWR WEALTH...DECISION GEN/LAWS NATO TERR/GP. PAGE 60 F1182 — INT/ORG ECO/TAC

B58
ATOMIC INDUSTRIAL FORUM,MANAGEMENT AND ATOMIC ENERGY. WOR+45 SEA LAW MARKET NAT/G TEC/DEV INSPECT INT/TRADE CONFER PEACE HEALTH...ANTHOL 20. PAGE 7 F0136 — NUC/PWR INDUS MGT ECO/TAC

B58
COLM G.,THE ECONOMY OF THE AMERICAN PEOPLE: PROGRESS, PROBLEMS, PROSPECTS. USA+45 INDUS MARKET LABOR TEC/DEV INCOME 20. PAGE 26 F0509 — WEALTH PRODUC CAP/ISM MGT

B58
CROWE S.,THE LANDSCAPE OF POWER. UK CULTURE SERV/IND NAT/G CONSULT PARTIC NUC/PWR LEISURE...SOC EXHIBIT 20. PAGE 29 F0559 — HABITAT TEC/DEV PLAN CONTROL

B58
EHRHARD J.,LE DESTIN DU COLONIALISME. AFR FRANCE ECO/UNDEV AGRI FINAN MARKET CREATE PLAN TEC/DEV BUDGET DIPLOM PRICE 20. PAGE 36 F0710 — COLONIAL FOR/AID INT/TRADE INDUS

B58
HANCE W.A.,AFRICAN ECONOMIC DEVELOPMENT. AGRI DIST/IND INDUS R+D ACT/RES PLAN CAP/ISM FOR/AID ...GOV/COMP BIBLIOG 20. PAGE 54 F1058 — AFR ECO/UNDEV PROB/SOLV TEC/DEV

B58
HIRSCHMAN A.O.,STRATEGY OF ECONOMIC DEVELOPMENT. WOR+45 WOR-45 CULTURE ECO/DEV NAT/G PLAN TEC/DEV INT/TRADE BAL/PAY ATTIT DRIVE RIGID/FLEX WEALTH ...CONCPT METH/CNCPT OBS CHARTS SIMUL GEN/LAWS TOT/POP VAL/FREE. PAGE 60 F1176 — ECO/UNDEV ECO/TAC CAP/ISM

B58
MIKESELL R.F.,FINANCING FREE WORLD TRADE WITH THE SINO-SOVIET BLOC. CHINA/COM COM USSR WOR+45 ECO/DEV AGRI DIST/IND EXTR/IND FINAN INDUS MARKET PROC/MFG NAT/G PLAN TEC/DEV ECO/TAC...CHARTS METH/GP EEC FOR/TRADE 20. PAGE 91 F1780 — STAT BAL/PAY

B58
NICULESCU B.,COLONIAL PLANNING: A COMPARATIVE STUDY. AFR AGRI LOC/G NAT/G DELIB/GP COLONIAL MUNICH 20. PAGE 98 F1927 — PLAN ECO/UNDEV TEC/DEV NAT/COMP

B58
PALYI M.,MANAGED MONEY AT THE CROSSROADS: THE — FINAN

EUROPEAN EXPERIENCE. AFR WOR+45 WOR-45 TEC/DEV DIPLOM INT/TRADE DEMAND WEALTH...CHARTS BIBLIOG 19/20 EUROPE SILVER. PAGE 103 F2022
ECO/TAC ECO/DEV PRODUC

B58
POLLOCK F.,AUTOMATION: A STUDY OF ITS ECONOMIC AND SOCIAL CONSEQUENCES. FUT USA+45 USA-45 SOCIETY ECO/DEV LABOR ACT/RES PLAN ECO/TAC AUTOMAT ROUTINE ALL/VALS...STAT TREND COMPUT/IR CHARTS SOC/EXP WORK 20. PAGE 107 F2099
TEC/DEV SOC CAP/ISM

B58
SILOW R.A.,THE POTENTIAL CONTRIBUTION OF ATOMIC ENERGY TO DEVELOPMENT IN AGRICULTURE AND RELATED INDUSTRIES (PAMPHLET). WOR+45 R+D TEC/DEV EFFICIENCY 20 UN. PAGE 122 F2403
NUC/PWR ECO/UNDEV AGRI

B58
US OPERATIONS MISSION TO VIET,BUILDING ECONOMIC STRENGTH (PAMPHLET). USA+45 VIETNAM/S INDUS TEC/DEV BUDGET ADMIN EATING HEALTH...STAT 20. PAGE 138 F2725
FOR/AID ECO/UNDEV AGRI EDU/PROP

L58
MASON E.S.,"ECONOMIC PLANNING IN UNDERDEVELOPED AREAS." FUT WOR+45 PLAN TEC/DEV EDU/PROP ATTIT RIGID/FLEX KNOWL...SOC CONCPT GEN/LAWS TOT/POP 20. PAGE 87 F1697
NAT/G ECO/UNDEV

B59
ALLEN R.L.,SOVIET INFLUENCE IN LATIN AMERICA. ECO/UNDEV FINAN PROC/MFG NAT/G TEC/DEV EDU/PROP EXEC ROUTINE ATTIT DRIVE PERSON ALL/VALS PWR...STAT CHARTS WORK FOR/TRADE 20. PAGE 4 F0071
L/A+17C ECO/TAC INT/TRADE USSR

B59
BARBASH J.,UNIONS AND UNION LEADERSHIP. NAT/G WORKER TEC/DEV ECO/TAC PARTIC GP/REL RACE/REL ORD/FREE CLASSIF. PAGE 10 F0183
LABOR VOL/ASSN CAP/ISM LEAD

B59
FELS R.,AMERICAN BUSINESS CYCLES 1865-1897. USA+45 ECO/DEV LG/CO SML/CO PROB/SOLV TEC/DEV CAP/ISM INT/TRADE DEMAND...POLICY CHARTS METH 19 DEPRESSION. PAGE 40 F0782
FINAN INDUS TREND ECO/TAC

B59
LI CHOH-MING,ECONOMIC DEVELOPMENT OF COMMUNIST CHINA. ASIA CHINA/COM AGRI FINAN TAX INCOME MARXISM ...MGT 20. PAGE 80 F1557
ECO/UNDEV INDUS ORD/FREE TEC/DEV

B59
MEYER A.J.,MIDDLE EASTERN CAPITALISM: NINE ESSAYS. ISLAM CULTURE ECO/UNDEV INDUS MARKET NAT/G PLAN ATTIT RIGID/FLEX...STAT OBS TREND GEN/LAWS. PAGE 90 F1767
TEC/DEV ECO/TAC ANTHOL

B59
NORTON P.L.,URBAN PROBLEMS AND TECHNIQUES. AIR AGRI INDUS MARKET TEC/DEV BUDGET LEISURE ALL/VALS ...ANTHOL MUNICH 20 URBAN/RNWL. PAGE 99 F1936
PLAN LOC/G HABITAT

B59
NOVE A.,COMMUNIST ECONOMIC STRATEGY: SOVIET GROWTH AND CAPABILITIES. USSR AGRI LABOR PLAN TEC/DEV CAP/ISM INT/TRADE EFFICIENCY MARXISM 20 THIRD/WRLD. PAGE 99 F1941
FOR/AID ECO/TAC DIPLOM INDUS

B59
STERNBERG F.,THE MILITARY AND INDUSTRIAL REVOLUTION OF OUR TIME. USA+45 USSR WOR+45 WORKER COMPUTER PLAN TEC/DEV NUC/PWR GP/REL...POLICY NAT/COMP 20. PAGE 126 F2481
DIPLOM FORCES INDUS CIVMIL/REL

B59
US GENERAL ACCOUNTING OFFICE,EXAM OF ECONOMIC AND TECHNICAL ASSISTANCE PROGRAM FOR INDIA INT'NAT'L COOP ADMIN REPORT TO CONGRESS 1955-1958. INDIA USA+45 ECO/UNDEV FINAN PLAN DIPLOM COST UTIL WEALTH ...CHARTS 20 CONGRESS AID. PAGE 136 F2679
FOR/AID EFFICIENCY ECO/TAC TEC/DEV

L59
BEGUIN B.,"ILO AND THE TRIPARTITE SYSTEM." EUR+WWI WOR+45 WOR-45 CONSTN ECO/DEV ECO/UNDEV INDUS INT/ORG NAT/G VOL/ASSN DELIB/GP PLAN TEC/DEV LEGIT ORD/FREE WEALTH...CONCPT TIME/SEQ WORK ILO 20. PAGE 12 F0228
LABOR

L59
WURFEL D.,"FOREIGN AID AND SOCIAL REFORM IN POLITICAL DEVELOPMENT" (BMR)" PHILIPPINE USA+45 WOR+45 SOCIETY POL/PAR ACT/RES TEC/DEV DIPLOM 20. PAGE 149 F2943
FOR/AID PROB/SOLV ECO/TAC ECO/UNDEV

S59
HOFFMAN P.,"OPERATION BREAKTHROUGH." AFR S/ASIA STRUCT INDUS CONSULT TEC/DEV ATTIT RIGID/FLEX SKILL WEALTH...TECHNIC CONCPT STYLE RECORD CHARTS ORG/CHARTS GEN/METH VAL/FREE 20. PAGE 61 F1190
ECO/UNDEV EDU/PROP FOR/AID

S59
STREETEN P.,"UNBALANCED GROWTH" UK ECO/DEV AGRI MARKET TEC/DEV CAP/ISM ECO/TAC FOR/AID INT/TRADE DEMAND ORD/FREE...CONCPT 20. PAGE 127 F2502
IDEA/COMP FINAN PRODUC EQUILIB

S59
TIPTON J.B.,"PARTICIPATION OF THE UNITED STATES IN THE INTERNATIONAL LABOR ORGANIZATION." USA+45 LAW STRUCT ECO/DEV ECO/UNDEV INDUS TEC/DEV ECO/TAC ADMIN PERCEPT ORD/FRFE SKILL...STAT HIST/WRIT GEN/METH ILO WORK 20. PAGE 131 F2577
LABOR INT/ORG

C59
KURIHARA K.L.,"THE KEYNESIAN THEORY OF ECONOMIC DEVELOPMENT." WOR+45 WOR-45 PLAN OPTIMAL PRODUC ...CONCPT BIBLIOG 20. PAGE 74 F1451
ECO/DEV ECO/UNDEV OP/RES TEC/DEV

B60
ALLEN R.L.,SOVIET ECONOMIC WARFARE. USSR FINAN INDUS NAT/G PLAN TEC/DEV FOR/AID DETER WEALTH ...TREND GEN/LAWS FOR/TRADE 20. PAGE 4 F0072
COM ECO/TAC

B60
BILLERBECK K.,SOVIET BLOC FOREIGN AID TO UNDERDEVELOPED COUNTRIES. COM FUT USSR FINAN FORCES TEC/DEV DIPLOM INT/TRADE EDU/PROP NUC/PWR...TREND 20. PAGE 15 F0285
FOR/AID ECO/UNDEV ECO/TAC MARXISM

B60
BLACK E.R.,THE DIPLOMACY OF ECONOMIC DEVELOPMENT. WOR+45 CONSULT PLAN TEC/DEV DIPLOM ECO/TAC FOR/AID ...CONCPT TREND 20. PAGE 15 F0290
ECO/UNDEV ACT/RES

B60
BRYCE M.D.,INDUSTRIAL DEVELOPMENT: A GUIDE FOR ACCELERATING ECONOMIC GROWTH. WOR+45 FINAN MARKET COST EFFICIENCY PRODUC. PAGE 20 F0378
INDUS PLAN ECO/UNDEV TEC/DEV

B60
DIA M.,REFLEXIONS SUR L'ECONOMIE DE L'AFRIQUE NOIRE (REV. ED.). CULTURE ECO/UNDEV CREATE TEC/DEV DIPLOM INT/TRADE OPTIMAL ATTIT...POLICY 20. PAGE 32 F0631
AFR ECO/TAC SOCISM PLAN

B60
HALL C.A. JR.,FISCAL POLICY FOR STABLE GROWTH. USA+45 FINAN TEC/DEV TAX COST DEMAND INCOME ...BIBLIOG 20. PAGE 53 F1045
ECO/TAC BUDGET NAT/G POLICY

B60
HOFFMANN P.G.,ONE HUNDRED COUNTRIES, ONE AND ONE QUARTER BILLION PEOPLE. MARKET INT/ORG TEC/DEV CAP/ISM...GEOG CHARTS METH/COMP 20 UN. PAGE 61 F1191
FOR/AID ECO/TAC ECO/UNDEV INT/TRADE

B60
LENCZOWSKI G.,OIL AND STATE IN THE MIDDLE EAST. FUT IRAN LAW ECO/UNDEV EXTR/IND NAT/G TOP/EX PLAN TEC/DEV ECO/TAC LEGIT ADMIN COERCE ATTIT ALL/VALS PWR...CHARTS 20. PAGE 78 F1519
ISLAM INDUS NAT/LISM

B60
MYRDAL G.,BEYOND THE WELFARE STATE: ECONOMIC PLANNING AND ITS IMPLICATIONS. EUR+WWI FUT USA+45 USSR ECO/DEV ECO/UNDEV TEC/DEV SKILL WEALTH...PSY TREND FOR/TRADE 20. PAGE 96 F1881
PLAN ECO/TAC CAP/ISM

B60
RAO V.K.R.,INTERNATIONAL AID FOR ECONOMIC DEVELOPMENT - POSSIBILITIES AND LIMITATIONS. FINAN PLAN TEC/DEV ADMIN TASK EFFICIENCY...POLICY SOC METH/CNCPT CHARTS 20 UN. PAGE 109 F2147
FOR/AID DIPLOM INT/ORG ECO/UNDEV

B60
SIEGEL B.N.,AGGREGATE ECONOMICS AND PUBLIC POLICY. ECO/DEV TEC/DEV ECO/TAC TASK DEMAND EQUILIB INCOME ...CHARTS 20. PAGE 121 F2396
ECOMETRIC WEALTH PRODUC MARKET

B60
SILK L.S.,THE RESEARCH REVOLUTION. USA+45 FINAN CAP/ISM ECO/TAC PRICE EQUILIB PRODUC...STAT TREND CHARTS. PAGE 122 F2402
ECO/DEV R+D TEC/DEV PROB/SOLV

B60
SMET G.,BIBLIOGRAPHIE DE LA CONTRIBUTION A L'ETUDE DE LA PROGRESSION ECONOMIQUE DE L'AFRIQUE. AFR DIST/IND EXTR/IND TEC/DEV 20. PAGE 123 F2427
BIBLIOG ECO/UNDEV INDUS AGRI

B60
STEIN E.,AMERICAN ENTERPRISE IN THE EUROPEAN COMMON MARKET: A LEGAL PROFILE. EUR+WWI FUT USA+45 SOCIETY STRUCT ECO/DEV NAT/G VOL/ASSN CONSULT PLAN TEC/DEV ECO/TAC INT/TRADE ADMIN ATTIT RIGID/FLEX PWR...MGT NEW/IDEA STAT TREND COMPUT/IR SIMUL EEC 20. PAGE 125 F2475
MARKET ADJUD INT/LAW

B60
UNESCO,SOUTHERN ASIA SOCIAL SCIENCE BIBLIOGRAPHY (WITH ANNOTATIONS AND ABSTRACTS), 1959 (PAMPHLET). S/ASIA...SOC 20. PAGE 132 F2609
BIBLIOG/A ECO/UNDEV TEC/DEV INDUS

B60
US GENERAL ACCOUNTING OFFICE,EXAMINATION OF ECONOMIC AND TECHNICAL ASSISTANCE PROGRAM FOR GUATEMALA. GUATEMALA L/A+17C USA+45 FINAN INDUS PLAN...POLICY STAT CHARTS 20 DEPT/STATE. PAGE 136 F2680
FOR/AID ECO/UNDEV TEC/DEV NAT/G

B60
US SENATE COMM ON COMMERCE,URBAN MASS TRANSPORTATION. FUT USA+45 AIR ECO/DEV FINAN LOC/G LEGIS CREATE PROB/SOLV TEC/DEV MUNICH 20 PUB/TRANS. PAGE 139 F2732
DIST/IND PLAN NAT/G LAW

B60
WENTHOLT W.,INFLATION OR SECURITY? EUR+WWI USA+45 INDUS CONSULT TEC/DEV CAP/ISM DIPLOM FOR/AID INT/TRADE MARXISM 20 EEC. PAGE 145 F2858
ECO/DEV ECO/TAC FINAN ORD/FREE

L60
SPENGLER J.J.,"ECONOMIC DEVELOPMENT: POLITICAL PRECONDITIONS AND POLITICAL CONSEQUENCE." WOR+45 STRUCT ECO/UNDEV NAT/G PLAN ECO/TAC EDU/PROP ATTIT ORD/FREE WEALTH SOCISM...SOC CONCPT TREND SIMUL GEN/METH WORK 20. PAGE 124 F2452
TEC/DEV METH/CNCPT CAP/ISM

S60
FRANKEL S.H.,"ECONOMIC ASPECTS OF POLITICAL INDEPENDENCE IN AFRICA." AFR FUT SOCIETY ECO/UNDEV COM/IND FINAN LEGIS PLAN TEC/DEV CAP/ISM ECO/TAC INT/TRADE ADMIN ATTIT DRIVE RIGID/FLEX PWR WEALTH ...MGT NEW/IDEA MATH TIME/SEQ VAL/FREE 20. PAGE 43 F0846
NAT/G FOR/AID

S60
GARNICK D.H.,"ON THE ECONOMIC FEASIBILITY OF A MIDDLE EASTERN COMMON MARKET." AFR ISLAM CULTURE INDUS NAT/G PLAN TEC/DEV ECO/TAC ADMIN ATTIT DRIVE RIGID/FLEX...PLURIST STAT TREND GEN/LAWS 20. PAGE 46 F0907
MARKET INT/TRADE

S60
GROSSMAN G.,"SOVIET GROWTH: ROUTINE, INERTIA, AND PRESSURE." COM STRATA NAT/G DELIB/GP PLAN TEC/DEV ECO/TAC EDU/PROP ADMIN ROUTINE DRIVE WEALTH 20. PAGE 52 F1007
POL/PAR ECO/DEV AFR USSR

S60
HERZ J.H.,"EAST GERMANY: PROGRESS AND PROSPECTS." COM AGRI FINAN INDUS LOC/G NAT/G FORCES PLAN TEC/DEV DOMIN ADMIN COERCE DRIVE PERCEPT RIGID/FLEX MORAL ORD/FREE PWR...MARXIST PSY SOC RECORD STERTYP WORK. PAGE 59 F1158
POL/PAR STRUCT GERMANY

S60
MAIR L.P.,"SOCIAL CHANGE IN SOUTH AFRICA." MOD/EUR SOUTH/AFR WOR+45 ECO/UNDEV EX/STRUC TEC/DEV ATTIT DRIVE PERCEPT ORD/FREE...MGT CONCPT TIME/SEQ IND 20. PAGE 84 F1641
AFR NAT/G REV SOVEREIGN

S60
MILLER A.S.,"SOME OBSERVATIONS ON THE POLITICAL ECONOMY OF POPULATION GROWTH." FUT USA+45 ECO/DEV R+D CONSULT PLAN TEC/DEV ECO/TAC ROUTINE BIO/SOC WEALTH...POLICY OBS. PAGE 91 F1790
SOCIETY GEOG

S60
OWEN C.F.,"US AND SOVIET RELATIONS WITH UNDERDEVELOPED COUNTRIES: LATIN AMERICA-A CASE STUDY." AFR COM L/A+17C USA+45 USSR EXTR/IND MARKET TEC/DEV DIPLOM ECO/TAC NAT/LISM ORD/FREE PWR ...TREND WORK 20. PAGE 102 F2005
ECO/UNDEV DRIVE INT/TRADE

S60
RIVKIN A.,"AFRICAN ECONOMIC DEVELOPMENT: ADVANCED TECHNOLOGY AND THE STAGES OF GROWTH." CULTURE ECO/UNDEV AGRI COM/IND EXTR/IND PLAN ECO/TAC ATTIT DRIVE RIGID/FLEX SKILL WEALTH...MGT SOC GEN/LAWS FOR/TRADE WORK TOT/POP 20. PAGE 111 F2195
AFR TEC/DEV FOR/AID

C60
HOSELITZ B.,"THE ROLE OF CITIES IN THE ECONOMIC GROWTH OF UNDERDEVELOPED COUNTRIES" IN "SOCIOLOGICAL ASPECTS OF ECONOMIC GROWTH"(BMR). CULTURE LOC/G ACT/RES...SOC IDEA/COMP METH/COMP METH MUNICH IND 14/20 REDFIELD/R. PAGE 62 F1218
METH/CNCPT TEC/DEV ECO/UNDEV

N60
ERDMAN P.E.,COMMON MARKETS AND FREE TRADE AREAS (PAMPHLET). USA+45 MARKET INT/ORG TEC/DEV DIPLOM UTIL...CON/ANAL CHARTS BIBLIOG 20 EEC OEEC. PAGE 38 F0743
TREND PROB/SOLV INT/TRADE ECO/DEV

B61
BONNEFOUS M.,EUROPE ET TIERS MONDE. EUR+WWI SOCIETY INT/ORG NAT/G VOL/ASSN ACT/RES TEC/DEV CAP/ISM ECO/TAC ATTIT ORD/FREE SOVEREIGN...POLICY CONCPT TREND TERR/GP COMMUN 20. PAGE 16 F0314
AFR ECO/UNDEV FOR/AID INT/TRADE

B61
BRAIBANTI R.,TRADITION, VALUES AND SOCIO-ECONOMIC DEVELOPMENT. WOR+45 ACT/RES TEC/DEV ATTIT ORD/FREE CONSERVE...POLICY SOC ANTHOL. PAGE 17 F0336
ALL/VALS ECO/UNDEV CONCPT METH/CNCPT

B61
CLARK J.M.,COMPETITION AS A DYNAMIC PROCESS. ECO/DEV EXTR/IND INDUS LG/CO TEC/DEV ECO/TAC PRICE EQUILIB PRODUC...NEW/IDEA CAP 20. PAGE 25 F0483
WEALTH GP/REL FINAN PROFIT

B61
DE VRIES E.,MAN IN RAPID SOCIAL CHANGE. WOR+45 SOCIETY ECO/DEV ECO/UNDEV AGRI INDUS FAM SECT TEC/DEV ATTIT...RECORD 20 CHRISTIAN. PAGE 31 F0607
CULTURE ALL/VALS SOC TASK

B61
DETHINE P.,BIBLIOGRAPHIE DES ASPECTS ECONOMIQUES ET SOCIAUX DE L'INDUSTRIALISATION EN AFRIQUE. AFR FINAN LABOR FOR/AID...SOC 20. PAGE 32 F0623
BIBLIOG/A ECO/UNDEV INDUS TEC/DEV

B61
ERASMUS C.J.,MAN TAKES CONTROL: CULTURAL DEVELOPMENT AND AMERICAN AID. STRUCT OWN DRIVE PERCEPT...SOC 20 MEXIC/AMER. PAGE 38 F0741
ORD/FREE CULTURE ECO/UNDEV TEC/DEV

B61
FILLOL T.R.,SOCIAL FACTORS IN ECONOMIC DEVELOPMENT: THE ARGENTINE CASE. STRUCT INDUS LABOR CREATE TEC/DEV EFFICIENCY PRODUC DRIVE...METH/CNCPT METH/COMP BIBLIOG/A 20 ARGEN. PAGE 41 F0795
ECO/UNDEV MGT PERS/REL TREND

B61
GOODWIN C.D.W.,CANADIAN ECONOMIC THOUGHT. CANADA STRATA TEC/DEV CAP/ISM TARIFFS TAX COST EFFICIENCY WEALTH...METH/CNCPT TREND 20 MARITIME ONTARIO. PAGE 49 F0952
INT/TRADE ECO/DEV FINAN DEMAND

B61
HENDERSON W.O.,THE INDUSTRIAL REVOLUTION IN EUROPE. FRANCE GERMANY MOD/EUR RUSSIA WORKER PROFIT PWR MARXISM SOCISM...SOC HIST/WRIT 19 INDUS/REV. PAGE 58 F1148
INDUS REV CAP/ISM TEC/DEV

B61
HODGKINS J.A.,SOVIET POWER: ENERGY RESOURCES, PRODUCTION AND POTENTIALS. USSR ECO/DEV INDUS MARKET...POLICY STAT CHARTS 20 RESOURCE/N. PAGE 60 F1188
GEOG EXTR/IND TEC/DEV

B61
INDUSTRIAL COUN SOC-ECO STU,THE SWEDISH ECONOMY AND THE UNDERDEVELOPED COUNTRIES. SWEDEN INDUS DELIB/GP TEC/DEV INT/TRADE EDU/PROP COLONIAL DRIVE...CHARTS 20. PAGE 64 F1264
FOR/AID ECO/UNDEV PLAN FINAN

B61
LAHAYE R.,LES ENTREPRISES PUBLIQUES AU MAROC. FRANCE MOROCCO LAW DIST/IND EXTR/IND FINAN CONSULT PLAN TEC/DEV ADMIN AGREE CONTROL OWN...POLICY 20. PAGE 74 F1460
NAT/G INDUS ECO/UNDEV ECO/TAC

B61
LONGRIGG S.H.,OIL IN THE MIDDLE EAST: ITS DISCOVERY AND DEVELOPMENT. ECO/UNDEV LG/CO LOC/G TEC/DEV WEALTH...STAT TIME/SEQ 20 OIL. PAGE 82 F1599
ISLAM EXTR/IND

B61
LUZ N.V.,A LUTA PELA INDUSTRIALIZACAO DO BRAZIL. BRAZIL L/A+17C AGRI NAT/G TEC/DEV COLONIAL 19/20. PAGE 82 F1615
ECO/UNDEV INDUS NAT/LISM POLICY

B61
MEZERIK A.G.,ECONOMIC DEVELOPMENT AIDS FOR UNDERDEVELOPED COUNTRIES. WOR+45 FINAN LEGIS PROB/SOLV TEC/DEV DIPLOM FOR/AID GIVE TASK WAR 20 UN. PAGE 91 F1776
ECO/UNDEV INT/ORG WEALTH PLAN

B61
MORLEY L.,THE PATCHWORK HISTORY OF FOREIGN AID. AFR KOREA/S USA+45 USSR LAW FINAN INT/ORG TEC/DEV BAL/PWR GIVE 20 NATO. PAGE 93 F1834
FOR/AID ECO/UNDEV FORCES DIPLOM

B61
MORRIS B.R.,PROBLEMS OF AMERICAN ECONOMIC GROWTH. USA+45 LABOR WORKER BUDGET ECO/TAC INT/TRADE EQUILIB 20. PAGE 94 F1836
ECO/DEV POLICY TEC/DEV DEMAND

B61
NORTH D.C.,THE ECONOMIC GROWTH OF THE UNITED STATES 1790-1860. USA-45 INDUS TEC/DEV CAP/ISM ECO/TAC PRICE COST DEMAND LAISSEZ...ECOMETRIC STAT TREND 19. PAGE 98 F1933
AGRI ECO/UNDEV

B61
PETCH G.A.,ECONOMIC DEVELOPMENT AND MODERN WEST AFRICA. AFR CONGO/BRAZ GHANA NIGER SIER/LEONE AGRI MARKET LABOR FOR/AID TAX COST EFFICIENCY EQUILIB PRODUC...GEOG TREND 20. PAGE 105 F2068
ECO/UNDEV TEC/DEV EXTR/IND ECO/TAC

B61
ROEPKE W.,JENSEITS VON ANGEBOT UND NACHFRAGE (DRITTE VERAENDERTE AUFLAGE). WOR+45 MARKET TEC/DEV ECO/TAC GP/REL INGP/REL NEW/LIB...POLICY SOC IDEA/COMP PERS/COMP 20. PAGE 113 F2233
SOCIETY STRANGE ECO/DEV STRUCT

B61
SCHWARTZ H.,THE RED PHOENIX: RUSSIA SINCE WORLD WAR II. USA+45 WOR+45 ELITES POL/PAR TEC/DEV ECO/TAC MARXISM. PAGE 118 F2325
DIPLOM NAT/G ECO/DEV

B61
SHARP W.R.,FIELD ADMINISTRATION IN THE UNITED NATION SYSTEM: THE CONDUCT OF INTERNATIONAL ECONOMIC AND SOCIAL PROGRAMS. FUT WOR+45 CONSTN SOCIETY ECO/UNDEV R+D DELIB/GP ACT/RES PLAN TEC/DEV EDU/PROP EXEC ROUTINE HEALTH WEALTH...HUM CONCPT CHARTS METH ILO UNESCO GP VAL/FREE UN 20. PAGE 120 F2369
INT/ORG CONSULT

B61
SHONFIELD A.,ECONOMIC GROWTH AND INFLATION; A STUDY OF INDIAN PLANNING. AFR INDIA AGRI INDUS TEC/DEV CONTROL DEMAND UTIL 20. PAGE 121 F2384
ECO/UNDEV PRICE PLAN BUDGET

B61
SLICHTER S.H.,ECONOMIC GROWTH IN THE UNITED STATES. FUT USA+45 USA-45 LABOR PAY INCOME PRODUC...MGT 19/20. PAGE 123 F2422
ECO/DEV TEC/DEV CAP/ISM DEMAND

B61
US GENERAL ACCOUNTING OFFICE,EXAMINATION OF ECONOMIC AND TECHNICAL ASSISTANCE PROGRAM FOR IRAN. IRAN USA+45 AGRI INDUS DIPLOM CONTROL COST 20. PAGE 136 F2681
FOR/AID ADMIN TEC/DEV ECO/UNDEV

S61
ANDREWS R.B.,"URBAN ECONOMICS: AN APPRAISAL OF PROGRESS." LOC/G PROB/SOLV TEC/DEV...CONCPT
PHIL/SCI ECOMETRIC

OBS/ENVIR METH/COMP HYPO/EXP SOC/EXP SIMUL GEN/METH METH MUNICH 20. PAGE 5 F0102

S61
DALTON G.,"ECONOMIC THEORY AND PRIMITIVE SOCIETY" (BMR)" UNIV AGRI KIN TEC/DEV ECO/TAC REGION HABITAT SKILL...METH/COMP BIBLIOG. PAGE 30 F0574
ECO/UNDEV METH PHIL/SCI SOC

S61
GORDON L.,"ECONOMIC REGIONALISM RECONSIDERED." FUT USA+45 WOR+45 INDUS NAT/G TEC/DEV DIPLOM ROUTINE PERCEPT WEALTH...WELF/ST METH/CNCPT WORK 20. PAGE 49 F0957
ECO/DEV ATTIT CAP/ISM REGION

S61
HAYTES W.,"THREE VIEWS ON THE SOVIET ECONOMIC THREAT." AFR COM USA+45 USA-45 USSR WOR+45 WOR-45 INDUS TEC/DEV ECO/TAC DOMIN ATTIT PERCEPT PWR FOR/TRADE 20. PAGE 57 F1128
ECO/DEV PLAN TOTALISM

S61
HEILBRONER R.L.,"DYNAMICS OF FOREIGN AID: PROBLEMS OF UNDERDEVELOPED NATIONS PLAGUE ASSISTANCE PROGRAM." FUT USA+45 WOR+45 STRATA NAT/G PLAN TEC/DEV ATTIT DRIVE WEALTH WORK 20. PAGE 58 F1135
ECO/UNDEV ECO/TAC FOR/AID

C61
FILLOL T.R.,"SOCIAL FACTORS IN ECONOMIC DEVELOPMENT: THE ARGENTINE CASE" INDUS LABOR CREATE TEC/DEV PERS/REL EFFICIENCY PRODUC DRIVE ...METH/CNCPT METH/COMP 20 ARGEN. PAGE 41 F0794
BIBLIOG ECO/UNDEV MGT TREND

B62
ROUND TABLE ON EUROPE'S ROLE IN LATIN AMERICAN DEVELOPMENT. EUR+WWI L/A+17C PLAN BAL/PAY UTIL ROLE WEALTH...CHARTS ANTHOL 20 UN INT/AM/DEV. PAGE 1 F0017
ECO/UNDEV FINAN TEC/DEV FOR/AID

B62
BACKMAN J.,THE ECONOMICS OF THE ELECTRICAL MACHINERY INDUSTRY. USA+45 PROC/MFG LABOR WORKER INT/TRADE TV PRICE COST...CHARTS 19/20. PAGE 8 F0147
PRODUC TEC/DEV TREND

B62
BROOKINGS INSTITUTION,DEVELOPMENT OF THE EMERGING COUNTRIES; AN AGENDA FOR RESEARCH. WOR+45 AGRI TEC/DEV FOR/AID EDU/PROP ADJUST HABITAT KNOWL...PSY SOC ANTHOL 20 THIRD/WRLD. PAGE 19 F0362
ECO/UNDEV R+D SOCIETY PROB/SOLV

B62
CAIRNCROSS A.K.,FACTORS IN ECONOMIC DEVELOPMENT. WOR+45 ECO/UNDEV INDUS R+D LG/CO NAT/G EX/STRUC PLAN TEC/DEV ECO/TAC ATTIT HEALTH KNOWL PWR WEALTH ...TIME/SEQ GEN/LAWS TOT/POP TRUE/GP VAL/FREE 20. PAGE 21 F0399
MARKET ECO/DEV

B62
CHAPIN F.S.,URBAN GROWTH DYNAMICS IN A REGIONAL CLUSTER OF CITIES. TEC/DEV ECO/TAC HABITAT...GEOG SOC MUNICH. PAGE 23 F0453
REGION PLAN

B62
CHRISTENSON C.L.,ECONOMIC REDEVELOPMENT IN BITUMINOUS COAL: THE SPECIAL CASE OF TECHNOLOGICAL ADVANCE IN US COAL MINES 1930-1960. USA+45 USA-45 ECO/TAC AUTOMAT INCOME PRODUC...CHARTS 20. PAGE 24 F0471
EXTR/IND LABOR TEC/DEV ECO/DEV

B62
DENISON E.F.,THE SOURCES OF ECONOMIC GROWTH IN THE UNITED STATES AND THE ALTERNATIVES BEFORE US. AGRI INDUS SCHOOL TEC/DEV CAP/ISM ECO/TAC PRICE COST WEALTH...STAT TREND CHARTS 20. PAGE 32 F0620
ECO/DEV WORKER PRODUC

B62
DUPRE J.S.,SCIENCE AND THE NATION: POLICY AND POLITICS. USA+45 LAW ACADEM FORCES ADMIN CIVMIL/REL GOV/REL EFFICIENCY PEACE...TREND 20 SCI/ADVSRY. PAGE 35 F0682
R+D INDUS TEC/DEV NUC/PWR

B62
FAO,FOOD AND AGRICULTURE ORGANIZATION AFRICAN SURVEY. AFR CONGO/BRAZ GHANA STRATA AGRI INT/ORG TEC/DEV FOR/AID INT/TRADE RACE/REL DEMAND EFFICIENCY PRODUC...GEOG 20 UN CONGO/LEOP. PAGE 39 F0763
ECO/TAC WEALTH EXTR/IND ECO/UNDEV

B62
FRIEDMANN W.,METHODS AND POLICIES OF PRINCIPAL DONOR COUNTRIES IN PUBLIC INTERNATIONAL DEVELOPMENT FINANCING: PRELIMINARY APPRAISAL. FRANCE GERMANY/W UK USA+45 USSR WOR+45 FINAN TEC/DEV CAP/ISM DIPLOM ECO/TAC ATTIT 20 EEC. PAGE 44 F0864
INT/ORG FOR/AID NAT/COMP ADMIN

B62
FRIEDRICH-EBERT-STIFTUNG,THE SOVIET BLOC AND DEVELOPING COUNTRIES. CHINA/COM COM GERMANY/E USSR WOR+45 ECO/UNDEV INT/ORG NAT/G TEC/DEV NEUTRAL PWR ...POLICY 20. PAGE 44 F0868
MARXISM DIPLOM ECO/TAC FOR/AID

B62
GERSCHENKRON A.,ECONOMIC BACKWARDNESS IN HISTORICAL PERSPECTIVE. WOR+45 WOR-45 ECO/DEV ECO/UNDEV INDUS NAT/G LEGIT DRIVE...WELF/ST DECISION QUANT TREND CHARTS 20. PAGE 47 F0919
TEC/DEV USSR

B62
GRANICK D.,THE EUROPEAN EXECUTIVE. BELGIUM FRANCE GERMANY/W UK INDUS LABOR LG/CO SML/CO EX/STRUC PLAN TEC/DEV CAP/ISM COST DEMAND...POLICY CHARTS 20. PAGE 50 F0977
MGT ECO/DEV ECO/TAC EXEC

B62
HATTERY L.H.,INFORMATION RETRIEVAL MANAGEMENT. CLIENT INDUS TOP/EX COMPUTER OP/RES TEC/DEV ROUTINE COST EFFICIENCY RIGID/FLEX...METH/COMP ANTHOL 20. PAGE 57 F1113
R+D COMPUT/IR MGT CREATE

B62
HOOVER C.B.,ECONOMIC SYSTEMS OF THE COMMONWEALTH. AFR CANADA INDIA UK ECO/DEV ECO/UNDEV AGRI INDUS TEC/DEV TARIFFS PRICE BAL/PAY DEMAND...SIMUL 20 AUSTRAL. PAGE 61 F1208
CAP/ISM SOCISM ECO/TAC PLAN

B62
KAUTSKY J.H.,POLITICAL CHANGE IN UNDERDEVELOPED COUNTRIES: NATIONALISM AND COMMUNISM. WOR+45 AGRI TEC/DEV EDU/PROP ATTIT...POLICY METH/CNCPT STYLE INT QU CENSUS TREND SOC/EXP GEN/LAWS 20. PAGE 69 F1365
ECO/UNDEV SOCIETY CAP/ISM REV

B62
LEVENSTEIN A.,WHY PEOPLE WORK; CHANGING INCENTIVES IN A TROUBLED WORLD. USA+45 SOCIETY PROB/SOLV TEC/DEV EDU/PROP ADJUST...CENSUS BIBLIOG 20. PAGE 79 F1538
DRIVE WORKER ECO/DEV ANOMIE

B62
LICHFIELD N.,COST-BENEFIT ANALYSIS IN URBAN REDEVELOPMENT. CONSTRUC LOC/G NEIGH ACT/RES PROB/SOLV TEC/DEV BUDGET TAX...DECISION STAT CHARTS SOC/EXP MUNICH 20. PAGE 80 F1558
PLAN COST GOV/REL

B62
LITWACK L.,THE AMERICAN LABOR MOVEMENT. USA-45 NAT/G CREATE TEC/DEV CAP/ISM ECO/TAC ADJUD AUTOMAT SKILL...TREND ANTHOL 19/20. PAGE 81 F1588
INDUS LABOR GP/REL METH/COMP

B62
MARTINS A.F.,REVOLUCAO BRANCA NO CAMPO. L/A+17C SERV/IND DEMAND EFFICIENCY PRODUC...POLICY METH/COMP. PAGE 86 F1685
AGRI ECO/UNDEV TEC/DEV NAT/COMP

B62
MOWITZ R.J.,PROFILE OF A METROPOLIS: A CASE BOOK. COM/IND CONSTRUC INDUS PUB/INST PLAN TEC/DEV LEAD GP/REL...POLICY TECHNIC WELF/ST MUNICH. PAGE 94 F1851
DECISION ADMIN

B62
NATIONAL BUREAU ECONOMIC RES,THE RATE AND DIRECTION OF INVENTIVE ACTIVITY: ECONOMIC AND SOCIAL FACTORS. STRUCT INDUS MARKET R+D CREATE OP/RES TEC/DEV EFFICIENCY PRODUC RATIONAL UTIL...WELF/ST PHIL/SCI METH/CNCPT TIME. PAGE 97 F1895
DECISION PROB/SOLV MGT

B62
PERROUX F.,L'ECONOMIE DES JEUNES NATIONS. EUR+WWI SOUTH/AFR FINAN MARKET TEC/DEV CAP/ISM FOR/AID INT/TRADE 20. PAGE 105 F2065
INDUS ECO/UNDEV ECO/TAC DIPLOM

B62
PONCET J.,LA COLONISATION ET L'AGRICULTURE EUROPEENNES EN TUNISIE DEPUIS 1881. FRANCE WORKER TEC/DEV ECO/TAC CONTROL EFFICIENCY ROLE WEALTH 19/20 TUNIS. PAGE 107 F2101
ECO/UNDEV AGRI COLONIAL FINAN

B62
RIMALOV V.V.,ECONOMIC COOPERATION BETWEEN USSR AND UNDERDEVELOPED COUNTRIES. USSR FINAN TEC/DEV INT/TRADE DOMIN EDU/PROP COLONIAL NAT/LISM DRIVE SOVEREIGN...AUD/VIS 20. PAGE 111 F2194
FOR/AID PLAN ECO/UNDEV DIPLOM

B62
ROBERTSON B.C.,REGIONAL DEVELOPMENT IN THE EUROPEAN ECONOMIC COMMUNITY. EUR+WWI FRANCE FUT ITALY UK ECO/UNDEV WORKER ACT/RES PROB/SOLV TEC/DEV ECO/TAC INT/TRADE EEC. PAGE 112 F2209
PLAN ECO/DEV INT/ORG REGION

B62
ROBINSON A.D.,DUTCH ORGANIZED AGRICULTURE IN INTERNATIONAL POLITICS, 1945-1960. EUR+WWI NETHERLAND STRUCT ECO/DEV NAT/G VOL/ASSN CONSULT DELIB/GP PLAN TEC/DEV INT/TRADE EDU/PROP ATTIT RIGID/FLEX ALL/VALS...NEW/IDEA TREND EEC COMMUN 20. PAGE 112 F2215
AGRI INT/ORG

B62
SCHILLING W.R.,STRATEGY, POLITICS, AND DEFENSE BUDGETS. AFR USA+45 CHIEF LEGIS PLAN TEC/DEV BAL/PWR BUDGET NUC/PWR WAR CIVMIL/REL GOV/REL PWR 20 EISNHWR/DD. PAGE 117 F2297
NAT/G POLICY FORCES DETER

B62
SCHMITT H.A.,THE PATH TO EUROPEAN UNITY. EUR+WWI USA+45 PLAN TEC/DEV DIPLOM FOR/AID CONFER...INT/LAW 20 EEC EURCOALSTL MARSHL/PLN UNIFICA. PAGE 117 F2300
INT/ORG INT/TRADE REGION ECO/DEV

B62
SEN S.R.,THE STRATEGY FOR AGRICULTURAL DEVELOPMENT AND OTHER ESSAYS ON ECONOMIC POLICY AND PLANNING. INDIA FINAN ACT/RES TEC/DEV CAP/ISM PRICE...STAT 20. PAGE 119 F2354
ECO/UNDEV PLAN AGRI POLICY

B62
SHINOHARA M.,GROWTH AND CYCLES IN THE JAPANESE ECONOMY. INDUS LABOR TEC/DEV CAP/ISM INT/TRADE PAY COST EFFICIENCY INCOME WEALTH...METH/COMP 20 CHINJAP. PAGE 121 F2380
PRODUC ECO/DEV EQUILIB ECOMETRIC

B62
UNECA LIBRARY,BOOKS ON AFRICA IN THE UNECA
BIBLIOG

LIBRARY. WOR+45 AGRI INT/ORG NAT/G PLAN WRITING REGION...SOC STAT UN. PAGE 132 F2605
AFR ECO/UNDEV TEC/DEV

B62
UNECA LIBRARY,NEW ACQUISITIONS IN THE UNECA LIBRARY. LAW NAT/G PLAN PROB/SOLV TEC/DEV ADMIN REGION...GEOG SOC 20 UN. PAGE 132 F2606
BIBLIOG AFR ECO/UNDEV INT/ORG

B62
US CONGRESS JOINT ECO COMM,ECONOMIC DEVELOPMENTS IN SOUTH AMERICA. USA+45 SOCIETY FINAN NAT/G PROB/SOLV TEC/DEV INT/TRADE TAX EFFICIENCY PRODUC ATTIT ...POLICY 20 ALL/PROG CONGRESS SOUTH/AMER. PAGE 135 F2654
L/A+17C ECO/UNDEV FOR/AID DIPLOM

B62
VIET J.,INTERNATIONAL COOPERATION AND PROGRAMMES OF ECONOMIC AND SOCIAL DEVELOPMENT. TEC/DEV FOR/AID DOMIN COLONIAL PEACE WEALTH 20 UNESCO. PAGE 141 F2784
BIBLIOG/A INT/ORG DIPLOM ECO/UNDEV

S62
BOONE A.,"THE FOREIGN TRADE OF CHINA." AFR ECO/DEV ECO/UNDEV INDUS MARKET NAT/G TEC/DEV WEALTH ...POLICY STAT TREND CHARTS FOR/TRADE. PAGE 17 F0318
ASIA ECO/TAC

C62
JOINT ECONOMIC COMMITTEE,"DIMENSIONS OF SOVIET ECONOMIC POWER." USSR R+D FORCES ACT/RES OP/RES TEC/DEV...GEOG STAT BIBLIOG 20. PAGE 68 F1337
ECO/DEV PLAN PRODUC LABOR

B63
BRITISH AID. UK AGRI DIST/IND INDUS SCHOOL TEC/DEV INT/TRADE COLONIAL DEMAND...TREND CHARTS 20. PAGE 1 F0018
FOR/AID ECO/UNDEV NAT/G FINAN

B63
ALPERT P.,ECONOMIC DEVELOPMENT. WOR+45 FINAN TEC/DEV ECO/TAC PRICE GOV/REL HABITAT...GEOG BIBLIOG T 20 THIRD/WRLD. PAGE 4 F0079
ECO/DEV ECO/UNDEV INT/TRADE FOR/AID

B63
BARNETT H.J.,SCARCITY AND GROWTH: THE ECONOMICS OF NATURAL RESOURCE AVAILABILITY. FUT WOR+45 AGRI INDUS PROB/SOLV TEC/DEV CONTROL PRODUC...SOC/WK IDEA/COMP METH/COMP SIMUL 20 RESOURCE/N MALTHUS RICARDO/D MILL/JS DARWIN/C. PAGE 10 F0191
DEMAND HABITAT CENSUS GEOG

B63
BERGSON A.,ECONOMIC TRENDS IN THE SOVIET UNION. USSR ECO/UNDEV AGRI NAT/G FORCES PLAN TEC/DEV INT/TRADE BAL/PAY...POLICY ANTHOL 20. PAGE 14 F0259
ECO/DEV NAT/COMP INDUS LABOR

B63
CONF ON FUTURE OF COMMONWEALTH,THE FUTURE OF THE COMMONWEALTH. AFR UK ECO/UNDEV AGRI EDU/PROP ADMIN SOC/INTEG 20. PAGE 27 F0522
DIPLOM RACE/REL ORD/FREE TEC/DEV

B63
COPPOCK J.,NORTH ATLANTIC POLICY - THE AGRICULTURAL GAP. EUR+WWI ELITES ECO/DEV DIST/IND MARKET PLAN WEALTH...STAT TREND GEN/LAWS OEEC TOT/POP VAL/FREE FAO 20. PAGE 27 F0535
AGRI TEC/DEV INT/TRADE

B63
ENKE S.,ECONOMICS FOR DEVELOPMENT. AGRI TEC/DEV CAP/ISM DIPLOM ECO/TAC TAX ATTIT DRIVE HABITAT WEALTH...GOV/COMP BIBLIOG 20. PAGE 38 F0737
ECO/UNDEV PHIL/SCI CON/ANAL

B63
FREITAG R.S.,AGRICULTURAL DEVELOPMENT SCHEMES IN SUB-SAHARAN AFRICA. AFR EDU/PROP 20. PAGE 44 F0852
BIBLIOG/A AGRI TEC/DEV KNOWL

B63
FURTADO C.,THE ECONOMIC GROWTH OF BRAZIL: A SURVEY FROM COLONIAL TO MODERN TIMES. L/A+17C AGRI DIST/IND EXTR/IND INDUS WORKER COLONIAL RACE/REL OWN GOV/COMP. PAGE 45 F0877
ECO/UNDEV TEC/DEV LABOR DOMIN

B63
GEERTZ C.,PEDDLERS AND PRINCES: SOCIAL DEVELOPMENT AND ECONOMIC CHANGE IN TWO INDONESIAN TOWNS. S/ASIA CULTURE SOCIETY STRATA FACE/GP CREATE TEC/DEV ECO/TAC ORD/FREE WEALTH...OBS INT CENSUS CHARTS WORK TOT/POP METH/GP TERR/GP VAL/FREE 20 MUNICH. PAGE 47 F0913
ECO/UNDEV SOC ELITES INDONESIA

B63
GORDON L.,A NEW DEAL FOR LATIN AMERICA. L/A+17C USA+45 CULTURE NAT/G TEC/DEV DIPLOM FOR/AID REGION TASK...POLICY 20 ALL/PROG DEPT/STATE. PAGE 49 F0958
ECO/UNDEV ECO/TAC INT/ORG PLAN

B63
HAUSMAN W.H.,MANAGING ECONOMIC DEVELOPMENT IN AFRICA. AFR USA+45 LAW FINAN WORKER TEC/DEV WEALTH ...ANTHOL 20. PAGE 57 F1116
ECO/UNDEV PLAN FOR/AID MGT

B63
INTERAMERICAN ECO AND SOC COUN,THE ALLIANCE FOR PROGRESS: ITS FIRST YEAR: 1961-1962. AGRI SCHOOL PLAN TEC/DEV INT/TRADE TAX GIVE ADMIN WEALTH...SOC 20 ALL/PROG SOUTH/AMER. PAGE 64 F1267
INT/ORG PROB/SOLV ECO/TAC L/A+17C

B63
INTERNATIONAL BANK RECONST DEV,THE WORLD BANK GROUP IN ASIA. ASIA S/ASIA INDUS TEC/DEV ECO/TAC...RECORD 20 IBRD WORLD/BANK. PAGE 65 F1273
INT/ORG DIPLOM ECO/UNDEV FINAN

B63
KAPP W.K.,SOCIAL COSTS OF BUSINESS ENTERPRISE. WOR+45 LABOR TEC/DEV CAP/ISM HABITAT...PHIL/SCI NEW/IDEA CON/ANAL 20. PAGE 69 F1354
COST SOCIETY INDUS RIGID/FLEX

B63
KATZ S.M.,A SELECTED LIST OF US READINGS ON DEVELOPMENT. AGRI COM/IND DIST/IND INDUS LABOR PLAN FOR/AID EDU/PROP HEALTH...POLICY SOC/WK 20. PAGE 69 F1361
BIBLIOG/A ECO/UNDEV TEC/DEV ACT/RES

B63
LAIRD R.D.,SOVIET AGRICULTURAL AND PEASANT AFFAIRS. FUT STRATA LOC/G DELIB/GP ACT/RES TEC/DEV ECO/TAC EDU/PROP ATTIT RIGID/FLEX ORD/FREE SKILL WEALTH ...STAT CON/ANAL ANTHOL MUNICH WORK VAL/FREE 20. PAGE 74 F1461
COM AGRI POLICY

B63
LEE M.W.,MACROECONOMICS: FLUCTUATIONS, GROWTH AND STABILITY (3RD ED.). MARKET LABOR TEC/DEV INT/TRADE TAX PRICE WAR PRODUC...POLICY ECOMETRIC CHARTS 19/20. PAGE 77 F1505
EQUILIB TREND WEALTH

B63
MAIZELS A.,INDUSTRIAL GROWTH AND WORLD TRADE. FUT WOR+45 ECO/DEV FINAN INT/ORG PLAN TEC/DEV ECO/TAC WEALTH...MATH STAT CHARTS VAL/FREE 19/20. PAGE 84 F1642
INDUS ECO/UNDEV INT/TRADE

B63
MANN D.E.,THE POLITICS OF WATER IN ARIZONA. AGRI EXTR/IND PROVS ACT/RES CREATE PLAN GOV/REL COST HABITAT...MGT CHARTS 20 ARIZONA WATER. PAGE 84 F1655
POLICY ECO/TAC TEC/DEV

B63
RAO V.K.R.,FOREIGN AID AND INDIA'S ECONOMIC DEVELOPMENT. INDIA INT/ORG PROB/SOLV TEC/DEV ECO/TAC CONTROL WEALTH...TREND 20. PAGE 109 F2148
FOR/AID ECO/UNDEV RECEIVE DIPLOM

B63
THEOBALD R.,FREE MEN AND FREE MARKETS. USA+45 USA-45 ECO/DEV NAT/G TEC/DEV DIPLOM INT/TRADE INCOME ORD/FREE WEALTH...TREND 19/20 KEYNES/JM. PAGE 130 F2556
CONCPT ECO/TAC CAP/ISM MARKET

B63
US ADVISORY COMN INTERGOV REL,PERFORMANCE OF URBAN FUNCTIONS: LOCAL AND AREAWIDE. TEC/DEV PARTIC REPRESENT PWR...DECISION GOV/COMP MUNICH. PAGE 133 F2633
REGION LOC/G ECO/TAC

B63
US ECON SURVEY TEAM INDONESIA,INDONESIA - PERSPECTIVE AND PROPOSALS FOR UNITED STATES ECONOMIC AID. INDONESIA AGRI MARKET TEC/DEV DIPLOM INT/TRADE EDU/PROP 20. PAGE 136 F2678
FOR/AID ECO/UNDEV PLAN INDUS

B63
US GOVERNMENT,REPORT TO INTER-AMERICAN ECONOMIC AND SOCIAL COUNCIL AT SECOND ANNUAL MEETING. L/A+17C USA+45 VOL/ASSN TEC/DEV DIPLOM TAX EATING EFFICIENCY HEALTH...STAT CHARTS 20 AID. PAGE 136 F2682
ECO/TAC FOR/AID FINAN PLAN

B63
US HOUSE,URBAN RENEWAL: HOUSE COMMITTEE ON BANKING AND CURRENCY. USA+45 FINAN LOC/G NAT/G NEIGH DELIB/GP TEC/DEV BUDGET GOV/REL COST...CHARTS MUNICH 20 CONGRESS URBAN/RNWL. PAGE 136 F2684
PLAN PROB/SOLV LEGIS

B63
WALINSKY L.J.,PLANNING AND EXECUTION OF ECONOMIC DEVELOPMENT. PROB/SOLV TEC/DEV BUDGET COST WEALTH ...CHARTS BIBLIOG 20. PAGE 142 F2802
PLAN ECO/UNDEV ECO/TAC OPTIMAL

B63
WIGHTMAN D.,TOWARD ECONOMIC CO-OPERATION IN ASIA. ASIA S/ASIA VOL/ASSN ACT/RES PLAN TEC/DEV ECO/TAC EDU/PROP RIGID/FLEX SKILL...POLICY METH/CNCPT OBS INT GEN/LAWS UN 20 ECAFE. PAGE 146 F2877
ECO/UNDEV CREATE

L63
ADERBIGDE A.,"SYMPOSIUM ON WEST AFRICA INTEGRATION." AFR EUR+WWI FUT CULTURE SOCIETY STRATA DIST/IND INDUS MARKET SERV/IND DELIB/GP PLAN TEC/DEV DOMIN EDU/PROP LEGIT COERCE ATTIT ALL/VALS ...POLICY STAT TREND CHARTS VAL/FREE. PAGE 2 F0040
FINAN ECO/TAC REGION

L63
OLSON M. JR.,"RAPID ECONOMIC GROWTH AS A DESTABILIZING FORCE." WOR+45 WOR-45 STRATA ECO/UNDEV FAM KIN CREATE TEC/DEV DIPLOM PEACE ATTIT PERSON RIGID/FLEX PWR RESPECT WEALTH...SOC 20. PAGE 101 F1989
SOCIETY FOR/AID

S63
ADAMS F.G.,"ECONOMIC CONSIDERATIONS OF AN ATLANTIC ENERGY POLICY." EUR+WWI FUT USA+45 DIST/IND EXTR/IND MARKET CONSULT LEGIS ECO/TAC WEALTH ...POLICY EEC FOR/TRADE OEEC 20. PAGE 2 F0037
ECO/DEV TEC/DEV NUC/PWR

S63
BARANSON J.,"ECONOMIC AND SOCIAL CONSIDERATIONS IN
ECO/UNDEV

ADAPTING TECHNOLOGIES FOR DEVELOPING COUNTRIES." TEC/DEV
WOR+45 PLAN WEALTH...TECHNIC SOC 20. PAGE 10 F0180

S63
BEGUIN H.,"ASPECTS STRUCTURELS DU COMMERCE MARKET
EXTERIEUR DES PAYS SOUS-DEVELOPPES." FUT WOR+45 ECO/UNDEV
STRUCT FINAN SERV/IND POL/PAR TEC/DEV PERCEPT FOR/AID
WEALTH FOR/TRADE 20. PAGE 12 F0229

S63
CLEMHOUT S.,"PRODUCTION FUNCTION ANALYSIS APPLIED ECO/DEV
TO THE LEONTIEF SCARCE-FACTOR PARADOX OF ECO/TAC
INTERNATIONAL TRADE." EUR+WWI USA+45 DIST/IND NAT/G
PLAN TEC/DEV DIPLOM PWR WEALTH...MGT METH/CNCPT
CONT/OBS CON/ANAL CHARTS SIMUL GEN/LAWS FOR/TRADE
20. PAGE 25 F0490

S63
DE FOREST J.D.,"LOW LEVELS OF TECHNOLOGY AND ECO/UNDEV
ECONOMIC DEVELOPMENT PROSPECTS." WOR+45 WOR-45 TEC/DEV
CULTURE ACT/RES CREATE PLAN ECO/TAC ROUTINE PERCEPT
WEALTH...METH/CNCPT GEN/LAWS 20. PAGE 31 F0597

S63
DUCROS B.,"MOBILISATION DES RESSOURCES PRODUCTIVES ECO/UNDEV
ET DEVELOPPEMENT." FUT INTELL SOCIETY COM/IND TEC/DEV
DIST/IND EXTR/IND FINAN INDUS ROUTINE WEALTH
...METH/CNCPT OBS 20. PAGE 34 F0670

S63
ETHERINGTON D.M.,"LAND RESETTLEMENT IN KENYA: ECO/UNDEV
POLICY AND PRACTICE" AFR TEC/DEV ECO/TAC FOR/AID AGRI
TAX PRODUC...CHARTS 20. PAGE 39 F0752 WORKER
PLAN

S63
GANDILHON J.,"LA SCIENCE ET LA TECHNIQUE A L'AIDE ECO/UNDEV
DES REGIONS PEU DEVELOPPEES." FRANCE FUT WOR+45 TEC/DEV
ECO/DEV R+D PROF/ORG ACT/RES PLAN...MGT TOT/POP FOR/AID
VAL/FREE 20 UN. PAGE 46 F0893

S63
HOOVER C.B.,"ECONOMIC REFORM VERSUS ECONOMIC GROWTH ECO/DEV
IN UNDERDEVELOPED COUNTRIES." FUT WOR+45 ELITES ECO/TAC
STRATA ECO/UNDEV DIST/IND INDUS TEC/DEV CAP/ISM
FOR/AID INT/TRADE ATTIT WEALTH...MYTH TREND STERTYP
GEN/LAWS WORK 20. PAGE 61 F1209

S63
LEDUC G.,"L'AIDE INTERNATIONALE AU DEVELOPPEMENT." FINAN
FUT WOR+45 ECO/DEV ECO/UNDEV R+D PROF/ORG TEC/DEV PLAN
ECO/TAC ROUTINE ATTIT ALL/VALS...MGT TIME/SEQ FOR/AID
FOR/TRADE TOT/POP 20. PAGE 77 F1503

S63
NADLER E.B.,"SOME ECONOMIC DISADVANTAGES OF THE ECO/DEV
ARMS RACE." AFR USA+45 INDUS R+D FORCES PLAN MGT
TEC/DEV ECO/TAC FOR/AID EDU/PROP PWR WEALTH...TREND BAL/PAY
FOR/TRADE 20. PAGE 96 F1886

S63
POLYANOV N.,"THE DOLLAR'S VENTURES IN EUROPE." FINAN
EUR+WWI FRANCE USA+45 ECO/DEV MARKET POL/PAR PLAN
TEC/DEV ECO/TAC EDU/PROP DRIVE PWR WEALTH...MARXIST BAL/PAY
MYTH STAT TREND EEC 20. PAGE 107 F2100 CAP/ISM

S63
REDDAWAY W.B.,"THE ECONOMICS OF UNDERDEVELOPED ECO/TAC
COUNTRIES." S/ASIA WOR+45 WOR-45 STRATA AGRI ECO/UNDEV
COM/IND DIST/IND MARKET PROC/MFG PLAN TEC/DEV INDIA
FOR/AID BAL/PAY ATTIT DRIVE SKILL WORK FOR/TRADE
20. PAGE 110 F2165

S63
STEFANIAK N.J.,"A REFINEMENT OF HAIG'S THEORY." GEOG
USA+45 INDUS PROB/SOLV TEC/DEV...CONCPT CHARTS GEN/LAWS
MUNICH 20 HAIG. PAGE 125 F2474 PLAN

S63
WILES P.J.D.,"WILL CAPITALISM AND COMMUNISM PLAN
SPONTANEOUSLY CONVERGE." COM FUT USA+45 ECO/DEV TEC/DEV
DIST/IND MARKET CAP/ISM ECO/TAC RIGID/FLEX WEALTH USSR
MARXISM SOCISM...MATH STAT TREND COMPUT/IR 20.
PAGE 146 F2885

S63
WOLFERS A.,"INTEGRATION IN THE WEST: THE CONFLICT RIGID/FLEX
OF PERSPECTIVES." AFR EUR+WWI USA+45 ECO/DEV ECO/TAC
INT/ORG DELIB/GP CREATE TEC/DEV DIPLOM ATTIT PWR
...CONCPT HIST/WRIT TREND GEN/LAWS EEC 20. PAGE 148
F2918

N63
NORTH CAROLINA U INST GOVT,COSTING URBAN BIBLIOG
DEVELOPMENT AND REDEVELOPMENT (PAMPHLET). USA+45 COST
USA-45 NEIGH PLAN TEC/DEV TAX OWN...GEOG MUNICH 20. FINAN
PAGE 98 F1934

B64
BALOGH T.,THE ECONOMIC IMPACT OF MONETARY AND TEC/DEV
COMMERCIAL INSTITUTIONS OF A EUROPEAN ORIGIN IN FINAN
AFRICA. AFR UAR INDUS FOR/AID COLONIAL CONTROL ECO/UNDEV
...NAT/COMP 20. PAGE 9 F0169 ECO/TAC

B64
BARKSDALE H.C.,MARKETING: CHANGE AND EXCHANGE. MARKET
USA+45 FINAN ACADEM TEC/DEV PRICE AUTOMAT WEALTH ECO/DEV
...CHARTS 20. PAGE 10 F0187 DEMAND
TREND

B64
BOWEN W.G.,ECONOMIC ASPECTS OF EDUCATION (NO. 104). EDU/PROP
EUR+WWI UK USA+45 PROF/ORG PLAN TEC/DEV PAY ACADEM
...POLICY STAT 20. PAGE 17 F0329 FINAN
METH/COMP

B64
BRIGHT J.R.,RESEARCH, DEVELOPMENT AND TECHNOLOGICAL TEC/DEV
INNOVATION. CULTURE R+D CREATE PLAN PROB/SOLV NEW/IDEA
AUTOMAT RISK PERSON...DECISION CONCPT PREDICT INDUS
BIBLIOG. PAGE 18 F0352 MGT

B64
CALDER R.,TWO-WAY PASSAGE. INT/ORG TEC/DEV WAR FOR/AID
PERSON ORD/FREE 20. PAGE 21 F0400 ECO/UNDEV
ECO/TAC
DIPLOM

B64
CASEY R.G.,THE FUTURE OF THE COMMONWEALTH. INDIA DIPLOM
PAKISTAN UK ECO/UNDEV INT/ORG TEC/DEV COLONIAL SOVEREIGN
SUPEGO 20 EEC AUSTRAL. PAGE 22 F0425 NAT/LISM
FOR/AID

B64
CEPEDE M.,POPULATION AND FOOD. USA+45 STRUCT FUT
ECO/UNDEV FAM PLAN TEC/DEV FOR/AID CONTROL...CATH GEOG
SOC TREND 19/20. PAGE 22 F0436 AGRI
CENSUS

B64
CHINITZ B.,CITY AND SUBURB: THE ECONOMICS OF TEC/DEV
METROPOLITAN GROWTH. DIST/IND BUDGET GOV/REL DEMAND PLAN
ATTIT HABITAT MUNICH PHILADELPH. PAGE 24 F0467

B64
COLUMBIA U SCHOOL OF LAW,PUBLIC INTERNATIONAL ECO/UNDEV
DEVELOPMENT FINANCING IN INDIA. GERMANY/W INDIA UK FINAN
USA+45 INDUS PLAN TEC/DEV DIPLOM ECO/TAC GIVE ADMIN FOR/AID
UTIL ATTIT 20. PAGE 26 F0512 INT/ORG

B64
COMPOS R.O.,A MOEDA, O GOVERNO E O TEMPO. AFR ECO/UNDEV
BRAZIL WOR+45 FINAN TEC/DEV FOR/AID REGION DEMAND PLAN
...ANTHOL 20. PAGE 27 F0520 DIPLOM
INT/TRADE

B64
FEI J.C.H.,DEVELOPMENT OF THE LABOR SURPLUS ECO/TAC
ECONOMY: THEORY AND POLICY. WOR+45 AGRI INDUS POLICY
MARKET PROB/SOLV TEC/DEV...STAT CHARTS GEN/LAWS WORKER
METH 20 THIRD/WRLD. PAGE 40 F0772 ECO/UNDEV

B64
FEIS H.,FOREIGN AID AND FOREIGN POLICY. USA+45 ECO/UNDEV
WOR+45 NAT/G VOL/ASSN ACT/RES TEC/DEV ATTIT HEALTH ECO/TAC
WEALTH...SOC GEN/LAWS 20. PAGE 40 F0775 FOR/AID
DIPLOM

B64
FIESER M.E.,ECONOMIC POLICY AND WAR POTENTIAL. AFR INT/TRADE
WOR+45 ECO/DEV INDUS NAT/G FORCES TEC/DEV NUC/PWR POLICY
CIVMIL/REL ORD/FREE 20. PAGE 40 F0791 ECO/TAC
DETER

B64
FITCH L.C.,URBAN TRANSPORTATION AND PUBLIC POLICY. DIST/IND
FINAN NAT/G LEGIS PROB/SOLV TEC/DEV PRICE COST PLAN
EFFICIENCY...DECISION STAT CHARTS METH/COMP MUNICH LOC/G
20 NEWYORK/C PHILADELPH LOS/ANG CHICAGO WASHING/DC.
PAGE 41 F0806

B64
HAAR C.M.,LAW AND LAND: ANGLO-AMERICAN PLANNING LAW
PRACTICE. UK USA+45 NAT/G TEC/DEV BUDGET CT/SYS PLAN
INGP/REL EFFICIENCY OWN...JURID MUNICH 20. PAGE 52 NAT/COMP
F1019

B64
HAGGER A.J.,THE THEORY OF INFLATION. AFR PLAN DEMAND
PROB/SOLV PAY COST INCOME 20. PAGE 53 F1035 TEC/DEV
FINAN

B64
HARBISON F.H.,EDUCATION, MANPOWER, AND ECONOMIC PLAN
GROWTH. WOR+45 ECO/DEV ECO/UNDEV ACADEM LABOR TEC/DEV
SCHOOL WORKER UTIL...IDEA/COMP NAT/COMP. PAGE 55 EDU/PROP
F1075 SKILL

B64
HAZLEWOOD A.,THE ECONOMICS OF DEVELOPMENT: AN BIBLIOG/A
ANNOTATED LIST OF BOOKS AND ARTICLES PUBLISHED ECO/UNDEV
1958-1962. AGRI FINAN INDUS LABOR NAT/G DIPLOM TEC/DEV
INT/TRADE INCOME...MGT 20. PAGE 58 F1130

B64
HEKHUIS D.J.,INTERNATIONAL STABILITY: MILITARY, TEC/DEV
ECONOMIC AND POLITICAL DIMENSIONS. FUT WOR+45 LAW DETER
ECO/UNDEV INT/ORG NAT/G VOL/ASSN FORCES ACT/RES REGION
BAL/PWR PWR WEALTH...STAT UN 20. PAGE 58 F1143

B64
HERSKOVITS M.J.,ECONOMIC TRANSITION IN AFRICA. FUT AFR
INT/ORG NAT/G WORKER PROB/SOLV TEC/DEV INT/TRADE ECO/UNDEV
EQUILIB INCOME...ANTHOL 20. PAGE 59 F1157 PLAN
ADMIN

B64
JACOBY N.H.,UNITED STATES MONETARY POLICY. UK ECO/DEV
USA+45 LAW NAT/G TEC/DEV TAX EQUILIB INCOME POLICY
...METH/COMP 20 FED/RESERV. PAGE 66 F1300 ECO/TAC
FINAN

B64
KAPLAN A.D.H.,BIG ENTERPRISE IN A COMPETITIVE FINAN
SYSTEM (REV. ED.). USA+45 INDUS MARKET WORKER GP/REL
TEC/DEV ECO/TAC PRICE ADJUD ADMIN CONTROL...MGT NAT/G
CHARTS 20 MONOPOLY. PAGE 69 F1351 LG/CO

B64
KUZNETS S.,POSTWAR ECONOMIC GROWTH: FOUR LECTURES. WOR+45 INDUS NAT/G WORKER TEC/DEV ECO/TAC RATION TARIFFS PRICE BAL/PAY COST DEMAND 20. PAGE 74 F1455
ECO/DEV ECO/UNDEV TREND FINAN

B64
LANG A.S.,URBAN RAIL TRANSIT. OP/RES PLAN PROB/SOLV TEC/DEV AUTOMAT COST...TECHNIC MATH CON/ANAL CHARTS METH/COMP SIMUL MUNICH 20 RAILROAD PUB/TRANS. PAGE 75 F1474
DIST/IND ECOMETRIC

B64
LI C.M.,INDUSTRIAL DEVELOPMENT IN COMMUNIST CHINA. CHINA/COM ECO/DEV ECO/UNDEV AGRI FINAN INDUS MARKET LABOR NAT/G ECO/TAC INT/TRADE EXEC ALL/VALS ...POLICY RELATIV TREND WORK TOT/POP VAL/FREE 20. PAGE 79 F1556
ASIA TEC/DEV

B64
LITTLE I.M.D.,AID TO AFRICA. AFR UK TEC/DEV DIPLOM ECO/TAC INCOME WEALTH 20. PAGE 81 F1583
FOR/AID ECO/UNDEV ADMIN POLICY

B64
LITVAK I.A.,MARKETING: CANADA. CANADA STRATA PROC/MFG LEGIS TEC/DEV DIPLOM INT/TRADE PRICE AUTOMAT ATTIT WEALTH...ANTHOL 20. PAGE 81 F1587
ECO/TAC MARKET ECO/DEV EFFICIENCY

B64
NAGEL P.C.,ONE NATION INDIVISIBLE: THE UNION IN AMERICAN THOUGHT 1776-1861. USA-45 INDUS TEC/DEV EDU/PROP DREAM...IDEA/COMP 18/19. PAGE 96 F1887
FEDERAL NAT/G ATTIT INGP/REL

B64
OECD,DEVELOPMENT ASSISTANCE EFFORTS - POLICIES OF THE MEMBERS. AGRI INDUS BUDGET...GEOG NAT/COMP 20 OECD. PAGE 100 F1967
INT/ORG FOR/AID ECO/UNDEV TEC/DEV

B64
ORGANIZATION AMERICAN STATES,ECONOMIC SURVEY OF LATIN AMERICA, 1962. L/A+17C AGRI DIST/IND INDUS MARKET PROC/MFG R+D PLAN TEC/DEV ECO/TAC REGION BAL/PAY ALL/VALS...CON/ANAL ORG/CHARTS GEN/METH OAS ALL/PROG 20 ALL/PROG. PAGE 102 F1998
ECO/UNDEV CHARTS

B64
PAWERA J.C.,ALGERIA'S INFRASTRUCTURE. ALGERIA PLAN WEALTH...METH/CNCPT 20. PAGE 104 F2041
ECO/UNDEV INDUS TEC/DEV COM/IND

B64
RAMAZANI R.K.,THE MIDDLE EAST AND THE EUROPEAN COMMON MARKET. EUR+WWI ISLAM ECO/DEV EXTR/IND MARKET PROC/MFG INT/ORG NAT/G TEC/DEV ECO/TAC REGION DRIVE WEALTH...STAT CHARTS EEC TOT/POP 20. PAGE 109 F2141
ECO/UNDEV ATTIT INT/TRADE

B64
RANIS G.,THE UNITED STATES AND THE DEVELOPING ECONOMIES. COM USA+45 AGRI FINAN TEC/DEV CAP/ISM ECO/TAC INT/TRADE...POLICY METH/COMP ANTHOL 20 AID. PAGE 109 F2145
ECO/UNDEV DIPLOM FOR/AID

B64
RIVKIN A.,AFRICA AND THE EUROPEAN COMMON MARKET (PAMPHLET). AFR MOD/EUR WOR+45 TEC/DEV FOR/AID TARIFFS BAL/PAY...POLICY 20 EEC. PAGE 111 F2196
INT/ORG INT/TRADE ECO/TAC ECO/UNDEV

B64
SOLOW R.M.,THE NATURE AND SOURCES OF UNEMPLOYMENT IN THE UNITED STATES (PAMPHLET). USA+45 INDUS LABOR TEC/DEV ECO/TAC SKILL WEALTH...TREND NAT/COMP 20. PAGE 124 F2439
ECO/DEV WORKER STAT PRODUC

B64
STONIER A.W.,EXERCISES IN ECONOMICS. FINAN INDUS TEC/DEV RENT PAY EQUILIB PRODUC PROFIT...METH/COMP T. PAGE 127 F2498
PRICE MARKET WORKER

B64
URQUIDI V.L.,THE CHALLENGE OF DEVELOPMENT IN LATIN AMERICA. L/A+17C FINAN INT/ORG TEC/DEV DIPLOM INT/TRADE PRICE REGION PRODUC...CHARTS 20 ALL/PROG. PAGE 133 F2628
ECO/UNDEV ECO/TAC NAT/G TREND

B64
US SENATE COMM ON FOREIGN REL,HEARING ON BILLS RELATING TO FOREIGN ASSISTANCE. USA+45 WOR+45 ECO/UNDEV FINAN INDUS 20 UN CONGRESS. PAGE 139 F2733
FOR/AID DIPLOM TEC/DEV INT/ORG

B64
ZEBOT C.A.,THE ECONOMICS OF COMPETITIVE COEXISTENCE. CHINA/COM USSR WOR+45 FINAN MARKET FOR/AID PRICE DEMAND EQUILIB WEALTH ALL/IDEOS 20. PAGE 150 F2961
TEC/DEV DIPLOM METH/COMP

L64
BHAGWATI J.,"THE PURE THEORY OF INTERNATIONAL TRADE: A SURVEY." WOR+45 ECO/DEV ECO/UNDEV FINAN MARKET PROC/MFG INT/ORG LABOR LG/CO NAT/G TEC/DEV ECO/TAC SKILL WEALTH...POLICY RELATIV MGT CONCPT NEW/IDEA MATH QUANT GEN/LAWS FOR/TRADE 20. PAGE 14 F0276
INDUS HYPO/EXP

L64
CARNEGIE ENDOWMENT INT. PEACE,"ECONOMIC AND SOCIAL QUESTION (ISSUES BEFORE THE NINETEENTH GENERAL ASSEMBLY)." WOR+45 ECO/DEV ECO/UNDEV INDUS R+D DELIB/GP CREATE PLAN TEC/DEV ECO/TAC FOR/AID BAL/PAY...RECORD UN 20. PAGE 21 F0414
INT/ORG INT/TRADE

S64
FLORINSKY M.T.,"TRENDS IN THE SOVIET ECONOMY." COM USA+45 USSR INDUS LABOR NAT/G PLAN TEC/DEV ECO/TAC ALL/VALS SOCISM...MGT METH/CNCPT STYLE CON/ANAL GEN/METH WORK 20. PAGE 42 F0817
ECO/DEV AGRI

S64
HUELIN D.,"ECONOMIC INTEGRATION IN LATIN AMERICAN: PROGRESS AND PROBLEMS." L/A+17C ECO/DEV AGRI DIST/IND FINAN INDUS NAT/G VOL/ASSN CONSULT DELIB/GP EX/STRUC ACT/RES PLAN TEC/DEV ECO/TAC ROUTINE BAL/PAY WEALTH FOR/TRADE WORK TERR/GP 20. PAGE 63 F1232
MARKET ECO/UNDEV INT/TRADE

S64
MC WILLIAM M.,"THE WORLD BANK AND THE TRANSFER OF POWER IN KENYA." AFR ECO/UNDEV CONSULT ACT/RES TEC/DEV PERCEPT PWR SKILL WEALTH...CONCPT OBS TREND 20. PAGE 88 F1715
NAT/G ECO/TAC

S64
NASH M.,"SOCIAL PREREQUISITES TO ECONOMIC GROWTH IN LATIN AMERICA AND SOUTHEAST ASIA." L/A+17C S/ASIA CULTURE SOCIETY ECO/UNDEV AGRI INDUS NAT/G PLAN TEC/DEV EDU/PROP ROUTINE ALL/VALS...POLICY RELATIV SOC NAT/COMP WORK TOT/POP 20. PAGE 96 F1894
ECO/DEV PERCEPT

S64
PATEL S.J.,"THE ECONOMIC DISTANCE BETWEEN NATIONS: ITS ORIGIN, MEASUREMENT AND OUTLOOK." WOR+45 ECO/DEV AGRI FINAN INDUS MARKET LABOR NAT/G CONSULT TEC/DEV ECO/TAC WEALTH...POLICY RELATIV MGT TREND WORK 20. PAGE 103 F2035
ECO/UNDEV PLAN

S64
READER D.H.,"A SURVEY OF CATEGORIES OF ECONOMIC ACTIVITIES AMONG THE PEOPLES OF AFRICA." AGRI INDUS MARKET KIN HEALTH SKILL WEALTH...GEOG METH/CNCPT CHARTS TERR/GP WORK TOT/POP VAL/FREE 20. PAGE 110 F2160
TEC/DEV ECO/UNDEV AFR

B65
PEACE RESEARCH ABSTRACTS. FUT WOR+45 R+D INT/ORG NAT/G PLAN TEC/DEV BAL/PWR DIPLOM FOR/AID NUC/PWR HEALTH. PAGE 1 F0022
BIBLIOG/A PEACE ARMS/CONT WAR

B65
ALDERSON W.,DYNAMIC MARKETING BEHAVIOR. USA+45 FINAN CREATE TEC/DEV EDU/PROP PRICE COST 20. PAGE 3 F0057
MGT MARKET ATTIT CAP/ISM

B65
ALEXANDER R.J.,ORGANIZED LABOR IN LATIN AMERICA. L/A+17C INT/ORG LEGIS WORKER TEC/DEV BARGAIN INT/TRADE REV...NAT/COMP BIBLIOG 20. PAGE 3 F0059
LABOR POL/PAR ECO/UNDEV POLICY

B65
ANDERSON C.A.,EDUCATION AND ECONOMIC DEVELOPMENT. INDUS R+D SCHOOL TEC/DEV ECO/TAC EDU/PROP AGE HEREDITY PERCEPT SKILL 20. PAGE 5 F0092
ANTHOL ECO/DEV ECO/UNDEV WORKER

B65
ARTEL R.,THE STRUCTURE OF THE STOCKHOLM ECONOMY. SWEDEN DIST/IND LABOR LOC/G TEC/DEV DEMAND MUNICH LOUISIANA 20. PAGE 7 F0125
ECO/DEV METH/COMP BAL/PAY

B65
BELASSA B.,ECONOMIC DEVELOPMENT AND INTEGRATION. LG/CO PROB/SOLV TEC/DEV INT/TRADE TARIFFS COST WEALTH...POLICY METH/COMP 20. PAGE 12 F0232
ECO/UNDEV ECO/TAC INT/ORG INDUS

B65
BRYCE M.D.,POLICIES AND METHODS FOR INDUSTRIAL DEVELOPMENT. WOR+45 FINAN MARKET CONSULT TARIFFS TAX COST. PAGE 20 F0379
INDUS PLAN ECO/DEV TEC/DEV

B65
CHAO K.,THE RATE AND PATTERN OF INDUSTRIAL GROWTH IN COMMUNIST CHINA. CHINA/COM ECO/UNDEV TEC/DEV PRICE...NAT/COMP BIBLIOG 20. PAGE 23 F0452
INDUS INDEX STAT PRODUC

B65
DODDY F.S.,INTRODUCTION TO THE USE OF ECONOMIC INDICATORS. FINAN LABOR PLAN COST...ECOMETRIC INDICATOR MATH PREDICT CHARTS METH 20. PAGE 33 F0649
TEC/DEV STAT PRODUC PRICE

B65
FERMAN L.A.,POVERTY IN AMERICA: A BOOK OF READINGS. USA+45 CULTURE ECO/DEV PROB/SOLV ALL/VALS...POLICY ANTHOL BIBLIOG 20 POVRTY/WAR. PAGE 40 F0785
WEALTH TEC/DEV CONCPT RECEIVE

B65
GORDON W.,THE POLITICAL ECONOMY OF LATIN AMERICA. L/A+17C FINAN MARKET PROB/SOLV TEC/DEV RECEIVE ADMIN WEALTH 20. PAGE 49 F0962
ECO/UNDEV INT/TRADE REGION POLICY

B65
HARBISON F.,MANPOWER AND EDUCATION. AFR CHINA/COM IRAN L/A+17C S/ASIA TEC/DEV ADJUST OPTIMAL SKILL
ECO/UNDEV EDU/PROP

...ANTHOL 20. PAGE 55 F1073 WORKER NAT/COMP

B65
HASSON J.A.,THE ECONOMICS OF NUCLEAR POWER. INDIA UK USA+45 WOR+45 INT/ORG TEC/DEV COST...SOC STAT CHARTS 20 EURATOM. PAGE 56 F1108 NUC/PWR INDUS ECO/DEV METH

B65
IANNI O.,ESTADO E CAPITALISMO. L/A+17C FINAN TEC/DEV ECO/TAC ORD/FREE WEALTH POLICY. PAGE 64 F1258 ECO/UNDEV STRUCT INDUS NAT/G

B65
INT. BANK RECONSTR. DEVELOP.,ECONOMIC DEVELOPMENT OF KUWAIT. ISLAM KUWAIT AGRI FINAN MARKET EX/STRUC TEC/DEV ECO/TAC ADMIN WEALTH...OBS CON/ANAL CHARTS 20. PAGE 64 F1266 INDUS NAT/G

B65
KANTOROVICH L.V.,THE BEST USE OF ECONOMIC RESOURCES. USSR SOCIETY FINAN ACT/RES TEC/DEV ECO/TAC PRICE CONTROL COST DEMAND EFFICIENCY OPTIMAL...MGT STAT. PAGE 69 F1350 PLAN MATH DECISION

B65
KASER M.,COMECON* INTEGRATION PROBLEMS OF THE PLANNED ECONOMIES. INT/ORG TEC/DEV INT/TRADE PRICE ADMIN ADJUST CENTRAL...STAT TIME/SEQ ORG/CHARTS COMECON. PAGE 69 F1359 PLAN ECO/DEV COM REGION

B65
LUTZ V.,FRENCH PLANNING. FRANCE TEC/DEV RIGID/FLEX ORD/FREE 20. PAGE 82 F1613 PLAN ADMIN FUT

B65
LYONS G.M.,AMERICA: PURPOSE AND POWER. UK USA+45 FINAN INDUS MARKET WORKER TEC/DEV DIPLOM AUTOMAT NUC/PWR WAR RACE/REL ORD/FREE 20 EEC CONGRESS SUPREME/CT CIV/RIGHTS. PAGE 82 F1617 PWR PROB/SOLV ECO/DEV TASK

B65
MAO J.C.T.,EFFICIENCY IN PUBLIC URBAN RENEWAL EXPENDITURES THROUGH CAPITAL BUDGETING. USA+45 FINAN LOC/G NAT/G NEIGH REGION UTIL...GEOG METH/CNCPT STAT SIMUL GEN/LAWS MUNICH 20 URBAN/RNWL. PAGE 85 F1662 TEC/DEV BUDGET PROB/SOLV

B65
MONCRIEFF A.,SECOND THOUGHTS ON AID. WOR+45 ECO/UNDEV AGRI FINAN VOL/ASSN PLAN TEC/DEV GIVE EDU/PROP ROLE WEALTH 20. PAGE 93 F1816 FOR/AID ECO/TAC INT/ORG IDEA/COMP

B65
MOORE W.E.,THE IMPACT OF INDUSTRY. CULTURE STRUCT ORD/FREE...TREND 20. PAGE 93 F1824 INDUS MGT TEC/DEV ECO/UNDEV

B65
MURUMBI J.,PROBLEMS OF ECONOMIC DEVELOPMENT IN EAST AFRICA. FINAN INDUS WORKER TEC/DEV INT/TRADE TAX DEMAND EFFICIENCY PRODUC SOCISM...TREND CHARTS 20 AFRICA/E. PAGE 95 F1869 AGRI ECO/TAC ECO/UNDEV PROC/MFG

B65
ONUOHA B.,THE ELEMENTS OF AFRICAN SOCIALISM. AFR FINAN SECT TEC/DEV FOR/AID GP/REL OWN LAISSEZ MARXISM...CONCPT BIBLIOG 20. PAGE 101 F1992 SOCISM ECO/UNDEV NAT/G EX/STRUC

B65
OXENFELDT A.R.,ECONOMIC SYSTEMS IN ACTION. FRANCE USA+45 USSR CULTURE PLAN PROB/SOLV TEC/DEV INCOME PRODUC WEALTH...METH/COMP 20. PAGE 102 F2007 ECO/DEV CAP/ISM MARXISM ECO/TAC

B65
SCHULER E.A.,THE PAKISTAN ACADEMIES FOR RURAL DEVELOPMENT COMILLA AND PESHAWAR 1959-1964. PAKISTAN S/ASIA SOCIETY STRUCT AGRI NAT/G TEC/DEV EDU/PROP 20. PAGE 117 F2314 BIBLIOG PLAN ECO/TAC ECO/UNDEV

B65
SIMMS R.P.,URBANIZATION IN WEST AFRICA; A REVIEW OF CURRENT LITERATURE. AFR PLAN TEC/DEV...SOC OBS NAT/COMP MUNICH 20. PAGE 122 F2405 BIBLIOG/A ECO/DEV ECO/UNDEV

B65
SMERK G.M.,URBAN TRANSPORTATION; THE FEDERAL ROLE. FUT USA+45 FINAN PROB/SOLV TEC/DEV AUTOMAT GOV/REL COST...STAT BIBLIOG MUNICH 20 PUB/TRANS. PAGE 123 F2426 PLAN DIST/IND NAT/G

B65
STEINER G.A.,THE CREATIVE ORGANIZATION. ELITES LG/CO PLAN PROB/SOLV TEC/DEV INSPECT CAP/ISM CONTROL EXEC PERSON...METH/COMP HYPO/EXP 20. PAGE 126 F2476 CREATE MGT ADMIN SOC

B65
THAYER F.C. JR.,AIR TRANSPORT POLICY AND NATIONAL SECURITY: A POLITICAL, ECONOMIC, AND MILITARY ANALYSIS. DIST/IND OP/RES PLAN TEC/DEV DIPLOM DETER WAR COST EFFICIENCY...POLICY BIBLIOG 20 DEPT/DEFEN FAA CAB. PAGE 129 F2548 AIR FORCES CIVMIL/REL ORD/FREE

B65
US SENATE COMM ON FOREIGN REL,HEARINGS ON THE FOREIGN ASSISTANCE PROGRAM. AFR ASIA L/A+17C USA+45 WOR+45 FORCES TEC/DEV BUDGET CONTROL WEAPON ORD/FREE 20 UN CONGRESS SEC/STATE. PAGE 139 F2734 FOR/AID DIPLOM INT/ORG ECO/UNDEV

B65
WARNER A.W.,THE IMPACT OF SCIENCE ON TECHNOLOGY. UNIV INTELL SOCIETY NAT/G ACT/RES PLAN PROB/SOLV BUDGET OPTIMAL GEN/METH. PAGE 143 F2821 DECISION TEC/DEV CREATE POLICY

B65
WEIL G.L.,A HANDBOOK ON THE EUROPEAN ECONOMIC COMMUNITY. BELGIUM EUR+WWI FRANCE GERMANY/W ITALY CONSTN ECO/DEV CREATE PARTIC GP/REL...DECISION MGT CHARTS 20 EEC. PAGE 144 F2846 INT/TRADE INT/ORG TEC/DEV INT/LAW

B65
WHITE J.,GERMAN AID. GERMANY/W FINAN PLAN TEC/DEV INT/TRADE ADMIN ATTIT...POLICY 20. PAGE 146 F2870 FOR/AID ECO/UNDEV DIPLOM ECO/TAC

B65
WISH J.R.,ECONOMIC DEVELOPMENT IN LATIN AMERICA: AN ANNOTATED BIBLIOGRAPHY. L/A+17C COM/IND MARKET R+D CREATE CAP/ISM ATTIT...STAT METH 20. PAGE 148 F2912 BIBLIOG/A ECO/UNDEV TEC/DEV AGRI

L65
WILLIAMS S.,"NEGOTIATING INVESTMENT IN EMERGING COUNTRIES." USA+45 WOR+45 INDUS MARKET NAT/G TOP/EX TEC/DEV CAP/ISM ECO/TAC ADMIN SKILL WEALTH...POLICY RELATIV MGT WORK 20. PAGE 147 F2894 FINAN ECO/UNDEV

L65
WIONCZEK M.,"LATIN AMERICA FREE TRADE ASSOCIATION." AGRI DIST/IND FINAN INDUS INT/ORG LABOR NAT/G TEC/DEV ECO/TAC HEALTH SKILL WEALTH...POLICY RELATIV MGT LAFTA 20. PAGE 148 F2909 L/A+17C MARKET REGION

S65
BALDWIN D.A.,"THE INTERNATIONAL BANK IN POLITICAL PERSPECTIVE" USA+45 TEC/DEV FOR/AID RENT GIVE COST ...IDEA/COMP GAME IBRD. PAGE 9 F0160 FINAN INT/ORG

S65
CHU K.,"A DYNAMIC MODEL OF THE FIRM." OP/RES PROB/SOLV...DECISION ECOMETRIC NEW/IDEA STAT GAME ORG/CHARTS SIMUL. PAGE 24 F0472 INDUS COMPUTER TEC/DEV

S65
MUNZI U.,"THE EUROPEAN SOCIAL FUND IN THE DEVELOPMENT OF THE MEDITERRANEAN REGIONS OF THE EEC." FUT GREECE ITALY PORTUGAL SPAIN TURKEY WORKER TEC/DEV ECO/TAC REGION...STAT EEC. PAGE 95 F1862 ECO/UNDEV PREDICT RECORD

S65
TENDLER J.D.,"TECHNOLOGY AND ECONOMIC DEVELOPMENT* THE CASE OF HYDRO VS THERMAL POWER." CONSTRUC DIST/IND CREATE TEC/DEV INT/TRADE CENTRAL PWR SKILL WEALTH...MGT NAT/COMP ARGEN. PAGE 129 F2544 BRAZIL INDUS ECO/UNDEV

S65
VAN DER HORST S.T.,"THE ECONOMICS OF DECENTRALISATION OF INDUSTRY." SOUTH/AFR ECO/DEV LG/CO AUTOMAT DISCRIM...POLICY MUNICH 20. PAGE 140 F2761 PLAN INDUS CENTRAL TEC/DEV

B66
ALEXANDER Y.,INTERNATIONAL TECHNICAL ASSISTANCE EXPERTS: A CASE STUDY OF THE U.N. EXPERIENCE. USA+45 WOR+45 WORKER CREATE PLAN PROB/SOLV ECO/TAC FOR/AID GIVE EDU/PROP...CHARTS BIBLIOG 20 UN. PAGE 3 F0062 SKILL INT/ORG TEC/DEV CONSULT

B66
BAKLANOFF E.N.,NEW PERSPECTIVES ON BRAZIL. BRAZIL SOCIETY INDUS DOMIN LEAD REV CIVMIL/REL...GEOG PSY LING ANTHOL 20. PAGE 8 F0156 ECO/UNDEV TEC/DEV DIPLOM ORD/FREE

B66
BALDWIN R.E.,ECONOMIC DEVELOPMENT AND EXPORT GROWTH: A STUDY OF NORTHERN RHODESIA, 1920-1960. AFR RHODESIA AGRI EXTR/IND FINAN MARKET LABOR WORKER ECO/TAC...CONCPT NEW/IDEA MUNICH 20. PAGE 9 F0166 ECO/UNDEV TEC/DEV INT/TRADE CAP/ISM

B66
BOWEN H.R.,AUTOMATION AND ECONOMIC PROGRESS. EUR+WWI USA+45 ECO/DEV INCOME ORD/FREE WEALTH ...POLICY ANTHOL 20. PAGE 17 F0327 AUTOMAT TEC/DEV WORKER LEISURE

B66
BROEKMEIJER M.W.J.,FICTION AND TRUTH ABOUT THE "DECADE OF DEVELOPMENT" WOR+45 AGRI FINAN INDUS NAT/G TEC/DEV DIPLOM EDU/PROP LEAD SKILL 20 THIRD/WRLD. PAGE 19 F0358 FOR/AID POLICY ECO/UNDEV PLAN

B66
CURRIE L.,ACCELERATING DEVELOPMENT: THE NECESSITY AND MEANS. COLOMBIA USA+45 INDUS DIPLOM EFFICIENCY WEALTH...METH/CNCPT NEW/IDEA 20. PAGE 29 F0564 PLAN ECO/UNDEV FOR/AID TEC/DEV

B66
DOBB M.,SOVIET ECONOMIC DEVELOPMENT SINCE 1917. USSR ECO/DEV ECO/UNDEV LABOR NAT/G TEC/DEV ECO/TAC ROUTINE PRODUC MARXISM 20. PAGE 33 F0647 PLAN INDUS WORKER

B66
FRIEDMANN W.G.,INTERNATIONAL FINANCIAL AID. USA+45 ECO/DEV ECO/UNDEV NAT/G VOL/ASSN EX/STRUC PLAN RENT GIVE BAL/PAY PWR...GEOG INT/LAW STAT TREND UN EEC COMECON. PAGE 44 F0866 INT/ORG FOR/AID TEC/DEV ECO/TAC

B66
GITTINGER J.P.,THE LITERATURE OF AGRICULTURAL PLANNING. UNIV INT/ORG CONSULT WORKER TEC/DEV ECO/TAC OPTIMAL...POLICY METH/COMP BIBLIOG/A 20. PAGE 47 F0927
ECO/UNDEV AGRI PLAN WRITING

B66
GOULD J.M.,THE TECHNICAL ELITE. INDUS LABOR TECHRACY...POLICY DECISION STAT CHARTS 20. PAGE 49 F0967
ECO/DEV TEC/DEV ELITES TECHNIC

B66
HAYER T.,FRENCH AID. AFR FRANCE AGRI FINAN BUDGET ADMIN WAR PRODUC...CHARTS 18/20 THIRD/WRLD OVRSEA/DEV. PAGE 57 F1125
TEC/DEV COLONIAL FOR/AID ECO/UNDEV

B66
HOROWITZ I.L.,THREE WORLDS OF DEVELOPMENT. COM USA+45 STRUCT ECO/DEV PLAN PROB/SOLV TEC/DEV CIVMIL/REL...PHIL/SCI IDEA/COMP 20. PAGE 62 F1216
ECO/UNDEV BAL/PWR POL/PAR REV

B66
HUNT C.L.,SOCIAL ASPECTS OF ECONOMIC DEVELOPMENT. S/ASIA AGRI FAM TEC/DEV RECEIVE EDU/PROP OWN...GEOG MUNICH 20. PAGE 63 F1243
SOC STRATA ATTIT ECO/UNDEV

B66
HUTTENBACH R.A.,BRITISH IMPERIAL EXPERIENCE. AFR S/ASIA UK WOR-45 INT/ORG TEC/DEV...CHARTS 16/20 MERCANTLST. PAGE 64 F1253
COLONIAL TIME/SEQ INT/TRADE

B66
INGRAM J.C.,INTERNATIONAL ECONOMIC PROBLEMS. ECO/DEV ECO/UNDEV INDUS MARKET TEC/DEV TARIFFS BAL/PAY CENTRAL...POLICY 20 EEC. PAGE 64 F1265
INT/TRADE INT/ORG FINAN

B66
KAREFA-SMART J.,AFRICA: PROGRESS THROUGH COOPERATION. AFR FINAN TEC/DEV DIPLOM FOR/AID EDU/PROP CONFER REGION GP/REL WEALTH...HEAL SOC/INTEG 20. PAGE 69 F1356
ORD/FREE ECO/UNDEV VOL/ASSN PLAN

B66
KEENLEYSIDE H.L.,INTERNATIONAL AID: A SUMMARY. AFR INDIA S/ASIA UK STRATA EXTR/IND TEC/DEV ADMIN RACE/REL DEMAND NAT/LISM WEALTH...TREND CHINJAP. PAGE 70 F1367
ECO/UNDEV FOR/AID DIPLOM TASK

B66
KOMIYA R.,POSTWAR ECONOMIC GROWTH IN JAPAN. ELITES NAT/G EX/STRUC TEC/DEV BUDGET DIPLOM CONTROL BAL/PAY PRODUC...BIBLIOG 20 CHINJAP. PAGE 73 F1424
ECO/DEV POLICY PLAN ADJUST

B66
KURAKOV I.G.,SCIENCE, TECHNOLOGY AND COMMUNISM; SOME QUESTIONS OF DEVELOPMENT (TRANS. BY CARIN DEDIJER). USSR INDUS PLAN PROB/SOLV COST PRODUC ...MGT MATH CHARTS METH 20. PAGE 74 F1450
CREATE TEC/DEV MARXISM ECO/TAC

B66
KUZNETS S.,MODERN ECONOMIC GROWTH. WOR+45 WOR-45 ECO/DEV ECO/UNDEV AGRI FINAN INDUS TEC/DEV EFFICIENCY INCOME...NAT/COMP 19/20. PAGE 74 F1456
TIME/SEQ WEALTH PRODUC

B66
LAMBERG R.F.,PRAG UND DIE DRITTE WELT. AFR ASIA CZECHOSLVK L/A+17C MARKET TEC/DEV ECO/TAC REV ATTIT 20 TREATY. PAGE 75 F1462
DIPLOM ECO/UNDEV INT/TRADE FOR/AID

B66
LILLEY S.,MEN, MACHINES AND HISTORY: THE STORY OF TOOLS AND MACHINES IN RELATION TO SOCIAL PROGRESS. PREHIST SPACE STRUCT COMPUTER AUTOMAT NUC/PWR ...POLICY SOC. PAGE 80 F1564
AGRI TEC/DEV SOCIETY

B66
MACFARQUHAR R.,CHINA UNDER MAO: POLITICS TAKES COMMAND. CHINA/COM COM AGRI INDUS CHIEF FORCES DIPLOM INT/TRADE EDU/PROP TASK REV ADJUST...ANTHOL 20 MAO. PAGE 83 F1628
ECO/UNDEV TEC/DEV ECO/TAC ADMIN

B66
MUNBY D.,ECONOMIC GROWTH IN WORLD PERSPECTIVE. AFR WOR+45 SOCIETY INDUS PLAN TEC/DEV ECO/TAC FOR/AID INT/TRADE COST CATHISM...ANTHOL 20 EUROPE/W CHURCH/STA. PAGE 95 F1859
SECT ECO/UNDEV ECO/DEV

B66
NATIONAL COUN APPLIED ECO RES,DEVELOPMENT WITHOUT AID. INDIA FINAN TEC/DEV EFFICIENCY...ANTHOL 20. PAGE 97 F1901
FOR/AID PLAN SOVEREIGN ECO/UNDEV

B66
ODEGARD P.H.,POLITICAL POWER AND SOCIAL CHANGE. UNIV NAT/G CREATE ALL/IDEOS...POLICY GEOG SOC CENSUS TREND. PAGE 100 F1962
PWR TEC/DEV IDEA/COMP

B66
OECD DEVELOPMENT CENTRE,CATALOGUE OF SOCIAL AND ECONOMIC DEVELOPMENT INSTITUTES AND PROGRAMMES* RESEARCH. ACT/RES PLAN TEC/DEV EDU/PROP...SOC GP/COMP NAT/COMP. PAGE 101 F1976
ECO/UNDEV ECO/DEV R+D ACADEM

B66
PERSALL E.S.,AN ECONOMETRIC STUDY OF FINANCIAL MARKETS. COMPUTER PROB/SOLV TEC/DEV...MATH STAT CHARTS METH/COMP BIBLIOG 20. PAGE 105 F2066
ECOMETRIC FINAN MARKET METH

B66
PFEFFER K.H.,WELT IM UMBRUCH. SOCIETY STRUCT INDUS PROF/ORG SECT TEC/DEV PARTIC SUPEGO WORSHIP 20 CHRISTIAN. PAGE 106 F2076
ORD/FREE STRATA CREATE

B66
RUPPENTHAL K.M.,TRANSPORTATION AND TOMORROW. FUT SPACE USA+45 SEA AIR FORCES TEC/DEV INT/TRADE ...ANTHOL 20 RAILROAD. PAGE 115 F2261
DIST/IND PLAN CIVMIL/REL PREDICT

B66
SHULTZ G.P.,STRATEGIES FOR THE DISPLACED WORKER. USA+45 COMPUTER TEC/DEV BARGAIN RECEIVE EDU/PROP CONFER GP/REL...MGT METH/COMP 20. PAGE 121 F2391
ECO/DEV WORKER PLAN AUTOMAT

B66
SMITH H.E.,READINGS IN ECONOMIC DEVELOPMENT AND ADMINISTRATION IN TANZANIA. TANZANIA FINAN INDUS LABOR NAT/G PLAN PROB/SOLV INT/TRADE COLONIAL REGION...ANTHOL BIBLIOG 20 AFRICA/E. PAGE 123 F2431
TEC/DEV ADMIN GOV/REL

B66
THIESENHUSEN W.C.,CHILE'S EXPERIMENTS IN AGRARIAN REFORM. CHILE STRUCT NAT/G ACT/RES ECO/TAC GOV/REL COST SOCISM...TREND CHARTS SOC/EXP 20. PAGE 130 F2558
AGRI ECO/UNDEV SOC TEC/DEV

B66
US DEPARTMENT OF LABOR,TECHNOLOGICAL TRENDS IN MAJOR AMERICAN INDUSTRIES. USA+45 R+D LABOR GP/REL PRODUC...MGT BIBLIOG 20. PAGE 135 F2669
TEC/DEV INDUS TREND AUTOMAT

B66
US DEPARTMENT OF STATE,RESEARCH ON THE USSR AND EASTERN EUROPE (EXTERNAL RESEARCH LIST NO 1-25). USSR LAW CULTURE SOCIETY NAT/G TEC/DEV DIPLOM EDU/PROP REGION...GEOG LING. PAGE 136 F2675
BIBLIOG/A EUR+WWI COM MARXISM

B66
US HOUSE COMM FOREIGN AFFAIRS,HEARINGS ON HR 12449 A BILL TO AMEND FURTHER THE FOREIGN ASSISTANCE ACT OF 1961. AFR ASIA L/A+17C USA+45 VIETNAM INT/ORG TEC/DEV INT/TRADE ATTIT ORD/FREE 20 UN NATO CONGRESS AID. PAGE 137 F2692
FOR/AID ECO/TAC ECO/UNDEV DIPLOM

B66
US SENATE COMM GOVT OPERATIONS,HEARINGS BEFORE SUBCOMMITTEE ON FOREIGN AID EXPENDITURES: POPULATION CRISIS VOLUMES 1-5 JUNE-SEPT 1965. STRATA ECO/UNDEV PLAN TEC/DEV EDU/PROP ATTIT HEALTH ...GEOG CHARTS 20 CONGRESS BIRTH/CON CASEBOOK. PAGE 138 F2729
ECO/DEV CENSUS FAM CONTROL

B66
US SENATE COMM GOVT OPERATIONS,INTERGOVERNMENTAL PERSONNEL ACT OF 1966. USA+45 NAT/G CONSULT DELIB/GP WORKER TEC/DEV PAY AUTOMAT UTIL 20 CONGRESS. PAGE 139 F2730
ADMIN LEGIS EFFICIENCY EDU/PROP

B66
WESTON J.F.,THE SCOPE AND METHODOLOGY OF FINANCE. PLAN TEC/DEV CONTROL EFFICIENCY INCOME UTIL...MGT CONCPT MATH STAT TREND METH 20. PAGE 145 F2863
FINAN ECO/DEV POLICY PRICE

B66
ZINKIN T.,CHALLENGES IN INDIA. INDIA PAKISTAN LAW AGRI FINAN INDUS TOP/EX TEC/DEV CONTROL ROUTINE ORD/FREE PWR 20 NEHRU/J SHASTRI/LB CIVIL/SERV. PAGE 150 F2964
NAT/G ECO/TAC POLICY ADMIN

L66
AFRICAN BIBLIOGRAPHIC CENTER,"AFRICAN ECONOMIC AFFAIRS: A SELECT BIBLIOGRAPHICAL SURVEY, 1965-1966." AFR FINAN INDUS INT/ORG LABOR PLAN BUDGET DIPLOM INT/TRADE ADMIN EFFICIENCY WEALTH 20. PAGE 3 F0046
BIBLIOG ECO/UNDEV TEC/DEV FOR/AID

L66
AFRICAN BIBLIOGRAPHIC CENTER,"AFRICAN ECONOMIC AFFAIRS: A SELECT BIBLIOGRAPHICAL SURVEY, 1965-1966; SUPPLEMENTS NUMBERS 1-3." AFR FINAN INDUS LABOR PLAN BUDGET CAP/ISM DIPLOM INT/TRADE ADMIN...GEOG 20. PAGE 3 F0047
BIBLIOG/A ECO/UNDEV FOR/AID TEC/DEV

L66
CHENERY H.B.,"FOREIGN ASSISTANCE AND ECONOMIC DEVELOPMENT" FUT WOR+45 NAT/G DIPLOM GIVE PRODUC ...METH/CNCPT CHARTS 20. PAGE 24 F0464
FOR/AID EFFICIENCY ECO/UNDEV TEC/DEV

S66
VERSLUYS J.D.N.,"SOME NOTES ON THE SOCIAL AND ECONOMIC EFFECTS OF RURAL ELECTRIFICATION IN BURMA" BURMA EDU/PROP PRODUC ORD/FREE...SOC QU MUNICH TIME 20. PAGE 141 F2782
TEC/DEV SOCIETY CREATE

N66
US ADVISORY COMN INTERGOV REL,CATALOGS AND OTHER INFORMATION SOURCES ON FEDERAL AND STATE AID PROGRAMS: A SECTED BIBLIOGRAPHY (PAPER). USA+45 LAW LOC/G NAT/G PROVS VOL/ASSN TEC/DEV ADMIN HEALTH ...WELF/ST SOC/WK MUNICH. PAGE 134 F2635
BIBLIOG/A GOV/REL FINAN ECO/DEV

B67
ALNASRAWI A.,FINANCING ECONOMIC DEVELOPMENT IN IRAQ. IRAQ INDUS CAP/ISM COST PRODUC...STAT CHARTS BIBLIOG 20. PAGE 4 F0076
ECO/UNDEV EXTR/IND TEC/DEV INT/TRADE

B67
BARANSON J.,TECHNOLOGY FOR UNDERDEVELOPED AREAS: AN ANNOTATED BIBLIOGRAPHY. FUT WOR+45 CULTURE INDUS INT/ORG CREATE PROB/SOLV INT/TRADE EDU/PROP AUTOMAT ...CONCPT METH. PAGE 10 F0181 BIBLIOG/A ECO/UNDEV TEC/DEV R+D

B67
BARNETT A.D.,CHINA AFTER MAO. ASIA CHINA/COM CULTURE ECO/UNDEV ECO/TAC CONTROL EFFICIENCY NAT/LISM MARXISM 20. PAGE 10 F0189 POL/PAR NAT/G TEC/DEV GP/REL

B67
CHAPIN F.S. JR.,SELECTED REFERENCES ON URBAN PLANNING METHODS AND TECHNIQUES. USA+45 LAW ECO/DEV LOC/G NAT/G SCHOOL CONSULT CREATE PROB/SOLV TEC/DEV ...SOC/WK MUNICH. PAGE 23 F0454 BIBLIOG NEIGH PLAN

B67
CLEMENT M.O.,THEORETICAL ISSUES IN INTERNATIONAL ECONOMICS. WOR+45 PLAN PROB/SOLV TEC/DEV ...ECOMETRIC METH/CNCPT MATH BIBLIOG T MONEY. PAGE 25 F0489 INT/TRADE FINAN CREATE BAL/PAY

B67
DONALD A.G.,MANAGEMENT, INFORMATION, AND SYSTEMS. WOR+45 LG/CO PROB/SOLV CONTROL FEEDBACK KNOWL MGT. PAGE 34 F0653 ROUTINE TEC/DEV CONCPT ADMIN

B67
DUN J.L.,THE ESSENCE OF CHINESE CIVILIZATION. ASIA FAM NAT/G TEC/DEV ADMIN SANCTION WAR HABITAT ...ANTHOL WORSHIP. PAGE 35 F0676 CULTURE SOCIETY

B67
ELDREDGE H.W.,TAMING MEGALOPOLIS; HOW TO MANAGE AN URBANIZED WORLD. WOR+45 SOCIETY ECO/DEV ECO/UNDEV NAT/G COMPUTER CREATE PARTIC EFFICIENCY WEALTH ...MGT ANTHOL MUNICH. PAGE 37 F0716 TEC/DEV PLAN PROB/SOLV

B67
ELDREDGE H.W.,TAMING MEGALOPOLIS; WHAT IT IS AND WHAT COULD BE (VOL. I). FUT USA+45 WOR+45 SOCIETY STRUCT ECO/DEV INDUS LEISURE WEALTH...ANTHOL MUNICH. PAGE 37 F0717 PROB/SOLV PLAN TEC/DEV

B67
GOODMAN P.,LIKE A CONQUERED PROVINCE: THE MORAL AMBIGUITY OF AMERICA. AFR USA+45 NAT/G PROB/SOLV EDU/PROP ADJUST EFFICIENCY 20. PAGE 49 F0950 SOCIETY TEC/DEV WAR MORAL

B67
GUTKIND E.A.,URBAN DEVELOPMENT IN SOUTHERN EUROPE* SPAIN AND PORTUGAL. CHRIST-17C EUR+WWI MOD/EUR PORTUGAL SPAIN CULTURE AGRI...SOC SAMP/SIZ BIBLIOG MUNICH. PAGE 52 F1015 TEC/DEV ECO/DEV

B67
HARDT J.P.,MATHEMATICS AND COMPUTERS IN SOVIET ECONOMIC PLANNING. COM USSR OP/RES PROB/SOLV OPTIMAL...MODAL SIMUL 20. PAGE 55 F1082 PLAN TEC/DEV MATH COMPUT/IR

B67
HEADLEY J.C.,PESTICIDE PROBLEM: AN ECONOMIC APPROACH TO PUBLIC POLICY. AGRI TEC/DEV GOV/REL COST ATTIT CHARTS. PAGE 58 F1131 HABITAT POLICY BIO/SOC CONTROL

B67
HEILBRONER R.L.,THE LIMITS OF AMERICAN CAPITALISM. FUT ECO/DEV INDUS LG/CO EX/STRUC LEAD PWR TECHRACY 20. PAGE 58 F1137 ELITES CREATE TEC/DEV CAP/ISM

B67
JOHNSON D.G.,THE STRUGGLE AGAINST WORLD HUNGER (HEADLINE SERIES, NO. 184) (PAMPHLET). PLAN TEC/DEV FOR/AID...CHARTS 20 FAO MEXIC/AMER. PAGE 67 F1322 AGRI PROB/SOLV ECO/UNDEV HEALTH

B67
KANNER L.,THE NEW YORK TIMES WORLD ECONOMIC REVIEW AND FORECAST: 1967. WOR+45 ECO/DEV ECO/UNDEV TEC/DEV...STAT PREDICT CHARTS 20. PAGE 69 F1349 INDUS FINAN TREND ECO/TAC

B67
KRANZBERG M.,TECHNOLOGY IN WESTERN CIVILIZATION VOLUME ONE. UNIV INDUS SKILL. PAGE 73 F1431 TEC/DEV ACT/RES AUTOMAT POLICY

B67
KULSKI J.E.,LAND OF URBAN PROMISE* CONTINUING THE GREAT TRADITION* A SEARCH FOR SIGNIFICANT URBAN SPACE IN URBANIZED NORTHEAST. USA+45 DIST/IND PUB/INST CONSULT CREATE TEC/DEV...SOC NEW/IDEA CHARTS BIBLIOG MUNICH. PAGE 74 F1448 PLAN PROB/SOLV ECO/DEV

B67
LINDER S.B.,TRADE AND TRADE POLICY FOR DEVELOPMENT. OP/RES DIPLOM TARIFFS UTIL WEALTH...BIBLIOG 20. PAGE 80 F1569 ECO/UNDEV ECO/TAC TEC/DEV INT/TRADE

B67
MCDOUGAL M.S.,THE INTERPRETATION OF AGREEMENTS AND WORLD PUBLIC ORDER: PRINCIPLES OF CONTENT AND PROCEDURE. WOR+45 CONSTN PROB/SOLV TEC/DEV ...CON/ANAL TREATY. PAGE 88 F1727 INT/LAW STRUCT ECO/UNDEV DIPLOM

B67
OGLESBY C.,CONTAINMENT AND CHANGE. AFR COM USA+45 ECO/UNDEV TEC/DEV ECO/TAC FOR/AID INT/TRADE DOMIN GUERRILLA REV PEACE 20 STALIN/J. PAGE 101 F1983 DIPLOM BAL/PWR MARXISM CULTURE

B67
ORLANS H.,CONTRACTING FOR ATOMS. AFR USA+45 LAW INTELL ACADEM LG/CO NAT/G PLAN TEC/DEV CONTROL DETER...TREND 20. PAGE 102 F1999 NUC/PWR R+D PRODUC PEACE

B67
OVERSEAS DEVELOPMENT INSTIT,EFFECTIVE AID. WOR+45 INT/ORG TEC/DEV DIPLOM INT/TRADE ADMIN. PAGE 102 F2004 FOR/AID ECO/UNDEV ECO/TAC NAT/COMP

B67
PEDLEY F.H.,EDUCATION AND SOCIAL WORK. USA+45 INTELL TEC/DEV. PAGE 104 F2047 GP/REL EDU/PROP SOC/WK EFFICIENCY

B67
ROACH J.R.,THE UNITED STATES AND THE ATLANTIC COMMUNITY; ISSUES AND PROSPECTS. AFR WOR+45 TEC/DEV ECO/TAC COLONIAL REGION PEACE ROLE...ANTHOL NATO EEC. PAGE 112 F2199 INT/ORG POLICY ADJUST DIPLOM

B67
SCHAEFER W.V.,THE SUSPECT AND SOCIETY: CRIMINAL PROCEDURE AND CONVERGING CONSTITUTIONAL DOCTRINES. USA+45 TEC/DEV LOBBY ROUTINE SANCTION...INT 20. PAGE 116 F2288 CRIME FORCES CONSTN JURID

B67
SCHON D.A.,TECHNOLOGY AND CHANGE* THE NEW HERACLITUS. TEC/DEV CONTROL COST DEMAND EFFICIENCY RIGID/FLEX...MYTH 20. PAGE 117 F2311 INDUS PROB/SOLV R+D CREATE

B67
STEARNS P.N.,EUROPEAN SOCIETY IN UPHEAVAL* SOCIAL HISTORY SINCE 1800. EUR+WWI MOD/EUR STRATA SECT WORKER TEC/DEV WAR...WELF/ST SOC TREND BIBLIOG 19/20. PAGE 125 F2472 REGION ECO/DEV SOCIETY INDUS

B67
TANSKY L.,US AND USSR AID TO DEVELOPING COUNTRIES. INDIA TURKEY UAR USA+45 USSR FINAN PLAN TEC/DEV ADMIN WEALTH...TREND METH/COMP 20. PAGE 128 F2535 FOR/AID ECO/UNDEV MARXISM CAP/ISM

B67
UNIVERSAL REFERENCE SYSTEM,ECONOMIC REGULATION, BUSINESS, AND GOVERNMENT (VOLUME VIII). WOR+45 WOR-45 ECO/DEV ECO/UNDEV FINAN LABOR TEC/DEV ECO/TAC INT/TRADE GOV/REL...POLICY COMPUT/IR. PAGE 133 F2617 BIBLIOG/A CONTROL NAT/G

B67
UNIVERSAL REFERENCE SYSTEM,PUBLIC POLICY AND THE MANAGEMENT OF SCIENCE (VOLUME IX). FUT SPACE WOR+45 LAW NAT/G TEC/DEV CONTROL NUC/PWR GOV/REL ...COMPUT/IR GEN/METH. PAGE 133 F2618 BIBLIOG/A POLICY MGT PHIL/SCI

B67
US AGENCY INTERNATIONAL DEV,PROPOSED FOREIGN AID PROGRAM FOR 1968: SUMMARY PRESENTATION TO THE CONGRESS. AFR S/ASIA USA+45 AGRI TEC/DEV DIPLOM ECO/TAC BAL/PAY COST HEALTH KNOWL SKILL 20 AID CONGRESS ALL/PROG. PAGE 134 F2640 ECO/UNDEV BUDGET FOR/AID STAT

B67
WILLS A.J.,AN INTRODUCTION TO THE HISTORY OF CENTRAL AFRICA. RHODESIA ZAMBIA CULTURE SOCIETY ECO/UNDEV TEC/DEV DOMIN WAR ALL/VALS...POLICY TREND BIBLIOG T 14/20 NYASALAND. PAGE 147 F2899 AFR COLONIAL ORD/FREE

B67
WISEMAN H.V.,BRITAIN AND THE COMMONWEALTH. EUR+WWI FUT UK ECO/DEV POL/PAR TEC/DEV INT/TRADE LEAD ROLE SOVEREIGN...SOC TREND 20 CMN/WLTH. PAGE 148 F2911 INT/ORG DIPLOM NAT/G NAT/COMP

B67
YAMAMURA K.,ECONOMIC POLICY IN POSTWAR JAPAN. ASIA FINAN POL/PAR DIPLOM LEAD NAT/LISM ATTIT NEW/LIB POPULISM 20 CHINJAP. PAGE 149 F2946 ECO/DEV POLICY NAT/G TEC/DEV

B67
ZONDAG C.H.,THE BOLIVIAN ECONOMY 1952-65. L/A+17C TEC/DEV FOR/AID ADMIN...OBS TREND CHARTS BIBLIOG 20 BOLIV. PAGE 151 F2969 ECO/UNDEV INDUS PRODUC

L67
BARRON J.A.,"ACCESS TO THE PRESS." USA+45 TEC/DEV PRESS TV ADJUD AUD/VIS. PAGE 10 F0196 ORD/FREE COM/IND EDU/PROP LAW

L67
LAMBERT J.D.,"CORPORATE POLITICAL SPENDING AND CAMPAIGN FINANCE." LAW CONSTN FINAN LABOR LG/CO LOC/G NAT/G VOL/ASSN TEC/DEV ADJUD ADMIN PARTIC. PAGE 75 F1463 USA+45 POL/PAR CHOOSE COST

L67
WHITNEY S.N.,"MERGERS, CONGLOMERATES, AND OLIGOPOLIES* A WIDENING OF ANTI TRUST TARGETS." LAW NAT/G TEC/DEV CAP/ISM GP/REL PWR...OLD/LIB 20. PAGE 146 F2873 ECO/TAC INDUS JURID

S67

ALLISON D.,"THE GROWTH OF IDEAS." USA+45 LG/CO ADMIN. PAGE 4 F0075
R+D OP/RES INDUS TEC/DEV

S67

AVTORKHANOV A.,"A NEW AGRARIAN REVOLUTION." COM USSR ECO/DEV PLAN TEC/DEV ADMIN CONTROL OPTIMAL WEALTH SOCISM 20 KHRUSH/N STALIN/J. PAGE 8 F0144
AGRI METH/COMP MARXISM OWN

S67

BARAN P.,"THE FUTURE COMPUTER UTILITY." USA+45 NAT/G PLAN CONTROL COST...POLICY 20. PAGE 9 F0177
COMPUTER UTIL FUT TEC/DEV

S67

BENN W.,"TECHNOLOGY HAS AN INEXORABLE EFFECT." FUT UK ECO/DEV INT/ORG CONSULT PLAN EDU/PROP ADMIN LEAD GP/REL PRODUC...INT 20 EEC. PAGE 13 F0246
R+D LG/CO TEC/DEV INDUS

S67

BRANCO R.,"LAND REFORM* THE ANSWER TO LATIN AMERICA'S AGRICULTURAL DEVELOPMENT?" L/A+17C NAT/G PLAN TEC/DEV BUDGET RENT EFFICIENCY 20. PAGE 18 F0339
ECO/UNDEV AGRI TAX OWN

S67

COSGROVE C.A.,"AGRICULTURE, FINANCE AND POLITICS IN THE EUROPEAN COMMUNITY." EUR+WWI DIST/IND MARKET INT/ORG VOL/ASSN DELIB/GP TEC/DEV BAL/PWR BARGAIN ECO/TAC RATION CONFER 20 EEC. PAGE 28 F0538
ECO/DEV DIPLOM AGRI INT/TRADE

S67

CROKER F.P.U.,"ECONOMIC PEACEKEEPING." UK PLAN PROB/SOLV TEC/DEV BAL/PWR DIPLOM COERCE PEACE ...POLICY DECISION 20. PAGE 28 F0553
FORCES WEAPON COST WAR

S67

GAUSSENS J.,"THE APPLICATIONS OF NUCLEAR ENERGY - TECHNICAL, ECONOMIC AND SOCIAL ASPECTS." WOR+45 INDUS R+D ACT/RES EFFICIENCY PRODUC SKILL PREDICT. PAGE 47 F0911
NUC/PWR TEC/DEV ECO/DEV ADJUST

S67

HADDOCK G.B.,"CORPORATE GROWTH AS AFFECTED BY THE FEDERAL ANTITRUST LAWS" ECO/DEV NAT/G PLAN TEC/DEV CAP/ISM ECO/TAC 20. PAGE 53 F1029
INDUS JURID ADJUD

S67

HEILBRONER R.L.,"BUILDING NEW NATIONS." AFR STRUCT PLAN TEC/DEV ADJUST MARXISM...POLICY 20. PAGE 58 F1138
PROB/SOLV REV NAT/LISM ECO/UNDEV

S67

HILTON G.W.,"FEDERAL PARTICIPATION IN THE SUPERSONIC TRANSPORT PROGRAM." USA+45 LEGIS PROB/SOLV BUDGET ATTIT 20. PAGE 60 F1172
DIST/IND TEC/DEV FINAN NAT/G

S67

KINGSLEY R.E.,"THE US BUSINESS IMAGE IN LATIN AMERICA." L/A+17C USA+45 NAT/G TEC/DEV CAP/ISM FOR/AID DOMIN EDU/PROP...CONCPT LING IDEA/COMP 20. PAGE 71 F1396
ATTIT LOVE DIPLOM ECO/UNDEV

S67

KRAUS J.,"A MARXIST IN GHANA." GHANA ELITES CHIEF PROB/SOLV TEC/DEV DIPLOM ECO/TAC COLONIAL PARTIC PWR 20 NKRUMAH/K. PAGE 73 F1432
MARXISM PLAN ATTIT CREATE

S67

LAZUTKIN Y.,"SOCIALISM AND SPARE TIME." ECO/DEV WORKER CREATE TEC/DEV ROUTINE TIME. PAGE 76 F1497
LEISURE PRODUC SOCISM SOCIALIST

S67

MAJSTRENKO I.W.,"PROBLEMS CONFRONTING SOVIET AGRICULTURE." COM USSR ECO/DEV ECO/TAC EFFICIENCY OPTIMAL WEALTH MARXISM 20. PAGE 84 F1643
AGRI PROB/SOLV CENTRAL TEC/DEV

S67

MALKIN A.,"BUSINESS BOOKS OF 1966." INDUS LABOR OP/RES TEC/DEV CAP/ISM ECO/TAC INCOME WEALTH 20. PAGE 84 F1649
BIBLIOG/A FINAN MARKET

S67

MEHTA A.,"INDIA* POVERTY AND CHANGE." STRATA INDUS CREATE ECO/TAC FOR/AID NEUTRAL GP/REL ADJUST INCOME ...NEW/IDEA 20. PAGE 89 F1746
INDIA SOCIETY ECO/UNDEV TEC/DEV

S67

MILLER C.H.,"B. TRAVEN Y EL 'PROBLEMA PETROLERO'." USA-45 ECO/UNDEV INDUS TEC/DEV INT/TRADE ATTIT ORD/FREE SOVEREIGN 20 MEXIC/AMER. PAGE 91 F1791
EXTR/IND DIPLOM ECO/TAC DOMIN

S67

MORTON J.A.,"A SYSTEMS APPROACH TO THE INNOVATION PROCESS: ITS USE IN THE BELL SYSTEM." USA+45 INTELL INDUS LG/CO CONSULT WORKER COMPUTER AUTOMAT DEMAND ...MGT CHARTS 20. PAGE 94 F1841
TEC/DEV GEN/METH R+D COM/IND

S67

MYERS S.,"TECHNOLOGY AND URBAN TRANSIT: THE ENORMOUS POTENTIAL OF BUS AND RAIL SYSTEMS." USA+45 FINAN LOC/G WORKER PLAN PROB/SOLV PRICE AUTOMAT MUNICH 20. PAGE 96 F1877
R+D TEC/DEV DIST/IND ACT/RES

S67

MYRDAL G.,"ECONOMIC DEVELOPMENT IN THE BACKWARD COUNTRIES." INT/ORG TEC/DEV CAP/ISM DIPLOM INT/TRADE PRODUC WEALTH 20. PAGE 96 F1883
ECO/UNDEV INDUS NAT/G ECO/TAC

S67

PECCEI A.,"DEVELOPED-UNDERDEVELOPED AND EAST-WEST RELATIONS." ECO/UNDEV TEC/DEV DIPLOM LEAD EFFICIENCY GEOG. PAGE 104 F2045
FOR/AID TREND REGION ECO/DEV

S67

PENNEY N.,"BANK STATEMENTS, CANCELLED CHECKS, AND ARTICLE FOUR IN THE ELECTRONIC AGE." USA+45 TEC/DEV COST EFFICIENCY WEALTH. PAGE 104 F2056
CREATE LAW ADJUD FINAN

S67

PRATT R.C.,"THE ADMINISTRATION OF ECONOMIC PLANNING IN A NEWLY INDEPEND ENT STATE* THE TANZANIAN EXPERIENCE 1963-1966." AFR TANZANIA ECO/UNDEV PLAN CONTROL ROUTINE TASK EFFICIENCY 20. PAGE 107 F2114
NAT/G DELIB/GP ADMIN TEC/DEV

S67

RICHMAN B.M.,"SOVIET MANAGEMENT IN TRANSITION." USSR FINAN MARKET EX/STRUC PLAN PROB/SOLV TEC/DEV CONTROL LEAD CENTRAL EFFICIENCY...METH/COMP 20 REFORMERS. PAGE 111 F2186
MGT MARXISM POLICY AUTHORIT

S67

SCHNEIDER E.,"DIE ENTPOLITISIERUNG DES DEUTSCHEN OSTHANDELS." AFR MARKET TEC/DEV OBJECTIVE 20. PAGE 117 F2307
ATTIT INT/TRADE ECO/TAC DIPLOM

S67

WAITS C.R.,"CRAFT GILDS AS AN INSTITUTIONAL BARRIER TO THE INDUSTRIAL REVOLUTION." CHRIST-17C MOD/EUR ECO/UNDEV CONTROL GP/REL ATTIT 16/19. PAGE 142 F2801
TEC/DEV INDUS REV PROF/ORG

S67

WILLMANN J.,"LA COMMUNAUTE EUROPEENNE ET LA GRANDE-BRETAGNE." UK PROB/SOLV TEC/DEV CAP/ISM DIPLOM CONFER FEDERAL...POLICY 20 EEC. PAGE 147 F2898
INT/ORG DRIVE NAT/LISM INT/TRADE

N67

US HOUSE COMM SCI ASTRONAUT,AUTHORIZING APPROPRIATIONS TO THE NATIONAL AERONAUTICS AND SPACE ADMINISTRATION (PAMPHLET). USA+45 NAT/G OP/RES TEC/DEV BUDGET NASA HOUSE/REP. PAGE 137 F2704
SPACE R+D PHIL/SCI NUC/PWR

N67

US HOUSE COMM SCI ASTRONAUT,GOVERNMENT, SCIENCE, AND INTERNATIONAL POLICY (PAMPHLET). INDIA NETHERLAND ECO/DEV ECO/UNDEV R+D ACADEM PLAN DIPLOM FOR/AID CONFER...PREDICT 20 CHINJAP. PAGE 137 F2705
NAT/G POLICY CREATE TEC/DEV

B88

BENTHAM J.,DEFENCE OF USURY (1787). UK LAW NAT/G TEC/DEV ECO/TAC CONTROL ATTIT...CONCPT IDEA/COMP 18 SMITH/ADAM. PAGE 13 F0255
TAX FINAN ECO/DEV POLICY

TECHNIC....TECHNOCRATIC

B15

VEBLEN T.,IMPERIAL GERMANY AND THE INDUSTRIAL REVOLUTION. GERMANY MOD/EUR UK USA-45 NAT/G TEC/DEV CAP/ISM...MAJORIT NAT/COMP 19/20 CHINJAP. PAGE 141 F2769
ECO/DEV INDUS TECHNIC BAL/PWR

B59

PANIKKAR K.M.,THE AFRO-ASIAN STATES AND THEIR PROBLEMS. COM CULTURE KIN POL/PAR SECT DIPLOM EDU/PROP COLONIAL SOVEREIGN...TECHNIC GOV/COMP 20. PAGE 103 F2025
AFR S/ASIA ECO/UNDEV

S59

HOFFMAN P.,"OPERATION BREAKTHROUGH." AFR S/ASIA STRUCT INDUS CONSULT TEC/DEV ATTIT RIGID/FLEX SKILL WEALTH...TECHNIC CONCPT STYLE RECORD CHARTS ORG/CHARTS GEN/METH VAL/FREE 20. PAGE 61 F1190
ECO/UNDEV EDU/PROP FOR/AID

B62

MOWITZ R.J.,PROFILE OF A METROPOLIS: A CASE BOOK. COM/IND CONSTRUC INDUS PUB/INST PLAN TEC/DEV LEAD GP/REL...POLICY TECHNIC WELF/ST MUNICH. PAGE 94 F1851
DECISION ADMIN

S63

BARANSON J.,"ECONOMIC AND SOCIAL CONSIDERATIONS IN ADAPTING TECHNOLOGIES FOR DEVELOPING COUNTRIES." WOR+45 PLAN WEALTH...TECHNIC SOC 20. PAGE 10 F0180
ECO/UNDEV TEC/DEV

B64

GARFIELD PJ LOVEJOY WF,PUBLIC UTILITY ECONOMICS. DIST/IND FINAN MARKET ADMIN COST DEMAND ...TECHNIC JURID MUNICH 20 MONOPOLY. PAGE 46 F0906
T ECO/TAC OWN SERV/IND

B64

LANG A.S.,URBAN RAIL TRANSIT. OP/RES PLAN PROB/SOLV TEC/DEV AUTOMAT COST...TECHNIC MATH CON/ANAL CHARTS METH/COMP SIMUL MUNICH 20 RAILROAD PUB/TRANS. PAGE 75 F1474
DIST/IND ECOMETRIC

B64 LETICHE J.M.,A HISTORY OF RUSSIAN ECONOMIC THOUGHT: NINTH THROUGH EIGHTEENTH CENTURIES. RUSSIA FINAN SECT CAP/ISM DOMIN DEMAND EFFICIENCY OWN MARXISM ...TECHNIC ANTHOL BIBLIOG 9/18. PAGE 78 F1536 — ECO/TAC TIME/SEQ IDEA/COMP ECO/UNDEV

B66 GOULD J.M.,THE TECHNICAL ELITE. INDUS LABOR TECHRACY...POLICY DECISION STAT CHARTS 20. PAGE 49 F0967 — ECO/DEV TEC/DEV ELITES TECHNIC

TECHNIQUES....SEE TEC/DEV, METHODOLOGICAL INDEXES, PP. XIII-XIV

TECHNOCRACY....SEE TECHRACY, TECHNIC

TECHNOLOGY....SEE ~~COMPUTER~~, ~~TECHNIC~~, TEC/DEV

TECHRACY....SOCIO-POLITICAL ORDER DOMINATED BY TECHNICIANS

B61 QURESHI S.,INCENTIVES IN AMERICAN EMPLOYMENT (THESIS, UNIVERSITY OF PENNSYLVANIA). DELIB/GP TOP/EX BUDGET ROUTINE SANCTION COST TECHRACY MGT. PAGE 108 F2134 — SERV/IND ADMIN PAY EX/STRUC

B65 COLLOQUE SUR LA PLANIFICATION,LA PLANIFICATION COMME PROCESSUS DE DECISION. FRANCE SOCIETY MARKET LABOR LEGIS GP/REL EFFICIENCY INCOME ATTIT TECHRACY ...MYTH IDEA/COMP 20. PAGE 26 F0508 — PLAN ECO/TAC PROB/SOLV

B66 GOULD J.M.,THE TECHNICAL ELITE. INDUS LABOR TECHRACY...POLICY DECISION STAT CHARTS 20. PAGE 49 F0967 — ECO/DEV TEC/DEV ELITES TECHNIC

S66 COHEN A.,"THE TECHNOLOGY/ELITE APPROACH TO THE DEVELOPMENTAL PROCESS* PERUVIAN CASE STUDY." L/A+17C STRUCT CREATE ECO/TAC FOR/AID CIVMIL/REL MARXISM TECHRACY HYPO/EXP. PAGE 26 F0496 — ECO/UNDEV ELITES PERU

B67 ELSNER H.,THE TECHNOCRATS, PROPHETS OF AUTOMATION. SOCIETY INDUS VOL/ASSN COST INCOME ATTIT 20. PAGE 37 F0726 — AUTOMAT TECHRACY PRODUC HIST/WRIT

B67 HEILBRONER R.L.,THE LIMITS OF AMERICAN CAPITALISM. FUT ECO/DEV INDUS LG/CO EX/STRUC LEAD PWR TECHRACY 20. PAGE 58 F1137 — ELITES CREATE TEC/DEV CAP/ISM

TEHERAN....TEHERAN CONFERENCE

TEITSWORTH C.S. F2541

TELLADO A. F2542

TELLER A. F2543

TEMPERANCE....TEMPERANCE MOVEMENTS

TENDLER J.D. F2544

TENNESSEE VALLEY AUTHORITY....SEE TVA

TENNESSEE....TENNESSEE

B66 GREENE L.E.,GOVERNMENT IN TENNESSEE (2ND ED.). USA+45 DIST/IND INDUS POL/PAR EX/STRUC LEGIS PLAN BUDGET GIVE CT/SYS...MGT T 20 TENNESSEE. PAGE 51 F0989 — PROVS LOC/G CONSTN ADMIN

TENNYSON L.B. F2545

TERR/GP

B38 HOBSON J.A.,IMPERIALISM. MOD/EUR UK WOR-45 CULTURE ECO/UNDEV NAT/G VOL/ASSN PLAN EDU/PROP LEGIT REGION COERCE ATTIT PWR...POLICY PLURIST TIME/SEQ GEN/LAWS TERR/GP 19/20. PAGE 60 F1187 — DOMIN ECO/TAC BAL/PWR COLONIAL

B49 PARMELEE M.,GEO-ECONOMIC REGIONAL AND WORLD FEDERATION. FUT WOR+45 WOR-45 SOCIETY VOL/ASSN PLAN ...METH/CNCPT SIMUL GEN/METH TERR/GP TOT/POP 20. PAGE 103 F2028 — INT/ORG GEOG REGION

L53 NELSON J.R.,"UNITED STATES FOREIGN ECONOMIC POLICY AND THE STERLING AREA." USA-45 WOR+45 WOR-45 NAT/G ECO/TAC WEALTH...STAT TIME/SEQ TREND CHARTS METH/GP TERR/GP CMN/WLTH 20. PAGE 97 F1911 — FINAN DIPLOM UK

B57 TRIFFIN R.,EUROPE AND THE MONEY MUDDLE. USA+45 INT/ORG NAT/G CONSULT PLAN ECO/TAC EXEC ROUTINE BAL/PAY WEALTH...METH/CNCPT OBS TREND CHARTS STERTYP GEN/METH EEC TERR/GP VAL/FREE ECSC. PAGE 131 F2587 — EUR+WWI ECO/DEV REGION

S57 HOAG M.W.,"ECONOMIC PROBLEMS OF ALLIANCE." AFR COM EUR+WWI WOR+45 ECO/DEV ECO/UNDEV NAT/G VOL/ASSN FORCES PLAN TEC/DEV DIPLOM COERCE ORD/FREE PWR WEALTH...DECISION GEN/LAWS NATO TERR/GP. PAGE 60 F1182 — INT/ORG ECO/TAC

B60 LISTER L.,EUROPE'S COAL AND STEEL COMMUNITY. FRANCE GERMANY STRUCT ECO/DEV EXTR/IND INDUS MARKET NAT/G DELIB/GP ECO/TAC INT/TRADE EDU/PROP ATTIT RIGID/FLEX ORD/FREE PWR WEALTH...CONCPT STAT TIME/SEQ CHARTS ECSC TERR/GP 20. PAGE 81 F1582 — EUR+WWI INT/ORG REGION

S60 HERRERA F.,"THE INTER-AMERICAN DEVELOPMENT BANK." USA+45 ECO/UNDEV INT/ORG CONSULT DELIB/GP PLAN ECO/TAC INT/TRADE ROUTINE WEALTH...STAT TERR/GP 20. PAGE 59 F1153 — L/A+17C FINAN FOR/AID REGION

S60 NICHOLS J.P.,"HAZARDS OF AMERICAN PRIVATE INVESTMENT IN UNDERDEVELOPED COUNTRIES." FUT L/A+17C USA+45 USA-45 EXTR/IND CONSULT BAL/PWR ECO/TAC DOMIN ADJUD ATTIT SOVEREIGN WEALTH ...HIST/WRIT TIME/SEQ TREND TERR/GP VAL/FREE 20. PAGE 98 F1924 — FINAN ECO/UNDEV CAP/ISM NAT/LISM

B61 BONNEFOUS M.,EUROPE ET TIERS MONDE. EUR+WWI SOCIETY INT/ORG NAT/G VOL/ASSN ACT/RES TEC/DEV CAP/ISM ECO/TAC ATTIT ORD/FREE SOVEREIGN...POLICY CONCPT TREND TERR/GP COMMUN 20. PAGE 16 F0314 — AFR ECO/UNDEV FOR/AID INT/TRADE

S61 LANFALUSSY A.,"EUROPE'S PROGRESS: DUE TO COMMON MARKET." EUR+WWI ECO/DEV DELIB/GP PLAN ECO/TAC ROUTINE WEALTH...GEOG TREND EEC TERR/GP 20. PAGE 75 F1473 — INT/ORG MARKET

S61 RAY J.,"THE EUROPEAN FREE-TRADE ASSOCIATION AND ITS IMPACT ON INDIA'S TRADE." EUR+WWI FRANCE GERMANY INDIA S/ASIA UK NAT/G VOL/ASSN PLAN INT/TRADE ROUTINE WEALTH...STAT CHARTS TERR/GP CMN/WLTH EEC FOR/TRADE OEEC 20 EFTA. PAGE 109 F2155 — ECO/DEV ECO/TAC

L62 GALBRAITH J.K.,"ECONOMIC DEVELOPMENT IN PERSPECTIVE." CAP/ISM ECO/TAC ROUTINE ATTIT WEALTH ...TREND CHARTS SOC/EXP WORK TERR/GP 20. PAGE 45 F0884 — ECO/UNDEV PLAN

L62 MACHLUP F.,"PLANS FOR REFORM OF THE INTERNATIONAL MONETARY SYSTEM. PRINCETON: U. PR., 1962, 70 PP., $0.25." WOR+45 INT/ORG ECO/TAC BAL/PAY HEALTH ORD/FREE WEALTH MID/EX TERR/GP VAL/FREE APPLIC 20. PAGE 83 F1631 — ECO/DEV STAT

L62 PRYOR F.L.,"FOREIGN TRADE IN THE COMMUNIST BLOC." COM ECO/DEV VOL/ASSN...METH/CNCPT GEN/LAWS FOR/TRADE TERR/GP 20. PAGE 108 F2129 — ECO/TAC STERTYP USSR

L62 WATERSTON A.,"PLANNING IN MOROCCO, ORGANIZATION AND IMPLEMENTATION. BALTIMORE: HOPKINS ECON. DEVELOP. INT. BANK FOR." ISLAM ECO/DEV AGRI DIST/IND INDUS PROC/MFG SERV/IND LOC/G EX/STRUC ECO/TAC PWR WEALTH TOT/POP TRUE/GP METH/GP TERR/GP VAL/FREE 20. PAGE 144 F2829 — NAT/G PLAN MOROCCO

S62 MILLIKEN M.,"NEW AND OLD CRITERIA FOR AID." WOR+45 ECO/DEV ECO/UNDEV ACT/RES PLAN ATTIT KNOWL...TREND CON/ANAL SIMUL GEN/METH TERR/GP 20. PAGE 92 F1796 — USA+45 ECO/TAC FOR/AID

S62 ZAUBERMAN A.,"SOVIET AND CHINESE STRATEGY FOR ECONOMIC GROWTH." ASIA CHINA/COM COM USSR STRATA VOL/ASSN PLAN ATTIT PWR...METH/CNCPT GEN/LAWS WORK TERR/GP 20. PAGE 150 F2959 — ECO/DEV EDU/PROP

B63 GEERTZ C.,PEDDLERS AND PRINCES: SOCIAL DEVELOPMENT AND ECONOMIC CHANGE IN TWO INDONESIAN TOWNS. S/ASIA CULTURE SOCIETY STRATA FACE/GP CREATE TEC/DEV ECO/TAC ORD/FREE WEALTH...OBS INT CENSUS CHARTS WORK TOT/POP METH/GP TERR/GP VAL/FREE 20 MUNICH. PAGE 47 F0913 — ECO/UNDEV SOC ELITES INDONESIA

B63 LINDBERG L.,POLITICAL DYNAMICS OF EUROPEAN ECONOMIC INTEGRATION. EUR+WWI ECO/DEV INT/ORG VOL/ASSN DELIB/GP ADMIN WEALTH...DECISION EEC TERR/GP 20. PAGE 80 F1567 — MARKET ECO/TAC

B63 NEUMARK S.D.,FOREIGN TRADE AND ECONOMIC DEVELOPMENT IN AFRICA: A HISTORICAL PERSPECTIVE. EUR+WWI MOD/EUR ECO/UNDEV AGRI COM/IND EXTR/IND PROC/MFG SKILL WEALTH...CONCPT TIME/SEQ TREND SIMUL FOR/TRADE WORK TOT/POP TERR/GP VAL/FREE 19/20. PAGE 98 F1916 — AFR

S63 AYAL E.B.,"VALUE SYSTEM AND ECONOMIC DEVELOPMENT IN JAPAN AND THAILAND." ASIA S/ASIA THAILAND CULTURE ECO/DEV CAP/ISM DOMIN NAT/LISM DRIVE RIGID/FLEX — ECO/UNDEV ALL/VALS

SOCISM...WELF/ST OBS TREND CON/ANAL GEN/LAWS TERR/GP 20 CHINJAP. PAGE 8 F0145

S63
MILLEN B.H.,"INTERNATIONAL TRADE AND POLITICAL INDEPENDENCE." WOR+45 ECO/DEV WEALTH...STAT CHARTS FOR/TRADE METH/GP TERR/GP VAL/FREE 20. PAGE 91 F1788
ECO/UNDEV ECO/TAC INT/TRADE

S63
SHWADRAN B.,"MIDDLE EAST OIL, 1962." ISLAM DIST/IND INDUS PLAN ATTIT DRIVE WEALTH...POLICY STAT CONT/OBS TREND CHARTS GEN/LAWS TERR/GP METH/GP 20 OIL. PAGE 121 F2393
PROC/MFG ECO/TAC ELITES REGION

S63
SHWADRAN B.,"MIDDLE EAST OIL, 1962." ISLAM USSR ECO/DEV DIST/IND INDUS PLAN BAL/PWR DISPL DRIVE ...POLICY STAT TREND GEN/LAWS TERR/GP METH/GP EEC OEEC 20 OIL. PAGE 121 F2394
MARKET ECO/TAC INT/TRADE

B64
MELADY T.,FACES OF AFRICA. AFR FUT ISLAM NAT/G POL/PAR SCHOOL DELIB/GP PLAN ECO/TAC EDU/PROP ATTIT ALL/VALS...CHARTS TOT/POP TERR/GP VAL/FREE 20. PAGE 89 F1752
ECO/UNDEV TREND NAT/LISM

B64
STOESSINGER J.G.,FINANCING THE UNITED NATIONS SYSTEM. FUT WOR+45 CONSTN NAT/G VOL/ASSN DELIB/GP EX/STRUC ECO/TAC LEGIT CT/SYS PWR WEALTH...STAT TIME/SEQ TREND CHARTS TRUE/GP METH/GP TERR/GP VAL/FREE. PAGE 126 F2493
FINAN INT/ORG

L64
HAAS E.B.,"ECONOMICS AND DIFFERENTIAL PATTERNS OF POLITICAL INTEGRATION: PROJECTIONS ABOUT UNITY IN LATIN AMERICA." SOCIETY NAT/G DELIB/GP ACT/RES CREATE PLAN ECO/TAC REGION ROUTINE ATTIT DRIVE PWR WEALTH...CONCPT TREND CHARTS LAFTA TERR/GP 20. PAGE 52 F1020
L/A+17C INT/ORG MARKET

S64
HUELIN D.,"ECONOMIC INTEGRATION IN LATIN AMERICAN: PROGRESS AND PROBLEMS." L/A+17C ECO/DEV AGRI DIST/IND FINAN INDUS NAT/G VOL/ASSN CONSULT DELIB/GP EX/STRUC ACT/RES PLAN TEC/DEV ECO/TAC ROUTINE BAL/PAY WEALTH FOR/TRADE WORK TERR/GP 20. PAGE 63 F1232
MARKET ECO/UNDEV INT/TRADE

S64
HUTCHINSON E.C.,"AMERICAN AID TO AFRICA." FUT USA+45 MARKET INT/ORG LOC/G NAT/G PUB/INST PLAN ECO/TAC ATTIT RIGID/FLEX...POLICY CONCPT TREND TERR/GP 20. PAGE 63 F1248
AFR ECO/UNDEV FOR/AID

S64
PADELFORD N.J.,"THE ORGANIZATION OF AFRICAN UNITY." ECO/UNDEV INT/ORG PLAN BAL/PWR DIPLOM ECO/TAC NAT/LISM ORD/FREE PWR WEALTH...CONCPT TREND STERTYP TERR/GP VAL/FREE 20. PAGE 102 F2013
AFR VOL/ASSN REGION

S64
READER D.H.,"A SURVEY OF CATEGORIES OF ECONOMIC ACTIVITIES AMONG THE PEOPLES OF AFRICA." AGRI INDUS MARKET KIN HEALTH SKILL WEALTH...GEOG METH/CNCPT CHARTS TERR/GP WORK TOT/POP VAL/FREE 20. PAGE 110 F2160
TEC/DEV ECO/UNDEV AFR

S64
RUSSETT B.M.,"INEQUALITY AND INSTABILITY: THE RELATION OF LAND TENURE TO POLITICS." WOR+45 ECO/DEV ECO/UNDEV AGRI NAT/G COERCE PWR...MATH STAT CHARTS GEN/LAWS TERR/GP TRUE/GP METH/GP VAL/FREE 20. PAGE 115 F2263
WEALTH GEOG ECO/TAC ORD/FREE

S65
SPAAK P.H.,"THE SEARCH FOR CONSENSUS: A NEW EFFORT TO BUILD EUROPE." FRANCE GERMANY ECO/DEV NAT/G CONSULT FORCES PLAN EDU/PROP REGION CONSEN ATTIT ...SOC METH/CNCPT OBS TREND EEC NATO WORK TERR/GP METH/GP 20. PAGE 124 F2447
EUR+WWI INT/ORG

TERRELL/G....GLENN TERRELL

TERRY....TERRY V. OHIO

TESTS....THEORY AND USES OF TESTS AND SCALES; SEE ALSO TESTS AND SCALES INDEX, P. XIV

S61
DEUTSCH K.W.,"NATIONAL INDUSTRIALIZATION AND THE DECLINING SHARE OF THE INTERNATIONAL ECONOMIC SECTOR." EUR+WWI FUT WOR+45 WOR-45 MARKET PLAN EDU/PROP WEALTH...WELF/ST OBS TESTS 20. PAGE 32 F0624
DIST/IND ECO/DEV INT/TRADE

B65
RIGBY P.H.,CONCEPTUAL FOUNDATIONS OF BUSINESS RESEARCH. COMPUTER PROB/SOLV OPTIMAL...MGT CONCPT MATH STAT TESTS SIMUL GEN/METH. PAGE 111 F2192
PROFIT R+D INDUS DECISION

TEW B. F2546

TEXAS....TEXAS

THAILAND....THAILAND; SEE ALSO S/ASIA

N
US LIBRARY OF CONGRESS,SOUTHERN ASIA ACCESSIONS LIST. BURMA CEYLON INDIA NEPAL PAKISTAN S/ASIA THAILAND AGRI INDUS SCHOOL WORKER...ART/METH GEOG HEAL PHIL/SCI LING 20. PAGE 137 F2710
BIBLIOG/A SOCIETY CULTURE ECO/UNDEV

B58
MASON J.B.,THAILAND BIBLIOGRAPHY. S/ASIA THAILAND CULTURE EDU/PROP ADMIN...GEOG SOC LING 20. PAGE 87 F1701
BIBLIOG/A ECO/UNDEV DIPLOM NAT/G

S63
AYAL E.B.,"VALUE SYSTEM AND ECONOMIC DEVELOPMENT IN JAPAN AND THAILAND." ASIA S/ASIA THAILAND CULTURE ECO/DEV CAP/ISM DOMIN NAT/LISM DRIVE RIGID/FLEX SOCISM...WELF/ST OBS TREND CON/ANAL GEN/LAWS TERR/GP 20 CHINJAP. PAGE 8 F0145
ECO/UNDEV ALL/VALS

S63
GORDON B.,"ECONOMIC IMPEDIMENTS TO REGIONALISM IN SOUTH EAST ASIA." BURMA FUT S/ASIA THAILAND USA+45 AGRI INDUS R+D NAT/G PLAN ECO/TAC WEALTH...STAT CONT/OBS 20. PAGE 49 F0954
VOL/ASSN ECO/UNDEV INT/TRADE REGION

B64
THAILAND NATIONAL ECO DEV,THE NATIONAL ECONOMIC DEVELOPMENT PLAN: 1961-66: SECOND PHASE 1964-66. THAILAND AGRI FINAN BUDGET EFFICIENCY INCOME...STAT CHARTS 20. PAGE 129 F2547
ECO/UNDEV ECO/TAC PLAN NAT/G

S65
KAUFMAN R.H.,"THE ASIAN GOLD TRADE." ASIA LAOS THAILAND UK CHARTS. PAGE 69 F1362
S/ASIA FINAN STAT INT/TRADE

S67
MCCOLL R.W.,"A POLITICAL GEOGRAPHY OF REVOLUTION: CHINA, VIETNAM, AND THAILAND." ASIA THAILAND VIETNAM FORCES CONTROL 20. PAGE 88 F1720
REV GEOG PLAN DECISION

S67
ROY E.V.,"AN INTERPRETATION OF NORTHERN THAI PEASANT ECONOMY." THAILAND CLIENT CULTURE AGRI PROC/MFG FACE/GP DEMAND INCOME 20. PAGE 114 F2254
STRUCT STRATA ECO/UNDEV INGP/REL

THAILAND NATIONAL ECO DEV F2547

THAYER F.C. F2548

THE ECONOMIST (LONDON) F2550

THEIL H. F2551,F2552

THEOBALD R. F2553,F2554,F2555,F2556

THERAPY....SEE SPECIFICS, SUCH AS PROJ/TEST, DEEP/INT, SOC/EXP; ALSO SEE DIFFERENT VALUES (E.G., LOVE) AND TOPICAL TERMS (E.G., PRESS)

THEROUX P. F2557

THIESENHUSEN W.C. F2558

THING/STOR....ARTIFACTS AND MATERIAL EVIDENCE

THIRD/WRLD....THIRD WORLD - NONALIGNED NATIONS

N19
MEZERIK A.G.,ECONOMIC AID FOR UNDERDEVELOPED COUNTRIES (PAMPHLET). AFR USSR WOR+45 FINAN LG/CO DELIB/GP NUC/PWR...GEOG CENSUS CHARTS 20 UN THIRD/WRLD. PAGE 90 F1775
FOR/AID ECO/UNDEV DIPLOM POLICY

N19
VELYAMINOV G.,AFRICA AND THE COMMON MARKET (P[illegible]PHLET). AFR MARKET VOL/ASSN ECO/TAC COLONIAL ORD/[illegible]REE...SOCIALIST 20 THIRD/WRLD. PAGE 141 F2775
INT/ORG INT/TRADE SOVEREIGN ECO/UNDEV

B54
KARTUN D.,AFRICA, AFRICA: A CONTINENT RISES TO ITS FEET. AFR SOUTH/AFR UK ELITES AGRI LABOR LOC/G POL/PAR EDU/PROP CONTROL COERCE DISCRIM AGE/Y NEGRO THIRD/WRLD GOLD/COAST. PAGE 69 F1358
COLONIAL ORD/FREE PROFIT EXTR/IND

B58
CLAIRMONTE F.,LE LIBERALISME ECONOMIQUE ET LES PAYS SOUS-DEVELOPPES: ETUDES SUR L'EVOLUTION D'UNE IDEE. ASIA INDIA UK FINAN INDUS PLAN CAP/ISM ECO/TAC COLONIAL NEW/LIB...BIBLIOG 20 THIRD/WRLD. PAGE 24 F0475
LAISSEZ ECO/UNDEV

B59
NOVE A.,COMMUNIST ECONOMIC STRATEGY: SOVIET GROWTH AND CAPABILITIES. USSR AGRI LABOR PLAN TEC/DEV CAP/ISM INT/TRADE EFFICIENCY MARXISM 20 THIRD/WRLD. PAGE 99 F1941
FOR/AID ECO/TAC DIPLOM INDUS

B62
BROOKINGS INSTITUTION,DEVELOPMENT OF THE EMERGING
ECO/UNDEV

COUNTRIES; AN AGENDA FOR RESEARCH. WOR+45 AGRI TEC/DEV FOR/AID EDU/PROP ADJUST HABITAT KNOWL...PSY SOC ANTHOL 20 THIRD/WRLD. PAGE 19 F0362 — R+D SOCIETY PROB/SOLV

B62
GOLDWIN R.A.,WHY FOREIGN AID? - TWO MESSAGES BY PRESIDENT KENNEDY AND ESSAYS. S/ASIA USA+45 ECO/UNDEV 20 KENNEDY/JF THIRD/WRLD. PAGE 48 F0942 — DIPLOM FOR/AID POLICY

B63
ALPERT P.,ECONOMIC DEVELOPMENT. WOR+45 FINAN TEC/DEV ECO/TAC PRICE GOV/REL HABITAT...GEOG BIBLIOG T 20 THIRD/WRLD. PAGE 4 F0079 — ECO/DEV ECO/UNDEV INT/TRADE FOR/AID

B63
MENEZES A.J.,SUBDESENVOLVIMENTO E POLITICA INTERNACIONAL. BRAZIL WOR+45 PLAN CONTROL LEAD NAT/LISM ORD/FREE 20 THIRD/WRLD. PAGE 90 F1759 — ECO/UNDEV DIPLOM POLICY BAL/PWR

B64
FEI J.C.H.,DEVELOPMENT OF THE LABOR SURPLUS ECONOMY: THEORY AND POLICY. WOR+45 AGRI INDUS MARKET PROB/SOLV TEC/DEV...STAT CHARTS GEN/LAWS METH 20 THIRD/WRLD. PAGE 40 F0772 — ECO/TAC POLICY WORKER ECO/UNDEV

B65
NKRUMAH K.,NEO-COLONIALISM: THE LAST STAGE OF IMPERIALISM. AFR INT/ORG WORKER FOR/AID INT/TRADE EDU/PROP GOV/REL NAT/LISM SOVEREIGN POPULISM SOCISM ...SOCIALIST 20 THIRD/WRLD INTRVN/ECO. PAGE 98 F1929 — COLONIAL DIPLOM ECO/UNDEV ECO/TAC

B66
BROEKMEIJER M.W.J.,FICTION AND TRUTH ABOUT THE "DECADE OF DEVELOPMENT" WOR+45 AGRI FINAN INDUS NAT/G TEC/DEV DIPLOM EDU/PROP LEAD SKILL 20 THIRD/WRLD. PAGE 19 F0358 — FOR/AID POLICY ECO/UNDEV PLAN

B66
HAYER T.,FRENCH AID. AFR FRANCE AGRI FINAN BUDGET ADMIN WAR PRODUC...CHARTS 18/20 THIRD/WRLD OVRSEA/DEV. PAGE 57 F1125 — TEC/DEV COLONIAL FOR/AID ECO/UNDEV

THOMAN R.S. F2559

THOMAS D.S. F2560

THOMAS J.A. F2561

THOMAS M.J. F2562

THOMAS R.G. F2563

THOMAS/FA....F.A. THOMAS

THOMAS/N....NORMAN THOMAS

THOMAS/TK....TREVOR K. THOMAS

THOMPSON C.D. F2564

THOMPSON J.H. F2565

THOMPSON V.A. F2566

THOMPSON W.R. F2567

THOMPSON W.S. F2568

THOMSON C.A. F1491

THORBECKE E. F0837,F2569

THOREAU/H....HENRY THOREAU

THORKELSON H. F2570

THORNTN/WT....WILLIAM T. THORNTON

THORNTON A.P. F2571

THUCYDIDES....THUCYDIDES

THURSTON/L....LOUIS LEON THURSTONE

TIBET....TIBET; SEE ALSO ASIA

TIEBOUT C.M. F2572

TILLETT P. F1159

TILLICH/P....PAUL TILLICH

TILLION G. F2573

TIME....TIMING, TIME FACTOR; SEE ALSO ANALYSIS OF TEMPORAL SEQUENCES INDEX, P. XIV

N19
HATANAKA M.,A SPECTRAL ANALYSIS OF BUSINESS CYCLE INDICATORS: LEAD-LAG IN TERMS OF ALL TIME POINTS (PAMPHLET). UNIV WORKER EFFICIENCY...REGRESS STAT CHARTS TIME 20. PAGE 56 F1110 — ECOMETRIC ADJUST PRODUC CON/ANAL

B41
HAYEK F.A.,THE PURE THEORY OF CAPITAL. UNIV ECO/DEV ECO/TAC COST EQUILIB PROFIT WEALTH...SIMUL GEN/LAWS BIBLIOG INDEX TIME 20. PAGE 57 F1120 — CAP/ISM METH/CNCPT PRODUC FINAN

B47
ISAAC J.,ECONOMICS OF MIGRATION. MOD/EUR CULTURE STRATA STRUCT NAT/G COLONIAL WEALTH...OLD/LIB TREND TIME 19/20 EUROPE/W MIGRATION. PAGE 65 F1289 — HABITAT SOC GEOG

B47
MILLETT J.D.,THE PROCESS AND ORGANIZATION OF GOVERNMENT PLANNING. USA+45 DELIB/GP ACT/RES LEAD LOBBY TASK...POLICY GEOG TIME 20 RESOURCE/N. PAGE 91 F1793 — ADMIN NAT/G PLAN CONSULT

S52
PHILLIPS C.,"THE HIGH COST OF OUR LOW-PAID CONGRESS" (NYT MAG. 2/24/52)" USA+45 FINAN WRITING TASK TIME CONGRESS. PAGE 106 F2082 — LEGIS INCOME COST EFFICIENCY

B58
MOULTON H.G.,CAN INFLATION BE CONTROLLED? ECO/DEV INDUS CAP/ISM RATION GOV/REL COST INCOME PEACE WEALTH...CHARTS TIME 20 KEYNES/JM MONEY. PAGE 94 F1847 — ECO/TAC CONTROL DEMAND FINAN

B59
MATTHEWS R.C.O.,THE BUSINESS CYCLE. AFR LABOR INT/TRADE TAX PRICE RISK ADJUST WEALTH...POLICY ECOMETRIC CHARTS SIMUL TIME 20. PAGE 87 F1705 — FINAN DEMAND TASK

B60
BIERMAN H.,THE CAPITAL BUDGETING DECISION. AFR ECO/DEV MARKET TAX PRICE RISK COST INCOME TIME 20. PAGE 15 F0282 — FINAN OPTIMAL BUDGET PROFIT

B62
DE GRAZIA S.,OF TIME, WORK, AND LEISURE. USA+45 ECO/DEV WORKER HAPPINESS UTOPIA ALL/VALS...SOC NEW/IDEA TIME. PAGE 31 F0599 — CULTURE LEISURE CONCPT

B62
NATIONAL BUREAU ECONOMIC RES,THE RATE AND DIRECTION OF INVENTIVE ACTIVITY: ECONOMIC AND SOCIAL FACTORS. STRUCT INDUS MARKET R+D CREATE OP/RES TEC/DEV EFFICIENCY PRODUC RATIONAL UTIL...WELF/ST PHIL/SCI METH/CNCPT TIME. PAGE 97 F1895 — DECISION PROB/SOLV MGT

B64
COLSTON RESEARCH SOCIETY,ECONOMETRIC ANALYSIS FOR NATIONAL ECONOMIC PLANNING (PROCEEDINGS OF SIXTEENTH SYMPOSIUM OF COLSTON RESEARCH SOCIETY). UK USA+45 FINAN FAM LABOR NAT/G PLAN PRICE ...METH/CNCPT TREND CHARTS TIME 20. PAGE 26 F0510 — ECOMETRIC DELIB/GP ECO/TAC PROB/SOLV

B64
TAEUBER I.B.,POPULATION TRENDS IN THE UNITED STATES: 1900 TO 1960. USA+45 USA-45 PROVS INCOME AGE...SOC TIME/SEQ TREND CHARTS MUNICH TIME 20 NEGRO. PAGE 128 F2522 — CENSUS GEOG STRATA STRUCT

B65
BRENNAN M.J.,PATTERNS OF MARKET BEHAVIOR. AFR USA+45 OP/RES CAP/ISM ECO/TAC INT/TRADE...CHARTS METH/COMP ANTHOL TIME 20. PAGE 18 F0346 — MARKET LABOR FINAN ECOMETRIC

B65
FLEMING R.W.,THE LABOR ARBITRATION PROCESS. USA+45 LAW BARGAIN ADJUD ROUTINE SANCTION COST...PREDICT CHARTS TIME 20. PAGE 41 F0809 — GP/REL LABOR CONSULT DELIB/GP

S65
SCHROEDER G.,"LABOR PLANNING IN THE USSR." COM USSR ECO/DEV INDUS SCHOOL PRODUC WEALTH...PREDICT TIME/SEQ TREND TIME 20. PAGE 117 F2313 — WORKER PLAN CENSUS

B66
BROWN R.T.,TRANSPORT AND THE ECONOMIC INTEGRATION OF SOUTH AMERICA. L/A+17C ECO/UNDEV NAT/G OP/RES DIPLOM INT/TRADE REGION WEALTH...ECOMETRIC GEOG STAT LAFTA TIME. PAGE 19 F0373 — MARKET DIST/IND SIMUL

B66
MACBEAN A.I.,EXPORT INSTABILITY AND ECONOMIC DEVELOPMENT. CHILE PAKISTAN PUERT/RICO TANZANIA UGANDA WOR+45 MARKET ECO/TAC...POLICY REGRESS CHARTS BIBLIOG TIME 20. PAGE 83 F1622 — INT/TRADE ECO/UNDEV ECOMETRIC INSPECT

S66
VERSLUYS J.D.N.,"SOME NOTES ON THE SOCIAL AND ECONOMIC EFFECTS OF RURAL ELECTRIFICATION IN BURMA" BURMA EDU/PROP PRODUC ORD/FREE...SOC QU MUNICH TIME 20. PAGE 141 F2782 — TEC/DEV SOCIETY CREATE

S67
LAZUTKIN Y.,"SOCIALISM AND SPARE TIME." ECO/DEV WORKER CREATE TEC/DEV ROUTINE TIME. PAGE 76 F1497 — LEISURE PRODUC SOCISM SOCIALIST

N67
NATIONAL COMN COMMUNITY HEALTH,ACTION - PLANNING FOR COMMUNITY HEALTH SERVICES (PAMPHLET). USA+45 — PLAN HEALTH

PROF/ORG DELIB/GP BUDGET ROUTINE GP/REL ATTIT ...HEAL SOC SOC/WK CHARTS MUNICH TIME 20. PAGE 97 F1898 — ADJUST

TIME/SEQ....CHRONOLOGY AND GENETIC SERIES

B12
HOBSON J.A.,THE EVOLUTION OF MODERN CAPITALISM. MOD/EUR UK STRATA ECO/DEV INDUS INCOME UTIL WEALTH ...SOC GEN/LAWS 7/20. PAGE 60 F1184 — CAP/ISM WORKER TEC/DEV TIME/SEQ

B14
VEBLEN T.,THE INSTINCT OF WORKMANSHIP. UNIV SOCIETY ECO/DEV ECO/UNDEV CREATE TEC/DEV ECO/TAC EDU/PROP ROUTINE PERSON...HUM CONCPT TIME/SEQ GEN/LAWS. PAGE 140 F2768 — DRIVE SKILL

B26
TAWNEY R.H.,RELIGION AND THE RISE OF CAPITALISM. UK CULTURE NAT/G TEC/DEV OWN LAISSEZ...POLICY SOC TIME/SEQ 16/19. PAGE 129 F2537 — SECT WEALTH INDUS CAP/ISM

B27
SIEGFRIED A.,AMERICA COMES OF AGE: A FRENCH ANALYSIS (TRANS. BY H.H. HEMMING AND DORIS HEMMING). FRANCE UK POL/PAR WORKER TEC/DEV DIPLOM REGION RACE/REL ADJUST PRODUC HEREDITY...TIME/SEQ GP/COMP SOC/INTEG 20 DEMOCRAT REPUBLICAN KKK. PAGE 122 F2398 — USA-45 CULTURE ECO/DEV SOC

B30
THOMPSON W.R.,POPULATION PROBLEMS. FUT UNIV WOR-45 STRUCT DIST/IND ACT/RES ECO/TAC BIO/SOC...CONCPT OBS TIME/SEQ TOT/POP 20. PAGE 130 F2567 — ECO/UNDEV GEOG

B31
CROOK W.H.,THE GENERAL STRIKE: A STUDY OF LABOR'S TRAGIC WEAPON IN THEORY AND PRACTICE. BELGIUM FRANCE SWEDEN UK WOR-45 PROB/SOLV ECO/TAC DOMIN PWR ...POLICY TIME/SEQ NAT/COMP GEN/LAWS 19/20 STRIKE. PAGE 29 F0555 — LABOR WORKER LG/CO BARGAIN

B35
STALEY E.,WAR AND THE PRIVATE INVESTOR. UNIV WOR-45 INTELL SOCIETY INT/ORG NAT/G TOP/EX CAP/ISM ECO/TAC WAR ATTIT ALL/VALS...INT TIME/SEQ TREND CON/ANAL WORK TOT/POP 20. PAGE 125 F2464 — FINAN INT/TRADE DIPLOM

B36
HUBERMAN L.,MAN'S WORLDLY GOODS: THE STORY OF THE WEALTH OF NATIONS. CHRIST-17C EUR+WWI MOD/EUR SOCIETY DOMIN REV ORD/FREE...TIME/SEQ METH/COMP. PAGE 63 F1231 — WEALTH CAP/ISM MARXISM CREATE

B37
BRESCIANI-TURRONI C,THE ECONOMICS OF INFLATION: A STUDY OF CURRENCY DEPRECIATION IN POST-WAR GERMANY. AFR GERMANY FINAN INT/TRADE PRICE TOTALISM...POLICY TIME/SEQ CHARTS GEN/LAWS 20 HITLER/A. PAGE 18 F0347 — ECO/TAC WEALTH SOCIETY

B37
ROBBINS L.,ECONOMIC PLANNING AND INTERNATIONAL ORDER. WOR-45 SOCIETY FINAN INDUS NAT/G ECO/TAC ROUTINE WEALTH...SOC TIME/SEQ GEN/METH WORK 20 KEYNES/JM. PAGE 112 F2202 — INT/ORG PLAN INT/TRADE

B38
HOBSON J.A.,IMPERIALISM. MOD/EUR UK WOR-45 CULTURE ECO/UNDEV NAT/G VOL/ASSN PLAN EDU/PROP LEGIT REGION COERCE ATTIT PWR...POLICY PLURIST TIME/SEQ GEN/LAWS TERR/GP 19/20. PAGE 60 F1187 — DOMIN ECO/TAC BAL/PWR COLONIAL

B41
ESTEY J.A.,BUSINESS CYCLES; THEIR NATURE, CAUSE, AND CONTROL. NAT/G BUDGET CAP/ISM TAX PRICE CONTROL INCOME...MODAL TIME/SEQ GEN/METH T 18/20 KEYNES/JM MONEY. PAGE 38 F0749 — INDUS FINAN ECO/TAC POLICY

B41
HANSEN A.H.,FISCAL POLICY AND BUSINESS CYCLES. UK INDUS PROB/SOLV DIPLOM INT/TRADE OPTIMAL...POLICY TIME/SEQ CHARTS 19/20. PAGE 54 F1062 — FINAN PLAN ECO/TAC GOV/REL

B43
WILMERDING L. JR.,THE SPENDING POWER: A HISTORY OF THE EFFORTS OF CONGRESS TO CONTROL EXPENDITURES. USA-45 POL/PAR DELIB/GP EX/STRUC TOP/EX TARIFFS ADMIN GOV/REL...TIME/SEQ SENATE HOUSE/REP. PAGE 147 F2900 — LEGIS BUDGET CONTROL

B47
TOWLE L.W.,INTERNATIONAL TRADE AND COMMERCIAL POLICY. WOR+45 LAW ECO/DEV FINAN INDUS NAT/G ECO/TAC WEALTH...TIME/SEQ ILO 20. PAGE 131 F2582 — MARKET INT/ORG INT/TRADE

B48
HICKS J.R.,VALUE AND CAPITAL. FINAN PRICE EQUILIB INCOME PRODUC WEALTH...TIME/SEQ 20 MARSHALL/A PARETO/V SAMUELSN/P. PAGE 59 F1165 — ECOMETRIC MATH DEMAND PROB/SOLV

B48
METZLER L.A.,INCOME, EMPLOYMENT, AND PUBLIC POLICY. FINAN INDUS LOC/G NAT/G TAX GIVE PAY COST PRODUC ...MGT TIME/SEQ 20. PAGE 90 F1765 — INCOME WEALTH POLICY ECO/TAC

B48
ROBERTSON D.H.,MONEY. AFR ECO/DEV NAT/G DIPLOM INT/TRADE BAL/PAY INCOME WEALTH...TIME/SEQ 20 DEPRESSION. PAGE 112 F2212 — FINAN MARKET COST PRICE

B50
LIPSET S.M.,AGRARIAN SOCIALISM. CANADA POL/PAR OP/RES ECO/TAC ADMIN ATTIT...TIME/SEQ NAT/COMP SOC/EXP 20 SASKATCH. PAGE 80 F1576 — SOCISM AGRI METH/COMP STRUCT

B52
ALEXANDROWICZ C.H.,INTERNATIONAL ECONOMIC ORGANIZATION. WOR+45 ECO/DEV ECO/UNDEV DIST/IND FINAN MARKET PLAN ECO/TAC LEGIT DRIVE WEALTH ...POLICY CONCPT QUANT OBS TIME/SEQ GEN/LAWS WORK METH/GP EEC ILO OEEC UNESCO 20. PAGE 4 F0063 — INT/ORG INT/TRADE

L53
NELSON J.R.,"UNITED STATES FOREIGN ECONOMIC POLICY AND THE STERLING AREA." USA-45 WOR+45 WOR-45 NAT/G ECO/TAC WEALTH...STAT TIME/SEQ TREND CHARTS METH/GP TERR/GP CMN/WLTH 20. PAGE 97 F1911 — FINAN DIPLOM UK

B54
MITCHELL W.G.,BUSINESS CYCLES. FINAN MARKET PRICE COST EQUILIB OPTIMAL PRODUC PROFIT...IDEA/COMP GEN/LAWS 19/20. PAGE 92 F1809 — INDUS TIME/SEQ METH/COMP STAT

B54
TINBERGEN J.,INTERNATIONAL ECONOMIC INTEGRATION. WOR+45 WOR-45 ECO/UNDEV NAT/G ECO/TAC BAL/PAY ...METH/CNCPT STAT TIME/SEQ GEN/METH OEEC 20. PAGE 130 F2574 — INT/ORG ECO/DEV INT/TRADE

B54
WASHBURNE N.F.,INTERPRETING SOCIAL CHANGE IN AMERICA. USA+45 STRATA FAM NAT/G SECT OP/RES ECO/TAC EDU/PROP HABITAT...SOC TIME/SEQ TREND 20 BUREAUCRCY. PAGE 143 F2826 — CULTURE STRUCT CREATE TEC/DEV

B55
BERNSTEIN M.H.,REGULATING BUSINESS BY INDEPENDENT COMMISSION. USA+45 USA-45 LG/CO CHIEF LEGIS PROB/SOLV ADJUD SANCTION GP/REL ATTIT...TIME/SEQ 19/20 MONOPOLY PRESIDENT CONGRESS. PAGE 14 F0268 — DELIB/GP CONTROL CONSULT

B55
PANT Y.P.,PLANNING IN UNDERDEVELOPED ECONOMIES. INDIA NEPAL INT/TRADE COLONIAL SOVEREIGN ALL/IDEOS ...TIME/SEQ METH/COMP 20. PAGE 103 F2026 — ECO/UNDEV PLAN ECO/TAC DIPLOM

B56
BROWN R.E.,CHARLES BEARD AND THE CONSTITUTION. USA-45 NAT/G ORD/FREE WEALTH...HUM TIME/SEQ METH/COMP 20 BEARD/CA. PAGE 19 F0372 — CONSTN ELITES HIST/WRIT

B57
DAY A.C.L.,OUTLINE OF MONETARY ECONOMICS. AFR WOR-45 INT/ORG WORKER DIPLOM BAL/PAY COST INCOME WEALTH...TIME/SEQ SIMUL 20. PAGE 31 F0594 — FINAN NAT/G EQUILIB PRICE

B57
LAVES W.H.C.,UNESCO. FUT WOR+45 NAT/G CONSULT DELIB/GP TEC/DEV ECO/TAC EDU/PROP PEACE ORD/FREE ...CONCPT TIME/SEQ TREND UNESCO VAL/FREE 20. PAGE 76 F1491 — INT/ORG KNOWL

B58
LESTER R.A.,AS UNIONS MATURE. POL/PAR BARGAIN LEAD PARTIC GP/REL CENTRAL...MAJORIT TIME/SEQ METH/COMP. PAGE 78 F1533 — LABOR INDUS POLICY MGT

B58
MYRDAL G.,RICH LANDS AND POOR: THE ROAD TO WORLD PROSPERITY. FUT WOR+45 WOR-45 ECO/DEV ECO/UNDEV INT/ORG PLAN ECO/TAC REGION...GEOG TIME/SEQ GEN/LAWS TOT/POP 20. PAGE 96 F1880 — WEALTH TREND FOR/AID INT/TRADE

B58
OGDEN F.D.,THE POLL TAX IN THE SOUTH. USA+45 USA-45 CONSTN ADJUD ADMIN PARTIC CRIME...TIME/SEQ GOV/COMP METH/COMP 18/20 SOUTH/US. PAGE 101 F1982 — TAX CHOOSE RACE/REL DISCRIM

S58
LANE F.C.,"ECONOMIC CONSEQUENCES OF ORGANIZED VIOLENCE." FUT WOR+45 WOR-45 ECO/DEV DIST/IND SERV/IND NAT/G PROVS EX/STRUC CHOOSE ORD/FREE PWR ...TIME/SEQ GEN/LAWS MUNICH 20. PAGE 75 F1472 — WEALTH COERCE

B59
DIEBOLD W. JR.,THE SCHUMAN PLAN: A STUDY IN ECONOMIC COOPERATION, 1950-1959. EUR+WWI FRANCE GERMANY USA+45 EXTR/IND CONSULT DELIB/GP PLAN DIPLOM ECO/TAC INT/TRADE ROUTINE ORD/FREE WEALTH ...METH/CNCPT STAT CONT/OBS INT TIME/SEQ ECSC 20. PAGE 33 F0635 — INT/ORG REGION

B59
MORGENSTERN O.,INTERNATIONAL FINANCIAL TRANSACTIONS AND BUSINESS CYCLES. FRANCE GERMANY UK USA+45 USA-45 WOR+45 WOR-45 ECO/DEV ECO/TAC WEALTH ...CONCPT STAT CON/ANAL CHARTS 19/20. PAGE 93 F1832 — FINAN TIME/SEQ INT/TRADE

L59
BEGUIN B.,"ILO AND THE TRIPARTITE SYSTEM." EUR+WWI WOR+45 WOR-45 CONSTN ECO/DEV ECO/UNDEV INDUS INT/ORG NAT/G VOL/ASSN DELIB/GP PLAN TEC/DEV LEGIT ORD/FREE WEALTH...CONCPT TIME/SEQ WORK ILO 20. PAGE 12 F0228 — LABOR

S59
ZAUBERMAN A.,"SOVIET BLOC ECONOMIC INTEGRATION." COM CULTURE INTELL ECO/DEV INDUS TOP/EX ACT/RES PLAN ECO/TAC INT/TRADE ROUTINE CHOOSE ATTIT ...TIME/SEQ 20. PAGE 150 F2958
MARKET INT/ORG USSR TOTALISM

B60
CAMPBELL R.W.,SOVIET ECONOMIC POWER. COM USA+45 DIST/IND MARKET TOP/EX ACT/RES CAP/ISM ECO/TAC DOMIN EDU/PROP ADMIN ROUTINE DRIVE...MATH TIME/SEQ CHARTS WORK 20. PAGE 21 F0409
ECO/DEV PLAN SOCISM USSR

B60
HARBERGER A.C.,THE DEMAND FOR DURABLE GOODS. AGRI FINAN COST EQUILIB...MATH STAT TIME/SEQ TREND CON/ANAL CHARTS SIMUL ANTHOL 20. PAGE 55 F1072
ECOMETRIC DEMAND PRICE

B60
HOSELITZ B.F.,THEORIES OF ECONOMIC GROWTH. UK WOR+45 WOR-45 ECO/UNDEV PLAN INT/TRADE KNOWL ...CONCPT METH/CNCPT TIME/SEQ GEN/LAWS TOT/POP. PAGE 62 F1220
ECO/DEV INTELL

B60
LISTER L.,EUROPE'S COAL AND STEEL COMMUNITY. FRANCE GERMANY STRUCT ECO/DEV EXTR/IND INDUS MARKET NAT/G DELIB/GP ECO/TAC INT/TRADE EDU/PROP ATTIT RIGID/FLEX ORD/FREE PWR WEALTH...CONCPT STAT TIME/SEQ CHARTS ECSC TERR/GP 20. PAGE 81 F1582
EUR+WWI INT/ORG REGION

B60
ROSTOW W.W.,THE STAGES OF ECONOMIC GROWTH. UK USA+45 USSR WOR+45 WOR-45 ECO/DEV PERSON MARXISM ...METH/CNCPT TIME/SEQ GEN/LAWS GEN/METH 20. PAGE 114 F2246
ECO/UNDEV NEW/IDEA CAP/ISM

S60
"THE EMERGING COMMON MARKETS IN LATIN AMERICA." FUT L/A+17C STRATA DIST/IND INDUS LABOR NAT/G LEGIS ECO/TAC ADMIN RIGID/FLEX HEALTH...NEW/IDEA TIME/SEQ OAS 20. PAGE 1 F0013
FINAN ECO/UNDEV INT/TRADE

S60
BARNETT H.J.,"RESEARCH AND DEVELOPMENT, ECONOMIC GROWTH, AND NATIONAL SECURITY." AFR USA+45 R+D CREATE ECO/TAC ATTIT DRIVE PWR...POLICY SOC METH/CNCPT QUANT STAT TIME/SEQ ORG/CHARTS LOG/LING 20. PAGE 10 F0190
ACT/RES PLAN

S60
DUNN J.M.,"AMERICAN DEPENDENCE ON MATERIALS IMPORTS: THE WORLD-WIDE RESOURCE BASE." USA+45 WOR+45 NAT/G ATTIT WEALTH...RECORD TIME/SEQ CHARTS FOR/TRADE 20. PAGE 35 F0680
ACT/RES ECO/TAC

S60
FRANKEL S.H.,"ECONOMIC ASPECTS OF POLITICAL INDEPENDENCE IN AFRICA." AFR FUT SOCIETY ECO/UNDEV COM/IND FINAN LEGIS PLAN TEC/DEV CAP/ISM ECO/TAC INT/TRADE ADMIN ATTIT DRIVE RIGID/FLEX PWR WEALTH ...MGT NEW/IDEA MATH TIME/SEQ VAL/FREE 20. PAGE 43 F0846
NAT/G FOR/AID

S60
MAIR L.P.,"SOCIAL CHANGE IN SOUTH AFRICA." MOD/EUR SOUTH/AFR WOR+45 ECO/UNDEV EX/STRUC TEC/DEV ATTIT DRIVE PERCEPT ORD/FREE...MGT CONCPT TIME/SEQ IND 20. PAGE 84 F1641
AFR NAT/G REV SOVEREIGN

S60
MORALES C.J.,"TRADE AND ECONOMIC INTEGRATION IN LATIN AMERICA." FUT L/A+17C LAW STRATA ECO/UNDEV DIST/IND INDUS LABOR NAT/G LEGIS ECO/TAC ADMIN RIGID/FLEX WEALTH...CONCPT NEW/IDEA CONT/OBS TIME/SEQ WORK 20. PAGE 93 F1825
FINAN INT/TRADE REGION

S60
MURPHEY R.,"ECONOMIC CONFLICTS IN SOUTH ASIA." ASIA CULTURE INTELL ECO/TAC REGION ATTIT DRIVE KNOWL ...METH/CNCPT TIME/SEQ STERTYP TOT/POP METH/GP VAL/FREE 20. PAGE 95 F1864
S/ASIA ECO/UNDEV

S60
NANES A.,"THE EUROPEAN COMMUNITY AND THE UNITED STATES: EVOLVING RELATIONS." EUR+WWI USA+45 WOR+45 ECO/UNDEV MARKET NAT/G DELIB/GP PLAN LEGIT ATTIT PWR WEALTH...CONCPT STAT TIME/SEQ CON/ANAL EEC METH/GP OEEC 20 EURATOM. PAGE 96 F1889
INT/ORG REGION

S60
NEISSER H.,"ECONOMIC IMPERALISM RECONSIDERED." WOR+45 WOR-45 ECO/DEV ECO/UNDEV DIST/IND LEGIT COLONIAL PWR WEALTH SOCISM...MYTH MATH TIME/SEQ 20. PAGE 97 F1909
ACT/RES ECO/TAC CAP/ISM INT/TRADE

S60
NICHOLS J.P.,"HAZARDS OF AMERICAN PRIVATE INVESTMENT IN UNDERDEVELOPED COUNTRIES." FUT L/A+17C USA+45 USA-45 EXTR/IND CONSULT BAL/PWR ECO/TAC DOMIN ADJUD ATTIT SOVEREIGN WEALTH ...HIST/WRIT TIME/SEQ TREND TERR/GP VAL/FREE 20. PAGE 98 F1924
FINAN ECO/UNDEV CAP/ISM NAT/LISM

B61
KATKOFF U.,SOVIET ECONOMY 1940-1965. COM WOR+45 WOR-45 INTELL NAT/G POL/PAR TOP/EX ATTIT PWR ...POLICY TIME/SEQ VAL/FREE 20. PAGE 69 F1360
AGRI PERSON TOTALISM USSR

B61
KITZINGER V.W.,THE CHALLENGE OF THE COMMON MARKET. EUR+WWI ECO/DEV DIST/IND PLAN ECO/TAC INT/TRADE LEGIT ATTIT PWR WEALTH...TIME/SEQ TREND CHARTS EEC 20. PAGE 71 F1403
MARKET INT/ORG UK

B61
LICHTHEIM G.,MARXISM. GERMANY SOCIETY WORKER CAP/ISM ECO/TAC NAT/LISM POPULISM...TIME/SEQ GOV/COMP NAT/COMP 18/20 COM/PARTY. PAGE 80 F1559
MARXISM SOCISM IDEA/COMP CULTURE

B61
LONGRIGG S.H.,OIL IN THE MIDDLE EAST: ITS DISCOVERY AND DEVELOPMENT. ECO/UNDEV LG/CO LOC/G TEC/DEV WEALTH...STAT TIME/SEQ 20 OIL. PAGE 82 F1599
ISLAM EXTR/IND

S61
BARALL M.,"THE UNITED STATES GOVERNMENT RESPONDS." L/A+17C USA+45 SOCIETY NAT/G CREATE PLAN DIPLOM ECO/TAC ATTIT DRIVE RIGID/FLEX KNOWL SKILL WEALTH ...METH/CNCPT TIME/SEQ GEN/METH 20. PAGE 9 F0176
ECO/UNDEV ACT/RES FOR/AID

B62
CAIRNCROSS A.K.,FACTORS IN ECONOMIC DEVELOPMENT. WOR+45 ECO/UNDEV INDUS R+D LG/CO NAT/G EX/STRUC PLAN TEC/DEV ECO/TAC ATTIT HEALTH KNOWL PWR WEALTH ...TIME/SEQ GEN/LAWS TOT/POP TRUE/GP VAL/FREE 20. PAGE 21 F0399
MARKET ECO/DEV

B62
DOBB M.,CAPITALISM YESTERDAY AND TODAY. UK WORKER WAR PRODUC PROFIT 18/20 MONOPOLY. PAGE 33 F0646
CAP/ISM TIME/SEQ CONCPT ECO/TAC

B62
EINZIG P.,THE HISTORY OF FOREIGN EXCHANGE. CHRIST-17C ISLAM MEDIT-7 PRE/AMER WOR+45 ECO/DEV FINAN PLAN ECO/TAC ATTIT KNOWL WEALTH...SIMUL GEN/LAWS. PAGE 37 F0714
MARKET TIME/SEQ INT/TRADE

B62
GWYN W.B.,DEMOCRACY AND THE COST OF POLITICS IN BRITAIN. UK BUDGET CRIME CHOOSE ORD/FREE WEALTH ...TIME/SEQ 18/20. PAGE 52 F1017
COST POL/PAR POPULISM PAY

B62
HENDERSON W.O.,THE GENESIS OF THE COMMON MARKET. EUR+WWI FRANCE MOD/EUR UK SEA COM/IND EXTR/IND COLONIAL DISCRIM...TIME/SEQ CHARTS BIBLIOG 18/20 EEC TREATY. PAGE 58 F1149
ECO/DEV INT/TRADE DIPLOM

B62
HIGGANS B.,UNITED NATIONS AND U.S. FOREIGN ECONOMIC POLICY. FUT USA+45 WOR+45 ECO/DEV ECO/UNDEV NAT/G ECO/TAC WEALTH...TIME/SEQ TOT/POP UN 20. PAGE 59 F1168
INT/ORG ACT/RES FOR/AID DIPLOM

B62
KLEIN L.R.,AN INTRODUCTION TO ECONOMETRICS. DIST/IND DEMAND PRODUC WEALTH...MATH TIME/SEQ T 20. PAGE 72 F1408
ECOMETRIC SIMUL PREDICT STAT

B62
SIRUGO F.,L'ECONOMIA DEGLI STAT' ITALIANI PRIMA DELL' UNIFICAZIONE (10 VOLS.). ITALY...TIME/SEQ 18/19. PAGE 122 F2417
BIBLIOG PROVS NAT/G

B62
WARD B.,THE RICH NATIONS AND THE POOR NATIONS. FUT WOR+45 CULTURE ECO/DEV ECO/UNDEV PLAN CAP/ISM EDU/PROP REV NAT/LISM ATTIT DRIVE SOCISM...POLICY CONCPT TIME/SEQ 20. PAGE 143 F2816
ECO/TAC GEN/LAWS

S62
BOKOR-SZEGO H.,"LA CONVENTION DE BELGRADE ET LE REGIME DU DANUBE." COM EUR+WWI WOR+45 STRUCT POL/PAR VOL/ASSN PLAN EDU/PROP WEALTH...TIME/SEQ METH/GP COMMUN 20. PAGE 16 F0308
INT/ORG TOTALISM YUGOSLAVIA

S62
MEAD W.,"SOME POLITICAL-ECONOMIC ISSUES DETERMINING USA TARIFF POLICY." USA+45 USA-45 ECO/DEV NAT/G TARIFFS ATTIT...TIME/SEQ TREND CHARTS 19/20. PAGE 89 F1736
ECO/TAC METH/CNCPT BAL/PAY

S62
RAZAFIMBAHINY J.,"L'ORGANISATION AFRICAINE ET MALGACHE DE COOPERATION ECONOMIQUE." AFR ISLAM MADAGASCAR NAT/G ACT/RES ECO/TAC ALL/VALS ...TIME/SEQ 20. PAGE 110 F2158
INT/ORG ECO/UNDEV

B63
GLADE W.P. JR.,THE POLITICAL ECONOMY OF MEXICO. FUT L/A+17C CULTURE SOCIETY AGRI INDUS DELIB/GP ACT/RES ECO/TAC ATTIT HEALTH ORD/FREE...STAT TIME/SEQ TREND MEXIC/AMER TOT/POP VAL/FREE 20. PAGE 48 F0928
FINAN ECO/UNDEV

B63
KAPP W.K.,HINDU CULTURE: ECONOMIC DEVELOPMENT AND ECONOMIC PLANNING IN INDIA. INDIA S/ASIA CULTURE ECO/TAC EDU/PROP ADMIN ALL/VALS...POLICY MGT TIME/SEQ TRUE/GP VAL/FREE 20. PAGE 69 F1353
SECT ECO/UNDEV

B63
NEUMARK S.D.,FOREIGN TRADE AND ECONOMIC DEVELOPMENT IN AFRICA: A HISTORICAL PERSPECTIVE. EUR+WWI MOD/EUR ECO/UNDEV AGRI COM/IND EXTR/IND PROC/MFG SKILL WEALTH...CONCPT TIME/SEQ TREND SIMUL FOR/TRADE WORK TOT/POP TERR/GP VAL/FREE 19/20. PAGE 98 F1916
AFR

B63
RAFUSE R.W. JR.,STATE AND LOCAL FISCAL BEHAVIOR OVER THE POSTWAR CYCLES (DISSERTATION). USA+45 TAX PRICE ATTIT...POLICY TIME/SEQ TREND CHARTS BIBLIOG
BUDGET LOC/G ECO/TAC

20. PAGE 109 F2135 — PROVS

L63
MOUSKHELY M.,"LE BLOC COMMUNISTE ET LA COMMUNAUTE ECONOMIQUE EUROPEENNE." AFR COM EUR+WWI FUT USSR WOR+45 INTELL ECO/UNDEV LABOR POL/PAR NUC/PWR RIGID/FLEX...TIME/SEQ ORG/CHARTS EEC TOT/POP 20. PAGE 94 F1849 — INT/ORG ECO/DEV

S63
DELWERT J.,"L'ECONOMIE CAMBODGIENNE ET SON EVOLUTION ACTUELLE." FUT S/ASIA ECO/UNDEV ACT/RES PLAN WEALTH...CONCPT OBS TIME/SEQ TREND 20. PAGE 32 F0617 — FINAN ATTIT CAMBODIA

S63
GALENSON W.,"ECONOMIC DEVELOPMENT AND THE SECTORAL EXPANSION OF EMPLOYMENT, INT." FUT WOR+45 ECO/UNDEV DIST/IND PROC/MFG SERV/IND ACT/RES HEALTH SKILL WEALTH...STAT TIME/SEQ VAL/FREE 20. PAGE 46 F0889 — INDUS ECO/TAC

S63
HALLSTEIN W.,"THE EUROPEAN COMMUNITY AND ATLANTIC PARTNERSHIP." EUR+WWI USA+45 MARKET NAT/G VOL/ASSN DELIB/GP ARMS/CONT NUC/PWR ATTIT PWR...CONCPT STAT TIME/SEQ TREND OEEC 20 EEC. PAGE 54 F1053 — INT/ORG ECO/TAC UK

S63
LEDUC G.,"L'AIDE INTERNATIONALE AU DEVELOPPEMENT." FUT WOR+45 ECO/DEV ECO/UNDEV R+D PROF/ORG TEC/DEV ECO/TAC ROUTINE ATTIT ALL/VALS...MGT TIME/SEQ FOR/TRADE TOT/POP 20. PAGE 77 F1503 — FINAN PLAN FOR/AID

S63
RAMERIE L.,"TENSION AU SEIN DU COMECON: LE CAS ROUMAIN." COM EUR+WWI USSR WOR+45 ECO/DEV DIST/IND NAT/G POL/PAR VOL/ASSN EDU/PROP TOTALISM ATTIT WEALTH...TIME/SEQ 20 COMECON. PAGE 109 F2142 — INT/ORG ECO/TAC INT/TRADE ROMANIA

S63
SCHOFLING J.A.,"EFTA: THE OTHER EUROPE." ECO/DEV MARKET CONSULT ECO/TAC WEALTH...TIME/SEQ EEC OEEC 20 EFTA. PAGE 117 F2310 — EUR+WWI INT/ORG REGION

B64
BALASSA B.,TRADE PROSPECTS FOR DEVELOPING COUNTRIES. WOR+45 ECO/DEV AGRI EXTR/IND INDUS CREATE PLAN PRICE...ECOMETRIC CLASSIF TIME/SEQ GEN/METH. PAGE 8 F0158 — INT/TRADE ECO/UNDEV TREND STAT

B64
CHANDLER A.D. JR.,GIANT ENTERPRISE: FORD, GENERAL MOTORS, AND THE AUTOMOBILE INDUSTRY; SOURCES AND READINGS. USA+45 USA-45 FINAN MARKET CREATE ADMIN ...TIME/SEQ ANTHOL 20 AUTOMOBILE. PAGE 23 F0447 — LG/CO DIST/IND LABOR MGT

B64
EINZIG P.,MONETARY POLICY: ENDS AND MEANS. AFR UK INDUS WORKER PLAN DIPLOM PRICE BAL/PAY COST WEALTH ...DECISION TIME/SEQ 20. PAGE 37 F0715 — FINAN POLICY ECO/TAC BUDGET

B64
GARDNER L.C.,ECONOMIC ASPECTS OF NEW DEAL DIPLOMACY. USA-45 WOR-45 LAW ECO/DEV INT/ORG NAT/G VOL/ASSN LEGIS TOP/EX EDU/PROP ORD/FREE PWR WEALTH ...POLICY TIME/SEQ VAL/FREE 20 ROOSEVLT/F. PAGE 46 F0901 — ECO/TAC DIPLOM

B64
LETICHE J.M.,A HISTORY OF RUSSIAN ECONOMIC THOUGHT: NINTH THROUGH EIGHTEENTH CENTURIES. RUSSIA FINAN SECT CAP/ISM DOMIN DEMAND EFFICIENCY OWN MARXISM ...TECHNIC ANTHOL BIBLIOG 9/18. PAGE 78 F1536 — ECO/TAC TIME/SEQ IDEA/COMP ECO/UNDEV

B64
MEYER J.R.,INVESTMENT DECISIONS, ECONOMIC FORECASTING, AND PUBLIC POLICY. ECO/DEV ECO/TAC ...DECISION REGRESS TIME/SEQ CHARTS GP/COMP SIMUL 20. PAGE 90 F1771 — FINAN PROB/SOLV PREDICT LG/CO

B64
RUSTAMJI R.F.,THE LAW OF INDUSTRIAL DISPUTES IN INDIA. INDIA LEGIS WORKER CONTROL GP/REL...JURID MGT TIME/SEQ 20. PAGE 115 F2264 — INDUS ADJUD BARGAIN LABOR

B64
SCHULTZ T.W.,TRANSFORMING TRADITIONAL AGRICULTURE. WOR+45 WOR-45 CULTURE STRATA FINAN ACT/RES ECO/TAC ATTIT KNOWL SKILL...MATH STAT TIME/SEQ GEN/LAWS VAL/FREE. PAGE 117 F2316 — AGRI ECO/UNDEV

B64
SEERS D.,CUBA: THE ECONOMIC AND SOCIAL REVOLUTION. L/A+17C USSR YUGOSLAVIA STRATA AGRI INDUS SCHOOL DELIB/GP PLAN ECO/TAC DOMIN EDU/PROP ATTIT RIGID/FLEX ALL/VALS...STAT OBS TIME/SEQ WORK VAL/FREE 20. PAGE 119 F2341 — ACT/RES COERCE CUBA REV

B64
STOESSINGER J.G.,FINANCING THE UNITED NATIONS SYSTEM. FUT WOR+45 CONSTN NAT/G VOL/ASSN DELIB/GP EX/STRUC ECO/TAC LEGIT CT/SYS PWR WEALTH...STAT TIME/SEQ TREND CHARTS TRUE/GP METH/GP TERR/GP VAL/FREE. PAGE 126 F2493 — FINAN INT/ORG

B64
TAEUBER I.B.,POPULATION TRENDS IN THE UNITED STATES: 1900 TO 1960. USA+45 USA-45 PROVS INCOME AGE...SOC TIME/SEQ TREND CHARTS MUNICH TIME 20 NEGRO. PAGE 128 F2522 — CENSUS GEOG STRATA STRUCT

B64
WERTHEIM W.F.,EAST-WEST PARALLELS. INDONESIA S/ASIA NAT/G SECT...TIME/SEQ METH REFORMERS S/EASTASIA. PAGE 145 F2860 — SOC ECO/UNDEV CULTURE NAT/LISM

B64
WILLIAMSON J.G.,AMERICAN GROWTH AND THE BALANCE OF PAYMENTS, 1820-1913: A STUDY OF THE LONG SWING. EUR+WWI MOD/EUR USA+45 USA-45 ECO/DEV NAT/G ECO/TAC ROUTINE ORD/FREE WEALTH...MATH STAT TIME/SEQ CHARTS SIMUL GEN/LAWS TRUE/GP METH/GP VAL/FREE 19/20. PAGE 147 F2896 — FINAN BAL/PAY

L64
STERN R.M.,"POLICIES FOR TRADE AND DEVELOPMENT." AFR FUT WOR+45 DIST/IND FINAN NAT/G DELIB/GP PLAN ECO/TAC ORD/FREE WEALTH...POLICY STAT TIME/SEQ CHARTS METH/GP 20. PAGE 126 F2480 — MARKET ECO/UNDEV INT/TRADE

S64
BEIM D.,"THE COMMUNIST BLOC AND THE FOREIGN-AID GAME." AFR WOR+45 NAT/G PLAN ROUTINE ATTIT KNOWL ORD/FREE...DECISION QUANT CONT/OBS TIME/SEQ CHARTS GAME SIMUL LOG/LING 20. PAGE 12 F0231 — COM ECO/UNDEV ECO/TAC FOR/AID

S64
FINLEY D.D.,"A POLITICAL PERSPECTIVE OF ECONOMIC RELATIONS IN THE COMMUNIST CAMP." COM USSR FACE/GP NAT/G ACT/RES PLAN DOMIN COERCE ATTIT ORD/FREE WEALTH...TIME/SEQ 20. PAGE 41 F0800 — VOL/ASSN ECO/TAC DIPLOM REGION

S64
HABERLER G.,"INTEGRATION AND GROWTH OF THE WORLD ECONOMY IN HISTORICAL PERSPECTIVE." FUT WOR+45 WOR-45 ECO/DEV ECO/UNDEV...TIME/SEQ TREND VAL/FREE 20. PAGE 52 F1023 — WEALTH INT/TRADE

S64
HOOVER C.B.,"THE ROLE OF THE NATURAL AND DEVELOPED RESOURCES OF THE NATION STATES." FUT WOR+45 ECO/DEV ECO/UNDEV NAT/G PWR RESPECT SKILL WEALTH...POLICY GEOG TIME/SEQ TREND RESOURCE/N VAL/FREE 20. PAGE 62 F1210 — EXTR/IND DOMIN

B65
KASER M.,COMECON* INTEGRATION PROBLEMS OF THE PLANNED ECONOMIES. INT/ORG TEC/DEV INT/TRADE PRICE ADMIN ADJUST CENTRAL...STAT TIME/SEQ ORG/CHARTS COMECON. PAGE 69 F1359 — PLAN ECO/DEV COM REGION

B65
O'BRIEN F.,CRISIS IN WORLD COMMUNISM* MARXISM IN SEARCH OF EFFICIENCY. AFR COM ECO/DEV PLAN INT/TRADE WAR ADJUST PEACE...STAT TIME/SEQ GOV/COMP NAT/COMP. PAGE 99 F1951 — MARXISM USSR DRIVE EFFICIENCY

B65
PHELPS E.S.,PRIVATE WANTS AND PUBLIC NEEDS - AN INTRODUCTION TO A CURRENT ISSUE OF PUBLIC POLICY (REV. ED.). USA+45 PLAN CAP/ISM INGP/REL ROLE ...DECISION TIME/SEQ 20. PAGE 106 F2081 — NAT/G POLICY DEMAND

S65
SCHROEDER G.,"LABOR PLANNING IN THE USSR." COM USSR ECO/DEV INDUS SCHOOL PRODUC WEALTH...PREDICT TIME/SEQ TREND TIME 20. PAGE 117 F2313 — WORKER PLAN CENSUS

B66
HUTTENBACH R.A.,BRITISH IMPERIAL EXPERIENCE. AFR S/ASIA UK WOR-45 INT/ORG TEC/DEV...CHARTS 16/20 MERCANTLST. PAGE 64 F1253 — COLONIAL TIME/SEQ INT/TRADE

B66
KUZNETS S.,MODERN ECONOMIC GROWTH. WOR+45 WOR-45 ECO/DEV ECO/UNDEV AGRI FINAN INDUS TEC/DEV EFFICIENCY INCOME...NAT/COMP 19/20. PAGE 74 F1456 — TIME/SEQ WEALTH PRODUC

B66
MIKESELL R.F.,PUBLIC INTERNATIONAL LENDING FOR DEVELOPMENT. WOR+45 WOR-45 DELIB/GP...TIME/SEQ CHARTS BIBLIOG 20. PAGE 91 F1783 — INT/ORG FOR/AID ECO/UNDEV FINAN

B67
ANDERSON S.V.,THE NORDIC COUNCIL: A STUDY OF SCANDINAVIAN REGIONALISM. DENMARK FINLAND ICELAND NORWAY SWEDEN MARKET NAT/G VOL/ASSN CONSULT PARL/PROC ATTIT...TIME/SEQ BIBLIOG 20. PAGE 5 F0098 — INT/ORG REGION DIPLOM LEGIS

B67
ANDERSON T.,RUSSIAN POLITICAL THOUGHT; AN INTRODUCTION. USSR NAT/G POL/PAR CHIEF MARXISM ...TIME/SEQ BIBLIOG 9/20. PAGE 5 F0099 — TREND CONSTN ATTIT

B67
APTHEKER H.,THE NATURE OF DEMOCRACY, FREEDOM AND REVOLUTION. WOR+45 PROB/SOLV COERCE COST...CONCPT TIME/SEQ METH/COMP. PAGE 6 F0111 — REV POPULISM MARXIST ORD/FREE

B67
DE TORRES J.,FINANCING LOCAL GOVERNMENT. USA+45 USA-45 NAT/G PROVS GIVE ADJUST PWR...TIME/SEQ CHARTS MUNICH 20. PAGE 31 F0606 — LOC/G BUDGET TAX TREND

B67
GARAUDY R.,KARL MARX: THE EVOLUTION OF HIS THOUGHT. SOCIETY...BIBLIOG 20 MARX/KARL STALIN/J. PAGE 46 F0899 — MARXIST GEN/LAWS CONCPT TIME/SEQ

B67
MEYNAUD J.,TRADE UNIONISM IN AFRICA; A STUDY OF ITS GROWTH AND ORIENTATION (TRANS. BY ANGELA BRENCH). INT/ORG PROB/SOLV COLONIAL PWR...TIME/SEQ TREND — LABOR AFR NAT/LISM

ILO. PAGE 90 F1774 — ORD/FREE

B67
MORRIS A.J.A.,PARLIAMENTARY DEMOCRACY IN THE NINETEENTH CENTURY. UK INDUS LOC/G NAT/G POL/PAR CONSULT LEGIS INT/TRADE ADMIN CHOOSE SUFF SOVEREIGN 19 PARLIAMENT. PAGE 93 F1835 — TIME/SEQ CONSTN PARL/PROC POPULISM

B67
NORTON H.S.,NATIONAL TRANSPORTATION POLICY: FORMATION AND IMPLEMENTATION. USA+45 USA-45 DELIB/GP LEAD...DECISION TIME/SEQ 19/20 PRESIDENT CONGRESS. PAGE 98 F1935 — POLICY DIST/IND NAT/G PROB/SOLV

B67
OFER G.,THE SERVICE INDUSTRIES IN A DEVELOPING ECONOMY: ISRAEL AS A CASE STUDY. ISRAEL ECO/TAC INT/TRADE PRODUC WEALTH SOCISM...TIME/SEQ TREND CHARTS 20. PAGE 101 F1979 — DIPLOM ECO/DEV SERV/IND

B67
WALLBANK T.W.,CIVILIZATION PAST AND PRESENT (3RD ED.). FUT WOR+45 WOR-45 SOCIETY...SOC CONCPT TIME/SEQ CHARTS BIBLIOG T. PAGE 143 F2809 — CULTURE STRUCT TREND

S67
PETRAS J.,"GUERRILLA MOVEMENTS IN LATIN AMERICA - I." GUATEMALA PERU VENEZUELA NAT/G COLONIAL LEAD ATTIT PWR...TIME/SEQ METH/COMP 20 COLOMB. PAGE 105 F2072 — GUERRILLA REV L/A+17C MARXISM

S67
WOLFE T.W.,"SOVIET MILITARY POLICY AT THE FIFTY YEAR MARK." USSR VIETNAM WOR+45 RATION AGREE WAR WEAPON CIVMIL/REL TREATY. PAGE 148 F2917 — FORCES POLICY TIME/SEQ PLAN

B98
MARSHALL A.,PRINCIPLES OF ECONOMICS. INDUS WORKER PRICE COST EQUILIB INCOME OPTIMAL PRODUC...TIME/SEQ METH RICARDO/D. PAGE 86 F1678 — WEALTH GEN/LAWS MARKET

TIMING....SEE TIME

TINBERGEN J. F2574,F2576

TIPTON J.B. F2577

TITO/MARSH....JOSIP BROZ TITO

TIVEY L.J. F2578

TIZARD/H....HENRY TIZARD

TRINIDAD

TOBIN J. F2579

TOCQUEVILL....ALEXIS DE TOCQUEVILLE

TOGO....SEE ALSO AFR

B64
WITHERELL J.W.,OFFICIAL PUBLICATIONS OF FRENCH EQUATORIAL AFRICA, FRENCH CAMEROONS, AND TOGO, 1946-1958 (PAMPHLET). CAMEROON CHAD FRANCE GABON TOGO LAW ECO/UNDEV EXTR/IND INT/TRADE...GEOG HEAL 20. PAGE 148 F2913 — BIBLIOG/A AFR NAT/G ADMIN

TOLEDO/O....TOLEDO, OHIO

TOMA P.A. F2580

TONG T. F2581

TONGA....TONGA

TOP/EX....TOP EXECUTIVES

B11
SCOTT W.D.,INFLUENCING MEN IN BUSINESS: THE PSYCHOLOGY OF ARGUMENT AND SUGGESTION. WOR-45 WORKER EDU/PROP DEMAND ATTIT PERSON 20. PAGE 118 F2336 — PSY MARKET SML/CO TOP/EX

N19
BUSINESS ECONOMISTS' GROUP,INCOME POLICIES (PAMPHLET). UK INDUS LABOR TOP/EX PAY COST PRODUC ...ECOMETRIC GOV/COMP SIMUL ANTHOL 20. PAGE 20 F0395 — INCOME WORKER WEALTH POLICY

B35
STALEY E.,WAR AND THE PRIVATE INVESTOR. UNIV WOR-45 INTELL SOCIETY INT/ORG NAT/G TOP/EX CAP/ISM ECO/TAC WAR ATTIT ALL/VALS...INT TIME/SEQ TREND CON/ANAL WORK TOT/POP 20. PAGE 125 F2464 — FINAN INT/TRADE DIPLOM

B43
WILMERDING L. JR.,THE SPENDING POWER: A HISTORY OF THE EFFORTS OF CONGRESS TO CONTROL EXPENDITURES. USA-45 POL/PAR DELIB/GP EX/STRUC TOP/EX TARIFFS ADMIN GOV/REL...TIME/SEQ SENATE HOUSE/REP. PAGE 147 F2900 — LEGIS BUDGET CONTROL

S45
MILLS C.W.,"THE TRADE UNION LEADER: A COLLECTIVE PORTRAIT." EX/STRUC TOP/EX INGP/REL...QU CON/ANAL CHARTS. PAGE 92 F1798 — LABOR LEAD STAT STRATA

S49
STEINMETZ H.,"THE PROBLEMS OF THE LANDRAT: A STUDY OF COUNTY GOVERNMENT IN THE US ZONE OF GERMANY." GERMANY/W USA+45 INDUS PLAN DIPLOM EDU/PROP CONTROL WAR GOV/REL FEDERAL WEALTH PLURISM...GOV/COMP 20 LANDRAT. PAGE 126 F2478 — LOC/G COLONIAL MGT TOP/EX

B51
HALEVY E.,IMPERIALISM AND THE RISE OF LABOR (2ND ED.). UK NAT/G POL/PAR TOP/EX ATTIT ORD/FREE PWR 19/20 PARLIAMENT LABOR/PAR. PAGE 53 F1042 — COLONIAL LABOR POLICY WAR

B52
MACARTHUR D.,REVITALIZING A NATION. ASIA COM FUT KOREA WOR+45 NAT/G FOR/AID TAX GIVE WAR ATTIT SOCISM 20 CHINJAP EUROPE. PAGE 83 F1619 — LEAD FORCES TOP/EX POLICY

S57
CUNNINGHAM E.M.,"THE BUSINESS MAN AND HIS LAWYER." USA+45 LG/CO SML/CO TOP/EX CHOOSE SKILL...JURID MGT 20. PAGE 29 F0561 — CONSULT LAW DECISION SERV/IND

B59
WORTHY J.C.,BIG BUSINESS AND FREE MEN. LG/CO EX/STRUC EDU/PROP LEAD CHOOSE GP/REL ATTIT DRIVE ROLE ORD/FREE...MAJORIT 20. PAGE 149 F2927 — ELITES LOC/G TOP/EX PARTIC

L59
FURASH E.A.,"PROBLEMS IN REVIEW: INDUSTRIAL ESPIONAGE." WORKER ECO/TAC PERS/REL OPTIMAL AGE ATTIT KNOWL...MGT DEEP/INT DEEP/QU GP/COMP IDEA/COMP. PAGE 45 F0875 — INDUS TOP/EX MAJORITY

S59
ZAUBERMAN A.,"SOVIET BLOC ECONOMIC INTEGRATION." COM CULTURE INTELL ECO/DEV INDUS TOP/EX ACT/RES PLAN ECO/TAC INT/TRADE ROUTINE CHOOSE ATTIT ...TIME/SEQ 20. PAGE 150 F2958 — MARKET INT/ORG USSR TOTALISM

B60
CAMPBELL R.W.,SOVIET ECONOMIC POWER. COM USA+45 DIST/IND MARKET TOP/EX ACT/RES CAP/ISM ECO/TAC DOMIN EDU/PROP ADMIN ROUTINE DRIVE...MATH TIME/SEQ CHARTS WORK 20. PAGE 21 F0409 — ECO/DEV PLAN SOCISM USSR

B60
LENCZOWSKI G.,OIL AND STATE IN THE MIDDLE EAST. FUT IRAN LAW ECO/UNDEV EXTR/IND NAT/G TOP/EX PLAN TEC/DEV ECO/TAC LEGIT ADMIN COERCE ATTIT ALL/VALS PWR...CHARTS 20. PAGE 78 F1519 — ISLAM INDUS NAT/LISM

B61
BENOIT E.,EUROPE AT SIXES AND SEVENS: THE COMMON MARKET, THE FREE TRADE ASSOCIATION AND THE UNITED STATES. EUR+WWI FUT USA+45 INDUS CONSULT DELIB/GP EX/STRUC TOP/EX ACT/RES ECO/TAC EDU/PROP ROUTINE CHOOSE PERCEPT WEALTH...MGT TREND EEC FOR/TRADE TOT/POP 20 EFTA. PAGE 13 F0249 — FINAN ECO/DEV VOL/ASSN

B61
DELEFORTRIE-SOU N.,LES DIRIGEANTS DE L'INDUSTRIE FRANCAISE. FRANCE CULTURE ELITES PROB/SOLV ...DECISION STAT CHARTS 20. PAGE 32 F0613 — INDUS STRATA TOP/EX LEAD

B61
KATKOFF U.,SOVIET ECONOMY 1940-1965. COM WOR+45 WOR-45 INTELL NAT/G POL/PAR TOP/EX ATTIT PWR ...POLICY TIME/SEQ VAL/FREE 20. PAGE 69 F1360 — AGRI PERSON TOTALISM USSR

B61
QURESHI S.,INCENTIVES IN AMERICAN EMPLOYMENT (THESIS, UNIVERSITY OF PENNSYLVANIA). DELIB/GP TOP/EX BUDGET ROUTINE SANCTION COST TECHRACY MGT. PAGE 108 F2134 — SERV/IND ADMIN PAY EX/STRUC

S61
SCHER S.,"REGULATORY AGENCY CONTROL THROUGH APPOINTMENT: THE CASE OF THE EISENHOWER ADMINISTRATION AND THE NLRB." USA+45 EX/STRUC GOV/REL 20 NLRB. PAGE 116 F2296 — CHIEF LOBBY CONTROL TOP/EX

S61
VALLET R.,"IRAN: KEY TO THE MIDDLE EAST." COM IRAQ ISLAM KUWAIT LEBANON SAUDI/ARAB TURKEY ELITES SOCIETY INDUS PROC/MFG POL/PAR TOP/EX PLAN BAL/PWR DIPLOM ECO/TAC ALL/VALS...TREND FOR/TRADE CENTO 20. PAGE 140 F2760 — NAT/G ECO/UNDEV IRAN

S61
VERNON R.,"A TRADE POLICY FOR THE 1960'S." COM FUT USA+45 WOR+45 ECO/DEV ECO/UNDEV FINAN TOP/EX ACT/RES...WELF/ST METH/CNCPT CONT/OBS TOT/POP 20. PAGE 141 F2781 — PLAN INT/TRADE

S61
VINER J.,"ECONOMIC FOREIGN POLICY ON THE NEW FRONTIER." USA+45 ECO/UNDEV AGRI FINAN INDUS MARKET INT/ORG NAT/G FOR/AID INT/TRADE ADMIN ATTIT PWR 20 KENNEDY/JF. PAGE 141 F2786 — TOP/EX ECO/TAC BAL/PAY TARIFFS

B62
HATTERY L.H.,INFORMATION RETRIEVAL MANAGEMENT. CLIENT INDUS TOP/EX COMPUTER OP/RES TEC/DEV ROUTINE COST EFFICIENCY RIGID/FLEX...METH/COMP ANTHOL 20. PAGE 57 F1113 — R+D COMPUT/IR MGT CREATE

B62
PRAKASH O.M.,THE THEORY AND WORKING OF STATE CORPORATIONS: WITH SPECIAL REFERENCE TO INDIA. INDIA UK USA+45 TOP/EX PRICE ADMIN EFFICIENCY...MGT METH/COMP 20 TVA. PAGE 107 F2112
LG/CO ECO/UNDEV GOV/REL SOCISM

B62
SMITH G.A. JR.,POLICY FORMULATION AND ADMINISTRATION: A CASEBOOK OF TOPMANAGEMENT PROBLEMS IN BUSINESS. EX/STRUC PLAN PROB/SOLV ADMIN CONTROL EXEC LEAD ROUTINE EFFICIENCY ATTIT MGT. PAGE 123 F2430
INDUS SOC/EXP TOP/EX DECISION

S62
IOVTCHOUK M.T.,"ON SOME THEORETICAL PRINCIPLES AND METHODS OF SOCIOLOGICAL INVESTIGATIONS (IN RUSSIAN)." FUT USA+45 STRATA R+D NAT/G POL/PAR TOP/EX ACT/RES PLAN ECO/TAC EDU/PROP ROUTINE ATTIT RIGID/FLEX MARXISM SOCISM...MARXIST METH/CNCPT OBS TREND NAT/COMP GEN/LAWS 20. PAGE 65 F1288
COM ECO/DEV CAP/ISM USSR

S62
MUELLER E.,"LOCATION DECISIONS OF MANUFACTURERS." USA+45 MARKET ATTIT...POLICY STAT INT CHARTS 20. PAGE 94 F1852
DECISION PROC/MFG GEOG TOP/EX

S62
PIQUEMAL M.,"LA COOPERATION FINANCIERE ENTRE LA FRANCE ET LES ETATS AFRICAINS ET MALGACHE." ISLAM INT/ORG TOP/EX ECO/TAC...JURID CHARTS 20. PAGE 106 F2089
AFR FINAN FRANCE MADAGASCAR

S62
READ W.H.,"UPWARD COMMUNICATION IN INDUSTRIAL HIERARCHIES." LG/CO TOP/EX PROB/SOLV DOMIN EXEC PERS/REL ATTIT DRIVE PERCEPT...CORREL STAT CHARTS 20. PAGE 110 F2159
ADMIN INGP/REL PSY MGT

B63
BAUER R.A.,AMERICAN BUSINESS AND PUBLIC POLICY: THE POLITICS OF FOREIGN TRADE. USA+45 COM/IND LG/CO NAT/G PROF/ORG SML/CO VOL/ASSN LEGIS TOP/EX ECO/TAC EDU/PROP CHOOSE HEALTH PWR WEALTH...CONCPT METH/CNCPT OBS INT QU SAMP FOR/TRADE TRUE/GP VAL/FREE HI. PAGE 11 F0217
ECO/DEV ATTIT

B63
GANGULY D.S.,PUBLIC CORPORATIONS IN A NATIONAL ECONOMY. INDIA WOR+45 FINAN INDUS TOP/EX PRICE EFFICIENCY...MGT STAT CHARTS BIBLIOG 20. PAGE 46 F0897
ECO/UNDEV LG/CO SOCISM GOV/REL

B63
JACOBS P.,STATE OF UNIONS. USA+45 STRATA TOP/EX GP/REL RACE/REL DEMAND DISCRIM ATTIT PWR 20 CONGRESS NEGRO HOFFA/J. PAGE 66 F1296
LABOR ECO/TAC BARGAIN DECISION

L63
RIDAH A.,"LE NEO-DESTOUR DEPUIS L'INDEPENDANCE." FUT ISLAM WOR+45 ECO/UNDEV INT/ORG SCHOOL DELIB/GP TOP/EX ACT/RES EDU/PROP LEGIT ATTIT ALL/VALS 20 TUNIS. PAGE 111 F2189
NAT/G CONSTN

S63
BALOGH T.,"L'INFLUENCE DES INSTITUTIONS MONETAIRES ET COMMERCIALES SUR LA STRUCTURE ECONOMIQUE AFRICAIN." AFR EUR+WWI FUT USA+45 USA-45 WOR+45 SERV/IND INT/ORG NAT/G TOP/EX ROUTINE...INDEX EEC METH/GP 20. PAGE 9 F0168
FINAN

S63
BELOFF M.,"BRITAIN, EUROPE AND THE ATLANTIC COMMUNITY." EUR+WWI ELITES NAT/G VOL/ASSN TOP/EX ATTIT ORD/FREE PWR SOVEREIGN WEALTH EEC TOT/POP VAL/FREE CMN/WLTH 20. PAGE 13 F0240
INT/ORG ECO/DEV UK

S63
MONROE A.D.,"BRITAIN AND THE EUROPEAN COMMUNITY." EUR+WWI FRANCE NAT/G DELIB/GP TOP/EX ECO/TAC DOMIN PWR...POLICY RECORD GEN/LAWS EEC EFTA 20 EFTA CMN/WLTH. PAGE 93 F1817
VOL/ASSN ATTIT UK

S63
POPPINO R.E.,"IMBALANCE IN BRAZIL." L/A+17C NAT/G TOP/EX PLAN DIPLOM LEGIT DRIVE WEALTH...CON/ANAL FOR/TRADE LAFTA 20. PAGE 107 F2105
POL/PAR ECO/TAC BRAZIL

S63
TENNYSON L.B.,"THE USA IN ATLANTIC COMMUNITY." EUR+WWI FRANCE UK USA+45 ECO/UNDEV VOL/ASSN DELIB/GP TOP/EX DIPLOM DOMIN PWR...POLICY CONCPT TREND GEN/LAWS EEC 20. PAGE 129 F2545
ATTIT ECO/TAC BAL/PWR

B64
CHEIT E.F.,THE BUSINESS ESTABLISHMENT. FRANCE WOR+45 PROF/ORG TOP/EX PROB/SOLV CAP/ISM ADMIN SUPEGO MORAL PWR...METH/CNCPT MYTH NEW/IDEA 20. PAGE 24 F0460
PERSON EX/STRUC MGT INDUS

B64
GARDNER L.C.,ECONOMIC ASPECTS OF NEW DEAL DIPLOMACY. USA-45 WOR-45 LAW ECO/DEV INT/ORG NAT/G VOL/ASSN LEGIS TOP/EX EDU/PROP ORD/FREE PWR WEALTH ...POLICY TIME/SEQ VAL/FREE 20 ROOSEVLT/F. PAGE 46 F0901
ECO/TAC DIPLOM

B64
IMAZ J.L.,LOS QUE MANDAN. INDUS LABOR NAT/G POL/PAR PROVS SECT CHIEF TOP/EX CONTROL 20 ARGEN. PAGE 64 F1261
LEAD FORCES ELITES ATTIT

B64
NOSSITER B.D.,THE MYTHMAKERS: AN ESSAY ON POWER AND WEALTH. USA+45 LG/CO NAT/G TOP/EX PROB/SOLV ADMIN GP/REL ORD/FREE 20. PAGE 99 F1937
ECO/TAC WEALTH FINAN PLAN

B65
FLASH E.S. JR.,ECONOMIC ADVICE AND PRESIDENTIAL LEADERSHIP: THE COUNCIL OF ECONOMIC ADVISORS. USA+45 NAT/G EX/STRUC LEGIS TOP/EX ACT/RES ADMIN PRESIDENT CONGRESS. PAGE 41 F0808
PLAN CONSULT CHIEF

B65
KISSINGER H.A.,THE TROUBLED PARTNERSHIP* RE-APPRAISAL OF THE WESTERN ALLIANCE. EUR+WWI USA+45 INT/ORG NAT/G VOL/ASSN TOP/EX DIPLOM ORD/FREE PWR NATO. PAGE 71 F1402
FRANCE NUC/PWR ECO/DEV

B65
MORTON H.C.,BROOKINGS PAPERS ON PUBLIC POLICY. USA+45 WOR+45 INDUS ACADEM INT/ORG LOC/G PROVS EDU/PROP MUNICH. PAGE 94 F1840
FINAN ECO/DEV TOP/EX NAT/G

L65
HAMMOND A.,"COMPREHENSIVE VERSUS INCREMENTAL BUDGETING IN THE DEPARTMENT OF AGRICULTURE" USA+45 GP/REL ATTIT...PSY INT 20 DEPT/AGRI. PAGE 54 F1057
TOP/EX EX/STRUC AGRI BUDGET

L65
LETICHE J.M.,"EUROPEAN INTEGRATION: AN AMERICAN VIEW." EUR+WWI FRANCE WOR+45 ECO/DEV DIST/IND EXTR/IND NAT/G DELIB/GP TOP/EX PLAN ECO/TAC ATTIT ...STAT CON/ANAL CHARTS EEC 20. PAGE 78 F1537
INDUS AGRI

L65
WILLIAMS S.,"NEGOTIATING INVESTMENT IN EMERGING COUNTRIES." USA+45 WOR+45 INDUS MARKET NAT/G TOP/EX TEC/DEV CAP/ISM ECO/TAC ADMIN SKILL WEALTH...POLICY RELATIV MGT WORK 20. PAGE 147 F2894
FINAN ECO/UNDEV

S65
HADDAD W.F.,"MR. SHRIVER AND THE SAVAGE POLITICS OF POVERTY" USA+45 LAW NAT/G DELIB/GP LEGIS GIVE LEAD CENTRAL PWR...SOC/WK CHARTS 20 CONGRESS POVRTY/WAR SHRIVER/S OEO. PAGE 53 F1028
WEALTH GOV/REL CONTROL TOP/EX

S65
WHITAKER A.P.,"ARGENTINA: STRUGGLE FOR RECOVERY." L/A+17C USA+45 NAT/G TOP/EX PLAN LEGIT COERCE REV RIGID/FLEX PWR WEALTH...RECORD ALL/PROG ARGEN FOR/TRADE 20. PAGE 146 F2867
POL/PAR ECO/TAC NAT/LISM

B66
DUNCOMBE H.S.,COUNTY GOVERNMENT IN AMERICA. USA+45 FINAN ADMIN ROUTINE GOV/REL...GOV/COMP MUNICH 20. PAGE 35 F0678
LOC/G PROVS CT/SYS TOP/EX

B66
LEE R.A.,TRUMAN AND TAFT-HARTLEY: A QUESTION OF MANDATE. USA+45 LAW CONSTN LG/CO CONTROL LOBBY GOV/REL PEACE NEW/LIB 20 TRUMAN/HS CONGRESS. PAGE 77 F1507
LEGIS TOP/EX ADJUD LABOR

B66
ZINKIN T.,CHALLENGES IN INDIA. INDIA PAKISTAN LAW AGRI FINAN INDUS TOP/EX TEC/DEV CONTROL ROUTINE ORD/FREE PWR 20 NEHRU/J SHASTRI/LB CIVIL/SERV. PAGE 150 F2964
NAT/G ECO/TAC POLICY ADMIN

S66
VENTRE F.T.,"LOCAL INITIATIVES IN URBAN INDUSTRIAL DEVELOPMENT." FINAN SERV/IND TOP/EX PLAN BUDGET RENT TAX...GP/COMP MUNICH 20. PAGE 141 F2777
ECO/TAC LOC/G INDUS

B67
ANDERSON C.W.,ISSUES OF POLITICAL DEVELOPMENT. BURMA WOR+45 CULTURE TOP/EX ECO/TAC MARXISM ...CHARTS NAT/COMP 20 COLOMB CONGO/LEOP. PAGE 5 F0094
NAT/LISM COERCE ECO/UNDEV SOCISM

B67
BAILY S.L.,LABOR, NATIONALISM, AND POLITICS IN ARGENTINA. POL/PAR TOP/EX GP/REL...BIBLIOG/A 19/20 MIGRATION PERON/JUAN ARGEN. PAGE 8 F0154
LABOR NAT/LISM

B67
BARDENS D.,CHURCHILL IN PARLIAMENT. UK DIPLOM ADJUD CONTROL AUTHORIT PERSON ORD/FREE 20 CHURCHLL/W PARLIAMENT. PAGE 10 F0186
TOP/EX LEGIS GOV/REL

B67
THOMAS M.J.,PRESIDENTIAL STATEMENTS ON EDUCATION: EXCERPTS FROM INAUGURAL AND STATE OF THE UNION MESSAGES 1789-1967. USA+45 USA-45 NAT/G BUDGET ...IDEA/COMP 18/20 PRESIDENT. PAGE 130 F2562
EDU/PROP TOP/EX LEGIS SCHOOL

S67
GREGORY R.,"THE MINISTER'S LINE: OR, THE M4 COMES TO BERKSHIRE. PART I." UK CONSTN DIST/IND LEGIS TOP/EX PLAN ADJUD...GEOG 20. PAGE 51 F0994
DECISION CONSTRUC NAT/G DELIB/GP

TORONTO....TORONTO, ONTARIO

TORY/PARTY....TORY PARTY

B64
RAISON T.,WHY CONSERVATIVE? UK FORCES DIPLOM ECO/TAC GIVE EDU/PROP ORD/FREE WEALTH LAISSEZ ...GOV/COMP 20 TORY/PARTY CONSRV/PAR. PAGE 109
PLURISM CONSERVE POL/PAR

F2137
NAT/G

TOTALISM....TOTALITARIANISM

N19
HAYEK FA V.O.N.,FREEDOM AND THE ECONOMIC SYSTEM. GERMANY USSR PLAN REPRESENT TOTALISM FASCISM POPULISM...MAJORIT METH/COMP GEN/LAWS 20. PAGE 57 F1123
ORD/FREE ECO/TAC CAP/ISM SOCISM

B37
BRESCIANI-TURRONI C,THE ECONOMICS OF INFLATION: A STUDY OF CURRENCY DEPRECIATION IN POST-WAR GERMANY. AFR GERMANY FINAN INT/TRADE PRICE TOTALISM...POLICY TIME/SEQ CHARTS GEN/LAWS 20 HITLER/A. PAGE 18 F0347
ECO/TAC WEALTH SOCIETY

B39
MARQUAND H.A.,ORGANIZED LABOUR IN FOUR CONTINENTS. EUR+WWI USA-45 INDUS NAT/G PAY GP/REL TOTALISM ATTIT WEALTH ALL/IDEOS...TREND NAT/COMP 20 ILO AFL/CIO EUROPE CHINJAP MEXIC/AMER. PAGE 85 F1673
LABOR WORKER CONCPT ANTHOL

B40
SIKES E.R.,CONTEMPORARY ECONOMIC SYSTEMS: THEIR ANALYSIS AND SOCIAL BACKGROUND. GERMANY ITALY USSR AGRI INDUS PLAN CAP/ISM ROUTINE TOTALISM FASCISM ...POLICY CON/ANAL BIBLIOG 20. PAGE 122 F2400
COM SOCISM CONCPT

B42
DRUCKER P.F.,THE FUTURE OF INDUSTRIAL MAN; A CONSERVATIVE APPROACH. USA-45 LOC/G PLAN WAR CENTRAL RATIONAL TOTALISM ORD/FREE LAISSEZ ...PLURIST IDEA/COMP 19/20 HITLER/A. PAGE 34 F0664
INDUS SOCIETY REGION PROB/SOLV

B47
BAERWALD F.,FUNDAMENTALS OF LABOR ECONOMICS. LAW INDUS LABOR LG/CO CONTROL GP/REL INCOME TOTALISM ...MGT CHARTS GEN/LAWS BIBLIOG 20. PAGE 8 F0150
ECO/DEV WORKER MARKET

B48
LAUTERBACH A.,ECONOMIC SECURITY AND INDIVIDUAL FREEDOM: CAN WE HAVE BOTH? COM EUR+WWI MOD/EUR UNIV WOR+45 CAP/ISM TOTALISM ALL/VALS...GOV/COMP BIBLIOG 20. PAGE 76 F1490
ORD/FREE ECO/DEV DECISION INGP/REL

B50
HUNT R.N.,THE THEORY AND PRACTICE OF COMMUNISM. STRUCT WORKER NAT/LISM TOTALISM...CONCPT TREND 19/20 STALIN/J EUROPE. PAGE 63 F1244
MARXISM SOCISM REV STRATA

B57
LOUCKS W.N.,COMPARATIVE ECONOMIC SYSTEMS (5TH ED.). COM UK USSR INDUS POL/PAR PLAN CAP/ISM TOTALISM MARXISM...PHIL/SCI BIBLIOG 19/20. PAGE 82 F1603
NAT/COMP IDEA/COMP SOCISM

B59
BARNETT A.D.,COMMUNIST ECONOMIC STRATEGY: THE RISE OF MAINLAND CHINA. CHINA/COM USSR WOR+45 AGRI INDUS FOR/AID INGP/REL ATTIT. PAGE 10 F0188
ECO/UNDEV INT/TRADE TOTALISM BAL/PWR

B59
HENDEL S.,THE SOVIET CRUCIBLE. USSR LEAD COERCE NAT/LISM UTOPIA PWR...POLICY CONCPT ANTHOL 20 STALIN/J LENIN/VI MARX/KARL BOLSHEVIK. PAGE 58 F1147
COM MARXISM REV TOTALISM

B59
HOOVER C.B.,THE ECONOMY, LIBERTY AND THE STATE. COM EUR+WWI USA+45 USA-45 USSR CAP/ISM EDU/PROP COERCE TOTALISM ORD/FREE...POLICY OBS INT TREND NAZI 20. PAGE 61 F1206
ECO/DEV ECO/TAC

B59
WARD B.,5 IDEAS THAT CHANGE THE WORLD. WOR+45 WOR-45 SOCIETY STRUCT AGRI INDUS INT/ORG NAT/G FORCES ACT/RES ARMS/CONT TOTALISM ATTIT DRIVE GEN/LAWS. PAGE 143 F2815
ECO/UNDEV ALL/VALS NAT/LISM COLONIAL

S59
ZAUBERMAN A.,"SOVIET BLOC ECONOMIC INTEGRATION." COM CULTURE INTELL ECO/DEV INDUS TOP/EX ACT/RES PLAN ECO/TAC INT/TRADE ROUTINE CHOOSE ATTIT ...TIME/SEQ 20. PAGE 150 F2958
MARKET INT/ORG USSR TOTALISM

B60
ARON R.,COLLOQUES DE RHEINFELDEN. AFR USA+45 USSR WOR+45 WOR-45 CULTURE ECO/UNDEV NAT/G POL/PAR DIPLOM NAT/LISM TOTALISM ATTIT DRIVE ALL/VALS ...PLURIST CONCPT STERTYP GEN/LAWS TOT/POP 20. PAGE 6 F0120
ECO/DEV SOCIETY CAP/ISM SOCISM

B61
KATKOFF U.,SOVIET ECONOMY 1940-1965. COM WOR+45 WOR-45 INTELL NAT/G POL/PAR TOP/EX ATTIT PWR ...POLICY TIME/SEQ VAL/FREE 20. PAGE 69 F1360
AGRI PERSON TOTALISM USSR

S61
HAYTES W.,"THREE VIEWS ON THE SOVIET ECONOMIC THREAT." AFR COM USA+45 USA-45 USSR WOR+45 WOR-45 INDUS TEC/DEV ECO/TAC DOMIN ATTIT PERCEPT PWR FOR/TRADE 20. PAGE 57 F1128
ECO/DEV PLAN TOTALISM

S62
BOKOR-SZEGO H.,"LA CONVENTION DE BELGRADE ET LE REGIME DU DANUBE." COM EUR+WWI WOR+45 STRUCT POL/PAR VOL/ASSN PLAN EDU/PROP WEALTH...TIME/SEQ METH/GP COMMUN 20. PAGE 16 F0308
INT/ORG TOTALISM YUGOSLAVIA

B63
PRYOR F.L.,THE COMMUNIST FOREIGN TRADE SYSTEM. COM CZECHOSLVK GERMANY YUGOSLAVIA LAW ECO/DEV DIST/IND POL/PAR PLAN DOMIN TOTALISM DRIVE RIGID/FLEX WEALTH ...STAT STAND/INT CHARTS FOR/TRADE 20. PAGE 108 F2130
ATTIT ECO/TAC

S63
FLOREA I.,"CU PRIVIRE LA OBIECTUL MATERIALISMULUI ISTORIC SI AL COMUNISMULUI STIINTIFIC SI LA RAPORTUL DINTRE ELE." EUR+WWI WOR+45 WOR-45 INTELL NAT/G POL/PAR WORKER EDU/PROP PERCEPT MARXISM ...MARXIST PHIL/SCI CONCPT TOT/POP 20. PAGE 42 F0812
COM ATTIT TOTALISM

S63
RAMERIE L.,"TENSION AU SEIN DU COMECON: LE CAS ROUMAIN." COM EUR+WWI USSR WOR+45 ECO/DEV DIST/IND NAT/G POL/PAR VOL/ASSN EDU/PROP TOTALISM ATTIT WEALTH...TIME/SEQ 20 COMECON. PAGE 109 F2142
INT/ORG ECO/TAC INT/TRADE ROMANIA

B64
DANIELS R.V.,RUSSIA. RUSSIA USSR STRUCT NAT/LISM TOTALISM ORD/FREE WEALTH...POLICY DECISION TREND. PAGE 30 F0579
MARXISM REV ECO/DEV DIPLOM

C64
GOLDMAN M.I.,"COMPARATIVE ECONOMIC SYSTEMS: A READER." COM ECO/UNDEV NAT/G BUDGET CAP/ISM ADMIN TOTALISM MARXISM SOCISM...MGT ANTHOL BIBLIOG 19/20. PAGE 48 F0938
NAT/COMP CONTROL IDEA/COMP

B66
ANDRESKI S.,PARASITISM AND SUBVERSION* THE CASE OF LATIN AMERICA. CULTURE ECO/UNDEV LABOR NAT/G SECT PROB/SOLV RACE/REL TOTALISM ATTIT WEALTH ALL/IDEOS. PAGE 5 F0100
L/A+17C GOV/COMP STRATA REV

B66
SPULBER N.,THE STATE AND ECONOMIC DEVELOPMENT IN EASTERN EUROPE. BULGARIA COM CZECHOSLVK HUNGARY POLAND YUGOSLAVIA CULTURE PLAN CAP/ISM INT/TRADE CONTROL...POLICY CHARTS METH/COMP BIBLIOG/A 19/20. PAGE 125 F2460
ECO/DEV ECO/UNDEV NAT/G TOTALISM

B66
US SENATE COMM ON FOREIGN REL,HEARINGS ON S 2859 AND S 2861. USA+45 WOR+45 FORCES BUDGET CAP/ISM ADMIN DETER WEAPON TOTALISM...NAT/COMP 20 UN CONGRESS. PAGE 139 F2735
FOR/AID DIPLOM ORD/FREE ECO/UNDEV

B66
WETTER G.A.,SOVIET IDEOLOGY TODAY. USSR ECO/UNDEV SECT WORKER CAP/ISM CONTROL TASK EFFICIENCY TOTALISM DRIVE WEALTH...TREND 18/20. PAGE 145 F2864
ALL/IDEOS MARXISM REV

B67
BURDEN H.T.,THE NUREMBERG PARTY RALLIES 1923-39. GERMANY POL/PAR SECT CREATE DOMIN WAR ATTIT ...AUD/VIS FILM 20. PAGE 20 F0384
EDU/PROP CONTROL CROWD TOTALISM

S67
CAMMETT J.M.,"COMMUNIST THEORIES OF FASCISM, 1920-35." ITALY POL/PAR PROF/ORG VOL/ASSN WORKER COLONIAL TOTALISM...SOCIALIST 20. PAGE 21 F0403
MARXISM FASCISM ATTIT

S67
CATTELL D.T.,"THE FIFTIETH ANNIVERSARY: A SOVIET WATERSHED?" USSR CONSTN ECO/DEV NAT/G LEAD TOTALISM 20 KHRUSH/N. PAGE 22 F0430
MARXISM CHIEF POLICY ADJUST

S67
GORMAN W.,"ELLUL - A PROPHETIC VOICE." WOR+45 ELITES SOCIETY ACT/RES PLAN BAL/PWR DOMIN CONTROL PARTIC TOTALISM PWR 20. PAGE 49 F0963
CREATE ORD/FREE EX/STRUC UTOPIA

S67
MCCORD W.,"ARMIES AND POLITICS; A PROBLEM IN THE THIRD WORLD." AFR ISLAM USA+45 ECO/UNDEV TOTALISM 20. PAGE 88 F1723
FOR/AID POLICY NAT/G FORCES

S67
WALZER M.,"THE CONDITION OF GREECE; TWENTY YEARS AFTER THE TRUMAN DOCTRINE." AFR GREECE FORCES CAP/ISM 20 TRUMAN/HS. PAGE 143 F2814
DIPLOM POLICY FOR/AID TOTALISM

S67
WILES P.J.,"THE POLITICAL AND SOCIAL PREREQUISITES FOR A SOVIET-TYPE ECONOMY." COM USSR LAW CULTURE CREATE ADMIN FEEDBACK ROUTINE COST OPTIMAL TOTALISM MARXISM 20. PAGE 146 F2883
ECO/DEV PLAN EX/STRUC EFFICIENCY

TOTALITARIANISM....SEE TOTALISM

TOTTEN G.O. F0499

TOURISM....SEE TRAVEL

TOUSSAIN/P....PIERRE DOMINIQUE TOUSSAINT L'OUVERTURE

TOWLE L.W. F2582

TOWNSD/PLN....TOWNSEND PLAN

TOYNBEE/A....ARNOLD TOYNBEE

TRADE, INTERNATIONAL....SEE INT/TRADE

TRADIT....TRADITIONAL AND ARISTOCRATIC

B52
DE JOUVENEL B.,THE ETHICS OF REDISTRIBUTION. UK ELITES MARKET WORKER GIVE PAY INCOME PERSON ...POLICY PSY GEN/LAWS 20. PAGE 31 F0602
WEALTH TAX SOCISM TRADIT

S64
WOOD N.,"THE FAMILY FIRM - BASE OF JAPAN'S GROWING ECONOMY." ECO/DEV ECO/UNDEV ECO/TAC WEALTH...POLICY TRADIT BIOG TREND 20 CHINJAP. PAGE 148 F2921
ASIA SML/CO FAM

TRADITIONAL....SEE CONSERVE, TRADIT

TRAGER F.N. F2583

TRAINING....SEE SCHOOL, ACADEM, SKILL, EDU/PROP

TRANSFER....TRANSFER

TRANSITIVITY OF CHOICE....SEE DECISION

TRANSKEI....TRANSKEI

TRANSPORTATION....SEE DIST/IND

TRAVEL....TRAVEL AND TOURISM

B65
US HOUSE COMM BANKING-CURR,INTERNATIONAL TRAVEL IN RELATION TO THE BALANCE OF PAYMENTS DEFICIT. USA+45 DELIB/GP...CHARTS 20 CONGRESS TRAVEL. PAGE 136 F2690
BAL/PAY ECO/TAC SERV/IND PROB/SOLV

TRAVERS H. F2584

TREASURY DEPARTMENT....SEE DEPT/TREAS

TREATY....TREATIES; INTERNATIONAL AGREEMENTS

B42
JACKSON M.V.,EUROPEAN POWERS AND SOUTH-EAST AFRICA: A STUDY OF INTERNATIONAL RELATIONS ON SOUTH-EAST COAST OF AFRICA, 1796-1856. AFR FRANCE PORTUGAL SOUTH/AFR UK USA-45 FORCES INT/TRADE PWR...CHARTS BIBLIOG 18/19 TREATY. PAGE 66 F1294
DOMIN POLICY ORD/FREE DIPLOM

B47
ENKE S.,INTERNATIONAL ECONOMICS. UK USA+45 USSR INT/ORG BAL/PWR BARGAIN CAP/ISM BAL/PAY...NAT/COMP 20 TREATY. PAGE 38 F0735
INT/TRADE FINAN TARIFFS ECO/TAC

B56
WATT D.C.,BRITAIN AND THE SUEZ CANAL. COM UAR UK ...INT/LAW 20 SUEZ TREATY. PAGE 144 F2835
DIPLOM INT/TRADE DIST/IND NAT/G

B58
MOSKOWITZ M.,HUMAN RIGHTS AND WORLD ORDER. INT/ORG PLAN GP/REL NAT/LISM SOVEREIGN...CONCPT 20 UN TREATY CIV/RIGHTS. PAGE 94 F1845
DIPLOM INT/LAW ORD/FREE

B59
ROBERTSON A.H.,EUROPEAN INSTITUTIONS: COOPERATION, INTEGRATION, UNIFICATION. EUR+WWI FINAN INT/ORG FORCES INT/TRADE TARIFFS 20 EEC EURATOM ECSC NATO TREATY. PAGE 112 F2208
ECO/DEV DIPLOM INDUS ECO/TAC

B60
HEYSE T.,PROBLEMS FONCIERS ET REGIME DES TERRES (ASPECTS ECONOMIQUES, JURIDIQUES ET SOCIAUX). AFR CONGO/BRAZ INT/ORG DIPLOM SOVEREIGN...GEOG TREATY 20. PAGE 59 F1161
BIBLIOG AGRI ECO/UNDEV LEGIS

B61
SEPULVEDA C.,A STATEMENT OF THE LAWS OF MEXICO IN MATTERS AFFECTING BUSINESS (3RD ED.). AGRI DIST/IND EXTR/IND FINAN INDUS WORKER TAX MARRIAGE OWN ORD/FREE...BIBLIOG 20 MEXIC/AMER TREATY MIGRATION MONOPOLY. PAGE 119 F2356
CONSTN NAT/G JURID LEGIS

B62
FATOUROS A.A.,GOVERNMENT GUARANTEES TO FOREIGN INVESTORS. WOR+45 ECO/UNDEV INDUS WORKER ADJUD ...NAT/COMP BIBLIOG TREATY. PAGE 39 F0767
NAT/G FINAN INT/TRADE ECO/DEV

B62
HENDERSON W.O.,THE GENESIS OF THE COMMON MARKET. EUR+WWI FRANCE MOD/EUR UK SEA COM/IND EXTR/IND COLONIAL DISCRIM...TIME/SEQ CHARTS BIBLIOG 18/20 EEC TREATY. PAGE 58 F1149
ECO/DEV INT/TRADE DIPLOM

B63
PAN AMERICAN UNION,THE EFFECTS OF THE EUROPEAN ECONOMIC COMMUNITY ON THE LATIN AMERICAN ECONOMIES (BMR). EUR+WWI L/A+17C ECO/UNDEV AGRI INDUS MARKET REGION 20 EEC TREATY. PAGE 103 F2024
INT/TRADE INT/ORG AGREE POLICY

B64
ESTHUS R.A.,FROM ENMITY TO ALLIANCE: US AUSTRALIAN RELATIONS. S/ASIA DIST/IND VOL/ASSN FORCES ATTIT 20 AUSTRAL TREATY CMN/WLTH. PAGE 39 F0751
DIPLOM WAR INT/TRADE FOR/AID

B64
TONG T.,UNITED STATES DIPLOMACY IN CHINA, 1844-1860. ASIA USA-45 ECO/UNDEV ECO/TAC COERCE GP/REL...INT/LAW 19 TREATY. PAGE 131 F2581
DIPLOM INT/TRADE COLONIAL

B65
HABERLER G.,A SURVEY OF INTERNATIONAL TRADE THEORY. CANADA FRANCE GERMANY ECO/TAC TARIFFS AGREE COST DEMAND WEALTH...ECOMETRIC 19/20 MONOPOLY TREATY. PAGE 52 F1024
INT/TRADE BAL/PAY DIPLOM POLICY

B65
LUGO-MARENCO J.J.,A STATEMENT OF THE LAWS OF NICARAGUA IN MATTERS AFFECTING BUSINESS. NICARAGUA AGRI DIST/IND EXTR/IND FINAN INDUS FAM WORKER INT/TRADE TAX MARRIAGE OWN BIO/SOC 20 TREATY RESOURCE/N MIGRATION. PAGE 82 F1606
CONSTN NAT/G LEGIS JURID

B65
MACDONALD R.W.,THE LEAGUE OF ARAB STATES: A STUDY IN THE DYNAMICS OF REGIONAL ORGANIZATION. ISRAEL UAR USSR FINAN INT/ORG DELIB/GP ECO/TAC AGREE NEUTRAL ORD/FREE PWR...DECISION BIBLIOG 20 TREATY UN. PAGE 83 F1626
ISLAM REGION DIPLOM ADMIN

B65
O'CONNELL D.P.,INTERNATIONAL LAW (2 VOLS.). WOR+45 WOR-45 ECO/DEV ECO/UNDEV INT/ORG NAT/G AGREE ...POLICY JURID CONCPT NAT/COMP 20 TREATY. PAGE 99 F1952
INT/LAW DIPLOM CT/SYS

B65
WEILER J.,L'ECONOMIE INTERNATIONALE DEPUIS 1950. WOR+45 DIPLOM TARIFFS CONFER...POLICY TREATY. PAGE 145 F2848
FINAN INT/TRADE REGION FOR/AID

B65
WINT G.,ASIA: A HANDBOOK. ASIA COM INDIA USSR CULTURE INTELL NAT/G...GEOG STAT CENSUS NAT/COMP WORSHIP 20 TREATY CHINJAP. PAGE 148 F2907
DIPLOM SOC

C65
WUORINEN J.H.,"SCANDINAVIA." DENMARK FINLAND ICELAND NORWAY SWEDEN SOCIETY AGRI POL/PAR DELIB/GP DIPLOM INT/TRADE NEUTRAL WAR...CHARTS IND TREATY 20. PAGE 149 F2942
BIBLIOG NAT/G POLICY

B66
LAMBERG R.F.,PRAG UND DIE DRITTE WELT. AFR ASIA CZECHOSLVK L/A+17C MARKET TEC/DEV ECO/TAC REV ATTIT 20 TREATY. PAGE 75 F1462
DIPLOM ECO/UNDEV INT/TRADE FOR/AID

B66
PASSIN H.,THE UNITED STATES AND JAPAN. USA+45 INDUS CAP/ISM...TREND 20 CHINJAP TREATY. PAGE 103 F2032
DIPLOM INT/TRADE ECO/DEV ECO/TAC

S66
LAURENS H.,"LES PAYS OCCIDENTAUX ET LE MARCHE CHINOIS." EUR+WWI FUT S/ASIA AGRI INDUS VOL/ASSN ECO/TAC BAL/PAY...RECORD PREDICT TREATY. PAGE 76 F1488
ASIA INT/TRADE TREND STAT

B67
MCDOUGAL M.S.,THE INTERPRETATION OF AGREEMENTS AND WORLD PUBLIC ORDER: PRINCIPLES OF CONTENT AND PROCEDURE. WOR+45 CONSTN PROB/SOLV TEC/DEV ...CON/ANAL TREATY. PAGE 88 F1727
INT/LAW STRUCT ECO/UNDEV DIPLOM

B67
WATT A.,THE EVOLUTION OF AUSTRALIAN FOREIGN POLICY 1938-65. ASIA S/ASIA USA+45 USA-45 INT/ORG NAT/G FORCES FOR/AID TREATY 20 AUSTRAL. PAGE 144 F2834
DIPLOM WAR

L67
MCALLISTER J.T. JR.,"THE POSSIBILITIES FOR DIPLOMACY IN SOUTHEAST ASIA." LAOS VIETNAM INT/ORG NAT/G PROVS BAL/PWR DOMIN AGREE COLONIAL WAR PWR 17/20 TREATY. PAGE 88 F1716
DIPLOM S/ASIA

S67
IBARRA J.,"EL EXPERIMENTO CUBANO." COM CUBA L/A+17C USA+45 ECO/UNDEV LEGIS INT/TRADE CONTROL REV NAT/LISM PWR 19/20 TREATY. PAGE 64 F1259
COLONIAL DIPLOM NAT/G POLICY

S67
OLIVIER G.,"ASPECTS JURIDIQUES DE L'ADOPTION DU TRAITE CECA A LA CRISE CHARBONNIERE (SUITE ET FIN)" LAW DIST/IND PLAN DIPLOM RATION PRICE ADMIN COST DEMAND...POLICY CON/ANAL ECSC TREATY. PAGE 101 F1988
INT/TRADE INT/ORG EXTR/IND CONSTN

S67
WEIL G.L.,"THE MERGER OF THE INSTITUTIONS OF THE EUROPEAN COMMUNITIES" EUR+WWI ECO/DEV INT/TRADE CONSEN PLURISM...DECISION MGT 20 EEC EURATOM ECSC TREATY. PAGE 145 F2847
ECO/TAC INT/ORG CENTRAL INT/LAW

S67
WOLFE T.W.,"SOVIET MILITARY POLICY AT THE FIFTY YEAR MARK." USSR VIETNAM WOR+45 RATION AGREE WAR WEAPON CIVMIL/REL TREATY. PAGE 148 F2917
FORCES POLICY TIME/SEQ PLAN

TREND....PROJECTION OF HISTORICAL TRENDS

B00
LIST F.,NATIONAL SYSTEM OF POLITICAL ECONOMY. ECO/DEV AGRI EXTR/IND FINAN INDUS TEC/DEV ECO/TAC ATTIT WEALTH...TREND GEN/LAWS FOR/TRADE 19. PAGE 81 F1581
MOD/EUR MARKET

B00
MILL J.S.,PRINCIPLES OF POLITICAL ECONOMY. WOR-45 CULTURE SOCIETY STRATA ECO/DEV AGRI EXTR/IND FINAN INDUS DELIB/GP ECO/TAC WEALTH...CONCPT MATH TREND 20. PAGE 91 F1786
MARKET INT/ORG INT/TRADE

B15
JONES J.H.,THE ECONOMICS OF WAR AND CONQUEST. WOR-45 ECO/DEV NAT/G WEALTH...STAT TREND STERTYP GEN/LAWS TOT/POP 20. PAGE 68 F1338
MYTH WAR

N19
CASSELL F.,INTERNATIONAL MONETARY PROBLEMS (PAMPHLET). AFR BAL/PWR CONTROL EFFICIENCY WEALTH 20 EEC. PAGE 22 F0427
INT/TRADE FINAN DIPLOM TREND

N19
MORGENSTERN O.,A NEW LOOK AT ECONOMIC TIMES SERIES ANALYSIS (PAMPHLET). WEALTH...BIBLIOG 20 NSF NAVAL/RES. PAGE 93 F1831
TREND IDEA/COMP EFFICIENCY

N19
PATRICK H.T.,CYCLICAL INSTABILITY AND FISCAL-MONETARY POLICY IN POST-WAR JAPAN (PAMPHLET). INDUS MARKET DIPLOM TAX PRICE BAL/PAY...TREND CHARTS EQULIB 20 CHINJAP. PAGE 104 F2036
ECO/DEV PRODUC STAT

B25
EDGEWORTH F.Y.,PAPERS RELATING TO POLITICAL ECONOMY. MOD/EUR SOCIETY STRATA DIST/IND INDUS MARKET NAT/G ACT/RES ECO/TAC EXEC WEALTH ...METH/CNCPT MATH TREND HYPO/EXP SIMUL GEN/METH FOR/TRADE VAL/FREE LOG/LING. PAGE 36 F0702
ECO/DEV CAP/ISM

B32
WRIGHT Q.,GOLD AND MONETARY STABILIZATION. FUT USA-45 WOR-45 INTELL ECO/DEV INT/ORG NAT/G CONSULT PLAN ECO/TAC ADMIN ATTIT WEALTH...CONCPT TREND 20. PAGE 149 F2935
FINAN POLICY

B34
GRAHAM F.D.,PROTECTIVE TARIFFS. FUT USA+45 WOR-45 INDUS MARKET VOL/ASSN PLAN CAP/ISM ECO/TAC PEACE ATTIT DRIVE HEALTH ORD/FREE...OBS TREND GEN/LAWS FOR/TRADE 20. PAGE 50 F0970
INT/ORG TARIFFS

B34
MARX K.,THE CLASS STRUGGLES IN FRANCE. FRANCE INDUS WORKER CONSERVE...TREND GEN/LAWS 19. PAGE 86 F1689
MARXIST STRATA REV INT/TRADE

B35
STALEY E.,WAR AND THE PRIVATE INVESTOR. UNIV WOR-45 INTELL SOCIETY INT/ORG NAT/G TOP/EX CAP/ISM ECO/TAC WAR ATTIT ALL/VALS...INT TIME/SEQ TREND CON/ANAL WORK TOT/POP 20. PAGE 125 F2464
FINAN INT/TRADE DIPLOM

B37
BROOKS R.R.,WHEN LABOR ORGANIZES. FINAN EDU/PROP ADMIN LOBBY PARTIC REPRESENT WEALTH TREND. PAGE 19 F0364
LABOR GP/REL POLICY

B37
MACKENZIE F.,PLANNED SOCIETY: YESTERDAY, TODAY, AND TOMORROW. ECO/DEV ECO/UNDEV AGRI FINAN INDUS PLAN INSPECT CONTROL ALL/IDEOS...TREND METH/COMP BIBLIOG 20 RESOURCE/N. PAGE 83 F1635
SOC CONCPT ANTHOL

B38
LANGE O.,ON THE ECONOMIC THEORY OF SOCIALISM. UNIV ECO/DEV FINAN INDUS INT/ORG PUB/INST ROUTINE ATTIT ALL/VALS...SOC CONCPT STAT TREND 20. PAGE 75 F1475
MARKET ECO/TAC INT/TRADE SOCISM

B39
MARQUAND H.A.,ORGANIZED LABOUR IN FOUR CONTINENTS. EUR+WWI USA-45 INDUS NAT/G PAY GP/REL TOTALISM ATTIT WEALTH ALL/IDEOS...TREND NAT/COMP 20 ILO AFL/CIO EUROPE CHINJAP MEXIC/AMER. PAGE 85 F1673
LABOR WORKER CONCPT ANTHOL

B39
ROBBINS L.,ECONOMIC CAUSES OF WAR. WOR-45 ECO/DEV ECO/UNDEV INT/ORG NAT/G TEC/DEV DIPLOM DOMIN COLONIAL ATTIT DRIVE PWR WEALTH...POLICY CONCPT OBS SAMP TREND CON/ANAL GEN/LAWS MARX/KARL 20. PAGE 112 F2203
COERCE ECO/TAC WAR

B39
STALEY E.,WORLD ECONOMY IN TRANSITION. WOR-45 SOCIETY INT/ORG PROF/ORG ECO/TAC ATTIT WEALTH ...METH/CNCPT TREND GEN/LAWS 20. PAGE 125 F2465
TEC/DEV INT/TRADE

B40
BATCHELOR B.,THE NEW OUTLOOK IN BUSINESS. LAW WORKER TAX LEAD ORD/FREE...POLICY TREND. PAGE 11 F0208
LG/CO GP/REL CAP/ISM LABOR

B41
YOUNG G.,FEDERALISM AND FREEDOM. EUR+WWI MOD/EUR RUSSIA USA-45 WOR-45 SOCIETY STRUCT ECO/DEV INT/ORG EXEC FEDERAL ATTIT PERSON ALL/VALS...OLD/LIB CONCPT OBS TREND LEAGUE/NAT TOT/POP. PAGE 150 F2950
NAT/G WAR

B43
BRADY R.A.,BUSINESS AS A SYSTEM OF POWER. EX/STRUC PLAN ECO/TAC CONTROL GP/REL PWR...TREND GP/COMP. PAGE 17 F0334
VOL/ASSN LOBBY POLICY

S43
GOLDEN C.S.,"NEW PATTERNS OF DEMOCRACY." NEIGH DELIB/GP EDU/PROP EXEC PARTIC...MGT METH/CNCPT OBS TREND. PAGE 48 F0935
LABOR REPRESENT LG/CO GP/REL

S43
HERBERG W.,"BUREAUCRACY AND DEMOCRACY IN LABOR UNIONS." LAW CONSTN STRUCT WORKER ADMIN CONTROL PARTIC RIGID/FLEX PWR TREND. PAGE 59 F1151
LABOR REPRESENT ROUTINE INGP/REL

B44
HAYEK F.A.,THE ROAD TO SERFDOM. NAT/G POL/PAR CREATE EDU/PROP ATTIT WEALTH LAISSEZ...OLD/LIB CONCPT TREND 20. PAGE 57 F1121
FUT PLAN ECO/TAC SOCISM

B46
HARRISON S.M.,AMERICAN FOUNDATIONS FOR SOCIAL WELFARE. OP/RES CONTROL...POLICY MGT METH/CNCPT STAT TREND BIBLIOG. PAGE 56 F1092
GIVE FINAN CLASSIF ADMIN

B47
ISAAC J.,ECONOMICS OF MIGRATION. MOD/EUR CULTURE STRATA STRUCT NAT/G COLONIAL WEALTH...OLD/LIB TREND TIME 19/20 EUROPE/W MIGRATION. PAGE 65 F1289
HABITAT SOC GEOG

B49
HANSEN A.H.,MONETARY THEORY AND FISCAL POLICY. CONSULT PLAN INT/TRADE BAL/PAY OPTIMAL...TREND CHARTS METH/COMP BIBLIOG T 19/20 MONEY. PAGE 54 F1063
FINAN GEN/LAWS POLICY ECO/TAC

B50
HUNT R.N.,THE THEORY AND PRACTICE OF COMMUNISM. STRUCT WORKER NAT/LISM TOTALISM...CONCPT TREND 19/20 STALIN/J EUROPE. PAGE 63 F1244
MARXISM SOCISM REV STRATA

B50
SURANYI-UNGER T.,PRIVATE ENTERPRISE AND GOVERNMENTAL PLANNING. STRUCT FINAN BAL/PWR HAPPINESS DRIVE NEW/LIB PLURISM...MATH QUANT STAT TREND BIBLIOG. PAGE 127 F2516
PLAN NAT/G LAISSEZ POLICY

B51
US DEPARTMENT OF STATE,POINT FOUR, NEAR EAST AND AFRICA, A SELECTED BIBLIOGRAPHY OF STUDIES ON ECONOMICALLY UNDERDEVELOPED COUNTRIES. AGRI COM/IND FINAN INDUS PLAN INT/TRADE...SOC TREND 20. PAGE 135 F2672
BIBLIOG/A AFR S/ASIA ISLAM

B52
EGLE W.P.,ECONOMIC STABILIZATION. USA+45 SOCIETY FINAN MARKET PLAN ECO/TAC DOMIN EDU/PROP LEGIT EXEC WEALTH...CONCPT METH/CNCPT TREND HYPO/EXP GEN/METH TOT/POP VAL/FREE 20. PAGE 36 F0708
NAT/G ECO/DEV CAP/ISM

B52
GALBRAITH J.K.,AMERICAN CAPITALISM: THE CONCEPT OF COUNTERVAILING POWER. AFR FUT USA+45 FINAN PRICE CENTRAL INCOME PEACE WEALTH...POLICY DECISION 20. PAGE 45 F0881
ECO/TAC CAP/ISM TREND NAT/G

B52
HOSELITZ B.F.,THE PROGRESS OF UNDERDEVELOPED AREAS. AFR FUT WOR+45 WOR-45 ECO/DEV ECO/TAC INT/TRADE WEALTH...SOC TREND GEN/LAWS TOT/POP VAL/FREE FOR/TRADE 20. PAGE 62 F1219
ECO/UNDEV PLAN FOR/AID

B53
BOULDING K.E.,THE ORGANIZATIONAL REVOLUTION. FUT CULTURE ECO/DEV LABOR PROF/ORG ECO/TAC MORAL...SOC CONCPT RECORD INT SOC/EXP 20. PAGE 17 F0321
SOCIETY TREND

B53
DAHL R.A.,POLITICS, ECONOMICS AND WELFARE: PLANNING AND POLITICOECONOMIC SYSTEMS RESOLVED INTO BASIC SOCIAL PROCESSES. WOR+45 WOR-45 ECO/DEV ECO/UNDEV R+D CREATE PLAN TEC/DEV EDU/PROP HEALTH WEALTH ...SOC SELF/OBS TREND CHARTS GEN/METH 20. PAGE 29 F0571
ECO/TAC PHIL/SCI

B53
FRANKEL S.H.,THE ECONOMIC IMPACT ON UNDERDEVELOPED SOCIETIES: ESSAYS ON INTERNATIONAL INVESTMENT AND SOCIAL CHANGE. AFR WOR+45 ECO/DEV FINAN INDUS NAT/G ACT/RES TEC/DEV COLONIAL ATTIT...CONCPT OBS TREND 20. PAGE 43 F0845
ECO/UNDEV FOR/AID INT/TRADE

B53
MENDE T.,WORLD POWER IN THE BALANCE. FUT USA+45 USSR WOR-45 ECO/DEV ECO/TAC INT/TRADE EDU/PROP UTOPIA ATTIT...HUM CONCPT TREND TOT/POP 20. PAGE 90 F1756
WOR+45 PWR BAL/PWR AFR

B53
MILLIKAN M.F.,INCOME STABILIZATION FOR A DEVELOPING DEMOCRACY. USA+45 ECO/DEV LABOR BUDGET ECO/TAC TAX ADMIN ADJUST PRODUC WEALTH...POLICY TREND 20. PAGE 91 F1794
ANTHOL MARKET EQUILIB EFFICIENCY

B53
WOYTINSKY W.S.,WORLD POPULATION AND PRODUCTION: TRENDS AND OUTLOOK. FUT WOR+45 WOR-45 CULTURE SOCIETY ECO/DEV AGRI INDUS TEC/DEV EDU/PROP SKILL WEALTH...SOC TREND. PAGE 149 F2928
ECO/UNDEV METH/CNCPT GEOG PERSON

L53
NELSON J.R.,"UNITED STATES FOREIGN ECONOMIC POLICY AND THE STERLING AREA." USA-45 WOR+45 WOR-45 NAT/G ECO/TAC WEALTH...STAT TIME/SEQ TREND CHARTS METH/GP TERR/GP CMN/WLTH 20. PAGE 97 F1911
FINAN DIPLOM UK

S53
LINCOLN G.,"FACTORS DETERMINING ARMS AID." COM FUT USA+45 USSR WOR+45 ECO/DEV NAT/G CONSULT PLAN TEC/DEV DIPLOM DOMIN EDU/PROP PERCEPT PWR ...DECISION CONCPT TREND MARX/KARL 20. PAGE 80 F1566
FORCES POLICY BAL/PWR FOR/AID

B54
EMERSON F.D.,SHAREHOLDER DEMOCRACY: A BROADER OUTLOOK FOR CORPORATIONS. DELIB/GP EX/STRUC LEGIS ADJUD CONTROL REPRESENT INGP/REL OWN PWR...POLICY STAT RECORD. PAGE 37 F0727
LG/CO PARTIC MAJORIT TREND

B54
POTTER D.M.,PEOPLE OF PLENTY: ECONOMIC ABUNDANCE AND THE AMERICAN CHARACTER. USA+45 USA-45 ECO/DEV ATTIT PERSON...PSY SOC CONCPT TREND GEN/METH TOT/POP 20. PAGE 107 F2108
CULTURE WEALTH

B54
TAFT P.,THE STRUCTURE AND GOVERNMENT OF LABOR UNIONS. SANCTION INGP/REL ORD/FREE PWR MARXISM ...MAJORIT STAT TREND. PAGE 128 F2524
LABOR ADJUD WORKER FINAN

B54
WASHBURNE N.F.,INTERPRETING SOCIAL CHANGE IN AMERICA. USA+45 STRATA FAM NAT/G SECT OP/RES ECO/TAC EDU/PROP HABITAT...SOC TIME/SEQ TREND 20 BUREAUCRCY. PAGE 143 F2826
CULTURE STRUCT CREATE TEC/DEV

L54
OPLER M.E.,"SOCIAL ASPECTS OF TECHNICAL ASSISTANCE IN OPERATION." WOR+45 VOL/ASSN CREATE PLAN TEC/DEV EDU/PROP ALL/VALS...METH/CNCPT OBS RECORD TREND UN 20. PAGE 101 F1993
INT/ORG CONSULT FOR/AID

B55
BUCHANAN N.S.,APPROACHES TO ECONOMIC DEVELOPMENT. FUT USA+45 WOR+45 STRATA ECO/DEV INT/ORG NAT/G TEC/DEV DIPLOM FOR/AID ATTIT KNOWL PWR WEALTH ...RELATIV METH/CNCPT SELF/OBS TREND CON/ANAL STERTYP GEN/LAWS FOR/TRADE COMMUN 20. PAGE 20 F0380
ECO/UNDEV ECO/TAC INT/TRADE

B56
FELLNER W.,TRENDS AND CYCLES IN ECONOMIC ACTIVITY: AN INTRODUCTION TO PROBLEMS OF ECONOMIC GROWTH. USA+45 INDUS ACT/RES CAP/ISM EQUILIB...MODAL METH/COMP BIBLIOG 20. PAGE 40 F0779
ECO/TAC TREND FINAN ECO/DEV

S56
BROWN J.S.,"UNION SIZE AS A FUNCTION OF INTRA-UNION CONFLICT." CLIENT CONTROL CHOOSE EFFICIENCY ATTIT TREND. PAGE 19 F0370
LABOR INGP/REL CONSEN DRIVE

S56
SPENGLER J.J.,"POPULATION THREATENS PROSPERITY" (BMR)" WOR+45 SOCIETY FINAN RATION COST INCOME ...SOC CHARTS 20 RESOURCE/N. PAGE 124 F2451
CENSUS GEOG WEALTH TREND

B57
ARON R.,L'UNIFICATION ECONOMIQUE DE L'EUROPE. EUR+WWI SWITZERLND UK INT/ORG NAT/G REGION NAT/LISM ORD/FREE PWR...CONCPT METH/CNCPT OBS TREND STERTYP GEN/LAWS EEC FOR/TRADE 20. PAGE 6 F0118
VOL/ASSN ECO/TAC

B57
DRUCKER P.F.,AMERICA'S NEXT TWENTY YEARS. USA+45 DIST/IND ACADEM SCHOOL DIPLOM ECO/TAC AUTOMAT HABITAT HEALTH...SOC/WK TREND MUNICH 20 URBAN/RNWL PUB/TRANS. PAGE 34 F0667
WORKER FOR/AID CENSUS GEOG

B57
FOUSEK P.G.,FOREIGN CENTRAL BANKING: THE INSTRUMENTS OF MONETARY POLICY. WOR+45 CONTROL ...TREND CHARTS 20 MONEY. PAGE 43 F0836
FINAN ECO/TAC ECO/DEV MARKET

B57
HARWOOD E.C.,CAUSE AND CONTROL OF THE BUSINESS CYCLE (5TH ED.). AFR USA-45 PRICE CONTROL WAR DEMAND INCOME WEALTH...TREND CHARTS 19. PAGE 56 F1107
PRODUC MARKET FINAN

B57
LAVES W.H.C.,UNESCO. FUT WOR+45 NAT/G CONSULT DELIB/GP TEC/DEV ECO/TAC EDU/PROP PEACE ORD/FREE ...CONCPT TIME/SEQ TREND UNESCO VAL/FREE 20. PAGE 76 F1491
INT/ORG KNOWL

B57
TRIFFIN R.,EUROPE AND THE MONEY MUDDLE. USA+45 INT/ORG NAT/G CONSULT PLAN ECO/TAC EXEC ROUTINE BAL/PAY WEALTH...METH/CNCPT OBS TREND CHARTS STERTYP GEN/METH EEC TERR/GP VAL/FREE ECSC. PAGE 131 F2587
EUR+WWI ECO/DEV REGION

B57
WARRINER D.,LAND REFORM AND DEVELOPMENT IN THE MIDDLE EAST: A STUDY OF EGYPT, SYRIA AND IRAQ. IRAQ ISLAM SYRIA UAR AGRI DIST/IND PLAN TEC/DEV DOMIN REV ATTIT WEALTH...SOC METH/CNCPT STAT OBS RECORD HIST/WRIT TREND GEN/LAWS FAO 20. PAGE 143 F2825
ECO/UNDEV CONCPT

S57
VERNON R.,"PRODUCTION AND DISTRIBUTION IN THE LARGE METROPOLIS" (BMR)" USA+45 PROC/MFG ECO/TAC HABITAT ...CENSUS TREND MUNICH 20. PAGE 141 F2779
PRODUC DIST/IND PROB/SOLV

B58
DEFENSE AGAINST INFLATION. USA+45 LEGIS WORKER TAX PRICE DEMAND INCOME PRODUC...POLICY TREND METH/COMP 20 GOLD/STAND. PAGE 1 F0012
ECO/TAC EQUILIB WEALTH PROB/SOLV

B58
BANCROFT G.,THE AMERICAN LABOR FORCE: ITS GROWTH AND CHANGING COMPOSITION. FUT USA+45 USA-45 ECO/DEV INDUS WORKER...GEOG CHARTS 19/20. PAGE 9 F0170
LABOR STAT TREND CENSUS

B58
BROWN B.,INCOME TRENDS IN THE UNITED STATES THROUGH 1975. USA+45 NAT/G WEALTH...GEOG CENSUS PREDICT CHARTS METH 20. PAGE 19 F0366
STAT INCOME TREND TAX

B58
GALBRAITH J.K.,THE AFFLUENT SOCIETY. EUR+WWI FUT USA+45 USSR CULTURE SERV/IND PEACE WEALTH SOCISM ...NEW/IDEA TREND VAL/FREE 20. PAGE 45 F0882
ATTIT ECO/TAC CAP/ISM

B58
KINDLEBERGER C.P.,INTERNATIONAL ECONOMICS. WOR+45 WOR-45 ECO/DEV ECO/UNDEV FINAN VOL/ASSN ACT/RES DIPLOM ECO/TAC LEGIT REGION ATTIT DRIVE ORD/FREE WEALTH...POLICY STAT TREND GEN/LAWS EEC ECSC OEEC 20. PAGE 71 F1391
INT/ORG BAL/PWR TARIFFS

B58
MYRDAL G.,RICH LANDS AND POOR: THE ROAD TO WORLD PROSPERITY. FUT WOR+45 WOR-45 ECO/DEV ECO/UNDEV INT/ORG PLAN ECO/TAC REGION...GEOG TIME/SEQ GEN/LAWS TOT/POP 20. PAGE 96 F1880
WEALTH TREND FOR/AID INT/TRADE

B58
PALMER E.E.,INDUSTRIAL MAN. USA+45 PERSON ORD/FREE POPULISM...PREDICT TREND ANTHOL 20. PAGE 103 F2020
INDUS ECO/UNDEV CULTURE WEALTH

B58
POLLOCK F.,AUTOMATION: A STUDY OF ITS ECONOMIC AND SOCIAL CONSEQUENCES. FUT USA+45 USA-45 SOCIETY ECO/DEV LABOR ACT/RES PLAN ECO/TAC AUTOMAT ROUTINE ALL/VALS...STAT TREND COMPUT/IR CHARTS SOC/EXP WORK 20. PAGE 107 F2099
TEC/DEV SOC CAP/ISM

B58
ROBERTS B.C.,NATIONAL WAGES POLICY IN WAR AND PEACE. EUR+WWI GERMANY S/ASIA SWEDEN UK USA+45 USA-45 STRATA ECO/DEV LABOR NAT/G DELIB/GP PLAN INT/TRADE WEALTH...STAT TREND CHARTS 20. PAGE 112 F2205
CREATE ECO/TAC

B58
US CONGRESS JOINT ECO COMM,THE RELATIONSHIP OF PRICES TO ECONOMIC STABILITY AND GROWTH. USA+45 MARKET TAX ADJUST COST DEMAND INCOME PRODUC ...POLICY TREND CHARTS ANTHOL 20 CONGRESS. PAGE 134 F2650
ECO/DEV PLAN EQUILIB PRICE

S58
LATTIN N.D.,"MINORITY AND DISSENTING SHAREHOLDERS' RIGHTS IN FUNDAMENTAL CHANGES." FINAN LEGIS ADJUD PARTIC ROUTINE CHOOSE REPRESENT INGP/REL TREND. PAGE 76 F1487
MAJORIT LG/CO LAW CREATE

S58
O'NEAL F.H.,"RECENT LEGISLATION AFFECTING CLOSE CORPORATIONS." LAW EX/STRUC ECO/TAC ROUTINE CHOOSE RIGID/FLEX...MAJORIT MGT TREND. PAGE 100 F1959
LG/CO LEGIS REPRESENT PARTIC

S58
THOMAS D.S.,"AGE AND ECONOMIC DIFFERENTIALS IN INTERSTATE MIGRATION." SEX...GEOG SAMP/SIZ TREND CON/ANAL CHARTS BIBLIOG. PAGE 130 F2560
AGE WEALTH HABITAT CENSUS

B59
AITKEN H.G.,THE AMERICAN ECONOMIC IMPACT ON CANADA. CANADA USA+45 AGRI FINAN INDUS LABOR INT/TRADE BAL/PAY...INT/LAW TREND 20. PAGE 3 F0055
DIPLOM ECO/TAC POLICY NAT/G

B59
FELS R.,AMERICAN BUSINESS CYCLES 1865-1897. USA+45 ECO/DEV LG/CO SML/CO PROB/SOLV TEC/DEV CAP/ISM INT/TRADE DEMAND...POLICY CHARTS METH 19 DEPRESSION. PAGE 40 F0782
FINAN INDUS TREND ECO/TAC

B59
HARTOG F.,EUROPEAN TRADE CYCLE POLICY. WORKER TAX PRICE WAR CENTRAL DEMAND...TREND CHARTS 20 UN. PAGE 56 F1103
EQUILIB EUR+WWI INT/TRADE

B59
HOOVER C.B.,THE ECONOMY, LIBERTY AND THE STATE. COM EUR+WWI USA+45 USA-45 USSR CAP/ISM EDU/PROP COERCE TOTALISM ORD/FREE...POLICY OBS INT TREND NAZI 20. PAGE 61 F1206
ECO/DEV ECO/TAC

B59
LEWIS J.P.,BUSINESS CONDITIONS ANALYSIS. USA+45 MARKET LABOR BUDGET TAX AUTOMAT WAR DEMAND PRODUC ...ECOMETRIC CHARTS BIBLIOG 19/20. PAGE 79 F1549
FINAN PRICE TREND

B59
MADHOK B.,POLITICAL TRENDS IN INDIA. INDIA PAKISTAN UK STRATA ECO/UNDEV POL/PAR LEGIS CAP/ISM DIPLOM
GEOG NAT/G

COLONIAL CHOOSE MARXISM...SOC TREND 20 GANDHI/M NEHRU/J. PAGE 84 F1639

MEYER A.J.,MIDDLE EASTERN CAPITALISM: NINE ESSAYS. ISLAM CULTURE ECO/UNDEV INDUS MARKET NAT/G PLAN ATTIT RIGID/FLEX...STAT OBS TREND GEN/LAWS. PAGE 90 F1767 — B59 TEC/DEV ECO/TAC ANTHOL

MURPHY J.C.,"SOME IMPLICATIONS OF EUROPE'S COMMON MARKET. IN (COOK P, ECONOMIC DEVELOPMENT AND INTERNATIONAL TRADE.," EUR+WWI ECO/DEV DIST/IND INDUS NAT/G PLAN ECO/TAC INT/TRADE WEALTH...STAT TREND OEEC TOT/POP 20 EEC. PAGE 95 F1866 — L59 MARKET INT/ORG REGION

ALLEN G.,"NATIONAL FARMERS UNION AS A PRESSURE GROUP: II." UK ECO/DEV MARKET POL/PAR DELIB/GP PROB/SOLV ECO/TAC LOBBY INCOME...POLICY METH/COMP 19/20 NAT/FARMER. PAGE 4 F0069 — S59 DIST/IND AGRI PROF/ORG TREND

KINDLEBERGER C.P.,"UNITED STATES ECONOMIC FOREIGN POLICY: RESEARCH REQUIREMENTS FOR 1965." FUT USA+45 WOR+45 DIST/IND MARKET INT/ORG ECO/TAC INT/TRADE WEALTH...OBS TREND CON/ANAL GEN/LAWS FOR/TRADE VAL/FREE 20. PAGE 71 F1392 — S59 FINAN ECO/DEV FOR/AID

PLAZA G.,"FOR A REGIONAL MARKET IN LATIN AMERICA." FUT L/A+17C CULTURE INDUS NAT/G ECO/TAC INT/TRADE ATTIT WEALTH...NEW/IDEA TREND OAS 20. PAGE 106 F2092 — S59 MARKET INT/ORG REGION

REUBENS E.D.,"THE BASIS FOR REORIENATION OF AMERICAN FOREIGN AID POLICY." USA+45 USSR STRUCT INT/ORG CONSULT ECO/TAC ADMIN DRIVE MORAL ORD/FREE PWR WEALTH...RELATIV MATH STAT TREND GEN/LAWS VAL/FREE 20. PAGE 111 F2180 — S59 ECO/UNDEV PLAN FOR/AID DIPLOM

SHEPPARD H.L.,"THE POLITICAL ATTITUDES AND PREFERENCES OF UNION MEMBERS: THE CASE OF THE DETROIT AUTO WORKERS." LOBBY CHOOSE ROLE...CLASSIF QU SAMP TREND. PAGE 120 F2376 — S59 LABOR ATTIT WORKER

SOLDATI A.,"EOCNOMIC DISINTEGRATION IN EUROPE." EUR+WWI FUT WOR+45 INDUS INT/ORG NAT/G CAP/ISM WEALTH...NEW/IDEA OBS TREND CHARTS EEC 20. PAGE 124 F2438 — S59 FINAN ECO/TAC

ALLEN R.L.,SOVIET ECONOMIC WARFARE. USSR FINAN INDUS NAT/G PLAN TEC/DEV FOR/AID DETER WEALTH ...TREND GEN/LAWS FOR/TRADE 20. PAGE 4 F0072 — B60 COM ECO/TAC

APTHEKER H.,DISARMAMENT AND THE AMERICAN ECONOMY: A SYMPOSIUM. FUT USA+45 ECO/DEV DIST/IND FINAN INDUS PROC/MFG LABOR NAT/G POL/PAR CONSULT PLAN CAP/ISM INT/TRADE PEACE ATTIT MORAL WEALTH...TREND GEN/LAWS TOT/POP 20. PAGE 6 F0110 — B60 MARXIST ARMS/CONT

BILLERBECK K.,SOVIET BLOC FOREIGN AID TO UNDERDEVELOPED COUNTRIES. COM FUT USSR FINAN FORCES TEC/DEV DIPLOM INT/TRADE EDU/PROP NUC/PWR...TREND 20. PAGE 15 F0285 — B60 FOR/AID ECO/UNDEV ECO/TAC MARXISM

BLACK E.R.,THE DIPLOMACY OF ECONOMIC DEVELOPMENT. WOR+45 CONSULT PLAN TEC/DEV DIPLOM ECO/TAC FOR/AID ...CONCPT TREND 20. PAGE 15 F0290 — B60 ECO/UNDEV ACT/RES

FRANCIS R.G.,THE PREDICTIVE PROCESS. PLAN MARXISM ...DECISION SOC CONCPT NAT/COMP 19/20. PAGE 43 F0840 — B60 PREDICT PHIL/SCI TREND

FRANCK P.G.,AFGHANISTAN: BETWEEN EAST AND WEST. AFGHANISTN AFR USA+45 USSR ECO/UNDEV PLAN ADMIN ROUTINE ATTIT PWR...STAT OBS CHARTS TOT/POP FOR/TRADE 20. PAGE 43 F0843 — B60 ECO/TAC TREND FOR/AID

HARBERGER A.C.,THE DEMAND FOR DURABLE GOODS. AGRI FINAN COST EQUILIB...MATH STAT TIME/SEQ TREND CON/ANAL CHARTS SIMUL ANTHOL 20. PAGE 55 F1072 — B60 ECOMETRIC DEMAND PRICE

KERR C.,INDUSTRIALISM AND INDUSTRIAL MAN. CULTURE SOCIETY ECO/UNDEV NAT/G ADMIN PRODUC WEALTH ...PREDICT TREND NAT/COMP 19/20. PAGE 70 F1381 — B60 WORKER MGT ECO/DEV INDUS

KRISTENSEN T.,THE ECONOMIC WORLD BALANCE. FUT WOR+45 CULTURE ECO/DEV BAL/PWR INT/TRADE REGION PWR WEALTH...STAT TREND CHARTS 20. PAGE 73 F1442 — B60 ECO/UNDEV ECO/TAC FOR/AID

MYRDAL G.,BEYOND THE WELFARE STATE: ECONOMIC PLANNING AND ITS IMPLICATIONS. EUR+WWI FUT USA+45 USSR ECO/DEV ECO/UNDEV TEC/DEV SKILL WEALTH...PSY TREND FOR/TRADE 20. PAGE 96 F1881 — B60 PLAN ECO/TAC CAP/ISM

ROBSON W.A.,NATIONALIZED INDUSTRY AND PUBLIC OWNERSHIP. UK ECO/DEV FINAN LABOR LG/CO POL/PAR LEGIS ACT/RES GP/REL...TREND IDEA/COMP 20. PAGE 113 F2227 — B60 NAT/G OWN INDUS ATTIT

ROEPKE W.,A HUMANE ECONOMY: THE SOCIAL FRAMEWORK OF THE FREE MARKET. FUT USSR WOR+45 CULTURE SOCIETY ECO/DEV PLAN ECO/TAC ADMIN ATTIT PERSON RIGID/FLEX SUPEGO MORAL WEALTH SOCISM...POLICY OLD/LIB CONCPT TREND GEN/LAWS 20. PAGE 113 F2232 — B60 DRIVE EDU/PROP CAP/ISM

SILK L.S.,THE RESEARCH REVOLUTION. USA+45 FINAN CAP/ISM ECO/TAC PRICE EQUILIB PRODUC...STAT TREND CHARTS. PAGE 122 F2402 — B60 ECO/DEV R+D TEC/DEV PROB/SOLV

STEIN E.,AMERICAN ENTERPRISE IN THE EUROPEAN COMMON MARKET: A LEGAL PROFILE. EUR+WWI FUT USA+45 SOCIETY STRUCT ECO/DEV NAT/G VOL/ASSN CONSULT PLAN TEC/DEV ECO/TAC INT/TRADE ADMIN ATTIT RIGID/FLEX PWR...MGT NEW/IDEA STAT TREND COMPUT/IR SIMUL EEC 20. PAGE 125 F2475 — B60 MARKET ADJUD INT/LAW

THEOBALD R.,THE RICH AND THE POOR: A STUDY OF THE ECONOMICS OF RISING EXPECTATIONS. WOR+45 CONSTN ECO/DEV ECO/UNDEV INT/ORG NAT/G PLAN FOR/AID ROUTINE BAL/PAY ORD/FREE PWR WEALTH...GEOG TREND WORK FOR/TRADE 20. PAGE 129 F2553 — B60 ECO/TAC INT/TRADE

SPENGLER J.J.,"ECONOMIC DEVELOPMENT: POLITICAL PRECONDITIONS AND POLITICAL CONSEQUENCE." WOR+45 STRUCT ECO/UNDEV NAT/G PLAN ECO/TAC EDU/PROP ATTIT ORD/FREE WEALTH SOCISM...SOC CONCPT TREND SIMUL GEN/METH WORK 20. PAGE 124 F2452 — L60 TEC/DEV METH/CNCPT CAP/ISM

BAUM M.,"THE CASE FOR BUSINESS CIVILIZATION." R+D CAP/ISM GIVE EDU/PROP HAPPINESS...SOC TREND. PAGE 12 F0218 — S60 MGT CULTURE WEALTH

GARNICK D.H.,"ON THE ECONOMIC FEASIBILITY OF A MIDDLE EASTERN COMMON MARKET." AFR ISLAM CULTURE INDUS NAT/G PLAN TEC/DEV ECO/TAC ADMIN ATTIT DRIVE RIGID/FLEX...PLURIST STAT TREND GEN/LAWS 20. PAGE 46 F0907 — S60 MARKET INT/TRADE

NICHOLS J.P.,"HAZARDS OF AMERICAN PRIVATE INVESTMENT IN UNDERDEVELOPED COUNTRIES." FUT L/A+17C USA+45 USA-45 EXTR/IND CONSULT BAL/PWR ECO/TAC DOMIN ADJUD ATTIT SOVEREIGN WEALTH ...HIST/WRIT TIME/SEQ TREND TERR/GP VAL/FREE 20. PAGE 98 F1924 — S60 FINAN ECO/UNDEV CAP/ISM NAT/LISM

OWEN C.F.,"US AND SOVIET RELATIONS WITH UNDERDEVELOPED COUNTRIES: LATIN AMERICA-A CASE STUDY." AFR COM L/A+17C USA+45 USSR EXTR/IND MARKET TEC/DEV DIPLOM ECO/TAC NAT/LISM ORD/FREE PWR ...TREND WORK 20. PAGE 102 F2005 — S60 ECO/UNDEV DRIVE INT/TRADE

POLLARD J.A.,"EMERGING PATTERNS OF CORPORATE GIVING." FINAN DELIB/GP PLAN EDU/PROP CENTRAL TREND. PAGE 107 F2098 — S60 GIVE LG/CO ADMIN MGT

PYE L.W.,"SOVIET AND AMERICAN STYLES IN FOREIGN AID." COM USA+45 USSR WOR+45 NAT/G PLAN ECO/TAC ROUTINE RIGID/FLEX...POLICY CONCPT TREND GEN/LAWS TOT/POP 20. PAGE 108 F2132 — S60 ECO/UNDEV ATTIT FOR/AID

ERDMAN P.E.,COMMON MARKETS AND FREE TRADE AREAS (PAMPHLET). USA+45 MARKET INT/ORG TEC/DEV DIPLOM UTIL...CON/ANAL CHARTS BIBLIOG 20 EEC OEEC. PAGE 38 F0743 — N60 TREND PROB/SOLV INT/TRADE ECO/DEV

ACKLEY G.,MACROECONOMIC THEORY. AFR FINAN WORKER ECO/TAC PRICE COST INCOME PRODUC...MATH TREND CHARTS IDEA/COMP T KEYNES/JM. PAGE 2 F0034 — B61 SIMUL ECOMETRIC WEALTH

ASCHHEIM J.,TECHNIQUES OF MONETARY CONTROL. UK USA+45 CONTROL WAR DEMAND INCOME WEALTH...TREND CHARTS 20 MONEY. PAGE 7 F0127 — B61 FINAN MARKET BUDGET CENTRAL

BENOIT E.,EUROPE AT SIXES AND SEVENS: THE COMMON MARKET, THE FREE TRADE ASSOCIATION AND THE UNITED STATES. EUR+WWI FUT USA+45 INDUS CONSULT DELIB/GP EX/STRUC TOP/EX ACT/RES ECO/TAC EDU/PROP ROUTINE CHOOSE PERCEPT WEALTH...MGT TREND EEC FOR/TRADE TOT/POP 20 EFTA. PAGE 13 F0249 — B61 FINAN ECO/DEV VOL/ASSN

BONNEFOUS M.,EUROPE ET TIERS MONDE. EUR+WWI SOCIETY INT/ORG NAT/G VOL/ASSN ACT/RES TEC/DEV CAP/ISM ECO/TAC ATTIT ORD/FREE SOVEREIGN...POLICY CONCPT TREND TERR/GP COMMUN 20. PAGE 16 F0314 — B61 AFR ECO/UNDEV FOR/AID INT/TRADE

EINZIG P.,A DYNAMIC THEORY OF FORWARD EXCHANGE. FUT WOR+45 WOR-45 INT/TRADE BAL/PAY WEALTH...OLD/LIB NEW/IDEA OBS TREND FOR/TRADE 20. PAGE 37 F0713 — B61 FINAN ECO/TAC

FEARN H.,AN AFRICAN ECONOMY. AFR EUR+WWI PLAN COLONIAL WEALTH...CONT/OBS TREND EEC VAL/FREE 20. — B61 ECO/UNDEV

PAGE 39 F0770

B61
FILLOL T.R.,SOCIAL FACTORS IN ECONOMIC DEVELOPMENT: THE ARGENTINE CASE. STRUCT INDUS LABOR CREATE TEC/DEV EFFICIENCY PRODUC DRIVE...METH/CNCPT METH/COMP BIBLIOG/A 20 ARGEN. PAGE 41 F0795 — ECO/UNDEV MGT PERS/REL TREND

B61
GOODWIN C.D.W.,CANADIAN ECONOMIC THOUGHT. CANADA STRATA TEC/DEV CAP/ISM TARIFFS TAX COST EFFICIENCY WEALTH...METH/CNCPT TREND 20 MARITIME ONTARIO. PAGE 49 F0952 — INT/TRADE ECO/DEV FINAN DEMAND

B61
HEMPSTONE S.,THE NEW AFRICA. AGRI INDUS KIN NAT/G COLONIAL MARXISM...SOC INT TREND NAT/COMP BIBLIOG/A 20. PAGE 58 F1146 — AFR ORD/FREE PERSON CULTURE

B61
KITZINGER V.W.,THE CHALLENGE OF THE COMMON MARKET. EUR+WWI ECO/DEV DIST/IND PLAN ECO/TAC INT/TRADE LEGIT ATTIT PWR WEALTH...TIME/SEQ TREND CHARTS EEC 20. PAGE 71 F1403 — MARKET INT/ORG UK

B61
KLEIN L.R.,AN ECONOMETRIC MODEL OF THE UNITED KINGDOM. UK PRICE COST...MATH PREDICT TREND CHARTS SIMUL METH 20. PAGE 72 F1407 — ECOMETRIC COMPUTER STAT COMPUT/IR

B61
NORTH D.C.,THE ECONOMIC GROWTH OF THE UNITED STATES 1790-1860. USA-45 INDUS TEC/DEV CAP/ISM ECO/TAC PRICE COST DEMAND LAISSEZ...ECOMETRIC STAT TREND 19. PAGE 98 F1933 — AGRI ECO/UNDEV

B61
NOVE A.,THE SOVIET ECONOMY. USSR ECO/DEV FINAN NAT/G ECO/TAC PRICE ADMIN EFFICIENCY MARXISM ...TREND BIBLIOG 20. PAGE 99 F1943 — PLAN PRODUC POLICY

B61
PETCH G.A.,ECONOMIC DEVELOPMENT AND MODERN WEST AFRICA. AFR CONGO/BRAZ GHANA NIGER SIER/LEONE AGRI MARKET LABOR FOR/AID TAX COST EFFICIENCY EQUILIB PRODUC...GEOG TREND 20. PAGE 105 F2068 — ECO/UNDEV TEC/DEV EXTR/IND ECO/TAC

B61
THEOBALD R.,THE CHALLENGE OF ABUNDANCE. USA+45 WOR+45 MARKET DIPLOM FOR/AID REV PRODUC UTOPIA SUPEGO...POLICY TREND BIBLIOG/A 20. PAGE 129 F2554 — WELF/ST ECO/UNDEV PROB/SOLV ECO/TAC

S61
DICKS-MIREAUX L.A.,"THE INTERRELATIONSHIP BETWEEN COST AND PRICE CHANGES 19461959: A STUDY OF INFLATION IN POST-WAR BRITAIN" AFR UK ECO/DEV INDUS WORKER ECO/TAC ORD/FREE WEALTH...ECOMETRIC REGRESS STAT TREND CHARTS 20. PAGE 33 F0634 — PRICE PAY DEMAND

S61
LANFALUSSY A.,"EUROPE'S PROGRESS: DUE TO COMMON MARKET." EUR+WWI ECO/DEV DELIB/GP PLAN ECO/TAC ROUTINE WEALTH...GEOG TREND EEC TERR/GP 20. PAGE 75 F1473 — INT/ORG MARKET

S61
VALLET R.,"IRAN: KEY TO THE MIDDLE EAST." COM IRAQ ISLAM KUWAIT LEBANON SAUDI/ARAB TURKEY ELITES SOCIETY INDUS PROC/MFG POL/PAR TOP/EX PLAN BAL/PWR DIPLOM ECO/TAC ALL/VALS...TREND FOR/TRADE CENTO 20. PAGE 140 F2760 — NAT/G ECO/UNDEV IRAN

C61
FILLOL T.R.,"SOCIAL FACTORS IN ECONOMIC DEVELOPMENT: THE ARGENTINE CASE" INDUS LABOR CREATE TEC/DEV PERS/REL EFFICIENCY PRODUC DRIVE ...METH/CNCPT METH/COMP 20 ARGEN. PAGE 41 F0794 — BIBLIOG ECO/UNDEV MGT TREND

B62
ARNOLD H.J.P.,AID FOR DEVELOPING COUNTRIES. COM EUR+WWI USA+45 USSR WOR+45 EDU/PROP ATTIT DRIVE PWR WEALTH...TREND CHARTS STERTYP NAT/ 20. PAGE 6 F0115 — ECO/UNDEV ECO/TAC FOR/AID

B62
BACKMAN J.,THE ECONOMICS OF THE ELECTRICAL MACHINERY INDUSTRY. USA+45 PROC/MFG LABOR WORKER INT/TRADE TV PRICE COST...CHARTS 19/20. PAGE 8 F0147 — PRODUC TEC/DEV TREND

B62
BARTELS R.,THE DEVELOPMENT OF MARKETING THOUGHT. USA+45 USA-45 FINAN ECO/TAC...CONCPT TREND. PAGE 11 F0199 — ECO/DEV MARKET MGT EDU/PROP

B62
DENISON E.F.,THE SOURCES OF ECONOMIC GROWTH IN THE UNITED STATES AND THE ALTERNATIVES BEFORE US. AGRI INDUS SCHOOL TEC/DEV CAP/ISM ECO/TAC PRICE COST WEALTH...STAT TREND CHARTS 20. PAGE 32 F0620 — ECO/DEV WORKER PRODUC

B62
DUPRE J.S.,SCIENCE AND THE NATION: POLICY AND POLITICS. USA+45 LAW ACADEM FORCES ADMIN CIVMIL/REL GOV/REL EFFICIENCY PEACE...TREND 20 SCI/ADVSRY. PAGE 35 F0682 — R+D INDUS TEC/DEV NUC/PWR

B62
GERSCHENKRON A.,ECONOMIC BACKWARDNESS IN HISTORICAL PERSPECTIVE. WOR+45 WOR-45 ECO/DEV ECO/UNDEV INDUS NAT/G LEGIT DRIVE...WELF/ST DECISION QUANT TREND CHARTS 20. PAGE 47 F0919 — TEC/DEV USSR

B62
GORT M.,DIVERSIFICATION AND INTEGRATION IN AMERICAN INDUSTRY. CLIENT DIST/IND PROC/MFG SERV/IND LG/CO CONTROL DEMAND PWR...METH/CNCPT STAT TREND CON/ANAL GP/COMP. PAGE 49 F0964 — CONCPT GP/REL CLASSIF

B62
GREEN L.P.,DEVELOPMENT IN AFRICA. AFR CENTRL/AFR GHANA RHODESIA SOUTH/AFR AGRI PROC/MFG INT/TRADE DEMAND NAT/LISM PRODUC WEALTH...GEOG METH/CNCPT CHARTS BIBLIOG 20. PAGE 50 F0987 — CULTURE ECO/UNDEV GOV/REL TREND

B62
HOOVER E.M.,ANATOMY OF A METROPOLIS. FUT USA+45 SOCIETY ECO/DEV DIST/IND INDUS WORKER ECO/TAC TAX GP/REL COST WEALTH MUNICH 20 NEWYORK/C. PAGE 62 F1212 — ROUTINE TREND INCOME

B62
HUMPHREY D.D.,THE UNITED STATES AND THE COMMON MARKET. USA+45 INDUS MARKET INT/ORG PLAN EDU/PROP BAL/PAY DRIVE PWR WEALTH...TREND STERTYP FOR/TRADE EEC 20. PAGE 63 F1241 — ATTIT ECO/TAC

B62
KAUTSKY J.H.,POLITICAL CHANGE IN UNDERDEVELOPED COUNTRIES: NATIONALISM AND COMMUNISM. WOR+45 AGRI TEC/DEV EDU/PROP ATTIT...POLICY METH/CNCPT STYLE INT QU CENSUS TREND SOC/EXP GEN/LAWS 20. PAGE 69 F1365 — ECO/UNDEV SOCIETY CAP/ISM REV

B62
LITWACK L.,THE AMERICAN LABOR MOVEMENT. USA-45 NAT/G CREATE TEC/DEV CAP/ISM ECO/TAC ADJUD AUTOMAT SKILL...TREND ANTHOL 19/20. PAGE 81 F1588 — INDUS LABOR GP/REL METH/COMP

B62
REES A.,THE ECONOMICS OF TRADE UNIONS. FUT ECO/DEV INDUS BARGAIN CAP/ISM PRICE SENIOR CONTROL GP/REL COST...TREND 20 AFL/CIO. PAGE 110 F2172 — LABOR WORKER ECO/TAC

B62
ROBINSON A.D.,DUTCH ORGANIZED AGRICULTURE IN INTERNATIONAL POLITICS, 1945-1960. EUR+WWI NETHERLAND STRUCT ECO/DEV NAT/G VOL/ASSN CONSULT DELIB/GP PLAN TEC/DEV INT/TRADE EDU/PROP ATTIT RIGID/FLEX ALL/VALS...NEW/IDEA TREND EEC COMMUN 20. PAGE 112 F2215 — AGRI INT/ORG

L62
DURAND-REVILLE L.,"LE REGIME DES INVESTISSEMENTS DANS LES ETATS AFRICAINS D'EXPRESSION FRANCAISE ET A MADAGASCAR." MADAGASCAR ECO/UNDEV CAP/ISM ECO/TAC WEALTH...SOC TREND CHARTS 20. PAGE 35 F0683 — AFR FINAN

L62
GALBRAITH J.K.,"ECONOMIC DEVELOPMENT IN PERSPECTIVE." CAP/ISM ECO/TAC ROUTINE ATTIT WEALTH ...TREND CHARTS SOC/EXP WORK TERR/GP 20. PAGE 45 F0884 — ECO/UNDEV PLAN

S62
BOONE A.,"THE FOREIGN TRADE OF CHINA." AFR ECO/DEV ECO/UNDEV INDUS MARKET NAT/G TEC/DEV WEALTH ...POLICY STAT TREND CHARTS FOR/TRADE. PAGE 17 F0318 — ASIA ECO/TAC

S62
IOVTCHOUK M.T.,"ON SOME THEORETICAL PRINCIPLES AND METHODS OF SOCIOLOGICAL INVESTIGATIONS (IN RUSSIAN)." FUT USA+45 STRATA R+D NAT/G POL/PAR TOP/EX ACT/RES PLAN ECO/TAC EDU/PROP ROUTINE ATTIT RIGID/FLEX MARXISM SOCISM...MARXIST METH/CNCPT OBS TREND NAT/COMP GEN/LAWS 20. PAGE 65 F1288 — COM ECO/DEV CAP/ISM USSR

S62
MEAD W.,"SOME POLITICAL-ECONOMIC ISSUES DETERMINING USA TARIFF POLICY." USA+45 USA-45 ECO/DEV NAT/G TARIFFS ATTIT...TIME/SEQ TREND CHARTS 19/20. PAGE 89 F1736 — ECO/TAC METH/CNCPT BAL/PAY

S62
MILLIKEN M.,"NEW AND OLD CRITERIA FOR AID." WOR+45 ECO/DEV ECO/UNDEV ACT/RES PLAN ATTIT KNOWL...TREND CON/ANAL SIMUL GEN/METH TERR/GP 20. PAGE 92 F1796 — USA+45 ECO/TAC FOR/AID

S62
MORGENTHAU H.J.,"A POLITICAL THEORY OF FOREIGN AID." ECO/UNDEV NAT/G DELIB/GP PLAN ECO/TAC EDU/PROP EXEC ORD/FREE RESPECT WEALTH...METH/CNCPT TREND 20. PAGE 93 F1833 — USA+45 PHIL/SCI FOR/AID

S62
PYE L.W.,"THE POLITICAL IMPULSES AND FANTASIES BEHIND FOREIGN AID." FUT USA+45 ECO/UNDEV DIPLOM ECO/TAC ROUTINE DRIVE KNOWL...SOC METH/CNCPT NEW/IDEA TREND HYPO/EXP STERTYP GEN/METH 20. PAGE 108 F2133 — ACT/RES ATTIT FOR/AID

S62
SCOTT J.B.,"ANGLO-SOVIET TRADE AND ITS EFFECTS ON THE COMMONWEALTH." COM FUT UK USSR WOR+45 ECO/DEV MARKET INT/ORG CONSULT WEALTH...POLICY TREND CMN/WLTH FOR/TRADE 20. PAGE 118 F2333 — NAT/G ECO/TAC

B63
BRITISH AID. UK AGRI DIST/IND INDUS SCHOOL TEC/DEV INT/TRADE COLONIAL DEMAND...TREND CHARTS 20. PAGE 1 F0018 — FOR/AID ECO/UNDEV NAT/G FINAN

B63
BERLE A.A. JR.,THE AMERICAN ECONOMIC REPUBLIC. — CAP/ISM

STRUCT FINAN MARKET LABOR NAT/G PLAN...POLICY WELF/ST DECISION. PAGE 14 F0262
ECO/TAC TREND CONCPT

B63
COPPOCK J.,NORTH ATLANTIC POLICY - THE AGRICULTURAL GAP. EUR+WWI ELITES ECO/DEV DIST/IND MARKET PLAN WEALTH...STAT TREND GEN/LAWS OEEC TOT/POP VAL/FREE FAO 20. PAGE 27 F0535
AGRI TEC/DEV INT/TRADE

B63
CORLEY R.N.,THE LEGAL ENVIRONMENT OF BUSINESS. CONSTN LEGIS TAX ADMIN CT/SYS DISCRIM ATTIT PWR ...TREND 18/20. PAGE 28 F0537
NAT/G INDUS JURID DECISION

B63
DE VRIES E.,SOCIAL ASPECTS OF ECONOMIC DEVELOPMENT IN LATIN AMERICA. CULTURE SOCIETY STRATA FINAN INDUS INT/ORG DELIB/GP ACT/RES ECO/TAC EDU/PROP ADMIN ATTIT SUPEGO HEALTH KNOWL ORD/FREE...SOC STAT TREND ANTHOL TOT/POP VAL/FREE. PAGE 31 F0608
L/A+17C ECO/UNDEV

B63
DEUTSCH K.W.,THE POLITICAL ROLE OF LABOR IN DEVELOPING COUNTRIES. AFR ASIA S/ASIA USA+45 WOR+45 ECO/UNDEV POL/PAR ECO/TAC EDU/PROP LEGIT COERCE ORD/FREE PWR WEALTH...OBS INT TREND VAL/FREE 20. PAGE 32 F0625
LABOR NAT/LISM

B63
FOX S.,ECONOMIC CONTROL AND FREE ENTERPRISE. PLAN BUDGET INT/TRADE TAX...TREND 20. PAGE 43 F0839
CONTROL FINAN ECO/TAC

B63
GLADE W.P. JR.,THE POLITICAL ECONOMY OF MEXICO. FUT L/A+17C CULTURE SOCIETY AGRI INDUS DELIB/GP ACT/RES ECO/TAC ATTIT HEALTH ORD/FREE...STAT TIME/SEQ TREND MEXIC/AMER TOT/POP VAL/FREE 20. PAGE 48 F0928
FINAN ECO/UNDEV

B63
INTERNATIONAL MONETARY FUND,COMPENSATORY FINANCING OF EXPORT FLUCTUATIONS (PAMPHLET). WOR+45 ECO/DEV ECO/UNDEV INT/ORG WEALTH...TREND 20 IMF MONEY. PAGE 65 F1281
BAL/PAY FINAN BUDGET INT/TRADE

B63
LAFEBER W.,THE NEW EMPIRE: AN INTERPRETATION OF AMERICAN EXPANSION, 1860-1898. USA-45 CONSTN NAT/LISM SOVEREIGN...TREND BIBLIOG 19/20. PAGE 74 F1457
INDUS NAT/G DIPLOM CAP/ISM

B63
LARY M.B.,PROBLEMS OF THE UNITED STATES AS WORLD TRADER AND BANKER. USA+45 NAT/G PLAN DIPLOM FOR/AID ...TREND CHARTS. PAGE 76 F1482
ECO/DEV FINAN BAL/PAY INT/TRADE

B63
LEE M.W.,MACROECONOMICS: FLUCTUATIONS, GROWTH AND STABILITY (3RD ED.). MARKET LABOR TEC/DEV INT/TRADE TAX PRICE WAR PRODUC...POLICY ECOMETRIC CHARTS 19/20. PAGE 77 F1505
EQUILIB TREND WEALTH

B63
MARCHAL J.,EXPANSION ET RECESSION. FRANCE OP/RES PROB/SOLV ROLE ORD/FREE...TREND SIMUL 20 DEPRESSION. PAGE 85 F1663
FINAN PLAN ECO/DEV

B63
NEUMARK S.D.,FOREIGN TRADE AND ECONOMIC DEVELOPMENT IN AFRICA: A HISTORICAL PERSPECTIVE. EUR+WWI MOD/EUR ECO/UNDEV AGRI COM/IND EXTR/IND PROC/MFG SKILL WEALTH...CONCPT TIME/SEQ TREND SIMUL FOR/TRADE WORK TOT/POP TERR/GP VAL/FREE 19/20. PAGE 98 F1916
AFR

B63
RAFUSE R.W. JR.,STATE AND LOCAL FISCAL BEHAVIOR OVER THE POSTWAR CYCLES (DISSERTATION). USA+45 TAX PRICE ATTIT...POLICY TIME/SEQ TREND CHARTS BIBLIOG 20. PAGE 109 F2135
BUDGET LOC/G ECO/TAC PROVS

B63
RAO V.K.R.,FOREIGN AID AND INDIA'S ECONOMIC DEVELOPMENT. INDIA INT/ORG PROB/SOLV TEC/DEV ECO/TAC CONTROL WEALTH...TREND 20. PAGE 109 F2148
FOR/AID ECO/UNDEV RECEIVE DIPLOM

B63
THEOBALD R.,FREE MEN AND FREE MARKETS. USA+45 USA-45 ECO/DEV NAT/G TEC/DEV DIPLOM INT/TRADE INCOME ORD/FREE WEALTH...TREND 19/20 KEYNES/JM. PAGE 130 F2556
CONCPT ECO/TAC CAP/ISM MARKET

B63
UN FAO,BIBLIOGRAPHY ON THE ANALYSIS AND PROJECTION OF DEMAND AND PRODUCTION, 1963. WOR+45 ECO/DEV ECO/UNDEV...PREDICT TREND 20. PAGE 132 F2601
BIBLIOG/A AGRI INDUS

L63
ADERBIGDE A.,"SYMPOSIUM ON WEST AFRICA INTEGRATION." AFR EUR+WWI FUT CULTURE SOCIETY STRATA DIST/IND INDUS MARKET SERV/IND DELIB/GP PLAN TEC/DEV DOMIN EDU/PROP LEGIT COERCE ATTIT ALL/VALS ...POLICY STAT TREND CHARTS VAL/FREE. PAGE 2 F0040
FINAN ECO/TAC REGION

L63
NASH M.,"PSYCHO-CULTURAL FACTORS IN ASIAN ECONOMIC GROWTH." ASIA ISLAM S/ASIA CULTURE ECO/UNDEV DELIB/GP EDU/PROP COERCE ATTIT PERSON HEALTH KNOWL ORD/FREE...PSY SOC STAT TREND ANTHOL VAL/FREE 20. PAGE 96 F1893
SOCIETY ECO/TAC

S63
AYAL E.B.,"VALUE SYSTEM AND ECONOMIC DEVELOPMENT IN JAPAN AND THAILAND." ASIA S/ASIA THAILAND CULTURE ECO/DEV CAP/ISM DOMIN NAT/LISM DRIVE RIGID/FLEX SOCISM...WELF/ST OBS TREND CON/ANAL GEN/LAWS TERR/GP 20 CHINJAP. PAGE 8 F0145
ECO/UNDEV ALL/VALS

S63
BILL J.A.,"THE SOCIAL AND ECONOMIC FOUNDATIONS OF POWER IN CONTEMPORARY IRAN." ISLAM CULTURE NAT/G ECO/TAC DOMIN COERCE ATTIT PWR WEALTH...TREND VAL/FREE 20. PAGE 15 F0284
SOCIETY STRATA IRAN

S63
CLARK P.G.,"TOWARDS MORE COMPREHENSIVE PLANNING IN EAST AFRICA" AFR OP/RES ECO/TAC RATION TAX EFFICIENCY INCOME...MATH TREND CHARTS 20 AFRICA/E. PAGE 25 F0484
ECO/UNDEV PLAN STAT METH/COMP

S63
DELWERT J.,"L'ECONOMIE CAMBODGIENNE ET SON EVOLUTION ACTUELLE." FUT S/ASIA ECO/UNDEV ACT/RES PLAN WEALTH...CONCPT OBS TIME/SEQ TREND 20. PAGE 32 F0617
FINAN ATTIT CAMBODIA

S63
DIEBOLD W. JR.,"THE NEW SITUATION OF INTERNATIONAL TRADE POLICY." EUR+WWI FRANCE FUT UK USA+45 WOR+45 DIST/IND PLAN INT/TRADE EDU/PROP PWR WEALTH ...RECORD TREND GEN/LAWS EEC TRUE/GP VAL/FREE APPLIC 20. PAGE 33 F0636
MARKET ECO/TAC

S63
DOSSER D.,"TOWARD A THEORY OF INTERNATIONAL PUBLIC FINANCE." WOR+45 ECO/DEV PLAN ECO/TAC WEALTH ...WELF/ST TREND GEN/LAWS TRUE/GP METH/GP 20. PAGE 34 F0654
FINAN INT/ORG FOR/AID

S63
EMERSON R.,"THE ATLANTIC COMMUNITY AND THE EMERGING COUNTRIES." FUT WOR+45 ECO/DEV ECO/UNDEV R+D NAT/G DELIB/GP BAL/PWR ECO/TAC EDU/PROP ROUTINE ORD/FREE PWR WEALTH...POLICY CONCPT TREND GEN/METH EEC 20 NATO. PAGE 37 F0729
ATTIT INT/TRADE

S63
FOURASTIE J.,"LES SCIENCES ECONOMIQUES ET SOCIALES EN EUROPE." EUR+WWI FUT MOD/EUR WOR+45 WOR-45 INTELL SOCIETY R+D PLAN ROUTINE ATTIT RIGID/FLEX KNOWL...OBS TREND. PAGE 43 F0833
ACT/RES CULTURE

S63
GERHARD H.,"COMMODITY TRADE STABILIZATION THROUGH INTERNATIONAL AGREEMENTS." WOR+45 ECO/DEV ECO/UNDEV NAT/G ROUTINE ORD/FREE...INT/LAW OBS TREND GEN/METH TOT/POP 20. PAGE 47 F0918
PLAN ECO/TAC INT/TRADE

S63
HALLSTEIN W.,"THE EUROPEAN COMMUNITY AND ATLANTIC PARTNERSHIP." EUR+WWI USA+45 MARKET NAT/G VOL/ASSN DELIB/GP ARMS/CONT NUC/PWR ATTIT PWR...CONCPT STAT TIME/SEQ TREND OEEC 20 EEC. PAGE 54 F1053
INT/ORG ECO/TAC UK

S63
HOOVER C.B.,"ECONOMIC REFORM VERSUS ECONOMIC GROWTH IN UNDERDEVELOPED COUNTRIES." FUT WOR+45 ELITES STRATA ECO/UNDEV DIST/IND INDUS TEC/DEV CAP/ISM FOR/AID INT/TRADE ATTIT WEALTH...MYTH TREND STERTYP GEN/LAWS WORK 20. PAGE 61 F1209
ECO/DEV ECO/TAC

S63
MATHUR P.N.,"GAINS IN ECONOMIC GROWTH FROM INTERNATIONAL TRADE." USA-45 ECO/DEV FINAN INDUS ATTIT WEALTH...MATH QUANT STAT BIOG TREND GEN/LAWS WORK 20. PAGE 87 F1704
MARKET ECO/TAC CAP/ISM INT/TRADE

S63
NADLER E.B.,"SOME ECONOMIC DISADVANTAGES OF THE ARMS RACE." AFR USA+45 INDUS R+D FORCES PLAN TEC/DEV ECO/TAC FOR/AID EDU/PROP PWR WEALTH...TREND FOR/TRADE 20. PAGE 96 F1886
ECO/DEV MGT BAL/PAY

S63
POLYANOV N.,"THE DOLLAR'S VENTURES IN EUROPE." EUR+WWI FRANCE USA+45 ECO/DEV MARKET POL/PAR TEC/DEV ECO/TAC EDU/PROP DRIVE PWR WEALTH...MARXIST MYTH STAT TREND EEC 20. PAGE 107 F2100
FINAN PLAN BAL/PAY CAP/ISM

S63
PRYBYLA J.,"THE QUEST FOR ECONOMIC RATIONALITY IN THE SOVIET BLOC." COM FUT WOR+45 WOR-45 DIST/IND MARKET PLAN ECO/TAC ATTIT...METH/CNCPT TOT/POP 20. PAGE 108 F2128
ECO/DEV TREND USSR

S63
SCHURMANN F.,"ECONOMIC POLICY AND POLITICAL POWER IN COMMUNIST CHINA." ASIA CHINA/COM USSR SOCIETY ECO/UNDEV AGRI INDUS CREATE ADMIN ROUTINE ATTIT DRIVE RIGID/FLEX PWR WEALTH...HIST/WRIT TREND CHARTS WORK 20. PAGE 118 F2323
PLAN ECO/TAC

S63
SHONFIELD A.,"AFTER BRUSSELS." EUR+WWI FRANCE GERMANY UK ECO/DEV DIST/IND MARKET VOL/ASSN DELIB/GP CREATE INT/TRADE ATTIT RIGID/FLEX...RECORD TREND GEN/LAWS EEC COMMUN CMN/WLTH 20. PAGE 121 F2385
PLAN ECO/TAC

S63
SHWADRAN B.,"MIDDLE EAST OIL, 1962." ISLAM DIST/IND INDUS PLAN ATTIT DRIVE WEALTH...POLICY STAT CONT/OBS TREND CHARTS GEN/LAWS TERR/GP METH/GP 20 OIL. PAGE 121 F2393
PROC/MFG ECO/TAC ELITES REGION

S63
SHWADRAN B.,"MIDDLE EAST OIL, 1962." ISLAM USSR ECO/DEV DIST/IND INDUS PLAN BAL/PWR DISPL DRIVE ...POLICY STAT TREND GEN/LAWS TERR/GP METH/GP EEC OEEC 20 OIL. PAGE 121 F2394
MARKET ECO/TAC INT/TRADE

S63
TENNYSON L.B.,"THE USA IN ATLANTIC COMMUNITY." EUR+WWI FRANCE UK USA+45 ECO/UNDEV VOL/ASSN DELIB/GP TOP/EX DIPLOM DOMIN PWR...POLICY CONCPT TREND GEN/LAWS EEC 20. PAGE 129 F2545
ATTIT ECO/TAC BAL/PWR

S63
WILES P.J.D.,"WILL CAPITALISM AND COMMUNISM SPONTANEOUSLY CONVERGE." COM FUT USA+45 ECO/DEV DIST/IND MARKET CAP/ISM ECO/TAC RIGID/FLEX WEALTH MARXISM SOCISM...MATH STAT TREND COMPUT/IR 20. PAGE 146 F2885
PLAN TEC/DEV USSR

S63
WOLFERS A.,"INTEGRATION IN THE WEST: THE CONFLICT OF PERSPECTIVES." AFR EUR+WWI USA+45 ECO/DEV INT/ORG DELIB/GP CREATE TEC/DEV DIPLOM ATTIT PWR ...CONCPT HIST/WRIT TREND GEN/LAWS EEC 20. PAGE 148 F2918
RIGID/FLEX ECO/TAC

B64
THE SPECIAL COMMONWEALTH AFRICAN ASSISTANCE PLAN. AFR CANADA INDIA NIGERIA UK FINAN SCHOOL...CHARTS 20 COMMONWLTH. PAGE 1 F0019
ECO/UNDEV TREND FOR/AID ADMIN

B64
BALASSA B.,TRADE PROSPECTS FOR DEVELOPING COUNTRIES. WOR+45 ECO/DEV AGRI EXTR/IND INDUS CREATE PLAN PRICE...ECOMETRIC CLASSIF TIME/SEQ GEN/METH. PAGE 8 F0158
INT/TRADE ECO/UNDEV TREND STAT

B64
BARKSDALE H.C.,MARKETING: CHANGE AND EXCHANGE. USA+45 FINAN ACADEM TEC/DEV PRICE AUTOMAT WEALTH ...CHARTS 20. PAGE 10 F0187
MARKET ECO/DEV DEMAND TREND

B64
CEPEDE M.,POPULATION AND FOOD. USA+45 STRUCT ECO/UNDEV FAM PLAN TEC/DEV FOR/AID CONTROL...CATH SOC TREND 19/20. PAGE 22 F0436
FUT GEOG AGRI CENSUS

B64
COLSTON RESEARCH SOCIETY,ECONOMETRIC ANALYSIS FOR NATIONAL ECONOMIC PLANNING (PROCEEDINGS OF SIXTEENTH SYMPOSIUM OF COLSTON RESEARCH SOCIETY). UK USA+45 FINAN FAM LABOR NAT/G PLAN PRICE ...METH/CNCPT TREND CHARTS TIME 20. PAGE 26 F0510
ECOMETRIC DELIB/GP ECO/TAC PROB/SOLV

B64
DANIELS R.V.,RUSSIA. RUSSIA USSR STRUCT NAT/LISM TOTALISM ORD/FREE WEALTH...POLICY DECISION TREND. PAGE 30 F0579
MARXISM REV ECO/DEV DIPLOM

B64
GREBLER L.,URBAN RENEWAL IN EUROPEAN COUNTRIES: ITS EMERGENCE AND POTENTIALS. EUR+WWI UK ECO/DEV LOC/G NEIGH CREATE ADMIN ATTIT...TREND NAT/COMP MUNICH 20 URBAN/RNWL. PAGE 50 F0981
PLAN CONSTRUC NAT/G

B64
HINSHAW R.,THE EUROPEAN COMMUNITY AND AMERICAN TRADE: A STUDY IN ATLANTIC ECONOMICS AND POLICY. EUR+WWI UK USA+45 ECO/DEV ECO/UNDEV AGRI INDUS INT/ORG NAT/G ECO/TAC TARIFFS REGION...STAT CHARTS EEC 20. PAGE 60 F1174
MARKET TREND INT/TRADE

B64
KUZNETS S.,POSTWAR ECONOMIC GROWTH: FOUR LECTURES. WOR+45 INDUS NAT/G WORKER TEC/DEV ECO/TAC RATION TARIFFS PRICE BAL/PAY COST DEMAND 20. PAGE 74 F1455
ECO/DEV ECO/UNDEV TREND FINAN

B64
LEWIN P.,THE FOREIGN TRADE OF COMMUNIST CHINA* ITS IMPACT ON THE FREE WORLD. AFR EUR+WWI L/A+17C S/ASIA ECO/UNDEV CREATE FOR/AID...STAT NET/THEORY TREND CHARTS. PAGE 79 F1546
ASIA INT/TRADE NAT/COMP USSR

B64
LI C.M.,INDUSTRIAL DEVELOPMENT IN COMMUNIST CHINA. CHINA/COM ECO/DEV ECO/UNDEV AGRI FINAN INDUS MARKET LABOR NAT/G ECO/TAC INT/TRADE EXEC ALL/VALS ...POLICY RELATIV TREND WORK TOT/POP VAL/FREE 20. PAGE 79 F1556
ASIA TEC/DEV

B64
MARKHAM J.W.,THE COMMON MARKET: FRIEND OR COMPETITOR. AFR EUR+WWI FUT USA+45 INT/ORG LG/CO NAT/G VOL/ASSN DELIB/GP EX/STRUC PLAN TARIFFS ORD/FREE PWR WEALTH...POLICY STAT TREND EEC VAL/FREE 20. PAGE 85 F1671
ECO/DEV ECO/TAC

B64
MAZA ZAVALA D.F.,VENEZUELA; UNA ECONOMIA DEPENDIENTE. L/A+17C VENEZUELA FINAN INDUS ...ECOMETRIC STAT TREND 20. PAGE 87 F1710
ECO/UNDEV BAL/PAY INT/TRADE PRICE

B64
MELADY T.,FACES OF AFRICA. AFR FUT ISLAM NAT/G POL/PAR SCHOOL DELIB/GP PLAN ECO/TAC EDU/PROP ATTIT ALL/VALS...CHARTS TOT/POP TERR/GP VAL/FREE 20. PAGE 89 F1752
ECO/UNDEV TREND NAT/LISM

B64
SOLOW R.M.,THE NATURE AND SOURCES OF UNEMPLOYMENT IN THE UNITED STATES (PAMPHLET). USA+45 INDUS LABOR TEC/DEV ECO/TAC SKILL WEALTH...TREND NAT/COMP 20. PAGE 124 F2439
ECO/DEV WORKER STAT PRODUC

B64
STOESSINGER J.G.,FINANCING THE UNITED NATIONS SYSTEM. FUT WOR+45 CONSTN NAT/G VOL/ASSN DELIB/GP EX/STRUC ECO/TAC LEGIT CT/SYS PWR WEALTH...STAT TIME/SEQ TREND CHARTS TRUE/GP METH/GP TERR/GP VAL/FREE. PAGE 126 F2493
FINAN INT/ORG

B64
SULLIVAN G.,THE STORY OF THE PEACE CORPS. USA+45 WOR+45 INTELL FACE/GP NAT/G SCHOOL VOL/ASSN CONSULT EX/STRUC PLAN EDU/PROP ADMIN ATTIT DRIVE ALL/VALS ...POLICY HEAL SOC CONCPT INT QU BIOG TREND SOC/EXP WORK. PAGE 127 F2511
INT/ORG ECO/UNDEV FOR/AID PEACE

B64
TAEUBER I.B.,POPULATION TRENDS IN THE UNITED STATES: 1900 TO 1960. USA+45 USA-45 PROVS INCOME AGE...SOC TIME/SEQ TREND CHARTS MUNICH TIME 20 NEGRO. PAGE 128 F2522
CENSUS GEOG STRATA STRUCT

B64
URQUIDI V.L.,THE CHALLENGE OF DEVELOPMENT IN LATIN AMERICA. L/A+17C FINAN INT/ORG TEC/DEV DIPLOM INT/TRADE PRICE REGION PRODUC...CHARTS 20 ALL/PROG. PAGE 133 F2628
ECO/UNDEV ECO/TAC NAT/G TREND

B64
YUDELMAN M.,AFRICANS ON THE LAND. RHODESIA MARKET LABOR OWN...ECOMETRIC TREND 20. PAGE 150 F2955
ECO/DEV AFR AGRI ECO/TAC

B64
ZOBER M.,MARKETING MANAGEMENT. FINAN BUDGET EDU/PROP PRICE PRODUC ATTIT...POLICY TREND CHARTS METH/COMP EQULIB 20. PAGE 150 F2966
ECO/DEV MGT CONTROL MARKET

L64
ARMENGALD A.,"ECONOMIE ET COEXISTENCE." COM EUR+WWI FUT USA+45 WOR+45 ECO/DEV ECO/UNDEV FINAN INT/ORG NAT/G EXEC CHOOSE ATTIT ALL/VALS...POLICY RELATIV DECISION TREND SOC/EXP WORK 20. PAGE 6 F0113
MARKET ECO/TAC AFR CAP/ISM

L64
HAAS E.B.,"ECONOMICS AND DIFFERENTIAL PATTERNS OF POLITICAL INTEGRATION: PROJECTIONS ABOUT UNITY IN LATIN AMERICA." SOCIETY NAT/G DELIB/GP ACT/RES CREATE PLAN ECO/TAC REGION ROUTINE ATTIT DRIVE PWR WEALTH...CONCPT TREND CHARTS LAFTA TERR/GP 20. PAGE 52 F1020
L/A+17C INT/ORG MARKET

S64
GALBRAITH V.,"JAPAN'S POSITION IN WORLD TRADE." ASIA AGRI INDUS CREATE ECO/TAC LEGIT DRIVE WEALTH ...TREND EEC GATT FOR/TRADE 20 CHINJAP. PAGE 45 F0885
ECO/DEV DELIB/GP

S64
GARDNER R.N.,"GATT AND THE UNITED NATIONS CONFERENCE ON TRADE AND DEVELOPMENT." USA+45 WOR+45 SOCIETY ECO/UNDEV MARKET NAT/G DELIB/GP ACT/RES PLAN ECO/TAC TARIFFS EDU/PROP ROUTINE DRIVE RIGID/FLEX WEALTH...DECISION MGT TREND UN TOT/POP 20 GATT. PAGE 46 F0905
INT/ORG INT/TRADE

S64
HABERLER G.,"INTEGRATION AND GROWTH OF THE WORLD ECONOMY IN HISTORICAL PERSPECTIVE." FUT WOR+45 WOR-45 ECO/DEV ECO/UNDEV...TIME/SEQ TREND VAL/FREE 20. PAGE 52 F1023
WEALTH INT/TRADE

S64
HERMAN L.M.,"THE ECONOMIC CONTENT OF SOVIET TRADE WITH THE WEST." WOR+45 ECO/DEV ECO/UNDEV AGRI COM/IND INDUS CAP/ISM ECO/TAC ATTIT RIGID/FLEX WEALTH...OBS TREND VAL/FREE MARX/KARL 20. PAGE 59 F1152
COM MARKET INT/TRADE USSR

S64
HOOVER C.B.,"THE ROLE OF THE NATURAL AND DEVELOPED RESOURCES OF THE NATION STATES." FUT WOR+45 ECO/DEV ECO/UNDEV NAT/G PWR RESPECT SKILL WEALTH...POLICY GEOG TIME/SEQ TREND RESOURCE/N VAL/FREE 20. PAGE 62 F1210
EXTR/IND DOMIN

S64
HUTCHINSON E.C.,"AMERICAN AID TO AFRICA." FUT USA+45 MARKET INT/ORG LOC/G NAT/G PUB/INST PLAN ECO/TAC ATTIT RIGID/FLEX...POLICY CONCPT TREND TERR/GP 20. PAGE 63 F1248
AFR ECO/UNDEV FOR/AID

S64
KOJIMA K.,"THE PATTERN OF INTERNATIONAL TRADE AMONG ADVANCED COUNTRIES." EUR+WWI UK USA+45 WOR+45 MARKET NAT/G ECO/TAC WEALTH...MATH STAT CON/ANAL CHARTS METH/GP EEC CHINJAP 20 CHINJAP. PAGE 72 F1419
ECO/DEV TREND INT/TRADE

S64
MC WILLIAM M.,"THE WORLD BANK AND THE TRANSFER OF POWER IN KENYA." AFR ECO/UNDEV CONSULT ACT/RES TEC/DEV PERCEPT PWR SKILL WEALTH...CONCPT OBS TREND 20. PAGE 88 F1715
NAT/G ECO/TAC

S64
PADELFORD N.J.,"THE ORGANIZATION OF AFRICAN UNITY." AFR

ECO/UNDEV INT/ORG PLAN BAL/PWR DIPLOM ECO/TAC NAT/LISM ORD/FREE PWR WEALTH...CONCPT TREND STERTYP TERR/GP VAL/FREE 20. PAGE 102 F2013 — VOL/ASSN REGION

S64
PATEL S.J.,"THE ECONOMIC DISTANCE BETWEEN NATIONS: ITS ORIGIN, MEASUREMENT AND OUTLOOK." WOR+45 ECO/DEV AGRI FINAN INDUS MARKET LABOR NAT/G CONSULT TEC/DEV ECO/TAC WEALTH...POLICY RELATIV MGT TREND WORK 20. PAGE 103 F2035 — ECO/UNDEV PLAN

S64
PESELT B.M.,"COMMUNIST ECONOMIC OFFENSIVE." WOR+45 SOCIETY INT/ORG PLAN ECO/TAC DOMIN EDU/PROP ATTIT PERSON PWR WEALTH...TREND CHARTS METH/GP 20. PAGE 105 F2067 — COM ECO/UNDEV FOR/AID USSR

S64
POLARIS J.,"THE SINO-SOVIET DISPUTE: ITS ECONOMIC IMPACT ON CHINA." ASIA CHINA/COM COM WOR+45 NAT/G ATTIT PWR WEALTH...STAT TREND FOR/TRADE 20. PAGE 107 F2095 — ECO/UNDEV ECO/TAC

S64
SCHMITT H.D.,"POLITICAL CONDITIONS FOR INTERNATIONAL CURRENCY REFORM." WOR+45 SOCIETY ECO/DEV PLAN ECO/TAC BAL/PAY ATTIT ORD/FREE WEALTH ...SOC CONCPT OBS TREND EEC VAL/FREE ECSC 20. PAGE 117 F2301 — FINAN VOL/ASSN REGION

S64
WOOD N.,"THE FAMILY FIRM - BASE OF JAPAN'S GROWING ECONOMY." ECO/DEV ECO/UNDEV ECO/TAC WEALTH...POLICY TRADIT BIOG TREND 20 CHINJAP. PAGE 148 F2921 — ASIA SML/CO FAM

B65
BOLLENS J.C.,THE METROPOLIS: ITS PEOPLE, POLITICS, AND ECONOMIC LIFE. USA+45 PLAN PROB/SOLV PERS/REL PWR...DECISION GEOG CENSUS TREND CON/ANAL MUNICH 20 NEWYORK/C LOS/ANG SAN/FRAN CHICAGO PHILADELPH. PAGE 16 F0309 — HABITAT SOC LOC/G

B65
CAMPBELL J.C.,AMERICAN POLICY TOWARDS COMMUNIST EASTERN EUROPE* THE CHOICES AHEAD. AFR USA+45 ECO/DEV BAL/PWR MARXISM TREND. PAGE 21 F0406 — POLAND YUGOSLAVIA DIPLOM COM

B65
CRABB C.V. JR.,THE ELEPHANTS AND THE GRASS* A STUDY OF NONALIGNMENT. ASIA INDIA S/ASIA USA+45 USSR BAL/PWR NEUTRAL ATTIT...TREND NAT/COMP. PAGE 28 F0549 — ECO/UNDEV AFR DIPLOM CONCPT

B65
HAPGOOD D.,AFRICA: FROM INDEPENDENCE TO TOMARROW. AFR GUINEA SENEGAL CULTURE ELITES ECO/UNDEV AGRI SCHOOL FOR/AID COLONIAL MARXISM...TREND 20. PAGE 55 F1070 — ECO/TAC SOCIETY NAT/G

B65
HLA MYINT U.,THE ECONOMICS OF THE DEVELOPING COUNTRIES. USA+45 WOR+45 AGRI FINAN NAT/G INT/TRADE ...CLASSIF CENSUS TREND NAT/COMP SIMUL GEN/LAWS. PAGE 60 F1180 — ECO/UNDEV FOR/AID GEOG

B65
HOLLER J.E.,POPULATION TRENDS AND ECONOMIC DEVELOPMENT IN THE FAR EAST (PAMPHLET). KOREA S/ASIA AGRI INDUS DELIB/GP PROB/SOLV RATIONAL ...POLICY CHARTS BIBLIOG 20 OUTER/MONG CHINJAP HONG/KONG. PAGE 61 F1197 — CENSUS TREND ECO/UNDEV ASIA

B65
LAZARUS S.,RESOLVING BUSINESS DISPUTES: THE POTENTIAL OF COMMERCIAL ARBITRATION. USA+45 INDUS LG/CO ACT/RES PROB/SOLV EDU/PROP CONSEN UTIL ...TREND 20. PAGE 76 F1496 — FINAN DELIB/GP CONSULT ADJUD

B65
MCCOLL G.D.,THE AUSTRALIAN BALANCE OF PAYMENTS. UK USA+45 AGRI WORKER DIPLOM EQUILIB PRODUC...STAT TREND CHARTS BIBLIOG/A 20 AUSTRAL. PAGE 88 F1719 — ECO/DEV BAL/PAY INT/TRADE COST

B65
MOORE W.E.,THE IMPACT OF INDUSTRY. CULTURE STRUCT ORD/FREE...TREND 20. PAGE 93 F1824 — INDUS MGT TEC/DEV ECO/UNDEV

B65
MURUMBI J.,PROBLEMS OF ECONOMIC DEVELOPMENT IN EAST AFRICA. FINAN INDUS WORKER TEC/DEV INT/TRADE TAX DEMAND EFFICIENCY PRODUC SOCISM...TREND CHARTS 20 AFRICA/E. PAGE 95 F1869 — AGRI ECO/TAC ECO/UNDEV PROC/MFG

B65
ORG FOR ECO COOP AND DEVEL,THE MEDITERRANEAN REGIONAL PROJECT: YUGOSLAVIA; EDUCATION AND DEVELOPMENT. YUGOSLAVIA SOCIETY FINAN PROF/ORG PLAN ADMIN COST DEMAND MARXISM...STAT TREND CHARTS METH 20 OECD. PAGE 102 F1996 — EDU/PROP ACADEM SCHOOL ECO/UNDEV

B65
PROCHNOW H.V.,WORLD ECONOMIC PROBLEMS AND POLICIES. INDIA ISRAEL WOR+45 AGRI LABOR PROB/SOLV FOR/AID TARIFFS CONTROL BAL/PAY NAT/LISM WEALTH...TREND CHARTS 20 CHINJAP EEC. PAGE 108 F2124 — MARKET ECO/TAC PRODUC IDEA/COMP

B65
SCHWARTZ G.,SCIENCE IN MARKETING. OP/RES PROB/SOLV INT/TRADE PRICE CONTROL ADJUST PRODUC...CONCPT 20. PAGE 118 F2324 — PHIL/SCI TREND ECO/DEV MARKET

B65
SHARIF A.,THE BALANCE OF PAYMENTS OF PAKISTAN, 1948-1958 (THESIS, UNIVERSITY OF TORONTO). PAKISTAN FINAN INDUS FOR/AID PRICE WEALTH...TREND CHARTS 20. PAGE 120 F2368 — BAL/PAY BUDGET INT/TRADE ECO/UNDEV

B65
SPENCE J.E.,REPUBLIC UNDER PRESSURE: A STUDY OF SOUTH AFRICAN FOREIGN POLICY. SOUTH/AFR ADMIN COLONIAL GOV/REL RACE/REL DISCRIM NAT/LISM ATTIT ROLE...TREND 20 NEGRO. PAGE 124 F2449 — DIPLOM POLICY AFR

L65
DAANE J.D.,"THE EVOLVING INTERNATIONAL MONETARY MECHANISM." VOL/ASSN CREATE PLAN FOR/AID INT/TRADE CONFER BAL/PAY...RECORD PREDICT IMF. PAGE 29 F0569 — INT/ORG ECO/TAC TREND GP/COMP

S65
SCHROEDER G.,"LABOR PLANNING IN THE USSR." COM USSR ECO/DEV INDUS SCHOOL PRODUC WEALTH...PREDICT TIME/SEQ TREND TIME 20. PAGE 117 F2313 — WORKER PLAN CENSUS

S65
SELLERS C.,"THE EQUILIBRIUM CYCLE IN TWO-PARTY POLITICS." USA+45 USA-45 CULTURE R+D GP/REL MAJORITY DECISION. PAGE 119 F2351 — CHOOSE TREND POL/PAR

S65
SPAAK P.H.,"THE SEARCH FOR CONSENSUS: A NEW EFFORT TO BUILD EUROPE." FRANCE GERMANY ECO/DEV NAT/G CONSULT FORCES PLAN EDU/PROP REGION CONSEN ATTIT ...SOC METH/CNCPT OBS TREND EEC NATO WORK TERR/GP METH/GP 20. PAGE 124 F2447 — EUR+WWI INT/ORG

B66
BEQIRAJ M.,PEASANTRY IN REVOLUTION. STRATA ECO/UNDEV AGRI ROUTINE REV HABITAT RIGID/FLEX ...EPIST GEOG NEW/IDEA TREND MUNICH 20. PAGE 13 F0256 — WORKER KNOWL NAT/LISM SOC

B66
FRIEDMANN W.G.,INTERNATIONAL FINANCIAL AID. USA+45 ECO/DEV ECO/UNDEV NAT/G VOL/ASSN EX/STRUC PLAN RENT GIVE BAL/PAY PWR...GEOG INT/LAW STAT TREND UN EEC COMECON. PAGE 44 F0866 — INT/ORG FOR/AID TEC/DEV ECO/TAC

B66
GORDON R.A.,PROSPERITY AND UNEMPLOYMENT. USA+45 PLAN ECO/TAC ADJUST DEMAND ALL/VALS...POLICY DECISION TREND CHARTS ANTHOL 20. PAGE 49 F0961 — WORKER INDUS ECO/DEV WEALTH

B66
HALLET R.,PEOPLE AND PROGRESS IN WEST AFRICA: AN INTRODUCTION TO THE PROBLEMS OF DEVELOPMENT. COM/IND INDUS KIN DIPLOM FOR/AID INT/TRADE HEALTH ...GEOG TREND CHARTS BIBLIOG/A 20 AFRICA/W. PAGE 54 F1050 — AFR SOCIETY ECO/UNDEV ECO/TAC

B66
INTERNATIONAL ECONOMIC ASSN,STABILITY AND PROGRESS IN THE WORLD ECONOMY: THE FIRST CONGRESS OF THE INTERNATIONAL ECONOMIC ASSOCIATION. WOR+45 ECO/DEV ECO/UNDEV DELIB/GP FOR/AID BAL/PAY...TREND CMN/WLTH 20. PAGE 65 F1276 — INT/TRADE

B66
KEENLEYSIDE H.L.,INTERNATIONAL AID: A SUMMARY. AFR INDIA S/ASIA UK STRATA EXTR/IND TEC/DEV ADMIN RACE/REL DEMAND NAT/LISM WEALTH...TREND CHINJAP. PAGE 70 F1367 — ECO/UNDEV FOR/AID DIPLOM TASK

B66
LANSING J.B.,TRANSPORTATION AND ECONOMIC POLICY. USA+45 COST DEMAND...ECOMETRIC TREND CHARTS IDEA/COMP T 20. PAGE 76 F1481 — DIST/IND OP/RES ECO/DEV UTIL

B66
MASON E.S.,ECONOMIC DEVELOPMENT IN INDIA AND PAKISTAN. INDIA PAKISTAN AGRI FINAN PLAN BUDGET INT/TRADE WEALTH...POLICY STAT TREND CHARTS 20. PAGE 87 F1700 — NAT/COMP ECO/UNDEV ECO/TAC FOR/AID

B66
ODEGARD P.H.,POLITICAL POWER AND SOCIAL CHANGE. UNIV NAT/G CREATE ALL/IDEOS...POLICY GEOG SOC CENSUS TREND. PAGE 100 F1962 — PWR TEC/DEV IDEA/COMP

B66
PASSIN H.,THE UNITED STATES AND JAPAN. USA+45 INDUS CAP/ISM...TREND 20 CHINJAP TREATY. PAGE 103 F2032 — DIPLOM INT/TRADE ECO/DEV ECO/TAC

B66
THIESENHUSEN W.C.,CHILE'S EXPERIMENTS IN AGRARIAN REFORM. CHILE STRUCT NAT/G ACT/RES ECO/TAC GOV/REL COST SOCISM...TREND CHARTS SOC/EXP 20. PAGE 130 F2558 — AGRI ECO/UNDEV SOC TEC/DEV

B66
US DEPARTMENT OF LABOR,TECHNOLOGICAL TRENDS IN MAJOR AMERICAN INDUSTRIES. USA+45 R+D LABOR GP/REL PRODUC...MGT BIBLIOG 20. PAGE 135 F2669 — TEC/DEV INDUS TREND AUTOMAT

B66
WESTON J.F.,THE SCOPE AND METHODOLOGY OF FINANCE. PLAN TEC/DEV CONTROL EFFICIENCY INCOME UTIL...MGT CONCPT MATH STAT TREND METH 20. PAGE 145 F2863 — FINAN ECO/DEV POLICY PRICE

B66
WETTER G.A.,SOVIET IDEOLOGY TODAY. USSR ECO/UNDEV SECT WORKER CAP/ISM CONTROL TASK EFFICIENCY TOTALISM DRIVE WEALTH...TREND 18/20. PAGE 145 F2864
ALL/IDEOS MARXISM REV

S66
DAVIS O.A.,"A THEORY OF THE BUDGETARY PROCESS." ECO/DEV FINAN LEGIS PROB/SOLV GOV/REL...ECOMETRIC METH/CNCPT STAT CONT/OBS TREND METH/COMP SIMUL 20 CONGRESS. PAGE 30 F0592
DECISION NAT/G BUDGET EFFICIENCY

S66
LAURENS H.,"LES PAYS OCCIDENTAUX ET LE MARCHE CHINOIS." EUR+WWI FUT S/ASIA AGRI INDUS VOL/ASSN ECO/TAC BAL/PAY...RECORD PREDICT TREATY. PAGE 76 F1488
ASIA INT/TRADE TREND STAT

N66
BRITISH DEVELOPMENT POLICIES: 1966 (PAMPHLET). UK AGRI TARIFFS BAL/PAY...TREND CHARTS 20 OVRSEA/DEV. PAGE 1 F0023
WEALTH DIPLOM INT/TRADE FOR/AID

B67
ANDERSON T.,RUSSIAN POLITICAL THOUGHT; AN INTRODUCTION. USSR NAT/G POL/PAR CHIEF MARXISM ...TIME/SEQ BIBLIOG 9/20. PAGE 5 F0099
TREND CONSTN ATTIT

B67
BANFIELD E.C.,THE MORAL BASIS OF A BACKWARD SOCIETY. EUR+WWI ITALY STRATA NEIGH PARTIC INGP/REL ...SOC QU PREDICT TREND HYPO/EXP MUNICH 20. PAGE 9 F0173
MORAL WEALTH ATTIT

B67
BEATON L.,THE STRUGGLE FOR PEACE. INT/ORG FORCES NUC/PWR COST PWR...POLICY TREND 20. PAGE 12 F0225
PEACE BAL/PWR DIPLOM WAR

B67
BREAK G.F.,INTERGOVERNMENTAL FISCAL RELATIONS IN THE UNITED STATES. USA+45 USA-45 DELIB/GP PLAN BUDGET TAX GOV/REL CENTRAL...TREND CHARTS MUNICH. PAGE 18 F0345
LOC/G NAT/G PROVS FINAN

B67
CARNEY D.,PATTERNS AND MECHANICS OF ECONOMIC GROWTH: A GENERAL THEORETICAL APPROACH. WOR+45 OP/RES INCOME...MATH TREND CHARTS 20. PAGE 21 F0416
PLAN ECO/DEV FINAN

B67
CHILCOTE R.H.,PORTUGUESE AFRICA. PORTUGAL CULTURE SOCIETY ECO/UNDEV DOMIN NAT/LISM...TREND IDEA/COMP NAT/COMP BIBLIOG 15/20. PAGE 24 F0465
AFR COLONIAL ORD/FREE PROB/SOLV

B67
COTTAM R.W.,COMPETITIVE INTERFERENCE AND TWENTIETH CENTURY DIPLOMACY. IRAN ACT/RES CREATE PLAN ECO/TAC EFFICIENCY ATTIT...DECISION NEW/IDEA TREND 20 CIA. PAGE 28 F0541
DIPLOM DOMIN GAME

B67
DE TORRES J.,FINANCING LOCAL GOVERNMENT. USA+45 USA-45 NAT/G PROVS GIVE ADJUST PWR...TIME/SEQ CHARTS MUNICH 20. PAGE 31 F0606
LOC/G BUDGET TAX TREND

B67
EBENSTEIN W.,TODAY'S ISMS: COMMUNISM, FASCISM, CAPITALISM, SOCIALISM (5TH ED.). COM WOR+45 PERCEPT PWR...SOC TREND IDEA/COMP NAT/COMP 20. PAGE 35 F0691
FASCISM MARXISM SOCISM CAP/ISM

B67
HALLE L.J.,THE COLD WAR AS HISTORY. AFR USSR WOR+45 ECO/TAC FOR/AID NUC/PWR WAR PEACE ORD/FREE ...MAJORIT TREND 20 KENNEDY/JF KHRUSH/N BERLIN/BLO. PAGE 54 F1048
DIPLOM BAL/PWR

B67
KANNER L.,THE NEW YORK TIMES WORLD ECONOMIC REVIEW AND FORECAST: 1967. WOR+45 ECO/DEV ECO/UNDEV TEC/DEV...STAT PREDICT CHARTS 20. PAGE 69 F1349
INDUS FINAN TREND ECO/TAC

B67
MEYNAUD J.,TRADE UNIONISM IN AFRICA; A STUDY OF ITS GROWTH AND ORIENTATION (TRANS. BY ANGELA BRENCH). INT/ORG PROB/SOLV COLONIAL PWR...TIME/SEQ TREND ILO. PAGE 90 F1774
LABOR AFR NAT/LISM ORD/FREE

B67
MONTGOMERY J.D.,FOREIGN AID IN INTERNATIONAL POLITICS. USA+45 USA-45 WOR+45 ECO/TAC EFFICIENCY ...SOC TREND CHARTS BIBLIOG/A 20 AID. PAGE 93 F1818
DIPLOM FOR/AID

B67
OFER G.,THE SERVICE INDUSTRIES IN A DEVELOPING ECONOMY: ISRAEL AS A CASE STUDY. ISRAEL ECO/TAC INT/TRADE PRODUC WEALTH SOCISM...TIME/SEQ TREND CHARTS 20. PAGE 101 F1979
DIPLOM ECO/DEV SERV/IND

B67
ORLANS H.,CONTRACTING FOR ATOMS. AFR USA+45 LAW INTELL ACADEM LG/CO NAT/G PLAN TEC/DEV CONTROL DETER...TREND 20. PAGE 102 F1999
NUC/PWR R+D PRODUC PEACE

B67
SPIRO H.S.,PATTERNS OF AFRICAN DEVLOPMENT: FIVE COMPARISONS. STRUCT ECO/UNDEV NAT/G CONSERVE SOCISM ...PREDICT NAT/COMP 20 CHINJAP. PAGE 125 F2457
AFR CONSTN NAT/LISM TREND

B67
STEARNS P.N.,EUROPEAN SOCIETY IN UPHEAVAL* SOCIAL HISTORY SINCE 1800. EUR+WWI MOD/EUR STRATA SECT WORKER TEC/DEV WAR...WELF/ST SOC TREND BIBLIOG 19/20. PAGE 125 F2472
REGION ECO/DEV SOCIETY INDUS

B67
TANSKY L.,US AND USSR AID TO DEVELOPING COUNTRIES. INDIA TURKEY UAR USA+45 USSR FINAN PLAN TEC/DEV ADMIN WEALTH...TREND METH/COMP 20. PAGE 128 F2535
FOR/AID ECO/UNDEV MARXISM CAP/ISM

B67
WALLBANK T.W.,CIVILIZATION PAST AND PRESENT (3RD ED.). FUT WOR+45 WOR-45 SOCIETY...SOC CONCPT TIME/SEQ CHARTS BIBLIOG T. PAGE 143 F2809
CULTURE STRUCT TREND

B67
WILLIAMS E.J.,LATIN AMERICAN CHRISTIAN DEMOCRATIC PARTIES. L/A+17C FAM LABOR FORCES...CATH TREND BIBLIOG 20. PAGE 147 F2890
POL/PAR GP/COMP CATHISM ALL/VALS

B67
WILLS A.J.,AN INTRODUCTION TO THE HISTORY OF CENTRAL AFRICA. RHODESIA ZAMBIA CULTURE SOCIETY ECO/UNDEV TEC/DEV DOMIN WAR ALL/VALS...POLICY TREND BIBLIOG T 14/20 NYASALAND. PAGE 147 F2899
AFR COLONIAL ORD/FREE

B67
WISEMAN H.V.,BRITAIN AND THE COMMONWEALTH. EUR+WWI FUT UK ECO/DEV POL/PAR TEC/DEV INT/TRADE LEAD ROLE SOVEREIGN...SOC TREND 20 CMN/WLTH. PAGE 148 F2911
INT/ORG DIPLOM NAT/G NAT/COMP

B67
ZONDAG C.H.,THE BOLIVIAN ECONOMY 1952-65. L/A+17C TEC/DEV FOR/AID ADMIN...OBS TREND CHARTS BIBLIOG 20 BOLIV. PAGE 151 F2969
ECO/UNDEV INDUS PRODUC

L67
MACDONALD R.M.,"COLLECTIVE BARGAINING IN THE POSTWAR PERIOD." WORKER PROB/SOLV ECO/TAC PARTIC RISK CENTRAL EFFICIENCY DRIVE WEALTH...TREND 20. PAGE 83 F1624
LABOR INDUS BARGAIN CAP/ISM

S67
ALPANDER G.G.,"ENTREPRENEURS AND PRIVATE ENTERPRISE IN TURKEY." TURKEY INDUS PROC/MFG EDU/PROP ATTIT DRIVE WEALTH...GEOG MGT SOC STAT TREND CHARTS 20. PAGE 4 F0077
ECO/UNDEV LG/CO NAT/G POLICY

S67
FERGUSON D.E.,"DETERMINING CAPACITY FOR CAPITAL EXPENDITURES." USA+45 LOC/G BUDGET TAX ADMIN CONTROL...TREND MUNICH 20. PAGE 40 F0784
FINAN PAY COST

S67
GAMARNIKOW M.,"THE NEW ROLE OF PRIVATE ENTERPRISE." ECO/DEV INDUS NAT/G SML/CO CREATE PROB/SOLV MARXISM ...POLICY TREND IDEA/COMP 20. PAGE 46 F0890
ECO/TAC ATTIT CAP/ISM COM

S67
HANCOCK J.L.,"PLANNERS IN THE CHANGING AMERICAN CITY, 1900-1940." USA-45 CONSTRUC NAT/G POL/PAR ...SOC/WK TREND MUNICH 20. PAGE 54 F1059
PLAN CONSULT LOC/G

S67
JANSSEN P.,"NEA: THE RELUCTANT DRAGON." NAT/G EXEC LOBBY PARTIC SANCTION RACE/REL ROLE TREND. PAGE 66 F1305
EDU/PROP PROF/ORG MGT POLICY

S67
JAVITS J.K.,"THE USE OF AMERICAN PLURALISM." USA+45 ECO/DEV BUDGET ADMIN ALL/IDEOS...DECISION TREND. PAGE 67 F1309
CENTRAL ATTIT POLICY NAT/G

S67
LEONTYEV L.,"THE LENINIST PRINCIPLES OF SOCIALIST ECONOMIC MANAGEMENT." USA+45 USSR POL/PAR WORKER PLAN ECO/TAC EFFICIENCY PRODUC MARXISM...POLICY SOCIALIST MGT TREND 20 LENIN/VI MARX/KARL. PAGE 78 F1529
SOCISM CAP/ISM IDEA/COMP ECO/DEV

S67
MEADE J.E.,"POPULATION EXPLOSION, THE STANDARD OF LIVING AND SOCIAL CONFLICT." DIPLOM FOR/AID OWN ...PREDICT TREND 20. PAGE 89 F1739
GEOG WEALTH PRODUC INCOME

S67
PECCEI A.,"DEVELOPED-UNDERDEVELOPED AND EAST-WEST RELATIONS." ECO/UNDEV TEC/DEV DIPLOM LEAD EFFICIENCY GEOG. PAGE 104 F2045
FOR/AID TREND REGION ECO/DEV

S67
PRASOW P.,"THE DEVELOPMENT OF JUDICIAL ARBITRATION IN LABOR-MANAGEMENT DISPUTES." LAW INDUS WORKER GP/REL ROLE...HIST/WRIT 20. PAGE 107 F2113
LABOR BARGAIN ADJUD TREND

S67
RAZA M.A.,"EMERGING TRENDS IN PUBLIC LABOR POLICIES AND UNION - GOVERN MENT RELATIONS IN ASIA AND AFRICA." LAW NAT/G POL/PAR COLONIAL COERCE GP/REL ATTIT 20. PAGE 110 F2157
LABOR CONTROL TREND

S67
SEIDLER G.L.,"MARXIST LEGAL THOUGHT IN POLAND." POLAND SOCIETY R+D LOC/G NAT/G ACT/RES ADJUD CT/SYS SUPEGO PWR...SOC TREND 20 MARX/KARL. PAGE 119 F2343
MARXISM LAW CONCPT

EFFICIENCY
S67
SHISTER J.,"THE DIRECTION OF UNIONISM 1947-1967: THRUST OF DRIFT?" INDUS CENTRAL EFFICIENCY INCOME ATTIT SOCISM...POLICY TREND 20 AFL/CIO. PAGE 121 F2382
LABOR PROF/ORG LEAD LAW

TREVES G. F2585

TRIBAL....SEE KIN

TRIBUTE....FORMAL PAYMENTS TO DOMINANT POWER BY MINOR GROUP; SEE ALSO SANCTION
POWER

N19
CARPER E.T.,LOBBYING AND THE NATURAL GAS BILL (PAMPHLET). USA+45 SERV/IND BARGAIN PAY DRIVE ROLE WEALTH 20 CONGRESS SENATE EISNHWR/DD. PAGE 22 F0418
LOBBY ADJUD TRIBUTE NAT/G

B56
ABELS J.,THE TRUMAN SCANDALS. USA+45 USA-45 POL/PAR TAX LEGIT CT/SYS CHOOSE PRIVIL MORAL WEALTH 20 TRUMAN/HS PRESIDENT CONGRESS. PAGE 2 F0031
CRIME ADMIN CHIEF TRIBUTE

B62
MCCLELLAN J.L.,CRIME WITHOUT PUNISHMENT. USA+45 LAW SOCIETY DELIB/GP TRIBUTE CONTROL LOBBY COERCE GP/REL ANOMIE MORAL...CRIMLGY 20 CONGRESS HOFFA/J. PAGE 88 F1718
CRIME ACT/RES LABOR PWR

TRIESTE....TRIESTE

TRIFFIN R. F2586,F2587,F2588,F2589,F2590

TRINIDAD....TRINIDAD AND TOBAGO; SEE ALSO L/A+17C

TROBRIAND....TROBRIAND ISLANDS AND ISLANDERS

S21
MALINOWSKI B.,"THE PRIMITIVE ECONOMICS OF THE TROBRIAND ISLANDERS" (BMR)" CULTURE SOCIETY NAT/G CHIEF LEAD OWN...SOC MYTH WORSHIP 20 NEW/GUINEA TROBRIAND RESOURCE/N. PAGE 84 F1647
ECO/UNDEV AGRI PRODUC STRUCT

TROTSKY/L....LEON TROTSKY

B55
MAYO H.B.,DEMOCRACY AND MARXISM. COM USSR STRATA NAT/G WORKER ECO/TAC REV MORAL...PHIL/SCI HIST/WRIT IDEA/COMP WORSHIP 20 MARX/KARL LENIN/VI STALIN/J TROTSKY/L. PAGE 87 F1708
MARXISM CAP/ISM

TROW M.A. F1577

TRUDEAU A.G. F1128

TRUE A.C. F2591

TRUE/GP

S60
MARTIN E.M.,"NEW TRENDS IN UNITED STATES ECONOMIC FOREIGN POLICY." USA+45 INTELL DELIB/GP FOR/AID INT/TRADE ROUTINE BAL/PAY...RELATIV TRUE/GP 20. PAGE 86 F1682
NAT/G PLAN DIPLOM

B62
CAIRNCROSS A.K.,FACTORS IN ECONOMIC DEVELOPMENT. WOR+45 ECO/UNDEV INDUS R+D LG/CO NAT/G EX/STRUC PLAN TEC/DEV ECO/TAC ATTIT HEALTH KNOWL PWR WEALTH ...TIME/SEQ GEN/LAWS TOT/POP TRUE/GP VAL/FREE 20. PAGE 21 F0399
MARKET ECO/DEV

L62
WATERSTON A.,"PLANNING IN MOROCCO, ORGANIZATION AND IMPLEMENTATION. BALTIMORE: HOPKINS ECON. DEVELOP. INT. BANK FOR." ISLAM ECO/DEV AGRI DIST/IND INDUS PROC/MFG SERV/IND LOC/G EX/STRUC ECO/TAC PWR WEALTH TOT/POP TRUE/GP METH/GP TERR/GP VAL/FREE 20. PAGE 144 F2829
NAT/G PLAN MOROCCO

B63
BAUER R.A.,AMERICAN BUSINESS AND PUBLIC POLICY: THE POLITICS OF FOREIGN TRADE. USA+45 COM/IND LG/CO NAT/G PROF/ORG SML/CO VOL/ASSN LEGIS TOP/EX ECO/TAC EDU/PROP CHOOSE HEALTH PWR WEALTH...CONCPT METH/CNCPT OBS INT QU SAMP FOR/TRADE TRUE/GP VAL/FREE HI. PAGE 11 F0217
ECO/DEV ATTIT

B63
KAPP W.K.,HINDU CULTURE: ECONOMIC DEVELOPMENT AND ECONOMIC PLANNING IN INDIA. INDIA S/ASIA CULTURE ECO/TAC EDU/PROP ADMIN ALL/VALS...POLICY MGT TIME/SEQ TRUE/GP VAL/FREE 20. PAGE 69 F1353
SECT ECO/UNDEV

B63
LAGOS G.,INTERNATIONAL STRATIFICATION AND UNDERDEVELOPED COUNTRIES. L/A+17C WOR+45 PLAN ECO/TAC PWR RESPECT WEALTH...METH/CNCPT STAT CHARTS SIMUL GEN/LAWS TRUE/GP METH/GP VAL/FREE 20. PAGE 74 F1459
ECO/UNDEV STRATA

S63
DIEBOLD W. JR.,"THE NEW SITUATION OF INTERNATIONAL TRADE POLICY." EUR+WWI FRANCE FUT UK USA+45 WOR+45 DIST/IND PLAN INT/TRADE EDU/PROP PWR WEALTH ...RECORD TREND GEN/LAWS EEC TRUE/GP VAL/FREE APPLIC 20. PAGE 33 F0636
MARKET ECO/TAC

S63
DOSSER D.,"TOWARD A THEORY OF INTERNATIONAL PUBLIC FINANCE." WOR+45 ECO/DEV PLAN ECO/TAC WEALTH ...WELF/ST TREND GEN/LAWS TRUE/GP METH/GP 20. PAGE 34 F0654
FINAN INT/ORG FOR/AID

B64
STOESSINGER J.G.,FINANCING THE UNITED NATIONS SYSTEM. FUT WOR+45 CONSTN NAT/G VOL/ASSN DELIB/GP EX/STRUC ECO/TAC LEGIT CT/SYS PWR WEALTH...STAT TIME/SEQ TREND CHARTS TRUE/GP METH/GP TERR/GP VAL/FREE. PAGE 126 F2493
FINAN INT/ORG

B64
WILLIAMSON J.G.,AMERICAN GROWTH AND THE BALANCE OF PAYMENTS, 1820-1913: A STUDY OF THE LONG SWING. EUR+WWI MOD/EUR USA+45 USA-45 ECO/DEV NAT/G ECO/TAC ROUTINE ORD/FREE WEALTH...MATH STAT TIME/SEQ CHARTS SIMUL GEN/LAWS TRUE/GP METH/GP VAL/FREE 19/20. PAGE 147 F2896
FINAN BAL/PAY

S64
RUSSETT B.M.,"INEQUALITY AND INSTABILITY: THE RELATION OF LAND TENURE TO POLITICS." WOR+45 ECO/DEV ECO/UNDEV AGRI NAT/G COERCE PWR...MATH STAT CHARTS GEN/LAWS TERR/GP TRUE/GP METH/GP VAL/FREE 20. PAGE 115 F2263
WEALTH GEOG ECO/TAC ORD/FREE

TRUJILLO/R....RAFAEL TRUJILLO

TRUMAN/DOC....TRUMAN DOCTRINE

TRUMAN/HS....PRESIDENT HARRY S. TRUMAN

N19
MCCONNELL G.,THE STEEL SEIZURE OF 1952 (PAMPHLET). USA+45 FINAN INDUS PROC/MFG LG/CO EX/STRUC ADJUD CONTROL GP/REL ORD/FREE PWR 20 TRUMAN/HS PRESIDENT CONGRESS. PAGE 88 F1721
DELIB/GP LABOR PROB/SOLV NAT/G

B56
ABELS J.,THE TRUMAN SCANDALS. USA+45 USA-45 POL/PAR TAX LEGIT CT/SYS CHOOSE PRIVIL MORAL WEALTH 20 TRUMAN/HS PRESIDENT CONGRESS. PAGE 2 F0031
CRIME ADMIN CHIEF TRIBUTE

B61
CANTERBERY E.R.,THE PRESIDENT'S COUNCIL OF ECONOMIC ADVISERS. AFR USA+45 FINAN LABOR NAT/G PLAN ADMIN OPTIMAL WEALTH 20 EISNHWR/DD PRESIDENT TRUMAN/HS KEYNES/JM. PAGE 21 F0413
ECO/TAC OP/RES EXEC CHIEF

B65
SCHECHTER A.,THE BUSINESSMAN IN GOVERNMENT (THESIS, COLUMBIA UNIVERSITY). USA+45 CONFER GP/REL PERSON ...QU 20 PRESIDENT TRUMAN/HS CABINET. PAGE 116 F2291
INDUS NAT/G EX/STRUC DELIB/GP

B66
FREIDEL F.,AMERICAN ISSUES IN THE TWENTIETH CENTURY. SOCIETY FINAN ECO/TAC FOR/AID CONTROL NUC/PWR WAR RACE/REL PEACE ATTIT...ANTHOL T 20 WILSON/W ROOSEVLT/F KENNEDY/JF TRUMAN/HS. PAGE 44 F0851
DIPLOM POLICY NAT/G ORD/FREE

B66
LEE R.A.,TRUMAN AND TAFT-HARTLEY: A QUESTION OF MANDATE. USA+45 LAW CONSTN LG/CO CONTROL LOBBY GOV/REL PEACE NEW/LIB 20 TRUMAN/HS CONGRESS. PAGE 77 F1507
LEGIS TOP/EX ADJUD LABOR

S67
WALZER M.,"THE CONDITION OF GREECE; TWENTY YEARS AFTER THE TRUMAN DOCTRINE." AFR GREECE FORCES CAP/ISM 20 TRUMAN/HS. PAGE 143 F2814
DIPLOM POLICY FOR/AID TOTALISM

TRUST, PERSONAL....SEE RESPECT, SUPEGO

TRUST/TERR....TRUST TERRITORY

TSHOMBE/M....MOISE TSHOMBE

TULANE/U....TULANE UNIVERSITY

TUMIN M.M. F2592

TUNISIA....SEE ALSO ISLAM, AFR

B62
PONCET J.,LA COLONISATION ET L'AGRICULTURE EUROPEENNES EN TUNISIE DEPUIS 1881. FRANCE WORKER TEC/DEV ECO/TAC CONTROL EFFICIENCY ROLE WEALTH 19/20 TUNIS. PAGE 107 F2101
ECO/UNDEV AGRI COLONIAL FINAN

L63
RIDAH A.,"LE NEO-DESTOUR DEPUIS L'INDEPENDANCE." FUT ISLAM WOR+45 ECO/UNDEV INT/ORG SCHOOL DELIB/GP TOP/EX ACT/RES EDU/PROP LEGIT ATTIT ALL/VALS 20 TUNIS. PAGE 111 F2189 — NAT/G CONSTN

S63
ARDANT G.,"A PLAN FOR FULL EMPLOYMENT IN THE DEVELOPING COUNTRIES." AFR FUT WOR+45 DELIB/GP ACT/RES PLAN ECO/TAC ATTIT ALL/VALS...POLICY STAT CHARTS TUNIS VAL/FREE 20. PAGE 6 F0112 — ECO/UNDEV SOCIETY MOROCCO

TURKESTAN....TURKESTAN

TURKEY....TURKEY; SEE ALSO ISLAM

B55
OECD,MARSHALL PLAN IN TURKEY. TURKEY USA+45 COM/IND CONSTRUC SERV/IND FORCES BUDGET...STAT 20 MARSHL/PLN. PAGE 100 F1964 — FOR/AID ECO/UNDEV AGRI INDUS

B60
US OPERATIONS MISSION - TURKEY,SOME POSSIBILITIES FOR ACCELERATING TURKEY'S ECONOMIC GROWTH. TURKEY USA+45 AGRI FINAN INDUS NAT/G ACT/RES BUDGET COST ...CHARTS 20. PAGE 138 F2724 — ECO/UNDEV ECO/TAC FOR/AID PRODUC

S61
VALLET R.,"IRAN: KEY TO THE MIDDLE EAST." COM IRAQ ISLAM KUWAIT LEBANON SAUDI/ARAB TURKEY ELITES SOCIETY INDUS PROC/MFG POL/PAR TOP/EX PLAN BAL/PWR DIPLOM ECO/TAC ALL/VALS...TREND FOR/TRADE CENTO 20. PAGE 140 F2760 — NAT/G ECO/UNDEV IRAN

B62
GALENSON W.,LABOR IN DEVELOPING COUNTRIES. BRAZIL INDONESIA ISRAEL PAKISTAN TURKEY AGRI INDUS WORKER PAY PRICE GP/REL WEALTH...MGT CHARTS METH/COMP NAT/COMP 20. PAGE 45 F0888 — LABOR ECO/UNDEV BARGAIN POL/PAR

B65
ANALYSIS AND ASSESSMENT OF THE ECONOMIC EFFECTS: PUBLIC LAW 480 TITLE I PROGRAM TURKEY. INDIA TURKEY USA+45 AGRI NAT/G PLAN BUDGET DIPLOM COST EFFICIENCY...CHARTS 20. PAGE 1 F0021 — ECO/TAC FOR/AID FINAN ECO/UNDEV

B65
OECD,MEDITERRANEAN REGIONAL PROJECT: TURKEY; EDUCATION AND DEVELOPMENT. FUT TURKEY SOCIETY STRATA FINAN NAT/G PROF/ORG PLAN PROB/SOLV ADMIN COST...STAT CHARTS 20 OECD. PAGE 100 F1969 — EDU/PROP ACADEM SCHOOL ECO/UNDEV

B65
ORG FOR ECO COOP AND DEVEL,THE MEDITERRANEAN REGIONAL PROJECT: AN EXPERIMENT IN PLANNING BY SIX COUNTRIES. FUT GREECE SPAIN TURKEY YUGOSLAVIA SOCIETY FINAN NAT/G PROF/ORG EDU/PROP ADMIN REGION COST...POLICY STAT CHARTS 20 OECD. PAGE 102 F1995 — PLAN ECO/UNDEV ACADEM SCHOOL

B65
RIVKIN M.D.,AREA DEVELOPMENT FOR NATIONAL GROWTH; THE TURKISH PRECEDENT. ISLAM TURKEY ACT/RES INGP/REL...POLICY CHARTS GP/COMP MUNICH 20 ATATURK/MK INONU/I. PAGE 112 F2197 — ECO/UNDEV REGION ECO/TAC PLAN

S65
MUNZI U.,"THE EUROPEAN SOCIAL FUND IN THE DEVELOPMENT OF THE MEDITERRANEAN REGIONS OF THE EEC." FUT GREECE ITALY PORTUGAL SPAIN TURKEY WORKER TEC/DEV ECO/TAC REGION...STAT EEC. PAGE 95 F1862 — ECO/UNDEV PREDICT RECORD

B67
TANSKY L.,US AND USSR AID TO DEVELOPING COUNTRIES. INDIA TURKEY USA+45 USSR INDUS PLAN CAP/ISM WAR PWR WEALTH MARXISM...CHARTS NAT/COMP BIBLIOG 20. PAGE 128 F2534 — ECO/UNDEV FOR/AID DIPLOM ECO/TAC

B67
TANSKY L.,US AND USSR AID TO DEVELOPING COUNTRIES. INDIA TURKEY UAR USA+45 USSR FINAN PLAN TEC/DEV ADMIN WEALTH...TREND METH/COMP 20. PAGE 128 F2535 — FOR/AID ECO/UNDEV MARXISM CAP/ISM

S67
ALPANDER G.G.,"ENTREPRENEURS AND PRIVATE ENTERPRISE IN TURKEY." TURKEY INDUS PROC/MFG EDU/PROP ATTIT DRIVE WEALTH...GEOG MGT SOC STAT TREND CHARTS 20. PAGE 4 F0077 — ECO/UNDEV LG/CO NAT/G POLICY

S67
SHERWOOD W.B.,"THE RISE OF THE JUSTICE PARTY IN TURKEY." FUT TURKEY LEAD ATTIT 20. PAGE 121 F2378 — POL/PAR ECO/UNDEV STRUCT SOCIETY

TURKIC....TURKIC PEOPLES

TURNBULL J.G. F1876

TURNER H.A. F2593

TURNER J.E. F1201

TUSKEGEE....TUSKEGEE, ALABAMA

TV....TELEVISION; SEE ALSO PRESS, COM/IND

B62
BACKMAN J.,THE ECONOMICS OF THE ELECTRICAL MACHINERY INDUSTRY. USA+45 PROC/MFG LABOR WORKER INT/TRADE TV PRICE COST...CHARTS 19/20. PAGE 8 F0147 — PRODUC TEC/DEV TREND

L67
BARRON J.A.,"ACCESS TO THE PRESS." USA+45 TEC/DEV PRESS TV ADJUD AUD/VIS. PAGE 10 F0196 — ORD/FREE COM/IND EDU/PROP LAW

S67
DAVIS O.A.,"ON THE DISTINCTION BETWEEN PUBLIC AND PRIVATE GOODS." USA+45 COM/IND LG/CO NAT/G TV DEBATE PRICE ADMIN ROLE...MATH IDEA/COMP. PAGE 31 F0593 — MARKET OWN CONCPT

S67
STEMPEL GH I.I.I.,"A NEW ANALYSIS OF MONOPOLY AND COMPETITION." USA+45 INDUS TV ATTIT MUNICH. PAGE 126 F2479 — PRESS COM/IND GP/REL

TVA....TENNESSEE VALLEY AUTHORITY

B49
SELZNICK P.,TVA AND THE GRASS ROOTS: A STUDY IN THE SOCIOLOGY OF FORMAL ORGANIZATION. USA-45 EX/STRUC PROB/SOLV CONFER PARTIC ROUTINE PWR 20 TVA. PAGE 119 F2353 — REPRESENT LOBBY CONSULT

B61
ALFRED H.,PUBLIC OWNERSHIP IN THE USA: GOALS AND PRIORITIES. LAW INDUS INT/TRADE ADJUD GOV/REL EFFICIENCY PEACE SOCISM...POLICY ANTHOL 20 TVA. PAGE 4 F0065 — CONTROL OWN ECO/DEV ECO/TAC

B61
HUBBARD P.J.,ORIGINS OF THE TVA: THE MUSCLE SHOALS CONTROVERSY, 1920-1932. USA-45 DELIB/GP LEGIS LEAD LOBBY GOV/REL GP/REL INGP/REL OWN PERSON...BIBLIOG 20 TVA CONGRESS WATER. PAGE 62 F1229 — SEA CONTROL NAT/G INDUS

B62
PRAKASH O.M.,THE THEORY AND WORKING OF STATE CORPORATIONS: WITH SPECIAL REFERENCE TO INDIA. INDIA UK USA+45 TOP/EX PRICE ADMIN EFFICIENCY...MGT METH/COMP 20 TVA. PAGE 107 F2112 — LG/CO ECO/UNDEV GOV/REL SOCISM

TWAIN/MARK....MARK TWAIN (SAMUEL CLEMENS)

TYBOUT R.A. F2594

TYLER G. F2595

TYLER/JOHN....PRESIDENT JOHN TYLER

TYPOLOGY....SEE CLASSIF

U

U.S. DEPARTMENT OF LABOR....SEE DEPT/LABOR

U OF MICHIGAN LAW SCHOOL F2596

U WISCONSIN BUREAU OF GOVT F2597

U/THANT....U THANT

UA/PAR....UNITED AUSTRALIAN PARTY

UAM....UNION AFRICAINE ET MALGACHE;

UAR....UNITED ARAB REPUBLIC (EGYPT AND SYRIA 1958-1961, EGYPT AFTER 1958); SEE ALSO EGYPT, ISLAM

N
BROCKWAY A.F.,AFRICAN SOCIALISM. EUR+WWI GHANA ISLAM UAR ECO/UNDEV CAP/ISM INT/TRADE COLONIAL COERCE GOV/REL DISCRIM 20 NEGRO NKRUMAH/K NASSER/G. PAGE 19 F0356 — AFR SOCISM MARXISM

B12
FOUAD M.,LE REGIME DE LA PRESSE EN EGYPTE: THESE POUR LE DOCTORAT. UAR LICENSE EDU/PROP ADMIN SANCTION CRIME SUPEGO PWR...ART/METH JURID 19/20. PAGE 43 F0832 — ORD/FREE LEGIS CONTROL PRESS

N19
KUWAIT ARABIA,KUWAIT FUND FOR ARAB ECONOMIC DEVELOPMENT (PAMPHLET). ISLAM KUWAIT UAR ECO/UNDEV LEGIS ECO/TAC WEALTH 20. PAGE 74 F1452 — FOR/AID DIPLOM FINAN ADMIN

B56
WATT D.C.,BRITAIN AND THE SUEZ CANAL. COM UAR UK ...INT/LAW 20 SUEZ TREATY. PAGE 144 F2835 — DIPLOM INT/TRADE DIST/IND NAT/G

B57
WARRINER D.,LAND REFORM AND DEVELOPMENT IN THE MIDDLE EAST: A STUDY OF EGYPT, SYRIA AND IRAQ. IRAQ ISLAM SYRIA UAR AGRI DIST/IND PLAN TEC/DEV DOMIN REV ATTIT WEALTH...SOC METH/CNCPT STAT OBS RECORD HIST/WRIT TREND GEN/LAWS FAO 20. PAGE 143 F2825 — ECO/UNDEV CONCPT

B58
SHAW S.J.,THE FINANCIAL AND ADMINISTRATIVE — FINAN

ORGANIZATION AND DEVELOPMENT OF OTTOMAN EGYPT 1517-1798. UAR LOC/G FORCES BUDGET INT/TRADE TAX EATING INCOME WEALTH...CHARTS BIBLIOG 16/18 OTTOMAN NAPOLEON/B. PAGE 120 F2371 — ADMIN GOV/REL CULTURE

B60
AUSTRUY J.,STRUCTURE ECONOMIQUE ET CIVILISATION: L'EGYPTE ET LE DESTIN ECONOMIQUE DE L'ISLAM. ISLAM UAR CREATE OP/RES ECO/TAC...SOC BIBLIOG 20 MUSLIM. PAGE 8 F0142 — ECO/UNDEV CULTURE STRUCT

B63
EL-NAGGAR S.,FOREIGN AID TO UNITED ARAB REPUBLIC. UAR USA+45 USSR AGRI FINAN INDUS FORCES EATING DEMAND...CHARTS METH/COMP 20 RESOURCE/N AID. PAGE 37 F0718 — FOR/AID ECO/UNDEV RECEIVE PLAN

B63
HYDE D.,THE PEACEFUL ASSAULT. COM UAR USSR ECO/DEV ECO/UNDEV NAT/G POL/PAR CAP/ISM PWR 20. PAGE 64 F1256 — MARXISM CONTROL ECO/TAC DIPLOM

B63
ISSAWI C.,EGYPT IN REVOLUTION: AN ECONOMIC ANALYSIS. ISLAM STRUCT ECO/UNDEV AGRI FINAN INDUS PLAN EXEC REV NAT/LISM ATTIT RIGID/FLEX WEALTH SOCISM...STAT FOR/TRADE WORK 20. PAGE 66 F1292 — NAT/G UAR

B63
LANGE O.,ECONOMIC DEVELOPMENT, PLANNING, AND INTERNATIONAL COOPERATION. UAR WOR+45 FINAN CAP/ISM PERS/REL 20. PAGE 75 F1476 — ECO/UNDEV DIPLOM INT/TRADE PLAN

B64
BALOGH T.,THE ECONOMIC IMPACT OF MONETARY AND COMMERCIAL INSTITUTIONS OF A EUROPEAN ORIGIN IN AFRICA. AFR UAR INDUS FOR/AID COLONIAL CONTROL ...NAT/COMP 20. PAGE 9 F0169 — TEC/DEV FINAN ECO/UNDEV ECO/TAC

B65
MACDONALD R.W.,THE LEAGUE OF ARAB STATES: A STUDY IN THE DYNAMICS OF REGIONAL ORGANIZATION. ISRAEL UAR USSR FINAN INT/ORG DELIB/GP ECO/TAC AGREE NEUTRAL ORD/FREE PWR...DECISION BIBLIOG 20 TREATY UN. PAGE 83 F1626 — ISLAM REGION DIPLOM ADMIN

B67
CHANDRASEKHAR S.,PROBLEMS OF ECONOMIC DEVELOPMENT. AFR INDIA PHILIPPINE UAR WOR+45 INDUS...GEOG SOC ANTHOL BIBLIOG 20 CHINJAP. PAGE 23 F0450 — ECO/UNDEV PLAN AGRI PROB/SOLV

B67
KARDOUCHE G.K.,THE UAR IN DEVELOPMENT. UAR ECO/TAC INT/TRADE BAL/PAY...STAT CHARTS BIBLIOG 20. PAGE 69 F1355 — FINAN MGT CAP/ISM ECO/UNDEV

B67
TANSKY L.,US AND USSR AID TO DEVELOPING COUNTRIES. INDIA TURKEY UAR USA+45 USSR FINAN PLAN TEC/DEV ADMIN WEALTH...TREND METH/COMP 20. PAGE 128 F2535 — FOR/AID ECO/UNDEV MARXISM CAP/ISM

S67
KENNY L.M.,"THE AFTERMATH OF DEFEAT IN EGYPT." ISLAM ISRAEL UAR UK USA+45 USSR INDUS FORCES ECO/TAC PRICE COERCE WEAPON COST ATTIT. PAGE 70 F1378 — WAR ECO/UNDEV DIPLOM POLICY

N67
US SENATE COMM ON FOREIGN REL,WAR OR PEACE IN THE MIDDLE EAST (PAMPHLET). GREECE ISLAM ISRAEL JORDAN UAR CHIEF PROB/SOLV FOR/AID WAR PWR 20 SENATE. PAGE 139 F2739 — DIPLOM FORCES PLAN

UAW....UNITED AUTO WORKERS

UDR....UNION POUR LA DEFENSE DE LA REPUBLIQUE (FRANCE)

UDY S.H. F2598

UGANDA....SEE ALSO AFR

S61
NYANZI S.,"THE EAST AFRICAN MARKET: FOR BETTER OF FOR WORSE." AFR TANZANIA UGANDA PROB/SOLV TARIFFS TAX BAL/PAY. PAGE 99 F1947 — ECO/TAC ECO/UNDEV INT/ORG INT/TRADE

S61
OCHENG D.,"ECONOMIC FORCES AND UGANDA'S FOREIGN POLICY." AFR UGANDA INT/TRADE TARIFFS INCOME SOVEREIGN WEALTH 20 EACM EEC TANGANYIKA. PAGE 100 F1961 — ECO/TAC DIPLOM ECO/UNDEV INT/ORG

L62
BELSHAW D.G.R.,"PUBLIC INVESTMENT IN AGRICULTURE AND ECONOMIC DEVELOPMENT OF UGANDA" UGANDA AGRI INDUS R+D ECO/TAC RATION TAX PAY COLONIAL 20 WORLD/BANK. PAGE 13 F0242 — ECO/UNDEV PLAN ADMIN CENTRAL

S62
GILL P.J.,"FUTURE TAXATION POLICY IN AN INDEPENDENT EAST AFRICA" UGANDA LOC/G ECO/TAC ADMIN EFFICIENCY INCOME PRODUC...CHARTS 20. PAGE 47 F0923 — ECO/UNDEV TAX AFR COLONIAL

S62
KRISHNA K.G.V.,"PLANNING AND ECONOMIC DEVELOPMENT" AFR UGANDA AGRI INDUS R+D BUDGET RATION TAX COLONIAL 20. PAGE 73 F1441 — ECO/UNDEV ECO/TAC NAT/LISM PLAN

C62
GREEN L.P.,"DEVELOPMENT IN AFRICA." RHODESIA SOUTH/AFR UGANDA MARKET PROC/MFG PRODUC WEALTH ...GEOG 20. PAGE 50 F0986 — BIBLIOG ECO/UNDEV AFR AGRI

S64
ROTHCHILD D.,"EAST AFRICAN FEDERATION." AFR TANZANIA UGANDA INDUS REGION 20. PAGE 114 F2249 — INT/ORG DIPLOM ECO/UNDEV ECO/TAC

B66
MACBEAN A.I.,EXPORT INSTABILITY AND ECONOMIC DEVELOPMENT. CHILE PAKISTAN PUERT/RICO TANZANIA UGANDA WOR+45 MARKET ECO/TAC...POLICY REGRESS CHARTS BIBLIOG TIME 20. PAGE 83 F1622 — INT/TRADE ECO/UNDEV ECOMETRIC INSPECT

B66
O'CONNER A.M.,AN ECONOMIC GEOGRAPHY OF EAST AFRICA. AFR TANZANIA UGANDA AGRI WORKER INT/TRADE COLONIAL GOV/REL...CHARTS METH/COMP 20 AFRICA/E. PAGE 99 F1953 — ECO/UNDEV EXTR/IND GEOG HABITAT

S66
FLEMING W.G.,"AUTHORITY, EFFICIENCY, AND ROLE STRESS: PROBLEMS IN THE DEVELOPMENT OF EAST AFRICAN BUREAUCRACIES." AFR UGANDA STRUCT PROB/SOLV ROUTINE INGP/REL ROLE...MGT SOC GP/COMP GOV/COMP 20 TANGANYIKA AFRICA/E. PAGE 41 F0810 — DOMIN EFFICIENCY COLONIAL ADMIN

S66
NEWLYN W.T.,"MONEY MARKETS IN EAST AFRICA." AFR TANZANIA UGANDA UK DIPLOM CENTRAL 20. PAGE 98 F1923 — FINAN WEALTH BAL/PAY ECO/UNDEV

S67
SCOTT R.,"TRADE UNIONS IN AFRICA." AFR UGANDA USA-45 ECO/UNDEV INDUS INT/ORG POL/PAR ECO/TAC WEALTH...GP/COMP 20 NKRUMAH/K. PAGE 118 F2335 — LABOR WORKER NAT/G

S67
THEROUX P.,"HATING THE ASIANS." TANZANIA UGANDA CONSTN INDUS NAT/G POL/PAR WORKER ECO/TAC HABITAT LOVE...POLICY GEOG 20 MIGRATION. PAGE 130 F2557 — AFR RACE/REL SOVEREIGN ATTIT

UK....UNITED KINGDOM; SEE ALSO APPROPRIATE TIME/SPACE/ CULTURE INDEX, COMMONWLTH

N
LONDON TIMES OFFICIAL INDEX. UK LAW ECO/DEV NAT/G DIPLOM LEAD ATTIT 20. PAGE 1 F0006 — BIBLIOG INDEX PRESS WRITING

N
MINISTRY OF OVERSEAS DEVELOPME,TECHNICAL CO-OPERATION -- A BIBLIOGRAPHY. UK LAW SOCIETY DIPLOM ECO/TAC FOR/AID...STAT 20 CMN/WLTH. PAGE 92 F1803 — BIBLIOG TEC/DEV ECO/DEV NAT/G

NCO
CARRINGTON C.E.,THE COMMONWEALTH IN AFRICA (PAMPHLET). UK STRUCT NAT/G COLONIAL REPRESENT GOV/REL RACE/REL NAT/LISM...MAJORIT 20 EEC NEGRO. PAGE 22 F0421 — ECO/UNDEV AFR DIPLOM PLAN

B02
MOREL E.D.,AFFAIRS OF WEST AFRICA. UK FINAN INDUS FAM KIN SECT CHIEF WORKER DIPLOM RACE/REL LITERACY HEALTH...CHARTS 18/20 AFRICA/W NEGRO. PAGE 93 F1826 — COLONIAL ADMIN AFR

B02
WEBB S.,THE HISTORY OF TRADE UNIONISM. UK PARTIC ...OBS CHARTS BIBLIOG/A 15/19 CASEBOOK. PAGE 144 F2837 — LABOR VOL/ASSN GP/REL

B03
MOREL E.D.,THE BRITISH CASE IN FRENCH CONGO. CONGO/BRAZ FRANCE UK COERCE MORAL WEALTH...POLICY INT/LAW 20 CONGO/LEOP. PAGE 93 F1827 — DIPLOM INT/TRADE COLONIAL AFR

B04
MARX K.,A CONTRIBUTION TO THE CRITIQUE OF POLITICAL ECONOMY (TRANS. FROM 2ND ED. BY N.I. STONE). UK STRATA ECO/DEV FINAN MARKET PLAN BARGAIN CAP/ISM ECO/TAC ATTIT WEALTH...METH/CNCPT BIOG 19. PAGE 86 F1687 — MARXIST NEW/IDEA MARXISM

B12
HOBSON J.A.,THE EVOLUTION OF MODERN CAPITALISM. MOD/EUR UK STRATA ECO/DEV INDUS INCOME UTIL WEALTH ...SOC GEN/LAWS 7/20. PAGE 60 F1184 — CAP/ISM WORKER TEC/DEV TIME/SEQ

B15
VEBLEN T.,IMPERIAL GERMANY AND THE INDUSTRIAL REVOLUTION. GERMANY MOD/EUR UK USA-45 NAT/G TEC/DEV CAP/ISM...MAJORIT NAT/COMP 19/20 CHINJAP. PAGE 141 F2769 — ECO/DEV INDUS TECHNIC BAL/PWR

N19
ADMINISTRATIVE STAFF COLLEGE,THE ACCOUNTABILITY OF GOVERNMENT DEPARTMENTS (PAMPHLET) (REV. ED.). UK CONSTN FINAN NAT/G CONSULT ADMIN INGP/REL CONSEN PRIVIL 20 PARLIAMENT. PAGE 2 F0043 — PARL/PROC ELITES SANCTION PROB/SOLV

N19
ANDERSON J.,THE ORGANIZATION OF ECONOMIC STUDIES IN RELATION TO THE PROBLEMS OF GOVERNMENT (PAMPHLET). UK FINAN INDUS DELIB/GP PLAN PROB/SOLV ADMIN 20. PAGE 5 F0095
ECO/TAC ACT/RES NAT/G CENTRAL

N19
BUSINESS ECONOMISTS' GROUP,INCOME POLICIES (PAMPHLET). UK INDUS LABOR TOP/EX PAY COST PRODUC ...ECOMETRIC GOV/COMP SIMUL ANTHOL 20. PAGE 20 F0395
INCOME WORKER WEALTH POLICY

N19
ENGELS F.,THE BRITISH LABOUR MOVEMENT (PAMPHLET). FRANCE GERMANY MOD/EUR UK USA-45 POL/PAR WORKER PAY EDU/PROP PRICE REPRESENT GP/REL 19. PAGE 37 F0730
ECO/TAC MARXISM LABOR STRATA

N19
GROSECLOSE E.,THE DECAY OF MONEY; A SURVEY OF WESTERN CURRENCIES 1912-1962 (PAMPHLET). AFR FRANCE GERMANY UK LAW INT/TRADE BAL/PAY COST EQUILIB ...POLICY 20 DEPRESSION. PAGE 51 F1004
FINAN NAT/G ECO/DEV ECO/TAC

B20
MALTHUS T.R.,PRINCIPLES OF POLITICAL ECONOMY. UK AGRI INDUS MARKET NAT/G DIPLOM PRICE CONTROL BAL/PAY COST OWN PWR LAISSEZ 18/19. PAGE 84 F1650
GEN/LAWS DEMAND WEALTH

B20
WEBB S.,INDUSTRIAL DEMOCRACY. UK PARTIC GP/REL ...SOC OBS RECORD CHARTS 18/20. PAGE 144 F2838
LABOR NAT/G VOL/ASSN MAJORIT

B23
FINER H.,REPRESENTATIVE GOVERNMENT AND A PARLIAMENT OF INDUSTRY. A STUDY OF THE GERMAN FEDERAL ECONOMIC COUNCIL. GERMANY UK CONSTN INDUS PARL/PROC ...NAT/COMP 20. PAGE 41 F0796
DELIB/GP ECO/TAC WAR REV

B24
HOLDSWORTH W.S.,A HISTORY OF ENGLISH LAW; THE COMMON LAW AND ITS RIVALS (VOL. VI). AFR UK STRATA EX/STRUC ADJUD ADMIN CONTROL CT/SYS...JURID CONCPT GEN/LAWS 17 PARLIAMENT ENGLSH/LAW COMMON/LAW. PAGE 61 F1194
LAW CONSTN LEGIS CHIEF

B24
HOLDSWORTH W.S.,A HISTORY OF ENGLISH LAW; THE COMMON LAW AND ITS RIVALS (VOL. IV). UK SEA AGRI CHIEF ADJUD CONTROL CRIME GOV/REL...INT/LAW JURID NAT/COMP 16/17 PARLIAMENT COMMON/LAW CANON/LAW ENGLSH/LAW. PAGE 61 F1195
LAW LEGIS CT/SYS CONSTN

B25
WILLIAMS B.,THE SELBORNE MEMORANDUM. AFR FUT SOUTH/AFR UK NAT/G BUDGET DIPLOM REGION GOV/REL SOVEREIGN...POLICY CHARTS 20 UNIFICA SELBORNE/W. PAGE 147 F2888
COLONIAL PROVS

B26
MCPHEE A.,THE ECONOMIC REVOLUTION IN BRITISH WEST AFRICA. AFR UK CULTURE DIST/IND FINAN INDUS PLAN GP/REL RACE/REL 20 AFRICA/W. PAGE 88 F1735
ECO/UNDEV INT/TRADE COLONIAL GEOG

B26
TAWNEY R.H.,RELIGION AND THE RISE OF CAPITALISM. UK CULTURE NAT/G TEC/DEV OWN LAISSEZ...POLICY SOC TIME/SEQ 16/19. PAGE 129 F2537
SECT WEALTH INDUS CAP/ISM

B27
BELLOC H.,THE SERVILE STATE (1912) (3RD ED.). PRUSSIA UK CULTURE STRATA INDUS NAT/G ECO/TAC CONTROL LEAD SUFF DISCRIM EQUILIB ORD/FREE WEALTH 20. PAGE 12 F0237
WORKER CAP/ISM DOMIN CATH

B27
SIEGFRIED A.,AMERICA COMES OF AGE: A FRENCH ANALYSIS (TRANS. BY H.H. HEMMING AND DORIS HEMMING). FRANCE UK POL/PAR WORKER TEC/DEV DIPLOM REGION RACE/REL ADJUST PRODUC HEREDITY...TIME/SEQ GP/COMP SOC/INTEG 20 DEMOCRAT REPUBLICAN KKK. PAGE 122 F2398
USA-45 CULTURE ECO/DEV SOC

B28
CASSEL G.,FOREIGN INVESTMENTS. GERMANY UK USA-45 WOR-45 ECO/DEV NAT/G VOL/ASSN CAP/ISM REPAR ATTIT WEALTH...METH/CNCPT STAT SIMUL STERTYP ANTHOL FOR/TRADE TOT/POP VAL/FREE 20. PAGE 22 F0426
FINAN ECO/TAC BAL/PAY

B30
FEIS H.,EUROPE, THE WORLD'S BANKER, 1871-1914. FRANCE GERMANY MOD/EUR UK WOR-45 NAT/G PLAN ECO/TAC EXEC ATTIT PWR WEALTH...CONCPT HIST/WRIT GEN/LAWS VAL/FREE 19/20. PAGE 40 F0773
FINAN DIPLOM INT/TRADE

B30
KEYNES J.M.,A TREATISE ON MONEY (2 VOLS.). UK USA-45 INDUS MARKET WORKER PRICE CONTROL COST OPTIMAL PROFIT WEALTH...POLICY 19/20 KEYNES/JM. PAGE 70 F1385
EQUILIB ECO/TAC FINAN GEN/LAWS

B31
CROOK W.H.,THE GENERAL STRIKE: A STUDY OF LABOR'S TRAGIC WEAPON IN THEORY AND PRACTICE. BELGIUM FRANCE SWEDEN UK WOR-45 PROB/SOLV ECO/TAC DOMIN PWR ...POLICY TIME/SEQ NAT/COMP GEN/LAWS 19/20 STRIKE. PAGE 29 F0555
LABOR WORKER LG/CO BARGAIN

B35
WADE J.,HISTORY OF THE MIDDLE AND WORKING CLASSES; WITH A POPULAR EXPOSITION OF THE ECONOMICAL AND POLITICAL PRINCIPLES.... FRANCE UK CONSTN FINAN INDUS LABOR INCOME PROFIT KNOWL MORAL ORD/FREE WEALTH...CHARTS 14/19. PAGE 142 F2797
WORKER STRATA CONCPT

B36
BELLOC H.,THE RESTORATION OF PROPERTY. UK STRATA NAT/G PROF/ORG DELIB/GP WORKER CREATE PROB/SOLV ECO/TAC PARTIC UTOPIA ORD/FREE SOCISM 20. PAGE 13 F0238
CONTROL MAJORIT CAP/ISM OWN

B38
DAVIES E.,"NATIONAL" CAPITALISM: THE GOVERNMENT'S RECORD AS PROTECTOR OF PRIVATE MONOPOLY. UK ELITES SOCIETY STRATA POL/PAR WORKER PROB/SOLV CONTROL SOCISM 20 MONOPOLY LABOR/PAR CHAMBRLN/N. PAGE 30 F0583
CAP/ISM NAT/G INDUS POLICY

B38
HOBSON J.A.,IMPERIALISM. MOD/EUR UK WOR-45 CULTURE ECO/UNDEV NAT/G VOL/ASSN PLAN EDU/PROP LEGIT REGION COERCE ATTIT PWR...POLICY PLURIST TIME/SEQ GEN/LAWS TERR/GP 19/20. PAGE 60 F1187
DOMIN ECO/TAC BAL/PWR COLONIAL

S38
HALL R.C.,"REPRESENTATION OF BIG BUSINESS IN THE HOUSE OF COMMONS." UK ECO/DEV INDUS PROF/ORG LEGIS CAP/ISM ECO/TAC LAISSEZ...POLICY OLD/LIB PLURIST MGT 20 HOUSE/CMNS. PAGE 53 F1047
LOBBY NAT/G

B39
JENNINGS W.I.,PARLIAMENT. UK POL/PAR OP/RES BUDGET LEAD CHOOSE GP/REL...MGT 20 PARLIAMENT HOUSE/LORD HOUSE/CMNS. PAGE 67 F1315
PARL/PROC LEGIS CONSTN NAT/G

B39
THOMAS J.A.,THE HOUSE OF COMMONS, 1832-1901; A STUDY OF ITS ECONOMIC AND FUNCTIONAL CHARACTER. UK LAW STRATA FINAN DIPLOM CONTROL LEAD LOBBY REPRESENT WEALTH...POLICY STAT BIBLIOG 19/20 PARLIAMENT. PAGE 130 F2561
PARL/PROC LEGIS POL/PAR ECO/DEV

B40
SPENCER H.,THE MAN VS. THE STATE (1892). UK POL/PAR LEGIS TARIFFS COERCE CRIME REPRESENT PWR SOCISM ...POLICY GEN/LAWS 19/20. PAGE 124 F2450
FASCISM POPULISM LAISSEZ ORD/FREE

B41
HANSEN A.H.,FISCAL POLICY AND BUSINESS CYCLES. UK INDUS PROB/SOLV DIPLOM INT/TRADE OPTIMAL...POLICY TIME/SEQ CHARTS 19/20. PAGE 54 F1062
FINAN PLAN ECO/TAC GOV/REL

B41
LESTER R.A.,ECONOMICS OF LABOR. UK USA-45 TEC/DEV BARGAIN PAY INGP/REL INCOME...MGT 19/20. PAGE 78 F1532
LABOR ECO/DEV INDUS WORKER

B42
JACKSON M.V.,EUROPEAN POWERS AND SOUTH-EAST AFRICA: A STUDY OF INTERNATIONAL RELATIONS ON SOUTH-EAST COAST OF AFRICA, 1796-1856. AFR FRANCE PORTUGAL SOUTH/AFR UK USA-45 FORCES INT/TRADE PWR...CHARTS BIBLIOG 18/19 TREATY. PAGE 66 F1294
DOMIN POLICY ORD/FREE DIPLOM

B44
FABIAN SOCIETY,CAN PLANNING BE DEMOCRATIC? UK CULTURE INDUS NAT/G BUDGET ORD/FREE...GEN/LAWS ANTHOL 20. PAGE 39 F0757
PLAN MAJORIT SOCIALIST ECO/DEV

B44
INTL CHAMBER OF COMMERCE,TERMS COMMONLY USED IN DISTRIBUTION AND ADVERTISING. PORTUGAL SPAIN UK WOR-45 SERV/IND 20. PAGE 65 F1284
DICTIONARY EDU/PROP DIST/IND INT/TRADE

B44
LOCKE J.,FURTHER CONSIDERATIONS CONCERNING RAISING THE VALUE OF MONEY. AFR UK NAT/G ECO/TAC INCOME WEALTH...METH/COMP GEN/LAWS 17 SILVER. PAGE 81 F1591
COST FINAN PRICE CONTROL

B44
MCFADYEAN A.,GOVERNMENT AND INDUSTRY (PAMPHLET). UK INDUS CONTROL REPRESENT 20. PAGE 88 F1728
POL/PAR SOCISM

B46
DAVIES E.,NATIONAL ENTERPRISE: THE DEVELOPMENT OF THE PUBLIC CORPORATION. UK LG/CO EX/STRUC WORKER PROB/SOLV COST ATTIT SOCISM 20. PAGE 30 F0584
ADMIN NAT/G CONTROL INDUS

B47
ENKE S.,INTERNATIONAL ECONOMICS. UK USA+45 USSR INT/ORG BAL/PWR BARGAIN CAP/ISM BAL/PAY...NAT/COMP 20 TREATY. PAGE 38 F0735
INT/TRADE FINAN TARIFFS ECO/TAC

S47
DAHL R.A.,"WORKERS' CONTROL OF INDUSTRY AND THE BRITISH LABOUR PARTY." UK STRATA STRUCT DELIB/GP BARGAIN CAP/ISM DEBATE CONTROL CHOOSE GP/REL ATTIT ROLE PWR 19/20 PARLIAMENT LABOR/PAR FABIAN. PAGE 29 F0570
INDUS LABOR WORKER SOCISM

B48
KEIR D.L.,CASES IN CONSTITUTIONAL LAW. UK CHIEF LEGIS DIPLOM TAX PARL/PROC CRIME GOV/REL...INT/LAW JURID 17/20. PAGE 70 F1368
CONSTN LAW ADJUD CT/SYS

B49
DE JOUVENEL B.,PROBLEMS OF SOCIALIST ENGLAND. AFR UK USSR BAL/PWR ECO/TAC INT/TRADE PRICE WAR BAL/PAY PEACE 20. PAGE 31 F0601
SOCISM NEW/LIB PROB/SOLV PLAN

B50
HUTCHISON K.,THE DECLINE AND FALL OF BRITISH CAPITALISM. UK ELITES STRATA ECO/DEV LABOR WORKER CONTROL WAR PWR...BIBLIOG/A 19/20. PAGE 63 F1249
CAP/ISM SOCISM LAISSEZ DOMIN

B51
COOKE C.A.,CORPORATION TRUST AND COMPANY: AN ESSAY IN LEGAL HISTORY. UK STRUCT LEGIS CAP/ISM GP/REL PROFIT 13/20 COMPNY/ACT. PAGE 27 F0531
LG/CO FINAN ECO/TAC JURID

B51
HALEVY E.,IMPERIALISM AND THE RISE OF LABOR (2ND ED.). UK NAT/G POL/PAR TOP/EX ATTIT ORD/FREE PWR 19/20 PARLIAMENT LABOR/PAR. PAGE 53 F1042
COLONIAL LABOR POLICY WAR

B51
HARROD R.F.,THE LIFE OF JOHN MAYNARD KEYNES. UK INTELL FAM CAP/ISM DIPLOM ECO/TAC WAR ATTIT PERSON ROLE 20 KEYNES/JM WWI. PAGE 56 F1094
BIOG FINAN GEN/LAWS

B52
DE JOUVENEL B.,THE ETHICS OF REDISTRIBUTION. UK ELITES MARKET WORKER GIVE PAY INCOME PERSON ...POLICY PSY GEN/LAWS 20. PAGE 31 F0602
WEALTH TAX SOCISM TRADIT

B52
GOLDSTEIN J.,THE GOVERNMENT OF BRITISH TRADE UNIONS. UK ECO/DEV EX/STRUC INGP/REL...BIBLIOG 20. PAGE 48 F0940
LABOR PARTIC

B52
JENNINGS W.I.,CONSTITUTIONAL LAWS OF THE COMMONWEALTH. AFR UK LAW CHIEF LEGIS TAX CT/SYS PARL/PROC GOV/REL...INT/LAW 18/20 ENGLSH/LAW COMMON/LAW. PAGE 67 F1316
CONSTN JURID ADJUD COLONIAL

C52
HUME D.,"OF TAXES" IN D. HUME, POLITICAL DISCOURSES (1752)" UK NAT/G COST INCOME LAISSEZ...GEN/LAWS 18. PAGE 63 F1236
TAX FINAN WEALTH POLICY

C52
HUME D.,"OF THE BALANCE OF TRADE" IN D. HUME, POLITICAL DISCOURSES (1752)" UK FINAN NAT/G TARIFFS PRICE PWR LAISSEZ...POLICY GEN/LAWS 18. PAGE 63 F1237
BAL/PAY INT/TRADE DIPLOM WEALTH

C52
HUME D.,"OF COMMERCE" IN D. HUME, POLITICAL DISCOURSES (1752)" UK FINAN DIPLOM WEALTH ...GEN/LAWS 18 MONEY. PAGE 63 F1238
INDUS INT/TRADE PWR AGRI

C52
HUME D.,"OF INTEREST" IN D. HUME, POLITICAL DISCOURSES (1752)" UK INDUS WORKER DIPLOM PAY DEMAND INCOME WEALTH...GEN/LAWS 18 MONEY. PAGE 63 F1239
PRICE COST FINAN INT/TRADE

C52
HUME D.,"OF MONEY" IN D. HUME, POLITICAL DISCOURSES (1752)" UK INDUS DIPLOM INT/TRADE...GEN/LAWS 18 MONEY. PAGE 63 F1240
FINAN COST PRICE WEALTH

B53
FLORENCE P.S.,THE LOGIC OF BRITISH AND AMERICAN INDUSTRY; A REALISTIC ANALYSIS OF ECONOMIC STRUCTURE AND GOVERNMENT. UK USA+45 USA-45 FINAN LABOR CAP/ISM INGP/REL EFFICIENCY...MGT CONCPT STAT CHARTS METH 20. PAGE 42 F0813
INDUS ECO/DEV NAT/G NAT/COMP

B53
NEISSER H.,NATIONAL INCOMES AND INTERNATIONAL TRADE. FRANCE GERMANY SWEDEN UK USA-45 EXTR/IND FINAN INDUS TEC/DEV PRICE BAL/PAY EQUILIB INCOME WEALTH...CHARTS METH 19 CHINJAP. PAGE 97 F1908
INT/TRADE PRODUC MARKET CON/ANAL

B53
ROBINSON E.A.G.,THE STRUCTURE OF COMPETITIVE INDUSTRY. UK ECO/DEV DIST/IND MARKET TEC/DEV DIPLOM EDU/PROP ADMIN EFFICIENCY WEALTH...MGT 19/20. PAGE 113 F2217
INDUS PRODUC WORKER OPTIMAL

L53
NELSON J.R.,"UNITED STATES FOREIGN ECONOMIC POLICY AND THE STERLING AREA." USA-45 WOR+45 WOR-45 NAT/G ECO/TAC WEALTH...STAT TIME/SEQ TREND CHARTS METH/GP TERR/GP CMN/WLTH 20. PAGE 97 F1911
FINAN DIPLOM UK

B54
KARTUN D.,AFRICA, AFRICA: A CONTINENT RISES TO ITS FEET. AFR SOUTH/AFR UK ELITES AGRI LABOR LOC/G POL/PAR EDU/PROP CONTROL COERCE DISCRIM AGE/Y NEGRO THIRD/WRLD GOLD/COAST. PAGE 69 F1358
COLONIAL ORD/FREE PROFIT EXTR/IND

B54
MEYER F.V.,INFLATION AND CAPITAL. AFR UK WOR+45 BUDGET GOV/REL INCOME PRODUC PROFIT WEALTH...CONCPT CHARTS 20. PAGE 90 F1768
ECO/DEV FINAN ECO/TAC DEMAND

B54
REYNOLDS P.A.,BRITISH FOREIGN POLICY IN THE INTER-WAR YEARS. CZECHOSLVK GERMANY POLAND UK USA-45 POL/PAR FORCES ECO/TAC ARMS/CONT WAR ATTIT 20. PAGE 111 F2182
DIPLOM POLICY NAT/G

B55
COLE G.D.H.,STUDIES IN CLASS STRUCTURE. UK NAT/G WORKER TEC/DEV EDU/PROP...CLASSIF CHARTS 20. PAGE 26 F0501
STRUCT STRATA ELITES CONCPT

B55
FLORINSKY M.T.,INTEGRATED EUROPE. EUR+WWI FRANCE ITALY NETHERLAND UK ECO/DEV INT/ORG FORCES LEGIT FEDERAL ATTIT PWR WEALTH...POLICY GEOG CONCPT GEN/LAWS TOT/POP EEC OEEC 20. PAGE 42 F0816
FUT ECO/TAC REGION

B55
FOGARTY M.P.,ECONOMIC CONTROL. FUT UK ECO/DEV FINAN CONSULT INT/TRADE...CHARTS BIBLIOG/A 20. PAGE 42 F0819
ECO/TAC NAT/G CONTROL PROB/SOLV

B56
BELL P.W.,THE STERLING AREA IN THE POSTWAR WORLD. EUR+WWI FUT S/ASIA UK ECO/DEV PLAN DIPLOM WEALTH ...STAT RECORD CHARTS GEN/LAWS FOR/TRADE TOT/POP 20. PAGE 12 F0235
FINAN ECO/TAC

B56
WATT D.C.,BRITAIN AND THE SUEZ CANAL. COM UAR UK ...INT/LAW 20 SUEZ TREATY. PAGE 144 F2835
DIPLOM INT/TRADE DIST/IND NAT/G

B57
ARON R.,L'UNIFICATION ECONOMIQUE DE L'EUROPE. EUR+WWI SWITZERLND UK INT/ORG NAT/G REGION NAT/LISM ORD/FREE PWR...CONCPT METH/CNCPT OBS TREND STERTYP GEN/LAWS EEC FOR/TRADE 20. PAGE 6 F0118
VOL/ASSN ECO/TAC

B57
INTL BANKING SUMMER SCHOOL,RELATIONS BETWEEN THE CENTRAL BANKS AND COMMERCIAL BANKS. EUR+WWI FRANCE GERMANY/W ITALY UK USA+45 USSR INDUS INT/ORG CAP/ISM CONTROL MONEY. PAGE 65 F1282
FINAN NAT/G GP/REL LG/CO

B57
LOUCKS W.N.,COMPARATIVE ECONOMIC SYSTEMS (5TH ED.). COM UK USSR INDUS POL/PAR PLAN CAP/ISM TOTALISM MARXISM...PHIL/SCI BIBLIOG 19/20. PAGE 82 F1603
NAT/COMP IDEA/COMP SOCISM

B57
MURDESHWAR A.K.,ADMINISTRATIVE PROBLEMS RELATING TO NATIONALISATION: WITH SPECIAL REFERENCE TO INDIAN STATE ENTERPRISES. CZECHOSLVK FRANCE INDIA UK USA+45 LEGIS WORKER PROB/SOLV BUDGET PRICE CONTROL ...MGT GEN/LAWS 20 PARLIAMENT. PAGE 95 F1863
NAT/G OWN INDUS ADMIN

B57
WATSON G.,THE UNSERVILE STATE: ESSAYS IN LIBERTY AND WELFARE. UK LEGIS RECEIVE EDU/PROP COLONIAL ...WELF/ST 20 LIB/PARTY. PAGE 144 F2833
POL/PAR ORD/FREE CONTROL NEW/LIB

B58
CLAIRMONTE F.,LE LIBERALISME ECONOMIQUE ET LES PAYS SOUS-DEVELOPPES: ETUDES SUR L'EVOLUTION D'UNE IDEE. ASIA INDIA UK FINAN INDUS PLAN CAP/ISM ECO/TAC COLONIAL NEW/LIB...BIBLIOG 20 THIRD/WRLD. PAGE 24 F0475
LAISSEZ ECO/UNDEV

B58
COLE G.D.H.,COMMUNISM AND SOCIAL DEMOCRACY (VOL. IV OF "HISTORY OF SOCIAL THOUGHT"). COM GERMANY ITALY UK AGRI INT/ORG WORKER DIPLOM COLONIAL NAT/LISM ALL/IDEOS...BIBLIOG 20 LEAGUE/NAT AUST/HUNG. PAGE 26 F0502
MARXISM REV POL/PAR SOCISM

B58
CROWE S.,THE LANDSCAPE OF POWER. UK CULTURE SERV/IND NAT/G CONSULT PARTIC NUC/PWR LEISURE...SOC EXHIBIT 20. PAGE 29 F0559
HABITAT TEC/DEV PLAN CONTROL

B58
FINER S.E.,PRIVATE INDUSTRY AND POLITICAL POWER (PAMPHLET). UK INDUS CONTROL LOBBY PWR. PAGE 41 F0797
PLURISM REPRESENT EX/STRUC

B58
ROBERTS B.C.,NATIONAL WAGES POLICY IN WAR AND PEACE. EUR+WWI GERMANY S/ASIA SWEDEN UK USA+45 USA-45 STRATA ECO/DEV LABOR NAT/G DELIB/GP PLAN INT/TRADE WEALTH...STAT TREND CHARTS 20. PAGE 112 F2205
CREATE ECO/TAC

B59
HICKS J.R.,ESSAYS IN WORLD ECONOMICS. AFR CEYLON NIGERIA WOR+45 SOCIETY ECO/DEV ORD/FREE WEALTH ...GEN/LAWS TOT/POP 20. PAGE 59 F1166
ECO/UNDEV ECO/TAC UK

B59
JENKINS C.,POWER AT THE TOP: A CRITICAL SURVEY OF THE NATIONALIZED INDUSTRIES. UK POL/PAR CONTROL ...WELF/ST CHARTS 20 LABOR/PAR. PAGE 67 F1313
NAT/G OWN INDUS NEW/LIB

B59
KELF-COHEN R.,NATIONALISATION IN BRITAIN: THE END OF DOGMA. EUR+WWI UK NAT/G POL/PAR WORKER ECO/TAC PARL/PROC WEALTH SOCISM...GOV/COMP 20. PAGE 70 F1369
NEW/LIB ECO/DEV INDUS OWN

B59
LINK R.G.,ENGLISH THEORIES OF ECONOMIC
IDEA/COMP

FLUCTUATIONS: 1815-1848. FRANCE UK AGRI WORKER DIPLOM PRICE TASK WAR DEMAND PRODUC...POLICY BIBLIOG 18 MALTHUS MILL/JS WILSON/J. PAGE 80 F1574
ECO/DEV WEALTH EQUILIB

B59
MADHOK B.,POLITICAL TRENDS IN INDIA. INDIA PAKISTAN UK STRATA ECO/UNDEV POL/PAR LEGIS CAP/ISM DIPLOM COLONIAL CHOOSE MARXISM...SOC TREND 20 GANDHI/M NEHRU/J. PAGE 84 F1639
GEOG NAT/G

B59
MARTIN K.,WAR, HISTORY, AND HUMAN NATURE. FRANCE GERMANY INDIA UK UNIV POL/PAR COLONIAL DETER REV MARXISM PACIFISM...PSY CONCPT PREDICT LENIN/VI GANDHI/M. PAGE 86 F1683
PERSON WAR ATTIT IDEA/COMP

B59
MORGENSTERN O.,INTERNATIONAL FINANCIAL TRANSACTIONS AND BUSINESS CYCLES. FRANCE GERMANY UK USA+45 USA-45 WOR+45 WOR-45 ECO/DEV ECO/TAC WEALTH ...CONCPT STAT CON/ANAL CHARTS 19/20. PAGE 93 F1832
FINAN TIME/SEQ INT/TRADE

B59
RAMANADHAM V.V.,PROBLEMS OF PUBLIC ENTERPRISE: THOUGHTS ON BRITISH EXPERIENCE. UK FINAN INDUS PLAN PRICE CENTRAL...POLICY 20. PAGE 109 F2140
SOCISM LG/CO ECO/DEV GOV/REL

B59
VERNEY D.V.,PUBLIC ENTERPRISE IN SWEDEN. FUT SWEDEN UK INDUS POL/PAR LEGIS PROB/SOLV CAP/ISM INT/TRADE CONTROL SOCISM...MGT CONCPT NAT/COMP 20 SOCDEM/PAR CIVIL/SERV. PAGE 141 F2778
ECO/DEV POLICY LG/CO NAT/G

B59
WIBBERLEY G.P.,AGRICULTURE AND URBAN GROWTH. UK USA+45 ECO/DEV FINAN PROB/SOLV INT/TRADE COST ...GEOG STAT CHARTS METH/COMP HYPO/EXP METH MUNICH 20. PAGE 146 F2876
AGRI PLAN

S59
ALLEN G.,"NATIONAL FARMERS UNION AS A PRESSURE GROUP: II." UK ECO/DEV MARKET POL/PAR DELIB/GP PROB/SOLV ECO/TAC LOBBY INCOME...POLICY METH/COMP 19/20 NAT/FARMER. PAGE 4 F0069
DIST/IND AGRI PROF/ORG TREND

S59
BENDIX R.,"INDUSTRIALIZATION, IDEOLOGIES, AND SOCIAL STRUCTURE" (BMR)" UK USA-45 USSR STRUCT WORKER GP/REL EFFICIENCY...IDEA/COMP 20. PAGE 13 F0243
INDUS ATTIT MGT ADMIN

S59
SHEENAN D.,"PUBLIC CORPORATIONS AND PUBLIC ACTION." UK ADMIN CONTROL REPRESENT SOCISM 20. PAGE 120 F2372
ECO/DEV EFFICIENCY EX/STRUC EXEC

S59
STREAT R.,"GOVERNMENT CONSULTATION WITH INDUSTRY." UK 20. PAGE 127 F2501
REPRESENT ADMIN EX/STRUC INDUS

S59
STREETEN P.,"UNBALANCED GROWTH" UK ECO/DEV AGRI MARKET TEC/DEV CAP/ISM ECO/TAC FOR/AID INT/TRADE DEMAND ORD/FREE...CONCPT 20. PAGE 127 F2502
IDEA/COMP FINAN PRODUC EQUILIB

B60
BELLAN R.C.,PRINCIPLES OF ECONOMICS AND THE CANADIAN ECONOMY (2ND ED.). CANADA UK USA+45 LABOR WORKER CAP/ISM INT/TRADE RISK BAL/PAY EQUILIB ALL/IDEOS 20. PAGE 12 F0236
ECO/DEV PRODUC WEALTH FINAN

B60
GRAMPP W.D.,THE MANCHESTER SCHOOL OF ECONOMICS. UK LAW ECO/DEV COERCE ATTIT ORD/FREE LAISSEZ ...PHIL/SCI IDEA/COMP 19/20 MANCHESTER CORN/LAWS. PAGE 50 F0973
ECO/TAC VOL/ASSN LOBBY NAT/G

B60
HOSELITZ B.F.,THEORIES OF ECONOMIC GROWTH. UK WOR+45 WOR-45 ECO/UNDEV PLAN INT/TRADE KNOWL ...CONCPT METH/CNCPT TIME/SEQ GEN/LAWS TOT/POP. PAGE 62 F1220
ECO/DEV INTELL

B60
KENEN P.B.,BRITISH MONETARY POLICY AND THE BALANCE OF PAYMENTS 1951-57. UK PLAN BUDGET ECO/TAC INT/TRADE PAY PRICE COST ATTIT 20. PAGE 70 F1377
BAL/PAY PROB/SOLV FINAN NAT/G

B60
LATIFI D.,INDIA AND UNITED STATES AID. ASIA INDIA UK USA+45 AGRI FINAN INDUS COLONIAL ORD/FREE SOVEREIGN WEALTH...METH/COMP 20. PAGE 76 F1486
FOR/AID DIPLOM ECO/UNDEV

B60
MARSHALL A.H.,FINANCIAL ADMINISTRATION IN LOCAL GOVERNMENT. UK DELIB/GP CONFER COST INCOME PERSON ...JURID 20. PAGE 86 F1679
FINAN LOC/G BUDGET ADMIN

B60
POOLEY B.J.,THE EVOLUTION OF BRITISH PLANNING LEGISLATION. UK ECO/DEV LOC/G CONSULT DELIB/GP ADMIN MUNICH 20 URBAN/RNWL. PAGE 107 F2104
PLAN LEGIS PROB/SOLV

B60
ROBERTSON D.,THE CONTROL OF INDUSTRY. UK MARKET LABOR WORKER PRICE CONTROL GP/REL COST DEMAND ORD/FREE WEALTH NEW/LIB SOCISM 20. PAGE 112 F2211
INDUS FINAN NAT/G ECO/DEV

B60
ROBSON W.A.,NATIONALIZED INDUSTRY AND PUBLIC OWNERSHIP. UK ECO/DEV FINAN LABOR LG/CO POL/PAR LEGIS ACT/RES GP/REL...TREND IDEA/COMP 20. PAGE 113 F2227
NAT/G OWN INDUS ATTIT

B60
ROSTOW W.W.,THE STAGES OF ECONOMIC GROWTH. UK USA+45 USSR WOR+45 WOR-45 ECO/DEV PERSON MARXISM ...METH/CNCPT TIME/SEQ GEN/LAWS GEN/METH 20. PAGE 114 F2246
ECO/UNDEV NEW/IDEA CAP/ISM

B60
WEINER H.E.,BRITISH LABOR AND PUBLIC OWNERSHIP. UK SERV/IND LG/CO WORKER CONTROL OWN 20. PAGE 145 F2850
LABOR NAT/G INDUS ATTIT

B60
WHEARE K.C.,THE CONSTITUTIONAL STRUCTURE OF THE COMMONWEALTH. UK EX/STRUC DIPLOM DOMIN ADMIN COLONIAL CONTROL LEAD INGP/REL SUPEGO 20 CMN/WLTH. PAGE 145 F2865
CONSTN INT/ORG VOL/ASSN SOVEREIGN

S60
KREININ M.E.,"THE 'OUTER-SEVEN' AND EUROPEAN INTEGRATION." EUR+WWI FRANCE GERMANY ITALY UK ECO/DEV DIST/IND INT/TRADE DRIVE WEALTH...MYTH CHARTS EEC OEEC 20. PAGE 73 F1436
ECO/TAC GEN/LAWS

B61
AGARWAL R.C.,STATE ENTERPRISE IN INDIA. FUT INDIA UK FINAN INDUS ADMIN CONTROL OWN...POLICY CHARTS BIBLIOG 20 RAILROAD. PAGE 3 F0048
ECO/UNDEV SOCISM GOV/REL LG/CO

B61
ASCHHEIM J.,TECHNIQUES OF MONETARY CONTROL. UK USA+45 CONTROL WAR DEMAND INCOME WEALTH...TREND CHARTS 20 MONEY. PAGE 7 F0127
FINAN MARKET BUDGET CENTRAL

B61
FLINN M.W.,AN ECONOMIC AND SOCIAL HISTORY OF BRITAIN, 1066-1939. UK LAW STRATA STRUCT AGRI DIST/IND INDUS WORKER INT/TRADE WAR...CENSUS 11/20. PAGE 42 F0811
SOCIETY SOC

B61
KITZINGER V.W.,THE CHALLENGE OF THE COMMON MARKET. EUR+WWI ECO/DEV DIST/IND PLAN ECO/TAC INT/TRADE LEGIT ATTIT PWR WEALTH...TIME/SEQ TREND CHARTS EEC 20. PAGE 71 F1403
MARKET INT/ORG UK

B61
KLEIN L.R.,AN ECONOMETRIC MODEL OF THE UNITED KINGDOM. UK PRICE COST...MATH PREDICT TREND CHARTS SIMUL METH 20. PAGE 72 F1407
ECOMETRIC COMPUTER STAT COMPUT/IR

B61
LANDSKROY W.A.,OFFICIAL SERIAL PUBLICATIONS RELATING TO ECONOMIC DEVELOPMENT IN AFRICA SOUTH OF THE SAHARA (PAMPHLET). AFR UK R+D ACT/RES 20 UN. PAGE 75 F1471
BIBLIOG ECO/UNDEV COLONIAL INT/ORG

B61
SCHNAPPER B.,LA POLITIQUE ET LE COMMERCE FRANCAIS DANS LE GOLFE DE GUINEE DE 1838 A 1871. FRANCE GUINEA UK SEA EXTR/IND NAT/G DELIB/GP LEGIS ADMIN ORD/FREE...POLICY GEOG CENSUS CHARTS BIBLIOG 19. PAGE 117 F2303
COLONIAL INT/TRADE DOMIN AFR

B61
STARNER F.L.,GENERAL OBLIGATION BOND FINANCING BY LOCAL GOVERNMENTS: A SURVEY OF STATE CONTROLS. CANADA UK USA+45 CONSTN PROVS...POLICY JURID METH/COMP 20 EUROPE CALIFORNIA. PAGE 125 F2471
FINAN LOC/G GOV/REL ADJUD

B61
WARD B.J.,INDIA AND THE WEST. INDIA UK USA+45 INT/TRADE GIVE COLONIAL ATTIT MARXISM 19/20. PAGE 143 F2817
PLAN ECO/UNDEV ECO/TAC FOR/AID

S61
DICKS-MIREAUX L.A.,"THE INTERRELATIONSHIP BETWEEN COST AND PRICE CHANGES 19461959: A STUDY OF INFLATION IN POST-WAR BRITAIN" AFR UK ECO/DEV INDUS WORKER ECO/TAC ORD/FREE WEALTH...ECOMETRIC REGRESS STAT TREND CHARTS 20. PAGE 33 F0634
PRICE PAY DEMAND

S61
RAY J.,"THE EUROPEAN FREE-TRADE ASSOCIATION AND ITS IMPACT ON INDIA'S TRADE." EUR+WWI FRANCE GERMANY INDIA S/ASIA UK NAT/G VOL/ASSN PLAN INT/TRADE ROUTINE WEALTH...STAT CHARTS TERR/GP CMN/WLTH EEC FOR/TRADE OEEC 20 EFTA. PAGE 109 F2155
ECO/DEV ECO/TAC

B62
DOBB M.,CAPITALISM YESTERDAY AND TODAY. UK WORKER WAR PRODUC PROFIT 18/20 MONOPOLY. PAGE 33 F0646
CAP/ISM TIME/SEQ CONCPT ECO/TAC

B62
FORD A.G.,THE GOLD STANDARD 1880-1914: BRITAIN AND ARGENTINA. AFR UK ECO/UNDEV INT/TRADE ADMIN GOV/REL DEMAND EFFICIENCY...STAT CHARTS 19/20 ARGEN. PAGE 42 F0823
FINAN ECO/TAC BUDGET BAL/PAY

B62
FRIEDMANN W.,METHODS AND POLICIES OF PRINCIPAL DONOR COUNTRIES IN PUBLIC INTERNATIONAL DEVELOPMENT
INT/ORG FOR/AID

FINANCING: PRELIMINARY APPRAISAL. FRANCE GERMANY/W NAT/COMP
UK USA+45 USSR WOR+45 FINAN TEC/DEV CAP/ISM DIPLOM ADMIN
ECO/TAC ATTIT 20 EEC. PAGE 44 F0864

B62

GRANICK D.,THE EUROPEAN EXECUTIVE. BELGIUM FRANCE MGT
GERMANY/W UK INDUS LABOR LG/CO SML/CO EX/STRUC PLAN ECO/DEV
TEC/DEV CAP/ISM COST DEMAND...POLICY CHARTS 20. ECO/TAC
PAGE 50 F0977 EXEC

B62

GROVE J.W.,GOVERNMENT AND INDUSTRY IN BRITAIN. UK ECO/TAC
FINAN LOC/G CONSULT DELIB/GP INT/TRADE ADMIN INDUS
CONTROL...BIBLIOG 20. PAGE 52 F1008 NAT/G
GP/REL

B62

GWYN W.B.,DEMOCRACY AND THE COST OF POLITICS IN COST
BRITAIN. UK BUDGET CRIME CHOOSE ORD/FREE WEALTH POL/PAR
...TIME/SEQ 18/20. PAGE 52 F1017 POPULISM
PAY

B62

HENDERSON W.O.,THE GENESIS OF THE COMMON MARKET. ECO/DEV
EUR+WWI FRANCE MOD/EUR UK SEA COM/IND EXTR/IND INT/TRADE
COLONIAL DISCRIM...TIME/SEQ CHARTS BIBLIOG 18/20 DIPLOM
EEC TREATY. PAGE 58 F1149

B62

HOOVER C.B.,ECONOMIC SYSTEMS OF THE COMMONWEALTH. CAP/ISM
AFR CANADA INDIA UK ECO/DEV ECO/UNDEV AGRI INDUS SOCISM
TEC/DEV TARIFFS PRICE BAL/PAY DEMAND...SIMUL 20 ECO/TAC
AUSTRAL. PAGE 61 F1208 PLAN

B62

LIPPMANN W.,WESTERN UNITY AND THE COMMON MARKET. DIPLOM
EUR+WWI FRANCE GERMANY/W UK USA+45 ECO/DEV AGRI INT/TRADE
FINAN MARKET INT/ORG NAT/G FOR/AID AGREE WEALTH 20 VOL/ASSN
EEC. PAGE 80 F1575

B62

MCCRONE G.,THE ECONOMICS OF SUBSIDING AGRICULTURE. AGRI
UK ECO/DEV MARKET PLAN TARIFFS PROFIT 20 EEC. BAL/PAY
PAGE 88 F1725 INT/TRADE
LABOR

B62

PAKISTAN MINISTRY OF FINANCE,FOREIGN ECONOMIC AID: FOR/AID
A REVIEW OF FOREIGN ECONOMIC AID TO PAKISTAN. RECEIVE
EUR+WWI PAKISTAN UK USA+45 USSR ECO/UNDEV INT/ORG WEALTH
DELIB/GP DIPLOM ECO/TAC...CHARTS CMN/WLTH CHINJAP. FINAN
PAGE 103 F2016

B62

PRAKASH O.M.,THE THEORY AND WORKING OF STATE LG/CO
CORPORATIONS: WITH SPECIAL REFERENCE TO INDIA. ECO/UNDEV
INDIA UK USA+45 TOP/EX PRICE ADMIN EFFICIENCY...MGT GOV/REL
METH/COMP 20 TVA. PAGE 107 F2112 SOCISM

B62

ROBERTSON B.C.,REGIONAL DEVELOPMENT IN THE EUROPEAN PLAN
ECONOMIC COMMUNITY. EUR+WWI FRANCE FUT ITALY UK ECO/DEV
ECO/UNDEV WORKER ACT/RES PROB/SOLV TEC/DEV ECO/TAC INT/ORG
INT/TRADE EEC. PAGE 112 F2209 REGION

B62

SRIVASTAVA G.L.,COLLECTIVE BARGAINING AND LABOR- LABOR
MANAGEMENT RELATIONS IN INDIA. INDIA UK USA+45 MGT
INDUS LEGIS WORKER ADJUD EFFICIENCY PRODUC BARGAIN
...METH/COMP 20. PAGE 125 F2462 GP/REL

B62

WENDT P.F.,HOUSING POLICY - THE SEARCH FOR PLAN
SOLUTIONS. GERMANY/W SWEDEN UK USA+45 OP/RES ADMIN
HABITAT WEALTH...SOC/WK CHARTS 20. PAGE 145 F2856 METH/COMP
NAT/G

S62

SCOTT J.B.,"ANGLO-SOVIET TRADE AND ITS EFFECTS ON NAT/G
THE COMMONWEALTH." COM FUT UK USSR WOR+45 ECO/DEV ECO/TAC
MARKET INT/ORG CONSULT WEALTH...POLICY TREND
CMN/WLTH FOR/TRADE 20. PAGE 118 F2333

B63

BRITISH AID. UK AGRI DIST/IND INDUS SCHOOL TEC/DEV FOR/AID
INT/TRADE COLONIAL DEMAND...TREND CHARTS 20. PAGE 1 ECO/UNDEV
F0018 NAT/G
FINAN

B63

BELOFF M.,THE UNITED STATES AND THE UNITY OF ECO/DEV
EUROPE. EUR+WWI UK USA+45 WOR+45 VOL/ASSN DIPLOM INT/ORG
REGION ATTIT PWR...CONCPT EEC OEEC 20 NATO. PAGE 13
F0239

B63

CONF ON FUTURE OF COMMONWEALTH,THE FUTURE OF THE DIPLOM
COMMONWEALTH. AFR UK ECO/UNDEV AGRI EDU/PROP ADMIN RACE/REL
SOC/INTEG 20. PAGE 27 F0522 ORD/FREE
TEC/DEV

B63

LEWIN J.,POLITICS AND LAW IN SOUTH AFRICA. NAT/LISM
SOUTH/AFR UK POL/PAR BAL/PWR ECO/TAC COLONIAL POLICY
CONTROL GP/REL DISCRIM PWR 20 NEGRO. PAGE 79 F1545 LAW
RACE/REL

B63

MEEK R.L.,THE ECONOMICS OF PHYSIOCRACY. FRANCE UK PRODUC
AGRI FINAN WORKER CAP/ISM TAX DEMAND EQUILIB INCOME WEALTH
HABITAT...CHARTS ANTHOL 17. PAGE 89 F1744 MARKET

B63

MINGAY G.E.,ENGLISH LANDED SOCIETY IN THE OWN
EIGHTEENTH CENTURY. UK ELITES STRUCT AGRI INDUS STRATA
CONTROL WEALTH 18. PAGE 92 F1802 PWR

B63

OLSON M. JR.,THE ECONOMICS OF WARTIME SHORTAGE. WAR
FRANCE GERMANY MOD/EUR UK AGRI PROB/SOLV ADMIN ADJUST
DEMAND WEALTH...POLICY OLD/LIB FOR/TRADE 17/20. ECO/TAC
PAGE 101 F1990 NAT/COMP

B63

PELLING H.M.,A HISTORY OF BRITISH TRADE UNIONISM. LABOR
UK ELITES ECO/DEV POL/PAR GP/REL PWR NEW/LIB 19/20. VOL/ASSN
PAGE 104 F2051 NAT/G

B63

PREST A.R.,PUBLIC FINANCE IN UNDERDEVELOPED FINAN
COUNTRIES. UK WOR+45 WOR-45 SOCIETY INT/ORG NAT/G ECO/UNDEV
LEGIS ACT/RES PLAN ECO/TAC ADMIN ROUTINE...CHARTS NIGERIA
20. PAGE 108 F2115

B63

RICARDO D.,THE PRINCIPLES OF POLITICAL ECONOMY AND GEN/LAWS
TAXATION (1817). UK INDUS MARKET ECO/TAC INT/TRADE TAX
TARIFFS PRICE COST DEMAND OPTIMAL WEALTH...CONCPT LAISSEZ
19 INTRVN/ECO. PAGE 111 F2183

B63

SALENT W.S.,THE UNITED STATES BALANCE OF PAYMENTS BAL/PAY
IN 1968. EUR+WWI UK USA+45 AGRI R+D LABOR FORCES DEMAND
PRODUC...GEOG CONCPT CHARTS 20 CHINJAP EEC. FINAN
PAGE 115 F2274 INT/TRADE

B63

SCHOECK H.,THE NEW ARGUMENT IN ECONOMICS. UK USA+45 WELF/ST
INDUS MARKET LABOR NAT/G ECO/TAC ADMIN ROUTINE FOR/AID
BAL/PAY PWR...POLICY BOLIV. PAGE 117 F2309 ECO/DEV
ALL/IDEOS

B63

SELF P.,THE STATE AND THE FARMER. UK ECO/DEV MARKET AGRI
WORKER PRICE CONTROL GP/REL...WELF/ST 20 DEPT/AGRI. NAT/G
PAGE 119 F2346 ADMIN
VOL/ASSN

B63

SHANKS M.,THE LESSONS OF PUBLIC ENTERPRISE. UK SOCISM
LEGIS WORKER ECO/TAC ADMIN PARL/PROC GOV/REL ATTIT OWN
...POLICY MGT METH/COMP NAT/COMP ANTHOL 20 NAT/G
PARLIAMENT. PAGE 120 F2364 INDUS

B63

VON BECKERATH E.,PROBLEME DER NORMATIVEN OKONOMIK ECO/TAC
UND DER WIRTSCHAFTSPOLITISCHEN BERATUNG. GERMANY UK DELIB/GP
ELITES CAP/ISM EFFICIENCY...CONCPT GOV/COMP ECO/DEV
IDEA/COMP 20. PAGE 142 F2789 CONSULT

S63

APPERT K.,"BERECHTIGE VORBEHALTE DER FINAN
SCHWEIZERISCHEN ZUR INTEGRATION." EUR+WWI UK MARKET ATTIT
SERV/IND NAT/G PLAN RIGID/FLEX OEEC 20 EEC. PAGE 6 SWITZERLND
F0108

S63

BELOFF M.,"BRITAIN, EUROPE AND THE ATLANTIC INT/ORG
COMMUNITY." EUR+WWI ELITES NAT/G VOL/ASSN TOP/EX ECO/DEV
ATTIT ORD/FREE PWR SOVEREIGN WEALTH EEC TOT/POP UK
VAL/FREE CMN/WLTH 20. PAGE 13 F0240

S63

DIEBOLD W. JR.,"THE NEW SITUATION OF INTERNATIONAL MARKET
TRADE POLICY." EUR+WWI FRANCE FUT UK USA+45 WOR+45 ECO/TAC
DIST/IND PLAN INT/TRADE EDU/PROP PWR WEALTH
...RECORD TREND GEN/LAWS EEC TRUE/GP VAL/FREE
APPLIC 20. PAGE 33 F0636

S63

HALLSTEIN W.,"THE EUROPEAN COMMUNITY AND ATLANTIC INT/ORG
PARTNERSHIP." EUR+WWI USA+45 MARKET NAT/G VOL/ASSN ECO/TAC
DELIB/GP ARMS/CONT NUC/PWR ATTIT PWR...CONCPT STAT UK
TIME/SEQ TREND OEEC 20 EEC. PAGE 54 F1053

S63

MONROE A.D.,"BRITAIN AND THE EUROPEAN COMMUNITY." VOL/ASSN
EUR+WWI FRANCE NAT/G DELIB/GP TOP/EX ECO/TAC DOMIN ATTIT
PWR...POLICY RECORD GEN/LAWS EEC EFTA 20 EFTA UK
CMN/WLTH. PAGE 93 F1817

S63

SHONFIELD A.,"AFTER BRUSSELS." EUR+WWI FRANCE PLAN
GERMANY UK ECO/DEV DIST/IND MARKET VOL/ASSN ECO/TAC
DELIB/GP CREATE INT/TRADE ATTIT RIGID/FLEX...RECORD
TREND GEN/LAWS EEC COMMUN CMN/WLTH 20. PAGE 121
F2385

S63

TENNYSON L.B.,"THE USA IN ATLANTIC COMMUNITY." ATTIT
EUR+WWI FRANCE UK USA+45 ECO/UNDEV VOL/ASSN ECO/TAC
DELIB/GP TOP/EX DIPLOM DOMIN PWR...POLICY CONCPT BAL/PWR
TREND GEN/LAWS EEC 20. PAGE 129 F2545

B64

THE SPECIAL COMMONWEALTH AFRICAN ASSISTANCE PLAN. ECO/UNDEV
AFR CANADA INDIA NIGERIA UK FINAN SCHOOL...CHARTS TREND
20 COMMONWLTH. PAGE 1 F0019 FOR/AID
ADMIN

B64

BOWEN W.G.,ECONOMIC ASPECTS OF EDUCATION (NO. 104). EDU/PROP
EUR+WWI UK USA+45 PROF/ORG PLAN TEC/DEV PAY ACADEM
...POLICY STAT 20. PAGE 17 F0329 FINAN
METH/COMP

B64

BROWN W.M.,THE EXTERNAL LIQUIDITY OF AN ADVANCED FINAN
COUNTRY. CANADA FRANCE GERMANY/W SWEDEN UK USA+45 INT/TRADE
ECO/DEV DIPLOM PRICE...CONCPT STAT NAT/COMP 20. COST

PAGE 20 F0376
INCOME

B64
CASEY R.G.,THE FUTURE OF THE COMMONWEALTH. INDIA PAKISTAN UK ECO/UNDEV INT/ORG TEC/DEV COLONIAL SUPEGO 20 EEC AUSTRAL. PAGE 22 F0425
DIPLOM SOVEREIGN NAT/LISM FOR/AID

B64
CLAIRBORN E.L.,FORECASTING THE BALANCE OF PAYMENTS: AN EVALUATION. AFR FUT UK USA+45 WOR+45 FINAN PLAN BUDGET PAY CONTROL...STAT CHARTS BIBLIOG 20. PAGE 24 F0474
PREDICT BAL/PAY ECO/DEV ECO/TAC

B64
COLSTON RESEARCH SOCIETY,ECONOMETRIC ANALYSIS FOR NATIONAL ECONOMIC PLANNING (PROCEEDINGS OF SIXTEENTH SYMPOSIUM OF COLSTON RESEARCH SOCIETY). UK USA+45 FINAN FAM LABOR NAT/G PLAN PRICE ...METH/CNCPT TREND CHARTS TIME 20. PAGE 26 F0510
ECOMETRIC DELIB/GP ECO/TAC PROB/SOLV

B64
COLUMBIA U SCHOOL OF LAW,PUBLIC INTERNATIONAL DEVELOPMENT FINANCING IN INDIA. GERMANY/W INDIA UK USA+45 INDUS PLAN TEC/DEV DIPLOM ECO/TAC GIVE ADMIN UTIL ATTIT 20. PAGE 26 F0512
ECO/UNDEV FINAN FOR/AID INT/ORG

B64
EINZIG P.,MONETARY POLICY: ENDS AND MEANS. AFR UK INDUS WORKER PLAN DIPLOM PRICE BAL/PAY COST WEALTH ...DECISION TIME/SEQ 20. PAGE 37 F0715
FINAN POLICY ECO/TAC BUDGET

B64
GREBLER L.,URBAN RENEWAL IN EUROPEAN COUNTRIES: ITS EMERGENCE AND POTENTIALS. EUR+WWI UK ECO/DEV LOC/G NEIGH CREATE ADMIN ATTIT...TREND NAT/COMP MUNICH 20 URBAN/RNWL. PAGE 50 F0981
PLAN CONSTRUC NAT/G

B64
HAAR C.M.,LAW AND LAND: ANGLO-AMERICAN PLANNING PRACTICE. UK USA+45 NAT/G TEC/DEV BUDGET CT/SYS INGP/REL EFFICIENCY OWN...JURID MUNICH 20. PAGE 52 F1019
LAW PLAN NAT/COMP

B64
HINSHAW R.,THE EUROPEAN COMMUNITY AND AMERICAN TRADE: A STUDY IN ATLANTIC ECONOMICS AND POLICY. EUR+WWI UK USA+45 ECO/DEV ECO/UNDEV AGRI INDUS INT/ORG NAT/G ECO/TAC TARIFFS REGION...STAT CHARTS EEC 20. PAGE 60 F1174
MARKET TREND INT/TRADE

B64
JACOBY N.H.,UNITED STATES MONETARY POLICY. UK USA+45 LAW NAT/G TEC/DEV TAX EQUILIB INCOME ...METH/COMP 20 FED/RESERV. PAGE 66 F1300
ECO/DEV POLICY ECO/TAC FINAN

B64
KOHNSTAMM M.,THE EUROPEAN COMMUNITY AND ITS ROLE IN THE WORLD. FUT MOD/EUR UK USA+45 ECO/DEV 20. PAGE 72 F1418
INT/ORG NAT/G REGION DIPLOM

B64
KRAUSE L.B.,THE COMMON MARKET: PROGRESS AND CONTROVERSY. EUR+WWI UK ECO/DEV REGION...ANTHOL NATO EEC. PAGE 73 F1433
DIPLOM MARKET INT/TRADE INT/ORG

B64
LITTLE I.M.D.,AID TO AFRICA. AFR UK TEC/DEV DIPLOM ECO/TAC INCOME WEALTH 20. PAGE 81 F1583
FOR/AID ECO/UNDEV ADMIN POLICY

B64
MARSH D.C.,THE FUTURE OF THE WELFARE STATE. UK CONSTN NAT/G POL/PAR...POLICY WELF/ST 20. PAGE 86 F1676
NEW/LIB ADMIN CONCPT INSPECT

B64
MILIBAND R.,THE SOCIALIST REGISTER: 1964. GERMANY/W ITALY UK LABOR POL/PAR ECO/TAC FOR/AID NUC/PWR ...POLICY SOCIALIST IDEA/COMP 20 MAO NASSER/G. PAGE 91 F1784
MARXISM SOCISM CAP/ISM PROB/SOLV

B64
RAISON T.,WHY CONSERVATIVE? UK FORCES DIPLOM ECO/TAC GIVE EDU/PROP ORD/FREE WEALTH LAISSEZ ...GOV/COMP 20 TORY/PARTY CONSRV/PAR. PAGE 109 F2137
PLURISM CONSERVE POL/PAR NAT/G

B64
TAWNEY R.H.,EQUALITY. UK CULTURE STRATA ECO/TAC EDU/PROP REPRESENT OWN NEW/LIB...MAJORIT WELF/ST SOC 20. PAGE 129 F2538
WEALTH STRUCT ELITES POPULISM

B64
WILSON T.,POLICIES FOR REGIONAL DEVELOPMENT. CANADA UK FINAN INDUS NAT/G BUDGET TAX GIVE COST ...NAT/COMP 20. PAGE 147 F2904
REGION PLAN ECO/DEV ECO/TAC

S64
HOWE M.,"THE TRANSPORT ACT, 1962, AND THE CONSUMERS' CONSULTATIVE COMMITTEES." UK CONFER EXEC PWR 20. PAGE 62 F1225
PARTIC REPRESENT DELIB/GP DIST/IND

S64
KOJIMA K.,"THE PATTERN OF INTERNATIONAL TRADE AMONG ADVANCED COUNTRIES." EUR+WWI UK USA+45 WOR+45 MARKET NAT/G ECO/TAC WEALTH...MATH STAT CON/ANAL CHARTS METH/GP EEC CHINJAP 20 CHINJAP. PAGE 72 F1419
ECO/DEV TREND INT/TRADE

B65
AMERICAN ECONOMIC ASSOCIATION,INDEX OF ECONOMIC JOURNALS 1886-1965 (7 VOLS.). UK USA+45 USA-45 AGRI FINAN PLAN ECO/TAC INT/TRADE ADMIN...STAT CENSUS 19/20. PAGE 5 F0087
BIBLIOG WRITING INDUS

B65
BARRY E.E.,NATIONALISATION IN BRITISH POLITICS: THE HISTORICAL BACKGROUND. UK AGRI DIST/IND EXTR/IND LABOR LG/CO ATTIT CONSERVE SOCISM 19/20 LABOR/PAR. PAGE 10 F0198
NAT/G OWN INDUS POL/PAR

B65
COLLINS H.,KARL MARX AND THE BRITISH LABOUR MOVEMENT; YEARS OF THE FIRST INTERNATIONAL. FRANCE SWITZERLND UK CAP/ISM WAR...MARXIST IDEA/COMP BIBLIOG 19. PAGE 26 F0506
MARXISM LABOR INT/ORG REV

B65
COLLINS H.,KARL MARX AND THE BRITISH LABOR MOVEMENT, YEARS OF THE FIRST INTERNATIONAL. EUR+WWI MOD/EUR UK STRATA INDUS NAT/G POL/PAR SOCISM ...CONCPT 19/20 MARX/KARL. PAGE 26 F0507
MARXISM LABOR INT/ORG WORKER

B65
EDELMAN M.,THE POLITICS OF WAGE-PRICE DECISIONS. GERMANY ITALY NETHERLAND UK INDUS LABOR POL/PAR PROB/SOLV BARGAIN PRICE ROUTINE BAL/PAY COST DEMAND 20. PAGE 36 F0699
GOV/COMP CONTROL ECO/TAC PLAN

B65
HASSON J.A.,THE ECONOMICS OF NUCLEAR POWER. INDIA UK USA+45 WOR+45 INT/ORG TEC/DEV COST...SOC STAT CHARTS 20 EURATOM. PAGE 56 F1108
NUC/PWR INDUS ECO/DEV METH

B65
LITTLE I.M.D.,INTERNATIONAL AID. UK WOR+45 AGRI INDUS GIVE RECEIVE COLONIAL BAL/PAY WEALTH...POLICY GOV/COMP METH/COMP 20. PAGE 81 F1584
FOR/AID DIPLOM ECO/UNDEV NAT/G

B65
LYONS G.M.,AMERICA: PURPOSE AND POWER. UK USA+45 FINAN INDUS MARKET WORKER TEC/DEV DIPLOM AUTOMAT NUC/PWR WAR RACE/REL ORD/FREE 20 EEC CONGRESS SUPREME/CT CIV/RIGHTS. PAGE 82 F1617
PWR PROB/SOLV ECO/DEV TASK

B65
MCCOLL G.D.,THE AUSTRALIAN BALANCE OF PAYMENTS. UK USA+45 AGRI WORKER DIPLOM EQUILIB PRODUC...STAT TREND CHARTS BIBLIOG/A 20 AUSTRAL. PAGE 88 F1719
ECO/DEV BAL/PAY INT/TRADE COST

B65
NATIONAL CENTRAL LIBRARY,LATIN AMERICAN ECONOMIC AND SOCIAL SERIALS. UK SOCIETY NAT/G PLAN PROB/SOLV ...SOC 20. PAGE 97 F1897
BIBLIOG INT/TRADE ECO/UNDEV L/A+17C

B65
OECD,TECHNIQUES OF ECONOMIC FORECASTING. CANADA FRANCE NETHERLAND SWEDEN UK USA+45 PROB/SOLV ROUTINE...CONCPT MATH CHARTS BIBLIOG METH 20. PAGE 100 F1974
PREDICT METH/COMP PLAN

B65
PARRIS H.W.,GOVERNMENT AND THE RAILWAYS IN NINETEENTH-CENTURY BRITAIN. UK DELIB/GP CONTROL LEAD CENTRAL 19 RAILROAD. PAGE 103 F2029
DIST/IND NAT/G PLAN GP/REL

B65
ROLFE S.E.,GOLD AND WORLD POWER. AFR UK USA+45 WOR-45 INDUS WORKER INT/TRADE DEMAND...MGT CHARTS 20. PAGE 113 F2234
BAL/PAY EQUILIB ECO/TAC DIPLOM

B65
SHEPHERD W.G.,ECONOMIC PERFORMANCE UNDER PUBLIC OWNERSHIP: BRITISH FUEL AND POWER. UK BUDGET GP/REL ...METH/CNCPT CHARTS BIBLIOG 20. PAGE 120 F2375
PROC/MFG NAT/G OWN FINAN

B65
SHONFIELD A.,MODERN CAPITALISM: THE CHANGING BALANCE OF PUBLIC AND PRIVATE POWER. FRANCE GERMANY/W UK USA+45 WOR+45 ECO/DEV INT/ORG NAT/G CONSULT INT/TRADE PRODUC...POLICY CONCPT METH/COMP 20. PAGE 121 F2386
CAP/ISM CONTROL BAL/PWR CREATE

B65
SIMON B.,EDUCATION AND THE LABOR MOVEMENT, 1870-1920. UK SOCIETY STRATA LABOR POL/PAR SCHOOL CONTROL PARTIC SOCISM...BIBLIOG 19/20. PAGE 122 F2406
EDU/PROP WORKER ADJUST LAW

B65
TEW B.,WEALTH AND INCOME. UK BUDGET INT/TRADE PRICE BAL/PAY DEMAND...CHARTS GOV/COMP 20 AUSTRAL. PAGE 129 F2546
FINAN ECO/DEV WEALTH INCOME

B65
WASSERMAN M.J.,THE BALANCE OF PAYMENTS: HISTORY, METHODOLOGY, THEORY. UK USA+45 USA-45 CAP/ISM DIPLOM EFFICIENCY...DECISION METH/CNCPT BIBLIOG 18/20 LEAGUE/NAT. PAGE 144 F2828
BAL/PAY ECO/TAC GEN/LAWS EQUILIB

S65
KAUFMAN R.H.,"THE ASIAN GOLD TRADE." ASIA LAOS
S/ASIA

THAILAND UK CHARTS. PAGE 69 F1362
FINAN STAT INT/TRADE

S65
SOPER T.,"THE EEC AND AID TO AFRICA." FRANCE UK ECO/UNDEV INT/TRADE TARIFFS REGION ROUTINE CENTRAL DISCRIM...DECISION RECORD EEC. PAGE 124 F2443
AFR FOR/AID COLONIAL

B66
CANNING HOUSE LIBRARY,AUTHOR AND SUBJECT CATALOGUES OF THE CANNING HOUSE LIBRARY (5 VOLS.). UK CULTURE LEAD...SOC 19/20. PAGE 21 F0411
BIBLIOG L/A+17C NAT/G DIPLOM

B66
CONAN A.R.,THE PROBLEM OF STERLING. UK WOR+45 BUDGET ECO/TAC...POLICY STAT CHARTS 20 SILVER. PAGE 27 F0521
FINAN ECO/DEV BAL/PAY DIPLOM

B66
CROWDER M.,A SHORT HISTORY OF NIGERIA. AFR NIGERIA UK ECO/UNDEV CHIEF INT/TRADE RACE/REL NAT/LISM ORD/FREE...GEOG SOC CHARTS BIBLIOG 14/20. PAGE 29 F0558
COLONIAL NAT/G CULTURE

B66
DILLEY M.R.,BRITISH POLICY IN KENYA COLONY (2ND ED.). AFR INDIA UK LABOR BUDGET TAX ADMIN PARL/PROC GP/REL...BIBLIOG 20 PARLIAMENT. PAGE 33 F0639
COLONIAL REPRESENT SOVEREIGN

B66
HACKETT J.,L'ECONOMIE BRITANNIQUE: PROBLEMES ET PERSPECTIVES. FRANCE UK LABOR NAT/G EX/STRUC PROB/SOLV BAL/PAY INCOME RIGID/FLEX...MGT PHIL/SCI CHARTS MUNICH 20. PAGE 53 F1027
ECO/DEV FINAN ECO/TAC PLAN

B66
HUTTENBACH R.A.,BRITISH IMPERIAL EXPERIENCE. AFR S/ASIA UK WOR-45 INT/ORG TEC/DEV...CHARTS 16/20 MERCANTLST. PAGE 64 F1253
COLONIAL TIME/SEQ INT/TRADE

B66
KEENLEYSIDE H.L.,INTERNATIONAL AID: A SUMMARY. AFR INDIA S/ASIA UK STRATA EXTR/IND TEC/DEV ADMIN RACE/REL DEMAND NAT/LISM WEALTH...TREND CHINJAP. PAGE 70 F1367
ECO/UNDEV FOR/AID DIPLOM TASK

B66
LENSKI G.E.,POWER AND PRIVILEGE: A THEORY OF SOCIAL STRATIFICATION. SWEDEN UK UNIV USSR CULTURE ECO/UNDEV PRIVIL PWR...PHIL/SCI CONCPT CHARTS IDEA/COMP HYPO/EXP METH MARX/KARL. PAGE 78 F1525
SOC STRATA STRUCT SOCIETY

B66
NEVITT A.A.,HOUSING, TAXATION AND SUBSIDIES; A STUDY OF HOUSING IN THE UNITED KINGDOM. UK FINAN GIVE CONTROL COST INCOME...CHARTS 20. PAGE 98 F1918
PLAN TAX HABITAT RENT

B66
ROBERTSON D.J.,THE BRITISH BALANCE OF PAYMENTS. UK WOR+45 INDUS BUDGET TAX ADJUST...CHARTS ANTHOL 20. PAGE 112 F2213
FINAN BAL/PAY ECO/DEV INT/TRADE

B66
SHULTZ G.P.,GUIDELINES, INFORMAL CONTROLS, AND THE MARKET PLACE: POLICY CHOICES IN A FULL EMPLOYMENT ECONOMY. UK ECO/DEV LABOR INT/TRADE CONFER GOV/REL BAL/PAY DEMAND INCOME...POLICY ANTHOL 20 PRESIDENT. PAGE 121 F2392
ECO/TAC CONTROL FINAN RATION

B66
SPICER K.,A SAMARITAN STATE? AFR CANADA INDIA PAKISTAN UK USA+45 FINAN INDUS PRODUC...CHARTS 20 NATO. PAGE 124 F2455
DIPLOM FOR/AID ECO/DEV ADMIN

B66
TIVEY L.J.,NATIONALISATION IN BRITISH INDUSTRY. UK LEGIS PARL/PROC GP/REL OWN ATTIT SOCISM 20. PAGE 131 F2578
NAT/G INDUS CONTROL LG/CO

B66
US DEPARTMENT OF STATE,RESEARCH ON WESTERN EUROPE, GREAT BRITAIN, AND CANADA (EXTERNAL RESEARCH LIST NO 3-25). CANADA GERMANY/W UK LAW CULTURE NAT/G POL/PAR FORCES EDU/PROP REGION MARXISM...GEOG SOC WORSHIP 20 CMN/WLTH. PAGE 136 F2676
BIBLIOG/A EUR+WWI DIPLOM

B66
WILCOX C.,ECONOMIES OF THE WORLD TODAY: THEIR ORGANIZATION, DEVELOPMENT, AND PERFORMANCE (2ND ED.). CHINA/COM COM INDIA NIGERIA UK WOR+45 WOR-45 INDUS MARKET PLAN ECO/TAC SOCISM...CHARTS METH/COMP 20. PAGE 146 F2878
ECO/DEV ECO/UNDEV MARXISM CAP/ISM

B66
WILLIAMS G.,MERTHYR POLITICS: THE MAKING OF A WORKING-CLASS TRADITION. UK CHIEF WORKER LEAD SOCISM...ANTHOL MUNICH 19/20 MERTHYR RICHARD/H. PAGE 147 F2891
LOC/G POL/PAR INDUS

S66
NEWLYN W.T.,"MONEY MARKETS IN EAST AFRICA." AFR TANZANIA UGANDA UK DIPLOM CENTRAL 20. PAGE 98 F1923
FINAN WEALTH BAL/PAY ECO/UNDEV

N66
BRITISH DEVELOPMENT POLICIES: 1966 (PAMPHLET). UK AGRI TARIFFS BAL/PAY...TREND CHARTS 20 OVRSEA/DEV. PAGE 1 F0023
WEALTH DIPLOM INT/TRADE FOR/AID

B67
BARDENS D.,CHURCHILL IN PARLIAMENT. UK DIPLOM ADJUD CONTROL AUTHORIT PERSON ORD/FREE 20 CHURCHLL/W PARLIAMENT. PAGE 10 F0186
TOP/EX LEGIS GOV/REL

B67
BARROW T.C.,TRADE AND EMPIRE: THE BRITISH CUSTOMS SERVICE IN COLONIAL AMERICA, 1660-1775. UK USA-45 ECO/UNDEV NAT/G ECO/TAC DOMIN REV 17/18. PAGE 10 F0197
COLONIAL TARIFFS ADMIN EX/STRUC

B67
COWLING M.,1867 DISRAELI, GLADSTONE, AND REVOLUTION; THE PASSING OF THE SECOND REFORM BILL. UK LEGIS LEAD LOBBY GP/REL INGP/REL...DECISION BIBLIOG 19 REFORMERS. PAGE 28 F0545
PARL/PROC POL/PAR ATTIT LAW

B67
FIELD G.L.,COMPARATIVE POLITICAL DEVELOPMENT: THE PRECEDENT OF THE WEST. FRANCE GERMANY SWEDEN UK USSR STRATA STRUCT POL/PAR...METH 20. PAGE 40 F0790
NAT/COMP CONCPT ECO/DEV SOCIETY

B67
HODGKINSON R.G.,THE ORIGINS OF THE NATIONAL HEALTH SERVICE: THE MEDICAL SERVICES OF THE NEW POOR LAW, 1834-1871. UK INDUS WORKER PROB/SOLV EFFICIENCY ATTIT HEALTH WEALTH SOCISM...JURID SOC/WK MUNICH 19/20. PAGE 60 F1189
HEAL NAT/G POLICY LAW

B67
JOHNSON H.G.,ECONOMIC NATIONALISM IN OLD AND NEW STATES. CANADA CHINA/COM MALI UK DIPLOM...SIMUL GEN/LAWS 19/20 MEXIC/AMER. PAGE 68 F1328
NAT/LISM ECO/UNDEV ECO/DEV NAT/COMP

B67
LANDEN R.G.,OMAN SINCE 1856: DISRUPTIVE MODERNIZATION IN A TRADITIONAL ARAB SOCIETY. UK DIST/IND EXTR/IND SECT DIPLOM INT/TRADE...SOC LING CHARTS BIBLIOG 19/20. PAGE 75 F1468
ISLAM CULTURE ECO/UNDEV NAT/G

B67
MORRIS A.J.A.,PARLIAMENTARY DEMOCRACY IN THE NINETEENTH CENTURY. UK INDUS LOC/G NAT/G POL/PAR CONSULT LEGIS INT/TRADE ADMIN CHOOSE SUFF SOVEREIGN 19 PARLIAMENT. PAGE 93 F1835
TIME/SEQ CONSTN PARL/PROC POPULISM

B67
ROBINSON E.A.G.,ECONOMIC PLANNING IN THE UNITED KINGDOM. UK WORKER PLAN PROB/SOLV BAL/PAY 20. PAGE 113 F2220
ECO/DEV INDUS PRODUC BUDGET

B67
SACKS B.,SOUTH AFRICA: AN IMPERIAL DILEMMA. SOUTH/AFR UK ECO/UNDEV KIN DOMIN DEBATE CONTROL REV DISCRIM ISOLAT...POLICY STAT BIBLIOG 20. PAGE 115 F2268
COLONIAL RACE/REL DIPLOM ORD/FREE

B67
VENKATESWARAN R.J.,CABINET GOVERNMENT IN INDIA. INDIA UK SOCIETY OP/RES COLONIAL LEAD EFFICIENCY ORD/FREE 20. PAGE 141 F2776
DELIB/GP ADMIN CONSTN NAT/G

B67
WISEMAN H.V.,BRITAIN AND THE COMMONWEALTH. EUR+WWI FUT UK ECO/DEV POL/PAR TEC/DEV INT/TRADE LEAD ROLE SOVEREIGN...SOC TREND 20 CMN/WLTH. PAGE 148 F2911
INT/ORG DIPLOM NAT/G NAT/COMP

L67
SEABERG G.P.,"THE DRUG ABUSE PROBLEMS AND SOME PROPOSALS." UK USA+45 MARKET SANCTION CRIME ...POLICY NEW/IDEA. PAGE 119 F2339
BIO/SOC LAW ADJUD PROB/SOLV

S67
BENN W.,"TECHNOLOGY HAS AN INEXORABLE EFFECT." FUT UK ECO/DEV INT/ORG CONSULT PLAN EDU/PROP ADMIN LEAD GP/REL PRODUC...INT 20 EEC. PAGE 13 F0246
R+D LG/CO TEC/DEV INDUS

S67
BROWN M.B.,"THE TRADE UNION QUESTION." UK INDUS OP/RES PRICE PROFIT 20. PAGE 19 F0371
WORKER LABOR GP/REL LAW

S67
BUTT R.,"THE COMMON MARKET AND CONSERVATIVE POLITICS, 1961-2." UK CHIEF DIPLOM ECO/TAC INT/TRADE CONFER DEBATE REGION ATTIT...POLICY 20 EEC. PAGE 21 F0398
EUR+WWI INT/ORG POL/PAR

S67
CROKER F.P.U.,"ECONOMIC PEACEKEEPING." UK PLAN PROB/SOLV TEC/DEV BAL/PWR DIPLOM COERCE PEACE ...POLICY DECISION 20. PAGE 28 F0553
FORCES WEAPON COST WAR

S67
CROMER EARL OF,"STERLING AND THE COMMON MARKET." UK ECO/DEV INT/ORG 20 EEC. PAGE 29 F0554
ECO/TAC FINAN CHARTS INT/TRADE

S67
GANZ G.,"THE CONTROL OF INDUSTRY BY ADMINISTRATIVE PROCESS." UK DELIB/GP WORKER 20. PAGE 46 F0898
INDUS LAW ADMIN

CONTROL

S67
GREGORY R.,"THE MINISTER'S LINE: OR, THE M4 COMES TO BERKSHIRE. PART I." UK CONSTN DIST/IND LEGIS TOP/EX PLAN ADJUD...GEOG 20. PAGE 51 F0994
DECISION CONSTRUC NAT/G DELIB/GP

S67
JENCKS C.E.,"COAL MINERS IN BRITAIN SINCE NATIONALIZATION." UK LABOR GP/REL ADJUST SOCISM ...INT 20. PAGE 67 F1311
EXTR/IND WORKER STRATA ATTIT

S67
JENCKS C.E.,"SOCIAL STATUS OF COAL MINERS IN BRITAIN SINCE NATIONALIZATION." UK STRATA STRUCT LABOR RECEIVE GP/REL INCOME OWN ATTIT HABITAT...MGT T 20. PAGE 67 F1312
EXTR/IND WORKER CONTROL NAT/G

S67
KENNY L.M.,"THE AFTERMATH OF DEFEAT IN EGYPT." ISLAM ISRAEL UAR UK USA+45 USSR INDUS FORCES ECO/TAC PRICE COERCE WEAPON COST ATTIT. PAGE 70 F1378
WAR ECO/UNDEV DIPLOM POLICY

S67
LEIFER M.,"ASTRIDE THE STRAITS OF JAHORE: THE BRITISH PRESENCE AND COMMONWEALTH RIVALRY IN SOUTHEAST ASIA." MALAYSIA UK FORCES PLAN ECO/TAC ...DECISION 20 CMN/WLTH. PAGE 77 F1515
DIPLOM NAT/LISM COLONIAL

S67
MITCHELL J.D.B.,"THE CONSTITUTIONAL IMPLICATIONS OF JUDICIAL CONTROL OF THE ADMINISTRATION IN THE UNITED KINGDOM." UK LAW ADJUD ADMIN GOV/REL ROLE ...GP/COMP 20. PAGE 92 F1808
CONSTN CT/SYS CONTROL EX/STRUC

S67
NEALE R.S.,"WORKING CLASS WOMEN AND WOMEN'S SUFFRAGE." UK LAW CONSTN LABOR NAT/G DELIB/GP LEGIS WORKER PAY PARTIC CHOOSE 19 FEMALE/SEX. PAGE 97 F1906
STRATA SEX SUFF DISCRIM

S67
SCRIPP J.,"CONTROLLING PREJUDICIAL PUBLICITY BY THE CONTEMPT POWER: THE BRITISH PRACTICE AND ITS PROSPECT IN AMERICAN LAW." UK USA+45 EDU/PROP CONTROL GP/REL ORD/FREE JURID. PAGE 119 F2338
METH/COMP LAW PRESS ADJUD

S67
SHEFFTZ M.C.,"THE TRADE DISPUTES AND TRADE UNIONS ACT OF 1927: THE AFTERMATH OF THE GENERAL STRIKE." UK FINAN WORKER ADJUD LEAD PARL/PROC 20. PAGE 120 F2373
LEGIS ATTIT LABOR GP/REL

S67
WARNER G.,"FRANCE, BRITAIN AND THE EEC." FRANCE UK INT/ORG DELIB/GP ECO/TAC CONTROL 20 EEC. PAGE 143 F2822
INT/TRADE BAL/PWR DIPLOM

S67
WILLMANN J.,"LA COMMUNAUTE EUROPEENNE ET LA GRANDE-BRETAGNE." UK PROB/SOLV TEC/DEV CAP/ISM DIPLOM CONFER FEDERAL...POLICY 20 EEC. PAGE 147 F2898
INT/ORG DRIVE NAT/LISM INT/TRADE

B76
SMITH A.,THE WEALTH OF NATIONS. UK STRUCT WORKER DIPLOM ECO/TAC OPTIMAL DRIVE PERSON ORD/FREE ...OLD/LIB GEN/LAWS 17/18. PAGE 123 F2428
WEALTH PRODUC INDUS LAISSEZ

B82
CUNNINGHAM W.,THE GROWTH OF ENGLISH INDUSTRY AND COMMERCE. FUT UK FINAN NAT/G CAP/ISM...POLICY 20 MERCANTLST CHRISTIAN POPE. PAGE 29 F0562
INDUS INT/TRADE SML/CO CONSERVE

C83
BURKE E.,"RESOLUTIONS FOR CONCILIATION WITH AMERICA" (1775), IN E. BURKE, COLLECTED WORKS, VOL. 2." UK USA-45 FORCES INT/TRADE TARIFFS TAX SANCTION PEACE...POLICY 18 PRE/US/AM. PAGE 20 F0387
COLONIAL WAR SOVEREIGN ECO/TAC

B84
MILL J.,ELEMENTS OF POLITICAL ECONOMY. UK LAW ELITES FINAN WORKER ECO/TAC RENT OWN WEALTH ...POLICY GEN/LAWS 19. PAGE 91 F1785
TAX TARIFFS NAT/G INCOME

B86
O'CONNOR T.P.,THE PARNELL MOVEMENT: WITH A SKETCH OF IRISH PARTIES FROM 1843. IRELAND UK USA-45 LEGIS WORKER ECO/TAC COERCE CRIME REV CHOOSE ORD/FREE CATHISM LAISSEZ...SOC 19/20 PARLIAMENT PARNELL/CS LAND/LEAG. PAGE 100 F1957
LEAD DOMIN POL/PAR POLICY

B88
BENTHAM J.,DEFENCE OF USURY (1787). UK LAW NAT/G TEC/DEV ECO/TAC CONTROL ATTIT...CONCPT IDEA/COMP 18 SMITH/ADAM. PAGE 13 F0255
TAX FINAN ECO/DEV POLICY

B92
ENGELS F.,THE CONDITION OF THE WORKING-CLASS IN ENGLAND (1848). UK INDUS LABOR PRICE CONTROL COST INCOME HEALTH MARXISM MUNICH 19. PAGE 38 F0733
WORKER WEALTH MARXIST CAP/ISM

B95
SELIGMAN E.R.A.,ESSAYS IN TAXATION. NEW/ZEALND PRUSSIA UK USA-45 MARKET LOC/G CREATE PRICE CONTROL INCOME OWN WEALTH...GOV/COMP METH/COMP 19. PAGE 119 F2349
TAX TARIFFS INDUS NAT/G

B96
SMITH A.,LECTURES ON JUSTICE, POLICE, REVENUE AND ARMS (1763). UK LAW FAM FORCES TARIFFS AGREE COERCE INCOME OWN WEALTH LAISSEZ...GEN/LAWS 17/18. PAGE 123 F2429
DIPLOM JURID OLD/LIB TAX

ULMAN L. F2599

UN....UNITED NATIONS; SEE ALSO INT/ORG, VOL/ASSN, INT/REL

N
UNITED NATIONS,OFFICIAL RECORDS OF THE ECONOMIC AND SOCIAL COUNCIL OF THE UNITED NATIONS. WOR+45 DIPLOM INT/TRADE CONFER...SOC SOC/WK 20 UN UNESCO. PAGE 132 F2611
INT/ORG DELIB/GP WRITING

N19
FRANCK P.G.,AFGHANISTAN BETWEEN EAST AND WEST: THE ECONOMICS OF COMPETITIVE COEXISTENCE (PAMPHLET). AFGHANISTN USA+45 USA-45 USSR INDUS ECO/TAC INT/TRADE CONTROL NEUTRAL ORD/FREE MARXISM...GEOG 20 UN. PAGE 43 F0842
FOR/AID PLAN DIPLOM ECO/UNDEV

N19
MEZERIK A.G.,ECONOMIC AID FOR UNDERDEVELOPED COUNTRIES (PAMPHLET). AFR USSR WOR+45 FINAN LG/CO DELIB/GP NUC/PWR...GEOG CENSUS CHARTS 20 UN THIRD/WRLD. PAGE 90 F1775
FOR/AID ECO/UNDEV DIPLOM POLICY

B50
US DEPARTMENT OF STATE,POINT FOUR: COOPERATIVE PROGRAM FOR AID IN THE DEVELOPMENT OF ECONOMICALLY UNDERDEVELOPED AREAS. WOR+45 AGRI INDUS INT/ORG PLAN TEC/DEV DIPLOM EDU/PROP ADMIN PEACE PRODUC WEALTH 20 CONGRESS UN. PAGE 135 F2671
ECO/UNDEV FOR/AID FINAN INT/TRADE

L52
HUTH A.G.,"COMMUNICATION AND ECONOMIC DEVELOPMENT." FUT WOR+45 CULTURE SOCIETY INT/ORG PLAN TEC/DEV EDU/PROP DRIVE KNOWL WEALTH...POLICY CONCPT RECORD STERTYP GEN/LAWS COMMUN TOT/POP UNESCO 20 UN CMN/WLTH. PAGE 64 F1250
ECO/UNDEV

L54
OPLER M.E.,"SOCIAL ASPECTS OF TECHNICAL ASSISTANCE IN OPERATION." WOR+45 VOL/ASSN CREATE PLAN TEC/DEV EDU/PROP ALL/VALS...METH/CNCPT OBS RECORD TREND UN 20. PAGE 101 F1993
INT/ORG CONSULT FOR/AID

B55
WOYTINSKY W.S.,WORLD COMMERCE AND GOVERNMENTS: TRENDS AND OUTLOOK. WOR+45 FINAN POL/PAR DIPLOM ECO/TAC FOR/AID DOMIN WAR CHOOSE...CHARTS BIBLIOG 20 LEAGUE/NAT UN ILO. PAGE 149 F2929
INT/TRADE DIST/IND NAT/COMP NAT/G

B56
UNITED NATIONS,BIBLIOGRAPHY ON INDUSTRIALIZATION IN UNDER-DEVELOPED COUNTRIES. WOR+45 R+D INT/ORG NAT/G FOR/AID ADMIN LEAD 20 UN. PAGE 132 F2612
BIBLIOG ECO/UNDEV INDUS TEC/DEV

B57
ASHER R.E.,THE UNITED NATIONS AND ECONOMIC AND SOCIAL COOPERATION. ECO/UNDEV COM/IND DIST/IND FINAN PLAN PROB/SOLV INT/TRADE TASK WEALTH...SOC 20 UN. PAGE 7 F0129
INT/ORG DIPLOM FOR/AID

B58
MOSKOWITZ M.,HUMAN RIGHTS AND WORLD ORDER. INT/ORG PLAN GP/REL NAT/LISM SOVEREIGN...CONCPT 20 UN TREATY CIV/RIGHTS. PAGE 94 F1845
DIPLOM INT/LAW ORD/FREE

B58
SILOW R.A.,THE POTENTIAL CONTRIBUTION OF ATOMIC ENERGY TO DEVELOPMENT IN AGRICULTURE AND RELATED INDUSTRIES (PAMPHLET). WOR+45 R+D TEC/DEV EFFICIENCY 20 UN. PAGE 122 F2403
NUC/PWR ECO/UNDEV AGRI

B59
HARTOG F.,EUROPEAN TRADE CYCLE POLICY. WORKER TAX PRICE WAR CENTRAL DEMAND...TREND CHARTS 20 UN. PAGE 56 F1103
EQUILIB EUR+WWI INT/TRADE

B59
MEZERK A.G.,FINANCIAL ASSISTANCE FOR ECONOMIC DEVELOPMENT. WOR+45 INDUS DIPLOM INT/TRADE...CHARTS GOV/COMP UN. PAGE 91 F1778
FOR/AID FINAN ECO/TAC ECO/UNDEV

B60
ASPREMONT-LYNDEN H.,RAPPORT SUR L'ADMINISTRATION BELGE DU RUANDA-URUNDI PENDANT L'ANNEE 1959. BELGIUM RWANDA AGRI INDUS DIPLOM ECO/TAC INT/TRADE DOMIN ADMIN RACE/REL...GEOG CENSUS 20 UN. PAGE 7 F0132
AFR COLONIAL ECO/UNDEV INT/ORG

B60
HOFFMANN P.G.,ONE HUNDRED COUNTRIES, ONE AND ONE QUARTER BILLION PEOPLE. MARKET INT/ORG TEC/DEV CAP/ISM...GEOG CHARTS METH/COMP 20 UN. PAGE 61 F1191
FOR/AID ECO/TAC ECO/UNDEV INT/TRADE

B60
RAO V.K.R.,INTERNATIONAL AID FOR ECONOMIC DEVELOPMENT - POSSIBILITIES AND LIMITATIONS. FINAN PLAN TEC/DEV ADMIN TASK EFFICIENCY...POLICY SOC METH/CNCPT CHARTS 20 UN. PAGE 109 F2147
FOR/AID DIPLOM INT/ORG ECO/UNDEV

B61
LANDSKROY W.A.,OFFICIAL SERIAL PUBLICATIONS RELATING TO ECONOMIC DEVELOPMENT IN AFRICA SOUTH OF THE SAHARA (PAMPHLET). AFR UK R+D ACT/RES 20 UN.
BIBLIOG ECO/UNDEV COLONIAL

PAGE 75 F1471 INT/ORG

B61
MEZERIK A.G.,ECONOMIC DEVELOPMENT AIDS FOR UNDERDEVELOPED COUNTRIES. WOR+45 FINAN LEGIS PROB/SOLV TEC/DEV DIPLOM FOR/AID GIVE TASK WAR 20 UN. PAGE 91 F1776
ECO/UNDEV INT/ORG WEALTH PLAN

B61
SCAMMEL W.M.,INTERNATIONAL MONETARY POLICY. WOR+45 WOR-45 ACT/RES ECO/TAC LEGIT WEALTH...GEN/METH UN 20. PAGE 116 F2286
INT/ORG FINAN BAL/PAY

B61
SHARP W.R.,FIELD ADMINISTRATION IN THE UNITED NATION SYSTEM: THE CONDUCT OF INTERNATIONAL ECONOMIC AND SOCIAL PROGRAMS. FUT WOR+45 CONSTN SOCIETY ECO/UNDEV R+D DELIB/GP ACT/RES PLAN TEC/DEV EDU/PROP EXEC ROUTINE HEALTH WEALTH...HUM CONCPT CHARTS METH ILO UNESCO GP VAL/FREE UN 20. PAGE 120 F2369
INT/ORG CONSULT

B62
ROUND TABLE ON EUROPE'S ROLE IN LATIN AMERICAN DEVELOPMENT. EUR+WWI L/A+17C PLAN BAL/PAY UTIL ROLE WEALTH...CHARTS ANTHOL 20 UN INT/AM/DEV. PAGE 1 F0017
ECO/UNDEV FINAN TEC/DEV FOR/AID

B62
ALEXANDROWICZ C.H.,WORLD ECONOMIC AGENCIES: LAW AND PRACTICE. WOR+45 DIST/IND FINAN LABOR CONSULT INT/TRADE TARIFFS REPRESENT HEALTH...JURID 20 UN GATT EEC OAS ECSC. PAGE 4 F0064
INT/LAW INT/ORG DIPLOM ADJUD

B62
FAO,FOOD AND AGRICULTURE ORGANIZATION AFRICAN SURVEY. AFR CONGO/BRAZ GHANA STRATA AGRI INT/ORG TEC/DEV FOR/AID INT/TRADE RACE/REL DEMAND EFFICIENCY PRODUC...GEOG 20 UN CONGO/LEOP. PAGE 39 F0763
ECO/TAC WEALTH EXTR/IND ECO/UNDEV

B62
HIGGANS B.,UNITED NATIONS AND U.S. FOREIGN ECONOMIC POLICY. FUT USA+45 WOR+45 ECO/DEV ECO/UNDEV NAT/G ECO/TAC WEALTH...TIME/SEQ TOT/POP UN 20. PAGE 59 F1168
INT/ORG ACT/RES FOR/AID DIPLOM

B62
LEVY H.V.,LIBERDADE E JUSTICA SOCIAL (2ND ED.). BRAZIL COM L/A+17C USSR INT/ORG PARTIC GP/REL WEALTH 20 UN COM/PARTY. PAGE 79 F1544
ORD/FREE MARXISM CAP/ISM LAW

B62
UNECA LIBRARY,BOOKS ON AFRICA IN THE UNECA LIBRARY. WOR+45 AGRI INT/ORG NAT/G PLAN WRITING REGION...SOC STAT UN. PAGE 132 F2605
BIBLIOG AFR ECO/UNDEV TEC/DEV

B62
UNECA LIBRARY,NEW ACQUISITIONS IN THE UNECA LIBRARY. LAW NAT/G PLAN PROB/SOLV TEC/DEV ADMIN REGION...GEOG SOC 20 UN. PAGE 132 F2606
BIBLIOG AFR ECO/UNDEV INT/ORG

B62
UNIVERSITY OF TENNESSEE,GOVERNMENT AND WORLD CRISIS. USA+45 FOR/AID ORD/FREE...ANTHOL 20 UN ALL/PROG. PAGE 133 F2622
ECO/DEV DIPLOM NAT/G INT/ORG

B63
UN SECRETARY GENERAL,PLANNING FOR ECONOMIC DEVELOPMENT. ECO/UNDEV FINAN BUDGET INT/TRADE TARIFFS TAX ADMIN 20 UN. PAGE 132 F2603
PLAN ECO/TAC MGT NAT/COMP

B63
UNITED NATIONS,THE GROWTH OF WORLD INDUSTRY, 1938-1961: NATIONAL TABLES. WOR+45 STRUCT ECO/DEV ECO/UNDEV NAT/G COST...CHARTS UN. PAGE 132 F2613
STAT INDUS PRODUC ORD/FREE

B63
WIGHTMAN D.,TOWARD ECONOMIC CO-OPERATION IN ASIA. ASIA S/ASIA VOL/ASSN ACT/RES PLAN TEC/DEV ECO/TAC EDU/PROP RIGID/FLEX SKILL...POLICY METH/CNCPT OBS INT GEN/LAWS UN 20 ECAFE. PAGE 146 F2877
ECO/UNDEV CREATE

L63
PADELFORD N.J.,"FINANCIAL CRISIS AND THE UNITED NATIONS." FUT USSR WOR+45 LAW CONSTN FINAN INT/ORG DELIB/GP FORCES PLAN BUDGET DIPLOM COST WEALTH ...STAT CHARTS UN CONGO 20. PAGE 102 F2012
CREATE ECO/TAC

S63
GANDILHON J.,"LA SCIENCE ET LA TECHNIQUE A L'AIDE DES REGIONS PEU DEVELOPPEES." FRANCE FUT WOR+45 ECO/DEV R+D PROF/ORG ACT/RES PLAN...MGT TOT/POP VAL/FREE 20 UN. PAGE 46 F0893
ECO/UNDEV TEC/DEV FOR/AID

S63
MARTHELOT P.,"PROGRES DE LA REFORME AGRAIRE." INTELL ECO/DEV R+D FOR/AID ADMIN KNOWL...OBS VAL/FREE UN 20. PAGE 86 F1680
AGRI INT/ORG

B64
FREYMOND J.,WESTERN EUROPE SINCE THE WAR. COM EUR+WWI USA+45 DIPLOM...BIBLIOG 20 NATO UN EEC. PAGE 44 F0854
INT/ORG POLICY ECO/DEV ECO/TAC

B64
HEKHUIS D.J.,INTERNATIONAL STABILITY: MILITARY, ECONOMIC AND POLITICAL DIMENSIONS. FUT WOR+45 LAW ECO/UNDEV INT/ORG NAT/G VOL/ASSN FORCES ACT/RES BAL/PWR PWR WEALTH...STAT UN 20. PAGE 58 F1143
TEC/DEV DETER REGION

B64
MEZERIK A.G.,TRADE, AID AND ECONOMIC DEVELOPMENT. WOR+45 FINAN INDUS MARKET PLAN BAL/PWR BARGAIN FOR/AID TARIFFS EDU/PROP WEALTH...GP/COMP 20 UN GATT IMF IBRD. PAGE 91 F1777
ECO/TAC ECO/DEV INT/ORG INT/TRADE

B64
NEWCOMER H.A.,INTERNATIONAL AIDS TO OVERSEAS INVESTMENTS AND TRADE. ECO/UNDEV TARIFFS PROFIT ...BIBLIOG 20 GATT UN. PAGE 98 F1921
INT/TRADE FINAN DIPLOM FOR/AID

B64
SEGAL R.,SANCTIONS AGAINST SOUTH AFRICA. AFR SOUTH/AFR NAT/G INT/TRADE RACE/REL PEACE PWR ...INT/LAW ANTHOL 20 UN. PAGE 119 F2342
SANCTION DISCRIM ECO/TAC POLICY

B64
US SENATE COMM ON FOREIGN REL,HEARING ON BILLS RELATING TO FOREIGN ASSISTANCE. USA+45 WOR+45 ECO/UNDEV FINAN INDUS 20 UN CONGRESS. PAGE 139 F2733
FOR/AID DIPLOM TEC/DEV INT/ORG

L64
CARNEGIE ENDOWMENT INT. PEACE,"ECONOMIC AND SOCIAL QUESTION (ISSUES BEFORE THE NINETEENTH GENERAL ASSEMBLY)." WOR+45 ECO/DEV ECO/UNDEV INDUS R+D DELIB/GP CREATE PLAN TEC/DEV ECO/TAC FOR/AID BAL/PAY...RECORD UN 20. PAGE 21 F0414
INT/ORG INT/TRADE

S64
CARNEGIE ENDOWMENT INT. PEACE,"ADMINISTRATION AND BUDGET (ISSUES BEFORE THE NINETEENTH GENERAL ASSEMBLY)." WOR+45 FINAN BUDGET ECO/TAC ROUTINE COST...STAT RECORD UN. PAGE 21 F0415
INT/ORG ADMIN

S64
GARDNER R.N.,"GATT AND THE UNITED NATIONS CONFERENCE ON TRADE AND DEVELOPMENT." USA+45 WOR+45 SOCIETY ECO/UNDEV MARKET NAT/G DELIB/GP ACT/RES PLAN ECO/TAC TARIFFS EDU/PROP ROUTINE DRIVE RIGID/FLEX WEALTH...DECISION MGT TREND UN TOT/POP 20 GATT. PAGE 46 F0905
INT/ORG INT/TRADE

B65
BALDWIN D.A.,SOFT LOANS AND AMERICAN FOREIGN POLICY: 1943-1962 (THESIS). USA+45 WOR+45 FINAN NAT/G FOR/AID BAL/PAY ATTIT...POLICY METH/COMP 20 UN CONGRESS. PAGE 9 F0161
DIPLOM ECO/TAC ECO/UNDEV

B65
MACDONALD R.W.,THE LEAGUE OF ARAB STATES: A STUDY IN THE DYNAMICS OF REGIONAL ORGANIZATION. ISRAEL UAR USSR FINAN INT/ORG DELIB/GP ECO/TAC AGREE NEUTRAL ORD/FREE PWR...DECISION BIBLIOG 20 TREATY UN. PAGE 83 F1626
ISLAM REGION DIPLOM ADMIN

B65
US SENATE COMM ON FOREIGN REL,HEARINGS ON THE FOREIGN ASSISTANCE PROGRAM. AFR ASIA L/A+17C USA+45 WOR+45 FORCES TEC/DEV BUDGET CONTROL WEAPON ORD/FREE 20 UN CONGRESS SEC/STATE. PAGE 139 F2734
FOR/AID DIPLOM INT/ORG ECO/UNDEV

B65
WEAVER J.N.,THE INTERNATIONAL DEVELOPMENT ASSOCIATION: A NEW APPROACH TO FOREIGN AID. USA+45 NAT/G OP/RES PLAN PROB/SOLV WEALTH...CHARTS BIBLIOG 20 UN. PAGE 144 F2836
FOR/AID INT/ORG ECO/UNDEV FINAN

S65
LECLERCQ H.,"ECONOMIC RESEARCH AND DEVELOPMENT IN TROPICAL AFRICA." ECO/UNDEV INT/ORG CREATE PLAN UN. PAGE 77 F1500
AFR R+D ACADEM ECO/TAC

B66
ALEXANDER Y.,INTERNATIONAL TECHNICAL ASSISTANCE EXPERTS* A CASE STUDY OF THE U.N. EXPERIENCE. ECO/UNDEV CONSULT EX/STRUC CREATE PLAN DIPLOM FOR/AID TASK EFFICIENCY...ORG/CHARTS UN. PAGE 3 F0061
ECO/TAC INT/ORG ADMIN MGT

B66
ALEXANDER Y.,INTERNATIONAL TECHNICAL ASSISTANCE EXPERTS: A CASE STUDY OF THE U.N. EXPERIENCE. USA+45 WOR+45 WORKER CREATE PLAN PROB/SOLV ECO/TAC FOR/AID GIVE EDU/PROP...CHARTS BIBLIOG 20 UN. PAGE 3 F0062
SKILL INT/ORG TEC/DEV CONSULT

B66
FRIEDMANN W.G.,INTERNATIONAL FINANCIAL AID. USA+45 ECO/DEV ECO/UNDEV NAT/G VOL/ASSN EX/STRUC PLAN RENT GIVE BAL/PAY PWR...GEOG INT/LAW STAT TREND UN EEC COMECON. PAGE 44 F0866
INT/ORG FOR/AID TEC/DEV ECO/TAC

B66
KIRDAR U.,THE STRUCTURE OF UNITED NATIONS ECONOMIC AID TO UNDERDEVELOPED COUNTRIES. AGRI FINAN INDUS NAT/G EX/STRUC PLAN GIVE TASK...POLICY 20 UN. PAGE 71 F1397
INT/ORG FOR/AID ECO/UNDEV ADMIN

B66
LEAGUE OF WOMEN VOTERS OF US,FOREIGN AID AT THE CROSSROADS. USA+45 WOR+45 DELIB/GP PROB/SOLV DIPLOM INT/TRADE RECEIVE BAL/PAY...CHARTS 20 UN ALL/PROG. PAGE 76 F1498
FOR/AID GIVE ECO/UNDEV PLAN

B66
MANGONE G.J.,UN ADMINISTRATION OF ECONOMIC AND AOCIAL PROGRAMS. CONSULT BUDGET INT/TRADE REGION 20
ADMIN MGT

UN. PAGE 84 F1653 — ECO/TAC DELIB/GP

B66
RUBIN S.J.,THE CONSCIENCE OF THE RICH NATIONS: THE DEVELOPMENT ASSISTANCE COMMITTEE AND THE COMMON AID EFFORT. EUR+WWI USA+45 ECO/UNDEV INT/ORG NAT/G VOL/ASSN ECO/TAC INT/TRADE...OBS UN AID DEV/ASSIST IBRD OECD. PAGE 114 F2256 — FOR/AID ECO/DEV CONFER CENTRAL

B66
SEWELL J.P.,FUNCTIONALISM AND WORLD POLITICS* A STUDY BASED ON UNITED NATIONS PROGRAMS FINANCING ECONOMICAL DEVELOPMENT. ECO/UNDEV FINAN PROB/SOLV DIPLOM ECO/TAC FEEDBACK REGION ADJUST ATTIT UN IBRD INTL/FINAN INTL/DEV UNSF. PAGE 120 F2360 — TASK INT/ORG IDEA/COMP GEN/LAWS

B66
SINGH L.P.,THE POLITICS OF ECONOMIC COOPERATION IN ASIA; A STUDY OF ASIAN INTERNATIONAL ORGANIZATIONS. ASIA INT/ORG ACT/RES PLAN GP/REL...POLICY GP/COMP BIBLIOG 20 UN SEATO. PAGE 122 F2414 — ECO/UNDEV ECO/TAC REGION DIPLOM

B66
UNITED NATIONS,YEARBOOK OF INTERNATIONAL TRADE STATISTICS, 1964 (15TH ISSUE). WOR+45 ECO/DEV ECO/UNDEV UN. PAGE 132 F2614 — STAT INT/TRADE DIPLOM CHARTS

B66
US HOUSE COMM FOREIGN AFFAIRS,HEARINGS ON HR 12449 A BILL TO AMEND FURTHER THE FOREIGN ASSISTANCE ACT OF 1961. AFR ASIA L/A+17C USA+45 VIETNAM INT/ORG TEC/DEV INT/TRADE ATTIT ORD/FREE 20 UN NATO CONGRESS AID. PAGE 137 F2692 — FOR/AID ECO/TAC ECO/UNDEV DIPLOM

B66
US SENATE COMM ON FOREIGN REL,HEARINGS ON S 2859 AND S 2861. USA+45 WOR+45 FORCES BUDGET CAP/ISM ADMIN DETER WEAPON TOTALISM...NAT/COMP 20 UN CONGRESS. PAGE 139 F2735 — FOR/AID DIPLOM ORD/FREE ECO/UNDEV

S66
ERB GF,"THE UNITED NATIONS CONFERENCE ON TRADE AND DEVELOPMENT (UNCTAD): A SELECTED CURRENT READING LIST." FINAN FOR/AID CONFER 20 UN. PAGE 38 F0742 — BIBLIOG/A INT/TRADE ECO/UNDEV INT/ORG

B67
BLAIR P.W.,THE MINISTATE DILEMMA. WOR+45 AGREE COLONIAL ORD/FREE...GEOG CHARTS MUNICH LEAGUE/NAT UN. PAGE 15 F0294 — INT/ORG NAT/G CENSUS

B67
CEFKIN J.L.,THE BACKGROUND OF CURRENT WORLD PROBLEMS. AFR NAT/G MARXISM...T 20 UN. PAGE 22 F0432 — DIPLOM NAT/LISM ECO/UNDEV

B67
JOHNSON H.G.,ECONOMIC POLICY TOWARD LESS DEVELOPED COUNTRIES. USA+45 ECO/DEV INT/ORG PLAN CAP/ISM FOR/AID TARIFFS GIVE WEALTH...NEW/IDEA CHARTS 20 UN GATT. PAGE 67 F1327 — ECO/UNDEV ECO/TAC METH/COMP

B67
MACCLOSKEY M.,PACTS FOR PEACE: UN, NATO, SEATO, CENTO, OAS. WOR+45 PLAN DIPLOM CONTROL PEACE ORD/FREE...ORG/CHARTS UN NATO SEATO OAS CENTO. PAGE 83 F1623 — FORCES INT/ORG LEAD POLICY

B67
MARTIN P.,CANADA AND THE QUEST FOR PEACE. CANADA VIETNAM ECO/UNDEV PLAN FOR/AID WAR 20 UN. PAGE 86 F1684 — DIPLOM PEACE INT/ORG POLICY

B67
MURTY B.S.,PROPAGANDA AND WORLD PUBLIC ORDER. FUT WOR+45 COM/IND INT/ORG PROB/SOLV ATTIT KNOWL ORD/FREE...POLICY UN. PAGE 95 F1868 — EDU/PROP DIPLOM CONTROL JURID

B67
NKRUMAH K.,CHALLENGE OF THE CONGO. FORCES ECO/TAC FOR/AID REGION MURDER REPRESENT 20 CONGO/LEOP UN. PAGE 98 F1930 — REV ECO/UNDEV ORD/FREE DIPLOM

L67
MACDONALD R.S.J.,"THE RESORT TO ECONOMIC COERCION BY INTERNATIONAL POLITICAL ORGANIZATIONS." CUBA ETHIOPIA RHODESIA SOUTH/AFR NAT/G FOR/AID INT/TRADE DOMIN CONTROL SANCTION...DECISION LEAGUE/NAT UN OAS 20. PAGE 83 F1625 — INT/ORG COERCE ECO/TAC DIPLOM

L67
MEIER G.M.,"UNCTAD PROPOSALS FOR INTERNATIONAL ECONOMIC REFORM." WOR+45 MARKET INT/ORG TARIFFS CONFER UN GATT IMF. PAGE 89 F1749 — INT/TRADE FINAN INT/LAW ECO/UNDEV

L67
TANDON Y.,"CONSENSUS AND AUTHORITY BEHIND UNITED NATIONS PEACEKEEPING OPERATIONS." FINAN VOL/ASSN BUDGET DIPLOM PAY DOMIN...CHARTS 20 UN. PAGE 128 F2528 — CONSEN INT/ORG PWR PEACE

S67
ISELIN J.J.,"THE TRUMAN DOCTRINE: ITS PASSAGE THROUGH CONGRESS AND THE AFTERMATH." USA+45 ECO/UNDEV R+D INT/ORG DELIB/GP BAL/PWR REV PEACE ...POLICY UN. PAGE 66 F1291 — DIPLOM COM FOR/AID AFR

S67
KELLY F.K.,"A PROPOSAL FOR AN ANNUAL REPORT ON THE STATE OF MANKIND." FUT INTELL COM/IND INT/ORG CREATE PROB/SOLV PERS/REL...CONCPT 20 UN. PAGE 70 F1371 — SOCIETY UNIV ATTIT NEW/IDEA

S67
KOHN W.S.G.,"THE SOVEREIGNTY OF LIECHTENSTEIN." LIECHTENST SWITZERLND USSR CONSTN DEBATE WAR CONSERVE 18/20 UN. PAGE 72 F1417 — SOVEREIGN NAT/G PWR DIPLOM

S67
MERON T.,"THE UN'S 'COMMON SYSTEM' OF SALARY, ALLOWANCE, AND BENEFITS: CRITICAL APPR'SAL OF COORD IN PERSONNEL MATTERS." VOL/ASSN PAY EFFICIENCY ...CHARTS 20 UN. PAGE 90 F1761 — ADMIN EX/STRUC INT/ORG BUDGET

S67
STYCOS J.M.,"POLITICS AND POPULATION CONTROL IN LATIN AMERICA." USA+45 FAM NAT/G GP/REL AGE/C ATTIT CATHISM MARXISM...POLICY UN WHO. PAGE 127 F2509 — PLAN CENSUS CONTROL L/A+17C

N67
US HOUSE COMM FOREIGN AFFAIRS,REPORT OF SPECIAL STUDY MISSION TO THE NEAR EAST (PAMPHLET). ISRAEL USA+45 YEMEN ECO/UNDEV INT/ORG FOR/AID ARMS/CONT WAR WEAPON NAT/LISM PEACE...GEOG 20 UN HOUSE/REP. PAGE 137 F2694 — ISLAM DIPLOM FORCES

N67
US HOUSE COMM FOREIGN AFFAIRS,FOREIGN ASSISTANCE ACT OF 1967 (PAMPHLET). USA+45 WOR+45 FINAN CONGRESS HOUSE/REP UN. PAGE 137 F2695 — FOR/AID POLICY INT/ORG ECO/UNDEV

N67
US SENATE COMM ON FOREIGN REL,THE UNITED NATIONS AT TWENTY-ONE (PAMPHLET). WOR+45 BUDGET ADMIN SENATE UN. PAGE 139 F2738 — INT/ORG DIPLOM PEACE

UN ECONOMIC COMN ASIA & FAR E F2600

UN FAO F2601

UN HEADQUARTERS LIBRARY F2602

UN SECRETARY GENERAL F2603

UN STATISTICAL OFFICE F2604

UN/ILC....UNITED NATIONS INTERNATIONAL LAW COMMISSION

UN/SEC/GEN....UNITED NATIONS SECRETARY GENERAL

UNCSAT....UNITED NATIONS CONFERENCE ON THE APPLICATION OF SCIENCE AND TECHNOLOGY FOR THE BENEFIT OF THE LESS DEVELOPED AREAS

UNCTAD....UNITED NATIONS COMMISSION ON TRADE, AID, AND DEVELOPMENT

UNDERDEVELOPED COUNTRIES....SEE ECO/UNDEV

UNDP....UNITED NATIONS DEVELOPMENT PROGRAM

UNECA LIBRARY F2605,F2606

UNEF....UNITED NATIONS EMERGENCY FORCE

UNESCO F2607,F2608,F2609

UNESCO....UNITED NATIONS EDUCATIONAL, SCIENTIFIC, AND CULTURAL ORGANIZATION; SEE ALSO UN, INT/ORG

N
UNITED NATIONS,OFFICIAL RECORDS OF THE ECONOMIC AND SOCIAL COUNCIL OF THE UNITED NATIONS. WOR+45 DIPLOM INT/TRADE CONFER...SOC SOC/WK 20 UN UNESCO. PAGE 132 F2611 — INT/ORG DELIB/GP WRITING

B52
ALEXANDROWICZ C.H.,INTERNATIONAL ECONOMIC ORGANIZATION. WOR+45 ECO/DEV ECO/UNDEV DIST/IND FINAN MARKET PLAN ECO/TAC LEGIT DRIVE WEALTH ...POLICY CONCPT QUANT OBS TIME/SEQ GEN/LAWS WORK METH/GP EEC ILO OEEC UNESCO 20. PAGE 4 F0063 — INT/ORG INT/TRADE

L52
HUTH A.G.,"COMMUNICATION AND ECONOMIC DEVELOPMENT." FUT WOR+45 CULTURE SOCIETY INT/ORG PLAN TEC/DEV EDU/PROP DRIVE KNOWL WEALTH...POLICY CONCPT RECORD STERTYP GEN/LAWS COMMUN TOT/POP UNESCO 20 UN CMN/WLTH. PAGE 64 F1250 — ECO/UNDEV

B57
LAVES W.H.C.,UNESCO. FUT WOR+45 NAT/G CONSULT DELIB/GP TEC/DEV ECO/TAC EDU/PROP PEACE ORD/FREE ...CONCPT TIME/SEQ TREND UNESCO VAL/FREE 20. PAGE 76 F1491 — INT/ORG KNOWL

B60
SHONFIELD A.,THE ATTACK ON WORLD POVERTY. WOR+45 ECO/DEV ECO/UNDEV FINAN VOL/ASSN PLAN EDU/PROP DRIVE KNOWL WEALTH...CONT/OBS STAND/INT ORG/CHARTS TOT/POP UNESCO 20. PAGE 121 F2383 — INT/ORG ECO/TAC FOR/AID INT/TRADE

B61
SHARP W.R.,FIELD ADMINISTRATION IN THE UNITED NATION SYSTEM: THE CONDUCT OF INTERNATIONAL ECONOMIC AND SOCIAL PROGRAMS. FUT WOR+45 CONSTN SOCIETY ECO/UNDEV R+D DELIB/GP ACT/RES PLAN TEC/DEV EDU/PROP EXEC ROUTINE HEALTH WEALTH...HUM CONCPT CHARTS METH ILO UNESCO GP VAL/FREE UN 20. PAGE 120 F2369
INT/ORG CONSULT

B62
VIET J.,INTERNATIONAL COOPERATION AND PROGRAMMES OF ECONOMIC AND SOCIAL DEVELOPMENT. TEC/DEV FOR/AID DOMIN COLONIAL PEACE WEALTH 20 UNESCO. PAGE 141 F2784
BIBLIOG/A INT/ORG DIPLOM ECO/UNDEV

UNIDO....UNITED NATIONS INDUSTRIAL DEVELOPMENT ORGANIZATION

UNIFICA....UNIFICATION AND REUNIFICATION OF GEOGRAPHIC-POLITICAL ENTITIES

B25
WILLIAMS B.,THE SELBORNE MEMORANDUM. AFR FUT SOUTH/AFR UK NAT/G BUDGET DIPLOM REGION GOV/REL SOVEREIGN...POLICY CHARTS 20 UNIFICA SELBORNE/W. PAGE 147 F2888
COLONIAL PROVS

B62
SCHMITT H.A.,THE PATH TO EUROPEAN UNITY. EUR+WWI USA+45 PLAN TEC/DEV DIPLOM FOR/AID CONFER...INT/LAW 20 EEC EURCOALSTL MARSHL/PLN UNIFICA. PAGE 117 F2300
INT/ORG INT/TRADE REGION ECO/DEV

UNIFORM NARCOTIC DRUG ACT....SEE NARCO/ACT

UNION AFRICAINE ET MALGACHE, ALSO OCAM....SEE UAM

UNION FOR THE NEW REPUBLIC....SEE UNR

UNION OF SOUTH AFRICA....SEE SOUTH/AFR

UNION OF SOVIET SOCIALIST REPUBLICS....SEE USSR

UNION POUR LA DEFENSE DE LA REPUBLIQUE (FRANCE)....SEE UDR

UNION OF SOUTH AFRICA F2610

UNIONS....SEE LABOR

UNITED ARAB REPUBLIC....SEE UAR

UNITED AUTO WORKERS....SEE UAW

UNITED KINGDOM....SEE UK, COMMONWLTH

UNITED NATIONS....SEE UN

UNITED NATIONS INTERNATIONAL LAW COMMISSION....SEE UN/ILC

UNITED NATIONS SECURITY COUNCIL....SEE SECUR/COUN

UNITED NATIONS SPECIAL FUND....SEE UNSF

UNITED STATES ARMS CONTROL AND DISARMAMENT AGENCY....SEE ACD

UNITED STATES FEDERAL POWER COMMISSION....SEE FPC

UNITED STATES HOUSING CORPORATION....SEE US/HOUSING

UNITED STATES MILITARY ACADEMY....SEE WEST/POINT

UNITED STATES SENATE COMMITTEE ON FOREIGN RELATIONS....SEE FOREIGNREL

UNITED NATIONS F2611,F2612,F2613,F2614

UNIV....UNIVERSAL TO MAN

UNIVERSAL REFERENCE SYSTEM F2615,F2616,F2617,F2618

UNIVERSES....SEE UNIVERSES AND SAMPLING INDEX, P. XIV

UNIVERSITIES....SEE ACADEM

UNIVERSITIES RESEARCH ASSOCIATION, INC.....SEE UNIVS/RES

UNIVERSITY OF CHICAGO F2619

UNIVERSITY OF FLORIDA F2620

UNIVERSITY OF LONDON F2621

UNIVERSITY OF TENNESSEE F2622

UNIVS/RES....UNIVERSITIES RESEARCH ASSOCIATION, INC.

UNIVS-NATL BUR COMM ECO RES F2623

UNLABR/PAR....UNION LABOR PARTY

UNPLAN/INT....IMPROMPTU INTERVIEW

B57
OLIVER H.M. JR.,ECONOMIC OPINION AND POLICY IN CEYLON. CEYLON FINAN POL/PAR WORKER INT/TRADE INCOME WEALTH...GEOG UNPLAN/INT BIBLIOG 20 CMN/WLTH. PAGE 101 F1987
ECO/UNDEV NAT/LISM POLICY COLONIAL

UNR....UNION FOR THE NEW REPUBLIC

UNRRA....UNITED NATIONS RELIEF AND REHABILITATION AGENCY

UNRWA....UNITED NATIONS RELIEF AND WORKS AGENCY

UNSF....UNITED NATIONS SPECIAL FUND

B66
SEWELL J.P.,FUNCTIONALISM AND WORLD POLITICS* A STUDY BASED ON UNITED NATIONS PROGRAMS FINANCING ECONOMICAL DEVELOPMENT. ECO/UNDEV FINAN PROB/SOLV DIPLOM ECO/TAC FEEDBACK REGION ADJUST ATTIT UN IBRD INTL/FINAN INTL/DEV UNSF. PAGE 120 F2360
TASK INT/ORG IDEA/COMP GEN/LAWS

UPHOFF W.H. F2624

UPPER VOLTA....SEE UPPER/VOLT

UPPER/VOLT....UPPER VOLTA; SEE ALSO AFR

URBAN/LEAG....URBAN LEAGUE

URBAN/RNWL....URBAN RENEWAL

B57
DRUCKER P.F.,AMERICA'S NEXT TWENTY YEARS. USA+45 DIST/IND ACADEM SCHOOL DIPLOM ECO/TAC AUTOMAT HABITAT HEALTH...SOC/WK TREND MUNICH 20 URBAN/RNWL PUB/TRANS. PAGE 34 F0667
WORKER FOR/AID CENSUS GEOG

B59
NORTON P.L.,URBAN PROBLEMS AND TECHNIQUES. AIR AGRI INDUS MARKET TEC/DEV BUDGET LEISURE ALL/VALS ...ANTHOL MUNICH 20 URBAN/RNWL. PAGE 99 F1936
PLAN LOC/G HABITAT

B60
POOLEY B.J.,THE EVOLUTION OF BRITISH PLANNING LEGISLATION. UK ECO/DEV LOC/G CONSULT DELIB/GP ADMIN MUNICH 20 URBAN/RNWL. PAGE 107 F2104
PLAN LEGIS PROB/SOLV

B61
NEW JERSEY LEGISLATURE-SENATE,PUBLIC HEARINGS BEFORE COMMITTEE ON REVISION AND AMENDMENT OF LAWS ON SENATE BILL NO. 8. USA+45 FINAN PROVS WORKER ACT/RES PLAN BUDGET TAX CRIME...IDEA/COMP MUNICH 20 NEW/JERSEY URBAN/RNWL. PAGE 98 F1919
LEGIS INDUS PROB/SOLV

B63
US HOUSE,URBAN RENEWAL: HOUSE COMMITTEE ON BANKING AND CURRENCY. USA+45 FINAN LOC/G NAT/G NEIGH DELIB/GP TEC/DEV BUDGET GOV/REL COST...CHARTS MUNICH 20 CONGRESS URBAN/RNWL. PAGE 136 F2684
PLAN PROB/SOLV LEGIS

B64
FRIEDEN B.J.,THE FUTURE OF OLD NEIGHBORHOODS: REBUILDING FOR A CHANGING POPULATION. CONSTRUC LOC/G NAT/G ACT/RES ECO/TAC REGION ATTIT...INT SAMP MUNICH 20 NEWYORK/C LOS/ANG HARTFORD URBAN/RNWL. PAGE 44 F0855
NEIGH PROB/SOLV PLAN BUDGET

B64
GREBLER L.,URBAN RENEWAL IN EUROPEAN COUNTRIES: ITS EMERGENCE AND POTENTIALS. EUR+WWI UK ECO/DEV LOC/G NEIGH CREATE ADMIN ATTIT...TREND NAT/COMP MUNICH 20 URBAN/RNWL. PAGE 50 F0981
PLAN CONSTRUC NAT/G

B65
DUGGAR G.S.,RENEWAL OF TOWN AND VILLAGE I: A WORLD-WIDE SURVEY OF LOCAL GOVERNMENT EXPERIENCE. WOR+45 CONSTRUC INDUS CREATE BUDGET REGION GOV/REL...QU NAT/COMP MUNICH 20 URBAN/RNWL. PAGE 35 F0673
NEIGH PLAN ADMIN

B65
FRYE R.J.,HOUSING AND URBAN RENEWAL IN ALABAMA. USA+45 NEIGH LEGIS BUDGET ADJUD ADMIN PARTIC...MGT MUNICH 20 ALABAMA URBAN/RNWL. PAGE 45 F0871
PROB/SOLV PLAN GOV/REL

B65
GREER S.,URBAN RENEWAL AND AMERICAN CITIES: THE DILEMMA OF DEMOCRATIC INTERVENTION. USA+45 R+D LOC/G VOL/ASSN ACT/RES BUDGET ADMIN GOV/REL...SOC INT SAMP MUNICH 20 BOSTON CHICAGO LOS/ANG MIAMI URBAN/RNWL. PAGE 51 F0992
PROB/SOLV PLAN NAT/G

B65
MAO J.C.T.,EFFICIENCY IN PUBLIC URBAN RENEWAL EXPENDITURES THROUGH CAPITAL BUDGETING. USA+45 FINAN LOC/G NAT/G NEIGH REGION UTIL...GEOG METH/CNCPT STAT SIMUL GEN/LAWS MUNICH 20 URBAN/RNWL. PAGE 85 F1662
TEC/DEV BUDGET PROB/SOLV

B66
LECHT L.,GOAL, PRIORITIES, AND DOLLARS: THE NEXT DECADE. SPACE USA+45 SOCIETY AGRI BUDGET FOR/AID ...HEAL SOC/WK STAT CHARTS 20 URBAN/RNWL PUB/TRANS. PAGE 76 F1499
IDEA/COMP POLICY CONSEN PLAN

US OFFICE OF THE PRESIDENT F2722,F2723

US OPERATIONS MISSION - TURKEY F2724

US OPERATIONS MISSION TO VIET F2725

US PRES COMM ECO IMPACT DEFENS F2726

US SENATE COMM APPROPRIATIONS F2727

US SENATE COMM GOVT OPERATIONS F2728,F2729,F2730

US SENATE COMM LABOR-PUB WELF F2731

US SENATE COMM ON COMMERCE F2732

US SENATE COMM ON FOREIGN REL F2733,F2734,F2735,F2736,F2737 , F2738,F2739,F2740,F2741,F2742,F2743,F2744,F2745,F2746,F2747

US SENATE COMM ON JUDICIARY F2748,F2749,F2750

US SUPERINTENDENT OF DOCUMENTS F2751,F2752,F2753,F2754

US/AID....UNITED STATES AGENCY FOR INTERNATIONAL DEVELOPMENT

US/HOUSING....UNITED STATES HOUSING CORPORATION

US/STEEL....UNITED STATES STEEL CORPORATION

US/WEST....WESTERN UNITED STATES

USA+45....UNITED STATES, 1945 TO PRESENT

USA-45....UNITED STATES, 1700 TO 1945

USIA....UNITED STATES INFORMATION AGENCY

USPNSKII/G....GLEB USPENSKII

USSR....UNION OF SOVIET SOCIALIST REPUBLICS; SEE ALSO RUSSIA, APPROPRIATE TIME/SPACE/CULTURE INDEX

N19
FRANCK P.G.,AFGHANISTAN BETWEEN EAST AND WEST: THE ECONOMICS OF COMPETITIVE COEXISTENCE (PAMPHLET). AFGHANISTN USA+45 USA-45 USSR INDUS ECO/TAC INT/TRADE CONTROL NEUTRAL ORD/FREE MARXISM...GEOG 20 UN. PAGE 43 F0842
FOR/AID PLAN DIPLOM ECO/UNDEV

N19
HAYEK FA V.O.N.,FREEDOM AND THE ECONOMIC SYSTEM. GERMANY USSR PLAN REPRESENT TOTALISM FASCISM POPULISM...MAJORIT METH/COMP GEN/LAWS 20. PAGE 57 F1123
ORD/FREE ECO/TAC CAP/ISM SOCISM

N19
MEZERIK A.G.,ECONOMIC AID FOR UNDERDEVELOPED COUNTRIES (PAMPHLET). AFR USSR WOR+45 FINAN LG/CO DELIB/GP NUC/PWR...GEOG CENSUS CHARTS 20 UN THIRD/WRLD. PAGE 90 F1775
FOR/AID ECO/UNDEV DIPLOM POLICY

N19
SENGHOR L.S.,AFRICAN SOCIALISM (PAMPHLET). AFR FRANCE MALI USSR ELITES ECO/UNDEV NAT/G DIPLOM DOMIN EDU/PROP ATTIT 20 NEGRO. PAGE 119 F2355
SOCISM MARXISM ORD/FREE NAT/LISM

B28
DE MAN H.,THE PSYCHOLOGY OF SOCIALISM. EUR+WWI USSR LABOR NAT/LISM PERSON WEALTH MARXISM...METH/COMP 20. PAGE 31 F0604
WORKER ATTIT SOC SOCISM

B38
HARPER S.N.,THE GOVERNMENT OF THE SOVIET UNION. COM USSR LAW CONSTN ECO/DEV PLAN TEC/DEV DIPLOM INT/TRADE ADMIN REV NAT/LISM...POLICY 20. PAGE 55 F1085
MARXISM NAT/G LEAD POL/PAR

B40
SIKES E.R.,CONTEMPORARY ECONOMIC SYSTEMS: THEIR ANALYSIS AND SOCIAL BACKGROUND. GERMANY ITALY USSR AGRI INDUS PLAN CAP/ISM ROUTINE TOTALISM FASCISM ...POLICY CON/ANAL BIBLIOG 20. PAGE 122 F2400
COM SOCISM CONCPT

B44
BIENSTOCK G.,MANAGEMENT IN RUSSIAN INDUSTRY AND AGRICULTURE. USSR CONSULT WORKER LEAD COST PROFIT ATTIT DRIVE PWR...MGT METH/COMP DICTIONARY ACCT 20. PAGE 15 F0281
ADMIN MARXISM SML/CO AGRI

B47
ENKE S.,INTERNATIONAL ECONOMICS. UK USA+45 USSR INT/ORG BAL/PWR BARGAIN CAP/ISM BAL/PAY...NAT/COMP 20 TREATY. PAGE 38 F0735
INT/TRADE FINAN TARIFFS ECO/TAC

B48
VON HAYEK F.A.,INDIVIDUALISM AND ECONOMIC ORDER. GERMANY USA-45 USSR FINAN MARKET INT/ORG ECO/TAC INT/TRADE PRICE REPRESENT ORD/FREE...PLURIST GEN/LAWS 20. PAGE 142 F2793
SOCISM CAP/ISM POPULISM FEDERAL

B49
DE JOUVENEL B.,PROBLEMS OF SOCIALIST ENGLAND. AFR UK USSR BAL/PWR ECO/TAC INT/TRADE PRICE WAR BAL/PAY PEACE 20. PAGE 31 F0601
SOCISM NEW/LIB PROB/SOLV PLAN

B49
US DEPARTMENT OF STATE,SOVIET BIBLIOGRAPHY (PAMPHLET). CHINA/COM COM USSR LAW AGRI INT/ORG ECO/TAC EDU/PROP...POLICY GEOG IND 20. PAGE 135 F2670
BIBLIOG/A MARXISM CULTURE DIPLOM

B50
SCHUMPETER J.A.,CAPITALISM, SOCIALISM, AND DEMOCRACY (3RD ED.). USA-45 USSR WOR+45 WOR-45 INTELL ECO/DEV ECO/UNDEV ECO/TAC WAR PRODUC ORD/FREE...MGT SOC 20 MARX/KARL. PAGE 118 F2321
SOCIALIST CAP/ISM MARXISM IDEA/COMP

B51
BROGAN D.W.,THE PRICE OF REVOLUTION. FRANCE USA+45 USA-45 USSR CONSTN NAT/G DIPLOM COLONIAL NAT/LISM ORD/FREE POPULISM...CONCPT 18/20 PRE/US/AM. PAGE 19 F0359
REV METH/COMP COST MARXISM

B53
MENDE T.,WORLD POWER IN THE BALANCE. FUT USA+45 USSR WOR-45 ECO/DEV ECO/TAC INT/TRADE EDU/PROP UTOPIA ATTIT...HUM CONCPT TREND TOT/POP 20. PAGE 90 F1756
WOR+45 PWR BAL/PWR AFR

B53
WILLIAMS J.H.,ECONOMIC STABILITY IN A CHANGING WORLD. FRANCE USA+45 USSR AGRI WORKER BUDGET INT/TRADE TAX WAR BAL/PAY COST EFFICIENCY ALL/IDEOS EQULIB 20 KEYNES/JM. PAGE 147 F2892
POLICY FINAN ECO/TAC WEALTH

S53
LINCOLN G.,"FACTORS DETERMINING ARMS AID." COM FUT USA+45 USSR WOR+45 ECO/DEV NAT/G CONSULT PLAN TEC/DEV DIPLOM DOMIN EDU/PROP PERCEPT PWR ...DECISION CONCPT TREND MARX/KARL 20. PAGE 80 F1566
FORCES POLICY BAL/PWR FOR/AID

B54
LENIN V.I.,SELECTED WORKS (12 VOLS.). USSR INTELL SOCIETY STRATA STRUCT NAT/G POL/PAR WORKER CAP/ISM REV WAR...MARXIST PHIL/SCI 20 MARX/KARL LENIN/VI. PAGE 78 F1520
COM MARXISM

B55
MAYO H.B.,DEMOCRACY AND MARXISM. COM USSR STRATA NAT/G WORKER ECO/TAC REV MORAL...PHIL/SCI HIST/WRIT IDEA/COMP WORSHIP 20 MARX/KARL LENIN/VI STALIN/J TROTSKY/L. PAGE 87 F1708
MARXISM CAP/ISM

B56
KNORR K.E.,RUBLE DIPLOMACY: CHALLENGE TO AMERICAN FOREIGN AID(PAMPHLET). AFR CHINA/COM USA+45 USSR PLAN TEC/DEV CAP/ISM INT/TRADE DOMIN EDU/PROP CONTROL LEAD 20. PAGE 72 F1413
ECO/UNDEV COM DIPLOM FOR/AID

B56
UNIVERSITY OF CHICAGO,BIBLIOGRAPHY OF UKRAINE (PAMPHLET). USSR...SOC 20. PAGE 133 F2619
BIBLIOG/A COM

B56
US OFFICE OF THE PRESIDENT,REPORT TO CONGRESS ON THE MUTUAL SECURITY PROGRAM FOR THE SIX MONTHS ENDED DECEMBER 31, 1955. ASIA USSR ECO/DEV ECO/UNDEV INT/ORG CREATE TEC/DEV BAL/PWR ECO/TAC AGREE DETER COST ORD/FREE 20 DEPT/STATE DEPT/DEFEN EISNHWR/DD. PAGE 138 F2723
DIPLOM FORCES PLAN FOR/AID

B56
WOLFF R.L.,THE BALKANS IN OUR TIME. ALBANIA FUT MOD/EUR USSR YUGOSLAVIA CULTURE INT/ORG SECT DIPLOM EDU/PROP COERCE WAR ORD/FREE...CHARTS 4/20 BALKANS COMINFORM. PAGE 148 F2919
GEOG COM

B57
INTL BANKING SUMMER SCHOOL,RELATIONS BETWEEN THE CENTRAL BANKS AND COMMERCIAL BANKS. EUR+WWI FRANCE GERMANY/W ITALY UK USA+45 USSR INDUS INT/ORG CAP/ISM CONTROL MONEY. PAGE 65 F1282
FINAN NAT/G GP/REL LG/CO

B57
LENIN V.I.,THE DEVELOPMENT OF CAPITALISM IN RUSSIA. MOD/EUR USSR AGRI MARKET POL/PAR TEC/DEV...CONCPT 19/20. PAGE 78 F1521
COM INDUS CAP/ISM

B57
LOUCKS W.N.,COMPARATIVE ECONOMIC SYSTEMS (5TH ED.). COM UK USSR INDUS POL/PAR PLAN CAP/ISM TOTALISM MARXISM...PHIL/SCI BIBLIOG 19/20. PAGE 82 F1603
NAT/COMP IDEA/COMP SOCISM

B58
BERLINER J.S.,SOVIET ECONOMIC AID: THE AID AND TRADE POLICY IN UNDERDEVELOPED COUNTRIES. AFR COM ISLAM L/A+17C S/ASIA USSR ECO/DEV DIST/IND FINAN MARKET INT/ORG ACT/RES PLAN BAL/PWR WEAPON PWR WEALTH...CHARTS FOR/TRADE 20. PAGE 14 F0263
ECO/UNDEV ECO/TAC FOR/AID

B58
GALBRAITH J.K.,THE AFFLUENT SOCIETY. EUR+WWI FUT USA+45 USSR CULTURE SERV/IND PEACE WEALTH SOCISM ...NEW/IDEA TREND VAL/FREE 20. PAGE 45 F0882
ATTIT ECO/TAC CAP/ISM

B58
MIKESELL R.F.,FINANCING FREE WORLD TRADE WITH THE SINO-SOVIET BLOC. CHINA/COM COM USSR WOR+45 ECO/DEV AGRI DIST/IND EXTR/IND FINAN INDUS MARKET PROC/MFG NAT/G PLAN TEC/DEV ECO/TAC...CHARTS METH/GP EEC FOR/TRADE 20. PAGE 91 F1780
STAT BAL/PAY

B58
SCOTT D.J.R.,RUSSIAN POLITICAL INSTITUTIONS. RUSSIA USSR CONSTN AGRI DELIB/GP PLAN EDU/PROP CONTROL CHOOSE EFFICIENCY ATTIT MARXISM...BIBLIOG/A IND 13/20. PAGE 118 F2332
NAT/G POL/PAR ADMIN DECISION

B59
ALLEN R.L.,SOVIET INFLUENCE IN LATIN AMERICA. ECO/UNDEV FINAN PROC/MFG NAT/G TEC/DEV EDU/PROP EXEC ROUTINE ATTIT DRIVE PERSON ALL/VALS PWR...STAT CHARTS WORK FOR/TRADE 20. PAGE 4 F0071
L/A+17C ECO/TAC INT/TRADE USSR

B59
BARNETT A.D.,COMMUNIST ECONOMIC STRATEGY: THE RISE OF MAINLAND CHINA. CHINA/COM USSR WOR+45 AGRI INDUS FOR/AID INGP/REL ATTIT. PAGE 10 F0188
ECO/UNDEV INT/TRADE TOTALISM BAL/PWR

B59
ETSCHMANN R.,DIE WAHRUNGS- UND DEVISENPOLITIK DES OSTBLOCKS UND IHRE AUSWIRKUNGEN AUF DIE WIRTSCHAFTSBEZIEHUNGEN ZWISCHEN OST U WEST. BULGARIA CZECHOSLVK HUNGARY POLAND USSR MARKET NAT/G PLAN DIPLOM...NAT/COMP 20. PAGE 39 F0753
ECO/TAC FINAN POLICY INT/TRADE

B59
HENDEL S.,THE SOVIET CRUCIBLE. USSR LEAD COERCE NAT/LISM UTOPIA PWR...POLICY CONCPT ANTHOL 20 STALIN/J LENIN/VI MARX/KARL BOLSHEVIK. PAGE 58 F1147
COM MARXISM REV TOTALISM

B59
HOOVER C.B.,THE ECONOMY, LIBERTY AND THE STATE. COM EUR+WWI USA+45 USA-45 USSR CAP/ISM EDU/PROP COERCE TOTALISM ORD/FREE...POLICY OBS INT TREND NAZI 20. PAGE 61 F1206
ECO/DEV ECO/TAC

B59
NOVE A.,COMMUNIST ECONOMIC STRATEGY: SOVIET GROWTH AND CAPABILITIES. USSR AGRI LABOR PLAN TEC/DEV CAP/ISM INT/TRADE EFFICIENCY MARXISM 20 THIRD/WRLD. PAGE 99 F1941
FOR/AID ECO/TAC DIPLOM INDUS

B59
STERNBERG F.,THE MILITARY AND INDUSTRIAL REVOLUTION OF OUR TIME. USA+45 USSR WOR+45 WORKER COMPUTER PLAN TEC/DEV NUC/PWR GP/REL...POLICY NAT/COMP 20. PAGE 126 F2481
DIPLOM FORCES INDUS CIVMIL/REL

B59
YRARRAZAVAL E.,AMERICA LATINE EN LA GUERRA FRIA. AFR EUR+WWI L/A+17C USA+45 USSR WOR+45 INDUS INT/ORG NAT/LISM POLICY. PAGE 150 F2953
REGION DIPLOM ECO/UNDEV INT/TRADE

S59
ALKHIMOV V.S.,"SOVIET FOREIGN TRADE CHANNELS." COM FUT USA+45 USSR ECO/DEV MARKET CONSULT PLAN WEALTH ...MARXIST OBS CON/ANAL FOR/TRADE 20. PAGE 4 F0068
FINAN ECO/TAC DIPLOM

S59
BENDIX R.,"INDUSTRIALIZATION, IDEOLOGIES, AND SOCIAL STRUCTURE" (BMR)" UK USA-45 USSR STRUCT WORKER GP/REL EFFICIENCY...IDEA/COMP 20. PAGE 13 F0243
INDUS ATTIT MGT ADMIN

S59
REUBENS E.D.,"THE BASIS FOR REORIENATION OF AMERICAN FOREIGN AID POLICY." USA+45 USSR STRUCT INT/ORG CONSULT ECO/TAC ADMIN DRIVE MORAL ORD/FREE PWR WEALTH...RELATIV MATH STAT TREND GEN/LAWS VAL/FREE 20. PAGE 111 F2180
ECO/UNDEV PLAN FOR/AID DIPLOM

S59
ZAUBERMAN A.,"SOVIET BLOC ECONOMIC INTEGRATION." COM CULTURE INTELL ECO/DEV INDUS TOP/EX ACT/RES PLAN ECO/TAC INT/TRADE ROUTINE CHOOSE ATTIT ...TIME/SEQ 20. PAGE 150 F2958
MARKET INT/ORG USSR TOTALISM

B60
ALLEN R.L.,SOVIET ECONOMIC WARFARE. USSR FINAN INDUS NAT/G PLAN TEC/DEV FOR/AID DETER WEALTH ...TREND GEN/LAWS FOR/TRADE 20. PAGE 4 F0072
COM ECO/TAC

B60
ARON R.,COLLOQUES DE RHEINFELDEN. AFR USA+45 USSR WOR+45 WOR-45 CULTURE ECO/UNDEV NAT/G POL/PAR DIPLOM NAT/LISM TOTALISM ATTIT DRIVE ALL/VALS ...PLURIST CONCPT STERTYP GEN/LAWS TOT/POP 20. PAGE 6 F0120
ECO/DEV SOCIETY CAP/ISM SOCISM

B60
BILLERBECK K.,SOVIET BLOC FOREIGN AID TO UNDERDEVELOPED COUNTRIES. COM FUT USSR FINAN FORCES TEC/DEV DIPLOM INT/TRADE EDU/PROP NUC/PWR...TREND 20. PAGE 15 F0285
FOR/AID ECO/UNDEV ECO/TAC MARXISM

B60
CAMPBELL R.W.,SOVIET ECONOMIC POWER. COM USA+45 DIST/IND MARKET TOP/EX ACT/RES CAP/ISM ECO/TAC DOMIN EDU/PROP ADMIN ROUTINE DRIVE...MATH TIME/SEQ CHARTS WORK 20. PAGE 21 F0409
ECO/DEV PLAN SOCISM USSR

B60
FRANCK P.G.,AFGHANISTAN: BETWEEN EAST AND WEST. AFGHANISTN AFR USA+45 USSR ECO/UNDEV PLAN ADMIN ROUTINE ATTIT PWR...STAT OBS CHARTS TOT/POP FOR/TRADE 20. PAGE 43 F0843
ECO/TAC TREND FOR/AID

B60
GRANICK D.,THE RED EXECUTIVE. COM USA+45 SOCIETY ECO/DEV INDUS NAT/G POL/PAR EX/STRUC PLAN ECO/TAC EDU/PROP ADMIN EXEC ATTIT DRIVE...GP/COMP 20. PAGE 50 F0976
PWR STRATA USSR ELITES

B60
MYRDAL G.,BEYOND THE WELFARE STATE: ECONOMIC PLANNING AND ITS IMPLICATIONS. EUR+WWI FUT USA+45 USSR ECO/DEV ECO/UNDEV TEC/DEV SKILL WEALTH...PSY TREND FOR/TRADE 20. PAGE 96 F1881
PLAN ECO/TAC CAP/ISM

B60
ROEPKE W.,A HUMANE ECONOMY: THE SOCIAL FRAMEWORK OF THE FREE MARKET. FUT USSR WOR+45 CULTURE SOCIETY ECO/DEV PLAN ECO/TAC ADMIN ATTIT PERSON RIGID/FLEX SUPEGO MORAL WEALTH SOCISM...POLICY OLD/LIB CONCPT TREND GEN/LAWS 20. PAGE 113 F2232
DRIVE EDU/PROP CAP/ISM

B60
ROSTOW W.W.,THE STAGES OF ECONOMIC GROWTH. UK USA+45 USSR WOR+45 WOR-45 ECO/DEV PERSON MARXISM ...METH/CNCPT TIME/SEQ GEN/LAWS GEN/METH 20. PAGE 114 F2246
ECO/UNDEV NEW/IDEA CAP/ISM

S60
BECKER A.S.,"COMPARISIONS OF UNITED STATES AND USSR NATIONAL OUTPUT: SOME RULES OF THE GAME." COM USA+45 ECO/DEV AGRI DIST/IND INDUS R+D CONSULT PLAN ECO/TAC RIGID/FLEX KNOWL...METH/CNCPT CHARTS 20. PAGE 12 F0227
STAT USSR

S60
GROSSMAN G.,"SOVIET GROWTH: ROUTINE, INERTIA, AND PRESSURE." COM STRATA NAT/G DELIB/GP PLAN TEC/DEV ECO/TAC EDU/PROP ADMIN ROUTINE DRIVE WEALTH 20. PAGE 52 F1007
POL/PAR ECO/DEV AFR USSR

S60
HOOVER C.B.,"NATIONAL POLICY AND RATES OF ECONOMIC GROWTH: THE US SOVIET RUSSIA AND WESTERN EUROPE." COM EUR+WWI USA+45 USSR NAT/G PLAN ECO/TAC PWR WEALTH...MATH STAT GEN/LAWS 20. PAGE 61 F1207
ECO/DEV ACT/RES

S60
JACOBSON H.K.,"THE USSR AND ILO." AFR COM STRUCT ECO/DEV ECO/UNDEV CONSULT DELIB/GP ECO/TAC ILO WORK 20. PAGE 66 F1298
INT/ORG LABOR USSR

S60
MIKESELL R.F.,"AMERICA'S ECONOMIC RESPONSIBILITY AS A GREAT POWER." COM FUT USA+45 USSR WOR+45 INT/ORG PLAN ECO/TAC FOR/AID EDU/PROP CHOOSE WEALTH ...POLICY 20. PAGE 91 F1781
ECO/UNDEV BAL/PWR CAP/ISM

S60
OWEN C.F.,"US AND SOVIET RELATIONS WITH UNDERDEVELOPED COUNTRIES: LATIN AMERICA-A CASE STUDY." AFR COM L/A+17C USA+45 USSR EXTR/IND MARKET TEC/DEV DIPLOM ECO/TAC NAT/LISM ORD/FREE PWR ...TREND WORK 20. PAGE 102 F2005
ECO/UNDEV DRIVE INT/TRADE

S60
PYE L.W.,"SOVIET AND AMERICAN STYLES IN FOREIGN AID." COM USA+45 USSR WOR+45 NAT/G PLAN ECO/TAC ROUTINE RIGID/FLEX...POLICY CONCPT TREND GEN/LAWS TOT/POP 20. PAGE 108 F2132
ECO/UNDEV ATTIT FOR/AID

B61
AUBREY H.G.,COEXISTENCE: ECONOMIC CHALLENGE AND RESPONSE. AFR USSR WOR+45 ACT/RES BAL/PWR CAP/ISM DIPLOM ECO/TAC FOR/AID INT/TRADE PEACE SOCISM ...METH/COMP NAT/COMP. PAGE 7 F0139
POLICY ECO/UNDEV PLAN COM

B61
DEWITT N.,EDUCATION AND PROFESSIONAL EMPLOYMENT IN THE USSR. USSR PROF/ORG WORKER PLAN ADMIN UTIL AGE/C AGE/Y MARXISM...STAT CHARTS 20. PAGE 32 F0629
EDU/PROP ACADEM SCHOOL INTELL

B61
HARDT J.P.,THE COLD WAR ECONOMIC GAP. AFR USA+45 USSR ECO/DEV FORCES INT/TRADE NUC/PWR PWR 20. PAGE 55 F1081
DIPLOM ECO/TAC NAT/COMP POLICY

B61
HODGKINS J.A.,SOVIET POWER: ENERGY RESOURCES, PRODUCTION AND POTENTIALS. USSR ECO/DEV INDUS MARKET...POLICY STAT CHARTS 20 RESOURCE/N. PAGE 60 F1188
GEOG EXTR/IND TEC/DEV

B61
KATKOFF U.,SOVIET ECONOMY 1940-1965. COM WOR+45 WOR-45 INTELL NAT/G POL/PAR TOP/EX ATTIT PWR ...POLICY TIME/SEQ VAL/FREE 20. PAGE 69 F1360
AGRI PERSON TOTALISM USSR

B61
KOVNER M.,THE CHALLENGE OF COEXISTENCE: A STUDY OF SOVIET ECONOMIC DIPLOMACY. COM FUT ECO/DEV ECO/UNDEV PLAN EDU/PROP DETER SKILL...OBS VAL/FREE 20. PAGE 73 F1430
PWR DIPLOM USSR AFR

B61
LHOSTE-LACHAUME P.,OU GIT LE DESACCORD ENTRE LIBERAUX ET SOCIALISTES. EUR+WWI USA+45 USA-45 USSR CAP/ISM EDU/PROP MARXISM...MAJORIT IDEA/COMP 20 KEYNES/JM NEW/DEAL DEPRESSION. PAGE 79 F1555
LAISSEZ SOCISM FINAN

B61
MORLEY L.,THE PATCHWORK HISTORY OF FOREIGN AID. AFR KOREA/S USA+45 USSR LAW FINAN INT/ORG TEC/DEV BAL/PWR GIVE 20 NATO. PAGE 93 F1834
FOR/AID ECO/UNDEV FORCES DIPLOM

B61
NOVE A.,THE SOVIET ECONOMY. USSR ECO/DEV FINAN NAT/G ECO/TAC PRICE ADMIN EFFICIENCY MARXISM ...TREND BIBLIOG 20. PAGE 99 F1943
PLAN PRODUC POLICY

B61
VEIT O.,GRUNDRISS DER WAHRUNGSPOLITIK. AFR FRANCE GERMANY USSR DIPLOM INT/TRADE...NAT/COMP 19/20 SILVER. PAGE 141 F2773
FINAN POLICY ECO/TAC CAP/ISM

S61
HAYTES W.,"THREE VIEWS ON THE SOVIET ECONOMIC THREAT." AFR COM USA+45 USA-45 USSR WOR+45 WOR-45 INDUS TEC/DEV ECO/TAC DOMIN ATTIT PERCEPT PWR FOR/TRADE 20. PAGE 57 F1128
ECO/DEV PLAN TOTALISM

S61
NOVE A.,"THE SOVIET MODEL AND UNDERDEVELOPED COUNTRIES." COM FUT USSR WOR+45 CULTURE ECO/DEV POL/PAR FOR/AID EDU/PROP ADMIN MORAL WEALTH ...POLICY RECORD HIST/WRIT 20. PAGE 99 F1942
ECO/UNDEV PLAN

B62
ARNOLD H.J.P.,AID FOR DEVELOPING COUNTRIES. COM EUR+WWI USA+45 USSR WOR+45 EDU/PROP ATTIT DRIVE PWR WEALTH...TREND CHARTS STERTYP NAT/ 20. PAGE 6 F0115
ECO/UNDEV ECO/TAC FOR/AID

B62
BRUMBERG A.,RUSSIA UNDER KHRUSHCHEV. FUT USSR SOCIETY ECO/DEV AGRI PERF/ART WORKER PWR...SOC ANTHOL 20 KHRUSH/N. PAGE 20 F0377
COM MARXISM NAT/G CHIEF

B62
ELLIOTT J.R.,THE APPEAL OF COMMUNISM IN THE UNDERDEVELOPED NATIONS. AFR USSR WOR+45 INT/ORG NAT/G DIPLOM DOMIN EDU/PROP ROUTINE ATTIT RIGID/FLEX ORD/FREE PWR WEALTH MARXISM...POLICY SOC METH/CNCPT MYTH TOT/POP METH/GP 20. PAGE 37 F0722
COM ECO/UNDEV

B62
FRIEDMANN W.,METHODS AND POLICIES OF PRINCIPAL DONOR COUNTRIES IN PUBLIC INTERNATIONAL DEVELOPMENT FINANCING: PRELIMINARY APPRAISAL. FRANCE GERMANY/W UK USA+45 USSR WOR+45 FINAN TEC/DEV CAP/ISM DIPLOM ECO/TAC ATTIT 20 EEC. PAGE 44 F0864
INT/ORG FOR/AID NAT/COMP ADMIN

B62
FRIEDRICH-EBERT-STIFTUNG,THE SOVIET BLOC AND DEVELOPING COUNTRIES. CHINA/COM COM GERMANY/E USSR WOR+45 ECO/UNDEV INT/ORG NAT/G TEC/DEV NEUTRAL PWR ...POLICY 20. PAGE 44 F0868
MARXISM DIPLOM ECO/TAC FOR/AID

B62
GERSCHENKRON A.,ECONOMIC BACKWARDNESS IN HISTORICAL PERSPECTIVE. WOR+45 WOR-45 ECO/DEV ECO/UNDEV INDUS NAT/G LEGIT DRIVE...WELF/ST DECISION QUANT TREND CHARTS 20. PAGE 47 F0919
TEC/DEV USSR

B62
KIRPICEVA I.K.,HANDBUCH DER RUSSISCHEN UND SOWJETISCHEN BIBLIOGRAPHIEN (5 VOLS.). USSR STRUCT ECO/DEV DIPLOM LEAD ATTIT 18/20. PAGE 71 F1400
BIBLIOG/A NAT/G MARXISM COM

B62
LEVY H.V.,LIBERDADE E JUSTICA SOCIAL (2ND ED.). BRAZIL COM L/A+17C USSR INT/ORG PARTIC GP/REL WEALTH 20 UN COM/PARTY. PAGE 79 F1544
ORD/FREE MARXISM CAP/ISM LAW

B62
PAKISTAN MINISTRY OF FINANCE,FOREIGN ECONOMIC AID: A REVIEW OF FOREIGN ECONOMIC AID TO PAKISTAN. EUR+WWI PAKISTAN UK USA+45 USSR ECO/UNDEV INT/ORG DELIB/GP DIPLOM ECO/TAC...CHARTS CMN/WLTH CHINJAP. PAGE 103 F2016
FOR/AID RECEIVE WEALTH FINAN

B62
PHELPS E.S.,THE GOAL OF ECONOMIC GROWTH: SOURCES, COSTS, BENEFITS. USA+45 USSR FINAN TAX CONTROL DEMAND WEALTH...POLICY NAT/COMP ANTHOL BIBLIOG 20. PAGE 106 F2079
ECO/TAC ECO/DEV NAT/G FUT

B62
RIMALOV V.V.,ECONOMIC COOPERATION BETWEEN USSR AND UNDERDEVELOPED COUNTRIES. USSR FINAN TEC/DEV INT/TRADE DOMIN EDU/PROP COLONIAL NAT/LISM DRIVE SOVEREIGN...AUD/VIS 20. PAGE 111 F2194
FOR/AID PLAN ECO/UNDEV DIPLOM

L62
PRYOR F.L.,"FOREIGN TRADE IN THE COMMUNIST BLOC." COM ECO/DEV VOL/ASSN...METH/CNCPT GEN/LAWS FOR/TRADE TERR/GP 20. PAGE 108 F2129
ECO/TAC STERTYP USSR

S62
IOVTCHOUK M.T.,"ON SOME THEORETICAL PRINCIPLES AND METHODS OF SOCIOLOGICAL INVESTIGATIONS (IN RUSSIAN)." FUT USA+45 STRATA R+D NAT/G POL/PAR TOP/EX ACT/RES PLAN ECO/TAC EDU/PROP ROUTINE ATTIT RIGID/FLEX MARXISM SOCISM...MARXIST METH/CNCPT OBS TREND NAT/COMP GEN/LAWS 20. PAGE 65 F1288
COM ECO/DEV CAP/ISM USSR

S62
SCOTT J.B.,"ANGLO-SOVIET TRADE AND ITS EFFECTS ON THE COMMONWEALTH." COM FUT UK USSR WOR+45 ECO/DEV MARKET INT/ORG CONSULT WEALTH...POLICY TREND CMN/WLTH FOR/TRADE 20. PAGE 118 F2333
NAT/G ECO/TAC

S62
ZAUBERMAN A.,"SOVIET AND CHINESE STRATEGY FOR ECONOMIC GROWTH." ASIA CHINA/COM COM USSR STRATA VOL/ASSN PLAN ATTIT PWR...METH/CNCPT GEN/LAWS WORK TERR/GP 20. PAGE 150 F2959
ECO/DEV EDU/PROP

C62
JOINT ECONOMIC COMMITTEE,"DIMENSIONS OF SOVIET ECONOMIC POWER." USSR R+D FORCES ACT/RES OP/RES TEC/DEV...GEOG STAT BIBLIOG 20. PAGE 68 F1337
ECO/DEV PLAN PRODUC LABOR

B63
BERGSON A.,ECONOMIC TRENDS IN THE SOVIET UNION. USSR ECO/UNDEV AGRI NAT/G FORCES PLAN TEC/DEV INT/TRADE BAL/PAY...POLICY ANTHOL 20. PAGE 14 F0259
ECO/DEV NAT/COMP INDUS LABOR

B63
CERAMI C.A.,ALLIANCE BORN OF DANGER. EUR+WWI USA+45 USSR ECO/DEV INDUS VOL/ASSN ECO/TAC REGION ATTIT MARXISM ATLAN/ALL 20 NATO EEC. PAGE 22 F0437
DIPLOM INT/ORG NAT/G POLICY

B63
EL-NAGGAR S.,FOREIGN AID TO UNITED ARAB REPUBLIC. UAR USA+45 USSR AGRI FINAN INDUS FORCES EATING DEMAND...CHARTS METH/COMP 20 RESOURCE/N AID. PAGE 37 F0718
FOR/AID ECO/UNDEV RECEIVE PLAN

B63
GOLDMAN M.I.,SOVIET MARKETING. USSR DIST/IND FINAN RATION OWN WEALTH...SOC BIBLIOG 20. PAGE 48 F0937
MARKET ECO/TAC CONTROL MARXISM

B63
HYDE D.,THE PEACEFUL ASSAULT. COM UAR USSR ECO/DEV ECO/UNDEV NAT/G POL/PAR CAP/ISM PWR 20. PAGE 64 F1256
MARXISM CONTROL ECO/TAC DIPLOM

B63
LETHBRIDGE H.J.,THE PEASANT AND THE COMMUNES. CHINA/COM COM USSR NEIGH PROB/SOLV ADJUST EFFICIENCY...POLICY METH/COMP NAT/COMP 20. PAGE 78 F1535
MARXISM ECO/TAC AGRI WORKER

L63
MOUSKHELY M.,"LE BLOC COMMUNISTE ET LA COMMUNAUTE ECONOMIQUE EUROPEENNE." AFR COM EUR+WWI FUT USSR WOR+45 INTELL ECO/UNDEV LABOR POL/PAR NUC/PWR RIGID/FLEX...TIME/SEQ ORG/CHARTS EEC TOT/POP 20. PAGE 94 F1849
INT/ORG ECO/DEV

L63
PADELFORD N.J.,"FINANCIAL CRISIS AND THE UNITED NATIONS." FUT USSR WOR+45 LAW CONSTN FINAN INT/ORG DELIB/GP FORCES PLAN BUDGET DIPLOM COST WEALTH ...STAT CHARTS UN CONGO 20. PAGE 102 F2012
CREATE ECO/TAC

S63
GRUSHIN B.A.,"PROBLEMS OF THE MOVEMENT OF COMMUNIST LABOR IN THE USSR." COM SOCIETY LABOR ECO/TAC EDU/PROP COERCE RIGID/FLEX ORD/FREE...POLICY MARXIST STAT QU WORK 20. PAGE 52 F1011
ATTIT USSR

S63
PRYBYLA J.,"THE QUEST FOR ECONOMIC RATIONALITY IN THE SOVIET BLOC." COM FUT WOR+45 WOR-45 DIST/IND MARKET PLAN ECO/TAC ATTIT...METH/CNCPT TOT/POP 20. PAGE 108 F2128
ECO/DEV TREND USSR

S63
RAMERIE L.,"TENSION AU SEIN DU COMECON: LE CAS ROUMAIN." COM EUR+WWI USSR WOR+45 ECO/DEV DIST/IND NAT/G POL/PAR VOL/ASSN EDU/PROP TOTALISM ATTIT WEALTH...TIME/SEQ 20 COMECON. PAGE 109 F2142
INT/ORG ECO/TAC INT/TRADE ROMANIA

S63
SCHURMANN F.,"ECONOMIC POLICY AND POLITICAL POWER IN COMMUNIST CHINA." ASIA CHINA/COM USSR SOCIETY ECO/UNDEV AGRI INDUS CREATE ADMIN ROUTINE ATTIT DRIVE RIGID/FLEX PWR WEALTH...HIST/WRIT TREND CHARTS WORK 20. PAGE 118 F2323
PLAN ECO/TAC

S63
SHWADRAN B.,"MIDDLE EAST OIL, 1962." ISLAM USSR ECO/DEV DIST/IND INDUS PLAN BAL/PWR DISPL DRIVE ...POLICY STAT TREND GEN/LAWS TERR/GP METH/GP EEC OEEC 20 OIL. PAGE 121 F2394
MARKET ECO/TAC INT/TRADE

S63
WILES P.J.D.,"WILL CAPITALISM AND COMMUNISM SPONTANEOUSLY CONVERGE." COM FUT USA+45 ECO/DEV DIST/IND MARKET CAP/ISM ECO/TAC RIGID/FLEX WEALTH MARXISM SOCISM...MATH STAT TREND COMPUT/IR 20. PAGE 146 F2885
PLAN TEC/DEV USSR

B64
DANIELS R.V.,RUSSIA. RUSSIA USSR STRUCT NAT/LISM TOTALISM ORD/FREE WEALTH...POLICY DECISION TREND. PAGE 30 F0579
MARXISM REV ECO/DEV DIPLOM

B64
GRIFFITH W.E.,COMMUNISM IN EUROPE (2 VOLS.). CZECHOSLVK USSR WOR+45 WOR-45 YUGOSLAVIA INGP/REL MARXISM SOCISM...ANTHOL 20 EUROPE/E. PAGE 51 F1000
COM POL/PAR DIPLOM GOV/COMP

B64
LEWIN P.,THE FOREIGN TRADE OF COMMUNIST CHINA* ITS IMPACT ON THE FREE WORLD. AFR EUR+WWI L/A+17C S/ASIA ECO/UNDEV CREATE FOR/AID...STAT NET/THEORY TREND CHARTS. PAGE 79 F1546
ASIA INT/TRADE NAT/COMP USSR

B64
SAKAI R.K.,STUDIES ON ASIA, 1964. ASIA CHINA/COM ISRAEL MALAYSIA S/ASIA USA+45 USSR ECO/UNDEV FAM POL/PAR SECT CONSULT NAT/LISM...POLICY SOC 20 CHINJAP. PAGE 115 F2272
PWR DIPLOM

B64
SEERS D.,CUBA: THE ECONOMIC AND SOCIAL REVOLUTION. L/A+17C USSR YUGOSLAVIA STRATA AGRI INDUS SCHOOL DELIB/GP PLAN ECO/TAC DOMIN EDU/PROP ATTIT RIGID/FLEX ALL/VALS...STAT OBS TIME/SEQ WORK VAL/FREE 20. PAGE 119 F2341
ACT/RES COERCE CUBA REV

B64
US HOUSE COMM BANKING-CURR,INTERNATIONAL DEVELOPMENT ASSOCIATION ACT AMENDMENT. CHINA/COM USA+45 USSR FINAN FORCES LEGIS DIPLOM CONFER EFFICIENCY...CHARTS GOV/COMP 20 PRESIDENT CONGRESS INTL/DEV. PAGE 136 F2689
BAL/PAY FOR/AID RECORD ECO/TAC

B64
WELLISZ S.,THE ECONOMICS OF THE SOVIET BLOC. COM USSR INDUS WORKER PLAN BUDGET INT/TRADE TAX PRICE PRODUC WEALTH MARXISM...METH/COMP 20. PAGE 145 F2854
EFFICIENCY ADMIN MARKET

B64
ZEBOT C.A.,THE ECONOMICS OF COMPETITIVE COEXISTENCE. CHINA/COM USSR WOR+45 FINAN MARKET FOR/AID PRICE DEMAND EQUILIB WEALTH ALL/IDEOS 20. PAGE 150 F2961
TEC/DEV DIPLOM METH/COMP

S64
FINLEY D.D.,"A POLITICAL PERSPECTIVE OF ECONOMIC RELATIONS IN THE COMMUNIST CAMP." COM USSR FACE/GP NAT/G ACT/RES PLAN DOMIN COERCE ATTIT ORD/FREE WEALTH...TIME/SEQ 20. PAGE 41 F0800
VOL/ASSN ECO/TAC DIPLOM REGION

S64
FLORINSKY M.T.,"TRENDS IN THE SOVIET ECONOMY." COM USA+45 USSR INDUS LABOR NAT/G PLAN TEC/DEV ECO/TAC ALL/VALS SOCISM...MGT METH/CNCPT STYLE CON/ANAL GEN/METH WORK 20. PAGE 42 F0817
ECO/DEV AGRI

S64
FYFE J.,"LIST OF CURRENT ACQUISITIONS OF PERIODICALS AND NEWSPAPERS DEALING WITH THE SOVIET UNION AND EAST EUROPEAN COUNTRIES." USSR WRITING GP/REL INGP/REL MARXISM 20. PAGE 45 F0879
BIBLIOG COM EDU/PROP PRESS

S64
HERMAN L.M.,"THE ECONOMIC CONTENT OF SOVIET TRADE WITH THE WEST." WOR+45 ECO/DEV ECO/UNDEV AGRI COM/IND INDUS CAP/ISM ECO/TAC ATTIT RIGID/FLEX WEALTH...OBS TREND VAL/FREE MARX/KARL 20. PAGE 59 F1152
COM MARKET INT/TRADE USSR

S64
HORECKY P.L.,"LIBRARY OF CONGRESS PUBLICATIONS IN AID OF USSR AND EAST EUROPEAN RESEARCH." BULGARIA CZECHOSLVK POLAND USSR YUGOSLAVIA NAT/G POL/PAR DIPLOM ADMIN GOV/REL...CLASSIF 20. PAGE 62 F1214
BIBLIOG/A COM MARXISM

S64
PESELT B.M.,"COMMUNIST ECONOMIC OFFENSIVE." WOR+45 SOCIETY INT/ORG PLAN ECO/TAC DOMIN EDU/PROP ATTIT PERSON PWR WEALTH...TREND CHARTS METH/GP 20. PAGE 105 F2067
COM ECO/UNDEV FOR/AID USSR

S64
WU Y.,"CHINA'S ECONOMY AND ITS PROSPECTS." ASIA CHINA/COM FUT USSR AGRI INDUS PLAN ECO/TAC LEGIT WEALTH...STAT CON/ANAL CHARTS GEN/LAWS FOR/TRADE 20. PAGE 149 F2938
ECO/DEV

C64
LOUFTY A.,"LA PLANIFICATION DE L'ECONOMIE." FRANCE USSR FINAN INDUS BUDGET INCOME PRODUC...BIBLIOG 20. PAGE 82 F1604
PLAN ECO/UNDEV ECO/DEV

B65
CRABB C.V. JR.,THE ELEPHANTS AND THE GRASS* A STUDY OF NONALIGNMENT. ASIA INDIA S/ASIA USA+45 USSR BAL/PWR NEUTRAL ATTIT...TREND NAT/COMP. PAGE 28 F0549
ECO/UNDEV AFR DIPLOM CONCPT

B65
JASNY H.,KHRUSHCHEV'S CROP POLICY. USSR ECO/DEV PLAN MARXISM...STAT 20 KHRUSH/N RESOURCE/N. PAGE 66 F1306
AGRI NAT/G POLICY ECO/TAC

B65
KANTOROVICH L.V.,THE BEST USE OF ECONOMIC RESOURCES. USSR SOCIETY FINAN ACT/RES TEC/DEV ECO/TAC PRICE CONTROL COST DEMAND EFFICIENCY OPTIMAL...MGT STAT. PAGE 69 F1350
PLAN MATH DECISION

B65
MACDONALD R.W.,THE LEAGUE OF ARAB STATES: A STUDY IN THE DYNAMICS OF REGIONAL ORGANIZATION. ISRAEL UAR USSR FINAN INT/ORG DELIB/GP ECO/TAC AGREE NEUTRAL ORD/FREE PWR...DECISION BIBLIOG 20 TREATY UN. PAGE 83 F1626
ISLAM REGION DIPLOM ADMIN

B65
O'BRIEN F.,CRISIS IN WORLD COMMUNISM* MARXISM IN SEARCH OF EFFICIENCY. AFR COM ECO/DEV PLAN INT/TRADE WAR ADJUST PEACE...STAT TIME/SEQ GOV/COMP NAT/COMP. PAGE 99 F1951
MARXISM USSR DRIVE EFFICIENCY

B65
OXENFELDT A.R.,ECONOMIC SYSTEMS IN ACTION. FRANCE USA+45 USSR CULTURE PLAN PROB/SOLV TEC/DEV INCOME PRODUC WEALTH...METH/COMP 20. PAGE 102 F2007
ECO/DEV CAP/ISM MARXISM ECO/TAC

B65
PLOSS S.I.,CONFLICT AND DECISION-MAKING IN SOVIET RUSSIA - A CASE STUDY OF AGRICULTURAL POLICY - 1953-1963. USSR DELIB/GP INGP/REL PWR MARXISM. PAGE 106 F2093
AGRI DECISION ATTIT

B65
SCHULTZ T.W.,ECONOMIC CRISES IN WORLD AGRICULTURE. ASIA INDIA USSR ECO/DEV ECO/UNDEV INDUS VOL/ASSN CAP/ISM RATION COLONIAL 20. PAGE 117 F2317
AGRI ECO/TAC INCOME WORKER

B65
SHAFFER H.G.,THE SOVIET SYSTEM IN THEORY AND PRACTICE: SELECTED WESTERN AND SOVIET VIEWS. USSR LAW SOCIETY CREATE FOR/AID EDU/PROP PRESS CHOOSE PEACE ORD/FREE...ANTHOL 20 STALIN/J. PAGE 120 F2362
MARXISM SOCISM IDEA/COMP

B65
WINT G.,ASIA: A HANDBOOK. ASIA COM INDIA USSR CULTURE INTELL NAT/G...GEOG STAT CENSUS NAT/COMP WORSHIP 20 TREATY CHINJAP. PAGE 148 F2907
DIPLOM SOC

B65
WU YUAN-LI,THE ECONOMY OF COMMUNIST CHINA. CHINA/COM USSR AGRI FINAN INDUS POL/PAR WORKER PROB/SOLV INT/TRADE PRICE EATING INCOME OWN WEALTH 20. PAGE 149 F2939
ECO/TAC MARXISM PLAN EFFICIENCY

S65
GOLDMAN M.I.,"A BALANCE SHEET OF SOVIET FOREIGN AID." USA+45 ECO/UNDEV BAL/PWR ECO/TAC RENT GIVE EDU/PROP CONTROL COST PROFIT GEN/METH. PAGE 48 F0939
USSR FOR/AID NAT/COMP EFFICIENCY

S65
SCHROEDER G.,"LABOR PLANNING IN THE USSR." COM USSR ECO/DEV INDUS SCHOOL PRODUC WEALTH...PREDICT TIME/SEQ TREND TIME 20. PAGE 117 F2313
WORKER PLAN CENSUS

B66
BRODERSEN A.,THE SOVIET WORKER: LABOR AND GOVERNMENT IN SOVIET SOCIETY. USSR STRUCT INDUS LABOR PLAN PAY INGP/REL PRODUC...POLICY GEN/LAWS BIBLIOG 20 STALIN/J LENIN/VI BOLSHEVISM KHRUSH/N. PAGE 19 F0357
WORKER ROLE NAT/G MARXISM

B66
DOBB M.,SOVIET ECONOMIC DEVELOPMENT SINCE 1917. USSR ECO/DEV ECO/UNDEV LABOR NAT/G TEC/DEV ECO/TAC ROUTINE PRODUC MARXISM 20. PAGE 33 F0647
PLAN INDUS WORKER

B66
ECKSTEIN A.,COMMUNIST CHINA'S ECONOMIC GROWTH AND FOREIGN TRADE* IMPLICATIONS FOR US POLICY. COM USA+45 USSR STRUCT INDUS MARKET DIPLOM ECO/TAC FOR/AID INT/TRADE...STAT CHARTS. PAGE 36 F0696
ASIA ECO/UNDEV CREATE PWR

B66
FELKER J.L.,SOVIET ECONOMIC CONTROVERSIES. USSR INDUS PLAN INT/TRADE GP/REL MARXISM SOCISM...POLICY 20. PAGE 40 F0778
ECO/DEV MARKET PROFIT PRICE

B66
GYORGY A.,ISSUES OF WORLD COMMUNISM. ALBANIA CHINA/COM COM USSR YUGOSLAVIA STRATA AGRI INT/ORG CHIEF FORCES WORKER WAR ALL/IDEOS...GEOG 20 MAO. PAGE 52 F1018
ECO/UNDEV REV MARXISM CON/ANAL

B66
KUENNE R.E.,THE POLARIS MISSILE STRIKE* A GENERAL ECONOMIC SYSTEMS ANALYSIS. USA+45 USSR NAT/G BAL/PWR ARMS/CONT WAR...MATH PROBABIL COMPUT/IR CHARTS HYPO/EXP SIMUL. PAGE 74 F1446
NUC/PWR FORCES DETER DIPLOM

B66
KURAKOV I.G.,SCIENCE, TECHNOLOGY AND COMMUNISM; SOME QUESTIONS OF DEVELOPMENT (TRANS. BY CARIN DEDIJER). USSR INDUS PLAN PROB/SOLV COST PRODUC ...MGT MATH CHARTS METH 20. PAGE 74 F1450
CREATE TEC/DEV MARXISM ECO/TAC

B66
LENSKI G.E.,POWER AND PRIVILEGE: A THEORY OF SOCIAL STRATIFICATION. SWEDEN UK UNIV USSR CULTURE ECO/UNDEV PRIVIL PWR...PHIL/SCI CONCPT CHARTS IDEA/COMP HYPO/EXP METH MARX/KARL. PAGE 78 F1525
SOC STRATA STRUCT SOCIETY

B66
LONDON K.,EASTERN EUROPE IN TRANSITION. CHINA/COM USSR DOMIN COLONIAL CENTRAL RIGID/FLEX PWR...SOC ANTHOL 20. PAGE 82 F1597
SOVEREIGN COM NAT/LISM DIPLOM

B66
MURPHY G.G.,SOVIET MONGOLIA: A STUDY OF THE OLDEST POLITICAL SATELLITE. USSR STRATA STRUCT COST INCOME ATTIT SOCISM 20. PAGE 95 F1865
DIPLOM ECO/TAC PLAN DOMIN

B66
US DEPARTMENT OF STATE,RESEARCH ON THE USSR AND EASTERN EUROPE (EXTERNAL RESEARCH LIST NO 1-25). USSR LAW CULTURE SOCIETY NAT/G TEC/DEV DIPLOM EDU/PROP REGION...GEOG LING. PAGE 136 F2675
BIBLIOG/A EUR+WWI COM MARXISM

B66
WETTER G.A.,SOVIET IDEOLOGY TODAY. USSR ECO/UNDEV SECT WORKER CAP/ISM CONTROL TASK EFFICIENCY TOTALISM DRIVE WEALTH...TREND 18/20. PAGE 145 F2864
ALL/IDEOS MARXISM REV

S66
DUROSELLE J.B.,"THE FUTURE OF THE ATLANTIC COMMUNITY." EUR+WWI USA+45 USSR NAT/G CAP/ISM REGION DETER NUC/PWR ATTIT MARXISM...INT/LAW 20 NATO. PAGE 35 F0686
FUT DIPLOM MYTH POLICY

S66
POSEN G.S.,"RECENT TRENDS IN SOVIET ECONOMIC
ECO/TAC

THOUGHT." USSR ECO/DEV PLAN CONTROL CENTRAL 20. PAGE 107 F2107
MARXISM INDUS PROFIT

B67

ANDERSON T.,RUSSIAN POLITICAL THOUGHT; AN INTRODUCTION. USSR NAT/G POL/PAR CHIEF MARXISM ...TIME/SEQ BIBLIOG 9/20. PAGE 5 F0099
TREND CONSTN ATTIT

B67

BROMKE A.,POLAND'S POLITICS: IDEALISM VS. REALISM. COM GERMANY POLAND RUSSIA USSR POL/PAR CATHISM ...BIBLIOG 19/20. PAGE 19 F0360
NAT/G DIPLOM MARXISM

B67

CHO S.S.,KOREA IN WORLD POLITICS 1940-1950; AN EVALUATION OF AMERICAN RESPONSIBILITY. KOREA USA+45 USSR CONSTN INT/ORG NAT/G FORCES FOR/AID ANOMIE SUPEGO MARXISM...DECISION BIBLIOG 20. PAGE 24 F0469
POLICY DIPLOM PROB/SOLV WAR

B67

DINERSTEIN H.S.,INTERVENTION AGAINST COMMUNISM (STUDIES IN INTERNATIONAL AFFAIRS NO. 1). CUBA DOMIN/REP GREECE USA+45 USSR VIETNAM OP/RES COERCE WAR 20. PAGE 33 F0643
MARXISM DIPLOM NAT/LISM

B67

FIELD G.L.,COMPARATIVE POLITICAL DEVELOPMENT: THE PRECEDENT OF THE WEST. FRANCE GERMANY SWEDEN UK USSR STRATA STRUCT POL/PAR...METH 20. PAGE 40 F0790
NAT/COMP CONCPT ECO/DEV SOCIETY

B67

FILENE P.G.,AMERICANS AND THE SOVIET EXPERIMENT, 1917-1933. USA-45 USSR INTELL NAT/G CAP/ISM DIPLOM EDU/PROP PRESS REV SOCISM...PSY 20. PAGE 41 F0793
ATTIT RIGID/FLEX MARXISM SOCIETY

B67

GRIFFITH W.E.,SINO-SOVIET RELATIONS, 1964-1965. CHINA/COM COM USSR CHIEF 20. PAGE 51 F1001
DIPLOM PWR DOMIN MARXISM

B67

GRIPP R.C.,PATTERNS OF SOVIET POLITICS (REV. ED.). USSR LAW ELITES LOC/G PLAN CONTROL CT/SYS CHOOSE ...POLICY BIBLIOG/A DICTIONARY 9/20. PAGE 51 F1003
COM ADJUD POL/PAR

B67

HALLE L.J.,THE COLD WAR AS HISTORY. AFR USSR WOR+45 ECO/TAC FOR/AID NUC/PWR WAR PEACE ORD/FREE ...MAJORIT TREND 20 KENNEDY/JF KHRUSH/N BERLIN/BLO. PAGE 54 F1048
DIPLOM BAL/PWR

B67

HARDT J.P.,MATHEMATICS AND COMPUTERS IN SOVIET ECONOMIC PLANNING. COM USSR OP/RES PROB/SOLV OPTIMAL...MODAL SIMUL 20. PAGE 55 F1082
PLAN TEC/DEV MATH COMPUT/IR

B67

MAZOUR A.G.,SOVIET ECONOMIC DEVELOPMENT: OPERATION OUTSTRIP: 1921-1965. USSR ECO/UNDEV FINAN CHIEF WORKER PROB/SOLV CONTROL PRODUC MARXISM...CHARTS ORG/CHARTS 20 STALIN/J. PAGE 87 F1711
ECO/TAC AGRI INDUS PLAN

B67

MENDEL A.P.,POLITICAL MEMOIRS 1905-1917 BY PAUL MILIUKOV (TRANS. BY CARL GOLDBERG). USSR AGRI DIPLOM ECO/TAC POPULISM...MAJORIT 20. PAGE 90 F1757
BIOG LEAD NAT/G CONSTN

B67

TANSKY L.,US AND USSR AID TO DEVELOPING COUNTRIES. INDIA TURKEY USA+45 USSR INDUS PLAN CAP/ISM WAR PWR WEALTH MARXISM...CHARTS NAT/COMP BIBLIOG 20. PAGE 128 F2534
ECO/UNDEV FOR/AID DIPLOM ECO/TAC

B67

TANSKY L.,US AND USSR AID TO DEVELOPING COUNTRIES. INDIA TURKEY UAR USA+45 USSR FINAN PLAN TEC/DEV ADMIN WEALTH...TREND METH/COMP 20. PAGE 128 F2535
FOR/AID ECO/UNDEV MARXISM CAP/ISM

B67

ZALESKI E.,PLANNING REFORMS IN THE SOVIET UNION 1962-1966. COM USSR NAT/G CONFER CONTROL EFFICIENCY MARXISM...POLICY DECISION 20. PAGE 150 F2957
ECO/DEV PLAN ADMIN CENTRAL

S67

"PROTEST AGAINST SOVIET INDUSTRIALIZATION ILLS IN LITHUANIA* A MEMORANDUM." USSR LITHUANIA NAT/G PROVS COST GEOG. PAGE 1 F0024
INDUS COLONIAL NAT/LISM PLAN

S67

ALEXANDER R.J.,"'THIRD FORCE' IN WORLD COMMUNISM?" CHINA/COM CUBA USSR INT/ORG DIPLOM TASK INGP/REL ATTIT PWR 20 CASTRO/F. PAGE 3 F0060
CHIEF MARXISM LEAD REV

S67

ANDERSON S.S.,"SOVIET RUSSIA AND THE TWO EUROPES." AFR USSR PROB/SOLV CENTRAL SOVEREIGN 20. PAGE 5 F0097
DIPLOM POLICY MARXISM

S67

AVTORKHANOV A.,"A NEW AGRARIAN REVOLUTION." COM USSR ECO/DEV PLAN TEC/DEV ADMIN CONTROL OPTIMAL WEALTH SOCISM 20 KHRUSH/N STALIN/J. PAGE 8 F0144
AGRI METH/COMP MARXISM OWN

S67

BASOV V.,"THE DEVELOPMENT OF PUBLIC EDUCATION AND THE BUDGET." USSR NAT/G CONTROL REV COST AGE...STAT 20. PAGE 11 F0204
BUDGET GIVE EDU/PROP SCHOOL

S67

CAMPBELL J.C.,"SOVIET-AMERICAN RELATIONS: CONFLICT AND COOPERATION." AFR USA+45 USSR AGREE WAR PEACE 20 KHRUSH/N KENNEDY/JF. PAGE 21 F0407
DIPLOM POLICY

S67

CATTELL D.T.,"THE FIFTIETH ANNIVERSARY: A SOVIET WATERSHED?" USSR CONSTN ECO/DEV NAT/G LEAD TOTALISM 20 KHRUSH/N. PAGE 22 F0430
MARXISM CHIEF POLICY ADJUST

S67

FEDYSHYN O.S.,"KHRUSHCHEV'S 'LEAP FORWARD': NATIONAL ASSIMILATION IN THE USSR AFTER STALIN." USSR PLAN NAT/LISM PERSON...POLICY 20 KHRUSH/N STALIN/J. PAGE 39 F0771
GP/REL INGP/REL MARXISM METH

S67

FRANKEL T.,"ECONOMIC REFORM* A TENTATIVE APPRAISAL." COM USSR OP/RES BUDGET CONFER EFFICIENCY PRODUC MARXISM SOCISM...MGT 20. PAGE 43 F0847
ECO/DEV INDUS PLAN WEALTH

S67

GEISS I.,"THE GERMANS AND THE MIDDLE EAST CRISIS." GERMANY/W ISLAM ISRAEL USSR POL/PAR RACE/REL MARXISM...GP/COMP 20 JEWS. PAGE 47 F0914
ATTIT DIPLOM WAR POLICY

S67

HUTCHINGS R.,"THE ENDING OF UNEMPLOYMENT IN THE USSR" USSR PLAN ECO/TAC PRICE INGP/REL...GEOG STAT CHARTS 20 MIGRATION. PAGE 63 F1247
WORKER AGRI INDUS MARXISM

S67

KENNY L.M.,"THE AFTERMATH OF DEFEAT IN EGYPT." ISLAM ISRAEL UAR UK USA+45 USSR INDUS FORCES ECO/TAC PRICE COERCE WEAPON COST ATTIT. PAGE 70 F1378
WAR ECO/UNDEV DIPLOM POLICY

S67

KOHN W.S.G.,"THE SOVEREIGNTY OF LIECHTENSTEIN." LIECHTENST SWITZERLND USSR CONSTN DEBATE WAR CONSERVE 18/20 UN. PAGE 72 F1417
SOVEREIGN NAT/G PWR DIPLOM

S67

LEONTYEV L.,"THE LENINIST PRINCIPLES OF SOCIALIST ECONOMIC MANAGEMENT." USA+45 USSR POL/PAR WORKER PLAN ECO/TAC EFFICIENCY PRODUC MARXISM...POLICY SOCIALIST MGT TREND 20 LENIN/VI MARX/KARL. PAGE 78 F1529
SOCISM CAP/ISM IDEA/COMP ECO/DEV

S67

MAJSTRENKO I.W.,"PROBLEMS CONFRONTING SOVIET AGRICULTURE." COM USSR ECO/DEV ECO/TAC EFFICIENCY OPTIMAL WEALTH MARXISM 20. PAGE 84 F1643
AGRI PROB/SOLV CENTRAL TEC/DEV

S67

NUSENBAUM A.A.,"ON THE QUESTION OF TENDENCIES IN AMERICAN EDUCATION." USA+45 USSR SOCIETY SCHOOL RATIONAL 20. PAGE 99 F1946
MARXIST IDEA/COMP GEN/LAWS EDU/PROP

S67

ORAZEM F.,"THE NEW SOVIET PLAN FOR AGRICULTURE (1960-1970)" USSR WORKER CAP/ISM ECO/TAC PRICE OWN HABITAT MARXISM...CHARTS 20. PAGE 101 F1994
AGRI PLAN COM ECO/DEV

S67

POWELL D.,"THE EFFECTIVENESS OF SOVIET ANTI-RELIGIOUS PROPAGANDA." USSR NAT/G DOMIN LEGIT NAT/LISM 20. PAGE 107 F2109
EDU/PROP ATTIT SECT CONTROL

S67

RICHMAN B.M.,"SOVIET MANAGEMENT IN TRANSITION." USSR FINAN MARKET EX/STRUC PLAN PROB/SOLV TEC/DEV CONTROL LEAD CENTRAL EFFICIENCY...METH/COMP 20 REFORMERS. PAGE 111 F2186
MGT MARXISM POLICY AUTHORIT

S67

STOLTE S.C.,"THREE PROBLEMS FACING THE SOVIET BLOC." ASIA COM USA+45 USSR FORCES MARXISM ...IDEA/COMP METH/COMP 20 NATO WARSAW/P. PAGE 127 F2496
ECO/TAC DIPLOM INT/ORG POLICY

S67

TABORSKY E.,"THE CLASS STRUGGLE, THE PROLETARIAT, AND THE DEVELOPING NATIONS." USSR LABOR POL/PAR FOR/AID COLONIAL GP/REL 20. PAGE 128 F2521
DIPLOM MARXISM ECO/UNDEV WORKER

S67

WILES P.J.,"THE POLITICAL AND SOCIAL PREREQUISITES FOR A SOVIET-TYPE ECONOMY." COM USSR LAW CULTURE CREATE ADMIN FEEDBACK ROUTINE COST OPTIMAL TOTALISM MARXISM 20. PAGE 146 F2883
ECO/DEV PLAN EX/STRUC EFFICIENCY

S67

WOLFE T.W.,"SOVIET MILITARY POLICY AT THE FIFTY YEAR MARK." USSR VIETNAM WOR+45 RATION AGREE WAR WEAPON CIVMIL/REL TREATY. PAGE 148 F2917
FORCES POLICY TIME/SEQ PLAN

B68

NENAROKOV A.P.,RUSSIA IN THE 20TH CENTURY: THE OFFICIAL SOVIET HISTORY. USSR SOCIETY REV...AUD/VIS
COM ADJUST

20. PAGE 97 F1913 — MARXISM

UTAH....UTAH

UTIL....UTILITY, USEFULNESS

B12
HOBSON J.A.,THE EVOLUTION OF MODERN CAPITALISM. MOD/EUR UK STRATA ECO/DEV INDUS INCOME UTIL WEALTH ...SOC GEN/LAWS 7/20. PAGE 60 F1184 — CAP/ISM WORKER TEC/DEV TIME/SEQ

B14
HOBSON J.A.,WORK AND WEALTH. CULTURE FINAN INDUS WORKER TEC/DEV ECO/TAC GIVE PAY PRICE COST PRODUC UTIL. PAGE 60 F1185 — WEALTH INCOME GEN/LAWS

N19
ARNDT H.W.,AUSTRALIAN FOREIGN AID POLICY (PAMPHLET). ECO/UNDEV DIPLOM GIVE GOV/REL COST UTIL PWR...CHARTS 20 AUSTRAL PAPUA NEW/GUINEA. PAGE 6 F0114 — FOR/AID POLICY ECO/TAC EFFICIENCY

N19
CHATTERS C.H.,NEW MUNICIPAL REVENUES FOR NEW MUNICIPAL EXPENDITURES (PAMPHLET). PLAN PRICE UTIL HABITAT...IDEA/COMP MUNICH 20. PAGE 23 F0457 — LOC/G BUDGET TAX

B31
JEVONS W.S.,THE THEORY OF POLITICAL ECONOMY (4TH ED.; 1ST ED. 1871). WOR-45 FINAN MARKET RENT WEALTH ...LOG MATH QUANT CON/ANAL IDEA/COMP BIBLIOG METH 17/19. PAGE 67 F1318 — GEN/LAWS UTIL LABOR

B32
ROBBINS L.,AN ESSAY ON THE NATURE AND SIGNIFICANCE OF ECONOMIC SCIENCE. DEMAND EQUILIB PRODUC UTIL ...ECOMETRIC 20. PAGE 112 F2201 — GEN/LAWS METH/COMP ECO/DEV

B48
SAMUELSON P.A.,FOUNDATIONS OF ECONOMIC ANALYSIS. MARKET RATION DEMAND UTIL...MATH METH T 20. PAGE 115 F2276 — EQUILIB GEN/LAWS ECO/DEV

S50
DREYFUS S.,"THE INDUSTRIAL DESIGNER AND THE BUSINESSMAN." SERV/IND PROB/SOLV ECO/TAC COST EFFICIENCY PROFIT RATIONAL...DECISION MGT. PAGE 34 F0662 — CONSULT INDUS PRODUC UTIL

B56
PARSONS T.,ECONOMY AND SOCIETY: A STUDY IN THE INTEGRATION OF ECONOMIC AND SOCIAL THEORY. UNIV ACT/RES...SOC CHARTS IDEA/COMP BIBLIOG/A. PAGE 103 F2031 — STRUCT METH/CNCPT UTIL PHIL/SCI

B57
OLIVECRONA K.,THE PROBLEM OF THE MONETARY UNIT. AFR UNIV PAY PRICE UTIL...MATH 20 MONEY SILVER. PAGE 101 F1986 — FINAN ECO/TAC ECO/DEV CONCPT

B59
US GENERAL ACCOUNTING OFFICE,EXAM OF ECONOMIC AND TECHNICAL ASSISTANCE PROGRAM FOR INDIA INT'NAT'L COOP ADMIN REPORT TO CONGRESS 1955-1958. INDIA USA+45 ECO/UNDEV FINAN PLAN DIPLOM COST UTIL WEALTH ...CHARTS 20 CONGRESS AID. PAGE 136 F2679 — FOR/AID EFFICIENCY ECO/TAC TEC/DEV

L59
SIMON H.A.,"THEORIES OF DECISION-MAKING IN ECONOMICS AND BEHAVIORAL SCIENCE" (BMR)" MARKET BARGAIN UTIL DRIVE...DECISION MGT PROBABIL HYPO/EXP SIMUL 20 BEHAVIORSM. PAGE 122 F2409 — PSY GEN/LAWS PROB/SOLV

S59
HARING J.E.,"UTILITY THEORY, DECISION THEORY, AND PROFIT MAXIMIZATION." PROB/SOLV GAMBLE UTIL ...DECISION CHARTS IDEA/COMP HYPO/EXP SIMUL GEN/METH. PAGE 55 F1083 — PROBABIL RISK GAME

S59
TEITSWORTH C.S.,"GROWING ROLE OF THE COMPANY ECONOMIST." USA+45 PLAN PROB/SOLV CAP/ISM ECO/TAC ADMIN ATTIT MGT. PAGE 129 F2541 — INDUS CONSULT UTIL DECISION

B60
ATOMIC INDUSTRIAL FORUM,ATOMS FOR INDUSTRY: WORLD FORUM. WOR+45 FINAN COST UTIL...JURID ANTHOL 20. PAGE 7 F0137 — NUC/PWR INDUS PLAN PROB/SOLV

B60
WALLACE R.A.,CONGRESSIONAL CONTROL OF FEDERAL SPENDING. USA+45 CONSTN NAT/G OP/RES CONFER DEBATE PERS/REL UTIL RIGID/FLEX PWR OBJECTIVE...OBS CHARTS. PAGE 143 F2808 — LEGIS DELIB/GP BUDGET

N60
ERDMAN P.E.,COMMON MARKETS AND FREE TRADE AREAS (PAMPHLET). USA+45 MARKET INT/ORG TEC/DEV DIPLOM UTIL...CON/ANAL CHARTS BIBLIOG 20 EEC OEEC. PAGE 38 F0743 — TREND PROB/SOLV INT/TRADE ECO/DEV

B61
DEWITT N.,EDUCATION AND PROFESSIONAL EMPLOYMENT IN THE USSR. USSR PROF/ORG WORKER PLAN ADMIN UTIL AGE/C AGE/Y MARXISM...STAT CHARTS 20. PAGE 32 F0629 — EDU/PROP ACADEM SCHOOL INTELL

B61
DOIG J.W.,THE POLITICS OF METROPOLITAN TRANSPORTATION. DELIB/GP WORKER DIPLOM TASK EFFICIENCY UTIL...CHARTS BIBLIOG MUNICH 20 NEW/YORK NEW/JERSEY PUB/TRANS RAILROAD. PAGE 34 F0652 — PROB/SOLV STRATA DIST/IND

B61
SHONFIELD A.,ECONOMIC GROWTH AND INFLATION; A STUDY OF INDIAN PLANNING. AFR INDIA AGRI INDUS TEC/DEV CONTROL DEMAND UTIL 20. PAGE 121 F2384 — ECO/UNDEV PRICE PLAN BUDGET

B61
UNIVS-NATL BUR COMM ECO RES,PUBLIC FINANCES: NEEDS, SOURCES, AND UTILIZATION. USA+45 FORCES PLAN TAX CONFER PRICE FEDERAL UTIL...ANTHOL MUNICH 20. PAGE 133 F2623 — NAT/G FINAN DECISION BUDGET

S61
BENNION E.G.,"ECONOMETRICS FOR MANAGEMENT." USA+45 INDUS EX/STRUC ACT/RES COMPUTER UTIL...MATH STAT PREDICT METH/COMP HYPO/EXP. PAGE 13 F0248 — ECOMETRIC MGT SIMUL DECISION

S61
HIRSHLEIFER J.,"THE BAYESIAN APPROACH TO STATISTICAL DECISION: AN EXPOSITION." OP/RES PROB/SOLV UTIL...PROBABIL CHARTS IDEA/COMP HYPO/EXP 20. PAGE 60 F1178 — DECISION GAME SIMUL STAT

B62
ROUND TABLE ON EUROPE'S ROLE IN LATIN AMERICAN DEVELOPMENT. EUR+WWI L/A+17C PLAN BAL/PAY UTIL ROLE WEALTH...CHARTS ANTHOL 20 UN INT/AM/DEV. PAGE 1 F0017 — ECO/UNDEV FINAN TEC/DEV FOR/AID

B62
NATIONAL BUREAU ECONOMIC RES,THE RATE AND DIRECTION OF INVENTIVE ACTIVITY: ECONOMIC AND SOCIAL FACTORS. STRUCT INDUS MARKET R+D CREATE OP/RES TEC/DEV EFFICIENCY PRODUC RATIONAL UTIL...WELF/ST PHIL/SCI METH/CNCPT TIME. PAGE 97 F1895 — DECISION PROB/SOLV MGT

B64
BOURGOIGNIE G.E.,JEUNE AFRIQUE MOBILISABLE; LES PROBLEMES DE LA JEUNESSE DESOEUVREE EN AFRIQUE NOIRE. INT/ORG VOL/ASSN ECO/TAC ROUTINE UTIL ATTIT 20. PAGE 17 F0324 — AGE/Y AFR CREATE ECO/UNDEV

B64
COLUMBIA U SCHOOL OF LAW,PUBLIC INTERNATIONAL DEVELOPMENT FINANCING IN INDIA. GERMANY/W INDIA UK USA+45 INDUS PLAN TEC/DEV DIPLOM ECO/TAC GIVE ADMIN UTIL ATTIT 20. PAGE 26 F0512 — ECO/UNDEV FINAN FOR/AID INT/ORG

B64
HARBISON F.H.,EDUCATION, MANPOWER, AND ECONOMIC GROWTH. WOR+45 ECO/DEV ECO/UNDEV ACADEM LABOR SCHOOL WORKER UTIL...IDEA/COMP NAT/COMP. PAGE 55 F1075 — PLAN TEC/DEV EDU/PROP SKILL

B64
MCNULTY J.E.,SOME ECONOMIC ASPECTS OF BUSINESS ORGANIZATION. ECO/DEV UTIL...MGT CHARTS BIBLIOG METH 20. PAGE 88 F1734 — ADMIN LG/CO GEN/LAWS

S64
NEWLYN W.T.,"MONETARY SYSTEMS AND INTEGRATION" AFR BUDGET ADMIN FEDERAL PRODUC PROFIT UTIL...CHARTS 20 AFRICA/E. PAGE 98 F1922 — ECO/UNDEV REGION METH/COMP FINAN

B65
BLAIR T.L.V.,AFRICA: A MARKET PROFILE. AFR COM/IND DIST/IND FINAN UTIL...DECISION CHARTS BIBLIOG 20. PAGE 15 F0295 — MARKET OP/RES ECO/UNDEV INDUS

B65
HICKMAN B.G.,QUANTITATIVE PLANNING OF ECONOMIC POLICY. FRANCE NETHERLAND OP/RES PRICE ROUTINE UTIL ...POLICY DECISION ECOMETRIC METH/CNCPT STAT STYLE CHINJAP. PAGE 59 F1162 — PROB/SOLV PLAN QUANT

B65
LAZARUS S.,RESOLVING BUSINESS DISPUTES: THE POTENTIAL OF COMMERCIAL ARBITRATION. USA+45 INDUS LG/CO ACT/RES PROB/SOLV EDU/PROP CONSEN UTIL ...TREND 20. PAGE 76 F1496 — FINAN DELIB/GP CONSULT ADJUD

B65
MAO J.C.T.,EFFICIENCY IN PUBLIC URBAN RENEWAL EXPENDITURES THROUGH CAPITAL BUDGETING. USA+45 FINAN LOC/G NAT/G NEIGH REGION UTIL...GEOG METH/CNCPT STAT SIMUL GEN/LAWS MUNICH 20 URBAN/RNWL. PAGE 85 F1662 — TEC/DEV BUDGET PROB/SOLV

B65
ROSS A.M.,EMPLOYMENT POLICY AND THE LABOR MARKET. USA+45 MARKET LABOR NAT/G PROB/SOLV PAY EDU/PROP PARTIC UTIL...POLICY 20. PAGE 114 F2242 — ECO/DEV WORKER WEALTH DEMAND

B65
WEIDENBAUM M.L.,CONGRESS AND THE FEDERAL BUDGET. FINAN ACT/RES DOMIN CONFER EXEC UTIL PWR NEW/LIB ...CHARTS CONGRESS. PAGE 144 F2844 — BUDGET LEGIS PLAN DECISION

B66
LANSING J.B.,TRANSPORTATION AND ECONOMIC POLICY. USA+45 COST DEMAND...ECOMETRIC TREND CHARTS IDEA/COMP T 20. PAGE 76 F1481 — DIST/IND OP/RES ECO/DEV UTIL

B66
US SENATE COMM GOVT OPERATIONS,INTERGOVERNMENTAL PERSONNEL ACT OF 1966. USA+45 NAT/G CONSULT — ADMIN LEGIS

DELIB/GP WORKER TEC/DEV PAY AUTOMAT UTIL 20 CONGRESS. PAGE 139 F2730 — EFFICIENCY EDU/PROP

B66
WESTON J.F.,THE SCOPE AND METHODOLOGY OF FINANCE. PLAN TEC/DEV CONTROL EFFICIENCY INCOME UTIL...MGT CONCPT MATH STAT TREND METH 20. PAGE 145 F2863 — FINAN ECO/DEV POLICY PRICE

B66
WOODMAN H.D.,SLAVERY AND THE SOUTHERN ECONOMY: SOURCES AND READINGS. USA-45 CULTURE STRUCT AGRI ECO/TAC LEAD RACE/REL DISCRIM EFFICIENCY...CHARTS ANTHOL MUNICH 18/19 NEGRO SOUTH/US. PAGE 148 F2922 — ECO/DEV STRATA WORKER UTIL

B67
ENKE S.,DEFENSE MANAGEMENT. USA+45 R+D FORCES WORKER PLAN ECO/TAC ADMIN NUC/PWR BAL/PAY UTIL WEALTH...MGT DEPT/DEFEN. PAGE 38 F0738 — DECISION DELIB/GP EFFICIENCY BUDGET

B67
LINDER S.B.,TRADE AND TRADE POLICY FOR DEVELOPMENT. OP/RES DIPLOM TARIFFS UTIL WEALTH...BIBLIOG 20. PAGE 80 F1569 — ECO/UNDEV ECO/TAC TEC/DEV INT/TRADE

B67
NELSON R.R.,TECHNOLOGY, ECONOMIC GROWTH, AND PUBLIC POLICY. USA+45 PLAN GP/REL UTIL KNOWL...POLICY PHIL/SCI CHARTS BIBLIOG 20. PAGE 97 F1912 — R+D CONSULT CREATE ACT/RES

S67
BARAN P.,"THE FUTURE COMPUTER UTILITY." USA+45 NAT/G PLAN CONTROL COST...POLICY 20. PAGE 9 F0177 — COMPUTER UTIL FUT TEC/DEV

UTILITAR....UTILITARIANISM

UTILITY....SEE UTIL

UTOPIA....ENVISIONED GENERAL SOCIAL CONDITIONS; SEE ALSO STERTYP

B22
FOURIER C.,TRAITE DE L'ASSOCIATION DOMESTIQUE-AGRICOLE (2 VOLS.). UNIV SOCIETY INDUS ECO/TAC PERSON MORAL ANARCH. PAGE 43 F0834 — VOL/ASSN AGRI UTOPIA CONCPT

B36
BELLOC H.,THE RESTORATION OF PROPERTY. UK STRATA NAT/G PROF/ORG DELIB/GP WORKER CREATE PROB/SOLV ECO/TAC PARTIC UTOPIA ORD/FREE SOCISM 20. PAGE 13 F0238 — CONTROL MAJORIT CAP/ISM OWN

B50
SOREL G.,REFLECTIONS ON VIOLENCE (1908) (TRANS. BY T.E. HULME AND J. ROTH). UNIV SOCIETY LABOR UTOPIA MORAL SOCISM...ANARCH SOCIALIST CONCPT 20. PAGE 124 F2445 — COERCE REV WORKER MYTH

C50
ROUSSEAU J.J.,"A DISCOURSE ON POLITICAL ECONOMY" (1755) IN THE SOCIAL CONTRACT AND DISCOURSES." UNIV SOCIETY STRATA STRUCT CONSEN EQUILIB HAPPINESS UTOPIA HEALTH WEALTH...POLICY WELF/ST. PAGE 114 F2252 — NAT/G ECO/TAC TAX GEN/LAWS

B53
MENDE T.,WORLD POWER IN THE BALANCE. FUT USA+45 USSR WOR-45 ECO/DEV ECO/TAC INT/TRADE EDU/PROP UTOPIA ATTIT...HUM CONCPT TREND TOT/POP 20. PAGE 90 F1756 — WOR+45 PWR BAL/PWR AFR

B55
GEORGE H.,PROGRESS AND POVERTY (1880). STRATA STRUCT INDUS TEC/DEV CAP/ISM EQUILIB INCOME OWN UTOPIA...WELF/ST CONCPT NEW/IDEA 19. PAGE 47 F0915 — ECO/DEV ECO/TAC TAX WEALTH

B59
ENGELS F.,SOCIALISM: UTOPIAN AND SCIENTIFIC (2ND ED.). SOCISM...CONCPT CON/ANAL GEN/LAWS 19 DUHRING/E. PAGE 38 F0732 — MARXISM PHIL/SCI UTOPIA IDEA/COMP

B59
HENDEL S.,THE SOVIET CRUCIBLE. USSR LEAD COERCE NAT/LISM UTOPIA PWR...POLICY CONCPT ANTHOL 20 STALIN/J LENIN/VI MARX/KARL BOLSHEVIK. PAGE 58 F1147 — COM MARXISM REV TOTALISM

B61
THEOBALD R.,THE CHALLENGE OF ABUNDANCE. USA+45 WOR+45 MARKET DIPLOM FOR/AID REV PRODUC UTOPIA SUPEGO...POLICY TREND BIBLIOG/A 20. PAGE 129 F2554 — WELF/ST ECO/UNDEV PROB/SOLV ECO/TAC

B62
DE GRAZIA S.,OF TIME, WORK, AND LEISURE. USA+45 ECO/DEV WORKER HAPPINESS UTOPIA ALL/VALS...SOC NEW/IDEA TIME. PAGE 31 F0599 — CULTURE LEISURE CONCPT

B63
MARX K.,THE POVERTY OF PHILOSOPHY (1847). SOCIETY STRATA INDUS WORKER OWN UTOPIA SOCISM...GEN/LAWS MARX/KARL. PAGE 86 F1692 — MARXIST PRODUC

B63
NOMAD M.,POLITICAL HERETICS: FROM PLATO TO MAO TSE-TUNG. UNIV INGP/REL...SOC IDEA/COMP. PAGE 98 F1931 — SOCIETY UTOPIA ALL/IDEOS CONCPT

S67
GORMAN W.,"ELLUL - A PROPHETIC VOICE." WOR+45 ELITES SOCIETY ACT/RES PLAN BAL/PWR DOMIN CONTROL PARTIC TOTALISM PWR 20. PAGE 49 F0963 — CREATE ORD/FREE EX/STRUC UTOPIA

B76
FOURIER C.,SOCIAL DESTINIES, IN A. BRISBANE, GENERAL INTRODUCTION TO SOCIAL SCIENCE. UNIV AGRI INDUS SECT PRODUC...PHIL/SCI CONCPT. PAGE 43 F0835 — UTOPIA SOCIETY PERSON VOL/ASSN

B99
KROPOTKIN P.,FIELDS, FACTORIES, AND WORKSHOPS. UNIV INTELL ECO/DEV LG/CO SCHOOL SML/CO ECO/TAC PRODUC UTOPIA...NEW/IDEA MUNICH. PAGE 74 F1445 — SOCIETY WORKER AGRI INDUS

UTTAR/PRAD....UTTAR PRADESH, INDIA

UYEHARA C.H. F0499,F2755

V

VACCARO J.R. F2756

VAID K.N. F2757

VAIZEY J.E. F2216,F2758

VAKIL C.N. F2759

VALIDITY (AS CONCEPT)....SEE METH/CNCPT

VALLET R. F2760

VALUE ADDED TAX....SEE VALUE/ADD

VALUE/ADD....VALUE ADDED TAX

VALUE-FREE THOUGHT....SEE OBJECTIVE

VALUES....SEE VALUES INDEX, P. XIII

VAN DER HORST S.T. F2761

VAN KLAVEREN J. F2762

VAN RENSBURG P. F2763

VAN SLYKE L.P. F2764

VANBUREN/M....PRESIDENT MARTIN VAN BUREN

VANDUSEN A.C. F1410

VANEK J. F2765,F2766,F2767

VATICAN....VATICAN

VEBLEN T.B. F2768,F2769,F2770,F2771,F2772

VEBLEN/T....THORSTEIN VEBLEN

VEIT L.A. F2096

VEIT O. F2773

VELEZ GARCIA J. F2774

VELYAMINOV G. F2775

VENEZUELA....VENEZUELA; SEE ALSO L/A+17C

B64
MAZA ZAVALA D.F.,VENEZUELA; UNA ECONOMIA DEPENDIENTE. L/A+17C VENEZUELA FINAN INDUS ...ECOMETRIC STAT TREND 20. PAGE 87 F1710 — ECO/UNDEV BAL/PAY INT/TRADE PRICE

S65
BRANDENBURG F.,"THE RELEVANCE OF MEXICAN EXPERIENCE TO LATIN AMERICAN DEVELOPMENT." BRAZIL CHILE VENEZUELA STRUCT ECO/UNDEV AGRI CREATE ECO/TAC ...STAT RECORD MEXIC/AMER ARGEN COLOMB. PAGE 18 F0340 — L/A+17C GOV/COMP

S67
PETRAS J.,"GUERRILLA MOVEMENTS IN LATIN AMERICA - I." GUATEMALA PERU VENEZUELA NAT/G COLONIAL LEAD ATTIT PWR...TIME/SEQ METH/COMP 20 COLOMB. PAGE 105 — GUERRILLA REV L/A+17C

F2072 MARXISM

VENICE....VENETIAN REPUBLIC

VENKATESWARAN R.J. F2776

VENTRE F.T. F2777

VERDOORN P.J. F0783

VERMONT....VERMONT

B64
COMMITTEE ECONOMIC DEVELOPMENT,COMMUNITY ECONOMIC DEVELOPMENT PROGRAMS. USA+45 FINAN INDUS LG/CO PROF/ORG CREATE GP/REL MUNICH NEW/YORK VERMONT PENNSYLVAN IN ARKANSAS. PAGE 27 F0519 — LOC/G LABOR PLAN

VERNEY D.V. F2778

VERNON R. F1212,F2779,F2780,F2781

VERSAILLES....VERSAILLES, FRANCE

VERSLUYS J.D.N. F2782

VERWOERD/H....HENDRIK VERWOERD

VETO....VETO AND VETOING

VIA J.W. F2783

VICE/PRES....VICE-PRESIDENCY (ALL NATIONS)

VICEREGAL....VICEROYALTY; VICEROY SYSTEM

VICHY....VICHY, FRANCE

VICTORIA/Q....QUEEN VICTORIA

VIENNA/CNV....VIENNA CONVENTION ON CONSULAR RELATIONS

VIET J. F2784

VIET MINH....SEE VIETNAM, GUERRILLA, COLONIAL

VIET/CONG....VIET CONG

VIETNAM....VIETNAM IN GENERAL; SEE ALSO S/ASIA, VIETNAM/N, VIETNAM/S

N19
DEANE H.,THE WAR IN VIETNAM (PAMPHLET). AFR CHINA/COM VIETNAM BAL/PWR DIPLOM ECO/TAC SOCISM INTERVENT INTERVENT. PAGE 31 F0610 — WAR SOCIALIST MORAL CAP/ISM

B66
US HOUSE COMM FOREIGN AFFAIRS,HEARINGS ON HR 12449 A BILL TO AMEND FURTHER THE FOREIGN ASSISTANCE ACT OF 1961. AFR ASIA L/A+17C USA+45 VIETNAM INT/ORG TEC/DEV INT/TRADE ATTIT ORD/FREE 20 UN NATO CONGRESS AID. PAGE 137 F2692 — FOR/AID ECO/TAC ECO/UNDEV DIPLOM

B67
DINERSTEIN H.S.,INTERVENTION AGAINST COMMUNISM (STUDIES IN INTERNATIONAL AFFAIRS NO. 1). CUBA DOMIN/REP GREECE USA+45 USSR VIETNAM OP/RES COERCE WAR 20. PAGE 33 F0643 — MARXISM DIPLOM NAT/LISM

B67
FALL B.B.,HO CHI MINH ON REVOLUTION: SELECTED WRITINGS, 1920-66. COM VIETNAM ELITES NAT/G COERCE GUERRILLA RACE/REL MARXISM...MARXIST ANTHOL 20. PAGE 39 F0761 — REV COLONIAL ECO/UNDEV S/ASIA

B67
GIAP V.N.,BIG VICTORY, GREAT TASK. VIETNAM WOR+45 FORCES PLAN DOMIN LEGIT RISK PEACE 20. PAGE 47 F0921 — WAR LEAD ATTIT INSPECT

B67
MARTIN P.,CANADA AND THE QUEST FOR PEACE. CANADA VIETNAM ECO/UNDEV PLAN FOR/AID WAR 20 UN. PAGE 86 F1684 — DIPLOM PEACE INT/ORG POLICY

B67
MCNELLY T.,SOURCES IN MODERN EAST ASIAN HISTORY AND POLITICS. KOREA VIETNAM CULTURE DIPLOM COLONIAL REV WAR PWR ALL/IDEOS MARXISM...ANTHOL 20 CHINJAP. PAGE 88 F1733 — NAT/COMP ASIA S/ASIA SOCIETY

B67
US SENATE COMM ON FOREIGN REL,FOREIGN ASSISTANCE ACT OF 1967. VIETNAM WOR+45 DELIB/GP CONFER CONTROL WAR WEAPON BAL/PAY...CENSUS CHARTS SENATE. PAGE 139 F2744 — FOR/AID LAW DIPLOM POLICY

L67
MCALLISTER J.T. JR.,"THE POSSIBILITIES FOR DIPLOMACY IN SOUTHEAST ASIA." LAOS VIETNAM INT/ORG NAT/G PROVS BAL/PWR DOMIN AGREE COLONIAL WAR PWR 17/20 TREATY. PAGE 88 F1716 — DIPLOM S/ASIA

S67
GONZALEZ M.P.,"CUBA, UNA REVOLUCION EN MARCHA." CUBA L/A+17C USA+45 VIETNAM ECO/UNDEV FORCES DIPLOM DOMIN...POLICY MARXIST NAT/COMP CASTRO/F. PAGE 48 F0946 — REV NAT/G COLONIAL SOVEREIGN

S67
MCCOLL R.W.,"A POLITICAL GEOGRAPHY OF REVOLUTION: CHINA, VIETNAM, AND THAILAND." ASIA THAILAND VIETNAM FORCES CONTROL 20. PAGE 88 F1720 — REV GEOG PLAN DECISION

S67
WOLFE T.W.,"SOVIET MILITARY POLICY AT THE FIFTY YEAR MARK." USSR VIETNAM WOR+45 RATION AGREE WAR WEAPON CIVMIL/REL TREATY. PAGE 148 F2917 — FORCES POLICY TIME/SEQ PLAN

VIETNAM/N....NORTH VIETNAM

B67
US SENATE COMM ON FOREIGN REL,HARRISON E. SALISBURY'S TRIP TO NORTH VIETNAM. CHINA/COM USA+45 VIETNAM/N PRESS TASK GUERRILLA CONSEN EFFICIENCY PEACE DRIVE...OBS SENATE. PAGE 139 F2743 — DIPLOM WAR FORCES ATTIT

VIETNAM/S....SOUTH VIETNAM

B58
US OPERATIONS MISSION TO VIET,BUILDING ECONOMIC STRENGTH (PAMPHLET). USA+45 VIETNAM/S INDUS TEC/DEV BUDGET ADMIN EATING HEALTH...STAT 20. PAGE 138 F2725 — FOR/AID ECO/UNDEV AGRI EDU/PROP

B62
JORDAN A.A. JR.,FOREIGN AID AND THE DEFENSE OF SOUTHEAST ASIA. PAKISTAN VIETNAM/S FINAN PLAN BUDGET ECO/TAC DETER WAR ORD/FREE...POLICY DECISION CENSUS CHARTS BIBLIOG 20. PAGE 68 F1341 — FOR/AID S/ASIA FORCES ECO/UNDEV

B64
LINDHOLM R.W.,ECONOMIC DEVELOPMENT POLICY WITH EMPHASIS ON VIET-NAM. KOREA/S PAKISTAN VIETNAM/S AGRI INDUS CONSULT DELIB/GP FOR/AID...METH 20. PAGE 80 F1571 — ECO/UNDEV TAX FINAN ECO/TAC

S67
BENNETT J.T.,"POLITICAL IMPLICATIONS OF ECONOMIC CHANGE: SOUTH VIETNAM." VIETNAM/S INGP/REL INCOME ATTIT 20 AID. PAGE 13 F0247 — ECO/UNDEV INDUS AGRI PRODUC

VILLA/P....PANCHO VILLA

VILLARD/OG....OSWALD GARRISON VILLARD

VINCENT W.S. F2785

VINER J. F2786,F2787,F2788

VINER/J....JACOB VINER

B59
STOVEL J.A.,CANADA IN THE WORLD ECONOMY. CANADA PRICE DEMAND...STAT CHARTS BIBLIOG 20 VINER/J. PAGE 127 F2499 — INT/TRADE BAL/PAY FINAN ECO/TAC

VIOLENCE....SEE COERCE, ALSO PROCESSES AND PRACTICES INDEX, PART G, PAGE XIII

VIRGIN/ISL....VIRGIN ISLANDS

VIRGINIA....VIRGINIA

B30
GREEN F.M.,CONSTITUTIONAL DEVELOPMENT IN THE SOUTH ATLANTIC STATES, 1776-1860; A STUDY IN THE EVOLUTION OF DEMOCRACY. USA-45 ELITES SOCIETY STRATA ECO/DEV AGRI POL/PAR EX/STRUC LEGIS CT/SYS REGION...BIBLIOG 18/19 MARYLAND VIRGINIA GEORGIA NORTH/CAR SOUTH/CAR. PAGE 50 F0984 — CONSTN PROVS PLURISM REPRESENT

VISTA....VOLUNTEERS IN SERVICE TO AMERICA (VISTA)

VOL/ASSN....VOLUNTARY ASSOCIATION

B02
WEBB S.,THE HISTORY OF TRADE UNIONISM. UK PARTIC ...OBS CHARTS BIBLIOG/A 15/19 CASEBOOK. PAGE 144 F2837 — LABOR VOL/ASSN GP/REL

N19
STEUBER F.A.,THE CONTRIBUTION OF SWITZERLAND TO THE ECONOMIC AND SOCIAL DEVELOPMENT OF LOW-INCOME COUNTRIES (PAMPHLET). SWITZERLND FINAN NAT/G VOL/ASSN INT/TRADE DRIVE...CHARTS 20. PAGE 126 — FOR/AID ECO/UNDEV PLAN DIPLOM

F2482

N19
STUTZ R.L.,COLLECTIVE DEALING BY UNITS OF LOCAL GOVERNMENT IN CONNECTICUT (PAMPHLET). USA+45 LOC/G PROVS...STAT MUNICH 20 CONNECTICT. PAGE 127 F2508
VOL/ASSN LABOR WORKER

N19
VELYAMINOV G.,AFRICA AND THE COMMON MARKET (PAMPHLET). AFR MARKET VOL/ASSN ECO/TAC COLONIAL ORD/FREE...SOCIALIST 20 THIRD/WRLD. PAGE 141 F2775
INT/ORG INT/TRADE SOVEREIGN ECO/UNDEV

B20
BUCK S.J.,THE AGRARIAN CRUSADE: A CHRONICLE OF THE FARMER IN POLITICS. USA-45 INDUS PROB/SOLV PWR WEALTH...GEOG CENSUS 19/20 GREENBACK GRANGE SILVER. PAGE 20 F0381
AGRI POPULISM VOL/ASSN POL/PAR

B20
WEBB S.,INDUSTRIAL DEMOCRACY. UK PARTIC GP/REL ...SOC OBS RECORD CHARTS 18/20. PAGE 144 F2838
LABOR NAT/G VOL/ASSN MAJORIT

B22
FOURIER C.,TRAITE DE L'ASSOCIATION DOMESTIQUE-AGRICOLE (2 VOLS.). UNIV SOCIETY INDUS ECO/TAC PERSON MORAL ANARCH. PAGE 43 F0834
VOL/ASSN AGRI UTOPIA CONCPT

B28
CASSEL G.,FOREIGN INVESTMENTS. GERMANY UK USA-45 WOR-45 ECO/DEV NAT/G VOL/ASSN CAP/ISM REPAR ATTIT WEALTH...METH/CNCPT STAT SIMUL STERTYP ANTHOL FOR/TRADE TOT/POP VAL/FREE 20. PAGE 22 F0426
FINAN ECO/TAC BAL/PAY

B28
TRUE A.C.,A HISTORY OF AGRICULTURAL EXTENSION WORK IN THE UNITED STATES, 1785-1923. USA-45 LAW SCHOOL WAR ADJUST...CHARTS BIBLIOG 18/20 SMITH/LEVR COUNTY/AGT. PAGE 131 F2591
EDU/PROP AGRI VOL/ASSN PLAN

B34
GRAHAM F.D.,PROTECTIVE TARIFFS. FUT USA+45 WOR-45 INDUS MARKET VOL/ASSN PLAN CAP/ISM ECO/TAC PEACE ATTIT DRIVE HEALTH ORD/FREE...OBS TREND GEN/LAWS FOR/TRADE 20. PAGE 50 F0970
INT/ORG TARIFFS

S35
BONNETT C.E.,"THE EVOLUTION OF BUSINESS GROUPINGS." ECO/TAC EDU/PROP PRICE LOBBY ORD/FREE. PAGE 16 F0315
VOL/ASSN GP/REL PROB/SOLV

B38
HOBSON J.A.,IMPERIALISM. MOD/EUR UK WOR-45 CULTURE ECO/UNDEV NAT/G VOL/ASSN PLAN EDU/PROP LEGIT REGION COERCE ATTIT PWR...POLICY PLURIST TIME/SEQ GEN/LAWS TERR/GP 19/20. PAGE 60 F1187
DOMIN ECO/TAC BAL/PWR COLONIAL

B43
BRADY R.A.,BUSINESS AS A SYSTEM OF POWER. EX/STRUC PLAN ECO/TAC CONTROL GP/REL PWR...TREND GP/COMP. PAGE 17 F0334
VOL/ASSN LOBBY POLICY

B44
MERRIAM C.E.,PUBLIC AND PRIVATE GOVERNMENT. VOL/ASSN EDU/PROP ADMIN REPRESENT EFFICIENCY PWR PLURISM...MAJORIT CONCPT. PAGE 90 F1762
NAT/G NEIGH MGT POLICY

B48
KILE O.M.,THE FARM BUREAU MOVEMENT: THE FARM BUREAU THROUGH THREE DECADES. NAT/G LEGIS LEAD LOBBY GP/REL INCOME POLICY. PAGE 71 F1387
AGRI STRUCT VOL/ASSN DOMIN

S48
CLEVELAND A.S.,"NAM: SPOKESMAN FOR INDUSTRY?" LEGIS PLAN LEAD LOBBY PARTIC CONSEN INCOME ATTIT ROLE ORD/FREE POLICY. PAGE 25 F0491
VOL/ASSN CLIENT REPRESENT INDUS

B49
LEE A.M.,SOCIAL PROBLEMS IN AMERICA: A SOURCE BOOK. STRATA STRUCT KIN NEIGH VOL/ASSN ACT/RES LEAD CRIME AGE SEX 20. PAGE 77 F1504
SOC SOCIETY PERSON EDU/PROP

B49
PARMELEE M.,GEO-ECONOMIC REGIONAL AND WORLD FEDERATION. FUT WOR+45 WOR-45 SOCIETY VOL/ASSN PLAN ...METH/CNCPT SIMUL GEN/METH TERR/GP TOT/POP 20. PAGE 103 F2028
INT/ORG GEOG REGION

S49
HART C.W.M.,"INDUSTRIAL RELATIONS RESEARCH AND SOCIAL THEORY." CANADA VOL/ASSN WORKER LEAD EFFICIENCY...MGT SOC METH/CNCPT METH/COMP MUNICH 20. PAGE 56 F1099
GEN/LAWS LABOR GP/REL

B50
LINCOLN G.,ECONOMICS OF NATIONAL SECURITY. USA+45 ELITES COM/IND DIST/IND INDUS NAT/G VOL/ASSN DELIB/GP EX/STRUC FOR/AID EDU/PROP COERCE NUC/PWR WAR ATTIT KNOWL ORD/FREE PWR TOT/POP VAL/FREE 20. PAGE 80 F1565
FORCES ECO/TAC AFR

B54
O.E.E.C.,PRIVATE UNITED STATES INVESTMENT IN EUROPE AND THE OVERSEAS TERRITORIES. EUR+WWI WOR+45 ECO/DEV ECO/UNDEV INT/ORG NAT/G VOL/ASSN ECO/TAC ATTIT WEALTH...GEOG STAT SYS/QU CHARTS VAL/FREE 20. PAGE 99 F1950
USA+45 FINAN BAL/PAY FOR/AID

L54
OPLER M.E.,"SOCIAL ASPECTS OF TECHNICAL ASSISTANCE IN OPERATION." WOR+45 VOL/ASSN CREATE PLAN TEC/DEV EDU/PROP ALL/VALS...METH/CNCPT OBS RECORD TREND UN 20. PAGE 101 F1993
INT/ORG CONSULT FOR/AID

B55
BERNAYS E.L.,THE ENGINEERING OF CONSENT. VOL/ASSN OP/RES ROUTINE INGP/REL ATTIT RESPECT...POLICY METH/CNCPT METH/COMP 20. PAGE 14 F0264
GP/REL PLAN ACT/RES ADJUST

L55
KISER M.,"ORGANIZATION OF AMERICAN STATES." L/A+17C USA+45 ECO/UNDEV INT/ORG NAT/G PLAN TEC/DEV DIPLOM ECO/TAC INT/TRADE EDU/PROP ADMIN ALL/VALS...POLICY MGT RECORD ORG/CHARTS OAS COMMUN 20. PAGE 71 F1401
VOL/ASSN ECO/DEV REGION

S55
HALLETT D.,"THE HISTORY AND STRUCTURE OF OEEC." EUR+WWI USA+45 CONSTN INDUS INT/ORG NAT/G DELIB/GP ACT/RES PLAN ORD/FREE WEALTH...CONCPT OEEC 20 CMN/WLTH. PAGE 54 F1051
VOL/ASSN ECO/DEV

B56
BONNETT C.E.,HISTORY OF EMPLOYERS' ASSOCIATIONS IN THE UNITED STATES (1ST ED.). MARKET DETER GP/REL ADJUST. PAGE 16 F0316
LABOR VOL/ASSN LG/CO

B56
MYRDAL G.,AN INTERNATIONAL ECONOMY. EUR+WWI USA+45 WOR+45 WOR-45 NAT/G DIPLOM ECO/TAC BAL/PAY...PSY CONCPT OEEC TOT/POP 20. PAGE 96 F1879
VOL/ASSN AFR

B56
WHYTE W.H. JR.,THE ORGANIZATION MAN. CULTURE FINAN VOL/ASSN DOMIN EDU/PROP EXEC DISPL HABITAT ROLE ...PERS/TEST STERTYP. PAGE 146 F2875
ADMIN LG/CO PERSON CONSEN

B56
WILCOX W.W.,SOCIAL RESPONSIBILITY IN FARM LEADERSHIP. CLIENT LEGIS EXEC LOBBY GP/REL ATTIT WEALTH. PAGE 146 F2880
AGRI LEAD VOL/ASSN WORKER

S56
GORDON L.,"THE ORGANIZATION FOR EUROPEAN ECONOMIC COOPERATION." EUR+WWI INDUS INT/ORG NAT/G CONSULT DELIB/GP ACT/RES CREATE PLAN TEC/DEV EDU/PROP LEGIT WEALTH OEEC 20. PAGE 49 F0956
VOL/ASSN ECO/DEV

B57
ARON R.,L'UNIFICATION ECONOMIQUE DE L'EUROPE. EUR+WWI SWITZERLND UK INT/ORG NAT/G REGION NAT/LISM ORD/FREE PWR...CONCPT METH/CNCPT OBS TREND STERTYP GEN/LAWS EEC FOR/TRADE 20. PAGE 6 F0118
VOL/ASSN ECO/TAC

B57
EHRMANN H.W.,ORGANIZED BUSINESS IN FRANCE. EUR+WWI MOD/EUR ECO/DEV VOL/ASSN LEGIT ATTIT PERCEPT PWR RESPECT...PLURIST SOC INT TOT/POP 20. PAGE 36 F0712
PROF/ORG ECO/TAC FRANCE

B57
UDY S.H. JR.,THE ORGANIZATION OF PRODUCTION IN NONINDUSTRIAL CULTURE. VOL/ASSN DELIB/GP TEC/DEV ...CHARTS BIBLIOG. PAGE 132 F2598
METH/COMP ECO/UNDEV PRODUC ADMIN

S57
HOAG M.W.,"ECONOMIC PROBLEMS OF ALLIANCE." AFR COM EUR+WWI WOR+45 ECO/DEV ECO/UNDEV NAT/G VOL/ASSN FORCES PLAN TEC/DEV DIPLOM COERCE ORD/FREE PWR WEALTH...DECISION GEN/LAWS NATO TERR/GP. PAGE 60 F1182
INT/ORG ECO/TAC

B58
COOK P.L.,EFFECTS OF MERGERS: SIX STUDIES. USA+45 ECO/DEV LABOR LG/CO SML/CO VOL/ASSN ADMIN EFFICIENCY 20 CASEBOOK. PAGE 27 F0529
INDUS FINAN EX/STRUC GP/REL

B58
HOOD W.C.,FINANCING OF ECONOMIC ACTIVITY IN CANADA. CANADA FUT VOL/ASSN WORKER ECO/TAC ADJUD ADMIN ...CHARTS 20. PAGE 61 F1204
BUDGET FINAN GP/REL ECO/DEV

B58
KINDLEBERGER C.P.,INTERNATIONAL ECONOMICS. WOR+45 WOR-45 ECO/DEV ECO/UNDEV FINAN VOL/ASSN ACT/RES DIPLOM ECO/TAC LEGIT REGION ATTIT DRIVE ORD/FREE WEALTH...POLICY STAT TREND GEN/LAWS EEC ECSC OEEC 20. PAGE 71 F1391
INT/ORG BAL/PWR TARIFFS

S58
ELKIN A.B.,"OEEC-ITS STRUCTURE AND POWERS." EUR+WWI CONSTN INDUS INT/ORG NAT/G VOL/ASSN DELIB/GP ACT/RES PLAN ORD/FREE WEALTH...CHARTS ORG/CHARTS OEEC 20. PAGE 37 F0719
ECO/DEV EX/STRUC

B59
BARBASH J.,UNIONS AND UNION LEADERSHIP. NAT/G WORKER TEC/DEV ECO/TAC PARTIC GP/REL RACE/REL ORD/FREE CLASSIF. PAGE 10 F0183
LABOR VOL/ASSN CAP/ISM LEAD

B59
SANNWALD R.E.,ECONOMIC INTEGRATION: THEORETICAL ASSUMPTIONS AND CONSEQUENCES OF EUROPEAN UNIFICATION. EUR+WWI FUT FINAN INDUS VOL/ASSN ACT/RES ECO/TAC...PLURIST EEC FOR/TRADE OEEC 20. PAGE 116 F2279
INT/ORG ECO/DEV INT/TRADE

B59
VINCENT W.S.,ROLES OF THE CITIZENS: PRINCIPLES AND PRACTICES. LOC/G POL/PAR VOL/ASSN CHOOSE ROLE ORD/FREE PWR...POLICY 20. PAGE 141 F2785
INGP/REL EDU/PROP CREATE LOBBY

L59
BEGUIN B.,"ILO AND THE TRIPARTITE SYSTEM." EUR+WWI WOR+45 WOR-45 CONSTN ECO/DEV ECO/UNDEV INDUS INT/ORG NAT/G VOL/ASSN DELIB/GP PLAN TEC/DEV LEGIT ORD/FREE WEALTH...CONCPT TIME/SEQ WORK ILO 20. PAGE 12 F0228
LABOR

B60
GILMORE D.R.,DEVELOPING THE "LITTLE" ECONOMIES. USA+45 FINAN LG/CO PROF/ORG VOL/ASSN CREATE ADMIN. PAGE 47 F0924
ECO/TAC LOC/G PROVS PLAN

B60
GRAMPP W.D.,THE MANCHESTER SCHOOL OF ECONOMICS. UK LAW ECO/DEV COERCE ATTIT ORD/FREE LAISSEZ ...PHIL/SCI IDEA/COMP 19/20 MANCHESTER CORN/LAWS. PAGE 50 F0973
ECO/TAC VOL/ASSN LOBBY NAT/G

B60
ILLINOIS U BUR COMMUNITY PLAN,PROCEEDINGS OF ILLINOIS STATEWIDE PLANNING CONFERENCE 1960. USA+45 FINAN LOC/G ACT/RES LEAD GOV/REL GP/REL WEALTH MUNICH 20 ILLINOIS. PAGE 64 F1260
PLAN DELIB/GP VOL/ASSN

B60
MOORE W.E.,LABOR COMMITMENT AND SOCIAL CHANGE IN DEVELOPING AREAS. SOCIETY STRATA ECO/UNDEV MARKET VOL/ASSN WORKER AUTHORIT SKILL...MGT NAT/COMP SOC/INTEG 20. PAGE 93 F1823
LABOR ORD/FREE ATTIT INDUS

B60
SHONFIELD A.,THE ATTACK ON WORLD POVERTY. WOR+45 ECO/DEV ECO/UNDEV FINAN VOL/ASSN PLAN EDU/PROP DRIVE KNOWL WEALTH...CONT/OBS STAND/INT ORG/CHARTS TOT/POP UNESCO 20. PAGE 121 F2383
INT/ORG ECO/TAC FOR/AID INT/TRADE

B60
STEIN E.,AMERICAN ENTERPRISE IN THE EUROPEAN COMMON MARKET: A LEGAL PROFILE. EUR+WWI FUT USA+45 SOCIETY STRUCT ECO/DEV NAT/G VOL/ASSN CONSULT PLAN TEC/DEV ECO/TAC INT/TRADE ADMIN ATTIT RIGID/FLEX PWR...MGT NEW/IDEA STAT TREND COMPUT/IR SIMUL EEC 20. PAGE 125 F2475
MARKET ADJUD INT/LAW

B60
WHEARE K.C.,THE CONSTITUTIONAL STRUCTURE OF THE COMMONWEALTH. UK EX/STRUC DIPLOM DOMIN ADMIN COLONIAL CONTROL LEAD INGP/REL SUPEGO 20 CMN/WLTH. PAGE 145 F2865
CONSTN INT/ORG VOL/ASSN SOVEREIGN

S60
KELLOGG C.E.,"TRANSFER OF BASIC SKILLS OF FOOD PRODUCTION." AFR FUT S/ASIA STRATA ECO/UNDEV LABOR VOL/ASSN RIGID/FLEX...OLD/LIB SOCIALIST NEW/IDEA STAT PROJ/TEST GEN/LAWS 20. PAGE 70 F1370
AGRI PLAN

B61
BALASSA B.,THE THEORY OF ECONOMIC INTEGRATION. EUR+WWI L/A+17C MOD/EUR WOR+45 ECO/UNDEV MARKET INT/ORG NAT/G VOL/ASSN DELIB/GP PLAN CAP/ISM ECO/TAC...MAJORIT FOR/TRADE OEEC 20. PAGE 8 F0157
ECO/DEV ACT/RES INT/TRADE

B61
BENOIT E.,EUROPE AT SIXES AND SEVENS: THE COMMON MARKET, THE FREE TRADE ASSOCIATION AND THE UNITED STATES. EUR+WWI FUT USA+45 INDUS CONSULT DELIB/GP EX/STRUC TOP/EX ACT/RES ECO/TAC EDU/PROP ROUTINE CHOOSE PERCEPT WEALTH...MGT TREND EEC FOR/TRADE TOT/POP 20 EFTA. PAGE 13 F0249
FINAN ECO/DEV VOL/ASSN

B61
BONNEFOUS M.,EUROPE ET TIERS MONDE. EUR+WWI SOCIETY INT/ORG NAT/G VOL/ASSN ACT/RES TEC/DEV CAP/ISM ECO/TAC ATTIT ORD/FREE SOVEREIGN...POLICY CONCPT TREND TERR/GP COMMUN 20. PAGE 16 F0314
AFR ECO/UNDEV FOR/AID INT/TRADE

B61
DE GRAZIA A.,AMERICAN WELFARE. CLIENT FINAN LABOR LOC/G NAT/G NEIGH EDU/PROP GP/REL...CLASSIF CON/ANAL CHARTS BIBLIOG. PAGE 31 F0598
GIVE WEALTH SECT VOL/ASSN

B61
FRIEDMANN W.G.,JOINT INTERNATIONAL BUSINESS VENTURES. ASIA ISLAM L/A+17C ECO/DEV DIST/IND FINAN PROC/MFG FACE/GP LG/CO NAT/G VOL/ASSN CONSULT EX/STRUC PLAN ADMIN ROUTINE WEALTH...OLD/LIB FOR/TRADE WORK 20. PAGE 44 F0865
ECO/UNDEV INT/TRADE

B61
STROUD G.S.,LABOR HISTORY IN THE UNITED STATES: A GENERAL BIBLIOGRAPHY. USA+45 USA-45 STRATA VOL/ASSN AUTOMAT GP/REL INGP/REL ATTIT HEALTH 18/20. PAGE 127 F2504
BIBLIOG WORKER LABOR

B61
ZEIGLER H.,THE POLITICS OF SMALL BUSINESS. USA+45 EX/STRUC ADMIN 20. PAGE 150 F2963
LOBBY REPRESENT EXEC VOL/ASSN

S61
RAY J.,"THE EUROPEAN FREE-TRADE ASSOCIATION AND ITS IMPACT ON INDIA'S TRADE." EUR+WWI FRANCE GERMANY INDIA S/ASIA UK NAT/G VOL/ASSN PLAN INT/TRADE ROUTINE WEALTH...STAT CHARTS TERR/GP CMN/WLTH EEC FOR/TRADE OEEC 20 EFTA. PAGE 109 F2155
ECO/DEV ECO/TAC

B62
BOGARDUS J.,OUTLINE FOR THE COURSE IN BUSINESS AND ECONOMICS LITERATURE (REV. ED; PAMPHLET). USA+45 FINAN INDUS NAT/G VOL/ASSN PRESS WRITING INDEX. PAGE 16 F0305
BIBLIOG/A STAT

B62
LIPPMANN W.,WESTERN UNITY AND THE COMMON MARKET. EUR+WWI FRANCE GERMANY/W UK USA+45 ECO/DEV AGRI FINAN MARKET INT/ORG NAT/G FOR/AID AGREE WEALTH 20 EEC. PAGE 80 F1575
DIPLOM INT/TRADE VOL/ASSN

B62
ROBINSON A.D.,DUTCH ORGANIZED AGRICULTURE IN INTERNATIONAL POLITICS, 1945-1960. EUR+WWI NETHERLAND STRUCT ECO/DEV NAT/G VOL/ASSN CONSULT DELIB/GP PLAN TEC/DEV INT/TRADE EDU/PROP ATTIT RIGID/FLEX ALL/VALS...NEW/IDEA TREND EEC COMMUN 20. PAGE 112 F2215
AGRI INT/ORG

B62
WOODS H.D.,LABOUR POLICY AND LABOUR ECONOMICS IN CANADA. CANADA FUT NAT/G VOL/ASSN WORKER BARGAIN ECO/TAC PAY CONFER GP/REL 20. PAGE 148 F2924
LABOR POLICY INDUS ECO/DEV

L62
PRYOR F.L.,"FOREIGN TRADE IN THE COMMUNIST BLOC." COM ECO/DEV VOL/ASSN...METH/CNCPT GEN/LAWS FOR/TRADE TERR/GP 20. PAGE 108 F2129
ECO/TAC STERTYP USSR

S62
BOKOR-SZEGO H.,"LA CONVENTION DE BELGRADE ET LE REGIME DU DANUBE." COM EUR+WWI WOR+45 STRUCT POL/PAR VOL/ASSN PLAN EDU/PROP WEALTH...TIME/SEQ METH/GP COMMUN 20. PAGE 16 F0308
INT/ORG TOTALISM YUGOSLAVIA

S62
ZAUBERMAN A.,"SOVIET AND CHINESE STRATEGY FOR ECONOMIC GROWTH." ASIA CHINA/COM COM USSR STRATA VOL/ASSN PLAN ATTIT PWR...METH/CNCPT GEN/LAWS WORK TERR/GP 20. PAGE 150 F2959
ECO/DEV EDU/PROP

B63
BAUER R.A.,AMERICAN BUSINESS AND PUBLIC POLICY: THE POLITICS OF FOREIGN TRADE. USA+45 COM/IND LG/CO NAT/G PROF/ORG SML/CO VOL/ASSN LEGIS TOP/EX ECO/TAC EDU/PROP CHOOSE HEALTH PWR WEALTH...CONCPT METH/CNCPT OBS INT QU SAMP FOR/TRADE TRUE/GP VAL/FREE HI. PAGE 11 F0217
ECO/DEV ATTIT

B63
BELOFF M.,THE UNITED STATES AND THE UNITY OF EUROPE. EUR+WWI UK USA+45 WOR+45 VOL/ASSN DIPLOM REGION ATTIT PWR...CONCPT EEC OEEC 20 NATO. PAGE 13 F0239
ECO/DEV INT/ORG

B63
BURNS T.G.,DEVELOPMENT BANKING BIBLIOGRAPHY (PAPER). WOR+45 SML/CO VOL/ASSN PLAN BUDGET. PAGE 20 F0391
BIBLIOG/A ECO/DEV FINAN ECO/UNDEV

B63
CERAMI C.A.,ALLIANCE BORN OF DANGER. EUR+WWI USA+45 USSR ECO/DEV INDUS VOL/ASSN ECO/TAC REGION ATTIT MARXISM ATLAN/ALL 20 NATO EEC. PAGE 22 F0437
DIPLOM INT/ORG NAT/G POLICY

B63
GODWIN F.W.,THE HIDDEN FORCE. PUERT/RICO WOR+45 STRUCT VOL/ASSN PROB/SOLV DIPLOM CONFER...BIBLIOG 20 PEACE/CORP. PAGE 48 F0931
ECO/UNDEV WORKER SKILL ECO/TAC

B63
LINDBERG L.,POLITICAL DYNAMICS OF EUROPEAN ECONOMIC INTEGRATION. EUR+WWI ECO/DEV INT/ORG VOL/ASSN DELIB/GP ADMIN WEALTH...DECISION EEC TERR/GP 20. PAGE 80 F1567
MARKET ECO/TAC

B63
PELLING H.M.,A HISTORY OF BRITISH TRADE UNIONISM. UK ELITES ECO/DEV POL/PAR GP/REL PWR NEW/LIB 19/20. PAGE 104 F2051
LABOR VOL/ASSN NAT/G

B63
SELF P.,THE STATE AND THE FARMER. UK ECO/DEV MARKET WORKER PRICE CONTROL GP/REL...WELF/ST 20 DEPT/AGRI. PAGE 119 F2346
AGRI NAT/G ADMIN VOL/ASSN

B63
US GOVERNMENT,REPORT TO INTER-AMERICAN ECONOMIC AND SOCIAL COUNCIL AT SECOND ANNUAL MEETING. L/A+17C USA+45 VOL/ASSN TEC/DEV DIPLOM TAX EATING EFFICIENCY HEALTH...STAT CHARTS 20 AID. PAGE 136 F2682
ECO/TAC FOR/AID FINAN PLAN

B63
WIGHTMAN D.,TOWARD ECONOMIC CO-OPERATION IN ASIA. ASIA S/ASIA VOL/ASSN ACT/RES PLAN TEC/DEV ECO/TAC EDU/PROP RIGID/FLEX SKILL...POLICY METH/CNCPT OBS INT GEN/LAWS UN 20 ECAFE. PAGE 146 F2877
ECO/UNDEV CREATE

L63
MCKERSIE R.B.,"NONPROFESSIONAL HOSPITAL WORKERS AND A UNION ORGANIZING DRIVE." PLAN GP/REL RACE/REL ATTIT DRIVE...CORREL STAT INT GP/COMP. PAGE 88 F1732
VOL/ASSN HEALTH INGP/REL LABOR

S63
BARZANSKI S.,"REGIONAL UNDERDEVELOPMENT IN THE
ECO/UNDEV

EUROPEAN ECONOMIC COMMUNITY." EUR+WWI ELITES DIST/IND MARKET VOL/ASSN CONSULT EX/STRUC ECO/TAC RIGID/FLEX WEALTH EEC OEEC 20. PAGE 11 F0202
PLAN
S63

BELOFF M.,"BRITAIN, EUROPE AND THE ATLANTIC COMMUNITY." EUR+WWI ELITES NAT/G VOL/ASSN TOP/EX ATTIT ORD/FREE PWR SOVEREIGN WEALTH EEC TOT/POP VAL/FREE CMN/WLTH 20. PAGE 13 F0240
INT/ORG ECO/DEV UK
S63

GANDOLFI A.,"LES ACCORDS DE COOPERATION EN MATIERE DE POLITIQUE ETRANGERE ENTRE LA FRANCE ET LES NOUVEAUX ETATS AFRICAINS ET." AFR ISLAM MADAGASCAR WOR+45 ECO/DEV INT/ORG NAT/G DELIB/GP ECO/TAC ALL/VALS...CON/ANAL 20. PAGE 46 F0894
VOL/ASSN ECO/UNDEV DIPLOM FRANCE
S63

GORDON B.,"ECONOMIC IMPEDIMENTS TO REGIONALISM IN SOUTH EAST ASIA." BURMA FUT S/ASIA THAILAND USA+45 AGRI INDUS R+D NAT/G PLAN ECO/TAC WEALTH...STAT CONT/OBS 20. PAGE 49 F0954
VOL/ASSN ECO/UNDEV INT/TRADE REGION
S63

HALLSTEIN W.,"THE EUROPEAN COMMUNITY AND ATLANTIC PARTNERSHIP." EUR+WWI USA+45 MARKET NAT/G VOL/ASSN DELIB/GP ARMS/CONT NUC/PWR ATTIT PWR...CONCPT STAT TIME/SEQ TREND OEEC 20 EEC. PAGE 54 F1053
INT/ORG ECO/TAC UK
S63

MONROE A.D.,"BRITAIN AND THE EUROPEAN COMMUNITY." EUR+WWI FRANCE NAT/G DELIB/GP TOP/EX ECO/TAC DOMIN PWR...POLICY RECORD GEN/LAWS EEC EFTA 20 EFTA CMN/WLTH. PAGE 93 F1817
VOL/ASSN ATTIT UK
S63

PINCUS J.,"THE COST OF FOREIGN AID." WOR+45 ECO/DEV FINAN NAT/G VOL/ASSN CREATE ECO/TAC EDU/PROP WEALTH ...METH/CNCPT STAT CHARTS HYPO/EXP TOT/POP VAL/FREE 20. PAGE 106 F2087
USA+45 ECO/UNDEV FOR/AID
S63

RAMERIE L.,"TENSION AU SEIN DU COMECON: LE CAS ROUMAIN." COM EUR+WWI USSR WOR+45 ECO/DEV DIST/IND NAT/G POL/PAR VOL/ASSN EDU/PROP TOTALISM ATTIT WEALTH...TIME/SEQ 20 COMECON. PAGE 109 F2142
INT/ORG ECO/TAC INT/TRADE ROMANIA
S63

SHONFIELD A.,"AFTER BRUSSELS." EUR+WWI FRANCE GERMANY UK ECO/DEV DIST/IND MARKET VOL/ASSN DELIB/GP CREATE INT/TRADE ATTIT RIGID/FLEX...RECORD TREND GEN/LAWS EEC COMMUN CMN/WLTH 20. PAGE 121 F2385
PLAN ECO/TAC
S63

TENNYSON L.B.,"THE USA IN ATLANTIC COMMUNITY." EUR+WWI FRANCE UK USA+45 ECO/UNDEV VOL/ASSN DELIB/GP TOP/EX DIPLOM DOMIN PWR...POLICY CONCPT TREND GEN/LAWS EEC 20. PAGE 129 F2545
ATTIT ECO/TAC BAL/PWR
S63

WALKER H.,"THE INTERNATIONAL LAW OF COMMODITY AGREEMENTS." FUT WOR+45 ECO/DEV ECO/UNDEV FINAN INT/ORG NAT/G CONSULT CREATE PLAN ECO/TAC ATTIT PERCEPT...CONCPT GEN/LAWS TOT/POP GATT 20. PAGE 142 F2804
MARKET VOL/ASSN INT/LAW INT/TRADE
B64

BOURGOIGNIE G.E.,JEUNE AFRIQUE MOBILISABLE; LES PROBLEMES DE LA JEUNESSE DESOEUVREE EN AFRIQUE NOIRE. INT/ORG VOL/ASSN ECO/TAC ROUTINE UTIL ATTIT 20. PAGE 17 F0324
AGE/Y AFR CREATE ECO/UNDEV
B64

ESTHUS R.A.,FROM ENMITY TO ALLIANCE: US AUSTRALIAN RELATIONS. S/ASIA DIST/IND VOL/ASSN FORCES ATTIT 20 AUSTRAL TREATY CMN/WLTH. PAGE 39 F0751
DIPLOM WAR INT/TRADE FOR/AID
B64

FEIS H.,FOREIGN AID AND FOREIGN POLICY. USA+45 WOR+45 NAT/G VOL/ASSN ACT/RES TEC/DEV ATTIT HEALTH WEALTH...SOC GEN/LAWS 20. PAGE 40 F0775
ECO/UNDEV ECO/TAC FOR/AID DIPLOM
B64

GARDNER L.C.,ECONOMIC ASPECTS OF NEW DEAL DIPLOMACY. USA-45 WOR-45 LAW ECO/DEV INT/ORG NAT/G VOL/ASSN LEGIS TOP/EX EDU/PROP ORD/FREE PWR WEALTH ...POLICY TIME/SEQ VAL/FREE 20 ROOSEVLT/F. PAGE 46 F0901
ECO/TAC DIPLOM
B64

HEKHUIS D.J.,INTERNATIONAL STABILITY: MILITARY, ECONOMIC AND POLITICAL DIMENSIONS. FUT WOR+45 LAW ECO/UNDEV INT/ORG NAT/G VOL/ASSN FORCES ACT/RES BAL/PWR PWR WEALTH...STAT UN 20. PAGE 58 F1143
TEC/DEV DETER REGION
B64

MARKHAM J.W.,THE COMMON MARKET: FRIEND OR COMPETITOR. AFR EUR+WWI FUT USA+45 INT/ORG LG/CO NAT/G VOL/ASSN DELIB/GP EX/STRUC PLAN TARIFFS ORD/FREE PWR WEALTH...POLICY STAT TREND EEC VAL/FREE 20. PAGE 85 F1671
ECO/DEV ECO/TAC
B64

STOESSINGER J.G.,FINANCING THE UNITED NATIONS SYSTEM. FUT WOR+45 CONSTN NAT/G VOL/ASSN DELIB/GP EX/STRUC ECO/TAC LEGIT CT/SYS PWR WEALTH...STAT TIME/SEQ TREND CHARTS TRUE/GP METH/GP TERR/GP VAL/FREE. PAGE 126 F2493
FINAN INT/ORG
B64

SULLIVAN G.,THE STORY OF THE PEACE CORPS. USA+45 WOR+45 INTELL FACE/GP NAT/G SCHOOL VOL/ASSN CONSULT EX/STRUC PLAN EDU/PROP ADMIN ATTIT DRIVE ALL/VALS ...POLICY HEAL SOC CONCPT INT QU BIOG TREND SOC/EXP WORK. PAGE 127 F2511
INT/ORG ECO/UNDEV FOR/AID PEACE
S64

FINLEY D.D.,"A POLITICAL PERSPECTIVE OF ECONOMIC RELATIONS IN THE COMMUNIST CAMP." COM USSR FACE/GP NAT/G ACT/RES PLAN DOMIN COERCE ATTIT ORD/FREE WEALTH...TIME/SEQ 20. PAGE 41 F0800
VOL/ASSN ECO/TAC DIPLOM REGION
S64

HUELIN D.,"ECONOMIC INTEGRATION IN LATIN AMERICAN: PROGRESS AND PROBLEMS." L/A+17C ECO/DEV AGRI DIST/IND FINAN INDUS NAT/G VOL/ASSN CONSULT DELIB/GP EX/STRUC ACT/RES PLAN TEC/DEV ECO/TAC ROUTINE BAL/PAY WEALTH FOR/TRADE WORK TERR/GP 20. PAGE 63 F1232
MARKET ECO/UNDEV INT/TRADE
S64

PADELFORD N.J.,"THE ORGANIZATION OF AFRICAN UNITY." ECO/UNDEV INT/ORG PLAN BAL/PWR DIPLOM ECO/TAC NAT/LISM ORD/FREE PWR WEALTH...CONCPT TREND STERTYP TERR/GP VAL/FREE 20. PAGE 102 F2013
AFR VOL/ASSN REGION
S64

SCHMITT H.D.,"POLITICAL CONDITIONS FOR INTERNATIONAL CURRENCY REFORM." WOR+45 SOCIETY ECO/DEV PLAN ECO/TAC BAL/PAY ATTIT ORD/FREE WEALTH ...SOC CONCPT OBS TREND EEC VAL/FREE ECSC 20. PAGE 117 F2301
FINAN VOL/ASSN REGION
N64

GREAT BRITAIN CENTRAL OFF INF,THE COLOMBO PLAN (PAMPHLET). AFR ASIA S/ASIA USA+45 VOL/ASSN ...CHARTS 20 RESOURCE/N. PAGE 50 F0980
FOR/AID PLAN INT/ORG ECO/UNDEV
B65

BRADLEY J.F.,THE ROLE OF TRADE ASSOCIATIONS AND PROFESSIONAL BUSINESS SOCIETIES IN AMERICA. USA+45 USA-45 STRUCT CONSULT DELIB/GP CREATE LOBBY GP/REL 20. PAGE 17 F0333
ECO/DEV PROF/ORG VOL/ASSN SOCIETY
B65

CERNY K.H.,NATO IN QUEST OF COHESION* A CONFRONTATION OF VIEWPOINTS. COM EUR+WWI USA+45 FORCES LEAD REGION DETER...ANTHOL NATO. PAGE 22 F0438
CENTRAL NUC/PWR VOL/ASSN
B65

CONLEY R.W.,THE ECONOMICS OF VOCATIONAL REHABILITATION. USA+45 VOL/ASSN CREATE EDU/PROP COST EFFICIENCY SOC/INTEG 20. PAGE 27 F0527
PUB/INST HEALTH GIVE GP/REL
B65

COUGHLIN B.J.,CHURCH AND STATE IN SOCIAL WELFARE. USA+45 RECEIVE GP/REL ORD/FREE WEALTH NEW/LIB. PAGE 28 F0542
CULTURE SECT VOL/ASSN GIVE
B65

CRANE E.,MARKETING COMMUNICATION: A BEHAVIORAL APPROACH TO MEN, MESSAGES, AND MEDIA. STRATA R+D VOL/ASSN CROWD DRIVE PERSON SKILL WEALTH. PAGE 28 F0551
EDU/PROP MARKET PERCEPT ATTIT
B65

GREER S.,URBAN RENEWAL AND AMERICAN CITIES: THE DILEMMA OF DEMOCRATIC INTERVENTION. USA+45 R+D LOC/G VOL/ASSN ACT/RES BUDGET ADMIN GOV/REL...SOC INT SAMP MUNICH 20 BOSTON CHICAGO LOS/ANG MIAMI URBAN/RNWL. PAGE 51 F0992
PROB/SOLV PLAN NAT/G
B65

KISSINGER H.A.,THE TROUBLED PARTNERSHIP* RE-APPRAISAL OF THE WESTERN ALLIANCE. EUR+WWI USA+45 INT/ORG NAT/G VOL/ASSN TOP/EX DIPLOM ORD/FREE PWR NATO. PAGE 71 F1402
FRANCE NUC/PWR ECO/DEV
B65

MONCRIEFF A.,SECOND THOUGHTS ON AID. WOR+45 ECO/UNDEV AGRI FINAN VOL/ASSN PLAN TEC/DEV GIVE EDU/PROP ROLE WEALTH 20. PAGE 93 F1816
FOR/AID ECO/TAC INT/ORG IDEA/COMP
B65

NATIONAL CONF SOCIAL WELFARE,THE SOCIAL WELFARE FORUM, 1965. LAW CULTURE VOL/ASSN CONTROL PERS/REL ADJUST POLICY. PAGE 97 F1899
CONSTN WEALTH ORD/FREE NEIGH
B65

PAYNE J.L.,LABOR AND POLITICS IN PERU; THE SYSTEM OF POLITICAL BARGAINING. PERU CONSTN VOL/ASSN EX/STRUC LEAD PWR...CHARTS 20. PAGE 104 F2042
LABOR POL/PAR BARGAIN GP/REL
B65

SCHULTZ T.W.,ECONOMIC CRISES IN WORLD AGRICULTURE. ASIA INDIA USSR ECO/DEV ECO/UNDEV INDUS VOL/ASSN CAP/ISM RATION COLONIAL 20. PAGE 117 F2317
AGRI ECO/TAC INCOME WORKER
L65

DAANE J.D.,"THE EVOLVING INTERNATIONAL MONETARY MECHANISM." VOL/ASSN CREATE PLAN FOR/AID INT/TRADE CONFER BAL/PAY...RECORD PREDICT IMF. PAGE 29 F0569
INT/ORG ECO/TAC TREND GP/COMP
S65

BERREBY J.J.,"IMPERATIFS STRATEGIQUES DU PETROLE." ECO/UNDEV VOL/ASSN ECO/TAC COLONIAL NUC/PWR WAR.
ISLAM EXTR/IND

PAGE 14 F0270 STAT OBS

S65

JOHNSON L.L.,"US BUSINESS INTERESTS IN CUBA AND THE RISE OF CASTRO." L/A+17C USA+45 ECO/UNDEV INDUS NAT/G VOL/ASSN ATTIT ORD/FREE PWR WEALTH ALL/PROG. PAGE 68 F1330 DIPLOM CUBA ECO/TAC INT/TRADE

S65

RUSINOW D.I.,"YUGOSLAV DEVELOPMENT BETWEEN EAST AND WEST." AGRI VOL/ASSN PLAN CAP/ISM ECO/TAC FOR/AID INT/TRADE BAL/PAY...MARXIST EEC COMECON. PAGE 115 F2262 YUGOSLAVIA ECO/UNDEV STAT

B66

BEUGEL E.V.D.,FROM MARSHALL AID TO ATLANTIC PARTNERSHIP* EUROPEAN INTEGRATION AS A CONCERN OF AMERICAN FOREIGN POLICY. USA+45 INT/ORG FORCES PERSON EEC NATO. PAGE 14 F0272 REGION DIPLOM EUR+WWI VOL/ASSN

B66

FRIEDMANN W.G.,INTERNATIONAL FINANCIAL AID. USA+45 ECO/DEV ECO/UNDEV NAT/G VOL/ASSN EX/STRUC PLAN RENT GIVE BAL/PAY PWR...GEOG INT/LAW STAT TREND UN EEC COMECON. PAGE 44 F0866 INT/ORG FOR/AID TEC/DEV ECO/TAC

B66

JACKSON G.D.,COMINTERN AND PEASANT IN EAST EUROPE 1919-1930. BULGARIA COM CZECHOSLVK EUR+WWI POLAND ROMANIA YUGOSLAVIA STRATA AGRI VOL/ASSN DIPLOM CONTROL CROWD WEALTH...POLICY NAT/COMP 20. PAGE 66 F1293 MARXISM ECO/UNDEV WORKER INT/ORG

B66

KAREFA-SMART J.,AFRICA: PROGRESS THROUGH COOPERATION. AFR FINAN TEC/DEV DIPLOM FOR/AID EDU/PROP CONFER REGION GP/REL WEALTH...HEAL SOC/INTEG 20. PAGE 69 F1356 ORD/FREE ECO/UNDEV VOL/ASSN PLAN

B66

OHLIN G.,FOREIGN AID POLICIES RECONSIDERED. ECO/DEV ECO/UNDEV VOL/ASSN CONSULT PLAN CONTROL ATTIT ...CONCPT CHARTS BIBLIOG 20. PAGE 101 F1985 FOR/AID DIPLOM GIVE

B66

RUBIN S.J.,THE CONSCIENCE OF THE RICH NATIONS: THE DEVELOPMENT ASSISTANCE COMMITTEE AND THE COMMON AID EFFORT. EUR+WWI USA+45 ECO/UNDEV INT/ORG NAT/G VOL/ASSN ECO/TAC INT/TRADE...OBS UN AID DEV/ASSIST IBRD OECD. PAGE 114 F2256 FOR/AID ECO/DEV CONFER CENTRAL

S66

JAVITS J.K.,"POLITICAL ACTION VITAL FOR LATIN AMERICAN INTEGRATION." ECO/UNDEV INT/ORG POL/PAR VOL/ASSN PLAN PROB/SOLV INT/TRADE EFFICIENCY 20 OAS LAFTA ALL/PROG. PAGE 66 F1308 L/A+17C ECO/TAC REGION

S66

LAURENS H.,"LES PAYS OCCIDENTAUX ET LE MARCHE CHINOIS." EUR+WWI FUT S/ASIA AGRI INDUS VOL/ASSN ECO/TAC BAL/PAY...RECORD PREDICT TREATY. PAGE 76 F1488 ASIA INT/TRADE TREND STAT

N66

US ADVISORY COMN INTERGOV REL,CATALOGS AND OTHER INFORMATION SOURCES ON FEDERAL AND STATE AID PROGRAMS: A SECTED BIBLIOGRAPHY (PAPER). USA+45 LAW LOC/G NAT/G PROVS VOL/ASSN TEC/DEV ADMIN HEALTH ...WELF/ST SOC/WK MUNICH. PAGE 134 F2635 BIBLIOG/A GOV/REL FINAN ECO/DEV

B67

ANDERSON S.V.,THE NORDIC COUNCIL: A STUDY OF SCANDINAVIAN REGIONALISM. DENMARK FINLAND ICELAND NORWAY SWEDEN MARKET NAT/G VOL/ASSN CONSULT PARL/PROC ATTIT...TIME/SEQ BIBLIOG 20. PAGE 5 F0098 INT/ORG REGION DIPLOM LEGIS

B67

ELSNER H.,THE TECHNOCRATS, PROPHETS OF AUTOMATION. SOCIETY INDUS VOL/ASSN COST INCOME ATTIT 20. PAGE 37 F0726 AUTOMAT TECHRACY PRODUC HIST/WRIT

B67

UNIVERSAL REFERENCE SYSTEM,ADMINISTRATIVE MANAGEMENT: PUBLIC AND PRIVATE BUREAUCRACY (VOLUME IV). WOR+45 WOR-45 ECO/DEV LG/CO LOC/G PUB/INST VOL/ASSN GOV/REL...COMPUT/IR GEN/METH. PAGE 133 F2616 BIBLIOG/A MGT ADMIN NAT/G

L67

LAMBERT J.D.,"CORPORATE POLITICAL SPENDING AND CAMPAIGN FINANCE." LAW CONSTN FINAN LABOR LG/CO LOC/G NAT/G VOL/ASSN TEC/DEV ADJUD ADMIN PARTIC. PAGE 75 F1463 USA+45 POL/PAR CHOOSE COST

L67

TANDON Y.,"CONSENSUS AND AUTHORITY BEHIND UNITED NATIONS PEACEKEEPING OPERATIONS." FINAN VOL/ASSN BUDGET DIPLOM PAY DOMIN...CHARTS 20 UN. PAGE 128 F2528 CONSEN INT/ORG PWR PEACE

S67

"THE SIERRA CLUB, POLITICAL ACTIVITY, AND TAX EXEMPT CHARITABLE STATUS." USA+45 LAW VOL/ASSN TAX PAY ADJUD LOBBY INGP/REL HABITAT 20. PAGE 2 F0027 ELITES GOV/REL FACE/GP ORD/FREE

S67

CAMMETT J.M.,"COMMUNIST THEORIES OF FASCISM, 1920-35." ITALY POL/PAR PROF/ORG VOL/ASSN WORKER COLONIAL TOTALISM...SOCIALIST 20. PAGE 21 F0403 MARXISM FASCISM ATTIT

S67

COSGROVE C.A.,"AGRICULTURE, FINANCE AND POLITICS IN THE EUROPEAN COMMUNITY." EUR+WWI DIST/IND MARKET INT/ORG VOL/ASSN DELIB/GP TEC/DEV BAL/PWR BARGAIN ECO/TAC RATION CONFER 20 EEC. PAGE 28 F0538 ECO/DEV DIPLOM AGRI INT/TRADE

S67

KESTENBAUM L.,"PRIMARY JURISDICTION TO DECIDE ANTITRUST JURISDICTION* A PRACTICAL APPROACH TO THE ALLOCATION OF FUNCTIONS." USA+45 ECO/DEV INDUS VOL/ASSN ECO/TAC. PAGE 70 F1383 JURID CT/SYS LABOR ADJUD

S67

LASLETT J.H.M.,"SOCIALISM AND THE AMERICAN LABOR MOVEMENT* SOME NEW REFLECTIONS." USA-45 VOL/ASSN LOBBY PARTIC CENTRAL ALL/VALS SOCISM...GP/COMP 20. PAGE 76 F1484 LABOR ROUTINE ATTIT GP/REL

S67

MERON T.,"THE UN'S 'COMMON SYSTEM' OF SALARY, ALLOWANCE, AND BENEFITS: CRITICAL APPR'SAL OF COORD IN PERSONNEL MATTERS." VOL/ASSN PAY EFFICIENCY ...CHARTS 20 UN. PAGE 90 F1761 ADMIN EX/STRUC INT/ORG BUDGET

B76

FOURIER C.,SOCIAL DESTINIES, IN A. BRISBANE, GENERAL INTRODUCTION TO SOCIAL SCIENCE. UNIV AGRI INDUS SECT PRODUC...PHIL/SCI CONCPT. PAGE 43 F0835 UTOPIA SOCIETY PERSON VOL/ASSN

VOLTAIRE....VOLTAIRE (FRANCOIS MARIE AROUET)

VOLUNTARY ASSOCIATIONS....SEE VOL/ASSN

VOLUNTEERS IN SERVICE TO AMERICA (VISTA)....SEE VISTA

VON BECKERATH E. F2789

VON DER MEHDEN F.R. F0094,F2790

VON ENGELIN O.D. F2791

VON HAYEK F.A. F1120,F1121,F1122,F1123,F1124,F2792,F2793

VON MISES L. F2794

VON PETERFRY G. F0530

VON RENESSE E.A. F2795

VON/TRESCK....VON TRESCKOW

VOSE C.E. F2796

VOTING....SEE CHOOSE, SUFF

VTOL....VERTICAL TAKE-OFF AND LANDING AIRCRAFT

W

WADE J. F2797

WAGES....SEE PRICE, WORKER, WEALTH

WAGLE S.S. F2798

WAGLEY C. F2799

WAGNER/A....ADOLPH WAGNER

WAHLKE J.C. F2800

WAITS C.R. F2801

WALES....WALES

WALINSKY L.J. F2802

WALKER F.V. F2803

WALKER H. F2804

WALKER R.L. F2805

WALKER/E....EDWIN WALKER

WALLACE H.M. F2806

WALLACE R.A. F2807,F2808

WALLACE/G....GEORGE WALLACE

WALLACE/HA....HENRY A. WALLACE

WALLBANK T.W. F2809

WALLICH H.C. F2810

WALSTON H. F2811

WALTER I. F1317

WALTON R.E. F2812

WALTON S.D. F2813

WALTZ/KN....KENNETH N. WALTZ

WALZER M. F2814

WAR....SEE ALSO COERCE

N
US LIBRARY OF CONGRESS,SELECTED AND ANNOTATED BIBLIOGRAPHY ON AGRICULTURAL PROBLEMS AND POLICIES IN A WARTIME ECONOMY (PAMPHLET). R+D WORKER PRODUC 20. PAGE 137 F2706
BIBLIOG/A WAR AGRI EXTR/IND

N
US LIBRARY OF CONGRESS,SELECTED AND ANNOTATED BIBLIOGRAPHY ON INDUSTRIAL PROBLEMS AND POLICIES IN WARTIME (PAMPHLET). WOR-45 CONSTRUC NAT/G PROB/SOLV COST DEMAND PRODUC 20. PAGE 137 F2707
BIBLIOG/A ECO/DEV INDUS WAR

N
US LIBRARY OF CONGRESS,SELECTED AND ANNOTATED BIBLIOGRAPHY ON LABOR PROBLEMS AND POLICIES IN A WARTIME ECONOMY (PAMPHLET). USA-45 INDUS LEGIS GP/REL DISCRIM PRODUC...SOC 20. PAGE 137 F2708
BIBLIOG/A WAR LABOR WORKER

N
US LIBRARY OF CONGRESS,SELECTED AND ANNOTATED BIBLIOGRAPHY ON RAW MATERIALS IN A WARTIME ECONOMY (PAMPHLET). WOR-45 NAT/G DEMAND PRODUC 20. PAGE 137 F2709
BIBLIOG/A ECO/DEV EXTR/IND WAR

B14
DE BLOCH J.,THE FUTURE OF WAR IN ITS TECHNICAL, ECONOMIC, AND POLITICAL RELATIONS (1899). MOD/EUR TEC/DEV BUDGET INT/TRADE DETER GUERRILLA WEAPON COST PEACE 20. PAGE 31 F0596
WAR BAL/PWR PREDICT FORCES

B15
JONES J.H.,THE ECONOMICS OF WAR AND CONQUEST. WOR-45 ECO/DEV NAT/G WEALTH...STAT TREND STERTYP GEN/LAWS TOT/POP 20. PAGE 68 F1338
MYTH WAR

N19
BROWN W.M.,THE DESIGN AND PERFORMANCE OF "OPTIMUM" BLAST SHELTER PROGRAMS (PAMPHLET). USA+45 ACT/RES PLAN DEATH COST EFFICIENCY OPTIMAL...POLICY CHARTS 20. PAGE 19 F0375
HABITAT NUC/PWR WAR HEALTH

N19
DEANE H.,THE WAR IN VIETNAM (PAMPHLET). AFR CHINA/COM VIETNAM BAL/PWR DIPLOM ECO/TAC SOCISM INTERVENT INTERVENT. PAGE 31 F0610
WAR SOCIALIST MORAL CAP/ISM

N19
FREEMAN H.A.,COERCION OF STATES IN FEDERAL UNIONS (PAMPHLET). WOR-45 DIPLOM CONTROL COERCE PEACE ORD/FREE...GOV/COMP METH/COMP NAT/COMP PACIFIST 20. PAGE 43 F0850
FEDERAL WAR INT/ORG PACIFISM

B23
FINER H.,REPRESENTATIVE GOVERNMENT AND A PARLIAMENT OF INDUSTRY. A STUDY OF THE GERMAN FEDERAL ECONOMIC COUNCIL. GERMANY UK CONSTN INDUS PARL/PROC ...NAT/COMP 20. PAGE 41 F0796
DELIB/GP ECO/TAC WAR REV

B28
TRUE A.C.,A HISTORY OF AGRICULTURAL EXTENSION WORK IN THE UNITED STATES, 1785-1923. USA-45 LAW SCHOOL WAR ADJUST...CHARTS BIBLIOG 18/20 SMITH/LEVR COUNTY/AGT. PAGE 131 F2591
EDU/PROP AGRI VOL/ASSN PLAN

B30
BEVERIDGE W.H.,UNEMPLOYMENT: A PROBLEM OF INDUSTRY (1909-1930). USA-45 LAW ECO/DEV MARKET DELIB/GP WAR DEMAND INCOME...POLICY STAT CHARTS 20. PAGE 14 F0274
WORKER ECO/TAC GEN/LAWS

B30
HAWTREY R.G.,ECONOMIC ASPECTS OF SOVEREIGNTY. UNIV WOR+45 WOR-45 ECO/DEV ECO/UNDEV AGRI COM/IND INDUS MARKET NAT/G TEC/DEV ECO/TAC EDU/PROP COERCE ATTIT KNOWL WEALTH...CONCPT CON/ANAL GEN/LAWS 20. PAGE 57 F1118
FORCES PWR SOVEREIGN WAR

B35
STALEY E.,WAR AND THE PRIVATE INVESTOR. UNIV WOR-45 INTELL SOCIETY INT/ORG NAT/G TOP/EX CAP/ISM ECO/TAC WAR ATTIT ALL/VALS...INT TIME/SEQ TREND CON/ANAL WORK TOT/POP 20. PAGE 125 F2464
FINAN INT/TRADE DIPLOM

B37
HAMILTON W.H.,THE POWER TO GOVERN. ECO/DEV FINAN INDUS ECO/TAC INT/TRADE TARIFFS TAX CONTROL CT/SYS WAR COST PWR 18/20 SUPREME/CT. PAGE 54 F1056
LING CONSTN NAT/G POLICY

B38
LAWLEY F.E.,THE GROWTH OF COLLECTIVE ECONOMY VOL. 1: NATIONAL. EUR+WWI AGRI INDUS NAT/G BARGAIN CAP/ISM ECO/TAC WAR OPTIMAL WEALTH...GOV/COMP METH/COMP 19/20 MONOPOLY. PAGE 76 F1492
SOCISM PRICE CONTROL OWN

B39
ENGELS F.,HERRN EUGEN DUHRING'S REVOLUTION IN SCIENCE (1878). CULTURE STRATA STRUCT FAM SECT ECO/TAC REV WAR SOCISM...MARXIST 19. PAGE 37 F0731
PWR SOCIETY WEALTH GEN/LAWS

B39
ROBBINS L.,ECONOMIC CAUSES OF WAR. WOR-45 ECO/DEV ECO/UNDEV INT/ORG NAT/G TEC/DEV DIPLOM DOMIN COLONIAL ATTIT DRIVE PWR WEALTH...POLICY CONCPT OBS WAR SAMP TREND CON/ANAL GEN/LAWS MARX/KARL 20. PAGE 112 F2203
COERCE ECO/TAC WAR

S39
COLE G.D.H.,"NAZI ECONOMICS: HOW DO THEY MANAGE IT?" GERMANY FORCES WORKER BUDGET INT/TRADE ROUTINE COERCE WAR 20 HITLER/A NAZI. PAGE 26 F0500
FASCISM ECO/TAC ATTIT PLAN

B40
FULLER G.H.,LIST OF REFERENCES ON PRIORITIES (MIMEOGRAPHED PAPER). WOR-45 NAT/G RATION 20. PAGE 45 F0874
BIBLIOG/A WAR ECO/TAC PLAN

B41
YOUNG G.,FEDERALISM AND FREEDOM. EUR+WWI MOD/EUR RUSSIA USA-45 WOR-45 SOCIETY STRUCT ECO/DEV INT/ORG EXEC FEDERAL ATTIT PERSON ALL/VALS...OLD/LIB CONCPT OBS TREND LEAGUE/NAT TOT/POP. PAGE 150 F2950
NAT/G WAR

S41
MUKERJEE R.,"POPULATION THEORY AND POLITICS (BMR)" WOR-45 NAT/G PLAN PROB/SOLV ECO/TAC INT/TRADE CONTROL WAR PEACE...CENSUS 20 BIRTH/CON RESOURCE/N. PAGE 94 F1854
GEOG OPTIMAL CONCPT

B42
DRUCKER P.F.,THE FUTURE OF INDUSTRIAL MAN; A CONSERVATIVE APPROACH. USA-45 LOC/G PLAN WAR CENTRAL RATIONAL TOTALISM ORD/FREE LAISSEZ ...PLURIST IDEA/COMP 19/20 HITLER/A. PAGE 34 F0664
INDUS SOCIETY REGION PROB/SOLV

B42
US LIBRARY OF CONGRESS,ECONOMICS OF WAR (APRIL 1941-MARCH 1942). WOR-45 FINAN INDUS LOC/G NAT/G PLAN BUDGET RATION COST DEMAND...POLICY 20. PAGE 138 F2712
BIBLIOG/A INT/TRADE ECO/TAC WAR

B42
US LIBRARY OF CONGRESS,THE WAR PRODUCTION PROGRAM: SELECTED DOCUMENTATION ON THE ECONOMICS OF WAR (PAMPHLET). USA-45 ECO/DEV AGRI FINAN NAT/G ECO/TAC RATION PRICE EFFICIENCY 20. PAGE 138 F2713
BIBLIOG/A WAR PRODUC INDUS

B42
WRIGHT D.M.,THE CREATION OF PURCHASING POWER. USA-45 NAT/G PRICE ADMIN WAR INCOME PRODUC...POLICY CONCPT IDEA/COMP BIBLIOG 20 MONEY. PAGE 149 F2930
FINAN ECO/TAC ECO/DEV CREATE

B44
LANDAUER C.,THEORY OF NATIONAL ECONOMIC PLANNING. USA-45 INDUS MARKET WORKER PROB/SOLV DIPLOM RATION PRICE CONTROL WAR COST 20. PAGE 75 F1465
ECO/TAC PLAN NAT/G ECO/DEV

B47
GORDON D.L.,THE HIDDEN WEAPON: THE STORY OF ECONOMIC WARFARE. EUR+WWI USA-45 LAW FINAN INDUS NAT/G CONSULT FORCES PLAN DOMIN PWR WEALTH ...INT/LAW CONCPT OBS TOT/POP NAZI 20. PAGE 49 F0955
INT/ORG ECO/TAC INT/TRADE WAR

B47
US LIBRARY OF CONGRESS,POSTWAR PLANNING AND RECONSTRUCTION: JANUARY-MARCH 1943. WOR+45 SOCIETY INT/ORG DIPLOM...SOC PREDICT 20. PAGE 138 F2714
BIBLIOG/A WAR PEACE PLAN

B48
CLYDE P.H.,THE FAR EAST: A HISTORY OF THE IMPACT OF THE WEST ON EASTERN ASIA. CHINA/COM CULTURE INT/TRADE DOMIN COLONIAL WAR PWR...CHARTS BIBLIOG 19/20 CHINJAP. PAGE 25 F0494
DIPLOM ASIA

B48
OSBORN F.,OUR PLUNDERED PLANET. UNIV DEATH WAR ...BIBLIOG RESOURCE/N. PAGE 102 F2001
HABITAT GEOG ADJUST AGRI

B48
TAYLOR P.E.,THE ECONOMICS OF PUBLIC FINANCE. USA+45 USA-45 ECO/DEV WORKER PLAN BUDGET WAR INCOME WEALTH ...CONCPT STAT BIBLIOG 20. PAGE 129 F2540
FINAN POLICY NAT/G TAX

B48
WHYTE W.F.,HUMAN RELATIONS IN THE RESTAURANT INDUSTRY (1ST ED). CLIENT WORKER WAR ATTIT...MGT OBS INT. PAGE 146 F2874
INGP/REL GP/REL SERV/IND LABOR

B48
WINSLOW E.M.,THE PATTERN OF IMPERIALISM; A STUDY IN THE THEORIES OF POWER. DOMIN WAR PWR MARXISM ...IDEA/COMP METH/COMP BIBLIOG 20. PAGE 147 F2906
SOCISM CAP/ISM COLONIAL ECO/TAC

B49
DE JOUVENEL B.,PROBLEMS OF SOCIALIST ENGLAND. AFR UK USSR BAL/PWR ECO/TAC INT/TRADE PRICE WAR BAL/PAY PEACE 20. PAGE 31 F0601
SOCISM NEW/LIB PROB/SOLV PLAN

B49
MACGREGOR D.H.,ECONOMIC THOUGHT AND POLICY. WOR-45 WORKER WAR DEMAND EFFICIENCY WEALTH LAISSEZ SOCISM ...MAJORIT BIBLIOG 19/20. PAGE 83 F1629
CONCPT POLICY ECO/TAC

S49
STEINMETZ H.,"THE PROBLEMS OF THE LANDRAT: A STUDY OF COUNTY GOVERNMENT IN THE US ZONE OF GERMANY."
LOC/G COLONIAL

GERMANY/W USA+45 INDUS PLAN DIPLOM EDU/PROP CONTROL WAR GOV/REL FEDERAL WEALTH PLURISM...GOV/COMP 20 LANDRAT. PAGE 126 F2478
MGT TOP/EX

B50

HUTCHISON K.,THE DECLINE AND FALL OF BRITISH CAPITALISM. UK ELITES STRATA ECO/DEV LABOR WORKER CONTROL WAR PWR...BIBLIOG/A 19/20. PAGE 63 F1249
CAP/ISM SOCISM LAISSEZ DOMIN

B50

LINCOLN G.,ECONOMICS OF NATIONAL SECURITY. USA+45 ELITES COM/IND DIST/IND INDUS NAT/G VOL/ASSN DELIB/GP EX/STRUC FOR/AID EDU/PROP COERCE NUC/PWR WAR ATTIT KNOWL ORD/FREE PWR TOT/POP VAL/FREE 20. PAGE 80 F1565
FORCES ECO/TAC AFR

B50

SCHUMPETER J.A.,CAPITALISM, SOCIALISM, AND DEMOCRACY (3RD ED.). USA-45 USSR WOR+45 WOR-45 INTELL ECO/DEV ECO/UNDEV ECO/TAC WAR PRODUC ORD/FREE...MGT SOC 20 MARX/KARL. PAGE 118 F2321
SOCIALIST CAP/ISM MARXISM IDEA/COMP

B51

CHANDLER L.V.,INFLATION IN THE UNITED STATES 1940-1948. AFR NAT/G BUDGET PAY PRICE CONTROL WAR INCOME PRODUC...POLICY BIBLIOG 20. PAGE 23 F0448
ECO/TAC FINAN PROB/SOLV WEALTH

B51

HALEVY E.,IMPERIALISM AND THE RISE OF LABOR (2ND ED.). UK NAT/G POL/PAR TOP/EX ATTIT ORD/FREE PWR 19/20 PARLIAMENT LABOR/PAR. PAGE 53 F1042
COLONIAL LABOR POLICY WAR

B51

HANSEN B.,A STUDY IN THE THEORY OF INFLATION. WOR-45 FINAN WAR DEMAND...CHARTS 20. PAGE 54 F1067
PRICE ECO/TAC EQUILIB PRODUC

B51

HARROD R.F.,THE LIFE OF JOHN MAYNARD KEYNES. UK INTELL FAM CAP/ISM DIPLOM ECO/TAC WAR ATTIT PERSON ROLE 20 KEYNES/JM WWI. PAGE 56 F1094
BIOG FINAN GEN/LAWS

B51

HART A.G.,DEFENSE WITHOUT INFLATION. AFR KOREA FINAN INDUS NAT/G WORKER DIPLOM RATION TAX PRICE COST OPTIMAL 20 RESOURCE/N. PAGE 56 F1098
ECO/TAC CONTROL WAR PLAN

B51

US HOUSE COMM APPROPRIATIONS,MUTUAL SECURITY PROGRAM APPROPRIATIONS FOR 1952: HEARINGS BEFORE A SUBCOMMITTEE OF THE COMMITTEE ON APPROPRIATIONS. AFR KOREA L/A+17C ECO/DEV ECO/UNDEV INT/ORG INSPECT BAL/PWR DIPLOM DEBATE WAR...POLICY STAT ASIA/S 20 CONGRESS NATO MID/EAST. PAGE 136 F2686
LEGIS FORCES BUDGET FOR/AID

B52

MACARTHUR D.,REVITALIZING A NATION. ASIA COM FUT KOREA WOR+45 NAT/G FOR/AID TAX GIVE WAR ATTIT SOCISM 20 CHINJAP EUROPE. PAGE 83 F1619
LEAD FORCES TOP/EX POLICY

B52

WU Y.,ECONOMIC WARFARE. MARKET PLAN PROB/SOLV FOR/AID CONTROL EFFICIENCY WEALTH...METH/COMP 20. PAGE 149 F2937
ECO/TAC WAR INT/TRADE DIPLOM

B53

WILLIAMS J.H.,ECONOMIC STABILITY IN A CHANGING WORLD. FRANCE USA+45 USSR AGRI WORKER BUDGET INT/TRADE TAX WAR BAL/PAY COST EFFICIENCY ALL/IDEOS EQULIB 20 KEYNES/JM. PAGE 147 F2892
POLICY FINAN ECO/TAC WEALTH

B54

CHILDS M.W.,ETHICS IN A BUSINESS SOCIETY. PROF/ORG LEAD WAR GP/REL ATTIT DRIVE PERSON KNOWL MORAL PWR ...WELF/ST BIBLIOG. PAGE 24 F0466
MGT SOCIETY

B54

LENIN V.I.,SELECTED WORKS (12 VOLS.). USSR INTELL SOCIETY STRATA STRUCT NAT/G POL/PAR WORKER CAP/ISM REV WAR...MARXIST PHIL/SCI 20 MARX/KARL LENIN/VI. PAGE 78 F1520
COM MARXISM

B54

MEYER A.G.,MARXISM. INTELL ECO/DEV WORKER CAP/ISM LEAD WAR ATTIT ALL/IDEOS...SOC 19/20 MARX/KARL. PAGE 90 F1766
MARXISM CONCPT ECO/TAC STRUCT

B54

REYNOLDS P.A.,BRITISH FOREIGN POLICY IN THE INTER-WAR YEARS. CZECHOSLVK GERMANY POLAND UK USA-45 POL/PAR FORCES ECO/TAC ARMS/CONT WAR ATTIT 20. PAGE 111 F2182
DIPLOM POLICY NAT/G

B55

WOYTINSKY W.S.,WORLD COMMERCE AND GOVERNMENTS: TRENDS AND OUTLOOK. WOR+45 FINAN POL/PAR DIPLOM ECO/TAC FOR/AID DOMIN WAR CHOOSE...CHARTS BIBLIOG 20 LEAGUE/NAT UN ILO. PAGE 149 F2929
INT/TRADE DIST/IND NAT/COMP NAT/G

B56

WOLFF R.L.,THE BALKANS IN OUR TIME. ALBANIA FUT MOD/EUR USSR YUGOSLAVIA CULTURE INT/ORG SECT DIPLOM EDU/PROP COERCE WAR ORD/FREE...CHARTS 4/20 BALKANS COMINFORM. PAGE 148 F2919
GEOG COM

B57

HARWOOD E.C.,CAUSE AND CONTROL OF THE BUSINESS CYCLE (5TH ED.). AFR USA-45 PRICE CONTROL WAR DEMAND INCOME WEALTH...TREND CHARTS 19. PAGE 56 F1107
PRODUC MARKET FINAN

B57

SINGH D.B.,INFLATIONARY PRICE TRENDS IN INDIA SINCE 1939. AFR INDIA ECO/TAC RATION CONTROL WAR GOV/REL BAL/PAY DEMAND INCOME PEACE PRODUC...POLICY CHARTS 20. PAGE 122 F2413
BUDGET ECO/UNDEV PRICE FINAN

B57

THOMAS R.G.,OUR MODERN BANKING AND MONETARY SYSTEM (3RD ED.). AFR USA+45 USA-45 ACT/RES PLAN PROB/SOLV INT/TRADE PRICE WAR BAL/PAY INCOME...POLICY METH/CNCPT 20 DEPRESSION. PAGE 130 F2563
FINAN SERV/IND ECO/TAC

B58

BIDWELL P.W.,RAW MATERIALS: A STUDY OF AMERICAN POLICY. USA+45 USA-45 ECO/UNDEV AGRI INDUS KIN CREATE PLAN ECO/TAC WAR PEACE ATTIT DRIVE WEALTH ...STAT CHARTS CONGRESS FOR/TRADE VAL/FREE. PAGE 15 F0279
EXTR/IND ECO/DEV

B58

CHANG C.,THE INFLATIONARY SPIRAL: THE EXPERIENCE IN CHINA 1939-50. CHINA/COM BUDGET INT/TRADE PRICE ADMIN CONTROL WAR DEMAND...POLICY CHARTS 20. PAGE 23 F0451
FINAN ECO/TAC BAL/PAY GOV/REL

B58

MCIVOR R.C.,CANADIAN MONETARY, BANKING, AND FISCAL DEVELOPMENT. CANADA INDUS LG/CO NAT/G SML/CO CONTROL WAR...GEN/LAWS BIBLIOG 17/20. PAGE 88 F1729
ECO/TAC FINAN ECO/DEV WEALTH

B59

HARTOG F.,EUROPEAN TRADE CYCLE POLICY. WORKER TAX PRICE WAR CENTRAL DEMAND...TREND CHARTS 20 UN. PAGE 56 F1103
EQUILIB EUR+WWI INT/TRADE

B59

KOREAN MINISTRY RECONSTRUCTION,KOREAN ECONOMY AND ITS REQUIREMENTS. KOREA USA+45 ECO/TAC EQUILIB INCOME WEALTH...CHARTS 20. PAGE 73 F1427
FOR/AID WAR FINAN DIPLOM

B59

LEWIS J.P.,BUSINESS CONDITIONS ANALYSIS. USA+45 MARKET LABOR BUDGET TAX AUTOMAT WAR DEMAND PRODUC ...ECOMETRIC CHARTS BIBLIOG 19/20. PAGE 79 F1549
FINAN PRICE TREND

B59

LINK R.G.,ENGLISH THEORIES OF ECONOMIC FLUCTUATIONS: 1815-1848. FRANCE UK AGRI WORKER DIPLOM PRICE TASK WAR DEMAND PRODUC...POLICY BIBLIOG 18 MALTHUS MILL/JS WILSON/J. PAGE 80 F1574
IDEA/COMP ECO/DEV WEALTH EQUILIB

B59

MARTIN K.,WAR, HISTORY, AND HUMAN NATURE. FRANCE GERMANY INDIA UK UNIV POL/PAR COLONIAL DETER REV MARXISM PACIFISM...PSY CONCPT PREDICT LENIN/VI GANDHI/M. PAGE 86 F1683
PERSON WAR ATTIT IDEA/COMP

B59

ROPKE W.,INTERNATIONAL ORDER AND ECONOMIC INTEGRATION. ECO/DEV ECO/UNDEV AGRI FINAN INDUS INT/ORG WAR PEACE ORD/FREE...SOC METH/COMP 20 EEC. PAGE 114 F2238
INT/TRADE DIPLOM BAL/PAY ALL/IDEOS

S59

THOMPSON W.S.,"POPULATION AND PROGRESS IN THE FAR EAST." ASIA S/ASIA DIST/IND CREATE ECO/TAC WAR LOVE SKILL WEALTH...CONT/OBS TOT/POP 20. PAGE 130 F2568
ECO/UNDEV BIO/SOC GEOG

B60

FIRESTONE J.M.,FEDERAL RECEIPTS AND EXPENDITURES DURING BUSINESS CYCLES, 1879-1958. USA+45 USA-45 INDUS PLAN ECO/TAC TAX WAR COST...CHARTS 19/20. PAGE 41 F0801
FINAN INCOME BUDGET NAT/G

B60

HEILPERIN M.A.,STUDIES IN ECONOMIC NATIONALISM. EUR+WWI MOD/EUR USA+45 ECO/DEV PLAN INT/TRADE TARIFFS WAR PRODUC PROFIT 18/20 KEYNES/JM. PAGE 58 F1140
ECO/TAC NAT/G NAT/LISM POLICY

B60

WODDIS J.,AFRICA: THE ROOTS OF REVOLT. SOUTH/AFR WORKER INT/TRADE RACE/REL DISCRIM ORD/FREE 20. PAGE 148 F2915
COLONIAL SOVEREIGN WAR ECO/UNDEV

B61

ASCHHEIM J.,TECHNIQUES OF MONETARY CONTROL. UK USA+45 CONTROL WAR DEMAND INCOME WEALTH...TREND CHARTS 20 MONEY. PAGE 7 F0127
FINAN MARKET BUDGET CENTRAL

B61

FLINN M.W.,AN ECONOMIC AND SOCIAL HISTORY OF BRITAIN, 1066-1939. UK LAW STRATA STRUCT AGRI DIST/IND INDUS WORKER INT/TRADE WAR...CENSUS 11/20. PAGE 42 F0811
SOCIETY SOC

B61

HOLMANS A.E.,UNITED STATES FISCAL POLICY 1945-1959. AFR USA+45 USA-45 ECO/DEV TAX PRICE WAR...BIBLIOG 20 DEMOCRAT REPUBLICAN. PAGE 61 F1200
POLICY BUDGET NAT/G ECO/TAC

B61

MEZERIK A.G.,ECONOMIC DEVELOPMENT AIDS FOR UNDERDEVELOPED COUNTRIES. WOR+45 FINAN LEGIS PROB/SOLV TEC/DEV DIPLOM FOR/AID GIVE TASK WAR 20 UN. PAGE 91 F1776
ECO/UNDEV INT/ORG WEALTH PLAN

B61
MOORE G.H.,BUSINESS CYCLE INDICATORS (TWO VOLS.). LABOR DIPLOM PRICE RISK TASK WAR PRODUC...CHARTS BIBLIOG 20. PAGE 93 F1822
MARKET FINAN WEALTH

B61
PROUDHON P.J.,LA GUERRE ET LA PAIX (2 VOLS.). UNIV STRATA PROB/SOLV EQUILIB INCOME ATTIT...CONCPT 19. PAGE 108 F2125
WAR PEACE WEALTH

B61
STANLEY C.J.,LATE CH'ING FINANCE: HU KUANG-YUNG AS AN INNOVATOR. ASIA NAT/G FORCES BUDGET TAX WAR GOV/REL COST...POLICY BIOG CHARTS BIBLIOG 19. PAGE 125 F2469
FINAN ECO/TAC CIVMIL/REL ADMIN

B62
DOBB M.,CAPITALISM YESTERDAY AND TODAY. UK WORKER WAR PRODUC PROFIT 18/20 MONOPOLY. PAGE 33 F0646
CAP/ISM TIME/SEQ CONCPT ECO/TAC

B62
HIRSCHFIELD R.S.,THE CONSTITUTION AND THE COURT. AFR SCHOOL WAR RACE/REL EQUILIB ORD/FREE...POLICY MAJORIT DECISION JURID 18/20 PRESIDENT CIVIL/LIB SUPREME/CT CONGRESS. PAGE 60 F1175
ADJUD PWR CONSTN LAW

B62
JORDAN A.A. JR.,FOREIGN AID AND THE DEFENSE OF SOUTHEAST ASIA. PAKISTAN VIETNAM/S FINAN PLAN BUDGET ECO/TAC DETER WAR ORD/FREE...POLICY DECISION CENSUS CHARTS BIBLIOG 20. PAGE 68 F1341
FOR/AID S/ASIA FORCES ECO/UNDEV

B62
SCHILLING W.R.,STRATEGY, POLITICS, AND DEFENSE BUDGETS. AFR USA+45 CHIEF LEGIS PLAN TEC/DEV BAL/PWR BUDGET NUC/PWR WAR CIVMIL/REL GOV/REL PWR 20 EISNHWR/DD. PAGE 117 F2297
NAT/G POLICY FORCES DETER

B62
SIEVERS A.M.,REVOLUTION, EVOLUTION AND THE ECONOMIC ORDER. INDUS LABOR TAX CONTROL REV WAR DEMAND PRODUC WEALTH...IDEA/COMP 19/20 KEYNES/JM. PAGE 122 F2399
EFFICIENCY ALL/IDEOS ECO/DEV WELF/ST

B63
LEE M.W.,MACROECONOMICS: FLUCTUATIONS, GROWTH AND STABILITY (3RD ED.). MARKET LABOR TEC/DEV INT/TRADE TAX PRICE WAR PRODUC...POLICY ECOMETRIC CHARTS 19/20. PAGE 77 F1505
EQUILIB TREND WEALTH

B63
OLSON M. JR.,THE ECONOMICS OF WARTIME SHORTAGE. FRANCE GERMANY MOD/EUR UK AGRI PROB/SOLV ADMIN DEMAND WEALTH...POLICY OLD/LIB FOR/TRADE 17/20. PAGE 101 F1990
WAR ADJUST ECO/TAC NAT/COMP

B63
OTERO L.M.,HONDURAS. HONDURAS SPAIN STRUCT SECT COLONIAL REV WAR ATTIT PWR...GEOG WORSHIP 16/20. PAGE 102 F2003
NAT/G SOCIETY NAT/LISM ECO/UNDEV

B63
PATTON R.,THE DEVELOPMENT OF THE AMERICAN ECONOMY: REVISED. USA+45 USA-45 INDUS LABOR NAT/G CAP/ISM DIPLOM INT/TRADE WAR WEALTH 16/20. PAGE 104 F2038
ECO/TAC ECO/DEV DEMAND

B63
US DEPARTMENT OF LABOR,THE ANVIL AND THE PLOW. KOREA USA+45 USA-45 INDUS WORKER BUDGET WAR ...POLICY AUD/VIS CHARTS 20 DEPT/LABOR. PAGE 135 F2667
ECO/DEV LABOR ECO/TAC NAT/G

B63
WILTZ J.E.,IN SEARCH OF PEACE: THE SENATE MUNITIONS INQUIRY, 1934-36. EUR+WWI USA-45 ELITES INDUS LG/CO LEGIS INT/TRADE LOBBY NEUTRAL ARMS/CONT...POLICY CONGRESS 20 LEAGUE/NAT PRESIDENT SENATE CONSCRIPTN. PAGE 147 F2905
DELIB/GP PROFIT WAR WEAPON

S63
BENOIT E.,"ECONOMIC ADJUSTMENTS TO ARMS CONTROL." FUT USA+45 NAT/G NUC/PWR WAR WEAPON 20. PAGE 13 F0251
ECO/DEV PWR ARMS/CONT

B64
CALDER R.,TWO-WAY PASSAGE. INT/ORG TEC/DEV WAR PERSON ORD/FREE 20. PAGE 21 F0400
FOR/AID ECO/UNDEV ECO/TAC DIPLOM

B64
DUSCHA J.,ARMS, MONEY, AND POLITICS. USA+45 INDUS POL/PAR ECO/TAC TAX DETER NUC/PWR WAR WEAPON GOV/REL ATTIT...BIBLIOG/A 20 CONGRESS MONEY DEPT/DEFEN. PAGE 35 F0687
NAT/G FORCES POLICY BUDGET

B64
ESTHUS R.A.,FROM ENMITY TO ALLIANCE: US AUSTRALIAN RELATIONS. S/ASIA DIST/IND VOL/ASSN FORCES ATTIT 20 AUSTRAL TREATY CMN/WLTH. PAGE 39 F0751
DIPLOM WAR INT/TRADE FOR/AID

B65
PEACE RESEARCH ABSTRACTS. FUT WOR+45 R+D INT/ORG NAT/G PLAN TEC/DEV BAL/PWR DIPLOM FOR/AID NUC/PWR HEALTH. PAGE 1 F0022
BIBLIOG/A PEACE ARMS/CONT WAR

B65
COLLINS H.,KARL MARX AND THE BRITISH LABOUR MOVEMENT; YEARS OF THE FIRST INTERNATIONAL. FRANCE SWITZERLND UK CAP/ISM WAR...MARXIST IDEA/COMP BIBLIOG 19. PAGE 26 F0506
MARXISM LABOR INT/ORG REV

B65
COX D.W.,THE PERILS OF PEACE* CONVERSION TO WHAT? FUT USA+45 ECO/DEV NAT/G ACT/RES CREATE PLAN NUC/PWR WAR DEMAND MGT. PAGE 28 F0546
PEACE WORKER FORCES MARKET

B65
LYONS G.M.,AMERICA: PURPOSE AND POWER. UK USA+45 FINAN INDUS MARKET WORKER TEC/DEV DIPLOM AUTOMAT NUC/PWR WAR RACE/REL ORD/FREE 20 EEC CONGRESS SUPREME/CT CIV/RIGHTS. PAGE 82 F1617
PWR PROB/SOLV ECO/DEV TASK

B65
O'BRIEN F.,CRISIS IN WORLD COMMUNISM* MARXISM IN SEARCH OF EFFICIENCY. AFR COM ECO/DEV PLAN INT/TRADE WAR ADJUST PEACE...STAT TIME/SEQ GOV/COMP NAT/COMP. PAGE 99 F1951
MARXISM USSR DRIVE EFFICIENCY

B65
RANSOM H.H.,AN AMERICAN FOREIGN POLICY READER. USA+45 FORCES EDU/PROP COERCE NUC/PWR WAR PEACE ...DECISION 20. PAGE 109 F2146
NAT/G DIPLOM POLICY

B65
THAYER F.C. JR.,AIR TRANSPORT POLICY AND NATIONAL SECURITY: A POLITICAL, ECONOMIC, AND MILITARY ANALYSIS. DIST/IND OP/RES PLAN TEC/DEV DIPLOM DETER WAR COST EFFICIENCY...POLICY BIBLIOG 20 DEPT/DEFEN FAA CAB. PAGE 129 F2548
AIR FORCES CIVMIL/REL ORD/FREE

B65
YOUNG A.N.,CHINA'S WARTIME FINANCE AND INFLATION. ASIA AGRI INDUS NAT/G ECO/TAC CONFER PRICE WAR COST 20. PAGE 150 F2949
FINAN FOR/AID TAX BUDGET

S65
BERREBY J.J.,"IMPERATIFS STRATEGIQUES DU PETROLE." ECO/UNDEV VOL/ASSN ECO/TAC COLONIAL NUC/PWR WAR. PAGE 14 F0270
ISLAM EXTR/IND STAT OBS

C65
WUORINEN J.H.,"SCANDINAVIA." DENMARK FINLAND ICELAND NORWAY SWEDEN SOCIETY AGRI POL/PAR DELIB/GP DIPLOM INT/TRADE NEUTRAL WAR...CHARTS IND TREATY 20. PAGE 149 F2942
BIBLIOG NAT/G POLICY

B66
BOLTON R.E.,DEFENSE AND DISARMAMENT: THE ECONOMICS OF TRANSITION. USA+45 R+D FORCES PLAN LOBBY DETER WAR COST PEACE...ANTHOL BIBLIOG 20. PAGE 16 F0310
ARMS/CONT POLICY INDUS

B66
BROWN J.F.,THE NEW EASTERN EUROPE. ALBANIA BULGARIA HUNGARY POLAND ROMANIA CULTURE AGRI POL/PAR WAR NAT/LISM MARXISM...CHARTS BIBLIOG 20. PAGE 19 F0369
DIPLOM COM NAT/G ECO/UNDEV

B66
FREIDEL F.,AMERICAN ISSUES IN THE TWENTIETH CENTURY. SOCIETY FINAN ECO/TAC FOR/AID CONTROL NUC/PWR WAR RACE/REL PEACE ATTIT...ANTHOL T 20 WILSON/W ROOSEVLT/F KENNEDY/JF TRUMAN/HS. PAGE 44 F0851
DIPLOM POLICY NAT/G ORD/FREE

B66
GYORGY A.,ISSUES OF WORLD COMMUNISM. ALBANIA CHINA/COM COM USSR YUGOSLAVIA STRATA AGRI INT/ORG CHIEF FORCES WORKER WAR ALL/IDEOS...GEOG 20 MAO. PAGE 52 F1018
ECO/UNDEV REV MARXISM CON/ANAL

B66
HAYER T.,FRENCH AID. AFR FRANCE AGRI FINAN BUDGET ADMIN WAR PRODUC...CHARTS 18/20 THIRD/WRLD OVRSEA/DEV. PAGE 57 F1125
TEC/DEV COLONIAL FOR/AID ECO/UNDEV

B66
KROOSS H.E.,AMERICAN ECONOMIC DEVELOPMENT (2ND ED.). USA+45 USA-45 AGRI INDUS LABOR WORKER INT/TRADE TAX WAR...CHARTS 18/20. PAGE 73 F1443
ECO/TAC NAT/G CAP/ISM ECO/DEV

B66
KUENNE R.E.,THE POLARIS MISSILE STRIKE* A GENERAL ECONOMIC SYSTEMS ANALYSIS. USA+45 USSR NAT/G BAL/PWR ARMS/CONT WAR...MATH PROBABIL COMPUT/IR CHARTS HYPO/EXP SIMUL. PAGE 74 F1446
NUC/PWR FORCES DETER DIPLOM

B66
RAYBACK J.G.,A HISTORY OF AMERICAN LABOR. USA+45 USA-45 ECO/DEV LEGIS COLONIAL WAR INGP/REL PWR WEALTH 17/20. PAGE 110 F2156
LABOR LOBBY ECO/UNDEV NAT/G

B66
US PRES COMM ECO IMPACT DEFENS,REPORT* JULY 1965. USA+45 ECO/DEV INDUS DELIB/GP FORCES OP/RES ARMS/CONT NUC/PWR WEAPON BAL/PAY...PREDICT SIMUL. PAGE 138 F2726
ACT/RES STAT WAR BUDGET

B66
ZISCHKA A.,WAR ES EIN WUNDER? GERMANY/W ECO/DEV FINAN LG/CO BARGAIN CAP/ISM FOR/AID RATION 20 MARSHL/PLN. PAGE 150 F2965
ECO/TAC INT/TRADE INDUS WAR

B67
BEATON L.,THE STRUGGLE FOR PEACE. INT/ORG FORCES NUC/PWR COST PWR...POLICY TREND 20. PAGE 12 F0225
PEACE BAL/PWR DIPLOM WAR

B67
BURDEN H.T.,THE NUREMBERG PARTY RALLIES 1923-39. GERMANY POL/PAR SECT CREATE DOMIN WAR ATTIT ...AUD/VIS FILM 20. PAGE 20 F0384
EDU/PROP CONTROL CROWD TOTALISM

B67
CHO S.S.,KOREA IN WORLD POLITICS 1940-1950; AN EVALUATION OF AMERICAN RESPONSIBILITY. KOREA USA+45 USSR CONSTN INT/ORG NAT/G FORCES FOR/AID ANOMIE SUPEGO MARXISM...DECISION BIBLIOG 20. PAGE 24 F0469
POLICY DIPLOM PROB/SOLV WAR

B67
DINERSTEIN H.S.,INTERVENTION AGAINST COMMUNISM (STUDIES IN INTERNATIONAL AFFAIRS NO. 1). CUBA DOMIN/REP GREECE USA+45 USSR VIETNAM OP/RES COERCE WAR 20. PAGE 33 F0643
MARXISM DIPLOM NAT/LISM

B67
DUN J.L.,THE ESSENCE OF CHINESE CIVILIZATION. ASIA FAM NAT/G TEC/DEV ADMIN SANCTION WAR HABITAT ...ANTHOL WORSHIP. PAGE 35 F0676
CULTURE SOCIETY

B67
GIAP V.N.,BIG VICTORY, GREAT TASK. VIETNAM WOR+45 FORCES PLAN DOMIN LEGIT RISK PEACE 20. PAGE 47 F0921
WAR LEAD ATTIT INSPECT

B67
GOODMAN P.,LIKE A CONQUERED PROVINCE: THE MORAL AMBIGUITY OF AMERICA. AFR USA+45 NAT/G PROB/SOLV EDU/PROP ADJUST EFFICIENCY 20. PAGE 49 F0950
SOCIETY TEC/DEV WAR MORAL

B67
HALLE L.J.,THE COLD WAR AS HISTORY. AFR USSR WOR+45 ECO/TAC FOR/AID NUC/PWR WAR PEACE ORD/FREE ...MAJORIT TREND 20 KENNEDY/JF KHRUSH/N BERLIN/BLO. PAGE 54 F1048
DIPLOM BAL/PWR

B67
MARTIN P.,CANADA AND THE QUEST FOR PEACE. CANADA VIETNAM ECO/UNDEV PLAN FOR/AID WAR 20 UN. PAGE 86 F1684
DIPLOM PEACE INT/ORG POLICY

B67
MCNELLY T.,SOURCES IN MODERN EAST ASIAN HISTORY AND POLITICS. KOREA VIETNAM CULTURE DIPLOM COLONIAL REV WAR PWR ALL/IDEOS MARXISM...ANTHOL 20 CHINJAP. PAGE 88 F1733
NAT/COMP ASIA S/ASIA SOCIETY

B67
MEYERS M.,SOURCES OF THE AMERICAN REPUBLIC; A DOCUMENTARY HISTORY OF POLITICS, SOCIETY, AND THOUGHT (VOL. I, REV. ED.). USA-45 CULTURE STRUCT NAT/G LEGIS LEAD ATTIT...JURID SOC ANTHOL 17/19 PRESIDENT. PAGE 90 F1772
COLONIAL REV WAR

B67
STEARNS P.N.,EUROPEAN SOCIETY IN UPHEAVAL* SOCIAL HISTORY SINCE 1800. EUR+WWI MOD/EUR STRATA SECT WORKER TEC/DEV WAR...WELF/ST SOC TREND BIBLIOG 19/20. PAGE 125 F2472
REGION ECO/DEV SOCIETY INDUS

B67
TANSKY L.,US AND USSR AID TO DEVELOPING COUNTRIES. INDIA TURKEY USA+45 USSR INDUS PLAN CAP/ISM WAR PWR WEALTH MARXISM...CHARTS NAT/COMP BIBLIOG 20. PAGE 128 F2534
ECO/UNDEV FOR/AID DIPLOM ECO/TAC

B67
US SENATE COMM ON FOREIGN REL,HARRISON E. SALISBURY'S TRIP TO NORTH VIETNAM. CHINA/COM USA+45 VIETNAM/N PRESS TASK GUERRILLA CONSEN EFFICIENCY PEACE DRIVE...OBS SENATE. PAGE 139 F2743
DIPLOM WAR FORCES ATTIT

B67
US SENATE COMM ON FOREIGN REL,FOREIGN ASSISTANCE ACT OF 1967. VIETNAM WOR+45 DELIB/GP CONFER CONTROL WAR WEAPON BAL/PAY...CENSUS CHARTS SENATE. PAGE 139 F2744
FOR/AID LAW DIPLOM POLICY

B67
WATT A.,THE EVOLUTION OF AUSTRALIAN FOREIGN POLICY 1938-65. ASIA S/ASIA USA+45 USA-45 INT/ORG NAT/G FORCES FOR/AID TREATY 20 AUSTRAL. PAGE 144 F2834
DIPLOM WAR

B67
WILLS A.J.,AN INTRODUCTION TO THE HISTORY OF CENTRAL AFRICA. RHODESIA ZAMBIA CULTURE SOCIETY ECO/UNDEV TEC/DEV DOMIN WAR ALL/VALS...POLICY TREND BIBLIOG T 14/20 NYASALAND. PAGE 147 F2899
AFR COLONIAL ORD/FREE

L67
MCALLISTER J.T. JR.,"THE POSSIBILITIES FOR DIPLOMACY IN SOUTHEAST ASIA." LAOS VIETNAM INT/ORG NAT/G PROVS BAL/PWR DOMIN AGREE COLONIAL WAR PWR 17/20 TREATY. PAGE 88 F1716
DIPLOM S/ASIA

L67
SCALAPINO R.A.,"A SURVEY OF ASIA IN 1966." ASIA S/ASIA CONSTN SOCIETY POL/PAR CHIEF WAR...ANTHOL 20. PAGE 116 F2285
DIPLOM

S67
CAMPBELL J.C.,"SOVIET-AMERICAN RELATIONS: CONFLICT AND COOPERATION." AFR USA+45 USSR AGREE WAR PEACE 20 KHRUSH/N KENNEDY/JF. PAGE 21 F0407
DIPLOM POLICY

S67
CROKER F.P.U.,"ECONOMIC PEACEKEEPING." UK PLAN PROB/SOLV TEC/DEV BAL/PWR DIPLOM COERCE PEACE ...POLICY DECISION 20. PAGE 28 F0553
FORCES WEAPON COST

WAR

S67
DRAPER A.P.,"UNIONS AND THE WAR IN VIETNAM." USA+45 CONFER ADMIN LEAD WAR ORD/FREE PACIFIST 20. PAGE 34 F0660
LABOR PACIFISM ATTIT ELITES

S67
GEISS I.,"THE GERMANS AND THE MIDDLE EAST CRISIS." GERMANY/W ISLAM ISRAEL USSR POL/PAR RACE/REL MARXISM...GP/COMP 20 JEWS. PAGE 47 F0914
ATTIT DIPLOM WAR POLICY

S67
GOSALVEZ R.B.,"PERFIL DEL GENERAL VINCENTE ROJO." SPAIN DIPLOM CIVMIL/REL EFFICIENCY PERSON SKILL 20 BOLIV. PAGE 49 F0966
WAR FORCES ELITES BIOG

S67
KENNY L.M.,"THE AFTERMATH OF DEFEAT IN EGYPT." ISLAM ISRAEL UAR UK USA+45 USSR INDUS FORCES ECO/TAC PRICE COERCE WEAPON COST ATTIT. PAGE 70 F1378
WAR ECO/UNDEV DIPLOM POLICY

S67
KOHN W.S.G.,"THE SOVEREIGNTY OF LIECHTENSTEIN." LIECHTENST SWITZERLND USSR CONSTN DEBATE WAR CONSERVE 18/20 UN. PAGE 72 F1417
SOVEREIGN NAT/G PWR DIPLOM

S67
MOLTMANN G.,"ZUR FORMULIERUNG DER AMERIKANISCHEN BESATZUNGSPOLITIK IN DEUTSCHLAND AM ENDE DES ZWEITEN WELTKRIEGES" GERMANY ECO/TAC ADMIN WAR CIVMIL/REL ORD/FREE FASCISM 20. PAGE 92 F1815
FORCES CONTROL POLICY INDUS

S67
WOLFE T.W.,"SOVIET MILITARY POLICY AT THE FIFTY YEAR MARK." USSR VIETNAM WOR+45 RATION AGREE WAR WEAPON CIVMIL/REL TREATY. PAGE 148 F2917
FORCES POLICY TIME/SEQ PLAN

N67
US HOUSE COMM FOREIGN AFFAIRS,REPORT OF SPECIAL STUDY MISSION TO THE NEAR EAST (PAMPHLET). ISRAEL USA+45 YEMEN ECO/UNDEV INT/ORG FOR/AID ARMS/CONT WAR WEAPON NAT/LISM PEACE...GEOG 20 UN HOUSE/REP. PAGE 137 F2694
ISLAM DIPLOM FORCES

N67
US SENATE COMM ON FOREIGN REL,WAR OR PEACE IN THE MIDDLE EAST (PAMPHLET). GREECE ISLAM ISRAEL JORDAN UAR CHIEF PROB/SOLV FOR/AID WAR PWR 20 SENATE. PAGE 139 F2739
DIPLOM FORCES PLAN

N67
US SENATE COMM ON FOREIGN REL,THE RIM OF ASIA (PAMPHLET). WAR MARXISM 20. PAGE 139 F2745
ASIA PROB/SOLV SOVEREIGN POLICY

C83
BURKE E.,"RESOLUTIONS FOR CONCILIATION WITH AMERICA" (1775), IN E. BURKE, COLLECTED WORKS, VOL. 2." UK USA-45 FORCES INT/TRADE TARIFFS TAX SANCTION PEACE...POLICY 18 PRE/US/AM. PAGE 20 F0387
COLONIAL WAR SOVEREIGN ECO/TAC

WAR/TRIAL....WAR TRIAL; SEE ALSO NUREMBERG

WAR/1812....WAR OF 1812

WARBURTON E.A. F1340

WARD B. F2815,F2816

WARD B.J. F2817

WARD R. F2818

WARD R.J. F2819

WARD....SEE LOC/G, POL/PAR

WARD/LEST....LESTER WARD

WARE R.M. F2828

WARNE C. F2038

WARNER A.W. F2820,F2821

WARNER G. F2822

WARNER K.O. F2823

WARNER L. F2278

WARNER W.L. F2824

WARRINER D. F2825

WARRN/EARL....EARL WARREN

B67
LYTLE C.M.,THE WARREN COURT AND ITS CRITICS. USA+45 CT/SYS

NAT/G PROVS FORCES LOBBY RACE/REL DISCRIM SOVEREIGN 20 SUPREME/CT WARRN/EARL. PAGE 83 F1618 — ADJUD PROB/SOLV ATTIT

WARSAW PACT....SEE WARSAW/PCT

WARSAW....WARSAW, POLAND

WARSAW/PCT....WARSAW PACT TREATY ORGANIZATION

S67
STOLTE S.C.,"THREE PROBLEMS FACING THE SOVIET BLOC." ASIA COM USA+45 USSR FORCES MARXISM ...IDEA/COMP METH/COMP 20 NATO WARSAW/P. PAGE 127 F2496 — ECO/TAC DIPLOM INT/ORG POLICY

WARSAW/PCT....WARSAW PACT TREATY ORGANIZATION

WASHBURNE N.F. F2826

WASHING/BT....BOOKER T. WASHINGTON

WASHING/DC....WASHINGTON, D.C.

B64
FITCH L.C.,URBAN TRANSPORTATION AND PUBLIC POLICY. FINAN NAT/G LEGIS PROB/SOLV TEC/DEV PRICE COST EFFICIENCY...DECISION STAT CHARTS METH/COMP MUNICH 20 NEWYORK/C PHILADELPH LOS/ANG CHICAGO WASHING/DC. PAGE 41 F0806 — DIST/IND PLAN LOC/G

WASHINGT/G....PRESIDENT GEORGE WASHINGTON

WASHINGTON....WASHINGTON, STATE OF

WASP....WHITE-ANGLO-SAXON-PROTESTANT ESTABLISHMENT

WASSERMAN M. F2827

WASSERMAN M.J. F2828

WATER....PERTAINING TO ALL NON-SALT WATER

B59
MAYER H.M.,READINGS IN URBAN GEOGRAPHY. WOR+45 SOCIETY DIST/IND INDUS MARKET HABITAT...CLASSIF CENSUS CHARTS ANTHOL MUNICH 20 WATER. PAGE 87 F1706 — GEOG STRUCT

B61
HUBBARD P.J.,ORIGINS OF THE TVA: THE MUSCLE SHOALS CONTROVERSY, 1920-1932. USA-45 DELIB/GP LEGIS LEAD LOBBY GOV/REL GP/REL INGP/REL OWN PERSON...BIBLIOG 20 TVA CONGRESS WATER. PAGE 62 F1229 — SEA CONTROL NAT/G INDUS

B63
MANN D.E.,THE POLITICS OF WATER IN ARIZONA. AGRI EXTR/IND PROVS ACT/RES CREATE PLAN GOV/REL COST HABITAT...MGT CHARTS 20 ARIZONA WATER. PAGE 84 F1655 — POLICY ECO/TAC TEC/DEV

WATERSTON A. F2829,F2830

WATKINS J.B. F2831

WATSON D.S. F0389,F2832

WATSON G. F2833

WATT A. F2834

WATT D.C. F2835

WATTS....WATTS, CALIFORNIA

WCC....WORLD COUNCIL CHURCHES

WCTU....WOMAN'S CHRISTIAN TEMPERANCE UNION

WEALTH....ACCESS TO GOODS AND SERVICES (ALSO POVERTY)

N
AMERICAN ECONOMIC REVIEW. FINAN INDUS LABOR OP/RES CAP/ISM INT/TRADE TAX WEALTH...CON/ANAL CHARTS 20. PAGE 1 F0001 — BIBLIOG/A USA+45 ECO/DEV NAT/G

LCA
GODFREY E.M.,"THE ECONOMICS OF AN AFRICAN UNIVERSITY." AFR SCHOOL PRICE EFFICIENCY INCOME WEALTH...ECOMETRIC CHARTS 20. PAGE 48 F0930 — ACADEM ECO/TAC COST EDU/PROP

B00
LIST F.,NATIONAL SYSTEM OF POLITICAL ECONOMY. ECO/DEV AGRI EXTR/IND FINAN INDUS TEC/DEV ECO/TAC ATTIT WEALTH...TREND GEN/LAWS FOR/TRADE 19. PAGE 81 F1581 — MOD/EUR MARKET

B00
MILL J.S.,PRINCIPLES OF POLITICAL ECONOMY. WOR-45 CULTURE SOCIETY STRATA ECO/DEV AGRI EXTR/IND FINAN INDUS DELIB/GP ECO/TAC WEALTH...CONCPT MATH TREND 20. PAGE 91 F1786 — MARKET INT/ORG INT/TRADE

B03
MOREL E.D.,THE BRITISH CASE IN FRENCH CONGO. CONGO/BRAZ FRANCE UK COERCE MORAL WEALTH...POLICY INT/LAW 20 CONGO/LEOP. PAGE 93 F1827 — DIPLOM INT/TRADE COLONIAL AFR

B04
MARX K.,A CONTRIBUTION TO THE CRITIQUE OF POLITICAL ECONOMY (TRANS. FROM 2ND ED. BY N.I. STONE). UK STRATA ECO/DEV FINAN MARKET PLAN BARGAIN CAP/ISM ECO/TAC ATTIT WEALTH...METH/CNCPT BIOG 19. PAGE 86 F1687 — MARXIST NEW/IDEA MARXISM

B04
VEBLEN T.B.,THE THEORY OF BUSINESS ENTERPRISE. USA-45 FINAN WORKER ECO/TAC PRICE GP/REL COST ...POLICY 19/20. PAGE 141 F2770 — TEC/DEV GEN/LAWS SOCIETY WEALTH

B12
HOBSON J.A.,THE EVOLUTION OF MODERN CAPITALISM. MOD/EUR UK STRATA ECO/DEV INDUS INCOME UTIL WEALTH ...SOC GEN/LAWS 7/20. PAGE 60 F1184 — CAP/ISM WORKER TEC/DEV TIME/SEQ

B13
DAVENPORT H.J.,THE ECONOMICS OF ENTERPRISE. UNIV FINAN SML/CO RENT COST WEALTH GEN/LAWS. PAGE 30 F0582 — CAP/ISM PRICE ECO/TAC LG/CO

B14
HOBSON J.A.,WORK AND WEALTH. CULTURE FINAN INDUS WORKER TEC/DEV ECO/TAC GIVE PAY PRICE COST PRODUC UTIL. PAGE 60 F1185 — WEALTH INCOME GEN/LAWS

B15
JONES J.H.,THE ECONOMICS OF WAR AND CONQUEST. WOR-45 ECO/DEV NAT/G WEALTH...STAT TREND STERTYP GEN/LAWS TOT/POP 20. PAGE 68 F1338 — MYTH WAR

B18
MARX K.,CAPITAL. FUT MOD/EUR STRATA DIST/IND PROC/MFG TEC/DEV WEALTH...MARXIST WORK 19. PAGE 86 F1688 — ECO/DEV CAP/ISM SOCISM

B19
VEBLEN T.B.,THE VESTED INTERESTS AND THE STATE OF THE INDUSTRIAL ARTS. USA-45 LAW FINAN WORKER PAY DOMIN PRICE COST SOCISM...MARXIST 19/20. PAGE 141 F2771 — INDUS CAP/ISM METH/COMP WEALTH

N19
BUSINESS ECONOMISTS' GROUP,INCOME POLICIES (PAMPHLET). UK INDUS LABOR TOP/EX PAY COST PRODUC ...ECOMETRIC GOV/COMP SIMUL ANTHOL 20. PAGE 20 F0395 — INCOME WORKER WEALTH POLICY

N19
CARPER E.T.,LOBBYING AND THE NATURAL GAS BILL (PAMPHLET). USA+45 SERV/IND BARGAIN PAY DRIVE ROLE WEALTH 20 CONGRESS SENATE EISNHWR/DD. PAGE 22 F0418 — LOBBY ADJUD TRIBUTE NAT/G

N19
CASSELL F.,INTERNATIONAL MONETARY PROBLEMS (PAMPHLET). AFR BAL/PWR CONTROL EFFICIENCY WEALTH 20 EEC. PAGE 22 F0427 — INT/TRADE FINAN DIPLOM TREND

N19
CONGRESSIONAL QUARTERLY SERV,FEDERAL ECONOMIC POLICY 1945-1965 (PAMPHLET). USA+45 FINAN OP/RES BAL/PWR ECO/TAC TAX BAL/PAY CENTRAL COST WEALTH ...CHARTS 20. PAGE 27 F0525 — NAT/G ECO/DEV BUDGET POLICY

N19
KUWAIT ARABIA,KUWAIT FUND FOR ARAB ECONOMIC DEVELOPMENT (PAMPHLET). ISLAM KUWAIT UAR ECO/UNDEV LEGIS ECO/TAC WEALTH 20. PAGE 74 F1452 — FOR/AID DIPLOM FINAN ADMIN

N19
LANGE O.R.,"DISARMAMENT ECONOMIC GROWTH AND INTERNATIONAL CO-OPERATION" (PAMPHLET). WOR+45 DIST/IND PLAN INT/TRADE GIVE TASK DETER WEALTH SOCISM 18/19 BOLIVAR/S. PAGE 75 F1477 — ARMS/CONT DIPLOM ECO/DEV ECO/UNDEV

N19
MORGENSTERN O.,A NEW LOOK AT ECONOMIC TIMES SERIES ANALYSIS (PAMPHLET). WEALTH...BIBLIOG 20 NSF NAVAL/RES. PAGE 93 F1831 — TREND IDEA/COMP EFFICIENCY

N19
RIDLEY C.E.,MEASURING MUNICIPAL ACTIVITIES (PAMPHLET). FINAN SERV/IND FORCES RECEIVE INGP/REL HABITAT...POLICY SOC/WK 20. PAGE 111 F2191 — MGT HEALTH WEALTH LOC/G

N19
ROBERTSON D.,GROWTH, WAGES, MONEY (PAMPHLET). UNIV WORKER BUDGET PRICE DEMAND PRODUC WEALTH...CONCPT MATH MONEY. PAGE 112 F2210 — FINAN ECO/DEV ECO/TAC PAY

B20
BUCK S.J.,THE AGRARIAN CRUSADE: A CHRONICLE OF THE FARMER IN POLITICS. USA-45 INDUS PROB/SOLV PWR WEALTH...GEOG CENSUS 19/20 GREENBACK GRANGE SILVER. — AGRI POPULISM VOL/ASSN

PAGE 20 F0381 POL/PAR

B20
MALTHUS T.R.,PRINCIPLES OF POLITICAL ECONOMY. UK AGRI INDUS MARKET NAT/G DIPLOM PRICE CONTROL BAL/PAY COST OWN PWR LAISSEZ 18/19. PAGE 84 F1650 GEN/LAWS DEMAND WEALTH

B20
PIGOU A.C.,THE ECONOMICS OF WELFARE. UNIV INDUS WORKER ACT/RES RECEIVE INCOME NEW/LIB...MAJORIT SOC/WK. PAGE 106 F2085 ECO/TAC WEALTH FINAN CONTROL

B20
TAWNEY R.H.,THE ACQUISITIVE SOCIETY. STRATA WORKER PROB/SOLV CAP/ISM ECO/TAC CONTROL GP/REL OWN PRIVIL ATTIT ORD/FREE WEALTH 20. PAGE 128 F2536 INDUS SOCIETY PRODUC MORAL

B23
HOBSON J.A.,INCENTIVES IN THE NEW INDUSTRIAL ORDER. USA-45 NAT/G PAY COST EFFICIENCY PRODUC WEALTH ...MAJORIT PSY SOC/WK 20. PAGE 60 F1186 INDUS LABOR INCOME OPTIMAL

B24
CLARK J.B.,THE DISTRIBUTION OF WEALTH (1899). WORKER OWN PRODUC PROFIT WEALTH LAISSEZ...IDEA/COMP GEN/LAWS. PAGE 25 F0478 ECO/TAC INDUS LABOR INCOME

B25
EDGEWORTH F.Y.,PAPERS RELATING TO POLITICAL ECONOMY. MOD/EUR SOCIETY STRATA DIST/IND INDUS MARKET NAT/G ACT/RES ECO/TAC EXEC WEALTH ...METH/CNCPT MATH TREND HYPO/EXP SIMUL GEN/METH FOR/TRADE VAL/FREE LOG/LING. PAGE 36 F0702 ECO/DEV CAP/ISM

B26
TAWNEY R.H.,RELIGION AND THE RISE OF CAPITALISM. UK CULTURE NAT/G TEC/DEV OWN LAISSEZ...POLICY SOC TIME/SEQ 16/19. PAGE 129 F2537 SECT WEALTH INDUS CAP/ISM

B27
BELLOC H.,THE SERVILE STATE (1912) (3RD ED.). PRUSSIA UK CULTURE STRATA INDUS NAT/G ECO/TAC CONTROL LEAD SUFF DISCRIM EQUILIB ORD/FREE WEALTH 20. PAGE 12 F0237 WORKER CAP/ISM DOMIN CATH

B28
CASSEL G.,FOREIGN INVESTMENTS. GERMANY UK USA-45 WOR-45 ECO/DEV NAT/G VOL/ASSN CAP/ISM REPAR ATTIT WEALTH...METH/CNCPT STAT SIMUL STERTYP ANTHOL FOR/TRADE TOT/POP VAL/FREE 20. PAGE 22 F0426 FINAN ECO/TAC BAL/PAY

B28
DE MAN H.,THE PSYCHOLOGY OF SOCIALISM. EUR+WWI USSR LABOR NAT/LISM PERSON WEALTH MARXISM...METH/COMP 20. PAGE 31 F0604 WORKER ATTIT SOC SOCISM

B30
BIEL G.,TREATISE ON THE POWER AND UTILITY OF MONEY (1484). INDUS MARKET LOC/G NAT/G SECT ECO/TAC PRODUC WEALTH 15. PAGE 15 F0280 FINAN COST PRICE GEN/LAWS

B30
FEIS H.,EUROPE, THE WORLD'S BANKER, 1871-1914. FRANCE GERMANY MOD/EUR UK WOR-45 NAT/G PLAN ECO/TAC EXEC ATTIT PWR WEALTH...CONCPT HIST/WRIT GEN/LAWS VAL/FREE 19/20. PAGE 40 F0773 FINAN DIPLOM INT/TRADE

B30
HAWTREY R.G.,ECONOMIC ASPECTS OF SOVEREIGNTY. UNIV WOR+45 WOR-45 ECO/DEV ECO/UNDEV AGRI COM/IND INDUS MARKET NAT/G TEC/DEV ECO/TAC EDU/PROP COERCE ATTIT KNOWL WEALTH...CONCPT CON/ANAL GEN/LAWS 20. PAGE 57 F1118 FORCES PWR SOVEREIGN WAR

B30
KEYNES J.M.,A TREATISE ON MONEY (2 VOLS.). UK USA-45 INDUS MARKET WORKER PRICE CONTROL COST OPTIMAL PROFIT WEALTH...POLICY 19/20 KEYNES/JM. PAGE 70 F1385 EQUILIB ECO/TAC FINAN GEN/LAWS

B31
JEVONS W.S.,THE THEORY OF POLITICAL ECONOMY (4TH ED.; 1ST ED. 1871). WOR-45 FINAN MARKET RENT WEALTH ...LOG MATH QUANT CON/ANAL IDEA/COMP BIBLIOG METH 17/19. PAGE 67 F1318 GEN/LAWS UTIL LABOR

B32
DICKINSON H.D.,INSTITUTIONAL REVENUE: A STUDY OF THE INFLUENCE OF SOCIAL INSTITUTIONS ON THE DISTRIBUTION OF WEALTH. SOCIETY STRATA FINAN ...NEW/IDEA IDEA/COMP 20. PAGE 33 F0632 WEALTH CONCPT METH/CNCPT MARKET

B32
WRIGHT Q.,GOLD AND MONETARY STABILIZATION. FUT USA-45 WOR-45 INTELL ECO/DEV INT/ORG NAT/G CONSULT PLAN ECO/TAC ADMIN ATTIT WEALTH...CONCPT TREND 20. PAGE 149 F2935 FINAN POLICY

S32
DODD E.M. JR.,"FOR WHOM ARE CORPORATE MANAGERS TRUSTEES'." SERV/IND CAP/ISM GIVE LEAD REPRESENT ORD/FREE WEALTH. PAGE 33 F0648 LG/CO ROLE NAT/G PLAN

B33
TANNENBAUM F.,PEACE BY REVOLUTION. ECO/UNDEV AGRI SECT WORKER DIPLOM EDU/PROP DISCRIM OWN WEALTH POPULISM 17/20 MEXIC/AMER INDIAN/AM. PAGE 128 F2532 CULTURE COLONIAL RACE/REL

REV

B34
ROBINSON J.,THE ECONOMICS OF IMPERFECT COMPETITION. FINAN ECO/TAC PRICE COST DEMAND EQUILIB OPTIMAL WEALTH...METH MONOPOLY. PAGE 113 F2221 MARKET WORKER INDUS

B35
HICKS J.R.,THE THEORY OF WAGES. INDUS NAT/G PAY PRICE CONTROL COST EFFICIENCY WEALTH 19/20 MARSHALL/A CLARK/JB. PAGE 59 F1164 INCOME WORKER LABOR PRODUC

B35
KEYNES J.M.,THE GENERAL THEORY OF EMPLOYMENT, INTEREST, AND MONEY. AGRI INDUS WORKER ECO/TAC DEMAND EQUILIB INCOME PRODUC PROFIT ATTIT WEALTH 20. PAGE 71 F1386 FINAN GEN/LAWS MARKET PRICE

B35
LASKI H.J.,THE STATE IN THEORY AND PRACTICE. ELITES ECO/TAC REPRESENT ORD/FREE PWR WEALTH POPULISM ...GOV/COMP GEN/LAWS 19/20. PAGE 76 F1483 CAP/ISM COERCE NAT/G FASCISM

B35
MARX K.,WAGE-LABOR AND CAPITAL -- VALUE, PRICE AND PROFIT. LABOR PAY PRICE COST INCOME OWN PROFIT WEALTH 19. PAGE 86 F1690 STRATA WORKER MARXIST MARXISM

B35
WADE J.,HISTORY OF THE MIDDLE AND WORKING CLASSES; WITH A POPULAR EXPOSITION OF THE ECONOMICAL AND POLITICAL PRINCIPLES.... FRANCE UK CONSTN FINAN INDUS LABOR INCOME PROFIT KNOWL MORAL ORD/FREE WEALTH...CHARTS 14/19. PAGE 142 F2797 WORKER STRATA CONCPT

B36
HUBERMAN L.,MAN'S WORLDLY GOODS: THE STORY OF THE WEALTH OF NATIONS. CHRIST-17C EUR+WWI MOD/EUR SOCIETY DOMIN REV ORD/FREE...TIME/SEQ METH/COMP. PAGE 63 F1231 WEALTH CAP/ISM MARXISM CREATE

B37
BRESCIANI-TURRONI C,THE ECONOMICS OF INFLATION: A STUDY OF CURRENCY DEPRECIATION IN POST-WAR GERMANY. AFR GERMANY FINAN INT/TRADE PRICE TOTALISM...POLICY TIME/SEQ CHARTS GEN/LAWS 20 HITLER/A. PAGE 18 F0347 ECO/TAC WEALTH SOCIETY

B37
BROOKS R.R.,WHEN LABOR ORGANIZES. FINAN EDU/PROP ADMIN LOBBY PARTIC REPRESENT WEALTH TREND. PAGE 19 F0364 LABOR GP/REL POLICY

B37
ROBBINS L.,ECONOMIC PLANNING AND INTERNATIONAL ORDER. WOR-45 SOCIETY FINAN INDUS NAT/G ECO/TAC ROUTINE WEALTH...SOC TIME/SEQ GEN/METH WORK 20 KEYNES/JM. PAGE 112 F2202 INT/ORG PLAN INT/TRADE

B38
LAWLEY F.E.,THE GROWTH OF COLLECTIVE ECONOMY VOL. 1: NATIONAL. EUR+WWI AGRI INDUS NAT/G BARGAIN CAP/ISM ECO/TAC WAR OPTIMAL WEALTH...GOV/COMP METH/COMP 19/20 MONOPOLY. PAGE 76 F1492 SOCISM PRICE CONTROL OWN

B38
LAWLEY F.E.,THE GROWTH OF COLLECTIVE ECONOMY VOL. 2: INTERNATIONAL. WOR-45 AGRI INDUS EQUILIB OPTIMAL OWN WEALTH...NAT/COMP 19/20 NAZI NEW/DEAL MONOPOLY. PAGE 76 F1493 ECO/TAC SOCISM NAT/LISM CONTROL

B39
ENGELS F.,HERRN EUGEN DUHRING'S REVOLUTION IN SCIENCE (1878). CULTURE STRATA STRUCT FAM SECT ECO/TAC REV WAR SOCISM...MARXIST 19. PAGE 37 F0731 PWR SOCIETY WEALTH GEN/LAWS

B39
FIRTH R.,PRIMITIVE POLYNESIAN ECONOMY. SOCIETY DIST/IND SECT CHIEF CAP/ISM PRODUC WEALTH...SOC OBS METH WORSHIP 20 POLYNESIA. PAGE 41 F0802 ECO/UNDEV CULTURE AGRI ECO/TAC

B39
FURNIVALL J.S.,NETHERLANDS INDIA. INDIA NETHERLAND CULTURE INDUS NAT/G DIPLOM ADMIN WEALTH...POLICY CHARTS 17/20. PAGE 45 F0876 COLONIAL ECO/UNDEV SOVEREIGN PLURISM

B39
MARQUAND H.A.,ORGANIZED LABOUR IN FOUR CONTINENTS. EUR+WWI USA-45 INDUS NAT/G PAY GP/REL TOTALISM ATTIT WEALTH ALL/IDEOS...TREND NAT/COMP 20 ILO AFL/CIO EUROPE CHINJAP MEXIC/AMER. PAGE 85 F1673 LABOR WORKER CONCPT ANTHOL

B39
ROBBINS L.,ECONOMIC CAUSES OF WAR. WOR-45 ECO/DEV ECO/UNDEV INT/ORG NAT/G TEC/DEV DIPLOM DOMIN COLONIAL ATTIT DRIVE PWR WEALTH...POLICY CONCPT OBS SAMP TREND CON/ANAL GEN/LAWS MARX/KARL 20. PAGE 112 F2203 COERCE ECO/TAC WAR

B39
STALEY E.,WORLD ECONOMY IN TRANSITION. WOR-45 SOCIETY INT/ORG PROF/ORG ECO/TAC ATTIT WEALTH ...METH/CNCPT TREND GEN/LAWS 20. PAGE 125 F2465 TEC/DEV INT/TRADE

B39
THOMAS J.A.,THE HOUSE OF COMMONS, 1832-1901; A STUDY OF ITS ECONOMIC AND FUNCTIONAL CHARACTER. UK LAW STRATA FINAN DIPLOM CONTROL LEAD LOBBY REPRESENT WEALTH...POLICY STAT BIBLIOG 19/20 PARLIAMENT. PAGE 130 F2561 PARL/PROC LEGIS POL/PAR ECO/DEV

B41
HAYEK F.A.,THE PURE THEORY OF CAPITAL. UNIV ECO/DEV ECO/TAC COST EQUILIB PROFIT WEALTH...SIMUL GEN/LAWS BIBLIOG INDEX TIME 20. PAGE 57 F1120
CAP/ISM METH/CNCPT PRODUC FINAN

B42
VEBLEN T.B.,THE THEORY OF THE LEISURE CLASS. USA-45 SOCIETY STRATA STRUCT NAT/G SECT WORKER CREATE EDU/PROP ATTIT...SOC GEN/LAWS 19. PAGE 141 F2772
WEALTH ELITES LEISURE PRODUC

C43
BENTHAM J.,"THE RATIONALE OF REWARD" IN J. BOWRING, ED., THE WORKS OF JEREMY BENTHAM (VOL. 2)" LAW WORKER CREATE INSPECT PAY ROUTINE HAPPINESS PRODUC SUPEGO WEALTH METH/CNCPT. PAGE 13 F0254
SANCTION ECO/TAC INCOME PWR

B44
HAYEK F.A.,THE ROAD TO SERFDOM. NAT/G POL/PAR CREATE EDU/PROP ATTIT WEALTH LAISSEZ...OLD/LIB CONCPT TREND 20. PAGE 57 F1121
FUT PLAN ECO/TAC SOCISM

B44
LOCKE J.,FURTHER CONSIDERATIONS CONCERNING RAISING THE VALUE OF MONEY. AFR UK NAT/G ECO/TAC INCOME WEALTH...METH/COMP GEN/LAWS 17 SILVER. PAGE 81 F1591
COST FINAN PRICE CONTROL

B46
CLOUGH S.B.,ECONOMIC HISTORY OF EUROPE. CHRIST-17C EUR+WWI MOD/EUR WOR-45 SOCIETY EXEC ATTIT WEALTH ...CONCPT GEN/LAWS WORK TOT/POP VAL/FREE 7/20. PAGE 25 F0493
ECO/TAC CAP/ISM

B47
GORDON D.L.,THE HIDDEN WEAPON: THE STORY OF ECONOMIC WARFARE. EUR+WWI USA-45 LAW FINAN INDUS NAT/G CONSULT FORCES PLAN DOMIN PWR WEALTH ...INT/LAW CONCPT OBS TOT/POP NAZI 20. PAGE 49 F0955
INT/ORG ECO/TAC INT/TRADE WAR

B47
HEILPERIN M.A.,THE TRADE OF NATIONS. USA+45 USA-45 WOR+45 WOR-45 CULTURE ECO/DEV NAT/G DELIB/GP EDU/PROP ATTIT DISPL ORD/FREE PWR WEALTH TOT/POP 20. PAGE 58 F1139
MARKET INT/ORG INT/TRADE PEACE

B47
ISAAC J.,ECONOMICS OF MIGRATION. MOD/EUR CULTURE STRATA STRUCT NAT/G COLONIAL WEALTH...OLD/LIB TREND TIME 19/20 EUROPE/W MIGRATION. PAGE 65 F1289
HABITAT SOC GEOG

B47
TOWLE L.W.,INTERNATIONAL TRADE AND COMMERCIAL POLICY. WOR+45 LAW ECO/DEV FINAN INDUS NAT/G ECO/TAC WEALTH...TIME/SEQ ILO 20. PAGE 131 F2582
MARKET INT/ORG INT/TRADE

B48
GRAHAM F.D.,THE THEORY OF INTERNATIONAL VALUES. FUT WOR+45 WOR-45 ECO/DEV FINAN INT/ORG PLAN TEC/DEV CAP/ISM DIPLOM ECO/TAC TARIFFS ROUTINE BAL/PAY DRIVE PWR WEALTH SOCISM...POLICY STAT HYPO/EXP GEN/LAWS 20. PAGE 50 F0971
NEW/IDEA INT/TRADE

B48
HART A.G.,MONEY, DEBT, AND ECONOMIC ACTIVITY. AFR WORKER DIPLOM PRICE CONTROL BAL/PAY COST OWN PRODUC ...METH/COMP 20 FED/RESERV. PAGE 56 F1097
FINAN WEALTH ECO/TAC NAT/G

B48
HICKS J.R.,VALUE AND CAPITAL. FINAN PRICE EQUILIB INCOME PRODUC WEALTH...TIME/SEQ 20 MARSHALL/A PARETO/V SAMUELSN/P. PAGE 59 F1165
ECOMETRIC MATH DEMAND PROB/SOLV

B48
METZLER L.A.,INCOME, EMPLOYMENT, AND PUBLIC POLICY. FINAN INDUS LOC/G NAT/G TAX GIVE PAY COST PRODUC ...MGT TIME/SEQ 20. PAGE 90 F1765
INCOME WEALTH POLICY ECO/TAC

B48
ROBERTSON D.H.,MONEY. AFR ECO/DEV NAT/G DIPLOM INT/TRADE BAL/PAY INCOME WEALTH...TIME/SEQ 20 DEPRESSION. PAGE 112 F2212
FINAN MARKET COST PRICE

B48
TAYLOR P.E.,THE ECONOMICS OF PUBLIC FINANCE. USA+45 USA-45 ECO/DEV WORKER PLAN BUDGET WAR INCOME WEALTH ...CONCPT STAT BIBLIOG 20. PAGE 129 F2540
FINAN POLICY NAT/G TAX

B49
MACGREGOR D.H.,ECONOMIC THOUGHT AND POLICY. WOR-45 WORKER WAR DEMAND EFFICIENCY WEALTH LAISSEZ SOCISM ...MAJORIT BIBLIOG 19/20. PAGE 83 F1629
CONCPT POLICY ECO/TAC

S49
STEINMETZ H.,"THE PROBLEMS OF THE LANDRAT: A STUDY OF COUNTY GOVERNMENT IN THE US ZONE OF GERMANY." GERMANY/W USA+45 INDUS PLAN DIPLOM EDU/PROP CONTROL WAR GOV/REL FEDERAL WEALTH PLURISM...GOV/COMP 20 LANDRAT. PAGE 126 F2478
LOC/G COLONIAL MGT TOP/EX

B50
CHAMBERLIN E.,THE THEORY OF MONOPOLISTIC COMPETITION (1933). INDUS PAY GP/REL COST DEMAND EFFICIENCY OPTIMAL PRODUC WEALTH...GEN/LAWS 20. PAGE 23 F0443
MARKET PRICE ECO/TAC EQUILIB

B50
CLARK J.M.,ALTERNATIVE TO SERFDOM. SOCIETY STRATA INDUS MARKET WORKER PRICE GP/REL PROFIT BIO/SOC PWR WEALTH...GEN/LAWS 20 KEYNES/JM. PAGE 25 F0481
ORD/FREE POPULISM ECO/TAC REPRESENT

B50
MARX H.L.,THE WELFARE STATE. USA+45 USA-45 CHIEF CAP/ISM CENTRAL ORD/FREE LAISSEZ...SOC ANTHOL 20. PAGE 86 F1686
ECO/DEV INDUS WEALTH WELF/ST

B50
SHAW E.S.,MONEY, INCOME, AND MONETARY POLICY. AFR USA-45 NAT/G DIPLOM PAY CONTROL COST INCOME PRODUC WEALTH...T 20 FED/RESERV DEPT/TREAS. PAGE 120 F2370
FINAN ECO/TAC ECO/DEV PRICE

B50
US DEPARTMENT OF STATE,POINT FOUR: COOPERATIVE PROGRAM FOR AID IN THE DEVELOPMENT OF ECONOMICALLY UNDERDEVELOPED AREAS. WOR+45 AGRI INDUS INT/ORG PLAN TEC/DEV DIPLOM EDU/PROP ADMIN PEACE PRODUC WEALTH 20 CONGRESS UN. PAGE 135 F2671
ECO/UNDEV FOR/AID FINAN INT/TRADE

C50
ROUSSEAU J.J.,"A DISCOURSE ON POLITICAL ECONOMY" (1755) IN THE SOCIAL CONTRACT AND DISCOURSES." UNIV SOCIETY STRATA STRUCT CONSEN EQUILIB HAPPINESS UTOPIA HEALTH WEALTH...POLICY WELF/ST. PAGE 114 F2252
NAT/G ECO/TAC TAX GEN/LAWS

B51
CHANDLER L.V.,INFLATION IN THE UNITED STATES 1940-1948. AFR NAT/G BUDGET PAY PRICE CONTROL WAR INCOME PRODUC...POLICY BIBLIOG 20. PAGE 23 F0448
ECO/TAC FINAN PROB/SOLV WEALTH

B51
CLARK C.,THE CONDITIONS OF ECONOMIC PROGRESS. EUR+WWI WOR+45 WOR-45 ECO/DEV INDUS CAP/ISM MORAL ...WELF/ST METH/CNCPT STAT TOT/POP VAL/FREE 20. PAGE 25 F0477
MARKET WEALTH

B51
POOLE K.,FISCAL POLICIES AND THE AMERICAN ECONOMY. AFR ECO/DEV FINAN INDUS WORKER OP/RES INT/TRADE TAX COST INCOME PROFIT WEALTH...GP/COMP 20. PAGE 107 F2102
NAT/G POLICY ANTHOL

B52
ALEXANDROWICZ C.H.,INTERNATIONAL ECONOMIC ORGANIZATION. WOR+45 ECO/DEV ECO/UNDEV DIST/IND FINAN MARKET PLAN ECO/TAC LEGIT DRIVE WEALTH ...POLICY CONCPT QUANT OBS TIME/SEQ GEN/LAWS WORK METH/GP EEC ILO OEEC UNESCO 20. PAGE 4 F0063
INT/ORG INT/TRADE

B52
BEVAN A.,IN PLACE OF FEAR. WOR+45 STRATA LEGIS REPRESENT OWN NEW/LIB POPULISM...CHARTS 20. PAGE 14 F0273
SOCISM SOCIALIST WEALTH MAJORIT

B52
DE JOUVENEL B.,THE ETHICS OF REDISTRIBUTION. UK ELITES MARKET WORKER GIVE PAY INCOME PERSON ...POLICY PSY GEN/LAWS 20. PAGE 31 F0602
WEALTH TAX SOCISM TRADIT

B52
EGLE W.P.,ECONOMIC STABILIZATION. USA+45 SOCIETY FINAN MARKET PLAN ECO/TAC DOMIN EDU/PROP LEGIT EXEC WEALTH...CONCPT METH/CNCPT TREND HYPO/EXP GEN/METH TOT/POP VAL/FREE 20. PAGE 36 F0708
NAT/G ECO/DEV CAP/ISM

B52
GALBRAITH J.K.,AMERICAN CAPITALISM: THE CONCEPT OF COUNTERVAILING POWER. AFR FUT USA+45 FINAN PRICE CENTRAL INCOME PEACE WEALTH...POLICY DECISION 20. PAGE 45 F0881
ECO/TAC CAP/ISM TREND NAT/G

B52
HOSELITZ B.F.,THE PROGRESS OF UNDERDEVELOPED AREAS. AFR FUT WOR+45 WOR-45 ECO/DEV ECO/TAC INT/TRADE WEALTH...SOC TREND GEN/LAWS TOT/POP VAL/FREE FOR/TRADE 20. PAGE 62 F1219
ECO/UNDEV PLAN FOR/AID

B52
ROSE A.M.,UNION SOLIDARITY: THE INTERNAL COHESION OF A LABOR UNION. SECT GP/REL RACE/REL ATTIT ROLE HEALTH WEALTH...INT QU. PAGE 114 F2241
LABOR INGP/REL PARTIC SUPEGO

B52
SURANYI-UNGER T.,COMPARATIVE ECONOMIC SYSTEMS. FINAN MARKET DIPLOM PRICE WEALTH...GEOG SOC BIBLIOG METH T 20. PAGE 128 F2517
LAISSEZ PLAN ECO/DEV IDEA/COMP

B52
WU Y.,ECONOMIC WARFARE. MARKET PLAN PROB/SOLV FOR/AID CONTROL EFFICIENCY WEALTH...METH/COMP 20. PAGE 149 F2937
ECO/TAC WAR INT/TRADE DIPLOM

L52
HUTH A.G.,"COMMUNICATION AND ECONOMIC DEVELOPMENT." FUT WOR+45 CULTURE SOCIETY INT/ORG PLAN TEC/DEV EDU/PROP DRIVE KNOWL WEALTH...POLICY CONCPT RECORD STERTYP GEN/LAWS COMMUN TOT/POP UNESCO 20 UN CMN/WLTH. PAGE 64 F1250
ECO/UNDEV

S52
HEBERLE R.,"ON POLITICAL ECOLOGY" (BMR)" INCOME
HABITAT

ATTIT WEALTH...GEOG METH SOC/INTEG 20. PAGE 58 F1133 — STRATA CHOOSE

C52
HUME D.,"OF TAXES" IN D. HUME, POLITICAL DISCOURSES (1752)" UK NAT/G COST INCOME LAISSEZ...GEN/LAWS 18. PAGE 63 F1236 — TAX FINAN WEALTH POLICY

C52
HUME D.,"OF THE BALANCE OF TRADE" IN D. HUME, POLITICAL DISCOURSES (1752)" UK FINAN NAT/G TARIFFS PRICE PWR LAISSEZ...POLICY GEN/LAWS 18. PAGE 63 F1237 — BAL/PAY INT/TRADE DIPLOM WEALTH

C52
HUME D.,"OF COMMERCE" IN D. HUME, POLITICAL DISCOURSES (1752)" UK FINAN DIPLOM WEALTH ...GEN/LAWS 18 MONEY. PAGE 63 F1238 — INDUS INT/TRADE PWR AGRI

C52
HUME D.,"OF INTEREST" IN D. HUME, POLITICAL DISCOURSES (1752)" UK INDUS WORKER DIPLOM PAY DEMAND INCOME WEALTH...GEN/LAWS 18 MONEY. PAGE 63 F1239 — PRICE COST FINAN INT/TRADE

C52
HUME D.,"OF MONEY" IN D. HUME, POLITICAL DISCOURSES (1752)" UK INDUS DIPLOM INT/TRADE...GEN/LAWS 18 MONEY. PAGE 63 F1240 — FINAN COST PRICE WEALTH

B53
BOEKE J.H.,ECONOMICS AND ECONOMIC POLICY OF DUAL SOCIETIES AS EXEMPLIFIED BY INDONESIA. INDIA INDONESIA SOCIETY CAP/ISM INT/TRADE GIVE PRICE GP/REL WEALTH SOCISM...POLICY NAT/COMP GEN/LAWS 20. PAGE 16 F0304 — ECO/TAC ECO/UNDEV NAT/G CONTROL

B53
BURNS A.E.,MODERN ECONOMICS. UNIV ECO/DEV INT/TRADE PRICE INCOME WEALTH...POLICY CHARTS T 20 KEYNES/JM. PAGE 20 F0389 — NAT/G ECO/TAC FINAN

B53
DAHL R.A.,POLITICS, ECONOMICS AND WELFARE: PLANNING AND POLITICOECONOMIC SYSTEMS RESOLVED INTO BASIC SOCIAL PROCESSES. WOR+45 WOR-45 ECO/DEV ECO/UNDEV R+D CREATE PLAN TEC/DEV EDU/PROP HEALTH WEALTH ...SOC SELF/OBS TREND CHARTS GEN/METH 20. PAGE 29 F0571 — ECO/TAC PHIL/SCI

B53
HARROD R.,THE DOLLAR. AFR USA+45 USA-45 ECO/DEV OPTIMAL WEALTH 18/20 FED/RESERV. PAGE 56 F1093 — FINAN DIPLOM BAL/PAY

B53
MILLIKAN M.F.,INCOME STABILIZATION FOR A DEVELOPING DEMOCRACY. USA+45 ECO/DEV LABOR BUDGET ECO/TAC TAX ADMIN ADJUST PRODUC WEALTH...POLICY TREND 20. PAGE 91 F1794 — ANTHOL MARKET EQUILIB EFFICIENCY

B53
NEISSER H.,NATIONAL INCOMES AND INTERNATIONAL TRADE. FRANCE GERMANY SWEDEN UK USA-45 EXTR/IND FINAN INDUS TEC/DEV PRICE BAL/PAY EQUILIB INCOME WEALTH...CHARTS METH 19 CHINJAP. PAGE 97 F1908 — INT/TRADE PRODUC MARKET CON/ANAL

B53
ROBINSON E.A.G.,THE STRUCTURE OF COMPETITIVE INDUSTRY. UK ECO/DEV DIST/IND MARKET TEC/DEV DIPLOM EDU/PROP ADMIN EFFICIENCY WEALTH...MGT 19/20. PAGE 113 F2217 — INDUS PRODUC WORKER OPTIMAL

B53
WILLIAMS J.H.,ECONOMIC STABILITY IN A CHANGING WORLD. FRANCE USA+45 USSR AGRI WORKER BUDGET INT/TRADE TAX WAR BAL/PAY COST EFFICIENCY ALL/IDEOS EQULIB 20 KEYNES/JM. PAGE 147 F2892 — POLICY FINAN ECO/TAC WEALTH

B53
WOYTINSKY W.S.,WORLD POPULATION AND PRODUCTION: TRENDS AND OUTLOOK. FUT WOR+45 WOR-45 CULTURE SOCIETY ECO/DEV AGRI INDUS TEC/DEV EDU/PROP SKILL WEALTH...SOC TREND. PAGE 149 F2928 — ECO/UNDEV METH/CNCPT GEOG PERSON

L53
NELSON J.R.,"UNITED STATES FOREIGN ECONOMIC POLICY AND THE STERLING AREA." USA-45 WOR+45 WOR-45 NAT/G ECO/TAC WEALTH...STAT TIME/SEQ TREND CHARTS METH/GP TERR/GP CMN/WLTH 20. PAGE 97 F1911 — FINAN DIPLOM UK

S53
BLOUGH R.,"THE ROLE OF THE ECONOMIST IN FEDERAL POLICY MAKING." USA+45 ELITES INTELL ECO/DEV NAT/G CONSULT EX/STRUC ACT/RES PLAN INT/TRADE BAL/PAY WEALTH...POLICY METH/GP CONGRESS 20. PAGE 16 F0301 — DELIB/GP ECO/TAC

B54
BERNSTEIN I.,ARBITRATION OF WAGES. USA+45 CONSULT PAY COST PRODUC WEALTH...CHARTS 20. PAGE 14 F0266 — DELIB/GP BARGAIN WORKER PRICE

B54
HAYEK FA V.O.N.,CAPITALISM AND THE HISTORIANS. MOD/EUR TEC/DEV GP/REL WEALTH...HIST/WRIT ANTHOL 19. PAGE 57 F1124 — CAP/ISM LABOR STRATA ECO/TAC

B54
MEYER F.V.,INFLATION AND CAPITAL. AFR UK WOR+45 BUDGET GOV/REL INCOME PRODUC PROFIT WEALTH...CONCPT CHARTS 20. PAGE 90 F1768 — ECO/DEV FINAN ECO/TAC DEMAND

B54
O.E.E.C.,PRIVATE UNITED STATES INVESTMENT IN EUROPE AND THE OVERSEAS TERRITORIES. EUR+WWI WOR+45 ECO/DEV ECO/UNDEV INT/ORG NAT/G VOL/ASSN ECO/TAC ATTIT WEALTH...GEOG STAT SYS/QU CHARTS VAL/FREE 20. PAGE 99 F1950 — USA+45 FINAN BAL/PAY FOR/AID

B54
POTTER D.M.,PEOPLE OF PLENTY: ECONOMIC ABUNDANCE AND THE AMERICAN CHARACTER. USA+45 USA-45 ECO/DEV ATTIT PERSON...PSY SOC CONCPT TREND GEN/METH TOT/POP 20. PAGE 107 F2108 — CULTURE WEALTH

B55
BUCHANAN N.S.,APPROACHES TO ECONOMIC DEVELOPMENT. FUT USA+45 WOR+45 STRATA ECO/DEV INT/ORG NAT/G TEC/DEV DIPLOM FOR/AID ATTIT KNOWL PWR WEALTH ...RELATIV METH/CNCPT SELF/OBS TREND CON/ANAL STERTYP GEN/LAWS FOR/TRADE COMMUN 20. PAGE 20 F0380 — ECO/UNDEV ECO/TAC INT/TRADE

B55
FLORINSKY M.T.,INTEGRATED EUROPE. EUR+WWI FRANCE ITALY NETHERLAND UK ECO/DEV INT/ORG FORCES LEGIT FEDERAL ATTIT PWR WEALTH...POLICY GEOG CONCPT GEN/LAWS TOT/POP EEC OEEC 20. PAGE 42 F0816 — FUT ECO/TAC REGION

B55
GEORGE H.,PROGRESS AND POVERTY (1880). STRATA STRUCT INDUS TEC/DEV CAP/ISM EQUILIB INCOME OWN UTOPIA...WELF/ST CONCPT NEW/IDEA 19. PAGE 47 F0915 — ECO/DEV ECO/TAC TAX WEALTH

B55
PEDLER F.J.,ECONOMIC GEOGRAPHY OF WEST AFRICA. GAMBIA NIGER SIER/LEONE STRATA EXTR/IND MARKET LABOR INT/TRADE DEMAND HABITAT WEALTH...CHARTS 20. PAGE 104 F2046 — ECO/UNDEV GEOG PRODUC EFFICIENCY

B55
UN ECONOMIC COMN ASIA & FAR E,ECONOMIC SURVEY OF ASIA AND THE FAR EAST, 1954. AFGHANISTN CEYLON INDIA PHILIPPINE S/ASIA ECO/DEV FINAN INDUS INT/TRADE PRODUC WEALTH...STAT CHARTS 20 CHINJAP. PAGE 132 F2600 — ECO/UNDEV PRICE NAT/COMP ASIA

B55
US ADVISORY COMN INTERGOV REL,THE COMMISSION ON INTERGOVERNMENTAL RELATIONS; A REPORT TO THE PRESIDENT FOR TRANSMITTAL TO THE CONGRESS. USA+45 ECO/DEV AGRI COM/IND FINAN FORCES PLAN EDU/PROP HEALTH WEALTH...STAT MUNICH 20 CIV/DEFENS. PAGE 133 F2630 — GOV/REL NAT/G LOC/G PROVS

S55
HALLETT D.,"THE HISTORY AND STRUCTURE OF OEEC." EUR+WWI USA+45 CONSTN INDUS INT/ORG NAT/G DELIB/GP ACT/RES PLAN ORD/FREE WEALTH...CONCPT OEEC 20 CMN/WLTH. PAGE 54 F1051 — VOL/ASSN ECO/DEV

B56
ABELS J.,THE TRUMAN SCANDALS. USA+45 USA-45 POL/PAR TAX LEGIT CT/SYS CHOOSE PRIVIL MORAL WEALTH 20 TRUMAN/HS PRESIDENT CONGRESS. PAGE 2 F0031 — CRIME ADMIN CHIEF TRIBUTE

B56
BELL P.W.,THE STERLING AREA IN THE POSTWAR WORLD. EUR+WWI FUT S/ASIA UK ECO/DEV PLAN DIPLOM WEALTH ...STAT RECORD CHARTS GEN/LAWS FOR/TRADE TOT/POP 20. PAGE 12 F0235 — FINAN ECO/TAC

B56
BROWN R.E.,CHARLES BEARD AND THE CONSTITUTION. USA-45 NAT/G ORD/FREE WEALTH...HUM TIME/SEQ METH/COMP 20 BEARD/CA. PAGE 19 F0372 — CONSTN ELITES HIST/WRIT

B56
GARDNER R.N.,STERLING-DOLLAR DIPLOMACY. EUR+WWI USA+45 INT/ORG NAT/G PLAN INT/TRADE EDU/PROP ADMIN KNOWL PWR WEALTH...POLICY SOC METH/CNCPT STAT CHARTS SIMUL GEN/LAWS 20. PAGE 46 F0902 — ECO/DEV DIPLOM

B56
POOLE K.E.,PUBLIC FINANCE AND ECONOMIC WELFARE. STRUCT ECO/DEV LOC/G NAT/G BUDGET PAY ROUTINE COST EQUILIB WEALTH...SOC/WK METH/COMP 20. PAGE 107 F2103 — FINAN TAX ORD/FREE

B56
WILCOX W.W.,SOCIAL RESPONSIBILITY IN FARM LEADERSHIP. CLIENT LEGIS EXEC LOBBY GP/REL ATTIT WEALTH. PAGE 146 F2880 — AGRI LEAD VOL/ASSN WORKER

S56
GORDON L.,"THE ORGANIZATION FOR EUROPEAN ECONOMIC COOPERATION." EUR+WWI INDUS INT/ORG NAT/G CONSULT DELIB/GP ACT/RES CREATE PLAN TEC/DEV EDU/PROP LEGIT WEALTH OEEC 20. PAGE 49 F0956 — VOL/ASSN ECO/DEV

S56
SPENGLER J.J.,"POPULATION THREATENS PROSPERITY" (BMR)" WOR+45 SOCIETY FINAN RATION COST INCOME ...SOC CHARTS 20 RESOURCE/N. PAGE 124 F2451 — CENSUS GEOG WEALTH TREND

B57
ASHER R.E.,THE UNITED NATIONS AND ECONOMIC AND SOCIAL COOPERATION. ECO/UNDEV COM/IND DIST/IND FINAN PLAN PROB/SOLV INT/TRADE TASK WEALTH...SOC 20 UN. PAGE 7 F0129 — INT/ORG DIPLOM FOR/AID

B57
BERLE A.A. JR.,ECONOMIC POWER AND FREE SOCIETY (PAMPHLET). CLIENT CONSTN EX/STRUC ECO/TAC CONTROL PARTIC PWR WEALTH MAJORIT. PAGE 14 F0261
LG/CO CAP/ISM INGP/REL LEGIT

B57
CLARK J.M.,ECONOMIC INSTITUTIONS AND HUMAN WELFARE. USA+45 SOCIETY ECO/DEV NAT/G WORKER PLAN PROB/SOLV CAP/ISM CONTROL...POLICY 20. PAGE 25 F0482
ECO/TAC ORD/FREE WEALTH

B57
DAY A.C.L.,OUTLINE OF MONETARY ECONOMICS. AFR WOR-45 INT/ORG WORKER DIPLOM BAL/PAY COST INCOME WEALTH...TIME/SEQ SIMUL 20. PAGE 31 F0594
FINAN NAT/G EQUILIB PRICE

B57
GOLD N.L.,REGIONAL ECONOMIC DEVELOPMENT AND NUCLEAR POWER IN INDIA. FUT INDIA FINAN FOR/AID INT/TRADE BAL/PAY EFFICIENCY OPTIMAL PRODUC WEALTH...PREDICT 20. PAGE 48 F0934
ECO/UNDEV TEC/DEV NUC/PWR INDUS

B57
HARWOOD E.C.,CAUSE AND CONTROL OF THE BUSINESS CYCLE (5TH ED.). AFR USA-45 PRICE CONTROL WAR DEMAND INCOME WEALTH...TREND CHARTS 19. PAGE 56 F1107
PRODUC MARKET FINAN

B57
LEIBENSTEIN H.,ECONOMIC BACKWARDNESS AND ECONOMIC GROWTH. WOR+45 SOCIETY AGRI INDUS TEC/DEV CAP/ISM FOR/AID COST DEMAND WEALTH...CHARTS IDEA/COMP 20. PAGE 77 F1513
ECO/UNDEV ECO/TAC PRODUC POLICY

B57
MASON E.S.,ECONOMIC CONCENTRATION AND THE MONOPOLY PROBLEM. USA+45 USA-45 LAW ELITES ECO/DEV LABOR RATION PRICE PWR WEALTH...CHARTS 20 MONOPOLY. PAGE 87 F1696
GP/REL LG/CO CONTROL MARKET

B57
MEIER G.M.,ECONOMIC DEVELOPMENT: THEORY, HISTORY, AND POLICY. WOR+45 WOR-45 ECO/DEV ECO/UNDEV PLAN CAP/ISM BAL/PAY ATTIT PWR WEALTH SOCISM...CHARTS TOT/POP FOR/TRADE 20. PAGE 89 F1748
ECO/TAC GEN/LAWS

B57
NANIWADA H.,STAAT UND WIRTSCHAFT; GRUNDLEGUNG DER NATIONALOEKONOMIE ALS DER LOGIK DER BURGERLICHEN GESELLSCHAFT. WOR+45 WOR-45 STRATA MARKET WORKER INGP/REL DEMAND EQUILIB WEALTH...POLICY IDEA/COMP GEN/LAWS 17/20 MARX/KARL KEYNES/JM LENIN/VI. PAGE 96 F1890
ALL/IDEOS ECO/TAC SOCIETY NAT/G

B57
OLIVER H.M. JR.,ECONOMIC OPINION AND POLICY IN CEYLON. CEYLON FINAN POL/PAR WORKER INT/TRADE INCOME WEALTH...GEOG UNPLAN/INT BIBLIOG 20 CMN/WLTH. PAGE 101 F1987
ECO/UNDEV NAT/LISM POLICY COLONIAL

B57
TRIFFIN R.,EUROPE AND THE MONEY MUDDLE. USA+45 INT/ORG NAT/G CONSULT PLAN ECO/TAC EXEC ROUTINE BAL/PAY WEALTH...METH/CNCPT OBS TREND CHARTS STERTYP GEN/METH EEC TERR/GP VAL/FREE ECSC. PAGE 131 F2587
EUR+WWI ECO/DEV REGION

B57
WARRINER D.,LAND REFORM AND DEVELOPMENT IN THE MIDDLE EAST: A STUDY OF EGYPT, SYRIA AND IRAQ. IRAQ ISLAM SYRIA UAR AGRI DIST/IND PLAN TEC/DEV DOMIN REV ATTIT WEALTH...SOC METH/CNCPT STAT OBS RECORD HIST/WRIT TREND GEN/LAWS FAO 20. PAGE 143 F2825
ECO/UNDEV CONCPT

L57
MASS. INST. TECH.,"THE CENTER FOR INTERNATIONAL STUDIES." AFR ASIA COM EUR+WWI ISLAM L/A+17C S/ASIA USA+45 USA-45 DIST/IND CONSULT FORCES ACT/RES TEC/DEV DIPLOM REV ATTIT WEALTH...CONCPT FOR/TRADE 20. PAGE 87 F1702
R+D ECO/UNDEV

S57
HOAG M.W.,"ECONOMIC PROBLEMS OF ALLIANCE." AFR COM EUR+WWI WOR+45 ECO/DEV ECO/UNDEV NAT/G VOL/ASSN FORCES PLAN TEC/DEV DIPLOM COERCE ORD/FREE PWR WEALTH...DECISION GEN/LAWS NATO TERR/GP. PAGE 60 F1182
INT/ORG ECO/TAC

B58
DEFENSE AGAINST INFLATION. USA+45 LEGIS WORKER TAX PRICE DEMAND INCOME PRODUC...POLICY TREND METH/COMP 20 GOLD/STAND. PAGE 1 F0012
ECO/TAC EQUILIB WEALTH PROB/SOLV

B58
BERLINER J.S.,SOVIET ECONOMIC AID: THE AID AND TRADE POLICY IN UNDERDEVELOPED COUNTRIES. AFR COM ISLAM L/A+17C S/ASIA USSR ECO/DEV DIST/IND FINAN MARKET INT/ORG ACT/RES PLAN BAL/PWR WEAPON PWR WEALTH...CHARTS FOR/TRADE 20. PAGE 14 F0263
ECO/UNDEV ECO/TAC FOR/AID

B58
BIDWELL P.W.,RAW MATERIALS: A STUDY OF AMERICAN POLICY. USA+45 USA-45 ECO/UNDEV AGRI INDUS KIN CREATE PLAN ECO/TAC WAR PEACE ATTIT DRIVE WEALTH ...STAT CHARTS CONGRESS FOR/TRADE VAL/FREE. PAGE 15 F0279
EXTR/IND ECO/DEV

B58
BROWN B.,INCOME TRENDS IN THE UNITED STATES THROUGH 1975. USA+45 NAT/G WEALTH...GEOG CENSUS PREDICT CHARTS METH 20. PAGE 19 F0366
STAT INCOME TREND

TAX

B58
CHAMBERLIN E.H.,LABOR UNIONS AND PUBLIC POLICY. PLAN BARGAIN SANCTION INGP/REL JURID. PAGE 23 F0444
LABOR WEALTH PWR NAT/G

B58
COALE A.J.,POPULATION GROWTH AND ECONOMIC DEVELOPMENT IN LOW-INCOME COUNTRIES: A CASE STUDY OF INDIA'S PROSPECTS. INDIA AGRI WORKER INCOME AGE WEALTH...CHARTS 20 MEXIC/AMER. PAGE 25 F0495
ECO/UNDEV GEOG CENSUS SEX

B58
COLM G.,THE ECONOMY OF THE AMERICAN PEOPLE: PROGRESS, PROBLEMS, PROSPECTS. USA+45 INDUS MARKET LABOR TEC/DEV INCOME 20. PAGE 26 F0509
WEALTH PRODUC CAP/ISM MGT

B58
DAVIS E.H.,OF THE PEOPLE, BY THE PEOPLE, FOR THE PEOPLE. INCOME WEALTH...METH/COMP MUNICH 20. PAGE 30 F0587
FINAN LOC/G TAX

B58
DOWNIE J.,THE COMPETITIVE PROCESS. ECO/TAC PRICE EFFICIENCY OPTIMAL PRODUC WEALTH...IDEA/COMP METH/COMP 20 MONOPOLY. PAGE 34 F0658
EQUILIB MARKET INDUS ECO/DEV

B58
GALBRAITH J.K.,THE AFFLUENT SOCIETY. EUR+WWI FUT USA+45 USSR CULTURE SERV/IND PEACE WEALTH SOCISM ...NEW/IDEA TREND VAL/FREE 20. PAGE 45 F0882
ATTIT ECO/TAC CAP/ISM

B58
HIRSCHMAN A.O.,STRATEGY OF ECONOMIC DEVELOPMENT. WOR+45 WOR-45 CULTURE ECO/DEV NAT/G PLAN TEC/DEV INT/TRADE BAL/PAY ATTIT DRIVE RIGID/FLEX WEALTH ...CONCPT METH/CNCPT OBS CHARTS SIMUL GEN/LAWS TOT/POP VAL/FREE. PAGE 60 F1176
ECO/UNDEV ECO/TAC CAP/ISM

B58
KINDLEBERGER C.P.,INTERNATIONAL ECONOMICS. WOR+45 WOR-45 ECO/DEV ECO/UNDEV FINAN VOL/ASSN ACT/RES DIPLOM ECO/TAC LEGIT REGION ATTIT DRIVE ORD/FREE WEALTH...POLICY STAT TREND GEN/LAWS EEC ECSC OEEC 20. PAGE 71 F1391
INT/ORG BAL/PWR TARIFFS

B58
MCIVOR R.C.,CANADIAN MONETARY, BANKING, AND FISCAL DEVELOPMENT. CANADA INDUS LG/CO NAT/G SML/CO CONTROL WAR...GEN/LAWS BIBLIOG 17/20. PAGE 88 F1729
ECO/TAC FINAN ECO/DEV WEALTH

B58
MOULTON H.G.,CAN INFLATION BE CONTROLLED? ECO/DEV INDUS CAP/ISM RATION GOV/REL COST INCOME PEACE WEALTH...CHARTS TIME 20 KEYNES/JM MONEY. PAGE 94 F1847
ECO/TAC CONTROL DEMAND FINAN

B58
MYRDAL G.,RICH LANDS AND POOR: THE ROAD TO WORLD PROSPERITY. FUT WOR+45 WOR-45 ECO/DEV ECO/UNDEV INT/ORG PLAN ECO/TAC REGION...GEOG TIME/SEQ GEN/LAWS TOT/POP 20. PAGE 96 F1880
WEALTH TREND FOR/AID INT/TRADE

B58
PALMER E.E.,INDUSTRIAL MAN. USA+45 PERSON ORD/FREE POPULISM...PREDICT TREND ANTHOL 20. PAGE 103 F2020
INDUS ECO/UNDEV CULTURE WEALTH

B58
PALYI M.,MANAGED MONEY AT THE CROSSROADS: THE EUROPEAN EXPERIENCE. AFR WOR+45 WOR-45 TEC/DEV DIPLOM INT/TRADE DEMAND WEALTH...CHARTS BIBLIOG 19/20 EUROPE SILVER. PAGE 103 F2022
FINAN ECO/TAC ECO/DEV PRODUC

B58
ROBERTS B.C.,NATIONAL WAGES POLICY IN WAR AND PEACE. EUR+WWI GERMANY S/ASIA SWEDEN UK USA+45 USA-45 STRATA ECO/DEV LABOR NAT/G DELIB/GP PLAN INT/TRADE WEALTH...STAT TREND CHARTS 20. PAGE 112 F2205
CREATE ECO/TAC

B58
SCITOUSKY T.,ECONOMIC THEORY AND WESTERN EUROPEAN INTEGRATION. EUR+WWI INT/ORG ACT/RES INT/TRADE REGION BAL/PAY WEALTH...METH/CNCPT STAT CHARTS GEN/METH ECSC TOT/POP EEC OEEC 20. PAGE 118 F2328
ECO/TAC

B58
SHAW S.J.,THE FINANCIAL AND ADMINISTRATIVE ORGANIZATION AND DEVELOPMENT OF OTTOMAN EGYPT 1517-1798. UAR LOC/G FORCES BUDGET INT/TRADE TAX EATING INCOME WEALTH...CHARTS BIBLIOG 16/18 OTTOMAN NAPOLEON/B. PAGE 120 F2371
FINAN ADMIN GOV/REL CULTURE

B58
TAFT P.,CORRUPTION AND RACKETEERING IN THE LABOR MOVEMENT (PAMPHLET). ADMIN SANCTION CENTRAL ROLE WEALTH...POLICY CLASSIF. PAGE 128 F2525
LABOR INGP/REL GP/REL CRIME

B58
TILLION G.,ALGERIA: THE REALITIES. ALGERIA FRANCE ISLAM CULTURE STRATA PROB/SOLV DOMIN REV NAT/LISM WEALTH MARXISM...GEOG 20. PAGE 130 F2573
ECO/UNDEV SOC COLONIAL DIPLOM

S58
ELKIN A.B.,"OEEC-ITS STRUCTURE AND POWERS." EUR+WWI CONSTN INDUS INT/ORG NAT/G VOL/ASSN DELIB/GP
ECO/DEV EX/STRUC

ACT/RES PLAN ORD/FREE WEALTH...CHARTS ORG/CHARTS OEEC 20. PAGE 37 F0719

S58 JOHNSON D.G.,"GOVERNMENT AND AGRICULTURE: IS AGRICULTURE A SPECIAL CASE?" PLAN ECO/TAC LOBBY WEALTH POLICY. PAGE 67 F1321
INDUS GP/REL INCOME NAT/G

S58 LANE F.C.,"ECONOMIC CONSEQUENCES OF ORGANIZED VIOLENCE." FUT WOR+45 WOR-45 ECO/DEV DIST/IND SERV/IND NAT/G PROVS EX/STRUC CHOOSE ORD/FREE PWR ...TIME/SEQ GEN/LAWS MUNICH 20. PAGE 75 F1472
WEALTH COERCE

S58 LOCKWOOD W.W.,"THE SOCIALISTIC SOCIETY: INDIA AND JAPAN." INDIA ECO/DEV ECO/UNDEV INDUS NAT/G CONTROL LEAD PRODUC WEALTH 20 CHINJAP. PAGE 81 F1593
ECO/TAC NAT/COMP FINAN SOCISM

S58 THOMAS D.S.,"AGE AND ECONOMIC DIFFERENTIALS IN INTERSTATE MIGRATION." SEX...GEOG SAMP/SIZ TREND CON/ANAL CHARTS BIBLIOG. PAGE 130 F2560
AGE WEALTH HABITAT CENSUS

B59 AITKEN H.,THE STATE AND ECONOMIC GROWTH. COM EUR+WWI MOD/EUR S/ASIA USA+45 FINAN NAT/G DELIB/GP PLAN PWR WEALTH 20. PAGE 3 F0054
DIST/IND ECO/DEV

B59 DIEBOLD W. JR.,THE SCHUMAN PLAN: A STUDY IN ECONOMIC COOPERATION, 1950-1959. EUR+WWI FRANCE GERMANY USA+45 EXTR/IND CONSULT DELIB/GP PLAN DIPLOM ECO/TAC INT/TRADE ROUTINE ORD/FREE WEALTH ...METH/CNCPT STAT CONT/OBS INT TIME/SEQ ECSC 20. PAGE 33 F0635
INT/ORG REGION

B59 HICKS J.R.,ESSAYS IN WORLD ECONOMICS. AFR CEYLON NIGERIA WOR+45 SOCIETY ECO/DEV ORD/FREE WEALTH ...GEN/LAWS TOT/POP 20. PAGE 59 F1166
ECO/UNDEV ECO/TAC UK

B59 KELF-COHEN R.,NATIONALISATION IN BRITAIN: THE END OF DOGMA. EUR+WWI UK NAT/G POL/PAR WORKER ECO/TAC PARL/PROC WEALTH SOCISM...GOV/COMP 20. PAGE 70 F1369
NEW/LIB ECO/DEV INDUS OWN

B59 KOREAN MINISTRY RECONSTRUCTION,KOREAN ECONOMY AND ITS REQUIREMENTS. KOREA USA+45 ECO/TAC EQUILIB INCOME WEALTH...CHARTS 20. PAGE 73 F1427
FOR/AID WAR FINAN DIPLOM

B59 LINK R.G.,ENGLISH THEORIES OF ECONOMIC FLUCTUATIONS: 1815-1848. FRANCE UK AGRI WORKER DIPLOM PRICE TASK WAR DEMAND PRODUC...POLICY BIBLIOG 18 MALTHUS MILL/JS WILSON/J. PAGE 80 F1574
IDEA/COMP ECO/DEV WEALTH EQUILIB

B59 MATTHEWS R.C.O.,THE BUSINESS CYCLE. AFR LABOR INT/TRADE TAX PRICE RISK ADJUST WEALTH...POLICY ECOMETRIC CHARTS SIMUL TIME 20. PAGE 87 F1705
FINAN DEMAND TASK

B59 MORGENSTERN O.,INTERNATIONAL FINANCIAL TRANSACTIONS AND BUSINESS CYCLES. FRANCE GERMANY UK USA+45 USA-45 WOR+45 WOR-45 ECO/DEV ECO/TAC WEALTH ...CONCPT STAT CON/ANAL CHARTS 19/20. PAGE 93 F1832
FINAN TIME/SEQ INT/TRADE

B59 NUNEZ JIMENEZ A.,LA LIBERACION DE LAS ISLAS. CUBA L/A+17C USA+45 LAW CHIEF PLAN DIPLOM FOR/AID OWN WEALTH 20 CASTRO/F. PAGE 99 F1945
AGRI REV ECO/UNDEV NAT/G

B59 SHACKLE G.L.S.,ECONOMICS FOR PLEASURE. FINAN MARKET NAT/G WORKER PLAN INT/TRADE TARIFFS PAY BAL/PAY COST PRODUC 20. PAGE 120 F2361
METH/CNCPT WEALTH INCOME

B59 US GENERAL ACCOUNTING OFFICE,EXAM OF ECONOMIC AND TECHNICAL ASSISTANCE PROGRAM FOR INDIA INT'NAT'L COOP ADMIN REPORT TO CONGRESS 1955-1958. INDIA USA+45 ECO/UNDEV FINAN PLAN DIPLOM COST UTIL WEALTH ...CHARTS 20 CONGRESS AID. PAGE 136 F2679
FOR/AID EFFICIENCY ECO/TAC TEC/DEV

L59 BEGUIN B.,"ILO AND THE TRIPARTITE SYSTEM." EUR+WWI WOR+45 WOR-45 CONSTN ECO/DEV ECO/UNDEV INDUS INT/ORG NAT/G VOL/ASSN DELIB/GP PLAN TEC/DEV LEGIT ORD/FREE WEALTH...CONCPT TIME/SEQ WORK ILO 20. PAGE 12 F0228
LABOR

L59 MURPHY J.C.,"SOME IMPLICATIONS OF EUROPE'S COMMON MARKET. IN (COOK P, ECONOMIC DEVELOPMENT AND INTERNATIONAL TRADE.." EUR+WWI ECO/DEV DIST/IND INDUS NAT/G PLAN ECO/TAC INT/TRADE WEALTH...STAT TREND OEEC TOT/POP 20 EEC. PAGE 95 F1866
MARKET INT/ORG REGION

S59 ALKHIMOV V.S.,"SOVIET FOREIGN TRADE CHANNELS." COM FUT USA+45 USSR ECO/DEV MARKET CONSULT PLAN WEALTH ...MARXIST OBS CON/ANAL FOR/TRADE 20. PAGE 4 F0068
FINAN ECO/TAC DIPLOM

S59 HOFFMAN P.,"OPERATION BREAKTHROUGH." AFR S/ASIA STRUCT INDUS CONSULT TEC/DEV ATTIT RIGID/FLEX SKILL WEALTH...TECHNIC CONCPT STYLE RECORD CHARTS ORG/CHARTS GEN/METH VAL/FREE 20. PAGE 61 F1190
ECO/UNDEV EDU/PROP FOR/AID

S59 KINDLEBERGER C.P.,"UNITED STATES ECONOMIC FOREIGN POLICY: RESEARCH REQUIREMENTS FOR 1965." FUT USA+45 WOR+45 DIST/IND MARKET INT/ORG ECO/TAC INT/TRADE WEALTH...OBS TREND CON/ANAL GEN/LAWS FOR/TRADE VAL/FREE 20. PAGE 71 F1392
FINAN ECO/DEV FOR/AID

S59 PLAZA G.,"FOR A REGIONAL MARKET IN LATIN AMERICA." FUT L/A+17C CULTURE INDUS NAT/G ECO/TAC INT/TRADE ATTIT WEALTH...NEW/IDEA TREND OAS 20. PAGE 106 F2092
MARKET INT/ORG REGION

S59 REUBENS E.D.,"THE BASIS FOR REORIENATION OF AMERICAN FOREIGN AID POLICY." USA+45 USSR STRUCT INT/ORG CONSULT ECO/TAC ADMIN DRIVE MORAL ORD/FREE PWR WEALTH...RELATIV MATH STAT TREND GEN/LAWS VAL/FREE 20. PAGE 111 F2180
ECO/UNDEV PLAN FOR/AID DIPLOM

S59 SOLDATI A.,"EOCNOMIC DISINTEGRATION IN EUROPE." EUR+WWI FUT WOR+45 INDUS INT/ORG NAT/G CAP/ISM WEALTH...NEW/IDEA OBS TREND CHARTS EEC 20. PAGE 124 F2438
FINAN ECO/TAC

S59 THOMPSON W.S.,"POPULATION AND PROGRESS IN THE FAR EAST." ASIA S/ASIA DIST/IND CREATE ECO/TAC WAR LOVE SKILL WEALTH...CONT/OBS TOT/POP 20. PAGE 130 F2568
ECO/UNDEV BIO/SOC GEOG

B60 ALLEN R.L.,SOVIET ECONOMIC WARFARE. USSR FINAN INDUS NAT/G PLAN TEC/DEV FOR/AID DETER WEALTH ...TREND GEN/LAWS FOR/TRADE 20. PAGE 4 F0072
COM ECO/TAC

B60 APTHEKER H.,DISARMAMENT AND THE AMERICAN ECONOMY: A SYMPOSIUM. FUT USA+45 ECO/DEV DIST/IND FINAN INDUS PROC/MFG LABOR NAT/G POL/PAR CONSULT PLAN CAP/ISM INT/TRADE PEACE ATTIT MORAL WEALTH...TREND GEN/LAWS TOT/POP 20. PAGE 6 F0110
MARXIST ARMS/CONT

B60 BELLAN R.C.,PRINCIPLES OF ECONOMICS AND THE CANADIAN ECONOMY (2ND ED.). CANADA UK USA+45 LABOR WORKER CAP/ISM INT/TRADE RISK BAL/PAY EQUILIB ALL/IDEOS 20. PAGE 12 F0236
ECO/DEV PRODUC WEALTH FINAN

B60 DALE W.B.,THE FOREIGN DEFICIT OF THE UNITED STATES. ECO/TAC TARIFFS PAY PRICE CONTROL COST WEALTH POLICY. PAGE 30 F0573
BAL/PAY DIPLOM FINAN INT/TRADE

B60 FORM W.H.,INDUSTRY, LABOR, AND COMMUNITY. STRUCT NEIGH SECT BAL/PWR EDU/PROP PARTIC ATTIT ROLE PWR WEALTH...METH/CNCPT CHARTS. PAGE 42 F0828
LABOR MGT GP/REL CONTROL

B60 GARBARINO J.W.,HEALTH PLANS AND COLLECTIVE BARGAINING. USA+45 LABOR BARGAIN GP/REL WEALTH ...WELF/ST CHARTS 20 DEPT/HEW SAN/FRAN. PAGE 46 F0900
HEAL PLAN FINAN SERV/IND

B60 HOSELITZ B.F.,SOCIOLOGICAL ASPECTS OF ECONOMIC GROWTH. WOR+45 WOR-45 ECO/UNDEV CAP/ISM RIGID/FLEX WEALTH...MATH CHARTS. PAGE 62 F1221
ECO/DEV SOC

B60 ILLINOIS U BUR COMMUNITY PLAN,PROCEEDINGS OF ILLINOIS STATEWIDE PLANNING CONFERENCE 1960. USA+45 FINAN LOC/G ACT/RES LEAD GOV/REL GP/REL WEALTH MUNICH 20 ILLINOIS. PAGE 64 F1260
PLAN DELIB/GP VOL/ASSN

B60 KENEN P.B.,GIANT AMONG NATIONS: PROBLEMS IN UNITED STATES FOREIGN ECONOMIC POLICY. AFR USA+45 FINAN DIPLOM TARIFFS BAL/PAY WEALTH 20. PAGE 70 F1376
FOR/AID ECO/UNDEV INT/TRADE PLAN

B60 KERR C.,INDUSTRIALISM AND INDUSTRIAL MAN. CULTURE SOCIETY ECO/UNDEV NAT/G ADMIN PRODUC WEALTH ...PREDICT TREND NAT/COMP 19/20. PAGE 70 F1381
WORKER MGT ECO/DEV INDUS

B60 KRISTENSEN T.,THE ECONOMIC WORLD BALANCE. FUT WOR+45 CULTURE ECO/DEV BAL/PWR INT/TRADE REGION PWR WEALTH...STAT TREND CHARTS 20. PAGE 73 F1442
ECO/UNDEV ECO/TAC FOR/AID

B60 LATIFI D.,INDIA AND UNITED STATES AID. ASIA INDIA UK USA+45 AGRI FINAN INDUS COLONIAL ORD/FREE SOVEREIGN WEALTH...METH/COMP 20. PAGE 76 F1486
FOR/AID DIPLOM ECO/UNDEV

B60 LERNER A.P.,THE ECONOMICS OF CONTROL. USA+45 ECO/UNDEV INT/ORG ACT/RES PLAN CAP/ISM INT/TRADE ATTIT WEALTH...SOC MATH STAT GEN/LAWS INDEX 20. PAGE 78 F1530
ECO/DEV ROUTINE ECO/TAC SOCISM

B60 LISTER L.,EUROPE'S COAL AND STEEL COMMUNITY. FRANCE GERMANY STRUCT ECO/DEV EXTR/IND INDUS MARKET NAT/G DELIB/GP ECO/TAC INT/TRADE EDU/PROP ATTIT RIGID/FLEX ORD/FREE PWR WEALTH...CONCPT STAT TIME/SEQ CHARTS ECSC TERR/GP 20. PAGE 81 F1582
EUR+WWI INT/ORG REGION

B60
MYRDAL G.,BEYOND THE WELFARE STATE: ECONOMIC PLANNING AND ITS IMPLICATIONS. EUR+WWI FUT USA+45 USSR ECO/DEV ECO/UNDEV TEC/DEV SKILL WEALTH...PSY TREND FOR/TRADE 20. PAGE 96 F1881
PLAN
ECO/TAC
CAP/ISM

B60
NEALE A.D.,THE FLOW OF RESOURCES FROM RICH TO POOR. WOR+45 ECO/DEV ECO/UNDEV FINAN INDUS NAT/G PLAN EFFICIENCY WEALTH...POLICY NAT/COMP 20 RESOURCE/N. PAGE 97 F1905
FOR/AID
DIPLOM
METH/CNCPT

B60
PETERSON W.C.,THE WELFARE STATE IN FRANCE. EUR+WWI FRANCE FUT STRATA PROB/SOLV TAX GIVE RECEIVE INCOME ORD/FREE PWR...CHARTS 20. PAGE 105 F2070
NEW/LIB
ECO/TAC
WEALTH
NAT/G

B60
ROBERTSON D.,THE CONTROL OF INDUSTRY. UK MARKET LABOR WORKER PRICE CONTROL GP/REL COST DEMAND ORD/FREE WEALTH NEW/LIB SOCISM 20. PAGE 112 F2211
INDUS
FINAN
NAT/G
ECO/DEV

B60
ROBINSON R.I.,FINANCIAL INSTITUTIONS. USA+45 PRICE GOV/REL DEMAND WEALTH...CHARTS T 20 MONEY. PAGE 113 F2226
FINAN
ECO/TAC
ECO/DEV
BUDGET

B60
ROEPKE W.,A HUMANE ECONOMY: THE SOCIAL FRAMEWORK OF THE FREE MARKET. FUT USSR WOR+45 CULTURE SOCIETY ECO/DEV PLAN ECO/TAC ADMIN ATTIT PERSON RIGID/FLEX SUPEGO MORAL WEALTH SOCISM...POLICY OLD/LIB CONCPT TREND GEN/LAWS 20. PAGE 113 F2232
DRIVE
EDU/PROP
CAP/ISM

B60
ROPKE W.,A HUMANE ECONOMY. CULTURE ECO/DEV FINAN INDUS GP/REL CENTRAL WEALTH...GEOG SOC IDEA/COMP 20 EEC. PAGE 114 F2239
ECO/TAC
INT/ORG
DIPLOM
ORD/FREE

B60
SHANNON D.A.,THE GREAT DEPRESSION. USA-45 FINAN LG/CO SCHOOL SML/CO DELIB/GP RECEIVE REV EATING INCOME...ANTHOL MUNICH 20 ROOSEVLT/F CONGRESS. PAGE 120 F2365
WEALTH
NAT/G
AGRI
INDUS

B60
SHONFIELD A.,THE ATTACK ON WORLD POVERTY. WOR+45 ECO/DEV ECO/UNDEV FINAN VOL/ASSN PLAN EDU/PROP DRIVE KNOWL WEALTH...CONT/OBS STAND/INT ORG/CHARTS TOT/POP UNESCO 20. PAGE 121 F2383
INT/ORG
ECO/TAC
FOR/AID
INT/TRADE

B60
SIEGEL B.N.,AGGREGATE ECONOMICS AND PUBLIC POLICY. ECO/DEV TEC/DEV ECO/TAC TASK DEMAND EQUILIB INCOME ...CHARTS 20. PAGE 121 F2396
ECOMETRIC
WEALTH
PRODUC
MARKET

B60
THEOBALD R.,THE RICH AND THE POOR: A STUDY OF THE ECONOMICS OF RISING EXPECTATIONS. WOR+45 CONSTN ECO/DEV ECO/UNDEV INT/ORG NAT/G PLAN FOR/AID ROUTINE BAL/PAY ORD/FREE PWR WEALTH...GEOG TREND WORK FOR/TRADE 20. PAGE 129 F2553
ECO/TAC
INT/TRADE

B60
THORBECKE E.,THE TENDENCY TOWARDS REGIONALIZATION IN INTERNATIONAL TRADE, 1928-1956. WOR+45 WOR-45 ECO/DEV FINAN ECO/TAC WEALTH...GEOG CHARTS TOT/POP FOR/TRADE 20. PAGE 130 F2569
STAT
BAL/PAY
REGION

B60
WATSON D.S.,ECONOMIC POLICY: BUSINESS AND GOVERNMENT. USA+45 FINAN LABOR PLAN BUDGET INT/TRADE GP/REL WEALTH LAISSEZ...CHARTS T. PAGE 144 F2832
ECO/TAC
NAT/G
POLICY
ECO/DEV

L60
SPENGLER J.J.,"ECONOMIC DEVELOPMENT: POLITICAL PRECONDITIONS AND POLITICAL CONSEQUENCE." WOR+45 STRUCT ECO/UNDEV NAT/G PLAN ECO/TAC EDU/PROP ATTIT ORD/FREE WEALTH SOCISM...SOC CONCPT TREND SIMUL GEN/METH WORK 20. PAGE 124 F2452
TEC/DEV
METH/CNCPT
CAP/ISM

S60
BAUM M.,"THE CASE FOR BUSINESS CIVILIZATION." R+D CAP/ISM GIVE EDU/PROP HAPPINESS...SOC TREND. PAGE 12 F0218
MGT
CULTURE
WEALTH

S60
BERG E.J.,"ECONOMIC BASIS OF POLITICAL CHOICE IN FRENCH WEST AFRICA." FRANCE ECO/UNDEV AGRI INDUS NAT/G PLAN LEGIT COLONIAL REGION ATTIT PWR WEALTH ...CONCPT FOR/TRADE 20. PAGE 13 F0257
AFR
ECO/TAC

S60
BUTLER W.F.,"ECONOMIC PROGRESS IN LATIN AMERICA." L/A+17C USA+45 ECO/UNDEV AGRI FINAN NAT/G PLAN ECO/TAC FOR/AID ADMIN WEALTH...OLD/LIB TOT/POP 20. PAGE 21 F0397
INDUS
ACT/RES

S60
DUNN J.M.,"AMERICAN DEPENDENCE ON MATERIALS IMPORTS: THE WORLD-WIDE RESOURCE BASE." USA+45 WOR+45 NAT/G ATTIT WEALTH...RECORD TIME/SEQ CHARTS FOR/TRADE 20. PAGE 35 F0680
ACT/RES
ECO/TAC

S60
ENKE S.,"THE ECONOMIES OF GOVERNMENT PAYMENTS TO LIMIT POPULATION." FUT INDIA WOR+45 CULTURE FINAN NAT/G CONSULT PLAN LEGIT CONTROL COST ATTIT RIGID/FLEX HEALTH WEALTH...STAT OBS CHARTS TOT/POP VAL/FREE 20. PAGE 38 F0736
FAM
ACT/RES

S60
FRANKEL S.H.,"ECONOMIC ASPECTS OF POLITICAL INDEPENDENCE IN AFRICA." AFR FUT SOCIETY ECO/UNDEV COM/IND FINAN LEGIS PLAN TEC/DEV CAP/ISM ECO/TAC INT/TRADE ADMIN ATTIT DRIVE RIGID/FLEX PWR WEALTH ...MGT NEW/IDEA MATH TIME/SEQ VAL/FREE 20. PAGE 43 F0846
NAT/G
FOR/AID

S60
GROSSMAN G.,"SOVIET GROWTH: ROUTINE, INERTIA, AND PRESSURE." COM STRATA NAT/G DELIB/GP PLAN TEC/DEV ECO/TAC EDU/PROP ADMIN ROUTINE DRIVE WEALTH 20. PAGE 52 F1007
POL/PAR
ECO/DEV
AFR
USSR

S60
HERRERA F.,"THE INTER-AMERICAN DEVELOPMENT BANK." USA+45 ECO/UNDEV INT/ORG CONSULT DELIB/GP PLAN ECO/TAC INT/TRADE ROUTINE WEALTH...STAT TERR/GP 20. PAGE 59 F1153
L/A+17C
FINAN
FOR/AID
REGION

S60
HOOVER C.B.,"NATIONAL POLICY AND RATES OF ECONOMIC GROWTH: THE US SOVIET RUSSIA AND WESTERN EUROPE." COM EUR+WWI USA+45 USSR NAT/G PLAN ECO/TAC PWR WEALTH...MATH STAT GEN/LAWS 20. PAGE 61 F1207
ECO/DEV
ACT/RES

S60
KREININ M.E.,"THE 'OUTER-SEVEN' AND EUROPEAN INTEGRATION." EUR+WWI FRANCE GERMANY ITALY UK ECO/DEV DIST/IND INT/TRADE DRIVE WEALTH...MYTH CHARTS EEC OEEC 20. PAGE 73 F1436
ECO/TAC
GEN/LAWS

S60
LINDHOLM R.W.,"ACCELERATED DEVELOPMENT WITH A MINIMUM OF FOREIGN AID AND ECONOMIC CONTROLS." SOCIETY INDUS ECO/TAC WEALTH...CONCPT 20. PAGE 80 F1570
ECO/DEV
FINAN
FOR/AID

S60
MIKESELL R.F.,"AMERICA'S ECONOMIC RESPONSIBILITY AS A GREAT POWER." COM FUT USA+45 USSR WOR+45 INT/ORG PLAN ECO/TAC FOR/AID EDU/PROP CHOOSE WEALTH ...POLICY 20. PAGE 91 F1781
ECO/UNDEV
BAL/PWR
CAP/ISM

S60
MILLER A.S.,"SOME OBSERVATIONS ON THE POLITICAL ECONOMY OF POPULATION GROWTH." FUT USA+45 ECO/DEV R+D CONSULT PLAN TEC/DEV ECO/TAC ROUTINE BIO/SOC WEALTH...POLICY OBS. PAGE 91 F1790
SOCIETY
GEOG

S60
MORALES C.J.,"TRADE AND ECONOMIC INTEGRATION IN LATIN AMERICA." FUT L/A+17C LAW STRATA ECO/UNDEV DIST/IND INDUS LABOR NAT/G LEGIS ECO/TAC ADMIN RIGID/FLEX WEALTH...CONCPT NEW/IDEA CONT/OBS TIME/SEQ WORK 20. PAGE 93 F1825
FINAN
INT/TRADE
REGION

S60
MURPHY J.C.,"INTERNATIONAL INVESTMENT AND THE NATIONAL INTEREST." AFR WOR+45 WOR-45 ECO/DEV ECO/UNDEV NAT/G ACT/RES...CHARTS TOT/POP FOR/TRADE 20. PAGE 95 F1867
FINAN
WEALTH
FOR/AID

S60
NANES A.,"THE EUROPEAN COMMUNITY AND THE UNITED STATES: EVOLVING RELATIONS." EUR+WWI USA+45 WOR+45 ECO/UNDEV MARKET NAT/G DELIB/GP PLAN LEGIT ATTIT PWR WEALTH...CONCPT STAT TIME/SEQ CON/ANAL EEC METH/GP OEEC 20 EURATOM. PAGE 96 F1889
INT/ORG
REGION

S60
NEISSER H.,"ECONOMIC IMPERALISM RECONSIDERED." WOR+45 WOR-45 ECO/DEV ECO/UNDEV DIST/IND LEGIT COLONIAL PWR WEALTH SOCISM...MYTH MATH TIME/SEQ 20. PAGE 97 F1909
ACT/RES
ECO/TAC
CAP/ISM
INT/TRADE

S60
NICHOLS J.P.,"HAZARDS OF AMERICAN PRIVATE INVESTMENT IN UNDERDEVELOPED COUNTRIES." FUT L/A+17C USA+45 USA-45 EXTR/IND CONSULT BAL/PWR ECO/TAC DOMIN ADJUD ATTIT SOVEREIGN WEALTH ...HIST/WRIT TIME/SEQ TREND TERR/GP VAL/FREE 20. PAGE 98 F1924
FINAN
ECO/UNDEV
CAP/ISM
NAT/LISM

S60
RICHTER J.H.,"TOWARDS AN INTERNATIONAL POLICY ON AGRICULTURAL TRADE." EUR+WWI USA+45 ECO/DEV NAT/G PLAN ECO/TAC ATTIT PWR WEALTH...CONCPT GEN/LAWS 20. PAGE 111 F2187
AGRI
INT/ORG

S60
RIVKIN A.,"AFRICAN ECONOMIC DEVELOPMENT: ADVANCED TECHNOLOGY AND THE STAGES OF GROWTH." CULTURE ECO/UNDEV AGRI COM/IND EXTR/IND PLAN ECO/TAC ATTIT DRIVE RIGID/FLEX SKILL WEALTH...MGT SOC GEN/LAWS FOR/TRADE WORK TOT/POP 20. PAGE 111 F2195
AFR
TEC/DEV
FOR/AID

S60
STOCKWELL E.G.,"THE MEASUREMENT OF ECONOMIC DEVELOPMENT." WOR+45 SOCIETY ECO/DEV ECO/UNDEV INDUS ECO/TAC HEALTH WEALTH...WELF/ST GEOG METH/CNCPT CHARTS METH METH/GP 20. PAGE 126 F2492
FAM
STAT

B61
ACKLEY G.,MACROECONOMIC THEORY. AFR FINAN WORKER ECO/TAC PRICE COST INCOME PRODUC...MATH TREND CHARTS IDEA/COMP T KEYNES/JM. PAGE 2 F0034
SIMUL
ECOMETRIC
WEALTH

B61
ASCHHEIM J.,TECHNIQUES OF MONETARY CONTROL. UK USA+45 CONTROL WAR DEMAND INCOME WEALTH...TREND
FINAN
MARKET

CHARTS 20 MONEY. PAGE 7 F0127 BUDGET CENTRAL

B61
ASHER R.E.,GRANTS, LOANS, AND LOCAL CURRENCIES; THEIR ROLE IN FOREIGN AID. AFR USA+45 ECO/UNDEV INT/ORG ACT/RES PLAN ECO/TAC GIVE CONTROL WEALTH 20. PAGE 7 F0130
FOR/AID FINAN NAT/G BUDGET

B61
BENOIT E.,EUROPE AT SIXES AND SEVENS: THE COMMON MARKET, THE FREE TRADE ASSOCIATION AND THE UNITED STATES. EUR+WWI FUT USA+45 INDUS CONSULT DELIB/GP EX/STRUC TOP/EX ACT/RES ECO/TAC EDU/PROP ROUTINE CHOOSE PERCEPT WEALTH...MGT TREND EEC FOR/TRADE TOT/POP 20 EFTA. PAGE 13 F0249
FINAN ECO/DEV VOL/ASSN

B61
BUSSCHAU W.J.,GOLD AND INTERNATIONAL LIQUIDITY. AFR WOR+45 PRICE EQUILIB WEALTH...CHARTS 20. PAGE 20 F0396
FINAN DIPLOM PROB/SOLV

B61
CANTERBERY E.R.,THE PRESIDENT'S COUNCIL OF ECONOMIC ADVISERS. AFR USA+45 FINAN LABOR NAT/G PLAN ADMIN OPTIMAL WEALTH 20 EISNHWR/DD PRESIDENT TRUMAN/HS KEYNES/JM. PAGE 21 F0413
ECO/TAC OP/RES EXEC CHIEF

B61
CARNEY D.E.,GOVERNMENT AND ECONOMY IN BRITISH WEST AFRICA. GAMBIA GHANA NIGERIA SIER/LEONE DOMIN ADMIN GOV/REL SOVEREIGN WEALTH LAISSEZ...BIBLIOG 20 CMN/WLTH. PAGE 21 F0417
METH/COMP COLONIAL ECO/TAC ECO/UNDEV

B61
CLARK J.M.,COMPETITION AS A DYNAMIC PROCESS. ECO/DEV EXTR/IND INDUS LG/CO TEC/DEV ECO/TAC PRICE EQUILIB PRODUC...NEW/IDEA CAP 20. PAGE 25 F0483
WEALTH GP/REL FINAN PROFIT

B61
DE GRAZIA A.,AMERICAN WELFARE. CLIENT FINAN LABOR LOC/G NAT/G NEIGH EDU/PROP GP/REL...CLASSIF CON/ANAL CHARTS BIBLIOG. PAGE 31 F0598
GIVE WEALTH SECT VOL/ASSN

B61
EINZIG P.,A DYNAMIC THEORY OF FORWARD EXCHANGE. FUT WOR+45 WOR-45 INT/TRADE BAL/PAY WEALTH...OLD/LIB NEW/IDEA OBS TREND FOR/TRADE 20. PAGE 37 F0713
FINAN ECO/TAC

B61
ESTEVEZ A.,ASPECTOS ECONOMICO-FINANCIEROS DE LA CAMPANA SANMARITANA. L/A+17C SPAIN FINAN COLONIAL LEAD ROLE ORD/FREE WEALTH 19 SOUTH/AMER SAN/MARTIN. PAGE 38 F0748
ECO/UNDEV REV BUDGET NAT/G

B61
FEARN H.,AN AFRICAN ECONOMY. AFR EUR+WWI PLAN COLONIAL WEALTH...CONT/OBS TREND EEC VAL/FREE 20. PAGE 39 F0770
ECO/UNDEV

B61
FERTIG L.,PROSPERITY THROUGH FREEDOM. COM INDUS LABOR CAP/ISM ECO/TAC PRODUC PROFIT ORD/FREE WEALTH SOCISM...METH/CNCPT 20. PAGE 40 F0788
NAT/G CONTROL POLICY

B61
FRIEDMANN W.G.,JOINT INTERNATIONAL BUSINESS VENTURES. ASIA ISLAM L/A+17C ECO/DEV DIST/IND FINAN PROC/MFG FACE/GP LG/CO NAT/G VOL/ASSN CONSULT EX/STRUC PLAN ADMIN ROUTINE WEALTH...OLD/LIB FOR/TRADE WORK 20. PAGE 44 F0865
ECO/UNDEV INT/TRADE

B61
GANGULI B.N.,ECONOMIC INTEGRATION. FINAN LABOR CAP/ISM DIPLOM WEALTH...NAT/COMP 20. PAGE 46 F0895
ECO/TAC METH/CNCPT EQUILIB ECO/UNDEV

B61
GARDNER R.N.,LEGAL-ECONOMIC PROBLEMS OF INTERNATIONAL TRADE. FUT WOR+45 INTELL ECO/DEV EX/STRUC INT/TRADE ROUTINE ATTIT WEALTH...GEN/LAWS ANTHOL FOR/TRADE 20. PAGE 46 F0904
FINAN ACT/RES

B61
GOODWIN C.D.W.,CANADIAN ECONOMIC THOUGHT. CANADA STRATA TEC/DEV CAP/ISM TARIFFS TAX COST EFFICIENCY WEALTH...METH/CNCPT TREND 20 MARITIME ONTARIO. PAGE 49 F0952
INT/TRADE ECO/DEV FINAN DEMAND

B61
GREY A.L.,ECONOMIC ISSUES AND POLICIES; READINGS IN INTRODUCTORY ECONOMICS (2ND ED.). WOR+45 ECO/UNDEV FINAN MARKET LABOR LG/CO INT/TRADE BAL/PAY WEALTH ...ANTHOL T. PAGE 51 F0996
ECO/TAC PROB/SOLV METH/COMP

B61
HARRIS S.E.,THE DOLLAR IN CRISIS. AFR USA+45 MARKET INT/ORG ECO/TAC PRICE CONTROL WEALTH...METH/COMP ANTHOL 20. PAGE 55 F1089
BAL/PAY DIPLOM FINAN INT/TRADE

B61
HICKS U.K.,FEDERALISM AND ECONOMIC GROWTH IN UNDERDEVELOPED COUNTRIES. WOR+45 WOR-45 FINAN NAT/G PLAN BUDGET DIPLOM INT/TRADE DEMAND WEALTH...ANTHOL 20. PAGE 59 F1167
ECO/UNDEV ECO/TAC FEDERAL CONSTN

B61
HORVATH B.,THE CHARACTERISTICS OF YUGOSLAV ECONOMIC DEVELOPMENT. COM ECO/UNDEV AGRI INDUS PLAN CAP/ISM ECO/TAC ROUTINE WEALTH...SOCIALIST STAT CHARTS STERTYP WORK 20. PAGE 62 F1217
ACT/RES YUGOSLAVIA

B61
INTL UNION LOCAL AUTHORITIES,METROPOLIS. WOR+45 DIST/IND FINAN GIVE EDU/PROP CRIME COST HEALTH WEALTH MUNICH 20. PAGE 65 F1286
GOV/COMP LOC/G BIBLIOG

B61
JAVITS B.A.,THE PEACE BY INVESTMENT CORPORATION. WOR+45 NAT/G LEGIS PROB/SOLV PERS/REL WEALTH ...POLICY 20. PAGE 66 F1307
ECO/UNDEV DIPLOM FOR/AID PEACE

B61
KELSO L.O.,THE NEW CAPITALISTS: A PROPOSAL TO FREE ECONOMIC GROWTH FROM THE SLAVERY OF SAVINGS. UNIV USA+45 ECO/DEV CAP/ISM PRODUC WEALTH SOCISM ...NEW/IDEA 20. PAGE 70 F1373
ECO/TAC WORKER FINAN GEN/LAWS

B61
KITZINGER V.W.,THE CHALLENGE OF THE COMMON MARKET. EUR+WWI ECO/DEV DIST/IND PLAN ECO/TAC INT/TRADE LEGIT ATTIT PWR WEALTH...TIME/SEQ TREND CHARTS EEC 20. PAGE 71 F1403
MARKET INT/ORG UK

B61
LONGRIGG S.H.,OIL IN THE MIDDLE EAST: ITS DISCOVERY AND DEVELOPMENT. ECO/UNDEV LG/CO LOC/G TEC/DEV WEALTH...STAT TIME/SEQ 20 OIL. PAGE 82 F1599
ISLAM EXTR/IND

B61
MEZERIK A.G.,ECONOMIC DEVELOPMENT AIDS FOR UNDERDEVELOPED COUNTRIES. WOR+45 FINAN LEGIS PROB/SOLV TEC/DEV DIPLOM FOR/AID GIVE TASK WAR 20 UN. PAGE 91 F1776
ECO/UNDEV INT/ORG WEALTH PLAN

B61
MOORE G.H.,BUSINESS CYCLE INDICATORS (TWO VOLS.). LABOR DIPLOM PRICE RISK TASK WAR PRODUC...CHARTS BIBLIOG 20. PAGE 93 F1822
MARKET FINAN WEALTH

B61
OECD,STATISTICS OF BALANCE OF PAYMENTS 1950-61. WOR+45 FINAN ECO/TAC INT/TRADE DEMAND WEALTH...STAT NAT/COMP 20 OEEC OECD. PAGE 100 F1965
BAL/PAY ECO/DEV INT/ORG CHARTS

B61
PROUDHON P.J.,LA GUERRE ET LA PAIX (2 VOLS.). UNIV STRATA PROB/SOLV EQUILIB INCOME ATTIT...CONCPT 19. PAGE 108 F2125
WAR PEACE WEALTH

B61
SCAMMEL W.M.,INTERNATIONAL MONETARY POLICY. WOR+45 WOR-45 ACT/RES ECO/TAC LEGIT WEALTH...GEN/METH UN 20. PAGE 116 F2286
INT/ORG FINAN BAL/PAY

B61
SHARP W.R.,FIELD ADMINISTRATION IN THE UNITED NATION SYSTEM: THE CONDUCT OF INTERNATIONAL ECONOMIC AND SOCIAL PROGRAMS. FUT WOR+45 CONSTN SOCIETY ECO/UNDEV R+D DELIB/GP ACT/RES PLAN TEC/DEV EDU/PROP EXEC ROUTINE HEALTH WEALTH...HUM CONCPT CHARTS METH ILO UNESCO GP VAL/FREE UN 20. PAGE 120 F2369
INT/ORG CONSULT

B61
US SENATE COMM ON FOREIGN RELS,INTERNATIONAL DEVELOPMENT AND SECURITY: HEARINGS ON BILL (2 VOLS.). ECO/UNDEV FINAN FORCES REV COST WEALTH ...CHARTS 20 AID PRESIDENT. PAGE 139 F2747
FOR/AID CIVMIL/REL ORD/FREE ECO/TAC

S61
BARALL M.,"THE UNITED STATES GOVERNMENT RESPONDS." L/A+17C USA+45 SOCIETY NAT/G CREATE PLAN DIPLOM ECO/TAC ATTIT DRIVE RIGID/FLEX KNOWL SKILL WEALTH ...METH/CNCPT TIME/SEQ GEN/METH 20. PAGE 9 F0176
ECO/UNDEV ACT/RES FOR/AID

S61
BENOIT E.,"THE PROPENSITY TO REDUCE THE NATIONAL DEBT OUT OF DEFENSE SAVINGS." FUT USA+45 SOCIETY R+D PLAN...WELF/ST SOC REC/INT STERTYP TOT/POP 20. PAGE 13 F0250
WEALTH ECO/TAC

S61
DELLA PORT G.,"PROBLEMI E PROSPETTIVE DI COESISTENZA FRA ORIENTE ED OCCIDENTE. (PART 3)." COM FUT WOR+45 NAT/G BAL/PWR FOR/AID BAL/PAY PWR WEALTH...SOC CONCPT GEN/LAWS 20. PAGE 32 F0616
AFR INT/TRADE

S61
DEUTSCH K.W.,"NATIONAL INDUSTRIALIZATION AND THE DECLINING SHARE OF THE INTERNATIONAL ECONOMIC SECTOR." EUR+WWI FUT WOR+45 WOR-45 MARKET PLAN EDU/PROP WEALTH...WELF/ST OBS TESTS 20. PAGE 32 F0624
DIST/IND ECO/DEV INT/TRADE

S61
DICKS-MIREAUX L.A.,"THE INTERRELATIONSHIP BETWEEN COST AND PRICE CHANGES 19461959: A STUDY OF INFLATION IN POST-WAR BRITAIN" AFR UK ECO/DEV INDUS WORKER ECO/TAC ORD/FREE WEALTH...ECOMETRIC REGRESS STAT TREND CHARTS 20. PAGE 33 F0634
PRICE PAY DEMAND

S61
GALBRAITH J.K.,"A POSITIVE APPROACH TO ECONOMIC AID." FUT USA+45 INTELL NAT/G CONSULT ACT/RES DIPLOM ECO/TAC EDU/PROP ATTIT KNOWL PWR WEALTH ...SOC STERTYP MID/EX METH/GP 20. PAGE 45 F0883
ECO/UNDEV ROUTINE FOR/AID

S61
GORDON L.,"ECONOMIC REGIONALISM RECONSIDERED." FUT USA+45 WOR+45 INDUS NAT/G TEC/DEV DIPLOM ROUTINE PERCEPT WEALTH...WELF/ST METH/CNCPT WORK 20. PAGE 49 F0957
ECO/DEV ATTIT CAP/ISM REGION

S61
HEILBRONER R.L.,"DYNAMICS OF FOREIGN AID: PROBLEMS OF UNDERDEVELOPED NATIONS PLAGUE ASSISTANCE PROGRAM." FUT USA+45 WOR+45 STRATA NAT/G PLAN TEC/DEV ATTIT DRIVE WEALTH WORK 20. PAGE 58 F1135
ECO/UNDEV ECO/TAC FOR/AID

S61
LANFALUSSY A.,"EUROPE'S PROGRESS: DUE TO COMMON MARKET." EUR+WWI ECO/DEV DELIB/GP PLAN ECO/TAC ROUTINE WEALTH...GEOG TREND EEC TERR/GP 20. PAGE 75 F1473
INT/ORG MARKET

S61
NOVE A.,"THE SOVIET MODEL AND UNDERDEVELOPED COUNTRIES." COM FUT USSR WOR+45 CULTURE ECO/DEV POL/PAR FOR/AID EDU/PROP ADMIN MORAL WEALTH ...POLICY RECORD HIST/WRIT 20. PAGE 99 F1942
ECO/UNDEV PLAN

S61
OCHENG D.,"ECONOMIC FORCES AND UGANDA'S FOREIGN POLICY." AFR UGANDA INT/TRADE TARIFFS INCOME SOVEREIGN WEALTH 20 EACM EEC TANGANYIKA. PAGE 100 F1961
ECO/TAC DIPLOM ECO/UNDEV INT/ORG

S61
RAY J.,"THE EUROPEAN FREE-TRADE ASSOCIATION AND ITS IMPACT ON INDIA'S TRADE." EUR+WWI FRANCE GERMANY INDIA S/ASIA UK NAT/G VOL/ASSN PLAN INT/TRADE ROUTINE WEALTH...STAT CHARTS TERR/GP CMN/WLTH EEC FOR/TRADE OEEC 20 EFTA. PAGE 109 F2155
ECO/DEV ECO/TAC

B62
ROUND TABLE ON EUROPE'S ROLE IN LATIN AMERICAN DEVELOPMENT. EUR+WWI L/A+17C PLAN BAL/PAY UTIL ROLE WEALTH...CHARTS ANTHOL 20 UN INT/AM/DEV. PAGE 1 F0017
ECO/UNDEV FINAN TEC/DEV FOR/AID

B62
ALTMAN G.T.,INVISIBLE BARRIER: THE OPTIMUM GROWTH CURVE. USA+45 USA-45 ECO/DEV PLAN PAY CONTROL DEMAND OPTIMAL PRODUC WEALTH...STAT CHARTS 20. PAGE 4 F0080
INDUS FINAN ECO/TAC TAX

B62
ARNOLD H.J.P.,AID FOR DEVELOPING COUNTRIES. COM EUR+WWI USA+45 USSR WOR+45 EDU/PROP ATTIT DRIVE PWR WEALTH...TREND CHARTS STERTYP NAT/ 20. PAGE 6 F0115
ECO/UNDEV ECO/TAC FOR/AID

B62
BERNSTEIN P.L.,THE PRICE OF PROSPERITY. USA+45 TAX CONTROL OPTIMAL WEALTH...PREDICT 20. PAGE 14 F0269
ECO/DEV ECO/TAC NAT/G DEMAND

B62
BUREAU OF NATIONAL AFFAIRS,FEDERAL-STATE REGULATION OF WELFARE FUNDS (REV. ED.). USA+45 LAW LEGIS DEBATE AGE/O 20 CONGRESS. PAGE 20 F0386
WELF/ST WEALTH PLAN SOC/WK

B62
CAIRNCROSS A.K.,FACTORS IN ECONOMIC DEVELOPMENT. WOR+45 ECO/UNDEV INDUS R+D LG/CO NAT/G EX/STRUC PLAN TEC/DEV ECO/TAC ATTIT HEALTH KNOWL PWR WEALTH ...TIME/SEQ GEN/LAWS TOT/POP TRUE/GP VAL/FREE 20. PAGE 21 F0399
MARKET ECO/DEV

B62
CONGRES ECONOMISTES LANG FRAN,MONNAIE ET EXPANSION. AFR FRANCE PROB/SOLV BUDGET CENTRAL COST OPTIMAL PRODUC WEALTH 20. PAGE 27 F0524
FINAN PLAN EUR+WWI

B62
COX O.C.,CAPITALISM AND AMERICAN LEADERSHIP. WOR+45 WOR-45 STRATA INDUS SECT INT/TRADE EXEC INGP/REL RACE/REL RATIONAL PWR WEALTH. PAGE 28 F0548
CAP/ISM LEAD ECO/DEV SOCIETY

B62
DEBUYST F.,LAS CLASES SOCIALES EN AMERICA LATINA. L/A+17C SOCIETY STRUCT WORKER EDU/PROP RACE/REL ATTIT HABITAT ROLE...GEOG SOC NAT/COMP SOC/INTEG 20. PAGE 32 F0612
STRATA GP/REL WEALTH

B62
DENISON E.F.,THE SOURCES OF ECONOMIC GROWTH IN THE UNITED STATES AND THE ALTERNATIVES BEFORE US. AGRI INDUS SCHOOL TEC/DEV CAP/ISM ECO/TAC PRICE COST WEALTH...STAT TREND CHARTS 20. PAGE 32 F0620
ECO/DEV WORKER PRODUC

B62
EINZIG P.,THE HISTORY OF FOREIGN EXCHANGE. CHRIST-17C ISLAM MEDIT-7 PRE/AMER WOR+45 ECO/DEV FINAN PLAN ECO/TAC ATTIT KNOWL WEALTH...SIMUL GEN/LAWS. PAGE 37 F0714
MARKET TIME/SEQ INT/TRADE

B62
ELLIOTT J.R.,THE APPEAL OF COMMUNISM IN THE UNDERDEVELOPED NATIONS. AFR USSR WOR+45 INT/ORG NAT/G DIPLOM DOMIN EDU/PROP ROUTINE ATTIT RIGID/FLEX ORD/FREE PWR WEALTH MARXISM...POLICY SOC METH/CNCPT MYTH TOT/POP METH/GP 20. PAGE 37 F0722
COM ECO/UNDEV

B62
FAO,FOOD AND AGRICULTURE ORGANIZATION AFRICAN SURVEY. AFR CONGO/BRAZ GHANA STRATA AGRI INT/ORG TEC/DEV FOR/AID INT/TRADE RACE/REL DEMAND EFFICIENCY PRODUC...GEOG 20 UN CONGO/LEOP. PAGE 39 F0763
ECO/TAC WEALTH EXTR/IND ECO/UNDEV

B62
FRIEDMAN M.,CAPITALISM AND FREEDOM. USA+45 FINAN LG/CO WORKER INT/TRADE RECEIVE EDU/PROP CONTROL DISCRIM INCOME WEALTH POLICY. PAGE 44 F0859
CAP/ISM ORD/FREE NAT/G

ECO/DEV

B62
GALENSON W.,LABOR IN DEVELOPING COUNTRIES. BRAZIL INDONESIA ISRAEL PAKISTAN TURKEY AGRI INDUS WORKER PAY PRICE GP/REL WEALTH...MGT CHARTS METH/COMP NAT/COMP 20. PAGE 45 F0888
LABOR ECO/UNDEV BARGAIN POL/PAR

B62
GEARY R.C.,EUROPE'S FUTURE IN FIGURES. FUT GOV/REL DEMAND PRODUC...STAT CHARTS METH/COMP ANTHOL METH 20 EUROPE. PAGE 47 F0912
FINAN ECO/DEV PREDICT WEALTH

B62
GREEN L.P.,DEVELOPMENT IN AFRICA. AFR CENTRL/AFR GHANA RHODESIA SOUTH/AFR AGRI PROC/MFG INT/TRADE DEMAND NAT/LISM PRODUC WEALTH...GEOG METH/CNCPT CHARTS BIBLIOG 20. PAGE 50 F0987
CULTURE ECO/UNDEV GOV/REL TREND

B62
GWYN W.B.,DEMOCRACY AND THE COST OF POLITICS IN BRITAIN. UK BUDGET CRIME CHOOSE ORD/FREE WEALTH ...TIME/SEQ 18/20. PAGE 52 F1017
COST POL/PAR POPULISM PAY

B62
HARRINGTON M.,THE OTHER AMERICA: POVERTY IN THE UNITED STATES. WORKER CREATE REPRESENT RACE/REL AGE/O DRIVE POLICY. PAGE 55 F1086
WEALTH WELF/ST INCOME CULTURE

B62
HIGGANS B.,UNITED NATIONS AND U.S. FOREIGN ECONOMIC POLICY. FUT USA+45 WOR+45 ECO/DEV ECO/UNDEV NAT/G ECO/TAC WEALTH...TIME/SEQ TOT/POP UN 20. PAGE 59 F1168
INT/ORG ACT/RES FOR/AID DIPLOM

B62
HOLMAN A.G.,SOME MEASURES AND INTERPRETATIONS OF EFFECTS OF US FOREIGN ENTERPRISES ON US BALANCE OF PAYMENTS. USA+45 COST INCOME WEALTH...MATH CHARTS 20. PAGE 61 F1199
BAL/PAY INT/TRADE FINAN ECO/TAC

B62
HOOVER E.M.,ANATOMY OF A METROPOLIS. FUT USA+45 SOCIETY ECO/DEV DIST/IND INDUS WORKER ECO/TAC TAX GP/REL COST WEALTH MUNICH 20 NEWYORK/C. PAGE 62 F1212
ROUTINE TREND INCOME

B62
HUHNE L.H.,FINANCING ECONOMIC DEVELOPMENT THROUGH NATIONAL AND INTERNATIONAL ORGANIZATIONS (THESIS; U OF WIS.). USA+45 INT/ORG PLAN GIVE GOV/REL WEALTH 20. PAGE 63 F1235
RATION FINAN FOR/AID ECO/UNDEV

B62
HUMPHREY D.D.,THE UNITED STATES AND THE COMMON MARKET. USA+45 INDUS MARKET INT/ORG PLAN EDU/PROP BAL/PAY DRIVE PWR WEALTH...TREND STERTYP FOR/TRADE EEC 20. PAGE 63 F1241
ATTIT ECO/TAC

B62
JOHNSON H.G.,MONEY, TRADE AND ECONOMIC GROWTH. ECO/DEV ECO/UNDEV FINAN COST WEALTH...POLICY SOC IDEA/COMP 20 KEYNES/JM MONEY. PAGE 67 F1324
PLAN BAL/PAY INT/TRADE ECO/TAC

B62
KLEIN L.R.,AN INTRODUCTION TO ECONOMETRICS. DIST/IND DEMAND PRODUC WEALTH...MATH TIME/SEQ T 20. PAGE 72 F1408
ECOMETRIC SIMUL PREDICT STAT

B62
KOLKO G.,WEALTH AND POWER IN AMERICA. USA+45 SOCIETY STRATA LG/CO ECO/TAC TAX PWR...SOC BIBLIOG 20 DEPRESSION. PAGE 72 F1420
STRUCT INCOME ECO/DEV WEALTH

B62
LEVY H.V.,LIBERDADE E JUSTICA SOCIAL (2ND ED.). BRAZIL COM L/A+17C USSR INT/ORG PARTIC GP/REL WEALTH 20 UN COM/PARTY. PAGE 79 F1544
ORD/FREE MARXISM CAP/ISM LAW

B62
LIPPMANN W.,WESTERN UNITY AND THE COMMON MARKET. EUR+WWI FRANCE GERMANY/W UK USA+45 ECO/DEV AGRI FINAN MARKET INT/ORG NAT/G FOR/AID AGREE WEALTH 20 EEC. PAGE 80 F1575
DIPLOM INT/TRADE VOL/ASSN

B62
LUTZ F.A.,THE PROBLEM OF INTERNATIONAL ECONOMIC EQUILIBRIUM. FINAN PRODUC WEALTH 20 MONEY. PAGE 82 F1611
DIPLOM EQUILIB BAL/PAY PROB/SOLV

B62
MEADE J.E.,CASE STUDIES IN EUROPEAN ECONOMIC UNION. BELGIUM EUR+WWI LUXEMBOURG NAT/G INT/TRADE REGION ROUTINE WEALTH...METH/CNCPT STAT CHARTS ECSC TOT/POP OEEC EEC FOR/TRADE 20. PAGE 89 F1738
INT/ORG ECO/TAC

B62
MEANS G.C.,PRICING POWER AND THE PUBLIC INTEREST. PLAN PROB/SOLV COST EFFICIENCY PROFIT RIGID/FLEX WEALTH. PAGE 89 F1741
LG/CO EX/STRUC PRICE ECO/TAC

B62
MOUSSA P.,THE UNDERPRIVILEGED NATIONS. FINAN INT/ORG PLAN PROB/SOLV CAP/ISM GIVE TASK WEALTH ...POLICY SOC IND 20. PAGE 94 F1850
ECO/UNDEV NAT/G DIPLOM FOR/AID

B62
PAKISTAN MINISTRY OF FINANCE,FOREIGN ECONOMIC AID: A REVIEW OF FOREIGN ECONOMIC AID TO PAKISTAN. EUR+WWI PAKISTAN UK USA+45 USSR ECO/UNDEV INT/ORG DELIB/GP DIPLOM ECO/TAC...CHARTS CMN/WLTH CHINJAP. PAGE 103 F2016
FOR/AID RECEIVE WEALTH FINAN

B62
PHELPS E.S.,THE GOAL OF ECONOMIC GROWTH: SOURCES, COSTS, BENEFITS. USA+45 USSR FINAN TAX CONTROL DEMAND WEALTH...POLICY NAT/COMP ANTHOL BIBLIOG 20. PAGE 106 F2079
ECO/TAC ECO/DEV NAT/G FUT

B62
PONCET J.,LA COLONISATION ET L'AGRICULTURE EUROPEENNES EN TUNISIE DEPUIS 1881. FRANCE WORKER TEC/DEV ECO/TAC CONTROL EFFICIENCY ROLE WEALTH 19/20 TUNIS. PAGE 107 F2101
ECO/UNDEV AGRI COLONIAL FINAN

B62
ROBINSON M.A.,AN INTRODUCTION TO ECONOMIC REASONING. FINAN MARKET LABOR DIPLOM INT/TRADE BAL/PAY INCOME PRODUC WEALTH...POLICY MGT 20. PAGE 113 F2223
ECO/TAC METH/CNCPT NAT/G

B62
SHINOHARA M.,GROWTH AND CYCLES IN THE JAPANESE ECONOMY. INDUS LABOR TEC/DEV CAP/ISM INT/TRADE PAY COST EFFICIENCY INCOME WEALTH...METH/COMP 20 CHINJAP. PAGE 121 F2380
PRODUC ECO/DEV EQUILIB ECOMETRIC

B62
SIEVERS A.M.,REVOLUTION, EVOLUTION AND THE ECONOMIC ORDER. INDUS LABOR TAX CONTROL REV WAR DEMAND PRODUC WEALTH...IDEA/COMP 19/20 KEYNES/JM. PAGE 122 F2399
EFFICIENCY ALL/IDEOS ECO/DEV WELF/ST

B62
THEOBALD R.,NATIONAL DEVELOPMENT EFFORTS (PAMPHLET). WOR+45 AGRI BUDGET FOR/AID INT/TRADE TAX 20. PAGE 129 F2555
ECO/UNDEV PLAN BAL/PAY WEALTH

B62
US ADVISORY COMN INTERGOV REL,STATE CONSTITUTIONAL AND STATUTORY RESTRICTIONS ON LOCAL TAXING POWERS. USA+45 USA-45 LAW CONSTN ACT/RES CONTROL WEALTH ...JURID CHARTS 20. PAGE 133 F2632
LOC/G PROVS GOV/REL TAX

B62
US CONGRESS,LEGISLATIVE HISTORY OF UNITED STATES TAX CONVENTIONS(VOL. 1). USA+45 USA-45 DELIB/GP WEALTH...CHARTS 20 CONGRESS. PAGE 134 F2649
TAX LEGIS LAW DIPLOM

B62
US CONGRESS JOINT ECO COMM,FACTORS AFFECTING THE UNITED STATES BALANCE OF PAYMENTS. USA+45 DELIB/GP PLAN DIPLOM FOR/AID PRODUC WEALTH...CHARTS 20 CONGRESS OEEC. PAGE 134 F2653
BAL/PAY INT/TRADE ECO/TAC FINAN

B62
VIET J.,INTERNATIONAL COOPERATION AND PROGRAMMES OF ECONOMIC AND SOCIAL DEVELOPMENT. TEC/DEV FOR/AID DOMIN COLONIAL PEACE WEALTH 20 UNESCO. PAGE 141 F2784
BIBLIOG/A INT/ORG DIPLOM ECO/UNDEV

B62
WENDT P.F.,HOUSING POLICY - THE SEARCH FOR SOLUTIONS. GERMANY/W SWEDEN UK USA+45 OP/RES HABITAT WEALTH...SOC/WK CHARTS 20. PAGE 145 F2856
PLAN ADMIN METH/COMP NAT/G

L62
DURAND-REVILLE L.,"LE REGIME DES INVESTISSEMENTS DANS LES ETATS AFRICAINS D'EXPRESSION FRANCAISE ET A MADAGASCAR." MADAGASCAR ECO/UNDEV CAP/ISM ECO/TAC WEALTH...SOC TREND CHARTS 20. PAGE 35 F0683
AFR FINAN

L62
GALBRAITH J.K.,"ECONOMIC DEVELOPMENT IN PERSPECTIVE." CAP/ISM ECO/TAC ROUTINE ATTIT WEALTH ...TREND CHARTS SOC/EXP WORK TERR/GP 20. PAGE 45 F0884
ECO/UNDEV PLAN

L62
MACHLUP F.,"PLANS FOR REFORM OF THE INTERNATIONAL MONETARY SYSTEM. PRINCETON: U. PR., 1962, 70 PP., $0.25." WOR+45 INT/ORG ECO/TAC BAL/PAY HEALTH ORD/FREE WEALTH MID/EX TERR/GP VAL/FREE APPLIC 20. PAGE 83 F1631
ECO/DEV STAT

L62
WATERSTON A.,"PLANNING IN MOROCCO, ORGANIZATION AND IMPLEMENTATION. BALTIMORE: HOPKINS ECON. DEVELOP. INT. BANK FOR." ISLAM ECO/DEV AGRI DIST/IND INDUS PROC/MFG SERV/IND LOC/G EX/STRUC ECO/TAC PWR WEALTH TOT/POP TRUE/GP METH/GP TERR/GP VAL/FREE 20. PAGE 144 F2829
NAT/G PLAN MOROCCO

S62
ADISESHIAN M.,"EDUCATION AND DEVELOPMENT." FUT WOR+45 SOCIETY ACT/RES INT/TRADE EDU/PROP KNOWL SKILL WEALTH...POLICY CONCPT CONT/OBS CENSUS CHARTS TOT/POP VAL/FREE APPLIC FAO FOR/TRADE 20. PAGE 2 F0041
SCHOOL ECO/UNDEV

S62
ALPERT P.,"ECONOMIC POLICIES AND PLANNING IN NEWLY INDEPENDENT AFRICA." PLAN ATTIT PWR WEALTH ...STERTYP GEN/LAWS VAL/FREE 20. PAGE 4 F0078
AFR ECO/DEV NAT/LISM COLONIAL

S62
BOKOR-SZEGO H.,"LA CONVENTION DE BELGRADE ET LE REGIME DU DANUBE." COM EUR+WWI WOR+45 STRUCT POL/PAR VOL/ASSN PLAN EDU/PROP WEALTH...TIME/SEQ METH/GP COMMUN 20. PAGE 16 F0308
INT/ORG TOTALISM YUGOSLAVIA

S62
BOONE A.,"THE FOREIGN TRADE OF CHINA." AFR ECO/DEV ECO/UNDEV INDUS MARKET NAT/G TEC/DEV WEALTH ...POLICY STAT TREND CHARTS FOR/TRADE. PAGE 17 F0318
ASIA ECO/TAC

S62
MORGENTHAU H.J.,"A POLITICAL THEORY OF FOREIGN AID." ECO/UNDEV NAT/G DELIB/GP PLAN ECO/TAC EDU/PROP EXEC ORD/FREE RESPECT WEALTH...METH/CNCPT TREND 20. PAGE 93 F1833
USA+45 PHIL/SCI FOR/AID

S62
SCOTT J.B.,"ANGLO-SOVIET TRADE AND ITS EFFECTS ON THE COMMONWEALTH." COM FUT UK USSR WOR+45 ECO/DEV MARKET INT/ORG CONSULT WEALTH...POLICY TREND CMN/WLTH FOR/TRADE 20. PAGE 118 F2333
NAT/G ECO/TAC

C62
GREEN L.P.,"DEVELOPMENT IN AFRICA." RHODESIA SOUTH/AFR UGANDA MARKET PROC/MFG PRODUC WEALTH ...GEOG 20. PAGE 50 F0986
BIBLIOG ECO/UNDEV AFR AGRI

N62
BANK INTERNATIONAL SETTLEMENTS,AUSTRIA: MONETARY AND ECONOMIC SITUATION 1952-61 (PAMPHLET). AUSTRIA WORKER BUDGET INT/TRADE PRICE BAL/PAY DEMAND EFFICIENCY INCOME PRODUC...STAT 20 SILVER. PAGE 9 F0174
FINAN ECO/DEV CHARTS WEALTH

B63
ABSHIRE D.M.,NATIONAL SECURITY: POLITICAL, MILITARY, AND ECONOMIC STRATEGIES IN THE DECADE AHEAD. ASIA COM USA+45 WOR+45 ECO/DEV ECO/UNDEV INT/ORG DELIB/GP FORCES ECO/TAC COERCE ATTIT RIGID/FLEX HEALTH ORD/FREE PWR WEALTH...POLICY STAT CHARTS ANTHOL COLD/WAR VAL/FREE APP/SCI. PAGE 2 F0032
FUT ACT/RES BAL/PWR

B63
BARBOUR V.,CAPITALISM IN AMSTERDAM IN THE 17TH CENTURY. NETHERLAND FINAN ECO/TAC...METH/COMP BIBLIOG MUNICH 16. PAGE 10 F0185
CAP/ISM INT/TRADE MARKET WEALTH

B63
BAUER R.A.,AMERICAN BUSINESS AND PUBLIC POLICY: THE POLITICS OF FOREIGN TRADE. USA+45 COM/IND LG/CO NAT/G PROF/ORG SML/CO VOL/ASSN LEGIS TOP/EX ECO/TAC EDU/PROP CHOOSE HEALTH PWR WEALTH...CONCPT METH/CNCPT OBS INT QU SAMP FOR/TRADE TRUE/GP VAL/FREE HI. PAGE 11 F0217
ECO/DEV ATTIT

B63
BRAIBANTI R.J.D.,ADMINISTRATION AND ECONOMIC DEVELOPMENT IN INDIA. INDIA S/ASIA SOCIETY STRATA ECO/TAC PERSON WEALTH...MGT GEN/LAWS TOT/POP VAL/FREE 20. PAGE 18 F0337
ECO/UNDEV ADMIN

B63
CHAMBERLAIN E.H.,THE ECONOMIC ANALYSIS OF LABOR UNION POWER (PAMPHLET). WORKER ECO/TAC DOMIN COERCE GP/REL DRIVE WEALTH POLICY. PAGE 23 F0441
LABOR PWR CONTROL

B63
CHATTERJEE I.K.,ECONOMIC DEVELOPMENT PAYMENTS DEFICIT AND PAYMENT RESTRICTION. INDIA WOR+45 FINAN INT/TRADE CONTROL BAL/PAY WEALTH...POLICY CONCPT STAT CHARTS IDEA/COMP BIBLIOG 20. PAGE 23 F0456
ECO/DEV ECO/TAC PAY GOV/REL

B63
COPPOCK J.,NORTH ATLANTIC POLICY - THE AGRICULTURAL GAP. EUR+WWI ELITES ECO/DEV DIST/IND MARKET PLAN WEALTH...STAT TREND GEN/LAWS OEEC TOT/POP VAL/FREE FAO 20. PAGE 27 F0535
AGRI TEC/DEV INT/TRADE

B63
COSSA L.,SAGGI BIBLIOGRAFICI DI ECONOMIA POLITICA. MOD/EUR LABOR PRICE COST INCOME 18/19. PAGE 28 F0539
BIBLIOG FINAN WEALTH

B63
COURNOT A.A.,RESEARCHES INTO THE MATHEMATICAL PRINCIPLES OF THE THEORY OF WEALTH (1838). UNIV ECO/DEV ECO/UNDEV AGRI INDUS MARKET PAY CONTROL COST INCOME 19. PAGE 28 F0544
ECOMETRIC GEN/LAWS WEALTH

B63
DEUTSCH K.W.,THE POLITICAL ROLE OF LABOR IN DEVELOPING COUNTRIES. AFR ASIA S/ASIA USA+45 WOR+45 ECO/UNDEV POL/PAR ECO/TAC EDU/PROP LEGIT COERCE ORD/FREE PWR WEALTH...OBS INT TREND VAL/FREE 20. PAGE 32 F0625
LABOR NAT/LISM

B63
ELLENDER A.J.,A REPORT ON UNITED STATES FOREIGN OPERATIONS IN AFRICA. SOUTH/AFR USA+45 STRATA EXTR/IND FORCES RACE/REL ISOLAT SOVEREIGN...CHARTS 20 NEGRO. PAGE 37 F0721
FOR/AID DIPLOM WEALTH ECO/UNDEV

B63
ENKE S.,ECONOMICS FOR DEVELOPMENT. AGRI TEC/DEV CAP/ISM DIPLOM ECO/TAC TAX ATTIT DRIVE HABITAT WEALTH...GOV/COMP BIBLIOG 20. PAGE 38 F0737
ECO/UNDEV PHIL/SCI CON/ANAL

B63
GEERTZ C.,PEDDLERS AND PRINCES: SOCIAL DEVELOPMENT
ECO/UNDEV

AND ECONOMIC CHANGE IN TWO INDONESIAN TOWNS. S/ASIA CULTURE SOCIETY STRATA FACE/GP CREATE TEC/DEV ECO/TAC ORD/FREE WEALTH...OBS INT CENSUS CHARTS WORK TOT/POP METH/GP TERR/GP VAL/FREE 20 MUNICH. PAGE 47 F0913
SOC ELITES INDONESIA

B63
GOLDMAN M.I.,SOVIET MARKETING. USSR DIST/IND FINAN RATION OWN WEALTH...SOC BIBLIOG 20. PAGE 48 F0937
MARKET ECO/TAC CONTROL MARXISM

B63
GORDON M.S.,THE ECONOMICS OF WELFARE POLICIES. INDUS LOC/G NAT/G LEGIS WORKER INCOME AGE/O SKILL WEALTH...METH/COMP NAT/COMP 20. PAGE 49 F0959
METH/CNCPT ECO/TAC POLICY

B63
GRIGSBY W.G.,HOUSING MARKETS AND PUBLIC POLICY. USA+45 FAM NEIGH PRICE DEMAND WEALTH...POLICY CHARTS BIBLIOG METH MUNICH 20. PAGE 51 F1002
MARKET RENT HABITAT PLAN

B63
GRUBEL H.G.,WORLD MONETARY REFORM: PLANS AND ISSUES. FUT WOR+45 ECO/DEV ECO/UNDEV R+D DELIB/GP CREATE ECO/TAC ATTIT RIGID/FLEX WEALTH...STAT ANTHOL VAL/FREE 20. PAGE 52 F1009
FINAN INT/ORG BAL/PAY INT/TRADE

B63
HARROD R.F.,INTERNATIONAL TRADE THEORY IN A DEVELOPING WORLD. COM WOR+45 FOR/AID REGION COST DEMAND WEALTH...POLICY 20 INTL/ECON. PAGE 56 F1095
INT/TRADE BAL/PAY ECO/UNDEV METH/COMP

B63
HAUSMAN W.H.,MANAGING ECONOMIC DEVELOPMENT IN AFRICA. AFR USA+45 LAW FINAN WORKER TEC/DEV WEALTH ...ANTHOL 20. PAGE 57 F1116
ECO/UNDEV PLAN FOR/AID MGT

B63
HIRSCHMAN A.O.,JOURNEYS TOWARD PROGRESS: STUDIES OF ECONOMIC POLICYMAKING IN LATIN AMERICA. CHILE FUT ECO/UNDEV AGRI FINAN INDUS CONSULT DELIB/GP PLAN ATTIT HEALTH ORD/FREE WEALTH...POLICY STAT VAL/FREE COLOMB 20. PAGE 60 F1177
L/A+17C ECO/TAC BRAZIL

B63
INTERAMERICAN ECO AND SOC COUN,THE ALLIANCE FOR PROGRESS: ITS FIRST YEAR: 1961-1962. AGRI SCHOOL PLAN TEC/DEV INT/TRADE TAX GIVE ADMIN WEALTH...SOC 20 ALL/PROG SOUTH/AMER. PAGE 64 F1267
INT/ORG PROB/SOLV ECO/TAC L/A+17C

B63
INTERNATIONAL ASSOCIATION RES,AFRICAN STUDIES IN INCOME AND WEALTH. AFR NAT/G PROB/SOLV DEMAND INCOME...ECOMETRIC METH/COMP 20. PAGE 64 F1270
WEALTH PLAN ECO/UNDEV BUDGET

B63
INTERNATIONAL MONETARY FUND,COMPENSATORY FINANCING OF EXPORT FLUCTUATIONS (PAMPHLET). WOR+45 ECO/DEV ECO/UNDEV INT/ORG WEALTH...TREND 20 IMF MONEY. PAGE 65 F1281
BAL/PAY FINAN BUDGET INT/TRADE

B63
ISSAWI C.,EGYPT IN REVOLUTION: AN ECONOMIC ANALYSIS. ISLAM STRUCT ECO/UNDEV AGRI FINAN INDUS PLAN EXEC REV NAT/LISM ATTIT RIGID/FLEX WEALTH SOCISM...STAT FOR/TRADE WORK 20. PAGE 66 F1292
NAT/G UAR

B63
LAGOS G.,INTERNATIONAL STRATIFICATION AND UNDERDEVELOPED COUNTRIES. L/A+17C WOR+45 PLAN ECO/TAC PWR RESPECT WEALTH...METH/CNCPT STAT CHARTS SIMUL GEN/LAWS TRUE/GP METH/GP VAL/FREE 20. PAGE 74 F1459
ECO/UNDEV STRATA

B63
LAIRD R.D.,SOVIET AGRICULTURAL AND PEASANT AFFAIRS. FUT STRATA LOC/G DELIB/GP ACT/RES TEC/DEV ECO/TAC EDU/PROP ATTIT RIGID/FLEX ORD/FREE SKILL WEALTH ...STAT CON/ANAL ANTHOL MUNICH WORK VAL/FREE 20. PAGE 74 F1461
COM AGRI POLICY

B63
LEE M.W.,MACROECONOMICS: FLUCTUATIONS, GROWTH AND STABILITY (3RD ED.). MARKET LABOR TEC/DEV INT/TRADE TAX PRICE WAR PRODUC...POLICY ECOMETRIC CHARTS 19/20. PAGE 77 F1505
EQUILIB TREND WEALTH

B63
LINDBERG L.,POLITICAL DYNAMICS OF EUROPEAN ECONOMIC INTEGRATION. EUR+WWI ECO/DEV INT/ORG VOL/ASSN DELIB/GP ADMIN WEALTH...DECISION EEC TERR/GP 20. PAGE 80 F1567
MARKET ECO/TAC

B63
MAIZELS A.,INDUSTRIAL GROWTH AND WORLD TRADE. FUT WOR+45 ECO/DEV FINAN INT/ORG PLAN TEC/DEV ECO/TAC WEALTH...MATH STAT CHARTS VAL/FREE 19/20. PAGE 84 F1642
INDUS ECO/UNDEV INT/TRADE

B63
MEEK R.L.,THE ECONOMICS OF PHYSIOCRACY. FRANCE UK AGRI FINAN WORKER CAP/ISM TAX DEMAND EQUILIB INCOME HABITAT...CHARTS ANTHOL 17. PAGE 89 F1744
PRODUC WEALTH MARKET

B63
MEIER G.,INTERNATIONAL TRADE AND DEVELOPMENT. FINAN BAL/PAY COST DEMAND DISCRIM EQUILIB WEALTH...POLICY ECOMETRIC MATH STAT BIBLIOG/A 20. PAGE 89 F1747
ECO/UNDEV ECO/TAC INT/TRADE IDEA/COMP

B63
MINGAY G.E.,ENGLISH LANDED SOCIETY IN THE EIGHTEENTH CENTURY. UK ELITES STRUCT AGRI INDUS CONTROL WEALTH 18. PAGE 92 F1802
OWN STRATA PWR

B63
MYRDAL G.,CHALLENGE TO AFFLUENCE. USA+45 WOR+45 FINAN INT/ORG NAT/G PLAN ECO/TAC INT/TRADE BAL/PAY ORD/FREE 20 EUROPE/W. PAGE 96 F1882
ECO/DEV WEALTH DIPLOM PRODUC

B63
NEUMARK S.D.,FOREIGN TRADE AND ECONOMIC DEVELOPMENT IN AFRICA: A HISTORICAL PERSPECTIVE. EUR+WWI MOD/EUR ECO/UNDEV AGRI COM/IND EXTR/IND PROC/MFG SKILL WEALTH...CONCPT TIME/SEQ TREND SIMUL FOR/TRADE WORK TOT/POP TERR/GP VAL/FREE 19/20. PAGE 98 F1916
AFR

B63
OECD,FOOD AID: ITS ROLE IN ECONOMIC DEVELOPMENT. FINAN NAT/G PLAN DIPLOM GIVE TASK WEALTH ...METH/COMP METH 20. PAGE 100 F1966
ECO/UNDEV FOR/AID INT/ORG POLICY

B63
OLSON M. JR.,THE ECONOMICS OF WARTIME SHORTAGE. FRANCE GERMANY MOD/EUR UK AGRI PROB/SOLV ADMIN DEMAND WEALTH...POLICY OLD/LIB FOR/TRADE 17/20. PAGE 101 F1990
WAR ADJUST ECO/TAC NAT/COMP

B63
PATTON R.,THE DEVELOPMENT OF THE AMERICAN ECONOMY: REVISED. USA+45 USA-45 INDUS LABOR NAT/G CAP/ISM DIPLOM INT/TRADE WAR WEALTH 16/20. PAGE 104 F2038
ECO/TAC ECO/DEV DEMAND

B63
PRYOR F.L.,THE COMMUNIST FOREIGN TRADE SYSTEM. COM CZECHOSLVK GERMANY YUGOSLAVIA LAW ECO/DEV DIST/IND POL/PAR PLAN DOMIN TOTALISM DRIVE RIGID/FLEX WEALTH ...STAT STAND/INT CHARTS FOR/TRADE 20. PAGE 108 F2130
ATTIT ECO/TAC

B63
RAO V.K.R.,FOREIGN AID AND INDIA'S ECONOMIC DEVELOPMENT. INDIA INT/ORG PROB/SOLV TEC/DEV ECO/TAC CONTROL WEALTH...TREND 20. PAGE 109 F2148
FOR/AID ECO/UNDEV RECEIVE DIPLOM

B63
REAGAN M.D.,THE MANAGED ECONOMY. USA+45 INDUS LG/CO BUDGET GP/REL ORD/FREE PWR WEALTH 20. PAGE 110 F2161
PLAN ECO/DEV NAT/G ROLE

B63
RICARDO D.,THE PRINCIPLES OF POLITICAL ECONOMY AND TAXATION (1817). UK INDUS MARKET ECO/TAC INT/TRADE TARIFFS PRICE COST DEMAND OPTIMAL WEALTH...CONCPT 19 INTRVN/ECO. PAGE 111 F2183
GEN/LAWS TAX LAISSEZ

B63
ROPKE W.,ECONOMICS OF THE FREE SOCIETY. FINAN INT/TRADE BAL/PAY COST DEMAND EFFICIENCY ORD/FREE WEALTH...CON/ANAL METH/COMP T 20 KEYNES/JM. PAGE 114 F2240
SOCIETY BUDGET ECO/DEV ECO/TAC

B63
STIFEL L.D.,THE TEXTILE INDUSTRY - A CASE STUDY OF INDUSTRIAL DEVELOPMENT IN THE PHILIPPINES (PAPER). PHILIPPINE WORKER CAP/ISM INT/TRADE TARIFFS RECEIVE PRICE ADMIN COST EFFICIENCY WEALTH...BIBLIOG 20. PAGE 126 F2486
S/ASIA ECO/UNDEV PROC/MFG NAT/G

B63
THEOBALD R.,FREE MEN AND FREE MARKETS. USA+45 USA-45 ECO/DEV NAT/G TEC/DEV DIPLOM INT/TRADE INCOME ORD/FREE WEALTH...TREND 19/20 KEYNES/JM. PAGE 130 F2556
CONCPT ECO/TAC CAP/ISM MARKET

B63
US BD GOVERNORS FEDL RESRV,THE FEDERAL RESERVE AND THE TREASURY. USA+45 WORKER PROB/SOLV PRICE COST DEMAND WEALTH...STAT INT CHARTS 20 FED/RESERV DEPT/TREAS. PAGE 134 F2641
FINAN GOV/REL CONTROL BUDGET

B63
US SENATE COMM GOVT OPERATIONS,REPORT OF A STUDY OF US FOREIGN AID IN TEN MIDDLE EASTERN AND AFRICAN COUNTRIES. AFR ISLAM USA+45 FORCES PLAN BUDGET DIPLOM TAX DETER WEALTH...STAT CHARTS 20 CONGRESS AID MID/EAST. PAGE 138 F2728
FOR/AID EFFICIENCY ECO/TAC FINAN

B63
VELEZ GARCIA J.,DEVALUACION 1962; HISTORIA DOCUMENTAL DE UN PROCESO ECONOMICO. AFR L/A+17C USA+45 FINAN FOR/AID PRODUC WEALTH...POLICY STAT CHARTS ANTHOL 20 COLOMB. PAGE 141 F2774
ECO/UNDEV ECO/TAC PLAN NAT/G

B63
WAGLEY C.,INTRODUCTION TO BRAZIL. BRAZIL L/A+17C FAM KIN SCHOOL SECT ATTIT WEALTH...GEOG SOC. PAGE 142 F2799
ECO/UNDEV ELITES HABITAT STRATA

B63
WALINSKY L.J.,PLANNING AND EXECUTION OF ECONOMIC DEVELOPMENT. PROB/SOLV TEC/DEV BUDGET COST WEALTH ...CHARTS BIBLIOG 20. PAGE 142 F2802
PLAN ECO/UNDEV ECO/TAC OPTIMAL

L63
KUZNETS S.,"QUANTITATIVE ASPECTS OF THE ECONOMIC GROWTH OF NATIONS: DISTRIBUTION OF INCOME BY SIZE."
WEALTH ECO/TAC

WOR+45 FINAN ACT/RES HEALTH...MATH STAT VAL/FREE 20. PAGE 74 F1454

L63
OLSON M. JR.,"RAPID ECONOMIC GROWTH AS A DESTABILIZING FORCE." WOR+45 WOR-45 STRATA ECO/UNDEV FAM KIN CREATE TEC/DEV DIPLOM PEACE ATTIT PERSON RIGID/FLEX PWR RESPECT WEALTH...SOC 20. PAGE 101 F1989 SOCIETY FOR/AID

L63
PADELFORD N.J.,"FINANCIAL CRISIS AND THE UNITED NATIONS." FUT USSR WOR+45 LAW CONSTN FINAN INT/ORG DELIB/GP FORCES PLAN BUDGET DIPLOM COST WEALTH ...STAT CHARTS UN CONGO 20. PAGE 102 F2012 CREATE ECO/TAC

S63
ADAMS F.G.,"ECONOMIC CONSIDERATIONS OF AN ATLANTIC ENERGY POLICY." EUR+WWI FUT USA+45 DIST/IND EXTR/IND MARKET CONSULT LEGIS ECO/TAC WEALTH ...POLICY EEC FOR/TRADE OEEC 20. PAGE 2 F0037 ECO/DEV TEC/DEV NUC/PWR

S63
BARANSON J.,"ECONOMIC AND SOCIAL CONSIDERATIONS IN ADAPTING TECHNOLOGIES FOR DEVELOPING COUNTRIES." WOR+45 PLAN WEALTH...TECHNIC SOC 20. PAGE 10 F0180 ECO/UNDEV TEC/DEV

S63
BARZANSKI S.,"REGIONAL UNDERDEVELOPMENT IN THE EUROPEAN ECONOMIC COMMUNITY." EUR+WWI ELITES DIST/IND MARKET VOL/ASSN CONSULT EX/STRUC ECO/TAC RIGID/FLEX WEALTH EEC OEEC 20. PAGE 11 F0202 ECO/UNDEV PLAN

S63
BEGUIN H.,"ASPECTS STRUCTURELS DU COMMERCE EXTERIEUR DES PAYS SOUS-DEVELOPPES." FUT WOR+45 STRUCT FINAN SERV/IND POL/PAR TEC/DEV PERCEPT WEALTH FOR/TRADE 20. PAGE 12 F0229 MARKET ECO/UNDEV FOR/AID

S63
BELOFF M.,"BRITAIN, EUROPE AND THE ATLANTIC COMMUNITY." EUR+WWI ELITES NAT/G VOL/ASSN TOP/EX ATTIT ORD/FREE PWR SOVEREIGN WEALTH EEC TOT/POP VAL/FREE CMN/WLTH 20. PAGE 13 F0240 INT/ORG ECO/DEV UK

S63
BILL J.A.,"THE SOCIAL AND ECONOMIC FOUNDATIONS OF POWER IN CONTEMPORARY IRAN." ISLAM CULTURE NAT/G ECO/TAC DOMIN COERCE ATTIT PWR WEALTH...TREND VAL/FREE 20. PAGE 15 F0284 SOCIETY STRATA IRAN

S63
CLEMHOUT S.,"PRODUCTION FUNCTION ANALYSIS APPLIED TO THE LEONTIEF SCARCE-FACTOR PARADOX OF INTERNATIONAL TRADE." EUR+WWI USA+45 DIST/IND NAT/G PLAN TEC/DEV DIPLOM PWR WEALTH...MGT METH/CNCPT CONT/OBS CON/ANAL CHARTS SIMUL GEN/LAWS FOR/TRADE 20. PAGE 25 F0490 ECO/DEV ECO/TAC

S63
COLLERY A.,"A FULL EMPLOYMENT, KEYNESIAN THEORY OF INTERNATIONAL TRADE." WOR+45 ECO/DEV ACT/RES ECO/TAC ROUTINE ORD/FREE WEALTH...MATH CHARTS 20 KEYNES/JM. PAGE 26 F0504 SIMUL INT/TRADE

S63
DE FOREST J.D.,"LOW LEVELS OF TECHNOLOGY AND ECONOMIC DEVELOPMENT PROSPECTS." WOR+45 WOR-45 CULTURE ACT/RES CREATE PLAN ECO/TAC ROUTINE PERCEPT WEALTH...METH/CNCPT GEN/LAWS 20. PAGE 31 F0597 ECO/UNDEV TEC/DEV

S63
DELWERT J.,"L'ECONOMIE CAMBODGIENNE ET SON EVOLUTION ACTUELLE." FUT S/ASIA ECO/UNDEV ACT/RES PLAN WEALTH...CONCPT OBS TIME/SEQ TREND 20. PAGE 32 F0617 FINAN ATTIT CAMBODIA

S63
DIEBOLD W. JR.,"THE NEW SITUATION OF INTERNATIONAL TRADE POLICY." EUR+WWI FRANCE FUT UK USA+45 WOR+45 DIST/IND PLAN INT/TRADE EDU/PROP PWR WEALTH ...RECORD TREND GEN/LAWS EEC TRUE/GP VAL/FREE APPLIC 20. PAGE 33 F0636 MARKET ECO/TAC

S63
DOSSER D.,"TOWARD A THEORY OF INTERNATIONAL PUBLIC FINANCE." WOR+45 ECO/DEV PLAN ECO/TAC WEALTH ...WELF/ST TREND GEN/LAWS TRUE/GP METH/GP 20. PAGE 34 F0654 FINAN INT/ORG FOR/AID

S63
DUCROS B.,"MOBILISATION DES RESSOURCES PRODUCTIVES ET DEVELOPPEMENT." FUT INTELL SOCIETY COM/IND DIST/IND EXTR/IND FINAN INDUS ROUTINE WEALTH ...METH/CNCPT OBS 20. PAGE 34 F0670 ECO/UNDEV TEC/DEV

S63
EMERSON R.,"THE ATLANTIC COMMUNITY AND THE EMERGING COUNTRIES." FUT WOR+45 ECO/DEV ECO/UNDEV R+D NAT/G DELIB/GP BAL/PWR ECO/TAC EDU/PROP ROUTINE ORD/FREE PWR WEALTH...POLICY CONCPT TREND GEN/METH EEC 20 NATO. PAGE 37 F0729 ATTIT INT/TRADE

S63
GALENSON W.,"ECONOMIC DEVELOPMENT AND THE SECTORAL EXPANSION OF EMPLOYMENT, INT." FUT WOR+45 ECO/UNDEV DIST/IND PROC/MFG SERV/IND ACT/RES HEALTH SKILL WEALTH...STAT TIME/SEQ VAL/FREE 20. PAGE 46 F0889 INDUS ECO/TAC

S63
GORDON B.,"ECONOMIC IMPEDIMENTS TO REGIONALISM IN SOUTH EAST ASIA." BURMA FUT S/ASIA THAILAND USA+45 AGRI INDUS R+D NAT/G PLAN ECO/TAC WEALTH...STAT CONT/OBS 20. PAGE 49 F0954 VOL/ASSN ECO/UNDEV INT/TRADE REGION

S63
HINDLEY D.,"FOREIGN AID TO INDONESIA AND ITS POLITICAL IMPLICATIONS." INDONESIA POL/PAR ATTIT SOVEREIGN...CHARTS 20. PAGE 60 F1173 FOR/AID NAT/G WEALTH ECO/TAC

S63
HOOVER C.B.,"ECONOMIC REFORM VERSUS ECONOMIC GROWTH IN UNDERDEVELOPED COUNTRIES." FUT WOR+45 ELITES STRATA ECO/UNDEV DIST/IND INDUS TEC/DEV CAP/ISM FOR/AID INT/TRADE ATTIT WEALTH...MYTH TREND STERTYP GEN/LAWS WORK 20. PAGE 61 F1209 ECO/DEV ECO/TAC

S63
MATHUR P.N.,"GAINS IN ECONOMIC GROWTH FROM INTERNATIONAL TRADE." USA-45 ECO/DEV FINAN INDUS ATTIT WEALTH...MATH QUANT STAT BIOG TREND GEN/LAWS WORK 20. PAGE 87 F1704 MARKET ECO/TAC CAP/ISM INT/TRADE

S63
MIKESELL R.F.,"COMMODITY AGREEMENTS AND AID TO DEVELOPING COUNTRIES." WOR+45 WOR-45 INT/ORG ECO/TAC ATTIT WEALTH WORK FOR/TRADE 20. PAGE 91 F1782 FINAN ECO/UNDEV BAL/PAY FOR/AID

S63
MILLEN B.H.,"INTERNATIONAL TRADE AND POLITICAL INDEPENDENCE." WOR+45 ECO/DEV WEALTH...STAT CHARTS FOR/TRADE METH/GP TERR/GP VAL/FREE 20. PAGE 91 F1788 ECO/UNDEV ECO/TAC INT/TRADE

S63
NADLER E.B.,"SOME ECONOMIC DISADVANTAGES OF THE ARMS RACE." AFR USA+45 INDUS R+D FORCES PLAN TEC/DEV ECO/TAC FOR/AID EDU/PROP PWR WEALTH...TREND FOR/TRADE 20. PAGE 96 F1886 ECO/DEV MGT BAL/PAY

S63
PINCUS J.,"THE COST OF FOREIGN AID." WOR+45 ECO/DEV FINAN NAT/G VOL/ASSN CREATE ECO/TAC EDU/PROP WEALTH ...METH/CNCPT STAT CHARTS HYPO/EXP TOT/POP VAL/FREE 20. PAGE 106 F2087 USA+45 ECO/UNDEV FOR/AID

S63
POLYANOV N.,"THE DOLLAR'S VENTURES IN EUROPE." EUR+WWI FRANCE USA+45 ECO/DEV MARKET POL/PAR TEC/DEV ECO/TAC EDU/PROP DRIVE PWR WEALTH...MARXIST MYTH STAT TREND EEC 20. PAGE 107 F2100 FINAN PLAN BAL/PAY CAP/ISM

S63
POPPINO R.E.,"IMBALANCE IN BRAZIL." L/A+17C NAT/G TOP/EX PLAN DIPLOM LEGIT DRIVE WEALTH...CON/ANAL FOR/TRADE LAFTA 20. PAGE 107 F2105 POL/PAR ECO/TAC BRAZIL

S63
RAMERIE L.,"TENSION AU SEIN DU COMECON: LE CAS ROUMAIN." COM EUR+WWI USSR WOR+45 ECO/DEV DIST/IND NAT/G POL/PAR VOL/ASSN EDU/PROP TOTALISM ATTIT WEALTH...TIME/SEQ 20 COMECON. PAGE 109 F2142 INT/ORG ECO/TAC INT/TRADE ROMANIA

S63
SCHOFLING J.A.,"EFTA: THE OTHER EUROPE." ECO/DEV MARKET CONSULT ECO/TAC WEALTH...TIME/SEQ EEC OEEC 20 EFTA. PAGE 117 F2310 EUR+WWI INT/ORG REGION

S63
SCHURMANN F.,"ECONOMIC POLICY AND POLITICAL POWER IN COMMUNIST CHINA." ASIA CHINA/COM USSR SOCIETY ECO/UNDEV AGRI INDUS CREATE ADMIN ROUTINE ATTIT DRIVE RIGID/FLEX PWR WEALTH...HIST/WRIT TREND CHARTS WORK 20. PAGE 118 F2323 PLAN ECO/TAC

S63
SHWADRAN B.,"MIDDLE EAST OIL, 1962." ISLAM DIST/IND INDUS PLAN ATTIT DRIVE WEALTH...POLICY STAT CONT/OBS TREND CHARTS GEN/LAWS TERR/GP METH/GP 20 OIL. PAGE 121 F2393 PROC/MFG ECO/TAC ELITES REGION

S63
VINER J.,"REPORT OF THE CLAY COMMITTEE ON FOREIGN AID: A SYMPOSIUM." USA+45 WOR+45 NAT/G CONSULT PLAN BAL/PWR ATTIT WEALTH...MGT CONCPT TOT/POP 20. PAGE 142 F2788 ACT/RES ECO/TAC FOR/AID

S63
WILES P.J.D.,"WILL CAPITALISM AND COMMUNISM SPONTANEOUSLY CONVERGE." COM FUT USA+45 ECO/DEV DIST/IND MARKET CAP/ISM ECO/TAC RIGID/FLEX WEALTH MARXISM SOCISM...MATH STAT TREND COMPUT/IR 20. PAGE 146 F2885 PLAN TEC/DEV USSR

B64
BALASSA B.,CHANGING PATTERNS IN FOREIGN TRADE AND PAYMENTS. AFR USA+45 USA-45 ECO/DEV NAT/G PLAN BAL/PWR...POLICY ANTHOL BIBLIOG 20. PAGE 8 F0159 ECO/TAC INT/TRADE BAL/PAY WEALTH

B64
BALL R.J.,INFLATION AND THE THEORY OF MONEY. MARKET TAX PAY PRICE TASK ADJUST BAL/PAY COST INCOME PRODUC WEALTH...METH/COMP 20 KEYNES/JM MONEY. PAGE 9 F0167 EQUILIB DEMAND POLICY

B64
BARKSDALE H.C.,MARKETING: CHANGE AND EXCHANGE. USA+45 FINAN ACADEM TEC/DEV PRICE AUTOMAT WEALTH ...CHARTS 20. PAGE 10 F0187 MARKET ECO/DEV DEMAND TREND

B64
BEARDSLEY R.K.,STUDIES ON ECONOMIC LIFE IN JAPAN (OCCASIONAL PAPERS NO. 8). INDUS FAM HABITAT...GEOG GOV/COMP 20 CHINJAP. PAGE 12 F0223 WEALTH PRESS PRODUC INCOME

B64
CENTRO ESTUDIOS MONETARIOS LAT,PROBLEMAS DE PAGOS EN AMERICA LATINA. L/A+17C MARKET BUDGET ECO/TAC EFFICIENCY WEALTH 20 CENTRAL/AM. PAGE 22 F0434
FINAN INT/TRADE BAL/PAY ECO/UNDEV

B64
COMMISSION ON MONEY AND CREDIT,INFLATION, GROWTH, AND EMPLOYMENT. AFR USA+45 PLAN PROB/SOLV PAY PRICE EFFICIENCY PRODUC WEALTH 20. PAGE 26 F0514
WORKER ECO/TAC OPTIMAL

B64
DANIELS R.V.,RUSSIA. RUSSIA USSR STRUCT NAT/LISM TOTALISM ORD/FREE WEALTH...POLICY DECISION TREND. PAGE 30 F0579
MARXISM REV ECO/DEV DIPLOM

B64
EINZIG P.,MONETARY POLICY: ENDS AND MEANS. AFR UK INDUS WORKER PLAN DIPLOM PRICE BAL/PAY COST WEALTH ...DECISION TIME/SEQ 20. PAGE 37 F0715
FINAN POLICY ECO/TAC BUDGET

B64
FEIS H.,FOREIGN AID AND FOREIGN POLICY. USA+45 WOR+45 NAT/G VOL/ASSN ACT/RES TEC/DEV ATTIT HEALTH WEALTH...SOC GEN/LAWS 20. PAGE 40 F0775
ECO/UNDEV ECO/TAC FOR/AID DIPLOM

B64
GARDNER L.C.,ECONOMIC ASPECTS OF NEW DEAL DIPLOMACY. USA-45 WOR-45 LAW ECO/DEV INT/ORG NAT/G VOL/ASSN LEGIS TOP/EX EDU/PROP ORD/FREE PWR WEALTH ...POLICY TIME/SEQ VAL/FREE 20 ROOSEVLT/F. PAGE 46 F0901
ECO/TAC DIPLOM

B64
GOWDA K.V.,INTERNATIONAL CURRENCY PLANS AND EXPANSION OF WORLD TRADE. INT/ORG CREATE BUDGET CONTROL BAL/PAY WEALTH 20 KEYNES/JM. PAGE 50 F0969
INT/TRADE FINAN METH/COMP

B64
GUTMANN P.M.,ECONOMIC GROWTH: AN AMERICAN PROBLEM. USA+45 FINAN R+D...POLICY NAT/COMP ANTHOL BIBLIOG 20. PAGE 52 F1016
WEALTH ECO/DEV CAP/ISM ORD/FREE

B64
HANSEN A.H.,BUSINESS CYCLES AND NATIONAL INCOME. USA+45 FINAN ECO/TAC COST OPTIMAL...POLICY METH 20 KEYNES/JM. PAGE 54 F1065
INCOME WEALTH PRODUC INDUS

B64
HANSEN B.,INTERNATIONAL LIQUIDITY. USA+45 INT/ORG ECO/TAC PRICE CONTROL WEALTH...POLICY 20. PAGE 54 F1068
BAL/PAY INT/TRADE DIPLOM FINAN

B64
HEKHUIS D.J.,INTERNATIONAL STABILITY: MILITARY, ECONOMIC AND POLITICAL DIMENSIONS. FUT WOR+45 LAW ECO/UNDEV INT/ORG NAT/G VOL/ASSN FORCES ACT/RES BAL/PWR PWR WEALTH...STAT UN 20. PAGE 58 F1143
TEC/DEV DETER REGION

B64
INTERNATIONAL LABOUR OFFICE,EMPLOYMENT AND ECONOMIC GROWTH. ECO/DEV ECO/UNDEV NAT/G PLAN DIPLOM INT/TRADE CONTROL INCOME PRODUC WEALTH...STAT NAT/COMP 20 ILO. PAGE 65 F1279
WORKER METH/COMP ECO/TAC OPTIMAL

B64
JUCKER-FLEETWOOD E.,MONEY AND FINANCE IN AFRICA. ISLAM ECO/UNDEV SERV/IND NAT/G EX/STRUC PLAN ECO/TAC ROUTINE WEALTH...MGT TOT/POP 20. PAGE 68 F1344
AFR FINAN

B64
KNIGHT R.,BIBLIOGRAPHY ON INCOME AND WEALTH, 1957-1960 (VOL VIII). WOR+45 ECO/DEV FINAN INT/TRADE...GOV/COMP METH/COMP. PAGE 72 F1412
BIBLIOG/A ECO/UNDEV WEALTH INCOME

B64
LITTLE I.M.D.,AID TO AFRICA. AFR UK TEC/DEV DIPLOM ECO/TAC INCOME WEALTH 20. PAGE 81 F1583
FOR/AID ECO/UNDEV ADMIN POLICY

B64
LITVAK I.A.,MARKETING: CANADA. CANADA STRATA PROC/MFG LEGIS TEC/DEV DIPLOM INT/TRADE PRICE AUTOMAT ATTIT WEALTH...ANTHOL 20. PAGE 81 F1587
ECO/TAC MARKET ECO/DEV EFFICIENCY

B64
LUTHULI A.,AFRICA'S FREEDOM. KIN LABOR POL/PAR SCHOOL DIPLOM NEUTRAL REGION REV NAT/LISM PWR WEALTH SOCISM SOC/INTEG 20. PAGE 82 F1608
AFR ECO/UNDEV COLONIAL

B64
MAGALHAES S.,PRATICA DA EMANCIPACAO NACIONAL. L/A+17C INDUS PLAN ECO/TAC CONTROL NAT/LISM ORD/FREE. PAGE 84 F1640
BAL/PAY ECO/UNDEV DIPLOM WEALTH

B64
MARKHAM J.W.,THE COMMON MARKET: FRIEND OR COMPETITOR. AFR EUR+WWI FUT USA+45 INT/ORG LG/CO NAT/G VOL/ASSN DELIB/GP EX/STRUC PLAN TARIFFS ORD/FREE PWR WEALTH...POLICY STAT TREND EEC VAL/FREE 20. PAGE 85 F1671
ECO/DEV ECO/TAC

B64
MEZERIK A.G.,TRADE, AID AND ECONOMIC DEVELOPMENT. WOR+45 FINAN INDUS MARKET PLAN BAL/PWR BARGAIN FOR/AID TARIFFS EDU/PROP WEALTH...GP/COMP 20 UN GATT IMF IBRD. PAGE 91 F1777
ECO/TAC ECO/DEV INT/ORG INT/TRADE

B64
NOSSITER B.D.,THE MYTHMAKERS: AN ESSAY ON POWER AND WEALTH. USA+45 LG/CO NAT/G TOP/EX PROB/SOLV ADMIN GP/REL ORD/FREE 20. PAGE 99 F1937
ECO/TAC WEALTH FINAN PLAN

B64
NOVACK D.E.,DEVELOPMENT AND SOCIETY; THE DYNAMICS OF ECONOMIC CHANGE. WOR+45 STRATA STRUCT ECO/TAC CONTROL CROWD REV GP/REL ADJUST PRODUC WEALTH PSY. PAGE 99 F1940
SOCIETY CULTURE SOC ECO/UNDEV

B64
ODEH H.S.,THE IMPACT OF INFLATION ON THE LEVEL OF ECONOMIC ACTIVITY. AFR BRAZIL CHILE BUDGET GOV/REL COST DEMAND INCOME WEALTH...STAT METH 20 MONEY. PAGE 100 F1963
ECOMETRIC ECO/TAC ECO/UNDEV FINAN

B64
PAWERA J.C.,ALGERIA'S INFRASTRUCTURE. ALGERIA PLAN WEALTH...METH/CNCPT 20. PAGE 104 F2041
ECO/UNDEV INDUS TEC/DEV COM/IND

B64
POWELSON J.P.,LATIN AMERICA: TODAY'S ECONOMIC AND SOCIAL REVOLUTION. L/A+17C INTELL SOCIETY STRUCT AGRI INDUS NAT/G DIPLOM ECO/TAC REV...POLICY 20. PAGE 107 F2110
ECO/UNDEV WEALTH ADJUST PLAN

B64
RAISON T.,WHY CONSERVATIVE? UK FORCES DIPLOM ECO/TAC GIVE EDU/PROP ORD/FREE WEALTH LAISSEZ ...GOV/COMP 20 TORY/PARTY CONSRV/PAR. PAGE 109 F2137
PLURISM CONSERVE POL/PAR NAT/G

B64
RAMAZANI R.K.,THE MIDDLE EAST AND THE EUROPEAN COMMON MARKET. EUR+WWI ISLAM ECO/DEV EXTR/IND MARKET PROC/MFG INT/ORG NAT/G TEC/DEV ECO/TAC REGION DRIVE WEALTH...STAT CHARTS EEC TOT/POP 20. PAGE 109 F2141
ECO/UNDEV ATTIT INT/TRADE

B64
SHANNON I.,INTERNATIONAL LIQUIDITY. AFR FUT USA+45 WOR+45 ECO/TAC PRICE DEMAND WEALTH...CONCPT 20. PAGE 120 F2367
FINAN DIPLOM BAL/PAY ECO/DEV

B64
SINGER H.W.,INTERNATIONAL DEVELOPMENT: GROWTH AND CHANGE. AFR BRAZIL L/A+17C WOR+45 CULTURE AGRI INDUS NAT/G ACT/RES ECO/TAC EDU/PROP WEALTH...GEOG CONCPT METH/CNCPT STAT HYPO/EXP WORK TOT/POP 20. PAGE 122 F2412
FINAN ECO/UNDEV FOR/AID INT/TRADE

B64
SOLOW R.M.,THE NATURE AND SOURCES OF UNEMPLOYMENT IN THE UNITED STATES (PAMPHLET). USA+45 INDUS LABOR TEC/DEV ECO/TAC SKILL WEALTH...TREND NAT/COMP 20. PAGE 124 F2439
ECO/DEV WORKER STAT PRODUC

B64
STOESSINGER J.G.,FINANCING THE UNITED NATIONS SYSTEM. FUT WOR+45 CONSTN NAT/G VOL/ASSN DELIB/GP EX/STRUC ECO/TAC LEGIT CT/SYS PWR WEALTH...STAT TIME/SEQ TREND CHARTS TRUE/GP METH/GP TERR/GP VAL/FREE. PAGE 126 F2493
FINAN INT/ORG

B64
TAWNEY R.H.,EQUALITY. UK CULTURE STRATA ECO/TAC EDU/PROP REPRESENT OWN NEW/LIB...MAJORIT WELF/ST SOC 20. PAGE 129 F2538
WEALTH STRUCT ELITES POPULISM

B64
TAX S.,EL CAPITALISMO DEL CENTAVO; UNA ECONOMIA INDIGENA DE GUATEMALA (2 VOLS.). GUATEMALA L/A+17C SOCIETY GP/REL DEMAND INCOME HABITAT...SOC MUNICH 20 INDIAN/AM. PAGE 129 F2539
ECO/UNDEV AGRI WEALTH COST

B64
VON DER MEHDEN F.R.,POLITICS OF THE DEVELOPING NATIONS. WOR+45 CONSTN PROB/SOLV ORD/FREE WEALTH OBJECTIVE. PAGE 142 F2790
ECO/UNDEV SOCIETY STRUCT

B64
WELLISZ S.,THE ECONOMICS OF THE SOVIET BLOC. COM USSR INDUS WORKER PLAN BUDGET INT/TRADE TAX PRICE PRODUC WEALTH MARXISM...METH/COMP 20. PAGE 145 F2854
EFFICIENCY ADMIN MARKET

B64
WILLIAMSON J.G.,AMERICAN GROWTH AND THE BALANCE OF PAYMENTS, 1820-1913: A STUDY OF THE LONG SWING. EUR+WWI MOD/EUR USA+45 USA-45 ECO/DEV NAT/G ECO/TAC ROUTINE ORD/FREE WEALTH...MATH STAT TIME/SEQ CHARTS SIMUL GEN/LAWS TRUE/GP METH/GP VAL/FREE 19/20. PAGE 147 F2896
FINAN BAL/PAY

B64
ZEBOT C.A.,THE ECONOMICS OF COMPETITIVE COEXISTENCE. CHINA/COM USSR WOR+45 FINAN MARKET FOR/AID PRICE DEMAND EQUILIB WEALTH ALL/IDEOS 20. PAGE 150 F2961
TEC/DEV DIPLOM METH/COMP

L64
BHAGWATI J.,"THE PURE THEORY OF INTERNATIONAL TRADE: A SURVEY." WOR+45 ECO/DEV ECO/UNDEV FINAN MARKET PROC/MFG INT/ORG LABOR LG/CO NAT/G TEC/DEV
INDUS HYPO/EXP

ECO/TAC SKILL WEALTH...POLICY RELATIV MGT CONCPT NEW/IDEA MATH QUANT GEN/LAWS FOR/TRADE 20. PAGE 14 F0276

L64

HAAS E.B.,"ECONOMICS AND DIFFERENTIAL PATTERNS OF POLITICAL INTEGRATION: PROJECTIONS ABOUT UNITY IN LATIN AMERICA." SOCIETY NAT/G DELIB/GP ACT/RES CREATE PLAN ECO/TAC REGION ROUTINE ATTIT DRIVE PWR WEALTH...CONCPT TREND CHARTS LAFTA TERR/GP 20. PAGE 52 F1020 — L/A+17C INT/ORG MARKET

L64

STERN R.M.,"POLICIES FOR TRADE AND DEVELOPMENT." AFR FUT WOR+45 DIST/IND FINAN NAT/G DELIB/GP PLAN ECO/TAC ORD/FREE WEALTH...POLICY STAT TIME/SEQ CHARTS METH/GP 20. PAGE 126 F2480 — MARKET ECO/UNDEV INT/TRADE

S64

CLELLAND D.A.,"ECONOMIC DOMINANTS AND COMMUNITY POWER: A COMPARATIVE ANALYSIS." ELITES ADJUST ATTIT WEALTH...DECISION MUNICH. PAGE 25 F0488 — LEAD MGT PWR

S64

DOE J.F.,"TROPICAL AFRICAN CONTRIBUTIONS TO FEDERAL FINANCE." AFR NAT/G PROVS CENTRAL RIGID/FLEX PWR WEALTH...STAT VAL/FREE 20 CMN/WLTH. PAGE 33 F0650 — FINAN ECO/TAC

S64

FINLEY D.D.,"A POLITICAL PERSPECTIVE OF ECONOMIC RELATIONS IN THE COMMUNIST CAMP." COM USSR FACE/GP NAT/G ACT/RES PLAN DOMIN COERCE ATTIT ORD/FREE WEALTH...TIME/SEQ 20. PAGE 41 F0800 — VOL/ASSN ECO/TAC DIPLOM REGION

S64

GALBRAITH V.,"JAPAN'S POSITION IN WORLD TRADE." ASIA AGRI INDUS CREATE ECO/TAC LEGIT DRIVE WEALTH ...TREND EEC GATT FOR/TRADE 20 CHINJAP. PAGE 45 F0885 — ECO/DEV DELIB/GP

S64

GARDNER R.N.,"GATT AND THE UNITED NATIONS CONFERENCE ON TRADE AND DEVELOPMENT." USA+45 WOR+45 SOCIETY ECO/UNDEV MARKET NAT/G DELIB/GP ACT/RES PLAN ECO/TAC TARIFFS EDU/PROP ROUTINE DRIVE RIGID/FLEX WEALTH...DECISION MGT TREND UN TOT/POP 20 GATT. PAGE 46 F0905 — INT/ORG INT/TRADE

S64

GERBET P.,"LA MISE EN OEUVRE DU MARCHE COMMUN AGRICOLE." ECO/DEV MARKET INT/ORG NAT/G PLAN EDU/PROP NAT/LISM WEALTH...OBS EEC VAL/FREE 20. PAGE 47 F0917 — EUR+WWI AGRI REGION

S64

HABERLER G.,"INTEGRATION AND GROWTH OF THE WORLD ECONOMY IN HISTORICAL PERSPECTIVE." FUT WOR+45 WOR-45 ECO/DEV ECO/UNDEV...TIME/SEQ TREND VAL/FREE 20. PAGE 52 F1023 — WEALTH INT/TRADE

S64

HERMAN L.M.,"THE ECONOMIC CONTENT OF SOVIET TRADE WITH THE WEST." WOR+45 ECO/DEV ECO/UNDEV AGRI COM/IND INDUS CAP/ISM ECO/TAC ATTIT RIGID/FLEX WEALTH...OBS TREND VAL/FREE MARX/KARL 20. PAGE 59 F1152 — COM MARKET INT/TRADE USSR

S64

HOOVER C.B.,"THE ROLE OF THE NATURAL AND DEVELOPED RESOURCES OF THE NATION STATES." FUT WOR+45 ECO/DEV ECO/UNDEV NAT/G PWR RESPECT SKILL WEALTH...POLICY GEOG TIME/SEQ TREND RESOURCE/N VAL/FREE 20. PAGE 62 F1210 — EXTR/IND DOMIN

S64

HUELIN D.,"ECONOMIC INTEGRATION IN LATIN AMERICAN: PROGRESS AND PROBLEMS." L/A+17C ECO/DEV AGRI DIST/IND FINAN INDUS NAT/G VOL/ASSN CONSULT DELIB/GP EX/STRUC ACT/RES PLAN TEC/DEV ECO/TAC ROUTINE BAL/PAY WEALTH FOR/TRADE WORK TERR/GP 20. PAGE 63 F1232 — MARKET ECO/UNDEV INT/TRADE

S64

KLEIN H.,"AMERICAN OIL COMPANIES IN LATIN AMERICA: THE BOLIVIAN EXPERIENCE." L/A+17C USA+45 USA-45 EXTR/IND LG/CO NAT/G ECO/TAC WEALTH...POLICY GEN/LAWS BOLIV TOT/POP 20 OIL. PAGE 72 F1405 — MARKET ECO/UNDEV NAT/LISM

S64

KOJIMA K.,"THE PATTERN OF INTERNATIONAL TRADE AMONG ADVANCED COUNTRIES." EUR+WWI UK USA+45 WOR+45 MARKET NAT/G ECO/TAC WEALTH...MATH STAT CON/ANAL CHARTS METH/GP EEC CHINJAP 20 CHINJAP. PAGE 72 F1419 — ECO/DEV TREND INT/TRADE

S64

MC WILLIAM M.,"THE WORLD BANK AND THE TRANSFER OF POWER IN KENYA." AFR ECO/UNDEV CONSULT ACT/RES TEC/DEV PERCEPT PWR SKILL WEALTH...CONCPT OBS TREND 20. PAGE 88 F1715 — NAT/G ECO/TAC

S64

NEISSER H.,"THE EXTERNAL EQUILIBRIUM OF THE UNITED STATES ECONOMY." FUT USA+45 NAT/G ACT/RES PLAN ECO/TAC ATTIT WEALTH...METH/CNCPT GEN/METH VAL/FREE FOR/TRADE 20. PAGE 97 F1910 — FINAN ECO/DEV BAL/PAY INT/TRADE

S64

PADELFORD N.J.,"THE ORGANIZATION OF AFRICAN UNITY." ECO/UNDEV INT/ORG PLAN BAL/PWR DIPLOM ECO/TAC NAT/LISM ORD/FREE PWR WEALTH...CONCPT TREND STERTYP TERR/GP VAL/FREE 20. PAGE 102 F2013 — AFR VOL/ASSN REGION

S64

PATEL S.J.,"THE ECONOMIC DISTANCE BETWEEN NATIONS: ITS ORIGIN, MEASUREMENT AND OUTLOOK." WOR+45 ECO/DEV AGRI FINAN INDUS MARKET LABOR NAT/G CONSULT TEC/DEV ECO/TAC WEALTH...POLICY RELATIV MGT TREND WORK 20. PAGE 103 F2035 — ECO/UNDEV PLAN

S64

PESELT B.M.,"COMMUNIST ECONOMIC OFFENSIVE." WOR+45 SOCIETY INT/ORG PLAN ECO/TAC DOMIN EDU/PROP ATTIT PERSON PWR WEALTH...TREND CHARTS METH/GP 20. PAGE 105 F2067 — COM ECO/UNDEV FOR/AID USSR

S64

POLARIS J.,"THE SINO-SOVIET DISPUTE: ITS ECONOMIC IMPACT ON CHINA." ASIA CHINA/COM COM WOR+45 NAT/G ATTIT PWR WEALTH...STAT TREND FOR/TRADE 20. PAGE 107 F2095 — ECO/UNDEV ECO/TAC

S64

READER D.H.,"A SURVEY OF CATEGORIES OF ECONOMIC ACTIVITIES AMONG THE PEOPLES OF AFRICA." AGRI INDUS MARKET KIN HEALTH SKILL WEALTH...GEOG METH/CNCPT CHARTS TERR/GP WORK TOT/POP VAL/FREE 20. PAGE 110 F2160 — TEC/DEV ECO/UNDEV AFR

S64

RUSSETT B.M.,"INEQUALITY AND INSTABILITY: THE RELATION OF LAND TENURE TO POLITICS." WOR+45 ECO/DEV ECO/UNDEV AGRI NAT/G COERCE PWR...MATH STAT CHARTS GEN/LAWS TERR/GP TRUE/GP METH/GP VAL/FREE 20. PAGE 115 F2263 — WEALTH GEOG ECO/TAC ORD/FREE

S64

SALVADORI M.,"EL CAPITALISMO EN LA EUROPA DE LA POSGUERRA." AFR INT/ORG NAT/G POL/PAR PLAN ECO/TAC ATTIT ORD/FREE WEALTH...HIST/WRIT EEC 20. PAGE 115 F2275 — EUR+WWI ECO/DEV CAP/ISM

S64

SCHMITT H.O.,"POLITICAL CONDITIONS FOR INTERNATIONAL CURRENCY REFORM." WOR+45 SOCIETY ECO/DEV PLAN ECO/TAC BAL/PAY ATTIT ORD/FREE WEALTH ...SOC CONCPT OBS TREND EEC VAL/FREE ECSC 20. PAGE 117 F2301 — FINAN VOL/ASSN REGION

S64

WOOD N.,"THE FAMILY FIRM - BASE OF JAPAN'S GROWING ECONOMY." ECO/DEV ECO/UNDEV ECO/TAC WEALTH...POLICY TRADIT BIOG TREND 20 CHINJAP. PAGE 148 F2921 — ASIA SML/CO FAM

S64

WU Y.,"CHINA'S ECONOMY AND ITS PROSPECTS." ASIA CHINA/COM FUT USSR AGRI INDUS PLAN ECO/TAC LEGIT WEALTH...STAT CON/ANAL CHARTS GEN/LAWS FOR/TRADE 20. PAGE 149 F2938 — ECO/DEV

N64

KENYA MINISTRY ECO PLAN DEV,AFRICAN SOCIALISM AND ITS APPLICATION TO PLANNING IN KENYA (PAMPHLET). AFR AGRI INDUS WORKER TAX COLONIAL WEALTH 20. PAGE 70 F1380 — NAT/G SOCISM PLAN ECO/UNDEV

B65

ALLEN W.R.,INTERNATIONAL TRADE THEORY: HUME TO OHLIN. FINAN LABOR TARIFFS TAX PRICE DEMAND PRODUC PROFIT...ANTHOL 18/20. PAGE 4 F0074 — INT/TRADE WEALTH METH/CNCPT

B65

BELASSA B.,ECONOMIC DEVELOPMENT AND INTEGRATION. LG/CO PROB/SOLV TEC/DEV INT/TRADE TARIFFS COST WEALTH...POLICY METH/COMP 20. PAGE 12 F0232 — ECO/UNDEV ECO/TAC INT/ORG INDUS

B65

BOWEN W.G.,UNEMPLOYMENT IN A PROSPEROUS ECONOMY. USA+45 ECO/DEV NAT/G ACT/RES PLAN PAY EDU/PROP DEMAND...POLICY IDEA/COMP ANTHOL 20. PAGE 17 F0330 — WORKER ECO/TAC WEALTH PROB/SOLV

B65

CASSELL F.,GOLD OR CREDIT? THE ECONOMICS AND POLITICS OF INTERNATIONAL MONEY. AFR WOR+45 PLAN PROB/SOLV BAL/PAY SOVEREIGN WEALTH 20 OEEC. PAGE 22 F0428 — FINAN INT/ORG DIPLOM ECO/TAC

B65

CLARK T.D.,THREE PATHS TO THE MODERN SOUTH: EDUCATION, AGRICULTURE, AND CONSERVATION. FUT USA-45 ECO/DEV ECO/TAC PEACE WEALTH...POLICY 20 SOUTH/US. PAGE 25 F0485 — AGRI EDU/PROP GOV/REL REGION

B65

COUGHLIN B.J.,CHURCH AND STATE IN SOCIAL WELFARE. USA+45 RECEIVE GP/REL ORD/FREE WEALTH NEW/LIB. PAGE 28 F0542 — CULTURE SECT VOL/ASSN GIVE

B65

CRANE E.,MARKETING COMMUNICATION: A BEHAVIORAL APPROACH TO MEN, MESSAGES, AND MEDIA. STRATA R+D VOL/ASSN CROWD DRIVE PERSON SKILL WEALTH. PAGE 28 F0551 — EDU/PROP MARKET PERCEPT ATTIT

B65

DEMAS W.G.,THE ECONOMICS OF DEVELOPMENT IN SMALL COUNTRIES WITH SPECIAL REFERENCE TO THE CARIBBEAN. WOR+45 BAL/PAY DEMAND EFFICIENCY PRODUC...GEOG CARIBBEAN. PAGE 32 F0618 — ECO/UNDEV PLAN WEALTH INT/TRADE

B65

FERMAN L.A.,POVERTY IN AMERICA: A BOOK OF READINGS. USA+45 CULTURE ECO/DEV PROB/SOLV ALL/VALS...POLICY ANTHOL BIBLIOG 20 POVRTY/WAR. PAGE 40 F0785 — WEALTH TEC/DEV CONCPT

RECEIVE

B65
FRIEDLANDER S.L.,LABOR MIGRATION AND ECONOMIC GROWTH: A CASE STUDY OF PUERTO RICO. PUERT/RICO AGRI WORKER PLAN PROB/SOLV...ECOMETRIC STAT PREDICT CHARTS HYPO/EXP SIMUL 20. PAGE 44 F0858 — CENSUS GEOG ECO/UNDEV WEALTH

B65
GORDON W.,THE POLITICAL ECONOMY OF LATIN AMERICA. L/A+17C FINAN MARKET PROB/SOLV TEC/DEV RECEIVE ADMIN WEALTH 20. PAGE 49 F0962 — ECO/UNDEV INT/TRADE REGION POLICY

B65
GRAMPP W.D.,ECONOMIC LIBERALISM; THE BEGINNINGS (VOL. I). USA-45 WOR-45 MARKET LABOR ATTIT WEALTH ...POLICY CONCPT BIBLIOG GREECE/ANC MERCANTLST REPUBLICAN FEDERALIST. PAGE 50 F0974 — ECO/DEV CAP/ISM IDEA/COMP ECO/TAC

B65
GRAMPP W.D.,ECONOMIC LIBERALISM; THE CLASSICAL VIEW (VOL. II). MOD/EUR SOCIETY MARKET INT/TRADE NAT/LISM WEALTH LAISSEZ...POLICY PSY CONCPT BIBLIOG 19 SMITH/ADAM HUME/D MILL/JS. PAGE 50 F0975 — ECO/DEV CAP/ISM IDEA/COMP ECO/TAC

B65
GRIFFIN C.E.,THE FREE SOCIETY. CONSTN SOCIETY MARKET FEDERAL RATIONAL WEALTH...MAJORIT 20 CIVIL/LIB. PAGE 51 F0999 — CONCPT ORD/FREE CAP/ISM POPULISM

B65
HABERLER G.,A SURVEY OF INTERNATIONAL TRADE THEORY. CANADA FRANCE GERMANY ECO/TAC TARIFFS AGREE COST DEMAND WEALTH...ECOMETRIC 19/20 MONOPOLY TREATY. PAGE 52 F1024 — INT/TRADE BAL/PAY DIPLOM POLICY

B65
HOSELITZ B.F.,ECONOMICS AND THE IDEA OF MANKIND. UNIV ECO/DEV ECO/UNDEV DIST/IND INDUS INT/ORG NAT/G ACT/RES ECO/TAC WEALTH...CONCPT STAT. PAGE 62 F1223 — CREATE INT/TRADE

B65
IANNI O.,ESTADO E CAPITALISMO. L/A+17C FINAN TEC/DEV ECO/TAC ORD/FREE WEALTH POLICY. PAGE 64 F1258 — ECO/UNDEV STRUCT INDUS NAT/G

B65
INT. BANK RECONSTR. DEVELOP.,ECONOMIC DEVELOPMENT OF KUWAIT. ISLAM KUWAIT AGRI FINAN MARKET EX/STRUC TEC/DEV ECO/TAC ADMIN WEALTH...OBS CON/ANAL CHARTS 20. PAGE 64 F1266 — INDUS NAT/G

B65
JOHNSTONE A.,UNITED STATES DIRECT INVESTMENT IN FRANCE: AN INVESTIGATION OF THE FRENCH CHARGES. FRANCE USA+45 ECO/DEV INDUS LG/CO NAT/G ECO/TAC CONTROL WEALTH...BIBLIOG 20 INTERVENT. PAGE 68 F1335 — FINAN DIPLOM POLICY SOVEREIGN

B65
KLEIN J.J.,MONEY AND THE ECONOMY. USA+45 NAT/G DIPLOM CONTROL...POLICY T 20 FED/RESERV. PAGE 72 F1406 — FINAN PLAN WEALTH BAL/PAY

B65
LITTLE I.M.D.,INTERNATIONAL AID. UK WOR+45 AGRI INDUS GIVE RECEIVE COLONIAL BAL/PAY WEALTH...POLICY GOV/COMP METH/COMP 20. PAGE 81 F1584 — FOR/AID DIPLOM ECO/UNDEV NAT/G

B65
MARCUS E.,INTERNATIONAL TRADE AND FINANCE. EFFICIENCY EQUILIB...CHARTS METH/COMP BIBLIOG METH T 20. PAGE 85 F1664 — INT/TRADE FINAN MARKET WEALTH

B65
MONCRIEFF A.,SECOND THOUGHTS ON AID. WOR+45 ECO/UNDEV AGRI FINAN VOL/ASSN PLAN TEC/DEV GIVE EDU/PROP ROLE WEALTH 20. PAGE 93 F1816 — FOR/AID ECO/TAC INT/ORG IDEA/COMP

B65
NATIONAL CONF SOCIAL WELFARE,THE SOCIAL WELFARE FORUM, 1965. LAW CULTURE VOL/ASSN CONTROL PERS/REL ADJUST POLICY. PAGE 97 F1899 — CONSTN WEALTH ORD/FREE NEIGH

B65
OFFICE OF ECONOMIC OPPORTUNITY,CATALOG OF FEDERAL PROGRAMS FOR INDIVIDUAL AND COMMUNITY IMPROVEMENT. USA+45 WEALTH NEW/LIB 20. PAGE 101 F1980 — INDEX ECO/UNDEV RECEIVE NAT/G

B65
ONSLOW C.,ASIAN ECONOMIC DEVELOPMENT. BURMA CEYLON INDIA MALAYSIA PAKISTAN S/ASIA AGRI INDUS MARKET PROB/SOLV CAP/ISM FOR/AID INT/TRADE DEMAND WEALTH ...POLICY ANTHOL 20. PAGE 101 F1991 — ECO/UNDEV ECO/TAC PLAN NAT/G

B65
OXENFELDT A.R.,ECONOMIC SYSTEMS IN ACTION. FRANCE USA+45 USSR CULTURE PLAN PROB/SOLV TEC/DEV INCOME PRODUC WEALTH...METH/COMP 20. PAGE 102 F2007 — ECO/DEV CAP/ISM MARXISM ECO/TAC

B65
PEARL A.,NEW CAREERS FOR THE POOR: THE NON-PROFESSIONAL IN HUMAN SERVICE. USA+45 SERV/IND NAT/G NEIGH WORKER EDU/PROP AUTOMAT SKILL...WELF/ST NEW/IDEA BIBLIOG SOC/INTEG 20. PAGE 104 F2044 — SOC/WK WEALTH STRATA POLICY

B65
PROCHNOW H.V.,WORLD ECONOMIC PROBLEMS AND POLICIES. INDIA ISRAEL WOR+45 AGRI LABOR PROB/SOLV FOR/AID TARIFFS CONTROL BAL/PAY NAT/LISM WEALTH...TREND CHARTS 20 CHINJAP EEC. PAGE 108 F2124 — MARKET ECO/TAC PRODUC IDEA/COMP

B65
REAGAN M.D.,"POLITICS, ECONOMICS, AND THE GENERAL WELFARE. USA+45 INDUS ECO/TAC TAX WEALTH...POLICY IDEA/COMP ANTHOL 20. PAGE 110 F2162 — NAT/G ECO/DEV R+D ACADEM

B65
ROOSA R.V.,MONETARY REFORM FOR THE WORLD ECONOMY. AFR EUR+WWI USA+45 WOR+45 CREATE BUDGET DIPLOM FOR/AID EQUILIB WEALTH IMF. PAGE 114 F2237 — FINAN INT/ORG INT/TRADE BAL/PAY

B65
ROSS A.M.,EMPLOYMENT POLICY AND THE LABOR MARKET. USA+45 MARKET LABOR NAT/G PROB/SOLV PAY EDU/PROP PARTIC UTIL...POLICY 20. PAGE 114 F2242 — ECO/DEV WORKER WEALTH DEMAND

B65
SHARIF A.,THE BALANCE OF PAYMENTS OF PAKISTAN, 1948-1958 (THESIS, UNIVERSITY OF TORONTO). PAKISTAN FINAN INDUS FOR/AID PRICE WEALTH...TREND CHARTS 20. PAGE 120 F2368 — BAL/PAY BUDGET INT/TRADE ECO/UNDEV

B65
SHOSTAK A.B.,NEW PERSPECTIVES ON POVERTY. USA+45 SCHOOL WORKER INGP/REL RACE/REL AGE/C AGE/Y ATTIT HEALTH...ANTHOL BIBLIOG 20 JOHNSON/LB POVRTY/WAR. PAGE 121 F2388 — WEALTH NAT/G RECEIVE INCOME

B65
TEW B.,WEALTH AND INCOME. UK BUDGET INT/TRADE PRICE BAL/PAY DEMAND...CHARTS GOV/COMP 20 AUSTRAL. PAGE 129 F2546 — FINAN ECO/DEV WEALTH INCOME

B65
US OFFICE ECONOMIC OPPORTUNITY,CATALOG OF FEDERAL PROGRAMS FOR INDIVIDUAL AND COMMUNITY IMPROVEMENT. USA+45 GIVE RECEIVE ADMIN HEALTH KNOWL SKILL WEALTH ...CHARTS MUNICH. PAGE 138 F2721 — BIBLIOG CLIENT ECO/TAC

B65
US SENATE COMM ON JUDICIARY,ANTITRUST EXEMPTIONS FOR AGREEMENTS RELATING TO BALANCE OF PAYMENTS. FINAN ECO/TAC CONTROL WEALTH...POLICY 20 CONGRESS. PAGE 140 F2750 — BAL/PAY ADJUD MARKET INT/TRADE

B65
WEAVER J.N.,THE INTERNATIONAL DEVELOPMENT ASSOCIATION: A NEW APPROACH TO FOREIGN AID. USA+45 NAT/G OP/RES PLAN PROB/SOLV WEALTH...CHARTS BIBLIOG 20 UN. PAGE 144 F2836 — FOR/AID INT/ORG ECO/UNDEV FINAN

B65
WEISBROD B.A.,THE ECONOMICS OF POVERTY: AN AMERICAN PARADOX. USA+45 NAT/G WORKER TASK INGP/REL DISCRIM POLICY. PAGE 145 F2852 — ECO/DEV WEALTH RECEIVE STRATA

B65
WRIGHT L.B.,THE DREAM OF PROSPERITY IN COLONIAL AMERICA. USA-45 ECO/UNDEV AGRI EXTR/IND PARLIAMENT 17/18. PAGE 149 F2934 — PROVS WEALTH MOD/EUR

B65
WU YUAN-LI,THE ECONOMY OF COMMUNIST CHINA. CHINA/COM USSR AGRI FINAN INDUS POL/PAR WORKER PROB/SOLV INT/TRADE PRICE EATING INCOME OWN WEALTH 20. PAGE 149 F2939 — ECO/TAC MARXISM PLAN EFFICIENCY

L65
LOFTUS M.L.,"INTERNATIONAL MONETARY FUND, 1962-1965: A SELECTED BIBLIOGRAPHY." WOR+45 PLAN BUDGET INCOME PROFIT WEALTH. PAGE 81 F1596 — BIBLIOG FINAN INT/TRADE INT/ORG

L65
WILLIAMS S.,"NEGOTIATING INVESTMENT IN EMERGING COUNTRIES." USA+45 WOR+45 INDUS MARKET NAT/G TOP/EX TEC/DEV CAP/ISM ECO/TAC ADMIN SKILL WEALTH...POLICY RELATIV MGT WORK 20. PAGE 147 F2894 — FINAN ECO/UNDEV

L65
WIONCZEK M.,"LATIN AMERICA FREE TRADE ASSOCIATION." AGRI DIST/IND FINAN INDUS INT/ORG LABOR NAT/G TEC/DEV ECO/TAC HEALTH SKILL WEALTH...POLICY RELATIV MGT LAFTA 20. PAGE 148 F2909 — L/A+17C MARKET REGION

S65
CECIL C.O.,"THE DETERMINANTS OF LIBYAN FOREIGN POLICY." AFR INTELL ECO/UNDEV EXTR/IND POL/PAR CREATE REGION SOVEREIGN CONSERVE MAGHREB NASSER/G. PAGE 22 F0431 — LIBYA DIPLOM WEALTH ISLAM

S65
HADDAD W.F.,"MR. SHRIVER AND THE SAVAGE POLITICS OF POVERTY" USA+45 LAW NAT/G DELIB/GP LEGIS GIVE LEAD CENTRAL PWR...SOC/WK CHARTS 20 CONGRESS POVRTY/WAR SHRIVER/S OEO. PAGE 53 F1028 — WEALTH GOV/REL CONTROL TOP/EX

S65
HUTT W.H.,"KEYNESIAN REVISIONS" SOUTH/AFR ECO/DEV FINAN NAT/G WORKER BUDGET TAX PRICE EQUILIB WEALTH 20 KEYNES/JM. PAGE 64 F1252 — ECO/TAC GEN/LAWS LOG

S65
JOHNSON H.G.,"A THEORETICAL MODEL OF ECONOMIC NATIONALISM IN NEW AND DEVELOPING STATES." ELITES — NAT/LISM ECO/UNDEV

INDUS INT/TRADE EDU/PROP COST OPTIMAL RATIONAL PWR GEN/LAWS
WEALTH SOCISM STERTYP. PAGE 67 F1325

S65
JOHNSON L.L.,"US BUSINESS INTERESTS IN CUBA AND THE DIPLOM
RISE OF CASTRO." L/A+17C USA+45 ECO/UNDEV INDUS CUBA
NAT/G VOL/ASSN ATTIT ORD/FREE PWR WEALTH ALL/PROG. ECO/TAC
PAGE 68 F1330 INT/TRADE

S65
KAUN D.E.,"THE FAIR LABOUR STANDARDS ACT: AN ECO/TAC
EVALUATION IN TERMS OF ITS STATED GOALS." SOUTH/AFR PRICE
LAW LABOR BARGAIN PAY INGP/REL WEALTH 20. PAGE 69 WORKER
F1364 LEGIS

S65
KEE W.S.,"CENTRAL CITY EXPENDITURES AND LOC/G
METROPOLITAN AREAS." PLAN BUDGET ECO/TAC TAX GP/REL GOV/COMP
WEALTH...CHARTS MUNICH 20. PAGE 70 F1366 NEIGH

S65
KORBONSKI A.,"USA POLICY IN EAST EUROPE." COM ACT/RES
EUR+WWI GERMANY USA+45 CULTURE ECO/UNDEV EDU/PROP ECO/TAC
RIGID/FLEX WEALTH FOR/TRADE 20. PAGE 73 F1426 FOR/AID

S65
SCHROEDER G.,"LABOR PLANNING IN THE USSR." COM USSR WORKER
ECO/DEV INDUS SCHOOL PRODUC WEALTH...PREDICT PLAN
TIME/SEQ TREND TIME 20. PAGE 117 F2313 CENSUS

S65
STEENKAMP W.F.J.,"THE PROBLEM OF WAGE REGULATION." ECO/TAC
SOUTH/AFR LAW ECO/DEV ECO/UNDEV LABOR NAT/G BARGAIN PRICE
PAY INGP/REL DISCRIM WEALTH...METH/COMP 20. WORKER
PAGE 125 F2473 RATION

S65
TENDLER J.D.,"TECHNOLOGY AND ECONOMIC DEVELOPMENT* BRAZIL
THE CASE OF HYDRO VS THERMAL POWER." CONSTRUC INDUS
DIST/IND CREATE TEC/DEV INT/TRADE CENTRAL PWR SKILL ECO/UNDEV
WEALTH...MGT NAT/COMP ARGEN. PAGE 129 F2544

S65
WHITAKER A.P.,"ARGENTINA: STRUGGLE FOR RECOVERY." POL/PAR
L/A+17C USA+45 NAT/G TOP/EX PLAN LEGIT COERCE REV ECO/TAC
RIGID/FLEX PWR WEALTH...RECORD ALL/PROG ARGEN NAT/LISM
FOR/TRADE 20. PAGE 146 F2867

N65
STUDY GP CREATE RESERVE ASSETS,REPORT TO DEPUTIES INT/ORG
(PAMPHLET). AFR FUT PLAN CONTROL DEMAND WEALTH INT/TRADE
...ANTHOL METH 20. PAGE 127 F2507 FINAN
BUDGET

B66
AMER ENTERPRISE INST PUB POL,SIGNIFICANT ISSUES IN ECO/UNDEV
ECONOMIC AID TO DEVELOPING COUNTRIES. FINAN INT/ORG FOR/AID
NAT/G PLAN PROB/SOLV GIVE TASK WEALTH...DECISION DIPLOM
20. PAGE 4 F0083 POLICY

B66
ANDRESKI S.,PARASITISM AND SUBVERSION* THE CASE OF L/A+17C
LATIN AMERICA. CULTURE ECO/UNDEV LABOR NAT/G SECT GOV/COMP
PROB/SOLV RACE/REL TOTALISM ATTIT WEALTH ALL/IDEOS. STRATA
PAGE 5 F0100 REV

B66
BOWEN H.R.,AUTOMATION AND ECONOMIC PROGRESS. AUTOMAT
EUR+WWI USA+45 ECO/DEV INCOME ORD/FREE WEALTH TEC/DEV
...POLICY ANTHOL 20. PAGE 17 F0327 WORKER
LEISURE

B66
BOYD H.W.,MARKETING MANAGEMENT: CASES FROM EMERGING MGT
COUNTRIES. BRAZIL GHANA ISRAEL WOR+45 ADMIN ECO/UNDEV
PERS/REL ATTIT HABITAT WEALTH...ANTHOL 20 ARGEN PROB/SOLV
CASEBOOK. PAGE 17 F0332 MARKET

B66
BROWN R.T.,TRANSPORT AND THE ECONOMIC INTEGRATION MARKET
OF SOUTH AMERICA. L/A+17C ECO/UNDEV NAT/G OP/RES DIST/IND
DIPLOM INT/TRADE REGION WEALTH...ECOMETRIC GEOG SIMUL
STAT LAFTA TIME. PAGE 19 F0373

B66
CURRIE L.,ACCELERATING DEVELOPMENT: THE NECESSITY PLAN
AND MEANS. COLOMBIA USA+45 INDUS DIPLOM EFFICIENCY ECO/UNDEV
WEALTH...METH/CNCPT NEW/IDEA 20. PAGE 29 F0564 FOR/AID
TEC/DEV

B66
ECONOMIC RESEARCH SERVICE,RESEARCH DATA ON MINORITY BIBLIOG/A
GROUPS: AN ANNOTATED BIBLIOGRAPHY OF ECONOMIC DISCRIM
RESEARCH SERVICE REPORTS: 1955-1965 (PAMPHLET). WEALTH
USA+45 STRATA ECO/DEV AGRI SCHOOL WORKER EDU/PROP RACE/REL
HEALTH NEW/LIB SOC. PAGE 36 F0697

B66
FELLNER W.,MAINTAINING AND RESTORING BALANCE IN BAL/PAY
INTERNATIONAL PAYMENTS. ECO/UNDEV MARKET ECO/TAC DIPLOM
PRICE INCOME WEALTH...POLICY METH/COMP 20 MONEY. FINAN
PAGE 40 F0781 INT/TRADE

B66
FUSFELD D.R.,THE AGE OF THE ECONOMIST. ECO/TAC PHIL/SCI
WEALTH LAISSEZ MARXISM...EPIST 18/20 KEYNES/JM. CAP/ISM
PAGE 45 F0878 POLICY

B66
GORDON R.A.,PROSPERITY AND UNEMPLOYMENT. USA+45 WORKER
PLAN ECO/TAC ADJUST DEMAND ALL/VALS...POLICY INDUS
DECISION TREND CHARTS ANTHOL 20. PAGE 49 F0961 ECO/DEV
WEALTH

B66
HOROWITZ D.,HEMISPHERES NORTH AND SOUTH: ECONOMIC ECO/TAC
DISPARITY AMONG NATIONS. WOR+45 ECO/DEV ECO/UNDEV FOR/AID
INT/ORG PLAN DIPLOM INT/TRADE GIVE PARTIC GP/REL STRATA
...WELF/ST 20. PAGE 62 F1215 WEALTH

B66
INTERNATIONAL ECO POLICY ASSN,THE UNITED STATES BAL/PAY
BALANCE OF PAYMENTS. INT/ORG NAT/G PROB/SOLV BUDGET ECO/TAC
DIPLOM INT/TRADE WEALTH 20. PAGE 65 F1274 POLICY
FINAN

B66
JACKSON G.D.,COMINTERN AND PEASANT IN EAST EUROPE MARXISM
1919-1930. BULGARIA COM CZECHOSLVK EUR+WWI POLAND ECO/UNDEV
ROMANIA YUGOSLAVIA STRATA AGRI VOL/ASSN DIPLOM WORKER
CONTROL CROWD WEALTH...POLICY NAT/COMP 20. PAGE 66 INT/ORG
F1293

B66
KAREFA-SMART J.,AFRICA: PROGRESS THROUGH ORD/FREE
COOPERATION. AFR FINAN TEC/DEV DIPLOM FOR/AID ECO/UNDEV
EDU/PROP CONFER REGION GP/REL WEALTH...HEAL VOL/ASSN
SOC/INTEG 20. PAGE 69 F1356 PLAN

B66
KEENLEYSIDE H.L.,INTERNATIONAL AID: A SUMMARY. AFR ECO/UNDEV
INDIA S/ASIA UK STRATA EXTR/IND TEC/DEV ADMIN FOR/AID
RACE/REL DEMAND NAT/LISM WEALTH...TREND CHINJAP. DIPLOM
PAGE 70 F1367 TASK

B66
KUZNETS S.,MODERN ECONOMIC GROWTH. WOR+45 WOR-45 TIME/SEQ
ECO/DEV ECO/UNDEV AGRI FINAN INDUS TEC/DEV WEALTH
EFFICIENCY INCOME...NAT/COMP 19/20. PAGE 74 F1456 PRODUC

B66
LEWIS W.A.,DEVELOPMENT PLANNING; THE ESSENTIALS OF PLAN
ECONOMIC POLICY. USA+45 FINAN INDUS NAT/G WORKER ECO/DEV
FOR/AID INT/TRADE ADMIN ROUTINE WEALTH...CONCPT POLICY
STAT. PAGE 79 F1552 CREATE

B66
LICHTMAN R.,TOWARD COMMUNITY (PAPER). PLAN NEW/LIB
PROB/SOLV WEALTH MARXISM...HEAL CONCPT 20. PAGE 80 EFFICIENCY
F1561 CAP/ISM
ADJUST

B66
MASON E.S.,ECONOMIC DEVELOPMENT IN INDIA AND NAT/COMP
PAKISTAN. INDIA PAKISTAN AGRI FINAN PLAN BUDGET ECO/UNDEV
INT/TRADE WEALTH...POLICY STAT TREND CHARTS 20. ECO/TAC
PAGE 87 F1700 FOR/AID

B66
OHLIN G.,AID AND INDEBTEDNESS. AUSTRIA FINAN FOR/AID
INT/ORG PLAN DIPLOM GIVE...POLICY MATH CHARTS 20. ECO/UNDEV
PAGE 101 F1984 ADMIN
WEALTH

B66
ORG FOR ECO COOP AND DEVEL,GEOGRAPHICAL FINAN
DISTRIBUTION OF FINANCIAL FLOWS TO LESS DEVELOPED ECO/UNDEV
COUNTRIES. WOR+45 DIPLOM INT/TRADE GIVE RECEIVE INT/ORG
REPAR REGION WEALTH...GEOG STAT CHARTS 20 OECD. FOR/AID
PAGE 102 F1997

B66
RAYBACK J.G.,A HISTORY OF AMERICAN LABOR. USA+45 LABOR
USA-45 ECO/DEV LEGIS COLONIAL WAR INGP/REL PWR LOBBY
WEALTH 17/20. PAGE 110 F2156 ECO/UNDEV
NAT/G

B66
SOMMERFELD R.M.,TAX REFORM AND THE ALLIANCE FOR TAX
PROGRESS. USA+45 ECO/DEV ECO/UNDEV FINAN NAT/G INT/ORG
INCOME ORD/FREE WEALTH...STAT CHARTS 20 ALL/PROG. L/A+17C
PAGE 124 F2442 FOR/AID

B66
TRIFFIN R.,THE WORLD MONEY MAZE. AFR INT/ORG BAL/PAY
ECO/TAC PRICE OPTIMAL WEALTH...METH/COMP 20 EEC FINAN
OEEC SILVER. PAGE 131 F2589 INT/TRADE
DIPLOM

B66
TURNER H.A.,PRICES, WAGES, AND INCOME POLICIES IN PRICE
INDUSTRIALIZED MARKET ECONOMIES. AFR WOR+45 ECO/DEV PAY
INDUS PROB/SOLV ECO/TAC CONTROL WEALTH...CHARTS 20 MARKET
INTRVN/ECO. PAGE 131 F2593 INCOME

B66
US SENATE COMM APPROPRIATIONS,FOREIGN ASSISTANCE BUDGET
AND RELATED AGENCIES APPROPRIATIONS FOR FISCAL YEAR FOR/AID
1967: HEARINGS... ON H. R. 17788. ECO/UNDEV INT/ORG DIPLOM
FORCES INSPECT ECO/TAC GIVE DEBATE WEAPON COST
CIVMIL/REL WEALTH...INT 20 CONGRESS DEPT/DEFEN
DEPT/STATE DEPT/HEW AID. PAGE 138 F2727

B66
WECHSBERG J.,THE MERCHANT BANKERS. EUR+WWI MOD/EUR FINAN
CONTROL...BIOG GP/COMP PERS/COMP 16/20. PAGE 144 PWR
F2842 WEALTH
FAM

B66
WETTER G.A.,SOVIET IDEOLOGY TODAY. USSR ECO/UNDEV ALL/IDEOS
SECT WORKER CAP/ISM CONTROL TASK EFFICIENCY MARXISM
TOTALISM DRIVE WEALTH...TREND 18/20. PAGE 145 F2864 REV

L66
AFRICAN BIBLIOGRAPHIC CENTER,"AFRICAN ECONOMIC BIBLIOG
AFFAIRS: A SELECT BIBLIOGRAPHICAL SURVEY, ECO/UNDEV
1965-1966." AFR FINAN INDUS INT/ORG LABOR PLAN TEC/DEV
BUDGET DIPLOM INT/TRADE ADMIN EFFICIENCY WEALTH 20. FOR/AID
PAGE 3 F0046

S66
ANGELL J.W.,"THE LONGER RUN PROSPECTS FOR THE US BALANCE OF PAYMENTS." USA+45 DIPLOM FOR/AID RATION ORD/FREE WEALTH...IDEA/COMP GATT. PAGE 6 F0104
BAL/PAY ECO/TAC INT/TRADE FINAN

S66
FROMM G.,"RECENT MONETARY POLICY: AN ECONOMETRIC VIEW" USA+45 ECO/DEV INDUS PAY PRICE PRODUC ORD/FREE WEALTH...STAT 20 FED/RESERV. PAGE 45 F0869
ECOMETRIC FINAN POLICY SIMUL

S66
JACOBS P.,"RE-RADICALIZING THE DE-RADICALIZED." USA+45 SOCIETY STRUCT FINAN PLAN PROB/SOLV CAP/ISM WEALTH CONSERVE NEW/LIB 20. PAGE 66 F1297
NAT/G POLICY MARXIST ADMIN

S66
NEWLYN W.T.,"MONEY MARKETS IN EAST AFRICA." AFR TANZANIA UGANDA UK DIPLOM CENTRAL 20. PAGE 98 F1923
FINAN WEALTH BAL/PAY ECO/UNDEV

N66
BRITISH DEVELOPMENT POLICIES: 1966 (PAMPHLET). UK AGRI TARIFFS BAL/PAY...TREND CHARTS 20 OVRSEA/DEV. PAGE 1 F0023
WEALTH DIPLOM INT/TRADE FOR/AID

B67
AARON H.J.,FINANCING URBAN DEVELOPMENT IN MEXICO CITY: A CASE STUDY OF PROPERTY TAX, LAND USE, HOUSING, AND URBAN PLANNING. LOC/G CREATE EFFICIENCY WEALTH...CHARTS MUNICH 20 MEXIC/AMER. PAGE 2 F0030
PLAN TAX PROB/SOLV

B67
BANFIELD E.C.,THE MORAL BASIS OF A BACKWARD SOCIETY. EUR+WWI ITALY STRATA NEIGH PARTIC INGP/REL ...SOC QU PREDICT TREND HYPO/EXP MUNICH 20. PAGE 9 F0173
MORAL WEALTH ATTIT

B67
BEAL E.F.,THE PRACTICE OF COLLECTIVE BARGAINING (3RD ED.). USA+45 WOR+45 ECO/DEV INDUS LG/CO PROF/ORG WORKER ECO/TAC GP/REL WEALTH...JURID METH/CNCPT. PAGE 12 F0221
BARGAIN MGT LABOR ADJUD

B67
BERGMANN D KAUN B.,STRUCTURAL UNEMPLOYMENT IN THE UNITED STATES. USA+45 ECO/DEV PRICE ADMIN INGP/REL DEMAND EQUILIB WEALTH...MATH REGRESS STAT 20 NEGRO. PAGE 13 F0258
ECOMETRIC METH WORKER ECO/TAC

B67
CLEGERN W.M.,BRITISH HONDURAS: COLONIAL DEAD END, 1859-1900. HONDURAS AGRI FINAN PROB/SOLV INT/TRADE PWR WEALTH...BIBLIOG/A 19. PAGE 25 F0487
COLONIAL POLICY ECO/UNDEV DOMIN

B67
COHEN M.R.,LAW AND THE SOCIAL ORDER: ESSAYS IN LEGAL PHILOSOPHY. USA-45 CONSULT WORKER ECO/TAC ATTIT WEALTH...POLICY WELF/ST SOC 20 NEW/DEAL DEPRESSION. PAGE 26 F0497
JURID LABOR IDEA/COMP

B67
ELDREDGE H.W.,TAMING MEGALOPOLIS; HOW TO MANAGE AN URBANIZED WORLD. WOR+45 SOCIETY ECO/DEV ECO/UNDEV NAT/G COMPUTER CREATE PARTIC EFFICIENCY WEALTH ...MGT ANTHOL MUNICH. PAGE 37 F0716
TEC/DEV PLAN PROB/SOLV

B67
ELDREDGE H.W.,TAMING MEGALOPOLIS; WHAT IT IS AND WHAT COULD BE (VOL. I). FUT USA+45 WOR+45 SOCIETY STRUCT ECO/DEV INDUS LEISURE WEALTH...ANTHOL MUNICH. PAGE 37 F0717
PROB/SOLV PLAN TEC/DEV

B67
ENKE S.,DEFENSE MANAGEMENT. USA+45 R+D FORCES WORKER PLAN ECO/TAC ADMIN NUC/PWR BAL/PAY UTIL WEALTH...MGT DEPT/DEFEN. PAGE 38 F0738
DECISION DELIB/GP EFFICIENCY BUDGET

B67
GREEN C.,NEGATIVE TAXES AND THE POVERTY PROBLEM. COST EFFICIENCY INCOME NEW/LIB...METH/CNCPT CHARTS METH/COMP BIBLIOG 20. PAGE 50 F0983
TAX RECEIVE WEALTH PLAN

B67
HODGKINSON R.G.,THE ORIGINS OF THE NATIONAL HEALTH SERVICE: THE MEDICAL SERVICES OF THE NEW POOR LAW, 1834-1871. UK INDUS WORKER PROB/SOLV EFFICIENCY ATTIT HEALTH WEALTH SOCISM...JURID SOC/WK MUNICH 19/20. PAGE 60 F1189
HEAL NAT/G POLICY LAW

B67
HOGAN J.,THE US BALANCE OF PAYMENTS AND CAPITAL FLOWS. MARKET INT/ORG ECO/TAC PRICE CONTROL WEALTH ...METH/COMP 20 EEC. PAGE 61 F1192
BAL/PAY FINAN DIPLOM INT/TRADE

B67
JOHNSON H.G.,ECONOMIC POLICY TOWARD LESS DEVELOPED COUNTRIES. USA+45 ECO/DEV INT/ORG PLAN CAP/ISM FOR/AID TARIFFS GIVE WEALTH...NEW/IDEA CHARTS 20 UN GATT. PAGE 67 F1327
ECO/UNDEV ECO/TAC METH/COMP

B67
KREININ M.E.,ALTERNATIVE COMMERCIAL POLICIES - THEIR EFFECT ON THE AMERICAN ECONOMY. USA+45 LAW ECO/DEV MARKET INT/ORG DIPLOM ECO/TAC TARIFFS PRICE DEMAND WEALTH...QUANT EEC AFTA. PAGE 73 F1437
INT/TRADE BAL/PAY NAT/G POLICY

B67
LINDER S.B.,TRADE AND TRADE POLICY FOR DEVELOPMENT. OP/RES DIPLOM TARIFFS UTIL WEALTH...BIBLIOG 20. PAGE 80 F1569
ECO/UNDEV ECO/TAC TEC/DEV INT/TRADE

B67
MARRIS P.,DILEMMAS OF SOCIAL REFORM: POVERTY AND COMMUNITY ACTION IN THE UNITED STATES. USA+45 NAT/G OP/RES ADMIN PARTIC EFFICIENCY WEALTH...SOC METH/COMP T MUNICH 20 REFORMERS. PAGE 85 F1674
STRUCT PROB/SOLV COST

B67
MOSS F.M.,THE WATER CRISIS. PROB/SOLV CONTROL ...POLICY NEW/IDEA. PAGE 94 F1846
GEOG ACT/RES PRODUC WEALTH

B67
NARVER J.C.,CONGLOMERATE MERGERS AND MARKET COMPETITION. USA+45 LAW STRUCT ADMIN LEAD RISK COST PROFIT WEALTH...POLICY CHARTS BIBLIOG. PAGE 96 F1892
DEMAND LG/CO MARKET MGT

B67
OFER G.,THE SERVICE INDUSTRIES IN A DEVELOPING ECONOMY: ISRAEL AS A CASE STUDY. ISRAEL ECO/TAC INT/TRADE PRODUC WEALTH SOCISM...TIME/SEQ TREND CHARTS 20. PAGE 101 F1979
DIPLOM ECO/DEV SERV/IND

B67
POLLACK N.,THE POPULIST MIND. USA-45 STRATA AGRI NAT/G POL/PAR LEGIS WORKER RACE/REL WEALTH...ANTHOL BIBLIOG 19 NEGRO. PAGE 107 F2097
POPULISM HIST/WRIT ATTIT INGP/REL

B67
POWLEDGE F.,BLACK POWER WHITE RESISTANCE. USA+45 STRUCT PLAN GP/REL DISCRIM HABITAT ORD/FREE WEALTH ...METH/COMP SOC/INTEG NEGRO. PAGE 107 F2111
RACE/REL ATTIT PWR

B67
ROBINSON R.D.,INTERNATIONAL MANAGEMENT. LAW MARKET LABOR PRICE CONTROL COST DEMAND OWN PRODUC WEALTH 20. PAGE 113 F2225
T OP/RES MGT DIPLOM

B67
ROSS A.M.,EMPLOYMENT, RACE, AND POVERTY. USA+45 LAW STRATA MARKET LABOR EDU/PROP ISOLAT SKILL...MGT ANTHOL 20 NEGRO. PAGE 114 F2244
RACE/REL WORKER WEALTH DISCRIM

B67
SCOTT J.C.,ANTITRUST AND TRADE REGULATION TODAY: 1967. USA+45 MARKET LG/CO DELIB/GP LEGIS CAP/ISM INT/TRADE TAX PRICE INGP/REL WEALTH 20 SUPREME/CT. PAGE 118 F2334
NAT/G INDUS CONTROL JURID

B67
SMITH T.L.,THE PROCESS OF RURAL DEVELOPMENT IN LATIN AMERICA (A MONOGRAPH). L/A+17C STRATA INDUS PLAN GP/REL PERS/REL RIGID/FLEX WEALTH...OBS CHARTS ORG/CHARTS ANTHOL 20 COLOMB. PAGE 123 F2434
IDEA/COMP SOC AGRI ECO/UNDEV

B67
TANSKY L.,US AND USSR AID TO DEVELOPING COUNTRIES. INDIA TURKEY USA+45 USSR INDUS PLAN CAP/ISM WAR PWR WEALTH MARXISM...CHARTS NAT/COMP BIBLIOG 20. PAGE 128 F2534
ECO/UNDEV FOR/AID DIPLOM ECO/TAC

B67
TANSKY L.,US AND USSR AID TO DEVELOPING COUNTRIES. INDIA TURKEY UAR USA+45 USSR FINAN PLAN TEC/DEV ADMIN WEALTH...TREND METH/COMP 20. PAGE 128 F2535
FOR/AID ECO/UNDEV MARXISM CAP/ISM

B67
TUMIN M.M.,SOCIAL STRATIFICATION; THE FORMS AND FUNCTIONS OF INEQUALITY. SENIOR SANCTION WEALTH ...SOC CLASSIF METH 20. PAGE 131 F2592
STRATA DISCRIM CONCPT SOCIETY

B67
US CONGRESS JOINT ECO COMM,AN ECONOMIC PROFILE OF MAINLAND CHINA, VOLUMES I AND II. CHINA/COM AGRI DIST/IND FINAN INDUS LABOR FORCES ACT/RES PLAN INT/TRADE INGP/REL BAL/PAY 20 CONGRESS. PAGE 135 F2664
ECO/UNDEV WEALTH ECO/TAC DELIB/GP

B67
WEINBERG M.,SCHOOL INTEGRATION: A COMPREHENSIVE CLASSIFIED BIBLIOGRAPHY OF 3,100 REFERENCES. USA+45 LAW NAT/G NEIGH SECT PLAN ROUTINE AGE/C WEALTH SOC/INTEG INDIAN/AM. PAGE 145 F2849
BIBLIOG SCHOOL DISCRIM RACE/REL

L67
GLAZER N.,"HOUSING PROBLEMS AND HOUSING POLICIES." USA+45 PLAN RENT ADJUST CONSEN DEMAND DISCRIM AGE ATTIT HEALTH WEALTH MUNICH NEGRO. PAGE 48 F0929
POLICY CONSTRUC CREATE HABITAT

L67
MACDONALD R.M.,"COLLECTIVE BARGAINING IN THE POSTWAR PERIOD." WORKER PROB/SOLV ECO/TAC PARTIC RISK CENTRAL EFFICIENCY DRIVE WEALTH...TREND 20. PAGE 83 F1624
LABOR INDUS BARGAIN CAP/ISM

L67
STRUVE G.M.,"THE LESS-RESTRICTIVE-ALTERNATIVE PRINCIPLE AND ECONOMIC DUE PROCESS." USA+45 ECO/DEV LABOR NAT/G CONSULT DELIB/GP OP/RES PLAN WEALTH. PAGE 127 F2505
JURID JUDGE SANCTION CAP/ISM

L67
VIA J.W. JR.,"ANTITRUST AND THE AMENDED BANK MERGER AND HOLDING COMPANY ACTS: THE SEARCH FOR STANDARDS." USA+45 CONTROL GP/REL WEALTH SUPREME/CT. PAGE 141 F2783
FINAN CT/SYS LAW EX/STRUC

S67
ALPANDER G.G.,"ENTREPRENEURS AND PRIVATE ENTERPRISE IN TURKEY." TURKEY INDUS PROC/MFG EDU/PROP ATTIT DRIVE WEALTH...GEOG MGT SOC STAT TREND CHARTS 20. PAGE 4 F0077
ECO/UNDEV LG/CO NAT/G POLICY

S67
AVTORKHANOV A.,"A NEW AGRARIAN REVOLUTION." COM USSR ECO/DEV PLAN TEC/DEV ADMIN CONTROL OPTIMAL WEALTH SOCISM 20 KHRUSH/N STALIN/J. PAGE 8 F0144
AGRI METH/COMP MARXISM OWN

S67
BAILEY S.L.,"THE ITALIANS AND ORGANIZED LABOR IN THE UNITED STATES AND ARGENTINA: 1880-1910." ITALY USA-45 PARTIC HABITAT PWR...GEOG GP/COMP 19/20 ARGEN. PAGE 8 F0153
LABOR LEAD WEALTH GP/REL

S67
BRAUCHER R.,"RECLAMATION OF GOODS FROM A FRAUDULENT BUYER." USA+45 CLIENT FINAN CT/SYS PERS/REL COST WEALTH. PAGE 18 F0341
LAW ADJUD GOV/REL INT/TRADE

S67
DANIEL C.,"FREEDOM, EQUITY, AND THE WAR ON POVERTY." USA+45 WORKER ECO/TAC JURID. PAGE 30 F0578
WEALTH INCOME SOCIETY ORD/FREE

S67
FADDEYEV N.,"CMEA CO-OPERATION OF EQUAL NATIONS." COM R+D PLAN CAP/ISM DIPLOM FOR/AID WEALTH...POLICY MARXIST. PAGE 39 F0758
MARXISM ECO/TAC INT/ORG ECO/UNDEV

S67
FOX R.G.,"FAMILY, CASTE, AND COMMERCE IN A NORTH INDIAN MARKET TOWN." INDIA STRATA AGRI FACE/GP FAM NEIGH OP/RES BARGAIN ADMIN ROUTINE WEALTH...SOC CHARTS 20. PAGE 43 F0838
CULTURE GP/REL ECO/UNDEV DIST/IND

S67
FRANKEL T.,"ECONOMIC REFORM* A TENTATIVE APPRAISAL." COM USSR OP/RES BUDGET CONFER EFFICIENCY PRODUC MARXISM SOCISM...MGT 20. PAGE 43 F0847
ECO/DEV INDUS PLAN WEALTH

S67
FRANKLIN N.N.,"THE CONCEPT AND MEASUREMENT OF 'MINIMUM LIVING STANDARDS'." UNIV OP/RES PAY INGP/REL DEMAND INCOME DRIVE WEALTH...SOC CHARTS METH/COMP. PAGE 43 F0849
CONCPT PHIL/SCI ALL/VALS HAPPINESS

S67
FRIEDEN B.J.,"THE CHANGING PROSPECTS FOR SOCIAL PLANNING." USA+45 PROB/SOLV RACE/REL WEALTH ...SOC/WK PREDICT MUNICH 20 NEGRO. PAGE 44 F0856
PLAN LOC/G POLICY

S67
FUCHS V.R.,"REDEFINING POVERTY AND REDISTRIBUTING INCOME." USA+45 NAT/G ECO/TAC GIVE COST...NEW/IDEA CHARTS. PAGE 45 F0873
WEALTH INCOME STRATA PROB/SOLV

S67
GATELL F.O.,"MONEY AND PARTY IN JACKSONIAN AMERICA* A QUANTITATIVE LOOK AT NEW YORK CITY'S MEN OF QUALITY." USA-45 STRATA SECT SUFF CONSEN MAJORITY ATTIT...CHARTS HYPO/EXP 19. PAGE 46 F0908
WEALTH POL/PAR PERSON IDEA/COMP

S67
GREEN C.,"SCHEMES FOR TRANSFERRING INCOME TO THE POOR." BUDGET GIVE RECEIVE DEBATE COST INCOME ...SOC/WK METH/COMP. PAGE 50 F0982
TAX WEALTH PLAN ACT/RES

S67
HILDEBRAND G.H.,"SECOND THOUGHTS ON THE NEGATIVE INCOME TAX." PLAN BUDGET ECO/TAC GIVE RECEIVE DEBATE EFFICIENCY INCOME...METH/COMP COSTS. PAGE 59 F1169
TAX WEALTH SOC/WK ACT/RES

S67
HILL L.W.,"FINANCING URBAN RENEWAL PROGRAMS." USA+45 ECO/DEV LOC/G EDU/PROP MUNICH 20. PAGE 60 F1171
FINAN NAT/G WEALTH

S67
KOTLER P.,"OPERATIONS RESEARCH IN MARKETING." USA+45 DIST/IND INDUS LG/CO CONSULT BUDGET TASK DEMAND EFFICIENCY PROFIT WEALTH DECISION. PAGE 73 F1429
ECOMETRIC OP/RES MARKET PLAN

S67
LEVIN T.,"PSYCHOANALYSIS AND SOCIAL CHANGE." SOCIETY ANOMIE DRIVE PWR 20. PAGE 79 F1541
PSY PHIL/SCI ADJUST WEALTH

S67
MAJSTRENKO I.W.,"PROBLEMS CONFRONTING SOVIET AGRICULTURE." COM USSR ECO/DEV ECO/TAC EFFICIENCY OPTIMAL WEALTH MARXISM 20. PAGE 84 F1643
AGRI PROB/SOLV CENTRAL TEC/DEV

S67
MALKIN A.,"BUSINESS BOOKS OF 1966." INDUS LABOR OP/RES TEC/DEV CAP/ISM ECO/TAC INCOME WEALTH 20. PAGE 84 F1649
BIBLIOG/A FINAN MARKET

S67
MEADE J.E.,"POPULATION EXPLOSION, THE STANDARD OF LIVING AND SOCIAL CONFLICT." DIPLOM FOR/AID OWN ...PREDICT TREND 20. PAGE 89 F1739
GEOG WEALTH PRODUC INCOME

S67
MENCHER S.,"THE PROBLEM OF MEASURING POVERTY." UNIV USA+45 STRATA PROB/SOLV...NEW/IDEA METH/COMP 20. PAGE 89 F1755
WEALTH CENSUS STAT GEN/LAWS

S67
MOONEY J.D.,"URBAN POVERTY AND LABOR FORCE PARTICIPATION." FAM DISCRIM...SOC/WK STAT CHARTS MUNICH. PAGE 93 F1820
INCOME WORKER WEALTH

S67
MUNDHEIM R.H.,"SOME THOUGHTS ON THE DUTIES AND RESPONSIBILITIES OF UNAFFILIATED DIRECTORS OF MUTUAL FUNDS." USA+45 LG/CO SML/CO CONSULT LEAD PARTIC. PAGE 95 F1861
FINAN WEALTH ECO/TAC ADMIN

S67
MYRDAL G.,"ECONOMIC DEVELOPMENT IN THE BACKWARD COUNTRIES." INT/ORG TEC/DEV CAP/ISM DIPLOM INT/TRADE PRODUC WEALTH 20. PAGE 96 F1883
ECO/UNDEV INDUS NAT/G ECO/TAC

S67
NOURSE E.G.,"EARLY FLOWERING OF THE EMPLOYMENT ACT" USA+45 LABOR CONSULT DELIB/GP LEGIS BUDGET GOV/REL PRODUC WEALTH 20 INTRVN/ECO. PAGE 99 F1939
NAT/G WORKER ECO/TAC CONTROL

S67
PAI G.A.,"TAXATION AND PLANNING IN INDIA: A BIRDS-EYE VIEW." INDIA ELITES NAT/G LEGIS BUDGET CONTROL LOBBY INCOME...STAT CHARTS 20. PAGE 102 F2015
TAX PLAN WEALTH STRATA

S67
PENNEY N.,"BANK STATEMENTS, CANCELLED CHECKS, AND ARTICLE FOUR IN THE ELECTRONIC AGE." USA+45 TEC/DEV COST EFFICIENCY WEALTH. PAGE 104 F2056
CREATE LAW ADJUD FINAN

S67
RICHMAN B.M.,"CAPITALISTS & MANAGERS IN COMMUNIST CHINA." ASIA CHINA/COM ECO/UNDEV NAT/G CONSULT EX/STRUC PLAN EFFICIENCY PRODUC WEALTH MARXISM ...MGT CHARTS 20. PAGE 111 F2185
CAP/ISM INDUS

S67
SCHWARZWELLER H.K.,"SOCIAL CLASS ORIGINS, RURAL-URBAN MIGRATION, AND ECONOMIC LIFE CHANGES." USA+45 SOCIETY STRUCT FAM NEIGH INCOME...SOC RECORD CHARTS MUNICH. PAGE 118 F2326
CLASSIF WEALTH AGRI

S67
SCOTT R.,"TRADE UNIONS IN AFRICA." AFR UGANDA USA-45 ECO/UNDEV INDUS INT/ORG POL/PAR ECO/TAC WEALTH...GP/COMP 20 NKRUMAH/K. PAGE 118 F2335
LABOR WORKER NAT/G

S67
SPITTMANN I.,"EAST GERMANY: THE SWINGING PENDULUM." COM GERMANY/E NAT/G EFFICIENCY MARXISM 20. PAGE 125 F2458
PRODUC POL/PAR WEALTH ATTIT

S67
THORKELSON H.,"FOOD STAMPS AND HUNGER IN AMERICA." USA+45 LAW DELIB/GP ADMIN COST DEMAND POLICY. PAGE 130 F2570
WEALTH RECEIVE EATING PLAN

B75
JEVONS W.S.,MONEY AND THE MECHANISM OF EXCHANGE. INDUS MARKET DIPLOM COST EQUILIB WEALTH LAISSEZ ...GEN/LAWS 19 MONEY. PAGE 67 F1319
PRICE FINAN ECO/TAC POLICY

B76
PROUDHON P.J.,WHAT IS PROPERTY? (TRANS. BY B.R. TUCKER). SOCIETY AGRI CAP/ISM CRIME GP/REL PERSON MORAL ORD/FREE WEALTH. PAGE 108 F2127
OWN WORKER PRODUC ANARCH

B76
SMITH A.,THE WEALTH OF NATIONS. UK STRUCT WORKER DIPLOM ECO/TAC OPTIMAL DRIVE PERSON ORD/FREE ...OLD/LIB GEN/LAWS 17/18. PAGE 123 F2428
WEALTH PRODUC INDUS LAISSEZ

B76
TAINE H.A.,THE ANCIENT REGIME. FRANCE STRATA FORCES PARTIC EQUILIB WEALTH CONSERVE POPULISM...GOV/COMP SOC/INTEG 18/19. PAGE 128 F2527
NAT/G GOV/REL TAX REV

B84
MILL J.,ELEMENTS OF POLITICAL ECONOMY. UK LAW ELITES FINAN WORKER ECO/TAC RENT OWN WEALTH ...POLICY GEN/LAWS 19. PAGE 91 F1785
TAX TARIFFS NAT/G INCOME

L86
OSGOOD H.L.,"SCIENTIFIC SOCIALISM: RODBERTUS" GERMANY CAP/ISM COST WEALTH...MAJORIT BIOG IDEA/COMP 19 RODBRTUS/C. PAGE 102 F2002
SOCISM MARXISM ECO/DEV ECO/TAC

S86
SMITH R.M.,"THE NATIONAL BUREAU OF LABOR AND
LABOR

INDUSTRIAL DEPRESSIONS" USA-45 DELIB/GP BARGAIN CONTROL COST INCOME WEALTH...STAT 19 DEPRESSION. PAGE 123 F2433
INDUS FINAN GOV/REL

B91
MILL J.S.,SOCIALISM (1859). MOD/EUR AGRI INDUS NAT/G REV INCOME PRODUC ORD/FREE POPULISM SOCISM ...GOV/COMP METH/COMP 19. PAGE 91 F1787
WEALTH SOCIALIST ECO/TAC OWN

B92
ENGELS F.,THE CONDITION OF THE WORKING-CLASS IN ENGLAND (1848). UK INDUS LABOR PRICE CONTROL COST INCOME HEALTH MARXISM MUNICH 19. PAGE 38 F0733
WORKER WEALTH MARXIST CAP/ISM

B95
SELIGMAN E.R.A.,ESSAYS IN TAXATION. NEW/ZEALND PRUSSIA UK USA-45 MARKET LOC/G CREATE PRICE CONTROL INCOME OWN WEALTH...GOV/COMP METH/COMP 19. PAGE 119 F2349
TAX TARIFFS INDUS NAT/G

B96
MARX K.,REVOLUTION AND COUNTER-REVOLUTION. GERMANY CONSTN ELITES INDUS NAT/G DIPLOM ECO/TAC WEALTH. PAGE 86 F1693
MARXIST REV PWR STRATA

B96
SCHMOLLER G.,THE MERCANTILE SYSTEM AND ITS HISTORICAL SIGNIFICANCE: ILLUSTRATED CHIEFLY FROM PRUSSIAN HISTORY (TRANS.). PRUSSIA CULTURE INDUS KIN NAT/G PROVS OP/RES ECO/TAC INT/TRADE SUPEGO PWR WEALTH MUNICH 19 MERCANTLST. PAGE 117 F2302
GEN/METH INGP/REL CONCPT

B96
SMITH A.,LECTURES ON JUSTICE, POLICE, REVENUE AND ARMS (1763). UK LAW FAM FORCES TARIFFS AGREE COERCE INCOME OWN WEALTH LAISSEZ...GEN/LAWS 17/18. PAGE 123 F2429
DIPLOM JURID OLD/LIB TAX

B98
MARSHALL A.,PRINCIPLES OF ECONOMICS. INDUS WORKER PRICE COST EQUILIB INCOME OPTIMAL PRODUC...TIME/SEQ METH RICARDO/D. PAGE 86 F1678
WEALTH GEN/LAWS MARKET

WEAPON....NON-NUCLEAR WEAPONS

B14
DE BLOCH J.,THE FUTURE OF WAR IN ITS TECHNICAL, ECONOMIC, AND POLITICAL RELATIONS (1899). MOD/EUR TEC/DEV BUDGET INT/TRADE DETER GUERRILLA WEAPON COST PEACE 20. PAGE 31 F0596
WAR BAL/PWR PREDICT FORCES

S53
HANSER P.M.,"EXPLODING POPULATIONS: INTERNATIONAL AND REGIONAL ASPECTS." AFR S/ASIA ECO/TAC WEAPON BIO/SOC LOVE ORD/FREE...NEW/IDEA CENSUS TOT/POP 20. PAGE 55 F1069
ECO/UNDEV GEOG

B58
BERLINER J.S.,SOVIET ECONOMIC AID: THE AID AND TRADE POLICY IN UNDERDEVELOPED COUNTRIES. AFR COM ISLAM L/A+17C S/ASIA USSR ECO/DEV DIST/IND FINAN MARKET INT/ORG ACT/RES PLAN BAL/PWR WEAPON PWR WEALTH...CHARTS FOR/TRADE 20. PAGE 14 F0263
ECO/UNDEV ECO/TAC FOR/AID

B63
WILTZ J.E.,IN SEARCH OF PEACE: THE SENATE MUNITIONS INQUIRY, 1934-36. EUR+WWI USA-45 ELITES INDUS LG/CO LEGIS INT/TRADE LOBBY NEUTRAL ARMS/CONT...POLICY CONGRESS 20 LEAGUE/NAT PRESIDENT SENATE CONSCRIPTN. PAGE 147 F2905
DELIB/GP PROFIT WAR WEAPON

S63
BENOIT E.,"ECONOMIC ADJUSTMENTS TO ARMS CONTROL." FUT USA+45 NAT/G NUC/PWR WAR WEAPON 20. PAGE 13 F0251
ECO/DEV PWR ARMS/CONT

S63
ENTHOVEN A.C.,"ECONOMIC ANALYSIS IN THE DEPARTMENT OF DEFENSE." USA+45 NAT/G DELIB/GP PROB/SOLV RATION NUC/PWR WEAPON COST...DECISION 20 DEPT/DEFEN RESOURCE/N. PAGE 38 F0739
PLAN BUDGET ECO/TAC FORCES

B64
DUSCHA J.,ARMS, MONEY, AND POLITICS. USA+45 INDUS POL/PAR ECO/TAC TAX DETER NUC/PWR WAR WEAPON GOV/REL ATTIT...BIBLIOG/A 20 CONGRESS MONEY DEPT/DEFEN. PAGE 35 F0687
NAT/G FORCES POLICY BUDGET

B64
HOLLEY I.B. JR.,US ARMY IN WORLD WAR II: SPECIAL STUDIES: BUYING AIRCRAFT: MATERIEL PROCUREMENT FOR THE ARMY AIR FORCES. USA+45 USA-45 BUDGET WEAPON GOV/REL PRODUC 20. PAGE 61 F1198
FORCES COST DIST/IND CIVMIL/REL

B65
BEAUFRE A.,AN INTRODUCTION TO STRATEGY, WITH PARTICULAR REFERENCE TO PROBLEMS OF DEFENSE, POLITICS, ECONOMICS IN THE NUCLEAR AGE. WOR+45 FORCES DIPLOM DETER CIVMIL/REL GP/REL...NEW/IDEA IDEA/COMP 20. PAGE 12 F0226
PLAN NUC/PWR WEAPON DECISION

B65
MELMANS S.,OUR DEPLETED SOCIETY. AFR SPACE USA+45 ECO/DEV FORCES BUDGET ECO/TAC ADMIN WEAPON EFFICIENCY 20. PAGE 89 F1753
CIVMIL/REL INDUS EDU/PROP CONTROL

B65
US SENATE COMM ON FOREIGN REL,HEARINGS ON THE FOREIGN ASSISTANCE PROGRAM. AFR ASIA L/A+17C USA+45 WOR+45 FORCES TEC/DEV BUDGET CONTROL WEAPON ORD/FREE 20 UN CONGRESS SEC/STATE. PAGE 139 F2734
FOR/AID DIPLOM INT/ORG ECO/UNDEV

B65
WARD R.,BACKGROUND MATERIAL ON ECONOMIC IMPACT OF FEDERAL PROCUREMENT - 1965: FOR JOINT ECONOMIC COMMITTEE US CONGRESS. FINAN ROUTINE WEAPON CIVMIL/REL EFFICIENCY...STAT CHARTS 20 CONGRESS. PAGE 143 F2818
ECO/DEV NAT/G OWN GOV/REL

B66
US PRES COMM ECO IMPACT DEFENS,REPORT* JULY 1965. USA+45 ECO/DEV INDUS DELIB/GP FORCES OP/RES ARMS/CONT NUC/PWR WEAPON BAL/PAY...PREDICT SIMUL. PAGE 138 F2726
ACT/RES STAT WAR BUDGET

B66
US SENATE COMM APPROPRIATIONS,FOREIGN ASSISTANCE AND RELATED AGENCIES APPROPRIATIONS FOR FISCAL YEAR 1967: HEARINGS... ON H. R. 17788. ECO/UNDEV INT/ORG FORCES INSPECT ECO/TAC GIVE DEBATE WEAPON CIVMIL/REL WEALTH...INT 20 CONGRESS DEPT/DEFEN DEPT/STATE DEPT/HEW AID. PAGE 138 F2727
BUDGET FOR/AID DIPLOM COST

B66
US SENATE COMM ON FOREIGN REL,HEARINGS ON S 2859 AND S 2861. USA+45 WOR+45 FORCES BUDGET CAP/ISM ADMIN DETER WEAPON TOTALISM...NAT/COMP 20 UN CONGRESS. PAGE 139 F2735
FOR/AID DIPLOM ORD/FREE ECO/UNDEV

S66
BENOIT J.,"WORLD DEFENSE EXPENDITURES." WOR+45 WEAPON COST PRODUC. PAGE 13 F0253
FORCES STAT NAT/COMP BUDGET

B67
US SENATE COMM ON FOREIGN REL,ARMS SALES TO NEAR EAST AND SOUTH ASIAN COUNTRIES. INDIA IRAN PAKISTAN WOR+45 PROC/MFG BAL/PWR DIPLOM...DECISION SENATE. PAGE 139 F2742
WEAPON FOR/AID FORCES POLICY

B67
US SENATE COMM ON FOREIGN REL,FOREIGN ASSISTANCE ACT OF 1967. VIETNAM WOR+45 DELIB/GP CONFER CONTROL WAR WEAPON BAL/PAY...CENSUS CHARTS SENATE. PAGE 139 F2744
FOR/AID LAW DIPLOM POLICY

S67
CROKER F.P.U.,"ECONOMIC PEACEKEEPING." UK PLAN PROB/SOLV TEC/DEV BAL/PWR DIPLOM COERCE PEACE ...POLICY DECISION 20. PAGE 28 F0553
FORCES WEAPON COST WAR

S67
KENNY L.M.,"THE AFTERMATH OF DEFEAT IN EGYPT." ISLAM ISRAEL UAR UK USA+45 USSR INDUS FORCES ECO/TAC PRICE COERCE WEAPON COST ATTIT. PAGE 70 F1378
WAR ECO/UNDEV DIPLOM POLICY

S67
WOLFE T.W.,"SOVIET MILITARY POLICY AT THE FIFTY YEAR MARK." USSR VIETNAM WOR+45 RATION AGREE WAR WEAPON CIVMIL/REL TREATY. PAGE 148 F2917
FORCES POLICY TIME/SEQ PLAN

N67
US HOUSE COMM FOREIGN AFFAIRS,REPORT OF SPECIAL STUDY MISSION TO THE NEAR EAST (PAMPHLET). ISRAEL USA+45 YEMEN ECO/UNDEV INT/ORG FOR/AID ARMS/CONT WAR WEAPON NAT/LISM PEACE...GEOG 20 UN HOUSE/REP. PAGE 137 F2694
ISLAM DIPLOM FORCES

WEATHER....WEATHER

WEATHERFORD W.D. F2878

WEAVER J.N. F2836

WEBB B. F2837,F2838

WEBB S. F2837,F2838

WEBER A.R. F2391

WEBER M. F2839,F2840,F2841

WEBER/MAX....MAX WEBER

S53
BIRNBAUM N.,"CONFLICTING INTERPRETATIONS OF THE RISE OF CAPITALISM: MARX AND WEBER" (BMR)" WOR-45 INTELL SOCIETY STRUCT INDUS WORKER...PHIL/SCI SOC PERS/COMP 19/20 MARX/KARL WEBER/MAX. PAGE 15 F0288
CAP/ISM IDEA/COMP ECO/DEV MARXISM

S59
STINCHCOMBE A.L.,"BUREAUCRATIC AND CRAFT ADMINISTRATION OF PRODUCTION: A COMPARATIVE STUDY" (BMR)" USA+45 STRUCT EX/STRUC ECO/TAC GP/REL ...CLASSIF GP/COMP IDEA/COMP GEN/LAWS 20 WEBER/MAX. PAGE 126 F2490
CONSTRUC PROC/MFG ADMIN PLAN

L65
HAGE J.,"AN AXIOMATIC THEORY OF ORGANIZATIONS" USA+45 STRUCT LABOR PRODUC DRIVE PERSON RIGID/FLEX 20 WEBER/MAX. PAGE 53 F1032
GP/REL EFFICIENCY PROF/ORG ATTIT

WECHSBERG J. F2842

WEIDENBAUM M.L. F2843,F2844

WEIGERT H.W. F2845

WEIL G.L. F2846,F2847

WEILER J. F2848

WEIMAR/REP....WEIMAR REPUBLIC

B38
REICH N.,LABOR RELATIONS IN REPUBLICAN GERMANY. GERMANY CONSTN ECO/DEV INDUS NAT/G ADMIN CONTROL GP/REL FASCISM POPULISM 20 WEIMAR/REP. PAGE 110 F2176
WORKER MGT LABOR BARGAIN

S58
SCHUMM S.,"INTEREST REPRESENTATION IN FRANCE AND GERMANY." EUR+WWI FRANCE GERMANY INSPECT PARL/PROC REPRESENT 20 WEIMAR/REP. PAGE 118 F2320
LOBBY DELIB/GP NAT/G

B64
LAURSEN K.,THE GERMAN INFLATION, 1918-23. EUR+WWI GERMANY/E GERMANY/W WOR-45 BUDGET TAX GOV/REL BAL/PAY DEMAND PEACE...POLICY CHARTS 20 WEIMAR/REP. PAGE 76 F1489
ECO/DEV FINAN REPAR ECO/TAC

WEIN H.H. F1658

WEINBERG M. F2849

WEINER H.E. F2850

WEINER M. F1222

WEISBROD B.A. F2851,F2852

WEISS S.F. F0453

WEISSKOPF W.A. F2853

WELF/ST....WELFARE STATE ADVOCATE

B50
MARX H.L.,THE WELFARE STATE. USA+45 USA-45 CHIEF CAP/ISM CENTRAL ORD/FREE LAISSEZ...SOC ANTHOL 20. PAGE 86 F1686
ECO/DEV INDUS WEALTH WELF/ST

C50
ROUSSEAU J.J.,"A DISCOURSE ON POLITICAL ECONOMY" (1755) IN THE SOCIAL CONTRACT AND DISCOURSES." UNIV SOCIETY STRATA STRUCT CONSEN EQUILIB HAPPINESS UTOPIA HEALTH WEALTH...POLICY WELF/ST. PAGE 114 F2252
NAT/G ECO/TAC TAX GEN/LAWS

B51
CLARK C.,THE CONDITIONS OF ECONOMIC PROGRESS. EUR+WWI WOR+45 WOR-45 ECO/DEV INDUS CAP/ISM MORAL ...WELF/ST METH/CNCPT STAT TOT/POP VAL/FREE 20. PAGE 25 F0477
MARKET WEALTH

B54
CHILDS M.W.,ETHICS IN A BUSINESS SOCIETY. PROF/ORG LEAD WAR GP/REL ATTIT DRIVE PERSON KNOWL MORAL PWR ...WELF/ST BIBLIOG. PAGE 24 F0466
MGT SOCIETY

B55
GEORGE H.,PROGRESS AND POVERTY (1880). STRATA STRUCT INDUS TEC/DEV CAP/ISM EQUILIB INCOME OWN UTOPIA...WELF/ST CONCPT NEW/IDEA 19. PAGE 47 F0915
ECO/DEV ECO/TAC TAX WEALTH

B57
WATSON G.,THE UNSERVILE STATE: ESSAYS IN LIBERTY AND WELFARE. UK LEGIS RECEIVE EDU/PROP COLONIAL ...WELF/ST 20 LIB/PARTY. PAGE 144 F2833
POL/PAR ORD/FREE CONTROL NEW/LIB

B59
JENKINS C.,POWER AT THE TOP: A CRITICAL SURVEY OF THE NATIONALIZED INDUSTRIES. UK POL/PAR CONTROL ...WELF/ST CHARTS 20 LABOR/PAR. PAGE 67 F1313
NAT/G OWN INDUS NEW/LIB

B60
GARBARINO J.W.,HEALTH PLANS AND COLLECTIVE BARGAINING. USA+45 LABOR BARGAIN GP/REL WEALTH ...WELF/ST CHARTS 20 DEPT/HEW SAN/FRAN. PAGE 46 F0900
HEAL PLAN FINAN SERV/IND

S60
STOCKWELL E.G.,"THE MEASUREMENT OF ECONOMIC DEVELOPMENT." WOR+45 SOCIETY ECO/DEV ECO/UNDEV INDUS ECO/TAC HEALTH WEALTH...WELF/ST GEOG METH/CNCPT CHARTS METH METH/GP 20. PAGE 126 F2492
FAM STAT

B61
MYRDAL G.,THE POLITICAL ELEMENT IN THE DEVELOPMENT OF ECONOMIC THEORY. FINAN LOBBY ATTIT...WELF/ST CONCPT IDEA/COMP GEN/LAWS 20. PAGE 95 F1875
ECO/DEV ECO/TAC SOCIETY

B61
THEOBALD R.,THE CHALLENGE OF ABUNDANCE. USA+45 WOR+45 MARKET DIPLOM FOR/AID REV PRODUC UTOPIA SUPEGO...POLICY TREND BIBLIOG/A 20. PAGE 129 F2554
WELF/ST ECO/UNDEV PROB/SOLV ECO/TAC

S61
BENOIT E.,"THE PROPENSITY TO REDUCE THE NATIONAL DEBT OUT OF DEFENSE SAVINGS." FUT USA+45 SOCIETY R+D PLAN...WELF/ST SOC REC/INT STERTYP TOT/POP 20. PAGE 13 F0250
WEALTH ECO/TAC

S61
DEUTSCH K.W.,"NATIONAL INDUSTRIALIZATION AND THE DECLINING SHARE OF THE INTERNATIONAL ECONOMIC SECTOR." EUR+WWI FUT WOR+45 WOR-45 MARKET PLAN EDU/PROP WEALTH...WELF/ST OBS TESTS 20. PAGE 32 F0624
DIST/IND ECO/DEV INT/TRADE

S61
GORDON L.,"ECONOMIC REGIONALISM RECONSIDERED." FUT USA+45 WOR+45 INDUS NAT/G TEC/DEV DIPLOM ROUTINE PERCEPT WEALTH...WELF/ST METH/CNCPT WORK 20. PAGE 49 F0957
ECO/DEV ATTIT CAP/ISM REGION

S61
VERNON R.,"A TRADE POLICY FOR THE 1960'S." COM FUT USA+45 WOR+45 ECO/DEV ECO/UNDEV FINAN TOP/EX ACT/RES...WELF/ST METH/CNCPT CONT/OBS TOT/POP 20. PAGE 141 F2781
PLAN INT/TRADE

B62
BUREAU OF NATIONAL AFFAIRS,FEDERAL-STATE REGULATION OF WELFARE FUNDS (REV. ED.). USA+45 LAW LEGIS DEBATE AGE/O 20 CONGRESS. PAGE 20 F0386
WELF/ST WEALTH PLAN SOC/WK

B62
GERSCHENKRON A.,ECONOMIC BACKWARDNESS IN HISTORICAL PERSPECTIVE. WOR+45 WOR-45 ECO/DEV ECO/UNDEV INDUS NAT/G LEGIT DRIVE...WELF/ST DECISION QUANT TREND CHARTS 20. PAGE 47 F0919
TEC/DEV USSR

B62
HARRINGTON M.,THE OTHER AMERICA: POVERTY IN THE UNITED STATES. WORKER CREATE REPRESENT RACE/REL AGE/O DRIVE POLICY. PAGE 55 F1086
WEALTH WELF/ST INCOME CULTURE

B62
MOWITZ R.J.,PROFILE OF A METROPOLIS: A CASE BOOK. COM/IND CONSTRUC INDUS PUB/INST PLAN TEC/DEV LEAD GP/REL...POLICY TECHNIC WELF/ST MUNICH. PAGE 94 F1851
DECISION ADMIN

B62
NATIONAL BUREAU ECONOMIC RES,THE RATE AND DIRECTION OF INVENTIVE ACTIVITY: ECONOMIC AND SOCIAL FACTORS. STRUCT INDUS MARKET R+D CREATE OP/RES TEC/DEV EFFICIENCY PRODUC RATIONAL UTIL...WELF/ST PHIL/SCI METH/CNCPT TIME. PAGE 97 F1895
DECISION PROB/SOLV MGT

B62
SIEVERS A.M.,REVOLUTION, EVOLUTION AND THE ECONOMIC ORDER. INDUS LABOR TAX CONTROL REV WAR DEMAND PRODUC WEALTH...IDEA/COMP 19/20 KEYNES/JM. PAGE 122 F2399
EFFICIENCY ALL/IDEOS ECO/DEV WELF/ST

B63
BERLE A.A. JR.,THE AMERICAN ECONOMIC REPUBLIC. STRUCT FINAN MARKET LABOR NAT/G PLAN...POLICY WELF/ST DECISION. PAGE 14 F0262
CAP/ISM ECO/TAC TREND CONCPT

B63
SCHOECK H.,THE NEW ARGUMENT IN ECONOMICS. UK USA+45 INDUS MARKET LABOR NAT/G ECO/TAC ADMIN ROUTINE BAL/PAY PWR...POLICY BOLIV. PAGE 117 F2309
WELF/ST FOR/AID ECO/DEV ALL/IDEOS

B63
SELF P.,THE STATE AND THE FARMER. UK ECO/DEV MARKET WORKER PRICE CONTROL GP/REL...WELF/ST 20 DEPT/AGRI. PAGE 119 F2346
AGRI NAT/G ADMIN VOL/ASSN

S63
AYAL E.B.,"VALUE SYSTEM AND ECONOMIC DEVELOPMENT IN JAPAN AND THAILAND." ASIA S/ASIA THAILAND CULTURE ECO/DEV CAP/ISM DOMIN NAT/LISM DRIVE RIGID/FLEX SOCISM...WELF/ST OBS TREND CON/ANAL GEN/LAWS TERR/GP 20 CHINJAP. PAGE 8 F0145
ECO/UNDEV ALL/VALS

S63
DOSSER D.,"TOWARD A THEORY OF INTERNATIONAL PUBLIC FINANCE." WOR+45 ECO/DEV PLAN ECO/TAC WEALTH ...WELF/ST TREND GEN/LAWS TRUE/GP METH/GP 20. PAGE 34 F0654
FINAN INT/ORG FOR/AID

B64
AHMAD M.,THE CIVIL SERVANT IN PAKISTAN. PAKISTAN ECO/UNDEV COLONIAL INGP/REL...SOC CHARTS BIBLIOG 20 CIVIL/SERV. PAGE 3 F0051
WELF/ST ADMIN ATTIT STRATA

B64
MARSH D.C.,THE FUTURE OF THE WELFARE STATE. UK CONSTN NAT/G POL/PAR...POLICY WELF/ST 20. PAGE 86 F1676
NEW/LIB ADMIN CONCPT INSPECT

B64
TAWNEY R.H.,EQUALITY. UK CULTURE STRATA ECO/TAC EDU/PROP REPRESENT OWN NEW/LIB...MAJORIT WELF/ST SOC 20. PAGE 129 F2538
WEALTH STRUCT ELITES POPULISM

B65
PEARL A.,NEW CAREERS FOR THE POOR: THE NON-PROFESSIONAL IN HUMAN SERVICE. USA+45 SERV/IND
SOC/WK WEALTH

NAT/G NEIGH WORKER EDU/PROP AUTOMAT SKILL...WELF/ST NEW/IDEA BIBLIOG SOC/INTEG 20. PAGE 104 F2044 — STRATA POLICY

B66
HOROWITZ D.,HEMISPHERES NORTH AND SOUTH: ECONOMIC DISPARITY AMONG NATIONS. WOR+45 ECO/DEV ECO/UNDEV INT/ORG PLAN DIPLOM INT/TRADE GIVE PARTIC GP/REL ...WELF/ST 20. PAGE 62 F1215 — ECO/TAC FOR/AID STRATA WEALTH

N66
US ADVISORY COMN INTERGOV REL,CATALOGS AND OTHER INFORMATION SOURCES ON FEDERAL AND STATE AID PROGRAMS: A SECTED BIBLIOGRAPHY (PAPER). USA+45 LAW LOC/G NAT/G PROVS VOL/ASSN TEC/DEV ADMIN HEALTH ...WELF/ST SOC/WK MUNICH. PAGE 134 F2635 — BIBLIOG/A GOV/REL FINAN ECO/DEV

B67
COHEN M.R.,LAW AND THE SOCIAL ORDER: ESSAYS IN LEGAL PHILOSOPHY. USA-45 CONSULT WORKER ECO/TAC ATTIT WEALTH...POLICY WELF/ST SOC 20 NEW/DEAL DEPRESSION. PAGE 26 F0497 — JURID LABOR IDEA/COMP

B67
STEARNS P.N.,EUROPEAN SOCIETY IN UPHEAVAL* SOCIAL HISTORY SINCE 1800. EUR+WWI MOD/EUR STRATA SECT WORKER TEC/DEV WAR...WELF/ST SOC TREND BIBLIOG 19/20. PAGE 125 F2472 — REGION ECO/DEV SOCIETY INDUS

WELFARE....SEE RECEIVE, NEW/LIB, WELF/ST

WELFARE STATE....SEE NEW/LIB, WELF/ST

WELLISZ S. F2854

WELLS S.J. F1738

WELTON H. F2855

WENDT P.F. F2856

WENTHOLT W. F2857,F2858

WERNETTE J.P. F2859

WERTHEIM W.F. F2860

WESSON R.G. F2861

WEST R.L. F1500

WEST AFRICA....SEE AFRICA/W

WEST GERMANY....SEE GERMANY/W

WEST/EDWRD....SIR EDWARD WEST

WEST/IND....WEST INDIES; SEE ALSO L/A+17C

WEST/POINT....UNITED STATES MILITARY ACADEMY

WEST/SAMOA....WESTERN SAMOA; SEE ALSO S/ASIA

WEST/VIRGN....WEST VIRGINIA

WESTERN EUROPE....SEE EUROPE/W

WESTERN UNITED STATES....SEE US/WEST

WESTIN A.F. F2122

WESTMINSTER HALL, COURTS OF....SEE CTS/WESTM

WESTON J.F. F2862,F2863

WESTPHALIA....PEACE OF WESTPHALIA

WETTER G.A. F2864

WHEARE K.C. F2865,F2866

WHIG/PARTY....WHIG PARTY (USE WITH SPECIFIC NATION)

WHINSTON A.B. F0593

WHIP....SEE LEGIS, CONG, ROUTINE

WHITAKER A.P. F2867

WHITAKER J.K. F1100

WHITE C.L. F2868

WHITE J. F2869,F2870

WHITE W.L. F2871

WHITE/SUP....WHITE SUPREMACY - PERSONS, GROUPS, AND IDEAS

WHITE/T....THEODORE WHITE

WHITE/WA....WILLIAM ALLEN WHITE

WHITEHD/AN....ALFRED NORTH WHITEHEAD

WHITEHEAD T.N. F2872

WHITMAN/W....WALT WHITMAN

WHITNEY S.N. F2873

WHO....WORLD HEALTH ORGANIZATION

S67
STYCOS J.M.,"POLITICS AND POPULATION CONTROL IN LATIN AMERICA." USA+45 FAM NAT/G GP/REL AGE/C ATTIT CATHISM MARXISM...POLICY UN WHO. PAGE 127 F2509 — PLAN CENSUS CONTROL L/A+17C

WHYTE W.F. F2874

WHYTE W.H. F2875

WHYTE/WF....WILLIAM FOOTE WHYTE

WIBBERLEY G.P. F2876

WICKERSHAM E.D. F0221

WIGGINS J.W. F2309

WIGHTMAN D. F2877

WILCOX C. F2878

WILCOX W.A. F2879

WILCOX W.W. F2880

WILDAVSKY A. F0592,F2881,F2882

WILES P.J. F2883

WILES P.J.D. F2883,F2885

WILHELM/I....WILHELM I (KAISER)

WILHELM/II....WILHELM II (KAISER)

WILKINS/R....ROY WILKINS

WILKINSON J.H. F2886

WILKINSON T.O. F2887

WILLIAM/3....WILLIAM III (PRINCE OF ORANGE)

WILLIAMS B. F2888

WILLIAMS C. F2889

WILLIAMS E.J. F2890

WILLIAMS G. F2891

WILLIAMS J.H. F2892

WILLIAMS M. F2893

WILLIAMS S. F2894

WILLIAMS/R....ROGER WILLIAMS

WILLIAMSON H.F. F2895

WILLIAMSON J.G. F2896

WILLIAMSON O.E. F2897

WILLMANN J. F2898

WILLOW/RUN....WILLOW RUN, MICHIGAN

WILLS A.J. F2899

WILLS....WILLS AND TESTAMENTS

WILMERDING L. F2900

WILSON C.E. F2901

B59

LINK R.G.,ENGLISH THEORIES OF ECONOMIC FLUCTUATIONS: 1815-1848. FRANCE UK AGRI WORKER DIPLOM PRICE TASK WAR DEMAND PRODUC...POLICY BIBLIOG 18 MALTHUS MILL/JS WILSON/J. PAGE 80 F1574
IDEA/COMP ECO/DEV WEALTH EQUILIB

B66

FREIDEL F.,AMERICAN ISSUES IN THE TWENTIETH CENTURY. SOCIETY FINAN ECO/TAC FOR/AID CONTROL NUC/PWR WAR RACE/REL PEACE ATTIT...ANTHOL T 20 WILSON/W ROOSEVLT/F KENNEDY/JF TRUMAN/HS. PAGE 44 F0851
DIPLOM POLICY NAT/G ORD/FREE

B18

MARX K.,CAPITAL. FUT MOD/EUR STRATA DIST/IND PROC/MFG TEC/DEV WEALTH...MARXIST WORK 19. PAGE 86 F1688
ECO/DEV CAP/ISM SOCISM

B35

STALEY E.,WAR AND THE PRIVATE INVESTOR. UNIV WOR-45 INTELL SOCIETY INT/ORG NAT/G TOP/EX CAP/ISM ECO/TAC WAR ATTIT ALL/VALS...INT TIME/SEQ TREND CON/ANAL WORK TOT/POP 20. PAGE 125 F2464
FINAN INT/TRADE DIPLOM

B37

ROBBINS L.,ECONOMIC PLANNING AND INTERNATIONAL ORDER. WOR-45 SOCIETY FINAN INDUS NAT/G ECO/TAC ROUTINE WEALTH...SOC TIME/SEQ GEN/METH WORK 20 KEYNES/JM. PAGE 112 F2202
INT/ORG PLAN INT/TRADE

B46

CLOUGH S.B.,ECONOMIC HISTORY OF EUROPE. CHRIST-17C EUR+WWI MOD/EUR WOR-45 SOCIETY EXEC ATTIT WEALTH ...CONCPT GEN/LAWS WORK TOT/POP VAL/FREE 7/20. PAGE 25 F0493
ECO/TAC CAP/ISM

B52

ALEXANDROWICZ C.H.,INTERNATIONAL ECONOMIC ORGANIZATION. WOR+45 ECO/DEV ECO/UNDEV DIST/IND FINAN MARKET PLAN ECO/TAC LEGIT DRIVE WEALTH ...POLICY CONCPT QUANT OBS TIME/SEQ GEN/LAWS WORK METH/GP EEC ILO OEEC UNESCO 20. PAGE 4 F0063
INT/ORG INT/TRADE

B58

POLLOCK F.,AUTOMATION: A STUDY OF ITS ECONOMIC AND SOCIAL CONSEQUENCES. FUT USA+45 USA-45 SOCIETY ECO/DEV LABOR ACT/RES PLAN ECO/TAC AUTOMAT ROUTINE ALL/VALS...STAT TREND COMPUT/IR CHARTS SOC/EXP WORK 20. PAGE 107 F2099
TEC/DEV SOC CAP/ISM

B59

ALLEN R.L.,SOVIET INFLUENCE IN LATIN AMERICA. ECO/UNDEV FINAN PROC/MFG NAT/G TEC/DEV EDU/PROP EXEC ROUTINE ATTIT DRIVE PERSON ALL/VALS PWR...STAT CHARTS WORK FOR/TRADE 20. PAGE 4 F0071
L/A+17C ECO/TAC INT/TRADE USSR

L59

BEGUIN B.,"ILO AND THE TRIPARTITE SYSTEM." EUR+WWI WOR+45 WOR-45 CONSTN ECO/DEV ECO/UNDEV INDUS INT/ORG NAT/G VOL/ASSN DELIB/GP PLAN TEC/DEV LEGIT ORD/FREE WEALTH...CONCPT TIME/SEQ WORK ILO 20. PAGE 12 F0228
LABOR

S59

TIPTON J.B.,"PARTICIPATION OF THE UNITED STATES IN THE INTERNATIONAL LABOR ORGANIZATION." USA+45 LAW STRUCT ECO/DEV ECO/UNDEV INDUS TEC/DEV ECO/TAC ADMIN PERCEPT ORD/FREE SKILL...STAT HIST/WRIT GEN/METH ILO WORK 20. PAGE 131 F2577
LABOR INT/ORG

B60

CAMPBELL R.W.,SOVIET ECONOMIC POWER. COM USA+45 DIST/IND MARKET TOP/EX ACT/RES CAP/ISM ECO/TAC DOMIN EDU/PROP ADMIN ROUTINE DRIVE...MATH TIME/SEQ CHARTS WORK 20. PAGE 21 F0409
ECO/DEV PLAN SOCISM USSR

B60

THEOBALD R.,THE RICH AND THE POOR: A STUDY OF THE ECONOMICS OF RISING EXPECTATIONS. WOR+45 CONSTN ECO/DEV ECO/UNDEV INT/ORG NAT/G PLAN FOR/AID ROUTINE BAL/PAY ORD/FREE PWR WEALTH...GEOG TREND WORK FOR/TRADE 20. PAGE 129 F2553
ECO/TAC INT/TRADE

L60

SPENGLER J.J.,"ECONOMIC DEVELOPMENT: POLITICAL PRECONDITIONS AND POLITICAL CONSEQUENCE." WOR+45 STRUCT ECO/UNDEV NAT/G PLAN ECO/TAC EDU/PROP ATTIT ORD/FREE WEALTH SOCISM...SOC CONCPT TREND SIMUL GEN/METH WORK 20. PAGE 124 F2452
TEC/DEV METH/CNCPT CAP/ISM

S60

HERZ J.H.,"EAST GERMANY: PROGRESS AND PROSPECTS." COM AGRI FINAN INDUS LOC/G NAT/G FORCES PLAN TEC/DEV DOMIN ADMIN COERCE DRIVE PERCEPT RIGID/FLEX MORAL ORD/FREE PWR...MARXIST PSY SOC RECORD STERTYP WORK. PAGE 59 F1158
POL/PAR STRUCT GERMANY

S60

JACOBSON H.K.,"THE USSR AND ILO." AFR COM STRUCT ECO/DEV ECO/UNDEV CONSULT DELIB/GP ECO/TAC ILO WORK 20. PAGE 66 F1298
INT/ORG LABOR USSR

S60

MORALES C.J.,"TRADE AND ECONOMIC INTEGRATION IN LATIN AMERICA." FUT L/A+17C LAW STRATA ECO/UNDEV DIST/IND INDUS LABOR NAT/G LEGIS ECO/TAC ADMIN RIGID/FLEX WEALTH...CONCPT NEW/IDEA CONT/OBS TIME/SEQ WORK 20. PAGE 93 F1825
FINAN INT/TRADE REGION

S60

OWEN C.F.,"US AND SOVIET RELATIONS WITH UNDERDEVELOPED COUNTRIES: LATIN AMERICA-A CASE STUDY." AFR COM L/A+17C USA+45 USSR EXTR/IND MARKET TEC/DEV DIPLOM ECO/TAC NAT/LISM ORD/FREE PWR ...TREND WORK 20. PAGE 102 F2005
ECO/UNDEV DRIVE INT/TRADE

S60

RIVKIN A.,"AFRICAN ECONOMIC DEVELOPMENT: ADVANCED TECHNOLOGY AND THE STAGES OF GROWTH." CULTURE ECO/UNDEV AGRI COM/IND EXTR/IND PLAN ECO/TAC ATTIT DRIVE RIGID/FLEX SKILL WEALTH...MGT SOC GEN/LAWS FOR/TRADE WORK TOT/POP 20. PAGE 111 F2195
AFR TEC/DEV FOR/AID

S60

SPINRAD W.,"CORRELATES OF TRADE UNION PARTICIPATION: A SUMMARY OF LITERATURE." ACT/RES
LABOR PARTIC

PERS/REL HAPPINESS HABITAT...BIBLIOG WORK. PAGE 125 F2456 — CORREL ROLE

B61
FRIEDMANN W.G.,JOINT INTERNATIONAL BUSINESS VENTURES. ASIA ISLAM L/A+17C ECO/DEV DIST/IND FINAN PROC/MFG FACE/GP LG/CO NAT/G VOL/ASSN CONSULT EX/STRUC PLAN ADMIN ROUTINE WEALTH...OLD/LIB FOR/TRADE WORK 20. PAGE 44 F0865 — ECO/UNDEV INT/TRADE

B61
HORVATH B.,THE CHARACTERISTICS OF YUGOSLAV ECONOMIC DEVELOPMENT. COM ECO/UNDEV AGRI INDUS PLAN CAP/ISM ECO/TAC ROUTINE WEALTH...SOCIALIST STAT CHARTS STERTYP WORK 20. PAGE 62 F1217 — ACT/RES YUGOSLAVIA

B61
MARX K.,THE COMMUNIST MANIFESTO. IN (MENDEL A. ESSENTIAL WORKS OF MARXISM, NEW YORK: BANTAM. FUT MOD/EUR CULTURE ECO/DEV ECO/UNDEV AGRI FINAN INDUS MARKET PROC/MFG LABOR POL/PAR CONSULT FORCES CREATE PLAN ADMIN ATTIT DRIVE RIGID/FLEX ORD/FREE PWR RESPECT MARX/KARL MUNICH WORK. PAGE 86 F1691 — COM NEW/IDEA CAP/ISM REV

S61
GORDON L.,"ECONOMIC REGIONALISM RECONSIDERED." FUT USA+45 WOR+45 INDUS NAT/G TEC/DEV DIPLOM ROUTINE PERCEPT WEALTH...WELF/ST METH/CNCPT WORK 20. PAGE 49 F0957 — ECO/DEV ATTIT CAP/ISM REGION

S61
HEILBRONER R.L.,"DYNAMICS OF FOREIGN AID: PROBLEMS OF UNDERDEVELOPED NATIONS PLAGUE ASSISTANCE PROGRAM." FUT USA+45 WOR+45 STRATA NAT/G PLAN TEC/DEV ATTIT DRIVE WEALTH WORK 20. PAGE 58 F1135 — ECO/UNDEV ECO/TAC FOR/AID

L62
GALBRAITH J.K.,"ECONOMIC DEVELOPMENT IN PERSPECTIVE." CAP/ISM ECO/TAC ROUTINE ATTIT WEALTH ...TREND CHARTS SOC/EXP WORK TERR/GP 20. PAGE 45 F0884 — ECO/UNDEV PLAN

S62
ZAUBERMAN A.,"SOVIET AND CHINESE STRATEGY FOR ECONOMIC GROWTH." ASIA CHINA/COM COM USSR STRATA VOL/ASSN PLAN ATTIT PWR...METH/CNCPT GEN/LAWS WORK TERR/GP 20. PAGE 150 F2959 — ECO/DEV EDU/PROP

B63
GEERTZ C.,PEDDLERS AND PRINCES: SOCIAL DEVELOPMENT AND ECONOMIC CHANGE IN TWO INDONESIAN TOWNS. S/ASIA CULTURE SOCIETY STRATA FACE/GP CREATE TEC/DEV ECO/TAC ORD/FREE WEALTH...OBS INT CENSUS CHARTS WORK TOT/POP METH/GP TERR/GP VAL/FREE 20 MUNICH. PAGE 47 F0913 — ECO/UNDEV SOC ELITES INDONESIA

B63
ISSAWI C.,EGYPT IN REVOLUTION: AN ECONOMIC ANALYSIS. ISLAM STRUCT ECO/UNDEV AGRI FINAN INDUS PLAN EXEC REV NAT/LISM ATTIT RIGID/FLEX WEALTH SOCISM...STAT FOR/TRADE WORK 20. PAGE 66 F1292 — NAT/G UAR

B63
LAIRD R.D.,SOVIET AGRICULTURAL AND PEASANT AFFAIRS. FUT STRATA LOC/G DELIB/GP ACT/RES TEC/DEV ECO/TAC EDU/PROP ATTIT RIGID/FLEX ORD/FREE SKILL WEALTH ...STAT CON/ANAL ANTHOL MUNICH WORK VAL/FREE 20. PAGE 74 F1461 — COM AGRI POLICY

B63
NEUMARK S.D.,FOREIGN TRADE AND ECONOMIC DEVELOPMENT IN AFRICA: A HISTORICAL PERSPECTIVE. EUR+WWI MOD/EUR ECO/UNDEV AGRI COM/IND EXTR/IND PROC/MFG SKILL WEALTH...CONCPT TIME/SEQ TREND SIMUL FOR/TRADE WORK TOT/POP TERR/GP VAL/FREE 19/20. PAGE 98 F1916 — AFR

S63
GRUSHIN B.A.,"PROBLEMS OF THE MOVEMENT OF COMMUNIST LABOR IN THE USSR." COM SOCIETY LABOR ECO/TAC EDU/PROP COERCE RIGID/FLEX ORD/FREE...POLICY MARXIST STAT QU WORK 20. PAGE 52 F1011 — ATTIT USSR

S63
HOOVER C.B.,"ECONOMIC REFORM VERSUS ECONOMIC GROWTH IN UNDERDEVELOPED COUNTRIES." FUT WOR+45 ELITES STRATA ECO/UNDEV DIST/IND INDUS TEC/DEV CAP/ISM FOR/AID INT/TRADE ATTIT WEALTH...MYTH TREND STERTYP GEN/LAWS WORK 20. PAGE 61 F1209 — ECO/DEV ECO/TAC

S63
MATHUR P.N.,"GAINS IN ECONOMIC GROWTH FROM INTERNATIONAL TRADE." USA-45 ECO/DEV FINAN INDUS ATTIT WEALTH...MATH QUANT STAT BIOG TREND GEN/LAWS WORK 20. PAGE 87 F1704 — MARKET ECO/TAC CAP/ISM INT/TRADE

S63
MIKESELL R.F.,"COMMODITY AGREEMENTS AND AID TO DEVELOPING COUNTRIES." WOR+45 WOR-45 INT/ORG ECO/TAC ATTIT WEALTH WORK FOR/TRADE 20. PAGE 91 F1782 — FINAN ECO/UNDEV BAL/PAY FOR/AID

S63
REDDAWAY W.B.,"THE ECONOMICS OF UNDERDEVELOPED COUNTRIES." S/ASIA WOR+45 WOR-45 STRATA AGRI COM/IND DIST/IND MARKET PROC/MFG PLAN TEC/DEV FOR/AID BAL/PAY ATTIT DRIVE SKILL WORK FOR/TRADE 20. PAGE 110 F2165 — ECO/TAC ECO/UNDEV INDIA

S63
SCHURMANN F.,"ECONOMIC POLICY AND POLITICAL POWER IN COMMUNIST CHINA." ASIA CHINA/COM USSR SOCIETY ECO/UNDEV AGRI INDUS CREATE ADMIN ROUTINE ATTIT DRIVE RIGID/FLEX PWR WEALTH...HIST/WRIT TREND CHARTS WORK 20. PAGE 118 F2323 — PLAN ECO/TAC

B64
LI C.M.,INDUSTRIAL DEVELOPMENT IN COMMUNIST CHINA. CHINA/COM ECO/DEV ECO/UNDEV AGRI FINAN INDUS MARKET LABOR NAT/G ECO/TAC INT/TRADE EXEC ALL/VALS ...POLICY RELATIV TREND WORK TOT/POP VAL/FREE 20. PAGE 79 F1556 — ASIA TEC/DEV

B64
SEERS D.,CUBA: THE ECONOMIC AND SOCIAL REVOLUTION. L/A+17C USSR YUGOSLAVIA STRATA AGRI INDUS SCHOOL DELIB/GP PLAN ECO/TAC DOMIN EDU/PROP ATTIT RIGID/FLEX ALL/VALS...STAT OBS TIME/SEQ WORK VAL/FREE 20. PAGE 119 F2341 — ACT/RES COERCE CUBA REV

B64
SINGER H.W.,INTERNATIONAL DEVELOPMENT: GROWTH AND CHANGE. AFR BRAZIL L/A+17C WOR+45 CULTURE AGRI INDUS NAT/G ACT/RES ECO/TAC EDU/PROP WEALTH...GEOG CONCPT METH/CNCPT STAT HYPO/EXP WORK TOT/POP 20. PAGE 122 F2412 — FINAN ECO/UNDEV FOR/AID INT/TRADE

B64
SULLIVAN G.,THE STORY OF THE PEACE CORPS. USA+45 WOR+45 INTELL FACE/GP NAT/G SCHOOL VOL/ASSN CONSULT EX/STRUC PLAN EDU/PROP ADMIN ATTIT DRIVE ALL/VALS ...POLICY HEAL SOC CONCPT INT QU BIOG TREND SOC/EXP WORK. PAGE 127 F2511 — INT/ORG ECO/UNDEV FOR/AID PEACE

L64
ARMENGALD A.,"ECONOMIE ET COEXISTENCE." COM EUR+WWI FUT USA+45 WOR+45 ECO/DEV ECO/UNDEV FINAN INT/ORG NAT/G EXEC CHOOSE ATTIT ALL/VALS...POLICY RELATIV DECISION TREND SOC/EXP WORK 20. PAGE 6 F0113 — MARKET ECO/TAC AFR CAP/ISM

S64
FLORINSKY M.T.,"TRENDS IN THE SOVIET ECONOMY." COM USA+45 USSR INDUS LABOR NAT/G PLAN TEC/DEV ECO/TAC ALL/VALS SOCISM...MGT METH/CNCPT STYLE CON/ANAL GEN/METH WORK 20. PAGE 42 F0817 — ECO/DEV AGRI

S64
HUELIN D.,"ECONOMIC INTEGRATION IN LATIN AMERICAN: PROGRESS AND PROBLEMS." L/A+17C ECO/DEV AGRI DIST/IND FINAN INDUS NAT/G VOL/ASSN CONSULT DELIB/GP EX/STRUC ACT/RES PLAN TEC/DEV ECO/TAC ROUTINE BAL/PAY WEALTH FOR/TRADE WORK TERR/GP 20. PAGE 63 F1232 — MARKET ECO/UNDEV INT/TRADE

S64
NASH M.,"SOCIAL PREREQUISITES TO ECONOMIC GROWTH IN LATIN AMERICA AND SOUTHEAST ASIA." L/A+17C S/ASIA CULTURE SOCIETY ECO/UNDEV AGRI INDUS NAT/G PLAN TEC/DEV EDU/PROP ROUTINE ALL/VALS...POLICY RELATIV SOC NAT/COMP WORK TOT/POP 20. PAGE 96 F1894 — ECO/DEV PERCEPT

S64
PATEL S.J.,"THE ECONOMIC DISTANCE BETWEEN NATIONS: ITS ORIGIN, MEASUREMENT AND OUTLOOK." WOR+45 ECO/DEV AGRI FINAN INDUS MARKET LABOR NAT/G CONSULT TEC/DEV ECO/TAC WEALTH...POLICY RELATIV MGT TREND WORK 20. PAGE 103 F2035 — ECO/UNDEV PLAN

S64
READER D.H.,"A SURVEY OF CATEGORIES OF ECONOMIC ACTIVITIES AMONG THE PEOPLES OF AFRICA." AGRI INDUS MARKET KIN HEALTH SKILL WEALTH...GEOG METH/CNCPT CHARTS TERR/GP WORK TOT/POP VAL/FREE 20. PAGE 110 F2160 — TEC/DEV ECO/UNDEV AFR

L65
WILLIAMS S.,"NEGOTIATING INVESTMENT IN EMERGING COUNTRIES." USA+45 WOR+45 INDUS MARKET NAT/G TOP/EX TEC/DEV CAP/ISM ECO/TAC ADMIN SKILL WEALTH...POLICY RELATIV MGT WORK 20. PAGE 147 F2894 — FINAN ECO/UNDEV

S65
SPAAK P.H.,"THE SEARCH FOR CONSENSUS: A NEW EFFORT TO BUILD EUROPE." FRANCE GERMANY ECO/DEV NAT/G CONSULT FORCES PLAN EDU/PROP REGION CONSEN ATTIT ...SOC METH/CNCPT OBS TREND EEC NATO WORK TERR/GP METH/GP 20. PAGE 124 F2447 — EUR+WWI INT/ORG

S67
LEWIS W.A.,"THE STATUTORY LANGUAGE OF LABOR DISQUALIFICATION IN STATE EMPLOYMENT SECURITY LAWS." LABOR WORKER WORK 20. PAGE 79 F1553 — METH/COMP LEGIS SOC PROVS

WORKER....WORKER, LABORER

B
BRITISH COMMONWEALTH BUR AGRI,WORLD AGRICULTURAL ECONOMICS AND RURAL SOCIOLOGY ABSTRACTS. NAT/G OP/RES PLAN TEC/DEV LEAD PRODUC...GEOG MGT NAT/COMP 20. PAGE 18 F0354 — BIBLIOG/A AGRI SOC WORKER

N
US LIBRARY OF CONGRESS,SELECTED AND ANNOTATED BIBLIOGRAPHY ON AGRICULTURAL PROBLEMS AND POLICIES IN A WARTIME ECONOMY (PAMPHLET). R+D WORKER PRODUC 20. PAGE 137 F2706 — BIBLIOG/A WAR AGRI EXTR/IND

N
US LIBRARY OF CONGRESS,SELECTED AND ANNOTATED BIBLIOGRAPHY ON LABOR PROBLEMS AND POLICIES IN A WARTIME ECONOMY (PAMPHLET). USA-45 INDUS LEGIS GP/REL DISCRIM PRODUC...SOC 20. PAGE 137 F2708 — BIBLIOG/A WAR LABOR WORKER

N
US LIBRARY OF CONGRESS,SOUTHERN ASIA ACCESSIONS LIST. BURMA CEYLON INDIA NEPAL PAKISTAN S/ASIA THAILAND AGRI INDUS SCHOOL WORKER...ART/METH GEOG HEAL PHIL/SCI LING 20. PAGE 137 F2710
BIBLIOG/A SOCIETY CULTURE ECO/UNDEV

N
US SUPERINTENDENT OF DOCUMENTS,LABOR (PRICE LIST 33). USA+45 LAW AGRI CONSTRUC INDUS NAT/G BARGAIN PRICE ADMIN AUTOMAT PRODUC MGT. PAGE 140 F2753
BIBLIOG/A WORKER LABOR LEGIS

B02
MOREL E.D.,AFFAIRS OF WEST AFRICA. UK FINAN INDUS FAM KIN SECT CHIEF WORKER DIPLOM RACE/REL LITERACY HEALTH...CHARTS 18/20 AFRICA/W NEGRO. PAGE 93 F1826
COLONIAL ADMIN AFR

B04
VEBLEN T.B.,THE THEORY OF BUSINESS ENTERPRISE. USA-45 FINAN WORKER ECO/TAC PRICE GP/REL COST ...POLICY 19/20. PAGE 141 F2770
TEC/DEV GEN/LAWS SOCIETY WEALTH

B08
LLOYD H.D.,THE SWISS DEMOCRACY. SWITZERLND INDUS NAT/G WORKER CHOOSE OWN ORD/FREE SOCISM...PLURIST 19/20 MONOPOLY. PAGE 81 F1590
NAT/COMP GOV/COMP REPRESENT POPULISM

B11
SCOTT W.D.,INFLUENCING MEN IN BUSINESS: THE PSYCHOLOGY OF ARGUMENT AND SUGGESTION. WOR-45 WORKER EDU/PROP DEMAND ATTIT PERSON 20. PAGE 118 F2336
PSY MARKET SML/CO TOP/EX

B11
SOREL G.,LES ILLUSIONS DU PROGRES (1906). UNIV SOCIETY STRATA INDUS GP/REL OWN PRODUC SOCISM 17/20. PAGE 124 F2444
WORKER POPULISM ECO/DEV ATTIT

B12
HOBSON J.A.,THE EVOLUTION OF MODERN CAPITALISM. MOD/EUR UK STRATA ECO/DEV INDUS INCOME UTIL WEALTH ...SOC GEN/LAWS 7/20. PAGE 60 F1184
CAP/ISM WORKER TEC/DEV TIME/SEQ

B13
KROPOTKIN P.,THE CONQUEST OF BREAD. SOCIETY STRATA AGRI INDUS WORKER REV HAPPINESS INCOME PRODUC HEALTH MORAL ORD/FREE. PAGE 74 F1444
ANARCH SOCIALIST OWN AGREE

B14
HOBSON J.A.,WORK AND WEALTH. CULTURE FINAN INDUS WORKER TEC/DEV ECO/TAC GIVE PAY PRICE COST PRODUC UTIL. PAGE 60 F1185
WEALTH INCOME GEN/LAWS

B19
VEBLEN T.B.,THE VESTED INTERESTS AND THE STATE OF THE INDUSTRIAL ARTS. USA-45 LAW FINAN WORKER PAY DOMIN PRICE COST SOCISM...MARXIST 19/20. PAGE 141 F2771
INDUS CAP/ISM METH/COMP WEALTH

N19
BUSINESS ECONOMISTS' GROUP,INCOME POLICIES (PAMPHLET). UK INDUS LABOR TOP/EX PAY COST PRODUC ...ECOMETRIC GOV/COMP SIMUL ANTHOL 20. PAGE 20 F0395
INCOME WORKER WEALTH POLICY

N19
ENGELS F.,THE BRITISH LABOUR MOVEMENT (PAMPHLET). FRANCE GERMANY MOD/EUR UK USA-45 POL/PAR WORKER PAY EDU/PROP PRICE REPRESENT GP/REL 19. PAGE 37 F0730
ECO/TAC MARXISM LABOR STRATA

N19
FIKS M.,PUBLIC ADMINISTRATION IN ISRAEL (PAMPHLET). ISRAEL SCHOOL EX/STRUC BUDGET PAY INGP/REL ...DECISION 20 CIVIL/SERV. PAGE 41 F0792
EDU/PROP NAT/G ADMIN WORKER

N19
HALL G.,MAIN STREET TO WALL STREET: END THE COLD WAR (PAMPHLET). AFR USA+45 LAW STRUCT POL/PAR WORKER INT/TRADE DOMIN INCOME...POLICY 20 COM/PARTY. PAGE 53 F1046
MARXIST CAP/ISM DIPLOM NAT/G

N19
HATANAKA M.,A SPECTRAL ANALYSIS OF BUSINESS CYCLE INDICATORS: LEAD-LAG IN TERMS OF ALL TIME POINTS (PAMPHLET). UNIV WORKER EFFICIENCY...REGRESS STAT CHARTS TIME 20. PAGE 56 F1110
ECOMETRIC ADJUST PRODUC CON/ANAL

N19
HOGARTY R.A.,NEW JERSEY FARMERS AND MIGRANT HOUSING RULES (PAMPHLET). USA+45 LAW ELITES FACE/GP LABOR PROF/ORG LOBBY PERS/REL RIGID/FLEX ROLE 20 NEW/JERSEY. PAGE 61 F1193
AGRI PROVS WORKER HEALTH

N19
INTERNATIONAL LABOUR OFFICE,EMPLOYMENT, UNEMPLOYMENT AND LABOUR FORCE STATISTICS (PAMPHLET). EUR+WWI STRATA AGRI INDUS NAT/G PROB/SOLV PAY AGE SEX...SAMP NAT/COMP METH 20 ILO. PAGE 65 F1278
WORKER LABOR STAT ECO/DEV

N19
MARSH J.F. JR.,THE FBI RETIREMENT BILL (PAMPHLET). USA+45 EX/STRUC WORKER PLAN PROB/SOLV BUDGET LEAD LOBBY PARL/PROC PERS/REL RIGID/FLEX...POLICY 20 FBI PRESIDENT BUR/BUDGET. PAGE 86 F1677
ADMIN NAT/G SENIOR GOV/REL

N19
PEGRUM D.F.,URBAN TRANSPORT AND THE LOCATION OF INDUSTRY IN METROPOLITAN LOS ANGELES (PAMPHLET). USA+45 WORKER...GEOG CHARTS MUNICH. PAGE 104 F2049
DIST/IND REGION INDUS

N19
ROBERTSON D.,GROWTH, WAGES, MONEY (PAMPHLET). UNIV WORKER BUDGET PRICE DEMAND PRODUC WEALTH...CONCPT MATH MONEY. PAGE 112 F2210
FINAN ECO/DEV ECO/TAC PAY

N19
STUTZ R.L.,COLLECTIVE DEALING BY UNITS OF LOCAL GOVERNMENT IN CONNECTICUT (PAMPHLET). USA+45 LOC/G PROVS...STAT MUNICH 20 CONNECTICT. PAGE 127 F2508
VOL/ASSN LABOR WORKER

B20
PIGOU A.C.,THE ECONOMICS OF WELFARE. UNIV INDUS WORKER ACT/RES RECEIVE INCOME NEW/LIB...MAJORIT SOC/WK. PAGE 106 F2085
ECO/TAC WEALTH FINAN CONTROL

B20
TAWNEY R.H.,THE ACQUISITIVE SOCIETY. STRATA WORKER PROB/SOLV CAP/ISM ECO/TAC CONTROL GP/REL OWN PRIVIL ATTIT ORD/FREE WEALTH 20. PAGE 128 F2536
INDUS SOCIETY PRODUC MORAL

B24
CLARK J.B.,THE DISTRIBUTION OF WEALTH (1899). WORKER OWN PRODUC PROFIT WEALTH LAISSEZ...IDEA/COMP GEN/LAWS. PAGE 25 F0478
ECO/TAC INDUS LABOR INCOME

B26
SUFRIN S.C.,A BRIEF ANNOTATED BIBLIOGRAPHY ON LABOR IN EMERGING SOCIETIES. WOR+45 CULTURE SOCIETY INDUS EDU/PROP GP/REL INGP/REL. PAGE 127 F2510
BIBLIOG/A LABOR ECO/UNDEV WORKER

B27
BELLOC H.,THE SERVILE STATE (1912) (3RD ED.). PRUSSIA UK CULTURE STRATA INDUS NAT/G ECO/TAC CONTROL LEAD SUFF DISCRIM EQUILIB ORD/FREE WEALTH 20. PAGE 12 F0237
WORKER CAP/ISM DOMIN CATH

B27
SIEGFRIED A.,AMERICA COMES OF AGE: A FRENCH ANALYSIS (TRANS. BY H.H. HEMMING AND DORIS HEMMING). FRANCE UK POL/PAR WORKER TEC/DEV DIPLOM REGION RACE/REL ADJUST PRODUC HEREDITY...TIME/SEQ GP/COMP SOC/INTEG 20 DEMOCRAT REPUBLICAN KKK. PAGE 122 F2398
USA-45 CULTURE ECO/DEV SOC

B28
DE MAN H.,THE PSYCHOLOGY OF SOCIALISM. EUR+WWI USSR LABOR NAT/LISM PERSON WEALTH MARXISM...METH/COMP 20. PAGE 31 F0604
WORKER ATTIT SOC SOCISM

B28
HARDMAN J.B.,AMERICAN LABOR DYNAMICS. WORKER ECO/TAC DOMIN ADJUD LEAD LOBBY PWR...POLICY MGT. PAGE 55 F1079
LABOR INGP/REL ATTIT GP/REL

B29
DE MAN H.,JOY IN WORK. STRATA ECO/DEV ECO/TAC PRODUC ANOMIE ROLE SOCISM...IDEA/COMP 20. PAGE 31 F0605
SOC WORKER HAPPINESS RESPECT

B30
BEVERIDGE W.H.,UNEMPLOYMENT: A PROBLEM OF INDUSTRY (1909-1930). USA-45 LAW ECO/DEV MARKET DELIB/GP WAR DEMAND INCOME...POLICY STAT CHARTS 20. PAGE 14 F0274
WORKER ECO/TAC GEN/LAWS

B30
KEYNES J.M.,A TREATISE ON MONEY (2 VOLS.). UK USA-45 INDUS MARKET WORKER PRICE CONTROL COST OPTIMAL PROFIT WEALTH...POLICY 19/20 KEYNES/JM. PAGE 70 F1385
EQUILIB ECO/TAC FINAN GEN/LAWS

B31
CROOK W.H.,THE GENERAL STRIKE: A STUDY OF LABOR'S TRAGIC WEAPON IN THEORY AND PRACTICE. BELGIUM FRANCE SWEDEN UK WOR-45 PROB/SOLV ECO/TAC DOMIN PWR ...POLICY TIME/SEQ NAT/COMP GEN/LAWS 19/20 STRIKE. PAGE 29 F0555
LABOR WORKER LG/CO BARGAIN

B33
TANNENBAUM F.,PEACE BY REVOLUTION. ECO/UNDEV AGRI SECT WORKER DIPLOM EDU/PROP DISCRIM OWN WEALTH POPULISM 17/20 MEXIC/AMER INDIAN/AM. PAGE 128 F2532
CULTURE COLONIAL RACE/REL REV

B34
MARX K.,THE CLASS STRUGGLES IN FRANCE. FRANCE INDUS WORKER CONSERVE...TREND GEN/LAWS 19. PAGE 86 F1689
MARXIST STRATA REV INT/TRADE

B34
ROBINSON J.,THE ECONOMICS OF IMPERFECT COMPETITION. FINAN ECO/TAC PRICE COST DEMAND EQUILIB OPTIMAL WEALTH...METH MONOPOLY. PAGE 113 F2221
MARKET WORKER INDUS

B35
HICKS J.R.,THE THEORY OF WAGES. INDUS NAT/G PAY PRICE CONTROL COST EFFICIENCY WEALTH 19/20 MARSHALL/A CLARK/JB. PAGE 59 F1164
INCOME WORKER LABOR PRODUC

B35
KEYNES J.M.,THE GENERAL THEORY OF EMPLOYMENT, INTEREST, AND MONEY. AGRI INDUS WORKER ECO/TAC
FINAN GEN/LAWS

DEMAND EQUILIB INCOME PRODUC PROFIT ATTIT WEALTH 20. PAGE 71 F1386 MARKET PRICE

B35
MARX K.,WAGE-LABOR AND CAPITAL -- VALUE, PRICE AND PROFIT. LABOR PAY PRICE COST INCOME OWN PROFIT WEALTH 19. PAGE 86 F1690 STRATA WORKER MARXIST MARXISM

B35
O'CONNOR H.,REVOLUTION IN SEATTLE. USA-45 STRATA WORKER GP/REL ATTIT SOCISM...OBS BIBLIOG/A 20 SEATTLE STRIKE COM/PARTY. PAGE 99 F1954 REV EDU/PROP LABOR MARXISM

B35
WADE J.,HISTORY OF THE MIDDLE AND WORKING CLASSES; WITH A POPULAR EXPOSITION OF THE ECONOMICAL AND POLITICAL PRINCIPLES.... FRANCE UK CONSTN FINAN INDUS LABOR INCOME PROFIT KNOWL MORAL ORD/FREE WEALTH...CHARTS 14/19. PAGE 142 F2797 WORKER STRATA CONCPT

B36
BELLOC H.,THE RESTORATION OF PROPERTY. UK STRATA NAT/G PROF/ORG DELIB/GP WORKER CREATE PROB/SOLV ECO/TAC PARTIC UTOPIA ORD/FREE SOCISM 20. PAGE 13 F0238 CONTROL MAJORIT CAP/ISM OWN

B38
DAVIES E.,"NATIONAL" CAPITALISM: THE GOVERNMENT'S RECORD AS PROTECTOR OF PRIVATE MONOPOLY. UK ELITES SOCIETY STRATA POL/PAR WORKER PROB/SOLV CONTROL SOCISM 20 MONOPOLY LABOR/PAR CHAMBRLN/N. PAGE 30 F0583 CAP/ISM NAT/G INDUS POLICY

B38
LEVINSON E.,LABOR ON THE MARCH. WORKER CREATE ECO/TAC ADJUD LEAD PARL/PROC PARTIC INGP/REL SKILL POLICY. PAGE 79 F1543 LABOR INCOME NAT/G PLAN

B38
REICH N.,LABOR RELATIONS IN REPUBLICAN GERMANY. GERMANY CONSTN ECO/DEV INDUS NAT/G ADMIN CONTROL GP/REL FASCISM POPULISM 20 WEIMAR/REP. PAGE 110 F2176 WORKER MGT LABOR BARGAIN

B39
MARQUAND H.A.,ORGANIZED LABOUR IN FOUR CONTINENTS. EUR+WWI USA-45 INDUS NAT/G PAY GP/REL TOTALISM ATTIT WEALTH ALL/IDEOS...TREND NAT/COMP 20 ILO AFL/CIO EUROPE CHINJAP MEXIC/AMER. PAGE 85 F1673 LABOR WORKER CONCPT ANTHOL

S39
COLE G.D.H.,"NAZI ECONOMICS: HOW DO THEY MANAGE IT?" GERMANY FORCES WORKER BUDGET INT/TRADE ROUTINE COERCE WAR 20 HITLER/A NAZI. PAGE 26 F0500 FASCISM ECO/TAC ATTIT PLAN

B40
BATCHELOR B.,THE NEW OUTLOOK IN BUSINESS. LAW WORKER TAX LEAD ORD/FREE...POLICY TREND. PAGE 11 F0208 LG/CO GP/REL CAP/ISM LABOR

B40
WUNDERLICH F.,LABOR UNDER GERMAN DEMOCRACY, ARBITRATION 1918-1933. GERMANY NAT/G PAY REPAR ADJUD CT/SYS GP/REL...MAJORIT 20. PAGE 149 F2941 LABOR WORKER INDUS BARGAIN

B41
LESTER R.A.,ECONOMICS OF LABOR. UK USA-45 TEC/DEV BARGAIN PAY INGP/REL INCOME...MGT 19/20. PAGE 78 F1532 LABOR ECO/DEV INDUS WORKER

B41
MACMAHON A.W.,THE ADMINISTRATION OF FEDERAL WORK RELIEF. USA-45 EX/STRUC WORKER BUDGET EFFICIENCY ...CONT/OBS CHARTS 20 WPA. PAGE 84 F1636 ADMIN NAT/G MGT GIVE

B41
SLICHTER S.H.,UNION POLICIES AND INDUSTRIAL MANAGEMENT. USA-45 INDUS TEC/DEV PAY GP/REL INGP/REL COST EFFICIENCY PRODUC...POLICY 20. PAGE 123 F2420 BARGAIN LABOR MGT WORKER

B42
VEBLEN T.B.,THE THEORY OF THE LEISURE CLASS. USA-45 SOCIETY STRATA STRUCT NAT/G SECT WORKER CREATE EDU/PROP ATTIT...SOC GEN/LAWS 19. PAGE 141 F2772 WEALTH ELITES LEISURE PRODUC

S43
HERBERG W.,"BUREAUCRACY AND DEMOCRACY IN LABOR UNIONS." LAW CONSTN STRUCT WORKER ADMIN CONTROL PARTIC RIGID/FLEX PWR TREND. PAGE 59 F1151 LABOR REPRESENT ROUTINE INGP/REL

C43
BENTHAM J.,"THE RATIONALE OF REWARD" IN J. BOWRING, ED., THE WORKS OF JEREMY BENTHAM (VOL. 2)" LAW WORKER CREATE INSPECT PAY ROUTINE HAPPINESS PRODUC SUPEGO WEALTH METH/CNCPT. PAGE 13 F0254 SANCTION ECO/TAC INCOME PWR

B44
BIENSTOCK G.,MANAGEMENT IN RUSSIAN INDUSTRY AND AGRICULTURE. USSR CONSULT WORKER LEAD COST PROFIT ATTIT DRIVE PWR...MGT METH/COMP DICTIONARY ACCT 20. PAGE 15 F0281 ADMIN MARXISM SML/CO AGRI

B44
LANDAUER C.,THEORY OF NATIONAL ECONOMIC PLANNING. USA-45 INDUS MARKET WORKER PROB/SOLV DIPLOM RATION PRICE CONTROL WAR COST 20. PAGE 75 F1465 ECO/TAC PLAN NAT/G ECO/DEV

B45
MILLIS H.A.,ORGANIZED LABOR (FIRST ED.). LAW STRUCT DELIB/GP WORKER ECO/TAC ADJUD CONTROL REPRESENT INGP/REL INCOME MGT. PAGE 92 F1797 LABOR POLICY ROUTINE GP/REL

B46
DAVIES E.,NATIONAL ENTERPRISE: THE DEVELOPMENT OF THE PUBLIC CORPORATION. UK LG/CO EX/STRUC WORKER PROB/SOLV COST ATTIT SOCISM 20. PAGE 30 F0584 ADMIN NAT/G CONTROL INDUS

B46
DRUCKER P.F.,CONCEPT OF CORPORATION. LAW LABOR WORKER PRICE CONTROL LEAD GP/REL POLICY. PAGE 34 F0665 LG/CO CENTRAL INGP/REL

B47
BAERWALD F.,FUNDAMENTALS OF LABOR ECONOMICS. LAW INDUS LABOR LG/CO CONTROL GP/REL INCOME TOTALISM ...MGT CHARTS GEN/LAWS BIBLIOG 20. PAGE 8 F0150 ECO/DEV WORKER MARKET

B47
WARNER W.L.,THE SOCIAL SYSTEM OF THE MODERN FACTORY; THE STRIKE: AN ANALYSIS. USA-45 STRATA WORKER ECO/TAC GP/REL INGP/REL...MGT SOC CHARTS 20 YANKEE/C. PAGE 143 F2824 ROLE STRUCT LABOR PROC/MFG

B47
WHITEHEAD T.N.,LEADERSHIP IN A FREE SOCIETY; A STUDY IN HUMAN RELATIONS BASED ON AN ANALYSIS OF PRESENT-DAY INDUSTRIAL CIVILIZATION. WOR-45 STRUCT R+D LABOR LG/CO SML/CO WORKER PLAN PROB/SOLV TEC/DEV DRIVE...MGT 20. PAGE 146 F2872 INDUS LEAD ORD/FREE SOCIETY

S47
DAHL R.A.,"WORKERS' CONTROL OF INDUSTRY AND THE BRITISH LABOUR PARTY." UK STRATA STRUCT DELIB/GP BARGAIN CAP/ISM DEBATE CONTROL CHOOSE GP/REL ATTIT ROLE PWR 19/20 PARLIAMENT LABOR/PAR FABIAN. PAGE 29 F0570 INDUS LABOR WORKER SOCISM

B48
HART A.G.,MONEY, DEBT, AND ECONOMIC ACTIVITY. AFR WORKER DIPLOM PRICE CONTROL BAL/PAY COST OWN PRODUC ...METH/COMP 20 FED/RESERV. PAGE 56 F1097 FINAN WEALTH ECO/TAC NAT/G

B48
HOOVER E.M.,THE LOCATION OF ECONOMIC ACTIVITY. WOR+45 MARKET WORKER PROB/SOLV INT/TRADE ADMIN COST ...POLICY CHARTS T MUNICH 20. PAGE 62 F1211 HABITAT INDUS ECO/TAC GEOG

B48
KESSELMAN L.C.,THE SOCIAL POLITICS OF THE FEPC. INDUS WORKER EDU/PROP GP/REL RACE/REL 20 NEGRO JEWS FEPC. PAGE 70 F1382 POLICY NAT/G ADMIN DISCRIM

B48
MCCABE D.A.,LABOR AND SOCIAL ORGANIZATION. LEGIS WORKER CAP/ISM ECO/TAC PAY MARXISM SOCISM SOC/INTEG 20 INTRVN/ECO. PAGE 88 F1717 LABOR STRATA NEW/LIB

B48
MILLS C.W.,THE NEW MEN OF POWER. ELITES INTELL STRUCT WORKER ANOMIE ATTIT PWR POLICY. PAGE 92 F1799 LABOR LEAD PLAN

B48
TAYLOR P.E.,THE ECONOMICS OF PUBLIC FINANCE. USA+45 USA-45 ECO/DEV WORKER PLAN BUDGET WAR INCOME WEALTH ...CONCPT STAT BIBLIOG 20. PAGE 129 F2540 FINAN POLICY NAT/G TAX

B48
WHYTE W.F.,HUMAN RELATIONS IN THE RESTAURANT INDUSTRY (1ST ED). CLIENT WORKER WAR ATTIT...MGT OBS INT. PAGE 146 F2874 INGP/REL GP/REL SERV/IND LABOR

B49
MACGREGOR D.H.,ECONOMIC THOUGHT AND POLICY. WOR-45 WORKER WAR DEMAND EFFICIENCY WEALTH LAISSEZ SOCISM ...MAJORIT BIBLIOG 19/20. PAGE 83 F1629 CONCPT POLICY ECO/TAC

B49
SHISTER J.,ECONOMICS OF THE LABOR MARKET. LOC/G NAT/G WORKER TEC/DEV BARGAIN PAY PRICE EXEC GP/REL INCOME...MGT T 20. PAGE 121 F2381 MARKET LABOR INDUS

S49
ECKLER A.R.,"IMMIGRATION AND THE LABOR FORCE." USA+45 USA-45 EXTR/IND FINAN PROC/MFG AGE/Y SKILL ...CHARTS 19/20 MIGRATION. PAGE 36 F0694 WORKER STRANGE INDUS ECO/TAC

S49
HART C.W.M.,"INDUSTRIAL RELATIONS RESEARCH AND SOCIAL THEORY." CANADA VOL/ASSN WORKER LEAD EFFICIENCY...MGT SOC METH/CNCPT METH/COMP MUNICH 20. PAGE 56 F1099 GEN/LAWS LABOR GP/REL

B50
CLARK J.M.,ALTERNATIVE TO SERFDOM. SOCIETY STRATA INDUS MARKET WORKER PRICE GP/REL PROFIT BIO/SOC PWR WEALTH...GEN/LAWS 20 KEYNES/JM. PAGE 25 F0481 ORD/FREE POPULISM ECO/TAC REPRESENT

B50
HUNT R.N.,THE THEORY AND PRACTICE OF COMMUNISM. MARXISM

STRUCT WORKER NAT/LISM TOTALISM...CONCPT TREND 19/20 STALIN/J EUROPE. PAGE 63 F1244
SOCISM REV STRATA

B50
HUTCHISON K.,THE DECLINE AND FALL OF BRITISH CAPITALISM. UK ELITES STRATA ECO/DEV LABOR WORKER CONTROL WAR PWR...BIBLIOG/A 19/20. PAGE 63 F1249
CAP/ISM SOCISM LAISSEZ DOMIN

B50
SOREL G.,REFLECTIONS ON VIOLENCE (1908) (TRANS. BY T.E. HULME AND J. ROTH). UNIV SOCIETY LABOR UTOPIA MORAL SOCISM...ANARCH SOCIALIST CONCPT 20. PAGE 124 F2445
COERCE REV WORKER MYTH

S50
DALTON M.,"CONFLICTS BETWEEN STAFF AND LINE MANAGERIAL OFFICERS" (BMR). USA+45 USA-45 ELITES LG/CO WORKER PROB/SOLV ADMIN EXEC EFFICIENCY PRODUC ...GP/COMP 20. PAGE 30 F0576
MGT ATTIT GP/REL INDUS

B51
HARBISON F.H.,GOALS AND STRATEGY IN COLLECTIVE BARGAINING. WORKER BAL/PWR PARTIC DRIVE...POLICY MGT. PAGE 55 F1074
LABOR BARGAIN GP/REL ADMIN

B51
HART A.G.,DEFENSE WITHOUT INFLATION. AFR KOREA FINAN INDUS NAT/G WORKER DIPLOM RATION TAX PRICE COST OPTIMAL 20 RESOURCE/N. PAGE 56 F1098
ECO/TAC CONTROL WAR PLAN

B51
PETERSON F.,SURVEY OF LABOR ECONOMICS (REV. ED.). STRATA ECO/DEV LABOR INSPECT BARGAIN PAY PRICE EXEC ROUTINE GP/REL ALL/VALS ORD/FREE 20 AFL/CIO DEPT/LABOR. PAGE 105 F2069
WORKER DEMAND IDEA/COMP T

B51
POOLE K.,FISCAL POLICIES AND THE AMERICAN ECONOMY. AFR ECO/DEV FINAN INDUS WORKER OP/RES INT/TRADE TAX COST INCOME PROFIT WEALTH...GP/COMP 20. PAGE 107 F2102
NAT/G POLICY ANTHOL

B51
PRINCETON U INDUSTRIAL REL SEC,COMPULSORY ARBITRATION OF UTILITY DISPUTES IN NEW JERSEY AND PENNSYLVANIA. USA+45 LEGIS WORKER ADJUD ORD/FREE ...POLICY MGT METH/COMP 20 NEW/JERSEY PENNSYLVAN. PAGE 108 F2118
BARGAIN PROVS INDUS LABOR

L51
SUMMERS C.W.,"UNION POWERS AND WORKERS RIGHTS." WORKER PROB/SOLV ECO/TAC PARTIC INGP/REL PWR. PAGE 127 F2513
LABOR CONSTN LAW REPRESENT

C51
HOMANS G.C.,"THE WESTERN ELECTRIC RESEARCHES" IN S. HOSLETT, ED., HUMAN FACTORS IN MANAGEMENT (BMR)" ACT/RES GP/REL HAPPINESS PRODUC DRIVE...MGT OBS 20. PAGE 61 F1202
OP/RES EFFICIENCY SOC/EXP WORKER

B52
DE JOUVENEL B.,THE ETHICS OF REDISTRIBUTION. UK ELITES MARKET WORKER GIVE PAY INCOME PERSON ...POLICY PSY GEN/LAWS 20. PAGE 31 F0602
WEALTH TAX SOCISM TRADIT

B52
TANNENBAUM F.,A PHILOSOPHY OF LABOR. SOCIETY STRATA INDUS LG/CO AGREE ADJUST OWN ORD/FREE PWR...CONCPT 20. PAGE 128 F2533
LABOR PHIL/SCI WORKER CREATE

S52
CHINOY E.,"THE TRADITION OF OPPORTUNITY AND THE ASPIRATIONS OF AUTOMOBILE WORKERS" (BMR)" STRATA ACT/RES ALL/VALS SKILL...INT 20. PAGE 24 F0468
WORKER ECO/DEV DRIVE INDUS

S52
KLUMB S.,"EMPLOYEE DETERMINATION OF MANAGERIAL FUNCTIONS AND CHARACTERISTICS." DELIB/GP WORKER PARTIC ROUTINE INGP/REL...CLASSIF OBS QU. PAGE 72 F1410
MGT INDUS EX/STRUC CHOOSE

C52
HUME D.,"OF INTEREST" IN D. HUME, POLITICAL DISCOURSES (1752)" UK INDUS WORKER DIPLOM PAY DEMAND INCOME WEALTH...GEN/LAWS 18 MONEY. PAGE 63 F1239
PRICE COST FINAN INT/TRADE

B53
PURCELL T.V.,THE WORKER SPEAKS HIS MIND ON COMPANY AND UNION. WORKER ADJUD LEAD RACE/REL ATTIT DRIVE MARXISM...MGT CLASSIF STAT OBS INT SAMP BIBLIOG. PAGE 108 F2131
LABOR PARTIC INGP/REL HAPPINESS

B53
ROBINSON E.A.G.,THE STRUCTURE OF COMPETITIVE INDUSTRY. UK ECO/DEV DIST/IND MARKET TEC/DEV DIPLOM EDU/PROP ADMIN EFFICIENCY WEALTH...MGT 19/20. PAGE 113 F2217
INDUS PRODUC WORKER OPTIMAL

B53
WILLIAMS J.H.,ECONOMIC STABILITY IN A CHANGING WORLD. FRANCE USA+45 USSR AGRI WORKER BUDGET INT/TRADE TAX WAR BAL/PAY COST EFFICIENCY ALL/IDEOS EQULIB 20 KEYNES/JM. PAGE 147 F2892
POLICY FINAN ECO/TAC WEALTH

S53
BIRNBAUM N.,"CONFLICTING INTERPRETATIONS OF THE RISE OF CAPITALISM: MARX AND WEBER" (BMR)" WOR-45 INTELL SOCIETY STRUCT INDUS WORKER...PHIL/SCI SOC PERS/COMP 19/20 MARX/KARL WEBER/MAX. PAGE 15 F0288
CAP/ISM IDEA/COMP ECO/DEV MARXISM

S53
DRUCKER P.F.,"THE EMPLOYEE SOCIETY." STRUCT BAL/PWR PARTIC REPRESENT PWR...DECISION CONCPT. PAGE 34 F0666
LABOR MGT WORKER CULTURE

B54
BERNSTEIN I.,ARBITRATION OF WAGES. USA+45 CONSULT PAY COST PRODUC WEALTH...CHARTS 20. PAGE 14 F0266
DELIB/GP BARGAIN WORKER PRICE

B54
INTERNATIONAL LABOUR OFF LIB,BIBLIOGRAPHY ON THE INTERNATIONAL LABOUR ORGANISATION. WORKER 20. PAGE 65 F1277
BIBLIOG LABOR INT/ORG CONFER

B54
LENIN V.I.,SELECTED WORKS (12 VOLS.). USSR INTELL SOCIETY STRATA STRUCT NAT/G POL/PAR WORKER CAP/ISM REV WAR...MARXIST PHIL/SCI 20 MARX/KARL LENIN/VI. PAGE 78 F1520
COM MARXISM

B54
MEYER A.G.,MARXISM. INTELL ECO/DEV WORKER CAP/ISM LEAD WAR ATTIT ALL/IDEOS...SOC 19/20 MARX/KARL. PAGE 90 F1766
MARXISM CONCPT ECO/TAC STRUCT

B54
TAFT P.,THE STRUCTURE AND GOVERNMENT OF LABOR UNIONS. SANCTION INGP/REL ORD/FREE PWR MARXISM ...MAJORIT STAT TREND. PAGE 128 F2524
LABOR ADJUD WORKER FINAN

S54
MACK R.W.,"ECOLOGICAL PATTERNS IN AN INDUSTRIAL SHOP" (BMR)" USA+45 CULTURE SOCIETY STRATA STRUCT LABOR NEIGH GP/REL ADJUST HABITAT...SOC SOC/INTEG 20. PAGE 83 F1634
INDUS DISCRIM WORKER

B55
BLOOM G.F.,ECONOMICS OF LABOR RELATIONS. USA+45 LAW CONSULT WORKER CAP/ISM PAY ADJUD CONTROL EFFICIENCY ORD/FREE...CHARTS 19/20 AFL/CIO NLRB DEPT/LABOR. PAGE 16 F0299
ECO/DEV ECO/TAC LABOR GOV/REL

B55
COLE G.D.H.,STUDIES IN CLASS STRUCTURE. UK NAT/G WORKER TEC/DEV EDU/PROP...CLASSIF CHARTS 20. PAGE 26 F0501
STRUCT STRATA ELITES CONCPT

B55
MAYO H.B.,DEMOCRACY AND MARXISM. COM USSR STRATA NAT/G WORKER ECO/TAC REV MORAL...PHIL/SCI HIST/WRIT IDEA/COMP WORSHIP 20 MARX/KARL LENIN/VI STALIN/J TROTSKY/L. PAGE 87 F1708
MARXISM CAP/ISM

B55
UYEHARA C.H.,COMPARATIVE PLATFORMS OF JAPAN'S MAJOR PARTIES... USA+45 AGRI LEGIS WORKER CAP/ISM ORD/FREE MARXISM SOCISM...IDEA/COMP 20 CHINJAP. PAGE 140 F2755
POLICY POL/PAR DIPLOM NAT/G

B55
WRONG D.H.,AMERICAN AND CANADIAN VIEWPOINTS. CANADA USA+45 CONSTN STRATA FAM SECT WORKER ECO/TAC EDU/PROP ADJUD MARRIAGE...IDEA/COMP 20. PAGE 149 F2936
DIPLOM ATTIT NAT/COMP CULTURE

B56
GREENHUT M.L.,PLANT LOCATION IN THEORY AND PRACTICE; THE ECONOMICS OF SPACE. WOR+45 WOR-45 MARKET WORKER COST DEMAND...CONCPT STAT CHARTS HYPO/EXP BIBLIOG 19/20. PAGE 51 F0991
SML/CO ECO/DEV CAP/ISM IDEA/COMP

B56
HICKMAN C.A.,INDIVIDUALS, GROUPS, AND ECONOMIC BEHAVIOR. WORKER PAY CONTROL EXEC GP/REL INGP/REL PERSON ROLE...PSY SOC PERS/COMP METH 20. PAGE 59 F1163
MGT ADMIN ECO/TAC PLAN

B56
LIPSET S.M.,UNION DEMOCRACY. STRUCT INDUS FACE/GP WORKER CONTROL LEAD PARTIC GP/REL ATTIT LAISSEZ ...INT QU CHARTS. PAGE 80 F1577
LABOR INGP/REL MAJORIT

B56
UPHOFF W.H.,UNDERSTANDING THE UNION MEMBER (PAMPHLET). STRATA R+D LEAD PARTIC...METH/CNCPT STAT QU. PAGE 133 F2624
LABOR WORKER ATTIT DRIVE

B56
WILCOX W.W.,SOCIAL RESPONSIBILITY IN FARM LEADERSHIP. CLIENT LEGIS EXEC LOBBY GP/REL ATTIT WEALTH. PAGE 146 F2880
AGRI LEAD VOL/ASSN WORKER

B57
BAUER P.T.,THE ECONOMICS OF UNDERDEVELOPED COUNTRIES. WOR+45 AGRI FINAN INDUS PROC/MFG WORKER CAP/ISM PAY PRICE INCOME MARXISM...METH/COMP 20 RESOURCE/N. PAGE 11 F0213
ECO/UNDEV ECO/TAC PROB/SOLV NAT/G

B57
CLARK J.M.,ECONOMIC INSTITUTIONS AND HUMAN WELFARE. USA+45 SOCIETY ECO/DEV NAT/G WORKER PLAN PROB/SOLV CAP/ISM CONTROL...POLICY 20. PAGE 25 F0482
ECO/TAC ORD/FREE WEALTH

B57
DAY A.C.L.,OUTLINE OF MONETARY ECONOMICS. AFR WOR-45 INT/ORG WORKER DIPLOM BAL/PAY COST INCOME WEALTH...TIME/SEQ SIMUL 20. PAGE 31 F0594
FINAN NAT/G EQUILIB PRICE

B57
DRUCKER P.F.,AMERICA'S NEXT TWENTY YEARS. USA+45 DIST/IND ACADEM SCHOOL DIPLOM ECO/TAC AUTOMAT HABITAT HEALTH...SOC/WK TREND MUNICH 20 URBAN/RNWL PUB/TRANS. PAGE 34 F0667
WORKER FOR/AID CENSUS GEOG

B57
DUNLOP J.T.,THE THEORY OF WAGE DETERMINATION; PROCEEDINGS OF CONFERENCE HELD BY INTERNATIONAL ECONOMIC ASSOCIATION. AFR ECO/DEV LABOR BARGAIN PAY CONFER...CHARTS ANTHOL 20. PAGE 35 F0679
PRICE WORKER GEN/LAWS INCOME

B57
MURDESHWAR A.K.,ADMINISTRATIVE PROBLEMS RELATING TO NATIONALISATION: WITH SPECIAL REFERENCE TO INDIAN STATE ENTERPRISES. CZECHOSLVK FRANCE INDIA UK USA+45 LEGIS WORKER PROB/SOLV BUDGET PRICE CONTROL ...MGT GEN/LAWS 20 PARLIAMENT. PAGE 95 F1863
NAT/G OWN INDUS ADMIN

B57
NANIWADA H.,STAAT UND WIRTSCHAFT; GRUNDLEGUNG DER NATIONALOEKONOMIE ALS DER LOGIK DER BURGERLICHEN GESELLSCHAFT. WOR+45 WOR-45 STRATA MARKET WORKER INGP/REL DEMAND EQUILIB WEALTH...POLICY IDEA/COMP GEN/LAWS 17/20 MARX/KARL KEYNES/JM LENIN/VI. PAGE 96 F1890
ALL/IDEOS ECO/TAC SOCIETY NAT/G

B57
NEUMARK S.D.,ECONOMIC INFLUENCES ON THE SOUTH AFRICAN FRONTIER, 1652-1836. SOUTH/AFR SEA AGRI NAT/G FORCES WORKER DIPLOM INT/TRADE PRICE DEMAND PRODUC...STAT CHARTS 17/19 FRONTIER. PAGE 97 F1915
COLONIAL ECO/UNDEV ECO/TAC MARKET

B57
OLIVER H.M. JR.,ECONOMIC OPINION AND POLICY IN CEYLON. CEYLON FINAN POL/PAR WORKER INT/TRADE INCOME WEALTH...GEOG UNPLAN/INT BIBLIOG 20 CMN/WLTH. PAGE 101 F1987
ECO/UNDEV NAT/LISM POLICY COLONIAL

S57
ROURKE F.E.,"THE POLITICS OF ADMINISTRATIVE ORGANIZATION: A CASE HISTORY." USA+45 LABOR WORKER PLAN ADMIN TASK EFFICIENCY 20 DEPT/LABOR CONGRESS. PAGE 114 F2251
POLICY ATTIT MGT GP/COMP

S57
TANNENBAUM A.S.,"ORGANIZATIONAL CONTROL STRUCTURE: A GENERAL DESCRIPTIVE TECHNIQUE AS APPLIED TO FOUR LOCAL UNIONS." LABOR PWR...METH/CNCPT CLASSIF QU CHARTS. PAGE 128 F2530
WORKER PARTIC STRUCT CONTROL

B58
DEFENSE AGAINST INFLATION. USA+45 LEGIS WORKER TAX PRICE DEMAND INCOME PRODUC...POLICY TREND METH/COMP 20 GOLD/STAND. PAGE 1 F0012
ECO/TAC EQUILIB WEALTH PROB/SOLV

B58
BANCROFT G.,THE AMERICAN LABOR FORCE: ITS GROWTH AND CHANGING COMPOSITION. FUT USA+45 USA-45 ECO/DEV INDUS WORKER...GEOG CHARTS 19/20. PAGE 9 F0170
LABOR STAT TREND CENSUS

B58
BUGEDA LANZAS J.,A STATEMENT OF THE LAWS OF CUBA IN MATTERS AFFECTING BUSINESS (2ND ED. REV., ENLARGED). CUBA L/A+17C LAW FINAN FAM LEGIS ACT/RES ADMIN GP/REL...BIBLIOG 20 OAS. PAGE 20 F0382
JURID NAT/G INDUS WORKER

B58
CHEEK G.,ECONOMIC AND SOCIAL IMPLICATIONS OF AUTOMATION: A BIBLIOGRAPHIC REVIEW (PAMPHLET). USA+45 LG/CO WORKER CREATE PLAN CONTROL ROUTINE PERS/REL EFFICIENCY PRODUC...METH/COMP 20. PAGE 24 F0459
BIBLIOG/A SOCIETY INDUS AUTOMAT

B58
COALE A.J.,POPULATION GROWTH AND ECONOMIC DEVELOPMENT IN LOW-INCOME COUNTRIES: A CASE STUDY OF INDIA'S PROSPECTS. INDIA AGRI WORKER INCOME AGE WEALTH...CHARTS 20 MEXIC/AMER. PAGE 25 F0495
ECO/UNDEV GEOG CENSUS SEX

B58
COLE G.D.H.,COMMUNISM AND SOCIAL DEMOCRACY (VOL. IV OF "HISTORY OF SOCIAL THOUGHT"). COM GERMANY ITALY UK AGRI INT/ORG WORKER DIPLOM COLONIAL NAT/LISM ALL/IDEOS...BIBLIOG 20 LEAGUE/NAT AUST/HUNG. PAGE 26 F0502
MARXISM REV POL/PAR SOCISM

B58
HOOD W.C.,FINANCING OF ECONOMIC ACTIVITY IN CANADA. CANADA FUT VOL/ASSN WORKER ECO/TAC ADJUD ADMIN ...CHARTS 20. PAGE 61 F1204
BUDGET FINAN GP/REL ECO/DEV

B58
JACOBSSON P.,SOME MONETARY PROBLEMS, INTERNATIONAL AND NATIONAL. WOR+45 WOR-45 ECO/DEV FORCES WORKER PROB/SOLV DIPLOM INT/TRADE...ANTHOL 20. PAGE 66 F1299
FINAN PLAN ECO/TAC NAT/COMP

B58
SEIDMAN J.I.,DEMOCRACY IN THE LABOR MOVEMENT (PAMPHLET). LAW CONSTN STRUCT DELIB/GP WORKER ADJUD PARTIC SANCTION POLICY. PAGE 119 F2345
LABOR INGP/REL PWR MAJORIT

B58
US HOUSE COMM POST OFFICE,MANPOWER UTILIZATION IN THE FEDERAL GOVERNMENT. USA+45 DIST/IND EX/STRUC LEGIS CONFER EFFICIENCY 20 CONGRESS CIVIL/SERV. PAGE 137 F2702
ADMIN WORKER DELIB/GP NAT/G

B58
US HOUSE COMM POST OFFICE,MANPOWER UTILIZATION IN THE FEDERAL GOVERNMENT. USA+45 DIST/IND EX/STRUC LEGIS CONFER EFFICIENCY 20 CONGRESS CIVIL/SERV. PAGE 137 F2703
ADMIN WORKER DELIB/GP NAT/G

L58
TRAGER F.N.,"A SELECTED AND ANNOTATED BIBLIOGRAPHY ON ECONOMIC DEVELOPMENT, 1953-1957." WOR+45 AGRI FINAN INDUS MARKET LABOR WORKER PLAN INT/TRADE PRODUC...CENSUS MUNICH. PAGE 131 F2583
BIBLIOG/A ECO/UNDEV ECO/DEV

S58
MANSFIELD E.,"A STUDY OF DECISION-MAKING WITHIN THE FIRM." LG/CO WORKER INGP/REL COST EFFICIENCY PRODUC ...CHARTS 20. PAGE 85 F1658
OP/RES PROB/SOLV AUTOMAT ROUTINE

N58
EUROPEAN COMM ECO-SOC PROG,EUROPEAN BUSINESS CYCLE POLICY (PAMPHLET). AFR EUR+WWI MARKET WORKER DIPLOM PRICE BAL/PAY 20 EUROPE. PAGE 39 F0754
ECO/DEV FINAN ECO/TAC PROB/SOLV

B59
BARBASH J.,UNIONS AND UNION LEADERSHIP. NAT/G WORKER TEC/DEV ECO/TAC PARTIC GP/REL RACE/REL ORD/FREE CLASSIF. PAGE 10 F0183
LABOR VOL/ASSN CAP/ISM LEAD

B59
BLACK J.D.,ECONOMICS FOR AGRICULTURE. USA+45 EXTR/IND FAM WORKER ACT/RES PLAN PRICE EATING INCOME...CENSUS BIBLIOG 20. PAGE 15 F0291
AGRI ECO/TAC MARKET POLICY

B59
CHECCHI V.,HONDURAS: A PROBLEM IN ECONOMIC DEVELOPMENT. HONDURAS AGRI FINAN INDUS LABOR WORKER INT/TRADE EDU/PROP PRICE HEALTH...GEOG CHARTS BIBLIOG 20. PAGE 24 F0458
ECO/UNDEV ECO/TAC PROB/SOLV PLAN

B59
GOMEZ ROBLES J.,A STATEMENT OF THE LAWS OF GUATEMALA IN MATTERS AFFECTING BUSINESS (2ND ED. REV., ENLARGED). GUATEMALA L/A+17C LAW FINAN FAM WORKER ACT/RES DIPLOM ADJUD ADMIN GP/REL 20 OAS. PAGE 48 F0945
JURID NAT/G INDUS LEGIT

B59
HARTOG F.,EUROPEAN TRADE CYCLE POLICY. WORKER TAX PRICE WAR CENTRAL DEMAND...TREND CHARTS 20 UN. PAGE 56 F1103
EQUILIB EUR+WWI INT/TRADE

B59
KELF-COHEN R.,NATIONALISATION IN BRITAIN: THE END OF DOGMA. EUR+WWI UK NAT/G POL/PAR WORKER ECO/TAC PARL/PROC WEALTH SOCISM...GOV/COMP 20. PAGE 70 F1369
NEW/LIB ECO/DEV INDUS OWN

B59
LINK R.G.,ENGLISH THEORIES OF ECONOMIC FLUCTUATIONS: 1815-1848. FRANCE UK AGRI WORKER DIPLOM PRICE TASK WAR DEMAND PRODUC...POLICY BIBLIOG 18 MALTHUS MILL/JS WILSON/J. PAGE 80 F1574
IDEA/COMP ECO/DEV WEALTH EQUILIB

B59
LOPEZ VILLAMIL H.,A STATEMENT OF THE LAWS OF THE HONDURAS IN MATTERS AFFECTING BUSINESS (2ND ED.). HONDURAS DIST/IND EXTR/IND FINAN WORKER TAX DEATH MARRIAGE OWN MARITIME 20 MIGRATION. PAGE 82 F1600
CONSTN INDUS LEGIS NAT/G

B59
SHACKLE G.L.S.,ECONOMICS FOR PLEASURE. FINAN MARKET NAT/G WORKER PLAN INT/TRADE TARIFFS PAY BAL/PAY COST PRODUC 20. PAGE 120 F2361
METH/CNCPT WEALTH INCOME

B59
STANFORD U. BOARD OF TRUSTEES,THE ALLOCATION OF ECONOMIC RESOURCES. WORKER PLAN BUDGET ECO/TAC TAX RECEIVE COST PRODUC...POLICY IDEA/COMP SIMUL ANTHOL 20. PAGE 125 F2468
INCOME PRICE FINAN

B59
STERNBERG F.,THE MILITARY AND INDUSTRIAL REVOLUTION OF OUR TIME. USA+45 USSR WOR+45 WORKER COMPUTER PLAN TEC/DEV NUC/PWR GP/REL...POLICY NAT/COMP 20. PAGE 126 F2481
DIPLOM FORCES INDUS CIVMIL/REL

B59
U OF MICHIGAN LAW SCHOOL,ATOMS AND THE LAW. USA+45 PROVS WORKER PROB/SOLV DIPLOM ADMIN GOV/REL ANTHOL. PAGE 132 F2596
NUC/PWR NAT/G CONTROL LAW

L59
FURASH E.A.,"PROBLEMS IN REVIEW: INDUSTRIAL ESPIONAGE." WORKER ECO/TAC PERS/REL OPTIMAL AGE ATTIT KNOWL...MGT DEEP/INT DEEP/QU GP/COMP IDEA/COMP. PAGE 45 F0875
INDUS TOP/EX MAJORITY

S59
BENDIX R.,"INDUSTRIALIZATION, IDEOLOGIES, AND SOCIAL STRUCTURE" (BMR)" UK USA-45 USSR STRUCT WORKER GP/REL EFFICIENCY...IDEA/COMP 20. PAGE 13 F0243
INDUS ATTIT MGT ADMIN

S59
CLONER A.,"THE CALIFORNIA LEGISLATOR AND THE
INCOME

PROBLEM OF COMPENSATION." USA+45 WORKER REPRESENT. PAGE 25 F0492
PROVS LEGIS SUPEGO

S59
MILLER A.S.,"CONSTITUTIONALIZING THE CORPORATION." LABOR NAT/G WORKER PWR...POLICY MGT. PAGE 91 F1789
CONSTN INGP/REL LG/CO CONTROL

S59
REES A.,"DO UNIONS CAUSE INFLATION?" CONTROL 20. PAGE 110 F2171
LABOR ECO/TAC PRICE WORKER

S59
SHEPPARD H.L.,"THE POLITICAL ATTITUDES AND PREFERENCES OF UNION MEMBERS: THE CASE OF THE DETROIT AUTO WORKERS." LOBBY CHOOSE ROLE...CLASSIF QU SAMP TREND. PAGE 120 F2376
LABOR ATTIT WORKER

N59
CHAMBER OF COMMERCE OF USA,ECONOMIC LESSONS OF POSTWAR RECESSIONS (PAMPHLET). AFR USA+45 LAW LEGIS WORKER TAX...CHARTS 20 CONGRESS FED/RESERV. PAGE 23 F0440
ECO/DEV PROB/SOLV FINAN ECO/TAC

B60
BELLAN R.C.,PRINCIPLES OF ECONOMICS AND THE CANADIAN ECONOMY (2ND ED.). CANADA UK USA+45 LABOR WORKER CAP/ISM INT/TRADE RISK BAL/PAY EQUILIB ALL/IDEOS 20. PAGE 12 F0236
ECO/DEV PRODUC WEALTH FINAN

B60
CROSSER P.K.,STATE CAPITALISM IN THE ECONOMY OF THE UNITED STATES. USA+45 USA-45 AGRI FINAN INDUS LABOR WORKER RATION CONTROL GOV/REL DEMAND...NEW/IDEA 20. PAGE 29 F0557
CAP/ISM ECO/DEV ECO/TAC NAT/G

B60
FRYE R.J.,GOVERNMENT AND LABOR: THE ALABAMA PROGRAM. USA+45 INDUS R+D LABOR WORKER BUDGET EFFICIENCY AGE/Y HEALTH...CHARTS 20 ALABAMA. PAGE 45 F0870
ADMIN LEGIS LOC/G PROVS

B60
KERR C.,INDUSTRIALISM AND INDUSTRIAL MAN. CULTURE SOCIETY ECO/UNDEV NAT/G ADMIN PRODUC WEALTH ...PREDICT TREND NAT/COMP 19/20. PAGE 70 F1381
WORKER MGT ECO/DEV INDUS

B60
MAYO H.B.,INTRODUCTION TO MARXIST THEORY. SECT WORKER POPULISM SOCISM 19/20. PAGE 87 F1709
MARXISM STRATA IDEA/COMP PHIL/SCI

B60
MOORE W.E.,LABOR COMMITMENT AND SOCIAL CHANGE IN DEVELOPING AREAS. SOCIETY STRATA ECO/UNDEV MARKET VOL/ASSN WORKER AUTHORIT SKILL...MGT NAT/COMP SOC/INTEG 20. PAGE 93 F1823
LABOR ORD/FREE ATTIT INDUS

B60
ROBERTSON D.,THE CONTROL OF INDUSTRY. UK MARKET LABOR WORKER PRICE CONTROL GP/REL COST DEMAND ORD/FREE WEALTH NEW/LIB SOCISM 20. PAGE 112 F2211
INDUS FINAN NAT/G ECO/DEV

B60
SLOTKIN J.S.,FROM FIELD TO FACTORY; NEW INDUSTRIAL EMPLOYEES. HABITAT...MGT NEW/IDEA NAT/COMP BIBLIOG SOC/INTEG 20. PAGE 123 F2423
INDUS LABOR CULTURE WORKER

B60
WEINER H.E.,BRITISH LABOR AND PUBLIC OWNERSHIP. UK SERV/IND LG/CO WORKER CONTROL OWN 20. PAGE 145 F2850
LABOR NAT/G INDUS ATTIT

B60
WODDIS J.,AFRICA: THE ROOTS OF REVOLT. SOUTH/AFR WORKER INT/TRADE RACE/REL DISCRIM ORD/FREE 20. PAGE 148 F2915
COLONIAL SOVEREIGN WAR ECO/UNDEV

B61
ACKLEY G.,MACROECONOMIC THEORY. AFR FINAN WORKER ECO/TAC PRICE COST INCOME PRODUC...MATH TREND CHARTS IDEA/COMP T KEYNES/JM. PAGE 2 F0034
SIMUL ECOMETRIC WEALTH

B61
AMERICAN MANAGEMENT ASSN,SUPERIOR-SUBORDINATE COMMUNICATION IN MANAGEMENT. STRATA FINAN INDUS SML/CO WORKER CONTROL EXEC ATTIT 20. PAGE 5 F0090
MGT ACT/RES PERS/REL LG/CO

B61
BARBASH J.,LABOR'S GRASS ROOTS. CONSTN NAT/G EX/STRUC LEGIS WORKER LEAD...MAJORIT BIBLIOG. PAGE 10 F0184
LABOR INGP/REL GP/REL LAW

B61
CAMPAIGNE J.G.,CHECK-OFF: LABOR BOSSES AND WORKING MEN. LEGIS WORKER EDU/PROP DEBATE COERCE REPRESENT GP/REL ORD/FREE CONSERVE. PAGE 21 F0404
LABOR ELITES PWR CONTROL

B61
CARROTHERS A.W.R.,LABOR ARBITRATION IN CANADA. CANADA LAW NAT/G CONSULT LEGIS WORKER ADJUD ADMIN CT/SYS 20. PAGE 22 F0422
LABOR MGT GP/REL BARGAIN

B61
DEWITT N.,EDUCATION AND PROFESSIONAL EMPLOYMENT IN THE USSR. USSR PROF/ORG WORKER PLAN ADMIN UTIL AGE/C AGE/Y MARXISM...STAT CHARTS 20. PAGE 32 F0629
EDU/PROP ACADEM SCHOOL INTELL

B61
DOIG J.W.,THE POLITICS OF METROPOLITAN TRANSPORTATION. DELIB/GP WORKER DIPLOM TASK EFFICIENCY UTIL...CHARTS BIBLIOG MUNICH 20 NEW/YORK NEW/JERSEY PUB/TRANS RAILROAD. PAGE 34 F0652
PROB/SOLV STRATA DIST/IND

B61
FELLNER W.,THE PROBLEM OF RISING PRICES. AGRI INDUS WORKER BUDGET CAP/ISM ECO/TAC INT/TRADE PAY DEMAND ...POLICY 20 EEC. PAGE 40 F0780
PRICE MARKET ECO/DEV COST

B61
FLINN M.W.,AN ECONOMIC AND SOCIAL HISTORY OF BRITAIN, 1066-1939. UK LAW STRATA STRUCT AGRI DIST/IND INDUS WORKER INT/TRADE WAR...CENSUS 11/20. PAGE 42 F0811
SOCIETY SOC

B61
FRIEDMANN G.,THE ANATOMY OF WORK. USA+45 SOCIETY CONTROL ROUTINE DRIVE SKILL...PSY SOC STAT OBS METH/COMP PERS/COMP 20. PAGE 44 F0862
AUTOMAT WORKER INDUS PERSON

B61
GALENSON W.,TRADE UNION DEMOCRACY IN WESTERN EUROPE. ECO/DEV INDUS PROF/ORG WORKER INCOME ...METH/COMP 20. PAGE 45 F0886
LABOR GP/REL ECO/TAC EUR+WWI

B61
HENDERSON W.O.,THE INDUSTRIAL REVOLUTION IN EUROPE. FRANCE GERMANY MOD/EUR RUSSIA WORKER PROFIT PWR MARXISM SOCISM...SOC HIST/WRIT 19 INDUS/REV. PAGE 58 F1148
INDUS REV CAP/ISM TEC/DEV

B61
KELSO L.O.,THE NEW CAPITALISTS: A PROPOSAL TO FREE ECONOMIC GROWTH FROM THE SLAVERY OF SAVINGS. UNIV USA+45 ECO/DEV CAP/ISM PRODUC WEALTH SOCISM ...NEW/IDEA 20. PAGE 70 F1373
ECO/TAC WORKER FINAN GEN/LAWS

B61
LENIN V.I.,WHAT IS TO BE DONE? (1902). RUSSIA LABOR NAT/G POL/PAR WORKER CAP/ISM ECO/TAC ADMIN PARTIC ...MARXIST IDEA/COMP GEN/LAWS 19/20. PAGE 78 F1522
EDU/PROP PRESS MARXISM METH/COMP

B61
LICHTHEIM G.,MARXISM. GERMANY SOCIETY WORKER CAP/ISM ECO/TAC NAT/LISM POPULISM...TIME/SEQ GOV/COMP NAT/COMP 18/20 COM/PARTY. PAGE 80 F1559
MARXISM SOCISM IDEA/COMP CULTURE

B61
LIEFMANN-KEIL E.,OKONOMISCHE THEORIE DER SOZIALPOLITIK. INT/ORG LABOR WORKER COST INCOME NEW/LIB...CONCPT SOC/INTEG 20. PAGE 80 F1562
ECO/DEV INDUS NAT/G SOC/WK

B61
MORRIS B.R.,PROBLEMS OF AMERICAN ECONOMIC GROWTH. USA+45 LABOR WORKER BUDGET ECO/TAC INT/TRADE EQUILIB 20. PAGE 94 F1836
ECO/DEV POLICY TEC/DEV DEMAND

B61
NEW JERSEY LEGISLATURE-SENATE,PUBLIC HEARINGS BEFORE COMMITTEE ON REVISION AND AMENDMENT OF LAWS ON SENATE BILL NO. 8. USA+45 FINAN PROVS WORKER ACT/RES PLAN BUDGET TAX CRIME...IDEA/COMP MUNICH 20 NEW/JERSEY URBAN/RNWL. PAGE 98 F1919
LEGIS INDUS PROB/SOLV

B61
SEPULVEDA C.,A STATEMENT OF THE LAWS OF MEXICO IN MATTERS AFFECTING BUSINESS (3RD ED.). AGRI DIST/IND EXTR/IND FINAN INDUS WORKER TAX MARRIAGE OWN ORD/FREE...BIBLIOG 20 MEXIC/AMER TREATY MIGRATION MONOPOLY. PAGE 119 F2356
CONSTN NAT/G JURID LEGIS

B61
STROUD G.S.,LABOR HISTORY IN THE UNITED STATES: A GENERAL BIBLIOGRAPHY. USA+45 USA-45 STRATA VOL/ASSN AUTOMAT GP/REL INGP/REL ATTIT HEALTH 18/20. PAGE 127 F2504
BIBLIOG WORKER LABOR

S61
CYERT R.M.,"TWO EXPERIMENTS ON BIAS AND CONFLICT IN ORGANIZATIONAL ESTIMATION." WORKER PROB/SOLV EFFICIENCY...MGT PSY STAT CHARTS. PAGE 29 F0568
LAB/EXP ROUTINE ADMIN DECISION

S61
DICKS-MIREAUX L.A.,"THE INTERRELATIONSHIP BETWEEN COST AND PRICE CHANGES 19461959: A STUDY OF INFLATION IN POST-WAR BRITAIN" AFR UK ECO/DEV INDUS WORKER ECO/TAC ORD/FREE WEALTH...ECOMETRIC REGRESS STAT TREND CHARTS 20. PAGE 33 F0634
PRICE PAY DEMAND

B62
BACKMAN J.,THE ECONOMICS OF THE ELECTRICAL MACHINERY INDUSTRY. USA+45 PROC/MFG LABOR WORKER INT/TRADE TV PRICE COST...CHARTS 19/20. PAGE 8 F0147
PRODUC TEC/DEV TREND

B62
BRUMBERG A.,RUSSIA UNDER KHRUSHCHEV. FUT USSR
COM

SOCIETY ECO/DEV AGRI PERF/ART WORKER PWR...SOC ANTHOL 20 KHRUSH/N. PAGE 20 F0377
MARXISM NAT/G CHIEF

B62
DE GRAZIA S.,OF TIME, WORK, AND LEISURE. USA+45 ECO/DEV WORKER HAPPINESS UTOPIA ALL/VALS...SOC NEW/IDEA TIME. PAGE 31 F0599
CULTURE LEISURE CONCPT

B62
DE LAVALLE H.,A STATEMENT OF THE LAWS OF PERU IN MATTERS AFFECTING BUSINESS (3RD ED.). PERU WORKER INT/TRADE INCOME ORD/FREE...INT/LAW 20. PAGE 31 F0603
CONSTN JURID FINAN TAX

B62
DEBUYST F.,LAS CLASES SOCIALES EN AMERICA LATINA. L/A+17C SOCIETY STRUCT WORKER EDU/PROP RACE/REL ATTIT HABITAT ROLE...GEOG SOC NAT/COMP SOC/INTEG 20. PAGE 32 F0612
STRATA GP/REL WEALTH

B62
DENISON E.F.,THE SOURCES OF ECONOMIC GROWTH IN THE UNITED STATES AND THE ALTERNATIVES BEFORE US. AGRI INDUS SCHOOL TEC/DEV CAP/ISM ECO/TAC PRICE COST WEALTH...STAT TREND CHARTS 20. PAGE 32 F0620
ECO/DEV WORKER PRODUC

B62
DOBB M.,CAPITALISM YESTERDAY AND TODAY. UK WORKER WAR PRODUC PROFIT 18/20 MONOPOLY. PAGE 33 F0646
CAP/ISM TIME/SEQ CONCPT ECO/TAC

B62
FATOUROS A.A.,GOVERNMENT GUARANTEES TO FOREIGN INVESTORS. WOR+45 ECO/UNDEV INDUS WORKER ADJUD ...NAT/COMP BIBLIOG TREATY. PAGE 39 F0767
NAT/G FINAN INT/TRADE ECO/DEV

B62
FRIEDMAN M.,CAPITALISM AND FREEDOM. USA+45 FINAN LG/CO WORKER INT/TRADE RECEIVE EDU/PROP CONTROL DISCRIM INCOME WEALTH POLICY. PAGE 44 F0859
CAP/ISM ORD/FREE NAT/G ECO/DEV

B62
GALENSON W.,LABOR IN DEVELOPING COUNTRIES. BRAZIL INDONESIA ISRAEL PAKISTAN TURKEY AGRI INDUS WORKER PAY PRICE GP/REL WEALTH...MGT CHARTS METH/COMP NAT/COMP 20. PAGE 45 F0888
LABOR ECO/UNDEV BARGAIN POL/PAR

B62
HARRINGTON M.,THE OTHER AMERICA: POVERTY IN THE UNITED STATES. WORKER CREATE REPRESENT RACE/REL AGE/O DRIVE POLICY. PAGE 55 F1086
WEALTH WELF/ST INCOME CULTURE

B62
HOOVER E.M.,ANATOMY OF A METROPOLIS. FUT USA+45 SOCIETY ECO/DEV DIST/IND INDUS WORKER ECO/TAC TAX GP/REL COST WEALTH MUNICH 20 NEWYORK/C. PAGE 62 F1212
ROUTINE TREND INCOME

B62
LEVENSTEIN A.,WHY PEOPLE WORK; CHANGING INCENTIVES IN A TROUBLED WORLD. USA+45 SOCIETY PROB/SOLV TEC/DEV EDU/PROP ADJUST...CENSUS BIBLIOG 20. PAGE 79 F1538
DRIVE WORKER ECO/DEV ANOMIE

B62
MEANS G.C.,THE CORPORATE REVOLUTION IN AMERICA: ECONOMIC REALITY VS. ECONOMIC THEORY. USA+45 USA-45 INDUS WORKER PLAN CAP/ISM ADMIN...IDEA/COMP 20. PAGE 89 F1742
LG/CO MARKET CONTROL PRICE

B62
MORGAN C.A.,LABOR ECONOMICS. LAW INDUS MARKET WORKER PLAN PROB/SOLV GOV/REL INCOME ROLE...T 20 DEPT/LABOR NLRB. PAGE 93 F1829
LABOR ECO/TAC ECO/DEV CAP/ISM

B62
PONCET J.,LA COLONISATION ET L'AGRICULTURE EUROPEENNES EN TUNISIE DEPUIS 1881. FRANCE WORKER TEC/DEV ECO/TAC CONTROL EFFICIENCY ROLE WEALTH 19/20 TUNIS. PAGE 107 F2101
ECO/UNDEV AGRI COLONIAL FINAN

B62
REES A.,THE ECONOMICS OF TRADE UNIONS. FUT ECO/DEV INDUS BARGAIN CAP/ISM PRICE SENIOR CONTROL GP/REL COST...TREND 20 AFL/CIO. PAGE 110 F2172
LABOR WORKER ECO/TAC

B62
ROBERTSON B.C.,REGIONAL DEVELOPMENT IN THE EUROPEAN ECONOMIC COMMUNITY. EUR+WWI FRANCE FUT ITALY UK ECO/UNDEV WORKER ACT/RES PROB/SOLV TEC/DEV ECO/TAC INT/TRADE EEC. PAGE 112 F2209
PLAN ECO/DEV INT/ORG REGION

B62
SRIVASTAVA G.L.,COLLECTIVE BARGAINING AND LABOR-MANAGEMENT RELATIONS IN INDIA. INDIA UK USA+45 INDUS LEGIS WORKER ADJUD EFFICIENCY PRODUC ...METH/COMP 20. PAGE 125 F2462
LABOR MGT BARGAIN GP/REL

B62
URQUIDI C.W.,A STATEMENT OF THE LAWS OF BOLIVIA IN MATTERS AFFECTING BUSINESS (3RD ED. REV., ENLARGED). L/A+17C LAW FINAN FAM WORKER ACT/RES DIPLOM ADJUD ADMIN GP/REL 20 BOLIV OAS. PAGE 133 F2626
JURID INDUS NAT/G LEGIT

B62
WOODS H.D.,LABOUR POLICY AND LABOUR ECONOMICS IN CANADA. CANADA FUT NAT/G VOL/ASSN WORKER BARGAIN ECO/TAC PAY CONFER GP/REL 20. PAGE 148 F2924
LABOR POLICY INDUS ECO/DEV

L62
SCHULTZ T.W.,"INVESTMENT IN HUMAN BEINGS." ECO/DEV ECO/TAC CONFER COST INCOME PRODUC HEALTH...GEOG ANTHOL. PAGE 117 F2315
FINAN WORKER EDU/PROP SKILL

N62
BANK INTERNATIONAL SETTLEMENTS,AUSTRIA: MONETARY AND ECONOMIC SITUATION 1952-61 (PAMPHLET). AUSTRIA WORKER BUDGET INT/TRADE PRICE BAL/PAY DEMAND EFFICIENCY INCOME PRODUC...STAT 20 SILVER. PAGE 9 F0174
FINAN ECO/DEV CHARTS WEALTH

B63
BURTT E.J. JR.,LABOR MARKETS, UNIONS, AND GOVERNMENT POLICIES. USA+45 MARKET NAT/G DELIB/GP CREATE BARGAIN GP/REL ORD/FREE PWR...POLICY CHARTS 20 AFL/CIO. PAGE 20 F0393
LABOR ECO/DEV CONTROL WORKER

B63
CHAMBERLAIN E.H.,THE ECONOMIC ANALYSIS OF LABOR UNION POWER (PAMPHLET). WORKER ECO/TAC DOMIN COERCE GP/REL DRIVE WEALTH POLICY. PAGE 23 F0441
LABOR PWR CONTROL

B63
FLORES E.,LAND REFORM AND THE ALLIANCE FOR PROGRESS (PAMPHLET). L/A+17C USA+45 STRUCT ECO/UNDEV NAT/G WORKER CREATE PLAN ECO/TAC COERCE REV 20 ALL/PROG. PAGE 42 F0815
AGRI INT/ORG DIPLOM POLICY

B63
FURTADO C.,THE ECONOMIC GROWTH OF BRAZIL: A SURVEY FROM COLONIAL TO MODERN TIMES. L/A+17C AGRI DIST/IND EXTR/IND INDUS WORKER COLONIAL RACE/REL OWN GOV/COMP. PAGE 45 F0877
ECO/UNDEV TEC/DEV LABOR DOMIN

B63
GODWIN F.W.,THE HIDDEN FORCE. PUERT/RICO WOR+45 STRUCT VOL/ASSN PROB/SOLV DIPLOM CONFER...BIBLIOG 20 PEACE/CORP. PAGE 48 F0931
ECO/UNDEV WORKER SKILL ECO/TAC

B63
GORDON M.S.,THE ECONOMICS OF WELFARE POLICIES. INDUS LOC/G NAT/G LEGIS WORKER INCOME AGE/O SKILL WEALTH...METH/COMP NAT/COMP 20. PAGE 49 F0959
METH/CNCPT ECO/TAC POLICY

B63
HAUSMAN W.H.,MANAGING ECONOMIC DEVELOPMENT IN AFRICA. AFR USA+45 LAW FINAN WORKER TEC/DEV WEALTH ...ANTHOL 20. PAGE 57 F1116
ECO/UNDEV PLAN FOR/AID MGT

B63
IANNI O.,INDUSTRIALIZACAO E DESENVOLVIMENTO SOCIAL NO BRASIL. BRAZIL L/A+17C STRATA STRUCT ECO/UNDEV EDU/PROP LEAD LOBBY NAT/LISM 20. PAGE 64 F1257
WORKER GP/REL INDUS PARTIC

B63
LETHBRIDGE H.J.,THE PEASANT AND THE COMMUNES. CHINA/COM COM USSR NEIGH PROB/SOLV ADJUST EFFICIENCY...POLICY METH/COMP NAT/COMP 20. PAGE 78 F1535
MARXISM ECO/TAC AGRI WORKER

B63
LEWIS G.K.,PUERTO RICO: FREEDOM AND POWER IN THE CARIBBEAN. PUERT/RICO USA+45 CULTURE STRUCT INDUS POL/PAR WORKER EDU/PROP CATHISM 20. PAGE 79 F1548
ECO/UNDEV COLONIAL NAT/LISM GEOG

B63
MARX K.,THE POVERTY OF PHILOSOPHY (1847). SOCIETY STRATA INDUS WORKER OWN UTOPIA SOCISM...GEN/LAWS MARX/KARL. PAGE 86 F1692
MARXIST PRODUC

B63
MEEK R.L.,THE ECONOMICS OF PHYSIOCRACY. FRANCE UK AGRI FINAN WORKER CAP/ISM TAX DEMAND EQUILIB INCOME HABITAT...CHARTS ANTHOL 17. PAGE 89 F1744
PRODUC WEALTH MARKET

B63
SELF P.,THE STATE AND THE FARMER. UK ECO/DEV MARKET WORKER PRICE CONTROL GP/REL...WELF/ST 20 DEPT/AGRI. PAGE 119 F2346
AGRI NAT/G ADMIN VOL/ASSN

B63
SHANKS M.,THE LESSONS OF PUBLIC ENTERPRISE. UK LEGIS WORKER ECO/TAC ADMIN PARL/PROC GOV/REL ATTIT ...POLICY MGT METH/COMP NAT/COMP ANTHOL 20 PARLIAMENT. PAGE 120 F2364
SOCISM OWN NAT/G INDUS

B63
STIFEL L.D.,THE TEXTILE INDUSTRY - A CASE STUDY OF INDUSTRIAL DEVELOPMENT IN THE PHILIPPINES (PAPER). PHILIPPINE WORKER CAP/ISM INT/TRADE TARIFFS RECEIVE PRICE ADMIN COST EFFICIENCY WEALTH...BIBLIOG 20. PAGE 126 F2486
S/ASIA ECO/UNDEV PROC/MFG NAT/G

B63
US BD GOVERNORS FEDL RESRV,THE FEDERAL RESERVE AND THE TREASURY. USA+45 WORKER PROB/SOLV PRICE COST DEMAND WEALTH...STAT INT CHARTS 20 FED/RESERV DEPT/TREAS. PAGE 134 F2641
FINAN GOV/REL CONTROL BUDGET

B63
US DEPARTMENT OF LABOR,THE ANVIL AND THE PLOW. KOREA USA+45 USA-45 INDUS WORKER BUDGET WAR ...POLICY AUD/VIS CHARTS 20 DEPT/LABOR. PAGE 135 F2667
ECO/DEV LABOR ECO/TAC NAT/G

B63
WALKER F.V.,GROWTH, EMPLOYMENT, AND THE PRICE
ECO/DEV

LEVEL. USA+45 NAT/G PLAN ECO/TAC DEMAND EFFICIENCY CHARTS. PAGE 142 F2803
FINAN PRICE WORKER

S63
ETHERINGTON D.M.,"LAND RESETTLEMENT IN KENYA: POLICY AND PRACTICE" AFR TEC/DEV ECO/TAC FOR/AID TAX PRODUC...CHARTS 20. PAGE 39 F0752
ECO/UNDEV AGRI WORKER PLAN

S63
FLOREA I.,"CU PRIVIRE LA OBIECTUL MATERIALISMULUI ISTORIC SI AL COMUNISMULUI STIINTIFIC SI LA RAPORTUL DINTRE ELE." EUR+WWI WOR+45 WOR-45 INTELL NAT/G POL/PAR WORKER EDU/PROP PERCEPT MARXISM ...MARXIST PHIL/SCI CONCPT TOT/POP 20. PAGE 42 F0812
COM ATTIT TOTALISM

S63
NYE J.,"TANGANYIKA'S SELF-HELP." TANZANIA NAT/G GIVE COST EFFICIENCY NAT/LISM 20. PAGE 99 F1948
ECO/TAC POL/PAR ECO/UNDEV WORKER

S63
REES A.,"THE EFFECTS OF UNIONS ON RESOURCE ALLOCATION." USA+45 WORKER PRICE CONTROL GP/REL ...MGT METH/COMP 20. PAGE 110 F2173
LABOR BARGAIN RATION INCOME

B64
BROWN E.H.P.,A COURSE IN APPLIED ECONOMICS (2ND ED.). ECO/DEV FINAN MARKET WORKER INT/TRADE RATION RENT PAY PRICE BAL/PAY...DECISION T RESOURCE/N. PAGE 19 F0368
POLICY ECO/TAC PROB/SOLV

B64
COMMISSION ON MONEY AND CREDIT,INFLATION, GROWTH, AND EMPLOYMENT. AFR USA+45 PLAN PROB/SOLV PAY PRICE EFFICIENCY PRODUC WEALTH 20. PAGE 26 F0514
WORKER ECO/TAC OPTIMAL

B64
EDWARDS E.O.,THE NATION'S ECONOMIC OBJECTIVES. INDUS WORKER BUDGET DIPLOM CONTROL ORD/FREE ...POLICY SOC METH/CNCPT ANTHOL 20. PAGE 36 F0704
NAT/G ECO/TAC

B64
EINZIG P.,MONETARY POLICY: ENDS AND MEANS. AFR UK INDUS WORKER PLAN DIPLOM PRICE BAL/PAY COST WEALTH ...DECISION TIME/SEQ 20. PAGE 37 F0715
FINAN POLICY ECO/TAC BUDGET

B64
FEI J.C.H.,DEVELOPMENT OF THE LABOR SURPLUS ECONOMY: THEORY AND POLICY. WOR+45 AGRI INDUS MARKET PROB/SOLV TEC/DEV...STAT CHARTS GEN/LAWS METH 20 THIRD/WRLD. PAGE 40 F0772
ECO/TAC POLICY WORKER ECO/UNDEV

B64
HARBISON F.H.,EDUCATION, MANPOWER, AND ECONOMIC GROWTH. WOR+45 ECO/DEV ECO/UNDEV ACADEM LABOR SCHOOL WORKER UTIL...IDEA/COMP NAT/COMP. PAGE 55 F1075
PLAN TEC/DEV EDU/PROP SKILL

B64
HERSKOVITS M.J.,ECONOMIC TRANSITION IN AFRICA. FUT INT/ORG NAT/G WORKER PROB/SOLV TEC/DEV INT/TRADE EQUILIB INCOME...ANTHOL 20. PAGE 59 F1157
AFR ECO/UNDEV PLAN ADMIN

B64
INTERNATIONAL LABOUR OFFICE,EMPLOYMENT AND ECONOMIC GROWTH. ECO/DEV ECO/UNDEV NAT/G PLAN DIPLOM INT/TRADE CONTROL INCOME PRODUC WEALTH...STAT NAT/COMP 20 ILO. PAGE 65 F1279
WORKER METH/COMP ECO/TAC OPTIMAL

B64
KAPLAN A.D.H.,BIG ENTERPRISE IN A COMPETITIVE SYSTEM (REV. ED.). USA+45 INDUS MARKET WORKER TEC/DEV ECO/TAC PRICE ADJUD ADMIN CONTROL...MGT CHARTS 20 MONOPOLY. PAGE 69 F1351
FINAN GP/REL NAT/G LG/CO

B64
KUZNETS S.,POSTWAR ECONOMIC GROWTH: FOUR LECTURES. WOR+45 INDUS NAT/G WORKER TEC/DEV ECO/TAC RATION TARIFFS PRICE BAL/PAY COST DEMAND 20. PAGE 74 F1455
ECO/DEV ECO/UNDEV TREND FINAN

B64
MORGAN H.W.,AMERICAN SOCIALISM 1900-1960. AFR USA+45 USA-45 INTELL AGRI LABOR WORKER BARGAIN ECO/TAC GP/REL RACE/REL 20 NEGRO MIGRATION. PAGE 93 F1830
SOCISM POL/PAR ECO/DEV STRATA

B64
NATIONAL COUN APPLIED ECO RES,A STRATEGY FOR THE FOURTH PLAN. INDIA DIST/IND EXTR/IND SERV/IND ECO/TAC RATION EDU/PROP EATING HEALTH...CHARTS 20. PAGE 97 F1900
ECO/UNDEV PLAN AGRI WORKER

B64
NEUFIELD M.F.,A REPRESENTATIVE BIBLIOGRAPHY OF AMERICAN LABOR HISTORY. USA+45 USA-45 20. PAGE 97 F1914
BIBLIOG LABOR WORKER INDUS

B64
PIERSON J.H.,INSURING FULL EMPLOYMENT. USA+45 LABOR DIPLOM ECO/TAC PAY BAL/PAY 20. PAGE 106 F2084
ECO/DEV INT/TRADE POLICY WORKER

B64
REDLICH F.,THE GERMAN MILITARY ENTERPRISER AND HIS WORK FORCE. CHRIST-17C GERMANY ELITES SOCIETY FINAN ECO/TAC CIVMIL/REL GP/REL INGP/REL...HIST/WRIT METH/COMP 14/17. PAGE 110 F2170
EX/STRUC FORCES PROFIT WORKER

B64
REUSS H.S.,THE CRITICAL DECADE - AN ECONOMIC POLICY FOR AMERICA AND THE FREE WORLD. AFR USA+45 FINAN POL/PAR WORKER PLAN DIPLOM ECO/TAC TARIFFS BAL/PAY ...POLICY 20 CONGRESS. PAGE 111 F2181
FOR/AID INT/TRADE LABOR LEGIS

B64
RUSTAMJI R.F.,THE LAW OF INDUSTRIAL DISPUTES IN INDIA. INDIA LEGIS WORKER CONTROL GP/REL...JURID MGT TIME/SEQ 20. PAGE 115 F2264
INDUS ADJUD BARGAIN LABOR

B64
SOLOW R.M.,THE NATURE AND SOURCES OF UNEMPLOYMENT IN THE UNITED STATES (PAMPHLET). USA+45 INDUS LABOR TEC/DEV ECO/TAC SKILL WEALTH...TREND NAT/COMP 20. PAGE 124 F2439
ECO/DEV WORKER STAT PRODUC

B64
STONIER A.W.,EXERCISES IN ECONOMICS. FINAN INDUS TEC/DEV RENT PAY EQUILIB PRODUC PROFIT...METH/COMP T. PAGE 127 F2498
PRICE MARKET WORKER

B64
STRONG A.L.,THE RISE OF THE CHINESE PEOPLE'S COMMUNES - AND SIX YEARS AFTER (2ND ED.). CHINA/COM AGRI INDUS FORCES WORKER PROB/SOLV EDU/PROP EFFICIENCY ISOLAT 20. PAGE 127 F2503
NEIGH ECO/TAC MARXISM METH/COMP

B64
TELLADO A.,A STATEMENT OF THE LAWS OF THE DOMINICAN REPUBLIC IN MATTERS AFFECTING BUSINESS (3RD ED.). DOMIN/REP AGRI DIST/IND EXTR/IND FINAN FAM WORKER ECO/TAC TAX CT/SYS MARRIAGE OWN...BIBLIOG 20 MIGRATION. PAGE 129 F2542
CONSTN LEGIS NAT/G INDUS

B64
US DEPT LABOR OFF SOLICITOR,LEGISLATIVE HISTORY OF THE LABOR-MANAGEMENT AND DISCLOSURE ACT OF 1959. DELIB/GP WORKER ADMIN LOBBY PARL/PROC SANCTION CHOOSE GOV/REL 20 CONGRESS PRESIDENT. PAGE 136 F2677
LABOR LEGIS DEBATE POLICY

B64
WELLISZ S.,THE ECONOMICS OF THE SOVIET BLOC. COM USSR INDUS WORKER PLAN BUDGET INT/TRADE TAX PRICE PRODUC WEALTH MARXISM...METH/COMP 20. PAGE 145 F2854
EFFICIENCY ADMIN MARKET

S64
TOBIN J.,"ECONOMIC GROWTH AS AN OBJECTIVE OF GOVERNMENT POLICY." FUT WOR+45 FINAN WORKER BUDGET INCOME...SOC 20. PAGE 131 F2579
ECO/DEV POLICY ECO/TAC IDEA/COMP

C64
NORGREN P.H.,"TOWARD FAIR EMPLOYMENT." USA+45 LAW STRATA LABOR NAT/G FORCES ACT/RES ADMIN ATTIT ...POLICY BIBLIOG 20 NEGRO. PAGE 98 F1932
RACE/REL DISCRIM WORKER MGT

N64
KENYA MINISTRY ECO PLAN DEV,AFRICAN SOCIALISM AND ITS APPLICATION TO PLANNING IN KENYA (PAMPHLET). AFR AGRI INDUS WORKER TAX COLONIAL WEALTH 20. PAGE 70 F1380
NAT/G SOCISM PLAN ECO/UNDEV

B65
ALEXANDER R.J.,ORGANIZED LABOR IN LATIN AMERICA. L/A+17C INT/ORG LEGIS WORKER TEC/DEV BARGAIN INT/TRADE REV...NAT/COMP BIBLIOG 20. PAGE 3 F0059
LABOR POL/PAR ECO/UNDEV POLICY

B65
ANDERSON C.A.,EDUCATION AND ECONOMIC DEVELOPMENT. INDUS R+D SCHOOL TEC/DEV ECO/TAC EDU/PROP AGE HEREDITY PERCEPT SKILL 20. PAGE 5 F0092
ANTHOL ECO/DEV ECO/UNDEV WORKER

B65
BOWEN W.G.,UNEMPLOYMENT IN A PROSPEROUS ECONOMY. USA+45 ECO/DEV NAT/G ACT/RES PLAN PAY EDU/PROP DEMAND...POLICY IDEA/COMP ANTHOL 20. PAGE 17 F0330
WORKER ECO/TAC WEALTH PROB/SOLV

B65
COLBERG M.R.,HUMAN CAPITAL IN SOUTHERN DEVELOPMENT. USA+45 AGRI ACADEM LABOR SCHOOL WORKER CAP/ISM DISCRIM. PAGE 26 F0498
PROVS RACE/REL GP/REL

B65
COLLINS H.,KARL MARX AND THE BRITISH LABOR MOVEMENT, YEARS OF THE FIRST INTERNATIONAL. EUR+WWI MOD/EUR UK STRATA INDUS NAT/G POL/PAR SOCISM ...CONCPT 19/20 MARX/KARL. PAGE 26 F0507
MARXISM LABOR INT/ORG WORKER

B65
COX D.W.,THE PERILS OF PEACE* CONVERSION TO WHAT? FUT USA+45 ECO/DEV NAT/G ACT/RES CREATE PLAN NUC/PWR WAR DEMAND MGT. PAGE 28 F0546
PEACE WORKER FORCES MARKET

B65
FRIEDLANDER S.L.,LABOR MIGRATION AND ECONOMIC GROWTH: A CASE STUDY OF PUERTO RICO. PUERT/RICO AGRI WORKER PLAN PROB/SOLV...ECOMETRIC STAT PREDICT CHARTS HYPO/EXP SIMUL 20. PAGE 44 F0858
CENSUS GEOG ECO/UNDEV WEALTH

B65
GOETZ-GIREY R.,LE MOUVEMENT DES GREVES EN FRANCE. FRANCE FINAN OP/RES PROB/SOLV ECO/TAC INCOME HABITAT...STAT CHARTS 19/20. PAGE 48 F0932
LABOR WORKER GP/REL

INDUS

HARBISON F.,MANPOWER AND EDUCATION. AFR CHINA/COM IRAN L/A+17C S/ASIA TEC/DEV ADJUST OPTIMAL SKILL ...ANTHOL 20. PAGE 55 F1073
B65 ECO/UNDEV EDU/PROP WORKER NAT/COMP

KLASSEN L.H.,AREA ECONOMIC AND SOCIAL REDEVELOPMENT. ECO/UNDEV INDUS NAT/G PLAN CAP/ISM TAX...ECOMETRIC SIMUL 20. PAGE 72 F1404
B65 OPTIMAL WORKER METH ECO/TAC

LUGO-MARENCO J.J.,A STATEMENT OF THE LAWS OF NICARAGUA IN MATTERS AFFECTING BUSINESS. NICARAGUA AGRI DIST/IND EXTR/IND FINAN INDUS FAM WORKER INT/TRADE TAX MARRIAGE OWN BIO/SOC 20 TREATY RESOURCE/N MIGRATION. PAGE 82 F1606
B65 CONSTN NAT/G LEGIS JURID

LYONS G.M.,AMERICA: PURPOSE AND POWER. UK USA+45 FINAN INDUS MARKET WORKER TEC/DEV DIPLOM AUTOMAT NUC/PWR WAR RACE/REL ORD/FREE 20 EEC CONGRESS SUPREME/CT CIV/RIGHTS. PAGE 82 F1617
B65 PWR PROB/SOLV ECO/DEV TASK

MCCOLL G.D.,THE AUSTRALIAN BALANCE OF PAYMENTS. UK USA+45 AGRI WORKER DIPLOM EQUILIB PRODUC...STAT TREND CHARTS BIBLIOG/A 20 AUSTRAL. PAGE 88 F1719
B65 ECO/DEV BAL/PAY INT/TRADE COST

MORRIS M.D.,THE EMERGENCE OF AN INDUSTRIAL LABOR FORCE IN INDIA: A STUDY OF THE BOMBAY COTTON MILLS, 1854-1947. INDIA WORKER OP/RES ADMIN 19/20. PAGE 94 F1837
B65 INDUS LABOR ECO/UNDEV CAP/ISM

MURUMBI J.,PROBLEMS OF ECONOMIC DEVELOPMENT IN EAST AFRICA. FINAN INDUS WORKER TEC/DEV INT/TRADE TAX DEMAND EFFICIENCY PRODUC SOCISM...TREND CHARTS 20 AFRICA/E. PAGE 95 F1869
B65 AGRI ECO/TAC ECO/UNDEV PROC/MFG

NKRUMAH K.,NEO-COLONIALISM: THE LAST STAGE OF IMPERIALISM. AFR INT/ORG WORKER FOR/AID INT/TRADE EDU/PROP GOV/REL NAT/LISM SOVEREIGN POPULISM SOCISM ...SOCIALIST 20 THIRD/WRLD INTRVN/ECO. PAGE 98 F1929
B65 COLONIAL DIPLOM ECO/UNDEV ECO/TAC

OECD,THE MEDITERRANEAN REGIONAL PROJECT: PORTUGAL; EDUCATION AND DEVELOPMENT. PORTUGAL SOCIETY STRATA FINAN PROF/ORG WORKER PLAN PROB/SOLV ADMIN...POLICY STAT CHARTS METH 20 OECD. PAGE 100 F1970
B65 EDU/PROP SCHOOL ACADEM ECO/UNDEV

OECD,THE MEDITERRANEAN REGIONAL PROJECT: ITALY; EDUCATION AND DEVELOPMENT. ITALY SOCIETY STRATA FINAN NAT/G PROF/ORG WORKER PLAN PROB/SOLV ADMIN ...STAT CHARTS METH 20 OECD. PAGE 100 F1971
B65 SCHOOL EDU/PROP ECO/UNDEV ACADEM

OECD,THE MEDITERRANEAN REGIONAL PROJECT: GREECE; EDUCATION AND DEVELOPMENT. FUT GREECE SOCIETY AGRI FINAN NAT/G PROF/ORG WORKER PLAN PROB/SOLV ADMIN DEMAND ATTIT 20 OECD. PAGE 100 F1972
B65 EDU/PROP SCHOOL ACADEM ECO/UNDEV

OECD,THE MEDITERRANEAN REGIONAL PROJECT: SPAIN; EDUCATION AND DEVELOPMENT. FUT SPAIN STRATA FINAN NAT/G WORKER PLAN PROB/SOLV ADMIN COST...POLICY STAT CHARTS 20 OECD. PAGE 100 F1973
B65 ECO/UNDEV EDU/PROP ACADEM SCHOOL

PEARL A.,NEW CAREERS FOR THE POOR: THE NON-PROFESSIONAL IN HUMAN SERVICE. USA+45 SERV/IND NAT/G NEIGH WORKER EDU/PROP AUTOMAT SKILL...WELF/ST NEW/IDEA BIBLIOG SOC/INTEG 20. PAGE 104 F2044
B65 SOC/WK WEALTH STRATA POLICY

ROLFE S.E.,GOLD AND WORLD POWER. AFR UK USA+45 WOR-45 INDUS WORKER INT/TRADE DEMAND...MGT CHARTS 20. PAGE 113 F2234
B65 BAL/PAY EQUILIB ECO/TAC DIPLOM

ROSS A.M.,EMPLOYMENT POLICY AND THE LABOR MARKET. USA+45 MARKET LABOR NAT/G PROB/SOLV PAY EDU/PROP PARTIC UTIL...POLICY 20. PAGE 114 F2242
B65 ECO/DEV WORKER WEALTH DEMAND

SCHULTZ T.W.,ECONOMIC CRISES IN WORLD AGRICULTURE. ASIA INDIA USSR ECO/DEV ECO/UNDEV INDUS VOL/ASSN CAP/ISM RATION COLONIAL 20. PAGE 117 F2317
B65 AGRI ECO/TAC INCOME WORKER

SHOSTAK A.B.,NEW PERSPECTIVES ON POVERTY. USA+45 SCHOOL WORKER INGP/REL RACE/REL AGE/C AGE/Y ATTIT HEALTH...ANTHOL BIBLIOG 20 JOHNSON/LB POVRTY/WAR. PAGE 121 F2388
B65 WEALTH NAT/G RECEIVE INCOME

SIMON B.,EDUCATION AND THE LABOR MOVEMENT, 1870-1920. UK SOCIETY STRATA LABOR POL/PAR SCHOOL CONTROL PARTIC SOCISM...BIBLIOG 19/20. PAGE 122 F2406
B65 EDU/PROP WORKER ADJUST LAW

SINHA M.R.,THE ECONOMICS OF MANPOWER PLANNING. FUT HUNGARY NAT/G CONTROL...POLICY GEOG ANTHOL 20 CHINJAP. PAGE 122 F2415
B65 ECO/UNDEV PLAN WORKER ECO/TAC

VAID K.N.,STATE AND LABOR IN INDIA. INDIA INDUS WORKER PAY PRICE ADJUD CONTROL PARL/PROC GP/REL ORD/FREE 20. PAGE 140 F2757
B65 LAW LABOR MGT NEW/LIB

WEISBROD B.A.,THE ECONOMICS OF POVERTY: AN AMERICAN PARADOX. USA+45 NAT/G WORKER TASK INGP/REL DISCRIM POLICY. PAGE 145 F2852
B65 ECO/DEV WEALTH RECEIVE STRATA

WISCONSIN HISTORICAL SOCIETY,LABOR PAPERS ON MICROFILM: A COMBINED LIST. USA+45 USA-45 WORKER 20. PAGE 148 F2910
B65 BIBLIOG LABOR PRESS

WU YUAN-LI,THE ECONOMY OF COMMUNIST CHINA. CHINA/COM USSR AGRI FINAN INDUS POL/PAR WORKER PROB/SOLV INT/TRADE PRICE EATING INCOME OWN WEALTH 20. PAGE 149 F2939
B65 ECO/TAC MARXISM PLAN EFFICIENCY

HUTT W.H.,"KEYNESIAN REVISIONS" SOUTH/AFR ECO/DEV FINAN NAT/G WORKER BUDGET TAX PRICE EQUILIB WEALTH 20 KEYNES/JM. PAGE 64 F1252
S65 ECO/TAC GEN/LAWS LOG

KAUN D.E.,"THE FAIR LABOUR STANDARDS ACT: AN EVALUATION IN TERMS OF ITS STATED GOALS." SOUTH/AFR LAW LABOR BARGAIN PAY INGP/REL WEALTH 20. PAGE 69 F1364
S65 ECO/TAC PRICE WORKER LEGIS

KINDLEBERGER C.P.,"MASS MIGRATION, THEN AND NOW." LAW ECO/DEV ECO/UNDEV INDUS LABOR INT/TRADE FEEDBACK REGION RIGID/FLEX...SOC NAT/COMP EEC. PAGE 71 F1394
S65 EUR+WWI USA-45 WORKER IDEA/COMP

MULLER A.L.,"THE ECONOMIC POSITION OF THE ASIANS IN AFRICA." AFR SOUTH/AFR ECO/UNDEV MARKET ECO/TAC GP/REL INCOME...CHARTS IND 20 MONOPOLY ASIANS. PAGE 95 F1856
S65 WORKER RACE/REL CAP/ISM DISCRIM

MUNZI U.,"THE EUROPEAN SOCIAL FUND IN THE DEVELOPMENT OF THE MEDITERRANEAN REGIONS OF THE EEC." FUT GREECE ITALY PORTUGAL SPAIN TURKEY WORKER TEC/DEV ECO/TAC REGION...STAT EEC. PAGE 95 F1862
S65 ECO/UNDEV PREDICT RECORD

SCHROEDER G.,"LABOR PLANNING IN THE USSR." COM USSR ECO/DEV INDUS SCHOOL PRODUC WEALTH...PREDICT TIME/SEQ TREND TIME 20. PAGE 117 F2313
S65 WORKER PLAN CENSUS

STEENKAMP W.F.J.,"THE PROBLEM OF WAGE REGULATION." SOUTH/AFR LAW ECO/DEV ECO/UNDEV LABOR NAT/G BARGAIN PAY INGP/REL DISCRIM WEALTH...METH/COMP 20. PAGE 125 F2473
S65 ECO/TAC PRICE WORKER RATION

ALEXANDER Y.,INTERNATIONAL TECHNICAL ASSISTANCE EXPERTS: A CASE STUDY OF THE U.N. EXPERIENCE. USA+45 WOR+45 WORKER CREATE PLAN PROB/SOLV ECO/TAC FOR/AID GIVE EDU/PROP...CHARTS BIBLIOG 20 UN. PAGE 3 F0062
B66 SKILL INT/ORG TEC/DEV CONSULT

BALDWIN R.E.,ECONOMIC DEVELOPMENT AND EXPORT GROWTH: A STUDY OF NORTHERN RHODESIA, 1920-1960. AFR RHODESIA AGRI EXTR/IND FINAN MARKET LABOR WORKER ECO/TAC...CONCPT NEW/IDEA MUNICH 20. PAGE 9 F0166
B66 ECO/UNDEV TEC/DEV INT/TRADE CAP/ISM

BEN-PORATH Y.,THE ARAB LABOR FORCE IN ISRAEL. ISLAM ISRAEL AGRI INDUS SCHOOL CAP/ISM PAY DEMAND...GEOG REGRESS STAT CHARTS 20 ARABS. PAGE 13 F0245
B66 WORKER CENSUS GP/REL STRUCT

BEQIRAJ M.,PEASANTRY IN REVOLUTION. STRATA ECO/UNDEV AGRI ROUTINE REV HABITAT RIGID/FLEX ...EPIST GEOG NEW/IDEA TREND MUNICH 20. PAGE 13 F0256
B66 WORKER KNOWL NAT/LISM SOC

BOWEN H.R.,AUTOMATION AND ECONOMIC PROGRESS. EUR+WWI USA+45 ECO/DEV INCOME ORD/FREE WEALTH ...POLICY ANTHOL 20. PAGE 17 F0327
B66 AUTOMAT TEC/DEV WORKER LEISURE

BRODERSEN A.,THE SOVIET WORKER: LABOR AND GOVERNMENT IN SOVIET SOCIETY. USSR STRUCT INDUS LABOR PLAN PAY INGP/REL PRODUC...POLICY GEN/LAWS BIBLIOG 20 STALIN/J LENIN/VI BOLSHEVISM KHRUSH/N. PAGE 19 F0357
B66 WORKER ROLE NAT/G MARXISM

DOBB M.,SOVIET ECONOMIC DEVELOPMENT SINCE 1917. USSR ECO/DEV ECO/UNDEV LABOR NAT/G TEC/DEV ECO/TAC ROUTINE PRODUC MARXISM 20. PAGE 33 F0647
B66 PLAN INDUS WORKER

EBONY,THE NEGRO HANDBOOK. ACADEM LABOR LOC/G SECT FORCES WORKER CT/SYS CRIME DISCRIM ORD/FREE...BIOG SOC/INTEG 19/20 NEGRO CIV/RIGHTS. PAGE 36 F0692
B66 RACE/REL EDU/PROP LAW STAT

B66
ECONOMIC RESEARCH SERVICE,RESEARCH DATA ON MINORITY GROUPS: AN ANNOTATED BIBLIOGRAPHY OF ECONOMIC RESEARCH SERVICE REPORTS: 1955-1965 (PAMPHLET). USA+45 STRATA ECO/DEV AGRI SCHOOL WORKER EDU/PROP HEALTH NEW/LIB SOC. PAGE 36 F0697
BIBLIOG/A DISCRIM WEALTH RACE/REL

B66
GITTINGER J.P.,THE LITERATURE OF AGRICULTURAL PLANNING. UNIV INT/ORG CONSULT WORKER TEC/DEV ECO/TAC OPTIMAL...POLICY METH/COMP BIBLIOG/A 20. PAGE 47 F0927
ECO/UNDEV AGRI PLAN WRITING

B66
GORDON R.A.,PROSPERITY AND UNEMPLOYMENT. USA+45 PLAN ECO/TAC ADJUST DEMAND ALL/VALS...POLICY DECISION TREND CHARTS ANTHOL 20. PAGE 49 F0961
WORKER INDUS ECO/DEV WEALTH

B66
GYORGY A.,ISSUES OF WORLD COMMUNISM. ALBANIA CHINA/COM COM USSR YUGOSLAVIA STRATA AGRI INT/ORG CHIEF FORCES WORKER WAR ALL/IDEOS...GEOG 20 MAO. PAGE 52 F1018
ECO/UNDEV REV MARXISM CON/ANAL

B66
HO YHI-MIN,AGRICULTURAL DEVELOPMENT OF TAIWAN: 1903-1960. FINAN WORKER EDU/PROP...STAT CHARTS BIBLIOG 20. PAGE 60 F1181
ECO/UNDEV AGRI PRODUC PLAN

B66
JACKSON G.D.,COMINTERN AND PEASANT IN EAST EUROPE 1919-1930. BULGARIA COM CZECHOSLVK EUR+WWI POLAND ROMANIA YUGOSLAVIA STRATA AGRI VOL/ASSN DIPLOM CONTROL CROWD WEALTH...POLICY NAT/COMP 20. PAGE 66 F1293
MARXISM ECO/UNDEV WORKER INT/ORG

B66
KROOSS H.E.,AMERICAN ECONOMIC DEVELOPMENT (2ND ED.). USA+45 USA-45 AGRI INDUS LABOR WORKER INT/TRADE TAX WAR...CHARTS 18/20. PAGE 73 F1443
ECO/TAC NAT/G CAP/ISM ECO/DEV

B66
LEWIS W.A.,DEVELOPMENT PLANNING; THE ESSENTIALS OF ECONOMIC POLICY. USA+45 FINAN INDUS NAT/G WORKER FOR/AID INT/TRADE ADMIN ROUTINE WEALTH...CONCPT STAT. PAGE 79 F1552
PLAN ECO/DEV POLICY CREATE

B66
MC CONNELL J.P.,LAW AND BUSINESS: PATTERNS AND ISSUES IN COMMERCIAL LAW. USA+45 USA-45 LOC/G WORKER LICENSE CRIME REPRESENT GP/REL 20. PAGE 87 F1713
ECO/DEV JURID ADJUD MGT

B66
MOSKOW M.H.,TEACHERS AND UNIONS. SCHOOL WORKER ADJUD LOBBY ATTIT ORD/FREE 20. PAGE 94 F1844
EDU/PROP PROF/ORG LABOR BARGAIN

B66
O'CONNER A.M.,AN ECONOMIC GEOGRAPHY OF EAST AFRICA. AFR TANZANIA UGANDA AGRI WORKER INT/TRADE COLONIAL GOV/REL...CHARTS METH/COMP 20 AFRICA/E. PAGE 99 F1953
ECO/UNDEV EXTR/IND GEOG HABITAT

B66
PEIRCE W.S.,SELECTIVE MANPOWER POLICIES AND THE TRADE-OFF BETWEEN RISING PRICES AND UNEMPLOYMENT (DISSERTATION). ECO/DEV WORKER ACT/RES...PHIL/SCI 20. PAGE 104 F2050
PRICE LABOR POLICY ECO/TAC

B66
ROSS A.M.,INDUSTRIAL RELATIONS AND ECONOMIC DEVELOPMENT. POL/PAR LEGIS WORKER BARGAIN PRICE EXEC LOBBY INCOME PWR...DECISION ANTHOL BIBLIOG 20. PAGE 114 F2243
ECO/UNDEV LABOR NAT/G GP/REL

B66
SHULTZ G.P.,STRATEGIES FOR THE DISPLACED WORKER. USA+45 COMPUTER TEC/DEV BARGAIN RECEIVE EDU/PROP CONFER GP/REL...MGT METH/COMP 20. PAGE 121 F2391
ECO/DEV WORKER PLAN AUTOMAT

B66
SOVERN M.I.,LEGAL RESTRAINTS ON RACIAL DISCRIMINATION IN EMPLOYMENT. USA+45 LAW INDUS LG/CO SML/CO DELIB/GP LEGIS SANCTION 20 NLRB PRESIDENT NEGRO CIV/RIGHTS RAILROAD. PAGE 124 F2446
DISCRIM RACE/REL WORKER JURID

B66
US SENATE COMM GOVT OPERATIONS,INTERGOVERNMENTAL PERSONNEL ACT OF 1966. USA+45 NAT/G CONSULT DELIB/GP WORKER TEC/DEV PAY AUTOMAT UTIL 20 CONGRESS. PAGE 139 F2730
ADMIN LEGIS EFFICIENCY EDU/PROP

B66
WETTER G.A.,SOVIET IDEOLOGY TODAY. USSR ECO/UNDEV SECT WORKER CAP/ISM CONTROL TASK EFFICIENCY TOTALISM DRIVE WEALTH...TREND 18/20. PAGE 145 F2864
ALL/IDEOS MARXISM REV

B66
WILLIAMS G.,MERTHYR POLITICS: THE MAKING OF A WORKING-CLASS TRADITION. UK CHIEF WORKER LEAD SOCISM...ANTHOL MUNICH 19/20 MERTHYR RICHARD/H. PAGE 147 F2891
LOC/G POL/PAR INDUS

B66
WOODMAN H.D.,SLAVERY AND THE SOUTHERN ECONOMY: SOURCES AND READINGS. USA-45 CULTURE STRUCT AGRI ECO/TAC LEAD RACE/REL DISCRIM EFFICIENCY...CHARTS ANTHOL MUNICH 18/19 NEGRO SOUTH/US. PAGE 148 F2922
ECO/DEV STRATA WORKER UTIL

L66
AMERICAN ECONOMIC REVIEW,"SIXTY-THIRD LIST OF DOCTORAL DISSERTATIONS IN POLITICAL ECONOMY IN AMERICAN UNIVERSITIES AND COLLEGES." ECO/DEV AGRI FINAN LABOR WORKER PLAN BUDGET INT/TRADE ADMIN DEMAND...MGT STAT 20. PAGE 5 F0088
BIBLIOG/A CONCPT ACADEM

N66
PRINCETON U INDUSTRIAL REL SEC,PUBLIC PROGRAMS TO CREATE JOBS (PAMPHLET NO. 125). USA+45 ECO/DEV INDUS PLAN ECO/TAC AGE/Y 20. PAGE 108 F2119
BIBLIOG/A NAT/G POLICY WORKER

N66
PRINCETON U INDUSTRIAL REL SEC,RECENT MATERIAL ON COLLECTIVE BARGAINING IN GOVERNMENT (PAMPHLET NO. 130). USA+45 ECO/DEV LABOR WORKER ECO/TAC GOV/REL ...MGT 20. PAGE 108 F2120
BIBLIOG/A BARGAIN NAT/G GP/REL

B67
BALDWIN G.B.,PLANNING AND DEVELOPMENT IN IRAN. IRAN AGRI INDUS CONSULT WORKER EDU/PROP BAL/PAY...CHARTS 20. PAGE 9 F0164
PLAN ECO/UNDEV ADMIN PROB/SOLV

B67
BEAL E.F.,THE PRACTICE OF COLLECTIVE BARGAINING (3RD ED.). USA+45 WOR+45 ECO/DEV INDUS LG/CO PROF/ORG WORKER ECO/TAC GP/REL WEALTH...JURID METH/CNCPT. PAGE 12 F0221
BARGAIN MGT LABOR ADJUD

B67
BERGMANN D KAUN B.,STRUCTURAL UNEMPLOYMENT IN THE UNITED STATES. USA+45 ECO/DEV PRICE ADMIN INGP/REL DEMAND EQUILIB WEALTH...MATH REGRESS STAT 20 NEGRO. PAGE 13 F0258
ECOMETRIC METH WORKER ECO/TAC

B67
BUREAU NATIONAL AFFAIRS,LABOR RELATIONS REFERENCE MANUAL VOL. 63. USA+45 CONSTN ECO/DEV PROVS WORKER DEBATE INGP/REL...DECISION 20. PAGE 20 F0385
LABOR ADJUD CT/SYS NAT/G

B67
COHEN M.R.,LAW AND THE SOCIAL ORDER: ESSAYS IN LEGAL PHILOSOPHY. USA-45 CONSULT WORKER ECO/TAC ATTIT WEALTH...POLICY WELF/ST SOC 20 NEW/DEAL DEPRESSION. PAGE 26 F0497
JURID LABOR IDEA/COMP

B67
EGGERT G.G.,RAILROAD LABOR DISPUTES. USA+45 USA-45 ELITES DIST/IND DELIB/GP FORCES JUDGE WORKER PROB/SOLV DOMIN PWR...POLICY 20. PAGE 36 F0707
GP/REL NAT/G LABOR BARGAIN

B67
ENKE S.,DEFENSE MANAGEMENT. USA+45 R+D FORCES WORKER PLAN ECO/TAC ADMIN NUC/PWR BAL/PAY UTIL WEALTH...MGT DEPT/DEFEN. PAGE 38 F0738
DECISION DELIB/GP EFFICIENCY BUDGET

B67
FONER P.S.,THE BOLSHEVIK REVOLUTION. USA-45 POL/PAR WORKER DIPLOM EDU/PROP MARXISM...STERTYP 20. PAGE 42 F0821
LABOR INTELL REV PRESS

B67
HERRESHOFF D.,AMERICAN DISCIPLES OF MARX: FROM THE AGE OF JACKSON TO THE PROGRESSIVE ERA. USA-45 AGRI POL/PAR 19/20. PAGE 59 F1155
MARXISM ATTIT WORKER CONCPT

B67
HODGKINSON R.G.,THE ORIGINS OF THE NATIONAL HEALTH SERVICE: THE MEDICAL SERVICES OF THE NEW POOR LAW, 1834-1871. UK INDUS WORKER PROB/SOLV EFFICIENCY ATTIT HEALTH WEALTH SOCISM...JURID SOC/WK MUNICH 19/20. PAGE 60 F1189
HEAL NAT/G POLICY LAW

B67
INTERNATIONAL LABOUR OFFICE,SUBJECT GUIDE TO PUBLICATIONS OF THE INTERNATIONAL LABOUR OFFICE, 1919-1964. DIPLOM 20. PAGE 65 F1280
BIBLIOG LABOR INT/ORG WORKER

B67
LEWIS L.J.,SOCIETY, SCHOOLS AND PROGRESS IN NIGERIA. NIGERIA WORKER ECO/TAC ADJUST 20. PAGE 79 F1550
EDU/PROP ECO/UNDEV SKILL SOCIETY

B67
MAZOUR A.G.,SOVIET ECONOMIC DEVELOPMENT: OPERATION OUTSTRIP: 1921-1965. USSR ECO/UNDEV FINAN CHIEF WORKER PROB/SOLV CONTROL PRODUC MARXISM...CHARTS ORG/CHARTS 20 STALIN/J. PAGE 87 F1711
ECO/TAC AGRI INDUS PLAN

B67
POLLACK N.,THE POPULIST MIND. USA-45 STRATA AGRI NAT/G POL/PAR LEGIS WORKER RACE/REL WEALTH...ANTHOL BIBLIOG 19 NEGRO. PAGE 107 F2097
POPULISM HIST/WRIT ATTIT INGP/REL

B67
REHMUS C.M.,LABOR AND AMERICAN POLITICS. POL/PAR WORKER EDU/PROP PARTIC ATTIT PWR. PAGE 110 F2175
LABOR ROLE LOBBY

B67
ROBINSON E.A.G.,ECONOMIC PLANNING IN THE UNITED KINGDOM. UK WORKER PLAN PROB/SOLV BAL/PAY 20. PAGE 113 F2220
ECO/DEV INDUS PRODUC BUDGET

B67
ROSS A.M.,EMPLOYMENT, RACE, AND POVERTY. USA+45 LAW STRATA MARKET LABOR EDU/PROP ISOLAT SKILL...MGT ANTHOL 20 NEGRO. PAGE 114 F2244
RACE/REL WORKER WEALTH DISCRIM

B67
SPURRIER R.B.,THE OVERPOPULATED SOCIETY. WORKER EATING PERS/REL DEMAND EQUILIB ILLEGIT INCOME HABITAT 20. PAGE 125 F2461
BIO/SOC FOR/AID DRIVE RECEIVE

B67
STEARNS P.N.,EUROPEAN SOCIETY IN UPHEAVAL* SOCIAL HISTORY SINCE 1800. EUR+WWI MOD/EUR STRATA SECT WORKER TEC/DEV WAR...WELF/ST SOC TREND BIBLIOG 19/20. PAGE 125 F2472
REGION ECO/DEV SOCIETY INDUS

B67
WOOTON G.,WORKERS, UNIONS, AND THE STATE. INDUS PROB/SOLV GP/REL DRIVE SUPEGO RESPECT...PSY SOC. PAGE 148 F2925
PARTIC WORKER NAT/G LABOR

L67
BONFIELD A.E.,"THE SUBSTANCE OF AMERICAN FAIR EMPLOYMENT PRACTICES LEGISLA TION II - EMPLOYMENT AGENCIES, LABOR ORGANIZATIONS, ETC." ACT/RES DISCRIM EFFICIENCY. PAGE 16 F0311
LAW WORKER LABOR SERV/IND

L67
DEALEY S.,"MONETARY RECOVERY UNDER FEDERAL TRANSPORTATION STATUTES." USA+45 SEA WORKER TAX PAY ADJUD DEATH GOV/REL OWN HEALTH ORD/FREE 20. PAGE 31 F0609
DIST/IND LAW CONTROL FINAN

L67
MACDONALD R.M.,"COLLECTIVE BARGAINING IN THE POSTWAR PERIOD." WORKER PROB/SOLV ECO/TAC PARTIC RISK CENTRAL EFFICIENCY DRIVE WEALTH...TREND 20. PAGE 83 F1624
LABOR INDUS BARGAIN CAP/ISM

L67
STILL C.H.,"MONETARY RECOVERY UNDER THE FAIR LABOR STANDARDS ACT." USA+45 USA-45 WORKER PAY ADJUD GOV/REL HEALTH ORD/FREE...MATH 20 NLRB. PAGE 126 F2487
LABOR CONTROL LAW FINAN

S67
BRIMMER A.F.,"EMPLOYMENT PATTERNS AND THE DILEMMA OF DESEGREGATION." USA+45 SOCIETY SKILL 20 NEGRO. PAGE 18 F0353
RACE/REL DISCRIM WORKER STRATA

S67
BROWN M.B.,"THE TRADE UNION QUESTION." UK INDUS OP/RES PRICE PROFIT 20. PAGE 19 F0371
WORKER LABOR GP/REL LAW

S67
CAMMETT J.M.,"COMMUNIST THEORIES OF FASCISM, 1920-35." ITALY POL/PAR PROF/ORG VOL/ASSN WORKER COLONIAL TOTALISM...SOCIALIST 20. PAGE 21 F0403
MARXISM FASCISM ATTIT

S67
DANIEL C.,"FREEDOM, EQUITY, AND THE WAR ON POVERTY." USA+45 WORKER ECO/TAC JURID. PAGE 30 F0578
WEALTH INCOME SOCIETY ORD/FREE

S67
DEWHURST A.,"THE WAGE MOVEMENT IN CANADA." CANADA AGRI NAT/G PARTIC COST PRODUC PROFIT 20. PAGE 32 F0627
WORKER MARXIST INDUS LABOR

S67
DEYRUP F.J.,"SOCIAL MOBILITY AS A MAJOR FACTOR IN ECONOMIC DEVELOPMENT." CHRIST-17C EUR+WWI MOD/EUR ECO/UNDEV DEMAND 20. PAGE 32 F0630
STRATA ECO/DEV INDUS WORKER

S67
EDGEWORTH A.B. JR.,"CIVIL RIGHTS PLUS THREE YEARS: BANKS AND THE ANTI-DISCRIMINATION LAW" USA+45 SOCIETY DELIB/GP RACE/REL EFFICIENCY 20 NEGRO CIV/RIGHTS. PAGE 36 F0701
WORKER DISCRIM FINAN LAW

S67
FLACKS R.,"CONSCRIPTION IN A DEMOCRATIC SOCIETY." USA+45 WORKER CONTROL SUFF SUPEGO. PAGE 41 F0807
POLICY FORCES ORD/FREE CIVMIL/REL

S67
GANZ G.,"THE CONTROL OF INDUSTRY BY ADMINISTRATIVE PROCESS." UK DELIB/GP WORKER 20. PAGE 46 F0898
INDUS LAW ADMIN CONTROL

S67
GRAYSON D.K.,"RISK ALLOCATIONS UNDER THE PERMITS AND RESPONSIBILITIES CLAUSE OF THE STANDARD GOVERNMENT CONSTRUCTION CONTRACT." USA+45 LAW WORKER. PAGE 50 F0979
CONSTRUC CONTROL RISK NAT/G

S67
HALL B.,"THE COALITION AGAINST DISHWASHERS." USA+45 POL/PAR PROB/SOLV BARGAIN LEAD CHOOSE REPRESENT GP/REL ORD/FREE PWR...POLICY 20. PAGE 53 F1044
LABOR ADMIN DOMIN WORKER

S67
HUTCHINGS R.,"THE ENDING OF UNEMPLOYMENT IN THE USSR" USSR PLAN ECO/TAC PRICE INGP/REL...GEOG STAT CHARTS 20 MIGRATION. PAGE 63 F1247
WORKER AGRI INDUS MARXISM

S67
JENCKS C.E.,"COAL MINERS IN BRITAIN SINCE NATIONALIZATION." UK LABOR GP/REL ADJUST SOCISM ...INT 20. PAGE 67 F1311
EXTR/IND WORKER STRATA ATTIT

S67
JENCKS C.E.,"SOCIAL STATUS OF COAL MINERS IN BRITAIN SINCE NATIONALIZATION." UK STRATA STRUCT LABOR RECEIVE GP/REL INCOME OWN ATTIT HABITAT...MGT T 20. PAGE 67 F1312
EXTR/IND WORKER CONTROL NAT/G

S67
LANDES W.M.,"THE EFFECT OF STATE FAIR EMPLOYMENT LAWS ON THE ECONOMIC POSITION OF NONWHITES." USA+45 PROVS SECT LEGIS ADMIN GP/REL RACE/REL...JURID CONCPT CHARTS HYPO/EXP NEGRO. PAGE 75 F1470
DISCRIM LAW WORKER

S67
LAZUTKIN Y.,"SOCIALISM AND SPARE TIME." ECO/DEV WORKER CREATE TEC/DEV ROUTINE TIME. PAGE 76 F1497
LEISURE PRODUC SOCISM SOCIALIST

S67
LEE R.L.,"THE PARADOX OF EQUALITY: A THREAT TO INDIVIDUAL AND SYSTEM FUNCTIONING." CHINA/COM ECO/UNDEV WORKER...SIMUL GEN/LAWS 20. PAGE 77 F1508
SOCIETY STRATA MARXISM IDEA/COMP

S67
LENS S.,"WALTER REUTHER TRIES TO BUILD A FIRE." WORKER LEAD DISCRIM AGE ORD/FREE NEW/LIB SOC. PAGE 78 F1523
LABOR PARTIC NEIGH PLAN

S67
LEONTYEV L.,"THE LENINIST PRINCIPLES OF SOCIALIST ECONOMIC MANAGEMENT." USA+45 USSR POL/PAR WORKER PLAN ECO/TAC EFFICIENCY PRODUC MARXISM...POLICY SOCIALIST MGT TREND 20 LENIN/VI MARX/KARL. PAGE 78 F1529
SOCISM CAP/ISM IDEA/COMP ECO/DEV

S67
LEWIS W.A.,"THE STATUTORY LANGUAGE OF LABOR DISQUALIFICATION IN STATE EMPLOYMENT SECURITY LAWS." LABOR WORKER WORK 20. PAGE 79 F1553
METH/COMP LEGIS SOC PROVS

S67
MOONEY J.D.,"URBAN POVERTY AND LABOR FORCE PARTICIPATION." FAM DISCRIM...SOC/WK STAT CHARTS MUNICH. PAGE 93 F1820
INCOME WORKER WEALTH

S67
MORTON J.A.,"A SYSTEMS APPROACH TO THE INNOVATION PROCESS: ITS USE IN THE BELL SYSTEM." USA+45 INTELL INDUS LG/CO CONSULT WORKER COMPUTER AUTOMAT DEMAND ...MGT CHARTS 20. PAGE 94 F1841
TEC/DEV GEN/METH R+D COM/IND

S67
MULLER A.L.,"ECONOMIC GROWTH AND MINORITIES." USA+45 SKILL...SOC GP/COMP NEGRO. PAGE 95 F1857
INCOME WORKER ECO/DEV RACE/REL

S67
MYERS S.,"TECHNOLOGY AND URBAN TRANSIT: THE ENORMOUS POTENTIAL OF BUS AND RAIL SYSTEMS." USA+45 FINAN LOC/G WORKER PLAN PROB/SOLV PRICE AUTOMAT MUNICH 20. PAGE 96 F1877
R+D TEC/DEV DIST/IND ACT/RES

S67
NEALE R.S.,"WORKING CLASS WOMEN AND WOMEN'S SUFFRAGE." UK LAW CONSTN LABOR NAT/G DELIB/GP LEGIS WORKER PAY PARTIC CHOOSE 19 FEMALE/SEX. PAGE 97 F1906
STRATA SEX SUFF DISCRIM

S67
NOURSE E.G.,"EARLY FLOWERING OF THE EMPLOYMENT ACT" USA+45 LABOR CONSULT DELIB/GP LEGIS BUDGET GOV/REL PRODUC WEALTH 20 INTRVN/ECO. PAGE 99 F1939
NAT/G WORKER ECO/TAC CONTROL

S67
ORAZEM F.,"THE NEW SOVIET PLAN FOR AGRICULTURE (1960-1970)" USSR WORKER CAP/ISM ECO/TAC PRICE OWN HABITAT MARXISM...CHARTS 20. PAGE 101 F1994
AGRI PLAN COM ECO/DEV

S67
PETRAS J.,"MINERS AND AGRARIAN RADICALISM." CHILE AGRI EXTR/IND WORKER CHOOSE ATTIT SOCISM MUNICH 20. PAGE 105 F2073
PARTIC EDU/PROP LABOR

S67
PIERPONT J.R.,"NEW STAGE IN THE LONGSHORE STRUGGLE." USA+45 SENIOR ADJUD RACE/REL...JURID 20 NEGRO. PAGE 106 F2083
LABOR DISCRIM WORKER CT/SYS

S67
PRASOW P.,"THE DEVELOPMENT OF JUDICIAL ARBITRATION IN LABOR-MANAGEMENT DISPUTES." LAW INDUS WORKER GP/REL ROLE...HIST/WRIT 20. PAGE 107 F2113
LABOR BARGAIN ADJUD TREND

S67
RONY V.,"HEARTBREAK IN TENNESSEE* POOR WHITES AND THE UNIONS." LAW STRUCT CAP/ISM ADJUD GP/REL. PAGE 113 F2236
LABOR LOC/G WORKER

PWR
S67
SANDMEYER R.L.,"METHODOLOGICAL ISSUES IN THE STUDY OF LABOR FORCE PARTICIPATION RATES." WOR+45 ...CLASSIF REGRESS CHARTS SIMUL. PAGE 116 F2278 METH CON/ANAL PARTIC WORKER
S67
SCHACHTER G.,"REGIONAL DEVELOPMENT IN THE ITALIAN DUAL ECONOMY" ITALY AGRI INDUS MARKET WORKER ECO/TAC CONTROL INCOME PRODUC 20. PAGE 116 F2287 REGION ECO/UNDEV NAT/G PROB/SOLV
S67
SCOTT R.,"TRADE UNIONS IN AFRICA." AFR UGANDA USA-45 ECO/UNDEV INDUS INT/ORG POL/PAR ECO/TAC WEALTH...GP/COMP 20 NKRUMAH/K. PAGE 118 F2335 LABOR WORKER NAT/G
S67
SHEFFTZ M.C.,"THE TRADE DISPUTES AND TRADE UNIONS ACT OF 1927: THE AFTERMATH OF THE GENERAL STRIKE." UK FINAN WORKER ADJUD LEAD PARL/PROC 20. PAGE 120 F2373 LEGIS ATTIT LABOR GP/REL
S67
TABORSKY E.,"THE CLASS STRUGGLE, THE PROLETARIAT, AND THE DEVELOPING NATIONS." USSR LABOR POL/PAR FOR/AID COLONIAL GP/REL 20. PAGE 128 F2521 DIPLOM MARXISM ECO/UNDEV WORKER
S67
THEROUX P.,"HATING THE ASIANS." TANZANIA UGANDA CONSTN INDUS NAT/G POL/PAR WORKER ECO/TAC HABITAT LOVE...POLICY GEOG 20 MIGRATION. PAGE 130 F2557 AFR RACE/REL SOVEREIGN ATTIT
S67
ZACK A.M.,"ARE STRIKES OF PUBLIC EMPLOYEES NECESSARY?" USA+45 DELIB/GP PROB/SOLV REPRESENT GP/REL MGT. PAGE 150 F2956 LABOR NAT/G WORKER BARGAIN
B68
PROUDHON P.J.,SYSTEME DES CONTRADICTIONS ECONOMIQUES, OU PHILOSOPHIE DA LA MISERE (2 VOLS.) (1846). SECT WORKER GP/REL ISOLAT PRODUC IDEA/COMP. PAGE 108 F2126 SOCIETY STRATA MORAL
B76
PROUDHON P.J.,WHAT IS PROPERTY? (TRANS. BY B.R. TUCKER). SOCIETY AGRI CAP/ISM CRIME GP/REL PERSON MORAL ORD/FREE WEALTH. PAGE 108 F2127 OWN WORKER PRODUC ANARCH
B76
SMITH A.,THE WEALTH OF NATIONS. UK STRUCT WORKER DIPLOM ECO/TAC OPTIMAL DRIVE PERSON ORD/FREE ...OLD/LIB GEN/LAWS 17/18. PAGE 123 F2428 WEALTH PRODUC INDUS LAISSEZ
B84
MILL J.,ELEMENTS OF POLITICAL ECONOMY. UK LAW ELITES FINAN WORKER ECO/TAC RENT OWN WEALTH ...POLICY GEN/LAWS 19. PAGE 91 F1785 TAX TARIFFS NAT/G INCOME
B86
O'CONNOR T.P.,THE PARNELL MOVEMENT: WITH A SKETCH OF IRISH PARTIES FROM 1843. IRELAND UK USA-45 LEGIS WORKER ECO/TAC COERCE CRIME REV CHOOSE ORD/FREE CATHISM LAISSEZ...SOC 19/20 PARLIAMENT PARNELL/CS LAND/LEAG. PAGE 100 F1957 LEAD DOMIN POL/PAR POLICY
B92
ENGELS F.,THE CONDITION OF THE WORKING-CLASS IN ENGLAND (1848). UK INDUS LABOR PRICE CONTROL COST INCOME HEALTH MARXISM MUNICH 19. PAGE 38 F0733 WORKER WEALTH MARXIST CAP/ISM
B98
MARSHALL A.,PRINCIPLES OF ECONOMICS. INDUS WORKER PRICE COST EQUILIB INCOME OPTIMAL PRODUC...TIME/SEQ METH RICARDO/D. PAGE 86 F1678 WEALTH GEN/LAWS MARKET
B99
KROPOTKIN P.,FIELDS, FACTORIES, AND WORKSHOPS. UNIV INTELL ECO/DEV LG/CO SCHOOL SML/CO ECO/TAC PRODUC UTOPIA...NEW/IDEA MUNICH. PAGE 74 F1445 SOCIETY WORKER AGRI INDUS

WORKING....SEE ROUTINE

WORLD COUNCIL OF CHURCHES....SEE WCC

WORLD HEALTH ORGANIZATION....SEE WHO

WORLD WAR I....SEE WWI

WORLD WAR II....SEE WWII

WORLD/BANK....WORLD BANK

L62
BELSHAW D.G.R.,"PUBLIC INVESTMENT IN AGRICULTURE AND ECONOMIC DEVELOPMENT OF UGANDA" UGANDA AGRI INDUS R+D ECO/TAC RATION TAX PAY COLONIAL 20 WORLD/BANK. PAGE 13 F0242 ECO/UNDEV PLAN ADMIN CENTRAL
B63
INTERNATIONAL BANK RECONST DEV,THE WORLD BANK GROUP IN ASIA. ASIA S/ASIA INDUS TEC/DEV ECO/TAC...RECORD 20 IBRD WORLD/BANK. PAGE 65 F1273 INT/ORG DIPLOM ECO/UNDEV FINAN
S67
AUBERT DE LA RUE P.,"PERSPECTIVES ECONOMIQUES ENTRE LES ETATS-UNIS ET L'EUROPE." FUT INDUS R+D INT/ORG ACT/RES ECO/TAC AGREE BAL/PAY PRODUC...CHARTS 20 EEC GATT WORLD/BANK. PAGE 7 F0138 INT/TRADE ECO/DEV FINAN TARIFFS

WORLD/CONG....WORLD CONGRESS

WORLD/CT....WORLD COURT; SEE ALSO ICJ

WORLDUNITY....WORLD UNITY, WORLD FEDERATION (EXCLUDING UN AND LEAGUE OF NATIONS)

WORSHIP....SEE ALSO SECT

S21
MALINOWSKI B.,"THE PRIMITIVE ECONOMICS OF THE TROBRIAND ISLANDERS" (BMR)" CULTURE SOCIETY NAT/G CHIEF LEAD OWN...SOC MYTH WORSHIP 20 NEW/GUINEA TROBRIAND RESOURCE/N. PAGE 84 F1647 ECO/UNDEV AGRI PRODUC STRUCT
B39
FIRTH R.,PRIMITIVE POLYNESIAN ECONOMY. SOCIETY DIST/IND SECT CHIEF CAP/ISM PRODUC WEALTH...SOC OBS METH WORSHIP 20 POLYNESIA. PAGE 41 F0802 ECO/UNDEV CULTURE AGRI ECO/TAC
B55
MAYO H.B.,DEMOCRACY AND MARXISM. COM USSR STRATA NAT/G WORKER ECO/TAC REV MORAL...PHIL/SCI HIST/WRIT IDEA/COMP WORSHIP 20 MARX/KARL LENIN/VI STALIN/J TROTSKY/L. PAGE 87 F1708 MARXISM CAP/ISM
B63
GAMBLE S.D.,NORTH CHINA VILLAGES: SOCIAL, POLITICAL, AND ECONOMIC ACTIVITIES BEFORE 1933. ASIA CULTURE STRUCT FAM DOMIN EDU/PROP MUNICH WORSHIP 20. PAGE 46 F0891 AGRI LEAD FINAN
B63
OTERO L.M.,HONDURAS. HONDURAS SPAIN STRUCT SECT COLONIAL REV WAR ATTIT PWR...GEOG WORSHIP 16/20. PAGE 102 F2003 NAT/G SOCIETY NAT/LISM ECO/UNDEV
B65
RATNAM K.J.,COMMUNALISM AND THE POLITICAL PROCESS IN MALAYA. MALAYSIA WOR+45 ECO/UNDEV PARTIC CHOOSE REPRESENT GP/REL CENTRAL ATTIT...CHARTS WORSHIP 20. PAGE 109 F2152 CONSTN GOV/REL REGION
B65
WINT G.,ASIA: A HANDBOOK. ASIA COM INDIA USSR CULTURE INTELL NAT/G...GEOG STAT CENSUS NAT/COMP WORSHIP 20 TREATY CHINJAP. PAGE 148 F2907 DIPLOM SOC
B66
HOWE R.W.,BLACK AFRICA: FROM PRE-HISTORY TO THE EVE OF THE COLONIAL ERA. ECO/UNDEV KIN PROVS SECT INT/TRADE EDU/PROP COLONIAL...BIBLIOG WORSHIP. PAGE 62 F1226 AFR CULTURE SOC
B66
PFEFFER K.H.,WELT IM UMBRUCH. SOCIETY STRUCT INDUS PROF/ORG SECT TEC/DEV PARTIC SUPEGO WORSHIP 20 CHRISTIAN. PAGE 106 F2076 ORD/FREE STRATA CREATE
B66
US DEPARTMENT OF STATE,RESEARCH ON WESTERN EUROPE, GREAT BRITAIN, AND CANADA (EXTERNAL RESEARCH LIST NO 3-25). CANADA GERMANY/W UK LAW CULTURE NAT/G POL/PAR FORCES EDU/PROP REGION MARXISM...GEOG SOC WORSHIP 20 CMN/WLTH. PAGE 136 F2676 BIBLIOG/A EUR+WWI DIPLOM
B67
DUN J.L.,THE ESSENCE OF CHINESE CIVILIZATION. ASIA FAM NAT/G TEC/DEV ADMIN SANCTION WAR HABITAT ...ANTHOL WORSHIP. PAGE 35 F0676 CULTURE SOCIETY
S67
RAMA C.M.,"PASADO Y PRESENTE DE LA RELIGION EN AMERICA LATINA." L/A+17C ELITES SOCIETY STRATA MARXISM...STAT WORSHIP PROTESTANT. PAGE 109 F2139 SECT CATHISM STRUCT NAT/COMP

WORTHY J.C. F2927

WOYTINSKY E.S. F2928,F2929

WOYTINSKY W.S. F2928,F2929

WPA....WORK PROJECTS ADMINISTRATION

B41
MACMAHON A.W.,THE ADMINISTRATION OF FEDERAL WORK RELIEF. USA-45 EX/STRUC WORKER BUDGET EFFICIENCY ...CONT/OBS CHARTS 20 WPA. PAGE 84 F1636 ADMIN NAT/G MGT GIVE

WRIGHT D.M. F2930,F2931

WRIGHT D.S. F1851

WRIGHT G. F2932

WRIGHT H.M. F2933

WRIGHT H.W. F1416

WRIGHT L.B. F2934

WRIGHT Q. F2935

WRITING....SEE ALSO HIST/WRIT

N
ECONOMIC ABSTRACTS. WOR+45 FINAN INDUS MARKET LABOR ACT/RES INT/TRADE WRITING GP/REL...MGT 20. PAGE 1 F0005 — BIBLIOG/A EDU/PROP

N
LONDON TIMES OFFICIAL INDEX. UK LAW ECO/DEV NAT/G DIPLOM LEAD ATTIT 20. PAGE 1 F0006 — BIBLIOG INDEX PRESS WRITING

N
ECONOMIC LIBRARY SELECTIONS. AGRI INDUS MARKET ADMIN...STAT NAT/COMP 20. PAGE 1 F0007 — BIBLIOG/A WRITING FINAN

N
UNITED NATIONS,OFFICIAL RECORDS OF THE ECONOMIC AND SOCIAL COUNCIL OF THE UNITED NATIONS. WOR+45 DIPLOM INT/TRADE CONFER...SOC SOC/WK 20 UN UNESCO. PAGE 132 F2611 — INT/ORG DELIB/GP WRITING

S52
PHILLIPS C.,"THE HIGH COST OF OUR LOW-PAID CONGRESS" (NYT MAG. 2/24/52)" USA+45 FINAN WRITING TASK TIME CONGRESS. PAGE 106 F2082 — LEGIS INCOME COST EFFICIENCY

B62
BOGARDUS J.,OUTLINE FOR THE COURSE IN BUSINESS AND ECONOMICS LITERATURE (REV. ED; PAMPHLET). USA+45 FINAN INDUS NAT/G VOL/ASSN PRESS WRITING INDEX. PAGE 16 F0305 — BIBLIOG/A STAT

B62
UNECA LIBRARY,BOOKS ON AFRICA IN THE UNECA LIBRARY. WOR+45 AGRI INT/ORG NAT/G PLAN WRITING REGION...SOC STAT UN. PAGE 132 F2605 — BIBLIOG AFR ECO/UNDEV TEC/DEV

B63
JOHNSTON J.,ECONOMETRIC METHODS. PROB/SOLV WRITING ...REGRESS CHARTS T. PAGE 68 F1333 — ECOMETRIC PHIL/SCI OP/RES STAT

S64
FYFE J.,"LIST OF CURRENT ACQUISITIONS OF PERIODICALS AND NEWSPAPERS DEALING WITH THE SOVIET UNION AND EAST EUROPEAN COUNTRIES." USSR WRITING GP/REL INGP/REL MARXISM 20. PAGE 45 F0879 — BIBLIOG COM EDU/PROP PRESS

B65
AMERICAN ECONOMIC ASSOCIATION,INDEX OF ECONOMIC JOURNALS 1886-1965 (7 VOLS.). UK USA+45 USA-45 AGRI FINAN PLAN ECO/TAC INT/TRADE ADMIN...STAT CENSUS 19/20. PAGE 5 F0087 — BIBLIOG WRITING INDUS

B65
CAMERON W.J.,NEW ZEALAND. NEW/ZEALND S/ASIA DIPLOM INT/TRADE WRITING COLONIAL PARL/PROC...GEOG CMN/WLTH. PAGE 21 F0402 — SOCIETY GP/REL STRUCT

B66
GITTINGER J.P.,THE LITERATURE OF AGRICULTURAL PLANNING. UNIV INT/ORG CONSULT WORKER TEC/DEV ECO/TAC OPTIMAL...POLICY METH/COMP BIBLIOG/A 20. PAGE 47 F0927 — ECO/UNDEV AGRI PLAN WRITING

WRONG D.H. F2936

WRONG M. F0590

WU YUAN-LI F2937,F2938,F2939

WUERTHNER J.J. F2940

WUNDERLICH F. F2941

WUORINEN J.H. F2942

WURFEL D. F2943

WURFEL S.W. F2944

WWI....WORLD WAR I

B51
HARROD R.F.,THE LIFE OF JOHN MAYNARD KEYNES. UK INTELL FAM CAP/ISM DIPLOM ECO/TAC WAR ATTIT PERSON ROLE 20 KEYNES/JM WWI. PAGE 56 F1094 — BIOG FINAN GEN/LAWS

WWII....WORLD WAR II

WYOMING....WYOMING

X

XENOPHOBIA....SEE NAT/LISM

XENOPHON....XENOPHON

XHOSA....XHOSA TRIBE (SOUTH AFRICA)

Y

YABUKI K. F2945

YALE/U....YALE UNIVERSITY

YALTA....YALTA CONFERENCE

YAMAMURA K. F2946

YAMEY B.S. F0213,F0803

YANKEE/C....YANKEE CITY - LOCATION OF W.L. WARNEROS STUDY OF SAME NAME

B47
WARNER W.L.,THE SOCIAL SYSTEM OF THE MODERN FACTORY; THE STRIKE: AN ANALYSIS. USA-45 STRATA WORKER ECO/TAC GP/REL INGP/REL...MGT SOC CHARTS 20 YANKEE/C. PAGE 143 F2824 — ROLE STRUCT LABOR PROC/MFG

YARBROGH/R....RALPH YARBOROUGH

YAZOO....YAZOO LAND SCANDAL

YEAGER L.B. F2947

YEMEN....SEE ALSO ISLAM

N67
US HOUSE COMM FOREIGN AFFAIRS,REPORT OF SPECIAL STUDY MISSION TO THE NEAR EAST (PAMPHLET). ISRAEL USA+45 YEMEN ECO/UNDEV INT/ORG FOR/AID ARMS/CONT WAR WEAPON NAT/LISM PEACE...GEOG 20 UN HOUSE/REP. PAGE 137 F2694 — ISLAM DIPLOM FORCES

YLVISAKER P.N. F2948

YORUBA....YORUBA TRIBE

YOUNG A.N. F2949

YOUNG C. F0094

YOUNG C.M. F1316

YOUNG G. F2950

YOUNG J.M. F2951

YOUNG S. F2952

YOUNG/TURK....YOUNG TURK POLITICAL PARTY

YOUTH....SEE AGE/Y

YRARRAZAVAL E. F2953

YUAN TUNG-LI F2954

YUDELMAN M. F2955

YUDELMAN/M....MONTEGU YUDELMAN

YUGOSLAVIA....YUGOSLAVIA; SEE ALSO COM

B56
WOLFF R.L.,THE BALKANS IN OUR TIME. ALBANIA FUT MOD/EUR USSR YUGOSLAVIA CULTURE INT/ORG SECT DIPLOM EDU/PROP COERCE WAR ORD/FREE...CHARTS 4/20 BALKANS COMINFORM. PAGE 148 F2919 — GEOG COM

B61
HORVATH B.,THE CHARACTERISTICS OF YUGOSLAV ECONOMIC DEVELOPMENT. COM ECO/UNDEV AGRI INDUS PLAN CAP/ISM ECO/TAC ROUTINE WEALTH...SOCIALIST STAT CHARTS STERTYP WORK 20. PAGE 62 F1217 — ACT/RES YUGOSLAVIA

S62
BOKOR-SZEGO H.,"LA CONVENTION DE BELGRADE ET LE REGIME DU DANUBE." COM EUR+WWI WOR+45 STRUCT POL/PAR VOL/ASSN PLAN EDU/PROP WEALTH...TIME/SEQ METH/GP COMMUN 20. PAGE 16 F0308 — INT/ORG TOTALISM YUGOSLAVIA

B63
PRYOR F.L.,THE COMMUNIST FOREIGN TRADE SYSTEM. COM CZECHOSLVK GERMANY YUGOSLAVIA LAW ECO/DEV DIST/IND POL/PAR PLAN DOMIN TOTALISM DRIVE RIGID/FLEX WEALTH ...STAT STAND/INT CHARTS FOR/TRADE 20. PAGE 108 F2130 — ATTIT ECO/TAC

B64
GRIFFITH W.E.,COMMUNISM IN EUROPE (2 VOLS.). CZECHOSLVK USSR WOR+45 WOR-45 YUGOSLAVIA INGP/REL MARXISM SOCISM...ANTHOL 20 EUROPE/E. PAGE 51 F1000 — COM POL/PAR DIPLOM GOV/COMP

B64
SEERS D.,CUBA: THE ECONOMIC AND SOCIAL REVOLUTION. ACT/RES
L/A+17C USSR YUGOSLAVIA STRATA AGRI INDUS SCHOOL COERCE
DELIB/GP PLAN ECO/TAC DOMIN EDU/PROP ATTIT CUBA
RIGID/FLEX ALL/VALS...STAT OBS TIME/SEQ WORK REV
VAL/FREE 20. PAGE 119 F2341

S64
HORECKY P.L.,"LIBRARY OF CONGRESS PUBLICATIONS IN BIBLIOG/A
AID OF USSR AND EAST EUROPEAN RESEARCH." BULGARIA COM
CZECHOSLVK POLAND USSR YUGOSLAVIA NAT/G POL/PAR MARXISM
DIPLOM ADMIN GOV/REL...CLASSIF 20. PAGE 62 F1214

B65
CAMPBELL J.C.,AMERICAN POLICY TOWARDS COMMUNIST POLAND
EASTERN EUROPE* THE CHOICES AHEAD. AFR USA+45 YUGOSLAVIA
ECO/DEV BAL/PWR MARXISM TREND. PAGE 21 F0406 DIPLOM
COM

B65
ORG FOR ECO COOP AND DEVEL,THE MEDITERRANEAN PLAN
REGIONAL PROJECT: AN EXPERIMENT IN PLANNING BY SIX ECO/UNDEV
COUNTRIES. FUT GREECE SPAIN TURKEY YUGOSLAVIA ACADEM
SOCIETY FINAN NAT/G PROF/ORG EDU/PROP ADMIN REGION SCHOOL
COST...POLICY STAT CHARTS 20 OECD. PAGE 102 F1995

B65
ORG FOR ECO COOP AND DEVEL,THE MEDITERRANEAN EDU/PROP
REGIONAL PROJECT: YUGOSLAVIA; EDUCATION AND ACADEM
DEVELOPMENT. YUGOSLAVIA SOCIETY FINAN PROF/ORG PLAN SCHOOL
ADMIN COST DEMAND MARXISM...STAT TREND CHARTS METH ECO/UNDEV
20 OECD. PAGE 102 F1996

S65
RUSINOW D.I.,"YUGOSLAV DEVELOPMENT BETWEEN EAST AND YUGOSLAVIA
WEST." AGRI VOL/ASSN PLAN CAP/ISM ECO/TAC FOR/AID ECO/UNDEV
INT/TRADE BAL/PAY...MARXIST EEC COMECON. PAGE 115 STAT
F2262

B66
GYORGY A.,ISSUES OF WORLD COMMUNISM. ALBANIA ECO/UNDEV
CHINA/COM COM USSR YUGOSLAVIA STRATA AGRI INT/ORG REV
CHIEF FORCES WORKER WAR ALL/IDEOS...GEOG 20 MAO. MARXISM
PAGE 52 F1018 CON/ANAL

B66
JACKSON G.D.,COMINTERN AND PEASANT IN EAST EUROPE MARXISM
1919-1930. BULGARIA COM CZECHOSLVK EUR+WWI POLAND ECO/UNDEV
ROMANIA YUGOSLAVIA STRATA AGRI VOL/ASSN DIPLOM WORKER
CONTROL CROWD WEALTH...POLICY NAT/COMP 20. PAGE 66 INT/ORG
F1293

B66
SPULBER N.,THE STATE AND ECONOMIC DEVELOPMENT IN ECO/DEV
EASTERN EUROPE. BULGARIA COM CZECHOSLVK HUNGARY ECO/UNDEV
POLAND YUGOSLAVIA CULTURE PLAN CAP/ISM INT/TRADE NAT/G
CONTROL...POLICY CHARTS METH/COMP BIBLIOG/A 19/20. TOTALISM
PAGE 125 F2460

YUKON....YUKON, CANADA

Z

ZACK A.M. F2956

ZALESKI E. F2957

ZAMBIA....SEE ALSO AFR

B67
WILLS A.J.,AN INTRODUCTION TO THE HISTORY OF AFR
CENTRAL AFRICA. RHODESIA ZAMBIA CULTURE SOCIETY COLONIAL
ECO/UNDEV TEC/DEV DOMIN WAR ALL/VALS...POLICY TREND ORD/FREE
BIBLIOG T 14/20 NYASALAND. PAGE 147 F2899

ZANDE....ZANDE, AFRICA

ZANZIBAR....SEE TANZANIA

ZAUBERMAN A. F2958,F2959

ZAWADZKI K.K.F. F2960

ZEBOT C.A. F2961

ZEIDBERG L.D. F2962

ZEIGLER H. F2963

ZEITLIN M. F2073

ZINKIN T. F2964

ZIONISM....SEE ISRAEL, NAT/LISM

ZISCHKA A. F2965

ZLATOVRT/N....NIKOLAI ZLATOVRATSKII

ZLOTNICK J. F0694

ZOBER M. F2966

ZOETEWEIJ B. F2967

ZOETEWEIJ H. F2593

ZOLLSCHAN G.K. F2968

ZONDAG C.H. F2969

ZONING....ZONING REGULATIONS

B64
MITAU G.T.,INSOLUBLE PROBLEMS: CASE PROBLEMS ON THE ADJUD
FUNCTIONS OF STATE AND LOCAL GOVERNMENT. USA+45 AIR LOC/G
FINAN LABOR POL/PAR PROB/SOLV TAX RECEIVE CONTROL PROVS
GP/REL 20 CASEBOOK ZONING. PAGE 92 F1807

Directory of Publishers

Abelard-Schuman Ltd., New York
Abeledo-Perrot, Buenos Aires
Abingdon Press, Nashville, Tenn.; New York
Academic Press, London; New York
Academy of the Rumanian People's Republic Scientific Documentation Center, Bucharest
Academy Publishers, New York
Accra Government Printer, Accra, Ghana
Acharya Book Depot, Baroda, India
Acorn Press, Phoenix, Ariz.
Action Housing, Inc., Pittsburgh, Pa.
Adams & Charles Black, London
Addison-Wesley Publishing Co., Inc., Reading, Mass.
Adelphi, Greenberg, New York
Adelphi Terrace, London
Advertising Research Foundation, New York
Advisory Committee on Intergovernmental Relations, Washington
Africa Bureau, London
Africa 1960 Committee, London
African Bibliographical Center, Inc., Washington
African Research Ltd., Exeter, England
Agarwal Press, Allahabad, India
Agathon Press, New York
Agency for International Development, Washington
Agrupacion Bibliotecalogica, Montevideo
Aguilar, S. A. de Ediciones, Madrid
Air University, Montgomery, Ala.
Akademiai Kiado, Budapest
Akademische Druck-und Verlagsanstalt, Graz, Austria
Akhil Bharat Sarva Seva Sangh, Rajghat, Varanasi, India; Rajghat, Kashi, India
Al Jadidah Press, Cairo
Alba House, New York
Eberhard Albert Verlag, Freiburg, Germany
Alcan, Paris
Aldine Publishing Co., Chicago
Aligarh Muslim University, Department of History, Aligarh, India
All-India Congress Committee, New Delhi
Allen and Unwin, Ltd., London
Howard Allen, Inc., Cleveland, Ohio
W. H. Allen & Co., Ltd., London
Alliance Inc., New York
Allied Publishers, Private, Ltd., Bombay; New Delhi
Allyn and Bacon, Inc., Boston
Almquist-Wiksell, Stockholm; Upsala
Ambassador Books, Ltd., Toronto, Ontario
American Academy of Arts and Sciences, Harvard University, Cambridge, Mass.
American Academy of Political and Social Science, Philadelphia
American Anthropological Association, Washington, D. C.
American Arbitration Association, New York
American-Asian Educational Exchange, New York
American Assembly, New York
American Association for the Advancement of Science, Washington, D. C.
American Association for the United Nations, New York
American Association of University Women, Washington, D. C.
American Bankers Association, New York
American Bar Association, Chicago
American Bar Foundation, Chicago
American Bibliographical Center-Clio Press, Santa Barbara, Calif.
American Bibliographic Service, Darien, Conn.
American Book Company, New York
American Civil Liberties Union, New York
American Council of Learned Societies, New York
American Council on Education, Washington
American Council on Public Affairs, Washington
American Data Processing, Inc., Detroit, Mich.
American Documentation Institute, Washington
American Economic Association, Evanston, Ill.
American Elsevier Publishing Co., Inc., New York
American Enterprise Institute for Public Policy Research, Washington, D. C.
American Features, New York
American Federation of Labor & Congress of Industrial Organizations, Washington, D. C.
American Foreign Law Association, Chicago
American Forest Products Industries, Washington, D. C.
American Friends of Vietnam, New York
American Friends Service Committee, New York
American Historical Association, Washington, D. C.
American Historical Society, New York
American Institute for Economic Research, Great Barrington, Mass.
American Institute of Consulting Engineers, New York
American Institute of Pacific Relations, New York
American International College, Springfield, Mass.
American Jewish Archives, Hebrew Union College—Jewish Institute of Religion, Cincinnati, Ohio
American Jewish Committee Institute of Human Relations, New York
American Judicature Society, Chicago
American Law Institute, Philadelphia
American Library Association, Chicago
American Management Association, New York
American Marketing Association, Inc., Chicago
American Municipal Association, Washington
American Museum of Natural History Press, New York
American Nepal Education Foundation, Eugene, Oregon
American Newspaper Publishers' Association, New York
American Opinion, Belmont, Mass.
American Philosophical Society, Philadelphia
American Political Science Association, Washington
American Psychiatric Association, New York
American Public Welfare Association, Chicago
American Research Council, Larchmont, N. Y.
American Society of African Culture, New York
American Society of International Law, Chicago
American Society for Public Administration, Chicago; Washington
American Textbook Publishers Council, New York
American Universities Field Staff, New York
American University, Washington, D. C.
American University of Beirut, Beirut
American University of Cairo, Cairo
American University Press, Washington
American University Press Services, Inc., New York
Ampersand Press, Inc., London, New York
Amsterdam Stock Exchange, Amsterdam
Anchor Books, New York
Anderson Kramer Association, Washington, D. C.
Anglo-Israel Association, London
Angus and Robertson, Sydney, Australia
Ann Arbor Publications, Ann Arbor, Mich.
Anthropological Publications, Oosterhout, Netherlands
Anti-Defamation League of B'nai B'rith, New York
Antioch Press, Yellow Springs, Ohio
Antwerp Institut Universitaire des Territoires d'Outre-Mer, Antwerp, Belgium
APEC Editora, Rio de Janeiro
Apollo Editions, New York
Ludwig Appel Verlag, Hamburg
Appleton-Century-Crofts, New York
Aqueduct Books, Rochester, N. Y.
Arbeitsgemeinschaft fur Forschung des Landes Nordrhein-Westfalen, Dusseldorf, Germany
Arcadia, New York
Architectural Press, London
Archon Books, Hamden, Conn.
Arco Publishing Company, New York
Arizona Department of Library and Archives, Tucson
Arizona State University, Bureau of Government Research, Tucson
Arlington House, New Rochelle, N. Y.
Arnold Foundation, Southern Methodist University, Dallas
Edward Arnold Publishers, Ltd., London
J. W. Arrowsmith, Ltd., London
Artes Graficas, Buenos Aires
Artes Graficas Industrias Reunidas SA, Rio de Janeiro
Asia Foundation, San Francisco
Asia Publishing House, Bombay; Calcutta; London; New York
Asia Society, New York
Asian Studies Center, Michigan State University, East Lansing, Mich.
Asian Studies Press, Bombay
Associated College Presses, New York

Associated Lawyers Publishing Co., Newark, N. J.
Association for Asian Studies, Ann Arbor
Association of National Advertisers, New York
Association of the Bar of the City of New York, New York
Association Press, New York
Associated University Bureaus of Business and Economic Research, Eugene, Ore.
M. L. Atallah, Rotterdam
Atheneum Publishers, New York
Atherton Press, New York
Athlone Press, London
Atlanta University Press, Atlanta, Ga.
The Atlantic Institute, Boulogne-sur-Seine
Atlantic Provinces Research Board, Fredericton, Newfoundland
Atma Ram & Sons, New Delhi
Atomic Industrial Forum, New York
Augustan Reprint Society, Los Angeles, Calif.
Augustana College Library, Rock Island, Ill.
Augustana Press, Rock Island, Ill.
J. J. Augustin, New York
Augustinus Verlag, Wurzburg
Australian National Research Council, Melbourne
Australian National University, Canberra
Australian Public Affairs Information Service, Sydney
Australian War Memorial, Canberra
Avi Publishing Co., Westport, Conn.
Avtoreferaty Dissertatsii, Moscow
N. W. Ayer and Sons, Inc., Philadelphia, Pa.
Aymon, Paris

La Baconniere, Neuchatel; Paris
Richard G. Badger, Boston
Baker Book House, Grand Rapids, Mich.
Baker, Vorhis, and Co., Boston
John Baker, London
A. A. Balkema, Capetown
Ballantine Books, Inc., New York
James Ballantine and Co., London
Baltimore Sun, Baltimore, Md.
Banco Central de Venezuela, Caracas
Bank for International Settlements, Basel
Bank of Finland Institute for Economic Research, Helsinki
Bank of Italy, Rome
Bankers Publishing Co., Boston
George Banta Publishing Co., Menasha, Wis.
Bantam Books, Inc., New York
A. S. Barnes and Co., Inc., Cranbury, N. J.
Barnes and Noble, Inc., New York
Barre Publishers, Barre, Mass.
Basic Books, Inc., New York
Batchworth Press Ltd., London
Bayerische Akademie der Wissenschaften, Munich
Bayerischer Schulbuch Verlag, Munich
Ebenezer Baylis and Son, Ltd., Worcester, England
Baylor University Press, Waco, Texas
Beacon Press, Boston
Bechte Verlag, Esslingen, Germany
H. Beck, Dresden
Bedminster Press, Inc., Totowa, N. J.
Beechhurst Press, New York
Behavioral Research Council, Great Barrington, Mass.
Belknap Press, Cambridge, Mass.
G. Bell & Sons, London
Bellman Publishing Co., Inc., Cambridge, Mass.
Matthew Bender and Co., Albany, New York
Bengal Publishers, Ltd., Calcutta
Marshall Benick, New York
Ernest Benn, Ltd., London
J. Bensheimer, Berlin; Leipzig; Mannheim
Benziger Brothers, New York
Berkley Publishing Corporation, New York
Bernard und Graefe Verlag fur Wehrwesen, Frankfurt
C. Bertelsmann Verlag, Gutersloh
Bharati Bhawan, Bankipore, India
Bharatiyi Vidya Bhavan, Bombay
G. R. Bhatkal for Popular Prakashan, Bombay
Bibliographical Society, London
Bibliographical Society of America, New York
Bibliographie des Staats, Dresden
Biblioteca de la II feria del libro exposicion nacional del periodismo, Panuco, Mexico
Biblioteca Nacional, Bogota
Biblioteka Imeni V. I. Lenina, Moscow
Bibliotheque des Temps Nouveaux, Paris
Bibliotheque Nationale, Paris
Adams & Charles Black, London
Basil Blackwell, Oxford
William Blackwood, Edinburgh
Blaisdell Publishing Co., Inc., Waltham, Mass.
Blanford Press, London
Blass, S. A., Madrid
Geoffrey Bles, London
BNA, Inc. (Bureau of National Affairs), Washington, D. C.
Board of Trade and Industry Estates Management Corp., London
T. V. Boardman and Co., London
Bobbs-Merrill Company, Inc., Indianapolis, Ind.
The Bodley Head, London
Bogen-Verlag, Munich
Bohlau-Verlag, Cologne; Graz; Tubingen
H. G. Bohn, London
Boni and Gaer, New York
Bonn University, Bonn
The Book of the Month Club, Johannesburg
Bookcraft, Inc., Salt Lake City, Utah
Bookfield House, New York
Bookland Private, Ltd., Calcutta; London
Bookmailer, New York
Bookman Associates, Record Press, New York
Books for Libraries, Inc., Freeport, N. Y.
Books International, Jullundur City, India
Borsenverein der deutschen Buchhandler, Leipzig
Bossange, Paris
Boston Book Co., Boston
Boston College Library, Chestnut Hill, Boston
Boston University, African Research Program, Boston
Boston University Press, Boston
H. Bouvier Verlag, Bonn
Bowes and Bowes, Ltd., Cambridge, England
R. R. Bowker Co., New York
John Bradburn, New York
George Braziller, Inc., New York
Brentano's, New York
Brigham Young University, Provo, Utah
E. J. Brill, Leyden
British Borneo Research Project, London
British Broadcasting Corp., London
British Council, London
British Liberal Party Organization, London
British Museum, London
Broadman Press, Nashville, Tenn.
The Brookings Institution, Washington
Brown University Press, Providence, R. I.
A. Brown and Sons, Ltd., London
William C. Brown Co., Dubuque, Iowa
Brown-White-Lowell Press, Kansas City
Bruce Publishing Co., Milwaukee, Wis.
Buchdruckerei Meier, Bulach, Germany
Buchhandler-Vereinigung, Frankfurt
Buijten & Schipperheijn, Amsterdam
Building Contractors Council, Chicago
Bureau of Public Printing, Manila
Bureau of Social Science Research, Washington, D. C.
Business Economists Group, Oxford
Business Publications, Inc., Chicago
Business Service Corp., Detroit, Mich.
Buttenheim Publishing Corp., New York
Butterworth's, London; Washington, D. C.; Toronto

Anne Cabbott, Manchester, England
California, Assembly of the State of, Sacramento, Calif.
California State Library, Sacramento
Calman Levy, Paris
Camara Oficial del Libro, Madrid
Cambridge Book Co., Inc., Bronxville, N. Y.
Cambridge University Press, Cambridge; London; New York
Camelot Press Ltd., London
Campion Press, London
M. Campos, Rio de Janeiro
Canada, Civil Service Commission, Ottawa
Canada, Civil Service Commission, Organization Division, Ottawa
Canada, Ministry of National Health and Welfare, Ottawa
Canada, National Joint Council of the Public Service, Ottawa

Canadian Dept. of Mines and Technical Surveys, Ottawa
Canadian Institute of International Affairs, Toronto
Canadian Peace Research Institute, Clarkson, Ont.
Canadian Trade Committee, Montreal
Candour Publishing Co., London
Jonathan Cape, London
Cape and Smith, New York
Capricorn Books, New York
Caribbean Commission, Port-of-Spain, Trinidad
Carleton University Library, Ottawa
Erich Carlsohn, Leipzig
Carnegie Endowment for International Peace, New York
Carnegie Endowment for International Peace, Washington, D. C.
Carnegie Foundation for the Advancement of Teaching, New York
Carnegie Press, Pittsburgh, Pa.
Carswell Co., Ltd., Toronto, Canada
Casa de las Americas, Havana
Case Institute of Technology, Cleveland, Ohio
Frank Cass & Co., Ltd., London
Cassell & Co., Ltd., London
Castle Press, Pasadena, Calif.
Catholic Historical Society of Philadelphia, Philadelphia
Catholic Press, Beirut
Catholic Students Mission Crusade Press, Cincinnati, Ohio
Catholic University Press, Washington
The Caxton Printers, Ltd., Caldwell, Idaho
Cedesa, Brussels
Cellar Book Shop, Detroit, Mich.
Center for Applied Research in Education, New York
Center for Applied Research in Education, Washington, D. C.
Center for Research on Economic Development, Ann Arbor, Mich.
Center for the Study of Democratic Institutions, Santa Barbara, Calif.
Center of Foreign Policy Research, Washington, D. C.
Center of International Studies, Princeton
Center of Planning and Economic Research, Athens, Greece; Washington, D. C.
Central Asian Research Centre, London
Central Bank of Egypt, Cairo
Central Book Co., Inc., Brooklyn, N. Y.
Central Book Department, Allahabad, India
Central Law Book Supply, Inc., Manila
Central News Agency, Ltd., Capetown, S. Afr.
Central Publicity Commission, Indian National Congress, New Delhi
Centre de Documentation CNRS, Paris
Centre de Documentation Economique et Sociale Africaine, Brussels
Centre d'Etudes de Politique Etrangere, Paris
Centre de Recherches sur l'URSS et les pays de l'est, Strasbourg
Centro de Estudios Monetarios Latino-Americanos, Mexico City
Centro Editorial, Guatemala City
Centro Mexicano de Escritores, Mexico City
Centro Para el "Desarrollo Economico y Social de America Latina", Santiago, Chile
The Century Co., New York
Century House, Inc., Watkins Glen, N. Y.
Cercle de la Librairie, Paris
Leon Chaillez Editeur, Paris
Chaitanya Publishing House, Allahabad, India
Chamber of Commerce of the United States, Washington, D. C.
S. Chand and Co., New Delhi
Chandler Publishing Co., San Francisco
Chandler-Davis, Lexington, Mass.
Chandler-Davis Publishing Co., West Trenton, N. J.
Channel Press, Inc., Great Neck, N. Y.
Chapman and Hall, London
Geoffrey Chapman, London
Chatham College, Pittsburgh, Pa.
Chatto and Windus, Ltd., London
F. W. Cheshire, London
Chestnut Hill, Boston College Library, Boston
Chicago Joint Reference Library, Chicago
Chilean Development Corp., New York
Chilmark Press, New York
Chilton Books, New York
China Viewpoints, Hong Kong
Chinese-American Publishing Co., Shanghai
Chiswick Press, London
Christian Crusade, Tulsa, Okla.
Georg Christiansen, Itzehoe, Germany
Christopher Publishing House, Boston
Chulalongkorn University, Bangkok
Church League of America, Wheaton, Ill.
C. I. Associates, New York
Cincinnati Civil Service, Cincinnati, Ohio
Citadel Press, New York
City of Johannesburg Public Library, Johannesburg
Citizens Research Foundation, Paris
Citizens Research Foundation, Princeton, N. J.
Ciudad Universitaria, San Jose, Calif.
Ciudad y Espiritu, Buenos Aires
Claremont Colleges, Claremont, Calif.
Clarendon Press, London
Clark, Irwin and Co., Ltd., Toronto
Clark University Press, Worcester, Mass.
Classics Press, New York
Clay and Sons, London
Cleveland Civil Service Commission, Cleveland
Clio Press, Santa Barbara, Calif.
William Clowes and Sons, Ltd., London
Colin (Librairie Armand) Paris
College and University Press, New Haven
Collet's Holdings, Ltd., London
Colliers, New York
F. Collin, Brussels
Collins, London
Colloquium Verlag, Berlin
Colombo Plan Bureau, Colombo, Ceylon
Colonial Press Inc., Northport, Ala.; New York
Colorado Bibliographic Institute, Denver
Colorado Legislature Council, Denver
Colorado State Board of Library Commissioners, Denver
Columbia University, New York
Columbia University, Bureau of Applied Social Research, New York
Columbia University, Center for Urban Education, New York
Columbia University, East Asian Institute, New York
Columbia University, Graduate School of Business, New York
Columbia University, Institute of French Studies, New York
Columbia University, Institute of Public Administration, New York
Columbia University, Institute of Russian Studies, New York
Columbia University, Institute of War-Peace Studies, New York
Columbia University, Law Library, New York
Columbia University, Parker School, New York
Columbia University, School of International Affairs, New York
Columbia University, School of Library Service, New York
Columbia University Press, New York
Columbia University Teachers College, New York
Combat Forces Press, Washington, D. C.
Comet Press, New York
Comision Nacional Ejecutiva, Buenos Aires
Commerce Clearing House, Chicago; Washington; New York
Commercial Credit Co., Baltimore, Md.
Commissao do iv Centenario de Ciudade, Sao Paulo
Commission for Technical Cooperation, Lahore
Commission to Study the Organization of Peace, New York
Committee for Economic Development, New York
Committee on Africa, New York
Committee on Federal Tax Policy, New York
Committee on Near East Studies, Washington
Committee on Public Administration, Washington, D. C.
Committee to Frame World Constitution, New York
Common Council for American Unity, New York
Commonwealth Agricultural Bureau, London
Commonwealth Economic Commission, London
Community Publications, Manila
Community Renewal Program, San Francisco
Community Studies, Inc., Kansas City
Companhia Editora Forense, Rio de Janeiro
Companhia Editora Nacional, Sao Paulo
Compass Books, New York
Concordia Publishing House, St. Louis, Mo.
Confederate Publishing Co., Tuscaloosa, Ala.
Conference on Economic Progress, Washington, D. C.
Conference on State and Economic Enterprise in Modern Japan, Estes Park, Colo.
Congress for Cultural Freedom, Prabhakar

Congressional Quarterly Service, Washington
Connecticut Personnel Department, Hartford
Connecticut State Civil Service Commission, Hartford
Conseil d'Etat, Paris
Conservative Political Centre, London
Constable and Co., London
Archibald Constable and Co., Edinburgh
Cooper Square Publishers, New York
U. Cooper and Partners, Ltd., London
Corinth Books, New York
Cornell University, Dept. of Asian Studies, Ithaca
Cornell University, Graduate School of Business and Public Administration, Ithaca
Cornell University Press, Ithaca
Cornell University, School of Industry and Labor Planning, Ithaca
Council for Economic Education, Bombay
Council of Education, Johannesburg
Council of Europe, Strasbourg
Council of State Governments, Chicago, Ill.
Council of the British National Bibliography, Ltd., London
Council on Foreign Relations, New York
Council on Public Affairs, Washington, D. C.
Council on Religion and International Affairs, New York
Council on Social Work Education, Washington, D. C.
Covici, Friede, Inc., New York
Coward-McCann, Inc., New York
Cresset Press, London
Crestwood Books, Springfield, Va.
Criterion Books, Inc., New York
S. Crofts and Co., New York
Crosby, Lockwood, and Sons, Ltd., London
Crosscurrents Press, New York
Thomas Y. Crowell Co., New York
Crowell-Collier and MacMillan, New York
Crown Publishers, Inc., New York
C.S.I.C., Madrid
Cuadernos de la Facultad de Derecho Universidad Veracruzana, Mexico City
Cuerpo Facultativo de Archiveros, Bibliotecarios y Argueologos, Madrid
Cultural Center of the French Embassy, New York
Current Scene, Hong Kong
Current Thought, Inc., Durham, N. C.
Czechoslovak Foreign Institute in Exile, Chicago

Da Capo Press, New York
Daguin Freres, Editeurs, Paris
Daily Telegraph, London
Daily Worker Publishing Co., Chicago
Dalloz, Paris
Damascus Bar Association, Damascus
Dangary Publishing Co., Baltimore
David Davies Memorial Institute of Political Studies, London
David-Stewart, New York
John Day Co., Inc., New York
John de Graff, Inc., Tuckahoe, N. Y.
La Decima Conferencia Interamericana, Caracas
Delacorte Press, New York
Dell Publishing Co., New York
T. S. Denison & Co., Inc., Minneapolis, Minn.
J. M. Dent, London
Departamento de Imprensa Nacional, Rio de Janeiro
Deseret Book Co., Salt Lake City, Utah
Desert Research Institute Publications' Office, Reno, Nev.
Deus Books, Paulist Press, Glen Rock, N. J.
Andre Deutsch, Ltd., London
Deutsche Afrika Gesellschaft, Bonn
Deutsche Bibliographie, Frankfurt am Main
Deutsche Bucherei, Leipzig
Deutsche Gesellschaft fur Volkerrecht, Karlsruhe
Deutsche Gesellschaft fur Auswartige Politik, Bonn
Deutsche Verlagsanstalt, Stuttgart
Deutscher Taschenbuch Verlag, Munich
Deva Datta Shastri, Hoshiarpur
Development Loan Fund, Washington, D. C.
Devin-Adair, Co., New York
Diablo Press, Inc., Berkeley, Calif.
Dial Press, Inc., New York
Dibco Press, San Jose, Cal.
Dickenson Publishing Co., Inc., Belmont, Calif.
Didier Publishers, New York

Firmin Didot Freres, Paris
Dietz Verlag, Berlin
Difusao Europeia do Livro, Sao Paulo
Diplomatic Press, London
Direccion General de Accion Social, Lisbon
District of Columbia, Office of Urban Renewal, Washington, D. C.
Djambatan, Amsterdam
Dennis Dobson, London
Dobunken Co., Ltd., Tokyo
La Documentation Francaise, Paris
Documents Index, Arlington, Virginia
Dodd, Mead and Co., New York
Octave Doin et Fils, Paris
Dolphin Books, Inc., New York
Dominion Press, Chicago
Walter Doon Verlag, Bremen
George H. Doran Co., New York
Dorrance and Co., Inc., Philadelphia, Pa.
Dorsey Press, Homewood, Illinois
Doubleday and Co., Inc., Garden City, N. Y.
Dover Publications, New York
Dow Jones and Co., Inc., New York
Dragonfly Books, Hong Kong
Drei Masken Verlag, Munich
Droemersche Verlagsanstalt, Zurich
Droste Verlag, Dusseldorf
Druck und Verlag von Carl Gerolds Sohn, Vienna
Guy Drummond, Montreal
The Dryden Press, New York
Dryfus Conference on Public Affairs, Hanover, N. H.
Duckworth, London
Duell, Sloan & Pearce, New York
Dufour Editions, Inc., Chester Springs, Pa.
Carl Duisburg-Gesellschaft fur Nachwuchsforderung, Cologne
Duke University, School of Law, Durham, N. C.
Duke University Press, Durham, N. C.
Dulau and Co., London
Duncker und Humblot, Berlin
Duquesne University Press, Pittsburgh, Pa.
R. Dutt, London
E. P. Dutton and Co., Inc., Garden City, N. Y.

E. P. & Commercial Printing Co., Durban, S. Africa
East Africa Publishing House, Nairobi
East European Fund, Inc., New York
East-West Center Press, Honolulu
Eastern Kentucky Regional Development Commission, Frankfort, Ky.
Eastern World, Ltd., London
Emil Ebering, Berlin
Echter-Verlag, Wurzburg
Ecole Francaise d'Extreme Orient, Paris
Ecole Nationale d'Administration, Paris
Econ Verlag, Dusseldorf; Vienna
Economic Research Corp., Ltd., Montreal
Economic Society of South Africa, Johannesburg
The Economist, London
Edicao Saraiva, Sao Paulo
Ediciones Ariel, Barcelona
Ediciones Cultura Hispanica, Madrid
Ediciones del Movimiento, Borgos, Spain
Ediciones Nuestro Tiempo, Montevideo
Ediciones Rialp, Madrid
Ediciones Riaz, Lima
Ediciones Siglo Veinte, Buenos Aires
Ediciones Tercer Mundo, Bogota
Edicoes de Revista de Estudes Politos, Rio de Janeiro
Edicoes Do Val, Rio de Janeiro
Edicoes GRD, Rio de Janeiro
Edicoes o Cruzeiro, Rio de Janeiro
Edicoes Tempo Brasileiro, Ltda., Rio de Janeiro
Edinburgh House Press, Edinburgh
Editions Albin Michel, Paris
Editions Alsatia, Paris
Editions Berger-Levrault, Paris
Editions Cujas, Paris
Editions de l'Epargne, Paris
Editions de l'Institut de Sociologie de l'Universite Libre de Bruxelles, Brussels
Editions d'Organisation, Paris
Editions Denoel, Paris
Editions John Didier, Paris

Editions du Carrefour, Paris
Editions du Cerf, Paris
Editions du Livre, Monte Carlo
Editions du Monde, Paris
Editions du Rocher, Monaco
Editions du Seuil, Paris
Editions du Tiers-Monde, Algiers
Editions du Vieux Colombier, Paris
Editions Eyrolles, Paris
Editions Internationales, Paris
Editions Mont Chrestien, Paris
Editions Nauwelaerts, Louvain
Editions Ouvrieres, Paris
Editions A. Pedone Paris
Editions Presence Africaine, Paris
Editions Rouff, Paris
Editions Sedif, Paris
Editions Sirey, Paris
Editions Sociales, Paris
Editions Techniques Nord Africaines, Rabat
Editions Universitaires, Paris
Editora Brasiliense, Sao Paulo
Editora Civilizacao Brasileira S. A., Rio de Janeiro
Editora Fulgor, Sao Paulo
Editora Saga, Rio de Janerio
Editores letras e artes, Rio de Janeiro
Editores Mexicanos, Mexico City
Editores Mexicanos Unidos, Mexico City
Editorial AIP, Miami
Editorial Amerinda, Buenos Aires
Editorial Columbia, Buenos Aires
Editorial Freeland, Buenos Aires
Editorial Gustavo Gili, Barcelona
Editorial Jus, Mexico City, Mexico
Editorial Lex, Havana
Editorial Losa da Buenos Aires, Buenos Aires
Editorial Marymar, Buenos Aires
Editorial Mentora, Barcelona
Editorial Nascimento, Santiago
Editorial Palestra, Buenos Aires
Editorial Patria, Mexico City
Editorial Pax, Bogota
Editorial Pax-Mexico, Mexico City
Editorial Platina, Buenos Aires
Editorial Porrua, Mexico City
Editorial Stylo Durangozgo, Mexico City
Editorial Universitaria de Buenos Aires, Buenos Aires
Editorial Universitaria de Puerto Rico, San Jose
Editorial Universitaria Santiago, Santiago
Le Edizioni de Favoro, Rome
Edizioni di Storia e Letteratura, Rome
Edizioni Scientifiche Italiane, Naples
Education and World Affairs, New York
Educational Heritage, Yonkers, N. Y.
Edwards Brothers, Ann Arbor
Effingham Wilson Publishers, London
Egyptian Library Press, Cairo
Egyptian Society of International Law, Cairo
Elex Books, London
Elsevier Publishing Co., Ltd., London
EMECE Editores, Buenos Aires
Emerson Books, New York
Empresa Editora Austral, Ltd., Santiago
Encyclopedia Britannica, Inc., Chicago
English Universities Press, London
Ferdinand Enke Verlag, Bonn; Erlangen; Stuttgart
Horst Erdmann Verlag, Schwarzwald
Paul Eriksson, Inc., New York
Escorpion, Buenos Aires
Escuela de Historia Moderna, Madrid
Escuela Nacional de Ciencias Politicas y Sociales, Mexico City
Escuela Superior de Administracion Publica America Central, San Jose, Costa Rica
Essener Verlagsanstalt, Essen
Essential Books, Ltd., London
Ethiopia, Ministry of Information, Addis Ababa
Etudes, Paris
Euroamerica, Madrid
Europa-Archiv, Frankfurt am Main
Europa Publications Ltd., London
Europa Verlag, Zurich; Vienna
Europaische Verlagsanstalt, Frankfurt
European Committee for Economic and Social Progress, Milan
European Free Trade Association, Geneva
Evangelischer Verlag, Zurich
Edward Evans and Sons, Shanghai
Everline Press, Princeton
Excerpta Criminologica Foundation, Leyden, Netherlands
Exchange Bibliographies, Eugene, Ore.
Export Press, Belgrade
Exposition Press, Inc., New York
Eyre and Spottiswoode, Ltd., London
Extending Horizon Books, Boston

F. and T. Publishers, Seattle, Washington
Faber and Faber, Ltd., London
Fabian Society, London
Facing Reality Publishing Corporation, Detroit, Mich.
Facts on File, Inc., New York
Fairchild Publishing, Inc., New York
Fairleigh Dickinson Press, Rutherford, N. J.
Falcon Press, London
Family Service Association of America, New York
Farrar and Rinehart, New York
Farrar, Strauss & Giroux, Inc., New York
Fawcett World Library, New York
F. W. Faxon Co., Inc., Boston
Fayard, Paris
Federal Legal Publications, Inc., New York
Federal Reserve Bank of New York, New York
Federal Trust for Education and Research, London
Fellowship Publications, New York
Feltrinelli Giangiacomo (Editore), Milan
Au Fil d'Ariadne, Paris
Filipiniana Book Guild, Manila
Financial Index Co., New York
Finnish Political Science Association, Helsinki
Fischer Bucherei, Frankfurt
Fischer Verlag, Stuttgart
Gustav Fischer Verlag, Jena
Flammarion, Paris
Fleet Publishing Co., New York
Fletcher School of Law and Diplomacy, Boston
R. Flint and Co., London
Florida State University, Tallahassee
Follett Publishing Co., Chicago
Fondation Nationale des Sciences Politiques, Paris
Fondo Historico y Bibliografico Jose Foribio, Medina, Santiago
Fondo de Cultura Economica, Mexico
B. C. Forbes and Sons, New York
Ford Foundation, New York
Fordham University Press, New York
Foreign Affairs Association of Japan, Tokyo
Foreign Affairs Bibliography, New York
Foreign Language Press, Peking
Foreign Language Publishing House, Moscow
Foreign Policy Association, New York
Foreign Policy Clearing House, Washington, D. C.
Foreign Policy Research Institute, University of Pennsylvania, Philadelphia, Pa.
Foreign Trade Library, Philadelphia
Arnold Forni Editore, Bologna
Forschungs-Berichte des Landes Nordrhein-Westfalen, Dusseldorf, Germany
Fortress Press, Philadelphia, Pa.
Foundation for Economic Education, Irvington-on-Hudson, N. Y.
Foundation for Social Research, Los Angeles, Calif.
Foundation Press, Inc., Brooklyn, N. Y.; Mineola, N. Y.
Foundation Press, Inc., Chicago
Foundation for Research on Human Behavior, New York
France Editions Nouvelles, Paris
France, Ministere de l'Education Nationale, Paris
France, Ministere d'Etat aux Affaires Culturelles, Paris
France, Ministere des Finances et des Affaires Economiques, Paris
Francois Maspera, Paris
Francke Verlag, Munich
Ben Franklin Press, Pittsfield, Mass.
Burt Franklin, New York
Free Europe Committee, New York
Free Press, New York
Free Press of Glencoe, Glencoe, Ill.; New York

Free Speech League, New York
Freedom Books, New York
Freedom Press, London
Ira J. Friedman, Inc., Port Washington, N. Y.
Friends General Conference, Philadelphia, Pa.
Friendship Press, New York
M. L. Fuert, Los Angeles
Fund for the Republic, New York
Fundacao Getulio Vargas, Rio de Janeiro
Funk and Wagnalls Co., Inc., New York
Orell Fuessli Verlag, Zurich

Galaxy Books, Oxford
Gale Research Co., Detroit
Galton Publishing Co., New York
A. R. Geoghegan, Buenos Aires
George Washington University, Population Research Project, Washington, D. C.
Georgetown University Press, Washington, D. C.
Georgia State College, Atlanta, Ga.
Georgia State Library, Atlanta, Ga.
Germany (Territory under Allied Occupation, 1945—U. S. Zone) Office of Public Information, Information Control Division, Bonn
Germany, Bundesministerium fur Vertriebene, Fluechtlinge, und Kriegsbeschadigte (Federal Ministry for Expellees, Refugees, and War Victims), Bonn
Gerold & Co. Verlag, Vienna, Austria
Ghana University Press, Accra, Ghana
Gideon Press, Beirut
Gustavo Gili, Barcelona
Ginn and Co., Boston
Glanville Publishing Co., New York
Glasgow University Press, Glasgow
Gleditsch Brockhaus, Leipzig
Glencoe Free Press, London
Golden Bell Press, Denver, Colo.
Victor Gollancz, Ltd., London
Gordon and Breach Science Publications, New York
Gothic Printing Co., Capetown, S. Afr.
Gould Publications, Jamaica, N. Y.
Government Affairs Foundation, Albany, N. Y.
Government Data Publications, New York
Government of India National Library, Calcutta
Government Printing Office, Washington
Government Publications of Political Literature, Moscow
Government Research Institute, Cleveland
Grafica Americana, Caracas
Grafica Editorial Souza, Rio de Janeiro
Graficas Gonzales, Madrid
Graficas Uguina, Madrid
Graphic, New York
H. W. Gray, Inc., New York
Great Britain, Administrative Staff College, London
Great Britain, Committee on Ministers' Powers, London
Great Britain, Department of Technical Cooperation, London
Great Britain, Foreign Office, London
Great Britain, Ministry of Overseas Development, London
Great Britain, Treasury, London
Greater Bridgeport Region, Planning Agency, Trumbull
W. Green and Son, Edinburgh
Green Pagoda Press, Hong Kong
Greenwich Book Publications, New York
Greenwood Periodicals, New York
Griffin Press, Adelaide, Australia
Grolier, Inc., New York
J. Groning, Hamburg
Grosset and Dunlap, Inc., New York
Grossman Publishers, New York
G. Grote'sche Verlagsbuchhandlung, Rastalt, Germany
Group for the Advancement of Psychiatry, New York
Grove Press, Inc., New York
Grune and Stratton, New York
Gruyter and Co., Walter de, Berlin
E. Guilmato, Paris
Democratic Party of Guinea, Guinea
Gulf Publishing Co., Houston, Texas
J. Chr. Gunderson Boktrykkeri og Bokbinderi, Oslo
Hans E. Gunther Verlag, Stuttgart
Gutersloher Verlagshaus, Gutersloh

Hadar Publishing Co., Tel-Aviv
Hafner Publishing Co., Inc., New York
G. K. Hall, Boston
Robert Hall, London
Charles Hallberg and Co., Chicago
Hamburgisches Wirtschafts Archiv, Hamburg
Hamilton & Co., London
Hamilton County Research Foundation, Cincinnati
Hamish Hamilton, London
Hanover House, New York
Hansard Society, London
Harcourt, Brace and World, New York
Harlo Press, Detroit, Mich.
Harper and Row Publishers, New York; London
George Harrap and Co., London
Otto Harrassowitz, Wiesbaden
Harrison Co., Atlanta, Ga.
Rupert Hart-Davis, London
Hartford Printing Co., Hartford, Conn.
Harvard Center for International Affairs, Cambridge, Mass.
Harvard Law School, Cambridge, Mass.
Harvard Law Review Association, Cambridge, Mass.
Harvard University Center for East Asian Studies, Cambridge, Mass.
Harvard University, Center for Russian Research and Studies, Cambridge, Mass.
Harvard University, Graduate School of Business Administration, Cambridge, Mass.
Harvard University, Peabody Museum, Cambridge, Mass.
Harvard University, Widener Library, Cambridge
Harvard University Press, Cambridge
V. Hase und Kohler Verlag, Mainz
Hastings House, New York
Hauser Press, New Orleans, La.
Hawthorne Books, Inc., New York
Hayden Book Company, New York
The John Randolph Haynes and Dora Haynes Foundation, Los Angeles
The Edward D. Hazen Foundation, New Haven, Conn.
D. C. Heath and Co., Boston
Hebrew University Press, Jerusalem
Heffer and Sons Ltd., Cambridge, England
William S. Hein and Co., Buffalo
James H. Heineman, Inc., New York
Heinemann Ltd., London
Heirsemann, Leipzig
A. Hepple, Johannesburg
Helicon Press, Inc., Baltimore, Md.
Herald Press, Scottdale, Penna.
Herder and Herder, New York
Herder Book Co., New York, St. Louis
Johann Gottfried Herder, Marburg, Germany
Heritage Foundation, Chicago
The Heritage Press, New York
Hermitage Press, Inc., New York
Heron House Winslow, Washington, D. C.
Herzl Press, New York
Carl Heymanns Verlag, Berlin
Hill and Wang, Inc., New York
Hillary House Publishers, Ltd., New York
Hind Kitabs, Ltd., Bombay
Hinds, Noble, and Eldridge, New York
Ferdinand Hirt, Kiel, Germany
Historical Society of New Mexico, Albuquerque, N. M.
H. M. Stationery Office, London
Hobart and William Smith Colleges, Geneva, N. Y.
Hobbs, Dorman and Co., New York
Hodden and Staughton, London
William Hodge and Co., Ltd., London
Hodges Figgis and Co., Ltd., Dublin
J. G. Hodgson, Fort Collins, Colo.
Hogarth Press, London
The Hokuseido Press, Tokyo
Holborn Publishing House, London
Hollis and Carter, London
Hollywood A.S.P. Council, Hollywood, Calif.
Holt and Williams, New York
Holt, Rinehart and Winston, New York
Henry Holt and Co., New York
Holzner Verlag, Wurzburg
Home and Van Thal, London
Hong Kong Government Press, Hong Kong
Hong Kong University Press, Hong Kong
Hoover Institute on War, Revolution and Peace, Stanford, Calif.

Hope College, Holland, Mich.
Horizon Press, Inc., New York
Houghton, Mifflin Co., Boston
Houlgate House, Los Angeles
Howard University Press, Washington
Howell, Sosbin and Co., New York
Hudson Institute, Inc., Harmon-on-Hudson, New York
B. W. Huebsch, Inc., New York
H. Hugendubel Verlag, Munich
Human Relations Area Files Press (HRAF), New Haven
Human Rights Publications, Caulfield, Victoria, Australia
Human Sciences Research, Inc., Arlington, Va.
Humanities Press, New York
Humon and Rousseau, Capetown
Hungarian Academy of Science, Publishing House of, Budapest
Hunter College Library, New York
R. Hunter, London
Huntington Library, San Marino, Calif.
Hutchinson and Co., London
Hutchinson University Library, London

Ibadan University Press, Ibadan, Nigeria
Iberia Publishing Company, New York
Ibero-American Institute, Stockholm
Illini Union Bookstore, Champaign, Ill.
Illinois State Publications, Springfield
Ilmgau Verlag, Pfaffenhofen
Imago Publishing Co., Ltd., London
Imprenta Calderon, Honduras
Imprenta Mossen Alcover, Mallorca
Imprenta Nacional, Caracas
Imprimerie d'Extreme Orient, Hanoi
Imprimerie Nationale, Paris
Imprimerie Sefan, Tunis
Imprimerie Fr. Van Muysewinkel, Brussels
Incentivist Publications, Greenwich, Conn.
Index Society, New York
India and Pakistan: Combined Interservice Historical Section, New Delhi
India, Government of, Press, New Delhi
India, Ministry of Community Development, New Delhi
India, Ministry of Finance, New Delhi
India, Ministry of Health, New Delhi
India, Ministry of Home Affairs, New Delhi
India, Ministry of Information and Broadcasting, Faridabad; New Delhi
India, Ministry of Law, New Delhi
Indian Council on World Affairs, New Delhi
Indian Institute of Public Administration, New Delhi
Indian Ministry of Information and Broadcasting, New Delhi
Indian Press, Ltd., Allahabad
Indian School of International Studies, New Delhi
Indiana University, Bureau of Government Research, Bloomington
Indiana University, Institute of Training for Public Service, Department of Government, Bloomington
Indiana University Press, Bloomington
Indraprastha Estate, New Delhi
Industrial Areas Foundations, Chicago
Industrial Council for Social and Economic Studies, Upsala
Industrial Press, New York
Infantry Journal Press, Washington, D. C.
Information Bulletin Ltd., London
Insel Verlag, Frankfurt
Institut Afro-Asiatique d'Etudes Syndicales, Tel Aviv
Institut de Droit International, Paris
Institut des Hautes Etudes de l'Amerique Latine, Rio de Janeiro
Institut des Relations Internationales, Brussels
Institut fur Kulturwissenschaftliche Forschung, Freiburg
Institut fur Politische Wissenschaft, Frankfurt
Institut International de Collaboration Philosophique, Paris
Institute for Comparative Study of Political Systems, Washington, D. C.
Institute for Defense Analyses, Washington, D. C.
Institute for International Politics and Economics, Prague
Institute for International Social Research, Princeton, N. J.
Institute for Mediterranean Affairs, New York
Institute for Monetary Research, Washington, D. C.
Institute for Social Science Research, Washington, D. C.
Institute of Brazilian Studies, Rio de Janeiro
Institute of Early American History and Culture, Williamsburg, Va.
Institute of Economic Affairs, London
Institute of Ethiopian Studies, Addis Ababa
Institute of Human Relations Press, New York
Institute of Islamic Culture, Lahore
Institute of Labor and Industrial Relations, Urbana, Ill.
Institute of Judicial Administration, New York
Institute of National Planning, Cairo
Institute of Pacific Relations, New York
Institute of Professional Civil Servants, London
Institute of Public Administration, Dublin
Instituto de Antropologia e Etnologia de Para, Belem, Para, Brazil
Instituto Brasileiro de Estudos Afro-Asiaticos, Rio de Janeiro
Instituto Caro y Cuervo, Bogota
Instituto de Derecho Comparedo, Barcelona
Instituto de Estudios Africanos, Madrid
Instituto de Estudios Politicos, Madrid
Instituto de Investigaciones Historicas, Mexico City
Instituto Guatemalteco-Americano, Guatemala City
Instituto Internacional de Ciencias Administrativas, Rio de Janeiro
Instituto Nacional do Livro, Rio de Janeiro
Instituto Nazionale di Cultura Fascista, Firenze
Instituto Pan Americano de Geografia e Historia, Mexico City
Integrated Education Associates, Chicago
Inter-American Bibliographical and Library Association, Gainesville, Fla.
Inter-American Development Bank, Buenos Aires
Inter-American Statistical Institute, Washington
Intercollegiate Case Clearing House, Boston
International African Institute, London
International Association for Research in Income and Wealth, New Haven, Conn.
International Atomic Energy Commission, Vienna
International Bank for Reconstruction and Development, Washington, D. C.
International Center for African Economic and Social Documentation, Brussels
International Chamber of Commerce, New York
International City Managers' Association, Chicago
International Commission of Jurists, Geneva
International Committee for Peaceful Investment, Washington, D. C.
International Congress of History of Discoveries, Lisbon
International Congress of Jurists, Rio de Janeiro
International Cotton Advisory Committee, Washington, D. C.
International Court of Justice, The Hague
International Development Association, Washington, D. C.
International Economic Policy Association, Washington, D. C.
International Editions, New York
International Federation for Documentation, The Hague
International Federation for Housing and Planning, The Hague
International Finance, Princeton, N. J.
International Institute of Administrative Science, Brussels
International Institute of Differing Civilizations, Brussels
International Labour Office, Geneva
International Managers' Association, Chicago
International Monetary Fund, Washington
International Press Institute, Zurich
International Publications Service, New York
International Publishers Co., New York
International Publishing House, Meerat, India
International Review Service, New York
International Textbook Co., Scranton, Penna.
International Union for Scientific Study of Population, New York
International Universities Press, Inc., New York
Interstate Printers and Publishers, Danville, Ill.
Iowa State University, Center for Agricultural and Economic Development, Ames
Iowa State University Press, Ames
Irish Manuscripts Commission, Dublin
Richard D. Irwin, Inc., Homewood, Ill.
Isar Verlag, Munich
Isbister and Co., London
Italian Library of Information, New York; Rome
Italy, Council of Ministers, Rome

Jacaranda Press, Melbourne
Mouriel Jacobs, Inc., Philadelphia
Al Jadidah Press, Cairo
Jain General House, Jullundur, India
Japan, Ministry of Education, Tokyo

Japan, Ministry of Justice, Tokyo
Japanese National Commission for UNESCO, Tokyo
Jarrolds Publishers, Ltd., London
Jewish Publication Society of America, Philadelphia, Pa.
Johns Hopkins Press, Baltimore
Johns Hopkins School of Advanced International Studies, Baltimore
Johns Hopkins School of Hygiene, Baltimore
Johnson Publishing Co., Chicago
Christopher Johnson Publishers, Ltd., London
Johnstone and Hunter, London
Joint Center for Urban Studies, Cambridge, Mass.
Joint Committee on Slavic Studies, New York
Joint Council on Economic Education, New York
Joint Library of IMF and IBRD, Washington
Joint Reference Library, Chicago
Jonathan Cape, London
Jones and Evans Book Shop, Ltd., London
Marshall Jones, Boston
Jornal do Commercio, Rio de Janeiro
Michael Joseph, Ltd., London
Jowett, Leeds, England
Juilliard Publishers, Paris
Junker und Dunnhaupt Verlag, Berlin
Juta and Co., Ltd., Capetown, South Africa

Kallman Publishing Co., Gainesville, Fla.
Karl Karusa, Washington, D. C.
Katzman Verlag, Tubingen
Kay Publishing Co., Salt Lake City
Nicholas Kaye, London
Calvin K. Kazanjian Economics Foundation, Westport, Conn.
Kegan, Paul and Co., Ltd., London
P. G. Keller, Winterthur, Switz.
Augustus M. Kelley, Publishers, New York
Kelly and Walsh, Ltd., Baltimore, Md.
P. J. Kenedy, New York
Kennikat Press, Port Washington, N. Y.
Kent House, Port-of-Spain
Kent State University Bureau of Economic and Business Research, Kent, Ohio
Kentucky State Archives and Records Service, Frankfort
Kentucky State Planning Commission, Frankfort
Kenya Ministry of Economic Planning and Development, Nairobi
Charles H. Kerr and Co., Chicago
Khadiand Village Industries Commission, Bombay
Khayat's, Beirut
Khun Aroon, Bangkok
P. S. King and Son, Ltd., London
King's College, Cambridge
King's Crown Press, New York
Kino Kuniva Bookstore Co., Ltd., Tokyo
Kitab Mahal, Allahabad, India
Kitabistan, Allahabad
B. Klein and Co., New York
Ernst Klett Verlag, Stuttgart
V. Klostermann, Frankfurt
Fritz Knapp Verlag, Frankfurt
Alfred Knopf, New York
John Knox Press, Richmond, Va.
Kodansha International, Ltd., Tokyo
W. Kohlhammer Verlag, Stuttgart; Berlin; Cologne; Mainz
Korea Researcher and Publisher, Inc., Seoul
Korea, Ministry of Reconstruction, Seoul
Korea, Republic of, Seoul
Korea University, Asiatic Research Center, Seoul
Korean Conflict Research Foundation, Albany, N. Y.
Kosel Verlag, Munich
Kossuth Foundation, New York
Guillermo Kraft, Ltd., Buenos Aires
John F. Kraft, Inc., New York
Krasnzi Proletarii, Moscow
Kraus, Ltd., Dresden
Kraus Reprint Co., Vaduz, Liechtenstein
Kreuz-Verlag, Stuttgart
Kumasi College of Technology, The Library, Kumasi, Ghana
Kuwait, Arabia, Government Printing Press, Kuwait

Labor News Co., New York
Robert Laffont, Paris
Lambarde Press, Sidcup, Kent, England
Albert D. and Mary Lasker Foundation, Washington, D. C.
Harold Laski Institute of Political Science, Ahmedabad
Guiseppe Laterza e Figli, Bari, Italy
T. Werner Laurie, Ltd., London
Lawrence Brothers, Ltd., London
Lawrence and Wishart, London
Lawyers Co-operative Publishing Co., Rochester, N. Y.
League for Industrial Democracy, New York
League of Independent Voters, New Haven
League of Nations, Geneva
League of Women Voters, Cambridge
League of Women Voters of U. S., Washington, D. C.
Leeds University Press, Leeds, Engand
J. F. Lehmanns Verlag, Munich
Leicester University Press, London
F. Leitz, Frankfurt
Lemcke, Lemcke and Beuchner, New York
Michel Levy Freres, Paris
Lexington Publishing Co., New York
Liberal Arts Press, Inc., New York
Liberia Altiplano, La Paz
Liberia Anticuaria, Barcelona
Liberia Campos, San Juan
Liberia Panamericana, Buenos Aires
Liberty Bell Press, Jefferson City, Mo.
Librairie Academique Perrin, Paris
Librairie Artheme Fayard, Paris
Librairie Beauchemin, Montreal
Librairie Armand Colin, Paris
Librairie Firmin Didot et Cie., Paris
Librairie Droz, Geneva
Librairie de Medicis, Paris
Librairie de la Societe du Recueil Sirey, Paris
Librairie des Sciences Politiques et Sociales, Paris
Librairie Felix Alcan, Paris
Librairie Gallimard, Paris
Librairie Hachette et Cie., Paris
Librairie Julius Abel, Greiswald
Librairie La Rose, Paris
Librairie Letouzey, Paris
Librairie Payot, Paris
Librairie Philosophique J. Vrin, Paris
Librairie Plon, Paris
Librairie Marcel Riviere et Cie., Paris
Librairie Stock Delamain et Boutelleau, Paris
Library, Kumasi College of Technology, Kumasi
Library Association, London
Library of Congress, Washington
Library House, London
Library of International Relations, Chicago
Libyan Publishing, Tripoli
Light and Life Press, Winona Lake, Ind.
Lincoln University, Lincoln, Pa.
J. B. Lippincott Co., New York, Philadelphia
Little, Brown and Co., Boston
Liverpool University Press, Liverpool
Horace Liveright, New York
Living Books, New York
Livraria Agir Editora, Rio de Janeiro
Livraria Editora da Casa di Estudante do Brazil, Sao Paulo
Livraria Jose Olympio Editora, Rio de Janeiro
Livraria Martins Editora, Sao Paulo
Lok Sabha Secretariat, New Delhi
London Conservative Political Centre, London
London Historical Association, London
London Institute of World Affairs, London
London Library Association, London
London School of Economics, London
London Times, Inc., London
London University, School of Oriental and African Studies, London
Roy Long and Richard R. Smith, Inc., New York
Long House, New Canaan, Conn.
Longmans, Green and Co., New York, London
Los Angeles Board of Civil Service Commissioners, Los Angeles
Louisiana State Legislature, Baton Rouge
Louisiana State University Press, Baton Rouge
Loyola University Press, Chicago
Lucas Brothers, Columbia
Herman Luchterhand Verlag, Neuwied am Rhein
Lyle Stuart, Inc., New York

MIT Center of International Studies, Cambridge

MIT Press, Cambridge
MIT School of Industrial Management, Cambridge
Macfadden-Bartwell Corp., New York
MacGibbon and Kee, Ltd., London
Macmillan Co., New York; London
Macmillan Co., of Canada, Ltd., Toronto
Macrae Smith Co., Philadelphia, Pa.
Magistrats Druckerei, Berlin
Magnes Press, Jerusalem
S. P. Maisonneuve et La Rose, Paris
Malaysia Publications, Ltd., Singapore
Malhorta Brothers, New Delhi
Manager Government of India Press, Kosib
Manaktalas, Bombay
Manchester University Press, Manchester, England
Manhattan Publishing Co., New York
Manzsche Verlag, Vienna
Marathon Oil Co., Findlay, Ohio
Marisal, Madrid
Marquette University Press, Milwaukee
Marshall Benick, New York
Marzani and Munsell, New York
Marzun Kabushiki Kaisha, Tokyo
Mascat Publications, Ltd., Calcutta
Francois Maspera, Paris
Massachusetts Mass Transportation Commission, Boston
Masses and McInstream, New York
Maurice Falk Institute for Economic Research, Jerusalem
Maxwell Air Force Base, Montgomery, Ala.
Robert Maxwell and Co., Ltd., London
McBride, Nast and Co., New York
McClelland and Stewart, Ltd., London
McClure and Co., Chicago
McClure, Phillips and Co., New York
McCutchan Publishing Corp., Berkeley
McDonald and Evans, Ltd., London
McDowell, Obolensky, New York
McFadden Bartwell Corp., New York
McGill University Industrial Relations Section, Montreal
McGill University, Institute of Islamic Studies, Montreal
McGill University Press, Montreal
McGraw Hill Book Co., New York
David McKay Co., Inc., New York
McKinley Publishing Co., Philadelphia
George J. McLeod, Ltd., Toronto
McMullen Books, Inc., New York
Meador Publishing Co., Boston
Mediaeval Academy of Americana, Cambridge
Felix Meiner Verlag, Hamburg
Melbourne University Press, Melbourne, Victoria, Australia
Mendonca, Lisbon
Mental Health Materials Center, New York
Mentor Books, New York
Meredith Press, Des Moines
Meridian Books, New York
Merit Publishers, New York
The Merlin Press, Ltd., London
Charles E. Merrill Publishing Co., Inc., Columbus
Methuen and Co., Ltd., London
Metropolitan Book Co., Ltd., New Delhi
Metropolitan Housing and Planning Council, Chicago
Metropolitan Police District, Scotland Yard, London
Alfred Metzner Verlag, Frankfurt
Meyer London Memorial Library, London
Miami University Press, Oxford, Ohio
Michie Co., Charlottesville, Va.
Michigan Municipal League, Ann Arbor
Michigan State University, Agricultural Experiment Station, East Lansing
Michigan State University, Bureau of Business and Economic Research, East Lansing
Michigan State University, Bureau of Social and Political Research, East Lansing
Michigan State University, Governmental Research Bureau, East Lansing
Michigan State University, Institute for Community Development and Services, East Lansing
Michigan State University, Institute for Social Research, East Lansing
Michigan State University, Labor and Industrial Relations Center, East Lansing
Michigan State University Press, East Lansing
Michigan State University School of Business Administration, East Lansing
Michigan State University, Vietnam Advisory Group, East Lansing
Mid-European Studies Center, Free European Committee, New York
Middle East Institute, Washington
Middle East Research Associates, Arlington, Va.
Middlebury College, Middlebury, Vt.
Midwest Administration Center, Chicago
Midwest Beach Co., Sioux Falls
Milbank Memorial Fund, New York
M. S. Mill and Co., Inc., Division of William Morrow and Co., Inc., New York
Ministere de l'Education Nationale, Paris
Ministere d'Etat aux Affaires Culturelles, Paris
Ministerio de Educacao e Cultura, Rio de Janeiro
Ministerio de Relaciones Exteriores, Havana
Minnesota Efficiency in Government Commission, St. Paul
Minton, Balch and Co., New York
Missionary Research Library, New York
Ernst Siegfried Mittler und Sohn, Berlin
Modern Humanities Research Association, Chicago
T. C. B. Mohr, Tubingen
Moira Books, Detroit
Monarch Books, Inc., Derby, Conn.
Monthly Review, New York
Mont Pelerin Society, University of Chicago, Chicago
Hugh Moore Fund, New York
T. G. Moran's Sons, Inc., Baton Rouge
William Morrow and Co., Inc., New York
Morus Verlag, Berlin
Mosaik Verlag, Hamburg
Motilal Banarsidass, New Delhi
Mouton and Co., The Hague; Paris
C. F. Mueller Verlag, Karlsruhe, Germany
Muhammad Mosque of Islam #2, Chicago
Firma K. L. Mukhopadhyaz, Calcutta
F. A. W. Muldener, Gottingen, Germany
Frederick Muller, Ltd., London
Municipal Finance Officers Association of the United States and Canada, Chicago
Munksgaard International Booksellers and Publishers, Copenhagen
John Murray, London
Museum fur Volkerkunde, Vienna
Museum of Honolulu, Honolulu
Musterschmidt Verlag, Gottingen

NA Tipographia do Panorama, Lisbon
Nassau County Planning Committee, Long Island
Natal Witness, Ltd., Pietermaritzburg
The Nation Associates, New York
National Academy of Sciences-National Research Council, Washington, D. C.
National Archives of Rhodesia and Nyasaland, Salisbury
National Assembly on Teaching The Principles of the Bill of Rights, Washington
National Association of Counties Research Foundation, Washington, D. C.
National Association of County Officials, Chicago
National Association of Home Builders, Washington, D. C.
National Association of Local Government Officers, London
National Association of State Libraries, Boston
National Bank of Egypt, Cairo
National Bank of Libya, Tripoli
National Board of YMCA, New York
National Book League, London
National Bureau of Economic Research, New York
National Capitol Publishers, Manassas, Va.
National Central Library, London
National Citizens' Commission on International Cooperation, Washington, D. C.
National Council for the Social Sciences, New York
National Council for the Social Studies, New York
National Council of Applied Economic Research, New Delhi
National Council of Churches of Christ in USA, New York
National Council of National Front of Democratic Germany, Berlin
National Council on Aging, New York
National Council on Crime and Delinquency, New York
National Economic and Social Planning Agency, Washington

National Education Association, Washington
National Home Library Foundation, Washington, D. C.
National Industrial Conference Board, New York
National Institute for Personnel Research, Johannesburg
National Institute of Administration, Saigon
National Institute of Economic Research, Stockholm
National Labor Relations Board Library, Washington
National Labour Press, London
National Library of Canada, Ottawa
National Library Press, Ottawa
National Municipal League, New York
National Observer, Silver Springs, Md.
National Opinion Research Center, Chicago
National Peace Council, London
National Planning Association, Washington, D. C.
National Press, Palo Alto, Calif.
National Review, New York
National Science Foundation Scientific Information, Washington, D. C.
Natural History Press, Garden City, N. Y.
Nauka Publishing House, Moscow
Navahind, Hyderabad
Navajiran Publishing House, Ahmedabad
Thomas Nelson and Sons, London; New York
Neukirchener Verlag des Erziehungsvereins, Neukirchen
New American Library, New York
New Century Publishers, New York
New Jersey Department of Agriculture, Rural Advisory Council, Trenton
New Jersey Department of Civil Service, Trenton
New Jersey Department of Conservation and Economic Development, Trenton
New Jersey Division of State and Regional Planning, Trenton
New Jersey Housing and Renewal, Trenton
New Jersey State Department of Education, Trenton
New Jersey State Legislature, Trenton
New Republic, Washington, D. C.
New School of Social Research, New York
New World Press, New York
New York City College Institute for Pacific Relations, New York
New York City Department of Correction, New York
New York City Temporary Committee on City Finance, New York
New York Public Library, New York
New York State College of Agriculture, Ithaca
New York State Library, Albany
New York State School of Industrial and Labor Relations, Cornell University, Ithaca
New York, State University of, at Albany, Albany
New York, State University of, State Education Department, Albany
New York, State University of, State Education Department, Office of Foreign Area Studies, Albany
New York Times, New York
New York University School of Commerce, Accounts and Finance, New York
New York University, School of Law, New York
New York University Press, New York
Newark Public Library, Newark
Newman Press, Westminster, Md.
Martinus Nijhoff, The Hague; Geneva
James Nisbet and Co., Ltd., Welwyn, Herts, England
Noonday Press, New York
North American Review Publishing Co., New York
North Atlantic Treaty Organization, Brussels
North Holland Publishing Co., Amsterdam, Holland
Northern California Friends Committee on Legislation, San Francisco
Northern Michigan University Press, Marquette
Northwestern University, Evanston
Northwestern University, African Department, Evanston, Ill.
Northwestern University, International Relations Conference, Chicago
Northwestern University Press, Evanston, Ill.
W. W. Norton and Co., Inc., New York
Norwegian Institute of International Affairs, Oslo
Norwegian University Press, Oslo
Nouvelle Librairie Nationale, Paris
John Nuveen and Co., Chicago
Novelty and Co., Patna, India
Novostii Press Agency Publishing House, Moscow
Nymphenburger Verlagsbuchhandlung, Munich

Oak Publications, New York
Oak Ridge Associated Universities, Oak Ridge, Tenn.
Oceana Publishing Co., Dobbs Ferry, N. Y.
Octagon Publishing Co., New York
Odyssey Press, New York
Oesterreichische Ethnologische Gesellschaft, Vienna
Oficina Internacional de Investigaciones Sociales de Freres, Madrid
W.E.R. O'Gorman, Glendale, Calif.
O'Hare, Flanders, N. J.
Ohio State University, Columbus
Ohio State University, College of Commerce and Administration, Bureau of Business Research, Columbus
Ohio State University Press, Columbus
Ohio University Press, Athens
Old Lyme Press, Old Lyme, Conn.
R. Oldenbourg, Munich
Oliver and Boyd, London, Edinburgh
Guenter Olzog Verlag, Munich
Open Court Publishing Co., La Salle, Ill.
Operation America, Inc., Los Angeles
Operations and Policy Research, Inc., Washington, D. C.
Oregon Historical Society, Portland
Organization for European Economic Cooperation and Development (OEEC), Paris
Organization of African Unity, Addis Ababa
Organization of American States, Rio de Janeiro
Organization of Economic Aid, Washington, D. C.
Orient Longman's, Bombay
Oriole Press, Berkeley Heights, N. J.
P. O'Shey, New York
Osaka University of Commerce, Tokyo
James R. Osgood and Co., Boston
Oslo University Press, Oslo
Oswald-Wolff, London
John Ousley, Ltd., London
George Outram Co., Ltd., Glasgow
Overseas Development Institute, Ltd., London
R. E. Owen, Wellington, N. Z.
Oxford Book Co., New York
Oxford University Press, Capetown; London; Madras; Melbourne; New York

Pacific Books, Palo Alto, Calif.
Pacific Coast Publishing Co., Menlo Park, Calif.
Pacific Philosophy Institute, Stockton, Calif.
Pacific Press Publishing Association, Mountain View, Calif.
Pacifist Research Bureau, Philadelphia
Padma Publications, Ltd., Bombay
Hermann Paetel Verlag, Berlin
Pageant Press, New York
Paine-Whitman, New York
Pakistan Academy for Rural Development, Peshawar
Pakistan Association for Advancement of Science, Lahore
Pakistan Bibliographical Working Group, Karachi
Pakistan Educational Publishers, Ltd., Karachi
Pakistan Ministry of Finance, Rawalpindi
Pall Mall Press, London
Pan American Union, Washington
Pantheon Books, Inc., New York
John W. Parker, London
Patna University Press, Madras
B. G. Paul and Co., Madras
Paulist Press, Glen Rock, N. J.
Payne Fund, New York
Peabody Museum, Cambridge
Peace Publications, New York
Peace Society, London
P. Pearlman, Washington
Pegasus, New York
Peking Review, Peking
Pelican Books, Ltd., Hammonsworth, England
Pemberton Press, Austin
Penguin Books, Baltimore
Penn.-N.J.-Del. Metropolitan Project, Philadelphia, Pa.
Pennsylvania German Society, Lancaster, Pa.
Pennsylvania Historical and Museum Commission, Harrisburg
Pennsylvania State University, Department of Religious Studies, University Park, Pa.

Pennsylvania State University, Institute of Public Administration, University Park, Pa.
Pennsylvania State University Press, University Park, Pa.
People's Publishing House, Ltd., New Delhi
Pergamon Press, Inc., New York
Permanent Secretariat, AAPS Conference, Cairo
Perrine Book Co., Minneapolis
Personnel Administration, Washington
Personnel Research Association, New York
George A. Pflaum Publishers, Inc., Dayton, Ohio
Phelps-Stokes Fund, Capetown; New York
Philadelphia Bibliographical Center, Philadelphia
George Philip & Son, London
Philippine Historical Society, Manila
Philippine Islands Bureau of Science, Manila
Philosophical Library Inc., New York
Phoenix House, Ltd., London
Pichon et Durand-Auzias, Paris
B. M. Pickering, London
Oskar Piest, New York
Pilot Press, London
Pioneer Publishers, New York
R. Piper and Co. Verlag, Munich
Pitman Publishing Corp., New York
Plimpton Press, Norwood, Mass.
PLJ Publications, Manila
Pocket Books, Inc., New York
Polish Scientific Publishers, Warsaw
Polygraphischer Verlag, Zurich
The Polynesian Society, Inc., Wellington, N. Z.
Popular Book Depot, Bombay
Popular Prakashan, Bombay
Population Association of America, Washington
Population Council, New York
Post Printing Co., New York
Post Publishing Co., Bangkok
Potomac Books, Washington, D. C.
Clarkson N. Potter, Inc., New York
Prabhakar Sahityalok, Lucknow, India
Practicing Law Institute, New York
Frederick A. Praeger, Inc., New York
Prager, Berlin
Prensa Latino Americana, Santiago
Prentice Hall, Inc., Englewood Cliffs, N. J.
Prentice-Hall International, London
Presence Afrique, Paris
President's Press, New Delhi
Press & Information Division of the French Embassy, New York
The Press of Case Western Reserve University, Cleveland
Presses de l'Ecole des Hautes Etudes Commerciales, Montreal
Presses Universitaires de Bruxelles, Brussels
Presses Universitaires de France, Paris
Presseverband der Evangelischen Kirche im Rheinland, Dusseldorf
Princeton Research Publishing Co., Princeton
Princeton University, Princeton, N. J.
Princeton University, Center of International Studies, Woodrow Wilson School of Public and International Affairs, Princeton, N. J.
Princeton University, Department of Economics, Princeton, N. J.
Princeton University, Department of History, Princeton, N. J.
Princeton University, Department of Oriental Studies, Princeton, N. J.
Princeton University, Department of Philosophy, Princeton, N. J.
Princeton University, Department of Politics, Princeton, N. J.
Princeton University, Department of Psychology, Princeton
Princeton University, Department of Sociology, Princeton, N. J.
Princeton University, Econometric Research Program, Princeton, N. J.
Princeton University, Firestone Library, Princeton, N. J.
Princeton University, Industrial Relations Center, Princeton
Princeton University, International Finance Section, Princeton, N. J.
Princeton University, Princeton Public Opinion Research Project, Princeton, N. J.
Princeton University Press, Princeton
Edouard Privat, Toulouse
Arthur Probsthain, London
Professional Library Press, West Haven, Conn.
Programa Interamericano de Informacion Popular, San Jose
Progress Publishing Co., Indianapolis
Progressive Education Association, New York
Prolog Research and Publishing Association, New York
Prometheus Press, New York
Psycho-Sociological Press, New York
Public Administration Clearing House, Chicago
Public Administration Institute, Ankara
Public Administration Service, Chicago
Public Affairs Forum, Bombay
Public Affairs Press, Washington
Public Enterprises, Tequcigalpa
Public Personnel Association, Chicago
Publications Centre, University of British Columbia, Vancouver
Publications de l'Institut Pedagogique National, Paris
Publications de l'Institut Universitaire des Hautes Etudes Internationales, Paris
Publications du CNRS, Paris
Publisher's Circular, Ltd., London, England
Publisher's Weekly, Inc., New York
Publishing House Jugoslavia, Belgrade
Punjab University, Pakistan
Punjab University Extension Library, Ludhiana, Punjab
Purdue University Press, Lafayette, Ind.
Purnell and Sons, Capetown
G. P. Putnam and Sons, New York

Quadrangle Books, Inc., Chicago
Bernard Quaritch, London
Queen's Printer, Ottawa
Queen's University, Belfast
Quell Verlag, Stuttgart, Germany
Quelle und Meyer, Heidelberg
Queromon Editores, Mexico City

Atma Ram and Sons, New Delhi
Ramsey-Wallace Corporation, Ramsey, New Jersey
Rand Corporation, Publications of the Social Science Department, New York
Rand McNally and Co., Skokie, Ill.
Random House, Inc., New York
Regents Publishing House, Inc., New York
Regional Planning Association, New York
Regional Science Research Institute, Philadelphia
Henry Regnery Co., Chicago
D. Reidel Publishing Co., Dordrecht, Holland
E. Reinhardt Verlag, Munich
Reinhold Publishing Corp., New York; London
Remsen Press, New York
La Renaissance de Loire, Paris
Eugen Rentsch Verlag, Stuttgart
Republican National Committee, Washington, D. C.
Research Institute on Sino-Soviet Bloc, Washington, D. C.
Research Microfilm Publications, Inc., Annapolis
Resources for the Future, Inc., Washington, D. C.
Revista de Occidente, Madrid
Revue Administrative, Paris
Renyal and Co., Inc., New York
Reynal & Hitchcock, New York
Rheinische Friedrich Wilhelms Universitat, Bonn
Rice University, Fondren Library, Houston
Richards Rosen Press, New York
The Ridge Press, Inc., New York
Rinehart, New York
Ring-Verlag, Stuttgart
Riverside Editions, Cambridge
Robinson and Co., Durban, South Africa
J. A. Rogers, New York
Roques Roman, Trujillo
Rudolf M. Rohrer, Leipzig
Ludwig Rohrscheid Verlag, Bonn
Walter Roming and Co., Detroit
Ronald Press Co., New York
Roper Public Opinion Poll Research Center, New York
Ross and Haine, Inc., Minneapolis, Minn.
Fred B. Rothman and Co., S. Hackensack, N. J.
Rotterdam University Press, Rotterdam
Routledge and Kegan Paul, London
George Routledge and Sons, Ltd., London
Row-Peterson Publishing Co., Evanston, Ill.

Rowohlt, Hamburg
Roy Publishers, Inc., New York
Royal African Society, London
Royal Anthropological Institute, London
Royal Colonial Institute, London
Royal Commission of Canada's Economic Prospects, Ottawa
Royal Commonwealth Society, London
Royal Geographical Society, London
Royal Greek Embassy Information Service, Washington, D. C.
Royal Institute of International Affairs, London; New York
Royal Institute of Public Administration, London
Royal Netherlands Printing Office, Schiedam
Royal Statistical Society, London
Rubin Mass, Jerusalem
Rule of Law Press, Durham
Rupert Hart-Davis, London
Russell and Russell, Inc., New York
Russell Sage College, Institute for Advanced Study in Crisis, NDEA Institute, Troy, N. Y.
Russell Sage Foundation, New York
Rutgers University, New Brunswick, N. J.
Rutgers University Bureau of Government Research, New Brunswick, N. J.
Rutgers University, Institute of Management and Labor Relations, New Brunswick, N. J.
Rutgers University, Urban Studies Conference, New Brunswick, N. J.
Rutgers University Press, New Brunswick, N. J.
Rutten und Loening Verlag, Munich
Ryerson Press, Toronto

Sage Publications, Beverly Hills, Calif.
Sahitya Akademi, Bombay
St. Andrews College, Drygrange, Scotland
St. Clement's Press, London
St. George Press, Los Angeles
St. John's University Bookstore, Annapolis
St. John's University Press, Jamaica, N. Y.
St. Louis Post-Dispatch, St. Louis
St. Martin's Press, New York
St. Michael's College, Toronto
San Diego State College Library, San Diego
San Francisco State College, San Francisco
The Sapir Memorial Publication Fund, Menasha, Wis.
Sarah Lawrence College, New York
Sarah Lawrence College, Institute for Community Studies, New York
Porter Sargent, Publishers, Boston, Mass.
Sauerlaender and Co., Aarau, Switz.
Saunders and Ottey, London
W. B. Saunders Co., Philadelphia, Pa.
Scandinavian University Books, Copenhagen
Scarecrow Press, Metuchen, N. J.
L. N. Schaffrath, Geldern, Germany
Robert Schalkenbach Foundation, New York
Schenkman Publishing Co., Cambridge
P. Schippers, N. V., Amsterdam
Schocken Books, Inc., New York
Henry Schuman, Inc., New York
Carl Schunemann Verlag, Bremen
Curt E. Schwab, Stuttgart
Otto Schwartz und Co., Gottingen
Science and Behavior Books, Palo Alto, Calif.
Science Council of Japan, Tokyo
Science of Society Foundation, Baltimore, Md.
Science Press, New York
Science Research Associates, Inc., Chicago
Scientia Verlag, Aalen, Germany
SCM Press, London
Scott, Foresman and Co., Chicago
Scottish League for European Freedom, Edinburgh
Chas. Scribner's Sons, New York
Seabury Press, New York
Sears Publishing Co., Inc., New York
Secker and Warburg, Ltd., London
Secretaria del Consejo Nacional Economia, Tegucigalpa
Securities Study Project, Vancouver, Wash.
Seewald Verlag, Munich; Stuttgart
Selbstverlag Jakob Rosner, Vienna
Seldon Society, London
Robert C. Sellers and Associates, Washington, D. C.
Thomas Seltzer Inc., New York
Seminar, New Delhi
C. Serbinis Press, Athens
Service Bibliographique des Messageries Hachette, Paris
Service Center for Teaching of History, Washington, D. C.
Servicos de Imprensa e Informacao da Exbaixada, Lisbon
Sheed and Ward, New York
Shoestring Press, Hamden, Conn.
Shuter and Shooter, Pietermaritzburg
Siam Society, Bangkok
Sidgewick and Jackson, London
K. G. Siegler & Co., Bonn
Signet Books, New York
A. W. Sijthoff, Leyden, Netherlands
Silver Burdett, Morristown, N. J.
Simmons Boardman Publishing Co., New York
Simon and Schuster, Inc., New York
Simpkin, Marshall, et al., London
Sino-American Cultural Society, Washington
William Sloane Associates, New York
Small, Maynard and Co., Boston
Smith-Brook Printing Co., Denver
Smith College, Northampton, Mass.
Smith, Elder and Co., London
Smith, Keynes and Marshall, Buffalo, N. Y.
Allen Smith Co., Indianapolis, Ind.
Peter Smith, Gloucester, Mass.
Richard R. Smith Co. Inc., Peterborough, N. H.
Smithsonian Institute, Washington, D. C.
Social Science Research Center, Rio Piedras, Puerto Rico
Social Science Research Council, New York
Social Science Research Council, Committee on the Economy of China, Berkeley, Calif.
Social Science Research Council of Australia, Sydney
The Social Sciences, Mexico City
Societa Editrice del "Foro Italiano", Rome
Societas Bibliographica, Lausanne, Switzerland
Societe d'Edition d'Enseignement Superieur, Paris
Societe Francaise d'Imprimerie et Librairie, Paris
Society for Advancement of Management, New York
Society for Promoting Christian Knowledge, London
Society for the Study of Social Problems, Kalamazoo, Mich.
Society of Comparative Legislative and International Law, London
Sociological Abstracts, New York
Solidaridad Publishing House, Manila
Somerset Press, Inc., Somerville, N. J.
Soney and Sage Co., Newark, N. J.
South Africa Commission on Future Government, Capetown
South Africa State Library, Pretoria
South African Congress of Democrats, Johannesburg
South African Council for Scientific and Industrial Research, Pretoria
South African Institute of International Affairs, Johannesburg
South African Institute of Race Relations, Johannesburg
South African Public Library, Johannesburg
South Carolina Archives, State Library, Columbia
South Pacific Commission, Noumea, New Caledonia
South Western Publishing Co., Cincinnati, Ohio
Southern Illinois University Press, Carbondale, Ill.
Southern Methodist University Press, Dallas, Tex.
Southern Political Science Association, New York
Southworth Anthoensen Press, Portland, Maine
Sovetskaia Rossiia, Moscow
Soviet and East European Research and Translation Service, New York
Spartan Books, Washington, D. C.
Special Libraries Association, New York
Specialty Press of South Africa, Johannesburg
Robert Speller and Sons, New York
Lorenz Spindler Verlag, Nuremberg
Julius Springer, Berlin
Springer-Verlag, New York; Stuttgart; Gottingen; Vienna
Stackpole Co., New York
Gerhard Stalling, Oldenburg, Germany
Stanford Bookstore, Stanford
Stanford University Comparative Education Center, Stanford, Calif.
Stanford University Institute for Communications Research, Stanford
Stanford University, Institute of Hispanic-American and Luso-Brazilian Studies, Stanford, Calif.
Stanford University, Project on Engineering-Economic Planning, Stanford, Calif.

Stanford University Research Institute, Menlo Park, Calif.
Stanford University, School of Business Administration, Stanford, Calif.
Stanford University, School of Education, Stanford, Calif.
Stanford University Press, Stanford, Cal.
Staples Press, New York
State University of New York at Albany, Albany
Stein & Day Publishers, New York
Franz Steiner Verlag, Wiesbaden
Ulrich Steiner Verlag, Wurttemburg
H. E. Stenfert Kroese, Leyden
Sterling Printing and Publishing Co., Ltd., Karachi
Sterling Publishers, Ltd., London
Stevens and Hayes, London
Stevens and Sons, Ltd., London
George W. Stewart, Inc., New York
George Stilke Berlin
Frederick A. Stokes Publishing Co., New York
C. Struik, Capetown
Stuttgarter Verlags Kantor, Stuttgart
Summy-Birchard Co., Evanston, Ill.
Swann Sonnenschein and Co., London
Philip Swartzwelder, Pittsburgh, Pa.
Sweet and Maxwell, Ltd., London
Swiss Eastern Institute, Berne
Sydney University Press, Sydney, Australia
Syracuse University, Maxwell School of Citizenship and Public Affairs, Syracuse, N. Y.
Syracuse University Press, Syracuse
Szczesnez Verlag, Munich

Talleres Graficos de Manuel Casas, Mexico City
Talleres de Impresion de Estampillas y Valores, Mexico City
Taplinger Publishing Co., New York
Tavistock, London
Tax Foundation, New York
Teachers' College, Bureau of Publications, Columbia University, New York
Technical Assistance Information Clearing House, New York
Technology Press, Cambridge
de Tempel, Bruges, Belgium
B. G. Teubner, Berlin; Leipzig
Texas College of Arts and Industries, Kingsville
Texas Western Press, Dallas
Texian Press, Waco, Texas
Thacker's Press and Directories, Ltd., Calcutta
Thailand, National Office of Statistics, Bangkok
Thailand National Economic Development Board, Bangkok
Thames and Hudson, Ltd., London
Thammasat University Institute of Public Administration, Bangkok, Thailand
E. J. Theisen, East Orange, N. J.
Charles C. Thomas, Publisher, Springfield, Ill.
Tilden Press, New York
Time, Inc., New York
Time-Life Books, New York
Times Mirror Printing and Binding, New York
Tipografia de Archivos, Madrid
Tipografia Mendonca, Lisbon
Tipografia Nacional, Guatemala, Guatemala City
Tipographia Nacional Guatemala, Guatemala City
H. D. Tjeenk Willink, Haarlem, Netherlands
J. C. Topping, Cambridge, Mass.
Transatlantic Arts, Inc., New York
Trejos Hermanos, San Jose
Trenton State College, Trenton
Tri-Ocean Books, San Francisco
Trident Press, New York
Trowitzsch and Son, Berlin
Truebner and Co., London
Tufts University Press, Medford, Mass.
Tulane University, School of Business Administration, New Orleans, La.
Tulane University Press, New Orleans
Turnstile Press, London
Tuskegee Institute, Tuskegee, Ala.
Charles E. Tuttle Co., Tokyo
Twayne Publishers Inc., New York
The Twentieth Century Fund, New York
Twin Circle Publishing Co., New York
Typographische Anstalt, Vienna
Tyrolia Verlag, Innsbruck

UNESCO, Paris
N. V. Uitgeverij W. Van Hoeve, The Hague
Frederick Ungar Publishing Co., Inc., New York
Union Federaliste Inter-Universitaire, Paris
Union of American Hebrew Congregations, New York
Union of International Associations, Brussels
Union of Japanese Societies of Law and Politics, Tokyo
Union of South Africa, Capetown
Union of South Africa, Government Information Office, New York
Union Press, Hong Kong
Union Research Institute, Hong Kong
United Arab Republic, Information Department, Cairo
United Nations Economic Commission for Asia and the Far East, Secretariat of Bangkok, Bangkok
United Nations Educational, Scientific and Cultural Organization, Paris
United Nations Food and Agriculture Organization, Rome
United Nations International Conference on Peaceful Uses of Atomic Energy, Geneva
United Nations Publishing Service, New York
United States Air Force Academy, Colorado Springs, Colo.
United States Bureau of the Census, Washington, D. C.
United States Business and Defense Services Administration, Washington D.C.
United States Civil Rights Commission, Washington, D. C.
United States Civil Service Commission, Washington, D. C.
United States Consulate General, Hong Kong
United States Department of Agriculture, Washington, D. C.
United States Department of the Army, Washington
United States Department of the Army, Office of Chief of Military History, Washington, D. C.
United States Department of Correction, New York
United States Department of State, Washington
United States Department of State, Government Printing Office, Washington, D. C.
United States Government Printing Office, Washington
United States Housing and Home Financing Agency, Washington, D. C.
United States Mutual Security Agency, Washington, D. C.
United States National Archives General Services, Washington, D. C.
United States National Referral Center for Science and Technology, Washington, D. C.
United States National Resources Committee, Washington, D. C.
United States Naval Academy, Annapolis, Md.
United States Naval Institute, Annapolis, Md.
United States Naval Officers Training School, China Lake, Cal.
United States Operations Mission to Vietnam, Washington, D. C.
United States President's Committee to Study Military Assistance, Washington, D. C.
United States Small Business Administration, Washington, D. C.
United World Federalists, Boston
Universal Reference System; see **Princeton Research Publishing Co.**, Princeton, N.J.
Universidad Central de Venezuela, Caracas
Universidad de Buenos Aires, Instituto Sociologia, Buenos Aires
Universidad de Chile, Santiago
Universidad de el Salvador, El Salvador
Universidad Nacional Autonomo de Mexico, Direccion General de Publicaciones, Mexico
Universidad Nacional de la Plata, Argentina
Universidad Nacional Instituto de Historia Antonoma de Mexico, Mexico City
Universidad Nacional Mayor de San Marcos, Lima
Universidad de Antioquia, Medellin, Colombia
Universite de Rabat, Rabat, Morocco
Universite Fouad I, Cairo
Universite Libre de Bruxelles, Brussels
Universite Mohammed V, Rabat, Morocco
University Books, Inc., Hyde Park, New York
University Bookstore, Hong Kong
University Microfilms, Inc., Ann Arbor
University of Alabama, Bureau of Public Administration, University, Ala.
University of Alabama Press, University, Ala.
University of Ankara, Ankara
University of Arizona Press, Tucson
University of Bombay, Bombay

University of Bonn, Bonn
University of British Columbia Press, Vancouver
University of California, Berkeley, Calif.
University of California at Los Angeles, Bureau of Government Research, Los Angeles
University of California at Los Angeles, Near Eastern Center, Los Angeles
University of California, Bureau of Business and Economic Research, Berkeley, Calif.
University of California, Bureau of Government Research, Los Angeles
University of California, Bureau of Public Administration, Berkeley
University of California, Department of Psychology, Los Angeles
University of California, Institute for International Studies, Berkeley, Calif.
University of California, Institute of East Asiatic Studies, Berkeley, Calif.
University of California, Institute of Governmental Affairs, Davis
University of California, Institute of Governmental Studies, Berkeley
University of California, Institute of Urban and Regional Development, Berkeley, Calif.
University of California, Latin American Center, Los Angeles
University of California Library, Berkeley, Calif.
University of California Press, Berkeley
University of California Survey Research Center, Berkeley, Calif.
University of Canterbury, Christchurch, New Zealand
University of Capetown, Capetown
University of Chicago, Chicago
University of Chicago, Center for Policy Study, Chicago
University of Chicago, Center for Program in Government Administration, Chicago
University of Chicago, Center of Race Relations, Chicago
University of Chicago, Graduate School of Business, Chicago
University of Chicago Law School, Chicago
University of Chicago, Politics Department, Chicago
University of Chicago Press, Chicago
University of Cincinnati, Cincinnati
University of Cincinnati, Center for Study of United States Foreign Policy, Cincinnati
University of Colorado Press, Boulder
University of Connecticut, Institute of Public Service, Storrs, Conn.
University of Dar es Salaam, Institute of Public Administration, Dar es Salaam
University of Denver, Denver
University of Detroit Press, Detroit
University of Edinburgh, Edinburgh, Scotland
University of Florida, Public Administration Clearing Service, Gainesville, Fla.
University of Florida, School of Inter-American Studies, Gainesville, Fla.
University of Florida Libraries, Gainesville
University of Florida Press, Gainesville
University of Georgia, Institute of Community and Area Development, Athens, Georgia
University of Georgia Press, Athens
University of Glasgow Press, Glasgow, Scotland
University of Glasgow Press, Fredericton, New Brunswick, Canada
University of Hawaii Press, Honolulu
University of Hong Kong Press, Hong Kong
University of Houston, Houston
University of Illinois, Champaign
University of Illinois, Graduate School of Library Science, Urbana
University of Illinois, Institute for Labor and Industrial Relations, Urbana
University of Illinois, Institute of Government and Public Affairs, Urbana, Ill.
University of Illinois Press, Urbana
University of Iowa, Center for Labor and Management, Iowa City
University of Iowa, School of Journalism, Iowa City
University of Iowa Press, Iowa City
University of Kansas, Bureau of Government Research, Lawrence, Kans.
University of Kansas Press, Lawrence
University of Karachi, Institute of Business and Public Administration, Karachi
University of Karachi Press, Karachi
University of Kentucky, Bureau of Governmental Research, Lexington
University of Kentucky Press, Lexington
University of London, Institute of Advanced Legal Studies, London
University of London, Institute of Commonwealth Studies, London
University of London, Institute of Education, London
University of London, School of Oriental and African Studies, London
University of London Press, London
University of Lund, Lund, Sweden
University of Maine Studies, Augusta, Me.
University of Malaya, Kualalumpur
University of Manchester Press, Manchester, England
University of Maryland, Bureau of Governmental Research, College of Business and Public Administration, College Park, Md.
University of Maryland, Department of Agriculture and Extension Education, College Park, Md.
University of Massachusetts, Bureau of Government Research, Amherst, Mass.
University of Massachusetts Press, Amherst
University of Melbourne Press, Melbourne, Australia
University of Miami Law Library, Coral Gables
University of Miami Press, Coral Gables
University of Michigan, Center for Research on Conflict Resolution, Ann Arbor
University of Michigan, Department of History and Political Science, Ann Arbor
University of Michigan, Graduate School of Business Administration, Ann Arbor
University of Michigan, Institute for Social Research, Ann Arbor
University of Michigan, Institute of Public Administration, Ann Arbor
University of Michigan Law School, Ann Arbor
University of Michigan, Survey Research Center, Ann Arbor
University of Michigan Press, Ann Arbor
University of Minnesota, St. Paul; Duluth
University of Minnesota, Industrial Relations Center, Minneapolis
University of Minnesota Press, Minneapolis
University of Mississippi, Bureau of Public Administration, University, Miss.
University of Missouri, Research Center, School of Business and Public Administration, Columbia
University of Missouri Press, Columbia
University of Natal Press, Pietermaritzburg
University of Nebraska Press, Lincoln
University of New England, Grafton, Australia
University of New Mexico, Department of Government, Albuquerque, N. Mex.
University of New Mexico, School of Law, Albuquerque
University of New Mexico Press, Albuquerque
University of North Carolina, Department of City and Regional Planning, Chapel Hill
University of North Carolina, Institute for International Studies, Chapel Hill
University of North Carolina, Institute for Research in the Social Sciences, Center for Urban and Regional Studies, Chapel Hill
University of North Carolina, Institute of Government, Chapel Hill
University of North Carolina Library, Chapel Hill
University of North Carolina Press, Chapel Hill
University of Notre Dame, Notre Dame, Ind.
University of Notre Dame Press, Notre Dame, Ind.
University of Oklahoma Press, Norman
University of Oregon Press, Eugene
University of Panama, Panama City
University of Paris (Conferences du Palais de la Decouverte), Paris
University of Pennsylvania, Philadelphia, Pa.
University of Pennsylvania, Department of Translations, Philadelphia
University of Pennsylvania Law School, Philadelphia, Pa.
University of Pennsylvania Press, Philadelphia
University of Pittsburgh, Institute of Local Government, Pittsburgh, Pa.
University of Pittsburgh Book Centers, Pittsburgh
University of Pittsburgh Press, Pittsburgh

University of Puerto Rico, San Juan
University of Rochester, Rochester, N. Y.
University of Santo Tomas, Manila
University of South Africa, Pretoria
University of South Carolina Press, Columbia
University of Southern California, Middle East and North Africa Program, Los Angeles
University of Southern California, School of International Relations, Los Angeles
University of Southern California Press, Los Angeles
University of Southern California, School of Public Administration, Los Angeles
University of State of New York, State Education Department, Albany
University of Sussex, Sussex, England
University of Sydney, Department of Government and Public Administration, Sydney
University of Tennessee, Knoxville
University of Tennessee, Bureau of Public Administration, Knoxville
University of Tennessee, Municipal Technical Advisory Service, Division of University Extension, Knoxville
University of Tennessee Press, Knoxville
University of Texas, Austin
University of Texas, Bureau of Business Research, Austin
University of Texas Press, Austin
University of the Philippines, Quezon City
University of the Punjab, Department of Public Administration, Lahore, Pakistan
University of the Witwatersrand, Johannesburg
University of Toronto, Toronto
University of Toronto Press, Toronto; Buffalo, N. Y.
University of Utah Press, Salt Lake City
University of Vermont, Burlington
University of Virginia, Bureau of Public Administration, Charlottesville
University of Wales Press, Cardiff
University of Washington, Bureau of Governmental Research and Services, Seattle
University of Washington Press, Seattle
University of Wisconsin, Madison
University of Wisconsin Press, Madison
University Press, University of the South, Sewanee, Tenn.
University Press of Virginia, Charlottesville
University Publishers, Inc., New York
University Publishing Co., Lincoln, Nebr.
University Society, Inc., Ridgewood, N. J.
Unwin University Books, London
T. Fisher Unwin, Ltd., London
Upjohn Institute for Employment Research, Kalamazoo, Mich; Los Angeles; Washington, D. C.
Urban America, New York
Urban Studies Center, New Brunswick, N. J.

VEB Verlag fur Buch-und Bibliothekwesen, Leipzig
Franz Vahlen, Berlin
Vallentine, Mitchell and Co., London
Van Nostrand Co., Inc., Princeton
Van Rees Press, New York
Vandenhoeck und Ruprecht, Gottingen
Vanderbilt University Press, Nashville, Tenn.
Vanguard Press, Inc., New York
E. C. Vann, Richmond, Va.
Vantage Press, New York
G. Velgaminov, New York
Verein fur Sozial Politik, Berlin
Vergara Editorial, Barcelona
Verlag Karl Alber, Freiburg
Verlag Georg D. W. Callwey, Munich
Verlag der Wiener Volksbuchhandlung, Vienna
Verlag der Wirtschaft, Berlin
Verlag Deutsche Polizei, Hamburg
Verlag Felix Dietrich, Osnabrueck
Verlag Kurt Dosch, Vienna
Verlag Gustav Fischer, Jena
Verlag Huber Frauenfeld, Stuttgart
Verlag fur Buch- und Bibliothekwesen, Leipzig
Verlag fur Literatur und Zeitgeschehen, Hannover, Germany
Verlag fur Recht und Gesellschaft, Basel
Verein fuer Sozialpolitik, Wirtschaft und Statistik, Berlin
Verlag Anton Hain, Meisenheim
Verlag Hans Krach, Mainz
Verlag Edward Krug, Wurttemburg
Verlag Helmut Kupper, Godesberg
Verlag August Lutzeyer, Baden-Baden
Verlag Mensch und Arbeit, Bruckmann, Munich
Verlag C. F. Muller, Karlsruhe
Verlag Anton Pustet, Munich
Verlag Rombach und Co., Freiburg
Verlag Heinrich Scheffler, Frankfurt
Verlag Hans Schellenberg, Winterthur, Switz.
Verlag P. Schippers, Amsterdam
Verlag Lambert Schneider, Heidelberg
Verlag K. W. Schutz, Gottingen
Verlag Styria, Graz, Austria
Lawrence Verry, Publishers, Mystic, Conn.
Viking Press, New York
Villanova Law School, Philadelphia
J. Villanueva, Buenos Aires
Vintage Books, New York
Virginia Commission on Constitutional Government, Richmond
Virginia State Library, Richmond
Vishveshvaranand Vedic Research Institute, Hoshiarpur
Vista Books, London
F. & J. Voglrieder, Munich
Voigt und Gleibner, Frankfurt
Voltaire Verlag, Berlin
Von Engelhorn, Stuttgart
Vora and Co. Publishers, Bombay
J. Vrin, Paris

Karl Wachholtz Verlag, Neumunster
Wadsworth Publishing Co., Belmont, Cal.
Walker and Co., New York
Ives Washburn, Inc., New York
Washington State University Press, Pullman
Washington University Libraries, Washington
Franklin Watts, Inc., New York
Waverly Press, Inc., Baltimore, Md.
Wayne State University Press, Detroit, Mich.
Christian Wegner Verlag, Hamburg
Weidenfield and Nicolson, London
R. Welch, Belmont, Mass.
Wellesley College, Wellesley, Mass.
Herbert Wendler & Co., Berlin
Wenner-Gren Foundation for Anthropological Research, New York
Wesleyan University Press, Middletown, Conn.
West Publishing Co., St. Paul, Minn.
Westdeutscher Verlag, Cologne
Western Islands Publishing Co., Belmont, Mass.
Western Publishing Co., Inc., Racine, Wis.
Western Reserve University Press, Cleveland
Westminster Press, Philadelphia, Pa.
J. Whitaker and Sons, Ltd., London
Whitcombe and Tombs, Ltd., Christchurch
Whiteside, Inc., New York
Thomas Wilcox, Los Angeles
John Wiley and Sons, Inc., New York
William-Frederick Press, New York
Williams and Vorgate, Ltd., London
Williams and Wilkins Co., Baltimore, Md.
Wilshire Book Co., Hollywood, Calif.
H. W. Wilson Co., New York
Winburn Press, Lexington, Ky.
Allan Wingate, Ltd., London
Carl Winters Universitats-Buchhandlung, Heidelberg
Wisconsin State University Press, River Falls
Wisconsin State Historical Society, Madison
Witwatersrand University Press, Capetown
Woking Muslim Mission and Literary Trust, Surrey
Wolters, Groningen, Netherlands
Woodrow Wilson Foundation, New York
Woodrow Wilson Memorial Library, New York
World Law Fund, New York
World Peace Foundation, Boston
World Press, Ltd., Calcutta
World Publishing Co., Cleveland
World Trade Academy Press, New York
World University Library, New York

Yale University, New Haven, Conn.
Yale University, Department of Industrial Administration, New Haven, Conn.

Yale University, Harvard Foundation, New Haven, Conn.
Yale University, Institute of Advanced Studies, New Haven, Conn.
Yale University Press, New Haven
Yale University, Southeast Asia Studies, New Haven
Yeshiva University Press, New York
Thomas Yoseloff, New York

T. L. Yuan, Tokyo

Zambia, Government Printer, Lusaka
Otto Zeller, Osnabruck, Germany
Zentral Verlag der NSDAP, Munich
Zwingli Verlag, Zurich

List of Periodicals Cited in this Volume

Academy of Political Science (Columbia University), Proceedings
Accounting Review
Administrative Science Quarterly
Africa
African Affairs
American Anthropologist
American Behavioral Scientist
American Economic Review
American Historical Review
American Journal of Comparative Law
American Journal of Economics and Sociology
American Journal of International Law
American Journal of Public Health
American Journal of Sociology
American Political Science Review
American Sociological Review
Annales Politiques et Economiques
Annals of the American Academy of Political and Social Science
Annuaire Europeen (European Yearbook)
Annuaire Francais de Droit International
Antioch Review
Anti-Trust Bulletin
Archives of Environmental Health
Asian Survey
Atlantic Community Quarterly
Aussenpolitik
Bankers' Magazine
Banking
Behavioral Science
British Journal of Sociology
Business Horizons
Business Topics
Cahiers de Bruges
Cahiers du Droit Europeen
California Management Review
Cambridge Law Journal
Canadian Journal of Economics and Political Science
Canadian Public Administration
Casa de las Americas
Center Magazine
Centro
Cercetari Filozofice
China Mainland Review
China Quarterly
Co-Existence
Colorado Quarterly
Columbia Journalism Review
Columbia Law Review
Commonweal
Comunita Internazionale
Congressional Record
Cornell Law Quarterly
Corporate Practice Commentator
Crisis
Cuadernos Americanos
Current History
Daedalus
Development Digest
Diogenes
Dissent
Dun's Review and Modern Industry
Duquesne Review
East African Economic Review
East Europe
Econometrica
Economic Development and Cultural Change
Economic Journal
Economica
Encounter
Foreign Affairs
Foreign Service Journal
Freedomways
Georgetown Law Journal
George Washington Law Review
Government and Opposition
Harvard Business Review
Harvard Law Review
Hitotsubashi Journal of Economics
Human Relations
India Quarterly
Indiana Law Journal
Industrial and Labor Relations Review
Industrial Relations
Institut zur Erforschung der UdSSR, Bulletin
Instituto de Ciencias Sociales, Revista (Barcelona)
Integrated Education
Inter-American Economic Affairs
International Affairs (U.K.)
International and Comparative Law Quarterly
International Conciliation
International Journal
International Labour Review
International Monetary Fund Staff Papers
International Organization
International Relations
International Review of Administrative Sciences
International Review of the Social Sciences
International Science and Technology

International Socialist Journal
International Studies
Journal of Abnormal and Social Psychology
Journal of Administration Overseas
Journal of the American Institute of Planners
Journal of Arms Control
Journal of Asian and African Studies
Journal of Asian Studies
Journal of Business
Journal of Commonwealth Political Studies
Journal of Conflict Resolution
Journal of Criminal Law, Criminology, and Police Science
Journal of Economic History
Journal of Educational Sociology
Journal of Farm Economics
Journal of Human Relations
Journal of Inter-American Studies
Journal of International Affairs
Journal of Law and Economics
Journal of Marketing
Journal of Modern African Studies
Journal of Philosophy
Journal of Political Economy
Journal of Politics
Journal of Social Issues
Journal of Social Psychology
Kyklos
Labor History
Labor Law Journal
Labour Review
Land Economics
Language
Latin American Research Review
Law and Contemporary Problems
Library Journal
Lloyd Bank Review
Management Science
Manchester Economic and Social Studies
Michigan Business Review
Michigan Law Review
Middle East Journal
Middle Eastern Affairs
Midstream
Midwestern Journal of Political Science
Military Review
Minnesota Law Review
Modern Age
Modern Asian Studies
Municipal Finance
National Real Estate and Building Journal
National Tax Journal
Neue Politische Literatur
New Individualist Review
New Politics
New York Times Magazine
Nigerian Journal of Economic and Social Studies
North Dakota Law Review
Notre Dame Lawyer
NYU Law Review
Operational Research Quarterly
Orbis
Orient/West
Oxford Economic Papers
Pacific Affairs
Personnel Psychology
Political Quarterly
Political Science Quarterly
Politique Etrangere
Population Index
Problems of Communism
Psychoanalytic Review
Public Administration
Public Administration Review
Public Interest
Public Law
Public Opinion Quarterly
Quarterly Journal of Economics
Reprints from the Soviet Press
Review of Economics and Statistics
Review of Politics
Revue d'Economie Politique
Revue de Psychologie des Peuples
Revue Economique
Revue Economique Francaise
Revue Francaise de Science Politique
Revue Juridique et Politique d'Outre-mer
Rocky Mountain Social Science Journal
Royal Central Asian Journal
Royal United Service Institution, Journal
Rural Sociology
Rutgers Law Review
Sales Management
Schweizerische Monatshefte
Science and Society
Science and Technology
Slavic Review
Social and Economic Studies
Social Forces
Social Research
Social Science
South African Journal of Economics
South Atlantic Quarterly
Southern California Law Review

Southern Economic Journal
Southwestern Social Science Quarterly
Soviet Education
Soviet Review
Soviet Studies
Stanford Law Review
Table Ronde
Technology and Culture
Texas Law Review
Tiers-Monde
Trans-Action
Transition
Tri-Quarterly Review
United Asia
University of Chicago Law Review
University of Illinois Bulletin
University of Kansas Law Journal
University of Pennsylvania Law Review
University of Toronto Law Journal
Urban Affairs Quarterly
Vanderbilt Law Review
Vierteljahrschrift fur Sozial- und Wirtschaftsgeschichte
Vierteljahrshefte fur Zeitgeschichte
Virginia Law Review
Virginia Quarterly Review
Voprosy Filosofii
Western Political Quarterly
World Marxist Review
World Politics
World Today

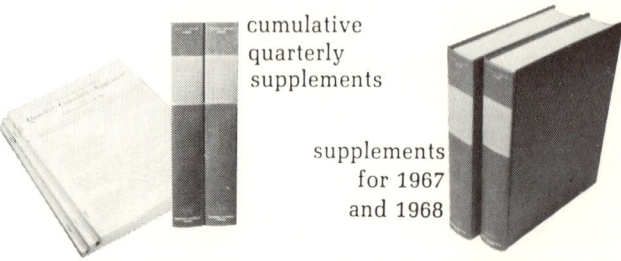